KU-018-300

COLLINS SHORTER ENGLISH DICTIONARY

COLLINS SHORTER ENGLISH DICTIONARY

HarperCollins Publishers
PO Box, Glasgow G4 ONB

First published in this edition 1993

©HarperCollins Publishers 1982, 1988, 1993

ISBN 0 00 470363-4

A catalogue record for this book is available from the British Library

All rights reserved. No part of this publication may be reproduced, stored in a retrieval system or transmitted, in any form or by any means, electronic, mechanical, photocopying, recording or otherwise, without the prior permission of the publisher. This book is sold subject to the conditions that it shall not, by way of trade or otherwise, be lent, re-sold, hired out or otherwise circulated without the publisher's prior consent in any form of binding or cover other than that in which it is published and without a similar condition including this condition being imposed on the subsequent purchaser.

Entered words that we have reason to believe constitute trademarks have been designated as such. However, neither the presence nor absence of such designation should be regarded as affecting the legal status of any trademark.

Printed and bound in Great Britain
by HarperCollins Manufacturing

Foreword

The new *Collins Shorter English Dictionary* has been prepared to take account of the fact that language today is developing more rapidly than at any time in the past. A continuous process of language monitoring is carried out by the dictionary editors, who note and record new words and terms and new uses of existing vocabulary as they come into use. They are collected from a variety of sources – national and local newspapers, TV and radio, books and magazines, and everyday conversation. At the last stage in the preparation of the dictionary a selection is made from the many hundreds of citations, and those new words and meanings judged to have established themselves in the language of today are included in the text.

The text of the dictionary is clearly arranged and all entries which need a definition are entered as headwords, so the required item, whether it be a single word, a compound word, an abbreviation or acronym, or a foreign word, is entered in its alphabetical position. The meanings are written in clear, explanatory English, and numbered to make it easy to find the one required. The core modern meaning is the one given first, with older, rare, or specialized senses following. Meanings which are regional, technical, or otherwise restricted in their area of use are clearly labelled. Special attention has been given to the English of Commonwealth countries and the United States, so that the dictionary covers the language not just of the United Kingdom but of all the main English-speaking regions of the world. Help is given on disputed or problematic points of usage, which are discussed in the many usage notes at the end of the relevant entries.

The text has been set in clear legible type, using the latest developments in computer technology. It provides a balanced view of today's English in a convenient and easy-to-use format.

The editors are indebted to the many consultants, specialist editors, organizations, and individuals who have contributed to and advised on the material contained in this book, and to those members of the public who have written with suggestions.

EDITORIAL STAFF

Managing Editors
William T. McLeod
Marian Makins

Editors
Diana Adams, Alice Grandison,
Danielle McGinley, Tom Shearer,
Lorna Knight

Australian Advisers
G.A. Wilkes
Challis Professor of English Literature
University of Sydney

W.A. Krebs
Bond University, Queensland

Canadian Adviser
Patrick Drysdale
Editor, *A Dictionary of Canadianisms on Historical Principles*

New Zealand Adviser
Professor Emeritus Ian A. Gordon
University of Wellington

South African Adviser
M. V. Aldridge
Professor of Phonetics and
General Linguistics
University of the Witwatersrand

Guide to the Use of the Dictionary

The Headword

The headwords are listed in strictly alphabetical order. This rule applies even if the headword consists of more than one word, or is an abbreviation, an acronym, or a symbol. Thus **bed** and the entries related to it are separated by intervening entries occurring in strict alphabetical order.

bed
BEd
bed and board
bed and breakfast
bedaub
bedazzle
bed bath
bedbug
bedchamber
bedclothes

Words that have the same spelling but are derived from different sources etymologically (homographs) are entered separately with superscript numbers after the headwords.

saw[1] (sɔː) *n.* **1.** any of various hand tools. . . .
saw[2] (sɔː) *vb.* the past tense of **see**[1].
saw[3] (sɔː) *n.* a wise saying, maxim, or proverb. . . .

Common acceptable variant spellings of English words are given as alternative forms of the headword.

characterize *or* **-ise** (ˈkærɪktəˌraɪz) *vb.* . . .

Where it is different, the U.S. spelling of a word is also recorded in the headword.

centre *or U.S.* **center** (ˈsɛntə) *n.* . . .

Prefixes (e.g. **in-**[1], **pre-**, **sub-**), suffixes (e.g. **-able, -ation, -ity**), and combining forms (e.g. **psycho-, -iatry**) have been entered as headwords if they are still used freely to produce new words in English.

The Pronunciation

Pronunciation of words in this dictionary represent those that are common in educated British English speech. They are transcribed in the International Phonetic Alphabet (IPA). A *Key to the Pronunciation Symbols* is printed at the end of this Guide. See also the article on *The Pronunciation of British English* by Professor Gimson on p. xiii.

When a headword has a common acceptable variant pronunciation or stress pattern, the variant is shown in full or by repeating only the syllable or syllables that change.

amok (əˈmʌk, əˈmɒk) . . . . *n*
lactose (ˈlæktəʊs, -təʊz) *n.* . . .

When two or more parts of speech of a word have different pronunciations, the pronunciations are shown in parentheses before the relevant group of senses.

record *n.* (ˈrɛkɔːd). **1.** an account in permanent form. . . ~*vb.* (rɪˈkɔːd). (*mainly tr.*) **18.** to set down in some permanent form. . . .

If one sense of a headword has a different pronunciation from that of the rest, that pronunciation is given in parentheses after the sense number.

conjure (ˈkʌndʒə) *vb.* **1.** (*intr.*) to practise conjuring. . . . **3.** (kənˈdʒʊə). (*tr.*) to appeal earnestly to: *I conjure you to help me.* . . .

Inflected Forms

Inflected forms are shown for the following:

Nouns and verbs whose inflections involve a change in internal spelling.

goose[1] (guːs) *n., pl.* **geese**. . . .
drive (draɪv) *vb.* **driving, drove, driven**. . . .

Nouns, verbs, and adjectives that end in a consonant plus *y*, where *y* is changed to *i* before inflectional endings.

augury (ˈɔːgjʊrɪ) *n., pl.* **-ries**. . . .

Nouns having identical singular and plural forms.

sheep (ʃiːp) *n., pl.* **sheep**. . . .

Nouns that closely resemble others that form their plurals differently.

mongoose (ˈmɒŋˌguːs) *n., pl.* **-gooses**. . . .

Nouns that end in *-ful, -o,* and *-us.*

handful (ˈhændfʊl) *n., pl.* **-fuls**. . . .
potato (pəˈteɪtəʊ) *n., pl.* **-toes**. . . .
prospectus (prəˈspɛktəs) *n., pl.* **-tuses**. . . .

Nouns whose plurals are not regular English inflections.

basis (ˈbeɪsɪs) *n., pl.* **-ses** (-siːz). . . .

Plural nouns whose singulars are not regular English forms.

bacteria (bækˈtɪərɪə) *pl. n., sing.* **-rium**. . . .

Nouns whose plurals have regular spellings but involve a change in pronunciation.

house *n.* (haʊs), *pl.* **houses** (ˈhaʊzɪz). . . .

Multiword nouns when it is not obvious which word takes a plural inflection.

attorney-at-law *n., pl.* **attorneys-at-law**. . . .

Adjectives that change their roots to form comparatives and superlatives.

good (gʊd) *adj.* **better, best**. . . .

Adjectives and verbs that double their final consonant before adding endings.

fat (fæt). . . .~*adj.* **fatter, fattest**. . . .
control (kənˈtrəʊl) *vb.* **-trolling, -trolled**

Verbs and adjectives that end in a vowel plus *e.*

canoe (kəˈnuː). . . ~*vb.* **-noeing, -noed**. . . .
free (friː) *adj.* **freer, freest**. . . . ~*vb.* **freeing, freed**. . . .

Parts of Speech

A part-of-speech label in italics precedes the account of the sense or senses relating to that part of speech.

Standard parts of speech

The following parts of speech, with abbreviations as shown, are standard and need no further explanation: adjective (*adj.*), adverb (*adv.*), conjunction (*conj.*), interjection (*interj.*), noun (*n.*), preposition (*prep.*), pronoun (*pron.*), verb (*vb.*).

Less traditional parts of speech

Certain other less traditional parts of speech have been adopted in this dictionary. They are as follows:

determiner. This denotes such words as *the, a, some, any, that, this,* possessives like *my, his,* and *your,* and the numerals. Many determiners can have a pronoun function without change of meaning, and this is shown thus:

some (sʌm; *unstressed* səm) *determiner*. . . . **2. a.** an unknown or unspecified quantity or amount of: *there's some rice on the table; he owns some horses.* **b.** (*as pron.; functioning as sing. or pl.*): *we'll buy some*. . . .

sentence connector. This denotes words like *however* and *therefore,* which have been traditionally classed as adverbs but which function as conjunctions, linking sentences, without being restricted, as are conjunctions, to the initial position in their clause.

sentence substitute. Sentence substitutes comprise words such as *yes, no, perhaps, definitely,* and *maybe,* which can stand as meaningful utterances by themselves.

If a word can be used as more than one part of speech, the account of the senses of one part of speech is separated from the others by a swung dash (~).

lure (lʊə) *vb.* (*tr.*). . . . **2.** *Falconry.* to entice (a hawk or falcon) from the air to the falconer by a lure. ~*n.* **3.** a person or thing that lures. . . .

Grammatical Information

Adjectives and Determiners

Some adjectives and determiners are restricted by usage to a particular position relative to the nouns they qualify. This is indicated by the following labels:

postpositive (used predicatively or after the noun, but not before the noun):

ablaze (əˈbleɪz) *adj.* (*postpositive*), *adv.* **1.** on fire; burning. . . .

immediately postpositive (always used immediately following the noun qualified and never used predicatively):

galore (gəˈlɔː) *determiner.* (*immediately postpositive*) in great numbers or quantity: *there were daffodils galore in the park.* . . .

prenominal (used before the noun, and never used predicatively):

chief (tʃiːf). . . . ~*adj.* **4.** (*prenominal*) **a.** most important; principal. **b.** highest in rank or authority . . . .

Intensifiers

Adjectives and adverbs that perform an exclusively intensifying function, with no addition of meaning, are described as (intensifier) without further explanation.

blooming (ˈbluːmɪŋ) *adv., adj. Brit. inf.* (intensifier): *a blooming genius; blooming painful.* . . .

Conjunctions

Conjunctions are divided into two classes, marked by the following labels placed in parentheses:

coordinating. Coordinating conjunctions connect words, phrases, or clauses that perform an identical function and are not dependent on each other. They include *and, but,* and *or.*

subordinating. Subordinating conjunctions introduce clauses that are dependent on a main clause in a complex sentence. Examples are *where, until,* and *before.*

Some conjunctions, such as *while* and *whether,* can function as either coordinating or subordinating conjunctions.

Singular and plural labelling

Headwords and senses that are apparently plural in form but that take a singular verb, etc., are marked "*functioning as sing.*"

physics (ˈfɪzɪks) *n.* (*functioning as sing.*) **1.** the branch of science. . . .

Headwords and senses that appear to be singular but take a plural verb, etc., are marked "*functioning as pl.*"

cattle (ˈkætᵊl) *n.* (*functioning as pl.*) **1.** bovid mammals of the tribe *Bovini.* . . .

Headwords and senses that may take either a singular or a plural verb, etc., are marked "*functioning as sing. or pl.*"

bellows (ˈbɛləʊz) *n.* (*functioning as sing. or pl.*) **1.** Also: **pair of bellows.** an instrument consisting of an air chamber. . . .

Modifiers

A noun that is commonly used with adjectival force is labelled *modifier.*

If the sense of the modifier is strictly inferable from the sense of the noun, the modifier is shown without further explanation, with an example to illustrate its use; otherwise an account of its meaning and/or usage is given in a separate numbered definition.

key[1] (kiː) *n.* . . . **18.** (*modifier*) of great importance: *a key issue.* . . .

Verbs

The account of the meaning of a verb is given without subdivision into separate groupings for transitive and intransitive senses. Instead, each definition is worded so as to take account of transitivity or intransitivity. When a sense of a verb (*vb.*) is restricted to transitive use, it is labelled (*tr.*); if it is intransitive only, it is labelled (*intr.*). If all the senses of a verb are either transitive or intransitive, the appropriate label appears before the first numbered sense and is not repeated. Absence of a label indicates that the sense or verb may be used both transitively and intransitively. If nearly all the senses of a verb are transitive, the label (*mainly tr.*) appears immediately before the first numbered sense. This indicates that, unless otherwise labelled, any given sense of the verb is transitive. Similarly, all the senses of a verb may be labelled (*mainly intr.*).

Copulas

A verb that takes a complement is labelled *copula.*

seem (siːm) *vb.* (*may take an infinitive*) **1.** (*copula*) to appear to the mind or eye;. . . .

Phrasal verbs

Verbal constructions consisting of a verb and a preposition or a verb and an adverbial particle are given headword status if the meaning of the phrasal verb cannot be deduced from the separate meanings of the verb and the particle.

Phrasal verbs are labelled to show four possible distinctions:

a transitive verb with an adverbial particle (*tr., adv.*); a transitive verb with a preposition (*tr., prep.*); an intransitive verb with an adverbial particle (*intr., adv.*); an intransitive verb with a preposition (*intr., prep.*):

turn on. . . . **1.** (*tr., adv.*) to cause (something) to operate by turning a knob, etc.

take for. . . . (*tr., prep.*) **1.** . . . . to consider or suppose to be, esp. mistakenly: *the fake coins were taken for genuine; who do you take me for?*

play up. . . . (*adv.*). . . . **3.** (*intr.*) *Brit. inf.* (of a machine, etc.) to function erratically: *the car is playing up again.*

turn on. . . . 2. (*intr., prep.*) to depend or hinge on: *the success of the party turns on you.*

As with the labelling of other verbs, the absence of a label is significant. If there is no label (*tr.*) or (*intr.*), the verb may be used either transitively or intransitively. If there is no label (*adv.*) or (*prep.*), the particle may be either adverbial or prepositional.

Any noun, adjective, or modifier formed from a phrasal verb is entered under the phrasal-verb headword. In some cases, where the noun or adjective is more common than the verb, the phrasal verb is entered after the noun/adjective form:

breakaway (ˈbreɪkəˌweɪ) *n.* **1. a.** loss or withdrawal of a group of members from an association, club, etc. **b.** (*as modifier*): *a breakaway faction*. . . . ~*vb.* **break away**. (*intr., adv.*). . . . **4.** to withdraw or secede.

Restrictive Labels

If a particular sense is restricted as to appropriateness, connotation, subject field, etc., an italicized label is placed immediately before the account of the relevant meaning.

hang on *vb.* (*intr.*). . . . **5.** (*adv.*) *Inf.* to wait: *hang on for a few minutes.*

If a label applies to all senses of one part of speech, it is placed immediately after the part-of-speech label.

assured (əˈʃʊəd) *adj.* . . . ~*n.* **4.** *Chiefly Brit.* **a.** the beneficiary. . . . **b.** the person whose life is insured.

If a label applies to all senses of a headword, it is placed immediately after the pronunciation (or inflections).

con[1] (kɒn) *Inf.* ~*n.* **1. a.** short for **confidence trick. b.** (*as modifier*): *con man.* ~*vb.* **conning, conned. 2.** (*tr.*) to swindle or defraud.

Arch. (*Archaic*). Denotes a word or sense that is no longer in common use but may be found in literary works or used to impart a historical colour to contemporary writing.

Obs. (*Obsolete*). Denotes a word or sense that is no longer in use. In specialist or technical fields the label often implies that the term has been superseded.

The word "formerly" is placed in parentheses before a sense or set of senses when the practice, concept, etc., being described, rather than the word itself, is obsolete or out-of-date.

Sl. (*Slang*). Refers to words or senses that are informal and restricted in context, for example, to members of a particular social or cultural group. Slang words are inappropriate in formal speech or writing.

Inf. (*Informal*). Applies to words or senses that may be widely used, especially in conversation, but are not common in formal writing. Such words are subject to fewer contextual restrictions than slang words.

Taboo. Indicates words that are not acceptable in polite use.

Not standard. Indicates words or senses that are frequently encountered but widely regarded as incorrect.

Derog. (*Derogatory*). Implies that the connotations of a word are unpleasant with intent on the part of the speaker or writer.

Offens. (*Offensive*). Indicates that a word may be regarded as offensive by the person described or referred to, even if the speaker uses the word without any malicious intention.

A number of other usage labels, such as *Facetious* and *Euphemistic*, are used where appropriate.

Various italicized labels are used to indicate that a word or sense is used in a particular specialist or technical field.

The Arrangement of Entries

As a general rule, where a headword has more than one sense, the first sense given is the one most common in current usage.

complexion (kəmˈplɛkʃən) *n.* **1.** the colour and general appearance of a person's skin, esp. of the face. **2.** aspect or nature: *the general complexion of a nation's finances.* **3.** *Obs.* temperament.

Where the editors consider that a current sense is the "core meaning", in that it illuminates the meaning of other senses, the core meaning may be placed first.

think (θɪŋk) *vb.* **thinking, thought. 1.** (*tr.; may take a clause as object*) to consider, judge, or believe: *he thinks my ideas impractical.* **2.** (*intr.;* often foll. by *about*) to exercise the mind as in order to make a decision; ponder. **3.** (*intr.*) to be capable of conscious thought: *man is the only animal that thinks.*

Subsequent senses are arranged so as to give a coherent account of the meaning of a headword. If a word is used as more than one part of speech, all the senses of each part of speech are grouped together in a single block. Within a part-of-speech block, closely related senses are grouped together; technical senses generally follow general senses; archaic and obsolete senses follow technical senses; idioms and fixed phrases are generally placed last.

Scientific definitions

Units, physical quantities, formulas, etc. In accordance with the recommendations of the International Standards Organization, all scientific measurements are expressed in SI units (*Système International d'Unités*). Measurements and quantities in more traditional units are often given as well as SI units.

Cross-references

Cross-references refer the reader to additional information elsewhere in the dictionary. If the cross-reference is preceded by a swung dash (~), it applies to all the senses of the headword that have gone before it, unless otherwise stated. If there is no swung dash, the cross-reference applies only to the sense immediately preceding it. Many cross-references include a sense number for the sake of clarity.

Variant spellings are generally entered as cross-references if their place in the alphabetical list is more than ten entries distant from the main entry.

aether (ˈi:θə) *n.* a variant spelling of **ether** (senses 3, 4).

Alternative names are printed in boldface type and introduced by the words "Also" or "Also called". If the alternative name is preceded by a swung dash (~), it applies to the entire entry.

Related adjectives

Certain nouns of Germanic origin have related adjectives that are derived from Greek, Latin, or French. For example, *mural* (from Latin) is an adjective related in meaning to *wall.* Such adjectives are shown in a number of cases after the sense (or part-of-speech block) to which they are related.

bishop (ˈbɪʃəp) *n.* **1.** a clergyman having spiritual and administrative powers. . . . Related adj.: **episcopal.**

Idioms

Placement

Fixed noun phrases, such as **dark horse,** and certain other idioms are given full headword status. Other idioms are placed under the key word of the idiom, as a separate sense, generally at the end of the appropriate part-of-speech block.

ground[1] (graʊnd) *n*. . . . **17. break new ground.** to do something that has not been done before. . . .

The Etymology

Placement and selection

Etymologies are placed in square brackets after the account of the meaning. They are given for most headwords except those that are derivative forms (consisting of a base word and a suffix or prefix), compound words, inflected forms, and some chemical compounds. Thus, the headword **manage** has been given an etymology but the related headwords **manageable** (equivalent to *manage* plus the suffix *-able*), **management** (*manage* plus *-ment*), **manager** (*manage* plus *-er*[1]), **manageress** (*manager* plus *-ess*), etc., do not have etymologies. Inflected forms such as **saw**[2] (the past tense of *see*[1]) and obvious compounds such as **mothball** are not given an etymology. Many headwords, such as **enlighten** and **prepossess,** consist of a prefix and a base word and are not accompanied by etymologies since the essential etymological information is shown for the component parts, all of which are entered in the dictionary as headwords in their own right (in this instance, **en-**[1], **light**[1], **-en**[1] and **pre-**, **possess**).

Words printed in SMALL CAPITALS within etymologies refer the reader to other headwords where additional information, either in the definition text or in the etymology, may be found or to words that are etymologically related.

Dating

The etymology records the first known occurrence (a written citation) of a word in English. Words first appearing in the language during the Middle English period or later are dated by century, abbreviated C.

mantis. . . . [C17: NL, < Gk: prophet, alluding to its praying posture]

This indicates that there is a written citation for *mantis* in the seventeenth century, when the word was in use as a New Latin term in the scientific vocabulary of the time. The absence of a New Latin or Greek form in the etymology means that the form of the word was the same in those languages as in English.

Native words from Old English are not dated, written records of Old English being comparatively scarce, but are simply identified as being of Old English origin.

Derived Words

Words derived from a base word by the addition of suffixes such as *-ly, -ness,* etc., are entered in boldface type at the end of the entry for the base word. The meanings of such words may be deduced from the meanings of the suffix and the headword. Where a derived word has developed a specialized or restricted meaning, it is entered as a headword and defined, e.g. **absolutely, arrangement.**

Abbreviations

Abbreviations and acronyms that are included as entries are styled in general without stops. Most abbreviations are, however, equally acceptable written with or without stops.

Listed Entries

In English many easily understood words are formed by adding productive prefixes such as *non-, over-, pre-, un-*, etc., to existing words. Such words are included, without definition, at the foot of the page on which they would occur in alphabetical sequence.

Usage Notes

A brief note introduced by the label **Usage** and the marginal sign ▷ has been added at the end of a number of entries in order to comment on matters of usage. These comments are based on the observed practice or preference of the majority of educated speakers and writers.

Pronunciation Key

The symbols used in the pronunciation transcriptions are those of the International Phonetic Alphabet. The following consonant symbols have their usual English values: *b, d, f, h, k, l, m, n, p, r, s, t, v, w, z*. The remaining symbols and their interpretations are listed below.

English Sounds

ɑː as in *father* (ˈfɑːðə), *alms* (ɑːmz), *clerk* (klɑːk), *heart* (hɑːt), *sergeant* (ˈsɑːdʒənt)

æ as in *act* (ækt), *Caedmon* (ˈkædmən), *plait* (plæt)

aɪ as in *dive* (daɪv), *aisle* (aɪl), *guy* (gaɪ), *might* (maɪt), *rye* (raɪ)

aɪə as in *fire* (ˈfaɪə), *buyer* (ˈbaɪə), *liar* (ˈlaɪə), *tyre* (ˈtaɪə)

aʊ as in *out* (aʊt), *bough* (baʊ), *crowd* (kraʊd), *slouch* (slaʊtʃ)

aʊə as in *flour* (ˈflaʊə), *cower* (ˈkaʊə), *flower* (ˈflaʊə), *sour* (ˈsaʊə)

ɛ as in *bet* (bɛt), *ate* (ɛt), *bury* (ˈbɛrɪ), *heifer* (ˈhɛfə), *said* (sɛd), *says* (sɛz)

eɪ as in *paid* (peɪd), *day* (deɪ), *deign* (deɪn), *gauge* (geɪdʒ), *grey* (greɪ), *neigh* (neɪ)

ɛə as in *bear* (bɛə), *dare* (dɛə), *prayer* (prɛə), *stairs* (stɛəz), *where* (wɛə)

g as in *get* (gɛt), *give* (gɪv), *ghoul* (guːl), *guard* (gɑːd), *examine* (ɪgˈzæmɪn)

ɪ as in *pretty* (ˈprɪtɪ), *build* (bɪld), *busy* (ˈbɪzɪ), *nymph* (nɪmf), *pocket* (ˈpɒkɪt), *sieve* (sɪv), *women* (ˈwɪmɪn)

iː as in *see* (siː), *aesthete* (ˈiːsθiːt), *evil* (ˈiːvᵊl), *magazine* (ˌmægəˈziːn), *receive* (rɪˈsiːv), *siege* (siːdʒ)

ɪə as in *fear* (fɪə), *beer* (bɪə), *mere* (mɪə), *tier* (tɪə)

j as in *yes* (jɛs), *onion* (ˈʌnjən), *vignette* (vɪˈnjɛt)

ɒ as in *pot* (pɒt), *botch* (bɒtʃ), *sorry* (ˈsɒrɪ)

əʊ as in *note* (nəʊt), *beau* (bəʊ), *dough* (dəʊ), *hoe* (həʊ), *slow* (sləʊ), *yeoman* (ˈjəʊmən)

ɔː as in *thaw* (θɔː), *broad* (brɔːd), *drawer* (ˈdrɔːə), *fault* (fɔːlt), *halt* (hɔːlt), *organ* (ˈɔːgən)

ɔɪ as in *void* (vɔɪd), *boy* (bɔɪ), *destroy* (dɪˈstrɔɪ)

ʊ as in *pull* (pʊl), *good* (gʊd), *should* (ʃʊd), *woman* (ˈwʊmən)

uː as in *zoo* (zuː), *do* (duː), *queue* (kjuː), *shoe* (ʃuː), *spew* (spjuː), *true* (truː), *you* (juː)

ʊə as in *poor* (pʊə), *skewer* (skjʊə), *sure* (ʃʊə)

ə as in *potter* (ˈpɒtə), *alone* (əˈləʊn), *furious* (ˈfjʊərɪəs), *nation* (ˈneɪʃən), *the* (ðə)

ɜː as in *fern* (fɜːn), *burn* (bɜːn), *fir* (fɜː), *learn* (lɜːn), *term* (tɜːm), *worm* (wɜːm)

ʌ as in *cut* (kʌt), *flood* (flʌd), *rough* (rʌf), *son* (sʌn)

ʃ as in *ship* (ʃɪp), *election* (ɪˈlɛkʃən), *machine* (məˈʃiːn), *mission* (ˈmɪʃən), *pressure* (ˈprɛʃə), *schedule* (ˈʃɛdjuːl), *sugar* (ˈʃʊgə)

ʒ as in *treasure* (ˈtrɛʒə), *azure* (ˈæʒə), *closure* (ˈkləʊʒə), *evasion* (ɪˈveɪʒən)

tʃ as in *chew* (tʃuː), *nature* (ˈneɪtʃə)

dʒ as in *jaw* (dʒɔː), *adjective* (ˈædʒɪktɪv), *lodge* (lɒdʒ), *soldier* (ˈsəʊldʒə), *usage* (ˈjuːsɪdʒ)

θ as in *thin* (θɪn), *strength* (strɛŋθ), *three* (θriː)

ð as in *these* (ðiːz), *bathe* (beɪð), *lather* (ˈlɑːðə)

ŋ as in *sing* (sɪŋ), *finger* (ˈfɪŋgə), *sling* (slɪŋ)

ᵊ indicates that the following consonant (*l* or *n*) is syllabic, as in *bundle* (ˈbʌndᵊl), *button* (ˈbʌtᵊn)

Foreign Sounds

The symbols above are also used to represent foreign sounds where these are similar to English sounds. However, certain common foreign sounds require symbols with markedly different values, as follows:

a *a* in French *ami*, German *Mann*, Italian *pasta*: a sound between English (æ) and (ɑː), similar to the vowel in Northern English *cat* or London *cut*.

ɑ *a* in French *bas*: a sound made with a tongue position similar to that of English (ɑː), but shorter.

e *é* in French *été*, *eh* in German *sehr*, *e* in Italian *che*: a sound similar to the first part of the English diphthong (eɪ) in *day* or to the Scottish vowel in *day*.

i *i* in French *il*, German *Idee*, Spanish *filo*, Italian *signor*: a sound made with a tongue position similar to that of English (iː), but shorter.

ɔ *o* in Italian *no*, French *bonne*, German *Sonne*: a vowel resembling English (ɒ), but with a higher tongue position and more rounding of the lips.

o *o* in French *rose*, German *so*, Italian *voce*: a sound between English (ɔː) and (uː) with closely rounded lips, similar to the Scottish vowel in *so*.

u *ou* in French *genou*, *u* in German *kulant*, Spanish *puna*: a sound made with a tongue position similar to that of English (uː), but shorter.

y *u* in French *tu*, *ü* in German *über* or *fünf*: a sound made with a tongue position similar to that of English (iː) but with closely rounded lips.

ø *eu* in French *deux*, *ö* in German *schön*: a sound made with the tongue position of (e) but with closely rounded lips.

œ *œu* in French *œuf*, *ö* in German *zwölf*: a sound made with a tongue position similar to that of English (ɛ) but with open rounded lips.

~ above a vowel indicates nasalization, as in French *un* (œ̃), *bon*, (bɔ̃), *vin* (vɛ̃), *blanc* (blɑ̃).

x *ch* in Scottish *loch*, German *Buch*, *j* in Spanish *Juan*.

ç *ch* in German *ich*: a (j) sound as in *yes*, said without voice; similar to the first sound in *huge*.

β *b* in Spanish *Habana*: a voiced fricative sound similar to (v), but made by the two lips.

ʎ *ll* in Spanish *llamar*, *gl* in Italian *consiglio*: similar to the (lj) sequence in *million*, but with the tongue tip lowered and the sounds said simultaneously.

ɥ *u* in French *lui*: a short (y).

ɲ *gn* in French *vigne*, Italian *gnocchi*, *ñ* in Spanish *España*: similar to the (nj) sequence in *onion*, but with the tongue tip lowered and the two sounds said simultaneously.

ɣ *g* in Spanish *luego*: a weak (g) made with voiced friction.

Length

The symbol ː denotes length and is shown together with certain vowel symbols when the vowels are typically long.

Pronunciation Key

Stress

Three grades of stress are shown in the transcriptions by the presence or absence of marks placed immediately *before* the affected syllable. Primary or strong stress is shown by ˈ, while secondary or weak stress is shown by ˌ. Unstressed syllables are not marked. In *photographic* (ˌfəʊtəˈɡræfɪk), for example, the first syllable carries secondary stress and the third primary stress, while the second and fourth are unstressed.

Notes

(i) Though words like *castle, path, fast* are shown as pronounced with an /ɑː/ sound, many speakers use an /æ/. Such variations are acceptable and are to be assumed by the reader.

(ii) The letter "r" in some positions is not sounded in the speech of Southern England and elsewhere. However, many speakers in other areas do sound the "r" in such positions with varying degrees of distinctness. Again, such variations are to be assumed, and in such words as *fern, fear, arm* the reader will sound or not sound the "r" according to his speech habits.

(iii) Though the widely received pronunciation of words like *which, why* is with a simple /w/ sound and is so shown in the dictionary, many speakers in Scotland and elsewhere, preserve an aspirated sound: /hw/. Once again this variation is to be assumed.

The Pronunciation of British English

by A. C. Gimson

Reprinted from Collins English Dictionary

The Origins

English has been spoken in Britain for some fourteen centuries. During this time, it has undergone such fundamental changes (affecting grammar, vocabulary, and pronunciation) that the speech of an inhabitant of the London region of the 7th century would be totally unintelligible to the modern Londoner. The earliest form of English, brought by Germanic invaders from the 5th century onwards, is known as *Old English* and extends up to about the 11th century. This general term itself embraces a number of separate dialects deriving from the different geographical origins of the invaders. It was the West-Saxon form of the South and the Southwest of the country that ultimately became regarded as a standard language, and it is in this form that most of the extant texts are written. From about the 7th century, Old English began to be written with the Latin alphabet, probably introduced into England by Irish missionaries. The Latin alphabet was, however, inadequate to express the more complex phonological system of the dialects of Old English. New letters, such as "æ", were added to indicate a value between that of Italian *e* and *a*; digraphs, such as "th", had to be used for consonant sounds that were unknown in Italian. Although there was a good deal of agreement about the orthography to be applied to the Old English sound system, there are in the texts of the period considerable variations in spelling forms as between one dialect and another and also between scribes. In fact, English has had a standardized form of spelling for not much more than two hundred years, the present apparent inconsistencies in our orthography reflecting the historical development of the language.

It can be said that the next major influence on our language — that of the French dominance from the 11th century onwards — affected spelling more than pronunciation (although it added enormously to our stock of words). During this period of *Middle English* (roughly 1100—1450), English remained the language of the people, but French was used by the aristocracy as well as in administrative and legal proceedings. It was not until the end of this era that English became re-established as the language used by all sections of society. By then, various French spelling forms had been taken over, e.g. *u* was replaced by *ou* in a word like *house* because of the different value attributed to *u* in French borrowings; and the *ch* sound of a word like *chin* (originally spelt with *c*) took on the French spelling of words such as *chamber*. By the time of Chaucer, the language began to look more like modern English and would be to a large extent intelligible to the modern ear.

In the following period, *Early Modern English* (1450—1600), the pronunciation of the language became increasingly similar to that of today. A modern Londoner would have little difficulty in understanding the speech used in the plays performed at Shakespeare's *Globe*, although it would make a somewhat rustic impression on his ear. Nevertheless, he would notice that there was still considerable variation in the spelling forms used, to some extent in printed works (where the styles depended upon the conventions adopted by individual printers) but more particularly in the handwritten letters of individuals (who continued to spell largely according to their own phonetic principles and thus provided us with a good deal of information about contemporary pronunciation). It is not until the end of the 18th century that English began to sound more completely like the language we speak today. What is more, with the appearance of the great dictionaries of that century, the orthography was standardized into a form almost identical with our present one. However, even in the last two centuries, there have been notable pronunciation changes, which demonstrate that the sound system of the language is constantly undergoing evolution. The ambiguities of spelling that reflect fourteen centuries of linguistic history remain to puzzle the native user and to frustrate the foreign learner.

The Present Situation

With so many influences at work on the language for so long, it is hardly surprising that the pronunciation of English in Britain today presents an extremely complex picture. It is possible to discern three main causes for variation, relating to the speaker's regional origin, his place in society, and his generation.

Elements of regional differences of pronunciation are evident today, to such an extent that a Cockney and a Glasgwegian may still have serious difficulties of communication in speech. Englishmen are still readily able to identify the part of the country from which a person comes simply by listening to his speech, despite the fears of those who predict that dialect forms will soon disappear completely. Indeed, these regional forms of speech are often related to gross statements of regional prejudice — the Southerner who regards the speech of the Northerner as overblunt, and the Northerner who characterizes the speaker with a Southern accent as affected. Dialect differences of pronunciation are therefore still important both for reasons of intelligibility and also in social terms. It is worth remarking too that, of all the various accents of British English, that of the London region has developed most rapidly, the speech of the other regions remaining closer to the historical origins of the language.

But the pronunciation of English in Britain has also a more purely social significance. As has been stated, at one time the upper classes would speak French whereas the rest of the people spoke English. In more recent centuries, when English was in universal use, there emerged different types of pronunciation in any region relating to the speaker's position in society, e.g. the popular speech forms of the working man, full of the historical characteristics of the region, as opposed to the pronunciation used by the professional and upper classes, which was modified towards a general standard. It can be said that the notion of a socially prestigious standard of pronunciation arose explicitly in the 16th century, when grammarians began to recommend that the only acceptable form of pronunciation was that used in London and at the Court, i.e. the speech of educated people in the Southeast of England. Such a notion of standard pronunciation, based on social criteria, became increasingly accepted during the next three centuries, so that in the middle of the 19th century the philologist Alexander J. Ellis was able to characterize it as "received pronunciation" — a term which is used to this day (often in an abbreviated form as RP). A century ago, persons of the ruling classes would pronounce English in the same way wherever they lived in Britain. This form of pronunciation had the advantage, therefore, of being widely intelligible. Moreover, it was important for the ambitious, who might wish to move upwards in society, to change their pronunciation. This was the sociolinguistic climate in which Bernard Shaw wrote his *Pygmalion*, a play which had a greater social significance at the time of its first production than it can possibly have now. In the first half of this century, this standard was adopted as a model by more and more of the population, despite vigorous opposition from a number of interests, notably the Poet Laureate, Robert Bridges, and his Society for Pure English, who advocated a standard based on a more Northern type. It was on the grounds of wide intelligibility that, in the 1930s, the B.B.C. decided to adopt "received pronunciation" as the form to be used by announcers. Indeed, the British public became so accustomed to this style of speech that they were suspicious of any attempt by the B.B.C. to introduce news readers with a regional pronunciation. Moreover, the broadcasting media exposed more and more of the population to the Southern-based standard, with the result that a greater number of people began to use it, at least in a modified form.

Within the last twenty-five years, however, a considerable change of attitude seems to have taken place. The social divisions in the country have become noticeably less rigid, and the movement between classes has become easier. In particular, the young tend to reject the former "received" pronunciation as the voice of outmoded authority, preferring new speech styles related to their own culture, such as the popular speech of London and Liverpool, as well as non-British accents such as those of America and Australia. It is too early to say whether this reaction by the young will have lasting consequences for the line of development of the traditional standard. But it is already clear that it is no longer possible to define the standard form as simply the variety of speech used by a particular section of society, since in a diluted form its use is more widespread than was the case even fifty years ago. It is no longer thought of as the "best" pronunciation, but as one which has advantages on account of its wide intelligibility; it is for this reason that it remains the form taught to foreign learners, although it is not the simplest system for them to acquire. It continues to have as its basis the speech of the London region, but, being no longer socially determined, must rely for definition on phonetic and phonological criteria. In the remarks on the sound system given below, 20 vowels and 24 consonants are listed. In addition, certain characteristics of usage identify the accent, e.g. different vowels are used in *cat* and *calm*; the vowels of *cot* and *caught* are distinguished; the vowel of *book* is the same as that in *good* rather than that in *food*; an *r* is not pronounced in words like *farm*, despite the spelling, nor is the final *g* sounded in *sing*, etc. Other characteristics are of a more phonetic kind, i.e. are concerned with the quality of the sounds, e.g. the vowels of *day* and *go* are clearly diphthongal, though the more open onset typical of Cockney is excluded; the two *l* sounds of *little* have different qualities, the first being "clear" and the second "dark", thus excluding some Scottish accents where both are "dark" and some Irish accents where both tend to be "clear", etc.

Nevertheless, even when a theoretical basis for the standard has been decided upon, account has to be taken of changes in pronunciation, especially in respect of vowels, reflected in the speech of different generations. Thus, older speakers (and those with conservative attitudes to life) use the vowel of *saw* in words like *off*, *cloth* and *cross*, rather than that of *hot*, which is of almost universal currency amongst the younger generation. Consonantal change is typified by the treatment of words beginning with *wh-*, such as *where*, *which* as opposed to *wear*, *witch*.

The distinction between such pairs began to be lost, on a large scale, in the London region as early as the 18th century. Today, it may be regarded as an optional extra to the system (often advocated by elocutionists) but almost totally abandoned by the young. The pronunciation shown in this dictionary represents the form used by the middle generations, avoiding the archaisms of the old and the possibly ephemeral eccentricities of the young.

It will be clear from what has been said that there remains a great diversity in the pronunciation of English in Britain, reflecting differences of region, social class, and generation. It is possible that modern facility of communication, in all its senses, is levelling out some of the extreme forms of pronunciation which even a century ago led to lack of intelligibility. But complete standardization is unlikely to be achieved. However far we proceed along the road to a standard pronunciation, there will always remain slight differences as between one individual and another, and between the various speech styles which an individual will use in different situations.

The Sound System

The infinite number of sounds produced in speaking a language can be reduced for linguistic purposes to a finite set of distinctive terms known as *phonemes*. Thus, the meaningful oppositions illustrated by the English series *seat*, *sit*, *set*, *sat*, etc., demonstrate the operation of vowel phonemes; similarly, *pin*, *tin*, *kin*, *bin*, *fin*, etc., exemplify the distinctive use of consonant phonemes. The realization of a phoneme may differ considerably according to its situation, e.g. the /p/ of *pin* is different from the /p/ of *nip*; the sound of /l/ in *leaf* differs from that in *feel*. But these differences of phonetic quality, of which the speaker is usually unaware, do not distinguish meaning. A phoneme may therefore be regarded as the smallest linguistic unit that can bring about a change of meaning. It should be noted, however, that English tolerates a certain degree of variability in the incidence of phonemes in particular words, even within the standard pronunciation, e.g. the short or long vowel in *room*. This dictionary recommends the form that has the most extensive current usage and is most widely understood. It is not a form which is intrinsically "better" than any other nor can it be thought of as synonymous with "educated": many highly educated people speak in a way that is easily identifiable as regional, e.g. with a type of Scottish, Northern, Southwestern, or even Cockney English.

(a) Vowels

The standard Southern English form of pronunciation operates with 20 basic vowel phonemes:

5 long vowels /iː/ *feed*, /uː/ *food*, /ɑː/ *calm*, /ɔː/ *saw*, /ɜː/ *bird* (where : indicates length)

7 short vowels: /ɪ/ *bit*, /ɛ/ *bet*, /æ/ *bat*, /ʌ/ *bud*, /ɒ/ *hot*, /ʊ/ *foot*; and the unstressed vowel /ə/ as in the first syllable of *above*

8 diphthongs: /eɪ/ *late*, /aɪ/ *five*, /ɔɪ/ *boy*, /əʊ/ *home*, /aʊ/ *house*, /ɪə/ *dear*, /ɛə/ *fair*, /ʊə/ *poor*

Notes:

(i) The length of so-called long vowels and diphthongs varies considerably. Thus, the /iː/ sound of *seat* is very much shorter than those in *seed* and *sea*; the diphthong in *plate* is shorter than those in *played* or *play*. In such cases, the duration of the vowel is a prime cue in distinguishing between a pair like *seat* and *seed* – more important than the final consonants. The actual length of long vowels and diphthongs is conditioned by the type of syllable closure involved:

when a "voiceless" consonant (e.g. /s/ or /t/) closes the syllable, the long vowel or diphthong is much shorter than when it is followed by a "voiced" consonant (e.g. /z/ or /d/) or when it is in an open syllable (e.g. in *see*). The result is that, in fact, the shortened "long" /iː/ of *seat* may be no longer than the short /ɪ/ of *sit*.

(ii) The vowels /iː, ɪ, uː, ʊ/ are traditionally paired as long and short. However, the difference of quality between /iː/ and /ɪ/ and between /uː/ and /ʊ/ is more important than that of length. In an opposition such as *bead – bid*, both length and quality operate as distinctive features; but, as was noted above, *seat* and *sit* exhibit an opposition which relies entirely upon a quality difference. In this dictionary, the notations /iː/-/ɪ/ and /uː/-/ʊ/ indicate the quality distinction by means of different symbols.

(iii) /ɪ/ frequently occurs in unstressed syllables, e.g. in *pocket, waited, savage*, etc. However, there is a tendency for the traditional /ɪ/ to be replaced by /ə/ in many cases, e.g. in words like *hopeless, goodness, secret*, etc. This use of /ə/, characteristic of regional forms of English, is extended by some even to cases like *boxers* v. *boxes*, where a meaningful opposition is lost. In this dictionary, the use of /ɪ/ in such cases, typical of the middle generations of English speakers, is retained.

(iv) Considerable variation between the use of /juː/ and /uː/ is found in words like *lurid, revolution*, and *suit*. The /j/-less form, which is increasingly common in such cases, is the first form given in this dictionary.

(v) Similarly, it is possible to use /æ/ or /ɑː/ in the prefix *trans-* (e.g. *translation*) or the suffix *-graph* (e.g. *telegraph*). The most common forms, shown in the dictionary, are /æ/ for the prefix and /ɑː/ for the suffix.

(vi) The old-fashioned /ɔː/ in words like *off, cloth, cross*, is abandoned in favour of /ɒ/.

(vii) Since the distinction between *pour* and *paw* is now rarely made, /ɔː/ is shown in both.

(viii) The sequences /aɪə, aʊə/ as in *tyre, tower* have, for at least a century, been reduced to /aə/ or /ɑː/, so that for many speakers the opposition is lost. Since this merger is by no means completely established in the language, the full forms /aɪə, aʊə/ are retained.

(ix) Certain monosyllables, having a grammatical function, e.g. *and, was, for*, have different pronunciations according to whether or not they carry stress, e.g. stressed /ænd, wɒz, fɔː/, unstressed /ən(d), wəz, fə/. The citation (stressed) form is given first in the dictionary, although in normal discourse the weaker form has a much higher frequency of occurrence.

(b) Consonants

There are 24 consonant phonemes:

/p/ *pin*, /t/ *tin*, /k/ *kin*
/b/ *bay*, /d/ *day*, /g/ *gay*
/tʃ/ *choke*, /dʒ/ *joke*
/m/ *some*, /n/ *sun*, /ŋ/ *sung*
/r/ *red*, /l/ *led*
/f/ *fine*, /v/ *vine*, /θ/ *thing*, /ð/ *this*
/s/ *seal*, /z/ *zeal*, /ʃ/ *shoe*, /ʒ/ *measure*, /h/ *hat*
/w/ *wet*, /j/ *yet*

Notes:

(i) Some consonant phonemes have a restricted distribution, e.g. /ŋ/ occurs only in syllable-final positions; /ʒ/ occurs typically only in medial positions. In the case of words borrowed comparatively recently from French, such as *prestige, beige, camouflage*, both /ʒ/ and /dʒ/ are possible, the more common form being given in the dictionary.

(ii) Words ending in *r*, e.g. *father, far*, have no /r/ in the pronunciation when a consonant or a pause follows. However, it is normal for a "linking" /r/ to be pronounced when a vowel follows, e.g. in *father and mother, far off*. (This usage is extended by many speakers to cases where no *r* exists in the spelling, e.g. *the idea*/r/ *of it*.)

(iii) Variant pronunciations occur in words like *issue* (/sj/ or /ʃ/), *actual* (/tj/ or /tʃ/). The commonest form is given.

(iv) /l/ and /n/, in particular, are frequently sounded as syllabic, without an accompanying vowel. Such cases are shown with raised ᵊ, e.g. *mutton* /ˈmʌtᵊn/.

(c) Stress

What is here referred to as "stress", for the sake of brevity, is in English a complex of several factors, including stress (i.e. intensity for the speaker and loudness for the listener), pitch, quality (some sounds being more prominent to the listener than others), and length. The effect of this combination of factors is to render a syllable more or less prominent amongst its neighbours. The situation of the stressed syllable has always been an important feature of English pronunciation both in the word and in connected speech. Indeed, there are some pairs of words that are distinguished entirely or mainly by the placing of the stress-accent, e.g. *insult* (*vb.*) v. *insult* (*n.*), *object* (*vb.*) v. *object* (*n.*). In short words, there is usually only one stress-accent, e.g. *over* and *above*. This is shown by placing ˈ before the stressed syllable, e.g. /ˈəʊvə/ and /əˈbʌv/. However, in addition to this type of primary (tonic) stress, there may occur secondary stresses, e.g. *consideration*, where the secondary stress on *-sid-* is shown by ˌ before the syllable, e.g. /kənˌsɪdəˈreɪʃən/.

The stress patterns given in the dictionary will always be those of the isolate, predicative forms, although in the case of double stressed words and compounds there may be a shift of primary and secondary stressing when the word or compound is used attributively, e.g. *afternoon* (predicative) /ˌ--ˈ-/; but attributive in *afternoon tea* /ˌ---ˈ-/.

Finally, as was the case with vowels and, to a lesser extent, with consonants, word stress patterns are liable to change in time; e.g. *character* was once stressed on the second syllable, whereas now the first syllable carries the stress-accent. Today, some instability of stressing may be observed in certain words, e.g. *controversy* (ˈkɒntrəˌvɜːsɪ, kənˈtrɒvəsɪ). There are also stressing variants that are characteristic of regional forms of English, e.g. Scottish English *realize* with /-ˈ-/ rather than the Southern /ˈ--/. As with the sounds, the most common Southern form is given.

Selected Bibliography

G. F. Arnold, *Stress in English Words* (North Holland Publishing Co.), 1957.

A. Campbell, *Old English Grammar* (Oxford University Press), 1959.

E. J. Dobson, *English Pronunciation 1500–1700* (Oxford University Press), 1957.

A. C. Gimson, *An Introduction to the Pronunciation of English* (Edward Arnold), 3rd edition 1980.

D. Jones, *The Pronunciation of English* (Cambridge University Press), 4th edition 1956.

D. Jones, *An English Pronouncing Dictionary*, ed. A. C. Gimson (Dent), 14th edition 1977.

R. Kingdon, *Groundwork of English Stress* (Longman), 1958.

H. C. Wyld, *A History of Modern Colloquial English* (Blackwell), 3rd edition 1936.

Abbreviations and Symbols used in the Dictionary

abbrev. abbreviation
Abor. Aboriginal
adj. adjective
adv. adverb(ial)
Afrik. Afrikaans
Amerind American Indian
Anat. Anatomy
approx. approximate(ly)
Ar. Arabic
Arch. Archaic
Archaeol. Archaeology
Archit. Architecture
Astrol. Astrology
Astron. Astronomy
Austral. Australian

Biol. Biology
Bot. Botany
Brit. Britain; British

C century (e.g. C14=14th century)
°C degrees Celsius
Canad. Canadian
cap. capital
cf. compare
Chem. Chemistry
comp. comparative
conj. conjunction

Derog. Derogatory
dim. diminutive
Du. Dutch

E east(ern): (in etymologies) English
Econ. Economics
e.g. for example
esp. especially

F French
fem. feminine
foll. followed

G German
Geog. Geography
Geol. Geology
Geom. Geometry
Gk Greek
Gmc Germanic

Heb. Hebrew

i.e. that is
imit. of imitative origin
Inf. Informal
infl. influence(d)
interj. interjection
intr. intransitive
It. Italian

L Late; Latin
lit. literally
LL Late Latin

M Middle
masc. masculine
Maths. Mathematics
Med. Medicine; (in etymologies) Medieval
MHG Middle High German
Mil. Military
Mod. Modern
Myth. Mythology

N North(ern)
n. noun
Naut. Nautical
NE Northeast(ern)
NL New Latin
no. number
NW Northwest(ern)
N.Z. New Zealand

O Old
Obs. Obsolete
Offens. Offensive
OHG Old High German
ON Old Norse
orig. originally

Photog. Photography
pl. plural
Port. Portuguese
p.p. past participle
prep. preposition(al)
prob. probably
pron. pronoun
Psychol. Psychology
p.t. past tense

rel. related

S south(ern)
S. African South African
Sansk. Sanskrit
Scand. Scandinavian
Scot. Scottish; Scots
SE southeast(ern)
sing. singular
Sl. Slang
Sp. Spanish
sup. superlative
SW southwest(ern)

Theol. Theology
tr. transitive

ult. ultimately
U.S. United States

var. variant
vb. verb

W west(ern)
wt. weight

Zool. Zoology

< from
<**?** of unknown or uncertain origin
? perhaps
?< perhaps from

a *or* **A** (eɪ) *n., pl.* **a's, A's,** *or* **As. 1.** the first letter and first vowel of the English alphabet. **2.** any of several speech sounds represented by this letter, as in *take, bag,* or *calm.* **3.** Also called: **alpha.** the first in a series, esp. the highest mark. **4. from A to Z.** from start to finish.

a[1] (ə; *emphatic* eɪ) *determiner.* (*indefinite article; used before an initial consonant.* Cf. **an**[1]) **1.** used preceding a singular countable noun, not previously specified: *a dog; a great pity.* **2.** used preceding a noun or determiner of quantity: *a dozen eggs; a great many; to read a lot.* **3.** (preceded by *once, twice, several times,* etc.) each or every; per: *once a day.* **4.** a certain; one: *a Mr Jones called.* **5.** (preceded by *not*) any at all: *not a hope.* ~Cf. **the**[1].

a[2] *symbol for:* **1.** acceleration. **2.** are(s) (metric measure of area). **3.** atto-.

A *symbol for:* **1.** *Music.* **a.** the sixth note of the scale of C major. **b.** the major or minor key having this note as its tonic. **2.** a human blood type of the ABO group, containing the A antigen. **3.** (in Britain) a major arterial road. **4.** ampere(s). **5.** absolute (temperature). **6.** area. **7.** (*in combination*) atomic: *an A-bomb; an A-plant.*

Å *symbol for* angstrom unit.

a. *abbrev. for:* **1.** acre(s). **2.** Also **A.** alto.

A. *abbrev. for:* **1.** acre(s). **2.** America(n). **3.** answer.

a-[1] *or before a vowel* **an-** *prefix.* not; without; opposite to: *atonal; asocial.* [< Gk *a-, an-* 'not, without]

a-[2] *prefix.* **1.** on; in; towards: *aground; aback.* **2.** in the state of: *afloat; asleep.*

A1, A-1, *or* **A-one** (ˈeɪˈwʌn) *adj.* **1.** physically fit. **2.** *Inf.* first class; excellent. **3.** (of a vessel) in first-class condition.

A4 *n.* a standard paper size, 297 × 210 mm.

AA *abbrev. for:* **1.** Alcoholics Anonymous. **2.** anti-aircraft. **3.** (in Britain) Automobile Association.

AAA *abbrev. for:* **1.** *Brit.* Amateur Athletic Association. **2.** *U.S.* Automobile Association of America.

A & R *abbrev. for* artists and repertoire.

AAP *abbrev. for* Australian Associated Press.

aardvark (ˈɑːdˌvɑːk) *n.* a nocturnal burrowing African mammal, which has long ears and snout, and feeds on termites. Also called: **ant bear.** [C19: < obs. Afrik., < *aarde* earth + *varken* pig]

aardwolf (ˈɑːdˌwʊlf) *n., pl.* **-wolves.** a nocturnal mammal of the hyena family that inhabits the plains of southern Africa and feeds on termites and insect larvae. [C19: < Afrik., < *aarde* earth + *wolf* wolf]

Aaron's beard (ˈɛərənz) *n.* another name for **rose of Sharon.**

Aaron's rod *n.* a widespread Eurasian plant having tall erect spikes of yellow flowers.

A'asia *abbrev. for* Australasia.

AB *abbrev. for:* **1.** Also: **a.b.** able-bodied seaman. **2.** (in the U.S.) Bachelor of Arts. ~**3.** *symbol for* a human blood type of the ABO group, containing both the A antigen and the B antigen.

ab-[1] *prefix.* away from; opposite to: *abnormal.* [< L *ab* away from]

ab-[2] *prefix.* a cgs unit of measurement in the electromagnetic system: *abampere, abwatt, abvolt.* [< ABSOLUTE]

aba (ˈæbə) *n.* **1.** a type of cloth from Syria, made of goat or camel hair. **2.** a sleeveless outer garment of such cloth. [< Ar.]

abaca (ˈæbəkə) *n.* **1.** a Philippine plant, the source of Manila hemp. **2.** another name for **Manila hemp.** [via Sp. < Tagalog *abaká*]

aback (əˈbæk) *adv.* **taken aback. a.** startled or disconcerted. **b.** *Naut.* (of a vessel or sail) having the wind against the forward side so as to prevent forward motion. [OE *on bæc* to the back]

abacus (ˈæbəkəs) *n., pl.* **-ci** (-ˌsaɪ) *or* **-cuses. 1.** a counting device that consists of a frame holding rods on which a number of beads are free to move. **2.** *Archit.* the flat upper part of the capital of a column. [C16: < L, < Gk *abax* board covered with sand, < Heb. *ābhāq* dust]

Abaddon (əˈbædᵊn) *n.* **1.** the Devil (Revelation 9:11). **2.** (in rabbinical literature) Hell. [Heb.: lit., destruction]

abaft (əˈbɑːft) *Naut.* ~*adv., adj.* (*postpositive*) **1.** closer to the stern than to another place on a vessel. ~*prep.* **2.** behind; aft of. [C13: *on baft; baft* < OE *beæftan,* < *be* by + *æftan* behind]

abalone (ˌæbəˈləʊnɪ) *n.* an edible marine mollusc having an ear-shaped shell perforated with a row of respiratory holes and lined with mother-of-pearl. Also called: **ear shell.** [C19: < American Sp. *abulón*]

abandon (əˈbændən) *vb.* (*tr.*) **1.** to forsake completely; desert; leave behind. **2.** to give up completely: *to abandon hope.* **3.** to give up (something begun) before completion: *the game was abandoned.* **4.** to surrender (oneself) to emotion without restraint. **5.** to give (insured property that has suffered partial loss or damage) to the insurers in order that a claim for a total loss may be made. ~*n.* **6.** freedom from inhibitions, restraint, or worry: *she danced with abandon.* [C14: *abandounen* (vb.), < OF, < *a bandon* under one's control, < *a* at, to + *bandon* control] —**aˈbandonment** *n.*

abandoned (əˈbændənd) *adj.* **1.** deserted: *an abandoned windmill.* **2.** forsaken: *an abandoned child.* **3.** uninhibited.

abase (əˈbeɪs) *vb.* (*tr.*) **1.** to humble or belittle (oneself, etc.). **2.** to lower or reduce, as in rank. [C15 *abessen,* < OF *abaissier* to make low. See BASE[2]] —**aˈbasement** *n.*

abash (əˈbæʃ) *vb.* (*tr.; usually passive*) to cause to feel ill at ease, embarrassed, or confused. [C14: < OF *esbair* to be astonished, < *es-* out + *bair* to gape] —**aˈbashed** *adj.*

abate (əˈbeɪt) *vb.* **1.** to make or become less in amount, intensity, degree, etc. **2.** (*tr.*) *Law.* **a.** to suppress or terminate (a nuisance). **b.** to suspend or extinguish (a claim or action). **c.** to annul (a writ). **3.** (*intr.*) *Law.* (of a writ, etc.) to become null and void. [C14: < OF *abatre* to beat down] —**aˈbatement** *n.*

abatis *or* **abattis** (ˈæbətɪs) *n.* **1.** a rampart of felled trees with their branches outwards. **2.** a barbed-wire entanglement before a position. [C18: < F, < *abattre* to fell]

abattoir (ˈæbəˌtwɑː) *n.* another name for **slaughterhouse.** [C19: F, < *abattre* to fell]

abbacy (ˈæbəsɪ) *n., pl.* **-cies.** the office, term of office, or jurisdiction of an abbot or abbess. [C15: < Church L *abbātia,* < *abbāt-* ABBOT]

abbatial (əˈbeɪʃəl) *adj.* of an abbot, abbess, or abbey. [C17: < Church L *abbātiālis,* < *abbāt-* ABBOT]

abbé (ˈæbeɪ) *n.* **1.** a French abbot. **2.** a title used in addressing any other French cleric, such as a priest.

abbess (ˈæbɪs) *n.* the female superior of a convent. [C13: < OF, < Church L *abbātissa*]

Abbevillian (æbˈvɪlɪən) *Archaeol.* ~*n.* **1.** the period represented by Lower Palaeolithic European sites containing the earliest hand axes. ~*adj.* **2.** of this period. [C20: after *Abbeville,* France, where the stone tools were discovered]

abbey (ˈæbɪ) *n.* **1.** a building inhabited by a community of monks or nuns. **2.** a church built in conjunction with such a building. **3.** a community of monks or nuns. [C13: via OF *abeie* < Church L *abbātia* ABBACY]

abbot (ˈæbət) *n.* the superior of an abbey of monks. [OE *abbod,* < Church L *abbāt-* (stem of *abbas*), ult. < Aramaic *abbā* father] —**ˈabbotˌship** *or* **ˈabbotcy** *n.*

abbreviate (əˈbriːvɪˌeɪt) *vb.* (*tr.*) **1.** to shorten (a word or phrase) by contraction or omission of some letters or words. **2.** to cut short; curtail. [C15: < p.p. of LL *abbreviāre*, < L *brevis* brief]

abbreviation (əˌbriːvɪˈeɪʃən) *n.* **1.** a shortened or contracted form of a word or phrase. **2.** the process or result of abbreviating.

ABC[1] *n.* **1.** (*pl. in U.S.*) the rudiments of a subject. **2.** an alphabetical guide. **3.** (*often pl. in U.S.*) the alphabet.

ABC[2] *abbrev. for:* **1.** Australian Broadcasting Corporation. **2.** American Broadcasting Company.

abdicate (ˈæbdɪˌkeɪt) *vb.* to renounce (a throne, rights, etc.), esp. formally. [C16: < L *abdicāre* to disclaim] —ˌ**abdiˈcation** *n.* —ˈ**abdiˌcator** *n.*

abdomen (ˈæbdəmən) *n.* **1.** the region of the body of a vertebrate that contains the viscera other than the heart and lungs. **2.** the front or surface of this region; belly. **3.** (in arthropods) the posterior part of the body behind the thorax. [C16: < L; <?] —**abdominal** (æbˈdɒmɪnᵊl) *adj.*

abduct (æbˈdʌkt) *vb.* (*tr.*) **1.** to remove (a person) by force or cunning; kidnap. **2.** (of certain muscles) to pull away (a leg, arm, etc.) from the median axis of the body. [C19: < L *abdūcere* to lead away] —**abˈduction** *n.* —**abˈductor** *n.*

abeam (əˈbiːm) *adv., adj.* (*postpositive*) at right angles to the length of a vessel or aircraft. [C19: A-[2] + BEAM]

abed (əˈbɛd) *adv. Arch.* in bed.

Aberdeen Angus (ˈæbədiːn ˈæŋgəs) *n.* a black hornless breed of beef cattle originating in Scotland. [< *Aberdeen*, former Scot. county]

aberrant (æˈbɛrənt) *adj.* **1.** deviating from the normal or usual type. **2.** behaving in an abnormal or untypical way. **3.** deviating from morality. [rare before C19: < L *aberrāre* to wander away] —**abˈerrance** *or* **abˈerrancy** *n.*

aberration (ˌæbəˈreɪʃən) *n.* **1.** deviation from what is normal, expected, or usual. **2.** departure from truth, morality, etc. **3.** a lapse in control of one's mental faculties. **4.** *Optics.* a defect in a lens or mirror that causes either a distorted image or one with coloured fringes. **5.** *Astron.* the apparent displacement of a celestial body due to the motion of the observer with the earth.

abet (əˈbɛt) *vb.* **abetting, abetted.** (*tr.*) to assist or encourage, esp. in wrongdoing. [C14: < OF *abeter* to lure on, < *beter* to bait] —**aˈbetment** *n.* —**aˈbetter** *or* (*esp. Law*) **aˈbettor** *n.*

abeyance (əˈbeɪəns) *n.* **1.** (usually preceded by *in* or *into*) a state of being suspended or put aside temporarily. **2.** (usually preceded by *in*) *Law.* an indeterminate state of ownership. [C16–17: < Anglo-F, < OF *abeance* expectation, lit. a gaping after]

abhor (əbˈhɔː) *vb.* **-horring, -horred.** (*tr.*) to detest vehemently; find repugnant. [C15: < L *abhorrēre*, < *ab-* away from + *horrēre* to shudder] —**abˈhorrer** *n.*

abhorrence (əbˈhɒrəns) *n.* **1.** a feeling of extreme loathing or aversion. **2.** a person or thing that is loathsome.

abhorrent (əbˈhɒrənt) *adj.* **1.** repugnant; loathsome. **2.** (when *postpositive*, foll. by *of*) feeling extreme aversion (for): *abhorrent of vulgarity.* **3.** (usually *postpositive* and foll. by *to*) conflicting (with): *abhorrent to common sense.*

abide (əˈbaɪd) *vb.* **abiding, abode** *or* **abided. 1.** (*tr.*) to tolerate; put up with. **2.** (*tr.*) to accept or submit to. **3.** (*intr.*; foll. by *by*) **a.** to comply (with): *to abide by the decision.* **b.** to remain faithful (to): *to abide by your promise.* **4.** (*intr.*) to remain or continue. **5.** (*intr.*) *Arch.* to dwell. **6.** (*tr.*) *Arch.* to await in expectation. [OE *ābīdan*, < a- (intensive) + *bīdan* to wait] —**aˈbider** *n.*

abiding (əˈbaɪdɪŋ) *adj.* permanent; enduring: *an abiding belief.*

ability (əˈbɪlɪtɪ) *n., pl.* **-ties. 1.** possession of necessary skill, competence, or power. **2.** considerable proficiency; natural capability: *a man of ability.* **3.** (*pl.*) special talents. [C14: < OF < L *habilitās* aptitude, < *habilis* ABLE]

ab initio *Latin.* (æb ɪˈnɪʃɪˌəʊ) from the start.

abiogenesis (ˌeɪbaɪəʊˈdʒɛnɪsɪs) *n.* the hypothetical process by which living organisms arise from inanimate matter. Also called: **spontaneous generation.** [C19: NL, < A-[1] + BIO- + GENESIS]

abject (ˈæbdʒɛkt) *adj.* **1.** utterly wretched or hopeless. **2.** forlorn; dejected. **3.** submissive: *an abject apology.* **4.** contemptible; despicable: *an abject liar.* [C14 (in the sense: rejected, cast out): < L *abjectus* thrown away, < *abjicere*, < *ab-* away + *jacere* to throw] —**abˈjection** *n.* —ˈ**abjectly** *adv.* —ˈ**abjectness** *n.*

abjure (əbˈdʒʊə) *vb.* (*tr.*) **1.** to renounce or retract, esp. formally or under oath. **2.** to abstain from. [C15: < OF *abjurer* or L *abjurāre* to deny on oath] —ˌ**abjuˈration** *n.* —**abˈjurer** *n.*

ablation (æbˈleɪʃən) *n.* **1.** the surgical removal of an organ, structure, or part. **2.** the melting or wearing away of a part, such as the heat shield of a space re-entry vehicle on passing through the earth's atmosphere. **3.** the wearing away of a rock or glacier. [C15: < LL *ablatiōn-*, < L *auferre* to carry away] —**ablate** (æbˈleɪt) *vb.*

ablative (ˈæblətɪv) *Grammar.* ~*adj.* **1.** (in certain inflected languages such as Latin) denoting a case of nouns, pronouns, and adjectives indicating the agent, or the instrument, manner, or place of the action. ~*n.* **2.** the ablative case or a speech element in it.

ablaut (ˈæblaʊt) *n. Linguistics.* vowel gradation, esp. in Indo-European languages. See **gradation** (sense 5). [G, coined 1819 by Jakob Grimm < *ab* off + *Laut* sound]

ablaze (əˈbleɪz) *adj.* (*postpositive*), *adv.* **1.** on fire; burning. **2.** brightly illuminated. **3.** emotionally aroused.

able (ˈeɪbᵊl) *adj.* **1.** (*postpositive*) having the necessary power, resources, skill, opportunity, etc., to do something. **2.** capable; talented. **3.** *Law.* competent or authorized. [C14: ult. < L *habilis* easy to hold, manageable, < *habēre* to have + *-ilis* -ILE]

-able *suffix forming adjectives.* **1.** capable of or deserving of (being acted upon as indicated): *enjoyable; washable.* **2.** inclined to; able to; causing: *comfortable; variable.* [via OF < L *-ābilis, -ībilis*, forms of *-bilis*, adjectival suffix] —**-ably** *suffix forming adverbs.* —**-ability** *suffix forming nouns.*

able-bodied *adj.* physically strong and healthy; robust.

able-bodied seaman *n.* a seaman, esp. one in the merchant navy, who has been trained in certain skills. Also: **able seaman.** Abbrev.: **AB, a.b.**

able rating *n.* (esp. in the Royal Navy) a rating who is qualified to perform certain duties of seamanship.

abloom (əˈbluːm) *adj.* (*postpositive*) in flower; blooming.

ablution (əˈbluːʃən) *n.* **1.** the ritual washing of a priest's hands or of sacred vessels. **2.** (*often pl.*) the act of washing: *perform one's ablutions.* **3.** (*pl.*) *Mil. inf.* a washing place. [C14: ult. < L *ablūere* to wash away] —**abˈlutionary** *adj.*

ably (ˈeɪblɪ) *adv.* in a competent or skilful manner.

ABM *abbrev. for* antiballistic missile.

abnegate (ˈæbnɪˌgeɪt) *vb.* (*tr.*) to deny to oneself; renounce. [C17: < L *abnegāre* to deny] —ˌ**abneˈgation** *n.* —ˈ**abneˌgator** *n.*

abnormal (æbˈnɔːməl) *adj.* **1.** not normal; deviating from the usual or typical. **2.** concerned with abnormal behaviour: *abnormal psychology.* **3.** *Inf.* odd; strange. [C19: AB-[1] + NORMAL, replacing earlier *anormal* < Med. L *anormalus*, a blend of LL *anōmalus* ANOMALOUS + L *abnormis* departing from a rule] —**abˈnormally** *adv.*

abnormality (ˌæbnɔːˈmælɪtɪ) *n., pl.* **-ties. 1.** an abnormal feature, event, etc. **2.** a physical malformation. **3.** deviation from the usual.

Abo (ˈæbəʊ) *n., pl.* **Abos.** (*sometimes not cap.*) *Austral. inf., often derog.* short for **Aborigine** (sense 1).

aboard (əˈbɔːd) *adv., adj. (postpositive), prep.* **1.** on, in, onto, or into (a ship, train, etc.). **2.** *Naut.* alongside. **3. all aboard!** a warning to passengers to board a vehicle, ship, etc.

abode[1] (əˈbəʊd) *n.* a place in which one lives; one's home. [C17: n. formed from ABIDE]

abode[2] (əˈbəʊd) *vb.* a past tense and past participle of **abide.**

abolish (əˈbɒlɪʃ) *vb. (tr.)* to do away with (laws, regulations, customs, etc.). [C15: < OF, ult. < L *abolēre* to destroy] —**aˈbolishable** *adj.* —**aˈbolisher** *n.* —**aˈbolishment** *n.*

abolition (ˌæbəˈlɪʃən) *n.* **1.** the act of abolishing or the state of being abolished; annulment. **2.** (*often cap.*) (in British territories) the ending of the slave trade (1807) or of slavery (1833). **3.** (*often cap.*) (in the U.S.) the emancipation of slaves, by the Emancipation Proclamation (1863, ratified 1865). [C16: < L *abolitio,* < *abolēre* to destroy] —ˌ**aboˈlitionary** *adj.* —ˌ**aboˈlitionism** *n.* —ˌ**aboˈlitionist** *n., adj.*

abomasum (ˌæbəˈmeɪsəm) *n.* the fourth and last compartment of the stomach of ruminants. [C18: NL, < AB-[1] + *omāsum* bullock's tripe]

A-bomb *n.* short for **atom bomb.**

abominable (əˈbɒmɪnəbᵊl) *adj.* **1.** offensive; loathsome; detestable. **2.** *Inf.* very bad or inferior: *abominable workmanship.* [C14: < L, < *abōminārī* to ABOMINATE] —**aˈbominably** *adv.*

abominable snowman *n.* a large manlike or apelike creature alleged to inhabit the Himalayas. Also called: **yeti.** [translation of Tibetan *metohkangmi,* < *metoh* foul + *kangmi* snowman]

abominate (əˈbɒmɪˌneɪt) *vb. (tr.)* to dislike intensely; detest. [C17: < L *abōminārī* to regard as an ill omen, < *ab-* away from + *ōmin-,* < OMEN] —**aˈbomiˌnator** *n.*

abomination (əˌbɒmɪˈneɪʃən) *n.* **1.** a person or thing that is disgusting or loathsome. **2.** an action that is vicious, vile, etc. **3.** intense loathing or disgust.

aboriginal (ˌæbəˈrɪdʒɪnᵊl) *adj.* existing in a place from the earliest known period; indigenous. —ˌ**aboˈriginally** *adv.*

Aboriginal (ˌæbəˈrɪdʒɪnᵊl) *adj.* **1.** of, relating to, or characteristic of the Aborigines of Australia. ~*n.* **2.** another word for **Aborigine** (sense 1).

aborigine (ˌæbəˈrɪdʒɪnɪ) *n.* an original inhabitant of a country or region. [C16: back formation from *aborigines,* < L: inhabitants of Latium in pre-Roman times, associated in folk etymology with *ab origine* from the beginning]

Aborigine (ˌæbəˈrɪdʒɪnɪ) *n.* **1.** Also called: **native Australian.** a member of a dark-skinned hunting and gathering people who were living in Australia when European settlers arrived. Often shortened to **Abo. 2.** any of the languages of this people.

abort (əˈbɔːt) *vb.* **1.** to undergo or cause (a woman) to undergo the termination of pregnancy before the fetus is viable. **2.** (*tr.*) to cause (a fetus) to be expelled from the womb before it is viable. **3.** (*intr.*) to fail to come to completion. **4.** (*tr.*) to interrupt the development of. **5.** (*intr.*) to give birth to a dead or nonviable fetus. **6.** (of a space flight or other undertaking) to fail or terminate prematurely. **7.** (*intr.*) (of an organism or part of an organism) to fail to develop into the mature form. ~*n.* **8.** the premature termination or failure of (a space flight, etc.) [C16: < L *abortāre,* < *aborīrī* to miscarry, < *ab-* wrongly + *orīrī* to be born]

abortifacient (əˌbɔːtɪˈfeɪʃənt) *adj.* **1.** causing abortion. ~*n.* **2.** a drug or agent that causes abortion.

abortion (əˈbɔːʃən) *n.* **1.** an operation or other procedure to terminate pregnancy before the fetus is viable. **2.** the premature termination of pregnancy by spontaneous or induced expulsion of a nonviable fetus from the uterus. **3.** an aborted fetus. **4.** a failure to develop to completion or maturity. **5.** a person or thing that is deformed.

abortionist (əˈbɔːʃənɪst) *n.* a person who performs abortions, esp. illegally.

abortive (əˈbɔːtɪv) *adj.* **1.** failing to achieve a purpose; fruitless. **2.** (of organisms) imperfectly developed. **3.** causing abortion.

ABO system *n.* a system for classifying human blood on the basis of the presence or absence of two antigens in the red cells: there are four such blood types (A, B, AB, and O).

aboulia (əˈbuːlɪə, -ˈbjuː-) *n.* a variant spelling of **abulia.**

abound (əˈbaʊnd) *vb. (intr.)* **1.** to exist or occur in abundance. **2.** (foll. by *with* or *in*) to be plentifully supplied (with): *the fields abound in corn.* [C14: via OF < L *abundāre* to overflow, < *undāre* to flow, < *unda* wave]

about (əˈbaʊt) *prep.* **1.** relating to; concerning. **2.** near or close to. **3.** carried on: *I haven't any money about me.* **4.** on every side of. **5.** active in or engaged in. ~*adv.* **6.** near in number, time, degree, etc.: *about 50 years old.* **7.** nearby. **8.** here and there: *walk about to keep warm.* **9.** all around; on every side. **10.** in or to the opposite direction. **11.** in rotation or revolution: *turn and turn about.* **12.** used in informal phrases to indicate understatement: *it's about time you stopped.* **13.** *Arch.* around. **14. about to. a.** on the point of; intending to: *she was about to jump.* **b.** (*with a negative*) determined not to: *nobody is about to miss it.* ~*adj.* **15.** (*predicative*) active; astir after sleep: *up and about.* **16.** (*predicative*) in existence, current, or in circulation: *there aren't many about nowadays.* [OE *abūtan, onbūtan,* < ON + *būtan* outside]

about turn *or U.S.* **about face** *sentence substitute.* **1.** a military command to a formation of men to reverse the direction in which they are facing. ~*n.* **about-turn** *or U.S.* **about-face. 2.** a complete change of opinion, direction, etc. ~*vb.* **about-turn** *or U.S.* **about-face. 3.** (*intr.*) to perform an about-turn.

above (əˈbʌv) *prep.* **1.** on top of or higher than; over. **2.** greater than in quantity or degree: *above average.* **3.** superior to or prior to: *to place honour above wealth.* **4.** too high-minded for: *above petty gossiping.* **5.** too respected for; beyond: *above suspicion.* **6.** too difficult to be understood by: *the talk was above me.* **7.** louder or higher than (other noise). **8.** in preference to. **9.** north of. **10.** upstream from. **11. above all.** most of all; especially. **12. above and beyond.** in addition to. ~*adv.* **13.** in or to a higher place: *the sky above.* **14. a.** in a previous place (in something written). **b.** (*in combination*): *the above-mentioned clause.* **15.** higher in rank or position. **16.** in or concerned with heaven. ~*n.* **17. the above.** something previously mentioned. ~*adj.* **18.** appearing in a previous place (in something written). [OE *abufan,* < *a-* on + *bufan* above]

above board *adj.* (**aboveboard** *when prenominal*), *adv.* in the open; without dishonesty, concealment, or fraud.

Abp *or* **abp** *abbrev. for* archbishop.

abracadabra (ˌæbrəkəˈdæbrə) *interj.* **1.** a spoken formula, used esp. by conjurors. ~*n.* **2.** a word used in incantations, etc., considered to possess magic powers. **3.** gibberish. [C17: magical word used in certain Gnostic writings, ? rel. to Gk *Abraxas,* a Gnostic deity]

abrade (əˈbreɪd) *vb. (tr.)* to scrape away or wear down by friction. [C17: < L *abrādere,* < AB- + *rādere* to scrape] —**aˈbrader** *n.*

abranchiate (əˈbræŋkɪɪt, -ˌeɪt) *or* **abranchial** *adj. Zool.* having no gills. [C19: A-[1] + BRANCHIATE]

abrasion (əˈbreɪʒən) *n.* **1.** the process of scraping or wearing down by friction. **2.** a scraped area or spot; graze. **3.** *Geog.* the effect of mechanical erosion of rock, esp. a river bed, by rock fragments scratching and scraping it. [C17: < Med. L *abrāsiōn-,* < L *abrādere* to ABRADE]

abrasive (əˈbreɪsɪv) *n.* **1.** a substance or material such as sandpaper, pumice, or emery, used for cleaning, smoothing, or polishing. ~*adj.* **2.** causing abrasion; rough. **3.** irritating in manner or personality.

abreaction (ˌæbrɪˈækʃən) *n. Psychoanal.* the release and expression of emotional tension associated with repressed ideas by bringing those ideas into consciousness.

abreast (əˈbrɛst) *adj.* (*postpositive*) **1.** alongside each other and facing in the same direction. **2.** (foll. by *of* or *with*) up to date (with).

abridge (əˈbrɪdʒ) *vb.* (*tr.*) **1.** to reduce the length of (a written work) by condensing. **2.** to curtail. [C14: via OF *abregier* < LL *abbreviāre* to shorten] —**aˈbridgable** *or* **aˈbridgeable** *adj.* —**aˈbridger** *n.*

abridgment *or* **abridgement** (əˈbrɪdʒmənt) *n.* **1.** a shortened version of a written work. **2.** the act of abridging or state of being abridged.

abroad (əˈbrɔːd) *adv.* **1.** to or in a foreign country or countries. ~*adj.* (*postpositive*) **2.** (of rumours, etc.) in general circulation. **3.** out in the open. **4.** over a wide area. [C13: < A-[2] + BROAD]

abrogate (ˈæbrəʊˌgeɪt) *vb.* (*tr.*) to cancel or revoke formally or officially. [C16: < L *abrogātus* repealed, < AB-[1] + *rogāre* to propose (a law)] —ˌ**abroˈgation** *n.* —ˈ**abroˌgator** *n.*

abrupt (əˈbrʌpt) *adj.* **1.** sudden; unexpected. **2.** brusque or brief in speech, manner, etc. **3.** (of a style of writing or speaking) disconnected. **4.** precipitous; steep. **5.** *Bot.* truncate. **6.** *Geol.* (of strata) cropping out suddenly. [C16: < L *abruptus* broken off, < AB-[1] + *rumpere* to break] —**abˈruptly** *adv.* —**abˈruptness** *n.*

abscess (ˈæbsɛs) *n.* **1.** a localized collection of pus formed as the product of inflammation. ~*vb.* **2.** (*intr.*) to form such a collection of pus. [C16: < L *abscessus*, < *abscēdere* to go away] —ˈ**abscessed** *adj.*

abscissa (æbˈsɪsə) *n., pl.* **-scissas** *or* **-scissae** (-ˈsɪsiː). the horizontal or *x*-coordinate of a point in a two-dimensional system of Cartesian coordinates. It is the distance from the *y*-axis measured parallel to the *x*-axis. Cf. **ordinate** (sense 1). [C17: NL, orig. *linea abscissa* a cut-off line]

abscission (æbˈsɪʒən) *n.* **1.** the separation of leaves, branches, flowers, and bark from plants. **2.** the act of cutting off. [C17: < L, < AB-[1] + *scissiō* a cleaving]

abscond (əbˈskɒnd) *vb.* (*intr.*) to run away secretly, esp. to avoid prosecution or punishment. [C16: < L *abscondere*, < *abs-* AB-[1] + *condere* to stow] —**abˈsconder** *n.*

abseil (ˈæbsaɪl) *Mountaineering.* ~*vb.* (*intr.*) **1.** to descend a steep slope or vertical drop by a rope secured from above and coiled around one's body. ~*n.* **2.** an instance or the technique of abseiling. [C20: < G *abseilen*, < *ab-* down + *Seil* rope]

absence (ˈæbsəns) *n.* **1.** the state of being away. **2.** the time during which a person or thing is away. **3.** the fact of being without something; lack. [C14: via OF < L *absentia*, < *absēns* a being away]

absent *adj.* (ˈæbsənt). **1.** away or not present. **2.** lacking. **3.** inattentive. ~*vb.* (æbˈsɛnt). **4.** (*tr.*) to remove (oneself) or keep away. [C14: < L *absent-*, < *abesse* to be away] —**abˈsenter** *n.*

absentee (ˌæbsənˈtiː) *n.* **a.** a person who is absent. **b.** (*as modifier*): *an absentee landlord.*

absenteeism (ˌæbsənˈtiːɪzəm) *n.* persistent absence from work, school, etc.

absent-minded *adj.* preoccupied; forgetful. —ˌ**absent-ˈmindedly** *adv.* —ˌ**absent-ˈmindedness** *n.*

absinthe *or* **absinth** (ˈæbsɪnθ) *n.* **1.** a potent green alcoholic drink, originally having high wormwood content. **2.** another name for **wormwood** (the plant). [C15: via F and L < Gk *apsinthion* wormwood]

absolute (ˈæbsəˌluːt) *adj.* **1.** complete; perfect. **2.** free from limitations, restrictions, or exceptions. **3.** despotic: *an absolute ruler.* **4.** undoubted; certain: *the absolute truth.* **5.** not dependent on, conditioned by, or relative to anything else; independent: *absolute humidity; absolute units.* **6.** pure; unmixed: *absolute alcohol.* **7.** (of a grammatical construction) syntactically independent of the main clause, as for example the construction *Joking apart* in the sentence *Joking apart, we'd better leave now.* **8.** *Grammar.* (of a transitive verb) used without a direct object, as the verb *intimidate* in the sentence *His intentions are good, but his rough manner tends to intimidate.* **9.** *Grammar.* (of an adjective) used as a noun, as for instance *young* and *aged* in the sentence *The young care little for the aged.* ~*n.* **10.** something that is absolute. [C14: < L *absolūtus* unconditional, < *absolvere.* See ABSOLVE]

Absolute (ˈæbsəˌluːt) *n.* (*sometimes not cap.*) *Philosophy.* **1.** the ultimate basis of reality. **2.** that which is totally unconditioned, unrestricted, pure, perfect, or complete.

absolutely (ˌæbsəˈluːtlɪ) *adv.* **1.** in an absolute manner, esp. completely or perfectly. ~*sentence substitute.* **2.** yes; certainly.

absolute magnitude *n.* the magnitude a given star would have if it were 10 parsecs (32.6 light years) from earth.

absolute majority *n.* a number of votes totalling over 50 per cent, such as the total number of votes or seats obtained by a party that beats the combined opposition.

absolute pitch *n.* **1.** Also called: **perfect pitch.** the ability to identify exactly the pitch of a note without comparing it with another. **2.** the exact pitch of a note determined by vibration per second.

absolute temperature *n.* another name for **thermodynamic temperature.**

absolute value *n.* **1.** the positive real number equal to a given real but disregarding its sign: written $|-x|$. **2.** also called: **modulus.** a measure of the magnitude of a complex number.

absolute zero *n.* the lowest temperature theoretically attainable, at which the particles constituting matter would be at rest: equivalent to −273.15°C or −459.67°F.

absolution (ˌæbsəˈluːʃən) *n.* **1.** the act of absolving or the state of being absolved; release from guilt, obligation, or punishment. **2.** *Christianity.* **a.** a formal remission of sin pronounced by a priest in the sacrament of penance. **b.** the form of words granting such a remission. [C12: < L *absolūtiōn-* acquittal, < *absolvere* to ABSOLVE]

absolutism (ˈæbsəluːˌtɪzəm) *n.* the principle or practice of a political system in which unrestricted power is vested in a monarch, dictator, etc.; despotism. —ˈ**absolutist** *n., adj.*

absolve (əbˈzɒlv) *vb.* (*tr.*) **1.** (usually foll. by *from*) to release from blame, sin, obligation, or responsibility. **2.** to pronounce not guilty. [C15: < L *absolvere*, < AB-[1] + *solvere* to make loose] —**abˈsolver** *n.*

absorb (əbˈsɔːb) *vb.* (*tr.*) **1.** to soak or suck up (liquids). **2.** to engage or occupy (the interest or time) of (someone). **3.** to receive or take in (the energy of an impact). **4.** *Physics.* to take in (all or part of incident radiated energy) and retain it. **5.** to take in or assimilate; incorporate. **6.** to pay for as part of a commercial transaction: *the distributor absorbed the cost of transport.* **7.** *Chem.* to cause to undergo a process in which one substance permeates into or is dissolved by a liquid or solid: *porous solids absorb water.* [C15: via OF < L *absorbēre*, < AB-[1] + *sorbēre* to suck] —**abˌsorbaˈbility** *n.* —**abˈsorbable** *adj.*

absorbed (əbˈsɔːbd) *adj.* engrossed; deeply interested.

absorbed dose *n.* the amount of energy transferred by radiation to a unit mass of absorbing material.

absorbent (əbˈsɔːbənt) *adj.* **1.** able to absorb. ~*n.* **2.** a substance that absorbs. —**abˈsorbency** *n.*

absorbing (əbˈsɔːbɪŋ) *adj.* occupying one's interest or attention. —**abˈsorbingly** *adv.*

absorptance (əbˈsɔːptəns) *or* **absorption factor** *n. Physics.* the ability of an object to absorb radiation, measured as the ratio of absorbed flux to incident flux. [C20: < ABSORPTION + -ANCE]

absorption (əbˈsɔːpʃən) *n.* **1.** the process of absorbing or the state of being absorbed. **2.** *Physiol.* **a.** normal assimilation by the tissues of the products of digestion. **b.** the process of taking up various fluids, drugs, etc., through the mucous membranes or skin. [C16: < L *absorptiōn-*, < *absorbēre* to ABSORB] —**ab'sorptive** *adj.*

absorption spectrum *n.* the characteristic pattern of dark lines or bands that occurs when electromagnetic radiation is passed through an absorbing medium into a spectroscope. See also **emission spectrum.**

abstain (əb'steɪn) *vb.* (*intr.;* usually foll. by *from*) **1.** to choose to refrain. **2.** to refrain from voting, esp. in a committee, legislature, etc. [C14: via OF < L *abstinēre,* < *abs-* AB-[1] + *tenēre* to hold] —**ab'stainer** *n.*

abstemious (əb'stiːmɪəs) *adj.* sparing, esp. in the consumption of alcohol or food. [C17: < L *abstēmius,* < *abs-* AB-[1] + *tēm-,* < *tēmētum* intoxicating drink] —**ab'stemiously** *adv.* —**ab'stemiousness** *n.*

abstention (əb'stɛnʃən) *n.* **1.** the act of refraining or abstaining. **2.** the act of withholding one's vote. [C16: < LL *abstentiōn;* see ABSTAIN]

abstinence ('æbstɪnəns) *n.* the act or practice of refraining from some action or from the use of something, esp. alcohol. [C13: via OF < L *abstinentia,* < *abstinēre* to ABSTAIN] —'**abstinent** *adj.*

abstract *adj.* ('æbstrækt). **1.** having no reference to material objects or specific examples. **2.** not applied or practical; theoretical. **3.** hard to understand. **4.** denoting art characterized by geometric, formalized, or otherwise nonrepresentational qualities. ~*n.* ('æbstrækt). **5.** a condensed version of a piece of writing, speech, etc.; summary. **6.** an abstract term or idea. **7.** an abstract painting, sculpture, etc. **8. in the abstract.** without reference to specific circumstances. ~*vb.* (æb'strækt). (*tr.*) **9.** to regard theoretically. **10.** to form a general idea of (something) by abstraction. **11.** ('æbstrækt). (*also intr.*) to summarize. **12.** to remove or extract. [C14 (in the sense: extracted): < L *abstractus* drawn off, < *abs-* AB-[1] + *trahere* to draw]

abstracted (æb'stræktɪd) *adj.* **1.** lost in thought; preoccupied. **2.** taken out or separated. —**ab'stractedly** *adv.*

abstract expressionism *n.* a school of painting in the 1940s that combined the spontaneity of expressionism with abstract forms in apparently random compositions.

abstraction (æb'strækʃən) *n.* **1.** preoccupation. **2.** the process of formulating generalized concepts by extracting common qualities from specific examples. **3.** a concept formulated in this way: *good and evil are abstractions.* **4.** an abstract painting, sculpture, etc. —**ab'stractive** *adj.*

abstract noun *n.* a noun that refers to an abstract concept, as peace, joy, etc.

abstract term *n.* in traditional logic, the name of an attribute of many individuals: *humanity is an abstract term.*

abstruse (əb'struːs) *adj.* not easy to understand. [C16: < L *abstrūsus,* < *abs-* AB-[1] + *trūdere* to thrust] —**ab'strusely** *adv.* —**ab'struseness** *n.*

absurd (əb'sɜːd) *adj.* **1.** incongruous; ridiculous. **2.** ludicrous. [C16: via F < L *absurdus,* < AB-[1] (intensive) + *surdus* dull-sounding, indistinct] —**ab'surdity** *or* **ab'surdness** *n.* —**ab'surdly** *adv.*

ABTA ('æbtə) *n. acronym for* Association of British Travel Agents.

abulia *or* **aboulia** (ə'buːlɪə, -'bjuː-) *n. Psychiatry.* a pathological inability to take decisions. [C19: NL, < Gk *aboulia* lack of resolution, < A-[1] + *boulē* will]

abundance (ə'bʌndəns) *n.* **1.** a copious supply; great amount. **2.** fullness or benevolence: *from the abundance of my heart.* **3.** degree of plentifulness: *the abundance of uranium-235 in natural uranium.* **4.** Also: **abondance.** a call in solo whist undertaking to make nine tricks. **5.** affluence. [C14: via OF < L, < *abundāre* to ABOUND]

abundant (ə'bʌndənt) *adj.* **1.** existing in plentiful supply. **2.** (*postpositive;* foll. by *in*) having a plentiful supply (of). [C14: < L *abundant-,* p.p. of *abundāre* to ABOUND] —**a'bundantly** *adv.*

abuse *vb.* (ə'bjuːz). (*tr.*) **1.** to use incorrectly or improperly; misuse. **2.** to maltreat. **3.** to speak insultingly or cruelly to. ~*n.* (ə'bjuːs). **4.** improper, incorrect, or excessive use. **5.** maltreatment of a person; injury. **6.** insulting or coarse speech. **7.** an evil, unjust, or corrupt practice. **8.** *Arch.* a deception. [C14 (vb.): via OF < L *abūsus,* p.p. of *abūtī* to misuse, < AB-[1] + *ūtī* to USE] —**a'buser** *n.*

abusive (ə'bjuːsɪv) *adj.* **1.** characterized by insulting or coarse language. **2.** characterized by maltreatment. **3.** incorrectly used. —**a'busively** *adv.* —**a'busiveness** *n.*

abut (ə'bʌt) *vb.* **abutting, abutted.** (usually foll. by *on, upon,* or *against*) to adjoin, touch, or border on (something) at one end. [C15: < OF *abouter* to join at the ends; infl. by *abuter* to touch at an end]

abutment (ə'bʌtmənt) *or* **abuttal** *n.* **1.** the state or process of abutting. **2. a.** something that abuts. **b.** the thing on which something abuts. **c.** the point of junction between them. **3.** a construction that supports the end of a bridge.

abutter (ə'bʌtə) *n. Property law.* the owner of adjoining property.

abuzz (ə'bʌz) *adj.* (*postpositive*) humming, as with conversation, activity, etc.; buzzing.

abysm (ə'bɪzəm) *n.* an archaic word for **abyss.** [C13: via OF < Med. L *abysmus* ABYSS]

abysmal (ə'bɪzməl) *adj.* **1.** immeasurable; very great. **2.** *Inf.* extremely bad. —**a'bysmally** *adv.*

abyss (ə'bɪs) *n.* **1.** a very deep gorge or chasm. **2.** anything that appears to be endless or immeasurably deep, such as time, despair, or shame. **3.** hell. [C16: via LL < Gk *abussos* bottomless, < A-[1] + *bussos* depth] —**a'byssal** *adj.*

Ac *the chemical symbol for* actinium.

AC *abbrev. for:* **1.** Air Corps. **2.** alternating current. Cf. **DC. 3.** ante Christum. [L: before Christ] **4.** athletic club. **5.** Companion of the Order of Australia.

a/c *Book-keeping. abbrev. for:* **1.** account. **2.** account current.

acacia (ə'keɪʃə) *n.* **1.** a tropical or subtropical shrub or tree, having small yellow or white flowers. In Australia the term is applied esp. to the wattle. **2. false acacia.** another name for **locust** (senses 2, 3). **3. gum acacia.** another name for **gum arabic.** [C16: < L, < Gk *akakia,* ? rel. to *akē* point]

academe ('ækəˌdiːm) *n. Literary.* any place of learning, such as a college or university. [C16: first used by Shakespeare in *Love's Labour's Lost* (1588); see ACADEMY]

academic (ˌækə'dɛmɪk) *adj.* **1.** belonging or relating to a place of learning, esp. a college, university, or academy. **2.** of purely theoretical or speculative interest. **3.** (esp. of pupils) having an aptitude for study. **4.** excessively concerned with intellectual matters. **5.** conforming to set rules and traditions: *an academic painter.* **6.** relating to studies such as languages and pure science rather than technical, applied, or professional studies. ~*n.* **7.** a member of a college or university. —ˌ**aca'demically** *adv.*

academician (əˌkædə'mɪʃən) *n.* a member of an academy (senses 1, 2).

academy (ə'kædəmɪ) *n., pl.* **-mies. 1.** an institution or society for the advancement of literature, art, or science. **2.** a school for training in a particular skill or profession: *a military academy.* **3.** a secondary school, esp. in Scotland: now only used as part of a name. [C16: via L < Gk *akadēmeia* the grove where Plato taught, named after the legendary hero *Akadēmos*] —ˌ**aca'demical** *adj.*

Academy Award *n.* the official name for an **Oscar.**

acanthus (ə'kænθəs) *n., pl.* **-thuses** *or* **-thi** (-θaɪ). **1.** a shrub or herbaceous plant, native to the Mediterranean region but widely cultivated as an ornamental plant, having large spiny leaves and spikes of white or purplish flowers. **2.** a carved ornament based on the leaves of the acanthus plant, esp. as used on the capital of a Corinthian column. [C17: NL, < Gk *akanthos*, < *akantha* thorn, spine]

a cappella (ɑː kəˈpɛlə) *adj., adv. Music.* without instrumental accompaniment. [It.: lit., according to (the style of the) chapel]

acariasis (ˌækəˈraɪəsɪs) *n.* infestation with mites or ticks. [C19: NL: see ACARID, -IASIS]

acarid (ˈækərɪd) *or* **acaridan** (əˈkærɪdᵊn) *n.* any of an order of small arachnids that includes the ticks and mites. [C19: < Gk *akari* a small thing, mite]

acarpous (eɪˈkɑːpəs) *adj.* (of plants) producing no fruit. [< Gk *akarpos*, < A-¹ + *karpos* fruit]

ACAS *or* **Acas** (ˈeɪkæs) *n.* (in Britain) *acronym for* Advisory Conciliation and Arbitration Service.

acc. *abbrev. for:* **1.** accompanied. **2.** according. **3.** *Book-keeping.* account. **4.** *Grammar.* accusative.

accede (ækˈsiːd) *vb.* (*intr.;* usually foll. by *to*) **1.** to assent or give one's consent. **2.** to enter upon or attain (to an office, right, etc.): *the prince acceded to the throne.* **3.** *International law.* to become a party (to an agreement between nations, etc.). [C15: < L *accēdere*, < *ad-* to + *cēdere* to yield] —**acˈcedence** *n.*

accelerando (ækˌsɛləˈrændəʊ) *adj., adv. Music.* (to be performed) with increasing speed. [It.]

accelerate (ækˈsɛləˌreɪt) *vb.* **1.** to go, occur, or cause to go or occur more quickly; speed up. **2.** (*tr.*) to cause to happen sooner than expected. **3.** (*tr.*) to increase the velocity of (a body, reaction, etc.). [C16: < L *accelerātus*, < *accelerāre*, < *ad-* (intensive) + *celerāre* to hasten, < *celer* swift] —**acˈcelerative** *adj.*

acceleration (ækˌsɛləˈreɪʃən) *n.* **1.** the act of accelerating or the state of being accelerated. **2.** the rate of increase of speed or the rate of change of velocity. **3.** the power to accelerate.

acceleration of free fall *n.* the acceleration of a body falling freely in a vacuum in the earth's gravitational field. Symbol: *g* Also called: **acceleration due to gravity.**

accelerator (ækˈsɛləˌreɪtə) *n.* **1.** a device for increasing speed, esp. a pedal for controlling the fuel intake in a motor vehicle; throttle. **2.** *Physics.* a machine for increasing the kinetic energy of subatomic particles or atomic nuclei. **3.** Also: **accelerant.** *Chem.* a substance that increases the speed of a chemical reaction; catalyst.

accelerometer (ækˌsɛləˈrɒmɪtə) *n.* an instrument for measuring acceleration, esp. of an aircraft or rocket.

accent *n.* (ˈæksənt). **1.** the characteristic mode of pronunciation of a person or group, esp. one that betrays social or geographical origin. **2.** the relative prominence of a spoken or sung syllable, esp. with regard to stress or pitch. **3.** a mark (such as ˈ, ˌ, ´, or `) used in writing to indicate the stress or prominence of a syllable. **4.** any of various marks or symbols conventionally used in writing certain languages to indicate the quality of a vowel. See **acute** (sense 8), **grave²** (sense 5), **circumflex. 5.** rhythmical stress in verse or prose. **6.** *Music.* **a.** stress placed on certain notes in a piece of music, indicated by a symbol printed over the note concerned. **b.** the rhythmical pulse of a piece or passage, usually represented as the stress on the first beat of each bar. **7.** a distinctive characteristic of anything, such as taste, pattern, style, etc. **8.** particular attention or emphasis: *an accent on learning.* **9.** a strongly contrasting detail. ~*vb.* (ækˈsɛnt). (*tr.*) **10.** to mark with an accent in writing, speech, music, etc. **11.** to lay particular emphasis or stress on. [C14: via OF < L *accentus*, < *ad-* to + *cantus* chant]

accentor (ækˈsɛntə) *n.* a small sparrow-like songbird, which inhabits mainly mountainous regions of Europe and Asia. See also **hedge sparrow.**

accentual (ækˈsɛntʃʊəl) *adj.* **1.** of, relating to, or having accents; rhythmical. **2.** *Prosody.* of or relating to verse based on the number of stresses in a line. —**acˈcentually** *adv.*

accentuate (ækˈsɛntʃʊˌeɪt) *vb.* (*tr.*) to stress or emphasize. —**acˌcentuˈation** *n.*

accept (əkˈsɛpt) *vb.* (*mainly tr.*) **1.** to take or receive (something offered). **2.** to give an affirmative reply to. **3.** to take on the responsibilities, duties, etc., of: *he accepted office.* **4.** to tolerate. **5.** to consider as true or believe in (a philosophy, theory, etc.). **6.** (*may take a clause as object*) to be willing to believe: *you must accept that he lied.* **7.** to receive with approval or admit, as into a community, group, etc. **8.** *Commerce.* to agree to pay (a bill, draft, etc.). **9.** to receive as adequate or valid. [C14: < L *acceptāre*, < *ad-* to + *capere* to take] —**acˈcepter** *n.*

acceptable (əkˈsɛptəbᵊl) *adj.* **1.** satisfactory; adequate. **2.** pleasing; welcome. **3.** tolerable. —**acˌceptaˈbility** *or* **acˈceptableness** *n.* —**acˈceptably** *adv.*

acceptance (əkˈsɛptəns) *n.* **1.** the act of accepting or the state of being accepted or acceptable. **2.** favourable reception. **3.** (often foll. by *of*) belief (in) or assent (to). **4.** *Commerce.* a formal agreement by a debtor to pay a draft, bill, etc. **5.** (*pl.*) *Austral. & N.Z.* a list of horses accepted as starters in a race.

acceptation (ˌæksɛpˈteɪʃən) *n.* the accepted meaning, as of a word, phrase, etc.

accepted (əkˈsɛptɪd) *adj.* commonly approved or recognized; customary; established.

acceptor (əkˈsɛptə) *n.* **1.** *Commerce.* the person or organization on which a draft or bill of exchange is drawn. **2.** *Electronics.* an impurity, such as gallium, added to a semiconductor material to increase its p-type conductivity.

access (ˈæksɛs) *n.* **1.** the act of approaching or entering. **2.** the condition of allowing entry, esp. (of a building, etc.) entry by prams, wheelchairs, etc. **3.** the right or privilege to approach, enter, or make use of something. **4.** a way or means of approach or entry. **5.** (*modifier*) designating programmes made by the general public: *access television.* **6.** a sudden outburst or attack, as of rage or disease. ~*vb.* (*tr.*) **7.** *Computers.* **a.** to obtain or retrieve (information) from a storage device. **b.** to place (information) in a storage device. **8.** to gain access to; make accessible or available. [C14: < OF or < L *accessus*, < *accēdere* to ACCEDE]

accessary (əkˈsɛsərɪ) *n., pl.* **-ries.** *Law.* a less common spelling of **accessory.**

accessible (əkˈsɛsəbᵊl) *adj.* **1.** easy to approach, enter, or use. **2. accessible to.** likely to be affected by. **3.** obtainable; available. —**acˌcesˈsiˈbility** *n.*

accession (əkˈsɛʃən) *n.* **1.** the act of attaining to an office, right, condition, etc. **2.** an increase due to an addition. **3.** an addition, as to a collection. **4.** *Property law.* an addition to land or property by natural increase or improvement. **5.** *International law.* the formal acceptance of a convention or treaty. **6.** agreement. ~*vb.* **7.** (*tr.*) to make a record of (additions to a collection). —**acˈcessional** *adj.*

accessory (əkˈsɛsərɪ) *n., pl.* **-ries. 1.** a supplementary part or object, as of a car, appliance, etc. **2.** (*often pl.*) a small accompanying item of dress, esp. of women's dress. **3.** (formerly) a person involved in a crime although absent during its commission. ~*adj.* **4.** supplementary; additional. **5.** assisting in or having knowledge of an act, esp. a crime. [C17: < LL *accessōrius*: see ACCESS] —**accessorial** (ˌæksɛˈsɔːrɪəl) *adj.* —**acˈcessorily** *adv.*

access road *n.* a road giving entry to a region or, esp., a motorway.

access time *n. Computers.* the time required to retrieve a piece of stored information.

acciaccatura (əˌtʃækəˈtʊərə) *n., pl.* **-ras** *or* **-re** (-reɪ). a small grace note melodically adjacent to a principal note and played simultaneously with or immediately before it. [C18: It.: lit., a crushing sound]

accidence (ˈæksɪdəns) *n.* the part of grammar

concerned with changes in the form of words for the expression of tense, person, case, number, etc. [C15: < L *accidentia* accidental matters, < *accidere* to happen. See ACCIDENT]

accident (ˈæksɪdənt) *n.* **1.** an unforeseen event or one without an apparent cause. **2.** anything that occurs unintentionally or by chance: *I met him by accident.* **3.** a misfortune or mishap, esp. one causing injury or death. **4.** *Geol.* a surface irregularity in a natural formation. [C14: via OF < L *accident-*, < the p.p. of *accidere* to happen, < *ad-* to + *cadere* to fall]

accidental (ˌæksɪˈdɛntəl) *adj.* **1.** occurring by chance, unexpectedly, or unintentionally. **2.** nonessential; incidental. **3.** *Music.* denoting sharps, flats, or naturals that are not in the key signature of a piece. ~*n.* **4.** an incidental or supplementary circumstance, factor, or attribute. **5.** *Music.* a symbol denoting that the following note is a sharp, flat, or natural that is not a part of the key signature. —ˌ**acciˈdentally** *adv.*

accident-prone *adj.* liable to become involved in accidents.

accidie (ˈæksɪdɪ) *or* **acedia** *n.* spiritual sloth; apathy; indifference. [in use C13 to C16 and revived C19: via LL < Gk *akēdia*, < A-[1] + *kēdos* care]

accipiter (ækˈsɪpɪtə) *n.* any of a genus of hawks having short rounded wings and a long tail. [C19: NL, < L: hawk] —**acˈcipitrine** *adj.*

acclaim (əˈkleɪm) *vb.* **1.** (*tr.*) to acknowledge publicly the excellence of (a person, act, etc.). **2.** to applaud. **3.** (*tr.*) to acknowledge publicly: *they acclaimed him king.* ~*n.* **4.** an enthusiastic expression of approval, etc. [C17: < L *acclāmāre*, < *ad-* to + *clamāre* to shout] —**acˈclaimer** *n.*

acclamation (ˌækləˈmeɪʃən) *n.* **1.** an enthusiastic reception or exhibition of welcome, approval, etc. **2.** an expression of approval with shouts or applause. **3.** *Canad.* an instance of electing or being elected without opposition. —**acclamatory** (əˈklæmətərɪ) *adj.*

acclimatize *or* **-tise** (əˈklaɪməˌtaɪz) *vb.* to adapt or become accustomed to a new climate or environment. —**acˈclimaˌtizable** *or* **-ˌtisable** *adj.* —**acˌclimatiˈzation** *or* **-tiˈsation** *n.*

acclivity (əˈklɪvɪtɪ) *n., pl.* **-ties.** an upward slope, esp. of the ground. Cf. **declivity.** [C17: < L, < *acclīvis* sloping up] —**acˈclivitous** *adj.*

accolade (ˈækəˌleɪd) *n.* **1.** strong praise or approval. **2.** an award or honour. **3.** the ceremonial gesture used to confer knighthood, a touch on the shoulder with a sword. **4.** a rare word for **brace** (sense 7). [C17: via F & It. < Vulgar L *accollāre* (unattested) to hug; rel. to L *collum* neck]

accommodate (əˈkɒməˌdeɪt) *vb.* **1.** (*tr.*) to supply or provide, esp. with lodging. **2.** (*tr.*) to oblige or do a favour for. **3.** to adapt. **4.** (*tr.*) to bring into harmony. **5.** (*tr.*) to allow room for. **6.** (*tr.*) to lend money to. [C16: < L *accommodāre*, < *ad-* to + *commodus* having the proper measure]

accommodating (əˈkɒməˌdeɪtɪŋ) *adj.* willing to help; kind; obliging.

accommodation (əˌkɒməˈdeɪʃən) *n.* **1.** adjustment, as of differences or to new circumstances; settlement or reconciliation. **2.** lodging or board and lodging. **3.** something fulfilling a need, want, etc. **4.** *Physiol.* the automatic or voluntary adjustment of the thickness of the lens of the eye for far or near vision. **5.** willingness to help or oblige. **6.** *Commerce.* a loan.

accommodation address *n.* an address on letters, etc., to a person or business that does not wish or is not able to receive post at a permanent or actual address.

accommodation ladder *n. Naut.* a flight of stairs or a ladder for lowering over the side of a ship for access to and from a small boat, pier, etc.

accompaniment (əˈkʌmpənɪmənt) *n.* **1.** something that accompanies or is served or used with something else. **2.** *Music.* a subordinate or supporting part for an instrument, voices, or an orchestra.

accompanist (əˈkʌmpənɪst) *n.* a person who plays a musical accompaniment for another performer.

accompany (əˈkʌmpənɪ) *vb.* **-nying, -nied.** **1.** (*tr.*) to go along with, so as to be in company with. **2.** (*tr.;* foll. by *with*) to supplement. **3.** (*tr.*) to occur or be associated with. **4.** to provide a musical accompaniment for (a soloist, etc.). [C15: < OF *accompaignier*, < *compaing* COMPANION[1]]

▷ **Usage.** *Accompany* is used with *by* for people, *with* for things: *she was accompanied by her husband; she accompanied her words with a broad wink.*

accomplice (əˈkɒmplɪs, əˈkʌm-) *n.* a person who has helped another in committing a crime. [C15: < *a complice*, interpreted as one word, < OF, < LL *complex* partner, < L *complicāre* to COMPLICATE]

accomplish (əˈkɒmplɪʃ, əˈkʌm-) *vb.* (*tr.*) **1.** to manage to do; achieve. **2.** to complete. [C14: < OF *acomplir*, ult. < L *complēre* to fill up. See COMPLETE]

accomplished (əˈkɒmplɪʃt, əˈkʌm-) *adj.* **1.** successfully completed; achieved. **2.** expert; proficient.

accomplishment (əˈkɒmplɪʃmənt, əˈkʌm-) *n.* **1.** the act of achieving. **2.** something successfully completed. **3.** (*often pl.*) skill or talent. **4.** (*often pl.*) social grace and poise.

accord (əˈkɔːd) *n.* **1.** agreement; accordance (esp. in **in accord with**). **2.** concurrence of opinion. **3. with one accord.** unanimously. **4.** pleasing relationship between sounds, colours, etc. **5. of one's own accord.** voluntarily. ~*vb.* **6.** to be or cause to be in harmony or agreement. **7.** (*tr.*) to grant; bestow. [C12: via OF < L *ad-* to + *cord-*, stem of *cor* heart]

accordance (əˈkɔːdəns) *n.* conformity; agreement; accord (esp. in **in accordance with**).

according (əˈkɔːdɪŋ) *adj.* **1.** (foll. by *to*) in proportion. **2.** (foll. by *to*) as stated (by). **3.** (foll. by *to*) in conformity (with). **4.** (foll. by *as*) depending (on whether).

accordingly (əˈkɔːdɪŋlɪ) *adv.* **1.** in an appropriate manner; suitably. ~*sentence connector.* **2.** consequently.

accordion (əˈkɔːdɪən) *n.* **1.** a portable box-shaped instrument consisting of metallic reeds that are made to vibrate by air from a set of bellows controlled by the player's hands. Notes are produced by means of studlike keys. **2.** short for **piano accordion.** [C19: < G, < *Akkord* harmony] —**acˈcordionist** *n.*

accordion pleats *pl. n.* tiny knife pleats.

accost (əˈkɒst) *vb.* (*tr.*) to approach, stop, and speak to (a person), as to ask a question, solicit sexually, etc. [C16: < LL *accostāre*, < L *costa* side, rib] —**acˈcostable** *adj.*

accouchement *French.* (akuʃmɑ̃) *n.* childbirth or the period of confinement. [C19: < *accoucher* to put to bed. See COUCH]

account (əˈkaʊnt) *n.* **1.** a verbal or written report, description, or narration of some occurrence, event, etc. **2.** an explanation of conduct, esp. one made to someone in authority. **3.** basis; consideration: *on this account.* **4.** importance, consequence, or value: *of little account.* **5.** assessment; judgment. **6.** profit or advantage: *to good account.* **7.** part or behalf (only in **on one's** *or* **someone's account**). **8.** *Finance.* **a.** a business relationship between a bank, department store, etc., and a depositor, customer, or client permitting the latter certain banking or credit services. **b.** the sum of money deposited at a bank. **c.** the amount of credit available to the holder of an account. **d.** a record of these. **9.** a statement of monetary transactions with the resulting balance. **10.** (on the London Stock Exchange) the period, ordinarily of a fortnight's duration, at the end of which settlements are made. **11.** *Chiefly U.S. & Canad.* **a.** a regular client or customer. **b.** an area of business assigned to another: *they transferred their publicity account to a new agent.* **12. call** (*or* **bring**) **to account. a.** to insist on explanation. **b.** to reprimand. **c.** to hold responsible. **13. give a good (bad,** etc.) **account of oneself.** to perform well (badly, etc.). **14. on account. a.** on credit. **b.** Also: **to account.** as partial payment. **15. on account of.** (*prep.*) because of. **16. take account of** *or* **take into account.** to take into consideration; allow for. **17. settle** *or* **square accounts with. a.** to pay or receive a balance due. **b.** to get revenge on (someone). **18.** See **bank account.** ~*vb.* **19.** (*tr.*) to consider or reckon: *he accounts himself poor.* [C13: < OF *acont,* < *conter* to COUNT[1]]

accountable (əˈkaʊntəbᵊl) *adj.* **1.** responsible to someone or for some action. **2.** able to be explained. —**acˌcountaˈbility** *n.* —**acˈcountably** *adv.*

accountancy (əˈkaʊntənsɪ) *n.* the profession or business of an accountant.

accountant (əˈkaʊntənt) *n.* a person concerned with the maintenance and audit of business accounts.

account for *vb.* (*intr., prep.*) **1.** to give reasons for (an event, act, etc.). **2.** to make or provide a reckoning of (expenditure, etc.). **3.** to be responsible for destroying or putting (people, aircraft, etc.) out of action.

accounting (əˈkaʊntɪŋ) *n.* the skill or practice of maintaining and auditing accounts and preparing reports on the assets, liabilities, etc., of a business.

accoutre *or U.S.* **accouter** (əˈkuːtə) *vb.* (*tr.; usually passive*) to provide with equipment or dress, esp. military. [C16: < OF *accoustrer,* ult. rel. to L *consuere* to sew together]

accoutrement (əˈkuːtrəmənt, əˈkuːtə-) *or U.S.* **accouterment** (əˈkuːtərmənt) *n.* **1.** equipment worn by soldiers in addition to their clothing and weapons. **2.** (*usually pl.*) clothing, equipment, etc.; trappings: *the correct accoutrements for any sport.*

accredit (əˈkrɛdɪt) *vb.* (*tr.*) **1.** to ascribe or attribute. **2.** to give official recognition to. **3.** to certify as meeting required standards. **4.** (*often foll. by at or to*) **a.** to send (an envoy, etc.) with official credentials. **b.** to appoint (someone) as an envoy, etc. **5.** to believe. **6.** *N.Z.* to pass a candidate for university entrance on school recommendation, without external examination. [C17: < F *accréditer,* < *mettre à crédit* to put to CREDIT] —**acˌcrediˈtation** *n.*

accredited (əˈkrɛdɪtɪd) *adj.* **1.** officially authorized; recognized. **2.** (of milk, cattle, etc.) certified as free from disease; meeting certain standards. **3.** *N.Z.* accepted for university entrance on school recommendation, without external examination.

accrete (əˈkriːt) *vb.* **1.** to grow or cause to grow together. **2.** to make or become bigger, as by addition. [C18: back formation < ACCRETION]

accretion (əˈkriːʃən) *n.* **1.** any gradual increase in size, as through growth or external addition. **2.** something added, esp. extraneously, to cause growth or an increase in size. **3.** the growing together of normally separate plant or animal parts. [C17: < L *accretiō* increase, < *accrēscere.* See ACCRUE] —**acˈcretive** *adj.*

accrue (əˈkruː) *vb.* **-cruing, -crued.** (*intr.*) **1.** to increase by growth or addition, esp. (of capital) to increase by periodic addition of interest. **2.** (*often foll. by to*) to fall naturally (to). [C15: < OF *accreue,* ult. < L *accrēscere,* < *ad-* to, in addition + *crēscere* to grow] —**acˈcrual** *n.*

acct *Book-keeping. abbrev. for* account.

acculturate (əˈkʌltʃəˌreɪt) *vb.* (of a cultural or social group) to assimilate the cultural traits of another group. [C20: < AD- + CULTURE + -ATE[1]] —**acˌculturˈation** *n.*

accumulate (əˈkjuːmjʊˌleɪt) *vb.* to gather or become gathered together in an increasing quantity; collect. [C16: < L *accumulāre* to heap up, < *cumulus* a heap] —**acˈcumulable** *adj.* —**acˈcumulative** *adj.*

accumulation (əˌkjuːmjʊˈleɪʃən) *n.* **1.** the act or process of collecting together or becoming collected. **2.** something that has been collected, gathered, heaped, etc. **3.** *Finance.* the continuous growth of capital by retention of interest or earnings.

accumulator (əˈkjuːmjʊˌleɪtə) *n.* **1.** Also called: **battery, storage battery.** a rechargeable device for storing electrical energy in the form of chemical energy. **2.** *Horse racing, Brit.* a collective bet on successive races, with both stake and winnings being carried forward to accumulate progressively. **3.** a register in a calculator or computer used for holding the results of a computation or data transfer.

accuracy (ˈækjʊrəsɪ) *n., pl.* **-cies.** faithful measurement or representation of the truth; correctness; precision.

accurate (ˈækjərɪt) *adj.* **1.** faithfully representing or describing the truth. **2.** showing a negligible or permissible deviation from a standard: *an accurate ruler.* **3.** without error; precise. **4.** *Maths.* (of a number) correctly represented to a specified number of decimal places or significant figures. [C16: < L *accūrāre* to perform with care, < *cūra* care] —**ˈaccurately** *adv.*

accursed (əˈkɜːsɪd, əˈkɜːst) *or* **accurst** (əˈkɜːst) *adj.* **1.** under or subject to a curse. **2.** (*prenominal*) hateful; detestable. [OE *ācursod,* p.p. of *ācursian* to put under a CURSE] —**accursedly** (əˈkɜːsɪdlɪ) *adv.* —**acˈcursedness** *n.*

accusation (ˌækjʊˈzeɪʃən) *n.* **1.** an allegation that a person is guilty of some fault or crime. **2.** a formal charge brought against a person.

accusative (əˈkjuːzətɪv) *adj.* **1.** *Grammar.* denoting a case of nouns, pronouns, and adjectives in inflected languages that is used to identify the direct object of a finite verb, of certain prepositions, and for certain other purposes. **2.** another word for **accusatorial.** ~*n.* **3.** *Grammar.* the accusative case or a speech element in it. [C15: < L; in grammar, < *cāsus accūsātīvus* accusative case, a mistaken translation of Gk *ptōsis aitiatikē* the case indicating causation. See ACCUSE] —**accusatival** (əˌkjuːzəˈtaɪvᵊl) *adj.* —**acˈcusatively** *adv.*

accusatorial (əˌkjuːzəˈtɔːrɪəl) *or* **accusatory** (əˈkjuːzətərɪ) *adj.* **1.** containing or implying blame or strong criticism. **2.** *Law.* denoting a legal system in which the defendant is prosecuted before a judge in public. Cf. **inquisitorial.**

accuse (əˈkjuːz) *vb.* to charge (a person or persons) with some fault, offence, crime, etc. [C13: via OF < L *accūsare* to call to account, < *ad-* to + *causa* lawsuit] —**acˈcuser** *n.* —**acˈcusing** *adj.* —**acˈcusingly** *adv.*

accused (əˈkjuːzd) *n.* (preceded by *the*) *Law.* the defendant or defendants on a criminal charge.

accustom (əˈkʌstəm) *vb.* (*tr.; usually foll. by to*) to make (oneself) familiar (with) or used (to), as by habit or experience. [C15: < OF *acostumer,* < *costume* CUSTOM]

accustomed (əˈkʌstəmd) *adj.* **1.** usual; customary. **2.** (*postpositive;* foll. by *to*) used (to). **3.** (*postpositive;* foll. by *to*) in the habit (of).

ace (eɪs) *n.* **1.** any die, domino, or any of four playing cards with one spot. **2.** a single spot or pip on a playing card, die, etc. **3.** *Tennis.* a winning serve that the opponent fails to reach. **4.** a fighter pilot accredited with destroying several enemy aircraft. **5.** *Inf.* an expert: *an ace at driving.* **6. an ace up one's sleeve.** a hidden and powerful advantage. ~*adj.* **7.** *Inf.* superb; excellent. [C13: via OF < L *as* a unit]

-acea *suffix forming plural proper nouns.* denoting animals belonging to a class or order: *Crustacea* (class); *Cetacea* (order). [NL, < L, neuter pl. of *-āceus* -ACEOUS]

-aceae *suffix forming plural proper nouns.* denoting plants belonging to a family: *Liliaceae.* [NL, < L, fem. pl. of *-āceus* -ACEOUS]

acedia (əˈsiːdɪə) *n.* another word for **accidie.**

-aceous *suffix forming adjectives.* relating to, having the nature of, or resembling: *herbaceous.* [NL, < L *-āceus* of a certain kind; rel. to *-āc, -āx,* adjectival suffix]

acephalous (əˈsɛfələs) *adj.* having no head or one that is reduced and indistinct, as certain insect larvae. [C18: via Med. L < Gk *akephalos.* See A-[1], -CEPHALIC]

acerbate (ˈæsəˌbeɪt) *vb.* (*tr.*) **1.** to embitter or exasperate. **2.** to make sour or bitter. [C18: < L *acerbāre* to make sour]

acerbic (əˈsɜːbɪk) *adj.* harsh, bitter, or astringent; sour. [C17: < L *acerbus* sour, bitter]

acerbity (əˈsɜːbɪtɪ) *n., pl.* **-ties.** **1.** vitriolic or embittered speech, temper, etc. **2.** sourness or bitterness of taste.

acetabulum (ˌæsɪˈtæbjʊləm) *n., pl.* **-la** (-lə). the deep cuplike cavity on the side of the hipbone that receives the head of the thighbone. [L: vinegar cup, hence a cuplike cavity, < *acētum* vinegar + *-abulum*, suffix denoting a container]

acetal (ˈæsɪˌtæl) *n.* a colourless volatile liquid used as a solvent and in perfumes. [C19: < G *Azetal,* < ACETO- + ALCOHOL]

acetaldehyde (ˌæsɪˈtældɪˌhaɪd) *n.* a colourless volatile pungent liquid, used in the manufacture of organic compounds and as a solvent. Formula: CH_3CHO.

acetanilide (ˌæsɪˈtænɪˌlaɪd) *n.* a white crystalline powder used in the manufacture of dyes and as an analgesic in medicine. [C19: < ACETO- + ANILINE + -IDE]

acetate (ˈæsɪˌteɪt) *n.* **1.** any salt or ester of acetic acid. **2.** short for **acetate rayon** *or* **cellulose acetate. 3.** an audio disc with an acetate lacquer coating: used for demonstration purposes, etc. [C19: < ACETIC + -ATE[1]]

acetate rayon *n.* a synthetic textile fibre made from cellulose acetate.

acetic (əˈsiːtɪk) *adj.* of, containing, producing, or derived from acetic acid or vinegar. [C19: < L *acētum* vinegar]

acetic acid *n.* a colourless pungent liquid widely used in the manufacture of plastics, pharmaceuticals, dyes, etc. Formula: CH_3COOH. See also **vinegar.**

acetify (əˈsɛtɪˌfaɪ) *vb.* **-fying, -fied.** to become or cause to become acetic acid or vinegar. —**aˌcetifiˈcation** *n.*

aceto- *or before a vowel* **acet-** *combining form.* containing an acetyl group or derived from acetic acid: *acetone.* [< L *acētum* vinegar]

acetone (ˈæsɪˌtəʊn) *n.* a colourless volatile pungent liquid used in the manufacture of chemicals and as a solvent for paints, varnishes, and lacquers. Formula: CH_3COCH_3. [C19: < G *Azeton,* < ACETO- + -ONE]

acetous (ˈæsɪtəs) *or* **acetose** (ˈæsɪˌtəʊs) *adj.* **1.** producing or resembling acetic acid or vinegar. **2.** tasting like vinegar. [C18: < LL *acētōsus* vinegary, < *acētum* vinegar]

acetyl (ˈæsɪˌtaɪl, əˈsiːtaɪl) *n.* (*modifier*) of or containing the monovalent group CH_3CO-. [C19: < ACET(IC) + -YL]

acetylcholine (ˌæsɪtaɪlˈkəʊliːn, -lɪn) *n.* a chemical substance secreted at the ends of many nerve fibres, responsible for the transmission of nervous impulses.

acetylene (əˈsɛtɪˌliːn) *n.* a colourless soluble flammable gas used in the manufacture of organic chemicals and in cutting and welding metals. Formula: C_2H_2.

acetylsalicylic acid (ˌæsɪtaɪlˌsælɪˈsɪlɪk) *n.* the chemical name for **aspirin.**

Achaean (əˈkiːən) *or* **Achaian** (əˈkaɪən) *n.* **1.** a member of a principal Greek tribe in the Mycenaean era. ~*adj.* **2.** of or relating to the Achaeans.

Achates (əˈkeɪtiːz) *n.* a loyal friend. [< Aeneas' faithful companion in Virgil's *Aeneid*]

ache (eɪk) *vb.* (*intr.*) **1.** to feel, suffer, or be the source of a continuous dull pain. **2.** to suffer mental anguish. ~*n.* **3.** a continuous dull pain. [OE *ācan* (vb.), *æce* (n.), ME *aken* (vb.), *ache* (n.)] —ˈ**aching** *adj.*

achene (əˈkiːn) *n.* a dry one-seeded indehiscent fruit with the seed distinct from the fruit wall. [C19: < NL *achaenium* that which does not open, < A-[1] + Gk *khainein* to yawn]

Acheulian *or* **Acheulean** (əˈʃuːlɪən) *Archaeol.* ~*n.* **1.** (in Europe) the period in the Lower Palaeolithic following the Abbevillian, represented by the use of soft hammerstones in hand-axe production. **2.** (in Africa) the period represented by every stage of hand-axe development. ~*adj.* **3.** of or relating to this period. [C20: after *St Acheul,* town in N France]

achieve (əˈtʃiːv) *vb.* (*tr.*) **1.** to bring to a successful conclusion. **2.** to gain as by hard work or effort: *to achieve success.* [C14: < OF *achever* to bring to an end, < *a chef* to a head] —**aˈchievable** *adj.* —**aˈchiever** *n.*

achievement (əˈtʃiːvmənt) *n.* **1.** something that has been accomplished, esp. by hard work, ability, or heroism. **2.** successful completion; accomplishment.

achillea (ˌækɪˈliːə) *n.* any of several cultivated varieties of yarrow. [NL, < Gk *akhilleios* plant used medicinally by *Achilles*]

Achilles heel (əˈkɪliːz) *n.* a small but fatal weakness. [< *Achilles,* hero of Gk myth., invulnerable except for his heel]

Achilles tendon *n.* the fibrous cord that connects the muscles of the calf to the heelbone.

achromat (ˈækrəˌmæt) *or* **achromatic lens** *n.* a lens designed to reduce chromatic aberration.

achromatic (ˌækrəˈmætɪk) *adj.* **1.** without colour. **2.** capable of reflecting or refracting light without chromatic aberration. **3.** *Music.* involving no sharps or flats. —ˌ**achroˈmatically** *adv.* —**achromatism** (əˈkrəʊməˌtɪzəm) *or* **achromaticity** (əˌkrəʊməˈtɪsɪtɪ) *n.*

acid (ˈæsɪd) *n.* **1.** any substance that dissociates in water to yield a sour corrosive solution containing hydrogen ions, and turning litmus red. **2.** a sour-tasting substance. **3.** a slang name for **LSD. 4. put the acid on (someone).** *Austral. & N.Z. inf.* to apply pressure to someone, usually when seeking a favour. ~*adj.* **5.** *Chem.* **a.** of, derived from, or containing acid. **b.** being or having the properties of an acid. **6.** sharp or sour in taste. **7.** cutting, sharp, or hurtful in speech, manner, etc. [C17: < F *acide* or L *acidus,* < *acēre* to be sour] —ˈ**acidly** *adv.* —ˈ**acidness** *n.*

acid-fast *adj.* (of bacteria and tissues) resistant to decolorization by mineral acids after staining.

acidic (əˈsɪdɪk) *adj.* another word for **acid.**

acidify (əˈsɪdɪˌfaɪ) *vb.* **-fying, -fied.** to convert into or become acid. —**aˈcidiˌfiable** *adj.* —**aˌcidifiˈcation** *n.*

acidity (əˈsɪdɪtɪ) *n., pl.* **-ties. 1.** the quality or state of being acid. **2.** the amount of acid present in a solution.

acidosis (ˌæsɪˈdəʊsɪs) *n.* a condition characterized by an abnormal increase in the acidity of the blood. —**acidotic** (ˌæsɪˈdɒtɪk) *adj.*

acid rain *n.* rain containing pollutants, chiefly sulphur dioxide and nitrogen oxide, released into the atmosphere by burning coal or oil.

acid rock *n.* rock music characterized by bizarre amplified instrumental effects. [C20: < ACID (LSD)]

acid test *n.* a rigorous and conclusive test to establish worth or value. [C19: < the testing of gold with nitric acid]

acidulate (əˈsɪdjʊˌleɪt) *vb.* (*tr.*) to make slightly acid or sour. [C18: ACIDULOUS + -ATE[1]] —**aˌciduˈlation** *n.*

acidulous (əˈsɪdjʊləs) *or* **acidulent** *adj.* **1.** rather sour. **2.** sharp or sour in speech, manner, etc.; acid. [C18: < L *acidulus* sourish, dim. of *acidus* sour]

acinus (ˈæsɪnəs) *n., pl.* **-ni** (-ˌnaɪ). **1.** *Anat.* any of the terminal saclike portions of a compound gland. **2.** *Bot.* any of the small drupes that make up the fruit of the raspberry, etc. **3.** *Bot., obs.* a collection of berries, such as a bunch of grapes. [C18: NL, < L: grape, berry]

ack-ack (ˈækˌæk) *n. Mil.* **a.** anti-aircraft fire. **b.** (*as modifier*): *ack-ack guns.* [C20: British Army World War I phonetic alphabet for AA, abbrev. of *anti-aircraft*]

acknowledge (əkˈnɒlɪdʒ) *vb.* (*tr.*) **1.** (*may take a clause as object*) to recognize or admit the existence, truth, or reality of. **2.** to indicate recognition or awareness of, as by a greeting, glance, etc. **3.** to express appreciation or thanks for. **4.** to make the receipt of known: *to acknowledge a letter.* **5.** to recognize, esp. in legal form, the authority, rights, or claims of. [C15: prob. < earlier *knowledge*, on the model of OE *oncnāwan*, ME *aknowen* to confess, recognize] —**ac'knowledgeable** *adj.*

acknowledgment *or* **acknowledgement** (ək'nɒlɪdʒmənt) *n.* **1.** the act of acknowledging or state of being acknowledged. **2.** something done or given as an expression of thanks. **3.** (*pl.*) an author's statement acknowledging his use of the works of other authors.

aclinic line (ə'klɪnɪk) *n.* another name for **magnetic equator.** [C19 *aclinic*, < Gk *aklinēs* not bending, < A-[1] + *klinein* to bend]

acme ('ækmɪ) *n.* the culminating point, as of achievement or excellence. [C16: < Gk *akmē*]

acne ('æknɪ) *n.* a chronic skin disease common in adolescence, characterized by pustules on the face. [C19: NL, < a misreading of Gk *akmē* eruption on the face. See ACME]

acolyte ('ækəˌlaɪt) *n.* **1.** a follower or attendant. **2.** *Christianity.* an officer who assists a priest. [C16: via OF & Med. L < Gk *akolouthos* a follower]

aconite ('ækəˌnaɪt) *n.* **1.** any of a genus of N temperate plants, such as monkshood and wolfsbane, many of which are poisonous. Cf. **winter aconite. 2.** the dried poisonous root of many of these plants, sometimes used as a narcotic. [C16: via OF or L < Gk *akoniton* aconite] —**aconitic** (ˌækə'nɪtɪk) *adj.*

acorn ('eɪkɔːn) *n.* the fruit of the oak tree, consisting of a smooth thick-walled nut in a woody scaly cuplike base. [C16: var. (infl. by *corn*) of OE *æcern* the fruit of a tree, acorn]

acoustic (ə'kuːstɪk) *or* **acoustical** *adj.* **1.** of or related to sound, hearing, or acoustics. **2.** designed to respond to or absorb sound: *an acoustic tile.* **3.** (of a musical instrument or recording) without electronic amplification: *an acoustic guitar.* [C17: < Gk *akoustikos*, < *akouein* to hear] —**a'coustically** *adv.*

acoustics (ə'kuːstɪks) *n.* **1.** (*functioning as sing.*) the scientific study of sound and sound waves. **2.** (*functioning as pl.*) the characteristics of a room, auditorium, etc., that determine the fidelity with which sound can be heard within it.

acquaint (ə'kweɪnt) *vb.* (*tr.*) (foll. by *with* or *of*) to make (a person) familiar (with). [C13: via OF & Med. L < L *accognitus*, < *accognōscere* to know perfectly, < *ad-* (intensive) + *cognōscere* to know]

acquaintance (ə'kweɪntəns) *n.* **1.** a person whom one knows but who is not a close friend. **2.** knowledge of a person or thing, esp. when slight. **3. make the acquaintance of.** to come into social contact with. **4.** those persons collectively whom one knows. —**ac'quaintanceˌship** *n.*

acquainted (ə'kweɪntɪd) *adj.* (*postpositive*) **1.** (sometimes foll. by *with*) on terms of familiarity but not intimacy. **2.** (foll. by *with*) familiar (with).

acquiesce (ˌækwɪ'ɛs) *vb.* (*intr.*; often foll. by *in* or *to*) to comply (with); assent (to) without protest. [C17: < L *acquiēscere*, < *ad-* at + *quiēscere* to rest, < *quiēs* QUIET] —ˌ**acqui'escence** *n.* —ˌ**acqui'escent** *adj.*

acquire (ə'kwaɪə) *vb.* (*tr.*) to get or gain (something, such as an object, trait, or ability). [C15: via OF < L *acquīrere*, < *ad-* in addition + *quaerere* to get, seek] —**ac'quirable** *adj.* —**ac'quirement** *n.*

acquired characteristic *n.* a characteristic of an organism resulting from the effects of the environment.

acquired taste *n.* **1.** a liking for something at first considered unpleasant. **2.** the thing liked.

acquisition (ˌækwɪ'zɪʃən) *n.* **1.** the act of acquiring or gaining possession. **2.** something acquired. **3.** a person or thing of special merit added to a group. [C14: < L *acquīsītiōn-*, < *acquīrere* to ACQUIRE]

acquisitive (ə'kwɪzɪtɪv) *adj.* inclined or eager to acquire things, esp. material possessions. —**ac'quisitively** *adv.* —**ac'quisitiveness** *n.*

acquit (ə'kwɪt) *vb.* **-quitting, -quitted.** (*tr.*) **1.** (foll. by *of*) **a.** to free or release (from a charge of crime). **b.** to pronounce not guilty. **2.** (foll. by *of*) to free or relieve (from an obligation, duty, etc.). **3.** to repay or settle (a debt or obligation). **4.** to conduct (oneself). [C13: < OF *aquiter*, < *quiter* to release, QUIT] —**ac'quittal** *n.* —**ac'quitter** *n.*

acquittance (ə'kwɪtəns) *n.* **1.** a release from or settlement of a debt, etc. **2.** a record of this, such as a receipt.

acre ('eɪkə) *n.* **1.** a unit of area used in certain English-speaking countries, equal to 4840 square yards or 4046.86 square metres. **2.** (*pl.*) **a.** land, esp. a large area. **b.** *Inf.* a large amount. **3. farm the long acre.** *N.Z.* to graze stock on the grass along a highway. [OE *æcer* field, acre]

acreage ('eɪkərɪdʒ) *n.* land area in acres.

acrid ('ækrɪd) *adj.* **1.** unpleasantly pungent or sharp to the smell or taste. **2.** sharp or caustic, esp. in speech or nature. [C18: < L *ācer* sharp, sour; prob. infl. by ACID] —**acridity** (ə'krɪdɪtɪ) *n.* —**'acridly** *adv.*

acridine ('ækrɪˌdiːn) *n.* a colourless crystalline solid used in the manufacture of dyes.

acriflavine (ˌækrɪ'fleɪvɪn) *n.* a brownish or orange-red powder used in medicine as an antiseptic. [C20: < ACRIDINE + FLAVIN]

acriflavine hydrochloride *n.* a red crystalline substance obtained from acriflavine and used as an antiseptic.

Acrilan ('ækrɪˌlæn) *n.* *Trademark.* an acrylic fibre or fabric, characterized by strength and resistance to creasing and used for clothing, carpets, etc.

acrimony ('ækrɪmənɪ) *n., pl.* **-nies.** bitterness or sharpness of manner, speech, temper, etc. [C16: < L *ācrimōnia*, < *ācer* sharp, sour] —**acrimonious** (ˌækrɪ'məʊnɪəs) *adj.*

acro- *combining form.* **1.** denoting something at a height, top, beginning, or end: *acropolis.* **2.** denoting an extremity of the human body: *acromegaly.* [< Gk *akros* extreme, topmost]

acrobat ('ækrəˌbæt) *n.* **1.** an entertainer who performs acts that require skill, agility, and coordination, such as swinging from a trapeze or walking a tightrope. **2.** a person noted for his frequent and rapid changes of position or allegiance. [C19: via F < Gk *akrobatēs*, one who walks on tiptoe, < ACRO- + *bat-*, < *bainein* to walk] —ˌ**acro'batic** *adj.* —ˌ**acro'batically** *adv.*

acrobatics (ˌækrə'bætɪks) *pl. n.* **1.** the skills or feats of an acrobat. **2.** any activity requiring agility and skill: *mental acrobatics.*

acrogen ('ækrədʒən) *n.* any flowerless plant, such as a fern or moss, in which growth occurs from the tip of the main stem. —**acrogenous** (ə'krɒdʒɪnəs) *adj.*

acromegaly (ˌækrəʊ'mɛgəlɪ) *n.* a chronic disease characterized by enlargement of the bones of the head, hands, and feet. It is caused by excessive secretion of growth hormone by the pituitary gland. [C19: < F *acromégalie*, < ACRO- + Gk *megal-*, stem of *megas* big] —**acromegalic** (ˌækrəʊmɪ'gælɪk) *adj., n.*

acronym ('ækrənɪm) *n.* a pronounceable name made from a series of initial letters or parts of a group of words; for example, *UNESCO* for the *United Nations Educational, Scientific, and Cultural Organization.* [C20: < ACRO- + -ONYM]

acrophobia (ˌækrə'fəʊbɪə) *n.* abnormal fear or dread of being at a great height. [C19: < ACRO- + -PHOBIA] —ˌ**acro'phobic** *adj., n.*

acropolis (ə'krɒpəlɪs) *n.* the citadel of an ancient Greek city. [C17: < Gk, < ACRO- + *polis* city]

Acropolis (ə'krɒpəlɪs) *n.* the citadel of Athens on which the Parthenon stands.

across (ə'krɒs) *prep.* **1.** from one side to the other side of. **2.** on or at the other side of. **3.** so as to transcend the boundaries or barriers of: *across religious divisions.* ~*adv.* **4.** from one side to the other. **5.** on or to the other side. [C13 *on croice, acros*, < OF *a croix* crosswise]

across-the-board *adj.* (of salary increases, taxation cuts, etc.) affecting all levels or classes equally.

acrostic (ə'krɒstɪk) *n.* a number of lines of writing, such as a poem, certain letters of which form a word, proverb, etc. A **single acrostic** is formed by the initial letters of the lines, a **double acrostic** by the initial and final letters, and a **triple acrostic** by the initial, middle, and final letters. [C16: via F < Gk, < ACRO- + *stikhos* line of verse] —**a'crostically** *adv.*

acrylic (ə'krɪlɪk) *adj.* **1.** of, derived from, or concerned with acrylic acid. ~*n.* **2.** short for **acrylic fibre, acrylic resin.** [C20: < L *ăcer* sharp + *olēre* to smell + -IC]

acrylic acid *n.* a colourless corrosive pungent liquid, used in the manufacture of acrylic resins. Formula: CH_2: CHCOOH.

acrylic fibre *n.* a man-made fibre used in blankets, knitwear, etc.

acrylic resin *n.* any of a group of polymers of acrylic acid, its esters, or amides, used as synthetic rubbers, paints, and as plastics such as Perspex.

act (ækt) *n.* **1.** something done or performed. **2.** the performance of some physical or mental process; action. **3.** (*cap. when part of a name*) the formally codified result of deliberation by a legislative body. **4.** (*often pl.*) a formal written record of transactions, proceedings, etc., as of a society, committee, or legislative body. **5.** a major division of a dramatic work. **6. a.** a short performance of skill, a comic sketch, dance, etc. **b.** those giving such a performance. **7.** an assumed attitude or pose, esp. one intended to impress. **8. get in on the act.** *Inf.* to become involved in a profitable situation in order to share in the benefit. **9. get one's act together.** *Inf.* to organize oneself. ~*vb.* **10.** (*intr.*) to do something. **11.** (*intr.*) to operate; react: *his mind acted quickly.* **12.** to perform (a part or role) in a play, etc. **13.** (*tr.*) to present (a play, etc.) on stage. **14.** (*intr.;* usually foll. by *for* or *as*) to be a substitute (for). **15.** (*intr.;* foll. by *as*) to serve the function or purpose (of). **16.** (*intr.*) to conduct oneself or behave (as if one were): *she usually acts like a lady.* **17.** (*intr.*) to behave in an unnatural or affected way. **18.** (*copula*) to play the part of: *to act the fool.* **19.** (*copula*) to behave in a manner appropriate to: *to act one's age.* ~See also **act on, act up.** [C14: < L *actus* a doing, & *actum* a thing done, < the p.p. of *agere* to do] —**'actable** *adj.* —**ˌacta'bility** *n.*

ACT *abbrev. for* Australian Capital Territory.

ACTH *n.* adrenocorticotropic hormone; a hormone, secreted by the anterior lobe of the pituitary gland, that stimulates growth of the adrenal gland. It is used in treating rheumatoid arthritis, allergic and skin diseases, etc.

acting ('æktɪŋ) *adj.* (*prenominal*) **1.** taking on duties temporarily, esp. as a substitute for another. **2.** performing the duties of though not yet holding the rank of: *acting lieutenant.* **3.** operating or functioning. **4.** intended for stage performance; provided with directions for actors: *an acting version of "Hedda Gabler".* ~*n.* **5.** the art or profession of an actor.

actinia (æk'tɪnɪə) *n., pl.* **-tiniae** (-'tɪnɪˌiː) *or* **-tinias.** a sea anemone common in rock pools. [C18: NL, lit.: things having a radial structure]

actinic (æk'tɪnɪk) *adj.* (of radiation) producing a photochemical effect. [C19: < ACTINO- + -IC] —**ac'tinically** *adv.* —**'actinˌism** *n.*

actinide series ('æktɪˌnaɪd) *n.* a series of 15 radioactive elements with increasing atomic numbers from actinium to lawrencium.

actinium (æk'tɪnɪəm) *n.* a radioactive element of the actinide series, occurring as a decay product of uranium. It is used in neutron production. Symbol: Ac; atomic no.: 89; half-life of most stable isotope, ^{227}Ac: 22 years. [C19: NL, < ACTINO- + -IUM]

actino- *or before a vowel* **actin-** *combining form.* **1.** indicating a radial structure: *actinomorphic.* **2.** indicating radioactivity or radiation: *actinometer.* [< Gk, < *aktis* ray]

actinoid ('æktɪˌnɔɪd) *adj.* having a radiate form, as a sea anemone or starfish.

actinometer (ˌæktɪ'nɒmɪtə) *n.* an instrument for measuring the intensity of radiation, esp. of the sun's rays.

actinomycin (ˌæktɪnəʊ'maɪsɪn) *n.* any of several toxic antibiotics obtained from soil bacteria, used in treating some cancers.

actinozoan (ˌæktɪnəʊ'zəʊən) *n., adj.* another word for **anthozoan.**

action ('ækʃən) *n.* **1.** the state or process of doing something or being active. **2.** something done, such as an act or deed. **3.** movement or posture during some physical activity. **4.** activity, force, or energy: *a man of action.* **5.** (*usually pl.*) conduct or behaviour. **6.** *Law.* a legal proceeding brought by one party against another; lawsuit. **7.** the operating mechanism, esp. in a piano, gun, watch, etc. **8.** the force applied to a body. **9.** the way in which something operates or works. **10. out of action.** not functioning. **11.** the events that form the plot of a story, play, or other composition. **12.** *Mil.* **a.** a minor engagement. **b.** fighting at sea or on land: *he saw action in the war.* **13.** *Inf.* the profits of an enterprise or transaction (esp. in **a piece of the action**). **14.** *Sl.* the main activity, esp. social activity. **15.** short for **industrial action.** ~*vb.* (*tr.*) **16.** to put into effect; take action concerning. ~*sentence substitute.* **17.** a command given by a film director to indicate that filming is to begin. [C14 *accioun,* ult. < L *āctiōn-,* < *agere* to do]

actionable ('ækʃənəbᵊl) *adj. Law.* affording grounds for legal action. —**'actionably** *adv.*

action committee *or* **group** *n.* a committee or group formed to pursue an end, usually political, using petitions, marches, etc.

action painting *n.* a development of abstract expressionism characterized by accidental effects of thrown, smeared, dripped, or spattered paint. Also called: **tachisme.**

action replay *n.* the rerunning of a small section of a television film or tape of a match or other sporting contest, often in slow motion.

action stations *pl. n.* **1.** *Mil.* the positions taken up by individuals in preparation for or during a battle. ~*sentence substitute.* **2.** a command to take up such positions. **3.** *Inf.* a warning to get ready for something.

activate ('æktɪˌveɪt) *vb.* (*tr.*) **1.** to make active or capable of action. **2.** *Physics.* to make radioactive. **3.** *Chem.* to increase the rate of (a reaction). **4.** to purify (sewage) by aeration. **5.** *U.S. mil.* to mobilize or organize (a unit). —**ˌacti'vation** *n.* —**'actiˌvator** *n.*

activated carbon *n.* a highly adsorptive form of carbon used to remove colour or impurities from liquids and gases.

activated sludge *n.* a mass of aerated precipitated sewage added to untreated sewage to bring about purification by hastening bacterial decomposition.

active ('æktɪv) *adj.* **1.** moving, working, or doing something. **2.** busy or involved: *an active life.* **3.** physically energetic. **4.** effective: *an active ingredient.* **5.** *Grammar.* denoting a voice of verbs used to indicate that the subject of a sentence is performing the action or causing the event or process described by the verb, as *kicked* in *The boy kicked the football.* **6.** being fully engaged in military service. **7.** (of a volcano) erupting periodically; not extinct. **8.** *Astron.* (of the sun) exhibiting a large number of sunspots, solar flares, etc., and a marked variation in intensity and frequency of radio emission. ~*n.* **9.** *Grammar.* **a.** the active voice. **b.** an active verb. [C14: < L *āctīvus.* See ACT, -IVE] —**'actively** *adv.* —**'activeness** *n.*

active list *n. Mil.* a list of officers available for full duty.

activism ('æktɪˌvɪzəm) *n.* a policy of taking direct and often militant action to achieve an end, esp. a political or social one. —**'activist** *n.*

activity (æk'tɪvɪtɪ) *n., pl.* **-ties.** **1.** the state or quality of being active. **2.** lively action or movement. **3.** any specific action, pursuit, etc.: *recreational activities.* **4.** the number of disintegrations of a radioactive substance in a given unit of time.

act of God *n. Law.* a sudden and inevitable

occurrence caused by natural forces, such as a flood or earthquake.

act on *or* **upon** *vb.* (*intr., prep.*) **1.** to regulate one's behaviour in accordance with (advice, information, etc.). **2.** to have an effect on (illness, a part of the body, etc.).

actor ('æktə) *or* (*fem.*) **actress** ('æktrɪs) *n.* a person who acts in a play, film, broadcast, etc.

actual ('æktʃʊəl) *adj.* **1.** existing in reality or as a matter of fact. **2.** real or genuine. **3.** existing at the present time; current. [C14 *actuel* existing, < LL, < L *āctus* ACT]

▷ **Usage.** The excessive use of *actual* and *actually* should be avoided. They are unnecessary in sentences such as *in actual fact, he is forty-two,* and *he did actually go to the play but did not enjoy it.*

actuality (ˌæktʃʊ'ælɪtɪ) *n., pl.* **-ties. 1.** true existence; reality. **2.** (*sometimes pl.*) a fact or condition that is real.

actualize *or* **-lise** ('æktʃʊəˌlaɪz) *vb.* (*tr.*) **1.** to make actual or real. **2.** to represent realistically. —ˌ**actuali'zation** *or* **-li'sation** *n.*

actually ('æktʃʊəlɪ) *adv.* **1. a.** as an actual fact; really. **b.** (*as sentence modifier*): *actually, I haven't seen him.* **2.** at present.

actuarius ('æktʃʊˌɛərɪəs) *n. S. African history.* an official of the synod of a Dutch Reformed Church. [< L; see ACTUARY]

actuary ('æktʃʊərɪ) *n., pl.* **-aries.** a statistician, esp. one employed by insurance companies to calculate risks, policy premiums, and dividends. [C16 (meaning: registrar): < L *āctuārius* one who keeps accounts, < *actum* public business, & *acta* documents] —**actuarial** (ˌæktʃʊ'ɛərɪəl) *adj.*

actuate ('æktʃʊˌeɪt) *vb.* (*tr.*) **1.** to put into action or mechanical motion. **2.** to motivate: *actuated by unworthy desires.* [C16: < Med. L *actuātus,* < *actuāre* to incite to action, < L *āctus* ACT] —ˌ**actu'ation** *n.* —'**actuˌator** *n.*

act up *vb.* (*intr., adv.*) *Inf.* to behave in a troublesome way: *the engine began to act up.*

acuity (ə'kjuːɪtɪ) *n.* keenness or acuteness, esp. in vision or thought. [C15: < OF, < L *acūtus* ACUTE]

aculeus (ə'kjuːlɪəs) *n.* **1.** a prickle, such as the thorn of a rose. **2.** a sting. [C19: < L, dim. of *acus* needle] —**a'culeate** *adj.*

acumen ('ækjʊˌmɛn, ə'kjuːmən) *n.* the ability to judge well; insight. [C16: < L: sharpness, < *acuere* to sharpen] —**a'cuminous** *adj.*

acuminate *adj.* (ə'kjuːmɪnɪt). **1.** narrowing to a sharp point, as some types of leaf. ~*vb.* (ə'kjuːmɪˌneɪt). **2.** (*tr.*) to make pointed or sharp. [C17: < L *acūmināre* to sharpen] —**aˌcumi'nation** *n.*

acupuncture ('ækjʊˌpʌŋktʃə) *n.* the insertion of the tips of needles into the skin at specific points for the purpose of treating various disorders by stimulating nerve impulses. [C17: < L *acus* needle + PUNCTURE] —'**acuˌpuncturist** *n.*

acute (ə'kjuːt) *adj.* **1.** penetrating in perception or insight. **2.** sensitive to details; keen. **3.** of extreme importance; crucial. **4.** sharp or severe; intense. **5.** having a sharp end or point. **6.** *Maths.* (of an angle) less than 90°. **7.** (of a disease) **a.** arising suddenly and manifesting intense severity. **b.** of relatively short duration. **8.** *Phonetics.* of or relating to an accent (´) placed over vowels, denoting that the vowel is pronounced with higher musical pitch (as in ancient Greek) or with certain special quality (as in French). ~*n.* **9.** an acute accent. [C14: < L *acūtus,* p.p. of *acuere* to sharpen, < *acus* needle] —**a'cutely** *adv.* —**a'cuteness** *n.*

acute accent *n.* the diacritical mark (´), used in some languages to indicate that the vowel over which it is placed has a special quality (as in French *été*) or that it receives the strongest stress in the word (as in Spanish *hablé*).

acute dose *n.* a fatal dose of radiation.

ad (æd) *n. Inf.* short for **advertisement.**

A.D. *or* **AD** (indicating years numbered from the supposed year of the birth of Christ) *abbrev. for* anno Domini: *70 A.D.* [L: in the year of the Lord]

▷ **Usage.** In strict usage, A.D. is only employed with specific years: *he died in 1621 A.D.,* but *he died in the 17th century.* Formerly the practice was to write A.D. preceding the date (*A.D. 1621*), and it is also strictly correct to omit *in* when A.D. is used, since this is already contained in the meaning of the Latin *anno Domini* (in the year of Our Lord), but this is no longer general practice. B.C. is used with both specific dates and indications of the period: *Heraclitus was born about 540 B.C.; the battle took place in the 4th century B.C.*

ad- *prefix.* **1.** to; towards: *adverb.* **2.** near; next to: *adrenal.* [< L: to, towards. As a prefix in words of L origin, *ad-* became *ac-, af-, ag-, al-, an-, acq-, ar-, as-,* and *at-* before *c, f, g, l, n, q, r, s,* and *t,* and became *a-* before *gn, sc, sp, st*]

adage ('ædɪdʒ) *n.* a traditional saying that is accepted by many as true; proverb. [C16: via OF < L *adagium;* rel. to *āio* I say]

adagio (ə'dɑːdʒɪˌəʊ) *Music.* ~*adj., adv.* **1.** (to be performed) slowly. ~*n., pl.* **-gios. 2.** a movement or piece to be performed slowly. [C18: It., < *ad* at + *agio* ease]

Adam[1] ('ædəm) *n.* **1.** *Bible.* the first man, created by God (Genesis 2–3). **2. not know (someone) from Adam.** to have no knowledge of or acquaintance with someone. **3. Adam's ale** *or* **wine.** water.

Adam[2] ('ædəm) *adj.* in the neoclassical style made popular by Robert Adam (1728-92), Scottish architect and furniture designer.

adamant ('ædəmənt) *adj.* **1.** unshakable in determination, purpose, etc.; inflexible. **2.** unbreakable; impenetrable. ~*n.* **3.** any extremely hard substance. **4.** a legendary stone said to be impenetrable. [OE: < L *adamas,* < Gk, lit.: unconquerable, < A-[1] + *daman* to conquer] —ˌ**ada'mantine** *adj.*

Adam's apple *n.* the visible projection of the thyroid cartilage of the larynx at the front of the neck.

adapt (ə'dæpt) *vb.* **1.** (often foll. by *to*) to adjust (someone or something) to different conditions. **2.** (*tr.*) to fit, change, or modify to suit a new or different purpose. [C17: < L *adaptāre,* < *ad-* to + *aptāre* to fit] —**a'daptable** *adj.* —**aˌdapta'bility** *n.* —**a'daptive** *adj.*

adaptation (ˌædəp'teɪʃən) *n.* **1.** the act or process of adapting or the state of being adapted. **2.** something that is produced by adapting something else. **3.** something that is changed or modified to suit new conditions. **4.** *Biol.* a modification in organisms that makes them better suited to survive and reproduce in a particular environment.

adapter *or* **adaptor** (ə'dæptə) *n.* **1.** a person or thing that adapts. **2.** any device for connecting two parts, esp. ones that are of different sizes. **3. a.** a plug used to connect an electrical device to a mains supply when they have different types of terminals. **b.** a device used to connect several electrical appliances to a single socket.

ADC *abbrev. for:* **1.** aide-de-camp. **2.** analogue-digital converter.

add (æd) *vb.* **1.** to combine (two or more numbers or quantities) by addition. **2.** (*tr.;* foll. by *to*) to increase (a number or quantity) by another number or quantity using addition. **3.** (*tr.;* often foll. by *to*) to join (something) to something else in order to increase the size, effect, or scope: *to add insult to injury.* **4.** (*intr.;* foll. by *to*) to have an extra and increased effect (on). **5.** (*tr.*) to say or write further. **6.** (*tr.;* foll. by *in*) to include. ~See also **add up.** [C14: < L *addere,* < *ad-* to + *-dere, dare* to put]

addax ('ædæks) *n.* a large light-coloured antelope having ribbed loosely spiralled horns and inhabiting desert regions in N Africa. [C17: L, < an unidentified ancient N African language]

addend ('ædɛnd) *n.* any of a set of numbers that is to be added. [C20: short for ADDENDUM]

addendum (ə'dɛndəm) *n., pl.* **-da** (-də). **1.** something added; an addition. **2.** a supplement or appendix to a book, magazine, etc. [C18: < L, gerundive of *addere* to ADD]

adder ('ædə) *n.* **1.** Also called: **viper.** a common viper that is widely distributed in Europe, including Britain, and Asia and is dark grey with a black zigzag pattern along the back. **2.** any of various similar venomous or nonvenomous snakes. ~See also **puff adder.** [OE *nǣdre* snake; in ME *a naddre* was mistaken for *an addre*]

adder's-tongue *n.* any of several ferns that grow in the N hemisphere and have a narrow spore-bearing body that sticks out like a spike from the leaf.

addict *vb.* (əˈdɪkt). **1.** (*tr.; usually passive;* often foll. by *to*) to cause (someone or oneself) to become dependent (on something, esp. a narcotic drug). ~*n.* (ˈædɪkt). **2.** a person who is addicted, esp. to narcotic drugs. **3.** *Inf.* a person devoted to something: *a jazz addict.* [C16 (as adj. and as vb.; n. use C20): < L *addictus* given over, < *addīcere*, < *ad-* to + *dīcere* to say] **—adˈdiction** *n.* **—adˈdictive** *adj.*

Addison's disease (ˈædɪsᵊnz) *n.* a disease characterized by bronzing of the skin, anaemia, and extreme weakness, caused by underactivity of the adrenal glands. [C19: after Thomas *Addison* (1793–1860), E physician who identified it]

addition (əˈdɪʃən) *n.* **1.** the act, process, or result of adding. **2.** a person or thing that is added or acquired. **3.** a mathematical operation in which the sum of two numbers or quantities is calculated. Usually indicated by the symbol +. **4.** *Obs.* a title. **5. in addition.** (*adv.*) also; as well. **6. in addition to.** (*prep.*) besides; as well as. [C15: < L *additiōn-*, < *addere* to ADD] **—adˈditional** *adj.*

additive (ˈædɪtɪv) *adj.* **1.** characterized or produced by addition. ~*n.* **2.** any substance added to something to improve it, prevent deterioration, etc. **3.** short for **food additive.** [C17: < LL *additīvus*, < *addere* to ADD]

addle (ˈædᵊl) *vb.* **1.** to make or become confused or muddled. **2.** to make or become rotten. ~*adj.* **3.** (*in combination*) indicating a confused or muddled state: *addle-brained.* [C18 (vb.), back formation < *addled*, < C13 *addle* rotten, < OE *adela* filth]

add-on *n. Computers.* a circuit, hardware, etc., that can be added to a computer to increase its capacity or performance.

address (əˈdrɛs) *n.* **1.** the conventional form by which the location of a building is described. **2.** the written form of this, as on a letter or parcel. **3.** the place at which someone lives. **4.** a speech or written communication, esp. one of a formal nature. **5.** skilfulness or tact. **6.** *Arch.* manner of speaking. **7.** *Computers.* a number giving the location of a piece of stored information. **8.** (*usually pl.*) expressions of affection made by a man in courting a woman. ~*vb.* (*tr.*) **9.** to mark (a letter, parcel, etc.) with an address. **10.** to speak to, refer to in speaking, or deliver a speech to. **11.** (used reflexively; foll. by *to*) **a.** to speak or write to. **b.** to apply oneself to: *he addressed himself to the task.* **12.** to direct (a message, warning, etc.) to the attention of. **13.** to adopt a position facing (the ball in golf, etc.). [C14 (in the sense: to make right, adorn) and C15 (in the modern sense: to direct words): via OF < Vulgar L *addrictiāre* (unattested), < L *ad-* to + *dīrectus* DIRECT] **—adˈdresser** *or* **adˈdressor** *n.*

addressee (ˌædrɛˈsiː) *n.* a person or organization to whom a letter, etc., is addressed.

adduce (əˈdjuːs) *vb.* (*tr.*) to cite (reasons, examples, etc.) as evidence or proof. [C15: < L *addūcere* to lead to] **—adˈducent** *adj.* **—adˈducible** *adj.* **—adduction** (əˈdʌkʃən) *n.*

adduct (əˈdʌkt) *vb.* (*tr.*) (of a muscle) to draw or pull (a leg, arm, etc.) towards the median axis of the body. [C19: < L *addūcere*; see ADDUCE] **—adˈduction** *n.* **—adˈductor** *n.*

add up *vb.* (*adv.*) **1.** to find the sum (of). **2.** (*intr.*) to result in a correct total. **3.** (*intr.*) *Inf.* to make sense. **4.** (*intr.;* foll. by *to*) to amount to.

-ade *suffix forming nouns.* a sweetened drink made of various fruits: *lemonade.* [< F, < L *-āta* made of, fem. p.p. of verbs ending in *-āre*]

adenine (ˈædənɪn) *n.* a purine base present in animal and plant tissues as a constituent of the nucleic acids DNA and RNA.

adeno- *or before a vowel* **aden-** *combining form.* gland or glandular: *adenoid; adenology.* [NL, < Gk *adēn* gland]

adenoidal (ˌædɪˈnɔɪdᵊl) *adj.* **1.** having the nasal tones or impaired breathing of one with enlarged adenoids. **2.** of adenoids.

adenoids (ˈædɪˌnɔɪdz) *pl. n.* a mass of lymphoid tissue at the back of the throat behind the uvula: when enlarged it often restricts nasal breathing, esp. in young children. [C19 : < Gk *adenoeidēs.* See ADENO-, -OID]

adenoma (ˌædɪˈnəʊmə) *n., pl.* **-mas** *or* **-mata** (-mətə). **1.** a tumour occurring in glandular tissue. **2.** a tumour having a glandlike structure.

adenosine (æˈdɛnəˌsiːn) *n. Biochem.* a compound formed by the condensation of adenine and ribose. It is present in all living cells in a combined form. [C20: a blend of ADENINE + RIBOSE]

adept *adj.* (əˈdɛpt). **1.** proficient in something requiring skill or manual dexterity. **2.** expert. ~*n.* (ˈædɛpt). **3.** a person who is skilled or proficient in something. [C17: < Med. L *adeptus*, < L *adipiscī*, < *ad-* to + *apiscī* to attain] **—aˈdeptness** *n.*

adequate (ˈædɪkwɪt) *adj.* able to fulfil a need without being abundant, outstanding, etc. [C17: < L *adaequāre*, < *ad-* to + *aequus* EQUAL] **—adequacy** (ˈædɪkwəsɪ) *n.* **—ˈadequately** *adv.*

à deux *French.* (a dø) *adj., adv.* of or for two persons.

adhere (ədˈhɪə) *vb.* (*intr.*) **1.** (usually foll. by *to*) to stick or hold fast. **2.** (foll. by *to*) to be devoted (to a political party, religion, etc.). **3.** (foll. by *to*) to follow exactly. [C16: via Med. L, < L *adhaerēre* to stick to]

adherent (ədˈhɪərənt) *n.* **1.** (usually foll. by *of*) a supporter or follower. ~*adj.* **2.** sticking, holding fast, or attached. **—adˈherence** *n.*

adhesion (ədˈhiːʒən) *n.* **1.** the quality or condition of sticking together or holding fast. **2.** ability to make firm contact without slipping. **3.** attachment, as to a political party, cause, etc. **4.** an attraction or repulsion between the molecules of unlike substances in contact. **5.** *Pathol.* abnormal union of structures or parts. [C17: < L *adhaesiōn-* a sticking. See ADHERE]

adhesive (ədˈhiːsɪv) *adj.* **1.** able or designed to adhere: *adhesive tape.* **2.** tenacious or clinging. ~*n.* **3.** a substance used for sticking, such as glue or paste. **—adˈhesively** *adv.* **—adˈhesiveness** *n.*

ad hoc (æd ˈhɒk) *adj., adv.* for a particular purpose only: *an ad hoc committee.* [L, lit.: to this]

ad hominem *Latin.* (æd ˈhɒmɪˌnɛm) *adj., adv.* directed against a person rather than his arguments. [lit.: to the man]

adiabatic (ˌædɪəˈbætɪk) *adj.* **1.** (of a thermodynamic process) taking place without loss or gain of heat. ~*n.* **2.** a curve on a graph representing the changes in a system undergoing an adiabatic process. [C19: < Gk, < A-¹ + *diabatos* passable]

adieu (əˈdjuː) *sentence substitute., n., pl.* **adieus** *or* **adieux** (əˈdjuːz). goodbye. [C14: < OF, < *a* to + *dieu* God]

ad infinitum (æd ˌɪnfɪˈnaɪtəm) *adv.* without end; endlessly; to infinity. Abbrev.: **ad inf.** [L]

ad interim (æd ˈɪntərɪm) *adj., adv.* for the meantime: *ad interim measures.* Abbrev.: **ad int.** [L]

adipocere (ˌædɪpəʊˈsɪə) *n.* a waxlike fatty substance sometimes formed during the decomposition of corpses. [C19: < NL *adiposus* fat + F *cire* wax]

adipose (ˈædɪˌpəʊs) *adj.* **1.** of, resembling, or containing fat; fatty. ~*n.* **2.** animal fat. [C18: < NL *adiposus*, < L *adeps* fat]

adit (ˈædɪt) *n.* an almost horizontal shaft into a mine, for access or drainage. [C17: < L *aditus*, < *adīre*, < *ad-* towards + *īre* to go]

adj. *abbrev. for:* **1.** adjective. **2.** adjunct. **3.** Also: **adjt.** adjutant.

adjacent (əˈdʒeɪsᵊnt) *adj.* being near or close, esp. having a common boundary; contiguous. [C15: <

L *adjacēre*, < *ad-* near + *jacēre* to lie] —**adˈjacency** *n.* —**adˈjacently** *adv.*

adjacent angles *pl. n.* two angles having the same vertex and a side in common.

adjective (ˈædʒɪktɪv) *n.* **1. a.** a word imputing a characteristic to a noun or pronoun. **b.** (*as modifier*): *an adjective phrase.* Abbrev.: **adj.** ~*adj.* **2.** additional or dependent. [C14: < LL, < L < *adjicere*, < *ad-* to + *jacere* to throw] —**adjectival** (ˌædʒɪkˈtaɪvᵊl) *adj.*

adjoin (əˈdʒɔɪn) *vb.* **1.** to be next to (an area of land, etc.). **2.** (*tr.;* foll. by *to*) to join; attach. [C14: via OF < L, < *ad-* to + *jungere* to join] —**adˈjoining** *adj.*

adjourn (əˈdʒɜːn) *vb.* **1.** (*intr.*) (of a court, etc.) to close at the end of a session. **2.** to postpone or be postponed, esp. temporarily. **3.** (*tr.*) to put off (a problem, discussion, etc.) for later consideration. **4.** (*intr.*) *Inf.* to move elsewhere: *let's adjourn to the kitchen.* [C14: < OF *ajourner* to defer to an arranged day, < *a-* to + *jour* day, < LL *diurnum*, < L *diēs* day] —**adˈjournment** *n.*

adjudge (əˈdʒʌdʒ) *vb.* (*tr.; usually passive*) **1.** to pronounce formally; declare. **2. a.** to judge. **b.** to decree: *he was adjudged bankrupt.* **c.** to award (costs, damages, etc.). **3.** *Arch.* to condemn. [C14: via OF < L *adjūdicāre.* See ADJUDICATE]

adjudicate (əˈdʒuːdɪˌkeɪt) *vb.* **1.** (when *intr.*, usually foll. by *upon*) to give a decision (on), esp. a formal or binding one. **2.** (*intr.*) to serve as a judge or arbiter, as in a competition. [C18: < L *adjūdicāre*, < *ad-* to + *jūdicāre* to judge, < *jūdex* judge] —**adˌjudiˈcation** *n.* —**adˈjudiˌcator** *n.*

adjunct (ˈædʒʌŋkt) *n.* **1.** something incidental or not essential that is added to something else. **2.** a person who is subordinate to another. **3.** *Grammar.* **a.** part of a sentence other than the subject or the predicate. **b.** a modifier. ~*adj.* **4.** added or connected in a secondary position. [C16: < L *adjunctus*, p.p. of *adjungere* to ADJOIN] —**adjunctive** (əˈdʒʌŋktɪv) *adj.* —**ˈadjunctly** *adv.*

adjure (əˈdʒʊə) *vb.* (*tr.*) **1.** to command, often by exacting an oath. **2.** to appeal earnestly to. [C14: < L *adjūrāre*, < *ad-* to + *jūrāre* to swear, < *jūs* oath] —**adjuration** (ˌædʒʊəˈreɪʃən) *n.* —**adˈjuratory** *adj.* —**adˈjurer** *or* **adˈjuror** *n.*

adjust (əˈdʒʌst) *vb.* **1.** (*tr.*) to alter slightly, esp. to achieve accuracy. **2.** to adapt, as to a new environment, etc. **3.** (*tr.*) to put into order. **4.** (*tr.*) *Insurance.* to determine the amount payable in settlement of (a claim). [C17: < OF *adjuster*, < *ad-* to + *juste* right, JUST] —**adˈjustable** *adj.* —**adˈjuster** *n.*

adjustment (əˈdʒʌstmənt) *n.* **1.** the act of adjusting or state of being adjusted. **2.** a control for regulating.

adjutant (ˈædʒətənt) *n.* an officer who acts as administrative assistant to a superior officer. [C17: < L *adjūtāre* to AID] —**ˈadjutancy** *n.*

adjutant bird *or* **stork** *n.* either of two large carrion-eating storks which are similar to the marabou and occur in S and SE Asia. [so called for its supposedly military gait]

adjutant general *n., pl.* **adjutants general. 1.** *Brit. Army.* a member of the Army Board responsible for personnel and administrative functions. **2.** *U.S. Army.* the adjutant of a military unit with general staff.

Adlerian (ædˈlɪərɪən) *adj.* of or relating to the work of Alfred Adler (1870-1937), Austrian psychiatrist.

ad-lib (ædˈlɪb) *vb.* **-libbing, -libbed. 1.** to improvise and deliver spontaneously (a speech, etc.). ~*adj.* (**ad lib** when predicative) **2.** improvised. ~*adv.* **ad lib. 3.** spontaneously; freely. ~*n.* **4.** an improvised performance, often humorous. [C18: short for L *ad libitum*, lit.: according to pleasure]

ad libitum (ˌæd ˈlɪbɪtəm) *adv., adj. Music.* at the performer's discretion. [L.: see AD-LIB]

Adm. *abbrev. for:* **1.** Admiral. **2.** Admiralty.

adman (ˈædˌmæn) *n., pl.* **-men.** *Inf.* a man who works in advertising.

admass (ˈædmæs) *n.* the section of the public that is susceptible to advertising, etc., and the processes involved in influencing them. [C20: < AD + MASS]

admeasure (ædˈmɛʒə) *vb.* to measure out (land, etc.) as a share; apportion. [C14 *amesuren*, < OF, < *mesurer* to MEASURE; the modern form derives < AD- + MEASURE]

admin (ˈædmɪn) *n. Inf.* short for **administration.**

administer (ədˈmɪnɪstə) *vb.* (*mainly tr.*) **1.** (*also intr.*) to direct or control (the affairs of a business, etc.). **2.** to dispense: *administer justice.* **3.** (when *intr.*, foll. by *to*) to give or apply (medicine, etc.). **4.** to supervise the taking of (an oath, etc.). **5.** to manage (an estate, property, etc.). [C14 *amynistre* via OF < L, < *ad-* to + *ministrāre* to MINISTER]

administrate (ədˈmɪnɪˌstreɪt) *vb.* to manage or direct (the affairs of a business, institution, etc.).

administration (ədˌmɪnɪˈstreɪʃən) *n.* **1.** management of the affairs of an organization, such as a business or institution. **2.** the duties of an administrator. **3.** the body of people who administer an organization. **4.** the conduct of the affairs of government. **5.** term of office: used of governments, etc. **6.** the government as a whole. **7.** (*often cap.*) *Chiefly U.S.* the political executive, esp. of the U.S. **8.** *Property law.* **a.** the conduct or disposal of the estate of a deceased person. **b.** the management by a trustee of an estate. **9. a.** the administering of something, such as a sacrament or medical treatment. **b.** the thing that is administered. —**adˈministrative** *adj.* —**adˈministratively** *adv.*

administrator (ədˈmɪnɪˌstreɪtə) *n.* **1.** a person who administers the affairs of an organization, official body, etc. **2.** *Property law.* a person authorized to manage an estate.

admirable (ˈædmərəbᵊl) *adj.* deserving or inspiring admiration; excellent. —**ˈadmirably** *adv.*

admiral (ˈædmərəl) *n.* **1.** the supreme commander of a fleet or navy. **2.** Also called: **admiral of the fleet, fleet admiral.** a naval officer of the highest rank. **3.** a senior naval officer entitled to fly his own flag. See also **rear admiral, vice admiral. 4.** *Chiefly Brit.* the master of a fishing fleet. **5.** any of various brightly coloured butterflies, esp. the red admiral or white admiral. [C13 *amyral*, < OF *amiral* emir, & < Med. L *admīrālis* (spelling prob. infl. by *admīrābilis* admirable); both < Ar. *amīr* emir, commander, esp. in *amīr-al* commander of] —**ˈadmiralˌship** *n.*

admiralty (ˈædmərəltɪ) *n., pl.* **-ties. 1.** the office or jurisdiction of an admiral. **2.** jurisdiction over naval affairs.

Admiralty Board *n.* **the.** a department of the British Ministry of Defence, responsible for the administration of the Royal Navy.

Admiralty House *n.* the official residence of the governor general of Australia, in Sydney.

admiration (ˌædməˈreɪʃən) *n.* **1.** pleasurable contemplation or surprise. **2.** a person or thing that is admired.

admire (ədˈmaɪə) *vb.* (*tr.*) **1.** to regard with esteem, approval, or pleased surprise. **2.** *Arch.* to wonder at. [C16: < L *admīrāri*, < *ad-* to, at + *mīrāri* to wonder] —**adˈmirer** *n.* —**adˈmiring** *adj.* —**adˈmiringly** *adv.*

admissible (ədˈmɪsəbᵊl) *adj.* **1.** able or deserving to be considered or allowed. **2.** deserving to be allowed to enter. **3.** *Law.* (esp. of evidence) capable of being admitted in a court of law. —**adˌmissiˈbility** *n.*

admission (ədˈmɪʃən) *n.* **1.** permission to enter or the right to enter. **2.** the price charged for entrance. **3.** acceptance for a position, etc. **4.** a confession, as of a crime, etc. **5.** an acknowledgment of the truth of something. [C15: < L *admissiōn-*, < *admittere* to ADMIT] —**adˈmissive** *adj.*

admit (ədˈmɪt) *vb.* **-mitting, -mitted.** (*mainly tr.*) **1.** (*may take a clause as object*) to confess or acknowledge (a crime, mistake, etc.). **2.** (*may take a clause as object*) to concede (the truth of something). **3.** to allow to enter. **4.** (foll. by *to*) to allow participation (in) or the right to be part (of).

5. (when *intr.*, foll. by *of*) to allow (of). [C14: < L *admittere*, < *ad-* to + *mittere* to send]
admittance (əd'mɪtᵊns) *n.* **1.** the right or authority to enter. **2.** the act of giving entrance. **3.** *Electricity.* the reciprocal of impedance.
admittedly (əd'mɪtɪdlɪ) *adv.* (*sentence modifier*) willingly conceded: *admittedly I am afraid.*
admix (əd'mɪks) *vb.* (*tr.*) *Rare.* to mix or blend. [C16: back formation < obs. *admixt*, < L *admīscēre* to mix with]
admixture (əd'mɪkstʃə) *n.* **1.** a less common word for **mixture.** **2.** an ingredient.
admonish (əd'mɒnɪʃ) *vb.* (*tr.*) **1.** to reprove firmly but not harshly. **2.** to warn; caution. [C14: via OF < Vulgar L *admonestāre* (unattested), < L *admonēre*, < *monēre* to advise] **—admonition** (ˌædmə'nɪʃən) *n.* **—ad'monitory** *adj.*
ad nauseam (æd 'nɔːzɪˌæm) *adv.* to a disgusting extent. [L: to (the point of) nausea]
ado (ə'duː) *n.* bustling activity; fuss; bother; delay (esp. in **without more ado, with much ado).** [C14: < *at do* a to-do, < ON *at* to (marking the infinitive) + DO[1]]
adobe (ə'dəʊbɪ) *n.* **1.** a sun-dried brick used for building. **2.** a building constructed of such bricks. **3.** the clayey material from which such bricks are made. [C19: < Sp.]
adolescence (ˌædə'lɛsəns) *n.* the period in human development that occurs between the beginning of puberty and adulthood. [C15: via OF < L, < *adolēscere* to grow up]
adolescent (ˌædə'lɛsᵊnt) *adj.* **1.** of or relating to adolescence. **2.** *Inf.* behaving in an immature way. ~*n.* **3.** an adolescent person.
Adonis (ə'dəʊnɪs) *n.* **1.** *Greek myth.* a handsome youth loved by Aphrodite. **2.** a handsome young man.
adopt (ə'dɒpt) *vb.* (*tr.*) **1.** *Law.* to take (another's child) as one's own child. **2.** to choose and follow (a plan, method, etc.). **3.** to take over (an idea, etc.) as if it were one's own. **4.** to assume: *to adopt a title.* **5.** to accept (a report, etc.). [C16: < L *adoptāre*, < *optāre* to choose] **—a'doption** *n.*
adopted (ə'dɒptɪd) *adj.* having been adopted.
adoptive (ə'dɒptɪv) *adj.* due to adoption: *an adoptive parent.*
adorable (ə'dɔːrəbᵊl) *adj.* **1.** very attractive; lovable. **2.** *Becoming rare.* deserving adoration. **—a'dorably** *adv.*
adoration (ˌædə'reɪʃən) *n.* **1.** deep love or esteem. **2.** the act of worshipping.
adore (ə'dɔː) *vb.* **1.** (*tr.*) to love intensely or deeply. **2.** to worship (a god) with religious rites. **3.** (*tr.*) *Inf.* to like very much. [C15: via F < L *adōrāre*, < *ad-* to + *ōrāre* to pray] **—a'dorer** *n.* **—a'doring** *adj.* **—a'doringly** *adv.*
adorn (ə'dɔːn) *vb.* (*tr.*) **1.** to decorate. **2.** to increase the beauty, distinction, etc., of. [C14: via OF < L *adōrnāre*, < *ōrnāre* to furnish] **—a'dornment** *n.*
ADP[1] *n. Biochem.* adenosine diphosphate; a substance derived from ATP with the liberation of energy that is then used in the performance of muscular work.
ADP[2], **A.D.P.,** *or* **a.d.p.** *abbrev. for* automatic data processing.
ad rem *Latin.* (æd 'rɛm) *adj., adv.* to the point; without digression.
adrenal (ə'driːnᵊl) *adj.* **1.** on or near the kidneys. **2.** of or relating to the adrenal glands or their secretions. ~*n.* **3.** an adrenal gland. [C19: < AD- (near) + RENAL]
adrenal gland *n.* an endocrine gland at the anterior end of each kidney. It secretes adrenaline. Also called: **suprarenal gland.**
adrenaline *or* **adrenalin** (ə'drɛnəlɪn) *n.* a hormone that is secreted by the adrenal medulla in response to stress and increases heart rate, pulse rate, and blood pressure. It is extracted from animals or synthesized for medical use. U.S. name: **epinephrine.**
adrift (ə'drɪft) *adj.* (*postpositive*), *adv.* **1.** floating without steering or mooring; drifting. **2.** without purpose; aimless. **3.** *Inf.* off course.
adroit (ə'drɔɪt) *adj.* **1.** skilful or dexterous. **2.** quick in thought or reaction. [C17: < F *à droit* rightly] **—a'droitly** *adv.* **—a'droitness** *n.*
adsorb (əd'sɔːb) *vb.* to undergo or cause to undergo a process in which a substance, usually a gas, accumulates on the surface of a solid forming a thin film. [C19: AD- + *-sorb* as in ABSORB] **—ad'sorbable** *adj.* **—ad'sorbent** *adj.* **—ad'sorption** *n.*
ADT (in the U.S. and Canada) *abbrev. for* Atlantic Daylight Time.
adulate ('ædjʊˌleɪt) *vb.* (*tr.*) to flatter or praise obsequiously. [C17: back formation < C15 *adulation*, < L *adūlārī* to flatter] **—ˌadu'lation** *n.* **—'aduˌlator** *n.* **—adulatory** (ˌædjʊ'leɪtərɪ) *adj.*
adult ('ædʌlt, ə'dʌlt) *adj.* **1.** having reached maturity; fully developed. **2.** of or intended for mature people: *adult education.* **3.** suitable only for adults because of being pornographic. ~*n.* **4.** a person who has attained maturity. **5.** a mature fully grown animal or plant. **6.** *Law.* a person who has attained the age of legal majority. [C16: < L *adultus*, < *adolēscere* to grow up] **—a'dulthood** *n.*
adulterant (ə'dʌltərənt) *n.* **1.** a substance that adulterates. ~*adj.* **2.** adulterating.
adulterate *vb.* (ə'dʌltəˌreɪt). **1.** (*tr.*) to debase by adding inferior material: *to adulterate milk with water.* ~*adj.* (ə'dʌltərɪt). **2.** debased or impure. [C16: < L *adulterāre* to corrupt, commit adultery, prob. < *alter* another] **—aˌdulter'ation** *n.* **—a'dulterˌator** *n.*
adulterer (ə'dʌltərə) *or* (*fem.*) **adulteress** *n.* a person who has committed adultery. [C16: orig. also *adulter*, < L *adulter*, back formation < *adulterāre* to ADULTERATE]
adulterous (ə'dʌltərəs) *adj.* of, characterized by, or inclined to adultery. **—a'dulterously** *adv.*
adultery (ə'dʌltərɪ) *n., pl.* **-teries.** voluntary sexual intercourse between a married man or woman and partner other than the legal spouse. [C15 *adulterie*, altered < C14 *avoutrie*, via OF < L *adulterium*, < *adulter*, back formation < *adulterāre*. See ADULTERATE]
adumbrate ('ædʌmˌbreɪt) *vb.* (*tr.*) **1.** to outline; give a faint indication of. **2.** to foreshadow. **3.** to obscure. [C16: < L *adumbrāre* to cast a shadow on, < *umbra* shadow] **—ˌadum'bration** *n.* **—adumbrative** (æd'ʌmbrətɪv) *adj.*
adv. *abbrev. for:* **1.** adverb. **2.** adverbial. **3.** adversus. [L: against] **4.** advertisement. **5.** advocate.
ad valorem (æd və'lɔːrəm) *adj., adv.* (of taxes) in proportion to the estimated value of the goods taxed. Abbrev.: **ad val., a.v., A/V.** [< L]
advance (əd'vɑːns) *vb.* **1.** to go or bring forward in position. **2.** (foll. by *on*) to move (towards) in a threatening manner. **3.** (*tr.*) to present for consideration. **4.** to improve; further. **5.** (*tr.*) to cause (an event) to occur earlier. **6.** (*tr.*) to supply (money, goods, etc.) beforehand, either for a loan or as an initial payment. **7.** to increase (a price, etc.) or (of a price, etc.) to be increased. **8.** (*intr.*) to be promoted. ~*n.* **9.** forward movement; progress in time or space. **10.** improvement; progress in development. **11.** *Commerce.* **a.** the supplying of commodities or funds before receipt of an agreed consideration. **b.** the commodities or funds supplied in this manner. **12.** Also called: **advance payment.** a money payment made before it is legally due. **13.** a loan of money. **14.** an increase in price, etc. **15. in advance. a.** beforehand: *payment in advance.* **b.** (foll. by *of*) ahead in time or development: *ideas in advance of the time.* **16.** (*modifier*) forward in position or time: *advance booking.* ~See also **advances.** [C15 *advauncen*, altered < C13 *avauncen*, via OF < L *abante*, < *ab-* away + *ante* before] **—ad'vancer** *n.*
advanced (əd'vɑːnst) *adj.* **1.** being ahead in development, knowledge, progress, etc. **2.** having reached a comparatively late stage: *a man of advanced age.* **3.** ahead of the times.
advanced gas-cooled reactor *n.* a nuclear reactor using carbon dioxide as the coolant, and

ceramic uranium dioxide cased in stainless steel as the fuel. Abbrev.: **AGR.**

Advanced level *n.* a formal name for **A level.**

advancement (əd'vɑːnsmənt) *n.* **1.** promotion in rank, status, etc. **2.** a less common word for **advance** (senses 9, 10).

advances (əd'vɑːnsɪz) *pl. n.* (*sometimes sing.;* often foll. by *to* or *towards*) overtures made in an attempt to become friendly, etc.

advantage (əd'vɑːntɪdʒ) *n.* **1.** (often foll. by *over* or *of*) a more favourable position; superiority. **2.** benefit or profit (esp. in **to one's advantage**). **3.** *Tennis.* the point scored after deuce. **4. take advantage of. a.** to make good use of. **b.** to impose upon the weakness, good nature, etc., of. **c.** to seduce. **5. to advantage.** to good effect. ~*vb.* **6.** (*tr.*) to put in a better position; favour. [C14 *avantage* (later altered to *advantage*), < OF *avant* before, < L *abante* from before. See ADVANCE]

advantageous (ˌædvən'teɪdʒəs) *adj.* producing advantage. —ˌ**advan'tageously** *adv.*

advection (əd'vɛkʃən) *n.* the transference of heat energy in a horizontal stream of gas, esp. of air. [C20: < L *advectiō*, < *advehere*, < *ad-* to + *vehere* to carry]

advent ('ædvɛnt, -vənt) *n.* an arrival or coming, esp. one which is awaited. [C12: < L *adventus*, < *advenīre*, < *ad-* to + *venīre* to come]

Advent ('ædvɛnt) *n.* the season including the four Sundays preceding Christmas.

Advent calendar *n.* a large card with small numbered doors for children to open on each of the days of Advent, revealing pictures beneath them.

Adventist ('ædvɛntɪst) *n.* a member of a Christian group that holds that the Second Coming of Christ is imminent.

adventitious (ˌædvɛn'tɪʃəs) *adj.* **1.** added or appearing accidentally. **2.** (of a plant or animal part) developing in an abnormal position. [C17: < L *adventīcius* coming from outside, < *adventus* a coming] —ˌ**adven'titiously** *adv.*

adventure (əd'vɛntʃə) *n.* **1.** a risky undertaking of unknown outcome. **2.** an exciting or unexpected event or course of events. **3.** a hazardous financial operation. ~*vb.* **4.** to take a risk or put at risk. **5.** (*intr.;* foll. by *into, on,* or *upon*) to dare to enter (into a place, dangerous activity, etc.). **6.** to dare to say (something): *he adventured his opinion.* [C13 *aventure* (later altered to *adventure*), via OF ult. < L *advenīre* to happen to (someone), arrive]

adventure playground *n. Brit.* a playground for children that contains building materials, etc., used to build with, climb on, etc.

adventurer (əd'vɛntʃərə) or (*fem.*) **adventuress** *n.* **1.** a person who seeks adventure, esp. one who seeks success or money through daring exploits. **2.** a person who seeks money or power by unscrupulous means. **3.** a speculator.

adventurism (əd'vɛntʃəˌrɪzəm) *n.* recklessness, esp. in politics and finance. —**ad'venturist** *n.*

adventurous (əd'vɛntʃərəs) *adj.* **1.** Also: **adventuresome.** daring or enterprising. **2.** dangerous; involving risk.

adverb ('ædˌvɜːb) *n.* **a.** a word or group of words that serves to modify a whole sentence, a verb, another adverb, or an adjective; for example, *easily, very,* and *happily* respectively in the sentence *They could easily envy the very happily married couple.* **b.** (*as modifier*): *an adverb marker.* Abbrev.: **adv.** [C15–C16: < L *adverbium* adverb, lit.: added word] —**ad'verbial** *adj.*

adversarial (ˌædvɜː'sɛərɪəl) *adj.* (of political parties) hostile to and opposing each other on party lines; antagonistic.

adversary ('ædvəsərɪ) *n., pl.* **-saries. 1.** a person or group that is hostile to someone. **2.** an opposing contestant in a sport. [C14: < L *adversārius*, < *adversus* against]

adversative (əd'vɜːsətɪv) *Grammar.* ~*adj.* **1.** (of a word, phrase, or clause) implying opposition. *But* and *although* are adversative conjunctions. ~*n.* **2.** an adversative word or speech element.

adverse ('ædvɜːs) *adj.* **1.** antagonistic; hostile: *adverse criticism.* **2.** unfavourable to one's interests: *adverse circumstances.* **3.** contrary or opposite: *adverse winds.* [C14: < L *adversus*, < *advertere*, < *ad-* towards + *vertere* to turn] —**ad'versely** *adv.* —**ad'verseness** *n.*

adversity (əd'vɜːsɪtɪ) *n., pl.* **-ties. 1.** distress; affliction; hardship. **2.** an unfortunate event.

advert[1] (əd'vɜːt) *vb.* (*intr.;* foll. by *to*) to draw attention (to). [C15: < L *advertere* to turn one's attention to]

advert[2] ('ædvɜːt) *n. Brit. inf.* short for **advertisement.**

advertise *or U.S.* (*sometimes*) **-tize** ('ædvəˌtaɪz) *vb.* **1.** to present or praise (goods, a service, etc.) to the public, esp. in order to encourage sales. **2.** to make (a vacancy, article for sale, etc.) publicly known: *to advertise a job.* **3.** (*intr.;* foll. by *for*) to make a public request (for): *she advertised for a cook.* [C15: < OF *avertir*, ult. < L *advertere* to turn one's attention to. See ADVERSE] —'**adverˌtiser** *or U.S.* (*sometimes*) '**adverˌtizer** *n.*

advertisement *or U.S.* (*sometimes*) **-tizement** (əd'vɜːtɪsmənt) *n.* any public notice, as a printed display in a newspaper, short film on television, etc., designed to sell goods, publicize an event, etc.

advertising *or U.S.* (*sometimes*) **-tizing** ('ædvəˌtaɪzɪŋ) *n.* **1.** the promotion of goods or services for sale through impersonal media such as television. **2.** the business that specializes in creating such publicity. **3.** advertisements collectively.

advertorial (ˌædvɜː'tɔːrɪəl) *n.* **1.** advertising presented under the guise of editorial material. ~*adj.* **2.** presented in such a manner. [C20: < blend of ADVERT[2] + EDITORIAL]

advice (əd'vaɪs) *n.* **1.** recommendation as to appropriate choice of action. **2.** (*sometimes pl.*) formal notification of facts. [C13 *avis* (later *advise*), via OF < Vulgar L, < L *ad* to + *vīsum* view]

advisable (əd'vaɪzəbᵊl) *adj.* worthy of recommendation; prudent. —**ad'visably** *adv.*

advise (əd'vaɪz) *vb.* (*when tr., may take a clause as object or an infinitive*) **1.** to offer advice (to a person or persons): *he advised caution.* **2.** (*tr.;* sometimes foll. by *of*) to inform or notify. **3.** (*intr.;* foll. by *with*) *Chiefly U.S., obs. in Britain.* to consult. [C14: via OF < Vulgar L *advīsāre* (unattested), < L *ad-* to + *vidēre* to see]

▷ **Usage.** *Advise* is often used in the same sense as *inform: as we advised you in our last communication, the order is being dealt with.* This use is common in business correspondence. Careful users of English prefer *inform, notify,* or *tell* in general English: *the police informed him that his car had been stolen.*

advised (əd'vaɪzd) *adj.* resulting from deliberation. See also **ill-advised, well-advised.** —**advisedly** (əd'vaɪzɪdlɪ) *adv.*

adviser *or* **advisor** (əd'vaɪzə) *n.* **1.** a person who advises. **2.** *Education.* a person responsible for advising students on career guidance, etc. **3.** *Brit. education.* a subject specialist who advises on current teaching methods and facilities.

advisory (əd'vaɪzərɪ) *adj.* empowered to make recommendations: *an advisory body.*

advocaat ('ædvəʊˌkɑː) *n.* a liqueur having a raw egg base. [C20: Du.]

advocacy ('ædvəkəsɪ) *n., pl.* **-cies.** active support, esp. of a cause.

advocate *vb.* ('ædvəˌkeɪt). **1.** (*tr.; may take a clause as object*) to support or recommend publicly. ~*n.* ('ædvəkɪt). **2.** a person who upholds or defends a cause. **3.** a person who intercedes on behalf of another. **4.** a person who pleads his client's cause in a court of law. **5.** *Scots Law.* the usual word for **barrister.** [C14: via OF < L *advocātus* legal witness, < *advocāre*, < *vocāre* to call]

advowson (əd'vaʊzᵊn) *n. English ecclesiastical law.* the right of presentation to a vacant benefice. [C13: via OF < L *advocātiōn-*, < *advocāre* to summon]

advt *abbrev. for* advertisement.

adze *or U.S.* **adz** (ædz) *n.* a hand tool with a steel blade attached at right angles to a wooden handle, used for dressing timber. [OE *adesa*]

AEA (in Britain) *abbrev. for* Atomic Energy Authority.

AEC (in the U.S.) *abbrev. for* Atomic Energy Commission.

aedes (eɪˈiːdiːz) *n.* a mosquito of tropical and subtropical regions which transmits yellow fever. [C20: NL, < Gk *aēdēs* unpleasant, < A-¹ + *ēdos* pleasant]

aedile *or U.S.* (*sometimes*) **edile** (ˈiːdaɪl) *n.* a magistrate of ancient Rome in charge of public works, games, buildings, and roads. [C16: < L *aedīlis*, < *aedēs* a building]

Aegean (iːˈdʒiːən) *adj.* of or relating to the Aegean Sea or Islands.

aegis *or U.S.* (*sometimes*) **egis** (ˈiːdʒɪs) *n.* **1.** sponsorship or protection (esp. in **under the aegis of**). **2.** *Greek myth.* the shield of Zeus. [C18: < L, < Gk *aigis* shield of Zeus]

aegrotat (ˈaɪgrəʊˌtæt, ˈiː-) *n.* **1.** (in British and certain other universities, and, sometimes, schools) a certificate allowing a candidate to pass an examination although he has missed all or part of it through illness. **2.** a degree or other qualification obtained in such circumstances. [C19: L, lit.: he is ill]

-aemia, -haemia, *or U.S.* **-emia, -hemia** *n. combining form.* denoting blood, esp. a specified condition of the blood in diseases: *leukaemia.* [NL, < Gk, < *haima* blood]

Aeneid (ɪˈniːɪd) *n.* an epic poem in Latin by Virgil relating the experiences of Aeneas after the fall of Troy.

aeolian harp (iːˈəʊlɪən) *n.* a stringed instrument that produces a musical sound when wind passes over the strings. Also called: **wind harp.** [after Aeolus, god of winds in Gk myth.]

aeolotropic (ˌiːələʊˈtrɒpɪk) *adj.* a less common word for **anisotropic.** [C19: < Gk *aiolos* fickle + -TROPIC] —**aeolotropy** (ˌiːəˈlɒtrəpɪ) *n.*

aeon *or U.S.* **eon** (ˈiːən, ˈiːɒn) *n.* **1.** an immeasurably long period of time. **2.** *Geol.* the longest division of geological time, comprising two or more eras. [C17: < Gk *aiōn* an infinitely long time]

aerate (ˈɛəreɪt) *vb.* (*tr.*) **1.** to charge (a liquid) with a gas, as in the manufacture of effervescent drink. **2.** to expose to the action or circulation of the air. —**aerˈation** *n.* —**ˈaerator** *n.*

aeri- *combining form.* a variant of **aero-.**

aerial (ˈɛərɪəl) *adj.* **1.** of or resembling air. **2.** existing, moving, or operating in the air: *aerial cable car.* **3.** ethereal; light and delicate. **4.** imaginary. **5.** extending high into the air. **6.** of or relating to aircraft: *aerial combat.* ~*n.* **7.** Also called: **antenna.** the part of a radio or television system by means of which radio waves are transmitted or received. [C17: via L < Gk *aērios*, < *aēr* air]

aerialist (ˈɛərɪəlɪst) *n.* a trapeze artist or tightrope walker.

aerie (ˈɛərɪ) *n.* a variant spelling (esp. U.S.) of **eyrie.**

aeriform (ˈɛərɪˌfɔːm) *adj.* **1.** having the form of air; gaseous. **2.** unsubstantial.

aero (ˈɛərəʊ) *n.* (*modifier*) of or relating to aircraft or aeronautics: *an aero engine.*

aero-, aeri-, *or before a vowel* **aer-** *combining form.* **1.** denoting air, atmosphere, or gas: *aerodynamics.* **2.** denoting aircraft: *aeronautics.* [ult. < Gk *aēr* air]

aerobatics (ˌɛərəʊˈbætɪks) *n.* (*functioning as sing. or pl.*) spectacular or dangerous manoeuvres, such as loops or rolls, performed in an aircraft or glider. [C20: < AERO- + (ACRO)BATICS]

aerobe (ˈɛərəʊb) *or* **aerobium** (ɛəˈrəʊbɪəm) *n., pl.* **-obes** *or* **-obia** (-ˈəʊbɪə). an organism that requires free oxygen or air for respiration. [C19: < AERO- + Gk *bios* life] —**aeˈrobic** *adj.*

aerobics (ɛəˈrəʊbɪks) *n.* (*functioning as sing.*) any system of exercises designed to increase the amount of oxygen in the blood.

aerodrome (ˈɛərəˌdrəʊm) *n.* a landing area that is smaller than an airport.

aerodynamics (ˌɛərəʊdaɪˈnæmɪks) *n.* (*functioning as sing.*) the study of the dynamics of gases, esp. of the forces acting on a body passing through air. —ˌ**aerodyˈnamic** *adj.* —ˌ**aerodyˈnamically** *adv.*

aeroembolism (ˌɛərəʊˈɛmbəˌlɪzəm) *n.* the presence in the blood of nitrogen bubbles, caused by an abrupt reduction in atmospheric pressure. See **decompression sickness.**

aero engine *n.* an engine for powering an aircraft.

aerofoil (ˈɛərəʊˌfɔɪl) *n.* a cross section of a wing, rotor blade, etc.

aerogram *or* **aerogramme** (ˈɛərəˌgræm) *n.* an air-mail letter written on a single sheet of lightweight paper that folds and is sealed to form an envelope. Also called: **air letter.**

aerolite (ˈɛərəˌlaɪt) *n.* a stony meteorite consisting of silicate minerals.

aerology (ɛəˈrɒlədʒɪ) *n.* the study of the atmosphere, including its upper layers. —**aerological** (ˌɛərəˈlɒdʒɪkᵊl) *adj.* —**aerˈologist** *n.*

aeromechanics (ˌɛərəʊmɪˈkænɪks) *n.* (*functioning as sing.*) the mechanics of gases, esp. air. —ˌ**aeromeˈchanical** *adj.*

aeronautics (ˌɛərəˈnɔːtɪks) *n.* (*functioning as sing.*) the study or practice of all aspects of flight through the air. —ˌ**aeroˈnautical** *adj.*

aeropause (ˈɛərəˌpɔːz) *n.* the region of the upper atmosphere above which aircraft cannot fly.

aeroplane (ˈɛərəˌpleɪn) *or U.S.* **airplane** (ˈɛəˌpleɪn) *n.* a heavier-than-air powered flying vehicle with fixed wings. [C19: < F *aéroplane*, < AERO- + Gk *-planos* wandering]

aerosol (ˈɛərəˌsɒl) *n.* **1.** a colloidal dispersion of solid or liquid particles in a gas. **2.** a substance, such as a paint or insecticide, dispensed from a small metal container by a propellant under pressure. **3.** Also called: **air spray.** such a substance together with its container. [C20: < AERO- + SOL(UTION)]

aerospace (ˈɛərəˌspeɪs) *n.* **1.** the atmosphere and space beyond. **2.** (*modifier*) of rockets, missiles, space vehicles, etc.: *the aerospace industry.*

aerostat (ˈɛərəˌstæt) *n.* a lighter-than-air craft, such as a balloon. [C18: < F *aérostat*, < AERO- + Gk *-statos* standing] —ˌ**aeroˈstatic** *adj.*

aerostatics (ˌɛərəˈstætɪks) *n.* (*functioning as sing.*) **1.** the study of gases in equilibrium and bodies held in equilibrium in gases. Cf. **aerodynamics. 2.** the study of lighter-than-air craft, such as balloons.

aerugo (ɪˈruːgəʊ) *n.* (esp. of old bronze) another name for **verdigris.** [C18: < L, < *aes* copper, bronze] —**aeruginous** (ɪˈruːdʒɪnəs) *adj.*

aery (ˈɛərɪ) *n., pl.* **aeries.** a variant spelling of **eyrie.**

Aeschylean (ˌiːskəˈliːən) *adj.* of or relating to the works of Aeschylus, 5th-century B.C. Greek dramatist.

Aesculapian (ˌiːskjʊˈleɪpɪən) *adj.* of or relating to Aesculapius, the Roman god of medicine, or to the art of medicine.

aesthesia *or U.S.* **esthesia** (iːsˈθiːzɪə) *n.* the normal ability to experience sensation. [C20: back formation < ANAESTHESIA]

aesthete *or U.S.* **esthete** (ˈiːsθiːt) *n.* a person who has or who affects a highly developed appreciation of beauty. [C19: back formation < AESTHETICS]

aesthetic (iːsˈθɛtɪk, ɪs-), **aesthetical** *or U.S.* (*sometimes*) **esthetic, esthetical** *adj.* **1.** connected with aesthetics. **2. a.** relating to pure beauty rather than to other considerations. **b.** artistic: *an aesthetic consideration.* [C19: < Gk *aisthētikos*, < *aisthanesthai* to perceive, feel] —**aesˈthetically** *or U.S.* (*sometimes*) **esˈthetically** *adv.* —**aesˈtheticism** *or U.S.* (*sometimes*) **esˈtheticism** *n.*

aesthetics *or U.S.* (*sometimes*) **esthetics** (iːsˈθɛtɪks) *n.* (*functioning as sing.*) **1.** the branch of philosophy concerned with the study of such concepts as beauty, taste, etc. **2.** the study of the rules and principles of art.

aestival *or U.S.* **estival** (iːˈstaɪvᵊl) *adj. Rare.* of or occurring in summer. [C14: < F, < LL *aestīvālis*, < L *aestās* summer]

aestivate *or U.S.* **estivate** (ˈiːstɪˌveɪt) *vb.* (*intr.*) **1.** to pass the summer. **2.** (of animals) to pass the summer or dry season in a dormant condition. [C17: < L, < *aestīvāre*, < *aestās* summer] —ˌ**estiˈvation** *or U.S.* ˌ**estiˈvation** *n.*

aet. *or* **aetat.** *abbrev. for* aetatis. [L: at the age of]

aether (ˈiːθə) *n.* a variant spelling of **ether** (senses 3, 4).

aetiology (ˌiːtɪˈɒlədʒɪ) *n., pl.* **-gies.** a variant spelling of **etiology.**

AEU (in Britain) *abbrev. for* Amalgamated Engineering Union.

a.f. *abbrev. for* audio frequency.

afar (əˈfɑː) *adv.* **1.** at, from, or to a great distance. ~*n.* **2.** a great distance (esp. in **from afar**). [C14 *a fer*, altered < earlier *on fer* & *of fer*; see A-[2], FAR]

AFC *abbrev. for:* **1.** Air Force Cross. **2.** Association Football Club. **3.** automatic frequency control.

afeard *or* **afeared** (əˈfɪəd) *adj.* (*postpositive*) an archaic or dialect word for **afraid.** [OE *āfǣred*, < *afǣran* to frighten]

affable (ˈæfəbᵊl) *adj.* **1.** showing warmth and friendliness. **2.** easy to converse with; approachable. [C16: < L *affābilis*, < *affārī*, < *ad-* to + *fārī* to speak] —ˌ**affaˈbility** *n.* —ˈ**affably** *adv.*

affair (əˈfɛə) *n.* **1.** a thing to be done or attended to; matter. **2.** an event or happening: *a strange affair.* **3.** (*qualified by an adjective or descriptive phrase*) something previously specified: *our house is a tumbledown affair.* **4.** a sexual relationship between two people who are not married to each other. [C13: < OF, < *à faire* to do]

affairs (əˈfɛəz) *pl. n.* **1.** personal or business interests. **2.** matters of public interest: *current affairs.*

affect[1] *vb.* (əˈfɛkt). (*tr.*) **1.** to act upon or influence, esp. in an adverse way. **2.** to move or disturb emotionally or mentally. **3.** (of pain, disease, etc.) to attack. ~*n.* (ˈæfɛkt). **4.** *Psychol.* the emotion associated with an idea or set of ideas. [C17: < L *affectus*, p.p. of *afficere*, < *ad-* to + *facere* to do]

affect[2] (əˈfɛkt) *vb.* (*mainly tr.*) **1.** to put on an appearance or show of: *to affect ignorance.* **2.** to imitate or assume, esp. pretentiously. **3.** to have or use by preference. **4.** to adopt the character, manner, etc., of. **5.** to incline habitually towards. [C15: < L *affectāre* to strive after; rel. to *afficere* to AFFECT[1]]

affectation (ˌæfɛkˈteɪʃən) *n.* **1.** an assumed manner of speech, dress, or behaviour, esp. one that is intended to impress others. **2.** (often foll. by *of*) deliberate pretence. [C16: < L *affectātiōn-*, < *affectāre*; see AFFECT[2]]

affected[1] (əˈfɛktɪd) *adj.* (*usually postpositive*) **1.** deeply moved, esp. by sorrow or grief. **2.** changed, esp. detrimentally. [C17: < AFFECT[1]]

affected[2] (əˈfɛktɪd) *adj.* **1.** behaving, speaking, etc., in an assumed way, esp. in order to impress others. **2.** feigned: *affected indifference.* [C16: < AFFECT[2]] —**afˈfectedly** *adv.*

affecting (əˈfɛktɪŋ) *adj.* evoking feelings of pity; moving. —**afˈfectingly** *adv.*

affection (əˈfɛkʃən) *n.* **1.** a feeling of fondness or tenderness for a person or thing. **2.** (*often pl.*) emotion, feeling, or sentiment: *to play on a person's affections.* **3.** *Pathol.* any disease or pathological condition. **4.** the act of affecting or the state of being affected. [C13: < L *affectiōn-*, < *afficere* to AFFECT[1]] —**afˈfectional** *adj.*

affectionate (əˈfɛkʃənɪt) *adj.* having or displaying tender feelings, affection, or warmth. —**afˈfectionately** *adv.*

affective (əˈfɛktɪv) *adj.* concerned with the emotions or affection. —**affectivity** (ˌæfɛkˈtɪvɪtɪ) *n.*

afferent (ˈæfərənt) *adj.* bringing or directing inwards to a part or an organ of the body, esp. towards the brain or spinal cord. [C19: < L *afferre*, < *ad-* to + *ferre* to carry]

affiance (əˈfaɪəns) *vb.* (*tr.*) to bind (a person or oneself) in a promise of marriage; betroth. [C14: via OF < Med. L *affīdāre* to trust (oneself) to, < *fīdāre* to trust]

affidavit (ˌæfɪˈdeɪvɪt) *n. Law.* a declaration in writing made upon oath before a person authorized to administer oaths. [C17: < Med. L, lit.: he declares on oath, < *affīdāre*; see AFFIANCE]

affiliate *vb.* (əˈfɪlɪˌeɪt). **1.** (*tr.;* foll. by *to* or *with*) to receive into close connection or association (with a larger body, group, organization, etc.). **2.** (foll. by *with*) to associate (oneself) or be associated, esp. as a subordinate or subsidiary. ~*n.* (əˈfɪlɪɪt). **3. a.** a person or organization that is affiliated with another. **b.** (*as modifier*): *an affiliate member.* [C18: < Med. L *affīliātus* adopted as a son, < *affīliāre*, < L *fīlius* son] —**afˌfiliˈation** *n.*

affiliation order *n. Law.* an order that a man adjudged to be the father of an illegitimate child shall contribute towards the child's maintenance.

affine (ˈæfaɪn) *adj. Maths.* denoting transformations which preserve collinearity, esp. those of translation, rotation, and reflection. [C16: < F: see AFFINITY]

affinity (əˈfɪnɪtɪ) *n., pl.* **-ties.** **1.** a natural liking, taste, or inclination for a person or thing. **2.** the person or thing so liked. **3.** a close similarity in appearance or quality. **4.** relationship by marriage. **5.** similarity in structure, form, etc., between different animals, plants, or languages. **6.** *Chem.* chemical attraction. [C14: via OF < L *affīnitāt-*, < *affīnis* bordering on, related] —**afˈfinitive** *adj.*

affirm (əˈfɜːm) *vb.* (*mainly tr.*) **1.** (*may take a clause as object*) to declare to be true. **2.** to uphold, confirm, or ratify. **3.** (*intr.*) *Law.* to make an affirmation. [C14: via OF < L *affirmāre*, < *ad-* to + *firmāre* to make FIRM[1]] —**afˈfirmer** *or* **afˈfirmant** *n.*

affirmation (ˌæfəˈmeɪʃən) *n.* **1.** the act of affirming or the state of being affirmed. **2.** a statement of the truth of something; assertion. **3.** *Law.* a solemn declaration permitted on grounds of conscientious objection to taking an oath.

affirmative (əˈfɜːmətɪv) *adj.* **1.** confirming or asserting something as true or valid. **2.** indicating agreement or assent. **3.** *Logic.* (of a categorical proposition) affirming the satisfaction by the subject of the predicate, as in the proposition *some men are married.* ~*n.* **4.** a positive assertion. **5.** a word or phrase stating agreement or assent, such as *yes: to answer in the affirmative.* ~*sentence substitute.* **6.** *Mil., etc.* a signal codeword used to express assent or confirmation. —**afˈfirmatively** *adv.*

affix *vb.* (əˈfɪks). (*tr.;* usually foll. by *to* or *on*) **1.** to attach, fasten, join, or stick. **2.** to add or append: *to affix a signature to a document.* **3.** to attach or attribute (guilt, blame, etc.). ~*n.* (ˈæfɪks). **4.** a linguistic element added to a word or root to produce a derived or inflected form, as *-ment* in *establishment.* See also **prefix, suffix, infix.** **5.** something fastened or attached. [C15: < Med. L *affixāre*, < *ad-* to + *fixāre* to FIX] —**affixture** (əˈfɪkstʃə) *n.*

afflatus (əˈfleɪtəs) *n.* an impulse of creative power or inspiration considered to be of divine origin. [C17: L, < *afflātus*, < *afflāre*, < *flāre* to blow]

afflict (əˈflɪkt) *vb.* (*tr.*) to cause suffering or unhappiness to; distress greatly. [C14: < L *afflictus*, p.p. of *affligere* to knock against, < *fligere* to strike] —**afˈflictive** *adj.*

affliction (əˈflɪkʃən) *n.* **1.** a condition of great distress or suffering. **2.** something responsible for physical or mental suffering.

affluence (ˈæfluəns) *n.* **1.** an abundant supply of money, goods, or property; wealth. **2.** *Rare.* abundance or profusion.

affluent (ˈæfluənt) *adj.* **1.** rich; wealthy. **2.** abundant; copious. **3.** flowing freely. ~*n.* **4.** a tributary stream. [C15: < L *affluent-*, present participle of *affluere*, < *fluere* to flow]

affluent society *n.* a society in which the material benefits of prosperity are widely available.

afflux (ˈæflʌks) *n.* a flowing towards a point: *an afflux of blood to the head.* [C17: < L *affluxus*, < *fluxus* FLUX]

afford (əˈfɔːd) *vb.* **1.** (preceded by *can, could,* etc.) to be able to do or spare something, esp. without incurring financial difficulties or without risk of undesirable consequences. **2.** to give, yield, or supply. [OE *geforthian* to further, promote, < *forth* FORTH] **—afˈfordable** *adj.*

afforest (əˈfɒrɪst) *vb.* (*tr.*) to plant trees on. [C15: < Med. L *afforestāre*, < *forestis* FOREST] **—afˌforestˈation** *n.*

affranchise (əˈfræntʃaɪz) *vb.* (*tr.*) to release from servitude or an obligation. [C15: < OF *afranchir*] **—afˈfranchisement** *n.*

affray (əˈfreɪ) *n.* a fight, noisy quarrel, or disturbance between two or more persons in a public place. [C14: via OF < Vulgar L *exfridāre* (unattested) to break the peace]

affricate (ˈæfrɪkɪt) *n.* a composite speech sound consisting of a stop and a fricative articulated at the same point, such as the sound written *ch*, as in *chair.* [C19: < L *affricāre*, < *fricāre* to rub]

affright (əˈfraɪt) *Arch. or poetic.* ~*vb.* **1.** (*tr.*) to frighten. ~*n.* **2.** a sudden terror. [OE *āfyrhtan*, < *a-* + *fyrhtan* to FRIGHT]

affront (əˈfrʌnt) *n.* **1.** a deliberate insult. ~*vb.* (*tr.*) **2.** to insult, esp. openly. **3.** to offend the pride or dignity of. [C14: < OF *afronter* to strike in the face, < L *ad frontem* to the face]

afghan (ˈæfgæn, -gən) *n.* **1.** a knitted or crocheted wool blanket or shawl, esp. one with a geometric pattern. **2.** a sheepskin coat, often embroidered. [< *Afghanistan*, country in central Asia]

Afghan (ˈæfgæn) *or* **Afghani** (æfˈgænɪ) *n.* **1.** a native, citizen, or inhabitant of Afghanistan. **2.** another name for **Pashto** (the language). ~*adj.* **3.** denoting Afghanistan, its people, or their language.

Afghan hound *n.* a tall graceful breed of hound with a long silky coat.

aficionado (əˌfɪʃjəˈnɑːdəʊ) *n., pl.* **-dos.** **1.** an ardent supporter or devotee: *a jazz aficionado.* **2.** a devotee of bullfighting. [Sp., < *aficionar*, < *afición* AFFECTION]

afield (əˈfiːld) *adv., adj.* (*postpositive*) **1.** away from one's usual surroundings or home (esp. in **far afield**). **2.** off the subject (esp. in **far afield**). **3.** in or to the field.

afire (əˈfaɪə) *adv., adj.* (*postpositive*) **1.** on fire. **2.** intensely interested or passionate: *he was afire with enthusiasm for the new plan.*

aflame (əˈfleɪm) *adv., adj.* (*postpositive*) **1.** in flames. **2.** deeply aroused, as with passion: *he was aflame with desire.*

aflatoxin (ˌæfləˈtɒksɪn) *n.* a toxin produced by a fungus growing on peanuts, maize, etc., thought to cause liver disease (esp. cancer) in man. [C20: < L name of fungus *A*(*spergillus*) *fla*(*vus*) + TOXIN]

afloat (əˈfləʊt) *adj.* (*postpositive*), *adv.* **1.** floating. **2.** aboard ship; at sea. **3.** covered with water. **4.** aimlessly drifting. **5.** in circulation: *nasty rumours were afloat.* **6.** free of debt.

aflutter (əˈflʌtə) *adj.* (*postpositive*), *adv.* in or into a nervous or excited state.

AFM *abbrev. for* Air Force Medal.

afoot (əˈfʊt) *adj.* (*postpositive*), *adv.* **1.** in operation; astir: *mischief was afoot.* **2.** on or by foot.

afore (əˈfɔː) *adv., prep., conj.* an archaic or dialect word for **before.**

aforementioned (əˈfɔːˌmɛnʃənd) *adj.* (*usually prenominal*) (chiefly in legal documents) stated or mentioned before.

aforesaid (əˈfɔːˌsɛd) *adj.* (*usually prenominal*) (chiefly in legal documents) spoken of or referred to previously.

aforethought (əˈfɔːˌθɔːt) *adj.* (*immediately postpositive*) premeditated (esp. in **malice aforethought**).

a fortiori (eɪ ˌfɔːtɪˈɔːraɪ) *adv.* for similar but more convincing reasons. [L]

Afr. *abbrev. for* Africa(n).

afraid (əˈfreɪd) *adj.* (*postpositive*) **1.** (often foll. by *of*) feeling fear or apprehension. **2.** reluctant (to do something), as through fear or timidity. **3.** (often foll. by *that;* used to lessen the effect of an unpleasant statement) regretful: *I'm afraid that I shall have to tell you to go.* [C14 *affraied*, p.p. of AFFRAY (*obs.*) to frighten]

afreet *or* **afrit** (ˈæfriːt, əˈfriːt) *n. Arabian myth.* a powerful evil demon. [C19: < Ar. *ʻifrīt*]

afresh (əˈfrɛʃ) *adv.* once more; again; anew.

African (ˈæfrɪkən) *adj.* **1.** denoting or relating to Africa or any of its peoples, languages, nations, etc. ~*n.* **2.** a native or inhabitant of any of the countries of Africa. **3.** a member or descendant of any of the peoples of Africa, esp. a Negro.

Africana (ˌafrɪˈkɑːnə, ˌæf-) *n.* objects of cultural or historical interest of southern African origin.

Africander (ˌafrɪˈkændə, ˌæf-) *n.* a breed of hump-backed beef cattle originally raised in southern Africa. [C19: < South African Du., formed on the model of *Hollander*]

African violet *n.* a tropical African plant cultivated as a house plant, with violet, white, or pink flowers and hairy leaves.

Afrikaans (ˌafrɪˈkɑːns, -ˈkɑːnz, æf-) *n.* an official language of all the Republic of South Africa, closely related to Dutch and Flemish. [C20: < Du.: African]

Afrikaner (afriˈkaːnə, ˌæfrɪˈkɑːnə) *n.* a White native of the Republic of South Africa whose mother tongue is Afrikaans. See also **Boer.**

Afro (ˈæfrəʊ) *n., pl.* **-ros.** a hairstyle in which the hair is shaped into a wide frizzy bush, popular esp. among Negroes. [C20: independent use of AFRO-]

Afro- *combining form.* indicating Africa or African: *Afro-Asiatic.*

Afro-American *n.* **1.** an American Negro. ~*adj.* **2.** denoting or relating to American Negroes, their history, or their culture.

afrormosia (ˌæfrɔːˈməʊzɪə) *n.* a hard teaklike wood obtained from a genus of tropical African trees. [C20: < AFRO- + *Ormosia* (genus name)]

aft (ɑːft) *adv., adj. Chiefly naut.* towards or at the stern or rear: *the aft deck.* [C17: ? shortened < earlier ABAFT]

after (ˈɑːftə) *prep.* **1.** following in time; in succession to: *after dinner.* **2.** following; behind. **3.** in pursuit or search of: *he's only after money.* **4.** concerning: *to inquire after his health.* **5.** considering: *after what you have done, you shouldn't complain.* **6.** next in excellence or importance to. **7.** in imitation of; in the manner of. **8.** in accordance with or in conformity to: *a man after her own heart.* **9.** with a name derived from. **10.** *U.S.* past (the hour of): *twenty after three.* **11. after all. a.** in spite of everything: *it's only a game after all.* **b.** in spite of expectations, efforts, etc. **12. after you.** please go, enter, etc., before me. ~*adv.* **13.** at a later time; afterwards. **14.** coming afterwards. **15.** *Naut.* further aft. ~*conj.* **16.** (*subordinating*) at a time later than that at which. ~*adj.* **17.** *Naut.* further aft: *the after cabin.* [OE *æfter*]

afterbirth (ˈɑːftəˌbɜːθ) *n.* the placenta and fetal membranes expelled from the uterus after the birth of offspring.

afterburner (ˈɑːftəˌbɜːnə) *n.* **1.** a device in the exhaust system of an internal-combustion engine for removing dangerous exhaust gases. **2.** a device in an aircraft jet engine to produce extra thrust by igniting additional fuel.

aftercare (ˈɑːftəˌkɛə) *n.* **1.** support services by a welfare agency for a person discharged from a hospital, prison, etc. **2.** *Med.* the care of a patient after a serious illness or operation.

afterdamp (ˈɑːftəˌdæmp) *n.* a poisonous gas, consisting mainly of carbon monoxide, formed after the explosion of firedamp in coal mines.

aftereffect (ˈɑːftərɪˌfɛkt) *n.* any result occurring some time after its cause.

afterglow (ˈɑːftəˌgləʊ) *n.* **1.** the glow left after a light has disappeared, such as that sometimes seen after sunset. **2.** the glow of an incandescent metal after the source of heat has been removed.

afterimage (ˈɑːftərˌɪmɪdʒ) *n.* a sustained or renewed sensation, esp. visual, after the original stimulus has ceased.

afterlife (ˈɑːftəˌlaɪf) *n.* life after death or at a later time in a person's lifetime.

aftermath (ˈɑːftəˌmæθ) *n.* **1.** signs or results of an event or occurrence considered collectively: *the aftermath of war.* **2.** *Agriculture.* a second crop of grass from land that has already yielded one crop earlier in the same year. [C16: AFTER + *math* a mowing, < OE *mæth*]

aftermost (ˈɑːftəˌməʊst) *adj.* closer or closest to the rear or (in a vessel) the stern; last.

afternoon (ˌɑːftəˈnuːn) *n.* **1. a.** the period between noon and evening. **b.** (*as modifier*): *afternoon tea.* **2.** a later part: *the afternoon of life.*

afternoons (ˌɑːftəˈnuːnz) *adv. Inf.* during the afternoon, esp. regularly.

afterpains (ˈɑːftəˌpeɪnz) *pl. n.* cramplike pains caused by contraction of the uterus after childbirth.

afters (ˈɑːftəz) *n.* (*functioning as sing. or pl.*) *Brit. inf.* dessert; sweet.

aftershave lotion (ˈɑːftəˌʃeɪv) *n.* a lotion, usually perfumed, for application to the face after shaving. Often shortened to **aftershave.**

aftertaste (ˈɑːftəˌteɪst) *n.* **1.** a taste that lingers on after eating or drinking. **2.** a lingering impression or sensation.

afterthought (ˈɑːftəˌθɔːt) *n.* **1.** a comment, reply, etc., that occurs to one after the opportunity to deliver it has passed. **2.** an addition to something already completed.

afterwards (ˈɑːftəwədz) *or* **afterward** *adv.* after an earlier event or time. [OE *æfterweard, æfteweard,* < AFT + WARD]

Ag *the chemical symbol for* silver. [< L *argentum*]

AG *abbrev. for:* **1.** Adjutant General. **2.** Attorney General.

aga *or* **agha** (ˈɑːgə) *n.* (in the Ottoman Empire) a title of respect, often used with the title of a senior position. [C17: Turkish, lit.: lord]

again (əˈgɛn, əˈgeɪn) *adv.* **1.** another or a second time: *he had to start again.* **2.** once more in a previously experienced state or condition: *he is ill again.* **3.** in addition to the original amount, quantity, etc. (esp. in **as much again; half as much again**). **4.** (*sentence modifier*) on the other hand. **5.** besides; also. **6.** *Arch.* in reply; back: *he answered again.* **7. again and again.** continuously; repeatedly. ~*sentence connector.* **8.** moreover; furthermore. [OE *ongegn* opposite to, < A-[2] + *gegn* straight]

against (əˈgɛnst, əˈgeɪnst) *prep.* **1.** opposed to; in conflict or disagreement with. **2.** standing or leaning beside: *a ladder against the wall.* **3.** coming in contact with. **4.** in contrast to: *silhouettes are outlines against a light background.* **5.** having an unfavourable effect on: *the system works against small companies.* **6.** as a protection from: *a safeguard against contaminated water.* **7.** in exchange for or in return for. **8.** *Now rare.* in preparation for: *he gave them warm clothing against their journey.* **9. as against.** as opposed to or as compared with. [C12 *ageines,* < *again, ageyn,* etc. AGAIN + -*es,* genitive ending]

Aga Khan (ˈɑːgə ˈkɑːn) *n.* the hereditary title of the head of the Ismaili Islamic sect.

agamic (əˈgæmɪk) *adj.* asexual; occurring or reproducing without fertilization. [C19: < Gk *agamos* unmarried, < A-[1] + *gamos* marriage]

agamogenesis (ˌægəməʊˈdʒɛnɪsɪs) *n.* asexual reproduction, such as fission or parthenogenesis. [C19: AGAMIC + GENESIS]

agapanthus (ˌægəˈpænθəs) *n.* any African plant of the genus *Agapanthus,* esp. the African lily. [C19: NL, < Gk *agape* love + *anthos* flower]

agape (əˈgeɪp) *adj.* (*postpositive*) **1.** (esp. of the mouth) wide open. **2.** very surprised, expectant, or eager. [C17: A-[2] + GAPE]

Agape (ˈægəpɪ) *n.* **1.** Christian love, esp. as contrasted with erotic love; charity. **2.** a communal meal in the early Church in commemoration of the Last Supper. [C17: Gk *agapē* love]

agar (ˈeɪgə) *n.* a gelatinous carbohydrate obtained from seaweeds, used as a culture medium for bacteria, as a laxative, a thickening agent (**E406**) in food, etc. Also called: **agar-agar.** [C19: Malay]

agaric (ˈægərɪk) *n.* a fungus having gills on the underside of the cap. The group includes the edible mushrooms and poisonous forms such as the fly agaric. [C16: via L < Gk *agarikon*]

agate (ˈægɪt) *n.* **1.** an impure form of quartz consisting of a variegated, usually banded chalcedony, used as a gemstone and in making pestles and mortars. **2.** a playing marble of this quartz or resembling it. [C16: via F < L, < Gk *akhatēs*]

agave (əˈgeɪvɪ) *n.* a plant native to tropical America with tall flower stalks rising from thick fleshy leaves. Some species are the source of fibres such as sisal. [C18: NL, < Gk *agauē,* fem. of *agauos* illustrious]

age (eɪdʒ) *n.* **1.** the period of time that a person, animal, or plant has lived or is expected to live. **2.** the period of existence of an object, material, group, etc.: *the age of this table is 200 years.* **3. a.** a period or state of human life: *he should know better at his age.* **b.** (*as modifier*): *age group.* **4.** the latter part of life. **5. a.** a period of history marked by some feature or characteristic. **b.** (*cap. when part of a name*): *the Middle Ages.* **6.** generation: *the Edwardian age.* **7.** *Geol., palaeontol.* **a.** a period of the earth's history distinguished by special characteristics: *the age of reptiles.* **b.** a subdivision of an epoch. **8.** (*often pl.*) *Inf.* a relatively long time: *I've been waiting ages.* **9.** *Psychol.* the level in years that a person has reached in any area of development, compared with the normal level for his chronological age. **10. of age.** adult and legally responsible for one's actions (usually at 18 years). ~*vb.* **ageing** *or* **aging, aged. 11.** to become or cause to become old or aged. **12.** (*intr.*) to begin to seem older: *to have aged a lot in the past year.* **13.** *Brewing.* to mature or cause to mature. [C13: via OF < Vulgar L, < L *aetās*]

-age *suffix forming nouns.* **1.** indicating a collection, set, or group: *baggage.* **2.** indicating a process or action or the result of an action: *breakage.* **3.** indicating a state or relationship: *bondage.* **4.** indicating a house or place: *orphanage.* **5.** indicating a charge or fee: *postage.* **6.** indicating a rate: *dosage.* [< OF, < LL *-āticum* belonging to]

aged (ˈeɪdʒɪd) *adj.* **1. a.** advanced in years; old. **b.** (*as collective n.;* preceded by *the*): *the aged.* **2.** of, connected with, or characteristic of old age. **3.** (eɪdʒd). (*postpositive*) having the age of: *a woman aged twenty.*

ageing *or* **aging** (ˈeɪdʒɪŋ) *n.* **1.** the process of growing old or developing the appearance of old age. ~*adj.* **2.** becoming or appearing older: *an ageing car.* **3.** giving the appearance of elderliness: *that dress is really ageing.*

ageism *or* **agism** (ˈeɪdʒɪzəm) *n.* discrimination against people on the grounds of age. —ˈ**ageist** *or* ˈ**agist** *adj.*

ageless (ˈeɪdʒlɪs) *adj.* **1.** apparently never growing old. **2.** timeless; eternal: *an ageless quality.*

agency (ˈeɪdʒənsɪ) *n., pl.* **-cies. 1.** a business or other organization providing a specific service: *an employment agency.* **2.** the place where an agent conducts business. **3.** the business, duties, or functions of an agent. **4.** action, power, or operation: *the agency of fate.* [C17: < Med. L *agentia,* < L *agere* to do]

agenda (əˈdʒɛndə) *n.* **1.** (*functioning as sing.*) Also: **agendum.** a schedule or list of items to be attended to. **2.** (*functioning as pl.*) Also: **agendas, agendums.** matters to be attended to, as at a meeting. [C17: L, lit.: things to be done, < *agere* to do]

agent (ˈeɪdʒənt) *n.* **1.** a person who acts on behalf of another person, business, government, etc. **2.** a person or thing that acts or has the power to act. **3.** a substance or organism that exerts some force or effect: *a chemical agent.* **4.** the means by which something occurs or is achieved. **5.** a person representing a business concern, esp. a travelling salesman. [C15: < L *agent-*, noun use of the present participle of *agere* to do] —**agential** (eɪˈdʒɛnʃəl) *adj.*

agent-general *n., pl.* **agents-general.** a representative in London of a Canadian province or an Australian state.

agent provocateur *French.* (aʒɑ̃ prɔvɔkatœr) *n., pl.* ***agents provocateurs*** (aʒɑ̃ prɔvɔkatœr). a secret agent employed to provoke suspected persons to commit illegal acts and so be discredited or liable to punishment.

age of consent *n.* the age at which a person, esp. a female, is considered legally competent to consent to marriage or sexual intercourse.

Age of Reason *n.* (usually preceded by *the*) the 18th century in W Europe. See also **Enlightenment.**

age-old *or* **age-long** *adj.* very old or of long duration; ancient.

ageratum (ˌædʒəˈreɪtəm) *n.* a tropical American plant with thick clusters of purplish-blue flowers. [C16: NL, via L < Gk *agēraton* that does not age, < A-[1] + *gērat-*, stem of *gēras* old age]

agglomerate *vb.* (əˈglɒməˌreɪt). **1.** to form or be formed into a mass or cluster. ~*n.* (əˈglɒmərɪt, -ˌreɪt). **2.** a confused mass. **3.** a volcanic rock consisting of angular fragments within a groundmass of lava. ~*adj.* (əˈglɒmərɪt, -ˌreɪt). **4.** formed into a mass. [C17: < L *agglomerāre*, < *glomerāre* to wind into a ball] —**agˌglomerˈation** *n.* —**agˈglomerative** *adj.*

agglutinate (əˈgluːtɪˌneɪt) *vb.* **1.** to adhere or cause to adhere, as with glue. **2.** *Linguistics.* to combine or be combined by agglutination. **3.** (*tr.*) to cause (bacteria, red blood cells, etc.) to clump together. [C16: < L *agglūtināre* to glue to, < *gluten* glue] —**agˈglutinable** *adj.* —**agˈglutinant** *adj.*

agglutination (əˌgluːtɪˈneɪʃən) *n.* **1.** the act or process of agglutinating. **2.** a united mass of parts. **3.** *Linguistics.* the building up of words from component morphemes in such a way that these undergo little or no change of form or meaning.

aggrandize *or* **-dise** (əˈgrændaɪz) *vb.* (*tr.*) **1.** to increase the power, wealth, prestige, scope, etc., of. **2.** to cause (something) to seem greater. [C17: < OF *aggrandiss-*, stem of *aggrandir*, < L *grandis* GRAND] —**aggrandizement** *or* **-disement** (əˈgrændɪzmənt) *n.* —**ˈaggranˌdizer** *or* **-ˌdiser** *n.*

aggravate (ˈægrəˌveɪt) *vb.* (*tr.*) **1.** to make (a disease, situation, problem, etc.) worse. **2.** *Inf.* to annoy. [C16: < L *aggravāre* to make heavier, < *gravis* heavy] —**ˈaggraˌvating** *adj.* —**ˌaggraˈvation** *n.*

▷ **Usage.** The use of *aggravate, aggravating,* and *aggravation* for *annoy, annoying,* and *annoyance* is usually avoided in formal English.

aggregate *adj.* (ˈægrɪgɪt). **1.** formed of separate units collected into a whole. **2.** (of fruits and flowers) composed of a dense cluster of florets. ~*n.* (ˈægrɪgɪt, -ˌgeɪt). **3.** a sum or assemblage of many separate units. **4.** *Geol.* a rock, such as granite, consisting of a mixture of minerals. **5.** the sand and stone mixed with cement and water to make concrete. **6. in the aggregate.** taken as a whole. ~*vb.* (ˈægrɪˌgeɪt). **7.** to combine or be combined into a body, etc. **8.** (*tr.*) to amount to (a number). [C16: < L *aggregāre* to add to a flock or herd, < *grex* flock] —**ˌaggreˈgation** *n.* —**aggregative** (ˈægrɪˌgeɪtɪv) *adj.*

aggress (əˈgrɛs) *vb.* (*intr.*) to attack first or begin a quarrel. [C16: < Med. L *aggressāre*, < L *aggredī* to attack] —**aggressor** (əˈgrɛsə) *n.*

aggression (əˈgrɛʃən) *n.* **1.** an attack or harmful action, esp. an unprovoked attack by one country against another. **2.** any offensive activity, practice, etc. **3.** *Psychol.* a hostile or destructive mental attitude. [C17: < L *aggression-*, < *aggredī* to attack]

aggressive (əˈgrɛsɪv) *adj.* **1.** quarrelsome or belligerent. **2.** assertive; vigorous. —**agˈgressively** *adv.* —**agˈgressiveness** *n.*

aggrieve (əˈgriːv) *vb.* (*tr.*) **1.** (*often impersonal or passive*) to grieve; distress; afflict. **2.** to injure unjustly, esp. by infringing a person's legal rights. [C14 *agreven*, via OF < L *aggravāre* to AGGRAVATE] —**agˈgrieved** *adj.* —**aggrievedly** (əˈgriːvɪdlɪ) *adv.*

aggro (ˈægrəʊ) *n. Brit. sl.* aggressive behaviour. [C20: < AGGRAVATION]

aghast (əˈgɑːst) *adj.* (*postpositive*) overcome with amazement or horror. [C13 *agast*, < OE *gæstan* to frighten]

agile (ˈædʒaɪl) *adj.* **1.** quick in movement; nimble. **2.** mentally quick or acute. [C15: < L *agilis*, < *agere* to do, act] —**ˈagilely** *adv.* —**agility** (əˈdʒɪlɪtɪ) *n.*

agin (əˈgɪn) *prep. Inf. or dialect.* against. [C19: < obs. *again* AGAINST]

agio (ˈædʒɪəʊ) *n., pl.* **-ios. a.** the difference between the nominal and actual values of a currency. **b.** the charge payable for conversion of the less valuable currency. [C17: < It., lit.: ease]

agitate (ˈædʒɪˌteɪt) *vb.* **1.** (*tr.*) to excite, disturb, or trouble (a person, the mind or feelings). **2.** (*tr.*) to shake, stir, or disturb. **3.** (*intr.; often foll. by for or against*) to attempt to stir up public opinion for or against something. [C16: < L *agitātus*, < *agitāre* to set into motion, < *agere* to act] —**ˈagiˌtated** *adj.* —**ˈagiˌtatedly** *adv.* —**ˌagiˈtation** *n.*

agitato (ˌædʒɪˈtɑːtəʊ) *adj., adv. Music.* (to be performed) in an agitated manner.

agitator (ˈædʒɪˌteɪtə) *n.* **1.** a person who agitates for or against a cause, etc. **2.** a device for mixing or shaking.

agitprop (ˈædʒɪtˌprɒp) *n.* **a.** any promotion, as in the arts, of political propaganda, esp. of a Communist nature. **b.** (*as modifier*): *agitprop theatre.* [C20: short for Russian *Agitpropbyuro*]

agleam (əˈgliːm) *adj.* (*postpositive*) glowing; gleaming.

aglet (ˈæglɪt) *or* **aiglet** *n.* **1.** a metal sheath or tag at the end of a shoelace, ribbon, etc. **2.** a variant spelling of **aiguillette.** [C15: < OF *aiguillette* a small needle]

agley (əˈgleɪ, əˈgliː, əˈglaɪ) *or* **aglee** (əˈgliː) *adv., adj. Scot.* awry; oblique(ly); askew. [< *gley* squint]

aglitter (əˈglɪtə) *adj.* (*postpositive*) sparkling; glittering.

aglow (əˈgləʊ) *adj.* (*postpositive*) glowing.

aglu *or* **agloo** (ˈægluː) *n. Canad.* a breathing hole made in ice by a seal. [C19: < Eskimo]

AGM *abbrev. for* annual general meeting.

agnail (ˈægˌneɪl) *n.* another name for **hangnail.**

agnate (ˈægneɪt) *adj.* **1.** related by descent from a common male ancestor. **2.** related in any way. ~*n.* **3.** a male or female descendant by male links from a common male ancestor. [C16: < L *agnātus* born in addition, < *agnāscī*, < *ad-* in addition + *gnāscī* to be born]

agnostic (ægˈnɒstɪk) *n.* **1.** a person who holds that knowledge of a Supreme Being, ultimate cause, etc., is impossible. **2.** a person who claims, with respect to any particular question, that the answer cannot be known with certainty. ~*adj.* **3.** of or relating to agnostics. [C19: coined 1869 by T. H. Huxley < A-[1] + GNOSTIC] —**agˈnosticism** *n.*

Agnus Dei (ˈægnʊs ˈdeɪɪ) *n.* **1.** the figure of a lamb bearing a cross or banner, emblematic of Christ. **2.** a chant beginning with these words or a translation of them, forming part of the Roman Catholic Mass. [L: Lamb of God]

ago (əˈgəʊ) *adv.* in the past: *five years ago; long ago.* [C14 *ago*, < OE *āgān* to pass away]

▷ **Usage.** The use of *ago* with *since* (*it's ten years ago since he wrote the novel*) is redundant and is therefore avoided in careful English. *Ago* should be followed by *that: it was ten years ago that he wrote the novel.*

agog (əˈgɒg) *adj.* (*postpositive*) eager or curious. [C15: ? < OF *en gogues* in merriments]

-agogue *or esp. U.S.* **-agog** *n. combining form.* indicating a person or thing that leads or incites to action: *demagogue.* [via LL < Gk *agōgos,* < *agein* to lead] **—-agogic** *adj. combining form.* **—-agogy** *n. combining form.*

agonic (əˈgɒnɪk) *adj.* forming no angle. [C19: < Gk *agōnos,* < A-¹ + *gōnia* angle]

agonic line *n.* an imaginary line on the surface of the earth connecting points of zero magnetic declination.

agonize *or* **-nise** (ˈægəˌnaɪz) *vb.* **1.** to suffer or cause to suffer agony. **2.** (*intr.*) to struggle; strive. [C16: via Med. L < Gk *agōnizesthai* to contend for a prize, < *agōn* contest] **—ˈagoˌnizingly** *or* **-ˌnisingly** *adv.*

agony (ˈægənɪ) *n., pl.* **-nies. 1.** acute physical or mental pain; anguish. **2.** the suffering or struggle preceding death. [C14: via LL < Gk *agōnia* struggle, < *agōn* contest]

agony aunt *n.* (*sometimes cap.*) a person who replies to readers' letters in an agony column.

agony column *n.* **1.** a newspaper or magazine feature offering sympathetic advice to readers on their personal problems. **2.** *Inf.* a newspaper or magazine column devoted to advertisements relating esp. to personal problems.

agora (ˈægərə) *n., pl.* **-rae** (-riː, -raɪ) *or* **-ras.** (*often cap.*) **a.** the marketplace in Athens, used for popular meetings in ancient Greece. **b.** the meeting itself. [< Gk, < *agorein* to gather]

agoraphobia (ˌægərəˈfəʊbɪə) *n.* a pathological fear of open spaces. **—ˌagoraˈphobic** *adj., n.*

agouti (əˈguːtɪ) *n., pl.* **-tis** *or* **-ties.** a rodent of Central and South America and the West Indies. Agoutis are agile and long-legged, with hooflike claws, and are valued for their meat. [C18: via F & Sp. < Guarani]

AGR *abbrev. for* advanced gas-cooled reactor.

agrarian (əˈgrɛərɪən) *adj.* **1.** of or relating to land or its cultivation. **2.** of or relating to rural or agricultural matters. *~n.* **3.** a person who favours the redistribution of landed property. [C16: < L *agrārius,* < *ager* field, land] **—aˈgrarianism** *n.*

agree (əˈgriː) *vb.* **agreeing, agreed.** (*mainly intr.*) **1.** (often foll. by *with*) to be of the same opinion. **2.** (*also tr.;* when *intr.,* often foll. by *to;* when *tr., takes a clause as object or an infinitive*) to give assent; consent. **3.** (*also tr.;* when *intr.,* foll. by *on* or *about;* when *tr., may take a clause as object*) to come to terms (about). **4.** (foll. by *with*) to be similar or consistent; harmonize. **5.** (foll. by *with*) to be agreeable or suitable (to one's health, etc.). **6.** (*tr.; takes a clause as object*) to concede: *they agreed that the price was too high.* **7.** *Grammar.* to undergo agreement. [C14: < OF *agreer,* < *a gre* at will or pleasure]

agreeable (əˈgriːəbᵊl) *adj.* **1.** pleasing; pleasant. **2.** prepared to consent. **3.** (foll. by *to* or *with*) in keeping. **4.** (foll. by *to*) to one's liking. **—aˈgreeableness** *n.* **—aˈgreeably** *adv.*

agreed (əˈgriːd) *adj.* **1.** determined by common consent: *the agreed price.* *~sentence substitute.* **2.** an expression of consent or agreement.

agreement (əˈgriːmənt) *n.* **1.** the act of agreeing. **2.** a settlement, esp. one that is legally enforceable. **3.** a contract or document containing such a settlement. **4.** the state of being of the same opinion. **5.** the state of being similar or consistent. **6.** *Grammar.* the determination of the inflectional form of one word by some grammatical feature, such as number or gender, of another word. [C14: < OF]

agribusiness (ˈægrɪˌbɪznɪs) *n.* the various businesses that process and distribute farm products. [C20: < AGRI(CULTURE) + BUSINESS]

agriculture (ˈægrɪˌkʌltʃə) *n.* the science or occupation of cultivating land and rearing crops and livestock; farming. [C17: < L *agricultūra,* < *ager* field, land + *cultūra* CULTURE] **—ˌagriˈcultural** *adj.* **—ˌagriˈculturist** *or* **ˌagriˈculturalist** *n.*

agrimony (ˈægrɪmənɪ) *n.* **1.** any of various plants of the rose family, which have compound leaves, long spikes of small yellow flowers, and bristly burlike fruits. **2.** any of several other plants, such as hemp agrimony. [C15: via OF < L, < Gk *argemōnē* poppy]

agro- *combining form.* denoting fields, soil, or agriculture: *agrobiology.* [< Gk *agros* field]

agrobiology (ˌægrəʊbaɪˈɒlədʒɪ) *n.* the science of plant growth and nutrition in relation to agriculture.

agronomics (ˌægrəˈnɒmɪks) *n.* (*functioning as sing.*) the branch of economy dealing with the distribution, management, and productivity of land. **—ˌagroˈnomic** *adj.*

agronomy (əˈgrɒnəmɪ) *n.* the science of cultivation of land, soil management, and crop production. **—aˈgronomist** *n.*

agrostemma (ˌægrəʊˈstɛmə) *n.* any cultivated variety of corncockle. [NL, < Gk *agros* field + *stemma* wreath]

aground (əˈgraʊnd) *adv., adj.* (*postpositive*) on or onto the ground or bottom, as in shallow water.

agterskot (ˈaxtəˌskɒt) *n.* (in South Africa) the final instalment of payment to a farmers' cooperative for a crop or wool clip. [< Afrik. *agter* afterwards + *skot* payment]

ague (ˈeɪgjuː) *n.* **1.** malarial fever with successive stages of fever and chills. **2.** a fit of shivering. [C14: < OF (*fievre*) *ague* acute fever; see ACUTE] **—ˈaguish** *adj.*

ah (ɑː) *interj.* an exclamation expressing pleasure, pain, sympathy, etc., according to the intonation of the speaker.

AH (indicating years in the Muslim system of dating, numbered from the Hegira (622 A.D.)) *abbrev. for* anno Hegirae. [L]

aha (ɑːˈhɑː) *interj.* an exclamation expressing triumph, surprise, etc., according to the intonation of the speaker.

ahead (əˈhɛd) *adj.* **1.** (*postpositive*) in front; in advance. *~adv.* **2.** at or in the front; before. **3.** forwards: *go straight ahead.* **4. ahead of. a.** in front of; at a further advanced position than. **b.** *Stock Exchange.* in anticipation of: *the share price rose ahead of the annual figures.* **5. be ahead.** *Inf.* to have an advantage; be winning. **6. get ahead.** to attain success.

ahem (əˈhɛm) *interj.* a clearing of the throat, used to attract attention, express doubt, etc.

ahimsa (ɑːˈhɪmsɑː) *n.* (in Hindu, Buddhist, and Jainist philosophy) the law of reverence for, and nonviolence to, every form of life. [Sansk., < *a* without + *himsā* injury]

ahoy (əˈhɔɪ) *interj. Naut.* a hail used to call a ship or to attract attention.

ai (ˈɑːɪ) *n., pl.* **ais.** another name for **three-toed sloth** (see **sloth** (sense 1)). [C17: < Port., < Tupi]

AI *abbrev. for:* **1.** Amnesty International. **2.** artificial insemination. **3.** artificial intelligence.

aid (eɪd) *vb.* **1.** to give support to (someone to do something); help or assist. **2.** (*tr.*) to assist financially. *~n.* **3.** assistance; help; support. **4.** a person, device, etc., that helps or assists. **5.** *Mountaineering.* a device such as a piton when used as a direct help in the ascent. **6.** (in medieval Europe) a feudal payment made to the king or any lord by his vassals on certain occasions such as the knighting of an eldest son. [C15: via OF *aidier* < L *adjūtāre,* < *juvāre* to help] **—ˈaider** *n.*

Aid *or* **-aid** *n. combining form.* denoting a charitable organization or function that raises money for a cause: *Band Aid; Ferryaid.*

AID *abbrev. for:* **1.** *U.S.* Agency for International Development. **2.** artificial insemination (by) donor.

aide (eɪd) *n.* **1.** an assistant. **2.** short for **aide-de-camp.**

aide-de-camp *or* **aid-de-camp** (ˈeɪd də ˈkɒŋ) *n., pl.* **aides-de-camp** *or* **aids-de-camp.** a military officer serving as personal assistant to a senior. Abbrev.: **ADC.** [C17: < F: camp assistant]

aide-mémoire (ˈeɪdmɛmˈwɑː) *n., pl.* **aides-mémoire** (ˈeɪdzmɛmˈwɑː). **1.** a note serving as a reminder. **2.** a summarized diplomatic communication. [F, < *aider* to help + *mémoire* memory]

AIDS (eɪdz) *n. acronym for* acquired immune (*or* immuno-) deficiency syndrome: a condition in which the body loses its ability to resist infection.

AIDS-related complex *n.* See **ARC.**

AIF *abbrev. for* Australian Imperial Force.

aiglet (ˈeɪglɪt) *n.* a variant of **aglet.**

aigrette *or* **aigret** (ˈeɪgrɛt) *n.* **1.** a long plume worn on hats or as a headdress, esp. one of long egret feathers. **2.** an ornament in imitation of a plume of feathers. [C17: < F; see EGRET]

aiguille (eɪˈgwiːl) *n.* **1.** a rock mass or peak shaped like a needle. **2.** an instrument for boring holes in rocks or masonry. [C19: F, lit.: needle]

aiguillette (ˌeɪgwɪˈlɛt) *n.* **1.** an ornamentation worn by certain military officers, consisting of cords with metal tips. **2.** a variant of **aglet.** [C19: F; see AGLET]

AIH *abbrev. for* artificial insemination (by) husband.

ail (eɪl) *vb.* **1.** (*tr.*) to trouble; afflict. **2.** (*intr.*) to feel unwell. [OE *eglan,* < *egle* painful]

ailanthus (eɪˈlænθəs) *n., pl.* **-thuses.** an E Asian deciduous tree having pinnate leaves, small greenish flowers, and winged fruits. Also called: **tree of heaven.** [C19: NL, < native name in the Moluccas in the Indian and Pacific Oceans]

aileron (ˈeɪlərɒn) *n.* a flap hinged to the trailing edge of an aircraft wing to provide lateral control. [C20: < F, dim. of *aile* wing]

ailing (ˈeɪlɪŋ) *adj.* unwell, esp. over a long period.

ailment (ˈeɪlmənt) *n.* a slight but often persistent illness.

aim (eɪm) *vb.* **1.** to point (a weapon, missile, etc.) or direct (a blow) at a particular person or object. **2.** (*tr.*) to direct (satire, criticism, etc.) at a person, object, etc. **3.** (*intr.;* foll. by *at* or an infinitive) to propose or intend. **4.** (*intr.;* often foll. by *at* or *for*) to direct one's efforts or strive (towards). ~*n.* **5.** the action of directing something at an object. **6.** the direction in which something is pointed: *to take aim.* **7.** the object at which something is aimed. **8.** intention; purpose. [C14: via OF *aesmer* < L *aestimāre* to ESTIMATE]

aimless (ˈeɪmlɪs) *adj.* having no purpose or direction. —**ˈaimlessly** *adv.* —**ˈaimlessness** *n.*

ain't (eɪnt) *Not standard. contraction of* am not, is not, are not, have not, *or* has not: *I ain't seen it.*

▷ **Usage.** Although the interrogative form *ain't I?* would be a natural contraction of *am not I?,* it is generally avoided in spoken English and never used in formal English.

Ainu (ˈaɪnuː) *n.* **1.** (*pl.* **-nus** *or* **-nu**) a member of the aboriginal people of Japan. **2.** the language of this people, sometimes tentatively associated with Altaic, still spoken in parts of Hokkaido. [Ainu: man]

air (ɛə) *n.* **1.** the mixture of gases that forms the earth's atmosphere. It consists chiefly of nitrogen, oxygen, argon, and carbon dioxide. **2.** the space above and around the earth; sky. Related adj.: **aerial. 3.** breeze; slight wind. **4.** public expression; utterance. **5.** a distinctive quality: *an air of mystery.* **6.** a person's distinctive appearance, manner, or bearing. **7.** *Music.* a simple tune for either vocal or instrumental performance. **8.** transportation in aircraft (esp. in **by air**). **9.** an archaic word for **breath** (senses 1–3). **10. in the air. a.** in circulation; current. **b.** unsettled. **11. into thin air.** leaving no trace behind. **12. on** (*or* **off**) **the air.** (not) in the act of broadcasting or (not) being broadcast on radio or television. **13. take the air.** to go out of doors, as for a short walk. **14. up in the air. a.** uncertain. **b.** *Inf.* agitated or excited. **15.** (*modifier*) *Astrol.* of or relating to a group of three signs of the zodiac, Gemini, Libra, and Aquarius. ~*vb.* **16.** to expose or be exposed to the air so as to cool or freshen. **17.** to expose or be exposed to warm or heated air so as to dry: *to air linen.* **18.** (*tr.*) to make known publicly: *to air one's opinions.* ~See also **airs.** [C13: via OF & L < Gk *aēr* the lower atmosphere]

air bag *n.* a safety device in a car, consisting of a bag that inflates automatically in an accident and prevents the passengers from being thrown forwards.

air base *n.* a centre from which military aircraft operate.

air bladder *n.* **1.** an air-filled sac, lying above the alimentary canal in bony fishes, that regulates buoyancy at different depths by a variation in the pressure of the air. **2.** any air-filled sac, such as one in seaweeds.

airborne (ˈɛəˌbɔːn) *adj.* **1.** conveyed by or through the air. **2.** (of aircraft) flying; in the air.

air brake *n.* **1.** a brake operated by compressed air, esp. in heavy vehicles and trains. **2.** an articulated flap or small parachute for reducing the speed of an aircraft.

airbrick (ˈɛəˌbrɪk) *n. Chiefly Brit.* a brick with holes in it, put into the wall of a building for ventilation.

airbrush (ˈɛəˌbrʌʃ) *n.* **1.** an atomizer for spraying paint or varnish by means of compressed air. ~*vb.* (*tr.*) **2.** to paint or varnish (something) by using an airbrush.

airbus (ˈɛəˌbʌs) *n.* an airliner operated over short distances.

air chief marshal *n.* a senior officer of the Royal Air Force and certain other air forces, of equivalent rank to admiral in the Royal Navy.

air commodore *n.* a senior officer of the Royal Air Force and certain other air forces, of equivalent rank to brigadier in the Army.

air conditioning *n.* a system or process for controlling the temperature and sometimes the humidity of the air in a house, etc. —**ˈair-conˌdition** *vb.* (*tr.*) —**air conditioner** *n.*

air-cool *vb.* (*tr.*) to cool (an engine) by a flow of air. Cf. **water-cool.**

aircraft (ˈɛəˌkrɑːft) *n., pl.* **-craft.** any machine capable of flying by means of buoyancy or aerodynamic forces, such as a glider, helicopter, or aeroplane.

aircraft carrier *n.* a warship with an extensive flat deck for the launch of aircraft.

aircraftman (ˈɛəˌkrɑːftmən) *n., pl.* **-men.** a serviceman of the most junior rank in the Royal Air Force. —**ˈaircraftˌwoman** *fem. n.*

air curtain *n.* an air stream across a doorway to exclude draughts, etc.

air cushion *n.* **1.** an inflatable cushion. **2.** the pocket of air that supports a hovercraft.

airdrop (ˈɛəˌdrɒp) *n.* **1.** a delivery of supplies, troops, etc., from an aircraft by parachute. ~*vb.* **-dropping, -dropped. 2.** (*tr.*) to deliver (supplies, etc.) by an airdrop.

Airedale (ˈɛəˌdeɪl) *n.* a large rough-haired tan-coloured breed of terrier with a black saddle-shaped patch covering most of the back. Also called: **Airedale terrier.** [C19: < district in Yorkshire]

airfield (ˈɛəˌfiːld) *n.* a landing and taking-off area for aircraft.

airfoil (ˈɛəˌfɔɪl) *n.* the U.S. and Canad. name for **aerofoil.**

air force *n.* **a.** the branch of a nation's armed services primarily responsible for air warfare. **b.** (*as modifier*): *an air-force base.*

airframe (ˈɛəˌfreɪm) *n.* the body of an aircraft, excluding its engines.

air gun *n.* a gun discharged by means of compressed air.

air hole *n.* **1.** a hole that allows the passage of air, esp. for ventilation. **2.** a section of open water in a frozen surface.

air hostess *n.* a stewardess on an airliner.

airily (ˈɛərɪlɪ) *adv.* **1.** in a jaunty or high-spirited manner. **2.** in a light or delicate manner.

airiness (ˈɛərɪnɪs) *n.* **1.** the quality or condition of being fresh, light, or breezy. **2.** gaiety.

airing (ˈɛərɪŋ) *n.* **1. a.** exposure to air or warmth, as for drying or ventilation. **b.** (*as modifier*): *airing cupboard.* **2.** an excursion in the open air. **3.** exposure to public debate.

airless (ˈɛəlɪs) *adj.* 1. lacking fresh air; stuffy or sultry. 2. devoid of air. —ˈ**airlessness** *n.*
air letter *n.* another name for **aerogram.**
airlift (ˈɛəˌlɪft) *n.* 1. the transportation by air of passengers, troops, cargo, etc., esp. when other routes are blocked. ~*vb.* 2. (*tr.*) to transport by an airlift.
airline (ˈɛəˌlaɪn) *n.* 1. a. a system or organization that provides scheduled flights for passengers or cargo. b. (*as modifier*): *an airline pilot.* 2. a hose or tube carrying air under pressure.
airliner (ˈɛəˌlaɪnə) *n.* a large passenger aircraft.
airlock (ˈɛəˌlɒk) *n.* 1. a bubble in a pipe causing an obstruction. 2. an airtight chamber with regulated air pressure used to gain access to a space that has air under pressure.
air mail *n.* 1. the system of conveying mail by aircraft. 2. mail conveyed by aircraft. ~*adj.* **airmail.** 3. of or for air mail.
airman (ˈɛəmən) *n., pl.* **-men.** an aviator, esp. one serving in the armed forces.
air marshal *n.* 1. a senior Royal Air Force officer of equivalent rank to a vice admiral in the Royal Navy. 2. a Royal Australian Air Force officer of the highest rank. 3. a Royal New Zealand Air Force officer of the highest rank when chief of defence forces.
air mass *n.* a large body of air having characteristics of temperature, moisture, and pressure that are approximately uniform horizontally.
airplane (ˈɛəˌpleɪn) *n.* the U.S. and Canad. name for **aeroplane.**
airplay (ˈɛəˌpleɪ) *n.* (of a gramophone record) radio exposure.
air pocket *n.* a localized region of low air density or a descending air current, causing an aircraft to suffer an abrupt decrease in height.
airport (ˈɛəˌpɔːt) *n.* a landing and taking-off area for civil aircraft, usually with runways and aircraft maintenance and passenger facilities.
air power *n.* the strength of a nation's air force.
air pump *n.* a device for pumping air into or out of something.
air raid *n.* a. an attack by hostile aircraft or missiles. b. (*as modifier*): *an air-raid shelter.*
air-raid warden *n.* a member of a civil defence organization responsible for enforcing regulations, etc., during an air attack.
air rifle *n.* a rifle discharged by compressed air.
airs (ɛəz) *pl. n.* affected manners intended to impress others: *to give oneself airs; put on airs.*
air sac *n.* any of the membranous air-filled extensions of the lungs of birds, which increase the efficiency of respiration.
airscrew (ˈɛəˌskruː) *n. Brit.* an aircraft propeller.
air-sea rescue *n.* an air rescue at sea.
air shaft *n.* a shaft for ventilation, esp. in a mine or tunnel.
airship (ˈɛəˌʃɪp) *n.* a lighter-than-air self-propelled craft. Also called: **dirigible.**
airshow (ˈɛəˌʃəʊ) *n.* an occasion when an air base is open to the public and a flying display and, usually, static exhibitions are held.
airsick (ˈɛəˌsɪk) *adj.* nauseated from travelling in an aircraft.
airspace (ˈɛəˌspeɪs) *n.* the atmosphere above the earth or part of the earth, esp. the atmosphere above a particular country.
airspeed (ˈɛəˌspiːd) *n.* the speed of an aircraft relative to the air in which it moves.
airstrip (ˈɛəˌstrɪp) *n.* a cleared area for the landing and taking-off of aircraft; runway. Also called: **landing strip.**
air terminal *n. Brit.* a building in a city from which air passengers are taken to an airport.
airtight (ˈɛəˌtaɪt) *adj.* 1. not permitting the passage of air. 2. having no weak points; rigid or unassailable.
air-to-air *adj.* operating between aircraft in flight.
air-traffic control *n.* an organization that determines the altitude, speed, and direction at which planes fly in a given area, giving instructions to pilots by radio. —**air-traffic controller** *n.*
air vice-marshal *n.* 1. a senior Royal Air Force officer of equivalent rank to a rear admiral in the Royal Navy. 2. a Royal Australian Air Force officer of the second highest rank. 3. a Royal New Zealand Air Force officer of the highest rank.
airwaves (ˈɛəˌweɪvz) *pl. n. Inf.* radio waves used in radio and television broadcasting.
airway (ˈɛəˌweɪ) *n.* 1. an air route, esp. one that is fully equipped with navigational aids, etc. 2. a passage for ventilation, esp. in a mine.
airworthy (ˈɛəˌwɜːðɪ) *adj.* (of an aircraft) safe to fly.
airy (ˈɛərɪ) *adj.* **airier, airiest.** 1. abounding in fresh air. 2. spacious or uncluttered. 3. nonchalant. 4. visionary; fanciful: *airy promises.* 5. of or relating to air. 6. weightless and insubstantial. 7. light and graceful in movement. 8. buoyant and gay; lively. 9. high up in the air.
aisle (aɪl) *n.* 1. a passageway separating seating areas in a theatre, church, etc. 2. a lateral division in a church flanking the nave or chancel. [C14 *ele* (later *aile, aisle,* through confusion with *isle*), via OF < L *āla* wing] —**aisled** *adj.*
aitch (eɪtʃ) *n.* the letter *h* or the sound represented by it. [C16: a phonetic spelling]
aitchbone (ˈeɪtʃˌbəʊn) *n.* 1. the rump bone in cattle. 2. a cut of beef from or including the rump bone. [C15 *hach-boon,* altered < earlier *nachebone* (*a nache* mistaken for *an ache, an aitch*); *nache* buttock, via OF < LL *natica,* < L *natis* buttock]
ajar (əˈdʒɑː) *adj.* (*postpositive*), *adv.* (esp. of a door) slightly open. [C18: altered form of obs. *on char,* lit.: on the turn; < OE *cierran* to turn]
a.k.a. *or* **AKA** *abbrev. for* also known as.
akene (əˈkiːn) *n.* a variant spelling of **achene.**
akimbo (əˈkɪmbəʊ) *adj.* (*postpositive*), *adv.* with hands on hips and elbows out. [C15 *in kenebowe,* lit.: in keen bow, that is, in a sharp curve]
akin (əˈkɪn) *adj.* (*postpositive*) 1. related by blood. 2. (often foll. by *to*) having similar characteristics, properties, etc.
Akkadian *or* **Accadian** (əˈkædɪən) *n.* 1. a member of an ancient Semitic people who lived in central Mesopotamia in the third millennium B.C. 2. the extinct language of this people.
Al *the chemical symbol for* aluminium.
-al[1] *suffix forming adjectives.* of; related to: *functional; sectional; tonal.* [< L *-ālis*]
-al[2] *suffix forming nouns.* the act or process of doing what is indicated by the verb stem: *renewal.* [via OF *-aille, -ail,* < L *-ālia,* neuter pl. used as substantive, < *-ālis* -AL[1]]
-al[3] *suffix forming nouns.* 1. (*not used systematically*) indicating any aldehyde: *salicylal.* 2. indicating a pharmaceutical product: *phenobarbital.* [shortened < ALDEHYDE]
ala (ˈeɪlə) *n., pl.* **alae** (ˈeɪliː). 1. *Zool.* a wing or flat winglike process or structure. 2. *Bot.* a winglike part, such as one of the wings of a sycamore seed. [C18: < L *āla* a wing]
à la (ɑː lɑː) *prep.* 1. in the manner or style of. 2. as prepared in (a particular place) or by or for (a particular person). [C17: < F, short for *à la mode de* in the style of]
alabaster (ˈæləˌbɑːstə) *n.* 1. a fine-grained usually white, opaque, or translucent variety of gypsum. 2. a variety of hard semitranslucent calcite. ~*adj.* 3. of or resembling alabaster. [C14: < OF *alabastre,* < L *alabaster,* < Gk *alabastros*] —ˌ**ala**ˈ**bastrine** *adj.*
à la carte (ɑː lɑː ˈkɑːt) *adj., adv.* (of a menu) having dishes listed separately and individually priced. Cf. **table d'hôte.** [C19: < F, lit.: according to the card]
alack (əˈlæk) *or* **alackaday** (əˈlækəˌdeɪ) *interj.* an archaic or poetic word for **alas.** [C15: < *a* ah! + *lack* loss, LACK]
alacrity (əˈlækrɪtɪ) *n.* liveliness or briskness. [C15: < L, < *alacer* lively]
à la mode (ɑː lɑː ˈməʊd) *adj.* 1. fashionable in style, design, etc. 2. (of meats) braised with

vegetables in wine. [C17: < F: according to the fashion]

alar (ˈeɪlə) *adj.* relating to, resembling, or having wings or alae. [C19: < L *āla* a wing]

alarm (əˈlɑːm) *vb.* (*tr.*) **1.** to fill with apprehension, anxiety, or fear. **2.** to warn about danger; alert. ~*n.* **3.** fear or terror aroused by awareness of danger. **4.** apprehension or uneasiness. **5.** a noise, signal, etc., warning of danger. **6.** any device that transmits such a warning: *a burglar alarm.* **7. a.** the device in an alarm clock that triggers off the bell or buzzer. **b.** short for **alarm clock. 8.** *Arch.* a call to arms. [C14: < OF *alarme,* < OIt. *all'arme* to arms; see ARM[2]] —**aˈlarming** *adj.*

alarm clock *n.* a clock with a mechanism that sounds at a set time: used esp. for waking a person up.

alarmist (əˈlɑːmɪst) *n.* **1.** a person who alarms or attempts to alarm others needlessly. **2.** a person who is easily alarmed. ~*adj.* **3.** characteristic of an alarmist.

alarum (əˈlærəm, -ˈlɑːr-) *n.* **1.** *Arch.* an alarm, esp. a call to arms. **2.** (used as a stage direction, esp. in Elizabethan drama) a loud disturbance or conflict (esp. in **alarums and excursions).** [C15: var. of ALARM]

alas (əˈlæs) *sentence connector.* **1.** unfortunately; regrettably: *there were, alas, none left.* ~*interj.* **2.** *Arch.* an exclamation of grief or alarm. [C13: < OF *ha las!* oh wretched!; *las* < L *lassus* weary]

alate (ˈeɪleɪt) *adj.* having wings or winglike extensions. [C17: < L, < *āla* wing]

alb (ælb) *n. Christianity.* a long white linen vestment with sleeves worn by priests and others. [OE *albe,* < Med. L *alba* (*vestis*) white (clothing)]

albacore (ˈælbəˌkɔː) *n.* a tunny occurring mainly in warm regions of the Atlantic and Pacific. It has very long pectoral fins and is a valued food fish. [C16: < Port., < Ar.]

Albanian (ælˈbeɪnɪən) *n.* **1.** the official language of Albania. **2.** a native, citizen, or inhabitant of Albania. ~*adj.* **3.** of or relating to Albania, its people, or their language.

albatross (ˈælbəˌtrɒs) *n.* **1.** a large bird of cool southern oceans, with long narrow wings and a powerful gliding flight. See also **wandering albatross. 2.** a constant and inescapable burden or handicap. **3.** *Golf.* a score of three strokes under par for a hole. [C17: < Port. *alcatraz* pelican, < Ar., < *al* the + *ghattās* white-tailed sea eagle; infl. by L *albus* white: C20 in sense 2, < Coleridge's poem *The Rime of the Ancient Mariner* (1798)]

albedo (ælˈbiːdəʊ) *n.* the ratio of the intensity of light reflected from an object, such as a planet, to that of the light it receives from the sun. [C19: < Church L: whiteness, < L *albus* white]

albeit (ɔːlˈbiːɪt) *conj.* even though. [C14 *al be it,* that is, although it be (that)]

albert (ˈælbət) *n.* a kind of watch chain usually attached to a waistcoat. [C19: after Prince *Albert* (1819-61), Consort of Queen Victoria]

Albertan (ælˈbɜːtən) *adj.* **1.** of or denoting Alberta, a province of W Canada. ~*n.* **2.** a native or inhabitant of Alberta.

albescent (ælˈbɛsᵊnt) *adj.* shading into or becoming white. [C19: < L *albēscere,* < *albus* white] —**alˈbescence** *n.*

Albigenses (ˌælbɪˈdʒɛnsiːz) *pl. n.* members of a Manichean sect that flourished in S France from the 11th to the 13th century. [< Med. L: inhabitants of *Albi,* S France] —ˌ**Albiˈgensian** *adj.* —ˌ**Albiˈgensianism** *n.*

albino (ælˈbiːnəʊ) *n., pl.* **-nos. 1.** a person with congenital absence of pigmentation in the skin, eyes, and hair. **2.** any animal or plant that is deficient in pigment. [C18: via Port. & Sp. < L *albus* white] —**albinism** (ˈælbɪˌnɪzəm) *n.* —**albinotic** (ˌælbɪˈnɒtɪk) *adj.*

Albion (ˈælbɪən) *n. Arch. or poetic.* Britain or England. [C13: < L, of Celtic origin]

albite (ˈælbaɪt) *n.* a white, bluish-green, or reddish-grey feldspar mineral used in the manufacture of glass and as a gemstone. [C19: < L *albus* white]

album (ˈælbəm) *n.* **1.** a book or binder consisting of blank pages, for keeping photographs, stamps, autographs, etc. **2.** one or more long-playing records released as a single item. **3.** a booklike holder containing sleeves for gramophone records. **4.** *Chiefly Brit.* an anthology. [C17: < L: blank tablet, < *albus* white]

albumen (ˈælbjʊmɪn) *n.* **1.** the white of an egg; the nutritive substance that surrounds the yolk. **2.** a variant spelling of **albumin.** [C16: < L: white of an egg, < *albus* white]

albumin *or* **albumen** (ˈælbjʊmɪn) *n.* any of a group of simple water-soluble proteins that are found in blood plasma, egg white, etc. [C19: < ALBUMEN + -IN] —**alˈbuminous** *adj.*

albuminuria (ælˌbjuːmɪˈnjʊərɪə) *n.* the presence of albumin in the urine. Also called: **proteinuria.**

albumose (ˈælbjʊˌməʊs) *n.* the U.S. name for **proteose.** [C19: < ALBUMIN + -OSE[2]]

alburnum (ælˈbɜːnəm) *n.* a former name for **sapwood.** [C17: < L: sapwood, < *albus* white]

Alcaic (ælˈkeɪɪk) *adj.* **1.** of a metre used by Alcaeus, consisting of a strophe of four lines each with four feet. ~*n.* **2.** (*usually pl.*) verse written in the Alcaic form. [C17: < LL *Alcaicus* of *Alcaeus,* 7th-cent. B.C. Gk poet]

alcalde (ælˈkældɪ) *or* **alcade** (ælˈkeɪd) *n.* (in Spain and Spanish America) the mayor or chief magistrate in a town. [C17: < Sp., < Ar. *al-qādī* the judge]

alcazar (ˌælkəˈzɑː; *Spanish* alˈkaθar) *n.* any of various palaces or fortresses built in Spain by the Moors. [C17: < Sp., < Ar. *al-qasr* the castle]

alchemist (ˈælkəmɪst) *n.* a person who practises alchemy.

alchemize *or* **-mise** (ˈælkəˌmaɪz) *vb.* (*tr.*) to alter (an element, metal, etc.) by alchemy.

alchemy (ˈælkəmɪ) *n., pl.* **-mies. 1.** the pseudoscientific predecessor of chemistry that sought a method of transmuting base metals into gold, and an elixir to prolong life indefinitely. **2.** a power like that of alchemy: *her beauty had a potent alchemy.* [C14 *alkamye,* via OF < Med. L, < Ar., < *al* the + *kīmiyā'* transmutation, < LGk *khēmeia* the art of transmutation] —**alchemic** (ælˈkɛmɪk) *or* **alˈchemical** *adj.*

alcheringa (ˌæltʃəˈrɪŋgə) *n.* (in the mythology of Australian Aboriginal peoples) a mythical Golden Age of the past, when the first men were created. Also called: **dream time.** [< Abor., lit.: dream time]

alcohol (ˈælkəˌhɒl) *n.* **1.** a colourless flammable liquid, the active principle of intoxicating drinks, produced by the fermentation of sugars. Formula: C_2H_5OH. Also called: **ethanol, ethyl alcohol. 2.** a drink or drinks containing this substance. **3.** *Chem.* any one of a class of organic compounds that contain one or more hydroxyl groups bound to carbon atoms that are not part of an aromatic ring. Cf. **phenol** (sense 2). [C16: via NL < Med. L, < Ar. *al-kuhl* powdered antimony]

alcoholic (ˌælkəˈhɒlɪk) *n.* **1.** a person affected by alcoholism. ~*adj.* **2.** of, relating to, containing, or resulting from alcohol.

Alcoholics Anonymous *n.* an association of alcoholics who try, esp. by mutual assistance, to overcome alcoholism.

alcoholism (ˈælkəhɒˌlɪzəm) *n.* a condition in which dependence on alcohol harms a person's health, family life, etc.

alcoholize *or* **-lise** (ˈælkəhɒˌlaɪz) *vb.* (*tr.*) to turn into alcoholic drink, as by fermenting or mixing with alcohol. —ˌ**alcoˌholiˈzation** *or* **-liˈsation** *n.*

alcove (ˈælkəʊv) *n.* **1.** a recess or niche in the wall of a room, as for a bed, books, etc. **2.** any recessed usually vaulted area, as in a garden wall. **3.** any covered or secluded spot. [C17: < F, < Sp. *alcoba,* < Ar. *al-qubbah* the vault]

aldehyde (ˈældɪˌhaɪd) *n.* **1.** any organic compound containing the group -CHO. Aldehydes are oxidized to carboxylic acids. **2.** (*modifier*) consisting of, containing, or concerned with the group -CHO. [C19: < NL *al*(*cohol*) *dehyd*(*rogenā-*

tum) dehydrogenated alcohol] —**aldehydic** (ˌældəˈhɪdɪk) *adj.*

al dente (ˌæl ˈdɛntə) *adj.* (of pasta) still firm after cooking. [It., lit: to the tooth]

alder (ˈɔːldə) *n.* **1.** a shrub or tree of the birch family, having toothed leaves and conelike fruits. The wood is used for bridges, etc., because it resists underwater rot. **2.** any of several similar trees or shrubs. [OE *alor*]

alderman (ˈɔːldəmən) *n., pl.* **-men.** **1.** (in England and Wales until 1974) one of the senior members of a local council, elected by other councillors. **2.** (in the U.S., Canada, etc.) a member of the governing body of a municipality. **3.** *History.* a variant spelling of **ealdorman.** [OE *aldormann,* < *ealdor* chief (comp. of *eald* OLD) + *mann* MAN] —**aldermanic** (ˌɔːldəˈmænɪk) *adj.*

Aldis lamp (ˈɔːldɪs) *n.* a portable signalling lamp. [C20: after its inventor A.C.W. *Aldis*]

aldrin (ˈɔːldrɪn) *n.* a poisonous crystalline solid, mostly $C_{12}H_8Cl_6$, used as an insecticide. [C20: after K. *Alder* (1902–58), G chemist]

ale (eɪl) *n.* **1.** an alcoholic drink made by fermenting a cereal, esp. barley, originally differing from beer by being unflavoured by hops. **2.** *Chiefly Brit.* another word for **beer.** [OE *alu, ealu*]

aleatory (ˈeɪlɪətərɪ) *or* **aleatoric** (ˌeɪlɪəˈtɒrɪk) *adj.* **1.** dependent on chance. **2.** (esp. of a musical composition) involving elements chosen at random by the performer. [C17: < L, < *āleātor* gambler, < *ālea* game of chance]

alec *or* **aleck** (ˈælɪk) *n.* **1.** *Austral. sl.* a fool. **2.** See **smart aleck.**

alee (əˈliː) *adv., adj.* (*postpositive*) *Naut.* on or towards the lee: *with the helm alee.*

alehouse (ˈeɪlˌhaʊs) *n.* **1.** *Arch.* a place where ale was sold; tavern. **2.** *Inf.* a pub.

alembic (əˈlɛmbɪk) *n.* **1.** an obsolete type of retort used for distillation. **2.** anything that distils or purifies. [C14: < Med. L, < Ar. *al-anbīq* the still, < Gk *ambix* cup]

aleph (ˈɑːlɪf; *Hebrew* ˈalɛf) *n.* the first letter in the Hebrew alphabet. [Heb.: ox]

aleph-null *or* **aleph-zero** *n.* the smallest infinite cardinal number; the cardinal number of the set of positive integers.

alert (əˈlɜːt) *adj.* (*usually postpositive*) **1.** vigilantly attentive: *alert to the problems.* **2.** brisk, nimble, or lively. ~*n.* **3.** an alarm or warning. **4.** the period during which such a warning remains in effect. **5. on the alert. a.** on guard against danger, attack, etc. **b.** watchful; ready. ~*vb.* (*tr.*) **6.** to warn or signal (troops, police, etc.) to prepare for action. **7.** to warn of danger, an attack, etc. [C17: < It. *all'erta* on the watch, < *erta* lookout post] —**aˈlertly** *adv.* —**aˈlertness** *n.*

alethic (əˈliːθɪk) *adj. Logic.* designating the branch of modal logic dealing with necessary, contingent, and impossible truths. [C20: < Gk *alētheia* truth]

aleurone (əˈlʊərən) *or* **aleuron** (əˈlʊərɒn) *n.* a protein that occurs in the form of storage granules in plant cells, esp. in seeds such as maize. [C19: < Gk *aleuron* flour]

Aleut (æˈluːt) *n.* **1.** a member of a people inhabiting the Aleutian Islands and SW Alaska, related to the Eskimos. **2.** the language of this people, related to Eskimo. [< Russian *aleút,* prob. of native origin] —**Aleutian** (əˈluːʃən) *n., adj.*

A level *n. Brit.* **1. a.** the advanced level of a subject taken for the General Certificate of Education. **b.** (*as modifier*): *A-level maths.* **2.** a pass in a subject at A level: *he has two A levels.*

alewife (ˈeɪlˌwaɪf) *n., pl.* **-wives.** a North American fish similar to the herring. [C19: ? < F *alose* shad]

Alexandrine (ˌælɪgˈzændraɪn) *n.* **1.** a line of verse having six iambic feet, usually with a caesura after the third foot. ~*adj.* **2.** of or written in Alexandrines. [C16: < F, < *Alexandre,* 15th-cent. poem in this metre]

alexandrite (ˌælɪgˈzændraɪt) *n.* a green variety of chrysoberyl used as a gemstone. [C19: after *Alexander* I of Russia; see -ITE[1]]

alexia (əˈlɛksɪə) *n.* a disorder of the central nervous system characterized by impaired ability to read. [C19: < NL, < A-[1] + Gk *lexis* speech]

alfalfa (ælˈfælfə) *n.* a leguminous plant of Europe and Asia, widely cultivated for forage. Also called: **lucerne.** [C19: < Sp., < Ar. *al-fasfasah*]

alfresco (ælˈfrɛskəʊ) *adj., adv.* in the open air. [C18: < It.: in the cool]

alg. *abbrev. for* algebra *or* algebraic.

algae (ˈældʒiː) *pl. n., sing.* **alga** (ˈælgə). unicellular or multicellular plants, occurring in water or moist ground, that have chlorophyll but lack true stems, roots, and leaves. [C16: < L, pl. of *alga* seaweed, <?] —**algal** (ˈælgəl) *or* **algoid** (ˈælgɔɪd) *adj.*

algebra (ˈældʒɪbrə) *n.* **1.** a branch of mathematics in which arithmetical operations and relationships are generalized by using symbols to represent numbers. **2.** any abstract calculus, a formal language in which functions and operations can be defined and their properties studied. [C14: < Med. L, < Ar. *al-jabr* the bone-setting, mathematical reduction] —**algebraic** (ˌældʒɪˈbreɪɪk) *or* ˌ**algeˈbraical** *adj.* —**algebraist** (ˌældʒɪˈbreɪɪst) *n.*

Algerian (ælˈdʒɪərɪən) *adj.* **1.** of or denoting Algeria, a republic in NW Africa, or its inhabitants, their customs, etc. ~*n.* **2.** a native or inhabitant of Algeria.

-algia *n. combining form.* denoting pain in the part specified: *neuralgia; odontalgia.* [< Gk *algos* pain] —**-algic** *adj. combining form.*

algid (ˈældʒɪd) *adj. Med.* chilly or cold. [C17: < L *algidus,* < *algēre* to be cold] —**alˈgidity** *n.*

alginate (ˈældʒɪˌneɪt) *n.* a salt or ester of alginic acid.

alginic acid (ælˈdʒɪnɪk) *n.* a white or yellowish powdery substance having hydrophilic properties. Extracted from kelp, it is used mainly in the food and textile industries.

ALGOL (ˈælgɒl) *n.* a computer programming language designed for mathematical and scientific purposes. [C20 *alg*(*orithmic*) *o*(*riented*) *l*(*anguage*)]

algolagnia (ˌælgəˈlægnɪə) *n.* sexual pleasure got from suffering or inflicting pain. [ML, < Gk *algos* pain + *lagneiā* lust]

Algonquian (ælˈgɒŋkɪən, -kwɪ-) *or* **Algonkian** *n.* **1.** a widespread family of North American Indian languages. **2.** (*pl.* **-ans** *or* **-an**) a member of any of the North American Indian peoples that speak any of these languages. ~*adj.* **3.** denoting or relating to this linguistic family or its speakers.

algorism (ˈælgəˌrɪzəm) *n.* **1.** the Arabic or decimal system of counting. **2.** the skill of computation. **3.** an algorithm. [C13: < OF, < Med. L, < Ar., < the name of abu-Ja'far Mohammed ibn-Mūsa *al-Khuwārizmi,* 9th-cent. Persian mathematician]

algorithm (ˈælgəˌrɪðəm) *n.* **1.** a logical arithmetical or computational procedure that if correctly applied ensures the solution of a problem. **2.** *Logic, maths.* a recursive procedure whereby an infinite sequence of terms can be generated. ~Also called: **algorism.** [C17: changed < ALGORISM, infl. by Gk *arithmos* number] —ˌ**algoˈrithmic** *adj.*

alias (ˈeɪlɪəs) *adv.* **1.** at another time or place known as or named: *Dylan, alias Zimmerman.* ~*n., pl.* **-ases.** **2.** an assumed name. [C16: < L *aliās* (adv.) otherwise, < *alius* other]

alibi (ˈælɪˌbaɪ) *n., pl.* **-bis.** **1.** *Law.* **a.** a defence by an accused person that he was elsewhere at the time the crime was committed. **b.** the evidence given to prove this. **2.** *Inf.* an excuse. ~*vb.* **3.** (*tr.*) to provide with an alibi. [C18: < L *alibī* elsewhere, < *alius* other + *-bī* as in *ubī* where]

▷ **Usage.** The noun *alibi* is often used informally to mean an excuse: *he was late but, as always, had a good alibi.* In formal English, however, only the legal sense is acceptable.

Alice-in-Wonderland *adj.* fantastic; irrational.

[C20: alluding to the absurdities of Wonderland in Lewis Carroll's book]

alicyclic (ˌælɪˈsaɪklɪk, -ˈsɪk-) *adj.* (of an organic compound) having essentially aliphatic properties, in spite of the presence of a ring of carbon atoms. [C19: < ALI(PHATIC) + CYCLIC]

alidade (ˈælɪˌdeɪd) *or* **alidad** (ˈælɪˌdæd) *n.* **1.** a surveying instrument used for drawing lines of sight on a distant object and taking angular measurements. **2.** the upper rotatable part of a theodolite. [C15: < F, < Med. L, < Ar. *al-'idāda* the revolving radius of a circle]

alien (ˈeɪlɪən) *n.* **1.** a person owing allegiance to a country other than that in which he lives. **2.** any being or thing foreign to its environment. **3.** (in science fiction) a being from another world. ~*adj.* **4.** unnaturalized; foreign. **5.** having foreign allegiance: *alien territory.* **6.** unfamiliar: *an alien quality.* **7.** (*postpositive;* foll. by *to*) repugnant or opposed (to): *war is alien to his philosophy.* **8.** (in science fiction) of or from another world. [C14: < L *aliēnus* foreign, < *alius* other]

alienable (ˈeɪlɪənəbᵊl) *adj. Law.* (of property) transferable to another owner. —ˌ**alienaˈbility** *n.*

alienate (ˈeɪlɪəˌneɪt) *vb.* (*tr.*) **1.** to cause (a friend, etc.) to become unfriendly or hostile. **2.** to turn away: *to alienate the affections of a person.* **3.** *Law.* to transfer the ownership of (property, etc.) to another person. —ˌ**alienˈation** *n.* —ˈ**alienˌator** *n.*

alienee (ˌeɪlɪəˈniː) *n. Law.* a person to whom a transfer of property is made.

alienist (ˈeɪlɪənɪst) *n. U.S.* a psychiatrist who specializes in the legal aspects of mental illness.

alienor (ˈeɪlɪənə) *n. Law.* a person who transfers property to another.

aliform (ˈælɪˌfɔːm) *adj.* wing-shaped. [C19: < NL *āliformis,* < L *āla* a wing]

alight[1] (əˈlaɪt) *vb.* **alighting, alighted** *or* **alit.** (*intr.*) **1.** (usually foll. by *from*) to step out (of): *to alight from a taxi.* **2.** to come to rest; land: *a thrush alighted on the wall.* [OE *ālīhtan,* < A-[2] + *līhtan* to make less heavy]

alight[2] (əˈlaɪt) *adj.* (*postpositive*), *adv.* **1.** burning; on fire. **2.** illuminated. [OE, < *ālīhtan* to light up]

align (əˈlaɪn) *vb.* **1.** to place or become placed in a line. **2.** to bring (components or parts) into proper coordination or relation. **3.** (*tr.;* usually foll. by *with*) to bring (a person, country, etc.) into agreement with the policy, etc., of another. [C17: < OF, < *à ligne* into line]

alignment (əˈlaɪnmənt) *n.* **1.** arrangement in a straight line. **2.** the line or lines formed in this manner. **3.** alliance with a party, cause, etc. **4.** proper coordination or relation of components. **5.** a ground plan of a railway, road, etc.

alike (əˈlaɪk) *adj.* (*postpositive*) **1.** possessing the same or similar characteristics: *they all look alike.* ~*adv.* **2.** in the same or a similar manner or degree: *they walk alike.* [OE *gelīc*]

aliment (ˈælɪmənt) *n.* something that nourishes or sustains the body or mind. [C15: < L *alimentum* food, < *alere* to nourish] —ˌ**aliˈmental** *adj.*

alimentary (ˌælɪˈmɛntərɪ) *adj.* **1.** of or relating to nutrition. **2.** providing sustenance or nourishment.

alimentary canal *n.* the tubular passage extending from the mouth to the anus, through which food is passed and digested.

alimentation (ˌælɪmɛnˈteɪʃən) *n.* **1.** nourishment. **2.** sustenance; support.

alimony (ˈælɪmənɪ) *n. Law.* (formerly) an allowance paid under a court order by one spouse to another when they are separated but not divorced. See also **maintenance.** [C17: < L, < *alere* to nourish]

aline (əˈlaɪn) *vb.* a rare spelling of **align.** —**aˈlinement** *n.*

A-line (ˈeɪˌlaɪn) *adj.* (of garments) flaring out slightly from the waist or shoulders.

aliphatic (ˌælɪˈfætɪk) *adj.* (of an organic compound) not aromatic, esp. having an open chain structure. [C19: < Gk *aleiphat-, aleiphar* oil]

aliquant (ˈælɪkwənt) *adj. Maths.* of or signifying a quantity or number that is not an exact divisor of a given quantity or number: *5 is an aliquant part of 12.* [C17: < NL, < L *aliquantus* somewhat, a certain quantity of]

aliquot (ˈælɪˌkwɒt) *adj. Maths.* of or signifying an exact divisor of a quantity or number: *3 is an aliquot part of 12.* [C16: < L: several, a few]

alit (əˈlɪt) *vb.* a rare past tense and past participle of **alight**[1].

alive (əˈlaɪv) *adj.* (*postpositive*) **1.** living; having life. **2.** in existence; active: *they kept hope alive.* **3.** (*immediately postpositive*) now living: *the happiest woman alive.* **4.** full of life; lively. **5.** (usually foll. by *with*) animated: *a face alive with emotion.* **6.** (foll. by *to*) aware (of); sensitive (to). **7.** (foll. by *with*) teeming (with): *the mattress was alive with fleas.* **8.** *Electronics.* another word for **live**[2] (sense 10). [OE *on līfe* in LIFE]

alizarin (əˈlɪzərɪn) *n.* a brownish-yellow powder or orange-red crystalline solid used as a dye. [C19: prob. < F, < Ar. *al-'asārah* the juice, < *'asara* to squeeze]

alkali (ˈælkəˌlaɪ) *n., pl.* **-lis** *or* **-lies. 1.** *Chem.* a soluble base or a solution of a base. **2.** a soluble mineral salt that occurs in arid soils. [C14: < Med. L, < Ar. *al-qili* the ashes (of saltwort)]

alkali metal *n.* any of the monovalent metals lithium, sodium, potassium, rubidium, caesium, and francium.

alkaline (ˈælkəˌlaɪn) *adj.* having the properties of or containing an alkali. —**alkalinity** (ˌælkəˈlɪnɪtɪ) *n.*

alkaline earth *n.* **1.** Also called: **alkaline earth metal.** any of the divalent electropositive metals beryllium, magnesium, calcium, strontium, barium, and radium. **2.** an oxide of one of the alkaline earth metals.

alkalize *or* **-lise** (ˈælkəˌlaɪz) *vb.* (*tr.*) to make alkaline. —ˈ**alkaˌlizable** *or* -ˌ**lisable** *adj.*

alkaloid (ˈælkəˌlɔɪd) *n.* any of a group of nitrogenous compounds found in plants. Many are poisonous and some are used as drugs.

alkane (ˈælkeɪn) *n.* any saturated aliphatic hydrocarbon with the general formula C_nH_{2n+2}. See **methane, methane series, paraffin.**

alkanet (ˈælkəˌnɛt) *n.* **1.** a European plant, the roots of which yield a red dye. **2.** the dye obtained. [C14: < Sp., < Med. L, < Ar. *al* the + *hinnā'* henna]

alkene (ˈælkiːn) *n.* any unsaturated aliphatic hydrocarbon with the general formula $C_n H_{2n}$.

Alkoran *or* **Alcoran** (ˌælkɒˈrɑːn) *n.* a less common name for the **Koran.**

alkyd resin (ˈælkɪd) *n.* any of several synthetic resins made from a dicarboxylic acid, used in paints and adhesives.

alkyl (ˈælkɪl) *n.* (*modifier*) of or containing the monovalent group C_nH_{2n+1}: *alkyl radical.* [C19: < G, < *Alk(ohol)* ALCOHOL + -YL]

all (ɔːl) *determiner.* **1. a.** the whole quantity or amount of: *all the rice.* **b.** (*as pronoun; functioning as sing. or pl.*): *all of it is nice; all are welcome.* **2.** every one of a class: *all men are mortal.* **3.** the greatest possible: *in all earnestness.* **4.** any whatever: *beyond all doubt.* **5. all along.** all the time. **6. all but.** nearly: *all but dead.* **7. all of.** no less or smaller than: *she's all of thirteen years.* **8. all over. a.** finished. **b.** everywhere (in, on, etc.): *all over England.* **c.** *Inf.* typically (in **that's me (him,** etc.) **all over).** **d.** unduly effusive towards. **9. all in all. a.** everything considered: *all in all, it was a great success.* **b.** the object of one's attention: *you are my all in all.* **10. all the.** (foll. by a comp. adj. or adv.) so much (more or less) than otherwise: *we must work all the faster now.* **11. at all. a.** (*used with a negative or in a question*) in any way or to any degree: *I didn't know that at all.* **b.** anyway: *I'm surprised you came at all.* **12. be all for.** *Inf.* to be strongly in favour of. **13. for all. a.** in so far as: *for all anyone knows, he was a baron.* **b.** notwithstanding: *for all my pushing, I still couldn't move it.* **14. for all that.** in spite of that: *he was a nice man for all that.* **15. in all.** altogether: *there were five in all.* ~*adv.* **16.** (in scores of games) apiece; each: *the score was three all.* ~*n.* **17.** (preceded by *my, his,* etc.) (one's) complete effort or interest: *to give your all.* **18.** totality or whole. [OE *eall*]

all- *combining form.* a variant of **allo-** before a vowel.

alla breve ('ælə 'breɪvɪ) *Music.* ~*adj., adv.* **1.** with two beats to the bar instead of four, i.e. twice as fast as written. ~*n.* **2.** (formerly) a time of two or four minims to the bar. Symbol: ¢ [C19: It., lit.: according to the breve]

Allah ('ælə) *n.* the name of God in Islam. [C16: < Ar., < *al* the + *Ilāh* god]

all-American *adj. U.S.* **1.** representative of the whole of the United States. **2.** composed exclusively of American members. **3.** (of a person) typically American.

allantois (ˌælən'təʊɪs, ə'læntɔɪs) *n.* a membranous sac growing out of the ventral surface of the hind gut of embryonic reptiles, birds, and mammals. [C17: NL, < Gk *allantoeidēs* sausage-shaped] —**allantoic** (ˌælən'təʊɪk) *adj.*

allay (ə'leɪ) *vb.* **1.** to relieve (pain, grief, etc.) or be relieved. **2.** (*tr.*) to reduce (fear, anger, etc.). [OE *ālecgan* to put down]

All Blacks *pl. n.* **the.** the international Rugby Union football team of New Zealand. [so named because of the players' black strip]

all clear *n.* **1.** a signal indicating that some danger, such as an air raid, is over. **2.** permission to proceed.

allegation (ˌælɪ'geɪʃən) *n.* **1.** the act of alleging. **2.** an unproved assertion, esp. an accusation.

allege (ə'lɛdʒ) *vb.* (*tr.; may take a clause as object*) **1.** to state without or before proof: *he alleged malpractice.* **2.** to put forward (an argument or plea) for or against an accusation, claim, etc. [C14 *aleggen,* ult. < L *allēgāre* to dispatch on a mission, < *lēx* law]

alleged (ə'lɛdʒd) *adj.* (*prenominal*) **1.** stated to be such: *the alleged murderer.* **2.** dubious: *an alleged miracle.* —**allegedly** (ə'lɛdʒɪdlɪ) *adv.*

allegiance (ə'liːdʒəns) *n.* **1.** loyalty, as of a subject to his sovereign. **2.** (in feudal society) the obligations of a vassal to his liege lord. [C14: < OF, < *lige* LIEGE]

allegorical (ˌælɪ'gɒrɪkᵊl) *or* **allegoric** *adj.* used in, containing, or characteristic of allegory.

allegorize *or* **-ise** ('ælɪgəˌraɪz) *vb.* **1.** to transform (a story, fable, etc.) into or compose in the form of allegory. **2.** (*tr.*) to interpret allegorically. —ˌ**allegori'zation** *or* **-i'sation** *n.*

allegory ('ælɪgərɪ) *n., pl.* **-ries.** **1.** a poem, play, picture, etc., in which the apparent meaning of the characters and events is used to symbolize a moral or spiritual meaning. **2.** use of such symbolism. **3.** anything used as a symbol. [C14: < OF, < L, < Gk, < *allēgorein* to speak figuratively, < *allos* other + *agoreuein* to make a speech in public] —'**allegorist** *n.*

allegretto (ˌælɪ'grɛtəʊ) *Music.* ~*adj., adv.* **1.** (to be performed) fairly quickly or briskly. ~*n., pl.* **-tos.** **2.** a piece or passage to be performed in this manner. [C19: dim. of ALLEGRO]

allegro (ə'leɪgrəʊ, -'lɛg-) *Music.* ~*adj., adv.* **1.** (to be performed) in a brisk lively manner. ~*n., pl.* **-gros.** **2.** a piece or passage to be performed in this manner. [C17: < It.: cheerful, < L *alacer* brisk, lively]

allele (ə'liːl) *n.* any of two or more genes that are responsible for alternative characteristics, such as smooth or wrinkled seeds in peas. Also called: **allelomorph** (ə'liːləˌmɔːf). [C20: < G *Allel,* < *Allelomorph,* < Gk *allēl-* one another + *morphē* form]

alleluia (ˌælɪ'luːjə) *interj.* praise the Lord! Used in liturgical contexts in place of *hallelujah.* [C14: via Med. L < Heb. *hallelūyāh*]

allemande ('ælɪmænd) *n.* **1.** the first movement of the classical suite, composed in a moderate tempo. **2.** any of several German dances. **3.** a figure in country dancing or square dancing by which couples change position in the set. [C17: < F *danse allemande* German dance]

allergen ('æləˌdʒɛn) *n.* any substance capable of inducing an allergy. —ˌ**aller'genic** *adj.*

allergic (ə'lɜːdʒɪk) *adj.* **1.** of, having, or caused by an allergy. **2.** (*postpositive;* foll. by *to*) *Inf.* having an aversion (to): *allergic to work.*

allergist ('ælədʒɪst) *n.* a physician skilled in the treatment of allergies.

allergy ('ælədʒɪ) *n., pl.* **-gies.** **1.** a hypersensitivity to a substance that causes the body to react to any contact with it. Hay fever is an allergic reaction to pollen. **2.** *Inf.* an aversion. [C20: < G *Allergie* (indicating a changed reaction), < Gk *allos* other + *ergon* activity]

alleviate (ə'liːvɪˌeɪt) *vb.* (*tr.*) to make (pain, sorrow, etc.) easier to bear; lessen. [C15: < LL, < L *levis* light] —**al**ˌ**levi'ation** *n.* —**al'levi**ˌ**ator** *n.*

alley[1] ('ælɪ) *n.* **1.** a narrow passage, esp. one between or behind buildings. **2.** See **bowling alley.** **3.** *Tennis, chiefly U.S.* the space between the singles and doubles sidelines. **4.** a walk in a garden, esp. one lined with trees. **5. up** (*or* **down**) **one's alley.** *Sl.* suited to one's abilities or interests. [C14: < OF, < *aler* to go, ult. < L *ambulāre* to walk]

alley[2] ('ælɪ) *n.* a large playing marble. [C18: shortened and changed < ALABASTER]

alleyway ('ælɪˌweɪ) *n.* a narrow passage; alley.

all found *adj.* (of charges for accommodation) inclusive of meals, heating, etc.

all hail *sentence substitute.* an archaic greeting or salutation. [C14, lit.: all health (to someone)]

Allhallows (ˌɔːl'hæləʊz) *n.* a less common term for **All Saints' Day.**

alliaceous (ˌælɪ'eɪʃəs) *adj.* **1.** of or relating to a genus of plants that have a strong smell and often have bulbs. The genus occurs in the N hemisphere and includes onion and garlic. **2.** tasting or smelling like garlic or onions. [C18: < L *allium* garlic]

alliance (ə'laɪəns) *n.* **1.** the act of allying or state of being allied; union. **2.** a formal agreement, esp. a military one, between two or more countries. **3.** the countries involved. **4.** a union between families through marriage. **5.** affinity or correspondence in characteristics. **6.** *Bot.* a taxonomic category consisting of a group of related families. [C13: < OF, < *alier* to ALLY]

Alliance (ə'laɪəns) *n.* (in Britain) **a. the.** the Social Democratic Party and the Liberal Party as a political entity. **b.** (*as modifier*): *an Alliance candidate.*

allied (ə'laɪd, 'ælaɪd) *adj.* **1.** joined, as by treaty or marriage; united. **2.** of the same type or class.

Allied ('ælaɪd) *adj.* of or relating to the Allies.

Allies ('ælaɪz) *pl. n.* **1.** (in World War I) the powers of the Triple Entente (France, Russia, and Britain) together with the nations allied with them. **2.** (in World War II) the countries that fought against the Axis and Japan, esp. Britain and the Commonwealth countries, the U.S., the Soviet Union, China, Poland, and France.

alligator ('ælɪˌgeɪtə) *n.* **1.** a large crocodilian of the southern U.S., having powerful jaws but differing from the crocodiles in having a shorter and broader snout. **2.** a similar but smaller species occurring in China. **3.** any of various tools or machines having adjustable toothed jaws. [C17: < Sp. *el lagarto* the lizard, < L *lacerta*]

alligator pear *n.* another name for **avocado.**

all-important *adj.* crucial; vital.

all in *adj.* **1.** (*postpositive*) *Inf.* completely exhausted. ~*adv., adj.* (**all-in** *when prenominal*). **2.** with all expenses included: *twenty pounds a week all in.* **3.** (of wrestling) in freestyle.

alliterate (ə'lɪtəˌreɪt) *vb.* **1.** to contain or cause to contain alliteration. **2.** (*intr.*) to speak or write using alliteration.

alliteration (əˌlɪtə'reɪʃən) *n.* the use of the same consonant (**consonantal alliteration**) or of a vowel (**vocalic alliteration**), at the beginning of each word or stressed syllable in a line of verse, as in *around the rock the ragged rascal ran.* [C17: < L *litera* letter] —**al'literative** *adj.*

allium ('ælɪəm) *n.* a genus of liliaceous plants that

includes the onion, garlic, shallot, leek, and chive. [C19: < L: garlic]

allo- *or before a vowel* **all-** *combining form.* indicating difference, variation, or opposition: *allopathy; allomorph.* [< Gk *allos* other, different]

allocate (ˈæləˌkeɪt) *vb.* (*tr.*) **1.** to assign for a particular purpose. **2.** a less common word for **locate** (sense 2). [C17: < Med. L, < L *locus* a place] —**ˈalloˌcatable** *adj.* —**ˌalloˈcation** *n.*

allocution (ˌæləˈkjuːʃən) *n. Rhetoric.* a formal or authoritative speech or address. [C17: < LL *allocūtiō*, < L *alloquī* to address]

allomerism (əˈlɒməˌrɪzəm) *n.* similarity of crystalline structure in substances of different chemical composition. —**alˈlomerous** *adj.*

allomorph (ˈæləˌmɔːf) *n.* **1.** *Linguistics.* any of the representations of a single morpheme. For example, the final (s) and (z) sounds of *bets* and *beds* are allomorphs. **2.** any of the different crystalline forms of a chemical compound, such as a mineral. —**ˌalloˈmorphic** *adj.*

allopath (ˈæləˌpæθ) *or* **allopathist** (əˈlɒpəθɪst) *n.* a person who practises or is skilled in allopathy.

allopathy (əˈlɒpəθɪ) *n.* the usual method of treating disease, by inducing a condition different from the cause of the disease. Cf. **homeopathy.** —**allopathic** (ˌæləˈpæθɪk) *adj.*

allophone (ˈæləˌfəʊn) *n.* any of several speech sounds regarded as variants of the same phoneme. In English the aspirated initial (p) in *pot* and the unaspirated (p) in *spot* are allophones of the phoneme /p/. —**allophonic** (ˌæləˈfɒnɪk) *adj.*

allot (əˈlɒt) *vb.* **-lotting, -lotted.** (*tr.*) **1.** to assign or distribute (shares, etc.). **2.** to designate for a particular purpose; apportion: *we allotted two hours to the case.* [C16: < OF, < *lot* portion]

allotment (əˈlɒtmənt) *n.* **1.** the act of allotting. **2.** a portion or amount allotted. **3.** *Brit.* a small piece of land rented by an individual for cultivation.

allotrope (ˈæləˌtrəʊp) *n.* any of two or more physical forms in which an element can exist: *diamond and graphite are allotropes of carbon.*

allotropy (əˈlɒtrəpɪ) *or* **allotropism** *n.* the existence of an element in two or more physical forms. —**allotropic** (ˌæləˈtrɒpɪk) *adj.*

all-out *Inf.* ~*adj.* **1.** using one's maximum powers: *an all-out effort.* ~*adv.* **all out. 2.** to one's maximum capacity: *he went all out.*

allow (əˈlaʊ) *vb.* **1.** (*tr.*) to permit (to do something). **2.** (*tr.*) to set aside: *five hours were allowed to do the job.* **3.** (*tr.*) to let enter or stay: *they don't allow dogs.* **4.** (*tr.*) to acknowledge (a point, claim, etc.). **5.** (*tr.*) to let have: *he was allowed few visitors.* **6.** (*intr.*; foll. by *for*) to take into account. **7.** (*intr.*; often foll. by *of*) to permit: *a question that allows of only one reply.* **8.** (*tr.*; *may take a clause as object*) *U.S. dialect.* to assert; maintain. [C14: < OF, < LL *allaudāre* to extol, infl. by Med. L *allocāre* to assign] —**alˈlowable** *adj.* —**alˈlowably** *adv.*

allowance (əˈlaʊəns) *n.* **1.** an amount of something, esp. money or food, given at regular intervals. **2.** a discount, as in consideration for something given in part exchange; rebate. **3.** (in Britain) an amount of a person's income that is not subject to income tax. **4.** a portion set aside to cover special expenses. **5.** admission; concession. **6.** the act of allowing; toleration. **7. make allowances** (*or* **allowance**). (usually foll. by *for*) **a.** to take mitigating circumstances into account. **b.** to allow (for). ~*vb.* (*tr.*) **8.** to supply (something) in limited amounts.

allowedly (əˈlaʊɪdlɪ) *adv.* (*sentence modifier*) by general admission or agreement; admittedly.

alloy *n.* (ˈælɔɪ, əˈlɔɪ). **1.** a metallic material, such as steel, consisting of a mixture of two or more metals or of metallic with nonmetallic elements. **2.** something that impairs the quality of the thing to which it is added. ~*vb.* (əˈlɔɪ). (*tr.*) **3.** to add (one metal or element to another) to obtain a substance with a desired property. **4.** to debase (a pure substance) by mixing with an inferior element. **5.** to diminish or impair. [C16: < OF *aloi* a mixture, < *aloier* to combine, < L *alligāre*]

all-purpose *adj.* useful for many things.

all right *adj.* (*postpositive except in slang use*), *adv.* **1.** adequate; satisfactory. **2.** unharmed; safe. **3. all-right.** *U.S. sl.* acceptable; reliable. ~*sentence substitute.* **4.** very well: used to express assent. ~*adv.* **5.** satisfactorily: *the car goes all right.* **6.** without doubt. ~Also **alright.**

▷ **Usage.** See at **alright.**

all-round *adj.* **1.** efficient in all respects, esp. in sport: *an all-round player.* **2.** comprehensive; many-sided: *an all-round education.*

all-rounder *n.* a versatile person, esp. in a sport.

All Saints' Day *n.* a Christian festival celebrated on Nov. 1 to honour all the saints.

All Souls' Day *n. R.C. Church.* a day of prayer (Nov. 2) for the dead in purgatory.

allspice (ˈɔːlˌspaɪs) *n.* **1.** a tropical American tree, having small white flowers and aromatic berries. **2.** the seeds of this berry used as a spice, having a flavour said to resemble a mixture of cinnamon, cloves, and nutmeg. ~Also called: **pimento.**

all-star *adj.* (*prenominal*) consisting of star performers.

all-time *adj.* (*prenominal*) *Inf.* unsurpassed.

▷ **Usage.** *All-time* is an imprecise superlative and is avoided by careful writers as being superfluous: *his high jump was a record* (not *an all-time record*).

all told *adv.* (*sentence modifier*) in all: *we were seven all told.*

allude (əˈluːd) *vb.* (*intr.*; foll. by *to*) **1.** to refer indirectly. **2.** (loosely) to mention. [C16: < L *allūdere*, < *lūdere* to sport, < *lūdus* a game]

allure (əˈlʊə) *vb.* **1.** (*tr.*) to entice or tempt (someone); attract. ~*n.* **2.** attractiveness; appeal. [C15: < OF *alurer*, < *lure* bait] —**alˈlurement** *n.* —**alˈluring** *adj.*

allusion (əˈluːʒən) *n.* **1.** the act of alluding. **2.** a passing reference. [C16: < LL *allūsiō*, < L *allūdere* to sport with]

allusive (əˈluːsɪv) *adj.* containing or full of allusions. —**alˈlusiveness** *n.*

alluvial (əˈluːvɪəl) *adj.* **1.** of or relating to alluvium. ~*n.* **2.** another name for **alluvium.**

alluvion (əˈluːvɪən) *n.* **1. a.** the wash of the sea or a river. **b.** a flood. **c.** sediment; alluvium. **2.** *Law.* the gradual formation of new land, as by the recession of the sea. [C16: < L *alluviō* an overflowing, < *luere* to wash]

alluvium (əˈluːvɪəm) *n.*, *pl.* **-viums** *or* **-via** (-vɪə). a fine-grained fertile soil consisting of mud, silt, and sand deposited by flowing water. [C17: < L; see ALLUVION]

ally *vb.* (əˈlaɪ). **-lying, -lied.** (usually foll. by *to* or *with*) **1.** to unite or be united, esp. formally, as by treaty. **2.** (*tr.*; *usually passive*) to be related, as through being similar. ~*n.* (ˈælaɪ), *pl.* **-lies. 3.** a country, person, or group allied with another. **4.** a plant, animal, etc., closely related to another in characteristics or form. [C14: < OF *alier* to join, < L *ligāre* to bind]

allyl resin (ˈælɪl) *n.* any of several thermosetting synthetic resins, containing the $CH_2{:}CHCH_2$– group, used as adhesives. [C19: < L *allium* garlic + -YL]

alma mater (ˈælmə ˈmɑːtə, ˈmeɪtə) *n.* (*often caps.*) one's school, college, or university. [C17: < L: bountiful mother]

almanac (ˈɔːlməˌnæk) *n.* a yearly calendar giving statistical information, such as the phases of the moon, tides, anniversaries, etc. Also (archaic): **almanack.** [C14: < Med. L *almanachus*, ? < LGk *almenikhiaka*]

almandine (ˈælməndɪn) *n.* a deep violet-red garnet. [C17: < F, < Med. L, < *Alabanda*, ancient city of Asia Minor where these stones were cut]

almighty (ɔːlˈmaɪtɪ) *adj.* **1.** omnipotent. **2.** *Inf.* (intensifier): *an almighty row.* ~*adv.* **3.** *Inf.* (intensifier): *an almighty loud bang.*

Almighty (ɔːlˈmaɪtɪ) *n.* **the.** another name for **God.**

almond (ˈɑːmənd) *n.* **1.** a small widely cultivated

rosaceous tree that is native to W Asia and has pink flowers and an edible nutlike seed. **2.** the seed, which has a yellowish-brown shell. **3.** (*modifier*) made of or containing almonds: *almond cake.* [C13: < OF *almande*, ult. < Gk *amugdalē*]

almond-eyed *adj.* having narrow oval eyes.

almoner (ˈɑːmənə) *n.* **1.** *Brit.* a former name for a trained hospital social worker. **2.** (formerly) a person who distributes charity on behalf of a household or institution. [C13: < OF, < *almosne* alms, ult. < LL *eleēmosyna*]

almost (ˈɔːlməʊst) *adv.* very nearly.

alms (ɑːmz) *pl. n.* charitable donations of money or goods to the poor or needy. [OE *ælmysse*, < LL, < Gk *eleēmosunē* pity]

almshouse (ˈɑːmzˌhaʊs) *n. Brit.* a privately supported house offering accommodation to the aged or needy.

almucantar *or* **almacantar** (ˌælməˈkæntə) *n.* **1.** a circle on the celestial sphere parallel to the horizon. **2.** an instrument for measuring altitudes. [C14: < F, < Ar. *almukantarāt* sundial]

aloe (ˈæləʊ) *n., pl.* **-oes. 1.** any plant of the genus *Aloe*, chiefly native to southern Africa, with fleshy spiny-toothed leaves. **2. American aloe.** Also called: **century plant.** a tropical American agave which blooms only once in 10 to 30 years. [C14: < L *aloē*, < Gk]

aloes (ˈæləʊz) *n.* (*functioning as sing.*) a bitter purgative drug made from the leaves of several species of aloe. Also called: **bitter aloes.**

aloft (əˈlɒft) *adv., adj.* (*postpositive*) **1.** in or into a high or higher place. **2.** *Naut.* in or into the rigging of a vessel. [C12: < ON *ā lopt* in the air]

alone (əˈləʊn) *adj.* (*postpositive*), *adv.* **1.** apart from another or others. **2.** without anyone or anything else: *one man alone could lift it.* **3.** without equal: *he stands alone in the field of microbiology.* **4.** to the exclusion of others: *she alone believed him.* **5. leave** *or* **let alone.** to refrain from annoying or interfering with. **6. leave well alone.** to refrain from interfering with something that is satisfactory. **7. let alone.** not to mention; much less: *he can't afford beer, let alone whisky.* [OE *al one*, lit.: all (entirely) one]

along (əˈlɒŋ) *prep.* **1.** over or for the length of: *along the road.* ~*adv.* **2.** continuing over the length of some specified thing. **3.** together with some specified person or people: *he'd like to come along.* **4.** forward: *the horse trotted along.* **5.** to a more advanced state: *he got the work moving along.* **6. along with.** together with: *consider the advantages along with the disadvantages.* [OE *andlang*, < *and-* against + *lang* LONG[1]]

▷ **Usage.** See at **plus.**

alongshore (əˌlɒŋˈʃɔː) *adv., adj.* (*postpositive*) close to, by, or along a shore.

alongside (əˈlɒŋˌsaɪd) *prep.* **1.** (often foll. by *of*) close beside: *alongside the quay.* ~*adv.* **2.** near the side of something: *come alongside.*

aloof (əˈluːf) *adj.* distant, unsympathetic, or supercilious in manner. [C16: < A-[1] + *loof*, var. of LUFF] —**aˈloofly** *adv.* —**aˈloofness** *n.*

alopecia (ˌæləˈpiːʃɪə) *n.* baldness. [C14: < L, < Gk *alōpekia*, orig.: mange in foxes]

aloud (əˈlaʊd) *adv., adj.* (*postpositive*) **1.** in a normal voice. **2.** in a spoken voice; not silently.

alp (ælp) *n.* **1.** (in Switzerland) a mountain pasture. **2.** a high mountain. **3. the Alps.** a high mountain range in S central Europe. [C16: < L *Alpes*]

ALP *abbrev. for* Australian Labor Party.

alpaca (ælˈpækə) *n.* **1.** a domesticated South American mammal related to the llama, with dark shaggy hair. **2.** the wool or cloth obtained from this hair. **3.** a glossy fabric simulating this. [C18: via Sp. < Aymara *allpaca*]

alpenhorn (ˈælpənˌhɔːn) *n.* another name for **alphorn.**

alpenstock (ˈælpənˌstɒk) *n.* a stout stick with an iron tip used by hikers, mountain climbers, etc. [C19: < G, < *Alpen* Alps + *Stock* STICK[1]]

alpha (ˈælfə) *n.* **1.** the first letter in the Greek alphabet (Α, α). **2.** *Brit.* the highest grade or mark, as in an examination. **3.** (*modifier*) **a.** involving helium nuclei. **b.** denoting an isomeric or allotropic form of a substance. [via L < Gk, of Phoenician origin]

alpha and omega *n.* the first and last, a phrase used in Revelation 1:8 to signify God's eternity.

alphabet (ˈælfəˌbɛt) *n.* **1.** a set of letters or other signs used in a writing system, each letter or sign being used to represent one or sometimes more than one phoneme in the language being transcribed. **2.** any set of characters, esp. one representing sounds of speech. **3.** basic principles or rudiments. [C15: < LL, < the first two letters of the Greek alphabet; see ALPHA, BETA]

alphabetical (ˌælfəˈbɛtɪkᵊl) *or* **alphabetic** *adj.* **1.** in the conventional order of the letters of an alphabet. **2.** of or expressed by an alphabet. —ˌ**alphaˈbetically** *adv.*

alphabetize *or* **-ise** (ˈælfəbəˌtaɪz) *vb.* (*tr.*) **1.** to arrange in conventional alphabetical order. **2.** to express by an alphabet. —ˌ**alphabetiˈzation** *or* **-iˈsation** *n.*

alphanumeric (ˌælfənjuːˈmɛrɪk) *or* **alphameric** *adj.* (of a character set or file of data) consisting of alphabetical and numerical symbols.

alpha particle *n.* a helium nucleus, containing two neutrons and two protons, emitted during some radioactive transformations.

alpha ray *n.* ionizing radiation consisting of a stream of alpha particles.

alpha rhythm *or* **wave** *n. Physiol.* the normal bursts of electrical activity from the cerebral cortex of a person at rest. See also **brain wave.**

alphorn (ˈælpˌhɔːn) *or* **alpenhorn** *n.* a wind instrument used in the Swiss Alps, made from a very long tube of wood. [C19: < G: Alps horn]

alpine (ˈælpaɪn) *adj.* **1.** of or relating to high mountains. **2.** (of plants) growing on mountains above the limit for tree growth. **3.** connected with mountaineering. **4.** *Skiing.* of racing events on steep prepared slopes, such as the slalom and downhill. Compare **nordic.** ~*n.* **5.** a plant grown in or native to high altitudes.

alpinist (ˈælpɪnɪst) *n.* a mountain climber.

already (ɔːlˈrɛdɪ) *adv.* **1.** by or before a stated or implied time: *he is already here.* **2.** at a time earlier than expected: *is it ten o'clock already?*

alright (ɔːlˈraɪt) *adv., sentence substitute, adj.* a variant spelling of **all right.**

▷ **Usage.** The form *alright*, though very commonly encountered, is still considered by many careful users of English to be wrong or less acceptable than *all right.*

Alsatian (ælˈseɪʃən) *n.* **1.** Also called: **German shepherd (dog).** a large wolflike breed of dog often used as a guard dog and by the police. **2.** a native or inhabitant of Alsace, a region of NE France. ~*adj.* **3.** of or relating to Alsace or its inhabitants.

also (ˈɔːlsəʊ) *adv.* **1.** (*sentence modifier*) in addition; as well; too. ~*sentence connector.* **2.** besides; moreover. [OE *alswā*; see ALL, SO[1]]

▷ **Usage.** Since *also* is not a conjunction, careful writers and speakers consider it poor style to use it alone as a connector in sentences like *he bought pens, paper, ink, also notebooks.* In such sentences, *and* or *and also* would be the appropriate words: *he bought pens, paper, ink, and notebooks.*

also-ran *n.* **1.** a contestant, horse, etc., failing to finish among the first three. **2.** a loser.

alstroemeria (ˌælstrəʊˈmɪərɪə) *n.* any of several plants with fleshy roots and brightly coloured flowers in summer, esp. the Peruvian lily. [C18: NL, after Claude *Alstroemer* (1736-96), Swedish naturalist]

alt. *abbrev. for:* **1.** alternate. **2.** altitude. **3.** alto.

Alta. *abbrev. for* Alberta.

Altaic (ælˈteɪɪk) *n.* **1.** a postulated family of languages of Asia and SE Europe, including the Turkic, Tungusic, and Mongolic subfamilies. See also **Ural-Altaic.** ~*adj.* **2.** denoting or relating to this linguistic family or its speakers.

altar (ˈɔːltə) *n.* **1.** a raised place or structure where sacrifices are offered and religious rites performed. **2.** (in Christian churches) the communion table. **3.** a step in the wall of a dry dock. [OE, ult. < L *altus* high]

altar boy *n. R.C. Church, Church of England.* a boy serving as an acolyte.

altarpiece (ˈɔːltəˌpiːs) *n.* a work of art set above and behind an altar; a reredos.

altazimuth (ælˈtæzɪməθ) *n.* an instrument for measuring the altitude and azimuth of a celestial body. [C19: < ALT(ITUDE) + AZIMUTH]

alter (ˈɔːltə) *vb.* **1.** to make or become different in some respect; change. **2.** (*tr.*) *Inf., chiefly U.S.* a euphemistic word for **castrate** or **spay.** [C14: < OF, ult. < L *alter* other] —ˈ**alterable** *adj.*

alteration (ˌɔːltəˈreɪʃən) *n.* **1.** a change or modification. **2.** the act of altering.

alterative (ˈɔːltərətɪv) *adj.* **1.** likely or able to produce alteration. **2.** (of a drug) able to restore health. ~*n.* **3.** such a drug.

altercate (ˈɔːltəˌkeɪt) *vb.* (*intr.*) to argue, esp. heatedly; dispute. [C16: < L *altercārī* to quarrel with another, < *alter* other]

altercation (ˌɔːltəˈkeɪʃən) *n.* an angry or heated discussion or quarrel; argument.

alter ego (ˈæltər ˈiːgəʊ, ˈɛgəʊ) *n.* **1.** a second self. **2.** a very close friend. [L: other self]

alternate *vb.* (ˈɔːltəˌneɪt). **1.** (often foll. by *with*) to occur or cause to occur by turns: *day and night alternate.* **2.** (*intr.;* often foll. by *between*) to swing repeatedly from one condition, action, etc., to another. **3.** (*tr.*) to interchange regularly or in succession. **4.** (*intr.*) (of an electric current, voltage, etc.) to reverse direction or sign at regular intervals. ~*adj.* (ɔːlˈtɜːnɪt). **5.** occurring by turns: *alternate feelings of love and hate.* **6.** every other or second one of a series: *he came on alternate days.* **7.** being a second choice; alternative. **8.** *Bot.* (of leaves, flowers, etc.) arranged singly at different heights on either side of the stem. ~*n.* (ˈɔːltənɪt, ɔːlˈtɜːnɪt). **9.** *U.S. & Canad.* a person who substitutes for another; stand-in. [C16: < L *alternāre* to do one thing and then another, ult. < *alter* other] —ˌ**alterˈnation** *n.*

alternate angles *pl. n.* two angles at opposite ends and on opposite sides of a transversal cutting two lines.

alternately (ɔːlˈtɜːnɪtlɪ) *adv.* in an alternating sequence or position.

alternating current *n.* an electric current that reverses direction with a frequency independent of the characteristics of the circuit through which it flows. Abbrev.: **AC.**

alternation of generations *n.* the occurrence in the life cycle of many plants and lower animals of alternating sexual and asexual reproductive forms.

alternative (ɔːlˈtɜːnətɪv) *n.* **1.** a possibility of choice, esp. between two things. **2.** either of such choices: *we took the alternative of walking.* ~*adj.* **3.** presenting a choice, esp. between two possibilities only. **4.** (of two things) mutually exclusive. **5.** denoting a lifestyle, culture, art form, etc., that is regarded as preferable to that of contemporary society because it is less conventional, materialistic, or institutionalized. —**alˈternatively** *adv.*

▷ **Usage.** The use of *alternative* with reference to more than two possibilities is commonly encountered, but is regarded as unacceptable by some people. Careful writers and speakers of English may prefer to restrict its use to instances where two choices only are mentioned. The addition of *other* before *alternative* is redundant: *there is no alternative* not *there is no other alternative.*

alternative medicine *n.* the treatment or alleviation of disease by techniques such as osteopathy and acupuncture, allied with attention to a person's general wellbeing. Also called: **complementary medicine.**

alternative society *n.* a group of people who agree in rejecting the traditional values of the society around them.

alternator (ˈɔːltəˌneɪtə) *n.* an electrical machine that generates an alternating current.

althaea *or U.S.* **althea** (ælˈθiːə) *n.* any Eurasian plant of the genus *Althaea,* such as the hollyhock, having tall spikes of showy flowers. [C17: < L, < Gk *althaia* marsh mallow]

althorn (ˈæltˌhɔːn) *n.* a valved brass musical instrument belonging to the saxhorn family.

although (ɔːlˈðəʊ) *conj.* (*subordinating*) even though: *although she was ill, she worked hard.*

altimeter (ælˈtɪmɪtə, ˈæltɪˌmiːtə) *n.* an instrument that indicates height above sea level, esp. one based on an aneroid barometer and fitted to an aircraft. [C19: < L *altus* high + -METER]

altitude (ˈæltɪˌtjuːd) *n.* **1.** the vertical height of an object, esp. above sea level. **2.** *Geom.* the perpendicular distance from the apex to the base of a triangle. **3.** Also called: **elevation.** *Astron., navigation.* the angular distance of a celestial body from the horizon. **4.** *Surveying.* the angle of elevation of a point above the horizontal plane of the observer. **5.** (*often pl.*) a high place or region. [C14: < L *altus* high, deep]

alto (ˈæltəʊ) *n., pl.* **-tos. 1.** (in choral singing) short for **contralto. 2.** the highest adult male voice; countertenor. **3.** a singer with such a voice. **4.** a flute, saxophone, etc., that is the third or fourth highest instrument in its group. ~*adj.* **5.** denoting such an instrument. [C18: < It.: high, < L *altus*]

alto clef *n.* the clef that establishes middle C as being on the third line of the staff.

altocumulus (ˌæltəʊˈkjuːmjʊləs) *n., pl.* **-li** (-laɪ). a globular cloud at an intermediate height of about 2400 to 6000 metres (8000 to 20 000 feet).

altogether (ˌɔːltəˈgɛðə, ˈɔːltəˌgɛðə) *adv.* **1.** with everything included: *altogether he owed me sixty pounds.* **2.** completely; utterly: *altogether mad.* **3.** on the whole: *altogether it was very good.* ~*n.* **4. in the altogether.** *Inf.* naked.

altostratus (ˌæltəʊˈstreɪtəs, -ˈstrɑː-) *n., pl.* **-ti** (-taɪ). a layer cloud at an intermediate height of about 2400 to 6000 metres (8000 to 20 000 feet).

altricial (ælˈtrɪʃəl) *adj.* **1.** denoting birds whose young, after hatching, are naked, blind, and dependent on the parents for food. ~*n.* **2.** an altricial bird. ~Cf. **precocial.** [C19: < NL, < L *altrix* a nurse]

altruism (ˈæltruːˌɪzəm) *n.* unselfish concern for the welfare of others. [C19: < F, < It. *altrui* others, < L] —ˈ**altruist** *n.* —ˌ**altruˈistic** *adj.* —ˌ**altruˈistically** *adv.*

ALU *Computers. abbrev. for* arithmetical and logical unit.

alum (ˈæləm) *n.* **1.** a colourless soluble hydrated double sulphate of aluminium and potassium used in manufacturing and in medicine. **2.** any of a group of compounds of a monovalent metal or group and a trivalent metal. [C14: < OF, < L *alūmen*]

alumina (əˈluːmɪnə) *n.* another name for **aluminium oxide.** [C18: < NL, pl. of L *alūmen* ALUM]

aluminium (ˌæljʊˈmɪnɪəm) *or U.S. & Canad.* **aluminum** (əˈluːmɪnəm) *n.* a light malleable silvery-white metallic element that resists corrosion; the third most abundant element in the earth's crust, occurring as a compound, principally in bauxite. Symbol: Al; atomic no.: 13; atomic wt.: 26.981.

aluminium oxide *n.* a powder occurring naturally as corundum and used in the production of aluminium, abrasives, glass, and ceramics. Also called: **alumina.**

aluminize *or* **-ise** (əˈluːmɪˌnaɪz) *vb.* (*tr.*) to cover with aluminium or aluminium paint.

aluminous (əˈluːmɪnəs) *adj.* resembling aluminium.

alumnus (əˈlʌmnəs) *or* (*fem.*) **alumna** (əˈlʌmnə) *n., pl.* **-ni** (-naɪ) *or* **-nae** (-niː). *Chiefly U.S. & Canad.* a graduate of a school, college, etc. [C17: < L: nursling, pupil, < *alere* to nourish]

alveolar (ælˈvɪələ, ˌælvɪˈəʊlə) *adj.* **1.** *Anat.* of an alveolus. **2.** denoting the part of the jawbone containing the roots of the teeth. **3.** (of a consonant) articulated with the tongue in contact with the part of the jawbone immediately behind the upper teeth. ~*n.* **4.** an alveolar consonant, such as *t, d,* and *s* in English.

alveolate (æl'vɪəlɪt, -ˌleɪt) *adj.* having many small cavities. [C19: < LL *alveolātus* hollowed, < L: ALVEOLUS] —ˌ**alveo'lation** *n.*

alveolus (æl'vɪələs) *n., pl.* **-li** (-ˌlaɪ). any small pit, cavity, or saclike dilation, such as a honeycomb cell, a tooth socket, or the tiny air sacs in the lungs. [C18: < L: a little hollow, dim. of *alveus*]

always ('ɔːlweɪz) *adv.* **1.** without exception; every time: *he always arrives on time.* **2.** continually; repeatedly. **3.** in any case: *you could always take a day off work.* ~Also (archaic): **alway.** [C13 *alles weiss,* < OE *ealne weg,* lit.: all the way]

alyssum ('ælɪsəm) *n.* a widely cultivated herbaceous garden plant, having clusters of small yellow or white flowers. [C16: < NL, < Gk *alusson,* < *alussos* (adj.) curing rabies]

Alzheimer's disease ('æltsˌhaɪməz) *n.* a disorder of the brain resulting in progressive decline and eventual senility. [C20: after A. *Alzheimer* (1864-1915), G physician who first identified it]

am (æm; *unstressed* əm) *vb.* (used with *I*) a form of the present tense of **be.** [OE *eam*]

Am *the chemical symbol for* americium.

AM *abbrev. for:* **1.** Also: **am.** amplitude modulation. **2.** *U.S.* Master of Arts. **3.** Member of the Order of Australia.

Am. *abbrev. for* America(n).

a.m., A.M., am, *or* **AM** (indicating the time period from midnight to midday) *abbrev. for* ante meridiem. [L: before noon]

Amadhlozi *or* **Amadlozi** (ˌæmæ'hlɒʒiː) *pl. n. S. African.* the ancestral spirits. [< Zulu. pl. *amadlozi*]

amadoda (ˌæmæ'dɒdə) *pl. n. S. African.* men, esp. Black men. [< Bantu *ama* (pl. prefix) + *doda* man]

amadou ('æməˌduː) *n.* a spongy substance got from some fungi, used (formerly) as tinder, a styptic, and by fishermen to dry flies. [C18: < F, < Provençal: lover, < L *amāre* to love (because easily set alight)]

amah ('ɑːmə) *n.* (in the East, esp. formerly) a nurse or maidservant. [C19: < Port. *ama* nurse]

amain (ə'meɪn) *adv. Arch. or poetic.* with great strength or haste. [C16: < A-[2] + MAIN[1]]

amalgam (ə'mælgəm) *n.* **1.** an alloy of mercury with another metal, esp. silver: *dental amalgam.* **2.** a blend or combination. [C15: < Med. L *amalgama,* <?]

amalgamate (ə'mælgəˌmeɪt) *vb.* **1.** to combine or cause to combine; unite. **2.** to alloy (a metal) with mercury.

amalgamation (əˌmælgə'meɪʃən) *n.* **1.** the process of amalgamating. **2.** the state of being amalgamated. **3.** a method of extracting precious metals by treatment with mercury. **4.** a merger.

amanuensis (əˌmænjʊ'ɛnsɪs) *n., pl.* **-ses** (-siːz). a person employed to take dictation or to copy manuscripts. [C17: < L, < *servus ā manū* slave at hand (that is, handwriting)]

amaranth ('æməˌrænθ) *n.* **1.** *Poetic.* an imaginary flower that never fades. **2.** any of numerous plants having tassel-like heads of small green, red, or purple flowers. **3.** a synthetic red food colouring (**E123**), used in packet soups, cake mixes, etc. [C17: < L *amarantus,* < Gk, < A-[1] + *marainein* to fade]

amaryllis (ˌæmə'rɪlɪs) *n.* **1.** a plant native to southern Africa having large lily-like reddish or white flowers. **2.** any of several related plants. [C18: < NL, < L: after *Amaryllis,* Gk conventional name for a shepherdess]

amass (ə'mæs) *vb.* **1.** (*tr.*) to accumulate or collect (esp. riches, etc.). **2.** to gather in a heap. [C15: < OF, < *masse* MASS] —**a'masser** *n.*

amateur ('æmətə) *n.* **1.** a person who engages in an activity, esp. a sport, as a pastime rather than for gain. **2.** a person unskilled in a subject or activity. **3.** a person who is fond of or admires something. **4.** (*modifier*) of or for amateurs: *an amateur event.* ~*adj.* **5.** not professional or expert: *an amateur approach.* [C18: < F, < L *amātor* lover, < *amāre* to love] —**'amateurism** *n.*

amateurish ('æmətərɪʃ) *adj.* lacking professional skill or expertise. —**'amateurishly** *adv.*

amative ('æmətɪv) *adj.* a rare word for **amorous.** [C17: < Med. L, < L *amāre* to love]

amatory ('æmətərɪ) *or* **amatorial** (ˌæmə'tɔːrɪəl) *adj.* of, relating to, or inciting sexual love or desire. [C16: < L *amātōrius,* < *amāre* to love]

amaurosis (ˌæmɔː'rəʊsɪs) *n.* blindness, esp. when occurring without observable damage to the eye. [C17: via NL < Gk: darkening, < *amauroun* to dim] —**amaurotic** (ˌæmɔː'rɒtɪk) *adj.*

amaze (ə'meɪz) *vb.* (*tr.*) **1.** to fill with incredulity or surprise; astonish. ~*n.* **2.** an archaic word for **amazement.** [OE *āmasian*] —**a'mazing** *adj.*

amazement (ə'meɪzmənt) *n.* incredulity or great astonishment; complete wonder.

Amazon ('æməzᵊn) *n.* **1.** *Greek myth.* one of a race of women warriors of Scythia near the Black Sea. **2.** (*often not cap.*) any tall, strong, or aggressive woman. [C14: via L < Gk *Amazōn,* <?] —**Amazonian** (ˌæmə'zəʊnɪən) *adj.*

ambassador (æm'bæsədə) *n.* **1.** a diplomat of the highest rank, accredited as permanent representative to another country. **2. ambassador extraordinary.** a diplomat of the highest rank sent on a special mission. **3. ambassador plenipotentiary.** a diplomat of the first rank with treaty-signing powers. **4. ambassador-at-large.** *U.S.* an ambassador with special duties who may be sent to more than one government. **5.** an authorized representative or messenger. [C14: < OF, < It., < OProvençal *ambaisador,* < *ambaisa* (unattested) mission, errand] —**am'bassadress** *fem. n.* —**ambassadorial** (æmˌbæsə'dɔːrɪəl) *adj.* —**am'bassadorˌship** *n.*

amber ('æmbə) *n.* **1.** a yellow translucent fossil resin derived from extinct coniferous trees and often containing trapped insects. **2. a.** a brownish-yellow colour. **b.** (*as adj.*): *an amber dress.* **3.** an amber traffic light used as a warning between red and green. [C14: < Med. L *ambar,* < Ar. *'anbar* ambergris]

ambergris ('æmbəˌgriːs, -grɪs) *n.* a waxy substance secreted by the intestinal tract of the sperm whale and often found floating in the sea: used in the manufacture of some perfumes. [C15: < OF *ambre gris* grey amber]

amberjack ('æmbəˌdʒæk) *n.* any of several large fishes occurring in tropical and subtropical Atlantic waters. [C19: < AMBER + JACK]

ambi- *combining form.* indicating both: *ambidextrous; ambivalence.* [< L: round, on both sides, both, < *ambo* both]

ambidextrous (ˌæmbɪ'dɛkstrəs) *adj.* **1.** equally expert with each hand. **2.** *Inf.* skilled or adept. **3.** underhanded. —**ambidexterity** (ˌæmbɪdɛk'stɛrɪtɪ) *or* ˌ**ambi'dextrousness** *n.*

ambience *or* **ambiance** ('æmbɪəns) *n.* the atmosphere of a place. [C19: < F, < *ambiant* surrounding]

ambient ('æmbɪənt) *adj.* surrounding. [C16: < L *ambiēns* going round, < AMBI- + *īre* to go]

ambiguity (ˌæmbɪ'gjuːɪtɪ) *n., pl.* **-ties. 1.** the possibility of interpreting an expression in more than one way. **2.** an instance or example of this, as in the sentence *they are cooking apples.* **3.** vagueness or uncertainty of meaning.

ambiguous (æm'bɪgjʊəs) *adj.* **1.** having more than one possible interpretation. **2.** difficult to understand; obscure. [C16: < L *ambiguus* going here and there, uncertain, < *ambigere* to go around] —**am'biguously** *adv.* —**am'biguousness** *n.*

ambit ('æmbɪt) *n.* **1.** scope or extent. **2.** limits or boundary. [C16: < L *ambitus* a going round, < *ambīre* to go round]

ambition (æm'bɪʃən) *n.* **1.** strong desire for success or distinction. **2.** something so desired; goal. [C14: < OF, < L *ambitiō* a going round (of candidates), < *ambīre* to go round]

ambitious (æm'bɪʃəs) *adj.* **1.** having a strong desire for success or achievement. **2.** necessitating extraordinary effort or ability: *an ambitious* *project.* **3.** (often foll. by *of*) having a great desire (for something or to do something). —**am'bitiousness** *n.*

ambivalence (æm'bɪvələns) *or* **ambivalency** *n.* the coexistence of two opposed and conflicting emotions, etc. —**am'bivalent** *adj.*

amble ('æmbᵊl) *vb.* (*intr.*) **1.** to walk at a leisurely relaxed pace. **2.** (of a horse) to move, lifting both legs on one side together. **3.** to ride a horse at an amble. ~*n.* **4.** a leisurely motion in walking. **5.** a leisurely walk. **6.** the ambling gait of a horse. [C14: < OF, < L *ambulāre* to walk]

amblyopia (ˌæmblɪ'əʊpɪə) *n.* impaired vision with no discernible damage to the eye or optic nerve. [C18: NL, < Gk *ambluōpia*, < *amblus* dull, dim + *ōps* eye] —**amblyopic** (ˌæmblɪ'ɒpɪk) *adj.*

amboyna *or* **amboina** (æm'bɔɪnə) *n.* the mottled curly-grained wood of an Indonesian tree, used in making furniture. [C19: after *Amboina*, island in Indonesia]

ambrosia (æm'brəʊzɪə) *n.* **1.** *Classical myth.* the food of the gods, said to bestow immortality. Cf. **nectar** (sense 2). **2.** anything particularly delightful to taste or smell. **3.** another name for **beebread.** [C16: via L < Gk: immortality, < A-¹ + *brotos* mortal] —**am'brosial** *or* **am'brosian** *adj.*

ambry ('æmbrɪ) *or* **aumbry** ('ɔːmbrɪ) *n., pl.* **-bries.** **1.** a recessed cupboard in the wall of a church near the altar, used to store sacred vessels, etc. **2.** *Obs.* a small cupboard. [C14: < OF *almarie*, ult. < L *armārium* chest for storage, < *arma* arms]

ambulance ('æmbjʊləns) *n.* a motor vehicle designed to carry sick or injured people. [C19: < F, based on (*hôpital*) *ambulant* mobile or field (hospital), < L *ambulāre* to walk]

ambulant ('æmbjʊlənt) *adj.* **1.** moving about from place to place. **2.** *Med.* another word for **ambulatory** (sense 3).

ambulate ('æmbjʊˌleɪt) *vb.* (*intr.*) to wander about or move from place to place. [C17: < L *ambulāre* to walk] —ˌ**ambu'lation** *n.*

ambulatory ('æmbjʊlətərɪ) *adj.* **1.** of or designed for walking. **2.** changing position; not fixed. **3.** Also: **ambulant.** able to walk. ~*n., pl.* **-ries.** **4.** a place for walking, such as an aisle or a cloister.

ambuscade (ˌæmbə'skeɪd) *n.* **1.** an ambush. ~*vb.* **2.** to ambush or lie in ambush. [C16: < F, < OIt. *imboscata*, prob. of Gmc origin; cf. AMBUSH]

ambush ('æmbʊʃ) *n.* **1.** the act of waiting in a concealed position in order to launch a surprise attack. **2.** a surprise attack from such a position. **3.** the concealed position from which such an attack is launched. **4.** the person or persons waiting to launch such an attack. ~*vb.* **5.** to lie in wait (for). **6.** (*tr.*) to attack suddenly from a concealed position. [C14: < OF *embuschier* to position in ambush, < *em-* IM- + *-buschier*, < *busche* piece of firewood, prob. of Gmc origin]

ameba (ə'miːbə) *n., pl.* **-bae** (-biː) *or* **-bas.** the usual U.S. spelling of **amoeba.** —**a'mebic** *adj.*

ameer (ə'mɪə) *n.* a variant spelling of **emir.**

ameliorate (ə'miːljəˌreɪt) *vb.* to make or become better. [C18: < F *améliorer* to improve, < OF, < *meillor* better, < L *melior*] —**aˌmelio'ration** *n.* —**a'meliorative** *adj.* —**a'melioˌrator** *n.*

amen (ˌeɪ'mɛn, ˌɑː'mɛn) *sentence substitute.* **1.** so be it!: a term used at the end of a prayer. ~*n.* **2.** the use of the word *amen.* [C13: via LL via Gk < Heb. *āmēn* certainly]

amenable (ə'miːnəbᵊl) *adj.* **1.** likely to listen, cooperate, etc. **2.** accountable to some authority; answerable. **3.** capable of being tested, judged, etc. [C16: < Anglo-F, < OF, < L *mināre* to drive (cattle), < *minārī* to threaten] —**aˌmena'bility** *or* **a'menableness** *n.* —**a'menably** *adv.*

amend (ə'mɛnd) *vb.* (*tr.*) **1.** to improve; change for the better. **2.** to correct. **3.** to alter or revise (legislation, etc.) by formal procedure. [C13: < OF, < L *ēmendāre* to EMEND] —**a'mendable** *adj.* —**a'mender** *n.*

▷ **Usage.** Confusion sometimes arises between *amend* and *emend. Amend* means to improve, and can be used of a situation, character, etc., as well as of making improvements to the substance of written or spoken material: *we will amend our lifestyle; they all participate in amending or adding to the text. Emend* should be used only of correcting errors in a manuscript or text.

amendment (ə'mɛndmənt) *n.* **1.** correction. **2.** an addition or alteration to a document, etc.

amends (ə'mɛndz) *n.* (*functioning as sing.*) recompense or compensation for some injury, insult, etc.: *to make amends.* [C13: < OF, < *amende* compensation, < *amender* to EMEND]

amenity (ə'miːnɪtɪ) *n., pl.* **-ties.** **1.** (*often pl.*) a useful or pleasant facility: *a swimming pool was one of the amenities.* **2.** the fact or condition of being agreeable. **3.** (*usually pl.*) a social courtesy. [C14: < L, < *amoenus* agreeable]

amenorrhoea *or esp. U.S.* **amenorrhea** (æˌmɛnə'rɪə, eɪ-) *n.* abnormal absence of menstruation. [C19: < A-¹ + MENO- + -RRHOEA]

ament ('æmənt) *n.* another name for **catkin.** Also called: **amentum** (ə'mɛntəm). [C18: < L *āmentum* thong] —ˌ**amen'taceous** *adj.*

amentia (ə'mɛnʃə) *n.* severe mental deficiency, usually congenital. [C14: < L: insanity, < *āmēns* mad, < *mēns* mind]

amerce (ə'mɜːs) *vb.* (*tr.*) *Obs.* **1.** *Law.* to punish by a fine. **2.** to punish with any arbitrary penalty. [C14: < Anglo-F, < OF *à merci* at the mercy; see MERCY] —**a'mercement** *n.*

American (ə'mɛrɪkən) *adj.* **1.** of or relating to the United States of America, its inhabitants, or their form of English. **2.** of or relating to the American continent. ~*n.* **3.** a native or citizen of the U.S. **4.** a native or inhabitant of any country of North, Central, or South America. **5.** the English language as spoken or written in the United States.

Americana (əˌmɛrɪ'kɑːnə) *n.* objects, such as documents, relics, etc., relating to America.

American aloe *n.* See **aloe** (sense 2).

American football *n.* **1.** a team game similar to rugby, with 11 players on each side. **2.** the oval-shaped inflated ball used in this game.

American Indian *n.* **1.** Also called: **Indian, Red Indian, Amerindian.** a member of any of the indigenous peoples of America, having straight black hair and a yellow-to-brown skin. ~*adj.* **2.** Also called: **Amerindian.** of or relating to any of these peoples, their languages, or their cultures.

Americanism (ə'mɛrɪkəˌnɪzəm) *n.* **1.** a custom, linguistic usage, or other feature peculiar to or characteristic of the United States. **2.** loyalty to the United States.

Americanize *or* **-ise** (ə'mɛrɪkəˌnaɪz) *vb.* to make or become American in outlook, attitudes, etc. —**Aˌmericani'zation** *or* **-i'sation** *n.*

americium (ˌæmə'rɪsɪəm) *n.* a white metallic transuranic element artificially produced from plutonium. It is used as an alpha-particle source. Symbol: Am; atomic no.: 95; half-life of most stable isotope, ^{243}Am: 7.4 × 10^3 years. [C20: < *America* (where it was first produced) + -IUM]

Amerindian (ˌæmə'rɪndɪən) *n. also* **Amerind** ('æmərɪnd), *adj.* another word for **American Indian.**

amethyst ('æmɪθɪst) *n.* **1.** a purple or violet variety of quartz used as a gemstone. **2.** a purple variety of sapphire. **3. a.** the purple colour of amethyst. **b.** (*as adj.*): *amethyst shadow.* [C13: < OF, < L, < Gk *amethustos*, lit.: not drunken, < A-¹ + *methuein* to make drunk; < the belief that the stone could prevent intoxication] —**amethystine** (ˌæmɪ'θɪstaɪn) *adj.*

AMF *abbrev. for* Australian Military Forces.

Amharic (æm'hærɪk) *n.* **1.** the official language of Ethiopia. ~*adj.* **2.** denoting this language.

amiable ('eɪmɪəbᵊl) *adj.* having or displaying a pleasant or agreeable nature; friendly. [C14: < OF, < LL *amīcābilis* AMICABLE] —ˌ**amia'bility** *or* '**amiableness** *n.* —'**amiably** *adv.*

amianthus (ˌæmɪ'ænθəs) *n.* any of the fine silky varieties of asbestos. [C17: < L *amiantus*, < Gk *amiantos* unsullied, < A-¹ + *miainein* to pollute]

amicable ('æmɪkəbᵊl) *adj.* characterized by friendliness: *an amicable agreement.* [C15: < LL *amīcābilis*, < L *amīcus* friend] —ˌ**amicaˈbility** *or* ˈ**amicableness** *n.* —ˈ**amicably** *adv.*

amice (ˈæmɪs) *n. Christianity.* a rectangular piece of white linen worn by priests around the neck and shoulders under the alb or, formerly, on the head. [C15: < OF, < L *amictus* cloak]

amicus curiae (æˈmiːkʊs ˈkjʊərɪˌiː) *n., pl.* **amici curiae** (æˈmiːkaɪ) *Law.* a person, not directly engaged in a case, who advises the court. [L, lit.: friend of the court]

amid (əˈmɪd) *or* **amidst** *prep.* in the middle of; among. [OE *on middan* in the middle]

amide (ˈæmaɪd) *n.* **1.** any organic compound containing the group $-CONH_2$. **2.** (*modifier*) containing the group $-CONH_2$: *amide group or radical.* **3.** an inorganic compound having the general formula $M(NH_2)_x$, where M is a metal atom. [C19: < AM(MONIA) + -IDE]

amidships (əˈmɪdʃɪps) *adv., adj.* (*postpositive*) *Naut.* at, near, or towards the centre of a vessel.

amigo (æˈmiːgəʊ, ə-) *n., pl.* **-gos.** a friend; comrade. [Sp., < L *amicus*]

amine (əˈmiːn, ˈæmɪn) *n.* an organic base formed by replacing one or more of the hydrogen atoms of ammonia by organic groups. [C19: < AM(MONIUM) + -INE²]

amino (əˈmiːnəʊ) *n.* (*modifier*) of or containing the group of atoms $-NH_2$: *amino radical.*

amino acid *n.* **1.** any of a group of organic compounds containing one or more amino groups, $-NH_2$, and one or more carboxyl groups, $-COOH$. **2.** any of a group of organic nitrogenous compounds that form the component molecules of proteins.

amino resin *n.* a thermosetting synthetic resin used as an adhesive and coating for paper and textiles.

amir (əˈmɪə) *n.* a variant spelling of **emir.** [C19: < Ar., var. of EMIR] —**aˈmirate** *n.*

Amish (ˈæmɪʃ, ˈɑː-) *adj.* of a U.S. and Canadian Mennonite sect. [C19: < G *Amisch*, after Jakob *Amman*, 17th-cent. Swiss Mennonite bishop]

amiss (əˈmɪs) *adv.* **1.** in an incorrect or defective manner. **2. take (something) amiss.** to be annoyed or offended by (something). ~*adj.* **3.** (*postpositive*) wrong or faulty. [C13 *a mis*, < *mis* wrong]

amitosis (ˌæmɪˈtəʊsɪs) *n.* a form of cell division in which the nucleus and cytoplasm divide without the formation of chromosomes. [C20: < A¹ + MITOSIS] —**amitotic** (ˌæmɪˈtɒtɪk) *adj.*

amity (ˈæmɪtɪ) *n., pl.* **-ties.** friendship; cordiality. [C15: < OF *amité*, ult. < L *amīcus* friend]

ammeter (ˈæmˌmiːtə) *n.* an instrument for measuring an electric current in amperes. [C19: AM(PERE) + -METER]

ammo (ˈæməʊ) *n. Inf.* short for **ammunition.**

ammonia (əˈməʊnɪə) *n.* **1.** a colourless pungent gas used in the manufacture of fertilizers and as a refrigerant and solvent. Formula: NH_3. **2.** short for **aqueous ammonia.** See **ammonium hydroxide.** [C18: < NL, < L (*sal*) *ammōniacus* (sal) AMMONIAC]

ammoniac (əˈməʊnɪˌæk) *n.* a gum resin obtained from the stems of an Asian plant and formerly used as a stimulant, perfume, and in porcelain cement. Also called: **gum ammoniac.** [C14: < L, < Gk *ammōniakos* belonging to Ammon (apparently the gum resin was extracted from plants found in Libya near the temple of Ammon)]

ammoniacal (ˌæməˈnaɪəkᵊl) *adj.* of, containing, or resembling ammonia.

ammoniate (əˈməʊnɪˌeɪt) *vb.* to unite or treat with ammonia. —**amˌmoniˈation** *n.*

ammonify (əˈmɒnɪˌfaɪ) *vb.* **-fying, -fied.** to treat or impregnate with ammonia or a compound of ammonia. —**amˌmonifiˈcation** *n.*

ammonite (ˈæməˌnaɪt) *n.* **1.** any extinct marine cephalopod mollusc of the order *Ammonoidea*, which were common in Mesozoic times and had a coiled partitioned shell. **2.** the shell of any of these animals, commonly occurring as a fossil. [C18: < L *cornū Ammōnis*, lit.: horn of Ammon]

ammonium (əˈməʊnɪəm) *n.* (*modifier*) of or containing the monovalent group NH_4- or the ion NH_4^+: *ammonium compounds.*

ammonium chloride *n.* a white soluble crystalline solid used as an electrolyte in dry batteries. Formula: NH_4Cl. Also called: **sal ammoniac.**

ammonium hydroxide *n.* a solution of ammonia and water used in the manufacture of rayon and plastics, in photography, and in pharmaceuticals. Formula: NH_4OH.

ammonium sulphate *n.* a white soluble crystalline solid used mainly as a fertilizer and in water purification. Formula: $(NH_4)_2SO_4$.

ammunition (ˌæmjʊˈnɪʃən) *n.* **1.** any projectiles, such as bullets, rockets, etc., that can be discharged from a weapon. **2.** bombs, missiles, chemicals, etc., capable of use as weapons. **3.** any means of defence or attack, as in an argument. [C17: < obs. F *amunition*, by mistaken division < earlier *la munition*; see MUNITION]

amnesia (æmˈniːzjə, -ʒjə, -zɪə) *n.* a defect in memory, esp. one resulting from a pathological cause. [C19: via NL < Gk: forgetfulness, prob. < *amnēstia* oblivion] —**amnesiac** (æmˈniːzɪˌæk) *or* **amnesic** (æmˈniːsɪk, -zɪk) *adj., n.*

amnesty (ˈæmnɪstɪ) *n., pl.* **-ties.** **1.** a general pardon, esp. for offences against a government. **2.** a period during which a law is suspended to allow offenders to admit their crime without fear of prosecution. ~*vb.* **-tying, -tied.** **3.** (*tr.*) to overlook or forget (an offence). [C16: < L, < Gk: oblivion, < A-¹ + *-mnēstos*, < *mnasthai* to remember]

Amnesty International *n.* an international organization that works to secure the release of people imprisoned for their beliefs, to ban the use of torture, and to abolish the death penalty. Abbrev.: **AI.**

amniocentesis (ˌæmnɪəʊsɛnˈtiːsɪs) *n., pl.* **-ses** (-siːz). removal of amniotic fluid for diagnostic purposes by the insertion into the womb of a hollow needle. [C20: < AMNION + *centesis* < Gk *kentēsis* < *kentein* to prick]

amnion (ˈæmnɪən) *n., pl.* **-nions** *or* **-nia** (-nɪə). the innermost of two membranes enclosing an embryonic reptile, bird, or mammal. [C17: via NL < Gk: a little lamb, < *amnos* a lamb] —**amniotic** (ˌæmnɪˈɒtɪk) *adj.*

amniotic fluid *n.* the fluid surrounding the fetus in the womb.

amoeba *or U.S.* **ameba** (əˈmiːbə) *n., pl.* **-bae** (-biː) *or* **-bas.** any of an order of protozoans able to change shape because of the movements of cell processes. They live in fresh water or soil or as parasites in man and animals. [C19: < NL, < Gk, < *ameibein* to change, exchange] —**aˈmoebic** *or U.S.* **aˈmebic** *adj.*

amok (əˈmʌk, əˈmɒk) *or* **amuck** (əˈmʌk) *n.* **1.** a state of murderous frenzy. ~*adv.* **2. run amok.** to run about as with a frenzied desire to kill. [C17: < Malay *amoq* furious assault]

among (əˈmʌŋ) *or* **amongst** *prep.* **1.** in the midst of: *he lived among the Indians.* **2.** to each of: *divide the reward among yourselves.* **3.** in the group, class, or number of: *among the greatest writers.* **4.** taken out of (a group): *he is one among many.* **5.** with one another within a group: *decide it among yourselves.* **6.** in the general opinion or practice of: *accepted among experts.* [OE *amang*, contracted < *on gemang* in the group of, < ON + *gemang* crowd]

▷ **Usage.** See at **between.**

amontillado (əˌmɒntɪˈlɑːdəʊ) *n.* a medium-dry sherry. [C19: < Sp. *vino amontillado* wine of *Montilla*, town in Spain]

amoral (ˌeɪˈmɒrəl) *adj.* **1.** having no moral quality; nonmoral. **2.** without moral standards or principles. —**amorality** (ˌeɪmɒˈrælɪtɪ) *n.*

▷ **Usage.** *Amoral* is frequently and incorrectly used where *immoral* is meant. In careful usage, *immoral* is used of that which infringes moral rules and *amoral* only of that to which considerations of morality are irrelevant or of persons who lack any moral code.

amorist (ˈæmərɪst) *n.* a lover or a writer about love.

amoroso (ˌæməˈrəʊsəʊ) *adj., adv.* **1.** *Music.* (to be played) tenderly. ~*n.* **2.** a rich sweet sherry. [< It. & Sp.: AMOROUS]

amorous (ˈæmərəs) *adj.* **1.** inclined towards or displaying love or desire. **2.** in love. **3.** of or relating to love. [C14: < OF, < Med. L, < L *amor* love] —ˈ**amorously** *adv.* —ˈ**amorousness** *n.*

amorphous (əˈmɔːfəs) *adj.* **1.** lacking a definite shape. **2.** of no recognizable character or type. **3.** (of rocks, etc.) not having a crystalline structure. [C18: < NL, < Gk, < A-¹ + *morphē* shape] —**aˈmorphism** *n.* —**aˈmorphousness** *n.*

amortize *or* **-tise** (əˈmɔːtaɪz) *vb.* (*tr.*) **1.** *Finance.* to liquidate (a debt, mortgage, etc.) by payments or by periodic transfers to a sinking fund. **2.** to write off (a wasting asset) by transfers to a sinking fund. **3.** *Property law.* (formerly) to transfer (lands, etc.) in mortmain. [C14: < Med. L, < OF *amortir* to reduce to the point of death, ult. < L *ad* to + *mors* death] —**aˌmortiˈzation** *or* **-tiˈsation** *n.*

amount (əˈmaʊnt) *n.* **1.** extent; quantity. **2.** the total of two or more quantities. **3.** the full value or significance of something. **4.** a principal sum plus the interest on it, as in a loan. ~*vb.* **5.** (*intr.;* usually foll. by *to*) to be equal or add up. [C13: < OF *amonter* to go up, < *amont* upwards, < *a* to + *mont* mountain (< L *mōns*)]

amour (əˈmʊə) *n.* a love affair, esp. a secret or illicit one. [C13: < OF, < L *amor* love]

amour-propre *French.* (amurprɔprə) *n.* self-respect.

amp (æmp) *n.* **1.** an ampere. **2.** *Inf.* an amplifier.

ampelopsis (ˌæmpɪˈlɒpsɪs) *n.* any of a genus of woody climbing plants of tropical and subtropical Asia and America. [C19: < NL, < Gk *ampelos* grapevine]

amperage (ˈæmpərɪdʒ) *n.* the strength of an electric current measured in amperes.

ampere (ˈæmpɛə) *n.* **1.** the basic SI unit of electric current; the constant current that, when maintained in two parallel conductors of infinite length and negligible cross section placed 1 metre apart in free space, produces a force of 2×10^{-7} newton per metre between them. **2.** a former unit of electric current (**international ampere**); the current that, when passed through a solution of silver nitrate, deposits silver at the rate of 0.001118 gram per second. ~Abbrev.: **amp.** Symbol: A [C19: after A. M. *Ampère* (1775-1836), F physicist & mathematician]

ampere-turn *n.* a unit of magnetomotive force; the magnetomotive force produced by a current of 1 ampere passing through one complete turn of a coil.

ampersand (ˈæmpəˌsænd) *n.* the character (&), meaning *and: John Brown & Co.* [C19: shortened < *and per se and,* that is, the symbol & by itself (represents) *and*]

amphetamine (æmˈfɛtəˌmiːn) *n.* a synthetic colourless liquid used medicinally, mainly for its stimulant action on the central nervous system. [C20: < A(LPHA) + M(ETHYL) + PH(ENYL) + ET(HYL) +-AMINE]

amphi- *prefix of nouns and adjectives.* **1.** on both sides; at both ends; of both kinds: *amphipod; amphibious.* **2.** around: *amphibole.* [< Gk]

amphibian (æmˈfɪbɪən) *n.* **1.** any cold-blooded vertebrate of the class *Amphibia,* typically living on land but breeding in water. The class includes newts, frogs, and toads. **2.** an aircraft able to land and take off from both water and land. **3.** any vehicle able to travel on both water and land. ~*adj.* **4.** another word for **amphibious. 5.** of or belonging to the class *Amphibia.*

amphibious (æmˈfɪbɪəs) *adj.* **1.** able to live both on land and in the water, as frogs, etc. **2.** designed for operation on or from both water and land. **3.** relating to military forces and operations launched from the sea against an enemy shore. **4.** having a dual or mixed nature. [C17: < Gk *amphibios,* lit.: having a double life, < AMPHI- + *bios* life] —**amˈphibiousness** *n.*

amphibole (ˈæmfɪˌbəʊl) *n.* any of a large group of minerals consisting of the silicates of calcium, iron, magnesium, sodium, and aluminium, which are common constituents of igneous rocks. [C17: < F, < Gk *amphibolos* uncertain; so called from the large number of varieties in the group]

amphibology (ˌæmfɪˈbɒlədʒɪ) *or* **amphiboly** (æmˈfɪbəlɪ) *n., pl.* **-gies** *or* **-lies.** ambiguity of expression, esp. when due to a grammatical construction, as in *save rags and waste paper.* [C14: < LL, ult. < Gk *amphibolos* ambiguous]

amphimixis (ˌæmfɪˈmɪksɪs) *n., pl.* **-mixes** (-ˈmɪksiːz). true sexual reproduction, esp. the fusion of gametes from two organisms. [C19: < AMPHI- + Gk *mixis* a blending] —**amphimictic** (ˌæmfɪˈmɪktɪk) *adj.*

amphioxus (ˌæmfɪˈɒksəs) *n., pl.* **-oxi** (-ˈɒksaɪ) *or* **-oxuses.** another name for the **lancelet.** [C19: < NL, < AMPHI- + Gk *oxus* sharp]

amphipod (ˈæmfɪˌpɒd) *n.* **1.** any marine or freshwater crustacean of the order *Amphipoda,* such as the sand hoppers, in which the body is laterally compressed. ~*adj.* **2.** of or belonging to the *Amphipoda.*

amphiprostyle (æmˈfɪprəˌstaɪl) *adj.* **1.** (esp. of a classical temple) having a set of columns at both ends but not at the sides. ~*n.* **2.** a temple of this kind.

amphisbaena (æmfɪsˈbiːnə) *n., pl.* **-nae** (-niː) *or* **-nas. 1.** a genus of wormlike lizards of tropical America. **2.** *Classical myth.* a fabulous serpent with a head at each end. [C16: < L, < Gk *amphisbaina,* < *amphis* both ways + *bainein* to go]

amphitheatre *or U.S.* **amphitheater** (ˈæmfɪˌθɪətə) *n.* **1.** a building, usually circular or oval, in which tiers of seats rise from a central open arena. **2.** a place where contests are held. **3.** any level circular area of ground surrounded by higher ground. **4.** a gallery in a theatre. **5.** a lecture room in which seats are tiered away from a central area.

amphora (ˈæmfərə) *n., pl.* **-phorae** (-fəˌriː) *or* **-phoras.** a Greek or Roman two-handled narrow-necked jar for oil, etc. [C17: < L, < Gk, < AMPHI- + *phoreus* bearer, < *pherein* to bear]

amphoteric (ˌæmfəˈtɛrɪk) *adj. Chem.* able to function as either a base or an acid. [C19: < Gk *amphoteros* each of two (< *amphō* both) + -IC]

ample (ˈæmpᵊl) *adj.* **1.** more than sufficient: *an ample helping.* **2.** large: *of ample proportions.* [C15: < OF, < L *amplus* spacious] —ˈ**ampleness** *n.*

amplexicaul (æmˈplɛksɪˌkɔːl) *adj.* (of some sessile leaves, stipules, etc.) having an enlarged base that encircles the stem. [C18: < NL, < L *amplectī* to embrace + *caulis* stalk]

amplification (ˌæmplɪfɪˈkeɪʃən) *n.* **1.** the act or result of amplifying. **2.** material added to a statement, story, etc., to expand or clarify it. **3.** a statement, story, etc., with such additional material. **4.** *Electronics.* the increase in strength of an electrical signal by means of an amplifier.

amplifier (ˈæmplɪˌfaɪə) *n.* **1.** an electronic device used to increase the strength of the current fed into it, esp. one for the amplification of sound signals in a radio, record player, etc. **2.** *Photog.* an additional lens for altering focal length. **3.** a person or thing that amplifies.

amplify (ˈæmplɪˌfaɪ) *vb.* **-fying, -fied. 1.** (*tr.*) to increase in size, extent, effect, etc., as by the addition of extra material. **2.** *Electronics.* to produce amplification of (electrical signals). **3.** (*intr.*) to expand a speech, narrative, etc. [C15: < OF, ult. < L *amplificāre* to enlarge, < *amplus* spacious + *facere* to make]

amplitude (ˈæmplɪˌtjuːd) *n.* **1.** greatness of extent; magnitude. **2.** abundance. **3.** breadth or scope, as of the mind. **4.** *Astron.* the angular distance along the horizon measured from true east or west to the point of intersection of the vertical circle passing through a celestial body. **5.** *Physics.* the maximum displacement from the zero or mean position of a periodic motion. [C16: < L, < *amplus* spacious]

amplitude modulation *n.* one of the principal

methods of transmitting information using radio waves, the relevant signal being superimposed onto a radio-frequency carrier wave. The frequency of the carrier wave remains unchanged but its amplitude is varied in accordance with the amplitude of the input signal. Cf. **frequency modulation.**

amply ('æmplɪ) *adv.* fully; generously.

ampoule ('æmpuːl, -pjuːl) *or esp. U.S.* **ampule** *n. Med.* a small glass vessel in which liquids for injection are hermetically sealed. [C19: < F, < L: see AMPULLA]

ampulla (æm'pʊlə) *n., pl.* **-pullae** (-'pʊliː). **1.** *Anat.* the dilated end part of certain ducts or canals. **2.** *Christianity.* **a.** a vessel for the wine and water used at the Eucharist. **b.** a small flask for consecrated oil. **3.** a Roman two-handled bottle for oil, wine, or perfume. [C16: < L, dim. of AMPHORA]

amputate ('æmpjʊˌteɪt) *vb. Surgery.* to remove (all or part of a limb). [C17: < L, < *am-* around + *putāre* to trim, prune] —ˌ**ampu'tation** *n.*

amputee (ˌæmpjʊ'tiː) *n.* a person who has had a limb amputated.

AMU *abbrev. for* atomic mass unit.

amuck (ə'mʌk) *n., adv.* a variant spelling of **amok.**

amulet ('æmjʊlɪt) *n.* a trinket or piece of jewellery worn as a protection against evil; charm. [C17: < L *amulētum,* <?]

amuse (ə'mjuːz) *vb. (tr.)* **1.** to entertain; divert. **2.** to cause to laugh or smile. [C15: < OF *amuser* to cause to be idle, < *muser* to MUSE[1]]

amusement (ə'mjuːzmənt) *n.* **1.** something that amuses, such as a game or pastime. **2.** a mechanical device used for entertainment, as at a fair. **3.** the act of amusing or the state or quality of being amused.

amusement arcade *n. Brit.* a covered area having coin-operated game machines.

amusing (ə'mjuːzɪŋ) *adj.* entertaining; causing a smile or laugh. —**a'musingly** *adv.*

amygdalin (ə'mɪgdəlɪn) *n.* a white soluble bitter-tasting glycoside extracted from bitter almonds. [C17: < Gk: ALMOND + -IN]

amyl ('æmɪl) *n.* (*modifier*) (no longer in technical usage) of or containing any of eight isomeric forms of the monovalent group $C_5H_{11}-$: *amyl group or radical.* [C19: < L: AMYLUM]

amylaceous (ˌæmɪ'leɪʃəs) *adj.* of or resembling starch.

amylase ('æmɪˌleɪz) *n.* any of several enzymes that hydrolyse starch and glycogen to simple sugars, such as glucose.

amyl nitrite *n.* an ester of amyl alcohol and nitrous acid used as a vasodilator, esp. to treat angina pectoris.

amyloid ('æmɪˌlɔɪd) *n.* **1.** any substance resembling starch. *~adj.* **2.** starchlike.

amylopsin (ˌæmɪ'lɒpsɪn) *n.* an enzyme of the pancreatic juice that converts starch into sugar; pancreatic amylase. [C19: < AMYL + (PE)PSIN]

amylum ('æmɪləm) *n.* another name for **starch** (senses 1,2). [L, < Gk *amulon* fine meal, starch]

Amytal ('æmɪˌtæl) *n. Trademark.* sodium amytal, used as a sedative and hypnotic.

an[1] (æn; *unstressed* ən) *determiner.* (*indefinite article*) a form of **a**[1], used before an initial vowel sound: *an old car; an elf; an hour.* [OE *ān* ONE]

▷ **Usage.** *An* was formerly often used before words that begin with *h* and are unstressed on the first syllable: *an hotel; an historic meeting:* sometimes the initial *h* was not pronounced. In British English this usage is now obsolescent.

an[2] *or* **an'** (æn; *unstressed* ən) *conj.* (*subordinating*) an obsolete or dialect word for **if.** See **and** (sense 8).

an. *abbrev. for* anno. [L: in the year]

an- *or before a consonant* **a-** *prefix.* not; without: *anaphrodisiac.* [< Gk]

-an, -ean, *or* **-ian** *suffix.* **1.** (*forming adjectives and nouns*) belonging to; coming from; typical of; adhering to: *European; Elizabethan; Christian.* **2.** (*forming nouns*) a person who specializes or is expert in: *dietitian.* [< L *-ānus,* suffix of adjectives]

ana- *or before a vowel* **an-** *prefix.* **1.** up; upwards: *anadromous.* **2.** again: *anagram.* **3.** back; backwards: *anapaest.* [< Gk *ana*]

-ana *or* **-iana** *suffix forming nouns.* denoting a collection of objects or information relating to a particular individual, subject or place: *Victoriana, Americana.* [NL, < L *-āna,* lit.: matters relating to, neuter pl. of *-ānus;* see -AN]

Anabaptist (ˌænə'bæptɪst) *n.* **1.** a member of any of various Protestant movements, esp. of the 16th century, that rejected infant baptism, insisted that adults be rebaptized, and sought to establish Christian communism. *~adj.* **2.** of these sects or their doctrines. [C16: < Ecclesiastical L, < *anabaptīzāre* to baptize again, < LGk *anabaptizein*] —ˌ**Ana'baptism** *n.*

anabas ('ænəˌbæs) *n.* any of several freshwater fishes, esp. the climbing perch, that can travel on land. [C19: < NL, < Gk *anabainein* to go up]

anabasis (ə'næbəsɪs) *n., pl.* **-ses** (-ˌsiːz). **1.** the march of Cyrus the Younger from Sardis to Cunaxa in Babylonia in 401 B.C., described by Xenophon in his *Anabasis.* **2.** any military expedition, esp. one from the coast to the interior. [C18: < Gk: a going up, < *anabainein* to go up]

anabatic (ˌænə'bætɪk) *adj. Meteorol.* (of air currents) rising upwards. [C19: < Gk *anabatikos* relating to ascents, < *anabainein* to go up]

anabiosis (ˌænəbaɪ'əʊsɪs) *n.* a return to life after apparent death. [C19: via NL < Gk, < *anabioein* to come back to life] —**anabiotic** (ˌænəbaɪ'ɒtɪk) *adj.*

anabolic steroid *n.* any of a group of synthetic steroid hormones (androgens) used to stimulate muscle and bone growth for athletic or therapeutic purposes.

anabolism (ə'næbəˌlɪzəm) *n.* a metabolic process in which complex molecules are synthesized from simpler ones with the storage of energy; constructive metabolism. [C19: < ANA- + (META)BOLISM] —**anabolic** (ˌænə'bɒlɪk) *adj.*

anachronism (ə'nækrəˌnɪzəm) *n.* **1.** the representation of an event, person, or thing in a historical context in which it could not have occurred or existed. **2.** a person or thing that belongs or seems to belong to another time. [C17: < L, < Gk *anakhronismos* a mistake in chronology, < ANA- + *khronos* time] —**aˌnachro'nistic** *adj.* —**aˌnachro'nistically** *adv.*

anacoluthon (ˌænəkə'luːθɒn) *n., pl.* **-tha** (-θə). a construction that involves the change from one grammatical sequence to another within a single sentence. [C18: < LL, < Gk, < *anakolouthos* not consistent, < AN- + *akolouthos* following]

anaconda (ˌænə'kɒndə) *n.* a very large nonvenomous arboreal and semiaquatic snake of tropical South America, which kills its prey by constriction. [C18: prob. changed < Sinhalese *henakandayā* whip snake; orig. referring to a snake of Sri Lanka]

anacrusis (ˌænə'kruːsɪs) *n., pl.* **-ses** (-siːz). **1.** *Prosody.* one or more unstressed syllables at the beginning of a line of verse. **2.** *Music.* an unstressed note or group of notes immediately preceding the strong first beat of the first bar. [C19: < Gk, < *anakrouein* to strike up, < ANA- + *krouein* to strike]

anadromous (ə'nædrəməs) *adj.* (of fishes such as the salmon) migrating up rivers from the sea in order to breed. [C18: < Gk *anadromos* running upwards]

anaemia *or U.S.* **anemia** (ə'niːmɪə) *n.* a deficiency in the number of red blood cells or in their haemoglobin content, resulting in pallor and lack of energy. [C19: < NL, < Gk *anaimia* lack of blood, < AN- + *haima* blood]

anaemic *or U.S.* **anemic** (ə'niːmɪk) *adj.* **1.** relating to or suffering from anaemia. **2.** pale and sickly looking; lacking vitality.

anaerobe (æ'nɛərəʊb, 'ænərəʊb) *or* **anaerobium** (ˌænɛə'rəʊbɪəm) *n., pl.* **-obes** *or* **-obia** (-'əʊbɪə). an organism that does not require, or requires the absence of, free oxygen or air. —ˌ**anaerˈobic** *adj.*

anaesthesia *or U.S.* **anesthesia** (ˌænɪsˈθiːzɪə) *n.* **1.** loss of bodily sensation, esp. of touch, as the result of nerve damage or other abnormality. **2.** loss of sensation, esp. of pain, induced by drugs: called **general anaesthesia** when consciousness is lost and **local anaesthesia** when only a specific area of the body is involved. [C19: < NL, < Gk *anaisthēsia* absence of sensation]

anaesthetic *or U.S.* **anesthetic** (ˌænɪsˈθɛtɪk) *n.* **1.** a substance that causes anaesthesia. *~adj.* **2.** causing or characterized by anaesthesia.

anaesthetics (ˌænisˈθɛtɪks) *n.* (*functioning as sing.*) the science of anaesthesia and its application. U.S. name: **anesthesiology.**

anaesthetist (əˈniːsθətɪst) *n.* **1.** *Brit.* a doctor specializing in the administration of anaesthetics. U.S. name: **anesthesiologist. 2.** *U.S.* See **anesthetist.**

anaesthetize, anaesthetise, *or U.S.* **anesthetize** (əˈniːsθəˌtaɪz) *vb.* (*tr.*) to render insensible to pain by administering an anaesthetic. —**aˌnaesthetiˈzation, aˌnaesthetiˈsation,** *or U.S.* **aˌnesthetiˈzation** *n.*

anaglyph (ˈænəˌglɪf) *n.* **1.** *Photog.* a stereoscopic picture consisting of two images of the same object, taken from slightly different angles, in two complementary colours. When viewed through coloured spectacles, the images merge to produce a stereoscopic sensation. **2.** anything cut to stand in low relief, such as a cameo. [C17: < Gk *anagluphē* carved in low relief, < ANA- + *gluphē* carving, < *gluphein* to carve] —ˌ**anaˈglyphic** *adj.*

Anaglypta (ˌænəˈglɪptə) *n. Trademark.* a type of thick embossed wallpaper designed to be painted. [C19: < Gk *anagluptos;* see ANAGLYPH]

anagram (ˈænəˌgræm) *n.* a word or phrase the letters of which can be rearranged into another word or phrase. [C16: < NL, < Gk, < *anagrammatizein* to transpose letters, < ANA- + *gramma* a letter] —**anagrammatic** (ˌænəgrəˈmætɪk) *or* ˌ**anagramˈmatical** *adj.*

anagrammatize *or* **-tise** (ˌænəˈgræməˌtaɪz) *vb.* to arrange into an anagram.

anal (ˈeɪnᵊl) *adj.* **1.** of or near the anus. **2.** *Psychoanal.* relating to a stage of psychosexual development during which the child's interest is concentrated on the anal region and excremental functions. [C18: < NL *ānālis;* see ANUS] —ˈ**anally** *adv.*

analects (ˈænəˌlɛkts) *or* **analecta** (ˌænəˈlɛktə) *pl. n.* selected literary passages from one or more works. [C17: via L < Gk, < *analegein* to collect up, < *legein* to gather]

analeptic (ˌænᵊˈlɛptɪk) *adj.* **1.** (of a drug, etc.) restorative or invigorating. *~n.* **2.** a restorative remedy or drug. [C17: < NL, < Gk *analēptikos* stimulating, < *analambanein* to take up]

anal fin *n.* an unpaired fin between the anus and tail fin in fishes that maintains equilibrium.

analgesia (ˌænᵊlˈdʒiːzɪə) *or* **analgia** (ænˈældʒɪə) *n.* inability to feel pain. [C18: via NL < Gk: insensibility, < AN- + *algēsis* sense of pain]

analgesic (ˌænᵊlˈdʒiːzɪk) *adj.* **1.** of or causing analgesia. *~n.* **2.** a substance that produces analgesia.

analog (ˈænəˌlɒg) *n.* a variant spelling of **analogue.**

▷ **Usage.** The spelling *analog* is a U.S. variant of *analogue* in all its senses, and is also the generally preferred spelling in the computer industry.

analog computer *n.* a computer that performs arithmetical operations by using some variable physical quantity, such as mechanical movement or voltage, to represent numbers.

analogize *or* **-gise** (əˈnæləˌdʒaɪz) *vb.* **1.** (*intr.*) to make use of analogy, as in argument. **2.** (*tr.*) to make analogous or reveal analogy in.

analogous (əˈnæləgəs) *adj.* **1.** similar or corresponding in some respect. **2.** *Biol.* (of organs and parts) having the same function but different evolutionary origin. **3.** *Linguistics.* formed by analogy: *an analogous plural.* [C17: < L, < Gk *analogos* proportionate, < ANA- + *logos* speech, ratio]

analogue *or U.S.* (*sometimes*) **analog** (ˈænᵊˌlɒg) *n.* **1. a.** a physical object or quantity used to measure or represent another quantity. **b.** (*as modifier*): *analogue watch; analogue recording.* **2.** something analogous to something else. **3.** *Biol.* an analogous part or organ.

▷ **Usage.** See at **analog.**

analogy (əˈnælədʒɪ) *n., pl.* **-gies. 1.** agreement or similarity, esp. in a limited number of features. **2.** a comparison made to show such a similarity: *an analogy between an atom and the solar system.* **3.** *Biol.* the relationship between analogous organs or parts. **4.** *Logic, maths, philosophy.* a form of reasoning in which a similarity between two or more things is inferred from a known similarity between them in other respects. **5.** *Linguistics.* imitation of existing models or regular patterns in the formation of words, etc.: *a child may use "sheeps" as the plural of "sheep" by analogy with "cat," "cats," etc.* [C16: < Gk *analogia* correspondence, < *analogos* ANALOGOUS]

analysand (əˈnælɪˌsænd) *n.* any person who is undergoing psychoanalysis. [C20: < ANALYSE + *-and,* on the model of *multiplicand*]

analyse *or U.S.* **-lyze** (ˈænᵊˌlaɪz) *vb.* **1.** (*tr.*) to examine in detail in order to discover meaning, essential features, etc. **2.** (*tr.*) to break down into components or essential features. **3.** (*tr.*) to make a mathematical, chemical, grammatical, etc., analysis of. **4.** another word for **psychoanalyse.** [C17: back formation < ANALYSIS] —ˈ**anaˌlyser** *or U.S.* **-ˌlyzer** *n.*

analysis (əˈnælɪsɪs) *n., pl.* **-ses** (-ˌsiːz). **1.** the division of a physical or abstract whole into its constituent parts to examine or determine their relationship. **2.** a statement of the results of this. **3.** short for **psychoanalysis. 4.** *Chem.* **a.** the decomposition of a substance in order to determine the kinds of constituents present (**qualitative analysis**) or the amount of each constituent (**quantitative analysis**). **b.** the result obtained by such a determination. **5.** *Linguistics.* the use of word order together with word function to express syntactic relations in a language, as opposed to the use of inflections. **6.** *Maths.* the branch of mathematics principally concerned with the properties of functions. **7. in the last, final, *or* ultimate analysis.** after everything has been given due consideration. [C16: < NL, < Gk *analusis,* lit.: a dissolving, < ANA- + *luein* to loosen]

analysis of variance *n. Statistics.* a technique for analysing the total variation of a set of observations as measured by the variance of the observations multiplied by their number.

analyst (ˈænəlɪst) *n.* **1.** a person who analyses or is skilled in analysis. **2.** short for **psychoanalyst.**

analytic (ˌænəˈlɪtɪk) *or* **analytical** *adj.* **1.** relating to analysis. **2.** capable of or given to analysing: *an analytic mind.* **3.** *Linguistics.* denoting languages characterized by analysis. **4.** *Logic.* (of a proposition) true or false by virtue of the meanings of the words alone: *all spinsters are unmarried* is analytically true. [C16: via LL < Gk *analutikos,* < *analuein* to dissolve, break down] —ˌ**anaˈlytically** *adv.* —**analyticity** (ˌænəlɪˈtɪsɪtɪ) *n.*

analytical geometry *n.* the branch of geometry that uses algebraic notation to locate a point; coordinate geometry.

analytic philosophy *n.* See **philosophical analysis.**

anandrous (ænˈændrəs) *adj.* (of flowers) having no stamens. [C19: < Gk *anandros* lacking males, < AN- + *anēr* man]

anapaest *or* **anapest** (ˈænəpɛst, -piːst) *n.* *Prosody.* a metrical foot of three syllables, the first two short, the last long (⏑⏑–). [C17: via L < Gk *anapaistos* reversed, < *ana-* back + *paiein* to strike] —ˌ**anaˈpaestic** *or* ˌ**anaˈpestic** *adj.*

anaphora (əˈnæfərə) *n.* **1.** *Grammar.* the use of a word such as a pronoun to avoid repetition, as for example *one* in *He offered me a drink but I didn't want one.* **2.** *Rhetoric.* the repetition of a word or phrase at the beginning of successive clauses. [C16: via L < Gk: repetition, < ANA- + *pherein* to bear]

anaphrodisiac (ˌænæfrəˈdɪzɪˌæk) *adj.* **1.** tending to lessen sexual desire. ~*n.* **2.** an anaphrodisiac drug.

anaphylaxis (ˌænəfɪˈlæksɪs) *n.* extreme sensitivity to an injected antigen following a previous injection. [C20: < ANA- + (PRO)PHYLAXIS]

anaptyxis (ˌænæpˈtɪksɪs) *n., pl.* **-tyxes** (-ˈtɪksiːz). the insertion of a short vowel between consonants in order to make a word more easily pronounceable. [C19: via NL < Gk *anaptuxis,* < *anaptussein* to unfold, < ANA- + *ptussein* to fold]

anarchism (ˈænəˌkɪzəm) *n.* **1.** *Political theory.* a doctrine advocating the abolition of government. **2.** the principles or practice of anarchists.

anarchist (ˈænəkɪst) *n.* **1.** a person who advocates the abolition of government and a social system based on voluntary cooperation. **2.** a person who causes disorder or upheaval.

anarchy (ˈænəkɪ) *n.* **1.** general lawlessness and disorder, esp. when thought to result from an absence or failure of government. **2.** the absence of government. **3.** the absence of any guiding or uniting principle; chaos. **4.** political anarchism. [C16: < Med. L, < Gk, < *anarkhos* without a ruler, < AN- + *arkh-* leader, < *arkhein* to rule] —**anarchic** (ænˈɑːkɪk) *or* **anˈarchical** *adj.*

anastigmat (æˈnæstɪgmæt, ˌænəˈstɪgmæt) *n.* a lens system designed to be free of astigmatism. [C19: < AN- + ASTIGMATIC] —ˌ**anastigˈmatic** *adj.*

anastomose (əˈnæstəˌməʊz) *vb.* to join (two parts of a blood vessel, etc.) by anastomosis.

anastomosis (əˌnæstəˈməʊsɪs) *n., pl.* **-ses** (-siːz). **1.** a natural connection between two tubular structures, such as blood vessels. **2.** the union of two hollow parts that are normally separate. [C16: via NL < Gk: opening, < *anastomoun* to equip with a mouth, < *stoma* mouth]

anastrophe (əˈnæstrəfɪ) *n. Rhetoric.* another term for **inversion** (sense 3). [C16: < Gk, < *anastrephein* to invert]

anathema (əˈnæθəmə) *n., pl.* **-mas. 1.** a detested person or thing: *he is anathema to me.* **2.** a formal ecclesiastical excommunication, or denunciation of a doctrine. **3.** the person or thing so cursed. **4.** a strong curse. [C16: via Church L < Gk: something accursed, < *anatithenai* to dedicate, < ANA- + *tithenai* to set]

anathematize *or* **-tise** (əˈnæθɪməˌtaɪz) *vb.* to pronounce an anathema (upon a person, etc.); curse.

anatomical (ˌænəˈtɒmɪkˀl) *adj.* of anatomy.

anatomist (əˈnætəmɪst) *n.* an expert in anatomy.

anatomize *or* **-mise** (əˈnætəˌmaɪz) *vb.* (*tr.*) **1.** to dissect (an animal or plant). **2.** to examine in minute detail.

anatomy (əˈnætəmɪ) *n., pl.* **-mies. 1.** the science concerned with the physical structure of animals and plants. **2.** the physical structure of an animal or plant or any of its parts. **3.** a book or treatise on this subject. **4.** dissection of an animal or plant. **5.** any detailed analysis: *the anatomy of a crime.* **6.** *Inf.* the human body. [C14: < L, < Gk *anatomē,* < ANA- + *temnein* to cut]

anatto (əˈnætəʊ) *n., pl.* **-tos.** a variant spelling of **annatto.**

ANC *abbrev. for* African National Congress.

-ance *or* **-ancy** *suffix forming nouns.* indicating an action, state or condition, or quality: *resemblance; tenancy.* [via OF < L *-antia*]

ancestor (ˈænsɛstə) *n.* **1.** a person from whom another is directly descended; forefather. **2.** an early animal or plant from which a later type has evolved. **3.** a person or thing regarded as a forerunner: *the ancestor of the modern camera.* [C13: < OF, < LL *antecēssor* one who goes before, < L *antecēdere*] —ˈ**ancestress** *fem. n.*

ancestral (ænˈsɛstrəl) *adj.* of or inherited from ancestors.

ancestry (ˈænsɛstrɪ) *n., pl.* **-tries. 1.** lineage or descent, esp. when noble or distinguished. **2.** ancestors collectively.

anchor (ˈæŋkə) *n.* **1.** a device attached to a vessel by a cable and dropped overboard so as to grip the bottom and restrict movement. **2.** an object used to hold something else firmly in place: *the rock provided an anchor for the rope.* **3.** a source of stability or security. **4.** short for **anchor man. 5. cast, come to,** *or* **drop anchor.** to anchor a vessel. **6. ride at anchor.** to be anchored. ~*vb.* **7.** to use an anchor to hold (a vessel) in one place. **8.** to fasten or be fastened securely; fix or become fixed firmly. [OE *ancor,* < L, < Gk *ankura*]

anchorage (ˈæŋkərɪdʒ) *n.* **1.** the act of anchoring. **2.** any place where a vessel is anchored. **3.** a place designated for vessels to anchor. **4.** a fee imposed for anchoring. **5.** anything used as an anchor. **6.** a source of security or strength.

anchorite (ˈæŋkəˌraɪt) *n.* a person who lives in seclusion, esp. a religious recluse; hermit. [C15: < Med. L, < LL, < Gk, < *anakhōrein* to retire, < *khōra* a space] —ˈ**anchoress** *fem. n.*

anchor man *n.* **1.** *Sport.* the last person in a team to compete, esp. in a relay race. **2.** (in broadcasting) a person in a central studio who links up and maintains contact with various outside camera units, reporters, etc.

anchovy (ˈæntʃəvɪ) *n., pl.* **-vies** *or* **-vy.** any of various small marine food fishes which have a salty taste and are often tinned or made into a paste or essence. [C16: < Sp. *anchova,* ? ult. < Gk *aphuē* small fish]

anchusa (æŋˈkjuːsə) *n.* any of several Eurasian plants having rough hairy stems and leaves and blue flowers. [C18: < L]

anchylose (ˈæŋkɪˌləʊz) *vb.* a variant spelling of **ankylose.**

ancien régime *French.* (ɑ̃sjɛ̃ reʒim) *n., pl.* **anciens régimes** (ɑ̃sjɛ̃ reʒim). the political and social system of France before the Revolution of 1789. [lit.: old regime]

ancient (ˈeɪnʃənt) *adj.* **1.** dating from very long ago: *ancient ruins.* **2.** very old. **3.** of the far past, esp. before the collapse of the Western Roman Empire (476 A.D.). ~*n.* **4.** (*often pl.*) a member of a civilized nation in the ancient world, esp. a Greek or Roman. **5.** (*often pl.*) one of the classical authors of Greek or Roman antiquity. **6.** *Arch.* an old man. [C14: < OF *ancien,* < Vulgar L *anteanus* (unattested), < L *ante* before] —ˈ**ancientness** *n.*

ancient lights *n.* (*usually functioning as sing.*) the legal right to receive, by a particular window or windows, adequate and unobstructed daylight.

anciently (ˈeɪnʃəntlɪ) *adv.* in ancient times.

ancillary (ænˈsɪlərɪ) *adj.* **1.** subsidiary. **2.** auxiliary; supplementary: *ancillary services.* ~*n., pl.* **-laries. 3.** a subsidiary or auxiliary thing or person. [C17: < L *ancillāris* concerning maidservants, ult. < *ancūla* female servant]

ancon (ˈæŋkɒn) *or* **ancone** (ˈæŋkəʊn) *n., pl.* **ancones** (æŋˈkəʊniːz). *Architect.* a projecting bracket or console supporting a cornice. [C18: < Gk *ankōn* a bend]

-ancy *suffix forming nouns.* a variant of **-ance,** indicating condition or quality: *poignancy.*

ancylostomiasis (ˌænsɪˌlɒstəˈmaɪəsɪs) *or* **ankylostomiasis** (ˌæŋkɪˌlɒstəˈmaɪəsɪs) *n.* infestation of the intestine with blood-sucking hookworms; hookworm disease. [< NL, ult. < Gk *ankulos* hooked + *stoma* mouth]

and (ænd; *unstressed* ənd, ən) *conj.* (*coordinating*) **1.** in addition to: *boys and girls.* **2.** as a consequence: *he fell down and cut his knee.* **3.** afterwards: *we pay and go through that door.* **4.** plus: *two and two equals four.* **5.** used to give emphasis or indicate repetition or continuity: *it rained and rained.* **6.** used to express a contrast between instances of what is named: *there are jobs and jobs.* **7.** *Inf.* used in place of *to* in infinitives after verbs such as *try, go,* and *come: try and see it my way.* **8.** an obsolete word for **if**: *and it please you.* [OE *and*]

▷ **Usage.** See at **to.**

-and *or* **-end** *suffix forming nouns.* indicating a person or thing that is to be dealt with in a specified way: *dividend; multiplicand.* [< L gerundives ending in *-andus, -endus*]

andante (æn'dæntɪ) *Music.* ~*adj., adv.* **1.** (to be performed) at a moderately slow tempo. ~*n.* **2.** a passage or piece to be performed in this manner. [C18: < It., < *andare* to walk, < L *ambulāre*]

andantino (ˌændæn'tiːnəʊ) *Music.* ~*adj., adv.* **1.** (to be performed) slightly faster or slower than andante. ~*n., pl.* **-nos. 2.** a passage or piece to be performed in this manner. [C19: dim. of ANDANTE]

AND circuit *or* **gate** (ænd) *n. Computers.* a logic circuit that has a high-voltage output signal if and only if all input signals are at a high voltage simultaneously. [C20: < similarity of operation of *and* in logical conjunctions]

andiron ('ændˌaɪən) *n.* either of a pair of metal stands for supporting logs in a hearth. [C14: < OF *andier,* <?; infl. by IRON]

and/or *conj.* (*coordinating*) used to join terms when either one or the other or both is indicated: *passports and/or other means of identification.*

▷ **Usage.** *And/or* is not universally accepted as being good usage outside legal and commercial contexts. It is never used by careful writers and speakers where *or* is meant: *he must bring his car or his bicycle* (not *his car and/or his bicycle*).

andro- *or before a vowel* **andr-** *combining form.* **1.** male; masculine: *androsterone.* **2.** (in botany) stamen or anther: *androecium.* [< Gk *anēr* (genitive *andros*) man]

androecium (æn'driːsɪəm) *n., pl.* **-cia** (-sɪə). the stamens of a flowering plant collectively. [C19: < NL, < ANDRO- + Gk *oikion* a little house]

androgen ('ændrədʒən) *n.* any of several steroids that promote development of male sexual characteristics. —**androgenic** (ˌændrə'dʒɛnɪk) *adj.*

androgyne ('ændrəˌdʒaɪn) *n.* another word for **hermaphrodite.** [C17: < OF, via L < Gk *androgunos,* < *anēr* man + *gunē* woman]

androgynous (æn'drɒdʒɪnəs) *adj.* **1.** *Bot.* having male and female flowers in the same inflorescence. **2.** having male and female characteristics; hermaphrodite. —**an'drogyny** *n.*

android ('ændrɔɪd) *n.* **1.** (in science fiction) a robot resembling a human being. ~*adj.* **2.** resembling a human being. [C18: < LGk *androeidēs* manlike; see ANDRO-, -OID]

androsterone (æn'drɒstəˌrəʊn) *n.* an androgenic steroid hormone produced in the testes.

-androus *adj. combining form.* (in botany) indicating number or type of stamens: *diandrous.* [< NL, < Gk *-andros,* < *anēr* man]

ane (eɪn) *determiner, pron., n.* a Scottish word for **one.**

-ane *suffix forming nouns.* indicating a hydrocarbon of the paraffin series: *hexane.* [coined to replace *-ene, -ine,* and *-one*]

anecdotage ('ænɪkˌdəʊtɪdʒ) *n.* (usually used humorously) garrulous old age. [< ANECDOTE + -AGE, with play on *dotage*]

anecdote ('ænɪkˌdəʊt) *n.* a short usually amusing account of an incident. [C17: < Med. L, < Gk *anekdotos* unpublished, < AN- + *ekdotos* published] —ˌ**anec'dotal** *or* ˌ**anec'dotic** *adj.* —ˌ**anec'dotalist** *or* '**anec**ˌ**dotist** *n.*

anechoic (ˌænɪ'kəʊɪk) *adj.* having a low degree of reverberation: *an anechoic recording studio.*

anemia (ə'niːmɪə) *n.* the usual U.S. spelling of **anaemia.** —**anemic** (ə'niːmɪk) *adj.*

anemo- *combining form.* indicating wind: *anemometer; anemophilous.* [< Gk *anemos* wind]

anemograph (ə'nɛməʊˌgrɑːf) *n.* a self-recording anemometer.

anemometer (ˌænɪ'mɒmɪtə) *n.* an instrument for recording the speed and often the direction of winds. Also called: **wind gauge.** —ˌ**ane'mometry** *n.* —**anemometric** (ˌænɪməʊ'mɛtrɪk) *adj.*

anemone (ə'nɛmənɪ) *n.* any woodland plant of the genus *Anemone* of N temperate regions, such as the white-flowered **wood anemone** or **windflower.** Some cultivated anemones have coloured flowers. [C16: via L < Gk: windflower, < *anemos* wind]

anemophilous (ˌænɪ'mɒfɪləs) *adj.* (of flowering plants such as grasses) pollinated by the wind.

anent (ə'nɛnt) *prep. Arch. or Scot.* **1.** lying against; alongside. **2.** concerning; about. [OE *on efen,* lit.: on even (ground)]

aneroid barometer ('ænəˌrɔɪd) *n.* a device for measuring atmospheric pressure without the use of fluids. It consists of a partially evacuated chamber, the lid of which is displaced by variations in air pressure. This displacement is magnified by levers and made to operate a pointer. [C19 *aneroid,* < F, < AN- + Gk *nēros* wet + -OID]

anesthesia (ˌænɪs'θiːzɪə) *n.* the usual U.S. spelling of **anaesthesia.**

anesthesiologist (ˌænɪsˌθiːzɪ'ɒlədʒɪst) *n.* the U.S. name for an **anaesthetist.**

anesthesiology (ˌænɪsˌθiːzɪ'ɒlədʒɪ) *n.* the U.S. name for **anaesthetics.**

anesthetic (ˌænɪs'θɛtɪk) *n., adj.* the usual U.S. spelling of **anaesthetic.**

anesthetist (ə'nɛsθətɪst) *n.* (in the U.S.) a person qualified to administer anaesthesia, often a nurse or someone other than a physician.

aneurysm *or* **aneurism** ('ænjəˌrɪzəm) *n.* a sac formed by abnormal dilation of the weakened wall of a blood vessel. [C15: < Gk *aneurusma,* < *aneurunein* to dilate]

anew (ə'njuː) *adv.* **1.** once more. **2.** in a different way; afresh. [OE *of nīwe;* see OF, NEW]

angary ('æŋgərɪ) *n. Law.* the right of a belligerent state to use the property of a neutral state or to destroy it subject to payment of compensation to the owners. [C19: < F, < LL *angaria* enforced service, < Gk *angaros* courier]

angel ('eɪndʒəl) *n.* **1.** one of a class of spiritual beings attendant upon God. In medieval angelology they are divided by rank into nine orders. **2.** a divine messenger from God. **3.** a guardian spirit. **4.** a conventional representation of any of these beings, depicted in human form with wings. **5.** *Inf.* a person who is kind, pure, or beautiful. **6.** *Inf.* an investor, esp. in a theatrical production. **7.** Also called: **angel-noble.** a former English gold coin with a representation of the archangel Michael on it. **8.** *Inf.* an unexplained signal on a radar screen. [OE, < LL *angelus,* < Gk *angelos* messenger]

angel cake *or esp. U.S.* **angel food cake** *n.* a very light sponge cake made without egg yolks.

angelfish ('eɪndʒəlˌfɪʃ) *n., pl.* **-fish** *or* **-fishes. 1.** any of various small tropical marine fishes which have a deep flattened brightly coloured body. **2.** a South American freshwater fish having a compressed body and large dorsal and anal fins: a popular aquarium fish. **3.** a shark with flattened pectoral fins.

angelic (æn'dʒɛlɪk) *adj.* **1.** of or relating to angels. **2.** Also: **angelical.** resembling an angel in beauty, etc. —**an'gelically** *adv.*

angelica (æn'dʒɛlɪkə) *n.* **1.** an umbelliferous plant, the aromatic seeds, leaves, and stems of which are used in medicine and cookery. **2.** the candied stems of this plant, used for decorating and flavouring sweet dishes. [C16: < Med. L (*herba*) *angelica* angelic herb]

Angelus ('ændʒɪləs) *n. R.C. Church.* **1.** a series of prayers recited in the morning, at midday, and in the evening. **2.** the bell (**Angelus bell**) signalling the times of these prayers. [C17: L, < *Angelus domini nuntiavit Mariae* the angel of the Lord brought tidings to Mary]

anger ('æŋgə) *n.* **1.** a feeling of great annoyance or antagonism as the result of some real or supposed grievance; rage; wrath. ~*vb.* (*tr.*) **2.** to make angry; enrage. [C12: < ON *angr* grief]

Angevin ('ændʒɪvɪn) *n.* **1.** a native or inhabitant of Anjou, in France. **2.** *History.* a member of the Plantagenet royal line, esp. one of the kings of England from Henry II to Richard II (1154–1216). ~*adj.* **3.** of Anjou or its inhabitants. **4.** of the Plantagenet kings of England.

angina (æn'dʒaɪnə) *n.* **1.** any disease marked by

painful attacks of spasmodic choking. **2.** short for **angina pectoris.** [C16: < L: quinsy, < Gk *ankhonē* a strangling]

angina pectoris (ˈpɛktərɪs) *n.* a sudden intense pain in the chest, caused by momentary lack of adequate blood supply to the heart muscle. Sometimes shortened to **angina.** [C18: NL: angina of the chest]

angioma (ˌændʒɪˈəʊmə) *n., pl.* **-mas** *or* **-mata** (-mətə). a tumour consisting of a mass of blood vessels or a mass of lymphatic vessels.

angiosperm (ˈændʒɪəˌspɜːm) *n.* any seed-bearing plant in which the ovules are enclosed in an ovary which develops into the fruit after fertilization; any flowering plant. Cf. **gymnosperm.**

angle[1] (ˈæŋgᵊl) *n.* **1.** the space between two straight lines or two planes that extend from a common point. **2.** the shape formed by two such lines or planes. **3.** the extent to which one such line or plane diverges from the other, measured in degrees or radians. **4.** a recess; corner. **5.** point of view: *look at the question from another angle.* **6.** See **angle iron.** ~*vb.* **7.** to move in or bend into angles or an angle. **8.** (*tr.*) to produce (an article, statement, etc.) with a particular point of view. **9.** (*tr.*) to present or place at an angle. **10.** (*intr.*) to turn in a different direction. [C14: < F, < OL *angulus* corner]

angle[2] (ˈæŋgᵊl) *vb.* (*intr.*) **1.** to fish with a hook and line. **2.** (often foll. by *for*) to attempt to get: *he angled for a compliment.* ~*n.* **3.** *Obs.* a fish-hook. [OE *angul* fish-hook]

Angle (ˈæŋgᵊl) *n.* a member of a people from N Germany who invaded and settled large parts of E and N England in the 5th and 6th centuries A.D. [< L *Anglus,* of Gmc origin, an inhabitant of *Angul,* a district in Schleswig, a name identical with OE *angul* hook, ANGLE[2], referring to its shape] —ˈ**Anglian** *adj., n.*

angle iron *n.* an iron or a steel structural bar that has an L-shaped cross section. Also called: **angle, angle bar.**

angle of incidence *n.* **1.** the angle that a line or beam of radiation makes with a line perpendicular to the surface at the point of incidence. **2.** the angle between the chord line of an aircraft wing or tailplane and the aircraft's longitudinal axis.

angle of reflection *n.* the angle that a beam of reflected radiation makes with the normal to a surface at the point of reflection.

angle of refraction *n.* the angle that a refracted beam of radiation makes with the normal to the surface between two media at the point of refraction.

angle of repose *n.* the maximum angle to the horizontal at which rock, soil, etc., will remain without sliding.

angler (ˈæŋglə) *n.* **1.** a person who fishes with a hook and line. **2.** Also called: **angler fish.** any of various spiny-finned fishes which live at the bottom of the sea and typically have a long movable dorsal fin with which they lure their prey.

Anglican (ˈæŋglɪkən) *adj.* **1.** denoting or relating to the Church of England or one of the churches in communion with it. ~*n.* **2.** a member of the Anglican Church. [C17: < Med. L, < *Anglicus* English, < L *Anglī* the Angles]

Anglicism (ˈæŋglɪˌsɪzəm) *n.* **1.** a word, or idiom peculiar to the English language, esp. as spoken in England. **2.** an English mannerism, custom, etc. **3.** the fact of being English.

anglicize *or* **-cise** (ˈæŋglɪˌsaɪz) *vb.* **-cizing, -cized** *or* **-cising, -cised.** (*sometimes cap.*) to make or become English in outlook, form, etc.

angling (ˈæŋglɪŋ) *n.* the art or sport of catching fish with a baited hook or other lure, such as a fly; fishing.

Anglo (ˈæŋgləʊ) *n., pl.* **-glos.** **1.** *U.S.* a White inhabitant of the U.S. who is not of Latin extraction. **2.** *Canad.* an English-speaking Canadian, esp. one of Anglo-Celtic origin; an Anglo-Canadian.

Anglo- *combining form.* denoting English or England: *Anglo-Saxon.* [< Med. L *Anglii*]

Anglo-American *adj.* **1.** of relations between England and the United States. ~*n.* **2.** *Chiefly U.S.* an inhabitant of the United States who was or whose ancestors were born in England.

Anglo-Catholic *adj.* **1.** of or relating to a group within the Anglican Church that emphasizes the Catholic elements in its teaching and practice. ~*n.* **2.** a member of this group. —ˌ**Anglo-Caˈtholiˌcism** *n.*

Anglo-French *adj.* **1.** of England and France. **2.** of Anglo-French. ~*n.* **3.** the Norman-French language of medieval England.

Anglo-Indian *adj.* **1.** of England and India. **2.** denoting or relating to Anglo-Indians. **3.** (of a word) introduced into English from an Indian language. ~*n.* **4.** a person of mixed English and Indian descent. **5.** an Englishman who lives or has lived for a long time in India.

Anglomania (ˌæŋgləʊˈmeɪnɪə) *n.* excessive respect for English customs, etc. —ˌ**Angloˈmaniˌac** *n.*

Anglo-Norman *adj.* **1.** relating to the Norman conquerors of England, their society, or their language. ~*n.* **2.** a Norman inhabitant of England after 1066. **3.** the Anglo-French language.

Anglophile (ˈæŋgləʊfɪl, -ˌfaɪl) *or* **Anglophil** *n.* a person having admiration for England or the English.

Anglophobe (ˈæŋgləʊˌfəʊb) *n.* a person who hates or fears England or its people.

Anglophone (ˈæŋgləˌfəʊn) (*often not cap.*) ~*n.* **1.** a person who speaks English. ~*adj.* **2.** speaking English.

Anglo-Saxon *n.* **1.** a member of any of the West Germanic tribes that settled in Britain from the 5th century A.D. **2.** the language of these tribes. See **Old English.** **3.** any White person whose native language is English. **4.** *Inf.* plain blunt English. ~*adj.* **5.** forming part of the Germanic element in Modern English: *"forget" is an Anglo-Saxon word.* **6.** of the Anglo-Saxons or the Old English language. **7.** of the White Protestant culture of Britain and the U.S.

angora (æŋˈgɔːrə) *n.* (*sometimes cap.*) **1.** the long soft hair of the Angora goat or the fur of the Angora rabbit. **2.** yarn, cloth, or clothing made from this hair or fur. **3.** (*as modifier*): *an angora sweater.* ~See also **mohair.** [< *Angora,* former name of Ankara, in Turkey]

Angora goat (æŋˈgɔːrə) *n.* a breed of domestic goat with long soft hair.

Angora rabbit *n.* a breed of rabbit with long silky fur.

angostura bark (ˌæŋgəˈstjʊərə) *n.* the bitter aromatic bark of certain South American trees, formerly used to reduce fever. [C18: < *Angostura,* former name for Ciudad Bolívar, town in Venezuela]

angostura bitters *pl. n.* (*often cap.*) *Trademark.* a bitter aromatic tonic, used as a flavouring in alcoholic drinks.

angry (ˈæŋgrɪ) *adj.* **-grier, -griest.** **1.** feeling or expressing annoyance, animosity, or resentment. **2.** suggestive of anger: *angry clouds.* **3.** severely inflamed: *an angry sore.* —ˈ**angrily** *adv.*

angst (æŋst) *n.* an acute but nonspecific sense of anxiety or remorse. [G]

angstrom (ˈæŋstrəm) *n.* a unit of length equal to 10^{-10} metre, used principally to express the wavelengths of electromagnetic radiations. Symbol: Å or A Also called: **angstrom unit.** [C20: after Anders J. *Ångström* (1814-74), Swedish physicist]

anguine (ˈæŋgwɪn) *adj.* of or similar to a snake. [C17: < L *anguīnus,* < *anguis* snake]

anguish (ˈæŋgwɪʃ) *n.* **1.** extreme pain or misery; mental or physical torture; agony. ~*vb.* **2.** to afflict or be afflicted with anguish. [C13: < OF *angoisse* a strangling, < L, < *angustus* narrow] —ˈ**anguished** *adj.*

angular (ˈæŋgjʊlə) *adj.* **1.** lean or bony. **2.** awkward or stiff. **3.** having an angle or angles. **4.**

placed at an angle. **5.** measured by an angle or by the rate at which an angle changes: *angular momentum; angular velocity.* [C15: < L *angulāris,* < *angulus* ANGLE[1]]

angularity (ˌæŋgjʊˈlærɪtɪ) *n., pl.* **-ties.** **1.** the condition of being angular. **2.** an angular shape.

anhedral (ænˈhiːdrəl) *n.* the downward inclination of an aircraft wing in relation to the lateral axis.

anhydride (ænˈhaɪdraɪd) *n.* **1.** a compound that has been formed from another compound by dehydration. **2.** a compound that forms an acid or base when added to water. [C19: < ANHYDR(OUS) + -IDE]

anhydrous (ænˈhaɪdrəs) *adj.* containing no water, esp. no water of crystallization. [C19: < Gk *anudros;* see AN-, HYDRO-]

anil (ˈænɪl) *n.* a leguminous West Indian shrub which is a source of indigo. Also called: **indigo.** [C16: < Port., < Ar. *an-nīl,* the indigo]

aniline (ˈænɪlɪn, -ˌliːn) *n.* a colourless oily poisonous liquid used in the manufacture of dyes, plastics, and explosives. Formula: $C_6H_5NH_2$.

aniline dye *n.* any synthetic dye originally made from aniline, found in coal tar.

anima (ˈænɪmə) *n.* (in Jungian psychology) **a.** the feminine principle as present in the male unconscious. **b.** the inner personality. [L: air, breath, spirit, fem. of ANIMUS]

animadversion (ˌænɪmædˈvɜːʃən) *n.* criticism or censure.

animadvert (ˌænɪmædˈvɜːt) *vb.* (*intr.*) **1.** (usually foll. by *on* or *upon*) to comment with strong criticism (upon); make censorious remarks (about). **2.** to make an observation or comment. [C16: < L *animadvertere* to notice, < *animus* mind + *advertere* to turn to]

animal (ˈænɪməl) *n.* **1.** *Zool.* any living organism characterized by voluntary movement, the possession of specialized sense organs enabling rapid response to stimuli, and the ingestion of complex organic substances. **2.** any mammal, esp. except man. **3.** a brutish person. **4.** *Facetious.* a person or thing (esp. in **no such animal**). ~*adj.* **5.** of, relating to, or derived from animals. **6.** of or relating to physical needs or desires; carnal; sensual. [C14: < L, < *animālis* (adj.) living, breathing; see ANIMA]

animalcule (ˌænɪˈmælkjuːl) *n.* a microscopic animal such as an amoeba or rotifer. [C16: < NL *animalculum* a small animal] —**ˌaniˈmalcular** *adj.*

animal husbandry *n.* the science of breeding, rearing, and caring for farm animals.

animalism (ˈænɪməˌlɪzəm) *n.* **1.** preoccupation with physical matters; sensuality. **2.** the doctrine that man lacks a spiritual nature. **3.** a mode of behaviour typical of animals.

animality (ˌænɪˈmælɪtɪ) *n.* **1.** the animal side of man, as opposed to the intellectual or spiritual. **2.** the characteristics of an animal.

animalize *or* **-ise** (ˈænɪməˌlaɪz) *vb.* (*tr.*) to rouse to brutality or sensuality or make brutal or sensual. —**ˌanimaliˈzation** *or* **-iˈsation** *n.*

animal magnetism *n.* **1.** the quality of being attractive, esp. to members of the opposite sex. **2.** *Obs.* hypnotism.

animal spirits *pl. n.* boisterous exuberance. [from a vital force once supposed to be dispatched by the brain to all points of the body]

animate *vb.* (ˈænɪˌmeɪt). (*tr.*) **1.** to give life to or cause to come alive. **2.** to make gay or lively. **3.** to encourage or inspire. **4.** to impart motion to. **5.** to record on film or video tape so as to give movement to. ~*adj.* (ˈænɪmɪt). **6.** having life. **7.** gay, spirited, or lively. [C16: < L *animāre* to make alive, < *anima* breath, spirit] —**ˈaniˌmatedly** *adv.*

animated cartoon *n.* a film produced by photographing a series of gradually changing drawings, etc., which give the illusion of movement when the series is projected rapidly.

animation (ˌænɪˈmeɪʃən) *n.* **1.** vivacity. **2.** the condition of being alive. **3.** the techniques used in the production of animated cartoons.

animato (ˌænɪˈmɑːtəʊ) *adj., adv. Music.* lively; animated. [It.]

animé (ˈænɪˌmeɪ, -mɪ) *n.* any of various resins, esp. that obtained from a tropical American leguminous tree. [F: <?]

animism (ˈænɪˌmɪzəm) *n.* **1.** the belief that natural objects possess souls. **2.** (in the philosophies of Plato and Pythagoras) the hypothesis that there is an immaterial force that animates the universe. [C19: < L *anima* vital breath, spirit] —**animistic** (ˌænɪˈmɪstɪk) *adj.*

animosity (ˌænɪˈmɒsɪtɪ) *n., pl.* **-ties.** a powerful and active dislike or hostility. [C15: < LL *animōsitās,* < ANIMUS]

animus (ˈænɪməs) *n.* **1.** intense dislike; hatred; animosity. **2.** motive or purpose. **3.** (in Jungian psychology) the masculine principle present in the female unconscious. [C19: < L: mind, spirit]

anion (ˈænˌaɪən) *n.* a negatively charged ion; an ion that is attracted to the anode during electrolysis. [C19: < ANA- + ION] —**anionic** (ˌænaɪˈɒnɪk) *adj.*

anise (ˈænɪs) *n.* a Mediterranean umbelliferous plant having clusters of small yellowish-white flowers and liquorice-flavoured seeds. [C13: < OF *anis,* via L < Gk *anison*]

aniseed (ˈænɪˌsiːd) *n.* the liquorice-flavoured aromatic seeds of the anise plant, used medicinally for expelling intestinal gas and in cookery.

anisette (ˌænɪˈzɛt, -ˈsɛt) *n.* a liquorice-flavoured liqueur made from aniseed. [C19: < F]

anisotropic (ænˌaɪsəʊˈtrɒpɪk) *adj.* **1.** having different physical properties in different directions: *anisotropic crystals.* **2.** (of a plant) responding unequally to an external stimulus in different parts. —**anˌisoˈtropically** *adv.* —**anisotropy** (ˌænaɪˈsɒtrəpɪ) *n.*

ankh (æŋk) *n.* a tau cross with a loop on the top, symbolizing eternal life: often appearing in Egyptian personal names, such as Tutankhamen. [< Egyptian *'nh* life, soul]

ankle (ˈæŋkəl) *n.* **1.** the joint connecting the leg and the foot. **2.** the part of the leg just above the foot. [C14: < ON]

ankle biter *n. Austral. sl.* a child.

anklebone (ˈæŋkəlˌbəʊn) *n.* the nontechnical name for **talus**[1].

anklet (ˈæŋklɪt) *n.* an ornamental chain worn around the ankle.

ankylose *or* **anchylose** (ˈæŋkɪˌləʊz) *vb.* (of bones in a joint, etc.) to fuse or stiffen by ankylosis.

ankylosis *or* **anchylosis** (ˌæŋkɪˈləʊsɪs) *n.* abnormal adhesion or immobility of the bones in a joint, as by a fibrous growth of tissues within the joint. [C18: < NL, < Gk *ankuloun* to crook] —**ankylotic** *or* **anchylotic** (ˌæŋkɪˈlɒtɪk) *adj.*

anna (ˈænə) *n.* a former Indian coin, worth one sixteenth of a rupee. [C18: < Hindi *ānā*]

annals (ˈænəlz) *pl. n.* **1.** yearly records of events. **2.** history in general. **3.** regular reports of the work of a society, learned body, etc. [C16: < L (*librī*) *annālēs* yearly (books), < *annus* year] —**ˈannalist** *n.* —**ˌannalˈistic** *adj.*

annates (ˈæneɪts, -əts) *pl. n. R.C. Church.* the first year's revenue of a see, etc., paid to the pope. [C16: < F, < Med. L *annāta,* < L *annus* year]

annatto *or* **anatto** (əˈnætəʊ) *n., pl.* **-tos.** **1.** a small tropical American tree having pulpy seeds that yield a dye. **2.** the yellowish-red dye obtained from the seeds of this tree, used for colouring fabrics, butter, varnish, etc. [< Carib]

anneal (əˈniːl) *vb.* **1.** to temper or toughen (something) by heat treatment to remove internal stress, crystal defects, and dislocations. **2.** (*tr.*) to toughen or strengthen (the will, determination, etc.). ~*n.* **3.** an act of annealing. [OE *onǣlan,* < ON + *ǣlan* to burn, < *āl* fire] —**anˈnealer** *n.*

annelid (ˈænəlɪd) *n.* **1.** a worm in which the body is divided into segments both externally and internally, as the earthworms. ~*adj.* **2.** of such worms. [C19: < NL *Annelida,* < OF, ult. < L *ānulus* ring] —**annelidan** (əˈnɛlɪdən) *n., adj.*

annex *vb.* (æˈnɛks). (*tr.*) **1.** to join or add, esp.

to something larger. **2.** to add (territory) by conquest or occupation. **3.** to add or append as a condition, etc. **4.** to appropriate without permission. ~*n.* ('ænɛks). **5.** a variant spelling (esp. U.S.) of **annexe.** [C14: < Med. L, < L *annectere* to attach to, < *nectere* to join] —**an'nexable** *adj.* —**,annex'ation** *n.*

annexe *or esp. U.S.* **annex** ('ænɛks) *n.* **1. a.** an extension to a main building. **b.** a building used as an addition to a main one nearby. **2.** something added, esp. a supplement to a document.

annihilate (ə'naɪə,leɪt) *vb.* (*tr.*) **1.** to destroy completely; extinguish. **2.** *Inf.* to defeat totally, as in argument. [C16: < LL, < L *nihil* nothing] —**an,nihi'lation** *n.* —**an'nihi,lator** *n.*

anniversary (,ænɪ'vɜːsərɪ) *n., pl.* **-ries. 1.** the date on which an event occurred in some previous year: *a wedding anniversary.* **2.** the celebration of this. ~*adj.* **3.** of or relating to an anniversary. [C13: < L *anniversārius* returning every year, < *annus* year + *vertere* to turn]

anno Domini ('ænəʊ 'dɒmɪ,naɪ, -,niː) **1.** the full form of **A.D. 2.** *Inf.* advancing old age. [L: in the year of our Lord]

annotate ('ænəʊ,teɪt, 'ænə,teɪt) *vb.* to supply (a written work) with critical or explanatory notes. [C18: < L *annotāre,* < *nota* mark] —**'anno,tative** *adj.* —**'anno,tator** *n.*

annotation (,ænəʊ'teɪʃən, ,ænə'teɪʃən) *n.* **1.** the act of annotating. **2.** a note added in explanation, etc., esp. of some literary work.

announce (ə'naʊns) *vb.* **1.** (*tr.; may take a clause as object*) to make known publicly. **2.** (*tr.*) to declare the arrival of: *to announce a guest.* **3.** (*tr.; may take a clause as object*) to presage: *the dark clouds announced rain.* **4.** (*intr.*) to work as an announcer, as on radio or television. [C15: < OF, < L *annuntiāre,* < *nuntius* messenger] —**an'nouncement** *n.*

announcer (ə'naʊnsə) *n.* a person who announces, esp. one who reads the news, etc., on radio or television.

annoy (ə'nɔɪ) *vb.* **1.** to irritate or displease. **2.** to harass with repeated attacks. [C13: < OF, < LL *inodiāre* to make hateful, < L *in odiō* (*esse*) (to be) hated, < *odium* hatred] —**an'noyer** *n.* —**an'noying** *adj.* —**an'noyingly** *adv.*

annoyance (ə'nɔɪəns) *n.* **1.** the feeling of being annoyed. **2.** the act of annoying. **3.** a person or thing that annoys.

annual ('ænjʊəl) *adj.* **1.** occurring, done, etc., once a year or every year; yearly: *an annual income.* **2.** lasting for a year: *an annual subscription.* ~*n.* **3.** a plant that completes its life cycle in one year. **4.** a book, magazine, etc., published once every year. [C14: < LL, < L *annuus* yearly, < *annus* year] —**'annually** *adv.*

annual general meeting *n.* the statutory meeting of the directors and shareholders of a company or of the members of a society, held once every financial year. Abbrev.: **AGM.**

annualize *or* **-ise** ('ænjʊə,laɪz) *vb.* (*tr.*) to calculate for a shorter period as though on the basis of a full year: *an annualized percentage rate.*

annual ring *n.* a ring indicating one year's growth, seen in the transverse section of stems and roots of woody plants. Also called: **tree ring.**

annuitant (ə'njuːɪtənt) *n.* a person in receipt of or entitled to an annuity.

annuity (ə'njuːɪtɪ) *n., pl.* **-ties.** a fixed sum payable at specified intervals over a period, such as the recipient's life, or in perpetuity, in return for a premium paid either in instalments or in a single payment. [C15: < F, < Med. L *annuitās,* < L *annuus* ANNUAL]

annul (ə'nʌl) *vb.* **-nulling, -nulled.** (*tr.*) to make (something, esp. a law or marriage) void; abolish. [C14: < OF, < LL *adnullāre* to bring to nothing, < L *nullus* not any] —**an'nullable** *adj.*

annular ('ænjʊlə) *adj.* ring-shaped. [C16: < L *annulāris,* < *annulus, ānulus* ring]

annular eclipse *n.* an eclipse of the sun in which the moon does not cover the entire disc of the sun, so that a ring of sunlight surrounds the shadow of the moon.

annular ligament *n. Anat.* any of various ligaments that encircle a part, such as the wrist.

annulate ('ænjʊlɪt, -,leɪt) *adj.* having, composed of, or marked with rings. [C19: < L *ānulātus,* < *ānulus* a ring] —**,annu'lation** *n.*

annulet ('ænjʊlɪt) *n.* **1.** *Archit.* a moulding in the form of a ring. **2.** *Heraldry.* a ring-shaped device on a shield. **3.** a little ring. [C16: < L *ānulus* ring + -ET]

annulment (ə'nʌlmənt) *n.* **1.** a formal invalidation, as of a marriage, judicial proceeding, etc. **2.** the act of annulling.

annulus ('ænjʊləs) *n., pl.* **-li** (-,laɪ) *or* **-luses. 1.** the area between two concentric circles. **2.** a ring-shaped part. [C16: < L, var. of *ānulus* ring]

annunciate (ə'nʌnsɪ,eɪt, -ʃɪ-) *vb.* (*tr.*) a less common word for **announce.** [C16: < Med L < L *annuntiāre;* see ANNOUNCE]

Annunciation (ə,nʌnsɪ'eɪʃən) *n.* **1. the.** the announcement of the Incarnation by the angel Gabriel to the Virgin Mary (Luke 1:26–38). **2.** Also called: **Annunciation Day.** the festival commemorating this, on March 25 (Lady Day).

annunciator (ə'nʌnsɪ,eɪtə) *n.* **1.** a device that gives a visual indication as to which of a number of electric circuits has operated, such as an indicator showing in which room a bell has been rung. **2.** a device giving an audible signal indicating the position of a train. **3.** an announcer.

annus mirabilis *Latin.* ('ænʊs mɪ'ræbɪlɪs) *n., pl.* ***anni mirabiles*** ('ænaɪ mɪ'ræbɪliːz). a year of wonders, catastrophes, or other notable events.

anoa (ə'nəʊə) *n.* the smallest of the cattle tribe, having small straight horns and inhabiting the island of Celebes in Indonesia. [< a native name in Celebes]

anode ('ænəʊd) *n.* **1.** the positive electrode in an electrolytic cell or in an electronic valve or tube. **2.** the negative terminal of a primary cell. Cf. **cathode.** [C19: < Gk *anodos* a way up, < *hodos* a way; alluding to the movement of the current] —**anodal** (eɪ'nəʊdᵊl) *or* **anodic** (ə'nɒdɪk) *adj.*

anodize *or* **-dise** ('ænə,daɪz) *vb.* to coat (a metal, such as aluminium) with a protective oxide film by electrolysis.

anodyne ('ænə,daɪn) *n.* **1.** a drug that relieves pain. **2.** anything that alleviates mental distress. ~*adj.* **3.** capable of relieving pain or distress. [C16: < L, < Gk *anōdunos* painless, < AN- + *odunē* pain]

anoint (ə'nɔɪnt) *vb.* (*tr.*) **1.** to smear or rub over with oil. **2.** to apply oil to as a sign of consecration or sanctification. [C14: < OF, < L *inunguere,* < IN-[2] + *unguere* to smear with oil] —**a'nointer** *n.* —**a'nointment** *n.*

anomalistic (ə,nɒmə'lɪstɪk) *adj.* **1.** *Astron.* **a.** (of a month) measured between successive perigees of the moon. **b.** (of a year) between successive perihelia of the earth. **2.** anomalous.

anomalous (ə'nɒmələs) *adj.* deviating from the normal or usual order, type, etc. [C17: < LL, < Gk *anōmalos* uneven, inconsistent, < AN- + *homalos* even, < *homos* one and the same] —**a'nomalousness** *n.*

anomaly (ə'nɒməlɪ) *n., pl.* **-lies. 1.** something anomalous. **2.** deviation from the normal; irregularity. **3.** *Astron.* the angle between a planet, the sun, and the previous perihelion of the planet.

anomie *or* **anomy** ('ænəʊmɪ) *n. Sociol.* lack of social or moral standards in an individual or society. [< Gk *anomia* lawlessness, < A-[1] + *nomos* law] —**anomic** (ə'nɒmɪk) *adj.*

anon (ə'nɒn) *adv. Arch. or literary.* **1.** soon. **2. ever and anon.** now and then. [OE *on āne,* lit.: in one, that is, immediately]

anon. *abbrev. for* anonymous.

anonym ('ænənɪm) *n.* **1.** a less common word for **pseudonym. 2.** an anonymous person or publication.

anonymous (ə'nɒnɪməs) *adj.* **1.** from or by a person, author, etc., whose name is unknown or withheld. **2.** having no known name. **3.** lacking individual characteristics. **4.** (*often cap.*) denoting an organization which provides help to applicants who remain anonymous: *Alcoholics Anonymous.* [C17: via LL < Gk *anōnumos,* < AN- + *onoma* name] **—anonymity** (ˌænəˈnɪmɪtɪ) *n.*

anopheles (əˈnɒfɪˌliːz) *n., pl.* **-les.** any of various mosquitoes constituting the genus *Anopheles,* some species of which transmit the malaria parasite to man. [C19: via NL < Gk *anōphelēs* useless, < AN- + *ōphelein* to help]

anorak (ˈænəˌræk) *n.* a warm waterproof hip-length jacket usually with a hood. [< Eskimo *ánorâq*]

anorexia (ˌænɒˈrɛksɪə) *n.* **1.** loss of appetite. **2.** Also called: **anorexia nervosa** (nɜːˈvəʊsə). a disorder characterized by fear of becoming fat and refusal of food, leading to debility and even death. [C17: via NL < Gk, < AN- + *orexis* appetite] **—ˌanoˈrectic** *or* **ˌanoˈrexic** *adj., n.*

anosmia (ænˈɒzmɪə, -ˈɒs-) *n.* loss of the sense of smell. [C19: < NL, < AN- + Gk *osmē* smell] **—anosmatic** (ˌænɒzˈmætɪk) *or* **anˈosmic** *adj.*

another (əˈnʌðə) *determiner.* **1. a.** one more: *another chance.* **b.** (*as pron.*): *help yourself to another.* **2. a.** a different: *another era from ours.* **b.** (*as pron.*): *to try one, then another.* **3. a.** a different example of the same sort. **b.** (*as pron.*): *we got rid of one, but I think this is another.* [C14: orig. *an other*]

A.N. Other *n. Brit.* an unnamed person: used in team lists, etc., to indicate a place that remains to be filled.

anoxia (ænˈɒksɪə) *n.* lack or deficiency of oxygen. [C20: < AN- + OX(YGEN) + -IA] **—anˈoxic** *adj.*

Anschluss (ˈænʃlʊs) *n.* a political or economic union, esp. the annexation of Austria by Nazi Germany (1938). [G, < *anschliessen* to join]

anserine (ˈænsəˌraɪn) *adj.* of or resembling a goose. [C19: < L *anserīnus,* < *anser* goose]

answer (ˈɑːnsə) *n.* **1.** a reply, either spoken or written, as to a question, request, letter, or article. **2.** a reaction or response: *drunkenness was his answer to disappointment.* **3.** a solution, esp. of a mathematical problem. *~vb.* **4.** (when *tr., may take a clause as object*) to reply or respond (to) by word or act: *to answer a question; to answer the door.* **5.** (*tr.*) to reply correctly to; solve: *I could answer only three questions.* **6.** (*intr.;* usually foll. by *to*) to respond or react: *the steering answers to the slightest touch.* **7. a.** (when *intr.,* often foll. by *for*) to meet the requirements (of); be satisfactory (for): *this will answer his needs.* **b.** to be responsible (to a person or for a thing). **8.** (when *intr.,* foll. by *to*) to match or correspond (esp. in **answer** (*or* **answer to**) **the description**). **9.** (*tr.*) to give a defence or refutation of (a charge) or in (an argument). [OE *andswaru* an answer; see SWEAR]

answerable (ˈɑːnsərəbᵊl) *adj.* **1.** (*postpositive;* foll. by *for* or *to*) responsible or accountable: *answerable to one's boss.* **2.** able to be answered.

answer back *vb.* (*adv.*) to reply rudely to (a person, esp. someone in authority) when one is expected to remain silent.

answering machine *n.* a device by which a telephone call is answered automatically and the caller leaves a recorded message. In full: **telephone answering machine.**

ant (ænt) *n.* **1.** a small social insect of a widely distributed hymenopterous family, typically living in highly organized colonies of winged males, wingless sterile females (workers), and fertile females (queens). Related adj.: **formic. 2. white ant.** another name for a **termite.** [OE *ǣmette*]

-ant *suffix forming adjectives and nouns.* causing or performing an action or existing in a certain condition: *pleasant; deodorant; servant.* [< L *-ant,* ending of present participles of the first conjugation]

antacid (æntˈæsɪd) *n.* **1.** a substance used to treat acidity, esp. in the stomach. *~adj.* **2.** having the properties of this substance.

antagonism (ænˈtægəˌnɪzəm) *n.* **1.** openly expressed and usually mutual opposition. **2.** the inhibiting or nullifying action of one substance or organism on another.

antagonist (ænˈtægənɪst) *n.* **1.** an opponent or adversary. **2.** any muscle that opposes the action of another. **3.** a drug that counteracts the effects of another drug. **—anˌtagoˈnistic** *adj.* **—anˌtagoˈnistically** *adv.*

antagonize *or* **-nise** (ænˈtægəˌnaɪz) *vb.* (*tr.*) **1.** to make hostile; annoy or irritate. **2.** to act in opposition to or counteract. [C17: < Gk, < ANTI- + *agōnizesthai* to strive, < *agōn* contest] **—anˌtagoniˈzation** *or* **-niˈsation** *n.*

antalkali (æntˈælkəˌlaɪ) *n., pl.* **-lis** *or* **-lies.** a substance that neutralizes alkalis.

Antarctic (æntˈɑːktɪk) *adj.* of or relating to the south polar regions. [C14: via L < Gk *antarktikos;* see ANTI-, ARCTIC]

Antarctic Circle *n.* the imaginary circle around the earth, parallel to the equator, at latitude 66° 32′ S.

ant bear *n.* another name for **aardvark.**

ante (ˈæntɪ) *n.* **1.** the gaming stake put up before the deal in poker by the players. **2.** *Inf.* a sum of money representing a person's share, as in a syndicate. *~vb.* **-teing, -ted** *or* **-teed. 3.** to place (one's stake) in poker. **4.** (usually foll. by *up*) *Inf.* to pay.

ante- *prefix.* before in time or position: *antedate; antechamber.* [< L]

anteater (ˈæntˌiːtə) *n.* any of several toothless mammals having a long tubular snout used for eating termites.

antebellum (ˌæntɪˈbɛləm) *adj.* of or during the period before a war, esp. the American Civil War. [L *ante bellum,* lit.: before the war]

antecede (ˌæntɪˈsiːd) *vb.* (*tr.*) to go before; precede. [C17: < L *antecēdere,* < *cēdere* to go]

antecedent (ˌæntɪˈsiːdᵊnt) *n.* **1.** an event, etc., that happens before another. **2.** *Grammar.* a word or phrase to which a pronoun refers. In "People who live in glass houses shouldn't throw stones," *people* is the antecedent of *who.* **3.** *Logic.* the first hypothetical clause in a conditional statement. *~adj.* **4.** preceding in time or order; prior. **—ˌanteˈcedence** *n.*

antecedents (ˌæntɪˈsiːdᵊnts) *pl. n.* **1.** ancestry. **2.** a person's past history.

antechamber (ˈæntɪˌtʃeɪmbə) *n.* an anteroom. [C17: < OF, < It. *anticamera;* see ANTE-, CHAMBER]

antedate (ˈæntɪˌdeɪt) *vb.* (*tr.*) **1.** to be or occur at an earlier date than. **2.** to affix or assign a date to (a document, event, etc.) that is earlier than the actual date. **3.** to cause to occur sooner. *~n.* **4.** an earlier date.

antediluvian (ˌæntɪdɪˈluːvɪən) *adj.* **1.** belonging to the ages before the biblical Flood. **2.** old-fashioned. *~n.* **3.** an antediluvian person or thing. [C17: < ANTE- + L *dīluvium* flood]

antelope (ˈæntɪˌləʊp) *n., pl.* **-lopes** *or* **-lope.** any of a group of mammals of Africa and Asia. They are typically graceful, having long legs and horns, and include the gazelles, springbok, impala, and dik-diks. [C15: < OF, < Med. L, < LGk *antholops* a legendary beast]

antemeridian (ˌæntɪməˈrɪdɪən) *adj.* before noon; in the morning. [C17: < L]

ante meridiem (ˈæntɪ məˈrɪdɪəm) the full form of **a.m.** [L, < ANTE- + *merīdiēs* midday]

antenatal (ˌæntɪˈneɪtᵊl) *adj.* occurring or present before birth; during pregnancy.

antenna (ænˈtɛnə) *n.* **1.** (*pl.* **-nae** (-niː)) one of a pair of mobile appendages on the heads of insects, crustaceans, etc., that often respond to touch and taste but may be specialized for swimming. **2.** (*pl.* **-nas**) an aerial. [C17: < L: sail yard, <?] **—anˈtennal** *or* **anˈtennary** *adj.*

antenuptial contract (ˌæntɪˈnʌpʃəl) *n.* (in South Africa) a marriage contract effected prior to the wedding giving each partner control over his or her property.

antependium (ˌæntɪˈpɛndɪəm) *n., pl.* **-dia** (-dɪə). a covering hung over the front of an altar. [C17: < Med. L, < L ANTE- + *pendēre* to hang]

antepenult (ˌæntɪpɪˈnʌlt) *n.* the third last syllable

in a word. [C16: shortened < L (*syllaba*) *antepaenultima;* see ANTE-, PENULT]

antepenultimate (ˌæntɪpɪˈnʌltɪmɪt) *adj.* **1.** third from last. ~*n.* **2.** anything that is third from last.

anterior (ænˈtɪərɪə) *adj.* **1.** at or towards the front. **2.** earlier. **3.** *Zool.* of or near the head end. **4.** *Bot.* (of part of a flower or leaf) farthest away from the main stem. [C17: < L, comp. of *ante* before]

anteroom (ˈæntɪˌruːm, -ˌrʊm) *n.* a room giving entrance to a larger room, often used as a waiting room.

anthelion (ænˈθiːlɪən) *n., pl.* **-lia** (-lɪə). **1.** a faint halo sometimes seen in high altitude regions around a shadow cast onto fog. **2.** a white spot occasionally appearing at the same height as and opposite to the sun. [C17: < LGk, < *anthēlios* opposite the sun, < ANTE- + *hēlios* sun]

anthelmintic (ˌænθelˈmɪntɪk) *or* **anthelminthic** (ˌænθelˈmɪnθɪk) *n. Med.* another name for **vermifuge.**

anthem (ˈænθəm) *n.* **1.** a song of loyalty or devotion: *a national anthem.* **2.** a musical composition for a choir, usually set to words from the Bible. **3.** a religious chant sung antiphonally. [OE *antemne,* < LL *antiphōna* ANTIPHON]

anthemis (ænˈθiːmɪs) *n.* any of several cultivated varieties of camomile. [NL, < L, < Gk *anthos* flower]

anther (ˈænθə) *n.* the terminal part of a stamen consisting of two lobes each containing two sacs in which the pollen matures. [C18: < NL, < L, < Gk *anthēros* flowery, < *anthos* flower]

antheridium (ˌænθəˈrɪdɪəm) *n., pl.* **-ia** (-ɪə). the male sex organ of algae, fungi, mosses, etc. [C19: < NL, dim. of *anthēra* ANTHER]

ant hill *n.* a mound of soil, leaves, etc., near the entrance of an ants' nest, deposited there by the ants while constructing the nest.

anthologize *or* **-gise** (ænˈθɒləˌdʒaɪz) *vb.* to compile or put into an anthology.

anthology (ænˈθɒlədʒɪ) *n., pl.* **-gies.** **1.** a collection of literary passages, esp. poems, by various authors. **2.** any printed collection of literary pieces, songs, etc. [C17: < Med. L, < Gk, lit.: a flower gathering, < *anthos* flower + *legein* to collect] —**anˈthologist** *n.*

anthozoan (ˌænθəˈzəʊən) *n.* **1.** any of the sessile marine coelenterates of the class *Anthozoa,* including corals and sea anemones, in which the body is in the form of a polyp. ~*adj.* **2.** Also: **actinozoan.** of or relating to these.

anthracene (ˈænθrəˌsiːn) *n.* a colourless crystalline solid, used in the manufacture of chemicals and as crystals in scintillation counters. [C19: < ANTHRAX + -ENE]

anthracite (ˈænθrəˌsaɪt) *n.* a hard coal that burns slowly with a nonluminous flame giving out intense heat. Also called: **hard coal.** [C19: < L, < Gk *anthrakitēs* coal-like, < *anthrax* coal] —**anthracitic** (ˌænθrəˈsɪtɪk) *adj.*

anthrax (ˈænθræks) *n., pl.* **-thraces** (-θrəˌsiːz). **1.** a highly infectious bacterial disease of animals, esp. cattle and sheep, which can be transmitted to man. **2.** a pustule caused by this disease. [C19: < LL, < Gk: carbuncle]

anthropo- *combining form.* indicating man or human: *anthropology.* [< Gk *anthrōpos*]

anthropocentric (ˌænθrəpəʊˈsentrɪk) *adj.* regarding man as the central factor in the universe.

anthropogenesis (ˌænθrəpəʊˈdʒenɪsɪs) *or* **anthropogeny** (ˌænθrəˈpɒdʒɪnɪ) *n.* the study of the origins of man.

anthropoid (ˈænθrəˌpɔɪd) *adj.* **1.** resembling man. **2.** resembling an ape; apelike. ~*n.* **3.** any primate of the suborder *Anthropoidea,* including monkeys, apes, and man.

anthropoid ape *n.* any of a group of primates having no tail, elongated arms, and a highly developed brain, including gibbons, orang-utans, chimpanzees, and gorillas.

anthropology (ˌænθrəˈpɒlədʒɪ) *n.* the study of man, his origins, institutions, religious beliefs, social relationships, etc. —**anthropological** (ˌænθrəpəˈlɒdʒɪkᵊl) *adj.* —ˌ**anthroˈpologist** *n.*

anthropometry (ˌænθrəˈpɒmɪtrɪ) *n.* the comparative study of sizes and proportions of the human body. —**anthropometric** (ˌænθrəpəˈmetrɪk) *or* ˌ**anthropoˈmetrical** *adj.*

anthropomorphic (ˌænθrəpəˈmɔːfɪk) *adj.* **1.** of or relating to anthropomorphism. **2.** resembling the human form.

anthropomorphism (ˌænθrəpəˈmɔːfɪzəm) *n.* the attribution of human form or behaviour to a deity, animal, etc.

anthropomorphous (ˌænθrəpəˈmɔːfəs) *adj.* **1.** shaped like a human being. **2.** another word for **anthropomorphic.**

anthropophagi (ˌænθrəˈpɒfəˌgaɪ) *pl. n., sing.* **-gus** (-gəs). cannibals. [C16: < L, < Gk *anthrōpophagos;* see ANTHROPO-, -PHAGE]

anthurium (ænˈθjʊərɪəm) *n.* any of various tropical American plants, many of which are cultivated as house plants for their showy foliage and their flowers. [C19: NL, < Gk *anthos* flower + *oura* a tail]

anti (ˈæntɪ) *Inf.* ~*adj.* **1.** opposed to a party, policy, attitude, etc.: *he won't join because he is rather anti.* ~*n.* **2.** an opponent.

anti- *prefix.* **1.** against; opposing: *anticlerical.* **2.** opposite to: *anticlimax.* **3.** rival; false: *antipope.* **4.** counteracting or neutralizing: *antifreeze; antihistamine.* **5.** designating the antiparticle of the particle specified: *antineutron.* [< Gk *anti*]

anti-aircraft (ˌæntɪˈeəkrɑːft) *n.* (*modifier*) of or relating to defence against aircraft attack: *anti-aircraft batteries.*

antiar (ˈæntɪˌɑː) *n.* another name for **upas** (senses 1, 2). [< Javanese]

antiballistic missile (ˌæntɪbəˈlɪstɪk) *n.* a ballistic missile designed to destroy another ballistic missile in flight.

antibiosis (ˌæntɪbaɪˈəʊsɪs) *n.* an association between two organisms, esp. microorganisms, that is harmful to one of them.

antibiotic (ˌæntɪbaɪˈɒtɪk) *n.* **1.** any of various chemical substances, such as penicillin, produced by microorganisms, esp. fungi, or made synthetically, and capable of destroying microorganisms, esp. bacteria. ~*adj.* **2.** of or relating to antibiotics.

antibody (ˈæntɪˌbɒdɪ) *n., pl.* **-bodies.** any of various proteins produced in the blood in response to an antigen. By becoming attached to antigens on infectious organisms antibodies can render them harmless.

antic (ˈæntɪk) *Arch.* ~*n.* **1.** an actor in a ludicrous or grotesque part; clown. ~*adj.* **2.** fantastic; grotesque. ~See also: **antics.** [C16: < It. *antico* something grotesque (from its application to fantastic carvings found in ruins of ancient Rome)]

anticathode (ˌæntɪˈkæθəʊd) *n.* the target electrode for the stream of electrons in a vacuum tube, esp. an x-ray tube.

Antichrist (ˈæntɪˌkraɪst) *n.* **1.** *Bible.* the antagonist of Christ, expected by early Christians to appear and reign over the world until overthrown at Christ's Second Coming. **2.** (*sometimes not cap.*) an enemy of Christ or Christianity.

anticipant (ænˈtɪsɪpənt) *adj.* **1.** operating in advance. ~*n.* **2.** a person who anticipates.

anticipate (ænˈtɪsɪˌpeɪt) *vb.* (*mainly tr.*) **1.** (*may take a clause as object*) to foresee and act in advance of; forestall: *I anticipated his punch.* **2.** (*also intr.*) to mention (something) before its proper time: *don't anticipate the climax of the story.* **3.** (*may take a clause as object*) to regard as likely; expect. **4.** to make use of in advance of possession: *he anticipated his salary in buying a leather jacket.* [C16: < L *anticipāre* to take before, < *anti-* ANTE- + *capere* to take] —**anˈticiˌpator** *n.* —**anˈticiˌpatory** *or* **anˈticipative** *adj.*

▷ **Usage.** The use of *anticipate* to mean *expect,* while very common, is avoided by careful writers and speakers of English.

anticipation (ænˌtɪsɪˈpeɪʃən) *n.* **1.** the act of anticipating; expectation, premonition, or foresight. **2.** *Music.* an unstressed, usually short note introduced before a downbeat.

anticlerical (ˌæntɪˈklɛrɪkᵊl) *adj.* **1.** opposed to the power and influence of the clergy, esp. in politics. ~*n.* **2.** a supporter of an anticlerical party. —ˌ**antiˈclericalism** *n.*

anticlimax (ˌæntɪˈklaɪmæks) *n.* **1.** a disappointing or ineffective conclusion to a series of events, etc. **2.** a sudden change from a serious subject to one that is disappointing or ludicrous. —**anticlimactic** (ˌæntɪklaɪˈmæktɪk) *adj.*

anticline (ˈæntɪˌklaɪn) *n.* a formation of stratified rock raised up, by folding, into a broad arch so that the strata slope down on both sides from a common crest. —ˌ**antiˈclinal** *adj.*

anticlockwise (ˌæntɪˈklɒkˌwaɪz) *adv., adj.* in the opposite direction to the rotation of the hands of a clock. U.S. equivalent: **counterclockwise.**

anticoagulant (ˌæntɪkəʊˈægjʊlənt) *adj.* **1.** acting to prevent or retard coagulation, esp. of blood. ~*n.* **2.** an agent that prevents or retards coagulation.

antics (ˈæntɪks) *pl. n.* absurd acts or postures.

anticyclone (ˌæntɪˈsaɪkləʊn) *n. Meteorol.* a body of moving air of higher pressure than the surrounding air, in which the pressure decreases away from the centre. Also called: **high.** —**anticyclonic** (ˌæntɪsaɪˈklɒnɪk) *adj.*

antidepressant (ˌæntɪdɪˈprɛsᵊnt) *n.* **1.** any of a class of drugs used to alleviate depression. ~*adj.* **2.** of this class of drugs.

antidote (ˈæntɪˌdəʊt) *n.* **1.** *Med.* a drug or agent that counteracts or neutralizes the effects of a poison. **2.** anything that counteracts or relieves a harmful condition. [C15: < L, < Gk *antidoton* something given as a countermeasure, < ANTI- + *didonai* to give] —ˌ**antiˈdotal** *adj.*

antifreeze (ˈæntɪˌfriːz) *n.* a liquid, usually ethylene glycol (ethanediol), added to water to lower its freezing point, esp. for use in an internal-combustion engine.

antigen (ˈæntɪdʒən, -ˌdʒɛn) *n.* a substance, usually a toxin produced by a bacterium, that stimulates the production of antibodies. [C20: < ANTI(BODY) + -GEN]

antihero (ˈæntɪˌhɪərəʊ) *n., pl.* **-roes.** a central character in a novel, play, etc., who lacks the traditional heroic virtues.

antihistamine (ˌæntɪˈhɪstəˌmiːn, -mɪn) *n.* any drug that neutralizes the effects of histamine, used esp. in the treatment of allergies.

antiknock (ˌæntɪˈnɒk) *n.* a compound, such as lead tetraethyl, added to petrol to reduce knocking in the engine.

antilogarithm (ˌæntɪˈlɒgəˌrɪðəm) *n.* a number whose logarithm to a given base is a given number: *100 is the antilogarithm of 2 to base 10.* Often shortened to **antilog.** —ˌ**antiˌlogaˈrithmic** *adj.*

antilogy (ænˈtɪlədʒɪ) *n., pl.* **-gies.** a contradiction in terms. [C17: < Gk *antilogia*]

antimacassar (ˌæntɪməˈkæsə) *n.* a cloth covering the back and arms of chairs, etc., to prevent soiling. [C19: < ANTI- + MACASSAR (OIL)]

antimagnetic (ˌæntɪmægˈnɛtɪk) *adj.* of a material that does not acquire permanent magnetism when exposed to a magnetic field.

antimalarial (ˌæntɪməˈlɛərɪəl) *adj.* **1.** effective in the treatment of malaria. ~*n.* **2.** an antimalarial drug or agent.

antimasque (ˈæntɪˌmɑːsk) *n.* a comic dance, presented between the acts of a masque.

antimatter (ˈæntɪˌmætə) *n.* a hypothetical form of matter composed of antiparticles.

antimissile (ˌæntɪˈmɪsaɪl) *adj.* **1.** relating to defensive measures against missile attack: *an antimissile system.* ~*n.* **2.** Also called: **antimissile missile.** a defensive missile used to intercept and destroy attacking missiles.

antimony (ˈæntɪmənɪ) *n.* a toxic metallic element that exists in two allotropic forms and is added to alloys to increase their strength and hardness. Symbol: Sb; atomic no.: 51; atomic wt.: 121.75. [C15: < Med. L *antimōnium,* <?] —**antimonial** (ˌæntɪˈməʊnɪəl) *adj.*

antinomian (ˌæntɪˈnəʊmɪən) *adj.* **1.** relating to the doctrine that by faith a Christian is released from the obligation of adhering to any moral law. ~*n.* **2.** a member of a Christian sect holding such a doctrine. —ˌ**antiˈnomianism** *n.*

antinomy (ænˈtɪnəmɪ) *n., pl.* **-mies.** **1.** opposition of one law, principle, or rule to another. **2.** *Philosophy.* contradiction existing between two apparently indubitable propositions. [C16: < L, < Gk: conflict between laws, < ANTI- + *nomos* law] —**antinomic** (ˌæntɪˈnɒmɪk) *adj.*

antinovel (ˈæntɪˌnɒvᵊl) *n.* a type of prose fiction in which conventional or traditional novelistic elements are rejected.

antinuclear (ˌæntɪˈnjuːklɪə) *adj.* opposed to nuclear weapons or nuclear power.

antiparticle (ˈæntɪˌpɑːtɪkᵊl) *n.* any of a group of elementary particles that have the same mass as their corresponding particle but have a charge of equal magnitude but opposite sign. When a particle collides with its antiparticle mutual annihilation occurs.

antipasto (ˌæntɪˈpɑːstəʊ, -ˈpæs-) *n., pl.* **-tos.** a course of hors d'oeuvres in an Italian meal. [It.: before food]

antipathetic (ænˌtɪpəˈθɛtɪk, ˌæntɪpə-) *or* **antipathetical** *adj.* (often foll. by *to*) having or arousing a strong aversion.

antipathy (ænˈtɪpəθɪ) *n., pl.* **-thies.** **1.** a feeling of dislike or hostility. **2.** the object of such a feeling. [C17: < L, < Gk, < ANTI- + *patheia* feeling]

antipersonnel (ˌæntɪˌpɜːsəˈnɛl) *adj.* (of weapons, etc.) designed to cause casualties to personnel rather than to destroy equipment.

antiperspirant (ˌæntɪˈpɜːspərənt) *n.* **1.** a substance applied to the skin to reduce or prevent perspiration. ~*adj.* **2.** reducing perspiration.

antiphlogistic (ˌæntɪfləˈdʒɪstɪk) *adj.* **1.** of or relating to the prevention or alleviation of inflammation. ~*n.* **2.** an antiphlogistic drug.

antiphon (ˈæntɪfən) *n.* **1.** a short passage, usually from the Bible, recited or sung as a response after certain parts of a liturgical service. **2.** a psalm, hymn, etc., chanted or sung in alternate parts. **3.** any response. [C15: < LL *antiphōna* sung responses, < LGk, pl. of *antiphōnon* (something) responsive, < ANTI- + *phōnē* sound] —**antiphonal** (ænˈtɪfənəl) *adj.*

antiphonary (ænˈtɪfənərɪ) *n., pl.* **-naries.** a bound collection of antiphons.

antiphony (ænˈtɪfənɪ) *n., pl.* **-nies.** **1.** antiphonal singing. **2.** any musical or other sound effect that answers or echoes another.

antipode (ˈæntɪpəʊd) *n.* the exact or direct opposite. —**antipodal** (ænˈtɪpədᵊl) *adj.*

antipodes (ænˈtɪpəˌdiːz) *pl. n.* **1.** either or both of two places that are situated diametrically opposite one another on the earth's surface. **2.** the people who live there. **3.** (*often cap.*) **the.** Australia and New Zealand. [C16: via LL < Gk, pl. of *antipous* having the feet opposite, < ANTI- + *pous* foot] —**antipodean** (ænˌtɪpəˈdiːən) *adj.*

antipope (ˈæntɪˌpəʊp) *n.* a rival pope elected in opposition to one who has been canonically chosen.

antipyretic (ˌæntɪpaɪˈrɛtɪk) *adj.* **1.** preventing or alleviating fever. ~*n.* **2.** an antipyretic remedy or drug.

antiquarian (ˌæntɪˈkwɛərɪən) *adj.* **1.** concerned with the study of antiquities or antiques. ~*n.* **2.** a less common name for **antiquary.** —ˌ**antiˈquarianism** *n.*

antiquary (ˈæntɪkwərɪ) *n., pl.* **-quaries.** a person who collects, deals in, or studies antiques or ancient works of art. Also called: **antiquarian.**

antiquate (ˈæntɪˌkweɪt) *vb.* (*tr.*) to make obsolete or old-fashioned. [C15: < L *antīquāre* to make old, < *antīquus* ancient] —ˈ**antiˌquated** *adj.*

antique (ænˈtiːk) *n.* **1. a.** a decorative object, piece of furniture, or other work of art created in an earlier period, that is valued for its beauty, workmanship, and age. **b.** (*as modifier*): *an antique shop.* **2.** any object made in an earlier period. **3. the.** the style of ancient art, esp. Greek or Roman. ~*adj.* **4.** made in or in the style of an earlier period. **5.** of or belonging to the distant past, esp. of ancient Greece or Rome. **6.** *Inf.* old-fashioned. **7.** *Arch.* aged or venerable. ~*vb.* **8.** (*tr.*) to give an antique appearance to. [C16: < L *antīquus* ancient, < *ante* before]

antiquities (æn'tɪkwɪtɪz) *pl. n.* remains or relics, such as statues, buildings, or coins, that date from ancient times.

antiquity (æn'tɪkwɪtɪ) *n., pl.* **-ties.** **1.** the quality of being ancient: *a vase of great antiquity.* **2.** the far distant past, esp. preceding the Middle Ages. **3.** the people of ancient times collectively.

antirrhinum (ˌæntɪ'raɪnəm) *n.* any plant of the genus *Antirrhinum,* esp. the snapdragon, which has two-lipped flowers of various colours. [C16: via L < Gk *antirrhinon,* < ANTI- (imitating) + *rhis* nose]

antiscorbutic (ˌæntɪskɔː'bjuːtɪk) *adj.* **1.** preventing or curing scurvy. ~*n.* **2.** an antiscorbutic agent.

anti-Semite *n.* a person who persecutes or discriminates against Jews. —ˌ**anti-Se'mitic** *adj.* —ˌ**anti-'Semitism** *n.*

antisepsis (ˌæntɪ'sɛpsɪs) *n.* **1.** destruction of undesirable microorganisms, such as those that cause disease or putrefaction. **2.** the state of being free from such microorganisms.

antiseptic (ˌæntɪ'sɛptɪk) *adj.* **1.** of or producing antisepsis. **2.** entirely free from contamination. **3.** *Inf.* lacking spirit or excitement. ~*n.* **4.** an antiseptic agent. —ˌ**anti'septically** *adv.*

antiserum (ˌæntɪ'sɪərəm) *n., pl.* **-rums** *or* **-ra** (-rə). blood serum containing antibodies against a specific antigen, used to treat or provide immunity to a disease.

antisocial (ˌæntɪ'səʊʃəl) *adj.* **1.** avoiding the company of other people; unsociable. **2.** contrary or injurious to the interests of society in general.

antispasmodic (ˌæntɪspæz'mɒdɪk) *adj.* **1.** preventing or arresting spasms. ~*n.* **2.** an antispasmodic drug.

antistatic (ˌæntɪ'stætɪk) *adj.* (of a substance, textile, etc.) retaining sufficient moisture to provide a conducting path, thus avoiding the effects of static electricity.

antistrophe (æn'tɪstrəfɪ) *n.* (in ancient Greek drama) **a.** the second of two movements made by a chorus during the performance of a choral ode. **b.** the second part of a choral ode sung during this movement. ~See **strophe.** [C17: via LL < Gk *antistrophē* an answering turn, < ANTI- + *strophē* a turning]

antitank (ˌæntɪ'tæŋk) *adj.* designed to immobilize or destroy armoured vehicles.

antithesis (æn'tɪθɪsɪs) *n., pl.* **-ses** (-ˌsiːz). **1.** the exact opposite. **2.** contrast or opposition. **3.** *Rhetoric.* the juxtaposition of contrasting ideas or words to produce an effect of balance, such as *my words fly up, my thoughts remain below.* [C15: via L < Gk: a setting against, < ANTI- + *tithenai* to place] —**antithetical** (ˌæntɪ'θɛtɪkᵊl) *adj.*

antitoxin (ˌæntɪ'tɒksɪn) *n.* **1.** an antibody that neutralizes a toxin. **2.** blood serum that contains a specific antibody. —ˌ**anti'toxic** *adj.*

antitrades ('æntɪˌtreɪdz) *pl. n.* winds in the upper atmosphere blowing in the opposite direction from and above the trade winds.

antitrust (ˌæntɪ'trʌst) *n.* (*modifier*) *Chiefly U.S.* regulating or opposing trusts, monopolies, cartels, or similar organizations.

antitype ('æntɪˌtaɪp) *n.* **1.** a person or thing that is foreshadowed or represented by a type or symbol. **2.** an opposite type. —**antitypical** (ˌæntɪ'tɪpɪkᵊl) *adj.*

antivenin (ˌæntɪ'vɛnɪn) *or* **antivenene** (ˌæntɪvɪ'niːn) *n.* an antitoxin that counteracts a specific venom, esp. snake venom. [C19: < ANTI- + VEN(OM) + -IN]

antler ('æntlə) *n.* one of a pair of bony outgrowths on the heads of male deer and some related species of either sex. [C14: < OF *antoillier*] —'**antlered** *adj.*

antlion ('æntˌlaɪən) *n.* **1.** any of various insects which resemble dragonflies and are most common in tropical regions. **2.** the larva of this insect, which buries itself in the sand to await its prey.

antonomasia (ˌæntənə'meɪzɪə) *n.* **1.** the substitution of a title or epithet for a proper name, such as *his highness.* **2.** the use of a proper name for an idea: *he is a Daniel come to judgment.* [C16: via L < Gk, < *antonomazein* to name differently, < *onoma* name]

antonym ('æntənɪm) *n.* a word that means the opposite of another. [C19: < Gk, < ANTI- + *onoma* name] —**antonymous** (æn'tɒnɪməs) *adj.*

antrum ('æntrəm) *n., pl.* **-tra** (-trə). *Anat.* a natural cavity, hollow, or sinus, esp. in a bone. [C14: < L: cave, < Gk *antron*] —'**antral** *adj.*

ANU *abbrev. for* Australian National University.

anuresis (ˌænjʊ'riːsɪs) *n.* inability to urinate. [C20: NL, < AN- + Gk *ouresis* urination]

anus ('eɪnəs) *n.* the excretory opening at the end of the alimentary canal. [C16: < L]

anvil ('ænvɪl) *n.* **1.** a heavy iron or steel block on which metals are hammered during forging. **2.** any part having a similar shape or function, such as the lower part of a telegraph key. **3.** *Anat.* the nontechnical name for **incus.** [OE *anfealt*]

anxiety (æŋ'zaɪɪtɪ) *n., pl.* **-ties.** **1.** a state of uneasiness or tension caused by apprehension of possible misfortune, danger, etc. **2.** intense desire; eagerness. **3.** *Psychol.* a state of intense apprehension, common in mental illness or after a very distressing experience. [C16: < L *anxietas*]

anxious ('æŋkʃəs, 'æŋʃəs) *adj.* **1.** worried and tense because of possible misfortune, danger, etc. **2.** causing anxiety; worrying; distressing: *an anxious time.* **3.** intensely desirous: *anxious for promotion.* [C17: < L *anxius;* rel. to L *angere* to torment] —'**anxiously** *adv.* —'**anxiousness** *n.*

any ('ɛnɪ) *determiner.* **1. a.** one, some, or several, as specified, no matter how much, what kind, etc.: *you may take any clothes you like.* **b.** (*as pron.; functioning as sing. or pl.*): *take any you like.* **2.** (*usually used with a negative*) **a.** even the smallest amount or even one: *I can't stand any noise.* **b.** (*as pron.; functioning as sing. or pl.*): *don't give her any.* **3.** whatever or whichever: *any dictionary will do.* **4.** an indefinite or unlimited (amount or number): *any number of friends.* ~*adv.* **5.** (*usually used with a negative*) (foll. by a comp. adj.) to even the smallest extent: *it isn't any worse.* [OE *ǣnig*]

▷ **Usage.** Educated speakers and writers avoid using *any* for *at all* in formal English: *a translation would not help at all* (not *would not help any*).

anybody ('ɛnɪˌbɒdɪ) *pron.* **1.** any person; anyone. **2.** (*usually used with a negative or a question*) a person of any importance: *he isn't anybody.* ~*n., pl.* **-bodies.** **3.** (often preceded by *just*) any person at random.

anyhow ('ɛnɪˌhaʊ) *adv.* **1.** in any case. **2.** by any means whatever. **3.** carelessly.

any more *or esp. U.S.* **anymore** (ˌɛnɪ'mɔː) *adv.* any longer; still; nowadays.

anyone ('ɛnɪˌwʌn) *pron.* **1.** any person; anybody. **2.** (*used with a negative or a question*) a person of any importance: *is he anyone?* **3.** (often preceded by *just*) any person at random.

anyplace ('ɛnɪˌpleɪs) *adv. U.S. & Canad. inf.* anywhere.

anything ('ɛnɪˌθɪŋ) *pron.* **1.** any object, event, action, etc., whatever: *anything might happen.* ~*n.* **2.** a thing of any kind: *have you anything to declare?* ~*adv.* **3.** in any way: *he wasn't anything like his father.* **4. anything but.** not in the least: *she was anything but happy.* **5. like anything.** (intensifier): *he ran like anything.*

anyway ('ɛnɪˌweɪ) *adv.* **1.** in any case; at any rate; nevertheless. **2.** in a careless manner. **3.** Usually **any way.** in any manner.

anywhere ('ɛnɪˌwɛə) *adv.* **1.** in, at, or to any place. **2. get anywhere.** to be successful.

anywise ('ɛnɪˌwaɪz) *adv. Chiefly U.S.* in any way.

ANZAAS ('ænzəs, -zæs) *n. acronym for* Australian and New Zealand Association for the Advancement of Science.

Anzac ('ænzæk) *n.* **1.** (in World War I) a soldier

serving with the Australian and New Zealand Army Corps. **2.** (now) any Australian or New Zealand soldier. **3.** the Anzac landing at Gallipoli in 1915.

Anzac Day *n.* April 25, a public holiday in Australia and New Zealand commemorating the Anzac landing at Gallipoli in 1915.

ANZUS (ˈænzəs) *n. acronym for* Australia, New Zealand, and the United States, with reference to the security alliance between them.

AO *abbrev. for* Officer of the Order of Australia.

A/O *or* **a/o** (accounting, etc.) *abbrev. for* account of.

AOB *or* **a.o.b.** *abbrev. for* any other business.

aorist (ˈeɪərɪst, ˈɛərɪst) *n. Grammar.* a tense of the verb, esp. in classical Greek, indicating past action without reference to whether the action involved was momentary or continuous. [C16: < Gk *aoristos* not limited, < A-¹ + *horistos*, < *horizein* to define]

aorta (eɪˈɔːtə) *n., pl.* **-tas** *or* **-tae** (-tiː). the main vessel in the arterial network, which conveys oxygen-rich blood from the heart. [C16: < NL, < Gk *aortē*, lit.: something lifted, < *aeirein* to raise] —**aˈortic** *or* **aˈortal** *adj.*

Aotearoa (ˈæɒˌtɪəˌroːə) *n. N.Z.* the Maori name for New Zealand. [Maori: the long white cloud]

aoudad (ˈɑːʊˌdæd) *n.* a wild mountain sheep of N Africa. Also called: **Barbary sheep.** [< F, < Berber *audad*]

apace (əˈpeɪs) *adv.* quickly; rapidly. [C14: prob. < OF *à pas*, at a (good) pace]

apache (əˈpæʃ) *n.* a Parisian gangster or ruffian. [< F: APACHE]

Apache (əˈpætʃɪ) *n.* **1.** (*pl.* **Apaches** *or* **Apache**) a member of a North American Indian people inhabiting the southwestern U.S. and N Mexico. **2.** the language of this people. [< Mexican Sp.]

apanage (ˈæpənɪdʒ) *n.* a variant spelling of **appanage.**

apart (əˈpɑːt) *adj.* (*postpositive*), *adv.* **1.** to or in pieces: *he had the television apart.* **2.** placed or kept separately or for a particular purpose, etc.; aside (esp. in **set** *or* **put apart**). **3.** separate in time, place, or position: *he stood apart from the group.* **4.** not being taken into account: *these difficulties apart, the project ran smoothly.* **5.** individual; distinct: *a race apart.* **6.** separately or independently: *considered apart, his reasoning was faulty.* **7. apart from.** (*prep.*) besides. ~See also **take apart, tell apart.** [C14: < OF *a part* at (the) side]

apartheid (əˈpɑːthaɪt, -heɪt) *n.* (in South Africa) the official government policy of racial segregation. [C20: Afrik., < *apart* APART + *-heid* -HOOD]

apartment (əˈpɑːtmənt) *n.* **1.** (*often pl.*) any room in a building, usually one of several forming a suite, used as living accommodation, offices, etc. **2. a.** another name (esp. U.S. and Canad.) for **flat²** (sense 1). **b.** (*as modifier*): *apartment house.* [C17: < F *appartement*, < It., < *appartare* to separate]

apathetic (ˌæpəˈθɛtɪk) *adj.* having or showing little or no emotion or interest. [C18: < APATHY + PATHETIC] —ˌ**apaˈthetically** *adv.*

apathy (ˈæpəθɪ) *n.* **1.** absence of interest in or enthusiasm for things generally considered interesting or moving. **2.** absence of emotion. [C17: < L, < Gk *apatheia*, < A-¹ + *pathos* feeling]

apatite (ˈæpəˌtaɪt) *n.* a common naturally occurring mineral consisting basically of calcium fluorophosphate. It is a source of phosphorus and is used in fertilizers. [C19: < G *Apatit*, < Gk *apatē* deceit; from its misleading similarity to other minerals]

ape (eɪp) *n.* **1.** any of various primates in which the tail is very short or absent. **2.** (not in technical use) any monkey. **3.** an imitator; mimic. ~*vb.* **4.** (*tr.*) to imitate. [OE *apa*] —ˈ**apeˌlike** *adj.*

APEC *Canad. abbrev. for* Atlantic Provinces Economic Council.

apeman (ˈeɪpˌmæn) *n., pl.* **-men.** any of various extinct apelike primates thought to have been the forerunners of modern man.

aperçu *French.* (apɛrsy) *n.* **1.** an outline. **2.** an insight. [< *apercevoir* to PERCEIVE]

aperient (əˈpɪərɪənt) *Med.* ~*adj.* **1.** laxative. ~*n.* **2.** a mild laxative. [C17: < L *aperīre* to open]

aperiodic (ˌeɪpɪərɪˈɒdɪk) *adj.* **1.** not periodic; not occurring at regular intervals. **2.** *Physics.* **a.** (of a system or instrument) being damped sufficiently to reach equilibrium without oscillation. **b.** (of an oscillation or vibration) not having a regular period. **c.** (of an electrical circuit) not having a measurable resonant frequency. —**aperiodicity** (ˌeɪpɪərɪəˈdɪsɪtɪ) *n.*

apéritif (əˌpɛrɪˈtiːf) *n.* an alcoholic drink before a meal to whet the appetite. [C19: < F, < Med. L, < L *aperīre* to open]

aperture (ˈæpətʃə) *n.* **1.** a hole; opening. **2.** *Physics.* a usually circular and often variable opening in an optical instrument or device that controls the quantity of radiation entering or leaving it. [C15: < LL *apertūra* opening, < *aperīre* to open]

apetalous (eɪˈpɛtələs) *adj.* (of flowering plants such as the wood anemone) having no petals. [C18: < NL; see A-¹, PETAL]

apex (ˈeɪpɛks) *n., pl.* **apexes** *or* **apices. 1.** the highest point; vertex. **2.** the pointed end or tip of something. **3.** a high point, as of a career. [C17: < L: point]

APEX (ˈeɪpɛks) *n. acronym for:* **1.** Advance Purchase Excursion, a reduced airline fare, paid for at least 30 days before departure. **2.** Association of Professional, Executive, Clerical, and Computer Staff.

Apex Club (ˈeɪpɛks) *n.* (in Australia) an association of business and professional men to promote community welfare. —**Apexian** (eɪˈpɛksɪən) *adj., n.*

aphaeresis *or* **apheresis** (əˈfɪərɪsɪs) *n.* the omission of a letter or syllable at the beginning of a word. [C17: via LL < Gk, < *aphairein* to remove]

aphasia (əˈfeɪzɪə) *n.* a disorder of the central nervous system characterized by loss of the ability to communicate, esp. in speech. [C19: via NL < Gk, < A-¹ + *-phasia*, < *phanai* to speak]

aphelandra (ˌæfɛlˈændrə) *n.* any of a genus of tropical American plants cultivated for their dark foliage and bright flowers or bracts. [NL, < Gk *aphelēs* simple + *-andra*, from the one-celled anthers]

aphelion (æpˈhiːlɪən, əˈfiː-) *n., pl.* **-lia** (-lɪə). the point in its orbit when a planet or comet is at its greatest distance from the sun. [C17: < NL *aphēlium*, < AP(O)- + Gk *hēlios* sun]

aphesis (ˈæfɪsɪs) *n.* the gradual disappearance of an unstressed vowel at the beginning of a word, as in *squire* from *esquire*. [C19: < Gk, < *aphienai* to set free] —**aphetic** (əˈfɛtɪk) *adj.*

aphid (ˈeɪfɪd) *n.* any of the small homopterous insects of the family Aphididae, which feed by sucking the juices from plants. [C19: < *aphides*, pl. of APHIS]

aphis (ˈeɪfɪs) *n., pl.* **aphides** (ˈeɪfɪˌdiːz). any of a genus of aphids, such as the blackfly. [C18: < NL (coined by Linnaeus for obscure reasons)]

aphonia (əˈfəʊnɪə) *or* **aphony** (ˈæfənɪ) *n.* loss of voice caused by damage to the vocal tract. [C18: NL, < Gk, < A-¹ + *phōnē* sound]

aphorism (ˈæfəˌrɪzəm) *n.* a short pithy saying expressing a general truth; maxim. [C16: < LL, < Gk *aphorismos*, < *aphorizein* to define] —ˈ**aphorist** *n.* —ˌ**aphoˈristic** *adj.*

aphrodisiac (ˌæfrəˈdɪzɪæk) *n.* **1.** a drug, food, etc., that excites sexual desire. ~*adj.* **2.** exciting sexual desire. [C18: < Gk, < *aphrodisios* belonging to *Aphrodite*, goddess of love]

aphyllous (əˈfɪləs) *adj.* (of plants) having no leaves. [C19: < NL, < Gk A-¹ + *phullon* leaf]

apian (ˈeɪpɪən) *adj.* of, relating to, or resembling bees. [C19: < L *apiānus*, < *apis* bee]

apiarist (ˈeɪpɪərɪst) *n.* a person who studies or keeps bees.

apiary (ˈeɪpɪərɪ) *n., pl.* **-aries.** a place where bees are kept. [C17: < L *apiārium*, < *apis* bee]

apical (ˈæpɪkᵊl, ˈeɪ-) *adj.* of, at, or being the apex. [C19: < NL *apicālis*] —**ˈapically** *adv.*

apices (ˈæpɪˌsiːz, ˈeɪ-) *n.* a plural of **apex.**

apiculture (ˈeɪpɪˌkʌltʃə) *n.* the breeding and care of bees. [C19: < L *apis* bee + CULTURE] —ˌ**apiˈcultural** *adj.* —ˌ**apiˈculturist** *n.*

apiece (əˈpiːs) *adv.* for, to, or from each one: *they were given two apples apiece.*

apish (ˈeɪpɪʃ) *adj.* **1.** stupid; foolish. **2.** resembling an ape. **3.** slavishly imitative. —**ˈapishly** *adv.* —**ˈapishness** *n.*

aplanatic (ˌæpləˈnætɪk) *adj.* (of a lens or mirror) free from spherical aberration. [C18: < Gk *aplanetos* free from error, < A-[1] + *planaein* to wander]

aplenty (əˈplɛntɪ) *adj.* (*postpositive*), *adv.* in plenty.

aplomb (əˈplɒm) *n.* equanimity, self-confidence, or self-possession. [C18: < F: uprightness, < *à plomb* according to the plumb line]

apnoea *or U.S.* **apnea** (æpˈnɪə) *n.* a temporary inability to breathe. [C18: < NL, < Gk *apnoia*, < A-[1] + *pnein* to breathe]

apo- *or* **ap-** *prefix.* **1.** away from; off: *apogee.* **2.** separation of: *apocarpous.* [< Gk *apo* away, off]

Apoc. *abbrev. for:* **1.** Apocalypse. **2.** Apocrypha *or* Apocryphal.

apocalypse (əˈpɒkəlɪps) *n.* **1.** a prophetic disclosure or revelation. **2.** an event of great importance, violence, etc., like the events described in the Apocalypse. [C13: < LL *apocalypsis*, < Gk, < APO- + *kaluptein* to hide] —**aˌpocaˈlyptic** *adj.*

Apocalypse (əˈpɒkəlɪps) *n. Bible.* another name for the Book of Revelation.

apocarpous (ˌæpəˈkɑːpəs) *adj.* (of the ovaries of flowering plants) consisting of separate carpels. [C19: < NL, < Gk APO- + *karpos* fruit]

apochromat (ˌæpəˈkrəʊmæt) *or* **apochromatic lens** (ˌæpəkrəˈmætɪk) *n.* a lens system designed to bring trichromatic light to a single focus and reduce chromatic aberration.

apocope (əˈpɒkəpɪ) *n.* omission of the final sound or sounds of a word. [C16: via LL < Gk, < *apokoptein* to cut off]

apocrine (ˈæpəkraɪn, -krɪn) *adj.* losing cellular tissue in the process of secreting, as in mammary glands. Cf. **eccrine.** [C20: < APO- + *-crine*, < Gk *krinein* to separate]

Apocrypha (əˈpɒkrɪfə) *n.* **the.** (*functioning as sing. or pl.*) the 14 books included as an appendix to the Old Testament in the Septuagint and the Vulgate but not in the Hebrew canon. [C14: via LL *apocrypha* (*scripta*) hidden (writings), < Gk, < *apokruptein* to hide away]

apocryphal (əˈpɒkrɪfəl) *adj.* **1.** of questionable authenticity. **2.** (*sometimes cap.*) of or like the Apocrypha. **3.** untrue; counterfeit.

apodal (ˈæpədᵊl) *adj.* without feet; having no pelvic fins. [C18: < Gk A-[1] + *pous* foot]

apodosis (əˈpɒdəsɪs) *n., pl.* **-ses** (-ˌsiːz). *Logic, grammar.* the consequent of a conditional statement, as *I won't go* in *if it rains I won't go.* [C17: via LL < Gk, < *apodidonai* to give back]

apogee (ˈæpəˌdʒiː) *n.* **1.** the point in its orbit around the earth when the moon or an artificial satellite is at its greatest distance from the earth. **2.** the highest point. [C17: < NL, < Gk, < *apogaios* away from the earth] —ˌ**apoˈgean** *adj.*

apolitical (ˌeɪpəˈlɪtɪkᵊl) *adj.* politically neutral; without political attitudes, content, or bias.

Apollyon (əˈpɒljən) *n.* the destroyer, a name given to the Devil (Revelation 9:11). [C14: via LL < Gk, < *apollunai* to destroy totally]

apologetic (əˌpɒləˈdʒɛtɪk) *adj.* **1.** expressing or anxious to make apology; contrite. **2.** defending in speech or writing. —**aˌpoloˈgetically** *adv.*

apologetics (əˌpɒləˈdʒɛtɪks) *n.* (*functioning as sing.*) **1.** the branch of theology concerned with the rational justification of Christianity. **2.** a defensive method of argument.

apologia (ˌæpəˈləʊdʒɪə) *n.* a formal written defence of a cause or one's beliefs or conduct.

apologist (əˈpɒlədʒɪst) *n.* a person who offers a defence by argument.

apologize *or* **-gise** (əˈpɒləˌdʒaɪz) *vb.* (*intr.*) **1.** to express or make an apology; acknowledge faults. **2.** to make a formal defence.

apologue (ˈæpəˌlɒg) *n.* an allegory or moral fable. [C17: < L, < Gk *apologos*]

apology (əˈpɒlədʒɪ) *n., pl.* **-gies. 1.** a verbal or written expression of regret or contrition for a fault or failing. **2.** a poor substitute. **3.** another word for **apologia.** [C16: < OF, < LL, < Gk: a verbal defence, < APO- + *logos* speech]

apophthegm *or* **apothegm** (ˈæpəˌθɛm) *n.* a short remark containing some general or generally accepted truth; maxim. [C16: < Gk *apophthegma*, < *apophthengesthai* to speak frankly]

apoplectic (ˌæpəˈplɛktɪk) *adj.* **1.** of apoplexy. **2.** *Inf.* furious. —ˌ**apoˈplectically** *adv.*

apoplexy (ˈæpəˌplɛksɪ) *n.* sudden loss of consciousness, often followed by paralysis, caused by rupture or occlusion of a blood vessel in the brain. [C14: < OF *apoplexie*, < LL, < Gk, < *apoplēssein* to cripple by a stroke]

aport (əˈpɔːt) *adv., adj.* (*postpositive*) *Naut.* on or towards the port side: *with the helm aport.*

apostasy (əˈpɒstəsɪ) *n., pl.* **-sies.** abandonment of one's religious faith, party, a cause, etc. [C14: < Church L *apostasia*, < Gk *apostasis* desertion]

apostate (əˈpɒsteɪt, -tɪt) *n.* **1.** a person who abandons his religion, party, etc. ~*adj.* **2.** guilty of apostasy. —**apostatical** (ˌæpəˈstætɪkᵊl) *adj.*

apostatize *or* **-tise** (əˈpɒstəˌtaɪz) *vb.* (*intr.*) to abandon one's belief, faith, or allegiance.

a posteriori (eɪ pɒsˌtɛrɪˈɔːraɪ, -rɪ; ɑː) *adj. Logic.* **1.** relating to inductive reasoning from particular facts to a general principle. **2.** derived from or requiring evidence for its validation; empirical. [C18: < L, lit.: from the latter]

apostle (əˈpɒsᵊl) *n.* **1.** (*often cap.*) one of the 12 disciples chosen by Christ to preach his gospel. **2.** any prominent Christian missionary, esp. one who first converts a people. **3.** an ardent early supporter of a cause, movement, etc. [OE *apostol*, < Church L, < Gk *apostolos* a messenger]

Apostles' Creed *n.* a concise statement of Christian beliefs dating from about 500 A.D., traditionally ascribed to the Apostles.

apostolate (əˈpɒstəlɪt, -ˌleɪt) *n.* the office, authority, or mission of an apostle.

apostolic (ˌæpəˈstɒlɪk) *adj.* **1.** of or relating to the Apostles or their teachings or practice. **2.** of or relating to the pope as successor of the Apostles. —ˌ**aposˈtolical** *adj.*

Apostolic See (ˌæpəˈstɒlɪk) *n.* the see of the pope.

Apostolic succession *n.* the doctrine that the authority of Christian bishops derives from the Apostles through an unbroken line of consecration.

apostrophe[1] (əˈpɒstrəfɪ) *n.* the punctuation mark ' used to indicate the omission of a letter or number, such as *he's* for *he has* or *he is*, also used in English to form the possessive, as in *John's father.* [C17: < LL, < Gk *apostrophos* mark of elision, < *apostrephein* to turn away]

apostrophe[2] (əˈpɒstrəfɪ) *n. Rhetoric.* a digression from a discourse, esp. an address to an imaginary or absent person or a personification. [C16: < L *apostrophē*, < Gk: a turning away]

apostrophize *or* **-phise** (əˈpɒstrəˌfaɪz) *vb.* (*tr.*) to address an apostrophe to.

apothecaries' measure *n.* a system of liquid volume measure used in pharmacy in which 20 fluid ounces equal 1 pint.

apothecaries' weight *n.* a system of weights formerly used in pharmacy based on the Troy ounce.

apothecary (əˈpɒθɪkərɪ) *n., pl.* **-caries. 1.** an archaic word for **chemist. 2.** *Law.* a chemist licensed by the Society of Apothecaries of London to prescribe, prepare, and sell drugs. [C14: < OF, < LL, < Gk *apothēkē* storehouse]

apothegm (ˈæpəˌθɛm) *n.* a variant spelling of **apophthegm.**

apothem (ˈæpəˌθɛm) *n.* the perpendicular from

the centre of a regular polygon to any of its sides. [C20: < APO- + Gk *thema*, < *tithenai* to place]

apotheosis (əˌpɒθɪˈəʊsɪs) *n., pl.* **-ses** (-siːz). **1.** elevation to the rank of a god; deification. **2.** glorification of a person or thing. **3.** a glorified ideal. [C17: via LL < Gk: deification]

apotheosize *or* **-ise** (əˈpɒθɪəˌsaɪz) *vb.* (*tr.*) **1.** to deify. **2.** to glorify or idealize.

app. *abbrev. for:* **1.** apparatus. **2.** appendix (of a book). **3.** applied. **4.** appointed. **5.** apprentice. **6.** approved. **7.** approximate.

appal *or U.S.* **appall** (əˈpɔːl) *vb.* **-palling, -palled.** (*tr.*) to fill with horror; shock or dismay. [C14: < OF *appalir* to turn pale]

appalling (əˈpɔːlɪŋ) *adj.* causing dismay, horror, or revulsion. **—apˈpallingly** *adv.*

Appaloosa (ˌæpəˈluːsə) *n.* a breed of horse, originally from America, having a spotted rump. [C19: ? < *Palouse*, river in Idaho]

appanage *or* **apanage** (ˈæpənɪdʒ) *n.* **1.** land or other provision granted by a king for the support of esp. a younger son. **2.** a customary accompaniment or perquisite, as to a job or position. [C17: < OF, < Med. L, < *appānāre* to provide for, < L *pānis* bread]

apparatchik (ˌæpəˈrɑːtʃɪk) *n.* **1.** a member of a Communist Party organization. **2.** a bureaucrat in any organization. [C20: < Russian, < *apparat* apparatus, instrument + *-ckik*, suffix denoting agent]

apparatus (ˌæpəˈreɪtəs, -ˈrɑːtəs) *n., pl.* **-ratus** *or* **-ratuses. 1.** a collection of equipment used for a particular purpose. **2.** a machine having a specific function: *breathing apparatus.* **3.** the means by which something operates; organization. **4.** *Anat.* any group of organs having a specific function. [C17: < L, < *apparāre* to make ready]

apparel (əˈpærəl) *n.* **1.** garments or clothing. **2.** *Naut.* a vessel's gear and equipment. ~*vb.* **-elling, -elled** *or U.S.* **-eling, -eled. 3.** (*tr.*) *Arch.* to clothe, adorn, etc. [C13: < OF *apareillier* to make ready, < Vulgar L *appariculāre* (unattested), < L *parāre* to prepare]

apparent (əˈpærənt) *adj.* **1.** readily seen or understood; obvious. **2.** (*usually prenominal*) seeming, as opposed to real: *his apparent innocence.* **3.** *Physics.* as observed but ignoring such factors as the motion of the observer, etc. [C14: < L *appārēns*, < *appārēre* to APPEAR] **—apˈparently** *adv.*

apparent magnitude *n.* See **magnitude** (sense 4).

apparition (ˌæpəˈrɪʃən) *n.* **1.** an appearance, esp. of a ghost or ghostlike figure. **2.** the figure so appearing; spectre. **3.** the act of appearing. [C15: < LL *appāritiō*, < L *appārēre* to APPEAR]

appassionato (əˌpæsjəˈnɑːtəʊ) *adj., adv. Music.* (to be performed) with passion. [It.]

appeal (əˈpiːl) *n.* **1.** a request for relief, aid, etc. **2.** the power to attract, please, stimulate, or interest. **3.** an application or resort to another authority, esp. a higher one, as for a decision. **4.** *Law.* **a.** the judicial review by a superior court of the decision of a lower tribunal. **b.** a request for such review. **5.** *Cricket.* a request to the umpire to declare a batsman out. ~*vb.* **6.** (*intr.*) to make an earnest request. **7.** (*intr.*) to attract, please, stimulate, or interest. **8.** *Law.* to apply to a superior court to review (a case or issue decided by a lower tribunal). **9.** (*intr.*) to resort (to), as for a decision. **10.** (*intr.*) *Cricket.* to ask the umpire to declare a batsman out. **11.** (*intr.*) to challenge the umpire's or referee's decision. [C14: < OF *appeler*, < L *appellāre* to entreat, < *pellere* to drive] **—apˈpealable** *adj.* **—apˈpealer** *n.* **—apˈpealing** *adj.* **—apˈpealingly** *adv.*

appear (əˈpɪə) *vb.* (*intr.*) **1.** to come into sight. **2.** (*copula; may take an infinitive*) to seem: *the evidence appears to support you.* **3.** to be plain or clear, as after further evidence, etc.: *it appears you were correct after all.* **4.** to develop; occur: *faults appeared during testing.* **5.** to be published: *his biography appeared last month.* **6.** to perform: *he has appeared in many London productions.* **7.** to be present in court before a magistrate or judge: *he appeared on two charges of theft.* [C13: < OF *aparoir*, < L *appārēre* to become visible, attend upon, < *pārēre* to appear]

appearance (əˈpɪərəns) *n.* **1.** the act or an instance of appearing. **2.** the outward aspect of a person or thing. **3.** an outward show; pretence: *he gave an appearance of working hard.* **4. keep up appearances.** to maintain the public impression of wellbeing or normality. **5. put in** *or* **make an appearance.** to attend briefly, as out of politeness. **6. to all appearances.** apparently.

appearance money *n.* money paid by a promoter of an event to a particular celebrity in order to ensure that the celebrity takes part in the event.

appease (əˈpiːz) *vb.* (*tr.*) **1.** to calm or pacify, esp. by acceding to the demands of. **2.** to satisfy or quell (a thirst, etc.). [C16: < OF *apaisier*, < *pais* peace, < L *pax*] **—apˈpeaser** *n.*

appeasement (əˈpiːzmənt) *n.* **1.** the policy of acceding to the demands of a potentially hostile nation in the hope of maintaining peace. **2.** the act of appeasing.

appellant (əˈpɛlənt) *n.* **1.** a person who appeals. **2.** *Law.* the party who appeals to a higher court from the decision of a lower tribunal. ~*adj.* **3.** *Law.* another word for **appellate.** [C14: < OF; see APPEAL]

appellate (əˈpɛlɪt) *adj. Law.* **1.** of appeals. **2.** (of a tribunal) having jurisdiction to review cases on appeal. [C18: < L *appellātus* summoned, < *appellāre* to APPEAL]

appellation (ˌæpɪˈleɪʃən) *n.* **1.** a name or title. **2.** the act of naming.

appellative (əˈpɛlətɪv) *n.* **1.** a name or title. **2.** *Grammar.* another word for **common noun.** ~*adj.* **3.** of or relating to a name. **4.** (of a proper noun) used as a common noun.

append (əˈpɛnd) *vb.* (*tr.*) **1.** to add as a supplement: *to append a footnote.* **2.** to attach; hang on. [C15: < LL *appendere* to hang (something) from, < L *pendere* to hang]

appendage (əˈpɛndɪdʒ) *n.* an ancillary or secondary part attached to a main part; adjunct, such as an organ that projects from the trunk of an animal.

appendant (əˈpɛndənt) *adj.* **1.** attached or added. **2.** attendant or associated as an accompaniment or result. ~*n.* **3.** a person or thing attached or added.

appendicectomy (əˌpɛndɪˈsɛktəmɪ) *or esp. U.S. & Canad.* **appendectomy** (ˌæpənˈdɛktəmɪ) *n., pl.* **-mies.** surgical removal of any appendage, esp. the vermiform appendix.

appendicitis (əˌpɛndɪˈsaɪtɪs) *n.* inflammation of the vermiform appendix.

appendix (əˈpɛndɪks) *n., pl.* **-dixes** *or* **-dices** (-dɪˌsiːz). **1.** a body of separate additional material at the end of a book, etc. **2.** any part that is dependent or supplementary. **3.** *Anat.* See **vermiform appendix.** [C16: < L: an appendage, < *appendere* to APPEND]

apperceive (ˌæpəˈsiːv) *vb.* (*tr.*) **1.** to be aware of perceiving. **2.** *Psychol.* to comprehend by assimilating (a perception) to ideas already in the mind. [C19: < OF, < L *percipere* to PERCEIVE]

apperception (ˌæpəˈsɛpʃən) *n.* **1.** *Psychol.* the attainment of full awareness of a sensation or idea. **2.** the act of apperceiving. **—ˌapperˈceptive** *adj.*

appertain (ˌæpəˈteɪn) *vb.* (*intr.*; usually foll. by *to*) to belong (to) as a part, function, right, etc.; relate (to) or be connected (with). [C14: < OF *apertenir*, < LL, < L AD- + *pertinēre* to PERTAIN]

appetence (ˈæpɪtəns) *or* **appetency** *n., pl.* **-tences** *or* **-tencies. 1.** a craving or desire. **2.** an attraction or affinity. [C17: < L *appetentia*, < *appetere* to crave]

appetite (ˈæpɪˌtaɪt) *n.* **1.** a desire for food or drink. **2.** a desire to satisfy a bodily craving, as for sexual pleasure. **3.** (usually foll. by *for*) a liking or willingness: *a great appetite for work.* [C14: < OF *apetit*, < L, < *appetere* to desire ardently] **—appetitive** (əˈpɛtɪtɪv) *adj.*

appetizer *or* **-iser** (ˈæpɪˌtaɪzə) *n.* **1.** a small amount of food or drink taken to stimulate the appetite. **2.** any stimulating foretaste.
appetizing *or* **-ising** (ˈæpɪˌtaɪzɪŋ) *adj.* pleasing or stimulating to the appetite; delicious; tasty.
applaud (əˈplɔːd) *vb.* **1.** to indicate approval of (a person, performance, etc.) by clapping the hands. **2.** (*usually tr.*) to express approval or praise of: *I applaud your decision.* [C15: < L *applaudere,* < *plaudere* to beat, applaud]
applause (əˈplɔːz) *n.* appreciation or praise, esp. as shown by clapping the hands.
apple (ˈæpᵊl) *n.* **1.** a rosaceous tree, widely cultivated in temperate regions in many varieties. **2.** the fruit of this tree, having red, yellow, or green skin and crisp whitish flesh. **3.** the wood of this tree. **4.** any of several unrelated trees that have fruit similar to the apple. **5. apple of one's eye.** a person or thing that is very much loved. [OE *æppel*]
apple green *n.* **a.** a bright light green. **b.** (*as adj.*): *an apple-green carpet.*
apple-pie bed *n. Brit.* a way of making a bed so as to prevent the person from entering it.
apple-pie order *n. Inf.* perfect order or condition.
appliance (əˈplaɪəns) *n.* **1.** a machine or device, esp. an electrical one used domestically. **2.** any piece of equipment having a specific function. **3.** another name for a **fire engine.**
applicable (ˈæplɪkəbᵊl, əˈplɪkə-) *adj.* being appropriate or relevant; able to be applied; fitting. —ˌ**applicaˈbility** *n.* —ˈ**applicably** *adv.*
applicant (ˈæplɪkənt) *n.* a person who applies, as for a job, grant, support, etc.; candidate. [C15: < L *applicāns,* < *applicāre* to APPLY]
application (ˌæplɪˈkeɪʃən) *n.* **1.** the act of applying to a particular use. **2.** relevance or value: *the practical applications of space technology.* **3.** the act of asking for something. **4.** a written request, as for a job, etc. **5.** diligent effort: *a job requiring application.* **6.** something, such as a lotion, that is applied, esp. to the skin.
applicator (ˈæplɪˌkeɪtə) *n.* a device, such as a spatula or rod, for applying a medicine, glue, etc.
applicatory (ˈæplɪkətərɪ) *adj.* suitable for application.
applied (əˈplaɪd) *adj.* put to practical use: *applied mathematics.* Cf. **pure** (sense 5).
appliqué (æˈpliːkeɪ) *n.* **1.** a decoration of one material sewn or fixed onto another. **2.** the practice of decorating in this way. ~*vb.* **-quéing, -quéd. 3.** (*tr.*) to sew or fix (a decoration) on as an appliqué. [C18: < F, lit.: applied]
apply (əˈplaɪ) *vb.* **-plying, -plied. 1.** (*tr.*) to put to practical use; employ. **2.** (*intr.*) to be relevant or appropriate. **3.** (*tr.*) to cause to come into contact with. **4.** (*intr.;* often foll. by *for*) to put in an application or request. **5.** (*tr.;* often foll. by *to*) to devote (oneself or one's efforts) with diligence. **6.** (*tr.*) to bring into use: *the police only applied the law to aliens.* [C14: < OF *aplier,* < L *applicāre* to attach to] —**apˈplier** *n.*
appoggiatura (əˌpɒdʒəˈtʊərə) *n., pl.* **-ras** *or* **-re** (-reɪ). *Music.* an ornament consisting of a nonharmonic note preceding a harmonic one either before or on the stress. [C18: < It., lit.: a propping]
appoint (əˈpɔɪnt) *vb.* (*mainly tr.*) **1.** (*also intr.*) to assign officially, as for a position, responsibility, etc. **2.** to establish by agreement or decree. **3.** to prescribe: *laws appointed by tribunal.* **4.** *Property law.* to nominate (a person) to take an interest in property. **5.** to equip with usual features; furnish: *a well-appointed hotel.* [C14: < OF *apointer* to put into a good state] —**appoinˈtee** *n.* —**apˈpointer** *n.*
appointive (əˈpɔɪntɪv) *adj. Chiefly U.S.* filled by appointment: *an appointive position.*
appointment (əˈpɔɪntmənt) *n.* **1.** an arrangement to meet a person or be at a place at a certain time. **2.** the act of placing in a job or position. **3.** the person who receives such a job. **4.** the job or position to which such a person is appointed. **5.** (*usually pl.*) a fixture or fitting.
apportion (əˈpɔːʃən) *vb.* (*tr.*) to divide, distribute, or assign shares of; allot proportionally. —**apˈportionable** *adj.* —**apˈportionment** *n.*
appose (əˈpəʊz) *vb.* (*tr.*) **1.** to place side by side. **2.** (usually foll. by *to*) to place (something) near or against another thing. [C16: < OF *apposer,* < *poser* to put, < L *pōnere*] —**apˈposable** *adj.*
apposite (ˈæpəzɪt) *adj.* appropriate; apt. [C17: < L *appositus,* < *appōnere,* < *pōnere* to put] —ˈ**appositely** *adv.* —ˈ**appositeness** *n.*
apposition (ˌæpəˈzɪʃən) *n.* **1.** a putting into juxtaposition. **2.** a grammatical construction in which a word, esp. a noun, is placed after another to modify its meaning. —ˌ**appoˈsitional** *adj.*
appositive (əˈpɒzɪtɪv) *Grammar.* ~*adj.* **1.** in, of, or relating to apposition. ~*n.* **2.** an appositive word or phrase. —**apˈpositively** *adv.*
appraisal (əˈpreɪzᵊl) *or* **appraisement** *n.* **1.** an assessment of the worth or quality of a person or thing. **2.** a valuation.
appraise (əˈpreɪz) *vb.* (*tr.*) **1.** to assess the worth, value, or quality of. **2.** to make a valuation of, as for taxation. [C15: < OF, < *prisier* to PRIZE²] —**apˈpraisable** *adj.* —**apˈpraiser** *n.*
appreciable (əˈpriːʃəbᵊl) *adj.* sufficient to be easily measured or noticed. —**apˈpreciably** *adv.*
appreciate (əˈpriːʃɪˌeɪt, -sɪ-) *vb.* (*mainly tr.*) **1.** to feel thankful or grateful for. **2.** (*may take a clause as object*) to take sufficient account of: *to appreciate a problem.* **3.** to value highly. **4.** (*usually intr.*) to increase in value. [C17: < Med. L *appretiāre* to value, < L *pretium* PRICE] —**apˈpreciˌator** *n.*
appreciation (əˌpriːʃɪˈeɪʃən, -sɪ-) *n.* **1.** thanks or gratitude. **2.** assessment of the true worth of persons or things. **3.** perceptive recognition of qualities, as in art. **4.** an increase in value. **5.** a review of a book, etc., esp. when favourable.
appreciative (əˈpriːʃɪətɪv) *or* **appreciatory** *adj.* feeling or expressing appreciation. —**apˈpreciatively** *adv.* —**apˈpreciativeness** *n.*
apprehend (ˌæprɪˈhɛnd) *vb.* **1.** (*tr.*) to arrest and escort into custody. **2.** to grasp mentally; understand. **3.** to await with fear or anxiety. [C14: < L *apprehendere* to lay hold of]
apprehensible (ˌæprɪˈhɛnsɪbᵊl) *adj.* capable of being comprehended or grasped mentally. —ˌ**appreˌhensiˈbility** *n.*
apprehension (ˌæprɪˈhɛnʃən) *n.* **1.** anxiety over what may happen. **2.** the act of arresting. **3.** understanding. **4.** a notion or conception.
apprehensive (ˌæprɪˈhɛnsɪv) *adj.* **1.** fearful or anxious. **2.** (*usually postpositive* and foll. by *of*) *Arch.* intelligent, perceptive. —ˌ**appreˈhensively** *adv.* —ˌ**appreˈhensiveness** *n.*
apprentice (əˈprɛntɪs) *n.* **1.** someone who works for a skilled or qualified person in order to learn a trade, esp. for a recognized period. **2.** any beginner or novice. ~*vb.* **3.** (*tr.*) to take, place, or bind as an apprentice. [C14: < OF *aprentis,* < *aprendre* to learn, < L *apprehendere* to APPREHEND] —**apˈprenticeˌship** *n.*
apprise *or* **-ize** (əˈpraɪz) *vb.* (*tr.;* often foll. by *of*) to make aware; inform. [C17: < F *appris,* < *apprendre* to teach; learn]
appro (ˈæprəʊ) *n.* an informal shortening of **approval:** *on appro.*
approach (əˈprəʊtʃ) *vb.* **1.** to come nearer in position, time, quality, character, etc., to (someone or something). **2.** (*tr.*) to make a proposal or suggestion to. **3.** (*tr.*) to begin to deal with. ~*n.* **4.** the act of drawing close or closer. **5.** a close approximation. **6.** the way or means of entering or leaving. **7.** (*often pl.*) an overture to a person. **8.** a means adopted in tackling a problem, job of work, etc. **9.** Also called: **approach path.** the course followed by an aircraft preparing for landing. **10.** Also called: **approach shot.** *Golf.* a shot made to or towards the green after a tee shot. [C14: < OF *aprochier,* < LL *appropiāre* to draw near, < L *prope* near] —**apˈproachable** *adj.* —**apˌproachaˈbility** *n.*
approbation (ˌæprəˈbeɪʃən) *n.* **1.** commendation; praise. **2.** official recognition. —ˈ**approˌbative** *or* ˈ**approˌbatory** *adj.*

appropriate *adj.* (əˈprəʊprɪɪt). **1.** right or suitable; fitting. ~*vb.* (əˈprəʊprɪˌeɪt). (*tr.*) **2.** to take for one's own use, esp. illegally. **3.** to put aside (funds, etc.) for a particular purpose or person. [C15: < LL *appropriāre* to make one's own, < L *proprius* one's own] —**apˈpropriately** *adv.* —**apˈpropriateness** *n.* —**apˈpropriˌator** *n.*

appropriation (əˌprəʊprɪˈeɪʃən) *n.* **1.** the act of setting apart or taking for one's own use. **2.** a sum of money set apart for a specific purpose.

approval (əˈpruːvᵊl) *n.* **1.** the act of approving. **2.** formal agreement. **3.** a favourable opinion. **4.** **on approval.** (of articles for sale) for examination with an option to buy or return.

approve (əˈpruːv) *vb.* **1.** (when *intr.*, often foll. by *of*) to consider fair, good, or right. **2.** (*tr.*) to authorize or sanction. [C14: < OF *aprover*, < L *approbāre* to approve, < *probāre* to test, PROVE]

approved school *n.* (in Britain) a former name for **community home.**

approx. *abbrev. for* approximate(ly).

approximate *adj.* (əˈprɒksɪmɪt). **1.** almost accurate or exact. **2.** inexact; rough; loose. **3.** much alike; almost the same. **4.** near; close together. ~*vb.* (əˈprɒksɪˌmeɪt). **5.** (usually foll. by *to*) to come or bring near or close; be almost the same (as). **6.** *Maths.* to find an expression for (some quantity) accurate to a specified degree. [C15: < LL *approximāre*, < L *proximus* nearest] —**apˈproximately** *adv.*

approximation (əˌprɒksɪˈmeɪʃən) *n.* **1.** the process or result of making a rough calculation, estimate, or guess. **2.** an imprecise or unreliable record or version. **3.** *Maths.* an inexact number, relationship, or theory that is sufficiently accurate for a specific purpose.

appurtenance (əˈpɜːtɪnəns) *n.* **1.** a less significant thing or part. **2.** (*pl.*) accessories. **3.** *Property law.* a minor right, interest, or privilege. [C14: < Anglo-F *apurtenance*, < OF *apartenance*, < *apartenir* to APPERTAIN]

APR *abbrev. for:* **1.** annualized percentage rate. **2.** Annual Purchase Rate (in hire-purchase).

Apr. *abbrev. for* April.

apraxia (əˈpræksɪə) *n.* a disorder of the central nervous system characterized by impaired ability to carry out certain purposeful muscular movements. [C19: via NL < Gk: inactivity, < A-[1] + *praxis* action]

après-ski (ˌæpreɪˈskiː) *n.* **a.** social activity following a day's skiing. **b.** (*as modifier*): *an après-ski outfit.* [F, lit.: after ski]

apricot (ˈeɪprɪˌkɒt) *n.* **1.** a tree native to Africa and W Asia, but widely cultivated for its edible fruit. **2.** the yellow juicy fruit of this tree, which resembles a small peach. [C16: < Port., < Ar., < LGk, < L *praecox* early-ripening]

April (ˈeɪprəl) *n.* the fourth month of the year, consisting of 30 days. [C14: < L *Aprīlis*]

April fool *n.* a victim of a practical joke performed on the first of April (**April Fools' Day** *or* **All Fools' Day**).

a priori (eɪ praɪˈɔːraɪ, ɑː prɪˈɔːrɪ) *adj.* **1.** *Logic.* relating to or involving deductive reasoning from a general principle to the expected facts or effects. **2.** known to be true independently of experience of the subject matter. [C18: < L, lit.: from the previous] —**apriority** (ˌeɪpraɪˈɒrɪtɪ) *n.*

apron (ˈeɪprən) *n.* **1.** a protective or sometimes decorative garment worn over the front of the body and tied around the waist. **2.** the part of a stage extending in front of the curtain. **3.** a hard-surfaced area in front of an aircraft hangar, terminal building, etc. **4.** a continuous conveyor belt composed of metal slats. **5.** a protective plate screening the operator of a machine, artillery piece, etc. **6.** *Geol.* a sheet of sand, gravel, etc., deposited at the front of a moraine. **7.** another name for **skirt** (sense 3). **8.** **tied to someone's apron strings.** dominated by someone, esp. a mother or wife. ~*vb.* **9.** (*tr.*) to protect or provide with an apron. [C16: mistaken division of *a napron*, < OF, < L *mappa* napkin]

apron stage *n.* a stage that projects into the auditorium so that the audience sits on three sides of it.

apropos (ˌæprəˈpəʊ) *adj.* **1.** appropriate. ~*adv.* **2.** appropriately. **3.** by the way; incidentally. **4.** **apropos of.** (*prep.*) in respect of. [C17: < F *à propos* to the purpose]

apse (æps) *n.* a domed or vaulted semicircular or polygonal recess, esp. at the east end of a church. Also called: **apsis.** [C19: < L *apsis*, < Gk: a fitting together, < *haptein* to fasten] —**apsidal** (ˈæpsɪdᵊl) *adj.*

apsis (ˈæpsɪs) *n., pl.* **apsides** (æpˈsaɪdiːz). either of two points lying at the extremities of an eccentric orbit of a planet, satellite, etc. Also called: **apse.** [C17: via L < Gk; see APSE] —**apsidal** (ˈæpsɪdᵊl) *adj.*

apt (æpt) *adj.* **1.** suitable; appropriate. **2.** (*postpositive;* foll. by an infinitive) having a tendency (to behave as specified). **3.** having the ability to learn and understand easily. [C14: < L *aptus* fitting, < *apere* to fasten] —**ˈaptly** *adv.* —**ˈaptness** *n.*

APT *abbrev. for* Advanced Passenger Train.

apterous (ˈæptərəs) *adj.* **1.** (of insects) without wings, as silverfish. **2.** without winglike expansions, as some seeds and fruits. [C18: < Gk, < A-[1] + *pteron* wing]

apteryx (ˈæptərɪks) *n.* another name for **kiwi** (the bird). [C19: < NL; see APTEROUS]

aptitude (ˈæptɪˌtjuːd) *n.* **1.** inherent or acquired ability. **2.** ease in learning or understanding. **3.** the quality of being apt. [C15: via OF < LL, < L *aptus* APT]

aqua (ˈækwə) *n., pl.* **aquae** (ˈækwiː) *or* **aquas. 1.** water: used in compound names of certain liquid substances or solutions of substances in water. ~*n., adj.* **2.** short for **aquamarine** (the colour). [L: water]

aquaculture (ˈækwəˌkʌltʃə) *or* **aquiculture** *n.* the cultivation of freshwater and marine organisms for human consumption or use.

aqua fortis (ˈfɔːtɪs) *n.* an obsolete name for **nitric acid.** [C17: < L, lit.: strong water]

aqualung (ˈækwəˌlʌŋ) *n.* breathing apparatus used by divers, etc., consisting of a mouthpiece attached to air cylinders strapped to the back.

aquamarine (ˌækwəməˈriːn) *n.* **1.** a pale greenish-blue transparent variety of beryl used as a gemstone. **2. a.** a pale blue to greenish-blue colour. **b.** (*as adj.*): *an aquamarine dress.* [C19: < NL, < L: sea water (referring to the gem's colour)]

aquanaut (ˈækwənɔːt) *n.* a person who works, swims, or dives underwater. [C20: < AQUA + *-naut*, as in ASTRONAUT]

aquaplane (ˈækwəˌpleɪn) *n.* **1.** a board on which a person stands and is towed by a motorboat. ~*vb.* (*intr.*) **2.** to ride on an aquaplane. **3.** (of a motor vehicle travelling at high speeds on wet roads) to rise up onto a thin film of water so that contact with the road is lost.

aqua regia (ˈriːdʒɪə) *n.* a mixture of nitric acid and hydrochloric acid. [C17: < NL: royal water; referring to its use in dissolving gold, the royal metal]

aquarist (ˈækwərɪst) *n.* **1.** the curator of an aquarium. **2.** a person who studies aquatic life.

aquarium (əˈkwɛərɪəm) *n., pl.* **aquariums** *or* **aquaria** (əˈkwɛərɪə). **1.** a tank, bowl, or pool in which aquatic animals and plants are kept for pleasure, study, or exhibition. **2.** a building housing a collection of aquatic life, as for exhibition. [C19: < L *aquārius* relating to water, on the model of VIVARIUM]

Aquarius (əˈkwɛərɪəs) *n., Latin genitive* **Aquarii** (əˈkwɛərɪˌaɪ). **1.** *Astron.* a S constellation. **2.** *Astrol.* also called: the **Water Carrier.** the eleventh sign of the zodiac. The sun is in this sign between about Jan. 20 and Feb. 18. [L]

aquatic (əˈkwætɪk) *adj.* **1.** growing, living, or found in water. **2.** *Sport.* performed in or on water. ~*n.* **3.** a marine animal or plant. [C15: < L *aquāticus*, < *aqua* water]

aquatics (əˈkwætɪks) *pl. n.* sports or pastimes performed in or on the water.

aquatint (ˈækwəˌtɪnt) *n.* **1.** a technique of etching copper with acid to produce an effect resembling watercolour. **2.** an etching made in this way. ~*vb.* **3.** (*tr.*) to etch (a block, etc.) in aquatint. [C18: < It. *acqua tinta* dyed water]

aquavit (ˈækwəˌvɪt) *n.* a grain- or potato-based spirit flavoured with aromatic seeds. Also called: **akvavit.** [of Scandinavian origin: see AQUA VITAE]

aqua vitae (ˈviːtaɪ, ˈvaɪtiː) *n.* an archaic name for **brandy.** [Med. L: water of life]

aqueduct (ˈækwɪˌdʌkt) *n.* **1.** a conduit used to convey water over a long distance. **2.** a structure, often a bridge, that carries such a conduit or a canal across a valley or river. **3.** a channel or conduit in the body. [C16: < L *aquaeductus,* < *aqua* water + *dūcere* to convey]

aqueous (ˈeɪkwɪəs) *adj.* **1.** of, like, or containing water. **2.** (of rocks, etc.) formed from material laid down in water. [C17: < Med. L *aqueus,* < L *aqua* water]

aqueous ammonia *n.* another name for **ammonium hydroxide.**

aqueous humour *n. Physiol.* the watery fluid within the eyeball between the cornea and the lens.

aquiculture (ˈeɪkwɪˌkʌltʃə, ˈækwɪ-) *n.* **1.** another name for **hydroponics. 2.** a variant of **aquaculture.** —ˈ**aquiˌculturist** *n.* —ˈ**aquiˌcultural** *adj.*

aquifer (ˈækwɪfə) *n.* a deposit or rock, such as a sandstone, containing water that can be used to supply wells.

aquilegia (ˌækwɪˈliːdʒɪə) *n.* another name for **columbine**[1]. [C19: < Med. L, <?]

aquiline (ˈækwɪˌlaɪn) *adj.* **1.** (of a nose) having the curved shape of an eagle's beak. **2.** of or like an eagle. [C17: < L, < *aquila* eagle]

Ar *the chemical symbol for* argon.

ar. *abbrev. for:* **1.** arrival. **2.** arrive(s).

Ar. *abbrev. for:* **1.** Arabia(n). **2.** Also: **Ar** Arabic. **3.** Aramaic.

a.r. *abbrev. for* anno regni. [L: in the year of the reign]

-ar *suffix forming adjectives.* of; belonging to; like: *linear; polar.* [via OF *-er* < L *-āris*]

ARA *abbrev. for:* **1.** (in Britain) Associate of the Royal Academy. **2.** (in New Zealand) Auckland Regional Authority.

Arab (ˈærəb) *n.* **1.** a member of a Semitic people originally inhabiting Arabia. **2.** a small breed of horse, used for riding. **3.** See **street Arab. 4.** (*modifier*) of or relating to the Arabs. [C14: < L, < Gk *Araps,* < Ar. *ʻArab*]

arabesque (ˌærəˈbɛsk) *n.* **1.** *Ballet.* a classical position in which the dancer has one leg raised behind. **2.** *Music.* a piece or movement with a highly ornamented melody. **3.** *Arts.* a type of curvilinear decoration in painting, metalwork, etc., with intricate intertwining designs. [C18: < F, < It. *arabesco* in the Arabic style]

Arabian (əˈreɪbɪən) *adj.* **1.** of or relating to Arabia or the Arabs. ~*n.* **2.** another word for **Arab.**

Arabian camel *n.* a domesticated camel with one hump on its back, used as a beast of burden in the deserts of N Africa and SW Asia.

Arabic (ˈærəbɪk) *n.* **1.** the Semitic language of the Arabs, which has its own alphabet and is spoken in Algeria, Egypt, Iraq, Jordan, Saudi Arabia, Syria, Tunisia, etc. ~*adj.* **2.** denoting or relating to this language, any of the peoples that speak it, or the countries in which it is spoken.

arabica bean (əˈræbɪkə) *n.* a type of coffee bean obtained from the tree *Coffea arabica.*

Arabic numeral *n.* one of the numbers 1,2,3,4,5,6,7,8,9,0 (opposed to *Roman numerals*).

arabis (ˈærəbɪs) *n.* any of several trailing plants having pink or white flowers in spring. Also called: **rock cress.** [C16: < Med. L, < Gk *arabis,* ult. < *Arābios* Arabian, prob. from growing in sandy or stony soil]

Arabist (ˈærəbɪst) *n.* a student of Arabic culture, language, history, etc.

arable (ˈærəbᵊl) *adj.* **1.** (of land) being or capable of being tilled for the production of crops. **2.** of, relating to, or using such land. [C15: < L *arābilis,* < *arāre* to plough]

Araby (ˈærəbɪ) *n.* an archaic or poetic name for Arabia.

arachnid (əˈræknɪd) *n.* any of a class of arthropods characterized by simple eyes and four pairs of legs, including the spiders, scorpions, and ticks. [C19: < NL *Arachnida,* < Gk *arakhnē* spider] —**aˈrachnidan** *adj., n.*

arachnoid (əˈræknɔɪd) *n.* **1.** the middle one of three membranes that cover the brain and spinal cord. ~*adj.* **2.** of or relating to this membrane. **3.** *Bot.* consisting of or covered with soft fine hairs or fibres.

arak (ˈærək) *n.* a variant spelling of **arrack.**

Araldite (ˈærəldaɪt) *n. Trademark.* an epoxy resin used as a glue for mending glass, plastic, and china.

Aram. *abbrev. for* Aramaic.

Aramaic (ˌærəˈmeɪɪk) *n.* **1.** an ancient Semitic language of the Middle East, still spoken in parts of Syria and the Lebanon. ~*adj.* **2.** of, relating to, or using this language.

Aran (ˈærən) *adj.* **1.** of or relating to the Aran Islands, off the W coast of Ireland. **2.** made of thick natural wool: *an Aran sweater.*

araucaria (ˌærɔːˈkɛərɪə) *n.* any of a group of coniferous trees of South America, Australia, and Polynesia, such as the monkey puzzle. [C19: < NL (*arbor*) *Araucaria* (tree) from *Arauco,* a province in Chile]

arbalest *or* **arbalist** (ˈɑːbəlɪst) *n.* a large medieval crossbow, usually cocked by mechanical means. [C11: < OF, < LL *arcuballista,* < L *arcus* bow + BALLISTA]

arbiter (ˈɑːbɪtə) *n.* **1.** a person empowered to judge in a dispute; referee. **2.** a person having control of something. [C15: < L, <?] —ˈ**arbitress** *fem. n.*

arbitrament (ɑːˈbɪtrəmənt) *n.* **1.** the decision or award made by an arbitrator upon a disputed matter. **2.** another word for **arbitration.**

arbitrary (ˈɑːbɪtrərɪ) *adj.* **1.** founded on or subject to personal whims, prejudices, etc. **2.** not absolute. **3.** (of a government, ruler, etc.) despotic or dictatorial. **4.** *Law.* (esp. of a penalty) within the court's discretion. [C15: < L *arbitrārius* arranged through arbitration] —ˈ**arbitrarily** *adv.* —ˈ**arbitrariness** *n.*

arbitrate (ˈɑːbɪˌtreɪt) *vb.* **1.** to achieve a settlement between parties. **2.** to submit to or settle by arbitration. [C16: < L *arbitrāri* to give judgment] —ˈ**arbiˌtrator** *n.*

arbitration (ˌɑːbɪˈtreɪʃən) *n.* the hearing and determination of a dispute, esp. an industrial one, by an impartial referee selected or agreed upon by the parties concerned.

arbor[1] (ˈɑːbə) *n.* the U.S. spelling of **arbour.**

arbor[2] (ˈɑːbə) *n.* **1.** a rotating shaft in a machine on which a milling cutter or grinding wheel is fitted. **2.** a rotating shaft. [C17: < L: tree]

arboraceous (ˌɑːbəˈreɪʃəs) *adj. Literary.* **1.** resembling a tree. **2.** wooded.

arboreal (ɑːˈbɔːrɪəl) *adj.* **1.** of or resembling a tree. **2.** living in or among trees.

arborescent (ˌɑːbəˈrɛsᵊnt) *adj.* having the shape or characteristics of a tree. —ˌ**arboˈrescence** *n.*

arboretum (ˌɑːbəˈriːtəm) *n., pl.* **-ta** (-tə) *or* **-tums.** a place where trees or shrubs are cultivated. [C19: < L, < *arbor* tree]

arboriculture (ˈɑːbərɪˌkʌltʃə) *n.* the cultivation of trees or shrubs. —ˌ**arboriˈculturist** *n.*

arbor vitae (ˈɑːbɔː ˈviːtaɪ, ˈvaɪtiː) *n.* any of several Asian and North American evergreen coniferous trees having tiny scalelike leaves and egglike cones. [C17: < NL, lit.: tree of life]

arbour (ˈɑːbə) *n.* a leafy glade or bower shaded by trees, vines, shrubs, etc. [C14 *erber,* < OF, < L *herba* grass]

arbutus (ɑːˈbjuːtəs) *n., pl.* **-tuses.** any of a genus of shrubs having clusters of white or pinkish flowers, broad evergreen leaves, and strawberry-like berries. [C16: < L; rel. to *arbor* tree]

arc (ɑːk) *n.* **1.** something curved in shape. **2.** part of an unbroken curved line. **3.** a luminous discharge that occurs when an electric current flows between two electrodes separated by a small gap. **4.** *Maths.* a section of a curve, graph, or geometric figure. ~*vb.* **arcing, arced** *or* **arcking, arcked. 5.** (*intr.*) to form an arc. ~*adj.* **6.** *Maths.* specifying an inverse trigonometric function: *arcsin, arccos, arctan.* [C14: < OF, < L *arcus* bow, arch]

ARC *abbrev. for* AIDS-related complex: a condition in which a person is infected with the AIDS virus at an early stage before the disease has reached its full development and may suffer from relatively mild symptoms such as loss of weight, fever, etc.

arcade (ɑːˈkeɪd) *n.* **1.** a set of arches and their supporting columns. **2.** a covered and sometimes arched passageway, usually with shops on one or both sides. [C18: < F, < It. *arcata,* < L *arcus* bow, arch]

Arcadian (ɑːˈkeɪdɪən) *adj.* **1.** of the idealized Arcadia of pastoral poetry. **2.** rustic or bucolic. ~*n.* **3.** a person who leads a quiet simple rural life. [C16: < *Arcadia,* rural district of Ancient Greece] —**Arˈcadianism** *n.*

arcane (ɑːˈkeɪn) *adj.* requiring secret knowledge to be understood; esoteric. [C16: < L *arcānus* secret, < *arcēre* to keep safe]

arcanum (ɑːˈkeɪnəm) *n., pl.* **-na** (-nə). (*sometimes pl.*) a secret or mystery. [C16: < L; see ARCANE]

arch[1] (ɑːtʃ) *n.* **1.** a curved structure that spans an opening. **2.** Also called: **archway.** a structure in the form of an arch that serves as a gateway. **3.** something curved like an arch. **4.** any of various parts or structures of the body having a curved or archlike outline, such as the raised vault formed by the tarsal and metatarsal bones (**arch of the foot**). ~*vb.* **5.** (*tr.*) to span (an opening) with an arch. **6.** to form or cause to form an arch or a curve resembling that of an arch. **7.** (*tr.*) to span or extend over. [C14: < OF *arche,* < L *arcus* bow, ARC]

arch[2] (ɑːtʃ) *adj.* **1.** (*prenominal*) chief; principal; leading. **2.** (*prenominal*) expert: *an arch criminal.* **3.** knowing or superior; coyly playful: *an arch look.* [C16: independent use of ARCH-] —**ˈarchly** *adv.* —**ˈarchness** *n.*

arch. *abbrev. for:* **1.** archaic. **2.** archaism. **3.** archipelago. **4.** architect. **5.** architectural. **6.** architecture.

arch- *or* **archi-** *combining form.* **1.** chief; principal: *archangel; archbishop.* **2.** eminent above all others of the same kind: *archenemy.* [ult. < Gk *arkhi-,* < *arkhein* to rule]

-arch *n. combining form.* leader; ruler; chief: *patriarch; monarch.* [< Gk *-arkhēs,* < *arkhein* to rule]

Archaean *or esp. U.S.* **Archean** (ɑːˈkiːən) *adj.* of the metamorphosed rocks formed in the early Precambrian era.

archaeology *or* **archeology** (ˌɑːkɪˈɒlədʒɪ) *n.* the study of man's past by scientific analysis of the material remains of his cultures. [C17: < LL, < Gk *arkhaiologia* study of what is ancient, < *arkhē* beginning] —**archaeological** *or* **archeological** (ˌɑːkɪəˈlɒdʒɪkᵊl) *adj.* —ˌ**archaeˈologist** *or* ˌ**archeˈologist** *n.*

archaeopteryx (ˌɑːkɪˈɒptərɪks) *n.* any of several extinct primitive birds which occurred in Jurassic times and had teeth, a long tail, and well-developed wings. [C19: < Gk *arkhaios* ancient + *pterux* winged creature]

archaic (ɑːˈkeɪɪk) *adj.* **1.** belonging to or characteristic of a much earlier period. **2.** out of date; antiquated. **3.** (of vocabulary, etc.) characteristic of an earlier period of a language. [C19: < F, < Gk *arkhaïkos,* < *arkhaios* ancient, < *arkhē* beginning, < *arkhein* to begin] —**arˈchaically** *adv.*

archaism (ˈɑːkeɪˌɪzəm) *n.* **1.** the adoption or imitation of archaic words or style. **2.** an archaic word, style, etc. [C17: < NL, < Gk, < *arkhaizein* to model one's style upon that of ancient writers; see ARCHAIC] —**ˈarchaist** *n.* —ˌ**archaˈistic** *adj.*

archangel (ˈɑːkˌeɪndʒəl) *n.* a principal angel. —**archangelic** (ˌɑːkænˈdʒɛlɪk) *adj.*

archbishop (ˈɑːtʃˈbɪʃəp) *n.* a bishop of the highest rank. Abbrev.: **abp, Abp, Arch., Archbp.**

archbishopric (ˈɑːtʃˈbɪʃəprɪk) *n.* the rank, office, or jurisdiction of an archbishop.

archdeacon (ˈɑːtʃˈdiːkən) *n.* **1.** an Anglican clergyman ranking just below a bishop. **2.** a clergyman of similar rank in other Churches. —**ˈarchˈdeaconry** *n.*

archdiocese (ˌɑːtʃˈdaɪəˌsiːs) *n.* the diocese of an archbishop. —**archdiocesan** (ˌɑːtʃdaɪˈɒsɪsᵊn) *adj.*

archducal (ˈɑːtʃˈdjuːkᵊl) *adj.* of or relating to an archduke, archduchess, or archduchy.

archduchess (ˈɑːtʃˈdʌtʃɪs) *n.* **1.** the wife or widow of an archduke. **2.** (since 1453) a princess of the Austrian imperial family.

archduchy (ˈɑːtʃˈdʌtʃɪ) *n., pl.* **-duchies.** the territory ruled by an archduke or archduchess.

archduke (ˈɑːtʃˈdjuːk) *n.* a chief duke, esp. (since 1453) a prince of the Austrian imperial dynasty.

Archean (ɑːˈkiːən) *adj.* a variant spelling (esp. U.S.) of **Archaean.**

archegonium (ˌɑːkɪˈgəʊnɪəm) *n., pl.* **-nia** (-nɪə). a female sex organ, occurring in mosses, ferns, etc. [C19: < NL, < Gk, < *arkhe-* chief, first + *gonos* seed, race]

archenemy (ˈɑːtʃˈɛnɪmɪ) *n., pl.* **-mies. 1.** a chief enemy. **2.** (*often cap.; preceded by the*) the devil.

archeology (ˌɑːkɪˈɒlədʒɪ) *n.* a variant spelling of **archaeology.**

archer (ˈɑːtʃə) *n.* a person skilled in the use of a bow and arrow. [C13: < OF, < LL, < L *arcus* bow]

Archer (ˈɑːtʃə) *n.* **the.** the constellation Sagittarius.

archerfish (ˈɑːtʃəˌfɪʃ) *n., pl.* **-fish** *or* **-fishes.** a freshwater fish, related to the perch, of SE Asia and Australia, that catches insects by spitting water at them.

archery (ˈɑːtʃərɪ) *n.* **1.** the art or sport of shooting with bows and arrows. **2.** archers or their weapons collectively.

archetype (ˈɑːkɪˌtaɪp) *n.* **1.** a perfect or typical specimen. **2.** an original model; prototype. **3.** *Psychoanal.* one of the inherited mental images postulated by Jung. **4.** a recurring symbol or motif in literature, etc. [C17: < L *archetypum* an original, < Gk, < *arkhetupos* first-moulded; see ARCH-, -TYPE] —ˌ**archeˈtypal** *adj.*

archfiend (ˌɑːtʃˈfiːnd) *n.* (*often cap.*) **the.** the devil; Satan.

archidiaconal (ˌɑːkɪdaɪˈækənᵊl) *adj.* of or relating to an archdeacon or his office. —ˌ**archidiˈaconate** *n.*

archiepiscopal (ˌɑːkɪɪˈpɪskəpᵊl) *adj.* of or associated with an archbishop. —ˌ**archieˈpiscopate** *n.*

archil (ˈɑːtʃɪl) *n.* a variant of **orchil.**

archimandrite (ˌɑːkɪˈmændraɪt) *n. Greek Orthodox Church.* the head of a monastery. [C16: < LL, < LGk *arkhimandritēs,* < ARCHI- + *mandra* monastery]

Archimedes' principle (ˌɑːkɪˈmiːdiːz) *n.* a law of physics stating that the apparent loss in weight of a body immersed in a fluid is equal to the weight of the displaced fluid. [after *Archimedes* (? 287-212 B.C.), Gk mathematician and physicist]

Archimedes' screw *or* **Archimedean screw** (ˌɑːkɪˈmiːdɪən) *n.* an ancient water-lifting device using a spiral passage in an inclined cylinder.

archipelago (ˌɑːkɪˈpɛləˌgəʊ) *n., pl.* **-gos** *or* **-goes. 1.** a group of islands. **2.** a sea studded with islands. [C16 (meaning: the Aegean Sea): < It., < L *pelagus,* < Gk, < ARCH- + *pelagos* sea] —**archipelagic** (ˌɑːkɪpəˈlædʒɪk) *adj.*

architect (ˈɑːkɪˌtɛkt) *n.* **1.** a person qualified to design buildings and to supervise their erection. **2.** a person similarly qualified in another form of construction: *a naval architect.* **3.** any planner or creator. [C16: < F, < L, < Gk *arkhitektōn* director of works, < ARCHI- + *tektōn* workman; rel. to *tekhnē* art, skill]

architectonic (ˌɑːkɪtɛkˈtɒnɪk) *adj.* **1.** denoting, relating to, or having architectural qualities. **2.** *Metaphysics.* of the systematic classification of knowledge. [C16: < LL *architectonicus* concerning architecture; see ARCHITECT]

architectonics (ˌɑːkɪtɛkˈtɒnɪks) *n.* (*functioning as sing.*) **1.** the science of architecture. **2.** *Metaphysics.* the scientific classification of knowledge.

architecture (ˈɑːkɪˌtɛktʃə) *n.* **1.** the art and science of designing and superintending the erection of buildings, etc. **2.** a style of building or structure. **3.** buildings or structures collectively. **4.** the structure or design of anything. —ˌ**archiˈtectural** *adj.*

architrave (ˈɑːkɪˌtreɪv) *n. Archit.* **1.** the lowest part of an entablature that bears on the columns. **2.** a moulding around a doorway, window opening, etc. [C16: via F < It., < ARCHI- + *trave* beam, < L *trabs*]

archive (ˈɑːkaɪv) *n.* (*often pl.*) **1.** a collection of records of an institution, family, etc. **2.** a place where such records are kept. [C17: < LL, < Gk *arkheion* repository of official records, < *arkhē* government] —**arˈchival** *adj.*

archivist (ˈɑːkɪvɪst) *n.* a person in charge of archives.

archon (ˈɑːkɒn) *n.* (in ancient Athens) one of the nine chief magistrates. [C17: < Gk *arkhōn* ruler, < *arkhein* to rule] —ˈ**archonˌship** *n.*

archpriest (ˈɑːtʃˈpriːst) *n.* **1.** (formerly) a chief assistant to a bishop. **2.** a senior priest.

archway (ˈɑːtʃˌweɪ) *n.* a passageway or entrance under an arch or arches.

-archy *n. combining form.* government; rule: *anarchy; monarchy.* [< Gk *-arkhia;* see -ARCH]

arc light *n.* a light source in which an arc between two electrodes produces intense white illumination. Also called: **arc lamp.**

arctic (ˈɑːktɪk) *adj.* **1.** of or relating to the Arctic. **2.** *Inf.* cold; freezing. ~*n.* **3.** (*modifier*) suitable for conditions of extreme cold: *arctic clothing.* [C14: < L *arcticus,* < Gk *arktikos* northern, lit.: pertaining to (the constellation of) the Bear, < *arktos* bear]

Arctic (ˈɑːktɪk) *adj.* of or relating to the regions north of the Arctic Circle.

Arctic Circle *n.* the imaginary circle round the earth, parallel to the equator, at latitude 66° 32′ N.

arctic hare *n.* a large hare of the Canadian Arctic whose fur is white in winter.

arctic willow *n.* a low-growing shrub of the Canadian tundra.

Arcturus (ɑːkˈtjʊərəs) *n.* the brightest star in the constellation Boötes: a red giant. [C14: < L, < Gk *Arktouros,* < *arktos* bear + *ouros* guard, keeper]

arcuate (ˈɑːkjʊɪt) *adj.* shaped or bent like an arc or bow. [C17: < L *arcuāre,* < *arcus* ARC]

arc welding *n.* a technique in which metal is welded by heat generated by an electric arc. —**arc welder** *n.*

-ard *or* **-art** *suffix forming nouns.* indicating a person who does something, esp. to excess: *braggart; drunkard.* [via OF, of Gmc origin]

ardent (ˈɑːdᵊnt) *adj.* **1.** expressive of or characterized by intense desire or emotion. **2.** intensely enthusiastic; eager. **3.** glowing or shining: *ardent eyes.* **4. ardent spirits.** alcoholic drinks. [C14: < L *ārdēre* to burn] —ˈ**ardency** *n.* —ˈ**ardently** *adv.*

ardour *or U.S.* **ardor** (ˈɑːdə) *n.* **1.** feelings of great intensity and warmth. **2.** eagerness; zeal. [C14: < OF, < L *ārdor,* < *ārdēre* to burn]

arduous (ˈɑːdjuːəs) *adj.* **1.** difficult to accomplish; strenuous. **2.** hard to endure; harsh. **3.** steep or difficult: *an arduous track.* [C16: < L *arduus* steep, difficult] —ˈ**arduously** *adv.* —ˈ**arduousness** *n.*

are[1] (ɑː; *unstressed* ə) *vb.* the plural form of the present tense of **be** and the singular form used with *you.* [OE *aron,* second person pl. of *bēon* to BE]

are[2] (ɑː) *n.* a unit of area equal to 100 square metres. [C19: < F, < L *ārea* piece of ground; see AREA]

area (ˈɛərɪə) *n.* **1.** any flat, curved, or irregular expanse of a surface. **2. a.** the extent of a two-dimensional surface: *the area of a triangle.* **b.** the two-dimensional extent of a plane or surface: *the area of a sphere.* **3.** a section or part. **4.** region; district. **5. a.** a geographical division of administrative responsibility. **b.** (*as modifier*): *area manager.* **6.** a part or section, as of a building, town, etc., having some specified function: *reception area; commercial area.* **7.** the range or scope of anything. **8.** a subject field or field of study. **9.** Also called: **areaway.** a sunken area, usually enclosed, giving light, air, and sometimes access to a cellar basement. [C16: < L: level ground, threshing-floor; rel. to *ārēre* to be dry] —ˈ**areal** *adj.*

arena (əˈriːnə) *n.* **1.** an enclosure or platform, usually surrounded by seats, in which sports events, entertainments, etc., take place: *a boxing arena.* **2.** the central area of an ancient Roman amphitheatre, in which gladiatorial contests were held. **3.** a sphere of intense activity: *the political arena.* [C17: < L *harēna* sand, place where sand was strewn for the combats]

arenaceous (ˌærɪˈneɪʃəs) *adj.* **1.** (of sedimentary rocks) composed of sand. **2.** (of plants) growing in a sandy soil. [C17: < L *harēnāceus* sandy, < *harēna* sand]

aren't (ɑːnt) **1.** *contraction of* are not. **2.** *Inf., chiefly Brit.* (used in interrogative sentences) *contraction of* am not.

areola (əˈrɪələ) *n., pl.* **-lae** (-ˌliː) *or* **-las.** **1.** *Biol.* a space outlined on a surface, such as an area between veins on a leaf. **2.** *Anat.* any small circular area, such as the pigmented ring around the human nipple. [C17: < L: dim. of AREA] —**aˈreolar** *or* **areolate** (əˈrɪəlɪt, -ˌleɪt) *adj.*

arête (əˈreɪt, əˈrɛt) *n.* a sharp ridge that separates glacial valleys. [C19: < F: fishbone, ridge, < L *arista* ear of corn, fishbone]

argali (ˈɑːgəlɪ) *or* **argal** *n., pl.* **-gali** *or* **-gals.** a wild sheep, with massive horns in the male, inhabiting semidesert regions in central Asia. [C18: < Mongolian]

argent (ˈɑːdʒənt) *n.* **a.** an archaic or poetic word for **silver. b.** (*as adj.; often postpositive, esp. in heraldry*): *a bend argent.* [C15: < OF, < L]

argentiferous (ˌɑːdʒənˈtɪfərəs) *adj.* containing or bearing silver.

argentine (ˈɑːdʒənˌtaɪn) *adj.* **1.** of or resembling silver. ~*n.* **2.** a small marine fish characterized by a long silvery body.

Argentine (ˈɑːdʒənˌtiːn, -ˌtaɪn) *or* **Argentinian** (ˌɑːdʒənˈtɪnɪən) *adj.* **1.** of or relating to Argentina, a republic in South America. ~*n.* **2.** a native or inhabitant of Argentina.

argillaceous (ˌɑːdʒɪˈleɪʃəs) *adj.* (of sedimentary rocks) composed of very fine-grained material, such as clay. [C18: < L *argilla* white clay, < Gk, < *argos* white]

Argive (ˈɑːdʒaɪv, -gaɪv) *adj.* **1.** of or relating to Argos, a city of ancient Greece. **2.** a literary word for **Greek.** ~*n.* **3.** an ancient Greek, esp. one from Argos.

argol (ˈɑːgɒl) *or* **argal** (ˈɑːgəl) *n.* crude potassium hydrogen tartrate. [C14: < Anglo-F *argoil,* <?]

argon (ˈɑːgɒn) *n.* an unreactive colourless odourless element of the rare gas series that forms almost 1 per cent of the atmosphere. It is used in electric lights. Symbol: Ar; atomic no.: 18; atomic wt.: 39.95. [C19: < Gk, < *argos* inactive, < A-[1] + *ergon* work]

argosy (ˈɑːgəsɪ) *n., pl.* **-sies.** *Arch. or poetic.* a large abundantly laden merchant ship, or a fleet of such ships. [C16: < It. *Ragusea* (*nave*) (ship) of Ragusa]

argot (ˈɑːgəʊ) *n.* slang or jargon peculiar to a particular group, esp. (formerly) a group of thieves. [C19: < F, <?]

arguable (ˈɑːgjʊəbᵊl) *adj.* **1.** capable of being disputed. **2.** plausible; reasonable. —ˈ**arguably** *adv.*

argue (ˈɑːgjuː) *vb.* **-guing, -gued.** **1.** (*intr.*) to quarrel; wrangle. **2.** (*intr.; often foll. by* for *or* against) to present supporting or opposing reasons or cases in a dispute. **3.** (*tr.; may take a clause as object*) to try to prove by presenting reasons. **4.** (*tr.; often passive*) to debate or discuss. **5.** (*tr.*) to persuade. **6.** (*tr.*) to suggest:

her looks argue despair. [C14: < OF *arguer* to assert, < L *arguere* to make clear, accuse] —ˈ**arguer** *n.*

argufy (ˈɑːgjʊˌfaɪ) *vb.* **-fying, -fied.** *Facetious or dialect.* to argue or quarrel, esp. over something trivial.

argument (ˈɑːgjʊmənt) *n.* **1.** a quarrel; altercation. **2.** a discussion in which reasons are put forward; debate. **3.** (*sometimes pl.*) a point or series of reasons presented to support or oppose a proposition. **4.** a summary of the plot or subject of a book, etc. **5.** *Logic.* **a.** a process of reasoning in which the conclusion can be shown to be true or false. **b.** the middle term of a syllogism. **6.** *Maths.* another name for **independent variable** of a function.

argumentation (ˌɑːgjʊmɛnˈteɪʃən) *n.* **1.** the process of reasoning methodically. **2.** argument; debate.

argumentative (ˌɑːgjʊˈmɛntətɪv) *adj.* **1.** given to arguing. **2.** characterized by argument; controversial.

Argus (ˈɑːgəs) *n.* **1.** *Greek myth.* a giant with a hundred eyes who was made guardian of the heifer Io. **2.** a vigilant person.

Argus-eyed *adj.* observant; vigilant.

argy-bargy *or* **argie-bargie** (ˈɑːdʒɪˈbɑːdʒɪ) *n., pl.* **-bargies.** *Brit. inf.* a wrangling argument or verbal dispute. [C19: < Scot., < dialect *argle,* prob. < ARGUE]

aria (ˈɑːrɪə) *n.* an elaborate accompanied song for solo voice from a cantata, opera, or oratorio. [C18: < It.: tune, AIR]

Arian (ˈɛərɪən) *adj.* **1.** of, or relating to Arius, 3rd-century A.D. Greek Christian theologian, or to Arianism. ~*n.* **2.** an adherent of Arianism.

-arian *suffix forming nouns.* indicating a person or thing that advocates, believes, or is associated with something: *vegetarian; librarian.* [< L *-ārius* -ARY + -AN]

Arianism (ˈɛərɪəˌnɪzəm) *n.* the doctrine of Arius, declared heretical, which asserted that Christ was not of one substance with the Father.

arid (ˈærɪd) *adj.* **1.** having little or no rain; dry. **2.** devoid of interest. [C17: < L *āridus,* < *ārēre* to be dry] —**aridity** (əˈrɪdɪtɪ) *or* ˈ**aridness** *n.*

Aries (ˈɛəriːz) *n., Latin genitive* **Arietis** (əˈraɪɪtɪs). **1.** *Astron.* a N constellation. **2.** *Astrol.* Also called: the **Ram.** the first sign of the zodiac. The sun is in this sign between about March 21 and April 19. [C14: < L: ram]

aright (əˈraɪt) *adv.* correctly; rightly; properly.

aril (ˈærɪl) *n.* an additional covering formed on certain seeds, such as those of the yew and nutmeg, after fertilization. [C18: < NL, < Med. L *arilli* raisins, pips of grapes] —ˈ**arilˌlate** *adj.*

arioso (ˌɑːrɪˈəʊzəʊ) *n., pl.* **-sos** *or* **-si** (-siː). *Music.* a recitative with the lyrical quality of an aria. [C18: < It., < ARIA]

arise (əˈraɪz) *vb.* **arising, arose, arisen** (əˈrɪzᵊn). (*intr.*) **1.** to come into being; originate. **2.** (foll. by *from*) to proceed as a consequence. **3.** to get or stand up, as from a sitting or lying position. **4.** to come into notice. **5.** to ascend. [OE *ārīsan*]

aristo (ˈærɪstəʊ, əˈrɪstəʊ) *n., pl.* **-tos.** *Inf.* short for **aristocrat.**

aristocracy (ˌærɪˈstɒkrəsɪ) *n., pl.* **-cies.** **1.** government by the best citizens. **2.** a privileged class of people; the nobility. **3.** government by such a class. **4.** a state governed by such a class. **5.** a class of people considered to be outstanding in a sphere of activity. [C16: < LL, < Gk *aristokratia* rule by the best-born, < *aristos* best; see -CRACY]

aristocrat (ˈærɪstəˌkræt) *n.* **1.** a member of the aristocracy. **2.** a person who has the manners or qualities of a member of a privileged class. **3.** a supporter of aristocracy as a form of government.

aristocratic (ˌærɪstəˈkrætɪk) *adj.* **1.** relating to or characteristic of aristocracy or an aristocrat. **2.** elegant or stylish in appearance and behaviour. —ˌ**aristoˈcratically** *adv.*

Aristotelian (ˌærɪstəˈtiːlɪən) *adj.* **1.** of or relating to Aristotle, 4th-century B.C. Greek philosopher, or to his philosophy. ~*n.* **2.** a follower of Aristotle.

Aristotelian logic *n.* **1.** traditional logic, esp. relying on the theory of syllogism. **2.** the logical method of Aristotle, esp. as developed in the Middle Ages.

arithmetic *n.* (əˈrɪθmətɪk). **1.** the branch of mathematics concerned with numerical calculations, such as addition, subtraction, multiplication, and division. **2.** calculations involving numerical operations. **3.** knowledge of or skill in using arithmetic. ~*adj.* (ˌærɪθˈmɛtɪk) *also* **arithmetical.** **4.** of, relating to, or using arithmetic. [C13: < L, < Gk *arithmētikē,* < *arithmein* to count, < *arithmos* number] —ˌ**arithˈmetically** *adv.* —**aˌrithmeˈtician** *n.*

arithmetic mean *n.* the average value of a set of terms or quantities, expressed as their sum divided by their number: *the arithmetic mean of 3, 4, and 8 is 5.* Also called: **average.**

arithmetic progression *n.* a sequence, each term of which differs from the succeeding term by a constant amount, such as 3,6,9,12.

-arium *suffix forming nouns.* indicating a place for or associated with something: *aquarium; solarium.* [< L *-ārium,* neuter of *-ārius* -ARY]

ark (ɑːk) *n.* **1.** the vessel that Noah built which survived the Flood (Genesis 6–9). **2.** a place or thing offering shelter or protection. **3.** *Dialect.* a box. [OE *arc,* < L *arca* box, chest]

Ark (ɑːk) *n. Judaism.* **1.** Also called: **Holy Ark.** the cupboard in a synagogue in which the Torah scrolls are kept. **2.** Also called: **Ark of the Covenant.** the most sacred symbol of God's presence among the Hebrew people, carried in their journey from Sinai to the Promised Land (Canaan).

arm[1] (ɑːm) *n.* **1.** (in man) either of the upper limbs from the shoulder to the wrist. Related adj.: **brachial.** **2.** the part of either of the upper limbs from the elbow to the wrist; forearm. **3. a.** the corresponding limb of any other vertebrate. **b.** an armlike appendage of some invertebrates. **4.** an object that covers or supports the human arm, esp. the sleeve of a garment or the side of a chair, etc. **5.** anything considered to resemble an arm in appearance, function, etc.: *an arm of the sea; the arm of a record player.* **6.** an administrative subdivision of an organization: *an arm of the government.* **7.** power; authority: *the arm of the law.* **8. arm in arm.** with arms linked. **9. at arm's length.** at a distance. **10. in the arms of Morpheus.** sleeping. **11. with open arms.** with great warmth and hospitality. [OE]

arm[2] (ɑːm) *vb.* **1.** to equip with weapons as a preparation for war. **2.** (*tr.*) to provide (a person or thing) with something that strengthens, protects, or increases efficiency. **3. a.** (*tr.*) to activate (a fuse) so that it will explode at the required time. **b.** to prepare (an explosive device) for use by introducing a detonator, etc. ~*n.* **4.** (*usually pl.*) a weapon, esp. a firearm. [C14: < OF *armes,* < L *arma* arms, equipment]

armada (ɑːˈmɑːdə) *n.* **1.** a large number of ships or aircraft. **2.** (*cap.*) **the.** Also called: **Spanish Armada.** the great fleet sent by Philip II of Spain against England in 1588. [C16: < Sp., < Med. L *armāta* fleet, armed forces, < L *armāre* to provide with arms]

armadillo (ˌɑːməˈdɪləʊ) *n., pl.* **-los.** a burrowing mammal of Central and South America with a covering of strong horny plates over most of the body. [C16: < Sp., dim. of *armado* armed (man), < L *armātus* armed; cf. ARMADA]

Armageddon (ˌɑːməˈgɛdᵊn) *n.* **1.** *New Testament.* the final battle between good and evil at the end of the world. **2.** a catastrophic and extremely destructive conflict. [C19: < LL, < Gk, < Heb. *har megiddōn,* mountain district of *Megiddo* (in N Palestine)]

armament (ˈɑːməmənt) *n.* **1.** the weapon equipment of a military vehicle, ship, or aircraft. **2.** a military force raised and armed ready for war. **3.** preparation for war. [C17: < L *armāmenta* utensils, < *armāre* to equip]

armature (ˈɑːmətjʊə) *n.* **1.** a revolving structure in an electric motor or generator, wound with the coils that carry the current. **2.** any part of an electric machine or device that vibrates under the influence of a magnetic field or within which an electromotive force is induced. **3.** Also called: **keeper.** a soft iron or steel bar placed across the poles of a magnet to close the magnetic circuit. **4.** *Sculpture.* a framework to support the clay or other material used in modelling. **5.** the protective outer covering of an animal or plant. [C15: < L *armātūra* armour, equipment, < *armāre* to furnish with equipment]

armchair (ˈɑːmˌtʃɛə) *n.* **1.** a chair, esp. an upholstered one, that has side supports for the arms or elbows. **2.** (*modifier*) taking or involving no active part: *an armchair strategist.*

armed[1] (ɑːmd) *adj.* **1.** equipped with or supported by arms, armour, etc. **2.** prepared for conflict or any difficulty. **3.** (of an explosive device) prepared for use.

armed[2] (ɑːmd) *adj.* **a.** having an arm or arms. **b.** (*in combination*): *long-armed; one-armed.*

armed forces *pl. n.* the military forces of a nation or nations, including the army, navy, air force, marines, etc.

Armenian (ɑːˈmiːnɪən) *n.* **1.** a native or inhabitant of Armenia, an ancient kingdom now divided among the Soviet Union, Turkey, and Iran. **2.** the Indo-European language of the Armenians. ~*adj.* **3.** of Armenia, its inhabitants, or their language.

armful (ˈɑːmfʊl) *n., pl.* **-fuls.** the amount that can be held by one or both arms.

armhole (ˈɑːmˌhəʊl) *n.* the opening in an article of clothing through which the arm passes.

armillary sphere (ɑːˈmɪlərɪ) *n.* a model of the celestial sphere formerly used in fixing the positions of heavenly bodies.

Arminian (ɑːˈmɪnɪən) *adj.* denoting, relating to, or believing in the Protestant doctrines of Jacobus Arminius, 16th-century Dutch theologian, which rejected absolute predestination and stressed free will in man. —**Arˈminianˌism** *n.*

armistice (ˈɑːmɪstɪs) *n.* an agreement between opposing armies to suspend hostilities; truce. [C18: < NL, < L *arma* arms + *sistere* to stop]

Armistice Day (ˈɑːmɪstɪs) *n.* the anniversary of the signing of the armistice that ended World War I, on Nov. 11, 1918. See also **Remembrance Sunday.**

armlet (ˈɑːmlɪt) *n.* **1.** a small arm, as of a lake. **2.** a band or bracelet worn round the arm.

armoire (ɑːmˈwɑː) *n.* a large cabinet, originally used for storing weapons. [C16: < F, < OF *armaire,* < L *armārium* chest, closet; see AMBRY]

armorial (ɑːˈmɔːrɪəl) *adj.* of or relating to heraldry or heraldic arms.

armour *or U.S.* **armor** (ˈɑːmə) *n.* **1.** any defensive covering, esp. that of metal, chain mail, etc., worn by medieval warriors. **2.** the protective metal plates on a tank, warship, etc. **3.** *Mil.* armoured fighting vehicles in general. **4.** any protective covering, such as the shell of certain animals. **5.** heraldic insignia; arms. ~*vb.* **6.** (*tr.*) to equip or cover with armour. [C13: < OF *armure,* < L *armātūrā* armour, equipment]

armoured *or U.S.* **armored** (ˈɑːməd) *adj.* **1.** having a protective covering. **2.** comprising units making use of armoured vehicles: *an armoured brigade.*

armourer *or U.S.* **armorer** (ˈɑːmərə) *n.* **1.** a person who makes or mends arms and armour. **2.** a person employed in the maintenance of small arms and weapons in a military unit.

armour plate *n.* a tough heavy steel often hardened on the surface, used for protecting warships, tanks, etc.

armoury *or U.S.* **armory** (ˈɑːmərɪ) *n., pl.* **-mouries** *or* **-mories. 1.** a secure place for the storage of weapons. **2.** armour generally; military supplies. **3.** resources, such as arguments, on which to draw: *a few choice terms from her armoury of invective.*

armpit (ˈɑːmˌpɪt) *n.* the small depression beneath the arm where it joins the shoulder. Technical name: **axilla.**

armrest (ˈɑːmˌrɛst) *n.* the part of a chair, sofa, etc., that supports the arm. Sometimes shortened to **arm.**

arms (ɑːmz) *pl. n.* **1.** weapons collectively. See also **small arms. 2.** military exploits: *prowess in arms.* **3.** the official heraldic symbols of a family, state, etc. **4. bear arms. a.** to carry weapons. **b.** to serve in the armed forces. **c.** to have a coat of arms. **5. in** *or* **under arms.** armed and prepared for war. **6. lay down one's arms.** to stop fighting; surrender. **7. take (up) arms.** to prepare to fight. **8. up in arms.** indignant; prepared to protest strongly. [C13: < OF, < L *arma;* see ARM[2]]

arm wrestling *n.* a contest of strength in which two people rest the elbow of one arm on a flat surface, grasp each other's hand, and try to force their opponent's forearm down flat.

army (ˈɑːmɪ) *n., pl.* **-mies. 1.** the military land forces of a nation. **2.** a military unit usually consisting of two or more corps with supporting arms and services. **3.** (*modifier*) of or characteristic of an army. **4.** any large body of people united for some specific purpose. **5.** a large number of people, animals, etc. [C14: < OF, < Med. L *armāta* armed forces]

army ant *n.* any of various tropical American predatory ants which travel in vast hordes preying on other animals. Also called: **legionary ant.**

army worm *n.* a type of caterpillar which travels in vast hordes and is a serious pest of cereal crops.

arnica (ˈɑːnɪkə) *n.* **1.** any of a genus of N temperate or arctic plants having yellow flowers. **2.** the tincture of the dried flower heads of any of these plants, used in treating bruises. [C18: < NL, <?]

aroha (ˈɑːrɒhə) *n. N.Z.* love, compassion, or affectionate regard. [Maori]

aroid (ˈærɔɪd, ˈɛər-) *adj.* of or relating to a plant family that includes the arum, calla, and anthurium. [C19: < ARUM + -OID]

aroint thee *or* **ye** (əˈrɔɪnt) *sentence substitute. Arch.* away! begone! [C17: <?]

aroma (əˈrəʊmə) *n.* **1.** a distinctive usually pleasant smell, esp. of spices, wines, and plants. **2.** a subtle pervasive quality or atmosphere. [C18: via L < Gk: spice]

aromatherapy (əˌrəʊməˈθɛrəpɪ) *n.* the massaging of the skin with fragrant oils in order to relieve tension.

aromatic (ˌærəˈmætɪk) *adj.* **1.** having a distinctive, usually fragrant smell. **2.** (of an organic compound) having an unsaturated ring, esp. containing a benzene ring. Cf. **aliphatic.** ~*n.* **3.** something, such as a plant or drug, giving off a fragrant smell. —**ˌaroˈmatically** *adv.* —**aˌromaˈticity** *n.*

aromatize *or* **-tise** (əˈrəʊməˌtaɪz) *vb.* (*tr.*) to make aromatic. —**aˌromatiˈzation** *or* **-iˈsation** *n.*

arose (əˈrəʊz) *vb.* the past tense of **arise.**

around (əˈraʊnd) *prep.* **1.** situated at various points in: *a lot of shelves around the house.* **2.** from place to place in: *driving around Ireland.* **3.** somewhere in or near. **4.** *Chiefly U.S.* approximately in: *it happened around 1957.* ~*adv.* **5.** in all directions from a point of reference: *he owns the land for ten miles around.* **6.** in the vicinity, esp. restlessly but idly: *to stand around.* **7.** in no particular place or direction: *dotted around.* **8.** *Inf.* (of people) active and prominent in a particular area or profession. **9.** *Inf.* present in some place (the exact location being unknown or unspecified). **10.** *Inf.* in circulation; available: *that type of phone has been around for some years now.* **11.** *Inf.* to many places, so as to have gained considerable experience, often of a worldly or social nature: *I've been around.* [C17 (rare earlier): < A-[2] + ROUND]

▷ **Usage.** In American English, *around* is usually used instead of *round* in adverbial and prepositional senses, except in a few fixed phrases such as *all year round.* Such uses of *around* are less common in British English.

arouse (əˈraʊz) *vb.* **1.** (*tr.*) to evoke or elicit (a reaction, emotion, or response). **2.** to awaken from sleep. —**aˈrousal** *n.* —**aˈrouser** *n.*

arpeggio (ɑːˈpɛdʒɪəʊ) *n., pl.* **-gios.** a chord whose notes are played or sung in rapid succession rather than simultaneously. [C18: < It., < *arpeggiare* to perform on the harp, < *arpa* HARP]

arquebus (ˈɑːkwɪbəs) *or* **harquebus** *n.* a portable long-barrelled gun dating from the 15th century. [C16: via OF < MDu. *hakebusse*, lit.: hook gun, from the shape of the butt, < *hake* hook + *busse* box, gun, < LL *busis* box]

arr. *abbrev. for:* **1.** arranged (by). **2.** arrival. **3.** arrive(d).

arrack *or* **arak** (ˈærək) *n.* a coarse spirit distilled in various Eastern countries from grain, rice, sugar cane, etc. [C17: < Ar. *ʿaraq* sweat, sweet juice, liquor]

arraign (əˈreɪn) *vb.* (*tr.*) **1.** to bring (a prisoner) before a court to answer an indictment. **2.** to call to account; accuse. [C14: < OF, < Vulgar L *ratiōnāre* (unattested) to talk, argue, < L *ratiō* a reasoning] —**arˈraigner** *n.* —**arˈraignment** *n.*

arrange (əˈreɪndʒ) *vb.* **1.** (*tr.*) to put into a proper or systematic order. **2.** (*tr.; may take a clause as object or an infinitive*) to arrive at an agreement about. **3.** (when *intr.*, often foll. by *for;* when *tr., may take a clause as object or an infinitive*) to make plans or preparations in advance (for something): *we arranged for her to be met.* **4.** (*tr.*) to adapt (a musical composition) for performance in a different way, esp. on different instruments. **5.** (*intr.; often foll. by with*) to come to an agreement. [C14: < OF *arangier*, < A-[2] + *rangier* to put in a row, RANGE] —**arˈrangeable** *adj.* —**arˈranger** *n.*

arrangement (əˈreɪndʒmənt) *n.* **1.** the act of arranging or being arranged. **2.** the form in which things are arranged. **3.** a thing composed of various ordered parts: *a flower arrangement.* **4.** (*often pl.*) a preparation. **5.** an understanding. **6.** an adaptation of a piece of music for performance in a different way, esp. on different instruments.

arrant (ˈærənt) *adj.* utter; out-and-out: *an arrant fool.* [C14: var. of ERRANT (wandering, vagabond)] —**ˈarrantly** *adv.*

arras (ˈærəs) *n.* a wall hanging, esp. of tapestry. [< *Arras*, a town in N France]

array (əˈreɪ) *n.* **1.** an impressive display or collection. **2.** an orderly arrangement, esp. of troops in battle order. **3.** *Poetic.* rich clothing. **4.** *Maths.* a set of numbers or symbols arranged in rows and columns, as in a determinant or matrix. **5.** *Law.* a panel of jurors. **6.** *Computers.* a regular data structure in which elements may be located by reference to index numbers. ~*vb.* (*tr.*) **7.** to dress in rich attire. **8.** to arrange in order (esp. troops for battle). **9.** *Law.* to draw up (a panel of jurors). [C13: < OF, < *arayer* to arrange, of Gmc origin] —**arˈrayal** *n.*

arrears (əˈrɪəz) *n.* (*sometimes sing.*) **1.** Also called: **arrearage.** something outstanding or owed. **2. in arrears** *or* **arrear.** late in paying a debt or meeting an obligation. [C18: < obs. *arrear* (adv.) behindhand, < OF, < Med. L *adretrō*, < L *ad* to + *retrō* backwards]

arrest (əˈrɛst) *vb.* (*tr.*) **1.** to deprive (a person) of liberty by taking him into custody, esp. under lawful authority. **2.** to seize (a ship) under lawful authority. **3.** to slow or stop the development of (a disease, growth, etc.). **4.** to catch and hold (one's attention, etc.). ~*n.* **5.** the act of taking a person into custody, esp. under lawful authority. **6.** the act of seizing and holding a ship under lawful authority. **7.** the state of being held: *under arrest.* **8.** the slowing or stopping of something: *a cardiac arrest.* [C14: < OF, < Vulgar L *arrestāre* (unattested), < L *ad* at, to + *restāre* to stand firm, stop]

arresting (əˈrɛstɪŋ) *adj.* attracting attention; striking. —**arˈrestingly** *adv.*

arrhythmia (əˈrɪðmɪə) *n.* any variation from the normal rhythm in the heartbeat. [C19: NL, < Gk *arrhuthmia*, < A-[1] + *rhuthmos* RHYTHM]

arrière-pensée *French.* (arjɛrpɑ̃se) *n.* an unrevealed thought or intention. [C19: lit.: behind thought]

arris (ˈærɪs) *n., pl.* **-ris** *or* **-rises.** a sharp edge at the meeting of two surfaces at an angle with one another. [C17: < OF *areste* beard of grain, sharp ridge; see ARÊTE]

arrival (əˈraɪvəl) *n.* **1.** the act or time of arriving. **2.** a person or thing that arrives or has arrived.

arrive (əˈraɪv) *vb.* (*intr.*) **1.** to come to a certain place during or after a journey. **2.** to reach: *to arrive at a decision.* **3.** to occur eventually: *the moment arrived when pretence was useless.* **4.** *Inf.* (of a baby) to be born. **5.** *Inf.* to attain success. [C13: < OF, < Vulgar L *arrīpāre* (unattested) to land, reach the bank, < L *ad* to + *rīpa* river bank]

arrivederci *Italian.* (arriveˈdertʃi) *sentence substitute.* goodbye.

arriviste (ˌæriːˈviːst) *n.* a person who is unscrupulously ambitious. [F: see ARRIVE, -IST]

arrogant (ˈærəgənt) *adj.* having or showing an exaggerated opinion of one's own importance, merit, ability, etc.: *an arrogant assumption.* [C14: < L *arrogāre* to claim as one's own; see ARROGATE] —**ˈarrogance** *n.* —**ˈarrogantly** *adv.*

arrogate (ˈærəˌgeɪt) *vb.* (*tr.*) **1.** to claim or appropriate for oneself without justification. **2.** to attribute or assign to another without justification. [C16: < L *arrogāre*, < *rogāre* to ask] —ˌ**arroˈgation** *n.* —**arrogative** (əˈrɒgətɪv) *adj.*

arrondissement (*French* arɔ̃dismɑ̃) *n.* (in France) **1.** the largest subdivision of a department. **2.** a municipal district of large cities, esp. Paris. [C19: < *arrondir* to make round]

arrow (ˈærəʊ) *n.* **1.** a long slender pointed weapon, usually having feathers fastened at the end as a balance, that is shot from a bow. **2.** any of various things that resemble an arrow in shape, function, or speed. [OE *arwe*]

arrowhead (ˈærəʊˌhɛd) *n.* **1.** the pointed tip of an arrow, often removable from the shaft. **2.** something that resembles the head of an arrow in shape. **3.** an aquatic herbaceous plant having arrow-shaped leaves.

arrowroot (ˈærəʊˌruːt) *n.* **1.** a white-flowered West Indian plant, whose rhizomes yield an easily digestible starch. **2.** the starch obtained from this plant.

arroyo (əˈrɔɪəʊ) *n., pl.* **-os.** *Chiefly southwestern U.S.* a stream or brook. [C19: < Sp., prob. rel. to L *arrūgia* shaft in a gold mine]

arse (ɑːs) *or U.S. & Canad.* **ass** *n. Taboo.* **1.** the buttocks. **2.** the anus. **3.** a stupid person; fool. ~Also called (for senses 2, 3): **arsehole,** (U.S. & Canad.) **asshole.** [OE]

arsenal (ˈɑːsənəl) *n.* **1.** a store for arms, ammunition, and other military items. **2.** a workshop that produces munitions. **3.** a store of anything regarded as weapons. [C16: < It. *arsenale* dockyard, < Ar., < *dār* house + *ṣinā'ah* manufacture]

arsenate (ˈɑːsəˌneɪt, -nɪt) *n.* a salt or ester of arsenic acid.

arsenic *n.* (ˈɑːsnɪk). **1.** a toxic metalloid element used in transistors, lead-based alloys, and high-temperature brasses. Symbol: As; atomic no.: 33; atomic wt.: 74.92. **2.** a nontechnical name for **arsenic trioxide,** used as rat poison and an insecticide. ~*adj.* (ɑːˈsɛnɪk). **3.** of or containing arsenic, esp. in the pentavalent state. [C14: < L, < Gk *arsenikon* yellow arsenic ore, < Syriac *zarnīg* (infl. by Gk *arsenikos* virile)]

arsenic acid *n.* a white poisonous soluble crystalline solid used in the manufacture of insecticides.

arsenical (ɑːˈsɛnɪkəl) *adj.* **1.** of or containing arsenic. ~*n.* **2.** a drug or insecticide containing arsenic.

arsenious (ɑːˈsiːnɪəs) *or* **arsenous** (ˈɑːsɪnəs) *adj.* of or containing arsenic in the trivalent state.

arson (ˈɑːsən) *n. Criminal law.* the act of intentionally or recklessly setting fire to property for some improper reason. [C17: < OF, < Med. L *ārsiō*, < L *ārdēre* to burn] —**ˈarsonist** *n.*

art[1] (ɑːt) *n.* **1. a.** the creation of works of beauty or other special significance. **b.** (*as modifier*): *an art movement.* **2.** the exercise of human skill (as distinguished from *nature*). **3.** imaginative skill as applied to representations of the natural world or figments of the imagination. **4. a.** works of art collectively, esp. of the visual arts. **b.** (*as modifier*): *an art gallery.* **5.** any branch of the visual arts, esp. painting. **6. a.** any field using the techniques of art to display artistic qualities. **b.** (*as modifier*): *art film.* **7.** method, facility, or knack: *the art of threading a needle.* **8.** skill governing a particular human activity: *the art of government.* **9.** cunning. **10. get something down to a fine art.** to become highly proficient at something through practice. ~See also **arts.** [C13: < OF, < L *ars* craftsmanship]

art[2] (ɑːt) *vb. Arch.* (used with the pronoun *thou*) a singular form of the present tense of **be.** [OE *eart,* part of *bēon* to BE]

art. *abbrev. for:* **1.** article. **2.** artificial. **3.** Also: **arty.** artillery.

-art *suffix forming nouns.* a variant of **-ard.**

Art Deco (ˈdɛkəʊ) *n.* a style of interior decoration, architecture, etc., at its height in the 1930s and characterized by geometrical shapes. [C20: < *art décoratif,* after the *Exposition des arts décoratifs* held in Paris in 1925]

artefact *or* **artifact** (ˈɑːtɪˌfækt) *n.* **1.** something made or given shape by man, such as a tool or a work of art, esp. an object of archaeological interest. **2.** *Cytology.* a structure seen in dead tissue that is not normally present in the living tissue. [C19: < L *arte factum,* < *ars* skill + *facere* to make]

artel (ɑːˈtɛl) *n.* (in the Soviet Union) a cooperative union or organization, esp. of producers, such as peasants. [< Russian *artel',* < It. *artieri* artisans, < *arte* work, < L *ars* ART[1]]

arterial (ɑːˈtɪərɪəl) *adj.* **1.** of or affecting an artery or arteries. **2.** denoting or relating to the bright red reoxygenated blood that circulates in the arteries. **3.** being a major route, esp. one with many minor branches. **—arˈterially** *adv.*

arterialize *or* **-lise** (ɑːˈtɪərɪəˌlaɪz) *vb.* (*tr.*) **1.** to change (venous blood) into arterial blood by replenishing the depleted oxygen. **2.** to provide with arteries. **—arˌterialiˈzation** *or* **-liˈsation** *n.*

arteriole (ɑːˈtɪərɪˌəʊl) *n. Anat.* any of the small subdivisions of an artery that form thin-walled vessels ending in capillaries. [C19: < NL, < L *artēria* ARTERY]

arteriosclerosis (ɑːˌtɪərɪəʊsklɪəˈrəʊsɪs) *n., pl.* **-ses** (-siːz). a thickening and loss of elasticity of the walls of the arteries. Nontechnical name: **hardening of the arteries. —arteriosclerotic** (ɑːˌtɪərɪəʊsklɪəˈrɒtɪk) *adj.*

artery (ˈɑːtərɪ) *n., pl.* **-teries. 1.** any of the tubular thick-walled muscular vessels that convey oxygenated blood from the heart to various parts of the body. Cf. **pulmonary artery, vein. 2.** a major road or means of communication. [C14: < L *artēria,* rel. to Gk *aortē* the great artery, AORTA]

artesian well (ɑːˈtiːzɪən) *n.* a well sunk through impermeable strata into strata receiving water from an area at a higher altitude than that of the well, so the water is forced to flow upwards. [C19: < F, < OF *Arteis* Artois, old province, where such wells were common]

Artex (ˈɑːtɛks) *n. Trademark.* a textured coating for walls and ceilings.

art form *n.* **1.** an accepted mode of artistic composition, such as the sonnet, symphony, etc. **2.** a recognized medium of artistic expression.

artful (ˈɑːtfʊl) *adj.* **1.** cunning or tricky. **2.** skilful in achieving a desired end. **—ˈartfully** *adv.* **—ˈartfulness** *n.*

arthralgia (ɑːˈθrældʒə) *n. Pathol.* pain in a joint. **—arˈthralgic** *adj.*

arthritis (ɑːˈθraɪtɪs) *n.* inflammation of a joint or joints characterized by pain and stiffness of the affected parts. [C16: via L < Gk *arthron* joint + -ITIS] **—arthritic** (ɑːˈθrɪtɪk) *adj., n.*

arthropod (ˈɑːθrəˌpɒd) *n.* an invertebrate having jointed limbs, a segmented body, and an exoskeleton made of chitin, as the crustaceans, insects, arachnids, and centipedes. [C19: < NL, < Gk *arthron* joint + *-podus* footed, < *pous* foot]

artic (ɑːˈtɪk) *n. Inf.* short for **articulated lorry.**

artichoke (ˈɑːtɪˌtʃəʊk) *n.* **1.** Also called: **globe artichoke.** a thistle-like Eurasian plant, cultivated for its large edible flower head. **2.** the unopened flower head of this plant, which can be cooked and eaten. **3.** See **Jerusalem artichoke.** [C16: < It., < OSp., < Ar. *al-kharshūf*]

article (ˈɑːtɪkᵊl) *n.* **1.** one of a class of objects; item. **2.** an unspecified or previously named thing, esp. a small object. **3.** a written composition on a subject, often being one of several found in a magazine, newspaper, etc. **4.** *Grammar.* a kind of determiner, occurring in many languages including English, that lacks independent meaning. See also **definite article, indefinite article. 5.** a clause or section in a written document. **6.** (*often cap.*) *Christianity.* See **Thirty-nine Articles.** ~*vb.* (*tr.*) **7.** to bind by a written contract, esp. one that governs a period of training: *an articled clerk.* [C13: < OF, < L *articulus* small joint, < *artus* joint]

articular (ɑːˈtɪkjʊlə) *adj.* of or relating to joints or to the structural components in a joint. [C15: < L *articulāris* concerning the joints, < *articulus* small joint]

articulate *adj.* (ɑːˈtɪkjʊlɪt). **1.** able to express oneself fluently and coherently. **2.** having the power of speech. **3.** distinct, clear, or definite: *an articulate document.* **4.** *Zool.* (of arthropods and higher vertebrates) possessing joints or jointed segments. ~*vb.* (ɑːˈtɪkjʊˌleɪt). **5.** to speak or enunciate (words, syllables, etc.) clearly and distinctly. **6.** (*tr.*) to express coherently in words. **7.** (*intr.*) *Zool.* to be jointed or form a joint. [C16: < L *articulāre* to divide into joints] **—arˈticulately** *adv.* **—arˈticulateness** *n.* **—arˈticuˌlator** *n.*

articulated lorry *n.* a large lorry made in two separate sections, a tractor and a trailer, connected by a pivoted bar.

articulation (ɑːˌtɪkjʊˈleɪʃən) *n.* **1.** the act or process of speaking or expressing in words. **2. a.** the process of articulating a speech sound. **b.** the sound so produced, esp. a consonant. **3.** the act or the state of being jointed together. **4.** *Zool.* **a.** a joint such as that between bones or arthropod segments. **b.** the way in which jointed parts are connected. **5.** *Bot.* the part of a plant at which natural separation occurs.

artifact (ˈɑːtɪˌfækt) *n.* a variant spelling of **artefact.**

artifice (ˈɑːtɪfɪs) *n.* **1.** a clever expedient. **2.** crafty or subtle deception. **3.** skill; cleverness. **4.** a skilfully contrived device. [C16: < OF, < L *artificium* skill, < *artifex* one possessed of a specific skill, < *ars* skill + *-fex,* < *facere* to make]

artificer (ɑːˈtɪfɪsə) *n.* **1.** a skilled craftsman. **2.** a clever or inventive designer. **3.** a serviceman trained in mechanics.

artificial (ˌɑːtɪˈfɪʃəl) *adj.* **1.** produced by man; not occurring naturally. **2.** made in imitation of a natural product: *artificial cream.* **3.** pretended; insincere. **4.** lacking in spontaneity; affected: *an artificial laugh.* [C14: < L *artificiālis* belonging to art, < *artificium* skill, ARTIFICE] **—artificiality** (ˌɑːtɪˌfɪʃɪˈælɪtɪ) *n.* **—ˌartiˈficially** *adv.*

artificial insemination *n.* introduction of spermatozoa into the vagina or uterus by means other than sexual union.

artificial intelligence *n.* the ability of a machine, such as a computer, to imitate intelligent human behaviour.

artificial respiration *n.* **1.** any of various methods of restarting breathing after it has stopped. **2.** any method of maintaining respiration, as by use of an iron lung.

artillery (ɑːˈtɪlərɪ) *n.* **1.** guns, cannon, mortars, etc., of calibre greater than 20mm. **2.** troops or military units specializing in using such guns. **3.** the science dealing with the use of guns. [C14: < OF, < *artillier* to equip with weapons, <?]

artiodactyl (ˌɑːtɪəʊˈdæktɪl) *n.* an ungulate with an even number of toes, as pigs, camels, deer, cattle, etc. [C19: < Gk *artios* even-numbered + *daktulos* finger]

artisan (ˈɑːtɪˌzæn, ˌɑːtɪˈzæn) *n.* a skilled workman; craftsman. [C16: < F, < OIt. *artigiano*, < *arte* ART[1]]

artist (ˈɑːtɪst) *n.* **1.** a person who practises or is skilled in an art, esp. painting, drawing, or sculpture. **2.** a person who displays in his work qualities required in art, such as sensibility and imagination. **3.** a person whose profession requires artistic expertise. **4.** a person skilled in some task or occupation. **5.** *Sl.* a person devoted to or proficient in something: *a con artist; a booze artist.* —**arˈtistic** *adj.* —**arˈtistically** *adv.*

artiste (ɑːˈtiːst) *n.* **1.** an entertainer, such as a singer or dancer. **2.** a person who is highly skilled in some occupation: *a hair artiste.* [F]

artistry (ˈɑːtɪstrɪ) *n.* **1.** artistic workmanship, ability, or quality. **2.** artistic pursuits. **3.** great skill.

artless (ˈɑːtlɪs) *adj.* **1.** free from deceit; ingenuous: *an artless remark.* **2.** natural; unpretentious. **3.** without art or skill. —ˈ**artlessly** *adv.*

Art Nouveau (ɑː nuːˈvəʊ; *French* ar nuvo) *n.* a style of art and architecture of the 1890s, characterized by sinuous outlines and stylized natural forms. [F, lit.: new art]

art paper *n.* a high-quality type of paper having a smooth coating of china clay or similar substance on it.

arts (ɑːts) *pl. n.* **1. a. the.** imaginative, creative, and nonscientific branches of knowledge considered collectively, esp. as studied academically. **b.** (*as modifier*): *an arts degree.* **2.** See **fine art. 3.** cunning actions or schemes.

art union *n. Austral. & N.Z.* an officially approved lottery for prizes of cash or (formerly) works of art.

arty (ˈɑːtɪ) *adj.* **artier, artiest.** *Inf.* having an affected interest in artists or art. —ˈ**artiness** *n.*

arum (ˈɛərəm) *n.* **1.** any of various aroid plants of Europe and the Mediterranean region, having arrow-shaped leaves and a typically white spathe, such as the cuckoopint. **2. arum lily.** another name for **calla** (sense 1). [C16: < L, var. of *aros* wake-robin, < Gk *aron*]

arvo (ˈɑːvəʊ) *n. Austral. inf.* afternoon.

-ary *suffix.* **1.** (*forming adjectives*) of; related to; belonging to: *cautionary.* **2.** (*forming nouns*) a person or thing connected with: *missionary; aviary.* [< L *-ārius, -āria, -ārium*]

Aryan (ˈɛərɪən) *n.* **1.** (in Nazi ideology) a Caucasian of non-Jewish descent. **2.** a member of any of the peoples supposedly descended from the Indo-Europeans. ~*adj.* **3.** of or characteristic of an Aryan or Aryans. ~*adj., n.* **4.** *Arch.* Indo-European. [C19: < Sansk. *ārya* of noble birth]

as[1] (æz; *unstressed* əz) *conj.* (*subordinating*) **1.** (often preceded by *just*) while; when: *he caught me as I was leaving.* **2.** in the way that: *dancing as only she can.* **3.** that which; what: *I did as I was told.* **4.** (of) which fact, event, etc. (referring to the previous statement): *to become wise, as we all know, is not easy.* **5. as it were.** in a way; as if it were really so. **6.** since; seeing that. **7.** in the same way that: *he died of cancer, as his father had done.* **8.** for instance: *capital cities, as London.* ~*adv., conj.* **9. a.** used to indicate identity of extent, amount, etc.: *she is as heavy as her sister.* **b.** used with this sense after a noun phrase introduced by *the same: the same height as her sister.* ~*prep.* **10.** in the role of; being: *as his friend, my opinions are probably biased.* **11. as for** *or* **to.** with reference to: *as for my past, I'm not telling you anything.* **12. as if** *or* **though.** as it would be if: *he talked as if he knew all about it.* **13. as (it) is.** in the existing state of affairs. **14. as was.** in a previous state. [OE *alswā* likewise]

as[2] (æs) *n.* **1.** an ancient Roman unit of weight approximately equal to 1 pound troy (373 grams). **2.** a copper coin of ancient Rome. [C17: < L *ās* unity]

As *symbol for:* **1.** altostratus. **2.** *Chem.* arsenic.

AS *abbrev. for:* **1.** Also: **A.S.** Anglo-Saxon. **2.** antisubmarine.

ASA *abbrev. for:* **1.** (in Britain) Amateur Swimming Association. **2.** (in the U.S.) American Standards Association.

ASA/BS *abbrev.* an expression of the speed of a photographic film. [C20: < *American Standards Association/British Standard*]

asafoetida *or* **asafetida** (ˌæsəˈfɛtɪdə) *n.* a bitter resin with an unpleasant onion-like smell, obtained from the roots of some umbelliferous plants: formerly used to treat flatulence, etc. [C14: < Med. L, < *asa* gum (cf. Persian *azā* mastic) + L *foetidus* evil-smelling]

a.s.a.p. *abbrev. for* as soon as possible.

asbestos (æsˈbɛstɒs) *n.* **a.** any of the fibrous amphibole minerals that are incombustible and resistant to chemicals. It was formerly widely used in the form of fabric or board as a heat-resistant structural material. **b.** (*as modifier*): *asbestos matting.* [C14: via L < Gk: < *asbestos* inextinguishable, < A-[1] + *sbennunai* to extinguish]

asbestosis (ˌæsbɛsˈtəʊsɪs) *n.* inflammation of the lungs resulting from chronic inhalation of asbestos particles.

ascarid (ˈæskərɪd) *n.* a parasitic nematode worm such as the common roundworm of man and pigs. [C14: < NL, < Gk *askarides*, pl. of *askaris*]

ascend (əˈsɛnd) *vb.* **1.** to go or move up (a ladder, hill, slope, etc.). **2.** (*intr.*) to slope or incline upwards. **3.** (*intr.*) to rise to a higher point, level, etc. **4.** to trace (a genealogy, etc.) back in time. **5.** to sing or play (a scale, etc.) from the lower to higher notes. **6. ascend the throne.** to become king or queen. [C14: < L *ascendere*, < *scandere*]

ascendancy, ascendency (əˈsɛndənsɪ) *or* **ascendance, ascendence** *n.* the condition of being dominant.

ascendant *or* **ascendent** (əˈsɛndənt) *adj.* **1.** proceeding upwards; rising. **2.** dominant or influential. ~*n.* **3.** a position or condition of dominance. **4.** *Astrol.* (*sometimes cap.*) **a.** a point on the ecliptic that rises on the eastern horizon at a particular moment. **b.** the sign of the zodiac containing this point. **5. in the ascendant.** increasing in influence, etc.

ascender (əˈsɛndə) *n.* **1.** *Printing.* **a.** the part of certain lower-case letters, such as *b* or *h*, that extends above the body of the letter. **b.** any letter having such a part. **2.** a person or thing that ascends.

ascension (əˈsɛnʃən) *n.* the act of ascending. —**asˈcensional** *adj.*

Ascension (əˈsɛnʃən) *n. Bible.* the passing of Jesus Christ from earth into heaven (Acts 1:9).

Ascension Day *n.* the 40th day after Easter, when the Ascension of Christ into heaven is celebrated.

ascent (əˈsɛnt) *n.* **1.** the act of ascending; upward movement. **2.** an upward slope. **3.** movement back through time (esp. in **line of ascent**).

ascertain (ˌæsəˈteɪn) *vb.* (*tr.*) **1.** to determine definitely. **2.** *Arch.* to make certain. [C15: < OF *acertener* to make certain] —ˌ**ascerˈtainable** *adj.* —ˌ**ascerˈtainment** *n.*

ascetic (əˈsɛtɪk) *n.* **1.** a person who practises great self-denial and abstains from worldly comforts and pleasures, esp. for religious reasons. ~*adj.* also **ascetical. 2.** rigidly abstinent or abstemious. **3.** of or relating to ascetics or asceticism. [C17: < Gk *askētikos*, < *askētēs*, < *askein* to exercise] —**asˈcetically** *adv.*

ascidian (əˈsɪdɪən) *n.* any of a class of minute marine invertebrate animals, such as the sea squirt, the adults of which are degenerate and sedentary.

ascidium (əˈsɪdɪəm) *n., pl.* **-cidia** (-ˈsɪdɪə). part of a plant that is shaped like a pitcher, such as the modified leaf of the pitcher plant. [C18: < NL, < Gk *askidion* a little bag, < *askos* bag]

ascomycete (ˌæskəmaɪˈsiːt) *n.* any of a class of fungi in which the spores (ascospores) are formed inside a club-shaped cell (ascus). The group includes yeast, penicillium, and certain mildews. —ˌ**ascomy'cetous** *adj.*

ascorbic acid (ə'skɔːbɪk) *n.* a white crystalline vitamin present in plants, esp. citrus fruits, tomatoes, and green vegetables. A deficiency in the diet of man leads to scurvy. Also called: **vitamin C.** [C20: < A-[1] + SCORBUTIC]

ascribe (ə'skraɪb) *vb.* (*tr.*) **1.** to credit or assign, as to a particular origin or period. **2.** to consider as belonging to: *to ascribe beauty to youth.* [C15: < L *ascrībere* to enrol, < *ad* in addition + *scrībere* to write] —**as'cribable** *adj.*

ascription (ə'skrɪpʃən) *n.* **1.** the act of ascribing. **2.** a statement ascribing something to someone. [C16: < L *ascrīptiō,* < *ascrībere* to ASCRIBE]

asdic ('æzdɪk) *n.* an early form of **sonar.** [C20: < *A(nti-)S(ubmarine) D(etection) I(nvestigation) C(ommittee)*]

-ase *suffix forming nouns.* indicating an enzyme: *oxidase.* [< DIASTASE]

ASEAN ('æsɪˌæn) *n. acronym for* Association of South-East Asian Nations.

asepsis (ə'sɛpsɪs, eɪ-) *n.* **1.** the state of being free from living pathogenic organisms. **2.** the methods of achieving a germ-free condition. —**a'septic** *adj.*

asexual (eɪ'sɛksjʊəl) *adj.* **1.** having no apparent sex or sex organs. **2.** (of reproduction) not involving the fusion of male and female gametes. —ˌ**asexu'ality** *n.* —**a'sexually** *adv.*

ash[1] (æʃ) *n.* **1.** the residue formed when matter is burnt. **2.** fine particles of lava thrown out by an erupting volcano. **3.** a light silvery-grey colour. ~See also **ashes.** [OE *æsce*]

ash[2] (æʃ) *n.* **1.** a tree having compound leaves, clusters of small greenish flowers, and winged seeds. **2.** the wood of this tree, used for tool handles, etc. **3.** any of several trees resembling the ash, such as the mountain ash. **4.** *Austral.* any of various eucalypts. [OE *æsc*]

ash[3] (æʃ) *n.* the digraph *æ,* as in Old English, representing a vowel approximately like that of the a in Modern English *hat.*

ASH (æʃ) *n.* (in Britain) *acronym for* Action on Smoking and Health.

ashamed (ə'ʃeɪmd) *adj.* (*usually postpositive*) **1.** overcome with shame or remorse. **2.** (foll. by *of*) suffering from feelings of shame in relation to (a person or deed). **3.** (foll. by *to*) unwilling through fear of humiliation, shame, etc. [OE *āscamod,* p.p. of *āscamian* to shame, < *scamu* SHAME] —**ashamedly** (ə'ʃeɪmɪdlɪ) *adv.*

A shares *pl. n.* ordinary shares in a company which carry restricted voting rights.

ash can *n.* a U.S. word for **dustbin.** Also called: **garbage can, ash bin, trash can.**

ashen[1] ('æʃən) *adj.* **1.** drained of colour. **2.** consisting of or resembling ashes. **3.** of a pale greyish colour.

ashen[2] ('æʃən) *adj.* of, relating to, or made from the ash tree or its timber.

ashes ('æʃɪz) *pl. n.* **1.** ruins or remains, as after burning. **2.** the remains of a human body after cremation.

Ashes ('æʃɪz) *pl. n.* **the.** a cremated cricket bail constituting a trophy competed for by England and Australia in test cricket since 1882. [from a mock obituary of English cricket after a great Australian victory]

Ashkenazi (ˌæʃkə'nɑːzɪ) *n., pl.* **-zim** (-zɪm). **1.** (*modifier*) of or relating to the Jews of Germany and E Europe. **2.** a Jew of German or E European descent. Cf. **Sephardi.** [C19: LHeb., < Heb. *Ashkenaz,* the son of Gomer (Genesis 10:3; I Chronicles 1:6)]

ashlar *or* **ashler** ('æʃlə) *n.* **1.** a square block of hewn stone for use in building. **2.** a thin dressed stone with straight edges, used to face a wall. **3.** masonry made of ashlar. [C14: < OF *aisselier* crossbeam, < *ais* board, < L *axis* axletree]

ashore (ə'ʃɔː) *adv.* **1.** towards or onto land from the water. ~*adj.* (*postpositive*), *adv.* **2.** on land: *a day ashore before sailing.*

ashram ('æʃrəm) *n.* a religious retreat or community where a Hindu holy man lives. [< Sansk. *āśrama,* < *ā-* near + *śrama* religious exertion]

ashtray ('æʃˌtreɪ) *n.* a receptacle for tobacco ash, cigarette butts, etc.

Ash Wednesday *n.* the first day of Lent, named from the former Christian custom of sprinkling ashes on penitents' heads.

ashy ('æʃɪ) *adj.* **ashier, ashiest. 1.** of a pale greyish colour; ashen. **2.** consisting of, covered with, or resembling ash.

Asian ('eɪʃən, 'eɪʒən) *adj.* **1.** of or relating to Asia, the largest of the continents, or to any of its people or languages. ~*n.* **2.** a native or inhabitant of Asia or a descendant of one.

▷ **Usage.** *Asian* is used in formal writing as a noun indicating a person from Asia. The use of the word *Asiatic* in this sense is regarded by some people as offensive.

Asian flu *n.* a type of influenza caused by a virus which apparently originated in China in 1957.

Asiatic (ˌeɪʃɪ'ætɪk, -zɪ-) *n., adj.* another word for **Asian.**

Asiatic cholera *n.* another name for **cholera.**

aside (ə'saɪd) *adv.* **1.** on or to one side. **2.** out of hearing; in or into seclusion. **3.** away from oneself: *he threw the book aside.* **4.** out of mind or consideration: *he put aside all fears.* **5.** in or into reserve: *to put aside money for old age.* ~*n.* **6.** something spoken by an actor, intended to be heard by the audience, but not by the others on stage. **7.** any confidential statement spoken in undertones. **8.** an incidental remark, note, etc.

A-side *n.* the side of a gramophone record regarded as more important.

asinine ('æsɪˌnaɪn) *adj.* **1.** obstinate or stupid. **2.** resembling an ass. [C16: < L *asinīnus,* < *asinus* ASS[1]] —'**asiˌninely** *adv.* —**asininity** (ˌæsɪ'nɪnɪtɪ) *n.*

ASIO *abbrev. for* Australian Security Intelligence Organization.

ask (ɑːsk) *vb.* **1.** (often foll. by *about*) to put a question (to); request an answer (from). **2.** (*tr.*) to inquire about: *she asked the way.* **3.** (*tr.*) to direct or put (a question). **4.** (*may take a clause as object or an infinitive;* often foll. by *for*) to make a request or demand: *they asked for a deposit.* **5.** (*tr.*) to demand or expect (esp. in **ask a lot of, ask too much of**). **6.** (*tr.*) Also: **ask out, ask over.** to request (a person) politely to come or go to a place: *he asked her to the party.* [OE *āscian*] —'**asker** *n.*

ask after *vb.* (*prep.*) to make inquiries about the health of (someone): *he asked after her mother.*

askance (ə'skæns) *or* **askant** (ə'skænt) *adv.* **1.** with an oblique glance. **2.** with doubt or mistrust. [C16: <?]

askew (ə'skjuː) *adv., adj.* at an oblique angle; towards one side; awry.

ask for *vb.* (*prep.*) **1.** to try to obtain by requesting. **2.** (*intr.*) *Inf.* to behave in a provocative manner that is regarded as inviting (trouble, etc.): *you're asking for it.*

asking price *n.* the price suggested by a seller but usually considered to be subject to bargaining.

aslant (ə'slɑːnt) *adv.* **1.** at a slant. ~*prep.* **2.** at a slant across or athwart.

asleep (ə'sliːp) *adj.* (*postpositive*) **1.** in or into a state of sleep. **2.** in or into a dormant or inactive state. **3.** (of limbs) numb; lacking sensation. **4.** *Euphemistic.* dead.

ASLEF ('æzlɛf) *n.* (in Britain) *acronym for* Associated Society of Locomotive Engineers and Firemen.

ASM *abbrev. for* air-to-surface missile.

asocial (eɪ'səʊʃəl) *adj.* **1.** avoiding contact. **2.** unconcerned about the welfare of others. **3.** hostile to society.

asp (æsp) *n.* **1.** the venomous snake that caused the death of Cleopatra. **2.** Also called: **asp viper.** a viper that occurs in S Europe and is very similar to but smaller than the adder. **3. horned asp.** another name for **horned viper.** [C15: < L *aspis,* < Gk]

asparagus (ə'spærəgəs) *n.* **1.** a plant of the lily family, having small scaly or needle-like leaves.

2. the succulent young shoots, which may be cooked and eaten. 3. **asparagus fern.** a fernlike species of asparagus, native to southern Africa. [C15: < L, < Gk *asparagos,* <?]

aspartame (ə'spɑːˌteɪm) *n.* an artificial sweetener produced from a nonessential amino acid. [C20: < *aspart(ic acid)* + *(phenyl)a(lanine) m(ethyl) e(ster)*]

aspect ('æspɛkt) *n.* 1. appearance to the eye; visual effect. 2. a distinct feature or element in a problem, situation, etc.; facet. 3. the way in which a problem, idea, etc., may be considered. 4. a facial expression: *a severe aspect.* 5. a position facing a particular direction: *the southern aspect of a house.* 6. a view in a certain direction. 7. *Astrol.* any of several specific angular distances between two planets. 8. *Grammar.* a category of verbal inflections that expresses such features as the continuity, repetition, or completedness of the action described. [C14: < L *aspectus* a sight, < *ad-* to, at + *specere* to look]

aspect ratio *n.* 1. the ratio of width to height of a picture on a television or cinema screen. 2. *Aeronautics.* the ratio of the span of a wing to its mean chord.

aspen ('æspən) *n.* a kind of poplar tree in which the leaves are attached to the stem by long flattened stalks so that they quiver in the wind. [OE *æspe*]

asperity (æ'spɛrɪtɪ) *n., pl.* **-ties.** 1. roughness or sharpness of temper. 2. roughness or harshness of a surface, sound, etc. [C16: < L *asperitās,* < *asper* rough]

asperse (ə'spɜːs) *vb.* (*tr.*) to spread false rumours about; defame. [C15: < L *aspersus,* < *aspergere* to sprinkle] —**as'perser** *n.* —**as'persive** *adj.*

aspersion (ə'spɜːʃən) *n.* 1. a disparaging or malicious remark (esp. in **cast aspersions (on)**). 2. the act of defaming.

asphalt ('æsfælt) *n.* 1. any of several black semisolid substances composed of bitumen and inert mineral matter. They occur naturally and as a residue from petroleum distillation. 2. a mixture of this substance with gravel, used in road-surfacing and roofing materials. 3. (*modifier*) containing or surfaced with asphalt. ~*vb.* 4. (*tr.*) to cover with asphalt. [C14: < LL *aspaltus,* < Gk *asphaltos,* prob. < A-[1] + *sphallein* to cause to fall; referring to its use as a binding agent] —**as'phaltic** *adj.*

asphodel ('æsfəˌdɛl) *n.* 1. any of various S European plants of the lily family having clusters of white or yellow flowers. 2. an unidentified flower of Greek legend said to cover the Elysian fields. [C16: < L *asphodelus,* < Gk *asphodelos,* <?]

asphyxia (æs'fɪksɪə) *n.* lack of oxygen in the blood due to restricted respiration; suffocation. [C18: < NL, < Gk *asphuxia* a stopping of the pulse, < A-[1] + *sphuxis* pulse, < *sphuzein* to throb] —**as'phyxial** *adj.* —**as'phyxiant** *adj.*

asphyxiate (æs'fɪksɪˌeɪt) *vb.* to cause asphyxia in or undergo asphyxia; smother; suffocate. —**asˌphyxi'ation** *n.* —**as'phyxiˌator** *n.*

aspic ('æspɪk) *n.* a savoury jelly based on meat or fish stock, used as a relish or as a mould for meat, vegetables, etc. [C18: < F: aspic (jelly), asp]

aspidistra (ˌæspɪ'dɪstrə) *n.* a popular house plant of the lily family with long tough evergreen leaves. [C19: < NL, < Gk *aspis* shield, on the model of *Tupistra,* genus of liliaceous plants]

aspirant ('æspɪrənt) *n.* 1. a person who aspires, as to a high position. ~*adj.* 2. aspiring.

aspirate *vb.* ('æspɪˌreɪt). (*tr.*) 1. *Phonetics.* **a.** to articulate (a stop) with some force, so that breath escapes audibly. **b.** to pronounce (a word or syllable) with an initial *h.* 2. to remove by inhalation or suction, esp. to suck (air or fluid) from a body cavity. ~*n.* ('æspɪrɪt). 3. *Phonetics.* **a.** a stop pronounced with an audible release of breath. **b.** the glottal fricative represented in English and several other languages as *h.* ~*adj.* ('æspɪrɪt). 4. *Phonetics.* (of a stop) pronounced with a forceful expulsion of breath.

aspiration (ˌæspɪ'reɪʃən) *n.* 1. strong desire to achieve something, such as success. 2. the aim of such desire. 3. the act of breathing. 4. *Phonetics.* **a.** the pronunciation of an aspirated consonant. **b.** an aspirated consonant. 5. *Med.* the sucking of fluid or foreign matter into the air passages of the body. —ˌ**aspi'rational** *adj.* —**aspiratory** (ə'spaɪrətərɪ) *adj.*

aspirator ('æspɪˌreɪtə) *n.* a device employing suction, such as a jet pump or one for removing fluids from a body cavity.

aspire (ə'spaɪə) *vb.* (*intr.*) 1. (usually foll. by *to* or *after*) to yearn (for), desire, or hope (to do or be something): *to aspire to be a great leader.* 2. to rise to a great height. [C15: < L *aspīrāre* to breathe upon, < *spīrāre* to breathe] —**as'piring** *adj.*

aspirin ('æsprɪn) *n., pl.* **-rin** *or* **-rins.** 1. a white crystalline compound widely used in the form of tablets to relieve pain, fever, and colds. Chemical name: **acetylsalicylic acid.** 2. a tablet of aspirin. [C19: < G, < *A(cetyl)* + *Spir(säure)* spiraeic acid (modern salicylic acid) + -IN]

Aspirin ('æsprɪn) *n.* (in Canada) a trademark for **aspirin.**

asquint (ə'skwɪnt) *adv., adj.* (*postpositive*) with a glance from the corner of the eye, esp. a furtive one. [C13: ? < Du. *schuinte* slant, <?]

ass[1] (æs) *n.* 1. a mammal related to the horse. It is hardy and sure-footed, having longer ears than the horse. 2. (not in technical use) the donkey. 3. a foolish or ridiculously pompous person. [OE *assa,* prob. < OIrish *asan,* < L *asinus;* rel. to Gk *onos* ass]

ass[2] (æs) *n.* the usual U.S. and Canad. word for **arse.** [OE *ærs*]

assagai ('æsəˌgaɪ) *n., pl.* **-gais.** a variant spelling of **assegai.**

assai (æ'saɪ) *adv. Music.* (usually preceded by a musical direction) very: *allegro assai.* [It.: enough]

assail (ə'seɪl) *vb.* (*tr.*) 1. to attack violently; assault. 2. to criticize or ridicule vehemently. 3. to beset or disturb: *his mind was assailed by doubts.* 4. to encounter with the intention of mastering. [C13: < OF *asalir,* < L *assilīre,* < *salīre* to leap] —**as'sailable** *adj.* —**as'sailer** *n.*

assailant (ə'seɪlənt) *n.* a person who attacks another, either physically or verbally.

assassin (ə'sæsɪn) *n.* a murderer, esp. one who kills a prominent political figure. [C16: < Med. L *assassīnus,* < Ar. *hashshāshīn,* pl. of *hashshāsh* one who eats HASHISH]

assassinate (ə'sæsɪˌneɪt) *vb.* (*tr.*) 1. to murder (a political figure). 2. to ruin or harm (a person's reputation, etc.) by slander. —**asˌsassi'nation** *n.*

assault (ə'sɔːlt) *n.* 1. a violent attack, either physical or verbal. 2. *Law.* an act that causes violence to another. 3. **a.** the culmination of a military attack. **b.** (*as modifier*): *assault troops.* 4. rape. ~*vb.* (*tr.*) 5. to make an assault upon. 6. to rape or attempt to rape. [C13: < OF *asaut,* < Vulgar L, < *assalīre* (unattested) to leap upon; see ASSAIL] —**as'saultive** *adj.*

assault and battery *n. Criminal law.* a threat of attack to another person followed by actual attack.

assault course *n.* an obstacle course designed to give soldiers practice in negotiating hazards.

assay *vb.* (ə'seɪ). 1. to subject (a substance, such as silver or gold) to chemical analysis, as in the determination of the amount of impurity. 2. (*tr.*) to attempt (something or to do something). ~*n.* (ə'seɪ, 'æseɪ). 3. **a.** an analysis, esp. a determination of the amount of metal in an ore or the amounts of impurities in a precious metal. **b.** (*as modifier*): *an assay office.* 4. a substance undergoing an analysis. 5. a written report on the results of an analysis. 6. a test. [C14: < OF *assai;* see ESSAY] —**as'sayer** *n.*

assegai *or* **assagai** ('æsəˌgaɪ) *n., pl.* **-gais.** 1. a southern African tree, the wood of which is used for making spears. 2. a sharp light spear. [C17: < Port. *azagaia,* < Ar. *az zaghāyah,* < *al* the + *zaghāyah* assegai, < Berber]

assemblage (ə'sɛmblɪdʒ) *n.* 1. a number of

things or persons assembled together. **2.** the act of assembling or the state of being assembled. **3.** (ˌæsəmˈblɑːʒ). a three-dimensional work of art that combines various objects.

assemble (əˈsɛmbᵊl) *vb.* **1.** to come or bring together; collect or congregate. **2.** to fit or join together (the parts of something, such as a machine). [C13: < OF *assembler,* < Vulgar L *assimulāre* (unattested) to bring together, < L *simul* together]

assembler (əˈsɛmblə) *n.* **1.** a person or thing that assembles. **2.** a computer program that converts a set of low-level symbolic data into machine language. Cf. **compiler. 3.** In full: **assembler language.** a symbolic language that uses an assembler program to convert to machine language.

assembly (əˈsɛmblɪ) *n., pl.* **-blies. 1.** a number of people gathered together, esp. for a formal meeting held at regular intervals. **2.** the act of assembling or the state of being assembled. **3.** the process of putting together a number of parts to make a machine. **4.** *Mil.* a signal for personnel to assemble.

Assembly (əˈsɛmblɪ) *n., pl.* **-blies. 1.** the lower chamber in various state legislatures, esp. in Australia and America. See also **House of Assembly, legislative assembly. 2.** *N.Z.* short for **General Assembly.**

assembly language *n. Computers.* a programming language that uses mnemonic instruction codes, labels, and names to refer directly to their machine code equivalents.

assembly line *n.* a sequence of machines, tools, operations, workers, etc., in a factory, arranged so that at each stage a further process is carried out.

assent (əˈsɛnt) *n.* **1.** agreement, as to a statement, proposal, etc. **2.** compliance. *~vb.* (*intr.;* usually foll. by *to*) **3.** to agree or express agreement. [C13: < OF *assenter,* < L *assentīrī,* < *sentīre* to think]

assert (əˈsɜːt) *vb.* (*tr.*) **1.** to insist upon (rights, etc.). **2.** (*may take a clause as object*) to state to be true; declare. **3.** to put (oneself) forward in an insistent manner. [C17: < L *asserere* to join to oneself, < *serere* to join] **—asˈserter** *or* **asˈsertor** *n.*

assertion (əˈsɜːʃən) *n.* **1.** a positive statement, usually made without evidence. **2.** the act of asserting.

assertion sign *n.* a sign ⊢ used in symbolic logic to introduce the conclusion of a valid argument: often read as "therefore."

assertive (əˈsɜːtɪv) *adj.* given to making assertions; dogmatic or aggressive. **—asˈsertively** *adv.* **—asˈsertiveness** *n.*

assess (əˈsɛs) *vb.* (*tr.*) **1.** to evaluate. **2.** (foll. by *at*) to estimate the value of (income, property, etc.) for taxation purposes. **3.** to determine the amount of (a fine, tax, etc.). **4.** to impose a tax, fine, etc., on (a person or property). [C15: < OF *assesser,* < L *assidēre* to sit beside, < *sedēre* to sit] **—asˈsessable** *adj.*

assessment (əˈsɛsmənt) *n.* **1.** the act of assessing. esp., (in Britain) the evaluation of a student's achievement on a course. **2.** an amount determined as payable. **3.** a valuation set on taxable property, etc. **4.** evaluation.

assessor (əˈsɛsə) *n.* **1.** a person who evaluates the merits of something. **2.** a person who values property for taxation. **3.** a person who estimates the value of damage to property for insurance purposes. **4.** a person with technical expertise called in to advise a court. **—assessorial** (ˌæsɛˈsɔːrɪəl) *adj.*

asset (ˈæsɛt) *n.* anything valuable or useful. [C19: back formation < ASSETS]

assets (ˈæsɛts) *pl. n.* **1.** *Accounting.* the property and claims against debtors that are shown balanced against liabilities. **2.** *Law.* the property available to an executor for settling a deceased person's estate. **3.** any property owned by a person or firm. [C16: < OF *asez* enough, < Vulgar L *ad satis* (unattested) < L *ad* up to + *satis* enough]

asset-stripping *n. Commerce.* the practice of taking over a failing company at a low price and then selling the assets piecemeal. **—ˈasset-ˌstripper** *n.*

asseverate (əˈsɛvəˌreɪt) *vb.* (*tr.*) to declare solemnly. [C18: < L *assevērāre* to do (something) earnestly, < *sevērus* SEVERE] **—asˌseverˈation** *n.*

assibilate (əˈsɪbɪˌleɪt) *vb.* (*tr.*) *Phonetics.* to pronounce (a speech sound) with or as a sibilant. [C19: < LL *assībilāre* to hiss at, < *sībilāre* to hiss] **—asˌsibiˈlation** *n.*

assiduity (ˌæsɪˈdjuːɪtɪ) *n., pl.* **-ties. 1.** constant and close application. **2.** (*often pl.*) devoted attention.

assiduous (əˈsɪdjʊəs) *adj.* **1.** hard-working; persevering. **2.** undertaken with perseverance and care. [C16: < L, < *assidēre* to sit beside, < *sedēre* to sit] **—asˈsiduousness** *n.*

assign (əˈsaɪn) *vb.* (*mainly tr.*) **1.** to select for and appoint to a post, etc. **2.** to give out or allot (a task, problem, etc.). **3.** to set apart (a place, person, time, etc.) for a particular function or event: *to assign a day for the meeting.* **4.** to attribute to a specified cause, origin, or source. **5.** to transfer (one's right, interest, or title to property) to someone else. *~n.* **6.** *Law.* a person to whom property is assigned; assignee. [C14: < OF, < L *assignāre,* < *signāre* to mark out] **—asˈsignable** *adj.* **—asˈsigner** *or* **ˌassignˈor** *n.*

assignation (ˌæsɪgˈneɪʃən) *n.* **1.** a secret or forbidden arrangement to meet, esp. one between lovers. **2.** the act of assigning; assignment. [C14: < OF, < L *assignātiō* a marking out]

assignee (ˌæsaɪˈniː) *n. Law.* a person to whom some right, interest, or property is transferred.

assignment (əˈsaɪnmənt) *n.* **1.** something that has been assigned, such as a mission or task. **2.** a position or post to which a person is assigned. **3.** the act of assigning or state of being assigned. **4.** *Law.* **a.** the transfer to another of a right, interest, or title to property. **b.** the document effecting such a transfer.

assimilate (əˈsɪmɪˌleɪt) *vb.* **1.** (*tr.*) to learn (information, etc.) and understand it thoroughly. **2.** (*tr.*) to absorb (food). **3.** (*intr.*) to become absorbed, incorporated, or learned and understood. **4.** (usually foll. by *into* or *with*) to adjust or become adjusted: *the new immigrants assimilated easily.* **5.** (usually foll. by *to* or *with*) to become or cause to become similar. **6.** (usually foll. by *to*) *Phonetics.* to change (a consonant) or (of a consonant) to be changed into another under the influence of one adjacent to it. [C15: < L *assimilāre* to make one thing like another, < *similis* like, SIMILAR] **—asˈsimilable** *adj.* **—asˌsimiˈlation** *n.* **—asˈsimilative** *or* **asˈsimilatory** *adj.* **—asˈsimiˌlator** *n.*

assist (əˈsɪst) *vb.* **1.** to give help or support to (a person, cause, etc.). **2.** to work or act as an assistant or subordinate to (another). *~n.* **3.** *U.S.* the act of helping. [C15: < F, < L *assistere* to stand by, < *sistere* to cause to stand, < *stāre* to stand] **—asˈsister** *n.*

assistance (əˈsɪstəns) *n.* **1.** help; support. **2.** the act of assisting. **3.** *Brit. inf.* See **national assistance.**

assistant (əˈsɪstənt) *n.* **1. a.** a person who assists, esp. in a subordinate position. **b.** (*as modifier*): *assistant manager.* **2.** See **shop assistant.**

assize (əˈsaɪz) *n. Scots Law.* **a.** trial by a jury. **b.** a jury. [C13: < OF *assise* session, < *asseoir* to seat, < L *assidēre* to sit beside]

assizes (əˈsaɪzɪz) *pl. n.* (formerly in England and Wales) the sessions of the principal court in each county, exercising civil and criminal jurisdiction: replaced in 1971 by crown courts.

assn *abbrev. for* association.

assoc. *abbrev. for:* **1.** associate(d). **2.** association.

associate *vb.* (əˈsəʊʃɪˌeɪt, -sɪ-). (usually foll. by *with*) **1.** (*tr.*) to link or connect in the mind or imagination. **2.** (*intr.*) to mix socially: *to associate with writers.* **3.** (*intr.*) to form or join an association, group, etc. **4.** (*tr.; usually passive*) to consider in conjunction: *rainfall is associated with* *humidity.* **5.** (*tr.*) to bring (a person, esp. oneself) into friendship, partnership, etc. **6.** (*tr.; often passive*) to express agreement (with): *Bertrand Russell was associated with the CND movement.* ~*n.* (əˈsəʊʃɪɪt, -sɪ-). **7.** a person joined with another or others in an enterprise, business, etc. **8.** a companion or friend. **9.** something that usually accompanies another thing. **10.** a person having a subordinate position in or admitted to only partial membership of an institution, association, etc. ~*adj.* (əˈsəʊʃɪɪt, -sɪ-). (*prenominal*) **11.** joined with another or others in an enterprise, business, etc.: *an associate director.* **12.** having partial rights or subordinate status: *an associate member.* **13.** accompanying; concomitant. [C14: < L *associāre* to ally with, < *sociāre* to join, < *socius* an ally] —**asˈsociable** *adj.* —**asˈsociator** *n.* —**asˈsociateˌship** *n.*

association (əˌsəʊsɪˈeɪʃən, -ʃɪ-) *n.* **1.** a group of people having a common purpose or interest; a society or club. **2.** the act of associating or the state of being associated. **3.** friendship or companionship: *their association will not last.* **4.** a mental connection of ideas, feelings, or sensations. **5.** *Chem.* the formation of groups of molecules and ions held together by weak chemical bonds. **6.** *Ecology.* a group of similar plants that grow in a uniform environment.

association football *n.* **1.** a more formal name for **soccer. 2.** (in Australia) Australian Rules played in a football association rather than a league.

associative (əˈsəʊʃɪətɪv, -sɪ-) *adj.* **1.** of, relating to, or causing association or union. **2.** *Maths, logic.* **a.** of an operation, such as multiplication or addition, in which the answer is the same regardless of the way in which the elements are grouped: $(2 \times 3) \times 4 = 2 \times (3 \times 4)$. **b.** referring to this property: *the associative laws of arithmetic.*

assonance (ˈæsənəns) *n.* **1.** the use of the same vowel sound with different consonants or the same consonant with different vowels, as in a line of verse. Examples are *time* and *light* or *mystery* and *mastery.* **2.** partial correspondence. [C18: < F, < L *assonāre* to sound, < *sonāre* to sound] —ˈ**assonant** *adj., n.*

assort (əˈsɔːt) *vb.* **1.** (*tr.*) to arrange or distribute into groups of the same type; classify. **2.** (*intr.; usually foll. by with*) to fit or fall into a class or group. **3.** (*tr.*) to supply with an assortment of merchandise. **4.** (*tr.*) to put in the same category as others. [C15: < OF *assorter,* < *sorte* SORT] —**asˈsortative** *adj.*

assorted (əˈsɔːtɪd) *adj.* **1.** consisting of various kinds mixed together. **2.** classified: *assorted categories.* **3.** matched (esp. in **well-assorted, ill-assorted**).

assortment (əˈsɔːtmənt) *n.* **1.** a collection or group of various things or sorts. **2.** the act of assorting.

ASSR *abbrev. for* Autonomous Soviet Socialist Republic.

asst *abbrev. for* assistant.

assuage (əˈsweɪdʒ) *vb.* (*tr.*) **1.** to soothe, moderate, or relieve (grief, pain, etc.). **2.** to give relief to (thirst, etc.). **3.** to pacify; calm. [C14: < OF, < Vulgar L *assuāviāre* (unattested) to sweeten, < L *suāvis* pleasant] —**asˈsuagement** *n.* —**asˈsuager** *n.*

assume (əˈsjuːm) *vb.* (*tr.*) **1.** (*may take a clause as object*) to take for granted; suppose. **2.** to undertake or take on or over (a position, responsibility, etc.): *to assume office.* **3.** to pretend to; feign: *he assumed indifference.* **4.** to take or put on; adopt: *the problem assumed gigantic proportions.* **5.** to appropriate or usurp (power, control, etc.). [C15: < L *assūmere* to take up, < *sūmere* to take up, < SUB- + *emere* to take] —**asˈsumable** *adj.* —**asˈsumer** *n.*

assumed (əˈsjuːmd) *adj.* **1.** false; fictitious: *an assumed name.* **2.** taken for granted. **3.** usurped.

assuming (əˈsjuːmɪŋ) *adj.* **1.** expecting too much; presumptuous. ~*conj.* **2.** (often foll. by *that*) if it is assumed or taken for granted.

assumption (əˈsʌmpʃən) *n.* **1.** the act of taking something for granted or something that is taken for granted. **2.** an assuming of power or possession. **3.** presumption. **4.** *Logic.* a statement that is used as the premise of a particular argument but may not be otherwise accepted. [C13: < L *assūmptiō* a taking up, < *assūmere* to ASSUME] —**asˈsumptive** *adj.*

Assumption (əˈsʌmpʃən) *n. Christianity.* **1.** the taking up of the Virgin Mary (body and soul) into heaven when her earthly life was ended. **2.** the feast commemorating this.

assurance (əˈʃʊərəns) *n.* **1.** a statement, assertion, etc., intended to inspire confidence. **2.** a promise or pledge of support. **3.** freedom from doubt; certainty. **4.** forwardness; impudence. **5.** *Chiefly Brit.* insurance providing for certainties such as death as contrasted with fire.

assure (əˈʃʊə) *vb.* (*tr.; may take a clause as object*) **1.** to convince: *to assure a person of one's love.* **2.** to promise; guarantee. **3.** to state positively. **4.** to make (an event) certain. **5.** *Chiefly Brit.* to insure against loss, esp. of life. [C14: < OF, < Med. L *assēcūrāre* to secure or make sure, < *sēcūrus* SECURE] —**asˈsurable** *adj.* —**asˈsurer** *n.*

assured (əˈʃʊəd) *adj.* **1.** sure; guaranteed. **2.** self-assured. **3.** *Chiefly Brit.* insured. ~*n.* **4.** *Chiefly Brit.* **a.** the beneficiary under a life assurance policy. **b.** the person whose life is insured. —**assuredly** (əˈʃʊərɪdlɪ) *adv.*

Assyrian (əˈsɪrɪən) *n.* **1.** an inhabitant of ancient Assyria, a kingdom of Mesopotamia. **2.** the extinct Semitic language of the Assyrians. ~*adj.* **3.** of or characteristic of the ancient Assyrians, their language, or culture.

AST *abbrev. for* Atlantic Standard Time.

astatic (æˈstætɪk, eɪ-) *adj.* **1.** not static; unstable. **2.** *Physics.* having no tendency to assume any particular position or orientation. [C19: < Gk *astatos* unsteady] —**aˈstatically** *adv.*

astatine (ˈæstəˌtiːn) *n.* a radioactive element that occurs naturally in minute amounts and is artificially produced by bombarding bismuth with alpha particles. Symbol: At; atomic no.: 85; half-life of most stable isotope, ^{210}At: 8.3 hours. [C20: < Gk *astatos* unstable]

aster (ˈæstə) *n.* **1.** a plant having white, blue, purple, or pink daisy-like flowers. **2. China aster.** a related Chinese plant widely cultivated for its showy brightly coloured flowers. [C18: < NL, < L *aster* star, < Gk]

-aster *suffix forming nouns.* a person or thing that is inferior to what is specified: *poetaster.* [< L]

asterisk (ˈæstərɪsk) *n.* **1.** a star-shaped character (*) used in printing or writing to indicate a cross-reference to a footnote, an omission, etc. ~*vb.* **2.** (*tr.*) to mark with an asterisk. [C17: < LL *asteriscus* a small star, < Gk, < *astēr* star]

asterism (ˈæstəˌrɪzəm) *n.* **1.** three asterisks arranged in a triangle (⁂ or ⁂), to draw attention to the text that follows. **2.** a cluster of stars or a constellation. [C16: < Gk *asterismos* arrangement of constellations, < *astēr* star]

astern (əˈstɜːn) *adv., adj.* (*postpositive*) *Naut.* **1.** at or towards the stern. **2.** with the stern first: *full speed astern!* **3.** aft of the stern of a vessel.

asteroid (ˈæstəˌrɔɪd) *n.* **1.** Also called: **minor planet, planetoid.** any of numerous small celestial bodies that move around the sun mainly between the orbits of Mars and Jupiter. **2.** a starfish. ~*adj.* also **ˌasteˈroidal. 3.** of a starfish. **4.** shaped like a star. [C19: < Gk *asteroeidēs* starlike, < *astēr* a star]

asthenia (æsˈθiːnɪə) *n. Pathol.* an abnormal loss of strength; debility. [C19: via NL < Gk *astheneia* weakness, < A-[1] + *sthenos* strength]

asthenic (æsˈθɛnɪk) *adj.* **1.** of or having asthenia; weak. **2.** referring to a physique characterized by long limbs and a small trunk. ~*n.* **3.** a person with long limbs and a small trunk.

asthma (ˈæsmə) *n.* a respiratory disorder, often of allergic origin, characterized by difficulty in breathing. [C14: < Gk: laborious breathing, < *azein* to breathe hard]

asthmatic (æsˈmætɪk) *adj.* **1.** of or having asthma. ~*n.* **2.** a person who has asthma. —**asthˈmatically** *adv.*

astigmatic (ˌæstɪgˈmætɪk) *adj.* of, having, corrected, or corrected for astigmatism. [C19: < A-[1] + Gk *stigmat-, stigma* spot, focus] —ˌ**astigˈmatically** *adv.*

astigmatism (əˈstɪgməˌtɪzəm) *or* **astigmia** (əˈstɪgmɪə) *n.* **1.** a defect of a lens resulting in the formation of distorted images, caused by light rays not meeting at a single focal point. **2.** faulty vision resulting from astigmatism of the lens of the eye.

astilbe (əˈstɪlbɪ) *n.* any perennial plant of the genus *Astilbe,* cultivated for its spikes of ornamental pink or white flowers. [C19: NL, < Gk A-[1] + *stilbē,* < *stilbein* to glitter; referring to its inconspicuous individual flowers]

astir (əˈstɜː) *adj.* (*postpositive*) **1.** awake and out of bed. **2.** in motion; on the move.

ASTMS (in Britain) *abbrev. for* Association of Scientific, Technical, and Managerial Staffs.

astonish (əˈstɒnɪʃ) *vb.* (*tr.*) to fill with amazement; surprise greatly. [C15: < earlier *astonyen,* < OF, < Vulgar L *extonāre* (unattested) to strike with thunder, < L *tonāre* to thunder] —**aˈstonishing** *adj.*

astonishment (əˈstɒnɪʃmənt) *n.* **1.** extreme surprise; amazement. **2.** a cause of amazement.

astound (əˈstaʊnd) *vb.* (*tr.*) to overwhelm with amazement; bewilder. [C17: < *astoned* amazed, < OF, < *estoner* to ASTONISH] —**aˈstounding** *adj.*

astraddle (əˈstrædᵊl) *adj.* **1.** (*postpositive*) with a leg on either side of something. ~*prep.* **2.** astride.

astragal (ˈæstrəgᵊl) *n.* **1.** *Archit.* Also called: **bead.** a small convex moulding, usually with a semicircular cross section. **2.** *Anat.* the ankle or anklebone. [C17: < L, < Gk *astragalos* anklebone, hence, small round moulding]

astragalus (æˈstrægələs) *n., pl.* **-li** (-ˌlaɪ). *Anat.* another name for **talus**[1]. [C16: via NL < L: ASTRAGAL]

astrakhan (ˌæstrəˈkæn) *n.* **1.** a fur, usually black or grey, made of the closely curled wool of lambs from Astrakhan, a city in the S Soviet Union. **2.** a cloth with curled pile resembling this. **3.** (*modifier*) made of such fur or cloth.

astral (ˈæstrəl) *adj.* **1.** relating to or resembling the stars. **2.** *Theosophy.* relating to a supposed supersensible substance taking the form of an aura discernible to certain gifted individuals. [C17: < LL *astrālis,* < L *astrum* star, < Gk *astron*]

astray (əˈstreɪ) *adj.* (*postpositive*), *adv.* **1.** out of the correct path or direction. **2.** out of the right or expected way. [C13: < OF, < *estraier* to STRAY]

astride (əˈstraɪd) *adj.* (*postpositive*) **1.** with a leg on either side. **2.** with the legs far apart. ~*prep.* **3.** with a leg on either side of. **4.** with a part on both sides of; spanning.

astringent (əˈstrɪndʒənt) *adj.* **1.** severe; harsh. **2.** sharp or invigorating. **3.** causing contraction of body tissues, checking blood flow; styptic. ~*n.* **4.** an astringent drug or lotion. [C16: < L *astringēns* drawing together] —**asˈtringency** *n.* —**asˈtringently** *adv.*

astro- *combining form.* indicating a star or star-shaped structure: *astrology.* [< Gk, < *astron* star]

astrobiology (ˌæstrəʊbaɪˈɒlədʒɪ) *n.* the branch of biology that investigates the possibility of life on other planets.

astrodome (ˈæstrəˌdəʊm) *n.* a transparent dome on the top of an aircraft, through which observations can be made.

astrol. *abbrev. for:* **1.** astrologer. **2.** astrological. **3.** astrology.

astrolabe (ˈæstrəˌleɪb) *n.* an instrument used by early astronomers to measure the altitude of stars and planets and also as a navigational aid. [C13: via OF & Med. L < Gk, < *astrolabos,* < *astron* star + *lambanein* to take]

astrology (əˈstrɒlədʒɪ) *n.* **1.** the study of the motions and relative positions of the planets, sun, and moon, interpreted in terms of human characteristics and activities. **2.** primitive astronomy. [C14: < OF, < L *astrologia,* < Gk, < *astrologos* (orig.: astronomer); see ASTRO-, -LOGY] —**asˈtrologer** *or* **asˈtrologist** *n.* —**astrological** (ˌæstrəˈlɒdʒɪkᵊl) *adj.*

astron. *abbrev. for:* **1.** astronomer. **2.** astronomical. **3.** astronomy.

astronaut (ˈæstrəˌnɔːt) *n.* a person trained for travelling in space. [C20: < ASTRO- + *-naut,* < Gk *nautēs* sailor, on the model of *aeronaut*]

astronautics (ˌæstrəˈnɔːtɪks) *n.* (*functioning as sing.*) the science and technology of space flight. —ˌ**astroˈnautical** *adj.*

astronomical (ˌæstrəˈnɒmɪkᵊl) *or* **astronomic** *adj.* **1.** enormously large. **2.** of or relating to astronomy. —ˌ**astroˈnomically** *adv.*

astronomical unit *n.* a unit of distance used in astronomy equal to the mean distance between the earth and the sun. 1 astronomical unit is equivalent to 1.495×10^{11} metres.

astronomy (əˈstrɒnəmɪ) *n.* the scientific study of the individual celestial bodies (excluding the earth) and of the universe as a whole. [C13: < OF, < L *astronomia,* < Gk; see ASTRO-, -NOMY] —**asˈtronomer** *n.*

astrophysics (ˌæstrəʊˈfɪzɪks) *n.* (*functioning as sing.*) the branch of physics concerned with the physical and chemical properties of the celestial bodies. —ˌ**astroˈphysicist** *n.*

Astroturf (ˈæstrəʊˌtɜːf) *n. Trademark.* a type of grasslike artificial surface used for playing fields and lawns. [C20: < *Astro(dome)* the baseball stadium in Texas where it was first used + *turf*]

astute (əˈstjuːt) *adj.* having insight or acumen; perceptive; shrewd. [C17: < L *astūtus* cunning, < *astus* (n.) cleverness] —**asˈtutely** *adv.* —**asˈtuteness** *n.*

asunder (əˈsʌndə) *adv., adj.* (*postpositive*) in or into parts or pieces; apart: *to tear asunder.* [OE *on sundran* apart]

asylum (əˈsaɪləm) *n.* **1.** shelter; refuge; sanctuary. **2.** a safe or inviolable place of refuge, esp. as formerly offered by the Christian Church. **3.** *International law.* refuge afforded to a person whose extradition is sought by a foreign government: *political asylum.* **4.** an institution for the care or confinement of individuals, esp. (formerly) a mental hospital. [C15: via L < Gk *asulon* refuge, < A-[1] + *sulon* right of seizure]

asymmetric (ˌæsɪˈmɛtrɪk, ˌeɪ-) *or* **asymmetrical** *adj.* **1.** not symmetrical; lacking symmetry; misproportioned. **2.** *Logic, maths.* (of a relation) never holding between a pair of values *x* and *y* when it holds between *y* and *x,* as in *John is the father of David.* —ˌ**asymˈmetrically** *adv.*

asymmetry (æˈsɪmɪtrɪ, eɪ-) *n.* lack or absence of symmetry.

asymptomatic (ˌeɪsɪmptəˈmætɪk) *adj.* not showing any symptoms of disease.

asymptote (ˈæsɪmˌtəʊt) *n.* a straight line that is closely approached by a curve so that the distance between them decreases to zero as the distance from the origin increases to infinity. [C17: < Gk *asumptōtos* not falling together, < A-[1] + SYN- + *ptōtos* inclined to fall, < *piptein* to fall] —**asymptotic** (ˌæsɪmˈtɒtɪk) *or* ˌ**asympˈtotical** *adj.*

at (æt) *prep.* **1.** used to indicate location or position: *are they at the table?* **2.** towards; in the direction of: *looking at television.* **3.** used to indicate position in time: *come at three o'clock.* **4.** engaged in; in a state of (being): *children at play.* **5.** (in expressions concerned with habitual activity) during the passing of: *he used to work at night.* **6.** for; in exchange for: *it's selling at four pounds.* **7.** used to indicate the object of an emotion: *shocked at his behaviour.* **8.** **where it's at.** *Sl.* the real place of action. [OE *æt*]

At *the chemical symbol for* astatine.

at. *abbrev. for:* **1.** atmosphere (unit of pressure). **2.** atomic.

ataractic (ˌætəˈræktɪk) *or* **ataraxic** (ˌætəˈræksɪk) *adj.* **1.** able to calm or tranquillize. ~*n.* **2.** an ataractic drug.

ataraxia (ˌætəˈræksɪə) *or* **ataraxy** (ˈætəˌræksɪ)

n. calmness or peace of mind; emotional tranquillity. [C17: < Gk: serenity, < A-[1] + *tarassein* to trouble]

atavism (ˈætəˌvɪzəm) *n.* **1.** the recurrence in a plant or animal of certain primitive characteristics that were present in an ancestor but have not occurred in intermediate generations. **2.** reversion to a former type. [C19: < F, < L *atavus* strictly: great-grandfather's grandfather, prob. < *atta* daddy + *avus* grandfather] —ˌ**ataˈvistic** *adj.*

ataxia (əˈtæksɪə) *or* **ataxy** (əˈtæksɪ) *n. Pathol.* lack of muscular coordination. [C17: via NL < Gk: lack of coordination, < A-[1] + *-taxia,* < *tassein* to put in order] —**aˈtaxic** *adj.*

ATC *abbrev. for:* **1.** air-traffic control. **2.** (in Britain) Air Training Corps.

ate (ɛt, eɪt) *vb.* the past tense of **eat.**

-ate[1] *suffix.* **1.** (*forming adjectives*) having the appearance or characteristics of: *fortunate.* **2.** (*forming nouns*) a chemical compound, esp. a salt or ester of an acid: *carbonate.* **3.** (*forming nouns*) the product of a process: *condensate.* **4.** forming verbs from nouns and adjectives: *hyphenate.* [< L *-ātus,* p.p. ending of verbs ending in *-āre*]

-ate[2] *suffix forming nouns.* denoting office, rank, or a group having a certain function: *episcopate.* [< L *-ātus,* suffix of collective nouns]

atelier (ˈætəlˌjeɪ) *n.* an artist's studio or workshop. [C17: < OF, < *astele* chip of wood, < L *astula* splinter, < *assis* board]

a tempo (ɑː ˈtɛmpəʊ) *Music.* ~*adj., adv.* **1.** to the original tempo. ~*n.* **2.** a passage thus marked. ~Also: **tempo primo.** [It.: in (the original) time]

Athanasian Creed (ˌæθəˈneɪʃən) *n. Christianity.* a profession of faith widely used in the Western Church formerly attributed to Athanasius, 4th-century A.D. patriarch of Alexandria.

Athapascan, Athapaskan (ˌæθəˈpæskən) *or* **Athabascan, Athabaskan** (ˌæθəˈbæskən) *n.* a group of North American Indian languages including Apache and Navaho. [< Cree *athapaskaaw* scattered grass]

atheism (ˈeɪθɪˌɪzəm) *n.* rejection of belief in God or gods. [C16: < F, < Gk *atheos* godless, < A-[1] + *theos* god] —ˈ**atheist** *n., adj.* —ˌ**atheˈistic** *adj.*

athematic (ˌæθɪˈmætɪk) *adj.* **1.** *Music.* not based on themes. **2.** *Linguistics.* (of verbs) having a suffix attached with no intervening vowel.

athenaeum *or U.S.* **atheneum** (ˌæθɪˈniːəm) *n.* **1.** an institution for the promotion of learning. **2.** a building containing a reading room or library. [C18: < LL, < Gk *Athēnaion* temple of Athene, frequented by poets and teachers]

Athenian (əˈθiːnɪən) *n.* **1.** a native or inhabitant of Athens, the capital of Greece. ~*adj.* **2.** of or relating to Athens.

atherosclerosis (ˌæθərəʊsklɪəˈrəʊsɪs) *n., pl.* **-ses** (-siːz). a degenerative disease of the arteries characterized by thickening of the arterial walls, caused by deposits of fatty material. [C20: < NL, < Gk *athērōma* tumour full of grainy matter + SCLEROSIS] —**atherosclerotic** (ˌæθərəʊsklɪəˈrɒtɪk) *adj.*

athirst (əˈθɜːst) *adj.* (*postpositive*) **1.** (often foll. by *for*) having an eager desire; longing. **2.** *Arch.* thirsty.

athlete (ˈæθliːt) *n.* **1.** a person trained to compete in sports or exercises. **2.** a person who has a natural aptitude for physical activities. **3.** *Chiefly Brit.* a competitor in track and field events. [C18: < L via Gk, < *athlein* to compete for a prize, < *athlos* a contest]

athlete's foot *n.* a fungal infection of the skin of the foot, esp. between the toes and on the soles.

athletic (æθˈlɛtɪk) *adj.* **1.** physically fit or strong. **2.** of, relating to, or suitable for an athlete or for athletics. —**athˈletically** *adv.* —**athˈleticism** *n.*

athletics (æθˈlɛtɪks) *n.* (*functioning as pl. or sing.*) **1. a.** track and field events. **b.** (*as modifier*): *an athletics meeting.* **2.** sports or exercises engaged in by athletes.

athletic support *n.* a more formal term for **jockstrap.**

at-home *n.* **1.** a social gathering in a person's home. **2.** another name for **open day.**

-athon *suffix forming nouns.* a variant of **-thon.**

athwart (əˈθwɔːt) *adv.* **1.** transversely; from one side to another. ~*prep.* **2.** across the path or line of (esp. a ship). **3.** in opposition to; against. [C15: < A-[2] + THWART]

-atic *suffix forming adjectives.* of the nature of the thing specified: *problematic.* [< F, < Gk *-atikos*]

atilt (əˈtɪlt) *adv., adj.* (*postpositive*) **1.** in a tilted or inclined position. **2.** *Arch.* in or as if in a joust.

-ation *suffix forming nouns.* indicating an action, process, state, condition, or result: *arbitration; hibernation.* [< L *-ātiōn-,* suffix of abstract nouns]

-ative *suffix forming adjectives.* of, relating to, or tending to: *authoritative; informative.* [< L *-ātīvus*]

Atlantean (ˌætlænˈtiːən) *adj. Literary.* of, relating to, or like Atlas; extremely strong.

atlantes (ətˈlæntiːz) *n.* the plural of **atlas** (sense 4).

Atlantic (ətˈlæntɪk) *n.* **1. the.** short for the **Atlantic Ocean,** the world's second largest ocean. ~*adj.* **2.** of, relating to, or bordering the Atlantic Ocean. **3.** of or relating to Atlas or the Atlas Mountains. [C15: < L, < Gk (*pelagos*) *Atlantikos* (the sea) of Atlas (so called because it lay beyond the Atlas Mountains)]

Atlantic Provinces *pl. n.* **the.** certain of the Canadian provinces with coasts facing the Gulf of St Lawrence or the Atlantic: New Brunswick, Nova Scotia, Prince Edward Island, and Newfoundland.

Atlantis (ətˈlæntɪs) *n.* (in ancient legend) a continent said to have sunk beneath the Atlantic west of Gibraltar.

atlas (ˈætləs) *n.* **1.** a collection of maps, usually in book form. **2.** a book of charts, graphs, etc.: *an anatomical atlas.* **3.** *Anat.* the first cervical vertebra, supporting the skull in man. **4.** (*pl.* **atlantes**) *Archit.* another name for **telamon.** [C16: via L < Gk; first applied to maps < depictions of Atlas, a Titan in Gk myth., supporting the heavens in 16th- cent. books of maps]

atm. *abbrev. for:* **1.** atmosphere (unit of pressure). **2.** atmospheric.

atman (ˈɑːtmən) *n. Hinduism.* **1.** the personal soul or self. **2.** Brahman considered as the Universal Soul. [< Sansk. *ātman* breath]

atmolysis (ætˈmɒlɪsɪs) *n., pl.* **-ses** (-ˌsiːz). the separation of gases by differential diffusion through a porous substance.

atmosphere (ˈætməsˌfɪə) *n.* **1.** the gaseous envelope surrounding the earth or any other celestial body. **2.** the air or climate in a particular place. **3.** a general pervasive feeling or mood. **4.** the prevailing tone or mood of a novel, symphony, painting, etc. **5.** any local gaseous environment or medium: *an inert atmosphere.* **6.** Abbrev.: **at., atm.** a unit of pressure; the pressure that will support a column of mercury 760 mm high at 0°C at sea level. —**atmospheric** (ˌætməsˈfɛrɪk) *adj.* —ˌ**atmosˈpherically** *adv.*

atmospheric pressure *n.* the pressure exerted by the atmosphere at the earth's surface. It has an average value of 1 atmosphere.

atmospherics (ˌætməsˈfɛrɪks) *pl. n.* radio interference, heard as crackling or hissing in receivers, caused by electrical disturbance.

at. no. *abbrev. for* atomic number.

atoll (ˈætɒl) *n.* a circular coral reef or string of coral islands surrounding a lagoon. [C17: *atollon,* native name in the Maldive Islands]

atom (ˈætəm) *n.* **1. a.** the smallest quantity of an element that can take part in a chemical reaction. **b.** this entity as a source of nuclear energy: *the power of the atom.* **2.** the hypothetical indivisible particle of matter postulated by certain ancient philosophers. **3.** a very small amount or quantity: *to smash something to atoms.* [C16: via OF & L, <

Gk, < *atomos* (adj.) that cannot be divided, < A-[1] + *temnein* to cut]

atom bomb *or* **atomic bomb** *n.* a type of bomb in which the energy is provided by nuclear fission. Also called: **A-bomb, fission bomb.** Cf. **fusion bomb.**

atomic (əˈtɒmɪk) *adj.* **1.** of, using, or characterized by atom bombs or atomic energy: *atomic warfare.* **2.** of or comprising atoms: *atomic hydrogen.* —**aˈtomically** *adv.*

atomic clock *n.* an extremely accurate clock in which an electrical oscillator is controlled by the natural vibrations of an atomic or molecular system such as caesium or ammonia.

atomic energy *n.* another name for **nuclear energy.**

atomicity (ˌætəˈmɪsɪtɪ) *n.* **1.** the state of being made up of atoms. **2.** the number of atoms in the molecules of an element. **3.** a less common name for **valency.**

atomic mass unit *n.* a unit of mass used to express atomic and molecular weights that is equal to one twelfth of the mass of an atom of carbon-12. Abbrev.: **AMU.**

atomic number *n.* the number of protons in the nucleus of an atom of an element. Abbrev.: **at. no.**

atomic pile *n.* the original name for a **nuclear reactor.**

atomic sentence *n. Logic.* a sentence consisting of one predicate and a finite number of terms: *"it is raining" is an atomic sentence.*

atomic structure *n.* the concept of an atom as a central positively charged nucleus consisting of protons and neutrons surrounded by a number of electrons. The number of electrons is equal to the number of protons: the whole entity is thus electrically neutral.

atomic theory *n.* **1.** any theory in which matter is regarded as consisting of atoms. **2.** the current concept of the atom as an entity with a definite structure. See **atomic structure.**

atomic weight *n.* the ratio of the average mass per atom of an element to one-twelfth the mass of an atom of carbon-12. Abbrev.: **at. wt.** Also called: **relative atomic mass.**

▷ **Usage.** Until 1961 *atomic weights* were based on the mass of an atom of oxygen-16. The carbon-12 atom is now the usual basis of calculations and *relative atomic mass* is the preferred term for the new atomic weights.

atomize *or* **-ise** (ˈætəˌmaɪz) *vb.* **1.** to separate or be separated into free atoms. **2.** to reduce (a liquid or solid) to fine particles or spray or (of a liquid or solid) to be reduced in this way. **3.** (*tr.*) to destroy by weapons, esp. nuclear weapons.

atomizer *or* **-iser** (ˈætəˌmaɪzə) *n.* a device for reducing a liquid to a fine spray, such as a bottle with a fine outlet used to spray perfumes.

atom smasher *n. Physics.* the nontechnical name for **accelerator** (sense 2).

atomy (ˈætəmɪ) *n., pl.* **-mies.** *Arch.* a minute particle or creature. [C16: < L *atomi* atoms, used as sing.]

atonal (eɪˈtəʊnᵊl) *adj. Music.* having no established key.

atonality (ˌeɪtəʊˈnælɪtɪ) *n.* **1.** absence of or disregard for an established musical key in a composition. **2.** the principles of composition embodying this.

atone (əˈtəʊn) *vb.* (*intr.;* foll. by *for*) to make amends or reparation (for a crime, sin, etc.). [C16: back formation < ATONEMENT] —**aˈtoner** *n.*

atonement (əˈtəʊnmənt) *n.* **1.** satisfaction, reparation, or expiation given for an injury or wrong. **2.** (*often cap.*) *Christian theology.* **a.** the reconciliation of man with God through the sacrificial death of Christ. **b.** the sufferings and death of Christ. [C16: < ME *at onement* in harmony]

atonic (eɪˈtɒnɪk, æ-) *adj.* **1.** (of a syllable, word, etc.) carrying no stress; unaccented. **2.** lacking body or muscle tone. ~*n.* **3.** an unaccented or unstressed syllable, word, etc. [C18: < L, < Gk *atonos* lacking tone]

atop (əˈtɒp) *adv.* **1.** on top; at the top. ~*prep.* **2.** on top of; at the top of.

-ator *suffix forming nouns.* a person or thing that performs a certain action: *agitator; radiator.* [< L *-ātor*]

-atory *suffix forming adjectives.* of, relating to, characterized by, or serving to: *circulatory; explanatory.* [< L *-ātōrius*]

ATP *n.* adenosine triphosphate; a substance found in all plant and animal cells. It is the major source of energy for cellular reactions.

atrium (ˈeɪtrɪəm, ˈɑː-) *n., pl.* **atria** (ˈeɪtrɪə, ˈɑː-). **1.** the open main court of a Roman house. **2.** a central often glass-roofed hall that extends through several storeys in a building, such as a shopping centre or hotel. **3.** a court in front of an early Christian or medieval church. **4.** *Anat.* a cavity or chamber in the body, esp. the upper chamber of each half of the heart. [C17: < L; rel. to *āter* black] —**ˈatrial** *adj.*

atrocious (əˈtrəʊʃəs) *adj.* **1.** extremely cruel or wicked: *atrocious deeds.* **2.** horrifying or shocking. **3.** *Inf.* very bad: *atrocious writing.* [C17: < L *ātrōx* dreadful, < *āter* black] —**aˈtrociousness** *n.*

atrocity (əˈtrɒsɪtɪ) *n., pl.* **-ties. 1.** behaviour or an action that is wicked or ruthless. **2.** the fact or quality of being atrocious. **3.** (*usually pl.*) acts of extreme cruelty.

atrophy (ˈætrəfɪ) *n., pl.* **-phies. 1.** a wasting away of an organ or part, or a failure to grow to normal size. **2.** any degeneration or diminution. ~*vb.* **-phying, -phied. 3.** to waste away or cause to waste away. [C17: < LL, < Gk, < *atrophos* ill-fed, < A-[1] + *-trophos,* < *trephein* to feed] —**atrophic** (əˈtrɒfɪk) *adj.*

atropine (ˈætrəˌpiːn) *n.* a poisonous alkaloid obtained from the deadly nightshade, used to treat peptic ulcers, biliary and renal colic, etc. [C19: < NL *atropa* deadly nightshade, < Gk *atropos* unchangeable, inflexible]

att. *abbrev. for:* **1.** attached. **2.** attorney.

attach (əˈtætʃ) *vb.* (*mainly tr.*) **1.** to join, fasten, or connect. **2.** (*reflexive or passive*) to become associated with or join. **3.** (*intr.;* foll. by *to*) to be connected (with): *responsibility attaches to the job.* **4.** to attribute or ascribe. **5.** to include or append: *a proviso is attached to the contract.* **6.** (*usually passive*) *Mil.* to place on temporary duty with another unit. **7.** to appoint officially. **8.** *Law.* to arrest or take (a person, property, etc.) with lawful authority. [C14: < OF *atachier* to fasten, changed < *estachier* to fasten with a stake] —**atˈtachable** *adj.* —**atˈtacher** *n.*

attaché (əˈtæʃeɪ) *n.* a specialist attached to a diplomatic mission: *military attaché.* [C19: < F: someone attached (to a mission)]

attaché case *n.* a small flat rectangular briefcase used for carrying documents, papers, etc.

attached (əˈtætʃt) *adj.* **1.** (foll. by *to*) fond (of). **2.** married, engaged, or associated in an exclusive sexual relationship.

attachment (əˈtætʃmənt) *n.* **1.** a fastening. **2.** (often foll. by *to*) affection or regard (for). **3.** an object to be attached: *an attachment for an electric drill.* **4.** the act of attaching or the state of being attached. **5. a.** the lawful seizure of property and placing of it under control of a court. **b.** a writ authorizing such seizure.

attack (əˈtæk) *vb.* **1.** to launch a physical assault (against) with or without weapons. **2.** (*intr.*) to take the initiative in a game, sport, etc. **3.** (*tr.*) to criticize or abuse vehemently. **4.** (*tr.*) to turn one's mind or energies to (a job, problem, etc.). **5.** (*tr.*) to begin to injure or affect adversely: *rust attacked the metal.* ~*n.* **6.** the act or an instance of attacking. **7.** strong criticism or abuse. **8.** an offensive move in a game, sport, etc. **9. the attack.** *Ball games.* the players in a team whose main role is to attack the opponents. **10.** commencement of a task, etc. **11.** any sudden and usually severe manifestation of a disease or disorder: *a heart attack.* **12.** *Music.* decisiveness in beginning a passage, movement, or piece.

[C16: < F, < OIt. *attaccare* to attack, attach, < *estaccare* to attach] —**at'tacker** *n.*

attain (ə'teɪn) *vb.* **1.** (*tr.*) to achieve or accomplish (a task, aim, etc.). **2.** (*tr.*) to reach in space or time. **3.** (*intr.*; often foll. by *to*) to arrive (at) with effort or exertion. [C14: < OF, < L *attingere* to reach, < *tangere* to touch] —**at'tainable** *adj.* —**at,taina'bility** *or* **at'tainableness** *n.*

attainder (ə'teɪndə) *n.* (formerly) the extinction of a person's civil rights resulting from a sentence of death or outlawry on conviction for treason or felony. [C15: < Anglo-F *attaindre* to convict, < OF *ateindre* to ATTAIN]

attainment (ə'teɪnmənt) *n.* an achievement or the act of achieving; accomplishment.

attaint (ə'teɪnt) *vb.* (*tr.*) *Arch.* **1.** to pass judgment of death or outlawry upon (a person). **2.** (of sickness) to affect or strike (somebody). ~*n.* **3.** a less common word for **attainder.** [C14: < OF *ateint* convicted, < *ateindre* to ATTAIN]

attar ('ætə), **otto** ('ɒtəʊ), *or* **ottar** ('ɒtə) *n.* an essential oil from flowers, esp. the damask rose: *attar of roses.* [C18: < Persian, < *'itr* perfume, < Ar.]

attempt (ə'tɛmpt) *vb.* (*tr.*) **1.** to make an effort (to do something) or to achieve (something); try. **2.** to try to surmount (an obstacle). **3.** to try to climb. ~*n.* **4.** an endeavour to achieve something; effort. **5.** a result of an attempt or endeavour. **6.** an attack, esp. with the intention to kill. [C14: < OF, < L *attemptāre* to strive after, < *tentāre* to try] —**at'temptable** *adj.*

attend (ə'tɛnd) *vb.* **1.** to be present at (an event, etc.). **2.** (when *intr.*, foll. by *to*) to give care (to); minister (to). **3.** (when *intr.*, foll. by *to*) to pay attention. **4.** (*tr.; often passive*) to accompany or follow: *a high temperature attended by a severe cough.* **5.** (*intr.;* foll. by *on* or *upon*) to follow as a consequence (of). **6.** (*intr.;* foll. by *to*) to apply oneself: *to attend to the garden.* **7.** (*tr.*) to escort or accompany. **8.** (*intr.;* foll. by *on* or *upon*) to provide for the needs (of): *to attend on a guest.* [C13: < OF, < L *attendere* to stretch towards, < *tendere* to extend]

attendance (ə'tɛndəns) *n.* **1.** the act or state of attending. **2.** the number of persons present.

attendant (ə'tɛndənt) *n.* **1.** a person who accompanies or waits upon another. **2.** a person employed to assist, guide, or provide a service for others. **3.** a person who is present. ~*adj.* **4.** being in attendance. **5.** associated: *attendant problems.*

attention (ə'tɛnʃən) *n.* **1.** concentrated direction of the mind, esp. to a problem or task. **2.** consideration, notice, or observation. **3.** detailed care or special treatment: *to pay attention to one's appearance.* **4.** (*usually pl.*) an act of courtesy or gallantry indicating affection or love. **5.** the motionless position of formal military alertness, an upright position with legs and heels together. ~*sentence substitute.* **6.** the order to be alert or to adopt a position of formal military alertness. [C14: < L, < *attendere* to apply the mind to]

attentive (ə'tɛntɪv) *adj.* **1.** paying attention; listening carefully. **2.** (*postpositive;* often foll. by *to*) careful to fulfil the needs or wants (of). —**at'tentively** *adv.* —**at'tentiveness** *n.*

attenuate *vb.* (ə'tɛnjʊ,eɪt). **1.** to weaken or become weak. **2.** to make or become thin or fine; extend. ~*adj.* (ə'tɛnjʊɪt, -,eɪt). **3.** weakened or reduced. **4.** *Bot.* tapering. [C16: < L *attenuāre* to weaken, < *tenuis* thin] —**at,tenu'ation** *n.*

attest (ə'tɛst) *vb.* **1.** (*tr.*) to affirm the correctness or truth of. **2.** (when *intr.*, usually foll. by *to*) to witness (an act, event, etc.) or bear witness (to an act, event, etc.). **3.** (*tr.*) to make evident; demonstrate. **4.** (*tr.*) to provide evidence for. [C16: < L, < *testārī* to bear witness, < *testis* a witness] —**at'testable** *adj.* —**at'testant, at'tester** *or esp. in legal usage* **at'testor** *n.* —**attestation** (,ætɛ'steɪʃən) *n.*

attested (ə'tɛstɪd) *adj. Brit.* (of cattle, etc.) certified to be free from a disease, esp. from tuberculosis.

attic ('ætɪk) *n.* **1.** a space or room within the roof of a house. **2.** *Archit.* a storey or low wall above the cornice of a classical façade. [C18: special use of ATTIC, from use of Attic-style pilasters on façade of top storey]

Attic ('ætɪk) *adj.* **1.** of or relating to Attica, the area around Athens, its inhabitants, or the dialect of Greek spoken there. **2.** (*often not cap.*) classically elegant, simple, or pure. ~*n.* **3.** the dialect of Ancient Greek spoken and written in Athens.

Atticism ('ætɪ,sɪzəm) *n.* **1.** the idiom or character of the Attic dialect of Ancient Greek. **2.** an elegant, simple expression.

Attic salt *or* **wit** *n.* refined incisive wit.

attire (ə'taɪə) *vb.* **1.** (*tr.*) to dress, esp. in fine elegant clothes; array. ~*n.* **2.** clothes or garments, esp. if fine or decorative. [C13: < OF *atirier* to put in order, < *tire* row]

attitude ('ætɪ,tju:d) *n.* **1.** the way a person views something or tends to behave towards it, often in an evaluative way. **2.** a theatrical pose created for effect (esp. in **strike an attitude**). **3.** a position of the body indicating mood or emotion. **4.** the orientation of an aircraft's axes or a spacecraft in relation to some plane or the direction of motion. [C17: < F, < It. *attitudine* disposition, < LL *aptitūdō* fitness, < L *aptus* APT] —,**atti'tudinal** *adj.*

attitudinize *or* **-nise** (,ætɪ'tju:dɪ,naɪz) *vb.* (*intr.*) to adopt a pose or opinion for effect; strike an attitude.

attn *abbrev. for* attention.

atto- *prefix.* denoting 10^{-18}: *attotesla.* Symbol: a [< Norwegian & Danish *atten* eighteen]

attorney (ə'tɜ:nɪ) *n.* **1.** a person legally appointed or empowered to act for another. **2.** *U.S.* a lawyer qualified to represent clients in legal proceedings. [C14: < OF, < *atourner* to direct to, < *tourner* to TURN] —**at'torney,ship** *n.*

attorney-at-law *n., pl.* **attorneys-at-law.** *Law, now chiefly U.S.* a lawyer.

attorney general *n., pl.* **attorneys general** *or* **attorney generals.** a chief law officer and senior legal adviser of some national and state governments.

attract (ə'trækt) *vb.* (*mainly tr.*) **1.** to draw (notice, a crowd of observers, etc.) to oneself (esp. in **attract attention**). **2.** (*also intr.*) to exert a force on (a body) that tends to oppose a separation: *the gravitational pull of the earth attracts objects to it.* **3.** to possess some property that pulls or draws (something) towards itself. **4.** (*also intr.*) to exert a pleasing or fascinating influence (upon). [C15: < L *attrahere* to draw towards, < *trahere* to pull] —**at'tractable** *adj.* —**at'tractor** *n.*

attraction (ə'trækʃən) *n.* **1.** the act or quality of attracting. **2.** a person or thing that attracts or is intended to attract. **3.** a force by which one object attracts another: *magnetic attraction.*

attractive (ə'træktɪv) *adj.* **1.** appealing to the senses or mind through beauty, form, character, etc. **2.** arousing interest: *an attractive opportunity.* **3.** possessing the ability to draw or pull: *an attractive force.* —**at'tractively** *adv.*

attrib. *abbrev. for:* **1.** attribute. **2.** attributive.

attribute *vb.* (ə'trɪbju:t). **1.** (*tr.;* usually foll. by *to*) to regard as belonging (to), produced (by), or resulting (from): *to attribute a painting to Picasso.* ~*n.* ('ætrɪ,bju:t). **2.** a property, quality, or feature belonging to or representative of a person or thing. **3.** an object accepted as belonging to a particular office or position. **4.** *Grammar.* **a.** an adjective or adjectival phrase. **b.** an attributive adjective. **5.** *Logic.* the property or feature that is affirmed or denied concerning the subject of a proposition. [C15: < L *attribuere* to associate with, < *tribuere* to give] —**at'tributable** *adj.* —**attribution** (,ætrɪ'bju:ʃən) *n.*

attributive (ə'trɪbjʊtɪv) *adj.* **1.** relating to an attribute. **2.** *Grammar.* (of an adjective or adjectival phrase) preceding the noun modified. Cf. **predicative.**

attrition (ə'trɪʃən) *n.* **1.** the act of wearing away or the state of being worn away, as by friction. **2.** constant wearing down to weaken or destroy (often in **war of attrition**). **3.** *Geog.* the grinding down of rock particles by friction. **4.** *Theol.* sorrow for sin arising from fear of damnation, esp. as contrasted with contrition. [C14: < LL *attrītiō* a rubbing against something, < L *atterere* to weaken, < *terere* to rub]

attune (ə'tjuːn) *vb.* (*tr.*) to adjust or accustom (a person or thing); acclimatize.

at. vol. *abbrev. for* atomic volume.

at. wt. *abbrev. for* atomic weight.

atypical (eɪ'tɪpɪkᵊl) *adj.* not typical; deviating from or not conforming to type. —**a'typically** *adv.*

Au *the chemical symbol for* gold. [< NL *aurum*]

aubade (əʊ'bɑːd) *n.* a poem or short musical piece to greet the dawn. [C19: F, < OProvençal *auba* dawn, ult. < L *albus* white]

aubergine ('əʊbəˌʒiːn) *n.* **1.** a tropical Old World plant widely cultivated for its egg-shaped typically dark purple fruit. U.S. and Canad. name: **eggplant.** **2.** the fruit of this plant, which is cooked and eaten as a vegetable. **3. a.** a dark purple colour. **b.** (*as adj.*): *an aubergine dress.* [C18: < F, < Catalan *alberginia,* < Ar. *al-bādindjān,* ult. < Sansk. *vatin-ganah,* <?]

aubrietia, aubrieta, *or* **aubretia** (ɔː'briːʃə) *n.* a trailing purple-flowered plant native to European mountains but widely planted in rock gardens. [C19: < NL, after Claude *Aubriet,* 18th-cent. F painter of flowers and animals]

auburn ('ɔːbᵊn) *n.* **a.** a moderate reddish-brown colour. **b.** (*as adj.*): *auburn hair.* [C15 (orig. meaning: blond): < OF *alborne* blond, < Med. L, < L *albus* white]

au courant *French.* (o kurɑ̃) *adj.* up-to-date, esp. in knowledge of current affairs. [lit.: in the current]

auction ('ɔːkʃən) *n.* **1.** a public sale of goods or property in which prospective purchasers bid until the highest price is reached. **2.** the competitive calls made in bridge before play begins. ~*vb.* **3.** (*tr.*; often foll. by *off*) to sell by auction. [C16: < L *auctiō* an increasing, < *augēre* to increase]

auction bridge *n.* a variety of bridge in which all the tricks made score towards game.

auctioneer (ˌɔːkʃə'nɪə) *n.* **1.** a person who conducts an auction. ~*vb.* **2.** (*tr.*) to sell by auction.

auctorial (ɔːk'tɔːrɪəl) *adj.* of or relating to an author. [C19: < L *auctor* AUTHOR]

audacious (ɔː'deɪʃəs) *adj.* **1.** recklessly bold or daring. **2.** impudent or presumptuous. [C16: < L *audāx* bold, < *audēre* to dare] —**au'daciousness** *or* **audacity** (ɔː'dæsɪtɪ) *n.*

audible ('ɔːdɪbᵊl) *adj.* perceptible to the hearing; loud enough to be heard. [C16: < LL, < L *audīre* to hear] —ˌ**audi'bility** *or* '**audibleness** *n.* —'**audibly** *adv.*

audience ('ɔːdɪəns) *n.* **1.** a group of spectators or listeners, esp. at a concert or play. **2.** the people reached by a book, film, or radio or television programme. **3.** the devotees or followers of a public entertainer, etc. **4.** a formal interview with a monarch or head of state. [C14: < OF, < L *audientia* a hearing, < *audīre* to hear]

audio ('ɔːdɪəʊ) *n.* (*modifier*) **1.** of or relating to sound or hearing: *audio frequency.* **2.** relating to or employed in the transmission or reproduction of sound. [C20: < L *audīre* to hear]

audio frequency *n.* a frequency in the range 20 hertz to 20 000 hertz. A sound wave of this frequency would be audible to the human ear.

audiology (ˌɔːdɪ'ɒlədʒɪ) *n.* the scientific study of hearing, often including the treatment of persons with hearing defects. —ˌ**audi'ologist** *n.*

audiometer (ˌɔːdɪ'ɒmɪtə) *n.* an instrument for testing hearing. —ˌ**audi'ometrist** *n.* —ˌ**audi'ometry** *n.*

audiophile ('ɔːdɪəʊˌfaɪl) *n.* a person who has a great interest in high-fidelity sound reproduction.

audiotypist ('ɔːdɪəʊˌtaɪpɪst) *n.* a typist trained to type from a dictating machine. —'**audio**ˌ**typing** *n.*

audiovisual (ˌɔːdɪəʊ'vɪʒʊəl) *adj.* (esp. of teaching aids) involving or directed at both hearing and sight. —ˌ**audio'visually** *adv.*

audit ('ɔːdɪt) *n.* **1. a.** an inspection, correction, and verification of business accounts by a qualified accountant. **b.** (*as modifier*): *audit report.* **2.** *U.S.* an audited account. **3.** any thoroughgoing examination or check. ~*vb.* **4.** to inspect, correct, and certify (accounts, etc.). [C15: < L *audītus* a hearing, < *audīre* to hear]

audition (ɔː'dɪʃən) *n.* **1.** a test at which a performer or musician is asked to demonstrate his ability for a particular role, etc. **2.** the act or power of hearing. ~*vb.* **3.** to judge by means of or be tested in an audition. [C16: < L *audītiō* a hearing, < *audīre* to hear]

auditor ('ɔːdɪtə) *n.* **1.** a person qualified to audit accounts. **2.** a person who hears or listens. [C14: < OF, < L *audītor* a hearer] —ˌ**audi'torial** *adj.*

Auditor General *n.* (in Canada) an officer appointed by the Governor General to audit the accounts of the Federal Government and report to Parliament.

auditorium (ˌɔːdɪ'tɔːrɪəm) *n., pl.* **-toriums** *or* **-toria** (-'tɔːrɪə). **1.** the area of a concert hall, theatre, etc., in which the audience sits. **2.** *U.S. & Canad.* a building for public meetings. [C17: < L: a judicial examination]

auditory ('ɔːdɪtərɪ) *adj.* of or relating to hearing or the sense of hearing. [C14: < L *audītōrius* relating to hearing, < *audīre* to hear]

AUEW (in Britain) *abbrev. for* Amalgamated Union of Engineering Workers: the former name of the AEU.

au fait *French.* (o fɛ) *adj.* fully informed; in touch or expert. [C18: lit.: to the point]

au fond *French.* (o fɔ̃) *adv.* fundamentally; essentially. [lit.: at the bottom]

auf Wiedersehen *German.* (auf 'viːdərzeːən) *sentence substitute.* goodbye, until we see each other again.

Aug. *abbrev. for* August.

Augean (ɔː'dʒiːən) *adj.* extremely dirty or corrupt. [C16: < *Augeas,* in Gk myth., king whose filthy stables Hercules cleaned in one day]

augend ('ɔːdʒɛnd, ɔː'dʒɛnd) *n.* a number to which another number, the addend, is added. [< L *augendum,* < *augēre* to increase]

auger ('ɔːgə) *n.* **1.** a hand tool with a bit shaped like a corkscrew, for boring holes in wood. **2.** a larger tool of the same kind for boring holes in the ground. [C15: *an augur,* mistaken division of *a nauger,* < OE *nafugār* nave (of a wheel) spear, < *nafu* NAVE[2] + *gār* spear]

aught *or* **ought** (ɔːt) (*used with a negative or in conditional or interrogative sentences or clauses*) *Arch. or literary.* ~*pron.* **1.** anything whatever (esp. in **for aught I know**). ~*adv.* **2.** *Dialect.* to any degree. [OE *āwiht,* < *ā* ever, + *wiht* thing]

augment (ɔːg'mɛnt) *vb.* to make or become greater in number, strength, etc. [C15: < LL, < *augmentum* growth, < L *augēre* to increase] —**aug'mentable** *adj.* —**aug'menter** *n.*

augmentation (ˌɔːgmɛn'teɪʃən) *n.* **1.** the act of augmenting or the state of being augmented. **2.** the amount by which something is increased.

augmentative (ɔːg'mɛntətɪv) *adj.* **1.** tending or able to augment. **2.** *Grammar.* denoting an affix that may be added to a word to convey the meaning *large* or *great.*

augmented (ɔːg'mɛntɪd) *adj.* **1.** *Music.* (of an interval) increased from being perfect or major by the raising of the higher note or the dropping of the lower note by one semitone: *C to G sharp is an augmented fifth.* **2.** having been increased, esp. in number: *an augmented orchestra.*

au gratin (*French* o gratɛ̃) *adj.* covered and cooked with browned breadcrumbs and sometimes cheese. [F, lit.: with the grating]

augur ('ɔːgə) *n.* **1.** (in ancient Rome) a religious

official who observed and interpreted omens and signs. **2.** any prophet or soothsayer. ~*vb.* **3.** to predict (some future event), as from signs or omens. **4.** (*tr.; may take a clause as object*) to be an omen (of). **5.** (*intr.*) to foreshadow future events: *this augurs well for us.* [C14: < L: a diviner, ? < *augēre* to increase] —**augural** (ˈɔːgjʊrəl) *adj.*

augury (ˈɔːgjʊrɪ) *n., pl.* **-ries. 1.** the art of or a rite conducted by an augur. **2.** a sign or portent; omen.

august (ɔːˈgʌst) *adj.* **1.** dignified or imposing. **2.** of noble birth or high rank: *an august lineage.* [C17: < L *augustus;* rel. to *augēre* to increase] —**auˈgustness** *n.*

August (ˈɔːgəst) *n.* the eighth month of the year, consisting of 31 days. [OE, < L, after the emperor *Augustus*]

Augustan (ɔːˈgʌstən) *adj.* **1.** characteristic of or relating to the Roman emperor Augustus Caesar (63 B.C.–14 A.D.), his period, or the poets writing during his reign. **2.** of or characteristic of any literary period noted for refinement and classicism, esp. the 18th century in England. ~*n.* **3.** an author in an Augustan Age.

Augustinian (ˌɔːgəˈstɪnɪən) *adj.* **1.** of Saint Augustine of Hippo (354-430 A.D.), his doctrines, or the Christian religious orders founded on his doctrines. ~*n.* **2.** a member of any of several religious orders which are governed by the rule of Saint Augustine. **3.** a person who follows the doctrines of Saint Augustine.

auk (ɔːk) *n.* **1.** a diving bird of northern oceans having a heavy body, short tail, narrow wings, and a black-and-white plumage. See also **great auk, razorbill. 2. little auk.** a small short-billed auk, abundant in Arctic regions. [C17: < ON *ālka*]

auklet (ˈɔːklɪt) *n.* any of various small auks.

au lait (əʊ ˈleɪ) *adj.* prepared or served with milk. [F, lit.: with milk]

auld (ɔːld) *adj.* a Scottish word for **old.** [OE *āld*]

auld lang syne (ˈɔːld læŋ ˈsaɪn) *n.* times past, esp. those remembered with nostalgia. [Scot., lit.: old long since]

au naturel *French.* (o natyrɛl) *adj., adv.* **1.** naked; nude. **2.** uncooked or plainly cooked. [lit.: in (a) natural (condition)]

aunt (ɑːnt) *n.* (*often cap., esp. as a term of address*) **1.** a sister of one's father or mother. **2.** the wife of one's uncle. **3.** a term of address used by children for a female friend of the parents. **4. my (sainted) aunt!** an exclamation of surprise. [C13: < OF, < L *amita* a father's sister]

auntie *or* **aunty** (ˈɑːntɪ) *n., pl.* **-ies.** a familiar or diminutive word for **aunt.**

Auntie (ˈɑːntɪ) *n. Brit. inf.* the BBC.

Aunt Sally (ˈsælɪ) *n., pl.* **-lies.** *Brit.* **1.** a figure of an old woman used in fairgrounds and fêtes as a target. **2.** any person who is a target for insults or criticism.

au pair (əʊ ˈpɛə) *n.* **a.** a young foreigner, usually a girl, who undertakes housework in exchange for board and lodging, esp. in order to learn the language. **b.** (*as modifier*): *an au pair girl.* [C20: < F: on an equal footing]

aura (ˈɔːrə) *n., pl.* **auras** *or* **aurae** (ˈɔːriː). **1.** a distinctive air or quality considered to be characteristic of a person or thing. **2.** any invisible emanation, esp. surrounding a person or object. **3.** *Pathol.* strange sensations, such as noises in the ears or flashes of light, that immediately precede an attack, esp. of epilepsy. [C18: via L < Gk: breeze]

aural (ˈɔːrəl) *adj.* of or relating to the sense or organs of hearing; auricular. [C19: < L *auris* ear] —ˈ**aurally** *adv.*

aureate (ˈɔːrɪɪt) *adj.* **1.** covered with gold; gilded. **2.** (of a style of writing or speaking) excessively elaborate. [C15: < LL, < L *aureus* golden, < *aurum* gold]

aureole (ˈɔːrɪˌəʊl) *or* **aureola** (ɔːˈriːələ) *n.* **1.** a border of light or radiance enveloping the head of a figure represented as holy. **2.** a less common word for **halo. 3.** another name for **corona** (sense 2). [C13: < OF, < Med. L (*corōna*) *aureola* golden (crown), < L, < *aurum* gold]

au revoir *French.* (o rəvwar) *sentence substitute.* goodbye. [lit.: to the seeing again]

auric (ˈɔːrɪk) *adj.* of or containing gold, esp. in the trivalent state. [C19: < L *aurum* gold]

auricle (ˈɔːrɪkᵊl) *n.* **1.** the upper chamber of the heart; atrium. **2.** Also called: **pinna.** *Anat.* the external part of the ear. **3.** *Biol.* an ear-shaped part or appendage. [C17: < L *auricula* the external ear, < *auris* ear] —ˈ**auricled** *adj.*

auricula (ɔːˈrɪkjʊlə) *n., pl.* **-lae** (-ˌliː) *or* **-las. 1.** Also called: **bear's-ear.** a widely cultivated alpine primrose with leaves shaped like a bear's ear. **2.** another word for **auricle** (sense 3). [C17: < NL, < L; see AURICLE]

auricular (ɔːˈrɪkjʊlə) *adj.* **1.** of, relating to, or received by the sense or organs of hearing; aural. **2.** shaped like an ear. **3.** of or relating to an auricle of the heart.

auriferous (ɔːˈrɪfərəs) *adj.* (of rock) containing gold; gold-bearing. [C18: < L, < *aurum* gold + *ferre* to bear]

Aurignacian (ˌɔːrɪgˈneɪʃən) *adj.* of or produced during a flint culture of the Upper Palaeolithic type characterized by the use of bone and antler tools, and also by cave art. [C20: after *Aurignac,* France, near the cave where remains were discovered]

aurochs (ˈɔːrɒks) *n., pl.* **-rochs.** a recently extinct member of the cattle tribe that inhabited forests in N Africa, Europe, and SW Asia. Also called: **urus.** [C18: < G, < OHG *ūrohso,* < *ūro* bison + *ohso* ox]

aurora (ɔːˈrɔːrə) *n., pl.* **-ras** *or* **-rae** (-riː). **1.** an atmospheric phenomenon consisting of bands, curtains, or streamers of light, that move across the sky, esp. in polar regions. **2.** *Poetic.* the dawn. [C14: < L: dawn] —**auˈroral** *adj.*

aurora australis (ɒˈstreɪlɪs) *n.* (*sometimes cap.*) the aurora seen around the South Pole. Also called: **southern lights.** [NL: southern aurora]

aurora borealis (ˌbɔːrɪˈeɪlɪs) *n.* (*sometimes cap.*) the aurora seen around the North Pole. Also called: **northern lights.** [C17: NL: northern aurora]

auscultation (ˌɔːskəlˈteɪʃən) *n.* **1.** the diagnostic technique in medicine of listening to the various internal sounds made by the body, usually with the aid of a stethoscope. **2.** the act of listening. [C19: < L, < *auscultāre* to listen attentively; rel. to L *auris* ear] —ˈ**auscultate** *vb.* —**auscultatory** (ɔːˈskʌltətərɪ) *adj.*

auspice (ˈɔːspɪs) *n.* **1.** (*usually pl.*) patronage (esp. in **under the auspices of**). **2.** (*often pl.*) an omen, esp. one that is favourable. [C16: < L *auspicium* augury from birds]

auspicious (ɔːˈspɪʃəs) *adj.* **1.** favourable or propitious. **2.** *Arch.* fortunate. —**ausˈpiciously** *adv.* —**ausˈpiciousness** *n.*

Aussie (ˈɒzɪ) *n., adj. Inf.* Australian.

Aust. *abbrev. for:* **1.** Australia(n). **2.** Austria(n).

austere (ɒˈstɪə) *adj.* **1.** stern or severe in attitude or manner. **2.** grave, sober, or serious. **3.** self-disciplined, abstemious, or ascetic: *an austere life.* **4.** severely simple or plain: *an austere design.* [C14: < OF, < L *austērus* sour, < Gk *austēros* astringent; rel. to Gk *hauein* to dry] —**ausˈterely** *adv.*

austerity (ɒˈstɛrɪtɪ) *n., pl.* **-ties. 1.** the state or quality of being austere. **2.** (*often pl.*) an austere habit, practice, or act. **3. a.** reduced availability of luxuries and consumer goods. **b.** (*as modifier*): *an austerity budget.*

austral (ˈɔːstrəl) *adj.* of or coming from the south: *austral winds.* [C14: < L *austrālis,* < *auster* the south wind]

Austral. *abbrev. for:* **1.** Australasia. **2.** Australia(n).

Australasian (ˌɒstrəˈleɪzɪən) *adj.* **1.** of or relating to Australia, New Zealand, and neighbouring islands. **2.** (of organizations) having members in Australia and New Zealand.

Australian (ɒˈstreɪlɪən) *n.* **1.** a native or inhabitant of Australia, the smallest continent. **2.**

the form of English spoken in Australia. ~*adj.* **3.** of, relating to, or characteristic of Australia, the Australians, or their form of English.

Australiana (ɒˌstreɪlɪˈɑːnə) *n.* objects, books, documents, etc. relating to Australia and its history and culture.

Australian Rules *n.* (*functioning as sing.*) a game resembling rugby, played in Australia between teams of 18 men each on an oval pitch, with a ball resembling a large rugby ball. Players attempt to kick the ball between posts (without crossbars) at either end of the pitch.

Australian terrier *n.* a small wire-haired breed of terrier similar to the cairn.

Australoid (ˈɒstrəˌlɔɪd) *adj.* **1.** denoting, relating to, or belonging to a racial group that includes the Australian Aborigines and certain other peoples of southern Asia and the Pacific islands. ~*n.* **2.** any member of this racial group.

australopithecine (ˌɒstrələʊˈpɪθɪˌsiːn) *n.* any of various extinct apelike primates whose remains have been found in southern and E Africa. Some species are estimated to be over 4.5 million years old. [C20: < NL, < L *austrālis* southern + Gk *pithēkos* ape]

Australorp (ˈɒstrəˌlɔːp) *n.* a heavy black breed of domestic fowl laying brown eggs. [shortened < *Austral(ian Black) Orp(ington)*]

Austrian (ˈɒstrɪən) *adj.* **1.** of or relating to Austria, a republic in Central Europe. ~*n.* **2.** a native or inhabitant of Austria.

Austro-[1] (ˈɒstrəʊ) *combining form.* southern: *Austro-Asiatic.* [< L *auster* the south wind]

Austro-[2] (ˈɒstrəʊ) *combining form.* Austrian: *Austro-Hungarian.*

AUT (in Britain) *abbrev. for* Association of University Teachers.

autarchy (ˈɔːtɑːkɪ) *n., pl.* **-chies.** unlimited rule; autocracy. [C17: < Gk *autarkhia,* < *autarkhos* autocratic] **—auˈtarchic** *or* **auˈtarchical** *adj.*

autarky (ˈɔːtɑːkɪ) *n., pl.* **-kies.** (esp. of a political unit) a system or policy of economic self-sufficiency. [C17: < Gk *autarkeia,* < *autarkēs* self-sufficient, < AUTO- + *arkein* to suffice] **—auˈtarkic** *adj.* **—ˈautarkist** *n.*

authentic (ɔːˈθɛntɪk) *adj.* **1.** of undisputed origin or authorship; genuine. **2.** trustworthy; reliable: *an authentic account.* **3.** (of a deed, etc.) duly executed. **4.** *Music.* commencing on the final and ending an octave higher. Cf. **plagal.** [C14: < LL *authenticus* coming from the author, < Gk, < *authentēs* one who acts independently, < AUTO- + *hentēs* a doer] **—auˈthentically** *adv.* **—authenticity** (ˌɔːθɛnˈtɪsɪtɪ) *n.*

authenticate (ɔːˈθɛntɪˌkeɪt) *vb.* (*tr.*) **1.** to establish as genuine or valid. **2.** to give authority or legal validity to. **—auˌthentiˈcation** *n.* **—auˈthentiˌcator** *n.*

author (ˈɔːθə) *n.* **1.** a person who composes a book, article, or other written work. Related adj.: **auctorial. 2.** a person who writes books as a profession; writer. **3.** an originator or creator: *the author of this plan.* ~*vb.* (*tr.*) **4.** to write or originate. [C14: < OF, < L *auctor* author, < *augēre* to increase] **—authorial** (ɔːˈθɔːrɪəl) *adj.*

authoritarian (ɔːˌθɒrɪˈtɛərɪən) *adj.* **1.** favouring or characterized by strict obedience to authority. **2.** favouring or relating to government by a small elite. **3.** dictatorial; domineering. ~*n.* **4.** a person who favours or practises authoritarian policies.

authoritative (ɔːˈθɒrɪtətɪv) *adj.* **1.** recognized or accepted as being true or reliable. **2.** commanding: *an authoritative manner.* **3.** possessing or supported by authority; official. **—auˈthoritatively** *adv.* **—auˈthoritativeness** *n.*

authority (ɔːˈθɒrɪtɪ) *n., pl.* **-ties. 1.** the power or right to control, judge, or prohibit the actions of others. **2.** (*often pl.*) a person or group of people having this power, such as a government, police force, etc. **3.** a position that commands such a power or right (often in **in authority**). **4.** such a power or right delegated: *she has his authority.* **5.** the ability to influence or control others. **6.** an expert or an authoritative written work in a particular field. **7.** evidence or testimony. **8.** confidence resulting from great expertise. **9.** (*cap. when part of a name*) a public board or corporation exercising governmental authority: *Independent Broadcasting Authority.* [C14: < OF, < L, < *auctor* author]

authorize *or* **-rise** (ˈɔːθəˌraɪz) *vb.* (*tr.*) **1.** to confer authority upon (someone to do something). **2.** to permit (someone to do or be something) with official sanction. **—ˌauthoriˈzation** *or* **-riˈsation** *n.*

Authorized Version *n.* **the.** an English translation of the Bible published in 1611 under James I. Also called: **King James Version.**

authorship (ˈɔːθəˌʃɪp) *n.* **1.** the origin or originator of a written work, plan, etc. **2.** the profession of writing books.

autism (ˈɔːtɪzəm) *n. Psychiatry.* abnormal self-absorption, usually affecting children, characterized by lack of response to people and limited ability to communicate. [C20: < Gk *autos* self + -ISM] **—auˈtistic** *adj.*

auto (ˈɔːtəʊ) *n., pl.* **-tos.** *U.S. & Canad. inf.* **a.** short for **automobile. b.** (*as modifier*): *auto parts.*

auto. *abbrev. for:* **1.** automatic. **2.** automobile. **3.** automotive.

auto- *or sometimes before a vowel* **aut-** *combining form.* **1.** self; same; of or by the same one: *autobiography.* **2.** self-caused: *autohypnosis.* **3.** self-propelling: *automobile.* [< Gk *autos* self]

autobahn (ˈɔːtəˌbɑːn) *n.* a German motorway. [C20: < G < *Auto* car + *Bahn* road, track]

autobiography (ˌɔːtəʊbaɪˈɒgrəfɪ) *n., pl.* **-phies.** an account of a person's life written or otherwise recorded by that person. **—ˌautobiˈographer** *n.* **—autobiographical** (ˌɔːtəˌbaɪəˈgræfɪkᵊl) *adj.*

autocephalous (ˌɔːtəʊˈsɛfələs) *adj.* (of an Eastern Christian Church) governed by its own national synods and appointing its own patriarchs or prelates.

autochthon (ɔːˈtɒkθən) *n., pl.* **-thons** *or* **-thones** (-θəˌniːz). **1.** (*often pl.*) one of the earliest known inhabitants of any country. **2.** an animal or plant that is native to a particular region. [C17: < Gk *autokhthōn* from the earth itself, < AUTO- + *khthōn* the earth] **—auˈtochthonous** *adj.*

autoclave (ˈɔːtəˌkleɪv) *n.* **1.** a strong sealed vessel used for chemical reactions at high pressure. **2.** an apparatus for sterilizing objects (esp. surgical instruments) by means of steam under pressure. [C19: < F AUTO- + *-clave,* < L *clāvis* key]

autocracy (ɔːˈtɒkrəsɪ) *n., pl.* **-cies. 1.** government by an individual with unrestricted authority. **2.** a country, society, etc., ruled by an autocrat.

autocrat (ˈɔːtəˌkræt) *n.* **1.** a ruler who possesses absolute and unrestricted authority. **2.** a domineering or dictatorial person. **—ˌautoˈcratic** *adj.* **—ˌautoˈcratically** *adv.*

autocross (ˈɔːtəʊˌkrɒs) *n.* a motor sport in which cars race over a half-mile circuit of rough grass.

Autocue (ˈɔːtəʊˌkjuː) *n. Trademark.* an electronic television prompting device whereby a script, unseen by the audience, is displayed for the speaker.

auto-da-fé (ˌɔːtəʊdəˈfeɪ) *n., pl.* **autos-da-fé. 1.** *History.* a ceremony of the Spanish Inquisition including the pronouncement and execution of sentences passed on sinners or heretics. **2.** the burning to death of people condemned as heretics by the Inquisition. [C18: < Port., lit.: act of the faith]

autoeroticism (ˌɔːtəʊɪˈrɒtɪˌsɪzəm) *or* **autoerotism** (ˌɔːtəʊˈɛrəˌtɪzəm) *n. Psychol.* the arousal and use of one's own body as a sexual object. **—ˌautoeˈrotic** *adj.*

autogamy (ɔːˈtɒgəmɪ) *n.* self-fertilization. **—auˈtogamous** *adj.*

autogenous (ɔːˈtɒdʒɪnəs) *adj.* **1.** originating within the body. **2.** self-produced. **3.** (of a joint between two parts) achieved without flux, adhesive, or solder: *autogenous welding.*

autogiro *or* **autogyro** (ˌɔːtəʊˈdʒaɪrəʊ) *n., pl.* **-ros.** a self-propelled aircraft supported in flight mainly by unpowered rotating horizontal blades. [C20: orig. a trademark]

autograph (ˈɔːtəˌɡrɑːf) *n.* **1. a.** a handwritten signature, esp. that of a famous person. **b.** (*as modifier*): *an autograph album.* **2.** a person's handwriting. **3. a.** a book, document, etc., handwritten by its author. **b.** (*as modifier*): *an autograph letter.* ~*vb.* (*tr.*) **4.** to write one's signature on or in; sign. **5.** to write with one's own hand. —**autographic** (ˌɔːtəˈɡræfɪk) *adj.* —ˌ**autoˈgraphically** *adv.*

autohypnosis (ˌɔːtəʊhɪpˈnəʊsɪs) *n. Psychol.* the process or result of self-induced hypnosis.

autointoxication (ˌɔːtəʊɪnˌtɒksɪˈkeɪʃən) *n.* self-poisoning caused by toxic products originating within the body.

autolysis (ɔːˈtɒlɪsɪs) *n.* the destruction of cells and tissues of an organism by enzymes produced by the cells themselves. —**autolytic** (ˌɔːtəˈlɪtɪk) *adj.*

automat (ˈɔːtəˌmæt) *n.* another name, esp. U.S., for **vending machine.**

automata (ɔːˈtɒmətə) *n.* a plural of **automaton.**

automate (ˈɔːtəˌmeɪt) *vb.* to make (a manufacturing process, factory, etc.) automatic, or (of a manufacturing process, etc.) to be made automatic.

automatic (ˌɔːtəˈmætɪk) *adj.* **1.** performed from force of habit or without conscious thought: *an automatic smile.* **2. a.** (of a device, mechanism, etc.) able to activate, move, or regulate itself. **b.** (of an act or process) performed by such automatic equipment. **3.** (of the action of a muscle, etc.) involuntary or reflex. **4.** occurring as a necessary consequence: *promotion is automatic after a year.* **5.** (of a firearm) utilizing some of the force of each explosion to eject the empty shell, replace it with a new one, and fire continuously until release of the trigger. ~*n.* **6.** an automatic firearm. **7.** a motor vehicle having automatic transmission. **8.** a machine that operates automatically. [C18: < Gk *automatos* acting independently] —ˌ**autoˈmatically** *adv.*

automatic data processing *n.* data processing performed by automatic electromechanical devices. Abbrev.: **ADP, A.D.P., a.d.p.** Cf. **electronic data processing.**

automatic gain control *n.* a control of a radio receiver which adjusts the magnitude of the input so that the output (or volume) remains approximately constant.

automatic pilot *n.* a device that automatically maintains an aircraft on a preset course. Also called: **autopilot.**

automatic transmission *n.* a transmission system in a motor vehicle in which the gears change automatically.

automation (ˌɔːtəˈmeɪʃən) *n.* **1.** the use of methods for controlling industrial processes automatically, esp. by electronically controlled systems. **2.** the extent to which a process is so controlled.

automatism (ɔːˈtɒməˌtɪzəm) *n.* **1.** the state or quality of being automatic; mechanical or involuntary action. **2.** *Psychol.* the performance of actions, such as sleepwalking, without conscious knowledge or control. —**auˈtomatist** *n.*

automatize *or* **-tise** (ɔːˈtɒməˌtaɪz) *vb.* to make (a process, etc) automatic or (of a process, etc.) to be made automatic. —**auˌtomatiˈzation** *or* **-tiˈsation** *n.*

automaton (ɔːˈtɒmətᵊn) *n., pl.* **-tons** *or* **-ta. 1.** a mechanical device operating under its own hidden power. **2.** a person who acts mechanically. [C17: < L, < Gk, < *automatos* spontaneous]

autometer (ˈɔːtəʊˌmiːtə) *n.* a small device inserted in a photocopier to enable copying to begin and to record the number of copies made.

automobile (ˈɔːtəməˌbiːl) *n.* another word (esp. U.S.) for **car** (sense 1). —ˌ**automoˈbilist** *n.*

automotive (ˌɔːtəˈməʊtɪv) *adj.* **1.** relating to motor vehicles. **2.** self-propelling.

autonomic (ˌɔːtəˈnɒmɪk) *adj.* **1.** occurring spontaneously. **2.** of or relating to the autonomic nervous system. **3.** Also: **autonomous.** (of plant movements) occurring as a result of internal stimuli. —ˌ**autoˈnomically** *adv.*

autonomic nervous system *n.* the section of the nervous system of vertebrates that controls the involuntary actions of the smooth muscles, heart, and glands.

autonomous (ɔːˈtɒnəməs) *adj.* **1.** (of a community, country, etc.) possessing a large degree of self-government. **2.** of or relating to an autonomous community. **3.** independent of others. **4.** *Biol.* existing as an organism independent of other organisms or parts. [C19: < Gk *autonomos* living under one's own laws, < AUTO- + *nomos* law] —**auˈtonomously** *adv.*

autonomy (ɔːˈtɒnəmɪ) *n., pl.* **-mies. 1.** the right or state of self-government, esp. when limited. **2.** a state or individual possessing autonomy. **3.** freedom to determine one's own actions, behaviour, etc. **4.** *Philosophy.* the doctrine that the individual human will is, or ought to be, governed only by its own principles and laws. [C17: < Gk *automonia* freedom to live by one's own laws]

autopilot (ˌɔːtəˈpaɪlət) *n.* short for **automatic pilot.**

autopsy (ˈɔːtəpsɪ, ɔːˈtɒp-) *n., pl.* **-sies. 1.** Also called: **postmortem examination.** dissection and examination of a dead body to determine the cause of death. **2.** an eyewitness observation. **3.** any critical analysis. [C17: < NL, < Gk: seeing with one's own eyes, < AUTO- + *opsis* sight]

autoroute (ˈɔːtəʊˌruːt) *n.* a French motorway. [C20: < F < *auto* car + *route* road]

autostrada (ˈɔːtəʊˌstrɑːdə) *n.* an Italian motorway. [C20: < It. < *auto* car + *strada* road]

autosuggestion (ˌɔːtəʊsəˈdʒɛstʃən) *n.* a process of suggestion in which the person unconsciously supplies the means of influencing his own behaviour or beliefs.

autotelic (ˌɔːtəʊˈtɛlɪk) *adj.* being or having an end or justification in itself. [C20: < AUTO- + Gk *telos* end]

auto-teller (ˈɔːtəʊˌtɛlə) *n. Banking.* a computerized dispenser that can provide cash or account information at any time.

autotomy (ɔːˈtɒtəmɪ) *n., pl.* **-mies.** the casting off by an animal of a part of its body, to facilitate escape when attacked. —**autotomic** (ˌɔːtəˈtɒmɪk) *adj.*

autotrophic (ˌɔːtəˈtrɒfɪk) *adj.* (of organisms such as green plants) capable of manufacturing complex organic nutritive compounds from simple inorganic sources.

autumn (ˈɔːtəm) *n.* **1.** (*sometimes cap.*) **a.** Also called (esp. U.S. and Canad.): **fall.** the season of the year between summer and winter, astronomically from the September equinox to the December solstice in the N hemisphere and from the March equinox to the June solstice in the S hemisphere. **b.** (*as modifier*): *autumn leaves.* **2.** a period of late maturity, esp. one followed by a decline. [C14: < L *autumnus*] —**autumnal** (ɔːˈtʌmnᵊl) *adj.*

autumn crocus *n.* a plant of the lily family having pink or purplish autumn flowers, found in Europe and N Africa.

aux. *abbrev. for* auxiliary.

auxanometer (ˌɔːksəˈnɒmɪtə) *n.* an instrument that measures the linear growth of plant shoots. [C19: < Gk *auxanein* to increase + -METER]

auxiliaries (ɔːɡˈzɪljərɪz, -ˈzɪlə-) *pl. n.* foreign troops serving another nation; mercenaries.

auxiliary (ɔːɡˈzɪljərɪ, -ˈzɪlə-) *adj.* **1.** secondary or supplementary. **2.** supporting. ~*n., pl.* **-ries. 3.** a person or thing that supports or supplements. **4.** *Naut.* **a.** a sailing vessel with an engine. **b.** the engine of such a vessel. [C17: < L, < *auxilium* help, < *augēre* to increase, strengthen]

auxiliary verb *n.* a verb used to indicate the tense, voice, or mood of another verb where this is not indicated by inflection, such as English *will* in *he will go.*

auxin (ˈɔːksɪn) *n.* a plant hormone that promotes growth. [C20: < Gk *auxein* to grow]

AV *abbrev. for* Authorized Version (of the Bible).

av. *abbrev. for:* **1.** average. **2.** avoirdupois.
Av. *or* **av.** *abbrev. for* avenue.
a.v. *or* **A/V** *abbrev. for* ad valorem.
avadavat (ˌævədəˈvæt) *or* **amadavat** (ˌæməˈdəˈvæt) *n.* either of two Asian weaverbirds having a red plumage: often kept as cagebirds. [C18: < *Ahmadabad,* Indian city from which these birds were brought to Europe]
avail (əˈveɪl) *vb.* **1.** to be of use, advantage, profit, or assistance (to). **2. avail oneself of.** to make use of to one's advantage. ~*n.* **3.** use or advantage (esp. in **of no avail, to little avail).** [C13 *availen,* < OF *valoir,* < L *valēre* to be strong]
available (əˈveɪləbᵊl) *adj.* **1.** obtainable or accessible; capable of being made use of. **2.** *Arch.* advantageous. —**aˌvailaˈbility** *or* **aˈvailableness** *n.* —**aˈvailably** *adv.*
avalanche (ˈævəˌlɑːntʃ) *n.* **1. a.** a fall of large masses of snow and ice down a mountain. **b.** a fall of rocks, sand, etc. **2.** a sudden or overwhelming appearance of a large quantity of things. ~*vb.* **3.** to come down overwhelmingly (upon). [C18: < F, by mistaken division < *la valanche,* < *valanche,* < dialect *lavantse*]
avant-garde (ˌævɒŋˈgɑːd) *n.* **1.** those artists, writers, musicians, etc., whose techniques and ideas are in advance of those generally accepted. ~*adj.* **2.** of such artists, etc., their ideas, or techniques. [< F: VANGUARD]
avarice (ˈævərɪs) *n.* extreme greed for riches. [C13: < OF, < L, < *avārus* covetous, < *avēre* to crave] —**avaricious** (ˌævəˈrɪʃəs) *adj.*
avast (əˈvɑːst) *sentence substitute. Naut.* stop! cease! [C17: ? < Du. *hou'vast* hold fast]
avatar (ˈævəˌtɑː) *n.* **1.** *Hinduism.* the manifestation of a deity in human or animal form. **2.** a visible manifestation of an abstract concept. [C18: < Sansk. *avatāra* a going down, < *ava* down + *tarati* he passes over]
avaunt (əˈvɔːnt) *sentence substitute. Arch.* go away! depart! [C15: < OF *avant!* forward! < LL *ab ante* forward, < L *ab* from + *ante* before]
avdp. *abbrev. for* avoirdupois.
ave (ˈɑːvɪ, ˈɑːveɪ) *sentence substitute.* welcome or farewell. [L]
Ave (ˈɑːvɪ) *n. R.C. Church.* short for **Ave Maria:** see **Hail Mary.** [C13: < L: hail!]
Ave *or* **ave** *abbrev. for* avenue.
Ave Maria (məˈriːə) *n.* another name for **Hail Mary.** [C14: < Med. L: hail, Mary!]
avenge (əˈvɛndʒ) *vb.* (*usually tr.*) to inflict a punishment in retaliation for (harm, injury, etc.) done to (a person or persons): *to avenge a crime; to avenge a murdered friend.* [C14: < OF, < *vengier,* < L *vindicāre;* see VENGEANCE, VINDICATE] —**aˈvenger** *n.*
avens (ˈævɪnz) *n., pl.* **-ens.** (*functioning as sing.*) **1.** any of a genus of plants, such as **water avens,** which has a purple calyx and orange-pink flowers. **2. mountain avens.** a trailing evergreen white-flowered shrub that grows on mountains in N temperate regions. [C15: < OF, < Med. L *avencia* variety of clover]
aventurine (əˈvɛntjʊrɪn) *or* **avanturine** (əˈvæntjʊrɪn) *n.* **1.** a dark-coloured glass, usually green or brown, spangled with fine particles of gold, copper, or some other metal. **2.** a variety of quartz containing red or greenish particles of iron oxide or mica. [C19: < F, < It., < *avventura* chance; so named because usually found by accident]
avenue (ˈævɪnjuː) *n.* **1. a.** a broad street, often lined with trees. **b.** (*cap. as part of a street name*) a road, esp. in a built-up area. **2.** a main approach road, as to a country house. **3.** a way bordered by two rows of trees. **4.** a line of approach: *explore every avenue.* [C17: < F, < *avenir* to come to, < L, < *venīre* to come]
aver (əˈvɜː) *vb.* **averring, averred.** (*tr.*) **1.** to state positively. **2.** *Law.* to allege as a fact or prove to be true. [C14: < OF, < Med. L *advērāre,* < L *vērus* true] —**aˈverment** *n.*
average (ˈævərɪdʒ, ˈævrɪdʒ) *n.* **1.** the typical or normal amount, quality, degree, etc.: *above average in intelligence.* **2.** Also called: **arithmetic mean.** the result obtained by adding the numbers or quantities in a set and dividing the total by the number of members in the set: *the average of 3, 4, and 8 is 5.* **3.** a similar mean for continuously variable ratios, such as speed. **4.** *Maritime law.* **a.** a loss incurred or damage suffered by a ship or its cargo at sea. **b.** the equitable apportionment of such loss among the interested parties. **5. on (the** *or* **an) average.** usually; typically. ~*adj.* **6.** usual or typical. **7.** mediocre or inferior: *his performance was only average.* **8.** constituting a numerical average: *an average speed.* **9.** approximately typical of a range of values: *the average contents of a matchbox.* ~*vb.* **10.** (*tr.*) to obtain or estimate a numerical average of. **11.** (*tr.*) to assess the general quality of. **12.** (*tr.*) to perform or receive a typical number of: *to average eight hours' work a day.* **13.** (*tr.*) to divide up proportionately. **14.** to amount to or be on average: *the children averaged 15 years of age.* [C15 *averay* loss arising from damage to ships, < OIt. *avaria,* ult. < Ar. *awār* damage, blemish] —**ˈaveragely** *adv.*
averse (əˈvɜːs) *adj.* (*postpositive;* usually foll. by *to*) opposed, disinclined, or loath. [C16: < L, < *āvertere* to turn from, < *vertere* to turn] —**aˈversely** *adv.* —**aˈverseness** *n.*
▷ **Usage.** *To* is the preposition now normally used with *averse* (*he was averse to giving any assistance*), although *from* is often used with *averse* and *aversion* and was at one time considered to be grammatically correct.
aversion (əˈvɜːʃən) *n.* **1.** (usually foll. by *to* or *for*) extreme dislike or disinclination. **2.** a person or thing that arouses this: *he is my pet aversion.*
aversion therapy *n. Psychiatry.* a way of suppressing an undesirable habit, such as smoking, by associating an unpleasant effect, such as an electric shock, with the habit.
avert (əˈvɜːt) *vb.* (*tr.*) **1.** to turn away or aside: *to avert one's gaze.* **2.** to ward off: *to avert danger.* [C15: < OF, < L *āvertere;* see AVERSE] —**aˈvertible** *or* **aˈvertable** *adj.*
Avesta (əˈvɛstə) *n.* a collection of sacred writings of Zoroastrianism, including the Songs of Zoroaster.
Avestan (əˈvɛstən) *n.* **1.** the earliest recorded form of the Iranian language, formerly called **Zend.** ~*adj.* **2.** of the Avesta or its language.
avg. *abbrev. for* average.
avian (ˈeɪvɪən) *adj.* of, relating to, or resembling a bird. [C19: < L *avis* bird]
aviary (ˈeɪvjərɪ) *n., pl.* **aviaries.** a large enclosure in which birds are kept. [C16: < L, < *aviārius* concerning birds, < *avis* bird]
aviation (ˌeɪvɪˈeɪʃən) *n.* **1.** the art or science of flying aircraft. **2.** the design, production, and maintenance of aircraft. [C19: < F, < L *avis* bird]
aviator (ˈeɪvɪˌeɪtə) *n. Old-fashioned.* the pilot of an aeroplane or airship; flier. —**ˈaviˌatrix** *or* **ˈaviˌatress** *fem. n.*
avid (ˈævɪd) *adj.* **1.** very keen; enthusiastic: *an avid reader.* **2.** (*postpositive;* often foll. by *for* or *of*) eager (for): *avid for revenge.* [C18: < L, < *avēre* to long for] —**avidity** (əˈvɪdɪtɪ) *n.* —**ˈavidly** *adv.*
avifauna (ˌeɪvɪˈfɔːnə) *n.* all the birds in a particular region. —**ˌaviˈfaunal** *adj.*
avionics (ˌeɪvɪˈɒnɪks) *n.* **1.** (*functioning as sing.*) the science and technology of electronics applied to aeronautics. **2.** (*functioning as pl.*) the electronic circuits and devices of an aerospace vehicle. [C20: < *avi(ation electr)onics*] —**ˌaviˈonic** *adj.*
avitaminosis (æˌvɪtəmɪnˈəʊsɪs) *n., pl.* **-ses** (-siːz). any disease caused by a vitamin deficiency in the diet.
avocado (ˌævəˈkɑːdəʊ) *n., pl.* **-dos. 1.** a pear-shaped fruit having a leathery green or blackish skin, a large stony seed, and a greenish-yellow edible pulp. **2.** the tropical American tree that bears this fruit. **3. a.** a dull greenish colour. **b.** (*as adj.*): *an avocado bathroom suite.* ~Also called (for senses 1 & 2): **avocado pear, alligator**

pear. [C17: < Sp. *aguacate,* < Nahuatl *ahuacatl* testicle, alluding to the shape of the fruit]

avocation (ˌævəˈkeɪʃən) *n. Arch.* **1.** a minor occupation undertaken as a diversion. **2.** a person's regular job. [C17: < L, < *āvocāre* to distract, < *vocāre* to call]

avocet (ˈævəˌsɛt) *n.* a long-legged shore bird having black-and-white plumage and a long slender upward-curving bill. [C18: < F, < It. *avocetta,* <?]

Avogadro constant *or* **number** (ˌævəˈgɑːdrəʊ) *n.* the number of atoms or molecules in a mole of a substance, equal to 6.02252 × 10^{23} per mole. [C19: after Amedo *Avogadro* (1776-1856), It. physicist]

Avogadro's law *or* **hypothesis** *n.* the principle that equal volumes of all gases contain the same number of molecules at the same temperature and pressure.

avoid (əˈvɔɪd) *vb. (tr.)* **1.** to keep out of the way of. **2.** to refrain from doing. **3.** to prevent from happening: *to avoid damage to machinery.* **4.** *Law.* to invalidate; quash. [C14: < Anglo-F, < OF *esvuidier,* < *vuidier* to empty] **—aˈvoidable** *adj.* **—aˈvoidably** *adv.* **—aˈvoidance** *n.* **—aˈvoider** *n.*

avoirdupois *or* **avoirdupois weight** (ˌævədəˈpɔɪz) *n.* a system of weights used in many English-speaking countries. It is based on the pound, which contains 16 ounces or 7000 grains. [C14: < OF *aver de peis* goods of weight]

avouch (əˈvaʊtʃ) *vb. (tr.) Arch.* **1.** to vouch for; guarantee. **2.** to acknowledge. **3.** to assert. [C16: < OF *avochier* to summon, call on, < L *advocāre;* see ADVOCATE] **—aˈvouchment** *n.*

avow (əˈvaʊ) *vb. (tr.)* **1.** to state or affirm. **2.** to admit openly. [C13: < OF *avouer* to confess, < L *advocāre* to appeal to, call upon] **—aˈvowal** *n.* **—aˈvowed** *adj.* **—avowedly** (əˈvaʊɪdlɪ) *adv.* **—aˈvower** *n.*

avuncular (əˈvʌŋkjʊlə) *adj.* **1.** of or concerned with an uncle. **2.** resembling an uncle; friendly. [C19: < L *avunculus* (maternal) uncle, dim. of *avus* grandfather]

AWACS *or* **Awacs** (ˈeɪwæks) *n. acronym for* Airborne Warning and Control System.

await (əˈweɪt) *vb.* **1.** *(tr.)* to wait for. **2.** *(tr.)* to be in store for. **3.** *(intr.)* to wait, esp. with expectation.

awake (əˈweɪk) *vb.* **awaking; awoke** *or* **awaked; awoken** *or* **awaked. 1.** to emerge or rouse from sleep. **2.** to become or cause to become alert. **3.** (usually foll. by *to*) to become or make aware (of). **4.** Also: **awaken.** *(tr.)* to arouse (feelings, etc.) or cause to remember (memories, etc.). ~*adj. (postpositive)* **5.** not sleeping. **6.** (sometimes foll. by *to*) lively or alert. [OE *awacian, awacan*]

▷ **Usage.** See at **wake**[1].

award (əˈwɔːd) *vb. (tr.)* **1.** to give (something due), esp. as a reward for merit: *to award prizes.* **2.** *Law.* to declare to be entitled, as by decision of a court or an arbitrator. ~*n.* **3.** something awarded, such as a prize or medal. **4.** *Austral. & N.Z.* the amount of an **award wage** (esp. in **above award**). **5.** *Law.* **a.** the decision of an arbitrator. **b.** a grant made by a court of law. [C14: < Anglo-F *awarder,* < OF *eswarder* to decide after investigation, < *es-* EX-[1] + *warder* to observe] **—aˈwarder** *n.*

award wage *n.* (in Australia and New Zealand) statutory minimum pay for a particular group of workers. Sometimes shortened to **award.**

aware (əˈwɛə) *adj.* **1.** *(postpositive;* foll. by *of)* having knowledge: *aware of his error.* **2.** informed of current developments: *politically aware.* [OE *gewær*] **—aˈwareness** *n.*

awash (əˈwɒʃ) *adv., adj. (postpositive) Naut.* **1.** at a level even with the surface of the sea. **2.** washed over by the waves.

away (əˈweɪ) *adv.* **1.** from a particular place: *to swim away.* **2.** in or to another, a usual, or a proper place: *to put toys away.* **3.** apart; at a distance: *to keep away from strangers.* **4.** out of existence: *the music faded away.* **5.** indicating motion, displacement, transfer, etc., from a normal or proper place: *to turn one's head away.* **6.** indicating activity that is wasteful or designed to get rid of something: *to sleep away the hours.* **7.** continuously: *laughing away.* **8. away with.** a command for a person to go or be removed: *away with him to prison!* ~*adj. (usually postpositive)* **9.** not present: *away from school.* **10.** distant: *he is a good way away.* **11.** having started; released: *he was away before sunrise.* **12.** *(also prenominal) Sport.* played on an opponent's ground. ~*n.* **13.** *Sport.* a game played or won at an opponent's ground. ~*sentence substitute.* **14.** an expression of dismissal. [OE *on weg* on way]

awayday (əˈweɪˌdeɪ) *n.* a day trip taken for pleasure, relaxation, etc.; day excursion. [C20: < *awayday ticket,* name applied to some special-rate railway day returns]

awe (ɔː) *n.* **1.** overwhelming wonder, respect, or dread. **2.** *Arch.* power to inspire fear or reverence. ~*vb.* **3.** *(tr.)* to inspire with reverence or dread. [C13: < ON *agi*]

aweigh (əˈweɪ) *adj. (postpositive) Naut.* (of an anchor) no longer hooked into the bottom; hanging by its rope or chain.

awe-inspiring *adj.* causing or worthy of admiration or respect; amazing or magnificent.

awesome (ˈɔːsəm) *adj.* inspiring or displaying awe. **—ˈawesomely** *adv.* **—ˈawesomeness** *n.*

awe-stricken *or* **awe-struck** *adj.* overcome or filled with awe.

awful (ˈɔːfʊl) *adj.* **1.** very bad; unpleasant. **2.** *Arch.* inspiring reverence or dread. **3.** *Arch.* overcome with awe. ~*adv.* **4.** *Not standard.* (intensifier): *an awful cold day.* [C13: see AWE, -FUL] **—ˈawfulness** *n.*

awfully (ˈɔːfəlɪ) *adv.* **1.** in an unpleasant, bad, or reprehensible manner. **2.** *Inf.* (intensifier): *I'm awfully keen to come.* **3.** *Arch.* so as to express or inspire awe.

awhile (əˈwaɪl) *adv.* for a brief period.

awkward (ˈɔːkwəd) *adj.* **1.** lacking dexterity, proficiency, or skill; clumsy. **2.** ungainly or inelegant in movements or posture. **3.** unwieldy; difficult to use. **4.** embarrassing: *an awkward moment.* **5.** embarrassed: *he felt awkward about leaving.* **6.** difficult to deal with; requiring tact: *an awkward customer.* **7.** deliberately unhelpful. **8.** dangerous or difficult. [C14: *awk,* < ON *öfugr* turned the wrong way round + -WARD] **—ˈawkwardly** *adv.* **—ˈawkwardness** *n.*

awl (ɔːl) *n.* a pointed hand tool with a fluted blade used for piercing wood, leather, etc. [OE *ǣl*]

awn (ɔːn) *n.* any of the bristles growing from the flowering parts of certain grasses and cereals. [OE *agen* ear of grain] **—awned** *adj.*

awning (ˈɔːnɪŋ) *n.* a roof of canvas or other material supported by a frame to provide protection from the weather, esp. one placed over a doorway or part of a deck of a ship. [C17: <?]

awoke (əˈwəʊk) *vb.* a past tense and (now rare or dialectal) past participle of **awake.**

AWOL (ˈeɪwɒl) *or* **A.W.O.L.** *adj. Mil.* absent without leave but without intending to desert.

awry (əˈraɪ) *adv., adj. (postpositive)* **1.** with a slant or twist to one side; askew. **2.** away from the appropriate or right course; amiss. [C14 *on wry;* see A-[2], WRY]

axe *or U.S.* **ax** (æks) *n., pl.* **axes. 1.** a hand tool with one side of its head forged and sharpened to a cutting edge, used for felling trees, splitting timber, etc. **2. an axe to grind. a.** an ulterior motive. **b.** a grievance. **c.** a pet subject. **3. the axe.** *Inf.* **a.** dismissal, esp. from employment (esp. in **get the axe**). **b.** *Brit.* severe cutting down of expenditure, esp. in a public service. ~*vb. (tr.)* **4.** to chop or trim with an axe. **5.** *Inf.* to dismiss (employees), restrict (expenditure or services), or terminate (a project, etc.). [OE *æx*]

axel (ˈæksəl) *n. Skating.* a jump of one and a half, two and a half, or three and a half turns, taking off from the forward outside edge of one skate and landing on the backward outside edge of the other. [C20: after *Axel* Paulsen (d. 1938), Norwegian skater]

axes[1] (ˈæksiːz) *n.* the plural of **axis**[1].

axes[2] (ˈæksɪz) *n.* the plural of **axe.**

axial (ˈæksɪəl) *adj.* **1.** forming or characteristic of an axis. **2.** situated in, on, or along an axis. —ˌ**axiˈality** *n.* —ˈ**axially** *adv.*

axil (ˈæksɪl) *n.* the upper angle between a branch or leafstalk and the stem from which it grows. [C18: < L *axilla* armpit]

axilla (ækˈsɪlə) *n., pl.* **-lae** (-liː). **1.** the technical name for the **armpit. 2.** the area under a bird's wing corresponding to the armpit. [C17: < L: armpit]

axillary (ækˈsɪlərɪ) *adj.* **1.** of, relating to, or near the armpit. **2.** *Bot.* growing in or related to the axil. ~*n., pl.* **-laries. 3.** (*usually pl.*) Also called: **axillar** (ækˈsɪlə). one of the feathers growing from the axilla of a bird's wing.

axiom (ˈæksɪəm) *n.* **1.** a generally accepted proposition or principle, sanctioned by experience. **2.** a universally established principle or law that is not a necessary truth. **3.** a self-evident statement. **4.** *Logic, maths.* a statement that is stipulated to be true for the purpose of a chain of reasoning. [C15: < L *axiōma* a principle, < Gk, < *axioun* to consider worthy, < *axios* worthy]

axiomatic (ˌæksɪəˈmætɪk) *adj.* **1.** self-evident. **2.** containing maxims; aphoristic. —ˌ**axioˈmatically** *adv.*

axis[1] (ˈæksɪs) *n., pl.* **axes. 1.** a real or imaginary line about which a body, such as an aircraft, can rotate or about which an object, form, composition, or geometrical construction is symmetrical. **2.** one of two or three reference lines used in coordinate geometry to locate a point in a plane or in space. **3.** *Anat.* the second cervical vertebra. **4.** *Bot.* the main central part of a plant, typically consisting of the stem and root. **5.** an alliance between a number of states to coordinate their foreign policy. **6.** Also called: **principal axis.** *Optics.* the line of symmetry of an optical system, such as the line passing through the centre of a lens. [C14: < L: axletree, earth's axis; rel. to Gk *axōn* axis]

axis[2] (ˈæksɪs) *n., pl.* **axises.** a S Asian deer with a reddish-brown white-spotted coat and slender antlers. [C18: < L: Indian wild animal, <?]

Axis (ˈæksɪs) *n.* **a. the.** the alliance (1936) of Nazi Germany and Fascist Italy, later joined by Japan and other countries, and lasting until their defeat in World War II. **b.** (*as modifier*): *the Axis powers.*

axle (ˈæksəl) *n.* a bar or shaft on which a wheel, pair of wheels, or other rotating member revolves. [C17: < ON *öxull*]

axletree (ˈæksəlˌtriː) *n.* a bar fixed across the underpart of a wagon or carriage that has rounded ends on which the wheels revolve.

Axminster carpet (ˈæksˌmɪnstə) *n.* a type of patterned carpet with a cut pile. Often shortened to **Axminster.** [after *Axminster* in Devon]

axolotl (ˌæksəˈlɒtᵊl) *n.* an aquatic salamander of N America, such as the **Mexican axolotl,** in which the larval form (including external gills) is retained throughout life under natural conditions. [C18: < Nahuatl, < *atl* water + *xolotl* servant, doll]

axon (ˈæksɒn) *n.* the long threadlike extension of a nerve cell that conducts nerve impulses from the cell body. [C19: via NL < Gk: axis, axle, vertebra]

ay *or* **aye** (eɪ) *adv. Arch., poetic* always.

ayah (ˈaɪə) *n.* (in parts of the former British Empire) a native maidservant or nursemaid. [C18: < Hindi *āyā*, < Port. *aia*, < L *avia* grandmother]

ayatollah (ˌaɪəˈtɒlə) *n.* one of a class of Shiite religious leaders in Iran. [via Persian < Ar., < *aya* creation + ALLAH]

aye *or* **ay** (aɪ) *sentence substitute.* **1.** yes: archaic or dialectal except in voting by voice. ~*n.* **2. a.** a person who votes in the affirmative. **b.** an affirmative vote. ~Cf. **nay.** [C16: prob. < pron. *I,* expressing assent]

aye-aye (ˈaɪˌaɪ) *n.* a rare nocturnal arboreal primate of Madagascar related to the lemurs. It has long bony fingers and rodent-like incisor teeth. [C18: < F, < Malagasy *aiay*, prob. imit.]

Aymara (ˌaɪməˈrɑː) *n.* **1.** (*pl.* **-ras** *or* **-ra**) a member of a S American Indian people of Bolivia and Peru. **2.** the language of this people. [< Sp. *aimará*, < Amerind]

Ayrshire (ˈɛəʃə) *n.* any one of a hardy breed of brown-and-white dairy cattle. [< *Ayrshire*, former Scot. county]

azalea (əˈzeɪljə) *n.* an ericaceous plant cultivated for its showy pink or purple flowers. [C18: via NL < Gk, < *azaleos* dry; < its supposed preference for a dry situation]

azeotrope (əˈziːəˌtrəʊp) *n.* a mixture of liquids that boils at a constant temperature, at a given pressure, without change of composition. [C20: < A-[1] + *zeo-*, < Gk *zein* to boil + -TROPE] —**azeotropic** (ˌeɪzɪəˈtrɒpɪk) *adj.*

azide (ˈeɪzaɪd) *n.* **a.** an acyl derivative or salt of hydrazoic acid, used as a coating to enhance electron emission. **b.** (*as modifier*) *an azide group or radical.*

Azilian (əˈzɪlɪən) *n.* **1.** a Palaeolithic culture of Spain and SW France that can be dated to the 10th millennium B.C., characterized by flat bone harpoons and schematically painted pebbles. ~*adj.* **2.** of or relating to this culture. [C19: after Mas d'*Azil*, France, where artefacts were found]

azimuth (ˈæzɪməθ) *n.* **1.** *Astron., navigation.* the angular distance usually measured clockwise from the south point of the horizon in astronomy or from the north point in navigation to the intersection with the horizon of the vertical circle passing through a celestial body. **2.** *Surveying.* the horizontal angle of a bearing clockwise from north. [C14: < OF *azimut*, < Ar. *as-sumūt*, pl. of *as-samt* the path, < L *semita* path] —**azimuthal** (ˌæzɪˈmʌθəl) *adj.*

azine (ˈeɪziːn) *n.* an organic compound having a six-membered ring with at least one nitrogen atom.

azo (ˈeɪzəʊ, ˈæ-) *adj.* of, consisting of, or containing the divalent group -N:N-: *an azo group or radical.* See also **diazo.** [< F *azote* nitrogen, < Gk *azōos* lifeless]

azoic (əˈzəʊɪk) *adj.* without life; characteristic of the ages that have left no evidence of life in the form of organic remains. [C19: < Gk *azōos* lifeless]

AZT *abbrev. for* azidothymidine: a drug that prolongs life and alleviates symptoms among some AIDS sufferers.

Aztec (ˈæztɛk) *n.* **1.** a member of a Mexican Indian people who established a great empire, centred on the valley of Mexico, that was overthrown by Cortés in the early 16th century. **2.** the language of the Aztecs. See also **Nahuatl.** ~*adj. also* **Aztecan. 3.** of, relating to, or characteristic of the Aztecs, their civilization, or their language. [C18: < Sp., < Nahuatl *Aztecatl*, < *Aztlan*, their traditional place of origin, lit.: near the cranes]

azure (ˈæʒə, ˈeɪ-) *n.* **1.** a deep blue similar to the colour of a clear blue sky. **2.** *Poetic.* a clear blue sky. ~*adj.* **3.** of the colour azure. **4.** (*usually postpositive*) *Heraldry.* of the colour blue. [C14: < OF, < OSp., < Ar. *lāzaward* lapis lazuli, < Persian *lāzhuward*]

azurite (ˈæʒʊˌraɪt) *n.* a deep blue mineral consisting of hydrated basic copper carbonate. It is used as an ore of copper and as a gemstone.

azygous (ˈæzɪgəs) *adj. Biol.* developing or occurring singly. [C17: via NL < Gk *azugos*, < A-[1] + *zugon* YOKE]

B

b *or* **B** (biː) *n., pl.* **b's, B's,** *or* **Bs.** **1.** the second letter of the English alphabet. **2.** a speech sound represented by this letter, as in *bell.* **3.** Also: **beta.** the second in a series, class, or rank.

B *symbol for:* **1.** *Music.* **a.** the seventh note of the scale of C major. **b.** the major or minor key having this note as its tonic. **2.** the less important of two things. **3.** a human blood type of the ABO group, containing the B antigen. **4.** (in Britain) a secondary road. **5.** *Chem.* boron. **6.** magnetic flux density. **7.** *Chess.* bishop. **8.** (on Brit. pencils, signifying degree of softness of lead) black. **9.** Also: **b** *Physics.* bel. **10.** *Physics.* baryon number.

b. *abbrev. for:* **1.** born. **2.** *Cricket.* **a.** bowled. **b.** bye.

b. *or* **B.** *abbrev. for:* **1.** *Music.* bass *or* basso. **2.** billion. **3.** book. **4.** breadth.

B. *abbrev. for:* **1.** (on maps, etc.) bay. **2.** Bible.

B- (of U.S. military aircraft) *abbrev. for* bomber.

Ba *the chemical symbol for* barium.

BA *abbrev. for:* **1.** Bachelor of Arts. **2.** British Academy. **3.** British Airways. **4.** British Association (for the Advancement of Science).

baa (bɑː) *vb.* **baaing, baaed.** **1.** (*intr.*) to make the cry of a sheep; bleat. *~n.* **2.** the cry made by sheep.

BAA *abbrev. for* British Airports Authority.

baas (bɑːs) *n.* a South African word for **boss:** used by Africans and Coloureds in addressing European managers or overseers. [C17: < Afrik., < MDu. *baes* master]

baaskap *or* **baasskap** (ˈbɑːsˌkap) *n.* (*sometimes cap.*) (in South Africa) control by Whites of non-Whites. [< Afrik., < BAAS + *-skap* -SHIP]

baba (ˈbɑːbɑː) *n.* a small cake, usually soaked in rum (**rum baba**). [C19: < F, < Polish, lit.: old woman]

babalas (ˈbæbəˌlæs) *n. S. African.* a hangover. [< Zulu *ibhabhalasi*]

babbitt (ˈbæbɪt) *vb.* (*tr.*) to line (a bearing) or face (a surface) with Babbitt metal.

Babbitt (ˈbæbɪt) *n. U.S. derog.* a narrow-minded and complacent member of the middle class. [C20: after George *Babbitt,* central character in the novel *Babbitt* (1922) by Sinclair Lewis] —ˈ**Babbittry** *n.*

Babbitt metal *n.* any of a number of alloys originally based on tin, antimony, and copper but now often including lead: used esp. in bearings. [C19: after Isaac *Babbitt* (1799–1862), U.S. inventor]

babble (ˈbæbᵊl) *vb.* **1.** to utter (words, sounds, etc.) in an incoherent jumble. **2.** (*intr.*) to talk foolishly, incessantly, or irrelevantly. **3.** (*tr.*) to disclose (secrets, etc.) carelessly. **4.** (*intr.*) (of streams, birds, etc.) to make a low murmuring sound. *~n.* **5.** incoherent or foolish speech. **6.** a murmuring sound. [C13: prob. imit.]

babbler (ˈbæblə) *n.* **1.** a person or thing that babbles. **2.** any of various birds of the Old World tropics and subtropics having an incessant song.

babe (beɪb) *n.* **1.** a baby. **2.** *Inf.* a naive or gullible person. **3.** *Sl., chiefly U.S.* a girl.

Babel (ˈbeɪbᵊl) *n.* **1.** *Old Testament.* Also called: **Tower of Babel.** a tower presumptuously intended to reach from earth to heaven, the building of which was frustrated when Jehovah confused the language of the builders (Genesis 11:1–10). **2.** (*often not cap.*) **a.** a confusion of noises or voices. **b.** a scene of noise and confusion. [< Heb. *Bābhél,* < Akkadian *Bāb-ilu,* lit.: gate of God]

babirusa (ˌbɑːbɪˈruːsə) *n.* a wild pig of Indonesia. It has an almost hairless wrinkled skin and enormous curved canine teeth. [C17: < Malay, < *bābī* hog + *rūsa* deer]

Babism (ˈbɑːbɪzəm) *n.* a pantheistic Persian religious sect, founded in 1844, forbidding polygamy, concubinage, begging, trading in slaves, and indulgence in alcohol and drugs. [C19: < the *Bab,* title of Mirza Ali Mohammed (1819–50), Persian religious leader]

baboon (bəˈbuːn) *n.* any of several medium-sized Old World monkeys. They have an elongated muzzle, large teeth, and a fairly long tail. [C14 *babewyn* gargoyle, later, baboon, < OF]

babu (ˈbɑːbuː) *n.* (in India) **1.** a form of address more or less equivalent to *Mr.* **2.** (formerly) an Indian clerk who could write English. [Hindi, lit.: father]

babushka (bəˈbuːʃkə) *n.* **1.** a headscarf tied under the chin, worn by Russian peasant women. **2.** (in Russia) an old woman. [Russian: grandmother, < *baba* old woman]

baby (ˈbeɪbɪ) *n., pl.* **-bies.** **1. a.** a newborn child; infant. **b.** (*as modifier*): *baby food.* **2.** an unborn child; fetus. **3.** the youngest or smallest of a family or group. **4.** a newborn or recently born animal. **5.** *Usually derog.* an immature person. **6.** *Sl.* a young woman or sweetheart. **7.** a project of personal concern. **8.** **be left holding the baby.** to be left with the responsibility. *~adj.* **9.** (*prenominal*) comparatively small of its type: *a baby car.* *~vb.* **-bying, -bied.** **10.** (*tr.*) to treat with love and attention. **11.** to treat (someone) like a baby; pamper or overprotect. [C14: prob. childish reduplication] —ˈ**babyhood** *n.* —ˈ**babyish** *adj.*

baby bonus *n. Canad. inf.* Family Allowance.

baby boomer *n.* a person who was born during the **baby boom,** the years immediately after World War II when there was a sharp increase in the birth rate.

baby carriage *n.* the U.S. and Canad. name for **pram**¹.

Babylon (ˈbæbɪlən) *n. Derog.* **1.** (in Protestant polemic) the Roman Catholic Church, regarded as the seat of luxury and corruption. **2.** any society or group in a society considered to be corrupt or a place of exile by another society or group. [< *Babylon,* ancient Mesopotamian city] —**Babylonian** (ˌbæbɪˈləʊnɪən) *adj.*

baby's-breath *or* **babies'-breath** *n.* **1.** a tall Eurasian plant, bearing small white or pink fragrant flowers. **2.** any of several other plants that have small scented flowers.

baby-sit *vb.* **-sitting, -sat.** (*intr.*) to act or work as a baby-sitter. —ˈ**baby-ˌsitting** *n., adj.*

baby-sitter *n.* a person who takes care of a child or children while the parents are out.

baby snatcher *n. Inf.* **1.** a person who steals a baby from its pram. **2.** someone who marries or has an affair with a much younger person.

baccalaureate (ˌbækəˈlɔːrɪɪt) *n.* the university degree of Bachelor of Arts. [C17: < Med. L *baccalaureātus,* < *baccalaureus* advanced student < *baccalārius* BACHELOR]

baccarat (ˈbækəˌrɑː, ˌbækəˈrɑː) *n.* a card game in which two or more punters gamble against the banker. [C19: < F *baccara* <?]

baccate (ˈbækeɪt) *adj. Bot.* **1.** like a berry. **2.** bearing berries. [C19: < L *bāca* berry]

bacchanal (ˈbækənᵊl) *n.* **1.** a follower of Bacchus, Greek god of wine. **2.** a drunken and riotous celebration. **3.** a participant in such a celebration. *~adj.* **4.** of or relating to Bacchus. [C16: < L *Bacchānālis*]

bacchanalia (ˌbækəˈneɪlɪə) *pl. n.* **1.** (*often cap.*) orgiastic rites associated with Bacchus. **2.** any drunken revelry. —ˌ**bacchaˈnalian** *adj., n.*

bacchant (ˈbækənt) *or* (*fem.*) **bacchante** (bəˈkæntɪ) *n., pl.* **bacchants** *or* **bacchantes** (bəˈkæntɪz). **1.** a priest, priestess, or votary of Bacchus. **2.** a drunken reveller. [C17: < L *bacchāns,* < *bacchārī* to celebrate the BACCHANALIA]

Bacchic (ˈbækɪk) *adj.* **1.** of or relating to Bacchus. **2.** (*often not cap.*) riotously drunk.

baccy ('bækɪ) *n.* a Brit. informal name for **tobacco.**

bach (bætʃ) *n. N.Z.* ~*n.* **1.** a seaside, bush, or country cottage. ~*vb.* **2.** a variant spelling of **batch**[2].

bachelor ('bætʃələ, 'bætʃlə) *n.* **1. a.** an unmarried man. **b.** (*as modifier*): *a bachelor flat.* **2.** a person who holds the degree of Bachelor of Arts, Bachelor of Science, etc. **3.** (in the Middle Ages) a young knight serving a great noble. **4. bachelor seal.** a young male seal that has not yet mated. [C13: < OF *bacheler* youth, squire, < Vulgar L *baccalāris* (unattested) farm worker] —'**bachelorhood** *n.*

bachelor girl *n.* a young unmarried woman, esp. one who is self-supporting.

Bachelor of Arts *n.* **1.** a degree conferred on a person who has successfully completed undergraduate studies in the liberal arts or humanities. **2.** a person who holds this degree.

Bachelor of Science *n.* **1.** a degree conferred on a person who has successfully completed undergraduate studies in a science. **2.** a person who holds this degree.

bachelor's-buttons *n.* (*functioning as sing. or pl.*) any of various plants with button-like flower heads, esp. a double-flowered buttercup.

bacillary (bə'sɪlərɪ) *or* **bacillar** (bə'sɪlə) *adj.* **1.** of, relating to, or caused by bacilli. **2.** Also: **bacilliform** (bə'sɪlɪˌfɔːm). shaped like a short rod.

bacillus (bə'sɪləs) *n., pl.* **-cilli** (-'sɪlaɪ). **1.** any rod-shaped bacterium. **2.** any of various rodlike spore-producing bacteria constituting the family Bacillaceae. [C19: < L, < *baculum* walking stick]

back (bæk) *n.* **1.** the posterior part of the human body, from the neck to the pelvis. **2.** the corresponding or upper part of an animal. **3.** the spinal column. **4.** the part or side of an object opposite the front. **5.** the part or side of anything less often seen or used. **6.** the part or side of anything that is furthest from the front or from a spectator: *the back of the stage.* **7.** something that supports, covers, or strengthens the rear of an object. **8.** *Ball games.* **a.** a mainly defensive player behind a forward. **b.** the position of such a player. **9.** the part of a book to which the pages are glued or that joins the covers. **10. at the back of one's mind.** not in one's conscious thoughts. **11. back of Bourke.** *Austral.* a remote or backward place. **12. behind one's back.** secretly or deceitfully. **13. break one's back.** to overwork or work very hard. **14. break the back of.** to complete the greatest or hardest part of (a task). **15. get off someone's back.** *Inf.* to stop criticizing or pestering someone. **16. put one's back into.** to devote all one's strength to (a task). **17. put** (*or* **get**) **someone's back up.** to annoy someone. **18. the back of beyond.** a very remote place. **19. turn one's back on. a.** to turn away from in anger or contempt. **b.** to refuse to help; abandon. ~*vb.* (*mainly tr.*) **20.** (*also intr.*) to move or cause to move backwards. **21. back water.** to reverse the direction of a boat, esp. to push the oars of a rowing boat. **22.** to provide support, money, or encouragement for (a person, enterprise, etc.). **23.** to bet on the success of: *to back a horse.* **24.** to provide with a back, backing, or lining. **25.** to provide with a musical accompaniment. **26.** to countersign or endorse. **27.** (*intr.*; foll. by *on* or *onto*) to have the back facing (towards): *the house backs onto a river.* **28.** (*intr.*) (of the wind) to change direction anticlockwise. Cf. **veer**[1] (sense 3). ~*adj.* (*prenominal*) **29.** situated behind: *a back lane.* **30.** of the past: *back issues of a magazine.* **31.** owing from an earlier date: *back rent.* **32.** remote: *a back road.* **33.** *Phonetics.* of or denoting a vowel articulated with the tongue retracted towards the soft palate, as for the vowels in English *hard, fall, hot, full, fool.* ~*adv.* **34.** at, to, or towards the rear; behind. **35.** in, to, or towards the original starting point, place, or condition: *to go back home; put the book back.* **36.** in or into the past: *to look back on one's childhood.* **37.** in reply, repayment, or retaliation: *to hit someone back.* **38.** in check: *the dam holds back the water.* **39.** in concealment; in reserve: *to keep something back.* **40. back and forth.** to and fro. **41. back to front. a.** in reverse. **b.** in disorder. ~See also **back down, back out, back up.** [OE *bæc*]

backbencher ('bæk'bɛntʃə) *n. Brit., Austral., N.Z., etc.* a Member of Parliament who does not hold office in the government or opposition.

backbite ('bækˌbaɪt) *vb.* **-biting, bit; bitten** *or* **bit.** to talk spitefully about (an absent person). —'**backˌbiter** *n.*

backboard ('bækˌbɔːd) *n.* **1.** a board that is placed behind something to form or support its back. **2.** a board worn to straighten or support the back, as after surgery. **3.** (in basketball) a flat upright surface supported on a high frame, under which the basket is attached.

back boiler *n.* a tank or series of pipes at the back of a fireplace for heating water.

backbone ('bækˌbəʊn) *n.* **1.** a nontechnical name for **spinal column. 2.** something that resembles the spinal column in function, position, or appearance. **3.** strength of character; courage.

backbreaking ('bækˌbreɪkɪŋ) *adj.* exhausting.

backburn ('bækˌbɜːn) *vb.* (*tr.*) *Austral. & N.Z.* **1.** to clear (an area of bush, etc.) by creating a new fire that burns in the opposite direction to the line of advancing fire. ~*n.* **2.** the act or result of backburning.

back-calculate *vb.* to estimate (the probable amount of alcohol in a person's blood) at an earlier time than that at which the blood test was taken, based on an average rate at which alcohol leaves the bloodstream: used to determine whether a driver had more than the legal limit of alcohol at the time of an accident. —'**backˌcalcu'lation** *n.*

backchat ('bækˌtʃæt) *n. Inf.* the act of answering back, esp. impudently.

backcloth ('bækˌklɒθ) *n.* a painted curtain at the back of a stage set. Also called: **backdrop.**

backcomb ('bækˌkəʊm) *vb.* to comb the under layers of (the hair) towards the roots to give more bulk to a hairstyle. Also: **tease.**

back country *n. Austral. & N.Z.* land remote from settled areas.

backdate (ˌbæk'deɪt) *vb.* (*tr.*) to make effective from an earlier date.

back door *n.* **1.** a door at the rear or side of a building. **2.** a means of entry to a job, etc., that is secret or obtained through influence.

back down *vb.* **1.** (*intr., adv.*) to withdraw an earlier claim. ~*n.* **backdown. 2.** abandonment of an earlier claim.

backed (bækt) *adj.* **a.** having a back or backing. **b.** (*in combination*): *high-backed; black-backed.*

backer ('bækə) *n.* **1.** a person who gives financial or other support. **2.** a person who bets on a competitor or contestant.

backfill ('bækˌfɪl) *vb.* (*tr.*) to refill an excavated trench, esp. (in archaeology) at the end of an investigation.

backfire (ˌbæk'faɪə) *vb.* (*intr.*) **1.** (of an internal-combustion engine) to emit a loud noise as a result of an explosion in the exhaust system. **2.** to fail to have the desired effect, and, instead, recoil upon the originator. **3.** to start a controlled fire in order to halt an advancing forest or prairie fire by creating a barren area. ~*n.* **4.** (in an internal-combustion engine) an explosion of unburnt gases in the exhaust system. **5.** a controlled fire started to create a barren area that will halt an advancing forest or prairie fire.

back formation *n.* **1.** the unwitting invention of a new word on the assumption that a familiar word is derived from it. The verbs *edit* and *burgle* in English were so created from *editor* and *burglar.* **2.** a word formed by this process.

backgammon ('bækˌgæmən) *n.* **1.** a game for two people played on a board with pieces moved according to throws of the dice. **2.** the most complete form of win in this game. [C17: BACK + *gammon*, var. of GAME[1]]

background ('bækˌgraʊnd) *n.* **1.** the part of a scene furthest from the viewer. **2. a.** an inconspicuous or unobtrusive position (esp. in **in the background**). **b.** (*as modifier*): *a background influence.* **3.** the plane or ground in a picture upon which all other planes or forms appear superimposed. **4.** a person's social class, education, or experience. **5. a.** the circumstances that lead up to or help to explain something. **b.** (*as modifier*): *background information.* **6. a.** a low level of sound, lighting, etc., whose purpose is to be an unobtrusive accompaniment to something else. **b.** (*as modifier*): *background music.* **7.** Also called: **background radiation.** *Physics.* low-intensity radiation from small amounts of radioisotopes in soil, air, etc. **8.** *Electronics.* unwanted effects, such as noise, occurring in a measuring instrument, electronic device, etc.

backhand (ˈbækˌhænd) *n.* **1.** *Tennis, etc.* a stroke made across the body with the back of the hand facing the direction of the stroke. **2.** the side on which backhand strokes are made. **3.** handwriting slanting to the left. ~*adv.* **4.** with a backhand stroke.

backhanded (ˌbækˈhændɪd) *adj.* **1.** (of a blow, shot, etc.) performed with the arm moving across the body. **2.** double-edged; equivocal: *a backhanded compliment.* **3.** (of handwriting) slanting to the left. ~*adv.* **4.** in a backhanded manner.

backhander (ˈbækˌhændə) *n.* **1.** a backhanded stroke or blow. **2.** *Inf.* an indirect attack. **3.** *Sl.* a bribe.

backing (ˈbækɪŋ) *n.* **1.** support. **2.** a body of supporters. **3.** something that forms, protects, or strengthens the back of something. **4.** musical accompaniment, esp. for a pop singer.

backing dog *n. N.Z.* a dog that moves a flock of sheep by jumping on their backs.

backlash (ˈbækˌlæʃ) *n.* **1.** a sudden and adverse reaction. **2.** a reaction or recoil between interacting worn or badly fitting parts in a mechanism. **3.** the excessive play between such parts.

backlog (ˈbækˌlɒg) *n.* an accumulation of uncompleted work, unsold stock, etc., to be dealt with.

back marker *n.* a competitor who is at the back of a field in a race.

back matter *n.* the parts of a book, such as the index and appendixes, that follow the text.

backmost (ˈbækˌməʊst) *adj.* furthest back.

back number *n.* **1.** an issue of a newspaper, magazine, etc., that appeared on a previous date. **2.** *Inf.* a person or thing considered to be old-fashioned.

back out *vb.* (*intr., adv.;* often foll. by *of*) to withdraw (from an agreement, etc.).

backpack (ˈbækˌpæk) *n.* **1.** a rucksack. **2.** a pack carried on the back of an astronaut, containing oxygen cylinders, etc. ~*vb.* (*intr.*) **3.** to travel about or go hiking with a backpack.

back passage *n.* the rectum.

back-pedal *vb.* **-pedalling, -pedalled** *or U.S.* **-pedaling, -pedaled.** (*intr.*) **1.** to turn the pedals of a bicycle backwards. **2.** to retract or modify a previous opinion, principle, etc.

back projection *n.* a method of projecting pictures onto a translucent screen so that they are viewed from the opposite side, used esp. in films to create the illusion that the actors in the foreground are moving.

back room *n.* **a.** a place where important and usually secret research or planning is done. **b.** (*as modifier*): *back-room boys.*

back seat *n.* **1.** a seat at the back, esp. of a vehicle. **2.** *Inf.* a subordinate or inconspicuous position (esp. in **take a back seat**).

back-seat driver *n. Inf.* **1.** a passenger in a car who offers unwanted advice to the driver. **2.** a person who offers advice on or tries to direct matters that are not his concern.

backsheesh (ˈbækʃiːʃ) *n.* a variant spelling of **baksheesh.**

backside (ˌbækˈsaɪd) *n. Inf.* the buttocks.

backslide (ˌbækˈslaɪd) *vb.* **-sliding, -slid.** (*intr.*) to relapse into former bad habits or vices. —ˌ**back**ˈ**slider** *n.*

backspace (ˈbækˌspeɪs) *vb.* to move (a typewriter carriage, etc.) backwards.

backspin (ˈbækˌspɪn) *n. Sport.* a backward spin imparted to a ball to reduce its speed at impact.

backstage (ˌbækˈsteɪdʒ) *adv.* **1.** behind the part of the theatre in view of the audience. **2.** towards the rear of the stage. ~*adj.* **3.** situated backstage. **4.** *Inf.* away from public view.

backstairs (ˌbækˈstɛəz) *pl. n.* **1.** a secondary staircase in a house, esp. one originally for the use of servants. ~*adj. also* **backstair.** **2.** underhand: *backstairs gossip.*

backstay (ˈbækˌsteɪ) *n. Naut.* a stay leading aft from the upper mast to the deck or stern.

backstreet (ˈbækˌstriːt) *n.* **1.** a street in a town remote from the main roads. **2.** (*modifier*) denoting illicit activities regarded as likely to take place in such a street: *a backstreet abortion.*

backstroke (ˈbækˌstrəʊk) *n. Swimming.* a stroke performed on the back, using backward circular strokes of each arm and flipper movements of the feet. Also called: **back crawl.**

back-to-back *adj.* (*usually postpositive*) **1.** facing in opposite directions, often with the backs touching. **2.** *Chiefly Brit.* (of urban houses) built so that their backs are adjacent or separated only by a narrow alley.

backtrack (ˈbækˌtræk) *vb.* (*intr.*) **1.** to return by the same route by which one has come. **2.** to retract or reverse one's opinion, policy, etc.

back up *vb.* (*adv.*) **1.** (*tr.*) to support. **2.** (*intr.*) *Cricket.* (of a nonstriking batsman) to move down the wicket in readiness for a run as a ball is bowled. **3.** (of water) to accumulate. **4.** *Computers.* to make a copy of (a data file), esp. as a security copy. **5.** (*intr.;* usually foll. by *on*) *Austral.* to repeat an action immediately. ~*n.* **backup.** **6.** a support or reinforcement. **7. a.** a reserve or substitute. **b.** (*as modifier*): *a backup copy.* **8.** the overflow from a blocked drain or pipe. **9.** *Austral.* a second helping.

backveld (ˈbækˌfɛlt, -ˌvɛlt) *n. S. African inf.* a remote sparsely populated rural area. [Afrik., < *back* BACK + *velt* field] —ˈ**back**ˌ**velder** *n.*

backward (ˈbækwəd) *adj.* **1.** (*usually prenominal*) directed towards the rear: *a backward glance.* **2.** retarded in physical, material, or intellectual development. **3. a.** conservative or reactionary. **b.** (*in combination*): *backward-looking.* **4.** reluctant or bashful: *a backward lover.* ~*adv.* **5.** a variant of **backwards.** —ˈ**backwardness** *n.*

backwardation (ˌbækwəˈdeɪʃən) *n.* **1.** (on the London Stock Exchange) postponement of delivery by a seller of securities until the next settlement period. **2.** the fee paid for such postponement. ~Cf. **contango.**

backwards (ˈbækwədz) *or* **backward** *adv.* **1.** towards the rear. **2.** with the back foremost. **3.** in the reverse of usual order or direction. **4.** to or towards the past. **5.** into a worse state. **6.** towards the point of origin. **7. bend, lean,** *or* **fall over backwards.** *Inf.* to make a special effort, esp. in order to please.

backwash (ˈbækˌwɒʃ) *n.* **1.** water washed backwards by the motion of oars or other propelling devices. **2.** the backward flow of air set up by aircraft engines. **3.** a repercussion.

backwater (ˈbækˌwɔːtə) *n.* **1.** a body of stagnant water connected to a river. **2.** an isolated or backward place or condition.

backwoods (ˈbækwʊdz) *pl. n.* **1.** partially cleared, sparsely populated forests. **2.** any remote sparsely populated place. **3.** (*modifier*) of or like the backwoods. **4.** (*modifier*) uncouth; rustic. —ˈ**back**ˌ**woodsman** *n.*

back yard *n.* **1.** a yard at the back of a house, etc. **2. in one's own back yard. a.** close at hand. **b.** involving or implicating one.

baclava (ˈbɑːkləˌvɑː) *n.* a variant spelling of **baklava.**

bacon (ˈbeɪkən) *n.* **1.** meat from the back and sides of a pig, dried, salted, and usually smoked. **2. bring home the bacon.** *Inf.* **a.** to achieve success. **b.** to provide material support. **3. save**

(someone's) bacon. *Brit. inf.* to help (someone) to escape from danger. [C12: < OF *bacon,* < OHG *bahho*]

Baconian (beɪˈkəʊnɪən) *adj.* **1.** of or relating to Francis Bacon (1561-1626), English philosopher, or his inductive method of reasoning. ~*n.* **2.** a follower of Bacon's philosophy. **3.** one who believes that plays attributed to Shakespeare were written by Bacon.

bacteria (bækˈtɪərɪə) *pl. n., sing.* **-rium.** a large group of typically unicellular microorganisms, many of which cause disease. [C19: NL, < Gk *baktērion,* < *baktron* rod, staff] —**bacˈterial** *adj.* —**bacˈterially** *adv.*

bactericide (bækˈtɪərɪˌsaɪd) *n.* a substance able to destroy bacteria. —**bacˌteriˈcidal** *adj.*

bacterio-, bacteri-, *or sometimes before a vowel* **bacter-** *combining form.* indicating bacteria or an action or condition relating to bacteria: *bacteriology; bactericide.*

bacteriology (bækˌtɪərɪˈɒlədʒɪ) *n.* the study of bacteria. —**bacteriological** (bækˌtɪərɪəˈlɒdʒɪkəl) *adj.* —**bacˌteriˈologist** *n.*

bacteriophage (bækˈtɪərɪəˌfeɪdʒ) *n.* a virus that is parasitic in a bacterium and destroys its host. Often shortened to **phage.**

bacterium (bækˈtɪərɪəm) *n.* the singular of **bacteria.**

Bactrian camel (ˈbæktrɪən) *n.* a two-humped camel, used in the cold deserts of central Asia. [< *Bactria,* ancient country of SW Asia]

bad[1] (bæd) *adj.* **worse, worst.** **1.** not good; of poor quality; inadequate. **2.** (often foll. by *at*) lacking skill or talent; incompetent. **3.** (often foll. by *for*) harmful. **4.** immoral; evil. **5.** naughty; mischievous. **6.** rotten; decayed: *a bad egg.* **7.** severe; intense: *a bad headache.* **8.** incorrect; faulty: *bad pronunciation.* **9.** ill or in pain (esp. in **feel bad**). **10.** sorry or upset (esp. in **feel bad about**). **11.** unfavourable; distressing: *bad news.* **12.** offensive; unpleasant: *bad language; bad temper.* **13.** not valid or sound: *a bad cheque.* **14.** not recoverable: *a bad debt.* **15.** (**badder, baddest**) *Sl.* good, excellent. **16. go bad.** to putrefy; spoil. **17. in a bad way.** *Inf.* **a.** seriously ill. **b.** in trouble. **18. make the best of a bad job.** to manage as well as possible in unfavourable circumstances. **19. not bad** *or* **not so bad.** *Inf.* passable; fairly good. **20. too bad.** *Inf.* (often used dismissively) regrettable. ~*n.* **21.** unfortunate or unpleasant events (often in **take the bad with the good**). **22.** an immoral or degenerate state (often in **go to the bad**). **23.** the debit side of an account: *£200 to the bad.* **24. go from bad to worse.** to deteriorate even more. ~*adv.* **25.** *Not standard.* badly: *to want something bad.* [C13: prob. < *bæd-,* as the first element of OE *bǣddel* hermaphrodite] —ˈ**baddish** *adj.* —ˈ**badness** *n.*

▷ **Usage.** See at **good.**

bad[2] (bæd) *vb.* a variant spelling of **bade.**

bad blood *n.* a feeling of intense hatred or hostility; enmity.

bade (bæd, beɪd) *or* **bad** *vb.* a past tense of **bid.**

badge (bædʒ) *n.* **1.** a distinguishing emblem or mark worn to signify membership, employment, achievement, etc. **2.** any revealing feature or mark. [C14: < OF *bage*]

badger (ˈbædʒə) *n.* **1.** any of various stocky omnivorous mammals occurring in Europe, Asia, and N America. They are large burrowing animals, with strong claws and a thick coat striped black and white on the head. ~*vb.* **2.** (*tr.*) to pester or harass. [C16: var. of *badgeard,* prob. < BADGE (< the white mark on its forehead) + -ARD]

badinage (ˈbædɪˌnɑːʒ) *n.* playful or frivolous repartee or banter. [C17: < F, < *badiner* to jest]

badlands (ˈbædˌlændz) *pl. n.* any deeply eroded barren area.

badly (ˈbædlɪ) *adv.* **worse, worst.** **1.** poorly; defectively; inadequately. **2.** unfavourably; unsuccessfully: *our scheme worked out badly.* **3.** severely; gravely: *badly hurt.* **4.** incorrectly or inaccurately: *to speak German badly.* **5.** improperly; wickedly: *to behave badly.* **6.** cruelly: *to treat badly.* **7.** very much (esp. in **need badly, want badly**). **8.** regretfully: *he felt badly about it.* **9. badly off.** poor; impoverished.

badminton (ˈbædmɪntən) *n.* **1.** a game played with rackets and a shuttlecock which is hit back and forth across a high net. **2.** Also called: **badminton cup.** a long drink of claret with soda water and sugar. [< *Badminton* House, Glos]

bad-mouth *vb.* (*tr.*) *Sl., chiefly U.S. & Canad.* to speak unfavourably about.

bad-tempered *adj.* angry; irritable.

BAe *abbrev. for* British Aerospace.

Baedeker (ˈbeɪdɪkə) *n.* any of a series of travel guidebooks issued by the German publisher Karl Baedeker (1801–59) or his firm.

baffle (ˈbæfəl) *vb.* (*tr.*) **1.** to perplex; bewilder; puzzle. **2.** to frustrate (plans, efforts, etc.). **3.** to check, restrain, or regulate (the flow of a fluid or the emission of sound or light). ~*n.* **4.** Also called: **baffle board, baffle plate.** a plate or mechanical device to restrain or regulate the flow of fluid, light, or sound, esp. in a loudspeaker or microphone. [C16: ? < Scot. dialect *bachlen* to condemn publicly] —ˈ**bafflement** *n.* —ˈ**baffler** *n.* —ˈ**baffling** *adj.* —ˈ**bafflingly** *adv.*

BAFTA (ˈbæftə) *n. acronym for* British Association of Film and Television Arts.

bag (bæg) *n.* **1.** a flexible container with an opening at one end. **2.** Also: **bagful.** the contents of or amount contained in such a container. **3.** a piece of portable luggage. **4.** short for **handbag. 5.** anything that sags, or is shaped like a bag, such as a loose fold of skin under the eyes. **6.** any pouch or sac forming part of the body of an animal. **7.** the quantity of quarry taken in a single hunting trip or by a single hunter. **8.** *Derog. sl.* an ugly or bad-tempered woman or girl (often in **old bag**). **9. bag and baggage.** *Inf.* **a.** with all one's belongings. **b.** entirely. **10. bag of bones.** a lean creature. **11. in the bag.** *Sl.* almost assured of succeeding or being obtained. **12. rough as bags.** *Austral. sl.* **a.** uncouth. **b.** shoddy. ~*vb.* **bagging, bagged. 13.** (*tr.*) to put into a bag. **14.** to bulge or cause to bulge. **15.** (*tr.*) to capture or kill, as in hunting. **16.** (*tr.*) to catch, seize, or steal. **17.** (*intr.*) to hang loosely; sag. **18.** (*tr.*) *Brit. inf.* to secure the right to do or to have: *he bagged the best chair.* ~ See also **bags.** [C13: prob. < ON *baggi*]

bagasse (bəˈgæs) *n.* the dry pulp remaining after the extraction of juice from sugar cane or similar plants: used as fuel, for making fibreboard, etc. [C19: < F, < Sp. *bagazo* dregs]

bagatelle (ˌbægəˈtɛl) *n.* **1.** something of little value; trifle. **2.** a board game in which balls are struck into holes, with pins as obstacles. **3.** a short light piece of music. [C17: < F, < It. *bagattella,* < (dialect) *bagatta* a little possession]

bagel *or* **beigel** (ˈbeɪgəl) *n.* a hard ring-shaped bread roll. [C20: < Yiddish *beygel*]

baggage (ˈbægɪdʒ) *n.* **1.** suitcases, bags, etc., packed for a journey; luggage. **2.** an army's portable equipment. **3.** *Inf., old-fashioned.* **a.** a pert young woman. **b.** an immoral woman. [C15: < OF *bagage,* < *bague* a bundle]

baggy (ˈbægɪ) *adj.* **-gier, -giest.** (of clothes) hanging loosely; puffed out. —ˈ**baggily** *adv.* —ˈ**bagginess** *n.*

bag lady *n.* a homeless woman who wanders city streets with all her possessions in shopping bags.

bagman (ˈbægmən) *n., pl.* **-men. 1.** *Brit. inf.* a travelling salesman. **2.** *Sl., chiefly U.S.* a person who collects or distributes money for racketeers. **3.** *Austral.* a tramp or swagman, esp. one on horseback. **4.** *Inf., chiefly Canad.* a person who solicits money for a political party.

bagnio (ˈbɑːnjəʊ) *n., pl.* **-ios. 1.** a brothel. **2.** *Obs.* an oriental prison for slaves. **3.** *Obs.* an Italian or Turkish bathhouse. [C16: < It. *bagno,* < L *balneum* bath]

bagpipes (ˈbægˌpaɪps) *pl. n.* any of a family of musical wind instruments in which sounds are produced in reed pipes by air from a bag inflated either by the player's mouth or by arm-operated bellows.

bags (bægz) *pl. n.* **1.** *Inf.* a lot. **2.** *Brit. inf.* trousers. ~*interj.* **3.** Also: **bags I.** *Children's sl., Brit.* an indication of the desire to do, be, or have something.

baguette *or* **baguet** (bæˈgɛt) *n.* **1.** a small gem cut as a long rectangle. **2.** *Archit.* a small moulding having a semicircular cross section. **3.** a narrow French stick loaf. [C18: < F, < It. *bacchetta* a little stick, < *bacchio* rod]

bah (bɑː, bæ) *interj.* an expression of contempt or disgust.

Bahai (bəˈhɑːɪ) *n.* **1.** an adherent of Bahaism. ~*adj.* **2.** of or relating to Bahaism. [< Persian *bahā'ī*, lit.: of glory]

Bahaism (bəˈhɑːˌɪzəm) *n.* a religious system founded in 1863, based on Babism and emphasizing the value of all religions and the spiritual unity of mankind. —**Baˈhaist** *or* **Baˈhaite** *adj., n.*

bail[1] (beɪl) *Law.* ~*n.* **1.** a sum of money by which a person is bound to take responsibility for the appearance in court of another person or himself, forfeited if the person fails to appear. **2.** the person or persons so binding themselves; surety. **3.** the system permitting release of a person from custody where such security has been taken: *he was released on bail.* **4. jump bail** *or* (*formal*) **forfeit bail.** to fail to appear in court to answer to a charge. **5. stand** *or* **go bail.** to act as surety (for someone). ~*vb.* (*tr.*) **6.** (often foll. by *out*) to release or obtain the release of (a person) from custody, security having been made. [C14: < OF: custody, < *baillier* to hand over, < L *bājulāre* to carry burdens]

bail[2] *or* **bale** (beɪl) *vb.* (often foll. by *out*) to remove (water) from (a boat). See also **bale out.** [C13: < OF *baille* bucket, < L *bājulus* carrier] —ˈ**bailer** *or* ˈ**baler** *n.*

bail[3] (beɪl) *n.* **1.** *Cricket.* either of two small wooden bars across the tops of the stumps. **2.** a partition between stalls in a stable or barn. **3.** *Austral. & N.Z.* a framework in a cowshed used to secure the head of a cow during milking. **4.** a movable bar on a typewriter that holds the paper against the platen. ~*vb.* **5.** See **bail up.** [C18: < OF *baile* stake, fortification, prob. < L *baculum* stick]

bail[4] *or* **bale** (beɪl) *n.* the semicircular handle of a kettle, bucket, etc. [C15: prob. of Scand. origin]

bailey (ˈbeɪlɪ) *n.* the outermost wall or court of a castle. [C13: < OF *baille* enclosed court, < *bailler* to enclose]

Bailey bridge (ˈbeɪlɪ) *n.* a temporary bridge made of prefabricated steel parts that can be rapidly assembled. [C20: after Sir Donald Coleman *Bailey* (1901-85), its E designer]

bailie (ˈbeɪlɪ) *n.* (in Scotland) a municipal magistrate. [C13: < OF *bailli*, < earlier *baillif* BAILIFF]

bailiff (ˈbeɪlɪf) *n.* **1.** *Brit.* the agent of a landlord or landowner. **2.** a sheriff's officer who serves writs and summonses, makes arrests, and ensures that the sentences of the court are carried out. **3.** *Chiefly Brit.* (formerly) a high official having judicial powers. **4.** *Chiefly U.S.* an official having custody of prisoners appearing in court. [C13: < OF *baillif*, < *bail* custody; see BAIL[1]]

bailiwick (ˈbeɪlɪwɪk) *n.* **1.** *Law.* the area over which a bailiff has jurisdiction. **2.** a person's special field of interest. [C15: < BAILIE + WICK[2]]

bail up *vb.* (*adv.*) **1.** *Austral. & N.Z.* to confine (a cow) or (of a cow) to be confined by the head in a bail. See **bail**[3]. **2.** (*tr.*) *Austral.* (of a bushranger) to tie up or hold under guard in order to rob. **3.** (*intr.*) *Austral.* to submit to robbery without offering resistance. **4.** (*tr.*) *Austral. inf.* to accost or detain, esp. in conversation.

bain-marie *French.* (bɛ̃mari) *n., pl.* ***bains-marie*** (bɛ̃mari). a vessel for holding hot water, in which sauces and other dishes are gently cooked or kept warm. [C19: < F, < Med. L *balneum Mariae*, lit.: bath of Mary, inaccurate translation of Med. Gk *kaminos Marios*, lit.: furnace of *Miriam*, alleged author of a treatise on alchemy]

Bairam (baɪˈræm, ˈbaɪræm) *n.* either of two Muslim festivals, one (**Lesser Bairam**) at the end of Ramadan, the other (**Greater Bairam**) at the end of the Islamic year. [< Turkish *bayrām*]

bairn (bɛən) *n. Scot. & N English.* a child. [OE *bearn*]

bait[1] (beɪt) *n.* **1.** something edible fixed to a hook or in a trap to attract fish or animals. **2.** an enticement; temptation. **3.** a variant spelling of **bate**[3]. **4.** *Arch.* a short stop for refreshment during a journey. ~*vb.* **5.** (*tr.*) to put a piece of food on or in (a hook or trap). **6.** (*tr.*) to persecute or tease. **7.** (*tr.*) to entice; tempt. **8.** (*tr.*) to set dogs upon (a bear, etc.). **9.** (*intr.*) *Arch.* to stop for rest and refreshment during a journey. [C13: < ON *beita* to hunt, persecute]

bait[2] (beɪt) *vb.* a variant spelling of **bate**[2].

baize (beɪz) *n.* a woollen fabric resembling felt, usually green, used mainly for the tops of billiard tables. [C16: < OF *baies*, pl. of *baie* baize, < *bai* reddish brown, BAY[5]]

bake (beɪk) *vb.* **1.** (*tr.*) to cook by dry heat as in an oven. **2.** (*intr.*) to cook bread, pastry, etc. **3.** to make or become hardened by heat. **4.** (*intr.*) *Inf.* to be extremely hot. ~*n.* **5.** a batch of things baked at one time. **6.** *Caribbean.* a small flat fried cake. [OE *bacan*]

baked Alaska (əˈlæskə) *n.* a dessert made of cake and ice cream covered with meringue and cooked very quickly.

baked beans *pl. n.* haricot beans, baked and tinned in tomato sauce.

Bakelite (ˈbeɪkəˌlaɪt) *n. Trademark.* any one of a class of thermosetting resins used as electric insulators and for making plastic ware, etc. [C20: after L. H. *Baekeland* (1863–1944), Belgian-born U.S. inventor]

baker (ˈbeɪkə) *n.* a person whose business or employment is to make or sell bread, cakes, etc.

baker's dozen *n.* thirteen. [C16: < the bakers' former practice of giving thirteen rolls where twelve were requested, to protect themselves against accusations of giving light weight]

bakery (ˈbeɪkərɪ) *n., pl.* **-eries.** **1.** a room or building equipped for baking. **2.** a shop in which bread, cakes, etc., are sold.

baking powder *n.* a powdered mixture that contains sodium bicarbonate and one or more acidic compounds, such as cream of tartar: used in baking as a substitute for yeast.

baklava *or* **baclava** (ˈbɑːkləˌvɑː) *n.* a rich cake consisting of thin layers of pastry filled with nuts and honey. [< Turkish]

baksheesh *or* **backsheesh** (ˈbækʃiːʃ) *n.* (in some Eastern countries, esp. formerly) money given as a tip, a present, or alms. [C17: < Persian *bakhshīsh*, < *bakhshīdan* to give]

bal. *Book-keeping. abbrev. for* balance.

Balaclava helmet (ˌbæləˈklɑːvə) *n.* a close-fitting woollen hood that covers the ears and neck, as originally worn by soldiers in the Crimean War.

balalaika (ˌbæləˈlaɪkə) *n.* a Russian plucked musical instrument, usually having a triangular body and three strings. [C18: < Russian]

balance (ˈbæləns) *n.* **1.** a weighing device, generally consisting of a horizontal beam pivoted at its centre, from the ends of which two pans are suspended. The substance to be weighed is placed in one pan and weights are placed in the other until the beam returns to the horizontal. **2.** a state of equilibrium. **3.** something that brings about such a state. **4.** equilibrium of the body; steadiness: *to lose one's balance.* **5.** emotional stability. **6.** harmony in the parts of a whole. **7.** the act of weighing factors, quantities, etc., against each other. **8.** the power to influence or control: *the balance of power.* **9.** something that remains: *the balance of what you owe.* **10.** *Accounting.* **a.** equality of debit and credit totals in an account. **b.** a difference between such totals. **11. in the balance.** in an uncertain or undecided condition. **12. on balance.** after weighing up all the factors. **13. strike a balance.** to make a compromise. ~*vb.* **14.** (*tr.*) to weigh in or as if in a balance. **15.** (*intr.*) to be or come into equilibrium. **16.** (*tr.*) to bring into or hold in equilibrium. **17.** (*tr.*) to compare the relative weight, importance, etc., of. **18.** (*tr.*) to be equal to. **19.** (*tr.*) to arrange so as to create a state of harmony. **20.** (*tr.*) *Accounting.* **a.** to compare the credit and debit totals of (an account). **b.** to equalize the credit and debit totals of (an account) by making certain entries. **c.** to settle or adjust (an account) by paying any money due. **21.** (*intr.*) (of a balance sheet, etc.) to have the debit and credit totals equal. [C13: < OF, < Vulgar L *bilancia* (unattested), < LL *bilanx* having two scales, < BI- + *lanx* scale] —ˈ**balanceable** *adj.* —ˈ**balancer** *n.*

balance of payments *n.* the difference over a given time between total payments to foreign nations and total receipts from foreign nations.

balance of power *n.* the distribution of power among countries so that no one nation can seriously threaten another.

balance of trade *n.* the difference in value between total exports and total imports of goods.

balance sheet *n.* a statement that shows the financial position of a business by listing the asset balances and the claims on such assets.

balance wheel *n.* a wheel oscillating against the hairspring of a timepiece, regulating its beat.

balata (ˈbælətə) *n.* **1.** a tropical American tree, yielding a latex-like sap. **2.** a rubber-like gum obtained from this sap: a substitute for gutta-percha. [< American Sp., of Carib origin]

balcony (ˈbælkənɪ) *n., pl.* **-nies. 1.** a platform projecting from a building with a balustrade along its outer edge, often with access from a door or window. **2.** a gallery in a theatre, above the dress circle. **3.** *U.S. & Canad.* any circle in a theatre. [C17: < It. *balcone,* prob. < OHG *balko* beam] —ˈ**balconied** *adj.*

bald (bɔːld) *adj.* **1.** having no hair or fur, esp. (of a man) having no hair on the scalp. **2.** lacking natural growth or covering. **3.** plain or blunt: *a bald statement.* **4.** bare or unadorned. **5.** Also: **baldfaced.** (of birds and animals) having white markings on the head and face. **6.** (of a tyre) having a worn tread. [C14 *ballede* (lit.: having a white spot)] —ˈ**baldish** *adj.* —ˈ**baldly** *adv.* —ˈ**baldness** *n.*

baldachin *or* **baldaquin** (ˈbɔːldəkɪn) *n.* **1.** a richly ornamented brocade. **2.** a canopy over an altar, shrine, or throne or carried in Christian religious processions over an object of veneration. [OE *baldekin,* < It. *baldacchino,* lit.: stuff from Baghdad]

bald eagle *n.* a large eagle of North America, having a white head and tail. It is the U.S. national bird.

balderdash (ˈbɔːldəˌdæʃ) *n.* stupid or illogical talk; senseless rubbish. [C16: <?]

balding (ˈbɔːldɪŋ) *adj.* somewhat bald or becoming bald.

baldric (ˈbɔːldrɪk) *n.* a sash or belt worn over the right shoulder to the left hip for carrying a sword, etc. [C13: < OF *baudrei,* of Frankish origin]

bale[1] (beɪl) *n.* **1.** a large bundle, package, or carton of goods bound by ropes, wires, etc., for storage or transportation. **2.** *U.S.* 500 pounds of cotton. ~*vb.* **3.** to make (hay, etc.) or put (goods) into a bale or bales. [C14: prob. < OF *bale,* < OHG *balla* BALL[1]]

bale[2] (beɪl) *n. Arch.* **1.** evil; injury. **2.** woe; suffering; pain. [OE *bealu*]

bale[3] (beɪl) *vb.* a variant spelling of **bail**[2].

bale[4] (beɪl) *n.* a variant spelling of **bail**[4].

baleen (bəˈliːn) *n.* whalebone. [C14: < L *bālaena* whale]

baleen whale *n.* another name for **whalebone whale.**

baleful (ˈbeɪlfʊl) *adj.* harmful, menacing, or vindictive. —ˈ**balefully** *adv.* —ˈ**balefulness** *n.*

bale out *or* **bail out** *vb.* (*adv.*) **1.** (*intr.*) to make an emergency parachute jump from an aircraft. **2.** (*tr.*) *Inf.* to help (a person, organization, etc.) out of a predicament.

baler (ˈbeɪlə) *n.* a machine for making bales of hay, etc. Also called: **baling machine.**

balk *or* **baulk** (bɔːk, bɔːlk) *vb.* **1.** (*intr.;* usually foll. by *at*) to stop short; jib: *the horse balked at the jump.* **2.** (*intr.;* foll. by *at*) to recoil: *he balked at the idea of murder.* **3.** (*tr.*) to thwart, check, or foil: *he was balked in his plans.* ~*n.* **4.** a roughly squared heavy timber beam. **5.** a timber tie beam of a roof. **6.** an unploughed ridge between furrows. **7.** an obstacle; hindrance; disappointment. **8.** *Baseball.* an illegal motion by a pitcher. ~See also **baulk.** [OE *balca*]

Balkan (ˈbɔːlkən) *adj.* of or denoting a large peninsula in SE Europe, between the Adriatic and Aegean Seas, or its inhabitants, countries, etc.

balky *or* **baulky** (ˈbɔːkɪ, ˈbɔːlkɪ) *adj.* **balkier, balkiest** *or* **baulkier, baulkiest.** inclined to stop abruptly and unexpectedly: *a balky horse.*

ball[1] (bɔːl) *n.* **1.** a spherical or nearly spherical body or mass. **2.** a round or roundish body, of a size and composition suitable for any of various games. **3.** a ball propelled in a particular way: *a high ball.* **4.** any rudimentary game with a ball: *to play ball.* **5.** a single delivery of the ball in cricket and other games. **6. a.** a solid nonexplosive projectile for a firearm, cannon, etc. **b.** such projectiles collectively. **7.** any more or less rounded part: *the ball of the foot.* **8. ball of muscle.** *Austral.* a very strong, fit person. **9. have the ball at one's feet.** to have the chance of doing something. **10. keep the ball rolling.** to maintain the progress of a project, plan, etc. **11. on the ball.** *Inf.* alert; informed. **12. play ball.** *Inf.* to cooperate. **13. start** *or* **set the ball rolling.** to initiate an action, discussion, etc. ~*vb.* **14.** to make, form, wind, gather, etc., into a ball or balls. ~ See also **balls, balls-up.** [C13: < ON *böllr*]

ball[2] (bɔːl) *n.* **1.** a social function for dancing, esp. one that is lavish or formal. **2.** *Inf.* a very enjoyable time (esp. in **have a ball**). [C17: < F *bal* (n.), < OF *baller* (vb.), < LL *ballāre* to dance]

ballad (ˈbæləd) *n.* **1.** a narrative song with a recurrent refrain. **2.** a narrative poem in short stanzas of popular origin. **3.** a slow sentimental song, esp. a pop song. [C15: < OF *balade,* < OProvençal *balada* song accompanying a dance]

ballade (bæˈlɑːd) *n.* **1.** *Prosody.* a verse form consisting of three stanzas and an envoy, all ending with the same line. **2.** *Music.* an instrumental composition based on or intended to evoke a narrative.

balladeer (ˌbæləˈdɪə) *n.* a singer of ballads.

ball-and-socket joint *n. Anat.* a joint in which a rounded head fits into a rounded cavity, allowing a wide range of movement.

ballast (ˈbæləst) *n.* **1.** any heavy material used to stabilize a vessel, esp. one that is not carrying cargo. **2.** crushed rock, broken stone, etc., used for the foundation of a road or railway track or in making concrete. **3.** anything that provides stability or weight. **4.** *Electronics.* a device for maintaining the current in a circuit. ~*vb.* (*tr.*) **5.** to give stability or weight to. [C16: prob. < Low G]

ball bearing *n.* **1.** a bearing consisting of steel balls rolling between a metal sleeve fitted over the rotating shaft and an outer sleeve held in the bearing housing, so reducing friction. **2.** a metal ball, esp. one used in such a bearing.

ball boy *or* (*fem.*) **ball girl** *n.* (esp. in tennis) a person who retrieves balls that go out of play.

ball cock *n.* a device for regulating the flow of a liquid into a tank, cistern, etc., consisting of a floating ball mounted at one end of an arm and a valve on the other end that opens and closes as the ball falls and rises.

ballerina (ˌbæləˈriːnə) *n.* a female ballet dancer. [C18: < It., fem. of *ballerino* dancing master, < *ballare* to dance]

ballet (ˈbæleɪ, bæˈleɪ) *n.* **1.** a classical style of expressive dancing based on precise conventional steps. **2.** a theatrical representation of a story or theme performed by ballet dancers. **3.** a troupe of ballet dancers. **4.** music written for a ballet. [C17: < F, < It. *balletto,* lit.: a little dance, < *ballare* to dance] —**balletic** (bæˈlɛtɪk) *adj.*

balletomane (ˈbælɪtəʊˌmeɪn) *n.* a ballet enthusiast.

balletomania (ˌbælɪtəʊˈmeɪnɪə) *n.* passionate enthusiasm for ballet.
ball game *n.* **1.** any game played with a ball. **2.** *U.S. & Canad.* a game of baseball. **3.** *Inf.* a situation; state of affairs (esp. in **a whole new ball game**).
ballista (bəˈlɪstə) *n., pl.* **-tae** (-tiː). an ancient catapult for hurling stones, etc. [C16: < L, ult. < Gk *ballein* to throw]
ballistic (bəˈlɪstɪk) *adj.* **1.** of or relating to ballistics. **2.** denoting or relating to the flight of projectiles moving under their own momentum and the force of gravity. **3.** (of a measurement or measuring instrument) depending on a brief impulse or current that causes a movement related to the quantity to be measured: *a ballistic pendulum.* —**balˈlistically** *adv.*
ballistic missile *n.* a missile that has no wings or fins and that follows a ballistic trajectory when its propulsive power is discontinued.
ballistics (bəˈlɪstɪks) *n.* (*functioning as sing.*) **1.** the study of the flight dynamics of projectiles. **2.** the study of the effects of firing on firearms and their projectiles.
ballocks (ˈbɒləks) *pl. n., interj.* a variant spelling of **bollocks.**
ball of fire *n. Inf.* a very lively person.
balloon (bəˈluːn) *n.* **1.** an inflatable rubber bag used as a plaything or party decoration. **2.** a large bag inflated with a lighter-than-air gas, designed to rise and float in the atmosphere. It may have a basket or gondola for carrying passengers, etc. **3.** an outline containing the words or thoughts of a character in a cartoon. **4.** a large rounded brandy glass. **5. when the balloon goes up.** *Inf.* when the action starts. ~*vb.* **6.** (*intr.*) to go up or fly in a balloon. **7.** to inflate or be inflated: *the wind ballooned the sails.* **8.** (*tr.*) *Brit.* to propel (a ball) high into the air. [C16 (in the sense: ball, ball game): < It. dialect *ballone*] —**balˈloonist** *n.* —**balˈloon-ˌlike** *adj.*
balloon loan *n.* a loan in respect of which interest and capital are paid off in instalments at regular intervals.
ballot (ˈbælət) *n.* **1.** the practice of selecting a representative, course of action, etc., by submitting the options to a vote of all qualified persons. **2.** an instance of voting, usually in secret. **3.** a list of candidates standing for office. **4.** the number of votes cast in an election. ~*vb.* **-loting, -loted. 5.** to vote or elicit a vote from: *we balloted the members on this issue.* **6.** (*tr.;* usually foll. by *for*) to vote for or decide on by lot or ballot. [C16: < It. *ballotta,* lit.: a little ball]
ballot box *n.* a box into which ballot papers are dropped after voting.
ballot paper *n.* a paper used for voting.
ballpark (ˈbɔːlˌpɑːk) *n.* **1.** *U.S. & Canad.* a stadium used for baseball games. **2.** *Inf.* approximate range: *in the right ballpark.*
ball-peen hammer *n.* a hammer with one end of the head rounded for beating metal.
ballpoint *or* **ballpoint pen** (ˈbɔːlˌpɔɪnt) *n.* a pen having a small ball bearing as a writing point.
ballroom (ˈbɔːlˌruːm, -ˌrʊm) *n.* a large hall for dancing.
ballroom dancing *n.* social dancing, popular since the beginning of the 20th century, to dances in conventional rhythms (**ballroom dances**).
balls (bɔːlz) *Taboo sl.* ~*pl. n.* **1.** the testicles. **2.** nonsense; rubbish. ~*interj.* **3.** an exclamation of disagreement, contempt, etc.
balls-up *Taboo sl.* ~*n.* **1.** something botched or muddled. ~*vb.* **balls up. 2.** (*tr., adv.*) to muddle or botch.
bally (ˈbælɪ) *adj., adv.* (intensifier) *Brit. sl.* a euphemistic word for **bloody** (sense 5).
ballyhoo (ˌbælɪˈhuː) *Inf. n.* **1.** a noisy, confused, or nonsensical situation. **2.** sensational or blatant advertising or publicity. ~*vb.* **-hooing, -hooed. 3.** (*tr.*) *Chiefly U.S.* to advertise by sensational or blatant methods. [C19: <?]
balm (bɑːm) *n.* **1.** any of various oily aromatic substances obtained from certain tropical trees and used for healing and soothing. See also balsam (sense 1). **2.** any plant yielding such a substance, esp. the balm of Gilead. **3.** something comforting or soothing. **4.** Also called: **lemon balm.** an aromatic Eurasian plant, having clusters of small fragrant white flowers. **5.** a pleasant odour. [C13: < OF *basme,* < L *balsamum* BALSAM]
balm of Gilead (ˈgɪlɪˌæd) *n.* **1.** any of several trees of Africa and W Asia that yield a fragrant oily resin. **2.** the resin exuded by these trees. **3.** a North American poplar tree. **4.** a fragrant resin obtained from the balsam fir.
Balmoral (bælˈmɒrəl) *n.* (*sometimes not cap.*) **1.** a laced walking shoe. **2.** a Scottish brimless hat usually with a cockade and plume. [< *Balmoral* Castle, Scotland]
balmy (ˈbɑːmɪ) *adj.* **balmier, balmiest. 1.** (of weather) mild and pleasant. **2.** having the qualities of balm; fragrant or soothing. **3.** a variant spelling of **barmy.** —ˈ**balmily** *adv.* —ˈ**balminess** *n.*
balneology (ˌbælnɪˈɒlədʒɪ) *n.* the branch of medical science concerned with the therapeutic value of baths, esp. with natural mineral waters. [C19: < L *balneum* bath] —**balneological** (ˌbælnɪəˈlɒdʒɪkᵊl) *adj.* —ˌ**balneˈologist** *n.*
baloney *or* **boloney** (bəˈləʊnɪ) *n. Inf.* foolish talk; nonsense. [C20: < *Bologna* (sausage)]
BALPA (ˈbælpə) *n. acronym for* British Airline Pilots' Association.
balsa (ˈbɔːlsə) *n.* **1.** a tree of tropical America. **2.** Also called: **balsawood.** the very light wood of this tree, used for making rafts, etc. **3.** a light raft. [C18: < Sp.: raft]
balsam (ˈbɔːlsəm) *n.* **1.** any of various fragrant oleoresins, such as balm, obtained from any of several trees and shrubs and used as a base for medicines and perfumes. **2.** any of various similar substances used as ointments. **3.** any of certain aromatic resinous turpentines. See **Canada balsam. 4.** any plant yielding balsam. **5.** Also called: **busy Lizzie.** any of several plants of the genus *Impatiens.* **6.** anything healing or soothing. [C15: < L *balsamum,* < Gk *balsamon,* < Heb. *bāśām* spice] —**balsamic** (bɔːlˈsæmɪk) *adj.*
balsam fir *n.* a fir tree of NE North America, that yields Canada balsam.
Baltic (ˈbɔːltɪk) *adj.* **1.** denoting or relating to the Baltic Sea in N Europe, or the states bordering it. **2.** of or characteristic of Baltic as a group of languages. ~*n.* **3.** a branch of the Indo-European family of languages consisting of Lithuanian, Latvian, and Old Prussian. **4.** Also called: **Baltic Exchange.** a commodities exchange in the City of London.
baluster (ˈbæləstə) *n.* any of a set of posts supporting a rail or coping. [C17: < F *balustre,* < It. *balaustro* pillar resembling a pomegranate flower, ult. < Gk *balaustion*]
balustrade (ˈbæləˌstreɪd) *n.* an ornamental rail or coping with its supporting set of balusters. [C17: < F, < *balustre* BALUSTER]
bambino (bæmˈbiːnəʊ) *n., pl.* **-nos** *or* **-ni** (-niː). *Inf.* a young child, esp. Italian. [C18: < It.]
bamboo (bæmˈbuː) *n.* **1.** a tall treelike tropical or semitropical grass having hollow stems with ringed joints. **2.** the stem, used for building, poles, and furniture. [C16: prob. < Malay *bambu*]
bamboozle (bæmˈbuːzᵊl) *vb.* (*tr.*) *Inf.* **1.** to cheat; mislead. **2.** to confuse. [C18: <?] —**bamˈboozlement** *n.* —**bamˈboozler** *n.*
ban (bæn) *vb.* **banning, banned. 1.** (*tr.*) to prohibit, esp. officially, from action, display, entrance, sale, etc.; forbid. ~*n.* **2.** an official prohibition or interdiction. **3.** a public proclamation, esp. of outlawry. **4.** *Arch.* a curse; imprecation. [OE *bannan* to proclaim]
banal (bəˈnɑːl) *adj.* lacking force or originality; trite; commonplace. [C18: < OF: relating to compulsory feudal service, hence common to all, commonplace] —**banality** (bəˈnælɪtɪ) *n.* —**baˈnally** *adv.*
banana (bəˈnɑːnə) *n.* **1.** any of several tropical and subtropical treelike plants, esp. a widely

cultivated species having hanging clusters of edible fruit. **2.** the crescent-shaped fruit of any of these plants. [C16: < Sp. or Port., of African origin]

banana republic *n. Inf. & derog.* a small country, esp. in Central America, that is politically unstable and has an economy dominated by foreign interest, usually dependent on one export.

banana skin *n.* **1.** the soft outer covering of a banana. **2.** *Inf.* something unforeseen that causes an obvious and embarrassing mistake. [sense 2 < the common slapstick joke of slipping on a banana skin]

band[1] (bænd) *n.* **1.** a company of people having a common purpose; group: *a band of outlaws.* **2.** a group of musicians playing either brass and percussion instruments only (**brass band**) or brass, woodwind, and percussion instruments (**concert band** or **military band**). **3.** a group of musicians who play popular music, jazz, etc., often for dancing. ~*vb.* **4.** (usually foll. by *together*) to unite; assemble. [C15: < F *bande,* prob. < OProvençal *banda,* of Gmc origin]

band[2] (bænd) *n.* **1.** a thin flat strip of some material, used esp. to encircle objects and hold them together: *a rubber band.* **2. a.** a strip of fabric or other material used as an ornament or to reinforce clothing. **b.** (*in combination*): *waistband; hatband.* **3.** a stripe of contrasting colour or texture. **4.** a driving belt in machinery. **5.** a range of values that are close or related in number, degree, or quality. **6.** *Physics.* a range of frequencies or wavelengths between two limits. **7.** short for **energy band. 8.** *Computers.* one or more tracks on a magnetic disk or drum. **9.** *Anat.* any structure resembling a ribbon or cord that connects, encircles, or binds different parts. **10.** *Archit.* a strip of flat panelling, such as a fascia, usually attached to a wall. **11.** either of a pair of hanging extensions of the collar, forming part of academic, legal, or (formerly) clerical dress. **12.** (of a gramophone record) another word for **track** (sense 10). ~*vb.* (*tr.*) **13.** to fasten or mark with a band. [C15: < OF *bende,* of Gmc origin]

bandage (ˈbændɪdʒ) *n.* **1.** a piece of material used to dress a wound, bind a broken limb, etc. ~*vb.* **2.** to cover or bind with a bandage. [C16: < F, < *bande* strip, BAND[2]]

bandanna *or* **bandana** (bænˈdænə) *n.* a large silk or cotton handkerchief or neckerchief. [C18: < Hindi *bāndhnū* tie-dyeing]

b. and b. *or* **B & B** *abbrev. for* bed and breakfast.

bandbox (ˈbændˌbɒks) *n.* a lightweight usually cylindrical box for small articles, esp. hats.

bandeau (ˈbændəʊ) *n., pl.* **-deaux** (-dəʊz). a narrow band of ribbon, velvet, etc., worn round the head. [C18: < F, < OF *bandel* a little BAND[2]]

banderole *or* **banderol** (ˈbændəˌrəʊl) *n.* **1.** a long narrow flag, usually with forked ends, esp. one attached to the mast of a ship. **2.** a ribbon-like scroll or sculptured band bearing an inscription. [C16: < OF, < It. *banderuola,* lit.: a little banner]

bandicoot (ˈbændɪˌkuːt) *n.* **1.** an agile terrestrial marsupial of Australia and New Guinea with a long pointed muzzle and a long tail. **2. bandicoot rat.** Also called: **mole rat.** any of three burrowing rats of S and SE Asia. [C18: < Telugu *pandikokku*]

banding (ˈbændɪŋ) *n. Brit.* the practice of putting schoolchildren into ability groups to ensure a balanced intake to secondary school.

bandit (ˈbændɪt) *n., pl.* **bandits** *or* **banditti** (bænˈdɪtɪ). a robber, esp. a member of an armed gang. [C16: < It. *bandito,* < *bandire* to proscribe, < *bando* edict] —ˈ**banditry** *n.*

bandmaster (ˈbændˌmɑːstə) *n.* the conductor of a band.

Band of Hope *n.* a society devoted to abstinence from alcohol.

bandoleer *or* **bandolier** (ˌbændəˈlɪə) *n.* a soldier's broad shoulder belt having small pockets or loops for cartridges. [C16: < OF *bandouliere*]

band-pass filter *n.* **1.** *Electronics.* a filter that transmits only currents having frequencies within specified limits. **2.** an optical device for transmitting waves of predetermined wavelengths.

band saw *n.* a power-operated saw consisting of an endless toothed metal band running over and driven by two wheels.

bandsman (ˈbændzmən) *n., pl.* **-men.** a player in a musical band, esp. a brass or military band.

bandstand (ˈbændˌstænd) *n.* a platform for a band, usually out of doors and roofed.

bandwagon (ˈbændˌwægən) *n.* **1.** *U.S.* a wagon for the band in a parade. **2. climb, jump,** *or* **get on the bandwagon.** to join or support a party or movement that seems assured of success.

bandwidth (ˈbændˌwɪdθ) *n.* the range of frequencies within a given waveband used for a particular radio transmission.

bandy (ˈbændɪ) *adj.* **-dier, -diest. 1.** Also: **bandy-legged.** having legs curved outwards at the knees. **2.** (of legs) curved thus. ~*vb.* **-dying, -died.** (*tr.*) **3.** to exchange (words) in a heated or hostile manner. **4.** to give and receive (blows). **5.** (often foll. by *about*) to circulate (a name, rumour, etc.). [C16: prob. < OF *bander* to hit the ball back and forth at tennis]

bane (beɪn) *n.* **1.** a person or thing that causes misery or distress (esp. in **bane of one's life**). **2.** something that causes death or destruction. **3. a.** a fatal poison. **b.** (*in combination*): *ratsbane.* **4.** *Arch.* ruin or distress. [OE *bana*] —ˈ**baneful** *adj.*

baneberry (ˈbeɪnbərɪ) *n., pl.* **-ries. 1.** Also called: **herb Christopher** (Brit.). a plant which has small white flowers and red or white poisonous berries. **2.** the berry.

bang[1] (bæŋ) *n.* **1.** a short loud explosive noise, as of the report of a gun. **2.** a hard blow or knock, esp. a noisy one. **3.** *Sl.* an injection of heroin or other narcotic. **4.** *Taboo sl.* an act of sexual intercourse. **5. with a bang.** successfully: *the party went with a bang.* ~*vb.* **6.** to hit or knock, esp. with a loud noise. **7.** to move noisily or clumsily: *to bang about the house.* **8.** to close (a door, window, etc.) or (of a door, etc.) be closed noisily; slam. **9.** (*tr.*) to cause to move by hitting vigorously: *he banged the ball over the fence.* **10.** to make or cause to make a loud noise, as of an explosion. **11.** *Taboo sl.* to have sexual intercourse (with). **12.** (*intr.*) *Sl.* to inject heroin, etc. **13. bang one's head against a brick wall.** to try to achieve something impossible. ~*adv.* **14.** with a sudden impact or effect: *the car drove bang into a lamppost.* **15.** precisely: *bang in the middle.* **16. go bang.** to burst, shut, etc., with a loud noise. [C16: < ON *bang, banga* hammer]

bang[2] (bæŋ) *n.* **1.** a fringe of hair cut straight across the forehead. ~*vb.* (*tr.*) **2.** to cut (the hair) in such a style. **3.** to dock (the tail of a horse, etc.). [C19: prob. short for *bangtail* short tail]

banger (ˈbæŋə) *n. Brit.* **1.** *Sl.* a sausage. **2.** *Inf.* an old decrepit car. **3.** a firework that explodes loudly.

bangle (ˈbæŋgəl) *n.* a bracelet, usually without a clasp, often worn round the arm or sometimes round the ankle. [C19: < Hindi *bangrī*]

bang on *adj., adv. Brit. inf.* **1.** with absolute accuracy. **2.** excellent or excellently.

bangtail (ˈbæŋˌteɪl) *n.* **1.** a horse's tail cut straight across but not through the bone. **2.** a horse with a tail cut in this way. [C19: < *bangtail* short tail]

banian (ˈbænjən) *n.* a variant spelling of **banyan.**

banish (ˈbænɪʃ) *vb.* (*tr.*) **1.** to expel from a place, esp. by an official decree as a punishment. **2.** to drive away: *to banish gloom.* [C14: < OF *banir,* of Gmc origin] —ˈ**banishment** *n.*

banisters *or* **bannisters** (ˈbænɪstəz) *pl. n.* the railing and supporting balusters on a staircase; balustrade. [C17: altered < BALUSTER]

banjo (ˈbændʒəʊ) *n., pl.* **-jos** *or* **-joes.** a stringed musical instrument with a long neck and a circular drumlike body overlaid with parchment, plucked with the fingers or a plectrum. [C18: var. (U.S. Southern pronunciation) of earlier *bandore,* ult. < Gk *pandora*] —ˈ**banjoist** *n.*

bank[1] (bæŋk) *n.* **1.** an institution offering certain financial services, such as the safekeeping of money and lending of money at interest. **2.** the building used by such an institution. **3.** a small container used at home for keeping money. **4.** the funds held by a banker or dealer in some gambling games. **5.** (in various games) **a.** the stock, as of money, etc., on which players may draw. **b.** the player holding this stock. **6.** any supply, store, or reserve: *a data bank.* ~*vb.* **7.** (*tr.*) to deposit (cash, cheques, etc.) in a bank. **8.** (*intr.*) to transact business with a bank. **9.** (*intr.*) to engage in banking. ~See also **bank on.** [C15: prob. < It. *banca* bench, moneychanger's table, of Gmc origin]

bank[2] (bæŋk) *n.* **1.** a long raised mass, esp. of earth; ridge. **2.** a slope, as of a hill. **3.** the sloping side of any hollow in the ground, esp. when bordering a river. **4.** the ground beside a river or canal. **5. a.** an elevated section of the bed of a sea, lake, or river. **b.** (*in combination*): *sandbank.* **6.** the face of a body of ore in a mine. **7.** the lateral inclination of an aircraft about its longitudinal axis during a turn. **8.** a bend on a road, athletics track, etc., having the outside built higher than the inside to reduce the effects of centrifugal force on vehicles, runners, etc., rounding it at speed. ~*vb.* **9.** (when *tr.*, often foll. by *up*) to form into a bank or mound. **10.** (*tr.*) to border or enclose (a road, etc.) with a bank. **11.** (*tr.;* sometimes foll. by *up*) to cover (a fire) with ashes, fresh fuel, etc., so that it will burn slowly. **12.** to cause (an aircraft) to tip laterally about its longitudinal axis or (of an aircraft) to tip in this way, esp. while turning. [C12: of Scand. origin]

bank[3] (bæŋk) *n.* **1.** an arrangement of similar objects in a row or in tiers: *a bank of dials.* **2.** a tier of oars in a galley. ~*vb.* **3.** (*tr.*) to arrange in a bank. [C17: < OF *banc* bench, of Gmc origin]

bank account *n.* **1.** an account created by the deposit of money at a bank by a customer. **2.** the amount credited to a depositor at a bank.

bank bill *n.* **1.** a bill of exchange drawn by one bank on another. **2.** *U.S.* a banknote.

bankbook (ˈbæŋkˌbʊk) *n.* a book held by depositors at certain banks, in which the bank enters a record of deposits, withdrawals, and earned interest. Also called: **passbook.**

bank card *n.* another name for **banker's card.**

banker[1] (ˈbæŋkə) *n.* **1.** a person who owns or is an executive in a bank. **2.** an official or player in charge of the bank in various games. **3.** a result that has been forecast identically in a series of entries on a football pool coupon. **4.** a person whose performance can be relied on.

banker[2] (ˈbæŋkə) *n. Austral. & N.Z. inf.* a stream almost overflowing its banks (esp. in **run a banker**).

banker's card *n.* a card issued by a bank, guaranteeing payment of the cheques of a customer up to a stated value.

banker's order *n.* another name for **standing order** (sense 1).

bank holiday *n.* (in Britain) any of several weekdays on which banks are closed by law and which are observed as national holidays.

banking (ˈbæŋkɪŋ) *n.* the business engaged in by a bank.

bank manager *n.* a person who directs the business of a local branch of a bank.

banknote (ˈbæŋkˌnəʊt) *n.* a promissory note, esp. one issued by a central bank, serving as money.

Bank of England *n.* the central bank of the United Kingdom, which acts as banker to the government and the commercial banks.

bank on *vb.* (*intr., prep.*) to expect or rely with confidence on: *you can bank on him.*

bankrupt (ˈbæŋkrʌpt, -rəpt) *n.* **1.** a person adjudged insolvent by a court, his property being administered for the benefit of his creditors. **2.** any person unable to discharge all his debts. **3.** a person whose resources in a certain field are exhausted: *a spiritual bankrupt.* ~*adj.* **4.** adjudged insolvent. **5.** financially ruined. **6.** depleted in resources: *spiritually bankrupt.* **7.** (foll. by *of*) *Brit.* lacking: *bankrupt of intelligence.* ~*vb.* **8.** (*tr.*) to make bankrupt. [C16: < OF *banqueroute,* < OIt. *bancarotta,* < *banca* BANK[1] + *rotta* broken, < L *ruptus*] —ˈ**bankruptcy** *n.*

banksia (ˈbæŋksɪə) *n.* any shrub or tree of the Australian genus *Banksia,* having dense cylindrical heads of flowers that are often yellowish. [C19: NL, after Sir Joseph *Banks* (1743-1820), E botanist]

bank statement *n.* a statement of transactions in a bank account, esp. one of a series sent at regular intervals to the depositor.

banner (ˈbænə) *n.* **1.** a long strip of material displaying a slogan, advertisement, etc. **2.** a placard carried in a procession or demonstration. **3.** something that represents a belief or principle. **4.** the flag of a nation, army, etc. **5.** Also called: **banner headline.** a large headline in a newspaper, etc., extending across the page. [C13: < OF *baniere,* of Gmc origin] —ˈ**bannered** *adj.*

bannisters (ˈbænɪstəz) *pl. n.* a variant spelling of **banisters.**

bannock (ˈbænək) *n.* a round flat cake originating in Scotland, made from oatmeal or barley and baked on a griddle. [OE *bannuc*]

banns *or* **bans** (bænz) *pl. n.* **1.** the public declaration of an intended marriage, usually on three successive Sundays in the parish churches of the betrothed. **2. forbid the banns.** to raise an objection to a marriage announced in this way. [C14: pl. of *bann* proclamation]

banquet (ˈbæŋkwɪt) *n.* **1.** a sumptuous meal; feast. **2.** a ceremonial meal for many people. ~*vb.* **-queting, -queted. 3.** (*intr.*) to hold or take part in a banquet. **4.** (*tr.*) to entertain (a person) with a banquet. [C15: < OF, < It. *banchetto,* < *banco* a table, of Gmc origin] —ˈ**banqueter** *n.*

banquette (bæŋˈkɛt) *n.* **1.** (formerly) a raised part behind a parapet. **2.** *Chiefly U.S. & Canad.* an upholstered bench. [C17: < F, < Provençal *banqueta,* lit.: a little bench]

banshee (ˈbænʃiː, bænˈʃiː) *n.* (in Irish folklore) a female spirit whose wailing warns of impending death. [C18: < Irish Gaelic *bean sídhe,* lit.: woman of the fairy mound]

bantam (ˈbæntəm) *n.* **1.** any of various very small breeds of domestic fowl. **2.** a small but aggressive person. **3.** *Boxing.* short for **bantamweight.** [C18: after *Bantam,* village in Java, said to be the original home of this fowl]

bantamweight (ˈbæntəmˌweɪt) *n.* **1. a.** a professional boxer weighing 112–118 pounds (51–53.5 kg). **b.** an amateur boxer weighing 51–54 kg (112–119 pounds). **2.** an amateur wrestler weighing usually 52–57 kg (115–126 pounds).

banter (ˈbæntə) *vb.* **1.** to speak or tease lightly or jokingly. ~*n.* **2.** teasing or joking language or repartee. [C17: <?] —ˈ**banterer** *n.*

Bantu (ˈbɑːntʊ) *n.* **1.** a group of languages of Africa, including most of the principal languages spoken from the equator to the Cape of Good Hope. **2.** (*pl.* **-tu** *or* **-tus**) *Derog.* a Black speaker of a Bantu language. ~*adj.* **3.** of or relating to this group of peoples or their languages. [C19: < Bantu *Ba-ntu* people]

Bantu beer *n.* (in South Africa) a malted drink of partially fermented and germinated kaffir corn.

Bantustan (ˈbɑːntʊˌstɑːn) *n. Derog.* (in South Africa) an area reserved for occupation by a Black African people, with limited self-government. Official name: **homeland.** [< BANTU + Hindi *-stan* country of]

banyan *or* **banian** (ˈbænjən) *n.* **1.** an Indian tree with aerial roots that grow down into the soil forming additional trunks. **2.** a member of the Hindu merchant caste of India. **3.** a loose-fitting shirt, jacket, or robe, worn originally in India. [C16: < Hindi *baniyā,* < Sansk. *vānija* merchant]

banzai (ˈbɑːnzaɪ, bɑːnˈzaɪ) *interj.* a patriotic cheer, battle cry, or salutation. [Japanese: lit.: (may you live for) ten thousand years]

baobab (ˈbeɪəʊˌbæb) *n.* a tropical African tree that has a very thick trunk, angular branches, and a gourdlike fruit with an edible pulp. [C17: prob. < a native African word]

BAOR *abbrev. for* British Army of the Rhine.

bap (bæp) *n. Brit.* a large soft bread roll. [<?]

baptism (ˈbæpˌtɪzəm) *n.* a Christian religious rite consisting of immersion in or sprinkling with water as a sign that the subject is cleansed from sin and constituted as a member of the Church. —**bapˈtismal** *adj.* —**bapˈtismally** *adv.*

baptism of fire *n.* **1.** a soldier's first experience of battle. **2.** any initiating ordeal.

Baptist (ˈbæptɪst) *n.* **1.** a member of any of various Christian sects that affirm the necessity of baptism (usually of adults and by immersion). **2. the Baptist.** John the Baptist, the cousin and forerunner of Jesus, whom he baptized. ~*adj.* **3.** denoting or characteristic of any Christian sect of Baptists.

baptistry *or* **baptistery** (ˈbæptɪstrɪ) *n., pl.* **-ries. 1.** a part of a Christian church in which baptisms are carried out. **2.** a tank in a Baptist church in which baptisms are carried out.

baptize *or* **-ise** (bæpˈtaɪz) *vb.* **1.** *Christianity.* to immerse (a person) in water or sprinkle water on (a person) as part of the rite of baptism. **2.** (*tr.*) to give a name to; christen. [C13: < LL *baptīzāre*, < Gk, < *baptein* to bathe, dip]

bar[1] (bɑː) *n.* **1.** a rigid usually straight length of metal, wood, etc., used esp. as a barrier or as a structural part: *a bar of a gate.* **2.** a solid usually rectangular block of any material: *a bar of soap.* **3.** anything that obstructs or prevents. **4.** an offshore ridge of sand, mud, or shingle across the mouth of a river, bay, or harbour. **5.** a counter or room where alcoholic drinks are served. **6.** a counter, room, or establishment where a particular range of goods, food, services, etc., are sold: *a coffee bar; a heel bar.* **7.** a narrow band or stripe, as of colour or light. **8.** a heating element in an electric fire. **9.** See **Bar. 10.** the place in a court of law where the accused stands during his trial. **11.** a particular court of law. **12.** *Brit.* (in Parliament) the boundary where nonmembers wishing to address either House appear and where persons are arraigned. **13.** a plea showing that a plaintiff has no cause of action. **14.** anything referred to as an authority or tribunal: *the bar of decency.* **15.** *Music.* a group of beats that is repeated with a consistent rhythm throughout a piece of music. The number of beats in the bar is indicated by the time signature. **16. a.** *Brit.* insignia added to a decoration indicating a second award. **b.** *U.S.* a strip of metal worn with uniform, esp. to signify rank or as an award for service. **17.** *Football, etc.* See **crossbar. 18.** *Gymnastics.* See **horizontal bar. 19.** *Heraldry.* a narrow horizontal line across a shield. **20. behind bars.** in prison. **21. won't have a bar of.** *Austral. & N.Z. inf.* cannot tolerate; dislike. ~*vb.* **barring, barred.** (*tr.*) **22.** to secure with a bar: *to bar the door.* **23.** to shut in or out with or as if with barriers: *to bar the entrances.* **24.** to obstruct: *the fallen tree barred the road.* **25.** (usually foll. by *from*) to prohibit; forbid: *to bar a couple from meeting.* **26.** (usually foll. by *from*) to keep out; exclude: *to bar a person from membership.* **27.** to mark with a bar or bars. **28.** *Law.* to prevent or halt (an action) by showing that the plaintiff has no cause. ~*prep.* **29.** except for. **30. bar none.** without exception. [C12: < OF *barre*, < Vulgar L *barra* (unattested) bar, rod, <?]

bar[2] (bɑː) *n.* a cgs unit of pressure equal to 10^6 dynes per square centimetre. [C20: < Gk *baros* weight]

Bar (bɑː) *n.* **the. 1.** (in England and elsewhere) barristers collectively. **2.** *U.S.* the legal profession collectively. **3. be called to the Bar.** *Brit.* to become a barrister. **4. be called within the Bar.** *Brit.* to be appointed as a Queen's Counsel.

bar. *abbrev. for:* **1.** barometric. **2.** barrel. **3.** barrister.

barathea (ˌbærəˈθɪə) *n.* a fabric made of silk and wool or cotton and rayon. [C19: <?]

barb[1] (bɑːb) *n.* **1.** a point facing in the opposite direction to the main point of a fish-hook, harpoon, etc., intended to make extraction difficult. **2.** any of various pointed parts. **3.** a cutting remark. **4.** any of the hairlike filaments that form the vane of a feather. **5.** a beardlike growth, hair, or projection. ~*vb.* **6.** (*tr.*) to provide with a barb or barbs. [C14: < OF *barbe* beard, point, < L *barba* beard] —**barbed** *adj.*

barb[2] (bɑːb) *n.* a breed of horse of North African origin, similar to the Arab but less spirited. [C17: < F *barbe*, < It. *barbero* a Barbary (horse)]

Barbadian (bɑːˈbeɪdɪən) *adj.* **1.** of Barbados, an island in the West Indies. ~*n.* **2.** a native or inhabitant of Barbados.

barbarian (bɑːˈbɛərɪən) *n.* **1.** a member of a primitive or uncivilized people. **2.** a coarse or uncultured person. **3.** a vicious person. ~*adj.* **4.** of an uncivilized culture. **5.** uncultured or brutal. [C16: see BARBAROUS]

barbaric (bɑːˈbærɪk) *adj.* **1.** of or characteristic of barbarians. **2.** primitive; unrestrained. **3.** brutal. [C15: < L *barbaricus* outlandish; see BARBAROUS] —**barˈbarically** *adv.*

barbarism (ˈbɑːbəˌrɪzəm) *n.* **1.** a brutal, coarse, or ignorant act. **2.** the condition of being backward, coarse, or ignorant. **3.** a substandard word or expression; solecism. **4.** any act or object that offends against accepted taste. [C16: < L *barbarismus* error of speech, < Gk *barbarismos*, < *barbaros* BARBAROUS]

barbarity (bɑːˈbærɪtɪ) *n., pl.* **-ties. 1.** the state of being barbaric or barbarous. **2.** a vicious act.

barbarize *or* **-ise** (ˈbɑːbəˌraɪz) *vb.* **1.** to make or become barbarous. **2.** to use barbarisms in (language). —ˌ**barbariˈzation** *or* **-iˈsation** *n.*

barbarous (ˈbɑːbərəs) *adj.* **1.** uncivilized; primitive. **2.** brutal or cruel. **3.** lacking refinement. [C15: via L < Gk *barbaros* barbarian, non-Greek, imit. of incomprehensible speech] —ˈ**barbarously** *adv.* —ˈ**barbarousness** *n.*

Barbary ape (ˈbɑːbərɪ) *n.* a tailless macaque that inhabits NW Africa and Gibraltar. [< *Barbary*, old name for region in N Africa]

barbate (ˈbɑːbeɪt) *adj. Biol.* having tufts of long hairs; bearded. [C19: < L *barba* a beard]

barbecue (ˈbɑːbɪˌkjuː) *n.* **1.** a meal cooked out of doors over an open fire. **2.** a grill or fireplace used in barbecuing. **3.** the food so cooked. **4.** a party or picnic at which barbecued food is served. ~*vb.* **-cuing, -cued.** (*tr.*) **5.** to cook (meat, fish, etc.) on a grill, usually over charcoal and often with a highly seasoned sauce. [C17: < American Sp. *barbacoa:* frame made of sticks]

barbed wire *n.* strong wire with sharply pointed barbs at close intervals.

barbel (ˈbɑːbᵊl) *n.* **1.** any of several slender tactile spines or bristles that hang from the jaws of certain fishes, such as the carp. **2.** any of several European cyprinid fishes that resemble the carp. [C14: < OF, < LL < L *barba* beard]

barbell (ˈbɑːˌbɛl) *n.* a metal rod to which heavy discs are attached at each end for weightlifting.

barber (ˈbɑːbə) *n.* **1.** a person whose business is cutting men's hair and shaving beards. ~*vb.* (*tr.*) **2.** to cut the hair of. [C13: < OF *barbeor*, < *barbe* beard, < L *barba*]

barberry (ˈbɑːbərɪ) *n., pl.* **-ries.** any spiny Asian shrub of the genus *Berberis*, having clusters of yellow flowers and orange or red berries. [C15: < OF *berberis*, < Ar. *barbāris*]

barbershop (ˈbɑːbəˌʃɒp) *n.* **1.** *Now chiefly U.S.* the premises of a barber. **2.** (*modifier*) denoting a type of close four-part harmony for male voices: *a barbershop quartet.*

barber's pole *n.* a barber's sign consisting of a pole painted with red-and-white spiral stripes.

barbican (ˈbɑːbɪkən) *n.* **1.** a walled outwork to protect a gate or drawbridge of a fortification. **2.** a watchtower projecting from a fortification. [C13: < OF *barbacane*, < Med. L, <?]

barbicel (ˈbɑːbɪˌsɛl) *n. Ornithol.* any of the minute hooks on the barbules of feathers that interlock with those of adjacent barbules. [C19: < NL *barbicella*, lit.: a small beard]

barbitone (ˈbɑːbɪˌtəʊn) *or U.S.* **barbital** (ˈbɑːbɪ-

ˌtæl) *n.* a long-acting barbiturate. [C20: < BARBIT(URIC ACID) + -ONE]

barbiturate (bɑːˈbɪtjʊrɪt, -ˌreɪt) *n.* a derivative of barbituric acid, such as barbitone, used in medicine as a sedative or hypnotic.

barbituric acid (ˌbɑːbɪˈtjʊərɪk) *n.* a white crystalline solid used in the preparation of barbiturate drugs. [C19: partial translation of G *Barbitursäure*]

barbule (ˈbɑːbjuːl) *n. Ornithol.* any of the minute hairs that project from a barb and in some feathers interlock. [C19: < L *barbula* a little beard]

barcarole *or* **barcarolle** (ˈbɑːkəˌrəʊl, -ˌrɒl; ˌbɑːkəˈrəʊl) *n.* **1.** a Venetian boat song. **2.** an instrumental composition resembling this. [C18: < F, < It. *barcarola,* < *barcaruolo* boatman, < *barca* boat]

bar chart *n.* another term for **bar graph.**

bar code *n. Commerce.* a machine-readable arrangement of numbers and parallel lines printed on a package, which can be electronically scanned at a checkout to register the price of the goods.

bard[1] (bɑːd) *n.* **1. a.** (formerly) one of an ancient Celtic order of poets. **b.** a poet who wins a verse competition at a Welsh eisteddfod. **2.** *Arch. or literary.* any poet. [C14: < Scot. Gaelic] —ˈ**bardic** *adj.*

bard[2] (bɑːd) *n.* **1.** a piece of bacon or pork fat placed on meat during roasting to prevent drying out. ~*vb.* (*tr.*) **2.** to place a bard on. [C15: < OF *barde,* < OIt. *barda,* < Ar. *barda'ah* packsaddle]

Bard (bɑːd) *n.* **the.** an epithet of William Shakespeare.

bardie (ˈbɑːdiː) *n.* **1.** an edible white wood-boring grub of Australia. **2. starve the bardies!** *Austral.* an exclamation of surprise or protest. [< a native Australian language]

bare[1] (bɛə) *adj.* **1.** unclothed: used esp. of a part of the body. **2.** without the natural, conventional, or usual covering. **3.** lacking appropriate furnishings, etc. **4.** unembellished; simple: *the bare facts.* **5.** (*prenominal*) just sufficient: *the bare minimum.* **6. with one's bare hands.** without a weapon or tool. ~*vb.* **7.** (*tr.*) to make bare; uncover. [OE *bær*] —ˈ**bareness** *n.*

bare[2] (bɛə) *vb. Arch.* a past tense of **bear**[1].

bareback (ˈbɛəˌbæk) *or* **barebacked** *adj., adv.* (of horse-riding) without a saddle.

barefaced (ˈbɛəˌfeɪst) *adj.* unconcealed or shameless: *a barefaced lie.* —**barefacedly** (ˈbɛəˌfeɪsɪdlɪ) *adv.* —ˈ**bareˌfacedness** *n.*

barefoot (ˈbɛəˌfʊt) *or* **barefooted** *adj., adv.* **1.** with the feet uncovered. ~*adj.* **2.** denoting a worker with basic training sent to help people in remote rural areas, esp. of China: *barefoot doctor.*

bareheaded (ˌbɛəˈhɛdɪd) *adj., adv.* with the head uncovered.

barely (ˈbɛəlɪ) *adv.* **1.** only just: *barely enough.* **2.** *Inf.* not quite: *barely old enough.* **3.** scantily: *barely furnished.* **4.** *Arch.* openly.

barf (bɑːf) *vb.* (*intr.*) *Sl.* to vomit. [C20: prob. imit.]

bargain (ˈbɑːgɪn) *n.* **1.** an agreement establishing what each party will give, receive, or perform in a transaction. **2.** something acquired or received in such an agreement. **3. a.** something bought or offered at a low price. **b.** (*as modifier*)*: a bargain price.* **4. into the bargain.** in excess; besides. **5. make** *or* **strike a bargain.** to agree on terms. ~*vb.* **6.** (*intr.*) to negotiate the terms of an agreement, transaction, etc. **7.** (*tr.*) to exchange, as in a bargain. **8.** to arrive at (an agreement or settlement). [C14: < OF *bargaigne,* < *bargaignier* to trade, of Gmc origin] —ˈ**bargainer** *n.*

bargain away *vb.* (*tr., adv.*) to lose (rights, etc.) in return for something valueless.

bargain for *vb.* (*intr., prep.*) to expect; anticipate: *he got more than he bargained for.*

bargain on *vb.* (*intr., prep.*) to rely or depend on (something): *he bargained on her support.*

barge (bɑːdʒ) *n.* **1.** a vessel, usually flat-bottomed and with or without its own power, used for transporting freight, esp. on canals. **2.** a vessel, often decorated, used in pageants, etc. **3.** *Navy.* a boat allocated to a flag officer, used esp. for ceremonial occasions. ~*vb.* **4.** (*intr.;* foll. by *into*) *Inf.* to bump (into). **5.** *Inf.* to push (someone or one's way) violently. **6.** (*intr.;* foll. by *into* or *in*) *Inf.* to interrupt rudely or clumsily: *to barge into a conversation.* [C13: < OF, < Med. L *barga,* prob. < LL *barca* a small boat]

bargeboard (ˈbɑːdʒˌbɔːd) *n.* a board, often decorated, along the gable end of a roof.

bargee (bɑːˈdʒiː) *n.* a person employed on or in charge of a barge.

bargepole (ˈbɑːdʒˌpəʊl) *n.* **1.** a long pole used to propel a barge. **2. not touch with a bargepole.** *Inf.* to refuse to have anything to do with.

bar graph *n.* a graph consisting of vertical or horizontal bars whose lengths are proportional to amounts or quantities.

barite (ˈbɛəraɪt) *n.* the usual U.S. and Canad. name for **barytes.** [C18: < BAR(IUM) + -ITE[1]]

baritone (ˈbærɪˌtəʊn) *n.* **1.** the second lowest adult male voice. **2.** a singer with such a voice. **3.** the second lowest instrument in the families of the saxophone, horn, oboe, etc. ~*adj.* **4.** relating to or denoting a baritone. [C17: < It., < Gk, < *barus* heavy, low + *tonos* TONE]

barium (ˈbɛərɪəm) *n.* a soft silvery-white metallic element of the alkaline earth group. Symbol: Ba; atomic no.: 56; atomic wt.: 137.34. [C19: < BAR(YTA) + -IUM]

barium meal *n.* a preparation of barium sulphate, which is opaque to x-rays, swallowed by a patient before x-ray examination of the upper part of his alimentary canal.

bark[1] (bɑːk) *n.* **1.** the loud abrupt usually harsh cry of a dog or certain other animals. **2.** a similar sound, such as one made by a person, gun, etc. **3. his bark is worse than his bite.** he is bad-tempered but harmless. ~*vb.* **4.** (*intr.*) (of a dog, etc.) to make its typical cry. **5.** (*intr.*) (of a person, gun, etc.) to make a similar loud harsh sound. **6.** to say or shout in a brusque or angry tone: *he barked an order.* **7. bark up the wrong tree.** *Inf.* to misdirect one's attention, efforts, etc.; be mistaken. [OE *beorcan*]

bark[2] (bɑːk) *n.* **1.** a protective layer of dead corky cells on the outside of the stems of woody plants. **2.** any of several varieties of this, used in tanning, dyeing, or in medicine. ~*vb.* (*tr.*) **3.** to scrape or rub off skin, as in an injury. **4.** to remove the bark or a circle of bark from (a tree). **5.** to tan (leather), principally by the tannins in barks. [C13: < ON *bǫrkr*]

bark[3] (bɑːk) *n.* a variant spelling of **barque.**

barkeeper (ˈbɑːˌkiːpə) *n.* another name (esp. U.S.) for **barman** *or* **barmaid.**

barkentine (ˈbɑːkənˌtiːn) *n.* the usual U.S. and Canad. spelling of **barquentine.**

barker (ˈbɑːkə) *n.* **1.** an animal or person that barks. **2.** a person at a fair booth, etc., who loudly addresses passers-by to attract customers.

barley (ˈbɑːlɪ) *n.* **1.** any of various annual temperate grasses that have dense bristly flower spikes and are widely cultivated for grain and forage. **2.** the grain of any of these grasses, used in making beer and whisky and for soups, puddings, etc. [OE *bærlīc* (adj.); rel. to *bere* barley]

barleycorn (ˈbɑːlɪˌkɔːn) *n.* **1.** a grain of barley, or barley itself. **2.** an obsolete unit of length equal to one third of an inch.

barley sugar *n.* a brittle clear amber-coloured sweet.

barley water *n.* a drink made from an infusion of barley.

barm (bɑːm) *n.* **1.** the yeasty froth on fermenting malt liquors. **2.** an archaic or dialect word for **yeast.** [OE *bearm*]

barmaid (ˈbɑːˌmeɪd) *n.* a woman who serves in a pub.

barman (ˈbɑːmən) *n., pl.* **-men.** a man who serves in a pub.

Barmecide (ˈbɑːmɪˌsaɪd) *adj.* lavish in imagination only; illusory; sham: *a Barmecide feast.* [C18: < a prince in the *Arabian Nights' Entertainment* who served empty plates to beggars, alleging that they held sumptuous food]

bar mitzvah (bɑː ˈmɪtsvə) (*sometimes caps.*) *Judaism.* ~*adj.* **1.** (of a Jewish boy) having assumed full religious obligations, being at least thirteen years old. ~*n.* **2.** the occasion or celebration of this. **3.** the boy himself. [Heb.: son of the law]

barmy (ˈbɑːmɪ) *adj.* **-mier, -miest.** *Sl.* insane. [C16: orig., full of BARM, hence frothing, excited]

barn[1] (bɑːn) *n.* **1.** a large farm outbuilding, chiefly for storing grain, etc., but also for livestock. **2.** *U.S. & Canad.* a large shed for railroad cars, trucks, etc. **3.** any large building, esp. an unattractive one. [OE *beren,* < *bere* barley + *ærn* room]

barn[2] (bɑːn) *n.* a unit of nuclear cross section equal to 10^{-28} square metres. Symbol: b [C20: < BARN[1]; so called because of the relatively large cross section]

barnacle (ˈbɑːnəkᵊl) *n.* **1.** any of various marine crustaceans that, as adults, live attached to rocks, ship bottoms, etc. **2.** a person or thing that is difficult to get rid of. [C16: < earlier *bernak,* < OF *bernac,* < LL, <?] —ˈ**barnacled** *adj.*

barnacle goose *n.* a N European goose that has a black-and-white head and body. [C13 *bernekke:* it was formerly believed that the goose developed from a shellfish]

barn dance *n.* **1.** *Brit.* a progressive round country dance. **2.** *Brit.* a disco or party held in a barn. **3.** *U.S. & Canad.* a party with hoedown music and square-dancing.

barney (ˈbɑːnɪ) *Inf.* ~*n.* **1.** a noisy fight or argument. ~*vb. (intr.) Chiefly Austral. & N.Z.* **2.** to argue or quarrel. [C19: <?]

barn owl *n.* an owl with a pale brown and white plumage and a heart-shaped face.

barnstorm (ˈbɑːnˌstɔːm) *vb.* (*intr.*) **1.** to tour rural districts putting on shows. **2.** *Chiefly U.S. & Canad.* to tour rural districts making speeches in a political campaign. —ˈ**barnˌstorming** *n., adj.*

barnyard (ˈbɑːnˌjɑːd) *n.* **1.** a yard adjoining a barn. **2.** (*modifier*) characteristic of a barnyard. **3.** (*modifier*) crude or earthy.

baro- *combining form.* indicating weight or pressure: *barometer.* [< Gk *baros* weight]

barogram (ˈbærəˌɡræm) *n. Meteorol.* the record of atmospheric pressure traced by a barograph or similar instrument.

barograph (ˈbærəˌɡrɑːf) *n. Meteorol.* a self-recording aneroid barometer. —**barographic** (ˌbærəˈɡræfɪk) *adj.*

barometer (bəˈrɒmɪtə) *n.* **1.** an instrument for measuring atmospheric pressure, usually to determine altitude or weather changes. **2.** anything that shows change. —**barometric** (ˌbærəˈmɛtrɪk) *or* ˌ**baroˈmetrical** *adj.* —**baˈrometry** *n.*

baron (ˈbærən) *n.* **1.** a member of a specific rank of nobility, esp. the lowest rank in the British Isles. **2.** (in Europe from the Middle Ages) originally any tenant-in-chief of a king or other overlord. **3.** a powerful businessman or financier: *a press baron.* [C12: < OF, of Gmc origin]

baronage (ˈbærənɪdʒ) *n.* **1.** barons collectively. **2.** the rank or dignity of a baron.

baroness (ˈbærənɪs) *n.* **1.** the wife or widow of a baron. **2.** a woman holding the rank of baron.

baronet (ˈbærənɪt, -ˌnɛt) *n.* (in Britain) a commoner who holds the lowest hereditary title of honour, ranking below a baron. Abbrev.: **Bart, Bt.** —ˈ**baronetage** *n.* —ˈ**baronetcy** *n.*

baronial (bəˈrəʊnɪəl) *adj.* of, relating to, or befitting a baron or barons.

baron of beef *n.* a cut of beef consisting of a double sirloin joined at the backbone.

barony (ˈbærənɪ) *n., pl.* **-nies. 1. a.** the domain of a baron. **b.** (in Ireland) a division of a county. **c.** (in Scotland) a large estate or manor. **2.** the rank or dignity of a baron.

baroque (bəˈrɒk, bəˈrəʊk) *n.* (*often cap.*) **1.** a style of architecture and decorative art in Europe from the late 16th to the early 18th century, characterized by extensive ornamentation. **2.** a 17th-century style of music characterized by extensive use of ornamentation. **3.** any ornate or heavily ornamented style. ~*adj.* **4.** denoting, in, or relating to the baroque. **5.** (of pearls) irregularly shaped. [C18: < F, < It. *barroco*]

baroscope (ˈbærəˌskəʊp) *n.* any instrument for measuring atmospheric pressure. —**baroscopic** (ˌbærəˈskɒpɪk) *adj.*

barouche (bəˈruːʃ) *n.* a four-wheeled horse-drawn carriage, popular in the 19th century, having a retractable hood over the rear half. [C19: < G (dialect) *Barutsche,* < It. *baroccio,* < LL *birotus,* < BI- + *rota* wheel]

barperson (ˈbɑːˌpɜːsᵊn) *n., pl.* **-persons.** a person who serves in a pub: used esp. in advertisements.

barque (bɑːk) *n.* **1.** a sailing ship of three or more masts having the foremasts rigged square and the aftermast rigged fore-and-aft. **2.** *Poetic.* any boat. [C15: < OF, < OProvençal *barca*]

barquentine *or* **barquantine** (ˈbɑːkənˌtiːn) *n.* a sailing ship of three or more masts rigged square on the foremast and fore-and-aft on the others. [C17: < BARQUE + (BRIG)ANTINE]

barrack[1] (ˈbærək) *vb.* to house (soldiers, etc.) in barracks.

barrack[2] (ˈbærək) *vb. Brit., Austral., & N.Z. inf.* **1.** to criticize loudly or shout against (a team, speaker, etc.); jeer. **2.** (*intr.;* foll. by *for*) to shout support (for). [C19: < Irish: to boast]

barracks (ˈbærəks) *pl. n.* (*sometimes sing.; when pl., sometimes functions as sing.*) **1.** a building or group of buildings used to accommodate military personnel. **2.** any large building used for housing people, esp. temporarily. **3.** a large and bleak building. [C17: < F *baraque,* < OCatalan *barraca* hut, <?]

barracouta (ˌbærəˈkuːtə) *n.* a large predatory Pacific fish. [C17: var. of BARRACUDA]

barracuda (ˌbærəˈkjuːdə) *n., pl.* **-da** *or* **-das.** a predatory marine mostly tropical fish, which attacks man. [C17: < American Sp., <?]

barrage (ˈbærɑːʒ) *n.* **1.** *Mil.* the firing of artillery to saturate an area, either to protect against an attack or to support an advance. **2.** an overwhelming and continuous delivery of something, as questions. **3.** a construction across a watercourse, esp. one to increase the depth. [C19: < F, < *barrer* to obstruct; see BAR[1]]

barrage balloon *n.* one of a number of tethered balloons with cables or net suspended from them, used to deter low-flying air attack.

barramundi (ˌbærəˈmʌndɪ) *n., pl.* **-dis, -dies, -di.** an Australian estuary fish of the perch family. [< Abor.]

barrator (ˈbærətə) *n.* a person guilty of barratry. [C14: < OF *barateor*]

barratry *or* **barretry** (ˈbærətrɪ) *n.* **1.** *Criminal law.* (formerly) the vexatious stirring up of quarrels or bringing of lawsuits. **2.** *Maritime law.* a fraudulent practice committed by the master or crew of a ship to the prejudice of the owner. **3.** the purchase or sale of public or Church offices. [C15: < OF *baraterie* deception, < *barater* to BARTER] —ˈ**barratrous** *or* ˈ**barretrous** *adj.*

barre *French.* (bar) *n.* a rail at hip height used for ballet practice. [lit.: bar]

barrel (ˈbærəl) *n.* **1.** a cylindrical container usually bulging outwards in the middle and held together by metal hoops. **2.** Also called: **barrelful.** the amount that a barrel can hold. **3.** a unit of capacity of varying amount in different industries. **4.** a thing shaped like a barrel, esp. a tubular part of a machine. **5.** the tube through which the projectile of a firearm is discharged. **6.** the trunk of a four-legged animal: *the barrel of a horse.* **7. over a barrel.** *Inf.* powerless. **8. scrape the barrel.** *Inf.* to be forced to use one's last and weakest resource. ~*vb.* **-relling, -relled** *or U.S.* **-reling, -reled. 9.** (*tr.*) to put into a barrel or barrels. [C14: < OF *baril,* ? < *barre* BAR[1]]

barrel-chested *adj.* having a large rounded chest.

barrel organ *n.* an instrument consisting of a cylinder turned by a handle and having pins on it that interrupt the air flow to certain pipes or pluck strings, thereby playing tunes.

barrel roll *n.* a flight manoeuvre in which an aircraft rolls about its longitudinal axis while following a spiral course in line with the direction of flight.

barrel vault *n. Archit.* a vault in the form of a half cylinder.

barren (ˈbærən) *adj.* **1.** incapable of producing offspring, seed, or fruit; sterile. **2.** unable to support the growth of crops, etc.: *barren land.* **3.** lacking in stimulation; dull. **4.** not producing worthwhile results; unprofitable: *a barren period.* **5.** (foll. by *of*) devoid (of): *barren of wit.* [C13: < OF *brahain*, <?] —ˈ**barrenness** *n.*

Barren Grounds *pl. n.* **the.** a sparsely inhabited region of tundras in N Canada, extending westwards from Hudson Bay. Also called: **Barren Lands.**

barricade (ˌbærɪˈkeɪd, ˈbærɪˌkeɪd) *n.* **1.** a barrier for defence, esp. one erected hastily, as during street fighting. ~*vb.* (*tr.*) **2.** to erect a barricade across (an entrance, etc.) or at points of access to (a room, district, etc.). [C17: < OF, < *barriquer* to barricade, < *barrique* a barrel, < Sp. *barrica*, < *barril* BARREL]

barrier (ˈbærɪə) *n.* **1.** anything serving to obstruct passage or to maintain separation, such as a fence or gate. **2.** anything that prevents progress. **3.** anything that separates or hinders union: *a language barrier.* [C14: < OF *barriere*, < *barre* BAR[1]]

barrier cream *n.* a cream used to protect the skin, esp. the hands.

barrier reef *n.* a long narrow coral reef near the shore, separated from it by deep water.

barring (ˈbɑːrɪŋ) *prep.* unless (something) occurs; except for.

barrister (ˈbærɪstə) *n.* **1.** Also called: **barrister-at-law.** (in England) a lawyer who has been called to the bar and is qualified to plead in the higher courts. Cf. **solicitor. 2.** (in Canada) a lawyer who pleads in court **3.** *U.S.* a less common word for **lawyer.** [C16: < BAR[1]]

barrow[1] (ˈbærəʊ) *n.* **1.** See **wheelbarrow, handbarrow. 2.** Also called: **barrowful.** the amount contained in or on a barrow. **3.** *Chiefly Brit.* a handcart with a canvas roof, used esp. by street vendors. [OE *bearwe*]

barrow[2] (ˈbærəʊ) *n.* a heap of earth placed over one or more prehistoric tombs, often surrounded by ditches. [OE *beorg*]

barrow boy *n. Brit.* a man who sells his wares from a barrow; street vendor.

bar sinister *n.* **1.** (not in heraldic usage) another name for **bend sinister. 2.** the condition or stigma of being of illegitimate birth.

Bart. *abbrev. for* Baronet.

bartender (ˈbɑːˌtɛndə) *n.* another name (esp. U.S. and Canad.) for **barman** or **barmaid.**

barter (ˈbɑːtə) *vb.* **1.** to trade (goods, services, etc.) in exchange for other goods, services, etc., rather than for money. **2.** (*intr.*) to haggle over such an exchange; bargain. ~*n.* **3.** trade by the exchange of goods. [C15: < OF *barater* to cheat]

bartizan (ˈbɑːtɪzən, ˌbɑːtɪˈzæn) *n.* a small turret projecting from a wall, parapet, or tower. [C19: var. of *bertisene*, erroneously for *bretising*, < *bretasce* parapet; see BRATTICE] —**bartizaned** (ˈbɑːtɪzənd, ˌbɑːtɪˈzænd) *adj.*

baryon (ˈbærɪˌɒn) *n.* any of a class of elementary particles that have a mass greater than or equal to that of the proton. Baryons are either nucleons or hyperons. The **baryon number** is the number of baryons in a system minus the number of antibaryons. [C20: < Gk *barus* heavy + -ON] —ˌ**baryˈonic** *adj.*

baryta (bəˈraɪtə) *n.* another name for barium oxide or barium hydroxide. [C19: NL, < Gk *barutēs* weight, < *barus* heavy]

barytes (bəˈraɪtiːz) *n.* a colourless or white mineral occurring in sedimentary rocks and with sulphide ores: a source of barium. [C18: < Gk *barus* heavy + *-itēs* -ITE[1]]

basal (ˈbeɪsᵊl) *adj.* **1.** at, of, or constituting a base. **2.** of or constituting a basis; fundamental.

basal metabolism *n.* the amount of energy required by an individual in the resting state, for such functions as breathing and blood circulation.

basalt (ˈbæsɔːlt) *n.* **1.** a dark basic igneous rock: the most common volcanic rock. **2.** a form of black unglazed pottery resembling basalt. [C18: < LL *basaltēs*, var. of *basanītēs*, < Gk *basanitēs* touchstone] —**baˈsaltic** *adj.*

bascule (ˈbæskjuːl) *n.* **1.** a bridge with a movable section hinged about a horizontal axis and counterbalanced by a weight. **2.** a movable roadway forming part of such a bridge. [C17: < F: seesaw, < *bas* low + *cul* rump]

base[1] (beɪs) *n.* **1.** the bottom or supporting part of anything. **2.** the fundamental principle or part. **3. a.** a centre of operations, organization, or supply. **b.** (*as modifier*): *base camp.* **4.** starting point: *the new discovery became the base for further research.* **5.** the main ingredient of a mixture: *to use rice as a base in cookery.* **6.** a chemical compound that combines with an acid to form a salt and water. A solution of a base in water turns litmus paper blue and produces hydroxyl ions. **7.** a medium such as oil or water in which the pigment is dispersed in paints, inks, etc. **8.** *Biol.* the point of attachment of an organ or part. **9.** the bottommost layer or part of anything. **10.** *Archit.* the part of a column between the pedestal and the shaft. **11.** the lower side or face of a geometric construction. **12.** *Maths.* the number of units in a counting system that is equivalent to one in the next higher counting place: *10 is the base of the decimal system.* **13.** *Maths.* the number that when raised to a certain power has a logarithm (based on that number) equal to that power: *the logarithm to the base 10 of 1000 is 3.* **14.** *Linguistics.* a root or stem. **15.** *Electronics.* the region in a transistor between the emitter and collector. **16.** a starting or finishing point in any of various games. ~*vb.* **17.** (*tr.*; foll. by *on* or *upon*) to use as a basis (for); found (on). **18.** (often foll. by *at* or *in*) to station, post, or place (a person or oneself). [C14: < OF, < L *basis* pedestal; see BASIS]

base[2] (beɪs) *adj.* **1.** devoid of honour or morality; contemptible. **2.** of inferior quality or value. **3.** debased; alloyed; counterfeit: *base currency.* **4.** *English history.* (of land tenure) held by villein or other ignoble service. **5.** *Arch.* born of humble parents. **6.** *Arch.* illegitimate. [C14: < OF *bas*, < LL *bassus* of low height] —ˈ**baseness** *n.*

baseball (ˈbeɪsˌbɔːl) *n.* **1.** a team game with nine players on each side, played on a field with four bases connected to form a diamond. The object is to score runs by batting the ball and running round the bases. **2.** the hard rawhide-covered ball used in this game.

baseborn (ˈbeɪsˌbɔːn) *adj. Arch.* **1.** born of humble parents. **2.** illegitimate.

base hospital *n. Austral.* a hospital serving a large rural area.

baseless (ˈbeɪslɪs) *adj.* not based on fact; unfounded. —ˈ**baselessness** *n.*

baseline (ˈbeɪsˌlaɪn) *n.* **1.** *Surveying.* a measured line through a survey area from which triangulations are made. **2.** a line at each end of a tennis court that marks the limit of play.

basement (ˈbeɪsmənt) *n.* **1. a.** a partly or wholly underground storey of a building, esp. one used for habitation rather than storage. **b.** (*as modifier*): *a basement flat.* **2.** the foundation of a wall or building.

base metal *n.* any of certain common metals, such as copper and lead, as distinct from precious metals.

basenji (bəˈsɛndʒɪ) *n.* a small African breed of dog having an inability to bark. [C20: < Bantu]

base rate *n. Brit.* the rate of interest used by individual commercial banks as a basis for their lending rates.

bases[1] (ˈbeɪsiːz) *n.* the plural of **basis.**

bases[2] (ˈbeɪsɪz) *n.* the plural of **base**[2].

bash (bæʃ) *Inf.* ~*vb.* **1.** (*tr.*) to strike violently or crushingly. **2.** (*tr.; often foll. by in, down, etc.*) to smash, break, etc., with a crashing blow. **3.** (*intr.; foll. by into*) to crash (into); collide (with). **4.** to dent or be dented. ~*n.* **5.** a heavy blow. **6.** a party. **7. have a bash.** *Inf.* to make an attempt. [C17: <?]

bashful (ˈbæʃfʊl) *adj.* **1.** shy or modest; diffident. **2.** indicating or characterized by shyness or modesty. [C16: < *bash*, short for ABASH + -FUL] —ˈ**bashfully** *adv.* —ˈ**bashfulness** *n.*

-bashing *n. and adj. combining form. Inf. or sl.* **a.** indicating a malicious attack on members of a group: *union-bashing.* **b.** indicating various other activities: *Bible-bashing.* —**-basher** *n. combining form.*

basic (ˈbeɪsɪk; *Austral. also* ˈbæsɪk) *adj.* **1.** of, relating to, or forming a base or basis; fundamental. **2.** elementary or simple: *a few basic facts.* **3.** excluding additions or extras: *basic pay.* **4.** *Chem.* of, denoting, or containing a base; alkaline. **5.** *Metallurgy.* of or made by a process in which the furnace or converter is made of a basic material, such as magnesium oxide. **6.** (of such igneous rocks as basalt) containing between 52 and 45 per cent silica. ~*n.* **7.** (*usually pl.*) a fundamental principle, fact, etc. —ˈ**basically** *adv.*

BASIC (ˈbeɪsɪk) *n.* a computer programming language that uses common English terms. [C20: *b(eginner's) a(ll-purpose) s(ymbolic) i(nstruction) c(ode)*]

basic English *n.* a simplified form of English with a vocabulary of approximately 850 common words, intended as an international language.

basic industry *n.* an industry which is highly important in a nation's economy.

basicity (beɪˈsɪsɪtɪ) *n. Chem.* **a.** the state of being a base. **b.** the extent to which a substance is basic.

basic slag *n.* a slag produced in steel-making, containing calcium phosphate.

basic wage *n.* **1.** a person's wage excluding overtime, bonuses, etc. **2.** *Austral.* the statutory minimum wage for any worker.

basidiomycete (bæˌsɪdɪəʊmaɪˈsiːt) *n.* any of a class of fungi, including puffballs and rusts, which produce spores at the tips of slender projecting stalks. [C19: see BASIS, -MYCETE] —**baˌsidiomyˈcetous** *adj.*

basil (ˈbæzᵊl) *n.* a Eurasian plant having spikes of small white flowers and aromatic leaves used as herbs for seasoning. Also called: **sweet basil.** [C15: < OF *basile*, < LL, < Gk *basilikos* royal]

basilar (ˈbæsɪlə) *adj. Chiefly anat.* of or at a base. Also: **basilary** (ˈbæsɪlərɪ, -sɪlrɪ). [C16: < NL *basilaris*]

basilica (bəˈzɪlɪkə) *n.* **1.** a Roman building, used for public administration, having a large rectangular central nave with an aisle on each side and an apse at the end. **2.** a Christian church of similar design. **3.** a Roman Catholic church having special ceremonial rights. [C16: < L, < Gk, < *basilikē oikia* the king's house] —**baˈsilican** *or* **baˈsilic** *adj.*

basilisk (ˈbæzɪˌlɪsk) *n.* **1.** (in classical legend) a serpent that could kill by its breath or glance. **2.** a small semiaquatic lizard of tropical America. The males have an inflatable head crest, used in display. [C14: < L *basiliscus*, < Gk *basiliskos* royal child]

basin (ˈbeɪsᵊn) *n.* **1.** a round container open and wide at the top with sides sloping inwards towards the bottom. **2.** Also called: **basinful.** the amount a basin will hold. **3.** a washbasin or sink. **4.** any partially enclosed or sheltered area where vessels may be moored. **5.** the catchment area of a particular river and its tributaries. **6.** a depression in the earth's surface. **7.** *Geol.* a part of the earth's surface consisting of rock strata that slope down to a common centre. [C13: < OF *bacin*, < LL *bacchīnon*]

basis (ˈbeɪsɪs) *n., pl.* **-ses** (-siːz). **1.** something that underlies, supports, or is essential to something else, esp. an idea. **2.** a principle on which something depends or from which something has issued. [C14: via L < Gk: step]

▷ **Usage.** The phrase *on the basis of* is inappropriate in contexts where *because of* can be used: *he agreed to come because of your promise to protect him*, not *he agreed to come on the basis of your promise to protect him. On the basis of* is correctly used of a criterion of choice: *the players were chosen on the basis of their weight.*

bask (bɑːsk) *vb.* (*intr.; usually foll. by in*) **1.** to lie in or be exposed to pleasant warmth, esp. that of the sun. **2.** to flourish or feel secure under some benevolent influence or favourable condition. [C14: < ON *bathask* to BATHE]

basket (ˈbɑːskɪt) *n.* **1.** a container made of interwoven strips of pliable materials, such as cane, and often carried by a handle. **2.** Also called: **basketful.** the amount a basket will hold. **3.** something resembling such a container, such as the structure suspended from a balloon. **4.** *Basketball.* **a.** the hoop fixed to the backboard, through which a player must throw the ball to score points. **b.** a point or points scored in this way. **5.** a group of similar or related things: *a basket of currencies.* **6.** *Inf.* a euphemism for **bastard** (senses 2, 3). [C13: prob. < OF *baskot* (unattested), < L *bascauda* wickerwork holder] —ˈ**basketry** *n.*

basketball (ˈbɑːskɪtˌbɔːl) *n.* **1.** a game played by two teams of five men (or six women), usually on an indoor court. Points are scored by throwing the ball through an elevated horizontal hoop. **2.** the ball used in this game.

basket chair *n.* a chair made of wickerwork.

basketry (ˈbɑːskɪtrɪ) *n.* **1.** the art or practice of making baskets. **2.** baskets collectively.

basket weave *n.* a weave of yarns, resembling that of a basket.

basketwork (ˈbɑːskɪtˌwɜːk) *n.* another word for **wickerwork.**

basking shark *n.* a very large plankton-eating shark, often floating at the sea surface.

basophil (ˈbeɪsəfɪl) *or* **basophile** *adj. also* **basophilic** (ˌbeɪsəˈfɪlɪk). **1.** (of cells or cell contents) easily stained by basic dyes. ~*n.* **2.** a basophil cell, esp. a leucocyte. [C19: < Gk; see BASIS, -PHILE]

basque (bæsk) *n.* a type of tight-fitting bodice for women. [< F, < BASQUE]

Basque (bæsk, bɑːsk) *n.* **1.** a member of a people living around the W Pyrenees in France and Spain. **2.** the language of this people, of no known relationship with any other language. ~*adj.* **3.** of or relating to this people or their language. [C19: < F, < L *Vascō* a Basque]

bas-relief (ˌbɑːrɪˈliːf, ˈbæsrɪˌliːf) *n.* sculpture in low relief, in which the forms project slightly from the background. [C17: < F, < It. *basso rilievo* low relief]

bass[1] (beɪs) *n.* **1.** the lowest adult male voice. **2.** a singer with such a voice. **3. the bass.** the lowest part in a piece of harmony. **4.** *Inf.* short for **bass guitar, double bass.** **5. a.** the low-frequency component of an electrical audio signal, esp. in a record player or tape recorder. **b.** the knob controlling this. ~*adj.* **6.** relating to or denoting the bass. [C15 *bas* BASE[1]; modern spelling infl. by BASSO]

bass[2] (bæs) *n.* **1.** any of various sea perches. **2.** a European spiny-finned freshwater fish. **3.** any of various predatory North American freshwater fishes. [C15: < BASE[2], infl. by It. *basso* low]

bass clef (beɪs) *n.* the clef that establishes F a fifth below middle C on the fourth line of the staff.

bass drum (beɪs) *n.* a large drum of low pitch.

basset (ˈbæsɪt) *n.* a smooth-haired breed of hound with short legs and long ears. Also: **basset hound.** [C17: < F, < *basset* short, < *bas* low]

basset horn *n.* an obsolete woodwind instrument. [C19: prob. < G *Bassetthorn*, < It. *bassetto*, dim. of BASSO + HORN]

bass guitar (beɪs) *n.* an electrically amplified guitar that has the same pitch and tuning as a double bass.

bassinet (ˌbæsɪˈnɛt) *n.* a wickerwork or wooden cradle or pram, usually hooded. [C19: < F: little basin; associated in folk etymology with F *barcelonnette* a little cradle]

bassist (ˈbeɪsɪst) *n.* a player of a double bass or bass guitar.

basso (ˈbæsəʊ) *n., pl.* **-sos** *or* **-si** (-sɪ). (esp. in operatic or solo singing) a singer with a bass voice. [C19: < It., < LL *bassus* low; see BASE²]

bassoon (bəˈsuːn) *n.* **1.** a woodwind instrument, the tenor of the oboe family. **2.** an orchestral musician who plays a bassoon. [C18: < F *basson*, < It., < *basso* deep] **—basˈsoonist** *n.*

basso rilievo (*Italian* ˈbasso riˈljɛːvo) *n., pl.* **-vos.** Italian name for **bas-relief.**

bass viol (beɪs) *n.* **1.** another name for **viola da gamba. 2.** *U.S.* a less common name for **double bass** (sense 1).

bast (bæst) *n.* **1.** *Bot.* another name for **phloem. 2.** fibrous material obtained from the phloem of jute, flax, etc., used for making rope, matting, etc. [OE *bæst*]

bastard (ˈbɑːstəd, ˈbæs-) *n.* **1.** a person born of parents not married to each other. **2.** *Inf., offens.* an obnoxious or despicable person. **3.** *Inf.* a person, esp. a man: *lucky bastard.* **4.** *Inf.* something extremely difficult or unpleasant. **5.** something irregular, abnormal, or inferior. **6.** a hybrid, esp. an accidental or inferior one. ~*adj.* (*prenominal*) **7.** illegitimate by birth. **8.** irregular, abnormal, or inferior. **9.** resembling a specified thing, but not actually being such: *a bastard cedar.* **10.** counterfeit; spurious. **11.** hybrid. [C13: < OF *bastart*, ? < *fils de bast* son of the packsaddle] **—ˈbastardy** *n.*

bastardize *or* **-ise** (ˈbɑːstəˌdaɪz, ˈbæs-) *vb.* (*tr.*) **1.** to debase. **2.** to declare illegitimate.

baste¹ (beɪst) *vb.* (*tr.*) to sew with loose temporary stitches. [C14: < OF *bastir* to build, of Gmc origin] **—ˈbasting** *n.*

baste² (beɪst) *vb.* to moisten (meat) during cooking with hot fat and the juices produced. [C15: <?]

baste³ (beɪst) *vb.* (*tr.*) to beat thoroughly; thrash. [C16: prob. < ON *beysta*]

Bastille (bæˈstiːl) *n.* a fortress in Paris: a prison until its destruction in 1789, at the beginning of the French Revolution. [C14: < OF *bastile* fortress, < OProvençal *bastida*, < *bastir* to build]

bastinado (ˌbæstɪˈneɪdəʊ) *n., pl.* **-does. 1.** punishment or torture in which the soles of the feet are beaten with a stick. ~*vb.* **-doing, -doed. 2.** (*tr.*) to beat (a person) thus. [C16: < Sp. *bastonada*, < *baston* stick]

bastion (ˈbæstɪən) *n.* **1.** a projecting part of a fortification, designed to permit fire to the flanks along the face of the wall. **2.** any fortified place. **3.** a thing or person regarded as defending a principle, etc. [C16: < F, < earlier *bastillon* bastion, < *bastille* BASTILLE]

bat¹ (bæt) *n.* **1.** any of various types of club with a handle, used to hit the ball in certain sports, such as cricket. **2.** a flat round club with a short handle used by a man on the ground to guide the pilot of an aircraft when taxiing. **3.** *Cricket.* short for **batsman. 4.** *Inf.* a blow from a stick. **5.** *Sl.* speed; pace: *they went at a fair bat.* **6. carry one's bat.** *Cricket.* (of a batsman) to reach the end of an innings without being dismissed. **7. off one's own bat. a.** of one's own accord. **b.** by one's own unaided efforts. ~*vb.* **batting, batted. 8.** (*tr.*) to strike with or as if with a bat. **9.** (*intr.*) *Cricket, etc.* (of a player or a team) to take a turn at batting. [OE *batt* club, prob. of Celtic origin]

bat² (bæt) *n.* **1.** a nocturnal mouselike animal flying with a pair of membranous wings. **2. blind as a bat.** having extremely poor eyesight. **3. have bats in the** (*or* **one's**) **belfry.** *Inf.* to be mad or eccentric. [C14 *bakke*, prob. of Scand. origin]

bat³ (bæt) *vb.* **batting, batted.** (*tr.*) **1.** to wink or flutter (one's eyelids). **2. not bat an eye** (*or* **eyelid**). *Inf.* to show no surprise or concern. [C17: prob. var. of BATE²]

batch¹ (bætʃ) *n.* **1.** a group or set of usually similar objects or people, esp. if sent off, handled, or arriving at the same time. **2.** the bread, cakes, etc., produced at one baking. **3.** the amount of a material needed for an operation. ~*vb.* **4.** to group (items) for efficient processing. **5.** to handle by batch processing. [C15 *bache*; rel. to OE *bacan* to BAKE]

batch² (bætʃ) *vb.* (*intr.*) *Austral. & N.Z.* to live as a bachelor. Also (N.Z.): **bach.**

batch processing *n.* a system by which the computer programs of a number of individual users are submitted as a single batch.

bate¹ (beɪt) *vb.* **1.** another word for **abate. 2. with bated breath.** in suspense or fear.

bate² (beɪt) *vb.* (*intr.*) (of a hawk) to jump violently from a perch or the falconer's fist, often hanging from the leash while struggling to escape. [C13: < OF *batre* to beat]

bate³ (beɪt) *n. Brit. Sl.* a bad temper or rage. [C19: < BAIT¹, alluding to the mood of a person who is being baited]

bateau (bæˈtəʊ) *n., pl.* **-teaux** (-ˈtəʊz). a light flat-bottomed boat used on rivers in Canada and the northern U.S. [C18: < F: boat]

bateleur eagle (ˈbætələː) *n.* an African short-tailed bird of prey. [C19: < F *bateleur* juggler]

bath (bɑːθ) *n., pl.* **baths** (bɑːðz). **1.** a large container used for washing the body. **2.** the act or an instance of washing in such a container. **3.** the amount of liquid contained in a bath. **4.** (*usually pl.*) a place having baths or a swimming pool for public use. **5. a.** a vessel in which something is immersed to maintain it at a constant temperature, to process it photographically, etc., or to lubricate it. **b.** the liquid used in such a vessel. ~*vb.* **6.** *Brit.* to wash in a bath. [OE *bæth*]

Bath bun (bɑːθ) *n. Brit.* a sweet bun containing spices and dried fruit. [C19: < *Bath*, city in England where orig. made]

Bath chair *n.* a wheelchair for invalids.

bath cube *n.* a cube of soluble scented material for use in a bath.

bathe (beɪð) *vb.* **1.** (*intr.*) to swim in a body of open water, esp. for pleasure. **2.** (*tr.*) to apply liquid to (skin, a wound, etc.) in order to cleanse or soothe. **3.** to immerse or be immersed in a liquid. **4.** *Chiefly U.S. & Canad.* to wash in a bath. **5.** (*tr.; often passive*) to suffuse. ~*n.* **6.** *Brit.* a swim in a body of open water. [OE *bathian*] **—ˈbather** *n.*

bathers (ˈbeɪðəz) *pl. n. Austral.* a swimming costume.

bathhouse (ˈbɑːθˌhaʊs) *n.* a building containing baths, esp. for public use.

bathing cap (ˈbeɪðɪŋ) *n.* a tight rubber cap worn by a swimmer to keep the hair dry.

bathing costume (ˈbeɪðɪŋ) *n.* another name for **swimming costume.**

bathing machine (ˈbeɪðɪŋ) *n.* a small hut, on wheels so that it could be pulled to the sea, used in the 18th and 19th centuries for bathers to change their clothes.

bathing suit (ˈbeɪðɪŋ) *n.* a garment worn for bathing, esp. an old-fashioned one that covers much of the body.

batho- *combining form.* a variant of **bathy-.**

batholith (ˌbæθəlɪθ) *or* **batholite** (ˈbæθəˌlaɪt) *n.* a very large irregular-shaped mass of igneous rock, esp. granite, formed from an intrusion of magma at great depth, esp. one exposed after erosion of less resistant overlying rocks. **—ˌbathoˈlithic** *or* **batholitic** (ˌbæθəˈlɪtɪk) *adj.*

Bath Oliver (ˈɒlɪvə) *n. Brit.* a kind of unsweetened biscuit [C19: after William *Oliver* (1695–1764), a physician at Bath]

bathometer (bəˈθɒmɪtə) *n.* an instrument for measuring the depth of water. **—bathometric** (ˌbæθəˈmɛtrɪk) *adj.* **—baˈthometry** *n.*

bathos (ˈbeɪθɒs) *n.* **1.** a sudden ludicrous descent from exalted to ordinary matters or style in speech or writing. **2.** insincere or excessive pathos. [C18: < Gk: depth] **—baˈthetic** *adj.*

bathrobe (ˈbɑːθˌrəʊb) *n.* **1.** a loose-fitting garment of towelling, for wear before or after a bath or swimming. **2.** *U.S. & Canad.* a dressing gown.

bathroom (ˈbɑːθˌruːm, -ˌrʊm) *n.* **1.** a room containing a bath or shower and usually a washbasin and lavatory. **2.** *U.S. & Canad.* another name for **lavatory.**

bath salts *pl. n.* soluble scented salts for use in a bath.

bathtub (ˈbɑːθˌtʌb) *n.* a bath, esp. one not permanently fixed.

bathy- *or* **batho-** *combining form.* indicating depth: *bathysphere.* [< Gk *bathus* deep]

bathyscaph(ˈbæθɪˌskæf), **bathyscaphe** (ˈbæθɪˌskeɪf, -ˌskæf), *or* **bathyscape** *n.* a submersible vessel with an observation capsule underneath, capable of reaching ocean depths of over 10 000 metres. [C20: < BATHY- + Gk *skaphē* light boat]

bathysphere (ˈbæθɪˌsfɪə) *n.* a strong steel deep-sea diving sphere, lowered by cable.

batik (ˈbætɪk) *n.* **a.** a process of printing fabric in which parts not to be dyed are covered by wax. **b.** fabric printed in this way. [C19: via Malay < Javanese: painted]

batiste (bæˈtiːst) *n.* a fine plain-weave cotton. [C17: < F, prob. after *Baptiste* of Cambrai, 13th-cent. F weaver, its reputed inventor]

batman (ˈbætmən) *n., pl.* **-men.** an officer's servant in the armed forces. [C18: < OF *bat, bast,* < Med. L *bastum* packsaddle]

baton (ˈbætən) *n.* **1.** a thin stick used by the conductor of an orchestra, choir, etc. **2.** *Athletics.* a short bar carried by a competitor in a relay race and transferred to the next runner at the end of each stage. **3.** a long stick with a knob on one end, carried, twirled, and thrown up and down by a drum major or majorette, esp. at the head of a parade. **4.** a police truncheon (esp. in **baton charge**). **5.** a staff or club carried as a symbol of authority. [C16: < F *bâton,* < LL *bastum* rod]

baton round *n.* the official name for **plastic bullet.**

batrachian (bəˈtreɪkɪən) *n.* **1.** any amphibian, esp. a frog or toad. *~adj.* **2.** of or relating to the frogs and toads. [C19: < NL *Batrachia,* < Gk *batrakhos* frog]

bats (bæts) *adj. Inf.* mad or eccentric.

batsman (ˈbætsmən) *n., pl.* **-men. 1.** *Cricket, etc.* **a.** a person who bats or whose turn it is to bat. **b.** a player who specializes in batting. **2.** a person on the ground who uses bats to guide the pilot of an aircraft when taxiing. —ˈ**batsmanˌship** *n.*

battalion (bəˈtæljən) *n.* **1.** a military unit comprised of three or more companies or formations of similar size. **2.** (*usually pl.*) any large array. [C16: < F *bataillon,* < OIt., < *battaglia* company of soldiers, BATTLE]

batten[1] (ˈbætᵊn) *n.* **1.** a sawn strip of wood used in building to cover joints, support lathing, etc. **2.** a long narrow board used for flooring. **3.** a lath used for holding a tarpaulin along the side of a hatch on a ship. **4.** *Theatre.* **a.** a row of lights. **b.** the bar supporting them. *~vb.* **5.** (*tr.*) to furnish or strengthen with battens. **6. batten down the hatches. a.** to use battens in securing a tarpaulin over a hatch on a ship. **b.** to prepare for action, a crisis, etc. [C15: < F *bâton* stick; see BATON]

batten[2] (ˈbætᵊn) *vb.* (*intr.*) (usually foll. by *on*) to thrive, esp. at the expense of someone else. [C16: prob. < ON *batna* to improve]

batter[1] (ˈbætə) *vb.* **1.** to hit (someone or something) repeatedly using heavy blows, as with a club. **2.** (*tr.; often passive*) to damage or injure, as by blows, heavy wear, etc. **3.** (*tr.*) to subject (a person, esp. a close relative) to repeated physical violence. [C14 *bateren,* prob. < *batten* to BAT[1]] —ˈ**batterer** *n.* —ˈ**battering** *n.*

batter[2] (ˈbætə) *n.* a mixture of flour, eggs, and milk, used to make cakes, pancakes, etc., and to coat certain foods before frying. [C15 *bater,* prob. < *bateren* to BATTER[1]]

batter[3] (ˈbætə) *n. Baseball, etc.* a player who bats.

batter[4] (ˈbætə) *n.* **1.** the slope of the face of a wall that recedes gradually backwards and upwards. *~vb.* **2.** (*intr.*) to have such a slope. [C16 (vb.: to incline): <?]

battering ram *n.* (esp. formerly) a large beam used to break down fortifications.

battery (ˈbætərɪ) *n., pl.* **-teries. 1.** two or more primary cells connected, usually in series, to provide a source of electric current. **2.** another name for **accumulator** (sense 1). **3.** a number of similar things occurring together: *a battery of questions.* **4.** *Criminal law.* unlawful beating or wounding of a person or mere touching in a hostile or offensive manner. **5.** a fortified structure on which artillery is mounted. **6.** a group of guns, missile launchers, etc., operated as a single entity. **7.** a small unit of artillery. **8.** *Chiefly Brit.* **a.** a large group of cages for intensive rearing of poultry and other farm animals. **b.** (*as modifier*): *battery hens.* **9.** *Baseball.* the pitcher and the catcher considered together. [C16: < OF *batterie* beating, < *battre* to beat, < L *battuere*]

batting (ˈbætɪŋ) *n.* **1.** cotton or woollen wadding used in quilts, etc. **2.** the action of a person or team that hits with a bat.

battle (ˈbætᵊl) *n.* **1.** a fight between large armed forces; military or naval engagement. **2.** conflict; struggle. **3. do, give,** *or* **join battle.** to engage in conflict or competition. *~vb.* **4.** (*intr.;* often foll. by *against, for,* or *with*) to fight in or as if in military combat. **5.** to struggle: *he battled through the crowd.* **6.** (*intr.*) *Austral.* to scrape a living. [C13: < OF *bataile,* < LL *battālia* exercises performed by soldiers, < *battuere* to beat] —ˈ**battler** *n.*

battle-axe *n.* **1.** (formerly) a large broad-headed axe. **2.** *Inf.* an argumentative domineering woman.

battle cruiser *n.* a high-speed warship of battleship size but with lighter armour.

battle cry *n.* **1.** a shout uttered by soldiers going into battle. **2.** a slogan used to rally the supporters of a campaign, movement, etc.

battledore (ˈbætᵊlˌdɔː) *n.* **1.** Also called: **battledore and shuttlecock.** an ancient racket game. **2.** a light racket used in this game. **3.** (formerly) a wooden utensil used for beating clothes, in baking, etc. [C15 *batyldoure,* ? < OProvençal *batedor* beater, < OF *battre* to beat]

battledress (ˈbætᵊlˌdrɛs) *n.* the ordinary uniform of a soldier.

battle fatigue *n. Psychol.* mental disorder, characterized by anxiety and depression, caused by the stress of warfare. Also: **combat fatigue.**

battlefield (ˈbætᵊlˌfiːld) *or* **battleground** *n.* the place where a battle is fought.

battlement (ˈbætᵊlmənt) *n.* a parapet or wall with indentations or embrasures, originally for shooting through. [C14: < OF *batailles,* pl. of *bataille* BATTLE] —ˈ**battlemented** *adj.*

battle royal *n.* **1.** a fight, esp. with fists or cudgels, involving more than two combatants; melee. **2.** a long violent argument.

battleship (ˈbætᵊlˌʃɪp) *n.* a heavily armoured warship of the largest type.

batty (ˈbætɪ) *adj.* **-tier, -tiest.** *Sl.* **1.** insane; crazy. **2.** odd; eccentric. [C20: < BAT[2]]

batwoman (ˈbætwʊmən) *n., pl.* **-women.** a female servant in any of the armed forces.

bauble (ˈbɔːbᵊl) *n.* **1.** a trinket of little value. **2.** (formerly) a mock staff of office carried by a jester. [C14: < OF *baubel* plaything, <?]

baud (bɔːd) *n.* a unit used to measure the speed of electronic code transmissions. [after J. M. E. *Baudot* (1845-1903), F inventor]

bauera (ˈbaʊərə) *n.* a small evergreen Australian shrub with pink or purple flowers. [C19: after Franz & Ferdinand *Bauer,* 19th-cent. Austrian botanical artists]

Bauhaus (ˈbaʊˌhaʊs) *n.* a German school of architecture and applied arts founded in 1919 on experimental principles of functionalism and truth to materials. [G, lit.: building house]

bauhinia (bɔːˈhɪnɪə, bəʊ-) *n.* a climbing leguminous plant of tropical and warm regions, cultivated for ornament. [C18: NL, after Jean & Gaspard *Bauhin,* 16th-cent. F herbalists]

baulk (bɔːk; *usually for sense 1* bɔːlk) *n.* **1.** Also: **balk.** *Billiards.* the space between the baulk line and the bottom cushion. **2.** *Archaeol.* a strip of earth left between excavation trenches for the study of the complete stratigraphy of a site. *~vb., n.* **3.** a variant spelling of **balk.**

baulk line *or* **balk line** *n. Billiards.* a straight line across a billiard table behind which the cue balls are placed at the start of a game. Also: **string line.**

baulky (ˈbɔːkɪ, ˈbɔːlkɪ) *adj.* a variant of **balky.**

bauxite (ˈbɔːksaɪt) *n.* an amorphous claylike substance consisting of hydrated alumina with iron and other impurities: the chief source of alumina and aluminium and also used as an abrasive and catalyst. [C19: < F, < (*Les*) *Baux* in southern France, where orig. found]

bawd (bɔːd) *n. Arch.* **1.** a person who runs a brothel, esp. a woman. **2.** a prostitute. [C14: < OF *baude*, fem. of *baud* merry]

bawdy (ˈbɔːdɪ) *adj.* **bawdier, bawdiest. 1.** (of language, plays, etc.) containing references to sex, esp. to be humorous. ~*n.* **2.** obscenity or eroticism, esp. in writing or drama. —**ˈbawdily** *adv.* —**ˈbawdiness** *n.* —**bawdry** (ˈbɑːdrɪ) *n.*

bawdyhouse (ˈbɔːdɪˌhaʊs) *n.* an archaic word for **brothel.**

bawl (bɔːl) *vb.* **1.** (*intr.*) to utter long loud cries, as from pain or frustration; wail. **2.** to shout loudly, as in anger. ~*n.* **3.** a loud shout or cry. [C15: imit.] —**ˈbawler** *n.* —**ˈbawling** *n.*

bawl out *vb.* (*tr., adv.*) *Inf.* to scold loudly.

bay[1] (beɪ) *n.* **1.** a wide semicircular indentation of a shoreline, esp. between two headlands. **2.** an extension of lowland into hills that partly surround it. [C14: < OF *baie*, ? < OF *baer* to gape, < Med. L *batāre* to yawn]

bay[2] (beɪ) *n.* **1.** an alcove or recess in a wall. **2.** any partly enclosed compartment. **3.** See **bay window. 4.** an area off a road in which vehicles may park or unload. **5.** a compartment in an aircraft: *the bomb bay.* **6.** *Naut.* a compartment in the forward part of a ship between decks, often used as the ship's hospital. **7.** *Brit.* a tracked recess in the platform of a railway station, esp. one forming the terminus of a branch line. [C14: < OF *baee* gap, < *baer* to gape; see BAY[1]]

bay[3] (beɪ) *n.* **1.** a deep howl, esp. of a hound on the scent. **2. at bay. a.** forced to turn and face attackers: *the dogs held the deer at bay.* **b.** at a distance. **3. bring to bay.** to force into a position from which retreat is impossible. ~*vb.* **4.** (*intr.*) to howl (at) in deep prolonged tones. **5.** (*tr.*) to utter in a loud prolonged tone. **6.** (*tr.*) to hold at bay. [C13: < OF, imit.]

bay[4] (beɪ) *n.* **1.** a Mediterranean laurel. See **laurel** (sense 1). **2.** any of certain other trees or shrubs, esp. bayberry. **3.** (*pl.*) a wreath of bay leaves. [C14: < OF *baie* laurel berry, < L *bāca* berry]

bay[5] (beɪ) *n., adj.* **1.** (of) a reddish-brown colour. ~*n.* **2.** an animal of this colour. [C14: < OF *bai*, < L *badius*]

bayberry (ˈbeɪbərɪ) *or* **bay** *n., pl.* **-ries. 1.** any of several North American aromatic shrubs or small trees that bear grey waxy berries. **2.** a tropical American tree that yields an oil used in making bay rum. **3.** the fruit of any of these plants.

bay leaf *n.* a leaf, usually dried, of the Mediterranean laurel, used in cooking to flavour soups and stews.

bayonet (ˈbeɪənɪt) *n.* **1.** a blade for stabbing that can be attached to the muzzle of a firearm. **2.** a type of fastening in which a cylindrical member is inserted into a socket against spring pressure and turned so that pins on its side engage in slots in the socket. ~*vb.* **-neting, -neted** *or* **-netting, -netted. 3.** (*tr.*) to stab or kill with a bayonet. [C17: < F *baïonnette*, < *Bayonne*, a port in SW France, where it originated]

bayou (ˈbaɪjuː) *n.* (in the southern U.S.) a sluggish marshy tributary of a lake or river. [C18: < Louisiana F, < Amerind *bayuk*]

bay rum *n.* an aromatic liquid, used in medicines and cosmetics, originally obtained by distilling the leaves of the bayberry tree with rum: now also synthesized.

bay window *n.* a window projecting from a wall and forming an alcove of a room.

bazaar *or* **bazar** (bəˈzɑː) *n.* **1.** (esp. in the Orient) a market area, esp. a street of small stalls. **2.** a sale in aid of charity, esp. of second-hand or handmade articles. **3.** a shop where a variety of goods is sold. [C16: < Persian *bāzār*]

bazooka (bəˈzuːkə) *n.* a portable tubular rocket-launcher, used by infantrymen as a short-range antitank weapon. [C20: after a comic pipe instrument]

BB *abbrev. for:* **1.** Boys' Brigade. **2.** (on British pencils, signifying degrees of softness of lead) double black.

BBC *abbrev. for* British Broadcasting Corporation.

bbl. *abbrev. for* barrel (container or measure).

BC *abbrev. for* British Columbia.

B.C. *or* **BC** *abbrev. for* (indicating years numbered back from the supposed year of the birth of Christ) before Christ.

▷ **Usage.** See at **A.D.**

BCal (ˈbiːˌkæl) *n. acronym for* British Caledonian (Airways).

BCE *abbrev. for:* **1.** Before Common Era (used, esp. by non-Christians, in numbering years B.C.). **2.** *Brit.* Board of Customs and Excise.

BCG *abbrev. for* Bacillus Calmette-Guérin (antituberculosis vaccine).

BCNZ *abbrev. for* Broadcasting Corporation of New Zealand.

BD *abbrev. for* Bachelor of Divinity.

bdellium (ˈdɛlɪəm) *n.* **1.** any of several African or W Asian trees that yield a gum resin. **2.** the aromatic gum resin produced by any of these trees. [C16: < L, < Gk *bdellion*,? < Heb. *bĕdhōlah*]

BDS *abbrev. for* Bachelor of Dental Surgery.

be (biː; *unstressed* bɪ) *vb. present sing. 1st person* **am;** *2nd person* **are;** *3rd person* **is.** *present pl.* **are.** *past sing. 1st person* **was;** *2nd person* **were;** *3rd person* **was.** *past pl.* **were.** *present participle* **being.** *past participle* **been.** (*intr.*) **1.** to have presence in perceived reality; exist; live: *I think, therefore I am.* **2.** (*used in the perfect tenses only*) to pay a visit; go: *have you been to Spain?* **3.** to take place: *my birthday was last Thursday.* **4.** (*copula*) used as a linking verb between the subject of a sentence and its noun or adjective complement. *Be* has no intrinsic meaning of its own but rather expresses relationship of equivalence or identity (*John is a man; John is a musician*) or specifies an attribute (*honey is sweet; Susan is angry*). It is also used with an adverbial complement to indicate a relationship in space or time (*Bill is at the office; the dance is on Saturday*). **5.** (*takes a present participle*) forms the progressive present tense: *the man is running.* **6.** (*takes a past participle*) forms the passive voice of all transitive verbs: *a good film is being shown on television tonight.* **7.** (*takes an infinitive*) expresses intention, expectation, or obligation: *the president is to arrive at 9.30.* [OE *bēon*]

Be *the chemical symbol for* beryllium.

BE *abbrev. for:* **1.** bill of exchange. **2.** Bachelor of Education. **3.** Bachelor of Engineering.

be- *prefix forming transitive verbs.* **1.** (*from nouns*) to surround or cover: *befog.* **2.** (*from nouns*) to affect completely: *bedazzle.* **3.** (*from nouns*) to consider as or cause to be: *befriend.* **4.** (*from nouns*) to provide or cover with: *bejewel.* **5.** (*from verbs*) at, for, against, on, or over: *bewail; berate.* [OE *be-*, *bi-*, unstressed var. of *bī* BY]

beach (biːtʃ) *n.* **1.** an area of sand or shingle sloping down to a sea or lake, esp. the area between the high- and low-water marks on a seacoast. ~*vb.* **2.** to run or haul (a boat) onto a beach. [C16: perhaps rel. to OE *bæce* river]

beachcomber (ˈbiːtʃˌkəʊmə) *n.* **1.** a person who searches shore debris for anything of worth. **2.** a long high wave rolling onto a beach.

beachhead (ˈbiːtʃˌhɛd) *n. Mil.* an area on a beach that has been captured from the enemy and on which troops and equipment are landed.

beacon (ˈbiːkən) *n.* **1.** a signal fire or light on a hill, tower, etc., esp. formerly as a warning of invasion. **2.** a hill on which such fires were lit. **3.**

a lighthouse, signalling buoy, etc. **4.** short for **radio beacon. 5.** a radio or other signal marking a flight course in air navigation. **6.** short for **Belisha beacon. 7.** a person or thing that serves as a guide, inspiration, or warning. [OE *beacen* sign]

bead (biːd) *n.* **1.** a small pierced usually spherical piece of glass, wood, plastic, etc., which may be strung with others to form a necklace, etc. **2. tell one's beads.** to pray with a rosary. **3.** a small drop of moisture. **4.** a small bubble in or on a liquid. **5.** a small metallic knob acting as the sight of a firearm. **6. to draw** *or* **hold a bead on.** to aim a rifle or pistol at. **7.** *Archit., furniture.* a small convex moulding having a semicircular cross section. ~*vb.* **8.** (*tr.*) to decorate with beads. **9.** to form into beads or drops. [OE *bed* prayer] —ˈ**beaded** *adj.*

beading (ˈbiːdɪŋ) *n.* **1.** another name for **bead** (sense 7). **2.** Also called: **beadwork** (ˈbiːdˌwɜːk). a narrow strip of some material used for edging or ornamentation.

beadle (ˈbiːdᵊl) *n.* **1.** *Brit.* (formerly) a minor parish official who acted as an usher and kept order. **2.** *Judaism.* a synagogue attendant. **3.** *Scot.* a church official who attends the minister. **4.** an official in certain British institutions. [OE *bydel*] —ˈ**beadleship** *n.*

beadsman *or* **bedesman** (ˈbiːdzmən) *n., pl.* **-men.** *Arch.* **1.** a person who prays for another's soul, esp. one paid or fed for doing so. **2.** a person kept in an almshouse.

beady (ˈbiːdɪ) *adj.* **beadier, beadiest. 1.** small, round, and glittering (esp. in **beady eyes**). **2.** resembling or covered with beads. —ˈ**beadiness** *n.*

beagle (ˈbiːgᵊl) *n.* **1.** a small sturdy breed of hound. **2.** *Arch.* a spy. ~*vb.* **3.** (*intr.*) to hunt with beagles. [C15: <?]

beak[1] (biːk) *n.* **1.** the projecting jaws of a bird, covered with a horny sheath. **2.** any beaklike mouthpart in other animals. **3.** *Sl.* a person's nose. **4.** any projecting part, such as the pouring lip of a bucket. **5.** *Naut.* another word for **ram** (sense 5). [C13: < OF *bec*, < L *beccus*, of Gaulish origin] —**beaked** *adj.* —ˈ**beaky** *adj.*

beak[2] (biːk) *n.* a Brit. slang word for **judge, magistrate, headmaster,** or **schoolmaster.** [C19: orig. thieves' jargon]

beaker (ˈbiːkə) *n.* **1.** a cup usually having a wide mouth. **2.** a cylindrical flat-bottomed container used in laboratories, usually made of glass and having a pouring lip. [C14: < ON *bikarr*]

Beaker folk (ˈbiːkə) *n.* a prehistoric people inhabiting Europe and Britain during the second millennium B.C. [after beakers found among their remains]

be-all and end-all *n. Inf.* the ultimate aim or justification.

beam (biːm) *n.* **1.** a long thick piece of wood, metal, etc., esp. one used as a horizontal structural member. **2.** the breadth of a ship or boat taken at its widest part. **3.** a ray or column of light, as from a beacon. **4.** a broad smile. **5.** one of two cylindrical rollers on a loom, which hold the warp threads and the finished work. **6.** the main stem of a deer's antler. **7.** the central shaft of a plough to which all the main parts are attached. **8.** a narrow unidirectional flow of electromagnetic radiation or particles: *an electron beam.* **9.** the horizontal centrally pivoted bar in a balance. **10. beam in one's eye.** a fault or grave error greater in oneself than in another person. **11. broad in the beam.** *Inf.* having wide hips. **12. off (the) beam. a.** not following a radio beam to maintain a course. **b.** *Inf.* mistaken or irrelevant. **13. on the beam. a.** following a radio beam to maintain a course. **b.** *Inf.* correct, relevant, or appropriate. ~*vb.* **14.** to send out or radiate. **15.** (*tr.*) to divert or aim (a radio signal, light, etc.) in a certain direction: *to beam a programme to Tokyo.* **16.** (*intr.*) to smile broadly. [OE] —ˈ**beaming** *adj.*

beam-ends *pl. n.* **1. on her beam-ends.** (of a vessel) heeled over through an angle of 90°. **2. on one's beam-ends.** out of resources; destitute.

bean (biːn) *n.* **1.** any of various leguminous plants producing edible seeds in pods. **2.** any of various other plants whose seeds are produced in pods or podlike fruits. **3.** the seed or pod of any of these plants. **4.** any of various beanlike seeds, as coffee. **5.** *U.S. & Canad. sl.* another word for **head. 6. full of beans.** *Inf.* full of energy and vitality. **7. not have a bean.** *Sl.* to be without money. [OE *bēan*]

beanbag (ˈbiːnˌbæg) *n.* **1.** a small cloth bag filled with dried beans and thrown in games. **2.** a very large cushion filled with foam rubber or polystyrene granules and used as a seat.

beanfeast (ˈbiːnˌfiːst) *n. Brit. inf.* **1.** an annual dinner given by employers to employees. **2.** any festive or merry occasion.

beano (ˈbiːnəʊ) *n., pl.* **beanos.** *Brit. sl.* a celebration, party, or other enjoyable time.

beanpole (ˈbiːnˌpəʊl) *n.* **1.** a tall stick used to support bean plants. **2.** *Sl.* a tall thin person.

bean sprout *n.* the sprout of a newly germinated mung bean, eaten esp. in Chinese dishes.

beanstalk (ˈbiːnˌstɔːk) *n.* the stem of a bean plant.

bear[1] (bɛə) *vb.* **bearing, bore, borne.** (*mainly tr.*) **1.** to support or hold up. **2.** to bring: *to bear gifts.* **3.** to accept or assume the responsibility of: *to bear an expense.* **4.** (**born** in passive use except when followed by *by*) to give birth to: *to bear children.* **5.** (*also intr.*) to produce as by natural growth: *to bear fruit.* **6.** to tolerate or endure. **7.** to admit of; sustain: *his story does not bear scrutiny.* **8.** to hold in the mind: *to bear a grudge.* **9.** to show or be marked with: *he still bears the scars.* **10.** to render or supply (esp. in **bear witness**). **11.** to conduct (oneself, the body, etc.). **12.** to have, be, or stand in (relation or comparison): *his account bears no relation to the facts.* **13.** (*intr.*) to move or lie in a specified direction. **14. bear a hand.** to give assistance. **15. bring to bear.** to bring into operation or effect. ~See also **bear down, bear on,** etc. [OE *beran*]

bear[2] (bɛə) *n., pl.* **bears** *or* **bear. 1.** a plantigrade mammal typically having a large head, a long shaggy coat, and strong claws. **2.** any of various bearlike animals, such as the koala. **3.** a clumsy, churlish, or ill-mannered person. **4.** a teddy bear. **5.** *Stock Exchange.* **a.** a speculator who sells in anticipation of falling prices to make a profit on repurchase. **b.** (*as modifier*): *a bear market.* Cf. **bull**[1] (sense 4). ~*vb.* **bearing, beared. 6.** (*tr.*) to lower or attempt to lower the price or prices of (a stock market or a security) by speculative selling. [OE *bera*]

Bear (bɛə) *n.* **the. 1.** the English name for either Ursa Major (Great Bear) or Ursa Minor (Little Bear). **2.** an informal name for Russia.

bearable (ˈbɛərəbᵊl) *adj.* endurable; tolerable.

bear-baiting *n.* (formerly) an entertainment in which dogs attacked a chained bear.

beard (bɪəd) *n.* **1.** the hair growing on the lower parts of a man's face. **2.** any similar growth in animals. **3.** a tuft of long hairs in plants such as barley; awn. **4.** a barb, as on a fish-hook. ~*vb.* (*tr.*) **5.** to oppose boldly or impertinently. [OE *beard*] —ˈ**bearded** *adj.*

beardless (ˈbɪədlɪs) *adj.* **1.** without a beard. **2.** too young to grow a beard; immature.

bear down *vb.* (*intr., adv.;* often foll. by *on* or *upon*) **1.** to press or weigh down. **2.** to approach in a determined or threatening manner.

bearer (ˈbɛərə) *n.* **1.** a person or thing that bears, presents, or upholds. **2.** a person who presents a note or bill for payment. **3.** (in Africa, India, etc., formerly) a native porter or servant. **4.** (*modifier*) *Finance.* payable to the person in possession: *bearer bonds.*

bear garden *n.* **1.** (formerly) a place where bear-baiting took place. **2.** a scene of tumult.

bear hug *n.* **1.** a wrestling hold in which the arms are locked tightly round an opponent's chest and arms. **2.** any similar tight embrace.

bearing (ˈbɛərɪŋ) *n.* **1.** a support for a rotating or reciprocating mechanical part. **2.** (foll. by *on* or *upon*) relevance (to): *it has no bearing on this* *problem.* **3.** a person's general social conduct. **4.** the act, period, or capability of producing fruit or young. **5.** anything that carries weight or acts as a support. **6.** the angular direction of a point or course measured from a known position. **7.** (*usually pl.*) the position, as of a ship, fixed with reference to two or more known points. **8.** (*usually pl.*) a sense of one's relative position; orientation (esp. in **lose, get,** *or* **take one's bearings**). **9.** *Heraldry.* **a.** a device on a heraldic shield. **b.** another name for **coat of arms.**

bearing rein *n. Chiefly Brit.* a rein from the bit to the saddle, designed to keep the horse's head in the desired position.

bearish (ˈbɛərɪʃ) *adj.* **1.** like a bear; rough; clumsy; churlish. **2.** *Stock Exchange.* causing, expecting, or characterized by a fall in prices: *a bearish market.* —ˈ**bearishness** *n.*

bear on *vb.* (*intr., prep.*) **1.** to be relevant to; relate to. **2.** to be burdensome to or afflict.

bear out *vb.* (*tr., adv.*) to show to be true or truthful; confirm: *the witness will bear me out.*

bearskin (ˈbɛəˌskɪn) *n.* **1.** the pelt of a bear, esp. when used as a rug. **2.** a tall helmet of black fur worn by certain British Army regiments.

bear up *vb.* (*intr., adv.*) to endure cheerfully.

bear with *vb.* (*intr., prep.*) to be patient with.

beast (biːst) *n.* **1.** any animal other than man, esp. a large wild quadruped. **2.** savage nature or characteristics: *the beast in man.* **3.** a brutal, uncivilized, or filthy person. [C13: < OF *beste,* < L *bestia,* <?]

beastly (ˈbiːstlɪ) *adj.* **-lier, -liest.** **1.** *Inf.* unpleasant; disagreeable. **2.** *Obs.* of or like a beast; bestial. ~*adv.* **3.** *Inf.* (intensifier): *the weather is so beastly hot.* —ˈ**beastliness** *n.*

beast of burden *n.* an animal, such as a donkey or ox, used for carrying loads.

beast of prey *n.* any animal that hunts other animals for food.

beat (biːt) *vb.* **beating, beat; beaten** *or* **beat.** **1.** (when *intr.,* often foll. by *against, on,* etc.) to strike with or as if with a series of violent blows. **2.** (*tr.*) to punish by striking; flog. **3.** to move up and down; flap: *the bird beat its wings heavily.* **4.** (*intr.*) to throb rhythmically; pulsate. **5.** (*tr.; sometimes foll. by up*) *Cookery.* to stir or whisk vigorously. **6.** (*tr.; sometimes foll. by out*) to shape, thin, or flatten (metal) by repeated blows. **7.** (*tr.*) *Music.* to indicate (time) by one's hand, baton, etc., or by a metronome. **8.** (when *tr.,* sometimes foll. by *out*) to produce (a sound or signal) by or as if by striking a drum. **9.** to overcome; defeat. **10.** (*tr.*) to form (a path, track, etc.) by repeatedly walking or riding over it. **11.** (*tr.*) to arrive, achieve, or finish before (someone or something). **12.** (*tr.; often foll. by back, down, off,* etc.) to drive, push, or thrust. **13.** to scour (woodlands or undergrowth) so as to rouse game for shooting. **14.** (*tr.*) *Sl.* to puzzle or baffle: *it beats me.* **15.** (*intr.*) *Naut.* to steer a sailing vessel as close as possible to the direction from which the wind is blowing. **16. beat a retreat.** to withdraw in haste. **17. beat it.** *Sl.* (*often imperative*) to go away. **18. beat the bounds.** *Brit.* (formerly) to define the boundaries of a parish by making a procession around them and hitting the ground with rods. **19. can you beat it** *or* **that?** *Sl.* an expression of surprise. ~*n.* **20.** a stroke or blow. **21.** the sound made by a stroke or blow. **22.** a regular throb. **23.** an assigned or habitual round or route, as of a policeman. **24.** the basic rhythmic unit in a piece of music. **25. a.** pop or rock music characterized by a heavy rhythmic beat. **b.** (*as modifier*): *a beat group.* **26.** *Physics.* one of the regular pulses produced by combining two sounds or electrical signals that have similar frequencies. **27.** *Prosody.* the accent or stress in a metrical foot. **28.** (*modifier*) (*often cap.*) of, characterized by, or relating to the Beat Generation. ~*adj.* **29.** (*postpositive*) *Sl.* totally exhausted. ~See also **beat down, beat up.** [OE *bēatan*] —ˈ**beatable** *adj.*

beatbox (ˈbiːtˌbɒks) *n.* another name for **drum machine.**

beat down *vb.* (*adv.*) **1.** (*tr.*) *Inf.* to force or persuade (a seller) to accept a lower price. **2.** (*intr.*) (of the sun) to shine intensely.

beaten (ˈbiːtᵊn) *adj.* **1.** defeated or baffled. **2.** shaped or made thin by hammering: *beaten gold.* **3.** much travelled; well trodden. **4. off the beaten track. a.** in unfamiliar territory. **b.** out of the ordinary; unusual. **5.** (of food) mixed by beating; whipped. **6.** tired out; exhausted.

beater (ˈbiːtə) *n.* **1.** a person who beats or hammers: *a panel beater.* **2.** a device used for beating: *a carpet beater.* **3.** a person who rouses wild game.

Beat Generation *n.* (*functioning as sing. or pl.*) members of the generation that came to maturity in the 1950s, whose rejection of the social and political systems of the West was expressed through contempt for regular work, possessions, traditional dress, etc.

beatific (ˌbiːəˈtɪfɪk) *adj.* **1.** displaying great happiness, calmness, etc. **2.** of or conferring a state of celestial happiness. [C17: < LL *beātificus,* < L *beātus,* < *beāre* to bless + *facere* to make] —ˌ**beaˈtifically** *adv.*

beatify (bɪˈætɪˌfaɪ) *vb.* **-fying, -fied.** (*tr.*) **1.** *R.C. Church.* (of the pope) to declare formally that (a deceased person) showed a heroic degree of holiness in life and is worthy of veneration: the first step towards canonization. **2.** to make extremely happy. [C16: < OF *beatifier;* see BEATIFIC] —**beatification** (bɪˌætɪfɪˈkeɪʃən) *n.*

beating (ˈbiːtɪŋ) *n.* **1.** a whipping or thrashing. **2.** a defeat or setback. **3. take some** *or* **a lot of beating.** to be difficult to improve upon.

beatitude (bɪˈætɪˌtjuːd) *n.* **1.** supreme blessedness or happiness. **2.** an honorific title of the Eastern Christian Church, applied to those of patriarchal rank. [C15: < L *beātitūdō,* < *beātus* blessed; see BEATIFIC]

Beatitude (bɪˈætɪˌtjuːd) *n. Christianity.* any of eight sayings of Jesus in the Sermon on the Mount (Matthew 5:1-8) in which he declares that the poor, the meek, etc., will, in various ways, receive the blessings of heaven.

beatnik (ˈbiːtnɪk) *n.* **1.** a member of the Beat Generation. **2.** *Inf.* any person with long hair and shabby clothes. [C20: < BEAT (n.) + -NIK]

beat up *Inf.* ~*vb.* **1.** (*tr., adv.*) to strike or kick repeatedly, so as to inflict severe physical damage. ~*adj.* **beat-up.** **2.** worn-out; dilapidated.

beau (bəʊ) *n., pl.* **beaus** (bəʊz) *or* **beaux.** **1.** a man who is greatly concerned with his clothes and appearance; dandy. **2.** *Chiefly U.S.* a boyfriend; sweetheart. [C17: < F, < OF *biau,* < L *bellus* handsome]

Beaufort scale (ˈbəʊfət) *n. Meteorol.* an international scale of wind velocities from 0 (calm) to 12 (hurricane) (0 to 17 in the U.S.). [C19: after Sir Francis *Beaufort* (1774–1857), E admiral who devised it]

beau geste *French.* (bo ʒɛst) *n., pl.* ***beaux gestes*** (bo ʒɛst). a noble or gracious gesture or act. [lit.: beautiful gesture]

beaujolais (ˈbəʊʒəˌleɪ) *n.* (*sometimes cap.*) a popular fresh-tasting red or white wine from southern Burgundy in France.

beau monde (ˈbəʊ ˈmɒnd) *n.* the world of fashion and society. [C18: F, lit.: fine world]

beaut (bjuːt) *Sl., chiefly Austral. & N.Z.* ~*n.* **1.** an outstanding person or thing. ~*adj., interj.* **2.** good or excellent.

beauteous (ˈbjuːtɪəs) *adj.* a poetic word for **beautiful.** —ˈ**beauteousness** *n.*

beautician (bjuːˈtɪʃən) *n.* a person who works in or manages a beauty salon.

beautiful (ˈbjuːtɪfʊl) *adj.* **1.** possessing beauty; aesthetically pleasing. **2.** highly enjoyable; very pleasant. —ˈ**beautifully** *adv.*

beautify (ˈbjuːtɪˌfaɪ) *vb.* **-fying, -fied.** to make or become beautiful. —**beautification** (ˌbjuːtɪfɪˈkeɪʃən) *n.* —ˈ**beautiˌfier** *n.*

beauty (ˈbjuːtɪ) *n., pl.* **-ties.** **1.** the combination of all the qualities of a person or thing that delight the senses and mind. **2.** a very attractive woman. **3.** *Inf.* an outstanding example of its kind. **4.** *Inf.*

an advantageous feature: *one beauty of the job is the short hours.* ~*interj.* **5.** (*N.Z.* ˈbjuːdɪ). *Austral. & N.Z. sl.* an expression of approval or agreement. [C13: < OF *biauté,* < *biau* beautiful; see BEAU]

beauty queen *n.* an attractive young woman, esp. one who has won a beauty contest.

beauty salon *or* **parlour** *n.* an establishment providing services such as hairdressing, facial treatment, and massage.

beauty sleep *n. Inf.* sleep, esp. sleep before midnight.

beauty spot *n.* **1.** a small dark-coloured patch or spot worn on a lady's face as an adornment. **2.** a mole or other similar natural mark on the skin. **3.** a place of outstanding beauty.

beaux (bəʊ, bəʊz) *n.* a plural of **beau.**

beaux-arts (bəʊˈzɑː) *pl. n.* **1.** another word for **fine art. 2.** (*modifier*) relating to the classical decorative style, esp. that of the École des Beaux-Arts in Paris: *beaux-arts influences.* [F]

beaver[1] (ˈbiːvə) *n.* **1.** a large amphibious rodent of Europe, Asia, and North America. It has soft brown fur, a broad flat hairless tail, and webbed hind feet, and constructs complex dams and houses (lodges) in rivers. **2.** its fur. **3.** a tall hat of beaver fur worn during the 19th century. **4.** a woollen napped cloth resembling beaver fur. **5.** *Obs.* a full beard. **6.** a bearded man. **7.** (*modifier*) made of beaver fur or similar material. ~*vb.* **8.** (*intr.;* usually foll. by *away*) to work industriously or steadily. [OE *beofor*]

beaver[2] (ˈbiːvə) *n.* a movable piece on a medieval helmet used to protect the lower face. [C15: < OF *baviere,* < *baver* to dribble]

bebop (ˈbiːbɒp) *n.* the full name for **bop** (sense 1). [C20: imit. of the rhythm] —ˈ**bebopper** *n.*

becalmed (bɪˈkɑːmd) *adj.* (of a sailing boat or ship) motionless through lack of wind.

became (bɪˈkeɪm) *vb.* the past tense of **become.**

because (bɪˈkɒz, -ˈkəz) *conj.* **1.** (*subordinating*) on account of the fact that; since: *because it's so cold we'll go home.* **2. because of.** (*prep.*) on account of: *I lost my job because of her.* [C14 *bi cause,* < *bi* BY + CAUSE]

▷ **Usage.** See at **reason.**

béchamel sauce (ˌbeɪʃəˈmɛl) *n.* a thick white sauce flavoured with onion and seasonings. [C18: after the Marquis of *Béchamel,* its F inventor]

bêche-de-mer (ˌbɛʃdəˈmɛə) *n., pl.* **bêches-de-mer** (ˌbɛʃdəˈmɛə) *or* **bêche-de-mer.** another name for **trepang.** [C19: quasi-F, < earlier E *biche de mer,* < Port. *bicho do mar* worm of the sea]

Bechuana (bɛˈtʃwɑːnə; ˌbɛkjʊˈɑːnə) *n., pl.* **-na** *or* **-nas.** a former name for a Bantu of Botswana, a republic in southern Africa.

beck[1] (bɛk) *n.* **1.** a nod, wave, or other gesture. **2. at (someone's) beck and call.** subject to (someone's) slightest whim. [C14: short for *becnen* to BECKON]

beck[2] (bɛk) *n.* (in N England) a stream. [OE *becc*]

beckon (ˈbɛkən) *vb.* **1.** to summon with a gesture of the hand or head. **2.** to entice or lure. ~*n.* **3.** a summoning gesture. [OE *bīecnan,* < *bēacen* sign] —ˈ**beckoner** *n.* —ˈ**beckoning** *adj., n.*

becloud (bɪˈklaʊd) *vb.* (*tr.*) **1.** to cover or obscure with a cloud. **2.** to confuse or muddle.

become (bɪˈkʌm) *vb.* **-coming, -came, -come.** (*mainly intr.*) **1.** (*copula*) to come to be; develop or grow into: *he became a monster.* **2.** (foll. by *of; usually used in a question*) to happen (to): *what became of him?* **3.** (*tr.*) to suit: *that dress becomes you.* **4.** (*tr.*) to be appropriate; to befit: *it ill becomes you to complain.* [OE *becuman* to happen]

becoming (bɪˈkʌmɪŋ) *adj.* suitable; appropriate. —**be**ˈ**comingly** *adv.* —**be**ˈ**comingness** *n.*

becquerel (ˌbɛkəˈrɛl) *n.* the SI unit of activity of a radioactive source. [after A.H. *Becquerel* (1852-1908), F physicist]

bed (bɛd) *n.* **1.** a piece of furniture on which to sleep. **2.** the mattress and bedclothes: *an unmade bed.* **3.** sleep or rest: *time for bed.* **4.** any place in which a person or animal sleeps or rests. **5.** *Inf.* sexual intercourse. **6.** a plot of ground in which plants are grown. **7.** the bottom of a river, lake, or sea. **8.** a part of this used for cultivation of a plant or animal: *oyster beds.* **9.** any underlying structure or part. **10.** a layer of rock, esp. sedimentary rock. **11. go to bed. a.** (often foll. by *with*) to have sexual intercourse (with). **b.** *Journalism, printing.* (of a newspaper, etc.) to go to press; start printing. **12. put to bed.** *Journalism.* to finalize work on (a newspaper, etc.) so that it is ready to go to press. **13. take to one's bed.** to remain in bed, esp. because of illness. ~*vb.* **bedding, bedded. 14.** (usually foll. by *down*) to go to or put into a place to sleep or rest. **15.** (*tr.*) to have sexual intercourse with. **16.** (*tr.*) to place firmly into position; embed. **17.** *Geol.* to form or be arranged in a distinct layer; stratify. **18.** (*tr.;* often foll. by *out*) to plant in a bed of soil. [OE *bedd*]

BEd *abbrev. for* Bachelor of Education.

bed and board *n.* sleeping accommodation and meals.

bed and breakfast *n. Chiefly Brit.* (in a hotel, boarding house, etc.) overnight accommodation and breakfast.

bedaub (bɪˈdɔːb) *vb.* (*tr.*) **1.** to smear all over with something thick, sticky, or dirty. **2.** to ornament in a gaudy or vulgar fashion.

bedazzle (bɪˈdæzᵊl) *vb.* (*tr.*) to dazzle or confuse, as with brilliance. —**be**ˈ**dazzlement** *n.*

bed bath *n.* another name for **blanket bath.**

bedbug (ˈbɛdˌbʌg) *n.* any of several bloodsucking wingless insects of temperate regions, infesting dirty houses.

bedchamber (ˈbɛdˌtʃeɪmbə) *n.* an archaic word for **bedroom.**

bedclothes (ˈbɛdˌkləʊðz) *pl. n.* sheets, blankets, and other coverings for a bed.

beddable (ˈbɛdəbᵊl) *adj.* sexually attractive.

bedding (ˈbɛdɪŋ) *n.* **1.** bedclothes, sometimes considered with a mattress. **2.** litter, such as straw, for animals. **3.** a foundation, such as mortar under a brick. **4.** the stratification of rocks.

bedding plant *n.* an immature plant that may be planted out in a garden bed.

bedeck (bɪˈdɛk) *vb.* (*tr.*) to cover with decorations; adorn.

bedevil (bɪˈdɛvᵊl) *vb.* **-illing, -illed** *or U.S.* **-iling, -iled.** (*tr.*) **1.** to harass or torment. **2.** to throw into confusion. **3.** to possess, as with a devil. —**be**ˈ**devilment** *n.*

bedew (bɪˈdjuː) *vb.* (*tr.*) to wet as with dew.

bedfellow (ˈbɛdˌfɛləʊ) *n.* **1.** a person with whom one shares a bed. **2.** a temporary ally or associate.

bedight (bɪˈdaɪt) *Arch.* ~*vb.* **-dighting, -dight** *or* **-dighted. 1.** (*tr.*) to array or adorn. ~*adj.* **2.** (*p.p.*) adorned or bedecked. [C14: < DIGHT]

bedim (bɪˈdɪm) *vb.* **-dimming, -dimmed.** (*tr.*) to make dim or obscure.

bedizen (bɪˈdaɪzᵊn, -ˈdɪzᵊn) *vb.* (*tr.*) *Arch.* to dress or decorate gaudily or tastelessly. [C17: < BE- + obs. *dizen* to dress up, <?] —**be**ˈ**dizenment** *n.*

bed jacket *n.* a woman's short upper garment worn over a nightgown when sitting up in bed.

bedlam (ˈbɛdləm) *n.* **1.** a noisy confused situation. **2.** *Arch.* a madhouse. [C13 *bedlem, bethlem,* < Hospital of St Mary of *Bethlehem* in London]

bed linen *n.* sheets, pillowcases, etc., for a bed.

Bedouin *or* **Beduin** (ˈbɛdʊɪn) *n.* **1.** (*pl.* **-ins** *or* **-in**) a nomadic Arab tribesman of the deserts of Arabia, Jordan, and Syria. **2.** a wanderer. ~*adj.* **3.** of or relating to the Bedouins. **4.** wandering. [C14: < OF *beduin,* < Ar. *badāwi,* pl. of *badwi,* < *badw* desert]

bedpan (ˈbɛdˌpæn) *n.* a vessel used by a bedridden patient to collect his faeces and urine.

bedraggle (bɪˈdrægᵊl) *vb.* (*tr.*) to make (hair, clothing, etc.) limp, untidy, or dirty, as with rain or mud. —**be**ˈ**draggled** *adj.*

bedridden (ˈbɛdˌrɪdᵊn) *adj.* confined to bed because of illness, esp. for a long or indefinite period. [OE *bedreda*]

bedrock (ˈbɛdˌrɒk) *n.* **1.** the solid rock beneath the surface soil, etc. **2.** basic principles or facts. **3.** the lowest point, level, or layer.

bedroll (ˈbɛdˌrəʊl) *n.* a portable roll of bedding.

bedroom (ˈbɛdˌruːm, -ˌrʊm) *n.* **1.** a room used for sleeping. **2.** (*modifier*) containing references to sex: *a bedroom comedy.*

Beds *abbrev. for* Bedfordshire.

bedside (ˈbɛdˌsaɪd) *n.* **a.** the space beside a bed, esp. a sickbed. **b.** (*as modifier*): *a bedside lamp.*

bedsitter (ˌbɛdˈsɪtə) *n.* a furnished sitting room containing sleeping accommodation. Also called: **bedsitting room, bedsit.**

bedsore (ˈbɛdˌsɔː) *n.* a chronic ulcer on the skin of a bedridden person, caused by prolonged pressure.

bedspread (ˈbɛdˌsprɛd) *n.* a top cover on a bed.

bedstead (ˈbɛdˌstɛd) *n.* the framework of a bed.

bedstraw (ˈbɛdˌstrɔː) *n.* any of numerous plants which have small white or yellow flowers and prickly or hairy fruits: formerly used as straw for beds.

bedtime (ˈbɛdˌtaɪm) *n.* **a.** the time when one usually goes to bed. **b.** (*as modifier*): *a bedtime story.*

bed-wetting *n.* the act of urinating in bed.

bee[1] (biː) *n.* **1.** any of various four-winged insects that collect nectar and pollen and make honey and wax. **2. busy bee.** a person who is industrious or has many things to do. **3. have a bee in one's bonnet.** to be obsessed with an idea. [OE *bīo*]

bee[2] (biː) *n. Chiefly U.S.* a social gathering for a specific purpose, as to carry out a communal task: *quilting bee.* [? < dialect *bean* neighbourly help, < OE *bēn* boon]

Beeb (biːb) *n.* **the.** an informal name for the **BBC.**

beebread (ˈbiːˌbrɛd) *n.* a mixture of pollen and nectar prepared by worker bees and fed to the larvae. Also called: **ambrosia.**

beech (biːtʃ) *n.* **1.** a European tree having smooth greyish bark. **2.** a similar tree of temperate Australasia and South America. **3.** the hard wood of either of these trees. **4.** See **copper beech.** [OE *bēce*] —ˈ**beechen** *or* ˈ**beechy** *adj.*

beechnut (ˈbiːtʃˌnʌt) *n.* the small brown triangular edible nut of the beech tree, collectively often termed **beech mast.**

bee-eater *n.* any of various insectivorous birds of the Old World tropics and subtropics.

beef (biːf) *n.* **1.** the flesh of various bovine animals, esp. the cow, when killed for eating. **2.** (*pl.* **beeves**) an adult ox, etc., reared for its meat. **3.** *Inf.* human flesh, esp. when muscular. **4.** (*pl.* **beefs**) *Sl.* a complaint. ~*vb.* **5.** (*intr.*) *Sl.* to complain, esp. repeatedly. **6.** (*tr.;* often foll. by *up*) *Inf.* to strengthen; reinforce. [C13: < OF *boef,* < L *bōs* ox]

beefburger (ˈbiːfˌbɜːɡə) *n.* a flat fried cake of minced beef; hamburger.

beefcake (ˈbiːfˌkeɪk) *n. Sl.* men displayed for their muscular bodies, esp. in photographs.

beefeater (ˈbiːfˌiːtə) *n.* a yeoman warder of the Tower of London.

beef road *n. Austral.* a road used for transporting cattle.

beefsteak (ˈbiːfˌsteɪk) *n.* a lean piece of beef that can be grilled, fried, etc.

beef tea *n.* a drink made by boiling pieces of lean beef.

beefy (ˈbiːfɪ) *adj.* **beefier, beefiest. 1.** like beef. **2.** *Inf.* muscular; brawny. —ˈ**beefiness** *n.*

beehive (ˈbiːˌhaɪv) *n.* **1.** a man-made receptacle used to house a swarm of bees. **2.** a dome-shaped structure. **3.** a place where busy people are assembled. **4. the Beehive.** the dome-shaped building which houses Parliament in Wellington, New Zealand.

beekeeper (ˈbiːˌkiːpə) *n.* a person who keeps bees for their honey. —ˈ**beeˌkeeping** *n.*

beeline (ˈbiːˌlaɪn) *n.* the most direct route between two places (esp. in **make a beeline for**).

Beelzebub (bɪˈɛlzɪˌbʌb) *n.* Satan or any devil. [OE *Belzebub,* ult. < Heb. *bá'al zebūb,* lit.: lord of flies]

bee moth *n.* any of various moths whose larvae live in the nests of bees or wasps, feeding on nest materials and host larvae.

been (biːn, bɪn) *vb.* the past participle of **be.**

beep (biːp) *n.* **1.** a short high-pitched sound, as made by a car horn or by electronic apparatus. ~*vb.* **2.** to make or cause to make such a noise. [C20: imit.] —ˈ**beeper** *n.*

beer (bɪə) *n.* **1.** an alcoholic drink brewed from malt, sugar, hops, and water. **2.** a slightly fermented drink made from the roots or leaves of certain plants: *ginger beer.* **3.** (*modifier*) relating to beer: *beer glass.* **4.** (*modifier*) in which beer is drunk, esp. (of licensed premises) having a licence to sell beer but not spirits: *beer house; beer garden.* [OE *beor*]

beer and skittles *n.* (*functioning as sing.*) *Inf.* enjoyment or pleasure.

beer parlour *n. Canad.* a licensed place in which beer is sold to the public.

beery (ˈbɪərɪ) *adj.* **beerier, beeriest. 1.** smelling or tasting of beer. **2.** given to drinking beer. —ˈ**beerily** *adv.* —ˈ**beeriness** *n.*

bee's knees *n.* **the** (*functioning as sing.*) *Inf.* an excellent or ideally suitable person or thing.

beestings, biestings, *or U.S.* **beastings** (ˈbiːstɪŋz) *n.* (*functioning as sing.*) the first milk secreted by a cow or similar animal after giving birth; colostrum. [OE *bȳsting*]

beeswax (ˈbiːzˌwæks) *n.* **1.** a wax secreted by honeybees for constructing honeycombs. **2.** this wax after refining, used in polishes, etc.

beeswing (ˈbiːzˌwɪŋ) *n.* a light filmy crust of tartar that forms in some wines after long keeping in the bottle.

beet (biːt) *n.* **1.** a plant of a genus widely cultivated in such varieties as the sugar beet, mangelwurzel, and beetroot. **2.** the leaves of any of several varieties of this plant, cooked and eaten as a vegetable. **3. red beet.** the U.S. name for **beetroot.** [OE *bēte,* < L *bēta*]

beetle[1] (ˈbiːtəl) *n.* **1.** an insect having biting mouthparts and forewings modified to form shell-like protective casings. **2.** a game in which the players draw or assemble a beetle-shaped form. ~*vb.* (*intr.;* foll. by *along, off,* etc.) **3.** *Inf.* to scuttle or scurry; hurry. [OE *bitela*]

beetle[2] (ˈbiːtəl) *n.* **1.** a heavy hand tool for pounding or beating. **2.** a machine used to finish cloth by stamping it with wooden hammers. [OE *bīetel,* < *bēatan* to BEAT]

beetle[3] (ˈbiːtəl) *vb.* **1.** (*intr.*) to overhang; jut. ~*adj.* **2.** overhanging; prominent. [C14: ? rel. to BEETLE[1]] —ˈ**beetling** *adj.*

beetle-browed *adj.* having bushy or overhanging eyebrows.

beetroot (ˈbiːtˌruːt) *n.* a variety of the beet plant that has a bulbous dark red root that may be eaten as a vegetable, in salads, or pickled.

beet sugar *n.* the sucrose obtained from sugar beet, identical in composition to cane sugar.

beeves (biːvz) *n.* the plural of **beef** (sense 2).

BEF *abbrev. for* British Expeditionary Force, the British army that served in France 1939-40.

befall (bɪˈfɔːl) *vb.* **-falling, -fell, -fallen.** *Arch. or literary.* **1.** (*intr.*) to take place. **2.** (*tr.*) to happen to. **3.** (*intr.;* usually foll. by *to*) to be due, as by right. [OE *befeallan;* see BE-, FALL]

befit (bɪˈfɪt) *vb.* **-fitting, -fitted.** (*tr.*) to be appropriate to or suitable for. [C15: < BE- + FIT[1]] —**beˈfitting** *adj.* —**beˈfittingly** *adv.*

befog (bɪˈfɒg) *vb.* **-fogging, -fogged.** (*tr.*) **1.** to surround with fog. **2.** to make confused.

before (bɪˈfɔː) *conj.* (*subordinating*) **1.** earlier than the time when. **2.** rather than: *he'll resign before he agrees to it.* ~*prep.* **3.** preceding in space or time; in front of; ahead of: *standing before the altar.* **4.** in the presence of: *to be brought before a judge.* **5.** in preference to: *to put friendship before money.* ~*adv.* **6.** at an earlier time; previously. **7.** in front. [OE *beforan*]

beforehand (bɪˈfɔːˌhænd) *adj.* (*postpositive*), *adv.* early; in advance; in anticipation.

befoul (bɪˈfaʊl) *vb.* (*tr.*) to make dirty or foul.

befriend (bɪˈfrɛnd) *vb.* (*tr.*) to be a friend to; assist; favour.

befuddle (bɪˈfʌdəl) *vb.* (*tr.*) **1.** to confuse. **2.** to make stupid with drink. —**beˈfuddlement** *n.*

beg (bɛg) *vb.* **begging, begged. 1.** (when *intr.*, often foll. by *for*) to solicit (for money, food, etc.), esp. in the street. **2.** to ask formally, humbly, or earnestly: *I beg forgiveness; I beg to differ.* **3.** (*intr.*) (of a dog) to sit up with forepaws raised expectantly. **4. beg the question. a.** to evade the issue. **b.** to assume the thing under examination as proved. **5. go begging.** to be unwanted or unused. ~See also **beg off.** [C13: prob. < OE *bedecian*]

began (bɪˈgæn) *vb.* the past tense of **begin.**

beget (bɪˈgɛt) *vb.* **-getting, -got** *or* **-gat; -gotten** *or* **-got.** (*tr.*) **1.** to father. **2.** to cause or create. [OE *begietan*; see BE-, GET] —**beˈgetter** *n.*

beggar (ˈbɛgə) *n.* **1.** a person who begs, esp. one who lives by begging. **2.** a person who has no money or resources; pauper. **3.** *Chiefly Brit.* a fellow: *lucky beggar!* ~*vb.* (*tr.*) **4.** to be beyond the resources of (esp. in **to beggar description**). **5.** to impoverish. —ˈ**beggardom** *n.*

beggarly (ˈbɛgəlɪ) *adj.* meanly inadequate; very poor. —ˈ**beggarliness** *n.*

beggar-my-neighbour *n.* a card game in which one player tries to win all the cards of the other player.

beggary (ˈbɛgərɪ) *n.* extreme poverty or need.

begin (bɪˈgɪn) *vb.* **-ginning, -gan, -gun. 1.** to start or cause to start (something or to do something). **2.** to bring or come into being; arise or originate. **3.** to start to say or speak. **4.** (*with a negative*) to have the least capacity (to do something): *he couldn't begin to compete.* **5. to begin with.** in the first place. [OE *beginnan*]

beginner (bɪˈgɪnə) *n.* a person who has just started to do or learn something; novice.

beginning (bɪˈgɪnɪŋ) *n.* **1.** a start; commencement. **2.** (*often pl.*) a first or early part or stage. **3.** the place where or time when something starts. **4.** an origin; source.

begird (bɪˈgɜːd) *vb.* **-girding, -girt** *or* **-girded.** (*tr.*) *Poetic.* **1.** to surround; gird around. **2.** to bind. [OE *begierdan*; see BE-, GIRD[1]]

beg off *vb.* (*intr.*, *adv.*) to ask to be released from an engagement, obligation, etc.

begone (bɪˈgɒn) *sentence substitute.* go away! [C14: < BE (imperative) + GONE]

begonia (bɪˈgəʊnjə) *n.* a plant of warm and tropical regions, having ornamental leaves and waxy flowers. [C18: NL, after Michel *Bégon* (1638–1710), F patron of science]

begorra (bɪˈgɔːrə) *interj.* an emphatic exclamation, regarded as characteristic of Irishmen. [C19: < *by God!*]

begot (bɪˈgɒt) *vb.* a past tense and past participle of **beget.**

begotten (bɪˈgɒtən) *vb.* a past participle of **beget.**

begrime (bɪˈgraɪm) *vb.* (*tr.*) to make dirty; soil.

begrudge (bɪˈgrʌdʒ) *vb.* (*tr.*) **1.** to give, admit, or allow unwillingly or with a bad grace. **2.** to envy (someone) the possession of (something). —**beˈgrudgingly** *adv.*

beguile (bɪˈgaɪl) *vb.* **-guiling, -guiled.** (*tr.*) **1.** to charm; fascinate. **2.** to delude; influence by slyness. **3.** (often foll. by *of* or *out of*) to cheat (someone) of. **4.** to pass pleasantly; while away. —**beˈguilement** *n.* —**beˈguiler** *n.* —**beˈguiling** *adj.* —**beˈguilingly** *adv.*

beguine (bɪˈgiːn) *n.* **1.** a dance of South American origin in bolero rhythm. **2.** a piece of music in the rhythm of this dance. [C20: < Louisiana F, < F *béguin* flirtation]

begum (ˈbeɪgəm) *n.* (in certain Muslim countries) a woman of high rank. [C18: < Urdu *begam*, < Turkish *begim*; see BEY]

begun (bɪˈgʌn) *vb.* the past participle of **begin.**

behalf (bɪˈhɑːf) *n.* interest, part, benefit, or respect (only in **on (someone's) behalf, on** *or U.S. & Canad.* **in behalf of, in this** (*or* **that**) **behalf**). [OE *be halfe*, < *be* by + *halfe* side]

behave (bɪˈheɪv) *vb.* **1.** (*intr.*) to act or function in a specified or usual way. **2.** to conduct (oneself) in a specified way: *he behaved badly.* **3.** to conduct (oneself) properly or as desired. [C15: see BE-, HAVE]

behaviour *or U.S.* **behavior** (bɪˈheɪvjə) *n.* **1.** manner of behaving. **2. on one's best behaviour.** behaving with careful good manners. **3.** *Psychol.* the response of an organism to a stimulus. **4.** the reaction or functioning of a machine, etc., under normal or specified circumstances. [C15: < BEHAVE; infl. by ME *havior*, < OF *havoir*, < L *habēre* to have] —**beˈhavioural** *or U.S.* **beˈhavioral** *adj.*

behavioural science *n.* the scientific study of the behaviour of organisms.

behaviourism *or U.S.* **behaviorism** (bɪˈheɪvjəˌrɪzəm) *n.* a school of psychology that regards objective observation of the behaviour of organisms as the only valid subject for study. —**beˈhaviourist** *or U.S.* **beˈhaviorist** *adj.*, *n.* —**beˌhaviourˈistic** *or U.S.* **beˌhaviorˈistic** *adj.*

behaviour therapy *n.* any of various means of treating psychological disorders, such as aversion therapy, that depend on the patient systematically learning new behaviour.

behead (bɪˈhɛd) *vb.* (*tr.*) to remove the head from. [OE *behēafdian*, < BE- + *heafod* HEAD]

beheld (bɪˈhɛld) *vb.* the past tense and past participle of **behold.**

behemoth (bɪˈhiːmɒθ) *n.* **1.** *Bible.* a gigantic beast described in Job 40:15. **2.** a huge or monstrous person or thing. [C14: < Heb. *bĕhēmōth*, pl. of *bĕhēmāh* beast]

behest (bɪˈhɛst) *n.* an order or earnest request. [OE *behǣs*, < *behātan*; see BE-, HEST]

behind (bɪˈhaɪnd) *prep.* **1.** in or to a position further back than. **2.** in the past in relation to: *I've got the exams behind me now.* **3.** late according to: *running behind schedule.* **4.** concerning the circumstances surrounding: *the reasons behind his departure.* **5.** supporting: *I'm right behind you in your application.* ~*adv.* **6.** in or to a position further back; following. **7.** remaining after someone's departure: *he left his books behind.* **8.** in debt; in arrears: *to fall behind with payments.* ~*adj.* **9.** (*postpositive*) in a position further back. ~*n.* **10.** *Inf.* the buttocks. **11.** *Australian Rules football.* a score of one point made by kicking the ball over the **behind line** between a goalpost and one of the smaller outer posts (**behind posts**). [OE *behindan*]

behindhand (bɪˈhaɪndˌhænd) *adj.* (*postpositive*), *adv.* **1.** remiss in fulfilling an obligation. **2.** in arrears. **3.** backward. **4.** late.

behold (bɪˈhəʊld) *vb.* **-holding, -held.** (often imperative) *Arch. or literary.* to look (at); observe. [OE *bihealdan*; see BE-, HOLD[1]] —**beˈholder** *n.*

beholden (bɪˈhəʊldən) *adj.* indebted; obliged. [OE *behealden*, p.p. of *behealdan* to BEHOLD]

behoof (bɪˈhuːf) *n.*, *pl.* **-hooves.** *Rare.* advantage or profit. [OE *behōf*; see BEHOVE]

behove (bɪˈhəʊv) *vb.* (*tr.*; *impersonal*) *Arch.* to be necessary or fitting for: *it behoves me to arrest you.* [OE *behōfian*]

beige (beɪʒ) *n.* **1. a.** a very light brown, sometimes with a yellowish tinge. **b.** (*as adj.*): *beige gloves.* **2.** a fabric made of undyed or unbleached wool. [C19: < OF, <?]

being (ˈbiːɪŋ) *n.* **1.** the state or fact of existing; existence. **2.** essential nature; self. **3.** something that exists or is thought to exist: *a being from outer space.* **4.** a person; human being.

bejabers (bɪˈdʒeɪbəz) *or* **bejabbers** (bɪˈdʒæbəz) *interj.* an exclamation of surprise, emphasis, etc., regarded as characteristic of Irishmen. [C19: < *by Jesus!*]

bejewel (bɪˈdʒuːəl) *vb.* **-elling, -elled** *or U.S.* **-eling, -eled.** (*tr.*) to decorate as with jewels.

bel (bɛl) *n.* a unit for comparing two power levels, equal to the logarithm to the base ten of the ratio of the two powers. [C20: after A. G. *Bell* (1847-1922), U.S. scientist]

belabour *or U.S.* **belabor** (bɪˈleɪbə) *vb.* (*tr.*) **1.** to beat severely; thrash. **2.** to attack verbally.

belated (bɪˈleɪtɪd) *adj.* late or too late: *belated greetings.* —**beˈlatedly** *adv.* —**beˈlatedness** *n.*

belay (bɪˈleɪ) *vb.* **-laying, -layed.** **1.** *Naut.* to secure (a line) to a pin, cleat, or bitt. **2.** (*usually imperative*) *Naut.* to stop. **3.** (ˈbiːˌleɪ). *Mountaineering.* to secure (a climber) by means of a belay. ~*n.* (ˈbiːlˌeɪ). **4.** *Mountaineering.* the attachment of a climber to a mountain by securing a rope round a rock, piton, etc., to safeguard the party in the event of a fall. [OE *belecgan*]

belaying pin *n. Naut.* a cylindrical metal or wooden pin used for belaying.

bel canto (ˈbɛl ˈkæntəʊ) *n. Music.* a style of singing characterized by beauty of tone rather than dramatic power. [It., lit.: beautiful singing]

belch (bɛltʃ) *vb.* **1.** (*usually intr.*) to expel wind from the stomach noisily through the mouth. **2.** to expel or be expelled forcefully from inside: *smoke belching from factory chimneys.* ~*n.* **3.** an act of belching. [OE *bialcan*]

beldam *or* **beldame** (ˈbɛldəm) *n. Arch.* an old woman. [C15: < *bel-* grand (as in *grandmother*), < OF *bel* beautiful, + *dam* mother]

beleaguer (bɪˈliːgə) *vb.* (*tr.*) **1.** to lay siege to. **2.** to harass. [C16: < BE- + obs. *leaguer* a siege]

belemnite (ˈbɛləmˌnaɪt) *n.* **1.** an extinct marine mollusc related to the cuttlefish. **2.** its long pointed conical internal shell: a common fossil. [C17: < Gk *belemnon* dart]

belfry (ˈbɛlfrɪ) *n., pl.* **-fries.** **1.** the part of a tower or steeple in which bells are hung. **2.** a tower or steeple. [C13: < OF *berfrei*, of Gmc origin]

Belg. *or* **Bel.** *abbrev. for:* **1.** Belgian. **2.** Belgium.

Belgian (ˈbɛldʒən) *n.* **1.** a native or inhabitant of Belgium, a kingdom in NW Europe. ~*adj.* **2.** of or relating to Belgium, the Belgians, or their languages.

Belgian hare *n.* a large red domestic rabbit.

Belial (ˈbiːlɪəl) *n.* the devil or Satan. [C13: < Heb. *bəlīyya'al*, < *bəlīy* without + *ya'al* worth]

belie (bɪˈlaɪ) *vb.* **-lying, -lied.** (*tr.*) **1.** to show to be untrue; contradict. **2.** to misrepresent; disguise the nature of. **3.** to fail to justify; disappoint. [OE *belēogan;* see BE-, LIE[1]]

belief (bɪˈliːf) *n.* **1.** a principle, etc., accepted as true, esp. without proof. **2.** opinion; conviction. **3.** religious faith. **4.** trust or confidence, as in a person's abilities, etc.

believe (bɪˈliːv) *vb.* **1.** (*tr.; may take a clause as object*) to accept (a statement or opinion) as true or real: *I believe God exists.* **2.** (*tr.*) to accept the statement or opinion of (a person) as true. **3.** (*intr.;* foll. by *in*) to be convinced of the truth or existence (of): *to believe in fairies.* **4.** (*intr.*) to have religious faith. **5.** (when *tr., takes a clause as object*) to think, assume, or suppose. **6.** (*tr.*) to think that someone is able to do (a particular action): *I wouldn't have believed it of him.* [OE *beliefan*] —**beˈlievable** *adj.* —**beˈliever** *n.*

belike (bɪˈlaɪk) *adv. Arch.* perhaps; maybe.

Belisha beacon (bəˈliːʃə) *n. Brit.* a flashing orange globe mounted on a post, indicating a pedestrian crossing on a road. [C20: after L. Hore-*Belisha* (1893-1957), Brit. politician]

belittle (bɪˈlɪtᵊl) *vb.* (*tr.*) **1.** to consider or speak of (something) as less valuable or important than it really is; disparage. **2.** to make small; dwarf. —**beˈlittlement** *n.* —**beˈlittler** *n.*

bell[1] (bɛl) *n.* **1.** a hollow, usually metal, cup-shaped instrument that emits a ringing sound when struck. **2.** the sound made by such an instrument, as for marking the beginning or end of a period of time. **3.** an electrical device that rings or buzzes as a signal. **4.** something shaped like a bell, as the tube of certain musical wind instruments, or the corolla of certain flowers. **5.** *Naut.* a signal rung on a ship's bell to count the number of half-hour intervals during each of six four-hour watches reckoned from midnight. **6.** *Brit. sl.* a telephone call. **7. bell, book, and candle.** instruments used formerly in excommunications. **8. ring a bell.** to sound familiar; recall something previously experienced. **9. sound as a bell.** in perfect condition. ~*vb.* **10.** to be or cause to be shaped like a bell. **11.** (*tr.*) to attach a bell or bells to. [OE *belle*]

bell[2] (bɛl) *n.* **1.** a bellowing or baying cry, esp. that of a stag in rut. ~*vb.* **2.** to utter (such a cry). [OE *bellan*]

belladonna (ˌbɛləˈdɒnə) *n.* **1.** either of two alkaloid drugs obtained from the leaves and roots of the deadly nightshade. **2.** another name for **deadly nightshade.** [C16: < It., lit.: beautiful lady; supposed to refer to its use as a cosmetic]

bellbird (ˈbɛlˌbɜːd) *n.* **1.** any of several tropical American birds having a bell-like call. **2.** either of two other birds with a bell-like call: an Australian flycatcher (**crested bellbird**) or a New Zealand honeyeater.

bell-bottoms *pl. n.* trousers that flare from the knee. —ˈ**bell-ˌbottomed** *adj.*

bellboy (ˈbɛlˌbɔɪ) *n. Chiefly U.S. & Canad.* a porter or page in a hotel, club, etc. Also called: **bellhop.**

bell buoy *n.* a navigational buoy with a bell which strikes when the waves move the buoy.

belle (bɛl) *n.* **1.** a beautiful woman. **2.** the most attractive woman at a function, etc. (esp. in **belle of the ball**). [C17: < F, fem. of BEAU]

belle époque *French.* (bɛl epɔk) *n.* the period of comfortable well-established life before World War I. [lit.: fine period]

belles-lettres (*French* bɛlletrə) *n.* (*functioning as sing.*) literary works, esp. essays and poetry, valued for their aesthetic content. [C17: < F: fine letters] —**belˈletrist** *n.*

bellflower (ˈbɛlˌflaʊə) *n.* another name for **campanula.**

bellfounder (ˈbɛlˌfaʊndə) *n.* a foundry worker who casts bells.

bellicose (ˈbɛlɪˌkəʊs, -ˌkəʊz) *adj.* warlike; aggressive; ready to fight. [C15: < L *bellicōsus*, < *bellum* war] —**bellicosity** (ˌbɛlɪˈkɒsɪtɪ) *n.*

belligerence (bɪˈlɪdʒərəns) *n.* the act or quality of being belligerent or warlike; aggressiveness.

belligerency (bɪˈlɪdʒərənsɪ) *n.* the state of being at war.

belligerent (bɪˈlɪdʒərənt) *adj.* **1.** marked by readiness to fight or argue; aggressive. **2.** relating to or engaged in a war. ~*n.* **3.** a person or country engaged in war. [C16: < L *belliger*, < *bellum* war + *gerere* to wage]

bell jar *n.* a bell-shaped glass cover to protect flower arrangements, etc., or to cover apparatus in experiments. Also called: **bell glass.**

bellman (ˈbɛlmən) *n., pl.* **-men.** a man who rings a bell; (formerly) a town crier.

bell metal *n.* an alloy of copper and tin, with some zinc and lead, used in casting bells.

bellow (ˈbɛləʊ) *vb.* **1.** (*intr.*) to make a loud deep cry like that of a bull; roar. **2.** to shout (something) unrestrainedly, as in anger or pain. ~*n.* **3.** the characteristic noise of a bull. **4.** a loud deep sound, as of pain or anger. [C14: prob. < OE *bylgan*]

bellows (ˈbɛləʊz) *n.* (*functioning as sing. or pl.*) **1.** Also: **pair of bellows.** an instrument consisting of an air chamber with flexible sides that is used to create a stream of air, as for producing a draught for a fire or for sounding organ pipes. **2.** a flexible corrugated part, as that connecting the lens system of some cameras to the body. [C16: < pl. of OE *belig* BELLY]

bell pull *n.* a handle, rope, or cord pulled to operate a doorbell or servant's bell.

bell push *n.* a button pressed to operate an electric bell.

bell-ringer *n.* a person who rings church bells or musical handbells. —ˈ**bell-ˌringing** *n.*

bell tent *n.* a cone-shaped tent having a single central supporting pole.

bellwether (ˈbɛlˌwɛðə) *n.* **1.** a sheep that leads the herd, often bearing a bell. **2.** a leader, esp. one followed blindly.

belly (ˈbɛlɪ) *n., pl.* **-lies.** **1.** the lower or front part of the body of a vertebrate, containing the intestines and other organs; abdomen. **2.** the stomach, esp. when regarded as the seat of gluttony. **3.** a part that bulges deeply: *the belly of a sail.* **4.** the inside or interior cavity of something. **5.** the front, lower, or inner part of something. **6.** the surface of a stringed musical instrument over which the strings are stretched. **7.** *Austral. & N.Z.* **a.** the wool from a sheep's belly. **b.** (*as modifier*): *belly wool.* **8.** an archaic word for **womb** (sense 1). ~*vb.* **-lying, -lied. 9.** to swell out or cause to swell out; bulge. [OE *belig*]

bellyache (ˈbɛlɪˌeɪk) *n.* **1.** an informal term for **stomachache.** ~*vb.* **2.** (*intr.*) *Sl.* to complain repeatedly. —ˈ**belly,acher** *n.*

bellyband (ˈbɛlɪˌbænd) *n.* a strap around the belly of a draught animal, holding the shafts of a vehicle.

bellybutton (ˈbɛlɪˌbʌtᵊn) *n.* an informal name for the **navel** (sense 1). Also called: **tummy button.**

belly dance *n.* **1.** a sensuous dance of Middle Eastern origin, performed by women, with undulating movements of the abdomen. ~*vb.* **belly-dance. 2.** (*intr.*) to dance thus. —**belly dancer** *n.*

belly flop *n.* **1.** a dive into water in which the body lands horizontally. ~*vb.* **belly-flop, -flopping, -flopped. 2.** (*intr.*) to perform a belly flop.

bellyful (ˈbɛlɪˌfʊl) *n.* **1.** as much as one wants or can eat. **2.** *Sl.* more than one can tolerate.

belly landing *n.* the landing of an aircraft on its fuselage without use of its landing gear.

belly laugh *n.* a loud deep hearty laugh.

belong (bɪˈlɒŋ) *vb.* (*intr.*) **1.** (foll. by *to*) to be the property or possession (of). **2.** (foll. by *to*) to be bound (to) by ties of affection, allegiance, etc. **3.** (foll. by *to, under, with,* etc.) to be classified (with): *this plant belongs to the daisy family.* **4.** (foll. by *to*) to be a part or adjunct (of). **5.** to have a proper or usual place. **6.** *Inf.* to be acceptable, esp. socially. [C14 *belongen,* < BE- (intensive) + *longen,* < OE *langian* to belong]

belonging (bɪˈlɒŋɪŋ) *n.* secure relationship; affinity (esp. in **a sense of belonging**).

belongings (bɪˈlɒŋɪŋz) *pl. n.* (*sometimes sing.*) the things that a person owns or has with him.

Belorussian (ˌbɛləʊˈrʌʃən) *adj., n.* a variant spelling of **Byelorussian.**

beloved (bɪˈlʌvɪd, -ˈlʌvd) *adj.* **1.** dearly loved. ~*n.* **2.** a person who is dearly loved.

below (bɪˈləʊ) *prep.* **1.** at or to a position lower than; under. **2.** less than. **3.** south of. **4.** downstream of. **5.** unworthy of; beneath. ~*adv.* **6.** at or to a lower position. **7.** at a later place (in something written). **8.** *Arch.* on earth or in hell. [C14 *bilooghe,* < *bi* BY + *looghe* LOW¹]

Bel Paese (ˈbɛl pɑːˈeɪzɪ) *n.* a mild creamy Italian cheese. [< It., lit.: beautiful country]

belt (bɛlt) *n.* **1.** a band of cloth, leather, etc., worn, usually around the waist, to support clothing, carry weapons, etc., or as decoration. **2.** a belt worn to show rank (as by a knight), to mark expertise (as in judo), or awarded as a prize (as in boxing). **3.** a narrow band, circle, or stripe, as of colour. **4.** an area where a specific thing is found; zone: *a belt of high pressure.* **5.** See **seat belt. 6.** a band of flexible material between rotating shafts or pulleys to transfer motion or transmit goods: *a fan belt; a conveyer belt.* **7.** *Inf.* a sharp blow. **8. below the belt. a.** *Boxing.* below the waist. **b.** *Inf.* in an unscrupulous or cowardly way. **9. tighten one's belt.** to take measures to reduce expenditure. **10. under one's belt. a.** in one's stomach. **b.** as part of one's experience: *he had a degree under his belt.* ~*vb.* **11.** (*tr.*) to fasten or attach with or as if with a belt. **12.** (*tr.*) to hit with a belt. **13.** (*tr.*) *Sl.* to give a sharp blow; punch. **14.** (*intr.;* often foll. by *along*) *Sl.* to move very fast, esp. in a car. **15.** (*tr.*) *Rare.* to encircle. [OE, < L *balteus*] —ˈ**belted** *adj.*

Beltane (ˈbɛlteɪn, -tən) *n.* an ancient Celtic festival with a sacrificial bonfire on May Day. [C15: < Scot. Gaelic *bealltainn*]

belting (ˈbɛltɪŋ) *n.* **1.** material for belts. **2.** belts collectively. **3.** *Inf.* a beating.

belt man *n. Austral. & N.Z.* the member of a beach life-saving team who swims out wearing a belt with a line attached.

belt out *vb.* (*tr., adv.*) *Inf.* to sing or emit sound loudly.

belt up *vb.* (*adv.*) **1.** *Sl.* to stop talking: often imperative. **2.** to fasten with a belt.

beluga (bɪˈluːgə) *n.* **1.** a large white sturgeon of the Black and Caspian Seas: a source of caviar and isinglass. **2.** another name for **white whale.** [C18: < Russian *byeluga,* < *byely* white]

belvedere (ˈbɛlvɪˌdɪə, ˌbɛlvɪˈdɪə) *n.* a building, such as a summerhouse, sited to command a fine view. [C16: < It.: beautiful sight]

BEM *abbrev. for* British Empire Medal.

bemire (bɪˈmaɪə) *vb.* (*tr.*) **1.** to soil as with mire. **2.** (*usually passive*) to stick fast in mire.

bemoan (bɪˈməʊn) *vb.* to mourn; lament (esp. in **bemoan one's fate**). [OE *bemǣnan;* see BE-, MOAN]

bemuse (bɪˈmjuːz) *vb.* (*tr.*) to confuse; bewilder.

bemused (bɪˈmjuːzd) *adj.* preoccupied; lost in thought.

ben¹ (bɛn) *Scot.* ~*n.* **1.** an inner room in a cottage. ~*prep., adv.* **2.** in; within; inside. ~Cf. **but².** [OE *binnan,* < BE- + *innan* inside]

ben² (bɛn) *n. Scot., Irish.* a mountain peak: *Ben Lomond.* [C18: < Gaelic beinn, < *beann*]

bench (bɛntʃ) *n.* **1.** a long seat for more than one person, usually lacking a back. **2.** a plain stout worktable. **3. the bench.** (*sometimes cap.*) **a.** a judge or magistrate sitting in court. **b.** judges or magistrates collectively. **4.** a ledge in a mine or quarry from which work is carried out. **5.** (in a gymnasium) a low table, which may be inclined, used for various exercises. **6.** a platform on which dogs, etc., are exhibited at shows. **7.** *N.Z.* a hollow formed by sheep on a hillside. ~*vb.* (*tr.*) **8.** to provide with benches. **9.** to exhibit (a dog, etc.) at a show. [OE *benc*]

bencher (ˈbɛntʃə) *n.* (*often pl.*) *Brit.* **1.** a member of the governing body of one of the Inns of Court. **2.** See **backbencher.**

bench mark *n.* **1.** a mark on a stone post or other permanent feature, used as a reference point in surveying. **2.** a criterion by which to measure something; reference point.

bench warrant *n.* a warrant issued by a judge or court directing that an offender be apprehended.

bend¹ (bɛnd) *vb.* **bending, bent. 1.** to form or cause to form a curve. **2.** to turn or cause to turn from a particular direction: *the road bends left.* **3.** (*intr.;* often foll. by *down,* etc.) to incline the body; stoop; bow. **4.** to submit or cause to submit: *to bend before superior force.* **5.** (*tr.*) to turn or direct (one's eyes, steps, attention, etc.). **6.** (*tr.*) *Naut.* to attach or fasten, as a sail to a boom. **7. bend the rules.** *Inf.* to ignore rules or change them to suit one's own convenience. ~*n.* **8.** a curved part. **9.** *Naut.* a knot in a line for joining it to another or to an object. **10.** the act of bending. **11. round the bend.** *Brit. sl.* mad. [OE *bendan*] —ˈ**bendable** *adj.* —ˈ**bendy** *adj.*

bend² (bɛnd) *n. Heraldry.* a diagonal line traversing a shield. [OE *bend* BAND²]

bender (ˈbɛndə) *n. Inf.* a drinking bout.

bends (bɛndz) *pl. n.* (*functioning as sing. or pl.*) **the.** a nontechnical name for **decompression sickness.**

bend sinister *n. Heraldry.* a diagonal line bisecting a shield from the top right to the bottom left, typically indicating a bastard line.

beneath (bɪˈniːθ) *prep.* **1.** below, esp. if covered, protected, or obscured by. **2.** not as great or good as would be demanded by: *beneath his dignity.* ~*adv.* **3.** below; underneath. [OE *beneothan,* < BE- + *neothan* low]

benedicite (ˌbɛnɪˈdaɪsɪtɪ) *n.* (esp. in Christian religious orders) a blessing or grace. [C13: < L, < *benedīcere,* < *bene* well + *dīcere* to speak]

Benedictine *n.* **1.** (ˌbɛnɪˈdɪktɪn, -taɪn). a monk or nun who is a member of the order of Saint Benedict, founded about 540 A.D. **2.** (ˌbɛnɪˈdɪktiːn). a greenish-yellow liqueur first made at the Benedictine monastery at Fécamp in France in about 1510. ~*adj.* (ˌbɛnɪˈdɪktɪn, -taɪn). **3.** of or relating to Saint Benedict or his order.

benediction (ˌbɛnɪˈdɪkʃən) *n.* **1.** an invocation of divine blessing. **2.** a Roman Catholic service in which the congregation is blessed with the sacrament. **3.** the state of being blessed. [C15: < L *benedictio,* < *benedīcere* to bless; see BENEDICITE] —ˌ**bene'dictory** *adj.*

Benedictus (ˌbɛnɪˈdɪktəs) *n.* (*sometimes not cap.*) *Christianity.* **1.** a canticle beginning *Benedictus qui venit in nomine Domini* in Latin and *Blessed is he that cometh in the name of the Lord* in English. **2.** a canticle beginning *Benedictus Dominus Deus Israel* in Latin and *Blessed be the Lord God of Israel* in English.

benefaction (ˌbɛnɪˈfækʃən) *n.* **1.** the act of doing good, esp. by giving a donation to charity. **2.** the donation or help given. [C17: < LL *benefactiō,* < L *bene* well + *facere* to do]

benefactor (ˈbɛnɪˌfæktə, ˌbɛnɪˈfæk-) *n.* a person who supports or helps a person, institution, etc., esp. by giving money. —ˈ**beneˌfactress** *fem. n.*

benefice (ˈbɛnɪfɪs) *n.* **1.** *Christianity.* an endowed Church office yielding an income to its holder; a Church living. **2.** the property or revenue attached to such an office. [C14: < OF, < L *beneficium* benefit, < *bene* well + *facere* to do] —ˈ**beneficed** *adj.*

beneficent (bɪˈnɛfɪsᵊnt) *adj.* charitable; generous. [C17: < L *beneficus;* see BENEFICE] —**be'neficence** *n.*

beneficial (ˌbɛnɪˈfɪʃəl) *adj.* **1.** (sometimes foll. by *to*) advantageous. **2.** *Law.* entitling a person to receive the profits or proceeds of property. [C15: < LL *beneficiālis,* < L *beneficium* kindness]

beneficiary (ˌbɛnɪˈfɪʃərɪ) *n., pl.* **-ciaries.** **1.** a person who gains or benefits. **2.** *Law.* a person entitled to receive funds or other property under a trust, will, etc. **3.** the holder of a benefice. **4.** *N.Z.* a person who receives government assistance: *social security beneficiary.* ~*adj.* **5.** of or relating to a benefice.

benefit (ˈbɛnɪfɪt) *n.* **1.** something that improves or promotes. **2.** advantage or sake. **3.** (*sometimes pl.*) a payment or series of payments made by an institution or government to a person who is ill, unemployed, etc. **4.** a theatrical performance, sports event, etc., to raise money for a charity. ~*vb.* **-fiting, -fited** *or U.S.* **-fitting, -fitted. 5.** to do or receive good; profit. [C14: < Anglo-F *benfet,* < L *benefactum,* < *bene facere* to do well]

benefit of clergy *n. Christianity.* **1.** sanction by the church: *marriage without benefit of clergy.* **2.** (in the Middle Ages) a privilege that placed the clergy outside the jurisdiction of secular courts.

benefit society *n.* a U.S. term for **friendly society.**

benevolence (bɪˈnɛvələns) *n.* **1.** inclination to do good; charity. **2.** an act of kindness.

benevolent (bɪˈnɛvələnt) *adj.* **1.** intending or showing goodwill; kindly; friendly. **2.** doing good rather than making profit; charitable: *a benevolent organization.* [C15: < L *benevolēns,* < *bene* well + *velle* to wish]

BEng *abbrev. for* Bachelor of Engineering.

Bengali (bɛnˈgɔːlɪ, bɛŋ-) *n.* **1.** a member of a people living chiefly in Bangladesh (a republic in S Asia) and in West Bengal (in NE India). **2.** their language. ~*adj.* **3.** of or relating to Bengal, the Bengalis, or their language.

Bengal light (bɛnˈgɔːl, bɛŋ-) *n.* a firework or flare that burns with a bright blue light, formerly used as a signal.

benighted (bɪˈnaɪtɪd) *adj.* **1.** lacking cultural, moral, or intellectual enlightenment. **2.** *Arch.* overtaken by night. —**be'nightedness** *n.*

benign (bɪˈnaɪn) *adj.* **1.** showing kindliness; genial. **2.** (of soil, climate, etc.) mild; gentle. **3.** favourable; propitious. **4.** *Pathol.* (of a tumour, etc.) not malignant. [C14: < OF *benigne,* < L *benignus,* < *bene* well + *gignere* to produce] —**be'nignly** *adv.*

benignant (bɪˈnɪgnənt) *adj.* **1.** kind; gracious. **2.** a less common word for **benign** (senses 3, 4). —**be'nignancy** *n.*

benignity (bɪˈnɪgnɪtɪ) *n., pl.* **-ties.** **1.** the quality of being benign. **2.** a kind or gracious act.

benison (ˈbɛnɪzᵊn, -sᵊn) *n. Arch.* a blessing. [C13: < OF *beneison,* < L *benedictiō* BENEDICTION]

bent[1] (bɛnt) *adj.* **1.** not straight; curved. **2.** (foll. by *on*) resolved (to); determined (to). **3.** *Sl.* **a.** dishonest; corrupt. **b.** (of goods) stolen. **c.** crazy. **d.** sexually deviant. ~*n.* **4.** personal inclination or aptitude. **5.** capacity of endurance (esp. in **to the top of one's bent**).

bent[2] (bɛnt) *n.* **1.** short for **bent grass.** **2.** *Arch.* any stiff grass or sedge. **3.** *Arch. or dialect.* heath or moorland. [OE *bionot*]

bent grass *n.* a perennial grass which has a spreading panicle of tiny flowers sometimes planted for hay or in lawns.

Benthamism (ˈbɛnθəmɪzəm) *n.* the utilitarian philosophy of Jeremy Bentham (1748-1832), English philosopher and jurist, which holds that the ultimate goal of society should be to promote the greatest happiness of the greatest number. —ˈ**Benthamite** *n, adj.*

benthos (ˈbɛnθɒs) *n.* the animals and plants living at the bottom of a sea or lake. [C19: < Gk: depth; rel. to *bathus* deep] —ˈ**benthic** *adj.*

bentonite (ˈbɛntəˌnaɪt) *n.* a clay that swells as it absorbs water: used as a filler in various industries. [after Fort *Benton,* Montana, U.S.A., where found]

bentwood (ˈbɛntˌwʊd) *n.* **a.** wood bent in moulds after being heated by steaming, used mainly for furniture. **b.** (*as modifier*): *a bentwood chair.*

benumb (bɪˈnʌm) *vb.* (*tr.*) **1.** to make numb or powerless; deaden, as by cold. **2.** (*usually passive*) to stupefy (the mind, senses, will, etc.).

Benzedrine (ˈbɛnzɪˌdriːn, -drɪn) *n.* a trademark for **amphetamine.**

benzene (ˈbɛnziːn) *n.* a colourless flammable poisonous liquid used in the manufacture of styrene, phenol, etc., as a solvent for fats, resins, etc., and as an insecticide. Formula: C_6H_6.

benzene ring *n.* the hexagonal ring of bonded carbon atoms in the benzene molecule.

benzine (ˈbɛnziːn, bɛnˈziːn) *or* **benzin** (ˈbɛnzɪn) *n.* **1.** a volatile mixture of the lighter hydrocarbon constituents of petroleum. **2.** *Austral. & N.Z.* a rare name for **petrol.**

benzo- *or* **benz-** *combining form.* **1.** indicating a fused benzene ring. **2.** indicating derivation from benzene or benzoic acid or the presence of phenyl groups. [< BENZOIN]

benzoate (ˈbɛnzəʊˌeɪt, -ɪt) *n.* a salt or ester of benzoic acid.

benzocaine (ˈbɛnzəʊˌkeɪn) *n.* a white crystalline ester used as a local anaesthetic.

benzoic (bɛnˈzəʊɪk) *adj.* of, containing, or derived from benzoic acid or benzoin.

benzoic acid *n.* a white crystalline solid occurring in many natural resins, used in plasticizers and dyes and as a food preservative (**E210**).

benzoin (ˈbɛnzɔɪn, -zəʊɪn) *n.* a gum resin containing benzoic acid, obtained from various tropical Asian trees and used in ointments, perfume, etc. [C16: < F *benjoin,* < OCatalan *benjui,* < Ar. *lubān jāwī,* lit.: frankincense of Java]

benzol *or* **benzole** (ˈbɛnzɒl) *n.* **1.** a crude form of benzene obtained from coal tar or coal gas and used as a fuel. **2.** an obsolete name for **benzene.**

bequeath (bɪˈkwiːð, -ˈkwiːθ) *vb.* (*tr.*) **1.** *Law.* to dispose of (property) by will. **2.** to hand down; pass on. [OE *becwethan*] —**be'queathal** *n.*

bequest (bɪˈkwɛst) *n.* **1.** the act of bequeathing. **2.** something that is bequeathed. [C14: BE- + OE *-cwiss* degree]

berate (bɪˈreɪt) *vb.* (*tr.*) to scold harshly.

Berber (ˈbɜːbə) *n.* **1.** a member of a Caucasoid Muslim people of N Africa. **2.** the language of this people. ~*adj.* **3.** of or relating to this people or their language.

berberis (ˈbɜːbərɪs) *n.* any of a genus of mainly N temperate shrubs. See **barberry.** [C19: < Med. L, <?]

berceuse (*French* bɛrsøz) *n.* **1.** a lullaby. **2.** an instrumental piece suggestive of this. [C19: < F: lullaby]

bereave (bɪˈriːv) *vb.* (*tr.*) (usually foll. by *of*) to deprive (of) something or someone valued, esp.

through death. [OE *bereafian*] —**be'reaved** *adj.* —**be'reavement** *n.*

bereft (bɪ'rɛft) *adj.* (usually foll. by *of*) deprived; parted (from): *bereft of hope.*

beret ('bɛreɪ) *n.* a round close-fitting brimless cap. [C19: < F *béret,* < OProvençal *berret*]

berg[1] (bɜːg) *n.* short for **iceberg.**

berg[2] (bɜːg) *n.* a South African word for **mountain.**

bergamot ('bɜːgəˌmɒt) *n.* **1.** a small Asian tree having sour pear-shaped fruit. **2. essence of bergamot.** a fragrant essential oil from the fruit rind of this plant, used in perfumery. **3.** a Mediterranean mint that yields a similar oil. [C17: < F *bergamote,* < It. *bergamotta,* of Turkic origin]

Bergie ('bɜːgiː) *n. S. African inf.* a vagabond, esp. one living on the slopes of Table Mountain in SW South Africa. [< Afrik. *berg* mountain]

bergschrund ('bɛrkʃrʊnt) *n.* a crevasse at the head of a glacier. [C19: G: mountain crack]

bergwind ('bɜːxvənt) *n.* a hot dry wind in South Africa blowing from the plateau down to the coast.

beriberi (ˌbɛrɪ'bɛrɪ) *n.* a disease, endemic in E and S Asia, caused by dietary deficiency of thiamine (vitamin B_1). [C19: < Sinhalese, by reduplication < *beri* weakness]

berk (bɜːk) *n. Brit. sl.* a variant spelling of **burk.**

berkelium (bɜː'kiːlɪəm, 'bɜːklɪəm) *n.* a radioactive transuranic element produced by bombardment of americium. Symbol: Bk; atomic no.: 97; half-life of most stable isotope, ^{247}Bk: 1400 years. [C20: after *Berkeley,* California, where it was discovered]

Berks (bɑːks) *abbrev. for* Berkshire.

berley *or* **burley** ('bɜːlɪ) *Austral.* ~*n.* **1.** groundbait. **2.** *Sl.* rubbish, nonsense. ~*vb.* **3.** (*tr.*) to scatter groundbait over. **4.** (*tr.*) to hurry (someone); urge on. [<?]

berlin (bə'lɪn, 'bɜːlɪn) *n.* **1.** (*sometimes cap.*) Also called: **berlin wool.** a fine wool yarn used for tapestry work, etc. **2.** a four-wheeled two-seated covered carriage, popular in the 18th century. [after *Berlin,* city in N Germany]

berm *or* **berme** (bɜːm) *n.* **1.** a narrow path or ledge as at the edge of a slope, road, or canal. **2.** *N.Z.* the grass verge of a suburban street, usually kept mown. [C18: < F *berme,* < Du. *berm*]

Bermuda shorts (bə'mjuːdə) *pl. n.* close-fitting shorts that come down to the knees. [after *Bermudas,* islands in NW Atlantic]

berretta (bɪ'rɛtə) *n.* a variant spelling of **biretta.**

berry ('bɛrɪ) *n., pl.* **-ries. 1.** any of various small edible fruits such as the blackberry and strawberry. **2.** *Bot.* a fruit with two or more seeds and a fleshy pericarp, such as the grape or gooseberry. **3.** any of various seeds or dried kernels, such as a coffee bean. **4.** the egg of a lobster, crayfish, or similar animal. ~*vb.* **-rying, -ried.** (*intr.*) **5.** to bear or produce berries. **6.** to gather or look for berries. [OE *berie*]

berserk (bə'zɜːk, -'sɜːk) *adj.* **1.** frenziedly violent or destructive (esp. in **go berserk**). ~*n.* **2.** Also called: **berserker.** one of a class of ancient Norse warriors who fought frenziedly. [C19: Icelandic *berserkr,* < *björn* bear + *serkr* shirt]

berth (bɜːθ) *n.* **1.** a bed or bunk in a vessel or train. **2.** *Naut.* a place assigned to a ship at a mooring. **3.** *Naut.* sufficient room for a ship to manoeuvre. **4. give a wide berth to.** to keep clear of. **5.** *Inf.* a job, esp. as a member of a ship's crew. ~*vb.* **6.** (*tr.*) *Naut.* to assign a berth to (a vessel). **7.** *Naut.* to dock (a vessel). **8.** (*tr.*) to provide with a sleeping place. **9.** (*intr.*) *Naut.* to pick up a mooring in an anchorage. [C17: prob. < BEAR[1] + -TH[1]]

bertha ('bɜːθə) *n.* a wide deep collar, often of lace, usually to cover a low neckline. [C19: < F *berthe,* < *Berthe,* 8th-cent. Frankish queen]

beryl ('bɛrɪl) *n.* a green, blue, yellow, pink, or white hard mineral consisting of beryllium aluminium silicate in hexagonal crystalline form. Emerald and aquamarine are transparent varieties. [C13: < OF, < L, < Gk *bērullos*] —'**beryline** *adj.*

beryllium (bɛ'rɪlɪəm) *n.* a corrosion-resistant toxic silvery-white metallic element used mainly in x-ray windows and alloys. Symbol: Be; atomic no.: 4; atomic wt.: 9.012. [C19: < L, < Gk *bērullos*]

beseech (bɪ'siːtʃ) *vb.* **-seeching, -sought** *or* **-seeched.** (*tr.*) to ask (someone) earnestly (to do something or for something); beg. [C12: see BE-, SEEK]

beseem (bɪ'siːm) *vb. Arch.* to be suitable for or worthy of; befit.

beset (bɪ'sɛt) *vb.* **-setting, -set.** (*tr.*) **1.** (esp. of dangers or temptations) to trouble or harass constantly. **2.** to surround or attack from all sides. **3.** *Arch.* to cover with, esp. with jewels.

besetting (bɪ'sɛtɪŋ) *adj.* tempting, harassing, or assailing (esp. in **besetting sin).**

beshrew (bɪ'ʃruː) *vb.* (*tr.*) *Arch.* to wish evil on; curse (used in mild oaths). [C14: see BE-, SHREW]

beside (bɪ'saɪd) *prep.* **1.** next to; at, by, or to the side of. **2.** as compared with. **3.** away from; wide of. **4.** *Arch.* besides. **5. beside oneself.** (*postpositive;* often foll. by *with*) overwhelmed; overwrought: *beside oneself with grief.* ~*adv.* **6.** at, by, to, or along the side of something or someone. [OE *be sīdan;* see BY, SIDE]

besides (bɪ'saɪdz) *prep.* **1.** apart from; even considering. ~ *sentence connector.* **2.** anyway; moreover. ~*adv.* **3.** as well.

besiege (bɪ'siːdʒ) *vb.* (*tr.*) **1.** to surround (a fortified area) with military forces to bring about its surrender. **2.** to crowd round; hem in. **3.** to overwhelm, as with requests. —**be'sieger** *n.*

besmear (bɪ'smɪə) *vb.* (*tr.*) **1.** to smear over; daub. **2.** to sully; defile (often in **besmear (a person's) reputation).**

besmirch (bɪ'smɜːtʃ) *vb.* (*tr.*) **1.** to make dirty; soil. **2.** to reduce the brightness of. **3.** to sully (often in **besmirch (a person's) name).**

besom[1] ('biːzəm) *n.* a broom, esp. one made of a bundle of twigs tied to a handle. [OE *besma*]

besom[2] ('bɪzəm) *n. Scot. & N English dialect.* a derogatory term for a **woman.** [? < OE *bysen* example; rel. to ON *bysn* wonder]

besotted (bɪ'sɒtɪd) *adj.* **1.** stupefied with drink. **2.** infatuated; doting. **3.** foolish; muddled.

besought (bɪ'sɔːt) *vb.* the past tense and past participle of **beseech.**

bespangle (bɪ'spæŋg'l) *vb.* (*tr.*) to cover or adorn with or as if with spangles.

bespatter (bɪ'spætə) *vb.* (*tr.*) **1.** to splash, as with dirty water. **2.** to defile; besmirch.

bespeak (bɪ'spiːk) *vb.* **-speaking, -spoke; -spoken** *or* **-spoke.** (*tr.*) **1.** to engage or ask for in advance. **2.** to indicate or suggest: *this act bespeaks kindness.* **3.** *Poetic.* to address.

bespectacled (bɪ'spɛktək'ld) *adj.* wearing spectacles.

bespoke (bɪ'spəʊk) *adj. Chiefly Brit.* **1.** (esp. of a suit, jacket, etc.) made to the customer's specifications. **2.** making or selling such suits, jackets, etc.: *a bespoke tailor.*

besprinkle (bɪ'sprɪŋk'l) *vb.* (*tr.*) to sprinkle all over with liquid, powder, etc.

Bessemer process ('bɛsɪmə) *n.* (formerly) a process for producing steel by blowing air through molten pig iron in a **Bessemer converter** (a refractory-lined furnace): impurities are removed and the carbon content is controlled. [C19: after Sir Henry *Bessemer* (1813–98), E engineer]

best (bɛst) *adj.* **1.** the superlative of **good. 2.** most excellent of a particular group, category, etc. **3.** most suitable, desirable, etc. **4. the best part of.** most of. ~*adv.* **5.** the superlative of **well**[1]. **6** in a manner surpassing all others; most excellently, attractively, etc. ~*n.* **7. the best.** the most outstanding or excellent person, thing, or group in a category. **8.** the utmost effort. **9.** a winning majority. **10.** Also: **all the best.** best wishes. **11.** a person's smartest outfit of clothing. **12. at best. a.** in the most favourable interpretation. **b.** under the most favourable conditions. **13. for the best. a.** for an ultimately good outcome. **b.** with good intentions. **14. get** *or* **have the best of.** to defeat or outwit. **15. give (someone) the best.** to concede (someone's) superiority. **16.**

make the best of. to cope as well as possible with. ~*vb.* 17. (*tr.*) to gain the advantage over or defeat. [OE *betst*]

bestead (bɪˈstɛd) *Arch.* ~*vb.* **-steading, -steaded; -steaded** *or* **-stead.** 1. (*tr.*) to help; avail. ~*adj.* *also* **bested.** 2. placed; situated. [C13: see BE-, STEAD]

bestial (ˈbɛstɪəl) *adj.* 1. brutal or savage. 2. sexually depraved. 3. lacking in refinement; brutish. 4. of or relating to a beast. [C14: < LL *bestiālis*, < L *bestia* BEAST]

bestiality (ˌbɛstɪˈælɪtɪ) *n., pl.* **-ties.** 1. bestial behaviour. 2. sexual activity between a person and an animal.

bestialize *or* **-ise** (ˈbɛstɪəˌlaɪz) *vb.* (*tr.*) to make bestial or brutal.

bestiary (ˈbɛstɪərɪ) *n., pl.* **-aries.** a moralizing medieval collection of descriptions of real and mythical animals.

bestir (bɪˈstɜː) *vb.* **-stirring, -stirred.** (*tr.*) to cause (oneself) to become active; rouse.

best man *n.* the male attendant of the bridegroom at a wedding.

bestow (bɪˈstəʊ) *vb.* (*tr.*) 1. to present (a gift) or confer (an honour). 2. *Arch.* to apply (energy, resources, etc.). 3. *Arch.* to house (a person) or store (goods). —**beˈstowal** *n.*

bestrew (bɪˈstruː) *vb.* **-strewing, -strewed; -strewn** *or* **-strewed.** (*tr.*) to scatter or lie scattered over (a surface).

bestride (bɪˈstraɪd) *vb.* **-striding, -strode** *or* (*Arch.*) **-strid; -stridden** *or* (*Arch.*) **-strid.** (*tr.*) 1. to have or put a leg on either side of. 2. to extend across; span. 3. to stride over or across.

best seller *n.* 1. a book or other product that has sold in great numbers. 2. the author of one or more such books, etc. —ˌ**best-ˈselling** *adj.*

bet (bɛt) *n.* 1. an agreement between two parties that a sum of money or other stake will be paid by the loser to the party who correctly predicts the outcome of an event. 2. the stake risked. 3. the predicted result in such an agreement. 4. a person, event, etc., considered as likely to succeed or occur. 5. a course of action (esp. in **one's best bet**). 6. *Inf.* an opinion: *my bet is that you've been up to no good.* ~*vb.* **betting, bet** *or* **betted.** 7. (when *intr.* foll. by *on* or *against*) to make or place a bet with (a person or persons). 8. (*tr.*) to stake (money, etc.) in a bet. 9. (*tr.; may take a clause as object*) *Inf.* to predict (a certain outcome). 10. **you bet.** *Inf.* of course; naturally. [C16: prob. short for ABET]

beta (ˈbiːtə) *n.* 1. the second letter in the Greek alphabet (Β or β). 2. the second in a group or series. [< Gk *bēta*, < Heb.; see BETH]

beta-blocker *n.* any of a class of drugs, such as propranolol, that decrease the activity of the heart: used in the treatment of high blood pressure and angina pectoris.

beta decay *n.* the radioactive change in an atomic nucleus accompanying the emission of an electron.

betake (bɪˈteɪk) *vb.* **-taking, -took, -taken.** (*tr.*) 1. **betake oneself.** to go; move. 2. *Arch.* to apply (oneself) to.

beta particle *n.* a high-speed electron or positron emitted by a nucleus during radioactive decay or nuclear fission.

beta ray *n.* a stream of beta particles.

beta rhythm *or* **wave** *n. Physiol.* the normal electrical activity of the cerebral cortex.

betatron (ˈbiːtəˌtrɒn) *n.* a type of particle accelerator for producing high-energy beams of electrons by magnetic induction.

betel (ˈbiːtᵊl) *n.* an Asian climbing plant, the leaves of which are chewed by the peoples of SE Asia. [C16: < Port., < Malayalam *vettila*]

betel nut *n.* the seed of the betel palm, chewed with betel leaves and lime by people in S and SE Asia as a digestive stimulant and narcotic.

betel palm *n.* a tropical Asian feather palm.

bête noire *French.* (bɛt nwar) *n., pl.* ***bêtes noires*** (bɛt nwar). a person or thing that one particularly dislikes or dreads. [lit.: black beast]

beth (bɛt) *n.* the second letter of the Hebrew alphabet. [< Heb. *bēth-*, *bayith* house]

bethink (bɪˈθɪŋk) *vb.* **-thinking, -thought.** *Arch. or dialect.* 1. to cause (oneself) to consider or meditate. 2. (*tr.; often foll. by of*) to remind (oneself).

betide (bɪˈtaɪd) *vb.* to happen or happen to (often in **woe betide (someone)**). [C13: < BE- + obs. *tide* to happen]

betimes (bɪˈtaɪmz) *adv. Arch.* 1. in good time; early. 2. soon. [C14 *bitimes;* see BY, TIME]

betoken (bɪˈtəʊkən) *vb.* (*tr.*) 1. to indicate; signify. 2. to portend; augur.

betony (ˈbɛtənɪ) *n., pl.* **-nies.** 1. a Eurasian plant with a spike of reddish-purple flowers, formerly used in medicine and dyeing. 2. any of several related plants. [C14: < OF, < L]

betray (bɪˈtreɪ) *vb.* (*tr.*) 1. to hand over or expose (one's nation, friend, etc.) treacherously to an enemy. 2. to disclose (a secret, confidence, etc.) treacherously. 3. to break (a promise) or be disloyal to (a person's trust). 4. to show signs of; indicate. 5. to reveal unintentionally: *his grin betrayed his satisfaction.* [C13: < BE- + *trayen*, < OF, < L *trādere* to hand over] —**beˈtrayal** *n.* —**beˈtrayer** *n.*

betroth (bɪˈtrəʊð) *vb.* (*tr.*) *Arch.* to promise to marry or to give in marriage. [C14 *betreuthen*, < BE- + *treuthe* TROTH, TRUTH]

betrothal (bɪˈtrəʊðəl) *n.* 1. engagement to be married. 2. a mutual promise to marry.

betrothed (bɪˈtrəʊðd) *adj.* 1. engaged to be married: *he was betrothed to her.* ~*n.* 2. the person to whom one is engaged; fiancé or fiancée.

better (ˈbɛtə) *adj.* 1. the comparative of **good.** 2. more excellent than others. 3. more suitable, advantageous, attractive, etc. 4. improved or fully recovered in health. 5. **better off.** in more favourable circumstances, esp. financially. 6. **the better part of.** a large part of. ~*adv.* 7. the comparative of **well**[1]. 8. in a more excellent manner; more advantageously, attractively, etc. 9. in or to a greater degree or extent; more. 10. **had better.** would be wise, sensible, etc., to: *I had better be off.* 11. **think better of. a.** to change one's mind about (a course of action, etc.) after reconsideration. **b.** to rate more highly. ~*n.* 12. **the better.** something that is the more excellent, useful, etc., of two such things. 13. (*usually pl.*) a person who is superior, esp. in social standing or ability. 14. **for the better.** by way of improvement. 15. **get the better of.** to defeat, outwit, or surpass. ~*vb.* 16. to make or become better. 17. (*tr.*) to improve upon; surpass. [OE *betera*]

better half *n. Humorous.* one's spouse.

betterment (ˈbɛtəmənt) *n.* 1. a change for the better; improvement. 2. *Property law.* an improvement effected on real property that enhances the value of the property.

betting shop *n.* (in Britain) a licensed bookmaker's premises not on a racecourse.

between (bɪˈtwiːn) *prep.* 1. at a point or in a region intermediate to two other points in space, times, degrees, etc. 2. in combination; together: *between them, they saved enough money to buy a car.* 3. confined or restricted to: *between you and me.* 4. indicating a reciprocal relation or comparison. 5. indicating two or more alternatives. ~*adv. also* **in between.** 6. between one specified thing and another. [OE *betwēonum;* see TWO, TWAIN]

▷ **Usage.** In careful usage, *between* is restricted to cases where only two people, objects, possibilities, etc., are concerned. Grammatically, *between you and I* is incorrect. The proper construction is *between you and me.*

betweentimes (bɪˈtwiːnˌtaɪmz) *or* **betweenwhiles** *adv.* between other activities; during intervals.

betwixt (bɪˈtwɪkst) *prep., adv.* 1. *Arch.* another word for **between.** 2. **betwixt and between.** in an intermediate or indecisive position. [OE *betwix*]

BeV (in the U.S.) *abbrev. for* gigaelectronvolts (GeV). [C20: < *b*(*illion*) *e*(*lectron*) *v*(*olts*)]

bevatron (ˈbɛvəˌtrɒn) *n.* a synchrotron used to accelerate protons. [C20: < BEV + -TRON]
bevel (ˈbɛvᵊl) *n.* **1.** Also called: **cant.** a surface that meets another at an angle other than a right angle. ~*vb.* **-elling, -elled** *or U.S.* **-eling, -eled. 2.** (*intr.*) to be inclined; slope. **3.** (*tr.*) to cut a bevel on (a piece of timber, etc.). [C16: < OF, < *baer* to gape; see BAY[1]]
bevel gear *n.* a gear having teeth cut into a conical surface. Two such gears mesh together to transmit power between two shafts at an angle.
bevel square *n.* a tool with an adjustable arm that can be set to mark out an angle.
beverage (ˈbɛvərɪdʒ, ˈbɛvrɪdʒ) *n.* any drink, usually other than water. [C13: < OF *bevrage*, < *beivre* to drink, < L *bibere*]
beverage room *n. Canad.* another name for **beer parlour.**
bevvy (ˈbɛvɪ) *n., pl.* **-vies.** *Dialect.* **1.** a drink, esp. an alcoholic one. **2.** a night of drinking. [prob. < OF *bevee, buvee* drinking]
bevy (ˈbɛvɪ) *n., pl.* **bevies. 1.** a flock of quails. **2.** a group, esp. of girls. [C15: <?]
bewail (bɪˈweɪl) *vb.* to express great sorrow over (a person or thing); lament. **—beˈwailer** *n.*
beware (bɪˈwɛə) *vb.* (*usually used in the imperative or infinitive;* often foll. by *of*) to be cautious or wary (of); be on one's guard (against). [C13 *be war*, < BE (imperative) + *war* WARY]
bewilder (bɪˈwɪldə) *vb.* (*tr.*) to confuse utterly; puzzle. [C17: see BE-, WILDER] **—beˈwildering** *adj.* **—beˈwilderingly** *adv.* **—beˈwilderment** *n.*
bewitch (bɪˈwɪtʃ) *vb.* (*tr.*) **1.** to attract and fascinate. **2.** to cast a spell over. [C13 *bewicchen;* see BE-, WITCH[1]] **—beˈwitching** *adj.*
bewray (bɪˈreɪ) *vb.* (*tr.*) an obsolete word for **betray.** [C13: < BE- + OE *wrēgan* to accuse]
bey (beɪ) *n.* **1.** (in the Ottoman Empire) a title given to provincial governors. **2.** (in modern Turkey) a title of address, corresponding to *Mr.* ~Also called: **beg.** [C16: Turkish: lord]
beyond (bɪˈjɒnd) *prep.* **1.** at or to a point on the other side of; at or to the further side of: *beyond those hills.* **2.** outside the limits or scope of. ~*adv.* **3.** at or to the other or far side of something. **4.** outside the limits of something. ~*n.* **5. the beyond.** the unknown, esp. life after death in certain religious beliefs. [OE *begeondan;* see BY, YONDER]
bezel (ˈbɛzᵊl) *n.* **1.** the sloping face adjacent to the working edge of a cutting tool. **2.** the upper oblique faces of a cut gem. **3.** a grooved ring or part holding a gem, watch crystal, etc. [C17: prob. < F *biseau*]
bezique (bɪˈziːk) *n.* **1.** a card game for two or more players using two packs with nothing below a seven. **2.** (in this game) the queen of spades and jack of diamonds declared together. [C19: < F *bésigue*, <?]
bf *abbrev. for:* **1.** *Brit. inf.* bloody fool. **2.** *Printing.* bold face.
B/F *or* **b/f** *Book-keeping. abbrev. for* brought forward.
BFPO *abbrev. for* British Forces Post Office.
bhang *or* **bang** (bæŋ) *n.* a preparation of the leaves and flower tops of Indian hemp having psychoactive properties: much used in India. [C16: < Hindi *bhāng*]
bharal *or* **burhel** (ˈbʌrəl) *n.* a wild Himalayan sheep with a bluish-grey coat. [Hindi]
bhindi (ˈbɪndɪ) *n.* the okra as used in Indian cooking. [Hindi]
bhp *abbrev. for* brake horsepower.
BHP *Austral. abbrev. for* Broken Hill Proprietary.
Bi *the chemical symbol for* bismuth.
bi- *or sometimes before a vowel* **bin-** *combining form.* **1.** two; having two: *bifocal.* **2.** occurring every two; lasting for two: *biennial.* **3.** on both sides, directions, etc.: *bilateral.* **4.** occurring twice during: *biweekly.* **5. a.** denoting a compound containing two identical cyclic hydrocarbon systems: *biphenyl.* **b.** (rare in technical usage) indicating an acid salt of a dibasic acid: *sodium bicarbonate.* **c.** (not in technical usage) equivalent of **di-**[1] (sense 2). [< L, < *bis* TWICE]
▷ **Usage.** In order to avoid ambiguity, care should be taken in observing the distinction between *bi-* and *semi-* in *biweekly, bimonthly, biyearly* (once in two weeks, months, years) and *semiweekly, semimonthly, semiyearly* (twice during one week, month, year). In strict usage, *biennial* (lasting or occurring once in two years) is distinguished from *biannual* (occurring twice in one year).
biannual (baɪˈænjʊəl) *adj.* occurring twice a year. Cf. **biennial. —biˈannually** *adv.*
bias (ˈbaɪəs) *n.* **1.** mental tendency or inclination, esp. irrational preference or prejudice. **2.** a diagonal line or cut across the weave of a fabric. **3.** *Electronics.* the voltage applied to an electrode of a transistor or valve to establish suitable working conditions. **4.** *Bowls.* **a.** a bulge or weight inside one side of a bowl. **b.** the curved course of such a bowl. **5.** *Statistics.* a latent influence that disturbs an analysis. ~*adv.* **6.** obliquely; diagonally. ~*vb.* **-asing, -ased** *or* **-assing, -assed. 7.** (*tr.; usually passive*) to cause to have a bias; prejudice; influence. [C16: < OF *biais*] **—ˈbiased** *or* **ˈbiassed** *adj.*
bias binding *n.* a strip of material cut on the bias, used for binding hems or for decoration.
biathlon (baɪˈæθlən, -lɒn) *n. Sport.* a contest in which skiers with rifles shoot at four targets along a 20-kilometre (12.5-mile) cross-country course.
biaxial (baɪˈæksɪəl) *adj.* (esp. of a crystal) having two axes.
bib (bɪb) *n.* **1.** a piece of cloth or plastic worn, esp. by babies, to protect their clothes while eating. **2.** the upper front part of some aprons, dungarees, etc. **3.** Also called: **pout, whiting pout.** a light brown European marine gadoid food fish with a barbel on its lower jaw. **4. stick one's bib in.** *Austral. inf.* to interfere. ~*vb.* **bibbing, bibbed. 5.** *Arch.* to drink (something). [C14 *bibben* to drink, prob. < L *bibere*]
Bib. *abbrev. for:* **1.** Bible. **2.** Biblical.
bib and tucker *n. Inf.* an outfit of clothes.
bibcock (ˈbɪbˌkɒk) *or* **bib** *n.* a tap with a nozzle bent downwards fed from a horizontal pipe.
bibelot (ˈbɪbləʊ) *n.* an attractive or curious trinket. [C19: < F, < OF *beubelet*]
bibl. *abbrev. for:* **1.** bibliographical. **2.** bibliography.
Bibl. *abbrev. for* Biblical.
Bible (ˈbaɪbᵊl) *n.* **1. a. the.** the sacred writings of the Christian religion, comprising the Old and New Testaments. **b.** (*as modifier*): *a Bible reading.* **2.** (*often not cap.*) the sacred writings of a religion. **3.** (*usually not cap.*) a book regarded as authoritative. [C13: < OF, < Med. L *biblia* books, < Gk, dim. of *biblos* papyrus]
▷ **Usage.** *The Bible* is written with a capital initial but should not be put in inverted commas. The adjective *biblical* is written without a capital initial: *a new translation of the Bible; life in biblical times.*
Bible-thumper *n. Sl.* an enthusiastic or aggressive exponent of the Bible. Also: **Bible-basher. —ˈBible-ˌthumping** *n., adj.*
biblical (ˈbɪblɪkᵊl) *adj.* **1.** of or referring to the Bible. **2.** resembling the Bible in written style.
▷ **Usage.** See at **Bible.**
Biblicist (ˈbɪblɪsɪst) *or* **Biblist** *n.* **1.** a biblical scholar. **2.** a person who takes the Bible literally.
biblio- *combining form.* indicating book or books: *bibliography.* [< Gk *biblion* book]
bibliography (ˌbɪblɪˈɒgrəfɪ) *n., pl.* **-phies. 1.** a list of books on a subject or by a particular author. **2.** a list of sources used in a book, thesis, etc. **3. a.** the study of the history, classification, etc., of literary material. **b.** a work on this subject. **—ˌbibliˈographer** *n.* **—bibliographic** (ˌbɪblɪəʊˈgræfɪk) *or* **ˌbiblioˈgraphical** *adj.*
bibliomancy (ˈbɪblɪəʊˌmænsɪ) *n.* prediction of the future by interpreting a passage chosen at random from a book, esp. the Bible.
bibliomania (ˌbɪblɪəʊˈmeɪnɪə) *n.* extreme fondness for books. **—ˌbiblioˈmaniˌac** *n., adj.*
bibliophile (ˈbɪblɪəˌfaɪl) *or* **bibliophil** (ˈbɪblɪəfɪl) *n.* a person who collects or is fond of books.

—**bibliophilism** (ˌbɪblɪˈɒfɪˌlɪzəm) *n.* —ˌ**bibli'ophily** *n.*

bibliopole (ˈbɪblɪəʊˌpəʊl) *or* **bibliopolist** (ˌbɪblɪˈɒpəlɪst) *n.* a dealer in books, esp. rare or decorative ones. [C18: < L, < Gk, < BIBLIO- + *pōlein* to sell] —ˌ**bibli'opoly** *n.*

bibulous (ˈbɪbjʊləs) *adj.* addicted to alcohol. [C17: < L *bibulus*, < *bibere* to drink] —'**bibulously** *adv.* —'**bibulousness** *n.*

bicameral (baɪˈkæmərəl) *adj.* (of a legislature) consisting of two chambers. [C19: < BI- + L *camera* CHAMBER] —**bi'cameral**ˌ**ism** *n.*

bicarb (ˈbaɪkɑːb) *n.* short for **bicarbonate of soda.**

bicarbonate (baɪˈkɑːbənɪt, -ˌneɪt) *n.* a salt of carbonic acid.

bicarbonate of soda *n.* sodium bicarbonate, esp. as medicine or a raising agent in baking.

bice (baɪs) *n.* **1.** Also called: **bice blue.** medium blue. **2.** Also called: **bice green.** a yellowish green. [C14: < OF *bis* dark grey, <?]

bicentenary (ˌbaɪsɛnˈtiːnərɪ) *or U.S.* **bicentennial** (ˌbaɪsɛnˈtɛnɪəl) *adj.* **1.** marking a 200th anniversary. **2.** occurring every 200 years. **3.** lasting 200 years. ~*n., pl.* **-naries. 4.** a 200th anniversary.

bicephalous (baɪˈsɛfələs) *adj.* **1.** *Biol.* having two heads. **2.** crescent-shaped.

biceps (ˈbaɪsɛps) *n., pl.* **-ceps.** *Anat.* any muscle having two heads or origins, esp. the muscle that flexes the forearm. [C17: < L, < BI- + *caput* head]

bichloride (baɪˈklɔːraɪd) *n.* another name for **dichloride.**

bichloride of mercury *n.* another name for **mercuric chloride.**

bichromate (baɪˈkrəʊˌmeɪt, -mɪt) *n.* another name for **dichromate.**

bicker (ˈbɪkə) *vb.* (*intr.*) **1.** to argue over petty matters; squabble. **2.** *Poetic.* **a.** (esp. of a stream) to run quickly. **b.** to flicker; glitter. ~*n.* **3.** a squabble. [C13: <?] —'**bickerer** *n.*

bicolour (ˈbaɪˌkʌlə), **bicoloured** *or U.S.* **bicolor, bicolored** *adj.* two-coloured.

biconcave (baɪˈkɒnkeɪv, ˌbaɪkɒnˈkeɪv) *adj.* (of a lens) having concave faces on both sides.

biconditional (ˌbaɪkənˈdɪʃənᵊl) *n.* **1.** *Logic, maths.* a relation, taken as meaning *if and only if*, between two propositions which are either both true or both false and such that each implies the other. **2.** *Logic.* a logical connective between two propositions whose truth table is true only if both propositions are true or both false. ~Also called (esp. sense 1): **equivalence.**

biconvex (baɪˈkɒnvɛks, ˌbaɪkɒnˈvɛks) *adj.* (of a lens) having convex faces on both sides.

bicuspid (baɪˈkʌspɪd) *or* **bicuspidate** (baɪˈkʌspɪˌdeɪt) *adj.* **1.** having two cusps or points. ~*n.* **2.** a bicuspid tooth; premolar.

bicycle (ˈbaɪsɪkᵊl) *n.* **1.** a vehicle with a tubular metal frame mounted on two spoked wheels, one behind the other. The rider sits on a saddle, propels the vehicle by means of pedals, and steers with handlebars on the front wheel. Often shortened to **bike** (inf.), **cycle.** ~*vb.* **2.** (*intr.*) to ride a bicycle. —'**bicyclist** *or* '**bicycler** *n.*

bicycle clip *n.* one of a pair of clips worn around the ankles by cyclists to keep the trousers tight and out of the chain.

bid (bɪd) *vb.* **bidding; bad, bade,** *or* (esp. for senses 1, 4, 5) **bid; bidden** *or* (esp. for senses 1, 4, 5) **bid. 1.** (often foll. by *for* or *against*) to offer (an amount) in attempting to buy something. **2.** (*tr.*) to say (a greeting, etc.): *to bid farewell.* **3.** to order; command: *do as you are bid!* **4.** (*intr.*; usually foll. by *for*) to attempt to attain power, etc. **5.** *Bridge, etc.* to declare before play how many tricks one expects to make. **6. bid defiance.** to resist boldly. **7. bid fair.** to seem probable. ~*n.* **8. a.** an offer of a specified amount. **b.** the price offered. **9. a.** the quoting by a seller of a price. **b.** the price quoted. **10.** an attempt, esp. to attain power. **11.** *Bridge, etc.* **a.** the number of tricks a player undertakes to make. **b.** a player's turn to make a bid. ~See also **bid up.** [OE *biddan*] —'**bidder** *n.*

▷ **Usage.** *Bid* in journalistic usage has become a noun used to refer to any kind of attempt to achieve something: *bid to climb Everest; doctor makes bid to save life.* This use of *bid* is avoided by careful writers, however, and the word is restricted to the sense of an offer of a price: *the auctioneer accepted a bid of £3000.*

biddable (ˈbɪdəbᵊl) *adj.* **1.** having sufficient value to be bid on, as a hand at bridge. **2.** docile; obedient. —'**biddableness** *n.*

bidding (ˈbɪdɪŋ) *n.* **1.** an order; command. **2.** an invitation; summons. **3.** bids or the act of making bids.

biddy[1] (ˈbɪdɪ) *n., pl.* **-dies.** a dialect word for **chicken** or **hen.** [C17: ? limit. of calling chickens]

biddy[2] (ˈbɪdɪ) *n., pl.* **-dies.** *Inf.* a woman, esp. an old gossipy one. [C18: < pet form of *Bridget*]

biddy-biddy (ˈbɪdɪˌbɪdɪ) *n., pl.* **-biddies. 1.** a low-growing rosaceous plant of New Zealand, having prickly burs. **2.** the burs of this plant. ~Also: **bidgee-widgee** (ˈbɪdʒɪˌwɪdʒɪ). [< Maori *piripiri*]

bide (baɪd) *vb.* **biding, bided** *or* **bode, bided. 1.** (*intr.*) *Arch. or dialect.* to continue in a certain place or state; stay. **2.** (*tr.*) *Arch. or dialect.* to tolerate; endure. **3. bide one's time.** to wait patiently for an opportunity. [OE *bīdan*]

bidentate (baɪˈdɛnˌteɪt) *adj.* having two teeth or toothlike parts or processes.

bidet (ˈbiːdeɪ) *n.* a small low basin for washing the genital area. [C17: < F: small horse]

bid up *vb.* (*adv.*) to increase the market price of (a commodity) by making artificial bids.

biennial (baɪˈɛnɪəl) *adj.* **1.** occurring every two years. **2.** lasting two years. Cf. **biannual.** ~*n.* **3.** a plant that completes its life cycle in two years. **4.** an event that takes place every two years. —**bi'ennially** *adv.*

bier (bɪə) *n.* a platform or stand on which a corpse or a coffin containing a corpse rests before burial. [OE *bǣr*; rel. to *beran* to BEAR[1]]

biestings (ˈbiːstɪŋz) *n.* a variant spelling of **beestings.**

biff (bɪf) *Sl.* ~*n.* **1.** a blow with the fist. ~*vb.* **2.** (*tr.*) to give (someone) such a blow. [C20: prob. imit.]

bifid (ˈbaɪfɪd) *adj.* divided into two lobes by a median cleft. [C17: < L, < BI- + *-fidus*, < *findere* to split] —**bi'fidity** *n.* —'**bifidly** *adv.*

bifocal (baɪˈfəʊkᵊl) *adj.* **1.** *Optics.* having two different focuses. **2.** relating to a compound lens permitting near and distant vision.

bifocals (baɪˈfəʊkᵊlz) *pl. n.* a pair of spectacles with bifocal lenses.

BIFU (in Britain) *abbrev. for* Banking, Insurance and Finance Union.

bifurcate *vb.* (ˈbaɪfəˌkeɪt). **1.** to fork or divide into two branches. ~*adj.* (ˈbaɪfəˌkeɪt, -kɪt). **2.** forked or divided into two branches. [C17: < Med. L, < L, < BI- + *furca* fork] —ˌ**bifur'cation** *n.*

big (bɪg) *adj.* **bigger, biggest. 1.** of great or considerable size, height, weight, number, power, or capacity. **2.** having great significance; important. **3.** important through having power, influence, wealth, authority, etc. **4.** *Inf.* considerable in extent or intensity (esp. in **in a big way**). **5. a.** elder: *my big brother.* **b.** grown-up. **6. a.** generous; magnanimous: *that's very big of you.* **b.** (*in combination*): *big-hearted.* **7.** extravagant; boastful: *big talk.* **8. too big for one's boots** *or* **breeches.** conceited; unduly self-confident. **9.** in an advanced stage of pregnancy (esp. in **big with child**). ~*adv. Inf.* **10.** boastfully; pretentiously (esp. in **talk big**). **11.** in an exceptional way; well: *his talk went over big.* **12.** on a grand scale (esp. in **think big**). [C13: ?< ON] —'**bigness** *n.*

bigamy (ˈbɪgəmɪ) *n., pl.* **-mies.** the crime of marrying a person while still legally married to someone else. [C13: via F < Med. L; see BI-, -GAMY] —'**bigamist** *n.* —'**bigamous** *adj.*

Big Apple *n.* **the** *inf.* New York City. [C20: prob. < U.S. jazzmen's earlier use to mean any big, esp. northern, city; < ?]

Big Bang *n.* the reorganization of the London Stock Exchange that took effect in October 1986 when operations became fully computerized, fixed commissions were abolished, and the functions of jobbers and brokers were merged.

big-bang theory *n.* a cosmological theory postulating that all the matter of the universe was hurled in all directions by a cataclysmic explosion and that the universe is still expanding. Cf. **steady-state theory.**

Big Brother *n.* a person, organization, etc., that exercises total dictatorial control. [C20: < George Orwell's novel *1984* (1949)]

big business *n.* large commercial organizations collectively, esp. when considered as exploitative or socially harmful.

big deal *interj. Sl.* an exclamation of scorn, derision, etc., used esp. to belittle a claim or offer.

big dipper *n.* (in amusement parks) a narrow railway with open carriages that run swiftly over a route of sharp curves and steep inclines.

big end *n. Brit.* the larger end of a connecting rod in an internal-combustion engine.

big game *n.* large animals that are hunted or fished for sport.

big gun *n. Inf.* an important person.

bighead (ˈbɪɡˌhɛd) *n. Inf.* a conceited person. —ˌ**bigˈheaded** *adj.* —ˌ**bigˈheadedness** *n.*

bighorn (ˈbɪɡˌhɔːn) *n., pl.* **-horns** *or* **-horn.** a large wild sheep inhabiting mountainous regions in North America.

bight (baɪt) *n.* **1.** a wide indentation of a shoreline, or the body of water bounded by such a curve. **2.** the slack middle part or loop in a rope. [OE *byht;* see BOW[2]]

Bight (baɪt) *n.* **the.** the major indentation of the S coast of Australia. In full: **the Great Australian Bight.**

bigmouth (ˈbɪɡˌmaʊθ) *n. Sl.* a noisy, indiscreet, or boastful person. —ˈ**big-**ˌ**mouthed** *adj.*

big noise *n. Brit. inf.* an important person.

bignonia (bɪɡˈnəʊnɪə) *n.* a tropical American climbing shrub cultivated for its trumpet-shaped yellow or reddish flowers. [C19: < NL, after the Abbé Jean-Paul *Bignon* (1662–1743)]

big-note *vb. (tr.) Austral. inf.* to boast about (oneself).

bigot (ˈbɪɡət) *n.* a person who is intolerant, esp. regarding religion, politics, or race. [C16: < OF: name applied contemptuously to the Normans by the French, <?] —ˈ**bigoted** *adj.* —ˈ**bigotry** *n.*

big shot *n. Inf.* an important person.

big smoke *n.* **the.** *Inf.* a large city, esp. London.

big stick *n. Inf.* force or the threat of force.

big time *n. Inf.* **a. the.** the highest level of a profession, esp. entertainment. **b.** (*as modifier*): *a big-time comedian.* —ˈ**big-**ˈ**timer** *n.*

big top *n. Inf.* **1.** the main tent of a circus. **2.** the circus itself.

bigwig (ˈbɪɡˌwɪɡ) *n. Inf.* an important person.

bijou (ˈbiːʒuː) *n., pl.* **-joux** (-ʒuːz). **1.** something small and delicately worked. **2.** (*modifier*) *Often ironic.* small but tasteful: *a bijou residence.* [C19: < F, < Breton *bizou* finger ring, < *biz* finger]

bijugate (ˈbaɪdʒʊˌɡeɪt, baɪˈdʒuːɡeɪt) *or* **bijugous** *adj.* (of compound leaves) having two pairs of leaflets.

bike (baɪk) *n.* **1.** *Inf.* short for **bicycle** or **motorcycle. 2.** *Sl.* a promiscuous woman. **3. get off one's bike.** *Austral. & N.Z. sl.* to lose one's self-control. ~*vb.* **4.** (*intr.*) to ride a bike.

biker (ˈbaɪkə) *n.* a member of a motorcycle gang. Also called (Austral. & N.Z.): **bikie.**

bikini (bɪˈkiːnɪ) *n.* a woman's very brief two-piece swimming costume. [C20: after *Bikini* atoll, < a comparison between the devastating effect of the atom-bomb test and the effect caused by women wearing bikinis]

bilabial (baɪˈleɪbɪəl) *adj.* **1.** of or denoting a speech sound articulated using both lips: (*p*) *is a bilabial stop.* ~*n.* **2.** a bilabial speech sound.

bilabiate (baɪˈleɪbɪˌeɪt, -ɪt) *adj. Bot.* divided into two lips: *the snapdragon has a bilabiate corolla.*

bilateral (baɪˈlætərəl) *adj.* **1.** having or involving two sides. **2.** affecting or undertaken by two parties; mutual. **3.** having identical sides or parts on each side of an axis; symmetrical.

bilateral symmetry *n.* symmetry in one plane only. Cf. **radial symmetry.**

bilberry (ˈbɪlbərɪ) *n., pl.* **-ries. 1.** any of several shrubs, such as the whortleberry, having edible blue or blackish berries. **2.** the fruit of any of these plants. [C16: prob. of Scand. origin]

bilboes (ˈbɪlbəʊz) *pl. n.* a long iron bar with sliding shackles, for the ankles of a prisoner. [C16: ?< *Bilbao,* Spain]

Bildungsroman *German.* (ˈbɪldʊŋsromaːn) *n.* a novel about a person's formative years.

bile (baɪl) *n.* **1.** a bitter greenish to golden brown alkaline fluid secreted by the liver and stored in the gall bladder. It aids digestion of fats. **2.** a health disorder due to faulty secretion of bile. **3.** irritability or peevishness. [C17: < F, < L *bīlis*]

bilge (bɪldʒ) *n.* **1.** *Naut.* the parts of a vessel's hull where the sides curve inwards to form the bottom. **2.** (*often pl.*) the parts of a vessel between the lowermost floorboards and the bottom. **3.** Also called: **bilge water.** the dirty water that collects in a vessel's bilge. **4.** *Inf.* silly rubbish; nonsense. **5.** the widest part of a cask. ~*vb.* **6.** (*intr.*) *Naut.* (of a vessel) to take in water at the bilge. **7.** (*tr.*) *Naut.* to damage (a vessel) in the bilge. [C16: prob. var. of BULGE]

bilharzia (bɪlˈhɑːtsɪə) *n.* **1.** another name for a **schistosome. 2.** another name for **schistosomiasis.** [C19: NL, after Theodor *Bilharz* (1825–62), G parasitologist who discovered schistosomes]

bilharziasis (ˌbɪlhɑːˈtsaɪəsɪs) *or* **bilharziosis** (bɪlˌhɑːtsɪˈəʊsɪs) *n.* another name for **schistosomiasis.**

biliary (ˈbɪlɪərɪ) *adj.* of or relating to bile, to the ducts that convey bile, or to the gall bladder.

bilingual (baɪˈlɪŋɡwəl) *adj.* **1.** able to speak two languages, esp. with fluency. **2.** expressed in two languages. ~*n.* **3.** a bilingual person. —**biˈlingualˌism** *n.*

bilious (ˈbɪlɪəs) *adj.* **1.** of or relating to bile. **2.** affected with or denoting any disorder related to secretion of bile. **3.** *Inf.* bad-tempered; irritable. [C16: < L *bīliōsus* full of BILE] —ˈ**biliousness** *n.*

bilk (bɪlk) *vb. (tr.)* **1.** to balk; thwart. **2.** (*often foll. by of*) to cheat or deceive, esp. to avoid making payment to. **3.** to escape from; elude. ~*n.* **4.** a swindle or cheat. **5.** a person who swindles or cheats. [C17: ? var. of BALK] —ˈ**bilker** *n.*

bill[1] (bɪl) *n.* **1.** money owed for goods or services supplied. **2.** a statement of money owed. **3.** *Chiefly Brit.* such an account for food and drink in a restaurant, hotel, etc. **4.** any list of items, events, etc., such as a theatre programme. **5.** a statute in draft, before it becomes law. **6.** a printed notice or advertisement. **7.** *U.S. & Canad.* a piece of paper money; note. **8.** an obsolete name for **promissory note. 9.** See **bill of exchange, bill of fare.** ~*vb. (tr.)* **10.** to send or present an account for payment to (a person). **11.** to enter (items, goods, etc.) on an account or statement. **12.** to advertise by posters. **13.** to schedule as a future programme. [C14: < Anglo-L *billa,* alteration of LL *bulla* document, BULL[3]]

bill[2] (bɪl) *n.* **1.** the projecting jaws of a bird, covered with a horny sheath; beak. **2.** any beaklike mouthpart in other animals. **3.** a narrow promontory. ~*vb. (intr.)* (esp. in **bill and coo**). **4.** (of birds, esp. doves) to touch bills together. **5.** (of lovers) to kiss and whisper amorously. [OE *bile*]

bill[3] (bɪl) *n.* **1.** a pike or halberd with a narrow hooked blade. **2.** short for **billhook.** [OE *bill* sword]

billabong (ˈbɪləˌbɒŋ) *n. Austral.* **1.** a stagnant pool in the bed of an intermittent stream. **2.** a branch of a river running to a dead end. [C19: < Abor., < *billa* river + *bong* dead]

billboard (ˈbɪlˌbɔːd) *n. Chiefly U.S. & Canad.* another name for **hoarding.** [C19: < BILL[1] + BOARD]

billet[1] (ˈbɪlɪt) *n.* **1.** accommodation, esp. for a soldier, in civilian lodgings. **2.** the official requisition for such lodgings. **3.** a space or berth in a ship. **4.** *Inf.* a job. ~*vb.* **5.** (*tr.*) to assign a lodging to (a soldier). **6.** to lodge or be lodged. [C15: < OF *billette*, < *bulle* a document; see BULL[3]]

billet[2] ('bɪlɪt) *n.* **1.** a chunk of wood, esp. for fuel. **2.** a small bar of iron or steel. [C15: < OF *billette* a little log, < *bille* log]

billet-doux (ˌbɪlɪ'duː) *n., pl.* **billets-doux** (ˌbɪlɪ'duːz). *Old-fashioned or jocular.* a love letter. [C17: < F, lit.: a sweet letter]

billhook ('bɪlˌhʊk) *n.* a tool with a curved blade terminating in a hook, used for pruning, chopping, etc. Also called: **bill.**

billiard ('bɪljəd) *n.* (*modifier*) of or relating to billiards: *a billiard table; a billiard cue.*

billiards ('bɪljədz) *n.* (*functioning as sing.*) any of various games in which long cues are used to drive balls on a rectangular table covered with a smooth cloth and having raised cushioned edges. [C16: < OF *billard* curved stick, < *bille* log; see BILLET[2]]

billing ('bɪlɪŋ) *n.* **1.** *Theatre.* the relative importance of a performer or act as reflected in the prominence given in programmes, advertisements, etc. **2.** *Chiefly U.S. & Canad.* public notice or advertising.

billingsgate ('bɪlɪŋzˌgeɪt) *n.* obscene or abusive language. [C17: after *Billingsgate*, a London fish market, notorious for such language]

billion ('bɪljən) *n., pl.* **-lions** *or* **-lion.** **1.** (in Britain, orig.) one million million: written as 1 000 000 000 000 or 10^{12}. U.S. word: **trillion.** **2.** (in the U.S., Canada, and increasingly in Britain and elsewhere) one thousand million: written as 1 000 000 000 or 10^{9}. **3.** (*often pl.*) any exceptionally large number. ~*determiner.* **4.** (preceded by *a* or a cardinal number) amounting to a billion. [C17: < F, < BI- + *-llion* as in *million*] —**'billionth** *adj., n.*

billionaire (ˌbɪljə'nɛə) *n.* a person whose wealth exceeds a billion monetary units of his country.

bill of attainder *n.* (formerly) a legislative act finding a person guilty without trial of treason or felony and declaring him attainted.

bill of exchange *n.* (now chiefly in foreign transactions) a document, usually negotiable, instructing a third party to pay a stated sum at a designated future date or on demand.

bill of fare *n.* another name for **menu.**

bill of health *n.* **1.** a certificate that attests to the health of a ship's company. **2. clean bill of health.** *Inf.* **a.** a good report of one's physical condition. **b.** a favourable account of a person's or a company's financial position.

bill of lading *n.* (in foreign trade) a document containing full particulars of goods shipped.

Bill of Rights *n.* **1.** an English statute of 1689 guaranteeing the rights and liberty of the individual subject. **2.** the first ten amendments to the U.S. Constitution which guarantee the liberty of the individual. **3.** (*usually not caps.*) any charter of basic human rights.

bill of sale *n. Law.* a deed transferring personal property.

billow ('bɪləʊ) *n.* **1.** a large sea wave. **2.** a swelling or surging mass, as of smoke or sound. ~*vb.* **3.** to rise up, swell out, or cause to rise up or swell out. [C16: < ON *bylgja*] —**'billowing** *adj., n.* —**'billowy** *adj.* —**'billowiness** *n.*

billposter ('bɪlˌpəʊstə) *or* **billsticker** *n.* a person who sticks advertising posters to walls, etc. —**'billˌposting** *or* **'billˌsticking** *n.*

billy ('bɪlɪ) *or* **billycan** ('bɪlɪˌkæn) *n., pl.* **-lies** *or* **-lycans.** **1.** a metal can or pot for boiling water, etc., over a campfire. **2.** *Austral. & N.Z.* (*as modifier*): *billy-tea.* **3. boil the billy.** *Austral. & N.Z. inf.* to make tea. [C19: < Scot. *billypot* cooking vessel]

billy goat *n.* a male goat.

bilobate (baɪ'ləʊˌbeɪt) *or* **bilobed** ('baɪˌləʊbd) *adj.* divided into or having two lobes.

biltong ('bɪlˌtɒŋ) *n. S. African.* strips of meat dried and cured in the sun. [C19: Afrik., < Du. *bil* buttock + *tong* TONGUE]

BIM *abbrev. for* British Institute of Management.

bimanous ('bɪmənəs, baɪ'meɪ-) *adj.* (of man and the higher primates) having two hands distinct in form and function from the feet. [C19: < NL, < BI- + L *manus* hand]

bimanual (ˌbaɪ'mænjʊəl) *adj.* using both hands.

bimetallic (ˌbaɪmɪ'tælɪk) *adj.* **1.** consisting of two metals. **2.** of or based on bimetallism.

bimetallic strip *n.* strips of two metals that expand differently welded together for use in a thermostat.

bimetallism (baɪ'mɛtəˌlɪzəm) *n.* the use of two metals, esp. gold and silver, in fixed relative values as the standard of value and currency. —**bi'metallist** *n.*

bimonthly (baɪ'mʌnθlɪ) *adj., adv.* **1.** every two months. **2.** twice a month. ~*n., pl.* **-lies.** **3.** a periodical published every two months.

bimorph ('baɪmɔːf) *or* **bimorph cell** *n. Electron.* two piezoelectric crystals cemented together so that their movement converts electrical signals into mechanical energy or vice versa: used in record-player pick-ups and loudspeakers.

bin (bɪn) *n.* **1.** a large container for storing something in bulk, such as coal, grain, or bottled wine. **2.** Also called: **bread bin.** a small container for bread. **3.** Also called: **dustbin, rubbish bin.** a container for rubbish, etc. ~*vb.* **binning, binned.** (*tr.*) **4.** to store in a bin. **5.** to put in a wastepaper bin. [OE *binne* basket]

binary ('baɪnərɪ) *adj.* **1.** composed of or involving two; dual. **2.** *Maths, computers.* of or expressed in binary notation or binary code. **3.** (of a compound or molecule) containing atoms of two different elements. ~*n., pl.* **-ries.** **4.** something composed of two parts. **5.** *Astron.* See **binary star.** [C16: < LL *bīnārius*; see BI-]

binary code *n. Computers.* the representation of each one of a set of numbers, letters, etc., as a unique group of bits.

binary notation *or* **system** *n.* a number system having a base of two, numbers being expressed by sequences of the digits 0 and 1: used in computing, as 0 and 1 can be represented electrically as *off* and *on.*

binary number *n.* a number expressed in binary notation.

binary star *n.* a double star system containing two associated stars revolving around a common centre of gravity in different orbits.

binary weapon *n.* a chemical weapon containing two substances separately that mix to produce a nerve gas when the projectile is fired.

binate ('baɪˌneɪt) *adj. Bot.* occurring in two parts or in pairs: *binate leaves.* [C19: < NL *bīnātus*, prob. < L *combīnātus* united] —**'biˌnately** *adv.*

binaural (baɪ'nɔːrəl, bɪn'ɔːrəl) *adj.* **1.** relating to, having, or hearing with both ears. **2.** employing two separate channels for recording or transmitting sound.

bind (baɪnd) *vb.* **binding, bound.** **1.** to make or become fast or secure with or as if with a tie or band. **2.** (*tr.*; often foll. by *up*) to encircle or enclose with a band: *to bind the hair.* **3.** (*tr.*) to place (someone) under obligation; oblige. **4.** (*tr.*) to impose legal obligations or duties upon (a person). **5.** (*tr.*) to make (a bargain, agreement, etc.) irrevocable; seal. **6.** (*tr.*) to restrain or confine with or as if with ties, as of responsibility or loyalty. **7.** (*tr.*) to place under certain constraints; govern. **8.** (*tr.*; often foll. by *up*) to bandage. **9.** to cohere or cause to cohere: *egg binds fat and flour.* **10.** to make or become compact, stiff, or hard: *frost binds the earth.* **11.** (*tr.*) to enclose and fasten (the pages of a book) between covers. **12.** (*tr.*) to provide (a garment, hem, etc.) with a border or edging. **13.** (*tr.*; sometimes foll. by *out* or *over*) to employ as an apprentice; indenture. **14.** (*intr.*) *Sl.* to complain. ~*n.* **15.** something that binds. **16.** *Inf.* a difficult or annoying situation. **17.** a situation in which freedom of action is restricted. ~See also **bind over.** [OE *bindan*]

binder ('baɪndə) *n.* **1.** a firm cover or folder for holding loose sheets of paper together. **2.** a material used to bind separate particles together. **3.** a person who binds books; bookbinder. **4.** something used to fasten or tie, such as rope or twine. **5.** Also called: **reaper binder.** *Obs.* a machine for cutting grain and binding it into sheaves. **6.** an informal agreement giving insurance coverage pending formal issue of a policy.

bindery (ˈbaɪndərɪ) *n., pl.* **-eries.** a place in which books are bound.

bindi-eye (ˈbɪndɪˌaɪ) *n. Austral.* **1.** any of various small weedy Australian herbaceous plants with burlike fruits. **2.** any bur or prickle. [C20: ? < Abor.]

binding (ˈbaɪndɪŋ) *n.* **1.** anything that binds or fastens. **2.** the covering within which the pages of a book are bound. **3.** the tape used for binding hems, etc. ~*adj.* **4.** imposing an obligation or duty. **5.** causing hindrance; restrictive.

bind over *vb.* (*tr., adv.*) to place (a person) under a legal obligation, such as one to keep the peace.

bindweed (ˈbaɪndˌwiːd) *n.* any of various plants that twine around a support. See also **convolvulus.**

bine (baɪn) *n.* the climbing or twining stem of any of various plants, such as the woodbine or bindweed. [C19: var. of BIND]

Binet-Simon scale (ˈbiːneɪˈsaɪmən) *n. Psychol.* a test used to determine the mental age of subjects, usually children. Also called: **Binet scale** *or* **test.** [C20: after Alfred *Binet* (1857–1911) + Théodore *Simon* (1873–1961), F psychologists]

binge (bɪndʒ) *Inf.* ~*n.* **1.** a bout of excessive drinking. **2.** excessive indulgence in anything. ~*vb.* **bingeing** *or* **binging, binged. 3.** (*intr.*) to indulge in a binge. [C19: prob. dial. *binge* to soak]

bingo (ˈbɪŋgəʊ) *n.* a gambling game, usually played with several people, in which random numbers are called out and the players cover the numbers on their individual cards. The first to cover a given arrangement of numbers is the winner. [C19: ? < *bing*, imit. of a bell ringing to mark the win]

binman (ˈbɪnˌmæn, ˈbɪnmən) *n., pl.* **-men.** another name for **dustman.**

binnacle (ˈbɪnək°l) *n.* a housing for a ship's compass. [C17: changed < C15 *bitakle*, < Port. < LL *habitāculum* dwelling-place, < L *habitāre* to inhabit]

binocular (bɪˈnɒkjʊlə, baɪ-) *adj.* involving, relating to, seeing with or intended for both eyes: *binocular vision.* [C18: < BI- + L *oculus* eye]

binoculars (bɪˈnɒkjʊləz, baɪ-) *pl. n.* an optical instrument for use with both eyes, consisting of two small telescopes joined together.

binomial (baɪˈnəʊmɪəl) *n.* **1.** a mathematical expression consisting of two terms, such as $3x + 2y$. **2.** a two-part taxonomic name for an animal or plant indicating genus and species. ~*adj.* **3.** referring to two names or terms. [C16: < Med. L, < BI- + L *nōmen* name] —**biˈnomially** *adv.*

binomial distribution *n.* a statistical distribution giving the probability of obtaining a specified number of independent trials of an experiment, with a constant probability of success in each.

binomial theorem *n.* a general mathematical formula that expresses any power of a binomial without multiplying out, as in $(a+b)^2 = a^2+2ab+b^2$.

bint (bɪnt) *n. Sl.* a derogatory term for **girl** or **woman.** [C19: < Ar., lit.: daughter]

binturong (ˈbɪntjʊˌrɒŋ, bɪnˈtjʊərɒŋ) *n.* a long-bodied short-legged arboreal SE Asian mammal having shaggy black hair. [< Malay]

bio- *or before a vowel* **bi-** *combining form.* **1.** indicating or involving life or living organisms: *biogenesis.* **2.** indicating a human life or career: *biography.* [< Gk *bios* life]

bioastronautics (ˌbaɪəʊˌæstrəˈnɔːtɪks) *n.* (*functioning as sing.*) the study of the effects of space flight on living organisms.

biochemistry (ˌbaɪəʊˈkɛmɪstrɪ) *n.* the study of the chemical compounds, reactions, etc., occurring in living organisms. —**biochemical** (ˌbaɪəʊˈkɛmɪk°l) *adj.* —ˌ**bioˈchemist** *n.*

biocide (ˈbaɪəˌsaɪd) *n.* a chemical capable of killing living organisms. —ˌ**bioˈcidal** *adj.*

biocoenosis (ˌbaɪəʊsiːˈnəʊsɪs) *n.* the relationships between animals and plants subsisting together. [C19: NL < BIO- + Gk *koinōsis* sharing]

biodegradable (ˌbaɪəʊdɪˈgreɪdəb°l) *adj.* (of sewage, packaging, etc.) capable of being decomposed by bacteria or other biological means.

bioengineering (ˌbaɪəʊˌɛndʒɪˈnɪərɪŋ) *n.* **1.** the design and manufacture of aids, such as artificial limbs, to rectify defective body functions. **2.** the design, manufacture, and maintenance of engineering equipment used in biosynthetic processes. —ˌ**bioˌengiˈneer** *n.*

bioethics (ˌbaɪəʊˈɛθɪks) *n.* (*functioning as sing.*) the study of ethical problems arising from scientific advances, esp. in biology and medicine.

biofeedback (ˌbaɪəʊˈfiːdˌbæk) *n. Physiol., psychol.* the technique of recording and presenting (usually visually) the activity of an autonomic function, such as the rate of heartbeat, in order to teach control of it.

biog. *abbrev. for:* **1.** biographical. **2.** biography.

biogenesis (ˌbaɪəʊˈdʒɛnɪsɪs) *n.* the principle that a living organism must originate from a parent organism similar to itself. —ˌ**biogeˈnetic** *or* ˌ**biogeˈnetical** *adj.*

biography (baɪˈɒgrəfɪ) *n., pl.* **-phies. 1.** an account of a person's life by another. **2.** such accounts collectively. —**biˈographer** *n.* —**biographical** (ˌbaɪəˈgræfɪk°l) *adj.*

biol. *abbrev. for:* **1.** biological. **2.** biology.

biological (ˌbaɪəˈlɒdʒɪk°l) *adj.* **1.** of or relating to biology. ~*n.* **2.** (*usually pl.*) a drug derived from a living organism.

biological clock *n.* **1.** an inherent periodicity in the physiological processes of living organisms that is independent of external periodicity. **2.** the hypothetical mechanism responsible for this. ~See also **circadian.**

biological control *n.* the control of destructive organisms by nonchemical means, such as introducing the natural enemy of a pest.

biological warfare *n.* the use of living organisms or their toxic products to induce death or incapacity in humans.

biology (baɪˈɒlədʒɪ) *n.* **1.** the study of living organisms. **2.** the animal and plant life of a particular region. —**biˈologist** *n.*

bioluminescence (ˌbaɪəʊˌluːmɪˈnɛsəns) *n.* the production of light by living organisms, such as the firefly. —ˌ**bioˌlumiˈnescent** *adj.*

biomass (ˈbaɪəʊˌmæs) *n.* the total number of living organisms in a given area, expressed in terms of living or dry weight per unit area.

biomedicine (ˌbaɪəʊˈmɛdɪsɪn) *n.* the medical and biological study of the effects of unusual environmental stress, esp. in connection with space travel.

biometry (baɪˈɒmɪtrɪ) *or* **biometrics** (ˌbaɪəˈmɛtrɪks) *n.* (*functioning as sing.*) the study of biological data by means of statistical analysis. —ˌ**bioˈmetric** *adj.*

bionic (baɪˈɒnɪk) *adj.* **1.** of or relating to bionics. **2.** (in science fiction) having physiological functions augmented by electronic equipment.

bionics (baɪˈɒnɪks) *n.* (*functioning as sing.*) **1.** the study of certain biological functions that are applicable to the development of electronic equipment designed to operate similarly. **2.** the replacement of limbs or body parts by artificial limbs or parts that are electronically or mechanically powered.

bionomics (ˌbaɪəˈnɒmɪks) *n.* (*functioning as sing.*) a less common name for **ecology.** [C19: < BIO- + *nomics* on pattern of ECONOMICS] —ˌ**bioˈnomic** *adj.* —**bionomist** (baɪˈɒnəmɪst) *n.*

biophysics (ˌbaɪəʊˈfɪzɪks) *n.* (*functioning as sing.*) the physics of biological processes and the application of methods used in physics to biology. —ˌ**bioˈphysical** *adj.* —ˌ**bioˈphysically** *adv.* —**biophysicist** (ˌbaɪəʊˈfɪzɪsɪst) *n.*

biopic (ˈbaɪəʊˌpɪk) *n. Inf.* a film based on the life of a famous person. [C20: < *bio(graphical)* + *pic(ture)*]

biopsy (ˈbaɪɒpsɪ) *n., pl.* **-sies.** examination, esp. under a microscope, of tissue from a living body to determine the cause or extent of a disease. [C20: < BIO- + Gk *opsis* sight]

biorhythm (ˈbaɪəʊˌrɪðəm) *n.* a cyclically recurring pattern of physiological states, believed by some to affect a person's physical, emotional, and mental states and behaviour.

bioscope (ˈbaɪəˌskəʊp) *n.* **1.** a kind of early film projector. **2.** a South African word for **cinema.**

bioscopy (baɪˈɒskəpɪ) *n., pl.* **-pies.** examination of a body to determine whether it is alive.

-biosis *n. combining form.* indicating a specified mode of life. [NL, < Gk *biōsis;* see BIO-, -OSIS] —**-biotic** *adj. combining form.*

biosphere (ˈbaɪəˌsfɪə) *n.* the part of the earth's surface and atmosphere inhabited by living things.

biosynthesis (ˌbaɪəʊˈsɪnθɪsɪs) *n.* the formation of complex compounds from simple substances by living organisms. —**biosynthetic** (ˌbaɪəʊsɪnˈθɛtɪk) *adj.*

biotechnology (ˌbaɪəʊtɛkˈnɒlədʒɪ) *n.* the use of microorganisms for beneficial effect, as to process waste matter.

biotic (baɪˈɒtɪk) *adj.* of or relating to living organisms. [C17: < Gk *biotikos,* < *bios* life]

biotin (ˈbaɪətɪn) *n.* a vitamin of the B complex, abundant in egg yolk and liver. [C20: < Gk *biotē* life, way of life + -IN]

bipartisan (ˌbaɪpɑːtɪˈzæn, baɪˈpɑːtɪˌzæn) *adj.* consisting of or supported by two political parties. —ˌ**bipartiˈsanship** *n.*

bipartite (baɪˈpɑːtaɪt) *adj.* **1.** consisting of or having two parts. **2.** affecting or made by two parties. **3.** *Bot.* (esp. of some leaves) divided into two parts almost to the base. —**biˈpartitely** *adv.* —**bipartition** (ˌbaɪpɑːˈtɪʃən) *n.*

biped (ˈbaɪpɛd) *n.* **1.** any animal with two feet. ~*adj. also* **bipedal** (baɪˈpiːdᵊl, -ˈpɛdᵊl). **2.** having two feet.

bipinnate (baɪˈpɪneɪt) *adj.* (of compound leaves) having both the leaflets and the stems bearing them arranged pinnately. —**biˈpinnately** *adv.*

biplane (ˈbaɪˌpleɪn) *n.* a type of aeroplane having two sets of wings, one above the other.

bipolar (baɪˈpəʊlə) *adj.* **1.** having two poles: *a bipolar dynamo.* **2.** of or relating to the North and South Poles. **3.** having or characterized by two opposed opinions, etc. **4.** (of a transistor) utilizing both majority and minority charge carriers. —ˌ**bipoˈlarity** *n.*

biquadratic (ˌbaɪkwɒˈdrætɪk) *Maths.* ~*adj.* **1.** of or relating to the fourth power. ~*n.* **2.** a biquadratic equation, such as $x^4 + x + 6 = 0$.

biracial (baɪˈreɪʃəl) *adj.* of or for members of two races. —**biˈracialism** *n.*

birch (bɜːtʃ) *n.* **1.** any catkin-bearing tree or shrub having thin peeling bark. See also **silver birch.** **2.** the hard close-grained wood of any of these trees. **3. the birch.** a bundle of birch twigs or a birch rod used, esp. formerly, for flogging offenders. ~*adj.* **4.** consisting or made of birch. ~*vb.* **5.** (*tr.*) to flog with a birch. [OE *bierce*] —ˈ**birchen** *adj.*

bird (bɜːd) *n.* **1.** any warm-blooded egg-laying vertebrate, characterized by a body covering of feathers and forelimbs modified as wings. **2.** *Inf.* a person, as in **rare bird, odd bird, clever bird.** **3.** *Sl., chiefly Brit.* a girl or young woman. **4.** *Sl.* prison or a term in prison (esp. in **do bird**). **5. a bird in the hand.** something definite or certain. **6. birds of a feather.** people with the same characteristics, ideas, interests, etc. **7. get the bird.** *Inf.* **a.** to be fired or dismissed. **b.** (esp. of a public performer) to be hissed at. **8. kill two birds with one stone.** to accomplish two things with one action. **9. (strictly) for the birds.** *Inf.* deserving of disdain or contempt; not important. [OE *bridd,* <?]

birdbath (ˈbɜːdˌbɑːθ) *n.* a small basin or trough for birds to bathe in, usually in a garden.

bird-brained *adj. Inf.* silly; stupid.

birdcage (ˈbɜːdˌkeɪdʒ) *n.* **1.** a wire or wicker cage for captive birds. **2.** *Austral. & N.Z.* an area on a racecourse where horses parade before a race. **3.** *N.Z. inf.* a second-hand car dealer's yard.

bird call *n.* **1.** the characteristic call or song of a bird. **2.** an imitation of this.

birdie (ˈbɜːdɪ) *n.* **1.** *Golf.* a score of one stroke under par for a hole. **2.** *Inf.* a bird, esp. a small bird.

birdlime (ˈbɜːdˌlaɪm) *n.* **1.** a sticky substance smeared on twigs to catch small birds. ~*vb.* **2.** (*tr.*) to smear (twigs) with birdlime to catch (small birds).

bird-nesting *or* **birds'-nesting** *n.* searching for birds' nests as a hobby, often to steal the eggs.

bird of paradise *n.* **1.** any of various songbirds of New Guinea and neighbouring regions, the males having brilliantly coloured plumage. **2. bird-of-paradise flower.** any of various plants native to tropical southern Africa and South America that have purple bracts and large orange or yellow flowers resembling birds' heads.

bird of passage *n.* **1.** a bird that migrates seasonally. **2.** a transient person.

bird of prey *n.* a bird, such as a hawk or owl, that hunts other animals for food.

birdseed (ˈbɜːdˌsiːd) *n.* a mixture of various kinds of seeds for feeding cagebirds.

bird's-eye *adj.* **1. a.** seen or photographed from high above. **b.** summarizing (esp. in **bird's-eye view**). **2.** having markings resembling birds' eyes.

bird's-foot *or* **bird-foot** *n., pl.* **-foots.** any of various plants whose flowers, leaves, or pods resemble a bird's foot or claw.

birdshot (ˈbɜːdˌʃɒt) *n.* small pellets designed for shooting birds.

bird strike *n.* a collision of an aircraft with a bird.

bird table *n.* a table or platform in the open on which food for birds may be placed.

bird-watcher *n.* a person who identifies and studies wild birds in their natural surroundings. —ˈ**bird-**ˌ**watching** *n.*

birefringence (ˌbaɪrɪˈfrɪndʒəns) *n.* another name for **double refraction.** —ˌ**bireˈfringent** *adj.*

bireme (ˈbaɪriːm) *n.* an ancient galley having two banks of oars. [C17: < L, < BI- + *-rēmus* oar]

biretta *or* **berretta** (bɪˈrɛtə) *n. R.C. Church.* a stiff square clerical cap. [C16: < It. *berretta,* < OProvençal, < LL *birrus* hooded cape]

birl (bɜːl) *vb.* **1.** *Scot.* to spin; twirl. **2.** *U.S. & Canad.* to cause (a floating log) to spin using the feet, esp. as a sport among lumberjacks. ~*n.* **3.** a variant spelling of **burl**[2]. [C18: prob. imit. & infl. by WHIRL & HURL]

Biro (ˈbaɪrəʊ) *n., pl.* **-ros.** *Trademark, Brit.* a kind of ballpoint.

birth (bɜːθ) *n.* **1.** the process of bearing young; childbirth. **2.** the act or fact of being born; nativity. **3.** the coming into existence of something; origin. **4.** ancestry; lineage: *of high birth.* **5.** natural or inherited talent: *an artist by birth.* **6. give birth (to).** **a.** to bear (offspring). **b.** to produce or originate (an idea, plan, etc.). ~*vb.* (*tr.*). **7.** *Rare.* to bear or bring forth (a child). [C12: < ON *byrth*]

birth certificate *n.* an official form giving details of the time and place of a person's birth.

birth control *n.* limitation of child-bearing by means of contraception.

birthday (ˈbɜːθˌdeɪ) *n.* **1. a.** an anniversary of the day of one's birth. **b.** (*as modifier*): *birthday present.* **2.** the day on which a person was born.

birthmark (ˈbɜːθˌmɑːk) *n.* a blemish on the skin formed before birth; naevus.

birthplace (ˈbɜːθˌpleɪs) *n.* the place where someone was born or where something originated.

birth rate *n.* the ratio of live births in a specified area, group, etc., to population, usually expressed per 1000 population per year.

birthright (ˈbɜːθˌraɪt) *n.* **1.** privileges or possessions that a person has or is believed to be entitled to as soon as he is born. **2.** the privileges or possessions of a first-born son. **3.** inheritance.

birthstone (ˈbɜːθˌstəʊn) *n.* a precious or semiprecious stone associated with a month or sign of the zodiac and thought to bring luck if worn by a person born in that month or under that sign.

biryani or **biriani** (ˌbɪrɪˈɑːnɪ) *n.* an Indian dish made with rice, highly flavoured and coloured, mixed with meat or fish. [< Urdu]

biscuit (ˈbɪskɪt) *n.* **1.** *Brit.* a small flat dry sweet or plain cake of many varieties. U.S. and Canad. word: **cookie.** **2. a.** a pale brown or yellowish-grey colour. **b.** (*as adj.*): *biscuit gloves.* **3.** Also called: **bisque.** earthenware or porcelain that has been fired but not glazed. **4. take the biscuit.** *Brit.* to be regarded (by the speaker) as most surprising. [C14: < OF, < (*pain*) *bescuit* twice-cooked (bread), < *bes* twice + *cuire* to cook]

bise (biːz) *n.* a cold dry northerly wind in Switzerland and the neighbouring parts of France and Italy. [C14: < OF, of Gmc origin]

bisect (baɪˈsɛkt) *vb.* **1.** (*tr.*) *Maths.* to divide into two equal parts. **2.** to cut or split into two. [C17: BI- + *-sect,* < L *secāre* to cut] —**bisection** (baɪˈsɛkʃən) *n.*

bisector (baɪˈsɛktə) *n. Maths.* a straight line or plane that bisects an angle, etc.

bisexual (baɪˈsɛksjuəl) *adj.* **1.** sexually attracted by both men and women. **2.** showing characteristics of both sexes. **3.** of or relating to both sexes. ~*n.* **4.** a bisexual organism; a hermaphrodite. **5.** a bisexual person. **bisexuality** (baɪˌsɛksjuˈælɪtɪ) *n.*

bishop (ˈbɪʃəp) *n.* **1.** a clergyman having spiritual and administrative powers over a diocese. See also **suffragan.** Related adj.: **episcopal.** **2.** a chesspiece, capable of moving diagonally. **3.** mulled wine, usually port, spiced with oranges, cloves, etc. [OE *biscop,* < LL, < Gk *episkopos,* < EPI- + *skopos* watcher]

bishopric (ˈbɪʃəprɪk) *n.* the see, diocese, or office of a bishop.

bismuth (ˈbɪzməθ) *n.* a brittle pinkish-white crystalline metallic element. It is widely used in alloys; its compounds are used in medicines. Symbol: Bi; atomic no.: 83; atomic wt.: 208.98. [C17: < NL *bisemūtum,* < G *Wismut,* <?]

bison (ˈbaɪsᵊn) *n., pl.* **-son.** **1.** Also called: **American bison, buffalo.** a member of the cattle tribe, formerly widely distributed over the prairies of W North America, with a massive head, shaggy forequarters, and a humped back. **2.** Also called: **wisent, European bison.** a closely related and similar animal formerly widespread in Europe. [C14: < L *bisōn,* of Gmc origin]

bisque[1] (bɪsk) *n.* a thick rich soup made from shellfish. [C17: < F]

bisque[2] (bɪsk) *n.* **1. a.** a pink to yellowish tan colour. **b.** (*as adj.*): *a bisque tablecloth.* **2.** *Ceramics.* another name for **biscuit** (sense 3). [C20: shortened < BISCUIT]

bisque[3] (bɪsk) *n. Tennis, golf, croquet.* an extra point, stroke, or turn allowed to an inferior player, usually taken when desired. [C17: < F, <?]

bistable (ˌbaɪˈsteɪbᵊl) *adj.* (of an electrical circuit switch, etc.) having two stable states.

bistort (ˈbɪstɔːt) *n.* **1.** Also called: **snakeweed.** a Eurasian plant having leaf stipules fused to form a tube around the stem and a spike of small pink flowers. **2.** Also called: **snakeroot.** a related plant of W North America, with oval clusters of pink or white flowers. **3.** any of several similar plants. [C16: < F, < L *bis* twice + *tortus* < *torquēre* to twist]

bistoury (ˈbɪstərɪ) *n., pl.* **-ies.** a long narrow-bladed surgical knife. [C15: < OF *bistorie* dagger, <?]

bistre or *U.S.* **bister** (ˈbɪstə) *n.* **1.** a transparent water-soluble brownish-yellow pigment made by boiling the soot of wood. **2. a.** a yellowish-brown to dark brown colour. **b.** (*as adj.*): *bistre paint.* [C18: < F, <?]

bistro (ˈbiːstrəʊ) *n., pl.* **-tros.** a small restaurant. [F: <?]

bisulphate (baɪˈsʌlˌfeɪt) *n.* a salt or ester of sulphuric acid containing the monovalent group $-HSO_4$ or the ion HSO_4^-. Also called: **hydrogen sulphate.**

bisulphide (baɪˈsʌlfaɪd) *n.* another name for **disulphide.**

bit[1] (bɪt) *n.* **1.** a small piece, portion, or quantity. **2.** a short time or distance. **3.** *U.S. & Canad. inf.* the value of an eighth of a dollar: spoken of only in units of two: *two bits.* **4.** any small coin. **5.** short for **bit part.** **6. a bit.** rather; somewhat: *a bit dreary.* **7. a bit of. a.** rather: *a bit of a dope.* **b.** a considerable amount: *that must take quite a bit of courage.* **8. bit by bit.** gradually. **9. do one's bit.** to make one's expected contribution. [OE *bite* action of biting; see BITE]

bit[2] (bɪt) *n.* **1.** a metal mouthpiece on a bridle for controlling a horse. **2.** anything that restrains or curbs. **3.** a cutting or drilling tool, part, or head in a brace, drill, etc. **4.** the part of a key that engages the levers of a lock. ~*vb.* **bitting, bitted.** (*tr.*) **5.** to put a bit in the mouth of (a horse). **6.** to restrain; curb. [OE *bita;* rel. to OE *bītan* to BITE]

bit[3] (bɪt) *vb.* the past tense of **bite.**

bit[4] (bɪt) *n. Maths, computers.* **1.** a single digit of binary notation, represented either by 0 or by 1. **2.** the smallest unit of information, indicating the presence or absence of a single feature. [C20: < B(INARY + DIG)IT]

bitch (bɪtʃ) *n.* **1.** a female dog or other female canine animal, such as a wolf. **2.** *Sl., derog.* a malicious, spiteful, or coarse woman. **3.** *Inf.* a difficult situation or problem. ~*vb. Inf.* **4.** (*intr.*) to complain; grumble. **5.** to behave (towards) in a spiteful manner. **6.** (*tr.;* often foll. by *up*) to botch; bungle. [OE *bicce*]

bitchy (ˈbɪtʃɪ) *adj.* **-ier, -iest.** *Sl.* of or like a bitch; malicious; snide. —ˈ**bitchiness** *n.*

bite (baɪt) *vb.* **biting, bit, bitten.** **1.** to grip, cut off, or tear as with the teeth or jaws. **2.** (of animals, insects, etc.) to injure by puncturing or tearing (the skin or flesh) with the teeth, fangs, etc. **3.** (*tr.*) to cut or penetrate, as with a knife. **4.** (of corrosive material such as acid) to eat away or into. **5.** to smart or cause to smart; sting. **6.** (*intr.*) *Angling.* (of a fish) to take or attempt to take the bait or lure. **7.** to take firm hold (of) or act effectively (upon). **8.** (*tr.*) *Sl.* to annoy or worry: *what's biting her?* **9.** (*tr.;* often foll. by *for*) *Austral. & N.Z. sl.* to ask (for); scrounge from. **10. bite the dust. a.** to fall down dead. **b.** to be rejected: *another good idea bites the dust.* ~*n.* **11.** the act of biting. **12.** a thing or amount bitten off. **13.** a wound, bruise, or sting inflicted by biting. **14.** *Angling.* an attempt by a fish to take the bait or lure. **15.** a light meal; snack. **16.** a cutting, stinging, or smarting sensation. **17.** *Dentistry.* the angle or manner of contact between the upper and lower teeth. **18. put the bite on.** *Sl.* to cadge or borrow from. [OE *bītan*] —ˈ**biter** *n.*

biting (ˈbaɪtɪŋ) *adj.* **1.** piercing; keen: *a biting wind.* **2.** sarcastic; incisive. —ˈ**bitingly** *adv.*

bit part *n.* a very small acting role with few lines to speak.

bitt (bɪt) *Naut.* ~*n.* **1.** one of a pair of strong posts on the deck of a ship for securing mooring and other lines. **2.** another word for **bollard** (sense 1). ~*vb.* **3.** (*tr.*) to secure (a line) by means of a bitt. [C14: prob. < ON]

bitten (ˈbɪtᵊn) *vb.* the past participle of **bite.**

bitter (ˈbɪtə) *adj.* **1.** having or denoting an unpalatable harsh taste, as the peel of an orange. **2.** showing or caused by strong unrelenting hostility or resentment. **3.** difficult or unpleasant to accept or admit: *a bitter blow.* **4.** cutting; sarcastic: *bitter words.* **5.** bitingly cold: *a bitter night.* ~*adv.* **6.** very; extremely (esp. in **bitter cold**). ~*n.* **7.** a thing that is bitter. **8.** *Brit.* draught beer with a slightly bitter taste. [OE *biter;* rel. to *bītan* to BITE] —ˈ**bitterly** *adv.* —ˈ**bitterness** *n.*

bitter end *n.* **1.** *Naut.* the end of a line, chain, or cable. **2. to the bitter end. a.** until the finish of a task, etc., however unpleasant or difficult. **b.** until final defeat or death. [C19: ?< BITT]

bittern (ˈbɪtən) *n.* a wading bird related and similar to the herons but with shorter legs and neck and a booming call. [C14: < OF *butor,* ?< L *būtiō* bittern + *taurus* bull]

bitters (ˈbɪtəz) *pl. n.* **1.** bitter-tasting spirits of varying alcoholic content flavoured with plant extracts. **2.** a similar liquid containing a bitter-tasting substance, used as a tonic.

bittersweet (ˈbɪtəˌswiːt) *n.* **1.** any of several North American woody climbing plants having orange capsules that open to expose scarlet-coated seeds. **2.** another name for **woody nightshade.** ~*adj.* **3.** tasting of or being a mixture of bitterness and sweetness. **4.** pleasant but tinged with sadness.

bitty (ˈbɪtɪ) *adj.* **-tier, -tiest. 1.** lacking unity; disjointed. **2.** containing bits, sediment, etc.

bitumen (ˈbɪtjʊmɪn) *n.* **1.** any of various viscous or solid impure mixtures of hydrocarbons that occur naturally in asphalt, tar, mineral waxes, etc.: used as a road surfacing and roofing material. **2. the bitumen.** *Austral. & N.Z. inf.* any road with a bitumen surface. [C15: < L *bitūmen*] —**bituminous** (bɪˈtjuːmɪnəs) *adj.*

bituminize *or* **-ise** (bɪˈtjuːmɪˌnaɪz) *vb.* (*tr.*) to treat with or convert into bitumen.

bituminous coal *n.* a soft black coal that burns with a smoky yellow flame.

bivalent (baɪˈveɪlənt, ˈbɪvə-) *adj.* **1.** *Chem.* another word for **divalent. 2.** (of homologous chromosomes) associated together in pairs. —**biˈvalency** *n.*

bivalve (ˈbaɪˌvælv) *n.* **1.** a marine or freshwater mollusc, having a laterally compressed body, a shell consisting of two hinged valves, and gills for respiration. The group includes clams, cockles, oysters, and mussels. ~*adj.* **2.** of or relating to these molluscs. ~ Also: **lamellibranch.**

bivouac (ˈbɪvʊˌæk, ˈbɪvwæk) *n.* **1.** a temporary encampment, as used by soldiers, mountaineers, etc. ~*vb.* **-acking, -acked. 2.** (*intr.*) to make such an encampment. [C18: < F *bivuac*, prob. < Swiss G *Beiwacht*, lit.: BY + WATCH]

biweekly (baɪˈwiːklɪ) *adj., adv.* **1.** every two weeks. **2.** twice a week. See **bi-.** ~*n., pl.* **-lies. 3.** a periodical published every two weeks.

biyearly (baɪˈjɪəlɪ) *adj., adv.* **1.** every two years; biennial or biennially. **2.** twice a year; biannual or biannually. See **bi-.**

biz (bɪz) *n. Inf.* short for **business.**

bizarre (bɪˈzɑː) *adj.* odd or unusual, esp. in an interesting or amusing way. [C17: < F, < It. *bizzarro* capricious, <?] —**biˈzarreness** *n.*

bk *abbrev. for:* **1.** bank. **2.** book.

Bk *the chemical symbol for* berkelium.

bkg *abbrev. for* banking.

BL *abbrev. for:* **1.** Bachelor of Law. **2.** Bachelor of Letters. **3.** Barrister-at-Law. **4.** British Library.

B/L, b/l, *or* **b.l.** *pl.* **Bs/L, bs/l,** *or* **bs.l.** *abbrev. for* bill of lading.

blab (blæb) *vb.* **blabbing, blabbed. 1.** to divulge (secrets, etc.) indiscreetly. **2.** (*intr.*) to chatter thoughtlessly; prattle. ~*n.* **3.** a less common word for **blabber.** [C14: of Gmc origin]

blabber (ˈblæbə) *n.* **1.** a person who blabs. **2.** idle chatter. ~*vb.* **3.** (*intr.*) to talk without thinking; chatter. [C15 *blabberen*, prob. imit.]

black (blæk) *adj.* **1.** of the colour of jet or carbon black, having no hue due to the absorption of all or nearly all incident light. **2.** without light; completely dark. **3.** without hope of alleviation; gloomy: *the future looked black.* **4.** very dirty or soiled. **5.** angry or resentful: *black looks.* **6.** (of a play or other work) dealing with the unpleasant realities of life, esp. in a cynical or macabre manner: *black comedy.* **7.** (of coffee or tea) without milk or cream. **8. a.** wicked or harmful: *a black lie.* **b.** (*in combination*): *black-hearted.* **9.** *Brit.* (of goods, jobs, works, etc.) being subject to boycott by trade unionists. ~*n.* **10.** a black colour. **11.** a dye or pigment of or producing this colour. **12.** black clothing, worn esp. as a sign of mourning. **13.** *Chess, draughts.* a black or dark-coloured piece or square. **14.** complete darkness: *the black of the night.* **15. in the black.** in credit or without debt. ~*vb.* **16.** another word for **blacken. 17.** (*tr.*) to polish (shoes, etc.) with blacking. **18.** (*tr.*) *Brit., Austral., & N.Z.* (of trade unionists) to organize a boycott of (specified goods, jobs, work, etc.). ~See also **blackout.** [OE *blæc*] —ˈ**blackness** *n.*

Black (blæk) *n.* **1.** a member of a dark-skinned race, esp. a Negro or an Australian Aborigine. ~*adj.* **2.** of or relating to a Black or Blacks.

blackamoor (ˈblækəˌmʊə, -ˌmɔː) *n. Arch.* a Negro or other person with dark skin. [C16: see BLACK, MOOR]

black-and-blue *adj.* **1.** (of the skin) discoloured, as from a bruise. **2.** feeling pain or soreness, as from a beating.

Black and Tan *n.* a member of the armed force sent to Ireland in 1921 by the British Government to combat Sinn Fein. [named after the colour of their uniforms]

black-and-white *n.* **1. a.** a photograph, picture, sketch, etc., in black, white, and shades of grey rather than in colour. **b.** (*as modifier*): *black-and-white film.* **2. in black and white. a.** in print or writing. **b.** in extremes: *he always saw things in black and white.*

black art *n.* **the.** another name for **black magic.**

black-backed gull *n.* either of two common black-and-white European coastal gulls, **lesser black-backed gull** and **great black-backed gull.**

blackball (ˈblækˌbɔːl) *n.* **1.** a negative vote or veto. **2.** a black wooden ball used to indicate disapproval or to veto in a vote. ~*vb.* (*tr.*) **3.** to vote against. **4.** to exclude (someone) from a group, profession, etc.; ostracize. [C18: < *black ball* used to veto]

black bean *n.* an Australian leguminous tree: used in furniture manufacture. Also called: **Moreton Bay chestnut.**

black bear *n.* **1. American black bear.** a bear inhabiting forests of North America. It is smaller and less ferocious than the brown bear. **2. Asiatic black bear.** a bear of central and E Asia, black with a pale V-shaped mark on the chest.

black belt *n. Judo, karate, etc.* **a.** a black belt worn by an instructor or expert. **b.** a person entitled to wear this.

blackberry (ˈblækbərɪ) *n., pl.* **-ries. 1.** Also called: **bramble.** any of several woody rosaceous plants that have thorny stems and black or purple edible berry-like fruits. **2.** the fruit of any of these plants. ~*vb.* **-rying, -ried. 3.** (*intr.*) to gather blackberries.

blackbird (ˈblækˌbɜːd) *n.* **1.** a common European thrush in which the male has black plumage and a yellow bill. **2.** any of various American orioles having dark plumage. **3.** (formerly) a person, esp. a South Sea Islander, who was kidnapped and sold as a slave, esp. in Australia. ~*vb.* **4.** (*tr.*) (formerly) to kidnap and sell into slavery.

blackboard (ˈblækˌbɔːd) *n.* a hard or rigid surface made of a smooth usually dark substance, used for writing or drawing on with chalk, esp. in teaching.

black body *n. Physics.* a hypothetical body capable of absorbing all the electromagnetic radiation falling on it. Also called: **full radiator.**

black book *n.* **1.** a book containing the names of people to be punished, blacklisted, etc. **2. in someone's black books.** *Inf.* out of favour with someone.

black box *n.* **1.** a self-contained unit in an electronic or computer system whose circuitry need not be known to understand its function. **2.** an informal name for **flight recorder.**

blackboy (ˈblækˌbɔɪ) *n.* another name for **grass tree** (sense 1).

blackbuck (ˈblækˌbʌk) *n.* an Indian antelope, the male of which has a dark back.

blackbutt (ˈblækˌbʌt) *n.* any of various Australian eucalyptus trees having rough fibrous bark and hard wood used as timber.

blackcap (ˈblækˌkæp) *n.* a brownish-grey Old World warbler, the male of which has a black crown.

blackcock (ˈblækˌkɒk) *n.* the male of the black grouse.

Black Country *n.* **the.** the heavily industrialized West Midlands of England.

blackcurrant (ˌblækˈkʌrənt) *n.* **1.** a N temperate shrub having red or white flowers and small edible black berries. **2.** its fruit.
blackdamp (ˈblækˌdæmp) *n.* air that is low in oxygen content and high in carbon dioxide as a result of an explosion in a mine. Also called: **chokedamp.**
Black Death *n.* **the.** a form of bubonic plague pandemic in Europe and Asia during the 14th century. See **bubonic plague.**
black disc *n.* a conventional black vinyl gramophone record as opposed to a compact disc.
black earth *n.* another name for **chernozem.**
black economy *n.* that portion of the income of a nation that remains illegally undeclared.
blacken (ˈblækən) *vb.* **1.** to make or become black or dirty. **2.** (*tr.*) to defame; slander (esp. in **blacken someone's name**).
black eye *n.* bruising round the eye.
black-eyed Susan (ˈsuːzᵊn) *n.* any of several North American plants having flower heads of orange-yellow rays and brown-black centres.
blackface (ˈblækˌfeɪs) *n.* **1.** a variety of sheep with a black face. **2.** the make-up used by a performer imitating a Negro.
blackfish (ˈblækˌfɪʃ) *n., pl.* **-fish** *or* **-fishes. 1.** any of various dark fishes, esp. a common edible Australian estuary fish. **2.** a female salmon that has recently spawned. Cf. **redfish** (sense 1).
black flag *n.* another name for the **Jolly Roger.**
blackfly (ˈblækˌflaɪ) *n., pl.* **-flies.** a black aphid that infests beans, sugar beet, and other plants. Also called: **bean aphid.**
Black Forest *n.* **the.** a hilly wooded region of SW West Germany.
Black Friar *n.* a Dominican friar.
black grouse *n.* **1.** a large N European grouse, the male of which has a bluish-black plumage. **2.** a related and similar species of W Asia.
blackguard (ˈblægɑːd, -gəd) *n.* **1.** an unprincipled contemptible person; scoundrel. ~*vb.* **2.** (*tr.*) to ridicule or denounce with abusive language. **3.** (*intr.*) to behave like a blackguard. [C16: see BLACK, GUARD] —**ˈblackguardism** *n.* —**ˈblackguardly** *adj.*
blackhead (ˈblækˌhɛd) *n.* **1.** a black-tipped plug of fatty matter clogging a pore of the skin. **2.** any of various birds with black plumage on the head.
black hole *n. Astron.* a hypothetical region of space resulting from the gravitational collapse of a star and surrounded by a gravitational field so high that neither matter nor radiation could escape from it.
black ice *n.* a thin transparent layer of new ice on a road or similar surface.
blacking (ˈblækɪŋ) *n.* any preparation for giving a black finish to shoes, metals, etc.
blackjack[1] (ˈblækˌdʒæk) *Chiefly U.S. & Canad.* ~*n.* **1.** a truncheon of leather-covered lead with a flexible shaft. ~*vb.* (*tr.*) **2.** to hit as with a blackjack. **3.** to compel (a person) by threats. [C19: < BLACK + JACK (implement)]
blackjack[2] (ˈblækˌdʒæk) *n.* pontoon or any similar card game. [C20: < BLACK + JACK (the knave)]
black lead (lɛd) *n.* another name for **graphite.**
blackleg (ˈblæklɛg) *n.* **1.** Also called **scab.** *Brit.* a person who acts against the interests of a trade union, as by continuing to work during a strike or taking over a striker's job. ~*vb.* **-legging, -legged. 2.** (*intr.*) *Brit.* to act against the interests of a trade union, esp. by refusing to join a strike.
black light *n.* the invisible electromagnetic radiation in the ultraviolet and infrared regions of the spectrum.
blacklist (ˈblækˌlɪst) *n.* **1.** a list of persons or organizations under suspicion, or considered untrustworthy, disloyal, etc. ~*vb.* **2.** (*tr.*) to put on a blacklist.
black magic *n.* magic used for evil purposes.
blackmail (ˈblækˌmeɪl) *n.* **1.** the act of attempting to obtain money by intimidation, as by threats to disclose discreditable information. **2.** the exertion of pressure, esp. unfairly, in an attempt to influence someone. ~*vb.* (*tr.*) **3.** to exact or attempt to exact (money or anything of value) from (a person) by threats or intimidation; extort. **4.** to attempt to influence (a person), esp. by unfair pressure. [C16: < BLACK + OE *māl* terms] —**ˈblackˌmailer** *n.*
Black Maria (məˈraɪə) *n.* a police van for transporting prisoners.
black mark *n.* an indication of disapproval, failure, etc.
black market *n.* **1.** any system in which goods or currencies are sold and bought illegally, esp. in violation of controls or rationing. **2.** the place where such a system operates. ~*vb.* **black-market. 3.** to sell (goods) on the black market. —**black marketeer** *n.*
black mass *n.* (*sometimes cap.*) a blasphemous travesty of the Christian Mass, performed by practitioners of black magic.
Black Muslim *n.* (esp. in the U.S.) a member of an Islamic political movement of Black people who seek to establish a new Black nation.
black nightshade *n.* a common poisonous weed in cultivated land, having small white flowers and black berry-like fruits.
blackout (ˈblækaʊt) *n.* **1.** the extinguishing or hiding of all artificial light, esp. in a city visible to an air attack. **2.** a momentary loss of consciousness, vision, or memory. **3.** a temporary electrical power failure or cut. **4.** the suspension of broadcasting, as by a strike or for political reasons. ~*vb.* **black out.** (*adv.*) **5.** (*tr.*) to obliterate or extinguish (lights). **6.** (*tr.*) to create a blackout in (a city, etc.). **7.** (*intr.*) to lose vision, consciousness, or memory temporarily. **8.** (*tr.*) to stop (news, a television programme, etc.) from being broadcast.
black pepper *n.* a pungent condiment made by grinding the dried unripe berries and husks of the pepper plant.
Black Power *n.* a social, economic, and political movement of Black people, esp. in the U.S. and Australia, to obtain equality with Whites.
black pudding *n.* a kind of black sausage made from minced pork fat, pig's blood, and other ingredients. Also called: **blood pudding.**
Black Rod *n.* (in Britain) an officer of the House of Lords and of the Order of the Garter, whose main duty is summoning the Commons at the opening and proroguing of Parliament.
black section *n.* (in Britain) an unofficial group within the Labour Party in any constituency which represents the interests of local Black people.
black sheep *n.* a person who is regarded as a disgrace or failure by his family or peer group.
Blackshirt (ˈblækˌʃɜːt) *n.* (in Europe) a member of a fascist organization, esp. the Italian Fascist party before and during World War II.
blacksmith (ˈblækˌsmɪθ) *n.* an artisan who works iron with a furnace, anvil, hammer, etc. [C14: see BLACK, SMITH]
black snake *n.* **1.** any of several Old World black venomous snakes, esp. the **Australian black snake. 2.** any of various dark nonvenomous snakes.
black spot *n.* **1.** a place on a road where accidents frequently occur. **2.** any dangerous or difficult place. **3.** a disease of roses that causes black blotches on the leaves.
black stump *n.* **the.** *Austral.* an imaginary marker of the extent of civilization (esp. in **beyond the black stump**).
black tea *n.* tea made from fermented tea leaves.
blackthorn (ˈblækˌθɔːn) *n.* a thorny Eurasian shrub with black twigs, white flowers, and small sour plumlike fruits. Also called: **sloe.**
black tie *n.* **1.** a black bow tie worn with a dinner jacket. **2.** (*modifier*) denoting an occasion when a dinner jacket should be worn.
blacktop (ˈblækˌtɒp) *n. Chiefly U.S. & Canad.* a bituminous mixture used for paving.
Black tracker *n. Austral.* an Aboriginal tracker working for the police.

black velvet *n.* a mixture of stout and champagne in equal proportions.

Black Watch *n.* **the.** the Royal Highland Regiment in the British Army.

blackwater fever ('blæk,wɔːtə) *n.* a rare and serious complication of malaria, characterized by massive destruction of red blood cells, producing dark red or blackish urine.

black widow *n.* an American spider, the female of which is highly venomous, and commonly eats its mate.

Blackwood ('blæk,wʊd) *n. Bridge.* a conventional bidding sequence of four and five no-trumps, which are requests to the partner to show aces and kings respectively. [C20: after E. F. *Blackwood*, its U.S. inventor]

bladder ('blædə) *n.* **1.** *Anat.* a distensible membranous sac, usually containing liquid or gas, esp. the urinary bladder. **2.** an inflatable part of something. **3.** a hollow saclike part in certain plants, such as the bladderwrack. [OE *blǣdre*] —'**bladdery** *adj.*

bladderwort ('blædə,wɜːt) *n.* an aquatic plant some of whose leaves are modified as small bladders to trap minute aquatic animals.

bladderwrack ('blædə,ræk) *n.* any of several seaweeds that grow in the intertidal regions of rocky shores and have branched brown fronds with air bladders.

blade (bleɪd) *n.* **1.** the part of a sharp weapon, tool, etc., that forms the cutting edge. **2.** the thin flattish part of various tools, implements, etc., as of a propeller. **3.** the flattened expanded part of a leaf, sepal, or petal. **4.** the long narrow leaf of a grass or related plant. **5.** the striking surface of a bat, club, stick, or oar. **6.** the metal runner on an ice skate. **7.** the upper part of the tongue lying directly behind the tip. **8.** *Arch.* a dashing or swaggering young man. **9.** short for **shoulder blade. 10.** a poetic word for a **sword** or **swordsman.** [OE *blæd*] —'**bladed** *adj.*

blaeberry ('bleɪbərɪ) *n., pl.* **-ries.** *Brit.* another name for **whortleberry** (senses 1, 2). [C15: < dialect *blae* bluish + BERRY]

blag (blæg) *Sl.* ~*n.* **1.** a robbery, esp. with violence. ~*vb.* **blagging, blagged.** (*tr.*) **2.** to snatch (wages, someone's handbag, etc.); steal. **3.** to rob (esp. a bank or post office). [C19: <?] —'**blagger** *n.*

blah *or* **blah blah** (blɑː) *n. Sl.* worthless or silly talk. [C20: imit.]

blain (bleɪn) *n.* a blister, blotch, or sore on the skin. [OE *blegen*]

blame (bleɪm) *n.* **1.** responsibility for something that is wrong; culpability. **2.** an expression of condemnation. ~*vb.* (*tr.*) **3.** (usually foll. by *for*) to attribute responsibility to: *I blame him for the failure.* **4.** (usually foll. by *on*) to ascribe responsibility for (something) to: *I blame the failure on him.* **5.** to find fault with. **6. be to blame.** to be at fault. [C12: < OF *blasmer*, ult. < LL *blasphēmāre* to blaspheme] —'**blamable** *or* '**blameable** *adj.* —'**blamably** *or* '**blameably** *adv.*

blameful ('bleɪmfʊl) *adj.* deserving blame; guilty. —'**blamefully** *adv.* —'**blamefulness** *n.*

blameless ('bleɪmlɪs) *adj.* free from blame; innocent. —'**blamelessness** *n.*

blameworthy ('bleɪm,wɜːðɪ) *adj.* deserving censure. —'**blame,worthiness** *n.*

blanch (blɑːntʃ) *vb.* (*mainly tr.*) **1.** to remove colour from; whiten. **2.** (*usually intr.*) to become or cause to become pale, as with sickness or fear. **3.** to prepare (meat, green vegetables, nuts, etc.) by plunging them in boiling water. **4.** to cause (celery, chicory, etc.) to grow free of chlorophyll by the exclusion of sunlight. [C14: < OF *blanchir*, < *blanc* white; see BLANK]

blancmange (blə'mɒnʒ) *n.* a jelly-like dessert of milk, stiffened usually with cornflour. [C14: < OF *blanc manger*, lit.: white food]

bland (blænd) *adj.* **1.** devoid of distinctive or stimulating characteristics; uninteresting. **2.** gentle and agreeable; suave. **3.** mild and soothing. [C15: < L *blandus* flattering] —'**blandly** *adv.* —'**blandness** *n.*

blandish ('blændɪʃ) *vb.* (*tr.*) to seek to persuade or influence by mild flattery; coax. [C14: < OF *blandir*, < L *blandīrī*]

blandishments ('blændɪʃmənts) *pl. n.* (*rarely sing.*) flattery intended to coax or cajole.

blank (blæŋk) *adj.* **1.** (of a writing surface) bearing no marks; not written on. **2.** (of a form, etc.) with spaces left for details to be filled in. **3.** without ornament or break. **4.** not filled in; empty. **5.** exhibiting no interest or expression: *a blank look.* **6.** lacking understanding; confused: *he looked blank.* **7.** absolute; complete: *blank rejection.* **8.** devoid of ideas or inspiration: *his mind went blank.* ~*n.* **9.** an emptiness; void; blank space. **10.** an empty space for writing in. **11.** a printed form containing such empty spaces. **12.** something characterized by incomprehension or confusion: *my mind went a complete blank.* **13.** a mark, often a dash, in place of a word, esp. a taboo word. **14.** short for **blank cartridge. 15.** a piece of material prepared for stamping, punching, forging, or some other operation. **16. draw a blank.** to get no results from something. ~*vb.* (*tr.*) **17.** (usually foll. by *out*) to cross out, blot, or obscure. [C15: < OF *blanc* white, of Gmc origin] —'**blankness** *n.*

blank cartridge *n.* a cartridge containing powder but no bullet.

blank cheque *n.* **1.** a cheque that has been signed but on which the amount payable has not been specified. **2.** complete freedom of action.

blanket ('blæŋkɪt) *n.* **1.** a large piece of thick cloth for use as a bed covering, animal covering, etc. **2.** a concealing cover, as of smoke, leaves, or snow. **3.** (*modifier*) applying to or covering a wide group or variety of people, conditions, situations, etc.: *blanket insurance against loss, injury, and theft.* **4.** (**born**) **on the wrong side of the blanket.** *Inf.* illegitimate. ~*vb.* (*tr.*) **5.** to cover as with a blanket; overlie. **6.** to cover a wide area; give blanket coverage. **7.** (usually foll. by *out*) to obscure or suppress. [C13: < OF *blancquete*, < *blanc*; see BLANK]

blanket bath *n.* an all-over wash given to a person confined to bed.

blanket stitch *n.* a strong reinforcing stitch for the edges of blankets and other thick material.

blankety ('blæŋkɪtɪ) *adj., adv.* a euphemism for any taboo word. [C20: < BLANK]

blank verse *n. Prosody.* unrhymed verse, esp. in iambic pentameters.

blare (blɛə) *vb.* **1.** to sound loudly and harshly. **2.** to proclaim loudly and sensationally. ~*n.* **3.** a loud harsh noise. [C14: < MDu. *bleren*; imit.]

blarney ('blɑːnɪ) *n.* **1.** flattering talk. ~*vb.* **2.** to cajole with flattery; wheedle. [C19: after the *Blarney* Stone in SW Ireland, said to endow whoever kisses it with skill in flattery]

blasé ('blɑːzeɪ) *adj.* **1.** indifferent to something because of familiarity. **2.** lacking enthusiasm; bored. [C19: < F, p.p. of *blaser* to cloy]

blaspheme (blæs'fiːm) *vb.* **1.** (*tr.*) to show contempt or disrespect for (God or sacred things), esp. in speech. **2.** (*intr.*) to utter profanities or curses. [C14: < LL, < Gk, < *blasphēmos* BLASPHEMOUS] —**blas'phemer** *n.*

blasphemous ('blæsfɪməs) *adj.* involving impiousness or gross irreverence towards God or something sacred. [C15: via LL, < Gk *blasphēmos* evil-speaking, < *blapsis* evil + *phēmē* speech]

blasphemy ('blæsfɪmɪ) *n., pl.* **-mies.** blasphemous behaviour or language.

blast (blɑːst) *n.* **1.** an explosion, as of dynamite. **2.** the rapid movement of air away from the centre of an explosion; shock wave. **3.** the charge used in a single explosion. **4.** a sudden strong gust of wind or air. **5.** a sudden loud sound, as of a trumpet. **6.** a violent verbal outburst, as of criticism. **7.** a forcible jet of air, esp. one used to intensify the heating effect of a furnace. **8.** any of several diseases of plants and animals. **9.** (**at**) **full blast.** at maximum speed, volume, etc. ~*interj.* **10.** *Sl.* an exclamation of annoyance. ~*vb.* **11.** (*tr.*) to destroy or blow up with explosives, shells, etc. **12.** to make or cause to make a loud harsh noise. **13.** to wither or cause to wither; blight or be blighted. **14.** (*tr.*) to criticize severely. [OE *blǣst*] —**ˈblaster** *n.*

-blast *n. combining form.* (in biology) indicating an embryonic cell or formative layer: *mesoblast.* [< Gk *blastos* bud]

blasted (ˈblɑːstɪd) *adj.* **1.** blighted or withered. ~*adj.* (*prenominal*), *adv.* **2.** *Sl.* (intensifier): *a blasted idiot.*

blast furnace *n.* a vertical cylindrical furnace for smelting into which a blast of preheated air is forced.

blasto- *combining form.* indicating an embryo or bud. [see BLAST]

blastoff (ˈblɑːstˌɒf) *n.* **1.** the launching of a rocket under its own power. **2.** the time at which this occurs. ~*vb.* **blast off.** **3.** (*adv.; when tr., usually passive*) to be launched.

blastula (ˈblæstjʊlə) *n., pl.* **-las** *or* **-lae** (-liː). an early form of an animal embryo that develops a sphere of cells with a central cavity. Also called: **blastosphere.** [C19: NL < Gk, < dim. of *blastos* bud] —**ˈblastular** *adj.*

blatant (ˈbleɪtᵊnt) *adj.* **1.** glaringly conspicuous or obvious: *a blatant lie.* **2.** offensively noticeable; obtrusive. **3.** offensively noisy. [C16: coined by Edmund Spenser (? 1552-99), E poet; prob. infl. by L *blatīre* to babble] —**ˈblatancy** *n.*

blather (ˈblæðə) *vb., n.* a variant of **blether.**

blatherskite (ˈblæðəˌskaɪt) *n.* **1.** a talkative silly person. **2.** foolish talk; nonsense. [C17: < BLATHER + Scot & N English dialect *skate* fellow]

blaze[1] (bleɪz) *n.* **1.** a strong fire or flame. **2.** a very bright light or glare. **3.** an outburst (of passion, acclaim, patriotism, etc.). **4.** brilliance; brightness. ~*vb.* (*intr.*) **5.** to burn fiercely. **6.** to shine brightly. **7.** (often foll. by *up*) to become stirred, as with anger or excitement. **8.** (usually foll. by *away*) to shoot continuously. ~See also **blazes.** [OE *blæse*]

blaze[2] (bleɪz) *n.* **1.** a mark, usually indicating a path, made on a tree. **2.** a light-coloured marking on the face of a domestic animal. ~*vb.* (*tr.*) **3.** to mark (a tree, path, etc.) with a blaze. **4. blaze a trail.** to explore new territories, areas of knowledge, etc., so that others can follow. [C17: prob. < MLow G *bles* white marking]

blaze[3] (bleɪz) *vb.* (*tr;* often foll. by *abroad*) to make widely known; proclaim. [C14: < MDu. *blāsen,* < OHG *blāsan*]

blazer (ˈbleɪzə) *n.* a fairly lightweight jacket, often in the colours of a sports club, school, etc.

blazes (ˈbleɪzɪz) *pl. n.* **1.** *Sl.* a euphemistic word for **hell.** **2.** *Inf.* (intensifier): *to run like blazes.*

blazon (ˈbleɪzᵊn) *vb.* (*tr.*) **1.** (often foll. by *abroad*) to proclaim publicly. **2.** *Heraldry.* to describe (heraldic arms) in proper terms. **3.** to draw and colour (heraldic arms) conventionally. ~*n.* **4.** *Heraldry.* a conventional description or depiction of heraldic arms. [C13: < OF *blason* coat of arms] —**ˈblazoner** *n.*

blazonry (ˈbleɪzənrɪ) *n., pl.* **-ries.** **1.** the art or process of describing heraldic arms in proper form. **2.** heraldic arms collectively. **3.** colourful or ostentatious display.

bldg *abbrev. for* building.

bleach (bliːtʃ) *vb.* **1.** to make or become white or colourless, as by exposure to sunlight, by the action of chemical agents, etc. ~*n.* **2.** a bleaching agent. **3.** the act of bleaching. [OE *blǣcan*] —**ˈbleacher** *n.*

bleaching powder *n.* a white powder consisting of chlorinated calcium hydroxide. Also called: **chloride of lime, chlorinated lime.**

bleak[1] (bliːk) *adj.* **1.** exposed and barren. **2.** cold and raw. **3.** offering little hope; dismal: *a bleak future.* [OE *blāc* bright, pale] —**ˈbleakness** *n.*

bleak[2] (bliːk) *n.* any of various European cyprinid fishes occurring in slow-flowing rivers. [C15: prob. < ON *bleikja* white colour]

blear (blɪə) *Arch.* ~*vb.* **1.** (*tr.*) to make (eyes or sight) dim as with tears; blur. ~*adj.* **2.** a less common word for **bleary.** [C13: *blere* to make dim]

bleary (ˈblɪərɪ) *adj.* **blearier, bleariest.** **1.** (of eyes or vision) dimmed or blurred, as by tears or tiredness. **2.** indistinct or unclear. —**ˈbleariness** *n.*

bleary-eyed *or* **blear-eyed** *adj.* with eyes blurred, as with old age or after waking.

bleat (bliːt) *vb.* **1.** (*intr.*) (of a sheep, goat, or calf) to utter its characteristic plaintive cry. **2.** (*intr.*) to speak with any similar sound. **3.** to whine; whimper. ~*n.* **4.** the characteristic cry of sheep, goats, and calves. **5.** any sound similar to this. **6.** a weak complaint or whine. [OE *blǣtan*] —**ˈbleater** *n.* —**ˈbleating** *n., adj.*

bleb (blɛb) *n.* **1.** a fluid-filled blister on the skin. **2.** a small air bubble. [C17: var. of BLOB]

bleed (bliːd) *vb.* **bleeding, bled** (blɛd). **1.** (*intr.*) to lose or emit blood. **2.** (*tr.*) to remove or draw blood from (a person or animal). **3.** (*intr.*) to be injured or die, as for a cause. **4.** (of plants) to exude (sap or resin), esp. from a cut. **5.** (*tr.*) *Inf.* to obtain money, etc., from, esp. by extortion. **6.** (*tr.*) to draw liquid or gas from (a container or enclosed system): *to bleed the hydraulic brakes.* **7.** (*intr.*) (of dye or paint) to run or become mixed, as when wet. **8.** to print or be printed so that text, illustrations, etc., run off the trimmed page. **9. one's heart bleeds.** used to express sympathetic grief, often ironically. [OE *blēdan*]

bleeder (ˈbliːdə) *n.* **1.** *Sl.* **a.** *Derog.* a despicable person. **b.** any person. **2.** *Pathol.* a nontechnical name for a **haemophiliac.**

bleeding (ˈbliːdɪŋ) *adj., adv. Brit. sl.* (intensifier): *a bleeding fool.*

bleeding heart *n.* **1.** any of several plants, esp. a widely cultivated Japanese species which has heart-shaped nodding pink flowers. **2.** *Inf.* **a.** an excessively softhearted person. **b.** (*as modifier*): *bleeding-heart liberals.*

bleep (bliːp) *n.* **1.** a single short high-pitched signal made by an electronic apparatus; beep. **2.** Also called: **bleeper.** a small portable radio receiver that makes a bleeping signal. ~*vb.* **3.** (*intr.*) to make such a noise. **4.** (*tr.*) to call (somebody) by means of a bleep. [C20: imit.]

blemish (ˈblɛmɪʃ) *n.* **1.** a defect; flaw; stain. ~*vb.* **2.** (*tr.*) to flaw the perfection of; spoil; tarnish. [C14: < OF *blemir* to make pale]

blench (blɛntʃ) *vb.* (*intr.*) to shy away, as in fear; quail. [OE *blencan* to deceive]

blend (blɛnd) *vb.* **1.** to mix or mingle (components) together thoroughly. **2.** (*tr.*) to mix (different grades or varieties of tea, whisky, etc.). **3.** (*intr.*) to look good together; harmonize. **4.** (*intr.*) (esp. of colours) to shade imperceptibly into each other. ~*n.* **5.** a mixture or type produced by blending. **6.** the act of blending. **7.** Also called: **portmanteau word.** a word formed by joining together the beginning and the end of two other words: *"brunch" is a blend of "breakfast" and "lunch."* [OE *blandan*]

blende (blɛnd) *n.* **1.** another name for **sphalerite.** **2.** any of several sulphide ores. [C17: G, < *blenden* to deceive, BLIND; so called because it is easily mistaken for galena]

blender (ˈblɛndə) *n.* **1.** a person or thing that blends. **2.** Also called: **liquidizer.** a kitchen appliance with blades used for puréeing vegetables, blending liquids, etc.

blenny (ˈblɛnɪ) *n., pl.* **-nies.** any of various small fishes of coastal waters having a tapering scaleless body, a long dorsal fin, and long raylike pelvic fins. [C18: < L, < Gk *blennos* slime]

blent (blɛnt) *vb. Arch. or literary.* a past participle of **blend.**

blepharitis (ˌblɛfəˈraɪtɪs) *n.* inflammation of the eyelids. [C19: < Gk *blephar*(*on*) eyelid + -ITIS]

blesbok *or* **blesbuck** (ˈblɛsˌbʌk) *n., pl.* **-boks, -bok** *or* **-bucks, -buck.** an antelope of southern Africa. The coat is reddish brown with a white blaze between the eyes; the horns are lyre-shaped. [C19: Afrik., < Du. *bles* BLAZE[2] + *bok* BUCK[1]]

bless (blɛs) *vb.* **blessing, blessed** *or* **blest.** (*tr.*) **1.** to consecrate or render holy by means of a religious rite. **2.** to give honour or glory to (a person or thing) as holy. **3.** to call upon God to protect; give a benediction to. **4.** to worship or adore (God). **5.** (*often passive*) to grant happiness, health, or prosperity to. **6.** (*usually passive*) to endow with a talent, beauty, etc. **7.** *Rare.* to protect against evil or harm. **8. bless you!** (*interj.*) **a.** a traditional phrase said to a person who has just sneezed. **b.** an exclamation of well-wishing or surprise. **9. bless me!** *or* **(God) bless my soul!** (*interj.*) an exclamation of surprise. [OE *blǣdsian* to sprinkle with sacrificial blood]

blessed (ˈblɛsɪd, blɛst) *adj.* **1.** made holy; consecrated. **2.** worthy of deep reverence or respect. **3.** *R.C. Church.* (of a person) beatified by the pope. **4.** characterized by happiness or good fortune. **5.** bringing great happiness or good fortune. **6.** a euphemistic word for **damned,** used in mild oaths: *I'm blessed if I know.* —ˈ**blessedly** *adv.* —ˈ**blessedness** *n.*

Blessed Sacrament *n. Chiefly R.C. Church.* the consecrated elements of the Eucharist.

blessing (ˈblɛsɪŋ) *n.* **1.** the act of invoking divine protection or aid. **2.** the words or ceremony used for this. **3.** a short prayer before or after a meal; grace. **4.** approval; good wishes. **5.** the bestowal of a divine gift or favour. **6.** a happy event.

blest (blɛst) *vb.* a past tense and past participle of **bless.**

blether (ˈblɛðə) *Scot.* ~vb. **1.** (*intr.*) to speak foolishly. ~*n.* **2.** foolish talk; nonsense. [C16: < ON *blathr* nonsense]

blew (bluː) *vb.* the past tense of **blow**[1] and **blow**[3].

blight (blaɪt) *n.* **1.** any plant disease characterized by withering and shrivelling without rotting. **2.** any factor that causes the symptoms of blight in plants. **3.** a person or thing that mars or prevents growth. **4.** an ugly urban district. ~*vb.* **5.** to cause or suffer a blight. **6.** (*tr.*) to frustrate or disappoint. **7.** (*tr.*) to spoil; destroy. [C17: ? rel. to OE *blǣce* rash]

blighter (ˈblaɪtə) *n. Brit. inf.* **1.** a fellow. **2.** a despicable or irritating person or thing.

Blighty (ˈblaɪtɪ) *n.* (*sometimes not cap.*) *Brit. sl.* (used esp. by troops serving abroad) **1.** England; home. **2.** (*pl.* **Blighties**) Also called: **a blighty one.** (esp. in World War I) a wound that causes the recipient to be sent home to England. [C20: < Hindi *bilāyatī* foreign land, England, < Ar. *wilāyat* country]

blimey (ˈblaɪmɪ) *interj. Brit. sl.* an exclamation of surprise or annoyance. [C19: short for *gorblimey* God blind me]

blimp[1] (blɪmp) *n.* **1.** a small nonrigid airship. **2.** *Films.* a soundproof cover fixed over a camera during shooting. [C20: prob. < (*type*) *B-limp*]

blimp[2] (blɪmp) *n.* (*often cap.*) *Chiefly Brit.* a person, esp. a military officer, who is stupidly complacent and reactionary. Also called: **Colonel Blimp.** [C20: < a character created by David Low (1891-1963), Brit. cartoonist, born N.Z.] —ˈ**blimpish** *adj.*

blind (blaɪnd) *adj.* **1. a.** unable to see; sightless. **b.** (*as collective n.; preceded by the*)*: the blind.* **2.** (usually foll. by *to*) unable or unwilling to understand or discern. **3.** not determined by reason: *blind hatred.* **4.** acting or performed without control or preparation. **5.** done without being able to see, relying on instruments for information. **6.** hidden from sight: *a blind corner.* **7.** closed at one end: *a blind alley.* **8.** completely lacking awareness or consciousness: *a blind stupor.* **9.** *Inf.* very drunk. **10.** having no openings or outlets: *a blind wall.* **11.** (intensifier): *not a blind bit of notice.* ~*adv.* **12.** without being able to see ahead or using only instruments: *to drive blind; flying blind.* **13.** without adequate knowledge or information; carelessly: *to buy a house blind.* **14. bake blind.** to bake (an empty pastry case) by half filling with dried peas, crusts, etc., to keep it in shape. ~*vb.* (*mainly tr.*) **15.** to deprive of sight permanently or temporarily. **16.** to deprive of good sense, reason, or judgment. **17.** to darken; conceal. **18.** (foll. by *with*) to overwhelm by showing detailed knowledge: *to blind somebody with science.* ~*n.* **19.** (*modifier*) for or intended to help the blind: *a blind school.* **20.** a shade for a window, usually on a roller. **21.** any obstruction or hindrance to sight, light, or air. **22.** a person, action, or thing that serves to deceive or conceal the truth. [OE *blind*] —ˈ**blindly** *adv.* —ˈ**blindness** *n.*

blind alley *n.* **1.** an alley open at one end only; cul-de-sac. **2.** *Inf.* a situation in which no further progress can be made.

blind date *n. Inf.* a social meeting between a man and a woman who have not met before.

blinders (ˈblaɪndəz) *pl. n.* the usual U.S. & Canad. word for **blinkers.**

blindfold (ˈblaɪndˌfəʊld) *vb.* (*tr.*) **1.** to prevent (a person or animal) from seeing by covering (the eyes). ~*n.* **2.** a piece of cloth, bandage, etc., used to cover the eyes. ~*adj., adv.* **3.** having the eyes covered with a cloth or bandage. **4.** rash; inconsiderate. [changed (C16) through association with FOLD[1] < OE *blindfellian* to strike blind; see BLIND, FELL[2]]

blind man's buff *n.* a game in which a blindfolded person tries to catch and identify the other players. [C16: *buff,* ? < OF *buffe* a blow; see BUFFET[2]]

blind spot *n.* **1.** a small oval-shaped area of the retina, where the optic nerve enters, in which vision is not experienced. **2.** a place or area where vision is obscured. **3.** a subject about which a person is ignorant or prejudiced.

blindworm (ˈblaɪndˌwɜːm) *n.* another name for **slowworm.**

blink (blɪŋk) *vb.* **1.** to close and immediately reopen (the eyes or an eye), usually involuntarily. **2.** (*intr.*) to look with the eyes partially closed. **3.** to shine intermittently or unsteadily. **4.** (*tr.;* foll. by *away, from,* etc.) to clear the eyes of (dust, tears, etc.). **5.** (when *tr.,* usually foll. by *at*) to be surprised or amazed. **6.** (when *intr.,* foll. by *at*) to pretend not to know or see (a fault, injustice, etc.). ~*n.* **7.** the act or an instance of blinking. **8.** a glance; glimpse. **9.** short for **iceblink** (sense 1). **10. on the blink.** *Sl.* not working properly. [C14: var. of BLENCH]

blinker[1] (ˈblɪŋkə) *n.* **1.** a flashing light for sending messages, as a warning device, etc., such as a direction indicator on a road vehicle. **2.** (*often pl.*) a slang word for **eye.**

blinker[2] (ˈblɪŋkə) *vb.* (*tr.*) **1.** to provide (a horse) with blinkers. **2.** to obscure or be obscured with or as with blinkers. —ˈ**blinkered** *adj.*

blinkers (ˈblɪŋkəz) *pl. n.* (*sometimes sing.*) *Chiefly Brit.* leather sidepieces attached to a horse's bridle to prevent sideways vision.

blinking (ˈblɪŋkɪŋ) *adj., adv. Inf.* (intensifier): *a blinking fool; a blinking good film.*

blip (blɪp) *n.* **1.** a repetitive sound, such as that produced by an electronic device. **2.** Also called: **pip.** the spot of light on a radar screen indicating the position of an object. ~*vb.* **blipping, blipped. 3.** (*intr.*) to produce such a noise. [C20: imit.]

bliss (blɪs) *n.* **1.** perfect happiness; serene joy. **2.** the ecstatic joy of heaven. [OE *blīths;* rel. to *blīthe* BLITHE]

blissful (ˈblɪsfʊl) *adj.* **1.** serenely joyful or glad. **2. blissful ignorance.** unawareness or inexperience of something unpleasant. —ˈ**blissfully** *adv.* —ˈ**blissfulness** *n.*

blister (ˈblɪstə) *n.* **1.** a small bubble-like elevation of the skin filled with serum, produced as a reaction to a burn, mechanical irritation, etc. **2.** a swelling containing air or liquid, as on a painted surface. **3. a.** *N.Z. sl.* a rebuke. **b.** *N.Z. & Austral. sl.* a summons to court. ~*vb.* **4.** to have or cause to have blisters. **5.** (*tr.*) to attack verbally with great scorn or sarcasm. [C13: < OF *blestre*] —ˈ**blistered** *adj.* —ˈ**blistery** *adj.*

blister pack *n.* a type of pack for small goods, consisting of a transparent dome on a firm backing. Also called: **bubble pack.**

BLit *abbrev. for* Bachelor of Literature.

blithe (blaɪð) *adj.* **1.** very happy or cheerful; gay. **2.** heedless; casual and indifferent. [OE *blīthe*] —ˈ**blithely** *adv.* —ˈ**blitheness** *n.*

blithering (ˈblɪðərɪŋ) *adj.* **1.** talking foolishly;

jabbering. **2.** *Inf.* stupid; foolish: *you blithering idiot.* [C19: var. of BLETHER + -ING[2]]

blithesome ('blaɪðsəm) *adj. Literary.* cheery; merry.

BLitt *abbrev. for* Bachelor of Letters. [L *Baccalaureus Litterarum*]

blitz (blɪts) *n.* **1.** a violent and sustained attack, esp. with intensive aerial bombardment. **2.** any sudden intensive attack or concerted effort. ~*vb.* **3.** (*tr.*) to attack suddenly and intensively. [C20: shortened < G *Blitzkrieg* lightning war]

Blitz (blɪts) *n.* **the.** the systematic bombing of Britain in 1940–41 by the German Luftwaffe.

blitzkrieg ('blɪts,kri:g) *n.* a swift intensive military attack designed to defeat the opposition quickly. [C20: < G: lightning war]

blizzard ('blɪzəd) *n.* a strong cold wind accompanied by widespread heavy snowfall. [C19: <?]

bloat (bləʊt) *vb.* **1.** to swell or cause to swell, as with a liquid or air. **2.** to become or cause to be puffed up, as with conceit. **3.** (*tr.*) to cure (fish, esp. herring) by half drying in smoke. [C17: prob. rel. to ON *blautr* soaked] —'**bloated** *adj.*

bloater ('bləʊtə) *n.* a herring that has been salted in brine, smoked, and cured.

blob (blɒb) *n.* **1.** a soft mass or drop. **2.** a spot, dab, or blotch of colour, ink, etc. **3.** an indistinct or shapeless form or object. [C15: ? imit.]

bloc (blɒk) *n.* a group of people or countries combined by a common interest. [< F: BLOCK]

block (blɒk) *n.* **1.** a large solid piece of wood, stone, or other material usually having at least one face fairly flat. **2.** such a piece on which particular tasks may be done, as chopping, cutting, or beheading. **3.** Also called: **building block.** one of a set of wooden or plastic cubes as a child's toy. **4.** a form on which things are shaped: *a wig block.* **5.** *Sl.* a person's head. **6. do one's block.** *Austral. & N.Z. sl.* to become angry. **7.** a dull, unemotional, or hardhearted person. **8.** a large building of offices, flats, etc. **9. a.** a group of buildings in a city bounded by intersecting streets on each side. **b.** the area or distance between such intersecting streets. **10.** *Austral. & N.Z.* an area of land, usually extensive, taken up for farming, settlement, etc. **11.** *N.Z.* an area of bush reserved by licence for a trapper or hunter. **12.** a piece of wood, metal, or other material having a design in relief, used for printing. **13.** *Austral. & N.Z.* a log, usually of willow, fastened to a timber base and used in a wood-chopping competition. **14.** a casing housing one or more freely rotating pulleys. See also **block and tackle. 15.** an obstruction or hindrance. **16.** *Pathol.* **a.** interference in the normal physiological functioning of an organ or part. **b.** See **heart block. 17.** *Psychol.* a short interruption of perceptual or thought processes. **18.** obstruction of an opponent in a sport. **19. a.** a quantity handled or considered as a single unit. **b.** (*as modifier*): *a block booking.* **20.** *Athletics.* short for **starting block.** ~*vb.* (*mainly tr.*) **21.** (often foll. by *up*) to obstruct (a passage, channel, etc.) or prevent or impede the motion or flow of (something or someone) by introducing an obstacle: *to block the traffic; to block up a pipe.* **22.** to impede, retard, or prevent (an action, procedure, etc.). **23.** to stamp (a title, design, etc.) on (a book cover, etc.) esp. using gold leaf. **24.** to shape by use of a block: *to block a hat.* **25.** (*also intr.*) *Sports.* to obstruct or impede movement by (an opponent). **26.** to interrupt a physiological function, as by use of an anaesthetic. **27.** (*also intr.*) *Cricket.* to play (a ball) defensively. ~See also **block in, block out.** [C14: < OF *bloc,* < Du. *blok*] —'**blocker** *n.*

blockade (blɒ'keɪd) *n.* **1.** *Mil.* the interdiction of a nation's sea lines of communications, esp. of an individual port by the use of sea power. **2.** something that prevents access or progress. ~*vb.* (*tr.*) **3.** to impose a blockade on. **4.** to obstruct the way to. [C17: < BLOCK + *-ade,* as in AMBUSCADE] —**block'ader** *n.*

blockage ('blɒkɪdʒ) *n.* **1.** the act of blocking or state of being blocked. **2.** an object causing an obstruction.

block and tackle *n.* a hoisting device in which a rope or chain is passed around a pair of blocks containing one or more pulleys.

blockboard ('blɒk,bɔ:d) *n.* a bonded board in which strips of soft wood are sandwiched between two layers of veneer.

blockbuster ('blɒk,bʌstə) *n. Inf.* **1.** a large bomb used to demolish extensive areas. **2.** a very successful, effective, or forceful person, thing, etc.

block diagram *n.* a diagram showing the interconnections between the parts of an industrial process or the components of an electronic or electrical system.

blockhead ('blɒk,hɛd) *n. Derog.* a stupid person. —'**block,headed** *adj.*

blockhouse ('blɒk,haʊs) *n.* **1.** (formerly) a wooden fortification with ports for defensive fire, observation, etc. **2.** a concrete structure strengthened to give protection against enemy fire, with apertures to allow defensive gunfire. **3.** a building constructed of logs or squared timber.

block in *vb.* (*tr., adv.*) to sketch or outline with little detail.

blockish ('blɒkɪʃ) *adj.* lacking vivacity or imagination; stupid. —'**blockishly** *adv.*

block letter *n.* **1.** *Printing.* a less common name for **sans serif. 2.** Also called: **block capital.** a plain capital letter.

block out *vb.* (*tr., adv.*) **1.** to plan or describe (something) in a general fashion. **2.** to prevent the entry or consideration of (something).

block release *n. Brit.* the release of industrial trainees from work for study at a college for several weeks.

block vote *n. Brit.* (at a trade-union conference) the system whereby each delegate's vote has a value in proportion to the number of people he represents.

bloke (bləʊk) *n. Brit.* an informal word for **man.** [C19: < Shelta]

blonde *or* (*masc.*) **blond** (blɒnd) *adj.* **1.** (of hair) of a light colour; fair. **2.** (of people or a race) having fair hair, a light complexion, and, typically, blue or grey eyes. ~*n.* **3.** a person having light-coloured hair and skin. [C15: < OF *blond* (fem. *blonde*), prob. of Gmc origin] —'**blondeness** *or* '**blondness** *n.*

blood (blʌd) *n.* **1.** a reddish fluid in vertebrates that is pumped by the heart through the arteries and veins. **2.** a similar fluid in invertebrates. **3.** bloodshed, esp. when resulting in murder. **4.** life itself; lifeblood. **5.** relationship through being of the same family, race, or kind; kinship. **6. flesh and blood. a.** near kindred or kinship, esp. that between a parent and child. **b.** human nature (esp. in **it's more than flesh and blood can stand**). **7. in one's blood.** as a natural or inherited characteristic or talent. **8. the blood.** royal or noble descent: *a prince of the blood.* **9.** temperament; disposition; temper. **10. a.** good or pure breeding; pedigree. **b.** (*as modifier*): *blood horses.* **11.** people viewed as members of a group, esp. as an invigorating force (**new blood, young blood**). **12.** *Chiefly Brit., rare.* a dashing young man. **13. in cold blood.** showing no passion; deliberately; ruthlessly. **14. make one's blood boil.** to cause to be angry or indignant. **15. make one's blood run cold.** to fill with horror. ~*vb.* (*tr.*) **16.** *Hunting.* to cause (young hounds) to taste the blood of a freshly killed quarry. **17.** to initiate (a person) to war or hunting. [OE *blōd*]

blood-and-thunder *adj.* denoting or relating to a melodramatic adventure story.

blood bank *n.* a place where whole blood or blood plasma is stored until required in transfusion.

blood bath *n.* indiscriminate slaughter; a massacre.

blood brother *n.* **1.** a brother by birth. **2.** a man or boy who has sworn to treat another as his brother, often in a ceremony in which their blood is mingled.

blood count *n.* determination of the number of

red and white blood corpuscles in a specific sample of blood.

bloodcurdling (ˈblʌdˌkɜːdlɪŋ) *adj.* terrifying; horrifying. —ˈ**blood,curdlingly** *adv.*

blood donor *n.* a person who gives his blood to be used for transfusion.

blooded (ˈblʌdɪd) *adj.* **1.** (of horses, cattle, etc.) of good breeding. **2.** (*in combination*) having blood or temperament as specified: *hot-blooded, cold-blooded, warm-blooded, red-blooded.*

blood group *n.* any one of the various groups into which human blood is classified on the basis of its specific agglutinating properties. Also called: **blood type.**

blood heat *n.* the normal temperature of the human body, 98.4°F. or 37°C.

bloodhound (ˈblʌdˌhaʊnd) *n.* a large breed of hound, formerly used in tracking and police work.

bloodless (ˈblʌdlɪs) *adj.* **1.** without blood. **2.** conducted without violence (esp. in **bloodless revolution**). **3.** anaemic-looking; pale. **4.** lacking vitality; lifeless. **5.** lacking in emotion; unfeeling. —ˈ**bloodlessly** *adv.* —ˈ**bloodlessness** *n.*

blood-letting (ˈblʌdˌlɛtɪŋ) *n.* **1.** the therapeutic removal of blood. See also **phlebotomy. 2.** bloodshed, esp. in a feud.

blood money *n.* **1.** compensation paid to the relatives of a murdered person. **2.** money paid to a hired murderer. **3.** a reward for information about a criminal, esp. a murderer.

blood orange *n.* a variety of orange all or part of the pulp of which is dark red when ripe.

blood poisoning *n.* a nontechnical term for **septicaemia.**

blood pressure *n.* the pressure exerted by the blood on the inner walls of the arteries, being relative to the elasticity and diameter of the vessels and the force of the heartbeat.

blood pudding *n.* another name for **black pudding.**

blood relation *or* **relative** *n.* a person related to another by birth, as distinct from one related by marriage.

bloodshed (ˈblʌdˌʃɛd) *n.* slaughter; killing.

bloodshot (ˈblʌdˌʃɒt) *adj.* (of an eye) inflamed.

blood sport *n.* any sport involving the killing of an animal, esp. hunting.

bloodstain (ˈblʌdˌsteɪn) *n.* a dark discoloration caused by blood, esp. dried blood. —ˈ**blood,stained** *adj.*

bloodstock (ˈblʌdˌstɒk) *n.* thoroughbred horses.

bloodstone (ˈblʌdˌstəʊn) *n.* a dark green variety of chalcedony with red spots: used as a gemstone. Also called: **heliotrope.**

bloodstream (ˈblʌdˌstriːm) *n.* the flow of blood through the vessels of a living body.

bloodsucker (ˈblʌdˌsʌkə) *n.* **1.** an animal that sucks blood, esp. a leech or mosquito. **2.** *Inf.* a person or thing that preys upon another person, esp. by extorting money. —ˈ**blood,sucking** *adj.*

bloodthirsty (ˈblʌdˌθɜːstɪ) *adj.* **-thirstier, -thirstiest. 1.** murderous; cruel. **2.** taking pleasure in bloodshed or violence. **3.** describing or depicting killing and violence; gruesome. —ˈ**blood,thirstily** *adv.* —ˈ**blood,thirstiness** *n.*

blood type *n.* another name for **blood group.**

blood vessel *n.* an artery, capillary, or vein.

bloodwood (ˈblʌdˌwʊd) *n.* any of several species of Australian eucalyptus with red sap.

bloody (ˈblʌdɪ) *adj.* **bloodier, bloodiest. 1.** covered or stained with blood. **2.** resembling or composed of blood. **3.** marked by much killing and bloodshed: *a bloody war.* **4.** cruel or murderous: *a bloody tyrant.* ~*adv., adj.* **5.** *Sl.* (intensifier): *a bloody fool.* ~*vb.* **bloodying, bloodied. 6.** (*tr.*) to stain with blood. —ˈ**bloodily** *adv.* —ˈ**bloodiness** *n.*

Bloody Mary (ˈmɛərɪ) *n.* a drink consisting of tomato juice and vodka.

bloody-minded *adj. Brit. inf.* deliberately obstructive and unhelpful.

bloom[1] (bluːm) *n.* **1.** a blossom on a flowering plant; a flower. **2.** the state, time, or period when flowers open. **3.** open flowers collectively. **4.** a healthy, vigorous, or flourishing condition; prime. **5.** youthful or healthy rosiness in the cheeks or face; glow. **6.** a fine whitish coating on the surface of fruits, leaves, etc. **7.** Also called: **chill.** a dull area on the surface of old gloss paint, lacquer, or varnish. ~*vb.* (*intr.*) **8.** (of flowers) to open; come into flower. **9.** to bear flowers; blossom. **10.** to flourish or grow. **11.** to be in a healthy, glowing, or flourishing condition. [C13: of Gmc origin; cf. ON *blōm* flower]

bloom[2] (bluːm) *n.* a rectangular mass of metal obtained by rolling or forging a cast ingot. [OE *blōma* lump of metal]

bloomer[1] (ˈbluːmə) *n.* a plant that flowers, esp. in a specified way: *a night bloomer.*

bloomer[2] (ˈbluːmə) *n. Brit. inf.* a stupid mistake; blunder. [C20: < BLOOMING]

bloomer[3] (ˈbluːmə) *n. Brit.* a medium-sized loaf, glazed and notched on top. [C20: <?]

bloomers (ˈbluːməz) *pl. n.* **1.** *Inf.* women's baggy knickers. **2.** (formerly) loose trousers gathered at the knee worn by women for cycling, etc. **3.** *History.* loose trousers gathered at the ankle and worn under a shorter skirt. [after Mrs A. *Bloomer* (1818–94), U.S. social reformer]

blooming (ˈbluːmɪŋ) *adv., adj. Brit. inf.* (intensifier): *a blooming genius; blooming painful.* [C19: euphemistic for BLOODY]

blossom (ˈblɒsəm) *n.* **1.** the flower or flowers of a plant, esp. producing edible fruit. **2.** the time or period of flowering. ~*vb.* (*intr.*) **3.** (of plants) to come into flower. **4.** to develop or come to a promising stage. [OE *blōstm*] —ˈ**blossomy** *adj.*

blot (blɒt) *n.* **1.** a stain or spot of ink, paint, dirt, etc. **2.** something that spoils. **3.** a blemish or stain on one's character or reputation. **4.** *Austral. sl.* the anus. ~*vb.* **blotting, blotted. 5.** (of ink, dye, etc.) to form spots or blobs on (a material) or (of a person) to cause such spots or blobs to form on (a material). **6.** (*intr.*) to stain or become stained or spotted. **7.** (*tr.*) to cause a blemish in or on; disgrace. **8.** to soak up (excess ink, etc.) by using blotting paper. **9.** (of blotting paper) to absorb (excess ink, etc.). **10.** (*tr.; often foll. by out*) **a.** to darken or hide completely; obscure; obliterate. **b.** to destroy; annihilate. [C14: prob. of Gmc origin]

blotch (blɒtʃ) *n.* **1.** an irregular spot or discoloration, esp. a dark and relatively large one. ~*vb.* **2.** to become or cause to become marked by such discoloration. [C17: prob. < BOTCH, infl. by BLOT] —ˈ**blotchy** *adj.*

blotter (ˈblɒtə) *n.* something used to absorb excess ink, esp. a sheet of blotting paper.

blotting paper *n.* a soft absorbent unsized paper, used esp. for soaking up surplus ink.

blotto (ˈblɒtəʊ) *adj. Sl.* unconscious, esp. through drunkenness. [C20: < BLOT (vb.)]

blouse (blaʊz) *n.* **1.** a woman's shirtlike garment. **2.** a waist-length belted jacket worn by soldiers. ~*vb.* **3.** to hang or make so as to hang in full loose folds. [C19: < F, <?]

blouson (ˈbluːzɒn) *n.* a tight-waisted jacket or top that blouses out. [C20: < F]

blow[1] (bləʊ) *vb.* **blowing, blew, blown. 1.** (of a current of air, the wind, etc.) to be or cause to be in motion. **2.** (*intr.*) to move or be carried by or as if by wind. **3.** to expel (air, cigarette smoke, etc.) through the mouth or nose. **4.** to force or cause (air, dust, etc.) to move (into, in, over, etc.) by using an instrument or by expelling breath. **5.** (*intr.*) to breathe hard; pant. **6.** (sometimes foll. by *up*) to inflate with air or the breath. **7.** (*intr.*) (of wind, a storm, etc.) to make a roaring sound. **8.** to cause (a whistle, siren, etc.) to sound by forcing air into it or (of a whistle, etc.) to sound thus. **9.** (*tr.*) to force air from the lungs through (the nose) to clear out mucus. **10.** (often foll. by *up, down, in,* etc.) to explode, break, or disintegrate completely. **11.** *Electronics.* to burn out (a fuse, valve, etc.) because of excessive current or (of a fuse, valve, etc.) to burn out. **12.** (*tr.*) to wind (a horse) by making it run excessively. **13.** to cause (a wind instrument) to sound by forcing one's breath into the mouthpiece or (of such an instrument) to sound in this way.

14. (*intr.*) (of flies) to lay eggs (in). 15. to shape (glass, ornaments, etc.) by forcing air or gas through the material when molten. 16. (*tr.*) *Sl.* to spend (money) freely. 17. (*tr.*) *Sl.* to use (an opportunity) ineffectively. 18. *Sl.* to go suddenly away (from). 19. (*tr.*) *Sl.* to expose or betray (a secret). 20. (p.p. **blowed**). *Inf.* another word for **damn.** 21. **blow hot and cold.** *Inf.* to vacillate. 22. **blow one's top.** *Inf.* to lose one's temper. ~*n.* 23. the act or an instance of blowing. 24. the sound produced by blowing. 25. a blast of air or wind. 26. *Austral. sl.* a brief rest; a breather. ~See also **blow in, blow out,** etc. [OE *blāwan*]

blow² (bləʊ) *n.* 1. a powerful or heavy stroke with the fist, a weapon, etc. 2. **at one** *or* **a blow.** by or with only one action. 3. a sudden setback. 4. **come to blows. a.** to fight. **b.** to result in a fight. 5. an attacking action: *a blow for freedom.* 6. *Austral. & N.Z.* a stroke of the shears in sheep-shearing. [C15: prob. of Gmc origin]

blow³ (bləʊ) *vb.* **blowing, blew, blown.** 1. (*intr.*) (of a plant or flower) to blossom or open out. ~*n.* 2. a mass of blossoms. 3. the state or period of blossoming. [OE *blōwan*]

blow-by-blow *adj.* (*prenominal*) explained in great detail: *a blow-by-blow account.*

blow-dry *vb.* **-drying, -dried.** 1. (*tr.*) to style (the hair) while drying it with a hand-held hair dryer. ~*n.* 2. this method of styling hair.

blower (ˈbləʊə) *n.* 1. a mechanical device, such as a fan, that blows. 2. a low-pressure compressor, esp. in a furnace or internal-combustion engine. 3. an informal name for **telephone.**

blowfish (ˈbləʊˌfɪʃ) *n., pl.* **-fish** *or* **-fishes.** a popular name for **puffer** (sense 2).

blowfly (ˈbləʊˌflaɪ) *n., pl.* **-flies.** any of various flies that lay their eggs in rotting meat, dung, carrion, and open wounds. Also called: **bluebottle.**

blowgun (ˈbləʊˌgʌn) *n.* the U.S. word for **blowpipe** (sense 1).

blowhard (ˈbləʊˌhɑːd) *Inf.* ~*n.* 1. a boastful person. ~*adj.* 2. blustering or boastful.

blowhole (ˈbləʊˌhəʊl) *n.* 1. the nostril of whales, situated far back on the skull. 2. a hole in ice through which whales, seals, etc., breathe. 3. a vent in a cliff connecting with a cave below, through which spray is forced. 4. **a.** a vent for air or gas. **b.** *N.Z.* a hole emitting gas or steam in a volcanic region.

blow in *Inf.* ~*vb.* 1. (*intr., adv.*) to arrive or enter suddenly. ~*n.* **blow-in.** 2. *Austral.* a newcomer.

blowlamp (ˈbləʊˌlæmp) *n.* a small burner that produces a very hot flame, used to remove old paint, melt soft metal, etc. U.S. and Canad. name: **blowtorch.**

blown (bləʊn) *vb.* the past participle of **blow¹** and **blow³.**

blow out *vb.* (*adv.*) 1. to extinguish (a flame, candle, etc.) or (of a flame, etc.) to become extinguished. 2. (*intr.*) (of a tyre) to puncture suddenly, esp. at high speed. 3. (*intr.*) (of a fuse) to melt suddenly. 4. (*tr.; often reflexive*) to diminish or use up the energy of: *the storm blew itself out.* 5. (*intr.*) (of an oil or gas well) to lose oil or gas in an uncontrolled manner. ~*n.* **blowout.** 6. the sudden melting of an electrical fuse. 7. a sudden burst in a tyre. 8. the uncontrolled escape of oil or gas from an oil or gas well. 9. *Sl.* a large filling meal or lavish entertainment.

blow over *vb.* (*intr., adv.*) 1. to cease or be finished: *the storm blew over.* 2. to be forgotten.

blowpipe (ˈbləʊˌpaɪp) *n.* 1. a long tube from which pellets, poisoned darts, etc., are shot by blowing. 2. Also called: **blow tube.** a tube for blowing air or oxygen into a flame to intensify its heat. 3. a long narrow iron pipe used to gather molten glass and blow it into shape.

blow through *vb.* (*intr., adv.*) *Austral. inf.* to leave; make off.

blowtorch (ˈbləʊˌtɔːtʃ) *n.* the U.S. and Canad. name for **blowlamp.**

blow up *vb.* (*adv.*) 1. to explode or cause to explode. 2. (*tr.*) to increase the importance of (something): *they blew the whole affair up.* 3. (*intr.*) to arise: *we lived very quietly before this affair blew up.* 4. (*intr.*) to come into existence with sudden force: *a storm had blown up.* 5. (*intr.*) *Inf.* to lose one's temper (with a person). 6. (*tr.*) *Inf.* to reprimand. 7. (*tr.*) *Inf.* to enlarge the size of (a photograph). ~*n.* **blow-up.** 8. an explosion. 9. *Inf.* an enlarged photograph or part of a photograph. 10. *Inf.* a fit of temper.

blowy (ˈbləʊɪ) *adj.* **blowier, blowiest.** another word for **windy** (sense 1).

blowzy *or* **blowsy** (ˈblaʊzɪ) *adj.* **blowzier, blowziest** *or* **blowsier, blowsiest.** 1. (esp. of a woman) untidy in appearance; slovenly or sluttish. 2. (of a woman) ruddy in complexion. [C18: < dialect *blowze* beggar girl, <?]

blub (blʌb) *vb.* **blubbing, blubbed.** *Brit.* a slang word for **blubber** (senses 1-3).

blubber (ˈblʌbə) *vb.* 1. to sob without restraint. 2. to utter while sobbing. 3. (*tr.*) to make (the face) wet and swollen by crying. ~*n.* 4. the fatty tissue of aquatic mammals such as the whale. 5. *Inf.* flabby body fat. 6. the act or an instance of weeping without restraint. ~*adj.* 7. (*often in combination*) swollen or fleshy: *blubber-faced.* [C12: ?< Low G *blubbern* to BUBBLE, imit.] —ˈ**blubberer** *n.* —ˈ**blubbery** *adj.*

bludge (blʌdʒ) *Austral. & N.Z. inf.* ~*vb.* 1. (when *intr.*, often foll. by *on*) to scrounge from (someone). 2. (*intr.*) to skive. ~*n.* 3. a very easy task. [C19: back formation < *bludger* pimp, < BLUDGEON]

bludgeon (ˈblʌdʒən) *n.* 1. a stout heavy club, typically thicker at one end. 2. a person, line of argument, etc., that is effective but unsubtle. ~*vb.* (*tr.*) 3. to hit as with a bludgeon. 4. (often foll. by *into*) to force; bully; coerce. [C18: <?]

bludger (ˈblʌdʒə) *n. Austral. & N.Z. inf.* 1. a person who scrounges. 2. a person who avoids work. 3. a person in authority regarded as ineffectual by those working under him.

blue (bluː) *n.* 1. any of a group of colours, such as that of a clear unclouded sky or the deep sea. 2. a dye or pigment of any of these colours. 3. blue cloth or clothing: *dressed in blue.* 4. a sportsman who represents or has represented Oxford or Cambridge University and has the right to wear the university colour. 5. *Brit.* an informal name for **Tory.** 6. any of numerous small blue-winged butterflies. 7. a blue substance used in laundering. 8. *Austral. & N.Z. sl.* an argument or fight: *he had a blue with a taxi driver.* 9. Also: **bluey.** *Austral. & N.Z. inf.* a court summons. 10. *Austral. & N.Z. inf.* a mistake; error. 11. **out of the blue.** apparently from nowhere; unexpectedly. ~*adj.* **bluer, bluest.** 12. of the colour blue. 13. (of the flesh) having a purple tinge, as from cold or contusion. 14. depressed, moody, or unhappy. 15. indecent, titillating, or pornographic: *blue films.* ~*vb.* **blueing** *or* **bluing, blued.** 16. to make, dye, or become blue. 17. (*tr.*) to treat (laundry) with blue. 18. (*tr.*) *Sl.* to spend extravagantly or wastefully; squander. ~See also **blues.** [C13: < OF *bleu*, of Gmc origin] —ˈ**blueness** *n.*

Blue (bluː) *n. Austral. inf.* a person with red hair.

blue baby *n.* a baby born with a bluish tinge to the skin because of lack of oxygen in the blood.

Bluebeard (ˈbluːˌbɪəd) *n.* 1. a villain in European folk tales who marries several wives and murders them in turn. 2. a man who has had several wives.

bluebell (ˈbluːˌbɛl) *n.* 1. Also called: **wild** or **wood hyacinth.** a European woodland plant having a one-sided cluster of blue bell-shaped flowers. 2. a Scottish name for **harebell.** 3. any of various other plants with blue bell-shaped flowers.

blueberry (ˈbluːbərɪ, -brɪ) *n., pl.* **-ries.** 1. Also called: **huckleberry.** any of several North American ericaceous shrubs that have blue-black edible berries with tiny seeds. See also **bilberry.** 2. the fruit of any of these plants.

bluebird (ˈbluːˌbɜːd) *n.* 1. a North American songbird of the thrush family having a blue or partly blue plumage. **2.** any of various other birds having a blue plumage.

blue blood *n.* royal or aristocratic descent. [C19: translation of Sp. *sangre azul*] —ˌ**blue-ˈblooded** *adj.*

bluebook (ˈbluːˌbʊk) *n.* **1.** (in Britain) a government publication bound in a stiff blue paper cover: usually the report of a royal commission or a committee. **2.** (in Canada) an annual statement of government accounts.

bluebottle (ˈbluːˌbɒtᵊl) *n.* **1.** another name for the **blowfly.** **2.** any of various blue-flowered plants, esp. the cornflower. **3.** *Brit.* an informal word for a **policeman.** **4.** *Austral. & N.Z.* an informal name for **Portuguese man-of-war.**

blue cheese *n.* cheese containing a blue mould, esp. Stilton, Roquefort, or Danish blue.

blue chip *n.* **1.** a gambling chip with the highest value. **2.** *Finance.* a stock considered reliable with respect to both dividend income and capital value. **3.** (*modifier*) denoting something considered to be a valuable asset.

blue-collar *adj.* of or designating manual industrial workers. Cf. **white-collar.**

blue-eyed boy *n. Inf., chiefly Brit.* the favourite or darling of a person or group.

bluefish (ˈbluːˌfɪʃ) *n., pl.* **-fish** *or* **-fishes.** **1.** Also called: **snapper.** a bluish marine food and game fish, related to the horse mackerel. **2.** any of various other bluish fishes.

blue fox *n.* **1.** a variety of the arctic fox that has a pale grey winter coat. **2.** the fur of this animal.

blue funk *n. Sl.* a state of great terror.

bluegill (ˈbluːˌgɪl) *n.* a common North American freshwater sunfish: an important food and game fish.

bluegrass (ˈbluːˌgrɑːs) *n.* **1.** any of several North American bluish-green grasses, esp. **Kentucky bluegrass,** grown for forage. **2.** a type of folk music originating in Kentucky.

blue-green algae *pl. n.* a family of algae that contain a blue pigment as well as chlorophyll.

blue ground *n. Mineralogy.* another name for **kimberlite.**

blue gum *n.* a tall fast-growing widely cultivated Australian eucalyptus, having bluish aromatic leaves containing a medicinal oil, bark that peels off in shreds, and hard timber.

blue heeler *n. Austral.* a type of dog with dark speckled markings: used for herding cattle.

bluejacket (ˈbluːˌdʒækɪt) *n.* a sailor in the Navy.

blue jay *n.* a common North American jay having bright blue plumage.

blue moon *n.* **once in a blue moon.** *Inf.* very rarely; almost never.

blue mould *n.* any fungus that forms a bluish mass on decaying food, leather, etc. Also called: **green mould.**

blue pencil *n.* **1.** deletion, alteration, or censorship of the contents of a book or other work. ~*vb.* **blue-pencil, -cilling, -cilled** *or U.S.* **-ciling, -ciled.** **2.** (*tr.*) to alter or delete parts of (a book, film, etc.), esp. to censor.

blue peter *n.* a signal flag of blue with a white square at the centre, displayed by a vessel about to leave port. [C19:< the name *Peter*]

blue pointer *n.* a large shark of Australian coastal waters, having a blue back and pointed snout.

blueprint (ˈbluːˌprɪnt) *n.* **1.** Also called: **cyanotype.** a photographic print of plans, technical drawings, etc., consisting of white lines on a blue background. **2.** an original plan or prototype. ~*vb.* **3.** (*tr.*) to make a blueprint of (a plan, etc.).

blue ribbon *n.* **1.** (in Britain) a badge of blue silk worn by members of the Order of the Garter. **2.** a badge awarded as the first prize in a competition.

blues (bluːz) *pl. n.* (*sometimes functioning as sing.*) **the.** **1.** a feeling of depression or deep unhappiness. **2.** a type of folk song originating among Black Americans, usually employing a basic 12-bar chorus and frequent minor intervals.

bluestocking (ˈbluːˌstɒkɪŋ) *n. Usually disparaging.* a scholarly or intellectual woman. [< the blue worsted stockings worn by members of an 18th-cent. literary society]

bluestone (ˈbluːˌstəʊn) *n.* **1.** a blue-grey sandstone containing much clay, used for building and paving. **2.** the blue crystalline form of copper sulphate.

bluetit (ˈbluːˌtɪt) *n.* a common European tit having a blue crown, wings, and tail, yellow underparts, and a black-and-grey head.

blue whale *n.* the largest mammal: a widely distributed bluish-grey whalebone whale, closely related and similar to the rorquals.

bluey (ˈbluːɪ) *n. Austral. inf.* **1.** a blanket. **2.** a swagman's bundle. **3.** **hump (one's) bluey.** to carry one's bundle; tramp. **4.** a variant of **blue** (sense 9). **5.** a cattle dog. **6.** a variant of **blue** (sense 11). [(for senses 1, 2, 4) C19: < BLUE (on account of their colour) + -Y²]

bluff¹ (blʌf) *vb.* **1.** to pretend to be confident about an uncertain issue in order to influence (someone). ~*n.* **2.** deliberate deception intended to create the impression of a stronger position than one actually has. **3.** **call someone's bluff.** to challenge someone to give proof of his claims. [C19: orig. U.S. poker-playing term, < Du. *bluffen* to boast] —ˈ**bluffer** *n.*

bluff² (blʌf) *n.* **1.** a steep promontory, bank, or cliff. **2.** *Canad.* a clump of trees on the prairie; copse. ~*adj.* **3.** good-naturedly frank and hearty. **4.** (of a bank, cliff, etc.) presenting a steep broad face. [C17 (in the sense: nearly perpendicular): ?< MDu. *blaf* broad] —ˈ**bluffly** *adv.* —ˈ**bluffness** *n.*

bluish *or* **blueish** (ˈbluːɪʃ) *adj.* somewhat blue.

blunder (ˈblʌndə) *n.* **1.** a stupid or clumsy mistake. **2.** a foolish tactless remark. ~*vb.* (*mainly intr.*) **3.** to make stupid or clumsy mistakes. **4.** to make foolish tactless remarks. **5.** (often foll. by *about, into,* etc.) to act clumsily; stumble. **6.** (*tr.*) to mismanage; botch. [C14: of Scand. origin; cf. ON *blunda* to close one's eyes] —ˈ**blunderer** *n.* —ˈ**blundering** *n., adj.*

blunderbuss (ˈblʌndəˌbʌs) *n.* an obsolete short musket with large bore and flared muzzle. [C17: changed (infl. by BLUNDER) < Du. *donderbus;* < *donder* THUNDER + obs. *bus* gun]

blunge (blʌndʒ) *vb.* (*tr.*) to mix (clay or a similar substance) with water in order to form a suspension for use in ceramics. [C19: prob. < BLEND + PLUNGE] —ˈ**blunger** *n.*

blunt (blʌnt) *adj.* **1.** (esp. of a knife or blade) lacking sharpness or keenness; dull. **2.** not having a sharp edge or point: *a blunt instrument.* **3.** (of people, manner of speaking, etc.) straightforward and uncomplicated. ~*vb.* (*tr.*) **4.** to make less sharp. **5.** to diminish the sensitivity or perception of; make dull. [C12: prob. of Scand. origin] —ˈ**bluntly** *adv.* —ˈ**bluntness** *n.*

blur (blɜː) *vb.* **blurring, blurred.** **1.** to make or become vague or less distinct. **2.** to smear or smudge. **3.** (*tr.*) to make (the judgment, memory, or perception) less clear; dim. ~*n.* **4.** something vague, hazy, or indistinct. **5.** a smear or smudge. [C16: ? var. of BLEAR] —**blurred** *adj.* —ˈ**blurry** *adj.*

blurb (blɜːb) *n.* a promotional description, as on the jackets of books. [C20: coined by G. Burgess (1866–1951), U.S. humorist & illustrator]

blurt (blɜːt) *vb.* (*tr.;* often foll. by *out*) to utter suddenly and involuntarily. [C16: prob. imit.]

blush (blʌʃ) *vb.* **1.** (*intr.*) to become suddenly red in the face from embarrassment, shame, modesty, or guilt; redden. **2.** to make or become reddish or rosy. ~*n.* **3.** a sudden reddening of the face from embarrassment, shame, modesty, or guilt. **4.** a rosy glow. **5.** **at first blush.** when first seen; as a first impression. [OE *blȳscan*]

blusher (ˈblʌʃə) *n.* a cosmetic applied to the cheeks to give a rosy colour.

bluster (ˈblʌstə) *vb.* **1.** to speak or say loudly or boastfully. **2.** to act in a bullying way. **3.** (*tr.;* foll. by *into*) to force or attempt to force (a person) into doing something by behaving thus. **4.** (*intr.*) (of the wind) to be noisy or gusty. ~*n.* **5.** boisterous talk or action; swagger. **6.** empty threats or protests. 7. a strong wind; gale. [C15: prob. < MLow G *blüsteren* to storm, blow violently] —ˈ**blusterer** *n.* —ˈ**blustery** *adj.*

Blvd *abbrev. for* Boulevard.

BM *abbrev. for:* 1. Bachelor of Medicine. 2. *Surveying.* bench mark. 3. British Museum.

BMA *abbrev. for* British Medical Association.

BMC *abbrev. for* British Medical Council.

B-movie *n.* a film originally made (esp. in the 1940s and 50s) as a supporting film, now often considered as a genre in its own right.

BMus *abbrev. for* Bachelor of Music.

BMX 1. *abbrev. for* bicycle motocross: stunt riding over an obstacle course on a bicycle. ~*n.* 2. a bicycle designed for bicycle motocross.

Bn *abbrev. for:* 1. Baron. 2. Battalion.

BNFL *abbrev. for* British Nuclear Fuels Limited.

bo *or* **boh** (bəʊ) *interj.* an exclamation to startle or surprise someone, esp. a child in a game.

BO *abbrev. for:* 1. *Inf.* body odour. 2. box office.

b.o. *abbrev. for:* 1. back order. 2. branch office. 3. broker's order. 4. buyer's option.

boa (ˈbəʊə) *n.* 1. any of various large non-venomous snakes of Central and South America and the West Indies. They kill their prey by constriction. 2. a woman's long thin scarf, usually of feathers or fur. [C19: < NL, < L]

boa constrictor *n.* a very large snake of tropical America and the West Indies that kills its prey by constriction.

boar (bɔː) *n.* 1. an uncastrated male pig. 2. See **wild boar.** [OE *bār*]

board (bɔːd) *n.* 1. a long wide flat piece of sawn timber. 2. **a.** a smaller flat piece of rigid material for a specific purpose: *ironing board.* **b.** (*in combination*): *breadboard.* 3. a person's meals, provided regularly for money. 4. *Arch.* a table, esp. when laden with food. 5. **a.** (*sometimes functioning as pl.*) a group of people who officially administer a company, trust, etc. **b.** (*as modifier*): *a board meeting.* 6. any other committee or council: *a board of interviewers.* 7. stiff cardboard or similar material, used for the outside covers of a book. 8. a flat thin rectangular sheet of composite material, such as plasterboard or chipboard. 9. *Chiefly U.S.* **a.** a list of stock-exchange prices. **b.** *Inf.* the stock exchange itself. 10. *Naut.* the side of a ship. 11. *Austral. & N.Z.* the part of the floor of a sheep-shearing shed where the shearers work. 12. any of various portable surfaces specially designed for indoor games such as chess, backgammon, etc. 13. **go by the board.** *Inf.* to be in disuse, neglected, or lost: *in these days courtesy goes by the board.* 14. **on board.** on or in a ship, boat, aeroplane, or other vehicle. 15. **the boards.** the stage. ~*vb.* 16. to go aboard (a vessel, train, aircraft, or other vehicle). 17. to attack (a ship) by forcing one's way aboard. 18. (*tr.;* often foll. by *up, in,* etc.) to cover or shut with boards. 19. (*intr.*) to receive meals or meals and lodging in return for money. 20. (sometimes foll. by *out*) to arrange for (someone, esp. a child) to receive food and lodging away from home. 21. (in ice hockey and box lacrosse) to bodycheck an opponent against the boards. ~See also **boards.** [OE *bord*]

boarder (ˈbɔːdə) *n.* 1. a pupil who lives at school during term time. 2. another word for **lodger.** 3. a person who boards a ship, esp. in an attack.

boarding (ˈbɔːdɪŋ) *n.* 1. a structure of boards. 2. timber boards collectively. 3. **a.** the act of embarking on an aircraft, train, ship, etc. **b.** (*as modifier*): *a boarding pass.* 4. (in ice hockey and box lacrosse) an act of bodychecking an opponent against the boards.

boarding house *n.* a private house in which accommodation and meals are provided for paying guests.

boarding school *n.* a school providing living accommodation for some or all of its pupils.

Board of Trade *n.* (in the United Kingdom) a ministry responsible for the supervision of commerce and the promotion of export trade.

boardroom (ˈbɔːdˌruːm, -ˌrʊm) *n.* a room where the board of directors of a company meets.

boards (bɔːdz) *pl. n.* a wooden wall about one metre high forming the enclosure in which ice hockey or box lacrosse is played.

board school *n.* (formerly) a school managed by a board of local ratepayers.

boardwalk (ˈbɔːdˌwɔːk) *n. U.S. & Canad.* a promenade, esp. along a beach, usually made of planks.

boast (bəʊst) *vb.* 1. (*intr.;* sometimes foll. by *of* or *about*) to speak in excessively proud terms of one's possessions, skills, or superior qualities; brag. 2. (*tr.*) to possess (something to be proud of): *the city boasts a fine cathedral.* ~*n.* 3. a bragging statement. 4. a possession, attribute, etc., that is or may be bragged about. [C13: <?] —ˈ**boaster** *n.* —ˈ**boasting** *n., adj.*

boastful (ˈbəʊstfʊl) *adj.* tending to boast; characterized by boasting. —ˈ**boastfully** *adv.* —ˈ**boastfulness** *n.*

boat (bəʊt) *n.* 1. a small vessel propelled by oars, paddle, sails, or motor. 2. (not in technical use) another word for **ship.** 3. a container for gravy, sauce, etc. 4. **in the same boat.** sharing the same problems. 5. **miss the boat.** to lose an opportunity. 6. **rock the boat.** *Inf.* to cause a disturbance in the existing situation. ~*vb.* 7. (*intr.*) to travel or go in a boat, esp. as a form of recreation. 8. (*tr.*) to transport or carry in a boat. [OE *bāt*]

boater (ˈbəʊtə) *n.* a stiff straw hat with a straight brim and flat crown.

boathook (ˈbəʊtˌhʊk) *n.* a pole with a hook at one end, used aboard a vessel for fending off other vessels or for catching a mooring buoy.

boathouse (ˈbəʊtˌhaʊs) *n.* a shelter by the edge of a river, lake, etc., for housing boats.

boatie (ˈbəʊtɪ) *n. Austral. & N.Z. inf.* a boating enthusiast.

boating (ˈbəʊtɪŋ) *n.* rowing, sailing, or cruising in boats as a form of recreation.

boatload (ˈbəʊtˌləʊd) *n.* the amount of cargo or number of people held by a boat or ship.

boatman (ˈbəʊtmən) *n., pl.* **-men.** a man who works on, hires out, or repairs a boat or boats.

boatswain, bo's'n, *or* **bosun** (ˈbəʊsᵊn) *n.* a petty officer or a warrant officer who is responsible for the maintenance of a ship and its equipment. [OE *bātswegen;* see BOAT, SWAIN]

boat train *n.* a train scheduled to take passengers to or from a particular ship.

bob[1] (bɒb) *vb.* **bobbing, bobbed.** 1. to move or cause to move up and down repeatedly, as while floating in water. 2. to move or cause to move with a short abrupt movement, as of the head. 3. (*intr.;* usually foll. by *up*) to appear or emerge suddenly. 4. (*intr.;* usually foll. by *for*) to attempt to get hold (of a floating or hanging object, esp. an apple) in the teeth as a game. ~*n.* 5. a short abrupt movement, as of the head. [C14: <?]

bob[2] (bɒb) *n.* 1. a hairstyle for women and children in which the hair is cut short evenly all round the head. 2. a dangling or hanging object, such as the weight on a pendulum or on a plumb line. 3. short for **bobsleigh.** 4. a docked tail, esp. of a horse. ~*vb.* **bobbing, bobbed.** 5. (*tr.*) to cut (the hair) in a bob. 6. (*tr.*) to cut short (something, esp. the tail of an animal); dock or crop. 7. (*intr.*) to ride on a bobsleigh. [C14 *bobbe* bunch of flowers]

bob[3] (bɒb) *n., pl.* **bob.** *Brit.* (formerly) an informal word for a **shilling.** [C19: <?]

bobbejaan (ˈbɒbəˌjɑːn) *n. S. African.* a baboon. [< Afrik., < MDu. *babiaen*]

bobbejaan spanner *n. S. African.* a monkey wrench.

bobbin (ˈbɒbɪn) *n.* a spool or reel on which thread or yarn is wound. [C16: < OF *bobine,* <?]

bobble (ˈbɒbᵊl) *n.* a tufted ball, usually for ornament, as on a knitted hat. [C19: < BOB[1] (vb.)]

bobby (ˈbɒbɪ) *n., pl.* **-bies.** *Inf.* a British policeman. [C19: < *Bobby,* after *Robert* Peel, who set up the Metropolitan Police Force in 1828]

bobby calf *n.* an unweaned calf culled for slaughter.

bobby-dazzler *n. Dialect.* anything outstanding,

striking, or showy. [C19: expanded < *dazzler* something striking or attractive]

bobby pin *n. U.S., Canad., Austral., & N.Z.* a metal hairpin bent in order to hold the hair in place.

bobby socks *pl. n.* ankle-length socks worn by teenage girls, esp. in the U.S. in the 1940s.

bobcat (ˈbɒbˌkæt) *n.* a North American feline mammal, closely related to but smaller than the lynx, having reddish-brown fur with dark spots or stripes, tufted ears, and a short tail. Also called: **bay lynx.** [C19: < BOB[2] + CAT]

bobolink (ˈbɒbəˌlɪŋk) *n.* an American songbird, the male of which has a white back and black underparts. [C18: imit.]

bobotie (bʊˈbʊtɪ) *n.* a South African dish consisting of curried mincemeat with a topping of beaten egg baked to a crust. [C19: < Afrik., prob. < Malay]

bobsleigh (ˈbɒbˌsleɪ) *n.* **1.** a racing sledge for two or more people, with a steering mechanism enabling the driver to direct it down a steeply banked ice-covered run. ~*vb.* **2.** (*intr.*) to ride on a bobsleigh. ~Also called (esp. U.S. and Canad.): **bobsled** (ˈbɒbˌslɛd). [C19: BOB[2] + SLEIGH]

bobstay (ˈbɒbˌsteɪ) *n.* a strong stay between a bowsprit and the stem of a vessel for holding down the bowsprit. [C18: ? < BOB[1] + STAY[3]]

bobsy-die (ˈbɒbzɪˌdaɪ) *n. N.Z. inf.* fuss; confusion (esp. in **kick up bobsy-die**). [< C19 *Bob's a-dying*]

bobtail (ˈbɒbˌteɪl) *n.* **1.** a docked or diminutive tail. **2.** an animal with such a tail. ~*adj. also* **bobtailed. 3.** having the tail cut short. ~*vb.* (*tr.*) **4.** to dock the tail of. **5.** to cut short; curtail.

bobwhite (ˈbɒbˌwaɪt) *n.* a brown North American quail: the male has white markings on the head. [C19: imit.]

Boche (bɒʃ) *n. Derog. sl.* (esp. in World Wars I and II) **1.** a German, esp. a German soldier. **2. the.** (*usually functioning as pl.*) Germans collectively, esp. German soldiers regarded as the enemy. [C20: < F, prob. shortened < *alboche* German, < *allemand* German + *caboche* pate]

bod (bɒd) *n. Inf.* a fellow; chap: *he's a queer bod.* [C18: short for BODY]

bode[1] (bəʊd) *vb.* **1.** to be an omen of (good or ill, esp. of ill); portend; presage. **2.** (*tr.*) *Arch.* to predict; foretell. [OE *bodian*] —ˈ**bodement** *n.*

bode[2] (bəʊd) *vb.* a past tense of **bide.**

bodega (bəʊˈdiːgə) *n.* a shop selling wine and sometimes groceries, esp. in a Spanish-speaking country. [C19: < Sp., ult. < Gk *apothēkē* storehouse]

bodge (bɒdʒ) *vb. Inf.* to make a mess of; botch. [C16: changed < BOTCH]

bodgie (ˈbɒdʒɪ) *Austral. & N.Z. sl.* ~*n.* **1.** an unruly or uncouth young man, esp. in the 1950s. ~*adj.* **2.** false, fraudulent. [C20: < BODGE]

Bodhisattva (ˌbəʊdɪˈsætvə, -wə, ˌbɒd-) *n.* (in Buddhism) a divine being worthy of nirvana who remains on the human plane to help men to salvation. [Sansk., < *bodhi* enlightenment + *sattva* essence]

bodice (ˈbɒdɪs) *n.* **1.** the upper part of a woman's dress, from the shoulder to the waist. **2.** a tight-fitting corset worn laced over a blouse, or (formerly) as a woman's undergarment. [C16: orig. Scot. *bodies*, pl. of BODY]

bodice ripper *n. Inf.* a romantic novel, usually on a historical theme, that involves some sex and violence.

-bodied *adj.* (*in combination*) having a body or bodies as specified: *able-bodied; long-bodied.*

bodiless (ˈbɒdɪlɪs) *adj.* having no body or substance; incorporeal or insubstantial.

bodily (ˈbɒdɪlɪ) *adj.* **1.** relating to or being a part of the human body. ~*adv.* **2.** by taking hold of the body: *he threw him bodily from the platform.* **3.** in person; in the flesh.

bodkin (ˈbɒdkɪn) *n.* **1.** a blunt large-eyed needle. **2.** *Arch.* a dagger. **3.** *Arch.* a long ornamental hairpin. [C14: prob. of Celtic origin]

body (ˈbɒdɪ) *n., pl.* **bodies. 1. a.** the entire physical structure of an animal or human being. Related adj.: **corporeal. b.** (*as modifier*): *body odour.* **2.** the trunk or torso. **3.** a dead human or animal; corpse. **4.** the flesh as opposed to the spirit. **5.** the largest or main part of anything: *the body of a vehicle; the body of a plant.* **6.** a separate or distinct mass of water or land. **7.** a number of individuals regarded as a single entity; group. **8.** the characteristic full quality of certain wines. **9.** firmness, esp. of cloth. **10. a.** the pigment contained in or added to paint, dye, etc. **b.** the opacity of a paint. **c.** (*as modifier*): *body colour.* **11.** an informal or dialect word for a **person. 12. keep body and soul together.** to manage to keep alive; survive. ~*vb.* **bodying, bodied.** (*tr.*) **13.** (usually foll. by *forth*) to give a body or shape to. [OE *bodig*]

body blow *n.* **1.** *Boxing.* a blow to an opponent's body **2.** a severe disappointment or setback.

body building *n.* the practice of exercises to make the muscles of the body conspicuous.

bodycheck (ˈbɒdɪˌtʃɛk) *Ice hockey, etc.* ~*n.* **1.** obstruction of another player. ~*vb.* **2.** (*tr.*) to deliver a bodycheck to (an opponent).

bodyguard (ˈbɒdɪˌgɑːd) *n.* a man or group of men who escort and protect someone.

body language *n.* the nonverbal imparting of information by means of conscious or subconscious bodily gestures, posture, etc.

body-line *adj. Cricket.* denoting or relating to fast bowling aimed at the batsman's body.

body politic *n.* **the.** the people of a nation or the nation itself considered as a political entity.

body popping *n.* a dance of the 1980s, characterized by schematic, rhythmic movements. —**body popper** *n.*

body shop *n.* a repair yard for vehicle bodywork.

body snatcher *n.* (formerly) a person who robbed graves and sold the corpses for dissection.

body stocking *n.* a one-piece undergarment for women, usually of nylon, covering the torso.

body warmer *n.* a sleeveless type of jerkin, usually quilted, worn as an outer garment.

bodywork (ˈbɒdɪˌwɜːk) *n.* the external shell of a motor vehicle.

Boeotian (bɪˈəʊʃɪən) *adj.* **1.** of Boeotia, a region in ancient Greece. **2.** dull or stupid. ~*n.* **3.** a person from Boeotia. **4.** a dull or stupid person.

Boer (bʊə) *n.* **a.** a descendant of any of the Dutch or Huguenot colonists who settled in South Africa. **b.** (*as modifier*): *a Boer farmer.* [C19: < Du. *Boer*; see BOOR]

boerbul (ˈbʊəbəl) *n. S. African.* a crossbred mastiff used esp. as a watchdog. [< Afrik. *boerboel*, < *boel* large dog]

boeremusiek (ˈbʊərəˌmœsɪk) *n. S. African.* light music associated with the culture of the Afrikaners. [< Afrik. *boere* country, folk + *musiek* music]

boer-goat (ˈbʊəˌgəʊt) *n. S. African.* a hardy indigenous breed of goat. [< Afrik < *boer* + GOAT]

boerperd (ˈbʊəˌpɜːt) *n.* a S. African breed of rugged horse, often palomino. [< Afrik. *boer* Afrikaner, indigenous + *perd*, < Du. *paard* horse]

boet (bʊt) *or* **boetie** *n. S. African inf.* a friend. [< Afrik.: brother]

boffin (ˈbɒfɪn) *n. Brit. inf.* a scientist, esp. one carrying out military research. [C20: <?]

Bofors gun (ˈbəʊfəz) *n.* an automatic double-barrelled anti-aircraft gun. [C20: after *Bofors*, Sweden, where it was first made]

bog (bɒg) *n.* **1.** wet spongy ground consisting of decomposing vegetation. **2.** an area of such ground. **3.** a slang word for **lavatory.** [C13: < Gaelic *bogach* swamp, < *bog* soft] —ˈ**boggy** *adj.* —ˈ**bogginess** *n.*

bogan (ˈbəʊgən) *n. Canad.* (esp. in the Maritime Provinces) a sluggish side stream. Also called: **logan, pokelogan.** [of Algonquian origin]

bogbean (ˈbɒgˌbiːn) *n.* another name for **buckbean.**

bog down *vb.* **bogging, bogged.** (*adv.*; when *tr., often passive*) to impede or be impeded physically or mentally.

bogey *or* **bogy** (ˈbəʊgɪ) *n.* **1.** an evil or mischievous spirit. **2.** something that worries or annoys. **3.** *Golf.* **a.** a standard score for a hole or course, regarded as one that a good player should make. **b.** *U.S.* a score of one stroke over par on a hole. Cf. **par** (sense 5). **4.** *Sl.* a piece of dried mucus discharged from the nose. [C19: prob. rel. to obs. *bug* an evil spirit & BOGLE]

bogeyman (ˈbəʊgɪˌmæn) *n., pl.* **-men.** a person, real or imaginary, used as a threat, esp. to children.

boggle (ˈbɒgᵊl) *vb.* (*intr.;* often foll. by *at*) **1.** to be surprised, confused, or alarmed (esp. in **the mind boggles**). **2.** to hesitate or be evasive when confronted with a problem. [C16: prob. var. of BOGLE]

bogie *or* **bogy** (ˈbəʊgɪ) *n.* **1.** an assembly of four or six wheels forming a pivoted support at either end of a railway coach. **2.** *Chiefly Brit.* a small railway truck of short wheelbase, used for conveying coal, ores, etc. [C19: <?]

bogle (ˈbəʊgᵊl, ˈbɒg-) *n.* a dialect or archaic word for **bogey** (sense 1). [C16: < Scot. *bogill*]

bog myrtle *n.* another name for **sweet gale.**

bog oak *n.* oak found preserved in peat bogs.

bogong (ˈbəʊˌgɒŋ) *or* **bugong** (ˈbuːˌgɒŋ) *n.* an edible dark-coloured Australian noctuid moth.

bogtrotter (ˈbɒgˌtrɒtə) *n.* a derogatory term for an Irishman, esp. an Irish peasant.

bogus (ˈbəʊgəs) *adj.* spurious or counterfeit; not genuine. [C19: < *bogus* apparatus for making counterfeit money] —ˈ**bogusly** *adv.* —ˈ**bogusness** *n.*

bogy (ˈbəʊgɪ) *n., pl.* **-gies.** a variant spelling of **bogey** or **bogie.**

bohea (bəʊˈhiː) *n.* a black Chinese tea, once regarded as the choicest, but now as an inferior grade. [C18: < Chinese *Wu-i Shan,* range of hills on which this tea was grown]

Bohemian (bəʊˈhiːmɪən) *n.* **1.** a native or inhabitant of Bohemia, a former kingdom; a Czech. **2.** (*often not cap.*) a person, esp. an artist or writer, who lives an unconventional life. **3.** the Czech language. ~*adj.* **4.** of, relating to, or characteristic of Bohemia, its people, or their language. **5.** unconventional in appearance, behaviour, etc.

Bohemianism (bəʊˈhiːmɪəˌnɪzəm) *n.* unconventional behaviour or appearance, esp. of an artist.

boil[1] (bɔɪl) *vb.* **1.** to change or cause to change from a liquid to a vapour so rapidly that bubbles of vapour are formed in the liquid. **2.** to reach or cause to reach boiling point. **3.** to cook or be cooked by the process of boiling. **4.** (*intr.*) to bubble and be agitated like something boiling; seethe: *the ocean was boiling.* **5.** (*intr.*) to be extremely angry or indignant. ~*n.* **6.** the state or action of boiling. ~See also **boil away, boil down, boil over.** [C13: < OF, < L, < *bulla* a bubble]

boil[2] (bɔɪl) *n.* a red painful swelling with a hard pus-filled core caused by bacterial infection of the skin. Technical name: **furuncle.** [OE *bȳle*]

boil away *vb.* (*adv.*) to cause (liquid) to evaporate completely by boiling or (of liquid) to evaporate completely.

boil down *vb.* (*adv.*) **1.** to reduce or be reduced in quantity by boiling. **2. boil down to. a.** (*intr.*) to be the essential element in something. **b.** (*tr.*) to summarize; reduce to essentials.

boiled shirt *n. Inf.* a dress shirt with a stiff front.

boiler (ˈbɔɪlə) *n.* **1.** a closed vessel in which water is heated to supply steam or provide heat. **2.** a domestic device to provide hot water, esp. for central heating. **3.** a large tub for boiling laundry.

boilermaker (ˈbɔɪləˌmeɪkə) *n.* a person who works with metal in heavy industry; plater or welder.

boiler suit *n. Brit.* a one-piece overall work garment.

boiling point *n.* **1.** the temperature at which a liquid boils at sea level. **2.** *Inf.* the condition of being angered or highly excited.

boiling-water reactor *n.* a nuclear reactor using water as coolant and moderator, steam being produced in the reactor itself. Abbrev.: **BWR.**

boil over *vb.* (*adv.*) **1.** to overflow or cause to overflow while boiling. **2.** (*intr.*) to burst out in anger or excitement.

boisterous (ˈbɔɪstərəs, -strəs) *adj.* **1.** noisy and lively; unruly. **2.** (of the wind, sea, etc.) turbulent or stormy. [C13 *boistuous,* <?] —ˈ**boisterously** *adv.* —ˈ**boisterousness** *n.*

bola (ˈbəʊlə) *or* **bolas** (ˈbəʊləs) *n., pl.* **-las** *or* **-lases.** a missile used by gauchos and Indians of South America, consisting of heavy balls on a cord. It is hurled at a running quarry, so as to entangle its legs. [Sp.: ball, < L *bulla* knob]

bold (bəʊld) *adj.* **1.** courageous, confident, and fearless; ready to take risks. **2.** showing or requiring courage: *a bold plan.* **3.** immodest or impudent: *she gave him a bold look.* **4.** standing out distinctly; conspicuous: *a figure carved in bold relief.* **5.** very steep: *the bold face of the cliff.* **6.** imaginative in thought or expression. [OE *beald*] —ˈ**boldly** *adv.* —ˈ**boldness** *n.*

bold face *Printing.* ~*n.* **1.** a weight of type characterized by thick heavy lines, as the entry words in this dictionary. ~*adj.* **boldface. 2.** (of type) having this weight.

bole (bəʊl) *n.* the trunk of a tree. [C14: < ON *bolr*]

bolero (bəˈlɛərəʊ) *n., pl.* **-ros. 1.** a Spanish dance, usually in triple time. **2.** a piece of music for or in the rhythm of this dance. **3.** (*also* ˈbɒlərəʊ) a short open bodice-like jacket not reaching the waist. [C18: < Sp.]

boll (bəʊl) *n.* the fruit of such plants as flax and cotton, consisting of a rounded capsule containing the seeds. [C13: < Du. *bolle;* rel. to OE *bolla* BOWL[1]]

bollard (ˈbɒlɑːd, ˈbɒləd) *n.* **1.** a strong wooden or metal post on a wharf, quay, etc., used for securing mooring lines. **2.** *Brit.* a small post placed on a kerb or traffic island to make it conspicuous to motorists. [C14: ?< BOLE + -ARD]

bollocking (ˈbɒləkɪŋ) *n. Sl.* a severe telling-off. [< *bollock* (vb.) in the sense "to reprimand"]

bollocks (ˈbɒləks) *or* **ballocks** *Taboo sl.* ~*pl. n.* **1.** another word for **testicles.** ~*interj.* **2.** an exclamation of annoyance, disbelief, etc. [OE *beallucas;* see BALL[1]]

boll weevil *n.* a greyish weevil of the southern U.S. and Mexico, whose larvae live in and destroy cotton bolls.

bologna sausage (bəˈləʊnjə) *n. Chiefly U.S. & Canad.* a large smoked sausage made of seasoned mixed meats. Also called: **baloney, boloney,** (esp. Brit.) **polony.**

bolometer (bəʊˈlɒmɪtə) *n.* a sensitive instrument for measuring radiant energy. [C19: < Gk *bolē* ray of light, < *ballein* to throw + -METER] —**bolometric** (ˌbəʊləˈmɛtrɪk) *adj.*

boloney (bəˈləʊnɪ) *n.* **1.** a variant of **baloney. 2.** another name for **bologna sausage.**

Bolshevik (ˈbɒlʃɪvɪk) *n., pl.* **-viks** *or* **-viki** (ˌbɒlʃɪˈviːkɪ). **1.** (formerly) a Russian Communist. Cf **Menshevik. 2.** any Communist. **3.** (*often not cap.*) *Inf. & derog.* any political radical, esp. a revolutionary. [C20: < Russian *Bol'shevik* majority, < *bol'shoi* great] —ˈ**BolsheˌVism** *n.* —ˈ**Bolshevist** *adj., n.*

bolshie *or* **bolshy** (ˈbɒlʃɪ) (*sometimes cap.*) *Brit. inf.* ~*adj.* **1.** difficult to manage; rebellious. **2.** politically radical or left-wing. ~*n., pl.* **-shies. 3.** *Derog.* any political radical. [C20: shortened < BOLSHEVIK]

bolster (ˈbəʊlstə) *vb.* (*tr.*) **1.** (often foll. by *up*) to support or reinforce; strengthen: *to bolster morale.* **2.** to prop up with a pillow or cushion. ~*n.* **3.** a long narrow pillow or cushion. **4.** any pad or padded support. **5.** a cold chisel used for cutting stone slabs, etc. [OE *bolster*]

bolt[1] (bəʊlt) *n.* **1.** a bar that can be slid into a socket to lock a door, gate, etc. **2.** a bar or rod that forms part of a locking mechanism and is moved by a key or a knob. **3.** a metal rod or pin that has a head and a screw thread to take a nut. **4.** a sliding bar in a breech-loading firearm that ejects the empty cartridge, replaces it with a new one, and closes the breech. **5.** a flash of lightning. **6. a bolt from the blue.** a sudden, unexpected, and usually unwelcome event. **7.** a sudden start or movement, esp. in order to escape. **8.** a roll of something, such as cloth, wallpaper, etc. **9.** an arrow, esp. for a crossbow. **10. shoot one's bolt.** to exhaust one's efforts. ~*vb.* **11.** (*tr.*) to secure or lock with or as with a bolt. **12.** (*tr.*) to eat hurriedly. **13.** (*intr.;* usually foll. by *from* or *out*) to move or jump suddenly: *he bolted from the chair.* **14.** (*intr.*) (esp. of a horse) to start hurriedly and run away without warning. **15.** (*tr.*) to roll (cloth, wallpaper, etc.) into bolts. **16.** (*intr.*) (of cultivated plants) to produce flowers and seeds prematurely. ~*adv.* **17.** stiffly, firmly, or rigidly (archaic except in **bolt upright**). [OE *bolt* arrow] —**'bolter** *n.*

bolt[2] *or* **boult** (bəʊlt) *vb.* (*tr.*) **1.** to pass (flour, a powder, etc.) through a sieve. **2.** to examine and separate. [C13: < OF *bulter,* prob. of Gmc origin] —**'bolter** *or* **'boulter** *n.*

bolt hole *n.* a place of escape from danger.

boltrope ('bəʊlt,rəʊp) *n. Naut.* a rope sewn to the foot or luff of a sail to strengthen it.

bolus ('bəʊləs) *n., pl.* **-luses. 1.** a small round soft mass, esp. of chewed food. **2.** a large pill or tablet used in veterinary and clinical medicine. [C17: < NL, < Gk *bōlos* clod, lump]

bomb (bɒm) *n.* **1. a.** a hollow projectile containing explosive, incendiary, or other destructive substance. **b.** (*as modifier*): *bomb disposal; a bomb bay.* **c.** (*in combination*): *bombproof.* **2.** an object in which an explosive device has been planted: *a car bomb; a letter bomb.* **3.** a round mass of volcanic rock, solidified from molten lava that has been thrown into the air. **4.** *Med.* a container for radioactive material, applied therapeutically to any part of the body: *a cobalt bomb.* **5.** *Brit. sl.* a large sum of money. **6.** *U.S. & Canad. sl.* a disastrous failure: *the new play was a total bomb.* **7.** *Austral. & N.Z. sl.* an old or dilapidated motorcar. **8. like a bomb.** *Brit. & N.Z. inf.* with great speed or success; very well. **9. the bomb.** a hydrogen or an atom bomb considered as the ultimate destructive weapon. ~*vb.* **10.** to attack with or as if with a bomb or bombs; drop bombs (on). **11.** (*intr.;* often foll. by *off, along,* etc.) *Inf.* to move or drive very quickly. **12.** (*intr.*) *U.S. sl.* to fail disastrously. [C17: < F, < It., < L, < Gk *bombos,* imit.]

bombard *vb.* (bɒm'bɑːd). (*tr.*) **1.** to attack with concentrated artillery fire or bombs. **2.** to attack with vigour and persistence. **3.** to attack verbally, esp. with questions. **4.** *Physics.* to direct high-energy particles or photons against (atoms, nuclei, etc.). ~*n.* ('bɒmbɑːd). **5.** an ancient type of cannon that threw stone balls. [C15: < OF, < *bombarde* stone-throwing cannon, prob. < L *bombus* booming sound; see BOMB] —**bom'bardment** *n.*

bombardier (,bɒmbə'dɪə) *n.* **1.** the member of a bomber aircrew responsible for aiming and releasing the bombs. **2.** *Brit.* a noncommissioned rank, below the rank of sergeant, in the Royal Artillery. **3.** *Canad. trademark.* a snow tractor, usually having caterpillar tracks at the rear and skis at the front. [C16: < OF; see BOMBARD]

bombast ('bɒmbæst) *n.* pompous and grandiloquent language. [C16: < OF, < Med. L *bombāx* cotton] —**bom'bastic** *adj.* —**bom'bastically** *adv.*

Bombay duck (bɒm'beɪ) *n.* a fish that is eaten dried with curry dishes as a savoury. Also called: **bummalo.** [C19: changed < *bombil* through association with *Bombay,* port in W India]

bombazine *or* **bombasine** (,bɒmbə'ziːn, 'bɒmbə,ziːn) *n.* a twilled fabric, esp. one of silk and worsted, formerly worn dyed black for mourning. [C16: < OF, < L, < *bombyx* silk]

bomber ('bɒmə) *n.* **1.** a military aircraft designed to carry out bombing missions. **2.** a person who plants bombs.

bomber jacket *n.* a short jacket finishing at the waist with an elasticated band, usually having a zip front.

bombora (bɒm'bɔːrə) *n. Austral.* **1.** a submerged reef. **2.** a turbulent area of sea over such a reef. [< Abor.]

bombshell ('bɒm,ʃɛl) *n.* **1.** (esp. formerly) a bomb or artillery shell. **2.** a shocking or unwelcome surprise.

bombsight ('bɒm,saɪt) *n.* a mechanical or electronic device in an aircraft for aiming bombs.

bona fide ('bəʊnə 'faɪdɪ) *adj.* **1.** real or genuine: *a bona fide manuscript.* **2.** undertaken in good faith: *a bona fide agreement.* [C16: < L]

bona fides ('bəʊnə 'faɪdiːz) *n. Law.* good faith; honest intention. [L]

bonanza (bə'nænzə) *n.* **1.** a source, usually sudden and unexpected, of luck or wealth. **2.** *U.S. & Canad.* a mine or vein rich in ore. [C19: < Sp., lit.: calm sea, hence, good luck, < Med. L, < L *bonus* good + *malacia* calm, < Gk *malakia* softness]

bonbon ('bɒnbɒn) *n.* a sweet. [C19: < F, orig. a children's word < *bon* good]

bonce (bɒns) *n. Brit. sl.* the head. [C19 (orig.: a large playing marble): <?]

bond (bɒnd) *n.* **1.** something that binds, fastens, or holds together, such as a chain or rope. **2.** (*often pl.*) something that brings or holds people together; tie: *a bond of friendship.* **3.** (*pl.*) something that restrains or imprisons; captivity or imprisonment. **4.** a written or spoken agreement, esp. a promise. **5.** *Finance.* a certificate of debt issued in order to raise funds. It is repayable with or without security at a specified future date. **6.** *Law.* a written acknowledgment of an obligation to pay a sum or to perform a contract. **7.** any of various arrangements of bricks or stones in a wall in which they overlap so as to provide strength. **8. chemical bond.** a mutual attraction between two atoms resulting from a redistribution of their outer electrons, determining chemical properties; shown in some formulae by a dot (.) or score (—). **9.** See **bond paper. 10. in bond.** *Commerce.* deposited in a bonded warehouse. ~*vb.* (*mainly tr.*) **11.** (*also intr.*) to hold or be held together, as by a rope or an adhesive; bind; connect. **12.** (*intr.*) to become emotionally attached. **13.** to put or hold (goods) in bond. **14.** *Law.* to place under bond. **15.** *Finance.* to issue bonds on; mortgage. [C13: < ON *band;* see BAND[2]]

bondage ('bɒndɪdʒ) *n.* **1.** slavery or serfdom; servitude. **2.** subjection to some influence or duty.

bonded ('bɒndɪd) *adj.* **1.** *Finance.* consisting of, secured by, or operating under a bond or bonds. **2.** *Commerce.* deposited in a bonded warehouse.

bonded warehouse *n.* a warehouse in which goods are deposited until duty is paid.

bondholder ('bɒnd,həʊldə) *n.* an owner of bonds issued by a company or other institution.

bonding ('bɒndɪŋ) *n.* the process by which individuals become emotionally attached to one another.

bondmaid ('bɒnd,meɪd) *n.* an unmarried female serf or slave.

bond paper *n.* a superior quality of strong white paper, used esp. for writing and typing.

bondservant ('bɒnd,sɜːvənt) *n.* a serf or slave.

bondsman ('bɒndzmən) *n., pl.* **-men. 1.** *Law.* a person bound by bond to act as surety for another. **2.** another word for **bondservant.**

bond washing *n.* a series of illegal deals in bonds made with the intention of avoiding taxation.

bone (bəʊn) *n.* **1.** any of the various structures that make up the skeleton in most vertebrates. **2.** the porous rigid tissue of which these parts are made. **3.** something consisting of bone or a bonelike substance. **4.** (*pl.*) the human skeleton or body. **5.** a thin strip of whalebone, plastic, etc., used to stiffen corsets and brassieres. **6.** (*pl.*) the essentials (esp. in **the bare bones**). **7.** (*pl.*) dice. **8. feel in one's bones.** to have an intuition of. **9. have a bone to pick.** to have grounds for a quarrel. **10. make no bones about. a.** to be direct and candid about. **b.** to have no scruples about. **11. near** *or* **close to the bone. a.** risqué or indecent. **b.** in poverty; destitute. **12. point the bone.** (often foll. by *at*) *Austral.* **a.** to wish bad luck (on). **b.** to cast a spell (on) in order to kill. ~*vb.* (*mainly tr.*) **13.** to remove the bones from (meat for cooking, etc.). **14.** to stiffen (a corset, etc.) by inserting bones. **15.** *Brit.* a slang word for **steal.** ~See also **bone up.** [OE *bān*] —ˈ**boneless** *adj.*

bone ash *n.* ash obtained when bones are burnt in air, consisting mainly of calcium phosphate.

bone china *n.* porcelain containing bone ash.

bone-dry *adj. Inf.* **a.** completely dry: *a bone-dry well.* **b.** (*postpositive*): *the well was bone dry.*

bonehead (ˈbəʊnˌhɛd) *n. Sl.* a stupid or obstinate person. —ˈ**boneˌheaded** *adj.*

bone idle *adj.* very idle; extremely lazy.

bone meal *n.* dried and ground animal bones, used as a fertilizer or in stock feeds.

boner (ˈbəʊnə) *n. Sl.* a blunder.

bonesetter (ˈbəʊnˌsɛtə) *n.* a person who sets broken or dislocated bones, esp. one who has no formal medical qualifications.

boneshaker (ˈbəʊnˌʃeɪkə) *n.* **1.** an early type of bicycle having solid tyres and no springs. **2.** *Sl.* any decrepit or rickety vehicle.

bone up *vb.* (*adv.;* when *intr.,* usually foll. by *on*) *Inf.* to study intensively.

bonfire (ˈbɒnˌfaɪə) *n.* a large outdoor fire. [C15: alteration (infl. by F *bon* good) of *bone-fire;* < the use of bones as fuel]

bong (bɒŋ) *n.* **1.** a deep reverberating sound, as of a large bell. ~*vb.* **2.** to make a deep reverberating sound. [C20: imit.]

bongo[1] (ˈbɒŋgəʊ) *n., pl.* **-go** *or* **-gos.** a rare spiral-horned antelope inhabiting forests of central Africa. The coat is bright red-brown with narrow vertical stripes. [of African origin]

bongo[2] (ˈbɒŋgəʊ) *n., pl.* **-gos** *or* **-goes.** a small bucket-shaped drum, usually one of a pair, played by beating with the fingers. [American Sp., prob. imit.]

bonhomie (ˈbɒnəmiː) *n.* exuberant friendliness. [C18: < F, < *bon* good + *homme* man]

bonito (bəˈniːtəʊ) *n., pl.* **-tos.** any of various small tunny-like marine food fishes of warm Atlantic and Pacific waters. [C16: < Sp., < L *bonus* good]

bonk (bɒŋk) *vb. Inf.* **1.** (*tr.*) to hit. **2.** to have sexual intercourse (with). [C20: prob. imit.] —ˈ**bonking** *n.*

bonkers (ˈbɒŋkəz) *adj. Sl., chiefly Brit.* mad; crazy. [C20: <?]

bon mot (*French* bɔ̃ mo) *n., pl.* **bons mots** (bɔ̃ mo). a clever and fitting remark. [F, lit.: good word]

bonnet (ˈbɒnɪt) *n.* **1.** any of various hats worn, esp. formerly, by women and girls, and tied with ribbons under the chin. **2.** (in Scotland) Also: **bunnet. a.** a soft cloth cap. **b.** (formerly) a flat brimless cap worn by men. **3.** the hinged metal part of a motor vehicle body that provides access to the engine. U.S. name: **hood. 4.** a cowl on a chimney. **5.** *Naut.* a piece of sail laced to the foot of a foresail to give it greater area in light winds. **6.** (in the U.S. and Canada) a headdress of feathers worn by some tribes of American Indians. [C14: < OF *bonet,* <?]

bonny (ˈbɒnɪ) *adj.* **-nier, -niest. 1.** *Scot. & N English dialect.* beautiful or handsome: *a bonny lass.* **2.** good or fine. **3.** (esp. of babies) plump. [C15: < OF *bon* good, < L *bonus*]

bonsai (ˈbɒnsaɪ) *n., pl.* **-sai. 1.** the art of growing dwarfed ornamental varieties of trees or shrubs in small shallow pots by selective pruning, etc. **2.** a tree or shrub grown by this method. [C20: < Japanese, < *bon* bowl + *sai* to plant]

bontebok (ˈbɒntɪˌbʌk) *n., pl.* **-boks** *or* **-bok.** an antelope of southern Africa, having a deep reddish-brown coat with a white blaze, tail, and rump patch. [C18: Afrik. < *bont* pied + *bok* BUCK[1]]

bonus (ˈbəʊnəs) *n.* **1.** something given, paid, or received above what is due or expected. **2.** *Chiefly Brit.* an extra dividend allotted to shareholders out of profits. **3.** *Insurance, Brit.* a dividend, esp. a percentage of net profits, distributed to policyholders. [C18: < L *bonus* (adj.) good]

bonus issue *n. Brit.* a free issue of shares distributed among shareholders pro rata with their holdings.

bon vivant *French.* (bɔ̃ vivɑ̃) *n., pl.* ***bons vivants*** (bɔ̃ vivɑ̃). a person who enjoys luxuries, esp. good food and drink. Also called (but not in French): **bon viveur** (ˌbɒn viːˈvɜː). [lit.: good-living (man)]

bon voyage (*French* bɔ̃ vwajaʒ) *sentence substitute.* a phrase used to wish a traveller a pleasant journey. [F, lit.: good journey]

bony (ˈbəʊnɪ) *adj.* **bonier, boniest. 1.** resembling or consisting of bone. **2.** having many bones. **3.** having prominent bones. **4.** thin or emaciated.

bony fish *n.* any of a class of fishes, including most of the extant species, having a skeleton of bone rather than cartilage.

bonze (bɒnz) *n.* a Chinese or Japanese Buddhist priest or monk. [C16: < F, < Port. *bonzo,* < Chinese *fan sêng,* < *fan* Buddhist + *sêng* MONK]

bonzer (ˈbɒnzə) *adj. Austral & N.Z. sl., arch.* very good; excellent. [C20: ? < BONANZA]

boo (buː) *interj.* **1.** an exclamation uttered to startle or surprise someone, esp. a child. **2.** a shout uttered to express disgust, dissatisfaction, or contempt. ~*vb.* **booing, booed. 3.** to shout "boo" at (someone or something), esp. as an expression of disapproval.

boob (buːb) *Sl.* ~*n.* **1.** an ignorant or foolish person. **2.** *Brit.* an embarrassing mistake; blunder. **3.** a female breast. ~*vb.* **4.** (*intr.*) *Brit.* to make a blunder. [C20: back formation < BOOBY]

boobialla (ˌbuːbɪˈælə) *n. Austral.* **1.** another name for **golden wattle** (sense 2). **2.** any of various trees or shrubs of the genus *Myoporum.*

boo-boo *n., pl.* **-boos.** an embarrassing mistake; blunder. [C20: ?< nursery talk]

boob tube *n. Sl.* **1.** a close-fitting strapless top, worn by women. **2.** *Chiefly U.S. & Canad.* a television receiver.

booby (ˈbuːbɪ) *n., pl.* **-bies. 1.** an ignorant or foolish person. **2.** *Brit.* the losing player in a game. **3.** any of several tropical marine birds related to the gannet. They have a straight stout bill and the plumage is white with darker markings. [C17: < Sp. *bobo,* < L *balbus* stammering]

booby prize *n.* a mock prize given to the person having the lowest score.

booby trap *n.* **1.** a hidden explosive device primed in such a way as to be set off by an unsuspecting victim. **2.** a trap for an unsuspecting person, esp. one intended as a practical joke. ~*vb.* **booby-trap, -trapping, -trapped. 3.** (*tr.*) to set a booby trap in or on (a building or object) or for (a person).

boodle (ˈbuːdᵊl) *n. Sl.* money or valuables, esp. when stolen, counterfeit, or used as a bribe. [C19: < Du. *boedel* possessions]

boogie (ˈbuːgɪ) *vb.* **-gieing, -gied.** (*intr.*) *Sl.* **1.** to dance to pop music. **2.** to make love. [C20: orig. American Negro slang, ?< Bantu *mbugi* devilishly good]

boogie-woogie (ˈbʊgɪˈwʊgɪ, ˈbuːgɪˈwuːgɪ) *n.* a style of piano jazz using a dotted bass pattern, usually with eight notes in a bar and the harmonies of the 12-bar blues. [C20: ? imit.]

boohai (buːˈhaɪ) *n. N.Z. inf.* **up the boohai.** thoroughly lost. [< remote township of *Puhoi*]

boohoo (ˌbuːˈhuː) *vb.* **-hooing, -hooed. 1.** to sob or pretend to sob noisily. ~*n., pl.* **-hoos. 2.** (*sometimes pl.*) distressed or pretended sobbing. [C20: nursery talk]

book (bʊk) *n.* **1.** a number of printed or written pages bound together along one edge and usually protected by covers. **2. a.** a written work or composition, such as a novel, technical manual, or dictionary. **b.** (*as modifier*): *book reviews.* **c.** (*in combination*): *bookseller; bookshop; bookshelf.* **3.** a number of blank or ruled sheets of paper bound together, used to record lessons, keep accounts, etc. **4.** (*pl.*) a record of the transactions of a business or society. **5.** the libretto of an opera, musical, etc. **6.** a major division of a written composition, as of a long novel or of the Bible. **7.** a number of tickets, stamps, etc., fastened together along one edge. **8.** a record of betting transactions. **9.** (in card games) the number of tricks that must be taken by a side or player before any trick has a scoring value. **10.** strict or rigid rules or standards (esp. in **by the book**). **11.** a source of knowledge or authority: *the book of life.* **12. a closed book.** a person or subject that is unknown or beyond comprehension: *chemistry is a closed book to him.* **13. an open book.** a person or subject that is thoroughly understood. **14. bring to book.** to reprimand or require (someone) to give an explanation of his conduct. **15. close the books.** *Book-keeping.* to balance accounts in order to prepare a statement or report. **16. in someone's good** (*or* **bad**) **books.** regarded by someone with favour (*or* disfavour). **17. keep the books.** to keep written records of the finances of a business. **18. on the books. a.** enrolled as a member. **b.** recorded. **19. the book.** (*sometimes cap.*) the Bible. **20. throw the book at. a.** to charge with every relevant offence. **b.** to inflict the most severe punishment on. ~*vb.* **21.** to reserve (a place, passage, etc.) or engage the services of (a performer, driver, etc.) in advance. **22.** (*tr.*) to take the name and address of (a person guilty of a minor offence) with a view to bringing a prosecution. **23.** (*tr.*) (of a football referee) to take the name of (a player) who grossly infringes the rules. **24.** (*tr.*) *Arch.* to record in a book. ~See also **book in.** [OE *bōc;* see BEECH (its bark was used as a writing surface)]

bookbinder (ˈbʊkˌbaɪndə) *n.* a person whose business is binding books. —ˈ**book,binding** *n.*

bookbindery (ˈbʊkˌbaɪndərɪ) *n., pl.* **-eries.** a place in which books are bound. Often shortened to **bindery.**

bookcase (ˈbʊkˌkeɪs) *n.* a piece of furniture containing shelves for books.

book club *n.* a club that sells books at low prices to members, usually by mail order.

book end *n.* one of a pair of usually ornamental supports for holding a row of books upright.

bookie (ˈbʊkɪ) *n. Inf.* short for **bookmaker.**

book in *vb.* (*adv.*) **1.** to reserve a room at a hotel. **2.** *Chiefly Brit.* to register, esp. one's arrival at a hotel.

booking (ˈbʊkɪŋ) *n.* **1.** *Chiefly Brit.* a reservation, as of a table, room, or seat. **2.** *Theatre.* an engagement of an actor or company.

bookish (ˈbʊkɪʃ) *adj.* **1.** fond of reading; studious. **2.** consisting of or forming opinions through reading rather than experience; academic. **3.** of or relating to books. —ˈ**bookishness** *n.*

book-keeping *n.* the skill or occupation of systematically recording business transactions. —ˈ**book-ˌkeeper** *n.*

book-learning *n.* knowledge gained from books rather than from experience.

booklet (ˈbʊklɪt) *n.* a thin book, esp. one having paper covers; pamphlet.

bookmaker (ˈbʊkˌmeɪkə) *n.* a person who as an occupation accepts bets, esp. on horseraces, and pays out to winning betters. —ˈ**book,making** *n.*

bookmark (ˈbʊkˌmɑːk) *or* **bookmarker** *n.* a strip of some material put between the pages of a book to mark a place.

Book of Common Prayer *n.* the official book of church services of the Church of England.

bookplate (ˈbʊkˌpleɪt) *n.* a label bearing the owner's name and a design, pasted into a book.

bookstall (ˈbʊkˌstɔːl) *n.* a stall or stand where periodicals, newspapers, or books are sold.

book token *n. Brit.* a gift token to be exchanged for books.

book value *n.* **1.** the value of an asset of a business according to its books. **2.** the net capital value of an enterprise as shown by the excess of book assets over book liabilities.

bookworm (ˈbʊkˌwɜːm) *n.* **1.** any of various small insects that feed on the binding paste of books. **2.** a person devoted to reading.

Boolean algebra (ˈbuːlɪən) *n.* a system of symbolic logic devised to codify nonmathematical logical operations. It is used in computers. [C19: after George *Boole* (1815-64), E mathematician]

boom[1] (buːm) *vb.* **1.** to make a deep prolonged resonant sound. **2.** to prosper or cause to prosper vigorously and rapidly: *business boomed.* ~*n.* **3.** a deep prolonged resonant sound. **4.** a period of high economic growth. [C15: ?< Du. *bommen,* imit.]

boom[2] (buːm) *n.* **1.** *Naut.* a spar to which a sail is fastened to control its position relative to the wind. **2.** a pole carrying an overhead microphone and projected over a film or television set. **3.** a barrier across a waterway, usually consisting of a chain of logs, to confine free-floating logs, protect a harbour from attack, etc. [C16: < Du. *boom* tree, BEAM]

boomer (ˈbuːmə) *n.* **1.** *Austral.* a large male kangaroo. **2.** *Austral. & N.Z. inf.* anything exceptionally large.

boomerang (ˈbuːməˌræŋ) *n.* **1.** a curved flat wooden missile of Australian Aborigines, which can be made to return to the thrower. **2.** an action or statement that recoils on its originator. ~*vb.* **3.** (*intr.*) to recoil or return unexpectedly, causing harm to its originator. [C19: < Abor.]

boomslang (ˈbuːmˌslæŋ) *n.* a large greenish venomous arboreal snake of southern Africa. [C18: < Afrik., < *boom* tree + *slang* snake]

boon[1] (buːn) *n.* **1.** something extremely useful, helpful, or beneficial; a blessing or benefit. **2.** *Arch.* a favour; request. [C12: < ON *bōn* request]

boon[2] (buːn) *adj.* **1.** close, special, or intimate (in **boon companion**). **2.** *Arch.* jolly or convivial. [C14: < OF *bon,* < L *bonus* good]

boondocks (ˈbuːnˌdɒks) *pl. n.* **the.** *U.S. & Canad. sl.* **1.** wild, desolate, or uninhabitable country. **2.** a remote rural or provincial area. [C20: < Tagalog *bundok* mountain]

boong (buːŋ) *n. Austral. offens.* a Black person. [C20: < Abor.]

boor (bʊə) *n.* an ill-mannered, clumsy, or insensitive person. [OE *gebūr* dweller, farmer; see NEIGHBOUR] —ˈ**boorish** *adj.* —ˈ**boorishly** *adv.* —ˈ**boorishness** *n.*

boost (buːst) *n.* **1.** encouragement, improvement, or help: *a boost to morale.* **2.** an upward thrust or push. **3.** an increase or rise. **4.** the amount by which the induction pressure of a supercharged internal-combustion engine is increased. ~*vb.* (*tr.*) **5.** to encourage, assist, or improve: *to boost morale.* **6.** to lift by giving a push from below or behind. **7.** to increase or raise: *to boost the voltage in an electrical circuit.* **8.** to cause to rise; increase: *to boost sales.* **9.** to advertise on a big scale. **10.** to increase the induction pressure of (an internal-combustion engine); supercharge. [C19: <?]

▷ **Usage.** Except in the terminology of rocketry, the word *boost* is regarded as slightly informal, esp. in a figurative sense: *a boost to the economy.*

booster (ˈbuːstə) *n.* **1.** a person or thing that supports, assists, or increases power. **2.** Also called: **launching vehicle.** the first stage of a multistage rocket. **3.** a radio-frequency amplifier to strengthen signals. **4.** another name for **supercharger.** **5.** short for **booster shot.**

booster shot *n. Inf.* a supplementary injection of a vaccine given to maintain the immunization provided by an earlier dose.

boot[1] (buːt) *n.* **1.** a strong outer covering for the foot; shoe that extends above the ankle, often to the knee. **2.** *Brit.* an enclosed compartment of a car for holding luggage, etc., usually at the rear. U.S. and Canad. name: **trunk.** **3.** an instrument of torture used to crush the foot and lower leg. **4.** *Inf.* a kick: *he gave the door a boot.* **5. boots and all.** *Austral. & N.Z.* making every effort. **6. die with one's boots on.** to die while still active. **7. lick the boots of.** to be servile towards. **8. put the boot in.** *Sl.* **a.** to kick a person, esp. when he is already down. **b.** to harass someone. **c.** to finish off (something) with unnecessary brutality. **9. the boot.** *Sl.* dismissal from employment; the sack. **10. the boot is on the other foot** *or* **leg.** the situation is or has now reversed. ~*vb.* (*tr.*) **11.** to kick. **12.** to equip with boots. **13.** *Inf.* **a.** (often foll. by *out*) to eject forcibly. **b.** to dismiss from employment. [C14 *bote,* < OF, <?]

boot[2] (buːt) *vb. (usually impersonal)* **1.** *Arch.* to be of advantage or use to (a person): *what boots it to complain?* ~*n.* **2.** *Obs.* an advantage. **3. to boot.** as well; in addition. [OE *bōt* compensation]

bootblack (ˈbuːtˌblæk) *n.* (esp. formerly) a person who shines boots and shoes.

bootee (ˈbuːtiː, buːˈtiː) *n.* **1.** a soft shoe for a baby, esp. a knitted one. **2.** a boot for women and children, esp. an ankle-length one.

Boötes (bəʊˈəʊtiːz) *n., Latin genitive* **Boötis** (bəʊˈəʊtɪs). a constellation in the N hemisphere containing the star Arcturus. [C17: via L < Gk: ploughman]

booth (buːð, buːθ) *n., pl.* **booths** (buːðz). **1.** a stall, esp. a temporary one at a fair or market. **2.** a small partially enclosed cubicle, such as one for telephoning (**telephone booth**) or for voting (**polling booth**). **3.** *Chiefly U.S. & Canad.* two high-backed benches with a table between, used esp. in bars and restaurants. **4.** (formerly) a temporary structure for shelter, dwelling, storage, etc. [C12: of Scand. origin]

bootjack (ˈbuːtˌdʒæk) *n.* a device that grips the heel of a boot to enable the foot to be withdrawn easily.

bootleg (ˈbuːtˌlɛg) *vb.* **-legging, -legged. 1.** to make, carry, or sell (illicit goods, esp. alcohol). ~*n.* **2.** something made or sold illicitly, such as alcohol. ~*adj.* **3.** produced, distributed, or sold illicitly. [C17: see BOOT[1], LEG; < smugglers carrying bottles of liquor concealed in their boots] —**ˈbootˌlegger** *n.*

bootless (ˈbuːtlɪs) *adj.* of little or no use; vain; fruitless. [OE *bōtlēas*, < *bōt* compensation]

bootlicker (ˈbuːtˌlɪkə) *n. Inf.* one who seeks favour by servile or ingratiating behaviour towards (someone, esp. in authority); toady.

boot sale *n.* a sale of goods from car boots in a car park hired for the occasion. Also called: **car-boot sale.**

bootstrap (ˈbuːtˌstræp) *n.* **1.** a loop on a boot for pulling it on. **2. by one's (own) bootstraps.** by one's own efforts; unaided. **3. a.** a technique for loading the first few program instructions into a computer main store to enable the rest of the program to be introduced from an input device. **b.** *(as modifier): a bootstrap loader.*

booty (ˈbuːtɪ) *n., pl.* **-ties.** any valuable article or articles, esp. when obtained as plunder. [C15: < OF, < MLow G *buite* exchange]

booze (buːz) *Inf.* ~*n.* **1.** alcoholic drink. **2.** a drinking bout. ~*vb.* **3.** *(usually intr.)* to drink (alcohol), esp. in excess. [C13: < MDu. *būsen*]

boozer (ˈbuːzə) *n. Inf.* **1.** a person who is fond of drinking. **2.** *Brit., Austral., & N.Z.* a bar or pub.

booze-up *n. Brit., Austral., & N.Z. sl.* a drinking spree.

boozy (ˈbuːzɪ) *adj.* **boozier, booziest.** *Inf.* inclined to or involving excessive drinking of alcohol; drunken: *a boozy lecturer; a boozy party.*

bop (bɒp) *n.* **1.** a form of jazz originating in the 1940s, characterized by rhythmic and harmonic complexity and instrumental virtuosity. Originally called: **bebop.** ~*vb.* **bopping, bopped. 2.** *(intr.) Inf.* to dance to pop music. [C20: shortened < BEBOP] —**ˈbopper** *n.*

bo-peep (ˌbəʊˈpiːp) *n.* a game for very young children, in which one hides (esp. hiding one's face in one's hands) and reappears suddenly.

bora[1] (ˈbɔːrə) *n. (sometimes cap.)* a violent cold north wind blowing from the Adriatic. [C19: < It. dialect., < L *boreās* the north wind]

bora[2] (ˈbɔːrə) *n.* an initiation ceremony of Australian Aborigines, introducing youths to manhood. [< Abor.]

boracic (bəˈræsɪk) *adj.* another word for **boric.**

borage (ˈbɒrɪdʒ, ˈbʌrɪdʒ) *n.* a Mediterranean plant with star-shaped blue flowers. The young leaves are sometimes used in salads. [C13: < OF, ? < Ar. *abū 'āraq*, lit.: father of sweat]

borate *n.* (ˈbɔːreɪt, -ɪt). **1.** a salt or ester of boric acid. ~*vb.* (ˈbɔːreɪt). **2.** *(tr.)* to treat with borax, boric acid, or borate.

borax (ˈbɔːræks) *n., pl.* **-raxes** *or* **-races** (-rəˌsiːz). a soluble readily fusible white mineral in monoclinic crystalline form, occurring in alkaline soils and salt deposits. Formula: $Na_2B_4O_7.10H_2O$. [C14: < OF, < Med. L, < Ar., < Persian *būrah*]

borazon (ˈbɔːrəˌzɒn) *n.* an extremely hard form of boron nitride. [C20: < BOR(ON) + AZO + -ON]

borborygmus (ˌbɔːbəˈrɪgməs) *n., pl.* **-mi** (-maɪ). rumbling of the stomach. [C18: < Gk]

Bordeaux (bɔːˈdəʊ) *n.* any of several red, white, or rosé wines produced around Bordeaux in SW France.

Bordeaux mixture *n. Horticulture.* a fungicide consisting of a solution of equal quantities of copper sulphate and quicklime.

border (ˈbɔːdə) *n.* **1.** a band or margin around or along the edge of something. **2.** the dividing line or frontier between political or geographic regions. **3.** a region straddling such a boundary. **4.** a design around the edge of something. **5.** a long narrow strip of ground planted with flowers, shrubs, etc.: *a herbaceous border.* ~*vb.* **6.** *(tr.)* to provide with a border. **7.** (when *intr.*, foll. by *on* or *upon*) **a.** to be adjacent (to); lie along the boundary (of). **b.** to be nearly the same (as); verge (on): *his stupidity borders on madness.* [C14: < OF, < *bort* side of a ship, of Gmc origin]

Border (ˈbɔːdə) *n.* **the.** *(often pl.)* the area straddling the border between England and Scotland.

borderer (ˈbɔːdərə) *n.* a person who lives in a border area.

borderland (ˈbɔːdəˌlænd) *n.* **1.** land located on or near a frontier or boundary. **2.** an indeterminate state or condition.

borderline (ˈbɔːdəˌlaɪn) *n.* **1.** a border; dividing line. **2.** an indeterminate position between two conditions: *the borderline between friendship and love.* ~*adj.* **3.** on the edge of one category and verging on another: *a borderline failure in the exam.*

bore[1] (bɔː) *vb.* **1.** to produce (a hole) in (a material) by use of a drill, auger, or rotary cutting tool. **2.** to increase the diameter of (a hole), as by turning. **3.** *(tr.)* to produce (a hole in the ground, tunnel, mine shaft, etc.) by digging, drilling, etc. **4.** *(intr.) Inf.* (of a horse or athlete in a race) to push other competitors out of the way. ~*n.* **5.** a hole or tunnel in the ground, esp. one drilled in search of minerals, oil, etc. **6.** *Austral.* an artesian well. **7. a.** the hollow part of a tube or cylinder, esp. of a gun barrel. **b.** the diameter of such a hollow part; calibre. [OE *borian*]

bore[2] (bɔː) *vb.* **1.** *(tr.)* to tire or make weary by being dull, repetitious, or uninteresting. ~*n.* **2.** a dull or repetitious person, activity, or state. [C18: <?] —**bored** *adj.* —**ˈboring** *adj.*

bore[3] (bɔː) *n.* a high steep-fronted wave moving up a narrow estuary, caused by the tide. [C17: < ON *bāra* wave, billow]

bore[4] (bɔː) *vb.* the past tense of **bear**[1].

boreal (ˈbɔːrɪəl) *adj.* of or relating to the north or the north wind. [C15: < L *boreās* the north wind]

Boreal (ˈbɔːrɪəl) *adj.* of or denoting the coniferous forests in the north of the N hemisphere.

boredom (ˈbɔːdəm) *n.* the state of being bored.

boree (ˈbɔːriː) *n. Austral.* another name for **myall.** [< Abor.]

borer (ˈbɔːrə) *n.* **1.** a tool for boring holes. **2.** any of various insects, insect larvae, molluscs, or crustaceans, that bore into plant material, esp. wood.

boric (ˈbɔːrɪk) *adj.* of or containing boron. Also: **boracic.**

boric acid *n.* a white soluble weakly acid crystalline solid used in the manufacture of heat-resistant glass and porcelain enamels, as a fireproofing material, and as a mild antiseptic. Formula: H_3BO_3. Also called: **orthoboric acid.**

born (bɔːn) *vb.* **1.** the past participle (in most passive uses) of **bear**[1] (sense 4). **2. not born yesterday.** not gullible or foolish. ~*adj.* **3.** possessing certain qualities from birth: *a born musician.* **4. a.** being at birth in a particular social status or other condition as specified: *ignobly born.* **b.** *(in combination): lowborn.* **5. in all one's born days.** *Inf.* so far in one's life.

born-again (ˈbɔːnəˌgɛn) *adj.* **1.** having experienced conversion, esp. to evangelical Christianity. **2.** showing the enthusiasm of one newly converted to any cause: *a born-again monetarist.*

borne (bɔːn) *vb.* **1.** the past participle of **bear**[1] (for all active uses of the verb; also for all passive uses except sense 4 unless foll. by *by*). **2. be borne in on** *or* **upon.** (of a fact, etc.) to be realized by (someone).

boron (ˈbɔːrɒn) *n.* a very hard almost colourless crystalline metalloid element that in impure form exists as a brown amorphous powder. It occurs principally in borax and is used in hardening steel. Symbol: B; atomic no.: 5; atomic wt.: 10.81. [C19: < BOR(AX) + (CARB)ON]

boron carbide *n.* a black extremely hard inert substance used as an abrasive and in control rods in nuclear reactors. Formula: B_4C.

boronia (bəˈrəʊnɪə) *n.* any aromatic shrub of the Australian genus *Boronia.*

boron nitride *n.* a white inert crystalline solid, used as a refractory, high-temperature lubricant and insulator, and heat shield.

borough (ˈbʌrə) *n.* **1.** a town, esp. (in Britain) one that forms the constituency of an MP or that was originally incorporated by royal charter. See also **burgh. 2.** any of the 32 constituent divisions of Greater London. **3.** any of the five constituent divisions of New York City. **4.** (in the U.S.) a self-governing incorporated municipality. [OE *burg*]

borrow (ˈbɒrəʊ) *vb.* **1.** to obtain or receive (something, such as money) on loan for temporary use, intending to give it, or something equivalent, back to the lender. **2.** to adopt (ideas, words, etc.) from another source; appropriate. **3.** *Not standard.* to lend. **4.** (*intr.*) *Golf.* to putt the ball uphill of the direct path to the hole: *make sure you borrow enough.* [OE *borgian*] —ˈ**borrower** *n.*

▷ **Usage.** See at **lend.**

borsch, borsh (bɔːʃ), **borscht** (bɔːʃt), *or* **borshch** (bɔːʃtʃ) *n.* a Russian and Polish soup based on beetroot. [< Russian *borshch*]

borstal (ˈbɔːstəl) *n.* (in Britain) an informal name for an establishment in which offenders aged 15 to 21 may be detained for corrective training. Official name: **youth custody centre.** [C20: after *Borstal,* village in Kent where the first institution was founded]

bort, boart (bɔːt), *or* **bortz** (bɔːts) *n.* an inferior grade of diamond used for cutting and drilling or, in powdered form, as an industrial abrasive. [OE *gebrot* fragment]

borzoi (ˈbɔːzɔɪ) *n., pl.* **-zois.** a tall fast-moving breed of dog with a long coat. Also called: **Russian wolfhound.** [C19: Russian, lit.: swift]

boscage *or* **boskage** (ˈbɒskɪdʒ) *n. Literary.* a mass of trees and shrubs; thicket. [C14: < OF *bosc,* prob. of Gmc origin; see BUSH[1], -AGE]

bosh (bɒʃ) *n. Inf.* empty or meaningless talk or opinions; nonsense. [C19: < Turkish *boş* empty]

bosk (bɒsk) *n. Literary.* a small wood of bushes and small trees. [C13: var. of *busk* BUSH[1]]

bosky (ˈbɒskɪ) *adj.* **boskier, boskiest.** *Literary.* containing or consisting of bushes or thickets.

bo's'n (ˈbəʊsᵊn) *n. Naut.* a variant spelling of **boatswain.**

bosom (ˈbʊzəm) *n.* **1.** the chest or breast of a person, esp. the female breasts. **2.** the part of a woman's dress, coat, etc., that covers the chest. **3.** a protective centre or part: *the bosom of the family.* **4.** the breast considered as the seat of emotions. **5.** (*modifier*) very dear; intimate: *a bosom friend.* ~*vb.* (*tr.*) **6.** to embrace. **7.** to conceal or carry in the bosom. [OE *bōsm*]

bosomy (ˈbʊzəmɪ) *adj.* (of a woman) having large breasts.

boson (ˈbəʊzɒn) *n.* any of a group of elementary particles, such as a photon or pion, that has zero or integral spin and does not obey the Pauli exclusion principle. Cf. **fermion.** [C20: after S. N. *Bose* (1894-1974), Indian physicist]

boss[1] (bɒs) *Inf.* ~*n.* **1.** a person in charge of or employing others. **2.** *Chiefly U.S.* a professional politician who controls a political organization, often using devious or illegal methods. ~*vb.* (*tr.*) **3.** to employ, supervise, or be in charge of. **4.** (usually foll. by *around* or *about*) to be domineering or overbearing towards (others). ~*adj.* **5.** *Sl.* excellent; fine: *a boss hand at carpentry; that's boss!* [C19: < Du. *baas* master]

boss[2] (bɒs) *n.* **1.** a knob, stud, or other circular rounded protuberance, esp. an ornamental one on a vault, a ceiling, or a shield. **2.** an area of increased thickness, usually cylindrical, that strengthens or provides room for a locating device on a shaft, hub of a wheel, etc. **3.** a rounded mass of igneous rock. ~*vb.* (*tr.*) **4.** to ornament with bosses; emboss. [C13: < OF *boce*; rel. to It. *bozza* metal knob, swelling]

bossa nova (ˈbɒsə ˈnəʊvə) *n.* **1.** a dance similar to the samba, originating in Brazil. **2.** a piece of music composed for or in the rhythm of this dance. [C20: < Port., lit.: new voice]

bossy (ˈbɒsɪ) *adj.* **bossier, bossiest.** *Inf.* domineering, overbearing, or authoritarian. —ˈ**bossily** *adv.* —ˈ**bossiness** *n.*

bosun (ˈbəʊsᵊn) *n. Naut.* a variant spelling of **boatswain.**

bot[1] *or* **bott** (bɒt) *n.* **1.** the larva of a botfly, which typically develops inside the body of a horse, sheep, or man. **2.** any similar larva. [C15: prob. < Low G; rel. to Du. *bot,* <?]

bot[2] (bɒt) *Austral. inf.* ~*vb.* **botting, botted. 1.** to scrounge or borrow. ~*n.* **2.** a scrounger. **3. on the bot (for).** wanting to scrounge. [C20: ?< BOTFLY, alluding to its bite; see BITE (sense 9)]

bot. *abbrev. for:* **1.** botanical. **2.** botany. **3.** bottle.

botanical (bəˈtænɪkᵊl) *or* **botanic** *adj.* **1.** of or relating to botany or plants. ~*n.* **2.** any drug that is made from parts of a plant. [C17: < Med. L, < Gk *botanē* plant, pasture] —**boˈtanically** *adv.*

botanize *or* **-ise** (ˈbɒtəˌnaɪz) *vb.* **1.** (*intr.*) to collect or study plants. **2.** (*tr.*) to explore and study the plants in (an area or region).

botany (ˈbɒtənɪ) *n., pl.* **-nies. 1.** the study of plants, including their classification, structure, physiology, ecology, and economic importance. **2.** the plant life of a particular region or time. **3.** the biological characteristics of a particular group of plants. [C17: < BOTANICAL; cf. ASTRONOMY, ASTRONOMICAL] —ˈ**botanist** *n.*

Botany wool *n.* fine wool from merino sheep. [C19: < *Botany* Bay, Australia]

botch (bɒtʃ) *vb.* (*tr.*; often foll. by *up*) **1.** to spoil through clumsiness or ineptitude. **2.** to repair badly or clumsily. ~*n.* **3.** a badly done piece of work or repair (esp. in **make a botch of**). [C14: <?] —ˈ**botcher** *n.* —ˈ**botchy** *adj.*

botfly (ˈbɒtˌflaɪ) *n., pl.* **-flies.** any of various stout-bodied hairy dipterous flies, the larvae of which are parasites of man, sheep, and horses.

both (bəʊθ) *determiner.* **1. a.** the two; two considered together: *both dogs were dirty.* **b.** (*as pron.*): *both are to blame.* ~*conj.* **2.** (*coordinating*) used preceding words, phrases, or clauses joined by *and*: *both Ellen and Keith enjoyed the play; both new and exciting.* [C12: < ON *bāthir*]

bother (ˈbɒðə) *vb.* **1.** (*tr.*) to give annoyance, pain, or trouble to. **2.** (*tr.*) to trouble (a person) by repeatedly disturbing; pester. **3.** (*intr.*) to take the time or trouble; concern oneself: *don't bother to come with me.* **4.** (*tr.*) to make (a person) alarmed or confused. ~*n.* **5.** a state of worry, trouble, or confusion. **6.** a person or thing that causes fuss, trouble, or annoyance. **7.** *Inf.* a disturbance or fight; trouble (esp. in **a spot of bother**). ~*interj.* **8.** *Chiefly Brit.* an exclamation of slight annoyance. [C18: ?< Irish Gaelic *bodhar* deaf, vexed]

botheration (ˌbɒðəˈreɪʃən) *n., interj. Inf.* another word for **bother** (senses 5, 8).

bothersome (ˈbɒðəsəm) *adj.* causing bother; troublesome.

bothy (ˈbɒθɪ) *n., pl.* **bothies.** *Chiefly Scot.* **1.** a cottage or hut. **2.** a farmworker's summer quarters. [C18: ? rel. to BOOTH]

bo tree (bəʊ) *n.* another name for the **peepul.**

[C19: < Sinhalese, < Pali *bodhitaru* tree of wisdom]

bott (bɒt) *n.* a variant spelling of **bot**[1].

bottle (ˈbɒtᵊl) *n.* **1. a.** a vessel, often of glass and typically cylindrical with a narrow neck, for containing liquids. **b.** (*as modifier*): *a bottle rack.* **2.** Also called: **bottleful.** the amount such a vessel will hold. **3.** *Brit. sl.* courage; nerve; initiative. **4. the bottle.** *Inf.* drinking of alcohol, esp. to excess. ~*vb.* (*tr.*) **5.** to put or place in a bottle or bottles. **6.** to store (gas) in a portable container under pressure. ~See also **bottle up.** [C14: < OF *botaille*, < Med. L *butticula*, < LL *buttis* cask]

bottlebrush (ˈbɒtᵊlˌbrʌʃ) *n.* **1.** any of various Australian shrubs or trees having dense spikes of large red flowers with protruding brushlike stamens. **2.** a cylindrical brush on a thin shaft, used for cleaning bottles.

bottle-feed *vb.* **-feeding, -fed.** to feed (a baby) with milk from a bottle.

bottle green *n., adj.* (of) a dark green colour.

bottle-jack *n. N.Z.* a large jack used for heavy lifts.

bottleneck (ˈbɒtᵊlˌnɛk) *n.* **1. a.** a narrow stretch of road or a junction at which traffic is or may be held up. **b.** the hold-up. **2.** something that holds up progress.

bottlenose dolphin (ˈbɒtᵊlˌnəʊz) *n.* a type of dolphin with a bottle-shaped snout.

bottle party *n.* a party to which guests bring drink.

bottler (ˈbɒtᵊlə) *n. Austral. & N.Z. inf.* an exceptional or outstanding person or thing.

bottle shop *n. Austral.* a shop where alcohol is sold in unopened containers for consumption elsewhere.

bottle store *n. S. African & N.Z.* an off-licence.

bottle tree *n.* any of several Australian trees that have a bottle-shaped swollen trunk.

bottle up *vb.* (*tr., adv.*) **1.** to restrain (powerful emotion). **2.** to keep (an army or other force) contained or trapped.

bottom (ˈbɒtəm) *n.* **1.** the lowest, deepest, or farthest removed part of a thing: *the bottom of a hill.* **2.** the least important or successful position: *the bottom of a class.* **3.** the ground underneath a sea, lake, or river. **4.** the inner depths of a person's true feelings (esp. in **from the bottom of one's heart**). **5.** the underneath part of a thing. **6.** *Naut.* the parts of a vessel's hull that are under water. **7.** (in literary or commercial contexts) a boat or ship. **8.** (esp. of horses) staying power; stamina. **9.** *Inf.* the buttocks. **10. at bottom.** in reality; basically. **11. be at the bottom of.** to be the ultimate cause of. **12. get to the bottom of.** to discover the real truth about. ~*adj.* (*prenominal*) **13.** lowest or last. **14. bet** (*or* **put**) **one's bottom dollar on.** to be absolutely sure of. **15.** of, relating to, or situated at the bottom. **16.** fundamental; basic. ~*vb.* **17.** (*tr.*) to provide (a chair, etc.) with a bottom or seat. **18.** (*tr.*) to discover the full facts or truth of; fathom. **19.** (usually foll. by *on* or *upon*) to base or be founded (on an idea, etc.). [OE *botm*]

bottom drawer *n. Brit.* a young woman's collection of linen, cutlery, etc., made in anticipation of marriage. U.S., Canad., and N.Z. equivalent: **hope chest.**

bottomless (ˈbɒtəmlɪs) *adj.* **1.** having no bottom. **2.** unlimited; inexhaustible. **3.** very deep.

bottom line *n.* **1.** the last line of a financial statement that shows the net profit or loss of a company or organization. **2.** the conclusion or main point of a process, discussion, etc.

bottom out *vb.* (*intr., adv.*) to reach the lowest point and level out.

bottomry (ˈbɒtəmrɪ) *n., pl.* **-ries.** *Maritime law.* a contract whereby the owner of a ship borrows money to enable the vessel to complete the voyage and pledges the ship as security for the loan. [C16: < Du. *bodemerij*, < *bodem* BOTTOM (hull of a ship) + *-erij* -RY]

botulism (ˈbɒtjʊˌlɪzəm) *n.* severe, often fatal, poisoning resulting from the potent bacterial toxin, **botulin,** produced in imperfectly preserved food, etc. [C19: < G *Botulismus*, lit.: sausage poisoning, < L *botulus* sausage]

bouclé (ˈbuːkleɪ) *n.* **1.** a curled or looped yarn or fabric giving a thick knobbly effect. ~*adj.* **2.** of or designating such a yarn or fabric. [C19: < F *bouclé* curly, < *boucle* a curl]

boudoir (ˈbuːdwɑː, -dwɔː) *n.* a woman's bedroom or private sitting room. [C18: < F, lit.: room for sulking in, < *bouder* to sulk]

bouffant (ˈbuːfɔːŋ) *adj.* **1.** (of a hairstyle) having extra height and width through backcombing; puffed out. **2.** (of sleeves, skirts, etc.) puffed out. [C20: < F, < *bouffer* to puff up]

bougainvillea (ˌbuːgənˈvɪlɪə) *n.* a tropical woody climbing plant having inconspicuous flowers surrounded by showy red or purple bracts. [C19: NL, after L. A. de *Bougainville* (1729–1811), F navigator]

bough (baʊ) *n.* any of the main branches of a tree. [OE *bōg* arm, twig]

bought (bɔːt) *vb.* the past tense and past participle of **buy.**

bougie (ˈbuːʒiː, buːˈʒiː) *n. Med.* a slender semiflexible instrument for inserting into body passages such as the rectum or urethra to dilate structures, introduce medication, etc. [C18: < F, orig. a wax candle from *Bougie* (Bujiya), Algeria]

bouillabaisse (ˌbuːjəˈbɛs) *n.* a rich stew or soup of fish and vegetables. [C19: < F, < Provençal *bouiabaisso*, lit.: boil down]

bouillon (ˈbuːjɒn) *n.* a plain unclarified broth or stock. [C18: < F, < *bouillir* to BOIL[1]]

boulder (ˈbəʊldə) *n.* a smooth rounded mass of rock that has been shaped by erosion. [C13: prob. < ON; cf. OSwedish *bulder* rumbling + *sten* STONE]

boulder clay *n.* an unstratified glacial deposit consisting of fine clay, boulders, and pebbles.

boule (ˈbuːliː) *n.* **1.** the senate of an ancient Greek city-state. **2.** the parliament in modern Greece. [C19: < Gk *boulē* senate]

boules *French.* (bul) *n.* (*functioning as sing.*) a game, popular in France, in which metal bowls are thrown to land as near as possible to a target ball. [pl. of *boule* BALL[1]: see BOWL[2]]

boulevard (ˈbuːlvɑː, -vɑːd) *n.* a wide usually tree-lined road in a city. [C18: < F, < MDu. *bolwerc* BULWARK; so called because orig. often built on the ruins of an old rampart]

boulle, boule, *or* **buhl** (buːl) *adj.* **1.** denoting or relating to a type of marquetry of patterned inlays of brass and tortoiseshell, etc. ~*n.* **2.** something ornamented with such marquetry. [C18: after A. C. *Boulle* (1642–1732), F cabinet-maker]

boult (bəʊlt) *vb.* a variant spelling of **bolt**[2].

bounce (baʊns) *vb.* **1.** (*intr.*) (of a ball, etc.) to rebound from an impact. **2.** (*tr.*) to cause (a ball, etc.) to hit a solid surface and spring back. **3.** to move or cause to move suddenly, excitedly, or violently; spring: *she bounced up from her chair.* **4.** *Sl.* (of a bank) to send (a cheque) back or (of a cheque) to be sent back by a bank to a payee unredeemed because of lack of funds in the drawer's account. **5.** (*tr.*) *Sl.* to force (a person) to leave a place or job; throw out; eject. ~*n.* **6.** the action of rebounding from an impact. **7.** a leap; jump; bound. **8.** the quality of being able to rebound; springiness. **9.** *Inf.* vitality; vigour; resilience. **10.** *Brit.* swagger or impudence. [C13: prob. imit.; cf. Low G *bunsen* to beat, Du. *bonken* to thump]

bounce back *vb.* (*intr., adv.*) to recover one's health, good spirits, confidence, etc., easily.

bouncer (ˈbaʊnsə) *n. Sl.* a man employed at a club, disco, etc., to eject drunks or troublemakers.

bouncing (ˈbaʊnsɪŋ) *adj.* (when *postpositive*, foll. by *with*) vigorous and robust (esp. in **a bouncing baby**).

bouncy (ˈbaʊnsɪ) *adj.* **bouncier, bounciest. 1.** lively, exuberant, or self-confident. **2.** having the capability or quality of bouncing: *a bouncy ball.* **3.** responsive to bouncing; springy: *a bouncy bed.*

bound[1] (baʊnd) *vb.* **1.** the past tense and past participle of **bind.** ~*adj.* **2.** in bonds or chains; tied as with a rope. **3.** (*in combination*) restricted; confined: *housebound.* **4.** (*postpositive;*

foll. by an infinitive) destined; sure; certain: *it's bound to happen.* **5.** (*postpositive;* often foll. by *by*) compelled or obliged. **6.** *Rare.* constipated. **7.** (of a book) secured within a cover or binding. **8.** *Logic.* (of a variable) occurring within the scope of a quantifier. Cf. **free** (sense 18). **9. bound up with.** closely or inextricably linked with.

bound[2] (baʊnd) *vb.* **1.** to move forwards by leaps or jumps. **2.** to bounce; spring away from an impact. ~*n.* **3.** a jump upwards or forwards. **4.** a bounce, as of a ball. [C16: < OF *bond* a leap]

bound[3] (baʊnd) *vb.* **1.** (*tr.*) to place restrictions on; limit. **2.** (when *intr.*, foll. by *on*) to form a boundary of. ~*n.* **3.** See **bounds.** [C13: < OF *bonde,* < Med. L *bodina*]

bound[4] (baʊnd) *adj.* **a.** (*postpositive;* often foll. by *for*) going or intending to go towards: *bound for Jamaica; homeward bound.* **b.** (*in combination*): *northbound traffic.* [C13: < ON *buinn,* p.p. of *būa* to prepare]

boundary (ˈbaʊndərɪ, -drɪ) *n., pl.* **-ries. 1.** something that indicates the farthest limit, as of an area; border. **2.** *Cricket.* **a.** the marked limit of the playing area. **b.** a stroke that hits the ball beyond this limit. **c.** the four or six runs scored with such a stroke.

boundary rider *n. Austral.* an employee on a sheep or cattle station whose job is to maintain fences in good repair.

bounden (ˈbaʊndən) *adj.* morally obligatory (arch. except in **bounden duty**). [arch. p.p. of BIND]

bounder (ˈbaʊndə) *n. Old-fashioned Brit. sl.* a morally reprehensible person; cad.

boundless (ˈbaʊndlɪs) *adj.* unlimited; vast: *boundless energy.* —ˈ**boundlessly** *adv.*

bounds (baʊndz) *pl. n.* **1.** (*sometimes sing.*) a limit; boundary (esp. in **know no bounds**). **2.** something that restrains or confines, esp. the standards of a society: *within the bounds of modesty.* ~See also **out of bounds.**

bounteous (ˈbaʊntɪəs) *adj. Literary.* **1.** giving freely; generous. **2.** plentiful; abundant. —ˈ**bounteously** *adv.* —ˈ**bounteousness** *n.*

bountiful (ˈbaʊntɪfʊl) *adj.* **1.** plentiful; ample (esp. in **a bountiful supply**). **2.** giving freely; generous. —ˈ**bountifully** *adv.*

bounty (ˈbaʊntɪ) *n., pl.* **-ties. 1.** generosity; liberality. **2.** a generous gift. **3.** a payment made by a government, as, formerly, to a sailor on enlisting or to a soldier after a campaign. **4.** any reward or premium. [C13 (in the sense: goodness): < OF, < L, < *bonus* good]

bouquet (buːˈkeɪ) *n.* **1.** a bunch of flowers, esp. a large carefully arranged one. **2.** the characteristic aroma or fragrance of a wine or liqueur. **3.** a compliment or expression of praise. [C18: < F: thicket, < OF *bosc* forest]

bouquet garni (ˈbuːkeɪ gɑːˈniː) *n., pl.* **bouquets garnis** (ˈbuːkeɪz gɑːˈniː). a bunch of herbs tied together and used for flavouring soups, stews, etc. [C19: < F, lit.: garnished bouquet]

bourbon (ˈbɜːbᵊn) *n.* a whiskey distilled, chiefly in the U.S., from maize, esp. one containing at least 51 per cent maize. [C19: after *Bourbon* county, Kentucky, where it was first made]

bourdon (ˈbʊədᵊn, ˈbɔːdᵊn) *n.* **1.** a bass organ stop. **2.** the drone of a bagpipe. [C14: < OF: drone (of a musical instrument), imit.]

bourgeois (ˈbʊəʒwɑː) *Often disparaging.* ~*n., pl.* **-geois. 1.** a member of the middle class, esp. one regarded as being conservative and materialistic or capitalistic. **2.** a mediocre, unimaginative, or materialistic person. ~*adj.* **3.** characteristic of, relating to, or comprising the middle class. **4.** conservative or materialistic in outlook. **5.** (in Marxist thought) dominated by capitalists or capitalist interests. [C16: < OF *borjois, burgeis* burgher, citizen; see BURGESS] —**bourgeoise** (ˈbʊəʒwɑːz, bʊəˈʒwɑːz) *fem. n.*

bourgeoisie (ˌbʊəʒwɑːˈziː) *n.* **the. 1.** the middle classes. **2.** (in Marxist thought) the capitalist ruling class. The bourgeoisie owns the means of production, through which it exploits the working class.

bourgeon (ˈbɜːdʒən) *n., vb.* a variant spelling of **burgeon.**

bourn[1] *or* **bourne** (bɔːn) *n. Arch.* **1.** a destination; goal. **2.** a boundary. [C16: < OF *borne;* see BOUND[3]]

bourn[2] (bɔːn) *n. Chiefly southern Brit.* a stream. [C16: < OF *bodne* limit; see BOUND[3]]

bourrée (ˈbʊəreɪ) *n.* **1.** a traditional French dance in fast duple time. **2.** a piece of music in the rhythm of this dance. [C18: < F]

Bourse (bʊəs) *n.* a stock exchange of continental Europe, esp. Paris. [C19: < F, lit.: purse, < Med. L *bursa,* ult. < Gk: leather]

boustrophedon (ˌbaʊstrəˈfiːdᵊn) *adj.* having alternate lines written from right to left and from left to right. [C17: < Gk, lit.: turning as in ploughing with oxen, < *bous* ox + *strephein* to turn]

bout (baʊt) *n.* **1. a.** a period of time spent doing something, such as drinking. **b.** a period of illness. **2.** a contest or fight, esp. a boxing or wrestling match. [C16: var. of obs. *bought* turn]

boutique (buːˈtiːk) *n.* a shop, esp. a small one selling fashionable clothes and other items. [C18: < F, ult. < Gk *apothēkē* storehouse]

boutonniere (ˌbuːtɒnɪˈɛə) *n.* another name for **buttonhole** (sense 2). [C19: < F: buttonhole]

bouzouki (buːˈzuːkɪ) *n.* a Greek long-necked stringed musical instrument related to the mandolin. [C20: < Mod. Gk, ? < Turkish *büjük* large]

bovine (ˈbəʊvaɪn) *adj.* **1.** of or relating to cattle. **2.** (of people) dull; sluggish; stolid. [C19: < LL *bovīnus,* < L *bōs* ox, cow] —ˈ**bovinely** *adv.*

Bovril (ˈbɒvrɪl) *n. Trademark.* a concentrated beef extract, used for flavouring, as a stock, etc.

bovver (ˈbɒvə) *n. Brit. sl.* **a.** rowdiness, esp. caused by gangs of teenage youths. **b.** (*as modifier*): *a bovver boy.* [C20: sl. pronunciation of BOTHER]

bow[1] (baʊ) *vb.* **1.** to lower (one's head) or bend (one's knee or body) as a sign of respect, greeting, assent, or shame. **2.** to bend or cause to bend. **3.** (*intr.;* usually foll. by *to* or *before*) to comply or accept: *bow to the inevitable.* **4.** (*tr.;* foll. by *in, out, to,* etc.) to usher (someone) in or out with bows and deference. **5.** (*tr.;* usually foll. by *down*) to bring (a person, nation, etc.) to a state of submission. **6. bow and scrape.** to behave in an excessively deferential or obsequious way. ~*n.* **7.** a lowering or inclination of the head or body as a mark of respect, greeting, or assent. **8. take a bow.** to acknowledge or receive applause or praise. ~See also **bow out.** [OE *būgan*]

bow[2] (bəʊ) *n.* **1.** a weapon for shooting arrows, consisting of an arch of flexible wood, plastic, etc., bent by a string fastened at each end. **2. a.** a long stick across which are stretched strands of horsehair, used for playing the strings of a violin, viola, cello, etc. **b.** a stroke with such a stick. **3. a.** a decorative interlacing of ribbon or other fabrics, usually having two loops and two loose ends. **b.** the knot forming such an interlacing. **4.** something that is curved, bent, or arched. ~*vb.* **5.** to form or cause to form a curve or curves. **6.** to make strokes of a bow across (violin strings). [OE *boga* arch, bow]

bow[3] (baʊ) *n.* **1.** *Chiefly Naut.* **a.** (*often pl.*) the forward end or part of a vessel. **b.** (*as modifier*): *the bow mooring line.* **2.** *Rowing.* the oarsman at the bow. [C15: prob. < Low G *boog*]

bow compass (bəʊ) *n. Geom.* a compass in which the legs are joined by a flexible metal bow-shaped spring rather than a hinge.

bowdlerize *or* **-ise** (ˈbaʊdləˌraɪz) *vb.* (*tr.*) to remove passages or words regarded as indecent from (a play, novel, etc.); expurgate. [C19: after Thomas *Bowdler* (1754–1825), E editor who expurgated Shakespeare] —ˌ**bowdleriˈzation** *or* **-iˈsation** *n.* —ˈ**bowdlerism** *n.*

bowel (ˈbaʊəl) *n.* **1.** an intestine, esp. the large intestine in man. **2.** (*pl.*) innards; entrails. **3.** (*pl.*) the deep or innermost part (esp. in **the bowels of the earth**). [C13: < OF *bouel,* < L *botellus* a little sausage]

bowel movement *n.* **1.** the discharge of faeces; defecation. **2.** the waste matter discharged; faeces.

bower[1] (ˈbaʊə) *n.* **1.** a shady leafy shelter or recess, as in a wood or garden; arbour. **2.** *Literary.* a lady's bedroom or apartments; boudoir. [OE *būr* dwelling]

bower[2] (ˈbaʊə) *n. Naut.* a vessel's bow anchor. [C18: < BOW[3] + -ER[1]]

bowerbird (ˈbaʊəˌbɜːd) *n.* **1.** any of various songbirds of Australia and New Guinea. The males build bower-like display grounds to attract the females. **2.** *Inf., chiefly Austral.* a collector of unconsidered trifles.

bowfin (ˈbəʊˌfɪn) *n.* a primitive North American freshwater bony fish with an elongated body and a very long dorsal fin.

bowhead (ˈbəʊˌhɛd) *n.* a large-mouthed arctic whale.

bowie knife (ˈbəʊɪ) *n.* a stout hunting knife with a short hilt and a guard for the hand. [C19: after Jim *Bowie* (1796–1836), Texan adventurer]

bowl[1] (bəʊl) *n.* **1.** a round container open at the top, used for holding liquid, serving food, etc. **2.** Also: **bowlful.** the amount a bowl will hold. **3.** the rounded or hollow part of an object, esp. of a spoon or tobacco pipe. **4.** any container shaped like a bowl, such as a sink or lavatory. **5.** a bowl-shaped building or other structure, such as an amphitheatre. **6.** *Chiefly U.S.* a bowl-shaped depression of the land surface. **7.** *Literary.* a drinking cup. [OE *bolla*]

bowl[2] (bəʊl) *n.* **1.** a wooden ball used in the game of bowls, having one flattened side in order to make it run on a curved course. **2.** a large heavy ball with holes for gripping, used in tenpin bowling. ~*vb.* **3.** to roll smoothly or cause to roll smoothly along the ground. **4.** (*intr.;* usually foll. by *along*) to move easily and rapidly, as in a car. **5.** *Cricket.* **a.** to send (a ball) from one's hand towards the batsman. **b.** Also: **bowl out.** to dismiss (a batsman) by delivering a ball that breaks his wicket. **6.** (*intr.*) to play bowls or tenpin bowling. ~See also **bowl over, bowls.** [C15: < F *boule,* ult. < L *bulla* bubble]

bow legs (bəʊ) *pl. n.* a condition in which the legs curve outwards like a bow between the ankle and the thigh. Also called: **bandy legs.** —**bow-legged** (bəʊˈlɛgɪd, bəʊˈlɛgd) *adj.*

bowler[1] (ˈbəʊlə) *n.* **1.** one who bowls in cricket. **2.** a player at the game of bowls.

bowler[2] (ˈbəʊlə) *n.* a stiff felt hat with a rounded crown and narrow curved brim. U.S. and Canad. name: **derby.** [C19: after John *Bowler,* 19th-cent. London hatter]

bowline (ˈbəʊlɪn) *n. Naut.* **1.** a line for controlling the weather leech of a square sail when a vessel is close-hauled. **2.** a knot used for securing a loop that will not slip at the end of a piece of rope. [C14: prob. < MLow G *bōlīne,* equivalent to BOW[3] + LINE[1]]

bowling (ˈbəʊlɪŋ) *n.* **1.** any of various games in which a heavy ball is rolled down a special alley at a group of wooden pins. **2.** the game of bowls. **3.** *Cricket.* the act of delivering the ball to the batsman.

bowling alley *n.* **1. a.** a long narrow wooden lane down which the ball is rolled in tenpin bowling. **b.** a similar lane or alley for playing skittles. **2.** a building having lanes for tenpin bowling.

bowling green *n.* an area of closely mown turf on which the game of bowls is played.

bowl over *vb.* (*tr., adv.*) **1.** *Inf.* to surprise (a person) greatly, esp. in a pleasant way; astound; amaze. **2.** to knock down.

bowls (bəʊlz) *n.* (*functioning as sing.*) **1.** a game played on a bowling green in which a small bowl (the jack) is pitched from a mark and two opponents take turns to roll biased wooden bowls as near the jack as possible. **2.** skittles or tenpin bowling.

bowman (ˈbəʊmən) *n., pl.* **-men.** *Arch.* an archer.

bow out (baʊ) *vb.* (*adv.; usually tr.;* often foll. by *of*) to retire or withdraw gracefully.

bowser (ˈbaʊzə) *n.* **1.** a tanker containing fuel for aircraft, military vehicles, etc. **2.** *Austral. & N.Z.* a petrol pump at a filling station. [orig. a U.S. proprietary name]

bowshot (ˈbəʊˌʃɒt) *n.* the distance an arrow travels from the bow.

bowsprit (ˈbəʊsprɪt) *n. Naut.* a spar projecting from the bow of a vessel, esp. a sailing vessel. [C13: < MLow G, < *bōch* BOW[3] + *sprēt* pole]

bowstring (ˈbəʊˌstrɪŋ) *n.* the string of an archer's bow.

bow tie (bəʊ) *n.* a man's tie tied in a bow, now chiefly in plain black for formal evening wear.

bow window (bəʊ) *n.* a bay window in the shape of a curve.

bow-wow (ˈbaʊˌwaʊ, -ˈwaʊ) *n.* **1.** a child's word for **dog.** **2.** an imitation of the bark of a dog. ~*vb.* **3.** (*intr.*) to bark or imitate a dog's bark.

bowyangs (ˈbəʊjæŋz) *pl. n. Austral. & N.Z. sl.* a pair of strings or straps worn around the trouser leg below the knee, orig. esp. by agricultural workers. [C19: < E dialect *bowy-yanks* leggings]

box[1] (bɒks) *n.* **1.** a receptacle or container made of wood, cardboard, etc., usually rectangular and having a removable or hinged lid. **2.** Also called: **boxful.** the contents of such a receptacle. **3.** (*often in combination*) any of various small cubicles, kiosks, or shelters: *a telephone box; a signal box.* **4.** a separate compartment in a public place for a small group of people, as in a theatre. **5.** an enclosure within a courtroom: *witness box.* **6.** a compartment for a horse in a stable or a vehicle. **7.** *Brit.* a small country house occupied by sportsmen when following a field sport, esp. shooting. **8. a.** a protective housing for machinery or mechanical parts. **b.** (*in combination*): *a gearbox.* **9.** a shaped device of light tough material worn by sportsmen to protect the genitals, esp. in cricket. **10.** a section of printed matter on a page, enclosed by lines, a border, etc. **11.** a central agency to which mail is addressed and from which it is collected or redistributed: *a post-office box; a box number in a newspaper advertisement.* **12.** short for **penalty box.** **13.** the raised seat on which the driver sits in a horse-drawn coach. **14.** *Austral. & N.Z.* an accidental mixing of herds or flocks. **15.** *Brit.* (esp. formerly) a present, esp. of money, given at Christmas to tradesmen, etc. **16.** *Austral. taboo sl.* the female genitals. **17. out of the box.** *Austral. inf.* outstanding or excellent. **18. the box.** *Brit. inf.* television. ~*vb.* **19.** (*tr.*) to put into a box. **20.** (*tr.;* usually foll. by *in* or *up*) to prevent from moving freely; confine. **21.** *Austral. & N.Z.* to mix (flocks or herds) or (of flocks) to become mixed accidentally. **22. box the compass.** *Naut.* to name the compass points in order. [OE *box,* < L *buxus,* < Gk *puxos* BOX[3]] —**ˈbox,like** *adj.*

box[2] (bɒks) *vb.* **1.** (*tr.*) to fight (an opponent) in a boxing match. **2.** (*intr.*) to engage in boxing. **3.** (*tr.*) to hit (a person) with the fist. ~*n.* **4.** a punch with the fist, esp. on the ear. [C14: <?]

box[3] (bɒks) *n.* **1.** a slow-growing evergreen tree or shrub with small shiny leaves: used for hedges. **2.** the wood of this tree. **3.** any of several trees the timber or foliage of which resembles this tree, esp. species of *Eucalyptus.* [OE, < L *buxus*]

box camera *n.* a simple box-shaped camera having an elementary lens, shutter, and view-finder.

boxer (ˈbɒksə) *n.* **1.** a man who boxes; pugilist. **2.** a medium-sized smooth-haired breed of dog with a short nose and a docked tail.

Boxer (ˈbɒksə) *n.* a member of a nationalistic Chinese secret society that led an unsuccessful rebellion in 1900 against foreign interests in China. [C18: rough translation of Chinese *I Ho Ch'üan,* lit.: virtuous harmonious fist]

boxer shorts *pl. n.* men's underpants shaped like shorts but having a front opening.

box girder *n.* a girder that is hollow and square or rectangular in shape.

boxing (ˈbɒksɪŋ) *n.* **a.** the act, art, or profession of fighting with the fists. **b.** (*as modifier*): *a boxing enthusiast.*

Boxing Day *n. Brit.* the first weekday after Christmas, observed as a holiday. [C19: < the custom of giving Christmas boxes to tradesmen and staff on this day]

boxing glove *n.* one of a pair of thickly padded mittens worn for boxing.

box junction *n.* (in Britain) a road junction having yellow cross-hatching painted on the road surface. Vehicles may only enter the hatched area when their exit is clear.

box kite *n.* a kite with a boxlike frame open at both ends.

box lacrosse *n. Canad.* lacrosse played indoors. Also called: **boxla.**

box number *n.* **1.** the number of an individual pigeonhole at a newspaper to which replies to an advertisement may be addressed. **2.** the number of an individual pigeonhole at a post office from which mail may be collected.

box office *n.* **1.** an office at a theatre, cinema, etc., where tickets are sold. **2. a.** the public appeal of an actor or production. **b.** (*as modifier*): *a box-office success.*

box pleat *n.* a flat double pleat made by folding under the fabric on either side of it.

boxroom (ˈbɒksˌruːm, -ˌrʊm) *n.* a small room or large cupboard in which boxes, cases, etc., may be stored.

box seat *n.* **1.** a seat in a theatre box. **2. in the box seat.** *Austral. & N.Z.* in the best position.

box spanner *n.* a spanner consisting of a steel cylinder with a hexagonal end that fits over a nut.

box spring *n.* a coiled spring contained in a boxlike frame, used for mattresses, chairs, etc.

boxwood (ˈbɒksˌwʊd) *n.* **1.** the hard close-grained yellow wood of the box tree, used to make tool handles, etc. **2.** the box tree.

boy (bɔɪ) *n.* **1.** a male child; lad; youth. **2.** a man regarded as immature or inexperienced. **3. the boys.** *Inf.* a group of men, esp. a group of friends. **4.** *S. African derog.* a Black male servant. ~*interj.* **5.** an exclamation of surprise, pleasure, contempt, etc. [C13 (in the sense: male servant; C14: young male): ? < Anglo-F *abuié* fettered (unattested), < L *boia* fetter] —ˈ**boyish** *adj.*

boycott (ˈbɔɪkɒt) *vb.* **1.** (*tr.*) to refuse to have dealings with (a person, organization, etc.) or refuse to buy (a product) as a protest or means of coercion. ~*n.* **2.** an instance or the use of boycotting. [C19: after Captain C. C. *Boycott* (1832–97), Irish land agent, a victim of such practices for refusing to reduce rents]

boyfriend (ˈbɔɪˌfrɛnd) *n.* a male friend with whom a person is romantically or sexually involved; sweetheart or lover.

boyhood (ˈbɔɪhʊd) *n.* the state or time of being a boy.

Boyle's law (bɔɪlz) *n.* the principle that the pressure of a gas varies inversely with its volume at constant temperature. [C18: after Robert *Boyle* (1627–91), Irish scientist]

Boys' Brigade *n.* (in Britain) an organization for boys, founded in 1883, with the aim of promoting discipline and self-respect.

boy scout *n.* See **Scout.**

boysenberry (ˈbɔɪzᵊnbərɪ) *n., pl.* **-ries. 1.** a type of bramble: a hybrid of the loganberry and various blackberries and raspberries. **2.** the large red edible fruit of this plant. [C20: after Rudolph *Boysen*, American botanist]

bp *abbrev. for:* **1.** (of alcoholic density) below proof. **2.** boiling point. **3.** bishop. **4.** Also: **B/P.** bills payable.

BP *abbrev. for:* **1.** British Petroleum. **2.** British Pharmacopoeia.

bp. *abbrev. for:* **1.** baptized. **2.** birthplace.

B/P *or* **bp** *abbrev. for* bills payable.

BPC *abbrev. for* British Pharmaceutical Codex.

BPhil *abbrev. for* Bachelor of Philosophy.

bpi *abbrev. for* bits per inch (used of a computer tape).

b.pt. *abbrev. for* boiling point.

Bq *Physics. symbol for* becquerel.

br *abbrev. for* brother.

Br 1. *abbrev. for* (in a religious order) Brother. ~**2.** *the chemical symbol for* bromine.

BR *abbrev. for* British Rail (British Railways).

br. *abbrev. for:* **1.** branch. **2.** bronze.

Br. *abbrev. for:* **1.** Breton. **2.** Britain. **3.** British.

bra (brɑː) *n.* a woman's undergarment for covering and supporting the breasts. [C20: < BRASSIERE]

braai (braɪ) *n.* short for **braaivleis.**

braaivleis (ˈbraɪˌfleɪs) *n. S. African.* a barbecue. [< Afrik. *braai* grill + *vleis* meat]

brace (breɪs) *n.* **1.** a hand tool for drilling holes, with a socket to hold the drill at one end and a cranked handle by which the tool can be turned. See also **brace and bit. 2.** something that steadies, binds, or holds up another thing. **3.** a structural member, such as a beam or prop, used to stiffen a framework. **4.** a pair, esp. of game birds. **5.** either of a pair of characters, { }, used for connecting lines of printing or writing. **6.** Also called: **accolade.** a line or bracket connecting two or more staves of music. **7.** (*often pl.*) an appliance of metal bands and wires for correcting uneven alignment of teeth. **8.** *Med.* any of various appliances for supporting the trunk or a limb. **9.** See **braces.** ~*vb.* (*mainly tr.*) **10.** to provide, strengthen, or fit with a brace. **11.** to steady or prepare (oneself or something) as before an impact. **12.** (*also intr.*) to stimulate; freshen; invigorate: *sea air is bracing.* [C14: < OF, < L *bracchia* arms]

brace and bit *n.* a hand tool for boring holes, consisting of a cranked handle into which a drilling bit is inserted.

bracelet (ˈbreɪslɪt) *n.* an ornamental chain worn around the arm or wrist. [C15: < OF, < L *bracchium* arm]

bracelets (ˈbreɪslɪts) *pl. n.* a slang name for **handcuffs.**

bracer (ˈbreɪsə) *n.* **1.** a person or thing that braces. **2.** *Inf.* a tonic, esp. an alcoholic drink taken as a tonic.

braces (ˈbreɪsɪz) *pl. n. Brit.* a pair of straps worn over the shoulders by men for holding up the trousers. U.S. and Canad. word: **suspenders.**

brachial (ˈbreɪkɪəl, ˈbræk-) *adj.* of or relating to the arm or to an armlike part or structure.

brachiate *adj.* (ˈbreɪkɪɪt, -ˌeɪt, ˈbræk-). **1.** *Bot.* having widely divergent paired branches. ~*vb.* (ˈbreɪkɪˌeɪt, ˈbræk-). **2.** (*intr.*) (of some arboreal apes and monkeys) to swing by the arms from one hold to the next. [C19: < L *bracchiātus* with armlike branches] —ˌ**brachiˈation** *n.*

brachio- *or before a vowel* **brachi-** *combining form.* indicating a brachium: *brachiopod.*

brachiopod (ˈbreɪkɪəˌpɒd, ˈbræk-) *n.* any marine invertebrate animal having a ciliated feeding organ and a shell consisting of dorsal and ventral valves. [C19: < NL *Brachiopoda;* see BRACHIUM, -POD]

brachiosaurus (ˌbreɪkɪəˈsɔːrəs, ˌbræk-) *n.* a dinosaur up to 30 metres long: the largest land animal ever known.

brachium (ˈbreɪkɪəm, ˈbræk-) *n., pl.* **-chia** (-kɪə). **1.** *Anat.* the arm, esp. the upper part. **2.** a corresponding part in an animal. **3.** *Biol.* a branching or armlike part. [C18: NL, < L *bracchium* arm]

brachy- *combining form.* indicating something short: *brachycephalic.* [< Gk *brakhus* short]

brachycephalic (ˌbrækɪsɪˈfælɪk) *adj.* having a head nearly as broad from side to side as from front to back. Also: **brachycephalous** (ˌbrækɪˈsɛfələs). —ˌ**brachyˈcephaly** *n.*

bracing (ˈbreɪsɪŋ) *adj.* **1.** refreshing; stimulating; invigorating. ~*n.* **2.** a system of braces used to strengthen or support.

bracken (ˈbrækən) *n.* **1.** Also called: **brake.** any of various large coarse ferns having large fronds with spore cases along the undersides. **2.** a clump of any of these ferns. [C14: < ON]

bracket (ˈbrækɪt) *n.* **1.** an L-shaped or other support fixed to a wall to hold a shelf, etc. **2.** one or more wall shelves carried on brackets. **3.** *Archit.* a support projecting from the side of a wall or other structure. **4.** Also called: **square bracket.** either of a pair of characters, [ ], used to enclose a section of writing or printing. **5.** a general name for **parenthesis** (sense 2), **square bracket,** and **brace** (sense 5). **6.** a group or category falling within certain defined limits: *the lower income bracket.* **7.** the distance between two preliminary shots of artillery fire in range-finding. ~*vb.* (*tr.*) **8.** to fix or support by means of brackets. **9.** to put (written or printed matter) in brackets. **10.** to couple or join (two lines of text, etc.) with a brace. **11.** (often foll. by *with*) to group or class together. **12.** to adjust (artillery fire) until the target is hit. [C16: < OF *braguette* codpiece, < OProvençal *braga,* < L *brāca* breeches]

brackish (ˈbrækɪʃ) *adj.* (of water) slightly briny or salty. [C16: < MDu. *brac* salty; see -ISH] —ˈ**brackishness** *n.*

bract (brækt) *n.* a specialized leaf with a single flower or inflorescence growing in its axil. [C18: < L *bractea* thin metal plate, gold leaf, <?] —ˈ**bracteal** *adj.* —**bracteate** (ˈbræktɪɪt) *adj.*

bracteole (ˈbræktɪˌəʊl) *n.* a secondary or small bract. Also called: **bractlet.** [C19: < NL *bracteola;* see BRACT]

brad (bræd) *n.* a small tapered nail with a small head. [OE *brord* point, prick]

bradawl (ˈbrædˌɔːl) *n.* an awl used to pierce wood, leather, etc.

Bradshaw (ˈbrædˌʃɔː) *n.* a British railway timetable, published annually from 1839 to 1961. [C19: after its original publisher, George *Bradshaw* (1801–53)]

bradycardia (ˌbrædɪˈkɑːdɪə) *n. Pathol.* an abnormally slow heartbeat. [C19: < Gk *bradus* slow + *kardia* heart]

brae (breɪ) *n. Scot.* **1.** a hill or hillside **2.** (*pl.*) an upland area. [C14 *bra;* rel to ON *brā* eyelash]

brag (bræg) *vb.* **bragging, bragged.** **1.** to speak arrogantly and boastfully. ~*n.* **2.** boastful talk or behaviour. **3.** something boasted of. **4.** a braggart; boaster. **5.** a card game: an old form of poker. [C13: <?] —ˈ**bragger** *n.*

braggadocio (ˌbrægəˈdəʊtʃɪˌəʊ) *n., pl.* **-os.** **1.** vain empty boasting. **2.** a person who boasts; braggart. [C16: < *Braggadocchio,* a boastful character in Spenser's *Faerie Queene;* prob. < BRAGGART + It. *-occhio* (augmentative suffix)]

braggart (ˈbrægət) *n.* **1.** a person who boasts loudly or exaggeratedly; bragger. ~*adj.* **2.** boastful. [C16: see BRAG]

Brahma (ˈbrɑːmə) *n.* **1.** a Hindu god, the Creator. **2.** another name for **Brahman** (sense 2). [< Sansk., < *brahman* praise]

Brahman (ˈbrɑːmən) *n., pl.* **-mans.** **1.** (*sometimes not cap.*) Also (esp. formerly): **Brahmin.** a member of the highest or priestly caste in the Hindu caste system. **2.** *Hinduism.* the ultimate and impersonal divine reality of the universe. **3.** another name for **Brahma.** [C14: < Sansk. *brahman* prayer] —**Brahmanic** (brɑːˈmænɪk) *or* **Brahˈmanical** *adj.*

Brahmanism (ˈbrɑːməˌnɪzəm) *or* **Brahminism** *n.* (*sometimes not cap.*) the religious and social system of orthodox Hinduism. —ˈ**Brahmanist** *or* ˈ**Brahminist** *n.*

Brahmin (ˈbrɑːmɪn) *n., pl.* **-min** *or* **-mins.** **1.** the older spelling of **Brahman** (a Hindu priest). **2.** *U.S.* a highly intelligent or socially exclusive person.

braid (breɪd) *vb.* (*tr.*) **1.** to interweave (hair, thread, etc.); plait. **2.** to decorate with an ornamental trim or border. ~*n.* **3.** a length of hair, fabric, etc., that has been braided; plait. **4.** narrow ornamental tape of woven silk, wool, etc. [OE *bregdan* to move suddenly, weave together] —ˈ**braider** *n.* —ˈ**braiding** *n.*

Braille (breɪl) *n.* **1.** a system of writing for the blind consisting of raised dots interpreted by touch. **2.** any writing produced by this method. ~*vb.* **3.** (*tr.*) to print or write using this method. [C19: after Louis *Braille* (1809–52), F inventor]

brain (breɪn) *n.* **1.** the soft convoluted mass of nervous tissue within the skull of vertebrates that is the controlling and coordinating centre of the nervous system and the seat of thought, memory, and emotion. Related adj.: **cerebral.** **2.** (*often pl.*) *Inf.* intellectual ability: *he's got brains.* **3.** *Inf.* shrewdness or cunning. **4.** *Inf.* an intellectual or intelligent person. **5.** (*usually pl.; functioning as sing.*) *Inf.* a person who plans and organizes. **6.** an electronic device, such as a computer, that performs similar functions to those of the human brain. **7. on the brain.** *Inf.* constantly in mind: *I had that song on the brain.* ~*vb.* (*tr.*) **8.** to smash the skull of. **9.** *Sl.* to hit hard on the head. [OE *brægen*]

brainchild (ˈbreɪnˌtʃaɪld) *n., pl.* **-children.** *Inf.* an idea or plan produced by creative thought.

brain death *n.* irreversible cessation of respiration due to irreparable brain damage: widely considered as the criterion of death. —**brain dead** *adj.*

brain drain *n. Inf.* the emigration of scientists, technologists, academics, etc.

brain fever *n.* inflammation of the brain.

brainless (ˈbreɪnlɪs) *adj.* stupid or foolish.

brainpan (ˈbreɪnˌpæn) *n. Inf.* the skull.

brainstorm (ˈbreɪnˌstɔːm) *n.* **1.** a severe outburst of excitement, often as the result of a transitory disturbance of cerebral activity. **2.** *Brit. inf.* a sudden mental aberration. **3.** *U.S. & Canad. inf.* another word for **brain wave** (sense 2).

brainstorming (ˈbreɪnˌstɔːmɪŋ) *n.* intensive discussion to solve problems or generate ideas.

brains trust *n.* a group of knowledgeable people who discuss topics in public or on radio or television.

brain-teaser *or* **brain-twister** *n. Inf.* a difficult problem.

brainwash (ˈbreɪnˌwɒʃ) *vb.* (*tr.*) to effect a radical change in the ideas and beliefs of (a person), esp. by methods based on isolation, sleeplessness, etc. —ˈ**brainˌwashing** *n.*

brain wave *n.* **1.** any of the fluctuations of electrical potential in the brain. **2.** *Inf.* a sudden idea or inspiration.

brainy (ˈbreɪnɪ) *adj.* **brainier, brainiest.** *Inf.* clever; intelligent. —ˈ**braininess** *n.*

braise (breɪz) *vb.* to cook (meat, vegetables, etc.) by lightly browning in fat and then cooking slowly in a closed pan with a small amount of liquid. [C18: < F *braiser,* < OF *brese* live coals]

brak (bræk) *n. S. African.* a crossbred dog; mongrel. [< Du. *brak* setter]

brake[1] (breɪk) *n.* **1.** (*often pl.*) a device for slowing or stopping a vehicle, wheel, shaft, etc., or for keeping it stationary, esp. by means of friction. **2.** a machine or tool for crushing or breaking flax or hemp to separate the fibres. **3.** Also called: **brake harrow.** a heavy harrow for breaking up clods. **4.** short for **shooting brake.** ~*vb.* **5.** to slow down or cause to slow down, by or as if by using a brake. **6.** (*tr.*) to crush or break up using a brake. [C18: < MDu. *braeke;* rel. to *breken* to BREAK] —ˈ**brakeless** *adj.*

brake[2] (breɪk) *n.* an area of dense undergrowth, shrubs, brushwood, etc.; thicket. [OE *bracu*]

brake[3] (breɪk) *n.* another name for **bracken** (sense 1).

brake[4] (breɪk) *vb. Arch., chiefly biblical.* a past tense of **break.**

brake horsepower *n.* the rate at which an engine does work, expressed in horsepower. It is measured by the resistance of an applied brake. Abbrev.: **bhp.**

brake light *n.* a red light at the rear of a motor vehicle that lights up when the brakes are applied.

brake lining *n.* a renewable strip of asbestos riveted to a brake shoe.

brake shoe *n.* the curved metal casting to which the brake lining is riveted in a drum brake.

brakesman (ˈbreɪksmən) *n., pl.* **-men.** **1.** a pithead winch operator. **2.** a brake operator on railway rolling stock.

brake van *n. Railways, Brit.* the coach or vehicle from which the guard applies the brakes; guard's van.

bramble (ˈbræmbᵊl) *n.* **1.** any of various prickly rosaceous plants or shrubs, esp. the blackberry. **2.** any of several similar and related shrubs, such as the dog rose. **3.** *Scot. & N English.* a blackberry. [OE *brǣmbel*] —ˈ**brambly** *adj.*

brambling (ˈbræmblɪŋ) *n.* a Eurasian finch with a speckled head and back and, in the male, a reddish-brown breast.

bran (bræn) *n.* **1.** husks of cereal grain separated from the flour. **2.** food prepared from these husks. [C13: < OF, prob. of Gaulish origin]

branch (brɑːntʃ) *n.* **1.** a secondary woody stem arising from the trunk or bough of a tree or the main stem of a shrub. **2.** an offshoot or secondary part: *a branch of a deer's antlers.* **3. a.** a subdivision or subsidiary section of something larger or more complex: *branches of learning; branch of the family.* **b.** (*as modifier*): *a branch office.* **4.** *U.S.* any small stream. ~*vb.* **5.** (*intr.*) (of a tree or other plant) to produce or possess branches. **6.** (*intr.;* usually foll. by *from*) (of stems, roots, etc.) to grow and diverge (from another part). **7.** to divide or be divided into subsidiaries or offshoots. **8.** (*intr.;* often foll. by *off*) to diverge from the main way, road, topic, etc. [C13: < OF *branche,* < LL *branca* paw, foot] —ˈ**branchˌlike** *adj.*

branchia (ˈbræŋkɪə) *n., pl.* **-chiae** (-kɪˌiː). a gill in aquatic animals. —ˈ**branchial** *or* ˈ**branchiate** *adj.*

branch out *vb.* (*intr., adv.;* often foll. by *into*) to expand or extend one's interests.

brand (brænd) *n.* **1.** a particular product or a characteristic that identifies a particular producer. **2.** a particular kind or variety. **3.** an identifying mark made, usually by burning, on the skin of animals or (formerly) slaves or criminals, esp. as a proof of ownership. **4.** an iron heated and used for branding animals, etc. **5.** a mark of disgrace or infamy; stigma. **6.** a burning or burnt piece of wood, as in a fire. **7.** *Arch. or poetic.* **a.** a flaming torch. **b.** a sword. **8.** a fungal disease of garden plants characterized by brown spots on the leaves. ~*vb.* (*tr.*) **9.** to label, burn, or mark with or as with a brand. **10.** to place indelibly in the memory: *the scene was branded in their minds.* **11.** to denounce; stigmatize: *they branded him a traitor.* [OE *brand-;* see BURN[1]] —ˈ**brander** *n.*

brandish (ˈbrændɪʃ) *vb.* **1.** (*tr.*) to wave or flourish (a weapon, etc.) in a triumphant, threatening, or ostentatious way. ~*n.* **2.** a threatening or defiant flourish. [C14: < OF *brandir,* of Gmc origin] —ˈ**brandisher** *n.*

brandling (ˈbrændlɪŋ) *n.* a small red earthworm, found in manure and used as bait by anglers. [C17: < BRAND (*n.*) + -LING[1]]

brand name *n.* the name used for a particular make of a commodity.

brand-new *adj.* absolutely new. [C16: < BRAND (n.) + NEW, likened to newly forged iron]

brandy (ˈbrændɪ) *n., pl.* **-dies. 1.** an alcoholic spirit distilled from grape wine. **2.** a distillation of wines made from other fruits: *plum brandy.* [C17: < earlier *brandewine,* < Du. *brandewijn,* burnt (or distilled) wine]

brandy butter *n.* another name for **hard sauce.**

brandy snap *n.* a crisp sweet biscuit, rolled into a cylinder and filled with whipped cream.

brant (brænt) *n., pl.* **brants** *or* **brant.** another name (esp. U.S. and Canad.) for **brent goose.**

bran tub *n. Brit.* a tub containing bran in which small wrapped gifts are hidden.

brash[1] (bræʃ) *adj.* **1.** tastelessly or offensively loud, showy, or bold. **2.** hasty; rash. **3.** impudent. [C19: ? infl. by RASH[1]] —ˈ**brashly** *adv.* —ˈ**brashness** *n.*

brash[2] (bræʃ) *n.* loose rubbish, such as broken rock, hedge clippings, etc. [C18: <?] —ˈ**brashy** *adj.*

brasier (ˈbreɪzɪə) *n.* a less common spelling of **brazier.**

brass (brɑːs) *n.* **1.** an alloy of copper and zinc containing more than 50 per cent of copper. Cf. **bronze** (sense 1). **2.** an object, ornament, or utensil made of brass. **3. a.** the large family of wind instruments including the trumpet, trombone, French horn, etc., made of brass. **b.** (*sometimes functioning as pl.*) instruments of this family forming a section in an orchestra. **4.** (*functioning as pl.*) *Inf.* important or high-ranking officials, esp. military officers: *the top brass.* See also **brass hat. 5.** *N English dialect.* money. **6.** *Brit.* an engraved brass memorial tablet or plaque in a church. **7.** *Inf.* bold self-confidence; cheek; nerve. **8.** (*modifier*) of, consisting of, or relating to brass or brass instruments: *a brass ornament; a brass band.* [OE *bræs*]

brassard (ˈbræsɑːd) *or* **brassart** (ˈbræsət) *n.* an identifying armband or badge. [C19: < F, < *bras* arm]

brass band *n.* See **band**[1] (sense 2).

brasserie (ˈbræsərɪ) *n.* **1.** a bar in which drinks and often food are served. **2.** a small and usually cheap restaurant. [C19: < F, < *brasser* to stir]

brass hat *n. Brit. inf.* a top-ranking official, esp. a military officer. [C20: < the gold decoration on the caps of officers of high rank]

brassica (ˈbræsɪkə) *n.* any plant of the genus *Brassica,* such as cabbage, rape, swede, turnip, and mustard. [C19: < L: cabbage]

brassie *or* **brassy** (ˈbræsɪ, ˈbrɑː-) *n., pl.* **brassies.** *Golf.* a former name for a club, a No. 2 wood, originally having a brass-plated sole.

brassiere (ˈbræsɪə, ˈbræz-) *n.* the full name for **bra.** [C20: < 17th-cent. F: bodice, < OF *braciere* a protector for the arm]

brass rubbing *n.* **1.** the taking of an impression of an engraved brass tablet or plaque by rubbing a paper placed over it with heelball, chalk, etc. **2.** an impression made in this way.

brass tacks *pl. n. Inf.* basic realities; hard facts (esp. in **get down to brass tacks).**

brassy (ˈbrɑːsɪ) *adj.* **brassier, brassiest. 1.** insolent; brazen. **2.** flashy; showy. **3.** (of sound) harsh and strident. **4.** like brass, esp. in colour. **5.** decorated with or made of brass. —ˈ**brassily** *adv.* —ˈ**brassiness** *n.*

brat (bræt) *n.* a child, esp. one who is dirty or unruly. [C16: ? < earlier *brat* rag, < OE *bratt* cloak]

brattice (ˈbrætɪs) *n.* **1.** a partition of wood or treated cloth used to control ventilation in a mine. **2.** *Medieval fortifications.* a fixed wooden tower or parapet. [C13: < OF *bretesche* wooden tower]

bravado (brəˈvɑːdəʊ) *n., pl.* **-does** *or* **-dos.** vaunted display of courage or self-confidence; swagger. [C16: < Sp. *bravada;* see BRAVE]

brave (breɪv) *adj.* **1. a.** having or displaying courage, resolution, or daring; not cowardly or timid. **b.** (*as collective n.;* preceded by *the*): *the brave.* **2.** fine; splendid: *a brave sight.* ~*n.* **3.** a warrior of a North American Indian tribe. ~*vb.* (*tr.*) **4.** to dare or defy: *to brave the odds.* **5.** to confront with resolution or courage: *to brave the storm.* [C15: < F, < It. *bravo* courageous, wild, ? ult. < L *barbarus* BARBAROUS] —ˈ**bravely** *adv.* —ˈ**braveness** *n.* —ˈ**bravery** *n.*

bravo *interj.* **1.** (brɑːˈvəʊ). well done! ~*n.* **2.** (brɑːˈvəʊ) *pl.* **-vos.** a cry of "bravo." **3.** (ˈbrɑːvəʊ) *pl.* **-voes** *or* **-vos.** a hired killer or assassin. [C18: < It.: splendid! see BRAVE]

bravura (brəˈvjʊərə, -ˈvʊərə) *n.* **1.** a display of boldness or daring. **2.** *Music.* brilliance of execution. [C18: < It.: spirit, courage; see BRAVE]

braw (brɔː, brɑː) *adj. Chiefly Scot.* fine or excellent, esp. in appearance or dress. [C16: Scot. var. of BRAVE]

brawl (brɔːl) *n.* **1.** a loud disagreement or fight. **2.** *U.S. & Canad. sl.* an uproarious party. ~*vb.* (*intr.*) **3.** to quarrel or fight noisily; squabble. **4.** (esp. of water) to flow noisily. [C14: prob. rel. to Du. *brallen* to boast, behave aggressively] —ˈ**brawler** *n.*

brawn (brɔːn) *n.* **1.** strong well-developed muscles. **2.** physical strength, esp. as opposed to intelligence. **3.** *Brit.* a seasoned jellied loaf made from the head of a pig or calf. [C14: < OF *braon* slice of meat, of Gmc origin]

brawny (ˈbrɔːnɪ) *adj.* **brawnier, brawniest.** muscular and strong. —ˈ**brawniness** *n.*

bray (breɪ) *vb.* **1.** (*intr.*) (of a donkey) to utter its characteristic loud harsh sound; heehaw. **2.** (*intr.*) to make a similar sound, as in laughing. **3.** (*tr.*) to utter with a loud harsh sound. ~*n.* **4.** the loud harsh sound uttered by a donkey. **5.** a similar loud cry or uproar. [C13: < OF *braire*, prob. of Celtic origin]

braze[1] (breɪz) *vb.* (*tr.*) **1.** to decorate with or make of brass. **2.** to make like brass, as in hardness. [OE *bræsen*, < *bræs* BRASS]

braze[2] (breɪz) *vb.* (*tr.*) to make a joint between (two metal surfaces) by fusing a layer of brass or high-melting solder between them. [C16: < OF: to burn, of Gmc origin; see BRAISE] —ˈ**brazer** *n.*

brazen (ˈbreɪzᵊn) *adj.* **1.** shameless and bold. **2.** made of or resembling brass. **3.** having a ringing metallic sound. ~*vb.* (*tr.*) **4.** (usually foll. by *out* or *through*) to face and overcome boldly or shamelessly. [OE *bræsen*, < *bræs* BRASS] —ˈ**brazenly** *adv.* —ˈ**brazenness** *n.*

brazier[1] *or* **brasier** (ˈbreɪzɪə) *n.* a person engaged in brass-working or brass-founding. [C14: < OE *bræsian* to work in brass + -ER[1]] —ˈ**braziery** *n.*

brazier[2] *or* **brasier** (ˈbreɪzɪə) *n.* a portable metal receptacle for burning charcoal or coal. [C17: < F *brasier*, < *braise* live coals; see BRAISE]

brazil (brəˈzɪl) *n.* **1.** Also called: **brazil wood.** the red wood obtained from various tropical trees of America: used for cabinetwork. **2.** the red or purple dye extracted from these woods. **3.** short for **brazil nut.** [C14: < OSp., < *brasa* glowing coals, of Gmc origin; referring to the redness of the wood]

Brazilian (brəˈzɪlɪən) *adj.* **1.** of or relating to Brazil, a republic in South America. ~*n.* **2.** a native or inhabitant of Brazil.

brazil nut *n.* **1.** a tropical South American tree producing large globular capsules, each containing several closely packed triangular nuts. **2.** the nut, having an edible oily kernel and a woody shell. ~Often shortened to **brazil.**

BRCS *abbrev. for* British Red Cross Society.

breach (briːtʃ) *n.* **1.** a crack, break, or rupture. **2.** a breaking, infringement, or violation of a promise, obligation, etc. **3.** any severance or separation. ~*vb.* (*tr.*) **4.** to break through or make an opening, hole, or incursion in. **5.** to break a promise, law, etc. [OE *bræc*]

breach of promise *n. Law.* (formerly) failure to carry out one's promise to marry.

breach of the peace *n. Law.* an offence against public order causing an unnecessary disturbance of the peace.

bread (brɛd) *n.* **1.** a food made from a dough of flour or meal mixed with water or milk, usually raised with yeast or baking powder and then baked. **2.** necessary food; nourishment. **3.** *Sl.* money. **4. cast one's bread upon the waters.** to do good without expectation of advantage or return. **5. know which side one's bread is buttered.** to know what to do in order to keep one's advantages. **6. take the bread out of (someone's) mouth.** to deprive of a livelihood. ~*vb.* **7.** (*tr.*) to cover with bread-crumbs before cooking. [OE *brēad*]

bread and butter *Inf.* ~*n.* **1.** a means of support or subsistence; livelihood. ~*modifier.* **bread-and-butter 2. a.** providing a basic means of subsistence. **b.** expressing gratitude, as for hospitality (esp. in **bread-and-butter letter**).

breadbasket (ˈbrɛdˌbɑːskɪt) *n.* **1.** a basket for carrying bread or rolls. **2.** *Sl.* stomach.

breadboard (ˈbrɛdˌbɔːd) *n.* **1.** a wooden board on which bread is sliced. **2.** an experimental arrangement of electronic circuits.

breadfruit (ˈbrɛdˌfruːt) *n., pl.* **-fruits** *or* **-fruit. 1.** a tree of the Pacific Islands, having edible round, usually seedless, fruit. **2.** the fruit, which is eaten baked or roasted and has a texture like bread.

breadline (ˈbrɛdˌlaɪn) *n.* **1.** a queue of people waiting for free food. **2. on the breadline.** impoverished; living at subsistence level.

breadth (brɛdθ, brɛtθ) *n.* **1.** the linear extent or measurement of something from side to side; width. **2.** a piece of fabric, etc., having a standard or definite width. **3.** distance, extent, size, or dimension. **4.** openness and lack of restriction, esp. of viewpoint or interest; liberality. [C16: < obs. *brede* (< OE *brǣdu*, < *brād* BROAD) + -TH[1]]

breadthways (ˈbrɛdθˌweɪz, ˈbrɛtθ-) *or esp. U.S.* **breadthwise** (ˈbrɛdθˌwaɪz, ˈbrɛtθ-) *adv.* from side to side.

breadwinner (ˈbrɛdˌwɪnə) *n.* a person supporting a family with his or her earnings.

break (breɪk) *vb.* **breaking, broke, broken. 1.** to separate or become separated into two or more pieces. **2.** to damage or become damaged so as to be inoperative: *my radio is broken.* **3.** to crack or become cracked without separating. **4.** to burst or cut the surface of (skin, etc.). **5.** to discontinue or become discontinued: *to break a journey.* **6.** to disperse or become dispersed: *the clouds broke.* **7.** (*tr.*) to fail to observe (an agreement, promise, law, etc.): *to break one's word.* **8.** (foll. by *with*) to discontinue an association (with). **9.** to disclose or be disclosed: *he broke the news gently.* **10.** (*tr.*) to fracture (a bone) in (a limb, etc.). **11.** (*tr.*) to divide (something complete or perfect): *to break a set of books.* **12.** to bring or come to an end: *the summer weather broke at last.* **13.** (*tr.*) to bring to an end as by force: *to break a strike.* **14.** (when *intr.*, often foll. by *out*) to escape (from): *he broke out of jail.* **15.** to weaken or overwhelm or be weakened or overwhelmed, as in spirit. **16.** (*tr.*) to cut through or penetrate: *a cry broke the silence.* **17.** (*tr.*) to improve on or surpass: *to break a record.* **18.** (*tr.*; often foll. by *in*) to accustom (a horse) to the bridle and saddle, to being ridden, etc. **19.** (*tr.*; often foll. by *of*) to cause (a person) to give up (a habit): *this cure will break you of smoking.* **20.** (*tr.*) to weaken the impact or force of: *this net will break his fall.* **21.** (*tr.*) to decipher: *to break a code.* **22.** (*tr.*) to lose the order of: *to break ranks.* **23.** (*tr.*) to reduce to poverty or the state of bankruptcy. **24.** (when *intr.*, foll. by *into*) to obtain, give, or receive smaller units in exchange for; change: *to break a pound note.* **25.** (*tr.*) *Chiefly mil.* to demote to a lower rank. **26.** (*intr.*; often foll. by *from* or *out of*) to proceed suddenly. **27.** (*intr.*) to come into being: *light broke over the mountains.* **28.** (*intr.*; foll. by *into* or *out into*) **a.** to burst into song, laughter, etc. **b.** to change to a faster pace. **29.** (*tr.*) to open with explosives: *to break a safe.* **30.** (*intr.*) (of waves) **a.** (often foll. by *against*) to strike violently. **b.** to collapse into foam or surf. **31.** (*intr.*) (of prices, esp. stock exchange quotations) to fall sharply. **32.** (*intr.*) to make a sudden effort, as in running, horse racing, etc. **33.** (*intr.*) *Cricket.* (of a ball) to change direction on bouncing. **34.** (*intr.*) *Billiards.* to scatter the balls at the start of a game. **35.** (*intr.*) *Boxing, wrestling.* (of two fighters) to separate from a clinch. **36.** (*intr.*) (of the male voice) to undergo a change in register, quality, and range at puberty. **37.** (*tr.*) to open the breech of (certain firearms) by snapping the barrel away from the butt on its hinge. **38.** (*tr.*) to interrupt the flow of current in (an electrical circuit). **39.** *Inf, chiefly U.S.* to become successful. **40. break camp.** to pack up and leave a camp. **41. break the bank.** to ruin financially or deplete the resources of a bank (as in gambling). **42. break service.** *Tennis.* to win a game in which an opponent is serving. ~*n.* **43.** the act or result of breaking; fracture. **44.** a crack formed as the result of breaking. **45.** a brief respite. **46.** a sudden rush, esp. to escape: *to make a break for freedom.* **47.** a breach in a relationship. **48.** any sudden interruption in a continuous action. **49.** *Brit.* a short period between classes at school. **50.** *Inf.* a fortunate opportunity, esp. to prove oneself. **51.** *Inf.* a piece of good or bad luck. **52.** (esp. in a stock exchange) a sudden and substantial decline in prices. **53.** *Billiards, snooker.* a series of successful shots during one turn. **54.** *Billiards, snooker.* the opening shot that scatters the placed balls. **55.** Also called: **service break, break of serve.** *Tennis.* the act or an instance of breaking an opponent's service. **56. a.** *Jazz.* a short usually improvised solo passage. **b.** an instrumental passage in a pop song. **57.** a discontinuity in an electrical circuit. **58.** access to a radio channel by a citizens' band radio operator. **59. break of day.** the dawn. *~interj.* **60.** *Boxing, wrestling.* a command by a referee for two opponents to separate. ~See also **breakaway, break down,** etc. [OE *brecan*]

breakable (ˈbreɪkəbᵊl) *adj.* **1.** capable of being broken. *~n.* **2.** (*usually pl.*) a fragile easily broken article.

breakage (ˈbreɪkɪdʒ) *n.* **1.** the act or result of breaking. **2.** the quantity or amount broken. **3.** compensation or allowance for goods damaged while in use, transit, etc.

breakaway (ˈbreɪkəˌweɪ) *n.* **1. a.** loss or withdrawal of a group of members from an association, club, etc. **b.** (*as modifier*): *a breakaway faction.* **2.** *Austral.* a stampede of animals, esp. at the smell of water. *~vb.* **break away.** (*intr., adv.*) **3.** (often foll. by *from*) to leave hastily or escape. **4.** to withdraw or secede.

break dance *n.* **1.** an acrobatic dance style of the 1980s. *~vb.* **break-dance.** (*intr.*) **2.** to perform a break dance. —**break dancer** *n.* —**break dancing** *n.*

break down *vb.* (*adv.*) **1.** (*intr.*) to cease to function; become ineffective. **2.** to yield or cause to yield, esp. to strong emotion or tears. **3.** (*tr.*) to crush or destroy. **4.** (*intr.*) to have a nervous breakdown. **5.** to analyse or be subjected to analysis. **6. break it down.** *Austral. & N.Z. inf.* **a.** stop it. **b.** don't expect me to believe that; come off it. *~n.* **breakdown. 7.** an act or instance of breaking down; collapse. **8.** short for **nervous breakdown. 9.** an analysis or classification of something into its component parts: *he prepared a breakdown of the report.*

breaker (ˈbreɪkə) *n.* **1.** a person or thing that breaks something, such as a person or firm that breaks up old cars, etc. **2.** a large wave with a white crest on the open sea or one that breaks into foam on the shore. **3.** a citizens' band radio operator.

break even *vb.* **1.** (*intr., adv.*) to attain a level of activity, as in commerce, or a point of operation, as in gambling, at which there is neither profit nor loss. *~n.* **breakeven. 2.** *Accounting.* the level of commercial activity at which the total cost and total revenue of a business enterprise are equal.

breakfast (ˈbrɛkfəst) *n.* **1.** the first meal of the day. **2.** the food at this meal. *~vb.* **3.** to eat or supply with breakfast. [C15: < BREAK + FAST[2]] —ˈ**breakfaster** *n.*

break in *vb.* (*adv.*) **1.** (sometimes foll. by *on*) to interrupt. **2.** (*intr.*) to enter a house, etc., illegally, esp. by force. **3.** (*tr.*) to accustom (a person or animal) to normal duties or practice. **4.** (*tr.*) to use or wear (shoes, new equipment, etc.) until comfortable or running smoothly. **5.** *Austral.* to bring new land under cultivation. *~n.* **break-in. 6.** the illegal entering of a building, esp. by thieves.

breaking and entering *n.* (formerly) the gaining of unauthorized access to a building with intent to commit a crime.

breaking point *n.* the point at which something or someone gives way under strain.

breakneck (ˈbreɪkˌnɛk) *adj.* (*prenominal*) (of speed, pace, etc.) excessive and dangerous.

break off *vb.* **1.** to sever or detach or be severed or detached. **2.** (*adv.*) to end (a relationship, association, etc.) or (of a relationship, etc.) to be ended. **3.** (*intr., adv.*) to stop abruptly: *he broke off in the middle of his speech.*

break out *vb.* (*intr., adv.*) **1.** to begin or arise suddenly. **2.** to make an escape, esp. from prison or confinement. **3.** (foll. by *in*) (of the skin) to erupt (in a rash, pimples, etc.). *~n.* **break-out. 4.** an escape, esp. from prison or confinement.

break through *vb.* **1.** (*intr.*) to penetrate. **2.** (*intr., adv.*) to achieve success, make a discovery, etc., esp. after lengthy efforts. *~n.* **breakthrough. 3.** a significant development or discovery, esp. in science. **4.** the penetration of an enemy's defensive position.

break up *vb.* (*adv.*) **1.** to separate or cause to separate. **2.** to put an end to (a relationship) or (of a relationship) to come to an end. **3.** to dissolve or cause to dissolve; disrupt or be disrupted: *the meeting broke up at noon.* **4.** (*intr.*) *Brit.* (of a school) to close for the holidays. **5.** *Inf.* to lose or cause to lose control of the emotions. **6.** *Sl.* to be or cause to be overcome with laughter. *~n.* **break-up. 7.** a separation or disintegration. **8. a.** in the Canadian north, the breaking up of the ice on a body of water that marks the beginning of spring. **b.** this season.

breakwater (ˈbreɪkˌwɔːtə) *n.* **1.** Also called: **mole.** a massive wall built out into the sea to protect a shore or harbour from the force of waves. **2.** another name for **groyne.**

bream[1] (briːm; *Austral.* brɪm) *or Austral.* **brim** (brɪm) *n., pl.* **bream** *or* **brim. 1.** any of several Eurasian freshwater cyprinid fishes having a deep compressed body covered with silvery scales. **2.** short for **sea bream. 3.** *Austral.* any of various marine fishes. [C14: < OF *bresme,* of Gmc origin]

bream[2] (briːm) *vb. Naut.* (formerly) to clean debris from (the bottom of a vessel) by heating to soften the pitch. [C15: prob. < MDu. *bremme* broom; < burning broom as a source of heat]

breast (brɛst) *n.* **1.** the front part of the body from the neck to the abdomen; chest. **2.** either of the two soft fleshy milk-secreting glands on the chest in sexually mature human females. **3.** a similar organ in certain other mammals. **4.** anything that resembles a breast in shape or position: *the breast of the hill.* **5.** a source of nourishment. **6.** the source of human emotions. **7.** the part of a garment that covers the breast. **8.** a projection from the side of a wall, esp. that formed by a chimney. **9. beat one's breast.** to display guilt and remorse publicly or ostentatiously. **10. make a clean breast of.** to make a confession of. *~vb.* (*tr.*) **11.** to confront boldly; face: *breast the storm.* **12.** to oppose with the breast or meet at breast level: *breasting the waves.* **13.** to reach the summit of: *breasting the mountain top.* [OE *brēost*]

breastbone (ˈbrɛstˌbəʊn) *n.* the nontechnical name for **sternum.**

breast-feed *vb.* **-feeding, -fed.** to feed (a baby) with milk from the breast; suckle.

breastpin (ˈbrɛstˌpɪn) *n.* a brooch worn on the breast, esp. to close a garment.

breastplate (ˈbrɛstˌpleɪt) *n.* a piece of armour covering the chest.

breaststroke (ˈbrɛstˌstrəʊk) *n.* a swimming stroke in which the arms are extended in front of the head and swept back on either side while the legs are drawn up beneath the body and thrust back together.

breastwork (ˈbrɛstˌwɜːk) *n. Fortifications.* a temporary defensive work, usually breast-high.

breath (brɛθ) *n.* **1.** the intake and expulsion of air during respiration. **2.** the air inhaled or exhaled during respiration. **3.** a single respiration or inhalation of air, etc. **4.** the vapour, heat, or odour of exhaled air. **5.** a slight gust of air. **6.** a short pause or rest. **7.** a brief time. **8.** a suggestion or slight evidence; suspicion: *a breath of scandal.* **9.** a whisper or soft sound. **10.** life, energy, or vitality: *the breath of new industry.* **11.** *Phonetics.* the exhalation of air without vibration of the vocal cords, as in pronouncing fricatives such as (f) or (h) or stops such as (p) or (k). **12. catch one's breath. a.** to rest until breathing is normal, esp. after exertion. **b.** to stop breathing momentarily from excitement, fear, etc. **13. in the same breath.** done or said at the same time. **14. out of breath.** gasping for air after exertion. **15. save one's breath.** to refrain from useless talk. **16. take one's breath away.** to overwhelm with surprise, etc. **17. under** *or* **below one's breath.** in a quiet voice or whisper. [OE *brǣth*]

Breathalyser *or* **-lyzer** (ˈbrɛθəˌlaɪzə) *n. Brit., trademark.* a device for estimating the amount of alcohol in the breath: used in testing people suspected of driving under the influence of alcohol. [C20: BREATH + (AN)ALYSER] —ˈ**breathaˌlyse** *or* **-ˌlyze** *vb.* (*tr.*)

breathe (briːð) *vb.* **1.** to take in oxygen and give out carbon dioxide; respire. **2.** (*intr.*) to exist; be alive. **3.** (*intr.*) to rest to regain breath, composure, etc. **4.** (*intr.*) (esp. of air) to blow lightly. **5.** (*intr.*) *Machinery.* to take in air, esp. for combustion. **6.** (*tr.*) *Phonetics.* to articulate (a speech sound) without vibration of the vocal cords. **7.** to exhale or emit: *the dragon breathed fire.* **8.** (*tr.*) to impart; instil: *to breathe confidence into the actors.* **9.** (*tr.*) to speak softly; whisper. **10.** (*tr.*) to permit to rest: *to breathe a horse.* **11. breathe again, freely,** *or* **easily.** to feel relief. **12. breathe one's last.** to die or be finished or defeated. [C13: < BREATH]

breather (ˈbriːðə) *n.* **1.** *Inf.* a short pause for rest. **2.** a person who breathes in a specified way: *a deep breather.* **3.** a vent in a container to equalize internal and external pressure.

breathing (ˈbriːðɪŋ) *n.* **1.** the passage of air into and out of the lungs to supply the body with oxygen. **2.** a single breath: *a breathing between words.* **3.** *Phonetics.* **a.** expulsion of breath (**rough breathing**) or absence of such expulsion (**smooth breathing**) preceding the pronunciation of an initial vowel or rho in ancient Greek. **b.** either of two symbols indicating this.

breathless (ˈbrɛθlɪs) *adj.* **1.** out of breath; gasping, etc. **2.** holding one's breath or having it taken away by excitement, etc. **3.** (esp. of the atmosphere) motionless and stifling. **4.** *Rare.* lifeless; dead. —ˈ**breathlessly** *adv.* —ˈ**breathlessness** *n.*

breathtaking (ˈbrɛθˌteɪkɪŋ) *adj.* causing awe or excitement. —ˈ**breathˌtakingly** *adv.*

breath test *n. Brit.* a chemical test of a driver's breath to determine the amount of alcohol he has consumed.

breathy (ˈbrɛθɪ) *adj.* **breathier, breathiest. 1.** (of the speaking voice) accompanied by an audible emission of breath. **2.** (of the singing voice) lacking resonance. —ˈ**breathily** *adv.* —ˈ**breathiness** *n.*

breccia (ˈbrɛtʃɪə) *n.* a rock consisting of angular fragments embedded in a finer matrix. [C18: < It.] —ˈ**brecciˌated** *adj.*

bred (brɛd) *vb.* the past tense and past participle of **breed.**

breech *n.* (briːtʃ). **1.** the buttocks; rump. **2.** the lower part or bottom of something. **3.** the part of a firearm behind the barrel or bore. ~*vb.* (briːtʃ, brɪtʃ). (*tr.*) **4.** to fit (a gun) with a breech. **5.** *Arch.* to clothe in breeches or any other clothing. [OE *brēc*, pl. of *brōc* leg covering]

breechblock (ˈbriːtʃˌblɒk) *n.* a metal block in breech-loading firearms that is withdrawn to insert the cartridge and replaced before firing.

breech delivery *n.* birth of a baby with the feet or buttocks appearing first.

breeches (ˈbrɪtʃɪz, ˈbriː-) *pl. n.* **1.** trousers extending to the knee or just below, worn for riding, etc. **2.** *Inf. or dialect.* any trousers or pants, esp. extending to the knee.

breeches buoy *n.* a ring-shaped life buoy with a support in the form of a pair of short breeches, in which a person is suspended for safe transfer from a ship.

breeching (ˈbrɪtʃɪŋ, ˈbriː-) *n.* the strap of a harness that passes behind a horse's haunches.

breechloader (ˈbriːtʃˌləʊdə) *n.* a firearm that is loaded at the breech. —ˈ**breech-ˌloading** *adj.*

breed (briːd) *vb.* **breeding, bred. 1.** to bear (offspring). **2.** (*tr.*) to bring up; raise. **3.** to produce or cause to produce by mating; propagate. **4.** to produce new or improved strains of (domestic animals and plants). **5.** to produce or be produced; generate: *to breed trouble.* ~*n.* **6.** a group of organisms within a species, esp. domestic animals, having clearly defined characteristics. **7.** a lineage or race. **8.** a kind, sort, or group. [OE *brēdan*, of Gmc origin; rel. to BROOD]

breeder (ˈbriːdə) *n.* **1.** a person who breeds plants or animals. **2.** something that reproduces. **3.** an animal kept for breeding purposes. **4.** a source or cause: *a breeder of discontent.* **5.** short for **breeder reactor.**

breeder reactor *n.* a type of nuclear reactor that produces more fissionable material than it consumes.

breeding (ˈbriːdɪŋ) *n.* **1.** the process of bearing offspring; reproduction. **2.** the process of producing plants or animals by hybridization, inbreeding, or other methods of reproduction. **3.** the result of good training, esp. the knowledge of correct social behaviour; refinement.

breeze[1] (briːz) *n.* **1.** a gentle or light wind. **2.** *Meteorol.* a wind of force two to six (4–31 mph) inclusive on the Beaufort scale. **3.** *U.S. & Canad. inf.* an easy task or state of ease. **4.** *Inf., chiefly Brit.* a disturbance, esp. a lively quarrel. ~*vb.* (*intr.*) **5.** to move quickly or casually: *he breezed into the room.* [C16: prob. < OSp. *briza* northeast wind]

breeze[2] (briːz) *n.* ashes of coal, coke, or charcoal used to make breeze blocks. [C18: < F *braise* live coals; see BRAISE]

breeze block *n.* a light building brick made from the ashes of coal, coke, etc., bonded together by cement.

breezeway (ˈbriːzˌweɪ) *n.* a roofed passageway connecting two buildings.

breezy (ˈbriːzɪ) *adj.* **breezier, breeziest. 1.** fresh; windy. **2.** casual or carefree; lively; light-hearted. —ˈ**breezily** *adv.* —ˈ**breeziness** *n.*

bremsstrahlung (ˈbrɛmzˌʃtrɑːlʊŋ) *n.* the x-radiation produced when an electrically charged particle, such as an electron, is slowed down by the electric field of an atomic nucleus. [G: braking radiation]

Bren gun (brɛn) *n.* an air-cooled gas-operated light machine gun: used by the British in World War II. [C20: after *Br*(*no*), Czechoslovakia, where it was first made and *En*(*field*), England, where manufacture was continued]

brent goose (brɛnt) *n.* a small goose that has a dark grey plumage and short neck and occurs in most northern coastal regions. Also called: **brent,** (esp. U.S. and Canad.) **brant.** [C16: ? of Scand. origin]

brethren (ˈbrɛðrɪn) *pl. n. Arch. except when referring to fellow members of a religion, society, etc.* a plural of **brother.**

Breton (ˈbrɛtᵊn) *adj.* **1.** of, relating to, or characteristic of Brittany, its people, or their language. ~*n.* **2.** a native or inhabitant of Brittany. **3.** the Celtic language of Brittany.

breve (briːv) *n.* **1.** an accent, ˘, placed over a vowel to indicate that it is short or is pronounced in a specified way. **2.** *Music.* a note, now rarely used, equivalent to two semibreves. **3.** *R.C. Church.* a less common word for **brief** (papal letter). [C13: < Med. L, < L *brevis* short]

brevet (ˈbrɛvɪt) *n.* **1.** a document entitling a commissioned officer to hold temporarily a higher military rank without the appropriate pay and allowances. ~*vb.* **-vetting, -vetted** *or* **-veting, -veted. 2.** (*tr.*) to promote by brevet. [C14: < OF, < *brief* letter; see BRIEF] —ˈ**brevetcy** *n.*

breviary (ˈbriːvjərɪ) *n., pl.* **-ries.** *R.C. Church.* a book of psalms, hymns, prayers, etc., to be recited daily by clerics and certain members of religious orders as part of the divine office. [C16: < L *breviārium* an abridged version, < *brevis* short]

brevity (ˈbrɛvɪtɪ) *n., pl.* **-ties. 1.** conciseness of expression; lack of verbosity. **2.** a short duration; brief time. [C16: < L, < *brevis* BRIEF]

brew (bruː) *vb.* **1.** to make (beer, ale, etc.) from malt and other ingredients by steeping, boiling, and fermentation. **2.** to prepare (a drink, such as tea) by boiling or infusing. **3.** (*tr.*) to devise or plan: *to brew a plot.* **4.** (*intr.*) to be in the process of being brewed. **5.** (*intr.*) to be impending or forming: *there's a storm brewing.* ~*n.* **6.** a beverage produced by brewing, esp. tea or beer. **7.** an instance or time of brewing: *last year's brew.* [OE *brēowan*] —ˈ**brewer** *n.*

brewery (ˈbrʊərɪ) *n., pl.* **-eries.** a place where beer, ale, etc., is brewed.

brewing (ˈbruːɪŋ) *n.* a quantity of a beverage brewed at one time.

briar[1] *or* **brier** (ˈbraɪə) *n.* **1.** Also called: **tree heath.** a shrub of S Europe, having a hard woody root (briarroot). **2.** a tobacco pipe made from the root of this plant. [C19: < F *bruyère* heath] —ˈ**briary** *or* ˈ**briery** *adj.*

briar[2] (ˈbraɪə) *n.* a variant spelling of **brier**[1].

briarroot *or* **brierroot** (ˈbraɪəˌruːt) *n.* the hard woody root of the briar, used for making tobacco pipes. Also called: **briarwood, brierwood.**

bribe (braɪb) *vb.* **1.** to promise, offer, or give something, often illegally, to (a person) to procure services or gain influence. ~*n.* **2.** a reward, such as money or favour, given or offered for this purpose. **3.** any persuasion or lure. [C14: < OF *briber* to beg, <?] —ˈ**bribery** *n.*

bric-a-brac (ˈbrɪkəˌbræk) *n.* miscellaneous small objects, esp. furniture and curios, kept because they are ornamental or rare. [C19: < F]

brick (brɪk) *n.* **1. a.** a rectangular block of clay mixed with sand and fired in a kiln or baked by the sun, used in building construction. **b.** (*as modifier*): *a brick house.* **2.** the material used to make such blocks. **3.** any rectangular block: *a brick of ice.* **4.** bricks collectively. **5.** *Inf.* a reliable, trustworthy, or helpful person. **6.** *Brit.* a child's building block. **7. drop a brick.** *Brit. inf.* to make a tactless or indiscreet remark. **8. like a ton of bricks.** *Inf.* with great force; severely. ~*vb.* **9.** (*tr.;* usually foll. by *in, up,* or *over*) to construct, line, pave, fill, or wall up with bricks: *to brick up a window.* [C15: < OF *brique,* < MDu. *bricke*] —ˈ**bricky** *adj.*

brickbat (ˈbrɪkˌbæt) *n.* **1.** a piece of brick or similar material, esp. one used as a weapon. **2.** blunt criticism.

brickie (ˈbrɪkɪ) *n. Inf.* a bricklayer.

bricklayer (ˈbrɪkˌleɪə) *n.* a person trained or skilled in laying bricks. —ˈ**brickˌlaying** *n.*

brick red *n., adj.* (of) a reddish-brown colour.

brickwork (ˈbrɪkˌwɜːk) *n.* **1.** a structure built of bricks. **2.** construction using bricks.

brickyard (ˈbrɪkˌjɑːd) *n.* a place in which bricks are made, stored, or sold.

bridal (ˈbraɪdᵊl) *adj.* of or relating to a bride or a wedding; nuptial. [OE *brȳdealu,* lit.: "bride ale", that is, wedding feast]

bride (braɪd) *n.* a woman who has just been or is about to be married. [OE *brȳd*]

bridegroom (ˈbraɪdˌgruːm, -ˌgrʊm) *n.* a man who has just been or is about to be married. [C14: changed (through infl. of GROOM) < OE *brȳdguma,* < *brȳd* BRIDE + *guma* man]

bride price *or* **wealth** *n.* (in some societies) money, property, or services given by a bridegroom to the kinsmen of his bride.

bridesmaid (ˈbraɪdzˌmeɪd) *n.* a girl or young unmarried woman who attends a bride at her wedding.

bridge[1] (brɪdʒ) *n.* **1.** a structure that spans and provides a passage over a road, railway, river, or some other obstacle. **2.** something that resembles this in shape or function. **3.** the hard ridge at the upper part of the nose, formed by the underlying nasal bones. **4.** the part of a pair of glasses that rests on the nose. **5.** Also called: **bridgework.** a dental plate containing one or more artificial teeth that is secured to the surrounding natural teeth. **6.** a platform from which a ship is piloted and navigated. **7.** a piece of wood, usually fixed, supporting the strings of a violin, guitar, etc., and transmitting their vibrations to the sounding board. **8.** Also called: **bridge passage.** a passage in a musical, literary, or dramatic work linking two or more important sections. **9.** Also called: **bridge circuit.** *Electronics.* any of several networks across which a device is connected for measuring resistance, capacitance, etc. **10.** *Billiards, snooker.* a support for a cue. **11. cross a bridge when (one) comes to it.** to deal with a problem only when it arises. ~*vb.* (*tr.*) **12.** to build or provide a bridge over something; span: *to bridge a river.* **13.** to connect or reduce the distance between: *let us bridge our differences.* [OE *brycg*] —ˈ**bridgeable** *adj.*

bridge[2] (brɪdʒ) *n.* a card game for four players, based on whist, in which one hand (the dummy) is exposed and the trump suit decided by bidding between the players. See also **contract bridge, auction bridge.** [C19: <?]

bridgehead (ˈbrɪdʒˌhɛd) *n.* **1.** *Mil.* an area of ground secured or to be taken on the enemy's side of an obstacle. **2.** *Mil.* a fortified or defensive position at the end of a bridge nearest to the enemy. **3.** an advantagous position gained for future expansion.

bridge roll *n.* a soft bread roll in a long thin shape. [C20: < BRIDGE[2] or ? BRIDGE[1]]

bridgework (ˈbrɪdʒˌwɜːk) *n.* a partial denture attached to the surrounding teeth.

bridging loan *n.* a loan made to cover the period between two transactions, such as the buying of another house before the sale of the first is completed.

bridle (ˈbraɪdᵊl) *n.* **1.** a headgear for a horse, etc., consisting of a series of buckled straps and a metal mouthpiece (bit) by which the animal is controlled through the reins. **2.** something that curbs or restrains; check. **3.** a Y-shaped cable, rope, or chain, used for holding, towing, etc. ~*vb.* **4.** (*tr.*) to put a bridle on (a horse, mule, etc.). **5.** (*tr.*) to restrain; curb: *he bridled his rage.* **6.** (*intr.;* often foll. by *at*) to show anger, scorn, or indignation. [OE *brigdels*]

bridle path *n.* a path suitable for riding or leading horses.

Brie (briː) *n.* a soft creamy white cheese. [C19: F, after *Brie,* region in N France where it originated]

brief (briːf) *adj.* **1.** short in duration. **2.** short in length or extent; scanty: *a brief bikini.* **3.** abrupt in manner; brusque: *the professor was brief with me.* **4.** terse or concise. ~*n.* **5.** a condensed statement or written synopsis; abstract. **6.** *Law.* a document containing all the facts and points of law of a case by which a solicitor instructs a barrister to represent a client. **7.** *R.C. Church.* a letter issuing from the Roman court written in modern characters, as contrasted with a papal bull; papal brief. **8.** Also called: **briefing.** instructions. **9. hold a brief for.** to argue for; champion. **10. in brief.** in short; to sum up. ~*vb.* (*tr.*) **11.** to prepare or instruct by giving a summary of relevant facts. **12.** to make a summary or synopsis of. **13.** *English law.* **a.** to instruct (a barrister) by brief. **b.** to retain (a barrister) as counsel. [C14: < OF *bref,* < L *brevis*] —ˈ**briefly** *adv.* —ˈ**briefness** *n.*

briefcase (ˈbriːfˌkeɪs) *n.* a flat portable case, often of leather, for carrying papers, books, etc.

briefing (ˈbriːfɪŋ) *n.* **1.** a meeting at which information and instructions are given. **2.** the facts presented at such a meeting.

briefless (ˈbriːflɪs) *adj.* (said of a barrister) without clients.

briefs (briːfs) *pl. n.* men's underpants or women's pants without legs.

brier[1] *or* **briar** (ˈbraɪə) *n.* any of various thorny shrubs or other plants, such as the sweetbrier. [OE *brēr, brǣr,* <?] —ˈ**briery** *or* ˈ**briary** *adj.*

brier[2] (ˈbraɪə) *n.* a variant spelling of **briar**[1].

brierroot (ˈbraɪəˌruːt) *n.* a variant spelling of **briarroot.** Also called: **brierwood.**

brig[1] (brɪg) *n.* **1.** *Naut.* a two-masted square-rigger. **2.** *Chiefly U.S.* a prison, esp. in a navy ship. [C18: shortened < BRIGANTINE]

brig[2] (brɪg) *n.* a Scot. and N English word for a **bridge**[1].

Brig. *abbrev. for* Brigadier.

brigade (brɪˈgeɪd) *n.* **1.** a military formation smaller than a division and usually commanded by a brigadier. **2.** a group of people organized for a certain task: *a rescue brigade.* ~*vb.* (*tr.*) **3.** to organize into a brigade. [C17: < OF, < OIt., < *brigare* to fight; see BRIGAND]

brigadier (ˌbrɪgəˈdɪə) *n.* **1.** an officer of the British Army or Royal Marines junior to a major general but senior to a colonel, usually commanding a brigade. **2.** an equivalent rank in other armed forces. [C17: < F, < BRIGADE]

brigalow (ˈbrɪgələʊ) *n. Austral.* **a.** any of various acacia trees, forming dense scrub. **b.** (*as modifier*): *brigalow country.* [C19: < Abor.]

brigand (ˈbrɪgənd) *n.* a bandit, esp. a member of a gang operating in mountainous areas. [C14: < OF, < OIt. *brigante* fighter, < *briga* strife] —ˈ**brigandage** *or* ˈ**brigandry** *n.*

brigantine (ˈbrɪgənˌtiːn, -ˌtaɪn) *n.* a two-masted sailing ship, rigged square on the foremast and fore-and-aft on the mainmast. [C16: < OIt. *brigantino* pirate ship, < *brigante* BRIGAND]

bright (braɪt) *adj.* **1.** emitting or reflecting much light; shining. **2.** (of colours) intense or vivid. **3.** full of promise: *a bright future.* **4.** full of animation; cheerful: *a bright face.* **5.** *Inf.* quick-witted or clever: *a bright child.* **6.** magnificent; glorious. **7.** polished; glistening. **8.** (of a liquid) translucent and clear. **9. bright and early.** very early in the morning. ~*adv.* **10.** brightly: *the fire was burning bright.* [OE *beorht*] —ˈ**brightly** *adv.* —ˈ**brightness** *n.*

brighten (ˈbraɪtᵊn) *vb.* **1.** to make or become bright or brighter. **2.** to make or become cheerful.

Bright's disease (braɪts) *n.* chronic inflammation of the kidneys; chronic nephritis. [C19: after Richard *Bright* (1789–1858), E physician]

brightwork (ˈbraɪtˌwɜːk) *n.* shiny metal trimmings or fittings on ships, cars, etc.

brill (brɪl) *n., pl.* **brill** *or* **brills.** a European flatfish similar to the turbot. [C15: prob. < Cornish *brȳthel* mackerel, < OCornish *brȳth* speckled]

brilliance (ˈbrɪljəns) *or* **brilliancy** *n.* **1.** great brightness; radiance. **2.** excellence or distinction in physical or mental ability; exceptional talent. **3.** splendour; magnificence.

brilliant (ˈbrɪljənt) *adj.* **1.** shining with light; sparkling. **2.** (of a colour) reflecting a considerable amount of light; vivid. **3.** outstanding; exceptional: *a brilliant success.* **4.** splendid; magnificent: *a brilliant show.* **5.** of outstanding intelligence or intellect: *a brilliant mind.* ~*n.* **6.** Also called: **brilliant cut. a.** a cut for diamonds and other gemstones in the form of two many-faceted pyramids joined at their bases. **b.** a diamond of this cut. [C17: < F *brillant* shining, < It., < *brillo* BERYL] —ˈ**brilliantly** *adv.*

brilliantine (ˈbrɪljənˌtiːn) *n.* a perfumed oil used to make the hair smooth and shiny. [C19: < F, < *brillant* shining]

brim (brɪm) *n.* **1.** the upper rim of a vessel: *the brim of a cup.* **2.** a projecting rim or edge: *the brim of a hat.* **3.** the brink or edge of something. ~*vb.* **brimming, brimmed. 4.** to fill or be full to the brim: *eyes brimming with tears.* [C13: < MHG *brem*] —ˈ**brimless** *adj.*

brimful *or* **brimfull** (ˌbrɪmˈfʊl) *adj.* (*postpositive;* foll. by *of*) filled up to the brim (with).

brimstone (ˈbrɪmˌstəʊn) *n.* **1.** an obsolete name for **sulphur. 2.** a common yellow butterfly of N temperate regions of the Old World. [OE *brynstān;* see BURN[1], STONE]

brindle (ˈbrɪndᵊl) *n.* **1.** a brindled animal. **2.** a brindled colouring. [C17: back formation < BRINDLED]

brindled (ˈbrɪndᵊld) *adj.* brown or grey streaked or patched with a darker colour: *a brindled dog.* [C17: changed < C15 *brended,* lit.: branded]

brine (braɪn) *n.* **1.** a strong solution of salt and water, used for salting and pickling meats, etc. **2.** the sea or its water. ~*vb.* **3.** (*tr.*) to soak in or treat with brine. [OE *brīne*] —ˈ**brinish** *adj.*

bring (brɪŋ) *vb.* **bringing, brought.** (*tr.*) **1.** to carry, convey, or take (something or someone) to a designated place or person: *bring that book to me.* **2.** to cause to happen or occur to (oneself or another): *to bring disrespect on oneself.* **3.** to cause to happen as a consequence: *responsibility brings maturity.* **4.** to cause to come to mind: *it brought back memories.* **5.** to cause to be in a certain state, position, etc.: *the punch brought him to his knees.* **6.** to force, persuade, or make (oneself): *I couldn't bring myself to do it.* **7.** to sell for; fetch: *the painting brought 20 pounds.* **8.** *Law.* **a.** to institute (proceedings, charges, etc.). **b.** to put (evidence, etc.) before a tribunal. **9. bring forth.** to give birth to. ~See also **bring about, bring down,** etc. [OE *bringan*] —ˈ**bringer** *n.*

bring about *vb.* (*tr., adv.*) **1.** to cause to happen. **2.** to turn (a ship) around.

bring-and-buy sale *n. Brit. & N.Z.* an informal sale, often for charity, to which people bring items for sale and buy those that others have brought.

bring down *vb.* (*tr., adv.*) to cause to fall.

bring forward *vb.* (*tr., adv.*) **1.** to present or introduce (a subject) for discussion. **2.** *Book-keeping.* to transfer (a sum) to the top of the next page or column.

bring in *vb.* (*tr., adv.*) **1.** to yield (income, profit, or cash). **2.** to produce or return (a verdict). **3.** to introduce (a legislative bill, etc.).

bring off *vb.* (*tr., adv.*) to succeed in achieving (something), esp. with difficulty.

bring out *vb.* (*tr., adv.*) **1.** to produce or publish or have published. **2.** to expose, reveal, or cause to be seen: *she brought out the best in me.* **3.** (foll. by *in*) to cause (a person) to become covered (with spots, a rash, etc.). **4.** *Brit.* to introduce (a girl) formally into society as a debutante.

bring over *vb.* (*tr., adv.*) to cause (a person) to change allegiances.

bring round *or* **around** *vb.* (*tr., adv.*) **1.** to restore (a person) to consciousness, esp. after a faint. **2.** to convince (another person, usually an opponent) of an opinion or point of view.

bring to *vb.* (*tr., adv.*) **1.** to restore (a person) to consciousness. **2.** to cause (a ship) to turn into the wind and reduce her headway.

bring up *vb.* (*tr., adv.*) **1.** to care for and train (a child); rear. **2.** to raise (a subject) for discussion; mention. **3.** to vomit (food).

brinjal (ˈbrɪndʒəl) *n.* (in India and Africa) another name for the **aubergine.** [C17: < Port. *berinjela,* < Ar.]

brink (brɪŋk) *n.* **1.** the edge, border, or verge of a steep place. **2.** the land at the edge of a body of water. **3.** the verge of an event or state: *the brink of disaster.* [C13: < MDu. *brinc,* of Gmc origin]

brinkmanship (ˈbrɪŋkmənˌʃɪp) *n.* the art or practice of pressing a dangerous situation, esp. in international affairs, to the limit of safety and peace in order to win an advantage.

briny (ˈbraɪnɪ) *adj.* **brinier, briniest. 1.** of or resembling brine; salty. ~*n.* **2.** (preceded by *the*) *Inf.* the sea. —ˈ**brininess** *n.*

brio (ˈbriːəʊ) *n.* liveliness or vigour; spirit. See also **con brio.** [C19: < It., of Celtic origin]

brioche (ˈbriːəʊʃ, -ɒʃ) *n.* a soft roll made from a very light yeast dough. [C19: < Norman dialect, < *brier* to knead, of Gmc origin]

briquette *or* **briquet** (brɪˈkɛt) *n.* a small brick made of compressed coal dust, sawdust, charcoal, etc., used for fuel. [C19: < F: a little brick, < *brique* BRICK]

brisk (brɪsk) *adj.* **1.** lively and quick; vigorous: *a brisk walk.* **2.** invigorating or sharp: *brisk weather.* ~*vb.* **3.** (often foll. by *up*) to enliven; make or become brisk. [C16: prob. var. of BRUSQUE] —ˈ**briskly** *adv.* —ˈ**briskness** *n.*

brisket (ˈbrɪskɪt) *n.* **1.** the breast of a four-legged animal. **2.** the meat from this part, esp. of beef. [C14: prob. < ON]

brisling (ˈbrɪslɪŋ) *n.* another name for a **sprat.** [C20: < Norwegian; rel. to obs. Danish *bretling*]

bristle (ˈbrɪsᵊl) *n.* **1.** any short stiff hair of an animal or plant, such as on a pig's back. **2.** something resembling these hairs: *toothbrush bristle.* ~*vb.* **3.** (when *intr.,* often foll. by *up*) to stand up or cause to stand up like bristles. **4.** (*intr.;* sometimes foll. by *up*) to show anger, indignation, etc.: *she bristled at the suggestion.* **5.** (*intr.*) to be thickly covered or set: *the target bristled with arrows.* [C13 *bristil, brustel,* < earlier *brust,* < OE *byrst*] —ˈ**bristly** *adj.*

Bristol board (ˈbrɪstᵊl) *n.* a heavy smooth cardboard of fine quality, used for drawing.

Bristol fashion *adv., adj.* (*postpositive*) in good order; efficiently arranged.

bristols (ˈbrɪstᵊlz) *pl. n. Brit. sl.* a woman's breasts. [C20: short for *Bristol Cities,* rhyming slang for *titties*]

Brit (brɪt) *n. Inf.* a British person.

Brit. *abbrev. for:* 1. Britain. 2. British.

Britannia (brɪˈtænɪə) *n.* 1. a female warrior carrying a trident and wearing a helmet, personifying Great Britain or the British Empire. 2. (in the ancient Roman Empire) the S part of Great Britain.

Britannia metal *n.* an alloy of tin with antimony and copper: used for decorative purposes and for bearings.

Britannic (brɪˈtænɪk) *adj.* of Britain; British (esp. in **His** *or* **Her Britannic Majesty**).

britches (ˈbrɪtʃɪz) *pl. n.* a variant spelling of **breeches.**

Briticism (ˈbrɪtɪˌsɪzəm) *n.* a custom, linguistic usage, or other feature peculiar to Britain or its people. Also: **Britishism.**

British (ˈbrɪtɪʃ) *adj.* 1. of or denoting Britain, a country of W Europe, consisting of the island of Great Britain (comprising England, Scotland, and Wales) and part of the island of Ireland (Northern Ireland). 2. relating to, denoting, or characteristic of the inhabitants of Britain. 3. relating to or denoting the English language as spoken and written in Britain. 4. of or relating to the Commonwealth: *British subjects.* ~*n.* 5. **the British.** (*functioning as pl.*) the natives or inhabitants of Britain. —ˈ**Britishness** *n.*

▷ **Usage.** See at **English.**

Britisher (ˈbrɪtɪʃə) *n.* (not used by the British) 1. a native or inhabitant of Great Britain. 2. any British subject.

British Legion *n. Brit.* an organization founded in 1921 to provide services and assistance for former members of the armed forces.

British thermal unit *n.* a unit of heat in the fps system equal to the quantity of heat required to raise the temperature of 1 pound of water by 1°F. 1 British thermal unit is equivalent to 1055.06 joules. Abbrev.: **btu, BThU.**

Briton (ˈbrɪtᵊn) *n.* 1. a native or inhabitant of Britain. 2. *History.* any of the early Celtic inhabitants of S Britain. [C13: < OF *Breton,* of Celtic origin]

brittle (ˈbrɪtᵊl) *adj.* 1. easily cracked, snapped, or broken; fragile. 2. curt or irritable. 3. hard or sharp in quality. ~*n.* 4. a crunchy sweet made with treacle and nuts: *peanut brittle.* [C14: ult. < OE *brēotan* to break] —ˈ**brittleness** *n.*

brittle-star *n.* an echinoderm occurring on the sea bottom and having long slender arms radiating from a small central disc.

bro. *abbrev. for* brother.

broach (brəʊtʃ) *vb.* (*tr.*) 1. to initiate (a topic) for discussion. 2. to tap or pierce (a container) to draw off (a liquid): *to broach a cask.* 3. to open in order to begin to use. ~*n.* 4. a long tapered toothed cutting tool for enlarging holes. 5. a spit for roasting meat, etc. [C14: < OF *broche,* < L *brochus* projecting]

broad (brɔːd) *adj.* 1. having relatively great breadth or width. 2. of vast extent; spacious: *a broad plain.* 3. (*postpositive*) from one side to the other: *four miles broad.* 4. of great scope or potential: *that invention had broad applications.* 5. not detailed; general: *broad plans.* 6. clear and open; full (esp. in **broad daylight**). 7. obvious or plain: *broad hints.* 8. liberal; tolerant: *a broad political stance.* 9. widely spread; extensive: *broad support.* 10. vulgar; coarse; indecent: *a broad joke.* 11. (of a dialect or pronunciation) consisting of a large number of speech sounds characteristic of a particular geographical area: *a broad Yorkshire accent.* 12. *Finance.* denoting an assessment of liquidity as including notes and coin in circulation with the public, banks' till money and balances, most private-sector bank deposits, and sterling bank-deposit certificates: *broad money. Cf.* **narrow** (sense 7). 13. *Phonetics.* the long vowel in English words such as *father, half,* as represented in Received Pronunciation. ~*n.* 14. the broad part of something. 15. *Sl., chiefly U.S. & Canad.* a. a girl or woman. b. a prostitute. 16. See **Broads.** [OE *brād*] —ˈ**broadly** *adv.*

B-road *n.* a secondary road in Britain.

broad arrow *n.* 1. a mark shaped like a broad arrowhead designating British government property and formerly used on prison clothing. 2. an arrow with a broad head.

broad bean *n.* 1. an erect annual Eurasian bean plant cultivated for its large edible flattened seeds. 2. the seed of this plant.

broadcast (ˈbrɔːdˌkɑːst) *vb.* **-casting, -cast** *or* **-casted.** 1. to transmit (announcements or programmes) on radio or television. 2. (*intr.*) to take part in a radio or television programme. 3. (*tr.*) to make widely known throughout an area: *to broadcast news.* 4. (*tr.*) to scatter (seed, etc.) over an area, esp. by hand. ~*n.* 5. a. a transmission or programme on radio or television. b. (*as modifier*): *a broadcast signal.* 6. the act of scattering seeds. ~*adj.* 7. dispersed over a wide area. ~*adv.* 8. far and wide. —ˈ**broadˌcaster** *n.* —ˈ**broadˌcasting** *n.*

Broad Church *n.* 1. a party within the Church of England which favours a broad and liberal interpretation of Anglican doctrine. ~*adj.* **Broad-Church.** 2. of or relating to this party.

broadcloth (ˈbrɔːdˌklɒθ) *n.* 1. fabric woven on a wide loom. 2. a closely woven fabric of wool, worsted, cotton, or rayon with lustrous finish, used for clothing.

broaden (ˈbrɔːdᵊn) *vb.* to make or become broad or broader; widen.

broad gauge *n.* 1. a railway track with a greater distance between the lines than the standard gauge of 56½ inches. ~*adj.* **broad-gauge.** 2. of or denoting a railway having this track.

broad-leaved *adj.* denoting trees other than conifers; having broad rather than needle-shaped leaves.

broadloom (ˈbrɔːdˌluːm) *n.* (*modifier*) of or designating carpets woven on a wide loom.

broad-minded *adj.* 1. tolerant of opposing viewpoints; not prejudiced; liberal. 2. not easily shocked by permissive sexual habits, pornography, etc. —ˌ**broad-ˈmindedly** *adv.* —ˌ**broad-ˈmindedness** *n.*

Broads (brɔːdz) *pl. n.* **the.** a group of shallow navigable lakes, connected by a network of rivers, in E England, in Norfolk and Suffolk.

broadsheet (ˈbrɔːdˌʃiːt) *n.* 1. a newspaper having a large format, approximately 15 by 24 inches (38 by 61 centimetres). 2. another word for **broadside** (sense 4).

broadside (ˈbrɔːdˌsaɪd) *n.* 1. *Naut.* the entire side of a vessel. 2. *Naval.* a. all the armament fired from one side of a warship. b. the simultaneous discharge of such armament. 3. a strong or abusive verbal or written attack. 4. Also called: **broadside ballad.** a ballad or popular song printed on one side of a sheet of paper, esp. in 16th-century England. ~*adv.* 5. with a broader side facing an object; sideways.

broad-spectrum *n.* (*modifier*) effective against a wide variety of diseases or microorganisms: *a broad-spectrum antibiotic.*

broadsword (ˈbrɔːdˌsɔːd) *n.* a broad-bladed sword used for cutting rather than stabbing.

broadtail (ˈbrɔːdˌteɪl) *n.* 1. the highly valued black wavy fur obtained from the skins of newly born karakul lambs; caracul. 2. another name for **karakul.**

Broadway (ˈbrɔːdˌweɪ) *n.* 1. a thoroughfare in New York City: the centre of the commercial theatre in the U.S. ~*adj.* 2. of, relating to, or suitable for the commercial theatre, esp. on Broadway.

brocade (brəʊˈkeɪd) *n.* 1. a rich fabric woven with a raised design, often using gold or silver threads. ~*vb.* 2. (*tr.*) to weave with such a design. [C17: < Sp. *brocado,* < It. *broccato* embossed fabric, < L *brochus* projecting]

broccoli (ˈbrɒkəlɪ) *n.* 1. a cultivated variety of cabbage having branched greenish flower heads. 2. the flower head, eaten as a vegetable before the buds have opened. [C17: < It., pl. of *broccolo* a little sprout, < *brocco* sprout]

broch (brɒk, brɒx) *n.* (in Scotland) a prehistoric circular dry-stone tower large enough to serve as a fortified home. [C17: < ON *borg;* rel. to OE *burh* settlement, burgh]

brochette (brɒˈʃɛt) *n.* a skewer or small spit, used for holding pieces of meat, etc., while roasting or grilling. [C19: < OF *brochete* small pointed tool; see BROACH]

brochure (ˈbrəʊʃjʊə, -ʃə) *n.* a pamphlet or booklet, esp. one containing summarized or introductory information or advertising. [C18: < F, < *brocher* to stitch (a book)]

brock (brɒk) *n.* a Brit. name for **badger** (sense 1). [OE *broc,* of Celtic origin]

brocket (ˈbrɒkɪt) *n.* a small deer of tropical America, having small unbranched antlers. [C15: < Anglo-F *broquet,* < *broque* horn]

broderie anglaise (ˈbrəʊdəriː ɑːŋˈglɛz) *n.* open embroidery on white cotton, fine linen, etc. [C19: < F: English embroidery]

Broederbond (ˈbrʊdəˌbɔːnt, ˈbruːdəˌbɒnt) *n.* (in South Africa) a secret society of Afrikaner Nationalists. [Afrik.: band of brothers]

brogue[1] (brəʊg) *n.* a broad gentle-sounding dialectal accent, esp. that used by the Irish in speaking English. [C18: <?]

brogue[2] (brəʊg) *n.* **1.** a sturdy walking shoe, often with ornamental perforations. **2.** an untanned shoe worn formerly in Ireland and Scotland. [C16: < Irish Gaelic *bróg* shoe]

broil[1] (brɔɪl) *vb.* **1.** the usual U.S. & Canad. word for **grill** (sense 1). **2.** to become or cause to become extremely hot. **3.** (*intr.*) to be furious. [C14: < OF *bruillir* to burn, <?]

broil[2] (brɔɪl) *Arch.* ~*n.* **1.** a loud quarrel or disturbance; brawl. ~*vb.* **2.** (*intr.*) to brawl; quarrel. [C16: < OF *brouiller* to mix]

broiler (ˈbrɔɪlə) *n.* **1.** a young tender chicken suitable for roasting. **2.** a pan, grate, etc., for broiling food. **3.** a very hot day.

broke (brəʊk) *vb.* **1.** the past tense of **break.** ~*adj.* **2.** *Inf.* having no money; bankrupt. **3. go for broke.** *Sl.* to risk everything in a gambling or other venture.

broken (ˈbrəʊkən) *vb.* **1.** the past participle of **break.** ~*adj.* **2.** fractured, smashed, or splintered: *a broken vase.* **3.** interrupted; disturbed; disconnected: *broken sleep.* **4.** intermittent or discontinuous: *broken sunshine.* **5.** not functioning. **6.** spoilt or ruined by divorce (esp. in **broken home, broken marriage**). **7.** (of a trust, promise, contract, etc.) violated; infringed. **8.** (of the speech of a foreigner) imperfect in grammar, vocabulary, and pronunciation: *broken English.* **9.** Also: **broken-in.** made tame or disciplined by training. **10.** exhausted or weakened, as through ill-health or misfortune. **11.** irregular or rough; uneven: *broken ground.* **12.** bankrupt. —ˈ**brokenly** *adv.*

broken chord *n.* another term for **arpeggio.**

broken-down *adj.* **1.** worn out, as by age or long use; dilapidated. **2.** not in working order.

brokenhearted (ˌbrəʊkənˈhɑːtɪd) *adj.* overwhelmed by grief or disappointment. —ˌ**broken**ˈ**heartedly** *adv.*

broken wind (wɪnd) *n. Vet. science.* another name for **heaves.** —ˌ**broken**ˈ**winded** *adj.*

broker (ˈbrəʊkə) *n.* **1.** an agent who, acting on behalf of a principal, buys or sells goods, securities, etc.: *insurance broker.* **2.** short for **stockbroker. 3.** a person who deals in second-hand goods. [C14: < Anglo-F *brocour* broacher (of casks, hence, one who sells, agent), < OF *broquier* to tap a cask]

brokerage (ˈbrəʊkərɪdʒ) *n.* **1.** commission charged by a broker. **2.** a broker's business or office.

brolga (ˈbrɒlgə) *n.* a large grey Australian crane having a red-and-green head and a trumpeting call. Also called: **native companion.** [C19: < Abor.]

brolly (ˈbrɒlɪ) *n., pl.* **-lies.** an informal Brit. name for **umbrella** (sense 1).

bromeliad (brəʊˈmiːlɪˌæd) *n.* any of a family of tropical American plants, typically epiphytes with a rosette of fleshy leaves, such as the pineapple and Spanish moss. [C19: < NL, after Olaf *Bromelius* (1639-1705), Swedish botanist]

bromide (ˈbrəʊmaɪd) *n.* **1.** any salt of hydrobromic acid. **2.** any compound containing a bromine atom. **3.** a dose of sodium or potassium bromide given as a sedative. **4. a.** a platitude. **b.** a boring person.

bromide paper *n.* a type of photographic paper coated with an emulsion of silver bromide.

bromine (ˈbrəʊmiːn, -mɪn) *n.* a pungent dark red volatile liquid element that occurs in brine and is used in the production of chemicals. Symbol: Br; atomic no.: 35; atomic wt.: 79.91. [C19: < F *brome* bromine, < Gk *brōmos* bad smell, <?]

bronchi (ˈbrɒŋkaɪ) *n.* the plural of **bronchus.**

bronchial (ˈbrɒŋkɪəl) *adj.* of or relating to the bronchi or the bronchial tubes. —ˈ**bronchially** *adv.*

bronchial tubes *pl. n.* the bronchi or their smaller divisions.

bronchiectasis (ˌbrɒŋkɪˈɛktəsɪs) *n.* chronic dilation and usually infection of the bronchi. [C19: < BRONCHO- + Gk *ektasis* a stretching]

bronchiole (ˈbrɒŋkɪˌəʊl) *n.* any of the smallest bronchial tubes. [C19: < NL; see BRONCHUS] —ˌ**bronchi**ˈ**olar** *adj.*

bronchitis (brɒŋˈkaɪtɪs) *n.* inflammation of the bronchial tubes, characterized by coughing, difficulty in breathing, etc. —**bronchitic** (brɒŋˈkɪtɪk) *adj., n.*

broncho- *or before a vowel* **bronch-** *combining form.* indicating or relating to the bronchi: *bronchitis.* [< Gk: BRONCHUS]

bronchopneumonia (ˌbrɒŋkəʊnjuːˈməʊnɪə) *n.* inflammation of the lungs, starting in the bronchioles.

bronchoscope (ˈbrɒŋkəˌskəʊp) *n.* an instrument for examining and providing access to the interior of the bronchial tubes.

bronchus (ˈbrɒŋkəs) *n., pl.* **-chi.** either of the two main branches of the trachea. [C18: < NL, < Gk *bronkhos* windpipe]

bronco *or* **broncho** (ˈbrɒŋkəʊ) *n., pl.* **-cos** *or* **-chos.** (in the U.S. and Canada) a wild or partially tamed pony or mustang of the western plains. [C19: < Mexican Sp., < Sp.: rough, wild]

brontosaurus (ˌbrɒntəˈsɔːrəs) *or* **brontosaur** (ˈbrɒntəˌsɔː) *n.* a very large herbivorous quadrupedal dinosaur, common in N America during late Jurassic times, having a long neck and long tail. [C19: < NL, < Gk *brontē* thunder + *sauros* lizard]

bronze (brɒnz) *n.* **1.** any hard water-resistant alloy consisting of copper and smaller proportions of tin and sometimes zinc and lead. **2.** a yellowish-brown colour or pigment. **3.** a statue, medal, or other object made of bronze. ~*adj.* **4.** made of or resembling bronze. **5.** of a yellowish-brown colour. ~*vb.* **6.** (esp. of the skin) to make or become brown; tan. **7.** (*tr.*) to give the appearance of bronze to. [C18: < F, < It. *bronzo*] —ˈ**bronzy** *adj.*

Bronze Age *n.* **a.** a technological stage between the Stone and Iron Ages, beginning in the Middle East about 4500 B.C. and lasting in Britain from about 2000 to 500 B.C., during which weapons and tools were made of bronze. **b.** (*as modifier*): *a Bronze-Age tool.*

bronze medal *n.* a medal awarded to a competitor who comes third in a contest or race.

brooch (brəʊtʃ) *n.* an ornament with a hinged pin and catch, worn fastened to clothing. [C13: < OF *broche;* see BROACH]

brood (bruːd) *n.* **1.** a number of young animals, esp. birds, produced at one hatching. **2.** all the offspring in one family: often used jokingly or contemptuously. **3.** a group of a particular kind; breed. **4.** (*modifier*) kept for breeding: *a brood mare.* ~*vb.* **5.** (of a bird) **a.** to sit on or hatch (eggs). **b.** (*tr.*) to cover (young birds) protectively with the wings. **6.** (when *intr.,* often foll. by *on,* *over,* or *upon*) to ponder morbidly or persistently. [OE *brōd*] —ˈ**brooding** *n., adj.*

brooder (ˈbruːdə) *n.* **1.** a structure, usually heated, used for rearing young chickens or other fowl. **2.** a person or thing that broods.

broody (ˈbruːdɪ) *adj.* **broodier, broodiest. 1.** moody; introspective. **2.** (of poultry) wishing to sit on or hatch eggs. **3.** *Inf.* (of a woman) wishing to have a baby. —ˈ**broodiness** *n.*

brook[1] (brʊk) *n.* a natural freshwater stream smaller than a river. [OE *brōc*]

brook[2] (brʊk) *vb.* (*tr.*) (*usually used with a negative*) to bear; tolerate. [OE *brūcan*]

brooklet (ˈbrʊklɪt) *n.* a small brook.

brooklime (ˈbrʊkˌlaɪm) *n.* either of two blue-flowered trailing plants, *Veronica americana* of North America or *V. beccabunga* of Europe and Asia, growing in moist places. See also **speedwell.** [C16: < BROOK[1] + *-lemk,* < OE *hleomoce*]

brook trout *n.* a North American trout, valued as a food and game fish.

broom (bruːm, brʊm) *n.* **1.** an implement for sweeping consisting of a long handle to which is attached either a brush of straw or twigs, bound together, or a solid head into which are set tufts of bristles or fibres. **2.** any of various yellow-flowered Eurasian leguminous shrubs. **3. new broom.** a newly appointed official, etc., eager to make radical changes. ~*vb.* **4.** (*tr.*) to sweep with a broom. [OE *brōm*]

broomrape (ˈbruːmˌreɪp, ˈbrʊm-) *n.* any of a genus of leafless fleshy parasitic plants growing on the roots of other plants, esp. on broom. [C16: adaptation & partial translation of Med. L *rāpum genistae* tuber (hence: root nodule) of Genista (a type of broom plant)]

broomstick (ˈbruːmˌstɪk, ˈbrʊm-) *n.* the long handle of a broom.

bros. *or* **Bros.** *abbrev. for* brothers.

brose (brəʊz) *n. Scot.* a porridge made by adding a boiling liquid to meal, esp. oatmeal. [C13 *broys,* < OF *broez,* < *breu* broth, of Gmc origin]

broth (brɒθ) *n.* **1.** a soup made by boiling meat, fish, vegetables, etc., in water. **2.** another name for **stock** (sense 19). [OE *broth*]

brothel (ˈbrɒθəl) *n.* **1.** a house where men pay to have sexual intercourse with prostitutes. **2.** *Austral. inf.* any untidy or messy place. [C16: short for *brothel-house,* < C14 *brothel* useless person, < OE *brēothan* to deteriorate]

brother (ˈbrʌðə) *n.* **1.** a male person having the same parents as another person. **2. a.** a male person belonging to the same group, profession, nationality, trade union, etc., as another or others; fellow member. **b.** (*as modifier*): *brother workers.* **3.** comrade; friend: used as a form of address. **4.** *Christianity.* a member of a male religious order. ~Related adj.: **fraternal.** [OE *brōthor*]

brotherhood (ˈbrʌðəˌhʊd) *n.* **1.** the state of being related as a brother or brothers. **2.** an association or fellowship, such as a trade union. **3.** all persons engaged in a particular profession, trade, etc. **4.** the belief, feeling, or hope that all men should treat one another as brothers.

brother-in-law *n., pl.* **brothers-in-law. 1.** the brother of one's wife or husband. **2.** the husband of one's sister. **3.** the husband of the sister of one's husband or wife.

brotherly (ˈbrʌðəlɪ) *adj.* of, resembling, or suitable to a brother, esp. in showing loyalty and affection; fraternal. —ˈ**brotherliness** *n.*

brougham (ˈbruːəm, bruːm) *n.* **1.** a four-wheeled horse-drawn closed carriage having a raised open driver's seat in front. **2.** *Obs.* a large car with an open compartment at the front for the driver. **3.** *Obs.* an early electric car. [C19: after Lord *Brougham* (1778–1868)]

brought (brɔːt) *vb.* the past tense and past participle of **bring.**

brouhaha (ˈbruːhɑːhɑː) *n.* a loud confused noise; commotion; uproar. [F, imit.]

brow (braʊ) *n.* **1.** the part of the face from the eyes to the hairline; forehead. **2.** short for **eyebrow. 3.** the expression of the face; countenance: *a troubled brow.* **4.** the jutting top of a hill, etc. [OE *brū*]

browbeat (ˈbraʊˌbiːt) *vb.* **-beating, -beat, -beaten.** (*tr.*) to discourage or frighten with threats or a domineering manner; intimidate.

brown (braʊn) *n.* **1.** any of various dark colours, such as those of wood or earth. **2.** a dye or pigment producing these colours. ~*adj.* **3.** of the colour brown. **4.** (of bread) made from a flour that has not been bleached or bolted, such as wheatmeal or wholemeal flour. **5.** deeply tanned or sunburnt. ~*vb.* **6.** to make (esp. food as a result of cooking) brown or (esp. of food) to become brown. [OE *brūn*] —ˈ**brownish** *or* ˈ**browny** *adj.* —ˈ**brownness** *n.*

brown bear *n.* a large ferocious brownish bear inhabiting temperate forests of North America, Europe, and Asia.

brown coal *n.* another name for **lignite.**

browned-off *adj. Inf., chiefly Brit.* thoroughly discouraged or disheartened; fed up.

Brownian movement (ˈbraʊnɪən) *n.* random movement of microscopic particles suspended in a fluid, caused by bombardment of the particles by molecules of the fluid. [C19: after Robert *Brown* (1773-1858), Scot. botanist]

brownie (ˈbraʊnɪ) *n.* **1.** (in folklore) an elf said to do helpful work at night, esp. household chores. **2.** a small square nutty chocolate cake. [C16: dim. of BROWN (that is, a small brown man)]

Brownie Guide *or* **Brownie** (ˈbraʊnɪ) *n.* a member of the junior branch of the Guides.

Brownie point *n.* a notional mark to one's credit for being seen to do the right thing. [C20: ? < the mistaken notion that Brownie Guides earn points for good deeds]

browning (ˈbraʊnɪŋ) *n. Brit.* a substance used to darken soups, gravies, etc.

brown paper *n.* a kind of coarse unbleached paper used for wrapping.

brown rice *n.* unpolished rice, in which the grains retain the outer yellowish-brown layer (bran).

Brown Shirt *n.* **1.** (in Nazi Germany) a storm trooper. **2.** a member of any fascist party or group.

brownstone (ˈbraʊnˌstəʊn) *n. U.S.* a reddish-brown iron-rich sandstone used for building.

brown sugar *n.* sugar that is unrefined or only partially refined.

brown trout *n.* a common brownish variety of the trout that occurs in the rivers of N Europe.

browse (braʊz) *vb.* **1.** to look through (a book, articles for sale in a shop, etc.) in a casual leisurely manner. **2.** (of deer, goats, etc.) to feed upon (vegetation) by continual nibbling. ~*n.* **3.** the act or an instance of browsing. **4.** the young twigs, shoots, leaves, etc., on which certain animals feed. [C15: < F *broust, brost* bud, of Gmc origin] —ˈ**browser** *n.*

BRS *abbrev. for* British Road Services.

brucellosis (ˌbruːsɪˈləʊsɪs) *n.* an infectious disease of cattle, goats, and pigs, caused by bacteria and transmittable to man. Also called: **undulant fever.** [C20: < NL *Brucella,* after Sir David *Bruce* (1855–1931), Australian bacteriologist & physician]

bruin (ˈbruːɪn) *n.* a name for a bear, used in children's tales, etc. [C17: < Du. *bruin* brown]

bruise (bruːz) *vb.* (*mainly tr.*) **1.** (*also intr.*) to injure (tissues) without breaking the skin, usually with discoloration, or (of tissues) to be injured in this way. **2.** to offend or injure (someone's feelings). **3.** to damage the surface of (something). **4.** to crush (food, etc.) by pounding. ~*n.* **5.** a bodily injury without a break in the skin, usually with discoloration; contusion. [OE *brȳsan*]

bruiser (ˈbruːzə) *n.* a strong tough person, esp. a boxer or a bully.

bruit (bruːt) *vb.* **1.** (*tr.; often passive;* usually foll. by *about*) to report; rumour. ~*n.* **2.** *Arch.* **a.** a rumour. **b.** a loud outcry; clamour. [C15: via F < Med. L *brūgītus,* prob. < L *rugīre* to roar]

brumby (ˈbrʌmbɪ) *n., pl.* **-bies.** *Austral.* **1.** a wild horse, esp. one descended from runaway stock. **2.** a disorderly person. [C19: <?]

brume (bruːm) *n. Poetic* heavy mist or fog. [C19: < F: mist, winter, < L *brūma,* contracted < *brevissima diēs* the shortest day]

brunch (brʌntʃ) *n.* a meal eaten late in the morning, combining breakfast with lunch. [C20: < BR(EAKFAST) + (L)UNCH]

brunette (bruːˈnɛt) *n.* **1.** a girl or woman with dark brown hair. *~adj.* **2.** dark brown: *brunette hair.* [C17: < F, fem. of *brunet* dark, brownish, < *brun* brown]

brunt (brʌnt) *n.* the main force or shock of a blow, attack, etc. (esp. in **bear the brunt of**). [C14: <?]

brush[1] (brʌʃ) *n.* **1.** a device made of bristles, hairs, wires, etc., set into a firm back or handle: used to apply paint, clean or polish surfaces, groom the hair, etc. **2.** the act or an instance of brushing. **3.** a light stroke made in passing; graze. **4.** a brief encounter or contact, esp. an unfriendly one; skirmish. **5.** the bushy tail of a fox. **6.** an electric conductor, esp. one made of carbon, that conveys current between stationary and rotating parts of a generator, motor, etc. *~vb.* **7.** (*tr.*) to clean, polish, scrub, paint, etc., with a brush. **8.** (*tr.*) to apply or remove with a brush or brushing movement. **9.** (*tr.*) to touch lightly and briefly. **10.** (*intr.*) to move so as to graze or touch something lightly. ~See also **brush aside, brush off, brush up.** [C14: < OF *broisse,* ? < *broce* BRUSH[2]] —**ˈbrusher** *n.*

brush[2] (brʌʃ) *n.* **1.** a thick growth of shrubs and small trees; scrub. **2.** land covered with scrub. **3.** broken or cut branches or twigs; brushwood. **4.** wooded sparsely populated country; backwoods. [C16 (dense undergrowth), C14 (cuttings of trees): < OF *broce,* < Vulgar L *bruscia* (unattested) brushwood] —**ˈbrushy** *adj.*

brush aside *or* **away** *vb.* (*tr., adv.*) to dismiss without consideration; disregard.

brush discharge *n.* a slightly luminous brushlike electrical discharge.

brushed (brʌʃt) *adj. Textiles.* treated with a brushing process to raise the nap and give a softer and warmer finish: *brushed nylon.*

brush off *Sl.* *~vb.* (*tr., adv.*) **1.** to dismiss and ignore (a person), esp. curtly. *~n.* **brushoff. 2.** an abrupt dismissal or rejection.

brush turkey *n.* any of several gallinaceous flightless birds of New Guinea and Australia, having a black plumage.

brush up *vb.* (*adv.*) **1.** (*tr.;* often foll. by *on*) to refresh one's knowledge, skill, or memory of (a subject). **2.** to make (a person or oneself) clean or neat as after a journey. *~n.* **brush-up. 3.** *Brit.* the act or an instance of tidying one's appearance (esp. in **wash and brush-up**).

brushwood (ˈbrʌʃˌwʊd) *n.* **1.** cut or broken-off tree branches, twigs, etc. **2.** another word for **brush**[2] (sense 1).

brushwork (ˈbrʌʃˌwɜːk) *n.* **1.** a characteristic manner of applying paint with a brush: *Rembrandt's brushwork.* **2.** work done with a brush.

brusque (bruːsk, brʊsk) *adj.* blunt or curt in manner or speech. [C17: < F, < It. *brusco* sour, rough, < Med. L *bruscus* butcher's broom] —**ˈbrusquely** *adv.* —**ˈbrusqueness** *n.*

Brussels carpet (ˈbrʌsᵊlz) *n.* a worsted carpet with a heavy pile formed by uncut loops of wool on a linen warp.

Brussels lace *n.* a fine lace with a raised or appliqué design.

Brussels sprout *n.* **1.** a variety of cabbage, having a stout stem studded with budlike heads resembling tiny cabbages. **2.** the head of this plant, eaten as a vegetable.

brutal (ˈbruːtᵊl) *adj.* **1.** cruel; vicious; savage. **2.** extremely honest or coarse in speech or manner. **3.** harsh; severe; extreme: *brutal cold.* —**bruˈtality** *n.* —**ˈbrutally** *adv.*

brutalize *or* **-ise** (ˈbruːtəˌlaɪz) *vb.* **1.** to make or become brutal. **2.** (*tr.*) to treat brutally. —ˌ**brutaliˈzation** *or* **-iˈsation** *n.*

brute (bruːt) *n.* **1. a.** any animal except man; beast; lower animal. **b.** (*as modifier*): *brute nature.* **2.** a brutal person. *~adj.* (*prenominal*) **3.** wholly instinctive or physical (esp. in **brute strength, brute force**). **4.** without reason or intelligence. **5.** coarse and grossly sensual. [C15: < L *brūtus* heavy, irrational]

brutish (ˈbruːtɪʃ) *adj.* **1.** of, relating to, or resembling a brute; animal. **2.** coarse; cruel; stupid. —**ˈbrutishly** *adv.* —**ˈbrutishness** *n.*

bryology (braɪˈɒlədʒɪ) *n.* the branch of botany concerned with the study of bryophytes. —**bryological** (ˌbraɪəˈlɒdʒɪkᵊl) *adj.* —**bryˈologist** *n.*

bryony *or* **briony** (ˈbraɪənɪ) *n., pl.* **-nies.** any of several herbaceous climbing plants of Europe and N Africa. [OE *bryōnia,* < L, < Gk *bruōnia*]

bryophyte (ˈbraɪəˌfaɪt) *n.* any plant of the division *Bryophyta,* esp. mosses and liverworts. [C19: < Gk *bruon* moss + -PHYTE] —**bryophytic** (ˌbraɪəˈfɪtɪk) *adj.*

bryozoan (ˌbraɪəˈzəʊən) *n.* any aquatic invertebrate animal forming colonies of polyps each having a ciliated feeding organ. Popular name: **sea mat.** [C19: < Gk *bruon* moss + *zōion* animal]

Brythonic (brɪˈθɒnɪk) *n.* **1.** the S group of Celtic languages, consisting of Welsh, Cornish, and Breton. *~adj.* **2.** of or relating to this group of languages. [C19: < Welsh; see BRITON]

bs *abbrev. for:* **1.** balance sheet. **2.** bill of sale.

BS *abbrev. for* British Standard(s).

BSc *abbrev. for* Bachelor of Science.

BSI *abbrev. for* British Standards Institution.

B-side *n.* the less important side of a gramophone record.

BST *abbrev. for:* **1.** British Standard Time. **2.** British Summer Time.

Bt *abbrev. for* Baronet.

BT *abbrev. for* British Telecom. [C20: shortened < TELECOMMUNICATIONS]

btu *or* **BThU** *abbrev. for* British thermal unit. U.S. abbrev.: **BTU.**

bu. *abbrev. for* bushel.

bubble (ˈbʌbᵊl) *n.* **1.** a thin film of liquid forming a hollow globule around air or a gas: *a soap bubble.* **2.** a small globule of air or a gas in a liquid or a solid. **3.** the sound made by a bubbling liquid. **4.** something lacking substance, stability, or seriousness. **5.** an unreliable scheme or enterprise. **6.** a dome, esp. a transparent glass or plastic one. *~vb.* **7.** to form or cause to form bubbles. **8.** (*intr.*) to move or flow with a gurgling sound. **9.** (*intr.;* often foll. by *over*) to overflow (with excitement, anger, etc.). [C14: prob. < ON; imit.]

bubble and squeak *n. Brit.* a dish of leftover boiled cabbage and potatoes fried together.

bubble bath *n.* **1.** a powder, liquid, or crystals used to scent, soften, and foam in bath water. **2.** a bath to which such a substance has been added.

bubble car *n. Brit.* a small car with a transparent bubble-shaped top.

bubble chamber *n.* a device that enables the tracks of ionizing particles to be photographed as a row of bubbles in a superheated liquid.

bubble gum *n.* a type of chewing gum that can be blown into large bubbles.

bubble memory *n. Computers.* a method of storing high volumes of data by using minute pockets of magnetism (bubbles) in a semiconducting material.

bubbly (ˈbʌblɪ) *adj.* **-blier, -bliest. 1.** full of or resembling bubbles. **2.** lively; animated; excited. *~n.* **3.** *Inf.* champagne.

bubo (ˈbjuːbəʊ) *n., pl.* **-boes.** *Pathol.* inflammation and swelling of a lymph node, esp. in the armpit or groin. [C14: < Med. L *bubō,* < Gk *boubōn* groin] —**bubonic** (bjuːˈbɒnɪk) *adj.*

bubonic plague *n.* an acute infectious febrile disease characterized by chills, prostration, delirium, and formation of buboes: caused by the bite of an infected rat flea.

buccal (ˈbʌkᵊl) *adj.* **1.** of or relating to the cheek. **2.** of or relating to the mouth; oral. [C19: < L *bucca* cheek]

buccaneer (ˌbʌkəˈnɪə) *n.* **1.** a pirate, esp. one who preyed on Spanish shipping in the Caribbean in the 17th and 18th centuries. ~*vb.* (*intr.*) **2.** to be or act like a buccaneer. [C17: < F *boucanier,* < *boucaner* to smoke meat]

buccinator (ˈbʌksɪˌneɪtə) *n.* either of two flat cheek muscles used in chewing. [C17: < L, < *buccina* a trumpet]

buck[1] (bʌk) *n.* **1. a.** the male of various animals including the goat, hare, kangaroo, rabbit, and reindeer. **b.** (*as modifier*): *a buck antelope.* **2.** *S. African.* an antelope or deer of either sex. **3.** *Arch.* a robust spirited young man. **4.** the act of bucking. ~*vb.* **5.** (*intr.*) (of a horse or other animal) to jump vertically, with legs stiff and back arched. **6.** (*tr.*) (of a horse, etc.) to throw (its rider) by bucking. **7.** (when *intr.*, often foll. by *against* or *at*) *Chiefly U.S., Canad., & Austral. inf.* to resist or oppose obstinately. **8.** (*tr.; usually passive*) *Inf.* to cheer or encourage: *I was very bucked at passing the exam.* ~See also **buck up.** [OE *bucca* he-goat] —ˈ**bucker** *n.*

buck[2] (bʌk) *n. U.S., Canad., & Austral. sl.* a dollar. [C19: <?]

buck[3] (bʌk) *n.* **1.** *Poker.* a marker in the jackpot to remind the winner of some obligation when his turn comes to deal. **2. pass the buck.** *Inf.* to shift blame or responsibility onto another. [C19: prob. < *buckhorn knife,* placed before a player in poker to indicate that he was the next dealer]

buckbean (ˈbʌkˌbiːn) *n.* a marsh plant with white or pink flowers. Also called: **bogbean.**

buckboard (ˈbʌkˌbɔːd) *n. U.S. & Canad.* an open four-wheeled horse-drawn carriage with the seat attached to a flexible board between the front and rear axles.

bucket (ˈbʌkɪt) *n.* **1.** an open-topped roughly cylindrical container; pail. **2.** Also called: **bucketful.** the amount a bucket will hold. **3.** any of various bucket-like parts of a machine, such as the scoop on a mechanical shovel. **4.** *Austral.* a small container for ice cream. **5. kick the bucket.** *Sl.* to die. ~*vb.* **6.** (*tr.*) to carry in or put into a bucket. **7.** (*intr.;* often foll. by *along*) *Chiefly Brit.* to travel or drive fast. **8.** (*tr.*) *Austral. sl.* to criticize severely. [C13: < Anglo-F *buket,* < OE *būc*]

bucket down *vb.* (*intr.*) (of rain) to fall very heavily.

bucket seat *n.* a seat in a car, aircraft, etc., having curved sides.

bucket shop *n.* **1.** an unregistered firm of stockbrokers that engages in fraudulent speculation. **2.** *Chiefly Brit.* a firm specializing in cheap airline tickets.

buckeye (ˈbʌkˌaɪ) *n.* any of several North American trees of the horse chestnut family having erect clusters of white or red flowers and prickly fruits.

buckhorn (ˈbʌkˌhɔːn) *n.* **a.** horn from a buck, used for knife handles, etc. **b.** (*as modifier*): *a buckhorn knife.*

buckjumper (ˈbʌkˌdʒʌmpə) *n. Austral.* an untamed horse.

buckle (ˈbʌkᵊl) *n.* **1.** a clasp for fastening together two loose ends, esp. of a belt or strap, usually consisting of a frame with an attached movable prong. **2.** an ornamental representation of a buckle, as on a shoe. **3.** a kink, bulge, or other distortion. ~*vb.* **4.** to fasten or be fastened with a buckle. **5.** to bend or cause to bend out of shape, esp. as a result of pressure or heat. [C14: < OF, < L *buccula* a little cheek, hence, cheek strap of a helmet]

buckle down *vb.* (*intr., adv.*) *Inf.* to apply oneself with determination.

buckler (ˈbʌklə) *n.* **1.** a small round shield worn on the forearm. **2.** a means of protection; defence. [C13: < OF *bocler,* < *bocle* shield boss]

Buckley's chance (ˈbʌklɪz) *n. Austral. & N.Z. sl.* no chance at all. Often shortened to **Buckley's.** [C19: <?]

bucko (ˈbʌkəʊ) *n., pl.* **buckoes.** *Irish.* a young fellow: often a term of address.

buckram (ˈbʌkrəm) *n.* **a.** cotton or linen cloth stiffened with size, etc., used in lining or stiffening clothes, bookbinding, etc. **b.** (*as modifier*): *a buckram cover.* [C14: < OF *boquerant,* ult. < *Bukhara,* USSR, once important for textiles]

Bucks (bʌks) *abbrev. for* Buckinghamshire.

buckshee (ˌbʌkˈʃiː) *adj. Brit. sl.* without charge; free. [C20: < BAKSHEESH]

buckshot (ˈbʌkˌʃɒt) *n.* lead shot of large size used in shotgun shells, esp. for hunting game.

buckskin (ˈbʌkˌskɪn) *n.* **1.** the skin of a male deer. **2. a.** a strong greyish-yellow suede leather, originally made from deerskin but now usually made from sheepskin. **b.** (*as modifier*): *buckskin boots.* **3.** a stiffly starched cotton cloth. **4.** a strong and heavy satin-woven woollen fabric.

buckthorn (ˈbʌkˌθɔːn) *n.* any of several thorny small-flowered shrubs whose berries were formerly used as a purgative. [C16: < BUCK[1] (< the spiny branches resembling antlers) + THORN]

bucktooth (ˈbʌkˌtuːθ) *n., pl.* **-teeth.** *Derog.* a projecting upper front tooth. [C18: < BUCK[1] (deer) + TOOTH]

buck up *vb.* (*adv.*) *Inf.* **1.** to make or cause to make haste. **2.** to make or become more cheerful, confident, etc.

buckwheat (ˈbʌkˌwiːt) *n.* **1.** a cereal plant with fragrant white flowers, cultivated, esp. in the U.S., for its seeds. **2.** the edible seeds of this plant, ground into flour or used as animal fodder. **3.** the flour obtained from these seeds. [C16: < MDu. *boecweite,* < *boeke* BEECH + *weite* WHEAT, < the resemblance of the seeds to beechnuts]

bucolic (bjuːˈkɒlɪk) *adj. also* **bucolical. 1.** of the countryside or country life; rustic. **2.** of or relating to shepherds; pastoral. ~*n.* **3.** (*sometimes pl.*) a pastoral poem. [C16: < L, < Gk, < *boukolos* cowherd, < *bous* ox] —**buˈcolically** *adv.*

bud (bʌd) *n.* **1.** a swelling on a plant stem consisting of overlapping immature leaves or petals. **2. a.** a partially opened flower. **b.** (*in combination*): *rosebud.* **3.** any small budlike outgrowth: *taste buds.* **4.** something small or immature. **5.** an asexually produced outgrowth in simple organisms such as yeasts that develops into a new individual. **6. nip in the bud.** to put an end to (an idea, movement, etc.) in its initial stages. ~*vb.* **budding, budded. 7.** (*intr.*) (of plants and some animals) to produce buds. **8.** (*intr.*) to begin to develop or grow. **9.** (*tr.*) *Horticulture.* to graft (a bud) from one plant onto another. [C14 *budde,* of Gmc origin]

Buddha (ˈbʊdə) *n.* **the.** ?563–483 B.C., a title applied to Gautama Siddhartha, a religious teacher of N India: the founder of Buddhism.

Buddhism (ˈbʊdɪzəm) *n.* a religious teaching propagated by the Buddha and his followers, which declares that by destroying greed, hatred, and delusion, which are the causes of all suffering, man can attain perfect enlightenment. —ˈ**Buddhist** *n., adj.*

buddleia (ˈbʌdlɪə) *n.* an ornamental shrub which has long spikes of mauve flowers. Also called: **butterfly bush.** [C19: after A. *Buddle* (died 1715), Brit. botanist]

buddy (ˈbʌdɪ) *n., pl.* **-dies. 1.** Also (as a term of address): **bud.** *Chiefly U.S. & Canad.* an informal word for **friend. 2.** a volunteer who visits and gives help and support to a person suffering from AIDS. ~ *vb.* **-dying, -died. 3.** (*intr.*) to act as a buddy to a person suffering from AIDS. [C19: prob. baby-talk var. (U.S.) of BROTHER]

budge (bʌdʒ) *vb.* (*usually used with a negative*) **1.** to move, however slightly. **2.** to change or cause to change opinions, etc. [C16: < OF *bouger,* < L *bullīre* to boil]

budgerigar (ˈbʌdʒərɪˌgɑː) *n.* a small green Australian parrot: a popular cagebird bred in many different-coloured varieties. [C19: < Abor., < *budgeri* good + *gar* cockatoo]

budget (ˈbʌdʒɪt) *n.* **1.** an itemized summary of expected income and expenditure over a specified period. **2.** (*modifier*) economical; inexpensive: *budget meals for a family.* **3.** the total amount of money allocated for a specific purpose during a specified period. ~*vb.* **4.** (*tr.*) to enter or provide for in a budget. **5.** to plan the expenditure of (money, time, etc.). **6.** (*intr.*) to make a budget. [C15 (meaning: leather pouch, wallet): < OF *bougette*, dim. of *bouge*, < L *bulga*] —**ˈbudgetary** *adj.*

Budget (ˈbʌdʒɪt) *n.* **the.** an estimate of British government expenditures and revenues and the financial plans for the ensuing fiscal year presented annually to the House of Commons by the Chancellor of the Exchequer.

budget account *n.* an account with a department store, etc., enabling a customer to make monthly payments to cover his past and future purchases.

budgie (ˈbʌdʒɪ) *n. Inf.* short for **budgerigar.**

buff[1] (bʌf) *n.* **1. a.** a soft thick flexible undyed leather made chiefly from the skins of buffalo, oxen, and elk. **b.** (*as modifier*): *a buff coat.* **2. a.** a dull yellow or yellowish-brown colour. **b.** (*as adj.*): *a buff envelope.* **3.** Also called: **buffer. a.** a cloth or pad of material used for polishing an object. **b.** a disc or wheel impregnated with a fine abrasive for polishing metals, etc. **4.** *Inf.* one's bare skin (esp. in **in the buff**). ~*vb.* **5.** to clean or polish (a metal, floor, shoes, etc.) with a buff. **6.** to remove the grain surface of (a leather). [C16: < OF, < OIt. *bufalo*, < LL *būfalus* BUFFALO]

buff[2] (bʌf) *n. Arch.* a blow or buffet (now only in **blind man's buff**). [C15: back formation < BUFFET[2]]

buff[3] (bʌf) *n. Inf.* an expert on or devotee of a given subject. [C20: orig. U.S.: an enthusiastic fire-watcher, < the buff-coloured uniforms worn by volunteer firemen in New York City]

buffalo (ˈbʌfəˌləʊ) *n., pl.* **-loes** *or* **-lo. 1.** a type of cattle, mostly found in game reserves in southern and eastern Africa and having upward-curving horns. **2.** short for **water buffalo. 3.** a U.S. & Canad. name for **bison** (sense 1). [C16: < It. *bufalo*, < LL *būfalus*, ult. < Gk *bous* ox]

buffalo grass *n.* **1.** a short grass growing on the dry plains of the central U.S. **2.** *Austral.* a grass, *Stenotaphrum americanum*, introduced from North America.

buffel grass (ˈbʌfᵊl) *n.* (in Australia) any of various grasses used for grazing or fodder, originally introduced from Africa.

buffer[1] (ˈbʌfə) *n.* **1.** one of a pair of spring-loaded steel pads attached at both ends of railway vehicles and at the end of a railway track to reduce shock due to contact. **2.** a person or thing that lessens shock or protects from damaging impact, circumstances, etc. **3.** *Chem.* **a.** an ionic compound added to a solution to resist changes in its acidity or alkalinity and thus stabilize its pH. **b.** Also called: **buffer solution.** a solution containing such a compound. **4.** *Computers.* a memory device for temporarily storing data. ~*vb.* (*tr.*) **5.** *Chem.* to add a buffer to (a solution). **6.** to insulate against or protect from shock. [C19: < BUFF[2]]

buffer[2] (ˈbʌfə) *n.* **1.** any device used to shine, polish, etc.; buff. **2.** a person who uses such a device.

buffer[3] (ˈbʌfə) *n. Brit. inf.* a stupid or bumbling man (esp. in **old buffer**). [C18: ? < ME *buffer* stammerer]

buffer state *n.* a small and usually neutral state between two rival powers.

buffet[1] *n.* **1.** (ˈbʊfeɪ). a counter where light refreshments are served. **2.** (ˈbʊfeɪ). **a.** a meal at which guests help themselves from a number of dishes. **b.** (*as modifier*): *a buffet lunch.* **3.** (ˈbʌfɪt, ˈbʊfeɪ). (formerly) a piece of furniture used for displaying plate, etc., and typically comprising cupboards and some open shelves. [C18: < F, <?]

buffet[2] (ˈbʌfɪt) *vb.* **-feting, -feted. 1.** (*tr.*) to knock against or about; batter. **2.** (*tr.*) to hit, esp. with the fist; cuff. **3.** to force (one's way), as through a crowd. **4.** (*intr.*) to struggle; battle. ~*n.* **5.** a blow, esp. with a fist or hand. [C13: < OF *buffet* a light blow, < *buffe*, imit.]

buffet car (ˈbʊfeɪ) *n. Brit.* a railway coach where light refreshments are served.

bufflehead (ˈbʌfᵊlˌhɛd) *n.* a small North American diving duck: the male has black-and-white plumage and a fluffy head. [C17 *buffle*, < obs. *buffle* wild ox, referring to the duck's head]

buffo (ˈbʊfəʊ) *n., pl.* **-fi** (-fɪ) *or* **-fos. 1.** (in Italian opera of the 18th century) a comic part, esp. one for a bass. **2.** Also called: **buffo bass, basso buffo.** a bass singer who performs such a part. [C18: < It. (adj.): comic, < *buffo* (n.) BUFFOON]

buffoon (bəˈfuːn) *n.* **1.** a person who amuses others by ridiculous or odd behaviour, jokes, etc. **2.** a foolish person. [C16: < F *bouffon*, < It. *buffone*, < Med. L *būfō*, < L: toad] —**bufˈfoonery** *n.*

bug (bʌg) *n.* **1.** an insect having piercing and sucking mouthparts specialized as a beak. **2.** *Chiefly U.S. & Canad.* any insect. **3.** *Inf.* **a.** a microorganism, esp. a bacterium, that produces disease. **b.** a disease, esp. a stomach infection, caused by a microorganism. **4.** *Inf.* an obsessive idea, hobby, etc.; craze. **5.** *Inf.* a person having such a craze. **6.** (*often pl.*) *Inf.* a fault, as in a machine. **7.** *Inf.* a concealed microphone used for recording conversations, as in spying. ~*vb.* **bugging, bugged.** *Inf.* **8.** (*tr.*) to irritate; bother. **9.** (*tr.*) to conceal a microphone in (a room, etc.). **10.** (*intr.*) *U.S.* (of eyes) to protrude. [C16: <?]

bugaboo (ˈbʌgəˌbuː) *n., pl.* **-boos.** an imaginary source of fear; bugbear; bogey. [C18: prob. of Celtic origin; cf. Cornish *buccaboo* the devil]

bugbear (ˈbʌgˌbɛə) *n.* **1.** a thing that causes obsessive anxiety. **2.** (in English folklore) a goblin in the form of a bear. [C16: < obs. *bug* an evil spirit + BEAR[2]]

bugger (ˈbʌgə) *n.* **1.** a person who practises buggery. **2.** *Taboo sl.* a person or thing considered to be contemptible, unpleasant, or difficult. **3.** *Sl.* a humorous or affectionate term for a man or child: *a friendly little bugger.* **4. bugger all.** *Sl.* nothing. ~*vb.* **5.** to practise buggery (with). **6.** (*tr.*) *Sl., chiefly Brit.* to ruin, complicate, or frustrate. **7.** (*tr.*) *Sl.* to tire; weary. ~*interj.* **8.** *Taboo sl.* an exclamation of annoyance or disappointment. [C16: < OF *bougre*, < Med. L *Bulgarus* Bulgarian; < the condemnation of the Eastern Orthodox Bulgarians as heretics]

bugger about *or* **around** *vb.* (*adv.*) *Sl.* **1.** (*intr.*) to fool about and waste time. **2.** (*tr.*) to create difficulties or complications for (a person).

bugger off *vb.* (*intr., adv.*) *Taboo sl.* to go away; depart.

buggery (ˈbʌgərɪ) *n.* anal intercourse between a man and another man, a woman, or an animal.

buggy[1] (ˈbʌgɪ) *n., pl.* **-gies. 1.** a light horse-drawn carriage having either four wheels (esp. in the U.S. and Canada) or two wheels (esp. in Britain and India). **2.** any small light cart or vehicle, such as a baby buggy or beach buggy. [C18: <?]

buggy[2] (ˈbʌgɪ) *adj.* **-gier, -giest.** infested with bugs.

bugle[1] (ˈbjuːgᵊl) *n.* **1.** *Music.* a brass instrument similar to the cornet but usually without valves: used for military fanfares, signal calls, etc. ~*vb.* **2.** (*intr.*) to play or sound (on) a bugle. [C14: short for *bugle horn* ox horn, < OF *bugle*, < L *būculus* young bullock, < *bōs* ox] —**ˈbugler** *n.*

bugle[2] (ˈbjuːgᵊl) *n.* any of several Eurasian plants having small blue or white flowers. [C13: < LL *bugula*, <?]

bugle[3] (ˈbjuːgᵊl) *n.* a tubular glass or plastic bead sewn onto clothes for decoration. [C16: <?]

bugloss (ˈbjuːglɒs) *n.* any of various hairy Eurasian plants having clusters of blue flowers. [C15: < L, < Gk *buglōssos* ox-tongued]

bugong (ˈbuːgɒŋ) *n.* another name for **bogong.**

buhl (buːl) *adj., n.* a variant spelling of **boulle.**

build (bɪld) *vb.* **building, built. 1.** to make, construct, or form by joining parts or materials: *to build a house.* **2.** (*tr.*) to order the building of: *the government builds most of our hospitals.* **3.** (foll. by *on* or *upon*) to base; found: *his theory was not built on facts.* **4.** (*tr.*) to establish and develop: *it took ten years to build a business.* **5.** (*tr.*) to make in a particular way or for a particular purpose: *the car was not built for speed.* **6.** (*intr.*; often foll. by *up*) to increase in intensity. ~*n.* **7.** physical form, figure, or proportions: *a man with an athletic build.* [OE *byldan*]

builder (ˈbɪldə) *n.* a person who builds, esp. one who contracts for and supervises the construction or repair of buildings.

building (ˈbɪldɪŋ) *n.* **1.** something built with a roof and walls. **2.** the act, business, occupation, or art of building houses, boats, etc.

building society *n.* a cooperative banking enterprise financed by deposits on which interest is paid and from which mortgage loans are advanced on homes and real property.

build up *vb.* (*adv.*) **1.** (*tr.*) to construct gradually, systematically, and in stages. **2.** to increase, accumulate, or strengthen, esp. by degrees: *the murmur built up to a roar.* **3.** (*tr.*) to improve the health or physique of (a person). **4.** (*intr.*) to prepare for or gradually approach a climax. ~*n.* **build-up. 5.** progressive increase in number, size, etc.: *the build-up of industry.* **6.** a gradual approach to a climax. **7.** extravagant publicity or praise, esp. in the form of a campaign. **8.** *Mil.* the process of attaining the required strength of forces and equipment.

built (bɪlt) *vb.* the past tense and past participle of **build.**

built-in *adj.* **1.** made or incorporated as an integral part: *a built-in cupboard.* **2.** essential; inherent. ~*n.* **3.** *Austral.* a built-in cupboard.

built-up *adj.* **1.** having many buildings (esp. in **built-up area**). **2.** increased by the addition of parts: *built-up heels.*

bulb (bʌlb) *n.* **1.** a rounded organ of vegetative reproduction in plants such as the tulip and onion: a flattened stem bearing a central shoot surrounded by fleshy nutritive inner leaves and thin brown outer leaves. **2.** a plant, such as a hyacinth or daffodil, that grows from a bulb. **3.** See **light bulb. 4.** any bulb-shaped thing. [C16: < L *bulbus,* < Gk *bolbos* onion] —ˈ**bulbous** *adj.*

bulbil (ˈbʌlbɪl) *n.* **1.** a small bulb produced from a parent bulb. **2.** a bulblike reproductive organ in a leaf axil of certain plants. [C19: < NL *bulbillus* BULB]

bulbul (ˈbʊlbʊl) *n.* a songbird of tropical Africa and Asia having brown plumage and, in many species, a distinct crest. [C18: via Persian < Ar.]

Bulgarian (bʌlˈgɛərɪən, bʊl-) *adj.* **1.** of or denoting Bulgaria, a country of SE Europe, on the Balkan Peninsula, its people, or their language. ~*n.* **2.** the official language of Bulgaria. **3.** a native or inhabitant of Bulgaria.

bulge (bʌldʒ) *n.* **1.** a swelling or an outward curve. **2.** a sudden increase in number, esp. of population. ~*vb.* **3.** to swell outwards. [C13: < OF *bouge,* < L *bulga* bag, prob. of Gaulish origin] —ˈ**bulging** *adj.* —ˈ**bulgy** *adj.*

bulimia (bjuːˈlɪmɪə) *n.* **1.** pathologically insatiable hunger. **2.** Also called: **bulimia nervosa.** a disorder characterized by compulsive overeating followed by vomiting. [C17: < NL, < Gk *bous* ox + *limos* hunger]

bulk (bʌlk) *n.* **1.** volume, size, or magnitude, esp. when great. **2.** the main part: *the bulk of the work is repetitious.* **3.** a large body, esp. of a person. **4.** the part of food which passes unabsorbed through the digestive system. **5. in bulk. a.** in large quantities. **b.** (of a cargo, etc.) unpackaged. ~*vb.* **6.** to cohere or cause to cohere in a mass. **7. bulk large.** to be or seem important or prominent. [C15: < ON *bulki* cargo]

bulk buying *n.* the purchase of goods in large amounts, often at reduced prices.

bulkhead (ˈbʌlkˌhɛd) *n.* any upright wall-like partition in a ship, aircraft, etc. [C15: prob. < *bulk* projecting framework < ON *bálkr* + HEAD]

bulk modulus *n.* a coefficient of elasticity of a substance equal to the ratio of the applied stress to the resulting fractional change in volume.

bulky (ˈbʌlkɪ) *adj.* **bulkier, bulkiest.** very large and massive, esp. so as to be unwieldy. —ˈ**bulkily** *adv.* —ˈ**bulkiness** *n.*

bull[1] (bʊl) *n.* **1.** any male bovine animal, esp. one that is sexually mature. Related adj.: **taurine. 2.** the male of various other animals including the elephant and whale. **3.** a very large, strong, or aggressive person. **4.** *Stock Exchange.* **a.** a speculator who buys in anticipation of rising prices in order to make a profit on resale. **b.** (*as modifier*): *a bull market.* Cf. **bear**[2] (sense 5). **5.** *Chiefly Brit.* short for **bull's-eye** (senses 1, 2). **6.** *Sl.* short for **bullshit. 7. a bull in a china shop.** a clumsy person. **8. take the bull by the horns.** to face and tackle a difficulty without shirking. ~*adj.* **9.** male; masculine: *a bull elephant.* **10.** large; strong. [OE *bula*]

bull[2] (bʊl) *n.* a ludicrously self-contradictory or inconsistent statement. [C17: <?]

bull[3] (bʊl) *n.* a formal document issued by the pope. [C13: < Med. L *bulla* seal attached to a bull, < L: round object]

Bull (bʊl) *n.* **the.** the constellation Taurus, the second sign of the zodiac.

Bullamakanka (ˌbuːləməˈkæŋkə) *n. Austral.* an imaginary very remote place.

bulldog (ˈbʊlˌdɒg) *n.* a sturdy thickset breed of dog with an undershot jaw, broad head, and a muscular body.

bulldog clip *n.* a clip for holding papers together, consisting of two T-shaped metal clamps held in place by a cylindrical spring.

bulldoze (ˈbʊlˌdəʊz) *vb.* (*tr.*) **1.** to move, demolish, flatten, etc., with a bulldozer. **2.** *Inf.* to force; push. **3.** *Inf.* to intimidate or coerce. [C19: prob. < BULL[1] + DOSE]

bulldozer (ˈbʊlˌdəʊzə) *n.* **1.** a powerful tractor fitted with caterpillar tracks and a blade at the front, used for moving earth, rocks, etc. **2.** *Inf.* a person who bulldozes.

bull dust *n. Austral.* **1.** fine dust, as on roads in outback Australia. **2.** *Sl.* nonsense.

bullet (ˈbʊlɪt) *n.* **1. a.** a small metallic missile enclosed in a cartridge, used as the projectile of a gun, rifle, etc. **b.** the entire cartridge. **2.** something resembling a bullet, esp. in shape or effect. [C16: < F *boulette,* dim. of *boule* ball; see BOWL[2]] —ˈ**bullet-ˌlike** *adj.*

bulletin (ˈbʊlɪtɪn) *n.* **1.** an official statement on a matter of public interest. **2.** a broadcast summary of the news. **3.** a periodical publication of an association, etc. ~*vb.* **4.** (*tr.*) to make known by bulletin. [C17: < F, < It., < *bulletta,* dim. of *bulla* papal edict, BULL[3]]

bulletin board *n.* the U.S. and Canad. name for **notice board.**

bullet loan *n.* a loan which is repaid with interest in a single payment at the end of a fixed term.

bulletproof (ˈbʊlɪtˌpruːf) *adj.* **1.** not penetrable by bullets. ~*vb.* **2.** (*tr.*) to make bulletproof.

bullfight (ˈbʊlˌfaɪt) *n.* a traditional Spanish, Portuguese, and Latin American spectacle in which a matador baits and usually kills a bull in an arena. —ˈ**bullˌfighter** *n.* —ˈ**bullˌfighting** *n.*

bullfinch (ˈbʊlˌfɪntʃ) *n.* **1.** a common European finch: the male has a bright red throat and breast. **2.** any of various similar finches. [C14: see BULL[1], FINCH]

bullfrog (ˈbʊlˌfrɒg) *n.* any of various large American frogs having a loud deep croak.

bullhead (ˈbʊlˌhɛd) *n.* any of various small northern mainly marine fishes that have a large head covered with bony plates and spines.

bull-headed *adj.* blindly obstinate; stupid. —ˌ**bull-ˈheadedly** *adv.* —ˌ**bull-ˈheadedness** *n.*

bullhorn (ˈbʊlˌhɔːn) *n.* the U.S. and Canad. name for **loud-hailer.**

bullion (ˈbʊljən) *n.* **1.** gold or silver in mass. **2.** gold or silver in the form of bars and ingots, suitable for further processing. [C14: < Anglo-F: mint, prob. < OF *bouillir* to boil, < L *bullīre*]

bullish (ˈbʊlɪʃ) *adj.* **1.** like a bull. **2.** *Stock Exchange.* causing, expecting, or characterized by a rise in prices. **3.** *Inf.* cheerful and optimistic.

bull-necked *adj.* having a short thick neck.

bullock (ˈbʊlək) *n.* **1.** a gelded bull; steer. ~*vb.* **2.** (*intr.*) *Austral. & N.Z. inf.* to work hard and long. [OE *bulluc;* see BULL[1], -OCK]

bullocky (ˈbʊləkɪ) *n., pl.* **-ockies.** *Austral. & N.Z.* a bullock driver; teamster.

bullring (ˈbʊlˌrɪŋ) *n.* an arena for bullfighting.

bullroarer (ˈbʊlˌrɔːrə) *n.* a wooden slat attached to a thong that makes a roaring sound when the thong is whirled: used esp. by Australian Aborigines in religious rites.

bull's-eye *n.* **1.** the small central disc of a target, usually the highest valued area. **2.** a shot hitting this. **3.** *Inf.* something that exactly achieves its aim. **4.** a small circular or oval window or opening. **5.** a thick disc of glass set into a ship's deck, etc., to admit light. **6.** the glass boss at the centre of a sheet of blown glass. **7. a.** a small thick plano-convex lens used as a condenser. **b.** a lamp or lantern containing such a lens. **8.** a peppermint-flavoured boiled sweet.

bullshit (ˈbʊlˌʃɪt) *Taboo sl.* ~*n.* **1.** exaggerated or foolish talk; nonsense. **2.** deceitful or pretentious talk. **3.** (in the British Army) exaggerated zeal, esp. for ceremonial drill, cleaning, polishing, etc. Usually shortened to **bull.** ~*vb.* **-shitting, -shitted. 4.** (*intr.*) to talk in an exaggerated or foolish manner. **5.** (*tr.*) to talk bullshit to.

bull terrier *n.* a breed of terrier having a muscular body and thick neck, with a short smooth coat.

bully (ˈbʊlɪ) *n., pl.* **-lies. 1.** a person who hurts, persecutes, or intimidates weaker people. **2.** a small New Zealand freshwater fish. ~*vb.* **-lying, -lied. 3.** (when *tr.*, often foll. by *into*) to hurt, intimidate, or persecute (a weaker or smaller person), esp. to make him do something. ~*adj.* **4.** dashing; jolly: *my bully boy.* **5.** *Inf.* very good; fine. ~*interj.* **6.** Also: **bully for you, him,** etc. *Inf.* well done! bravo! [C16 (in the sense: sweetheart, hence fine fellow, hence swaggering coward): prob. < MDu. *boele* lover, < MHG *buole*]

bully beef *n.* canned corned beef. Often shortened to **bully.** [C19 *bully,* anglicized version of F *bouilli,* < *boeuf bouilli* boiled beef]

bully-off *Hockey.* ~*n.* **1.** the method by which a game is started. Two opposing players stand with the ball between them and alternately strike their sticks together and against the ground three times before trying to hit the ball. ~*vb.* **bully off. 2.** (*intr., adv.*) to start play with a bully-off. ~Often shortened to **bully.** [C19: < ?]

bullyrag (ˈbʊlɪˌræg) *vb.* **-ragging, -ragged.** (*tr.*) to bully, esp. by means of cruel practical jokes. Also: **ballyrag.** [C18: < ?]

bulrush (ˈbʊlˌrʌʃ) *n.* **1.** a popular name for **reed mace. 2.** a grasslike marsh plant used for making mats, chair seats, etc. **3.** a biblical word for **papyrus** (the plant). [C15 *bulrish, bul-* ? < BULL[1] + *rish* RUSH[2]]

bulwark (ˈbʊlwək) *n.* **1.** a wall or similar structure used as a fortification; rampart. **2.** a person or thing acting as a defence. **3.** (*often pl.*) *Naut.* a solid vertical fencelike structure along the outward sides of a deck. **4.** a breakwater or mole. ~*vb.* **5.** (*tr.*) to defend or fortify with or as if with a bulwark. [C15: via Du. < MHG *bolwerk,* < *bol* plank, BOLE + *werk* WORK]

bum[1] (bʌm) *n. Brit. sl.* the buttocks or anus. [C14: <?]

bum[2] (bʌm) *Inf., chiefly U.S. & Canad.* ~*n.* **1.** a disreputable loafer or idler. **2.** a tramp; hobo. ~*vb.* **bumming, bummed. 3.** (*tr.*) to get by begging; cadge: *to bum a lift.* **4.** (*intr.;* often foll. by *around*) to live by begging or as a vagrant or loafer. **5.** (*intr.;* usually foll. by *around*) to spend time to no good purpose; loaf; idle. ~*adj.* **6.** (*prenominal*) of poor quality; useless. [C19: prob. shortened < earlier *bummer* a loafer, prob. < G *bummeln* to loaf]

bumbailiff (ˌbʌmˈbeɪlɪf) *n. Brit. derog.* (formerly) an officer employed to collect debts and arrest debtors. [C17: < BUM[1] + *bailiff,* so called because he follows hard behind debtors]

bumble (ˈbʌmbᵊl) *vb.* **1.** to speak or do in a clumsy, muddled, or inefficient way. **2.** (*intr.*) to proceed unsteadily. [C16: ? a blend of BUNGLE + STUMBLE] —ˈ**bumbler** *n.* —ˈ**bumbling** *adj., n.*

bumblebee (ˈbʌmbᵊlˌbiː) *or* **humblebee** *n.* any large hairy social bee of temperate regions. [C16: < *bumble* to buzz + BEE]

bumf (bʌmf) *n.* a variant spelling of **bumph.**

bump (bʌmp) *vb.* **1.** (when *intr.,* usually foll. by *against* or *into*) to knock or strike with a jolt. **2.** (*intr.;* often foll. by *along*) to travel or proceed in jerks and jolts. **3.** (*tr.*) to hurt by knocking. **4.** *Cricket.* to bowl (a ball) so that it bounces high on pitching or (of a ball) to bounce high when bowled. ~*n.* **5.** an impact; knock; jolt; collision. **6.** a dull thud or other noise from an impact or collision. **7.** the shock of a blow or collision. **8.** a lump on the body caused by a blow. **9.** a protuberance, as on a road surface. **10.** any of the natural protuberances of the human skull, said by phrenologists to indicate underlying faculties and character. ~See also **bump into, bump off, bump up.** [C16: prob. imit.]

bumper[1] (ˈbʌmpə) *n.* **1.** a horizontal usually metal bar attached to the front or rear end of a car, lorry, etc., to protect against damage from impact. **2.** *Cricket.* a ball bowled so that it bounces high on pitching; bouncer.

bumper[2] (ˈbʌmpə) *n.* **1.** a glass, tankard, etc., filled to the brim, esp. as a toast. **2.** an unusually large or fine example of something. ~*adj.* **3.** unusually large, fine, or abundant: *a bumper crop.* [C17 (in the sense: a brimming glass): prob. < *bump* (obs. vb.) to bulge; see BUMP]

bumph *or* **bumf** (bʌmf) *n. Brit.* **1.** *Inf., derog.* official documents, forms, etc. **2.** *Sl.* toilet paper. [C19: short for earlier *bumfodder;* see BUM[1]]

bump into *vb.* (*intr., prep.*) *Inf.* to meet by chance; encounter unexpectedly.

bumpkin (ˈbʌmpkɪn) *n.* an awkward simple rustic person (esp. in **country bumpkin**). [C16: ? < Du. *boomken* small tree, or < MDu. *boomekijn* small barrel]

bump off *vb.* (*tr., adv.*) *Sl.* to murder; kill.

bumptious (ˈbʌmpʃəs) *adj.* offensively self-assertive or conceited. [C19: ? < BUMP + FRACTIOUS] —ˈ**bumptiously** *adv.* —ˈ**bumptiousness** *n.*

bump up *vb.* (*tr., adv.*) *Inf.* to raise or increase.

bumpy (ˈbʌmpɪ) *adj.* **bumpier, bumpiest. 1.** having an uneven surface. **2.** full of jolts; rough. —ˈ**bumpily** *adv.* —ˈ**bumpiness** *n.*

bun (bʌn) *n.* **1.** a small roll, similar to bread but usually containing sweetening, currants, etc. **2.** *Chiefly Scot. & N English.* any of various small round cakes. **3.** a hairstyle in which long hair is gathered into a bun shape at the back of the head. [C14: <?]

bunch (bʌntʃ) *n.* **1.** a number of things growing, fastened, or grouped together: *a bunch of grapes; a bunch of keys.* **2.** a collection; group: *a bunch of queries.* **3.** *Inf.* a group or company: *a bunch of boys.* ~*vb.* **4.** (sometimes foll. by *up*) to group or be grouped into a bunch. [C14: <?]

bunchy (ˈbʌntʃɪ) *adj.* **bunchier, bunchiest. 1.** composed of or resembling bunches. **2.** bulging.

buncombe (ˈbʌŋkəm) *n.* a variant spelling (esp. U.S.) of **bunkum.**

bundle (ˈbʌndᵊl) *n.* **1.** a number of things or a quantity of material gathered or loosely bound together: *a bundle of sticks.* Related adj.: **fascicular. 2.** something wrapped or tied for carrying; package. **3.** *Sl.* a large sum of money. **4. go a bundle on.** *Sl.* to be extremely fond of. **5.** *Biol.* a collection of strands of specialized tissue such as nerve fibres. **6.** *Bot.* short for **vascular bundle. 7. drop one's bundle.** *Austral. & N.Z. sl.* to panic or give up hope. ~*vb.* **8.** (*tr.;* often foll. by *up*) to make into a bundle. **9.** (foll. by *out, off, into,* etc.) to go or cause to go, esp. roughly or unceremoniously. **10.** (*tr.;* usually foll. by *into*) to push or throw, esp. quickly and untidily. **11.** (*intr.*) to sleep or lie in one's clothes on the same bed as one's betrothed: formerly a custom in New England, Wales, and elsewhere. [C14: prob. < MDu. *bundel;* rel. to OE *bindele* bandage; see BIND, BOND] —ˈ**bundler** *n.*

bundle up *vb.* (*adv.*) **1.** to dress (somebody) warmly and snugly. **2.** (*tr.*) to make (something) into a bundle or bundles, esp. by tying.

bundu (ˈbʊndʊ) *n. S. African & Zimbabwean sl.* a

largely uninhabited wild region far from towns. [C20: < a Bantu language]

bun fight *n. Brit. sl.* **1.** a tea party. **2.** *Ironic.* an official function.

bung[1] (bʌŋ) *n.* **1.** a stopper, esp. of cork or rubber, for a cask, etc. **2.** short for **bunghole.** ~*vb.* (*tr.*) **3.** (often foll. by *up*) *Inf.* to close or seal with or as with a bung. **4.** *Brit. sl.* to throw; sling. **5. bung it on.** *Austral. sl.* to behave in a pretentious manner. [C15: < MDu. *bonghe*]

bung[2] (bʌŋ) *adj. Austral. & N.Z. sl.* **1.** dead. **2.** destroyed. **3.** useless. **4. go bung. a.** to fail or collapse. **b.** to die. [C19: < Abor.]

bungalow (ˈbʌŋɡəˌləʊ) *n.* a one-storey house, sometimes with an attic. [C17: < Hindi *banglā* (house) of the Bengal type]

bunghole (ˈbʌŋˌhəʊl) *n.* a hole in a cask, barrel, etc., through which liquid can be drained.

bungle (ˈbʌŋɡᵊl) *vb.* **1.** (*tr.*) to spoil (an operation) through clumsiness, incompetence, etc.; botch. ~*n.* **2.** a clumsy or unsuccessful performance; mistake; botch. [C16: ? of Scand. origin] —ˈ**bungler** *n.* —ˈ**bungling** *adj., n.*

bunion (ˈbʌnjən) *n.* an inflamed swelling of the first joint of the big toe. [C18: ? < obs. *bunny* a swelling, <?]

bunk[1] (bʌŋk) *n.* **1.** a narrow shelflike bed fixed along a wall. **2.** short for **bunk bed. 3.** *Inf.* any place where one sleeps. ~*vb.* **4.** (*intr.;* often foll. by *down*) to prepare to sleep: *he bunked down on the floor.* **5.** (*intr.*) to occupy a bunk or bed. [C19: prob. short for BUNKER]

bunk[2] (bʌŋk) *n. Inf.* short for **bunkum** (sense 1).

bunk[3] (bʌŋk) *n. Brit. sl.* a hurried departure, usually under suspicious circumstances (esp. in **do a bunk).** [C19: ? < BUNK[1] (in the sense: to occupy a bunk, hence a hurried departure)]

bunk bed *n.* one of a pair of beds constructed one above the other to save space.

bunker (ˈbʌŋkə) *n.* **1.** a large storage container or tank, as for coal. **2.** Also called (esp. U.S. and Canad.): **sand trap.** an obstacle on a golf course, usually a sand-filled hollow bordered by a ridge. **3.** an underground shelter with a bank and embrasures for guns above ground. ~*vb.* **4.** (*tr.*) *Golf.* **a.** to drive (the ball) into a bunker. **b.** (*passive*) to have one's ball trapped in a bunker. [C16 (in the sense: chest, box): < Scot. *bonkar,* <?]

bunkhouse (ˈbʌŋkˌhaʊs) *n.* (in the U.S. and Canada) a building containing the sleeping quarters of workers on a ranch.

bunkum *or* **buncombe** (ˈbʌŋkəm) *n.* **1.** empty talk; nonsense. **2.** *Chiefly U.S.* empty or insincere speechmaking by a politician. [C19: after *Buncombe,* a county in North Carolina, alluded to in an inane speech by its Congressional representative Felix Walker (about 1820)]

bunny (ˈbʌnɪ) *n., pl.* **-nies. 1.** Also called: **bunny rabbit.** a child's word for **rabbit** (sense 1). **2.** Also called: **bunny girl.** a night-club hostess whose costume includes rabbit-like tail and ears. **3.** *Austral. sl.* a mug; dupe. [C17: < Scot. Gaelic *bun* scut of a rabbit]

Bunsen burner (ˈbʌnsᵊn) *n.* a gas burner consisting of a metal tube with an adjustable air valve at the base. [C19: after R. W. *Bunsen* (1811-99), G chemist]

bunting[1] (ˈbʌntɪŋ) *n.* **1.** a coarse, loosely woven cotton fabric used for flags, etc. **2.** decorative flags, pennants, and streamers. [C18: <?]

bunting[2] (ˈbʌntɪŋ) *n.* any of numerous seed-eating songbirds of the Old World and North America having short stout bills. [C13: <?]

buntline (ˈbʌntlɪn, -ˌlaɪn) *n. Naut.* one of several lines fastened to the foot of a square sail for hauling it up to the yard when furling. [C17: < *bunt* centre of a sail + LINE[1] (sense 11)]

bunya-bunya (ˈbʌnjəˈbʌnjə) *or* **bunya** *n.* a tall dome-shaped Australian coniferous tree having edible seeds and thickish flattened needles. [C19: < Abor.]

bunyip (ˈbʌnjɪp) *n. Austral.* a legendary monster said to inhabit swamps and lagoons. [C19: < Abor.]

buoy (bɔɪ; *U.S.* ˈbuːɪ) *n.* **1.** a distinctively shaped and coloured float, anchored to the bottom, for designating moorings, navigable channels, or obstructions in a body of water. See also **life buoy.** ~*vb.* **2.** (*tr.;* usually foll. by *up*) to prevent from sinking: *the life belt buoyed him up.* **3.** (*tr.;* usually foll. by *up*) to raise the spirits of; hearten. **4.** (*tr.*) *Naut.* to mark (a channel or obstruction) with a buoy or buoys. **5.** (*intr.*) to rise to the surface; float. [C13: prob. of Gmc origin]

buoyancy (ˈbɔɪənsɪ) *n.* **1.** the ability to float in a liquid or to rise in liquid, air, or other gas. **2.** the tendency of a fluid to keep a body afloat. **3.** the ability to recover quickly after setbacks; resilience. **4.** cheerfulness.

buoyant (ˈbɔɪənt) *adj.* **1.** able to float in or rise to the surface of a liquid. **2.** (of a liquid or gas) able to keep a body afloat. **3.** cheerful or resilient. [C16: prob. < Sp. *boyante,* < *boyar* to float]

BUPA (ˈbjuːpə, ˈbuːpə) *n. acronym for* British United Provident Association.

bur (bɜː) *n.* **1.** a seed vessel or flower head having hooks or prickles. **2.** any plant that produces burs. **3.** a person or thing that clings like a bur. **4.** a small surgical or dental drill. ~*vb.* **burring, burred. 5.** (*tr.*) to remove burs from. ~Also: **burr.** [C14: prob. < ON]

burble (ˈbɜːbᵊl) *vb.* **1.** to make or utter with a bubbling sound; gurgle. **2.** (*intr.;* often foll. by *away* or *on*) to talk quickly and excitedly. ~*n.* **3.** a bubbling or gurgling sound. **4.** a flow of excited speech. [C14: prob. imit.] —ˈ**burbler** *n.*

burbot (ˈbɜːbət) *n., pl.* **-bots** *or* **-bot.** a freshwater gadoid food fish that has barbels around its mouth and occurs in Europe, Asia, and North America. [C14: < OF *bourbotte,* < *bourbeter* to wallow in mud, < *bourbe* mud]

burden[1] (ˈbɜːdᵊn) *n.* **1.** something that is carried; load. **2.** something that is exacting, oppressive, or difficult to bear. Related adj.: **onerous. 3.** *Naut.* **a.** the cargo capacity of a ship. **b.** the weight of a ship's cargo. ~*vb.* (*tr.*) **4.** (sometimes foll. by *up*) to put or impose a burden on; load. **5.** to weigh down; oppress. [OE *byrthen*]

burden[2] (ˈbɜːdᵊn) *n.* **1.** a line of words recurring at the end of each verse of a song; chorus or refrain. **2.** the theme of a speech, book, etc. **3.** another word for **bourdon.** [C16: < OF *bourdon* bass horn, droning sound, imit.]

burden of proof *n. Law.* the obligation to provide evidence that will convince the court or jury of the truth of one's contention.

burdensome (ˈbɜːdᵊnsəm) *adj.* hard to bear.

burdock (ˈbɜːˌdɒk) *n.* a coarse weedy Eurasian plant having large heart-shaped leaves, tiny purple flowers surrounded by hooked bristles, and burlike fruits. [C16: < BUR + DOCK[4]]

bureau (ˈbjʊərəʊ) *n., pl.* **-reaus** *or* **-reaux. 1.** *Chiefly Brit.* a writing desk with pigeonholes, drawers, etc., against which the writing surface can be closed when not in use. **2.** *U.S.* a chest of drawers. **3.** an office or agency, esp. one providing services for the public. **4.** a government department. [C17: < F, orig.: type of cloth used for covering desks, < OF *burel*]

bureaucracy (bjʊəˈrɒkrəsɪ) *n., pl.* **-cies. 1.** a system of administration based upon organization into bureaus, division of labour, a hierarchy of authority, etc. **2.** government by such a system. **3.** government or other officials collectively. **4.** any administration in which action is impeded by unnecessary official procedures.

bureaucrat (ˈbjʊərəˌkræt) *n.* **1.** an official in a bureaucracy. **2.** an official who adheres to bureaucracy, esp. rigidly. —ˌ**bureauˈcratic** *adj.* —ˌ**bureauˈcratically** *adv.*

bureaucratize *or* **-tise** (bjʊəˈrɒkrəˌtaɪz) *vb.* (*tr.*) to administer by or transform into a bureaucracy. —**buˌreaucratiˈzation** *or* **-tiˈsation** *n.*

bureaux (ˈbjʊərəʊz) *n.* a plural of **bureau.**

burette *or U.S.* **buret** (bjʊˈrɛt) *n.* a graduated glass tube with a stopcock on one end for dispensing and transferring known volumes of fluids, esp. liquids. [C15: < F, < OF *buire* ewer]

burg (bɜːɡ) *n.* **1.** *History.* a fortified town. **2.** *U.S.*

inf. a town or city. [C18 (in the sense: fortress): < OHG *burg*]

burgage ('bɜːgɪdʒ) *n. History.* **1.** (in England) tenure of land or tenement in a town or city, which originally involved a fixed money rent. **2.** (in Scotland) the tenure of land direct from the crown in Scottish royal burghs in return for watching and warding. [C14: < Med. L *burgāgium,* < OE *burg*]

burgeon *or* **bourgeon** ('bɜːdʒən) *vb.* **1.** (often foll. by *forth* or *out*) (of a plant) to sprout (buds). **2.** (*intr.;* often foll. by *forth* or *out*) to develop or grow rapidly; flourish. [C13: < OF *burjon*]

burger ('bɜːgə) *n. Inf.* **a.** short for **hamburger.** **b.** (*in combination*): *a cheeseburger.*

burgess ('bɜːdʒɪs) *n.* **1.** (in England) a citizen, freeman, or inhabitant of a borough. **2.** *English history.* a Member of Parliament from a borough, corporate town, or university. [C13: < OF *burgeis;* see BOROUGH]

burgh ('bʌrə) *n.* **1.** (in Scotland until 1975) a town, esp. one incorporated by charter, that enjoyed a degree of self-government. **2.** an archaic form of **borough.** [C14: Scot. form of BOROUGH] —**burghal** ('bɜːgᵊl) *adj.*

burgher ('bɜːgə) *n.* **1.** a member of the trading or mercantile class of a medieval city. **2.** a respectable citizen; bourgeois. **3.** *Arch.* a citizen or inhabitant of a corporate town, esp on the Continent. **4.** *S. African history.* a citizen of the Cape Colony or of one of the Transvaal and Free State republics. [C16: < G *Bürger* or Du. *burger* freeman of a BOROUGH]

burglar ('bɜːglə) *n.* a person who commits burglary; housebreaker. [C15: < Anglo-F, < Med. L *burglātor,* prob. < *burgāre* to thieve]

burglary ('bɜːglərɪ) *n., pl.* **-ries.** the crime of entering a building as a trespasser to commit theft or another offence. —**burglarious** (bɜː'glɛərɪəs) *adj.* —'**burgla,rize** *or* **-ise** *vb.* (*tr.*)

burgle ('bɜːgᵊl) *vb.* to commit burglary upon (a house, etc.).

burgomaster ('bɜːgə,mɑːstə) *n.* the chief magistrate of a town in Austria, Belgium, Germany, or the Netherlands; mayor. [C16: partial translation of Du. *burgemeester;* see BOROUGH, MASTER]

burial ('bɛrɪəl) *n.* the act of burying, esp. the interment of a dead body. [OE *byrgels* burial place, tomb; see BURY, -AL[2]]

burial ground *n.* a graveyard or cemetery.

burin ('bjʊərɪn) *n.* **1.** a chisel of tempered steel used for engraving metal, wood, or marble. **2.** *Archaeol.* a prehistoric flint tool. [C17: < F, ? < It. *burino,* of Gmc origin]

burk *or* **berk** (bɜːk) *n. Brit. sl.* a stupid person; fool. [C20: shortened < *Berkeley* or *Berkshire Hunt,* rhyming slang for *cunt*]

burl[1] (bɜːl) *n.* **1.** a small knot or lump in wool. **2.** a roundish warty outgrowth from certain trees. ~*vb.* **3.** (*tr.*) to remove the burls from (cloth). [C15: < OF *burle* tuft of wool, prob. ult. < LL *burra* shaggy cloth] —'**burler** *n.*

burl[2] *or* **birl** (bɜːl) *n. Inf.* **1.** *Scot., Austral., & N.Z.* an attempt; try (esp. in **give it a burl**). **2.** *Austral. & N.Z.* a ride in a car. [C20: ? < BIRL in Scots sense: to spin or turn]

burlap ('bɜːlæp) *n.* a coarse fabric woven from jute, hemp, or the like. [C17: < *borel* coarse cloth, < OF *burel* (see BUREAU) + LAP[1]]

burlesque (bɜː'lɛsk) *n.* **1.** an artistic work, esp. literary or dramatic, satirizing a subject by caricaturing it. **2.** a ludicrous imitation or caricature. **3.** Also: **burlesk.** *U.S. & Canad. theatre.* a bawdy comedy show of the late 19th and early 20th centuries: the striptease eventually became one of its chief elements. ~*adj.* **4.** of, relating to, or characteristic of a burlesque. ~*vb.* **-lesquing, -lesqued.** **5.** to represent or imitate (a person or thing) in a ludicrous way; caricature. [C17: < F, < It., < *burla* a jest, piece of nonsense] —**bur'lesquer** *n.*

burley ('bɜːlɪ) *n.* a variant spelling of **berley.**

burly ('bɜːlɪ) *adj.* **-lier, -liest.** large and thick of build; sturdy. [C13: of Gmc origin] —'**burliness** *n.*

Burmese (bɜː'miːz) *adj. also* **Burman.** **1.** of or denoting Burma, a country of SE Asia, or its inhabitants, their customs, etc. ~*n.* **2.** (*pl.* **-mese**) a native or inhabitant of Burma. **3.** the language of the Burmese.

burn[1] (bɜːn) *vb.* **burning, burnt** *or* **burned.** **1.** to undergo or cause to undergo combustion. **2.** to destroy or be destroyed by fire. **3.** (*tr.*) to damage, injure, or mark by heat: *he burnt his hand; she was burnt by the sun.* **4.** to die or put to death by fire. **5.** (*intr.*) to be or feel hot: *my forehead burns.* **6.** to smart or cause to smart: *brandy burns one's throat.* **7.** (*intr.*) to feel strong emotion, esp. anger or passion. **8.** (*tr.*) to use for the purposes of light, heat, or power: *to burn coal.* **9.** (*tr.*) to form by or as if by fire: *to burn a hole.* **10.** to char or become charred: *the potatoes are burning.* **11.** (*tr.*) to brand or cauterize. **12.** to produce by or subject to heat as part of a process: *to burn charcoal.* **13.** **burn one's boats** *or* **bridges.** to commit oneself to a particular course of action with no possibility of turning back. **14.** **burn one's fingers.** to suffer from having meddled or interfered. ~*n.* **15.** an injury caused by exposure to heat, electrical, chemical, or radioactive agents. **16.** a mark, e.g. on wood, caused by burning. **17.** a controlled use of rocket propellant, esp. for a course correction. **18.** a hot painful sensation in a muscle, experienced during vigorous exercise. **19.** *Sl.* tobacco or a cigarette. ~See also **burn out.** [OE *beornan* (intr.), *bærnan* (tr.)]

burn[2] (bɜːn) *n. Scot.* a small stream; brook. [OE *burna;* rel. to ON *brunnr* spring]

burner ('bɜːnə) *n.* **1.** the part of a stove, lamp, etc., that produces flame or heat. **2.** an apparatus for burning something, as fuel or refuse.

burnet ('bɜːnɪt) *n.* **1.** a plant of the rose family which has purple-tinged green flowers and leaves. **2.** **burnet rose.** a very prickly Eurasian rose with white flowers and purplish-black fruits. **3.** a moth with red-spotted dark green wings and antennae with enlarged tips. [C14: < OF *burnete,* var. of *brunete* BRUNETTE]

burning ('bɜːnɪŋ) *adj.* **1.** intense; passionate. **2.** urgent; crucial: *a burning problem.*

burning bush *n.* **1.** any of several shrubs or trees that have bright red fruits or seeds. **2.** any of several plants with a bright red autumn foliage. **3.** *Bible.* the bush that burned without being consumed, from which God spoke to Moses (Exodus 3:2–4).

burning glass *n.* a convex lens for concentrating the sun's rays to produce fire.

burnish ('bɜːnɪʃ) *vb.* **1.** to make or become shiny or smooth by friction; polish. ~*n.* **2.** a shiny finish; lustre. [C14 *burnischen,* < OF *brunir* to make brown, < *brun* BROWN] —'**burnisher** *n.*

burnoose, burnous, *or* **burnouse** (bɜː'nuːs, -'nuːz) *n.* a long circular cloak with a hood attached, worn esp. by Arabs. [C20: via F *burnous* < Ar. *burnus,* < Gk *birros* cloak]

burn out *vb.* (*adv.*) **1.** to become or cause to become inoperative as a result of heat or friction: *the clutch burnt out.* **2.** (*intr.*) (of a rocket, jet engine, etc.) to cease functioning as a result of exhaustion of the fuel supply. **3.** (*tr.; usually passive*) to destroy by fire. **4.** to become or cause to become exhausted through overwork or dissipation.

burnt (bɜːnt) *vb.* **1.** a past tense and past participle of **burn**[1]. ~*adj.* **2.** affected by or as if by burning; charred.

burnt offering *n.* a sacrificial offering burnt, usually on an altar, to honour, propitiate, or supplicate a deity.

burnt sienna *n.* **1.** a reddish-brown pigment obtained by roasting raw sienna. ~*n., adj.* **2.** (of) a reddish-brown colour.

burnt umber *n.* **1.** a brown pigment obtained by heating umber. ~*n., adj.* **2.** (of) a dark brown colour.

burp (bɜːp) *n.* **1.** *Inf.* a belch. ~*vb.* **2.** (*intr.*) *Inf.* to belch. **3.** (*tr.*) to cause (a baby) to burp. [C20: imit.]

burr[1] (bɜː) *n.* **1.** a small power-driven hand-operated rotary file, esp. for removing burrs or for machining recesses. **2.** a rough edge left on a workpiece after cutting, drilling, etc. **3.** a rough or irregular protuberance, such as a burl on a tree. **4.** a variant spelling of **bur.** [C14: var. of BUR]

burr[2] (bɜː) *n.* **1.** an articulation of (r) characteristic of certain English dialects, esp. the uvular fricative trill of Northumberland or the retroflex *r* of the West of England. **2.** a whirring sound. ~*vb.* **3.** to pronounce (words) with a burr. **4.** (*intr.*) to make a whirring sound. [C18: either special use of BUR (in the sense: rough sound) or imit.]

burro (ˈbʊrəʊ) *n., pl.* **-ros.** a donkey, esp. one used as a pack animal. [C19: Sp., < Port., < *burrico*]

burrow (ˈbʌrəʊ) *n.* **1.** a hole dug in the ground by a rabbit or other small animal. **2.** a small snug place affording shelter or retreat. ~*vb.* **3.** to dig (a burrow) in, through, or under (ground). **4.** (*intr.;* often foll. by *through*) to move through by or as by digging. **5.** (*intr.*) to hide or live in a burrow. **6.** (*intr.*) to delve deeply: *he burrowed into his pockets.* **7.** to hide (oneself). [C13: prob. var. of BOROUGH] —ˈ**burrower** *n.*

burry (ˈbɜːrɪ) *adj.* **-rier, -riest.** **1.** full of or covered in burs. **2.** resembling burs; prickly.

bursa (ˈbɜːsə) *n., pl.* **-sae** (-siː) *or* **-sas.** *Anat.* a small fluid-filled sac that reduces friction, esp. at joints. [C19: < Med. L: bag, pouch, < Gk: skin, hide; see PURSE] —ˈ**bursal** *adj.*

bursar (ˈbɜːsə) *n.* **1.** a treasurer of a school, college, or university. **2.** *Chiefly Scot. & N.Z.* a student holding a bursary. [C13: < Med. L *bursārius* keeper of the purse, < *bursa* purse]

bursary (ˈbɜːsərɪ) *n., pl.* **-ries.** **1.** Also called: ˈ**bursar,ship.** a scholarship awarded esp. in Scottish and New Zealand schools and universities. **2.** *Brit.* the treasury of a college, etc. —**bursarial** (bɜːˈsɛərɪəl) *adj.*

bursitis (bɜːˈsaɪtɪs) *n.* inflammation of a bursa.

burst (bɜːst) *vb.* **bursting, burst.** **1.** to break or cause to break open or apart suddenly and noisily; explode. **2.** (*intr.*) to come, go, etc., suddenly and forcibly: *he burst into the room.* **3.** (*intr.*) to be full to the point of breaking open. **4.** (*intr.*) to give vent (to) suddenly or loudly: *to burst into song.* **5.** (*tr.*) to cause or suffer the rupture of: *to burst a blood vessel.* ~*n.* **6.** a sudden breaking open; explosion. **7.** a break; breach; rupture. **8.** a sudden display or increase of effort; spurt: *a burst of speed.* **9.** a sudden and violent emission, occurrence, or outbreak: *a burst of applause.* **10.** a volley of fire from a weapon. [OE *berstan*]

burthen (ˈbɜːðən) *n., vb.* an archaic word for **burden**[1]. —ˈ**burthensome** *adj.*

burton (ˈbɜːtᵊn) *n.* **go for a burton.** *Brit. sl.* **a.** to be broken, useless, or lost. **b.** to die. [C20: <?]

bury (ˈbɛrɪ) *vb.* **burying, buried.** (*tr.*) **1.** to place (a corpse) in a grave; inter. **2.** to place in the earth and cover with soil. **3.** to cover from sight; hide. **4.** to embed; sink: *to bury a nail in plaster.* **5.** to occupy (oneself) with deep concentration; engross: *to be buried in a book.* **6.** to dismiss from the mind; abandon: *to bury old hatreds.* [OE *byrgan*]

bus (bʌs) *n., pl.* **buses** *or* **busses.** **1.** a large motor vehicle designed to carry passengers between stopping places along a regular route. More formal name: **omnibus.** **2.** (*modifier*) of or relating to a bus or buses: *a bus driver; a bus station.* **3.** *Inf.* a car or aircraft, esp. one that is old and shaky. **4.** *Electronics, computers.* short for **busbar.** **5. miss the bus.** to miss an opportunity. ~*vb.* **busing, bused** *or* **bussing, bussed.** **6.** to travel or transport by bus. **7.** *Chiefly U.S. & Canad.* to transport (children) by bus from one area to another in order to create racially integrated schools. [C19: short for OMNIBUS]

bus. *abbrev. for* business.

busbar (ˈbʌz,bɑː) *n.* **1.** an electrical conductor usually used to make a common connection between several circuits. **2.** a group of such electrical conductors maintained at a low voltage, used for carrying data in binary form between the various parts of a computer or its peripherals.

busby (ˈbʌzbɪ) *n., pl.* **-bies.** **1.** a tall fur helmet worn by hussars. **2.** (not in official usage) another name for **bearskin** (the hat). [C18: ? < a proper name]

bush[1] (bʊʃ) *n.* **1.** a dense woody plant, smaller than a tree, with many branches arising from the lower part of the stem; shrub. **2.** a dense cluster of such shrubs; thicket. **3.** something resembling a bush, esp. in density: *a bush of hair.* **4.** (often preceded by *the*) an uncultivated or sparsely settled area, covered with trees or shrubs, which can vary from open, shrubby country to dense rainforest. **5.** a forested area; woodland. **6.** *Canad.* Also called: **bush lot, woodlot.** an area on a farm on which timber is grown and cut. **7.** (often preceded by *the*) *Inf.* the countryside, as opposed to the city: *out in the bush.* **8.** *Obs.* a bunch of ivy hung as a vintner's sign in front of a tavern. **9. beat about the bush.** to avoid the point at issue; prevaricate. ~*adj.* **10.** *Austral. & N.Z. inf.* rough-and-ready. **11. go bush.** *Inf.* **a.** *Austral.* to go off into the bush. **b.** *Austral.* to go into hiding. **c.** *N.Z.* to abandon city amenities and live rough. ~*vb.* **12.** (*intr.*) to grow thick and bushy. **13.** (*tr.*) to cover, decorate, support, etc., with bushes. **14. bush it.** *Austral.* to camp out in the bush. [C13: of Gmc origin]

bush[2] (bʊʃ) *n.* **1.** a thin metal sleeve or tubular lining serving as a bearing. ~*vb.* **2.** to fit a bush to (a casing, bearing, etc.). [C15: < MDu. *busse* box, bush; rel. to LL *buxis* BOX[1]]

bushbaby (ˈbʊʃ,beɪbɪ) *n., pl.* **-babies.** an agile nocturnal arboreal primate occurring in Africa south of the Sahara. It has large eyes and ears and a long tail. Also called: **galago.**

bushbuck (ˈbʊʃ,bʌk) *or* **boschbok** (ˈbɒʃ,bʌk) *n., pl.* **-bucks, -buck** *or* **-boks, -bok.** a small nocturnal spiral-horned antelope of the bush and tropical forest of Africa.

bush carpenter *n. Austral. & N.Z.* a rough-and-ready unskilled workman.

bushed (bʊʃt) *adj. Inf.* **1.** (*postpositive*) extremely tired; exhausted. **2.** *Canad.* mentally disturbed from living in isolation. **3.** *Austral. & N.Z.* lost or bewildered, as in the bush.

bushel (ˈbʊʃəl) *n.* **1.** a British unit of dry or liquid measure equal to 8 Imperial gallons. 1 Imperial bushel is equivalent to 0.036 37 cubic metres. **2.** a U.S. unit of dry measure equal to 64 U.S. pints. 1 U.S. bushel is equivalent to 0.035 24 cubic metres. **3.** a container with a capacity equal to either of these quantities. **4.** *U.S. inf.* a large amount. **5. hide one's light under a bushel.** to conceal one's abilities or good qualities. [C14: < OF *boissel*]

bushfire (ˈbʊʃ,faɪə) *n.* a wild fire in the bush; a scrub or forest fire.

bushfly (ˈbʊʃ,flaɪ) *n. pl.* **-flies.** any of various small black dipterous flies of Australia that breed in faeces and dung.

bush house *n. Chiefly Austral.* a shed or hut in the bush or a garden.

Bushido (,buːʃɪˈdəʊ) *n.* (*sometimes not cap.*) the feudal code of the Japanese samurai. [C19: < Japanese *bushi* warrior + *dō* way]

bushie (ˈbʊʃɪ) *n.* a variant spelling of **bushy**[2].

bushing (ˈbʊʃɪŋ) *n.* **1.** another word for **bush**[2]. **2.** an adapter used to connect pipes of different sizes. **3.** a layer of electrical insulation enabling a live conductor to pass through an earthed wall, etc.

bush jacket *or* **shirt** *n.* a casual jacket or shirt having four patch pockets and a belt.

bush lawyer *n. Austral. & N.Z.* **1.** a trailing plant with sharp hooks. **2.** *Inf.* a person who gives legal opinions but is not qualified to do so.

bush line *n.* an airline operating in the bush country of Canada's northern regions.

bushman (ˈbʊʃmən) *n., pl.* **-men.** *Austral. & N.Z.* a person who lives or travels in the bush, esp. one versed in bush lore.

Bushman (ˈbʊʃmən) *n., pl.* **-men.** a member of a hunting and gathering people of southern Africa. [C18: < Afrik. *boschjesman*]

bushmaster (ˈbʊʃ,mɑːstə) *n.* a large greyish-brown highly venomous snake inhabiting wooded regions of tropical America.

bush pilot *n. Canad.* a pilot who operates in the bush country.

bushranger (ˈbʊʃˌreɪndʒə) *n.* **1.** *Austral.* (formerly) an outlaw living in the bush. **2.** *U.S.* a person who lives away from civilization.

bush sickness *n. N.Z.* an animal disease caused by mineral deficiency in old bush country. —ˈ**bush-ˌsick** *adj.*

bush tea *n.* **1.** a leguminous shrub of southern Africa. **2.** a beverage prepared from the dried leaves of such a plant.

bush telegraph *n.* a means of spreading rumour, gossip, etc.

bushveld (ˈbʊʃˌfɛlt) *n. S. African.* bushy countryside. [< Afrik. *bosveld*]

bushwhack (ˈbʊʃˌwæk) *vb.* **1.** (*tr.*) *U.S. & Canad.* to ambush. **2.** (*intr.*) *U.S. & Canad.* to cut or beat one's way through thick woods. **3.** (*intr.*) *U.S., Canad., & Austral.* to range or move around in woods or the bush. **4.** (*intr.*) *N.Z.* to work in the bush. **5.** (*intr.*) *U.S. & Canad.* to fight as a guerrilla in wild regions.

bushwhacker (ˈbʊʃˌwækə) *n.* **1.** *U.S., Canad., & Austral.* a person who travels around or lives in thinly populated woodlands. **2.** *Austral. sl.* an unsophisticated person. **3.** *N.Z.* a person who works in the bush. **4.** a Confederate guerrilla in the American Civil War. **5.** *U.S.* any guerrilla.

bushy[1] (ˈbʊʃɪ) *adj.* **bushier, bushiest.** **1.** covered or overgrown with bushes. **2.** thick and shaggy. —ˈ**bushily** *adv.* —ˈ**bushiness** *n.*

bushy[2] *or* **bushie** (ˈbʊʃɪ) *n., pl.* **bushies.** *Austral. inf.* **1.** a person who lives in the bush. **2.** an unsophisticated uncouth person.

business (ˈbɪznɪs) *n.* **1.** a trade or profession. **2.** the purchase and sale of goods and services. **3.** a commercial or industrial establishment. **4.** commercial activity; dealings (esp. in **do business**). **5.** volume of commercial activity: *business is poor today.* **6.** commercial policy: *overcharging is bad business.* **7.** proper or rightful concern or responsibility (often in **mind one's own business**). **8.** a special task; assignment. **9.** an affair; matter. **10.** serious work or activity: *get down to business.* **11.** a difficult or complicated matter. **12.** *Theatre.* an incidental action performed by an actor for dramatic effect. **13. mean business.** to be in earnest. [OE *bisignis* solicitude, < *bisig* BUSY + *-nis* -NESS]

business college *n.* a college providing courses in secretarial studies, business management, accounting, commerce, etc.

businesslike (ˈbɪznɪsˌlaɪk) *adj.* efficient and methodical.

businessman (ˈbɪznɪsˌmæn, -mən) *or* (*fem.*) **businesswoman** *n., pl.* **-men** *or* **-women.** a person engaged in commercial or industrial business, esp. as an owner or executive.

business park *n.* an area specially designated and landscaped to accommodate business offices, warehouses, light industry, etc.

business school *n.* an institution that offers courses in aspects of business, such as marketing, finance, and law, designed to train managers in industry and commerce to do their jobs effectively.

busker (ˈbʌskə) *n.* a person who entertains for money in public places, as in front of theatre queues. [C20: <?] —**busk** *vb.* (*intr.*)

buskin (ˈbʌskɪn) *n.* **1.** (formerly) a sandal-like covering for the foot and leg, reaching the calf. **2.** a thick-soled laced half-boot worn esp. by actors of ancient Greece. **3.** (usually preceded by *the*) *Chiefly literary.* tragic drama. [C16: ? < Sp. *borzeguí*; rel. to OF *bouzequin*]

busman's holiday (ˈbʌsmənz) *n. Inf.* a holiday spent doing the same as one does at work. [C20: < a bus driver having a driving holiday]

buss (bʌs) *n., vb.* an archaic or dialect word for **kiss.** [C16: prob. imit.]

bust[1] (bʌst) *n.* **1.** the chest of a human being, esp. a woman's bosom. **2.** a sculpture of the head, shoulders, and upper chest of a person. [C17: < F, < It. *busto* a sculpture, <?]

bust[2] (bʌst) *Inf.* ~*vb.* **busting, busted** *or* **bust.** **1.** to burst or break. **2.** to make or become bankrupt. **3.** (*tr.*) (of the police) to raid, search, or arrest. **4.** (*tr.*) *U.S. & Canad.* to demote, esp. in military rank. ~*n.* **5.** a raid, search, or arrest by the police. **6.** *Chiefly U.S.* a punch. **7.** *U.S. & Canad.* a failure, esp. bankruptcy. **8.** a drunken party. ~*adj.* **9.** broken. **10.** bankrupt. **11. go bust.** to become bankrupt.

bustard (ˈbʌstəd) *n.* a large terrestrial bird inhabiting open regions of the Old World. It has long strong legs, a heavy body, a long neck, and speckled plumage. [C15: < OF *bistarde*, < L *avis tarda* slow bird]

bustier (ˈbuːstɪeɪ) *n.* a type of close-fitting usually strapless top worn by women, esp. with a puffball skirt.

bustle[1] (ˈbʌsᵊl) *vb.* **1.** (when *intr.*, often foll. by *about*) to hurry or cause to hurry with a great show of energy or activity. ~*n.* **2.** energetic and noisy activity. [C16: prob. < obs. *buskle* to make energetic preparation] —ˈ**bustling** *adj.*

bustle[2] (ˈbʌsᵊl) *n.* a cushion or framework worn by women in the late 19th century at the back in order to expand the skirt. [C18: <?]

bust-up *Inf.* ~*n.* **1.** a quarrel, esp. a serious one ending a friendship, etc. **2.** *Brit.* a disturbance or brawl. ~*vb.* **bust up** (*adv.*) **3.** (*intr.*) to quarrel and part. **4.** (*tr.*) to disrupt (a meeting), esp. violently.

busy (ˈbɪzɪ) *adj.* **busier, busiest.** **1.** actively or fully engaged; occupied. **2.** crowded with or characterized by activity. **3.** *Chiefly U.S. & Canad.* (of a room, telephone line, etc.) in use; engaged. **4.** overcrowded with detail: *a busy painting.* **5.** meddlesome; inquisitive. ~*vb.* **busying, busied.** **6.** (*tr.*) to make or keep (someone, esp. oneself) busy; occupy. [OE *bisig*] —ˈ**busily** *adv.* —ˈ**busyness** *n.*

busybody (ˈbɪzɪˌbɒdɪ) *n., pl.* **-bodies.** a meddlesome, prying, or officious person.

busy Lizzie (ˈlɪzɪ) *n.* a flowering plant that has pink, red, or white flowers and is often grown as a pot plant.

but[1] (bʌt; *unstressed* bət) *conj.* (*coordinating*) **1.** contrary to expectation: *he cut his knee but didn't cry.* **2.** in contrast; on the contrary: *I like opera but my husband doesn't.* **3.** (*usually used after a negative*) other than: *we can't do anything but wait.* **4.** only: *I can but try.* ~*conj.* (*subordinating*) **5.** (*usually used after a negative*) without it happening: *we never go out but it rains.* **6.** (foll. by *that*) except that: *nothing is impossible but that we live forever.* **7.** *Arch.* if not; unless. ~*prep.* **8.** except; save: *they saved all but one.* **9. but for.** were it not for: *but for you, we couldn't have managed.* ~*adv.* **10.** just; merely: *he was but a child.* **11.** *Dialect & Austral.* though; however: *it's a rainy day; warm, but.* ~*n.* **12.** an objection (esp. in **ifs and buts**). [OE *būtan* without, outside, except, < *be* BY + *ūtan* OUT]

but[2] (bʌt) *n. Scot.* the outer room of a two-roomed cottage. Cf. **ben**[1]. [C18: < *but* (adv.) outside; see BUT[1]]

butadiene (ˌbjuːtəˈdaɪiːn) *n.* a colourless flammable gas used mainly in the manufacture of synthetic rubbers. Formula: CH_2:CHCH:CH_2. [C20: < BUTA(NE) + DI-[1] + -ENE]

butane (ˈbjuːteɪn, bjuːˈteɪn) *n.* a colourless flammable gaseous alkane used mainly in the manufacture of rubber and fuels. Formula: C_4H_{10}. [C20: < BUT(YL) + -ANE]

butanol (ˈbjuːtəˌnɒl) *n.* a colourless substance existing in four isomeric forms. The three liquid isomers are used as solvents and in the manufacture of organic compounds. Formula: C_4H_9OH. Also called: **butyl alcohol.**

butanone (ˈbjuːtəˌnəʊn) *n.* a colourless flammable liquid used as a resin solvent, and paint remover, and in lacquers, adhesives, etc. Formula: $CH_3COC_2H_5$.

butch (bʊtʃ) *Sl.* ~*adj.* **1.** (of a woman or man) markedly or aggressively masculine. ~*n.* **2.** a lesbian who is noticeably masculine. **3.** a strong rugged man. [C18: back formation < BUTCHER]

butcher (ˈbʊtʃə) *n.* **1.** a retailer of meat. **2.** a person who slaughters or dresses meat. **3.** an indiscriminate or brutal murderer. ~*vb.* (*tr.*) **4.** to slaughter or dress (animals) for meat. **5.** to kill indiscriminately or brutally. **6.** to make a mess of; botch. [C13: < OF *bouchier*, < *bouc* he-goat]

butcherbird (ˈbʊtʃəˌbɜːd) *n.* **1.** a shrike, esp. of the genus *Lanius*. **2.** any of several Australian magpies that impale their prey on thorns.

butcher's-broom *n.* an evergreen shrub with stiff prickle-tipped flattened green stems, formerly used for making brooms.

butchery (ˈbʊtʃərɪ) *n., pl.* **-eries.** **1.** the business of a butcher. **2.** wanton and indiscriminate slaughter. **3.** a slaughterhouse.

butler (ˈbʌtlə) *n.* the male servant of a household in charge of the wines, table, etc.: usually the head servant. [C13: < OF, < *bouteille* BOTTLE]

butlery (ˈbʌtlərɪ) *n., pl.* **-leries.** **1.** a butler's room. **2.** another name for **buttery**[2].

butt[1] (bʌt) *n.* **1.** the thicker or blunt end of something, such as the end of the stock of a rifle. **2.** the unused end of something, esp. of a cigarette; stub. **3.** *U.S.* a slang word for **cigarette.** **4.** *Building.* short for **butt joint.** [C15 (in the sense: thick end of something, buttock): rel. to OE *buttuc* end, ridge]

butt[2] (bʌt) *n.* **1.** a person or thing that is the target of ridicule, wit, etc. **2.** *Shooting, archery.* **a.** a mound of earth behind the target that stops bullets or wide shots. **b.** the target itself. **c.** (*pl.*) the target range. **3.** a low barrier behind which sportsmen shoot game birds, esp. grouse. ~*vb.* **4.** (usually foll. by *on* or *against*) to lie or be placed end on to; abut. [C14 (in the sense: mark for archery practice): < OF *but*]

butt[3] (bʌt) *vb.* **1.** to strike or push (something) with the head or horns. **2.** (*intr.*) to project; jut. **3.** (*intr.*; foll. by *in* or *into*) to intrude, esp. into a conversation; interfere. ~*n.* **4.** a blow with the head or horns. [C12: < OF *boter*, of Gmc origin]

butt[4] (bʌt) *n.* a large cask for storing wine or beer. [C14: < OF *botte*, < LL *buttis* cask]

butte (bjuːt) *n. U.S. & Canad.* an isolated steep flat-topped hill. [C19: F, < OF *bute* mound behind a target; see BUTT[2]]

butter (ˈbʌtə) *n.* **1.** an edible fatty whitish-yellow solid made from cream by churning. **2.** any substance with a butter-like consistency, such as peanut butter. **3. look as if butter wouldn't melt in one's mouth.** to look innocent, although probably not so. ~*vb.* (*tr.*) **4.** to put butter on or in. **5.** to flatter. ~See also **butter up.** [OE *butere*, < L, < Gk *bouturon*, < *bous* cow + *turos* cheese]

butter bean *n.* a variety of lima bean that has large pale flat edible seeds.

butterbur (ˈbʌtəˌbɜː) *n.* a plant of the composite family with fragrant whitish or purple flowers, and large leaves formerly used to wrap butter.

buttercup (ˈbʌtəˌkʌp) *n.* any of various yellow-flowered plants of the genus *Ranunculus* of Europe, Asia, and North America.

butterfat (ˈbʌtəˌfæt) *n.* the fatty substance of milk from which butter is made, consisting of a mixture of glycerides.

butterfingers (ˈbʌtəˌfɪŋgəz) *n.* (*functioning as sing.*) *Inf.* a person who drops things inadvertently or fails to catch things. —ˈ**butterˌfingered** *adj.*

butterfish (ˈbʌtəˌfɪʃ) *n., pl.* **-fish** *or* **-fishes.** any of several species of fishes having a slippery skin.

butterflies (ˈbʌtəˌflaɪz) *pl. n. Inf.* tremors in the stomach region due to nervousness.

butterfly (ˈbʌtəˌflaɪ) *n., pl.* **-flies.** **1.** any diurnal insect that has a slender body with clubbed antennae and typically rests with the wings (often brightly coloured) closed over the back. **2.** a person who never settles with one interest or occupation for long. **3.** a swimming stroke in which the arms are plunged forward together in large circular movements. [OE *buttorflēoge*]

butterfly nut *n.* another name for **wing nut.**

buttermilk (ˈbʌtəˌmɪlk) *n.* the sourish liquid remaining after the butter has been separated from milk.

butter muslin *n.* a fine loosely woven cotton material originally used for wrapping butter.

butternut (ˈbʌtəˌnʌt) *n.* **1.** *Austral. & N.Z.* a type of small edible pumpkin. **2. a.** a walnut tree of North America. **b.** its oily edible nut.

butterscotch (ˈbʌtəˌskɒtʃ) *n.* **1.** a kind of hard brittle toffee made with butter, brown sugar, etc. **2.** a flavouring made from these ingredients. [C19: ? first made in Scotland]

butter up *vb.* (*tr., adv.*) to flatter.

butterwort (ˈbʌtəˌwɜːt) *n.* a plant that grows in wet places and has violet-blue spurred flowers and fleshy greasy glandular leaves on which insects are trapped and digested.

buttery[1] (ˈbʌtərɪ) *adj.* containing, like, or coated with butter. —ˈ**butteriness** *n.*

buttery[2] (ˈbʌtərɪ) *n., pl.* **-teries.** **1.** a room for storing foods or wines. **2.** *Brit.* (in some universities) a room in which food and drink are supplied or sold to students. [C14: < Anglo-F *boterie*, prob. < L *butta* cask, BUTT[4]]

butt joint *n.* a joint between two plates, planks, etc., fastened end to end without overlapping or interlocking. Sometimes shortened to **butt.**

buttock (ˈbʌtək) *n.* **1.** either of the two large fleshy masses of thick muscular tissue that form the human rump. See also **gluteus.** Related adj.: **gluteal.** **2.** the analogous part in some mammals. [C13: ? < OE *buttuc* round slope]

button (ˈbʌtˀn) *n.* **1.** a disc or knob of plastic, wood, etc., attached to a garment, etc., usually for fastening two surfaces together by passing it through a buttonhole or loop. **2.** a small round object, such as any of various sweets, decorations, or badges. **3.** a small disc that completes an electric circuit when pushed, as one that operates a doorbell or machine. **4.** *Biol.* any rounded knoblike part or organ, such as an unripe mushroom. **5.** *Fencing.* the protective knob fixed to the point of a foil. **6.** *Brit.* an object of no value (esp. in **not worth a button**). ~*vb.* **7.** to fasten with a button or buttons. **8.** (*tr.*) to provide with buttons. [C14: < OF *boton*, < *boter* to thrust, butt; see BUTT[3]] —ˈ**buttoner** *n.* —ˈ**buttonless** *adj.*

buttonhole (ˈbʌtˀnˌhəʊl) *n.* **1.** a slit in a garment, etc., through which a button is passed to fasten two surfaces together. **2.** a flower or small bunch of flowers worn pinned to the lapel or in the buttonhole, esp. at weddings. U.S. name: **boutonniere.** ~*vb.* (*tr.*) **3.** to detain (a person) in conversation. **4.** to make buttonholes in.

buttonhook (ˈbʌtˀnˌhʊk) *n.* a thin tapering hooked instrument formerly used for pulling buttons through the buttonholes of shoes.

button up *vb.* (*tr., adv.*) **1.** to fasten (a garment) with a button or buttons. **2.** *Inf.* to conclude (business) satisfactorily. **3. button up one's lip** *or* **mouth.** *Sl.* to be silent.

buttress (ˈbʌtrɪs) *n.* **1.** Also called: **pier.** a construction, usually of brick or stone, built to support a wall. **2.** any support or prop. **3.** something shaped like a buttress, such as a projection from a mountainside. ~*vb.* (*tr.*) **4.** to support (a wall) with a buttress. **5.** to support or sustain. [C13: < OF *bouterez*, < *bouter* to thrust, BUTT[3]]

butty[1] (ˈbʌtɪ) *n., pl.* **-ties.** *Chiefly N English dialect.* a sandwich: *a jam butty.* [C19: < *buttered* (bread)]

butty[2] (ˈbʌtɪ) *n., pl.* **-ties.** *English dialect.* (esp. in mining parlance) a friend or workmate. [C19: ? < obs. *booty* sharing, < BOOT[2]]

butyl (ˈbjuːˌtaɪl, -tɪl) *n.* (*modifier*) of or containing any of four isomeric forms of the group C_4H_9—: *butyl rubber.* [C19: < BUT(YRIC ACID) + -YL]

butyl alcohol *n.* another name for **butanol.**

butyric acid (bjuːˈtɪrɪk) *n.* a carboxylic acid which produces the smell in rancid butter. Formula: $CH_3(CH_2)_2COOH$. [C19 *butyric*, < L *būtyrum* BUTTER]

buxom (ˈbʌksəm) *adj.* **1.** (esp. of a woman) healthily plump, attractive, and vigorous. **2.** (of a woman) full-bosomed. [C12: *buhsum* compliant,

pliant, < OE būgan to bend, BOW[1]] —'**buxomness** *n.*

buy (baɪ) *vb.* **buying, bought.** (*mainly tr.*) **1.** to acquire by paying or promising to pay a sum of money; purchase. **2.** to be capable of purchasing: *money can't buy love.* **3.** to acquire by any exchange or sacrifice: *to buy time by equivocation.* **4.** to bribe or corrupt; hire by or as by bribery. **5.** *Sl.* to accept as true, practical, etc. **6.** (*intr.;* foll. by *into*) to purchase shares of (a company). ~*n.* **7.** a purchase (often in **good** or **bad buy**). ~See also **buy in, buy into,** etc. [OE *bycgan*]

buyer ('baɪə) *n.* **1.** a person who buys; customer. **2.** a person employed to buy merchandise, materials, etc., as for a shop or factory.

buy in *vb.* (*adv.*) **1.** (*tr.*) to buy back for the owner (an item in an auction) at or below the reserve price. **2.** (*intr.*) to purchase shares in a company. **3.** (*tr.*) Also: **buy into.** *U.S. inf.* to pay money to secure a position or place for (someone, esp. oneself) in some organization, esp. a business or club. **4.** to purchase (goods, etc.) in large quantities.

buy into *vb.* (*intr., prep.*) *Austral. & N.Z.* to get involved in (an argument, fight, etc.)

buy off *vb.* (*tr., adv.*) to pay (a person or group) to drop a charge, end opposition, etc.

buy out *vb.* (*tr., adv.*) **1.** to purchase the ownership, controlling interest, shares, etc., of (a company, etc.). **2.** to gain the release of (a person) from the armed forces by payment. **3.** to pay (a person) to give up ownership of (property, etc.). ~*n.* **buy-out. 4.** the purchase of a company, esp. by its former workers.

buy up *vb.* (*tr., adv.*) **1.** to purchase all, or all that is available, of (something). **2.** to purchase a controlling interest in (a company, etc.).

buzz (bʌz) *n.* **1.** a rapidly vibrating humming sound, as of a bee. **2.** a low sound, as of many voices in conversation. **3.** a rumour; report; gossip. **4.** *Inf.* a telephone call. **5.** *Inf.* **a.** a pleasant sensation. **b.** a sense of excitement; kick. **6.** *modifier*) fashionable, trendy. ~*vb.* **7.** (*intr.*) to make a vibrating sound like that of a prolonged *z.* **8.** (*intr.*) to talk or gossip with an air of excitement: *the town buzzed with the news.* **9.** (*tr.*) to utter or spread (a rumour). **10.** (*intr.;* often foll. by *about*) to move around quickly and busily. **11.** (*tr.*) to signal or summon with a buzzer. **12.** (*tr.*) *Inf.* to call by telephone. **13.** (*tr.*) *Inf.* to fly an aircraft very low over (an object). **14.** (*tr.*) (esp. of insects) to make a buzzing sound with (wings, etc.). [C16: imit.]

buzzard ('bʌzəd) *n.* a diurnal bird of prey of the hawk family, typically having broad wings and tail and a soaring flight. [C13: < OF *buisard,* < L *būteō* hawk]

buzzer ('bʌzə) *n.* **1.** a device that produces a buzzing sound, esp. one similar to an electric bell. **2.** *N.Z.* a wood-planing machine.

buzz off *vb.* (*intr., adv.; often imperative*) *Inf., chiefly Brit.* to go away; leave; depart.

buzz word *n. Inf.* a word, originally from a particular jargon, which becomes a popular vogue word. [C20: <?]

BVM *abbrev. for* Beata Virgo Maria. [L: Blessed Virgin Mary]

bwana ('bwɑːnə) *n.* (in E Africa) a master, often used as a form of address corresponding to *sir.* [Swahili, < Ar. *abūna* our father]

by (baɪ) *prep.* **1.** used to indicate the agent after a passive verb: *seeds eaten by the birds.* **2.** used to indicate the person responsible for a creative work: *this song is by Schubert.* **3.** via; through: *enter by the back door.* **4.** foll. by a gerund to indicate a means used: *he frightened her by hiding behind the door.* **5.** beside; next to; near: a *tree by the house.* **6.** passing the position of; past: *he drove by the old cottage.* **7.** not later than; before: *return the books by Tuesday.* **8.** used to indicate extent, after a comparative: *it is hotter by five degrees.* **9.** (esp. in oaths) invoking the name of: *I swear by all the gods.* **10.** multiplied by: *four by three equals twelve.* **11.** during the passing of (esp. in **by day, by night**). **12.** placed between measurements of the various dimensions of something: *a plank fourteen inches by seven.* ~*adv.* **13.** near: *the house is close by.* **14.** away; aside: *he put some money by each week.* **15.** passing a point near something; past: *he drove by.* ~*n., pl.* **byes. 16.** a variant spelling of **bye.** [OE *bī*]

by- *or* **bye-** *prefix.* **1.** near: *bystander.* **2.** secondary or incidental: *by-election; by-product.* [< BY]

by and by *adv.* presently or eventually.

by and large *adv.* in general; on the whole. [C17: orig. nautical: to the wind and off it]

bye (baɪ) *n.* **1.** *Sport.* the situation in which a player or team wins a preliminary round by virtue of having no opponent. **2.** *Golf.* one or more holes that are left unplayed after the match has been decided. **3.** *Cricket.* a run scored off a ball not struck by the batsman. **4.** something incidental or secondary. **5. by the bye.** incidentally; by the way. [C16: var. of BY]

bye-bye *sentence substitute. Brit. inf.* goodbye.

bye-byes *n.* (*functioning as sing.*) an informal word for **sleep,** used esp. to children (as in **go to bye-byes**).

by-election *or* **bye-election** *n.* (in Great Britain and other countries of the Commonwealth) an election held during the life of a parliament to fill a vacant seat.

Byelorussian *or* **Belorussian** (ˌbjɛləʊˈrʌʃən, ˌbɛl-) *adj.* **1.** of Byelorussia, an administrative division of the W Soviet Union. **2.** relating to, or characteristic of Byelorussia, its people, or their language. ~*n.* **3.** the official language of the Byelorussian SSR. **4.** a native or inhabitant of Byelorussia. ~Also called: **White Russian.**

bygone ('baɪˌgɒn) *adj.* **1.** (*usually prenominal*) past; former. ~*n.* **2.** (*often pl.*) a past occurrence. **3.** an artefact, implement, etc., of former domestic or industrial use. **4. let bygones be bygones.** to agree to forget past quarrels.

bylaw *or* **bye-law** ('baɪˌlɔː) *n.* **1.** a rule made by a local authority. **2.** a regulation of a company, society, etc. [C13: prob. of Scand. origin; cf. ON *bȳr* dwelling, town]

by-line *n.* **1.** a line under the title of a newspaper or magazine article giving the author's name. **2.** another word for **touchline.**

BYO(G) *n. Austral. & N.Z.* an unlicensed restaurant at which diners may drink their own wine, etc. [C20: < *bring your own (grog)*]

bypass ('baɪˌpɑːs) *n.* **1.** a main road built to avoid a city or other congested area. **2.** a means of redirecting the flow of a substance around an appliance through which it would otherwise pass. **3.** *Electronics.* an electrical circuit connected in parallel around one or more components, providing an alternative path for certain frequencies. ~*vb.* (*tr.*) **4.** to go around or avoid (a city, obstruction, problem, etc.). **5.** to cause (traffic, fluid, etc.) to go through a bypass. **6.** to proceed without reference to (regulations, a superior, etc.); get round; avoid.

bypass engine *n.* a gas turbine in which part of the compressor delivery bypasses the combustion zone, flowing directly into or around the exhaust to provide additional thrust.

bypath ('baɪˌpɑːθ) *n.* a little-used path or track.

by-play *n.* secondary action or talking carried on apart while the main action proceeds, esp. in a play.

by-product *n.* **1.** a secondary or incidental product of a manufacturing process. **2.** a side effect.

byre ('baɪə) *n. Brit.* a shelter for cows. [OE *bȳre;* rel. to *būr* hut, cottage]

byroad ('baɪˌrəʊd) *n.* a secondary or side road.

Byronic (baɪˈrɒnɪk) *adj.* of, like, or characteristic of Byron, his poetry, or his style. [C19: < Lord *Byron* (1788–1824), E poet]

byssinosis (ˌbɪsɪˈnəʊsɪs) *n.* a lung disease caused by prolonged inhalation of fibre dust. [C19: < NL, < Gk *bussinos* of linen + -OSIS]

bystander (ˈbaɪˌstændə) *n.* a person present but not involved; onlooker; spectator.

byte (baɪt) *n. Computers.* **1.** a group of bits processed as one unit of data. **2.** the storage space allocated to such a group of bits. **3.** a subdivision of a word. [C20: prob. a blend of BIT[4] + BITE]

byway (ˈbaɪˌweɪ) *n.* **1.** a secondary or side road, esp. in the country. **2.** an area, field of study, etc., that is very obscure or of secondary importance.

byword (ˈbaɪˌwɜːd) *n.* **1.** a person or thing regarded as a perfect or proverbial example of something: *their name is a byword for good service.* **2.** an object of scorn or derision. **3.** a common saying; proverb. [OE *bīwyrde;* see BY, WORD]

Byzantine (bɪˈzænˌtaɪn, -ˌtiːn, baɪ-; ˈbɪzənˌtiːn, -ˌtaɪn) *adj.* **1.** of or relating to Byzantium, an ancient Greek city on the Bosphorus. **2.** of or relating to the Byzantine Empire, the continuation of the Roman Empire in the East. **3.** of, relating to, or characterizing the Orthodox Church. **4.** of or relating to the highly coloured stylized form of religious art developed in the Byzantine Empire. **5.** of or relating to the style of architecture developed in the Byzantine Empire, characterized by massive domes, rounded arches, spires and minarets, and mosaics. **6.** (of attitudes, etc.) inflexible or complicated. ~*n.* **7.** an inhabitant of Byzantium.

Bz *or* **bz.** *abbrev. for* benzene.

C

c *or* **C** (siː) *n., pl.* **c's, C's,** *or* **Cs.** **1.** the third letter of the English alphabet. **2.** a speech sound represented by this letter, usually either as in *cigar* or as in *case.* **3.** the third in a series, esp. the third highest grade in an examination. **4.** something shaped like a C.

c *symbol for:* **1.** centi-. **2.** *Maths.* constant. **3.** cubic. **4.** cycle. **5.** specific heat capacity. **6.** the speed of light and other types of electromagnetic radiation in free space.

C *symbol for:* **1.** *Music.* **a.** the first degree of a major scale containing no sharps or flats (**C major**). **b.** the major or minor key having this note as its tonic. **c.** a time signature denoting four crotchet beats to the bar. See also **alla breve** (sense 2), **common time.** **2.** *Chem.* carbon. **3.** capacitance. **4.** heat capacity. **5.** cold (water). **6.** *Physics.* compliance. **7.** Celsius. **8.** centigrade. **9.** century: *C20.* **10.** coulomb. ~ **11.** *the Roman numeral for* 100.

c. *abbrev. for:* **1.** carat. **2.** carbon (paper). **3.** *Cricket.* caught. **4.** cent(s). **5.** century *or* centuries. **6.** (*pl.* **cc.**) chapter. **7.** (used esp. preceding a date) circa: *c. 1800.* [L: about] **8.** colt. **9.** contralto. **10.** copyright. **11.** coulomb.

C. *abbrev. for:* **1.** (on maps as part of name) Cape. **2.** Catholic. **3.** Celtic. **4.** Conservative. **5.** Corps.

c/- (in Australia) *abbrev. for* care of.

Ca *the chemical symbol for* calcium.

CA *abbrev. for:* **1.** Central America. **2.** chartered accountant. **3.** Civil Aviation. **4.** (in Britain) Consumers' Association.

ca. *abbrev. for* circa. [L: about]

CAA (in Britain) *abbrev. for* Civil Aviation Authority.

Caaba (ˈkɑːbə) *n.* a variant spelling of **Kaaba.**

cab (kæb) *n.* **1. a.** a taxi. **b.** (*as modifier*): *a cab rank.* **2.** the enclosed compartment of a lorry, crane, etc., from which it is driven. **3.** (formerly) a horse-drawn vehicle used for public hire. [C19: < CABRIOLET]

cabal (kəˈbæl) *n.* **1.** a small group of intriguers, esp. one formed for political purposes. **2.** a secret plot; conspiracy. **3.** a clique. ~*vb.* **-balling, -balled.** **4.** (*intr.*) to form a cabal; plot. [C17: < F *cabale,* < Med. L *cabala*]

cabala (kəˈbɑːlə) *n.* a variant spelling of **cabbala.**

caballero (ˌkæbəˈljɛərəʊ) *n., pl.* **-ros** (-rəʊz). a Spanish gentleman. [C19: < Sp.: gentleman, < LL *caballārius* rider, < *caballus* horse]

cabana (kəˈbɑːnə) *n. Chiefly U.S.* a tent used as a dressing room by the sea. [< Sp. *cabaña:* CABIN]

cabaret (ˈkæbəˌreɪ) *n.* **1.** a floor show of dancing, singing, etc., at a nightclub or restaurant. **2.** *Chiefly U.S.* a nightclub or restaurant providing such entertainment. [C17: < Norman F: tavern, prob. < LL *camera* an arched roof]

cabbage (ˈkæbɪdʒ) *n.* **1.** Also called: **cole.** any of various cultivated varieties of a plant of the genus *Brassica* having a short thick stalk and a large head of green or reddish edible leaves. See also **brassica.** **2. a.** the head of a cabbage. **b.** the edible leaf bud of the cabbage palm. **3.** *Inf.* a dull or unimaginative person. **4.** *Inf.* a person who has no mental faculties and is dependent on others. [C14: < Norman F *caboche* head]

cabbage palm *n.* **1.** a West Indian palm whose leaf buds are eaten like cabbage. **2.** a similar Brazilian palm.

cabbage rose *n.* a rose with a round compact full-petalled head.

cabbage tree *n.* **1.** a tall palmlike ornamental New Zealand tree. **2.** a tall palm tree of Eastern Australia.

cabbage white *n.* a large white butterfly, the larvae of which feed on the leaves of cabbages and related vegetables.

cabbala, cabala, kabbala, *or* **kabala** (kəˈbɑːlə) *n.* **1.** an ancient Jewish mystical tradition. **2.** any secret or occult doctrine. [C16: < Med. L, < Heb. *qabbālāh* tradition, < *qābal* to receive] —**cabbalism, cabalism, kabbalism,** *or* **kabalism** (ˈkæbəˌlɪzəm) *n.* —ˈ**cabbalist,** ˈ**cabalist,** ˈ**kabbalist,** *or* ˈ**kabalist** *n.* —ˌ**cabbaˈlistic,** ˌ**cabaˈlistic,** ˌ**kabbaˈlistic,** *or* ˌ**kabaˈlistic** *adj.*

cabby *or* **cabbie** (ˈkæbɪ) *n., pl.* **-bies.** *Inf.* a cab driver.

caber (ˈkeɪbə) *n. Scot.* a heavy section of trimmed tree trunk thrown in competition at Highland games (**tossing the caber**). [C16: < Gaelic *cabar* pole]

cabin (ˈkæbɪn) *n.* **1.** a small simple dwelling; hut. **2.** a simple house providing accommodation for travellers or holiday-makers. **3.** a room used as an office or living quarters in a ship. **4.** a covered compartment used for shelter in a small boat. **5.** *Brit.* another name for **signal box.** **6. a.** the enclosed part of a light aircraft in which the pilot and passengers sit. **b.** the part of an aircraft for passengers or cargo. ~*vb.* **7.** (*tr.*) to confine in a small space. [C14: < OF *cabane,* < OProvençal *cabana,* < LL *capanna* hut]

cabin boy *n.* a boy who waits on the officers and passengers of a ship.

cabin cruiser *n.* a power boat fitted with a cabin for pleasure cruising or racing.

cabinet (ˈkæbɪnɪt) *n.* **1.** a piece of furniture containing shelves, cupboards, or drawers for storage or display. **2.** the outer case of a television, radio, etc. **3. a.** (*often cap.*) the executive and policy-making body of a country, consisting of senior government ministers. **b.** (*sometimes cap.*) an advisory council to a president, governor, etc. **c.** (*as modifier*): *a cabinet reshuffle.* **4. a.** a standard size of paper, 6 × 4 inches (15 × 10 cm), for mounted photographs. **b.** (*as modifier*): *a cabinet photograph.* **5.** *Arch.* a private room. [C16: < OF, dim. of *cabine,* <?]

cabinet-maker *n.* a craftsman specializing in making fine furniture. —ˈ**cabinet-ˌmaking** *n.*

cabinetwork (ˈkæbɪnɪtˌwɜːk) *n.* **1.** the making of furniture, esp. of fine quality. **2.** an article made by a cabinet-maker.

cabin fever *n. Canad.* acute depression resulting from being isolated or sharing cramped quarters in the wilderness.

cable (ˈkeɪbᵊl) *n.* **1.** a strong thick rope, usually of twisted hemp or steel wire. **2.** *Naut.* an anchor chain or rope. **3.** Also called: **cable length, cable's length.** a unit of length in nautical use that has various values. It is most commonly taken as 120 fathoms (720 feet) in the U.S. and one tenth of a nautical mile (608 feet) in Britain. **4.** a wire or bundle of wires that conducts electricity: *a submarine cable.* **5.** Also called: **cablegram.** a telegram sent abroad by submarine cable, telephone line, etc. **6.** Also called: **cable stitch.** a knitting pattern resembling a twisted rope. ~*vb.* **7.** to send (a message) to (someone) by cable. **8.** (*tr.*) to fasten or provide with a cable or cables. **9.** (*tr.*) to supply (a place) with cable television. [C13: < OF, < LL *capulum* halter]

cable car *n.* **1.** a cabin suspended from and moved by an overhead cable in a mountain area. **2.** the passenger car on a **cable railway,** drawn along by a strong cable operated by a motor.

cablegram (ˈkeɪbᵊlˌgræm) *n.* a more formal name for **cable** (sense 5).

cable television *n.* a television service in which the subscriber's television is connected to the supplier by cable, enabling a much greater choice of channels to be provided.

cabochon (ˈkæbəˌʃɒn) *n.* a smooth domed gem, polished but unfaceted. [C16: < OF, < *caboche* head]

caboodle (kəˈbuːdᵊl) *n. Inf.* a lot, bunch, or group

(esp. in **the whole caboodle**). [C19: prob. contraction of KIT[1] & BOODLE]

caboose (kəˈbuːs) *n.* **1.** *U.S. inf.* short for **calaboose.** **2.** *Railways. U.S. & Canad.* a guard's van. **3.** *Naut.* **a.** a deckhouse for a galley aboard ship. **b.** *Chiefly Brit.* the galley itself. **4.** *Canad.* **a.** a mobile bunkhouse used by lumbermen, etc. **b.** an insulated cabin on runners, equipped with a stove. [C18: < Du. *cabūse,* <?]

cabotage (ˈkæbəˌtɑːʒ) *n.* **1.** *Naut.* coastal navigation or shipping. **2.** reservation to a country's carriers of its internal traffic, esp. air traffic. [C19: < F, < *caboter* to sail near the coast, apparently < Sp. *cabo* CAPE[2]]

cabriole (ˈkæbrɪˌəʊl) *n.* a type of curved furniture leg, popular in the first half of the 18th century. Also called: **cabriole leg.** [C18: < F, < *cabrioler* to caper; from its being based on the leg of a capering animal]

cabriolet (ˌkæbrɪəʊˈleɪ) *n.* **1.** a small two-wheeled horse-drawn carriage with two seats and a folding hood. **2.** a type of motorcar with a folding top. [C18: < F, lit.: a little skip, < L, < *caper* goat; referring to the lightness of movement]

cacao (kəˈkɑːəʊ, -ˈkeɪəʊ) *n.* **1.** a small tropical American evergreen tree having reddish-brown seed pods from which cocoa and chocolate are prepared. **2. cacao bean.** the seed pod; cocoa bean. **3. cacao butter.** another name for **cocoa butter.** [C16: < Sp., < Nahuatl *cacauatl* cacao beans]

cachalot (ˈkæʃəˌlɒt) *n.* another name for **sperm whale.** [C18: < F, < Port., *cachalote,* <?]

cache (kæʃ) *n.* **1.** a hidden store of provisions, weapons, treasure, etc. **2.** the place where such a store is hidden. ~*vb.* **3.** (*tr.*) to store in a cache. [C19: < F, < *cacher* to hide]

cachepot (ˈkæʃˌpɒt, kæʃˈpəʊ) *n.* an ornamental container for a flowerpot. [F: pot-hider]

cachet (ˈkæʃeɪ) *n.* **1.** an official seal on a document, letter, etc. **2.** a distinguishing mark. **3.** prestige; distinction. **4.** *Philately.* a mark stamped by hand on mail for commemorative purposes. **5.** a hollow wafer, formerly used for enclosing an unpleasant-tasting medicine. [C17: < OF, < *cacher* to hide]

cachexia (kəˈkɛksɪə) *or* **cachexy** *n.* a weakened condition of body or mind resulting from any debilitating disease. [C16: < LL, < Gk, < *kakos* bad + *hexis* condition]

cachinnate (ˈkækɪˌneɪt) *vb.* (*intr.*) to laugh loudly. [C19: < L *cacchināre,* prob. imit.] —ˌ**cachinˈnation** *n.* —ˌ**cachinˈnatory** *adj.*

cachou (ˈkæʃuː, kæˈʃuː) *n.* **1.** a lozenge eaten to sweeten the breath. **2.** another name for **catechu.** [C18: via F < Port., < Malay *kāchu*]

cacique (kəˈsiːk) *or* **cazique** (kəˈziːk) *n.* **1.** an American Indian chief in a Spanish-speaking region. **2.** (esp. in Spanish America) a local political boss. [C16: < Sp., of Amerind origin]

cack-handed (ˌkækˈhændɪd) *adj. Inf.* **1.** left-handed. **2.** clumsy. [< dialect *cack* excrement]

cackle (ˈkækᵊl) *vb.* **1.** (*intr.*) (esp. of a hen) to squawk with shrill broken notes. **2.** (*intr.*) to laugh or chatter raucously. **3.** (*tr.*) to utter in a cackling manner. ~*n.* **4.** the noise or act of cackling. **5.** noisy chatter. **6. cut the cackle.** *Inf.* to be quiet. [C13: prob. < MLow G *kākelen,* imit.]

caco- *combining form.* bad, unpleasant, or incorrect: *cacophony.* [< Gk *kakos* bad]

cacodyl (ˈkækəˌdaɪl) *n.* an oily poisonous liquid with a strong garlic smell; tetramethyldiarsine. [C19: <Gk, < *kakos* CACO- + *ozein* to smell + -YL]

cacoethes (ˌkækəʊˈiːθiːz) *n.* an uncontrollable urge or desire: *a cacoethes for smoking.* [C16: < L *cacoēthes* malignant disease, < Gk, < *kakos* CACO- + *ēthos* character]

cacography (kæˈkɒgrəfɪ) *n.* **1.** bad handwriting. **2.** incorrect spelling. —**cacographic** (ˌkækəˈgræfɪk) *adj.*

cacophony (kəˈkɒfənɪ) *n., pl.* **-nies.** harsh discordant sound. —**caˈcophonous** *adj.*

cactus (ˈkæktəs) *n., pl.* **-tuses** *or* **-ti** (-taɪ). **1.** any of a family of spiny succulent plants of the arid regions of America with swollen tough stems and leaves reduced to spines. **2. cactus dahlia.** a double-flowered variety of dahlia. [C17: < L: prickly plant, < Gk *kaktos* cardoon] —**cactaceous** (kækˈteɪʃəs) *adj.*

cacuminal (kæˈkjuːmɪnᵊl) *Phonetics.* ~*adj.* **1.** denoting a consonant articulated with the tip of the tongue turned back towards the hard palate. ~*n.* **2.** a consonant articulated in this manner. [C19: < L *cacūmen* point]

cad (kæd) *n. Brit. inf. old-fashioned.* a man who does not behave in a gentlemanly manner towards others. [C18: < CADDIE] —ˈ**caddish** *adj.*

cadaver (kəˈdeɪvə, -ˈdɑːv-) *n. Med.* a corpse. [C16: < L, < *cadere* to fall] —**cadaveric** (kəˈdævərɪk) *adj.*

cadaverous (kəˈdævərəs) *adj.* **1.** of or like a corpse, esp. in being deathly pale. **2.** thin and haggard. —**caˈdaverousness** *n.*

caddie *or* **caddy** (ˈkædɪ) *Golf.* ~*n., pl.* **-dies.** **1.** an attendant who carries clubs, etc., for a player. ~*vb.* **-dying, -died.** **2.** (*intr.*) to act as a caddie. [C17 (C18 (Scot.): an errand-boy): < F CADET]

caddis fly *n.* a small mothlike insect having two pairs of hairy wings and aquatic larvae (caddis worms). [C17: <?]

caddis worm *or* **caddis** (ˈkædɪs) *n.* the aquatic larva of a caddis fly, which constructs a protective case around itself made of silk, sand, stones, etc. Also called: **caseworm, strawworm.**

caddy[1] (ˈkædɪ) *n., pl.* **-dies.** *Chiefly Brit.* a small container, esp. for tea. [C18: < Malay *kati*]

caddy[2] (ˈkædɪ) *n., pl.* **-dies,** *vb.* **-dying, -died.** a variant spelling of **caddie.**

cadence (ˈkeɪdᵊns) *or* **cadency** *n., pl.* **-dences** *or* **-dencies.** **1.** the beat or measure of something rhythmic. **2.** a fall in the pitch of the voice, as at the end of a sentence. **3.** intonation. **4.** rhythm in verse or prose. **5.** the close of a musical phrase. [C14: < OF, < OIt. *cadenza,* lit.: a falling, < L *cadere* to fall]

cadenza (kəˈdɛnzə) *n.* a virtuoso solo passage occurring near the end of a piece of music, formerly improvised by the soloist. [C19: < It.; see CADENCE]

cadet (kəˈdɛt) *n.* **1.** a young person undergoing preliminary training, usually before full entry to the uniformed services, police, etc. **2.** (in England and in France before 1789) a gentleman who entered the army to prepare for a commission. **3.** a younger son. **4. cadet branch.** the family of a younger son. **5.** (in New Zealand, formerly) a person learning sheep farming on a sheep station. [C17: < F, < dialect *capdet* captain, ult. < L *caput* head] —**caˈdetship** *n.*

cadge (kædʒ) *vb.* **1.** to get (food, money, etc.) by sponging or begging. ~*n.* **2.** *Brit.* a person who cadges. [C17: <?] —ˈ**cadger** *n.*

cadi *or* **kadi** (ˈkɑːdɪ, ˈkeɪdɪ) *n., pl.* **-dis.** a judge in a Muslim community. [C16: < Ar. *qāḍī* judge]

Cadmean victory (ˈkædmɪən) *n.* another name for **Pyrrhic victory.** [after *Cadmus,* in Gk myth., who sowed dragon's teeth from which sprang soldiers who began to kill each other]

cadmium (ˈkædmɪəm) *n.* a malleable bluish-white metallic element that occurs in association with zinc ores. It is used in electroplating and alloys. Symbol: Cd; atomic no.: 48; atomic wt.: 112.4. [C19: < NL, < L *cadmīa* zinc ore, CALAMINE: both calamine and cadmium are found in the ore]

cadmium yellow *n.* an orange or yellow insoluble solid used as a pigment in paints, etc.

cadre (ˈkɑːdə) *n.* **1.** the nucleus of trained professional servicemen forming the basis for military expansion. **2.** a group of activists, esp. in the Communist Party. **3.** a basic unit or structure; nucleus. **4.** a member of a cadre. [C19: < F, < It. *quadro,* < L *quadrum* square]

caduceus (kəˈdjuːsɪəs) *n., pl.* **-cei** (-sɪˌaɪ). **1.** *Classical myth.* a winged staff entwined with two serpents carried by Hermes (Mercury) as messenger of the gods. **2.** an insignia resembling this staff used as an emblem of the medical profession. [C16: < L, < Doric Gk *karukeion,* < *karux* herald]

caducous (kəˈdjuːkəs) *adj. Biol.* (of parts of a plant or animal) shed during the life of the organism. [C17: < L, < *cadere* to fall]

CAE (in Australia) *abbrev. for* College of Advanced Education.

caecilian (siːˈsɪlɪən) *n.* a tropical limbless cylindrical amphibian resembling the earthworm and inhabiting moist soil. [C19: < L, < *caecus* blind]

caecum *or U.S.* **cecum** (ˈsiːkəm) *n., pl.* **-ca** (-kə). *Anat.* any structure that ends in a blind sac or pouch, esp. that at the beginning of the large intestine. [C18: short for L *intestinum caecum* blind intestine, translation of Gk *tuphlon enteron*] —ˈ**caecal** *or U.S.* ˈ**cecal** *adj.*

Caenozoic (ˌsiːnəˈzəʊɪk) *adj.* a variant spelling of **Cenozoic.**

Caerphilly (kɛəˈfɪlɪ) *n.* a creamy white mild-flavoured cheese, orig. made in Caerphilly in SE Wales.

Caesar (ˈsiːzə) *n.* **1.** any Roman emperor. **2.** (*sometimes not cap.*) any emperor, autocrat, or dictator. **3.** a title of the Roman emperors from Augustus to Hadrian. [after Gaius Julius *Caesar* (100–44 B.C.), Roman general & statesman]

Caesarean, Caesarian, *or U.S.* **Cesarean, Cesarian** (sɪˈzɛərɪən) *adj.* **1.** of or relating to any of the Caesars, esp. Julius Caesar. ~*n.* **2.** (*sometimes not cap.*) *Surgery.* **a.** a Caesarean section. **b.** (*as modifier*): *Caesarean operation.*

Caesarean section *n.* surgical incision through the abdominal and uterine walls in order to deliver a baby. [C17: from the belief that Julius Caesar was so delivered, the name allegedly being derived < *caedere* to cut]

caesium *or U.S.* **cesium** (ˈsiːzɪəm) *n.* a ductile silvery-white element of the alkali metal group. It is used in photocells and in an atomic clock (**caesium clock**) that uses the frequency of radiation from changing the spin of electrons. The radioisotope **caesium-137,** with a half-life of 30.2 years, is used in radiotherapy. Symbol: Cs; atomic no.: 55; atomic wt.: 132.905.

caesura (sɪˈzjʊərə) *n., pl.* **-ras** *or* **-rae** (-riː). **1.** (in modern prosody) a pause, esp. for sense, usually near the middle of a verse line. **2.** (in classical prosody) a break between words within a metrical foot. [C16: < L, lit.: a cutting, < *caedere* to cut] —**cae'sural** *adj.*

café (ˈkæfeɪ, ˈkæfɪ) *n.* a small or inexpensive restaurant serving light or easily prepared meals and refreshments. [C19: < F: COFFEE]

café au lait *French.* (kafe o lɛ) *n.* **1.** coffee with milk. **2. a.** a light brown colour. **b.** (*as adj.*): *café au lait brocade.*

café noir *French.* (kafe nwar) *n.* black coffee.

cafeteria (ˌkæfɪˈtɪərɪə) *n.* a self-service restaurant. [C20: < American Sp.: coffee shop]

caff (kæf) *n.* a slang word for **café.**

caffeine *or* **caffein** (ˈkæfiːn) *n.* a white crystalline bitter alkaloid responsible for the stimulant action of tea, coffee, and cocoa. [C19: < G *Kaffein,* < *Kaffee* COFFEE]

caftan (ˈkæfˌtæn, -ˌtɑːn) *n.* a variant spelling of **kaftan.**

cage (keɪdʒ) *n.* **1. a.** an enclosure, usually made with bars or wire, for keeping birds, monkeys, etc. **b.** (*as modifier*): *cagebird.* **2.** a thing or place that confines. **3.** something resembling a cage in function or structure: *the rib cage.* **4.** the enclosed platform of a lift, esp. as used in a mine. ~*vb.* **5.** (*tr.*) to confine in or as in a cage. [C13: < OF, < L *cavea* enclosure, < *cavus* hollow]

cagey *or* **cagy** (ˈkeɪdʒɪ) *adj.* **cagier, cagiest.** *Inf.* not frank; wary. [C20: <?] —ˈ**caginess** *n.*

cagoule (kəˈguːl) *n.* a lightweight usually knee-length type of anorak. [C20: < F]

cahoots (kəˈhuːts) *pl. n.* (*sometimes sing.*) *Inf.* **1.** *U.S.* partnership; league. **2. in cahoots.** in collusion. [C19: <?]

caiman (ˈkeɪmən) *n., pl.* **-mans.** a variant spelling of **cayman.**

Cainozoic (ˌkaɪnəʊˈzəʊɪk, ˌkeɪ-) *adj.* a variant spelling of **Cenozoic.**

caïque (kaɪˈiːk) *n.* **1.** a long rowing skiff used on the Bosporus. **2.** a sailing vessel of the E Mediterranean with a square topsail. [C17: < F, < It. *caicco,* < Turkish *kayik*]

cairn (kɛən) *n.* **1.** a mound of stones erected as a memorial or marker. **2.** Also called: **cairn terrier.** a small rough-haired breed of terrier orig. from Scotland. [C15: < Gaelic *carn*]

cairngorm (ˌkɛənˈgɔːm) *n.* a smoky yellow or brown variety of quartz, used as a gemstone. Also called: **smoky quartz.** [C18: < *Cairn Gorm* (lit.: blue cairn), mountain in Scotland]

caisson (kəˈsuːn, ˈkeɪsᵊn) *n.* **1.** a watertight chamber open at the bottom and containing air under pressure, used to carry out construction work under water. **2.** a watertight float filled with air, used to raise sunken ships. **3.** a watertight structure placed across the entrance of a dry dock, etc., to exclude water. **4. a.** a box containing explosives formerly used as a mine. **b.** an ammunition chest. [C18: < F, assimilated to *caisse* CASE[2]]

caisson disease *n.* another name for **decompression sickness.**

caitiff (ˈkeɪtɪf) *Arch. or poetic.* ~*n.* **1.** a cowardly or base person. ~*adj.* **2.** cowardly. [C13: < OF, < L *captīvus* CAPTIVE]

cajole (kəˈdʒəʊl) *vb.* to persuade (someone) by flattery to do what one wants; wheedle; coax. [C17: < F *cajoler* to coax, <?] —**caˈjolement** *n.* —**caˈjoler** *n.* —**caˈjolery** *n.*

cake (keɪk) *n.* **1.** a baked food, usually in loaf or layer form, made from a mixture of flour, sugar, and eggs. **2.** a flat thin mass of bread, esp. unleavened bread. **3.** a shaped mass of dough or other food: *a fish cake.* **4.** a mass, slab, or crust of a solidified substance, as of soap. **5. go** *or* **sell like hot cakes.** *Inf.* to be sold very quickly. **6. have one's cake and eat it.** to enjoy both of two desirable but incompatible alternatives. **7. piece of cake.** *Inf.* something that is easily achieved or obtained. **8. take the cake.** *Inf.* to surpass all others, esp. in stupidity, folly, etc. **9.** *Inf.* the whole of something that is to be shared or divided: *a larger slice of the cake.* ~*vb.* **10.** (*tr.*) to encrust: *the hull was caked with salt.* **11.** to form or be formed into a hardened mass. [C13: < ON *kaka*]

cakewalk (ˈkeɪkˌwɔːk) *n.* **1.** a dance based on a march with intricate steps, orig. performed by American Negroes for the prize of a cake. **2.** a piece of music for this dance. **3.** *Inf.* an easy task.

cal. *abbrev. for:* **1.** calendar. **2.** calibre. **3.** calorie (small).

Cal. *abbrev. for* Calorie (large).

calabash (ˈkæləˌbæʃ) *n.* **1.** Also called: **calabash tree.** a tropical American evergreen tree that produces large round gourds. **2.** the gourd. **3.** the dried hollow shell of a gourd used as the bowl of a tobacco pipe, a bottle, etc. **4. calabash nutmeg.** a tropical African shrub whose seeds can be used as nutmegs. [C17: < obs. F *calabasse,* < Sp., ? < Ar., < *qar'ah* gourd + *yābisah* dry]

calaboose (ˈkæləˌbuːs) *n. U.S. inf.* a prison. [C18: < Creole F, < Sp. *calabozo* dungeon, <?]

calabrese (ˌkæləˈbreɪzɪ) *n.* a variety of green sprouting broccoli. [C20: < It.: Calabrian]

calamander (ˈkæləˌmændə) *n.* the hard black-and-brown striped wood of several trees of India and Ceylon, used in making furniture. See also **ebony** (sense 2). [C19: metathetic var. of *Coromandel,* coast in SE India]

calamine (ˈkæləˌmaɪn) *n.* a pink powder consisting of zinc oxide and ferric oxide, used medicinally in the form of soothing lotions or ointments. [C17: < OF, < Med. L *calamīna,* < L *cadmīa;* see CADMIUM]

calamint (ˈkæləmɪnt) *n.* an aromatic Eurasian plant having clusters of purple or pink flowers. [C14: < OF *calament,* < Med. L *calamentum,* < Gk *kalaminthē*]

calamitous (kəˈlæmɪtəs) *adj.* causing, involving, or resulting in a calamity; disastrous.

calamity (kəˈlæmɪtɪ) *n., pl.* **-ties. 1.** a disaster or misfortune, esp. one causing distress or misery.

2. a state or feeling of deep distress or misery. [C15: < F *calamité*, < L *calamitās*]

calamus (ˈkæləməs) *n., pl.* **-mi** (-ˌmaɪ). **1.** any of a genus of tropical Asian palms, some of which are a source of rattan and canes. **2.** another name for **sweet flag. 3.** *Ornithol.* a quill. [C14: < L, < Gk *kalamos* reed, stem]

calandria (kəˈlændrɪə) *n.* a cylindrical vessel through which vertical tubes pass, esp. one forming part of a heat exchanger or nuclear reactor. [C20: arbitrarily named, < Sp., lit.: lark]

calash (kəˈlæʃ) *or* **calèche** *n.* **1.** a horse-drawn carriage with low wheels and a folding top. **2.** a woman's folding hooped hood worn in the 18th century. [C17: < F, < G, < Czech *kolesa* wheels]

calcaneus (kælˈkeɪnɪəs) *or* **calcaneum** *n., pl.* **-nei** (-nɪˌaɪ). the largest tarsal bone, forming the heel in man. Nontechnical name: **heel bone.** [C19: < LL: heel, < L *calx* heel]

calcareous (kælˈkɛərɪəs) *adj.* of, containing, or resembling calcium carbonate; chalky. [C17: < L *calcārius*, < *calx* lime]

calceolaria (ˌkælsɪəˈlɛərɪə) *n.* a tropical American plant cultivated for its speckled slipper-shaped flowers. Also called: **slipperwort.** [C18: < L *calceolus* small shoe, < *calceus*]

calces (ˈkælsiːz) *n.* a plural of **calx.**

calci- *or before a vowel* **calc-** *combining form.* indicating lime or calcium: *calcify.* [< L *calx*, *calc-* limestone]

calciferol (kælˈsɪfərɒl) *n.* a fat-soluble steroid, found esp. in fish-liver oils and used in the treatment of rickets. Also called: **vitamin D_2.** [C20: < CALCIF(EROUS + ERGOST)EROL]

calciferous (kælˈsɪfərəs) *adj.* producing salts of calcium, esp. calcium carbonate.

calcify (ˈkælsɪˌfaɪ) *vb.* **-fying, -fied. 1.** to convert or be converted into lime. **2.** to harden or become hardened by impregnation with calcium salts. —ˌ**calcifiˈcation** *n.*

calcimine (ˈkælsɪˌmaɪn) *n.* **1.** a white or tinted wash for walls. ~*vb.* **2.** (*tr.*) to cover with calcimine. [C19: < *Kalsomine*, a trademark]

calcine (ˈkælsaɪn, -sɪn) *vb.* **1.** (*tr.*) to heat (a substance) so that it is oxidized, is reduced, or loses water. **2.** (*intr.*) to oxidize as a result of heating. [C14: < Med. L *calcināre* to heat, < L *calx* lime] —**calcination** (ˌkælsɪˈneɪʃən) *n.*

calcite (ˈkælsaɪt) *n.* a colourless or white mineral consisting of crystalline calcium carbonate: the transparent variety is Iceland spar. Formula: $CaCO_3$.

calcium (ˈkælsɪəm) *n.* a malleable silvery-white metallic element of the alkaline earth group, occurring esp. as forms of calcium carbonate. It is an essential constituent of bones and teeth. Symbol: Ca; atomic no.: 20; atomic wt.: 40.08. [C19: < NL, < L *calx* lime]

calcium carbide *n.* a grey salt of calcium used in the production of acetylene. Formula: CaC_2. Sometimes shortened to **carbide.**

calcium carbonate *n.* a white crystalline salt occurring in limestone, chalk, and pearl: used in the production of lime. Formula: $CaCO_3$.

calcium chloride *n.* a white deliquescent salt occurring naturally in seawater and used in the de-icing of roads. Formula: $CaCl_2$.

calcium hydroxide *n.* a white crystalline slightly soluble alkali with many uses, esp. in cement, water softening, and the neutralization of acid soils. Formula: $Ca(OH)_2$. Also called: **lime, slaked lime, caustic lime.**

calcium oxide *n.* a white crystalline base used in the production of calcium hydroxide and in the manufacture of glass and steel. Formula: CaO. Also called: **lime, quicklime, calx.**

calcium phosphate *n.* an insoluble nonacid calcium salt that occurs in bones and is the main constituent of bone ash.

calcspar (ˈkælkˌspɑː) *n.* another name for **calcite.** [C19: < Swedish *kalkspat*, < *kalk* lime (ult. < L *calx*) + *spat* SPAR[3]]

calculable (ˈkælkjʊləbᵊl) *adj.* **1.** that may be computed or estimated. **2.** predictable. —ˌ**calculaˈbility** *n.* —ˈ**calculably** *adv.*

calculate (ˈkælkjʊˌleɪt) *vb.* **1.** to solve (one or more problems) by a mathematical procedure. **2.** (*tr.; may take a clause as object*) to determine beforehand by judgment, etc.; estimate. **3.** (*tr.; usually passive*) to aim: *the car was calculated to appeal to women.* **4.** (*intr.;* foll. by *on* or *upon*) to rely. **5.** (*tr.; may take a clause as object*) *U.S. dialect.* to suppose. [C16: < LL *calculāre*, < *calculus* pebble used as a counter] —**calculative** (ˈkælkjʊlətɪv) *adj.*

calculated (ˈkælkjʊˌleɪtɪd) *adj.* (*usually prenominal*) **1.** undertaken after considering the likelihood of success or failure. **2.** premeditated: *a calculated insult.*

calculating (ˈkælkjʊˌleɪtɪŋ) *adj.* **1.** selfishly scheming. **2.** shrewd. —ˈ**calcuˌlatingly** *adv.*

calculation (ˌkælkjʊˈleɪʃən) *n.* **1.** the act, process, or result of calculating. **2.** a forecast. **3.** careful planning, esp. for selfish motives.

calculator (ˈkælkjʊˌleɪtə) *n.* **1.** a device for performing mathematical calculations, esp. an electronic device that can be held in the hand. **2.** a person or thing that calculates. **3.** a set of tables used as an aid to calculations.

calculous (ˈkælkjʊləs) *adj. Pathol.* of or suffering from a calculus.

calculus (ˈkælkjʊləs) *n., pl.* **-luses. 1.** a branch of mathematics, developed independently by Newton and Leibnitz. Both **differential calculus** and **integral calculus** are concerned with the effect on a function of an infinitesimal change in the independent variable. **2.** any mathematical system of calculation involving the use of symbols. **3.** (*pl.* **-li** (-ˌlaɪ)). *Pathol.* a stonelike concretion of minerals found in organs of the body. [C17: < L: pebble, < *calx* small stone, counter]

caldera (kælˈdɛərə) *n.* a large basin-shaped crater at the top of a volcano, formed by the collapse of the cone. [C19: < Sp. *caldera*, lit.: CAULDRON]

caldron (ˈkɔːldrən) *n.* a variant spelling of **cauldron.**

calèche (*French* kalɛʃ) *n.* a variant of **calash.**

Caledonia (ˌkælɪˈdəʊnɪə) *n.* the Roman name for Scotland.

Caledonian (ˌkælɪˈdəʊnɪən) *adj.* **1.** relating to Scotland. **2.** of a period of mountain building in NW Europe in the Palaeozoic era. ~*n.* **3.** *Literary.* a native or inhabitant of Scotland.

calefacient (ˌkælɪˈfeɪʃənt) *adj.* **1.** causing warmth. ~*n.* **2.** *Med.* an agent that warms, such as a mustard plaster. [C17: < L, < *calefacere* to heat]

calendar (ˈkælɪndə) *n.* **1.** a system for determining the beginning, length, and order of years and their divisions. **2.** a table showing any such arrangement, esp. as applied to one or more successive years. **3.** a list or schedule of pending court cases, appointments, etc. ~*vb.* **4.** (*tr.*) to enter in a calendar; schedule. [C13: via Norman F < Med. L *kalendārium* account book, < *Kalendae* the CALENDS] —**calendrical** (kæˈlɛndrɪkᵊl) *or* **caˈlendric** *adj.*

calendar month *n.* See **month** (sense 1).

calendar year *n.* See **year** (sense 1).

calender (ˈkælɪndə) *n.* **1.** a machine in which paper or cloth is smoothed by passing between rollers. ~*vb.* **2.** (*tr.*) to subject (material) to such a process. [C17: < F *calandre*, <?]

calends *or* **kalends** (ˈkælɪndz) *pl. n.* the first day of each month in the ancient Roman calendar. [C14: < L *kalendae*]

calendula (kæˈlɛndjʊlə) *n.* any of a genus of Eurasian plants, esp. the pot marigold, having orange-and-yellow rayed flowers. [C19: < Med. L, < L *kalendae* CALENDS]

calf[1] (kɑːf) *n., pl.* **calves. 1.** the young of cattle, esp. domestic cattle. **2.** the young of certain other mammals, such as the buffalo and whale. **3.** a large piece of ice detached from an iceberg, etc. **4. kill the fatted calf.** to celebrate lavishly, esp. as a welcome. [OE *cealf*]

calf[2] (kɑːf) *n., pl.* **calves.** the thick fleshy part of the back of the leg between the ankle and the knee. [C14: < ON *kalfi*]

calf love *n.* temporary infatuation of an adolescent for a member of the opposite sex.
calf's-foot jelly *n.* a jelly made from the stock of boiled calves' feet and flavourings.
calfskin (ˈkɑːfˌskɪn) *n.* **1.** the skin or hide of a calf. **2.** Also called: **calf. a.** fine leather made from this skin. **b.** (*as modifier*): *calfskin boots.*
calibrate (ˈkælɪˌbreɪt) *vb.* (*tr.*) **1.** to measure the calibre of (a gun, etc.). **2.** to mark (the scale of a measuring instrument) so that readings can be made in appropriate units. **3.** to determine the accuracy of (a measuring instrument, etc.). —ˌ**caliˈbration** *n.* —ˈ**caliˌbrator** *n.*
calibre *or U.S.* **caliber** (ˈkælɪbə) *n.* **1.** the diameter of a cylindrical body, esp. the internal diameter of a tube or the bore of a firearm. **2.** the diameter of a shell or bullet. **3.** ability; distinction. **4.** personal character: *a man of high calibre.* [C16: < OF, < It. *calibro,* < Ar. *qālib* shoemaker's last] —ˈ**calibred** *or U.S.* ˈ**calibered** *adj.*
calices (ˈkælɪˌsiːz) *n.* the plural of **calix.**
calico (ˈkælɪˌkəʊ) *n., pl.* **-coes** *or* **-cos. 1.** a white or unbleached cotton fabric. **2.** *Chiefly U.S.* a coarse printed cotton fabric. [C16: based on *Calicut,* town in India]
calif (ˈkeɪlɪf, ˈkæl-) *n.* a variant spelling of **caliph.**
californium (ˌkælɪˈfɔːnɪəm) *n.* a transuranic element artificially produced from curium. Symbol: Cf; atomic no.: 98; half-life of most stable isotope, ^{251}Cf: 800 years (approx.). [C20: NL; discovered at the University of *California*]
calipash *or* **callipash** (ˈkælɪˌpæʃ) *n.* the greenish glutinous edible part of the turtle found next to the upper shell. [C17: ? changed < Sp. *carapacho* CARAPACE]
calipee (ˈkælɪˌpiː) *n.* the yellow glutinous edible part of the turtle found next to the lower shell. [C17: ? a var. of CALIPASH]
caliper (ˈkælɪpə) *n.* the usual U.S. spelling of **calliper.**
caliph, calif, *or* **khalif** (ˈkeɪlɪf, ˈkæl-) *n. Islam.* the title of the successors of Mohammed as rulers of the Islamic world. [C14: < OF, < Ar. *khalīfa* successor]
caliphate, califate, *or* **khalifate** (ˈkeɪlɪˌfeɪt) *n.* the office, jurisdiction, or reign of a caliph.
calisthenics (ˌkælɪsˈθɛnɪks) *n.* a variant spelling (esp. U.S.) of **callisthenics.**
calix (ˈkeɪlɪks, ˈkæ-) *n., pl.* **calices.** a cup; chalice. [C18: < L: CHALICE]
calk[1] (kɔːk) *vb.* a variant spelling of **caulk.**
calk[2] (kɔːk) *or* **calkin** (ˈkɔːkɪn, ˈkæl-) *n.* **1.** a metal projection on a horse's shoe to prevent slipping. ~*vb.* (*tr.*) **2.** to provide with calks. [C17: < L *calx* heel]
call (kɔːl) *vb.* **1.** (often foll. by *out*) to speak or utter (words, sounds, etc.) loudly so as to attract attention: *he called out her name.* **2.** (*tr.*) to ask or order to come: *to call a policeman.* **3.** (*intr.;* sometimes foll. by *on*) to make a visit (to): *she called on him.* **4.** (often foll. by *up*) to telephone (a person). **5.** (*tr.*) to summon to a specific office, profession, etc. **6.** (of animals or birds) to utter (a characteristic sound or cry). **7.** (*tr.*) to summon (a bird or animal), as by imitating its cry. **8.** (*tr.*) to name or style: *they called the dog Rover.* **9.** (*tr.*) to designate: *they called him a coward.* **10.** (*tr.*) to regard in a specific way: *I call it a foolish waste of time.* **11.** (*tr.*) to attract (attention). **12.** (*tr.*) to read (a list, etc.) aloud to check for omissions or absentees. **13.** (when *tr.,* usually foll. by *for*) to give an order (for): *to call a strike.* **14.** (*intr.*) to try to predict the result of tossing a coin. **15.** (*tr.*) to awaken: *I was called early this morning.* **16.** (*tr.*) to cause to assemble. **17.** (*tr.*) *Sport.* (of an umpire, etc.) to pass judgment upon (a shot, etc.) with a call. **18.** (*tr.*) *Austral. & N.Z.* to broadcast a commentary on (a horse race, etc.). **19.** (*tr.*) to demand repayment of (a loan, security, etc.). **20.** (*tr.*) *Brit.* to award (a student at an Inn of Court) the degree of barrister (esp. in **call to the bar**). **21.** (*tr.*) *Poker.* to demand that (a player) expose his hand, after equalling his bet. **22.** (*intr.*) *Bridge.* to make a bid. **23.** (*tr.*) to expose (a person's misleading statements, etc.): *I called his bluff.* **24.** (in square-dancing) to call out (instructions) to the dancers. **25.** (*intr.;* foll. by *for*) **a.** to require: *this problem calls for study.* **b.** to come or go (for) in order to fetch. **26.** (*intr.;* foll. by *on* or *upon*) to make an appeal or request (to): *they called upon him to reply.* **27. call into being.** to create. **28. call to mind.** to remember or cause to be remembered. ~*n.* **29.** a cry or shout. **30.** the characteristic cry of a bird or animal. **31.** a device, such as a whistle, intended to imitate the cry of a bird or animal. **32.** a summons or invitation. **33.** a summons or signal sounded on a horn, bugle, etc. **34.** a short visit: *the doctor made six calls this morning.* **35.** an inner urge to some task or profession; vocation. **36.** allure or fascination, esp. of a place: *the call of the forest.* **37.** need, demand, or occasion: *there is no call to shout.* **38.** demand or claim (esp. in **the call of duty**). **39.** *Theatre.* a notice to actors informing them of times of rehearsals. **40.** a conversation or a request for a connection by telephone. **41.** *Commerce.* **a.** a demand for repayment of a loan. **b.** (*as modifier*): *call money.* **42.** *Finance.* a demand for redeemable bonds or shares to be presented for repayment. **43.** *Poker.* a demand for a hand or hands to be exposed. **44.** *Bridge.* a bid or a player's turn to bid. **45.** *Sport.* a decision of an umpire or referee regarding a shot, pitch, etc. **46.** *Austral.* a broadcast commentary on a horse race, etc. **47.** Also called: **call option.** *Stock Exchange.* an option to buy a stated amount of securities at a specified price during a specified period. **48. on call. a.** (of a loan, etc.) repayable on demand. **b.** (of a doctor, etc.) available for duty. **49. within call.** accessible. ~See also **call down, call forth,** etc. [OE *ceallian*]
calla (ˈkælə) *n.* **1.** Also called: **calla lily, arum lily.** a southern African plant which has a white funnel-shaped spathe enclosing a yellow spadix. **2.** a plant that grows in wet places and has a white spathe and red berries. [C19: < NL, prob. < Gk *kalleia* wattles on a cock, prob. < *kallos* beauty]
call box *n.* a soundproof enclosure for a public telephone. Also called: **telephone kiosk.**
callboy (ˈkɔːlˌbɔɪ) *n.* a person who notifies actors when it is time to go on stage.
call down *vb.* (*tr., adv.*) to request or invoke: *to call down God's anger.*
caller (ˈkɔːlə) *n.* **1.** a person or thing that calls, esp. a person who makes a brief visit. **2.** *Austral.* a racing commentator.
call forth *vb.* (*tr., adv.*) to cause (something) to come into action or existence.
call girl *n.* a prostitute with whom appointments are made by telephone.
calligraphy (kəˈlɪgrəfɪ) *n.* handwriting, esp. beautiful handwriting. —**calˈligrapher** *or* **calˈligraphist** *n.* —**calligraphic** (ˌkælɪˈgræfɪk) *adj.*
call in *vb.* (*adv.*) **1.** (*intr.;* often foll. by *on*) to pay a visit, esp. a brief one: *call in if you are in the neighbourhood.* **2.** (*tr.*) to demand payment of: *to call in a loan.* **3.** (*tr.*) to take (something) out of circulation, because it is defective. **4.** to summon to one's assistance: *to call in a specialist.*
calling (ˈkɔːlɪŋ) *n.* **1.** a strong inner urge to follow an occupation, etc.; vocation. **2.** an occupation, profession, or trade.
calling card *n.* the usual U.S. and Canad. term for **visiting card.**
calliope (kəˈlaɪəpɪ) *n. U.S. & Canad.* a steam organ. [after CALLIOPE (lit.: beautiful-voiced)]
Calliope (kəˈlaɪəpɪ) *n. Greek myth.* the Muse of epic poetry.
calliper *or U.S.* **caliper** (ˈkælɪpə) *n.* **1.** (*often pl.*) Also called: **calliper compasses.** an instrument for measuring internal or external dimensions, consisting of two steel legs hinged together. **2.** Also called: **calliper splint.** *Med.* a metal splint for supporting the leg. ~*vb.* **3.** (*tr.*) to measure with callipers. [C16: var. of CALIBRE]
calliper rule *n.* a measuring instrument having two parallel jaws, one fixed and the other sliding.
callisthenics *or* **calisthenics** (ˌkælɪsˈθɛnɪks) *n.*

1. (*functioning as pl.*) light exercises designed to promote general fitness. 2. (*functioning as sing.*) the practice of callisthenic exercises. [C19: < Gk *kalli-* beautiful + Gk *sthenos* strength] —ˌ**callisˈthenic** *or* ˌ**calisˈthenic** *adj.*

call loan *n.* a loan that is repayable on demand. Also called: **demand loan.**

call off *vb.* (*tr., adv.*) 1. to cancel or abandon: *the game was called off.* 2. to order (an animal or person) to desist: *the man called off his dog.* 3. to stop (something).

callosity (kəˈlɒsɪtɪ) *n., pl.* **-ties.** 1. hard-heartedness. 2. a callus.

callous (ˈkæləs) *adj.* 1. insensitive. 2. (of skin) hardened and thickened. ~*vb.* 3. *Pathol.* to make or become callous. [C16: < L *callōsus;* see CALLUS] —ˈ**callously** *adv.* —ˈ**callousness** *n.*

call out *vb.* (*adv.*) 1. to utter aloud, esp. loudly. 2. (*tr.*) to summon: *call out the troops.* 3. (*tr.*) to order (workers) to strike. 4. (*tr.*) to challenge to a duel.

callow (ˈkæləʊ) *adj.* lacking experience of life; immature. [OE *calu*] —ˈ**callowness** *n.*

call sign *n.* a group of letters and numbers identifying a radio transmitting station.

call up *vb.* (*tr., adv.*) 1. to summon to report for active military service, as in time of war. 2. to recall (something); evoke. 3. to bring or summon (people, etc.) into action. 4. to telephone. ~*n.* **call-up.** 5. a. a general order to report for military service. b. the number of men so summoned.

callus (ˈkæləs) *n., pl.* **-luses.** 1. Also called: **callosity.** an area of skin that is hard or thick, esp. on the sole of the foot. 2. an area of bony tissue formed during the healing of a fractured bone. 3. *Bot.* a mass of hard protective tissue produced in woody plants at the site of an injury. [C16: < L, var. of *callum* hardened skin]

calm (kɑːm) *adj.* 1. still: *a calm sea.* 2. *Meteorol.* without wind, or with wind of less than 1 mph. 3. not disturbed, agitated, or excited. 4. tranquil; serene: *a calm voice.* ~*n.* 5. an absence of disturbance or rough motion. 6. absence of wind. 7. tranquillity. ~*vb.* 8. (often foll. by *down*) to make or become calm. [C14: < OF *calme,* < OIt., < LL *cauma* heat, hence a rest during the heat of the day, < Gk, < *kaiein* to burn] —ˈ**calmly** *adv.* —ˈ**calmness** *n.*

calmative (ˈkælmətɪv, ˈkɑːmə-) *adj.* (of a remedy or agent) sedative.

calomel (ˈkæləˌmɛl, -məl) *n.* a colourless tasteless powder consisting chiefly of mercurous chloride, used medicinally, esp. as a cathartic. [C17: ? < NL *calomelas* (unattested), lit.: beautiful black, < Gk *kalos* beautiful + *melas* black]

Calor Gas (ˈkælə) *n. Trademark.* butane gas liquefied under pressure in portable containers for domestic use.

caloric (kəˈlɒrɪk) *adj.* 1. of or concerned with heat or calories. ~*n.* 2. *Obs.* a hypothetical elastic fluid, the embodiment of heat.

calorie *or* **calory** (ˈkælərɪ) *n., pl.* **-ries.** a unit of heat, equal to 4.1868 joules (**International Table calorie**): formerly defined as the quantity of heat required to raise the temperature of 1 gram of water by 1°C. Abbrev.: **cal.** Also called: **small calorie.** [C19: < F, < L *calor* heat]

Calorie (ˈkælərɪ) *n.* 1. Also called: **kilogram calorie, large calorie.** a unit of heat, equal to one thousand calories. Abbrev.: **Cal.** 2. the amount of a specific food capable of producing one thousand calories of energy.

calorific (ˌkæləˈrɪfɪk) *adj.* of, concerning, or generating heat. —ˌ**caloˈrifically** *adv.*

calorific value *n.* the quantity of heat produced by the complete combustion of a given mass of a fuel.

calorimeter (ˌkæləˈrɪmɪtə) *n.* an apparatus for measuring amounts of heat, esp. to find calorific values, etc. —**calorimetric** (ˌkælərɪˈmɛtrɪk) *adj.* —ˌ**caloˈrimetry** *n.*

calque (kælk) *n.* another word for **loan translation.** [C20: < F: a tracing, < L *calcāre* to tread]

calumet (ˈkæljʊˌmɛt) *n.* the peace pipe. [C18: < Canad. F, < F: straw, < LL *calamellus* a little reed, < L: CALAMUS]

calumniate (kəˈlʌmnɪˌeɪt) *vb.* (*tr.*) to slander. —**caˌlumniˈation** *n.* —**caˈlumniˌator** *n.*

calumny (ˈkæləmnɪ) *n., pl.* **-nies.** 1. the malicious utterance of false charges or misrepresentation. 2. such a false charge or misrepresentation. [C15: < L *calumnia* deception, slander] —**calumnious** (kəˈlʌmnɪəs) *or* **caˈlumniatory** *adj.*

Calvados (ˈkælvəˌdɒs) *n.* an apple brandy distilled from cider in Calvados in Normandy, France.

Calvary (ˈkælvərɪ) *n.* the place just outside the walls of Jerusalem where Jesus was crucified. Also called: **Golgotha.** [< LL *Calvāria,* translation of Gk *kranion* skull, translation of Aramaic *gulgulta* Golgotha]

calve (kɑːv) *vb.* 1. to give birth to (a calf). 2. (of a glacier or iceberg) to release (masses of ice) in breaking up.

calves (kɑːvz) *n.* the plural of **calf**[1] and **calf**[2].

Calvinism (ˈkælvɪˌnɪzəm) *n.* the theological system of Calvin, 16th-century French theologian, and his followers, characterized by emphasis on predestination and justification by faith. —ˈ**Calvinist** *n., adj.* —ˌ**Calvinˈistic** *or* ˌ**Calvinˈistical** *adj.*

calx (kælks) *n., pl.* **calxes** *or* **calces.** 1. the powdery metallic oxide formed when an ore or mineral is roasted. 2. calcium oxide. [C15: < L: lime, < Gk *khalix* pebble]

calypso (kəˈlɪpsəʊ) *n., pl.* **-sos.** a popular type of satirical West Indian ballad, esp. from Trinidad, usually extemporized to a syncopated accompaniment. [C20: prob. < *Calypso,* sea nymph in Gk myth.]

calyx (ˈkeɪlɪks, ˈkælɪks) *n., pl.* **calyxes** *or* **calyces** (ˈkælɪˌsiːz, ˈkeɪlɪ-). 1. the sepals of a flower collectively that protect the developing flower bud. 2. any cup-shaped cavity or structure. [C17: < L, < Gk *kalux* shell, < *kaluptein* to cover]

cam (kæm) *n.* a rotating cylinder attached to a revolving shaft to give a reciprocating motion to a part in contact with it. [C16: < Du. *kam* comb]

camaraderie (ˌkæməˈrɑːdərɪ) *n.* a spirit of familiarity and trust existing between friends. [C19: < F, < *camarade* COMRADE]

camarilla (ˌkæməˈrɪlə) *n.* a group of confidential advisers, esp. formerly, to the Spanish kings. [C19: < Sp., lit.: a little room]

camber (ˈkæmbə) *n.* 1. a slight upward curve to the centre of the surface of a road, ship's deck, etc. 2. another name for **bank**[2] (sense 8). 3. an outward inclination of the front wheels of a road vehicle so that they are slightly closer together at the bottom. 4. aerofoil curvature expressed by the ratio of the maximum height of the aerofoil mean line to its chord. ~*vb.* 5. to form or be formed with a surface that curves upwards to its centre. [C17: < OF *cambre* curved, < L *camurus*]

cambium (ˈkæmbɪəm) *n., pl.* **-biums** *or* **-bia** (-bɪə). *Bot.* a layer of cells that increases the girth of stems and roots. [C17: < Med. L: exchange, < LL *cambiāre* to exchange] —ˈ**cambial** *adj.*

Cambodian (kæmˈbəʊdɪən) *adj.* 1. of or relating to Kampuchea (formerly Cambodia) in SE Asia, or its people. ~*n.* 2. a native or inhabitant of Kampuchea.

Cambrian (ˈkæmbrɪən) *adj.* 1. of or formed in the first 100 million years of the Palaeozoic era. 2. of or relating to Wales. ~*n.* 3. **the.** the Cambrian period or rock system. 4. a Welshman.

cambric (ˈkeɪmbrɪk) *n.* a fine white linen fabric. [C16: < Flemish *Kamerijk* Cambrai]

Cambs *abbrev. for* Cambridgeshire.

camcorder (ˈkæmˌkɔːdə) *n.* a video camera and recorder combined in a portable unit.

came (keɪm) *vb.* the past tense of **come.**

camel (ˈkæməl) *n.* 1. either of two cud-chewing, humped mammals (see **Arabian camel, Bactrian camel**) that are adapted for surviving long periods without food or water in desert regions. 2. a float attached to a vessel to increase its buoyancy. 3. a. a fawn colour. b. (*as adj.*): *a* *camel coat.* [OE, < L, < Gk *kamēlos*, of Semitic origin]

cameleer (ˌkæmɪˈlɪə) *n.* a camel driver.

camellia (kəˈmiːlɪə) *n.* any of a genus of ornamental shrubs having glossy evergreen leaves and showy white, pink, or red flowers. Also called: **japonica.** [C18: NL, after Georg Josef *Kamel* (1661–1706), Moravian Jesuit missionary]

camelopard (ˈkæmɪləˌpɑːd, kəˈmɛl-) *n.* an obsolete word for **giraffe.** [C14: < Med. L, < Gk, < *kamēlos* CAMEL + *pardalis* LEOPARD, because the giraffe was thought to have a head like a camel's and spots like a leopard's]

camel's hair *or* **camelhair** (ˈkæməlˌhɛə) *n.* **1.** the hair of a camel, used in rugs, etc. **2.** soft cloth made of this hair, usually tan in colour. **3.** (*modifier*) (of a painter's brush) made from the tail hairs of squirrels.

Camembert (ˈkæməmˌbɛə) *n.* a soft creamy cheese. [F, < *Camembert*, a village in Normandy]

cameo (ˈkæmɪˌəʊ) *n., pl.* **cameos. 1.** a medallion, as on a brooch or ring, with a profile head carved in relief. **2.** an engraving upon a gem or other stone so that the background is of a different colour from the raised design. **3.** a stone with such an engraving. **4. a.** a brief dramatic scene played by a well-known actor or actress in a film or television play. **b.** (*as modifier*): *a cameo performance.* **5.** a short literary work. [C15: < It. *cammeo*, <?]

camera (ˈkæmərə) *n.* **1.** an optical device consisting of a lens system set in a light-proof construction inside which a light-sensitive film or plate can be positioned. **2.** *Television.* the equipment used to convert the optical image of a scene into the corresponding electrical signals. **3.** (*pl.* **-erae** (-əˌriː)). a judge's private room. **4. in camera. a.** *Law.* relating to a hearing from which members of the public are excluded. **b.** in private. [C18: < L: vault, < Gk *kamara*]

cameraman (ˈkæmərəˌmæn) *n., pl.* **-men.** a person who operates a film or television camera.

camera obscura (ɒbˈskjʊərə) *n.* a darkened chamber with an aperture, in which images of outside objects are projected onto a flat surface. [NL: dark chamber]

camera-shy *adj.* having an aversion to being photographed or filmed.

camiknickers (ˈkæmɪˌnɪkəz) *pl. n.* women's knickers attached to a camisole top.

camisole (ˈkæmɪˌsəʊl) *n.* **1.** a woman's under-bodice with shoulder straps, originally designed as a cover for a corset. **2.** a woman's short negligee. [C19: < F, < Provençal *camisola*, < *camisa* shirt, < LL *camīsia*]

camomile *or* **chamomile** (ˈkæməˌmaɪl) *n.* **1.** any of a genus of aromatic plants whose finely dissected leaves and daisy-like flowers are used medicinally. **2.** any plant of a related genus as **German** or **wild camomile. 3. camomile tea.** a medicinal beverage made from the fragrant leaves and flowers of any of these plants. [C14: < OF, < Med. L, < Gk *khamaimēlon* lit., earth-apple (referring to the scent of the flowers)]

camouflage (ˈkæməˌflɑːʒ) *n.* **1.** the exploitation of natural surroundings or artificial aids to conceal or disguise the presence of military units, etc. **2.** the means by which animals escape the notice of predators. **3.** a device or expedient designed to conceal or deceive. ~*vb.* **4.** (*tr.*) to conceal by camouflage. [C20: < F, < *camoufler*, < It. *camuffare* to disguise, <?]

camp[1] (kæmp) *n.* **1.** a place where tents, cabins, etc., are erected for the use of military troops, etc. **2.** tents, cabins, etc., used as temporary lodgings by holiday-makers, Scouts, Gypsies, etc. **3.** the group of people living in such lodgings. **4.** a group supporting a given doctrine: *the socialist camp.* **5.** (*modifier*) suitable for use in temporary quarters, on holiday, etc.: *a camp bed; a camp chair.* **6.** *S. African.* a field or pasture. **7.** *Austral.* a place where sheep or cattle gather to rest. ~*vb.* (*intr.*) **8.** (often foll. by *down*) to establish or set up a camp. **9.** (often foll. by *out*) to live temporarily in or as if in a tent. [C16: < OF, ult. < L *campus* field] —ˈ**camping** *n.*

camp[2] (kæmp) *Inf.* ~*adj.* **1.** effeminate; affected. **2.** homosexual. **3.** consciously artificial, vulgar, or mannered. ~*vb.* **4.** (*tr.*) to perform or invest with a camp quality. **5. camp it up. a.** to overact. **b.** to flaunt one's homosexuality. [C20: <?] —ˈ**campy** *adj.*

campaign (kæmˈpeɪn) *n.* **1.** a series of coordinated activities, such as public speaking, designed to achieve a social, political, or commercial goal: *a presidential campaign.* **2.** *Mil.* a number of operations aimed at achieving a single objective. ~*vb.* **3.** (*intr.*; often foll. by *for*) to conduct, serve in, or go on a campaign. [C17: < F *campagne* open country, < It., < LL, < L *campus* field] —**camˈpaigner** *n.*

campanile (ˌkæmpəˈniːlɪ) *n.* (esp. in Italy) a bell tower, not usually attached to another building. [C17: < It., < *campana* bell]

campanology (ˌkæmpəˈnɒlədʒɪ) *n.* the art or skill of ringing bells. [C19: < NL, < LL *campāna* bell] —**campanological** (ˌkæmpənəˈlɒdʒɪkᵊl) *adj.* —ˌ**campaˈnologist** *or* ˌ**campaˈnologer** *n.*

campanula (kæmˈpænjʊlə) *n.* any of a genus of N temperate plants having blue or white bell-shaped flowers. Also called: **bellflower.** [C17: < NL: a little bell, < LL *campāna* bell]

camp drafting *n. Austral.* a competitive test of horsemen's skill in drafting cattle.

camper (ˈkæmpə) *n.* **1.** a person who lives or temporarily stays in a tent, cabin, etc. **2.** *U.S. & Canad.* a vehicle equipped for camping out.

camp follower *n.* **1.** any civilian, esp. a prostitute, who unofficially provides services to military personnel. **2.** a nonmember who is sympathetic to a particular group, theory, etc.

camphor (ˈkæmfə) *n.* a whitish crystalline aromatic ketone obtained from the wood of an Asian or Australian laurel (**camphor tree**): used in medicine as a liniment. [C15: < OF *camphre*, < Med. L *camphora*, < Ar. *kāfūr*, < Malay *kāpūr* chalk] —**camphoric** (kæmˈfɒrɪk) *adj.*

camphorate (ˈkæmfəˌreɪt) *vb.* (*tr.*) to apply, treat with, or impregnate with camphor.

camphor ball *n.* another name for **mothball** (sense 1).

camphor ice *n.* an ointment consisting of camphor, white wax, spermaceti, and castor oil, used to treat skin ailments, esp. chapped skin.

camphor wood *n. Austral.* a popular name for any of several trees with pungent smelling wood.

campion (ˈkæmpɪən) *n.* any of various plants related to the pink, having red, pink, or white flowers. [C16: prob. < *campion*, obs. var. of CHAMPION]

camp oven *n. Austral. & N.Z.* a metal pot or box with a heavy lid, used for baking over an open fire.

camp site *n.* an area on which holiday-makers may pitch a tent, etc. Also called: **camping site.**

campus (ˈkæmpəs) *n., pl.* **-puses. 1.** the grounds and buildings of a university. **2.** *Chiefly U.S.* the outside area of a college, etc. [C18: < L: field]

campylobacter (ˈkæmpɪləʊˌbæktə) *n.* a rod-shaped bacterium that causes infections in animals and man: a common cause of gastroenteritis. [< Gk *kampulos* bent + BACTER(IUM)]

camshaft (ˈkæmˌʃɑːft) *n.* a shaft having one or more cams attached to it.

can[1] (kæn; *unstressed* kən) *vb. past* **could.** (takes an infinitive without *to* or an implied infinitive) used as an auxiliary: **1.** to indicate ability, skill, or fitness to perform a task: *I can run.* **2.** to indicate permission or the right to something: *can I have a drink?* **3.** to indicate knowledge of how to do something: *he can speak three languages.* **4.** to indicate the possibility, opportunity, or likelihood: *my trainer says I can win the race.* [OE *cunnan*]

▷ **Usage.** See at **may**[1].

can[2] (kæn) *n.* **1.** a container, esp. for liquids, usually of thin metal: *a petrol can.* **2.** a tin (metal container): *a beer can.* **3.** Also: **canful.** the contents of a can or the amount a can will hold. **4.** a slang word for **prison. 5.** *U.S. & Canad.* a slang word for **toilet.** **6.** a shallow cylindrical metal container used for storing and handling film. **7. can of worms.** *Inf.* a complicated problem. **8. in the can. a.** (of a film, piece of music, etc.) having been recorded, edited, etc. **b.** *Inf.* agreed: *the contract is in the can.* ~*vb.* **canning, canned. 9.** to put (food, etc.) into a can or cans. [OE *canne*] —ˈ**canner** *n.*

Can. *abbrev. for:* **1.** Canada. **2.** Canadian.

Canaan (ˈkeɪnən) *n.* an ancient region between the River Jordan and the Mediterranean: the Promised Land of the Israelites.

Canaanite (ˈkeɪnəˌnaɪt) *n.* a member of an ancient Semitic people who occupied the land of Canaan before the Israelite conquest.

Canada balsam *n.* **1.** a yellow transparent resin obtained from the balsam fir. Because its refractive index is similar to that of glass, it is used as a mounting medium for microscope specimens. **2.** another name for **balsam fir.**

Canada Day *n.* (in Canada) July 1, the anniversary of the day in 1867 when Canada received dominion status: a public holiday.

Canada goose *n.* a large common greyish-brown North American goose with a black neck and head and a white throat patch.

Canada jay *n.* a grey crestless jay, notorious in northern parts of N America for its stealing. Also called: **camp robber, whisky-jack.**

Canadian (kəˈneɪdɪən) *adj.* **1.** of or relating to Canada or its people. ~*n.* **2.** a native, citizen, or inhabitant of Canada.

Canadiana (kəˌneɪdɪˈɑːnə; *Canad.* -ˈænə) *n.* objects, such as books, furniture, and antiques, relating to Canadian history and culture.

Canadian football *n.* a game like American football played on a grass pitch between teams of 12 players.

Canadianism (kəˈneɪdɪəˌnɪzəm) *n.* **1.** the Canadian national character or spirit. **2.** a linguistic usage, custom, or other feature peculiar to Canada, its people, or their culture.

Canadianize *or* **-ise** (kəˈneɪdɪəˌnaɪz) *vb.* to make or become Canadian by changing customs, ownership, character, content, etc.

Canadian Shield *n.* the wide area of Precambrian rock extending over most of E and central Canada: rich in minerals. Also called: **Laurentian Shield.**

Canadien (*French* kanadjɛ̃; *English* kəˌnædɪˈɛn) *or* (*fem.*) **Canadienne** (*French* kanadjɛn; *English* kəˌnædɪˈɛn) *n.* a French Canadian.

canaille *French.* (kanɑj) *n.* the masses; mob; rabble. [C17: < F, < It. *canaglia* pack of dogs]

canakin (ˈkænɪkɪn) *n.* a variant spelling of **cannikin.**

canal (kəˈnæl) *n.* **1.** an artificial waterway constructed for navigation, irrigation, etc. **2.** any of various passages or ducts: *the alimentary canal.* **3.** any of various intercellular spaces in plants. **4.** *Astron.* any of the indistinct surface features of Mars orig. thought to be a network of channels. ~*vb.* **-nalling, -nalled** *or U.S.* **-naling, -naled.** (*tr.*) **5.** to dig a canal through. **6.** to provide with a canal or canals. [C15 (in the sense: pipe, tube): < L *canālis* channel, < *canna* reed]

canal boat *n.* a long narrow boat used on canals, esp. for carrying freight.

canaliculus (ˌkænəˈlɪkjʊləs) *n., pl.* **-li** (-ˌlaɪ). a small channel or groove, as in some bones. [C16: < L: a little channel, < *canālis* CANAL] —ˌ**canaˈlicular** *or* ˌ**canaˈliculate** *adj.*

canalize *or* **-lise** (ˈkænəˌlaɪz) *vb.* (*tr.*) **1.** to provide with or convert into a canal or canals. **2.** to give a particular direction to or provide an outlet for. —ˌ**canaliˈzation** *or* **-liˈsation** *n.*

canal ray *n. Physics.* a stream of positive ions produced in a discharge tube by allowing them to pass through holes in the cathode.

canapé (ˈkænəpɪ, -ˌpeɪ) *n.* a small piece of bread, toast, etc., spread with a savoury topping. [C19: < F: sofa]

canard (kæˈnɑːd) *n.* **1.** a false report; rumour or hoax. **2.** an aircraft in which the tailplane is mounted in front of the wing. [C19: < F: a duck, < OF *caner* to quack, imit.]

canary (kəˈnɛərɪ) *n., pl.* **-naries. 1.** a small finch of the Canary Islands and Azores: a popular cagebird noted for its singing. **2. canary yellow. a.** a light yellow. **b.** (*as adj.*): *a canary-yellow car.* **3.** a sweet wine similar to Madeira. **4.** *Arch.* a sweet wine from the Canary Islands. [C16: < OSp. *canario* of or from the Canary Islands]

canasta (kəˈnæstə) *n.* **1.** a card game for two to six players who seek to amass points by declaring sets of cards. **2.** Also called: **meld.** a declared set in this game, containing seven or more like cards. [C20: < Sp.: basket (because two packs of cards are required), < L *canistrum;* see CANISTER]

canaster (ˈkænəstə) *n.* coarsely broken dried tobacco leaves. [C19: (meaning: basket in which tobacco was packed): < Sp.; see CANISTER]

cancan (ˈkænˌkæn) *n.* a high-kicking dance performed by a female chorus, originating in the music halls of 19th-century Paris. [C19: < F, <?]

cancel (ˈkænsᵊl) *vb.* **-celling, -celled** *or U.S.* **-celing, -celed.** (*mainly tr.*) **1.** to order (something already arranged, such as a meeting or event) to be postponed indefinitely; call off. **2.** to revoke or annul: *the order was cancelled.* **3.** to delete (writing, numbers, etc.); cross out. **4.** to mark (a cheque, stamp, etc.) with an official stamp to prevent further use. **5.** (*also intr.;* usually foll. by *out*) to counterbalance: *his generosity cancelled out his past unkindness.* **6.** *Maths.* to eliminate (numbers or terms) as common factors from both the numerator and denominator of a fraction or as equal terms from opposite sides of an equation. ~*n.* **7.** a new leaf or section of a book replacing one containing errors, or one that has been omitted. **8.** a cancellation. **9.** *Music.* a U.S. word for **natural** (sense 15). [C14: < OF *canceller,* < Med. L, < LL: to make like a lattice, < L *cancellī* lattice] —ˈ**canceller** *or U.S.* ˈ**canceler** *n.*

cancellate (ˈkænsɪˌleɪt) *or* **cancellated** *adj.* **1.** *Anat.* having a spongy internal structure: *cancellate bones.* **2.** *Bot.* forming a network. [C17: < L *cancellāre* to make like a lattice]

cancellation (ˌkænsɪˈleɪʃən) *n.* **1.** the fact or an instance of cancelling. **2.** something that has been cancelled, such as a theatre ticket: *we have a cancellation in the balcony.* **3.** the marks made by cancelling.

cancer (ˈkænsə) *n.* **1.** any type of malignant growth or tumour, caused by abnormal and uncontrolled cell division. **2.** the condition resulting from this. **3.** an evil influence that spreads dangerously. [C14: < L: crab, a creeping tumour] —ˈ**cancerous** *adj.*

Cancer (ˈkænsə) *n., Latin genitive* **Cancri** (ˈkæŋkriː). **1.** *Astron.* Also called: the **Crab.** a small N constellation. **2.** *Astrol.* the fourth sign of the zodiac. The sun is in this sign between about June 21 and July 22. **3. tropic of Cancer.** See **tropic** (sense 1).

cancroid (ˈkæŋkrɔɪd) *adj.* **1.** resembling a cancerous growth. **2.** resembling a crab. ~*n.* **3.** a skin cancer.

candela (kænˈdiːlə, -ˈdeɪlə) *n.* the basic SI unit of luminous intensity; the intensity, in a perpendicular direction, of a surface of 1/600 000 square metre of a black body at the temperature of freezing platinum under a pressure of 101 325 newtons per square metre. Symbol: cd [C20: < L: CANDLE]

candelabrum (ˌkændɪˈlɑːbrəm) *or* **candelabra** *n., pl.* **-bra** (-brə), **-brums,** *or* **-bras.** a large, branched table candleholder. [C19: < L, < *candēla* CANDLE]

candescent (kænˈdɛsᵊnt) *adj. Rare.* glowing or starting to glow with heat. [C19: < L, < *candēre* to be white, shine] —**canˈdescence** *n.*

c & f *abbrev. for* cost and freight.

C & G *abbrev. for* City and Guilds.

candid (ˈkændɪd) *adj.* **1.** frank and outspoken. **2.** without partiality; unbiased. **3.** unposed or informal: *a candid photograph.* [C17: < L, <

candēre to be white] —ˈ**candidly** *adv.* —ˈ**candidness** *n.*

candida (ˈkændɪdə) *n.* any of a genus of yeastlike parasitic fungi, esp. one that causes thrush (**candidiasis**).

candidate (ˈkændɪˌdeɪt) *n.* **1.** a person seeking or nominated for election to a position of authority or selection for a job, etc. **2.** a person taking an examination or test. **3.** a person or thing regarded as suitable or likely for a particular fate or position. [C17: < L *candidātus* clothed in white (because the candidate wore a white toga), < *candidus* white] —**candidacy** (ˈkændɪdəsɪ) *or* **candidature** (ˈkændɪdətʃə) *n.*

candid camera *n.* a small camera that may be used to take informal photographs of people.

candied (ˈkændɪd) *adj.* impregnated or encrusted with or as if with sugar: *candied peel.*

candle (ˈkændᵊl) *n.* **1.** a cylindrical piece of wax, tallow, or other fatty substance surrounding a wick, which is burned to produce light. **2.** *Physics.* another name for **candela. 3. burn the candle at both ends.** to exhaust oneself by doing too much, esp. by being up late and getting up early to work. **4. not hold a candle to.** *Inf.* to be inferior or contemptible in comparison with. **5. not worth the candle.** *Inf.* not worth the price or trouble entailed. ~*vb.* **6.** (*tr.*) to examine (eggs) for freshness or the likelihood of being hatched by viewing them against a bright light. [OE *candel,* < L *candēla,* < *candēre* to glitter] —ˈ**candler** *n.*

candleberry (ˈkændᵊlbərɪ) *n., pl.* **-ries.** another name for **wax myrtle.**

candlelight (ˈkændᵊlˌlaɪt) *n.* **1. a.** the light from a candle or candles. **b.** (*as modifier*): *a candlelight dinner.* **2.** dusk; evening.

Candlemas (ˈkændᵊlməs) *n. Christianity.* Feb. 2, the Feast of the Purification of the Virgin Mary and the presentation of Christ in the Temple.

candlenut (ˈkændᵊlˌnʌt) *n.* **1.** a tree of tropical Asia and Polynesia. **2.** the nut of this tree, which yields an oil used in paints. In their native regions the nuts are burned as candles.

candlepower (ˈkændᵊlˌpaʊə) *n.* the luminous intensity of a source of light in a given direction: now expressed in candelas.

candlestick (ˈkændᵊlˌstɪk) *or* **candleholder** (ˈkændᵊlˌhəʊldə) *n.* a holder, usually ornamental, with a spike or socket for a candle.

candlewick (ˈkændᵊlˌwɪk) *n.* **1.** unbleached cotton or muslin into which loops of yarn are hooked and then cut to give a tufted pattern. **2.** (*modifier*) being or made of candlewick fabric.

candour *or U.S.* **candor** (ˈkændə) *n.* **1.** the quality of being open and honest; frankness. **2.** fairness; impartiality. [C17: < L *candor,* < *candēre* to be white]

C & W *abbrev. for* country and western.

candy (ˈkændɪ) *n., pl.* **-dies. 1.** *Chiefly U.S. & Canad.* sweets, chocolate, etc. ~*vb.* **-dying, -died. 2.** to cause (sugar, etc.) to become crystalline or (of sugar) to become crystalline. **3.** (*tr.*) to preserve (fruit peel, ginger, etc.) by boiling in sugar. **4.** (*tr.*) to cover with any crystalline substance, such as ice or sugar. [C18: < OF *sucre candi* candied sugar, < Ar. *qandi* candied, < *qand* cane sugar]

candyfloss (ˈkændɪˌflɒs) *n. Brit.* a very light fluffy confection made from coloured spun sugar, usually held on a stick. U.S. and Canad. name: **cotton candy.**

candy-striped *adj.* (esp. of clothing fabric) having narrow coloured stripes on a white background. —**candy stripe** *n.*

candytuft (ˈkændɪˌtʌft) *n.* either of two species of *Iberis* having clusters of white, red, or purplish flowers. [C17 *Candy,* obs. var. of *Candia* (former name of city in Crete) + TUFT]

cane (keɪn) *n.* **1. a.** the long jointed pithy or hollow flexible stem of the bamboo, rattan, or any similar plant. **b.** any plant having such a stem. **2. a.** strips of such stems, woven or interlaced to make wickerwork, etc. **b.** (*as modifier*): *a cane chair.* **3.** the woody stem of a reed, blackberry, or loganberry. **4.** a flexible rod with which to administer a beating. **5.** a slender rod used as a walking stick. **6.** see **sugar cane.** ~*vb.* (*tr.*) **7.** to whip or beat with or as if with a cane. **8.** to make or repair with cane. **9.** *Inf.* to defeat: *we got well caned in the match.* [C14: < OF, < L *canna,* < Gk *kanna,* of Semitic origin] —ˈ**caner** *n.*

canebrake (ˈkeɪnˌbreɪk) *n. U.S.* a thicket of canes.

cane sugar *n.* **1.** the sucrose obtained from sugar cane. **2.** another name for **sucrose.**

cangue *or* **cang** (kæŋ) *n.* (formerly in China) a large wooden collar worn by petty criminals as a punishment. [C18: < F, < Port. *canga* yoke]

canikin (ˈkænɪkɪn) *n.* a variant spelling of **cannikin.**

canine (ˈkeɪnaɪn, ˈkæn-) *adj.* **1.** of or resembling a dog. **2.** of or belonging to the Canidae, a family of mammals, including dogs, wolves, and foxes, typically having a bushy tail, erect ears, and a long muzzle. **3.** of or relating to any of the four teeth, two in each jaw, situated between the incisors and the premolars. ~*n.* **4.** any animal of the family Canidae. **5.** a canine tooth. [C17: < L *canīnus,* < *canis* dog]

caning (ˈkeɪnɪŋ) *n. Inf.* a severe defeat or punishment.

Canis Major (ˈkeɪnɪs) *n., Latin genitive* **Canis Majoris** (məˈdʒɔːrɪs). a S constellation containing Sirius, the brightest star in the sky. Also called: the **Great Dog.** [L: the greater dog]

Canis Minor *n., Latin genitive* **Canis Minoris** (maɪˈnɔːrɪs). a small N constellation. Also called: the **Little Dog.** [L: the lesser dog]

canister (ˈkænɪstə) *n.* **1.** a container, usually made of metal, in which dry food, such as tea or coffee, is stored. **2.** (formerly) **a.** a type of shrapnel shell for firing from a cannon. **b.** Also called: **canister shot.** the shot or shrapnel packed inside this. [C17: < L *canistrum* basket woven from reeds, < Gk, < *kanna* reed]

canker (ˈkæŋkə) *n.* **1.** an ulceration, esp. of the lips. **2.** *Vet. science.* **a.** a disease of horses in which the horn of the hoofs becomes spongy. **b.** an ulcerative disease of the lining of the external ear, esp. in dogs and cats. **3.** an open wound in the stem of a tree or shrub. **4.** something evil that spreads and corrupts. ~*vb.* **5.** to infect or become infected with or as if with canker. [OE *cancer,* < L *cancer* cancerous sore] —ˈ**cankerous** *adj.*

cankerworm (ˈkæŋkəˌwɜːm) *n.* the larva of either of two moths, which feed on and destroy fruit and shade trees in North America.

canna (ˈkænə) *n.* any of a genus of tropical plants having broad leaves and red or yellow showy flowers. [C17: < NL CANE]

cannabis (ˈkænəbɪs) *n.* **1.** another name for **hemp** (the plant), esp. Indian hemp. **2.** the drug obtained from the dried leaves and flowers of the hemp plant, which is smoked or chewed for its psychoactive properties. See also **hashish, marijuana. 3. cannabis resin.** a poisonous resin obtained from the hemp plant. [C18: < L, < Gk *kannabis*]

canned (kænd) *adj.* **1.** preserved and stored in airtight cans or tins. **2.** *Inf.* prepared or recorded in advance: *canned music.* **3.** *Sl.* drunk.

cannel coal *or* **cannel** (ˈkænᵊl) *n.* a dull coal burning with a smoky luminous flame. [C16: < N English dialect *cannel* candle]

cannelloni *or* **canneloni** (ˌkænɪˈləʊnɪ) *pl. n.* tubular pieces of pasta filled with meat or cheese. [It., pl. of *cannellone,* < *cannello* stalk]

cannery (ˈkænərɪ) *n., pl.* **-neries.** a place where foods are canned.

cannibal (ˈkænɪbᵊl) *n.* **1.** a person who eats the flesh of other human beings. **2.** an animal that feeds on the flesh of others of its kind. [C16: < Sp. *Canibales,* the name used by Columbus to designate the Caribs of Cuba and Haiti] —ˈ**cannibaˌlism** *n.*

cannibalize *or* **-lise** (ˈkænɪbəˌlaɪz) *vb.* (*tr.*) to use (serviceable parts from one machine or vehicle) to repair another. —ˌ**cannibaliˈzation** *or* **-liˈsation** *n.*

cannikin, canakin, *or* **canikin** (ˈkænɪkɪn) *n.* a small can, esp. one used as a drinking vessel. [C16: < MDu. *kanneken;* see CAN², -KIN]

canning (ˈkænɪŋ) *n.* the process or business of sealing food in cans or tins to preserve it.

cannon (ˈkænən) *n., pl.* **-nons** *or* **-non.** **1.** an automatic aircraft gun. **2.** *History.* a heavy artillery piece consisting of a metal tube mounted on a carriage. **3.** a heavy tube or drum, esp. one that can rotate freely. **4.** See **cannon bone. 5.** *Billiards.* a shot in which the cue ball is caused to contact one object ball after another. Usual U.S. and Canad. word: **carom.** ~*vb.* **6.** (*intr.*) to rebound; collide (*with* into). **7.** (*intr.*) *Billiards.* to make a cannon. [C16: < OF *canon,* < It. *cannone* cannon, < *canna* tube]

cannonade (ˌkænəˈneɪd) *n.* **1.** an intense and continuous artillery bombardment. ~*vb.* **2.** to attack (a target) with cannon.

cannonball (ˈkænənˌbɔːl) *n.* **1.** a projectile fired from a cannon: usually a solid round metal shot. ~*vb.* (*intr.*) **2.** (often foll. by *along,* etc.) to rush along. ~*adj.* **3.** very fast or powerful.

cannon bone *n.* a bone in the legs of horses and other hoofed animals consisting of greatly elongated fused metatarsals or metacarpals.

cannoneer (ˌkænəˈnɪə) *n.* (formerly) a soldier who served and fired a cannon; artilleryman.

cannon fodder *n.* men regarded as expendable in war because they are part of a huge army.

cannonry (ˈkænənrɪ) *n., pl.* **-ries.** *Rare* **1.** a volley of artillery fire. **2.** artillery in general.

cannot (ˈkænɒt, kæˈnɒt) an auxiliary verb expressing incapacity, inability, withholding permission, etc.; can not.

cannula *or* **canula** (ˈkænjʊlə) *n., pl.* **-las** *or* **-lae** (-ˌliː). *Surgery.* a narrow tube for draining fluid from or introducing medication into the body. [C17: < L: a small reed, < *canna* a reed]

canny (ˈkænɪ) *adj.* **-nier, -niest. 1.** shrewd, esp. in business. **2.** *Scot. & NE English dialect.* good or nice: used as a general term of approval. **3.** *Scot.* lucky or fortunate. [C16: < CAN¹ (in the sense: to know how) + -Y¹] —ˈ**cannily** *adv.* —ˈ**canniness** *n.*

canoe (kəˈnuː) *n.* **1.** a light narrow open boat, propelled by one or more paddles. ~*vb.* **-noeing, -noed. 2.** to go in or transport by canoe. [C16: < Sp. *canoa,* of Carib origin] —**caˈnoeist** *n.*

canon¹ (ˈkænən) *n.* **1.** *Christianity.* a Church decree enacted to regulate morals or religious practices. **2.** (*often pl.*) a general rule or standard, as of judgment, morals, etc. **3.** (*often pl.*) a principle or criterion applied in a branch of learning or art. **4.** *R.C. Church.* the list of the canonized saints. **5.** *R.C. Church.* Also called: **Eucharistic Prayer.** the prayer in the Mass in which the Host is consecrated. **6.** a list of writings, esp. sacred writings, recognized as genuine. **7.** a piece of music in which an extended melody in one part is imitated successively in one or more other parts. **8.** a list of the works of an author that are accepted as authentic. [OE, < L, < Gk *kanōn* rule, rod for measuring]

canon² (ˈkænən) *n.* **1.** a priest who is a member of a cathedral chapter. **2.** *R.C. Church.* Also called: **canon regular.** a member of either of two religious orders living communally as monks but performing clerical duties.. [C13: < Anglo-F, < LL *canonicus* one living under a rule, < CANON¹]

canonical (kəˈnɒnɪkᵊl) *or* **canonic** *adj.* **1.** included in a canon of sacred or other officially recognized writings. **2.** in conformity with canon law. **3.** accepted; authoritative. **4.** *Music.* in the form of a canon. **5.** of or relating to a cathedral chapter. **6.** of a canon (clergyman). —**caˈnonically** *adv.*

canonical hour *n.* **1.** *R.C. Church.* one of the seven prayer times appointed for each day by canon law. **2.** *Church of England.* any time at which marriages may lawfully be celebrated.

canonicals (kəˈnɒnɪkᵊlz) *pl. n.* the vestments worn by clergy when officiating.

canonicity (ˌkænəˈnɪsɪtɪ) *n.* the fact or quality of being canonical.

canonist (ˈkænənɪst) *n.* a specialist in canon law.

canonize *or* **-ise** (ˈkænəˌnaɪz) *vb.* (*tr.*) **1.** *R.C. Church.* to declare (a person) to be a saint. **2.** to regard as a saint. **3.** to sanction by canon law. —ˌ**canoniˈzation** *or* **-iˈsation** *n.*

canon law *n.* the codified body of laws enacted by the supreme authorities of a Christian Church.

canonry (ˈkænənrɪ) *n., pl.* **-ries. 1.** the office, benefice, or status of a canon. **2.** canons collectively. [C15: < CANON² + -RY]

canoodle (kəˈnuːdᵊl) *vb.* (*intr.;* often foll. by *with*) *Sl.* to kiss and cuddle. [C19: <?]

Canopic jar, urn, *or* **vase** (kəˈnəʊpɪk) *n.* (in ancient Egypt) one of four containers for holding the entrails of a mummy. [C19: < *Canopus* a port in ancient Egypt]

canopy (ˈkænəpɪ) *n., pl.* **-pies. 1.** an ornamental awning above a throne, bed, person, etc. **2.** a rooflike covering over an altar, niche, etc. **3.** a roofed structure serving as a sheltered passageway. **4.** a large or wide covering: *the sky was a grey canopy.* **5.** the hemisphere that forms the supporting surface of a parachute. **6.** the transparent cover of an aircraft cockpit. **7.** the highest level of foliage in a forest, formed by the crowns of the trees. ~*vb.* **-pying, -pied. 8.** (*tr.*) to cover with or as with a canopy. [C14: < Med. L *canōpeum* mosquito net, < L, < Gk *kōnōpeion* bed with protective net]

canst (kænst) *vb. Arch.* the form of **can**¹ used with the pronoun *thou* or its relative form.

cant¹ (kænt) *n.* **1.** insincere talk, esp. concerning religion or morals. **2.** phrases that have become meaningless through repetition. **3.** specialized vocabulary of a particular group, such as thieves, journalists, or lawyers. ~*vb.* **4.** (*intr.*) to speak in or use cant. [C16: prob. via Norman F *canter* to sing, < L *cantāre;* used disparagingly, from the 12th cent., of chanting in religious services] —ˈ**cantingly** *adv.*

cant² (kænt) *n.* **1.** inclination from a vertical or horizontal plane. **2.** a sudden movement that tilts or turns something. **3.** the angle or tilt thus caused. **4.** a corner or outer angle. **5.** an oblique or slanting surface, edge, or line. ~*vb.* (*tr.*) **6.** to tip, tilt, or overturn. **7.** to set in an oblique position. **8.** another word for **bevel** (sense 1). ~*adj.* **9.** oblique; slanting. **10.** having flat surfaces. [C14 (in the sense: edge): ? < L *canthus* iron hoop round a wheel, <?]

can't (kɑːnt) *contraction of* cannot.

Cantab. (kænˈtæb) *abbrev. for* Cantabrigiensis. [L: of Cambridge]

cantabile (kænˈtɑːbɪlɪ) *Music.* ~*adj., adv.* **1.** (to be performed) flowingly and melodiously. ~*n.* **2.** a piece or passage performed in this way. [It., < LL, < L *cantāre* to sing]

Cantabrigian (ˌkæntəˈbrɪdʒɪən) *adj.* **1.** of or characteristic of Cambridge or Cambridge University. ~*n.* **2.** a member or graduate of Cambridge University. **3.** an inhabitant or native of Cambridge. [C17: < Med. L *Cantabrigia*]

cantaloupe *or* **cantaloup** (ˈkæntəˌluːp) *n.* **1.** a cultivated variety of muskmelon with ribbed warty rind and orange flesh. **2.** any of several other muskmelons. [C18: < F, < *Cantaluppi,* near Rome, where first cultivated in Europe]

cantankerous (kænˈtæŋkərəs) *adj.* quarrelsome; irascible. [C18: ? < C14 (obs.) *conteckour* a contentious person, < Anglo-F *contek* strife, <?] —**canˈtankerously** *adv.* —**canˈtankerousness** *n.*

cantata (kænˈtɑːtə) *n.* a musical setting of a text, esp. a religious text, consisting of arias, duets, and choruses. [C18: < It., < *cantare* to sing, < L]

canteen (kænˈtiːn) *n.* **1.** a restaurant attached to a factory, school, etc., providing meals for large numbers. **2. a.** a small shop that provides a limited range of items to a military unit. **b.** a recreation centre for military personnel. **3.** a temporary or mobile stand at which food is provided. **4. a.** a box in which a set of cutlery is laid out. **b.** the cutlery itself. **5.** a flask for carrying water or other liquids. [C18: < F, < It.

cantina wine cellar, < *canto* corner, < L *canthus* iron hoop encircling chariot wheel]

canter ('kæntə) *n.* **1.** a gait of horses, etc., between a trot and a gallop in speed. **2. at a canter.** easily; without effort. ~*vb.* **3.** to move or cause to move at a canter. [C18: short for *Canterbury trot,* the supposed pace at which pilgrims rode to Canterbury]

Canterbury bell ('kæntəbərı) *n.* a biennial European plant related to the campanula and widely cultivated for its blue, violet, or white flowers.

cantharides (kæn'θærı,di:z) *pl. n., sing.* **cantharis** ('kænθərıs). a diuretic and urogenital stimulant prepared from the dried bodies of Spanish fly. Also called: **Spanish fly.** [C15: < L, pl. of *cantharis,* < Gk *kantharis* Spanish fly]

cant hook *or* **dog** *n. Forestry.* a wooden pole with an adjustable hook at one end, used for handling logs.

canthus ('kænθəs) *n., pl.* **-thi** (-,θaı). the inner or outer corner of the eye, formed by the natural junction of the eyelids. [C17: < NL, < L: iron tyre]

canticle ('kæntık'l) *n.* a nonmetrical hymn, derived from the Bible and used in the liturgy of certain Christian churches. [C13: < L *canticulum,* dim. of *canticus* a song, < *canere* to sing]

cantilena (,kæntı'leınə) *n.* a smooth flowing style in the writing of vocal music. [C18: It.]

cantilever ('kæntı,li:və) *n.* **1.** a beam, girder, or structural framework that is fixed at one end only. **2.** a part of a beam or a structure projecting outwards beyond its support. [C17: ? < CANT² + LEVER]

cantilever bridge *n.* a bridge having spans that are constructed as cantilevers.

cantillate ('kæntı,leıt) *vb.* **1.** to chant (passages of the Hebrew Scriptures) according to the traditional Jewish melody. **2.** to intone or chant. [C19: < LL *cantillāre* to sing softly, < L *cantāre* to sing] —,**cantil'lation** *n.*

cantle ('kænt'l) *n.* **1.** the back part of a saddle that slopes upwards. **2.** a broken-off piece. [C14: < OF *cantel,* < *cant* corner]

canto ('kæntəʊ) *n., pl.* **-tos.** a main division of a long poem. [C16: < It.: song, < L, < *canere* to sing]

canto fermo ('kæntəʊ 'fɜ:məʊ) *or* **cantus firmus** ('kæntəs 'fɜ:məs) *n.* **1.** a melody that is the basis to which other parts are added in polyphonic music. **2.** the traditional Church plainchant as prescribed by use and regulation. [It., < Med L: fixed song]

canton *n.* **1.** ('kæntɒn, kæn'tɒn). a political division of Switzerland. **2.** ('kæntən). *Heraldry.* a small square charge on a shield, usually in the top left corner. ~*vb.* **3.** (kæn'tɒn). (*tr.*) to divide into cantons. **4.** (kən'tu:n). (esp. formerly) to allocate accommodation to (military personnel, etc.). [C16: < OF: corner, < It., < *canto* corner, < L *canthus* iron rim] —'**cantonal** *adj.*

Cantonese (,kæntə'ni:z) *n.* **1.** the Chinese language spoken in Canton, and elsewhere inside and outside China. **2.** (*pl.* **-ese**) a native or inhabitant of Canton. ~*adj.* **3.** of or relating to Canton or the Chinese language spoken there.

cantonment (kən'tu:nmənt) *n. Mil.* (esp. formerly) **1.** a large training camp. **2.** the winter quarters of a campaigning army. **3.** *History.* a permanent military camp in British India.

cantor ('kæntɔ:) *n.* **1.** *Judaism.* a man employed to lead synagogue services. **2.** *Christianity.* the leader of the singing in a church choir. [C16: < L: singer, < *canere* to sing]

cantorial (kæn'tɔ:rıəl) *adj.* **1.** of a precentor. **2.** (of part of a choir) on the same side of a cathedral, etc., as the precentor.

cantoris (kæn'tɔ:rıs) *adj.* (in antiphonal music) to be sung by the cantorial side of a choir. Cf. **decani.** [L: genitive of *cantor* precentor]

Canuck (kə'nʌk) *n., adj. U.S. & Canad. inf.* Canadian. [C19: < ?]

canvas ('kænvəs) *n.* **1. a.** a heavy cloth made of cotton, hemp, or jute, used for sails, tents, etc. **b.** (*as modifier*): *a canvas bag.* **2. a.** a piece of canvas, etc., on which a painting is done, usually in oils. **b.** an oil painting. **3.** a tent or tents collectively. **4.** *Naut.* the sails of a vessel collectively. **5.** any coarse loosely woven cloth on which tapestry, etc., is done. **6.** (preceded by *the*) the floor of a boxing or wrestling ring. **7.** *Rowing.* the covered part at either end of a racing boat: *to win by a canvas.* **8. under canvas. a.** in tents. **b.** *Naut.* with sails unfurled. [C14: < Norman F *canevas,* ult. < L *cannabis* hemp]

canvasback ('kænvəs,bæk) *n., pl.* **-backs** *or* **-back.** a North American diving duck, the male of which has a reddish-brown head.

canvass ('kænvəs) *vb.* **1.** to solicit votes, orders, etc., (from). **2.** to determine the opinions of (voters before an election, etc.), esp. by conducting a survey. **3.** to investigate (something) thoroughly, esp. by discussion. **4.** *Chiefly U.S.* to inspect (votes) to determine their validity. ~*n.* **5.** a solicitation of opinions, votes, etc. [C16: prob. < obs. sense of CANVAS (to toss someone in a canvas sheet, hence, to criticize)] —'**canvasser** *n.*

canyon *or* **cañon** ('kænjən) *n.* a gorge or ravine, esp. in North America, usually formed by a river. [C19: < Sp., < *caña* tube, < L *canna* cane]

canzonetta (,kænzə'nɛtə) *or* **canzonet** (,kænzə'nɛt) *n.* a short, lively song, typically of the 16th to 18th centuries. [C16: It.: dim. of *canzone,* < L *canere* to sing]

caoutchouc ('kaʊtʃʊk) *n.* another name for **rubber**¹ (sense 1). [C18: < F, < obs. Sp., < Quechua]

cap (kæp) *n.* **1.** a covering for the head, esp. a small close-fitting one. **2.** such a covering serving to identify the wearer's rank, occupation, etc.: a *nurse's cap.* **3.** something that protects or covers: *lens cap.* **4.** an uppermost surface or part: *the cap of a wave.* **5. a.** See **percussion cap. b.** a small amount of explosive enclosed in paper and used in a toy gun. **6.** *Sport, chiefly Brit.* **a.** an emblematic hat or beret given to someone chosen for a representative team. **b.** a player chosen for such a team. **7.** any part like a cap in shape. **8.** *Bot.* the pileus of a mushroom or toadstool. **9.** *Hunting.* money contributed to the funds of a hunt by a follower who is neither a subscriber nor a farmer, in return for a day's hunting. **10.** *Anat.* **a.** the natural enamel covering a tooth. **b.** an artificial protective covering for a tooth. **11.** Also: **Dutch cap, diaphragm.** a contraceptive membrane placed over the mouth of the cervix. **12.** a mortarboard worn at an academic ceremony (esp. in **cap and gown**). **13. set one's cap at.** (of a woman) to be determined to win as a husband or lover. **14. cap in hand.** humbly, as when asking a favour. ~*vb.* **capping, capped.** (*tr.*) **15.** to cover, as with a cap: *snow capped the mountain tops.* **16.** to seal off (an oil or gas well). **17.** to impose an upper level on the rate of increase of (a tax): *rate-capping.* **18.** *Inf.* to outdo; excel. **19. cap it all.** to provide the finishing touch. **20.** *Sport, Brit.* to select (a player) for a representative team. **21.** *Chiefly Scot. & N.Z.* to award a degree to. [OE *cæppe,* < LL *cappa* hood, ? < L *caput* head]

cap. *abbrev. for:* **1.** capacity. **2.** capital. **3.** capitalize. **4.** capital letter.

capability (,keıpə'bılıtı) *n., pl.* **-ties. 1.** the quality of being capable; ability. **2.** the quality of being susceptible to the use or treatment indicated: *the capability of a metal to be fused.* **3.** (*usually pl.*) potential aptitude.

capable ('keıpəb'l) *adj.* **1.** having ability; competent. **2.** (*postpositive;* foll. by *of*) able or having the skill (to do something): *she is capable of hard work.* **3.** (*postpositive;* foll. by *of*) having the temperament or inclination (to do something): *he seemed capable of murder.* [C16: < F, < LL *capābilis* able to take in, < L *capere* to take] —'**capableness** *n.* —'**capably** *adv.*

capacious (kə'peıʃəs) *adj.* capable of holding much; roomy. [C17: < L, < *capere* to take] —**ca'paciously** *adv.* —**ca'paciousness** *n.*

capacitance (kə'pæsıtəns) *n.* **1.** the property of

a system that enables it to store electric charge. **2.** a measure of this, equal to the charge that must be added to such a system to raise its electrical potential by one unit. Former name: **capacity.** [C20: < CAPACIT(Y) + -ANCE] —**ca'pacitive** *adj.*

capacitor (kə'pæsıtə) *n.* a device for accumulating electric charge, usually consisting of two conducting surfaces separated by a dielectric. Former name: **condenser.**

capacity (kə'pæsıtı) *n., pl.* **-ties. 1.** the ability or power to contain, absorb, or hold. **2.** the amount that can be contained: *a capacity of six gallons.* **3. a.** the maximum amount something can contain or absorb (esp. in **filled to capacity**). **b.** (*as modifier*): *a capacity crowd.* **4.** the ability to understand or learn: *he has a great capacity for Greek.* **5.** the ability to do or produce: *the factory's output was not at capacity.* **6.** a specified position or function. **7.** a measure of the electrical output of a piece of apparatus such as a generator or accumulator. **8.** *Electronics.* a former name for **capacitance. 9.** *Computers.* **a.** the number of words or characters that can be stored in a storage device. **b.** the range of numbers that can be processed in a register. **10.** legal competence: *the capacity to make a will.* [C15: < OF *capacite,* < L, < *capāx* spacious, < *capere* to take]

cap and bells *n.* the traditional garb of a court jester, including a cap with bells.

cap-a-pie (ˌkæpə'pi:) *adv.* (dressed, armed, etc.) from head to foot. [C16: < OF]

caparison (kə'pærıs°n) *n.* **1.** a decorated covering for a horse. **2.** rich or elaborate clothing and ornaments. ~*vb.* **3.** (*tr.*) to put a caparison on. [C16: via obs. F < OSp. *caparazón* saddle-cloth, prob. < *capa* CAPE[1]]

cape[1] (keıp) *n.* a sleeveless garment like a cloak but usually shorter. [C16: < F, < Provençal *capa,* < LL *cappa;* see CAP]

cape[2] (keıp) *n.* a headland or promontory. [C14: < OF *cap,* < OProvençal, < L *caput* head]

Cape (keıp) *n.* **the. 1.** the Cape of Good Hope. **2.** the SW region of the Cape Province of South Africa.

Cape Coloured *n.* (in South Africa) another name for a **Coloured** (sense 2).

Cape doctor *n. S. African inf.* a strong fresh SE wind blowing in the vicinity of Cape Town, esp. in the summer.

Cape Dutch *n.* **1.** (in South Africa) a distinctive style in furniture or buildings. **2.** an obsolete name for **Afrikaans.**

Cape gooseberry *n.* another name for **strawberry tomato.**

capelin ('kæpəlın) *or* **caplin** ('kæplın) *n.* a small marine food fish of northern and Arctic seas. [C17: < F *capelan,* < OProvençal, lit.: chaplain]

capellmeister *or* **kapellmeister** (kæ'pɛlˌmaıstə) *n.* a person in charge of an orchestra, esp. in an 18th-century princely household. [< G, < *Kapelle* chapel + *Meister* MASTER]

Cape pigeon *n.* a kind of petrel common in S Africa.

caper[1] ('keıpə) *n.* **1.** a playful skip or leap. **2.** a high-spirited escapade. **3. cut a caper** *or* **capers.** to skip, leap, or frolic. **4.** *U.S & Canad. sl.* a crime. ~*vb.* **5.** (*intr.*) to leap or dance about in a light-hearted manner. [C16: prob. < CAPRIOLE]

caper[2] ('keıpə) *n.* **1.** a spiny trailing Mediterranean shrub with edible flower buds. **2.** its pickled flower buds, used in sauces. [C15: < earlier *capers, capres* (assumed to be pl.), < L, < Gk *kapparis*]

capercaillie *or* **capercailzie** (ˌkæpə'keılјı) *n.* a large European woodland grouse having a black plumage. [C16: < Scot. Gaelic *capull coille* horse of the woods]

Cape sparrow *n.* a sparrow very common in southern Africa. Also called (esp. S. African): **mossie.**

capias ('keıpıˌæs, 'kæp-) *n. Law.* a writ directing a sheriff or other officer to arrest a named person. [C15: < L, lit.: you must take, < *capere*]

capillarity (ˌkæpı'lærıtı) *n.* a phenomenon caused by surface tension and resulting in the elevation or depression of the surface of a liquid in contact with a solid. Also called: **capillary action.**

capillary (kə'pılərı) *adj.* **1.** resembling a hair; slender. **2.** (of tubes) having a fine bore. **3.** *Anat.* of the delicate thin-walled blood vessels that interconnect between the arterioles and the venules. **4.** *Physics.* of or relating to capillarity. ~*n., pl.* **-laries. 5.** *Anat.* any of the capillary blood vessels. [C17: < L *capillāris,* < *capillus* hair]

capital[1] ('kæpıt°l) *n.* **1. a.** the seat of government of a country. **b.** (*as modifier*): *a capital city.* **2.** material wealth owned by an individual or business enterprise. **3.** wealth available for or capable of use in the production of further wealth, as by industrial investment. **4. make capital (out) of.** to get advantage from. **5.** (*sometimes cap.*) the capitalist class or their interests: *capital versus labour.* **6.** *Accounting.* **a.** the ownership interests of a business as represented by the excess of assets over liabilities. **b.** the nominal value of the issued shares. **7.** any assets or resources. **8. a.** a capital letter. Abbrev.: **cap. b.** (*as modifier*): *capital B.* ~*adj.* **9.** (*prenominal*) *Law.* involving or punishable by death: *a capital offence.* **10.** very serious: *a capital error.* **11.** primary, chief, or principal: *our capital concern.* **12.** of, relating to, or designating the large letter used chiefly as the initial letter in personal names and place names and often for abbreviations and acronyms. See also **upper case. 13.** *Chiefly Brit.* excellent; first-rate: *a capital idea.* [C13: < L *capitālis* (adj.) concerning the head, < *caput* head]

capital[2] ('kæpıt°l) *n.* the upper part of a column or pier that supports the entablature. [C14: < OF, < LL *capitellum,* dim. of *caput* head]

capital account *n.* **1.** *Econ.* that part of a balance of payments composed of movements of capital. **2.** *Accounting.* a financial statement showing the net value of a company at a specified date.

capital expenditure *n.* expenditure to increase fixed assets.

capital gain *n.* the amount by which the selling price of a financial asset exceeds its cost.

capital gains tax *n.* a tax on the profit made from sale of an asset.

capital goods *pl. n. Econ.* goods that are themselves utilized in the production of other goods.

capitalism ('kæpıtəˌlızəm) *n.* an economic system based on the private ownership of the means of production, distribution, and exchange. Also called: **free enterprise, private enterprise.** Cf. **socialism** (sense 1).

capitalist ('kæpıtəlıst) *n.* **1.** a person who owns capital, esp. capital invested in a business. **2.** *Politics.* a supporter of capitalism. ~*adj.* **3.** relating to capital, capitalists, or capitalism. —ˌ**capital'istic** *adj.*

capitalization *or* **-isation** (ˌkæpıtəlaı'zeıʃən) *n.* **1. a.** the act of capitalizing. **b.** the sum so derived. **2.** *Accounting.* the par value of the total share capital issued by a company. **3.** the act of estimating the present value of future payments, etc.

capitalize *or* **-ise** ('kæpıtəˌlaız) *vb.* (*mainly tr.*) **1.** (*intr.; foll. by on*) to take advantage (of). **2.** to write or print (text) in capital letters. **3.** to convert (debt or earnings) into capital stock. **4.** to authorize (a business enterprise) to issue a specified amount of capital stock. **5.** to provide with capital. **6.** *Accounting.* to treat (expenditures) as assets. **7. a.** to estimate the present value of (a periodical income). **b.** to compute the present value of (a business) from actual or potential earnings.

capital levy *n.* a tax on capital or property as contrasted with a tax on income.

capitally ('kæpıtəlı) *adv. Chiefly Brit.* in an excellent manner; admirably.

capital punishment *n.* the punishment of death for a crime; death penalty.

capital ship *n.* one of the largest and most heavily armed ships in a naval fleet.

capital stock *n.* **1.** the par value of the total share capital that a company is authorized to issue. **2.** the total physical capital existing in an economy at any moment of time.

capital transfer tax *n.* (in Britain) a tax payable on the cumulative total of gifts of money or property made during the donor's lifetime or after his death.

capitation (ˌkæpɪˈteɪʃən) *n.* **1.** a tax levied on the basis of a fixed amount per head. **2. capitation grant.** a grant of money given to every person who qualifies under certain conditions. [C17: < LL, < L *caput* head]

Capitol (ˈkæpɪtᵊl) *n.* **1.** the temple of Jupiter in ancient Rome. **2. the.** the main building of the U.S. Congress. [C14: < L *Capitōlium,* < *caput* head]

capitulate (kəˈpɪtjʊˌleɪt) *vb.* (*intr.*) to surrender, esp. under agreed conditions. [C16 (meaning: to draw up in order): < Med. L *capitulare* to draw up under heads, < *capitulum* CHAPTER] —**caˈpituˌlator** *n.*

capitulation (kəˌpɪtjʊˈleɪʃən) *n.* **1.** the act of capitulating. **2.** a document containing terms of surrender. **3.** a statement summarizing the main divisions of a subject. —**caˈpitulatory** *adj.*

capitulum (kəˈpɪtjʊləm) *n., pl.* **-la** (-lə). an inflorescence in the form of a disc, the youngest at the centre. It occurs in the daisy and related plants. [C18: < L, lit.: a little head, < *caput* head]

capo (ˈkæpəʊ) *n., pl.* **-pos.** a device fitted across all the strings of a guitar, lute, etc., so as to raise the pitch of each string simultaneously. Also called: **capo tasto** (ˈtæstəʊ). [< It. *capo tasto* head stop]

capon (ˈkeɪpən) *n.* a castrated cock fowl fattened for eating. [OE *capun,* < L *cāpō* capon] —**ˈcaponˌize** *or* **-ˌise** *vb.*

capote (kəˈpəʊt) *n.* a long cloak or soldier's coat, usually with a hood. [C19: < F: cloak, < *cape*]

capping (ˈkæpɪŋ) *n.* **a.** *Scot. & N.Z.* the act of conferring an academic degree. **b.** (*as modifier*): *Capping Day.*

cappuccino (ˌkæpʊˈtʃiːnəʊ) *n., pl.* **-nos.** coffee with steamed milk, usually sprinkled with powdered chocolate. [It.: CAPUCHIN]

capriccio (kəˈprɪtʃɪˌəʊ) *or* **caprice** *n., pl.* **-priccios, -pricci** (-ˈpriːtʃɪ), *or* **-prices.** *Music.* a lively piece of irregular musical form. [C17: < It.: CAPRICE]

capriccioso (kəˌprɪtʃɪˈəʊzəʊ) *adv. Music.* to be played in a free and lively style. [It.: < *capriccio* CAPRICE]

caprice (kəˈpriːs) *n.* **1.** a sudden change of attitude, behaviour, etc. **2.** a tendency to such changes. **3.** another word for **capriccio.** [C17: < F, < It. *capriccio* a shiver, caprice, < *capo* head + *riccio* lit.: hedgehog]

capricious (kəˈprɪʃəs) *adj.* characterized by or liable to sudden unpredictable changes in attitude or behaviour. —**caˈpriciously** *adv.*

Capricorn (ˈkæprɪˌkɔːn) *n.* **1.** *Astrol.* Also called: the **Goat, Capricornus.** the tenth sign of the zodiac. The sun is in this sign between about Dec. 22 and Jan. 19. **2.** *Astron.* a S constellation. **3. tropic of Capricorn.** See **tropic** (sense 1). [C14: < L *Capricornus,* < *caper* goat + *cornū* horn]

caprine (ˈkæpraɪn) *adj.* of or resembling a goat. [C17: < L *caprīnus,* < *caper* goat]

capriole (ˈkæprɪˌəʊl) *n.* **1.** *Dressage.* a high upward but not forward leap made by a horse with all four feet off the ground. ~*vb.* **2.** (*intr.*) to perform a capriole. [C16: < F, < OIt., < *capriolo* roebuck, < L *capreolus, caper* goat]

caps. *abbrev. for:* **1.** capital letters. **2.** capsule.

capsicum (ˈkæpsɪkəm) *n.* **1.** any of a genus of tropical American plants related to the potato, having mild or pungent seeds enclosed in a bell-shaped fruit. **2.** the fruit of any of these plants, used as a vegetable or ground to produce a condiment. ~See also **pepper** (sense 4). [C18: < NL, < L *capsa* box]

capsid[1] (ˈkæpsɪd) *n.* a bug related to the water bug that feeds on plant tissues, causing damage to crops. [C19: < NL *Capsus* (genus)]

capsid[2] (ˈkæpsɪd) *n.* the outer protein coat of a mature virus. [C20: < F *capside,* < L *capsa* box]

capsize (kæpˈsaɪz) *vb.* to overturn accidentally; upset. [C18: <?] —**capˈsizal** *n.*

capstan (ˈkæpstən) *n.* **1.** a windlass with a drum equipped with a ratchet, used on ships for hauling in ropes, etc. **2.** the rotating shaft in a tape recorder that pulls the tape past the head. [C14: < OProvençal *cabestan,* < L *capistrum* a halter, < *capere* to seize]

capstan lathe *n.* a lathe for repetitive work, having a rotatable turret to hold tools for successive operations. Also called: **turret lathe.**

capstone (ˈkæpˌstəʊn) *n.* another word for **copestone** (sense 2).

capsule (ˈkæpsjuːl) *n.* **1.** a soluble case of gelatin enclosing a dose of medicine. **2.** a thin metal cap, seal, or cover. **3.** *Bot.* **a.** a dry fruit that liberates its seeds by splitting, as in the violet, or through pores, as in the poppy. **b.** the spore-producing organ of mosses and liverworts. **4.** *Anat.* a membranous envelope surrounding any of certain organs or parts. **5.** See **space capsule.** **6.** an aeroplane cockpit that can be ejected in a flight emergency, complete with crew, instruments, etc. **7.** (*modifier*) in a highly concise form: *a capsule summary.* [C17: < F, < L *capsula,* dim. of *capsa* box] —**ˈcapsuˌlate** *adj.*

capsulize *or* **-ise** (ˈkæpsjʊˌlaɪz) *vb.* (*tr.*) **1.** to state (information, etc.) in a highly condensed form. **2.** to enclose in a capsule.

Capt. *abbrev. for* Captain.

captain (ˈkæptɪn) *n.* **1.** the person in charge of a vessel. **2.** an officer of the navy who holds a rank junior to a rear admiral. **3.** an officer of the army, certain air forces, and the marines who holds a rank junior to a major. **4.** the officer in command of a civil aircraft. **5.** the leader of a team in games. **6.** a person in command over a group, organization, etc.: *a captain of industry.* **7.** *U.S.* a policeman in charge of a precinct. **8.** *U.S. & Canad.* a head waiter. ~*vb.* **9.** (*tr.*) to be captain of. [C14: < OF, < LL *capitāneus* chief, < L *caput* head] —**ˈcaptaincy** *or* **ˈcaptainˌship** *n.*

Captain Cooker (ˈkʊkə) *n. N.Z.* a wild pig. [< Captain James *Cook* (1728–79), E navigator, who first released pigs in the New Zealand bush]

caption (ˈkæpʃən) *n.* **1.** a title, brief explanation, or comment accompanying an illustration. **2.** a heading or title of a chapter, article, etc. **3.** graphic material used in television presentation. **4.** another name for **subtitle** (sense 2). **5.** the formal heading of a legal document. ~*vb.* **6.** to provide with a caption or captions. [C14 (meaning: seizure): < L *captiō* a seizing, < *capere* to take]

captious (ˈkæpʃəs) *adj.* apt to make trivial criticisms. [C14 (meaning: catching in error): < L *captiōsus,* < *captiō* a seizing] —**ˈcaptiously** *adv.* —**ˈcaptiousness** *n.*

captivate (ˈkæptɪˌveɪt) *vb.* (*tr.*) to hold the attention of by fascinating; enchant. [C16: < LL *captivāre,* < *captīvus* CAPTIVE] —**ˈcaptiˌvating** *adj.* —**ˌcaptiˈvation** *n.*

captive (ˈkæptɪv) *n.* **1.** a person or animal that is confined or restrained. **2.** a person whose behaviour is dominated by some emotion: *a captive of love.* ~*adj.* **3.** held as prisoner. **4.** held under restriction or control; confined. **5.** captivated. **6.** unable to avoid speeches, advertisements, etc.: *a captive audience.* [C14: < L *captīvus,* < *capere* to take]

captivity (kæpˈtɪvɪtɪ) *n., pl.* **-ties.** **1.** imprisonment. **2.** the period of imprisonment.

captor (ˈkæptə) *n.* a person or animal that holds another captive. [C17: < L, < *capere* to take]

capture (ˈkæptʃə) *vb.* (*tr.*) **1.** to take prisoner or gain control over: *to capture a town.* **2.** (in a game) to win possession of: *to capture a pawn in chess.* **3.** to succeed in representing (something elusive): *the artist captured her likeness.* **4.** *Physics.* (of an atom, etc.) to acquire (an additional particle). ~*n.* **5.** the act of taking by force. **6.** the person or thing captured. **7.** *Physics.* a process by which an atom, etc., acquires an additional particle. **8.** *Geog.* the process by which the headwaters of one river are diverted into another. **9.** *Computers.* the collection of data for processing. [C16: < L *captūra* a catching, that which is caught, < *capere* to take] —**'capturer** *n.*

capuchin ('kæpjʊtʃɪn, -jʊʃɪn) *n.* **1.** an agile intelligent S American monkey having a cowl of thick hair on the top of the head. **2.** a woman's hooded cloak. **3.** (*sometimes cap.*) a variety of domestic fancy pigeon. [C16: < F, < It., < *cappuccio* hood]

Capuchin ('kæpjʊtʃɪn, -jʊʃɪn) *n.* **1.** a friar belonging to a branch of the Franciscan Order founded in 1525. ~*adj.* **2.** of or relating to this order. [C16: < F, < It. *cappuccio* hood]

capybara (ˌkæpɪ'bɑːrə) *n.* the largest rodent, resembling a guinea pig and native to Central and South America. [C18: < Port. *capibara*, < Tupi]

car (kɑː) *n.* **1. a.** Also called: **motorcar, automobile.** a self-propelled road vehicle designed to carry passengers, that is powered by an internal-combustion engine. **b.** (*as modifier*): *car coat.* **2.** a conveyance for passengers, freight, etc., such as a cable car or the carrier of an airship or balloon. **3.** *Brit.* a railway vehicle for passengers only. **4.** *Chiefly U.S. & Canad.* a railway carriage or van. **5.** a poetic word for **chariot.** [C14: < Anglo-F *carre*, ult. rel. to L *carra, carrum* two-wheeled wagon, prob. of Celtic origin]

carabineer *or* **carabinier** (ˌkærəbɪ'nɪə) *n.* variants of **carbineer.**

carabiner (ˌkærə'biːnə) *n.* a variant of **karabiner.**

caracal ('kærəˌkæl) *n.* **1.** a lynxlike feline mammal inhabiting deserts of N Africa and S Asia, having a smooth coat of reddish fur. **2.** this fur. [C18: < F, < Turkish *kara kūlāk*, lit.: black ear]

caracara (ˌkɑːrə'kɑːrə) *n.* a large carrion-eating bird of prey of Central and South America, having long legs. [C19: < Sp. or Port., < Tupi; imit.]

caracole ('kærəˌkəʊl) *or* **caracol** ('kærəˌkɒl) *Dressage.* ~*n.* **1.** a half turn to the right or left. ~*vb.* (*intr.*) **2.** to execute a half turn. [C17: < F, < Sp. *caracol* snail, spiral staircase]

caracul ('kærəˌkʌl) *n.* **1.** Also called: **Persian lamb.** the black loosely curled fur obtained from the skins of newly born lambs of the karakul sheep. **2.** a variant spelling of **karakul.**

carafe (kə'ræf, -'rɑːf) *n.* an open-topped glass container for serving water or wine at table [C18: < F, < It., < Sp., < Ar. *gharrāfah* vessel]

carageen ('kærəˌgiːn) *n.* a variant spelling of **carrageen.**

carambola (ˌkærəm'bəʊlə) *n.* the yellow edible star-shaped fruit of a Brazilian tree. Also called: **star fruit.** [Sp., < Port.]

caramel ('kærəməl) *n.* **1.** burnt sugar, used for colouring and flavouring food. **2.** a chewy sweet made from sugar, milk, etc. [C18: < F, < Sp. *caramelo*, <?]

caramelize *or* **-ise** ('kærəməˌlaɪz) *vb.* to convert or be converted into caramel.

carapace ('kærəˌpeɪs) *n.* the thick hard shield that covers part of the body of crabs, tortoises, etc. [C19: < F, < Sp. *carapacho*, <?]

carat ('kærət) *n.* **1.** a measure of the weight of precious stones, esp. diamonds, now standardized as 0.20 grams. **2.** Usual U.S. spelling: **karat.** a measure of the gold in an alloy, expressed as the number of parts of gold in 24 parts of the alloy. [C16: < OF, < Med. L, < Ar. *qīrāt* weight of four grains, < Gk, < *keras* horn]

caravan ('kærəˌvæn) *n.* **1. a.** a large enclosed vehicle capable of being pulled by a car and equipped to be lived in. U.S. and Canad. name: **trailer. b.** (*as modifier*): *a caravan site.* **2.** (esp. in some parts of Asia and Africa) a company of traders or other travellers journeying together. **3.** a large covered vehicle, esp. a gaily coloured one used by Gypsies, circuses, etc. ~*vb.* **-vanning, -vanned. 4.** (*intr.*) *Brit.* to travel or have a holiday in a caravan. [C16: < It. *caravana*, < Persian *kārwān*]

caravanserai (ˌkærə'vænsəˌraɪ) *or* **caravansary** (ˌkærə'vænsərɪ) *n., pl.* **-rais** *or* **-ries.** (in some Eastern countries) a large inn enclosing a courtyard, providing accommodation for caravans. [C16: < Persian *kārwānsarāī* caravan inn]

caravel ('kærəˌvɛl) *or* **carvel** *n.* a two- or three-masted sailing ship used by the Spanish and Portuguese in the 15th and 16th centuries. [C16: < Port. *caravela*, dim. of *caravo* ship, ult. < Gk *karabos* crab]

caraway ('kærəˌweɪ) *n.* **1.** an umbelliferous Eurasian plant having finely divided leaves and clusters of small whitish flowers. **2. caraway seed.** the pungent aromatic fruit of this plant, used in cooking. [C14: prob. < Med. L *carvi*, < Ar. *karawyā*, < Gk *karon*]

carbide ('kɑːbaɪd) *n.* **1.** a binary compound of carbon with a metal **2.** See **calcium carbide.**

carbine ('kɑːbaɪn) *n.* **1.** a light automatic or semiautomatic rifle. **2.** a light short-barrelled rifle formerly used by cavalry. [C17: < F *carabine*, < OF *carabin* carabineer]

carbineer (ˌkɑːbɪ'nɪə), **carabineer,** *or* **carabinier** (ˌkærəbɪ'nɪə) *n.* (formerly) a soldier equipped with a carbine.

carbo- *or before a vowel* **carb-** *combining form.* carbon: *carbohydrate; carbonate.*

carbohydrate (ˌkɑːbəʊ'haɪdreɪt) *n.* any of a large group of organic compounds, including sugars and starch, that contain carbon, hydrogen, and oxygen, with the general formula $C_m(H_2O)_n$: a source of food and energy for animals.

carbolic acid (kɑː'bɒlɪk) *n.* another name for **phenol,** esp. when it is used as a disinfectant. [C19: < CARBO- + -OL[1] + -IC]

carbon ('kɑːbᵊn) *n.* **1. a.** a nonmetallic element existing in the three allotropic forms: amorphous carbon, graphite, and diamond: occurring in all organic compounds. The isotope **carbon-12** is the standard for atomic wt.; **carbon-14** is used in radiocarbon dating and as a tracer. Symbol: C; atomic no.: 6; atomic wt.: 12.011 15. **b.** (*as modifier*): *a carbon compound.* **2.** short for **carbon paper** or **carbon copy. 3.** a carbon electrode used in a carbon-arc light. **4.** a rod or plate, made of carbon, used in some types of battery. [C18: < F, < L *carbō* charcoal]

carbonaceous (ˌkɑːbə'neɪʃəs) *adj.* of, resembling, or containing carbon.

carbonade (ˌkɑːbə'neɪd, -'nɑːd) *n.* beef and onions stewed in beer. [C20: F]

carbonado (ˌkɑːbə'neɪdəʊ) *n., pl.* **-dos** *or* **-does.** an inferior variety of diamond used in industry. Also called: **black diamond.** [Port., lit.: carbonated]

carbon arc *n.* an electric arc between two carbon electrodes or between a carbon electrode and materials to be welded.

carbonate *n.* ('kɑːbəˌneɪt, -nɪt). **1.** a salt or ester of carbonic acid. ~*vb.* ('kɑːbəˌneɪt). **2.** to turn into a carbonate. **3.** (*tr.*) to treat with carbon dioxide, as in the manufacture of soft drinks. [C18: < F, < *carbone* CARBON]

carbon black *n.* a finely divided form of carbon produced by incomplete combustion of natural gas or petroleum: used in pigments and ink.

carbon copy *n.* **1.** a duplicate copy of writing, typewriting, or drawing obtained by using carbon paper. **2.** *Inf.* a person or thing that is identical to another.

carbon dating *n.* a technique for determining the age of organic materials, such as wood, based on their content of the radioisotope ^{14}C acquired from the atmosphere when they formed part of a living plant.

carbon dioxide *n.* a colourless odourless incombustible gas present in the atmosphere and formed during respiration, etc.: used in fire extinguishers, and as dry ice for refrigeration. Formula: CO_2. Also called: **carbonic-acid gas.**

carbonette (ˌkɑːbə'nɛt) *n.* *N.Z.* a ball of compressed coal dust used as fuel.

carbon fibre *n.* a thread of pure carbon used because of its lightness and strength at high temperatures for reinforcing resins, ceramics, and metals, and for fishing rods.

carbon-14 dating *n.* another name for **carbon dating.**

carbonic (kɑːˈbɒnɪk) *adj.* (of a compound) containing carbon, esp. tetravalent carbon.

carbonic acid *n.* a weak acid formed when carbon dioxide combines with water. Formula: H_2CO_3.

carboniferous (ˌkɑːbəˈnɪfərəs) *adj.* yielding coal or carbon.

Carboniferous (ˌkɑːbəˈnɪfərəs) *adj.* **1.** of, denoting, or formed in the fifth period of the Palaeozoic era during which coal measures were formed. ~*n.* **2. the.** the Carboniferous period or rock system divided into the **Upper Carboniferous** period and the **Lower Carboniferous** period.

carbonize *or* **-ise** (ˈkɑːbəˌnaɪz) *vb.* **1.** to turn into carbon as a result of heating. **2.** (*tr.*) to coat (a substance) with carbon. —ˌ**carboniˈzation** *or* **-iˈsation** *n.*

carbon monoxide *n.* a colourless odourless poisonous gas formed when carbon compounds burn in insufficient air. Formula: CO.

carbon paper *n.* a thin sheet of paper coated on one side with a dark waxy pigment, often containing carbon, that is transferred by pressure onto the copying surface below.

carbon tetrachloride *n.* a colourless volatile nonflammable liquid made from chlorine and used as a solvent, cleaning fluid, and insecticide. Formula: CCl_4.

car-boot sale *n.* another name for **boot sale.**

Carborundum (ˌkɑːbəˈrʌndəm) *n. Trademark.* any of various abrasive materials, esp. one consisting of silicon carbide.

carboxyl group *or* **radical** (kɑːˈbɒksaɪl) *n.* the monovalent group -COOH: the functional group in organic acids. [C19 *carboxyl,* < CARBO- + OXY-[2] + -YL]

carboxylic acid (ˌkɑːbɒkˈsɪlɪk) *n.* any of a class of organic acids containing the carboxyl group. See also **fatty acid.**

carboy (ˈkɑːˌbɔɪ) *n.* a large bottle, usually protected by a basket or box, used for containing corrosive liquids. [C18: < Persian *qarāba*]

carbuncle (ˈkɑːˌbʌŋkᵊl) *n.* **1.** an extensive skin eruption, similar to a boil, with several openings. **2.** a rounded gemstone, esp. a garnet cut without facets. [C13: < L *carbunculus,* dim. of *carbō* coal] —**carbuncular** (kɑːˈbʌŋkjʊlə) *adj.*

carburation (ˌkɑːbjʊˈreɪʃən) *n.* the process of mixing a hydrocarbon fuel with air to make an explosive mixture for an internal-combustion engine.

carburet (ˈkɑːbjʊˌrɛt, ˌkɑːbjʊˈrɛt) *vb.* **-retting, -retted** *or U.S.* **-reting, -reted.** (*tr.*) to combine or mix (a gas, etc.) with carbon or carbon compounds. [C18: < CARB(ON) + -URET]

carburettor, carburetter (ˌkɑːbjʊˈrɛtə, ˈkɑːbjʊˌrɛtə), *or U.S.* **carburetor** (ˈkɑːbjʊˌreɪtə) *n.* a device used in petrol engines for mixing atomized petrol with air, and regulating the intake of the mixture into the engine.

carcajou (ˈkɑːkəˌdʒuː, -kəˌʒuː) *n.* a North American name for **wolverine.** [C18: < Canad. F, < Algonquian *karkajou*]

carcass *or* **carcase** (ˈkɑːkəs) *n.* **1.** the dead body of an animal, esp. one that has been slaughtered for food. **2.** *Inf., usually facetious or derog.* a person's body. **3.** the skeleton or framework of a structure. **4.** the remains of anything when its life or vitality is gone. [C14: < OF *carcasse,* <?]

carcinogen (kɑːˈsɪnədʒən) *n. Pathol.* any substance that produces cancer. [C20: < Gk *karkinos* CANCER + -GEN] —ˌ**carcinoˈgenic** *adj.*

carcinoma (ˌkɑːsɪˈnəʊmə) *n., pl.* **-mas** *or* **-mata** (-mətə). *Pathol.* any malignant tumour derived from epithelial tissue, esp. a cancer. [C18: < L, < Gk, < *karkinos* CANCER]

card[1] (kɑːd) *n.* **1.** a piece of stiff paper or thin cardboard, usually rectangular, with varied uses, as for bearing a written notice for display, etc. **2.** such a card used for identification, reference, proof of membership, etc.: *identity card.* **3.** such a card used for sending greetings, messages, or invitations: *birthday card.* **4. a.** one of a set of small pieces of cardboard, marked with figures, symbols, etc., used for playing games or for fortune-telling. See also **playing card. b.** (*as modifier*): *a card game.* **5.** a small rectangle of stiff plastic with identifying numbers, issued by banks and other organizations, and signed by the holder, for use as a credit card, banker's card, etc. **6.** *Inf.* a witty or eccentric person. **7.** See **compass card. 8.** Also called: **racecard.** *Horse racing.* a daily programme of all the races at a meeting. **9. a card up one's sleeve.** a thing or action used in order to gain an advantage, esp. one kept in reserve until needed. **10.** *Computers.* See **punched card.** ~See also **cards.** [C15: < OF *carte,* < L *charta* leaf of papyrus, < Gk *khartēs,* prob. of Egyptian origin]

card[2] (kɑːd) *n.* **1.** a machine for combing fibres of cotton, wool, etc., to remove small unwanted fibres before spinning. **2.** a comblike tool for raising the nap on cloth. ~*vb.* **3.** (*tr.*) to process with such a machine or tool. [C15: < OF *carde* card, teasel, < L *carduus* thistle] —ˈ**carder** *n.*

cardamom *or* **cardamum** (ˈkɑːdəməm) *n.* **1.** a tropical Asian plant that has large hairy leaves. **2.** the seeds of this plant, used esp. as a spice or condiment. [C15: < L, < Gk, < *kardamon* cress + *amōmon* an Indian spice]

cardboard (ˈkɑːdˌbɔːd) *n.* **1. a.** a thin stiff board made from paper pulp. **b.** (*as modifier*): *cardboard boxes.* ~*adj.* **2.** (*prenominal*) without substance.

card-carrying *adj.* being an official member of an organization: *a card-carrying Communist.*

cardiac (ˈkɑːdɪˌæk) *adj.* **1.** of or relating to the heart. **2.** of or relating to the portion of the stomach connected to the oesophagus. ~*n.* **3.** a person with a heart disorder. [C17: < L *cardiacus,* < Gk, < *kardia* heart]

cardie *or* **cardy** (ˈkɑːdɪ) *n., pl.* **-dies.** *Inf.* short for **cardigan.**

cardigan (ˈkɑːdɪgən) *n.* a knitted jacket or sweater with buttons up the front. [C19: after 7th Earl of *Cardigan* (1797–1868)]

cardinal (ˈkɑːdɪnᵊl) *n.* **1.** *R.C. Church.* any of the members of the Sacred College who elect the pope and act as his chief counsellors. **2.** Also called: **cardinal red.** a deep red colour. **3.** See **cardinal number. 4.** Also called (U.S.): **redbird.** a crested North American bunting, the male of which has a bright red plumage. **5.** a woman's hooded shoulder cape worn in the 17th and 18th centuries. ~*adj.* **6.** (*usually prenominal*) fundamentally important; principal. **7.** of a deep red. [C13: < L *cardinālis,* lit.: relating to a hinge, < *cardō* hinge] —ˈ**cardinally** *adv.*

cardinalate (ˈkɑːdɪnᵊˌleɪt) *or* **cardinalship** *n.* **1.** the rank, office, or term of office of a cardinal. **2.** the cardinals collectively.

cardinal flower *n.* a lobelia of E North America that has brilliant scarlet flowers.

cardinal number *or* **numeral** *n.* a number denoting quantity but not order in a group. Sometimes shortened to **cardinal.** Cf. **ordinal number.**

cardinal points *pl. n.* the four main points of the compass: north, south, east, and west.

cardinal virtues *pl. n.* the most important moral qualities, traditionally justice, prudence, temperance, and fortitude.

card index *or* **file** *n.* **1.** an index in which each item is separately listed on systematically arranged cards. ~*vb.* **card-index.** (*tr.*) **2.** to make such an index of (a book, etc.).

cardio- *or before a vowel* **cardi-** *combining form.* heart: *cardiogram.* [< Gk *kardia* heart]

cardiogram (ˈkɑːdɪəʊˌgræm) *n.* short for **electrocardiogram.** See **electrocardiograph.**

cardiograph (ˈkɑːdɪəʊˌgrɑːf) *n.* **1.** an instrument for recording heart movements. **2.** short for electrocardiograph. —cardiographer (ˌkɑːdɪˈɒgrəfə) *n.* —ˌcardiˈography *n.*

cardiology (ˌkɑːdɪˈɒlədʒɪ) *n.* the branch of medical science concerned with the heart and its diseases. —ˌcardiˈologist *n.*

cardiovascular (ˌkɑːdɪəʊˈvæskjʊlə) *adj.* of or relating to the heart and the blood vessels.

cardoon (kɑːˈduːn) *n.* a thistle-like relative of the artichoke with an edible leafstalk. [C17: < F, < L *carduus* thistle, artichoke]

card punch *n.* a device, controlled by a computer, for transferring information from the central processing unit onto punched cards which can then be read by a **card reader.**

cards (kɑːdz) *n.* **1.** (*usually functioning as sing.*) **a.** any game played with cards, esp. playing cards. **b.** the playing of such a game. **2.** an employee's tax and national insurance documents or information held by the employer. **3. ask for** *or* **get one's cards.** to ask *or* be told to terminate one's employment. **4. on the cards.** possible. **5. play one's cards (right).** to manoeuvre (cleverly). **6. put** *or* **lay one's cards on the table.** to declare one's intentions, etc.

cardsharp (ˈkɑːdˌʃɑːp) *or* **cardsharper** *n.* a professional card player who cheats.

card vote *n. Brit.* a vote by delegates, esp. at a trade-union conference, in which each delegate's vote counts as a vote by all his constituents.

care (kɛə) *vb.* **1.** (when *tr., may take a clause as object*) to be troubled or concerned: *he is dying, and she doesn't care.* **2.** (*intr.;* foll. by *for* or *about*) to have regard or consideration (for): *he cares more for his hobby than his job.* **3.** (*intr.;* foll. by *for*) to have a desire or taste (for): *would you care for tea?* **4.** (*intr.;* foll. by *for*) to provide physical needs, help, or comfort (for). **5.** (*tr.*) to agree or like (to do something): *would you care to sit down?* **6. for all I care** *or* **I couldn't care less.** I am completely indifferent. ~*n.* **7.** careful or serious attention: *he does his work with care.* **8.** protective or supervisory control: *in the care of a doctor.* **9.** (*often pl.*) trouble; worry. **10.** an object of or cause for concern. **11.** caution: *handle with care.* **12. care of.** at the address of: written on envelopes. Usual abbrev.: **c/o. 13. in** (*or* **into**) **care.** *Brit.* made the legal responsibility of a local authority by order of a court. [OE *cearu* (n.), *cearian* (vb.), of Gmc origin] —ˈ**carer** *n.*

CARE (kɛə) *n. acronym for:* **1.** *N.Z.* Citizens' Association for Racial Equality. **2.** Cooperative for American Relief Everywhere.

careen (kəˈriːn) *vb.* **1.** to sway or cause to sway over to one side. **2.** (*tr.*) *Naut.* to cause (a vessel) to keel over to one side, esp. in order to clean its bottom. **3.** (*intr.*) *Naut.* (of a vessel) to keel over to one side. [C17: < F, < It., < L *carīna* keel] —**caˈreenage** *n.*

career (kəˈrɪə) *n.* **1.** a path through life or history. **2. a.** a profession or occupation chosen as one's life's work. **b.** (*as modifier*): *a career diplomat.* **3.** a course or path, esp. a headlong one. ~*vb.* **4.** (*intr.*) to rush in an uncontrolled way. [C16: < F, < LL *carrāria* carriage road, < L *carrus* two-wheeled wagon]

career girl *or* **woman** *n.* a woman, often unmarried, who follows a profession.

careerist (kəˈrɪərɪst) *n.* a person who seeks to advance his career by any possible means.

carefree (ˈkɛəˌfriː) *adj.* without worry or responsibility. —ˈ**careˌfreeness** *n.*

careful (ˈkɛəfʊl) *adj.* **1.** cautious in attitude or action. **2.** painstaking in one's work; exact and thorough. **3.** (*usually postpositive;* foll. by *of, in,* or *about*) solicitous; protective. **4.** *Brit.* mean or miserly. —ˈ**carefully** *adv.* —ˈ**carefulness** *n.*

careless (ˈkɛəlɪs) *adj.* **1.** done with or acting with insufficient attention. **2.** (often foll. by *in, of,* or *about*) unconcerned in attitude or action. **3.** (*usually prenominal*) carefree. **4.** (*usually prenominal*) unstudied: *careless elegance.* —ˈ**carelessly** *adv.* —ˈ**carelessness** *n.*

caress (kəˈrɛs) *n.* **1.** a gentle touch or embrace, esp. one given to show affection. ~*vb.* **2.** (*tr.*) to touch or stroke gently with or as with affection. [C17: < F, < It., < L *cārus* dear]

caret (ˈkærɪt) *n.* a symbol (‸) used to indicate the place in written or printed matter at which something is to be inserted. [C17: < L, lit.: there is missing, < *carēre* to lack]

caretaker (ˈkɛəˌteɪkə) *n.* **1.** a person who is in charge of a place or thing, esp. in the owner's absence. **2.** (*modifier*) interim: *a caretaker government.*

careworn (ˈkɛəˌwɔːn) *adj.* showing signs of care, stress, worry, etc.: *a careworn face.*

cargo (ˈkɑːgəʊ) *n., pl.* **-goes** *or esp. U.S.* **-gos. 1. a.** goods carried by a ship, aircraft, or other vehicle; freight. **b.** (*as modifier*): *a cargo vessel.* **2.** any load: *a cargo of new arrivals.* [C17: < Sp.: < *cargar* to load, < LL, < L *carrus* CAR]

Carib (ˈkærɪb) *n.* **1.** (*pl.* **-ibs** *or* **-ib**) a member of a group of American Indian peoples of NE South America and the Lesser Antilles. **2.** the family of languages spoken by these peoples. [C16: < Sp. *Caribe,* < Amerind]

Caribbean (ˌkærɪˈbiːən) *adj.* **1.** of the Caribbean Sea and its islands. **2.** of the Carib or any of their languages. ~*n.* **3.** the Caribbean Sea. **4.** a member of any of the peoples inhabiting the islands of the Caribbean Sea, such as a West Indian or a Carib.

caribou (ˈkærɪˌbuː) *n., pl.* **-bous** *or* **-bou.** a large North American reindeer. [C18: < Canad. F, of Algonquian origin]

caricature (ˈkærɪkəˌtjʊə) *n.* **1.** a pictorial, written, or acted representation of a person, which exaggerates his characteristic traits for comic effect. **2.** an inadequate or inaccurate imitation. ~*vb.* **3.** (*tr.*) to represent in caricature or produce a caricature of. [C18: < It. *caricatura* a distortion, < *caricare* to load, exaggerate] —ˈ**caricaˌturist** *n.*

caries (ˈkɛərɪiːz) *n., pl.* **-ies.** progressive decay of a bone or a tooth. [C17: < L: decay]

carillon (kəˈrɪljən) *n. Music.* **1.** a set of bells usually hung in a tower. **2.** a tune played on such bells. **3.** a mixture stop on an organ giving the effect of a bell. [C18: < F: set of bells, < OF *quarregnon,* ult. < L *quattuor* four]

carina (kəˈriːnə, -ˈraɪ-) *n., pl.* **-nae** (-niː) *or* **-nas.** a keel-like part or ridge, as in the breastbone of birds. [C18: < L: keel]

carinate (ˈkærɪˌneɪt) *or* **carinated** *adj. Biol.* having a keel or ridge. [C17: < L *carīnāre,* < *carīna* keel]

caring (kɛərɪŋ) *adj.* **1.** showing care and compassion: *a caring attitude.* **2.** of or relating to professional social or medical care: *nursing is a caring job.* ~*n.* **3.** the practice of providing care.

carioca (ˌkærɪˈəʊkə) *n.* **1.** a Brazilian dance similar to the samba. **2.** a piece of music for this dance. [C19: < Brazilian Port.]

cariole *or* **carriole** (ˈkærɪˌəʊl) *n.* **1.** a small open two-wheeled horse-drawn vehicle. **2.** a covered cart. [C19: < F, ult. < L *carrus;* see CAR]

carious (ˈkɛərɪəs) *adj.* (of teeth or bone) affected with caries; decayed.

carl *or* **carle** (kɑːl) *n. Arch. or Scot.* another word for **churl.** [OE, < ON *karl*]

Carlovingian (ˌkɑːləʊˈvɪndʒɪən) *adj., n. History.* a variant of **Carolingian.**

carmagnole (ˌkɑːmənˈjəʊl) *n.* **1.** a dance and song popular during the French Revolution. **2.** the costume worn by many French Revolutionaries. [C18: < F, prob. after *Carmagnola,* Italy]

Carmelite (ˈkɑːməˌlaɪt) *n. R.C. Church.* **1.** a member of an order of mendicant friars founded about 1154. **2.** a member of a corresponding order of nuns founded in 1452. ~*adj.* **3.** of or relating to either of these orders. [C14: < F, after Mount *Carmel,* where the order was founded]

carminative (ˈkɑːmɪnətɪv) *adj.* **1.** able to relieve flatulence. ~*n.* **2.** a carminative drug. [C15: < F, < L *carmināre* to card wool]

carmine (ˈkɑːmaɪn) *n.* **1. a.** a vivid red colour. **b.** (*as adj.*): *carmine paint.* **2.** a pigment of this colour obtained from cochineal. [C18: < Med. L *carmīnus,* < Ar. *qirmiz* KERMES]

carnage (ˈkɑːnɪdʒ) *n.* extensive slaughter. [C16: < F, < It., < Med. L, < L *carō* flesh]

carnal (ˈkɑːnᵊl) *adj.* relating to the appetites and passions of the body. [C15: < LL, < L *carō* flesh] —**carˈnality** *n.* —**ˈcarnally** *adv.*

carnal knowledge *n. Chiefly law.* sexual intercourse.

carnation (kɑːˈneɪʃən) *n.* **1.** Also called: **clove pink.** a Eurasian plant cultivated in many varieties for its white, pink, or red flowers, which have a fragrant scent of cloves. **2.** the flower of this plant. **3. a.** a pink or reddish-pink colour. **b.** (*as adj.*): *a carnation dress.* [C16: < F: flesh colour, < LL, < L *carō* flesh]

carnauba (kɑːˈnaʊbə) *n.* **1.** Also called: **wax palm.** a Brazilian fan palm. **2.** Also called: **carnauba wax.** the wax obtained from the young leaves of this tree. [< Brazilian Port., prob. of Tupi origin]

carnelian (kɑːˈniːljən) *n.* a reddish-yellow translucent variety of chalcedony, used as a gemstone. [C17: var. of *cornelian,* < OF, <?]

carnet (ˈkɑːneɪ) *n.* **1.** a customs licence authorizing the temporary importation of a motor vehicle. **2.** an official document permitting motorists to cross certain frontiers. [F: notebook, < OF, ult. < L *quaternī* four at a time]

carnival (ˈkɑːnɪvᵊl) *n.* **1. a.** a festive period marked by merrymaking, etc.: esp. in some Roman Catholic countries, the period just before Lent. **b.** (*as modifier*): *a carnival atmosphere.* **2.** a travelling fair having sideshows, merry-go-rounds, etc. **3.** a show or display arranged as an amusement. **4.** *Austral.* a sports meeting. [C16: < It., < OIt. *carnelevare* a removing of meat (referring to the Lenten fast)]

carnivore (ˈkɑːnɪˌvɔː) *n.* **1.** any of an order of mammals having large pointed canine teeth specialized for eating flesh. The order includes cats, dogs, bears, and weasels. **2.** any other animal or any plant that feeds on animals. [C19: prob. back formation < CARNIVOROUS]

carnivorous (kɑːˈnɪvərəs) *adj.* **1.** (esp. of animals) feeding on flesh. **2.** (of plants such as the pitcher plant and sundew) able to trap and digest insects. **3.** of or relating to the carnivores. [C17: < L, < *carō* flesh + *vorāre* to consume] —**carˈnivorousness** *n.*

carob (ˈkærəb) *n.* **1.** an evergreen Mediterranean tree with compound leaves and edible pods. **2.** the long blackish sugary pod of this tree, used for animal fodder and sometimes for human food. [C16: < OF, < Med. L *carrūbium,* < Ar. *al kharrūbah*]

carol (ˈkærəl) *n.* **1.** a joyful hymn or religious song, esp. one (a **Christmas carol**) celebrating the birth of Christ. ~*vb.* **-olling, -olled** *or U.S.* **-oling, -oled. 2.** (*intr.*) to sing carols at Christmas. **3.** to sing (something) in a joyful manner. [C13: < OF, <?]

Caroline (ˈkærəˌlaɪn) *or* **Carolean** (ˌkærəˈliːən) *adj.* characteristic of or relating to Charles I or Charles II (kings of England, Scotland, and Ireland), the society over which they ruled, or their government. Also called: **Carolinian.**

Carolingian (ˌkærəˈlɪndʒɪən) *adj.* **1.** of or relating to the Frankish dynasty founded by Pepin the Short which ruled in France from 751–987 A.D. and in Germany until 911 A.D. ~*n.* **2.** a member of the dynasty of the Carolingian Franks. ~Also: **Carlovingian, Carolinian.**

carom (ˈkærəm) *n. Billiards.* another word (esp. U.S. and Canad.) for **cannon** (sense 5). [C18: < earlier *carambole* (taken as *carom ball*), < Sp. *carambola* CARAMBOLA]

carotene (ˈkærəˌtiːn) *or* **carotin** (ˈkærətɪn) *n.* any of four orange-red isomers of a hydrocarbon present in many plants and converted to vitamin A in the liver. [C19 *carotin,* < L *carōta* CARROT]

carotenoid *or* **carotinoid** (kəˈrɒtɪˌnɔɪd) *n.* any of a group of red or yellow pigments, including carotenes, found in plants and certain animal tissues.

carotid (kəˈrɒtɪd) *n.* **1.** either of the two principal arteries that supply blood to the head and neck. ~*adj.* **2.** of either of these arteries. [C17: < F, < Gk, < *karoun* to stupefy; so named because pressure on them produced unconsciousness]

carousal (kəˈraʊzᵊl) *n.* a merry drinking party.

carouse (kəˈraʊz) *vb.* **1.** (*intr.*) to have a merry drinking spree. ~*n.* **2.** another word for **carousal.** [C16: via F *carrousser* < G (*trinken*) *gar aus* (to drink) right out] —**caˈrouser** *n.*

carousel (ˌkærəˈsɛl, -ˈzɛl) *n.* **1.** a circular tray in which slides for a projector are held in slots from which they can be released in turn. **2.** a revolving luggage conveyor, as at an airport. **3.** *U.S. & Canad.* a merry-go-round. **4.** *History.* a tournament in which horsemen took part in races. [C17: < F, < It. *carosello,* <?]

carp¹ (kɑːp) *n., pl.* **carp** *or* **carps. 1.** a freshwater food fish having one long dorsal fin, and two barbels on each side of the mouth. **2.** a cyprinid. [C14: < OF *carpe,* of Gmc origin]

carp² (kɑːp) *vb.* (*intr.*; often foll. by *at*) to complain or find fault. [C13: < ON *karpa* to boast] —**ˈcarper** *n.* —**ˈcarping** *adj., n.*

-carp *n. combining form.* (in botany) fruit or a reproductive structure that develops into a particular part of the fruit: *epicarp.* [< NL *-carpium,* < Gk *-karpion,* < *karpos* fruit]

carpal (ˈkɑːpᵊl) *n.* **a.** any bone of the wrist. **b.** (*as modifier*): *carpal bones.* [C18: < NL *carpālis,* < Gk *karpos* wrist]

car park *n.* an area or building reserved for parking cars. Usual U.S. and Canad. term: **parking lot.**

carpe diem *Latin.* (ˈkɑːpɪ ˈdiːɛm) *sentence substitute.* enjoy the pleasures of the moment, without concern for the future. [lit.: seize the day!]

carpel (ˈkɑːpᵊl) *n.* the female reproductive organ of flowering plants, consisting of an ovary, style, and stigma. [C19: < NL *carpellum,* < Gk *karpos* fruit] —**ˈcarpellary** *adj.*

carpenter (ˈkɑːpɪntə) *n.* **1.** a person skilled in woodwork, esp. in buildings, ships, etc. ~*vb.* **2.** (*intr.*) to do the work of a carpenter. **3.** (*tr.*) to make or fit together by or as if by carpentry. [C14: < Anglo-F, < L, < *carpentum* wagon]

carpentry (ˈkɑːpɪntrɪ) *n.* **1.** the art or technique of working wood. **2.** the work produced by a carpenter; woodwork.

carpet (ˈkɑːpɪt) *n.* **1.** a heavy fabric for covering floors. **2.** a covering like a carpet: *a carpet of leaves.* **3. on the carpet.** *Inf.* **a.** before authority to be reproved. **b.** under consideration. ~*vb.* (*tr.*) **4.** to cover with or as if with a carpet. **5.** *Inf.* to reprimand. [C14: < OF, < OIt., < LL *carpeta,* < L *carpere* to pluck, card]

carpetbag (ˈkɑːpɪtˌbæg) *n.* a travelling bag originally made of carpeting.

carpetbagger (ˈkɑːpɪtˌbægə) *n.* a politician who seeks public office in a locality where he has no real connections.

carpet beetle *or U.S.* **carpet bug** *n.* any of various beetles, the larvae of which feed on carpets, furnishing fabrics, etc.

carpeting (ˈkɑːpɪtɪŋ) *n.* carpet material or carpets in general.

carpet slipper *n.* one of a pair of slippers, originally one made with woollen uppers resembling carpeting.

carpet snake *or* **python** *n.* a large nonvenomous Australian snake having a carpet-like pattern on its back.

carpet-sweeper *n.* a household device with a revolving brush for sweeping carpets.

car phone *n.* a telephone that operates by cellular radio for use in a car.

carpo- *combining form.* (in botany) indicating fruit or a seed. [< Gk *karpos* fruit]

carport (ˈkɑːˌpɔːt) *n.* a shelter for a car usually consisting of a roof built out from the side of a building and supported by posts.

-carpous *or* **-carpic** *adj. combining form.* (in botany) indicating a certain kind or number of fruit: *apocarpous.* [< NL, < Gk *karpos* fruit]

carpus (ˈkɑːpəs) *n., pl.* **-pi** (-paɪ). **1.** the technical name for **wrist.** **2.** the eight small bones of the human wrist. [C17: NL, < Gk *karpos*]

carrack ('kærək) *n.* a galleon sailed in the Mediterranean as a merchantman in the 15th and 16th centuries. [C14: < OF *caraque,* < OSp. *carraca,* < Ar. *qarāqīr* merchant ships]

carrageen, carragheen, *or* **carageen** ('kærəˌgiːn) *n.* an edible red seaweed, of rocky shores of North America and N Europe, used to make a beverage, medicine, and jelly, and as an emulsifying and gelling agent (**E407**). Also called: **Irish moss.** [C19: < *Carragheen,* near Waterford, Ireland]

carrel *or* **carrell** ('kærəl) *n.* a small individual study room or private desk, often in a library. [C20: < obs. *carrel* study area, var. of CAROL]

carriage ('kærɪdʒ) *n.* **1.** *Brit.* a railway coach for passengers. **2.** the manner in which a person holds and moves his head and body. **3.** a four-wheeled horse-drawn vehicle for persons. **4.** the moving part of a machine that bears another part: *a typewriter carriage.* **5.** ('kærɪdʒ, 'kærɪɪdʒ). **a.** the act of conveying. **b.** the charge made for conveying (esp. in **carriage forward,** when the charge is to be paid by the receiver, and **carriage paid**). [C14: < OF *cariage,* < *carier* to CARRY]

carriage clock *n.* a portable clock, usually in a rectangular case, originally used by travellers.

carriage trade *n.* trade from the wealthy part of society.

carriageway ('kærɪdʒˌweɪ) *n. Brit.* the part of a road along which traffic passes in a single line moving in one direction only: *a dual carriageway.*

carrier ('kærɪə) *n.* **1.** a person, thing, or organization employed to carry goods, etc. **2.** a mechanism by which something is carried or moved, such as a device for transmitting rotation from the faceplate of a lathe to the workpiece. **3.** *Pathol.* another name for **vector** (sense 2). **4.** *Pathol.* a person or animal that, without having any symptoms of a disease, is capable of transmitting it to others. **5.** Also called: **charge carrier.** *Physics.* an electron or hole that carries the charge in a conductor or semiconductor. **6.** short for **carrier wave.** **7.** *Chem.* **a.** an inert substance used to absorb a dyestuff, transport a sample through a gas chromatography column, contain a radioisotope for radioactive tracing, etc. **b.** a catalyst or substance used to support a catalyst. **8.** See **aircraft carrier.**

carrier bag *n. Brit.* a large paper or plastic bag for carrying shopping, etc.

carrier pigeon *n.* any homing pigeon, esp. one used for carrying messages.

carrier wave *n. Radio.* a wave of fixed amplitude and frequency that is modulated in order to carry a signal in radio transmission, etc.

carriole ('kærɪˌəʊl) *n.* a variant spelling of **cariole.**

carrion ('kærɪən) *n.* **1.** dead and rotting flesh. **2.** (*modifier*) eating carrion. **3.** something rotten. [C13: < Anglo-F *caroine,* ult. < L *carō* flesh]

carrion crow *n.* a common predatory and scavenging European crow similar to the rook but having a pure black bill.

carrot ('kærət) *n.* **1.** an umbelliferous plant with finely divided leaves. **2.** the long tapering orange root of this plant, eaten as a vegetable. **3.** something offered as a lure or incentive. [C16: < OF *carotte,* < LL *carōta,* < Gk *karōton*]

carroty ('kærətɪ) *adj.* **1.** of a reddish or yellowish-orange colour. **2.** having red hair.

carrousel (ˌkærə'sɛl, -'zɛl) *n.* a variant spelling of **carousel.**

carry ('kærɪ) *vb.* **-rying, -ried.** (*mainly tr.*) **1.** (*also intr.*) to take or bear (something) from one place to another. **2.** to transfer for consideration: *he carried his complaints to her superior.* **3.** to have on one's person: *he carries a watch.* **4.** (*also intr.*) to be transmitted or serve as a medium for transmitting: *sound carries over water.* **5.** to bear or be able to bear the weight, pressure, or responsibility of: *her efforts carry the whole production.* **6.** to have as an attribute or result: *this crime carries a heavy penalty.* **7.** to bring or communicate: *to carry news.* **8.** (*also intr.*) to be pregnant with (young). **9.** to bear (the head, body, etc.) in a specified manner: *she carried her head high.* **10.** to conduct or bear (oneself) in a specified manner: *she carried herself well.* **11.** to continue or extend: *the war was carried into enemy territory.* **12.** to cause to move or go: *desire for riches carried him to the city.* **13.** to influence, esp. by emotional appeal: *his words carried the crowd.* **14.** to secure the passage of (a bill, motion, etc.). **15.** to win (an election). **16.** to obtain victory for (a candidate). **17.** *Chiefly U.S.* to win a majority of votes in (a district, etc.): *the candidate carried 40 states.* **18.** to capture: *our troops carried the town.* **19.** (of communications media) to include as the content: *this newspaper carries no book reviews.* **20.** Also (esp. U.S.): **carry over.** *Book-keeping.* to transfer (an item) to another account, esp. to transfer to the following year's account: *to carry a loss.* **21.** *Maths.* to transfer (a number) from one column of figures to the next. **22.** (of a shop, trader, etc.) to keep in stock: *to carry confectionery.* **23.** to support (a musical part or melody) against the other parts. **24.** (*intr.*) (of a ball, projectile, etc.) to travel through the air or reach a specified point: *his first drive carried to the green.* **25.** *Inf.* to imbibe (alcoholic drink) without showing ill effects. **26.** (*intr.*) *Sl.* to have drugs on one's person. **27. carry all before (one).** to win unanimous support or approval for (oneself). **28. carry the can (for).** *Inf.* to take responsibility for some misdemeanour, etc. (on behalf of). **29. carry the day.** to be successful. ~*n., pl.* **-ries.** **30.** the act of carrying. **31.** *U.S. & Canad.* a portion of land over which a boat must be portaged. **32.** the range of a firearm or its projectile. **33.** *Golf.* the distance from where the ball is struck to where it first touches the ground. ~See also **carry away, carry forward,** etc. [C14 *carien,* < OF *carier* to move by vehicle, < *car,* < L *carrum* transport wagon]

carryall ('kærɪˌɔːl) *n.* the usual U.S. and Canad. name for a **holdall.**

carry away *vb.* (*tr., adv.*) **1.** to remove forcefully. **2.** (*usually passive*) to cause (a person) to lose self-control. **3.** (*usually passive*) to delight: *he was carried away by the music.*

carrycot ('kærɪˌkɒt) *n.* a light cot with handles, similar to but smaller than the body of a pram.

carry forward *vb.* (*tr., adv.*) **1.** *Book-keeping.* to transfer (a balance) to the next column, etc. **2.** *Tax accounting.* to apply (a legally permitted credit, esp. an operating loss) to the taxable income of following years. ~Also: **carry over.**

carrying-on *n., pl.* **carryings-on.** *Inf.* **1.** unconventional behaviour. **2.** excited or flirtatious behaviour.

carry off *vb.* (*tr., adv.*) **1.** to remove forcefully. **2.** to win. **3.** to handle (a situation) successfully: *he carried off the introductions well.* **4.** to cause to die: *he was carried off by pneumonia.*

carry on *vb.* (*adv.*) **1.** (*intr.*) to continue or persevere. **2.** (*tr.*) to conduct: *to carry on a business.* **3.** (*intr.;* often foll. by *with*) *Inf.* to have an affair. **4.** (*intr.*) *Inf.* to cause a fuss or commotion. ~*n.* **carry-on.** **5.** *Inf., chiefly Brit.* a fuss.

carry out *vb.* (*tr., adv.*) **1.** to perform or cause to be implemented: *I wish he could afford to carry out his plan.* **2.** to accomplish. ~*n.* **carry-out.** *Chiefly Scot.* **3.** alcohol bought at an off-licence, etc., for consumption elsewhere. **4. a.** a shop which sells hot cooked food for consumption away from the premises. **b.** (*as modifier*): *a carry-out shop.*

carry over *vb.* (*tr., adv.*) **1.** to postpone or defer. **2.** *Book-keeping, tax accounting.* another term for **carry forward.** ~*n.* **carry-over.** **3.** something left over for future use, esp. goods to be sold. **4.** *Book-keeping.* a sum or balance carried forward.

carry through *vb.* (*tr., adv.*) **1.** to bring to completion. **2.** to enable to endure (hardship, trouble, etc.); support.

carse (kɑːs) *n. Scot.* a riverside area of flat fertile alluvium. [C14: <?]

carsick (ˈkɑːˌsɪk) *adj.* nauseated from riding in a car or other vehicle. —**ˈcarˌsickness** *n.*

cart (kɑːt) *n.* **1.** a heavy open vehicle, usually having two wheels and drawn by horses. **2.** a light open horse-drawn vehicle for business or pleasure. **3.** any small vehicle drawn or pushed by hand, such as a trolley. **4. in the cart. a.** in an awkward situation. **b.** in the lurch. **5. put the cart before the horse.** to reverse the usual order of things. ~*vb.* **6.** (*usually tr.*) to use or draw a cart to convey (goods, etc.). **7.** (*tr.*) to carry with effort: *to cart wood home.* [C13: < ON *kartr*] —**ˈcarter** *n.*

cartage (ˈkɑːtɪdʒ) *n.* the process or cost of carting.

carte blanche (ˈkɑːt ˈblɑːntʃ) *n., pl.* **cartes blanches** (ˈkɑːts ˈblɑːntʃ). complete discretion or authority: *the government gave their negotiator carte blanche.* [C18: < F: blank paper]

cartel (kɑːˈtɛl) *n.* **1.** Also called: **trust.** a collusive association of independent enterprises formed to monopolize production and distribution of a product or service. **2.** *Politics.* an alliance of parties to further common aims. [C20: < G *Kartell,* < F, < It. *cartello* public notice, dim. of *carta* CARD[1]]

Cartesian (kɑːˈtiːzɪən) *adj.* **1.** of or relating to the works of Descartes, 17th-century French philosopher and mathematician. **2.** of or used in Descartes' mathematical system. —**Carˈtesianˌism** *n.*

Cartesian coordinates *pl. n.* a system of coordinates that defines the location of a point in space in terms of its perpendicular distance from each of a set of mutually perpendicular axes.

carthorse (ˈkɑːtˌhɔːs) *n.* a large heavily built horse kept for pulling carts or carriages.

Carthusian (kɑːˈθjuːzɪən) *R.C. Church.* ~*n.* **1.** a member of a monastic order founded by Saint Bruno in 1084 near Grenoble, France. ~*adj.* **2.** of or relating to this order. [C14: < Med. L, < L *Carthusia* Chartreuse, near Grenoble]

cartilage (ˈkɑːtɪlɪdʒ) *n.* a tough elastic tissue composing most of the embryonic skeleton of vertebrates. In the adults of higher vertebrates it is mostly converted into bone. Nontechnical name: **gristle.** [C16: < L *cartilāgō*] —**cartilaginous** (ˌkɑːtɪˈlædʒɪnəs) *adj.*

cartilaginous fish *n.* any of a class of fish including the sharks and rays, having a skeleton composed entirely of cartilage.

cartload (ˈkɑːtˌləʊd) *n.* the amount a cart can hold.

cart off, away, *or* **out** *vb.* (*tr., adv.*) *Inf.* to carry or remove brusquely or by force.

cartogram (ˈkɑːtəˌgræm) *n.* a map showing statistical information in diagrammatic form. [C20: < F *cartogramme,* < *carte* map, CHART]

cartography (kɑːˈtɒgrəfɪ) *n.* the art, technique, or practice of compiling or drawing maps or charts. [C19: < F *cartographie,* < *carte* map, CHART] —**carˈtographer** *n.* —**cartographic** (ˌkɑːtəˈgræfɪk) *or* **ˌcartoˈgraphical** *adj.*

carton (ˈkɑːtᵊn) *n.* **1.** a cardboard box for containing goods. **2.** a container of waxed paper in which liquids, such as milk, are sold. [C19: < F, < It. *cartone* pasteboard, < *carta* CARD[1]]

cartoon (kɑːˈtuːn) *n.* **1.** a humorous or satirical drawing, esp. one in a newspaper or magazine. **2.** Also called: **comic strip.** a sequence of drawings in a newspaper, magazine, etc. **3.** See **animated cartoon. 4.** a full-size preparatory sketch for a fresco, tapestry, mosaic, etc. [C17: < It. *cartone* pasteboard] —**carˈtoonist** *n.*

cartouche *or* **cartouch** (kɑːˈtuːʃ) *n.* **1.** a carved or cast ornamental tablet or panel in the form of a scroll. **2.** an oblong figure enclosing characters expressing royal or divine names in Egyptian hieroglyphics. [C17: < F: scroll, cartridge, < It., < *carta* paper]

cartridge (ˈkɑːtrɪdʒ) *n.* **1.** a metal casing containing an explosive charge and often a bullet, for a rifle or other small arms. **2.** a stylus unit in the pick-up of a record player, either containing a piezoelectric crystal (**crystal cartridge**) or an electromagnet (**magnetic cartridge**). **3.** an enclosed container of magnetic tape, photographic film, ink, etc., for insertion into a tape deck, camera, pen, etc. [C16: < earlier *cartage,* var. of CARTOUCHE (cartridge)]

cartridge belt *n.* a belt with pockets for cartridge clips or loops for cartridges.

cartridge clip *n.* a metallic container holding cartridges for an automatic firearm.

cartridge paper *n.* **1.** an uncoated type of drawing or printing paper. **2.** a heavy paper used in making cartridges or as drawing or printing paper.

cartwheel (ˈkɑːtˌwiːl) *n.* **1.** the wheel of a cart, usually having wooden spokes. **2.** an acrobatic movement in which the body makes a revolution supported on the hands with legs outstretched.

caruncle (ˈkærəŋkᵊl, kəˈrʌŋ-) *n.* **1.** a fleshy outgrowth on the heads of certain birds, such as a cock's comb. **2.** an outgrowth near the hilum on the seeds of some plants. [C17: < obs. F *caruncule,* < L *caruncula* a small piece of flesh, < *carō* flesh] —**caruncular** (kəˈrʌŋkjʊlə) *or* **caˈrunculous** *adj.*

carve (kɑːv) *vb.* **1.** (*tr.*) to cut or chip in order to form something: *to carve wood.* **2.** to form (something) by cutting or chipping: *to carve statues.* **3.** to slice (meat) into pieces. ~See also **carve out, carve up.** [OE *ceorfan*]

carvel (ˈkɑːvᵊl) *n.* another word for **caravel.**

carvel-built *adj.* (of a vessel) having a hull with planks made flush at the seams. Cf. **clinker-built.**

carven (ˈkɑːvᵊn) *vb.* an archaic or literary past participle of **carve.**

carve out *vb.* (*tr., adv.*) *Inf.* to make or create (a career): *he carved out his own future.*

carver (ˈkɑːvə) *n.* **1.** a carving knife. **2.** (*pl.*) a large matched knife and fork for carving meat. **3.** *Brit.* a chair having arms that forms part of a set of dining chairs.

carvery (ˈkɑːvərɪ) *n., pl.* **-veries.** an eating establishment at which customers pay a set price for unrestricted helpings from a variety of meats, salads, etc.

carve up *vb.* (*tr., adv.*) **1.** to cut (something) into pieces. **2.** to divide (land, etc.). ~*n.* **carve-up. 3.** *Inf.* an act or instance of dishonestly prearranging the result of a competition. **4.** *Sl.* the distribution of something.

carving (ˈkɑːvɪŋ) *n.* a figure or design produced by carving stone, wood, etc.

carving knife *n.* a long-bladed knife for carving cooked meat for serving.

caryatid (ˌkærɪˈætɪd) *n., pl.* **-ids** *or* **-ides** (-ɪˌdiːz). a column, used to support an entablature, in the form of a draped female figure. [C16: < L, < Gk *Karuatides* priestesses of Artemis at *Karuai* (Caryae), in Laconia]

Casanova (ˌkæsəˈnəʊvə) *n.* any man noted for his amorous adventures. [after Giovanni *Casanova,* (1725–98), It. adventurer]

casbah (ˈkæzbɑː) *n.* (*sometimes cap.*) a variant spelling of **kasbah.**

cascade (kæsˈkeɪd) *n.* **1.** a waterfall or series of waterfalls over rocks. **2.** something resembling this, such as folds of lace. **3.** a consecutive sequence of chemical or physical processes. **4.** a series of stages in the processing chain of an electrical signal where each operates the next in turn. ~*vb.* **5.** (*intr.*) to flow or fall in or like a cascade. [C17: < F, < It., ult. < L *cadere* to fall]

cascara (kæsˈkɑːrə) *n.* **1.** Also called: **cascara sagrada.** the dried bark of the cascara buckthorn, used as a laxative and stimulant. **2.** Also called: **cascara buckthorn.** a shrub or small tree of NW North America. [C19: < Sp.: bark]

case[1] (keɪs) *n.* **1.** a single instance or example of something. **2.** an instance of disease, injury, etc. **3.** a question or matter for discussion. **4.** a specific condition or state of affairs; situation. **5.** a set of arguments supporting a particular action, cause, etc. **6. a.** a person attended or served by a doctor, social worker, solicitor, etc. **b.** (*as *modifier): a case study.* **7. a.** an action or suit at law: *he has a good case.* **b.** the evidence offered in court to support a claim. **8.** *Grammar.* **a.** a set of grammatical categories of nouns, pronouns, and adjectives indicating the relation of the noun, adjective, or pronoun to other words in the sentence. **b.** any one of these categories: *the nominative case.* **9.** *Inf.* an eccentric. **10. in any case.** (*adv.*) no matter what. **11. in case.** (*adv.*) **a.** in order to allow for eventualities. **b.** (*conj.*) in order to allow for the possibility that: *take your coat in case it rains.* **12. in case of.** (*prep.*) in the event of. **13. in no case.** (*adv.*) under no circumstances. [OE *casus* (grammatical) case, associated also with OF *cas* a happening; both < L *cāsus*, a befalling, < *cadere* to fall]

case[2] (keɪs) *n.* **1. a.** a container, such as a box or chest. **b.** (*in combination*)*: suitcase.* **2.** an outer cover, esp. for a watch. **3.** a receptacle and its contents: *a case of ammunition.* **4.** *Archit.* another word for **casing** (sense 3). **5.** a cover ready to be fastened to a book to form its binding. **6.** *Printing.* a tray in which a compositor keeps individual metal types of a particular size and style. Cases were originally used in pairs, one (the **upper case**) for capitals, the other (the **lower case**) for small letters. ~*vb.* (*tr.*) **7.** to put into or cover with a case. **8.** *Sl.* to inspect carefully (esp. a place to be robbed). [C13: < OF *casse*, < L, < *capere* to take, hold]

case-harden *vb.* (*tr.*) **1.** *Metallurgy.* to form a hard surface layer of high carbon content on (a steel component). **2.** to make callous: *experience had case-hardened the judge.*

case history *n.* a record of a person's background, medical history, etc.

casein (ˈkeɪsɪɪn, -siːn) *n.* a protein, precipitated from milk by the action of rennin, forming the basis of cheese. [C19: < L *cāseus* cheese + -IN]

case law *n.* law established by following judicial decisions given in earlier cases. Cf. **statute law.**

casemate (ˈkeɪsˌmeɪt) *n.* an armoured compartment in a ship or fortification in which guns are mounted. [C16: < F, < It. *casamatta*, ? < Gk *khasmata* apertures]

casement (ˈkeɪsmənt) *n.* **1.** a window frame that is hinged on one side. **2.** a window containing frames hinged at the side. **3.** a poetic word for **window.** [C15: prob. < OF *encassement* frame, < *encasser* to encase, < *casse* framework]

caseous (ˈkeɪsɪəs) *adj.* of or like cheese. [C17: < L *cāseus* CHEESE]

casern *or* **caserne** (kəˈzɜːn) *n.* (formerly) a billet or accommodation for soldiers in a town. [C17: < F *caserne*, < OProvençal *cazerna* group of four men, ult. < L *quattuor* four]

casework (ˈkeɪsˌwɜːk) *n.* social work based on close study of the personal histories and circumstances of individuals and families. —ˈ**caseˌworker** *n.*

cash[1] (kæʃ) *n.* **1.** banknotes and coins, esp. in hand or readily available. **2.** immediate payment for goods or services (esp. in **cash down**). **3.** (*modifier*) of, for, or paid by cash: *a cash transaction.* ~*vb.* **4.** (*tr.*) to obtain or pay ready money for. ~See also **cash in, cash up.** [C16: < OIt. *cassa* money box, < L *capsa* CASE[2]] —ˈ**cashable** *adj.*

cash[2] (kæʃ) *n., pl.* **cash.** any of various Chinese or Indian coins of low value. [C16: < Port. *caixa*, < Tamil *kāsu*, < Sansk. *karsa* weight of gold]

cash-and-carry *adj., adv.* sold or operated on a basis of cash payment for merchandise that is not delivered but removed by the purchaser.

cash-book *n. Book-keeping.* a journal in which all receipts and disbursements are recorded.

cash crop *n.* a crop grown for sale rather than for subsistence.

cash desk *n.* a counter or till in a shop where purchases are paid for.

cash discount *n.* a discount granted to a purchaser who pays before a stipulated date.

cash dispenser *n.* a computerized device outside a bank that supplies cash when the user inserts his personal card and keys in his identification number.

cashew (ˈkæʃuː, kæˈʃuː) *n.* **1.** a tropical American evergreen tree, bearing kidney-shaped nuts. **2.** Also called: **cashew nut.** the nut of this tree, edible only when roasted. [C18: < Port. *cajú*, < Tupi *acajú*]

cash flow *n.* the movement of money into and out of a business.

cashier[1] (kæˈʃɪə) *n.* **1.** a person responsible for receiving payments for goods, services, etc., as in a shop. **2.** an employee of a bank responsible for receiving deposits, cashing cheques, etc.: bank clerk. **3.** any person responsible for handling cash in a business. [C16: < Du. or F, < *casse* money chest]

cashier[2] (kæˈʃɪə) *vb.* (*tr.*) to dismiss with dishonour, esp. from the armed forces. [C16: < MDu., < OF, < L *quassāre* to QUASH]

cash in *vb.* (*adv.*) **1.** (*tr.*) to give (something) in exchange. **2.** (*intr.;* often foll. by *on*) *Inf.* **a.** to profit (from). **b.** to take advantage (of).

cashmere (ˈkæʃmɪə) *n.* **1.** a fine soft wool from goats of the Kashmir area. **2. a.** cloth or knitted material made from this or similar wool. **b.** (*as modifier*)*: a cashmere sweater.*

cash on delivery *n.* a service entailing cash payment to the carrier on delivery of merchandise.

cash register *n.* a till with a keyboard that operates a mechanism for displaying and adding the amounts of cash received in individual sales.

cash up *vb.* (*intr., adv.*) *Brit.* (of cashiers, shopkeepers, etc.) to add up the money taken, esp. at the end of a working day.

casing (ˈkeɪsɪŋ) *n.* **1.** a protective case or cover. **2.** material for a case or cover. **3.** Also called: **case.** a frame containing a door or window.

casino (kəˈsiːnəʊ) *n., pl.* **-nos. 1.** a public building or room in which gaming takes place. **2.** a variant spelling of **cassino.** [C18: < It., dim. of *casa* house, < L]

cask (kɑːsk) *n.* **1.** a strong wooden barrel used mainly to hold alcoholic drink: *a wine cask.* **2.** any barrel. **3.** the quantity contained in a cask. [C15: < Sp. *casco* helmet]

casket (ˈkɑːskɪt) *n.* **1.** a small box or chest for valuables, esp. jewels. **2.** another word for **coffin.** (sense 1). [C15: prob. < OF *cassette* little box]

casque (kæsk) *n. Zool.* a helmet or a helmet-like structure, as on the bill of most hornbills. [C17: < F, < Sp. *casco*] —**casqued** *adj.*

Cassandra (kəˈsændrə) *n.* **1.** *Greek myth.* a daughter of Priam and Hecuba, endowed with the gift of prophecy but fated never to be believed. **2.** anyone whose prophecies of doom are unheeded.

cassava (kəˈsɑːvə) *n.* **1.** Also called: **manioc.** any of various tropical plants, esp. the widely cultivated American species (**bitter cassava, sweet cassava**). **2.** a starch derived from the root of this plant: a source of tapioca. [C16: < Sp. *cazabe* cassava bread, < Taino *caçábi*]

casserole (ˈkæsəˌrəʊl) *n.* **1.** a covered dish of earthenware, glass, etc., in which food is cooked and served. **2.** any food cooked and served in such a dish: *chicken casserole.* ~*vb.* **3.** to cook or be cooked in a casserole. [C18: < F, < OF *casse* ladle, < OProvençal, < LL *cattia* dipper, < Gk *kuathion*, dim. of *kuathos* cup]

cassette (kæˈsɛt) *n.* **1. a.** a plastic container for magnetic tape, inserted into a tape deck to be played or used. **b.** (*as modifier*)*: a cassette recorder.* **2.** *Photog.* another term for **cartridge** (sense 3). [C18: < F: little box]

cassia (ˈkæsɪə) *n.* **1.** any of a genus of tropical plants whose pods yield **cassia pulp,** a mild laxative. See also **senna. 2.** a lauraceous tree of tropical Asia. **3. cassia bark.** the cinnamon-like bark of this tree, used as a spice. [OE, < L *casia*, < Gk *kasia*, of Semitic origin]

cassino *or* **casino** (kəˈsiːnəʊ) *n.* a card game for two to four players in which players pair cards with those exposed on the table.

Cassiopeia (ˌkæsɪəˈpiːə) *n., Latin genitive* **Cassio-**

peiae (ˌkæsɪəˈpiːiː). a very conspicuous W-shaped constellation near the Pole Star.

cassis (kɑːˈsiːs) *n.* a blackcurrant cordial. [C19: < F]

cassiterite (kəˈsɪtəˌraɪt) *n.* a hard heavy brownish-black mineral, the chief ore of tin. Formula: SnO_2. Also called: **tinstone.** [C19: < Gk *kassiteros* tin]

cassock (ˈkæsək) *n.* an ankle-length garment, usually black, worn by Christian priests. [C16: < OF, < It. *casacca* a long coat, <?]

cassowary (ˈkæsəˌwɛərɪ) *n., pl.* **-waries.** a large flightless bird inhabiting forests in NE Australia, New Guinea, and adjacent islands, having a horny head crest, black plumage, and brightly coloured neck. [C17: < Malay *kĕsuari*]

cast (kɑːst) *vb.* **casting, cast.** (*mainly tr.*) **1.** to throw or expel with force. **2.** to throw off or away: *she cast her clothes to the ground.* **3.** to reject: *he cast the idea from his mind.* **4.** to shed or drop: *the horse cast a shoe.* **5.** to cause to appear: *to cast a shadow.* **6.** to express (doubts, etc.) or cause (them) to be felt. **7.** to direct (a glance, etc.): *cast your eye over this.* **8.** to place, esp. violently: *he was cast into prison.* **9.** (*also intr.*) *Angling.* to throw (a line) into the water. **10.** to draw or choose (lots). **11.** to give or deposit (a vote). **12.** to select (actors) to play parts in (a play, etc.). **13. a.** to shape (molten metal, glass, etc.) by pouring into a mould. **b.** to make (an object) by such a process. **14.** (*also intr.; often foll. by up*) to compute (figures or a total). **15.** *Astrol.* to draw on (a horoscope) details concerning the positions of the planets in the signs of the zodiac at a particular time for interpretation. **16.** to contrive (esp. in **cast a spell**). **17.** to formulate: *he cast his work in the form of a chart.* **18.** (*also intr.*) to twist or cause to twist. **19.** (*intr.*) (of birds of prey) to eject from the crop and bill a pellet consisting of the indigestible parts of birds or animals previously eaten. **20.** *Printing.* to stereotype or electrotype. **21. be cast.** *N.Z.* (of sheep) to have fallen and been unable to rise. ~*n.* **22.** the act of casting or throwing. **23. a.** Also called: **casting.** something that is shed, dropped, or egested, such as the coil of earth left by an earthworm. **b.** another name for **pellet** (sense 4). **24.** the distance an object is or may be thrown. **25. a.** a throw at dice. **b.** the resulting number shown. **26.** *Angling.* the act or an instance of casting a line. **27.** the wide sweep made by a sheepdog to get behind a flock of sheep or by a hunting dog in search of a scent. **28. a.** the actors in a play collectively. **b.** (*as modifier*): *a cast list.* **29. a.** an object made of metal, glass, etc., that has been shaped in a molten state by being poured or pressed into a mould. **b.** the mould used to shape such an object. **30.** form or appearance. **31.** a sort, kind, or style. **32.** a fixed twist or defect, esp. in the eye. **33.** a distortion of shape. **34.** *Surgery.* a rigid encircling casing, often made of plaster of Paris, **plaster cast,** for immobilizing broken bones while they heal. **35.** a slight tinge or trace, as of colour. **36.** fortune or stroke of fate. ~See also **cast about, castaway,** etc. [C13: < ON *kasta*]

cast about *vb.* (*intr., adv.*) to make a mental or visual search: *to cast about for a plot.*

castanets (ˌkæstəˈnɛts) *pl. n.* curved pieces of hollow wood, usually held between the fingers and thumb and made to click together: used esp. by Spanish dancers. [C17 *castanet,* < Sp. *castañeta,* dim. of *castaña* CHESTNUT]

castaway (ˈkɑːstəˌweɪ) *n.* **1.** a person who has been shipwrecked. ~*adj.* (*prenominal*) **2.** shipwrecked. **3.** thrown away or rejected. ~*vb.* **cast away. 4.** (*tr., adv.; often passive*) to cause (a ship, person, etc.) to be shipwrecked.

cast back *vb.* (*adv.*) to turn (the mind) to the past.

cast down *vb.* (*tr., adv.*) to make (a person) discouraged or dejected.

caste (kɑːst) *n.* **1. a.** any of the four major hereditary classes, namely the **Brahman, Kshatriya, Vaisya,** and **Sudra,** into which Hindu society is divided. **b.** Also called: **caste system.** the system or basis of such classes. **2.** any social class or system based on such distinctions as heredity, rank, wealth, etc. **3.** the position conferred by such a system. **4. lose caste.** *Inf.* to lose one's social position. **5.** *Entomol.* any of various types of individual, such as the worker, in social insects. [C16: < Port. *casta* race, < *casto* pure, chaste, < L *castus*]

castellan (ˈkæstɪlən) *n. Rare.* a keeper or governor of a castle. Also called: **chatelain.** [C14: < L *castellānus,* < *castellum* CASTLE]

castellated (ˈkæstɪˌleɪtɪd) *adj.* **1.** having turrets and battlements, like a castle. **2.** having indentations similar to battlements: *a castellated nut.* [C17: < Med. L *castellātus,* < *castellāre* to fortify as a CASTLE] —ˌ**castelˈlation** *n.*

caster (ˈkɑːstə) *n.* **1.** a person or thing that casts. **2.** a bottle with a perforated top for sprinkling sugar, etc. **3.** a small wheel mounted on a swivel so that the wheel tends to turn into its plane of rotation. ~ Also (for senses 2, 3): **castor.**

caster sugar (ˈkɑːstə) *n.* finely ground white sugar.

castigate (ˈkæstɪˌgeɪt) *vb.* (*tr.*) to rebuke or criticize in a severe manner. [C17: < L *castīgāre* to correct, < *castum* pure + *agere* to compel (to be)] —ˌ**castiˈgation** *n.* —ˈ**castiˌgator** *n.*

Castile soap (kæˈstiːl) *n.* a hard soap made from olive oil and sodium hydroxide.

Castilian (kæˈstɪljən) *n.* **1.** the Spanish dialect of Castile; the standard form of European Spanish. **2.** a native or inhabitant of Castile. ~*adj.* **3.** denoting or of Castile, its inhabitants, or the standard form of European Spanish.

casting (ˈkɑːstɪŋ) *n.* **1.** an object that has been cast, esp. in metal from a mould. **2.** the process of transferring molten steel to a mould. **3.** the choosing of actors for a production. **4.** *Zool.* another word for **cast** (sense 23) or **pellet** (sense 4).

casting couch *n. Inf.* a couch on which a casting director is said to seduce girls seeking a part in a film or play.

casting vote *n.* the deciding vote used by the presiding officer of an assembly when votes cast on both sides are equal in number.

cast iron *n.* **1.** iron containing so much carbon that it cannot be wrought and must be cast into shape. ~*adj.* **cast-iron. 2.** made of cast iron. **3.** rigid or unyielding: *a cast-iron decision.*

castle (ˈkɑːsᵊl) *n.* **1.** a fortified building or set of buildings as in medieval Europe. **2.** any fortified place or structure. **3.** a large magnificent house, esp. when the present or former home of a nobleman or prince. **4.** *Chess.* another name for **rook**[2]. ~*vb.* **5.** *Chess.* to move (the king) two squares laterally on the first rank and place the nearest rook on the square passed over by the king. [C11: < L *castellum,* dim. of *castrum* fort]

castle in the air *or* **in Spain** *n.* a hope or desire unlikely to be realized; daydream.

cast-off *adj.* **1.** (*prenominal*) abandoned: *cast-off shoes.* ~*n.* **castoff. 2.** a person or thing that has been discarded or abandoned. **3.** *Printing.* an estimate of the amount of space that a piece of copy will occupy. ~*vb.* **cast off.** (*adv.*) **4.** to remove (mooring lines) that hold (a vessel) to a dock. **5.** to knot (a row of stitches, esp. the final row) in finishing off knitted or woven material. **6.** *Printing.* to estimate the amount of space that will be taken up by (a book, piece of copy, etc.).

cast on *vb.* (*adv.*) to form (the first row of stitches) in knitting and weaving.

castor[1] (ˈkɑːstə) *n.* **1.** the aromatic secretion of a beaver, used in perfumery and medicine. **2.** the fur of the beaver. **3.** a hat made of beaver or similar fur. [C14: < L, < Gk *kastōr* beaver]

castor[2] (ˈkɑːstə) *n.* a variant spelling of **caster** (senses 2, 3).

castor oil *n.* an oil obtained from the seeds of the castor-oil plant and used as a lubricant and cathartic.

castor-oil plant *n.* a tall Indian plant cultivated

for its poisonous seeds, from which castor oil is extracted.

castrate (kæˈstreɪt) *vb.* (*tr.*) **1.** to remove the testicles of. **2.** to deprive of vigour, masculinity, etc. **3.** to remove the ovaries of; spay. [C17: < L *castrāre* to emasculate, geld] —**casˈtration** *n.*

castrato (kæˈstrɑːtəʊ) *n., pl.* **-ti** (-tɪ) *or* **-tos.** (in 17th- and 18th-century opera, etc.) a male singer whose testicles were removed before puberty, allowing the retention of a soprano or alto voice. [C18: < It., < L *castrātus* castrated]

cast steel *n.* steel containing varying amounts of carbon, manganese, etc., that is cast into shape rather than wrought.

casual (ˈkæʒjʊəl) *adj.* **1.** happening by accident or chance. **2.** offhand: *a casual remark.* **3.** shallow or superficial: *a casual affair.* **4.** being or seeming unconcerned or apathetic: *he assumed a casual attitude.* **5.** (esp. of dress) for informal wear: *a casual coat.* **6.** occasional or irregular: *a casual labourer.* ~*n.* **7.** (*usually pl.*) an informal article of clothing or footwear. **8.** an occasional worker. **9.** (*usually pl.*) a young man dressed in expensive casual clothes who goes to football matches in order to start fights. [C14: < LL *cāsuālis* happening by chance, < L *cāsus* event, < *cadere* to fall] —ˈ**casually** *adv.* —ˈ**casualness** *n.*

casualty (ˈkæʒjʊəltɪ) *n., pl.* **-ties.** **1.** a serviceman who is killed, wounded, captured, or missing as a result of enemy action. **2.** a person who is injured or killed in an accident. **3.** the hospital department treating victims of accidents. **4.** anything that is lost, damaged, or destroyed as the result of an accident, etc.

casuarina (ˌkæsjʊəˈraɪnə) *n.* any of a genus of trees of Australia and the East Indies, having jointed leafless branches. [C19: < NL, < Malay *kĕsuari* CASSOWARY, referring to the resemblance of the branches to the feathers of the cassowary]

casuist (ˈkæzjʊɪst) *n.* **1.** a person, esp. a theologian, who attempts to resolve moral dilemmas by the application of general rules and the careful distinction of special cases. **2.** a sophist. [C17: < F, < Sp. *casuista,* < L *cāsus* CASE[1]] —ˌ**casuˈistic** *or* ˌ**casuˈistical** *adj.*

casuistry (ˈkæzjʊɪstrɪ) *n., pl.* **-ries.** **1.** *Philosophy.* the resolution of particular moral dilemmas, esp. those arising from conflicting general moral rules, by the careful distinction of the cases to which these rules apply. **2.** reasoning that is specious or oversubtle.

cat (kæt) *n.* **1.** Also called: **domestic cat.** a small domesticated feline mammal having thick soft fur and occurring in many breeds in which the colour of the fur varies greatly: kept as a pet or to catch rats and mice. **2.** Also called: **big cat.** any of the larger felines, such as a lion or tiger. **3.** any wild feline mammal such as the lynx or serval, resembling the domestic cat. **4.** *Inf.* a woman who gossips maliciously. **5.** *Sl.* a man. **6.** *Naut.* a heavy tackle for hoisting an anchor to the cathead. **7.** *Austral. sl.* a coward. **8.** *Inf.* short for **caterpillar** (the vehicle). **9.** short for **cat-o'-nine-tails.** **10. fight like Kilkenny cats.** to fight until both parties are destroyed. **11. let the cat out of the bag.** to disclose a secret, often by mistake. **12. like a cat on a hot tin roof** *or* **on hot bricks.** in an uneasy or agitated state. **13. put, set,** etc., **the cat among the pigeons.** to introduce some violently disturbing new element. **14. rain cats and dogs.** to rain very heavily. ~*vb.* **catting, catted.** **15.** (*tr.*) *Naut.* to hoist (an anchor) to the cathead. **16.** (*intr.*) *Sl.* to vomit. [OE *catte,* < L *cattus*] —ˈ**catˌlike** *adj.* —ˈ**cattish** *adj.*

cat. *abbrev. for:* **1.** catalogue. **2.** catamaran.

cata-, kata-, *before an aspirate* **cath-,** *or before a vowel* **cat-** *prefix.* **1.** down; downwards; lower in position: *catadromous.* **2.** indicating reversal, opposition, degeneration, etc.: *catatonia.* [< Gk *kata-,* < *kata.* In compound words borrowed from Gk *kata-* means: down, away, off, against, according to, and thoroughly]

catabolism *or* **katabolism** (kəˈtæbəˌlɪzəm) *n.* a metabolic process in which complex molecules are broken down into simple ones with the release of energy; destructive metabolism. [C19: < Gk *katabolē* a throwing down, < *kata-* down + *ballein* to throw] —**catabolic** *or* **katabolic** (ˌkætəˈbɒlɪk) *adj.*

catachresis (ˌkætəˈkriːsɪs) *n.* the incorrect use of words, as *luxuriant* for *luxurious.* [C16: < L, < Gk *katakhrēsis* a misusing, < *khrēsthai* to use] —**catachrestic** (ˌkætəˈkrɛstɪk) *adj.*

cataclysm (ˈkætəˌklɪzəm) *n.* **1.** a violent upheaval, esp. of a political, military, or social nature. **2.** a disastrous flood. [C17: via F < L, < Gk, < *katakluzein* to flood, < *kluzein* to wash] —ˌ**cataˈclysmic** *or* ˌ**cataˈclysmal** *adj.* —ˌ**cataˈclysmically** *adv.*

catacomb (ˈkætəˌkəʊm) *n.* **1.** (*usually pl.*) an underground burial place, esp. in Rome, consisting of tunnels with niches leading off them for tombs. **2.** a series of underground tunnels or caves. [OE *catacumbe,* < LL *catacumbas* (sing.), name of the cemetery under the Basilica of St Sebastian, near Rome; <?]

catadromous (kəˈtædrəməs) *adj.* (of fishes such as the eel) migrating down rivers to the sea in order to breed. Cf. **anadromous.** [C19: < Gk, < *kata-* down + *dromos,* < *dremein* to run]

catafalque (ˈkætəˌfælk) *n.* a temporary raised platform on which a body lies in state before or during a funeral. [C17: < F, < It. *catafalco,* <?]

Catalan (ˈkætəˌlæn) *n.* **1.** a language of Catalonia, closely related to Spanish and Provençal. **2.** a native or inhabitant of Catalonia. ~*adj.* **3.** denoting or characteristic of Catalonia, its inhabitants, or their language.

catalepsy (ˈkætəˌlɛpsɪ) *n.* a state of prolonged rigid posture, occurring for example in schizophrenia. [C16: < LL *catalēpsis,* < Gk *katalēpsis,* lit.: a seizing, < *kata-* down + *lambanein* to grasp] —ˌ**cataˈleptic** *adj.*

catalogue *or U.S.* **catalog** (ˈkætəˌlɒg) *n.* **1.** a complete, usually alphabetical, list of items. **2.** a book, usually illustrated, containing details of items for sale. **3.** a list of all the books of a library. **4.** *U.S. and Canad.* a list of courses offered by a university, etc. ~*vb.* **5.** to compile a catalogue of (a library, etc.). **6.** to add (books, items, etc.) to an existing catalogue. [C15: < LL *catalogus,* < Gk, < *katalegein* to list, < *kata-* completely + *legein* to collect] —ˈ**cataˌloguer** *n.*

catalpa (kəˈtælpə) *n.* any of a genus of trees of North America and Asia, having large leaves, bell-shaped whitish flowers, and long slender pods. [C18: NL, < Carolina Creek *kutuhlpa,* lit.: winged head]

catalyse *or U.S.* **catalyze** (ˈkætəˌlaɪz) *vb.* (*tr.*) to influence (a chemical reaction) by catalysis.

catalysis (kəˈtælɪsɪs) *n., pl.* **-ses** (-ˌsiːz). acceleration of a chemical reaction by the action of a catalyst. [C17: < NL, < Gk, < *kataluein* to dissolve] —**catalytic** (ˌkætəˈlɪtɪk) *adj.*

catalyst (ˈkætəlɪst) *n.* **1.** a substance that increases the rate of a chemical reaction without itself suffering any permanent chemical change. **2.** a person or thing that causes a change.

catalytic cracker *n.* a unit in an oil refinery in which mineral oils with high boiling points are converted to fuels with lower boiling points by a catalytic process.

catamaran (ˌkætəməˈræn) *n.* **1.** a sailing vessel with twin hulls held parallel by a rigid framework. **2.** a primitive raft made of logs lashed together. **3.** *Inf.* a quarrelsome woman. [C17: < Tamil *kattumaram* tied timber]

catamite (ˈkætəˌmaɪt) *n.* a boy kept for homosexual purposes. [C16: < L *Catamītus,* var. of *Ganymēdēs* Ganymede, cupbearer to the Gods in Gk myth.]

catamount (ˈkætəˌmaʊnt) *or* **catamountain** *n.* any of various felines, such as the puma or lynx. [C17: short for *cat of the mountain*]

catananche (kætənˈæŋkɪ) *n.* any herb of the genus *Catananche,* having blue or yellow flowers. [C18: NL, < L, < Gk *kata* down + *anagkē* compulsion (< its use by ancient Greeks as a philtre)]

cataplexy (ˈkætəˌplɛksɪ) *n.* **1.** sudden temporary

paralysis, brought on by severe shock. **2.** a state assumed by animals while shamming death. [C19: < Gk *kataplēxis* amazement, < *kataplēssein*, < *kata-* down + *plēssein* to strike] —**ˌcataˈplectic** *adj.*

catapult (ˈkætəˌpʌlt) *n.* **1.** a Y-shaped implement with a loop of elastic fastened to the ends of the prongs, used mainly by children for shooting stones, etc. U.S. and Canad. name: **slingshot. 2.** a war engine used formerly for hurling stones, etc. **3.** a device installed in warships to launch aircraft. ~*vb.* **4.** (*tr.*) to shoot forth from or as if from a catapult. **5.** (foll. by *over, into,* etc.) to move precipitately. [C16: < L, < Gk *katapeltēs*, < *kata-* down + *pallein* to hurl]

cataract (ˈkætəˌrækt) *n.* **1.** a large waterfall or rapids. **2.** a downpour. **3.** *Pathol.* **a.** partial or total opacity of the lens of the eye. **b.** the opaque area. [C15: < L, < Gk, < *katarassein* to dash down, < *arassein* to strike]

catarrh (kəˈtɑː) *n.* inflammation of a mucous membrane with increased production of mucus, esp. affecting the nose and throat. [C16: via F < LL, < Gk, < *katarrhein* to flow down, < *kata-* down + *rhein* to flow] —**caˈtarrhal** *adj.*

catarrhine (ˈkætəˌraɪn) *adj.* **1.** (of apes and Old World monkeys) having the nostrils set close together and opening to the front of the face. ~*n.* **2.** an animal with this characteristic. [C19: ult. < Gk *katarrhin* having a hooked nose, < *kata-* down + *rhis* nose]

catastrophe (kəˈtæstrəfɪ) *n.* **1.** a sudden, extensive disaster or misfortune. **2.** the denouement of a play. **3.** a final decisive event, usually causing a disastrous end. [C16: < Gk, < *katastrephein* to overturn, < *strephein* to turn] —**catastrophic** (ˌkætəˈstrɒfɪk) *adj.* —**ˌcataˈstrophically** *adv.*

catastrophism (kəˈtæstrəˌfɪzəm) *n.* **1.** a former doctrine that the earth was formed by sudden divine acts rather than by evolutionary processes. **2.** a modern doctrine that the evolutionary processes shaping the earth have in the past been supplemented by the effects of huge natural catastrophes.

catatonia (ˌkætəˈtəʊnɪə) *n.* a form of schizophrenia characterized by stupor, with outbreaks of excitement. [C20: NL, < G *Katatonie*, < CATA- + Gk *tonos* tension] —**catatonic** (ˌkætəˈtɒnɪk) *adj., n.*

catbird (ˈkætˌbɜːd) *n.* **1.** any of several North American songbirds whose call resembles the mewing of a cat. **2.** any of several Australian bowerbirds having a catlike call.

catboat (ˈkætˌbəʊt) *n.* a sailing vessel with a single mast, set well forward, and a large sail. Shortened form: **cat.**

cat burglar *n.* a burglar who enters buildings by climbing through upper windows, etc.

catcall (ˈkætˌkɔːl) *n.* **1.** a shrill whistle or cry expressing disapproval, as at a public meeting, etc. ~*vb.* **2.** to utter such a call (at).

catch (kætʃ) *vb.* **catching, caught. 1.** (*tr.*) to take hold of so as to retain or restrain. **2.** (*tr.*) to take or capture, esp. after pursuit. **3.** (*tr.*) to ensnare or deceive. **4.** (*tr.*) to surprise or detect in an act: *he caught the dog rifling the larder.* **5.** (*tr.*) to reach with a blow: *the stone caught him on the side of the head.* **6.** (*tr.*) to overtake or reach in time to board. **7.** (*tr.*) to see or hear; attend. **8.** (*tr.*) to be infected with: *to catch a cold.* **9.** to hook or entangle or become hooked or entangled. **10.** to fasten or be fastened with or as if with a latch or other device. **11.** (*tr.*) to attract: *she tried to catch his eye.* **12.** (*tr.*) to comprehend: *I didn't catch his meaning.* **13.** (*tr.*) to hear accurately: *I didn't catch what you said.* **14.** (*tr.*) to captivate or charm. **15.** (*tr.*) to reproduce accurately: *the painter managed to catch his model's beauty.* **16.** (*tr.*) to hold back or restrain: *he caught his breath in surprise.* **17.** (*intr.*) to become alight: *the fire won't catch.* **18.** (*tr.*) *Cricket.* to dismiss (a batsman) by intercepting and holding a ball struck by him before it touches the ground. **19.** (*intr.;* often foll. by *at*) **a.** to grasp or attempt to grasp. **b.** to take advantage (of): *he caught at the chance.* **20. catch it.** *Inf.* to be scolded or reprimanded. ~*n.* **21.** the act of catching or grasping. **22.** a device that catches and fastens, such as a latch. **23.** anything that is caught. **24.** the amount or number caught. **25.** *Inf.* an eligible matrimonial prospect. **26.** a check or break in the voice. **27.** *Inf.* **a.** a concealed, unexpected, or unforeseen drawback. **b.** (*as modifier*): *a catch question.* **28.** *Cricket.* the catching of a ball struck by a batsman before it touches the ground, resulting in him being out. **29.** *Music.* a type of round having a humorous text that is often indecent or bawdy and hard to articulate. ~See also **catch on, catch out, catch up.** [C13 *cacchen* to pursue, < OF *cachier*, < L *captāre* to snatch, < *capere* to seize] —**ˈcatchable** *adj.*

catch-as-catch-can *n.* a style of wrestling in which trips, holds below the waist, etc., are allowed.

catchfly (ˈkætʃˌflaɪ) *n., pl.* **-flies.** any of various plants that have sticky calyxes and stems on which insects are sometimes trapped.

catching (ˈkætʃɪŋ) *adj.* **1.** infectious. **2.** attractive; captivating.

catching pen *n. Austral. & N.Z.* a pen adjacent to a shearer's stand containing the sheep ready for shearing.

catchment (ˈkætʃmənt) *n.* **1.** the act of catching or collecting water. **2.** a structure in which water is collected. **3.** the water so collected. **4.** *Brit.* the intake of a school from one catchment area.

catchment area *n.* **1.** the area of land bounded by watersheds draining into a river, basin, or reservoir. **2.** the area from which people are allocated to a particular school, hospital, etc.

catch on *vb.* (*intr., adv.*) *Inf.* **1.** to become popular or fashionable. **2.** to understand.

catch out *vb.* (*tr., adv.*) *Inf., chiefly Brit.* to trap (a person), esp. in an error.

catchpenny (ˈkætʃˌpɛnɪ) *adj.* (*prenominal*) designed to have instant appeal, esp. in order to sell quickly: *catchpenny ornaments.*

catch phrase *n.* a well-known frequently used phrase, esp. one associated with a particular group, etc.

catch-22 *n.* a situation in which a person is frustrated by a set of circumstances that preclude any attempt to escape from them. [C20: from the title of a novel (1961) by J. Heller]

catch up *vb.* (*adv.*) **1.** (*tr.*) to seize and take up (something) quickly. **2.** (when *intr.*, often foll. by *with*) to reach or pass (someone or something): *he caught him up.* **3.** (*intr.;* usually foll. by *on* or *with*) to make up for lost ground or deal with a backlog. **4.** (*tr.; often passive*) to absorb or involve: *she was caught up in her reading.* **5.** (*tr.*) to raise by or as if by fastening.

catchweight (ˈkætʃˌweɪt) *adj. Wrestling.* of or relating to a contest in which normal weight categories have been waived by agreement.

catchword (ˈkætʃˌwɜːd) *n.* **1.** a word or phrase made temporarily popular; slogan. **2.** a word printed as a running head in a book. **3.** *Theatre.* an actor's cue to speak or enter. **4.** the first word of a page repeated at the bottom of the page preceding.

catchy (ˈkætʃɪ) *adj.* **catchier, catchiest. 1.** (of a tune, etc.) pleasant and easily remembered. **2.** deceptive: *a catchy question.* **3.** irregular: *a catchy breeze.*

cat cracker *n.* an informal name for **catalytic cracker.**

catechetical (ˌkætɪˈkɛtɪkᵊl) *or* **catechetic** *adj.* of or relating to teaching by question and answer. —**ˌcateˈchetically** *adv.*

catechism (ˈkætɪˌkɪzəm) *n.* instruction by a series of questions and answers, esp. a book containing such instruction on the religious doctrine of a Christian Church. [C16: < LL, ult. < Gk *katēkhizein* to CATECHIZE] —**ˌcateˈchismal** *adj.*

catechize *or* **-ise** (ˈkætɪˌkaɪz) *vb.* (*tr.*) **1.** to teach or examine by means of questions and answers. **2.** to give oral instruction in Christianity, esp. by using a catechism. **3.** to put questions to (someone). [C15: < LL, < Gk *katēkhizein*, < *katēkhein* to instruct orally, < *kata-* down + *ēkhein* to sound] —**ˈcatechist, ˈcateˌchizer** *or* **-iser** *n.*

catechu (ˈkætɪˌtʃuː) *or* **cachou** *n.* an astringent resinous substance obtained from certain tropical plants, and used in medicine, tanning, and dyeing. [C17: prob. < Malay *kachu*]

catechumen (ˌkætɪˈkjuːmɛn) *n. Christianity.* a person, esp. in the early Church, undergoing instruction prior to baptism. [C15: via OF, < LL, < Gk *katēkhoumenos* one being instructed verbally]

categorial (ˌkætɪˈgɔːrɪəl) *adj.* **1.** of or relating to a category. **2.** *Logic.* (of a statement) consisting of a subject, S, and a predicate, P, each of which denote a class, as in: *all S are P.*

categorical (ˌkætɪˈgɒrɪkᵊl) *or* **categoric** *adj.* **1.** unqualified; unconditional: *a categorical statement.* **2.** relating to or included in a category. **3.** another word for **categorial** (sense 2). —ˌ**cateˈgorically** *adv.*

categorize *or* **-ise** (ˈkætɪgəˌraɪz) *vb.* (*tr.*) to place in a category. —ˌ**categoriˈzation** *or* **-iˈsation** *n.*

category (ˈkætɪgərɪ) *n., pl.* **-ries.** **1.** a class or group of things, people, etc., possessing some quality or qualities in common. **2.** *Metaphysics.* one of the most basic classes into which objects and concepts can be analysed. **3. a.** (in the philosophy of Aristotle) any one of ten most fundamental modes of being, such as quantity, quality, and substance. **b.** (in the philosophy of Kant) one of twelve concepts required by human beings to interpret the empirical world. [C15: < LL, < Gk *katēgoria*, < *kategorein* to accuse, assert]

catena (kəˈtiːnə) *n., pl.* **-nae** (-niː). a connected series, esp. of patristic comments on the Bible. [C17: < L: chain]

catenary (kəˈtiːnərɪ) *n., pl.* **-ries.** **1.** the curve formed by a heavy uniform flexible cord hanging freely from two points. **2.** the hanging cable between pylons along a railway track, from which the trolley wire is suspended. ~*adj.* **3.** of, resembling, relating to, or constructed using a catenary or suspended chain. [C18: < L *catēnārius* relating to a chain]

catenate (ˈkætɪˌneɪt) *vb. Biol.* to arrange or be arranged in a series of chains or rings. [C17: < L *catēnāre* to bind with chains] —ˌ**cateˈnation** *n.*

cater (ˈkeɪtə) *vb.* **1.** (*intr.*; foll. by *for* or *to*) to provide what is required or desired (for). **2.** (when *intr.*, foll. by *for*) to provide food, services, etc. (for): *we cater for parties.* [C16: < earlier *catour* purchaser, var. of *acatour*, < Anglo-Norman *acater* to buy] —**ˈcatering** *n.*

cater-cornered (ˈkætəˌkɔːnəd) *adj., adv. U.S. & Canad. inf.* diagonal. Also: **catty-cornered.** [C16: < dialect *cater* (adv.) diagonally, < obs. *cater* (n.) four-spot of dice, < OF *quatre* four, < L *quattuor*]

caterer (ˈkeɪtərə) *n.* one who as a profession provides food for large social events, etc.

caterpillar (ˈkætəˌpɪlə) *n.* **1.** the wormlike larva of butterflies and moths, having numerous pairs of legs and powerful biting jaws. **2.** an endless track, driven by sprockets or wheels, used to propel a heavy vehicle. **3.** a vehicle, such as a tractor, tank, etc., driven by such tracks. [C15 *catyrpel*, prob. < OF *catepelose*, lit.: hairy cat]

caterwaul (ˈkætəˌwɔːl) *vb.* (*intr.*) **1.** to make a yowling noise, as a cat on heat. ~*n.* **2.** a yell made by or sounding like a cat on heat. [C14: imit.]

catfish (ˈkætˌfɪʃ) *n., pl.* **-fish** *or* **-fishes.** **1.** any of numerous mainly freshwater fishes having whisker-like barbels around the mouth. **2.** another name for **wolffish.**

cat flap *or* **door** *n.* a small flap or door in a larger door through which a cat can pass.

catgut (ˈkætˌgʌt) *n.* a strong cord made from the dried intestines of sheep and other animals that is used for stringing certain musical instruments and sports rackets.

Cath. *abbrev. for:* **1.** Cathedral. **2.** Catholic.

cath- *prefix.* a variant of **cata-** before an aspirate: *cathode.*

Cathar (ˈkæθə) *or* **Catharist** (ˈkæθərɪst) *n., pl.* **-ars, -ari** (-ərɪ) *or* **-arists.** a member of a Christian sect in Provence in the 12th and 13th centuries who believed the material world was evil and only the spiritual was good. [< Med. L, < Gk *katharoi* the pure] —**ˈCatharˌism** *n.*

catharsis (kəˈθɑːsɪs) *n.* **1.** the purging or purification of the emotions through the evocation of pity and fear, as in tragedy. **2.** *Psychoanal.* the bringing of repressed ideas or experiences into consciousness, thus relieving tensions. **3.** purgation, esp. of the bowels. [C19: NL, < Gk *katharsis*, < *kathairein* to purge, purify]

cathartic (kəˈθɑːtɪk) *adj.* **1.** purgative. **2.** effecting catharsis. ~*n.* **3.** a purgative drug or agent. —**caˈthartically** *adv.*

Cathay (kæˈθeɪ) *n.* a literary or archaic name for China. [C14: < Med. L *Cataya*]

cathead (ˈkætˌhɛd) *n.* a fitting at the bow of a vessel for securing the anchor when raised.

cathedral (kəˈθiːdrəl) *n.* **a.** the principal church of a diocese, containing the bishop's official throne. **b.** (*as modifier*): *a cathedral city.* [C13: < LL (*ecclesia*) *cathedrālis* cathedral (church), < Gk *kathedra* seat]

Catherine wheel (ˈkæθrɪn) *n.* **1.** a firework which rotates, producing sparks and coloured flame. **2.** a circular window having ribs radiating from the centre. [C16: after St *Catherine* of Alexandria, martyred on a spiked wheel, 307 A.D.]

catheter (ˈkæθɪtə) *n. Med.* a long slender flexible tube for inserting into a bodily cavity for introducing or withdrawing fluid. [C17: < LL, < Gk *kathetēr*, < *kathienai* to insert]

catheterize *or* **-ise** (ˈkæθɪtəˌraɪz) *vb.* (*tr.*) to insert a catheter into.

cathexis (kəˈθɛksɪs) *n., pl.* **-thexes** (-ˈθɛksiːz). *Psychoanal.* concentration of psychic energy on a single goal. [C20: < NL, < Gk *kathexis*, < *katekhein* to hold fast]

cathode (ˈkæθəʊd) *n.* **1.** the negative electrode in an electrolytic cell. **2.** the negatively charged electron source in an electronic valve. **3.** the positive terminal of a primary cell. ~Cf. **anode.** [C19: < Gk *kathodos* a descent, < *kata-* down + *hodos* way] —**cathodal** (kæˈθəʊdᵊl) *or* **cathodic** (kæˈθɒdɪk, -ˈθəʊ-) *adj.*

cathode rays *pl. n.* a stream of electrons emitted from the surface of a cathode in a vacuum tube.

cathode-ray tube *n.* a vacuum tube in which a beam of electrons is focused onto a fluorescent screen to give a visible spot of light. The device is used in television receivers, visual display units, etc.

catholic (ˈkæθəlɪk, ˈkæθlɪk) *adj.* **1.** universal; relating to all men. **2.** broad-minded; liberal. [C14: < L, < Gk *katholikos* universal, < *kata-* according to + *holos* whole] —**catholically** *or* **catholicly** (kəˈθɒlɪklɪ) *adv.*

Catholic (ˈkæθəlɪk, ˈkæθlɪk) *Christianity.* ~*adj.* **1.** denoting or relating to the entire body of Christians, esp. to the Church before separation into the Eastern and Western Churches. **2.** denoting or relating to the Latin or Western Church after this separation. **3.** denoting or relating to the Roman Catholic Church. ~*n.* **4.** a member of the Roman Catholic Church.

Catholicism (kəˈθɒlɪˌsɪzəm) *n.* **1.** short for **Roman Catholicism.** **2.** the beliefs, practices, etc., of any Catholic Church.

catholicity (ˌkæθəˈlɪsɪtɪ) *n.* **1.** a wide range of interests, tastes, etc. **2.** comprehensiveness.

catholicize *or* **-cise** (kəˈθɒlɪˌsaɪz) *vb.* **1.** to make or become catholic. **2.** (*often cap.*) to convert to or become converted to Catholicism.

cation (ˈkætaɪən) *n.* a positively charged ion; an ion that is attracted to the cathode during electrolysis. Cf. **anion.** [C19: < CATA- + ION] —**cationic** (ˌkætaɪˈɒnɪk) *adj.*

catkin (ˈkætkɪn) *n.* an inflorescence consisting of a hanging spike of much reduced flowers of either sex: occurs in birch, hazel, etc. [C16: < obs. Du. *katteken* kitten]

cat litter *n.* absorbent material used to line a receptacle in which a domestic cat can urinate and defecate.

catmint (ˈkætˌmɪnt) *n.* a Eurasian plant having spikes of purple-spotted white flowers and scented leaves of which cats are fond. Also called: **catnip.**

catnap (ˈkætˌnæp) *n.* **1.** a short sleep or doze. ~*vb.* **-napping, -napped. 2.** (*intr.*) to sleep or doze for a short time or intermittently.

cat-o'-nine-tails *n., pl.* **-tails.** a rope whip consisting of nine knotted thongs, used formerly to flog prisoners. Often shortened to **cat.**

CAT scanner (kæt) *n.* an x-ray machine that can produce stereoscopic pictures. [C20: < *C*omputerized *A*xial *T*omography]

cat's cradle *n.* a game played by making patterns with a loop of string between the fingers.

Catseye (ˈkætsaɪ) *n. Trademark, Brit.* a glass reflector set into a small fixture, placed at intervals along roads to indicate traffic lanes at night.

cat's-eye *n.* any of a group of gemstones that reflect a streak of light when cut in a rounded unfaceted shape.

cat's-paw *n.* **1.** a person used by another as a tool; dupe. **2.** a pattern of ripples on the surface of water caused by a light wind. [(sense 1) C18: so called from the tale of the monkey who used a cat's paw to draw chestnuts out of a fire]

catsup (ˈkætsəp) *n.* a variant spelling (esp. U.S.) of **ketchup.**

cat's whisker *n.* a pointed wire formerly used to make contact with the crystal in a crystal radio receiver.

cat's whiskers *or* **cat's pyjamas** *n.* **the.** *Sl.* a person or thing that is excellent or superior.

cattery (ˈkætərɪ) *n., pl.* **-teries.** a place where cats are bred or looked after.

cattle (ˈkætᵊl) *n.* (*functioning as pl.*) **1.** bovid mammals of the tribe *Bovini* (bovines). **2.** Also called: **domestic cattle.** any domesticated bovine mammals. [C13: < OF *chatel* CHATTEL]

cattle-cake *n.* concentrated food for cattle in the form of cakes.

cattle-grid *n.* a grid of metal bars covering a hole dug in a roadway intended to prevent the passage of livestock while allowing vehicles, etc., to pass unhindered.

cattleman (ˈkætᵊlmən) *n., pl.* **-men. 1.** a person who breeds, rears, or tends cattle. **2.** *Chiefly U.S. & Canad.* a person who rears cattle on a large scale.

cattle-stop *n.* the New Zealand name for a **cattle-grid.**

catty (ˈkætɪ) *or* **cattish** *adj.* **-tier, -tiest. 1.** *Inf.* spiteful: *a catty remark.* **2.** of or resembling a cat. —ˈ**cattily** *or* ˈ**cattishly** *adv.* —ˈ**cattiness** *or* ˈ**cattishness** *n.*

catwalk (ˈkætˌwɔːk) *n.* a narrow pathway over the stage of a theatre, along a bridge, etc.

Caucasian (kɔːˈkeɪzɪən) *adj.* **1.** another word for **Caucasoid. 2.** of or relating to the Caucasus in the SW Soviet Union. ~*n.* **3.** a member of the Caucasoid race; a White person. **4.** a native or inhabitant of the Caucasus.

Caucasoid (ˈkɔːkəˌzɔɪd) *adj.* **1.** denoting or belonging to the light-complexioned racial group of mankind, which includes the peoples indigenous to Europe, N Africa, SW Asia, and the Indian subcontinent. ~*n.* **2.** a member of this racial group.

caucus (ˈkɔːkəs) *n., pl.* **-cuses. 1.** *Chiefly U.S. & Canad.* a closed meeting of the members of one party in a legislative chamber, etc., to coordinate policy, choose candidates, etc. **2.** *Chiefly U.S.* a local meeting of party members. **3.** *Brit.* a group or faction within a larger group, esp. a political party, who discuss tactics, choose candidates, etc. **4.** *N.Z.* a formal meeting of all MPs of one party. **5.** *Austral.* a group of MPs from one party who meet to discuss tactics, etc. ~*vb.* **6.** (*intr.*) to hold a caucus. [C18: prob. of Algonquian origin]

caudal (ˈkɔːdᵊl) *adj.* **1.** *Anat.* of the posterior part of the body. **2.** *Zool.* resembling or in the position of the tail. [C17: < NL, < L *cauda* tail] —ˈ**caudally** *adv.*

caudal fin *n.* the tail fin of fishes and some other aquatic vertebrates, used for propulsion.

caudate (ˈkɔːdeɪt) *or* **caudated** *adj.* having a tail or a tail-like appendage. [C17: < NL *caudātus*, < L *cauda* tail] —**cauˈdation** *n.*

caudillo (kɔːˈdiːljəʊ) *n., pl.* **-los** (-ljəʊz). (in Spanish-speaking countries) a military or political leader. [Sp., < LL *capitellum*, dim. of L *caput* head]

caudle (ˈkɔːdᵊl) *n.* a hot spiced wine drink made with gruel, formerly used medicinally. [C13: < OF *caudel*, < Med. L, < L *calidus* warm]

caught (kɔːt) *vb.* the past tense and past participle of **catch.**

caul (kɔːl) *n. Anat.* a portion of the amniotic sac sometimes covering a child's head at birth. [C13: < OF *cale*, back formation < *calotte* close-fitting cap, of Gmc origin]

cauldron *or* **caldron** (ˈkɔːldrən) *n.* a large pot used for boiling, esp. one with handles. [C13: < Anglo-F, < L *caldārium* hot bath, < *calidus* warm]

cauliflower (ˈkɒlɪˌflaʊə) *n.* **1.** a variety of cabbage having a large edible head of crowded white flowers on a very short thick stem. **2.** the flower head of this plant, used as a vegetable. [C16: < It. *caoli fiori*, lit.: cabbage flowers]

cauliflower ear *n.* permanent swelling and distortion of the external ear as the result of ruptures of the blood vessels: usually caused by blows received in boxing.

caulk *or* **calk** (kɔːk) *vb.* **1.** to stop up (cracks, crevices, etc.) with a filler. **2.** *Naut.* to pack (the seams) between the planks of the bottom of (a vessel) with waterproof material to prevent leakage. [C15: < OF *cauquer* to press down, < L *calcāre* to trample, < *calx* heel]

causal (ˈkɔːzᵊl) *adj.* **1.** acting as or being a cause. **2.** stating, involving, or implying a cause: *the causal part of the argument.* —ˈ**causally** *adv.*

causality (kɔːˈzælɪtɪ) *n., pl.* **-ties. 1. a.** the relationship of cause and effect. **b.** the principle that nothing can happen without being caused. **2.** causal agency or quality.

causation (kɔːˈzeɪʃən) *n.* **1.** the production of an effect by a cause. **2.** the relationship of cause and effect. —**cauˈsational** *adj.*

causative (ˈkɔːzətɪv) *adj.* **1.** *Grammar.* relating to a form or class of verbs, such as *persuade*, that express causation. **2.** (*often postpositive* and foll. by *of*) producing an effect. ~*n.* **3.** the causative form or class of verbs. —ˈ**causatively** *adv.*

cause (kɔːz) *n.* **1.** a person, thing, event, state, or action that produces an effect. **2.** grounds for action; justification: *she had good cause to shout like that.* **3.** the ideals, etc., of a group or movement: *the Communist cause.* **4.** the welfare or interests of a person or group in a dispute: *they fought for the miners' cause.* **5. a.** a ground for legal action; matter giving rise to a lawsuit. **b.** the lawsuit itself. **6.** *Arch.* a subject of debate or discussion. **7. make common cause with.** to join with (a person, group, etc.) for a common objective. ~*vb.* **8.** (*tr.*) to be the cause of; bring about. [C13: < L *causa* cause, reason, motive] —ˈ**causeless** *adj.*

cause célèbre (ˈkɔːz səˈlɛbrə) *n., pl.* **causes célèbres** (ˈkɔːz səˈlɛbrəz). a famous lawsuit, trial, or controversy. [C19: < F: famous case]

causerie (ˈkəʊzərɪ) *n.* an informal talk or conversational piece of writing. [C19: < F, < *causer* to chat]

causeway (ˈkɔːzˌweɪ) *n.* **1.** a raised path or road crossing water, marshland, etc. **2.** a paved footpath. [C15 *cauciwey* (< *cauci* + WAY); *cauci* paved road, < Med. L, < L *calx* limestone]

caustic (ˈkɔːstɪk) *adj.* **1.** capable of burning or corroding by chemical action: *caustic soda.* **2.** sarcastic; cutting: *a caustic reply.* ~*n.* **3.** Also called: **caustic surface.** a surface that envelops the light rays reflected or refracted by a curved surface. **4.** Also called: **caustic curve.** a curve formed by the intersection of a caustic surface with a plane. **5.** *Chem.* a caustic substance, esp. an alkali. [C14: < L, < Gk *kaustikos*, < *kaiein* to burn] —**ˈcaustically** *adv.* —**causticity** (kɔːˈstɪsɪtɪ) *n.*

caustic potash *n.* another name for **potassium hydroxide.**

caustic soda *n.* another name for **sodium hydroxide.**

cauterize *or* **-ise** (ˈkɔːtəˌraɪz) *vb.* (*tr.*) (esp. in the treatment of a wound) to burn or sear (body tissue) with a hot iron or caustic agent. [C14: < OF, < LL, < *cautērium* branding iron, < Gk *kautērion*, < *kaiein* to burn] —**ˌcauteriˈzation** *or* **-iˈsation** *n.*

cautery (ˈkɔːtərɪ) *n., pl.* **-teries. 1.** the coagulation of blood or destruction of body tissue by cauterizing. **2.** an instrument or agent for cauterizing. [C14: < OF *cautère*, < L *cautērium*]

caution (ˈkɔːʃən) *n.* **1.** care, forethought, or prudence, esp. in the face of danger. **2.** something intended or serving as a warning. **3.** *Law, chiefly Brit.* a formal warning given to a person suspected of an offence that his words will be taken down and may be used in evidence. **4.** *Inf.* an amusing or surprising person or thing. ~*vb.* **5.** (*tr.*) to warn (a person) to be careful. **6.** (*tr.*) *Law, chiefly Brit.* to give a caution to (a person). **7.** (*intr.*) to warn, urge, or advise: *he cautioned against optimism.* [C13: < OF, < L *cautiō*, < *cavēre* to beware]

cautionary (ˈkɔːʃənərɪ) *adj.* serving as a warning; intended to warn: *a cautionary tale.*

cautious (ˈkɔːʃəs) *adj.* showing or having caution. —**ˈcautiously** *adv.* —**ˈcautiousness** *n.*

cavalcade (ˌkævəlˈkeɪd) *n.* **1.** a procession of people on horseback, in cars, etc. **2.** any procession. [C16: < F, < It., < *cavalcare* to ride on horseback, < LL, < *caballus* horse]

cavalier (ˌkævəˈlɪə) *adj.* **1.** supercilious; offhand. ~*n.* **2.** a courtly gentleman, esp. one acting as a lady's escort. **3.** *Arch.* a horseman, esp. one who is armed. [C16: < It., < OProvençal, < LL *caballārius* rider, < *caballus* horse, <?] —**ˌcavaˈlierly** *adv.*

Cavalier (ˌkævəˈlɪə) *n.* a supporter of Charles I during the English Civil War.

cavalry (ˈkævəlrɪ) *n., pl.* **-ries. 1.** (esp. formerly) the part of an army composed of mounted troops. **2.** the armoured element of a modern army. **3.** (*as modifier*): *a cavalry unit.* [C16: < F *cavallerie*, < It., < *cavaliere* horseman] —**ˈcavalryman** *n.*

cavatina (ˌkævəˈtiːnə) *n., pl.* **-ne** (-nɪ). **1.** a simple solo song. **2.** an instrumental composition reminiscent of this. [C19: < It.]

cave[1] (keɪv) *n.* **1.** an underground hollow with access from the ground surface or from the sea. **2.** *Brit. history.* a secession or a group seceding from a political party on some issue. **3.** (*modifier*) living in caves. ~*vb.* **4.** (*tr.*) to hollow out. [C13: < OF, < L *cava*, pl. of *cavum* cavity, < *cavus* hollow]

cave[2] (ˈkeɪvɪ) *Brit. school sl.* ~*n.* **1.** lookout: *keep cave.* ~*sentence substitute.* **2.** watch out! [< L *cavē* beware!]

caveat (ˈkeɪvɪˌæt, ˈkæv-) *n.* **1.** *Law.* a formal notice requesting the court not to take a certain action without warning the person lodging the caveat. **2.** a caution. [C16: < L, lit.: let him beware]

caveat emptor (ˈɛmptɔː) *n.* the principle that the buyer must bear the risk for the quality of goods purchased. [L: let the buyer beware]

cave in *vb.* (*intr., adv.*) **1.** to collapse; subside. **2.** *Inf.* to yield completely, esp. under pressure. ~*n.* **cave-in. 3.** the sudden collapse of a roof, piece of ground, etc. **4.** the site of such a collapse, as at a mine or tunnel.

cavel (ˈkeɪvᵊl) *n. N.Z.* a drawing of lots among miners for an easy and profitable place at the coalface. [C19: < E dialect *cavel* to cast lots, apportion]

caveman (ˈkeɪvˌmæn) *n., pl.* **-men. 1.** a man of the Palaeolithic age; cave dweller. **2.** *Inf.* a man who is primitive or brutal in behaviour, etc.

cavendish (ˈkævəndɪʃ) *n.* tobacco that has been sweetened and pressed into moulds to form bars. [C19: ? from the name of the first maker]

cavern (ˈkævᵊn) *n.* **1.** a cave, esp. when large. ~*vb.* (*tr.*) **2.** to shut in or as if in a cavern. **3.** to hollow out. [C14: < OF *caverne*, < L *caverna*, < *cavus* hollow]

cavernous (ˈkævənəs) *adj.* **1.** suggestive of a cavern in vastness, etc.: *cavernous eyes.* **2.** filled with small cavities. **3.** (of rocks) containing caverns.

caviar *or* **caviare** (ˈkævɪˌɑː, ˌkævɪˈɑː) *n.* the salted roe of sturgeon, usually served as an hors d'oeuvre. [C16: < earlier *cavery*, < OIt. *caviari*, pl. of *caviaro* caviar, < Turkish *havyār*]

cavil (ˈkævɪl) *vb.* **-illing, -illed** *or U.S.* **-iling, -iled. 1.** (*intr.*; foll. by *at* or *about*) to raise annoying petty objections. ~*n.* **2.** a trifling objection. [C16: < OF, < L *cavillārī* to jeer, < *cavilla* raillery] —**ˈcaviller** *n.*

caving (ˈkeɪvɪŋ) *n.* the sport of climbing in and exploring caves. —**ˈcaver** *n.*

cavity (ˈkævɪtɪ) *n., pl.* **-ties. 1.** a hollow space. **2.** *Dentistry.* a decayed area on a tooth. **3.** any empty or hollow space within the body. [C16: < F, < LL *cavitās*, < L *cavus* hollow]

cavity wall *n.* a wall that consists of two separate walls with an airspace between them.

cavort (kəˈvɔːt) *vb.* (*intr.*) to prance; caper. [C19: ? < CURVET] —**caˈvorter** *n.*

cavy (ˈkeɪvɪ) *n., pl.* **-vies.** a small South American rodent having a thickset body and very small tail. See also **guinea pig.** [C18: < NL *Cavia*, < Carib *cabiai*]

caw (kɔː) *n.* **1.** the cry of a crow, rook, or raven. ~*vb.* **2.** (*intr.*) to make this cry. [C16: imit.]

CAWU *abbrev. for* Clerical and Administrative Workers' Union.

cay (keɪ, kiː) *n.* a small low island or bank composed of sand and coral fragments. [C18: < Sp. *cayo*, prob. < OF *quai* QUAY]

cayenne pepper (keɪˈɛn) *n.* a very hot red condiment made from the dried seeds of various capsicums. Often shortened to **cayenne.** Also called: **red pepper.** [C18: ult. < Tupi *quiynha*]

cayman *or* **caiman** (ˈkeɪmən) *n., pl.* **-mans.** a tropical American crocodilian similar to alligators but with a more heavily armoured belly. [C16: < Sp. *caimán*, < Carib *cayman*]

CB *abbrev. for:* **1.** Citizens' Band. **2.** Companion of the (Order of the) Bath (a Brit. title). **3.** County Borough.

CBC *abbrev. for* Canadian Broadcasting Corporation.

CBE *abbrev. for* Commander of the (Order of the) British Empire.

CBI *abbrev. for:* **1.** *U.S.* Central Bureau of Investigation. **2.** Confederation of British Industry.

cc *or* **c.c.** *abbrev. for:* **1.** carbon copy *or* copies. **2.** cubic centimetre(s).

CC *abbrev. for:* **1.** City Council. **2.** County Council. **3.** Cricket Club.

cc. *abbrev. for* chapters.

C clef *n. Music.* a symbol (𝄡), placed at the beginning of the staff, establishing the position of middle C: see **alto clef, soprano clef, tenor clef.**

CCTV *abbrev. for* closed-circuit television.

cd *symbol for* candela.

Cd *the chemical symbol for* cadmium.

CD *abbrev. for:* **1.** Civil Defence (Corps). **2.** compact disc. **3.** Corps Diplomatique (Diplomatic Corps).

CDI *abbrev. for* compact disc interactive.

Cdn *abbrev. for* Canadian.

Cdr *Mil. abbrev. for* Commander.

CD-ROM (-rɒm) *abbrev. for* compact disc read only memory: a compact disc used for storing written information to be displayed on a visual display unit.

CDT (in the U.S. and Canada) *abbrev. for* Central Daylight Time.

CDV *abbrev. for* compact disc video.

Ce *the chemical symbol for* cerium.

CE *abbrev. for:* **1.** Church of England. **2.** civil engineer. **3.** Common Era.

cease (siːs) *vb.* **1.** (when *tr.*, may take a gerund or an infinitive as object) to bring or come to an end. *~n.* **2. without cease.** without stopping. [C14: < OF, < L *cessāre*, frequentative of *cēdere* to yield]

cease-fire *Chiefly mil.* *~n.* **1.** a period of truce, esp. one that is temporary. *~sentence substitute, n.* **2.** the order to stop firing.

ceaseless (ˈsiːslɪs) *adj.* without stop or pause; incessant. —ˈ**ceaselessly** *adv.*

cecum (ˈsiːkəm) *n., pl.* **-ca** (-kə). *U.S.* a variant spelling of **caecum.** —ˈ**cecal** *adj.*

cedar (ˈsiːdə) *n.* **1.** any of a genus of Old World coniferous trees having needle-like evergreen leaves, and erect barrel-shaped cones. See also **cedar of Lebanon, deodar. 2.** any of various other conifers, such as the red cedars and white cedars. **3.** the wood of any of these trees. *~adj.* **4.** made of the wood of a cedar tree. [C13: < OF, < L *cedrus*, < Gk *kedros*]

cedar of Lebanon (ˈlɛbənən) *n.* a cedar of SW Asia with level spreading branches and fragrant wood.

cede (siːd) *vb.* **1.** (when *intr.*, often foll. by *to*) to transfer, make over, or surrender (something, esp. territory or legal rights). **2.** (*tr.*) to allow or concede (a point in an argument, etc.). [C17: < L *cēdere* to yield] —ˈ**ceder** *n.*

cedilla (sɪˈdɪlə) *n.* a character (¸) placed underneath a *c* before *a*, *o*, or *u*, esp. in French, Spanish, or Portuguese, denoting that it is to be pronounced (s), not (k). [C16: < Sp.: little *z*, < *ceda* zed, < LL *zeta*]

Ceefax (ˈsiːfæks) *n. Trademark.* the BBC teletext service.

CEGB (in Britain) *abbrev. for* Central Electricity Generating Board.

ceil (siːl) *vb.* (*tr.*) **1.** to line (a ceiling) with plaster, etc. **2.** to provide with a ceiling. [C15 *celen*, ? back formation < CEILING]

ceilidh (ˈkeɪlɪ) *n.* (esp. in Scotland and Ireland) an informal social gathering with singing, dancing, and storytelling. [C19: < Gaelic]

ceiling (ˈsiːlɪŋ) *n.* **1.** the inner upper surface of a room. **2.** an upper limit, such as one set by regulation on prices or wages. **3.** the upper altitude to which an aircraft can climb measured under specified conditions. **4.** *Meteorol.* the highest level in the atmosphere from which the earth's surface is visible at a particular time, usually the base of a cloud layer. [C14: <?]

celadon (ˈsɛləˌdɒn) *n.* **1.** a type of porcelain having a greyish-green glaze: mainly Chinese. **2. a.** a pale greyish-green colour. **b.** (*as adj.*): *a celadon jar.* [C18: < F, < the name of the shepherd hero of *L'Astrée* (1610), a romance by Honoré d'Urfé]

celandine (ˈsɛlənˌdaɪn) *n.* either of two unrelated plants, **greater celandine** or **lesser celandine,** with yellow flowers. [C13: earlier *celydon*, < L, < Gk *khelidōn* swallow; the plant's season was believed to parallel the migration of swallows]

-cele *n. combining form.* tumour or hernia: *hydrocele.* [< Gk *kēlē* tumour]

celebrant (ˈsɛlɪbrənt) *n.* a person participating in a religious ceremony, esp. at the Eucharist.

celebrate (ˈsɛlɪˌbreɪt) *vb.* **1.** to rejoice in or have special festivities to mark (a happy day, event, etc.). **2.** (*tr.*) to observe (a birthday, anniversary, etc.). **3.** (*tr.*) to perform (a solemn or religious ceremony), esp. to officiate at (Mass). **4.** (*tr.*) to praise publicly; proclaim. [C15: < L, < *celeber* numerous, renowned] —ˌ**celeˈbration** *n.* —ˈ**celeˌbrator** *n.* —ˈ**celeˌbratory** *adj.*

celebrated (ˈsɛlɪˌbreɪtɪd) *adj.* (*usually prenominal*) famous: *a celebrated pianist.*

celebrity (sɪˈlɛbrɪtɪ) *n., pl.* **-ties. 1.** a famous person. **2.** fame or notoriety.

celeriac (sɪˈlɛrɪˌæk) *n.* a variety of celery with a large turnip-like root, used as a vegetable. [C18: < CELERY + *-ac*, <?]

celerity (sɪˈlɛrɪtɪ) *n.* rapidity; swiftness; speed. [C15: < OF *celerite*, < L *celeritās*, < *celer* swift]

celery (ˈsɛlərɪ) *n.* **1.** an umbelliferous Eurasian plant whose blanched leafstalks are used in salads or cooked as a vegetable. **2. wild celery.** a related and similar plant. [C17: < F *céleri*, < It. (Lombardy) dialect *selleri* (pl.), < Gk *selinon* parsley]

celesta (sɪˈlɛstə) *or* **celeste** (sɪˈlɛst) *n. Music.* a keyboard percussion instrument consisting of a set of steel plates of graduated length that are struck with key-operated hammers. [C19: < F, Latinized var. of *céleste* heavenly]

celestial (sɪˈlɛstɪəl) *adj.* **1.** heavenly; divine: *celestial peace.* **2.** of or relating to the sky: *celestial bodies.* **3.** of or connected with the celestial sphere: *celestial pole.* [C14: < Med. L, < L *caelestis*, < *caelum* heaven] —**ceˈlestially** *adv.*

celestial equator *n.* the great circle lying on the celestial sphere the plane of which is perpendicular to the line joining the north and south celestial poles. Also called: **equinoctial, equinoctial circle.**

celestial sphere *n.* an imaginary sphere of infinitely large radius enclosing the universe so that all celestial bodies appear to be projected onto its surface.

celiac (ˈsiːlɪˌæk) *adj. Anat.* the usual U.S. spelling of **coeliac.**

celibate (ˈsɛlɪbɪt) *n.* **1.** a person who is unmarried, esp. one who has taken a religious vow of chastity. *~adj.* **2.** unmarried. [C17: < L, < *caelebs* unmarried, <?] —ˈ**celibacy** *n.*

cell (sɛl) *n.* **1.** a small simple room, as in a prison, convent, etc. **2.** any small compartment: *the cells of a honeycomb.* **3.** *Biol.* the smallest unit of an organism that is able to function independently. It consists of a nucleus, containing the genetic material, surrounded by the cytoplasm. **4.** *Biol.* any small cavity, such as the cavity containing pollen in an anther. **5.** a device for converting chemical energy into electrical energy, usually consisting of a container with two electrodes immersed in an electrolyte. See also **dry cell, fuel cell. 6.** in full **electrolytic cell.** a device in which electrolysis occurs. **7.** a small religious house dependent upon a larger one. **8.** a small group of persons operating as a nucleus of a larger organization: *Communist cell.* [C12: < Med. L *cella* monk's cell, < L: room, storeroom]

cellar (ˈsɛlə) *n.* **1.** an underground room, or storey of a building, usually used for storage. **2.** a place where wine is stored. **3.** a stock of bottled wines. *~vb.* **4.** (*tr.*) to store in a cellar. [C13: < Anglo-F, < L *cellārium* foodstore, < *cella* cell]

cellarage (ˈsɛlərɪdʒ) *n.* **1.** an area of a cellar. **2.** a charge for storing goods in a cellar, etc.

cellarer (ˈsɛlərə) *n.* a monastic official responsible for food, drink, etc.

cellaret (ˌsɛləˈrɛt) *n.* a cabinet or sideboard with compartments for holding wine bottles.

Cellnet (ˈsɛlˌnɛt) *n. Trademark.* a British Telecom car phone.

cello (ˈtʃɛləʊ) *n., pl.* **-los.** *Music.* a bowed stringed instrument of the violin family. It has four strings, is held between the knees, and has a metal spike at the lower end, which acts as a support. Full name: **violoncello.** —ˈ**cellist** *n.*

Cellophane (ˈsɛləˌfeɪn) *n. Trademark.* a flexible thin transparent sheeting made from wood pulp and used as a moisture-proof wrapping. [C20: < CELLULOSE + -PHANE]

cellphone (ˈsɛlˌfəʊn) *n.* a portable telephone operated by cellular radio. In full: **cellular telephone.**

cellular (ˈsɛljʊlə) *adj.* **1.** of, relating to, or resembling a cell. **2.** consisting of or having cells or small cavities; porous. **3.** *Textiles.* woven with an open texture: *a cellular blanket.* **4** designed for or involving cellular radio.

cellular radio *n.* radio communication based on a network of transmitters each serving a small area known as a 'cell': used esp. in car phones in which the receiver switches frequencies automatically as it passes from one cell to another.

cellule (ˈsɛljuːl) *n.* a very small cell. [C17: < L *cellula*, dim. of *cella* CELL]

cellulite (ˈsɛljʊˌlaɪt) *n.* subcutaneous fat alleged to resist dieting.

cellulitis (ˌsɛljʊˈlaɪtɪs) *n.* inflammation of body tissue, with fever, pain, and swelling. [C19: < L *cellula* CELLULE + -ITIS]

celluloid (ˈsɛljʊˌlɔɪd) *n.* **1.** a flammable material consisting of cellulose nitrate and camphor: used in sheets, rods, etc. **2. a.** a cellulose derivative used for coating film. **b.** cinema film.

cellulose (ˈsɛljʊˌləʊz, -ˌləʊs) *n.* a substance which is the main constituent of plant cell walls and used in making paper, rayon, and film. [C18: < F *cellule* cell (see CELLULE) + -OSE[2]]

cellulose acetate *n.* nonflammable material used in the manufacture of film, dopes, lacquers, and artificial fibres.

cellulose nitrate *n.* cellulose treated with nitric and sulphuric acids, used in plastics, lacquers, and explosives. See also **guncotton.**

Celsius (ˈsɛlsɪəs) *adj.* denoting a measurement on the Celsius scale. Symbol: C [C18: after Anders *Celsius* (1701–44), Swedish astronomer who invented it]

Celsius scale *n.* a scale of temperature in which 0° represents the melting point of ice and 100° represents the boiling point of water. Also called: **centigrade scale.** Cf. **Fahrenheit scale.**

celt (sɛlt) *n. Archaeol.* a stone or metal axelike instrument. [C18: < LL *celtes* chisel, <?]

Celt (kɛlt, sɛlt) *or* **Kelt** *n.* **1.** a person who speaks a Celtic language. **2.** a member of an Indo-European people who in pre-Roman times inhabited Britain, Gaul, and Spain.

Celtic (ˈkɛltɪk, ˈsɛl-) *or* **Keltic** *n.* **1.** a branch of the Indo-European family of languages that includes Gaelic, Welsh, and Breton. Modern Celtic is divided into the Brythonic (southern) and Goidelic (northern) groups. ~*adj.* **2.** of, relating to, or characteristic of the Celts or the Celtic languages. —**Celticism** (ˈkɛltɪˌsɪzəm, ˈsɛl-) *or* **ˈKeltiˌcism** *n.*

Celtic cross *n.* a Latin cross with a broad ring surrounding the point of intersection.

cembalo (ˈtʃɛmbələʊ) *n., pl.* **-li** (-lɪ) *or* **-los.** another word for **harpsichord.** [C19: < It. *clavicembalo* < Med. L *clāvis* key + *cymbalum* CYMBAL]

cement (sɪˈmɛnt) *n.* **1.** a fine grey powder made of a mixture of limestone and clay, used with water and sand to make mortar, or with water, sand, and aggregate, to make concrete. **2.** a binder, glue, or adhesive. **3.** something that unites or joins. **4.** *Dentistry.* any of various materials used in filling teeth. **5.** another word for **cementum.** ~*vb.* (*tr.*) **6.** to join, bind, or glue together with or as if with cement. **7.** to coat or cover with cement. [C13: < OF, < L *caementum* stone from the quarry, < *caedere* to hew]

cementum (sɪˈmɛntəm) *n.* a thin bonelike tissue that covers the dentine in the root of a tooth. [C19: NL, < L: CEMENT]

cemetery (ˈsɛmɪtrɪ) *n., pl.* **-teries.** a place where the dead are buried, esp. one not attached to a church. [C14: < LL, < Gk *koimētērion*, < *koiman* to put to sleep]

-cene *n. and adj. combining form.* denoting a recent geological period. [< Gk *kainos* new]

cenobite (ˈsiːnəʊˌbaɪt) *n.* a variant spelling of **coenobite.**

cenotaph (ˈsɛnəˌtɑːf) *n.* a monument honouring a dead person or persons buried elsewhere. [C17: < L, < Gk, < *kenos* empty + *taphos* tomb]

Cenozoic, Caenozoic (ˌsiːnəʊˈzəʊɪk), *or* **Cainozoic** *adj.* **1.** of, denoting, or relating to the most recent geological era characterized by the development and increase of the mammals. ~*n.* **2. the.** the Cenozoic era. [C19: < Gk *kainos* recent + *zōikos*, < *zōion* animal]

censer (ˈsɛnsə) *n.* a container for burning incense. Also called: **thurible.**

censor (ˈsɛnsə) *n.* **1.** a person authorized to examine publications, films, letters, etc., in order to suppress in whole or part those considered obscene, politically unacceptable, etc. **2.** any person who controls or suppresses the behaviour of others, usually on moral grounds. **3.** (in republican Rome) either of two senior magistrates elected to keep the list of citizens up to date, and supervise public morals. **4.** *Psychoanal.* the postulated factor responsible for regulating the translation of ideas and desires from the unconscious to the conscious mind. ~*vb.* (*tr.*) **5.** to ban or cut portions of (a film, letter, etc.). **6.** to act as a censor of (behaviour, etc.). [C16: < L, < *cēnsēre* to consider] —**censorial** (sɛnˈsɔːrɪəl) *adj.*

censorious (sɛnˈsɔːrɪəs) *adj.* harshly critical; fault-finding. —**cenˈsoriously** *adv.*

censorship (ˈsɛnsəˌʃɪp) *n.* **1.** a policy or programme of censoring. **2.** the act or system of censoring.

censure (ˈsɛnʃə) *n.* **1.** severe disapproval. ~*vb.* **2.** to criticize (someone or something) severely. [C14: < L *cēnsūra*, < *cēnsēre*: see CENSOR] —**ˈcensurable** *adj.*

census (ˈsɛnsəs) *n., pl.* **-suses.** **1.** an official periodic count of a population including such information as sex, age, occupation, etc. **2.** any official count: *a traffic census.* **3.** (in ancient Rome) a registration of the population and a property evaluation for taxation. [C17: < L, < *cēnsēre* to assess]

cent (sɛnt) *n.* a monetary unit of Australia, Barbados, Botswana, Canada, Hong Kong, Kenya, Malaysia, New Zealand, Singapore, South Africa, Tanzania, Trinidad and Tobago, Uganda, the United States, etc. It is worth one hundredth of their respective standard units. [C16: < L *centēsimus* hundredth, < *centum* hundred]

cent. *abbrev. for:* **1.** centigrade. **2.** central. **3.** century.

centaur (ˈsɛntɔː) *n. Greek myth.* one of a race of creatures with the head, arms, and torso of a man, and the lower body and legs of a horse. [C14: < L, < Gk *kentauros*, <?]

centaurea (sɛntɔːˈrɪə, sɛnˈtɔːrɪə) *n.* any plant of the genus *Centaurea* which includes the cornflower and knapweed. [C19: ult. < Gk *Kentauros* the Centaur; see CENTAURY]

centaury (ˈsɛntɔːrɪ) *n., pl.* **-ries.** **1.** any of a genus of Eurasian plants having purplish-pink flowers and formerly believed to have medicinal properties. **2.** another name for **centaurea.** [C14: ult. < Gk *Kentauros* the Centaur; from the legend that Chiron the Centaur divulged its healing properties]

centavo (sɛnˈtɑːvəʊ) *n., pl.* **-vos.** a monetary unit of Argentina, Brazil, Colombia, Ecuador, El Salvador, Mexico, Nicaragua, Peru, the Philippines, Portugal, etc. It is worth one hundredth of their respective standard units. [Sp.: one hundredth part]

centenarian (ˌsɛntɪˈnɛərɪən) *n.* **1.** a person who is at least 100 years old. ~*adj.* **2.** being at least 100 years old. **3.** of or relating to a centenarian.

centenary (sɛnˈtiːnərɪ) *adj.* **1.** of or relating to a period of 100 years. **2.** occurring once every 100 years. ~*n., pl.* **-naries.** **3.** a 100th anniversary or its celebration. [C17: < L, < *centēnī* a hundred each, < *centum* hundred]

centennial (sɛnˈtɛnɪəl) *adj.* **1.** relating to or completing a period of 100 years. **2.** occurring every 100 years. ~*n.* **3.** *U.S. & Canad.* another name for **centenary.** [C18: < L *centum* hundred, on the model of BIENNIAL]

center (ˈsɛntə) *n., vb.* the U.S. spelling of **centre.**

centesimal (sɛnˈtɛsɪməl) *n.* **1.** hundredth. ~*adj.* **2.** relating to division into hundredths. [C17: < L, < *centum* hundred] —**cenˈtesimally** *adv.*

centesimo (sɛnˈtɛsɪˌməʊ) *n., pl.* **-mos.** a monetary unit of Chile, Italy, etc. It is worth one hundredth of their respective standard units. [C19: < Sp. & It., < L, < *centum* hundred]

centi- *or before a vowel* **cent-** *prefix.* **1.** denoting one hundredth: *centimetre.* Symbol: c **2.** *Rare.* denoting a hundred: *centipede.* [< F, < L *centum* hundred]

centiare (ˈsɛntɪˌɛə) *or* **centare** (ˈsɛntɛə) *n.* a unit of area equal to one square metre. [F, < CENTI- + *are* < L *ārea*]

centigrade (ˈsɛntɪˌgreɪd) *adj.* **1.** another name for **Celsius.** ~*n.* **2.** a unit of angle equal to one hundredth of a grade.

▷ **Usage.** *Centigrade*, when indicating the Celsius scale of temperature, is now usually avoided in scientific contexts because of possible confusion with the hundredth part of a grade.

centigram *or* **centigramme** (ˈsɛntɪˌgræm) *n.* one hundredth of a gram.

centilitre *or U.S.* **centiliter** (ˈsɛntɪˌliːtə) *n.* one hundredth of a litre.

centime (ˈsɒnˌtiːm; *French* sɑ̃tim) *n.* a monetary unit of Algeria, Belgium, the Central African Republic, France, Guinea, Haiti, Liechtenstein, Luxembourg, Mali, Mauritania, Switzerland, Tahiti, Togo, etc. It is worth one hundredth of their respective standard units. [C18: < F, < OF, < L, < *centum* hundred]

centimetre *or U.S.* **centimeter** (ˈsɛntɪˌmiːtə) *n.* one hundredth of a metre.

centimetre-gram-second *n.* See **cgs units.**

céntimo (ˈsɛntɪˌməʊ) *n., pl.* **-mos.** a monetary unit of Costa Rica, Spain, Venezuela, etc. It is worth one hundredth of their respective standard currency units. [< Sp.; see CENTIME]

centipede (ˈsɛntɪˌpiːd) *n.* a carnivorous arthropod having a body of between 15 and 190 segments, each bearing one pair of legs.

cento (ˈsɛntəʊ) *n., pl.* **-tos.** a piece of writing, esp. a poem, composed of quotations from other authors. [C17: < L, lit.: patchwork garment]

CENTO (ˈsɛntəʊ) *n. acronym for* Central Treaty Organization; an organization for military and economic cooperation formed in 1959 by the U.K., Iran, Pakistan, and Turkey: disbanded 1979.

central (ˈsɛntrəl) *adj.* **1.** in, at, of, from, containing, or forming the centre of something: *the central street in a city.* **2.** main, principal, or chief: *the central cause of a problem.* —**centrality** (sɛnˈtrælɪtɪ) *n.* —**ˈcentrally** *adv.*

central bank *n.* a national bank that does business mainly with a government and with other banks: it regulates the volume of credit.

central heating *n.* a system for heating the rooms of a building by means of radiators or air vents connected to a central source of heat.

centralism (ˈsɛntrəˌlɪzəm) *n.* the principle or act of bringing something under central control. —**ˈcentralist** *n., adj.*

centralize *or* **-lise** (ˈsɛntrəˌlaɪz) *vb.* **1.** to draw or move (something) to or towards a centre. **2.** to bring or come under central, esp. governmental, control. —**ˌcentraliˈzation** *or* **-liˈsation** *n.*

central limit theorem *n. Statistics.* the fundamental result that the sum of independent identically distributed random variables with finite variance approaches a normally distributed random variable as their number increases.

central nervous system *n.* the mass of nerve tissue that controls and coordinates the activities of an animal. In vertebrates it consists of the brain and spinal cord.

central processing unit *n.* the part of a computer that performs logical and arithmetical operations on the data. Abbrev.: **CPU.**

central reserve *or* **reservation** *n. Brit.* the strip, often covered with grass, that separates the two sides of a motorway or dual carriageway.

central tendency *n. Statistics.* the tendency of the values of a random variable to cluster around the mean, median, and mode.

centre *or U.S.* **center** (ˈsɛntə) *n.* **1.** *Geom.* **a.** the midpoint of any line or figure, esp. the point within a circle or sphere that is equidistant from any point on the circumference or surface. **b.** the point within a body through which a specified force may be considered to act, such as the centre of gravity. **2.** the point, axis, or pivot about which a body rotates. **3.** a point, area, or part that is approximately in the middle of a larger area or volume. **4.** a place at which some specified activity is concentrated: *a shopping centre.* **5.** a person or thing that is a focus of interest. **6.** a place of activity or influence: *a centre of power.* **7.** a person, group, or thing in the middle. **8.** (*usually cap.*) *Politics.* a political party or group favouring moderation. **9.** a bar with a conical point upon which a workpiece or part may be turned or ground. **10.** *Football, hockey, etc.* **a.** a player who plays in the middle of the forward line. **b.** an instance of passing the ball from a wing to the middle of the field, etc. ~*vb.* **11.** to move towards, mark, put, or be at a centre. **12.** (*tr.*) to focus or bring together: *to centre one's thoughts.* **13.** (*intr.;* often foll. by *on*) to have as a main theme: *the novel centred on crime.* **14.** (*intr.;* foll. by *on* or *round*) to have as a centre. **15.** (*tr.*) *Football, hockey, etc.* to pass (the ball) into the middle of the field or court. [C14: < L *centrum* the stationary point of a compass, < Gk *kentron* needle, < *kentein* to prick]

▷ **Usage.** *To centre round* is considered illogical by many writers and speakers, who prefer the more precise phrase *to centre on.*

Centre (ˈsɛntə) *n.* **the.** the sparsely inhabited central region of Australia. Also called: **Centralia** (arch.), **the Red Centre.**

centre bit *n.* a drilling bit with a central point and two side cutters.

centreboard (ˈsɛntəˌbɔːd) *n.* a supplementary keel for a sailing vessel.

centrefold *or U.S.* **centerfold** (ˈsɛntəˌfəʊld) *n.* a large coloured illustration folded so that it forms the central spread of a magazine.

centre forward *n. Soccer, hockey, etc.* the central forward in the attack.

centre half *or* **centre back** *n. Soccer.* a defender who plays in the middle of the defence.

centre of gravity *n.* the point through which the resultant of the gravitational forces on a body always acts.

centrepiece (ˈsɛntəˌpiːs) *n.* an object used as the centre of something, esp. for decoration.

centre spread *n.* the pair of two facing pages in the middle of a magazine, newspaper, etc.

centri- *combining form.* a variant of **centro-.**

centric (ˈsɛntrɪk) *or* **centrical** *adj.* **1.** being central or having a centre. **2.** relating to a nerve centre. —**centricity** (sɛnˈtrɪsɪtɪ) *n.*

-centric *suffix forming adjectives.* having a centre as specified: *heliocentric.* [abstracted < ECCENTRIC, CONCENTRIC, etc.]

centrifugal (sɛnˈtrɪfjʊgᵊl, ˈsɛntrɪˌfjuːgᵊl) *adj.* **1.** acting, moving, or tending to move away from a centre. Cf. **centripetal. 2.** of, concerned with, or operated by centrifugal force: *centrifugal pump.* [C18: < NL, < CENTRI- + L *fugere* to flee] —**cenˈtrifugally** *adv.*

centrifugal force *n.* a force that acts outwards on any body that rotates or moves along a curved path.

centrifuge (ˈsɛntrɪˌfjuːdʒ) *n.* **1.** any of various rotating machines that separate liquids from solids or other liquids by the action of centrifugal force. **2.** any of various rotating devices for subjecting human beings or animals to varying accelerations. ~*vb.* **3.** (*tr.*) to subject to the action of a centrifuge. —**centrifugation** (ˌsɛntrɪfjʊˈgeɪʃən) *n.*

centring (ˈsɛntrɪŋ) *or U.S.* **centering** (ˈsɛntərɪŋ) *n.* a temporary structure, esp. one made of timber, used to support an arch during construction.

centripetal (sɛnˈtrɪpɪtᵊl, ˈsɛntrɪˌpiːtᵊl) *adj.* **1.** acting, moving, or tending to move towards a centre. Cf. **centrifugal. 2.** of, concerned with, or operated by centripetal force. [C17: < NL *centripetus* seeking the centre] —**cenˈtripetally** *adv.*

centripetal force *n.* a force that acts inwards on any body that rotates or moves along a curved path.

centrist (ˈsɛntrɪst) *n.* a person holding moderate political views. —**ˈcentrism** *n.*

centro-, centri-, *or before a vowel* **centr-** *combining form.* denoting a centre: *centrosome; centrist.* [< Gk *kentron* CENTRE]

centrosome (ˈsɛntrəˌsəʊm) *n.* a small protoplasmic body found near the cell nucleus.

centuplicate *vb.* (sɛnˈtjuːplɪˌkeɪt). **1.** (*tr.*) to increase 100 times. ~*adj.* (sɛnˈtjuːplɪkɪt). **2.** increased a hundredfold. ~*n.* (sɛnˈtjuːplɪkɪt). **3.** one hundredfold. ~Also **centuple** (ˈsɛntjʊpᵊl).

[C17: < LL, < *centuplex* hundredfold, < L *centum* hundred + *-plex* -fold]

centurion (sɛn'tjʊərɪən) *n.* the officer commanding a Roman century. [C14: < L *centuriō*, < *centuria* CENTURY]

century ('sɛntʃərɪ) *n., pl.* **-ries. 1.** a period of 100 years. **2.** one of the successive periods of 100 years dated before or after an epoch or event, esp. the birth of Christ. **3.** a score or grouping of 100: *to score a century in cricket.* **4.** (in ancient Rome) a unit of foot soldiers, originally consisting of 100 men. **5.** (in ancient Rome) a division of the people for purposes of voting. [C16: < L *centuria*, < *centum* hundred]

▷ **Usage.** In strict usage, the dating of any century begins with a year ending -01 and ends with a year ending -00: *the nineteenth century covers the years 1801 to 1900.* This is because the system of dating by *A.D.* is based on the supposed year in which Christ was born, so that it begins with A.D. 1. In popular practice, however, the dating of a century is often moved back by one year so that it includes all the years starting with the same number: *the nineteenth century covers the years 1800 to 1899.*

cep (sɛp) *n.* an edible woodland fungus with a brown shining cap and a rich nutty flavour. [C19: < F, < Gascon dialect *cep*, < L *cippus* stake]

cephalic (sɪ'fælɪk) *adj.* **1.** of or relating to the head. **2.** situated in, on, or near the head.

-cephalic *or* **-cephalous** *adj. combining form.* indicating skull or head; -headed: *brachycephalic.* [< Gk *-kephalos*] **—-cephaly** *or* **-cephalism** *n. combining form.*

cephalic index *n.* the ratio of the greatest width of the human head to its greatest length, multiplied by 100.

cephalo- *or before a vowel* **cephal-** *combining form.* indicating the head: *cephalopod.* [via L < Gk, < *kephate* head]

cephalopod ('sɛfələˌpɒd) *n.* any of various marine molluscs, characterized by well-developed head and eyes and a ring of sucker-bearing tentacles, including the octopuses, squids, and cuttlefish. **—ˌcepha'lopodan** *adj., n.*

cephalothorax (ˌsɛfələʊ'θɔːræks) *n., pl.* **-raxes** *or* **-races** (-rəˌsiːz). the anterior part of many crustaceans and some other arthropods consisting of a united head and thorax.

-cephalus *n. combining form.* denoting a cephalic abnormality: *hydrocephalus.* [NL *-cephalus;* see -CEPHALIC]

Cepheid variable ('siːfɪɪd) *n. Astron.* any of a class of variable stars with regular cycles of variations in luminosity, which are used for measuring distances.

ceramic (sɪ'ræmɪk) *n.* **1.** a hard brittle material made by firing clay and similar substances. **2.** an object made from such a material. ~*adj.* **3.** of or made from a ceramic. **4.** of or relating to ceramics: *ceramic arts.* [C19: < Gk, < *keramos* potter's clay]

ceramic hob *n.* (on an electric cooker) a flat ceramic cooking surface having heating elements fitted on the underside.

ceramic oxide *n.* a compound of oxygen with nonorganic material: recently discovered to act as a high-temperature superconductor.

ceramics (sɪ'ræmɪks) *n.* (*functioning as sing.*) the art and techniques of producing articles of clay, porcelain, etc. **—ceramist** ('sɛrəmɪst) *n.*

cere (sɪə) *n.* a soft waxy swelling, containing the nostrils, at the base of the upper beak, as in the parrot. [C15: < OF *cire* wax, < L *cēra*]

cereal ('sɪərɪəl) *n.* **1.** any grass that produces an edible grain, such as oat, wheat, rice, maize, and millet. **2.** the grain produced by such a plant. **3.** any food made from this grain, esp. breakfast food. **4.** (*modifier*) of or relating to any of these plants or their products. [C19: < L *cereālis* concerning agriculture]

cerebellum (ˌsɛrɪ'bɛləm) *n., pl.* **-lums** *or* **-la** (-lə). one of the major divisions of the vertebrate brain whose function is coordination of voluntary movements. [C16: < L, dim. of CEREBRUM]

cerebral ('sɛrɪbrəl; *U.S. also* sə'riːbrəl) *adj.* **1.** of or relating to the cerebrum or to the entire brain. **2.** involving intelligence rather than emotions or instinct. **3.** *Phonetics.* another word for **cacuminal.** **—'cerebrally** *adv.*

cerebral palsy *n.* an impairment of muscular function and weakness of the limbs, caused by damage to the brain before or during birth.

cerebrate ('sɛrɪˌbreɪt) *vb.* (*intr.*) *Usually facetious.* to use the mind; think; ponder; consider. **—ˌcere'bration** *n.*

cerebro- *or before a vowel* **cerebr-** *combining form.* indicating the brain: *cerebrospinal.* [< CEREBRUM]

cerebrospinal (ˌsɛrɪbrəʊ'spaɪnᵊl) *adj.* of or relating to the brain and spinal cord: *cerebrospinal fluid.*

cerebrovascular (ˌsɛrɪbrəʊ'væskjʊlə) *adj.* of or relating to the blood vessels and the blood supply of the brain.

cerebrum ('sɛrɪbrəm) *n., pl.* **-brums** *or* **-bra** (-brə). **1.** the anterior portion of the brain of vertebrates, consisting of two lateral hemispheres: the dominant part of the brain in man, associated with intellectual function, emotion, and personality. **2.** the brain considered as a whole. [C17: < L: the brain] **—'cerebric** *adj.*

cerecloth ('sɪəˌklɒθ) *n.* waxed waterproof cloth of a kind formerly used as a shroud. [C15: < earlier *cered cloth*, < L *cērāre* to wax]

cerement ('sɪəmənt) *n.* **1.** cerecloth. **2.** any burial clothes. [C17: < F, < *cirer* to wax]

ceremonial (ˌsɛrɪ'məʊnɪəl) *adj.* **1.** involving or relating to ceremony or ritual. ~*n.* **2.** the observance of formality, esp. in etiquette. **3.** a plan for formal observances; ritual. **4.** *Christianity.* **a.** the prescribed order of rites and ceremonies. **b.** a book containing this. **—ˌcere'monialism** *n.* **—ˌcere'monialist** *n.* **—ˌcere'monially** *adv.*

ceremonious (ˌsɛrɪ'məʊnɪəs) *adj.* **1.** especially or excessively polite or formal. **2.** involving formalities. **—ˌcere'moniously** *adv.*

ceremony ('sɛrɪmənɪ) *n., pl.* **-nies. 1.** a formal act or ritual, often set by custom or tradition, performed in observation of an event or anniversary. **2.** a religious rite or series of rites. **3.** a courteous gesture or act: *the ceremony of toasting the Queen.* **4.** ceremonial observances or gestures collectively. **5. stand on ceremony.** to insist on or act with excessive formality. [C14: < Med. L, < L *caerimōnia* what is sacred]

cerise (sə'riːz, -'riːs) *n., adj.* (of) a moderate to dark red colour. [C19: < F: CHERRY]

cerium ('sɪərɪəm) *n.* a malleable ductile steel-grey element of the lanthanide series of metals, used in lighter flints. Symbol: Ce; atomic no.: 58; atomic wt.: 140.12. [C19: NL, < *Ceres* (the asteroid) + -IUM]

cermet ('sɜːmɪt) *n.* any of several materials consisting of a metal and ceramic particles. They are hard and resistant to high temperatures. [C20: < CER(AMIC) + MET(AL)]

CERN (sɜːn) *n. acronym for* Conseil Européen pour la Recherche Nucléaire; an organization of European states with a centre in Geneva, for research in high-energy particle physics.

cerography (sɪə'rɒgrəfɪ) *n.* the art of engraving on a waxed plate on which a printing surface is created by electrotyping.

ceroplastic (ˌsɪərəʊ'plæstɪk) *adj.* **1.** relating to wax modelling. **2.** modelled in wax.

cert (sɜːt) *n. Inf.* something that is a certainty, esp. a horse that is certain to win a race.

cert. *abbrev. for:* **1.** certificate. **2.** certification. **3.** certified.

certain ('sɜːtᵊn) *adj.* **1.** (*postpositive*) positive and confident about the truth of something; convinced: *I am certain that he wrote a book.* **2.** (*usually postpositive*) definitely known: *it is certain that they were on the bus.* **3.** (*usually postpositive*) sure; bound: *he was certain to fail.* **4.** fixed: *the date is already certain for the invasion.* **5.** reliable: *his judgment is certain.* **6.** moderate or minimum: *to a certain extent.* **7. for**

certain. without a doubt. ~*determiner.* **8. a.** known but not specified or named: *certain people.* **b.** (*as pron.; functioning as pl.*): *certain of the members have not paid.* **9.** named but not known: *he had written to a certain Mrs Smith.* [C13: < OF, < L *certus* sure, < *cernere* to decide]

certainly (ˈsɜːtᵊnlɪ) *adv.* **1.** without doubt: *he certainly rides very well.* ~ *sentence substitute.* **2.** by all means; definitely.

certainty (ˈsɜːtᵊntɪ) *n., pl.* **-ties. 1.** the condition of being certain. **2.** something established as inevitable. **3. for a certainty.** without doubt.

CertEd (in Britain) *abbrev. for* Certificate in Education.

certes (ˈsɜːtɪz) *adv. Arch.* with certainty; truly. [C13: < OF, ult. < L *certus* CERTAIN]

certificate *n.* (səˈtɪfɪkɪt). **1.** an official document attesting the truth of the facts stated, as of birth, death, completion of an academic course, etc. **2.** short for **share certificate.** ~*vb.* (səˈtɪfɪˌkeɪt). **3.** (*tr.*) to authorize by or present with an official document. [C15: < OF, < *certifier* to CERTIFY] —**cerˈtificatory** *adj.*

Certificate of Secondary Education *n.* the full name for **CSE.**

certification (ˌsɜːtɪfɪˈkeɪʃən) *n.* **1.** the act of certifying or state of being certified. **2.** *Law.* a document attesting the truth of a fact or statement.

certified (ˈsɜːtɪˌfaɪd) *adj.* **1.** holding or guaranteed by a certificate. **2.** endorsed or guaranteed: *a certified cheque.* **3.** (of a person) declared legally insane.

certify (ˈsɜːtɪˌfaɪ) *vb.* **-fying, -fied. 1.** to confirm or attest (to), usually in writing. **2.** (*tr.*) to endorse or guarantee that certain required standards have been met. **3.** to give reliable information or assurances: *he certified that it was Walter's handwriting.* **4.** (*tr.*) to declare legally insane. [C14: < OF, < Med. L, < L *certus* CERTAIN + *facere* to make] —**ˈcertiˌfiable** *adj.*

certiorari (ˌsɜːtɪɔːˈrɛəraɪ) *n. Law.* an order of a superior court directing that a record of proceedings in a lower court be sent up for review. [C15: < legal L: to be informed]

certitude (ˈsɜːtɪˌtjuːd) *n.* confidence; certainty. [C15: < Church L *certitūdō*, < L *certus* CERTAIN]

cerulean (sɪˈruːlɪən) *n., adj.* (of) a deep blue colour. [C17: < L *caeruleus*, prob. < *caelum* sky]

cerumen (sɪˈruːmɛn) *n.* the soft brownish-yellow wax secreted by glands in the external ear. Nontechnical name: **earwax.** [C18: < NL, < L *cēra* wax + ALBUMEN] —**ceˈruminous** *adj.*

cervelat (ˈsɜːvəˌlæt, -ˌlɑː) *n.* a smoked sausage made from pork and beef. [C17: via obs. F < It. *cervellata*]

cervical (səˈvaɪkᵊl, ˈsɜːvɪkᵊl) *adj.* of or relating to the neck or cervix. [C17: < NL, < L *cervīx* neck]

cervical smear *n. Med.* a smear taken from the neck (cervix) of the uterus for detection of cancer. See also **Pap test.**

cervine (ˈsɜːvaɪn) *adj.* resembling or relating to a deer. [C19: < L *cervīnus*, < *cervus* a deer]

cervix (ˈsɜːvɪks) *n., pl.* **cervixes** *or* **cervices** (səˈvaɪsiːz). **1.** the technical name for **neck. 2.** any necklike part, esp. the lower part of the uterus that extends into the vagina. [C18: < L]

cesium (ˈsiːzɪəm) *n.* the usual U.S. spelling of **caesium.**

cess[1] (sɛs) *n. Brit.* any of several special taxes, such as a land tax in Scotland. [C16: short for ASSESSMENT]

cess[2] (sɛs) *n.* an Irish slang word for **luck** (esp. in **bad cess to you!**). [C19: prob. < CESS[1]]

cessation (sɛˈseɪʃən) *n.* a ceasing or stopping; pause: *temporary cessation of hostilities.* [C14: < L, < *cessāre* to be idle, < *cēdere* to yield]

cession (ˈsɛʃən) *n.* **1.** the act of ceding. **2.** something that is ceded, esp. land or territory. [C14: < L *cessiō*, < *cēdere* to yield]

cessionary (ˈsɛʃənərɪ) *n., pl.* **-aries.** *Law.* a person to whom something is transferred.

cesspit (ˈsɛsˌpɪt) *n.* a pit for the disposal of refuse, esp. sewage. [C19: see CESSPOOL]

cesspool (ˈsɛsˌpuːl) *n.* **1.** Also called: **sink, sump.** a covered cistern, etc., for collecting and storing sewage or waste water. **2.** a filthy or corrupt place: *a cesspool of iniquity.* [C17: ? changed < earlier *cesperalle*, < OF *souspirail* vent, air, < *soupirer* to sigh]

cestoid (ˈsɛstɔɪd) *adj.* (esp. of tapeworms and similar animals) ribbon-like in form.

cesura (sɪˈzjʊərə) *n., pl.* **-ras** *or* **-rae** (-riː). *Prosody.* a variant spelling of **caesura.**

cetacean (sɪˈteɪʃən) *adj. also* **cetaceous. 1.** of or belonging to an order of aquatic placental mammals having no hind limbs and a blowhole for breathing: includes toothed whales (dolphins, porpoises, etc.) and whalebone whales (rorquals, etc.). ~*n.* **2.** a whale. [C19: < NL, ult. < L *cētus* whale, < Gk *kētos*]

cetane (ˈsiːteɪn) *n.* a colourless insoluble liquid hydrocarbon used in the determination of the cetane number of diesel fuel. Also called: **hexadecane.** [C19: < L *cētus* whale + -ANE]

cetane number *n.* a measure of the quality of a diesel fuel expressed as the percentage of cetane. Also called: **cetane rating.** Cf. **octane number.**

Cf *the chemical symbol for* californium.

CF *abbrev. for* Canadian Forces.

cf. *abbrev. for:* **1.** (in bookbinding, etc.) calfskin. **2.** confer. [L: compare]

CFB *abbrev. for* Canadian Forces Base.

CFL *abbrev. for* Canadian Football League.

cg *abbrev. for* centigram.

cgs units *pl. n.* a metric system of units based on the centimetre, gram, and second. For scientific and technical purposes these units have been replaced by SI units.

CGT *abbrev. for* Capital Gains Tax.

CH *abbrev. for* Companion of Honour (a Brit. title).

ch. *abbrev. for:* **1.** chain (unit of measure). **2.** chapter. **3.** *Chess.* check. **4.** chief. **5.** church.

chablis (ˈʃæblɪ) *n.* (*sometimes cap.*) a dry white wine made around Chablis, France.

cha-cha-cha (ˌtʃɑːtʃɑːˈtʃɑː) *or* **cha-cha** *n.* **1.** a modern ballroom dance from Latin America with small steps and swaying hip movements. **2.** a piece of music composed for this dance. ~*vb.* (*intr.*) **3.** to perform this dance. [C20: < American (Cuban) Sp.]

chaconne (ʃəˈkɒn) *n.* **1.** a musical form consisting of a set of continuous variations upon a ground bass. **2.** *Arch.* a dance in slow triple time probably originating in Spain. [C17: < F, < Sp. *chacona*]

chafe (tʃeɪf) *vb.* **1.** to make or become sore or worn by rubbing. **2.** (*tr.*) to warm (the hands, etc.) by rubbing. **3.** to irritate or be irritated or impatient. **4.** (*intr.; often foll. by on, against, etc.*) to rub. ~*n.* **5.** a soreness or irritation caused by friction. [C14: < OF *chaufer* to warm, ult. < L, < *calēre* to be warm + *facere* to make]

chafer (ˈtʃeɪfə) *n.* any of various beetles, such as the cockchafer. [OE *ceafor*]

chaff[1] (tʃɑːf) *n.* **1.** the mass of husks, etc., separated from the seeds during threshing. **2.** finely cut straw and hay used to feed cattle. **3.** something of little worth; rubbish: *to separate the wheat from the chaff.* **4.** thin strips of metallic foil released into the earth's atmosphere to deflect radar signals and prevent detection. [OE *ceaf*] —**ˈchaffy** *adj.*

chaff[2] (tʃɑːf) *n.* **1.** light-hearted teasing or joking; banter. ~*vb.* **2.** to tease good-naturedly. [C19: prob. slang var. of CHAFE] —**ˈchaffer** *n.*

chaffer (ˈtʃæfə) *vb.* **1.** (*intr.*) to haggle or bargain. **2.** to chatter, talk, or say idly. ~*n.* **3.** haggling or bargaining. [C13 *chaffare*, < *chep* bargain + *fare* journey] —**ˈchafferer** *n.*

chaffinch (ˈtʃæfɪntʃ) *n.* a common European finch with black-and-white wings and, in the male, a reddish body and blue-grey head. [OE *ceaffinc*, < *ceaf* CHAFF[1] + *finc* FINCH]

chafing dish *n.* a vessel with a heating apparatus beneath it, for cooking or keeping food warm at the table.

chagrin (ˈʃægrɪn) *n.* **1.** a feeling of annoyance or

mortification. ~*vb.* **2.** to embarrass and annoy. [C17: < F *chagrin, chagriner,* <?]

chain (tʃeɪn) *n.* **1.** a flexible length of metal links, used for confining, connecting, etc., or in jewellery. **2.** (*usually pl.*) anything that confines or restrains: *the chains of poverty.* **3.** (*usually pl.*) a set of metal links that fit over the tyre of a motor vehicle to reduce skidding on an icy surface. **4.** a series of related or connected facts, events, etc. **5. a.** a number of establishments such as hotels, shops, etc., having the same owner or management. **b.** (*as modifier*): *a chain store.* **6.** Also called: **Gunter's chain.** a unit of length equal to 22 yards. **7.** Also called: **engineer's chain.** a unit of length equal to 100 feet. **8.** Also called: **nautical chain.** a unit of length equal to 15 feet. **9.** *Austral. & N.Z.* **a.** the rail along which carcasses are moved in a slaughterhouse. **b.** the team of workers who slaughter, skin, and otherwise process carcasses in a slaughterhouse. **10.** *Chem.* two or more atoms or groups bonded together so that the resulting molecule, ion, or radical resembles a chain. **11.** *Geog.* a series of natural features, esp. mountain ranges. ~*vb.* **12.** (*tr.*; often foll. by *up*) to confine, tie, or make fast with or as if with a chain. [C13: < OF, ult. < L; see CATENA]

chain gang *n. U.S.* a group of convicted prisoners chained together.

chain letter *n.* a letter, often with a request for and promise of money, that is sent to many people who add to or recopy it and send it on.

chain mail *n.* **a.** another term for **mail**[2] (sense 1). **b.** (*as modifier*): *a chain-mail hood.*

chain printer *n.* a line printer in which the type is on a continuous chain.

chain reaction *n.* **1.** a process in which a neutron colliding with an atomic nucleus causes fission and the ejection of one or more other neutrons. **2.** a chemical reaction in which the product of one step is a reactant in the following step. **3.** a series of events, each of which precipitates the next. —ˌ**chain-reˈact** *vb.* (*intr.*).

chain saw *n.* a motor-driven saw in which the cutting teeth form links in a continuous chain.

chain-smoke *vb.* to smoke (cigarettes, etc.) continually, esp. lighting one from the preceding one. —**chain smoker** *n.*

chain stitch *n.* **1.** a looped embroidery stitch resembling the links of a chain. ~*vb.* **chain-stitch. 2.** to sew (something) with this stitch.

chainwheel (ˈtʃeɪnˌwiːl) *n.* (esp. on a bicycle) a toothed wheel that transmits drive via the chain.

chair (tʃɛə) *n.* **1.** a seat with a back on which one person sits, typically having four legs and often having arms. **2.** an official position of authority. **3.** a person holding an office of authority: *questions are to be addressed to the chair.* **4.** a professorship. **5.** *Railways.* an iron or steel cradle bolted to a sleeper in which the rail is locked in position. **6.** short for **sedan chair. 7. take the chair.** to preside as chairman for a meeting, etc. **8. the chair.** *Inf.* the electric chair. ~*vb.* (*tr.*) **9.** to preside over (a meeting). **10.** *Brit.* to carry aloft in a sitting position after a triumph. **11.** to provide with a chair of office. **12.** to install in a chair. [C13: < OF, < L *cathedra,* < Gk *kathedra,* < *kata-* down + *hedra* seat]

chair lift *n.* a series of chairs suspended from a power-driven cable for conveying people, esp. skiers, up a mountain.

chairman (ˈtʃɛəmən) *n., pl.* **-men.** a person who presides over a company's board of directors, a committee, a debate, etc. Also: **chairperson** *or* (*fem.*) **chairwoman.**

chaise (ʃeɪz) *n.* **1.** a light open horse-drawn carriage, esp. one with two wheels. **2.** short for **post chaise** and **chaise longue.** [C18: < F, var. of OF *chaiere* CHAIR]

chaise longue (ˈʃeɪz ˈlɒŋ) *n., pl.* **chaise longues** *or* **chaises longues** (ˈʃeɪz ˈlɒŋ). a long low chair with a back and single armrest. [C19: < F: long chair]

chalaza (kəˈleɪzə) *n., pl.* **-zas** *or* **-zae** (-ziː). one of a pair of spiral threads holding the yolk of a bird's egg in position. [C18: NL, < Gk: hailstone]

chalcedony (kælˈsɛdənɪ) *n., pl.* **-nies.** a form of quartz with crystals arranged in parallel fibres: a gemstone. [C15: < LL, < Gk *khalkēdōn* a precious stone, ? after *Khalkēdōn* Chalcedon, town in Asia Minor] —**chalcedonic** (ˌkælsɪˈdɒnɪk) *adj.*

chalcolithic (ˌkælkəˈlɪθɪk) *adj. Archaeol.* of or relating to the period in which both stone and bronze tools were used. [C19: < Gk *khalkos* copper + *lithos* stone]

chalcopyrite (ˌkælkəˈpaɪraɪt) *n.* a common ore of copper, a crystalline sulphide of copper and iron. Formula: $CuFeS_2$. Also called: **copper pyrites.**

chaldron (ˈtʃɔːldrən) *n.* a unit of capacity equal to 36 bushels. [C17: < OF *chauderon* CAULDRON]

chalet (ˈʃæleɪ) *n.* **1.** a type of wooden house of Swiss origin, with wide projecting eaves. **2.** a similar house used as a ski lodge, etc. [C19: < F (Swiss dialect)]

chalice (ˈtʃælɪs) *n.* **1.** *Poetic.* a drinking cup; goblet. **2.** *Christianity.* a gold or silver cup containing the wine at Mass. **3.** a cup-shaped flower. [C13: < OF, < L *calix* cup]

chalk (tʃɔːk) *n.* **1.** a soft fine-grained white sedimentary rock consisting of nearly pure calcium carbonate, containing minute fossil fragments of marine organisms. **2.** a piece of chalk, or substance like chalk, often coloured, used for writing and drawing on blackboards. **3. as alike** (*or* **different**) **as chalk and cheese.** *Inf.* totally different in essentials. **4. by a long chalk.** *Brit. inf.* by far. **5. not by a long chalk.** *Brit. inf.* by no means. **6.** (*modifier*) made of chalk. ~*vb.* **7.** to draw or mark (something) with chalk. **8.** (*tr.*) to mark, rub, or whiten with or as with chalk. [OE *cealc,* < L *calx* limestone, < Gk *khalix* pebble] —ˈ**chalk**ˌ**like** *adj.* —ˈ**chalky** *adj.* —ˈ**chalkiness** *n.*

chalk out *vb.* (*tr., adv.*) to outline (a plan, scheme, etc.); sketch.

chalkpit (ˈtʃɔːkˌpɪt) *n.* a quarry for chalk.

chalk up *vb.* (*tr., adv.*) *Inf.* **1.** to score or register (something). **2.** to credit (money) to an account, etc. (esp. in **chalk it up**).

challenge (ˈtʃælɪndʒ) *vb.* (*mainly tr.*) **1.** to invite or summon (someone to do something, esp. to take part in a contest). **2.** (*also intr.*) to call (something) into question. **3.** to make demands on; stimulate: *the job challenges his ingenuity.* **4.** to order (a person) to halt and be identified. **5.** *Law.* to make formal objection to (a juror or jury). **6.** to lay claim to (attention, etc.). **7.** to inject (an experimental animal immunized with a test substance) with disease microorganisms to test for immunity to the disease. ~*n.* **8.** a call to engage in a fight, argument, or contest. **9.** a questioning of a statement or fact. **10.** a demanding or stimulating situation, career, etc. **11.** a demand by a sentry, etc., for identification or a password. **12.** *Law.* a formal objection to a person selected to serve on a jury or to the whole body of jurors. [C13: < OF *chalenge,* < L *calumnia* CALUMNY] —ˈ**challengeable** *adj.* —ˈ**challenger** *n.* —ˈ**challenging** *adj.*

challis (ˈʃælɪ, -lɪs) *or* **challie** (ˈʃælɪ) *n.* a lightweight fabric of wool, cotton, etc., usually with a printed design. [C19: prob. < a surname]

chalybeate (kəˈlɪbɪɪt) *adj.* containing or impregnated with iron salts. [C17: < NL *chalybēātus,* ult. < Gk *khalups* iron]

chamber (ˈtʃeɪmbə) *n.* **1.** a meeting hall, esp. one used for a legislative or judicial assembly. **2.** a reception room in an official residence, palace, etc. **3.** *Arch. or poetic.* a room in a private house, esp. a bedroom. **4. a.** a legislative, judicial, or administrative assembly. **b.** any of the houses of a legislature. **5.** an enclosed space; compartment; cavity. **6.** an enclosure for a cartridge in the cylinder of a revolver or for a shell in the breech of a cannon. **7.** short for **chamber pot. 8.** (*modifier*) of, relating to, or suitable for chamber music: *a chamber concert.* **9.** (*modifier*) on a small, quasi-domestic scale. ~ See also **chambers.**

[C13: < OF, < LL *camera* room, L: vault, < Gk *kamara*]

chamberlain (ˈtʃeɪmbəlɪn) *n.* **1.** an officer who manages the household of a king. **2.** the steward of a nobleman or landowner. **3.** the treasurer of a municipal corporation. [C13: < OF *chamberlayn*, of Frankish origin]

chambermaid (ˈtʃeɪmbəˌmeɪd) *n.* a woman employed to clean bedrooms, esp. in hotels.

chamber music *n.* music for performance by a small group of instrumentalists.

chamber of commerce *n.* (*sometimes cap.*) an organization composed mainly of local businessmen to promote, regulate, and protect their interests.

chamber orchestra *n.* a small orchestra of about 25 players, used for the authentic performance of baroque and early classical music as well as modern music.

chamber organ *n. Music.* a small compact organ used esp. for the authentic performance of preclassical music.

chamber pot *n.* a vessel for urine, used in bedrooms.

chambers (ˈtʃeɪmbəz) *pl. n.* **1.** a judge's room for hearing private cases not taken in open court. **2.** (in England) the set of rooms occupied by barristers where clients are interviewed.

chambray (ˈʃæmbreɪ) *n.* a smooth light fabric of cotton, linen, etc., with white weft and a coloured warp. [C19: after *Cambrai;* see CAMBRIC]

chameleon (kəˈmiːlɪən) *n.* **1.** a lizard of Africa and Madagascar, having long slender legs, a prehensile tail and tongue, and the ability to change colour. **2.** a changeable or fickle person. [C14: < L, < Gk *khamaileōn,* < *khamai* on the ground + *leōn* LION] —**chameleonic** (kəˌmiːlɪˈɒnɪk) *adj.*

chamfer (ˈtʃæmfə) *n.* **1.** a narrow flat surface at the corner of a beam, post, etc. ~*vb.* (*tr.*) **2.** to cut such a surface on (a beam, etc.). [C16: back formation < *chamfering,* < OF, < *chant* edge (see CANT[2]) + *fraindre* to break, < L *frangere*]

chamois (ˈʃæmɪ; *for senses 1 and 4* ˈʃæmwɑː) *n., pl.* **-ois. 1.** a sure-footed goat antelope of Europe and SW Asia, having vertical horns with backward-pointing tips. **2.** a soft suede leather formerly made from this animal, now obtained from the skins of sheep and goats. **3.** Also called: **chamois leather, shammy (leather), chammy (leather).** a piece of such leather or similar material used for polishing, etc. **4. a.** a greyish-yellow colour. **b.** (*as adj.*): *a chamois stamp.* ~*vb.* (*tr.*) **5.** to dress (leather or skin) like chamois. **6.** to polish with a chamois. [C16: < OF, < LL *camox,* <?]

chamomile (ˈkæməˌmaɪl) *n.* a variant spelling of **camomile.**

champ[1] (tʃæmp) *vb.* **1.** to munch (food) noisily like a horse. **2.** (when *intr.,* often foll. by *on, at,* etc.) to bite (something) nervously or impatiently. **3. champ (*or* chafe) at the bit.** *Inf.* to be impatient to start work, a journey, etc. ~*n.* **4.** the act or noise of champing. [C16: prob. imit.]

champ[2] (tʃæmp) *n. Inf.* short for **champion.**

champagne (ʃæmˈpeɪn) *n.* **1.** (*sometimes cap.*) a white sparkling wine produced around Reims and Épernay, France. **2.** (loosely) any effervescent white wine. **3. a.** a pale tawny colour. **b.** (*as adj.*): *champagne tights.*

champers (ˈʃæmpəz) *n.* (*functioning as sing.*) *Sl.* champagne.

champerty (ˈtʃæmpətɪ) *n., pl.* **-ties.** *Law.* (formerly) an illegal bargain between a party to litigation and an outsider whereby the latter agrees to pay for the action and thereby share in any proceeds recovered. [C14: < Anglo-F *champartie,* < OF *champart* share of produce, < *champ* field + *part* share]

champion (ˈtʃæmpɪən) *n.* **1. a.** a person, plant, or animal that has defeated all others in a competition: *a chess champion.* **b.** (*as modifier*): *a champion team; a champion marrow.* **2.** a person who defends a person or cause: *champion of the underprivileged.* **3.** (formerly) a knight who did battle for another, esp. a king or queen. ~*adj.* **4.** *N English dialect.* excellent. ~*adv.* **5.** *N English dialect.* very well. ~*vb.* (*tr.*) **6.** to support: *we champion the cause of liberty.* [C13: < OF, < LL *campiō,* < L *campus* field]

championship (ˈtʃæmpɪənˌʃɪp) *n.* **1.** (*sometimes pl.*) any of various contests held to determine a champion. **2.** the title of being a champion. **3.** support for a cause, person, etc.

champlevé *French.* (ʃɑ̃lve) *adj.* **1.** of a process of enamelling by which grooves are cut into a metal base and filled with enamel colours. ~*n.* **2.** an object enamelled by this process. [C19: < *champ* field (level surface) + *levé* raised]

Chanc. *abbrev. for:* **1.** Chancellor. **2.** Chancery.

chance (tʃɑːns) *n.* **1. a.** the unknown and unpredictable element that causes an event to result in a certain way rather than another, spoken of as a real force. **b.** (*as modifier*): *a chance meeting.* Related adj.: **fortuitous. 2.** fortune; luck; fate. **3.** an opportunity or occasion. **4.** a risk; gamble. **5.** the extent to which an event is likely to occur; probability. **6.** an unpredicted event, esp. a fortunate one. **7. by chance.** accidentally: *he slipped by chance.* **8. on the (off) chance.** acting on the (remote) possibility. ~*vb.* **9.** (*tr.*) to risk; hazard. **10.** (*intr.*) to happen by chance: *I chanced to catch sight of her.* **11. chance on (*or* upon).** to come upon by accident. **12. chance one's arm.** to attempt to do something although the chance of success may be slight. [C13: < OF, < *cheoir* to occur, < L *cadere*] —ˈ**chanceful** *adj.*

chancel (ˈtʃɑːnsəl) *n.* the part of a church containing the altar, sanctuary, and choir. [C14: < OF, < L *cancellī* (pl.) lattice]

chancellery *or* **chancellory** (ˈtʃɑːnsələrɪ) *n., pl.* **-leries** *or* **-lories. 1.** the building or room occupied by a chancellor's office. **2.** the position or office of a chancellor. **3.** *U.S.* the office of an embassy or legation. [C14: < Anglo-F *chancellerie,* < OF *chancelier* CHANCELLOR]

chancellor (ˈtʃɑːnsələ) *n.* **1.** the head of the government in several European countries. **2.** *U.S.* the president of a university. **3.** *Brit. & Canad.* the honorary head of a university. Cf. **vice chancellor. 4.** *Christianity.* a clergyman acting as the law officer of a bishop. [C11: < Anglo-F *chanceler,* < LL *cancellārius* porter, < L *cancellī* lattice] —ˈ**chancellor**ˌ**ship** *n.*

Chancellor of the Exchequer *n. Brit.* the cabinet minister responsible for finance.

chance-medley *n. Law.* a sudden quarrel in which one party kills another. [C15: < Anglo-F *chance medlee* mixed chance]

chancer (ˈtʃɑːnsə) *n. Sl.* an unscrupulous or dishonest opportunist. [C19: < CHANCE + -ER[1]]

chancery (ˈtʃɑːnsərɪ) *n., pl.* **-ceries.** (*usually cap.*) **1.** Also called: **Chancery Division.** (in England) the Lord Chancellor's court, now a division of the High Court of Justice. **2.** Also called: **court of chancery.** (in the U.S.) a court of equity. **3.** *Brit.* the political section or offices of an embassy or legation. **4.** another name for **chancellery. 5.** a court of public records. **6.** *Christianity.* a diocesan office under the supervision of a bishop's chancellor. **7. in chancery. a.** *Law.* (of a suit) pending in a court of equity. **b.** in an awkward situation. [C14: shortened < CHANCELLERY]

chancre (ˈʃæŋkə) *n. Pathol.* a small hard growth, which is the first sign of syphilis. [C16: < F, < L: CANCER] —ˈ**chancrous** *adj.*

chancroid (ˈʃæŋkrɔɪd) *n.* **1.** a soft venereal ulcer, esp. of the male genitals. ~*adj.* **2.** relating to or resembling a chancroid or chancre.

chancy *or* **chancey** (ˈtʃɑːnsɪ) *adj.* **chancier, chanciest.** *Inf.* uncertain; risky.

chandelier (ˌʃændɪˈlɪə) *n.* an ornamental hanging light with branches and holders for several candles or bulbs. [C17: < F: candleholder, < L CANDELABRUM]

chandler (ˈtʃɑːndlə) *n.* **1.** a dealer in a specified trade or merchandise: *ship's chandler.* **2.** a person who makes or sells candles. [C14: < OF *chandelier* one who makes or deals in candles, < *chandelle* CANDLE] —ˈ**chandlery** *n.*

change (tʃeɪndʒ) *vb.* **1.** to make or become different; alter. **2.** (*tr.*) to replace with or exchange for another: *to change one's name.* **3.** (sometimes foll. by *to* or *into*) to transform or convert or be transformed or converted. **4.** to give and receive (something) in return: *to change places.* **5.** (*tr.*) to give or receive (money) in exchange for the equivalent sum in a smaller denomination or different currency. **6.** (*tr.*) to remove or replace the coverings of: *to change a baby.* **7.** (when *intr.*, may be foll. by *into* or *out of*) to put on other clothes. **8.** to operate (the gear lever of a motor vehicle): *to change gear.* **9.** to alight from (one bus, train, etc.) and board another. ~*n.* **10.** the act or fact of changing or being changed. **11.** a variation or modification. **12.** the substitution of one thing for another. **13.** anything that is or may be substituted for something else. **14.** variety or novelty (esp. in **for a change**). **15.** a different set, esp. of clothes. **16.** money given or received in return for its equivalent in a larger denomination or in a different currency. **17.** the balance of money when the amount tendered is larger than the amount due. **18.** coins of a small denomination. **19.** (*often cap.*) *Arch.* a place where merchants meet to transact business. **20.** the act of passing from one state or phase to another. **21.** the transition from one phase of the moon to the next. **22.** the order in which a peal of bells may be rung. **23. get no change out of (someone).** *Sl.* not to be successful in attempts to exploit (someone). **24. ring the changes.** to vary the manner or performance of an action that is often repeated. ~See also **change down, changeover, change up.** [C13: < OF, < L *cambīre* to exchange, barter] —'**changeful** *adj.* —'**changeless** *adj.* —'**changer** *n.*

changeable ('tʃeɪndʒəbᵊl) *adj.* **1.** able to change or be changed: *changeable weather.* **2.** varying in colour as when viewed from different angles. —ˌ**changea'bility** *n.* —'**changeably** *adv.*

change down *vb.* (*intr., adv.*) to select a lower gear when driving.

changeling ('tʃeɪndʒlɪŋ) *n.* a child believed to have been exchanged by fairies for the parents' true child.

change of life *n.* a nontechnical name for **menopause.**

changeover ('tʃeɪndʒˌəʊvə) *n.* **1.** an alteration or complete reversal from one method, system, or product to another. **2.** a reversal of a situation, attitude, etc. **3.** *Sport.* the act of transferring to or being relieved by a team-mate in a relay race, as by handing over a baton, etc. ~*vb.* **change over.** (*adv.*) **4.** to adopt (a different position or attitude): *the driver and navigator changed over.*

change-ringing *n.* the art of bell-ringing in which a set of bells is rung in an established order which is then changed.

change up *vb.* (*intr., adv.*) to select a higher gear when driving.

channel ('tʃænᵊl) *n.* **1.** a broad strait connecting two areas of sea. **2.** the bed or course of a river, stream, or canal. **3.** a navigable course through a body of water. **4.** (*often pl.*) a means or agency of access, communication, etc.: *through official channels.* **5.** a course into which something can be directed or moved. **6.** *Electronics.* **a.** a band of radio frequencies assigned for a particular purpose, esp. the broadcasting of a television signal. **b.** a path for an electrical signal: *a stereo set has two channels.* **7.** a tubular passage for fluids. **8.** a groove, as in the shaft of a column. **9.** *Computers.* **a.** a path along which data can be transmitted. **b.** one of the lines along the length of a paper tape on which information can be stored in the form of punched holes. ~*vb.* **-nelling, -nelled** *or U.S.* **-neling, -neled. 10.** to make or cut channels in (something). **11.** (*tr.*) to guide into or convey through a channel or channels: *information was channelled through to them.* [C13: < OF, < L *canālis* pipe, groove, conduit]

Channel ('tʃænᵊl) *n.* **the.** the English Channel, between England and France.

chanson de geste *French.* (ʃɑ̃sɔ̃ də ʒɛst) *n.* one of a genre of Old French epic poems, the most famous of which is the *Chanson de Roland.* [lit.: song of exploits]

chant (tʃɑːnt) *n.* **1.** a simple song. **2.** a short simple melody in which several words or syllables are assigned to one note. **3.** a psalm or canticle performed by using such a melody. **4.** a rhythmic or repetitious slogan, usually spoken or sung, as by sports supporters, etc. ~*vb.* **5.** to sing or recite (a psalm, etc.) as a chant. **6.** to intone (a slogan). [C14: < OF *chanter* to sing, < L *cantāre,* frequentative of *canere* to sing] —'**chanting** *n., adj.*

chanter ('tʃɑːntə) *n.* the pipe on a set of bagpipes on which the melody is played.

chanterelle (ˌtʃæntə'rɛl) *n.* any of a genus of fungi having an edible yellow funnel-shaped mushroom. [C18: < F, < L *cantharus* drinking vessel, < Gk *kantharos*]

chanteuse (*French* ʃɑ̃tøz) *n.* a female singer, esp. in a nightclub or cabaret. [F: singer]

chanticleer (ˌtʃæntɪ'klɪə) *n.* a name for a cock, used esp. in fables. [C13: < OF, < *chanter cler* to sing clearly]

chantry ('tʃɑːntrɪ) *n., pl.* **-tries.** *Christianity.* **1.** an endowment for the singing of Masses for the soul of the founder. **2.** a chapel or altar so endowed. [C14: < OF, < *chanter* to sing; see CHANT]

chanty ('ʃæntɪ, 'tʃæn-) *n., pl.* **-ties.** a variant of **shanty**[2].

Chanukah *or* **Hanukkah** ('hɑːnəkə, -nʊˌkɑː) *n.* the eight-day Jewish festival of lights commemorating the rededication of the temple by Judas Maccabeus in 165 B.C. Also called: **Feast of Dedication, Feast of Lights.** [< Heb., lit.: a dedication]

chaos ('keɪɒs) *n.* **1.** (*usually cap.*) the disordered formless matter supposed to have existed before the ordered universe. **2.** complete disorder; utter confusion. [C15: < L, < Gk *khaos*] —**chaotic** (keɪ'ɒtɪk) *adj.* —**cha'otically** *adv.*

chap[1] (tʃæp) *vb.* **chapping, chapped. 1.** (of the skin) to make or become raw and cracked, esp. by exposure to cold. ~*n.* **2.** (*usually pl.*) a cracked patch on the skin. [C14: prob. of Gmc origin]

chap[2] (tʃæp) *n. Inf.* a man or boy; fellow. [C16 (in the sense: buyer): shortened < CHAPMAN]

chap[3] (tʃɒp, tʃæp) *n.* a less common word for **chop**[3].

chaparejos *or* **chaparajos** (ˌʃæpə'reɪəʊs) *pl. n.* another name for **chaps.** [< Mexican Sp.]

chaparral (ˌtʃæpə'ræl, ˌʃæp-) *n.* (in the southwestern U.S.) a dense growth of shrubs and trees. [C19: < Sp., < *chaparra* evergreen oak]

chapatti *or* **chapati** (tʃə'pætɪ, -'pɑːtɪ) *n., pl.* **-ti, -tis,** *or* **-ties.** (in Indian cookery) a flat unleavened bread resembling a pancake. [< Hindi]

chapbook ('tʃæpˌbʊk) *n.* a book of popular ballads, stories, etc., formerly sold by chapmen.

chapel ('tʃæpᵊl) *n.* **1.** a place of Christian worship, esp. with a separate altar, in a church or cathedral. **2.** a similar place of worship in a large house or institution, such as a college. **3.** a church subordinate to a parish church. **4.** (in Britain) **a.** a Nonconformist place of worship. **b.** Nonconformist religious practices or doctrine. **5. a.** the members of a trade union in a particular newspaper office, printing house, etc. **b.** a meeting of these members. [C13: < OF, < LL *cappella,* dim. of *cappa* cloak (see CAP); orig. the sanctuary where the cloak of St Martin was kept]

chaperon *or* **chaperone** ('ʃæpəˌrəʊn) *n.* **1.** (esp. formerly) an older or married woman who accompanies or supervises a young unmarried woman on social occasions. ~*vb.* **2.** to act as a chaperon to. [C14: < OF, < *chape* hood; see CAP] —**chaperonage** ('ʃæpərənɪdʒ) *n.*

chapfallen ('tʃæpˌfɔːlən) *or* **chopfallen** *adj.* dejected; downhearted. [C16: < CHOPS + FALLEN]

chaplain ('tʃæplɪn) *n.* a Christian clergyman

attached to a chapel of an institution or ministering to a military body, etc. [C12: < OF, < LL, < *cappella* CHAPEL] —**'chaplaincy** *n.*

chaplet ('tʃæplɪt) *n.* **1.** an ornamental wreath of flowers worn on the head. **2.** a string of beads. **3.** *R.C. Church.* **a.** a string of prayer beads constituting one third of the rosary. **b.** the prayers counted on this string. **4.** a narrow moulding in the form of a string of beads; astragal. [C14: < OF, < *chapel* hat] —**'chapleted** *adj.*

chapman ('tʃæpmən) *n., pl.* **-men.** *Arch.* a trader, esp. an itinerant pedlar. [OE *cēapman,* < *cēap* buying and selling]

chappie ('tʃæpɪ) *n. Inf.* another word for **chap**[2].

chaps (tʃæps, ʃæps) *pl. n.* leather overleggings without a seat, worn by cowboys. Also called: **chaparajos, chaparejos.** [C19: shortened < CHAPAREJOS]

chapter ('tʃæptə) *n.* **1.** a division of a written work. **2.** a sequence of events: *a chapter of disasters.* **3.** a period in a life, history, etc. **4.** a numbered reference to that part of a Parliamentary session which relates to a specified Act of Parliament. **5.** a branch of some societies, clubs, etc. **6.** the collective body or a meeting of the canons of a cathedral or of the members of a monastic or knightly order. **7. chapter and verse.** exact authority for an action or statement. ~*vb.* **8.** (*tr.*) to divide into chapters. [C13: < OF *chapitre,* < L *capitulum,* lit.: little head, hence, section of writing, < *caput* head]

chapterhouse ('tʃæptəˌhaʊs) *n.* **1.** the building in which a chapter meets. See **chapter** (sense 6). **2.** *U.S.* the meeting place of a college fraternity or sorority.

char[1] (tʃɑː) *vb.* **charring, charred. 1.** to burn or be burned partially; scorch. **2.** (*tr.*) to reduce (wood) to charcoal by partial combustion. [C17: short for CHARCOAL]

char[2] *or* **charr** (tʃɑː) *n., pl.* **char, chars** *or* **charr, charrs.** any of various troutlike fishes occurring in cold lakes and northern seas. [C17: <?]

char[3] (tʃɑː) *n.* **1.** *Inf.* short for **charwoman.** ~*vb.* **charring, charred. 2.** (*intr.*) *Brit. inf.* to do cleaning as a job. [C18: < OE *cęrran*]

char[4] (tʃɑː) *n. Brit.* a slang word for **tea.** [< Chinese *ch'a*]

charabanc ('ʃærəˌbæŋ) *n. Brit.* a coach, esp. for sightseeing. [C19: < F: wagon with seats]

character ('kærɪktə) *n.* **1.** the combination of traits and qualities distinguishing the individual nature of a person or thing. **2.** one such distinguishing quality; characteristic. **3.** moral force: *a man of character.* **4. a.** reputation, esp. a good reputation. **b.** (*as modifier*): *character assassination.* **5.** a person represented in a play, film, story, etc.; role. **6.** an outstanding person: *one of the great characters of the century.* **7.** *Inf.* an odd, eccentric, or unusual person: *he's quite a character.* **8.** an informal word for **person:** *a shady character.* **9.** a symbol used in a writing system, such as a letter of the alphabet. **10.** Also called: **sort.** *Printing.* any single letter, numeral, etc., cast as a type. **11.** *Computers.* any such letter, numeral, etc., which can be represented uniquely by a binary pattern. **12.** a style of writing or printing. **13.** *Genetics.* any structure, function, attribute, etc., in an organism that is determined by a gene or group of genes. **14.** a short prose sketch of a distinctive type of person. **15. in** (*or* **out of**) **character.** typical (*or* not typical) of the apparent character of a person. [C14: < L: distinguishing mark, < Gk *kharaktēr* engraver's tool] —**'characterful** *adj.* —**'characterless** *adj.*

character actor *n.* an actor who specializes in playing odd or eccentric characters.

characteristic (ˌkærɪktə'rɪstɪk) *n.* **1.** a distinguishing quality, attribute, or trait. **2.** *Maths.* **a.** the integral part of a common logarithm: *the characteristic of 2.4771 is 2.* **b.** another name for **exponent** (sense 4). ~*adj.* **3.** indicative of a distinctive quality, etc.; typical. —ˌ**character'istically** *adv.*

characterize *or* **-ise** ('kærɪktəˌraɪz) *vb.* (*tr.*) **1.** to be a characteristic of. **2.** to distinguish or mark as a characteristic. **3.** to describe or portray the character of. —ˌ**characteri'zation** *or* **-i'sation** *n.*

charade (ʃə'rɑːd) *n.* **1.** an act in the game of charades. **2.** *Chiefly Brit.* an absurd act; travesty.

charades (ʃə'rɑːdz) *n.* (*functioning as sing.*) a parlour game in which one team acts out each syllable of a word, the other team having to guess the word. [C18: < F, < Provençal *charrado* chat, < *charra* chatter]

charcoal ('tʃɑːˌkəʊl) *n.* **1.** a black amorphous form of carbon made by heating wood or other organic matter in the absence of air. **2.** a stick of this for drawing. **3.** a drawing done in charcoal. **4.** Also: **charcoal grey. a.** a dark grey colour. **b.** (*as adj.*): *a charcoal suit.* ~*vb.* **5.** (*tr.*) to write, draw, or blacken with charcoal. [C14: < *char* (<?) + COAL]

chard (tʃɑːd) *n.* a variety of beet with large succulent leaves and thick stalks, used as a vegetable. Also called: **Swiss chard.** [C17: prob. < F *carde,* ult. < L *carduus* thistle]

charge (tʃɑːdʒ) *vb.* **1.** to set or demand (a price). **2.** (*tr.*) to enter a debit against a person or his account. **3.** (*tr.*) to accuse or impute a fault to (a person, etc.), as formally in a court of law. **4.** (*tr.*) to command; place a burden upon or assign responsibility to: *I was charged to take the message to headquarters.* **5.** to make a rush at or sudden attack upon (a person or thing). **6.** (*tr.*) to fill (a receptacle) with the proper quantity. **7.** (often foll. by *up*) to cause (an accumulator, capacitor, etc.) to take or store electricity or (of an accumulator) to have electricity fed into it. **8.** to fill or be filled with matter by dispersion, solution, or absorption: *to charge water with carbon dioxide.* **9.** (*tr.*) to fill or suffuse with feeling, emotion, etc.: *the atmosphere was charged with excitement.* **10.** (*tr.*) *Law.* (of a judge) to address (a jury) authoritatively. **11.** (*tr.*) to load (a firearm). **12.** (*tr.*) *Heraldry.* to paint (a shield, banner, etc.) with a charge. ~*n.* **13.** a price charged for some article or service; cost. **14.** a financial liability, such as a tax. **15.** a debt or a book entry recording it. **16.** an accusation or allegation, such as a formal accusation of a crime in law. **17. a.** an onrush, attack, or assault. **b.** the call to such an attack in battle. **18.** custody or guardianship. **19.** a person or thing committed to someone's care. **20. a.** a cartridge or shell. **b.** the explosive required to discharge a firearm. **c.** an amount of explosive to be detonated at any one time. **21.** the quantity of anything that a receptacle is intended to hold. **22.** *Physics.* **a.** the attribute of matter responsible for all electrical phenomena, existing in two forms: *negative charge; positive charge.* **b.** an excess or deficiency of electrons in a system. **c.** a quantity of electricity determined by the product of an electric current and the time for which it flows, measured in coulombs. **d.** the total amount of electricity stored in a capacitor or an accumulator. **23.** a load or burden. **24.** a duty or responsibility; control. **25.** a command, injunction, or order. **26.** *Heraldry.* a design depicted on heraldic arms. **27. in charge.** in command. **28. in charge of. a.** having responsibility for. **b.** *U.S.* under the care of. [C13: < OF *chargier* to load, < LL *carricāre;* see CARRY]

chargeable ('tʃɑːdʒəbᵊl) *adj.* **1.** liable to be charged. **2.** liable to result in a legal charge.

charge account *n.* another term for **credit account.**

charge card *n.* a card issued by a chain store, shop, or organization, that enables customers to obtain goods and services for which they pay at a later date.

chargé d'affaires ('ʃɑːʒeɪ dæ'fɛə) *n., pl.* **chargés d'affaires** ('ʃɑːʒeɪ, -ʒeɪz). **1.** the temporary head of a diplomatic mission in the absence of the ambassador or minister. **2.** the head of a diplomatic mission of the lowest level. [C18: < F: (one) charged with affairs]

charge hand *n. Brit.* a workman whose grade of responsibility is just below that of a foreman.

charge nurse *n. Brit.* a nurse in charge of a ward in a hospital. Male equivalent of **sister.**

charger[1] (ˈtʃɑːdʒə) *n.* **1.** a person or thing that charges. **2.** a horse formerly ridden into battle. **3.** a device for charging an accumulator.

charger[2] (ˈtʃɑːdʒə) *n. Antiques.* a large dish. [C14 *chargeour,* < *chargen* to CHARGE]

charge sheet *n. Brit.* a document on which a police officer enters details of the charge against a prisoner and the court in which he will appear.

charily (ˈtʃɛərɪlɪ) *adv.* **1.** cautiously; carefully. **2.** sparingly.

chariness (ˈtʃɛərɪnɪs) *n.* the state of being chary.

chariot (ˈtʃærɪət) *n.* **1.** a two-wheeled horse-drawn vehicle used in ancient wars, races, etc. **2.** a light four-wheeled horse-drawn ceremonial carriage. **3.** *Poetic.* any stately vehicle. [C14: < OF, augmentative of *char* CAR]

charioteer (ˌtʃærɪəˈtɪə) *n.* the driver of a chariot.

charisma (kəˈrɪzmə) *or* **charism** (ˈkærɪzəm) *n.* **1.** a special personal quality or power of an individual making him capable of influencing or inspiring large numbers of people. **2.** a quality inherent in a thing, such as a particular type of car, which inspires great enthusiasm and devotion. **3.** *Christianity.* a divinely bestowed power or talent. [C17: < Church L, < Gk *kharisma,* < *kharis* grace, favour] —**charismatic** (ˌkærɪzˈmætɪk) *adj.*

charismatic movement *n. Christianity.* any of various groups, within existing denominations, emphasizing the charismatic gifts of speaking in tongues, healing, etc.

charitable (ˈtʃærɪtəbᵊl) *adj.* **1.** generous in giving to the needy. **2.** kind or lenient in one's attitude towards others. **3.** of or for charity. —ˈ**charitableness** *n.* —ˈ**charitably** *adv.*

charity (ˈtʃærɪtɪ) *n., pl.* **-ties. 1. a.** the giving of help, money, food, etc., to those in need. **b.** (*as modifier*): *a charity show.* **2.** an institution or organization set up to provide help, money, etc., to those in need. **3.** the help, money, etc., given to the needy; alms. **4.** a kindly attitude towards people. **5.** love of one's fellow men. [C13: < OF, < L *cāritās* affection, < *cārus* dear]

charivari (ˌʃɑːrɪˈvɑːrɪ), **shivaree,** *or esp. U.S.* **chivaree** *n.* **1.** a discordant mock serenade to newlyweds, made with pans, kettles, etc. **2.** a confused noise; din. [C17: < F, < LL, < Gk *karēbaria,* < *karē* head + *barus* heavy]

charlady (ˈtʃɑːˌleɪdɪ) *n., pl.* **-dies.** another name for **charwoman.**

charlatan (ˈʃɑːlətᵊn) *n.* someone who professes expertise, esp. in medicine, that he does not have; quack. [C17: < F, < It., < *ciarlare* to chatter] —ˈ**charlatanˌism** *or* ˈ**charlatanry** *n.*

Charles's Wain (weɪn) *n.* another name for the **Plough.** [OE *Carles wægn,* < *Carl* Charlemagne + *wægn* WAIN]

charleston (ˈtʃɑːlstən) *n.* a fast rhythmic dance of the 1920s, characterized by kicking and by twisting of the legs from the knee down. [named after *Charleston,* South Carolina]

charley horse (ˈtʃɑːlɪ) *n. U.S. & Canad. inf.* cramp following strenuous athletic exercise. [C19: <?]

charlie (ˈtʃɑːlɪ) *n. Brit. inf.* a silly person; fool.

charlock (ˈtʃɑːlɒk) *n.* a weedy Eurasian plant with hairy stems and foliage and yellow flowers. Also called: **wild mustard.** [OE *cerlic,* <?]

charlotte (ˈʃɑːlət) *n.* **1.** a dessert made with fruit and layers or a casing of bread or cake crumbs, sponge cake, etc.: *apple charlotte.* **2.** short for **charlotte russe.** [C19: < F, < the name *Charlotte*]

charlotte russe (ruːs) *n.* a cold dessert made with sponge fingers enclosing a mixture of cream, custard, etc. [F.: Russian charlotte]

charm (tʃɑːm) *n.* **1.** the quality of pleasing, fascinating, or attracting people. **2.** a pleasing or attractive feature. **3.** a small object worn for supposed magical powers; amulet. **4.** a trinket worn on a bracelet. **5.** a magic spell. **6.** a formula used in casting such a spell. **7.** *Physics.* a property of certain elementary particles, used to explain some scattering experiments. **8. like a charm.** perfectly; successfully. ~*vb.* **9.** to attract or fascinate; delight greatly. **10.** to cast a magic spell on. **11.** to protect, influence, or heal, supposedly by magic. **12.** (*tr.*) to influence or obtain by personal charm. [C13: < OF, < L *carmen* song] —ˈ**charmer** *n.*

charming (ˈtʃɑːmɪŋ) *adj.* delightful; pleasant; attractive. —ˈ**charmingly** *adv.*

charnel (ˈtʃɑːnᵊl) *n.* **1.** short for **charnel house.** ~*adj.* **2.** ghastly; sepulchral; deathly. [C14: < OF: burial place, < L *carnālis* fleshly, CARNAL]

charnel house *n.* (esp. formerly) a building or vault where corpses or bones are deposited.

Charon (ˈkɛərən) *n. Greek myth.* the ferryman who brought the dead across the rivers Styx or Acheron to Hades.

chart (tʃɑːt) *n.* **1.** a map designed to aid navigation by sea or air. **2.** an outline map, esp. one on which weather information is plotted. **3.** a sheet giving graphical, tabular, or diagrammatical information. **4. the charts.** *Inf.* the lists produced weekly of the best-selling pop singles and albums. ~*vb.* **5.** (*tr.*) to make a chart of. **6.** (*tr.*) to plot or outline the course of. **7.** (*intr.*) (of a record) to appear in the charts. [C16: < L, < Gk *khartēs* papyrus] —ˈ**chartless** *adj.*

charter (ˈtʃɑːtə) *n.* **1.** a formal document from the sovereign or state incorporating a city, bank, college, etc., and specifying its purposes and rights. **2.** (*sometimes cap.*) a formal document granting or demanding certain rights or liberties. **3.** a document issued by a society or an organization authorizing the establishment of a local branch or chapter. **4.** a special privilege or exemption. **5.** (*often cap.*) the fundamental principles of an organization; constitution. **6. a.** the hire or lease of transportation. **b.** (*as modifier*): *a charter flight.* ~*vb.* (*tr.*) **7.** to lease or hire by charter. **8.** to hire (a vehicle, etc.). **9.** to grant a charter to (a group or person). [C13: < OF, < L *chartula,* dim. of *charta* leaf of papyrus; see CHART] —ˈ**charterer** *n.*

chartered accountant *n.* (in Britain) an accountant who has passed the examinations of the Institute of Chartered Accountants.

chartered bank *n. Canad.* a privately owned bank that has been incorporated by Parliament to operate in the commercial banking system.

Chartism (ˈtʃɑːtɪzəm) *n. English history.* a movement (1838-48) to achieve certain political reforms, demand for which was embodied in charters presented to Parliament. —ˈ**Chartist** *n., adj.*

chartreuse (ʃɑːˈtrɜːz; *French* ʃartrøz) *n.* **1.** either of two liqueurs, green or yellow, made from herbs. **2. a.** a yellowish-green colour. **b.** (*as adj.*): *a chartreuse dress.* [C19: < F, after *La Grande Chartreuse,* monastery near Grenoble, where the liqueur is produced]

charwoman (ˈtʃɑːˌwʊmən) *n., pl.* **-women.** *Brit.* a woman who is hired to clean a house.

chary (ˈtʃɛərɪ) *adj.* **charier, chariest. 1.** wary; careful. **2.** choosy; finicky. **3.** shy. **4.** sparing; mean. [OE *cearig;* rel. to *caru* CARE]

Charybdis (kəˈrɪbdɪs) *n.* a ship-devouring monster in classical mythology, identified with a whirlpool off the coast of Sicily. Cf. **Scylla.**

chase[1] (tʃeɪs) *vb.* **1.** to follow or run after (a person, animal, or goal) persistently or quickly. **2.** (*tr.;* often foll. by *out, away,* or *off*) to force to run (away); drive (out). **3.** (*tr.*) *Inf.* to court (a member of the opposite sex) in an unsubtle manner. **4.** (*tr.;* often foll. by *up*) *Inf.* to pursue persistently and energetically in order to obtain results, information, etc. **5.** (*intr.*) *Inf.* to hurry; rush. ~*n.* **6.** the act of chasing; pursuit. **7.** any quarry that is pursued. **8.** *Brit.* an unenclosed area of land where wild animals are preserved to be hunted. **9.** *Brit.* the right to hunt a particular quarry over the land of others. **10. the chase.** the act or sport of hunting. **11.** short for **steeplechase. 12. give chase.** to pursue (a person, animal, or thing) actively. [C13: < OF *chacier,* < Vulgar L *captiāre* (unattested), < L, < *capere* to take; see CATCH]

chase[2] (tʃeɪs) *n.* **1.** *Letterpress printing.* a rectangular steel frame into which metal type and blocks are locked for printing. **2.** the part of a gun barrel from the trunnions to the muzzle. **3.** a groove or channel, esp. to take a pipe, cable, etc. ~*vb.* (*tr.*) **4.** Also: **chamfer.** to cut a groove, furrow, or flute in (a surface, column, etc.). [C17: prob. < F *châsse* frame, < OF *chas* enclosure, < LL *capsus* pen for animals; both < L *capsa* CASE[2]]

chase[3] (tʃeɪs) *vb.* (*tr.*) to ornament (metal) by engraving or embossing. Also: **enchase.** [C14: < OF *enchasser* ENCHASE]

chaser (ˈtʃeɪsə) *n.* **1.** a person or thing that chases. **2.** a drink drunk after another of a different kind, as beer after spirits.

chasm (ˈkæzəm) *n.* **1.** a deep cleft in the ground; abyss. **2.** a break in continuity; gap. **3.** a wide difference in interests, feelings, etc. [C17: < L, < Gk *khasma;* rel. to *khainein* to gape] —**chasmal** (ˈkæzməl) *or* ˈ**chasmic** *adj.*

chasseur (ʃæˈsɜː) *n.* **1.** *French Army.* a member of a unit specially trained for swift deployment. **2.** a uniformed attendant. ~*adj.* **3.** (*often postpositive*) designating or cooked in a sauce consisting of white wine and mushrooms. [C18: < F: huntsman]

Chassid *or* **Hassid** (ˈhæsɪd) *n., pl.* **Chassidim** *or* **Hassidim** (ˈhæsɪˌdiːm, -dɪm). **1.** a sect of Jewish mystics founded in Poland about 1750, characterized by religious zeal and a spirit of prayer, joy and charity. **2.** a Jewish sect of the 2nd century B.C., formed to combat Hellenistic influences. —**Chassidic** *or* **Hassidic** (həˈsɪdɪk) *adj.*

chassis (ˈʃæsɪ) *n., pl.* **-sis** (-sɪz). **1.** the steel frame, wheels, and mechanical parts of a motor vehicle. **2.** *Electronics.* a mounting for the circuit components of an electrical or electronic device, such as a radio or television. **3.** the landing gear of an aircraft. **4.** the frame on which a cannon carriage moves. [C17 (meaning: window frame): < F *châssis,* < Vulgar L *capsicum* (unattested), ult. < L *capsa* CASE[2]]

chaste (tʃeɪst) *adj.* **1.** not having experienced sexual intercourse; virginal. **2.** abstaining from unlawful sexual intercourse. **3.** abstaining from all sexual intercourse. **4.** (of conduct, speech, etc.) pure; decent; modest. **5.** (of style) simple; restrained. [C13: < OF, < L *castus* pure] —ˈ**chastely** *adv.* —ˈ**chasteness** *n.*

chasten (ˈtʃeɪsᵊn) *vb.* (*tr.*) **1.** to bring to submission; subdue. **2.** to discipline or correct by punishment. **3.** to moderate; restrain. [C16: < OF, < L *castigāre;* see CASTIGATE] —ˈ**chastener** *n.*

chastise (tʃæsˈtaɪz) *vb.* (*tr.*) **1.** to punish, esp. by beating. **2.** to scold severely. [C14 *chastisen,* irregularly < *chastien* to CHASTEN] —**chastisement** (ˈtʃæstɪzment, tʃæsˈtaɪz-) *n.* —**chasˈtiser** *n.*

chastity (ˈtʃæstɪtɪ) *n.* **1.** the state of being chaste; purity. **2.** abstention from sexual intercourse; virginity or celibacy. [C13: < OF, < L, < *castus* CHASTE]

chasuble (ˈtʃæzjʊbᵊl) *n.* *Christianity.* a long sleeveless outer vestment worn by a priest when celebrating Mass. [C13: < F, < LL *casubla* garment with a hood]

chat (tʃæt) *n.* **1.** informal conversation or talk in an easy familiar manner. **2.** an Old World songbird of the thrush family, having a harsh chattering cry. **3.** any of various North American warblers. **4.** any of various Australian wrens. ~*vb.* **chatting, chatted. 5.** (*intr.*) to talk in an easy familiar way. ~See also **chat up.** [C16: short for CHATTER]

chateau *or* **château** (ˈʃætəʊ) *n., pl.* **-teaux** (-təʊ, -təʊz) *or* **-teaus. 1.** a country house or castle, esp. in France. **2.** (in the name of a wine) estate or vineyard. [C18: < F, < OF, < L *castellum* CASTLE]

Chateaubriand (*French* ʃɑtobrijɑ̃) *n.* a thick steak cut from the fillet of beef. [C19: after F.R. *Chateaubriand* (1768-1848), F writer & statesman]

chatelaine (ˈʃætəˌleɪn) *n.* **1.** (esp. formerly) the mistress of a castle or large household. **2.** a chain or clasp worn at the waist by women in the 16th to the 19th centuries, with handkerchief, keys, etc., attached. [< F, < OF, ult. < L *castellum* CASTLE]

chat show *n. Brit.* a television or radio show in which guests are interviewed informally.

chattel (ˈtʃætᵊl) *n.* **1.** (*often pl.*) *Property law.* **a. chattel personal.** an item of movable personal property, such as furniture, etc. **b. chattel real.** an interest in land less than a freehold. **2. goods and chattels.** personal property. [C13: < OF *chatel* personal property, < Med. L *capitāle* wealth]

chatter (ˈtʃætə) *vb.* **1.** to speak (about unimportant matters) rapidly and incessantly. **2.** (*intr.*) (of birds, monkeys, etc.) to make rapid repetitive high-pitched noises. **3.** (*intr.*) (of the teeth) to click together rapidly through cold or fear. **4.** (*intr.*) to make rapid intermittent contact with a component, as in machining. ~*n.* **5.** idle or foolish talk; gossip. **6.** the high-pitched repetitive noise made by a bird, monkey, etc. **7.** the rattling of objects, such as parts of a machine. [C13: imit.] —ˈ**chatterer** *n.*

chatterbox (ˈtʃætəˌbɒks) *n. Inf.* a person who talks constantly, esp. about trivial matters.

chatty (ˈtʃætɪ) *adj.* **-tier, -tiest. 1.** full of trivial conversation; talkative. **2.** informal and friendly; gossipy. —ˈ**chattily** *adv.* —ˈ**chattiness** *n.*

chat up *vb.* (*tr., adv.*) *Brit. inf.* **1.** to talk persuasively to (a person), esp. with an ulterior motive. **2.** to talk flirtatiously to (a person of the opposite sex).

chauffeur (ˈʃəʊfə, ʃəʊˈfɜː) *n.* **1.** a person employed to drive a car. ~*vb.* **2.** to act as driver for (a person, etc.): *he chauffeured me to the stadium.* [C20: < F, lit.: stoker, < *chauffer* to heat] —**chauffeuse** (ʃəʊˈfɜːz) *fem. n.*

chaunt (tʃɔːnt) *n.* a less common variant of **chant.** —ˈ**chaunter** *n.*

chauvinism (ˈʃəʊvɪˌnɪzəm) *n.* **1.** aggressive or fanatical patriotism; jingoism. **2.** enthusiastic devotion to a cause. **3.** smug irrational belief in the superiority of one's own race, party, sex, etc.: *male chauvinism.* [C19: < F, after Nicolas *Chauvin,* F soldier under Napoleon, noted for his unthinking patriotism] —ˈ**chauvinist** *n., adj.* —ˌ**chauvinˈistic** *adj.* —ˌ**chauvinˈistically** *adv.*

cheap (tʃiːp) *adj.* **1.** costing relatively little; inexpensive; of good value. **2.** charging low prices: *a cheap hairdresser.* **3.** of poor quality; shoddy: *cheap furniture.* **4.** worth relatively little: *promises are cheap.* **5.** not worthy of respect; vulgar. **6.** ashamed; embarrassed: *to feel cheap.* **7.** stingy; miserly. **8.** *Inf.* mean; despicable: *a cheap liar.* ~*n.* **9. on the cheap.** *Brit. inf.* at a low cost. ~*adv.* **10.** at very little cost. [OE *ceap* barter, bargain, price, property] —ˈ**cheaply** *adv.* —ˈ**cheapness** *n.*

cheapen (ˈtʃiːpᵊn) *vb.* **1.** to make or become lower in reputation, quality, etc. **2.** to make or become cheap or cheaper. —ˈ**cheapener** *n.*

cheap-jack *Inf.* ~*n.* **1.** a person who sells cheap and shoddy goods. ~*adj.* **2.** shoddy or inferior. [C19: < CHEAP + JACK]

cheapo (ˈtʃiːpəʊ) *adj. Inf.* very cheap and possibly shoddy.

cheapskate (ˈtʃiːpˌskeɪt) *n. Inf.* a miserly person.

cheat (tʃiːt) *vb.* **1.** to deceive or practise deceit, esp. for one's own gain; trick or swindle (someone). **2.** (*intr.*) to obtain unfair advantage by trickery, as in a game of cards. **3.** (*tr.*) to escape or avoid (something unpleasant) by luck or cunning: *to cheat death.* **4.** (when *intr.*, usually foll. by *on*) *Inf.* to be sexually unfaithful to (one's wife, husband, or lover). ~*n.* **5.** a person who cheats. **6.** a deliberately dishonest transaction, esp. for gain; fraud. **7.** *Inf.* sham. **8.** *Law.* the obtaining of another's property by fraudulent means. [C14: short for ESCHEAT] —ˈ**cheater** *n.*

check (tʃɛk) *vb.* **1.** to pause or cause to pause, esp. abruptly. **2.** (*tr.*) to restrain or control: *to check one's tears.* **3.** (*tr.*) to slow the growth or progress of; retard. **4.** (*tr.*) to rebuke or rebuff. **5.** (when *intr.*, often foll. by *on* or *up on*) to examine, investigate, or make an inquiry into (facts, a product, etc.) for accuracy, quality, or progress. **6.** (*tr.*) *Chiefly U.S. & Canad.* to mark off so as to indicate approval, correctness, or preference. **7.**

(*intr.;* often foll. by *with*) *Chiefly U.S. & Canad.* to correspond or agree: *this report checks with the other.* **8.** (*tr.*) *Chiefly U.S., Canad., & N.Z.* to leave in or accept for temporary custody. **9.** *Chess.* to place (an opponent's king) in check. **10.** (*tr.*) to mark with a pattern of squares or crossed lines. **11.** to crack or cause to crack. **12.** (*tr.*) *Ice hockey.* to impede (an opponent). **13.** (*intr.*) *Hunting.* (of hounds) to pause while relocating a lost scent. ~*n.* **14.** a break in progress; stoppage. **15.** a restraint or rebuff. **16.** a person or thing that restrains, halts, etc. **17.** a control, esp. a rapid or informal one, to ensure accuracy, progress, etc. **18.** a means or standard to ensure against fraud or error. **19.** the U.S. word for **tick**[1]. **20.** the U.S. spelling of **cheque.** **21.** *U.S. & Canad.* the bill in a restaurant. **22.** *Chiefly U.S. & Canad.* a tag used to identify property deposited for custody. **23.** a pattern of squares or crossed lines. **24.** a single square in such a pattern. **25.** fabric with a pattern of squares or crossed lines. **26.** *Chess.* the state or position of a king under direct attack. **27.** a small crack, as one that occurs in timber during drying. **28.** a chip or counter used in some card and gambling games. **29.** *Hunting.* a pause by the hounds owing to loss of the scent. **30.** *Ice hockey.* the act of impeding an opponent with one's body or stick. **31. in check.** under control or restraint. ~*sentence substitute.* **32.** *Chess.* a call made to an opponent indicating that his king is in check. **33.** *Chiefly U.S. & Canad.* an expression of agreement. ~See also **check in, check out, checkup.** [C14: < OF *eschec* a check at chess, via Ar. < Persian *shāh* the king] —ˈ**checkable** *adj.*

checked (tʃɛkt) *adj.* having a pattern of squares.

checker[1] (ˈtʃɛkə) *n., vb.* **1.** the usual U.S. spelling of **chequer.** ~*n.* **2.** *Textiles.* a variant spelling of **chequer** (sense 2). **3.** the U.S. name for **draughtsman** (sense 3).

checker[2] (ˈtʃɛkə) *n. Chiefly U.S.* **1.** a cashier, esp. in a supermarket. **2.** an attendant in a cloakroom, left-luggage office, etc.

checkerboard (ˈtʃɛkəˌbɔːd) *n.* the U.S. and Canad. name for a **draughtboard.**

checkers (ˈtʃɛkəz) *n.* (*functioning as sing.*) the U.S. and Canad. name for **draughts.**

check in *vb.* (*adv.*) **1.** (*intr.*) to record one's arrival, as at a hotel or for work; sign in or report. **2.** (*tr.*) to register the arrival of (passengers, etc.). ~*n.* **check-in.** **3.** the formal registration of arrival, as at an airport or a hotel. **4.** the place where one registers arrival at an airport, etc.

check list *n.* a list of items, names, etc., to be referred to for identification or verification.

checkmate (ˈtʃɛkˌmeɪt) *n.* **1.** *Chess.* **a.** the winning position in which an opponent's king is under attack and unable to escape. **b.** the move by which this position is achieved. **2.** utter defeat. ~*vb.* (*tr.*) **3.** *Chess.* to place (an opponent's king) in checkmate. **4.** to thwart or render powerless. ~*sentence substitute.* **5.** *Chess.* a call made when placing an opponent's king in checkmate. [C14: < OF, < Ar. *shāh māt* the king is dead; see CHECK]

check out *vb.* (*adv.*) **1.** (*intr.*) to pay the bill and depart, esp. from a hotel. **2.** (*intr.*) to depart from a place; record one's departure from work. **3.** (*tr.*) to investigate or prove to be in order after investigation: *the police checked out all the statements.* ~*n.* **checkout.** **4.** the latest time for vacating a room in a hotel, etc. **5.** a counter, esp. in a supermarket, where customers pay.

checkpoint (ˈtʃɛkˌpɔɪnt) *n.* a place, as at a frontier, where vehicles or travellers are stopped for official identification, inspection, etc.

checkup (ˈtʃɛkˌʌp) *n.* **1.** an examination to see if something is in order. **2.** *Med.* a medical examination, esp. one taken at regular intervals. ~*vb.* **check up.** **3.** (*intr., adv.;* sometimes foll. by *on*) to investigate or make an inquiry into (a person's character, evidence, etc.).

Cheddar (ˈtʃɛdə) *n.* (*sometimes not cap.*) any of several types of smooth hard yellow or whitish cheese. [C17: < *Cheddar,* village in Somerset, where it was orig. made]

cheek (tʃiːk) *n.* **1.** either side of the face, esp. that part below the eye. **2.** *Inf.* impudence; effrontery. **3.** (*often pl.*) *Inf.* either side of the buttocks. **4.** (*often pl.*) a side of a door jamb. **5.** one of the jaws of a vice. **6. cheek by jowl.** close together; intimately linked. **7. turn the other cheek.** to be submissive and refuse to retaliate. ~*vb.* **8.** (*tr.*) *Inf.* to speak or behave disrespectfully to. [OE *ceace*]

cheekbone (ˈtʃiːkˌbəʊn) *n.* the nontechnical name for **zygomatic bone.**

cheeky (ˈtʃiːkɪ) *adj.* **cheekier, cheekiest.** disrespectful in speech or behaviour; impudent. —ˈ**cheekily** *adv.* —ˈ**cheekiness** *n.*

cheep (tʃiːp) *n.* **1.** the short weak high-pitched cry of a young bird; chirp. ~*vb.* **2.** (*intr.*) (of young birds) to utter such sounds. —ˈ**cheeper** *n.*

cheer (tʃɪə) *vb.* **1.** (usually foll. by *up*) to make or become happy or hopeful; comfort or be comforted. **2.** to applaud with shouts. **3.** (when *tr.,* sometimes foll. by *on*) to encourage (a team, etc.) with shouts. ~*n.* **4.** a shout or cry of approval, encouragement, etc., often using **hurrah!** **5. three cheers.** three shouts of hurrah given in unison to honour someone or celebrate something. **6.** happiness; good spirits. **7.** state of mind; spirits (archaic, except in **be of good cheer, with good cheer**). **8.** *Arch.* provisions for a feast; fare. [C13 (in the sense: face, welcoming aspect): < OF *chere,* < LL *cara* face, < Gk *kara* head]

cheerful (ˈtʃɪəfʊl) *adj.* **1.** having a happy disposition; in good spirits. **2.** pleasantly bright: *a cheerful room.* **3.** ungrudging: *cheerful help.* —ˈ**cheerfully** *adv.* —ˈ**cheerfulness** *n.*

cheerio (ˌtʃɪərɪˈəʊ) *Inf.* ~*sentence substitute.* **1.** *Chiefly Brit.* a farewell greeting. **2.** *Chiefly Brit.* a drinking toast. ~*n., pl.* **cheerios.** **3.** *N.Z.* a type of small sausage.

cheerleader (ˈtʃɪəˌliːdə) *n. U.S. & Canad.* a person who leads a crowd in cheers, esp. at sports events.

cheerless (ˈtʃɪəlɪs) *adj.* dreary or gloomy. —ˈ**cheerlessly** *adv.* —ˈ**cheerlessness** *n.*

cheers (tʃɪəz) *sentence substitute. Inf., chiefly Brit.* **1.** a drinking toast. **2.** goodbye! cheerio! **3.** thanks!

cheery (ˈtʃɪərɪ) *adj.* **cheerier, cheeriest.** showing or inspiring cheerfulness; gay. —ˈ**cheerily** *adv.* —ˈ**cheeriness** *n.*

cheese (tʃiːz) *n.* **1.** the curd of milk separated from the whey and variously prepared as a food. **2.** a mass or cake of this substance. **3.** any of various substances of similar consistency, etc.: *lemon cheese.* **4.** *Sl.* an important person (esp. in **big cheese**). [OE *cēse,* < L *cāseus* cheese]

cheeseburger (ˈtʃiːzˌbɜːgə) *n.* a hamburger cooked with a slice of cheese on top of it.

cheesecake (ˈtʃiːzˌkeɪk) *n.* **1.** a rich tart filled with cheese, esp. cream cheese, cream, sugar, etc. **2.** *Sl.* women displayed for their sex appeal, as in photographs in magazines or films.

cheesecloth (ˈtʃiːzˌklɒθ) *n.* a loosely woven cotton cloth formerly used for wrapping cheese.

cheesed off *adj.* (*usually postpositive*) *Brit. sl.* bored, disgusted, or angry. [C20: <?]

cheeseparing (ˈtʃiːzˌpɛərɪŋ) *adj.* **1.** penny-pinching. ~*n.* **2. a.** a paring of cheese rind. **b.** anything similarly worthless. **3.** stinginess.

cheesy (ˈtʃiːzɪ) *adj.* **cheesier, cheesiest.** like cheese in flavour, smell, or consistency. —ˈ**cheesiness** *n.*

cheetah *or* **chetah** (ˈtʃiːtə) *n.* a large feline of Africa and SW Asia: the swiftest mammal, having very long legs, and a black-spotted coat. [C18: < Hindi *cītā,* < Sansk. *citra* speckled]

chef (ʃɛf) *n.* a cook, esp. the principal cook in a restaurant. [C19: < F, < OF *chief* head, CHIEF]

chef-d'œuvre *French.* (ʃɛdœvrə) *n., pl.* ***chefs-d'œuvre*** (ʃɛdœvrə). a masterpiece.

chela[1] (ˈkiːlə) *n., pl.* **-lae** (-liː). a large pincer-like claw of such arthropods as the crab and scorpion. [C17: NL, < Gk *khēlē* claw]

chela[2] (ˈtʃeɪlə) *n. Hinduism.* a disciple of a religious teacher. [C19: < Hindi *celā,* < Sansk. *ceta* servant, slave]

chelate (ˈkiːleɪt) *n.* **1.** *Chem.* a chemical compound whose molecules contain a closed ring of atoms of which one is a metal atom. ~*adj.* **2.** *Zool.* of or possessing chelae. **3.** *Chem.* of a chelate. ~*vb.* **4.** (*intr.*) *Chem.* to form a chelate. [C20: < CHELA[1]] —**cheˈlation** *n.*

chelicera (kɪˈlɪsərə) *n., pl.* **-erae** (-əˌriː). one of a pair of appendages on the head of spiders and other arachnids: often modified as food-catching claws. [C19: < NL, < Gk *khēle* claw+ *keras* horn]

cheloid (ˈkiːlɔɪd) *n. Pathol.* a variant spelling of **keloid.** —**cheˈloidal** *adj.*

chelonian (kɪˈləʊnɪən) *n.* **1.** any reptile of the order *Chelonia,* including the tortoises and turtles, in which most of the body is enclosed in a bony capsule. ~*adj.* **2.** of or belonging to the *Chelonia.* [C19: < NL, < Gk *khelōnē* tortoise]

Chelsea Pensioner (ˈtʃɛlsɪ) *n.* an inhabitant of the Chelsea Royal Hospital in SW London, a home for old and infirm soldiers.

chem. *abbrev. for:* **1.** chemical. **2.** chemist. **3.** chemistry.

chem- *combining form.* a variant of **chemo-** before a vowel.

chemical (ˈkɛmɪkᵊl) *n.* **1.** any substance used in or resulting from a reaction involving changes to atoms or molecules. ~*adj.* **2.** of or used in chemistry. **3.** of, made from, or using chemicals: *chemical fertilizer.* —ˈ**chemically** *adv.*

chemical engineering *n.* the branch of engineering concerned with the design and manufacture of the plant used in industrial chemical processes. —**chemical engineer** *n.*

chemical warfare *n.* warfare using asphyxiating or nerve gases, poisons, defoliants, etc.

chemiluminescence (ˌkɛmɪˌluːmɪˈnɛsəns) *n.* the phenomenon in which a chemical reaction leads to the emission of light without incandescence. —ˌ**chemiˌlumiˈnescent** *adj.*

chemin de fer (ʃəˈmæn də ˈfɛə) *n.* a gambling game, a variation of baccarat. [F: railway, referring to the fast tempo of the game]

chemise (ʃəˈmiːz) *n.* **1.** an unwaisted loose-fitting dress hanging straight from the shoulders. **2.** a loose shirtlike undergarment. ~Also called: **shift.** [C14: < OF: shirt, < LL *camisa*]

chemist (ˈkɛmɪst) *n.* **1.** *Brit.* a shop selling medicines, cosmetics, etc. **2.** *Brit.* a qualified dispenser of prescribed medicines. **3.** a person studying, trained in, or engaged in chemistry. [C16: < earlier *chimist,* < NL, shortened < Med. L *alchimista* ALCHEMIST]

chemistry (ˈkɛmɪstrɪ) *n., pl.* **-tries. 1.** the branch of physical science concerned with the composition, properties, and reactions of substances. **2.** the composition, properties, and reactions of a particular substance. **3.** the nature and effects of any complex phenomenon: *the chemistry of humour.* [C17: < earlier *chimistrie,* < *chimist* CHEMIST]

chemo-, chemi-, *or before a vowel* **chem-** *combining form.* indicating that chemicals or chemical reactions are involved: *chemotherapy.* [NL, < LGk *khēmeia;* see ALCHEMY]

chemoreceptor (ˌkɛməʊrɪˈsɛptə) *or* **chemoceptor** *n.* a sensory receptor in a biological cell membrane to which an external molecule binds to generate a smell or taste sensation.

chemosynthesis (ˌkɛməʊˈsɪnθɪsɪs) *n.* the formation of organic material by some bacteria using energy from simple chemical reactions.

chemotherapy (ˌkɛməʊˈθɛrəpɪ) *n.* treatment of disease by means of chemical agents. —ˌ**chemoˈtherapist** *n.*

chemurgy (ˈkɛmɜːdʒɪ) *n.* the branch of chemistry concerned with the industrial use of organic raw materials, esp. of agricultural origin. —**chemˈurgic** *or* **chemˈurgical** *adj.*

chenille (ʃəˈniːl) *n.* **1.** a thick soft tufty silk or worsted velvet cord or yarn used in embroidery and for trimmings, etc. **2.** a fabric of such yarn. **3.** a carpet of such fabric. [C18: < F, lit.: hairy caterpillar, < L *canicula,* dim. of *canis* dog]

cheongsam (ˈtʃɔːŋˈsæm) *n.* a straight dress with a stand-up collar and a slit in one side of the skirt, worn by Chinese women. [< Chinese *ch'ang shan* long jacket]

cheque *or U.S.* **check** (tʃɛk) *n.* **1.** a bill of exchange drawn on a bank by the holder of a current account. **2.** *Austral. & N.Z.* the total sum of money received for contract work or a crop. [C18: < CHECK, in the sense: means of verification]

chequebook *or U.S.* **checkbook** (ˈtʃɛkˌbʊk) *n.* a book of detachable blank cheques issued by a bank to holders of current accounts.

chequebook journalism *n.* the practice of securing exclusive rights to material for newspaper stories by paying a high price, regardless of any moral implications.

cheque card *n.* another name for **banker's card.**

chequer *or U.S.* **checker** (ˈtʃɛkə) *n.* **1.** any of the marbles, pegs, or other pieces used in the game of Chinese chequers. **2. a.** a pattern of squares. **b.** one of the squares in such a pattern. ~*vb.* (*tr.*) **3.** to make irregular in colour or character; variegate. **4.** to mark off with alternating squares of colour. ~See also **chequers.** [C13: chessboard, < Anglo-F *escheker,* < *eschec* CHECK]

chequered *or esp. U.S.* **checkered** (ˈtʃɛkəd) *adj.* marked by fluctuations of fortune (esp. in **a chequered career**).

chequers (ˈtʃɛkəz) *n.* (*functioning as sing.*) another name for **draughts.**

cherish (ˈtʃɛrɪʃ) *vb.* (*tr.*) **1.** to feel or show great tenderness or care for. **2.** to cling fondly to (a hope, idea, etc.); nurse: *to cherish ambitions.* [C14: < OF, < *cher* dear, < L *cārus*]

chernozem (ˈtʃɜːnəʊˌzɛm) *n.* a rich black soil found in temperate semiarid regions, such as the grasslands of Russia. [< Russian *chernaya zemlya* black earth]

Cherokee (ˈtʃɛrəˌkiː) *n.* **1.** (*pl.* **-kees** *or* **-kee**) a member of a North American Indian people formerly living in the Appalachian Mountains. **2.** the Iroquois language of this people.

cheroot (ʃəˈruːt) *n.* a cigar with both ends cut off squarely. [C17: < Tamil *curuttu* curl, roll]

cherry (ˈtʃɛrɪ) *n., pl.* **-ries. 1.** any of several trees of the genus *Prunus,* having a small fleshy rounded fruit containing a hard stone. **2.** the fruit or wood of any of these trees. **3.** any of various unrelated plants, such as the ground cherry and Jerusalem cherry. **4. a.** a bright red colour; cerise. **b.** (*as adj.*): *a cherry coat.* **5.** *Taboo sl.* virginity or the hymen as its symbol. [C14: back formation < OE *ciris* (mistakenly thought to be pl.), ult. < LL *ceresia,* ?< L *cerasus* cherry tree, < Gk *kerasios*]

cherry tomato *n.* a miniature tomato not much bigger than a cherry.

chert (tʃɜːt) *n.* an impure black or grey microcrystalline variety of quartz that resembles flint. [C17: <?] —ˈ**cherty** *adj.*

cherub (ˈtʃɛrəb) *n., pl.* **cherubs** *or* (*for sense 1*) **cherubim** (ˈtʃɛrəbɪm, -ʊbɪm). **1.** a member of the second order of angels, often represented as a winged child. **2.** an innocent or sweet child. [OE, < Heb. *kĕrūbh*] —**cherubic** (tʃəˈruːbɪk) *or* **cheˈrubical** *adj.* —**cheˈrubically** *adv.*

chervil (ˈtʃɜːvɪl) *n.* an aromatic umbelliferous Eurasian plant with small white flowers and aniseed-flavoured leaves used as herbs in soups and salads. [OE *cerfelle,* < L, < Gk, < *khairein* to enjoy + *phullon* leaf]

Cheshire (ˈtʃɛʃə) *n.* (*sometimes not cap.*) a mild-flavoured crumbly chesse. [C16: < the county of *Cheshire,* where it was orig. made]

chess (tʃɛs) *n.* a game of skill for two players using a chessboard on which chessmen are moved. The object is to checkmate the opponent's king. [C13: < OF *esches,* pl. of *eschec* CHECK]

chessboard (ˈtʃɛsˌbɔːd) *n.* a square board divided into 64 squares of two alternating colours, used for playing chess or draughts.

chessman (ˈtʃɛsˌmæn, -mən) *n., pl.* **-men.** any of the pieces and pawns used in a game of chess.

[C17: < *chessmen*, < ME *chessemeyne* chess company]

chest (tʃɛst) *n.* **1. a.** the front part of the trunk from the neck to the belly. Related adj.: **pectoral.** **b.** (*as modifier*): *a chest cold.* **2. get (something) off one's chest.** *Inf.* to unburden oneself of troubles, worries, etc., by talking about them. **3.** a box used for storage or shipping: *a tea chest.* [OE *cest*, < L, < Gk *kistē* box] —**'chested** *adj.*

chesterfield ('tʃɛstə,fi:ld) *n.* **1.** a man's overcoat, usually with a velvet collar. **2.** a large tightly stuffed sofa, with straight upholstered arms of the same height as the back. [C19: after a 19th-cent. Earl of *Chesterfield*]

chestnut ('tʃɛs,nʌt) *n.* **1.** a N temperate tree such as the **sweet** or **Spanish chestnut**, which produces flowers in long catkins and nuts in a prickly bur. Cf. **horse chestnut. 2.** the edible nut of any of these trees. **3.** the hard wood of any of these trees, used in making furniture, etc. **4. a.** a reddish-brown colour. **b.** (*as adj.*): *chestnut hair.* **5.** a horse of a golden-brown colour. **6.** *Inf.* an old or stale joke. [C16: < earlier *chesten nut*: *chesten*, < OF, < L, < Gk *kastanea*]

chest of drawers *n.* a piece of furniture consisting of a set of drawers in a frame.

chesty ('tʃɛstɪ) *adj.* **chestier, chestiest.** *Inf.* **1.** *Brit.* suffering from or symptomatic of chest disease: *a chesty cough.* **2.** having a large well-developed chest or bosom. —**'chestiness** *n.*

cheval glass (ʃə'væl) *n.* a full-length mirror mounted so as to swivel within a frame. [C19: < F *cheval* support (lit.: horse)]

chevalier (,ʃɛvə'lɪə) *n.* **1.** a member of certain orders of merit, such as the French Legion of Honour. **2.** the lowest title of rank in the old French nobility. **3.** an archaic word for **knight. 4.** a chivalrous man; gallant. [C14: < OF, < Med. L *caballārius* horseman, CAVALIER]

Cheviot ('tʃi:vɪət, 'tʃɛv-) *n.* **1.** a large British breed of sheep reared for its wool. **2.** (*often not cap.*) a rough twill-weave woollen suiting fabric. [< *Cheviot* Hills on borders of England & Scotland]

chevron ('ʃɛvrən) *n.* **1.** *Mil.* a badge or insignia consisting of one or more V-shaped stripes to indicate a noncommissioned rank or length of service. **2.** *Heraldry.* an inverted V-shaped charge on a shield. **3.** any V-shaped pattern or device. [C14: < OF, ult. < L *caper* goat; cf. L *capreoli* pair of rafters (lit.: little goats)]

chevrotain ('ʃɛvrə,teɪn, -tɪn) *n.* a small timid ruminant mammal of S and SE Asia. Also called: **mouse deer.** [C18: < F, < OF *chevrot* kid, < *chèvre* goat, ult. < L *caper* goat]

chevy ('tʃɛvɪ) *n., vb.* a variant spelling of **chivy.**

chew (tʃu:) *vb.* **1.** to work the jaws and teeth in order to grind (food); masticate. **2.** to bite repeatedly: *she chewed her nails anxiously.* **3.** (*intr.*) to use chewing tobacco. **4. chew the fat** *or* **rag.** *Sl.* **a.** to argue over a point. **b.** to talk idly; gossip. ~*n.* **5.** the act of chewing. **6.** something that is chewed. [OE *ceowan*] —**'chewable** *adj.* —**'chewer** *n.*

chewing gum *n.* a preparation for chewing, usually made of flavoured and sweetened chicle.

chew over *vb.* (*tr., adv.*) to consider carefully.

chewy ('tʃu:ɪ) *adj.* **chewier, chewiest.** of a consistency requiring chewing.

chez *French.* (ʃe) *prep.* **1.** at the home of. **2.** with, among, or in the manner of.

chi (kaɪ) *n.* the 22nd letter of the Greek alphabet (Χ, χ).

chiack *or* **chyack** ('tʃaɪæk) *Austral inf.* ~*vb.* **1.** (*tr.*) to tease or banter. ~*n.* **2.** Also called: **chiacking.** good-humoured banter. [C19: < *chi-hike*, a shout of greeting]

chianti (kɪ'æntɪ) *n.* (*sometimes cap.*) a dry red or white wine produced in Tuscany, Italy.

chiaroscuro (kɪ,ɑ:rə'skʊərəʊ) *n., pl.* **-ros. 1.** the artistic distribution of light and dark masses in a picture. **2.** monochrome painting using light and dark only. [C17: < It., < *chiaro* CLEAR + *oscuro* OBSCURE]

chiasma (kaɪ'æzmə) *n., pl.* **-mas, -mata** (-mətə) **1.** *Cytology.* the cross-shaped connection produced by the crossing over of pairing chromosomes during meiosis. **2.** *Anat.* the crossing over of two parts or structures. [C19: < Gk *khiasma*, < *khi* CHI]

chiasmus (kaɪ'æzməs) *n., pl.* **-mi** (-maɪ). *Rhetoric.* reversal of word order in the second of two parallel phrases: *he came in triumph and in defeat departs.* [NL < Gk: see CHIASMA] —**chiastic** (kaɪ'æstɪk) *adj.*

chic (ʃi:k, ʃɪk) *adj.* **1.** (esp. of fashionable clothes, women, etc.) stylish or elegant. ~*n.* **2.** stylishness, esp. in dress; modishness; fashionable good taste. [C19: < F, <?] —**'chicly** *adv.*

chicane (ʃɪ'keɪn) *n.* **1.** a bridge or whist hand without trumps. **2.** *Motor racing.* a short section of sharp narrow bends formed by barriers placed on a motor-racing circuit. **3.** a less common word for **chicanery.** ~*vb.* **4.** (*tr.*) to deceive or trick by chicanery. **5.** (*intr.*) to use tricks or chicanery. [C17: < F *chicaner* to quibble, <?] —**chi'caner** *n.*

chicanery (ʃɪ'keɪnərɪ) *n., pl.* **-eries. 1.** verbal deception or trickery, dishonest or sharp practice. **2.** a trick, deception, or quibble.

chicano (tʃɪ'kɑ:nəʊ) *n., pl.* **-nos.** *U.S.* an American citizen of Mexican origin. [C20: < Sp. *mejicano* Mexican]

chichi ('ʃi:,ʃi:) *adj.* **1.** affectedly pretty or stylish. ~*n.* **2.** the quality of being affectedly pretty or stylish. [C20: < F]

chick (tʃɪk) *n.* **1.** the young of a bird, esp. of a domestic fowl. **2.** *Sl.* a girl or young woman, esp. an attractive one. **3.** a young child: used as a term of endearment. [C14: short for CHICKEN]

chickadee ('tʃɪkə,di:) *n.* any of various small North American songbirds, typically having grey-and-black plumage. [C19: imit.]

chicken ('tʃɪkɪn) *n.* **1.** a domestic fowl bred for its flesh or eggs. **2.** the flesh of such a bird used for food. **3.** any of various similar birds, such as a prairie chicken. **4.** *Sl.* a cowardly person. **5.** *Sl.* a young inexperienced person. **6. count one's chickens before they are hatched.** to be over-optimistic in acting on expectations which are not yet fulfilled. ~*adj.* **7.** *Sl.* easily scared; cowardly; timid. [OE *ciecen*]

chicken feed *n. Sl.* a trifling amount of money.

chicken-hearted *or* **chicken-livered** *adj.* easily frightened; cowardly.

chicken out *vb.* (*intr., adv.*) *Inf.* to fail to do something through fear or lack of conviction.

chickenpox ('tʃɪkɪn,pɒks) *n.* a highly communicable viral disease most commonly affecting children, characterized by slight fever and the eruption of a rash.

chicken wire *n.* wire netting with a hexagonal mesh.

chickpea ('tʃɪk,pi:) *n.* **1.** a bushy leguminous plant, cultivated for its edible pealike seeds. **2.** the seed of this plant. [C16 *ciche peasen*, < *ciche* (< F, < L *cicer* chickpea) + *peasen*; see PEA]

chickweed ('tʃɪk,wi:d) *n.* any of various plants of the pink family, esp. a common garden weed with small white flowers.

chicle ('tʃɪkᵊl) *n.* a gumlike substance obtained from the sapodilla; the main ingredient of chewing gum. [< Sp., < Nahuatl *chictli*]

chicory ('tʃɪkərɪ) *n., pl.* **-ries. 1.** a blue-flowered plant, cultivated for its leaves, which are used in salads, and for its roots. **2.** the root of this plant, roasted, dried, and used as a coffee substitute. ~Cf. **endive.** [C15: < OF, < L *cichorium*, < Gk *kikhōrion*]

chide (tʃaɪd) *vb.* **chiding, chided** *or* **chid** (tʃɪd); **chided, chid** *or* **chidden** ('tʃɪdᵊn). **1.** to rebuke or scold. **2.** (*tr.*) to goad into action. [OE *cīdan*] —**'chider** *n.* —**'chidingly** *adv.*

chief (tʃi:f) *n.* **1.** the head or leader of a group or body of people. **2.** *Heraldry.* the upper third of a shield. **3. in chief.** primarily; especially. ~*adj.* **4.** (*prenominal*) **a.** most important; principal. **b.** highest in rank or authority. ~*adv.* **5.** *Arch.* principally. [C13: < OF, < L *caput* head]

chief justice *n.* **1.** (in any of several Commonwealth countries) the judge presiding over a supreme court. **2.** (in the U.S.) the presiding judge of a court composed of a number of members. ~See also **Lord Chief Justice.**

chiefly ('tʃiːflɪ) *adv.* **1.** especially or essentially; above all. **2.** in general; mainly; mostly. ~*adj.* **3.** of or relating to a chief or chieftain.

Chief of Staff *n.* **1.** the senior staff officer under the commander of a major military formation or organization. **2.** the senior officer of each service of the armed forces.

chief petty officer *n.* the senior naval rank for personnel without commissioned or warrant rank.

chieftain ('tʃiːftən, -tɪn) *n.* the head or leader of a tribe or clan. [C14: < OF, < LL *capitāneus* commander; see CAPTAIN] —'**chieftaincy** *or* '**chieftain,ship** *n.*

chief technician *n.* a noncommissioned officer in the Royal Air Force, junior to a flight sergeant.

chiffchaff ('tʃɪf,tʃæf) *n.* a common European warbler with a yellowish-brown plumage. [C18: imit.]

chiffon (ʃɪ'fɒn, 'ʃɪfɒn) *n.* **1.** a fine almost transparent fabric of silk, nylon, etc. **2.** (*often pl.*) *Now rare.* feminine finery. ~*adj.* **3.** made of chiffon. **4.** (of soufflés, pies, cakes, etc.) having a very light fluffy texture. [C18: < F, < *chiffe* rag]

chiffonier *or* **chiffonnier** (,ʃɪfə'nɪə) *n.* **1.** a tall, elegant chest of drawers. **2.** a wide low open-fronted cabinet. [C19: < F, < *chiffon* rag]

chigetai (,tʃɪgɪ'taɪ) *n.* a variety of the Asiatic wild ass of Mongolia. Also spelled: **dziggetai.** [< Mongolian *tchikhitei* long-eared, < *tchikhi* ear]

chigger ('tʃɪgə) *n.* **1.** *U.S. & Canad.* the parasitic larva of a mite, which causes intense itching. **2.** another name for **chigoe.**

chignon ('ʃiːnjɒn) *n.* an arrangement of long hair in a roll or knot at the back of the head. [C18: < F, < OF *chaignon* link, < *chaine* CHAIN; infl. also by OF *tignon* coil of hair]

chigoe ('tʃɪgəʊ) *n.* **1.** a tropical flea, the female of which burrows into the skin of its host, which includes man. **2.** another name for **chigger.** [C17: < Carib *chigo*]

Chihuahua (tʃɪ'wɑːwɑː, -wə) *n.* a breed of tiny dog originally from Mexico, having short hair and protruding eyes. [after *Chihuahua*, state in Mexico]

chilblain ('tʃɪl,bleɪn) *n.* (*usually pl.*) an inflammation of the fingers or toes, caused by exposure to cold. [C16: < CHILL (n.) + BLAIN] —'**chil,blained** *adj.*

child (tʃaɪld) *n., pl.* **children.** **1.** **a.** a boy or girl between birth and puberty. **b.** (*as modifier*): *child labour.* **2.** a baby or infant. **3.** an unborn baby. **4.** **with child.** an old-fashioned term for **pregnant.** **5.** a human offspring; a son or daughter. Related adj.: **filial.** **6.** a childish or immature person. **7.** a member of a family or tribe; descendant: *a child of Israel.* **8.** a person or thing regarded as the product of an influence or environment: *a child of nature.* [OE *cild*] —'**childless** *adj.* —'**childlessness** *n.*

child abuse *n.* physical, sexual, or emotional ill-treatment of a child by its parents or other adults responsible for its welfare.

child-bearing *n.* **a.** the act or process of carrying and giving birth to a child. **b.** (*as modifier*): *of child-bearing age.*

childbed ('tʃaɪld,bɛd) *n.* (often preceded by *in*) the condition of giving birth to a child.

child benefit *n.* (in Britain and New Zealand) a regular government payment to parents of children up to a certain age. In New Zealand more commonly called: **family benefit.** Austral. equivalent: **child endowment.**

childbirth ('tʃaɪld,bɜːθ) *n.* the act of giving birth to a child.

childhood ('tʃaɪldhʊd) *n.* the condition of being a child; the period of life before puberty.

childish ('tʃaɪldɪʃ) *adj.* **1.** in the manner of or suitable to a child. **2.** foolish or petty: *childish fears.* —'**childishly** *adv.* —'**childishness** *n.*

childlike ('tʃaɪld,laɪk) *adj.* like or befitting a child, as in being innocent, trustful, etc.

child minder *n.* a person who looks after children, esp. those whose parents are working.

children ('tʃɪldrən) *n.* the plural of **child.**

Children of Israel *pl. n.* the Jewish people or nation.

child's play *n. Inf.* something easy to do.

chile ('tʃɪlɪ) *n.* a variant spelling of **chilli.**

Chilean ('tʃɪlɪən) *adj.* **1.** of or relating to Chile, a republic in South America. ~*n.* **2.** a native or inhabitant of Chile.

Chile pine *n.* another name for the **monkey puzzle.**

Chile saltpetre *or* **nitre** *n.* a naturally occurring form of sodium nitrate.

chiliad ('kɪlɪ,æd) *n.* **1.** a group of one thousand. **2.** one thousand years. [C16: < Gk, < *khilioi* a thousand]

chill (tʃɪl) *n.* **1.** a moderate coldness. **2.** a sensation of coldness resulting from a cold or damp environment, or from a sudden emotional reaction. **3.** a feverish cold. **4.** a check on enthusiasm or joy. ~*adj.* **5.** another word for **chilly.** ~*vb.* **6.** to make or become cold. **7.** (*tr.*) to cool or freeze (food, drinks, etc.). **8.** (*tr.*) **a.** to depress (enthusiasm, etc.). **b.** to discourage. [OE *ciele*] —'**chilling** *adj.* —'**chillingly** *adv.* —'**chillness** *n.*

chiller ('tʃɪlə) *n.* **1.** short for **spine-chiller.** **2.** *N.Z.* a refrigerated storage area for meat.

chilli *or* **chili** ('tʃɪlɪ) *n., pl.* **chillies** *or* **chilies.** the small red hot-tasting pod of a type of capsicum used for flavouring sauces, etc. [C17: < Sp., < Nahuatl *chilli*]

chilli con carne ('tʃɪlɪ kɒn 'kɑːnɪ) *n.* a highly seasoned Mexican dish of meat, onions, beans, and chilli powder. [< Sp.: chilli with meat]

chilli powder *n.* ground chilli blended with other spices.

chilli sauce *n.* a highly seasoned sauce made of tomatoes cooked with chilli and other spices.

chilly ('tʃɪlɪ) *adj.* **-lier, -liest.** **1.** causing or feeling cool or moderately cold. **2.** without warmth; unfriendly. **3.** (of people) sensitive to cold. —'**chilliness** *n.*

chilly bin *n. N.Z. inf.* a portable insulated container with provision for packing food and drink in ice.

Chiltern Hundreds ('tʃɪltən) *pl. n.* (in Britain) short for **Stewardship of the Chiltern Hundreds;** a nominal office that an MP applies for in order to resign his seat.

chime[1] (tʃaɪm) *n.* **1.** an individual bell or the sound it makes when struck. **2.** (*often pl.*) the machinery employed to sound a bell in this way. **3.** Also called: **bell.** a percussion instrument consisting of a set of vertical metal tubes of graduated length, suspended in a frame and struck with a hammer. **4.** agreement; concord. ~*vb.* **5.** **a.** to sound (a bell) or (of a bell) to be sounded by a clapper or hammer. **b.** to produce (music or sounds) by chiming. **6.** (*tr.*) to indicate or show (time or the hours) by chiming. **7.** (*intr.*; foll. by *with*) to agree or harmonize. [C13: prob. shortened < earlier *chymbe bell,* ult. < L *cymbalum* CYMBAL] —'**chimer** *n.*

chime[2], **chimb** (tʃaɪm), *or* **chine** *n.* the projecting rim of a cask or barrel. [OE *cimb-*]

chime in *vb.* (*intr., adv.*) *Inf.* **1.** to join in or interrupt (a conversation), esp. repeatedly and unwelcomely. **2.** to voice agreement.

chimera *or* **chimaera** (kaɪ'mɪərə, kɪ-) *n.* **1.** (*often cap.*) *Greek myth.* a fire-breathing monster with the head of a lion, body of a goat, and tail of a serpent. **2.** a fabulous beast made up of parts taken from various animals. **3.** a grotesque product of the imagination. **4.** *Biol.* an organism consisting of at least two genetically different kinds of tissue as a result of mutation, grafting, etc. [C16: < L, < Gk *khimaira* she-goat]

chimerical (kaɪ'mɛrɪkᵊl, kɪ-) *or* **chimeric** *adj.* **1.** wildly fanciful; imaginary. **2.** given to or indulging in fantasies. —**chi'merically** *adv.*

chimney ('tʃɪmnɪ) *n.* **1.** a vertical structure of brick, masonry, or steel that carries smoke or steam away from a fire, engine, etc. **2.** another name for **flue**[1] (sense 1). **3.** short for **chimney stack.** **4.** an open-ended glass tube fitting around the flame of an oil or gas lamp in order to exclude draughts. **5.** *Brit.* a fireplace, esp. an old and large one. **6.** the vent of a volcano. **7.** *Mountaineering.* a vertical fissure large enough for a person's body to enter. [C14: < OF *cheminée,* < LL *camīnāta,* < L *camīnus* furnace, < Gk *kaminos* oven]

chimney breast *n.* the wall or walls that surround the base of a chimney or fireplace.

chimneypot (ˈtʃɪmnɪˌpɒt) *n.* a short pipe on the top of a chimney.

chimney stack *n.* the part of a chimney that rises above the roof of a building.

chimney sweep *or* **sweeper** *n.* a person who cleans soot from chimneys.

chimp (tʃɪmp) *n. Inf.* short for **chimpanzee.**

chimpanzee (ˌtʃɪmpænˈziː) *n.* a gregarious and intelligent anthropoid ape, inhabiting forests in central W Africa. [C18: < Central African dialect]

chin (tʃɪn) *n.* **1.** the protruding part of the lower jaw. **2.** the front part of the face below the lips. **3. keep one's chin up.** *Inf.* to keep cheerful under difficult circumstances. **4. take it on the chin.** *Inf.* to face squarely up to a defeat, adversity, etc. ~*vb.* **chinning, chinned. 5.** *Gymnastics.* to raise one's chin to (a horizontal bar, etc.) when hanging by the arms. [OE *cinn*]

Chin. *abbrev. for:* **1.** China. **2.** Chinese.

china (ˈtʃaɪnə) *n.* **1.** ceramic ware of a type originally from China. **2.** any porcelain or similar ware. **3.** cups, saucers, etc., collectively. **4.** (*modifier*) made of china. [C16 *chiny,* < Persian *chīnī*]

china clay *n.* another name for **kaolin.**

Chinagraph (ˈtʃaɪnəˌgrɑːf) *n. Trademark.* a coloured pencil used for writing on china, glass, etc.

Chinaman (ˈtʃaɪnəmən) *n., pl.* **-men. 1.** a native or inhabitant of China. **2.** (*often not cap.*) *Cricket.* a ball bowled by a left-handed bowler to a right-handed batsman that spins from off to leg.

Chinatown (ˈtʃaɪnəˌtaʊn) *n.* a quarter of any city or town outside China with a predominantly Chinese population.

chinaware (ˈtʃaɪnəˌwɛə) *n.* articles made of china, esp. those made for domestic use.

chincherinchee (ˌtʃɪntʃərɪnˈtʃiː, -ˈrɪntʃɪ) *n.* a bulbous South African liliaceous plant having long spikes of white or yellow long-lasting flowers. [<?]

chinchilla (tʃɪnˈtʃɪlə) *n.* **1.** a small gregarious rodent inhabiting mountainous regions of South America. It is bred in captivity for its soft silvery grey fur. **2.** the highly valued fur of this animal. **3.** a thick napped woollen cloth used for coats. [C17: < Sp., ?< Aymara]

chin-chin *sentence substitute. Inf.* a greeting or toast. [C18: < Chinese (Peking) *ch'ing-ch'ing,* please-please]

Chindit (ˈtʃɪndɪt) *n.* a member of the Allied forces fighting behind the Japanese lines in Burma (1943–45). [C20: < Burmese *chinthé* a fabulous lion]

chine[1] (tʃaɪn) *n.* **1.** the backbone. **2.** the backbone of an animal with adjoining meat, cut for cooking. **3.** a ridge or crest of land. ~*vb.* **4.** (*tr.*) to cut (meat) along or across the backbone. [C14: < OF *eschine,* of Gmc origin; see SHIN]

chine[2] (tʃaɪn) *n. S English dialect.* a deep fissure in the wall of a cliff. [OE *cīnan* to crack]

Chinese (tʃaɪˈniːz) *adj.* **1.** of, relating to, or characteristic of China, its people, or their languages. ~*n.* **2.** (*pl.* **-nese**) a native or inhabitant of China or a descendant of one. **3.** any of the languages of China.

Chinese cabbage *n.* a Chinese plant that is related to the cabbage and has crisp edible leaves growing in a loose cylindrical head.

Chinese chequers *n.* (*functioning as sing.*) a board game played with marbles or pegs.

Chinese gooseberry *n.* another name for **kiwi fruit.**

Chinese lantern *n.* **1.** a collapsible lantern made of thin coloured paper. **2.** an Asian plant, cultivated for its attractive orange-red inflated calyx.

Chinese leaves *pl. n.* the edible leaves of a Chinese cabbage.

Chinese puzzle *n.* **1.** an intricate puzzle, esp. one consisting of boxes within boxes. **2.** a complicated problem.

Chinese wall *n.* (esp. in financial institutions) a notional barrier between departments in the same company in order to avoid conflicts of interest between them.

chink[1] (tʃɪŋk) *n.* **1.** a small narrow opening, such as a fissure or crack. **2. chink in one's armour.** a small but fatal weakness. [C16: ? var. of earlier *chine,* < OE *cine* crack]

chink[2] (tʃɪŋk) *vb.* **1.** to make or cause to make a light ringing sound, as by the striking of glasses or coins. ~*n.* **2.** such a sound. [C16: imit.]

chinless wonder (ˈtʃɪnlɪs) *n. Brit. inf.* a person, esp. upper-class, lacking strength of character.

chinoiserie (ʃiːnˌwɑːzəˈriː, -ˈwɑːzərɪ) *n.* **1.** a style of decorative or fine art based on imitations of Chinese motifs. **2.** an object or objects in this style. [F, < *chinois* CHINESE; see -ERY]

chinook (tʃɪˈnuːk, -ˈnʊk) *n.* **1.** a warm dry southwesterly wind blowing down the eastern slopes of the Rocky Mountains. **2.** a warm moist wind blowing onto the Washington and Oregon coasts from the sea. [C19: < Amerind]

Chinook (tʃɪˈnuːk, -ˈnʊk) *n.* **1.** (*pl.* **-nook** *or* **-nooks**) a North American Indian people of the Pacific coast near the Columbia River. **2.** the language of this people.

Chinook Jargon *n.* a pidgin language containing elements of North American Indian languages, English, and French: formerly used among fur traders and Indians on the NW coast of North America.

Chinook salmon *n.* a Pacific salmon valued as a food fish.

chintz (tʃɪnts) *n.* a printed, patterned cotton fabric, with glazed finish. [C17: < Hindi *chīnt,* < Sansk. *citra* gaily-coloured]

chintzy (ˈtʃɪntsɪ) *adj.* **chintzier, chintziest. 1.** of, resembling, or covered with chintz. **2.** *Brit. inf.* typical of the décor associated with the use of chintz soft furnishings.

chinwag (ˈtʃɪnˌwæg) *n. Brit. inf.* a chat.

chip (tʃɪp) *n.* **1.** a small piece removed by chopping, cutting, or breaking. **2.** a mark left after a small piece has been broken off something. **3.** (in some games) a counter used to represent money. **4.** a thin strip of potato fried in deep fat. **5.** the U.S. and Canad. name for **crisp** (sense 10). **6.** *Sport.* a shot, kick, etc., lofted into the air, and travelling only a short distance. **7.** *Electronics.* a tiny wafer of semiconductor material, such as silicon, processed to form a type of integrated circuit or component such as a transistor. **8.** a thin strip of wood or straw used for making woven hats, baskets, etc. **9.** *N.Z.* a container for soft fruit, made of thin sheets of wood; punnet. **10. chip off the old block.** *Inf.* a person who resembles one of his or her parents in behaviour. **11. have a chip on one's shoulder.** *Inf.* to be aggressive or bear a grudge. **12. have had one's chips.** *Brit. inf.* to be defeated, condemned to die, killed, etc. **13. when the chips are down.** *Inf.* at a time of crisis. ~*vb.* **chipping, chipped. 14.** to break small pieces from or become broken off in small pieces: *will the paint chip?* **15.** (*tr.*) to break or cut into small pieces: *to chip ice.* **16.** (*tr.*) to shape by chipping. **17.** *Austral.* to dig or weed (a crop) with a hoe. **18.** *Sport.* to strike or kick (a ball) in a high arc. [OE *cipp* (n.), *cippian* (vb.), <?]

chip-based *adj.* using or incorporating microchips in electronic equipment.

chipboard (ˈtʃɪpˌbɔːd) *n.* a thin rigid sheet made of compressed wood particles.

chip heater *n. Austral. & N.Z.* a domestic water heater that burns chips of wood.

chip in *vb.* (*adv.*) *Inf.* **1.** to contribute (money, time, etc.) to a cause or fund. **2.** (*intr.*) to interpose a remark or interrupt with a remark.

chipmunk (ˈtʃɪpˌmʌŋk) *n.* a burrowing rodent of North America and Asia, typically having black-striped yellowish fur and cheek pouches for storing food. [C19: of Algonquian origin]

chipolata (ˌtʃɪpəˈlɑːtə) *n. Chiefly Brit.* a small sausage. [via F < It., < *cipolla* onion]

Chippendale (ˈtʃɪpᵊnˌdeɪl) *adj.* (of furniture) designed by, made by, or in the style of Thomas Chippendale (?1718-79), characterized by the use of Chinese and Gothic motifs, cabriole legs, and massive carving.

chipper (ˈtʃɪpə) *adj. Inf.* **1.** cheerful; lively. **2.** smartly dressed.

chippy (ˈtʃɪpɪ) *n., pl.* **-pies.** **1.** *Brit. inf.* a fish-and-chip shop. **2.** *N.Z.* a potato crisp.

chip shot *n. Golf.* a short approach shot to the green, esp. one that is lofted.

chiro- *or* **cheiro-** *combining form.* of or by means of the hand: *chiromancy; chiropractic.* [via L < Gk *kheir* hand]

chirography (kaɪˈrɒgrəfɪ) *n.* another name for **calligraphy.** —**chiˈrographer** *n.* —**chirographic** (ˌkaɪrəˈgræfɪk) *or* ˌ**chiroˈgraphical** *adj.*

chiromancy (ˈkaɪrəˌmænsɪ) *n.* another word for **palmistry.** —ˈ**chiroˌmancer** *n.*

chiropody (kɪˈrɒpədɪ) *n.* the treatment of the feet, esp. corns, verrucas, etc. —**chiˈropodist** *n.*

chiropractic (ˌkaɪrəˈpræktɪk) *n.* a system of treating bodily disorders by manipulation of the spine and other parts. [C20: < CHIRO- + Gk *praktikos* PRACTICAL] —ˈ**chiroˌpractor** *n.*

chirp (tʃɜːp) *vb.* (*intr.*) **1.** (esp. of some birds and insects) to make a short high-pitched sound. **2.** to speak in a lively fashion. ~*n.* **3.** a chirping sound. [C15 (as *chirpinge*, gerund): imit.] —ˈ**chirper** *n.*

chirpy (ˈtʃɜːpɪ) *adj.* **chirpier, chirpiest.** *Inf.* cheerful; lively. —ˈ**chirpily** *adv.* —ˈ**chirpiness** *n.*

chirr *or* **churr** (tʃɜː) *vb.* **1.** (*intr.*) (esp. of certain insects, such as crickets) to make a shrill trilled sound. ~*n.* **2.** such a sound. [C17: imit.]

chirrup (ˈtʃɪrəp) *vb.* (*intr.*) **1.** (esp. of some birds) to chirp repeatedly. **2.** to make clucking sounds with the lips. ~*n.* **3.** such a sound. [C16: var. of CHIRP] —ˈ**chirruper** *n.* —ˈ**chirrupy** *adj.*

chisel (ˈtʃɪzᵊl) *n.* **1. a.** a hand tool for working wood, consisting of a flat steel blade with a handle. **b.** a similar tool without a handle for working stone or metal. ~*vb.* **-elling, -elled** *or U.S.* **-eling, -eled.** **2.** to carve (wood, stone, metal, etc.) or form (an engraving, statue, etc.) with or as with a chisel. **3.** *Sl.* to cheat or obtain by cheating. [C14: via OF, < Vulgar L *cīsellus* (unattested), < L *caesus* cut] —ˈ**chiseller** *n.*

chi-square distribution *n. Statistics.* a continuous single-parameter distribution used esp. to measure goodness of fit and to test hypotheses.

chi-square test *n. Statistics.* a test derived from the chi-square distribution to compare the goodness of fit of theoretical and observed frequency distributions.

chit[1] (tʃɪt) *n.* **1.** a voucher for a sum of money owed, esp. for food or drink. **2.** Also called: **chitty.** *Chiefly Brit.* **a.** a note or memorandum. **b.** a requisition or receipt. [C18: < earlier *chitty*, < Hindi *cittha* note, < Sansk. *citra* marked]

chit[2] (tʃɪt) *n. Facetious or derog.* a pert, impudent, or self-confident girl or child. [C14 (in the sense: young of an animal, kitten): <?]

chital (ˈtʃiːtᵊl) *n.* another name for **axis**[2] (the deer). [< Hindi]

chitchat (ˈtʃɪtˌtʃæt) *n.* **1.** gossip. ~*vb.* **-chatting, -chatted.** **2.** (*intr.*) to gossip.

chitin (ˈkaɪtɪn) *n.* a polysaccharide that is the principal component of the exoskeletons of arthropods and of the bodies of fungi. [C19: < F, < Gk *khitōn* CHITON + -IN] —ˈ**chitinous** *adj.*

chiton (ˈkaɪtᵊn, -tɒn) *n.* **1.** (in ancient Greece) a loose woollen tunic worn by men and women. **2.** any small primitive marine mollusc having an elongated body covered with eight overlapping shell plates. [C19: < Gk *khitōn* coat of mail]

chitterlings (ˈtʃɪtəlɪŋz) *or* **chitlings** (ˈtʃɪtlɪŋz) *pl. n.* (*sometimes sing.*) the intestines of a pig or other animal prepared as a dish. [C13: <?]

chiv (tʃɪv, ʃɪv) *or* **shiv** (ʃɪv) *Sl.* ~*n.* **1.** a knife. ~*vb.* **chivving, chivved** *or* **shivving, shivved.** **2.** to stab (someone). [C17: ? < Romany *chiv* blade]

chivalrous (ˈʃɪvəlrəs) *adj.* **1.** gallant; courteous. **2.** involving chivalry. [C14: < OF, < CHEVALIER] —ˈ**chivalrously** *adv.* —ˈ**chivalrousness** *n.*

chivalry (ˈʃɪvəlrɪ) *n., pl.* **-ries.** **1.** the combination of qualities expected of an ideal knight, esp. courage, honour, justice, and a readiness to help the weak. **2.** courteous behaviour, esp. towards women. **3.** the medieval system and principles of knighthood. **4.** knights, noblemen, etc., collectively. [C13: < OF *chevalerie*, < CHEVALIER] —ˈ**chivalric** *adj.*

chive (tʃaɪv) *n.* a small Eurasian purple-flowered alliaceous plant, whose long slender hollow leaves are used in cooking. Also called: **chives.** [C14: < OF *cive*, ult. < L *caepa* onion]

chivy, chivvy (ˈtʃɪvɪ), *or* **chevy** *Brit.* ~*vb.* **chivying, chivied, chivvying, chivvied,** *or* **chevying, chevied.** **1.** (*tr.*) to harass or nag. **2.** (*tr.*) to hunt. **3.** (*intr.*) to run about. ~*n., pl.* **chivies, chivvies,** *or* **chevies.** **4.** a hunt. **5.** *Obs.* a hunting cry. [C19: var. of *chevy*, prob. < *Chevy Chase*, a Scottish border ballad]

chlamydia (kləˈmɪdɪə) *n.* a microorganism of a type midway between a virus and a bacterium that causes trachoma and inflammation of the genital organs in women and of the urinary passage in men. [C20: NL, < Gk *khlamus* mantle + -IA]

chloral (ˈklɔːrəl) *n.* **1.** a colourless oily liquid with a pungent odour, made from chlorine and acetaldehyde and used in preparing chloral hydrate and DDT. **2.** short for **chloral hydrate.**

chloral hydrate *n.* a colourless crystalline soluble solid produced by the reaction of chloral with water and used as a sedative and hypnotic.

chloramphenicol (ˌklɔːræmˈfɛnɪˌkɒl) *n.* a broad-spectrum antibiotic used esp. in treating typhoid fever and rickettsial infections. [C20: < CHLORO- + AM(IDE) + PHE(NO)- + NI(TRO)- + (GLY)COL]

chlorate (ˈklɔːreɪt, -rɪt) *n.* any salt of chloric acid, containing the monovalent ion ClO_3^-.

chlordane (ˈklɔːdeɪn) *or* **chlordan** *n.* a white insoluble toxic solid used as an insecticide. [C20: < CHLORO- + (IN)D(OLE + -ENE) + -ANE]

chloric (ˈklɔːrɪk) *adj.* of or containing chlorine in the pentavalent state.

chloric acid *n.* a strong acid with a pungent smell, known only in solution and in the form of chlorate salts. Formula: $HClO_3$.

chloride (ˈklɔːraɪd) *n.* **1.** any salt of hydrochloric acid, containing the chloride ion Cl^-. **2.** any compound containing a chlorine atom, such as methyl chloride, CH_3Cl.

chloride of lime *or* **chlorinated lime** *n.* another name for **bleaching powder.**

chlorinate (ˈklɔːrɪˌneɪt) *vb.* (*tr.*) **1.** to combine or treat (a substance) with chlorine. **2.** to disinfect (water) with chlorine. —ˌ**chlorinˈation** *n.* —ˈ**chlorinˌator** *n.*

chlorine (ˈklɔːriːn) *or* **chlorin** (ˈklɔːrɪn) *n.* a toxic pungent greenish-yellow gas of the halogen group; occurring only in the combined state, mainly in common salt: used in the manufacture of many organic chemicals, in water purification, and as a disinfectant and bleaching agent. Symbol: Cl; atomic no.: 17; atomic wt.: 35.453. [C19 (coined by Sir Humphrey Davy): < CHLORO- + -INE[2], referring to its colour]

chlorite[1] (ˈklɔːraɪt) *n.* any of a group of green soft secondary minerals consisting of the hydrated silicates of aluminium, iron, and magnesium. [C18: < L, < Gk, < *khlōros* greenish yellow] —**chloritic** (klɔːˈrɪtɪk) *adj.*

chlorite[2] (ˈklɔːraɪt) *n.* any salt of chlorous acid.

chloro- *or before a vowel* **chlor-** *combining form.* **1.** indicating the colour green: *chlorophyll.* **2.** chlorine: *chloroform.*

chlorofluorocarbon (ˌklɔːrəˌflʊərəʊˈkɑːbᵊn) *n. Chem.* any of various gaseous compounds of carbon, hydrogen, chlorine, and fluorine, used as refrigerants, aerosol propellants, solvents, and in foam: some cause a breakdown of ozone in the earth's atmosphere.

chloroform (ˈklɔːrəˌfɔːm) *n.* a heavy volatile liquid with a sweet taste and odour, used as a solvent and cleansing agent and in refrigerants: formerly used as an inhalation anaesthetic. Formula: $CHCl_3$. [C19: < CHLORO- + *formyl* < FORMIC]

Chloromycetin (ˌklɔːrəʊmaɪˈsiːtɪn) *n. Trademark.* a brand of **chloramphenicol.**

chlorophyll *or U.S.* **chlorophyl** (ˈklɔːrəfɪl) *n.* the green pigment of plants, occurring in chloroplasts, that traps the energy of sunlight for photosynthesis: used as a colouring agent (**E140**) in medicines and food. —**ˈchloroˌphylloid** *adj.* —**ˌchloroˈphyllous** *adv.*

chloroplast (ˈklɔːrəʊˌplæst) *n.* a plastid containing chlorophyll and other pigments, occurring in plants that carry out photosynthesis.

chlorosis (kləˈrəʊsɪs) *n.* a once-common iron-deficiency disease of adolescent girls, characterized by greenish-yellow skin colour, weakness, and palpitation. Also called: **greensickness.** [C17: < CHLORO- + -OSIS]

chlorous (ˈklɔːrəs) *adj.* **1.** of or containing chlorine in the trivalent state. **2.** of or containing chlorous acid.

chlorous acid *n.* an unstable acid that is a strong oxidizing agent. Formula: $HClO_2$.

chlorpromazine (klɔːˈprɒməˌziːn) *n.* a drug used as a sedative and tranquillizer. [C20: < CHLORO- + PRO(PYL + A)M(INE) + AZINE]

chlortetracycline (klɔːˌtɛtrəˈsaɪkliːn) *n.* an antibiotic used in treating many bacterial and rickettsial infections and some viral infections.

chock (tʃɒk) *n.* **1.** a block or wedge of wood used to prevent the sliding or rolling of a heavy object. **2.** *Naut.* **a.** a ringlike device with an opening at the top through which a rope is placed. **b.** a cradle-like support for a boat, barrel, etc. ~*vb.* (*tr.*) **3.** (usually foll. by *up*) *Brit.* to cram full. **4.** to fit with or secure by a chock. **5.** to support (a boat, barrel, etc.) on chocks. ~*adv.* **6.** as closely or tightly as possible: *chock against the wall.* [C17: <?; ? rel. to OF *çoche* log]

chock-a-block *adj., adv.* **1.** filled to capacity; in a crammed state. **2.** *Naut.* with the blocks brought close together, as when a tackle is pulled as tight as possible.

chocker (ˈtʃɒkə) *adj.* **1.** *Austral. & N.Z. inf.* full up; packed. **2.** *Brit. sl.* irritated; fed up. [C20: < CHOCK-A-BLOCK]

chock-full *or* **choke-full** *adj.* (*postpositive*) completely full. [C17 *choke-full;* see CHOKE, FULL[1]]

choco *or* **chocko** (ˈtʃɒkəʊ) *n., pl.* **chocos** *or* **chockos.** *Austral. sl.* a conscript or militiaman. [< *chocolate soldier*]

chocolate (ˈtʃɒkəlɪt, ˈtʃɒklɪt, -lət) *n.* **1.** a food preparation made from roasted ground cacao seeds, usually sweetened and flavoured. **2.** a drink or sweetmeat made from this. **3. a.** a deep brown colour. **b.** (*as adj.*): *a chocolate carpet.* [C17: < Sp., < Aztec *xocolatl,* < *xococ* sour + *atl* water] —**ˈchocolaty** *adj.*

chocolate-box *n.* (*modifier*) *Inf.* sentimentally pretty or appealing.

Choctaw (ˈtʃɒktɔː) *n.* **1.** (*pl.* **-taws** *or* **-taw**) a member of a N American people originally of Alabama. **2.** their language. [C18: < Choctaw *Chahta*]

choice (tʃɔɪs) *n.* **1.** the act or an instance of choosing or selecting. **2.** the opportunity or power of choosing. **3.** a person or thing chosen or that may be chosen: *he was a possible choice.* **4.** an alternative action or possibility: *what choice did I have?* **5.** a supply from which to select. ~*adj.* **6.** of superior quality; excellent: *choice wine.* [C13: < OF, < *choisir* to CHOOSE] —**ˈchoicely** *adv.* —**ˈchoiceness** *n.*

choir (ˈkwaɪə) *n.* **1.** an organized group of singers, esp. for singing in church services. **2.** the part of a cathedral, abbey, or church in front of the altar and used by the choir and clergy. **3.** a number of instruments of the same family playing together: *a brass choir.* **4.** Also called: **choir organ.** one of the manuals on an organ controlling a set of soft sweet-toned pipes. [C13 *quer,* < OF *cuer,* < L CHORUS]

choirboy (ˈkwaɪəˌbɔɪ) *n.* a young boy who sings the treble part in a church choir.

choir school *n.* (in Britain) a school attached to a cathedral, college, etc., offering general education to boys whose singing ability is good.

choke (tʃəʊk) *vb.* **1.** (*tr.*) to hinder or stop the breathing of (a person or animal), esp. by constricting the windpipe or by asphyxiation. **2.** (*intr.*) to have trouble or fail in breathing, swallowing, or speaking. **3.** (*tr.*) to block or clog up (a passage, pipe, street, etc.). **4.** (*tr.*) to retard the growth or action of: *the weeds are choking my plants.* **5.** (*tr.*) to enrich the petrol-air mixture by reducing the air supply to (a carburettor, petrol engine, etc.). ~*n.* **6.** the act or sound of choking. **7.** a device in the carburettor of a petrol engine that enriches the petrol-air mixture by reducing the air supply. **8.** any mechanism for reducing the flow of a fluid in a pipe, tube, etc. **9.** Also called: **choke coil.** *Electronics.* an inductor having a relatively high impedance, used to prevent the passage of high frequencies or to smooth the output of a rectifier. [OE *āceōcian*] —**ˈchoky** *or* **ˈchokey** *adj.*

choke back *or* **down** *vb.* (*tr., adv.*) to suppress (anger, tears, etc.).

choke chain *n.* a collar and lead for a dog so designed that if the dog drags on the lead the collar tightens round its neck.

choked (tʃəʊkt) *adj. Brit. inf.* annoyed or disappointed.

choker (ˈtʃəʊkə) *n.* **1.** a woman's high collar. **2.** any neckband or necklace worn tightly around the throat. **3.** a high clerical collar; stock. **4.** a person or thing that chokes.

choke up *vb.* (*tr., adv.*) **1.** to block (a drain, pipe, etc.) completely. **2.** *Inf.* (*usually passive*) to overcome (a person) with emotion.

chokey *or* **choky** (ˈtʃəʊkɪ) *n. Brit. sl.* prison. [C17: < Anglo-Indian, < Hindi *caukī* a lockup]

choko (ˈtʃəʊkəʊ) *n., pl.* **-kos.** *Austral. & N.Z.* the cucumber-like fruit of a tropical American vine. [C18: < Brazilian Indian]

chole- *or before a vowel* **chol-** *combining form.* bile or gall: *cholesterol.* [< Gk *kholē*]

choler (ˈkɒlə) *n.* **1.** anger or ill humour. **2.** *Arch.* one of the four bodily humours; yellow bile. [C14: < OF, < Med. L, < L: jaundice, CHOLERA]

cholera (ˈkɒlərə) *n.* an acute intestinal infection characterized by severe diarrhoea, cramp, etc.: caused by ingestion of water or food contaminated with the bacterium *Vibrio comma.* [C14: < L, < Gk *kholera* jaundice, < *kholē* bile] —**choleraic** (ˌkɒləˈreɪɪk) *adj.*

choleric (ˈkɒlərɪk) *adj.* **1.** bad-tempered. **2.** *Obs.* bilious or causing biliousness. —**ˈcholerically** *adv.*

cholesterol (kəˈlɛstəˌrɒl) *or* **cholesterin** (kəˈlɛstərɪn) *n.* a sterol found in all animal tissues, blood, bile, and animal fats. A high level of cholesterol is implicated in some cases of atherosclerosis. [C19: < CHOLE- + Gk *stereos* solid]

choline (ˈkəʊliːn, -ɪn, ˈkɒl-) *n.* a colourless viscous soluble alkaline substance present in animal tissues, esp. as a constituent of lecithin. [C19: < CHOLE- + -INE[2]]

chomp (tʃɒmp) *or* **chump** *vb.* **1.** to chew (food) noisily; champ. ~*n.* **2.** the act or sound of chewing in this manner. [var. of CHAMP[1]]

chondrite (ˈkɒndraɪt) *n.* a stony meteorite consisting mainly of silicate minerals in small spherical masses.

choof off (tʃʊf) *vb.* (*intr., adv.*) *Austral. sl.* to go away; make off.

chook (tʃʊk) *n. Inf., chiefly Austral. & N.Z.* a hen or chicken. Also called: **chookie.**

choose (tʃuːz) *vb.* **choosing, chose, chosen. 1.** to select (a person, thing, course of action, etc.) from a number of alternatives. **2.** (*tr.; takes a clause as object or an infinitive*) to consider it desirable or proper: *I don't choose to read that book.* **3.** (*intr.*) to like; please: *you may stand if you choose.* [OE *ceosan*] —ˈ**chooser** *n.*

choosy (ˈtʃuːzɪ) *adj.* **choosier, choosiest.** *Inf.* particular in making a choice; difficult to please.

chop[1] (tʃɒp) *vb.* **chopping, chopped. 1.** (often foll. by *down* or *off*) to cut (something) with a blow from an axe or other sharp tool. **2.** (*tr.;* often foll. by *up*) to cut into pieces. **3.** (*tr.*) *Brit. inf.* to dispense with or reduce. **4.** (*intr.*) to move quickly or violently. **5.** *Tennis, cricket, etc.* to hit (a ball) sharply downwards. **6.** *Boxing, karate, etc.* to punch or strike (an opponent) with a short sharp blow. ~*n.* **7.** a cutting blow. **8.** the act or an instance of chopping. **9.** a piece chopped off. **10.** a slice of mutton, lamb, or pork, generally including a rib. **11.** *Austral. & N.Z. sl.* a share (esp. in **get** *or* **hop in for one's chop**). **12.** *Austral. & N.Z.* a competition of skill and speed in chopping logs. **13.** *Sport.* a sharp downward blow or stroke. **14. not much chop.** *Austral. & N.Z. inf.* not much good; poor. **15. the chop.** *Sl., chiefly Brit.* dismissal from employment. [C16: var. of CHAP[1]]

chop[2] (tʃɒp) *vb.* **chopping, chopped. 1.** (*intr.*) to change direction suddenly; vacillate (esp. in **chop and change**). **2. chop logic.** use excessively subtle or involved argument. [OE *ceapian* to barter]

chop[3] (tʃɒp) *n.* a design stamped on goods as a trademark, esp. in the Far East. [C17: < Hindi *chhāp*]

chop chop *adv.* pidgin English for **quickly.** [C19: < Chinese dialect]

chophouse (ˈtʃɒpˌhaʊs) *n.* a restaurant specializing in steaks, grills, chops, etc.

choplogic (ˈtʃɒpˌlɒdʒɪk) *n.* fallacious reasoning. [C16: < CHOP[2] + LOGIC]

chopper (ˈtʃɒpə) *n.* **1.** *Chiefly Brit.* a small hand axe. **2.** a butcher's cleaver. **3.** a person or thing that cuts or chops. **4.** an informal name for a **helicopter. 5.** a device for periodically interrupting an electric current or beam of radiation to produce a pulsed current or beam. **6.** a type of bicycle or motorcycle with very high handlebars. **7.** *N.Z.* a child's bicycle. **8.** *Sl., chiefly U.S.* a submachine-gun.

choppy (ˈtʃɒpɪ) *adj.* **-pier, -piest.** (of the sea, weather, etc.) fairly rough. —ˈ**choppily** *adv.* —ˈ**choppiness** *n.*

chops (tʃɒps) *pl. n.* **1.** the jaws or cheeks; jowls. **2.** the mouth. **3. lick one's chops.** *Inf.* to anticipate with pleasure. [C16: <?]

chopsticks (ˈtʃɒpstɪks) *pl. n.* a pair of thin sticks, of ivory, wood, etc., used as eating utensils by the Chinese, Japanese, etc. [C17: < pidgin E, < *chop* quick, < Chinese dialect + STICK[1]]

chop suey (ˈsuːɪ) *n.* a Chinese-style dish originating in the U.S., consisting of meat, bean sprouts, etc., stewed and served with rice. [C19: < Chinese *tsap sui* odds and ends]

choral (ˈkɔːrəl) *adj.* relating to, sung by, or designed for a chorus or choir. —ˈ**chorally** *adv.*

chorale *or* **choral** (kɒˈrɑːl) *n.* **1.** a slow stately hymn tune. **2.** *Chiefly U.S.* a choir or chorus. [C19: < G *Choralgesang,* translation of L *cantus chorālis* choral song]

chord[1] (kɔːd) *n.* **1.** *Maths.* a straight line connecting two points on a curve or curved surface. **2.** *Engineering.* one of the principal members of a truss, esp. one that lies along the top or the bottom. **3.** *Anat.* a variant spelling of **cord. 4.** an emotional response, esp. one of sympathy: *the story struck the right chord.* [C16: < L, < Gk *khordē* gut, string; see CORD]

chord[2] (kɔːd) *n.* **1.** the simultaneous sounding of a group of musical notes, usually three or more in number. ~*vb.* **2.** (*tr.*) to provide (a melodic line) with chords. [C15: short for ACCORD; spelling infl. by CHORD[1]] —ˈ**chordal** *adj.*

chordate (ˈkɔːdeɪt) *n.* **1.** an animal with a backbone or notochord. ~*adj.* **2.** of or relating to the chordates. [C19: < Med. L *chordata:* see CHORD[1] & -ATE[1]]

chore (tʃɔː) *n.* **1.** a small routine task, esp. a domestic one. **2.** an unpleasant task. [C19: < ME *chare,* < OE *cierr* a job]

-chore *n. combining form.* (in botany) indicating a plant that is distributed by a certain means: *anemochore.* [< Gk *khōrein* to move] —**-chorous** *or* **-choric** *adj. combining form.*

chorea (kɒˈrɪə) *n.* a disorder of the central nervous system characterized by uncontrollable irregular brief jerky movements. Nontechnical name: **Saint Vitus's dance.** [C19: < NL, < L: dance, < Gk *khoreia;* see CHORUS]

choreograph (ˈkɒrɪəˌgrɑːf) *vb.* (*tr.*) to compose the steps and dances for (a ballet, etc.)

choreography (ˌkɒrɪˈɒgrəfɪ) *or* **choregraphy** (kɒˈrɛgrəfɪ) *n.* **1.** the composition of dance steps and sequences for ballet and stage and film dancing. **2.** the steps and sequences of a ballet or dance. **3.** the notation representing such steps. **4.** the art of dancing. [C18: < Gk *khoreia* dance + -GRAPHY] —ˌ**choreˈographer** *or* **choˈregrapher** *n.* —**choreographic** (ˌkɒrɪəˈgræfɪk) *or* **choregraphic** (ˌkɒrəˈgræfɪk) *adj.* —ˌ**choreoˈgraphically** *or* ˌ**choreˈgraphically** *adv.*

choric (ˈkɒrɪk) *adj.* of, like, or for a chorus, esp. of singing, dancing, or the speaking of verse.

chorion (ˈkɔːrɪən) *n.* the outer membrane surrounding an embryo. [C16: < Gk *khorion* afterbirth] —**chorionic** (ˌkɔːrɪˈɒnɪk) *adj.*

chorister (ˈkɒrɪstə) *n.* a singer in a choir, esp. a choirboy. [C14: < Med. L *chorista*]

choroid (ˈkɔːrɔɪd) *or* **chorioid** (ˈkɔːrɪˌɔɪd) *adj.* **1.** resembling the chorion, esp. in being vascular. ~*n.* **2.** the vascular membrane of the eyeball between the sclera and the retina. [C18: < Gk *khoroeidēs,* erroneously for *khorioeidēs,* < CHORION]

chortle (ˈtʃɔːtᵊl) *vb.* **1.** (*intr.*) to chuckle gleefully. ~*n.* **2.** a gleeful chuckle. [C19: coined (1871) by Lewis Carroll; prob. a blend of CHUCKLE + SNORT] —ˈ**chortler** *n.*

chorus (ˈkɔːrəs) *n., pl.* **-ruses. 1.** a large choir of singers or a piece of music composed for such a choir. **2.** a body of singers or dancers who perform together. **3.** a section of a song in which a soloist is joined by a group of singers, esp. in a recurring refrain. **4.** an intermediate section of a pop song, blues, etc., as distinct from the verse. **5.** *Jazz.* any of a series of variations on a theme. **6.** (in ancient Greece) **a.** a lyric poem sung by a group of dancers, originally as a religious rite. **b.** an ode or series of odes sung by a group of actors. **c.** the actors who sang the chorus and commented on the action of the play. **7. a.** (esp. in Elizabethan drama) the actor who spoke the prologue, etc. **b.** the part spoken by this actor. **8.** a group of people or animals producing words or sounds simultaneously. **9.** any speech, song, or utterance produced by a group of people or animals simultaneously: *the dawn chorus.* **10. in chorus.** in unison. ~*vb.* **11.** to speak, sing, or utter (words, sounds, etc.) in unison. [C16: < L, < Gk *khoros*]

chorus girl *n.* a girl who dances or sings in the chorus of a musical comedy, revue, etc.

chose (tʃəʊz) *vb.* the past tense of **choose.**

chosen (ˈtʃəʊzᵊn) *vb.* **1.** the past participle of **choose.** ~*adj.* **2.** selected or picked out, esp. for some special quality.

chough (tʃʌf) *n.* a large black passerine bird of parts of Europe, Asia, and Africa, with a long downward-curving red bill: family Corvidae (crows). [C14: <?]

choux pastry (ʃuː) *n.* a very light pastry made with eggs, used for éclairs, etc. [partial translation of F *pâte choux* cabbage dough]

chow (tʃaʊ) *n.* **1.** *Inf.* food. **2.** short for **chow-chow** (sense 1). **3. Chow.** *Austral. & N.Z. obs.* a derogatory term for **Chinese** (sense 2).

chow-chow *n.* **1.** a thick-coated breed of dog with a curled tail, originally from China. Often shortened to **chow. 2.** a Chinese preserve of ginger, orange peel, etc., in syrup. **3.** a mixed vegetable pickle. [C19: < pidgin E, prob. based on Chinese *cha* miscellaneous]

chowder (ˈtʃaʊdə) *n. Chiefly U.S. & Canad.* a thick

soup or stew containing clams or fish. [C18: < F *chaudière* kettle, < LL *caldāria;* see CAULDRON]

chow mein (meɪn) *n.* a Chinese-American dish, consisting of mushrooms, meat, shrimps, etc., served with fried noodles. [< Chinese *ch'ao mien* fried noodles]

Chr. *abbrev. for:* **1.** Christ. **2.** Christian.

chrism *or* **chrisom** (ˈkrɪzəm) *n.* a mixture of olive oil and balsam used for sacramental anointing in the Greek Orthodox and Roman Catholic Churches. [OE, < Med. L, < Gk, < *khriein* to anoint] —**chrismal** (ˈkrɪzməl) *adj.*

Christ (kraɪst) *n.* **1.** Jesus of Nazareth (Jesus Christ), regarded by Christians as fulfilling Old Testament prophecies of the Messiah. **2.** the Messiah or anointed one of God as the subject of Old Testament prophecies. **3.** an image or picture of Christ. *~interj.* **4.** *Taboo sl.* an oath expressing annoyance, surprise, etc. ~See also **Jesus.** [OE *Crīst,* < L *Chrīstus,* < Gk *khristos* anointed one (< *khriein* to anoint), translating Heb. *māshīah* MESSIAH] —ˈ**Christly** *adj.*

Christadelphian (ˌkrɪstəˈdɛlfɪən) *n.* **1.** a member of a Christian millenarian sect founded in the U.S. about 1848, holding that only the just will enter eternal life, and that the ignorant and unconverted will not be raised from the dead. *~adj.* **2.** of or relating to this body or its beliefs and practices. [C19: < LGk *khristadelphos, khristos* CHRIST + *adelpos* brother]

christen (ˈkrɪsᵊn) *vb.* (*tr.*) **1.** to give a Christian name to in baptism as a sign of incorporation into a Christian Church. **2.** another word for **baptize.** **3.** to give a name to anything, esp. with some ceremony. **4.** *Inf.* to use for the first time. [OE *cristnian,* < *Crīst* CHRIST] —ˈ**christening** *n.*

Christendom (ˈkrɪsᵊndəm) *n.* the collective body of Christians throughout the world.

Christian (ˈkrɪstʃən) *n.* **1. a.** a person who believes in and follows Jesus Christ. **b.** a member of a Christian Church or denomination. **2.** *Inf.* a person who possesses Christian virtues. *~adj.* **3.** of, relating to, or derived from Jesus Christ, his teachings, example, or followers. **4.** (*sometimes not cap.*) exhibiting kindness or goodness. —ˈ**christianly** *adj., adv.*

Christian Era *n.* the period beginning with the year of Christ's birth.

Christianity (ˌkrɪstɪˈænɪtɪ) *n.* **1.** the Christian religion. **2.** Christian beliefs or practices. **3.** a less common word for **Christendom.**

Christianize *or* **-ise** (ˈkrɪstʃəˌnaɪz) *vb.* (*tr.*) **1.** to make Christian or convert to Christianity. **2.** to imbue with Christian principles, spirit, or outlook. —ˌ**Christianiˈzation** *or* **-iˈsation** *n.* —ˈ**Christianˌizer** *or* **-ˌiser** *n.*

Christian name *n. Brit.* a personal name formally given to Christians at christening: loosely used to mean any person's first name.

Christian Science *n.* the religious system of the Church of Christ, Scientist, founded by Mary Baker Eddy (1866), and emphasizing spiritual healing. —**Christian Scientist** *n.*

Christlike (ˈkraɪstˌlaɪk) *adj.* resembling the spirit of Jesus Christ. —ˈ**Christˌlikeness** *n.*

Christmas (ˈkrɪsməs) *n.* **1. a.** the annual commemoration by Christians of the birth of Jesus Christ, on Dec. 25. **b.** Also called: **Christmas Day.** Dec. 25, observed as a day of secular celebrations when gifts and greetings are exchanged. **c.** (*as modifier*): *Christmas celebrations.* **2.** another name for **Christmastide.** [OE *Crīstes mæsse* MASS OF CHRIST] —ˈ**Christmassy** *adj.*

Christmas box *n.* a tip or present given at Christmas, esp. to postmen, tradesmen, etc.

Christmas Eve *n.* the evening or the whole day before Christmas Day.

Christmas pudding *n. Brit.* a rich steamed pudding containing suet, dried fruit, spices, etc. Also called: **plum pudding.**

Christmas rose *n.* an evergreen plant of S Europe and W Asia with white or pinkish winter-blooming flowers. Also called: **hellebore, winter rose.**

Christmastide (ˈkrɪsməsˌtaɪd) *n.* the season of Christmas, extending from Dec. 24 (Christmas Eve) to Jan. 6 (the festival of the Epiphany or Twelfth Night).

Christmas tree *n.* **1.** an evergreen tree or an imitation of one, decorated as part of Christmas celebrations. **2.** Also called: **Christmas bush.** *Austral.* any of various trees or shrubs flowering at Christmas and used for decoration. **3.** *N.Z.* another name for the **pohutukawa.**

Christy *or* **Christie** (ˈkrɪstɪ) *n., pl.* **-ties.** *Skiing.* a turn in which the body is swung sharply round with the skis parallel: used for stopping or changing direction quickly. [C20: < *Christiania,* former name of Oslo]

chroma (ˈkrəʊmə) *n.* the attribute of a colour that enables an observer to judge how much chromatic colour it contains. See also **saturation** (sense 4). [C19: < Gk *khrōma* colour]

chromate (ˈkrəʊmeɪt) *n.* any salt or ester of chromic acid.

chromatic (krəˈmætɪk) *adj.* **1.** of, relating to, or characterized by a colour or colours. **2.** *Music.* **a.** involving the sharpening or flattening of notes or the use of such notes in chords and harmonic progressions. **b.** of or relating to the chromatic scale or an instrument capable of producing it. [C17: < Gk, < *khrōma* colour] —**chroˈmatically** *adv.* —**chroˈmaticism** *n.* —**chromaticity** (ˌkrəʊməˈtɪsɪtɪ) *n.*

chromatic aberration *n.* a defect in a lens system in which different wavelengths of light are focused at different distances because they are refracted through different angles. It produces a blurred image with coloured fringes.

chromatics (krəʊˈmætɪks) *n.* (*functioning as sing.*) the science of colour.

chromatic scale *n.* a twelve-note scale including all the semitones of the octave.

chromatin (ˈkrəʊmətɪn) *n.* the part of the nucleus that consists of DNA, RNA, and proteins, forms the chromosomes, and stains with basic dyes.

chromato- *or before a vowel* **chromat-** *combining form.* **1.** indicating colour or coloured: *chromatophore.* **2.** indicating chromatin: *chromatolysis.* [< Gk *khrōma, khrōmat-* colour]

chromatography (ˌkrəʊməˈtɒgrəfɪ) *n.* the technique of separating and analysing the components of a mixture of liquids or gases by selective adsorption.

chrome (krəʊm) *n.* **1. a.** another word for **chromium,** esp. when present in a pigment or dye. **b.** (*as modifier*): *a chrome dye.* **2.** anything plated with chromium. **3.** a pigment or dye that contains chromium. *~vb.* **4.** to plate or be plated with chromium. **5.** to treat or be treated with a chromium compound, as in dyeing or tanning. [C19: via F < Gk *khrōma* colour]

-chrome *n. and adj. combining form.* colour, coloured, or pigment: *monochrome.* [< Gk *khrōma* colour]

chrome dioxide *n.* a chemical compound, chromium dioxide, which is used as the sensitive coating on some cassette tapes. Formula: CrO_2.

chrome steel *n.* any of various hard rust-resistant steels containing chromium.

chrome yellow *n.* any yellow pigment consisting of lead chromate.

chromic (ˈkrəʊmɪk) *adj.* **1.** of or containing chromium in the trivalent state. **2.** of or derived from chromic acid.

chromic acid *n.* an unstable dibasic oxidizing acid known only in solution and in the form of chromate salts. Formula: H_2CrO_4.

chromite (ˈkrəʊmaɪt) *n.* a brownish-black mineral consisting of a ferrous chromic oxide in crystalline form: the only commercial source of chromium. Formula: $FeCr_2O_4$.

chromium (ˈkrəʊmɪəm) *n.* a hard grey metallic element, used in steel alloys and electroplating to increase hardness and corrosion-resistance. Symbol: Cr; atomic no.: 24; atomic wt.: 51.996. [C19: < NL, < F: CHROME]

chromium steel *n.* another name for **chrome steel.**

chromo ('krəuməu) *n., pl.* **-mos.** short for **chromolithograph.**

chromo- *or before a vowel* **chrom-** *combining form.* **1.** indicating colour, coloured, or pigment: *chromogen.* **2.** indicating chromium: *chromyl.* [< Gk *khrōma* colour]

chromolithograph (ˌkrəuməu'lɪθəˌgrɑːf) *n.* a picture produced by chromolithography.

chromolithography (ˌkrəuməulɪ'θɒgrəfɪ) *n.* the process of making coloured prints by lithography. —**chromoli'thographer** *n.* —**chromolithographic** (ˌkrəuməulɪθə'græfɪk) *adj.*

chromosome ('krəuməˌsəum) *n.* any of the microscopic rod-shaped structures that appear in a cell nucleus during cell division, consisting of nucleoprotein arranged into units (genes) that are responsible for the transmission of hereditary characteristics. —ˌ**chromo'somal** *adj.*

chromosphere ('krəuməˌsfɪə) *n.* a gaseous layer of the sun's atmosphere extending from the photosphere to the corona. —**chromospheric** (ˌkrəumə'sfɛrɪk) *adj.*

chromous ('krəuməs) *adj.* of or containing chromium in the divalent state.

chron. *or* **chronol.** *abbrev. for:* **1.** chronological. **2.** chronology.

Chron. *Bible. abbrev. for* Chronicles.

chronic ('krɒnɪk) *adj.* **1.** continuing for a long time; constantly recurring. **2.** (of a disease) developing slowly, or of long duration. Cf. **acute** (sense 7). **3.** inveterate; habitual: *a chronic smoker.* **4.** *Inf.* **a.** very bad: *the play was chronic.* **b.** very serious: *he left her in a chronic condition.* [C15: < L, < Gk, < *khronos* time] —'**chronically** *adv.* —**chronicity** (krɒ'nɪsɪtɪ) *n.*

chronicle ('krɒnɪk°l) *n.* **1.** a record or register of events in chronological order. ~*vb.* **2.** (*tr.*) to record in or as if in a chronicle. [C14: < Anglo-F, via L *chronica* (pl.), < Gk *khronika* annals; see CHRONIC] —'**chronicler** *n.*

chrono- *or before a vowel* **chron-** *combining form.* time: *chronology.* [< Gk *khronos* time]

chronograph ('krɒnəˌgrɑːf, 'krəunə-) *n.* an accurate instrument for recording small intervals of time. —**chronographic** (ˌkrɒnə'græfɪk) *adj.*

chronological (ˌkrɒnə'lɒdʒɪk°l, ˌkrəu-) *or* **chronologic** *adj.* **1.** (esp. of a sequence of events) arranged in order of occurrence. **2.** relating to or in accordance with chronology. —ˌ**chrono'logically** *adv.*

chronology (krə'nɒlədʒɪ) *n., pl.* **-gies.** **1.** the determination of the proper sequence of past events. **2.** the arrangement of dates, events, etc., in order of occurrence. **3.** a table of events arranged in order of occurrence. —**chro'nologist** *n.*

chronometer (krə'nɒmɪtə) *n.* a timepiece designed to be accurate in all conditions of temperature, pressure, etc., used esp. at sea. —**chronometric** (ˌkrɒnə'mɛtrɪk) *or* ˌ**chrono'metrical** *adj.* —ˌ**chrono'metrically** *adv.*

chronometry (krə'nɒmɪtrɪ) *n.* the science of measuring time with extreme accuracy.

chronon ('krəunɒn) *n.* a unit of time equal to the time that a photon would take to traverse the diameter of an electron: about 10^{-24} seconds.

chrysalid ('krɪsəlɪd) *n.* **1.** another name for **chrysalis.** ~*adj.* **2.** of or relating to a chrysalis.

chrysalis ('krɪsəlɪs) *n., pl.* **chrysalises** *or* **chrysalides** (krɪ'sælɪˌdiːz). **1.** the pupa of a moth or butterfly, in a case or cocoon. **2.** anything in the process of developing. [C17: < L, < Gk *khrusallis,* < *khrusos* gold]

chrysanthemum (krɪ'sænθəməm) *n.* **1.** any of various widely cultivated plants of the composite family, having brightly coloured showy flower heads in autumn. **2.** any other plant of the genus *Chrysanthemum,* such as the oxeye daisy. [C16: < L: marigold, < Gk, < *khrusos* gold + *anthemon* flower]

chryselephantine (ˌkrɪsɛlɪ'fæntɪn) *adj.* (of ancient Greek statues, etc.) made of or overlaid with gold and ivory. [C19: < Gk, < *khrusos* gold + *elephas* ivory]

chrysoberyl ('krɪsəˌbɛrɪl) *n.* a rare very hard greenish-yellow mineral consisting of beryllium aluminate: used as a gemstone. Formula: $BeAl_2O_4$. [C17: < L, < Gk, < *khrusos* gold + *bērullos* beryl]

chrysolite ('krɪsəˌlaɪt) *n.* a brown or yellowish-green olivine: used as a gemstone. [C14 *crisolite,* < OF, < L, < Gk, < *khrusos* gold + *lithos* stone]

chrysoprase ('krɪsəˌpreɪz) *n.* an apple-green variety of chalcedony: used as a gemstone. [C13 *crisopace,* < OF, < L, < Gk, < *khrusos* gold + *prason* leek]

chthonian ('θəunɪən) *or* **chthonic** ('θɒnɪk) *adj.* of or relating to the underworld. [C19: < Gk *khthonios* in or under the earth, < *khthōn* earth]

chub (tʃʌb) *n., pl.* **chub** *or* **chubs.** **1.** a common European freshwater cyprinid game fish, having a cylindrical dark greenish body. **2.** any of various North American fishes, esp. certain whitefishes and minnows. [C15: <?]

chubby ('tʃʌbɪ) *adj.* **-bier, -biest.** (esp. of the human form) plump and round. [C17: ?< CHUB] —'**chubbiness** *n.*

chuck[1] (tʃʌk) *vb.* (*mainly tr.*) **1.** *Inf.* to throw. **2.** to pat affectionately, esp. under the chin. **3.** *Inf.* (sometimes foll. by *in* or *up*) to give up; reject: *he chucked up his job.* ~*n.* **4.** a throw or toss. **5.** a pat under the chin. **6.** **the chuck.** *Inf.* dismissal. ~See also **chuck in, chuck off, chuck out.** [C16: <?]

chuck[2] (tʃʌk) *n.* **1.** Also called: **chuck steak.** a cut of beef from the neck to the shoulder blade. **2.** a device that holds a workpiece in a lathe or tool in a drill. [C17: var. of CHOCK]

chuck[3] (tʃʌk) *n.* *W Canad.* **1.** a large body of water. **2.** In full: **saltchuck.** the sea. [C19: < Chinook Jargon, of Amerind origin, < *chauk*]

chuck in *vb.* (*adv.*) **1.** (*tr.*) *Brit inf.* to abandon or give up: *to chuck in a hopeless attempt.* **2.** (*intr.*) *Austral. inf.* to contribute to the cost of something. ~*n.* **chuck-in.** **3.** *Austral. inf.* a contribution to the cost of something.

chuckle ('tʃʌk°l) *vb.* (*intr.*) **1.** to laugh softly or to oneself. **2.** (of animals, esp. hens) to make a clucking sound. ~*n.* **3.** a partly suppressed laugh. [C16: prob. < *chuck* cluck + *le*]

chucklehead ('tʃʌk°lˌhɛd) *n.* *Inf.* a stupid person; blockhead; dolt.

chuck off *vb.* (*intr., adv.;* often foll. by *at*) *Austral. & N.Z. inf.* to sneer.

chuck out *vb.* (*tr., adv.;* often foll. by *of*) *Inf.* to eject forcibly (from); throw out (of).

chuddy ('tʃʌdɪ) *n.* *Austral. & N.Z. inf.* chewing gum.

chuff[1] (tʃʌf) *n.* **1.** a puffing sound as of a steam engine. ~*vb.* **2.** (*intr.*) to move while emitting such sounds. [C20: imit.]

chuff[2] (tʃʌf) *vb.* (*tr.; usually passive*) *Brit. sl.* to please or delight: *he was chuffed by his pay rise.* [prob. < *chuff* (adj.) pleased, happy]

chug (tʃʌg) *n.* **1.** a short dull sound, such as that made by an engine. ~*vb.* **chugging, chugged.** **2.** (*intr.*) (of an engine, etc.) to operate while making such sounds. [C19: imit.]

chukar (tʃʌ'kɑː) *n.* a common Indian partridge having a red bill and black-barred sandy plumage. [< Hindi *cakor,* < Sansk. *cakora,* prob. imit.]

chukka boot ('tʃʌkə) *or* **chukka** *n.* an ankle-high boot worn for playing polo. [C19: < CHUKKER]

chukker *or* **chukka** ('tʃʌkə) *n.* *Polo.* a period of continuous play, generally lasting 7½ minutes. [C20: < Hindi *cakkar,* < Sansk. *cakra* wheel]

chum (tʃʌm) *n.* **1.** *Inf.* a close friend. ~*vb.* **chumming, chummed.** **2.** (*intr.;* usually foll. by *up with*) to be or become an intimate friend (of). [C17 (meaning: a person sharing rooms with another): prob. shortened < *chamber fellow*]

chummy ('tʃʌmɪ) *adj.* **-mier, -miest.** *Inf.* friendly. —'**chummily** *adv.* —'**chumminess** *n.*

chump (tʃʌmp) *n.* **1.** *Inf.* a stupid person. **2.** a thick heavy block of wood. **3.** the thick blunt end of anything, esp. of a piece of meat. **4.** *Brit. sl.* the head (esp. in **off one's chump**). [C18: ? a blend of CHUNK + LUMP[1]]

chunder (ˈtʃʌndə) *Sl., chiefly Austral.* ~*vb.* (*intr.*) **1.** to vomit. ~*n.* **2.** vomit. [C20: <?]

chunk (tʃʌŋk) *n.* **1.** a thick solid piece, as of meat, wood, etc. **2.** a considerable amount. [C17: var. of CHUCK²]

chunky (ˈtʃʌŋkɪ) *adj.* **chunkier, chunkiest. 1.** thick and short. **2.** containing thick pieces. **3.** *Chiefly Brit.* (of clothes, esp. knitwear) made of thick bulky material. —ˈ**chunkiness** *n.*

Chunnel (ˈtʃʌnᵊl) *n. Inf.* the tunnel to be built under the English Channel, linking England and France. [C20: < CH(ANNEL) + T(UNNEL)]

chunter (ˈtʃʌntə) *vb.* (*intr.*) *Brit. inf.* to mutter or grumble. [C16: prob. imit.]

church (tʃɜːtʃ) *n.* **1.** a building for public worship, esp. Christian worship. **2.** an occasion of public worship. **3.** the clergy as distinguished from the laity. **4.** (*usually cap.*) institutionalized forms of religion as a political or social force: *conflict between Church and State.* **5.** (*usually cap.*) the collective body of all Christians. **6.** (*often cap.*) a particular Christian denomination or group. **7.** (*often cap.*) the Christian religion. ~Related adj.: **ecclesiastical.** ~*vb.* (*tr.*) **8.** *Church of England.* to bring (someone, esp. a woman after childbirth) to church for special ceremonies. [OE *cirice,* < LGk, < Gk *kuriakon* (*dōma*) the Lord's (house), < *kurios* master, < *kuros* power]

Church Army *n.* a voluntary Anglican organization founded to assist the parish clergy.

Church Commissioners *pl. n. Brit.* a group of representatives of Church and State that administers the property of the Church of England.

churchgoer (ˈtʃɜːtʃˌgəʊə) *n.* a person who attends church regularly. —ˈ**churchˌgoing** *adj., n.*

churchly (ˈtʃɜːtʃlɪ) *adj.* appropriate to or associated with the church. —ˈ**churchliness** *n.*

churchman (ˈtʃɜːtʃmən) *n., pl.* **-men. 1.** a clergyman. **2.** a male member of a church.

Church of Christ, Scientist *n.* the official name for the **Christian Scientists.**

Church of England *n.* the reformed established state Church in England, with the Sovereign as its temporal head.

Church of Jesus Christ of Latter-Day Saints *n.* the official name for the Mormon Church.

churchwarden (ˌtʃɜːtʃˈwɔːdᵊn) *n.* **1.** *Church of England, Episcopal Church.* one of two assistants of a parish priest who administer the secular affairs of the church. **2.** a long-stemmed tobacco pipe made of clay.

churchwoman (ˈtʃɜːtʃˌwʊmən) *n., pl.* **-women.** a female member of a church.

churchyard (ˈtʃɜːtʃˌjɑːd) *n.* the grounds round a church, used as a graveyard.

churinga (tʃəˈrɪŋgə) *n., pl.* **-ga** *or* **-gas.** a sacred amulet of the Australian Aborigines. [< Abor.]

churl (tʃɜːl) *n.* **1.** a surly ill-bred person. **2.** *Arch.* a farm labourer. **3.** *Arch.* a miserly person. [OE *ceorl*] —ˈ**churlish** *adj.*

churn (tʃɜːn) *n.* **1.** *Brit.* a large container for milk. **2.** a vessel or machine in which cream or whole milk is vigorously agitated to produce butter. ~*vb.* **3. a.** to agitate (milk or cream) to make butter. **b.** to make (butter) by this process. **4.** (sometimes foll. by *up*) to move or cause to move with agitation. [OE *ciern*]

churn out *vb.* (*tr., adv.*) *Inf.* **1.** to produce (something) at a rapid rate: *to churn out ideas.* **2.** to perform (something) mechanically: *to churn out a song.*

churr (tʃɜː) *vb., n.* a variant spelling of **chirr.**

chute¹ (ʃuːt) *n.* **1.** an inclined channel or vertical passage down which water, parcels, coal, etc., may be dropped. **2.** a steep slope, used as a slide as for toboggans. **3.** a slide into a swimming pool. **4.** a rapid or waterfall. [C19: < OF *cheoite,* fem. p.p. of *cheoir* to fall, < L *cadere;* in some senses, var. spelling of SHOOT]

chute² (ʃuːt) *n., vb. Inf.* short for **parachute.** —ˈ**chutist** *n.*

chutney (ˈtʃʌtnɪ) *n.* a pickle of Indian origin, made from fruit, vinegar, spices, sugar, etc.: *mango chutney.* [C19: < Hindi *catnī,* <?]

chutzpah (ˈxʊtspə) *n. U.S. & Canad. inf.* shameless audacity; impudence. [C20: < Yiddish]

chyack (ˈtʃaɪæk) *vb., n.* a variant spelling of **chiack.**

chyle (kaɪl) *n.* a milky fluid composed of lymph and emulsified fat globules, formed in the small intestine during digestion. [C17: < LL, < Gk *khulos* juice] —**chylaceous** (kaɪˈleɪʃəs) *or* ˈ**chylous** *adj.*

chyme (kaɪm) *n.* the thick fluid mass of partially digested food that leaves the stomach. [C17: < LL, < Gk *khumos* juice] —ˈ**chymous** *adj.*

chypre *French.* (ʃiprə) *n.* a perfume made from sandalwood. [lit.: Cyprus, ? where it originated]

Ci *symbol for* curie.

CI *abbrev. for* Channel Islands.

CIA *abbrev. for* Central Intelligence Agency; a federal U.S. bureau created in 1947 to coordinate and conduct espionage and intelligence activities.

CIB *abbrev. for* Criminal Investigation Branch (of the New Zealand and Australian police).

ciborium (sɪˈbɔːrɪəm) *n., pl.* **-ria** (-rɪə). *Christianity.* **1.** a goblet-shaped lidded vessel used to hold consecrated wafers in Holy Communion. **2.** a canopy fixed over an altar. [C17: < Med. L, < L, < Gk *kibōrion* cup-shaped seed vessel of the Egyptian lotus]

cicada (sɪˈkɑːdə) *or* **cicala** *n., pl.* **-das, -dae** (-diː) *or* **-las, -le** (-leɪ). any large broad insect, most common in warm regions, having membranous wings: the males produce a high-pitched drone by vibration of a pair of drumlike abdominal organs. [C19: < L]

cicatrix (ˈsɪkətrɪks) *n., pl.* **cicatrices** (ˌsɪkəˈtraɪsiːz). **1.** the tissue that forms in a wound during healing; scar. **2.** a scar on a plant indicating the former point of attachment of a part, esp. a leaf. [C17: < L: scar, <?] —**cicatricial** (ˌsɪkəˈtrɪʃəl) *adj.*

cicatrize *or* **-trise** (ˈsɪkəˌtraɪz) *vb.* (of a wound or defect in tissue) to be closed by scar formation; heal. —ˌ**cicatriˈzation** *or* **-triˈsation** *n.*

cicely (ˈsɪsəlɪ) *n., pl.* **-lies.** short for **sweet cicely.** [C16: < L *seselis,* < Gk, <?]

cicerone (ˌsɪsəˈrəʊnɪ, ˌtʃɪtʃ-) *n., pl.* **-nes** *or* **-ni** (-nɪ). a person who conducts and informs sightseers. [C18: < It.: antiquarian scholar, guide, after *Cicero* (106–43 B.C.), Roman orator & writer]

CID (in Britain) *abbrev. for* Criminal Investigation Department; the detective division of a police force.

-cide *n. combining form.* **1.** indicating a person or thing that kills: *insecticide.* **2.** indicating a killing; murder: *homicide.* [< L *-cīda* (agent), *-cīdium* (act), < *caedere* to kill] —**-cidal** *adj. combining form.*

cider *or* **cyder** (ˈsaɪdə) *n.* **1.** an alcoholic drink made from the fermented juice of apples. **2.** Also called: **sweet cider.** *U.S. & Canad.* an unfermented drink made from apple juice. [C14: < OF, via Med. L, < LGk *sikera* strong drink, < Heb. *shēkhār*]

c.i.f. *or* **CIF** *abbrev. for* cost, insurance, and freight (included in the price quoted).

cig (sɪg) *or* **ciggy** (ˈsɪgɪ) *n., pl.* **cigs** *or* **ciggies.** *Inf.* a cigarette.

cigar (sɪˈgɑː) *n.* a cylindrical roll of cured tobacco leaves, for smoking. [C18: < Sp. *cigarro*]

cigarette *or U.S.* (*sometimes*) **cigaret** (ˌsɪgəˈrɛt) *n.* a short tightly rolled cylinder of tobacco, wrapped in thin paper for smoking. [C19: < F, lit.: a little CIGAR]

cigarette card *n.* a small picture card, formerly given away with cigarettes, now collected as a hobby.

cigarillo (ˌsɪgəˈrɪləʊ) *n., pl.* **-los.** a small cigar, often only slightly larger than a cigarette.

ciliary (ˈsɪlɪərɪ) *adj.* of or relating to cilia.

ciliary body *n.* the part of the eye that joins the choroid to the iris.

cilium (ˈsɪlɪəm) *n., pl.* **cilia** (ˈsɪlɪə). **1.** any of the short threads projecting from the surface of a cell, organism, etc., whose rhythmic beating causes movement. **2.** the technical name for **eyelash.**

[C18: NL, < L: (lower) eyelid, eyelash] —**ciliate** (ˈsɪlɪɪt, -eɪt) *or* ˈ**cili,ated** *adj.*
C in C *or* **C.-in-C.** *Mil. abbrev. for* Commander in Chief.
cinch (sɪntʃ) *n.* **1.** *Sl.* an easy task. **2.** *Sl.* a certainty. **3.** a U.S. and Canad. name for **girth** (sense 2). **4.** *U.S. inf.* a firm grip. ~*vb.* **5.** (often foll. by *up*) *U.S. & Canad.* to fasten a girth around (a horse). **6.** (*tr.*) *Inf.* to make sure of. **7.** (*tr.*) *Inf., chiefly U.S.* to get a firm grip on. [C19: < Sp., < L, < *cingere* to encircle]
cinchona (sɪŋˈkəʊnə) *n.* **1.** any tree or shrub of the South American genus *Cinchona*, having medicinal bark. **2.** the dried bark of any of these trees, which yields quinine. **3.** any of the drugs derived from cinchona bark. [C18: NL, after the Countess of *Chinchón* (1576–1639), vicereine of Peru] —**cinchonic** (sɪŋˈkɒnɪk) *adj.*
cincture (ˈsɪŋktʃə) *n.* something that encircles, esp. a belt or girdle. [C16: < L, < *cingere* to gird]
cinder (ˈsɪndə) *n.* **1.** a piece of incombustible material left after the combustion of coal, coke, etc.; clinker. **2.** a piece of charred material that burns without flames; ember. **3.** any solid waste from smelting or refining. **4.** (*pl.*) fragments of volcanic lava; scoriae. [OE *sinder*] —ˈ**cindery** *adj.*
Cinderella (ˌsɪndəˈrɛlə) *n.* **1.** a girl who achieves fame after being obscure. **2.** a poor, neglected, or unsuccessful person or thing. [C19: after *Cinderella*, the heroine of a fairy tale]
cine- *combining form.* indicating motion picture or cinema: *cine camera; cinephotography.*
cineaste (ˈsɪnɪˌæst) *n.* an enthusiast for films. [C20: F]
cinema (ˈsɪnɪmə) *n.* **1.** *Chiefly Brit.* a place designed for the exhibition of films. **2. the cinema. a.** the art or business of making films. **b.** films collectively. [C19 (earlier spelling: *kinema*): shortened < CINEMATOGRAPH] —**cinematic** (ˌsɪnɪˈmætɪk) *adj.* —ˌ**cineˈmatically** *adv.*
cinematograph (ˌsɪnɪˈmætəˌgrɑːf) *Chiefly Brit.* ~*n.* **1.** a combined camera, printer, and projector. ~*vb.* **2.** to take (pictures) with a film camera. [C19 (earlier spelling: *kinematograph*): < Gk *kinēma* motion + -GRAPH] —**cinematographer** (ˌsɪnɪməˈtɒgrəfə) *n.* —**cinematographic** (ˌsɪnɪˌmætəˈgræfɪk) *adj.* —ˌ**cineˌmatoˈgraphically** *adv.* —ˌ**cinemaˈtography** *n.*
cinéma vérité (*French* sinema verite) *n.* films characterized by subjects, actions, etc., that have the appearance of real life. [F, lit.: truth cinema]
cineraria (ˌsɪnəˈrɛərɪə) *n.* a plant of the Canary Islands, widely cultivated for its blue, purple, red, or variegated daisy-like flowers. [C16: < NL, < L, < *cinis* ashes; < its downy leaves]
cinerarium (ˌsɪnəˈrɛərɪəm) *n., pl.* **-raria** (-ˈrɛərɪə). a place for keeping the ashes of the dead after cremation. [C19: < L, < *cinerārius* relating to ashes] —**cinerary** (ˈsɪnərərɪ) *adj.*
cinerator (ˈsɪnəˌreɪtə) *n. Chiefly U.S.* a furnace for cremating corpses. —ˌ**cineˈration** *n.*
cinnabar (ˈsɪnəˌbɑː) *n.* **1.** a heavy red mineral consisting of mercuric sulphide: the chief ore of mercury. Formula: HgS. **2.** the red form of mercuric sulphide, esp. when used as a pigment. **3. a.** a bright red; vermilion. **b.** (*as adj.*): *a cinnabar tint.* **4.** a large red-and-black European moth. [C15: < OF, < L, < Gk *kinnabari*, of Oriental origin]
cinnamon (ˈsɪnəmən) *n.* **1.** a tropical Asian tree, having aromatic yellowish-brown bark. **2.** the spice obtained from the bark of this tree, used for flavouring food and drink. **3. a.** a light yellowish brown. **b.** (*as adj.*): *a cinnamon coat.* [C15: < OF, via L & Gk, < Heb. *qinnāmōwn*]
cinque (sɪŋk) *n.* the number five in cards, dice, etc. [C14: < OF *cinq* five]
cinquecento (ˌtʃɪŋkwɪˈtʃɛntəʊ) *n.* the 16th century, esp. in reference to Italian art, architecture, or literature. [C18: It., shortened < *milcinquecento* 1500]
cinquefoil (ˈsɪŋkˌfɔɪl) *n.* **1.** any plant of the N temperate rosaceous genus *Potentilla*, typically having five-lobed compound leaves. **2.** an ornamental carving in the form of five arcs arranged in a circle and separated by cusps. [C13 *sink foil*, < OF, < L *quinquefolium* plant with five leaves]
Cinque Ports (sɪŋk) *pl. n.* an association of ports on the SE coast of England, which from late Anglo-Saxon times until 1685 provided ships for the king's service in return for the profits of justice in their courts.
cipher *or* **cypher** (ˈsaɪfə) *n.* **1.** a method of secret writing using substitution of letters according to a key. **2.** a secret message. **3.** the key to a secret message. **4.** an obsolete name for **zero** (sense 1). **5.** any of the Arabic numerals or the Arabic system of numbering **6.** a person or thing of no importance; nonentity. **7.** a design consisting of interwoven letters; monogram. ~*vb.* **8.** to put (a message) into secret writing. **9.** *Rare.* to perform (a calculation) arithmetically. [C14: < OF *cifre* zero, < Med. L, < Ar. *sifr* zero]
circa (ˈsɜːkə) *prep.* (used with a date) at the approximate time of: *circa 1182* B.C. Abbrev.: **c, ca.** [L: about]
circadian (sɜːˈkeɪdɪən) *adj.* of or relating to biological processes that occur regularly at 24-hour intervals. See also **biological clock.** [C20: < L *circa* about + *diēs* day]
circle (ˈsɜːkᵊl) *n.* **1.** a closed plane curve every point of which is equidistant from a given fixed point, the centre. **2.** the figure enclosed by such a curve. **3.** *Theatre.* the section of seats above the main level of the auditorium, usually comprising the dress circle and the upper circle. **4.** something formed or arranged in the shape of a circle. **5.** a group of people sharing an interest, activity, upbringing, etc.; set: *golf circles; a family circle.* **6.** a domain or area of activity, interest, or influence. **7.** a circuit. **8.** a process or chain of events or parts that forms a connected whole; cycle. **9.** a parallel of latitude. See also **great circle, small circle. 10.** one of a number of Neolithic or Bronze Age rings of standing stones, such as Stonehenge. **11. come full circle.** to arrive back at one's starting point. See also **vicious circle.** ~*vb.* **12.** to move in a circle (around). **13.** (*tr.*) to enclose in a circle; encircle. [C14: < L *circulus*, < *circus* ring, circle] —ˈ**circler** *n.*
circlet (ˈsɜːklɪt) *n.* a small circle or ring, esp. a circular ornament worn on the head. [C15: < OF *cerclet* a little CIRCLE]
circuit (ˈsɜːkɪt) *n.* **1. a.** a complete route or course, esp. one that is curved or circular or that lies around an object. **b.** the area enclosed within such a route. **2.** the act of following such a route: *we made three circuits of the course.* **3. a.** a complete path through which an electric current can flow. **b.** (*as modifier*): *a circuit diagram.* **4. a.** a periodical journey around an area, as made by judges, salesmen, etc. **b.** the places visited on such a journey. **c.** the persons making such a journey. **5.** an administrative division of the Methodist Church comprising a number of neighbouring churches. **6.** a number of theatres, cinemas, etc., under one management. **7.** *Sport.* **a.** a series of tournaments in which the same players regularly take part: *the international tennis circuit.* **b.** (usually preceded by *the*) the contestants who take part in such a series. **8.** *Chiefly Brit.* a motor-racing track, usually of irregular shape. ~*vb.* **9.** to make or travel in a circuit around (something). [C14: < L *circuitus*, < *circum* around + *īre* to go] —ˈ**circuital** *adj.*
circuit breaker *n.* a device that under abnormal conditions, such as a short circuit, stops the flow of current in an electrical circuit.
circuitous (səˈkjuːɪtəs) *adj.* indirect and lengthy; roundabout: *a circuitous route.* —**cirˈcuitously** *adv.* —**cirˈcuitousness** *n.*
circuitry (ˈsɜːkɪtrɪ) *n.* **1.** the design of an electrical circuit. **2.** the system of circuits used in an electronic device.
circuity (səˈkjuːɪtɪ) *n., pl.* **-ties.** (of speech, reasoning, etc.) a roundabout or devious quality.
circular (ˈsɜːkjʊlə) *adj.* **1.** of, involving, resem-

bling, or shaped like a circle. **2.** circuitous. **3.** (of arguments) futile because the truth of the premises cannot be established independently of the conclusion. **4.** travelling or occurring in a cycle. **5.** (of letters, announcements, etc.) intended for general distribution. ~*n.* **6.** a printed advertisement or notice for mass distribution. —**circularity** (ˌsɜːkjʊˈlærɪtɪ) *n.* —ˈ**circularly** *adv.*

circularize *or* **-ise** (ˈsɜːkjʊləˌraɪz) *vb.* (*tr.*) **1.** to distribute circulars to. **2.** to canvass or petition (people), as for support, votes, etc., by distributing letters, etc. **3.** to make circular. —ˌ**circulariˈzation** *or* **-iˈsation** *n.*

circular saw *n.* a power-driven saw in which a circular disc with a toothed edge is rotated at high speed.

circulate (ˈsɜːkjʊˌleɪt) *vb.* **1.** to send, go, or pass from place to place or person to person: *don't circulate the news.* **2.** to distribute or be distributed over a wide area. **3.** to move or cause to move through a circuit, system, etc., returning to the starting point: *blood circulates through the body.* **4.** to move in a circle. [C15: < L *circulārī*, < *circulus* CIRCLE] —ˈ**circuˌlative** *adj.* —ˈ**circuˌlator** *n.* —ˈ**circulatory** *adj.*

circulating library *n.* **1.** another word (esp. U.S.) for **lending library.** **2.** a small library circulated in turn to a group of institutions.

circulation (ˌsɜːkjʊˈleɪʃən) *n.* **1.** the transport of oxygenated blood through the arteries, and the return of oxygen-depleted blood through the veins to the heart, where the cycle is renewed. **2.** the flow of sap through a plant. **3.** any movement through a closed circuit. **4.** the spreading or transmission of something to a wider group of people or area. **5.** (of air and water) free movement within an area or volume. **6. a.** the distribution of newspapers, magazines, etc. **b.** the number of copies of an issue that are distributed. **7. in circulation. a.** (of currency) serving as a medium of exchange. **b.** (of people) active in a social or business context.

circum- *prefix.* around; surrounding; on all sides: *circumlocution; circumpolar.* [< L *circum* around, < *circus* circle]

circumambient (ˌsɜːkəmˈæmbɪənt) *adj.* surrounding. [C17: < LL, < L CIRCUM- + *ambīre* to go round] —ˌ**circumˈambience** *or* ˌ**circumˈambiency** *n.*

circumambulate (ˌsɜːkəmˈæmbjʊˌleɪt) *vb.* **1.** to walk around (something). **2.** (*intr.*) to avoid the point. [C17: < LL, < L CIRCUM- + *ambulāre* to walk] —ˌ**circumˌambuˈlation** *n.*

circumcise (ˈsɜːkəmˌsaɪz) *vb.* (*tr.*) **1.** to remove the foreskin of (a male). **2.** to incise surgically the skin over the clitoris of (a female). **3.** to remove the clitoris of (a female). **4.** to perform such an operation as a religious rite on (someone). [C13: < L < CIRCUM- + *caedere* to cut] —**circumcision** (ˌsɜːkəmˈsɪʒən) *n.*

circumference (səˈkʌmfərəns) *n.* **1.** the boundary of a specific area or figure, esp. of a circle. **2.** the length of a closed geometric curve, esp. of a circle. [C14: < OF, < L < CIRCUM- + *ferre* to bear] —**circumferential** (səˌkʌmfəˈrɛnʃəl) *adj.* —**cirˌcumferˈentially** *adv.*

circumflex (ˈsɜːkəmˌflɛks) *n.* **1.** a mark (ˆ) placed over a vowel to show that it is pronounced with rising and falling pitch, as in ancient Greek, or as a long vowel, as in French. ~*adj.* **2.** (of nerves, arteries, etc.) bending or curving around. [C16: < L, < CIRCUM- + *flectere* to bend] —ˌ**circumˈflexion** *n.*

circumfluous (səˈkʌmfluəs) *adj.* flowing all around. Also: **circumfluent.** [C17: < L CIRCUM- + *fluere* to flow] —**cirˈcumfluence** *n.*

circumfuse (ˌsɜːkəmˈfjuːz) *vb.* (*tr.*) **1.** to pour or spread (a liquid, powder, etc.) around. **2.** to surround with a substance, such as a liquid. [C16: < L *circumfūsus*, < CIRCUM- + *fundere* to pour] —**circumfusion** (ˌsɜːkəmˈfjuːʒən) *n.*

circumlocution (ˌsɜːkəmləˈkjuːʃən) *n.* **1.** an indirect way of expressing something. **2.** an indirect expression. —**circumlocutory** (ˌsɜːkəmˈlɒkjətərɪ, -trɪ) *adj.*

circumnavigate (ˌsɜːkəmˈnævɪˌgeɪt) *vb.* (*tr.*) to sail or fly completely around. —ˌ**circumˌnaviˈgation** *n.* —ˌ**circumˈnaviˌgator** *n.*

circumscribe (ˌsɜːkəmˈskraɪb, ˈsɜːkəmˌskraɪb) *vb.* (*tr.*) **1.** to restrict within limits. **2.** to mark or set the bounds of. **3.** to draw a geometric construction around (another construction) so that the two are in contact but do not intersect. **4.** to draw a line round. [C15: < L < CIRCUM- + *scrībere* to write] —ˌ**circumˈscribable** *adj.* —ˌ**circumˈscriber** *n.* —**circumscription** (ˌsɜːkəmˈskrɪpʃən) *n.*

circumspect (ˈsɜːkəmˌspɛkt) *adj.* cautious, prudent, or discreet. [C15: < L, < CIRCUM- + *specere* to look] —ˌ**circumˈspection** *n.* —ˈ**circumˌspectly** *adv.*

circumstance (ˈsɜːkəmstəns) *n.* **1.** (*usually pl.*) a condition of time, place, etc., that accompanies or influences an event or condition. **2.** an incident or occurrence, esp. a chance one. **3.** accessory information or detail. **4.** formal display or ceremony (archaic except in **pomp and circumstance).** **5. under** *or* **in no circumstances.** in no case; never. **6. under the circumstances.** because of conditions; this being the case. ~*vb.* (*tr.*) **7.** to place in a particular condition or situation. [C13: < OF, < L *circumstantia*, < CIRCUM- + *stāre* to stand]

circumstantial (ˌsɜːkəmˈstænʃəl) *adj.* **1.** of or dependent on circumstances. **2.** fully detailed. **3.** incidental. —**circumstantiality** (ˌsɜːkəmˌstænʃɪˈælɪtɪ) *n.* —ˌ**circumˈstantially** *adv.*

circumstantial evidence *n.* indirect evidence that tends to establish a conclusion by inference.

circumstantiate (ˌsɜːkəmˈstænʃɪˌeɪt) *vb.* (*tr.*) to support by giving particulars. —ˌ**circumˌstantiˈation** *n.*

circumvallate (ˌsɜːkəmˈvæleɪt) *vb.* (*tr.*) to surround with a defensive fortification. [C19: < L, < CIRCUM- + *vallum* rampart] —ˌ**circumvalˈlation** *n.*

circumvent (ˌsɜːkəmˈvɛnt) *vb.* (*tr.*) **1.** to evade or go around. **2.** to outwit. **3.** to encircle (an enemy) so as to intercept or capture. [C15: < L, < CIRCUM- + *venīre* to come] —ˌ**circumˈvention** *n.*

circus (ˈsɜːkəs) *n., pl.* **-cuses. 1.** a travelling company of entertainers such as acrobats, clowns, trapeze artists, and trained animals. **2.** a public performance given by such a company. **3.** an arena, usually tented, in which such a performance is held. **4.** a travelling group of professional sportsmen: *a cricket circus.* **5.** (in ancient Rome) **a.** an open-air stadium, usually oval or oblong, for chariot races or public games. **b.** the games themselves. **6.** *Brit.* **a.** an open place, usually circular, where several streets converge. **b.** (*cap. when part of a name*): *Piccadilly Circus.* **7.** *Inf.* noisy or rowdy behaviour. **8.** *Inf.* a group of people travelling together and putting on a display. [C16: < L, < Gk *kirkos* ring]

ciré (ˈsɪəreɪ) *adj.* **1.** (of fabric) treated with a heat or wax process to make it smooth. ~*n.* **2.** such a surface on a fabric. **3.** a fabric having such a surface. [C20: F, < L *cēra* wax]

cirque (sɜːk) *n.* a steep-sided semicircular or crescent-shaped depression found in mountainous regions. [C17: < F, < L *circus* ring]

cirrhosis (sɪˈrəʊsɪs) *n.* any of various chronic progressive diseases of the liver, characterized by death of liver cells, irreversible fibrosis, etc. [C19: NL, < Gk *kirrhos* orange-coloured + -OSIS; referring to the appearance of the diseased liver] —**cirrhotic** (sɪˈrɒtɪk) *adj.*

cirripede (ˈsɪrɪˌpiːd) *or* **cirriped** (ˈsɪrɪˌpɛd) *n.* **1.** any marine crustacean of the subclass *Cirripedia*, including the barnacles. ~*adj.* **2.** of, relating to, or belonging to the *Cirripedia*.

cirrocumulus (ˌsɪrəʊˈkjuːmjʊləs) *n., pl.* **-li** (-ˌlaɪ). a high cloud of ice crystals grouped into small separate globular masses.

cirrostratus (ˌsɪrəʊˈstrɑːtəs) *n., pl.* **-ti** (-taɪ). a uniform layer of cloud above about 6000 metres.

cirrus (ˈsɪrəs) *n., pl.* **-ri** (-raɪ). **1.** a thin wispy fibrous cloud at high altitudes, composed of ice particles. **2.** a plant tendril or similar part. **3.** a slender tentacle or filament in barnacles and other marine invertebrates. [C18: < L: curl]

cis- *prefix.* on this side of, as in **cismontane** on this side of the mountains. Often retains the original Latin sense of 'side nearest Rome', as in **cispadane** on this (the southern) side of the Po. [< L]

cisalpine (sɪsˈælpaɪn) *adj.* on this (the southern) side of the Alps, as viewed from Rome.

cisco (ˈsɪskəʊ) *n., pl.* **-coes** *or* **-cos.** any of various whitefish, esp. the lake herring of cold deep lakes of North America. [C19: short for Canad. F *ciscoette,* of Algonquian origin]

cislunar (sɪsˈluːnə) *adj.* of or relating to the space between the earth and the moon.

cissy (ˈsɪsɪ) *n.* a variant spelling of **sissy.**

cist[1] (sɪst) *n.* a wooden box for holding ritual objects used in ancient Rome and Greece. [C19: < L *cista* box, < Gk *kistē*]

cist[2] (sɪst) *or* **kist** *n.* a box-shaped burial chamber made from stone slabs or a hollowed tree trunk. [C19: < Welsh: chest, < L; see CIST[1]]

Cistercian (sɪˈstɜːʃən) *n.* **1.** Also called: **White Monk.** a member of a Christian order of monks and nuns founded in 1098, which follows an especially strict form of the Benedictine rule. ~*adj.* **2.** of or relating to this order [C17: < F, < Med. L, < *Cistercium* (modern *Cîteaux*), original home of the order]

cistern (ˈsɪstən) *n.* **1.** a tank for the storage of water, esp. on or within the roof of a house or connected to a WC. **2.** an underground reservoir for the storage of a liquid, esp. rainwater. **3.** Also called: **cisterna.** *Anat.* a sac or partially enclosed space containing body fluid. [C13: < OF, < L *cisterna* underground tank, < *cista* box]

cistus (ˈsɪstəs) *n.* any plant of the genus *Cistus.* See **rockrose.** [C16: NL, < Gk *kistos*]

citadel (ˈsɪtədᵊl, -ˌdɛl) *n.* **1.** a stronghold within or close to a city. **2.** any strongly fortified building or place of safety; refuge. [C16: < OF, < OIt. *cittadella* a little city, < L *cīvitās*]

citation (saɪˈteɪʃən) *n.* **1.** the quoting of a book or author. **2.** a passage or source cited. **3. a.** an official commendation or award, esp. for bravery or outstanding service. **b.** a formal public statement of this. **4.** *Law.* **a.** an official summons to appear in court. **b.** the document containing such a summons. —**citatory** (ˈsaɪtətərɪ) *adj.*

cite (saɪt) *vb.* (*tr.*) **1.** to quote or refer to (a passage, book, or author). **2.** to mention or commend (a soldier, etc.) for outstanding bravery or meritorious action. **3.** to summon to appear before a court of law. **4.** to enumerate: *he cited the king's virtues.* [C15: < OF *citer* to summon, ult. < L *ciēre* to excite] —ˈ**citable** *or* ˈ**citeable** *adj.*

cithara (ˈsɪθərə) *or* **kithara** (ˈkɪθərə) *n.* a stringed musical instrument of ancient Greece, similar to the lyre. [C18: < Gk *kithara*]

cither (ˈsɪθə) *or* **cithern** (ˈsɪθən) *n.* a variant spelling of **cittern.** [C17: < L, < Gk *kithara*]

citified *or* **cityfied** (ˈsɪtɪˌfaɪd) *adj. Often derog.* having the customs, manners, or dress of city people.

citizen (ˈsɪtɪzᵊn) *n.* **1.** a native registered or naturalized member of a state, nation, or other political community. **2.** an inhabitant of a city or town. **3.** a civilian, as opposed to a soldier, public official, etc. [C14: < Anglo-F *citesein,* < OF *citeien,* < *cité* CITY]

citizenry (ˈsɪtɪzənrɪ) *n., pl.* **-ries.** citizens collectively.

Citizens' Band *n.* a range of radio frequencies assigned officially for use by the public for private communication.

citizenship (ˈsɪtɪzənˌʃɪp) *n.* **1.** the condition or status of a citizen, with its rights and duties. **2.** a person's conduct as a citizen.

citrate (ˈsɪtreɪt, -rɪt; ˈsaɪtreɪt) *n.* any salt or ester of citric acid. [C18: < CITR(US) + -ATE[1]]

citric (ˈsɪtrɪk) *adj.* of or derived from citrus fruits or citric acid.

citric acid *n.* a water-soluble weak tribasic acid found in many fruits, esp. citrus fruits, and used in pharmaceuticals and as a flavouring (**E330**). Formula: $CH_2(COOH)C(OH)(COOH)CH_2COOH$.

citrine (ˈsɪtrɪn) *n.* **1.** a brownish-yellow variety of quartz: a gemstone; false topaz. **2. a.** the yellow colour of a lemon. **b.** (*as adj.*): *citrine hair.*

citron (ˈsɪtrən) *n.* **1.** a small Asian tree, having lemon-like fruit with a thick aromatic rind. **2.** the fruit of this tree. **3.** the rind of this fruit candied and used for decoration and flavouring of foods. [C16: < OF, < L *citrus* citrus tree]

citronella (ˌsɪtrəˈnɛlə) *n.* **1.** a tropical Asian grass with bluish-green lemon-scented leaves. **2.** Also called: **citronella oil.** the yellow aromatic oil obtained from this grass, used in insect repellents, soaps, perfumes, etc. [C19: NL, < F, < *citron* lemon]

citrus (ˈsɪtrəs) *n., pl.* **-ruses. 1.** any tree or shrub of the tropical and subtropical genus *Citrus,* which includes the orange, lemon, and lime. ~*adj. also* **citrous. 2.** of or relating to the genus *Citrus* or to the fruits of plants of this genus. [C19: < L: citrus tree]

cittern (ˈsɪtɜːn), **cither,** *or* **cithern** *n.* a medieval stringed instrument resembling a lute but having wire strings and a flat back. [C16: ? a blend of CITHER + GITTERN]

city (ˈsɪtɪ) *n., pl.* **cities. 1.** any large town or populous place. **2.** (in Britain) a large town that has received this title from the Crown: usually the seat of a bishop. **3.** (in the U.S.) an incorporated urban centre with its own government and administration established by state charter. **4.** (in Canada) a similar urban municipality incorporated by the provincial government **5.** the people of a city collectively. **6.** (*modifier*) in or characteristic of a city: *city habits.* ~Related adjs.: **civic, urban, municipal.** [C13: < OF *cité,* < L *cīvitās* state, < *cīvis* citizen]

City (ˈsɪtɪ) *n.* **the. 1.** the area in central London in which the United Kingdom's major financial business is transacted. **2.** the various financial institutions located in this area.

City and Guilds Institute *n.* (in Britain) an examining body for technical and craft skills.

city chambers *n.* (*functioning as sing.*) (in Scotland) the municipal buildings of a city; town hall.

city desk *n.* the editorial section of a newspaper dealing in Britain with financial news, in the U.S. and Canada with local news.

city editor *n.* (on a newspaper) **1.** *Brit.* the editor in charge of financial and commercial news. **2.** *U.S. & Canad.* the editor in charge of local news.

city father *n.* a person who is active or prominent in the public affairs of a city.

cityscape (ˈsɪtɪskeɪp) *n.* an urban landscape; view of a city.

city-state *n. Ancient history.* a state consisting of a sovereign city and its dependencies.

civet (ˈsɪvɪt) *n.* **1.** a catlike mammal of Africa and S Asia, typically having spotted fur and secreting a powerfully smelling fluid from anal glands. **2.** the yellowish fatty secretion of such an animal, used as a fixative in the manufacture of perfumes. **3.** the fur of such an animal. [C16: < OF, < It., < Ar. *zabād* civet perfume]

civic (ˈsɪvɪk) *adj.* of or relating to a city, citizens, or citizenship. [C16: < L, < *cīvis* citizen] —ˈ**civically** *adv.*

civic centre *n. Brit.* the public buildings of a town, including recreational facilities and offices of local administration.

civics (ˈsɪvɪks) *n.* (*functioning as sing.*) the study of the rights and responsibilities of citizenship.

civies (ˈsɪvɪz) *pl. n. Inf.* a variant spelling of **civvies.**

civil (ˈsɪvᵊl) *adj.* **1.** of the ordinary life of citizens as distinguished from military, legal, or ecclesiastical affairs. **2.** of or relating to the citizen as an individual: *civil rights.* **3.** of or occurring within the state or between citizens: *civil strife.* **4.** polite or courteous: *a civil manner.* **5.** of or in accordance with Roman law. [C14: < OF, < L *cīvīlis,* < *cīvis* citizen] —**ˈcivilly** *adv.*

civil defence *n.* the organizing of civilians to deal with enemy attacks.

civil disobedience *n.* a refusal to obey laws, pay taxes, etc.: a nonviolent means of protesting.

civil engineer *n.* a person qualified to design and construct public works, such as roads, bridges, harbours, etc. —**civil engineering** *n.*

civilian (sɪˈvɪljən) *n.* **a.** a person whose occupation is civil or nonmilitary. **b.** (*as modifier*): *civilian life.* [C14 (orig.: a practitioner of civil law): < *civile* (< L *jūs cīvīle* civil law) + -IAN]

civility (sɪˈvɪlɪtɪ) *n., pl.* **-ties.** **1.** politeness or courtesy. **2.** (*often pl.*) an act of politeness.

civilization *or* **-isation** (ˌsɪvɪlaɪˈzeɪʃən) *n.* **1.** a human society that has a complex cultural, political, and legal organization; an advanced state in social development. **2.** the peoples or nations collectively who have achieved such a state. **3.** the total culture and way of life of a particular people, nation, region, or period. **4.** the process of bringing or achieving civilization. **5.** intellectual, cultural, and moral refinement. **6.** cities or populated areas, as contrasted with sparsely inhabited areas, deserts, etc.

civilize *or* **-ise** (ˈsɪvɪˌlaɪz) *vb.* (*tr.*) **1.** to bring out of savagery or barbarism into a state characteristic of civilization. **2.** to refine, educate, or enlighten. —**ˈciviˌlizable** *or* **-isable** *adj.* —**ˈciviˌlized** *or* **-ised** *adj.*

civil law *n.* **1.** the law of a state relating to private and civilian affairs. **2.** the body of law in ancient Rome, esp. as applicable to private citizens. **3.** law based on the Roman system as distinguished from common law and canon law.

civil liberty *n.* the right of an individual to certain freedoms of speech and action.

civil list *n.* (in Britain) the annuities voted by Parliament for the support of the royal household and the royal family.

civil marriage *n. Law.* a marriage performed by an official other than a clergyman.

civil rights *pl. n.* **1.** the personal rights of the individual citizen. **2.** (*modifier*) of, relating to, or promoting equality in social, economic, and political rights.

civil servant *n.* a member of the civil service.

civil service *n.* **1.** the service responsible for the public administration of the government of a country. It excludes the legislative, judicial, and military branches. **2.** the members of the civil service collectively.

civil war *n.* war between parties or factions within the same nation.

civvy (ˈsɪvɪ) *n., pl.* **civvies** *or* **civies.** *Sl.* **1.** a civilian. **2.** (*pl.*) civilian dress as opposed to uniform. **3. civvy street.** civilian life.

CJ *abbrev. for* Chief Justice.

Cl *the chemical symbol for* chlorine.

clachan (*Gaelic* ˈklaxən; *English* ˈklæ-) *n. Scot. & Irish dialect.* a small village; hamlet. [C15: < Scot. Gaelic: prob. < *clach* stone]

clack (klæk) *vb.* **1.** to make or cause to make a sound like that of two pieces of wood hitting each other. **2.** (*intr.*) to jabber. ~*n.* **3.** a short sharp sound. **4.** chatter. **5.** Also called: **clack valve.** a simple nonreturn valve using a hinged flap or a ball. [C13: prob. < ON *klaka* to twitter, imit.] —**ˈclacker** *n.*

clad[1] (klæd) *vb.* a past tense and past participle of **clothe.** [OE *clāthode* clothed, < *clāthian* to CLOTHE]

clad[2] (klæd) *vb.* **cladding, clad.** (*tr.*) to bond a metal to (another metal), esp. to form a protective coating. [C14: special use of CLAD[1]]

cladding (ˈklædɪŋ) *n.* **1.** the process of protecting one metal by bonding a second metal to its surface. **2.** the protective coating so bonded to metal. **3.** the material used for the outside facing of a building, etc.

cladistics (kləˈdɪstɪks) *n.* (*functioning as sing.*) a method of grouping animals by measurable likenesses or homologues. [C20: NL < Gk *klādos* branch, shoot] —**cladism** (ˈklædɪzəm) *n.*

claim (kleɪm) *vb.* (*mainly tr.*) **1.** to demand as being due or as one's property; assert one's title or right to: *he claimed the record.* **2.** (*takes a clause as object or an infinitive*) to assert as a fact; maintain against denial: *he claimed to be telling the truth.* **3.** to call for or need; deserve: *this problem claims our attention.* **4.** to take: *the accident claimed four lives.* ~*n.* **5.** an assertion of a right; a demand for something as due. **6.** an assertion of something as true, real, or factual. **7.** a right or just title to something; basis for demand: *a claim to fame.* **8.** anything that is claimed, such as a piece of land staked out by a miner. **9. a.** a demand for payment in connection with an insurance policy, etc. **b.** the sum of money demanded. [C13: < OF *claimer* to call, < L *clāmāre* to shout] —**ˈclaimable** *adj.* —**ˈclaimant** *or* **ˈclaimer** *n.*

▷ **Usage.** It is sometimes maintained that *claim* should be used only in the sense of asserting or declaring one's right to something: *he claimed his share of the profits.* Nevertheless, even the most careful users of English do not hesitate to employ the verb in the sense of asserting something to be true or declaring something to be a fact: *he claimed that he had seen the man before; she claimed that the witness had lied.*

clairvoyance (klɛəˈvɔɪəns) *n.* **1.** the alleged power of perceiving things beyond the natural range of the senses. **2.** keen intuitive understanding. [C19: < F: clear-seeing, < *clair* clear + *voyance,* < *voir* to see]

clairvoyant (klɛəˈvɔɪənt) *adj.* **1.** of or possessing clairvoyance. **2.** having great insight. ~*n.* **3.** a person claiming to have the power to foretell future events. —**clairˈvoyantly** *adv.*

clam (klæm) *n.* **1.** any of various burrowing bivalve molluscs. **2.** the edible flesh of such a mollusc. **3.** *Inf.* a reticent person. ~*vb.* **clamming, clammed.** **4.** (*intr.*) *Chiefly U.S.* to gather clams. ~See also **clam up.** [C16: < earlier *clamshell,* that is, shell that clamps]

clamant (ˈkleɪmənt) *adj.* **1.** noisy. **2.** calling urgently. [C17: < L, < *clāmāre* to shout]

clamber (ˈklæmbə) *vb.* **1.** (usually foll. by *up, over,* etc.) to climb (something) awkwardly, esp. by using both hands and feet. ~*n.* **2.** a climb performed in this manner. [C15: prob. var. of CLIMB] —**ˈclamberer** *n.*

clammy (ˈklæmɪ) *adj.* **-mier, -miest.** **1.** unpleasantly sticky; moist. **2.** (of the weather) close; humid. [C14: < OE *clǣman* to smear] —**ˈclammily** *adv.* —**ˈclamminess** *n.*

clamour *or U.S.* **clamor** (ˈklæmə) *n.* **1.** a loud persistent outcry. **2.** a vehement expression of collective feeling or outrage: *a clamour against higher prices.* **3.** a loud and persistent noise: *the clamour of traffic.* ~*vb.* **4.** (*intr.;* often foll. by *for* or *against*) to make a loud noise or outcry; make a public demand. **5.** (*tr.*) to move or force by outcry. [C14: < OF, < L, < *clāmāre* to cry out] —**ˈclamorous** *adj.* —**ˈclamorously** *adv.* —**ˈclamorousness** *n.*

clamp[1] (klæmp) *n.* **1.** a mechanical device with movable jaws with which an object can be secured to a bench or with which two objects may be secured together. **2.** See **wheel clamp.** ~*vb.* (*tr.*) **3.** to fix or fasten with or as if with a clamp **4.** to immobilize (a car) by means of a wheel clamp. **5.** to inflict or impose forcefully: *they clamped a curfew on the town.* [C14: < Du. or Low G *klamp*]

clamp[2] (klæmp) *n.* **1.** a mound of a harvested root crop, covered with straw and earth to protect it from winter weather. ~*vb.* **2.** (*tr.*) to enclose (a harvested root crop) in a mound. [C16: < MDu. *klamp* heap]

clamp down *vb.* (*intr., adv.;* often foll. by *on*) **1.** to behave repressively; attempt to suppress something regarded as undesirable. ~*n.* **clampdown.** **2.** a sudden restrictive measure.

clam up *vb.* (*intr., adv.*) *Inf.* to keep or become silent or withhold information.

clan (klæn) *n.* **1.** a group of people interrelated by ancestry or marriage. **2.** a group of families with a common surname and a common ancestor, esp. among the Scots and the Irish. **3.** a group of people united by common characteristics, aims, or interests. [C14: < Scot. Gaelic *clann* family, descendants, < L *planta* sprout]

clandestine (klæn'dɛstɪn) *adj.* secret and concealed, often for illicit reasons; furtive. [C16: < L, < *clam* secretly] —**clan'destinely** *adv.*

clang (klæŋ) *vb.* **1.** to make or cause to make a loud resounding noise, as metal when struck. **2.** (*intr.*) to move or operate making such a sound. ~*n.* **3.** a resounding metallic noise. **4.** the harsh cry of certain birds. [C16: < L *clangere*]

clanger ('klæŋə) *n.* **1.** *Inf.* a conspicuous mistake (esp. in **drop a clanger**). **2.** something that clangs or causes a clang. [C20: < CLANG]

clangour *or U.S.* **clangor** ('klæŋgə, 'klæŋə) *n.* **1.** a loud resonant often-repeated noise. **2.** an uproar. ~*vb.* **3.** (*intr.*) to make or produce a loud resonant noise. —**'clangorous** *adj.* —**'clangorously** *adv.*

clank (klæŋk) *n.* **1.** an abrupt harsh metallic sound. ~*vb.* **2.** to make or cause to make such a sound. **3.** (*intr.*) to move or operate making such a sound. [C17: imit.] —**'clankingly** *adv.*

clannish ('klænɪʃ) *adj.* **1.** of or characteristic of a clan. **2.** tending to associate closely within a group to the exclusion of outsiders; cliquish. —**'clannishly** *adv.* —**'clannishness** *n.*

clansman ('klænzmən) *or* (*fem.*) **clanswoman** *n., pl.* **-men** *or* **-women.** a person belonging to a clan.

clap[1] (klæp) *vb.* **clapping, clapped. 1.** to make or cause to make a sharp abrupt sound, as of two nonmetallic objects struck together. **2.** to applaud (someone or something) by striking the palms of the hands together sharply. **3.** (*tr.*) to strike (a person) lightly with an open hand, in greeting, etc. **4.** (*tr.*) to place or put quickly or forcibly: *they clapped him into jail.* **5.** (of certain birds) to flap (the wings) noisily. **6.** (*intr.*; foll. by *up* or *together*) to contrive or put together hastily. **7. clap eyes on.** *Inf.* to catch sight of. **8. clap hold of.** *Inf.* to grasp suddenly or forcibly. ~*n.* **9.** the sharp abrupt sound produced by striking the hands together. **10.** the act of clapping, esp. in applause. **11.** a sudden sharp sound, esp. of thunder. **12.** a light blow. **13.** *Arch.* a sudden action or mishap. [OE *clæppan;* imit.]

clap[2] (klæp) *n.* (usually preceded by *the*) a slang word for **gonorrhoea.** [C16: < OF *clapoir* venereal sore, < *clapier* brothel, <?]

clapboard ('klæp,bɔːd, 'klæbəd) *n.* **1.** a long thin timber board, used esp. in the U.S. and Canada in wood-frame construction by lapping each board over the one below. ~*vb.* **2.** (*tr.*) to cover with such boards. [C16: partial translation of Low G *klappholt,* < *klappen* to crack + *holt* wood]

clapped out *adj.* (**clapped-out** *when prenominal*). *Inf.* **1.** *Brit., Austral., & N.Z.* worn out; dilapidated. **2.** *Austral. & N.Z.* extremely tired; exhausted.

clapper ('klæpə) *n.* **1.** a person or thing that claps. **2.** Also called: **tongue.** a small piece of metal suspended within a bell that causes it to sound when made to strike against its side. **3. go (run, move) like the clappers.** *Brit.. inf.* to move extremely fast.

clapperboard ('klæpə,bɔːd) *n.* a pair of hinged boards clapped together during film shooting to aid in synchronizing sound and picture prints.

claptrap ('klæp,træp) *n. Inf.* **1.** contrived but foolish talk. **2.** insincere and pretentious talk: *politicians' claptrap.* [C18: < CLAP[1] + TRAP[1]]

claque (klæk) *n.* **1.** a group of people hired to applaud. **2.** a group of fawning admirers. [C19: < F, < *claquer* to clap, imit.]

claret ('klærət) *n.* **1.** a red wine, esp. one from the Bordeaux district of France. **2. a.** a purplish-red colour. **b.** (*as adj.*): *a claret football strip.* [C14: < OF (*vin*) *claret* clear (wine), < Med. L *clārātum,* < L *clārus* clear]

clarify ('klærɪ,faɪ) *vb.* **-fying, -fied. 1.** to make or become clear or easy to understand. **2.** to make or become free of impurities. **3.** to make (fat, butter, etc.) clear by heating, etc., or (of fat, etc.) to become clear as a result of such a process. [C14: < OF, < LL, < L *clārus* clear + *facere* to make] —,**clarifi'cation** *n.* —**'clari,fier** *n.*

clarinet (,klærɪ'nɛt) *n. Music.* **1.** a keyed woodwind instrument with a cylindrical bore and a single reed. **2.** an orchestral musician who plays the clarinet. [C18: < F, prob. < It., < *clarino* trumpet] —,**clari'nettist** *or U.S. sometimes* ,**clari'netist** *n.*

clarion ('klærɪən) *n.* **1.** a stop of trumpet quality on an organ. **2.** an obsolete, high-pitched, small-bore trumpet. **3.** the sound of such an instrument or any similar sound. ~*adj.* **4.** (*prenominal*) clear and ringing; inspiring: *a clarion call to action.* ~*vb.* **5.** to proclaim loudly. [C14: < Med. L *clāriō* trumpet, < L *clārus* clear]

clarity ('klærɪtɪ) *n.* **1.** clearness, as of expression. **2.** clearness, as of water. [C16: < L *clāritās,* < *clārus* clear]

clarkia ('klɑːkɪə) *n.* any North American plant of the genus *Clarkia:* cultivated for their red, purple, or pink flowers. [C19: NL, after William *Clark* (1770–1838), American explorer]

clary ('klɛərɪ) *n., pl.* **claries.** any of several European plants having aromatic leaves and blue flowers. [C14: < earlier *sclarreye,* < Med. L *sclareia,* <?]

-clase *n. combining form.* (in mineralogy) indicating a particular type of cleavage: *plagioclase.* [via F < Gk *klasis* a breaking]

clash (klæʃ) *vb.* **1.** to make or cause to make a loud harsh sound, esp. by striking together. **2.** (*intr.*) to be incompatible. **3.** (*intr.*) to engage together in conflict. **4.** (*intr.*) (of dates or events) to coincide. **5.** (*intr.*) (of colours) to look inharmonious together. ~*n.* **6.** a loud harsh noise. **7.** a collision or conflict. [C16: imit.] —**'clasher** *n.*

clasp (klɑːsp) *n.* **1.** a fastening, such as a catch or hook, for holding things together. **2.** a firm grasp or embrace. **3.** *Mil.* a bar on a medal ribbon, to indicate either a second award or the battle, campaign, or reason for its award. ~*vb.* (*tr.*) **4.** to hold in a firm grasp. **5.** to grasp firmly with the hand. **6.** to fasten together with or as if with a clasp. [C14: <?] —**'clasper** *n.*

clasp knife *n.* a large knife with one or more blades or other devices folding into the handle.

class (klɑːs) *n.* **1.** a collection or division of people or things sharing a common characteristic. **2.** a group of persons sharing a similar social and economic position. **3. a.** the pattern of divisions that exist within a society on the basis of rank, economic status, etc. **b.** (*as modifier*): *the class struggle; class distinctions.* **4. a.** a group of pupils or students who are taught together. **b.** a meeting of a group of students for tuition. **5.** *U.S.* a group of students who graduated in a specified year: *the class of '53.* **6.** (*in combination and as modifier*) *Brit.* a grade of attainment in a university honours degree: *second-class honours.* **7.** one of several standards of accommodation in public transport. **8.** *Inf.* excellence or elegance, esp. in dress, design, or behaviour. **9.** *Biol.* any of the taxonomic groups into which a phylum is divided and which contains one or more orders. **10.** *Maths.* another name for **set**[2] (sense 3). **11. in a class by oneself** *or* **in a class of its own.** unequalled; unparalleled. ~*vb.* **12.** to have or assign a place within a group, grade, or class. [C17: < L *classis* class, rank, fleet]

class. *abbrev. for:* **1.** classic(al). **2.** classification. **3.** classified.

class-conscious *adj.* aware of belonging to a particular social rank. —,**class-'consciousness** *n.*

classic ('klæsɪk) *adj.* **1.** of the highest class, esp. in art or literature. **2.** serving as a standard or model of its kind. **3.** adhering to an established set of principles in the arts or sciences: *a classic* *proof.* **4.** characterized by simplicity, balance, regularity, and purity of form; classical. **5.** of lasting interest or significance. **6.** continuously in fashion because of its simple style: *a classic dress.* ~*n.* **7.** an author, artist, or work of art of the highest excellence. **8.** a creation or work considered as definitive. **9.** *Horse racing.* any of the five principal races for three-year-old horses in Britain, namely the One Thousand Guineas, Two Thousand Guineas, Derby, Oaks, and Saint Leger. [C17: < L *classicus* of the first rank, < *classis* division, rank, class]

▷ **Usage.** The adjectives *classic* and *classical* can often be treated as synonyms, but there are two contexts in which they should be carefully distinguished. *Classic* is applied to that which is of the first rank, esp. in art and literature, as in: *Lewis Carroll's classic works for children. Classical* is used to refer to Greek and Roman culture.

classical (ˈklæsɪkᵊl) *adj.* **1.** of, relating to, or characteristic of the ancient Greeks and Romans or their civilization. **2.** designating, following, or influenced by the art or culture of ancient Greece or Rome: *classical architecture.* **3.** *Music.* **a.** of, relating to, or denoting any music or its period of composition marked by stability of form, intellectualism, and restraint. Cf. **romantic** (sense 5). **b.** accepted as a standard: *the classical suite.* **c.** denoting serious art music in general. Cf. **pop**[2]. **4.** denoting or relating to a style in any of the arts characterized by emotional restraint and conservatism: *a classical style of painting.* **5.** (of an education) based on the humanities and the study of Latin and Greek. **6.** *Physics.* not involving the quantum theory or the theory of relativity: *classical mechanics.* —ˌ**classiˈcality** *or* ˈ**classicalness** *n.* —ˈ**classically** *adv.*

▷ **Usage.** See at **classic.**

classicism (ˈklæsɪˌsɪzəm) *or* **classicalism** (ˈklæsɪkəˌlɪzəm) *n.* **1.** a style based on the study of Greek and Roman models, characterized by emotional restraint and regularity of form; the antithesis of romanticism. **2.** knowledge of the culture of ancient Greece and Rome. **3. a.** a Greek or Latin expression. **b.** an expression in a modern language that is modelled on a Greek or Latin form. —ˈ**classicist** *n.*

classicize *or* **-cise** (ˈklæsɪˌsaɪz) *vb.* **1.** (*tr.*) to make classic. **2.** (*intr.*) to imitate classical style.

classics (ˈklæsɪks) *n.* **1. the.** a body of literature regarded as great or lasting, esp. that of ancient Greece or Rome. **2. the.** the ancient Greek and Latin languages. **3.** (*functioning as sing.*) ancient Greek and Roman culture as a subject for academic study.

classification (ˌklæsɪfɪˈkeɪʃən) *n.* **1.** systematic placement in categories. **2.** one of the divisions in a system of classifying. **3.** *Biol.* **a.** the placing of animals and plants in a series of increasingly specialized groups because of similarities in structure, origin, etc., that indicate a common relationship. **b.** the study of the principles and practice of this process; taxonomy. [C18: < F; see CLASS, -IFY, -ATION] —ˌ**classifiˈcatory** *adj.*

classified (ˈklæsɪˌfaɪd) *adj.* **1.** arranged according to some system of classification. **2.** *Government.* (of information) not available to people outside a restricted group, esp. for reasons of national security. **3.** *U.S. & Canad. inf.* (of information) closely concealed or secret. **4.** (of advertisements in newspapers, etc.) arranged according to type. **5.** *Brit.* (of newspapers) containing sports results. **6.** (of British roads) having a number in the national road system.

classify (ˈklæsɪˌfaɪ) *vb.* **-fying, -fied.** (*tr.*) **1.** to arrange or order by classes; categorize. **2.** *Government.* to declare (information, documents, etc.) of possible aid to an enemy and therefore not available to people outside a restricted group. [C18: back formation < CLASSIFICATION] —ˈ**classiˌfiable** *adj.* —ˈ**classiˌfier** *n.*

classless (ˈklɑːslɪs) *adj.* **1.** not belonging to a class. **2.** characterized by the absence of economic and social distinctions. —ˈ**classlessness** *n.*

class list *n.* (in Britain) a list categorizing students according to the class of honours they have obtained in their degree examination.

classmate (ˈklɑːsˌmeɪt) *n.* a friend or contemporary of the same class in a school.

classroom (ˈklɑːsˌruːm, -ˌrʊm) *n.* a room in which classes are conducted, esp. in a school.

class struggle *n.* **the.** *Marxism.* the continual conflict between the capitalist and working classes for economic and political power.

classy (ˈklɑːsɪ) *adj.* **classier, classiest.** *Sl.* elegant; stylish. —ˈ**classiness** *n.*

clatter (ˈklætə) *vb.* **1.** to make or cause to make a rattling noise, esp. as a result of movement. **2.** (*intr.*) to chatter. ~*n.* **3.** a rattling sound or noise. **4.** a noisy commotion, such as loud chatter. [OE *clatrung* clattering (gerund)] —ˈ**clatterer** *n.* —ˈ**clatteringly** *adv.*

clause (klɔːz) *n.* **1.** *Grammar.* a group of words, consisting of a subject and a predicate including a finite verb, that does not necessarily constitute a sentence. See also **main clause, subordinate clause. 2.** a section of a legal document such as a contract, will, or draft statute. [C13: < OF, < Med. L *clausa* a closing (of a rhetorical period), < L, < *claudere* to close] —ˈ**clausal** *adj.*

claustrophobia (ˌklɔːstrəˈfəʊbɪə, ˌklɒs-) *n.* an abnormal fear of being in a confined space. [C19: NL < L *claustrum* CLOISTER + -PHOBIA] —ˈ**claustroˌphobe** *n.* —ˌ**claustroˈphobic** *adj.*

clavate (ˈkleɪveɪt, -vɪt) *or* **claviform** (ˈklævɪˌfɔːm) *adj. Biol.* shaped like a club. [C19: < L *clāva* club] —ˈ**clavately** *adv.*

clave[1] (kleɪv, klɑːv) *n. Music.* one of a pair of hardwood sticks struck together to make a hollow sound. [C20: < American Sp., < L *clavis* key]

clave[2] (kleɪv) *vb. Arch.* a past tense of **cleave.**

clavichord (ˈklævɪˌkɔːd) *n.* a keyboard instrument consisting of a number of thin wire strings struck from below by brass tangents. [C15: < Med. L, < L *clāvis* key + *chorda* CHORD[1]]

clavicle (ˈklævɪkᵊl) *n.* **1.** either of the two bones connecting the shoulder blades with the upper part of the breastbone. Nontechnical name: **collarbone. 2.** the corresponding structure in other vertebrates. [C17: < Med. L *clāvicula*, < L *clāvis* key] —**clavicular** (kləˈvɪkjʊlə) *adj.*

clavier (kləˈvɪə, ˈklævɪə) *n.* **a.** any keyboard instrument. **b.** the keyboard itself. [C18: < F: keyboard, < L *clāvis* key]

claw (klɔː) *n.* **1.** a curved pointed horny process on the end of each digit in birds, some reptiles, and certain mammals. **2.** a corresponding structure in some invertebrates, such as the pincer of a crab. **3.** a part or member like a claw in function or appearance. ~*vb.* **4.** to scrape, tear, or dig (something or someone) with claws, etc. **5.** (*tr.*) to create by scratching as with claws: *to claw an opening.* [OE *clawu*] —ˈ**clawer** *n.*

claw back *vb.* (*tr., adv.*) **1.** to get back (something) with difficulty. **2.** to recover (a part of a tax, duty, etc.) in the form of an allowance. ~*n.* **clawback. 3.** the recovery of part of a tax, etc., in the form of an allowance. **4.** the sum so recovered.

claw hammer *n.* a hammer with a cleft at one end of the head for extracting nails.

clay (kleɪ) *n.* **1.** a very fine-grained material that occurs as sedimentary rocks, soils, and other deposits. It becomes plastic when moist but hardens on heating and is used in the manufacture of bricks, ceramics, etc. **2.** earth or mud. **3.** *Poetic.* the material of the human body. [OE *clǣg*] —ˈ**clayey,** ˈ**clayish,** *or* ˈ**clayˌlike** *adj.*

claymore (ˈkleɪˌmɔː) *n.* a large two-edged broadsword used formerly by Scottish Highlanders. [C18: < Gaelic *claidheamh mōr* great sword]

clay pigeon *n.* a disc of baked clay hurled into the air from a machine as a target to be shot at.

clay road *n. N.Z.* an unmetalled road in a rural area.

CLC *abbrev. for* Canadian Labour Congress.

-cle *suffix forming nouns.* indicating smallness: *cubicle; particle.* [via OF < L *-culus.* See -CULE]

clean (kliːn) *adj.* **1.** without dirt or other impurities; unsoiled. **2.** without anything in it or on it: *a clean page.* **3.** recently washed; fresh. **4.** without extraneous or foreign materials. **5.** without defect, difficulties, or problems. **6.** (of a nuclear weapon) producing little or no radioactive fallout or contamination. **7.** (of a wound, etc.) having no pus or other sign of infection. **8.** pure; morally sound. **9.** without objectionable language or obscenity. **10.** thorough or complete: *a clean break.* **11.** dexterous or adroit: *a clean throw.* **12.** *Sport.* played fairly and without fouls. **13.** simple in design: *a ship's clean lines.* **14.** *Aeronautics.* causing little turbulence; streamlined. **15.** honourable or respectable. **16.** habitually neat. **17.** (esp. of a driving licence) showing or having no record of offences. **18.** *Sl.* **a.** innocent; not guilty. **b.** not carrying illegal drugs, weapons, etc. ~*vb.* **19.** to make or become free of dirt, filth, etc.: *the stove cleans easily.* **20.** (*tr.*) to remove in making clean: *to clean marks off the wall.* **21.** (*tr.*) to prepare (fish, poultry, etc.) for cooking: *to clean a chicken.* ~*adv.* **22.** in a clean way; cleanly. **23.** *Not standard.* (intensifier): *clean forgotten.* **24.** **come clean.** *Inf.* to make a revelation or confession. ~*n.* **25.** the act or an instance of cleaning: *he gave his shoes a clean.* ~ See also **clean out, clean up.** [OE *clǣne*] —ˈ**cleanable** *adj.* —ˈ**cleanness** *n.*

clean-cut *adj.* **1.** clearly outlined; neat: *clean-cut lines of a ship.* **2.** definite.

cleaner (ˈkliːnə) *n.* **1.** a person, device, chemical agent, etc., that removes dirt, as from clothes or carpets. **2.** (*usually pl.*) a shop, etc., that provides a dry-cleaning service. **3. take (a person) to the cleaners.** *Inf.* to rob or defraud (a person).

cleanly *adv.* (ˈkliːnlɪ). **1.** in a fair manner. **2.** easily or smoothly. ~*adj.* (ˈklɛnlɪ), **-lier, -liest.** **3.** habitually clean or neat. —**cleanlily** (ˈklɛnlɪlɪ) *adv.* —**cleanliness** (ˈklɛnlɪnɪs) *n.*

clean out *vb.* (*tr., adv.*) **1.** (foll. by *of* or *from*) *Sl.* to remove (something) (from or away from). **2.** *Sl.* to leave (someone) with no money. **3.** *Inf.* to exhaust (stocks, goods, etc.) completely.

cleanse (klɛnz) *vb.* (*tr.*) **1.** to remove dirt, filth, etc., from. **2.** to remove guilt from. **3.** *Arch.* to cure. [OE *clǣnsian;* see CLEAN]

cleanser (ˈklɛnzə) *n.* a cleansing agent.

clean-shaven *adj.* (of men) having the facial hair shaved off.

clean up *vb.* (*adv.*) **1.** to rid (something) of dirt, filth, or other impurities. **2.** to make (someone or something) orderly or presentable. **3.** (*tr.*) to rid (a place) of undesirable people or conditions. **4.** *Inf., chiefly U.S. & Canad.* to make (a great profit). ~*n.* **cleanup.** **5.** the process of cleaning up. **6.** *Inf., chiefly U.S.* a great profit.

clear (klɪə) *adj.* **1.** free from darkness or obscurity; bright. **2.** (of weather) free from dullness or clouds. **3.** transparent: *clear water.* **4.** even and pure in tone or colour. **5.** without blemish, or defect: *a clear skin.* **6.** easy to see or hear; distinct. **7.** free from doubt or confusion. **8.** (*postpositive*) certain in the mind; sure: *are you clear?* **9.** (*in combination*) perceptive, alert: *clear-eyed; clear-headed; clear-sighted.* **10.** evident or obvious: *it is clear that he won't come now.* **11.** (of sounds or the voice) not harsh or hoarse. **12.** serene; calm. **13.** without qualification or limitation; complete: *a clear victory.* **14.** free of suspicion, guilt, or blame: *a clear conscience.* **15.** free of obstruction; open: *a clear passage.* **16.** free from debt or obligation. **17.** (of money, profits, etc.) without deduction; net. **18.** emptied of freight or cargo. **19.** *Showjumping.* (of a round) ridden without any points being lost. ~*adv.* **20.** in a clear or distinct manner. **21.** completely or utterly. **22.** (*postpositive;* often foll. by *of*) not in contact (with); free: *stand clear of the gates.* ~*n.* **23.** a clear space. **24. in the clear. a.** free of suspicion, guilt, or blame. **b.** *Sport.* able to receive a pass without being tackled. ~*vb.* **25.** to make or become free from darkness, obscurity, etc. **26.** (*intr.*) **a.** (of the weather) to become free from dullness, fog, rain, etc. **b.** (of mist, fog, etc.) to disappear. **27.** (*tr.*) to free from impurity or blemish. **28.** (*tr.*) to free from doubt or confusion. **29.** (*tr.*) to rid of objects, obstructions, etc. **30.** (*tr.*) to make or form (a path, way, etc.) by removing obstructions. **31.** (*tr.*) to free or remove (a person or thing) from something, as of suspicion, blame, or guilt. **32.** (*tr.*) to move or pass by or over without contact: *he cleared the wall easily.* **33.** (*tr.*) to rid (the throat) of phlegm. **34.** (*tr.*) to make or gain (money) as profit. **35.** (*tr.;* often foll. by *off*) to discharge or settle (a debt). **36.** (*tr.*) to free (a debtor) from obligation. **37.** (*intr.*) (of a cheque) to pass through one's bank and be charged against one's account. **38.** *Banking.* to settle accounts by exchanging (commercial documents) in a clearing house. **39.** to permit (ships, aircraft, cargo, passengers, etc.) to unload, disembark, depart, etc., or (of ships, etc.) to be permitted to unload, etc. **40.** to obtain or give (clearance). **41.** (*tr.*) to obtain clearance from. **42.** (*tr.*) to permit (a person, company, etc.) to see or handle classified information. **43.** (*tr.*) *Mil., etc.* to decode (a message, etc.). **44.** (*tr.*) *Computers.* to remove data from a storage device and revert to zero. **45. clear the air.** to dispel tension, confusion, etc., by settling misunderstandings, etc. ~See also **clear away, clear off,** etc. [C13: *clere,* < OF *cler,* < L *clārus* clear] —ˈ**clearer** *n.* —ˈ**clearly** *adv.* —ˈ**clearness** *n.*

clearance (ˈklɪərəns) *n.* **1. a.** the process or an instance of clearing: *slum clearance.* **b.** (*as modifier*): *a clearance order.* **2.** space between two parts in motion or in relative motion. **3.** permission for an aircraft, ship, passengers, etc., to proceed. **4.** official permission to have access to secret information, projects, areas, etc. **5.** *Banking.* the exchange of commercial documents drawn on the members of a clearing house. **6. a.** the disposal of merchandise at reduced prices. **b.** (*as modifier*): *a clearance sale.* **7.** the act of clearing an area of land by mass eviction: *the Highland Clearances.*

clear away *vb.* (*adv.*) to remove (objects) from (the table) after a meal.

clear-cut *adj.* (**clear cut** *when postpositive*). **1.** definite; not vague: *a clear-cut proposal.* **2.** clearly outlined.

clearing (ˈklɪərɪŋ) *n.* an area with few or no trees or shrubs in wooded or overgrown land.

clearing bank *n.* (in Britain) any bank that makes use of the central clearing house in London.

clearing house *n.* **1.** *Banking.* an institution where cheques and other commercial papers drawn on member banks are cancelled against each other so that only net balances are payable. **2.** a central agency for the collection and distribution of information or materials.

clear off *vb.* (*intr., adv.*) *Inf.* to go away: often used imperatively.

clear out *vb.* (*adv.*) **1.** (*intr.*) *Inf.* to go away: often used imperatively. **2.** (*tr.*) to remove and sort the contents of (a room, container, etc.). **3.** (*tr.*) *Sl.* to leave (someone) with no money. **4.** (*tr.*) *Sl.* to exhaust (stocks, goods, etc.) completely.

clearstory (ˈklɪəˌstɔːrɪ) *n.* a variant of **clerestory.**

clear up *vb.* (*adv.*) **1.** (*tr.*) to explain or solve (a mystery, misunderstanding, etc.). **2.** to put (a place or thing that is disordered) in order. **3.** (*intr.*) (of the weather) to become brighter.

clearway (ˈklɪəˌweɪ) *n.* **1.** *Brit.* a stretch of road on which motorists may stop only in an emergency. **2.** an area at the end of a runway over which an aircraft taking off makes its initial climb.

cleat (kliːt) *n.* **1.** a wedge-shaped block attached to a structure to act as a support. **2.** a device consisting of two hornlike prongs projecting horizontally in opposite directions from a central base, used for securing lines on vessels, wharves, etc. ~*vb.* (*tr.*) **3.** to supply or support with a cleat or cleats. **4.** to secure (a line) on a cleat. [C14: of Gmc origin]

cleavage (ˈkliːvɪdʒ) *n.* **1.** *Inf.* the separation between a woman's breasts, esp. as revealed by a low-cut dress. **2.** a division or split. **3.** (of crystals) the act of splitting or the tendency to split along definite planes so as to yield smooth surfaces. **4.** (in animals) the repeated division of a fertilized ovum into a solid ball of cells. **5.** the breaking of a chemical bond in a molecule to give smaller molecules or radicals.

cleave[1] (kliːv) *vb.* **cleaving; cleft, cleaved,** *or* **clove; cleft, cleaved,** *or* **cloven.** **1.** to split or cause to split, esp. along a natural weakness. **2.** (*tr.*) to make by or as if by cutting: *to cleave a path.* **3.** (when *intr.*, foll. by *through*) to penetrate or traverse. [OE *clēofan*] —ˈ**cleavable** *adj.*

cleave[2] (kliːv) *vb.* (*intr.;* foll. by *to*) to cling or adhere. [OE *cleofian*]

cleaver (ˈkliːvə) *n.* a heavy knife or long-bladed hatchet, esp. one used by butchers.

cleavers (ˈkliːvəz) *n.* (*functioning as sing.*) a Eurasian plant, having small white flowers and prickly stems and fruits. Also called: **goosegrass, hairif.** [OE *clīfe;* see CLEAVE[2]]

clef (klɛf) *n.* one of several symbols placed on the left-hand side beginning of each stave indicating the pitch of the music written after it. [C16: < F: key, clef, < L *clāvis*]

cleft (klɛft) *vb.* **1.** a past tense and past participle of **cleave**[1]. ~*n.* **2.** a fissure or crevice. **3.** an indentation or split in something, such as the chin, palate, etc. ~*adj.* **4.** split; divided. [OE *geclyft* (n.); see CLEAVE[1]]

cleft palate *n.* a congenital crack or fissure in the midline of the hard palate, often associated with a harelip.

cleg (klɛg) *n.* another name for a **horsefly.** [C15: < ON *kleggi*]

clematis (ˈklɛmətɪs, kləˈmeɪtɪs) *n.* any N temperate climbing plant of the genus *Clematis.* Many species are cultivated for their large colourful flowers. [C16: < L, < Gk, < *klēma* vine twig]

clemency (ˈklɛmənsɪ) *n., pl.* **-cies.** **1.** mercy or leniency. **2.** mildness, esp. of the weather. [C15: < L, < *clēmēns* gentle]

clement (ˈklɛmənt) *adj.* **1.** merciful. **2.** (of the weather) mild. [C15: < L *clēmēns* mild]

clementine (ˈklɛmənˌtiːn, -ˌtaɪn) *n.* a citrus fruit thought to be either a variety of tangerine or a hybrid between a tangerine and sweet orange. [C20: < F *clémentine*]

clench (klɛntʃ) *vb.* (*tr.*) **1.** to close or squeeze together (the teeth, a fist, etc.) tightly. **2.** to grasp or grip firmly. ~*n.* **3.** a firm grasp or grip. **4.** a device that grasps or grips. ~*n., vb.* **5.** another word for **clinch.** [OE *beclencan*]

clepsydra (ˈklɛpsɪdrə) *n., pl.* **-dras** *or* **-drae** (-ˌdriː). an ancient device for measuring time by the flow of water or mercury through a small aperture. Also called: **water clock.** [C17: < L, < Gk, < *kleptein* to steal + *hudōr* water]

cleptomania (ˌklɛptəʊˈmeɪnɪə) *n.* a variant spelling of **kleptomania.**

clerestory *or* **clearstory** (ˈklɪəˌstɔːrɪ) *n., pl.* **-ries.** **1.** a row of windows in the upper part of the wall of a church that divides the nave from the aisle. **2.** the part of the wall in which these windows are set. [C15: < CLEAR + STOREY] —ˈ**cléreˌstoried** *or* ˈ**clearˌstoried** *adj.*

clergy (ˈklɜːdʒɪ) *n., pl.* **-gies.** the collective body of men and women ordained as ministers of the Christian Church. [C13: < OF; see CLERK]

clergyman (ˈklɜːdʒɪmən) *n., pl.* **-men.** a member of the clergy.

cleric (ˈklɛrɪk) *n.* a member of the clergy. [C17: < Church L *clēricus* priest, CLERK]

clerical (ˈklɛrɪkᵊl) *adj.* **1.** relating to or associated with the clergy: *clerical dress.* **2.** of or relating to office clerks or their work: *a clerical error.* **3.** supporting or advocating clericalism. —ˈ**clerically** *adv.*

clerical collar *n.* a stiff white collar with no opening at the front that buttons at the back of the neck; the distinctive mark of the clergy in certain Churches. Informal name: **dog collar.**

clericalism (ˈklɛrɪkᵊˌlɪzəm) *n.* **1.** a policy of upholding the power of the clergy. **2.** the power of the clergy. —ˈ**clericalist** *n.*

clericals (ˈklɛrɪkᵊlz) *pl. n.* the distinctive dress of a clergyman.

clerihew (ˈklɛrɪˌhjuː) *n.* a form of comic or satiric verse, consisting of two couplets of metrically irregular lines, containing the name of a well-known person. [C20: after E. *Clerihew* Bentley (1875–1956), E writer who invented it]

clerk (klɑːk; *U.S.* klɜːrk) *n.* **1.** a worker, esp. in an office, who keeps records, files, etc. **2.** an employee of a court, legislature, board, corporation, etc., who keeps records and accounts, etc.: *a town clerk.* **3.** Also called: **clerk in holy orders.** a cleric. **4.** *U.S. & Canad.* short for **salesclerk.** **5.** Also called: **desk clerk.** *U.S. & Canad.* a hotel receptionist. **6.** *Arch.* a scholar. ~*vb.* **7.** (*intr.*) to serve as a clerk. [OE *clerc,* < Church L *clēricus,* < Gk *klērikos* cleric, < *klēros* heritage] —ˈ**clerkess** *n.* (*chiefly Scot.*) —ˈ**clerkish** *adj.* —ˈ**clerkship** *n.*

clerk of the works *n.* an employee who supervises building work in progress.

clever (ˈklɛvə) *adj.* **1.** displaying sharp intelligence or mental alertness. **2.** adroit or dexterous, esp. with the hands. **3.** smart in a superficial way. **4.** *Brit. inf.* sly; cunning. [C13 *cliver* (in the sense: quick to seize, adroit), <?] —ˈ**cleverly** *adv.* —ˈ**cleverness** *n.*

clevis (ˈklɛvɪs) *n.* the U-shaped component of a shackle. [C16: rel. to CLEAVE[1]]

clew (kluː) *n.* **1.** a ball of thread, yarn, or twine. **2.** *Naut.* either of the lower corners of a square sail or the after lower corner of a fore-and-aft sail. ~*vb.* **3.** (*tr.*) to coil into a ball. [OE *cliewen* (vb.)]

clianthus (klɪˈænθəs) *n.* a leguminous plant of Australia and New Zealand with ornamental clusters of slender flowers. [C19: NL, prob. < Gk *klei-, kleos* glory + *anthos* flower]

cliché (ˈkliːʃeɪ) *n.* **1.** a word or expression that has lost much of its force through overexposure. **2.** an idea, action, or habit that has become trite from overuse. **3.** *Printing, chiefly Brit.* a stereotype or electrotype plate. [C19: < F, < *clicher* to stereotype; imit.] —ˈ**clichéd** *or* ˈ**cliché'd** *adj.*

click (klɪk) *n.* **1.** a short light often metallic sound. **2.** the locking member of a ratchet mechanism, such as a pawl or detent. **3.** *Phonetics.* any of various stop consonants that are produced by the suction of air into the mouth. ~*vb.* **4.** to make or cause to make a clicking sound: *to click one's heels.* **5.** (*intr.*) *Sl.* to be a great success: *that idea really clicked.* **6.** (*intr.*) *Inf.* to become suddenly clear: *it finally clicked when her name was mentioned.* **7.** (*intr.*) *Sl.* to go or fit together with ease: *they clicked from their first meeting.* [C17: imit.] —ˈ**clicker** *n.*

client (ˈklaɪənt) *n.* **1.** a person, company, etc., that seeks the advice of a professional man or woman. **2.** a customer. **3.** a person for whom a social worker, etc., is responsible. [C14: < L *cliēns* retainer, dependent] —**cliental** (klaɪˈɛntᵊl) *adj.*

clientele (ˌkliːɒnˈtɛl) *or* **clientage** (ˈklaɪəntɪdʒ) *n.* customers or clients collectively. [C16: < L, < *cliēns* CLIENT]

cliff (klɪf) *n.* a steep high rock face, esp. one that runs along the seashore. [OE *clif*] —ˈ**cliffy** *adj.*

cliffhanger (ˈklɪfˌhæŋə) *n.* **1. a.** a situation of imminent disaster usually occurring at the end of each episode of a serialized film. **b.** the serialized film itself. **2.** a situation that is dramatic or uncertain. —ˈ**cliffˌhanging** *adj.*

climacteric (klaɪˈmæktərɪk, ˌklaɪmækˈtɛrɪk) *n.* **1.** a critical event or period. **2.** another name for **menopause.** **3.** the period in the life of a man corresponding to the menopause, chiefly characterized by diminished sexual activity. ~*adj. also* **climacterical** (ˌklaɪmækˈtɛrɪkᵊl). **4.** involving a crucial event or period. [C16: < L, < Gk, < *klimaktēr* rung of a ladder < *klimax* ladder]

climactic (klaɪˈmæktɪk) *or* **climactical** *adj.* consisting of, involving, or causing a climax. —**cliˈmactically** *adv.*

climate (ˈklaɪmɪt) *n.* **1.** the long-term prevalent weather conditions of an area, determined by latitude, altitude, etc. **2.** an area having a particular kind of climate. **3.** a prevailing trend: *the political climate.* [C14: < LL, < Gk *klima* inclination, region] —**climatic** (klaɪˈmætɪk), **cliˈmatical,** *or* **ˈclimatal** *adj.* —**cliˈmatically** *adv.*

climatology (ˌklaɪməˈtɒlədʒɪ) *n.* the study of climates. —**climatologic** (ˌklaɪmətəˈlɒdʒɪk) *or* **ˌclimatoˈlogical** *adj.* —**ˌclimaˈtologist** *n.*

climax (ˈklaɪmæks) *n.* **1.** the most intense or highest point of an experience or of a series of events: *the party was the climax of the week.* **2.** a decisive moment in a dramatic or other work. **3.** a rhetorical device by which a series of sentences, clauses, or phrases are arranged in order of increasing intensity. **4.** *Ecology.* the stage in the development of a community during which it remains stable under the prevailing environmental conditions. **5.** another word for **orgasm.** ~*vb.* **6.** to reach or bring to a climax. [C16: < LL, < Gk *klimax* ladder]

▷ **Usage.** In formal English careful writers avoid the use of *climax* as a verb. The phrase *reach a climax* is preferred.

climb (klaɪm) *vb.* (*mainly intr.*) **1.** (*also tr.;* often foll. by *up*) to go up or ascend (stairs, a mountain, etc.). **2.** (often foll. by *along*) to progress with difficulty: *to climb along a ledge.* **3.** to rise to a higher point or intensity: *the temperature climbed.* **4.** to incline or slope upwards: *the road began to climb.* **5.** to ascend in social position. **6.** (of plants) to grow upwards by twining, using tendrils or suckers, etc. **7.** *Inf.* (foll. by *into*) to put (on) or get (into). **8.** to be a climber or mountaineer. ~*n.* **9.** the act or an instance of climbing. **10.** a place or thing to be climbed, esp. a route in mountaineering. [OE *climban*] —**ˈclimbable** *adj.*

climb down *vb.* (*intr., adv.*) **1.** to descend. **2.** (often foll. by *from*) to retreat (from an opinion, position, etc.). ~*n.* **climb-down. 3.** a retreat from an opinion, etc.

climber (ˈklaɪmə) *n.* **1.** a person or thing that climbs, esp. a mountaineer. **2.** a plant that grows upwards by twining or clinging with tendrils and suckers. **3.** *Chiefly Brit.* short for **social climber.**

clime (klaɪm) *n. Poetic.* a region or its climate. [C16: < LL *clima;* see CLIMATE]

clinch (klɪntʃ) *vb.* **1.** (*tr.*) to secure (a driven nail), by bending the protruding point over. **2.** (*tr.*) to hold together in such a manner. **3.** (*tr.*) to settle (something, such as an argument, bargain, etc.) in a definite way. **4.** (*tr.*) *Naut.* to fasten by means of a clinch. **5.** (*intr.*) to engage in a clinch, as in boxing or wrestling. ~*n.* **6.** the act of clinching. **7. a.** a nail with its point bent over. **b.** the part of such a nail, etc., that has been bent over. **8.** *Boxing, wrestling, etc.* an act or an instance in which one or both competitors hold on to the other to avoid punches, regain wind, etc. **9.** *Sl.* a lovers' embrace. **10.** *Naut.* a loop or eye formed in a line. ~Also (for senses 1, 2, 4, 7, 8, 10): **clench.** [C16: var. of CLENCH]

clincher (ˈklɪntʃə) *n.* **1.** *Inf.* something decisive, such as fact, score, etc. **2.** a person or thing that clinches.

cline (klaɪn) *n.* the range of variation of form displayed within a species. [C20: < Gk *klinein* to lean] —**ˈclinal** *adj.*

-cline *n. combining form.* indicating a slope: *anticline.* [back formation < INCLINE] —**-clinal** *adj. combining form.*

cling (klɪŋ) *vb.* **clinging, clung.** (*intr.*) **1.** (often foll. by *to*) to hold fast or adhere closely (to something), as by gripping or sticking. **2.** (foll. by *together*) to remain in contact (with each other). **3.** to be or remain physically or emotionally close. ~*n.* **4.** short for **clingstone.** [OE *clingan*] —**ˈclinging** *adj.* —**ˈclingingly** *adv.* —**ˈclingy** *adj.* —**ˈclinginess** *or* **ˈclingingness** *n.*

clingfilm (ˈklɪŋˌfɪlm) *n.* a thin polythene material having the power to adhere closely: used for wrapping food.

clingstone (ˈklɪŋˌstəʊn) *n.* **a.** a fruit, such as certain peaches, in which the flesh adheres to the stone. **b.** (*as modifier*): *a clingstone peach.*

clinic (ˈklɪnɪk) *n.* **1.** a place in which outpatients are given medical treatment or advice. **2.** a similar place staffed by specialist physicians or surgeons: *eye clinic.* **3.** *Brit.* a private hospital or nursing home. **4.** the teaching of medicine to students at the bedside. **5.** *Chiefly U.S. & Canad.* a group or centre that offers advice or instruction. [C17: < L *clīnicus* one on a sickbed, < Gk, < *klinē* bed]

clinical (ˈklɪnɪkᵊl) *adj.* **1.** of or relating to a clinic. **2.** of or relating to the observation and treatment of patients directly: *clinical medicine.* **3.** scientifically detached; strictly objective: *a clinical attitude to life.* **4.** plain, simple, and usually unattractive. —**ˈclinically** *adv.*

clinical thermometer *n.* a thermometer for determining the temperature of the body.

clinician (klɪˈnɪʃən) *n.* a physician, psychiatrist, etc., who specializes in clinical work as opposed to one engaged in experimental studies.

clink[1] (klɪŋk) *vb.* **1.** to make or cause to make a light and sharply ringing sound. ~*n.* **2.** such a sound. [C14: ?< MDu. *klinken*]

clink[2] (klɪŋk) *n.* a slang word for **prison.** [C16: after *Clink*, a prison in Southwark, London]

clinker (ˈklɪŋkə) *n.* **1.** the ash and partially fused residues from a coal-fired furnace or fire. **2.** a partially vitrified brick or mass of brick. **3.** *U.S. sl.* a mistake or fault, esp. a wrong note in music. ~*vb.* **4.** (*intr.*) to form clinker during burning. [C17: < Du. *klinker* a type of brick, < *klinken* to CLINK[1]]

clinker-built *or* **clincher-built** *adj.* (of a boat or ship) having a hull constructed with each plank overlapping that below. [C18 *clinker* a nailing together, prob. < CLINCH]

clinometer (klaɪˈnɒmɪtə) *n.* an instrument used in surveying for measuring an angle of inclination. —**clinometric** (ˌklaɪnəˈmɛtrɪk) *or* **ˌclinoˈmetrical** *adj.* —**cliˈnometry** *n.*

Clio (ˈklaɪəʊ) *n. Greek myth.* the Muse of history. [C19: < L, < Gk *Kleiō*, < *kleein* to celebrate]

clip[1] (klɪp) *vb.* **clipping, clipped.** (*mainly tr.*) **1.** (*also intr.*) to cut, snip, or trim with or as if with scissors or shears, esp. in order to shorten or remove a part. **2.** *Brit.* to punch (a hole) in something, esp. a ticket. **3.** to curtail or cut short. **4.** to move a short section from (a film, etc.). **5.** to shorten (a word). **6.** *Inf.* to strike with a sharp, often slanting, blow. **7.** *Sl.* to defraud or swindle, esp. by overcharging. ~*n.* **8.** the act or process of clipping. **9.** something clipped off. **10.** a short extract from a film, newspaper, etc. **11.** *Inf.* a sharp, often slanting, blow. **12.** *Inf.* speed: *a rapid clip.* **13.** *Austral. & N.Z.* the total quantity of wool shorn, as in one place, season, etc. **14.** another word for **clipped form.** [C12: < ON *klippa* to cut]

clip[2] (klɪp) *n.* **1.** any of various small implements used to hold loose articles together or to attach one article to another. **2.** an article of jewellery that can be clipped onto a dress, hat, etc. **3.** short for **paperclip** or **cartridge clip.** ~*vb.* **clipping, clipped.** (*tr.*) **4.** to hold together tightly, as with a clip. [OE *clyppan* to embrace]

clipboard (ˈklɪpˌbɔːd) *n.* a portable writing board with a clip at the top for holding paper.

clip joint *n. Sl.* a place, such as a nightclub or restaurant, in which customers are overcharged.

clipped (klɪpt) *adj.* (of speech or tone of voice) abrupt, terse, and distinct.

clipped form *n.* a shortened form of a word.

clipper (ˈklɪpə) *n.* **1.** any fast sailing ship. **2.** a person or thing that cuts or clips.

clippers (ˈklɪpəz) *or* **clips** *pl. n.* **1.** a hand tool for clipping fingernails, veneers, etc. **2.** a hairdresser's tool for cutting short hair.

clippie (ˈklɪpɪ) *n. Brit. inf.* a bus conductress.

clipping (ˈklɪpɪŋ) *n.* something cut out, esp. an article from a newspaper; cutting.

clique (kliːk, klɪk) *n.* a small exclusive group of friends or associates. [C18: < F, ?< OF: latch, < *cliquer* to click] —ˈ**cliquey** *or* ˈ**cliquy** *adj.* —ˈ**cliquish** *adj.* —ˈ**cliquishly** *adv.* —ˈ**cliquishness** *n.*

clitoris (ˈklɪtərɪs, ˈklaɪ-) *n.* a part of the female genitalia consisting of a small elongated highly sensitive erectile organ at the front of the vulva: homologous with the penis. [C17: < NL, < Gk *kleitoris*] —ˈ**clitoral** *adj.*

Cllr *abbrev. for* Councillor.

cloaca (kləʊˈeɪkə) *n., pl.* **-cae** (-kiː). **1.** a cavity in most vertebrates, except higher mammals, and certain invertebrates, into which the alimentary canal and the genital and urinary ducts open. **2.** a sewer. [C18: < L: sewer] —**cloˈacal** *adj.*

cloak (kləʊk) *n.* **1.** a wraplike outer garment fastened at the throat and falling straight from the shoulders. **2.** something that covers or conceals. ~*vb.* (*tr.*) **3.** to cover with or as if with a cloak. **4.** to hide or disguise. [C13: < OF *cloque,* < Med. L *clocca* cloak, bell]

cloak-and-dagger *n.* (*modifier*) characteristic of or concerned with intrigue and espionage.

cloakroom (ˈkləʊkˌruːm, -rʊm) *n.* **1.** a room in which hats, coats, etc., may be temporarily deposited. **2.** *Brit.* a euphemistic word for **lavatory.**

clobber[1] (ˈklɒbə) *vb.* (*tr.*) *Sl.* **1.** to batter. **2.** to defeat utterly. **3.** to criticize severely. [C20: <?]

clobber[2] (ˈklɒbə) *n. Brit. sl.* personal belongings, such as clothes. [C19: <?]

clobbering machine *n. N.Z. inf.* pressure to conform with accepted standards.

cloche (klɒʃ) *n.* **1.** a bell-shaped cover used to protect young plants. **2.** a woman's close-fitting hat. [C19: < F: bell, < Med. L *clocca*]

clock[1] (klɒk) *n.* **1.** a timepiece having mechanically or electrically driven pointers that move constantly over a dial showing the numbers of the hours. Cf. **watch** (sense 7). **2.** any clocklike device for recording or measuring, such as a taximeter or pressure gauge. **3.** the downy head of a dandelion that has gone to seed. **4.** short for **time clock. 5.** (usually preceded by *the*) an informal word for **speedometer** or **mileometer. 6.** *Brit.* a slang word for **face. 7. around** *or* **round the clock.** all day and all night. ~*vb.* (*tr.*) **8.** *Brit., Austral., & N.Z. sl.* to strike, esp. on the face or head. **9.** to record time as with a stopwatch, esp. in the calculation of speed. **10.** *Inf.* to turn back the mileometer on (a car) illegally so that its mileage appears less. [C14: < MDu. *clocke* clock, < Med. L *clocca* bell, ult. of Celtic origin]

clock[2] (klɒk) *n.* an ornamental design on the side of a stocking. [C16: see CLOCK[1]]

clock off *or* **out** *vb.* (*intr., adv.*) to depart from work, esp. when it involves registering the time of departure on a card.

clock on *or* **in** *vb.* (*intr., adv.*) to arrive at work, esp. when it involves registering the time of arrival on a card.

clock up *vb.* (*tr., adv.*) to record or register: *this car has clocked up 80 000 miles.*

clock-watcher *n.* an employee who frequently checks the time in anticipation of a break or of the end of the working day.

clockwise (ˈklɒkˌwaɪz) *adv., adj.* in the direction that the hands of a clock rotate; from top to bottom towards the right when seen from the front.

clockwork (ˈklɒkˌwɜːk) *n.* **1.** the mechanism of a clock. **2.** any similar mechanism, as in a wind-up toy. **3. like clockwork.** with complete regularity and precision; smoothly.

clod (klɒd) *n.* **1.** a lump of earth or clay. **2.** earth, esp. when heavy or in hard lumps. **3.** Also called: **clod poll, clodpate.** a dull or stupid person. [OE *clod-* (occurring in compound words) lump] —ˈ**cloddy** *adj.* —ˈ**cloddish** *adj.* —ˈ**cloddishly** *adv.* —ˈ**cloddishness** *n.*

clodhopper (ˈklɒdˌhɒpə) *n. Inf.* **1.** a clumsy person; lout. **2.** (*usually pl.*) a large heavy shoe.

clog (klɒg) *vb.* **clogging, clogged. 1.** to obstruct or become obstructed with thick or sticky matter. **2.** (*tr.*) to encumber; hinder; impede. **3.** (*intr.*) to adhere or stick in a mass. ~*n.* **4. a.** any of various wooden or wooden-soled shoes. **b.** (*as modifier*): *clog dance.* **5.** a heavy block, esp. of wood, fastened to the leg of a person or animal to impede motion. **6.** something that impedes motion or action; hindrance. [C14 (in the sense: block of wood): <?] —ˈ**cloggy** *adj.*

cloisonné (klwɑːˈzɒneɪ) *n.* **1. a.** a design made by filling in with coloured enamel an outline of flattened wire put on edge. **b.** the method of doing this. ~*adj.* **2.** of or made by cloisonné. [C19: < F, < *cloisonner* to divide into compartments, ult. < L *claudere* to close]

cloister (ˈklɔɪstə) *n.* **1.** a covered walk, usually around a quadrangle in a religious institution, having an open colonnade on the inside. **2.** (*sometimes pl.*) a place of religious seclusion, such as a monastery. **3.** life in a monastery or convent. ~*vb.* **4.** (*tr.*) to confine or seclude in or as if in a monastery. [C13: < OF *cloistre,* < Med. L *claustrum* monastic cell, < L *claudere* to close] —ˈ**cloistered** *adj.* —ˈ**cloistral** *adj.*

clomb (kləʊm) *vb. Arch.* a past tense and past participle of **climb.**

clomp (klɒmp) *n., vb.* a less common word for **clump** (senses 2, 7).

clone (kləʊn) *n.* **1.** a group of organisms or cells of the same genetic constitution that are descended from a common ancestor by asexual reproduction, as by cuttings, grafting, etc. **2.** a segment of DNA that has been isolated and replicated by laboratory manipulation. **3.** *Inf.* a person or thing that closely resembles another. ~*vb.* **4.** to produce or cause to produce a clone. **5.** *Inf.* to produce near copies of (a person or thing). [C20: < Gk *klōn* twig, shoot] —ˈ**cloning** *n.*

clonk (klɒŋk) *vb.* (*intr.*) **1.** to make a loud dull thud. **2.** (*tr.*) *Inf.* to hit. ~*n.* **3.** a loud thud. [C20: imit.]

clonus (ˈkləʊnəs) *n.* a type of convulsion characterized by rapid contraction and relaxation of a muscle. [C19: < NL, < Gk *klonos* turmoil] —**clonic** (ˈklɒnɪk) *adj.* —**clonicity** (klɒˈnɪsɪtɪ) *n.*

clop (klɒp) *vb.* **clopping, clopped. 1.** (*intr.*) to make or move along with a sound as of a horse's hooves striking the ground. ~*n.* **2.** a sound of this nature. [C20: imit.]

close[1] (kləʊs) *adj.* **1.** near in space or time; in proximity. **2.** having the parts near together; dense: *a close formation.* **3.** near to the surface; short: *a close haircut.* **4.** near in relationship: *a close relative.* **5.** intimate: *a close friend.* **6.** almost equal: *a close contest.* **7.** not deviating or varying greatly from a model or standard: *a close resemblance; a close translation.* **8.** careful, strict, or searching: *a close study.* **9.** confined or enclosed. **10.** shut or shut tight. **11.** oppressive, heavy, or airless: *a close atmosphere.* **12.** strictly guarded: *a close prisoner.* **13.** neat or tight in fit. **14.** secretive or reticent. **15.** miserly; not generous, esp. with money. **16.** (of money or credit) hard to obtain. **17.** restricted as to public admission or membership. **18.** hidden or secluded. **19** Also: **closed.** restricted or prohibited as to the type of game or fish able to be taken. ~*adv.* **20.** closely; tightly. **21.** near or in proximity. **22. close to the wind.** *Naut.* sailing as nearly as possible towards the direction from which the wind is blowing. See also **wind**[1] (sense 23). [C13: < OF *clos,* < L *clausus,* < *claudere* to close] —ˈ**closely** *adv.* —ˈ**closeness** *n.*

close[2] (kləʊz) *vb.* **1.** to put or be put in such a position as to cover an opening; shut: *the door closed behind him.* **2.** (*tr.*) to bar, obstruct, or fill up (an entrance, a hole, etc.): *to close a road.* **3.** to bring the parts or edges of (a wound, etc.) together or (of a wound, etc.) to be brought together. **4.** (*intr.;* foll. by *on, over,* etc.) to take hold: *his hand closed over the money.* **5.** to bring or be brought to an end; terminate. **6.** (of agreements, deals, etc.) to complete or be completed successfully. **7.** to cease or cause to cease to render service: *the shop closed at six.* **8.**

(*intr.*) *Stock Exchange.* to have a value at the end of a day's trading, as specified: *steels closed two points down.* **9.** (*tr.*) *Arch.* to enclose or shut in. ~*n.* **10.** the act of closing. **11.** the end or conclusion: *the close of the day.* **12.** (kləʊs). *Brit.* a courtyard or quadrangle enclosed by buildings or an entry leading to such a courtyard. **13.** (kləʊs). *Brit.* (*cap. when part of a street name*) a small quiet residential road: *Hillside Close.* **14.** (kləʊs). the precincts of a cathedral or similar building. **15.** (klɑʊs). *Scot.* the entry from the street to a tenement building. ~See also **close down, close in,** etc. [C13: < OF *clos,* < L *clausus,* < *claudere* to close] —**'closer** *n.*

closed (kləʊzd) *adj.* **1.** blocked against entry; shut. **2.** restricted; exclusive. **3.** not open to question or debate. **4.** (of a hunting season, etc.) close. **5.** *Maths.* **a.** (of a curve or surface) completely enclosing an area or volume. **b.** (of a set) having members that can be produced by a specific operation on other members of the same set. **6.** *Phonetics.* denoting a syllable that ends in a consonant. **7.** not open to public entry or membership: *a closed society.*

closed chain *n. Chem.* another name for **ring**[1] (sense 17).

closed circuit *n.* a complete electrical circuit through which current can flow.

closed-circuit television *n.* a television system in which signals are transmitted from the television camera to the receivers by cables or telephone links.

close down (kləʊz) *vb.* (*adv.*) **1.** to cease or cause to cease operations. ~*n.* **close-down. 2.** a closure or stoppage, esp. in a factory. **3.** *Brit. radio, television.* the end of a period of broadcasting, esp. late at night.

closed shop *n.* an industrial establishment in which there exists a contract between a trade union and the employer permitting the employment of the union's members only.

close-fisted (ˌkləʊs'fɪstɪd) *adj.* very careful with money; mean. —ˌ**close-'fistedness** *n.*

close harmony (kləʊs) *n.* a type of singing in which all the parts except the bass lie close together.

close-hauled (ˌkləʊs'hɔːld) *adj. Naut.* with the sails flat, so as to sail as close to the wind as possible.

close in (kləʊz) *vb.* (*intr., adv.*) **1.** (of days) to become shorter with the approach of winter. **2.** (foll. by *on* or *upon*) to advance (on) so as to encircle or surround.

close out (kləʊz) *vb.* (*adv.*) to terminate (a client's or other account) usually by sale of securities to realize cash.

close punctuation (kləʊs) *n.* punctuation in which many commas, full stops, etc., are used. Cf. **open punctuation.**

close quarters (kləʊs) *pl. n.* **1.** a narrow cramped space or position. **2. at close quarters. a.** engaged in hand-to-hand combat. **b.** in close proximity; very near together.

close season (kləʊs) *or* **closed season** *n.* the period of the year when it is prohibited to kill certain game or fish.

close shave (kləʊs) *n. Inf.* a narrow escape.

closet ('klɒzɪt) *n.* **1.** a small cupboard or recess. **2.** a small private room. **3.** short for **water closet. 4.** (*modifier*) private or secret. ~*vb.* **5.** (*tr.*) to shut up or confine in a small private room, esp. for conference or meditation. [C14: < OF, < *clos* enclosure; see CLOSE[1]]

close-up ('kləʊsˌʌp) *n.* **1.** a photograph or film or television shot taken at close range. **2.** a detailed or intimate view or examination. ~*vb.* **close up** (kləʊz). (*adv.*) **3.** to shut entirely. **4.** (*intr.*) to draw together: *the ranks closed up.* **5.** (*intr.*) (of wounds) to heal completely.

close with (kləʊz) *vb.* (*intr., prep.*) to engage in battle with (an enemy).

closure ('kləʊʒə) *n.* **1.** the act of closing or the state of being closed. **2.** an end or conclusion. **3.** something that closes or shuts, such as a cap or seal for a container. **4.** (in a deliberative body) a procedure by which debate may be halted and an immediate vote taken. ~*vb.* **5.** (*tr.*) (in a deliberative body) to end (debate) by closure. [C14: < OF, < LL, < L *claudere* to close]

clot (klɒt) *n.* **1.** a soft thick lump or mass. **2.** *Brit. inf.* a stupid person; fool. ~*vb.* **clotting, clotted. 3.** to form or cause to form into a soft thick lump or lumps. [OE *clott,* of Gmc origin]

cloth (klɒθ) *n., pl.* **cloths** (klɒθs, klɒðz). **1. a.** a fabric formed by weaving, felting or knitting wool, cotton, etc. **b.** (*as modifier*): *a cloth bag.* **2.** a piece of such fabric used for a particular purpose, as for a dishcloth. **3.** (usually preceded by *the*) the clergy. [OE *clāth*]

clothe (kləʊð) *vb.* **clothing, clothed** *or* **clad.** (*tr.*) **1.** to dress or attire (a person). **2.** to provide with clothing. **3.** to conceal or disguise. **4.** to endow or invest. [OE *clāthian,* < *clāth* cloth]

clothes (kləʊðz) *pl. n.* **1.** articles of dress. **2.** *Chiefly Brit.* short for **bedclothes.** [OE *clāthas,* pl. of *clāth* cloth]

clotheshorse ('kləʊðzˌhɔːs) *n.* **1.** a frame on which to hang laundry for drying or airing. **2.** *Inf.* an excessively fashionable person.

clothesline ('kləʊðzˌlaɪn) *n.* a piece of rope or wire on which clean washing is hung to dry.

clothes peg *n.* a small wooden or plastic clip for attaching washing to a clothesline.

clothes pole *n.* a post to which a clothesline is attached. Also called: **clothes post.**

clothes-press *n.* a piece of furniture for storing clothes, usually containing wide drawers.

clothes prop *n.* a long wooden pole with a forked end used to raise a line of washing to enable it to catch the breeze.

clothier ('kləʊðɪə) *n.* a person who makes, sells, or deals in clothes or cloth.

clothing ('kləʊðɪŋ) *n.* **1.** garments collectively. **2.** something that covers or clothes.

Clotho ('kləʊθəʊ) *n. Greek myth.* one of the three Fates, spinner of the thread of life. [L, < Gk *Klōtho,* one who spins, < *klōthein* to spin]

cloth of gold *n.* cloth woven from silk threads interspersed with gold.

clotted cream *n. Brit.* a thick cream made from scalded milk, esp. in SW England.

cloture ('kləʊtʃə) *n.* **1.** closure in the U.S. Senate. ~*vb.* **2.** (*tr.*) to end (debate) by cloture. [C19: < F *clôture,* < OF CLOSURE]

cloud (klaʊd) *n.* **1.** a mass of water or ice particles visible in the sky. **2.** any collection of particles visible in the air, esp. of smoke or dust. **3.** a large number of insects or other small animals in flight. **4.** something that darkens, threatens, or carries gloom. **5.** *Jewellery.* a cloudlike blemish in a transparent stone. **6. in the clouds.** not in contact with reality. **7. on cloud nine.** *Inf.* elated; very happy. **8. under a cloud. a.** under reproach or suspicion. **b.** in a state of gloom or bad temper. ~*vb.* **9.** (when *intr.,* often foll. by *over* or *up*) to make or become cloudy, overcast, or indistinct. **10.** (*tr.*) to make obscure; darken. **11.** to make or become gloomy or depressed. **12.** (*tr.*) to place under or render liable to suspicion or disgrace. **13.** to render (liquids) milky or dull or (of liquids) to become milky or dull. [C13 (in the sense: a mass of vapour): < OE *clūd* rock, hill] —**'cloudless** *adj.* —**'cloudlessly** *adv.* —**'cloudlessness** *n.*

cloudburst ('klaʊdˌbɜːst) *n.* a heavy downpour.

cloud chamber *n. Physics.* an apparatus for detecting high-energy particles by observing their tracks through a chamber containing a supersaturated vapour.

cloud-cuckoo-land *n.* a realm of fantasy, dreams, or impractical notions.

cloudy ('klaʊdɪ) *adj.* **cloudier, cloudiest. 1.** covered with cloud or clouds. **2.** of or like clouds. **3.** streaked or mottled like a cloud. **4.** opaque or muddy. **5.** obscure or unclear. **6.** troubled or gloomy. —**'cloudily** *adv.* —**'cloudiness** *n.*

clough (klʌf) *n. Dialect.* a ravine. [OE *clōh*]

clout (klaʊt) *n.* **1.** *Inf.* a blow with the hand or a hard object. **2.** power or influence, esp. political. **3.** Also called: **clout nail.** a short, flat-headed nail.

4. *Dialect.* **a.** a piece of cloth: *a dish clout.* **b.** a garment. ~*vb.* (*tr.*) **5.** *Inf.* to give a hard blow to, esp. with the hand. [OE *clūt* piece of metal or cloth, *clūtian* to patch (C14: to strike with the hand)]

clove[1] (kləʊv) *n.* **1.** a tropical evergreen tree of the myrtle family. **2.** the dried unopened flower buds of this tree, used as a pungent fragrant spice. [C14: < OF, lit.: nail of clove, *clou* < L *clāvus* nail + *girofle* clove tree]

clove[2] (kləʊv) *n.* any of the segments of a compound bulb that arise from the axils of the scales of a large bulb. [OE *clufu* bulb; see CLEAVE[1]]

clove[3] (kləʊv) *vb.* a past tense of **cleave**[1].

clove hitch *n.* a knot or hitch used for securing a rope to a spar, post, or larger rope.

cloven (ˈkləʊvᵊn) *vb.* **1.** a past participle of **cleave**[1]. ~*adj.* **2.** split; cleft; divided.

cloven hoof *or* **foot** *n.* **1.** the divided hoof of a pig, goat, cow, deer, or related animal. **2.** the mark or symbol of Satan. —ˌ**cloven-ˈhoofed** *or* ˌ**cloven-ˈfooted** *adj.*

clover (ˈkləʊvə) *n.* **1.** a leguminous fodder plant having trifoliate leaves and dense flower heads. **2.** any of various similar or related plants. **3. in clover.** *Inf.* in a state of ease or luxury. [OE *clāfre*]

cloverleaf (ˈkləʊvəˌliːf) *n., pl.* **-leaves. 1.** an arrangement of connecting roads, resembling a four-leaf clover in form, that joins two intersecting main roads. **2.** (*modifier*) in the shape or pattern of a leaf of clover.

clown (klaʊn) *n.* **1.** a comic entertainer, usually grotesquely costumed and made up, appearing in the circus. **2.** a person who acts in a comic or buffoon-like manner. **3.** a clumsy rude person; boor. **4.** *Arch.* a countryman or rustic. ~*vb.* (*intr.*) **5.** to perform as a clown. **6.** to play jokes or tricks. **7.** to act foolishly. [C16: ? < Low G] —ˈ**clownery** *n.* —ˈ**clownish** *adj.* —ˈ**clownishly** *adv.* —ˈ**clownishness** *n.*

cloy (klɔɪ) *vb.* to make weary or cause weariness through an excess of something initially pleasurable or sweet. [C14 (orig.: to nail, hence, to obstruct): < earlier *acloyen*, < OF, < Med. L *inclavāre*, < L, < *clāvus* a nail] —ˈ**cloyingly** *adv.*

cloze test (kləʊz) *n.* a test of the ability to comprehend text in which the reader has to supply the missing words that have been removed from the text. [altered < *close* to complete a pattern (in Gestalt theory)]

club (klʌb) *n.* **1.** a stout stick, usually with one end thicker than the other, esp. one used as a weapon. **2.** a stick or bat used to strike the ball in various sports, esp. golf. See **golf club. 3.** short for **Indian club. 4.** a group or association of people with common aims or interests. **5.** the room, building, or facilities used by such a group. **6.** a building in which elected, fee-paying members go to meet, dine, read, etc. **7.** a commercial establishment providing drinks, food, etc. See also **nightclub. 8.** *Chiefly Brit.* an organization, esp. in a shop, set up as a means of saving. **9.** *Brit.* an informal word for **friendly society. 10. a.** the black trefoil symbol on a playing card. **b.** a card with one or more of these symbols or (*when pl.*) the suit of cards so marked. **11. in the club.** *Brit. sl.* pregnant. ~*vb.* **clubbing, clubbed. 12.** (*tr.*) to beat with or as if with a club. **13.** (often foll. by *together*) to gather or become gathered into a group. **14.** (often foll. by *together*) to unite or combine (resources, efforts, etc.) for a common purpose. [C13: < ON *klubba*, rel. to CLUMP] —ˈ**clubber** *n.*

club foot *n.* **1.** a congenital deformity of the foot, esp. one in which the foot is twisted so that most of the weight rests on the heel. Technical name: **talipes. 2.** a foot so deformed. —ˌ**club-ˈfooted** *adj.*

clubhouse (ˈklʌbˌhaʊs) *n.* the premises of a sports or other club, esp. a golf club.

clubman (ˈklʌbmən) *or* (*fem.*) **clubwoman** *n., pl.* **-men** *or* **-women.** a person who is an enthusiastic member of a club or clubs.

club root *n.* a fungal disease of cabbages and related plants, in which the roots become thickened and distorted.

cluck (klʌk) *n.* **1.** the low clicking sound made by a hen or any similar sound. ~*vb.* **2.** (*intr.*) (of a hen) to make a clicking sound. **3.** (*tr.*) to call or express (a feeling) by making a similar sound. [C17: imit.]

clucky (ˈklʌkɪ) *adj. Austral. sl.* **1.** pregnant. **2.** preoccupied with the idea of having children.

clue (kluː) *n.* **1.** something that helps to solve a problem or unravel a mystery. **2. not have a clue. a.** to be completely baffled. **b.** to be ignorant or incompetent. ~*vb.* **cluing, clued. 3.** (*tr.;* usually foll. by *in* or *up*) to provide with helpful information. [C15: var. of CLEW]

clueless (ˈkluːlɪs) *adj. Sl.* helpless; stupid.

clump (klʌmp) *n.* **1.** a cluster, as of trees or plants. **2.** a dull heavy tread or any similar sound. **3.** an irregular mass. **4.** an inactive mass of microorganisms, esp. a mass of bacteria produced as a result of agglutination. **5.** an extra sole on a shoe. **6.** *Sl.* a blow. ~*vb.* **7.** (*intr.*) to walk or tread heavily. **8.** to gather or be gathered into clumps, clusters, clots, etc. **9.** to cause (bacteria, blood cells, etc.) to collect together or (of bacteria, etc.) to collect together. See also **agglutination** (sense 3). **10.** (*tr.*) *Sl.* to punch (someone). [OE *clympe*] —ˈ**clumpy** *adj.*

clumsy (ˈklʌmzɪ) *adj.* **-sier, -siest. 1.** lacking in skill or physical coordination. **2.** awkwardly constructed or contrived. [C16 (in obs. sense: benumbed with cold; hence, awkward): ? < C13 dialect *clumse* to benumb, prob. of Scand. origin] —ˈ**clumsily** *adv.* —ˈ**clumsiness** *n.*

clung (klʌŋ) *vb.* the past tense and past participle of **cling.**

clunk (klʌŋk) *n.* **1.** a blow or the sound of a blow. **2.** a dull metallic sound. ~*vb.* **3.** to make or cause to make such a sound. [C19: imit.]

cluster (ˈklʌstə) *n.* **1.** a number of things growing, fastened, or occurring close together. **2.** a number of persons or things grouped together. ~*vb.* **3.** to gather or be gathered in clusters. [OE *clyster*] —ˈ**clustered** *adj.* —ˈ**clustery** *adj.*

clutch[1] (klʌtʃ) *vb.* **1.** (*tr.*) to seize with or as if with hands or claws. **2.** (*tr.*) to grasp or hold firmly. **3.** (*intr.;* usually foll. by *at*) to attempt to get hold or possession (of). ~*n.* **4.** a device that enables two revolving shafts to be joined or disconnected, esp. one that transmits the drive from the engine to the gearbox in a vehicle. **5.** a device for holding fast. **6.** a firm grasp. **7.** a hand, claw, or talon in the act of clutching: *in the clutches of a bear.* **8.** (*often pl.*) power or control: *in the clutches of the Mafia.* [OE *clyccan*]

clutch[2] (klʌtʃ) *n.* **1.** a hatch of eggs laid by a particular bird or laid in a single nest. **2.** a brood of chickens. **3.** *Inf.* a group or cluster. ~*vb.* **4.** (*tr.*) to hatch (chickens). [C17 (N English dialect) *cletch*, < ON *klekja* to hatch]

clutter (ˈklʌtə) *vb.* **1.** (*usually tr.;* often foll. by *up*) to strew or amass (objects) in a disorderly manner. **2.** (*intr.*) to move about in a bustling manner. ~*n.* **3.** a disordered heap or mass of objects. **4.** a state of disorder. **5.** unwanted echoes that confuse the observation of signals on a radar screen. [C15 *clotter*, < *clotteren* to CLOT]

Clydesdale (ˈklaɪdzˌdeɪl) *n.* a heavy powerful breed of carthorse, originally from Scotland.

clypeus (ˈklɪpɪəs) *n., pl.* **clypei** (ˈklɪpɪˌaɪ). a cuticular plate on the head of some insects. [C19: < NL, < L *clipeus* round shield] —ˈ**clypeal** *adj.* —**clypeate** (ˈklɪpɪˌeɪt) *adj.*

clyster (ˈklɪstə) *n. Med.* a former name for **enema.** [C14: < Gk *klustēr*, < *kluzein* to rinse]

cm *symbol for* centimetre.

Cm *the chemical symbol for* curium.

Cmdr *Mil. abbrev. for* Commander.

CMG *abbrev. for* Companion of St Michael and St George (a Brit. title).

CNAA *abbrev. for* Council for National Academic Awards.

CND (in Britain) *abbrev. for* Campaign for Nuclear Disarmament.

Co *the chemical symbol for* cobalt.
CO *abbrev. for:* **1.** Commanding Officer. **2.** conscientious objector.
Co. *or* **co.** *abbrev. for:* **1.** (esp. in names of business organizations) Company. **2. and co.** (kəʊ) *Inf.* and the rest of them: *Harold and co.*
Co. *abbrev. for* County.
co- *prefix.* **1.** together; joint or jointly; mutual or mutually: *coproduction.* **2.** indicating partnership or equality: *costar; copilot.* **3.** to the same or a similar degree: *coextend.* **4.** (in mathematics and astronomy) of the complement of an angle: *cosecant.* [< L, reduced form of COM-]
c/o *abbrev. for:* **1.** care of. **2.** *Book-keeping.* carried over.
coach (kəʊtʃ) *n.* **1.** a vehicle for several passengers, used for transport over long distances, sightseeing, etc. **2.** a large four-wheeled enclosed carriage, usually horse-drawn. **3.** a railway carriage. **4.** a trainer or instructor: *a drama coach.* **5.** a tutor who prepares students for examinations. ~*vb.* **6.** to give tuition or instruction to (a pupil). **7.** (*tr.*) to transport in a bus or coach. [C16: < F *coche,* < Hungarian *kocsi szekér* wagon of Kocs, village in Hungary where coaches were first made] —**ˈcoacher** *n.*
coach-built *adj.* (of a vehicle) having specially built bodywork. —**ˈcoach-ˌbuilder** *n.*
coach dog *n.* a former name for **Dalmatian.**
coachman (ˈkəʊtʃmən) *n., pl.* **-men.** the driver of a coach or carriage.
coachwork (ˈkəʊtʃˌwɜːk) *n.* **1.** the design and manufacture of car bodies. **2.** the body of a car.
coadjutor (kəʊˈædʒʊtə) *n.* **1.** a bishop appointed as assistant to a diocesan bishop. **2.** *Rare.* an assistant. [C15: via OF < L *co-* together + *adjūtor* helper, < *adjūtāre* to assist]
coagulate *vb.* (kəʊˈægjʊˌleɪt). **1.** to cause (a fluid, such as blood) to change into a soft semisolid mass or (of such a fluid) to change into such a mass; clot; curdle. ~*n.* (kəʊˈægjʊlɪt, -ˌleɪt). **2.** the solid or semisolid substance produced by coagulation. [C16: < L *coāgulāre,* < *coāgulum* rennet, < *cōgere* to drive together] —**coˈagulant** *or* **coˈaguˌlator** *n.* —**coˌaguˈlation** *n.* —**coagulative** (kəʊˈægjʊlətɪv) *adj.*
coal (kəʊl) *n.* **1. a.** a compact black or dark brown carbonaceous rock consisting of layers of partially decomposed vegetation deposited in the Carboniferous period: a fuel and a source of coke, coal gas, and coal tar. **b.** (*as modifier*): *coal cellar; coal mine; coal dust.* **2.** one or more lumps of coal. **3.** short for **charcoal. 4. coals to Newcastle.** something supplied where it is already plentiful. ~*vb.* **5.** to take in, provide with, or turn into coal. [OE *col*] —**ˈcoaly** *adj.*
coaler (ˈkəʊlə) *n.* a ship, train, etc., used to carry or supply coal.
coalesce (ˌkəʊəˈlɛs) *vb.* (*intr.*) to unite or come together in one body or mass; merge; fuse; blend. [C16: < L CO- + *alēscere* to increase, < *alere* to nourish] —**ˌcoaˈlescence** *n.* —**ˌcoaˈlescent** *adj.*
coalface (ˈkəʊlˌfeɪs) *n.* the exposed seam of coal in a mine.
coalfield (ˈkəʊlˌfiːld) *n.* an area rich in deposits of coal.
coalfish (ˈkəʊlˌfɪʃ) *n., pl.* **-fish** *or* **-fishes.** a dark-coloured gadoid food fish occurring in northern seas. Also called (Brit.): **saithe, coley.**
coal gas *n.* a mixture of gases produced by the distillation of bituminous coal and used for heating and lighting.
coalition (ˌkəʊəˈlɪʃən) *n.* **1. a.** an alliance between groups or parties, esp. for some temporary and specific reason. **b.** (*as modifier*): *a coalition government.* **2.** a fusion or merging into one body or mass. [C17: < Med. L *coalitiō,* < L *coalēscere* to COALESCE] —**ˌcoaˈlitionist** *n.*
Coal Measures *pl. n.* **the.** a series of coal-bearing rocks formed in the upper Carboniferous period.
coal scuttle *n.* a container to supply coal to a domestic fire.
coal tar *n.* a black tar, produced by the distillation of bituminous coal, that can be further distilled to yield benzene, toluene, etc.
coal tit *n.* a small European songbird having a black head with a white patch on the nape.
coaming (ˈkəʊmɪŋ) *n.* a raised frame round a ship's hatchway for keeping out water. [C17: <?]
coarse (kɔːs) *adj.* **1.** rough in texture, structure, etc.; not fine: *coarse sand.* **2.** lacking refinement or taste; indelicate; vulgar: *coarse jokes.* **3.** of inferior quality. **4.** (of a metal) not refined. [C14: <?] —**ˈcoarsely** *adv.* —**ˈcoarseness** *n.*
coarse fish *n.* a freshwater fish that is not of the salmon family. —**coarse fishing** *n.*
coarsen (ˈkɔːsᵊn) *vb.* to make or become coarse.
coast (kəʊst) *n.* **1.** the line or zone where the land meets the sea. Related adj.: **littoral. 2.** *Brit.* the seaside. **3.** *U.S.* **a.** a slope down which a sledge may slide. **b.** the act or an instance of sliding down a slope. **4. the coast is clear.** *Inf.* the obstacles or dangers are gone. ~*vb.* **5.** to move or cause to move by momentum or force of gravity. **6.** (*intr.*) to proceed without great effort: *to coast to victory.* **7.** to sail along (a coast). [C13: < OF *coste,* < L *costa* side, rib] —**ˈcoastal** *adj.*
coaster (ˈkəʊstə) *n.* **1.** *Brit.* a vessel engaged in coastal commerce. **2.** a small tray for holding a decanter, wine bottle, etc. **3.** a person or thing that coasts. **4.** a protective mat for glasses. **5.** *U.S.* short for **roller coaster.**
Coaster (ˈkəʊstə) *n. N.Z.* a person from the West Coast of the South Island, New Zealand.
coastguard (ˈkəʊstˌgɑːd) *n.* **1.** a maritime force which aids shipping, saves lives at sea, prevents smuggling, etc. **2.** Also called: **coastguardsman.** a member of such a force.
coastline (ˈkəʊstˌlaɪn) *n.* the outline of a coast.
coat (kəʊt) *n.* **1.** an outdoor garment with sleeves, covering the body from the shoulders to waist, knees, or feet. **2.** any similar garment, esp. one forming the top to a suit. **3.** a layer that covers or conceals a surface: *a coat of dust.* **4.** the hair, wool, or fur of an animal. ~*vb.* (*tr.*) **5.** (often foll. by *with*) to cover (with) a layer or covering. **6.** to provide with a coat. [C16: < OF *cote,* of Gmc origin]
coat hanger *n.* a curved piece of wood, wire, etc., with a hook, used to hang up clothes.
coati (kəʊˈɑːtɪ), **coati-mondi,** *or* **coati-mundi** (kəʊˌɑːtɪˈmʌndɪ) *n., pl.* **-tis** *or* **-dis.** an omnivorous mammal of Central and South America, related to but larger than the raccoons, having a long flexible snout and a brindled coat. [C17: < Port., < Tupi, lit.: belt-nosed, < *cua* belt + *tim* nose]
coating (ˈkəʊtɪŋ) *n.* **1.** a layer or film spread over a surface. **2.** fabric suitable for coats.
coat of arms *n.* the heraldic bearings of a person, family, or corporation.
coat of mail *n.* a protective garment made of linked metal rings or overlapping metal plates.
coat-tail *n.* the long tapering tails at the back of a man's tailed coat.
coauthor (kəʊˈɔːθə) *n.* **1.** a person who shares the writing of a book, etc., with another. ~*vb.* **2.** (*tr.*) to be the joint author of (a book, etc.).
coax (kəʊks) *vb.* **1.** to seek to manipulate or persuade (someone) by tenderness, flattery, pleading, etc. **2.** (*tr.*) to obtain by persistent coaxing. **3.** (*tr.*) to work on (something) carefully and patiently so as to make it function as desired: *he coaxed the engine into starting.* [C16: verb formed < obs. noun *cokes* fool, <?] —**ˈcoaxer** *n.* —**ˈcoaxingly** *adv.*
coaxial (kəʊˈæksɪəl) *or* **coaxal** (kəʊˈæksᵊl) *adj.* **1.** having or mounted on a common axis. **2.** *Geom.* (of a set of circles) having the same radical axis. **3.** *Electronics.* formed from, using, or connected to a coaxial cable.
coaxial cable *n.* a cable consisting of an inner insulated core of stranded or solid wire surrounded by an outer insulated flexible wire braid, used esp. as a transmission line for radio-frequency signals. Often shortened to **coax** (ˈkəʊæks).

cob (kɒb) *n.* **1.** a male swan. **2.** a thickset type of riding and draught horse. **3.** short for **corncob** or **cobnut.** **4.** *Brit.* another name for **hazel** (sense 1). **5.** a small rounded lump or heap of coal, ore, etc. **6.** *Brit. & N.Z.* a building material consisting of a mixture of clay and chopped straw. **7.** *Brit.* a round loaf of bread. [C15: <?]

cobalt (ˈkəʊbɔːlt) *n.* a brittle hard silvery-white element that is a ferromagnetic metal: used in alloys. The radioisotope **cobalt-60** is used in radiotherapy and as a tracer. Symbol: Co; atomic no.: 27; atomic wt.: 58.933. [C17: G *Kobalt,* < MHG *kobolt* goblin; from the miners' belief that goblins placed it in the silver ore]

cobalt blue *n.* **1.** any greenish-blue pigment containing cobalt aluminate. **2. a.** a deep blue colour. **b.** (*as adj.*): *a cobalt-blue car.*

cobalt bomb *n.* **1.** a cobalt-60 device used in radiotherapy. **2.** a nuclear weapon consisting of a hydrogen bomb encased in cobalt, which releases large quantities of radioactive cobalt-60 into the atmosphere.

cobber (ˈkɒbə) *n. Austral. arch. & N.Z.* a friend; mate: used as a term of address to males. [C19: < E dialect *cob* to take a liking to someone]

cobble[1] (ˈkɒbᵊl) *n.* **1.** short for **cobblestone.** ~*vb.* **2.** (*tr.*) to pave (a road, etc.) with cobblestones. [C15 (in *cobblestone*): < COB]

cobble[2] (ˈkɒbᵊl) *vb.* (*tr.*) **1.** to make or mend (shoes). **2.** to put together clumsily. [C15: back formation < COBBLER[1]]

cobbler[1] (ˈkɒblə) *n.* a person who makes or mends shoes. [C13 (as surname): <?]

cobbler[2] (ˈkɒblə) *n.* **1.** a sweetened iced drink, usually made from fruit and wine. **2.** *Chiefly U.S.* a hot dessert made of fruit covered with a rich cakelike crust. [C19: (for sense 1) ? shortened < *cobbler's punch*]

cobblers (ˈkɒbləz) *pl. n. Brit. taboo sl.* **1.** another word for **testicles.** **2. (a load of old) cobblers.** rubbish; nonsense. [C20: < rhyming sl. *cobblers' awls* balls]

cobblestone (ˈkɒbᵊlˌstəʊn) *n.* a rounded stone used for paving. Sometimes shortened to **cobble.**

cobelligerent (ˌkəʊbɪˈlɪdʒərənt) *n.* a country fighting in a war on the side of another country.

cobia (ˈkəʊbɪə) *n.* a large dark-striped percoid game fish of tropical and subtropical seas. [<?]

cobnut (ˈkɒbˌnʌt) *or* **cob** *n.* other names for a **hazelnut.** [C16: < earlier *cobylle nut*]

COBOL (ˈkəʊˌbɒl) *n.* a high-level computer programming language designed for general commercial use. [C20: *co(mmon) b(usiness) o(riented) l(anguage)*]

cobra (ˈkəʊbrə) *n.* any of several highly venomous snakes of tropical Africa and Asia. When alarmed they spread the skin of the neck region into a hood. [C19: < Port. *cobra (de capello)* snake (with a hood), < L *colubra* snake]

cobweb (ˈkɒbˌwɛb) *n.* **1.** a web spun by certain spiders. **2.** a single thread of such a web. **3.** something like a cobweb, as in its flimsiness or ability to trap. [C14: *cob,* < OE *(ātor)coppe* spider] —ˈ**cobˌwebbed** *adj.* —ˈ**cobˌwebby** *adj.*

cobwebs (ˈkɒbˌwɛbz) *pl. n.* **1.** mustiness, confusion, or obscurity. **2.** *Inf.* stickiness of the eyelids experienced upon first awakening.

coca (ˈkəʊkə) *n.* either of two shrubs, native to the Andes, the dried leaves of which contain cocaine and are chewed for their stimulating effects. [C17: < Sp., < Quechuan *kúka*]

Coca-Cola (ˌkəʊkəˈkəʊlə) *n. Trademark.* a carbonated soft drink flavoured with coca leaves, cola nuts, caramel, etc.

cocaine *or* **cocain** (kəˈkeɪn) *n.* an addictive narcotic drug derived from coca leaves or synthesized, used medicinally as a topical anaesthetic. [C19: < COCA + -INE[1]]

coccus (ˈkɒkəs) *n., pl.* **-ci** (-kaɪ, -saɪ). any spherical or nearly spherical bacterium, such as a staphylococcus. [C18: < NL, < Gk *kokkos* berry, grain] —ˈ**coccoid** *or* ˈ**coccal** *adj.*

coccyx (ˈkɒksɪks) *n., pl.* **coccyges** (kɒkˈsaɪdʒiːz). a small triangular bone at the end of the spinal column in man and some apes. [C17: < NL, < Gk *kokkux* cuckoo, imit.; from its likeness to a cuckoo's beak] —**coccygeal** (kɒkˈsɪdʒɪəl) *adj.*

cochineal (ˌkɒtʃɪˈniːl, ˈkɒtʃɪˌniːl) *n.* **1.** a Mexican insect that feeds on cacti. **2.** a crimson substance obtained from the crushed bodies of these insects, used for colouring food and for dyeing. **3.** the colour of this dye. [C16: < OSp. *cochinilla,* < L *coccineus* scarlet-coloured, < Gk *kokkos* kermes berry]

cochlea (ˈkɒklɪə) *n., pl.* **-leae** (-lɪˌiː). the spiral tube that forms part of the internal ear, converting sound vibrations into nerve impulses. [C16: < L: snail, spiral, < Gk *kokhlias*] —ˈ**cochlear** *adj.*

cochleate (ˈkɒklɪˌeɪt, -lɪɪt) *or* **cochleated** *adj. Biol.* shaped like a snail's shell.

cock[1] (kɒk) *n.* **1.** the male of the domestic fowl. **2. a.** any other male bird. **b.** the male of certain other animals, such as the lobster. **c.** (*as modifier*): *a cock sparrow.* **3.** short for **stopcock** or **weathercock.** **4.** a taboo slang word for **penis.** **5. a.** the hammer of a firearm. **b.** its position when the firearm is ready to be discharged. **6.** *Brit. inf.* a friend, mate, or fellow. **7.** a jaunty or significant tilting upwards: *a cock of the head.* ~*vb.* **8.** (*tr.*) to set the firing pin, hammer, or breech block of (a firearm) so that a pull on the trigger will release it and thus fire the weapon. **9.** (*tr.;* sometimes foll. by *up*) to raise in an alert or jaunty manner. **10.** (*intr.*) to stick or stand up conspicuously. ~See also **cockup.** [OE *cocc,* ult. imit.]

cock[2] (kɒk) *n.* **1.** a small, cone-shaped heap of hay, straw, etc. ~*vb.* **2.** (*tr.*) to stack (hay, etc.) in such heaps. [C14: ? of Scand. origin]

cockabully (ˌkɒkəˈbʊlɪ) *n., pl.* **-lies.** any of several small freshwater fish of New Zealand. [Maori *kokopu*]

cockade (kɒˈkeɪd) *n.* a feather or ribbon worn on military headwear. [C18: changed < earlier *cockard,* < F, < *coq* COCK[1]] —**cockˈaded** *adj.*

cock-a-doodle-doo (ˌkɒkəˌduːdᵊlˈduː) *interj.* an imitation or representation of a cock crowing.

cock-a-hoop *adj.* (*usually postpositive*) **1.** in very high spirits. **2.** boastful. **3.** askew; confused. [C16: ?< *set the cock a hoop*: to put a cock on a *hoop,* a full measure of grain]

cockalorum (ˌkɒkəˈlɔːrəm) *n.* **1.** a self-important little man. **2.** bragging talk. [C18: < COCK[1] + *-alorum,* var. of L genitive pl. ending; ? intended to suggest: the cock of all cocks]

cock-and-bull story *n. Inf.* an obviously improbable story, esp. one used as an excuse.

cockatoo (ˌkɒkəˈtuː, ˈkɒkəˌtuː) *n., pl.* **-toos.** **1.** any of a genus of parrots having an erectile crest and light-coloured plumage. **2.** *Austral. & N.Z.* a small farmer or settler. **3.** *Austral. inf.* a lookout during some illegal activity. [C17: < Du., < Malay *kakatua*]

cockatrice (ˈkɒkətrɪs, -ˌtraɪs) *n.* **1.** a legendary monster, part snake and part cock, that could kill with a glance. **2.** another name for **basilisk** (sense 1). [C14: < OF, ult. < L *calcāre* to tread, < *calx* heel]

cockboat (ˈkɒkˌbəʊt) *or* **cockleboat** *n.* any small boat. [C15 *cokbote,* ? ult. < LL *caudica* dugout canoe, < L *caudex* tree trunk]

cockchafer (ˈkɒkˌtʃeɪfə) *n.* any of various Old World beetles, whose larvae feed on crops and grasses. Also called: **May beetle, May bug.** [C18: < COCK[1] + CHAFER]

cockcrow (ˈkɒkˌkrəʊ) *n.* daybreak.

cocked hat *n.* **1.** a hat with brims turned up and caught together in order to give two points (bicorn) or three points (tricorn). **2. knock into a cocked hat.** *Sl.* to outdo or defeat.

cockerel (ˈkɒkərəl, ˈkɒkrəl) *n.* a young domestic cock, less than a year old. [C15: dim. of COCK[1]]

cocker spaniel (ˈkɒkə) *n.* a small compact breed of spaniel. [C19: < *cocking* hunting woodcocks]

cockeyed (ˈkɒkˌaɪd) *adj. Inf.* **1.** afflicted with strabismus or squint. **2.** physically or logically abnormal, absurd, etc.; crooked; askew: *cockeyed ideas.* **3.** drunk.

cockfight (ˈkɒkˌfaɪt) *n.* a fight between two

gamecocks fitted with sharp metal spurs. —ˈ**cock**ˌ**fighting** *n.*

cockhorse (ˌkɒkˈhɔːs) *n.* another name for **rocking horse** or **hobbyhorse.**

cockieleekie, cockyleeky, *or* **cock-a-leekie** (ˈkɒkəˈliːkɪ) *n. Scot.* a soup made from a fowl boiled with leeks.

cockle[1] (ˈkɒkᵊl) *n.* **1.** any edible sand-burrowing bivalve mollusc of Europe, typically having a rounded shell with radiating ribs. **2.** any of certain similar or related molluscs. **3.** short for **cockleshell** (sense 1). **4.** a wrinkle or puckering. **5.** one's deepest feelings (esp. in **warm the cockles of one's heart**). ~*vb.* **6.** to contract or cause to contract into wrinkles. [C14: < OF *coquille* shell, < L *conchȳlium* shellfish, < Gk *konkhule* mussel; see CONCH]

cockle[2] (ˈkɒkᵊl) *n.* any of several plants, esp. the corn cockle, that grow as weeds in cornfields.

cocklebur (ˈkɒkᵊlˌbɜː) *n.* **1.** a coarse weed of the composite family having spiny burs. **2.** the bur of this plant.

cockleshell (ˈkɒkᵊlˌʃɛl) *n.* **1.** the shell of the cockle. **2.** any of the shells of certain other molluscs. **3.** any small light boat.

cockney (ˈkɒknɪ) (*often cap.*) ~*n.* **1.** a native of London, esp. of the East End, speaking a characteristic dialect of English. Traditionally defined as someone born within the sound of the bells of St Mary-le-Bow church. **2.** the urban dialect of London or its East End. ~*adj.* **3.** characteristic of cockneys or their dialect of English. [C14: < *cokeney,* lit.: cock's egg, later applied contemptuously to townsmen, < *cokene,* genitive pl. of *cok* COCK[1] + *ey* EGG[1]] —ˈ**cockneyish** *adj.* —ˈ**cockney**ˌ**ism** *n.*

cock of the walk *n. Inf.* a person who asserts himself in a strutting pompous way.

cockpit (ˈkɒkˌpɪt) *n.* **1.** the compartment in a small aircraft in which the pilot, crew, and sometimes the passengers sit. Cf. **flight deck** (sense 1). **2.** the driver's compartment in a racing car. **3.** *Naut.* an enclosed area towards the stern of a small vessel containing the wheel and tiller. **4.** the site of numerous battles or campaigns. **5.** an enclosure used for cockfights.

cockroach (ˈkɒkˌrəʊtʃ) *n.* an insect having an oval flattened body with long antennae and biting mouthparts: a household pest. [C17: < Sp. *cucaracha,* <?]

cockscomb *or* **coxcomb** (ˈkɒksˌkəʊm) *n.* **1.** the comb of a domestic cock. **2.** a garden plant with yellow, crimson, or purple feathery plumelike flowers in a broad spike resembling the comb of a cock. **3.** *Inf.* a conceited dandy.

cockshy (ˈkɒkˌʃaɪ) *n., pl.* **-shies.** *Brit.* **1.** a target aimed at in throwing games. **2.** the throw itself. ~Often shortened to **shy.** [C18: < shying at a cock, the prize for the person who hit it]

cocksure (ˌkɒkˈʃʊə, -ˈʃɔː) *adj.* overconfident; arrogant. [C16: <?] —ˌ**cock**ˈ**sureness** *n.*

cocktail (ˈkɒkˌteɪl) *n.* **1. a.** any mixed drink with a spirit base. **b.** (*as modifier*): *the cocktail hour.* **2.** an appetizer of seafood, mixed fruits, etc. **3.** any combination of diverse elements, esp. one considered potent. **4.** (*modifier*) appropriate for formal occasions: *a cocktail dress.* [C19: <?]

cockup (ˈkɒkˌʌp) *n.* **1.** *Brit. sl.* something done badly. ~*vb.* **cock up.** (*tr., adv.*) **2.** (of an animal) to raise (its ears etc.), esp. in an alert manner. **3.** *Brit. sl.* to botch.

cocky[1] (ˈkɒkɪ) *adj.* **cockier, cockiest.** excessively proud of oneself. —ˈ**cockily** *adv.* —ˈ**cockiness** *n.*

cocky[2] (ˈkɒkɪ) *n., pl* **cockies.** *Austral. & N.Z. inf.* short for **cockatoo** (sense 2).

coco (ˈkəʊkəʊ) *n., pl.* **-cos.** short for **coconut** or **coconut palm.** [C16: < Port. *coco* grimace; < the likeness of the three holes of the nut to a face]

cocoa (ˈkəʊkəʊ) *or* **cacao** *n.* **1.** a powder made from cocoa beans after they have been roasted and ground. **2.** a hot or cold drink made from cocoa and milk or water. **3. a.** a light to moderate brown colour. **b.** (*as adj.*): *cocoa paint.* [C18: altered < CACAO]

cocoa bean *n.* the seed of the cacao.

cocoa butter *n.* a yellowish-white waxy solid that is obtained from cocoa beans and used for confectionery, soap, etc.

coconut *or* **cocoanut** (ˈkəʊkəˌnʌt) *n.* **1.** the fruit of the coconut palm, consisting of a thick fibrous oval husk inside which is a thin hard shell enclosing edible white meat. The hollow centre is filled with a milky fluid (**coconut milk**). **2.** the meat of the coconut, often shredded and used in cakes, curries, etc. [C18: see COCO]

coconut matting *n.* a form of coarse matting made from the fibrous husk of the coconut.

coconut oil *n.* the oil obtained from the meat of the coconut and used for making soap, etc.

coconut palm *n.* a tall palm tree, widely planted throughout the tropics, having coconuts as fruits. Also called: **coco palm, coconut tree.**

cocoon (kəˈkuːn) *n.* **1.** a silky protective envelope secreted by silkworms and certain other insect larvae, in which the pupae develop. **2.** a protective spray covering used as a seal on machinery. **3.** a cosy warm covering. ~*vb.* **4.** (*tr.*) to wrap in a cocoon. [C17: < F, < Provençal *coucoun* eggshell, < *coco* shell]

cocopan (ˈkəʊkəʊˌpæn) *n.* (in South Africa) a small wagon running on narrow-gauge railway lines used in mines. Also called: **hopper.** [C20: < Zulu *'ngkumbana* short truck]

cocotte (kəʊˈkɒt, kə-) *n.* **1.** a small fireproof dish in which individual portions of food are cooked and served. **2.** a prostitute or promiscuous woman. [C19: < F, < fem. of *coq* COCK[1]]

cod[1] (kɒd) *n., pl.* **cod** *or* **cods. 1.** any of the gadoid food fishes which occur in the North Atlantic and have a long body with three rounded dorsal fins. **2.** any of various Australian fishes of fresh or salt water, such as the Murray cod or the red cod. [C13: prob. of Gmc origin]

cod[2] (kɒd) *n.* **1.** *Brit. & U.S. dialect.* a pod or husk. **2.** *Taboo.* an obsolete word for **scrotum.** [OE *codd* husk, bag]

cod[3] (kɒd) *Brit. sl.* ~*vb.* **codding, codded.** (*tr.*) **1.** to make fun of; tease. **2.** to play a trick on; befool. ~*n.* **3.** a hoax or trick. [C19: ?< earlier *cod* a fool]

COD *abbrev. for:* **1.** cash on delivery. **2.** (in the U.S.) collect on delivery.

coda (ˈkəʊdə) *n.* **1.** *Music.* the final part of a musical structure. **2.** a concluding part of a literary work that rounds off the main work but is independent of it. [C18: < It.: tail, < L *cauda*]

coddle (ˈkɒdᵊl) *vb.* (*tr.*) **1.** to treat with indulgence. **2.** to cook (something, esp. eggs) in water just below the boiling point. [C16: <?; ? rel. to CAUDLE] —ˈ**coddler** *n.*

code (kəʊd) *n.* **1.** a system of letters or symbols, by which information can be communicated secretly, briefly, etc.: *binary code; Morse code.* See also **genetic code. 2.** a message in code. **3.** a symbol used in a code. **4.** a conventionalized set of principles or rules: *a code of behaviour.* **5.** a system of letters or digits used for identification purposes. ~*vb.* (*tr.*) **6.** to translate or arrange into a code. [C14: < F, < L *cōdex* book, CODEX] —ˈ**coder** *n.*

codeine (ˈkəʊdiːn) *n.* a white crystalline alkaloid prepared mainly from morphine. It is used as an analgesic, a sedative, and to relieve coughing. [C19: < Gk *kōdeia* head of a poppy, < *kōos* hollow place + -INE[2]]

codex (ˈkəʊdɛks) *n., pl.* **codices** (ˈkəʊdɪˌsiːz, ˈkɒdɪ-). **1.** a volume of manuscripts of an ancient text. **2.** *Obs.* a legal code. [C16: < L: tree trunk, wooden block, book]

codfish (ˈkɒdˌfɪʃ) *n., pl.* **-fish** *or* **-fishes.** a cod.

codger (ˈkɒdʒə) *n. Inf.* a man, esp. an old or eccentric one: often in **old codger.** [C18: prob. var. of CADGER]

codicil (ˈkɒdɪsɪl) *n.* **1.** *Law.* a supplement modifying a will or revoking some provision of it. **2.** an additional provision; appendix. [C15: < LL dim. of CODEX] —ˌ**codi**ˈ**cillary** *adj.*

codify (ˈkəʊdɪˌfaɪ, ˈkɒ-) *vb.* **-fying, -fied.** (*tr.*) to organize or collect together (laws, rules, procedures, etc.) into a system or code. —ˈ**codiˌfier** *n.* —ˌ**codifiˈcation** *n.*

codling[1] (ˈkɒdlɪŋ) *or* **codlin** (ˈkɒdlɪn) *n.* **1.** any of several varieties of long tapering apples. **2.** any unripe apple. [C15 *querdlyng,* <?]

codling[2] (ˈkɒdlɪŋ) *n.* a codfish, esp. a young one.

cod-liver oil *n.* an oil extracted from the livers of cod and related fish, rich in vitamins A and D.

codpiece (ˈkɒdˌpiːs) *n.* a bag covering the male genitals, attached to breeches: worn in the 15th and 16th centuries. [C15: < COD[2] + PIECE]

codswallop (ˈkɒdzˌwɒləp) *n. Brit. sl.* nonsense. [C20: <?]

co-ed (ˌkəʊˈɛd) *adj.* **1.** coeducational. ~*n.* **2.** *U.S.* a female student in a coeducational college or university. **3.** *Brit.* a school or college providing coeducation.

coeducation (ˌkəʊɛdjʊˈkeɪʃən) *n.* instruction in schools, colleges, etc., attended by both sexes. —ˌ**coeduˈcational** *adj.* —ˌ**coeduˈcationally** *adv.*

coefficient (ˌkəʊɪˈfɪʃənt) *n.* **1.** *Maths.* a numerical or constant factor in an algebraic term: *the coefficient of the term 3xyz is 3.* **2.** *Physics.* a number that is the value of a given substance under specified conditions. [C17: < NL, < L *co-* together + *efficere* to EFFECT]

coefficient of variation *n. Statistics.* a measure of the relative variation of distributions independent of the units of measurement; the standard deviation divided by the mean, sometimes expressed as a percentage.

coel- *prefix.* indicating a cavity within a body or a hollow organ or part: *coelacanth; coelenterate.* [NL, < Gk *koilos* hollow]

coelacanth (ˈsiːləˌkænθ) *n.* a primitive marine bony fish, having fleshy limblike pectoral fins: thought to be extinct until a living specimen was discovered in 1938. [C19: < NL, < COEL- + Gk *akanthos* spine]

coelenterate (sɪˈlɛntəˌreɪt, -rɪt) *n.* any of various invertebrates having a saclike body with a single opening (mouth), such as jellyfishes, sea anemones, and corals. [C19: < NL *Coelenterata,* hollow-intestined (creatures)]

coeliac *or U.S.* **celiac** (ˈsiːlɪˌæk) *adj.* of the abdomen. [C17: < L, < Gk, < *koilia* belly]

coelom *or esp. U.S.* **celom** (ˈsiːləʊm, -ləm) *n.* the body cavity of many multicellular animals, containing the digestive tract and other visceral organs. [C19: < Gk, < *koilos* hollow]

coeno- *or before a vowel* **coen-** *combining form.* common: *coenobite.* [NL, < Gk *koinos*]

coenobite *or* **cenobite** (ˈsiːnəʊˌbaɪt) *n.* a member of a religious order following a communal rule of life. [C17: < OF or ecclesiastical L, < Gk *koinobion* convent, < *koinos* common + *bios* life] —**coenobitic** (ˌsiːnəʊˈbɪtɪk), ˌ**coenoˈbitical** *or* ˌ**cenoˈbitic,** ˌ**cenoˈbitical** *adj.*

coequal (kəʊˈiːkwəl) *adj.* **1.** of the same size, rank, etc. ~*n.* **2.** a person or thing equal with another. —**coequality** (ˌkəʊɪˈkwɒlɪtɪ) *n.*

coerce (kəʊˈɜːs) *vb.* (*tr.*) to compel or restrain by force or authority without regard to individual wishes or desires. [C17: < L, < *co-* together + *arcēre* to enclose] —**coˈercer** *n.* —**coˈercible** *adj.*

coercion (kəʊˈɜːʃən) *n.* **1.** the act or power of coercing. **2.** government by force. —**coercive** (kəʊˈɜːsɪv) *adj.* —**coˈercively** *adv.*

coeval (kəʊˈiːvəl) *adj.* **1.** of or belonging to the same age or generation. ~*n.* **2.** a contemporary. [C17: < LL, < L *co-* + *aevum* age] —**coevality** (ˌkəʊɪˈvælɪtɪ) *n.* —**coˈevally** *adv.*

coexecutor (ˌkəʊɪgˈzɛkjʊtə) *n. Law.* a person acting jointly with another or others as executor.

coexist (ˌkəʊɪgˈzɪst) *vb.* (*intr.*) **1.** to exist together at the same time or in the same place. **2.** to exist together in peace. —ˌ**coexˈistence** *n.* —ˌ**coexˈistent** *adj.*

coextend (ˌkəʊɪkˈstɛnd) *vb.* to extend or cause to extend equally in space or time. —ˌ**coexˈtension** *n.* —ˌ**coexˈtensive** *adj.*

C of C *abbrev. for* Chamber of Commerce.

C of E *abbrev. for* Church of England.

coffee (ˈkɒfɪ) *n.* **1. a.** a drink consisting of an infusion of the roasted and ground seeds of the coffee tree. **b.** (*as modifier*): *coffee grounds.* **2.** Also called: **coffee beans.** the beanlike seeds of the coffee tree, used to make this beverage. **3.** the tree yielding these seeds. **4. a.** a light brown colour. **b.** (*as adj.*): *a coffee carpet.* [C16: < It. *caffè,* < Turkish *kahve,* < Ar. *qahwah* coffee, wine]

coffee bar *n.* a café; snack bar.

coffee cup *n.* a small cup for serving coffee.

coffee house *n.* a place where coffee is served, esp. one that was a fashionable meeting place in 18th-century London.

coffee mill *n.* a machine for grinding roasted coffee beans.

coffeepot (ˈkɒfɪˌpɒt) *n.* a pot in which coffee is brewed or served.

coffee shop *n.* a shop where coffee is sold or drunk.

coffee table *n.* a low table on which coffee may be served.

coffee-table book *n.* a book, usually glossily illustrated, designed chiefly to be looked at, rather than read.

coffer (ˈkɒfə) *n.* **1.** a chest, esp. for storing valuables. **2.** (*usually pl.*) a store of money. **3.** an ornamental sunken panel in a ceiling, dome, etc. **4.** a watertight box or chamber. **5.** short for **cofferdam.** ~*vb* (*tr.*) **6.** to store, as in a coffer. **7.** to decorate (a ceiling, dome, etc.) with coffers. [C13: < OF *coffre,* < L, < Gk *kophinos* basket]

cofferdam (ˈkɒfəˌdæm) *n.* **1.** a watertight structure that encloses an area under water, pumped dry to enable construction work to be carried out. **2.** (on a ship) a compartment separating two bulkheads, as for insulation or to serve as a barrier against the escape of gas, etc. ~Often shortened to **coffer.**

coffin (ˈkɒfɪn) *n.* **1.** a box in which a corpse is buried or cremated. **2.** the bony part of a horse's foot. ~*vb.* **3.** (*tr.*) to place in or as in a coffin. [C14: < OF *cofin,* < L *cophinus* basket]

coffin nail *n.* a slang term for **cigarette.**

coffle (ˈkɒfəl) *n.* a line of slaves, beasts, etc., fastened together. [C18: < Ar. *qāfilah* caravan]

C of S *abbrev. for* Church of Scotland.

cog[1] (kɒg) *n.* **1.** any of the teeth or projections on the rim of a gearwheel. **2.** a gearwheel, esp. a small one. **3.** a person or thing playing a small part in a large organization or process. [C13: of Scand. origin]

cog[2] (kɒg) *n.* **1.** a tenon that projects from the end of a timber beam for fitting into a mortise. ~*vb.* **cogging, cogged. 2.** (*tr.*) to join (pieces of wood) with cogs. [C19: <?]

cogent (ˈkəʊdʒənt) *adj.* compelling belief or assent; forcefully convincing. [C17: < L *cōgent-, cōgēns,* < *co-* together + *agere* to drive] —ˈ**cogency** *n.* —ˈ**cogently** *adv.*

cogitate (ˈkɒdʒɪˌteɪt) *vb.* to think deeply about (a problem, possibility, etc.); ponder. [C16: < L, < *co-* (intensive) + *agitāre* to turn over] —ˌ**cogiˈtation** *n.* —ˈ**cogitative** *adj.* —ˈ**cogiˌtator** *n.*

Cognac (ˈkɒnjæk) *n.* (*sometimes not cap.*) a high-quality grape brandy, distilled near Cognac in SW France.

cognate (ˈkɒgneɪt) *adj.* **1.** akin; related: *cognate languages.* **2.** related by blood or descended from a common maternal ancestor. ~*n.* **3.** something that is cognate with something else. [C17: < L, < *co-* same + *gnātus* born, var. of *nātus,* p.p. of *nāscī* to be born] —ˈ**cognately** *adv.* —ˈ**cognateness** *n.* —**cogˈnation** *n.*

cognition (kɒgˈnɪʃən) *n.* **1.** the mental act or process by which knowledge is acquired, including perception, intuition, and reasoning. **2.** the knowledge that results from such an act or process. [C15: < L, < *co-* (intensive) + *nōscere* to learn] —**cogˈnitional** *adj.* —**cognitive** (ˈkɒgnɪtɪv) *adj.*

cognizable *or* **cognisable** (ˈkɒgnɪzəbəl, ˈkɒnɪ-) *adj.* **1.** perceptible. **2.** *Law.* susceptible to the jurisdiction of a court.

cognizance *or* **cognisance** (ˈkɒgnɪzəns, ˈkɒnɪ-)

n. **1.** knowledge; acknowledgment. **2. take cognizance of.** to take notice of; acknowledge, esp. officially. **3.** the range or scope of knowledge or perception. **4.** *Law.* the right of a court to hear and determine a cause or matter. **5.** *Heraldry.* a distinguishing badge or bearing. [C14: < OF, < L *cognōscere* to learn; see COGNITION]

cognizant *or* **cognisant** (ˈkɒgnɪzənt, ˈkɒnɪ-) *adj.* (usually foll. by *of*) aware; having knowledge.

cognomen (kɒgˈnəʊmɛn) *n., pl.* **-nomens** *or* **-nomina** (-ˈnɒmɪnə, -ˈnəʊ-). (originally) an ancient Roman's third name or nickname, which later became his family name. [C19: < L: additional name, < *co-* together + *nōmen* name] —**cognominal** (kɒgˈnɒmɪnᵊl, -ˈnəʊ-) *adj.*

cognoscenti (ˌkɒnjəʊˈʃɛntɪ, ˌkɒgnəʊ-) *or* **conoscenti** (ˌkɒnəʊˈʃɛntɪ) *pl. n., sing.* **-te** (-tiː). (*sometimes sing.*) people with informed appreciation of a particular field, esp. in the fine arts; connoisseurs. [C18: < obs. It., < L *cognōscere* to learn]

cogwheel (ˈkɒgˌwiːl) *n.* another name for **gearwheel.**

cohabit (kəʊˈhæbɪt) *vb.* (*intr.*) to live together as husband and wife, esp. without being married. [C16: < L *co-* together + *habitāre* to live] —**coˈhabitant** *or* **coˈhabiter** *n.* —**coˌhabiˈtation** *n.*

coheir (kəʊˈɛə) *n.* a person who inherits jointly with others. —**coˈheiress** *fem. n.*

cohere (kəʊˈhɪə) *vb.* (*intr.*) **1.** to hold or stick firmly together. **2.** to be connected logically; be consistent. **3.** *Physics.* to be held together by the action of molecular forces. [C16: < L *co-* together + *haerēre* to cling]

coherence (kəʊˈhɪərəns) *or* **coherency** *n.* **1.** logical or natural connection or consistency. **2.** another word for **cohesion** (sense 1).

coherent (kəʊˈhɪərənt) *adj.* **1.** capable of intelligible speech. **2.** logical; consistent and orderly. **3.** cohering or sticking together. **4.** *Physics.* (of two or more waves) having the same frequency and the same phase or a fixed phase difference: *coherent light.* —**coˈherently** *adv.*

cohesion (kəʊˈhiːʒən) *n.* **1.** the act or state of cohering; tendency to unite. **2.** *Physics.* the force that holds together the atoms or molecules in a solid or liquid, as distinguished from adhesion. **3.** *Bot.* the fusion in some plants of flower parts, such as petals, that are usually separate. [C17: < L *cohaesus,* p.p. of *cohaerēre* to COHERE] —**coˈhesive** *adj.*

coho (ˈkəʊhəʊ) *n., pl.* **-ho** *or* **-hos.** a Pacific salmon. Also called: **silver salmon.** [<?]

cohort (ˈkəʊhɔːt) *n.* **1.** one of the ten units of an ancient Roman Legion. **2.** any band of warriors or associates: *the cohorts of Satan.* **3.** *Chiefly U.S.* an associate or follower. [C15: < L *cohors* yard, company of soldiers]

COHSE (ˈkəʊzɪ) *n.* (in Britain) *acronym for* Confederation of Health Service Employees.

COI (in Britain) *abbrev. for* Central Office of Information.

coif (kɔɪf) *n.* **1.** a close-fitting cap worn under a veil in the Middle Ages. **2.** a leather cap worn under a chain-mail hood. **3.** (kwɑːf). a less common word for **coiffure** (sense 1). ~*vb.* **coiffing, coiffed.** (*tr.*) **4.** to cover with or as if with a coif. **5.** (kwɑːf). to arrange (the hair). [C14: < OF *coiffe,* < LL *cofea* helmet, cap, <?]

coiffeur (kwɑːˈfɜː) *n.* a hairdresser. —**coiffeuse** (kwɑːˈfɜːz) *fem. n.*

coiffure (kwɑːˈfjʊə) *n.* **1.** a hairstyle. **2.** an obsolete word for **headdress.** ~*vb.* **3.** (*tr.*) to dress or arrange (the hair).

coign of vantage (kɔɪn) *n.* an advantageous position for observation or action.

coil[1] (kɔɪl) *vb.* **1.** to wind or gather (ropes, hair, etc.) into loops or (of ropes, hair, etc.) to be formed in such loops. **2.** (*intr.*) to move in a winding course. ~*n.* **3.** something wound in a connected series of loops. **4.** a single loop of such a series. **5.** an arrangement of pipes in a spiral or loop, as in a condenser. **6.** an electrical conductor wound into the form of a spiral, to provide inductance or a magnetic field. **7.** an intrauterine contraceptive device in the shape of a coil. **8.** the transformer in a petrol engine that supplies the high voltage to the sparking plugs. [C16: < OF *coillir* to collect together; see CULL]

coil[2] (kɔɪl) *n.* the troubles of the world (in Shakespeare's phrase **this mortal coil**). [C16: <?]

coin (kɔɪn) *n.* **1.** a metal disc or piece used as money. **2.** metal currency, as opposed to paper currency, etc. **3.** *Archit.* a variant spelling of **quoin. 4. pay (a person) back in (his) own coin.** to treat (a person) in the way that he has treated others. ~*vb.* (*tr.*) **5.** to make or stamp (coins). **6.** to make into a coin. **7.** to fabricate or invent (words, etc.). **8.** *Inf.* to make (money) rapidly (esp. in **coin it in**). [C14: < OF: stamping die, < L *cuneus* wedge]

coinage (ˈkɔɪnɪdʒ) *n.* **1.** coins collectively. **2.** the act of striking coins. **3.** the currency of a country. **4.** the act of inventing something, esp. a word or phrase. **5.** a newly invented word, phrase, usage, etc.

coincide (ˌkəʊɪnˈsaɪd) *vb.* (*intr.*) **1.** to occur or exist simultaneously. **2.** to be identical in nature, character, etc. **3.** to agree. [C18: < Med. L, < L *co-* together + *incidere* to occur, befall, < *cadere* to fall]

coincidence (kəʊˈɪnsɪdəns) *n.* **1.** a chance occurrence of events remarkable either for being simultaneous or for apparently being connected. **2.** the fact, condition, or state of coinciding. **3.** (*modifier*) *Electronics.* of or relating to a circuit that produces an output pulse only when both its input terminals receive pulses within a specified interval: *coincidence gate.*

coincident (kəʊˈɪnsɪdənt) *adj.* **1.** having the same position in space or time. **2.** (usually *postpositive* and foll. by *with*) in exact agreement. —**coˌinciˈdental** *adj.* —**coˌinciˈdentally** *adv.*

coin-op (ˈkɔɪnˌɒp) *n.* a launderette or other installation in which the machines are operated by insertion of a coin. —ˈ**coin-ˌoperˌated** *adj.*

Cointreau (ˈkwɑːntrəʊ) *n. Trademark.* a colourless liqueur with orange flavouring.

coir (ˈkɔɪə) *n.* the fibre from the husk of the coconut, used in making rope and matting. [C16: < Malayalam *kāyar* rope, < *kāyaru* to be twisted]

coitus (ˈkəʊɪtəs) *or* **coition** (kəʊˈɪʃən) *n.* a technical term for **sexual intercourse.** [C18: < L, < *coīre* to meet, < *īre* to go] —ˈ**coital** *adj.*

coke[1] (kəʊk) *n.* **1.** a solid-fuel product produced by distillation of coal to drive off its volatile constituents: used as a fuel. **2.** the layer formed in the cylinders of a car engine by incomplete combustion of the fuel. ~*vb.* **3.** to become or convert into coke. [C17: prob. var. of C14 N English dialect *colk* core, <?]

coke[2] (kəʊk) *n. Sl.* short for **cocaine.**

Coke (kəʊk) *n. Trademark.* short for **Coca-Cola.**

col (kɒl) *n.* **1.** the lowest point of a ridge connecting two mountain peaks. **2.** *Meteorol.* a low-pressure region between two anticyclones. [C19: < F: neck, col, < L *collum* neck]

Col. *abbrev. for:* **1.** Colombia(n). **2.** Colonel. **3.** *Bible.* Colossians.

col- *prefix.* a variant of **com-** before *l: collateral.*

cola *or* **kola** (ˈkəʊlə) *n.* **1.** either of two trees widely cultivated in tropical regions for their seeds (see **cola nut). 2.** a sweet carbonated drink flavoured with cola nuts. [C18: < *kola,* prob. var. of W African *kolo* nut]

colander (ˈkɒləndə, ˈkʌl-) *or* **cullender** *n.* a pan with a perforated bottom for straining or rinsing foods. [C14 *colyndore,* prob. < OProvençal *colador,* < LL, < L *cōlum* sieve]

cola nut *n.* any of the seeds of the cola tree, which contain caffeine and theobromine and are used medicinally and in soft drinks.

colchicine (ˈkɒltʃɪˌsiːn, -sɪn, ˈkɒlkɪ-) *n.* a pale yellow crystalline alkaloid extracted from seeds or corms of the autumn crocus and used in the treatment of gout. [C19: < COLCHICUM + -INE[2]]

colchicum (ˈkɒltʃɪkəm, ˈkɒlkɪ-) *n.* **1.** any Eurasian plant of the lily family, such as the autumn crocus. **2.** the dried seeds or corms of the autumn crocus. [C16: < L, < Gk, < *kolkhikos* of *Colchis*, ancient country on the Black Sea]

cold (kəʊld) *adj.* **1.** having relatively little warmth; of a rather low temperature: *cold weather; cold hands.* **2.** without proper warmth: *this meal is cold.* **3.** lacking in affection or enthusiasm: *a cold manner.* **4.** not affected by emotion: *cold logic.* **5.** dead. **6.** sexually unresponsive or frigid. **7.** lacking in freshness: *a cold scent; cold news.* **8.** chilling to the spirit; depressing. **9.** (of a colour) having violet, blue, or green predominating; giving no sensation of warmth. **10.** *Sl.* unconscious. **11.** *Inf.* (of a seeker) far from the object of a search. **12. cold comfort.** little or no comfort. **13. leave (someone) cold.** *Inf.* to fail to excite: *the performance left me cold.* **14. throw cold water on.** *Inf.* to be unenthusiastic about or discourage. ~*n.* **15.** the absence of heat regarded as a positive force: *the cold took away our breath.* **16.** the sensation caused by loss or lack of heat. **17.** (out) **in the cold.** *Inf.* neglected; ignored. **18.** an acute viral infection of the upper respiratory passages characterized by discharge of watery mucus from the nose, sneezing, etc. **19. catch a cold.** *Inf.* to make a financial loss. ~*adv.* **20.** *Inf.* without preparation: *he played his part cold.* [OE *ceald*] —**ˈcoldish** *adj.* —**ˈcoldly** *adv.* —**ˈcoldness** *n.*

cold-blooded *adj.* **1.** having or showing a lack of feeling or pity. **2.** *Inf.* particularly sensitive to cold. **3.** (of all animals except birds and mammals) having a body temperature that varies with that of the surroundings. —**ˌcold-ˈbloodedly** *adv.* —**ˌcold-ˈbloodedness** *n.*

cold cathode *n. Electronics.* a cathode from which electrons are emitted at an ambient temperature.

cold chisel *n.* a toughened steel chisel.

cold cream *n.* an emulsion of water and fat used for softening and cleansing the skin.

cold cuts *pl. n.* cooked meats sliced and served cold.

cold feet *n. Inf.* loss or lack of confidence.

cold frame *n.* an unheated wooden frame with a glass top, used to protect young plants.

cold front *n. Meteorol.* the boundary line between a warm air mass and the cold air pushing it from beneath and behind as it moves.

cold-hearted *adj.* lacking in feeling or warmth; unkind. —**ˌcold-ˈheartedly** *adv.* —**ˌcold-ˈheartedness** *n.*

cold pack *n.* a tinning process in which raw food is packed in cans or jars and then heated.

cold shoulder *Inf.* ~*n.* **1.** (often preceded by *the*) a show of indifference; a slight. ~*vb.* **cold-shoulder.** (*tr.*) **2.** to treat with indifference.

cold sore *n.* a cluster of blisters at the margin of the lips, caused by a viral infection. Technical name: **herpes labialis.**

cold storage *n.* **1.** the storage of things in an artificially cooled place for preservation. **2.** *Inf.* a state of temporary suspension: *to put an idea into cold storage.*

cold sweat *n. Inf.* a bodily reaction to fear or nervousness, characterized by chill and moist skin.

cold turkey *n. Sl.* a method of curing drug addiction by abrupt withdrawal of all doses.

cold war *n.* a state of political hostility and military tension between two countries or power blocs, involving propaganda, threats, etc.

cold wave *n.* **1.** *Meteorol.* a sudden spell of low temperatures over a wide area. **2.** *Hairdressing.* a permanent wave made by chemical agents applied at normal temperatures.

cole (kəʊl) *n.* any of various plants such as the cabbage and rape. Also called: **colewort.** [OE *cāl*, < L *caulis* cabbage]

coleopteran (ˌkɒlɪˈɒptərən) *n. also* **coleopteron. 1.** any of the order of insects in which the forewings are modified to form shell-like protective elytra. It includes the beetles and weevils. ~*adj. also* **coleopterous. 2.** of, relating to, or belonging to this order. [C18: < NL, < Gk, < *koleon* sheath + *pteron* wing]

coleslaw (ˈkəʊlˌslɔː) *n.* a salad of shredded cabbage, mayonnaise, carrots, onions, etc. [C19: < Du. *koolsla*, < *koolsalade*, lit.: cabbage salad]

coletit (ˈkəʊltɪt) *n.* another name for **coal tit.**

coleus (ˈkəʊlɪəs) *n., pl.* **-uses.** any plant of the Old World genus *Coleus:* cultivated for their variegated leaves. [C19: < NL, < Gk, var. of *koleon* sheath]

coley (ˈkəʊlɪ, ˈkɒlɪ) *n. Brit.* any of various edible fishes, esp. the coalfish.

colic (ˈkɒlɪk) *n.* a condition characterized by acute spasmodic abdominal pain, esp. that caused by inflammation, distention, etc., of the gastrointestinal tract. [C15: < OF, < LL, < Gk *kōlon*, var. of *kolon* COLON[2]] —**ˈcolicky** *adj.*

coliform bacteria (ˈkɒlɪfɔːm) *pl. n.* a large group of bacteria that inhabit the intestinal tract of man.

coliseum (ˌkɒlɪˈsɪəm) *or* **colosseum** (ˌkɒləˈsɪəm) *n.* a large building, such as a stadium, used for entertainments, sports, etc. [C18: < Med. L, var. of *Colosseum*, amphitheatre in Rome]

colitis (kɒˈlaɪtɪs) *n.* inflammation of the colon.

collaborate (kəˈlæbəˌreɪt) *vb.* (*intr.*) **1.** (often foll. by *on, with,* etc.) to work with another or others on a joint project. **2.** to cooperate as a traitor, esp. with an enemy occupying one's own country. [C19: < LL, < L *com-* together + *labōrāre* to work] —**colˌlaboˈration** *n.* —**colˈlaborative** *adj.* —**colˈlaboˌrator** *n.*

collage (kəˈlɑːʒ, kɒ-) *n.* **1.** an art form in which compositions are made out of pieces of paper, cloth, photographs, etc., pasted on a dry ground. **2.** a composition made in this way. **3.** any collection of unrelated things. [C20: F, < *colle* glue, < Gk *kolla*] —**colˈlagist** *n.*

collagen (ˈkɒlədʒən) *n.* a fibrous protein of connective tissue and bones that yields gelatin on boiling. [C19: < Gk *kolla* glue + -GEN]

collapsar (kɒˈlæpsɑː) *n. Astron.* another name for **black hole.**

collapse (kəˈlæps) *vb.* **1.** (*intr.*) to fall down or cave in suddenly: *the whole building collapsed.* **2.** (*intr.*) to fail completely. **3.** (*intr.*) to break down or fall down from lack of strength. **4.** to fold (furniture, etc.) compactly or (of furniture, etc.) to be designed to fold compactly. ~*n.* **5.** the act or instance of suddenly falling down, caving in, or crumbling. **6.** a sudden failure or breakdown. [C18: < L, < *collābī* to fall in ruins, < *lābī* to fall] —**colˈlapsible** *or* **colˈlapsable** *adj.* —**colˌlapsiˈbility** *n.*

collar (ˈkɒlə) *n.* **1.** the part of a garment around the neck and shoulders, often detachable or folded over. **2.** any band, necklace, garland, etc., encircling the neck. **3.** a band or chain of leather, rope, or metal placed around an animal's neck. **4.** *Biol.* a marking resembling a collar, such as that found around the necks of some birds. **5.** a section of a shaft or rod having a locally increased diameter to provide a bearing seat or a locating ring. **6.** a cut of meat, esp. bacon, taken from around the neck of an animal. ~*vb.* (*tr.*) **7.** to put a collar on; furnish with a collar. **8.** to seize by the collar. **9.** *Inf.* to seize; arrest; detain. [C13: < L *collāre* neckband, < *collum* neck]

collarbone (ˈkɒləˌbəʊn) *n.* the nontechnical name for **clavicle.**

collard (ˈkɒləd) *n.* a variety of the cabbage, having a crown of edible leaves. See also **kale.** [C18: var. of *colewort*, < COLE + WORT]

collate (kɒˈleɪt, kə-) *vb.* (*tr.*) **1.** to examine and compare (texts, statements, etc.) in order to note points of agreement and disagreement. **2.** to check the number and order of (the pages of a book). **3.** *Bookbinding.* **a.** to check the sequence of (the sections of a book) after gathering. **b.** a nontechnical word for **gather** (sense 8). **4.** (often foll. by *to*) *Christianity.* to appoint (an incumbent) to a benefice. [C16: < L, < *com-* together + *lātus*, p.p. of *ferre* to bring] —**colˈlator** *n.*

collateral (kɒˈlætərəl, kə-) *n.* **1. a.** security pledged for the repayment of a loan. **b.** (*as* *modifier): a collateral loan.* **2.** a person, animal, or plant descended from the same ancestor as another but through a different line. *~adj.* **3.** situated or running side by side. **4.** descended from a common ancestor but through different lines. **5.** serving to support or corroborate. [C14: < Med. L, < L *com-* together + *laterālis* of the side, < *latus* side] **—col'laterally** *adv.*

collation (kɒ'leɪʃən, kə-) *n.* **1.** the act or process of collating. **2.** a description of the technical features of a book. **3.** *R.C. Church.* a light meal permitted on fast days. **4.** any light informal meal.

colleague ('kɒliːg) *n.* a fellow worker or member of a staff, department, profession, etc. [C16: < F, < L *collēga,* < *com-* together + *lēgāre* to choose]

collect[1] (kə'lɛkt) *vb.* **1.** to gather together or be gathered together. **2.** to accumulate (stamps, books, etc.) as a hobby or for study. **3.** (*tr.*) to call for or receive payment of (taxes, dues, etc.). **4.** (*tr.*) to regain control of (oneself, one's emotions, etc.) as after a shock or surprise: *he collected his wits.* **5.** (*tr.*) to fetch: *collect your own post.* **6.** (*intr.;* sometimes foll. by *on*) *Sl.* to receive large sums of money. **7.** (*tr.*) *Austral. & N.Z. inf.* to collide with; be hit by. *~adv., adj.* **8.** *U.S.* (of telephone calls, etc.) on a reverse-charge basis. [C16: < L, < *com-* together + *legere* to gather] **—col'lectable** *or* **col'lectible** *adj.*

collect[2] ('kɒlɛkt) *n. Christianity.* a short Church prayer in Communion and other services. [C13: < Med. L *collecta* (< *ōrātiō ad collēctam* prayer at the assembly), < L *colligere* to COLLECT[1]]

collected (kə'lɛktɪd) *adj.* **1.** in full control of one's faculties; composed. **2.** assembled in totality or brought together into one volume or a set of volumes: *the collected works of Dickens.* **—col'lectedly** *adv.* **—col'lectedness** *n.*

collection (kə'lɛkʃən) *n.* **1.** the act or process of collecting. **2.** a number of things collected or assembled together. **3.** something gathered into a mass or pile; accumulation: *a collection of rubbish.* **4.** a sum of money collected or solicited, as in church. **5.** removal, esp. regular removal of letters from a postbox. **6.** (*often pl.*) (at Oxford University) a college examination or an oral report by a tutor.

collective (kə'lɛktɪv) *adj.* **1.** formed or assembled by collection. **2.** forming a whole or aggregate. **3.** of, done by, or characteristic of individuals acting in cooperation. *~n.* **4. a.** a cooperative enterprise or unit, such as a collective farm. **b.** the members of such a cooperative. **5.** short for **collective noun.** **—col'lectively** *adv.* **—col'lectiveness** *n.* **—ˌcollec'tivity** *n.*

collective bargaining *n.* negotiation between a trade union and an employer or an employers' organization on the incomes and working conditions of the employees.

collective noun *n.* a noun that is singular in form but that refers to a group of people or things.

▷ **Usage.** Collective nouns are usually used with singular verbs: *the family is on holiday; General Motors is mounting a big sales campaign.* In British usage, however, plural verbs are sometimes employed in this context, esp. where reference is being made to a collection of individual objects or persons rather than to the group as a unit: *the family are all on holiday.* Care should be taken that the same collective noun is not treated as both singular and plural in the same sentence: *the family is well and sends its best wishes* or *the family are all well and send their best wishes,* but not *the family is well and send their best wishes.*

collective ownership *n.* ownership by a group for the benefit of members of that group.

collective unconscious *n.* (in Jungian psychological theory) a part of the unconscious mind incorporating patterns of memories, instincts, and experiences common to all mankind.

collectivism (kə'lɛktɪˌvɪzəm) *n.* the principle of ownership of the means of production by the state or the people. **—col'lectivist** *n.* **—colˌlectiv'istic** *adj.*

collectivize *or* **-vise** (kə'lɛktɪˌvaɪz) *vb.* (*tr.*) to organize according to the principles of collectivism. **—colˌlectivi'zation** *or* **-vi'sation** *n.*

collector (kə'lɛktə) *n.* **1.** a person or thing that collects. **2.** a person employed to collect debts, rents, etc. **3.** a person who collects objects as a hobby. **4.** (in India, formerly) the head of a district administration. **5.** *Electronics.* the region in a transistor into which charge carriers flow from the base.

colleen ('kɒliːn, kɒ'liːn) *n.* an Irish word for **girl.** [C19: < Irish Gaelic *cailīn*]

college ('kɒlɪdʒ) *n.* **1.** an institution of higher education; part of a university. **2.** a school or an institution providing specialized courses: *a college of music.* **3.** the buildings in which a college is housed. **4.** the staff and students of a college. **5.** an organized body of persons with specific rights and duties: *an electoral college.* **6.** a body organized within a particular profession, concerned with regulating standards. **7.** *Brit.* a name given to some secondary schools. [C14: < L, < *collēga;* see COLLEAGUE]

College of Cardinals *n. R.C. Church.* the collective body of cardinals having the function of electing and advising the pope.

college of education *n. Brit.* a professional training college for teachers.

collegian (kə'liːdʒɪən) *n.* a member of a college.

collegiate (kə'liːdʒɪɪt) *adj.* **1.** Also: **col'legial.** of or relating to a college or college students. **2.** (of a university) composed of various colleges of equal standing.

collegiate church *n.* **1.** *R.C. Church, Church of England.* a church that has an endowed chapter of canons and prebendaries attached to it but that is not a cathedral. **2.** *U.S. Protestantism.* one of a group of churches presided over by a body of pastors. **3.** *Scot. Protestantism.* a church served by two or more ministers.

col legno ('kɒl 'lɛgnəʊ, 'leɪnjəʊ) *adv. Music.* to be played (on a stringed instrument) with the back of the bow. [It.: with the wood]

Colles' fracture ('kɒlɪs) *n.* a fracture of the radius just above the wrist with backward and outward displacement of the hand. [C19: after Abraham *Colles* (d. 1843), Irish surgeon]

collet ('kɒlɪt) *n.* **1.** (in a jewellery setting) a band or coronet-shaped claw that holds an individual stone. **2.** *Mechanical engineering.* an externally tapered sleeve made in two or more segments and used to grip a shaft passed through its centre. **3.** *Horology.* a small metal collar that supports the inner end of the hairspring. [C16: < OF: a little collar, < *col,* < L *collum* neck]

collide (kə'laɪd) *vb.* (*intr.*) **1.** to crash together with a violent impact. **2.** to conflict; clash; disagree. [C17: < L, < *com-* together + *laedere* to strike]

collie ('kɒlɪ) *n.* any of several silky-coated breeds of dog developed for herding sheep and cattle. [C17: Scot., prob. < earlier *colie* black < *cole* coal]

collier ('kɒlɪə) *n. Chiefly Brit.* **1.** a coal miner. **2. a.** a ship designed to transport coal. **b.** a member of its crew. [C14: < COAL + -IER]

colliery ('kɒljərɪ) *n., pl.* **-lieries.** *Chiefly Brit.* a coal mine.

collimate ('kɒlɪˌmeɪt) *vb.* (*tr.*) **1.** to adjust the line of sight of (an optical instrument). **2.** to use a collimator on (a beam of radiation). **3.** to make parallel or bring into line. [C17: < NL *collimāre,* erroneously for L *collīneāre* to aim, < *com-* (intensive) + *līneāre,* < *līnea* line] **—ˌcolli'mation** *n.*

collimator ('kɒlɪˌmeɪtə) *n.* **1.** a small telescope attached to a larger optical instrument as an aid in fixing its line of sight. **2.** an optical system of lenses and slits producing a nondivergent beam of light. **3.** any device for limiting the size and angle of spread of a beam of radiation or particles.

collinear (kɒ'lɪnɪə) *adj.* lying on the same straight line. **—collinearity** (ˌkɒlɪnɪ'ærɪtɪ) *n.*

collins ('kɒlɪnz) *n.* (*functioning as sing.*) an iced

drink made with gin, vodka, rum, etc., mixed with fruit juice, soda water, and sugar. [C20: prob. < the name *Collins*]

collision (kəˈlɪʒən) *n.* **1.** a violent impact of moving objects; crash. **2.** the conflict of opposed ideas, wishes, attitudes, etc. [C15: < LL, < L *collīdere* to COLLIDE]

collocate (ˈkɒləˌkeɪt) *vb.* (*tr.*) to group or place together in some system or order. [C16: < L, < *com-* together + *locāre* to place] —ˌ**colloˈcation** *n.*

collocutor (ˈkɒləˌkjuːtə) *n.* a person who talks or engages in conversation with another.

collodion (kəˈləʊdɪən) *or* **collodium** (kəˈləʊdɪəm) *n.* a syrupy liquid that consists of a solution of pyroxylin in ether and alcohol: used in medicine and in the manufacture of photographic plates, lacquers, etc. [C19: < NL, < Gk *kollōdēs* glutinous, < *kolla* glue]

collogue (kɒˈləʊg) *vb.* **colloguing, collogued.** (*intr.;* usually foll. by *with*) to confer confidentially; conspire. [C16: ? < obs. *colleague* (vb.) to conspire, infl. by L *colloquī* to talk with]

colloid (ˈkɒlɔɪd) *n.* **1.** a mixture having particles of one component suspended in a continuous phase of another component. The mixture has properties between those of a solution and a fine suspension. **2.** *Physiol.* a gelatinous substance of the thyroid follicles that holds the hormonal secretions of the thyroid gland. [C19: < Gk *kolla* glue + -OID] —**colˈloidal** *adj.*

collop (ˈkɒləp) *n. Dialect.* **1.** a slice of meat. **2.** a small piece of anything. [C14: of Scand. origin]

colloq. *abbrev. for* colloquial(ly).

colloquial (kəˈləʊkwɪəl) *adj.* **1.** of or relating to conversation. **2.** denoting or characterized by informal or conversational idiom or vocabulary. —**colˈloquially** *adv.* —**colˈloquialness** *n.*

colloquialism (kəˈləʊkwɪəˌlɪzəm) *n.* **1.** a word or phrase appropriate to conversation and other informal situations. **2.** the use of colloquial words and phrases.

colloquium (kəˈləʊkwɪəm) *n., pl.* **-quiums** *or* **-quia** (-kwɪə). **1.** a gathering for discussion. **2.** an academic seminar. [C17: < L: COLLOQUY]

colloquy (ˈkɒləkwɪ) *n., pl.* **-quies. 1.** a formal conversation or conference. **2.** an informal conference on religious or theological matters. [C16: < L *colloquium,* < *com-* together + *loquī* to speak] —ˈ**colloquist** *n.*

collotype (ˈkɒləʊˌtaɪp) *n.* **1.** a method of lithographic printing (usually of high-quality reproductions) from a plate of hardened gelatin. **2.** a print so made.

collude (kəˈluːd) *vb.* (*intr.*) to conspire together, esp. in planning a fraud. [C16: < L, < *com-* together + *lūdere* to play] —**colˈluder** *n.*

collusion (kəˈluːʒən) *n.* **1.** secret agreement for a fraudulent purpose; conspiracy. **2.** a secret agreement between opponents at law for some improper purpose. [C14: < L, < *collūdere* to COLLUDE] —**colˈlusive** *adj.*

collywobbles (ˈkɒlɪˌwɒbᵊlz) *pl. n.* (usually preceded by *the*) *Sl.* **1.** an upset stomach. **2.** an intense feeling of nervousness. [C19: prob. < NL *cholera morbus,* infl. through folk etymology by COLIC and WOBBLE]

colobus (ˈkɒləbəs) *n.* any leaf-eating arboreal Old World monkey of W and central Africa, having long silky fur and reduced or absent thumbs. [C19: NL, < Gk *kolobos* cut short; referring to its thumb]

cologarithm (kəʊˈlɒgəˌrɪðəm) *n.* the logarithm of the reciprocal of a number; the negative value of the logarithm: *the cologarithm of 4 is log ¼.* Abbrev.: **colog.**

cologne (kəˈləʊn) *n.* a perfumed liquid or solid made of fragrant essential oils and alcohol. Also called: **Cologne water, eau de cologne.** [C18 *Cologne water* < Cologne, where it was first manufactured (1709)]

colon¹ (ˈkəʊlən) *n., pl.* **-lons. 1.** the punctuation mark : , usually preceding an explanation or an example, a list, or an extended quotation. **2.** this mark used for certain other purposes, such as when a ratio is given in figures, as in *5:3.* [C16: < L, < Gk *kōlon* limb, clause]

colon² (ˈkəʊlən) *n., pl.* **-lons** *or* **-la** (-lə). the part of the large intestine between the caecum and the rectum. [C16: < L: large intestine, < Gk *kolon*] —**colonic** (kəˈlɒnɪk) *adj.*

colón³ (kəʊˈləʊn; *Spanish* koˈlon) *n., pl.* **-lons** *or* **-lones** (*Spanish* -ˈlones). **1.** the standard monetary unit of Costa Rica, divided into 100 céntimos. **2.** the standard monetary unit of El Salvador, divided into 100 centavos. [C19: American Sp., < Sp., after Cristóbal *Colón* Christopher Columbus]

colonel (ˈkɜːnᵊl) *n.* an officer of land or air forces junior to a brigadier but senior to a lieutenant colonel. [C16: via OF, < OIt. *colonnello* column of soldiers, < *colonna* COLUMN] —ˈ**colonelcy** *or* ˈ**colonelˌship** *n.*

colonial (kəˈləʊnɪəl) *adj.* **1.** of, characteristic of, relating to, possessing, or inhabiting a colony or colonies. **2.** (*often cap.*) characteristic of or relating to the 13 British colonies that became the United States of America (1776). **3.** (*often cap.*) of or relating to the colonies of the British Empire. **4.** denoting or having the style of Neoclassical architecture used in the British colonies in America in the 17th and 18th centuries. **5.** (of animals and plants) having become established in a community in a new environment. ~*n.* **6.** a native of a colony. —**coˈlonially** *adv.*

colonial goose *n. N.Z.* an old-fashioned name for stuffed roast mutton.

colonialism (kəˈləʊnɪəˌlɪzəm) *n.* the policy and practice of a power in extending control over weaker peoples or areas. Also called: **imperialism.** —**coˈlonialist** *n., adj.*

Colonies (ˈkɒlənɪz) *pl. n.* **the. 1.** *Brit.* the subject territories formerly in the British Empire. **2.** *U.S. history.* the 13 states forming the original United States of America when they declared their independence (1776).

colonist (ˈkɒlənɪst) *n.* **1.** a person who settles or colonizes an area. **2.** an inhabitant of a colony.

colonize *or* **-ise** (ˈkɒləˌnaɪz) *vb.* **1.** to send colonists to or establish a colony in (an area). **2.** to settle in (an area) as colonists. **3.** (*tr.*) to transform (a community, etc.) into a colony. **4.** (of plants and animals) to become established in (a new environment). —ˌ**coloniˈzation** *or* **-iˈsation** *n.* —ˈ**coloˌnizer** *or* **-iser** *n.*

colonnade (ˌkɒləˈneɪd) *n.* **1.** a set of evenly spaced columns. **2.** a row of regularly spaced trees. [C18: < F, < *colonne* COLUMN; on the model of It. *colonnato*] —ˌ**colonˈnaded** *adj.*

colony (ˈkɒlənɪ) *n., pl.* **-nies. 1.** a body of people who settle in a country distant from their homeland but maintain ties with it. **2.** the community formed by such settlers. **3.** a subject territory occupied by a settlement from the ruling state. **4. a.** a community of people who form a national, racial, or cultural minority concentrated in a particular place: *an artists' colony.* **b.** the area itself. **5.** *Zool.* a group of the same type of animal or plant living or growing together. **6.** *Bacteriol.* a group of bacteria, fungi, etc., derived from one or a few spores, esp. when grown on a culture medium. [C16: < L, < *colere* to cultivate, inhabit]

colophon (ˈkɒləˌfɒn, -fən) *n.* **1.** a publisher's emblem on a book. **2.** (formerly) an inscription at the end of a book showing the title, printer, date, etc. [C17: via LL, < Gk *kolophōn* a finishing stroke]

colophony (kɒˈlɒfənɪ) *n.* another name for **rosin** (sense 1). [C14: < L: resin from Colophon]

color (ˈkʌlə) *n., vb.* the U.S. spelling of **colour.**

Colorado beetle (ˌkɒləˈrɑːdəʊ) *n.* a black-and-yellow beetle that is a serious pest of potatoes, feeding on the leaves. [< *Colorado,* state of central U.S.]

colorant (ˈkʌlərənt) *n.* any substance that imparts colour, such as a pigment, dye, or ink.

coloration *or* **colouration** (ˌkʌləˈreɪʃən) *n.* **1.** arrangement of colour; colouring. **2.** the colouring or markings of insects, birds, etc.

coloratura (ˌkɒlərəˈtʊərə) *n. Music.* **1.** (in 18th-

and 19th-century arias) a florid virtuoso passage. **2.** Also called: **coloratura soprano.** a soprano who specializes in such music. [C19: < obs. It., lit.: colouring.]

colorific (ˌkʌləˈrɪfɪk) *adj.* producing, imparting, or relating to colour.

colorimeter (ˌkʌləˈrɪmɪtə) *n.* apparatus for measuring the quality of a colour by comparison with standard colours or combinations of colours. —**colorimetric** (ˌkʌlərɪˈmɛtrɪk) *adj.* —ˌ**colorˈimetry** *n.*

colossal (kəˈlɒsᵊl) *adj.* **1.** of immense size; huge; gigantic. **2.** (in figure sculpture) approximately twice life-size. **3.** *Archit.* of the order of columns that extend more than one storey in a façade. —**coˈlossally** *adv.*

colossus (kəˈlɒsəs) *n., pl.* **-si** (-saɪ) *or* **-suses.** something very large, esp. a statue. [C14: < L, < Gk *kolossos*]

colostomy (kəˈlɒstəmɪ) *n., pl.* **-mies.** the surgical formation of an opening from the colon onto the surface of the body, which functions as an anus.

colostrum (kəˈlɒstrəm) *n.* the thin milky secretion from the nipples that precedes and follows true lactation. [C16: < L, <?]

colotomy (kəˈlɒtəmɪ) *n., pl.* **-mies.** a colonic incision. [C19: COLON² + -TOMY]

colour *or U.S.* **color** (ˈkʌlə) *n.* **1. a.** an attribute of things that results from the light they reflect or emit in so far as this causes a visual sensation that depends on its wavelengths. **b.** the aspect of visual perception by which an observer recognizes this attribute. **c.** the quality of the light producing this visual perception. **2.** Also called: **chromatic colour. a.** a colour, such as red or green, that possesses hue, as opposed to achromatic colours such as white or black. **b.** (*as modifier*): *colour television.* **3.** a substance, such as a dye or paint, that imparts colour. **4. a.** the skin complexion of a person, esp. as determined by his race. **b.** (*as modifier*): *colour prejudice.* **5.** the use of all the hues in painting as distinct from composition, form, and light and shade. **6.** the quantity and quality of ink used in a printing process. **7.** the distinctive tone of a musical sound. **8.** vividness or authenticity: *period colour.* **9.** semblance or pretext: *under colour of.* ~*vb.* **10.** (*tr.*) to apply colour to (something). **11.** (*tr.*) to give a convincing appearance to: *to colour an alibi.* **12.** (*tr.*) to influence or distort: *anger coloured her judgment.* **13.** (*intr.*; often foll. by *up*) to become red in the face, esp. when embarrassed or annoyed. ~See also **colours.** [C13 < OF *colour* < L *color* tint, hue]

colourable (ˈkʌlərəbᵊl) *adj.* **1.** capable of being coloured. **2.** appearing to be true; plausible. **3.** pretended; feigned.

colour bar *n.* discrimination against people of a different race, esp. as practised by Whites against Blacks.

colour-blind *adj.* of or relating to any defect in the normal ability to distinguish certain colours. —**colour blindness** *n.*

colour code *n.* a system of easily distinguishable colours, as for the identification of electrical wires or resistors.

coloured (ˈkʌləd) *adj.* **1.** possessing colour. **2.** having a strong element of fiction or fantasy; distorted (esp. in **highly coloured**).

Coloured (ˈkʌləd) *n.* **1.** an individual who is not a White, esp. a Negro. **2.** Also called: **Cape Coloured.** (in South Africa) a person of racially mixed parentage or descent. ~*adj.* **3.** designating or relating to a Coloured or Coloureds.

colourfast (ˈkʌləˌfɑːst) *adj.* (of a fabric) having a colour that does not run or change when washed or worn. —ˈ**colourˌfastness** *n.*

colourful (ˈkʌləfʊl) *adj.* **1.** having intense colour or richly varied colours. **2.** vivid, rich, or distinctive in character. —ˈ**colourfully** *adv.*

colour guard *n.* a military guard in a parade, ceremony, etc., that carries and escorts the flag.

colouring (ˈkʌlərɪŋ) *n.* **1.** the process or art of applying colour. **2.** anything used to give colour, such as paint. **3.** appearance with regard to shade and colour. **4.** arrangements of colours, as in the markings of birds. **5.** the colour of a person's complexion. **6.** a false or misleading appearance.

colourist (ˈkʌlərɪst) *n.* a person who uses colour, esp. an artist.

colourless (ˈkʌləlɪs) *adj.* **1.** without colour. **2.** lacking in interest: *a colourless individual.* **3.** grey or pallid in tone or hue. **4.** without prejudice; neutral. —ˈ**colourlessly** *adv.*

colours (ˈkʌləz) *pl. n.* **1. a.** the flag that indicates nationality. **b.** *Mil.* the ceremony of hoisting or lowering the colours. **2.** a pair of silk flags borne by a military unit and showing its crest and battle honours. **3.** true nature or character (esp. in **show one's colours**). **4.** a distinguishing badge or flag. **5.** *Sport, Brit.* a badge or other symbol denoting membership of a team, esp. at a school or college. **6. nail one's colours to the mast. a.** to commit oneself publicly and irrevocably to some party, course of action, etc. **b.** to refuse to admit defeat.

colour sergeant *n.* a sergeant who carries the regimental, battalion, or national colours.

colour supplement *n.* *Brit.* an illustrated magazine accompanying a newspaper.

colourway (ˈkʌləˌweɪ) *n.* one of several different combinations of colours in which a given pattern is printed on fabrics or wallpapers, etc.

colposcope (ˈkɒlpəˌskəʊp) *n.* an instrument for examining the cervix. [C20: < Gk *kolpos* womb + -SCOPE]

colt (kəʊlt) *n.* **1.** a male horse or pony under the age of four. **2.** *Sport.* **a.** a young and inexperienced player. **b.** a member of a junior team. [OE *colt* young ass]

colter (ˈkəʊltə) *n.* a variant spelling (esp. U.S.) of **coulter.**

coltish (ˈkəʊltɪʃ) *adj.* **1.** inexperienced; unruly. **2.** playful and lively. —ˈ**coltishness** *n.*

coltsfoot (ˈkəʊltsˌfʊt) *n., pl.* **-foots.** a European plant with yellow daisy-like flowers and heart-shaped leaves: a common weed.

colubrine (ˈkɒljʊˌbraɪn) *adj.* **1.** of or resembling a snake. **2.** of or belonging to the Colubrinae, a subfamily of harmless snakes. [C16: < L *colubrīnus,* < *coluber* snake]

columbine (ˈkɒləmˌbaɪn) *n.* any plant of the genus *Aquilegia,* having flowers with five spurred petals. Also called: **aquilegia.** [C13: < Med. L *columbīna herba* dovelike plant]

Columbine (ˈkɒləmˌbaɪn) *n.* the sweetheart of Harlequin in English pantomime.

column (ˈkɒləm) *n.* **1.** an upright pillar usually having a cylindrical shaft, a base, and a capital. **2. a.** a form or structure in the shape of a column: *a column of air.* **b.** a monument. **3.** a line, as of people in a queue. **4.** *Mil.* a narrow formation in which individuals or units follow one behind the other. **5.** *Journalism.* **a.** a single row of type on a newspaper. **b.** a regular feature in a paper: *the fashion column.* **6.** a vertical array of numbers. [C15: < L *columna,* < *columen* top, peak] —**columnar** (kəˈlʌmnə) *adj.* —ˈ**columned** *adj.*

columniation (kəˌlʌmnɪˈeɪʃən) *n.* the arrangement of architectural columns.

column inch *n.* a unit of measurement for advertising space, one inch deep and one column wide.

columnist (ˈkɒləmnɪst, -əmɪst) *n.* a journalist who writes a regular feature in a newspaper.

colure (kəˈlʊə, ˈkəʊlʊə) *n.* either of two great circles on the celestial sphere, one passing through the poles and the equinoxes, the other through the poles and the solstices. [C16: < LL, < Gk *kolourai,* dock-tailed, < *kolos* docked + *oura* tail (because the lower portion is not visible)]

colza (ˈkɒlzə) *n.* another name for **rape².** [C18: via F (Walloon) < Du., < *kool* cabbage, COLE + *zaad* SEED]

COM (kɒm) *n.* direct conversion of computer output to microfiche or film. [C20: *C(omputer) O(utput on) M(icrofilm)*]

Com. *abbrev. for:* **1.** Commander. **2.** Committee. **3.** Commodore. **4.** Communist.

com- *or* **con-** *prefix.* together; with; jointly: *commingle.* [< L *com-;* rel. to *cum* with. In compound words of L origin, *com-* becomes *col-* and *cor-* before *l* and *r, co-* before *gn, h,* and most vowels, and *con-* before consonants other than *b, p,* and *m*]

coma[1] ('kəʊmə) *n., pl.* **-mas.** a state of unconsciousness from which a person cannot be aroused, caused by injury, narcotics, poisons, etc. [C17: < medical L, < Gk *kōma* heavy sleep]

coma[2] ('kəʊmə) *n., pl.* **-mae** (-miː). **1.** *Astron.* the luminous cloud surrounding the nucleus in the head of a comet. **2.** *Bot.* **a.** a tuft of hairs attached to the seed coat of some seeds. **b.** the terminal crown of leaves of palms and moss stems. [C17: < L: hair of the head, < Gk *komē*]

comanche (kə'mæntʃɪ) *n.* **1.** (*pl.* **-ches** *or* **-che**) a member of a North American Indian people formerly inhabiting the W plains of the U.S. **2.** the language of this people.

comatose ('kəʊməˌtəʊs) *adj.* **1.** in a state of coma. **2.** torpid; lethargic.

comb (kəʊm) *n.* **1.** a toothed device for disentangling or arranging hair. **2.** a tool or machine that cleans and straightens wool, cotton, etc. **3.** *Austral. & N.Z.* the fixed cutter on a sheep-shearing machine. **4.** anything resembling a comb in form or function. **5.** the fleshy serrated outgrowth on the heads of certain birds, esp. the domestic fowl. **6.** a honeycomb. ~*vb.* **7.** (*tr.*) to use a comb on. **8.** (when *tr.,* often foll. by *through*) to search with great care: *the police combed the woods.* ~See also **comb out.** [OE *camb*]

combat *n.* ('kɒmbæt, -bət, 'kʌm-). **1.** a fight, conflict, or struggle. **2.** **a.** an action fought between two military forces. **b.** (*as modifier*): *a combat jacket.* **3.** **single combat.** a duel. ~*vb.* (kəm'bæt; 'kɒmbæt, 'kʌm-). **4.** (*tr.*) to fight. **5.** (*intr.;* often foll. by *with* or *against*) to struggle or strive (against): *to combat against disease.* [C16: < F, < OF *combattre,* < Vulgar L *combattere* (unattested), < L *com-* with + *battuere* to beat]

combatant ('kɒmbətᵊnt, 'kʌm-) *n.* **1.** a person or group engaged in or prepared for a fight. ~*adj.* **2.** engaged in or ready for combat.

combat fatigue *n.* another term for **battle fatigue.**

combative ('kɒmbətɪv, 'kʌm-) *adj.* eager or ready to fight, argue, etc. —'**combativeness** *n.*

combe *or* **comb** (kuːm) *n.* variant spellings of **coomb.**

comber ('kəʊmə) *n.* **1.** a person, tool, or machine that combs wool, flax, etc. **2.** a long curling wave; roller.

combination (ˌkɒmbɪ'neɪʃən) *n.* **1.** the act of combining or state of being combined. **2.** a union of separate parts, qualities, etc. **3.** an alliance of people or parties. **4.** the set of numbers that opens a combination lock. **5.** *Brit.* a motorcycle with a sidecar attached. **6.** *Maths.* an arrangement of the numbers, terms, etc., of a set into specified groups without regard to order in the group. **7.** the chemical reaction of two or more compounds, usually to form one other compound. **8.** *Chess.* a tactical manoeuvre involving a sequence of moves and more than one piece. —ˌ**combi'national** *adj.*

combination lock *n.* a type of lock that can only be opened when a set of dials is turned to show a specific sequence of numbers.

combinations (ˌkɒmbɪ'neɪʃənz) *pl. n. Brit.* a one-piece undergarment with long sleeves and legs. Often shortened to **combs** or **coms.**

combine *vb.* (kəm'baɪn). **1.** to join together. **2.** to unite or cause to unite to form a chemical compound. ~*n.* ('kɒmbaɪn). **3.** short for **combine harvester.** **4.** an association of enterprises, esp. in order to gain a monopoly of a market. **5.** an association of related bodies, such as business corporations or sports clubs, for a common purpose. [C15: < LL *combīnāre,* < L *com-* together + *bīnī* two by two] —**com'binable** *adj.* —**comˌbina'bility** *n.* —**combinative** ('kɒmbɪˌneɪtɪv) *or* **combinatory** ('kɒmbɪˌneɪtərɪ) *adj.*

combine harvester ('kɒmbaɪn) *n.* a machine that simultaneously cuts, threshes, and cleans a standing crop of grain.

combings ('kəʊmɪŋz) *pl. n.* **1.** the loose hair removed by combing. **2.** the unwanted fibres removed in combing cotton, etc.

combining form *n.* a linguistic element that occurs only as part of a compound word, such as *anthropo-* in *anthropology* and *anthropomorph.*

combo ('kɒmbəʊ) *n., pl.* **-bos.** **1.** a small group of jazz musicians. **2.** *Inf.* any combination.

comb out *vb.* (*tr., adv.*) **1.** to remove (tangles) from (the hair) with a comb. **2.** to remove for a purpose. **3.** to examine systematically.

combustible (kəm'bʌstɪbᵊl) *adj.* **1.** capable of igniting and burning. **2.** easily annoyed; excitable. ~*n.* **3.** a combustible substance. —**comˌbusti'bility** *or* **com'bustibleness** *n.*

combustion (kəm'bʌstʃən) *n.* **1.** the process of burning. **2.** any process in which a substance reacts to produce a significant rise in temperature and the emission of light. **3.** a process in which a compound reacts slowly with oxygen to produce little heat and no light. [C15: < OF, < L *combūrere* to burn up] —**com'bustive** *n., adj.*

combustion chamber *n.* an enclosed space in which combustion takes place, such as the space above the piston in the cylinder head of an internal-combustion engine.

combustor (kəm'bʌstə) *n.* the combustion system of a jet engine or ramjet.

Comdr *Mil. abbrev. for* Commander.

Comdt *Mil. abbrev. for* Commandant.

come (kʌm) *vb.* **coming, came, come.** (*mainly intr.*) **1.** to move towards a specified person or place. **2.** to arrive by movement or by making progress. **3.** to become perceptible: *light came into the sky.* **4.** to occur: *Christmas comes but once a year.* **5.** to happen as a result: *no good will come of this.* **6.** to be derived: *good may come of evil.* **7.** to occur to the mind: *the truth suddenly came to me.* **8.** to reach: *she comes up to my shoulder.* **9.** to be produced: *that dress comes in red.* **10.** to arrive at or be brought into a particular state: *you will soon come to grief.* **11.** (foll. by *from*) to be or have been a resident or native (of): *I come from London.* **12.** to become: *your wishes will come true.* **13.** (*tr.; takes an infinitive*) to be given awareness: *I came to realize its value.* **14.** *Taboo sl.* to have an orgasm. **15.** (*tr.*) *Brit. inf.* to play the part of: *don't come the fine gentleman with me.* **16.** (*tr.*) *Brit. inf.* to cause or produce: *don't come that nonsense.* **17.** (*subjunctive use*): *come next August, he will be fifty years old:* when next August arrives. **18.** **as ... as they come.** the most characteristic example of a type. **19.** **come again?** *Inf.* what did you say? **20.** **come good.** to recover and perform well after a setback or poor start. **21.** **come to light.** to be revealed. **22.** **come to light with.** *Austral. & N.Z. inf.* to find or produce. ~*interj.* **23.** an exclamation expressing annoyance, etc.: *come now!* ~See also **come about, come across,** etc. [OE *cuman*]

come about *vb.* (*intr., adv.*) **1.** to take place; happen. **2.** *Naut.* to change tacks.

come across *vb.* (*intr.*) **1.** (*prep.*) to meet or find by accident. **2.** (*adv.*) to communicate the intended meaning or impression. **3.** (often foll. by *with*) to provide what is expected.

come at *vb.* (*intr., prep.*) **1.** to discover (facts, the truth, etc.). **2.** to attack: *he came at me with an axe.* **3.** (*usually used with a negative*) *Austral. sl.* to agree to do (something).

comeback ('kʌmˌbæk) *n. Inf.* **1.** a return to a former position, status, etc. **2.** a response, esp. recriminatory. **3.** a quick retort. ~*vb.* **come back.** (*intr., adv.*) **4.** to return, esp. to the memory. **5.** to become fashionable again.

come between *vb.* (*intr., prep.*) to cause the estrangement or separation of (two people).

come by *vb.* (*intr., prep.*) to find or obtain, esp. accidentally: *do you ever come by any old books?*

Comecon ('kɒmɪˌkɒn) *n.* an association of Soviet-oriented Communist nations, founded in 1949 to coordinate economic development, etc. [C20: *Co(uncil for) M(utual) Econ(omic Aid)*]

comedian (kəˈmiːdɪən) *n.* **1.** an entertainer who specializes in jokes, comic skits, etc. **2.** an actor in comedy. **3.** an amusing person: sometimes used ironically.

comedienne (kəˌmiːdɪˈɛn) *n.* a female comedian.

comedo (ˈkɒmɪˌdəʊ) *n., pl.* **comedos** *or* **comedones** (ˌkɒmɪˈdəʊniːz). *Pathol.* the technical name for **blackhead.** [C19: < NL, < L: glutton]

comedown (ˈkʌmˌdaʊn) *n.* **1.** a decline in status or prosperity. **2.** *Inf.* a disappointment. ~*vb.* **come down.** (*intr., adv.*) **3.** to come to a place regarded as lower. **4.** to lose status, etc. (esp. in **come down in the world**). **5.** (of prices) to become lower. **6.** to reach a decision: *the report came down in favour of a pay increase.* **7.** (often foll. by *to*) to be handed down by tradition or inheritance. **8.** *Brit.* to leave university. **9.** (foll. by *with*) to succumb (to illness). **10.** (foll. by *on*) to rebuke harshly. **11.** (foll. by *to*) to amount in essence (to): *it comes down to two choices.*

comedy (ˈkɒmɪdɪ) *n., pl.* **-dies. 1.** a dramatic or other work of light and amusing character. **2.** the genre of drama represented by works of this type. **3.** (in classical literature) a play in which the main characters triumph over adversity. **4.** the humorous aspect of life or of events. **5.** an amusing event or sequence of events. **6.** humour: *the comedy of Chaplin.* [C14: < OF, < L, < Gk *kōmōidia,* < *kōmos* village festival + *aeidein* to sing] —**comedic** (kəˈmiːdɪk) *adj.*

comedy of manners *n.* a comedy dealing with the way of life and foibles of a social group.

come forward *vb.* (*intr., adv.*) **1.** to offer one's services; volunteer. **2.** to present oneself.

come-hither *adj.* (*usually prenominal*) *Inf.* alluring; seductive: *a come-hither look.*

come in *vb.* (*intr., mainly adv.*) **1.** to enter. **2.** to prove to be: *it came in useful.* **3.** to become fashionable or seasonable. **4.** *Cricket.* to begin an innings. **5.** to finish a race (in a certain position). **6.** to be received: *news is coming in of a big fire in Glasgow.* **7.** (of money) to be received as income. **8.** to play a role: *where do I come in?* **9.** (foll. by *for*) to be the object of: *the Chancellor came in for a lot of criticism.*

come into *vb.* (*intr., prep.*) **1.** to enter. **2.** to inherit.

comely (ˈkʌmlɪ) *adj.* **-lier, -liest. 1.** good-looking; attractive. **2.** *Arch.* suitable; fitting. [OE *cȳmlic* beautiful] —ˈ**comeliness** *n.*

come of *vb.* (*intr., prep.*) **1.** to be descended from. **2.** to result from: *nothing came of it.*

come off *vb.* (*intr., mainly adv.*) **1.** (*also prep.*) to fall (from). **2.** to become detached. **3.** (*prep.*) to be removed from (a price, tax, etc.): *will anything come off income tax in the budget?* **4.** (*copula*) to emerge from or as if from a contest: *he came off the winner.* **5.** *Inf.* to happen. **6.** *Inf.* to have the intended effect: *his jokes did not come off.* **7.** *Taboo sl.* to have an orgasm.

come-on *n.* **1.** *Inf.* anything that serves as a lure. ~*vb.* **come on** (*intr., mainly adv.*) **2.** (of power, water, etc.) to start running or functioning. **3.** to progress: *my plants are coming on nicely.* **4.** to advance, esp. in battle. **5.** to begin: *a new bowler has come on.* **6.** to make an entrance on stage.

come out *vb.* (*intr., adv.*) **1.** to be made public or revealed: *the news of her death came out last week.* **2.** to make a debut in society. **3.** Also: **come out of the closet. a.** to declare openly that one is a homosexual. **b.** to reveal or declare any practice or habit formerly concealed. **4.** *Chiefly Brit.* to go on strike. **5.** to declare oneself: *the government came out in favour of scrapping the project.* **6.** to be shown clearly: *you came out very well in the photos.* **7.** to yield a satisfactory solution: *these sums just won't come out.* **8.** to be published: *the paper comes out on Fridays.* **9.** (foll. by *in*) to become covered (with). **10.** (foll. by *with*) to declare openly: *you can rely on him to come out with the facts.*

come over *vb.* (*intr., adv.*) **1.** to communicate the intended meaning or impression: *he came over very well.* **2.** to change allegiances. **3.** *Inf.* to feel a particular sensation: *I came over funny.*

comer (ˈkʌmə) *n.* **1.** (*in combination*) a person who comes: *all-comers; newcomers.* **2.** *Inf.* a potential success.

come round *vb.* (*intr., adv.*) **1.** to be restored to consciousness. **2.** to modify one's opinion.

comestible (kəˈmɛstɪbᵊl) *n.* (*usually pl.*) food. [C15: < LL *comestibilis,* < *comedere* to eat up]

comet (ˈkɒmɪt) *n.* a celestial body that travels around the sun, usually in a highly elliptical orbit: thought to consist of a frozen nucleus, part of which vaporizes on approaching the sun to form a long luminous tail. [C13: < OF, < L, < Gk *komētēs* long-haired] —ˈ**cometary** *or* **cometic** (kɒˈmɛtɪk) *adj.*

come through *vb.* (*intr.*) **1.** (*adv.*) to emerge successfully. **2.** (*prep.*) to survive (an illness, etc.).

come to *vb.* (*intr.*) **1.** (*adv.* or *prep. and reflexive*) to regain consciousness. **2.** (*adv.*) *Naut.* to slow a vessel or bring her to a stop. **3.** (*prep.*) to amount to (a sum of money). **4.** (*prep.*) to arrive at: *what is the world coming to?*

come up *vb.* (*intr., adv.*) **1.** to come to a place regarded as higher. **2.** (of the sun) to rise. **3.** to present itself: *that question will come up again.* **4.** *Brit.* to begin a term at a university. **5.** to appear from out of the ground: *my beans have come up early.* **6.** *Inf.* to win: *have your premium bonds ever come up?* **7. come up against.** to come into conflict with. **8. come up to.** to meet a standard. **9. come up with.** to produce.

come upon *vb.* (*intr., prep.*) to meet or encounter unexpectedly.

comeuppance (ˌkʌmˈʌpəns) *n. Inf.* just retribution. [C19: from *come up* (in the sense): to appear before a court]

comfit (ˈkʌmfɪt, ˈkɒm-) *n.* a sugar-coated sweet containing a nut or seed. [C15: < OF, < L *confectum* something prepared]

comfort (ˈkʌmfət) *n.* **1.** a state of ease or well-being. **2.** relief from affliction, grief, etc. **3.** a person, thing, or event that brings solace or ease. **4.** (*usually pl.*) something that affords physical ease and relaxation. ~*vb.* (*tr.*) **5.** to soothe; cheer. **6.** to bring physical ease to. [C13: < OF *confort,* < LL *confortāre* to strengthen, < L *con-* (intensive) + *fortis* strong] —ˈ**comforting** *adj.* —ˈ**comfortless** *adj.*

comfortable (ˈkʌmftəbᵊl) *adj.* **1.** giving comfort. **2.** at ease. **3.** free from affliction or pain. **4.** (of a person or situation) relaxing. **5.** *Inf.* having adequate income. **6.** *Inf.* (of income, etc.) adequate to provide comfort. —ˈ**comfortably** *adv.*

comforter (ˈkʌmfətə) *n.* **1.** a person or thing that comforts. **2.** *Chiefly Brit.* a woollen scarf. **3.** a baby's dummy. **4.** *U.S.* a quilted bed covering.

Comforter (ˈkʌmfətə) *n. Christianity.* an epithet of the Holy Spirit. [C14: translation of L *consolātor,* representing Gk *paraklētos* advocate]

comfrey (ˈkʌmfrɪ) *n.* a hairy Eurasian plant having blue, purplish-pink, or white flowers. [C15: < OF *cunfirie,* < L *conferva* water plant]

comfy (ˈkʌmfɪ) *adj.* **-fier, -fiest.** *Inf.* short for **comfortable.**

comic (ˈkɒmɪk) *adj.* **1.** of, characterized by, or characteristic of comedy. **2.** (*prenominal*) acting in or composing comedy: *a comic writer.* **3.** humorous; funny. ~*n.* **4.** a person who is comic; comedian. **5.** a book or magazine containing comic strips. [C16: < L *cōmicus,* < Gk *kōmikos*]

comical (ˈkɒmɪkᵊl) *adj.* **1.** causing laughter. **2.** ludicrous; laughable. —ˈ**comically** *adv.*

comic opera *n.* a play largely set to music, employing comic effects or situations.

comic strip *n.* a sequence of drawings in a newspaper, magazine, etc., relating a humorous story or an adventure.

coming (ˈkʌmɪŋ) *adj.* **1.** (*prenominal*) (of time, events, etc.) approaching or next. **2.** promising (esp. in **up and coming**). **3.** of future importance: *this is the coming thing.* **4. have it coming to one.**

Inf. to deserve what one is about to suffer. ~*n.* **5.** arrival or approach.

Comintern *or* **Komintern** (ˈkɒmɪnˌtɜːn) *n.* short for **Communist International;** an international Communist organization founded by Lenin in 1919 and dissolved in 1943; it degenerated under Stalin into an instrument of Soviet politics. Also called: **Third International.**

comity (ˈkɒmɪtɪ) *n., pl.* **-ties. 1.** mutual civility; courtesy. **2.** short for **comity of nations.** [C16: < L *cōmitās,* < *cōmis* affable]

comity of nations *n.* the friendly recognition accorded by one nation to the laws and usages of another.

comm. *abbrev. for:* **1.** commerce. **2.** commercial. **3.** committee. **4.** commonwealth.

comma (ˈkɒmə) *n.* **1.** the punctuation mark , indicating a slight pause and used where there is a listing of items or to separate a nonrestrictive clause from a main clause. **2.** *Music.* a minute interval. [C16: < L, < Gk *komma* clause, < *koptein* to cut]

comma bacillus *n.* a comma-shaped bacterium that causes cholera in man.

command (kəˈmɑːnd) *vb.* **1.** (when *tr.*, may take a clause as object or an infinitive) to order or compel. **2.** to have or be in control or authority over. **3.** (*tr.*) to receive as due: *his nature commands respect.* **4.** to dominate (a view, etc.) as from a height. ~*n.* **5.** an order. **6.** the act of commanding. **7.** the right to command. **8.** the exercise of the power to command. **9.** knowledge; control: *a command of French.* **10.** *Chiefly mil.* the jurisdiction of a commander. **11.** a military unit or units commanding a specific function, as in the RAF. **12.** *Brit.* **a.** an invitation from the monarch. **b.** (*as modifier*): *a command performance.* **13.** *Computers.* another name for **instruction** (sense 3). [C13: < OF *commander,* < L *com-* (intensive) + *mandāre* to enjoin]

commandant (ˈkɒmənˌdænt, -ˌdɑːnt) *n.* an officer commanding a group or establishment.

commandeer (ˌkɒmənˈdɪə) *vb.* (*tr.*) **1.** to seize for public or military use. **2.** to seize arbitrarily. [C19: < Afrik. *kommandeer,* < F *commander* to COMMAND]

commander (kəˈmɑːndə) *n.* **1.** an officer in command of a military formation or operation. **2.** a naval commissioned rank junior to captain but senior to lieutenant commander. **3.** the second in command of larger British warships. **4.** someone who holds authority. **5.** a high-ranking member of some knightly orders. **6.** an officer responsible for a district of the Metropolitan Police in London. —**comˈmanderˌship** *n.*

commander in chief *n., pl.* **commanders in chief.** the officer holding supreme command of the forces in an area or operation.

commanding (kəˈmɑːndɪŋ) *adj.* (*usually prenominal*) **1.** being in command. **2.** having the air of authority: *a commanding voice.* **3.** (of a situation) exerting control. **4.** (of a viewpoint, etc.) overlooking; advantageous. —**comˈmandingly** *adv.*

commanding officer *n.* an officer in command of a military unit.

commandment (kəˈmɑːndmənt) *n.* **1.** a divine command, esp. one of the Ten Commandments of the Old Testament. **2.** *Literary.* any command.

command module *n.* the module used as the living quarters in an Apollo spacecraft and functioning as the splashdown vehicle.

commando (kəˈmɑːndəʊ) *n., pl.* **-dos** *or* **-does. 1. a.** an amphibious military unit trained for raiding. **b.** a member of such a unit. **2.** the basic unit of the Royal Marine Corps. **3.** (originally) an armed force raised by Boers during the Boer War. **4.** (*modifier*) denoting or relating to commandos: *a commando unit.* [C19: < Afrik. *kommando,* < Du. *commando* command]

command paper *n.* (in Britain) a government document that is presented to Parliament, in theory by royal command.

command post *n. Mil.* the position from which a commander exercises command.

commedia dell'arte (*Italian* kɔmˈmeːdia delˈlarte) *n.* a form of popular improvised comedy in Italy during the 16th to 18th centuries, with stock characters such as Punchinello, Harlequin, and Columbine. [It., lit.: comedy of art]

comme il faut *French.* (kɔm il fo) correct or correctly.

commemorate (kəˈmɛməˌreɪt) *vb.* (*tr.*) to honour or keep alive the memory of. [C16: < L *commemorāre,* < *com-* (intensive) + *memorāre* to remind] —**comˌmemoˈration** *n.* —**comˈmemorative** *adj.* —**comˈmemoˌrator** *n.*

commence (kəˈmɛns) *vb.* to begin; come or cause to come into being, operation, etc. [C14: < OF *comencer,* < Vulgar L *cominitiāre* (unattested), < L *com-* (intensive) + *initiāre* to begin]

commencement (kəˈmɛnsmənt) *n.* **1.** the beginning; start. **2.** *U.S.* a ceremony for the conferment of academic degrees. **3.** *U.S. & Canad.* a ceremony for the presentation of awards at secondary schools.

commend (kəˈmɛnd) *vb.* (*tr.*) **1.** to represent as being worthy of regard, confidence, etc.; recommend. **2.** to give in charge; entrust. **3.** to praise. **4.** to give the regards of: *commend me to your aunt.* [C14: < L *commendāre,* < *com-* (intensive) + *mandāre* to entrust] —**comˈmendable** *adj.* —**comˈmendably** *adv.* —**comˈmendatory** *adj.*

commendation (ˌkɒmɛnˈdeɪʃən) *n.* **1.** the act of commending; praise. **2.** *U.S.* an award.

commensal (kəˈmɛnsəl) *adj.* **1.** (of two different species of plant or animal) living in close association without being interdependent. **2.** *Rare.* of or relating to eating together, esp. at the same table. ~*n.* **3.** a commensal plant or animal. **4.** *Rare.* a companion at table. [C14: < Med. L *commensālis,* < L *com-* together + *mensa* table] —**comˈmensalism** *n.* —**commensality** (ˌkɒmɛnˈsælɪtɪ) *n.*

commensurable (kəˈmɛnsərəbəl, -ʃə-) *adj.* **1.** *Maths.* **a.** having a common factor. **b.** having units of the same dimensions and being related by whole numbers. **2.** proportionate. —**comˌmensuraˈbility** *n.* —**comˈmensurably** *adv.*

commensurate (kəˈmɛnsərɪt, -ʃə-) *adj.* **1.** having the same extent or duration. **2.** corresponding in degree, amount, or size; proportionate. **3.** commensurable. [C17: < LL *commēnsūrātus,* < L *com-* same + *mēnsurāre* to MEASURE] —**comˈmensurately** *adv.*

comment (ˈkɒmɛnt) *n.* **1.** a remark, criticism, or observation. **2.** talk or gossip. **3.** a note explaining or criticizing a passage in a text. **4.** explanatory or critical matter added to a text. ~*vb.* **5.** (when *intr.*, often foll. by *on;* when *tr.*, takes a clause as object) to remark or express an opinion. **6.** (*intr.*) to write notes explaining or criticizing a text. [C15: < L *commentum* invention, < *comminiscī* to contrive] —**ˈcommenter** *n.*

commentary (ˈkɒməntərɪ) *n., pl.* **-taries. 1.** an explanatory series of notes. **2.** a spoken accompaniment to a broadcast, film, etc. **3.** an explanatory treatise on a text. **4.** (*usually pl.*) a personal record of events: *the commentaries of Caesar.*

commentate (ˈkɒmənˌteɪt) *vb.* **1.** (*intr.*) to serve as a commentator. **2.** (*tr.*) *U.S.* to make a commentary on.

▷ **Usage.** The verb *commentate,* derived from *commentator,* is sometimes used as a synonym for *comment on* or *provide a commentary for.* It is not yet fully accepted as standard, though widespread in sports reporting and journalism.

commentator (ˈkɒmənˌteɪtə) *n.* **1.** a person who provides a spoken commentary for a broadcast, film, etc., esp. of a sporting event. **2.** a person who writes notes on a text, etc.

commerce (ˈkɒmɜːs) *n.* **1.** the activity embracing all forms of the purchase and sale of goods and services. **2.** social relations. **3.** *Arch.* sexual intercourse. [C16: < L *commercium,* < *commercārī,* < *mercārī* to trade, < *merx* merchandise]

commercial (kəˈmɜːʃəl) *adj.* **1.** of or engaged in

commerce. **2.** sponsored or paid for by an advertiser: *commercial television.* **3.** having profit as the main aim: *commercial music.* **4.** (of chemicals, etc.) unrefined and produced in bulk for use in industry. ~*n.* **5.** a commercially sponsored advertisement on radio or television. —**commerciality** (kəˌmɜːʃɪˈælɪtɪ) *n.* —**comˈmercially** *adv.*

commercial art *n.* graphic art for commercial uses such as advertising, packaging, etc.

commercial bank *n.* a bank primarily engaged in making short-term loans from funds deposited in current accounts.

commercialism (kəˈmɜːʃəˌlɪzəm) *n.* **1.** the spirit, principles, or procedure of commerce. **2.** exclusive or inappropriate emphasis on profit.

commercialize *or* **-lise** (kəˈmɜːʃəˌlaɪz) *vb.* (*tr.*) **1.** to make commercial. **2.** to exploit for profit, esp. at the expense of quality. —**comˌmercialiˈzation** *or* **-liˈsation** *n.*

commercial paper *n. Chiefly U.S.* a short-term negotiable document, such as a bill of exchange, calling for the transference of a specified sum of money at a designated date.

commercial traveller *n.* another name for a **travelling salesman.**

commercial vehicle *n.* a vehicle for carrying goods or (less commonly) passengers.

commie *or* **commy** (ˈkɒmɪ) *n., pl.* **-mies,** *adj. Inf. & derog.* short for **communist.**

commination (ˌkɒmɪˈneɪʃən) *n.* **1.** the act of threatening punishment or vengeance. **2.** *Church of England.* a recital of prayers, including a list of God's judgments against sinners, in the office for Ash Wednesday. [C15: < L *comminātiō,* < *com-* (intensive) + *minārī* to threaten] —**comminatory** (ˈkɒmɪnətərɪ) *adj.*

commingle (kɒˈmɪŋgəl) *vb.* to mix or be mixed.

comminute (ˈkɒmɪˌnjuːt) *vb.* **1.** to break (a bone) into small fragments. **2.** to divide (property) into small lots. [C17: < L *comminuere,* < *com-* (intensive) + *minuere* to reduce] —ˌ**commiˈnution** *n.*

commis (ˈkɒmɪs, ˈkɒmɪ) *n., pl.* **-mis. 1.** an agent or deputy. **2.** an apprentice waiter or chef. [C16 (meaning: deputy): < F, < *commettre* to employ]

commiserate (kəˈmɪzəˌreɪt) *vb.* (when *intr.,* usually foll. by *with*) to feel or express sympathy or compassion (for). [C17: < L *commiserārī,* < *com-* together + *miserārī* to bewail] —**comˌmiserˈation** *n.* —**comˈmiserˌator** *n.*

commissar (ˈkɒmɪˌsɑː, ˌkɒmɪˈsɑː) *n.* (in the Soviet Union) **1.** an official of the Communist Party responsible for political education. **2.** (before 1946) the head of a government department. [C20: < Russian *kommissar*]

commissariat (ˌkɒmɪˈsɛərɪət) *n.* **1.** (in the Soviet Union) a government department before 1946. **2.** a military department in charge of food supplies, etc. [C17: < NL *commissāriātus,* < Med. L *commissārius* COMMISSARY]

commissary (ˈkɒmɪsərɪ) *n., pl.* **-saries. 1.** *U.S.* a shop supplying food or equipment, as in a military camp. **2.** *U.S. army.* an officer responsible for supplies. **3.** *U.S.* a restaurant in a film studio. **4.** a representative or deputy, esp. of a bishop. [C14: < Med. L *commissārius* official in charge, < L *committere* to COMMIT] —**commissarial** (ˌkɒmɪˈsɛərɪəl) *adj.*

commission (kəˈmɪʃən) *n.* **1.** a duty committed to a person or group to perform. **2.** authority to perform certain duties. **3.** a document granting such authority. **4.** *Mil.* **a.** a document conferring a rank on an officer. **b.** the rank granted. **5.** a group charged with certain duties: *a commission of inquiry.* **6.** a government board empowered to exercise administrative, judicial, or legislative authority. See also **Royal Commission. 7. a.** the authority given to a person or organization to act as an agent to a principal in commercial transactions. **b.** the fee allotted to an agent for services rendered. **8.** the state of being charged with specific responsibilities. **9.** the act of committing a sin, crime, etc. **10.** good working condition or (esp. of a ship) active service (esp. in **in commission, out of commission**). ~*vb.* (*mainly tr.*) **11.** to grant authority to. **12.** *Mil.* to confer a rank on. **13.** to equip and test (a ship) for active service. **14.** to place an order for (something): *to commission a portrait.* **15.** to make or become operative or operable: *the plant is due to commission next year.* [C14: < OF, < L *commissiō* a bringing together, < *committere* to COMMIT]

commissionaire (kəˌmɪʃəˈnɛə) *n. Chiefly Brit.* a uniformed doorman at a hotel, theatre, etc. [C18: < F, < COMMISSION]

commissioned officer *n.* a military officer holding a commission, such as Second Lieutenant in the British Army, Acting Sub-Lieutenant in the Royal Navy, Pilot Officer in the Royal Air Force, and officers of all ranks senior to these.

commissioner (kəˈmɪʃənə) *n.* **1.** a person endowed with certain powers. **2.** any of several types of civil servant. **3.** a member of a commission. —**comˈmissionerˌship** *n.*

commissioner for oaths *n.* a solicitor authorized to authenticate oaths on sworn statements.

commit (kəˈmɪt) *vb.* **-mitting, -mitted.** (*tr.*) **1.** to hand over, as for safekeeping; entrust. **2. commit to memory.** to memorize. **3.** to take into custody: *to commit someone to prison.* **4.** (*usually passive*) to pledge or align (oneself), as to a particular cause: *a committed radical.* **5.** to order (forces) into action. **6.** to perform (a crime, error, etc.). **7.** to surrender, esp. for destruction: *she committed the letter to the fire.* **8.** to refer (a bill, etc.) to a committee. [C14: < L *committere* to join, < *com-* together + *mittere* to send] —**comˈmittable** *adj.* —**comˈmitter** *n.*

commitment (kəˈmɪtmənt) *n.* **1.** the act of committing or pledging. **2.** the state of being committed or pledged. **3.** an obligation, promise, etc., that restricts freedom of action. **4.** Also called (esp. formerly): **mittimus.** *Law.* a written order of a court directing that a person be imprisoned. **5.** a future financial obligation or contingent liability. ~Also called (esp. for sense 4): **committal** (kəˈmɪtəl).

committee *n.* **1.** (kəˈmɪtɪ). a group of people appointed to perform a specified service or function. **2.** (ˌkɒmɪˈtiː). (formerly) a person to whom the care of a mentally incompetent person or his property was entrusted by a court. [C15: < *committen* to entrust + -EE]

committeeman (kəˈmɪtɪmən, -ˌmæn) *n., pl.* **-men.** *Chiefly U.S.* a member of one or more committees. —**comˈmitteeˌwoman** *fem. n.*

Committee of the Whole House *n.* (in Britain) an informal sitting of the House of Commons to discuss and amend a bill.

commode (kəˈməʊd) *n.* **1.** a piece of furniture, usually highly ornamented, containing drawers or shelves. **2.** a bedside table with a cabinet for a chamber pot or washbasin. **3.** a chair with a hinged flap concealing a chamber pot. [C17: < F, < L *commodus* COMMODIOUS]

commodious (kəˈməʊdɪəs) *adj.* **1.** roomy; spacious. **2.** *Arch.* convenient. [C15: < Med. L, < L *commodus* convenient, < *com-* with + *modus* measure] —**comˈmodiousness** *n.*

commodity (kəˈmɒdɪtɪ) *n., pl.* **-ties. 1.** an article of commerce. **2.** something of use or profit. **3.** *Econ.* an exchangeable unit of economic wealth, such as a primary product. [C14: < OF *commodité,* < L *commoditās* suitability; see COMMODIOUS]

commodo (kəˈməʊdəʊ) *adv.* a variant spelling of **comodo.**

commodore (ˈkɒməˌdɔː) *n.* **1.** *Brit.* a naval rank junior to rear admiral and senior to captain. **2.** the captain of a shipping line. **3.** the officer in command of a merchant convoy. **4.** the titular head of a yacht club. [C17: prob. < Du. *commandeur,* < F, < OF *commander* to COMMAND]

common (ˈkɒmən) *adj.* **1.** belonging to two or more people: *common property.* **2.** belonging to members of one or more communities; public: *a common culture.* **3.** of ordinary standard;

average. **4.** prevailing; widespread: *common opinion.* **5.** frequently encountered; ordinary: *a common brand of soap.* **6.** notorious: *a common nuisance.* **7.** *Derog.* considered by the speaker to be low-class, vulgar, or coarse. **8.** (*prenominal*) having no special distinction: *the common man.* **9.** *Maths.* having a specified relationship with a group of numbers or quantities: *common denominator.* **10.** *Prosody.* (of a syllable) able to be long or short. **11.** *Grammar.* (in certain languages) denoting or belonging to a gender of nouns that includes both masculine and feminine referents. **12. common or garden.** *Inf.* ordinary; unexceptional. ~*n.* **13.** a tract of open public land. **14.** *Law.* the right to go onto someone else's property and remove natural products, as by pasturing cattle (esp. in **right of common**). **15.** *Christianity.* **a.** a form of the proper of the Mass used on festivals that have no special proper of their own. **b.** the ordinary of the Mass. **16. in common.** mutually held or used. ~See also **commons.** [C13: < OF *commun,* < L *commūnis* general] —ˈ**commonly** *adv.* —ˈ**commonness** *n.*

commonage (ˈkɒmənɪdʒ) *n.* **1.** *Chiefly law.* **a.** the use of something, esp. a pasture, in common with others. **b.** the right to such use. **2.** the state of being held in common. **3.** another word for **commonalty** (sense 1).

commonality (ˌkɒməˈnælɪtɪ) *n., pl.* **-ties. 1.** the fact of being common. **2.** another word for **commonalty** (sense 1).

commonalty (ˈkɒmənəltɪ) *n., pl.* **-ties. 1.** the ordinary people as distinct from those with rank or title. **2.** the members of an incorporated society. [C13: < OF *comunalte,* < *comunal* communal]

common carrier *n.* a person or firm engaged in the business of transporting goods or passengers.

common chord *n. Music.* a chord consisting of the keynote, a major or minor third, and a perfect fifth.

common cold *n.* a mild viral infection of the upper respiratory tract, characterized by sneezing, coughing, etc.

commoner (ˈkɒmənə) *n.* **1.** a person who does not belong to the nobility. **2.** a person who has a right in or over common land. **3.** *Brit.* a student at a university who is not on a scholarship.

common fraction *n.* another name for **simple fraction.**

common knowledge *n.* something widely or generally known.

common law *n.* the body of law based on judicial decisions and custom, as distinct from statute law.

common-law marriage *n.* a state of marriage deemed to exist between a man and a woman after a number of years of cohabitation.

Common Market *n.* **the.** a European economic association, originally composed (1958) of Belgium, France, West Germany, Italy, Luxembourg, and the Netherlands, joined in 1973 by the United Kingdom, the Irish Republic, and Denmark, in 1981 by Greece, and in 1986 by Spain and Portugal. Officially called: **European Economic Community.**

common noun *n. Grammar.* a noun that refers to each member of a whole class sharing the features connoted by the noun, as for example *orange* and *drum.* Cf. **proper noun.**

commonplace (ˈkɒmənˌpleɪs) *adj.* **1.** ordinary; everyday. **2.** dull; trite: *commonplace prose.* ~*n.* **3.** a platitude; truism. **4.** a passage in a book marked for inclusion in a commonplace book, etc. **5.** an ordinary thing. [C16: translation of L *locus commūnis* argument of wide application] —ˈ**commonˌplaceness** *n.*

commonplace book *n.* a notebook in which quotations, poems, etc., that catch the owner's attention are entered.

common room *n. Chiefly Brit.* a sitting room in schools, colleges, etc.

commons (ˈkɒmənz) *n.* **1.** (*functioning as pl.*) the lower classes as contrasted with the ruling or noble classes of society. **2.** (*functioning as sing.*) *Brit.* a hall for dining, recreation, etc., usually attached to a college, etc. **3.** (*usually functioning as pl.*) *Brit.* food or rations (esp. in **short commons**).

Commons (ˈkɒmənz) *n.* **the.** See **House of Commons.**

common sense *n.* **1.** sound practical sense. ~*adj.* **common-sense;** *also* **common-sensical. 2.** inspired by or displaying this.

common time *n. Music.* a time signature indicating four crotchet beats to the bar; four-four time. Symbol: **C**

commonweal (ˈkɒmənˌwiːl) *n. Arch.* **1.** the public good. **2.** another name for **commonwealth.**

commonwealth (ˈkɒmənˌwɛlθ) *n.* **1.** the people of a state or nation viewed politically; body politic. **2.** a state in which the people possess sovereignty; republic. **3.** a group of persons united by some common interest.

Commonwealth (ˈkɒmənˌwɛlθ) *n.* **the. 1.** Official name: **the Commonwealth of Nations.** an association of sovereign states that are or at some time have been ruled by Britain. **2.** the republic that existed in Britain from 1649 to 1660. **3.** the official designation of Australia, four states of the U.S., and Puerto Rico.

Commonwealth Day *n.* the anniversary of Queen Victoria's birth, May 24, celebrated (now on the second Monday in March) in many parts of the Commonwealth. Former name: **Empire Day.**

commotion (kəˈməʊʃən) *n.* **1.** violent disturbance; upheaval. **2.** political insurrection. **3.** a confused noise; din. [C15: < L *commōtiō,* < *commovēre,* < *com-* (intensive) + *movēre* to MOVE]

communal (ˈkɒmjʊnᵊl) *adj.* **1.** belonging to a community as a whole. **2.** of a commune or a religious community. —**communality** (ˌkɒmjʊˈnælɪtɪ) *n.* —ˈ**communally** *adv.*

communalism (ˈkɒmjʊnəˌlɪzəm) *n.* **1.** a system or theory of government in which the state is seen as a loose federation of self-governing communities. **2.** the practice or advocacy of communal living or ownership. —ˈ**communalist** *n.* —ˌ**communalˈistic** *adj.*

communalize *or* **-lise** (ˈkɒmjʊnəˌlaɪz) *vb.* (*tr.*) to render (something) the property of a commune or community. —ˌ**communaliˈzation** *or* **-liˈsation** *n.*

commune[1] *vb.* (kəˈmjuːn). (*intr.;* usually foll. by *with*) **1.** to talk intimately. **2.** to experience strong emotion (for): *to commune with nature.* ~*n.* (ˈkɒmjuːn). **3.** intimate conversation; communion. [C13: < OF *comuner* to hold in common, < *comun* COMMON]

commune[2] (ˈkɒmjuːn) *n.* **1.** a group of families or individuals living together and sharing possessions and responsibilities. **2.** any small group of people having common interests or responsibilities. **3.** the smallest administrative unit in Belgium, France, Italy, and Switzerland. **4.** a medieval town enjoying a large degree of autonomy. [C18: < F, < Med. L *commūnia,* < L: things held in common]

Commune (ˈkɒmjuːn) *n. French history.* **1.** See **Paris Commune. 2.** a committee that governed Paris during the French Revolution: suppressed 1794.

communicable (kəˈmjuːnɪkəbᵊl) *adj.* **1.** capable of being communicated. **2.** (of a disease) capable of being passed on readily. —**comˌmunicaˈbility** *n.* —**comˈmunicably** *adv.*

communicant (kəˈmjuːnɪkənt) *n.* **1.** *Christianity.* a person who receives Communion. **2.** a person who communicates or informs.

communicate (kəˈmjuːnɪˌkeɪt) *vb.* **1.** to impart (knowledge) or exchange (thoughts) by speech, writing, gestures, etc. **2.** (*tr.;* usually foll. by *to*) to transmit (to): *the dog communicated his fear to the other animals.* **3.** (*intr.*) to have a sympathetic mutual understanding. **4.** (*intr.;* usually foll. by *with*) to make or have a connecting passage: *the kitchen communicates with the dining room.* **5.** (*tr.*) to transmit (a disease). **6.** (*intr.*) *Christianity.* to receive Communion. [C16: < L *commūnicāre* to share, <

commūnis COMMON] —**com'muni,cator** *n.* —**com'municatory** *adj.*

communication (kə,mju:nɪ'keɪʃən) *n.* **1.** the imparting or exchange of information, ideas, or feelings. **2.** something communicated, such as a message. **3.** (*usually pl.; sometimes functioning as sing.*) the study of ways in which human beings communicate. **4.** a connecting route or link. **5.** (*pl.*) *Mil.* the system of routes by which forces, supplies, etc., are moved within an area of operations.

communication cord *n. Brit.* a cord or chain in a train which may be pulled by a passenger to stop the train in an emergency.

communications satellite *n.* an artificial satellite used to relay radio, television, and telephone signals around the earth's surface.

communicative (kə'mju:nɪkətɪv) *adj.* **1.** inclined or able to communicate readily; talkative. **2.** of or relating to communication.

communion (kə'mju:njən) *n.* **1.** an exchange of thoughts, emotions, etc. **2.** sharing in common; participation. **3.** (foll. by *with*) strong feelings (for): *communion with nature.* **4.** a religious group or denomination having common beliefs and practices. **5.** spiritual union. [C14: < L *commūniō,* < *commūnis* COMMON]

Communion (kə'mju:njən) *n. Christianity.* **1.** the act of participating in the Eucharist. **2.** the celebration of the Eucharist. **3.** the consecrated elements of the Eucharist. ~Also called: **Holy Communion.**

communiqué (kə'mju:nɪ,keɪ) *n.* an official communication or announcement, esp. to the press or public. [C19: < F]

communism ('kɒmjʊ,nɪzəm) *n.* **1.** advocacy of a classless society in which private ownership has been abolished and the means of production belong to the community. **2.** any movement or doctrine aimed at achieving such a society. **3.** (*usually cap.*) a political movement based upon the writings of Marx that considers history in terms of class conflict and revolutionary struggle. **4.** (*usually cap.*) a system of government established by a ruling Communist Party, esp. in the Soviet Union. **5.** communal living. [C19: < F *communisme,* < *commun* COMMON]

communist ('kɒmjʊnɪst) *n.* **1.** a supporter of communism. **2.** (*often cap.*) a supporter of a Communist movement or state. **3.** (*often cap.*) a member of a Communist party. **4.** (*often cap.*) *Chiefly U.S.* any person holding left-wing views, esp. when considered subversive. **5.** a person who practises communal living. ~*adj.* **6.** of, favouring, or relating to communism. —,**commu'nistic** *adj.*

community (kə'mju:nɪtɪ) *n., pl.* **-ties. 1. a.** the people living in one locality. **b.** the locality in which they live. **c.** (*as modifier*): *community spirit.* **2.** a group of people having cultural, religious, or other characteristics in common: *the Protestant community.* **3.** a group of nations having certain interests in common. **4.** the public; society. **5.** common ownership. **6.** similarity or agreement: *community of interests.* **7.** (in Wales and Scotland) the smallest unit of local government. **8.** *Ecology.* a group of interdependent plants and animals inhabiting the same region. [C14: < L *commūnitās,* < *commūnis* COMMON]

community centre *n.* a building used by a community for social gatherings, etc.

community charge *n.* the formal name for **poll tax.**

community chest *n. U.S.* a fund raised by voluntary contribution for local welfare activities.

community council *n.* (in Scotland and Wales) an independent voluntary local body set up to attend to local interests and organize community activities.

community home *n.* (in Britain) **1.** a home provided by a local authority for children who cannot remain with their parents. **2.** a boarding school for young offenders.

community policing *n.* the assigning of the same one or two policemen to a particular area so that they become familiar with the residents and they with them, as a way of reducing crime.

communize *or* **-ise** ('kɒmjʊ,naɪz) *vb.* (*tr.*) (*sometimes cap.*) **1.** to make (property) public; nationalize. **2.** to make (a person or country) communist. —,**communi'zation** *or* **-i'sation** *n.*

commutate ('kɒmjʊ,teɪt) *vb.* (*tr.*) **1.** to reverse the direction of (an electric current). **2.** to convert (an alternating current) into a direct current.

commutation (,kɒmjʊ'teɪʃən) *n.* **1.** a substitution or exchange. **2.** the replacement of one method of payment by another. **3.** the reduction in severity of a penalty imposed by law. **4.** the process of commutating an electric current.

commutative (kə'mju:tətɪv, 'kɒmjʊ,teɪtɪv) *adj.* **1.** relating to or involving substitution. **2.** *Maths, logic.* **a.** giving the same result irrespective of the order of the arguments; thus addition is commutative but subtraction is not. **b.** relating to this property: *the commutative law of addition.*

commutator ('kɒmjʊ,teɪtə) *n.* **1.** a device used to reverse the direction of flow of an electric current. **2.** the segmented metal cylinder or disc of an electric motor, generator, etc., used to make electrical contact with the rotating coils.

commute (kə'mju:t) *vb.* **1.** (*intr.*) to travel some distance regularly between one's home and one's place of work. **2.** (*tr.*) to substitute. **3.** (*tr.*) *Law.* to reduce (a sentence) to one less severe. **4.** to pay (an annuity, etc.) at one time, instead of in instalments. **5.** to change: *to commute base metal into gold.* [C17: < L *commūtāre,* < *com-* mutually + *mūtāre* to change] —**com'mutable** *adj.* —**com,muta'bility** *n.*

commuter (kə'mju:tə) *n.* a person who travels to work over an appreciable distance, usually from the suburbs to the centre of a city.

comodo *or* **commodo** (kə'məʊdəʊ) *adv. Music.* in a convenient tempo. [It.: comfortable, < L *commodus* convenient: see COMMODIOUS]

comose ('kəʊməʊs, kəʊ'məʊs) *adj. Bot.* having tufts of hair; hairy. Also: **comate.** [C18: < L *comōsus* hairy]

comp (kɒmp) *Inf.* ~*n.* **1.** a compositor. **2.** an accompaniment. **3.** a competition. ~*vb.* **4.** (*intr.*) to work as a compositor in the printing industry. **5.** to play an accompaniment (to).

comp. *abbrev. for:* **1.** companion. **2.** comparative. **3.** compare. **4.** compiled. **5.** composer. **6.** composition. **7.** compositor. **8.** compound. **9.** comprehensive. **10.** comprising.

compact[1] *adj.* (kəm'pækt). **1.** closely packed together. **2.** neatly fitted into a restricted space. **3.** concise; brief. **4.** well constructed; solid; firm. **5.** (foll. by *of*) composed (of). ~*vb.* (kəm'pækt). (*tr.*) **6.** to pack closely together; compress. **7.** (foll. by *of*) to form by pressing together: *sediment compacted of three types of clay.* **8.** *Metallurgy.* to compress (a metal powder) to form a stable product suitable for sintering. ~*n.* ('kɒmpækt). **9.** a small flat case containing a mirror, face powder, etc., designed to be carried in a woman's handbag. **10.** *U.S. & Canad.* a small and economical car. [C16: < L *compactus,* < *compingere,* < *com-* together + *pangere* to fasten] —**com'pactly** *adv.* —**com'pactness** *n.*

compact[2] ('kɒmpækt) *n.* an official contract or agreement. [C16: < L *compactum,* < *compacīscī,* < *com-* together + *pacīscī* to contract]

compact disc ('kɒmpækt) *n.* a small digital audio disc on which sound is recorded as a series of metallic pits enclosed in PVC and read by an optical laser system. Also called: **compact audio disc.** Abbrev.: **CD, CAD.**

compages (kəm'peɪdʒi:z) *n.* (*functioning as sing.*) a structure or framework. [C17: < L: < *com-* together + *pangēre* to fasten]

companion[1] (kəm'pænjən) *n.* **1.** a person who is an associate of another or others; comrade. **2.** (esp. formerly) an employee, usually a woman, who provides company for an employer. **3. a.** one of a pair. **b.** (*as modifier*): *a companion volume.* **4.** a guidebook or handbook. **5.** a member of the lowest rank of certain orders of knighthood. **6.** *Astron.* the fainter of the two components of a double star. ~*vb.* **7.** (*tr.*) to accompany. [C13: < LL *compāniō,* lit.: one who eats bread with another, < L *com-* with + *pānis* bread] —**com'panion,ship** *n.*

companion² (kəm'pænjən) *n. Naut.* a raised frame on an upper deck with windows to give light to the deck below. [C18: < Du. *kompanje* quarterdeck, < OF *compagne,* < OIt. *compagna* pantry, ? ult. < L *pānis* bread]

companionable (kəm'pænjənəbᵊl) *adj.* sociable. —**com'panionableness** *n.* —**com'panionably** *adv.*

companionate (kəm'pænjənɪt) *adj.* **1.** resembling, appropriate to, or acting as a companion. **2.** harmoniously suited.

companionway (kəm'pænjən,weɪ) *n.* a ladder from one deck to another in a ship.

company ('kʌmpənɪ) *n., pl.* **-nies. 1.** a number of people gathered together; assembly. **2.** the fact of being with someone; companionship: *I enjoy her company.* **3.** a guest or guests. **4.** a business enterprise. **5.** the members of an enterprise not specifically mentioned in the enterprise's title. Abbrev.: **Co., co. 6.** a group of actors. **7.** a small unit of troops. **8.** the officers and crew of a ship. **9.** a unit of Girl Guides. **10.** *English history.* a medieval guild. **11. keep company. a.** to accompany (someone). **b.** (esp. of lovers) to spend time together. ~*vb.* **-nying, -nied. 12.** *Arch.* to associate (with someone). [C13: < OF *compaignie,* < LL *compāniō;* see COMPANION¹]

company sergeant-major *n. Mil.* the senior noncommissioned officer in a company.

compar. *abbrev. for* comparative.

comparable ('kɒmpərəbᵊl) *adj.* **1.** worthy of comparison. **2.** able to be compared (with). —,**compara'bility** *or* '**comparableness** *n.*

comparative (kəm'pærətɪv) *adj.* **1.** denoting or involving comparison: *comparative literature.* **2.** relative: *a comparative loss of prestige.* **3.** *Grammar.* denoting the form of an adjective that indicates that the quality denoted is possessed to a greater extent. In English the comparative is marked by the suffix *-er* or the word *more.* ~*n.* **4.** the comparative form of an adjective. —**com'paratively** *adv.* —**com'parativeness** *n.*

compare (kəm'pɛə) *vb.* **1.** (*tr.;* foll. by *to*) to regard as similar; liken: *the general has been compared to Napoleon.* **2.** (*tr.*) to examine in order to observe resemblances or differences: *to compare rum and gin.* **3.** (*intr.;* usually foll. by *with*) to be the same or similar: *gin compares with rum in alcoholic content.* **4.** (*intr.*) to bear a specified relation when examined: *this car compares badly with the other.* **5.** (*tr.*) *Grammar.* to give the positive, comparative, and superlative forms of (an adjective). **6. compare notes.** to exchange opinions. ~*n.* **7.** comparison (esp. in **beyond compare**). [C15: < OF, < L *comparāre,* < *compar,* < *com-* together + *par* equal]

▷ **Usage.** In careful usage, *compare* is followed by *to* when it is used in the sense of "liken, point out a resemblance": *I don't know how to describe it — I haven't anything to compare it to;* and by *with* when some account of points of resemblance is meant: *in my next lecture I shall compare seventeenth-century French drama with classical Greek theatre.*

comparison (kəm'pærɪsᵊn) *n.* **1.** the act of comparing. **2.** the state of being compared. **3.** likeness: *there was no comparison between them.* **4.** a rhetorical device involving comparison, such as a simile. **5.** Also called: **degrees of comparison.** *Grammar.* the listing of the positive, comparative, and superlative forms of an adjective or adverb. **6. bear** *or* **stand comparison (with).** to be sufficiently similar to be compared with (something else), esp. favourably.

compartment (kəm'pɑːtmənt) *n.* **1.** one of the sections into which an area, esp. an enclosed space, is partitioned. **2.** any separate section: *a compartment of the mind.* **3.** a small storage space. [C16: < F *compartiment,* ult. < LL *compartīrī* to share] —**compartmental** (,kɒmpɑːt'mɛntᵊl) *adj.* —,**compart'mentally** *adv.*

compartmentalize *or* **-lise** (,kɒmpɑːt'mɛntᵊ,laɪz) *vb.* (*usually tr.*) to put into categories, etc., esp. to an excessive degree. —,**compart,mentali'zation** *or* **-li'sation** *n.*

compass ('kʌmpəs) *n.* **1.** Also called: **magnetic compass.** an instrument for finding direction, having a magnetized needle which points to magnetic north. **2.** (*often pl.*) Also called: **pair of compasses.** an instrument used for drawing circles, measuring distances, etc., that consists of two arms, joined at one end. **3.** limits or range: *within the compass of education.* **4.** *Music.* the interval between the lowest and highest note attainable. ~*vb.* (*tr.*) **5.** to surround; hem in. **6.** to grasp mentally. **7.** to achieve; accomplish. **8.** *Obs.* to plot. [C13: < OF *compas,* < Vulgar L *compassāre* (unattested) to pace out, ult. < L *passus* step] —'**compassable** *adj.*

compass card *n.* a compass in the form of a card that rotates so that "0°" or "North" points to magnetic north.

compassion (kəm'pæʃən) *n.* a feeling of distress and pity for the suffering or misfortune of another. [C14: < OF, < LL *compassiō,* < L *com-* with + *patī* to suffer]

compassionate (kəm'pæʃənɪt) *adj.* showing or having compassion. —**com'passionately** *adv.*

compassionate leave *n.* leave granted on the grounds of bereavement, family illness, etc.

compass rose *n.* a circle or decorative device printed on a map or chart showing the points of the compass.

compass saw *n.* a hand saw with a narrow tapered blade for making a curved cut.

compatible (kəm'pætɪbᵊl) *adj.* **1.** (usually foll. by *with*) able to exist together harmoniously. **2.** (usually foll. by *with*) consistent: *her deeds were not compatible with her ideology.* **3.** (of pieces of machinery, etc.) capable of being used together without modification or adaptation. [C15: < Med. L *compatibilis,* < LL *compatī;* see COMPASSION] —**com,pati'bility** *n.* —**com'patibly** *adv.*

compatriot (kəm'pætrɪət) *n.* a fellow countryman. [C17: < F *compatriote,* < LL; see PATRIOT] —**com,patri'otic** *adj.*

compeer ('kɒmpɪə) *n.* **1.** a person of equal rank, status, or ability. **2.** a comrade. [C13: < OF *comper,* < Med. L *compater* godfather]

compel (kəm'pɛl) *vb.* **-pelling, -pelled.** (*tr.*) **1.** to cause (someone) by force (to be or do something). **2.** to obtain by force; exact: *to compel obedience.* [C14: < L *compellere,* < *com-* together + *pellere* to drive] —**com'pellable** *adj.*

compelling (kəm'pɛlɪŋ) *adj.* arousing or denoting strong interest, esp. admiring interest.

compendious (kəm'pɛndɪəs) *adj.* stating the essentials of a subject in a concise form. —**com'pendiously** *adv.* —**com'pendiousness** *n.*

compendium (kəm'pɛndɪəm) *n., pl.* **-diums** *or* **-dia** (-dɪə). **1.** *Brit.* a book containing a collection of useful hints. **2.** *Brit.* a selection, esp. of different games in one container. **3.** a summary. [C16: < L: a saving, lit.: something weighed]

compensate ('kɒmpɛn,seɪt) *vb.* **1.** to make amends to (someone), esp. for loss or injury. **2.** (*tr.*) to serve as compensation or damages for (injury, loss, etc.). **3.** to counterbalance the effects of (a force, weight, etc.) so as to produce equilibrium. **4.** (*intr.*) to attempt to conceal one's shortcomings by the exaggerated exhibition of qualities regarded as desirable. [C17: < L *compēnsāre,* < *pendere* to weigh] —**compensative** ('kɒmpɛn,seɪtɪv, kəm'pɛnsə-) *or* **compensatory** ('kɒmpɛn,seɪtərɪ, kəm'pɛnsətərɪ) *adj.*

compensation (,kɒmpɛn'seɪʃən) *n.* **1.** the act of making amends for something. **2.** something given as reparation for loss, injury, etc. **3.** the attempt to conceal one's shortcomings by the exaggerated exhibition of qualities regarded as desirable. —,**compen'sational** *adj.*

compere ('kɒmpɛə) *Brit.* ~*n.* **1.** a master of ceremonies who introduces cabaret, television acts, etc. ~*vb.* **2.** to act as a compere (for). [C20: < F, lit.: godfather]

compete (kəmˈpiːt) *vb.* (*intr.*; often foll. by *with*) to contend (against) for profit, an award, etc. [C17: < LL *competere,* < L, < *com-* together + *petere* to seek]

competence (ˈkɒmpɪtəns) *or* **competency** *n.* **1.** the condition of being capable; ability. **2.** a sufficient income to live on. **3.** the state of being legally competent or qualified.

competent (ˈkɒmpɪtənt) *adj.* **1.** having sufficient skill, knowledge, etc.; capable. **2.** suitable or sufficient for the purpose: *a competent answer.* **3.** *Law.* (of a witness, etc.) qualified to testify, etc. [C14: < L *competēns,* < *competere;* see COMPETE] —ˈ**competently** *adv.*

competition (ˌkɒmpɪˈtɪʃən) *n.* **1.** the act of competing. **2.** a contest in which a winner is selected from among two or more entrants. **3.** a series of games, sports events, etc. **4.** the opposition offered by competitors. **5.** competitors offering opposition.

competitive (kəmˈpɛtɪtɪv) *adj.* **1.** involving rivalry: *competitive sports.* **2.** sufficiently low in price or high in quality to be successful against commercial rivals. **3.** characterized by an urge to compete: *a competitive personality.* —**comˈpetitiveness** *n.*

competitor (kəmˈpɛtɪtə) *n.* a person, group, team, firm, etc., that vies or competes; rival.

compile (kəmˈpaɪl) *vb.* (*tr.*) **1.** to make or compose from other sources: *to compile a list of names.* **2.** to collect for a book, hobby, etc. **3.** *Computers.* to create (a set of machine instructions) from a high-level programming language, using a compiler. [C14: < L *compīlāre,* < *com-* together + *pīlāre* to thrust down, pack] —**compilation** (ˌkɒmpɪˈleɪʃən) *n.*

compiler (kəmˈpaɪlə) *n.* **1.** a person who compiles something. **2.** a computer program by which a high-level programming language is converted into machine language that can be acted upon by a computer. Cf. **assembler.**

complacency (kəmˈpleɪsənsɪ) *or* **complacence** *n.* extreme self-satisfaction; smugness.

complacent (kəmˈpleɪsᵊnt) *adj.* extremely self-satisfied. [C17: < L *complacēns* very pleasing, < *complacēre,* < *com-* (intensive) + *placēre* to please] —**comˈplacently** *adv.*

complain (kəmˈpleɪn) *vb.* (*intr.*) **1.** to express resentment, displeasure, etc.; grumble. **2.** (foll. by *of*) to state the presence of pain, illness, etc.: *she complained of a headache.* [C14: < OF *complaindre,* < Vulgar L *complangere* (unattested), < L *com-* (intensive) + *plangere* to bewail] —**comˈplainer** *n.* —**comˈplainingly** *adv.*

complainant (kəmˈpleɪnənt) *n. Law.* a plaintiff.

complaint (kəmˈpleɪnt) *n.* **1.** the act of complaining. **2.** a cause for complaining; grievance. **3.** a mild ailment.

complaisant (kəmˈpleɪzᵊnt) *adj.* showing a desire to comply or oblige; polite. [C17: < F *complaire,* < L *complacēre* to please greatly; cf. COMPLACENT] —**comˈplaisance** *n.*

complement *n.* (ˈkɒmplɪmənt). **1.** a person or thing that completes something. **2.** a complete amount, number, etc. (often in **full complement**). **3.** the officers and crew needed to man a ship. **4.** *Grammar.* a word, phrase, or clause that completes the meaning of the predicate, as *an idiot* in *He is an idiot* or *that he would be early* in *I hoped that he would be early.* **5.** *Maths.* the angle that when added to a specified angle produces a right angle. **6.** *Logic.* the class of all the things that are not members of a given class. **7.** a group of proteins in the blood serum that, when activated by antibodies, destroys alien cells, such as bacteria. ~*vb.* (ˈkɒmplɪˌmɛnt). **8.** (*tr.*) to complete or form a complement to. [C14: < L *complēmentum,* < *complēre,* < *com-* (intensive) + *plēre* to fill]

complementary (ˌkɒmplɪˈmɛntərɪ) *adj.* **1.** forming a complement. **2.** forming a satisfactory or balanced whole. —ˌ**compleˈmentarily** *adv.* —ˌ**compleˈmentariness** *n.*

complementary angle *n.* either of two angles whose sum is 90°.

complementary colour *n.* one of any pair of colours, such as yellow and blue, that give white or grey when mixed in the correct proportions.

complementary medicine *n.* another name for **alternative medicine.**

complete (kəmˈpliːt) *adj.* **1.** having every necessary part; entire. **2.** finished. **3.** (*prenominal*) thorough: *he is a complete rogue.* **4.** perfect in quality or kind: *he is a complete scholar.* **5.** (of a logical system) constituted such that a contradiction or inconsistency arises on the addition of an axiom that cannot be deduced from the axioms of the system. **6.** *Arch.* skilled; accomplished. ~*vb.* (*tr.*) **7.** to make perfect. **8.** to finish. [C14: < L *complētus,* p.p. of *complēre* to fill up; see COMPLEMENT] —**comˈpletely** *adv.* —**comˈpleteness** *n.* —**comˈpletion** *n.*

complex (ˈkɒmplɛks) *adj.* **1.** made up of interconnected parts. **2.** (of thoughts, writing, etc.) intricate. **3.** *Maths.* **a.** of or involving complex numbers. **b.** consisting of a real and an imaginary part, either of which can be zero. ~*n.* **4.** a whole made up of related parts: *a building complex.* **5.** *Psychoanal.* a group of emotional impulses that have been banished from the conscious mind but continue to influence a person's behaviour. **6.** *Inf.* an obsession: *he's got a complex about cats.* **7.** any chemical compound in which one molecule is linked to another by a coordinate bond. [C17: < L *complexus,* < *complectī,* < *com-* together + *plectere* to braid] —ˈ**complexness** *n.*

complex fraction *n. Maths.* a fraction in which the numerator or denominator or both contain fractions. Also called: **compound fraction.**

complexion (kəmˈplɛkʃən) *n.* **1.** the colour and general appearance of a person's skin, esp. of the face. **2.** aspect or nature: *the general complexion of a nation's finances.* **3.** *Obs.* temperament. [C14: < L *complexiō* a combination, < *complectī* to embrace; see COMPLEX] —**comˈplexional** *adj.*

complexioned (kəmˈplɛkʃənd) *adj.* of a specified complexion: *light-complexioned.*

complexity (kəmˈplɛksɪtɪ) *n., pl.* **-ties. 1.** the state or quality of being intricate or complex. **2.** something intricate or complex; complication.

complex number *n.* any number of the form $a + bi$, where a and b are real numbers and $i = \sqrt{-1}$.

complex sentence *n. Grammar.* a sentence containing at least one main clause and one subordinate clause.

compliance (kəmˈplaɪəns) *or* **compliancy** *n.* **1.** acquiescence. **2.** a disposition to yield to others. **3.** a measure of the ability of a mechanical system to respond to an applied vibrating force.

compliance officer *or* **lawyer** *n.* a specialist, usually a lawyer, employed by a financial group operating in a variety of fields and for multiple clients to ensure that no conflict of interest arises and that all obligations and regulations are complied with.

compliant (kəmˈplaɪənt) *adj.* complying, obliging, or yielding. —**comˈpliantly** *adv.*

complicate *vb.* (ˈkɒmplɪˌkeɪt). **1.** to make or become complex, etc. ~*adj.* (ˈkɒmplɪkɪt). **2.** *Biol.* folded on itself: *a complicate leaf.* [C17: < L *complicāre* to fold together]

complicated (ˈkɒmplɪˌkeɪtɪd) *adj.* made up of intricate parts or aspects that are difficult to understand or analyse. —ˈ**compliˌcatedly** *adv.*

complication (ˌkɒmplɪˈkeɪʃən) *n.* **1.** a condition, event, etc., that is complex or confused. **2.** the act of complicating. **3.** an event or condition that complicates or frustrates: *her coming was a serious complication.* **4.** a disease arising as a consequence of another.

complicity (kəmˈplɪsɪtɪ) *n., pl.* **-ties. 1.** the fact of being an accomplice, esp. in a criminal act. **2.** a less common word for **complexity.**

compliment *n.* (ˈkɒmplɪmənt). **1.** a remark or act expressing respect, admiration, etc. **2.**

(*usually pl.*) a greeting of respect or regard. ~*vb.* (ˈkɒmplɪˌmɛnt). (*tr.*) **3.** to express admiration for; congratulate. **4.** to express or show regard for, esp. by a gift. [C17: < F, < It. *complimento,* < Sp. *cumplimiento,* < *cumplir* to complete]

complimentary (ˌkɒmplɪˈmɛntərɪ) *adj.* **1.** conveying a compliment. **2.** flattering. **3.** given free, esp. as a courtesy or for publicity purposes. —ˌ**compliˈmentarily** *adv.*

compline (ˈkɒmplɪn, -plaɪn) *or* **complin** (ˈkɒmplɪn) *n. R.C. Church.* the last of the seven canonical hours of the divine office. [C13: < OF *complie,* < Med. L *hōra complēta,* lit.: the completed hour]

comply (kəmˈplaɪ) *vb.* **-plying, -plied.** (*intr.*) (usually foll. by *with*) to act in accordance with rules, wishes, etc.; be obedient (to). [C17: < It. *complire,* < Sp. *cumplir* to complete]

compo (ˈkɒmpəʊ) *n., pl.* **-pos. 1.** a mixture of materials, such as mortar, plaster, etc. **2.** *Austral. & N.Z. inf.* compensation, esp. for injury or loss of work. ~*adj.* **3.** *Mil.* intended to last for several days: *a compo pack.* [short for *composition, compensation, composite*]

component (kəmˈpəʊnənt) *n.* **1.** a constituent part or aspect of something more complex. **2.** any electrical device that has distinct electrical characteristics and may be connected to other devices to form a circuit. **3.** *Maths.* one of a set of two or more vectors whose resultant is a given vector. **4.** See **phase rule.** ~*adj.* **5.** forming or functioning as a part or aspect; constituent. [C17: < L *compōnere* to put together] —**componential** (ˌkɒmpəˈnɛnʃəl) *adj.*

comport (kəmˈpɔːt) *vb.* **1.** (*tr.*) to conduct or bear (oneself) in a specified way. **2.** (*intr.;* foll. by *with*) to agree (with). [C16: < L *comportāre* collect, < *com-* together + *portāre* to carry] —**comˈportment** *n.*

compose (kəmˈpəʊz) *vb.* (*mainly tr.*) **1.** to put together or make up. **2.** to be the component elements of. **3.** to create (a musical or literary work). **4.** (*intr.*) to write music. **5.** to calm (someone, esp. oneself); make quiet. **6.** to adjust or settle (a quarrel, etc.). **7.** to order the elements of (a painting, sculpture, etc.); design. **8.** *Printing.* to set up (type). [C15: < OF *composer,* < L *compōnere* to put in place]

composed (kəmˈpəʊzd) *adj.* (of people) calm; tranquil. —**composedly** (kəmˈpəʊzɪdlɪ) *adv.*

composer (kəmˈpəʊzə) *n.* **1.** a person who composes music. **2.** a person or machine that composes anything, esp. type for printing.

composite *adj.* (ˈkɒmpəzɪt). **1.** composed of separate parts; compound. **2.** of or belonging to the plant family Compositae. **3.** *Maths.* capable of being factorized: *a composite function.* **4.** (*sometimes cap.*) denoting one of the five classical orders of architecture: characterized by a combination of the Ionic and Corinthian styles. ~*n.* (ˈkɒmpəzɪt). **5.** something composed of separate parts; compound. **6.** any plant of the family Compositae, having flower heads composed of many small flowers (e.g. dandelion, daisy). **7.** a material, such as reinforced concrete, made of two or more distinct materials. **8.** a proposal that has been composited. ~*vb.* (*tr.*) (ˈkɒmpəˌzaɪt). **9.** to merge related motions from local branches (of a political party, trade union, etc.) so as to produce a manageable number of proposals for discussion at national level. [C16: < L *compositus* well arranged, < *compōnere* to arrange] —ˈ**compositely** *adv.* —ˈ**compositeness** *n.*

composite photograph *n.* a photograph formed by superimposing two or more separate photographs.

composite school *n. Canad.* a secondary school offering both academic and nonacademic courses.

composition (ˌkɒmpəˈzɪʃən) *n.* **1.** the act of putting together or making up by combining parts. **2.** something formed in this manner; a mixture. **3.** the parts of which something is composed; constitution. **4.** a work of music, art, or literature. **5.** the harmonious arrangement of the parts of a work of art in relation to each other. **6.** a piece of writing undertaken as an academic exercise; an essay. **7.** *Printing.* the act or technique of setting up type. **8.** a settlement by mutual consent, esp. a legal agreement whereby the creditors agree to accept partial payment of a debt in full settlement. [C14: < OF, < L *compositus;* see COMPOSITE, -ION]

compositor (kəmˈpɒzɪtə) *n. Printing.* a person who sets and corrects type.

compos mentis *Latin.* (ˈkɒmpəs ˈmɛntɪs) *adj.* (*postpositive*) of sound mind; sane.

compost (ˈkɒmpɒst) *n.* **1.** a mixture of organic residues such as decomposed vegetation, manure, etc., used as a fertilizer. **2.** *Rare.* a mixture. ~*vb.* (*tr.*) **3.** to make (vegetable matter) into compost. **4.** to fertilize with compost. [C14: < OF *compost,* < L *compositus* put together]

composure (kəmˈpəʊʒə) *n.* calmness, esp. of the mind; tranquillity; serenity.

compote (ˈkɒmpəʊt) *n.* a dish of fruit stewed with sugar or in a syrup. [C17: < F *composte,* < L *compositus* put in place]

compound[1] *n.* (ˈkɒmpaʊnd). **1.** a substance that contains atoms of two or more chemical elements held together by chemical bonds. **2.** any combination of two or more parts, aspects, etc. **3.** a word formed from two existing words or combining forms. ~*vb.* (kəmˈpaʊnd). (*mainly tr.*) **4.** to combine so as to create a compound. **5.** to make by combining parts, aspects, etc.: *to compound a new plastic.* **6.** to intensify by an added element: *his anxiety was compounded by her crying.* **7.** (*also intr.*) to come to an agreement in (a dispute, etc.) or to settle (a debt, etc.) for less than what is owed; compromise. **8.** *Law.* to agree not to prosecute in return for a consideration: *to compound a crime.* ~*adj.* (ˈkɒmpaʊnd). **9.** composed of two or more parts, elements, etc. **10.** (of a word) consisting of elements that are also words or combining forms. **11.** *Grammar.* (of tense, mood, etc.) formed by using an auxiliary verb in addition to the main verb. **12.** *Music.* **a.** denoting a time in which the number of beats per bar is a multiple of three: *six-four is an example of compound time.* **b.** (of an interval) greater than an octave. **13.** (of a steam engine, etc.) having multiple stages in which the steam or working fluid from one stage is used in a subsequent stage. **14.** (of a piston engine) having a supercharger powered by a turbine in the exhaust stream. [C14: < earlier *compounen,* < OF *compondre* to set in order, < L *compōnere*] —**comˈpoundable** *adj.*

compound[2] (ˈkɒmpaʊnd) *n.* **1.** (esp. in South Africa) an enclosure, esp. on the mines, containing the living quarters for Black workers. **2.** any similar enclosure, such as a camp for prisoners of war. [C17: < Malay *kampong* village]

compound eye *n.* the convex eye of insects and some crustaceans, consisting of numerous separate light-sensitive units (ommatidia).

compound fraction *n.* another name for **complex fraction.**

compound fracture *n.* a fracture in which the broken bone pierces the skin.

compound interest *n.* interest calculated on both the principal and its accrued interest.

compound leaf *n.* a leaf consisting of two or more leaflets borne on the same leafstalk.

compound number *n.* a quantity expressed in two or more different but related units: *3 hours 10 seconds is a compound number.*

compound sentence *n.* a sentence containing at least two coordinate clauses.

compound time *n.* See **compound**[1] (sense 12).

comprehend (ˌkɒmprɪˈhɛnd) *vb.* **1.** to understand. **2.** (*tr.*) to comprise; include. [C14: < L *comprehendere,* < *prehendere* to seize]

comprehensible (ˌkɒmprɪˈhɛnsəbᵊl) *adj.* capable of being comprehended. —ˌ**compreˌhensiˈbility** *n.* —ˌ**compreˈhensibly** *adv.*

comprehension (ˌkɒmprɪˈhɛnʃən) *n.* **1.** the act

or capacity of understanding. **2.** the state of including; comprehensiveness.

comprehensive (ˌkɒmprɪˈhɛnsɪv) *adj.* **1.** of broad scope or content. **2.** (of a car insurance policy) providing protection against most risks, including third-party liability, fire, theft, and damage. **3.** of or being a comprehensive school. ~*n.* **4.** short for **comprehensive school.** —ˌ**comprеˈhensively** *adv.* —ˌ**compreˈhensiveness** *n.*

comprehensive school *n. Chiefly Brit.* a secondary school for children of all abilities from the same district.

compress *vb.* (kəmˈprɛs). **1.** (*tr.*) to squeeze together; condense. ~*n.* (ˈkɒmprɛs). **2.** a cloth or gauze pad applied firmly to some part of the body to relieve discomfort, reduce fever, etc. [C14: < LL *compressāre,* < L *comprimere,* < *premere* to press] —**comˈpressible** *adj.* —**com**ˌ**pressiˈbility** *n.* —**comˈpressive** *adj.*

compressed air *n.* air at a higher pressure than atmospheric pressure: used esp. as a source of power for machines.

compression (kəmˈprɛʃən) *n.* **1.** the act of compressing or the condition of being compressed. **2.** an increase in pressure of the charge in an engine or compressor obtained by reducing its volume.

compressor (kəmˈprɛsə) *n.* **1.** any device that compresses a gas. **2.** the part of a gas turbine that compresses the air before it enters the combustion chambers. **3.** any muscle that causes compression. **4.** an electronic device for reducing the variation in signal amplitude in a transmission system.

comprise (kəmˈpraɪz) *vb.* (*tr.*) **1.** to be made up of. **2.** to constitute the whole of; consist of: *her singing comprised the entertainment.* [C15: < F *compris* included, < *comprendre* to COMPREHEND] —**comˈprisable** *adj.*

▷ **Usage.** *Comprise* in the sense "to consist of" is not itself followed by *of*: *the work comprises the following duties.* It differs from *include* in being comprehensive; the above example means that all the duties are about to be mentioned, whereas *the work includes the following duties* implies that there may be others in addition to those about to be mentioned.

compromise (ˈkɒmprəˌmaɪz) *n.* **1.** settlement of a dispute by concessions on both or all sides. **2.** the terms of such a settlement. **3.** something midway between different things. ~*vb.* **4.** to settle (a dispute) by making concessions. **5.** (*tr.*) to expose (oneself or another) to disrepute. [C15: < OF *compromis,* < L, < *comprōmittere,* < *prōmittere* to promise] —**ˈcompro**ˌ**miser** *n.* —**ˈcompro**ˌ**misingly** *adv.*

compte rendu *French.* (kɔ̃t rɑ̃dy) *n., pl.* ***comptes rendus*** (kɔ̃t rɑ̃dy). **1.** a review or notice. **2.** an account. [lit.: account rendered]

Comptometer (kɒmpˈtɒmɪtə) *n. Trademark.* a high-speed calculating machine.

comptroller (kənˈtrəʊlə) *n.* a variant spelling of **controller** (sense 2), esp. as a title of any of various financial executives.

compulsion (kəmˈpʌlʃən) *n.* **1.** the act of compelling or the state of being compelled. **2.** something that compels. **3.** *Psychiatry.* an inner drive that causes a person to perform actions, often repetitive, against his will. See also **obsession.** [C15: < OF, < L *compellere* to COMPEL]

compulsive (kəmˈpʌlsɪv) *adj.* relating to or involving compulsion. —**comˈpulsively** *adv.*

compulsory (kəmˈpʌlsərɪ) *adj.* **1.** required by regulations or laws; obligatory. **2.** involving or employing compulsion; compelling; essential. —**comˈpulsorily** *adv.* —**comˈpulsoriness** *n.*

compulsory purchase *n.* purchase of a property by a local authority or government department for public use or development, regardless of whether or not the owner wishes to sell.

compunction (kəmˈpʌŋkʃən) *n.* a feeling of remorse, guilt, or regret. [C14: < Church L *compunctiō,* < L *compungere* to sting] —**comˈpunctious** *adj.* —**comˈpunctiously** *adv.*

computation (ˌkɒmpjʊˈteɪʃən) *n.* a calculation involving numbers or quantities. —ˌ**compuˈtational** *adj.*

compute (kəmˈpjuːt) *vb.* to calculate (an answer, result, etc.), often with the aid of a computer. [C17: < L *computāre,* < *putāre* to think] —**comˈputable** *adj.* —**com**ˌ**putaˈbility** *n.*

computer (kəmˈpjuːtə) *n.* **1. a.** a device, usually electronic, that processes data according to a set of instructions. The **digital computer** stores data in discrete units and performs operations at very high speed. The **analog computer** has no memory and is slower than the digital computer but has a continuous rather than a discrete input. **b.** (*as modifier*): *computer technology.* **2.** a person who computes or calculates.

computerize *or* **-ise** (kəmˈpjuːtəˌraɪz) *vb.* **1.** (*tr.*) to cause (certain operations) to be performed by a computer, esp. as a replacement for human labour. **2.** (*intr.*) to install a computer. **3.** (*tr.*) to control or perform (operations) by means of a computer. **4.** (*tr.*) to process or store (information) by or in a computer. —**com**ˌ**puteriˈzation** *or* **-iˈsation** *n.*

computer language *n.* another term for **programming language.**

comrade (ˈkɒmreɪd, -rɪd) *n.* **1.** a companion. **2.** a fellow member of a political party, esp. a fellow Communist. [C16: < F *camarade,* < Sp. *camarada* group of soldiers sharing a billet, < *cámara* room, < L] —**ˈcomradely** *adj.* —**ˈcomrade**ˌ**ship** *n.*

comsat (ˈkɒmsæt) *n.* short for **communications satellite.**

con[1] (kɒn) *Inf.* ~*n.* **1. a.** short for **confidence trick. b.** (*as modifier*): *con man.* ~*vb.* **conning, conned. 2.** (*tr.*) to swindle or defraud. [C19: < CONFIDENCE]

con[2] (kɒn) *n.* (*usually pl.*) an argument or vote against a proposal, motion, etc. See also **pros and cons.** [< L *contrā* against]

con[3] *or esp. U.S.* **conn** (kɒn) *vb.* **conning, conned.** (*tr.*) *Naut.* to direct the steering of (a vessel). [C17 *cun,* < earlier *condien* to guide, < OF *conduire,* < L *condūcere;* see CONDUCT]

con[4] (kɒn) *vb.* **conning, conned.** (*tr.*) *Arch.* to study attentively or learn. [C15: var. of CAN[1] in the sense: to come to know]

con[5] (kɒn) *prep. Music.* with. [It.]

con. *abbrev. for:* **1.** concerto. **2.** conclusion. **3.** connection. **4.** consolidated. **5.** continued.

con- *prefix.* a variant of **com-.**

con amore (kɒn æˈmɔːrɪ) *adj., adv. Music.* (to be performed) lovingly. [C19: < It.: with love]

con brio (kɒn ˈbriːəʊ) *adj., adv. Music.* (to be performed) with liveliness or spirit. [It.: with energy]

concatenate (kɒnˈkætɪˌneɪt) *vb.* (*tr.*) to link or join together, esp. in a chain or series. [C16: < LL *concatēnāre,* < L *com-* together + *catēna* CHAIN] —ˌ**concateˈnation** *n.*

concave (ˈkɒnkeɪv, kɒnˈkeɪv) *adj.* **1.** curving inwards; having the shape of a section of the interior of a sphere, paraboloid, etc.: *a concave lens.* ~*vb.* **2.** (*tr.*) to make concave. [C15: < L *concavus* arched, < *cavus* hollow] —**ˈconcavely** *adv.* —**ˈconcaveness** *n.*

concavity (kɒnˈkævɪtɪ) *n., pl.* **-ties. 1.** the state of being concave. **2.** a concave surface or thing.

concavo-concave (kɒnˌkeɪvəʊkɒnˈkeɪv) *adj.* (esp. of a lens) having both sides concave.

concavo-convex *adj.* **1.** having one side concave and the other side convex. **2.** (of a lens) having a concave face with greater curvature than the convex face.

conceal (kənˈsiːl) *vb.* (*tr.*) **1.** to keep from discovery; hide. **2.** to keep secret. [C14: < OF *conceler,* < L *concēlāre,* < *com-* (intensive) + *cēlāre* to hide] —**conˈcealer** *n.* —**conˈcealment** *n.*

concede (kənˈsiːd) *vb.* **1.** (when *tr., may take a clause as object*) to admit or acknowledge (something) as true or correct. **2.** to yield or allow (something, such as a right). **3.** (*tr.*) to admit as certain in outcome: *to concede an election.* [C17: < L *concēdere,* < *cēdere* to give way] —**con'ceder** *n.*

conceit (kən'siːt) *n.* **1.** a high, often exaggerated, opinion of oneself or one's accomplishments. **2.** *Literary.* an elaborate image or far-fetched comparison. **3.** *Arch.* **a.** a witty expression. **b.** fancy; imagination. **c.** an idea. ~*vb.* (*tr.*) **4.** *Obs.* to think. [C14: < CONCEIVE]

conceited (kən'siːtɪd) *adj.* having an exaggerated opinion of oneself or one's accomplishments. —**con'ceitedly** *adv.* —**con'ceitedness** *n.*

conceivable (kən'siːvəbᵊl) *adj.* capable of being understood, believed, or imagined; possible. —**con,ceiva'bility** *n.* —**con'ceivably** *adv.*

conceive (kən'siːv) *vb.* **1.** (when *intr.,* foll. by *of;* when *tr., often takes a clause as object*) to have an idea (of); imagine; think. **2.** (*tr.; takes a clause as object or an infinitive*) to believe. **3.** (*tr.*) to develop: *she conceived a passion for music.* **4.** to become pregnant with (a child). **5.** (*tr.*) *Rare.* to express in words. [C13: < OF *conceivre,* < L *concipere* to take in, < *capere* to take]

concelebrate (kən'sɛlɪ,breɪt) *vb. Christianity.* to celebrate (the Eucharist or Mass) jointly with one or more other priests. [C16: < L *concelebrāre*] —**con,cele'bration** *n.*

concentrate ('kɒnsən,treɪt) *vb.* **1.** to come or cause to come to a single purpose or aim: *to concentrate one's hopes on winning.* **2.** to make or become denser or purer by the removal of certain elements. **3.** (*intr.;* often foll. by *on*) to think intensely (about). ~*n.* **4.** a concentrated material or solution. [C17: back formation < CONCENTRATION, ult. < L *com-* same + *centrum* CENTRE] —**'concen,trative** *adj.* —**'concen,trator** *n.*

concentration (,kɒnsən'treɪʃən) *n.* **1.** intense mental application. **2.** the act of concentrating. **3.** something that is concentrated. **4.** the strength of a solution, esp. the amount of dissolved substance in a given volume of solvent. **5.** *Mil.* **a.** the act of bringing together military forces. **b.** the application of fire from a number of weapons against a target.

concentration camp *n.* a guarded prison camp for nonmilitary prisoners, esp. one in Nazi Germany.

concentre (kɒn'sɛntə) *vb.* to converge or cause to converge on a common centre; concentrate. [C16: < F *concentrer*]

concentric (kən'sɛntrɪk) *adj.* having a common centre: *concentric circles.* [C14: < Med. L *concentricus,* < L *com-* same + *centrum* CENTRE] —**con'centrically** *adv.*

concept ('kɒnsɛpt) *n.* **1.** an idea, esp. an abstract idea: *the concepts of biology.* **2.** *Philosophy.* a general idea that corresponds to some class of entities and consists of the essential features of the class. **3.** a new idea; invention. [C16: < L *conceptum,* < *concipere* to CONCEIVE]

conception (kən'sɛpʃən) *n.* **1.** something conceived; notion, idea, or plan. **2.** the description under which someone considers something: *a strange conception of freedom.* **3.** the state of an ovum being fertilized by a sperm in the womb. **4.** origin or beginning. [C13: < L *conceptiō,* < *concipere* to CONCEIVE] —**con'ceptional** *or* **con'ceptive** *adj.*

conceptual (kən'sɛptjʊəl) *adj.* of or characterized by concepts. —**con'ceptually** *adv.*

conceptualize *or* **-lise** (kən'sɛptjʊə,laɪz) *vb.* to form (a concept or concepts) out of observations, experience, data, etc. —**con,ceptuali'zation** *or* **-li'sation** *n.*

concern (kən'sɜːn) *vb.* (*tr.*) **1.** to relate to; affect. **2.** (usually foll. by *with* or *in*) to involve or interest (oneself): *he concerns himself with other people's affairs.* ~*n.* **3.** something that affects a person; affair; business. **4.** regard or interest: *he felt a strong concern for her.* **5.** anxiety or solicitude. **6.** important relation: *his news has great concern for us.* **7.** a commercial company. **8.** *Inf.* a material thing, esp. one of which one has a low opinion. [C15: < LL *concernere,* < L *com-* together + *cernere* to sift]

concerned (kən'sɜːnd) *adj.* **1.** (*postpositive*) interested, guilty, or involved: *I shall find the boy concerned and punish him.* **2.** worried or solicitous. —**concernedly** (kən'sɜːnɪdlɪ) *adv.*

concerning (kən'sɜːnɪŋ) *prep.* **1.** about; regarding. ~*adj.* **2.** worrying or troublesome.

concernment (kən'sɜːnmənt) *n. Rare.* affair or business; concern.

concert *n.* ('kɒnsɜːt). **1. a.** a performance of music by players or singers that does not involve theatrical staging. **b.** (*as modifier*): *a concert version of an opera.* **2.** agreement in design, plan, or action. **3. in concert. a.** acting with a common purpose. **b.** (of musicians, etc.) performing live. ~*vb.* (kən'sɜːt). **4.** to arrange or contrive (a plan) by mutual agreement. [C16: < F *concerter* to bring into agreement, < It., < LL *concertāre* to work together, < L *certāre* to contend]

concertante (,kɒntʃə'tæntɪ) *adj. Music.* characterized by contrasting alternating tutti and solo passages. [It.: < *concertare* to perform a CONCERT]

concerted (kən'sɜːtɪd) *adj.* **1.** mutually contrived, planned, or arranged; combined: *a concerted effort.* **2.** *Music.* arranged in parts for a group of singers or players.

concert grand *n.* a grand piano of the largest size.

concertina (,kɒnsə'tiːnə) *n.* **1.** a hexagonal musical instrument similar to the accordion, in which metallic reeds are vibrated by air from a set of bellows operated by the player's hands. ~*vb.* **-naing, -naed. 2.** (*intr.*) to collapse or fold up like the bellows of a concertina. [C19: CONCERT + *-ina*] —**,concer'tinist** *n.*

concertino (,kɒntʃə'tiːnəʊ) *n., pl.* **-ni** (-nɪ). *Music.* **1.** the solo group in a concerto grosso. **2.** a short concerto. [It.: a little CONCERTO]

concertmaster ('kɒnsət,mɑːstə) *n.* a U.S. and Canad. word for **leader** (of an orchestra).

concerto (kən'tʃɛətəʊ) *n., pl.* **-tos** *or* **-ti** (-tɪ). a composition for an orchestra and one or more soloists. [C18: < It.: CONCERT]

concerto grosso ('grɒsəʊ) *n., pl.* **concerti grossi** ('grɒsɪ) *or* **concerto grossos.** a composition for an orchestra and a group of soloists. [It., lit.: big concerto]

concert party *n.* **1.** esp. formerly, a social gathering for music-making. **2.** *Stock Exchange inf.* a group of individuals or companies who secretly agree together to purchase shares separately in a particular company which they plan to amalgamate later into a single holding: a malpractice which is illegal in some countries.

concert pitch *n.* **1.** the frequency of 440 hertz assigned to the A above middle C. **2.** *Inf.* a state of extreme readiness.

concession (kən'sɛʃən) *n.* **1.** the act of yielding or conceding. **2.** something conceded. **3.** any grant of rights, land, or property by a government, local authority, corporation, or individual. **4.** the right, esp. an exclusive right, to market a particular product in a given area. **5.** *Canad.* **a.** a land subdivision in a township survey. **b.** another name for a **concession road.** [C16: < L *concessiō,* < *concēdere* to CONCEDE] —**con'cessible** *adj.* —**con'cessive** *adj.*

concessionaire (kən,sɛʃə'nɛə), **concessioner** (kən'sɛʃənə), *or* **concessionary** *n.* someone who holds or operates a concession.

concessionary (kən'sɛʃənərɪ) *adj.* **1.** of, granted, or obtained by a concession. ~*n., pl.* **-aries. 2.** another word for **concessionaire.**

concession road *n. Canad.* one of a series of roads separating concessions in a township.

conch (kɒŋk, kɒntʃ) *n., pl.* **conchs** (kɒŋks) *or* **conches** ('kɒntʃɪz). **1.** any of various tropical marine gastropod molluscs characterized by a large brightly coloured spiral shell. **2.** the shell of such a mollusc, used as a trumpet. [C16: < L *concha,* < Gk *konkhē* shellfish]

conchie *or* **conchy** ('kɒntʃɪ) *n., pl.* **-chies.** *Inf.* short for **conscientious objector.**

conchology (kɒŋˈkɒlədʒɪ) *n.* the study of mollusc shells. —**conˈchologist** *n.*

concierge (ˌkɒnsɪˈɛəʒ) *n.* (esp. in France) a caretaker of a block of flats, hotel, etc., esp. one who lives on the premises. [C17: < F, ult. < L *conservus*, < *servus* slave]

conciliar (kənˈsɪlɪə) *adj.* of, from, or by means of a council, esp. an ecclesiastical one.

conciliate (kənˈsɪlɪˌeɪt) *vb.* (*tr.*) **1.** to overcome the hostility of; win over. **2.** to gain (favour, regard, etc.), esp. by making friendly overtures. [C16: < L *conciliāre* to bring together, < *concilium* COUNCIL] —**conˈciliable** *adj.* —**conˌciliˈation** *n.* —**conˈciliˌator** *n.*

conciliatory (kənˈsɪljətərɪ) *or* **conciliative** (kənˈsɪljətɪv) *adj.* intended to placate or reconcile. —**conˈciliatorily** *adv.*

concise (kənˈsaɪs) *adj.* brief and to the point. [C16: < L *concīsus* cut short, < *concīdere*, < *caedere* to cut, strike down] —**conˈcisely** *adv.* —**conˈciseness** *or* **concision** (kənˈsɪʒən) *n.*

conclave (ˈkɒnkleɪv) *n.* **1.** a secret meeting. **2.** *R.C. Church.* **a.** the closed apartments where the college of cardinals elects a new pope. **b.** a meeting of the college of cardinals for this purpose. [C14: < Med. L *conclāve*, < L: place that may be locked, < *clāvis* key]

conclude (kənˈkluːd) *vb.* (*mainly tr.*) **1.** (*also intr.*) to come or cause to come to an end. **2.** (*takes a clause as object*) to decide by reasoning; deduce: *the judge concluded that the witness had told the truth.* **3.** to settle: *to conclude a treaty.* **4.** *Obs.* to confine. [C14: < L *conclūdere*, < *claudere* to close]

conclusion (kənˈkluːʒən) *n.* **1.** end or termination. **2.** the last main division of a speech, essay, etc. **3.** outcome or result (esp. in **a foregone conclusion**). **4.** a final decision or judgment (esp. in **come to a conclusion**). **5.** *Logic.* **a.** a statement that purports to follow from another or others (the **premises**) by means of an argument. **b.** a statement that does validly follow from given premises. **6.** *Law.* **a.** an admission or statement binding on the party making it; estoppel. **b.** the close of a pleading or of a conveyance. **7. in conclusion.** lastly; to sum up. **8. jump to conclusions.** to come to a conclusion prematurely, without sufficient thought or on incomplete evidence. [C14: via OF < L; see CONCLUDE, -ION]

conclusive (kənˈkluːsɪv) *adj.* **1.** putting an end to doubt; decisive; final. **2.** approaching or involving an end. —**conˈclusively** *adv.*

concoct (kənˈkɒkt) *vb.* (*tr.*) **1.** to make by combining different ingredients. **2.** to invent; make up; contrive. [C16: < L *concoctus* cooked together, < *coquere* to cook] —**conˈcocter** *or* **conˈcoctor** *n.* —**conˈcoction** *n.*

concomitance (kənˈkɒmɪtəns) *n.* **1.** existence together. **2.** *Christianity.* the doctrine that the body and blood of Christ are present in the Eucharist.

concomitant (kənˈkɒmɪtənt) *adj.* **1.** existing or occurring together. ~*n.* **2.** a concomitant act, person, etc. [C17: < LL *concomitārī* to accompany, < *com-* with + *comes* companion]

concord (ˈkɒnkɔːd) *n.* **1.** agreement or harmony. **2.** a treaty establishing peaceful relations between nations. **3.** *Music.* a combination of musical notes, esp. one containing a series of consonant intervals. **4.** *Grammar.* another word for **agreement** (sense 6). [C13: < OF *concorde*, < L *concordia*, < *com-* same + *cors* heart]

concordance (kənˈkɔːdᵊns) *n.* **1.** a state of harmony. **2.** a book that indexes the principal words in a literary work, often with the immediate context and an account of the meaning. **3.** an index produced by computer or machine.

concordant (kənˈkɔːdᵊnt) *adj.* being in agreement; harmonious. —**conˈcordantly** *adv.*

concordat (kɒnˈkɔːdæt) *n.* a pact or treaty, esp. one between the Vatican and another state concerning the interests of religion in that state. [C17: via F, < Med. L *concordātum*, < L: something agreed; see CONCORD]

concourse (ˈkɒnkɔːs) *n.* **1.** a crowd; throng. **2.** a coming together; confluence. **3.** a large open space for the gathering of people in a public place. [C14: < OF *concours*, ult. < L *concurrere* to run together]

concrete (ˈkɒnkriːt) *n.* **1.** a construction material made of cement, sand, stone and water that hardens to a stonelike mass. ~*adj.* **2.** relating to a particular instance; specific as opposed to general. **3.** relating to things capable of being perceived by the senses, as opposed to abstractions. **4.** formed by the coalescence of particles; condensed; solid. ~*vb.* **5.** (*tr.*) to construct in or cover with concrete. **6.** (kənˈkriːt). to become or cause to become solid; coalesce. [C14: < L *concrētus*, < *concrēscere* to grow together] —ˈ**concretely** *adv.* —ˈ**concreteness** *n.*

concrete music *n.* music consisting of an electronically modified montage of tape-recorded sounds.

concrete noun *n.* a noun that refers to a material object.

concrete poetry *n.* poetry in which the visual form of the poem is used to convey meaning.

concretion (kənˈkriːʃən) *n.* **1.** the act of growing together; coalescence. **2.** a solidified mass. **3.** something made real, tangible, or specific. **4.** a rounded or irregular mineral mass different in composition from the sedimentary rock that surrounds it. **5.** *Pathol.* another word for **calculus.** —**conˈcretionary** *adj.*

concretize *or* **-tise** (ˈkɒnkrɪˌtaɪz) *vb.* (*tr.*) to render concrete; make real or specific.

concubine (ˈkɒŋkjʊˌbaɪn, ˈkɒn-) *n.* **1.** (in polygamous societies) a secondary wife. **2.** a woman who cohabits with a man, esp. (formerly) the mistress of a king, nobleman, etc. [C13: < OF, < L *concubīna*, < *concumbere* to lie together] —**concubinage** (kɒnˈkjuːbɪnɪdʒ) *n.* —**conˈcubinary** *n., adj.*

concupiscence (kənˈkjuːpɪsəns) *n.* strong desire, esp. sexual desire. [C14: < Church L *concupiscentia*, < L *concupiscere* to covet] —**conˈcupiscent** *adj.*

concur (kənˈkɜː) *vb.* **-curring, -curred.** (*intr.*) **1.** to agree; be in accord. **2.** to combine or cooperate. **3.** to occur simultaneously; coincide. [C15: < L *concurrere* to run together]

concurrence (kənˈkʌrəns) *n.* **1.** the act of concurring. **2.** agreement; accord. **3.** cooperation or combination. **4.** simultaneous occurrence.

concurrent (kənˈkʌrənt) *adj.* **1.** taking place at the same time or in the same location. **2.** cooperating. **3.** meeting at, approaching, or having a common point: *concurrent lines.* **4.** in agreement; harmonious. —**conˈcurrently** *adv.*

concuss (kənˈkʌs) *vb.* (*tr.*) **1.** to injure (the brain) by a violent blow, fall, etc. **2.** to shake violently. [C16: < L *concussus*, < *concutere* to disturb greatly, < *quatere* to shake]

concussion (kənˈkʌʃən) *n.* **1.** a jarring of the brain, caused by a blow or a fall, usually resulting in loss of consciousness. **2.** any violent shaking.

condemn (kənˈdɛm) *vb.* (*tr.*) **1.** to express strong disapproval of. **2.** to pronounce judicial sentence on. **3.** to demonstrate the guilt of: *his secretive behaviour condemned him.* **4.** to judge or pronounce unfit for use. **5.** to force into a particular state: *his disposition condemned him to boredom.* [C13: < OF *condempner*, < L *condemnāre*, < *damnāre* to condemn] —**conˈdemnable** *adj.* —ˌ**condemˈnation** *n.* —ˌ**condemˈnatory** *adj.*

condensate (kənˈdɛnseɪt) *n.* a substance formed by condensation.

condensation (ˌkɒndɛnˈseɪʃən) *n.* **1.** the act or process of condensing, or the state of being condensed. **2.** anything that has condensed from a vapour, esp. on a window. **3.** *Chem.* a type of reaction in which two organic molecules combine to form a larger molecule as well as a simple molecule such as water, etc. **4.** an abridged version of a book. —ˌ**condenˈsational** *adj.*

condensation trail *n.* another name for **vapour trail.**

condense (kənˈdɛns) *vb.* **1.** (*tr.*) to increase the density of; compress. **2.** to reduce or be reduced in volume or size. **3.** to change or cause to change from a gaseous to a liquid or solid state. **4.** *Chem.* to undergo or cause to undergo condensation. [C15: < L *condēnsāre,* < *dēnsāre* to make thick, < *dēnsus* DENSE] **—conˈdensable** *or* **conˈdensible** *adj.*

condensed milk *n.* milk reduced by evaporation to a thick concentration, with sugar added.

condenser (kənˈdɛnsə) *n.* **1. a.** an apparatus for reducing gases to their liquid or solid form by the abstraction of heat. **b.** a device for abstracting heat, as in a refrigeration unit. **2.** a lens that concentrates light. **3.** another name for **capacitor. 4.** a person or device that condenses.

condescend (ˌkɒndɪˈsɛnd) *vb.* (*intr.*) **1.** to act graciously towards another or others regarded as being on a lower level; behave patronizingly. **2.** to do something that one regards as below one's dignity. [C14: < Church L *condēscendere,* < L *dēscendere* to DESCEND] **—ˌcondeˈscending** *adj.* **—ˌcondeˈscendingly** *adv.* **—ˌcondeˈscension** *n.*

condign (kənˈdaɪn) *adj.* (esp. of a punishment) fitting; deserved. [C15: < OF *condigne,* < L *condignus,* < *dignus* worthy] **—conˈdignly** *adv.*

condiment (ˈkɒndɪmənt) *n.* any spice or sauce such as salt, pepper, mustard, etc. [C15: < L *condīmentum* seasoning, < *condīre* to pickle]

condition (kənˈdɪʃən) *n.* **1.** a particular state of being or existence: *the human condition.* **2.** something that limits or restricts; a qualification. **3.** (*pl.*) circumstances: *conditions were right for a takeover.* **4.** state of physical fitness, esp. good health: *out of condition.* **5.** an ailment: *a heart condition.* **6.** something indispensable: *your happiness is a condition of mine.* **7.** something required as part of an agreement; term: *the conditions of the lease are set out.* **8.** *Law.* **a.** a provision in a will, contract, etc., that makes some right or liability contingent upon the happening of some event. **b.** the event itself. **9.** *Logic.* a statement whose truth is either required for the truth of a given statement (a **necessary condition**) or sufficient to guarantee the truth of the given statement (a **sufficient condition**). **10.** rank, status, or position. **11. on condition that.** (*conj.*) provided that. ~*vb.* (*mainly tr.*) **12.** *Psychol.* **a.** to alter the response of (a person or animal) to a particular stimulus or situation. **b.** to establish a conditioned response in. **13.** to put into a fit condition. **14.** to improve the condition of (one's hair) by use of special cosmetics. **15.** to accustom or inure. **16.** to subject to a condition. [C14: < L *conditiō,* < *condīcere* to discuss, < *con-* together + *dīcere* to say] **—conˈditioner** *n.* **—conˈditioning** *n., adj.*

conditional (kənˈdɪʃənᵊl) *adj.* **1.** depending on other factors. **2.** *Grammar.* expressing a condition on which something else is contingent: "*If he comes*" *is a conditional clause in the sentence* "*If he comes I shall go*". **3.** *Logic.* (of a proposition) consisting of two component propositions associated by the words *if...then* so that the proposition is false only when the antecedent is true and the consequent false. ~*n.* **4.** a conditional verb form, clause, sentence, etc. **—conˌditionˈality** *n.* **—conˈditionally** *adv.*

conditioned response *n. Psychol.* a response that is transferred from the second to the first of a pair of stimuli. A well-known Pavlovian example is salivation by a dog when it hears a bell ring, because food has always been presented when the bell has been rung previously. Also called (esp. formerly): **conditioned reflex.**

condole (kənˈdəʊl) *vb.* (*intr.;* foll. by *with*) to express sympathy with someone in grief, pain, etc. [C16: < Church L *condolēre,* < L *com-* together + *dolēre* to grieve] **—conˈdolence** *n.*

condom (ˈkɒndəm) *n.* a rubber sheath worn on the penis during sexual intercourse to prevent conception or infection. [C18: <?]

condominium (ˌkɒndəˈmɪnɪəm) *n., pl.* **-ums. 1.** joint rule or sovereignty. **2.** a country ruled by two or more foreign powers. **3.** *U.S. & Canad.* an apartment building in which each apartment is individually owned and the common areas are jointly owned. [C18: < NL, < L *com-* together + *dominium* ownership]

condone (kənˈdəʊn) *vb.* (*tr.*) **1.** to overlook or forgive (an offence, etc.). **2.** *Law.* (esp. of a spouse) to pardon or overlook (an offence, usually adultery). [C19: < L *condōnāre,* < *com-* (intensive) + *dōnāre* to donate] **—condonation** (ˌkɒndəʊˈneɪʃən) *n.* **—conˈdoner** *n.*

condor (ˈkɒndɔː) *n.* either of two very large rare New World vultures, the **Andean condor,** which has black plumage with white around the neck, and the **California condor,** which is nearly extinct. [C17: < Sp. *cóndor,* < Quechuan *kuntur*]

condottiere (ˌkɒndɒˈtjɛərɪ) *n., pl.* **-ri** (-riː). a commander or soldier in a professional mercenary company in Europe from the 13th to the 16th centuries. [C18: < It., < *condotto* leadership, < *condurre* to lead, < L *condūcere*]

conduce (kənˈdjuːs) *vb.* (*intr.;* foll. by *to*) to lead or contribute (to a result). [C15: < L *condūcere,* < *com-* together + *dūcere* to lead]

conducive (kənˈdjuːsɪv) *adj.* (when *postpositive,* foll. by *to*) contributing, leading, or tending.

conduct *n.* (ˈkɒndʌkt). **1.** behaviour. **2.** the way of managing a business, affair, etc.; handling. **3.** *Rare.* the act of leading. ~*vb.* (kənˈdʌkt). **4.** (*tr.*) to accompany and guide (people, a party, etc.) (esp. in **conducted tour**). **5.** (*tr.*) to direct (affairs, business, etc.); control. **6.** (*tr.*) to carry out; organize: *conduct a survey.* **7.** (*tr.*) to behave (oneself). **8.** to control (an orchestra, etc.) by the movements of the hands or a baton. **9.** to transmit (heat, electricity, etc.). [C15: < Med. L *conductus* escorted, < L, < *condūcere* to CONDUCE] **—conˈductible** *adj.* **—conˌductiˈbility** *n.*

conductance (kənˈdʌktəns) *n.* the ability of a system to conduct electricity, measured by the ratio of the current flowing through the system to the potential difference across it. Symbol: G

conduction (kənˈdʌkʃən) *n.* **1.** the transfer of heat or electricity through a medium. **2.** the transmission of an impulse along a nerve fibre. **3.** the act of conveying or conducting, as through a pipe. **4.** *Physics.* another name for **conductivity** (sense 1). **—conˈductional** *adj.*

conductive (kənˈdʌktɪv) *adj.* of, denoting, or having the property of conduction.

conductivity (ˌkɒndʌkˈtɪvɪtɪ) *n., pl.* **-ties. 1.** the property of transmitting heat, electricity, or sound. **2.** a measure of the ability of a substance to conduct electricity. Symbol: κ

conductor (kənˈdʌktə) *n.* **1.** an official on a bus who collects fares. **2.** a person who conducts an orchestra, choir, etc. **3.** a person who leads or guides. **4.** *U.S. & Canad.* a railway official in charge of a train. **5.** a substance, body, or system that conducts electricity, heat, etc. **6.** See **lightning conductor. —conˈductorˌship** *n.* **—conductress** (kənˈdʌktrɪs) *fem. n.*

conduit (ˈkɒndɪt, -djʊɪt) *n.* **1.** a pipe or channel for carrying a fluid. **2.** a rigid tube for carrying electrical cables. [C14: < OF, < Med. L *conductus* channel, < L *condūcere* to lead]

condyle (ˈkɒndɪl) *n.* the rounded projection on the articulating end of a bone. [C17: < L *condylus,* < Gk *kondulos*] **—ˈcondylar** *adj.*

cone (kəʊn) *n.* **1.** a geometric solid consisting of a plane base bounded by a closed curve, usually a circle or an ellipse, every point of which is joined to a fixed point lying outside the plane of the base. **2.** anything that tapers from a circular section to a point, such as a wafer shell used to contain ice cream. **3. a.** the reproductive body of conifers and related plants, made up of overlapping scales. **b.** a similar structure in horsetails, club mosses, etc. **4.** a small cone used as a temporary traffic marker on roads. **5.** any one of the cone-shaped cells in the retina of the eye, sensitive to colour and bright light. ~*vb.* **6.** (*tr.*) to shape like a cone. [C16: < L *cōnus,* < Gk *kōnus* pine cone, geometrical cone]

cone off *vb.* (*tr., adv.*) *Brit.* to close one carriageway of a motorway by placing warning cones across it.

coney (ˈkəʊnɪ) *n.* a variant spelling of **cony.**

confab (ˈkɒnfæb) *Inf.* ~*n.* **1.** a conversation. ~*vb.* **-fabbing, -fabbed. 2.** (*intr.*) to converse.

confabulate (kənˈfæbjʊˌleɪt) *vb.* (*intr.*) **1.** to talk together; chat. **2.** *Psychiatry.* to replace the gaps left by a disorder of the memory with imaginary remembered experiences consistently believed to be true. [C17: < L *cōnfābulārī,* < *fābulārī* to talk, < *fābula* a story] —**conˌfabuˈlation** *n.*

confect (kənˈfɛkt) *vb.* (*tr.*) **1.** to prepare by combining ingredients. **2.** to make; construct. [C16: < L *confectus* prepared, < *conficere,* < *com-* (intensive) + *facere* to make]

confection (kənˈfɛkʃən) *n.* **1.** the act of compounding or mixing. **2.** any sweet preparation, such as a preserve or a sweet. **3.** *Old-fashioned.* an elaborate article of clothing, esp. for women. [C14: < OF, < L *confectiō* a preparing, < *conficere;* see CONFECT]

confectioner (kənˈfɛkʃənə) *n.* a person who makes or sells sweets or confections.

confectionery (kənˈfɛkʃənərɪ) *n., pl.* **-eries. 1.** sweets and other confections collectively. **2.** the art or business of a confectioner.

confederacy (kənˈfɛdərəsɪ) *n., pl.* **-cies. 1.** a union of states, etc.; alliance; league. **2.** a combination of groups or individuals for unlawful purposes. [C14: < OF *confederacie,* < LL *confoederātiō* agreement]

confederate *n.* (kənˈfɛdərɪt). **1.** a nation, state, or individual that is part of a confederacy. **2.** someone who is part of a conspiracy. ~*adj.* (kənˈfɛdərɪt). **3.** united; allied. ~*vb.* (kənˈfɛdəˌreɪt). **4.** to form into or become part of a confederacy. [C14: < LL *confoederātus,* < *confoederāre* to unite by a league]

Confederate (kənˈfɛdərɪt) *adj.* **1.** of or supporting the **Confederate States of America,** that seceded from the Union in 1861. ~*n.* **2.** a supporter of the Confederate States.

confederation (kənˌfɛdəˈreɪʃən) *n.* **1.** the act of confederating or the state of being confederated. **2.** a loose alliance of political units. **3.** (esp. in Canada) another name for a **federation.** —**conˌfederˈationist** *n.*

confer (kənˈfɜː) *vb.* **-ferring, -ferred. 1.** (*tr.;* foll. by *on* or *upon*) to grant or bestow (an honour, gift, etc.). **2.** (*intr.*) to consult together. [C16: < L *conferre,* < *com-* together + *ferre* to bring] —**conˈferment** *or* **conˈferral** *n.* —**conˈferrable** *adj.*

conferee *or* **conferree** (ˌkɒnfɜːˈriː) *n.* **1.** a person who takes part in a conference. **2.** a person on whom an honour or gift is conferred.

conference (ˈkɒnfərəns) *n.* **1.** a meeting for consultation or discussion, esp. one with a formal agenda. **2.** an assembly of the clergy or of clergy and laity of any of certain Protestant Churches acting as representatives of their denomination. **3.** *Sport, U.S. & Canad.* a league of clubs or teams. [C16: < Med. L *conferentia,* < L *conferre* to bring together] —**conferential** (ˌkɒnfəˈrɛnʃəl) *adj.*

conference call *n.* a special telephone facility by which three or more people using conventional or cellular phones can be linked up to speak to one another.

conferencing (ˈkɒnfərənsɪŋ) *n.* a telephone facility enabling geographically separated groups of people to hold a meeting via the telephone network.

confess (kənˈfɛs) *vb.* (when *tr., may take a clause as object*) **1.** (when *intr.,* often foll. by *to*) to make an admission (of faults, crimes, etc.). **2.** (*tr.*) to admit to be true; concede. **3.** *Christianity.* to declare (one's sins) to God or to a priest as his representative, so as to obtain pardon and absolution. [C14: < OF *confesser,* < LL, < L *confessus* confessed, < *confitērī* to admit]

confessedly (kənˈfɛsɪdlɪ) *adv.* (*sentence modifier*) by admission or confession; avowedly.

confession (kənˈfɛʃən) *n.* **1.** the act of confessing. **2.** something confessed. **3.** an acknowledgment, esp. of one's faults or crimes. **4.** *Christianity.* the act of a penitent accusing himself of his sins. **5. confession of faith.** a formal public avowal of religious beliefs. **6.** a religious sect united by common beliefs. —**conˈfessionary** *adj.*

confessional (kənˈfɛʃənᵊl) *adj.* **1.** of or suited to a confession. ~*n.* **2.** *Christianity.* a small stall where a priest hears confessions.

confessor (kənˈfɛsə) *n.* **1.** *Christianity.* a priest who hears confessions and sometimes acts as a spiritual counsellor. **2.** *History.* a person who bears witness to his Christian religious faith by the holiness of his life, but does not suffer martyrdom. **3.** a person who makes a confession.

confetti (kənˈfɛtɪ) *n.* small pieces of coloured paper thrown on festive occasions, esp. at weddings. [C19: < It., pl. of *confetto,* orig., a bonbon]

confidant *or* (*fem.*) **confidante** (ˌkɒnfɪˈdænt, ˈkɒnfɪˌdænt) *n.* a person to whom private matters are confided. [C17: < F *confident,* < It. *confidente,* n. use of adj.: trustworthy]

confide (kənˈfaɪd) *vb.* **1.** (usually foll. by *in;* when *tr., may take a clause as object*) to disclose (secret or personal matters) in confidence (to). **2.** (*intr.;* foll. by *in*) to have complete trust. **3.** (*tr.*) to entrust into another's keeping. [C15: < L *confidere,* < *fīdere* to trust] —**conˈfider** *n.*

confidence (ˈkɒnfɪdəns) *n.* **1.** trust in a person or thing. **2.** belief in one's own abilities; self-assurance. **3.** trust or a trustful relationship: *take me into your confidence.* **4.** something confided; secret. **5. in confidence.** as a secret.

confidence trick *or U.S. & Canad.* **confidence game** *n.* a swindle involving money in which the victim's trust is won by the swindler.

confident (ˈkɒnfɪdənt) *adj.* **1.** (*postpositive;* foll. by *of*) having or showing certainty; sure: *confident of success.* **2.** sure of oneself. **3.** presumptuous. [C16: < L *confidens,* < *confīdere* to have complete trust in] —ˈ**confidently** *adv.*

confidential (ˌkɒnfɪˈdɛnʃəl) *adj.* **1.** spoken or given in confidence; private. **2.** entrusted with another's secret affairs: *a confidential secretary.* **3.** suggestive of intimacy: *a confidential approach.* —ˌ**confiˌdentiˈality** *n.* —ˌ**confiˈdentially** *adv.*

confiding (kənˈfaɪdɪŋ) *adj.* unsuspicious; trustful. —**conˈfidingly** *adv.* —**conˈfidingness** *n.*

configuration (kənˌfɪgjʊˈreɪʃən) *n.* **1.** the arrangement of the parts of something. **2.** the external form or outline achieved by such an arrangement. **3.** *Psychol.* the unit or pattern in perception studied by Gestalt psychologists. [C16: < LL *configūrātiō,* < *configūrāre* to model on something, < *figūrāre* to shape, fashion] —**conˌfiguˈrational** *or* **conˈfigurative** *adj.*

confine *vb.* (kənˈfaɪn). (*tr.*) **1.** to keep within bounds; limit; restrict. **2.** to restrict the free movement of: *arthritis confined him to bed.* ~*n.* (ˈkɒnfaɪn). **3.** (*often pl.*) a limit; boundary. [C16: < Med. L *confīnāre,* < L *confīnis* adjacent, < *fīnis* boundary] —**conˈfiner** *n.*

confined (kənˈfaɪnd) *adj.* **1.** enclosed; limited. **2.** in childbed; undergoing childbirth.

confinement (kənˈfaɪnmənt) *n.* **1.** the act of confining or the state of being confined. **2.** the period of the birth of a child.

confirm (kənˈfɜːm) *vb.* (*tr.*) **1.** (*may take a clause as object*) to prove to be true or valid; corroborate. **2.** (*may take a clause as object*) to assert for a further time, so as to make more definite: *he confirmed that he would appear in court.* **3.** to strengthen: *his story confirmed my doubts.* **4.** to make valid by a formal act; ratify. **5.** to administer the rite of confirmation to. [C13: < OF *confermer,* < L *confirmāre,* < *firmus* FIRM[1]] —**conˈfirmatory** *or* **conˈfirmative** *adj.*

confirmation (ˌkɒnfəˈmeɪʃən) *n.* **1.** the act of confirming. **2.** something that confirms. **3.** a rite in several Christian churches that confirms a baptized person in his faith and admits him to full participation in the church.

confirmed (kən'fɜːmd) *adj.* **1.** (*prenominal*) long-established in a habit, way of life, etc. **2.** having received the rite of confirmation.

confiscate ('kɒnfɪˌskeɪt) *vb.* (*tr.*) **1.** to seize (property), esp. for public use and esp. by way of a penalty. ~*adj.* **2.** confiscated; forfeit. [C16: < L *confiscāre* to seize for the public treasury, < *fiscus* treasury] —ˌ**confis'cation** *n.* —'**confisˌcator** *n.* —**confiscatory** (kən'fɪskətərɪ) *adj.*

Confiteor (kən'fɪtɪˌɔː) *n. R.C. Church.* a prayer consisting of a general confession of sinfulness and an entreaty for forgiveness. [C13: < L: I confess]

conflagration (ˌkɒnflə'greɪʃən) *n.* a large destructive fire. [C16: < L *conflagrātiō,* < *conflagrāre,* < *com-* (intensive) + *flagrāre* to burn]

conflate (kən'fleɪt) *vb.* (*tr.*) to combine or blend (two things, esp. two versions of a text) so as to form a whole. [C16: < L *conflāre* to blow together, < *flāre* to blow] —**con'flation** *n.*

conflict *n.* ('kɒnflɪkt). **1.** a struggle between opposing forces; battle. **2.** opposition between ideas, interests, etc.; controversy. **3.** *Psychol.* opposition between two simultaneous but incompatible wishes or drives, sometimes leading to emotional tension. ~*vb.* (kən'flɪkt). (*intr.*) **4.** to come into opposition; clash. **5.** to fight. [C15: < L *conflictus,* < *confligere* to combat, < *fligere* to strike] —**con'flicting** *adj.* —**con'flictingly** *adv.* —**con'fliction** *n.*

confluence ('kɒnflʊəns) *or* **conflux** ('kɒnflʌks) *n.* **1.** a flowing together, esp. of rivers. **2.** a gathering. —'**confluent** *adj.*

conform (kən'fɔːm) *vb.* **1.** (*intr.;* usually foll. by *to*) to comply in actions, behaviour, etc., with accepted standards. **2.** (*intr.;* usually foll. by *with*) to be in accordance: *he conforms with my idea of a teacher.* **3.** to make or become similar. **4.** (*intr.*) to comply with the practices of an established church, esp. the Church of England. [C14: < OF *conformer,* < L *confirmāre* to strengthen, < *firmāre* to make firm] —**con'former** *n.* —**con'formist** *n., adj.*

conformable (kən'fɔːməbᵊl) *adj.* **1.** corresponding in character; similar. **2.** obedient; submissive. **3.** (foll. by *to*) consistent (with). **4.** (of rock strata) lying in a parallel arrangement so that their original relative positions have remained undisturbed. —**conˌforma'bility** *n.* —**con'formably** *adv.*

conformal (kən'fɔːməl) *adj.* (of a map projection) maintaining true shape over a small area and scale in every direction. [C17: < LL *conformālis,* < L *com-* same + *forma* shape]

conformation (ˌkɒnfɔː'meɪʃən) *n.* **1.** the general shape of an object; configuration. **2.** the arrangement of the parts of an object.

conformity (kən'fɔːmɪtɪ) *or* **conformance** *n., pl.* **-ities** *or* **-ances. 1.** compliance in actions, behaviour, etc., with certain accepted standards. **2.** likeness; congruity; agreement. **3.** compliance with the practices of an established church.

confound (kən'faʊnd) *vb.* (*tr.*) **1.** to astound; bewilder. **2.** to confuse. **3.** to treat mistakenly as similar to or identical with. **4.** (kɒn'faʊnd). to curse (usually in **confound it!**). **5.** to contradict or refute (an argument, etc.). **6.** to rout or defeat (an enemy). [C13: < OF *confondre,* < L *confundere* to mingle, pour together] —**con'founder** *n.*

confounded (kən'faʊndɪd) *adj.* **1.** bewildered; confused. **2.** (*prenominal*) *Inf.* execrable; damned. —**con'foundedly** *adv.*

confraternity (ˌkɒnfrə'tɜːnɪtɪ) *n., pl.* **-ties.** a group of men united for some particular purpose, esp. Christian laymen organized for religious or charitable service; brotherhood. [C15: < Med. L *confrāternitās,* ult. < L *frāter* brother]

confrère ('kɒnfrɛə) *n.* a fellow member of a profession, etc. [C15: < OF, < Med. L *confrāter*]

confront (kən'frʌnt) *vb.* (*tr.*) **1.** (usually foll. by *with*) to present (with something), esp. in order to accuse or criticize. **2.** to face boldly; oppose in hostility. **3.** to be face to face with. [C16: < Med. L *confrontārī,* < *frons* forehead] —**confrontation** (ˌkɒnfrʌn'teɪʃən) *n.* —ˌ**confron'tational** *adj.*

Confucian (kən'fjuːʃən) *adj.* **1.** of or relating to the doctrines of Confucius. ~*n.* **2.** a follower of Confucius.

Confucianism (kən'fjuːʃəˌnɪzəm) *n.* the ethical system of Confucius (551–479 B.C.), Chinese philosopher, emphasizing moral order, the virtue of China's ancient rules, and gentlemanly education. —**Con'fucianist** *n.*

confuse (kən'fjuːz) *vb.* (*tr.*) **1.** to bewilder; perplex. **2.** to mix up (things, ideas, etc.). **3.** to make unclear: *he confused his talk with irrelevant details.* **4.** to mistake (one thing) for another. **5.** to disconcert; embarrass. **6.** to cause to become disordered: *the enemy ranks were confused by gas.* [C18: back formation < *confused,* < L *confūsus,* < *confundere* to pour together] —**con'fusable** *adj.* —**confusedly** (kən'fjuːzɪdlɪ, -'fjuːzd-) *adv.* —**con'fusing** *adj.* —**con'fusingly** *adv.*

confusion (kən'fjuːʒən) *n.* **1.** the act of confusing or the state of being confused. **2.** disorder. **3.** bewilderment; perplexity. **4.** lack of clarity. **5.** embarrassment; abashment.

confute (kən'fjuːt) *vb.* (*tr.*) to prove (a person or thing) wrong, invalid, or mistaken; disprove. [C16: < L *confūtāre* to check, silence] —**con'futable** *adj.* —**confutation** (ˌkɒnfjʊ'teɪʃən) *n.*

conga ('kɒŋgə) *n.* **1.** a Latin American dance of three steps and a kick to each bar, performed by a number of people in single file. **2.** Also called: **conga drum.** a large tubular bass drum, usually played with the hands. ~*vb.* **-gaing, -gaed. 3.** (*intr.*) to perform this dance. [C20: < American Sp., fem. of *congo* belonging to the *Congo*]

congé ('kɒnʒeɪ) *n.* **1.** permission to depart or dismissal, esp. when formal. **2.** a farewell. [C16: < OF *congié,* < L *commeātus* leave of absence, < *meāre* to go]

congeal (kən'dʒiːl) *vb.* **1.** to change or cause to change from a soft or fluid state to a firm state. **2.** to form or cause to form into a coagulated mass; jell. [C14: < OF *congeler,* < L *congelāre,* < *com-* together + *gelāre* to freeze] —**con'gealable** *adj.* —**con'gealment** *n.*

congelation (ˌkɒndʒɪ'leɪʃən) *n.* **1.** the process of congealing. **2.** something formed by this process.

congener (kən'dʒiːnə, 'kɒndʒɪnə) *n.* a member of a class, group, or other category, esp. any animal of a specified genus. [C18: < L, < *com-* same + *genus* kind]

congenial (kən'dʒiːnjəl) *adj.* **1.** friendly, pleasant, or agreeable: *a congenial atmosphere to work in.* **2.** having a similar disposition, tastes, etc.; compatible. [C17: < CON- (same) + GENIAL¹] —**congeniality** (kənˌdʒiːnɪ'ælɪtɪ) *n.*

congenital (kən'dʒɛnɪtᵊl) *adj.* **1.** denoting any nonhereditary condition, esp. an abnormal condition, existing at birth: *congenital blindness.* **2.** *Inf.* complete, as if from birth: *a congenital idiot.* [C18: < L *congenitus,* < *genitus* born, < *gignere* to bear] —**con'genitally** *adv.*

conger ('kɒŋgə) *n.* a large marine eel occurring in temperate and tropical coastal waters. [C14: < OF *congre,* < L *conger,* < Gk *gongros*]

congeries (kɒn'dʒɪəriːz) *n.* (*functioning as sing. or pl.*) a collection; mass; heap. [C17: < L, < *congerere* to pile up, < *gerere* to carry]

congest (kən'dʒɛst) *vb.* **1.** to crowd or become crowded to excess; overfill. **2.** to clog (an organ) with blood or (of an organ) to become clogged with blood. **3.** (*tr.; usually passive*) to block (the nose) with mucus. [C16: < L *congestus,* < *congerere;* see CONGERIES] —**con'gestion** *n.*

conglomerate *n.* (kən'glɒmərɪt). **1.** a thing composed of heterogeneous elements. **2.** any coarse-grained sedimentary rock consisting of rounded fragments of rock embedded in a finer matrix. **3.** a large corporation consisting of a group of companies dealing in widely diversified goods, services, etc. ~*vb.* (kən'glɒməˌreɪt). **4.** to form into a mass. ~*adj.* (kən'glɒmərɪt). **5.** made up of heterogeneous elements. **6.** (of sedimentary rocks) consisting of rounded fragments within a finer matrix. [C16: < L *conglomerāre* to roll up, < *glomerāre*, < *glomus* ball of thread] —**con͵glomer'ation** *n.*

congrats (kən'græts) *pl. n., sentence substitute.* informal shortened form of **congratulations.**

congratulate (kən'grætjʊ͵leɪt) *vb.* (*tr.*) **1.** (usually foll. by *on*) to communicate pleasure, approval, or praise to; compliment. **2.** (often foll. by *on*) to consider (oneself) clever or fortunate (as a result of): *she congratulated herself on her tact.* **3.** *Obs.* to greet; salute. [C16: < L *congrātulārī*, < *grātulārī* to rejoice, < *grātus* pleasing] —**con͵gratu'lation** *n.* —**con'gratulatory** *or* **con'gratulative** *adj.*

congratulations (kən͵grætjʊ'leɪʃənz) *pl. n., sentence substitute.* expressions of pleasure or joy on another's success, good fortune, etc.

congregate ('kɒŋgrɪ͵geɪt) *vb.* to collect together in a body or crowd; assemble. [C15: < L *congregāre* to collect into a flock, < *grex* flock]

congregation (͵kɒŋgrɪ'geɪʃən) *n.* **1.** a group of persons gathered for worship, prayer, etc., esp. in a church. **2.** the act of congregating together. **3.** a group collected together; assemblage. **4.** the group of persons habitually attending a given church, chapel, etc. **5.** *R.C. Church.* **a.** a society of persons who follow a common rule of life but who are bound only by simple vows. **b.** an administrative subdivision of the papal curia. **6.** *Chiefly Brit.* an assembly of senior members of a university.

congregational (͵kɒŋgrɪ'geɪʃənᵊl) *adj.* **1.** of or relating to a congregation. **2.** (*usually cap.*) of or denoting Congregationalism.

Congregationalism (͵kɒŋgrɪ'geɪʃənə͵lɪzəm) *n.* a system of Christian doctrines and ecclesiastical government in which each congregation is self-governing. —͵**Congre'gationalist** *adj., n.*

congress ('kɒŋgrɛs) *n.* **1.** a meeting or conference, esp. of representatives of sovereign states. **2.** a national legislative assembly. **3.** a society or association. [C16: < L *congressus*, < *congredī*, < *com-* together + *gradī* to walk]

Congress ('kɒŋgrɛs) *n.* **1.** the bicameral federal legislature of the U.S., consisting of the House of Representatives and the Senate. **2.** Also called: **Congress Party.** (in India) a major political party. —**Con'gressional** *adj.*

congressional (kən'grɛʃənᵊl) *adj.* of or relating to a congress. —**con'gressionalist** *n.*

Congressman ('kɒŋgrɛsmən) *or* (*fem.*) **Congresswoman** *n., pl.* **-men** *or* **-women.** (in the U.S.) a member of Congress, esp. of the House of Representatives.

congruence ('kɒŋgrʊəns) *or* **congruency** *n.* **1.** the quality or state of corresponding, agreeing, or being congruent. **2.** *Maths.* the relationship between two integers, *x* and *y*, such that their difference, with respect to another integer called the modulus, *n*, is a multiple of the modulus.

congruent ('kɒŋgrʊənt) *adj.* **1.** agreeing; corresponding. **2.** having identical shapes so that all parts correspond: *congruent triangles.* **3.** of or concerning two integers related by a congruence. [C15: < L *congruere* to agree]

congruous ('kɒŋgrʊəs) *adj.* **1.** corresponding or agreeing. **2.** appropriate. [C16: < L *congruus*; see CONGRUENT] —**congruity** (kən'gruːɪtɪ) *n.*

conic ('kɒnɪk) *adj. also* **conical. 1. a.** having the shape of a cone. **b.** of a cone. ~*n.* **2.** another name for **conic section.** —'**conically** *adv.*

conics ('kɒnɪks) *n.* (*functioning as sing.*) the geometry of the parabola, ellipse, and hyperbola.

conic section *n.* one of a group of curves formed by the intersection of a plane and a right circular cone. It is either a circle, ellipse, parabola, or hyperbola.

conidium (kəʊ'nɪdɪəm) *n., pl.* **-nidia** (-'nɪdɪə). an asexual spore formed at the tip of a specialized hypha in fungi such as *Penicillium.* [C19: < NL, < Gk *konis* dust + -IUM]

conifer ('kəʊnɪfə, 'kɒn-) *n.* any tree or shrub of the group *Coniferae*, typically bearing cones and evergreen leaves. The group includes the pines, spruces, firs, larches, etc. [C19: < L, < *cōnus* CONE + *ferre* to bear] —**co'niferous** *adj.*

conj. *abbrev. for:* **1.** conjugation. **2.** conjunction.

conjectural (kən'dʒɛktʃərəl) *adj.* involving or inclined to conjecture. —**con'jecturally** *adv.*

conjecture (kən'dʒɛktʃə) *n.* **1.** the formation of conclusions from incomplete evidence; guess. **2.** the conclusion so formed. ~*vb.* **3.** to infer or arrive at (an opinion, conclusion, etc.) from incomplete evidence. [C14: < L *conjectūra*, < *conjicere* to throw together, < *jacere* to throw] —**con'jecturable** *adj.*

conjoin (kən'dʒɔɪn) *vb.* to join or become joined. [C14: < OF *conjoindre*, < L *conjungere*, < *jungere* to JOIN] —**con'joiner** *n.*

conjoint (kən'dʒɔɪnt) *adj.* united, joint, or associated. —**con'jointly** *adv.*

conjugal ('kɒndʒʊgᵊl) *adj.* of or relating to marriage or the relationship between husband and wife: *conjugal rights.* [C16: < L *conjugālis*, < *conjunx* wife or husband] —**conjugality** (͵kɒndʒʊ'gælɪtɪ) *n.* —'**conjugally** *adv.*

conjugate *vb.* ('kɒndʒʊ͵geɪt). **1.** (*tr.*) *Grammar.* to state or set out the conjugation of (a verb). **2.** (*intr.*) (of a verb) to undergo inflection according to a specific set of rules. **3.** (*intr.*) *Biol.* to undergo conjugation. **4.** (*tr.*) *Obs.* to join together, esp. in marriage. ~*adj.* ('kɒndʒʊgɪt, -͵geɪt). **5.** joined together in pairs. **6.** *Maths.* **a.** (of two angles) having a sum of 360°. **b.** (of two complex numbers) differing only in the sign of the imaginary part as $4 + 3i$ and $4 - 3i$. **7.** *Chem.* of the state of equilibrium in which two liquids can exist as separate phases that are both solutions. **8.** *Chem.* (of acids and bases) related by loss or gain of a proton. **9.** (of a compound leaf) having one pair of leaflets. **10.** (of words) cognate; related in origin. ~*n.* ('kɒndʒʊgɪt). **11.** one of a pair or set of conjugate substances, values, quantities, words, etc. [C15: < L *conjugāre*, < *com-* together + *jugāre* to connect, < *jugum* a yoke] —'**conju͵gative** *adj.* —'**conju͵gator** *n.*

conjugation (͵kɒndʒʊ'geɪʃən) *n.* **1.** *Grammar.* **a.** inflection of a verb for person, number, tense, voice, mood, etc. **b.** the complete set of the inflections of a given verb. **2.** a joining. **3.** a type of sexual reproduction in ciliate protozoans involving the temporary union of two individuals and the subsequent migration and fusion of the gametic nuclei. **4.** the union of gametes, as in some fungi. **5.** the pairing of chromosomes in the early phase of a meiotic division. —͵**conju'gational** *adj.*

conjunct ('kɒndʒʌŋkt, kən'dʒʌŋkt) *n. Logic.* one of the propositions or formulas in a conjunction.

conjunction (kən'dʒʌŋkʃən) *n.* **1.** the act of joining together; union. **2.** simultaneous occurrence of events; coincidence. **3.** any word or group of words, other than a relative pronoun, that connects words, phrases, or clauses; for example *and* and *while.* **4.** *Astron.* **a.** the position of a planet when it is in line with the sun as seen from the earth. **b.** the apparent proximity or coincidence of two celestial bodies on the celestial sphere. **5.** *Logic.* **a.** the operator that forms a compound sentence from two given sentences, and corresponds to the English *and.* **b.** a sentence so formed: it is true only when both the component sentences are true. **c.** the relation between such sentences. —**con'junctional** *adj.*

conjunctiva (͵kɒndʒʌŋk'taɪvə) *n., pl.* **-vas** *or* **-vae** (-viː). the delicate mucous membrane that covers the eyeball and the under surface of the eyelid. [C16: < NL *membrāna conjunctīva* the conjunctive membrane] —͵**conjunc'tival** *adj.*

conjunctive (kən'dʒʌŋktɪv) *adj.* **1.** joining; connective. **2.** joined. **3.** of or relating to conjunctions. ~*n.* **4.** a less common word for **conjunction** (sense 3). [C15: < LL *conjunctīvus*, < L *conjungere* to CONJOIN]

conjunctivitis (kən͵dʒʌŋktɪ'vaɪtɪs) *n.* inflammation of the conjunctiva.

conjuncture (kən'dʒʌŋktʃə) *n.* a combination of events, esp. a critical one.

conjuration (͵kɒndʒʊ'reɪʃən) *n.* **1.** a magic spell;

incantation. **2.** a less common word for **conjuring. 3.** *Arch.* supplication; entreaty.

conjure ('kʌndʒə) *vb.* **1.** (*intr.*) to practise conjuring. **2.** (*intr.*) to call upon supposed supernatural forces by spells and incantations. **3.** (kən'dʒʊə). (*tr.*) to appeal earnestly to: *I conjure you to help me.* **4. a name to conjure with. a.** a person thought to have great power or influence. **b.** any name that excites the imagination. [C13: < OF *conjurer* to plot, < L *conjūrāre* to swear together]

conjurer *or* **conjuror** ('kʌndʒərə) *n.* **1.** a person who practises conjuring, esp. for people's entertainment. **2.** a sorcerer.

conjure up *vb.* (*tr., adv.*) **1.** to present to the mind; evoke or imagine: *he conjured up a picture of his childhood.* **2.** to call up or command (a spirit or devil) by an incantation.

conjuring ('kʌndʒərɪŋ) *n.* **1.** the performance of tricks that appear to defy natural laws. *~adj.* **2.** denoting or of such tricks or entertainment.

conk (kɒŋk) *Sl.* *~vb.* **1.** to strike (someone) a blow, esp. on the head or nose. *~n.* **2.** a punch or blow, esp. on the head or nose. **3.** the head or nose. [C19: prob. changed < CONCH]

conker ('kɒŋkə) *n.* an informal name for the **horse chestnut** (sense 2).

conkers ('kɒŋkəz) *n.* (*functioning as sing.*) *Brit.* a game in which a player swings a horse chestnut (conker), threaded onto a string, against that of another player to try to break it. [C19: < dialect *conker* snail shell, orig. used in the game]

conk out *vb.* (*intr., adv.*) *Inf.* **1.** (of machines, cars, etc.) to fail suddenly. **2.** to tire suddenly or collapse. [C20: < ?]

con man *n. Inf.* a person who swindles another by means of a confidence trick. More formal term: **confidence man.**

con moto (kɒn 'məʊtəʊ) *adj., adv. Music.* (to be performed) in a brisk or lively manner. [It., lit.: with movement]

conn (kɒn) *vb., n.* a variant spelling (esp. U.S.) of **con³**.

connate ('kɒneɪt) *adj.* **1.** existing from birth; congenital or innate. **2.** allied in nature or origin. **3.** *Biol.* (of similar parts or organs) closely joined or united by growth. **4.** *Geol.* (of fluids) produced at the same time as the rocks surrounding them; *connate water.* [C17: < LL *connātus* born at the same time]

connect (kə'nɛkt) *vb.* **1.** to link or be linked. **2.** (*tr.*) to associate: *I connect him with my childhood.* **3.** (*tr.*) to establish telephone communications with or between. **4.** (*intr.*) to be meaningful or meaningfully related. **5.** (*intr.*) (of two public vehicles, such as trains or buses) to have the arrival of one timed to occur just before the departure of the other, for the convenient transfer of passengers. **6.** (*intr.*) *Inf.* to hit, punch, kick, etc., solidly. [C17: < L *connectere* to bind together, < *nectere* to tie] **—con'nectible** *or* **con'nectable** *adj.* **—con'nector** *or* **con'necter** *n.*

connecting rod *n.* **1.** a rod or bar for transmitting motion, esp. one that connects a rotating part to a reciprocating part. **2.** such a rod that connects the piston to the crankshaft in an internal-combustion engine.

connection *or* **connexion** (kə'nɛkʃən) *n.* **1.** the act of connecting; union. **2.** something that connects or relates; link or bond. **3.** a relationship or association. **4.** logical sequence in thought or expression; coherence. **5.** the relation of a word or phrase to its context: *in this connection the word has no political significance.* **6.** (*often pl.*) an acquaintance, esp. one who is influential. **7.** a relative, esp. if distant and related by marriage. **8. a.** an opportunity to transfer from one train, bus, etc., to another. **b.** the vehicle scheduled to provide such an opportunity. **9.** a link, usually a wire or metallic strip, between two components in an electric circuit. **10.** a communications link, esp. by telephone. **11.** *Sl.* a supplier of illegal drugs, such as heroin. **12.** *Rare.* sexual intercourse. **—con'nectional** *or* **con'nexional** *adj.*

connective (kə'nɛktɪv) *adj.* **1.** connecting. *~n.* **2.** a thing that connects. **3.** *Grammar, logic.* **a.** any word that connects phrases, clauses, or individual words. **b.** a symbol used in a formal language in the construction of compound sentences, corresponding to terms such as *or, and,* etc., in ordinary speech. **4.** *Bot.* the tissue of a stamen that connects the two lobes of the anther.

connective tissue *n.* an animal tissue that supports organs, fills the spaces between them, and forms tendons and ligaments.

conning tower ('kɒnɪŋ) *n.* **1.** a superstructure of a submarine, used as the bridge when the vessel is on the surface. **2.** the armoured pilot house of a warship. [C19: see CON³]

connivance (kə'naɪvəns) *n.* **1.** the act or fact of conniving. **2.** *Law.* the tacit encouragement of or assent to another's wrongdoing.

connive (kə'naɪv) *vb.* (*intr.*) **1.** to plot together; conspire. **2.** (foll. by *at*) *Law.* to give assent or encouragement (to the commission of a wrong). [C17: < F *conniver,* < L *connīvēre* to blink, hence, leave uncensured] **—con'niver** *n.*

connoisseur (ˌkɒnɪ'sɜː) *n.* a person with special knowledge or appreciation of a field, esp. in the arts. [C18: < F, < OF *conoiseor,* < *connoistre* to know, < L *cognōscere*] **—ˌconnois'seurship** *n.*

connotation (ˌkɒnə'teɪʃən) *n.* **1.** an association or idea suggested by a word or phrase. **2.** the act of connoting. **3.** *Logic.* the characteristic or set of characteristics that determines to which object the common name properly applies. In traditional logic synonymous with **intension. —connotative** ('kɒnəˌteɪtɪv, kə'nəʊtə-) *or* **con'notive** *adj.*

connote (kɒ'nəʊt) *vb.* (*tr.; often takes a clause as object*) **1.** (of a word, phrase, etc.) to imply or suggest (associations or ideas) other than the literal meaning: *the word "maiden" connotes modesty.* **2.** to involve as a consequence or condition. [C17: < Med. L *connotāre,* < L *notāre* to mark, note, < *nota* sign, note]

connubial (kə'njuːbɪəl) *adj.* of or relating to marriage: *connubial bliss.* [C17: < L *cōnūbiālis,* < *cōnūbium* marriage] **—conˌnubi'ality** *n.*

conoid ('kəʊnɔɪd) *n.* **1.** a cone-shaped object. *~adj. also* **conoidal** (kəʊ'nɔɪdᵊl). **2.** cone-shaped. [C17: < Gk *kōnoeidēs,* < *kōnos* CONE] **—co'noidally** *adv.*

conquer ('kɒŋkə) *vb.* **1.** to overcome (an enemy, army, etc.); defeat. **2.** to overcome (an obstacle, desire, etc.); surmount. **3.** (*tr.*) to gain possession or control of as by force or war; win. [C13: < OF *conquerre,* < Vulgar L *conquērere* (unattested) to obtain, < L *conquīrere* to search for, < *quaerere* to seek] **—'conquerable** *adj.* **—'conquering** *adj.* **—'conqueror** *n.*

Conqueror ('kɒŋkərə) *n.* **William the.** epithet of William I, duke of Normandy, and king of England (1066–87).

conquest ('kɒnkwɛst) *n.* **1.** the act of conquering or the state of having been conquered; victory. **2.** a person, thing, etc., that has been conquered. **3.** a person, whose compliance, love, etc., has been won. [C13: < OF *conqueste,* < Vulgar L *conquēsta* (unattested), < L *conquīsīta,* fem. p.p. of *conquīrere;* see CONQUER]

Conquest ('kɒnkwɛst) *n.* **the.** See **Norman Conquest.**

conquistador (kɒn'kwɪstəˌdɔː) *n., pl.* **-dors** *or* **conquistadores** (kɒnˌkwɪstə'dɔːrɛs). an adventurer or conqueror, esp. one of the Spanish conquerors of the New World in the 16th century. [C19: < Sp., < *conquistar* to conquer]

cons. *abbrev. for:* **1.** consecrated. **2.** consigned. **3.** consignment. **4.** consolidated. **5.** consonant. **6.** constitutional. **7.** construction.

Cons. *abbrev. for* Conservative.

consanguinity (ˌkɒnsæŋ'gwɪnɪtɪ) *n.* **1.** relationship by blood; kinship. **2.** close affinity or connection. [C14: see CON-, SANGUINE] **—ˌconsan'guineous** *or* **con'sanguine** *adj.*

conscience ('kɒnʃəns) *n.* **1.** the sense of right and wrong that governs a person's thoughts and actions. **2.** conscientiousness; diligence. **3.** a feeling of guilt or anxiety: *he has a conscience about his unkind action.* **4. in (all) conscience. a.**

with regard to truth and justice. **b.** certainly. **5. on one's conscience.** causing feelings of guilt or remorse. [C13: < OF, < L *conscientia* knowledge, < *conscīre* to know; see CONSCIOUS]

conscience clause *n.* a clause in a law or contract exempting persons with moral scruples.

conscience money *n.* money paid voluntarily to compensate for dishonesty, esp. for taxes formerly evaded.

conscience-stricken *adj.* feeling anxious or guilty. Also: **conscience-smitten.**

conscientious (ˌkɒnʃɪˈɛnʃəs) *adj.* **1.** involving or taking great care; painstaking. **2.** governed by or done according to conscience. —ˌ**consci'entiously** *adv.* —ˌ**consci'entiousness** *n.*

conscientious objector *n.* a person who refuses to serve in the armed forces on the grounds of conscience.

conscious (ˈkɒnʃəs) *adj.* **1.** alert and awake. **2.** aware of one's surroundings, one's own motivations and thoughts, etc. **3. a.** aware (of) and giving value and emphasis (to a particular fact): *I am conscious of your great kindness to me.* **b.** (*in combination*): *clothes-conscious.* **4.** deliberate or intended: *a conscious effort; conscious rudeness.* **5. a.** denoting a part of the human mind that is aware of a person's self, environment, and mental activity and that to a certain extent determines his choices of action. **b.** (*as n.*): *the conscious is only a small part of the mind.* [C17: < L *conscius* sharing knowledge, < *com-* with + *scīre* to know] —'**consciously** *adv.* —'**consciousness** *n.*

conscript *n.* (ˈkɒnskrɪpt). **1. a.** a person who is enrolled for compulsory military service. **b.** (*as modifier*): *a conscript army.* ~*vb.* (kənˈskrɪpt). **2.** (*tr.*) to enrol (youths, civilians, etc.) for compulsory military service. [C15: < L *conscrīptus,* p.p. of *conscrībere* to enrol, < *scrībere* to write]

conscription (kənˈskrɪpʃən) *n.* compulsory military service.

consecrate (ˈkɒnsɪˌkreɪt) *vb.* (*tr.*) **1.** to make or declare sacred or holy. **2.** to dedicate (one's life, time, etc.) to a specific purpose. **3.** *Christianity.* to sanctify (bread and wine) for the Eucharist to be received as the body and blood of Christ. **4.** to cause to be respected or revered: *time has consecrated this custom.* [C15: < L *consecrāre,* < *com-* (intensive) + *sacrāre* to devote, < *sacer* sacred] —ˌ**conse'cration** *n.* —'**conseˌcrator** *n.* —ˌ**conse'cratory** *adj.*

Consecration (ˌkɒnsɪˈkreɪʃən) *n. R.C. Church.* the part of the Mass after the sermon in which the bread and wine to be used in the Mass are ritually offered to God.

consecutive (kənˈsɛkjʊtɪv) *adj.* **1.** (of a narrative, account, etc.) following chronological sequence. **2.** following one another without interruption; successive. **3.** characterized by logical sequence. **4.** *Grammar.* expressing consequence or result: *consecutive clauses.* **5.** *Music.* another word for **parallel** (sense 3). [C17: < F *consécutif,* < L *consecūtus,* < *consequī* to pursue] —**con'secutively** *adv.* —**con'secutiveness** *n.*

consensual (kənˈsɛnsjʊəl) *adj.* **1.** *Law.* (of a contract, etc.) existing by consent. **2.** (of reflex actions of the body) responding to stimulation of another part. —**con'sensually** *adv.*

consensus (kənˈsɛnsəs) *n.* general or widespread agreement (esp. in **consensus of opinion**). [C19: < L, < *consentīre*; see CONSENT]

▷ **Usage.** Since *consensus* refers to a collective opinion, the words *of opinion* in the phrase *consensus of opinion* are redundant and are therefore avoided in careful usage.

consent (kənˈsɛnt) *vb.* **1.** to give assent or permission; agree. ~*n.* **2.** acquiescence to or acceptance of something done or planned by another. **3.** harmony in opinion; agreement (esp. in **with one consent**). [C13: < OF *consentir,* < L *consentīre* to agree, < *sentīre* to feel] —**con'senting** *adj.*

consequence (ˈkɒnsɪkwəns) *n.* **1.** a result or effect. **2.** an unpleasant result (esp. in **take the consequences**). **3.** an inference reached by reasoning; conclusion. **4.** significance or importance: *it's of no consequence; a man of consequence.* **5. in consequence.** as a result.

consequent (ˈkɒnsɪkwənt) *adj.* **1.** following as an effect. **2.** following as a logical conclusion. **3.** (of a river) flowing in the direction of the original slope of the land. ~*n.* **4.** something that follows something else, esp. as a result. **5.** *Logic.* the resultant clause in a conditional sentence. [C15: < L *consequēns* following closely, < *consequī* to pursue]

▷ **Usage.** See at **consequential.**

consequential (ˌkɒnsɪˈkwɛnʃəl) *adj.* **1.** important or significant. **2.** self-important. **3.** following as a consequence, esp. indirectly: *consequential loss.* —ˌ**conseˌquenti'ality** *n.* —ˌ**conse'quentially** *adv.*

▷ **Usage.** Although both *consequential* and *consequent* can refer to that which follows as a result, *consequent* is more frequently used in this sense in general contexts, while *consequential* is often used in commercial or legal contexts.

consequently (ˈkɒnsɪkwəntlɪ) *adv., sentence connector.* as a result or effect; therefore; hence.

conservancy (kənˈsɜːvənsɪ) *n., pl.* **-cies. 1.** (in Britain) a court or commission with jurisdiction over a river, port, area of countryside, etc. **2.** another word for **conservation** (sense 2).

conservation (ˌkɒnsəˈveɪʃən) *n.* **1.** the act of conserving or keeping from change, loss, injury, etc. **2. a.** protection, preservation, and careful management of natural resources. **b.** (*as modifier*): *a conservation area.* **3.** *Physics, etc.* the preservation of a specified aspect or value of a system, as in **conservation of charge, conservation of momentum, conservation of parity.** —ˌ**conser'vational** *adj.* —ˌ**conser'vationist** *n.*

conservation of energy *n.* the principle that the total energy of any isolated system is constant and independent of any changes occurring within the system.

conservation of mass *n.* the principle that the total mass of any isolated system is constant and is independent of any chemical and physical changes taking place within the system.

conservatism (kənˈsɜːvəˌtɪzəm) *n.* **1.** opposition to change and innovation. **2.** a political philosophy advocating the preservation of the best of the established order in society.

conservative (kənˈsɜːvətɪv) *adj.* **1.** favouring the preservation of established customs, values, etc., and opposing innovation. **2.** of conservatism. **3.** moderate or cautious: *a conservative estimate.* **4.** conventional in style: *a conservative suit.* ~*n.* **5.** a person who is reluctant to change or consider new ideas; conformist. **6.** a supporter of conservatism. —**con'servatively** *adv.* —**con'servativeness** *n.*

Conservative (kənˈsɜːvətɪv) (in Britain and elsewhere) ~*adj.* **1.** of, supporting, or relating to a Conservative Party. **2.** (in Canada) of, supporting, or relating to the Progressive Conservative Party. **3.** of, relating to, or characterizing Conservative Judaism. ~*n.* **4.** a supporter or member of a Conservative Party, or, (in Canada) of the Progressive Conservative Party.

Conservative Judaism *n.* a movement rejecting extreme change and advocating moderate relaxations of traditional Jewish law.

Conservative Party *n.* **1.** (in Britain) the major right-wing party, which developed from the Tories in the 1830s. It advocates a mixed economy, and encourages property owning and free enterprise. **2.** (in Canada) short for Progressive Conservative Party. **3.** (in other countries) any of various political parties generally opposing change.

conservatoire (kənˈsɜːvəˌtwɑː) *n.* an institution or school for instruction in music. Also called: **conservatory.** [C18: < F: CONSERVATORY]

conservator (ˈkɒnsəˌveɪtə, kənˈsɜːvə-) *n.* a custodian, guardian, or protector.

conservatorium (kənˌsɜːvəˈtɔːrɪəm) *n. Austral.* the usual term for **conservatoire.**

conservatory (kənˈsɜːvətrɪ) *n., pl.* **-tories.** **1.** a greenhouse, esp. one attached to a house. **2.** another word for **conservatoire.**

conserve *vb.* (kənˈsɜːv). (*tr.*) **1.** to keep or protect from harm, decay, loss, etc. **2.** to preserve (a foodstuff, esp. fruit) with sugar. ~*n.* (ˈkɒnsɜːv, kənˈsɜːv). **3.** a preparation similar to jam but containing whole pieces of fruit. [(vb.) C14: < L *conservāre* to keep safe, < *servāre* to save; (n.) C14: < Med. L *conserva,* < L *conservāre*]

consider (kənˈsɪdə) *vb.* (*mainly tr.*) **1.** (*also intr.*) to think carefully about (a problem, decision, etc.). **2.** (*may take a clause as object*) to judge; deem: *I consider him a fool.* **3.** to have regard for: *consider your mother's feelings.* **4.** to look at: *he considered her face.* **5.** (*may take a clause as object*) to bear in mind: *when buying a car consider this make.* **6.** to describe or discuss. [C14: < L *consīderāre* to inspect closely]

considerable (kənˈsɪdərəbᵊl) *adj.* **1.** large enough to reckon with: *a considerable quantity.* **2.** a lot of; much: *he had considerable courage.* **3.** worthy of respect: *a considerable man in the scientific world.* —**conˈsiderably** *adv.*

considerate (kənˈsɪdərɪt) *adj.* **1.** thoughtful towards other people; kind. **2.** *Rare.* carefully thought out; considered. —**conˈsiderately** *adv.*

consideration (kənˌsɪdəˈreɪʃən) *n.* **1.** deliberation; contemplation. **2. take into consideration.** to bear in mind; consider. **3. under consideration.** being currently discussed. **4.** a fact to be taken into account when making a judgment or decision. **5.** thoughtfulness for other people; kindness. **6.** payment for a service. **7.** thought resulting from deliberation; opinion. **8.** *Law.* the promise, object, etc., given by one party to persuade another to enter into a contract. **9.** esteem. **10. in consideration of. a.** because of. **b.** in return for.

considered (kənˈsɪdəd) *adj.* **1.** presented or thought out with care: *a considered opinion.* **2.** (*qualified by a preceding adverb*) esteemed: *highly considered.*

considering (kənˈsɪdərɪŋ) *prep.* **1.** in view of. ~*adv.* **2.** *Inf.* all in all; taking into account the circumstances: *it's not bad considering.* ~*conj.* **3.** (*subordinating*) in view of the fact that.

consign (kənˈsaɪn) *vb.* (*mainly tr.*) **1.** to give into the care or charge of; entrust. **2.** to commit irrevocably: *he consigned the papers to the flames.* **3.** to commit: *to consign someone to jail.* **4.** to address or deliver (goods): *it was consigned to his London address.* [C15: < OF *consigner,* < L *consignāre* to put one's seal to, sign, < *signum* mark] —**conˈsignable** *adj.* —ˌ**consignˈee** *n.* —**conˈsignor** *or* **conˈsigner** *n.*

consignment (kənˈsaɪnmənt) *n.* **1.** the act of consigning; commitment. **2.** a shipment of goods consigned. **3. on consignment.** for payment by the consignee after sale.

consist (kənˈsɪst) *vb.* (*intr.*) **1.** (foll. by *of* or *in*) to be composed (of). **2.** (foll. by *in* or *of*) to have its existence (in): *his religion consists only in going to church.* **3.** to be consistent; accord. [C16: < L *consistere* to stand firm, < *sistere* to stand]

consistency (kənˈsɪstənsɪ) *or* **consistence** *n., pl.* **-encies** *or* **-ences.** **1.** agreement or accordance. **2.** degree of viscosity or firmness. **3.** the state or quality of holding or sticking together and retaining shape. **4.** conformity with previous attitudes, behaviour, practice, etc.

consistent (kənˈsɪstənt) *adj.* **1.** (usually foll. by *with*) showing consistency or harmony. **2.** steady; even: *consistent growth.* **3.** *Logic.* (of a logical system) constituted so that the propositions deduced from different axioms of the system do not contradict each other. —**conˈsistently** *adv.*

consistory (kənˈsɪstərɪ) *n., pl.* **-ries.** **1.** *Church of England.* the court of a diocese (other than Canterbury) administering ecclesiastical law. **2.** *R.C. Church.* an assembly of the cardinals and the pope. **3.** (in certain Reformed Churches) the governing body of a local congregation. **4.** *Arch.* a council. [C14: < OF, < Med. L *consistōrium* ecclesiastical tribunal, ult. < L *consistere* to stand still] —**consistorial** (ˌkɒnsɪˈstɔːrɪəl) *adj.*

consolation (ˌkɒnsəˈleɪʃən) *n.* **1.** the act of consoling or state of being consoled. **2.** a person or thing that is a comfort in a time of grief, disappointment, etc. —**consolatory** (kənˈsɒlətərɪ) *adj.*

consolation prize *n.* a prize given to console a loser of a game.

console[1] (kənˈsəʊl) *vb.* to serve as a comfort to (someone) in disappointment, sadness, etc. [C17: < L *consōlārī,* < *sōlārī* to comfort] —**conˈsolable** *adj.* —**conˈsoler** *n.* —**conˈsolingly** *adv.*

console[2] (ˈkɒnsəʊl) *n.* **1.** an ornamental bracket used to support a wall fixture, etc. **2.** the part of an organ comprising the manuals, pedals, stops, etc. **3.** a desk or table on which the controls of an electronic system are mounted. **4.** a cabinet for a television, etc., designed to stand on the floor. **5.** See **console table.** [C18: < F, < OF *consolateur* one that provides support; see CONSOLE[1]]

console table (ˈkɒnsəʊl) *n.* a table with one or more curved legs of bracket-like construction, designed to stand against a wall.

consolidate (kənˈsɒlɪˌdeɪt) *vb.* **1.** to form or cause to form into a whole. **2.** to make or become stronger or more stable. **3.** *Mil.* to strengthen one's control over (a situation, area, etc.). [C16: < L *consolidare* to make firm, < *solidus* strong] —**conˌsoliˈdation** *n.* —**conˈsoliˌdator** *n.*

consolidated fund *n. Brit.* a fund maintained from tax revenue to meet standing charges, esp. national debt interest.

consols (ˈkɒnsɒlz, kənˈsɒlz) *pl. n.* irredeemable British government securities carrying annual interest. [short for *consolidated stock*]

consommé (kənˈsɒmeɪ) *n.* a clear soup made from meat stock. [C19: < F, < *consommer* to use up]

consonance (ˈkɒnsənəns) *n.* **1.** agreement, harmony, or accord. **2.** *Prosody.* similarity between consonants, but not between vowels, as between the *s* and *t* sounds in *sweet silent thought.* **3.** *Music.* a combination of notes which can sound together without harshness.

consonant (ˈkɒnsənənt) *n.* **1.** a speech sound or letter of the alphabet other than a vowel. ~*adj.* **2.** (*postpositive;* foll. by *with* or *to*) consistent; in agreement. **3.** harmonious. **4.** *Music.* characterized by the presence of a consonance. [C14: < L *consonāns,* < *consonāre* to sound at the same time, < *sonāre* to sound] —ˈ**consonantly** *adv.*

consonantal (ˌkɒnsəˈnæntᵊl) *adj.* relating to, functioning as, or characterized by consonants.

consort *vb.* (kənˈsɔːt). (*intr.*) **1.** (usually foll. by *with*) to keep company (with undesirable people); associate. **2.** to harmonize. ~*n.* (ˈkɒnsɔːt). **3.** (esp. formerly) a small group of instruments, either of the same type (**a whole consort**) or of different types (**a broken consort**). **4.** the husband or wife of a reigning monarch. **5.** a husband or wife. **6.** a ship that escorts another. [C15: < OF, < L *consors* partner, < *sors* lot, portion]

consortium (kənˈsɔːtɪəm) *n., pl.* **-tia** (-tɪə). **1.** an association of financiers, companies, etc., esp. for a particular purpose. **2.** *Law.* the right of husband or wife to the company and affection of the other. [C19: < L: partnership; see CONSORT]

conspectus (kənˈspɛktəs) *n.* **1.** an overall view; survey. **2.** a summary; résumé. [C19: < L: a viewing, < *conspicere,* < *specere* to look]

conspicuous (kənˈspɪkjʊəs) *adj.* **1.** clearly visible. **2.** attracting attention because of a striking feature: *conspicuous stupidity.* [C16: < L *conspicuus,* < *conspicere* to perceive; see CONSPECTUS] —**conˈspicuously** *adv.* —**conˈspicuousness** *n.*

conspiracy (kənˈspɪrəsɪ) *n., pl.* **-cies.** **1.** a secret plan to carry out an illegal or harmful act, esp. with political motivation; plot. **2.** the act of making such plans in secret. —**conˈspirator** *n.* —**conˌspiraˈtorial** *adj.*

conspire (kən'spaɪə) *vb.* (when *intr.*, sometimes foll. by *against*) **1.** to plan (a crime) together in secret. **2.** (*intr.*) to act together as if by design: *the elements conspired to spoil our picnic.* [C14: < OF, < L *conspīrāre* to plot together, lit.: to breathe together, < *spīrāre* to breathe]

con spirito (kɒn 'spɪrɪtəʊ) *adj., adv. Music.* (to be performed) in a spirited or lively manner. [It.: with spirit]

constable ('kʌnstəbᵊl, 'kɒn-) *n.* **1.** (in Britain, Australia, New Zealand, Canada, etc.) a police officer of the lowest rank. **2.** any of various officers of the peace, esp. one who arrests offenders, serves writs, etc. **3.** the keeper of a royal castle. **4.** (in medieval Europe) the chief military officer and functionary of a royal household. **5.** an officer of a hundred in medieval England. [C13: < OF, < LL *comes stabulī* officer in charge of the stable] —**'constable,ship** *n.*

constabulary (kən'stæbjulərɪ) *Chiefly Brit.* ~*n., pl.* **-laries.** **1.** the police force of a town or district. ~*adj.* **2.** of or relating to constables.

constant ('kɒnstənt) *adj.* **1.** unchanging. **2.** incessant: *constant interruptions.* **3.** resolute; loyal. ~*n.* **4.** something that is unchanging. **5.** a specific quantity that is invariable: *the velocity of light is a constant.* **6.** **a.** *Maths.* a symbol representing an unspecified number that remains invariable throughout a particular series of operations. **b.** *Physics.* a quantity or property that is considered invariable throughout a particular series of experiments. [C14: < OF, < L *constāns*, < *constāre* to be steadfast, < *stāre* to stand] —**'constancy** *n.* —**'constantly** *adv.*

constellate ('kɒnstɪ,leɪt) *vb.* to form into clusters in or as if in constellations.

constellation (,kɒnstɪ'leɪʃən) *n.* **1.** any of the 88 groups of stars as seen from the earth, many of which were named by the ancient Greeks after animals, objects, or mythological persons. **2.** a gathering of brilliant people or things. **3.** *Psychoanalysis.* a group of ideas felt to be related. [C14: < LL *constellātiō*, < L *com-* together + *stella* star] —**constellatory** (kən'stɛlətərɪ) *adj.*

consternate ('kɒnstə,neɪt) *vb.* (*tr.; usually passive*) to fill with anxiety, dismay, dread, or confusion. [C17: < L *consternāre*, < *sternere* to lay low]

consternation (,kɒnstə'neɪʃən) *n.* a feeling of anxiety, dismay, dread, or confusion.

constipate ('kɒnstɪ,peɪt) *vb.* (*tr.*) to cause constipation in. [C16: < L *constīpāre* to press closely together] —**'consti,pated** *adj.*

constipation (,kɒnstɪ'peɪʃən) *n.* infrequent or difficult evacuation of the bowels.

constituency (kən'stɪtjʊənsɪ) *n., pl.* **-cies.** **1.** the whole body of voters who elect one representative to a legislature or all the residents represented by one deputy. **2.** a district that sends one representative to a legislature.

constituent (kən'stɪtjʊənt) *adj.* (*prenominal*) **1.** forming part of a whole; component. **2.** having the power to frame a constitution or to constitute a government: *constituent assembly.* ~*n.* **3.** a component part; ingredient. **4.** a resident of a constituency, esp. one entitled to vote. **5.** *Chiefly law.* a person who appoints another to act for him. [C17: < L *constituēns*, < *constituere* to establish, CONSTITUTE] —**con'stituently** *adv.*

constitute ('kɒnstɪ,tjuːt) *vb.* (*tr.*) **1.** to form; compose: *the people who constitute a jury.* **2.** to appoint to an office: *a legally constituted officer.* **3.** to set up (an institution) formally; found. **4.** *Law.* to give legal form to (a court, assembly, etc.). [C15: < L *constituere*, < *com-* (intensive) + *statuere* to place] —**'consti,tutor** *n.*

constitution (,kɒnstɪ'tjuːʃən) *n.* **1.** the act of constituting or state of being constituted. **2.** physical make-up; structure. **3.** the fundamental principles on which a state is governed, esp. when considered as embodying the rights of the subjects. **4.** (*often cap.*) (in certain countries, esp. the U.S.) a statute embodying such principles. **5.** a person's state of health. **6.** a person's temperament.

constitutional (,kɒnstɪ'tjuːʃənᵊl) *adj.* **1.** of a constitution. **2.** authorized by or subject to a constitution: *constitutional monarchy.* **3.** inherent in the nature of a person or thing: *a constitutional weakness.* **4.** beneficial to one's physical wellbeing. ~*n.* **5.** a regular walk taken for the benefit of one's health. —**,consti,tution'ality** *n.* —**,consti'tutionally** *adv.*

constitutionalism (,kɒnstɪ'tjuːʃənə,lɪzəm) *n.* **1.** the principles or system of government in accord with a constitution. **2.** adherence to or advocacy of such a system. —**,consti'tutionalist** *n.*

constitutive ('kɒnstɪ,tjuːtɪv) *adj.* **1.** having power to enact or establish. **2.** another word for **constituent** (sense 1). —**'consti,tutively** *adv.*

constrain (kən'streɪn) *vb.* (*tr.*) **1.** to compel, esp. by circumstances, etc. **2.** to restrain as by force. [C14: < OF, < L *constringere* to bind together] —**con'strainer** *n.*

constrained (kən'streɪnd) *adj.* embarrassed, unnatural, or forced: *a constrained smile.*

constraint (kən'streɪnt) *n.* **1.** compulsion or restraint. **2.** repression of natural feelings. **3.** a forced unnatural manner. **4.** something that serves to constrain; restrictive condition.

constrict (kən'strɪkt) *vb.* (*tr.*) **1.** to make smaller or narrower, esp. by contracting at one place. **2.** to hold in or inhibit; limit. [C18: < L *constrictus*, < *constringere* to tie up together]

constriction (kən'strɪkʃən) *n.* **1.** a feeling of tightness in some part of the body, such as the chest. **2.** the act of constricting or condition of being constricted. **3.** something that is constricted. —**con'strictive** *adj.*

constrictor (kən'strɪktə) *n.* **1.** any of various very large nonvenomous snakes, such as the boas, that coil around and squeeze their prey to kill it. **2.** any muscle that constricts; sphincter.

construct *vb.* (kən'strʌkt). (*tr.*) **1.** to put together substances or parts systematically; build; assemble. **2.** to frame mentally (an argument, sentence, etc.). **3.** *Geom.* to draw (a line, angle, or figure) so that certain requirements are satisfied. ~*n.* ('kɒnstrʌkt). **4.** something formulated or built systematically. **5.** a complex idea resulting from a synthesis of simpler ideas. [C17: < L *constructus*, < *construere* to build, < *struere* to arrange, erect] —**con'structor** *or* **con'structer** *n.*

construction (kən'strʌkʃən) *n.* **1.** the act of constructing or manner in which a thing is constructed. **2.** a structure. **3.** **a.** the business or work of building dwellings, offices, etc. **b.** (*as modifier*): *a construction site.* **4.** an interpretation: *they put a sympathetic construction on her behaviour.* **5.** *Grammar.* a group of words that make up one of the constituents into which a sentence may be analysed; a phrase or clause. **6.** an abstract work of art in three dimensions. —**con'structional** *adj.* —**con'structionally** *adv.*

constructive (kən'strʌktɪv) *adj.* **1.** serving to improve; positive: *constructive criticism.* **2.** *Law.* deduced by inference; not expressed. **3.** another word for **structural.** —**con'structively** *adv.*

constructivism (kən'strʌktɪ,vɪzəm) *n.* a movement in abstract art evolved after World War I, which explored the use of movement and machine-age materials in sculpture. —**con'structivist** *adj., n.*

construe (kən'struː) *vb.* **-struing, -strued.** (*mainly tr.*) **1.** to interpret the meaning of (something): *you can construe that in different ways.* **2.** (*may take a clause as object*) to infer; deduce. **3.** to analyse the grammatical structure of; parse (esp. a Latin or Greek text as a preliminary to translation). **4.** to combine words syntactically. **5.** (*also intr.*) *Old-fashioned.* to translate literally, esp. aloud. [C14: < L *construere*; see CONSTRUCT] —**con'struable** *adj.*

consubstantial (,kɒnsəb'stænʃəl) *adj. Christian theol.* (esp. of the three persons of the Trinity) regarded as identical in essence though different in aspect. [C15: < Church L, < L *com-* COM- + *substantia* SUBSTANCE] —**,consub,stanti'ality** *n.*

consubstantiation (,kɒnsəb,stænʃɪ'eɪʃən) *n.*

Christian theol. (in the Lutheran branch of Protestantism) the doctrine that after the consecration of the Eucharist the substance of the body and blood of Christ coexists within the substance of the consecrated bread and wine. Cf. **transubstantiation.**

consuetude (ˈkɒnswɪˌtjuːd) *n.* an established custom or usage, esp. one having legal force. [C14: < L *consuētūdō*, < *consuēscere*, < CON- + *suēscere* to be wont]

consul (ˈkɒnsᵊl) *n.* **1.** an official appointed by a sovereign state to protect its commercial interests and aid its citizens in a foreign city. **2.** (in ancient Rome) either of two annually elected magistrates who jointly exercised the highest authority in the republic. **3.** (in France from 1799 to 1804) any of the three chief magistrates of the First Republic. [C14: < L, < *consulere* to CONSULT] —**consular** (ˈkɒnsjʊlə) *adj.* —ˈ**consulˌship** *n.*

consulate (ˈkɒnsjʊlɪt) *n.* **1.** the premises of a consul. **2.** government by consuls. **3.** the office or period of office of a consul. **4.** (*often cap.*) **a.** the government of France by the three consuls from 1799 to 1804. **b.** this period. **5.** (*often cap.*) the consular government of the Roman republic.

consul general *n., pl.* **consuls general.** a consul of the highest grade, usually stationed in a city of considerable commercial importance.

consult (kənˈsʌlt) *vb.* **1.** (when *intr.*, often foll. by *with*) to ask advice from (someone). **2.** (*tr.*) to refer to for information: *to consult a map.* **3.** (*tr.*) to have regard for (a person's feelings, interests, etc.); consider. [C17: < F, < L *consultāre*, < *consulere* to consult]

consultant (kənˈsʌltᵊnt) *n.* **1. a.** a specialist physician who is asked to confirm a diagnosis. **b.** a physician or surgeon holding the highest appointment in a particular branch of medicine or surgery in a hospital. **2.** a specialist who gives expert advice or information. **3.** a person who asks advice in a consultation. —**conˈsultancy** *n.*

consultation (ˌkɒnsᵊlˈteɪʃən) *n.* **1.** the act of consulting. **2.** a conference for discussion or the seeking of advice. —**consultative** (kənˈsʌltətɪv) *adj.*

consulting (kənˈsʌltɪŋ) *adj.* (*prenominal*) acting in an advisory capacity on professional matters: *a consulting engineer.*

consulting room *n.* a room in which a doctor sees his patients.

consume (kənˈsjuːm) *vb.* **1.** (*tr.*) to eat or drink. **2.** (*tr.; often passive*) to obsess. **3.** (*tr.*) to use up; expend. **4.** to destroy or be destroyed by: *fire consumed the forest.* **5.** (*tr.*) to waste. **6.** (*tr.; passive*) to waste away. [C14: < L *consūmere*, < *com-* (intensive) + *sūmere* to take up] —**conˈsumable** *adj.* —**conˈsuming** *adj.*

consumedly (kənˈsjuːmɪdlɪ) *adv. Old-fashioned.* (intensifier): *consumedly fascinating.*

consumer (kənˈsjuːmə) *n.* **1.** a person who purchases goods and services for his own personal needs. Cf. **producer** (sense 5). **2.** a person or thing that consumes.

consumer durable *n.* a manufactured product that has a relatively long useful life, such as a car or a television.

consumer goods *pl. n.* goods that satisfy personal needs rather than those required for the production of other goods or services.

consumerism (kənˈsjuːməˌrɪzəm) *n.* **1.** protection of the interests of consumers. **2.** advocacy of a high rate of consumption as a basis for a sound economy. —**conˈsumerist** *n., adj.*

consummate *vb.* (ˈkɒnsəˌmeɪt). (*tr.*) **1.** to bring to completion; fulfil. **2.** to complete (a marriage) legally by sexual intercourse. ~*adj.* (kənˈsʌmɪt, ˈkɒnsəmɪt). **3.** supremely skilled: *a consummate artist.* **4.** (*prenominal*) (intensifier): *a consummate fool.* [C15: < L *consummāre* to complete, < *summus* utmost] —**conˈsummately** *adv.* —ˌ**consumˈmation** *n.*

consumption (kənˈsʌmpʃən) *n.* **1.** the act of consuming or the state of being consumed, esp. by eating, burning, etc. **2.** *Econ.* expenditure on goods and services for final personal use. **3.** the quantity consumed. **4.** a wasting away of the tissues of the body, esp. in tuberculosis of the lungs. [C14: < L *consumptiō*, < *consūmere* to CONSUME]

consumptive (kənˈsʌmptɪv) *adj.* **1.** causing consumption; wasteful; destructive. **2.** relating to or affected with tuberculosis of the lungs. ~*n.* **3.** *Pathol.* a person who suffers from consumption. —**conˈsumptively** *adv.* —**conˈsumptiveness** *n.*

cont. *abbrev. for:* **1.** contents. **2.** continued.

contact *n.* (ˈkɒntækt). **1.** the act or state of touching. **2.** the state or fact of communication (esp. in **in contact, make contact**). **3. a.** a junction of electrical conductors. **b.** the part of the conductors that makes the junction. **c.** the part of an electrical device to which such connections are made. **4.** an acquaintance, esp. one who might be useful in business, etc. **5.** any person who has been exposed to a contagious disease. **6.** (*modifier*) caused by touching the causative agent: *contact dermatitis.* **7.** (*modifier*) of or maintaining contact. ~*vb.* (ˈkɒntækt, kənˈtækt). **8.** (when *intr.*, often foll. by *with*) to put, come, or be in association, touch, or communication. [C17: < L *contactus*, < *contingere* to touch on all sides, < *tangere* to touch] —**contactual** (kɒnˈtæktjʊəl) *adj.*

contact lens *n.* a lens placed directly on the surface of the eye to correct defects of vision.

contact print *n.* a photographic print made by exposing the printing paper through a negative placed directly on to it.

contagion (kənˈteɪdʒən) *n.* **1.** the transmission of disease from one person to another by contact. **2.** a contagious disease. **3.** a corrupting influence that tends to spread. **4.** the spreading of an emotional or mental state among a number of people: *the contagion of mirth.* [C14: < L *contāgiō* infection, < *contingere;* see CONTACT]

contagious (kənˈteɪdʒəs) *adj.* **1.** (of a disease) capable of being passed on by direct contact with a diseased individual or by handling his clothing, etc. **2.** (of an organism) harbouring the causative agent of a transmissible disease. **3.** causing or likely to cause the same reaction in several people: *her laughter was contagious.*

contain (kənˈteɪn) *vb.* (*tr.*) **1.** to hold or be capable of holding: *this contains five pints.* **2.** to restrain (feelings, behaviour, etc.). **3.** to consist of: *the book contains three sections.* **4.** *Mil.* to prevent (enemy forces) from operating beyond a certain area. **5.** to be a multiple of, leaving no remainder: *6 contains 2 and 3.* [C13: < OF, < L *continēre*, < *com-* together + *tenēre* to hold] —**conˈtainable** *adj.*

container (kənˈteɪnə) *n.* **1.** an object used for or capable of holding, esp. for transport or storage. **2. a.** a large cargo-carrying standard-sized container that can be loaded from one mode of transport to another. **b.** (*as modifier*): *a container ship.*

containerize *or* **-ise** (kənˈteɪnəˌraɪz) *vb.* (*tr.*) **1.** to convey (cargo) in standard-sized containers. **2.** to adapt (a port or transportation system) to the use of standard-sized containers. —**conˌtaineriˈzation** *or* **-iˈsation** *n.*

containment (kənˈteɪnmənt) *n.* the act of containing, esp. of restraining the power of a hostile country or the operations of a hostile military force.

contaminate (kənˈtæmɪˌneɪt) *vb.* (*tr.*) **1.** to make impure; pollute. **2.** to make radioactive by the addition of radioactive material. [C15: < L *contamināre* to defile] —**conˈtaminable** *adj.* —**conˈtaminant** *n.* —**conˌtamiˈnation** *n.* —**conˈtamiˌnator** *n.*

contango (kənˈtæŋgəʊ) *n., pl.* **-gos. 1.** (on the London Stock Exchange) postponement of payment for and delivery of stock from one account day to the next. **2.** the fee paid for such a postponement. ~Also called: **carry-over, continuation.** Cf. **backwardation.** [C19: apparently an arbitrary coinage]

conte *French.* (kɔ̃t) *n.* a tale or short story.

contemn (kən'tɛm) *vb.* (*tr.*) *Formal.* to regard with contempt; scorn. [C15: < L *contemnere*, < *temnere* to slight] —**contemner** (kən'tɛmnə, -'tɛmə) *n.*

contemplate ('kɒntɛm,pleɪt) *vb.* (*mainly tr.*) **1.** to think about intently and at length. **2.** (*intr.*) to think intently and at length, esp. for spiritual reasons; meditate. **3.** to look at thoughtfully. **4.** to have in mind as a possibility. [C16: < L *contemplāre*, < *templum* TEMPLE¹] —,**contem'plation** *n.* —'**contem,plator** *n.*

contemplative ('kɒntɛm,pleɪtɪv, -təm-; kən'tɛmplə-) *adj.* **1.** denoting, concerned with, or inclined to contemplation; meditative. ~*n.* **2.** a person dedicated to religious contemplation.

contemporaneous (kən,tɛmpə'reɪnɪəs) *adj.* existing, beginning, or occurring in the same period of time. —**contemporaneity** (kən,tɛmpərə'niːɪtɪ) *or* **con,tempo'raneousness** *n.*

contemporary (kən'tɛmprərɪ) *adj.* **1.** living or occurring in the same period. **2.** existing or occurring at the present time. **3.** conforming to modern ideas in style, fashion, etc. **4.** having approximately the same age as one another. ~*n., pl.* **-raries. 5.** a person living at the same time or of approximately the same age as another. **6.** something that is contemporary. [C17: < Med. L *contemporārius*, < L *com-* together + *temporārius* relating to time, < *tempus* time] —**con'temporarily** *adv.* —**con'temporariness** *n.*

▷ **Usage.** *Contemporary* is most acceptable when used to mean of the same period, in a sentence like *it is useful to compare Shakespeare's plays with those of contemporary* (that is, other Elizabethan) *playwrights.* The word is, however, often used to mean modern or up-to-date in contexts such as *the furniture was of a contemporary design.* The second use should be avoided where ambiguity is likely to arise, as in *a production of* Othello *in contemporary dress.*

contemporize *or* **-ise** (kən'tɛmpə,raɪz) *vb.* to be or make contemporary.

contempt (kən'tɛmpt) *n.* **1.** the feeling of a person towards a person or thing that he considers despicable; scorn. **2.** the state of being scorned; disgrace (esp. in **hold in contempt**). **3.** wilful disregard of the authority of a court of law or legislative body: *contempt of court.* [C14: < L *contemptus*, < *contemnere* to CONTEMN]

contemptible (kən'tɛmptɪbᵊl) *adj.* deserving or worthy of contempt. —**con,tempti'bility** *or* **con'temptibleness** *n.* —**con'temptibly** *adv.*

contemptuous (kən'tɛmptjʊəs) *adj.* (when *predicative*, often foll. by *of*) showing or feeling contempt; disdainful. —**con'temptuously** *adv.*

contend (kən'tɛnd) *vb.* **1.** (*intr.*; often foll. by *with*) to struggle in rivalry, battle, etc.; vie. **2.** to argue earnestly. **3.** (*tr.*; *may take a clause as object*) to assert. [C15: < L *contendere* to strive, < *com-* with + *tendere* to stretch] —**con'tender** *n.*

content[1] ('kɒntɛnt) *n.* **1.** (*often pl.*) everything inside a container. **2.** (*usually pl.*) **a.** the chapters or divisions of a book. **b.** a list of these printed at the front of a book. **3.** the meaning or significance of a work of art, as distinguished from its style or form. **4.** all that is contained or dealt with in a piece of writing, etc.; substance. **5.** the capacity or size of a thing. **6.** the proportion of a substance contained in an alloy, mixture, etc.: *the lead content of petrol.* [C15: < L *contentus* contained, < *continēre* to CONTAIN]

content[2] (kən'tɛnt) *adj.* (*postpositive*) **1.** satisfied with things as they are. **2.** assenting to or willing to accept circumstances, a proposed course of action, etc. ~*vb.* **3.** (*tr.*) to make (oneself or another person) satisfied. ~*n.* **4.** peace of mind. [C14: < OF, < L *contentus* contented, having restrained desires, < *continēre* to restrain] —**con'tentment** *n.*

contented (kən'tɛntɪd) *adj.* accepting one's situation or life with equanimity and satisfaction. —**con'tentedly** *adv.* —**con'tentedness** *n.*

contention (kən'tɛnʃən) *n.* **1.** a struggling between opponents; competition. **2.** a point of dispute (esp. in **bone of contention**). **3.** a point asserted in argument. [C14: < L *contentiō*, < *contendere* to CONTEND]

contentious (kən'tɛnʃəs) *adj.* **1.** tending to quarrel. **2.** causing or characterized by dispute; controversial. —**con'tentiousness** *n.*

conterminous (kən'tɜːmɪnəs) *or* **coterminous** (kəʊ'tɜːmɪnəs) *adj.* **1.** enclosed within a common boundary. **2.** without a break or interruption. [C17: < L *conterminus*, < CON- + *terminus* boundary]

contest *n.* ('kɒntɛst). **1.** a formal game or match in which people, teams, etc., compete. **2.** a struggle for victory between opposing forces. ~*vb.* (kən'tɛst). **3.** (*tr.*) to try to disprove; call in question. **4.** (when *intr.*, foll. by *with* or *against*) to dispute or contend (with): *to contest an election.* [C16: < L *contestārī* to introduce a lawsuit, < *testis* witness] —**con'testable** *adj.* —**con'tester** *n.*

contestant (kən'tɛstənt) *n.* a person who takes part in a contest; competitor.

context ('kɒntɛkst) *n.* **1.** the parts of a piece of writing, speech, etc., that precede and follow a word or passage and contribute to its full meaning: *it is unfair to quote out of context.* **2.** the circumstances that are relevant to an event, fact, etc. [C15: < L *contextus* a putting together, < *contexere*, < *com-* together + *texere* to weave] —**con'textual** *adj.*

contiguous (kən'tɪgjʊəs) *adj.* **1.** touching along the side or boundary; in contact. **2.** neighbouring. **3.** preceding or following in time. [C17: < L *contiguus*, < *contingere* to touch; see CONTACT] —**con'tiguously** *adv.*

continent[1] ('kɒntɪnənt) *n.* **1.** one of the earth's large land masses (Asia, Australia, Africa, Europe, North and South America, and Antarctica). **2.** *Obs.* **a.** mainland. **b.** a continuous extent of land. [C16: < the L phrase *terra continens* continuous land] —**continental** (,kɒntɪ'nɛntᵊl) *adj.* —,**conti'nentally** *adv.*

continent[2] ('kɒntɪnənt) *adj.* **1.** able to control urination and defecation. **2.** exercising self-restraint, esp. from sexual activity; chaste. [C14: < L *continēre*; see CONTAIN] —'**continence** *n.*

Continent ('kɒntɪnənt) *n.* **the.** the mainland of Europe as distinguished from the British Isles.

Continental (,kɒntɪ'nɛntᵊl) *adj.* **1.** of or characteristic of Europe, excluding the British Isles. **2.** of or relating to the 13 original British North American colonies during the War of American Independence. ~*n.* **3.** (*sometimes not cap.*) an inhabitant of Europe, excluding the British Isles. **4.** a regular soldier of the rebel army during the War of American Independence.

continental breakfast *n.* a light breakfast of coffee and rolls.

continental climate *n.* a climate characterized by hot summers, cold winters, and little rainfall, typical of the interior of a continent.

continental drift *n. Geol.* the theory that the earth's continents move gradually over the surface of the planet on a substratum of magma.

continental quilt *n. Brit.* a quilt, usually stuffed with down, used as a bed cover in place of the top sheet and blankets. Also called: **duvet.**

continental shelf *n.* the sea bed surrounding a continent at depths of up to about 200 metres (100 fathoms), at the edge of which the **continental slope** drops steeply.

contingency (kən'tɪndʒənsɪ) *or* **contingence** (kən'tɪndʒəns) *n., pl.* **-cies** *or* **-ces. 1. a.** a possible but not very likely future event or condition. **b.** (*as modifier*): *a contingency plan.* **2.** something dependent on a possible future event. **3.** a fact, event, etc., incidental to something else. **4.** *Logic.* the state of being contingent. **5.** uncertainty. **6.** *Statistics.* **a.** the degree of association between theoretical and observed common frequencies of two graded or classified variables. **b.** (*as modifier*): *a contingency table.*

contingent (kən'tɪndʒənt) *adj.* **1.** (when *postpositive*, often foll. by *on* or *upon*) dependent on events, conditions, etc., not yet known; conditional. **2.** *Logic.* (of a proposition) true under certain conditions, false under others; not logically necessary. **3.** happening by chance; accidental. **4.** uncertain. ~*n.* **5.** a part of a military force, parade, etc. **6.** a group distinguished by common interests, etc., that is part of a larger group. **7.** a chance occurrence. [C14: < L *contingere* to touch, befall]

continual (kən'tɪnjʊəl) *adj.* **1.** recurring frequently, esp. at regular intervals. **2.** occurring without interruption; continuous in time. [C14: < OF *continuel,* < L *continuus* uninterrupted, < *continēre* to CONTAIN] —**con'tinually** *adv.*

continuance (kən'tɪnjʊəns) *n.* **1.** the act of continuing. **2.** the duration of an action, etc. **3.** *U.S.* the adjournment of a legal proceeding.

continuant (kən'tɪnjʊənt) *Phonetics.* ~*n.* **1.** a speech sound, such as (l), (r), (f), or (s), in which the closure of the vocal tract is incomplete, allowing the continuous passage of the breath. ~*adj.* **2.** relating to or denoting a continuant.

continuation (kən,tɪnjʊ'eɪʃən) *n.* **1.** a part or thing added, esp. to a book or play; sequel. **2.** a renewal of an interrupted action, process, etc.; resumption. **3.** the act of continuing; prolongation. **4.** another word for **contango.**

continue (kən'tɪnju:) *vb.* **-uing, -ued.** **1.** (when *tr., may take an infinitive*) to remain or cause to remain in a particular condition or place. **2.** (when *tr., may take an infinitive*) to carry on uninterruptedly (a course of action): *he continued running.* **3.** (when *tr., may take an infinitive*) to resume after an interruption: *we'll continue after lunch.* **4.** to prolong or be prolonged: *continue the chord until it meets the tangent.* **5.** (*tr.*) *Law, chiefly Scots.* to adjourn (legal proceedings). [C14: < OF *continuer,* < L *continuāre* to join together] —**con'tinuer** *n.*

continuity (,kɒntɪ'nju:ɪtɪ) *n., pl.* **-ties.** **1.** logical sequence. **2.** a continuous or connected whole. **3.** the comprehensive script or scenario of detail in a film or broadcast. **4.** the continuous projection of a film.

continuity girl *or* **man** *n.* a woman or man whose job is to ensure continuity and consistency in successive shots of a film.

continuo (kən'tɪnjʊəʊ) *n., pl.* **-os.** **1.** *Music.* **a.** a shortened form of **basso continuo** (see **thorough bass**). **b.** (*as modifier*)*: a continuo accompaniment.* **2.** the thorough-bass part as played on a keyboard instrument. [It., lit.: continuous]

continuous (kən'tɪnjʊəs) *adj.* **1.** unceasing: *a continuous noise.* **2.** in an unbroken series or pattern. **3.** *Statistics.* (of a variable) having a continuum of possible values so that its distribution requires integration rather than summation to determine its cumulative probability. **4.** *Grammar.* another word for **progressive** (sense 7). [C17: < L *continuus,* < *continēre* to CONTAIN] —**con'tinuously** *adv.*

continuous creation *n.* the theory that matter is created continuously in the universe. See **steady-state theory.**

continuum (kən'tɪnjʊəm) *n., pl.* **-tinua** (-'tɪnjʊə) *or* **-tinuums.** a continuous series or whole, no part of which is perceptibly different from the adjacent parts. [C17: < L, neuter of *continuus* CONTINUOUS]

contort (kən'tɔ:t) *vb.* to twist or bend out of place or shape. [C15: < L *contortus* intricate, < *contorquēre* to whirl around, < *torquēre* to twist] —**con'tortion** *n.* —**con'tortive** *adj.*

contortionist (kən'tɔ:ʃənɪst) *n.* **1.** a performer who contorts his body for the entertainment of others. **2.** a person who twists or warps meaning.

contour ('kɒntʊə) *n.* **1.** the outline of a mass of land, figure, or body; a defining line. **2. a.** See **contour line. b.** (*as modifier*)*: a contour map.* **3.** (*often pl.*) the shape of a curving form: *the contours of her body were full and round.* ~*vb.* (*tr.*) **4.** to shape so as to form the contour of something. **5.** to mark contour lines on. **6.** to construct (a road, railway, etc.) to follow the outline of the land. [C17: < F, < It. *contorno,* < *contornare* to sketch, < *tornare* to TURN]

contour line *n.* a line on a map or chart joining points of equal height or depth.

contour ploughing *n.* ploughing along the contours of the land to minimize erosion.

contra- *prefix.* **1.** against; contrary; opposing; contrasting: *contraceptive.* **2.** (in music) pitched below: *contrabass.* [< L, < *contrā* against]

contraband ('kɒntrə,bænd) *n.* **1. a.** goods that are prohibited by law from being exported or imported. **b.** illegally imported or exported goods. **2.** illegal traffic in such goods; smuggling. **3.** Also called: **contraband of war.** goods that a neutral country may not supply to a belligerent. ~*adj.* **4.** (of goods) **a.** forbidden by law from being imported or exported. **b.** illegally imported or exported. [C16: < Sp. *contrabanda,* < It., < Med. L, < CONTRA- + *bannum* ban] —'**contra,bandist** *n.*

contrabass (,kɒntrə'beɪs) *n.* **1.** another name for **double bass.** ~*adj.* **2.** denoting the instrument of a family that is lower than the bass.

contrabassoon (,kɒntrəbə'su:n) *n.* the largest instrument in the oboe family, pitched an octave below the bassoon; double bassoon.

contraception (,kɒntrə'sɛpʃən) *n.* the intentional prevention of conception by artificial or natural means. [C19: < CONTRA- + CONCEPTION] —,**contra'ceptive** *adj., n.*

contract *vb.* (kən'trækt). **1.** to make or become smaller, narrower, shorter, etc. **2.** ('kɒntrækt). (when *intr.,* sometimes foll. by *for;* when *tr., may take an infinitive*) to enter into an agreement with (a person, company, etc.) to deliver (goods or services) or to do (something) on mutually agreed terms. **3.** to draw or be drawn together. **4.** (*tr.*) to incur or become affected by (a disease, debt, etc.). **5.** (*tr.*) to shorten (a word or phrase) by the omission of letters or syllables, usually indicated in writing by an apostrophe. **6.** (*tr.*) to wrinkle (the brow or a muscle). **7.** (*tr.*) to arrange (a marriage) for; betroth. ~*n.* ('kɒntrækt). **8.** a formal agreement between two or more parties. **9.** a document that states the terms of such an agreement. **10.** the branch of law treating of contracts. **11.** marriage considered as a formal agreement. **12.** See **contract bridge.** **13.** *Bridge.* **a.** the highest bid, which determines trumps and the number of tricks one side must make. **b.** the number and suit of these tricks. [C16: < L *contractus* agreement, < *contrahere* to draw together, < *trahere* to draw] —**con'tractible** *adj.*

contract bridge ('kɒntrækt) *n.* the most common variety of bridge, in which the declarer receives points counting towards game and rubber only for tricks he bids as well as makes. Cf. **auction bridge.**

contractile (kən'træktaɪl) *adj.* having the power to contract or to cause contraction.

contraction (kən'trækʃən) *n.* **1.** an instance of contracting or the state of being contracted. **2.** a shortening of a word or group of words, often marked by an apostrophe: *I've come* for *I have come.* —**con'tractive** *adj.*

contractor (kən'træktə) *n.* **1.** a person or firm that contracts to supply materials or labour, esp. for building. **2.** something that contracts.

contract out ('kɒntrækt) *vb.* (*intr., adv.*) *Brit.* to agree not to participate in something, esp. the state pension scheme.

contractual (kən'træktjʊəl) *adj.* of the nature of or assured by a contract.

contradance ('kɒntrə,dɑ:ns) *n.* a variant spelling of **contredanse.**

contradict (,kɒntrə'dɪkt) *vb.* **1.** (*tr.*) to affirm the opposite of (a statement, etc.). **2.** (*tr.*) to declare (a statement, etc.) to be false or incorrect; deny. **3.** (*tr.*) to be inconsistent with: *the facts contradicted his theory.* **4.** (*intr.*) to be at variance; be in contradiction. [C16: < L *contrādīcere,* < CONTRA- + *dīcere* to speak]

contradiction (,kɒntrə'dɪkʃən) *n.* **1.** opposition; denial. **2.** a declaration of the opposite. **3.** a statement that is at variance with itself (often in a **contradiction in terms**). **4.** conflict or inconsistency, as between events, qualities, etc. **5.** a person or thing containing conflicting qualities. **6.** *Logic.* a statement that is false under all circumstances; necessary falsehood.

contradictory (ˌkɒntrəˈdɪktərɪ) *adj.* **1.** inconsistent; incompatible. **2.** given to argument and contention: *a contradictory person.* **3.** *Logic.* (of a pair of statements) unable both to be true or both to be false under the same circumstances. —ˌ**contraˈdictorily** *adv.* —ˌ**contraˈdictoriness** *n.*

contradistinction (ˌkɒntrədɪˈstɪŋkʃən) *n.* a distinction made by contrasting different qualities. —ˌ**contradisˈtinctive** *adj.*

contraflow (ˈkɒntrəˌfləʊ) *n. Brit.* two-way traffic on one carriageway of a motorway.

contrail (ˈkɒntreɪl) *n.* another name for **vapour trail.** [C20: < CON(DENSATION) + TRAIL]

contralto (kənˈtræltəʊ) *n., pl.* **-tos** *or* **-ti** (-tɪ). **1.** the lowest female voice: in the context of a choir often shortened to **alto.** **2.** a singer with such a voice. ~*adj.* **3.** of or denoting a contralto: *the contralto part.* [C18: < It.; see CONTRA-, ALTO]

contraposition (ˌkɒntrəpəˈzɪʃən) *n.* **1.** the act of placing opposite or against. **2.** *Logic.* (esp. in traditional logic) the conclusion drawn from a subject-predicate proposition by negating its terms and changing their order.

contraption (kənˈtræpʃən) *n. Inf., often facetious or derog.* a device or contrivance, esp. one considered strange, unnecessarily intricate, or improvised. [C19: ? < CON(TRIVANCE) + TRAPˡ + (INVEN)TION]

contrapuntal (ˌkɒntrəˈpʌntᵊl) *adj. Music.* characterized by counterpoint. [C19: < It. *contrappunto*] —ˌ**contraˈpuntally** *adv.* —ˌ**contraˈpuntist** *or* ˌ**contraˈpuntalist** *n.*

contrariety (ˌkɒntrəˈraɪətɪ) *n., pl.* **-ties.** **1.** opposition between one thing and another; disagreement. **2.** an instance of such opposition; inconsistency; discrepancy.

contrariwise (ˈkɒntrərɪˌwaɪz) *adv.* **1.** from a contrasting point of view. **2.** in the reverse way. **3.** (kənˈtrɛərɪˌwaɪz). in a contrary manner.

contrary (ˈkɒntrərɪ) *adj.* **1.** opposed in nature, position, etc.: *contrary ideas.* **2.** (kənˈtrɛərɪ). perverse; obstinate. **3.** (esp. of wind) adverse; unfavourable. **4.** (of plant parts) situated at right angles to each other. **5.** *Logic.* (of a pair of propositions) related so they cannot both be true, although they may both be false. ~*n., pl.* **-ries.** **6.** the exact opposite (esp. in **to the contrary**). **7.** **on the contrary.** quite the reverse. **8.** either of two exactly opposite objects, facts, or qualities. ~*adv.* (usually foll. by *to*) **9.** in an opposite or unexpected way: *contrary to usual belief.* **10.** in conflict (with): *contrary to nature.* [C14: < L *contrārius* opposite, < *contrā* against] —**conˈtrarily** *adv.* —**conˈtrariness** *n.*

contrast *vb.* (kənˈtrɑːst). **1.** (often foll. by *with*) to distinguish or be distinguished by comparison of unlike or opposite qualities. ~*n.* (ˈkɒntrɑːst). **2.** distinction by comparison of opposite or dissimilar things, qualities, etc. (esp. in **by contrast, in contrast to** *or* **with**). **3.** a person or thing showing differences when compared with another. **4.** the effect of the juxtaposition of different colours, tones, etc. **5.** the extent to which adjacent areas of an optical image, esp. on a television screen or in a photograph, differ in brightness. [C16: (n.): via F < It., < *contrastare* (vb.), < L *contra-* against + *stare* to stand] —**conˈtrasting** *adj.* —**conˈtrastive** *adj.*

contravene (ˌkɒntrəˈviːn) *vb.* (*tr.*) **1.** to infringe (rules, laws, etc.). **2.** to dispute or contradict (a statement, proposition, etc.). [C16: < LL *contrāvenīre,* < L CONTRA- + *venīre* to come] —ˌ**contraˈvener** *n.* —**contravention** (ˌkɒntrəˈvɛnʃən) *n.*

contredanse *or* **contradance** (ˈkɒntrəˌdɑːns) *n.* **1.** a courtly Continental version of the English country dance, similar to the quadrille. **2.** music for this. [C19: < F, changed < E *country dance; country* altered to F *contre* (opposite) (because the dancers face each other)]

contretemps (ˈkɒntrəˌtɑːn) *n., pl.* **-temps.** an awkward or difficult situation or mishap. [C17: < F, < *contre* against + *temps* time]

contribute (kənˈtrɪbjuːt) *vb.* (often foll. by *to*) **1.** to give (support, money, etc.) for a common purpose or fund. **2.** to supply (ideas, opinions, etc.). **3.** (*intr.*) to be partly responsible (for): *drink contributed to the accident.* **4.** to write (articles, etc.) for a publication. [C16: < L *contribuere* to collect, < *tribuere* to grant] —**conˈtributive** *adj.* —**conˈtributor** *n.*

contribution (ˌkɒntrɪˈbjuːʃən) *n.* **1.** the act of contributing. **2.** something contributed, such as money. **3.** an article, etc., contributed to a newspaper or other publication. **4.** *Arch.* a levy.

contributory (kənˈtrɪbjʊtərɪ, -trɪ) *adj.* **1.** (often foll. by *to*) being partly responsible: *a contributory factor.* **2.** giving to a common purpose or fund. **3.** of or designating an insurance or pension scheme in which the premiums are paid partly by the employer and partly by the employees who benefit from it. ~*n., pl.* **-ries.** **4.** a person or thing that contributes. **5.** *Company law.* a member or former member of a company liable to contribute to the assets on the winding-up of the company.

contrite (kənˈtraɪt, ˈkɒntraɪt) *adj.* **1.** full of guilt or regret; remorseful. **2.** arising from a sense of shame or guilt: *contrite promises.* [C14: < L *contrītus* worn out, < *conterere* to bruise, < *terere* to grind] —**conˈtritely** *adv.* —**conˈtriteness** *or* **contrition** (kənˈtrɪʃən) *n.*

contrivance (kənˈtraɪvəns) *n.* **1.** something contrived, esp. an ingenious device; contraption. **2.** inventive skill or ability. **3.** an artificial rather than natural arrangement of details, parts, etc. **4.** an elaborate or deceitful plan; stratagem.

contrive (kənˈtraɪv) *vb.* **1.** (*tr.*) to manage (something or to do something), esp. by a trick: *he contrived to make them meet.* **2.** (*tr.*) to think up or adapt ingeniously: *he contrived a new mast for the boat.* **3.** to plot or scheme. [C14: < OF *controver,* < LL *contropāre* to represent by figures of speech, compare] —**conˈtriver** *n.*

contrived (kənˈtraɪvd) *adj.* obviously planned; artificial; forced; unnatural.

control (kənˈtrəʊl) *vb.* **-trolling, -trolled.** (*tr.*) **1.** to command, direct, or rule. **2.** to check, limit, or restrain: *to control one's emotions.* **3.** to regulate or operate (a machine). **4.** to verify (a scientific experiment) by conducting a parallel experiment in which the variable being investigated is held constant or is compared with a standard. **5. a.** to regulate (financial affairs). **b.** to examine (financial accounts). ~*n.* **6.** power to direct: *under control.* **7.** a curb; check: *a frontier control.* **8.** (*often pl.*) a mechanism for operating a car, aircraft, etc. **9. a.** a standard of comparison used in a statistical analysis, etc. **b.** (*as modifier*): *a control group.* **10. a.** a device that regulates the operation of a machine. **b.** (*as modifier*): *control room.* [C15: < OF *conteroller* to regulate, < *contrerolle* duplicate register, < *contre-* COUNTER- + *rolle* ROLL] —**conˈtrollable** *adj.* —**conˌtrollaˈbility** *n.* —**conˈtrollably** *adv.*

control experiment *n.* an experiment designed to check or correct the results of another experiment by removing the variable or variables operating in that other experiment.

controller (kənˈtrəʊlə) *n.* **1.** a person who directs. **2.** Also called: **comptroller.** a business executive or government officer responsible for financial planning, control, etc. **3.** the equipment concerned with controlling the operation of an electrical device. —**conˈtrollerˌship** *n.*

controlling interest *n.* a quantity of shares in a business that is sufficient to ensure control over its direction.

control tower *n.* a tower at an airport from which air traffic is controlled.

controversy (ˈkɒntrəˌvɜːsɪ, kənˈtrɒvəsɪ) *n., pl.* **-sies.** dispute, argument, or debate, esp. one concerning a matter about which there is strong disagreement and esp. one carried on in public or in the press. [C14: < L *contrōversia,* < *contrōversus,* < CONTRA- + *vertere* to turn] —**contro-**

versial (ˌkɒntrəˈvɜːʃəl) *adj.* —ˌ**controˈversialˌism** *n.* —ˌ**controˈversialist** *n.*

controvert (ˈkɒntrəˌvɜːt, ˌkɒntrəˈvɜːt) *vb.* (*tr.*) **1.** to deny, refute, or oppose (argument or opinion). **2.** to argue about. [C17: < L *contrōversus;* see CONTROVERSY] —ˌ**controˈvertible** *adj.*

contumacious (ˌkɒntjʊˈmeɪʃəs) *adj.* stubbornly resistant to authority. —ˌ**contuˈmaciously** *adv.*

contumacy (ˈkɒntjʊməsɪ) *n., pl.* **-cies.** obstinate and wilful resistance to authority, esp. refusal to comply with a court order. [C14: < L *contumācia,* < *contumāx* obstinate]

contumely (ˈkɒntjʊmɪlɪ) *n., pl.* **-lies.** **1.** scornful or insulting language or behaviour. **2.** a humiliating insult. [C14: < L *contumēlia,* < *tumēre* to swell, as with wrath] —**contumelious** (ˌkɒntjʊˈmiːlɪəs) *adj.* —ˌ**contuˈmeliously** *adv.*

contuse (kənˈtjuːz) *vb.* (*tr.*) to injure (the body) without breaking the skin; bruise. [C15: < L *contūsus* bruised, < *contundere* to grind, < *tundere* to beat] —**conˈtusion** *n.*

conundrum (kəˈnʌndrəm) *n.* **1.** a riddle, esp. one whose answer makes a play on words. **2.** a puzzling question or problem. [C16: <?]

conurbation (ˌkɒnɜːˈbeɪʃən) *n.* a large densely populated urban sprawl formed by the growth and coalescence of individual towns or cities. [C20: < CON- + *-urbation,* < L *urbs* city]

convalesce (ˌkɒnvəˈlɛs) *vb.* (*intr.*) to recover from illness, injury, or the aftereffects of a surgical operation. [C15: < L *convalēscere,* < *com-* (intensive) + *valēscere* to grow strong]

convalescence (ˌkɒnvəˈlɛsəns) *n.* **1.** gradual return to health after illness, injury, or an operation. **2.** the period during which such recovery occurs. —ˌ**convaˈlescent** *n., adj.*

convection (kənˈvɛkʃən) *n.* **1.** the process of heat transfer caused by movement of molecules from cool regions to warmer regions of lower density. **2.** *Meteorol.* the process by which masses of relatively warm air are raised into the atmosphere, often cooling and forming clouds, with compensatory downward movements of cooler air. [C19: < LL *convectiō,* < L *convehere* to bring together, < *vehere* to carry] —**conˈvectional** *adj.* —**conˈvective** *adj.*

convector (kənˈvɛktə) *n.* a space-heating device from which heat is transferred to the surrounding air by convection.

convene (kənˈviːn) *vb.* **1.** to gather, call together or summon, esp. for a formal meeting. **2.** (*tr.*) to order to appear before a court of law, judge, tribunal, etc. [C15: < L *convenīre* to assemble, < *venīre* to come] —**conˈvenable** *adj.*

convener *or* **convenor** (kənˈviːnə) *n.* a person who convenes or chairs a meeting, committee, etc., esp. one who is specifically elected to do so: *a convener of shop stewards.*

convenience (kənˈviːnɪəns) *n.* **1.** the quality of being suitable or opportune. **2.** a convenient time or situation. **3. at your convenience.** at a time suitable to you. **4.** usefulness, comfort, or facility. **5.** an object that is useful, esp. a labour-saving device. **6.** *Euphemistic, chiefly Brit.* a lavatory, esp. a public one. **7. make a convenience of.** to take advantage of; impose upon.

convenience food *n.* food that needs little preparation and can be used at any time.

convenient (kənˈviːnɪənt) *adj.* **1.** suitable; opportune. **2.** easy to use. **3.** close by; handy. [C14: < L *conveniēns,* < *convenīre* to be in accord with, < *venīre* to come] —**conˈveniently** *adv.*

convent (ˈkɒnvənt) *n.* **1.** a building inhabited by a religious community, usually of nuns. **2.** the religious community inhabiting such a building. **3.** Also called: **convent school.** a school in which the teachers are nuns. [C13: < OF, < L *conventus* meeting, < *convenīre;* see CONVENE]

conventicle (kənˈvɛntɪkᵊl) *n.* **1.** a secret or unauthorized assembly for worship. **2.** a small meeting house or chapel, esp. of Dissenters. [C14: < L *conventiculum,* < *conventus;* see CONVENT]

convention (kənˈvɛnʃən) *n.* **1.** a large formal assembly of a group with common interests, such as a trade union. **2.** *U.S. politics.* an assembly of delegates of one party to select candidates for office. **3.** an international agreement second only to a treaty in formality. **4.** any agreement or contract. **5.** the established view of what is thought to be proper behaviour, good taste, etc. **6.** an accepted rule, usage, etc.: *a convention used by printers.* **7.** *Bridge.* a bid or play not to be taken at its face value, which one's partner can interpret according to a prearranged bidding system. [C15: < L *conventiō* an assembling]

conventional (kənˈvɛnʃənᵊl) *adj.* **1.** following the accepted customs and proprieties, esp. in a way that lacks originality. **2.** established by accepted usage or general agreement. **3.** of a convention or assembly. **4.** *Visual arts.* conventionalized. **5.** (of weapons, warfare, etc.) not nuclear. —**conˈventionalism** *n.* —**conˈventionally** *adv.*

conventionality (kənˌvɛnʃəˈnælɪtɪ) *n., pl.* **-ties.** **1.** the quality of being conventional. **2.** (*often pl.*) something conventional.

conventionalize *or* **-lise** (kənˈvɛnʃənəˌlaɪz) *vb.* (*tr.*) **1.** to make conventional. **2.** to simplify or stylize (a design, decorative device, etc.). —**conˌventionaliˈzation** *or* **-liˈsation** *n.*

conventual (kənˈvɛntjʊəl) *adj.* **1.** of, belonging to, or characteristic of a convent. ~*n.* **2.** a member of a convent. —**conˈventually** *adv.*

converge (kənˈvɜːdʒ) *vb.* **1.** to move or cause to move towards the same point. **2.** to meet or join. **3.** (*intr.*) (of opinions, effects, etc.) to tend towards a common conclusion or result. **4.** (*intr.*) *Maths.* (of an infinite series) to approach a finite limit as the number of terms increases. **5.** (*intr.*) (of animals and plants) to undergo convergence. [C17: < LL *convergere,* < L *com-* together + *vergere* to incline] —**conˈvergent** *adj.*

convergence (kənˈvɜːdʒəns) *n.* **1.** Also: **convergency.** the act, degree, or a point of converging. **2.** Also called: **convergent evolution.** the evolutionary development of a superficial resemblance between unrelated animals that occupy a similar environment, as in the evolution of wings in birds and bats.

convergent thinking *n. Psychol.* analytical, usually deductive, thinking in which ideas are examined for their logical validity or in which a set of rules is followed, for example in arithmetic.

conversable (kənˈvɜːsəbᵊl) *adj.* **1.** easy or pleasant to talk to. **2.** able or inclined to talk.

conversant (kənˈvɜːsᵊnt) *adj.* (*usually postpositive* and foll. by *with*) experienced (in), familiar (with), or acquainted (with). —**conˈversance** *or* **conˈversancy** *n.* —**conˈversantly** *adv.*

conversation (ˌkɒnvəˈseɪʃən) *n.* the interchange through speech of information, ideas, etc.; spoken communication.

conversational (ˌkɒnvəˈseɪʃənᵊl) *adj.* **1.** of, using, or in the manner of conversation. **2.** inclined to conversation; conversable. —ˌ**converˈsationalist** *n.* —ˌ**converˈsationally** *adv.*

conversation piece *n.* **1.** something, esp. an unusual object, that provokes conversation. **2.** (esp. in 18th-century Britain) a group portrait in a landscape or domestic setting.

converse[1] *vb.* (kənˈvɜːs). (*intr.;* often foll. by *with*) **1.** to engage in conversation (with). **2.** to commune spiritually (with). ~*n.* (ˈkɒnvɜːs). **3.** conversation (often in **hold converse with**). [C16: < OF *converser,* < L *conversārī* to keep company with, < *conversāre* to turn constantly, < *vertere* to turn] —**conˈverser** *n.*

converse[2] (ˈkɒnvɜːs) *adj.* **1.** (*prenominal*) reversed; opposite; contrary. ~*n.* **2.** something that is opposite or contrary. **3.** *Logic.* a categorial proposition obtained from another by the transposition of the subject and predicate, as *all bald men are bad* from *all bad men are bald.* [C16: < L *conversus* turned around; see CONVERSE[1]] —**conˈversely** *adv.*

conversion (kənˈvɜːʃən) *n.* **1. a.** a change or adaptation in form, character, or function. **b.** something changed in one of these respects. **2.** a change to another belief, as in a change of religion. **3.** alteration to the structure or fittings of a building undergoing a change in function or legal status. **4.** *Maths.* a change in the units or form of a number or expression: *the conversion of miles to kilometres.* **5.** *Rugby.* a score made after a try by kicking the ball over the crossbar from a place kick. **6.** *Physics.* a change of fertile material to fissile material in a reactor. **7.** an alteration to a car engine to improve its performance. [C14: < L *conversiō* a turning around; see CONVERT]

convert *vb.* (kən'vɜːt). (*mainly tr.*) **1.** to change or adapt the form, character, or function of. **2.** to cause (someone) to change in opinion, belief, etc. **3.** (*intr.*) to admit of being changed (into): *the table converts into a tray.* **4.** (*also intr.*) to change or be changed into another state: *to convert water into ice.* **5.** *Law.* to assume unlawful proprietary rights over (personal property). **6.** (*also intr.*) *Rugby.* to make a conversion after (a try). **7.** *Logic.* to transpose the subject and predicate of (a proposition). **8.** to change (a value or measurement) from one system of units to another. **9.** to exchange (a security or bond) for something of equivalent value. ~*n.* ('kɒnvɜːt). **10.** a person who has been converted to another belief, religion, etc. [C13: < OF, < L *convertere* to turn around, alter, < *vertere* to turn]

converter *or* **convertor** (kən'vɜːtə) *n.* **1.** a person or thing that converts. **2.** *Physics.* **a.** a device for converting alternating current to direct current or vice versa. **b.** a device for converting a signal from one frequency to another. **3.** a vessel in which molten metal is refined, using a blast of air or oxygen.

converter reactor *n.* a nuclear reactor for converting one fuel into another, esp. fertile material into fissionable material.

convertible (kən'vɜːtɪbᵊl) *adj.* **1.** capable of being converted. **2.** (of a car) having a folding or removable roof. **3.** *Finance.* **a.** (of a currency) freely exchangeable into other currencies. **b.** (of a paper currency) exchangeable on demand for precious metal to an equivalent value. ~*n.* **4.** a car with a folding or removable roof. —**con,verti'bility** *n.* —**con'vertibly** *adv.*

convex ('kɒnvɛks, kɒn'vɛks) *adj.* **1.** curving outwards. **2.** having one or two surfaces curved or ground in the shape of a section of the exterior of a sphere, ellipsoid, etc.: *a convex lens.* [C16: < L *convexus* vaulted, rounded] —**con'vexity** *n.* —**'convexly** *adv.*

convexo-concave (kən,vɛksəʊkɒn'keɪv) *adj.* **1.** having one side convex and the other side concave. **2.** (of a lens) having a convex face with greater curvature than the concave face.

convexo-convex *adj.* (esp. of a lens) having both sides convex; biconvex.

convey (kən'veɪ) *vb.* (*tr.*) **1.** to take, carry, or transport from one place to another. **2.** to communicate (a message, information, etc.). **3.** (of a channel, path, etc.) to conduct or transfer. **4.** *Law.* to transfer (the title to property). [C13: < OF *conveier,* < Med. L *conviāre* to escort, < L *com-* with + *via* way] —**con'veyable** *adj.*

conveyance (kən'veɪəns) *n.* **1.** the act of conveying. **2.** a means of transport. **3.** *Law.* **a.** a transfer of the legal title to property. **b.** the document effecting such a transfer. —**con'veyancer** *n.* —**con'veyancing** *n.*

conveyor *or* **conveyer** (kən'veɪə) *n.* **1.** a person or thing that conveys. **2.** short for **conveyor belt.**

conveyor belt *n.* a flexible endless strip of fabric or linked plates driven by rollers and used to transport objects, esp. in a factory.

convict *vb.* (kən'vɪkt). (*tr.*) **1.** to pronounce (someone) guilty of an offence. ~*n.* ('kɒnvɪkt). **2.** a person found guilty of an offence against the law. **3.** a person serving a prison sentence. [C14: < L *convictus* convicted, < *convincere* to prove guilty, CONVINCE]

conviction (kən'vɪkʃən) *n.* **1.** the state of being convinced. **2.** a firmly held belief, opinion, etc. **3.** the act of convincing. **4.** the act of convicting or the state of being convicted. **5.** **carry conviction.** to be convincing. —**con'victional** *adj.* —**con'victive** *adj.*

convince (kən'vɪns) *vb.* (*tr.*) (*may take a clause as object*) to make (someone) agree, understand, or realize the truth or validity of something; persuade. [C16: < L *convincere* to demonstrate incontrovertibly, < *com-* (intensive) + *vincere* to overcome] —**con'vincer** *n.* —**con'vincible** *adj.* —**con'vincing** *adj.* —**con'vincingly** *adv.*

convivial (kən'vɪvɪəl) *adj.* sociable; jovial or festive: *a convivial atmosphere.* [C17: < LL *convīviālis,* < L *convīvium,* a living together, banquet, < *vīvere* to live] —**con,vivi'ality** *n.*

convocation (,kɒnvə'keɪʃən) *n.* **1.** a large formal assembly. **2.** the act of convoking or state of being convoked. **3.** *Church of England.* either of the synods of the provinces of Canterbury or York. **4.** *Episcopal Church.* an assembly of the clergy and part of the laity of a diocese. **5.** (*sometimes cap.*) (in some British universities) a legislative assembly. **6.** (in Australia and New Zealand) the graduate membership of a university. —,**convo'cational** *adj.*

convoke (kən'vəʊk) *vb.* (*tr.*) to call (a meeting, assembly, etc.) together; summon. [C16: < L *convocāre,* < *vocāre* to call] —**con'voker** *n.*

convolute ('kɒnvə,luːt) *vb.* (*tr.*) **1.** to form into a twisted, coiled, or rolled shape. ~*adj.* **2.** *Bot.* rolled longitudinally upon itself: *a convolute petal.* [C18: < L *convolūtus,* < *convolvere* to roll together, < *volvere* to turn]

convoluted ('kɒnvə,luːtɪd) *adj.* **1.** (esp. of meaning, style, etc.) difficult to comprehend; involved. **2.** coiled. —**'convo,lutedly** *adv.*

convolution (,kɒnvə'luːʃən) *n.* **1.** a turn, twist, or coil. **2.** an intricate or confused matter or condition. **3.** any of the numerous convex folds of the surface of the brain. —,**convo'lutional** *or* ,**convo'lutionary** *adj.*

convolve (kən'vɒlv) *vb.* to wind or roll together; coil; twist. [C16: < L *convolvere;* see CONVOLUTE]

convolvulus (kən'vɒlvjʊləs) *n., pl.* **-luses** *or* **-li** (-,laɪ). a twining herbaceous plant having funnel-shaped flowers and triangular leaves. [C16: < L: bindweed; see CONVOLUTE]

convoy ('kɒnvɔɪ) *n.* **1.** a group of merchant ships with an escort of warships. **2.** a group of land vehicles assembled to travel together. **3.** the act of travelling or escorting by convoy (esp. in **in convoy**). ~*vb.* **4.** (*tr.*) to escort while in transit. [C14: < OF *convoier* to CONVEY]

convulse (kən'vʌls) *vb.* **1.** (*tr.*) to shake or agitate violently. **2.** (*tr.*) to cause (muscles) to undergo violent spasms or contractions. **3.** (*intr.; often foll. by with*) *Inf.* to shake or be overcome (with violent emotion, esp. laughter). [C17: < L *convulsus,* < *convellere,* < *vellere* to pluck, pull] —**con'vulsive** *adj.* —**con'vulsively** *adv.*

convulsion (kən'vʌlʃən) *n.* **1.** a violent involuntary muscular contraction. **2.** a violent upheaval, esp. a social one. **3.** (*usually pl.*) *Inf.* uncontrollable laughter: *I was in convulsions.*

cony *or* **coney** ('kəʊnɪ) *n., pl.* **-nies** *or* **-neys.** **1.** a rabbit or fur made from the skin of a rabbit. **2.** (in the Bible) another name for the **hyrax.** [C13: back formation < *conies,* < OF *conis,* pl. of *conil,* < L *cunīculus* rabbit]

coo (kuː) *vb.* **cooing, cooed.** **1.** (*intr.*) (of doves, pigeons, etc.) to make a characteristic soft throaty call. **2.** (*tr.*) to speak in a soft murmur. **3.** (*intr.*) to murmur lovingly (esp. in **bill and coo**). ~*n.* **4.** the sound of cooing. ~*interj.* **5.** *Brit. sl.* an exclamation of surprise, awe, etc. —**'cooing** *adj., n.* —**'cooingly** *adv.*

cooee *or* **cooey** ('kuːiː) *interj.* **1.** a call used to attract attention, esp. a long loud high-pitched call on two notes. ~*vb.* **cooeeing, cooeed** *or* **cooeying, cooeyed.** **2.** (*intr.*) to utter this call. ~*n.* **3.** *Austral. & N.Z. inf.* calling distance (esp. in **within (a) cooee (of)**). [C19: < Abor.]

cook (kʊk) *vb.* **1.** to prepare (food) by the action of heat, or (of food) to become ready for eating through such a process. Related adj.: **culinary.** **2.** to subject or be subjected to intense heat: *the town cooked in the sun.* **3.** (*tr.*) *Sl.* to alter or falsify (figures, accounts, etc.): *to cook the books.* **4.** (*tr.*) *Sl.* to spoil (something). **5.** (*intr.*) *Sl.* to happen (esp. in **what's cooking?**). ~*n.* **6.** a person who prepares food for eating. ~See also **cook up.** [OE *cōc* (n.), < L *coquus* a cook, < *coquere* to cook] —ˈ**cookable** *adj.*

cooker (ˈkʊkə) *n.* **1.** an apparatus heated by gas, electricity, oil, or solid fuel, for cooking food. **2.** *Brit.* another name for **cooking apple.**

cookery (ˈkʊkərɪ) *n.* **1.** the art, study, or practice of cooking. **2.** *U.S.* a place for cooking.

cookery book *or* **cookbook** (ˈkʊkˌbʊk) *n.* a book containing recipes.

cook-general *n., pl.* **cooks-general.** *Brit.* (formerly, esp. in the 1920s and 30s) a domestic servant who did cooking and housework.

cookie *or* **cooky** (ˈkʊkɪ) *n., pl.* **cookies. 1.** the U.S. and Canad. word for **biscuit. 2.** *Inf., chiefly U.S. & Canad.* a person: *smart cookie.* **3. that's the way the cookie crumbles.** *Inf., chiefly U.S. & Canad.* matters are inevitably so. [C18: < Du. *koekje*, dim. of *koek* cake]

cooking apple *n.* any large sour apple used in cooking.

Cook's tour (kʊks) *n. Inf.* a rapid but extensive tour or survey of anything. [C19: after Thomas *Cook* (1808–92), E travel agent]

cook up *vb.* (*tr., adv.*) **1.** *Inf.* to concoct or invent (a story, alibi, etc.). **2.** to prepare (a meal), esp. quickly. **3.** *Sl.* to prepare (a drug) for use by heating, as by dissolving heroin in a spoon.

cool (kuːl) *adj.* **1.** moderately cold: *a cool day.* **2.** comfortably free of heat: *a cool room.* **3.** calm: *a cool head.* **4.** lacking in enthusiasm, cordiality, etc.: *a cool welcome.* **5.** calmly impudent. **6.** *Inf.* (of sums of money, etc.) without exaggeration; actual: *a cool ten thousand.* **7.** (of a colour) having violet, blue, or green predominating; cold. **8.** (of jazz) economical and rhythmically relaxed. **9.** *Inf.* sophisticated or elegant; unruffled. **10.** *Inf., chiefly U.S. & Canad.* marvellous. ~*n.* **11.** coolness: *the cool of the evening.* **12.** *Sl.* calmness; composure (esp. in **keep** *or* **lose one's cool**). **13.** *Sl.* unruffled elegance or sophistication. ~*vb.* **14.** (usually foll. by *down* or *off*) to make or become cooler. **15.** (usually foll. by *down* or *off*) to lessen the intensity of (anger or excitement) or (of anger or excitement) to become less intense; calm down. **16. cool it.** (*usually imperative*) *Sl.* to calm down. [OE *cōl*] —ˈ**coolly** *adv.* —ˈ**coolness** *n.*

coolabah *or* **coolibar** (ˈkuːləˌbɑː) *n.* an Australian eucalyptus that grows along rivers and has smooth bark and long narrow leaves. [< Abor.]

coolant (ˈkuːlənt) *n.* **1.** a fluid used to cool a system or to transfer heat from one part of it to another. **2.** a liquid used to lubricate and cool the workpiece and cutting tool during machining.

cool bag *or* **box** *n.* an insulated container for keeping food cool.

cool drink *n. S. African.* a soft drink.

cooler (ˈkuːlə) *n.* **1.** a container, vessel, or apparatus for cooling, such as a heat exchanger. **2.** a slang word for **prison. 3.** a drink consisting of wine, fruit juice, and carbonated water.

coolie *or* **cooly** (ˈkuːlɪ) *n., pl.* **-ies.** an unskilled Oriental labourer. [C17: < Hindi *kulī*]

cooling tower *n.* a tall, hollow structure, designed to permit free passage of air, inside which hot water trickles down, becoming cool as it does so: the water is normally reused as part of an industrial process.

coomb, combe, coombe, *or* **comb** (kuːm) *n.* **1.** *Chiefly southeastern English.* a short valley or deep hollow. **2.** *Chiefly northern English.* another name for a **cirque.** [OE *cumb*]

coon (kuːn) *n.* **1.** *Inf.* short for **raccoon. 2.** *Derog. sl.* a Negro or Australian Aborigine.

coonskin (ˈkuːnˌskɪn) *n.* **1.** the pelt of a raccoon. **2.** a raccoon cap with the tail hanging at the back. **3.** *U.S.* an overcoat made of raccoon.

coop[1] (kuːp) *n.* **1.** a cage or small enclosure for poultry or small animals. **2.** a small narrow place of confinement, esp. a prison cell. **3.** a wicker basket for catching fish. ~*vb.* **4.** (*tr.;* often foll. by *up* or *in*) to confine in a restricted area. [C15: prob. < MLow G *kūpe* basket]

coop[2] *or* **co-op** (ˈkəʊˌɒp) *n.* a cooperative society or a shop run by a cooperative society.

cooper (ˈkuːpə) *n.* **1.** a person skilled in making and repairing barrels, casks, etc. ~*vb.* **2.** (*tr.*) to make or mend (barrels, casks, etc.). [C13: < MDu. *cūper* or MLow G *kūper;* see COOP[1]]

cooperage (ˈkuːpərɪdʒ) *n.* **1.** Also called: **coopery.** the craft, place of work, or products of a cooper. **2.** the labour fee charged by a cooper.

cooperate *or* **co-operate** (kəʊˈɒpəˌreɪt) *vb.* (*intr.*) **1.** to work or act together. **2.** to be of assistance or be willing to assist. **3.** *Econ.* to engage in economic cooperation. [C17: < LL *cooperārī* to combine, < L *operārī* to work] —**coˈoperˌator** *or* **co-ˈoperˌator** *n.*

cooperation *or* **co-operation** (kəʊˌɒpəˈreɪʃən) *n.* **1.** joint operation or action. **2.** assistance or willingness to assist. **3.** *Econ.* the combination of consumers, workers, etc., in activities usually embracing production, distribution, or trade. —**coˌoperˈationist** *or* **co-ˌoperˈationist** *n.*

cooperative *or* **co-operative** (kəʊˈɒpərətɪv, -ˈɒprə-) *adj.* **1.** willing to cooperate; helpful. **2.** acting in conjunction with others; cooperating. **3. a.** (of an enterprise, farm, etc.) owned collectively and managed for joint economic benefit. **b.** (of an economy) based on collective ownership and cooperative use of the means of production and distribution. ~*n.* **4.** a cooperative organization, such as a farm.

cooperative society *n.* a commercial enterprise owned and managed by and for the benefit of customers or workers.

coopt *or* **co-opt** (kəʊˈɒpt) *vb.* (*tr.*) to add (someone) to a committee, board, etc., by the agreement of the existing members. [C17: < L *cooptāre,* < *optāre* to choose] —**coˈoption, co-ˈoption** *or* **ˌcoopˈtation, ˌco-opˈtation** *n.*

coordinate *or* **co-ordinate** *vb.* (kəʊˈɔːdɪˌneɪt). **1.** (*tr.*) to integrate (diverse elements) in a harmonious operation. **2.** to place (things) in the same class, or (of things) to be placed in the same class, etc. **3.** (*intr.*) to work together harmoniously. **4.** (*intr.*) to take or be in the form of a harmonious order. ~*n.* (kəʊˈɔːdɪnɪt). **5.** *Maths.* any of a set of numbers that defines the location of a point with reference to a system of axes. **6.** a person or thing equal in rank, type, etc. ~*adj.* (kəʊˈɔːdɪnɪt). **7.** of or involving coordination. **8.** of the same rank, type, etc. **9.** of or involving the use of coordinates: *coordinate geometry.* **10.** *Chem.* denoting a type of covalent bond in which both the shared electrons are provided by one of the atoms. —**coˈordinative** *or* **co-ˈordinative** *adj.* —**coˈordiˌnator** *or* **co-ˈordiˌnator** *n.*

coordinate clause *n.* one of two or more clauses in a sentence having the same status and introduced by coordinating conjunctions.

coordinates (kəʊˈɔːdɪnɪts) *pl. n.* clothes of matching or harmonious colours and design, suitable for wearing together.

coordinating conjunction *n.* a conjunction that introduces coordinate clauses, such as *and, but,* and *or.*

coordination *or* **co-ordination** (kəʊˌɔːdɪˈneɪʃən) *n.* balanced and effective interaction of movement, actions, etc. [C17: < LL *coordinātiō,* < L *ordinātiō* an arranging]

coot (kuːt) *n.* **1.** an aquatic bird of Europe and Asia, having dark plumage, and a white bill with a frontal shield: family Rallidae (rails, etc.). **2.** a foolish person, esp. an old man. [C14: prob. < Low G]

cootie (ˈkuːtɪ) *n. U.S. & N.Z.* a slang name for the body louse. [C20: < Maori & ? (for U.S.) Malay *kutu* louse]

cop[1] (kɒp) *Sl.* ~*n.* **1.** another name for **policeman. 2.** *Brit.* an arrest (esp. in **a fair cop**). ~*vb.* **copping, copped.** (*tr.*) **3.** to catch. **4.** to steal. **5.** to suffer (a punishment): *you'll cop a clout if you do that!* **6.** *Sl.* **cop this!** just look at this! ~See also **cop out.** [C18: (vb.) ? < obs. *cap* to arrest, < OF *caper* to seize]

cop[2] (kɒp) *n.* **1.** a conical roll of thread wound on a spindle. **2.** *Now chiefly dialect.* the top or crest, as of a hill. [OE *cop, copp* top, summit]

cop[3] (kɒp) *n. Brit. sl.* (*usually used with a negative*) value: *not much cop.* [C19: n. use of COP[1]]

copal (ˈkəʊpᵊl, -pæl) *n.* a hard aromatic resin obtained from various tropical trees and used in making varnishes and lacquers. [C16: < Sp., < Nahuatl *copalli*]

copartner (kəʊˈpɑːtnə) *n.* a partner or associate, esp. an equal partner in business. —**coˈpartnership** *n.*

cope[1] (kəʊp) *vb.* (*intr.*) **1.** (foll. by *with*) to contend (against). **2.** to deal successfully (with); manage: *she coped well with the problem.* [C14: < OF *coper* to strike, cut, < *coup* blow]

cope[2] (kəʊp) *n.* **1.** a large ceremonial cloak worn at liturgical functions by priests of certain Christian sects. **2.** any covering shaped like a cope. ~*vb.* **3.** (*tr.*) to dress (someone) in a cope. [OE *cāp,* < Med. L *cāpa,* < LL *cappa* hooded cloak]

cope[3] (kəʊp) *vb.* (*tr.*) **1.** to provide (a wall, etc.) with a coping. ~*n.* **2.** another name for **coping.** [C17: prob. < F *couper* to cut]

copeck (ˈkəʊpɛk) *n.* a variant spelling of **kopeck.**

copepod (ˈkəʊpɪˌpɒd) *n.* a minute marine or freshwater crustacean, an important constituent of plankton. [C19: < NL *copepoda,* < Gk *kōpē* oar + *pous* foot]

coper (ˈkəʊpə) *n.* a horse dealer. [C17 (a dealer): < dialect *cope* to buy, barter, < Low G]

Copernican system (kəˈpɜːnɪkən) *n.* the theory published in 1543 by Copernicus which stated that the earth and the planets rotated round the sun.

copestone (ˈkəʊpˌstəʊn) *n.* **1.** Also called: **coping stone.** a stone used to form a coping. **2.** the stone at the top of a building, wall, etc.

copier (ˈkɒpɪə) *n.* a person or device that copies.

copilot (ˈkəʊˌpaɪlət) *n.* a second or relief pilot of an aircraft.

coping (ˈkəʊpɪŋ) *n.* the sloping top course of a wall, usually made of masonry or brick.

coping saw *n.* a handsaw with a U-shaped frame used for cutting curves in a material too thick for a fret saw.

copious (ˈkəʊpɪəs) *adj.* **1.** abundant; extensive. **2.** having an abundant supply. **3.** full of words, ideas, etc.; profuse. [C14: < L *cōpiōsus,* < *cōpia* abundance] —ˈ**copiously** *adv.* —ˈ**copiousness** *n.*

coplanar (kəʊˈpleɪnə) *adj.* lying in the same plane: *coplanar lines.* —ˌ**coplaˈnarity** *n.*

copolymer (kəʊˈpɒlɪmə) *n.* a chemical compound of high molecular weight formed by uniting the molecules of two or more different compounds (monomers).

cop out *Sl.* ~ *vb.* **1.** (*intr., adv.*) to fail to assume responsibility or fail to perform. ~*n.* **cop-out. 2.** a way or an instance of avoiding responsibility or commitment. [C20: prob. < COP[1]]

copper[1] (ˈkɒpə) *n.* **1.** a malleable reddish metallic element occurring as the free metal, copper glance, and copper pyrites: used in such alloys as brass and bronze. Symbol: Cu; atomic no.: 29; atomic wt.: 63.54. Related adjs.: **cupric, cuprous. 2. a.** the reddish-brown colour of copper. **b.** (*as adj.*): *copper hair.* **3.** *Inf.* any copper or bronze coin. **4.** *Chiefly Brit.* a large vessel, formerly of copper, used for boiling or washing. **5.** any of various small widely distributed butterflies having reddish-brown wings. ~*vb.* **6.** (*tr.*) to coat or cover with copper. [OE *coper,* < L *Cyprium aes* Cyprian metal, < Gk *Kupris* Cyprus]

copper[2] (ˈkɒpə) *n.* a slang word for **policeman.** Often shortened to **cop.** [C19: < COP[1] (vb.)]

copperas (ˈkɒpərəs) *n.* a less common name for **ferrous sulphate.** [C14 *coperose,* via OF < Med. L *cuperosa,* ? orig. in *aqua cuprosa* copper water]

copper beech *n.* a cultivated variety of European beech that has reddish leaves.

Copper Belt *n.* a region of Central Africa, along the Zambia-Zaïre border: rich in deposits of copper.

copper-bottomed *adj.* reliable, esp. financially reliable. [< the practice of coating bottom of ships with copper to prevent the timbers rotting]

copperhead (ˈkɒpəˌhɛd) *n.* **1.** a venomous pit viper of the U.S., with a reddish-brown head. **2.** a venomous marsh snake of Australia, with a reddish band behind the head.

copperplate (ˈkɒpəˌpleɪt) *n.* **1.** a polished copper plate on which a design has been etched or engraved. **2.** a print taken from such a plate. **3.** a fine handwriting based upon that used on copperplate engravings.

copper pyrites (ˈpaɪraɪts) *n.* (*functioning as sing.*) another name for **chalcopyrite.**

coppersmith (ˈkɒpəˌsmɪθ) *n.* a person who works in copper.

copper sulphate *n.* a copper salt found naturally and made by the action of sulphuric acid on copper oxide: used as a mordant, in electroplating, and in plant sprays. Formula: $CuSO_4$.

coppice (ˈkɒpɪs) *n.* **1.** a dense growth of small trees or bushes, esp. one regularly trimmed back so that a continual supply of small poles and firewood is obtained. ~*vb.* **2.** (*tr.*) to trim back (trees or bushes) to form a coppice. [C14: < OF *copeiz*] —ˈ**coppiced** *adj.*

copra (ˈkɒprə) *n.* the dried, oil-yielding kernel of the coconut. [C16: < Port., < Malayalam *koppara* coconut]

copro- *or before a vowel* **copr-** *combining form.* indicating dung or obscenity, as in **copˈrology** *n.* preoccupation with excrement, **copˈrophagous** *adj.* feeding on dung. [< Gk *kopros* dung]

copse (kɒps) *n.* another word for **coppice** (sense 1). [C16: < COPPICE]

Copt (kɒpt) *n.* **1.** a member of the Coptic Church. **2.** an Egyptian descended from the ancient Egyptians. [C17: < Ar., < Coptic *kyptios* Egyptian, < Gk *Aiguptios,* < *Aiguptos* Egypt]

Coptic (ˈkɒptɪk) *n.* **1.** an Afro-Asiatic language, written in the Greek alphabet but descended from ancient Egyptian. Extinct as a spoken language, it survives in the Coptic Church. ~*adj.* **2.** of this language. **3.** of the Copts.

Coptic Church *n.* the ancient Christian Church of Egypt.

copula (ˈkɒpjʊlə) *n., pl.* **-las** *or* **-lae** (-ˌliː). **1.** a verb, such as *be, seem,* or *taste,* that is used to identify or link the subject with the complement of a sentence, as in *he became king, sugar tastes sweet.* **2.** anything that serves as a link. [C17: < L: bond, < *co-* together + *apere* to fasten] —ˈ**copular** *adj.*

copulate (ˈkɒpjʊˌleɪt) *vb.* (*intr.*) to perform sexual intercourse. [C17: < L *copulāre* to join together; see COPULA] —ˌ**copuˈlation** *n.* —ˈ**copulatory** *adj.*

copulative (ˈkɒpjʊlətɪv) *adj.* **1.** serving to join or unite. **2.** of copulation. **3.** *Grammar.* (of a verb) having the nature of a copula.

copy (ˈkɒpɪ) *n., pl.* **copies. 1.** an imitation or reproduction of an original. **2.** a single specimen of something that occurs in a multiple edition, such as a book. **3. a.** matter to be reproduced in print. **b.** written matter or text as distinct from graphic material in books, etc. **4.** the words used to present a promotional message in an advertisement. **5.** *Journalism, inf.* suitable material for an article: *disasters are always good copy.* **6.** *Arch.* a model to be copied, esp. an example of penmanship. ~*vb.* **copying, copied. 7.** (when *tr.,* often foll. by *out*) to make a copy (of). **8.** (*tr.*) to imitate as a model. **9.** to imitate unfairly. [C14: < Med. L *cōpia* an imitation, < L: abundance]

copybook (ˈkɒpɪˌbʊk) *n.* **1.** a book of specimens, esp. of penmanship, for imitation. **2.** *Chiefly U.S.* a book for or containing documents. **3. blot one's copybook.** *Inf.* to spoil one's reputation by a mistake or indiscretion. **4.** (*modifier*) trite or unoriginal.

copycat (ˈkɒpɪˌkæt) *n. Inf.* **a.** a person, esp. a child, who imitates or copies another. **b.** (*as modifier*): *copycat murders.*

copyhold (ˈkɒpɪˌhəʊld) *n. Law.* (formerly) a

tenure less than freehold of land in England evidenced by a copy of the Court roll.
copyist (ˈkɒpɪɪst) *n.* **1.** a person who makes written copies. **2.** a person who imitates.
copyreader (ˈkɒpɪˌriːdə) *n. U.S.* a person who edits and prepares newspaper copy for publication; subeditor.
copyright (ˈkɒpɪˌraɪt) *n.* **1.** the exclusive right to produce copies and to control an original literary, musical, or artistic work, granted by law for a specified number of years. ~*adj.* **2.** (of a work, etc.) subject to copyright. ~*vb.* **3.** (*tr.*) to take out a copyright on.
copy typist *n.* a typist whose job is to type from written or typed drafts rather than dictation.
copywriter (ˈkɒpɪˌraɪtə) *n.* a person employed to write advertising copy. —ˈ**copyˌwriting** *n.*
coquet (kəʊˈkɛt, kɒ-) *vb.* **-quetting, -quetted.** (*intr.*) **1.** to behave flirtatiously. **2.** to dally or trifle. [C17: < F: a gallant, lit.: a little cock, < *coq* cock] —ˈ**coquetry** *n.*
coquette (kəʊˈkɛt, kɒˈkɛt) *n.* **1.** a woman who flirts. **2.** any hummingbird of the genus *Lophornis.* [C17: < F, fem. of COQUET] —**coˈquettish** *adj.* —**coˈquettishness** *n.*
Cor. *Bible. abbrev. for* Corinthians.
coracle (ˈkɒrək^əl) *n.* a small roundish boat made of waterproofed hides stretched over a wicker frame. [C16: < Welsh *corwgl*]
coracoid (ˈkɒrəˌkɔɪd) *n.* a paired ventral bone of the pectoral girdle in vertebrates. In mammals it is reduced to a peg (the **coracoid process**) on the scapula. [C18: < NL *coracoīdēs,* < Gk *korakoeidēs* like a raven, < *korax* raven]
coral (ˈkɒrəl) *n.* **1.** any of a class of marine colonial coelenterates having a calcareous, horny, or soft skeleton. **2. a.** the calcareous or horny material forming the skeleton of certain of these animals. **b.** (*as modifier*): *a coral reef.* **3.** a rocklike aggregation of certain of these animals or their skeletons, forming an island or reef. **4. a.** something made of coral. **b.** (*as modifier*): *a coral necklace.* **5. a.** a yellowish-pink colour. **b.** (*as adj.*): *coral lipstick.* **6.** the roe of a lobster or crab, which becomes pink when cooked. [C14: < OF, < L *corāllium,* < Gk *korallion,* prob. of Semitic origin]
coral reef *n.* a marine reef consisting of coral consolidated into limestone.
coralroot (ˈkɒrəlˌruːt) *n.* a N temperate leafless orchid with branched roots resembling coral.
coral snake *n.* **1.** a venomous snake of tropical and subtropical America, marked with red, black, yellow, and white transverse bands. **2.** any of various other brightly coloured snakes of Africa and SE Asia.
cor anglais (ˈkɔːr ˈɑːŋgleɪ) *n., pl.* **cors anglais** (ˈkɔːz ˈɑːŋgleɪ). *Music.* a woodwind instrument, the alto of the oboe family. Also called: **English horn.** [C19: < F: English horn]
corbel (ˈkɔːb^əl) *Archit.* ~*n.* **1.** a bracket, usually of stone or brick. ~*vb.* **-belling, -belled** *or U.S.* **-beling, -beled. 2.** (*tr.*) to lay (a stone) so that it forms a corbel. [C15: < OF, lit.: a little raven, < Med. L *corvellus,* < L *corvus* raven]
corbie (ˈkɔːbɪ) *n.* a Scot. name for **raven**[1] or **crow**[1]. [C15: < OF *corbin,* < L *corvīnus* CORVINE]
corbie-step *or* **corbel step** *n. Archit.* any of a set of steps on the top of a gable. Also called: **crow step.**
cord (kɔːd) *n.* **1.** string or thin rope made of twisted strands. **2.** a length of woven or twisted strands of silk, etc., used as a belt, etc. **3.** a ribbed fabric, esp. corduroy. **4.** the U.S. and Canad. name for **flex** (sense 1). **5.** *Anat.* any part resembling a rope: *the spinal cord.* **6.** a unit for measuring cut wood, equal to 128 cubic feet. ~*vb.* (*tr.*) **7.** to bind or furnish with a cord or cords. ~See also **cords.** [C13: < OF *corde,* < L *chorda,* < Gk *khordē*] —ˈ**cordˌlike** *adj.*
cordage (ˈkɔːdɪdʒ) *n.* **1.** *Naut.* the lines and rigging of a vessel. **2.** an amount of wood measured in cords.
cordate (ˈkɔːdeɪt) *adj.* heart-shaped.
corded (ˈkɔːdɪd) *adj.* **1.** bound or fastened with cord. **2.** (of a fabric) ribbed. **3.** (of muscles) standing out like cords.
cordial (ˈkɔːdɪəl) *adj.* **1.** warm and friendly: *a cordial greeting.* **2.** stimulating. ~*n.* **3.** a drink with a fruit base: *lime cordial.* **4.** another word for **liqueur.** [C14: < Med. L *cordiālis,* < L *cor* heart] —ˈ**cordially** *adv.*
cordiality (ˌkɔːdɪˈælɪtɪ) *n., pl.* **-ties.** warmth of feeling.
cordillera (ˌkɔːdɪlˈjɛərə) *n.* a series of parallel ranges of mountains, esp. in the northwestern U.S. [C18: < Sp., < *cordilla,* lit.: a little cord]
cordite (ˈkɔːdaɪt) *n.* any of various explosive materials containing cellulose nitrate, sometimes mixed with nitroglycerin. [C19: < CORD + -ITE[1], from its stringy appearance]
cordless (ˈkɔːdlɪs) *adj.* (of an electrical device) operated by an internal battery so that no connection to mains supply is needed.
cordon (ˈkɔːd^ən) *n.* **1.** a chain of police, soldiers, ships, etc., stationed around an area. **2.** a ribbon worn as insignia of honour. **3.** a cord or ribbon worn as an ornament. **4.** *Archit.* another name for **string course. 5.** *Horticulture.* a fruit tree consisting of a single stem bearing fruiting spurs, produced by cutting back all lateral branches. ~*vb.* **6.** (*tr.;* often foll. by *off*) to put or form a cordon (around); close (off). [C16: < OF, lit.: a little cord, < *corde* CORD]
cordon bleu (*French* kɔrdɔ̃ blø) *n.* **1.** *French history.* the sky-blue ribbon worn by members of the highest order of knighthood under the Bourbon monarchy. **2.** any very high distinction. ~*adj.* **3.** of or denoting food prepared to a very high standard. [F, lit.: blue ribbon]
cordon sanitaire *French.* (kɔrdɔ̃ sanitɛr) *n.* **1.** a guarded line isolating an infected area. **2.** a line of buffer states shielding a country. [C19: lit.: sanitary line]
cordovan (ˈkɔːdəv^ən) *n.* a fine leather now made principally from horsehide. [C16: < *cordobán* of Córdoba, in Spain]
cords (kɔːdz) *pl. n.* trousers made of corduroy.
corduroy (ˈkɔːdəˌrɔɪ, ˌkɔːdəˈrɔɪ) *n.* a heavy cotton pile fabric with lengthways ribs. [C18: ? < the proper name *Corderoy*]
corduroys (ˌkɔːdəˈrɔɪz, ˈkɔːdəˌrɔɪz) *pl. n.* trousers or breeches of corduroy.
cordwainer (ˈkɔːdˌweɪnə) *n. Arch.* a shoemaker or worker in leather. [C12: *cordwaner,* < OF, < OSp. *cordován* CORDOVAN]
cordwood (ˈkɔːdˌwʊd) *n.* wood that has been cut into lengths of four feet so that it can be stacked in cords.
core (kɔː) *n.* **1.** the central part of certain fleshy fruits, such as the apple, consisting of the seeds. **2.** the central or essential part of something: *the core of the argument.* **3.** a piece of magnetic material, such as soft iron, inside an electromagnet or transformer. **4.** *Geol.* the central part of the earth. **5.** a cylindrical sample of rock, soil, etc., obtained by the use of a hollow drill. **6.** *Physics.* the region of a nuclear reactor in which the reaction takes place. **7.** *Computers.* **a.** a ferrite ring used in a computer memory to store one bit of information. **b.** the whole memory of a computer when made up of such rings. **c.** (*as modifier*): *core memory.* **8.** *Archaeol.* a stone or flint from which flakes have been removed. ~*vb.* **9.** (*tr.*) to remove the core from (fruit). [C14: <?]
coreligionist (ˌkəʊrɪˈlɪdʒənɪst) *n.* an adherent of the same religion as another.
coreopsis (ˌkɒrɪˈɒpsɪs) *n.* a plant of America and Africa, with yellow, brown, or yellow-and-red daisy-like flowers. [C18: < NL, < Gk *koris* bedbug + -OPSIS; so called from the appearance of the seed]
co-respondent (ˌkəʊrɪˈspɒndənt) *n. Law.* a person cited in divorce proceedings, alleged to have committed adultery with the respondent.
core time *n.* See **flexitime.**
corf (kɔːf) *n., pl.* **corves.** *Brit.* a wagon or basket used formerly in mines. [C14: < MDu. *corf* or MLow G *korf,* prob. < L *corbis* basket]
corgi (ˈkɔːgɪ) *n.* either of two short-legged sturdy

breeds of dog, the Cardigan and the Pembroke. [C20: < Welsh, < *cor* dwarf + *ci* dog]

coriander (ˌkɒrɪˈændə) *n.* **1.** a European umbelliferous plant, cultivated for its aromatic seeds. **2.** the dried seeds of this plant used in flavouring food, etc. [C14: < OF *coriandre*, < L *coriandrum*, < Gk *koriannon*, <?]

Corinthian (kəˈrɪnθɪən) *adj.* **1.** of Corinth. **2.** denoting one of the five classical orders of architecture: characterized by a bell-shaped capital having carved ornaments based on acanthus leaves. **3.** *Obs.* given to luxury; dissolute. ~*n.* **4.** a native or inhabitant of Corinth.

Coriolis force (ˌkɒrɪˈəʊlɪs) *n.* a hypothetical force postulated to explain a deflection in the path of a body moving relative to the earth: it is due to the earth's rotation and is to the left in the S hemisphere and to the right in the N hemisphere. [C19: after Gaspard G. *Coriolis* (1792–1843), F civil engineer]

corium (ˈkɔːrɪəm) *n., pl.* **-ria** (-rɪə). the deep inner layer of the skin, beneath the epidermis, containing connective tissue, blood vessels, and fat. Also called: **derma, dermis.** [C19: < L: rind, skin]

cork (kɔːk) *n.* **1.** the thick light porous outer bark of the cork oak. **2.** a piece of cork used as a stopper. **3.** an angling float. **4.** Also called: **phellem.** *Bot.* a protective layer of dead impermeable cells on the outside of the stems and roots of woody plants. ~*vb.* (*tr.*) **5.** to stop up (a bottle, etc.) with or as with a cork. **6.** (often foll. by *up*) to restrain. **7.** to black (the face, hands, etc.) with burnt cork. [C14: prob. < Ar. *qurq*, < L *cortex* bark] —**ˈcorkˌlike** *adj.*

corkage (ˈkɔːkɪdʒ) *n.* a charge made at a restaurant for serving wine, etc., bought off the premises.

corked (kɔːkt) *adj.* tainted through having a cork containing excess tannin.

corker (ˈkɔːkə) *n. Old-fashioned sl.* **1.** something or somebody striking or outstanding. **2.** an irrefutable remark that puts an end to discussion.

cork oak *n.* an evergreen Mediterranean oak whose porous bark yields cork.

corkscrew (ˈkɔːkˌskruː) *n.* **1.** a device for drawing corks from bottles, typically consisting of a pointed metal spiral attached to a handle or screw mechanism. **2.** (*modifier*) resembling a corkscrew in shape. ~*vb.* **3.** to move or cause to move in a spiral or zigzag course.

corm (kɔːm) *n.* an organ of vegetative reproduction in plants such as the crocus, consisting of a globular stem base swollen with food and surrounded by papery scale leaves. [C19: < NL *cormus*, < Gk *kormos* tree trunk from which the branches have been lopped]

cormorant (ˈkɔːmərənt) *n.* an aquatic bird having a dark plumage, a long neck and body, and a slender hooked beak. [C13: < OF *cormareng*, < *corp* raven + *-mareng* of the sea]

corn[1] (kɔːn) *n.* **1.** *Brit.* **a.** any of various cereal plants, esp. the predominant crop of a region, such as wheat in England and oats in Scotland. **b.** the seeds of such plants, esp. after harvesting. **c.** a single seed of such plants; a grain. **2.** the usual U.S., Canad., & N.Z. name for **maize. 3.** *Sl.* an idea, song, etc., regarded as banal or sentimental. ~*vb.* (*tr.*) **4. a.** to preserve in brine. **b.** to salt. [OE *corn*]

corn[2] (kɔːn) *n.* **1.** a hardening of the skin, esp. of the toes, caused by pressure. **2. tread on (someone's) corns.** *Brit. inf.* to offend or hurt (someone) by touching on a sensitive subject. [C15: < OF *corne* horn, < L *cornū*]

corn borer *n.* the larva of a moth native to Europe: in E North America a serious pest of maize.

corn bread *n. Chiefly U.S.* bread made from maize meal. Also called: **Indian bread.**

corn bunting *n.* a heavily built European songbird with a streaked brown plumage.

corncob (ˈkɔːnˌkɒb) *n.* the core of an ear of maize, to which kernels are attached.

corncob pipe *n.* a pipe made from a dried corncob.

corncockle (ˈkɔːnˌkɒkᵊl) *n.* a European plant that has reddish-purple flowers and grows in cornfields and by roadsides.

corncrake (ˈkɔːnˌkreɪk) *n.* a common Eurasian rail with a buff speckled plumage and reddish wings.

corn dolly *n.* a decorative figure made by plaiting straw.

cornea (ˈkɔːnɪə) *n., pl.* **-neas** *or* **-neae** (-nɪˌiː). the convex transparent membrane that forms the anterior covering of the eyeball. [C14: < Med. L *cornea tēla* horny web, < L *cornū* HORN] —**ˈcorneal** *adj.*

corned (kɔːnd) *adj.* (esp. of beef) cooked and then preserved or pickled in salt or brine.

cornel (ˈkɔːnᵊl) *n.* any shrub of the genus *Cornus*, such as the dogwood. [C16: prob. < MLow G *kornelle*, ult. < L *cornus*]

cornelian (kɔːˈniːlɪən) *n.* a variant spelling of **carnelian.**

corner (ˈkɔːnə) *n.* **1.** the place or angle formed by the meeting of two converging lines or surfaces. **2.** a projecting angle of a solid object. **3.** the place where two streets meet. **4.** any small, secluded, or private place. **5.** a dangerous position from which escape is difficult: *a tight corner.* **6.** any region, esp. a remote place. **7.** something used to protect or mark a corner, as of the hard cover of a book. **8.** *Commerce.* a monopoly over the supply of a commodity so that its market price can be controlled. **9.** *Soccer, hockey, etc.* a free kick or shot from the corner of the field, taken against a defending team when the ball goes out of play over their goal line after last touching one of their players. **10.** either of two opposite angles of a boxing ring in which the opponents take their rests. **11. cut corners.** to take the shortest or easiest way, esp. at the expense of high standards. **12. turn the corner.** to pass the critical point (in an illness, etc.). **13.** (*modifier*) on a corner: *a corner shop.* ~*vb.* **14.** (*tr.*) to manoeuvre (a person or animal) into a position from which escape is difficult or impossible. **15.** (*tr.*) **a.** to acquire enough of (a commodity) to attain control of the market. **b.** Also: **engross.** to attain control of (a market) in such a manner. **16.** (*intr.*) (of vehicles, etc.) to turn a corner. **17.** (*intr.*) (in soccer, etc.) to take a corner. [C13: < OF *corniere*, < L *cornū* point, HORN]

cornerstone (ˈkɔːnəˌstəʊn) *n.* **1.** a stone at the corner of a wall, uniting two intersecting walls. **2.** a stone placed at the corner of a building during a ceremony to mark the start of construction. **3.** a person or thing of prime importance: *the cornerstone of the whole argument.*

cornerwise (ˈkɔːnəˌwaɪz) *or* **cornerways** (ˈkɔːnəˌweɪz) *adv., adj.* with a corner in front; diagonally.

cornet (ˈkɔːnɪt) *n.* **1.** a three-valved brass instrument of the trumpet family. **2.** a person who plays the cornet. **3.** a cone-shaped paper container for sweets, etc. **4.** *Brit.* a cone-shaped wafer container for ice cream. **5.** (formerly) the lowest rank of commissioned cavalry officer in the British Army. **6.** the large white headdress of some nuns. [C14: < OF, < L *cornū* HORN] —**corˈnetist** *or* **corˈnettist** *n.*

corn exchange *n.* a building where corn is bought and sold.

cornfield (ˈkɔːnˌfiːld) *n.* a field planted with cereal crops.

cornflakes (ˈkɔːnˌfleɪks) *pl. n.* a breakfast cereal made from toasted maize.

cornflour (ˈkɔːnˌflaʊə) *n.* a fine maize flour, used for thickening sauces. U.S. and Canad. name: **cornstarch.**

cornflower (ˈkɔːnˌflaʊə) *n.* a herbaceous plant, with blue, purple, pink, or white flowers, formerly a common weed in cornfields.

cornice (ˈkɔːnɪs) *n.* **1.** *Archit.* **a.** the top projecting mouldings of an entablature. **b.** a continuous horizontal projecting course or moulding at the top of a wall, building, etc. **2.** an overhanging ledge of snow. [C16: < OF, < It., ? < L *cornix* crow, but infl. also by L *corōnis* decorative flourish]

corniche (ˈkɔːnɪʃ) *n.* a coastal road, esp. one built into the face of a cliff. [C19: < *corniche road;* see CORNICE]

Cornish (ˈkɔːnɪʃ) *adj.* **1.** of Cornwall or its inhabitants. ~*n.* **2.** a former language of Cornwall: extinct by 1800. **3. the.** (*functioning as pl.*) the natives or inhabitants of Cornwall. —ˈ**Cornishman** *n.*

Cornish pasty (ˈpæstɪ) *n. Cookery.* a pastry case with a filling of meat and vegetables.

corn meal *n.* meal made from maize. Also called: **Indian meal.**

corn salad *n.* a plant which often grows in cornfields and whose leaves are sometimes used in salads. Also called: **lamb's lettuce.**

cornstarch (ˈkɔːnˌstɑːtʃ) *n.* the U.S. and Canad. name for **cornflour.**

cornucopia (ˌkɔːnjʊˈkəʊpɪə) *n.* **1.** a representation of a horn in painting, sculpture, etc., overflowing with fruit, vegetables, etc.; horn of plenty. **2.** a great abundance. **3.** a horn-shaped container. [C16: < LL, < L *cornū cōpiae* horn of plenty] —ˌ**cornuˈcopian** *adj.*

corn whisky *n.* whisky made from maize.

corny (ˈkɔːnɪ) *adj.* **cornier, corniest.** *Sl.* **1.** trite or banal. **2.** sentimental or mawkish. **3.** abounding in corn. [C16 (C20 in the sense banal): < CORN[1] + -Y[1]]

corolla (kəˈrɒlə) *n.* the petals of a flower collectively, forming an inner floral envelope. [C17: dim. of L *corōna* crown]

corollary (kəˈrɒlərɪ) *n., pl.* **-laries. 1.** a proposition that follows directly from the proof of another proposition. **2.** an obvious deduction. **3.** a natural consequence. [C14: < L *corollārium* money paid for a garland, < L *corolla* garland]

corona (kəˈrəʊnə) *n., pl.* **-nas** *or* **-nae** (-niː). **1.** a circle of light around a luminous body, usually the moon. **2.** Also called: **aureole.** the outermost region of the sun's atmosphere, visible as a faint halo during a solar eclipse. **3.** *Archit.* the flat vertical face of a cornice. **4.** a circular chandelier. **5.** *Bot.* **a.** the trumpet-shaped part of the corolla of daffodils and similar plants. **b.** a crown of leafy outgrowths from inside the petals of some flowers. **6.** *Anat.* a crownlike structure. **7.** a long cigar with blunt ends. **8.** *Physics.* an electrical discharge appearing around the surface of a charged conductor. [C16: < L: crown]

coronach (ˈkɒrənəx) *n. Scot. & Irish.* a dirge or lamentation for the dead. [C16: < Scot. Gaelic *corranach*]

coronary (ˈkɒrənərɪ) *adj.* **1.** *Anat.* designating blood vessels, nerves, ligaments, etc., that encircle a part or structure. ~*n., pl.* **-naries. 2.** short for **coronary thrombosis.** [C17: < L *corōnārius* belonging to a wreath or crown]

coronary thrombosis *n.* a condition of interrupted blood flow to the heart due to a blood clot in a coronary artery.

coronation (ˌkɒrəˈneɪʃən) *n.* the act or ceremony of crowning a monarch. [C14: < OF, < *coroner* to crown, < L *corōnāre*]

coroner (ˈkɒrənə) *n.* a public official responsible for the investigation of violent, sudden, or suspicious deaths. [C14: < Anglo-F *corouner,* < OF *corone* CROWN] —ˈ**coronerˌship** *n.*

coronet (ˈkɒrənɪt) *n.* **1.** any small crown, esp. one worn by princes or peers. **2.** a woman's jewelled circlet for the head. **3.** the margin between the skin of a horse's pastern and the horn of the hoof. [C15: < OF *coronete*]

corp. *abbrev. for:* **1.** corporation. **2.** corporal.

corporal[1] (ˈkɔːpərəl, ˈkɔːprəl) *adj.* of or relating to the body. [C14: < L *corporālis,* < *corpus* body] —ˌ**corpoˈrality** *n.* —ˈ**corporally** *adv.*

corporal[2] (ˈkɔːpərəl) *n.* **1.** a noncommissioned officer junior to a sergeant in the army, air force, or marines. **2.** (in the Royal Navy) a petty officer who assists the master-at-arms. [C16: < OF, via It., < L *caput* head; ? also infl. in OF by *corps* body (of men)]

corporal[3] (ˈkɔːpərəl) *or* **corporale** (ˌkɔːpəˈreɪlɪ) *n.* a white linen cloth on which the bread and wine are placed during the Eucharist. [C14: < Med. L *corporāle pallium* eucharistic altar cloth, < L *corporālis,* < *corpus* body (of Christ)]

Corporal of Horse *n.* a noncommissioned rank in the British Army, above that of sergeant and below that of staff sergeant.

corporal punishment *n.* punishment of a physical nature, such as caning.

corporate (ˈkɔːpərɪt) *adj.* **1.** forming a corporation; incorporated. **2.** of a corporation. **3.** of or belonging to a united group; joint. [C15: < L *corporātus,* < *corpus* body] —ˈ**corporatism** *n.*

corporation (ˌkɔːpəˈreɪʃən) *n.* **1.** a group of people authorized by law to act as an individual and having its own powers, duties, and liabilities. **2.** Also called: **municipal corporation.** the municipal authorities of a city or town. **3.** a group of people acting as one body. **4.** See **public corporation. 5.** *Brit. inf.* a large paunch. —ˈ**corporative** *adj.*

corporeal (kɔːˈpɔːrɪəl) *adj.* **1.** of the nature of the physical body; not spiritual. **2.** of a material nature; physical. [C17: < L *corporeus,* < *corpus* body] —**corˌporeˈality** *or* **corporeity** (ˌkɔːpəˈriːɪtɪ) *n.* —**corˈporeally** *adv.*

corps (kɔː) *n., pl.* **corps** (kɔːz). **1.** a military formation that comprises two or more divisions. **2.** a military body with a specific function: *medical corps.* **3.** a body of people associated together: *the diplomatic corps.* [C18: < F, < L *corpus* body]

corps de ballet (ˈkɔː də ˈbæleɪ) *n.* the members of a ballet company who dance together in a group.

corps diplomatique (ˌdɪpləʊmæˈtiːk) *n.* another name for **diplomatic corps.**

corpse (kɔːps) *n.* a dead body, esp. of a human being. [C14: < OF *corps,* < L *corpus*]

corpulent (ˈkɔːpjʊlənt) *adj.* physically bulky; fat. [C14: < L *corpulentus*] —ˈ**corpulence** *n.*

corpus (ˈkɔːpəs) *n., pl.* **-pora** (-pərə). **1.** a body of writings, esp. by a single author or on a specific topic: *the corpus of Dickens' works.* **2.** the main body or substance of something. **3.** *Anat.* **a.** any distinct mass or body. **b.** the main part of an organ or structure. **4.** *Obs.* a corpse. [C14: < L: body]

Corpus Christi (ˈkrɪstɪ) *n. Chiefly R.C. Church.* a festival in honour of the Eucharist, observed on the Thursday after Trinity Sunday. [C14: < L: body of Christ]

corpuscle (ˈkɔːpʌsᵊl) *n.* **1.** any cell or similar minute body that is suspended in a fluid, esp. any of the **red blood corpuscles** (see **erythrocyte**) or **white blood corpuscles** (see **leucocyte**). **2.** Also: **corpuscule** (kɔːˈpʌskjuːl). any minute particle. [C17: < L *corpusculum* a little body, < *corpus* body] —**corpuscular** (kɔːˈpʌskjʊlə) *adj.*

corpuscular theory *n.* the theory, originally proposed by Newton, that light consists of a stream of particles. Cf. **wave theory.**

corpus delicti (dɪˈlɪktaɪ) *n. Law.* the body of facts that constitute an offence. [NL, lit.: the body of the crime]

corpus juris (ˈdʒʊərɪs) *n.* a body of law, esp. of a nation or state. [< LL, lit.: a body of law]

corpus luteum (ˈluːtɪəm) *n., pl.* **corpora lutea** (ˈluːtɪə). a mass of tissue that forms in a Graafian follicle following release of an ovum. [NL, lit.: yellow body]

corral (kɒˈrɑːl) *n.* **1.** *Chiefly U.S. & Canad.* an enclosure for cattle or horses. **2.** *Chiefly U.S.* (formerly) a defensive enclosure formed by a ring of covered wagons. ~*vb.* **-ralling, -ralled.** (*tr.*) *U.S. & Canad.* **3.** to drive into a corral. **4.** *Inf.* to capture. [C16: < Sp., ult. < L *currere* to run]

corrasion (kəˈreɪʒən) *n.* erosion of a rock surface by rock fragments transported over it by water, wind, or ice. [C17: < L *corrādere* to scrape together]

correa (ˈkɒrɪə, kəˈriːə) *n.* an Australian evergreen

shrub with large showy tubular flowers. [C19: after Jose Francesco *Correa* da Serra (1750-1823), Portuguese botanist]

correct (kəˈrɛkt) *vb.* (*tr.*) **1.** to make free from errors. **2.** to indicate the errors in. **3.** to rebuke or punish in order to improve: *to stand corrected.* **4.** to rectify (a malfunction, ailment, etc.). **5.** to adjust or make conform, esp. to a standard. *~adj.* **6.** true; accurate: *the correct version.* **7.** in conformity with accepted standards: *correct behaviour.* [C14: < L *corrigere* to make straight, < *com-* (intensive) + *regere* to rule] **—corˈrectly** *adv.* **—corˈrectness** *n.*

correction (kəˈrɛkʃən) *n.* **1.** the act of correcting. **2.** something substituted for an error; an improvement. **3.** a reproof. **4.** a quantity added to or subtracted from a scientific calculation or observation to increase its accuracy. **—corˈrectional** *adj.*

corrective (kəˈrɛktɪv) *adj.* **1.** tending or intended to correct. *~n.* **2.** something that tends or is intended to correct.

correlate (ˈkɒrɪˌleɪt) *vb.* **1.** to place or be placed in a complementary or reciprocal relationship. **2.** (*tr.*) to establish or show a correlation between. *~n.* **3.** either of two things mutually related.

correlation (ˌkɒrɪˈleɪʃən) *n.* **1.** a mutual relationship between two or more things. **2.** the act of correlating or the state of being correlated. **3.** *Statistics.* the extent of correspondence between the ordering of two variables. [C16: < Med. L *correlātiō*, < *com-* together + *relātiō* RELATION] **—ˌcorreˈlational** *adj.*

correlation coefficient *n. Statistics.* a statistic measuring the degree of correlation between two variables.

correlative (kɒˈrɛlətɪv) *adj.* **1.** in complementary or reciprocal relationship; corresponding. **2.** denoting words, usually conjunctions, occurring together though not adjacently in certain grammatical constructions, as *neither* and *nor.* *~n.* **3.** either of two things that are correlative. **4.** a correlative word. **—corˈrelatively** *adv.* **—corˌrelaˈtivity** *n.*

correspond (ˌkɒrɪˈspɒnd) *vb.* (*intr.*) **1.** (usually foll. by *with* or *to*) to be consistent or compatible (with); tally (with). **2.** (usually foll. by *to*) to be similar in character or function. **3.** (usually foll. by *with*) to communicate by letter. [C16: < Med. L *corrēspondēre*, < L *rēspondēre* to RESPOND] **—ˌcorreˈsponding** *adj.* **—ˌcorreˈspondingly** *adv.*

▷ **Usage.** See at **similar.**

correspondence (ˌkɒrɪˈspɒndəns) *n.* **1.** the condition of agreeing or corresponding. **2.** similarity. **3.** agreement or conformity. **4. a.** communication by letters. **b.** the letters so exchanged.

correspondence school *n.* an educational institution that offers tuition (**correspondence courses**) by post.

correspondent (ˌkɒrɪˈspɒndənt) *n.* **1.** a person who communicates by letter. **2.** a person employed by a newspaper, etc., to report on a special subject or from a foreign country. **3.** a person or firm that has regular business relations with another, esp. one abroad. *~adj.* **4.** similar or analogous.

corrida (koˈrriða) *n.* the Spanish word for **bullfight.** [Sp., < *corrida de toros*, lit.: a running of bulls]

corridor (ˈkɒrɪˌdɔː) *n.* **1.** a passage connecting parts of a building. **2.** a strip of land or airspace that affords access, either from a landlocked country to the sea or from a state to an exclave. **3.** a passageway connecting the compartments of a railway coach. **4. corridors of power.** the higher echelons of government, the Civil Service, etc., considered as the location of power and influence. [C16: < OF, < OIt. *corridore*, lit.: place for running]

corrie (ˈkɒrɪ) *n.* **1.** (in Scotland) a circular hollow on a hillside. **2.** *Geol.* another name for **cirque.** [C18: < Gaelic *coire* cauldron]

corrigendum (ˌkɒrɪˈdʒɛndəm) *n., pl.* **-da** (-də). **1.** an error to be corrected. **2.** (*sometimes pl.*) Also called: **erratum.** a slip of paper inserted into a book after printing, listing corrections. [C19: < L: that which is to be corrected]

corrigible (ˈkɒrɪdʒɪbᵊl) *adj.* **1.** capable of being corrected. **2.** submissive. [C15: < OF, < Med. L *corrigibilis*, < L *corrigere* to CORRECT]

corroborate (kəˈrɒbəˌreɪt) *vb.* (*tr.*) to confirm or support (facts, opinions, etc.), esp. by providing fresh evidence. [C16: < L *corrōborāre*, < *rōborāre* to make strong, < *rōbur* strength] **—corˌroboˈration** *n.* **—corroborative** (kəˈrɒbərətɪv) *adj.* **—corˈroboˌrator** *n.*

corroboree (kəˈrɒbərɪ) *n. Austral.* **1.** a native assembly of sacred, festive, or warlike character. **2.** any noisy gathering. [C19: < Abor.]

corrode (kəˈrəʊd) *vb.* **1.** to eat away or be eaten away, esp. as in the oxidation or rusting of a metal. **2.** (*tr.*) to destroy gradually: *his jealousy corroded his happiness.* [C14: < L *corrōdere* to gnaw to pieces, < *rōdere* to gnaw] **—corˈrodible** *adj.*

corrosion (kəˈrəʊʒən) *n.* **1.** a process in which a solid, esp. a metal, is eaten away and changed by a chemical action, as in the oxidation of iron. **2.** slow deterioration by being eaten or worn away. **3.** the product of corrosion.

corrosive (kəˈrəʊsɪv) *adj.* **1.** tending to eat away or consume. *~n.* **2.** a corrosive substance, such as a strong acid **—corˈrosively** *adv.* **—corˈrosiveness** *n.*

corrosive sublimate *n.* another name for **mercuric chloride.**

corrugate (ˈkɒrʊˌgeɪt) *vb.* (*usually tr.*) to fold or be folded into alternate furrows and ridges. [C18: < L *corrūgāre*, < *rūga* a wrinkle] **—ˈcorruˌgated** *adj.* **—ˌcorruˈgation** *n.*

corrugated iron *n.* a thin sheet of iron or steel, formed with alternating ridges and troughs.

corrupt (kəˈrʌpt) *adj.* **1.** open to or involving bribery or other dishonest practices: *a corrupt official; corrupt practices.* **2.** morally depraved. **3.** putrid or rotten. **4.** (of a text or manuscript) made meaningless or different in meaning by scribal errors or alterations. *~vb.* **5.** to become or cause to become dishonest or disloyal. **6.** (*tr.*) to deprave. **7.** (*tr.*) to infect or contaminate. **8.** (*tr.*) to cause to become rotten. **9.** (*tr.*) to alter (a text, etc.) from the original. [C14: < L *corruptus* spoiled, < *corrumpere* to ruin, < *rumpere* to break] **—corˈrupter** *or* **corˈruptor** *n.* **—corˈruptly** *adv.* **—corˈruptness** *n.*

corruptible (kəˈrʌptɪbᵊl) *adj.* capable of being corrupted. **—corˈruptibly** *adv.*

corruption (kəˈrʌpʃən) *n.* **1.** the act of corrupting or state of being corrupt. **2.** depravity. **3.** dishonesty, esp. bribery. **4.** decay. **5.** alteration, as of a manuscript. **6.** an altered form of a word.

corsage (kɔːˈsɑːʒ) *n.* **1.** a small bunch of flowers worn pinned to the lapel, bosom, etc. **2.** the bodice of a dress. [C15: < OF, < *cors* body, < L *corpus*]

corsair (ˈkɔːsɛə) *n.* **1.** a pirate. **2.** a privateer, esp. of the Barbary Coast. [C15: < OF *corsaire*, < Med. L *cursārius*, < L *cursus* a running]

corse (kɔːs) *n.* an archaic word for **corpse.**

corselet (ˈkɔːslɪt) *n.* **1.** Also spelt: **corslet.** a piece of armour for the top part of the body. **2.** a one-piece foundation garment. [C15: < OF, < *cors* bodice, < L *corpus* body]

corset (ˈkɔːsɪt) *n.* **1. a.** a stiffened, elasticated, or laced foundation garment, worn esp. by women. **b.** a similar garment worn because of injury, weakness, etc., by either sex. **2.** *Inf.* a restriction or limitation, esp. government control of bank lending. *~vb.* **3.** (*tr.*) to dress or enclose in, or as in, a corset. [C14: < OF, lit.: a little bodice] **—corsetière** (ˌkɔːsɛtɪˈɛə) *n.* **—ˈcorsetry** *n.*

cortege *or* **cortège** (kɔːˈteɪʒ) *n.* **1.** a formal procession, esp. a funeral procession. **2.** a train of attendants; retinue. [C17: < F, < It. *corteggio*, < *corteggiare* to attend]

cortex (ˈkɔːtɛks) *n., pl.* **-tices** (-tɪˌsiːz). **1.** *Anat.* the outer layer of any organ or part, such as the grey matter in the brain that covers the cerebrum (**cerebral cortex**). **2.** *Bot.* **a.** the tissue in plant stems and roots between the vascular bundles and the epidermis. **b.** the outer layer of a part such as the bark of a stem. [C17: < L: bark, outer layer] —**cortical** (ˈkɔːtɪkᵊl) *adj.*

corticate (ˈkɔːtɪkɪt, -ˌkeɪt) *or* **corticated** *adj.* (of plants, seeds, etc.) having a bark, husk, or rind. [C19: < L *corticātus*]

cortisone (ˈkɔːtɪˌzəʊn) *n.* a steroid hormone, the synthetic form of which has been used in treating rheumatoid arthritis, allergic and skin diseases, leukaemia, etc. [C20: < *corticosterone,* a hormone]

corundum (kəˈrʌndəm) *n.* a hard mineral consisting of aluminium oxide: used as an abrasive. Precious varieties include ruby and sapphire. Formula: Al_2O_3. [C18: < Tamil *kuruntam;* rel. to Sansk. *kuruvinda* ruby]

coruscate (ˈkɒrəˌskeɪt) *vb.* (*intr.*) to emit flashes of light; sparkle. [C18: < L *coruscāre* to flash] —ˌ**corusˈcation** *n.*

corvée (ˈkɔːveɪ) *n.* **1.** *European history.* a day's unpaid labour owed by a feudal vassal to his lord. **2.** the practice or an instance of forced labour. [C14: < OF, < LL *corrogāta* contribution, < L *corrogāre* to collect, < *rogāre* to ask]

corvette (kɔːˈvɛt) *n.* a lightly armed escort warship. [C17: < OF, ?< MDu. *corf*]

corvine (ˈkɔːvaɪn) *adj.* **1.** of or resembling a crow. **2.** of the passerine bird family Corvidae, which includes the crows, ravens, rooks, jackdaws, magpies, and jays. [C17: < L *corvīnus,* < *corvus* a raven]

Corybant (ˈkɒrɪˌbænt) *n., pl.* **Corybants** *or* **Corybantes** (ˌkɒrɪˈbæntiːz). *Classical myth.* a wild attendant of the goddess Cybele. [C14: < L *Corybās,* < Gk *Korubas*] —ˌ**Coryˈbantic** *adj.*

corymb (ˈkɒrɪmb, -rɪm) *n.* an inflorescence in the form of a flat-topped flower cluster with the oldest flowers at the periphery. [C18: < L *corymbus,* < Gk *korumbos* cluster]

coryza (kəˈraɪzə) *n.* acute inflammation of the mucous membrane of the nose, with discharge of mucus; a head cold. [C17: < LL: catarrh, < Gk *koruza*]

cos[1] *or* **cos lettuce** (kɒs) *n.* a variety of lettuce with a long slender head and crisp leaves. Usual U.S. and Canad. name: **romaine.** [C17: after *Kos,* the Aegean island of its origin]

cos[2] (kɒz) *abbrev. for* cosine.

Cos. *or* **cos.** *abbrev. for:* **1.** Companies. **2.** Counties.

Cosa Nostra (ˈkəʊzə ˈnɒstrə) *n.* the branch of the Mafia that operates in the U.S. [It.: our thing]

cosec (ˈkəʊsɛk) *abbrev. for* cosecant.

cosecant (kəʊˈsiːkənt) *n.* (of an angle) a trigonometric function that in a right-angled triangle is the ratio of the length of the hypotenuse to that of the opposite side.

coset (ˈkəʊˌsɛt) *n. Maths.* a set that produces a specified larger set when added to another set.

cosh[1] (kɒʃ) *Brit.* ~*n.* **1.** a blunt weapon, often made of hard rubber; bludgeon. **2.** an attack with such a weapon. ~*vb.* **3.** to hit with such a weapon, esp. on the head. [C19: < Romany *kosh*]

cosh[2] (kɒʃ, kɒsˈeɪtʃ) *n.* hyperbolic cosine. [C19: < COS(INE) + H(YPERBOLIC)]

cosignatory (kəʊˈsɪgnətərɪ, -trɪ) *n., pl.* **-ries.** **1.** a person, country, etc., that signs a document jointly with others. ~*adj.* **2.** signing jointly.

cosine (ˈkəʊˌsaɪn) *n.* (of an angle) a trigonometric function that in a right-angled triangle is the ratio of the length of the adjacent side to that of the hypotenuse. [C17: < NL *cosinus;* see CO-, SINE[1]]

cosmetic (kɒzˈmɛtɪk) *n.* **1.** any preparation applied to the body, esp. the face, with the intention of beautifying it. ~*adj.* **2.** serving or designed to beautify the body, esp. the face. **3.** having no other function than to beautify: *cosmetic illustrations in a book.* [C17: < Gk *kosmētikos,* < *kosmein* to arrange, < *kosmos* order] —**cosˈmetically** *adv.*

cosmic (ˈkɒzmɪk) *adj.* **1.** of or relating to the whole universe: *cosmic laws.* **2.** occurring or originating in outer space, esp. as opposed to the vicinity of the earth: *cosmic rays.* **3.** immeasurably extended; vast. —ˈ**cosmically** *adv.*

cosmic dust *n.* fine particles of solid matter occurring throughout interstellar space and often collecting into clouds of extremely low density.

cosmic rays *pl. n.* radiation consisting of atomic nuclei, esp. protons, of very high energy, that reach the earth from outer space. Also called: **cosmic radiation.**

cosmo- *or before a vowel* **cosm-** *combining form.* indicating the world or universe: *cosmology; cosmonaut.* [< Gk: COSMOS]

cosmogony (kɒzˈmɒgənɪ) *n., pl.* **-nies.** the study of the origin and development of the universe or of a particular system in the universe, such as the solar system. [C17: < Gk *kosmogonia,* < COSMO- + *gonos* creation] —**cosmogonic** (ˌkɒzməˈgɒnɪk) *or* ˌ**cosmoˈgonical** *adj.* —**cosˈmogonist** *n.*

cosmography (kɒzˈmɒgrəfɪ) *n.* **1.** a representation of the world or the universe. **2.** the science dealing with the whole order of nature. —**cosˈmographer** *n.* —**cosmographic** (ˌkɒzməˈgræfɪk) *or* ˌ**cosmoˈgraphical** *adj.*

cosmology (kɒzˈmɒlədʒɪ) *n.* **1.** the study of the origin and nature of the universe. **2.** a particular account of the origin or structure of the universe. —**cosmological** (ˌkɒzməˈlɒdʒɪkᵊl) *or* ˌ**cosmoˈlogic** *adj.* —**cosˈmologist** *n.*

cosmonaut (ˈkɒzməˌnɔːt) *n.* a Soviet astronaut. [C20: < Russian *kosmonavt,* < COSMO- + Gk *nautēs* sailor]

cosmopolitan (ˌkɒzməˈpɒlɪtᵊn) *n.* **1.** a person who has lived and travelled in many countries, esp. one who is free of national prejudices. ~*adj.* **2.** familiar with many parts of the world. **3.** sophisticated or urbane. **4.** composed of people or elements from all parts of the world or from many different spheres. [C17: < F, ult. < Gk *kosmopolitēs,* < *kosmo-* COSMO- + *politēs* citizen] —ˌ**cosmoˈpolitanism** *n.*

cosmopolite (kɒzˈmɒpəˌlaɪt) *n.* **1.** a less common word for **cosmopolitan** (sense 1). **2.** an animal or plant that occurs in most parts of the world. —**cosˈmopolitˌism** *n.*

cosmos (ˈkɒzmɒs) *n.* **1.** the universe considered as an ordered system. **2.** any ordered system. **3.** (*pl.* **-mos** *or* **-moses**) any tropical American plant of the genus *Cosmos* cultivated as garden plants for their brightly coloured flowers. [C17: < Gk *kosmos* order]

Cossack (ˈkɒsæk) *n.* **1.** (formerly) any of the free warrior-peasants of chiefly East Slavonic descent who served as cavalry under the tsars. ~*adj.* **2.** of, relating to, or characteristic of the Cossacks: *a Cossack dance.* [C16: < Russian *kazak* vagabond, of Turkic origin]

cosset (ˈkɒsɪt) *vb.* **1.** (*tr.*) to pamper; pet. ~*n.* **2.** any pet animal, esp. a lamb. [C16: <?]

cost (kɒst) *n.* **1.** the price paid or required for acquiring, producing, or maintaining something, measured in money, time, or energy; outlay. **2.** suffering or sacrifice: *I know to my cost.* **3. a.** the amount paid for a commodity by its seller: *to sell at cost.* **b.** (*as modifier*): *the cost price.* **4.** (*pl.*) *Law.* the expenses of judicial proceedings. **5. at all costs.** regardless of sacrifice involved. **6. at the cost of.** at the expense of losing. ~*vb.* **costing, cost. 7.** (*tr.*) to be obtained or obtainable in exchange for: *the ride cost one pound.* **8.** to cause or require the loss or sacrifice (of): *the accident cost him dearly.* **9.** to estimate the cost of (a product, process, etc.) for the purposes of pricing, budgeting, control, etc. [C13: < OF (n.), < *coster* to cost, < L *constāre* to stand at, cost, < *stāre* to stand]

costa (ˈkɒstə) *n., pl.* **-tae** (-tiː). **1.** the technical name for **rib**[1] (sense 1). **2.** a riblike part. [C19: < L: rib, side] —ˈ**costal** *adj.*

cost accounting *n.* the recording and controlling of all the expenditures of an enterprise in order to facilitate control of separate activities. Also called: **management accounting.** —**cost accountant** *n.*

costermonger (ˈkɒstəˌmʌŋgə) *or* **coster** *n.* *Brit., rare.* a person who sells fruit, vegetables, etc., from a barrow. [C16: < *costard* a kind of apple + MONGER]

costive (ˈkɒstɪv) *adj.* 1. constipated. 2. niggardly. [C14: < OF *costivé*, < L *constipātus*; see CONSTIPATE] —ˈ**costiveness** *n.*

costly (ˈkɒstlɪ) *adj.* **-lier, -liest.** 1. expensive. 2. entailing great loss or sacrifice: *a costly victory.* 3. splendid; lavish. —ˈ**costliness** *n.*

cost of living *n.* **a.** the basic cost of the food, clothing, shelter, and fuel necessary to maintain life, esp. at a standard of living regarded as basic. **b.** (*as modifier*): *the cost-of-living index.*

cost-plus *n.* a method of establishing a selling price in which an agreed percentage is added to the cost price to cover profit.

costume (ˈkɒstjuːm) *n.* 1. a style of dressing, including all the clothes, accessories, etc., worn at one time, as in a particular country or period. 2. *Old-fashioned.* a woman's suit. 3. a set of clothes, esp. unusual or period clothes: *a jester's costume.* 4. short for **swimming costume.** ~*vb.* (*tr.*) 5. to furnish the costumes for (a show, film, etc.). 6. to dress (someone) in a costume. [C18: < F, < It.: dress, habit, CUSTOM]

costumier (kɒˈstjuːmɪə) *or* **costumer** *n.* a person or firm that makes or supplies theatrical or fancy costumes.

cosy *or U.S.* **cozy** (ˈkəʊzɪ) *adj.* **-sier, -siest** *or U.S.* **-zier, -ziest.** 1. warm and snug. 2. intimate; friendly. ~*n., pl.* **-sies** *or U.S.* **-zies.** 3. a cover for keeping things warm: *egg cosy.* [C18: < Scot., <?] —ˈ**cosily** *or U.S.* ˈ**cozily** *adv.* —ˈ**cosiness** *or U.S.* ˈ**coziness** *n.*

cot[1] (kɒt) *n.* 1. a child's boxlike bed, usually incorporating vertical bars. 2. a portable bed. 3. a light bedstead. 4. *Naut.* a hammock-like bed. [C17: < Hindi *khāt* bedstead]

cot[2] (kɒt) *n.* 1. *Literary or arch.* a small cottage. 2. Also called: **cote. a.** a small shelter, esp. one for pigeons, sheep, etc. **b.** (*in combination*): *dovecot.* [OE *cot*]

cot[3] (kɒt) *abbrev. for* cotangent.

cotangent (kəʊˈtændʒənt) *n.* (of an angle) a trigonometric function that in a right-angled triangle is the ratio of the length of the adjacent side to that of the opposite side.

COTC *abbrev. for* Canadian Officers Training Corps.

cot death *n.* the unexplained sudden death of an infant during sleep.

cote (kəʊt) *or* **cot** *n.* 1. a small shelter for pigeons, sheep, etc. 2. (*in combination*): *dovecote.* [OE *cote*]

cotenant (kəʊˈtɛnənt) *n.* a person who holds property jointly or in common with others. —**coˈtenancy** *n.*

coterie (ˈkəʊtərɪ) *n.* a small exclusive group of friends or people with common interests; clique. [C18: < F, < OF: association of tenants, < *cotier* (unattested) cottager]

coterminous (kəʊˈtɜːmɪnəs) *or* **conterminous** *adj.* 1. having a common boundary. 2. coextensive or coincident in range, time, etc.

coth (kɒθ, ˈkɒtˈeɪtʃ) *n.* hyperbolic cotangent. [C20: < COT(ANGENT) + H(YPERBOLIC)]

cotillion *or* **cotillon** (kəˈtɪljən, kəʊ-) *n.* 1. a French formation dance of the 18th century. 2. *U.S.* a quadrille. 3. *U.S.* a formal ball. [C18: < F *cotillon* dance, < OF: petticoat]

cotinga (kəˈtɪŋgə) *n.* a tropical American passerine bird having a broad slightly hooked bill.

cotoneaster (kəˌtəʊnɪˈæstə) *n.* any Old World shrub of the rosaceous genus *Cotoneaster*: cultivated for their ornamental flowers and red or black berries. [C18: < NL, < L *cotōneum* QUINCE]

cotta (ˈkɒtə) *n. R.C. Church.* a short form of surplice. [C19: < It.: tunic]

cottage (ˈkɒtɪdʒ) *n.* a small simple house, esp. in a rural area. [C14: < COT[2]]

cottage cheese *n.* a mild loose soft white cheese made from skimmed milk curds.

cottage hospital *n. Brit.* a small rural hospital.

cottage industry *n.* an industry in which employees work in their own homes, often using their own equipment.

cottage pie *n. Brit.* another term for **shepherd's pie.**

cottager (ˈkɒtɪdʒə) *n.* 1. a person who lives in a cottage. 2. a rural labourer.

cotter[1] (ˈkɒtə) *n. Machinery.* 1. any part, such as a pin, wedge, key, etc., that is used to secure two other parts so that relative motion between them is prevented. 2. short for **cotter pin.** [C14: shortened < *cotterel,* <?]

cotter[2] (ˈkɒtə) *n.* 1. *English history.* a villein in late Anglo-Saxon and early Norman times occupying a cottage and land in return for labour. 2. Also called: **cottar.** a peasant occupying a cottage and land in the Scottish Highlands. [C14: < Med. L *cotārius,* < ME *cote* COT[2]]

cotter pin *n. Machinery.* a split pin secured, after passing through holes in the parts to be attached, by spreading the ends.

cotton (ˈkɒtᵊn) *n.* 1. any of various herbaceous plants and shrubs cultivated in warm climates for the fibre surrounding the seeds and the oil within the seeds. 2. the soft white downy fibre of these plants, used to manufacture textiles. 3. cotton plants collectively, as a cultivated crop. 4. a cloth or thread made from cotton fibres. [C14: < OF *coton,* < Ar. *qutn*] —ˈ**cottony** *adj.*

cotton grass *n.* any of various N temperate and arctic grasslike bog plants whose clusters of long silky hairs resemble cotton tufts.

cotton on *vb.* (*intr., adv.;* often foll. by *to*) *Inf.* to perceive the meaning (of).

cotton-picking *adj. U.S. & Canad. sl.* (intensifier qualifying something undesirable): *you cotton-picking layabout!*

cottonseed (ˈkɒtᵊnˌsiːd) *n., pl.* **-seeds** *or* **-seed.** the seed of the cotton plant: a source of oil and fodder.

cottontail (ˈkɒtᵊnˌteɪl) *n.* any of several common rabbits of American woodlands.

cottonwood (ˈkɒtᵊnˌwʊd) *n.* any of several North American poplars, whose seeds are covered with cottony hairs.

cotton wool *n.* 1. *Chiefly Brit.* bleached and sterilized cotton from which the impurities, such as the seeds, have been removed. Usual U.S. term: **absorbent cotton.** 2. cotton in the natural state. 3. *Brit. inf.* a state of pampered comfort and protection.

cotyledon (ˌkɒtɪˈliːdᵊn) *n.* a simple embryonic leaf in seed-bearing plants, which, in some species, forms the first green leaf after germination. [C16: < L: a plant, navelwort, < Gk *kotulēdōn,* < *kotulē* cup, hollow] —ˌ**cotyˈledonous** *adj.* —ˌ**cotyˈledonal** *adj.*

coucal (ˈkuːkæl) *n.* any ground-living bird of the genus *Centropus* of Africa, S Asia, and Australia. [C19: < F, ?< *couc*(*ou*) cuckoo + *al*(*ouette*) lark]

couch (kaʊtʃ) *n.* 1. a piece of upholstered furniture, usually having a back and armrests, for seating more than one person. 2. a bed, esp. one used in the daytime by the patients of a doctor or a psychoanalyst. ~*vb.* 3. (*tr.*) to express in a particular style of language: *couched in an archaic style.* 4. (when *tr., usually reflexive or passive*) to lie down or cause to lie down for or as for sleep. 5. (*intr.*) *Arch.* to crouch. 6. (*intr.*) *Arch.* to lie in ambush; lurk. 7. (*tr.*) *Surgery.* to remove (a cataract) by downward displacement of the lens of the eye. 8. (*tr.*) *Arch.* to lower (a lance) into a horizontal position. [C14: < OF *couche* a bed, lair, < *coucher* to lay down, < L *collocāre* to arrange, < *locāre* to place]

couchant (ˈkaʊtʃənt) *adj.* (*usually postpositive*) *Heraldry.* in a lying position: *a lion couchant.* [C15: < F: lying]

couchette (kuːˈʃɛt) *n.* a bed or berth in a railway carriage, esp. one converted from seats. [C20: < F, dim. of *couche* bed]

couch grass (kaʊtʃ, kuːtʃ) *n.* a grass with a yellowish-white creeping underground stem by which it spreads quickly: a troublesome weed. Also called: **twitch grass, quitch grass.**

cougar (ˈkuːgə) *n.* another name for **puma.** [C18: < F *couguar,* < Port., < Tupi]

cough (kɒf) *vb.* 1. (*intr.*) to expel air abruptly and explosively through the partially closed vocal chords. **2.** (*intr.*) to make a sound similar to this. **3.** (*tr.*) to utter or express with a cough or coughs. ~*n.* **4.** an act or sound of coughing. **5.** a condition of the lungs or throat which causes frequent coughing. [OE *cohhetten*] —ˈ**cougher** *n.*

cough drop *n.* a lozenge to relieve a cough.

cough mixture *n.* any medicine that relieves coughing.

cough up *vb.* (*adv.*) **1.** *Inf.* to surrender (money, information, etc.), esp. reluctantly. **2.** (*tr.*) to bring into the mouth or eject (phlegm, food, etc.) by coughing.

could (kʊd) *vb.* (takes an infinitive without *to* or an implied infinitive) used as an auxiliary: **1.** to make the past tense of **can**[1]. **2.** to make the subjunctive mood of **can**[1], esp. used in polite requests or in conditional sentences: *could I see you tonight?* **3.** to indicate suggestion of a course of action: *you could take the car if it's raining.* **4.** (often foll. by *well*) to indicate a possibility: *he could well be a spy.* [OE *cūthe*]

couldn't (ˈkʊdᵊnt) *contraction of* could not.

couldst (kʊdst) *vb. Arch.* the form of **could** used with the pronoun *thou* or its relative form.

coulee (ˈkuːleɪ, -lɪ) *n.* **1. a.** a flow of molten lava. **b.** such lava when solidified. **2.** *Western U.S. & Canad.* a steep-sided ravine. [C19: < Canad. F *coulée* a flow, < F, < *couler* to flow, < L *cōlāre* to sift]

coulomb (ˈkuːlɒm) *n.* the derived SI unit of electric charge; the quantity of electricity transported in one second by a current of 1 ampere. Symbol: C [C19: after C.A. de *Coulomb* (1736–1806), F physicist]

coulter (ˈkəʊltə) *n.* a blade or sharp-edged disc attached to a plough so that it cuts through the soil vertically in advance of the ploughshare. Also (esp. U.S.): **colter.** [OE *culter,* < L: ploughshare, knife]

coumarin *or* **cumarin** (ˈkuːmərɪn) *n.* a white vanilla-scented crystalline ester, used in perfumes and flavouring. [C19: < F, < *coumarou* tonka-bean tree, < Sp., < Tupi]

council (ˈkaʊnsəl) *n.* **1.** an assembly of people meeting for discussion, consultation, etc. **2. a.** a body of people elected or appointed to serve in an administrative, legislative, or advisory capacity: *a student council.* **b.** short for **legislative council. 3.** (*sometimes cap.; often preceded by the*) *Brit.* the local governing authority of a town, county, etc. **4.** a meeting of a council. **5.** (*modifier*) of, provided for, or used by a local council: *a council chamber; council offices.* **6.** (*modifier*) *Brit.* provided by a local council, esp. (of housing) at a subsidized rent: *a council house; a council estate; a council school.* **7.** *Christianity.* an assembly of bishops, etc., convened for regulating matters of doctrine or discipline. [C12: < OF *concile,* < L *concilium* assembly, < *com-* together + *calāre* to call]

councillor *or U.S.* **councilor** (ˈkaʊnsələ) *n.* a member of a council.

councilman (ˈkaʊnsəlmən) *n., pl.* **-men.** *Chiefly U.S.* a councillor.

counsel (ˈkaʊnsəl) *n.* **1.** advice or guidance on conduct, behaviour, etc. **2.** discussion; consultation: *to take counsel with a friend.* **3.** a person whose advice is sought. **4.** a barrister or group of barristers engaged in conducting cases in court and advising on legal matters. **5.** *Christianity.* any of the **counsels of perfection,** namely poverty, chastity, and obedience. **6. counsel of perfection.** excellent but unrealizable advice. **7.** private opinions (esp. in **keep one's own counsel**). **8.** *Arch.* wisdom; prudence. ~*vb.* **-selling, -selled** *or U.S.* **-seling, -seled. 9.** (*tr.*) to give advice or guidance to. **10.** (*tr.; often takes a clause as object*) to recommend; urge. **11.** (*intr.*) *Arch.* to take counsel; consult. [C13: < OF *counseil,* < L *consilium* deliberating body; rel. to CONSULT]

counselling *or U.S.* **counseling** (ˈkaʊnsəlɪŋ) *n.* systematic guidance offered by social workers, doctors, etc., in which a person's problems are discussed and advice is given.

counsellor *or U.S.* **counselor** (ˈkaʊnsələ) *n.* **1.** a person who gives counsel; adviser. **2.** Also called: **counselor-at-law.** *U.S.* a lawyer, esp. one who conducts cases in court. **3.** a senior diplomatic officer.

count[1] (kaʊnt) *vb.* **1.** to add up or check (each unit in a collection) in order to ascertain the sum: *count your change.* **2.** (*tr.*) to recite numbers in ascending order up to and including. **3.** (*tr.; often* foll. by *in*) to take into account or include: *we must count him in.* **4. not counting.** excluding. **5.** (*tr.*) to consider; deem: *count yourself lucky.* **6.** (*intr.*) to have importance: *this picture counts as a rarity.* **7.** (*intr.*) *Music.* to keep time by counting beats. ~*n.* **8.** the act of counting. **9.** the number reached by counting; sum: *a blood count.* **10.** *Law.* a paragraph in an indictment containing a separate charge. **11. keep** *or* **lose count.** to keep or fail to keep an accurate record of items, events, etc. **12.** *Boxing, wrestling.* the act of telling off a number of seconds by the referee, as when a boxer has been knocked down by his opponent. **13. out for the count.** *Boxing.* knocked out and unable to continue after a count of ten by the referee. ~See also **count against, countdown,** etc. [C14: < Anglo-F *counter,* < OF *conter,* < L *computāre* to calculate] —ˈ**countable** *adj.*

count[2] (kaʊnt) *n.* **1.** a nobleman in any of various European countries having a rank corresponding to that of a British earl. **2.** any of various officials in the late Roman Empire and in the early Middle Ages. [C16: < OF *conte,* < L *comes* associate, < COM- with + *īre* to go]

count against *vb.* (*intr., prep.*) to have influence to the disadvantage of.

countdown (ˈkaʊntˌdaʊn) *n.* **1.** the act of counting backwards to time a critical operation exactly, such as the launching of a rocket. ~*vb.* **count down.** (*intr., adv.*) **2.** to count thus.

countenance (ˈkaʊntɪnəns) *n.* **1.** the face, esp. when considered as expressing a person's character or mood. **2.** support or encouragement; sanction. **3.** composure; self-control (esp. in **keep** *or* **lose one's countenance**). ~*vb.* (*tr.*) **4.** to support or encourage; sanction. **5.** to tolerate; endure. [C13: < OF *contenance* mien, behaviour, < L *continentia* restraint, control; see CONTAIN]

counter[1] (ˈkaʊntə) *n.* **1.** a horizontal surface, as in a shop or bank, over which business is transacted. **2.** (in some cafeterias) a long table on which food is served. **3. a.** a small flat disc of wood, metal, or plastic, used in various board games. **b.** a similar disc or token used as an imitation coin. **4.** a person or thing that may be used or manipulated. **5. under the counter.** (**under-the-counter** *when prenominal*) (of the sale of goods) clandestine or illegal. **6. over the counter.** (**over-the-counter** *when prenominal*) (of security transactions) through a broker rather than on a stock exchange. [C14: < OF *comptouer,* ult. < L *computāre* to COMPUTE]

counter[2] (ˈkaʊntə) *n.* **1.** a person who counts. **2.** an apparatus that records the number of occurrences of events. [C14: < OF *conteor,* < L *computātor;* see COUNT[1]]

counter[3] (ˈkaʊntə) *adv.* **1.** in a contrary direction or manner. **2.** in a wrong or reverse direction. **3. run counter to.** to have a contrary effect or action to. ~*adj.* **4.** opposing; opposite; contrary. ~*n.* **5.** something that is contrary or opposite to some other thing. **6.** an act, effect, or force that opposes another. **7.** a return attack, such as a blow in boxing. **8.** *Fencing.* a parry in which the foils move in a circular fashion. **9.** the portion of the stern of a boat or ship that overhangs the water aft of the rudder. **10.** a piece of leather forming the back of a shoe. ~*vb.* **11.** to say or do (something) in retaliation or response. **12.** (*tr.*) to move, act, or perform in a manner or direction opposite to (a person or thing). **13.** to return the attack of (an opponent). [C15: < OF *contre,* < L *contrā* against]

counter- *prefix.* **1.** against; opposite; contrary: *counterattack.* **2.** complementary; corresponding: *counterfoil.* **3.** duplicate or substitute:

counterfeit. [via OF < L *contrā* against, opposite; see CONTRA-]

counteract (ˌkaʊntərˈækt) *vb.* (*tr.*) to oppose or neutralize by contrary action; check. —ˌ**counter'action** *n.* —ˌ**counter'active** *adj.*

counterattack (ˈkaʊntərəˌtæk) *n.* **1.** an attack in response to an attack. ~*vb.* **2.** to make a counterattack (against).

counterbalance *n.* (ˈkaʊntəˌbæləns). **1.** a weight or force that balances or offsets another. ~*vb.* (ˌkaʊntəˈbæləns). (*tr.*) **2.** to act as a counterbalance to. ~Also: **counterpoise.**

counterblast (ˈkaʊntəˌblɑːst) *n.* an aggressive response to a verbal attack.

countercheck *n.* (ˈkaʊntəˌtʃɛk). **1.** a check or restraint, esp. one that acts in opposition to another. **2.** a double check, as for accuracy. ~*vb.* (ˌkaʊntəˈtʃɛk). (*tr.*) **3.** to oppose by counteraction. **4.** to double-check.

counterclaim (ˈkaʊntəˌkleɪm) *Chiefly law.* ~*n.* **1.** a claim set up in opposition to another. ~*vb.* **2.** to set up (a claim) in opposition to another claim. —ˌ**counter'claimant** *n.*

counterclockwise (ˌkaʊntəˈklɒkˌwaɪz) *adv., adj.* the U.S. and Canad. equivalent of **anticlockwise.**

counterculture (ˈkaʊntəˌkʌltʃə) *n.* an alternative culture, deliberately at variance with the social norm.

counterespionage (ˌkaʊntərˈɛspɪəˌnɑːʒ) *n.* activities to counteract enemy espionage.

counterfeit (ˈkaʊntəfɪt) *adj.* **1.** made in imitation of something genuine with the intent to deceive or defraud; forged. **2.** simulated; sham: *counterfeit affection.* ~*n.* **3.** an imitation designed to deceive or defraud. ~*vb.* **4.** (*tr.*) to make a fraudulent imitation of. **5.** (*intr.*) to make counterfeits. **6.** to feign; simulate. [C13: < OF *contrefait,* < *contrefaire* to copy, < *contre-* COUNTER- + *faire* to make] —ˈ**counterˌfeiter** *n.*

counterfoil (ˈkaʊntəˌfɔɪl) *n. Brit.* the part of a cheque, receipt, etc., retained as a record. Also called (esp. in the U.S. and Canada): **stub.**

counterinsurgency (ˌkaʊntərɪnˈsɜːdʒənsɪ) *n.* action taken by a government against rebels, guerrillas, etc.

counterintelligence (ˌkaʊntərɪnˈtɛlɪdʒəns) *n.* activities designed to frustrate enemy espionage.

counterirritant (ˌkaʊntərˈɪrɪtᵊnt) *n.* **1.** an agent that causes a superficial irritation of the skin and thereby relieves inflammation of deep structures. ~*adj.* **2.** producing a counterirritation. —ˌ**counterˌirri'tation** *n.*

countermand *vb.* (ˌkaʊntəˈmɑːnd). (*tr.*) **1.** to revoke or cancel (a command, order, etc.). **2.** to order (forces, etc.) to retreat; recall. ~*n.* (ˈkaʊntəˌmɑːnd). **3.** a command revoking another. [C15: < OF *contremander,* < *contre-* COUNTER- + *mander* to command, < L *mandāre*]

countermarch (ˈkaʊntəˌmɑːtʃ) *Chiefly mil.* ~*vb.* **1.** to march or cause to march back or in the opposite direction. ~*n.* **2.** the act or an instance of countermarching.

countermeasure (ˈkaʊntəˌmɛʒə) *n.* action taken to oppose, neutralize, or retaliate against some other action.

countermove (ˈkaʊntəˌmuːv) *n.* **1.** an opposing move. ~*vb.* **2.** to make or do (something) as an opposing move. —ˈ**counterˌmovement** *n.*

counteroffensive (ˈkaʊntərəˌfɛnsɪv) *n.* a series of attacks by a defending force against an attacking enemy.

counterpane (ˈkaʊntəˌpeɪn) *n.* another word for **bedspread.** [C17: < obs. *counterpoint* (infl. by *pane* coverlet), changed < OF *coutepointe* quilt, < Med. L *culcita puncta* quilted mattress]

counterpart (ˈkaʊntəˌpɑːt) *n.* **1.** a person or thing identical to or closely resembling another. **2.** one of two parts that complement or correspond to each other. **3.** a duplicate, esp. of a legal document; copy.

counterplot (ˈkaʊntəˌplɒt) *n.* **1.** a plot designed to frustrate another plot. ~*vb.* **-plotting, -plotted.** **2.** (*tr.*) to oppose with a counterplot.

counterpoint (ˈkaʊntəˌpɔɪnt) *n.* **1.** the technique involving the simultaneous sounding of two or more parts or melodies. **2.** a melody or part combined with another melody or part. **3.** the musical texture resulting from the simultaneous sounding of two or more melodies or parts. ~*vb.* **4.** (*tr.*) to set in contrast. ~Related adj.: **contrapuntal.** [C15: < OF *contrepoint,* < *contre-* COUNTER- + *point* dot, note in musical notation, i.e. an accompaniment set against the notes of a melody]

counterpoise (ˈkaʊntəˌpɔɪz) *n.* **1.** a force, influence, etc., that counterbalances another. **2.** a state of balance; equilibrium. **3.** a weight that balances another. ~*vb.* (*tr.*) **4.** to oppose with something of equal effect, weight, or force; offset. **5.** to bring into equilibrium.

counterproductive (ˌkaʊntəprəˈdʌktɪv) *adj.* tending to hinder the achievement of an aim; having effects contrary to those intended.

counterproposal (ˈkaʊntəprəˌpəʊzᵊl) *n.* a proposal offered as an alternative to a previous proposal.

Counter-Reformation (ˌkaʊntəˌrɛfəˈmeɪʃən) *n.* the reform movement of the Roman Catholic Church in the 16th and early 17th centuries considered as a reaction to the Reformation.

counter-revolution (ˌkaʊntəˌrɛvəˈluːʃən) *n.* a revolution opposed to a previous revolution. —ˌ**counter-ˌrevo'lutionist** *n.* —**counter-ˌrevo'lutionary** *n., adj.*

countershaft (ˈkaʊntəˌʃɑːft) *n.* an intermediate shaft driven by a main shaft, esp. in a gear train.

countersign *vb.* (ˈkaʊntəˌsaɪn, ˌkaʊntəˈsaɪn). **1.** (*tr.*) to sign (a document already signed by another). ~*n.* (ˈkaʊntəˌsaɪn). **2.** Also called: **countersignature.** the signature so written. **3.** a secret sign given in response to another sign. **4.** *Chiefly mil.* a password.

countersink (ˈkaʊntəˌsɪŋk) *vb.* **-sinking, -sank, -sunk.** (*tr.*) **1.** to enlarge the upper part of (a hole) in timber, metal, etc., so that the head of a bolt or screw can be sunk below the surface. **2.** to drive (a screw) or sink (a bolt) into such a hole. ~*n.* **3.** Also called: **countersink bit.** a tool for countersinking. **4.** a countersunk hole.

counterspy (ˈkaʊntəˌspaɪ) *n., pl.* **-spies.** a spy working against enemy espionage.

countertenor (ˌkaʊntəˈtɛnə) *n.* **1.** an adult male voice with an alto range. **2.** a singer with such a voice.

countervail (ˌkaʊntəˈveɪl, ˈkaʊntəˌveɪl) *vb.* **1.** (when *intr.,* usually foll. by *against*) to act or act against with equal power or force. **2.** (*tr.*) to make up for; compensate; offset. [C14: < OF *contrevaloir,* < L *contrā valēre,* < *contrā* against + *valēre* to be strong]

counterweigh (ˌkaʊntəˈweɪ) *vb.* another word for **counterbalance** (sense 2).

counterweight (ˈkaʊntəˌweɪt) *n.* a counterbalancing weight, influence, or force.

countess (ˈkaʊntɪs) *n.* **1.** the wife or widow of a count or earl. **2.** a woman of the rank of count or earl.

counting house *n. Rare, chiefly Brit.* a room or building used by the accountants of a business.

countless (ˈkaʊntlɪs) *adj.* innumerable; myriad.

count noun *n.* a noun that can be qualified by the indefinite article and may be used in the plural, as *telephone* and *thing* but not *airs and graces* or *bravery.* Cf. **mass noun.**

count on *vb.* (*intr., prep.*) to rely or depend on.

count out *vb.* (*tr., adv.*) **1.** *Inf.* to leave out; exclude. **2.** (of a boxing referee) to judge (a floored boxer) to have failed to recover within the specified time.

count palatine *n., pl.* **counts palatine.** *History.* **1.** (in the Holy Roman Empire) a count who exercised royal authority in his own domain. **2.** (in England and Ireland) the lord of a county palatine.

countrified *or* **countryfied** (ˈkʌntrɪˌfaɪd) *adj.* in the style, manners, etc., of the country; rural.

country (ˈkʌntrɪ) *n., pl.* **-tries.** **1.** a territory distinguished by its people, culture, geography, etc. **2.** an area of land distinguished by its political autonomy; state. **3.** the people of a territory or state. **4. a.** the part of the land that is away from cities or industrial areas; rural districts. **b.** (*as modifier*): *country cottage.* Related adj.: **pastoral, rural. 5.** short for **country music. 6. across country.** not keeping to roads, etc. **7. go** *or* **appeal to the country.** *Chiefly Brit.* to dissolve Parliament and hold an election. **8. up country.** away from the coast or the capital. **9.** one's native land or nation of citizenship. [C13: < OF *contrée,* < Med. L *contrāta,* lit.: that which lies opposite, < L *contrā* opposite]

country and western *n.* another name for **country music.**

country club *n.* a club in the country, having sporting and social facilities.

country dance *n.* a type of folk dance in which couples face one another in a line.

country house *n.* a large house in the country, esp. belonging to a wealthy family.

countryman (ˈkʌntrɪmən) *n., pl.* **-men. 1.** a person who lives in the country. **2.** a person from a particular country or from one's own country. —ˈ**country,woman** *fem. n.*

country music *n.* a type of 20th-century popular music based on White folk music of the southeastern U.S.

country park *n. Brit.* an area of countryside set aside for public recreation.

country seat *n.* a large estate or property in the country.

countryside (ˈkʌntrɪˌsaɪd) *n.* a rural area or its population.

county (ˈkaʊntɪ) *n., pl.* **-ties. 1. a.** any of various administrative, political, or judicial subdivisions of certain English-speaking countries or states. **b.** (*as modifier*): *county cricket.* ~*adj.* **2.** *Brit. inf.* upper class; of or like the landed gentry. [C14: < OF *conté* land belonging to a count, < LL *comes* COUNT[2]]

county palatine *n., pl.* **counties palatine. 1.** the lands of a count palatine. **2.** (in England and Ireland) a county in which the earl (or other lord) exercised many royal powers, esp. judicial authority.

county town *n.* the town in which a county's affairs are or were administered.

coup (kuː) *n.* **1.** a brilliant and successful stroke or action. **2.** short for **coup d'état.** [C18: < F: blow, < L *colaphus* blow with the fist, < Gk *kolaphos*]

coup de grâce *French.* (ku də grɑs) *n., pl.* ***coups de grâce*** (ku də grɑs). **1.** a mortal or finishing blow, esp. one delivered as an act of mercy to a sufferer. **2.** a final or decisive stroke. [lit.: blow of mercy]

coup d'état (ˈkuː deɪˈtɑː) *n., pl.* **coups d'état** (ˈkuːz deɪˈtɑː). a sudden violent or illegal seizure of government. [F, lit.: stroke of state]

coupe (kuːp) *n.* **1.** a dessert of fruit and ice cream. **2.** a dish or stemmed glass bowl designed for this dessert. [C19: < F: goblet, CUP]

coupé (ˈkuːpeɪ) *n.* **1.** a four-seater car with a sloping back, and usually two doors. **2.** a four-wheeled horse-drawn carriage with two seats inside and one outside for the driver. [C19: < F, short for *carosse coupé,* lit.: cut-off carriage]

couple (ˈkʌpᵊl) *n.* **1.** two people who regularly associate with each other or live together: *an engaged couple.* **2.** (*functioning as sing. or pl.*) two people considered as a pair, for or as if for dancing, games, etc. **3.** a pair of equal and opposite parallel forces that have a tendency to produce rotation. **4.** a connector or link between two members, such as a tie connecting a pair of rafters in a roof. **5. a couple of.** (*functioning as sing. or pl.*) **a.** a combination of two; a pair of: *a couple of men.* **b.** *Inf.* a small number of; a few: *a couple of days.* ~*pron.* **6.** (usually preceded by *a; functioning as sing. or pl.*) two; a pair: *give him a couple.* ~*vb.* **7.** (*tr.*) to connect (two things) together or to connect (one thing) to (another): *to couple railway carriages.* **8.** to form or be formed into a pair or pairs. **9.** to associate, put, or connect together. **10.** (*intr.*) to have sexual intercourse. [C13: < OF: a pair, < L *cōpula* a bond; see COPULA]

coupler (ˈkʌplə) *n. Music.* a device on an organ or harpsichord connecting two keys, two manuals, etc., so that both may be played at once.

couplet (ˈkʌplɪt) *n.* two successive lines of verse, usually rhymed and of the same metre. [C16: < F, lit.: a little pair; see COUPLE]

coupling (ˈkʌplɪŋ) *n.* **1.** a mechanical device that connects two things. **2.** a device for connecting railway cars or trucks together.

coupon (ˈkuːpɒn) *n.* **1. a.** a detachable part of a ticket or advertisement entitling the holder to a discount, free gift, etc. **b.** a detachable slip usable as a commercial order form. **c.** a voucher given away with certain goods, a certain number of which are exchangeable for goods offered by the manufacturers. **2.** one of a number of detachable certificates attached to a bond, the surrender of which entitles the bearer to receive interest payments. **3.** *Brit.* a detachable entry form for any of certain competitions, esp. football pools. [C19: < F, < OF *colpon* piece cut off, < *colper* to cut, var. of *couper*]

courage (ˈkʌrɪdʒ) *n.* **1.** the power or quality of dealing with or facing danger, fear, pain, etc. **2. the courage of one's convictions.** the confidence to act in accordance with one's beliefs. [C13: < OF *corage,* < *cuer* heart, < L *cor*]

courageous (kəˈreɪdʒəs) *adj.* possessing or expressing courage. —**couˈrageously** *adv.* —**couˈrageousness** *n.*

courante (kʊˈrɑːnt) *n. Music.* **1.** an old dance in quick triple time. **2.** a movement of a (mostly) 16th- to 18th-century suite based on this. [C16: < F, lit.: running, < *courir* to run, < L *currere*]

coureur de bois (*French* kurœr də bwa) *n., pl.* **coureurs de bois** (kurœr də bwa). *Canad. history.* a French Canadian woodsman or Métis who traded with Indians for furs. [Canad. F: trapper (lit.: wood-runner)]

courgette (kʊəˈʒɛt) *n.* a small variety of vegetable marrow. U.S. and Canad. name: **zucchini.** [< F, dim. of *courge* marrow, gourd]

courier (ˈkʊərɪə) *n.* **1.** a special messenger, esp. one carrying diplomatic correspondence. **2.** a person who makes arrangements for or accompanies a group of travellers on a journey or tour. [C16: < OF *courrier,* < OIt. *correre* to run, < L *currere*]

course (kɔːs) *n.* **1.** a continuous progression in time or space; onward movement. **2.** a route or direction followed. **3.** the path or channel along which something moves: *the course of a river.* **4.** an area or stretch of land or water on which a sport is played or a race is run: *a golf course.* **5.** a period of time; duration: *in the course of the next hour.* **6.** the usual order of and time required for a sequence of events; regular procedure: *the illness ran its course.* **7.** a mode of conduct or action: *if you follow that course, you will fail.* **8.** a connected series of events, actions, etc. **9. a.** a prescribed number of lessons, lectures, etc., in an educational curriculum. **b.** the material covered in such a curriculum. **10.** a regimen prescribed for a specific period of time: *a course of treatment.* **11.** a part of a meal served at one time. **12.** a continuous, usually horizontal, layer of building material, such as a row of bricks, tiles, etc. **13. as a matter of course.** as a natural or normal consequence, mode of action, or event. **14. in course of.** in the process of. **15. in due course.** at some future time, esp. the natural or appropriate time. **16. of course. a.** (*adv.*) as expected; naturally. **b.** (*sentence substitute*) certainly; definitely. **17. the course of nature.** the ordinary course of events. ~*vb.* **18.** (*intr.*) to run, race, or flow. **19.** to cause (hounds) to hunt by sight rather than scent or (of hounds) to hunt (a quarry) thus. [C13: < OF *cours,* < L *cursus* a running, < *currere* to run]

courser[1] (ˈkɔːsə) *n.* **1.** a person who courses hounds or dogs, esp. greyhounds. **2.** a hound or dog trained for coursing.

courser[2] (ˈkɔːsə) *n. Literary.* a swift horse; steed. [C13: < OF *coursier,* < *cours* COURSE]

courser[3] (ˈkɔːsə) *n.* a terrestrial plover-like shore bird of desert and semidesert regions of the Old World.

coursing (ˈkɔːsɪŋ) *n.* **1.** hunting with hounds or dogs that follow their quarry by sight. **2.** a sport in which hounds are matched against one another in pairs for the hunting of hares by sight.

court (kɔːt) *n.* **1.** an area of ground wholly or partly surrounded by walls or buildings. **2.** *Brit.* **a.** a block of flats. **b.** a mansion or country house. **c.** a short street, sometimes closed at one end. **3. a.** the residence, retinues, or household of a sovereign or nobleman. **b.** (*as modifier*): *a court ball.* **4.** a sovereign or prince and his retinue, advisers, etc. **5.** any formal assembly held by a sovereign or nobleman. **6.** homage, flattering attention, or amorous approaches (esp. in **pay court to someone**). **7.** *Law.* **a.** a tribunal having power to adjudicate in civil, criminal, military, or ecclesiastical matters. **b.** the regular sitting of such a judicial tribunal. **c.** the room or building in which such a tribunal sits. **8. a.** a marked outdoor or enclosed area used for any of various ball games, such as tennis, squash, etc. **b.** a marked section of such an area. **9. go to court.** to take legal action. **10. hold court.** to preside over admirers, attendants, etc. **11. out of court.** without a trial or legal case. **12. the ball is in your court.** you are obliged to make the next move. ~*vb.* **13.** to attempt to gain the love of; woo. **14.** (*tr.*) to pay attention to (someone) in order to gain favour. **15.** (*tr.*) to try to obtain (fame, honour, etc.). **16.** (*tr.*) to invite, usually foolishly, as by taking risks. [C12: < OF, < L *cohors* COHORT]

court-bouillon (ˈkʊətˈbuːjɒn) *n.* a stock made from root vegetables, water, and wine or vinegar, used primarily for poaching fish. [< F, < *court* short, + *bouillon* broth, < *bouillir* to BOIL[1]]

court card *n.* (in a pack of playing cards) a king, queen, or jack of any suit. [C17: altered < earlier *coat-card,* < the decorative coats worn by the figures depicted]

court circular *n.* a daily report of the activities, engagements, etc., of the sovereign, published in a national newspaper.

Courtelle (kɔːˈtɛl) *n. Trademark.* a synthetic acrylic fibre resembling wool.

courteous (ˈkɜːtɪəs) *adj.* polite and considerate in manner. [C13 *corteis,* lit.: with courtly manners, < OF; see COURT] —ˈ**courteously** *adv.* —ˈ**courteousness** *n.*

courtesan *or* **courtezan** (ˌkɔːtɪˈzæn) *n.* (esp. formerly) a prostitute, or the mistress of a man of rank. [C16: < OF *courtisane,* < It. *cortigiana* female courtier, < *corte* COURT]

courtesy (ˈkɜːtɪsɪ) *n., pl.* **-sies. 1.** politeness; good manners. **2.** a courteous gesture or remark. **3.** favour or consent (esp. in **by courtesy of**). **4.** common consent as opposed to right (esp. in **by courtesy**). [C13 *curteisie,* < OF, < *corteis* COURTEOUS]

courtesy light *n.* the interior light in a motor vehicle.

courtesy title *n.* any of several titles having no legal significance, such as those borne by the children of peers.

courthouse (ˈkɔːtˌhaʊs) *n.* a public building in which courts of law are held.

courtier (ˈkɔːtɪə) *n.* **1.** an attendant at a court. **2.** a person who seeks favour in an ingratiating manner. [C13: < Anglo-F *courteour* (unattested), < OF *corteier* to attend at court]

courtly (ˈkɔːtlɪ) *adj.* **-lier, -liest. 1.** of or suitable for a royal court. **2.** refined in manner. **3.** ingratiating. —ˈ**courtliness** *n.*

court martial *n., pl.* **court martials** *or* **courts martial. 1.** a military court that tries persons subject to military law. ~*vb.* **court-martial, -tialling, -tialled** *or U.S.* **-tialing, -tialed. 2.** (*tr.*) to try by court martial.

Court of Appeal *n.* a court that hears appeals from the High Court and from the county and crown courts.

Court of St James's *n.* the official name of the royal court of Britain.

court plaster *n.* a plaster, composed of isinglass on silk, formerly used to cover superficial wounds. [C18: so called because formerly used by court ladies for beauty spots]

courtroom (ˈkɔːtˌruːm, -ˌrʊm) *n.* a room in which the sittings of a law court are held.

courtship (ˈkɔːtʃɪp) *n.* **1.** the act, period, or art of seeking the love of someone with intent to marry. **2.** the seeking or soliciting of favours.

court shoe *n.* a low-cut shoe for women, without any laces or straps.

courtyard (ˈkɔːtˌjɑːd) *n.* an open area of ground surrounded by walls or buildings; court.

couscous (ˈkuːskuːs) *n.* a spicy dish, originating in North Africa, consisting of steamed semolina served with a meat stew. [C17: via F < Ar. *kouskous,* < *kaskasa* to pound until fine]

cousin (ˈkʌzᵊn) *n.* **1.** Also called: **first cousin, cousin-german, full cousin.** the child of one's aunt or uncle. **2.** a relative descended from one of one's common ancestors. **3.** a title used by a sovereign when addressing another sovereign or a nobleman. [C13: < OF *cosin,* < L *consōbrīnus,* < *sōbrīnus* cousin on the mother's side] —ˈ**cousinˌhood** *or* ˈ**cousinˌship** *n.* —ˈ**cousinly** *adj., adv.*

couture (kuːˈtʊə) *n.* high-fashion designing and dressmaking. [< F: sewing, < OF *cousture* seam, < L *consuere* to stitch together]

couturier (kuːˈtʊərɪˌeɪ) *n.* a person who designs, makes, and sells fashion clothes for women. [< F: dressmaker; see COUTURE] —**couturière** (kuːˌtuːrɪˈɛə) *fem. n.*

couvade (kuːˈvɑːd) *n. Anthropol.* the custom in certain cultures of treating the husband of a woman giving birth as if he were bearing the child. [C19: < F, < *couver* to hatch, < L *cubāre* to lie down]

covalency (kəʊˈveɪlənsɪ) *or U.S.* **covalence** *n.* **1.** the formation and nature of covalent bonds, that is, chemical bonds involving the sharing of electrons between atoms in a molecule. **2.** the number of covalent bonds that a particular atom can make with other atoms in forming a molecule. —**coˈvalent** *adj.* —**coˈvalently** *adv.*

cove[1] (kəʊv) *n.* **1.** a small bay or inlet. **2.** a narrow cavern in the side of a cliff, mountain, etc. **3.** Also called: **coving.** *Archit.* a concave curved surface between the wall and ceiling of a room. [OE *cofa*]

cove[2] (kəʊv) *n. Sl., Brit. old-fashioned & Austral.* a fellow; chap. [C16: prob. < Romany *kova* thing, person]

coven (ˈkʌvᵊn) *n.* a meeting of witches. [C16: prob. < OF *covin* group, ult. < L *convenīre* to come together]

covenant (ˈkʌvənənt) *n.* **1.** a binding agreement; contract. **2.** *Law.* an agreement in writing under seal, as to pay a stated annual sum to a charity. **3.** *Bible.* God's promise to the Israelites and their commitment to worship him alone. ~*vb.* **4.** to agree to a covenant (concerning). [C13: < OF, < *covenir* to agree, < L *convenīre* to come together, make an agreement; see CONVENE] —**covenantal** (ˌkʌvəˈnæntᵊl) *adj.* —ˈ**covenantor** *or* ˈ**covenanter** *n.*

Covenanter (ˈkʌvənəntə, ˌkʌvəˈnæntə) *n. Scot. history.* a person upholding either of two 17th-century covenants to establish and defend Presbyterianism.

Coventry (ˈkɒvəntrɪ) *n.* **send to Coventry.** to ostracize or ignore. [after *Coventry,* a city in England, in the W Midlands]

cover (ˈkʌvə) *vb.* (*mainly tr.*) **1.** to place or spread something over so as to protect or conceal. **2.** to provide with a covering; clothe. **3.** to put a garment, esp. a hat, on (the body or head). **4.** to extend over or lie thickly on the surface of: *snow covered the fields.* **5.** to bring upon (oneself); invest (oneself) as if with a covering: *covered with shame.* **6.** (sometimes foll. by *up*) to act as a screen or concealment for; hide from view. **7.** *Mil.* to protect (an individual, formation, or place) by taking up a position from which fire may be returned if those being protected are fired upon. **8.** (*also intr.*, sometimes foll. by *for*) to assume responsibility for (a person or thing). **9.** (*intr.;* foll. by *for* or *up for*) to provide an alibi (for). **10.** to have as one's territory: *this salesman covers your area.* **11.** to travel over. **12.** to have or place in the aim and within the range of (a firearm). **13.** to include or deal with. **14.** (of an asset or income) to be sufficient to meet (a liability or expense). **15. a.** to insure against loss, risk, etc. **b.** to provide for (loss, risk, etc.) by insurance. **16.** to deposit (an equivalent stake) in a bet. **17.** to act as reporter or photographer on (a news event, etc.) for a newspaper or magazine: *to cover sports events.* **18.** *Music.* to record a cover version of. **19.** *Sport.* to guard or protect (an opponent, team-mate, or area). **20.** (of a male animal, esp. a horse) to copulate with (a female animal). ~*n.* **21.** anything that covers, spreads over, protects, or conceals. **22. a.** a blanket used on a bed for warmth. **b.** another word for **bedspread. 23.** a pretext, disguise, or false identity: *the thief sold brushes as a cover.* **24.** an envelope or package for sending through the post: *under plain cover.* **25. a.** an individual table setting, esp. in a restaurant. **b.** (*as modifier*): *a cover charge.* **26.** Also called: **cover version.** a version by a different artist of a previously recorded musical item. **27.** *Cricket.* **a.** (*often pl.*) the area more or less at right angles to the pitch on the off side and usually about halfway to the boundary. **b.** (*as modifier*): *a cover drive.* **28.** *Philately.* an entire envelope that has been postmarked. **29. break cover.** to come out from a shelter or hiding place. **30. take cover.** to make for a place of safety or shelter. **31. under cover.** protected, concealed, or in secret. ~ See also **cover-up.** [C13: < OF *covrir,* < L *cooperīre* to cover completely, < *operīre* to cover over] —ˈ**coverable** *adj.* —ˈ**coverer** *n.*

coverage (ˈkʌvərɪdʒ) *n.* **1.** the amount or extent to which something is covered. **2.** *Journalism.* the amount and quality of reporting or analysis given to a particular subject or event. **3.** the extent of the protection provided by insurance.

cover crop *n.* a crop planted between main crops to prevent leaching or soil erosion or to provide green manure.

covered wagon *n. U.S. & Canad.* a large horse-drawn wagon with an arched canvas top, used formerly for prairie travel.

cover girl *n.* a glamorous girl whose picture appears on the cover of a magazine.

covering letter *n.* an accompanying letter sent as an explanation, introduction, or record.

coverlet (ˈkʌvəlɪt) *n.* another word for **bedspread.**

cover note *n. Brit.* a certificate issued by an insurance company stating that a policy is operative: used as a temporary measure between the commencement of cover and the issue of the policy.

cover point *n. Cricket.* **a.** a fielding position in the covers. **b.** a fielder in this position.

covert (ˈkʌvət) *adj.* **1.** concealed or secret. ~*n.* **2.** a shelter or disguise. **3.** a thicket or woodland providing shelter for game. **4.** short for **covert cloth. 5.** *Ornithol.* any of the small feathers on the wings and tail of a bird that surround the bases of the larger feathers. [C14: < OF: covered, < *covrir* to COVER] —ˈ**covertly** *adv.*

covert cloth *n.* a twill-weave cotton or worsted suiting fabric.

coverture (ˈkʌvətʃə) *n. Rare.* shelter, concealment, or disguise. [C13: < OF, < *covert* covered; see COVERT]

cover-up *n.* **1.** concealment or attempted concealment of a mistake, crime, etc. ~*vb.* **cover up.** (*adv.*) **2.** (*tr.*) to cover completely. **3.** (when *intr.*, often foll. by *for*) to attempt to conceal (a mistake or crime).

cover version *n.* another name for **cover** (sense 26).

covet (ˈkʌvɪt) *vb.* (*tr.*) to wish, long, or crave for (something, esp. the property of another person). [C13: < OF *coveitier,* < *coveitié* eager desire, ult. < L *cupiditās* CUPIDITY] —ˈ**covetable** *adj.*

covetous (ˈkʌvɪtəs) *adj.* (*usually postpositive* and foll. by *of*) jealously eager for the possession of something (esp. the property of another person). —ˈ**covetously** *adv.* —ˈ**covetousness** *n.*

covey (ˈkʌvɪ) *n.* **1.** a small flock of grouse or partridge. **2.** a small group, as of people. [C14: < OF *covee,* < *cover* to sit on, hatch]

cow[1] (kaʊ) *n.* **1.** the mature female of any species of cattle, esp. domesticated cattle. **2.** the mature female of various other mammals, such as the elephant, whale, and seal. **3.** (not in technical use) any domestic species of cattle. **4.** *Inf.* a disagreeable woman. **5.** *Austral. & N.Z. sl.* something objectionable (esp. in **a fair cow**). [OE *cū*]

cow[2] (kaʊ) *vb.* (*tr.*) to frighten or overawe, as with threats. [C17: < ON *kūga* to oppress]

coward (ˈkaʊəd) *n.* a person who shrinks from or avoids danger, pain, or difficulty. [C13: < OF *cuard,* < *coue* tail, < L *cauda;* ? suggestive of a frightened animal with its tail between its legs]

cowardice (ˈkaʊədɪs) *n.* lack of courage in facing danger, pain, or difficulty.

cowardly (ˈkaʊədlɪ) *adj.* of or characteristic of a coward; lacking courage. —ˈ**cowardliness** *n.*

cowbell (ˈkaʊˌbɛl) *n.* a bell hung around a cow's neck so that the cow can be easily located.

cowberry (ˈkaʊbərɪ, -brɪ) *n., pl.* **-ries. 1.** a creeping evergreen shrub of N temperate and arctic regions, with pink or red flowers and edible slightly acid berries. **2.** the berry of this plant.

cowbird (ˈkaʊˌbɜːd) *n.* any of various American orioles, having dark plumage and a short bill.

cowboy (ˈkaʊˌbɔɪ) *n.* **1.** Also called: **cowhand.** a hired man who herds and tends cattle, usually on horseback, esp. in the western U.S. **2.** a conventional character of Wild West folklore, films, etc., esp. one involved in fighting Indians. **3.** *Inf.* an irresponsible or unscrupulous operator in business, etc. —ˈ**cowˌgirl** *fem. n.*

cowcatcher (ˈkaʊˌkætʃə) *n. U.S. & Canad.* a metal frame on the front of a locomotive to clear the track of animals or other obstructions.

cow-cocky *n., pl.* **-cockies.** *Austral. & N.Z.* a one-man dairy farmer.

cower (ˈkaʊə) *vb.* (*intr.*) to crouch or cringe, as in fear. [C13: < MLow G *kūren* to lie in wait; rel. to Swedish *kura*]

cowherd (ˈkaʊˌhɜːd) *n.* a person employed to tend cattle.

cowhide (ˈkaʊˌhaɪd) *n.* **1.** the hide of a cow. **2.** the leather made from such a hide.

cowl (kaʊl) *n.* **1.** a hood, esp. a loose one. **2.** the hooded habit of a monk. **3.** a cover fitted to a chimney to increase ventilation and prevent draughts. **4.** the part of a car body that supports the windscreen and the bonnet. ~*vb.* (*tr.*) **5.** to cover or provide with a cowl. [OE *cugele,* < LL *cuculla* cowl, < L *cucullus* hood]

cowlick (ˈkaʊˌlɪk) *n.* a tuft of hair over the forehead.

cowling (ˈkaʊlɪŋ) *n.* a streamlined metal covering, esp. around an aircraft engine.

cowman (ˈkaʊmən) *n., pl.* **-men. 1.** *Brit.* another name for **cowherd. 2.** *U.S. & Canad.* a man who owns cattle; rancher.

co-worker *n.* a fellow worker; associate.

cow parsley *n.* a common Eurasian umbelliferous hedgerow plant having umbrella-shaped clusters of white flowers.

cowpat (ˈkaʊˌpæt) *n.* a single dropping of cow dung.

cowpea (ˈkaʊˌpiː) *n.* **1.** a leguminous tropical climbing plant producing pods containing edible pealike seeds. **2.** the seed of this plant.

cowpox (ˈkaʊˌpɒks) *n.* a contagious viral disease of cows characterized by vesicles, esp. on the teats and udder. Inoculation of humans with this virus provides temporary immunity to smallpox.

cowpuncher (ˈkaʊˌpʌntʃə) *or* **cowpoke** (ˈkaʊˌpəʊk) *n. U.S. & Canad.* an informal word for **cowboy.**

cowrie *or* **cowry** (ˈkaʊrɪ) *n., pl.* **-ries. 1.** any marine gastropod mollusc of a mostly tropical family having a glossy brightly marked shell. **2.** the shell of any of these molluscs, esp. the money cowrie, used as money in parts of Africa and S Asia. [C17: < Hindi *kaurī*, < Sansk. *kaparda*]

cowslip (ˈkaʊˌslɪp) *n.* **1.** a primrose native to temperate regions of the Old World, having yellow flowers. **2.** *U.S. & Canad.* another name for **marsh marigold.** [OE *cūslyppe;* see COW[1], SLIP[3]]

cox (kɒks) *n.* **1.** a coxswain. ~*vb.* **2.** to act as coxswain of (a boat). —ˈ**coxless** *adj.*

coxa (ˈkɒksə) *n., pl.* **coxae** (ˈkɒksiː). **1.** a technical name for the hipbone or hip joint. **2.** the basal segment of the leg of an insect. [C18: < L: hip] —ˈ**coxal** *adj.*

coxalgia (kɒkˈsældʒɪə) *n.* **1.** pain in the hip joint. **2.** disease of the hip joint causing pain. [C19: < COXA + -ALGIA] —**coxˈalgic** *adj.*

coxcomb (ˈkɒksˌkəʊm) *n.* **1.** a variant spelling of **cockscomb. 2.** *Obs.* the cap, resembling a cock's comb, worn by a jester. —ˈ**coxˌcombry** *n.*

coxswain (ˈkɒksən, -ˌsweɪn) *n.* the helmsman of a lifeboat, racing shell, etc. Also called: **cockswain.** [C15: < *cock* a ship's boat + SWAIN]

coy (kɔɪ) *adj.* **1.** affectedly demure, esp. in a playful or provocative manner. **2.** shy; modest. **3.** evasive, esp. in an annoying way. [C14: < OF *coi* reserved, < L *quiētus* QUIET] —ˈ**coyly** *adv.* —ˈ**coyness** *n.*

Coy. *Mil. abbrev. for* company.

coyote (ˈkɔɪəʊt, kɔɪˈəʊtɪ; *esp. U.S.* ˈkaɪəʊt, kaɪˈəʊtɪ) *n., pl.* **-otes** *or* **-ote.** a predatory canine mammal of the deserts and prairies of North America. Also called: **prairie wolf.** [C19: < Mexican Sp., < Nahuatl *coyotl*]

coypu (ˈkɔɪpuː) *n., pl.* **-pus** *or* **-pu. 1.** an aquatic South American rodent, naturalized in Europe. It resembles a small beaver and is bred for its fur. **2.** the fur of this animal. ~Also called: **nutria.** [C18: < American Sp. *coipú*, < Amerind *kóypu*]

coz (kʌz) *n.* an archaic word for **cousin.**

cozen (ˈkʌzᵊn) *vb.* to cheat or trick (someone). [C16: cant term ? rel. to COUSIN] —ˈ**cozenage** *n.*

cozy (ˈkəʊzɪ) *adj., n.* the usual U.S. spelling of **cosy.**

cp *abbrev. for* candle power.

CP *abbrev. for:* **1.** Canadian Pacific Ltd. **2.** Common Prayer. **3.** Communist Party. **4.** (in Australia) Country Party.

cp. *abbrev. for* compare.

CPAG *abbrev. for* Child Poverty Action Group.

cpd *abbrev. for* compound.

Cpl *abbrev. for* Corporal.

CPO *abbrev. for* Chief Petty Officer.

cps *Physics. abbrev. for* cycles per second.

CPSA *abbrev. for* Civil and Public Services Association.

CQ a symbol transmitted by an amateur radio operator requesting communication with any other amateur radio operator.

Cr **1.** *abbrev. for* Councillor. **2.** *the chemical symbol for* chromium.

cr. *abbrev. for:* **1.** credit. **2.** creditor.

crab[1] (kræb) *n.* **1.** any chiefly marine decapod crustacean having a broad flattened carapace covering the cephalothorax, beneath which is folded the abdomen. The first pair of limbs are pincers. **2.** any of various similar or related arthropods. **3.** short for **crab louse. 4.** a mechanical lifting device, esp. the travelling hoist of a gantry crane. **5. catch a crab.** *Rowing.* to make a stroke in which the oar either misses the water or digs too deeply, causing the rower to fall backwards. ~*vb.* **crabbing, crabbed. 6.** (*intr.*) to hunt or catch crabs. [OE *crabba*]

crab[2] (kræb) *Inf.* ~*vb.* **crabbing, crabbed. 1.** (*intr.*) to find fault; grumble. ~*n.* **2.** an irritable person. [C16: prob. back formation < CRABBED]

crab[3] (kræb) *n.* short for **crab apple.** [C15: ? of Scand. origin; cf. Swedish *skrabbe* crab apple]

Crab (kræb) *n.* **the.** the constellation Cancer, the fourth sign of the zodiac.

crab apple *n.* **1.** any of several rosaceous trees that have white, pink, or red flowers and small sour apple-like fruits. **2.** the fruit of any of these trees, used to make jam.

crabbed (ˈkræbɪd) *adj.* **1.** surly; irritable; perverse. **2.** (esp. of handwriting) cramped and hard to decipher. **3.** *Rare.* abstruse. [C13: prob. < CRAB[1] (< its wayward gait), infl. by CRAB (APPLE) (< its tartness)] —ˈ**crabbedly** *adv.* —ˈ**crabbedness** *n.*

crabby (ˈkræbɪ) *adj.* **-bier, -biest.** bad-tempered.

crab louse *n.* a parasitic louse that infests the pubic region in man.

crabwise (ˈkræbˌwaɪz) *adj., adv.* (of motion) sideways; like a crab.

crack (kræk) *vb.* **1.** to break or cause to break without complete separation of the parts. **2.** to break or cause to break with a sudden sharp sound; snap. **3.** to make or cause to make a sudden sharp sound: *to crack a whip.* **4.** to cause (the voice) to change tone or become harsh or (of the voice) to change tone, esp. to a higher register; break. **5.** *Inf.* to fail or cause to fail. **6.** to yield or cause to yield. **7.** (*tr.*) to hit with a forceful or resounding blow. **8.** (*tr.*) to break into or force open: *to crack a safe.* **9.** (*tr.*) to solve or decipher (a code, problem, etc.). **10.** (*tr.*) *Inf.* to tell (a joke, etc.). **11.** to break (a molecule) into smaller molecules or radicals by the action of heat, as in the distillation of petroleum. **12.** (*tr.*) to open (a bottle) for drinking. **13.** (*intr.*) *Scot. & N English dialect.* to chat; gossip. **14.** (*tr.*) *Inf.* to achieve (esp. in **crack it**). **15. crack a smile.** *Inf.* to break into a smile. **16. crack hardy** *or* **hearty.** *Austral. & N.Z. inf.* to disguise one's discomfort, etc.; put on a bold front. ~*n.* **17.** a sudden sharp noise. **18.** a break or fracture without complete separation of the two parts. **19.** a narrow opening or fissure. **20.** *Inf.* a resounding blow. **21.** a physical or mental defect; flaw. **22.** a moment or specific instant: *the crack of day.* **23.** a broken or cracked tone of voice, as a boy's during puberty. **24.** (often foll. by *at*) *Inf.* an attempt; opportunity to try. **25.** *Sl.* a gibe; wisecrack; joke. **26.** *Sl.* a person that excels. **27.** *Scot. & N English dialect.* a talk; chat. **28.** *Sl.* a concentrated highly addictive form of cocaine made into pellets or powder and smoked. **29. a fair crack of the whip.** *Inf.* a fair chance or opportunity. **30. crack of doom.** doomsday; the end of the world; the Day of Judgment. ~*adj.* **31.** (*prenominal*) *Sl.* first-class; excellent: *a crack shot.* ~See also **crack down, crack up.** [OE *cracian*]

crackbrained (ˈkrækˌbreɪnd) *adj.* insane, idiotic, or crazy.

crack down *vb.* (*intr., adv.;* often foll. by *on*) **1.** to take severe measures (against); become stricter (with). ~*n.* **crackdown. 2.** severe or repressive measures.

cracked (krækt) *adj.* **1.** damaged by cracking. **2.** *Inf.* crazy.

cracker (ˈkrækə) *n.* **1.** a decorated cardboard tube that emits a bang when pulled apart, releasing a toy, a joke, or a paper hat. **2.** short for **firecracker. 3.** a thin crisp biscuit, usually unsweetened. **4.** a person or thing that cracks. **5.** *Brit. sl.* a thing or person of notable qualities or abilities. **6.** See **catalytic cracker.**

crackerjack (ˈkrækəˌdʒæk) *Inf.* ~*adj.* **1.** excellent. ~*n.* **2.** a person or thing of exceptional quality or ability. [C20: changed < CRACK (first-class) + JACK (man)]

crackers (ˈkrækəz) *adj.* (*postpositive*) *Brit.* a slang word for **insane.**

cracking (ˈkrækɪŋ) *adj.* **1.** (*prenominal*) *Inf.* fast; vigorous (esp. in **a cracking pace**). **2. get cracking.** *Inf.* to start doing something quickly or with increased speed. ~*adv., adj.* **3.** *Brit. inf.* first-class; excellent. ~*n.* **4.** the process in which molecules are cracked, esp. the oil-refining process in which heavy oils are broken down into hydrocarbons of lower molecular weight by heat or catalysis.

crackjaw (ˈkrækˌdʒɔː) *Inf.* ~*adj.* **1.** difficult to pronounce. ~*n.* **2.** a word or phrase that is difficult to pronounce.

crackle (ˈkrækᵊl) *vb.* **1.** to make or cause to

make a series of slight sharp noises, as of paper being crushed. **2.** (*tr.*) to decorate (porcelain or pottery) by causing fine cracks to appear in the glaze. **3.** (*intr.*) to abound in vivacity or energy. ~*n.* **4.** the act or sound of crackling. **5.** intentional crazing in the glaze of porcelain or pottery. **6.** Also called: **crackleware.** porcelain or pottery so decorated. —ˈ**crackly** *adj.*

crackling (ˈkræklɪŋ) *n.* the crisp browned skin of roast pork.

crackpot (ˈkrækˌpɒt) *Inf.* ~*n.* **1.** an eccentric person; crank. ~*adj.* **2.** eccentric; crazy.

crack up *vb.* (*adv.*) **1.** (*intr.*) to break into pieces. **2.** (*intr.*) *Inf.* to undergo a physical or mental breakdown. **3.** (*tr.*) *Inf.* to present or report, esp. in glowing terms: *it's not all it's cracked up to be.* ~*n.* **crackup. 4.** *Inf.* a physical or mental breakdown.

-cracy *n. combining form.* indicating a type of government or rule: *plutocracy; mobocracy.* See also **-crat.** [< Gk *-kratia,* < *kratos* power]

cradle (ˈkreɪdᵊl) *n.* **1.** a baby's bed, often with rockers. **2.** a place where something originates. **3.** a frame, rest, or trolley made to support a piece of equipment, aircraft, ship, etc. **4.** a platform or trolley in which workmen are suspended on the side of a building or ship. **5.** *Agriculture.* **a.** a framework of several wooden fingers attached to a scythe to gather the grain into bunches as it is cut. **b.** a scythe with such a cradle. **6.** Also called: **rocker.** a boxlike apparatus for washing rocks, sand, etc., containing gold or gemstones. **7. rob the cradle.** *Inf.* to take for a lover, husband, or wife a person much younger than oneself. ~*vb.* (*tr.*) **8.** to rock or place in or as if in a cradle; hold tenderly. **9.** to nurture in or bring up from infancy. **10.** to wash (soil bearing gold, etc.) in a cradle. [OE *cradol*]

cradle snatcher *n. Inf.* another name for **baby snatcher** (sense 2).

cradlesong (ˈkreɪdᵊlˌsɒŋ) *n.* a lullaby.

craft (krɑːft) *n.* **1.** skill or ability. **2.** skill in deception and trickery. **3.** an occupation or trade requiring special skill, esp. manual dexterity. **4. a.** the members of such a trade, regarded collectively. **b.** (*as modifier*): *a craft union.* **5.** a single vessel, aircraft, or spacecraft. **6.** (*functioning as pl.*) ships, boats, aircraft, or spacecraft collectively. ~*vb.* **7.** (*tr.*) to make or fashion with skill, esp. by hand. [OE *cræft* skill, strength]

craftsman (ˈkrɑːftsmən) *n., pl.* **-men. 1.** a member of a skilled trade; someone who practises a craft; artisan. **2.** an artist skilled in an art or craft. —ˈ**craftsmanˌship** *n.*

crafty (ˈkrɑːftɪ) *adj.* **-tier, -tiest. 1.** skilled in deception; shrewd; cunning. **2.** *Arch.* skilful. —ˈ**craftily** *adv.* —ˈ**craftiness** *n.*

crag (kræg) *n.* a steep rugged rock or peak. [C13: of Celtic origin]

craggy (ˈkrægɪ) *or U.S.* **cragged** (ˈkrægɪd) *adj.* **-gier, -giest. 1.** having many crags. **2.** (of the face) rugged; rocklike. —ˈ**cragginess** *n.*

crake (kreɪk) *n. Zool.* any of several rails of the Old World, such as the corncrake. [C14: < ON *krāka* crow or *krākr* raven, imit.]

cram (kræm) *vb.* **cramming, crammed. 1.** (*tr.*) to force more (people, material, etc.) into (a room, container, etc.) than it can hold; stuff. **2.** to eat or cause to eat more than necessary. **3.** *Inf.* to study or cause to study (facts, etc.), esp. for an examination, by hastily memorizing. ~*n.* **4.** the act or condition of cramming. **5.** a crush. [OE *crammian*]

crambo (ˈkræmbəʊ) *n., pl.* **-boes.** a word game in which one team says a rhyme or rhyming line for a word or line given by the other team. [C17: < earlier *crambe,* prob. < L *crambē repetīta* cabbage repeated, hence an old story]

crammer (ˈkræmə) *n.* a person or school that prepares pupils for an examination.

cramp[1] (kræmp) *n.* **1.** a painful involuntary contraction of a muscle, typically caused by overexertion, heat, or chill. **2.** temporary partial paralysis of a muscle group: *writer's cramp.* **3.** (*usually pl. in the U.S. and Canada*) severe abdominal pain. ~*vb.* **4.** (*tr.*) to affect with or as if with a cramp. [C14: < OF *crampe,* of Gmc origin]

cramp[2] (kræmp) *n.* **1.** Also called: **cramp iron.** a strip of metal with its ends bent at right angles, used to bind masonry. **2.** a device for holding pieces of wood while they are glued; clamp. **3.** something that confines or restricts. ~*vb.* (*tr.*) **4.** to hold with a cramp. **5.** to confine or restrict. **6. cramp (someone's) style.** *Inf.* to prevent (a person) from using his abilities or acting freely and confidently. [C15: < MDu. *crampe* cramp, hook, of Gmc origin]

cramped (kræmpt) *adj.* **1.** closed in; restricted. **2.** (esp. of handwriting) small and irregular.

crampon (ˈkræmpən) *or* **crampoon** (kræmˈpuːn) *n.* **1.** one of a pair of pivoted steel levers used to lift heavy objects; grappling iron. **2.** (*often pl.*) one of a pair of frames each with 10 or 12 metal spikes, strapped to boots for climbing or walking on ice or snow. [C15: < F, < MDu. *crampe* hook; see CRAMP[2]]

cran (kræn) *n.* a unit of capacity used for fresh herring, equal to 37.5 gallons. [C18: <?]

cranberry (ˈkrænbərɪ, -brɪ) *n., pl.* **-ries. 1.** any of several trailing shrubs that bear sour edible red berries. **2.** the berry of this plant. [C17: < Low G *kraanbere,* < *kraan* CRANE + *bere* BERRY]

crane (kreɪn) *n.* **1.** a large long-necked long-legged wading bird inhabiting marshes and plains in most parts of the world. **2.** (not in ornithological use) any similar bird, such as a heron. **3.** a device for lifting and moving heavy objects, typically consisting of a pivoted boom rotating about a vertical axis with lifting gear suspended from the end of the boom. ~*vb.* **4.** (*tr.*) to lift or move (an object) by or as if by a crane. **5.** to stretch out (esp. the neck), as to see over other people's heads. [OE *cran*]

crane fly *n.* a dipterous fly having long legs, slender wings, and a narrow body. Also called (Brit.): **daddy-longlegs.**

cranesbill (ˈkreɪnzˌbɪl) *n.* any of various plants of the genus *Geranium,* having pink or purple flowers and long slender beaked fruits.

cranial (ˈkreɪnɪəl) *adj.* of or relating to the skull. —ˈ**cranially** *adv.*

cranial index *n.* the ratio of the greatest length to the greatest width of the cranium, multiplied by 100.

cranial nerve *n.* any of the 12 paired nerves that have their origin in the brain.

craniate (ˈkreɪnɪɪt, -ˌeɪt) *adj.* **1.** having a skull or cranium. ~*adj., n.* **2.** another word for **vertebrate.**

cranio- *or before a vowel* **crani-** *combining form.* indicating the cranium or cranial.

craniology (ˌkreɪnɪˈɒlədʒɪ) *n.* the branch of science concerned with the shape and size of the human skull. —**craniological** (ˌkreɪnɪəˈlɒdʒɪkᵊl) *adj.* —ˌ**cranioˈlogically** *adv.* —ˌ**craniˈologist** *n.*

craniometry (ˌkreɪnɪˈɒmɪtrɪ) *n.* the study and measurement of skulls. —**craniometric** (ˌkreɪnɪəˈmɛtrɪk) *or* ˌ**cranioˈmetrical** *adj.* —ˌ**cranioˈmetrically** *adv.* —ˌ**craniˈometrist** *n.*

craniotomy (ˌkreɪnɪˈɒtəmɪ) *n., pl.* **-mies. 1.** surgical incision into the skull. **2.** surgical crushing of a fetal skull to extract a dead fetus.

cranium (ˈkreɪnɪəm) *n., pl.* **-niums** *or* **-nia** (-nɪə). **1.** the skull of a vertebrate. **2.** the part of the skull that encloses the brain. [C16: < Med. L *crānium* skull, < Gk *kranion*]

crank (kræŋk) *n.* **1.** a device for communicating or converting motion, consisting of an arm projecting from a shaft, often with a second member attached to it parallel to the shaft. **2.** Also called: **crank handle, starting handle.** a handle incorporating a crank, used to start an engine or motor. **3.** *Inf.* **a.** an eccentric or odd person. **b.** *U.S. & Canad.* a bad-tempered person. ~*vb.* (*tr.*) **4.** to rotate (a shaft) by means of a crank. **5.** to start (an engine, motor, etc.) by means of a crank handle. [OE *cranc*]

crankcase (ˈkræŋkˌkeɪs) *n.* the metal housing

that encloses the crankshaft, connecting rods, etc., in an internal-combustion engine.

crankpin (ˈkræŋkˌpɪn) *n.* a short cylindrical surface fitted between two arms of a crank parallel to the main shaft of the crankshaft.

crankshaft (ˈkræŋkˌʃɑːft) *n.* a shaft having one or more cranks, to which the connecting rods are attached.

crank up *vb.* (*tr., adv.*) **1.** to start (an engine, motor, etc.) with a crank handle. **2.** *Sl.* to speed up.

cranky (ˈkræŋkɪ) *adj.* **crankier, crankiest. 1.** *Inf.* eccentric. **2.** *U.S., Canad., & Irish inf.* fussy and bad-tempered. **3.** shaky; out of order. —ˈ**crankily** *adv.* —ˈ**crankiness** *n.*

crannog (ˈkrænəg) *n.* an ancient Celtic lake or bog dwelling. [C19: < Irish Gaelic *crannóg,* < OIrish *crann* tree]

cranny (ˈkrænɪ) *n., pl.* **-nies.** a narrow opening, as in a wall or rock face; chink; crevice (esp. in **every nook and cranny**). [C15: < OF *cran* notch, fissure; cf. CRENEL] —ˈ**crannied** *adj.*

crap[1] (kræp) *n.* **1.** a losing throw in the game of craps. **2.** another name for **craps.** [C20: back formation < CRAPS]

crap[2] (kræp) *Sl.* ~*n.* **1.** nonsense. **2.** rubbish **3.** a taboo word for **faeces.** ~*vb.* **crapping, crapped. 4.** (*intr.*) a taboo word for **defecate.** [C15 *crappe* chaff, < MDu., prob. < *crappen* to break off]

crape (kreɪp) *n.* **1.** a variant spelling of **crepe. 2.** crepe, esp. when used for mourning clothes. **3.** a band of black crepe worn in mourning.

crap out *vb.* (*intr., adv.*) *Sl.* **1.** *U.S.* to make a losing throw in craps. **2.** *U.S.* to fail; withdraw. **3.** to fail to attempt something through fear.

craps (kræps) *n.* (*usually functioning as sing.*) **1.** a gambling game using two dice. **2. shoot craps.** to play this game. [C19: prob. < *crabs* lowest throw at dice, pl. of CRAB[1]] —ˈ**crapˌshooter** *n.*

crapulent (ˈkræpjʊlənt) *or* **crapulous** (ˈkræpjʊləs) *adj.* **1.** given to or resulting from intemperance. **2.** suffering from intemperance; drunken. [C18: < LL *crāpulentus* drunk, < L *crāpula,* < Gk *kraipalē* drunkenness, headache resulting therefrom] —ˈ**crapulence** *n.*

crash[1] (kræʃ) *vb.* **1.** to make or cause to make a loud noise as of solid objects smashing or clattering. **2.** to fall or cause to fall with force, breaking in pieces with a loud noise. **3.** (*intr.*) to break or smash in pieces with a loud noise. **4.** (*intr.*) to collapse or fail suddenly. **5.** to cause (an aircraft) to land violently resulting in severe damage or (of an aircraft) to land in this way. **6.** to cause (a car, etc.) to collide with another car or other object or (of two or more cars) to be involved in a collision. **7.** to move or cause to move violently or noisily. **8.** (*intr.*) (of a computer system or program) to fail suddenly because of a malfunction. **9.** *Brit. inf.* short for **gate-crash.** ~*n.* **10.** an act or instance of breaking and falling to pieces. **11.** a sudden loud noise. **12.** a collision, as between vehicles. **13.** a sudden descent of an aircraft as a result of which it hits land or water. **14.** the sudden collapse of a business, stock exchange, etc. **15.** (*modifier*) requiring or using intensive effort and all possible resources in order to accomplish something quickly: *a crash course.* [C14: prob. < *crasen* to smash, shatter + *dasshen* to strike violently, DASH[1]; see CRAZE]

crash[2] (kræʃ) *n.* a coarse cotton or linen cloth. [C19: < Russian *krashenina* coloured linen]

crash barrier *n.* a barrier erected along the centre of a motorway, around a racetrack, etc., for safety purposes.

crash dive *n.* **1.** a sudden steep dive from the surface by a submarine. ~*vb.* **crash-dive. 2.** (*intr.*) (usually of an aircraft) to descend steeply and rapidly, before hitting the ground. **3.** to perform or cause to perform a crash dive.

crash helmet *n.* a padded helmet worn for motorcycling, flying, etc., to protect the head.

crashing (ˈkræʃɪŋ) *adj.* (*prenominal*) *Inf.* (intensifier) (esp. in **a crashing bore**).

crash-land *vb.* to land (an aircraft) causing some damage to it or (of an aircraft) to land in this way. —ˈ**crash-ˌlanding** *n.*

crass (kræs) *adj.* **1.** stupid; gross. **2.** *Rare.* thick or coarse. [C16: < L *crassus* thick, dense, gross] —ˈ**crassly** *adv.* —ˈ**crassness** *or* ˈ**crassiˌtude** *n.*

-crat *n. combining form.* indicating a person who takes part in or is a member of a form of government or class. [< Gk *-kratēs,* < *-kratia* -CRACY] —**-cratic** *or* **-cratical** *adj. combining form.*

crate (kreɪt) *n.* **1.** a fairly large container, usually made of wooden slats or wickerwork, used for packing, storing, or transporting goods. **2.** *Sl.* an old car, aeroplane, etc. ~*vb.* **3.** (*tr.*) to pack or place in a crate. [C16: < L *crātis* wickerwork, hurdle] —ˈ**crater** *n.* —ˈ**crateful** *n.*

crater (ˈkreɪtə) *n.* **1.** the bowl-shaped opening in a volcano or a geyser. **2.** a similar depression formed by the impact of a meteorite or exploding bomb. **3.** any of the roughly circular or polygonal walled formations on the moon and some other planets. **4.** a large open bowl with two handles, used for mixing wines, esp. in ancient Greece. ~*vb.* **5.** to make or form craters in (a surface, such as the ground). [C17: < L: mixing bowl, crater, < Gk *kratēr,* < *kerannunai* to mix] —ˈ**crater-ˌlike** *adj.* —ˈ**craterous** *adj.*

cravat (krəˈvæt) *n.* a scarf worn round the neck instead of a tie, esp. by men. [C17: < F *cravate,* < Serbo-Croatian *Hrvat* Croat; so called because worn by Croats in the French army during the Thirty Years' War]

crave (kreɪv) *vb.* **1.** (when *intr.*, foll. by *for* or *after*) to desire intensely; long (for). **2.** (*tr.*) to need greatly or urgently. **3.** (*tr.*) to beg or plead for. [OE *crafian*] —ˈ**craver** *n.* —ˈ**craving** *n.*

craven (ˈkreɪvᵊn) *adj.* **1.** cowardly. ~*n.* **2.** a coward. [C13 *cravant,* prob. < OF *crevant* bursting, < *crever* to burst, die, < L *crepāre* to burst, crack] —ˈ**cravenly** *adv.* —ˈ**cravenness** *n.*

craw (krɔː) *n.* **1.** a less common word for **crop** (sense 6). **2.** the stomach of an animal. **3. stick in one's craw.** *Inf.* to be difficult, or against one's conscience, for one to accept, utter, etc. [C14: rel. to MHG *krage,* MDu. *crāghe* neck, Icelandic *kragi* collar]

crawfish (ˈkrɔːˌfɪʃ) *n., pl.* **-fish** *or* **-fishes.** a variant of **crayfish** (esp. sense 2).

crawl[1] (krɔːl) *vb.* (*intr.*) **1.** to move slowly, either by dragging the body along the ground or on the hands and knees. **2.** to proceed very slowly or laboriously. **3.** to act in a servile manner; fawn. **4.** to be or feel as if overrun by crawling creatures: *the pile of refuse crawled with insects.* **5.** (of insects, worms, snakes, etc.) to move with the body close to the ground. **6.** to swim the crawl. ~*n.* **7.** a slow creeping pace or motion. **8.** *Swimming.* a stroke in which the feet are kicked like paddles while the arms reach forward and pull back through the water. [C14: prob. < ON *krafla* to creep] —ˈ**crawlingly** *adv.*

crawl[2] (krɔːl) *n.* an enclosure in shallow, coastal water for fish, lobsters, etc. [C17: < Du. KRAAL]

crawly (ˈkrɔːlɪ) *adj.* **crawlier, crawliest.** *Inf.* feeling or causing a sensation like creatures crawling on one's skin.

crayfish (ˈkreɪˌfɪʃ) *or esp. U.S.* **crawfish** *n., pl.* **-fish** *or* **-fishes. 1.** a freshwater decapod crustacean resembling a small lobster. **2.** any of various similar crustaceans, esp. the spiny lobster. [C14: *cray,* by folk etymology, < OF *crevice* crab, < OHG *krebiz* + fish]

crayon (ˈkreɪən, -ɒn) *n.* **1.** a small stick or pencil of charcoal, wax, clay, or chalk mixed with coloured pigment. **2.** a drawing made with crayons. ~*vb.* **3.** to draw or colour with crayons. [C17: < F, < *craie,* < L *crēta* chalk] —ˈ**crayonist** *n.*

craze (kreɪz) *n.* **1.** a short-lived fashion. **2.** a wild or exaggerated enthusiasm. ~*vb.* **3.** to make or become mad. **4.** *Ceramics, metallurgy.* to develop or cause to develop fine cracks. [C14 (in the sense: to break, shatter): prob. < ON]

crazy (ˈkreɪzɪ) *adj.* **-zier, -ziest. 1.** *Inf.* insane. **2.** fantastic; strange; ridiculous. **3.** (*postpositive;* foll.

by *about* or *over*) *Inf.* extremely fond (of). —ˈ**crazily** *adv.* —ˈ**craziness** *n.*

crazy paving *n. Brit.* a form of paving, as for a path, made of irregular slabs of stone.

creak (kriːk) *vb.* **1.** to make or cause to make a harsh squeaking sound. **2.** (*intr.*) to make such sounds while moving: *the old car creaked along.* ~*n.* **3.** a harsh squeaking sound. [C14: var. of CROAK, imit.] —ˈ**creaky** *adj.* —ˈ**creakily** *adv.* —ˈ**creakiness** *n.* —ˈ**creakingly** *adv.*

cream (kriːm) *n.* **1. a.** the fatty part of milk, which rises to the top. **b.** (*as modifier*): *cream buns.* **2.** anything resembling cream in consistency. **3.** the best one or most essential part of something; pick. **4.** a soup containing cream or milk: *cream of chicken soup.* **5.** any of various foods resembling or containing cream. **6. a.** a yellowish-white colour. **b.** (*as adj.*): *cream wallpaper.* ~*vb.* (*tr.*) **7.** to skim or otherwise separate the cream from (milk). **8.** to beat (foodstuffs) to a light creamy consistency. **9.** to add or apply cream or any creamlike substance to. **10.** (sometimes foll. by *off*) to take away the best part of. **11.** to prepare or cook (vegetables, chicken, etc.) with cream or milk. [C14: < OF *cresme,* < LL *crāmum* cream, of Celtic origin; infl. by Church L *chrisma* unction, CHRISM] —ˈ**creamˌlike** *adj.*

cream cheese *n.* a smooth soft white cheese made from soured cream or milk.

cream cracker *n. Brit.* a crisp unsweetened biscuit, often eaten with cheese.

creamer (ˈkriːmə) *n.* **1.** a vessel or device for separating cream from milk. **2.** *Now chiefly U.S. & Canad.* a small jug or pitcher for serving cream.

creamery (ˈkriːmərɪ) *n., pl.* **-eries. 1.** an establishment where milk and cream are made into butter and cheese. **2.** a place where dairy products are sold.

cream of tartar *n.* potassium hydrogen tartrate, esp. when used in baking powders.

cream puff *n.* a shell of light pastry with a custard or cream filling.

cream soda *n.* a soft drink flavoured with vanilla.

cream tea *n.* afternoon tea including bread or scones served with clotted cream and jam.

creamy (ˈkriːmɪ) *adj.* **creamier, creamiest. 1.** resembling cream in colour, taste, or consistency. **2.** containing cream. —ˈ**creaminess** *n.*

crease (kriːs) *n.* **1.** a line or mark produced by folding, pressing, or wrinkling. **2.** a wrinkle or furrow, esp. on the face. **3.** *Cricket.* any three lines near each wicket marking positions for the bowler or batsman. ~*vb.* **4.** to make or become wrinkled or furrowed. **5.** (*tr.*) to graze with a bullet. [C15: < earlier *crēst;* prob. rel. to OF *cresté* wrinkled] —ˈ**creaser** *n.* —ˈ**creasy** *adj.*

create (kriːˈeɪt) *vb.* **1.** (*tr.*) to cause to come into existence. **2.** (*tr.*) to invest with a new honour, office, or title; appoint. **3.** (*tr.*) to be the cause of. **4.** (*tr.*) to act (a role) in the first production of a play. **5.** (*intr.*) *Brit. sl.* to make a fuss or uproar. [C14 *creat* created, < L *creātus,* < *creāre* to produce, make]

creatine (ˈkriːəˌtiːn, -tɪn) *n.* an important compound involved in many biochemical reactions and present in many types of living cells. [C19: < Gk *kreas* flesh + -INE²]

creation (kriːˈeɪʃən) *n.* **1.** the act or process of creating. **2.** the fact of being created or produced. **3.** something brought into existence or created. **4.** the whole universe.

Creation (kriːˈeɪʃən) *n. Christianity.* **1.** (often preceded by *the*) God's act of bringing the universe into being. **2.** the universe as thus brought into being by God.

creative (kriːˈeɪtɪv) *adj.* **1.** having the ability to create. **2.** characterized by originality of thought; having or showing imagination. **3.** designed to or tending to stimulate the imagination. —**creˈatively** *adv.* —**creˈativeness** *n.* —ˌ**creaˈtivity** *n.*

creator (kriːˈeɪtə) *n.* a person or thing that creates; originator. —**creˈatorˌship** *n.*

Creator (kriːˈeɪtə) *n.* (usually preceded by *the*) an epithet of God.

creature (ˈkriːtʃə) *n.* **1.** a living being, esp. an animal. **2.** something that has been created, whether animate or inanimate. **3.** a human being; person: used as a term of scorn, pity, or endearment. **4.** a person who is dependent upon another; tool. [C13: < Church L *creātūra,* < L *creāre* to create] —ˈ**creatural** *or* ˈ**creaturely** *adj.*

crèche (krɛʃ, kreɪʃ) *n.* **1.** *Chiefly Brit.* a day nursery for very young children. **2.** a tableau of Christ's Nativity. [C19: < OF: manger, crib, ult. of Gmc origin]

credence (ˈkriːdᵊns) *n.* **1.** acceptance or belief, esp. with regard to the evidence of others. **2.** something supporting a claim to belief; credential (esp. in **letters of credence**). **3.** short for **credence table.** [C14: < Med. L *crēdentia* trust, credit, < L *crēdere* to believe]

credence table *n. Christianity.* a small table on which the Eucharistic bread and wine are placed.

credential (krɪˈdɛnʃəl) *n.* **1.** something that entitles a person to confidence, authority, etc. **2.** (*pl.*) a letter or certificate giving evidence of the bearer's identity or competence. [C16: < Med. L *crēdentia* credit, trust; see CREDENCE]

credenza (krɪˈdɛnzə) *n.* another name for **credence table.** [It.: see CREDENCE]

credibility gap *n.* a disparity between claims or statements made and the evident facts of the situation or circumstances to which they relate.

credible (ˈkrɛdɪbᵊl) *adj.* **1.** capable of being believed. **2.** trustworthy. [C14: < L *crēdibilis,* < L *crēdere* to believe] —ˈ**credibleness** *or* ˌ**crediˈbility** *n.* —ˈ**credibly** *adv.*

credit (ˈkrɛdɪt) *n.* **1.** commendation or approval, as for an act or quality. **2.** a person or thing serving as a source of good influence, repute, etc. **3.** influence or reputation coming from the good opinion of others. **4.** belief in the truth, reliability, quality, etc., of someone or something. **5.** a sum of money or equivalent purchasing power, available for a person's use. **6. a.** the positive balance in a person's bank account. **b.** the sum of money that a bank makes available to a client in excess of any deposit. **7. a.** the practice of permitting a buyer to receive goods or services before payment. **b.** the time permitted for paying for such goods or services. **8.** reputation for solvency and probity, inducing confidence among creditors. **9.** *Accounting.* **a.** acknowledgment of an income, liability, or capital item by entry on the right-hand side of an account. **b.** the right-hand side of an account. **c.** an entry on this side. **d.** the total of such entries. **e.** (*as modifier*): *credit entries.* **10.** *Education.* **a.** a distinction awarded to an examination candidate obtaining good marks. **b.** a section of an examination syllabus satisfactorily completed. **11. on credit.** with payment to be made at a future date. ~*vb.* (*tr.*) **12.** (foll. by *with*) to ascribe (to); give credit (for). **13.** to accept as true; believe. **14.** to do credit to. **15.** *Accounting.* **a.** to enter (an item) as a credit in an account. **b.** to acknowledge (a payer) by making such an entry. ~See also **credits.** [C16: < OF *crédit,* < It. *credito,* < L *crēditum* loan, < *crēdere* to believe]

creditable (ˈkrɛdɪtəbᵊl) *adj.* deserving credit, honour, etc.; praiseworthy. —ˈ**creditableness** *or* ˌ**creditaˈbility** *n.* —ˈ**creditably** *adv.*

credit account *n. Brit.* a credit system by means of which customers may obtain goods and services before payment.

credit card *n.* a card issued by banks, businesses, etc., enabling the holder to obtain goods and services on credit.

Creditiste (ˌkrɛdɪˈtiːst) *Canad.* ~*adj.* **1.** of, supporting, or relating to the Social Credit Rally of Quebec. ~*n.* **2.** a supporter or member of this organization.

creditor (ˈkrɛdɪtə) *n.* a person or commercial enterprise to whom money is owed.

credit rating *n.* an evaluation of the creditworthiness of an individual or business.

credits (ˈkrɛdɪts) *pl. n.* a list of those responsible for the production of a film or a television programme.

creditworthy (ˈkrɛdɪtˌwɜːðɪ) *adj.* (of an individual or business) adjudged as meriting credit on the basis of earning power, previous record of debt repayment, etc. —ˈ**creditˌworthiness** *n.*

credo (ˈkriːdəʊ, ˈkreɪ-) *n., pl.* **-dos.** any formal statement of beliefs, principles, or opinions.

Credo (ˈkriːdəʊ, ˈkreɪ-) *n., pl.* **-dos. 1.** the Apostles' or Nicene Creed. **2.** a musical setting of the Creed. [C12: < L, lit.: I believe; first word of the Apostles' and Nicene Creeds]

credulity (krɪˈdjuːlɪtɪ) *n.* disposition to believe something on little evidence; gullibility.

credulous (ˈkrɛdjʊləs) *adj.* **1.** tending to believe something on little evidence. **2.** arising from or characterized by credulity: *credulous beliefs.* [C16: < L *crēdulus,* < *crēdere* to believe] —ˈ**credulously** *adv.* —ˈ**credulousness** *n.*

Cree (kriː) *n.* **1.** (*pl.* **Cree** *or* **Crees**) a member of a N American Indian people living in Ontario, Saskatchewan, and Manitoba. **2.** the language of this people.

creed (kriːd) *n.* **1.** a concise, formal statement of the essential articles of Christian belief, such as the Apostles' Creed or the Nicene Creed. **2.** any statement or system of beliefs or principles. [OE *crēda,* < L *crēdo* I believe] —ˈ**creedal** *or* ˈ**credal** *adj.*

creek (kriːk) *n.* **1.** *Chiefly Brit.* a narrow inlet or bay, esp. of the sea. **2.** *U.S., Canad., Austral., & N.Z.* a small stream or tributary. **3. up the creek.** *Sl.* in trouble; in a difficult position. [C13: < ON *kriki* nook; rel. to MDu. *krēke* creek, inlet]

Creek (kriːk) *n.* **1.** (*pl.* **Creek** *or* **Creeks**) a member of a confederacy of N American Indian tribes formerly living in Georgia and Alabama. **2.** any of their languages.

creel (kriːl) *n.* **1.** a wickerwork basket, esp. one used to hold fish. **2.** a wickerwork trap for catching lobsters, etc. [C15: < Scot., <?]

creep (kriːp) *vb.* **creeping, crept.** (*intr.*) **1.** to crawl with the body near to or touching the ground. **2.** to move slowly, quietly, or cautiously. **3.** to act in a servile way; fawn; cringe. **4.** to move or slip out of place, as from pressure or wear. **5.** (of plants) to grow along the ground or over rocks. **6.** to develop gradually: *creeping unrest.* **7.** to have the sensation of something crawling over the skin. ~*n.* **8.** the act of creeping or a creeping movement. **9.** *Sl.* a person considered to be obnoxious or servile. **10.** *Geol.* the gradual downward movement of loose rock material, soil, etc., on a slope. [OE *crēopan*]

creeper (ˈkriːpə) *n.* **1.** a person or animal that creeps. **2.** a plant, such as the ivy, that grows by creeping. **3.** the U.S. and Canad. name for the **tree creeper. 4.** a hooked instrument for dragging deep water. **5.** *Inf.* a shoe with a soft sole.

creeps (kriːps) *pl. n.* (preceded by *the*) *Inf.* a feeling of fear, repulsion, disgust, etc.

creepy (ˈkriːpɪ) *adj.* **-ier, -iest. 1.** *Inf.* having or causing a sensation of repulsion or fear, as of creatures crawling on the skin. **2.** creeping; slow-moving. —ˈ**creepily** *adv.* —ˈ**creepiness** *n.*

creepy-crawly *Brit. inf.* ~*n., pl.* **-crawlies. 1.** a small crawling creature. ~*adj.* **2.** feeling or causing a sensation as of creatures crawling on one's skin.

cremate (krɪˈmeɪt) *vb.* (*tr.*) to burn up (something, esp. a corpse) and reduce to ash. [C19: < L *cremāre*] —**creˈmation** *n.* —**creˈmator** *n.* —**crematory** (ˈkrɛmətərɪ, -trɪ) *adj.*

crematorium (ˌkrɛməˈtɔːrɪəm) *n., pl.* **-riums** *or* **-ria** (-rɪə). *Brit.* a building in which corpses are cremated. Also called (esp. U.S.): **crematory.**

crème (krɛm, kriːm, kreɪm; *French* krɛm) *n.* **1.** cream. **2.** any of various sweet liqueurs: *crème de moka.* ~*adj.* **3.** (of a liqueur) rich and sweet.

crème de la crème *French.* (krɛm də la krɛm) *n.* the very best. [lit.: cream of the cream]

crème de menthe (ˈkrɛm də ˈmɛnθ, ˈmɪnt; ˈkriːm, ˈkreɪm) *n.* a liqueur flavoured with peppermint. [F, lit.: cream of mint]

crenate (ˈkriːneɪt) *or* **crenated** *adj.* having a scalloped margin, as certain leaves. [C18: < NL *crēnātus,* < Med. L, prob. < LL *crēna* a notch] —ˈ**crenately** *adv.* —**crenation** (krɪˈneɪʃən) *n.*

crenel (ˈkrɛnᵊl) *or* **crenelle** (krɪˈnɛl) *n.* any of a set of openings formed in the top of a wall or parapet and having slanting sides, as in a battlement. [C15: < OF, lit.: a little notch, < *cren* notch, < LL *crēna*]

crenellate *or U.S.* **crenelate** (ˈkrɛnɪˌleɪt) *vb.* (*tr.*) to supply with battlements. [C19: < OF *creneler,* < CRENEL] —ˈ**crenelˌlated** *or U.S.* ˈ**crenelˌated** *adj.* —ˌ**crenelˈlation** *or U.S.* ˌ**crenelˈation** *n.*

creole (ˈkriːəʊl) *n.* **1.** a language that has its origin in extended contact between two language communities, one of which is European. ~*adj.* **2.** of or relating to creole. **3.** (of a sauce or dish) containing or cooked with tomatoes, green peppers, onions, etc. [C17: via F & Sp., prob. < Port. *crioulo* slave born in one's household, prob. < *criar* to bring up, < L *creāre* to CREATE]

Creole (ˈkriːəʊl) *n.* **1.** (*sometimes not cap.*) (in the West Indies and Latin America) **a.** a native-born person of European ancestry. **b.** a native-born person of mixed European and Negro ancestry who speaks a creole. **2.** (in Louisiana and other Gulf States of the U.S.) a native-born person of French ancestry. **3.** the French Creole spoken in Louisiana. ~*adj.* **4.** of or relating to any of these peoples.

creosol (ˈkriːəˌsɒl) *n.* a colourless or pale yellow insoluble oily liquid with a smoky odour and a burning taste. [C19: < CREOS(OTE) + -OL[1]]

creosote (ˈkrɪəˌsəʊt) *n.* **1.** a colourless or pale yellow liquid with a burning taste and penetrating odour distilled from wood tar. It is used as an antiseptic. **2.** a thick dark liquid mixture prepared from coal tar: used as a preservative for wood. ~*vb.* **3.** to treat (wood) with creosote. [C19: < Gk *kreas* flesh + *sōtēr* preserver, < *sōzein* to keep safe] —**creosotic** (ˌkrɪəˈsɒtɪk) *adj.*

crepe *or* **crape** (kreɪp) *n.* **1. a.** a light cotton, silk, or other fabric with a fine ridged or crinkled surface. **b.** (*as modifier*): *a crepe dress.* **2.** a black armband originally made of this, worn as a sign of mourning. **3.** a very thin pancake, often folded around a filling. **4.** short for **crepe paper** or **crepe rubber.** [C19: < F *crêpe,* < L *crispus* curled, uneven, wrinkled]

crepe de Chine (kreɪp də ʃiːn) *n.* a very thin crepe of silk or a similar light fabric. [C19: < F: Chinese crepe]

crepe paper *n.* thin crinkled coloured paper, resembling crepe and used for decorations.

creperie (ˈkrɛpərɪ, ˈkreɪp-) *n.* an eating establishment that specializes in pancakes.

crepe rubber *n.* a type of rubber in the form of colourless or pale yellow crinkled sheets: used for the soles of shoes.

crêpe suzette (kreɪp suːˈzɛt) *n., pl.* **crêpes suzettes.** (*sometimes pl.*) an orange-flavoured pancake flambéed in a liqueur or brandy.

crepitate (ˈkrɛpɪˌteɪt) *vb.* (*intr.*) to make a rattling or crackling sound. [C17: < L *crepitāre*] —ˈ**crepitant** *adj.* —ˌ**crepiˈtation** *n.*

crepitus (ˈkrɛpɪtəs) *n.* **1.** a crackling chest sound heard in pneumonia, etc. **2.** the grating sound of two ends of a broken bone rubbing together. [C19: < L, < *crepāre* to crack, creak]

crept (krɛpt) *vb.* the past tense and past participle of **creep.**

crepuscular (krɪˈpʌskjʊlə) *adj.* **1.** of or like twilight; dim. **2.** (of certain creatures) active at twilight or just before dawn. [C17: < L *crepusculum* dusk, < *creper* dark]

crepy *or* **crepey** (ˈkreɪpɪ) *adj.* **crepier, crepiest.** (esp. of the skin) having a dry wrinkled appearance.

Cres. *abbrev. for* Crescent.

crescendo (krɪˈʃɛndəʊ) *n., pl.* **-dos** *or* **-di** (-dɪ). **1.** *Music.* **a.** a gradual increase in loudness or the musical direction or symbol indicating this.

Abbrev.: **cresc.** Symbol: < **b.** (*as modifier*): *a crescendo passage.* **2.** any similar gradual increase in loudness. ~*vb.* **-doing, -doed.** **3.** (*intr.*) to increase in loudness or force. ~*adv.* **4.** with a crescendo. [C18: < It., lit.: increasing, < *crescere* to grow, < L]

crescent (ˈkrɛsᵊnt, -zᵊnt) *n.* **1.** the biconcave shape of the moon in its first or last quarter. **2.** any shape or object resembling this. **3.** *Chiefly Brit.* a crescent-shaped street. **4.** (*often cap.* and preceded by *the*) **a.** the emblem of Islam or Turkey. **b.** Islamic or Turkish power. ~*adj.* **5.** *Arch. or poetic.* increasing or growing. [C14: < L *crescēns* increasing, < *crescere* to grow]

cresol (ˈkriːsɒl) *n.* an aromatic compound found in coal tar and creosote and used in making synthetic resins and as an antiseptic and disinfectant.

cress (krɛs) *n.* any of various plants having pungent-tasting leaves often used in salads and as a garnish. [OE *cressa*]

cresset (ˈkrɛsɪt) *n. History.* a metal basket mounted on a pole in which oil or pitch was burned for illumination. [C14: < OF *craisset,* < *craisse* GREASE]

crest (krɛst) *n.* **1.** a tuft or growth of feathers, fur, or skin along the top of the heads of some birds, reptiles, and other animals. **2.** something resembling or suggesting this. **3.** the top, highest point, or highest stage of something. **4.** an ornamental piece, such as a plume, on top of a helmet. **5.** *Heraldry.* a symbol of a family or office, borne in addition to a coat of arms and used in medieval times to decorate the helmet. ~*vb.* **6.** (*intr.*) to come or rise to a high point. **7.** (*tr.*) to lie at the top of; cap. **8.** (*tr.*) to reach the top of (a hill, wave, etc.). [C14: < OF *creste,* < L *crista*] —ˈ**crested** *adj.* —ˈ**crestless** *adj.*

crestfallen (ˈkrɛstˌfɔːlən) *adj.* dejected or disheartened. —ˈ**crestˌfallenly** *adv.*

cretaceous (krɪˈteɪʃəs) *adj.* consisting of or resembling chalk. [C17: < L *crētāceus,* < *crēta,* lit.: Cretan earth, that is, chalk]

Cretaceous (krɪˈteɪʃəs) *adj.* **1.** of, denoting, or formed in the last period of the Mesozoic era, during which chalk deposits were formed. ~*n.* **2. the.** the Cretaceous period or rock system.

Cretan (ˈkriːtən) *adj.* **1.** of or relating to the island of Crete in the W Mediterranean. **2.** of the inhabitants of Crete. ~*n.* **3.** a native or inhabitant of Crete.

cretin (ˈkrɛtɪn) *n.* **1.** a person afflicted with cretinism. **2.** a person considered to be extremely stupid. [C18: < F *crétin,* < Swiss F *crestin,* < L *Chrīstiānus* Christian, alluding to the humanity of such people, despite their handicaps] —ˈ**cretinous** *adj.*

cretinism (ˈkrɛtɪˌnɪzəm) *n.* a condition arising from a deficiency of thyroid hormone, present from birth, characterized by dwarfism and mental retardation. See also **myxoedema.**

cretonne (krɛˈtɒn, ˈkrɛtɒn) *n.* a heavy cotton or linen fabric with a printed design, used for furnishing. [C19: < F, < *Creton,* Norman village where it originated]

crevasse (krɪˈvæs) *n.* **1.** a deep crack or fissure, esp. in the ice of a glacier. **2.** *U.S.* a break in a river embankment. ~*vb.* **3.** (*tr.*) *U.S.* to make a break or fissure in (a dyke, wall, etc.). [C19: < F: CREVICE]

crevice (ˈkrɛvɪs) *n.* a narrow fissure or crack; split; cleft. [C14: < OF *crevace,* < *crever* to burst, < L *crepāre* to crack]

crew[1] (kruː) *n.* (*sometimes functioning as pl.*) **1.** the men who man a ship, boat, aircraft, etc. **2.** *Naut.* a group of people assigned to a particular job or type of work. **3.** *Inf.* a gang, company, or crowd. ~*vb.* **4.** to serve on (a ship) as a member of the crew. [C15 *crue* (military) reinforcement, < OF *creue* augmentation, < OF *creistre* to increase, < L *crescere*]

crew[2] (kruː) *vb. Arch.* a past tense of **crow**[2].

crew cut *n.* a closely cropped haircut for men. [C20: < the style of haircut worn by the boat crews at Harvard and Yale Universities]

crewel (ˈkruːɪl) *n.* a loosely twisted worsted yarn, used in fancy work and embroidery. [C15: <?] —ˈ**crewelist** *n.* —ˈ**crewelˌwork** *n.*

crew neck *n.* a plain round neckline in sweaters. —ˈ**crew-ˌneck** *or* ˈ**crew-ˌnecked** *adj.*

crib (krɪb) *n.* **1.** a child's bed with slatted wooden sides; cot. **2.** a cattle stall or pen. **3.** a fodder rack or manger. **4.** a small crude cottage or room. **5.** *N.Z.* a weekend cottage: term is South Island usage only. **6.** any small confined space. **7.** a representation of the manger in which the infant Jesus was laid at birth. **8.** *Inf.* a theft, esp. of another's writing or thoughts. **9.** *Inf., chiefly Brit.* a translation of a foreign text or a list of answers used by students, often illicitly, as an aid in lessons, examinations, etc. **10.** short for **cribbage.** **11.** *Cribbage.* the discard pile. **12.** Also called: **cribwork.** a framework of heavy timbers used in the construction of foundations, mines, etc. ~*vb.* **cribbing, cribbed.** **13.** (*tr.*) to put or enclose in or as if in a crib; furnish with a crib. **14.** (*tr.*) *Inf.* to steal (another's writings or thoughts). **15.** (*intr.*) *Inf.* to copy either from a crib or from someone else during a lesson or examination. **16.** (*intr.*) *Inf.* to grumble. [OE *cribb*] —ˈ**cribber** *n.*

cribbage (ˈkrɪbɪdʒ) *n.* a game of cards for two to four, in which players try to win a set number of points before their opponents. [C17: <?]

cribbage board *n.* a board, with pegs and holes, used for scoring at cribbage.

crib-biting *n.* a harmful habit of horses in which the animal leans on the manger or seizes it with the teeth and swallows a gulp of air.

crick (krɪk) *Inf.* ~*n.* **1.** a painful muscle spasm or cramp, esp. in the neck or back. ~*vb.* **2.** (*tr.*) to cause a crick in. [C15: <?]

cricket[1] (ˈkrɪkɪt) *n.* an insect having long antennae and, in the males, the ability to produce a chirping sound by rubbing together the leathery forewings. [C14: < OF *criquet,* < *criquer* to creak, imit.]

cricket[2] (ˈkrɪkɪt) *n.* **1. a.** a game played by two teams of eleven players on a field with a wicket at either end of a 22-yard pitch, the object being for one side to score runs by hitting a hard leather-covered ball with a bat while the other side tries to dismiss them by bowling, catching, running them out, etc. **b.** (*as modifier*): *a cricket bat.* **2. not cricket.** *Inf.* not fair play. ~*vb.* (*intr.*) **3.** to play cricket. [C16: < OF *criquet* goal post, wicket, <?] —ˈ**cricketer** *n.*

cricket[3] (ˈkrɪkɪt) *n.* a small low stool. [C17: <?]

cricoid (ˈkraɪkɔɪd) *adj.* **1.** of or relating to the ring-shaped lowermost cartilage of the larynx. ~*n.* **2.** this cartilage. [C18: < NL *cricoīdes,* < Gk *krikoeidēs* ring-shaped, < *krikos* ring]

cri de coeur (kriː də kɜː) *n., pl.* **cris de coeur.** (kriː də kɜː). a heartfelt or impassioned appeal. [C20: altered < F *cri du coeur*]

crier (ˈkraɪə) *n.* **1.** a person or animal that cries. **2.** (formerly) an official who made public announcements, esp. in a town or court.

crime (kraɪm) *n.* **1.** an act or omission prohibited and punished by law. **2.** unlawful acts in general. **3.** an evil act. **4.** *Inf.* something to be regretted. [C14: < OF, < L *crīmen* verdict, accusation, crime]

criminal (ˈkrɪmɪnᵊl) *n.* **1.** a person charged with and convicted of crime. **2.** a person who commits crimes for a living. ~*adj.* **3.** of, involving, or guilty of crime. **4.** (*prenominal*) of or relating to crime or its punishment. **5.** *Inf.* senseless or deplorable. [C15: < LL *crīminālis;* see CRIME, -AL[1]] —ˈ**criminally** *adv.* —ˌ**crimiˈnality** *n.*

criminal conversation *n.* another term for **adultery.**

criminal law *n.* the body of law dealing with offences and offenders.

criminate (ˈkrɪmɪˌneɪt) *vb.* (*tr.*) *Rare.* **1.** to charge with a crime; accuse. **2.** short for **incriminate.** [C17: < L *crīminārī* to accuse] —ˌ**crimiˈnation** *n.* —ˈ**criminative** *or* **criminatory** (ˈkrɪmɪnətərɪ, -trɪ) *adj.* —ˈ**crimiˌnator** *n.*

criminology (ˌkrɪmɪˈnɒlədʒɪ) *n.* the scientific study of crime. [C19: < L *crimin-* CRIME, + -LOGY]

—**criminological** (ˌkrɪmɪnəˈlɒdʒɪkˀl) *or* ˌ**crimino'logic** *adj.* —ˌ**crimino'logically** *adv.* —ˌ**crimi'nologist** *n.*

crimp (krɪmp) *vb.* (*tr.*) **1.** to fold or press into ridges. **2.** to fold and pinch together (something, such as two pieces of metal). **3.** to curl or wave (the hair) tightly, esp. with curling tongs. **4.** *U.S. inf.* to hinder. ~*n.* **5.** the act or result of folding or pressing together or into ridges. **6.** a tight wave or curl in the hair. [OE *crympan;* rel. to *crump* bent; see CRAMP[2]] —**'crimper** *n.* —**'crimpy** *adj.*

Crimplene (ˈkrɪmpliːn) *n. Trademark.* a synthetic material similar to Terylene, characterized by its crease-resistance.

crimson (ˈkrɪmzən) *n.* **1. a.** a deep or vivid red colour. **b.** (*as adj.*): *a crimson rose.* ~*vb.* **2.** to make or become crimson. **3.** (*intr.*) to blush. [C14: < OSp. *cremesin,* < Ar. *qirmizi* red of the kermes, < *qirmiz* KERMES] —**'crimsonness** *n.*

cringe (krɪndʒ) *vb.* (*intr.*) **1.** to shrink or flinch, esp. in fear or servility. **2.** to behave in a servile or timid way. **3.** *Inf.* to experience a sudden feeling of embarrassment or distaste. ~*n.* **4.** the act of cringing. [OE *cringan* to yield in battle] —**'cringer** *n.*

cringle (ˈkrɪŋgˀl) *n.* an eyelet at the edge of a sail. [C17: < Low G *Kringel* small ring]

crinkle (ˈkrɪŋkˀl) *vb.* **1.** to form or cause to form wrinkles, twists, or folds. **2.** to make or cause to make a rustling noise. ~*n.* **3.** a wrinkle, twist, or fold. **4.** a rustling noise. [OE *crincan* to bend, give way] —**'crinkly** *adj.*

crinoid (ˈkraɪnɔɪd, ˈkrɪn-) *n.* **1.** a primitive echinoderm having delicate feathery arms radiating from a central disc. ~*adj.* **2.** of, relating to, or belonging to the *Crinoidea.* **3.** shaped like a lily. [C19: < Gk *krinoeidēs* lily-like] —**cri'noidal** *adj.*

crinoline (ˈkrɪnˀlɪn) *n.* **1.** a stiff fabric, originally of horsehair and linen used in lining garments. **2.** a petticoat stiffened with this, worn to distend skirts, esp. in the mid-19th century. **3.** a framework of steel hoops worn for the same purpose. [C19: < F, < It. *crinolino,* < *crino* horsehair, < L *crīnis* hair + *lino* flax, < L *līnum*]

cripple (ˈkrɪpˀl) *n.* **1.** a person who is lame. **2.** a person who is or seems disabled or deficient in some way: *a mental cripple.* ~*vb.* **3.** (*tr.*) to make a cripple of; disable. [OE *crypel;* rel. to *crēopan* to creep] —**'crippler** *n.*

crisis (ˈkraɪsɪs) *n., pl.* **-ses** (-siːz). **1.** a crucial stage or turning point, esp. in a sequence of events or a disease. **2.** an unstable period, esp. one of extreme trouble or danger. **3.** *Pathol.* a sudden change in the course of a disease. [C15: < L: decision, < Gk *krisis,* < *krinein* to decide]

crisp (krɪsp) *adj.* **1.** dry and brittle. **2.** fresh and firm. **3.** invigorating or bracing: *a crisp breeze.* **4.** clear; sharp: *crisp reasoning.* **5.** lively or stimulating. **6.** clean and orderly. **7.** concise and pithy. **8.** wrinkled or curly: *crisp hair.* ~*vb.* **9.** to make or become crisp. ~*n.* **10.** *Brit.* a very thin slice of potato fried and eaten cold as a snack. **11.** something that is crisp. [OE, < L *crispus* curled, uneven, wrinkled] —**'crisply** *adv.* —**'crispness** *n.*

crispbread (ˈkrɪspˌbrɛd) *n.* a thin dry biscuit made of wheat or rye.

crisper (ˈkrɪspə) *n.* a compartment in a refrigerator for storing salads, vegetables, etc., in order to keep them fresh.

crispy (ˈkrɪspɪ) *adj.* **crispier, crispiest. 1.** crisp. **2.** having waves or curls. —**'crispiness** *n.*

crisscross (ˈkrɪsˌkrɒs) *vb.* **1.** to move or cause to move in a crosswise pattern. **2.** to mark with or consist of a pattern of crossing lines. ~*adj.* **3.** (esp. of lines) crossing one another in different directions. ~*n.* **4.** a pattern made of crossing lines. ~*adv.* **5.** in a crosswise manner or pattern.

crit. *abbrev. for:* **1.** *Med.* critical. **2.** criticism.

criterion (kraɪˈtɪərɪən) *n., pl.* **-ria** (-rɪə) *or* **-rions.** a standard by which something can be judged or decided. [C17: < Gk *kritērion,* < *kritēs* judge, < *krinein* to decide]

▷ **Usage.** *Criteria,* the plural of *criterion,* is not acceptable as a singular noun in careful English.

critic (ˈkrɪtɪk) *n.* **1.** a person who judges something. **2.** a professional judge of art, music, literature, etc. **3.** a person who often finds fault and criticizes. [C16: < L *criticus,* < Gk *kritikos* capable of judging, < *kritēs* judge; see CRITERION]

critical (ˈkrɪtɪkˀl) *adj.* **1.** containing or making severe or negative judgments. **2.** containing analytical evaluations. **3.** of a critic or criticism. **4.** of or forming a crisis; crucial. **5.** urgently needed. **6.** *Physics.* of, denoting, or concerned with a state in which the properties of a system undergo an abrupt change. **7. go critical.** (of a nuclear power station or reactor) to reach a state in which a nuclear-fission chain reaction becomes self-sustaining. —ˌ**criti'cality** *n.* —**'critically** *adv.* —**'criticalness** *n.*

critical mass *n.* the minimum mass of fissionable material that can sustain a nuclear chain reaction.

critical path analysis *n.* a technique for planning projects with reference to the critical path, which is the sequence of stages requiring the longest time.

critical temperature *n.* the temperature of a substance in its critical state. A gas can only be liquefied at temperatures below this.

criticism (ˈkrɪtɪˌsɪzəm) *n.* **1.** the act or an instance of making an unfavourable or severe judgment, comment, etc. **2.** the analysis or evaluation of a work of art, literature, etc. **3.** the occupation of a critic. **4.** a work that sets out to evaluate or analyse.

criticize *or* **-ise** (ˈkrɪtɪˌsaɪz) *vb.* **1.** to judge (something) with disapproval; censure. **2.** to evaluate or analyse (something). —**'critiˌcizable** *or* **-ˌcisable** *adj.* —**'critiˌcizer** *or* **-ˌciser** *n.*

critique (krɪˈtiːk) *n.* **1.** a critical essay or commentary. **2.** the act or art of criticizing. [C17: < F, < Gk *kritikē,* < *kritikos* able to discern]

croak (krəʊk) *vb.* **1.** (*intr.*) (of frogs, crows, etc.) to make a low, hoarse cry. **2.** to utter (something) in this manner. **3.** (*intr.*) to grumble or be pessimistic. **4.** *Sl.* **a.** (*intr.*) to die. **b.** (*tr.*) to kill. ~*n.* **5.** a low hoarse utterance or sound. [OE *crācettan*] —**'croaky** *adj.* —**'croakiness** *n.*

croaker (ˈkrəʊkə) *n.* **1.** an animal, bird, etc., that croaks. **2.** a grumbling person.

Croat (ˈkrəʊæt) *n.* **1. a.** a native or inhabitant of Croatia, a constituent republic of Yugoslavia. **b.** a speaker of Croatian. ~*n., adj.* **2.** another word for **Croatian.**

Croatian (krəʊˈeɪʃən) *adj.* **1.** of or relating to Croatia, its people, or their dialect of Serbo-Croatian. ~*n.* **2.** the dialect of Croatia. **3. a.** a native or inhabitant of Croatia. **b.** a speaker of Croatian.

crochet (ˈkrəʊʃeɪ, -ʃɪ) *vb.* **-cheting** (-ʃeɪɪŋ, -ʃɪɪŋ), **-cheted** (-ʃeɪd, -ʃɪd). **1.** to make (a piece of needlework, a garment, etc.) by looping and intertwining thread with a hooked needle (**crochet hook**). ~*n.* **2.** work made by crocheting. [C19: < F *crochet,* dim. of *croc* hook, prob. of Scand. origin] —**'crocheter** *n.*

crock[1] (krɒk) *n.* **1.** an earthen pot, jar, etc. **2.** a piece of broken earthenware. [OE *crocc* pot]

crock[2] (krɒk) *n. Sl., chiefly Brit.* a person or thing that is old or decrepit (esp. in **old crock**). [C15: orig. Scot.; rel. to Norwegian *krake* unhealthy animal, Du. *kraak* decrepit person or animal]

crockery (ˈkrɒkərɪ) *n.* china dishes, earthen vessels, etc., collectively.

crocket (ˈkrɒkɪt) *n.* a carved ornament in the form of a curled leaf or cusp, used in Gothic architecture. [C17: < Anglo-F *croket* a little hook, < *croc* hook, of Scand. origin]

crocodile (ˈkrɒkəˌdaɪl) *n.* **1.** a large tropical reptile having a broad head, tapering snout, massive jaws, and a thick outer covering of bony plates. **2. a.** leather made from the skin of any of these animals. **b.** (*as modifier*): *crocodile shoes.* **3.** *Brit. inf.* a line of schoolchildren walking two by two. [C13: via OF, < L *crocodīlus,* < Gk *krokodeilos* lizard, ult. < *krokē* pebble + *drilos* worm; referring to its basking on shingle]

crocodile clip *n.* a clasp with serrated interlocking edges used for making electrical connections, etc.

crocodile tears *pl. n.* an insincere show of grief; false tears. [< the belief that crocodiles wept over their prey to allure further victims]

crocodilian (ˌkrɒkəˈdɪlɪən) *n.* **1.** any large predatory reptile of the order *Crocodilia,* which includes the crocodiles, alligators, and caymans. ~*adj.* **2.** of, relating to, or belonging to the *Crocodilia.* **3.** of, relating to, or resembling a crocodile.

crocus (ˈkrəʊkəs) *n., pl.* **-cuses.** any plant of the iridaceous genus *Crocus,* having white, yellow, or purple flowers. [C17: < NL, < L *crocus,* < Gk *krokos* saffron]

Croesus (ˈkriːsəs) *n.* any very rich man. [after *Croesus* (died ? 546 B.C.) the last king of Lydia, noted for his great wealth]

croft (krɒft) *n. Brit.* a small enclosed plot of land, adjoining a house, worked by the occupier and his family, esp. in Scotland. [OE *croft*] —ˈ**crofter** *n.* —ˈ**crofting** *adj., n.*

croissant (ˈkrwʌsɒŋ) *n.* a flaky crescent-shaped bread roll. [F, lit.: crescent]

Croix de Guerre *French.* (krwa də gɛr) *n.* a French military decoration awarded for gallantry in battle: established 1915. [lit.: cross of war]

Cro-Magnon man (ˈkrəʊˈmænjɒn, -ˈmægnɒn) *n.* an early type of modern man, *Homo sapiens,* who lived in Europe during late Palaeolithic times. [C19: after the cave (Cro-Magnon), Dordogne, France, where the remains were first found]

cromlech (ˈkrɒmlɛk) *n.* **1.** a circle of prehistoric standing stones. **2.** (no longer in technical usage) a megalithic chamber tomb or dolmen. [C17: < Welsh, < *crom,* fem. of *crwm* bent, arched + *llech* flat stone]

crone (krəʊn) *n.* a witchlike old woman. [C14: < OF *carogne* carrion, ult. < L *caro* flesh]

cronk (krɒŋk) *adj. Austral. sl.* **1.** unfit; unsound. **2.** dishonest. [C19: ?< G *krank* ill]

crony (ˈkrəʊnɪ) *n., pl.* **-nies.** a friend or companion. [C17: student sl. (Cambridge), < Gk *khronios* of long duration, < *khronos* time]

crook (krʊk) *n.* **1.** a curved or hooked thing. **2.** a staff with a hooked end, such as a bishop's crosier or shepherd's staff. **3.** a turn or curve; bend. **4.** *Inf.* a dishonest person, esp. a swindler or thief. ~*vb.* **5.** to bend or curve or cause to bend or curve. ~*adj.* **6.** *Austral. & N.Z. sl.* **a.** ill. **b.** of poor quality. **c.** unpleasant; bad. **7. go (off) crook.** *Austral. & N.Z. sl.* to lose one's temper. **8. go crook at** *or* **on.** *Austral. & N.Z. sl.* to rebuke or upbraid. [C12: < ON *krokr* hook]

crooked (ˈkrʊkɪd) *adj.* **1.** bent, angled or winding. **2.** set at an angle; not straight. **3.** deformed or contorted. **4.** *Inf.* dishonest or illegal. **5. crooked on.** (*also* krʊkt) *Austral. inf.* hostile or averse to. —ˈ**crookedly** *adv.* —ˈ**crookedness** *n.*

croon (kruːn) *vb.* **1.** to sing or speak in a soft low tone. ~*n.* **2.** a soft low singing or humming. [C14: via MDu. *crōnen* to groan] —ˈ**crooner** *n.*

crop (krɒp) *n.* **1.** the produce of cultivated plants, esp. cereals, vegetables, and fruit. **2. a.** the amount of such produce in any particular season. **b.** the yield of some other farm produce: *the lamb crop.* **3.** a group of products, thoughts, people, etc., appearing at one time or in one season. **4.** the stock of a thonged whip. **5.** short for **riding crop. 6.** a pouchlike part of the oesophagus of birds, in which food is stored or partially digested before passing on to the gizzard. **7.** a short cropped hairstyle. **8.** a notch in or a piece cut out of the ear of an animal. **9.** the act of cropping. ~*vb.* **cropping, cropped.** (*mainly tr.*) **10.** to cut (hair, grass, etc.) very short. **11.** to cut and collect (mature produce) from the land or plant on which it has been grown. **12.** to clip part of (the ear or ears) of (an animal), esp. as a means of identification. **13.** (of herbivorous animals) to graze on (grass or similar vegetation). ~See also **crop out, crop up.** [OE *cropp*]

crop-dusting *n.* the spreading of fungicide, etc., on crops in the form of dust, often from an aircraft.

crop-eared *adj.* having the ears or hair cut short.

crop out *vb.* (*intr., adv.*) (of a formation of rock strata) to appear or be exposed at the surface.

cropper (ˈkrɒpə) *n.* **1.** a person who cultivates or harvests a crop. **2. come a cropper.** *Inf.* **a.** to fall heavily. **b.** to fail completely.

crop rotation *n.* the system of growing a sequence of different crops on the same ground so as to maintain or increase its fertility.

crop up *vb.* (*intr., adv.*) *Inf.* to occur or appear unexpectedly.

croquet (ˈkrəʊkeɪ, -kɪ) *n.* a game for two to four players who hit a wooden ball through iron hoops with mallets in order to hit a peg. [C19: ? < F dialect, var. of CROCHET (little hook)]

croquette (krəʊˈkɛt, krɒ-) *n.* a savoury cake of minced meat, fish, etc., fried in breadcrumbs. [C18: < F, < *croquer* to crunch, imit.]

crosier *or* **crozier** (ˈkrəʊʒə) *n.* a staff surmounted by a crook or cross, carried by bishops as a symbol of pastoral office. [C14: < OF *crossier* staff bearer, < *crosse* pastoral staff]

cross (krɒs) *n.* **1.** a structure or symbol consisting of two intersecting lines or pieces at right angles to one another. **2.** a wooden structure used as a means of execution, consisting of an upright post with a transverse piece to which people were nailed or tied. **3.** a representation of the Cross used as an emblem of Christianity or as a reminder of Christ's death. **4.** any mark or shape consisting of two intersecting lines, esp. such a symbol (×) used as a signature, error mark, etc. **5.** a sign representing the Cross made either by tracing a figure in the air or by touching the forehead, breast, and either shoulder in turn. **6.** any variation of the Christian symbol, such as a Maltese or Greek cross. **7.** a cruciform emblem awarded to indicate membership of an order or as a decoration for distinguished service. **8.** (*sometimes cap.*) Christianity or Christendom, esp. as contrasted with non-Christian religions. **9.** the place in a town or village where a cross has been set up. **10.** *Biol.* **a.** the process of crossing; hybridization. **b.** an individual produced as a result of this process. **11.** a mixture of two qualities or types. **12.** an opposition, hindrance, or misfortune; affliction (esp. in **bear one's cross**). **13.** *Boxing.* a straight punch delivered from the side, esp. with the right hand. **14.** *Football.* the act or an instance of passing the ball from a wing to the middle of the field. ~*vb.* **15.** (sometimes foll. by *over*) to move or go across (something); traverse or intersect. **16. a.** to meet and pass. **b.** (of each of two letters in the post) to be dispatched before receipt of the other. **17.** (*tr.;* usually foll. by *out, off,* or *through*) to cancel with a cross or with lines; delete. **18.** (*tr.*) to place or put in a form resembling a cross: *to cross one's legs.* **19.** (*tr.*) to mark with a cross or crosses. **20.** (*tr.*) *Brit.* to draw two parallel lines across the face of (a cheque) and so make it payable only into a bank account. **21.** (*tr.*) **a.** to trace the form of the Cross upon (someone or something) in token of blessing. **b.** to make the sign of the Cross upon (oneself). **22.** (*intr.*) (of telephone lines) to interfere with each other so that several callers are connected together at one time. **23.** to cause fertilization between (plants or animals of different breeds, races, varieties, etc.). **24.** (*tr.*) to oppose the wishes or plans of; thwart. **25.** *Football.* to pass (the ball) from a wing to the middle of the field. **26. cross one's fingers.** to fold one finger across another in the hope of bringing good luck. **27. cross one's heart.** to promise or pledge, esp. by making the sign of a cross over one's heart. **28. cross one's mind.** to occur to one briefly or suddenly. **29. cross the path (of).** to meet or thwart (someone). **30. cross swords.** to argue or fight. ~*adj.* **31.** angry; ill-humoured; vexed. **32.** lying or placed across; transverse: *a cross timber.* **33.** involving interchange; reciprocal. **34.** contrary or unfavourable. **35.** another word for **crossbred.** [OE *cros,* < OIrish *cross* (unattested), < L *crux;* see CRUX] —ˈ**crossly** *adv.* —ˈ**crossness** *n.*

Cross (krɒs) *n.* **the. 1.** the cross on which Jesus Christ was crucified. **2.** the Crucifixion of Jesus.

cross- *combining form.* **1.** indicating action from one individual, group, etc., to another: *cross-cultural; cross-fertilize; cross-refer.* **2.** indicating movement, position, etc., across something: *crosscurrent; crosstalk.* **3.** indicating a crosslike figure or intersection: *crossbones.* [< CROSS (in various senses)]

crossbar (ˈkrɒsˌbɑː) *n.* **1.** a horizontal bar, line, stripe, etc. **2.** a horizontal beam across a pair of goal posts. **3.** the horizontal bar on a man's bicycle.

crossbeam (ˈkrɒsˌbiːm) *n.* a beam that spans from one support to another.

cross-bench *n.* (*usually pl.*) *Brit.* a seat in Parliament occupied by a neutral or independent member. —ˈ**cross-ˌbencher** *n.*

crossbill (ˈkrɒsˌbɪl) *n.* any of various widely distributed finches that occur in coniferous woods and have a bill with crossed tips.

crossbones (ˈkrɒsˌbəʊnz) *pl. n.* See **skull and crossbones.**

crossbow (ˈkrɒsˌbəʊ) *n.* a type of medieval bow fixed transversely on a stock grooved to direct a square-headed arrow. —ˈ**crossˌbowman** *n.*

crossbred (ˈkrɒsˌbrɛd) *adj.* **1.** (of plants or animals) produced as a result of crossbreeding. ~*n.* **2.** a crossbred plant or animal.

crossbreed (ˈkrɒsˌbriːd) *vb.* **-breeding, -bred. 1.** Also: **interbreed.** to breed (animals or plants) using parents of different races, varieties, breeds, etc. ~*n.* **2.** the offspring produced by such a breeding.

crosscheck (ˌkrɒsˈtʃɛk) *vb.* **1.** to verify (a fact, report, etc.) by considering conflicting opinions or consulting other sources. ~*n.* **2.** the act or an instance of crosschecking.

cross-country *adj., adv.* **1.** by way of fields, etc., as opposed to roads. **2.** across a country. ~*n.* **3.** a long race held over open ground.

crosscurrent (ˈkrɒsˌkʌrənt) *n.* **1.** a current flowing across another current. **2.** a conflicting tendency moving counter to the usual trend.

crosscut (ˈkrɒsˌkʌt) *adj.* **1.** cut at right angles or obliquely to the major axis. ~*n.* **2.** a transverse cut or course. **3.** *Mining.* a tunnel through a vein of ore or from the shaft to a vein. ~*vb.* **-cutting, -cut. 4.** to cut across.

crosscut saw *n.* a saw for cutting timber across the grain.

crosse (krɒs) *n.* a light staff with a triangular frame to which a network is attached, used in playing lacrosse. [F, < OF *croce* CROSIER]

cross-examine *vb.* (*tr.*) **1.** *Law.* to examine (a witness for the opposing side), as in attempting to discredit his testimony. **2.** to examine closely or relentlessly. —ˈ**cross-exˌamiˈnation** *n.* —ˌ**cross-exˈaminer** *n.*

cross-eye *n.* a turning inwards towards the nose of one or both eyes, caused by abnormal alignment. —ˈ**cross-ˌeyed** *adj.*

cross-fertilize *vb.* **1.** to fertilize by fusion of male and female gametes from different individuals of the same species. **2.** a non-technical term for **cross-pollinate.** —ˈ**cross-ˌfertiliˈzation** *n.*

crossfire (ˈkrɒsˌfaɪə) *n.* **1.** *Mil., etc.* converging fire from one or more positions. **2.** a lively exchange of ideas, opinions, etc.

cross-grained *adj.* **1.** (of timber) having the fibres arranged irregularly or across the axis of the piece. **2.** perverse, cantankerous, or stubborn.

crosshatch (ˈkrɒsˌhætʃ) *vb. Drawing.* to shade or hatch with two or more sets of parallel lines that cross one another.

crossing (ˈkrɒsɪŋ) *n.* **1.** the place where one thing crosses another. **2.** a place where a street, railway, etc., may be crossed. **3.** the act or an instance of travelling across something, esp. the sea. **4.** the act or process of crossbreeding.

crossing over *n. Biol.* the interchange of sections between pairing chromosomes during meiosis that produces variations in inherited characteristics by rearranging genes.

cross-legged (ˈkrɒsˈlɛgɪd, -ˈlɛgd) *adj.* standing or sitting with one leg crossed over the other.

cross-match *vb. Immunol.* to test the compatibility of (a donor's and recipient's blood) by checking that the red cells of each do not agglutinate in the other's serum.

crossover network *n. Electronics.* an arrangement in a loudspeaker system that separates the signal into two or more frequency bands for feeding into different speakers.

crosspatch (ˈkrɒsˌpætʃ) *n. Inf.* a bad-tempered person. [C18: < CROSS + obs. *patch* fool]

crosspiece (ˈkrɒsˌpiːs) *n.* a transverse beam, joist, etc.

cross-ply *adj.* (of a motor tyre) having the fabric cords in the outer casing running diagonally to stiffen the sidewalls.

cross-pollinate *vb.* to transfer pollen from the anthers of one flower to the stigma of another. —ˌ**cross-polliˈnation** *n.*

cross-purpose *n.* **1.** a contrary aim or purpose. **2. at cross-purposes.** conflicting; opposed; disagreeing.

cross-question *vb.* **1.** to cross-examine. ~*n.* **2.** a question asked in cross-examination.

cross-refer *vb.* to refer from one part of something, esp. a book, to another.

cross-reference *n.* **1.** a reference within a text to another part of the text. ~*vb.* **2.** to cross-refer.

crossroad (ˈkrɒsˌrəʊd) *n. U.S. & Canad.* **1.** a road that crosses another road. **2.** Also called: **crossway.** a road that crosses from one main road to another.

crossroads (ˈkrɒsˌrəʊdz) *n.* (*functioning as sing.*) **1.** the point at which two or more roads cross each other. **2.** the point at which an important choice has to be made (esp. in **at the crossroads**).

crossruff (ˈkrɒsˌrʌf) *Bridge, whist.* ~*n.* **1.** the alternate trumping of each other's leads by two partners, or by declarer and dummy. ~*vb.* **2.** (*intr.*) to trump alternately in this way.

cross section *n.* **1.** *Maths.* a plane surface formed by cutting across a solid, esp. perpendicular to its longest axis. **2.** a section cut off in this way. **3.** the act of cutting anything in this way. **4.** a random sample, esp. one regarded as representative. —ˌ**cross-ˈsectional** *adj.*

cross-stitch *n.* **1.** an embroidery stitch made by two stitches forming a cross. **2.** embroidery worked with this stitch. ~*vb.* **3.** to embroider (a piece of needlework) with cross-stitch.

crosstalk (ˈkrɒsˌtɔːk) *n.* **1.** unwanted signals in one channel of a communications system as a result of a transfer of energy from other channels. **2.** *Brit.* rapid or witty talk.

crosstree (ˈkrɒsˌtriː) *n. Naut.* either of a pair of wooden or metal braces on the head of a lower mast to support the topmast, etc.

crosswise (ˈkrɒsˌwaɪz) *or* **crossways** (ˈkrɒsˌweɪz) *adj., adv.* **1.** across; transversely. **2.** in the shape of a cross.

crossword puzzle (ˈkrɒsˌwɜːd) *n.* a puzzle in which the solver guesses words suggested by numbered clues and writes them into a grid to form a vertical and horizontal pattern.

crotch (krɒtʃ) *n.* **1.** Also called (Brit.): **crutch. a.** the angle formed by the legs where they join the human trunk. **b.** the human genital area. **c.** the corresponding part of a pair of trousers, pants, etc. **2.** a forked region formed by the junction of two members. **3.** a forked pole or stick. [C16: prob. var. of CRUTCH] —**crotched** *adj.*

crotchet (ˈkrɒtʃɪt) *n.* **1.** *Music.* a note having the time value of a quarter of a semibreve. **2.** a perverse notion. [C14: < OF *crochet,* lit.: little hook, < *croche* hook; see CROCKET]

crotchety (ˈkrɒtʃɪtɪ) *adj.* **1.** *Inf.* irritable; contrary. **2.** full of crotchets. —ˈ**crotchetiness** *n.*

croton (ˈkrəʊtᵊn) *n.* **1.** any shrub or tree of the chiefly tropical genus *Croton,* esp. *C. tiglium,* the seeds of which yield croton oil, formerly used as a purgative. **2.** any of various tropical plants of the related genus *Codiaeum*. [C18: < NL, < Gk *krotōn* tick, castor-oil plant (whose berries resemble ticks)]

crouch (krautʃ) *vb.* (*intr.*) **1.** to bend low with the limbs pulled up close together, esp. (of an animal) in readiness to pounce. **2.** to cringe, as in humility or fear. ~*n.* **3.** the act of stooping or bending. [C14: ? < OF *crochir* to become bent like a hook, < *croche* hook]

croup[1] (kru:p) *n.* a throat condition, occurring usually in children, characterized by a hoarse cough and laboured breathing, resulting from inflammation of the larynx. [C16 *croup* to cry hoarsely, prob. imit.] —**'croupous** *or* **'croupy** *adj.*

croup[2] (kru:p) *n.* the hindquarters, esp. of a horse. [C13: < OF *croupe;* rel. to G *Kruppe*]

croupier ('kru:pɪə) *n.* a person who deals cards, collects bets, etc., at a gaming table. [C18: lit.: one who rides behind another, < *croupe* CROUP[2]]

crouton ('kru:tɒn) *n.* a small piece of fried or toasted bread, usually served in soup. [F: dim. of *croûte* CRUST]

crow[1] (krəʊ) *n.* **1.** any large gregarious songbird of the genus *Corvus* of Europe and Asia, such as the raven, rook, and jackdaw. All have a heavy bill, glossy black plumage, and rounded wings. **2.** any of various similar birds. **3.** *Sl.* an old or ugly woman. **4. as the crow flies.** as directly as possible. **5. eat crow.** *U.S. & Canad. inf.* to be forced to do something humiliating. **6. stone the crows.** (*interj.*) *Brit. & Austral. sl.* an expression of surprise, dismay, etc. [OE *crāwa*]

crow[2] (krəʊ) *vb.* (*intr.*) **1.** (p.t. **crowed** *or* **crew**) to utter a shrill squawking sound, as a cock. **2.** (often foll. by *over*) to boast one's superiority. **3.** (esp. of babies) to utter cries of pleasure. ~*n.* **4.** an act or instance of crowing. [OE *crāwan;* rel. to OHG *krāen*, Du. *kraaien*] —**'crowingly** *adv.*

crowbar ('krəʊˌbɑ:) *n.* a heavy iron lever with one end forged into a wedge shape.

crowd[1] (kraʊd) *n.* **1.** a large number of things or people gathered or considered together. **2.** a particular group of people, esp. considered as a set: *the crowd from the office.* **3.** (preceded by *the*) the common people; the masses. ~*vb.* **4.** (*intr.*) to gather together in large numbers; throng. **5.** (*tr.*) to press together into a confined space. **6.** (*tr.*) to fill to excess; fill by pushing into. **7.** (*tr.*) *Inf.* to urge or harass by urging. [OE *crūdan*] —**'crowded** *adj.* —**'crowdedness** *n.*

crowd[2] (kraʊd) *n. Music.* an ancient bowed stringed instrument. [C13: < Welsh *crwth*]

crowfoot ('krəʊˌfʊt) *n., pl.* **-foots.** any of several plants that have yellow or white flowers and divided leaves resembling the foot of a crow.

crown (kraʊn) *n.* **1.** an ornamental headdress denoting sovereignty, usually made of gold embedded with precious stones. **2.** a wreath or garland for the head, awarded as a sign of victory, success, honour, etc. **3.** (*sometimes cap.*) monarchy or kingship. **4.** an award, distinction, or title, given as an honour to reward merit, victory, etc. **5.** anything resembling or symbolizing a crown. **6. a.** a coin worth 25 pence (five shillings). **b.** any of several continental coins, such as the krona or krone, with a name meaning *crown.* **7.** the top or summit of something: *crown of a hill.* **8.** the centre part of a road, esp. when it is cambered. **9.** the outstanding quality, achievement, state, etc.: *the crown of his achievements.* **10. a.** the enamel-covered part of a tooth above the gum. **b. artificial crown.** a substitute crown, usually of gold, porcelain, or acrylic resin, fitted over a decayed or broken tooth. **11.** the part of an anchor where the arms are joined to the shank. ~*vb.* (*tr.*) **12.** to put a crown on the head of, symbolically vesting with royal title, powers, etc. **13.** to place a crown, wreath, garland, etc., on the head of. **14.** to place something on or over the head or top of. **15.** to confer a title, dignity, or reward upon. **16.** to form the summit or topmost part of. **17.** to cap or put the finishing touch to (a series of events): *to crown it all it rained, too.* **18.** *Draughts.* to promote (a draught) to a king by placing another draught on top of it. **19.** to attach a crown to (a tooth). **20.** *Sl.* to hit over the head. [C12: < OF *corone,* < L *corōna* wreath, crown, < Gk *korōnē* crown, something curved]

Crown (kraʊn) *n.* (*sometimes not cap.;* usually preceded by *the*) **1.** the sovereignty or realm of a monarch. **2. a.** the government of a monarchy. **b.** (*as modifier*): *Crown property.*

crown colony *n.* a British colony whose administration is controlled by the Crown.

crown court *n. English law.* a court of criminal jurisdiction holding sessions in towns throughout England and Wales.

Crown Derby *n.* **1.** a type of porcelain manufactured at Derby from 1784–1848. **2.** *Trademark.* shortened form of Royal Crown Derby.

crown glass *n.* **1.** another name for **optical crown. 2.** an old form of window glass made by blowing a globe and spinning it until it forms a flat disc.

crown green *n.* a type of bowling green in which the sides are lower than the middle.

crown jewels *pl. n.* the jewellery, including the regalia, used by a sovereign on a state occasion.

Crown Office *n.* (in Britain) an administrative office of the Queen's Bench Division of the High Court, where actions are entered for trial.

crown prince *n.* the male heir to a sovereign throne.

crown princess *n.* **1.** the wife of a crown prince. **2.** the female heir to a sovereign throne.

crown wheel *n.* **1.** *Horology.* a wheel that has one set of teeth at right angles to another. **2.** the larger of two wheels in a bevel gear.

crow's-foot *n., pl.* **-feet.** (*often pl.*) a wrinkle at the outer corner of the eye.

crow's-nest *n.* a lookout platform high up on a ship's mast.

crow step *n.* another term for **corbie-step.**

crozier ('krəʊʒə) *n.* a variant spelling of **crosier.**

CRT *abbrev. for:* **1.** cathode-ray tube. **2.** (in Britain) composite rate tax: a system of paying interest to savers by which a rate of tax for a period is determined in advance and interest is paid net of tax which is deducted at source.

crucial ('kru:ʃəl) *adj.* **1.** involving a final or supremely important decision or event; decisive; critical. **2.** *Inf.* very important. **3.** *Sl.* very good. [C18: < F, < L *crux* CROSS] —**'crucially** *adv.*

crucible ('kru:sɪbᵊl) *n.* **1.** a vessel in which substances are heated to high temperatures. **2.** the hearth at the bottom of a metallurgical furnace in which the metal collects. **3.** a severe trial or test. [C15 *corusible,* < Med. L *crūcibulum* night lamp, crucible, <?]

crucifix ('kru:sɪfɪks) *n.* a cross or image of a cross with a figure of Christ upon it. [C13: < Church L *crucifixus* the crucified Christ, < *crucifigere* to CRUCIFY]

crucifixion (ˌkru:sɪ'fɪkʃən) *n.* a method of putting to death by nailing or binding to a cross, normally by the hands and feet.

Crucifixion (ˌkru:sɪ'fɪkʃən) *n.* **1.** (usually preceded by *the*) the crucifying of Christ. **2.** a picture or representation of this.

cruciform ('kru:sɪˌfɔ:m) *adj.* shaped like a cross. [C17: < L *crux* cross + -FORM] —**'cruciˌformly** *adv.*

crucify ('kru:sɪˌfaɪ) *vb.* **-fying, -fied.** (*tr.*) **1.** to put to death by crucifixion. **2.** *Sl.* to defeat, ridicule, etc., totally. **3.** to treat very cruelly; torment. [C13: < OF *crucifier,* < LL *crucifigere* to crucify, to fasten to a cross, < L *crux* cross + *figere* to fasten] —**'cruciˌfier** *n.*

crud (krʌd) *n.* **1.** *Sl.* **a.** a sticky substance, esp. when dirty and encrusted. **b.** a despicable person. **2.** an undesirable residue, esp. one inside a nuclear reactor. [C14: earlier form of CURD] —**'cruddy** *adj.*

crude (kru:d) *adj.* **1.** lacking taste, tact, or refinement; vulgar. **2.** in a natural or unrefined state. **3.** lacking care, knowledge, or skill. **4.**

(*prenominal*) stark; blunt. ~*n.* **5.** short for **crude oil.** [C14: < L *crūdus* bloody, raw; rel. to L *cruor* blood] —ˈ**crudely** *adv.* —ˈ**crudity** *or* ˈ**crudeness** *n.*

crude oil *n.* unrefined petroleum.

cruel (ˈkruːəl) *adj.* **1.** causing or inflicting pain without pity. **2.** causing pain or suffering. ~*vb.* **-elling, -elled.** (*tr.*) **3. cruel someone's pitch.** *Austral. sl.* to ruin someone's chances. [C13: < OF, < L *crūdēlis,* < *crūdus* raw, bloody] —ˈ**cruelly** *adv.* —ˈ**cruelness** *n.*

cruelty (ˈkruːəltɪ) *n., pl.* **-ties. 1.** deliberate infliction of pain or suffering. **2.** the quality or characteristic of being cruel. **3.** a cruel action. **4.** *Law.* conduct that causes danger to life or limb or a threat to bodily or mental health.

cruet (ˈkruːɪt) *n.* **1.** a small container for holding pepper, salt, vinegar, oil, etc., at table. **2.** a set of such containers, esp. on a stand. [C13: < Anglo-F, dim. of OF *crue* flask, of Gmc origin]

cruise (kruːz) *vb.* **1.** (*intr.*) to make a trip by sea for pleasure, usually calling at a number of ports. **2.** to sail or travel over (a body of water) for pleasure. **3.** (*intr.*) to search for enemy vessels in a warship. **4.** (*intr.*) (of a vehicle, aircraft, or vessel) to travel at a moderate and efficient speed. ~*n.* **5.** an act or instance of cruising, esp. a trip by sea. [C17: < Du. *kruisen* to cross, < *cruis* CROSS]

cruise missile *n.* a low-flying subsonic missile that is guided throughout its flight.

cruiser (ˈkruːzə) *n.* **1.** a high-speed, long-range warship armed with medium-calibre weapons. **2.** Also called: **cabin cruiser.** a pleasure boat, esp. one that is power-driven and has a cabin. **3.** any person or thing that cruises.

cruiserweight (ˈkruːzəˌweɪt) *n. Boxing.* another term (esp. Brit.) for **light heavyweight.**

crumb (krʌm) *n.* **1.** a small fragment of bread, cake, or other baked foods. **2.** a small piece or bit. **3.** the soft inner part of bread. **4.** *Sl.* a contemptible person. ~*vb.* **5.** (*tr.*) to prepare or cover (food) with breadcrumbs. **6.** to break into small fragments. [OE *cruma*]

crumble (ˈkrʌmbᵊl) *vb.* **1.** to break or be broken into crumbs or fragments. **2.** (*intr.*) to fall apart or away. ~*n.* **3.** *Brit.* a baked pudding consisting of a crumbly mixture of flour, fat, and sugar over stewed fruit: *apple crumble.* [C16: var. of *crimble,* of Gmc origin]

crumbly (ˈkrʌmblɪ) *adj.* **-blier, -bliest.** easily crumbled or crumbling. —ˈ**crumbliness** *n.*

crumby (ˈkrʌmɪ) *adj.* **crumbier, crumbiest. 1.** full of or littered with crumbs. **2.** soft, like the inside of bread. **3.** a variant spelling of **crummy.**

crummy (ˈkrʌmɪ) *adj.* **-mier, -miest.** *Sl.* **1.** of little value; contemptible. **2.** unwell or depressed: *to feel crummy.* [C19: var. spelling of CRUMBY]

crumpet (ˈkrʌmpɪt) *n. Chiefly Brit.* **1.** a light soft yeast cake, eaten toasted and buttered. **2.** *Sl.* women collectively. [C17: <?]

crumple (ˈkrʌmpᵊl) *vb.* **1.** (when *intr.,* often foll. by *up*) to collapse or cause to collapse. **2.** (when *tr.,* often foll. by *up*) to crush or cause to be crushed so as to form wrinkles or creases. ~*n.* **3.** a loose crease or wrinkle. [C16: < obs. *crump* to bend] —ˈ**crumply** *adj.*

crunch (krʌntʃ) *vb.* **1.** to bite or chew with a crushing or crackling sound. **2.** to make or cause to make a crisp or brittle sound. ~*n.* **3.** the sound or act of crunching. **4. the crunch.** *Inf.* the critical moment or situation. ~*adj.* **5.** *Inf.* critical; decisive: *crunch time.* [C19: changed (through infl. of MUNCH) < earlier *craunch,* imit.] —ˈ**crunchy** *adj.* —ˈ**crunchily** *adv.* —ˈ**crunchiness** *n.*

crupper (ˈkrʌpə) *n.* **1.** a strap from the back of a saddle that passes under a horse's tail. **2.** the horse's rump. [C13: < OF *crupiere,* < *crupe* CROUP²]

crusade (kruːˈseɪd) *n.* **1.** (*often cap.*) any of the military expeditions undertaken in the 11th, 12th, and 13th centuries by the Christian powers of Europe to recapture the Holy Land from the Muslims. **2.** (formerly) any holy war. **3.** a vigorous and dedicated action or movement in favour of a cause. ~*vb.* (*intr.*) **4.** to campaign vigorously for something. **5.** to go on a crusade. [C16: < earlier *croisade,* < OF *crois* cross, < L *crux;* infl. also by Sp. *cruzada,* < *cruzar* to take up the cross] —**cruˈsader** *n.*

cruse (kruːz) *n.* a small earthenware container used, esp. formerly, for liquids. [OE *crūse*]

crush (krʌʃ) *vb.* (*mainly tr.*) **1.** to press, mash, or squeeze so as to injure, break, crease, etc. **2.** to break or grind into small particles. **3.** to put down or subdue, esp. by force. **4.** to extract (juice, water, etc.) by pressing. **5.** to oppress harshly. **6.** to hug or clasp tightly. **7.** to defeat or humiliate utterly, as in argument or by a cruel remark. **8.** (*intr.*) to crowd; throng. **9.** (*intr.*) to become injured, broken, or distorted by pressure. ~*n.* **10.** a dense crowd, esp. at a social occasion. **11.** the act of crushing; pressure. **12.** a drink or pulp prepared by or as if by crushing fruit: *orange crush.* **13.** *Inf.* **a.** an infatuation: *she had a crush on him.* **b.** the person with whom one is infatuated. [C14: < OF *croissir,* of Gmc origin] —ˈ**crushable** *adj.* —ˈ**crusher** *n.*

crush barrier *n.* a barrier erected to separate sections of large crowds.

crust (krʌst) *n.* **1. a.** the hard outer part of bread. **b.** a piece of bread consisting mainly of this. **2.** the baked shell of a pie, tart, etc. **3.** any hard or stiff outer covering or surface: *a crust of ice.* **4.** the solid outer shell of the earth. **5.** the dry covering of a skin sore or lesion; scab. **6.** *Sl.* impertinence. **7.** *Brit., Austral., & N.Z. sl.* a living (esp. in **earn a crust**). ~*vb.* **8.** to cover with or acquire a crust. **9.** to form or be formed into a crust. [C14: < L *crūsta* hard surface, rind, shell]

crustacean (krʌˈsteɪʃən) *n.* **1.** any arthropod of the mainly aquatic class *Crustacea,* typically having a carapace and including the lobsters, crabs, woodlice, and water fleas. ~*adj. also* **crustaceous. 2.** of, relating to, or belonging to the *Crustacea.* [C19: < NL *crūstāceus* hard-shelled, < L *crūsta* shell]

crustal (ˈkrʌstᵊl) *adj.* of or relating to the earth's crust.

crusty (ˈkrʌstɪ) *adj.* **crustier, crustiest. 1.** having or characterized by a crust. **2.** having a rude or harsh character or exterior. —ˈ**crustily** *adv.* —ˈ**crustiness** *n.*

crutch (krʌtʃ) *n.* **1.** a long staff having a rest for the armpit, for supporting the weight of the body. **2.** something that supports, helps, or sustains. **3.** *Brit.* another word for **crotch** (sense 1). ~*vb.* **4.** (*tr.*) to support or sustain (a person or thing) as with a crutch. **5.** *Austral. & N.Z.* to clip (wool) from the hindquarters of a sheep. [OE *crycc*]

crutchings (ˈkrʌtʃɪŋz) *pl. n. Austral. & N.Z.* wool clipped from a sheep's hindquarters.

crux (krʌks) *n., pl.* **cruxes** *or* **cruces** (ˈkruːsiːz). **1.** a vital or decisive stage, point, etc. (often in **the crux of the matter**). **2.** a baffling problem or difficulty. [C18: < L: cross]

cruzeiro (kruːˈzɛərəʊ) *n., pl.* **-ros** (-rəʊz). the standard monetary unit of Brazil. [Port.: < *cruz* CROSS]

cry (kraɪ) *vb.* **crying, cried. 1.** (*intr.*) to utter inarticulate sounds, esp. when weeping; sob. **2.** (*intr.*) to shed tears; weep. **3.** (*intr.;* usually foll. by *out*) to scream or shout in pain, terror, etc. **4.** (*tr.;* often foll. by *out*) to utter or shout (words of appeal, exclamation, fear, etc.). **5.** (*intr.;* often foll. by *out*) (of animals, birds, etc.) to utter loud characteristic sounds. **6.** (*tr.*) to hawk or sell by public announcement: *to cry newspapers.* **7.** to announce (something) publicly or in the streets. **8.** (*intr.;* foll. by *for*) to clamour or beg. **9. cry for the moon.** to desire the unattainable. **10. cry one's eyes** *or* **heart out.** to weep bitterly. ~*n., pl.* **cries. 11.** the act or sound of crying; a shout, scream, or wail. **12.** the characteristic utterance of an animal or bird. **13.** a fit of weeping. **14.** *Hunting.* the baying of a pack of hounds hunting their quarry by scent. **15. a far cry. a.** a long way. **b.** something very different. **16. in full cry.** (esp. of a pack of hounds) in hot pursuit of a quarry.

~See also **cry down, cry off,** etc. [C13: < OF *crier,* < L *quirītāre* to call for help]
crybaby (ˈkraɪˌbeɪbɪ) *n., pl.* **-bies.** a person, esp. a child, given to frequent crying or complaint.
cry down *vb.* (*tr., adv.*) to belittle; disparage.
crying (ˈkraɪɪŋ) *adj.* (*prenominal*) notorious; lamentable (esp. in **crying shame**).
cryo- *combining form.* cold or freezing: *cryogenics.* [< Gk *kruos* icy cold, frost]
cryobiology (ˌkraɪəʊbaɪˈɒlədʒɪ) *n.* the biology of the effects of very low temperatures on organisms. —ˌ**cryobiˈologist** *n.*
cry off *vb.* (*intr.*) *Inf.* to withdraw from or cancel (an agreement or arrangement).
cryogen (ˈkraɪədʒən) *n.* a substance used to produce low temperatures; a freezing mixture.
cryogenics (ˌkraɪəˈdʒɛnɪks) *n.* (*functioning as sing.*) the branch of physics concerned with very low temperatures and the phenomena occurring at these temperatures. —ˌ**cryoˈgenic** *adj.*
cryolite (ˈkraɪəˌlaɪt) *n.* a white or colourless fluoride of sodium and aluminium: used in the production of aluminium, glass, and enamel.
cryonics (kraɪˈɒnɪks) *n.* (*functioning as sing.*) the practice of freezing a human corpse in the hope of restoring it to life later.
cryostat (ˈkraɪəˌstæt) *n.* an apparatus for maintaining a constant low temperature.
cryosurgery (ˌkraɪəʊˈsɜːdʒərɪ) *n.* surgery involving quick freezing for therapeutic benefit.
cry out *vb.* (*intr., adv.*) **1.** to scream or shout aloud, esp. in pain, terror, etc. **2.** (often foll. by *for*) *Inf.* to demand in an obvious manner.
crypt (krɪpt) *n.* a vault or underground chamber, esp. beneath a church, often used as a chapel, burial place, etc. [C18: < L *crypta,* < Gk *kruptē* vault, secret place, ult. < *kruptein* to hide]
cryptanalysis (ˌkrɪptəˈnælɪsɪs) *n.* the study of codes and ciphers; cryptography. [C20: < CRYPTO- + ANALYSIS] —**cryptanalytic** (ˌkrɪptænəˈlɪtɪk) *adj.* —**cryptˈanalyst** *n.*
cryptic (ˈkrɪptɪk) *adj.* **1.** hidden; secret. **2.** esoteric or obscure in meaning. **3.** (of coloration) effecting camouflage or concealment. [C17: < LL *crypticus,* < Gk *kruptikos,* < *kruptos* concealed; see CRYPT] —ˈ**cryptically** *adv.*
crypto- *or before a vowel* **crypt-** *combining form.* secret, hidden, or concealed. [NL, < Gk *kruptos* hidden, < *kruptein* to hide]
cryptocrystalline (ˌkrɪptəʊˈkrɪstəlaɪn) *adj.* (of rocks) composed of crystals visible only under a polarizing microscope.
cryptogam (ˈkrɪptəʊˌgæm) *n.* (in former classification schemes) any plant that does not produce seeds, including algae, fungi, mosses, and ferns. [C19: < NL *Cryptogamia,* < CRYPTO- + Gk *gamos* marriage] —ˌ**cryptoˈgamic** *or* **cryptogamous** (krɪpˈtɒgəməs) *adj.*
cryptograph (ˈkrɪptəʊˌgrɑːf) *n.* **1.** something written in code or cipher. **2.** a code using secret symbols (**cryptograms**).
cryptography (krɪpˈtɒgrəfɪ) *n.* the science or study of analysing and deciphering codes, ciphers, etc. Also called: **cryptanalysis.** —**crypˈtographer** *or* **crypˈtographist** *n.* —**cryptographic** (ˌkrɪptəˈgræfɪk) *or* ˌ**cryptoˈgraphical** *adj.* —ˌ**cryptoˈgraphically** *adv.*
crystal (ˈkrɪstᵊl) *n.* **1.** a solid, such as quartz, with a regular shape in which plane faces intersect at definite angles. **2.** a single grain of a crystalline substance. **3.** anything resembling a crystal, such as a piece of cut glass. **4. a.** a highly transparent and brilliant type of glass. **b.** (*as modifier*): *a crystal chandelier.* **5.** something made of or resembling crystal. **6.** crystal glass articles collectively. **7.** *Electronics.* **a.** a crystalline element used in certain electronic devices as a detector, oscillator, etc. **b.** (*as modifier*): *crystal pick-up.* **8.** a transparent cover for the face of a watch. **9.** (*modifier*) of or relating to a crystal or the regular atomic arrangement of crystals: *crystal structure.* ~*adj.* **10.** resembling crystal; transparent: *crystal water.* [OE *cristalla,* < L *crystallum,* < Gk *krustallos* ice, crystal, < *krustainein* to freeze]
crystal ball *n.* the glass globe used in crystal gazing.
crystal class *n. Crystallography.* any of 32 possible types of crystals, classified according to their rotational symmetry about axes through a point. Also called: **point group.**
crystal detector *n. Electronics.* a demodulator, used esp. in early radio receivers, incorporating a semiconductor crystal.
crystal gazing *n.* **1.** the act of staring into a crystal ball supposedly in order to arouse visual perceptions of the future, etc. **2.** the act of trying to foresee or predict. —**crystal gazer** *n.*
crystal lattice *n.* the regular array of points about which the atoms, ions, or molecules composing a crystal are centred.
crystalline (ˈkrɪstəˌlaɪn) *adj.* **1.** having the characteristics or structure of crystals. **2.** consisting of or containing crystals. **3.** made of or like crystal; transparent; clear.
crystalline lens *n.* a biconvex transparent elastic lens in the eye.
crystallize *or* **-ise** (ˈkrɪstəˌlaɪz) *vb.* **1.** to form or cause to form crystals; assume or cause to assume a crystalline form or structure. **2.** to coat or become coated with sugar. **3.** to give a definite form or expression to (an idea, argument, etc.) or (of an idea, argument, etc.) to assume a definite form. —ˈ**crystalˌlizable** *or* **-isable** *adj.* —ˌ**crystalliˈzation** *or* **-iˈsation** *n.*
crystallo- *or before a vowel* **crystall-** *combining form.* crystal: *crystallography.*
crystallography (ˌkrɪstəˈlɒgrəfɪ) *n.* the science of crystal structure. —ˌ**crystalˈlographer** *n.* —**crystallographic** (ˌkrɪstələʊˈgræfɪk) *adj.*
crystalloid (ˈkrɪstəˌlɔɪd) *adj.* **1.** resembling or having the properties of a crystal. ~*n.* **2.** a substance that in solution can pass through a semipermeable membrane.
crystal pick-up *n.* a gramophone pick-up incorporating a piezoelectric crystal.
crystal set *n.* an early form of radio receiver having a crystal detector.
cry up *vb.* (*tr., adv.*) to praise highly; extol.
Cs *the chemical symbol for* caesium.
CS *abbrev. for:* **1.** Also: **cs.** capital stock. **2.** chartered surveyor. **3.** Christian Science. **4.** Civil Service. **5.** Also: **cs.** Court of Session.
csc *abbrev. for* cosecant.
CSC *abbrev. for* Civil Service Commission.
CSE (in Britain) *abbrev. for* Certificate of Secondary Education; an examination the first grade pass of which is an equivalent to a GCE O level.
CSEU *abbrev. for* Confederation of Shipbuilding and Engineering Unions.
CS gas *n.* a gas causing tears, salivation, and painful breathing, used in civil disturbances. [C20: < the surname initials of its U.S. inventors, Ben Carson and Roger Staughton]
CSIRO (in Australia) *abbrev. for* Commonwealth Scientific and Industrial Research Organization.
CSM (in Britain) *abbrev. for* Company Sergeant-Major.
CST (in the U.S. and Canada) *abbrev. for* Central Standard Time.
CSU *abbrev. for* Civil Service Union.
ct *abbrev. for:* **1.** carat. **2.** cent. **3.** court.
CTC (in Britain) *abbrev. for* city technology college.
ctenophore (ˈtɛnəˌfɔː, ˈtiːnə-) *n.* any marine invertebrate of the phylum *Ctenophora,* whose body bears eight rows of fused cilia, for locomotion. [C19: < NL *ctenophorus,* < Gk *kteno-, kteis* comb + -PHORE]
ctn *abbrev. for* cotangent.
CTT *abbrev. for* Capital Transfer Tax.
CTV *abbrev. for* Canadian Television (Network Limited).
Cu *the chemical symbol for* copper. [< LL *cuprum*]
cu. *abbrev. for* cubic.
cub (kʌb) *n.* **1.** the young of certain animals, such as the lion, bear, etc. **2.** a young or inexperienced person. ~*vb.* **cubbing, cubbed. 3.** to give birth

to (cubs). [C16: ? < ON *kubbi* young seal] —ˈ**cubbish** *adj.*

Cub (kʌb) *n.* short for **Cub scout.**

Cuban (ˈkjuːbən) *adj.* **1.** of or relating to Cuba, a republic and the largest island in the Caribbean. ~*n.* **2.** a native or inhabitant of Cuba.

cubby (ˈkʌbɪ) *n., pl.* **-bies.** *Austral.* a small room or enclosed area, esp. one used as a child's play area. Also: **cubbyhole, cubby-house.**

cubbyhole (ˈkʌbɪˌhəʊl) *n.* a small enclosed space or room. [C19: < dialect *cub* cattle pen]

cube (kjuːb) *n.* **1.** a solid having six plane square faces in which the angle between two adjacent sides is a right angle. **2.** the product of three equal factors. **3.** something in the form of a cube. ~*vb.* **4.** to raise (a number or quantity) to the third power. **5.** (*tr.*) to make, shape, or cut (something) into cubes. [C16: < L *cubus* die, cube, < Gk *kubos*] —ˈ**cuber** *n.*

cubeb (ˈkjuːbɛb) *n.* **1.** a SE Asian treelike climbing plant. **2.** its spicy fruit, dried and used as a stimulant and diuretic and sometimes smoked in cigarettes. [C14: < OF *cubebe,* < Med. L *cubēba,* < Ar. *kubābah*]

cube root *n.* the number or quantity whose cube is a given number or quantity: 2 is the cube root of 8 (usually written $\sqrt[3]{8}$ or $8^{1/3}$).

cubic (ˈkjuːbɪk) *adj.* **1.** having the shape of a cube. **2. a.** having three dimensions. **b.** denoting or relating to a linear measure that is raised to the third power: *a cubic metre.* **3.** *Maths.* of, relating to, or containing a variable to the third power or a term in which the sum of the exponents of the variables is three. —ˈ**cubical** *adj.*

cubicle (ˈkjuːbɪkᵊl) *n.* a partially or totally enclosed section of a room, as in a dormitory. [C15: < L *cubiculum,* < *cubāre* to lie down]

cubic measure *n.* a system of units for the measurement of volumes.

cubiform (ˈkjuːbɪˌfɔːm) *adj.* having the shape of a cube.

cubism (ˈkjuːbɪzəm) *n.* (*often cap.*) a French school of art, initiated in 1907 by Picasso and Braque, which amalgamated viewpoints of natural forms into a multifaceted surface of geometrical planes. —ˈ**cubist** *adj., n.* —**cuˈbistic** *adj.*

cubit (ˈkjuːbɪt) *n.* an ancient measure of length based on the length of the forearm. [C14: < L *cubitum* elbow, cubit]

cuboid (ˈkjuːbɔɪd) *adj. also* **cuboidal** (kjuːˈbɔɪdᵊl). **1.** shaped like a cube; cubic. **2.** of or denoting the cuboid bone. ~*n.* **3.** the cubelike bone of the foot. **4.** *Maths.* a geometric solid whose six faces are rectangles.

Cub Scout *or* **Cub** *n.* a member of the junior branch of the Scout Association.

cucking stool (ˈkʌkɪŋ) *n. History.* a stool to which suspected witches, scolds, etc., were tied and pelted or ducked into water. [C13 *cucking stol,* lit.: defecating chair, < *cukken* to defecate]

cuckold (ˈkʌkəld) *n.* **1.** a man whose wife has committed adultery. ~*vb.* **2.** (*tr.*) to make a cuckold of. [C13 *cukeweld,* < OF *cucuault,* < *cucu* CUCKOO; ? an allusion to cuckoos that lay eggs in the nests of other birds] —ˈ**cuckoldry** *n.*

cuckoo (ˈkʊkuː) *n., pl.* **-oos. 1.** any bird of the family Cuculidae, having pointed wings and a long tail. Many species, including the **European cuckoo,** lay their eggs in the nests of other birds and have a two-note call. **2.** *Inf.* an insane or foolish person. ~*adj.* **3.** *Inf.* insane or foolish. ~*interj.* **4.** an imitation or representation of the call of a cuckoo. ~*vb.* **-ooing, -ooed. 5.** (*intr.*) to make the sound imitated by the word *cuckoo.* [C13: < OF *cucu,* imit.]

cuckoo clock *n.* a clock in which a mechanical cuckoo pops out with a sound like a cuckoo's call when the clock strikes.

cuckoopint (ˈkʊkuːˌpaɪnt) *n.* a European plant with arrow-shaped leaves, a spathe marked with purple, a pale purple spadix, and scarlet berries. Also called: **lords-and-ladies.**

cuckoo spit *n.* a white frothy mass on the stems and leaves of many plants, produced by froghopper larvae.

cucullate (ˈkjuːkəˌleɪt, -lɪt) *adj.* shaped like a hood or having a hoodlike part: *cucullate sepals.* [C18: < LL *cucullātus,* < L *cucullus* hood, cap]

cucumber (ˈkjuːˌkʌmbə) *n.* **1.** a creeping plant cultivated in many forms for its edible fruit. **2.** the cylindrical fruit of this plant, which has hard thin green rind and white crisp flesh. [C14: < L *cucumis,* <?]

cucurbit (kjuːˈkɜːbɪt) *n.* any of a family of creeping flowering plants that includes the pumpkin, cucumber, and gourds. [C14: < OF, < L *cucurbita* gourd, cup] —**cuˌcurbiˈtaceous** *adj.*

cud (kʌd) *n.* **1.** partially digested food regurgitated from the first stomach of ruminants to the mouth for a second chewing. **2. chew the cud.** to reflect or think over something. [OE *cudu,* < *cwidu* what has been chewed]

cuddle (ˈkʌdᵊl) *vb.* **1.** to hold close or (of two people, etc.) to hold each other close, as for affection or warmth; hug. **2.** (*intr.;* foll. by *up*) to curl or snuggle up into a comfortable or warm position. ~*n.* **3.** a close embrace, esp. when prolonged. [C18: <?] —ˈ**cuddlesome** *adj.* —ˈ**cuddly** *adj.*

cuddy (ˈkʌdɪ) *n., pl.* **-dies.** a small cabin in a boat. [C17: ? < Du. *kajute*]

cudgel (ˈkʌdʒəl) *n.* **1.** a short stout stick used as a weapon. **2. take up the cudgels.** (often foll. by *for* or *on behalf of*) to join in a dispute, esp. to defend oneself or another. ~*vb.* **-elling, -elled** *or U.S.* **-eling, -eled. 3.** (*tr.*) to strike with a cudgel. **4. cudgel one's brains.** to think hard. [OE *cycgel*]

cudgerie (ˈkʌdʒərɪ) *n. Austral.* any of various large rainforest trees, such as the pink poplar or blush cudgerie, with pink wood. [< Abor.]

cudweed (ˈkʌdˌwiːd) *n.* any of various temperate woolly plants having clusters of whitish or yellow button-like flowers.

cue[1] (kjuː) *n.* **1. a.** (in the theatre, films, music, etc.) anything that serves as a signal to an actor, musician, etc., to follow with specific lines or action. **b. on cue.** at the right moment. **2.** a signal or reminder to do something. ~*vb.* **cueing, cued. 3.** (*tr.*) to give a cue or cues to (an actor). **4.** (usually foll. by *in* or *into*) to signal (to something or somebody) at a specific moment in a musical or dramatic performance. [C16: prob. < name of the letter *q,* used in an actor's script to represent L *quando* when]

cue[2] (kjuː) *n.* **1.** *Billiards, etc.* a long tapered shaft used to drive the balls. **2.** hair caught at the back forming a tail or braid. ~*vb.* **cueing, cued. 3.** to drive (a ball) with a cue. [C18: var. of QUEUE]

cue ball *n. Billiards, etc.* the ball struck by the cue, as distinguished from the object balls.

cuesta (ˈkwɛstə) *n.* a long low ridge with a steep scarp slope and a gentle back slope. [Sp.: shoulder, < L *costa* side, rib]

cuff[1] (kʌf) *n.* **1.** the end of a sleeve, sometimes turned back. **2.** the part of a glove that extends past the wrist. **3.** the U.S., Canad., and Austral. name for **turn-up** (sense 5). **4. off the cuff.** *Inf.* improvised; extemporary. [C14 *cuffe* glove, <?]

cuff[2] (kʌf) *vb.* **1.** (*tr.*) to strike with an open hand. ~*n.* **2.** a blow of this kind. [C16: <?]

cuff link *n.* one of a pair of linked buttons, used to join the buttonholes on the cuffs of a shirt.

cui bono *Latin.* (kwiː ˈbəʊnəʊ) for whose benefit? for what purpose?

cuirass (kwɪˈræs) *n.* **1.** a piece of armour covering the chest and back. ~*vb.* **2.** (*tr.*) to equip with a cuirass. [C15: < F *cuirasse,* < LL *coriacea,* < *coriaceus* made of leather]

cuirassier (ˌkwɪərəˈsɪə) *n.* a mounted soldier, esp. of the 16th century, who wore a cuirass.

Cuisenaire rod (ˌkwɪzəˈnɛə) *n. Trademark.* one of a set of rods of various colours and lengths representing different numbers, used to teach arithmetic to young children. [C20: after Emil-Georges *Cuisenaire* (?1891–1976), Belgian educationalist]

cuisine (kwɪˈziːn) *n.* **1.** a style or manner of cooking: *French cuisine.* **2.** the food prepared by a restaurant, household, etc. [C18: < F, lit.: kitchen, < LL *coquīna*, < L *coquere* to cook]

cuisse (kwɪs) *or* **cuish** (kwɪʃ) *n.* a piece of armour for the thigh. [C15: back formation < *cuisses* (pl.), < OF *cuisseaux*, < *cuisse* thigh]

cul-de-sac (ˈkʌldəˌsæk, ˈkʊl-) *n., pl.* **culs-de-sac** *or* **cul-de-sacs.** 1. a road with one end blocked off; dead end. 2. an inescapable position. [C18: < F, lit.: bottom of the bag]

-cule *suffix forming nouns.* indicating smallness. [< L *-culus*, dim. suffix]

culex (ˈkjuːlɛks) *n., pl.* **-lices** (-lɪˌsiːz). any mosquito of the genus *Culex*, such as *C. pipiens*, the common mosquito. [C15: < L: midge, gnat]

culinary (ˈkʌlɪnərɪ) *adj.* of, relating to, or used in the kitchen or in cookery. [C17: < L *culīnārius*, < *culīna* kitchen] —ˈ**culinarily** *adv.*

cull (kʌl) *vb. (tr.)* 1. to choose or gather the best or required examples of. 2. to take out (an animal, esp. an inferior one) from a herd. 3. to reduce the size of (a herd, etc.) by killing a proportion of its members. 4. to gather (flowers, fruit, etc.). ~*n.* 5. the act or product of culling. 6. an inferior animal taken from a herd. [C15: < OF *coillir* to pick, < L *colligere*; see COLLECT[1]] —ˈ**culler** *n.*

culm[1] (kʌlm) *n. Mining.* 1. coal-mine waste. 2. inferior anthracite. [C14: prob. rel. to COAL]

culm[2] (kʌlm) *n.* the hollow jointed stem of a grass or sedge. [C17: < L *culmus* stalk; see HAULM]

culminate (ˈkʌlmɪˌneɪt) *vb.* 1. (when *intr.*, usually foll. by *in*) to reach or bring to a final or climactic stage. 2. (*intr.*) (of a celestial body) to cross the meridian. [C17: < LL *culmināre* to reach the highest point, < L *culmen* top] —ˈ**culminant** *adj.*

culmination (ˌkʌlmɪˈneɪʃən) *n.* 1. the final or highest point. 2. the act of culminating.

culottes (kjuːˈlɒts) *pl. n.* women's flared trousers cut to look like a skirt. [C20: < F, lit.: breeches, < *cul* bottom]

culpable (ˈkʌlpəbˀl) *adj.* deserving censure; blameworthy. [C14: < OF *coupable*, < L *culpābilis*, < *culpāre* to blame, < *culpa* fault] —ˌ**culpaˈbility** *n.* —ˈ**culpably** *adv.*

culprit (ˈkʌlprɪt) *n.* 1. *Law.* a person awaiting trial. 2. the person responsible for a particular offence, misdeed, etc. [C17: < Anglo-F *cul-*, short for *culpable* guilty + *prit* ready, indicating that the prosecution was ready to prove the guilt of the one charged]

cult (kʌlt) *n.* 1. a specific system of religious worship. 2. a sect devoted to the beliefs of a cult. 3. intense interest in and devotion to a person, idea, or activity. 4. the person, idea, etc., arousing such devotion. 5. any popular fashion; craze. 6. (*modifier*) of, relating to, or characteristic of a cult or cults: *a cult figure.* [C17: < L *cultus* cultivation, refinement, < *colere* to till] —ˈ**cultic** *adj.* —ˈ**cultism** *n.* —ˈ**cultist** *n.*

cultivable (ˈkʌltɪvəbˀl) *or* **cultivatable** (ˈkʌltɪˌveɪtəbˀl) *adj.* (of land) capable of being cultivated. [C17: < F, < OF *cultiver* to CULTIVATE] —ˌ**cultivaˈbility** *n.*

cultivar (ˈkʌltɪˌvɑː) *n.* a variety of a plant produced from a natural species and maintained by cultivation. [C20: < CULTI(VATED) + VAR(IETY)]

cultivate (ˈkʌltɪˌveɪt) *vb. (tr.)* 1. to prepare (land or soil) for the growth of crops. 2. to plant, tend, harvest, or improve (plants). 3. to break up (land or soil) with a cultivator or hoe. 4. to improve (the mind, body, etc.) as by study, education, or labour. 5. to give special attention to: *to cultivate a friendship.* [C17: < Med. L *cultivāre* to till, < *cultīvus* cultivable, < L *cultus* cultivated, < *colere* to till, toil over] —ˈ**cultiˌvated** *adj.*

cultivation (ˌkʌltɪˈveɪʃən) *n.* 1. *Agriculture.* a. the cultivating of crops or plants. b. the preparation of ground to promote their growth. 2. development, esp. through education, training, etc. 3. culture or sophistication.

cultivator (ˈkʌltɪˌveɪtə) *n.* 1. a farm implement used to break up soil and remove weeds. 2. a person or thing that cultivates.

cultural (ˈkʌltʃərəl) *adj.* 1. of or relating to artistic or social pursuits or events considered valuable or enlightened. 2. of or relating to a culture. 3. obtained by specialized breeding.

culture (ˈkʌltʃə) *n.* 1. the total of the inherited ideas, beliefs, values, and knowledge, which constitute the shared bases of social action. 2. the total range of activities and ideas of a people. 3. a particular civilization at a particular period. 4. the artistic and social pursuits, expression, and tastes valued by a society or class. 5. the enlightenment or refinement resulting from these pursuits. 6. the cultivation of plants to improve stock or to produce new ones. 7. the rearing and breeding of animals, esp. with a view to improving the strain. 8. the act or practice of tilling or cultivating the soil. 9. *Biol.* a. the experimental growth of microorganisms in a nutrient substance. b. a group of microorganisms grown in this way. ~*vb. (tr.)* 10. to cultivate (plants or animals). 11. to grow (microorganisms) in a culture medium. [C15: < OF, < L *cultūra* a cultivating, < *colere* to till; see CULT] —ˈ**culturist** *n.*

cultured (ˈkʌltʃəd) *adj.* 1. showing or having good taste, manners, and education. 2. artificially grown or synthesized: *cultured pearls.* 3. treated by a culture of microorganisms.

cultured pearl *n.* a pearl induced to grow in the shell of an oyster or clam, by the insertion of a small object.

culture shock *n. Sociol.* the feelings of isolation, rejection, etc., experienced when one culture is brought into sudden contact with another.

culture vulture *n. Inf.* a person considered to be excessively eager to acquire culture.

cultus (ˈkʌltəs) *n., pl.* **-tuses** *or* **-ti** (-taɪ). another word for **cult** (sense 1). [C17: < L: a toiling over something, refinement, CULT]

culverin (ˈkʌlvərɪn) *n.* 1. a medium-to-heavy cannon used during the 15th, 16th, and 17th centuries. 2. a medieval musket. [C15: < OF *coulevrine*, < *couleuvre*, < L *coluber* serpent]

culvert (ˈkʌlvət) *n.* 1. a drain or covered channel that crosses under a road, railway, etc. 2. a channel for an electric cable. [C18: <?]

cum (kʌm) *prep.* used between nouns to designate a combined nature: *a kitchen-cum-dining room.* [L: with, together with]

cumber (ˈkʌmbə) *vb. (tr.)* 1. to obstruct or hinder. 2. *Obs.* to inconvenience. [C13: prob. < OF *combrer* to impede, prevent, < *combre* barrier; see ENCUMBER]

cumbersome (ˈkʌmbəsəm) *or* **cumbrous** (ˈkʌmbrəs) *adj.* 1. awkward because of size, weight, or shape. 2. difficult because of extent or complexity: *cumbersome accounts.* [C14: *cumber*, short for ENCUMBER + -SOME[1]] —ˈ**cumbersomeness** *or* ˈ**cumbrousness** *n.*

cumbrance (ˈkʌmbrəns) *n.* 1. a burden, obstacle, or hindrance. 2. trouble or bother.

cumin *or* **cummin** (ˈkʌmɪn) *n.* 1. an umbelliferous Mediterranean plant with small white or pink flowers. 2. the aromatic seeds (collectively) of this plant, used as a condiment and a flavouring. [C12: < OF, < L *cumīnum*, < Gk *kuminon*, of Semitic origin]

cummerbund (ˈkʌməˌbʌnd) *n.* a wide sash, worn with a dinner jacket. [C17: < Hindi *kamarband*, < Persian, < *kamar* loins, waist + *band* band]

cumquat (ˈkʌmkwɒt) *n.* a variant spelling of **kumquat.**

cumulate *vb.* (ˈkjuːmjʊˌleɪt). 1. to accumulate. 2. (*tr.*) to combine (two or more sequences) into one. ~*adj.* (ˈkjuːmjʊlɪt). 3. heaped up. [C16: < L *cumulāre* < *cumulus* heap] —ˌ**cumuˈlation** *n.*

cumulative (ˈkjuːmjʊlətɪv) *adj.* 1. growing in quantity, strength, or effect by successive additions. 2. (of dividends or interest) intended to be accumulated. 3. *Statistics.* a. (of a frequency) including all values of a variable either below or above a specified value. b. (of error) tending to increase as the sample size is increased. —ˈ**cumulatively** *adv.* —ˈ**cumulativeness** *n.*

cumulonimbus (ˌkjuːmjʊləʊˈnɪmbəs) *n., pl.* **-bi** (-baɪ) *or* **-buses.** *Meteorol.* a cumulus cloud of great vertical extent, the bottom being dark-coloured, indicating rain or hail.

cumulus (ˈkjuːmjʊləs) *n., pl.* **-li** (-ˌlaɪ). a bulbous or billowing white or dark grey cloud. [C17: < L: mass] —ˈ**cumulous** *adj.*

cuneate (ˈkjuːnɪɪt, -ˌeɪt) *adj.* wedge-shaped. [C19: < L *cuneāre* to make wedge-shaped, < *cuneus* a wedge] —ˈ**cuneately** *adv.* —ˈ**cuneal** *adj.*

cuneiform (ˈkjuːnɪˌfɔːm) *adj.* **1.** Also: **cuneal.** wedge-shaped. **2.** of, relating to, or denoting the wedge-shaped characters in several ancient languages of Mesopotamia and Persia. **3.** of or relating to a tablet in which this script is employed. ~*n.* **4.** cuneiform characters. [C17: prob. < OF *cunéiforme,* < L *cuneus* wedge]

cunjevoi (ˈkʌndʒɪˌvɔɪ) *n. Austral.* **1.** an arum of tropical Asia and Australia, cultivated for its edible rhizome. **2.** a sea squirt. Often shortened to **cunjie, cunjy.** [C19: < Abor.]

cunnilingus (ˌkʌnɪˈlɪŋgəs) *or* **cunnilinctus** (ˌkʌnɪˈlɪŋktəs) *n.* a sexual activity in which the female genitalia are stimulated by the partner's lips and tongue. Cf. **fellatio.** [C19: < NL, < L *cunnus* vulva + *lingere* to lick]

cunning (ˈkʌnɪŋ) *adj.* **1.** crafty and shrewd, esp. in deception. **2.** made with or showing skill; ingenious. ~*n.* **3.** craftiness, esp. in deceiving. **4.** skill or ingenuity. [OE *cunnende;* rel. to *cunnan* to know (see CAN[1])] —ˈ**cunningly** *adv.* —ˈ**cunningness** *n.*

cunt (kʌnt) *n. Taboo.* **1.** the female genitals. **2.** *Offens. sl.* a woman considered sexually. **3.** *Offens. sl.* a mean or obnoxious person. [C13: of Gmc origin; rel. to ON *kunta,* MLow G *kunte*]

cup (kʌp) *n.* **1.** a small open container, usually having one handle, used for drinking from. **2.** the contents of such a container. **3.** Also called: **teacup, cupful.** a unit of capacity used in cooking. **4.** something resembling a cup. **5.** either of two cup-shaped parts of a brassiere. **6.** a cup-shaped trophy awarded as a prize. **7.** *Brit.* **a.** a sporting contest in which a cup is awarded to the winner. **b.** (*as modifier*): *a cup competition.* **8.** a mixed drink with one ingredient as a base: *claret cup.* **9.** *Golf.* the hole or metal container in the hole on a green. **10.** the chalice or the consecrated wine used in the Eucharist. **11.** one's lot in life. **12. in one's cups.** drunk. **13. one's cup of tea.** *Inf.* one's chosen or preferred thing, task, company, etc. ~*vb.* **cupping, cupped.** (*tr.*) **14.** to form (something, such as the hands) into the shape of a cup. **15.** to put into or as if into a cup. **16.** to draw blood to the surface of the body of (a person) by cupping. [OE *cuppe,* < LL *cuppa* cup, alteration of L *cūpa* cask]

cupbearer (ˈkʌpˌbɛərə) *n.* an attendant who fills and serves wine cups, as in a royal household.

cupboard (ˈkʌbəd) *n.* a piece of furniture or a recessed area of a room, with a door concealing storage space.

cupboard love *n.* a show of love inspired only by some selfish or greedy motive.

cupcake (ˈkʌpˌkeɪk) *n.* a small cake baked in a cup-shaped foil or paper case.

cupel (ˈkjuːpᵊl, kjʊˈpɛl) *n.* **1.** a refractory pot in which gold or silver is refined. **2.** a small bowl in which gold and silver are recovered during assaying. ~*vb.* **-pelling, -pelled** *or U.S.* **-peling, -peled.** **3.** (*tr.*) to refine (gold or silver) using a cupel. [C17: < F *coupelle,* dim. of *coupe* CUP] —ˌ**cupelˈlation** *n.*

Cup Final *n.* **1.** (often preceded by *the*) the annual final of the FA or Scottish Cup soccer competition. **2.** (*often not cap.*) the final of any cup competition.

Cupid (ˈkjuːpɪd) *n.* **1.** the Roman god of love, represented as a winged boy with a bow and arrow. Greek counterpart: **Eros.** **2.** (*not cap.*) any similar figure. [C14: < L *Cupīdō,* < *cupīdō* desire, < *cupidus* desirous; see CUPIDITY]

cupidity (kjuːˈpɪdɪtɪ) *n.* strong desire, esp. for wealth; greed. [C15: < L *cupiditās,* < *cupidus* eagerly desiring, < *cupere* to long for]

cupola (ˈkjuːpələ) *n.* **1.** a roof or ceiling in the form of a dome. **2.** a small structure, usually domed, on the top of a roof or dome. **3.** a protective dome for a gun on a warship. **4.** a furnace in which metals are remelted. [C16: < It., < LL *cūpula* a small cask, < L *cūpa* tub] —ˈ**cupoˌlated** *adj.*

cuppa *or* **cupper** (ˈkʌpə) *n. Brit. inf.* a cup of tea.

cupping (ˈkʌpɪŋ) *n. Med.* formerly, the use of an evacuated glass cup to draw blood to the surface of the skin for blood-letting.

cupreous (ˈkjuːprɪəs) *adj.* **1.** of, containing, or resembling copper. **2.** of the colour of copper. [C17: < LL *cupreus,* < *cuprum* COPPER[1]]

cupressus (kəˈprɛsəs) *n.* any evergreen tree of the genus *Cupressus.*

cupric (ˈkjuːprɪk) *adj.* of or containing copper in the divalent state. [C18: < LL *cuprum* copper]

cupriferous (kjuːˈprɪfərəs) *adj.* (of a substance such as an ore) containing or yielding copper.

cupro-, cupri-, *or before a vowel* **cupr-** *combining form.* indicating copper. [< L *cuprum*]

cupronickel (ˌkjuːprəʊˈnɪkᵊl) *n.* any copper alloy containing up to 40 per cent nickel.

cuprous (ˈkjuːprəs) *adj.* of or containing copper in the monovalent state.

cup tie *n. Sport.* an eliminating match or round between two teams in a cup competition.

cupule (ˈkjuːpjuːl) *n. Biol.* a cup-shaped part or structure. [C19: < LL *cūpula;* see CUPOLA]

cur (kɜː) *n.* **1.** any vicious dog, esp. a mongrel. **2.** a despicable or cowardly person. [C13: < *kurdogge;* prob. rel. to ON *kurra* to growl]

curable (ˈkjʊərəbᵊl) *adj.* capable of being cured. —ˌ**curaˈbility** *or* ˈ**curableness** *n.*

curaçao (ˌkjʊərəˈsəʊ) *n.* an orange-flavoured liqueur originally made in Curaçao, a Caribbean island.

curacy (ˈkjʊərəsɪ) *n., pl.* **-cies.** the office or position of a curate.

curare *or* **curari** (kjʊˈrɑːrɪ) *n.* **1.** black resin obtained from certain tropical South American trees, which causes muscular paralysis: used medicinally as a muscle relaxant and by South American Indians as an arrow poison. **2.** any of various trees from which this resin is obtained. [C18: < Port. & Sp., < Carib *kurari*]

curassow (ˈkjʊərəˌsəʊ) *n.* any of various ground-nesting birds of S North, Central, and South America, having long legs and tail and a crest of curled feathers. [C17: anglicized < *Curaçao,* the Caribbean island]

curate (ˈkjʊərɪt) *n.* a clergyman appointed to assist a parish priest. [C14: < Med. L *cūrātus,* < *cūra* spiritual oversight, CURE]

curate's egg *n.* something that is bad but may be euphemistically described as being only partly so. [C20: simile from a cartoon in *Punch* (Nov., 1895) in which a timid curate, who has been served a bad egg while dining with his bishop, says that parts of the egg are excellent]

curative (ˈkjʊərətɪv) *adj.* **1.** able or tending to cure. ~*n.* **2.** anything able to heal or cure. —ˈ**curatively** *adv.* —ˈ**curativeness** *n.*

curator (kjʊəˈreɪtə) *n.* the administrative head of a museum, art gallery, etc. [C14: < L: one who cares, < *cūrāre* to care for, < *cūra* care] —**curatorial** (ˌkjʊərəˈtɔːrɪəl) *adj.* —**cuˈratorˌship** *n.*

curb (kɜːb) *n.* **1.** something that restrains or holds back. **2.** any enclosing framework, such as a wall around the top of a well. **3.** Also called: **curb bit.** a horse's bit with an attached chain or strap, which checks the horse. ~*vb.* (*tr.*) **4.** to control with or as if with a curb; restrain. ~See also **kerb.** [C15: < OF *courbe* curved piece of wood or metal, < L *curvus* curved]

curcuma (ˈkɜːkjʊmə) *n.* any tropical Asian tuberous plant of the genus *Curcuma,* such as *C. longa,* which is the source of turmeric. [C17: < NL, < Ar. *kurkum* turmeric]

curd (kɜːd) *n.* **1.** (*often pl.*) a substance formed from the coagulation of milk, used in making cheese or eaten as a food. **2.** something similar in consistency. ~*vb.* **3.** to turn into or become curd. [C15: < earlier *crud,* <?] —ˈ**curdy** *adj.*

curdle (ˈkɜːdᵊl) *vb.* **1.** to turn or cause to turn into curd. **2. curdle someone's blood.** to fill someone with fear. [C16 (*crudled*, p.p.): < CURD]

cure (kjʊə) *vb.* **1.** (*tr.*) to get rid of (an ailment or problem); heal. **2.** (*tr.*) to restore to health or good condition. **3.** (*intr.*) to bring about a cure. **4.** (*tr.*) to preserve (meat, fish, etc.) by salting, smoking, etc. **5.** (*tr.*) **a.** to treat or finish (a substance) by chemical or physical means. **b.** to vulcanize (rubber). **6.** (*tr.*) to assist the hardening of (concrete, mortar, etc.) by keeping it moist. ~*n.* **7.** a return to health. **8.** any course of medical therapy, esp. one proved effective. **9.** a means of restoring health or improving a situation, etc. **10.** the spiritual and pastoral charge of a parish. **11.** a process or method of preserving meat, fish, etc. [(n.) C13: < OF, < L *cūra* care; in ecclesiastical sense, < Med. L *cūra* spiritual charge; (vb.) C14: < OF *curer*, < L *cūrāre* to attend to, heal, < *cūra* care] —**'cureless** *adj.* —**'curer** *n.*

curé ('kjʊəreɪ) *n.* a parish priest in France. [F, < Med. L *cūrātus*; see CURATE]

cure-all *n.* something reputed to cure all ailments.

curet *or* **curette** (kjʊə'rɛt) *n.* **1.** a surgical instrument for removing dead tissue, growths, etc., from the walls of body cavities. ~*vb.* **-retting, -retted.** **2.** (*tr.*) to scrape or clean with such an instrument. [C18: < F *curette*, < *curer* to heal, make clean; see CURE]

curettage (ˌkjʊərɪ'tɑːʒ, kjʊə'rɛtɪdʒ) *or* **curettement** (kjʊə'rɛtmənt) *n.* the process of using a curet. See also **D and C.**

curfew ('kɜːfjuː) *n.* **1.** an official regulation setting restrictions on movement, esp. after a specific time at night. **2.** the time set as a deadline by such a regulation. **3.** (in medieval Europe) **a.** the ringing of a bell to prompt people to extinguish fires and lights. **b.** the time at which the curfew bell was rung. **c.** the bell itself. [C13: < OF *cuevrefeu*, lit.: cover the fire]

curia ('kjʊərɪə) *n., pl.* **-riae** (-rɪˌiː). **1.** (*sometimes cap.*) the papal court and government of the Roman Catholic Church. **2.** (in the Middle Ages) a court held in the king's name. [C16: < L, < OL *coviria* (unattested), < CO- + *vir* man] —**'curial** *adj.*

curie ('kjʊərɪ, -riː) *n.* a unit of radioactivity equal to 3.7×10^{10} disintegrations per second. [C20: after Marie *Curie* (1867–1934) & her husband Pierre (1859–1906), F physicists & chemists]

curio ('kjʊərɪˌəʊ) *n., pl.* **-rios.** a small article valued as a collector's item, esp. something unusual. [C19: shortened < CURIOSITY]

curiosity (ˌkjʊərɪ'ɒsɪtɪ) *n., pl.* **-ties.** **1.** an eager desire to know; inquisitiveness. **2.** the quality of being curious; strangeness. **3.** something strange or fascinating.

curious ('kjʊərɪəs) *adj.* **1.** eager to learn; inquisitive. **2.** overinquisitive; prying. **3.** interesting because of oddness or novelty. [C14: < L *cūriōsus* taking pains over something, < *cūra* care] —**'curiously** *adv.* —**'curiousness** *n.*

curium ('kjʊərɪəm) *n.* a silvery-white metallic transuranic element artificially produced from plutonium. Symbol: Cm; at. no.: 96; half-life of most stable isotope, ^{247}Cm: 1.6×10^7 years. [C20: NL, after Pierre & Marie *Curie*]

curl (kɜːl) *vb.* **1.** (*intr.*) (esp. of hair) to grow into curves or ringlets. **2.** (*tr.*; sometimes foll. by *up*) to twist or roll (esp. hair) into coils or ringlets. **3.** (often foll. by *up*) to become or cause to become spiral-shaped or curved. **4.** (*intr.*) to move in a curving or twisting manner. **5.** (*intr.*) to play the game of curling. **6. curl one's lip.** to show contempt, as by raising a corner of the lip. ~*n.* **7.** a curve or coil of hair. **8.** a curved or spiral shape or mark. **9.** the act of curling or state of being curled. ~See also **curl up.** [C14: prob. < MDu. *crullen* to curl]

curler ('kɜːlə) *n.* **1.** any of various pins, clasps, or rollers used to curl or wave hair. **2.** a person or thing that curls. **3.** a person who plays curling.

curlew ('kɜːljuː) *n.* any of certain large shore birds of Europe and Asia. They have a long downward-curving bill and occur in northern and arctic regions. [C14: < OF *corlieu*, ? imit.]

curlicue ('kɜːlɪˌkjuː) *n.* an intricate ornamental curl or twist. [C19: < CURLY + CUE[2]]

curling ('kɜːlɪŋ) *n.* a game played on ice, esp. in Scotland, in which heavy stones with handles (**curling stones**) are slid towards a target (**tee**).

curling tongs *pl. n.* a metal scissor-like device that is heated, so that strands of hair may be twined around it in order to form curls. Also called: **curling iron, curling irons, curling pins.**

curl up *vb.* (*adv.*) **1.** (*intr.*) to adopt a reclining position with the legs close to the body and the back rounded. **2.** to become or cause to become spiral-shaped or curved. **3.** (*intr.*) to retire to a quiet cosy setting: *to curl up with a good novel.* **4.** *Brit. inf.* to be or cause to be disgusted.

curly ('kɜːlɪ) *adj.* **curlier, curliest.** **1.** tending to curl; curling. **2.** having curls. **3.** (of timber) having waves in the grain. —**'curliness** *n.*

curmudgeon (kɜː'mʌdʒən) *n.* a surly or miserly person. [C16: <?] —**cur'mudgeonly** *adj.*

currach *or* **curragh** *Gaelic.* ('kʌrəx, 'kʌrə) *n.* a Scottish or Irish name for **coracle.** [C15: < Irish Gaelic *currach*; Cf. CORACLE]

currajong ('kʌrəˌdʒɒŋ) *n.* a variant spelling of **kurrajong.**

currant ('kʌrənt) *n.* **1.** a small dried seedless grape of the Mediterranean region. **2.** any of several mainly N temperate shrubs, esp. redcurrant and blackcurrant. **3.** the small acid fruit of any of these plants. [C16: shortened < *rayson of Corannte* raisin of Corinth]

currawong ('kʌrəˌwɒŋ) *n.* any Australian crowlike songbird of the genus *Strepera*, having black, grey, and white plumage. Also called: **bell-magpie.** [< Abor.]

currency ('kʌrənsɪ) *n., pl.* **-cies.** **1.** a metal or paper medium of exchange in current use in a particular country. **2.** general acceptance or circulation; prevalence. **3.** the period of time during which something is valid, accepted, or in force. ~*adj.* **4.** *Austral. inf.* native-born as distinct from immigrant: *a currency lad.* [C17: < Med. L *currentia*, lit.: a flowing, < L *currere* to run, flow]

current ('kʌrənt) *adj.* **1.** of the immediate present; in progress. **2.** most recent; up-to-date. **3.** commonly known, practised, or accepted. **4.** circulating and valid at present: *current coins.* ~*n.* **5.** (esp. of water or air) a steady, usually natural, flow. **6.** a mass of air, body of water, etc., that has a steady flow in a particular direction. **7.** the rate of flow of such a mass. **8.** *Physics.* **a.** a flow of electric charge through a conductor. **b.** the rate of flow of this charge. **9.** a general trend or drift: *currents of opinion.* [C13: < OF *corant*, lit.: running, < *corre* to run, < L *currere*] —**'currently** *adv.* —**'currentness** *n.*

current account *n.* a bank account that usually carries no interest and against which cheques may be drawn at any time.

curricle ('kʌrɪk°l) *n.* a two-wheeled open carriage drawn by two horses side by side. [C18: < L *curriculum* < *currus* chariot, < *currere* to run]

curriculum (kə'rɪkjʊləm) *n., pl.* **-la** (-lə) *or* **-lums.** **1.** a course of study in one subject at a school or college. **2.** a list of all the courses of study offered by a school or college. **3.** any programme or plan of activities. [C19: < L: course, < *currere* to run] —**cur'ricular** *adj.*

curriculum vitae (kə'rɪkjʊləm 'viːtaɪ, 'vaɪtiː) *n., pl.* **curricula vitae** (kə'rɪkjʊlə). an outline of a person's educational and professional history, usually prepared for job applications. [L, lit.: the course of one's life]

currish ('kɜːrɪʃ) *adj.* of or like a cur; rude or bad-tempered. —**'currishly** *adv.* —**'currishness** *n.*

curry[1] ('kʌrɪ) *n., pl.* **-ries.** **1.** a spicy dish of oriental, esp. Indian, origin that usually consists of meat or fish prepared in a hot piquant sauce. **2.** curry seasoning or sauce. **3. give someone curry.** *Austral. sl.* to assault (a person) verbally or physically. ~*vb.* **-rying, -ried.** **4.** (*tr.*) to prepare (food) with curry powder or sauce. [C16: < Tamil *kari* sauce, relish]

curry[2] (ˈkʌrɪ) *vb.* **-rying, -ried. 1.** to beat vigorously, as in order to clean. **2.** to dress and finish (leather) after it has been tanned. **3.** to groom (a horse). **4. curry favour.** to ingratiate oneself, esp. with superiors. [C13: < OF *correer* to make ready]

currycomb (ˈkʌrɪˌkəʊm) *n.* a square comb used for grooming horses.

curry powder *n.* a mixture of finely ground pungent spices, such as turmeric, cumin, coriander, ginger, etc., used in making curries.

curse (kɜːs) *n.* **1.** a profane or obscene expression of anger, disgust, surprise, etc.; oath. **2.** an appeal to a supernatural power for harm to come to a specific person, group, etc. **3.** harm resulting from an appeal to a supernatural power. **4.** something that brings or causes great trouble or harm. **5.** (preceded by *the*) *Inf.* menstruation or a menstrual period. ~*vb.* **cursing, cursed** *or* (*Arch.*) **curst. 6.** (*intr.*) to utter obscenities or oaths. **7.** (*tr.*) to abuse (someone) with obscenities or oaths. **8.** (*tr.*) to invoke supernatural powers to bring harm to (someone or something). **9.** (*tr.*) to bring harm upon. [OE *cursian* to curse, < *curs* a curse] —ˈ**curser** *n.*

cursed (ˈkɜːsɪd, kɜːst) *or* **curst** *adj.* **1.** under a curse. **2.** deserving to be cursed; detestable; hateful. —ˈ**cursedly** *adv.* —ˈ**cursedness** *n.*

cursive (ˈkɜːsɪv) *adj.* **1.** of or relating to handwriting in which letters are joined in a flowing style. **2.** *Printing.* of or relating to typefaces that resemble handwriting. ~*n.* **3.** a cursive letter or printing type. [C18: < Med. L *cursīvus* running, ult. < L *currere* to run] —ˈ**cursively** *adv.*

cursor (ˈkɜːsə) *n.* **1.** the sliding part of a measuring instrument, esp. on a slide rule. **2.** a movable point of light, etc., that identifies a specific position on a visual display unit.

cursorial (kɜːˈsɔːrɪəl) *adj. Zool.* adapted for running: *a cursorial skeleton; cursorial birds.*

cursory (ˈkɜːsərɪ) *adj.* hasty and usually superficial; quick. [C17: < LL *cursōrius* of running, < L *cursus* a course, < *currere* to run] —ˈ**cursorily** *adv.* —ˈ**cursoriness** *n.*

curst (kɜːst) *vb.* **1.** *Arch.* a past tense and past participle of **curse.** ~*adj.* **2.** a variant of **cursed.**

curt (kɜːt) *adj.* **1.** rudely blunt and brief. **2.** short or concise. [C17: < L *curtus* cut short, mutilated] —ˈ**curtly** *adv.* —ˈ**curtness** *n.*

curtail (kɜːˈteɪl) *vb.* (*tr.*) to cut short; abridge. [C16: changed (through infl. of TAIL[1]) < obs. *curtal* to dock] —**cur**ˈ**tailer** *n.* —**cur**ˈ**tailment** *n.*

curtain (ˈkɜːtᵊn) *n.* **1.** a piece of material that can be drawn across an opening or window, to shut out light or to provide privacy. **2.** a barrier to vision, access, or communication. **3.** a hanging cloth or similar barrier for concealing all or part of a theatre stage from the audience. **4.** (often preceded by *the*) the end of a scene of a play, opera, etc., marked by the fall or closing of the curtain. **5.** the rise or opening of the curtain at the start of a performance. ~*vb.* **6.** (*tr.;* sometimes foll. by *off*) to shut off or conceal as with a curtain. **7.** (*tr.*) to provide (a window, etc.) with curtains. [C13: < OF *courtine,* < LL *cortīna* enclosed place, curtain, prob. < L *cohors* courtyard]

curtain call *n.* the appearance of performers at the end of a theatrical performance to acknowledge applause.

curtain lecture *n.* a scolding or rebuke given in private, esp. by a wife to her husband. [alluding to the curtained beds where such rebukes were once given]

curtain-raiser *n.* **1.** *Theatre.* a short dramatic piece presented before the main play. **2.** any preliminary event.

curtains (ˈkɜːtᵊnz) *pl. n. Inf.* death or ruin: the end.

curtain wall *n.* a non-load-bearing external wall attached to a framed structure.

curtsy *or* **curtsey** (ˈkɜːtsɪ) *n., pl.* **-sies** *or* **-seys. 1.** a formal gesture of greeting and respect made by women, in which the knees are bent and the head slightly bowed. ~*vb.* **-sying, -sied** *or* **-seying, -seyed. 2.** (*intr.*) to make a curtsy. [C16: var. of COURTESY]

curvaceous (kɜːˈveɪʃəs) *adj. Inf.* (of a woman) having a well-rounded body.

curvature (ˈkɜːvətʃə) *n.* **1.** something curved or a curved part of a thing. **2.** any curving of a bodily part. **3.** the act of curving or the state or degree of being curved or bent.

curve (kɜːv) *n.* **1.** a continuously bending line that has no straight parts. **2.** something that curves or is curved. **3.** the act or extent of curving; curvature. **4.** *Maths.* a system of points whose coordinates satisfy a given equation. **5.** a line representing data on a graph. ~*vb.* **6.** to take or cause to take the shape or path of a curve; bend. [C15: < L *curvāre* to bend, < *curvus* crooked] —ˈ**curvedness** *n.* —ˈ**curvy** *adj.*

curvet (kɜːˈvɛt) *n.* **1.** *Dressage.* a low leap with all four feet off the ground. ~*vb.* **-vetting, -vetted** *or* **-veting, -veted. 2.** *Dressage.* to make or cause to make such a leap. **3.** (*intr.*) to prance or frisk about. [C16: < OIt. *corvetta,* < OF *courbette,* < *courber* to bend, < L *curvāre*]

curvilinear (ˌkɜːvɪˈlɪnɪə) *or* **curvilineal** *adj.* consisting of, bounded by, or characterized by a curved line.

cuscus (ˈkʌskʌs) *n., pl.* **-cuses.** any of several large nocturnal phalangers of N Australia, New Guinea, and adjacent islands, having dense fur, prehensile tails, large eyes, and a yellow nose. [C17: NL, prob. < a native name in New Guinea]

cusec (ˈkjuːsɛk) *n.* a unit of flow equal to 1 cubic foot per second. [C20: < *cu*(*bic foot per*) *sec*(*ond*)]

cushat (ˈkʌʃət) *n.* another name for **wood pigeon.** [OE *cūscote;* ? rel. to *sceōtan* to shoot]

cushion (ˈkʊʃən) *n.* **1.** a bag filled with a yielding substance, used for sitting on, leaning against, etc. **2.** something resembling a cushion in function or appearance, esp. one to support or pad or to absorb shock. **3.** the resilient felt-covered rim of a billiard table. ~*vb.* (*tr.*) **4.** to place on or as on a cushion. **5.** to provide with cushions. **6.** to protect. **7.** to lessen or suppress the effects of. **8.** to provide with a means of absorbing shock. [C14: < OF *coussin,* < Vulgar L *coxīnus* (unattested) hip-pillow, < L *coxa* hip] —ˈ**cushiony** *adj.*

Cushitic (kʊˈʃɪtɪk) *n.* **1.** a group of languages of Somalia, Ethiopia, and adjacent regions. ~*adj.* **2.** of or relating to this group of languages.

cushy (ˈkʊʃɪ) *adj.* **cushier, cushiest.** *Inf.* easy; comfortable. [C20: < Hindi *khush* pleasant, < Persian *khōsh*]

CUSO (ˈkjuːsəʊ) *n. acronym for* Canadian University Services Overseas; an organization that sends students to work as volunteers in developing countries.

cusp (kʌsp) *n.* **1.** any of the small elevations on the grinding or chewing surface of a tooth. **2.** any of the triangular flaps of a heart valve. **3.** a point or pointed end. **4.** *Geom.* a point at which two arcs of a curve intersect and at which the two tangents are coincident. **5.** *Archit.* a carving at the meeting place of two arcs. **6.** *Astron.* either of the points of a crescent moon. **7.** *Astrol.* any division between houses or signs of the zodiac. [C16: < L *cuspis* point, pointed end] —ˈ**cuspate** *adj.*

cuspid (ˈkʌspɪd) *n.* a tooth having one point; canine tooth.

cuspidate (ˈkʌspɪˌdeɪt), **cuspidated,** *or* **cuspidal** (ˈkʌspɪdᵊl) *adj.* **1.** having a cusp or cusps. **2.** (esp. of leaves) narrowing to a point. [C17: < L *cuspidāre* to make pointed, < *cuspis* a point]

cuspidor (ˈkʌspɪˌdɔː) *n.* another name (esp. U.S.) for **spittoon.** [C18: < Port., < *cuspir* to spit, < L *conspuere,* < *spuere* to spit]

cuss (kʌs) *Inf.* ~*n.* **1.** a curse; an oath. **2.** a person or animal, esp. an annoying one. ~*vb.* **3.** another word for **curse** (senses 6, 7).

cussed (ˈkʌsɪd) *adj. Inf.* **1.** another word for

cursed. **2.** obstinate. **3.** annoying: *a cussed nuisance.* —ˈ**cussedly** *adv.* —ˈ**cussedness** *n.*

custard (ˈkʌstəd) *n.* **1.** a baked sweetened mixture of eggs and milk. **2.** a sauce made of milk and sugar thickened with cornflour. [C15: alteration of ME *crustade* kind of pie]

custard apple *n.* **1.** a West Indian tree. **2.** its large heart-shaped fruit, which has a fleshy edible pulp.

custard pie *n.* **a.** a flat, open pie filled with real or artificial custard, as thrown in slapstick comedy. **b.** (*as modifier*): *custard-pie humour.*

custodian (kʌˈstəʊdɪən) *n.* **1.** a person who has custody, as of a prisoner, ward, etc. **2.** a keeper of an art collection, etc. —**cusˈtodianˌship** *n.*

custody (ˈkʌstədɪ) *n., pl.* **-dies.** **1.** the act of keeping safe or guarding. **2.** the state of being held by the police; arrest. [C15: < L *custōdia,* < *custōs* guard, defender] —**custodial** (kʌˈstəʊdɪəl) *adj.*

custom (ˈkʌstəm) *n.* **1.** a usual or habitual practice; typical mode of behaviour. **2.** the long-established habits or traditions of a society collectively; convention. **3. a.** a practice which by long-established usage has come to have the force of law. **b.** such practices collectively (esp. in **custom and practice**). **4.** habitual patronage, esp. of a shop or business. **5.** the customers of a shop or business collectively. ~*adj.* **6.** made to the specifications of an individual customer. ~See also **customs.** [C12: < OF *costume,* < L *consuētūdō,* < *consuēscere* to grow accustomed to]

customary (ˈkʌstəmərɪ, -təmrɪ) *adj.* **1.** in accordance with custom or habitual practice; usual. **2.** *Law.* **a.** founded upon long-continued practices and usage. **b.** (of land) held by custom. ~*n., pl.* **-aries.** **3.** a statement in writing of customary laws and practices. —ˈ**customarily** *adv.* —ˈ**customariness** *n.*

custom-built *adj.* (of cars, houses, etc.) made according to the specifications of an individual buyer.

customer (ˈkʌstəmə) *n.* **1.** a person who buys. **2.** *Inf.* a person with whom one has dealings.

custom house *n.* a government office, esp. at a port, where customs are collected and ships cleared for entry.

customize *or* **-ise** (ˈkʌstəˌmaɪz) *vb.* (*tr.*) to make (something) according to a customer's individual requirements.

custom-made *adj.* (of suits, dresses, etc.) made according to the specifications of an individual buyer.

customs (ˈkʌstəmz) *n.* (*functioning as sing. or pl.*) **1.** duty on imports or exports. **2.** the government department responsible for the collection of these duties. **3.** the part of a port, airport, etc., where baggage and freight are examined for dutiable goods and contraband.

cut (kʌt) *vb.* **cutting, cut.** **1.** to open up or incise (a person or thing) with a sharp edge or instrument. **2.** (of a sharp instrument) to penetrate or incise (a person or thing). **3.** to divide or be divided with or as if with a sharp instrument. **4.** (*intr.*) to use an instrument that cuts. **5.** (*tr.*) to trim or prune by or as if by clipping. **6.** (*tr.*) to reap or mow (a crop, grass, etc.). **7.** (*tr.; sometimes* foll. by *out*) to make, form, or shape by cutting. **8.** (*tr.*) to hollow or dig out; excavate. **9.** to strike (an object) sharply. **10.** *Cricket.* to hit (the ball) to the off side with a roughly horizontal bat. **11.** to hurt the feelings of (a person). **12.** (*tr.*) *Inf.* to refuse to recognize; snub. **13.** (*tr.*) *Inf.* to absent oneself from, esp. without permission or in haste: *to cut a class.* **14.** (*tr.*) to abridge or shorten. **15.** (*tr.; often* foll. by *down*) to lower, reduce, or curtail. **16.** (*tr.*) to dilute or weaken: *to cut whisky with water.* **17.** (*tr.*) to dissolve or break up: *to cut fat.* **18.** (when *intr.,* foll. by *across* or *through*) to cross or traverse. **19.** (*intr.*) to make a sharp or sudden change in direction; veer. **20.** to grow (teeth) through the gums or (of teeth) to appear through the gums. **21.** (*intr.*) *Films.* **a.** to call a halt to a shooting sequence. **b.** (foll. by *to*) to move quickly to another scene. **22.** *Films.* to edit (film). **23.** to switch off (a light, car engine, etc.). **24.** (*tr.*) to make (a record or tape of a song, performance, etc.). **25.** *Cards.* **a.** to divide (the pack) at random into two parts after shuffling. **b.** (*intr.*) to pick cards from a spread pack to decide dealer, partners, etc. **26.** (*tr.*) (of a tool) to bite into (an object). **27. cut a dash.** to make a stylish impression. **28. cut (a person) dead.** *Inf.* to ignore (a person) completely. **29. cut a (good, poor,** etc.) **figure.** to appear or behave in a specified manner. **30. cut and run.** *Inf.* to make a rapid escape. **31. cut both ways. a.** to have both good and bad effects. **b.** to affect both sides, as two parties in an argument, etc. **32. cut it fine.** *Inf.* to allow little margin of time, space etc. **33. cut loose.** to free or become freed from restraint, custody, anchorage, etc. **34. cut no ice.** *Inf.* to fail to make an impression. **35. cut one's teeth on.** *Inf.* **a.** to use at an early age or stage. **b.** to practise on. ~*adj.* **36.** detached, divided, or separated by cutting. **37.** made, shaped, or fashioned by cutting. **38.** reduced or diminished as by cutting: *cut prices.* **39.** weakened or diluted. **40.** *Brit.* a slang word for **drunk:** *half cut.* **41. cut and dried.** *Inf.* settled or arranged in advance. ~*n.* **42.** the act of cutting. **43.** a stroke or incision made by cutting; gash. **44.** a piece or part cut off: *a cut of meat.* **45.** the edge of anything cut or sliced. **46.** a passage, channel, path, etc., cut or hollowed out. **47.** an omission or deletion, esp. in a text, film, or play. **48.** a reduction in price, salary, etc. **49.** a decrease in government finance in a particular department or area. **50.** *Inf.* a portion or share. **51.** *Inf.* a straw, slip of paper, etc., used in drawing lots. **52.** the manner or style in which a thing, esp. a garment, is cut. **53.** a direct route; short cut. **54.** the U.S. name for **block** (sense 13). **55.** *Cricket.* a stroke made with the bat in a roughly horizontal position. **56.** *Films.* an immediate transition from one shot to the next. **57.** words or an action that hurt another person's feelings. **58.** a refusal to recognize an acquaintance; snub. **59.** *Brit.* a stretch of water, esp. a canal. **60. a cut above.** *Inf.* superior to; better than. ~See also **cut across, cutback,** etc. [C13: prob. < ON]

cut across *vb.* (*intr., prep.*) **1.** to be contrary to ordinary procedure or limitations. **2.** to cross or traverse, making a shorter route.

cutaneous (kjuːˈteɪnɪəs) *adj.* of or relating to the skin. [C16: < NL *cutāneus,* < L *cutis* skin]

cutaway (ˈkʌtəˌweɪ) *n.* **1.** a man's coat cut diagonally from the front waist to the back of the knees. **2. a.** a drawing or model of a machine, engine, etc., in which part of the casing is omitted to reveal the workings. **b.** (*as modifier*): *a cutaway model.* **3.** *Films, television.* a shot separate from the main action of a scene.

cutback (ˈkʌtˌbæk) *n.* **1.** a decrease or reduction. ~*vb.* **cut back** (*adv.*) **2.** (*tr.*) to shorten by cutting off the end; prune. **3.** (when *intr.,* foll. by *on*) to reduce or make a reduction (in).

cut down *vb.* (*adv.*) **1.** (*tr.*) to fell. **2.** (when *intr.,* often foll. by *on*) to reduce or make a reduction (in). **3.** (*tr.*) to remake (an old garment) in order to make a smaller one. **4.** (*tr.*) to kill. **5. cut (a person) down to size.** to reduce in importance or decrease the conceit of (a person).

cute (kjuːt) *adj.* **1.** appealing or attractive, esp. in a pretty way. **2.** *Inf., chiefly U.S. & Canad.* affecting cleverness or prettiness. **3.** clever; shrewd. [C18 (in the sense: clever): shortened < ACUTE] —ˈ**cutely** *adv.* —ˈ**cuteness** *n.*

cut glass *n.* **1. a.** glass, esp. bowls, vases, etc., decorated by facet-cutting or grinding. **b.** (*as modifier*): *a cut-glass vase.* **2.** (*modifier*) (of an accent) upper-class; refined.

cuticle (ˈkjuːtɪkᵊl) *n.* **1.** dead skin, esp. round the base of a fingernail or toenail. **2.** another name for **epidermis.** **3.** the protective layer that covers the epidermis of higher plants. **4.** the protective layer covering the epidermis of many invertebrates. [C17: < L *cutīcula* dim. of *cutis* skin] **—cuticular** (kjuːˈtɪkjʊlə) *adj.*

cut in *vb.* (*adv.*) **1.** (*intr.;* often foll. by *on*) Also: **cut into.** to break in or interrupt. **2.** (*intr.*) to interrupt a dancing couple to dance with one of them. **3.** (*intr.*) (of a driver, motor vehicle, etc.) to draw in front of another vehicle leaving too little space. **4.** (*tr.*) *Inf.* to allow to have a share. **5.** (*intr.*) to take the place of a person in a card game.

cutis (ˈkjuːtɪs) *n., pl.* **-tes** (-tiːz) *or* **-tises.** *Anat.* a technical name for the **skin.** [C17: < L: skin]

cutlass (ˈkʌtləs) *n.* a curved, one-edged sword formerly used by sailors. [C16: < F *coutelas,* < *coutel* knife, ult. < L *culter* knife]

cutler (ˈkʌtlə) *n.* a person who makes or sells cutlery. [C14: < F *coutelier,* ult. < L *culter* knife]

cutlery (ˈkʌtlərɪ) *n.* **1.** implements used for eating, such as knives, forks, and spoons. **2.** instruments used for cutting. **3.** the art or business of a cutler.

cutlet (ˈkʌtlɪt) *n.* **1.** a piece of meat taken esp. from the best end of neck of lamb, pork, etc. **2.** a flat croquette of minced chicken, lobster, etc. [C18: < OF *costelette,* lit.: a little rib, < *coste* rib, < L *costa*]

cut off *vb.* (*tr., adv.*) **1.** to remove by cutting. **2.** to intercept or interrupt something, esp. a telephone conversation. **3.** to discontinue the supply of. **4.** to bring to an end. **5.** to deprive of rights; disinherit: *cut off without a penny.* **6.** to sever or separate. **7.** to occupy a position so as to prevent or obstruct (a retreat or escape). *~n.* **cutoff.** **8. a.** the act of cutting off; limit or termination. **b.** (*as modifier*): *the cutoff point.* **9.** *Chiefly U.S.* a short cut. **10.** a device to terminate the flow of a fluid in a pipe or duct.

cut out *vb.* (*adv.*) **1.** (*tr.*) to delete or remove. **2.** (*tr.*) to shape or form by cutting. **3.** (*tr.; usually passive*) to suit or equip for: *you're not cut out for this job.* **4.** (*intr.*) (of an engine, etc.) to cease to operate suddenly. **5.** (*intr.*) (of an electrical device) to switch off, usually automatically. **6.** (*tr.*) *Inf.* to oust and supplant (a rival). **7.** (*intr.*) (of a person) to be excluded from a card game. **8.** (*tr.*) *Inf.* to cease doing something, esp. something undesirable (esp. in **cut it out**). **9.** (*tr.*) *Soccer.* to intercept (a pass). **10.** (*tr.*) to separate (cattle) from a herd. **11.** (*intr.*) *Austral.* to end or finish: *the road cuts out at the creek.* **12. have one's work cut out.** to have as much work as one can manage. *~n.* **cutout.** **13.** something that has been or is intended to be cut out from something else. **14.** a device that switches off or interrupts an electric circuit, esp. as a safety device. **15.** *Austral. sl.* the end of shearing.

cut-price *or esp. U.S.* **cut-rate** *adj.* **1.** available at prices or rates below the standard price or rate. **2.** (*prenominal*) offering goods or services at prices below the standard price.

cutpurse (ˈkʌtˌpɜːs) *n.* an archaic word for **pickpocket.**

cutter (ˈkʌtə) *n.* **1.** a person or thing that cuts, esp. a person who cuts cloth for clothing. **2.** a sailing boat with its mast stepped further aft than that of a sloop. **3.** a ship's boat, powered by oars or sail, for carrying passengers or light cargo. **4.** a small lightly armed boat, as used in the enforcement of customs regulations.

cutthroat (ˈkʌtˌθrəʊt) *n.* **1.** a person who cuts throats; murderer. **2.** Also called: **cutthroat razor.** *Brit.* a razor with a long blade that usually folds into the handle. *~adj.* **3.** bloodthirsty or murderous; cruel. **4.** fierce or relentless in competition: *cutthroat prices.* **5.** (of some games) played by three people: *cutthroat poker.*

cutting (ˈkʌtɪŋ) *n.* **1.** a piece cut off from something. **2.** *Horticulture.* **a.** a method of propagation in which a part of a plant is induced to form its own roots. **b.** a part separated for this purpose. **3.** Also called (esp. U.S. and Canad.): **clipping.** an article, photograph, etc., cut from a publication. **4.** the editing process of a film. **5.** an excavation in a piece of high land for a road, railway, etc. **6.** (*modifier*) designed for or adapted to cutting; sharp: *a cutting tool.* *~adj.* **7.** keen; piercing. **8.** tending to hurt the feelings: *a cutting remark.* **—ˈcuttingly** *adv.*

cuttlebone (ˈkʌtᵊlˌbəʊn) *n.* the internal calcareous shell of the cuttlefish, used as a mineral supplement to the diet of cagebirds and as a polishing agent. [C16: OE *cudele* + BONE]

cuttlefish (ˈkʌtᵊlˌfɪʃ) *n., pl.* **-fish** *or* **-fishes.** a cephalopod mollusc which occurs near the bottom of inshore waters and has a broad flattened body. Sometimes shortened to **cuttle.**

cut up *vb.* (*tr., adv.*) **1.** to cut into pieces. **2.** to inflict injuries on. **3.** (*usually passive*) *Inf.* to affect the feelings of deeply. **4.** *Inf.* to subject to severe criticism. **5. cut up rough.** *Brit. inf.* to become angry or bad-tempered.

cutwater (ˈkʌtˌwɔːtə) *n.* the forward part of the stem of a vessel, which cuts through the water.

cutworm (ˈkʌtˌwɜːm) *n.* the caterpillar of various noctuid moths, which is a pest of young crop plants in North America.

cuvée (kuːˈveɪ) *n.* an individual batch or blend of wine. [C19: < F, lit.: put in a cask, < *cuve* cask]

CV *abbrev. for* curriculum vitae.

Cwlth *abbrev. for* Commonwealth.

cwm (kuːm) *n.* **1.** (in Wales) a valley. **2.** *Geol.* another name for **cirque.**

c.w.o. *or* **CWO** *abbrev. for* cash with order.

CWS *abbrev. for* Cooperative Wholesale Society.

cwt *abbrev. for* hundredweight. [*c,* < the L numeral *C* one hundred (*centum*)]

-cy *suffix.* **1.** indicating state, quality, or condition: *plutocracy; lunacy.* **2.** rank or office: *captaincy.* [via OF < L *-cia, -tia,* Gk *-kia, -tia,* abstract noun suffixes]

cyan (ˈsaɪæn, ˈsaɪən) *n.* **1.** a green-blue colour. *~adj.* **2.** of this colour. [C19: < Gk *kuanos* dark blue]

cyanate (ˈsaɪəˌneɪt) *n.* any salt or ester of cyanic acid.

cyanic (saɪˈænɪk) *adj.* **1.** of or containing cyanogen. **2.** blue.

cyanic acid *n.* a colourless poisonous volatile liquid acid.

cyanide (ˈsaɪəˌnaɪd) *or* **cyanid** (ˈsaɪənɪd) *n.* any salt of hydrocyanic acid. Cyanides are extremely poisonous. **—ˌcyaniˈdation** *n.*

cyanite (ˈsaɪəˌnaɪt) *n.* a grey, green, or blue mineral consisting of aluminium silicate in crystalline form. **—cyanitic** (ˌsaɪəˈnɪtɪk) *adj.*

cyano- *or before a vowel* **cyan-** *combining form.* **1.** blue or dark blue. **2.** indicating cyanogen. **3.** indicating cyanide. [< Gk *kuanos* (adj.) dark blue, (n.) dark blue enamel, lapis lazuli]

cyanocobalamin (ˌsaɪənəʊkəʊˈbæləmɪn) *n.* vitamin B_{12}, a complex crystalline compound of cobalt and cyanide, lack of which leads to pernicious anaemia. [C20: < CYANO- + COBAL(T) + (VIT)AMIN]

cyanogen (saɪˈænədʒɪn) *n.* an extremely poisonous colourless flammable gas. [C19: < F *cyanogène;* see CYANO-, -GEN; so named because it is one of the constituents of Prussian blue]

cyanosis (ˌsaɪəˈnəʊsɪs) *n. Pathol.* a bluish-purple discoloration of skin and mucous membranes usually resulting from a deficiency of oxygen in the blood. **—cyanotic** (ˌsaɪəˈnɒtɪk) *adj.*

cybernate (ˈsaɪbəˌneɪt) *vb.* to control with a servomechanism or to be controlled by a servomechanism. [C20: < CYBER(NETICS) + -ATE[1]] **—ˌcyberˈnation** *n.*

cybernetics (ˌsaɪbəˈnɛtɪks) *n.* (*functioning as sing.*) the branch of science concerned with control systems and comparisons between man-made and biological systems. [C20: < Gk *kubernētēs* steersman, < *kubernan* to steer] **—ˌcyberˈnetic** *adj.* **—ˌcyberˈneticist** *n.*

cycad (ˈsaɪkæd) *n.* a tropical or subtropical plant, having an unbranched stem with fernlike leaves crowded at the top. [C19: < NL *Cycas* name of genus, < Gk *kukas,* scribe's error for *koïkas,* < *koïx* a kind of palm] **—ˌcycaˈdaceous** *adj.*

cyclamate (ˈsaɪkləˌmeɪt, ˈsɪkləmeɪt) *n.* any of certain compounds formerly used as food additives and sugar substitutes. [C20: *cycl(ohexylsulph)amate*]

cyclamen (ˈsɪkləmən, -ˌmɛn) *n.* **1.** any Old World plant of the genus *Cyclamen,* having white, pink, or red flowers, with reflexed petals. *~adj.* **2.** of a dark reddish-purple colour. [C16: < Med. L, < L *cyclamīnos,* < Gk *kuklaminos,* prob. < *kuklos* circle, referring to the bulblike roots]

cycle (ˈsaɪkᵊl) *n.* **1.** a recurring period of time in which certain events or phenomena occur and reach completion. **2.** a completed series of events that follows or is followed by another series of similar events occurring in the same sequence. **3.** the time taken or needed for one such series. **4.** a vast period of time; age; aeon. **5.** a group of poems or prose narratives about a central figure or event: *the Arthurian cycle.* **6.** short for **bicycle, motorcycle,** etc. **7.** a recurrent series of events or processes in plants and animals: *a life cycle.* **8.** one of a series of repeated changes in the magnitude of a periodically varying quantity, such as current or voltage. *~vb.* **9.** (*tr.*) to process through a cycle or system. **10.** (*intr.*) to move in or pass through cycles. **11.** to travel by or ride a bicycle or tricycle. [C14: < LL *cyclus,* < Gk *kuklos* cycle, circle, ring, wheel]

cyclic (ˈsaɪklɪk, ˈsɪklɪk) *or* **cyclical** *adj.* **1.** recurring or revolving in cycles. **2.** (of an organic compound) containing a closed saturated or unsaturated ring of atoms. **3.** *Bot.* **a.** arranged in whorls: *cyclic petals.* **b.** having parts arranged in this way: *cyclic flowers.* —**ˈcyclically** *adv.*

cyclist (ˈsaɪklɪst) *or U.S.* **cycler** *n.* a person who rides or travels by bicycle, motorcycle, etc.

cyclo- *or before a vowel* **cycl-** *combining form.* **1.** indicating a circle or ring: *cyclotron.* **2.** denoting a cyclic compound: *cyclopropane.* [< Gk *kuklos* CYCLE]

cycloid (ˈsaɪklɔɪd) *adj.* **1.** resembling a circle. *~n.* **2.** *Geom.* the curve described by a point on the circumference of a circle as the circle rolls along a straight line. —**cyˈcloidal** *adj.*

cyclometer (saɪˈklɒmɪtə) *n.* a device that records the number of revolutions made by a wheel and hence the distance travelled.

cyclone (ˈsaɪkləʊn) *n.* **1.** another name for **depression** (sense 6). **2.** a violent tropical storm; hurricane. *~adj.* **3.** *Austral. & N.Z.* (of fencing) made of interlaced wire and metal. [C19: < Gk *kuklōn* a turning around, < *kuklos* wheel] —**cyclonic** (saɪˈklɒnɪk) *adj.* —**cyˈclonically** *adv.*

Cyclopean (ˌsaɪkləʊˈpiːən, saɪˈkləʊpɪən) *adj.* **1.** of, relating to, or resembling the Cyclops. **2.** denoting or having the kind of masonry used in preclassical Greek architecture, characterized by large undressed blocks of stone.

cyclopedia *or* **cyclopaedia** (ˌsaɪkləʊˈpiːdɪə) *n.* a less common word for **encyclopedia.**

cyclopropane (ˌsaɪkləʊˈprəʊpeɪn) *n.* a colourless gaseous hydrocarbon, used as an anaesthetic. Formula: C_3H_6.

Cyclops (ˈsaɪklɒps) *n., pl.* **Cyclopes** (saɪˈkləʊpiːz) *or* **Cyclopses.** *Classical myth.* one of a race of giants having a single eye in the middle of the forehead. [C15: < L *Cyclōps,* < Gk *Kuklōps,* lit.: round eye, < *kuklos* circle + *ōps* eye]

cyclorama (ˌsaɪkləʊˈrɑːmə) *n.* **1.** a large picture on the interior wall of a cylindrical room, designed to appear in natural perspective to a spectator. **2.** *Theatre.* a curtain or wall curving along the back of a stage, usually painted to represent the sky. [C19: CYCLO- + Gk *horama* view, sight, on the model of *panorama*] —**cycloramic** (ˌsaɪkləʊˈræmɪk) *adj.*

cyclosporin-A (ˌsaɪkləʊˈspɔːrɪn-) *n.* a drug extracted from a fungus and used in transplant surgery to suppress the body's immune mechanisms, and so prevent rejection of an organ.

cyclostome (ˈsaɪkləˌstəʊm, ˈsɪk-) *n.* any primitive aquatic jawless vertebrate, such as the lamprey, having a round sucking mouth. —**cyclostomate** (saɪˈklɒstəmɪt, -ˌmeɪt) *or* **cyclostomatous** (ˌsaɪkləʊˈstɒmətəs, -ˈstəʊmə-, ˌsɪk-) *adj.*

cyclostyle (ˈsaɪkləˌstaɪl) *n.* **1.** a kind of pen with a small toothed wheel, used for cutting holes in a specially prepared stencil. **2.** an office duplicator using such a stencil. *~vb.* **3.** (*tr.*) to print using such a stencil. —**ˈcycloˌstyled** *adj.*

cyclothymia (ˌsaɪkləʊˈθaɪmɪə) *n. Psychiatry.* a condition characterized by alternating periods of excitement and depression. [< CYCLO- + Gk *thumos,* cast of mind + -IA] —**ˌcycloˈthymic** *adj.*

cyclotron (ˈsaɪkləˌtrɒn) *n.* a type of particle accelerator in which the particles spiral under the effect of a strong vertical magnetic field.

cyder (ˈsaɪdə) *n.* a variant spelling of **cider.**

cygnet (ˈsɪgnɪt) *n.* a young swan. [C15 *sygnett,* < OF *cygne* swan, < L *cygnus,* < Gk *kuknos*]

cylinder (ˈsɪlɪndə) *n.* **1.** a solid consisting of two parallel planes bounded by identical closed curves, usually circles, that are interconnected at every point by a set of parallel lines, usually perpendicular to the planes. **2.** a surface formed by a line moving round a closed plane curve at a fixed angle to it. **3.** any object shaped like a cylinder. **4.** the chamber in a reciprocating internal-combustion engine, pump, or compressor within which the piston moves. The cylinders are housed in the metal **cylinder block,** which is topped by the **cylinder head. 5.** the rotating mechanism of a revolver, containing cartridge chambers. **6.** *Printing.* any of the rotating drums on a printing press. **7.** Also called: **cylinder seal.** an ancient cylindrical seal found in the Middle East and Balkans. [C16: < L *cylindrus,* < Gk *kulindros* a roller, < *kulindein* to roll] —**ˈcylinder-ˌlike** *adj.*

cylindrical (sɪˈlɪndrɪkᵊl) *or* **cylindric** *adj.* of, shaped like, or characteristic of a cylinder. —**cyˌlindriˈcality** *n.* —**cyˈlindrically** *adv.*

cymbal (ˈsɪmbᵊl) *n.* a percussion instrument consisting of a thin circular piece of brass, which vibrates when clashed together with another cymbal or struck with a stick. [OE *cymbala,* < L *cymbalum,* < Gk *kumbalon,* < *kumbē* something hollow] —**ˈcymbalist** *n.*

cyme (saɪm) *n.* an inflorescence in which the first flower is the terminal bud of the main stem and subsequent flowers develop as terminal buds of lateral stems. [C18: < L *cȳma* cabbage sprout, < Gk *kuma* anything swollen] —**cymiferous** (saɪˈmɪfərəs) *adj.* —**cymose** (ˈsaɪməʊs, -məʊz, saɪˈməʊs) *adj.*

Cymric *or* **Kymric** (ˈkɪmrɪk) *n.* **1.** the Welsh language. **2.** the Brythonic group of Celtic languages. *~adj.* **3.** of or relating to the Cymry, any of their languages, Wales, or the Welsh.

Cymry *or* **Kymry** (ˈkɪmrɪ) *n.* **the.** (*functioning as pl.*) **1.** the Brythonic Celts, comprising the present-day Welsh, Cornish, and Bretons. **2.** the Welsh people. [Welsh: the Welsh]

cynic (ˈsɪnɪk) *n.* **1.** a person who believes the worst about people or the outcome of events. *~adj.* **2.** a less common word for **cynical.** [C16: via L < Gk *Kunikos,* < *kuōn* dog]

Cynic (ˈsɪnɪk) *n.* a member of an ancient Greek sect that scorned worldly things.

cynical (ˈsɪnɪkᵊl) *adj.* **1.** believing the worst of others, esp. that all acts are selfish. **2.** sarcastic; mocking. **3.** showing contempt for accepted standards, esp. of honesty or morality. —**ˈcynically** *adv.* —**ˈcynicalness** *n.*

cynicism (ˈsɪnɪˌsɪzəm) *n.* **1.** the attitude or beliefs of a cynic. **2.** a cynical action, idea, etc.

Cynicism (ˈsɪnɪˌsɪzəm) *n.* the doctrines of the Cynics.

cynosure (ˈsɪnəˌzjʊə, -ʃʊə) *n.* **1.** a person or thing that attracts notice. **2.** something that serves as a guide. [C16: < L *Cynosūra* the constellation of Ursa Minor, < Gk *Kunosoura,* < *kuōn* dog + *oura* tail]

cypher (ˈsaɪfə) *n., vb.* a variant spelling of **cipher.**

cypress (ˈsaɪprəs) *n.* **1.** any coniferous tree of a N temperate genus having dark green scalelike leaves and rounded cones. **2.** any of several similar and related trees. **3.** the wood of any of these trees. **4.** cypress branches used as a symbol of mourning. [OE *cypresse,* < L *cyparissus,* < Gk *kuparissos;* rel. to L *cupressus*]

cypress pine *n.* any coniferous tree of an Australian genus yielding valuable timber.

cyprinid (sɪˈpraɪnɪd, ˈsɪprɪnɪd) *n.* **1.** any teleost fish of the mainly freshwater family Cyprinidae, typically having toothless jaws and including the carp, tench, and dace. ~*adj.* **2.** of, relating to, or belonging to the Cyprinidae. **3.** resembling a carp; cyprinoid. [C19: < NL *Cyprīnidae,* < L *cyprīnus* carp, < Gk *kuprinos*]

cyprinoid (ˈsɪprɪˌnɔɪd, sɪˈpraɪnɔɪd) *adj.* **1.** of or relating to the Cyprinoidea, a large suborder of teleost fishes including the cyprinids, electric eels, and loaches. **2.** of, relating to, or resembling the carp. ~*n.* **3.** any fish belonging to the Cyprinoidea. [C19: < L *cyprīnus* carp]

Cypriot (ˈsɪprɪət) *or* **Cypriote** (ˈsɪprɪˌəʊt) *n.* **1.** a native or inhabitant of Cyprus, an island in the E Mediterranean. **2.** the dialect of Greek spoken in Cyprus. ~*adj.* **3.** denoting or relating to Cyprus, its inhabitants, or dialects.

cypripedium (ˌsɪprɪˈpiːdɪəm) *n.* any orchid of a genus having large flowers with an inflated pouchlike lip. See also **lady's-slipper.** [C18: < NL, < L *Cypria* the Cyprian, that is, Venus + *pēs* foot (that is, Venus' slipper)]

Cyrenaic (ˌsaɪrəˈneɪɪk, ˌsɪrə-) *adj.* **1.** of or relating to the ancient Greek city of Cyrene in N Africa. **2.** of or relating to the philosophical school founded by Aristippus in Cyrene that held pleasure to be the highest good. ~*n.* **3.** a follower of the Cyrenaic school of philosophy.

Cyrillic (sɪˈrɪlɪk) *adj.* **1.** denoting or relating to the alphabet devised supposedly by Saint Cyril, for Slavonic languages: now used primarily for Russian and Bulgarian. ~*n.* **2.** this alphabet.

cyst (sɪst) *n.* **1.** *Pathol.* any abnormal membranous sac or blister-like pouch containing fluid or semisolid material. **2.** *Anat.* any normal sac in the body. **3.** a protective membrane enclosing a cell, larva, or organism. [C18: < NL *cystis,* < Gk *kustis* pouch, bag, bladder]

-cyst *n. combining form.* indicating a bladder or sac: *otocyst.* [< Gk *kustis* bladder]

cystectomy (sɪˈstɛktəmɪ) *n., pl.* **-mies. 1.** surgical removal of the gall bladder or part of the urinary bladder. **2.** surgical removal of a cyst.

cystic (ˈsɪstɪk) *adj.* **1.** of, relating to, or resembling a cyst. **2.** having or enclosed within a cyst; encysted. **3.** relating to the gall bladder or urinary bladder.

cysticercus (ˌsɪstɪˈsɜːkəs) *n., pl.* **-ci** (-saɪ). an encysted larval form of many tapeworms, consisting of a head inverted in a fluid-filled bladder. [C19: < NL, < Gk *kustis* pouch, bladder + *kerkos* tail]

cystic fibrosis *n.* a congenital disease of the exocrine glands, usually affecting young children, characterized by chronic infection of the respiratory tract and by pancreatic insufficiency.

cystitis (sɪˈstaɪtɪs) *n.* inflammation of the urinary bladder.

cysto- *or before a vowel* **cyst-** *combining form.* indicating a cyst or bladder: *cystoscope.*

cystoid (ˈsɪstɔɪd) *adj.* **1.** resembling a cyst or bladder. ~*n.* **2.** a tissue mass that resembles a cyst but lacks an outer membrane.

cystoscope (ˈsɪstəˌskəʊp) *n.* a slender tubular medical instrument for examining the interior of the urethra and urinary bladder. —**cystoscopic** (ˌsɪstəˈskɒpɪk) *adj.* —**cystoscopy** (sɪsˈtɒskəpɪ) *n.*

-cyte *n. combining form.* indicating a cell. [< NL *-cyta,* < Gk *kutos* vessel]

cyto- *combining form.* indicating a cell: *cytoplasm.* [< Gk *kutos* vessel]

cytogenetics (ˌsaɪtəʊdʒɪˈnɛtɪks) *n.* (*functioning as sing.*) the branch of genetics that correlates the structure of chromosomes with heredity and variation. —ˌ**cytogeˈnetic** *adj.*

cytology (saɪˈtɒlədʒɪ) *n.* the study of plant and animal cells. —**cytological** (ˌsaɪtəˈlɒdʒɪkᵊl) *adj.* —ˌ**cytoˈlogically** *adv.* —**cyˈtologist** *n.*

cytoplasm (ˈsaɪtəʊˌplæzəm) *n.* the protoplasm of a cell excluding the nucleus. —ˌ**cytoˈplasmic** *adj.*

cytosine (ˈsaɪtəsɪn) *n.* a white crystalline base occurring in nucleic acids. [C19: < CYTO- + -OSE[2] + -INE[2]]

cytotoxin (ˌsaɪtəʊˈtɒksɪn) *n.* any substance that is poisonous to living cells.

czar (zɑː) *n.* a variant spelling (esp. U.S.) of **tsar.** —**ˈczardom** *n.* —**ˈCzarevitch, czaˈrevna, czaˈrina, ˈczarism, ˈczarist:** see **ts-** spellings.

czardas (ˈtʃɑːdæʃ) *n.* **1.** a Hungarian national dance of alternating slow and fast sections. **2.** music for this dance. [< Hungarian *csárdás*]

Czech (tʃɛk) *adj.* **1.** of, relating to, or characteristic of Bohemia, Moravia, and, loosely, of Czechoslovakia, a republic of central Europe, of which Bohemia and Moravia (with Slovakia) are constituent parts, or their people or language. ~*n.* **2.** one of the two official languages of Czechoslovakia. Czech and Slovak are closely related and mutually intelligible. **3. a.** a native or inhabitant of Bohemia or Moravia. **b.** (loosely) a native or inhabitant of Czechoslovakia. [C19: < Polish, < Czech *Čech*]

Czech. *abbrev. for:* **1.** Czechoslovak. **2.** Czechoslovakia. **3.** Czechoslovakian.

Czechoslovak (ˌtʃɛkəʊˈsləʊvæk) *or* **Czechoslovakian** (ˌtʃɛkəʊsləʊˈvækɪən) *adj.* **1.** of or relating to Czechoslovakia, its peoples, or languages. ~*n.* **2.** (loosely) either of the two languages of Czechoslovakia: Czech or Slovak.

D

d *or* **D** (diː) *n., pl.* **d's, D's,** *or* **Ds.** **1.** the fourth letter of the modern English alphabet. **2.** a speech sound represented by this letter.

d *symbol for Physics.* density.

D *symbol for:* **1.** *Music.* **a.** the second note of the scale of C major. **b.** the major or minor key having this note as its tonic. **2.** *Chem.* deuterium. ~ **3.** *the Roman numeral for* 500.

d. *abbrev. for:* **1.** date. **2.** daughter. **3.** degree. **4.** delete. **5.** *Brit. currency before decimalization.* penny *or* pennies. [L *denarius* or *denarii*] **6.** depart(s). **7.** diameter. **8.** died.

D. *abbrev. for:* **1.** *U.S.* Democrat(ic). **2.** Department. **3.** Deus. [L: God] **4.** *Optics.* diopter. **5.** Director. **6.** Dominus. [L: Lord] **7.** Dutch.

'd *contraction for* would *or* had: *I'd; you'd.*

DA (in the U.S.) *abbrev. for* District Attorney.

dab[1] (dæb) *vb.* **dabbing, dabbed.** **1.** to touch or pat lightly and quickly. **2.** (*tr.*) to daub with short tapping strokes: *to dab the wall with paint.* **3.** (*tr.*) to apply (paint, cream, etc.) with short tapping strokes. ~*n.* **4.** a small amount, esp. of something soft or moist. **5.** a light stroke or tap, as with the hand. **6.** (*often pl.*) *Chiefly Brit.* a slang word for **fingerprint.** [C14: imit.] —**'dabber** *n.*

dab[2] (dæb) *n.* **1.** a small common European flatfish covered with rough toothed scales. **2.** any of various other small flatfish. [C15: < Anglo-F *dabbe,* <?]

dabble ('dæbᵊl) *vb.* **1.** to dip, move, or splash (the fingers, feet, etc.) in a liquid. **2.** (*intr.;* usually foll. by *in, with,* or *at*) to deal (with) or work (at) frivolously or superficially. **3.** (*tr.*) to splash or smear. [C16: prob. < Du. *dabbelen*] —**'dabbler** *n.*

dabchick ('dæbˌtʃɪk) *n.* any of several small grebes. [C16: prob. < OE *dop* to dive + CHICK]

dab hand *n. Brit. inf.* a person who is particularly skilled at something: *a dab hand at chess.* [? < DAB[1]]

da capo (dɑː 'kɑːpəʊ) *adj., adv. Music.* to be repeated from the beginning. [C18: < It., lit.: from the head]

dace (deɪs) *n., pl.* **dace** *or* **daces.** **1.** a European freshwater fish of the carp family. **2.** any of various similar fishes. [C15: < OF *dars* DART]

dacha *or* **datcha** ('dætʃə) *n.* a country house or cottage in Russia. [< Russian: a giving, gift]

dachshund ('dæksˌhʊnd) *n.* a long-bodied short-legged breed of dog. [C19: < G, < *Dachs* badger + *Hund* dog]

dacoit (də'kɔɪt) *n.* (in India and Burma) a member of a gang of armed robbers. [C19: < Hindi *dakait,* < *dākā* robbery]

Dacron ('deɪkrɒn, 'dæk-) *n.* the U.S. name (trademark) for **Terylene.**

dactyl ('dæktɪl) *n. Prosody.* a metrical foot of three syllables, one long followed by two short (¯˘˘). [C14: via L < Gk *daktulos* finger, comparing the finger's three joints to the three syllables]

dactylic (dæk'tɪlɪk) *adj.* **1.** of, relating to, or having a dactyl: *dactylic verse.* ~*n.* **2.** a variant of **dactyl.** —**dac'tylically** *adv.*

dad (dæd) *n.* an informal word for **father.** [C16: childish word]

Dada ('dɑːdɑː) *or* **Dadaism** ('dɑːdɑːˌɪzəm) *n.* a nihilistic artistic movement of the early 20th century, founded on principles of irrationality, incongruity, and irreverence towards accepted aesthetic criteria. [C20: < F, < children's word for hobbyhorse] —**'Dadaist** *n., adj.* —**ˌDada'istic** *adj.*

daddy ('dædɪ) *n., pl.* **-dies.** **1.** an informal word for **father.** **2. the daddy.** *Sl., chiefly U.S., Canad., & Austral.* the supreme or finest example.

daddy-longlegs *n.* **1.** *Brit.* an informal name for **crane fly.** **2.** *U.S. & Canad.* an informal name for **harvestman** (sense 2).

dado ('deɪdəʊ) *n., pl.* **-does** *or* **-dos.** **1.** the lower part of an interior wall that is decorated differently from the upper part. **2.** *Archit.* the part of a pedestal between the base and the cornice. ~*vb.* **3.** (*tr.*) to provide with a dado. [C17: < It.: die, die-shaped pedestal]

daemon ('diːmən) *or* **daimon** *n.* **1.** a demigod. **2.** the guardian spirit of a place or person. **3.** a variant spelling of **demon** (sense 3). —**daemonic** (diː'mɒnɪk) *adj.*

daff (dæf) *n. Inf.* short for **daffodil.**

daffodil ('dæfədɪl) *n.* **1.** Also called: **Lent lily.** a widely cultivated Eurasian plant, *Narcissus pseudonarcissus,* having spring-blooming yellow nodding flowers. **2.** any other plant of the genus *Narcissus.* **3. a.** a brilliant yellow colour. **b.** (*as adj.*): *daffodil paint.* **4.** a daffodil as a national emblem of Wales. [C14: < Med. L *affodillus,* var. of L *asphodelus* ASPHODEL]

daffy ('dæfɪ) *adj.* **daffier, daffiest.** *Inf.* another word for **daft** (senses 1, 2). [C19: < obs. *daff* fool]

daft (dɑːft) *adj. Chiefly Brit.* **1.** *Inf.* foolish, simple, or stupid. **2.** a slang word for **insane.** **3.** (*postpositive;* foll. by *about*) *Inf.* extremely fond (of). **4.** *Sl.* frivolous; giddy. [OE *gedæfte* gentle, foolish] —**'daftness** *n.*

daftie ('dɑːftɪ) *n. Inf.* a daft person.

dag[1] (dæg) *n.* **1.** short for **daglock.** ~*vb.* **dagging, dagged.** **2.** to cut the daglock away from (a sheep). [C18: <?] —**'dagger** *n.*

dag[2] (dæg) *n. Inf.* **1.** *Austral.* a character; eccentric. **2.** *Austral.* a person who is untidily dressed. **3.** *Austral.* a conventional person. **4.** *N.Z.* a person with a good sense of humour. [back formation < DAGGY]

dagga ('daxə, 'dɑːgə) *n.* hemp smoked as a narcotic. [C19: < Afrik., < Hottentot *dagab*]

dagger ('dægə) *n.* **1.** a short stabbing weapon with a pointed blade. **2.** Also called: **obelisk.** a character (†) used in printing to indicate a cross reference. **3. at daggers drawn.** in a state of open hostility. **4. look daggers.** to glare with hostility; scowl. [C14: <?]

daggy ('dægɪ) *adj.* **-gier, -giest.** *Austral. & N.Z. inf.* untidy; dishevelled. [< DAG[1]]

daglock ('dægˌlɒk) *n.* a dung-caked lock of wool around the hindquarters of a sheep. [C17: see DAG[1], LOCK[2]]

dago ('deɪgəʊ) *n., pl.* **-gos** *or* **-goes.** *Derog.* a foreigner, esp. a Spaniard or Portuguese. [C19: < *Diego,* a common Sp. name]

daguerreotype (də'gɛrəʊˌtaɪp) *n.* **1.** one of the earliest photographic processes, in which the image was produced on iodine-sensitized silver and developed in mercury vapour. **2.** a photograph formed by this process. [C19: after L. *Daguerre* (1789-1851), F inventor] —**da'guerreoˌtypy** *n.*

dahlia ('deɪljə) *n.* **1.** any herbaceous perennial plant of the Mexican genus *Dahlia,* having showy flowers and tuberous roots. **2.** the flower or root of any of these plants. [C19: after Anders *Dahl,* 18th-cent. Swedish botanist]

Dáil Eireann ('dɑːl 'ɛːrɪn) *or* **Dáil** *n.* (in the Republic of Ireland) the lower chamber of parliament. [< Irish *dáil* assembly + *Eireann* of Eire]

daily ('deɪlɪ) *adj.* **1.** of or occurring every day or every weekday. ~*n., pl.* **-lies.** **2.** a daily newspaper. **3.** *Brit.* a charwoman. ~*adv.* **4.** every day. **5.** constantly; often. [OE *dæglīc*]

daimon ('daɪmɒn) *n.* a variant spelling of **daemon** or **demon** (sense 3). —**dai'monic** *adj.*

daimyo *or* **daimio** ('daɪmjəʊ) *n., pl.* **-myo, -myos** *or* **-mio, -mios.** (in Japan) one of the territorial magnates who formerly dominated much of the country. [< Japanese, < Ancient Chinese *d'âi miăng* great name]

dainty ('deɪntɪ) *adj.* **-tier, -tiest.** **1.** delicate or elegant. 2. choice; delicious: *a dainty morsel.* 3. excessively genteel; fastidious. ~*n., pl.* **-ties.** 4. a choice piece of food; delicacy. [C13: < OF *deintié,* < L *dignitās* DIGNITY] —ˈ**daintily** *adv.*

daiquiri (ˈdaɪkɪrɪ, ˈdæk-) *n., pl.* **-ris.** an iced drink containing rum, lime juice, and sugar. [C20: after *Daiquiri,* town in Cuba]

dairy (ˈdɛərɪ) *n., pl.* **dairies.** 1. a company that supplies milk and milk products. 2. a room or building where milk and cream are stored or made into butter and cheese. 3. a. (*modifier*) of milk and milk products. b. (*in combination*): *a dairymaid.* 4. a general shop, selling provisions, esp. milk and milk products. [C13 *daierie,* < OE *dǣge* servant girl, one who kneads bread]

dairying (ˈdɛərɪɪŋ) *n.* the business of producing, processing, and selling dairy products.

dairyman (ˈdɛərɪmən) *n., pl.* **-men.** a man who works in a dairy.

dais (ˈdeɪɪs, deɪs) *n.* a raised platform, usually at one end of a hall, used by speakers, etc. [C13: < OF *deis,* < L *discus* DISCUS]

daisy (ˈdeɪzɪ) *n., pl.* **-sies.** 1. a small low-growing European plant having flower heads with a yellow centre and pinkish-white outer rays. 2. any of various other composite plants having conspicuous ray flowers. 3. *Sl.* an excellent person or thing. 4. **pushing up the daisies.** dead and buried. [OE *dægesēge* day's eye] —ˈ**daisied** *adj.*

daisy chain *n.* a garland made, esp. by children, by threading daisies together.

daisycutter (ˈdeɪzɪˌkʌtə) *n. Cricket.* a ball bowled so that it rolls along the ground.

daisywheel (ˈdeɪzɪˌwiːl) *n. Computers.* a component of a computer printer shaped like a wheel with many spokes that prints using a disk with characters around the circumference. Also called: **printwheel.**

daks (dæks) *pl. n. Austral. inf.* trousers. [C20: < trade name *Daks*]

dal (dɑːl) *n.* 1. split grain, a common foodstuff in India; pulse. 2. a variant spelling of **dhal.**

Dalai Lama (ˈdælaɪ ˈlɑːmə) *n.* 1. (until 1959) the chief lama and ruler of Tibet. 2. the 14th holder of this office (1940), who fled to India (1959). [< Mongolian *dalai* ocean; see LAMA]

dale (deɪl) *n.* an open valley. [OE *dæl*]

Dalek (ˈdɑːlɛk) *n.* a fictional robot-like creation that is aggressive, mobile, and produces rasping staccato speech. [C20: < a children's television series, *Dr Who*]

dalesman (ˈdeɪlzmən) *n., pl.* **-men.** a person living in a dale, esp. in the dales of N England.

dalliance (ˈdælɪəns) *n.* waste of time in frivolous action or in dawdling.

dally (ˈdælɪ) *vb.* **-lying, -lied.** (*intr.*) 1. to waste time idly; dawdle. 2. (usually foll. by *with*) to deal frivolously; trifle: *to dally with someone's affections.* [C14: < Anglo-F *dalier* to gossip, <?]

Dalmatian (dælˈmeɪʃən) *n.* 1. a large breed of dog having a short smooth white coat with black or brown spots. 2. a native or inhabitant of Dalmatia. ~*adj.* 3. of Dalmatia or its inhabitants.

dalmatic (dælˈmætɪk) *n.* a wide-sleeved tunic-like vestment open at the sides, worn by deacons and bishops, and by a king at his coronation. [C15: < LL *dalmatica* (*vestis*) Dalmatian (robe) (orig. made of Dalmatian wool)]

dal segno (ˈdæl ˈsɛnjəʊ) *adj., adv. Music.* to be repeated from the point marked with a sign to the word *fine.* [It., lit.: from the sign]

daltonism (ˈdɔːltəˌnɪzəm) *n.* colour blindness, esp. the confusion of red and green. [C19: < F *daltonisme,* after J. *Dalton* (1766-1844), E scientist]

dam[1] (dæm) *n.* 1. a barrier of concrete, earth, etc., built across a river to create a body of water. 2. a reservoir of water created by such a barrier. 3. something that resembles or functions as a dam. ~*vb.* **damming, dammed.** 4. (*tr.;* often foll. by *up*) to restrict by a dam. [C12: prob. < MLow G]

dam[2] (dæm) *n.* the female parent of an animal, esp. of domestic livestock. [C13: var. of DAME]

damage (ˈdæmɪdʒ) *n.* 1. injury or harm impairing the function or condition of a person or thing. 2. loss of something desirable. 3. *Inf.* cost; expense. ~*vb.* 4. (*tr.*) to cause damage to. 5. (*intr.*) to suffer damage. [C14: < OF, < L *damnum* injury, loss] —ˈ**damaging** *adj.*

damages (ˈdæmɪdʒɪz) *pl. n. Law.* money to be paid as compensation for injury, loss, etc.

damascene (ˈdæməˌsiːn) *vb.* 1. (*tr.*) to ornament (metal, esp. steel) by etching or by inlaying other metals, usually gold or silver. ~*n.* 2. a design or article produced by this process. ~*adj.* 3. of or relating to this process. [C14: < L *damascēnus* of Damascus]

Damascene (ˈdæməˌsiːn) *adj.* 1. of Damascus. ~*n.* 2. a native or inhabitant of Damascus.

Damascus steel (dəˈmɑːskəs) *or* **damask steel** *n. History.* a hard flexible steel with wavy markings, used for sword blades.

damask (ˈdæməsk) *n.* 1. a. a reversible fabric, usually silk or linen, with a pattern woven into it. It is used for table linen, curtains, etc. b. table linen made from this. c. (*as modifier*): *a damask tablecloth.* 2. short for **Damascus steel.** 3. the wavy markings on such steel. 4. a. the greyish-pink colour of the damask rose. b. (*as adj.*): *damask wallpaper.* ~*vb.* 5. (*tr.*) another word for **damascene.** [C14: < Med. L *damascus,* < Damascus, where fabric orig. made]

damask rose *n.* a rose with fragrant flowers, which are used to make the perfume attar. [C16: < Med. L *rosa damascēna* rose of Damascus]

dame (deɪm) *n.* 1. (formerly) a woman of rank or dignity; lady. 2. *Arch., chiefly Brit.* an elderly woman. 3. *Sl., chiefly U.S. & Canad.* a woman. 4. *Brit.* the role of a comic old woman in a pantomime, usually played by a man. [C13: < OF, < L *domina* lady, mistress of household]

Dame (deɪm) *n.* (in Britain) 1. the title of a woman who has been awarded the Order of the British Empire or any of certain other orders of chivalry. 2. the title of the wife of a knight or baronet.

dame school *n.* (formerly) a small school, offering basic education, usually run by an elderly woman in her own home.

damn (dæm) *interj.* 1. *Sl.* an exclamation of annoyance. 2. *Inf.* an exclamation of surprise or pleasure. ~*adj.* 3. (*prenominal*) *Sl.* deserving damnation. ~*adv., adj.* (*prenominal*) 4. *Sl.* (intensifier): *a damn good pianist.* ~*adv.* 5. **damn all.** *Sl.* absolutely nothing. ~*vb.* (*mainly tr.*) 6. to condemn as bad, worthless, etc. 7. to curse. 8. to condemn to eternal damnation. 9. (*often passive*) to doom to ruin. 10. (*also intr.*) to prove (someone) guilty: *damning evidence.* 11. **damn with faint praise.** to praise so unenthusiastically that the effect is condemnation. ~*n.* 12. *Sl.* something of negligible value (esp. in **not worth a damn**). 13. **not give a damn.** *Inf.* not care. [C13: < OF *dampner,* < L *damnāre,* < *damnum* loss, injury]

damnable (ˈdæmnəbᵊl) *adj.* 1. execrable; detestable. 2. liable to or deserving damnation. —ˈ**damnableness** *or* ˌ**damnaˈbility** *n.*

damnation (dæmˈneɪʃən) *n.* 1. the act of damning or state of being damned. ~*interj.* 2. an exclamation of anger, disappointment, etc.

damnatory (ˈdæmnətərɪ) *adj.* threatening or occasioning condemnation.

damned (dæmd) *adj.* 1. a. condemned to hell. b. (*as collective n.;* preceded by *the*): *the damned.* ~*adv., adj. Sl.* 2. (intensifier): *a damned good try.* 3. used to indicate amazement, disavowal, or refusal (as in **damned if I care**).

damnify (ˈdæmnɪˌfaɪ) *vb.* **-fying, -fied.** (*tr.*) *Law.* to cause loss or damage to (a person); injure. [C16: < OF *damnifier,* ult. < L *damnum* harm, + *facere* to make] —ˌ**damnifiˈcation** *n.*

damoiselle, damosel, *or* **damozel** (ˌdæməˈzɛl) *n.* archaic variants of **damsel.**

damp (dæmp) *adj.* 1. slightly wet. ~*n.* 2. slight wetness; moisture. 3. rank air or poisonous gas, esp. in a mine. 4. a discouragement; damper. ~*vb.* (*tr.*) 5. to make slightly wet. 6. (often foll. by *down*) to stifle or deaden: *to damp one's* *ardour.* **7.** (often foll. by *down*) to reduce the flow of air to (a fire) to make it burn more slowly. **8.** *Physics.* to reduce the amplitude of (an oscillation or wave). **9.** *Music.* to muffle (the sound of an instrument). [C14: < MLow G *damp* steam] —ˈ**dampness** *n.*

dampcourse (ˈdæmpˌkɔːs) *n.* a layer of impervious material in a wall, to stop moisture rising. Also called: **damp-proof course.**

dampen (ˈdæmpən) *vb.* **1.** to make or become damp. **2.** (*tr.*) to stifle; deaden. —ˈ**dampener** *n.*

damper (ˈdæmpə) *n.* **1.** a person, event, or circumstance that depresses or discourages. **2. put a damper on.** to produce a depressing or stultifying effect on. **3.** a movable plate to regulate the draught in a stove or furnace flue. **4.** a device to reduce electronic, mechanical, acoustic, or aerodynamic oscillations in a system. **5.** the pad in a piano or harpsichord that deadens the vibration of each string as its key is released. **6.** *Chiefly Austral. & N.Z.* any of various unleavened loaves and scones, typically cooked on an open fire.

damping off *n.* any of various diseases of plants caused by fungi in conditions of excessive moisture.

damsel (ˈdæmzᵊl) *n. Arch. or poetic.* a young unmarried woman; maiden. [C13: < OF *damoisele,* < Vulgar L *domnicella* (unattested) young lady, < L *domina* mistress]

damselfly (ˈdæmzᵊlˌflaɪ) *n., pl.* **-flies.** any of various insects similar to dragonflies but usually resting with the wings closed over the back.

damson (ˈdæmzən) *n.* **1.** a small tree cultivated for its blue-black edible plumlike fruit. **2.** the fruit of this tree. [C14: < L *prūnum damascēnum* Damascus plum]

dan (dæn) *n. Judo, karate.* **1.** any one of the 10 black-belt grades of proficiency. **2.** a competitor entitled to dan grading. [Japanese]

Dan. *abbrev. for:* **1.** *Bible.* Daniel. **2.** Danish.

dance (dɑːns) *vb.* **1.** (*intr.*) to move the feet and body rhythmically, esp. in time to music. **2.** (*tr.*) to perform (a particular dance). **3.** (*intr.*) to skip or leap. **4.** to move or cause to move in a rhythmical way. **5. dance attendance on (someone).** to attend (someone) solicitously or obsequiously. ~*n.* **6.** a series of rhythmical steps and movements, usually in time to music. **7.** an act of dancing. **8. a.** a social meeting arranged for dancing. **b.** (*as modifier*): *a dance hall.* **9.** a piece of music in the rhythm of a particular dance form. **10.** dancelike movements. **11. lead (someone) a dance.** *Brit. inf.* to cause (someone) continued worry and exasperation. [C13: < OF *dancier*] —ˈ**danceable** *adj.* —ˈ**dancer** *n.* —ˈ**dancing** *n., adj.*

dance floor *n.* **a.** an area of floor in a disco, nightclub, etc., where patrons may dance. **b.** (*as modifier*): *dancefloor music.*

dance of death *n.* a medieval representation of a dance in which people are led off to their graves, by a personification of death. Also called (French): **danse macabre.**

dancing girl *n.* a professional female dancer.

D and C *n. Med.* dilation (of the cervix) and curettage (of the uterus).

dandelion (ˈdændɪˌlaɪən) *n.* **1.** a plant native to Europe and Asia and naturalized as a weed in North America, having yellow rayed flowers and deeply notched leaves. **2.** any of several similar plants. [C15: < OF *dent de lion,* lit.: tooth of a lion, referring to its leaves]

dander (ˈdændə) *n.* **1.** small particles of hair or feathers. **2. get one's** (*or* **someone's**) **dander up.** *Inf.* to become (*or* cause to become) annoyed or angry. [C19: < DANDRUFF]

dandify (ˈdændɪˌfaɪ) *vb.* **-fying, -fied.** (*tr.*) to dress like or cause to resemble a dandy.

dandle (ˈdændᵊl) *vb.* (*tr.*) **1.** to move (a young child) up and down (on the knee or in the arms). **2.** to pet; fondle. [C16: <?] —ˈ**dandler** *n.*

dandruff (ˈdændrəf) *n.* loose scales of dry dead skin shed from the scalp. [C16: *dand-* <? + *-ruff,* prob. < ME *roufe* scab, < ON *hrūfa*]

dandy (ˈdændɪ) *n., pl.* **-dies. 1.** a man greatly concerned with smartness of dress. ~*adj.* **-dier, -diest. 2.** *Inf.* very good or fine. [C18: ? short for *jack-a-dandy*] —ˈ**dandyish** *adj.*

dandy-brush *n.* a stiff brush used for grooming a horse.

dandy roll *or* **roller** *n.* a roller used in the manufacture of paper to produce watermarks.

Dane (deɪn) *n.* **1.** a native, citizen, or inhabitant of Denmark. **2.** any of the Vikings who invaded England from the late 8th to the 11th century A.D.

Danegeld (ˈdeɪnˌgɛld) *or* **Danegelt** (ˈdeɪnˌgɛlt) *n.* the tax levied in Anglo-Saxon England to provide protection money for or to finance forces to oppose Viking invaders. [C11: < *Dan* Dane + *geld* tribute; see YIELD]

Danelaw (ˈdeɪnˌlɔː) *n.* the parts of Anglo-Saxon England in which Danish law and custom were observed. [OE *Dena lagu* Danes' law]

danger (ˈdeɪndʒə) *n.* **1.** the state of being vulnerable to injury, loss, or evil; risk. **2.** a person or thing that may cause injury, pain, etc. **3. in danger of.** liable to. **4. on the danger list.** critically ill in hospital. [C13 *daunger* power, hence power to inflict injury, < OF *dongier* < L *dominium* ownership] —ˈ**dangerless** *adj.*

danger money *n.* extra money paid to compensate for the risks involved in certain dangerous jobs.

dangerous (ˈdeɪndʒərəs) *adj.* causing danger; perilous. —ˈ**dangerously** *adv.*

dangle (ˈdæŋgᵊl) *vb.* **1.** to hang or cause to hang freely: *his legs dangled over the wall.* **2.** (*tr.*) to display as an enticement. [C16: ? < Danish *dangle,* prob. imit.] —ˈ**dangler** *n.*

Danish (ˈdeɪnɪʃ) *adj.* **1.** of Denmark, its people, or their language. ~*n.* **2.** the official language of Denmark.

Danish blue *n.* a strong-tasting white cheese with blue veins.

Danish pastry *n.* a rich puff pastry filled with apple, almond paste, icing, etc.

dank (dæŋk) *adj.* (esp. of cellars, caves, etc.) unpleasantly damp and chilly. [C14: prob. < ON] —ˈ**dankly** *adv.* —ˈ**dankness** *n.*

danseur *French.* (dɑ̃sœr) *or* (*fem.*) ***danseuse*** (dɑ̃søz) *n.* a ballet dancer.

dap (dæp) *vb.* **dapping, dapped. 1.** *Angling.* to fly-fish so that the fly bobs on and off the water. **2.** (*intr.*) to dip lightly into water. **3.** to bounce or cause to bounce. [C17: imit.]

daphne (ˈdæfnɪ) *n.* any of various Eurasian ornamental shrubs with shiny evergreen leaves and clusters of small bell-shaped flowers. [via L < Gk: laurel]

daphnia (ˈdæfnɪə) *n.* any of several waterfleas having a rounded body enclosed in a transparent shell. [C19: prob. < *Daphne,* a nymph in Gk mythology]

dapper (ˈdæpə) *adj.* **1.** neat in dress and bearing. **2.** small and nimble. [C15: < MDu.: active, nimble] —ˈ**dapperly** *adv.* —ˈ**dapperness** *n.*

dapple (ˈdæpᵊl) *vb.* **1.** to mark or become marked with spots of a different colour; mottle. ~*n.* **2.** mottled or spotted markings. **3.** a dappled horse, etc. ~*adj.* **4.** marked with dapples or spots. [C14: <?]

dapple-grey *n.* a horse with a grey coat having spots of darker colour.

darbies (ˈdɑːbɪz) *pl. n. Brit.* a slang term for **handcuffs.** [C16: ?< *Father Derby's* (or *Darby's*) *bonds,* a rigid agreement between a usurer and his client]

Darby and Joan (ˈdɑːbɪ; dʒəʊn) *n.* **1.** an ideal elderly married couple living in domestic harmony. **2. Darby and Joan Club.** a club for elderly people. [C18: couple in 18th-cent. English ballad]

dare (dɛə) *vb.* **1.** (*tr.*) to challenge (a person to do something) as proof of courage. **2.** (can take an infinitive with or without *to*) to be courageous enough to try (to do something). **3.** (*tr.*) *Rare.* to oppose without fear; defy. **4. I dare say. a.** (it is) quite possible (that). **b.** probably. ~*n.* **5.** a challenge to do something as proof of courage. **6.**

something done in response to such a challenge. [OE *durran*] —'**darer** *n.*

▷ **Usage.** When used negatively or interrogatively and not followed by an infinitive with *to, dare* does not add *-s: he dare not; dare she come?*

daredevil ('dɛəˌdɛvᵊl) *n.* **1.** a recklessly bold person. ~*adj.* **2.** reckless; daring; bold. —'**dareˌdevilry** *or* '**dareˌdeviltry** *n.*

daring ('dɛərɪŋ) *adj.* **1.** bold or adventurous. ~*n.* **2.** courage in taking risks; boldness.

Darjeeling (dɑː'dʒiːlɪŋ) *n.* a high-quality black tea grown in the mountains around Darjeeling, a town in NE India.

dark (dɑːk) *adj.* **1.** having little or no light. **2.** (of a colour) reflecting or transmitting little light: *dark brown.* **3.** (of complexion, hair colour, etc.) not fair; swarthy; brunette. **4.** gloomy or dismal. **5.** sinister; evil: *a dark purpose.* **6.** sullen or angry. **7.** ignorant or unenlightened: *a dark period in our history.* **8.** secret or mysterious. ~*n.* **9.** absence of light; darkness. **10.** night or nightfall. **11.** a dark place. **12.** a state of ignorance (esp. in **in the dark**). [OE *deorc*] —'**darkish** *adj.* —'**darkly** *adv.* —'**darkness** *n.*

Dark Ages *pl. n. European history.* the period from about the late 5th century A.D. to about 1000 A.D., once considered an unenlightened period.

Dark Continent *n.* **the.** a term for Africa when it was relatively unexplored by Europeans.

darken ('dɑːkən) *vb.* **1.** to make or become dark or darker. **2.** to make or become gloomy, angry, or sad. **3. darken (someone's) door.** (*usually used with a negative*) to visit someone: *never darken my door again!* —'**darkener** *n.*

dark horse *n.* **1.** a competitor in a race or contest about whom little is known. **2.** a person who reveals little about himself, esp. one who has unexpected talents. **3.** *U.S. politics.* a candidate who is unexpectedly nominated or elected.

dark lantern *n.* a lantern having a sliding shutter or panel to dim or hide the light.

darkling ('dɑːklɪŋ) *adv., adj. Poetic.* in the dark or night. [C15: < DARK + -LING²]

dark matter *n. Astron.* matter, as in galaxies, that is assumed to exist, but which is invisible at any wavelength of the electromagnetic spectrum.

darkroom ('dɑːkˌruːm, -ˌrʊm) *n.* a room in which photographs are processed in darkness or safe light.

darksome ('dɑːksəm) *adj. Literary.* dark or darkish.

dark star *n.* an invisible star known to exist only from observation of its radio, infrared, or other spectrum or of its gravitational effect.

darling ('dɑːlɪŋ) *n.* **1.** a person very much loved. **2.** a favourite. ~*adj.* (*prenominal*) **3.** beloved. **4.** much admired; pleasing: *a darling hat.* [OE *dēorling*; see DEAR, -LING¹]

darn¹ (dɑːn) *vb.* **1.** to mend (a hole or a garment) with a series of crossing or interwoven stitches. ~*n.* **2.** a patch of darned work on a garment. [C16: prob. < F (dialect) *darner*] —'**darner** *n.*

darn² (dɑːn) *interj., adj., adv., n.* a euphemistic word for **damn** (senses 1-4).

darnel ('dɑːnᵊl) *n.* any of several grasses that grow as weeds in grain fields in Europe and Asia. [C14: prob. rel. to F (dialect) *darnelle*, <?]

darning ('dɑːnɪŋ) *n.* **1.** the act of mending a hole using interwoven stitches. **2.** garments needing to be darned.

darning needle *n.* **1.** a long needle with a large eye used for darning. **2.** *U.S. & Canad.* a dialect name for a **dragonfly.**

dart (dɑːt) *n.* **1.** a small narrow pointed missile that is thrown or shot, as in the game of darts. **2.** a sudden quick movement. **3.** *Zool.* a slender pointed structure, as in snails for aiding copulation. **4.** a tapered tuck made in dressmaking. ~*vb.* **5.** to move or throw swiftly and suddenly; shoot. [C14: < OF *dars*, of Gmc origin] —'**darting** *adj.*

dartboard ('dɑːtˌbɔːd) *n.* a circular piece of wood, cork, etc., used as the target in the game of darts.

darter ('dɑːtə) *n.* **1.** Also called: **anhinga, snakebird.** any of various aquatic birds of tropical and subtropical inland waters, having a long slender neck and bill. **2.** any of various small brightly coloured North American freshwater fish.

darts (dɑːts) *n.* (*functioning as sing.*) any of various competitive games in which darts are thrown at a dartboard.

Darwinian (dɑː'wɪnɪən) *adj.* **1.** of or relating to Charles Darwin, (1809-82), English naturalist, or his theory of evolution. ~*n.* **2.** a person who supports or uses this theory.

Darwinism ('dɑːwɪˌnɪzəm) *or* **Darwinian theory** *n.* the theory of the origin of animal and plant species by evolution through a process of natural selection. —'**Darwinist** *n., adj.*

dash¹ (dæʃ) *vb.* (*mainly tr.*) **1.** to hurl; crash: *he dashed the cup to the floor.* **2.** to mix: *white paint dashed with blue.* **3.** (*intr.*) to move hastily or recklessly; rush. **4.** (usually foll. by *off* or *down*) to write (down) or finish (off) hastily. **5.** to frustrate: *his hopes were dashed.* **6.** to daunt (someone); discourage. ~*n.* **7.** a sudden quick movement. **8.** a small admixture: *coffee with a dash of cream.* **9.** a violent stroke or blow. **10.** the sound of splashing or smashing. **11.** panache; style: *he rides with dash.* **12.** the punctuation mark —, used to indicate a sudden change of subject or to enclose a parenthetical remark. **13.** the symbol (-) used, in combination with the symbol *dot* (·), in the written representation of Morse and other telegraphic codes. **14.** *Athletics.* another word (esp. U.S. and Canad.) for **sprint.** [ME *daschen, dassen*, ?< ON]

dash² (dæʃ) *interj., adj., adv., vb. Inf.* a euphemistic word for **damn** (senses 1, 3, 4).

dashboard ('dæʃˌbɔːd) *n.* **1.** Also called (Brit.): **fascia.** the instrument panel in a car, boat, or aircraft. **2.** *Obs.* a board at the side of a carriage or boat to protect against splashing.

dasher ('dæʃə) *n.* **1.** one that dashes. **2.** *Canad.* the ledge along the top of the boards of an ice hockey rink.

dashiki (dɑː'ʃiːkɪ) *n.* a large loose-fitting upper garment worn esp. by Negroes in the U.S., Africa, and the Caribbean. [C20: of W African origin]

dashing ('dæʃɪŋ) *adj.* **1.** spirited; lively: *a dashing young man.* **2.** stylish; showy.

dashlight ('dæʃˌlaɪt) *n.* a light that illuminates the dashboard of a car, esp. at night.

dassie ('dæsɪ) *n.* another name for a **hyrax,** esp. the rock hyrax. [C19: < Afrik.]

dastard ('dæstəd) *n. Arch.* a contemptible sneaking coward. [C15 (in the sense: dullard): prob. < ON *dæstr* exhausted, out of breath]

dastardly ('dæstədlɪ) *adj.* mean and cowardly. —'**dastardliness** *n.*

dasyure ('dæsɪˌjʊə) *n.* **1.** any of several small carnivorous marsupials of Australia, New Guinea, and adjacent islands. **2.** the ursine dasyure. See **Tasmanian devil.** [C19: < NL, < Gk *dasus* shaggy + *oura* tail]

DAT *abbrev. for* digital audio tape.

dat. *abbrev. for* dative.

data ('deɪtə, 'dɑːtə) *n.* **1.** a series of observations, measurements, or facts; information. **2.** Also called: **information.** *Computers.* the information operated on by a computer program. [C17: < L, lit.: (things) given, < *dare* to give]

▷ **Usage.** Although now generally used as a singular noun, *data* is properly a plural.

data base *or* **data bank** *n.* a store of a large amount of information, esp. in a form that can be handled by a computer.

data capture *n.* any process for converting information into a form that can be handled by a computer.

data pen *n.* a device for reading or scanning magnetically coded data on labels, packets, etc.

data processing *n.* **a.** a sequence of operations performed on data, esp. by a computer, in order to extract information, reorder files, etc. **b.** (*as modifier*): *a data-processing centre.*

data set *n. Computers.* another name for **file**¹ (sense 6).

date[1] (deɪt) *n.* **1.** a specified day of the month. **2.** the particular day or year of an event. **3.** an inscription on a coin, letter, etc., stating when it was made or written. **4. a.** an appointment for a particular time, esp. with a person of the opposite sex. **b.** the person with whom the appointment is made. **5.** the present moment; now (esp. in **to date, up to date**). ~*vb* **6.** (*tr.*) to mark (a letter, coin, etc.) with the day, month, or year. **7.** (*tr.*) to assign a date of occurrence or creation to. **8.** (*intr.;* foll. by *from* or *back to*) to have originated (at a specified time). **9.** (*tr.*) to reveal the age of: *that dress dates her.* **10.** to make or become old-fashioned: *some good films hardly date at all.* **11.** *Inf., chiefly U.S. & Canad.* **a.** to be a boyfriend or girlfriend of (someone of the opposite sex). **b.** to accompany (a member of the opposite sex) on a date. [C14: < OF, < L *dare* to give, as in *epistula data Romae* letter handed over at Rome] —**ˈdatable** *or* **ˈdateable** *adj.*

▷ **Usage.** See at **year.**

date[2] (deɪt) *n.* **1.** the fruit of the date palm, having sweet edible flesh and a single large woody seed. **2.** short for **date palm.** [C13: < OF, < L, < Gk *daktulos* finger]

dated (ˈdeɪtɪd) *adj.* unfashionable; outmoded.

dateless (ˈdeɪtlɪs) *adj.* likely to remain fashionable, good, or interesting regardless of age.

dateline (ˈdeɪtˌlaɪn) *n. Journalism.* the date and location of a story, placed at the top of an article.

date line *n.* (*often caps.*) short for **International Date Line.**

date palm *n.* a tall feather palm grown in tropical regions for its sweet edible fruit.

date stamp *n.* **1.** an adjustable rubber stamp for recording the date. **2.** an inked impression made by this.

dative (ˈdeɪtɪv) *Grammar.* ~*adj.* **1.** denoting a case of nouns, pronouns, and adjectives used to express the indirect object, to identify the recipients, and for other purposes. ~*n.* **2. a.** the dative case. **b.** a word or speech element in this case. [C15: < L *datīvus,* < *dare* to give] —**datival** (deɪˈtaɪvᵊl) *adj.* —**ˈdatively** *adv.*

datum (ˈdeɪtəm, ˈdɑːtəm) *n., pl.* **-ta. 1.** a single piece of information; fact. **2.** a proposition taken as unquestionable, often in order to construct some theoretical framework upon it. See also **sense datum.** [C17: < L: something given; see DATA]

datura (dəˈtjʊərə) *n.* any of various chiefly Indian plants and shrubs with large trumpet-shaped flowers. [C16: < NL, < Hindi]

daub (dɔːb) *vb.* **1.** (*tr.*) to smear or spread (paint, mud, etc.), esp. carelessly. **2.** (*tr.*) to cover or coat (with paint, plaster, etc.) carelessly. **3.** to paint (a picture) clumsily or badly. ~*n.* **4.** an unskilful or crude painting. **5.** something daubed on, esp. as a wall covering. **6.** a smear (of paint, mud, etc.) [C14: < OF *dauber* to paint, whitewash, < L *dealbāre,* < *albāre* to whiten] —**ˈdauber** *n.*

daughter (ˈdɔːtə) *n.* **1.** a female offspring; a girl or woman in relation to her parents. **2.** a female descendant. **3.** a female from a certain country, etc., or one closely connected with a certain environment, etc.: *a daughter of the church.* ~(*modifier*) **4.** *Biol.* denoting a cell or unicellular organism produced by the division of one of its own kind. **5.** *Physics.* (of a nuclide) formed from another nuclide by radioactive decay. [OE *dohtor*] —**ˈdaughterhood** *n.* —**ˈdaughterless** *adj.* —**ˈdaughterly** *adj.*

daughter-in-law *n., pl.* **daughters-in-law.** the wife of one's son.

daunt (dɔːnt) *vb.* (*tr.; often passive*) **1.** to intimidate. **2.** to dishearten. [C13: < OF *danter,* changed < *donter* to conquer, < L *domitāre* to tame] —**ˈdaunting** *adj.* —**ˈdauntingly** *adv.*

dauntless (ˈdɔːntlɪs) *adj.* bold; fearless; intrepid. —**ˈdauntlessly** *adv.* —**ˈdauntlessness** *n.*

dauphin (ˈdɔːfɪn; *French* dofɛ̃) *n.* (from 1349–1830) the title of the eldest son of the king of France. [C15: < OF: orig. a family name]

dauphine (ˈdɔːfiːn; *French* dofin) *or* **dauphiness** (ˈdɔːfɪnɪs) *n. French history.* the wife of a dauphin.

davenport (ˈdævənˌpɔːt) *n.* **1.** *Chiefly Brit.* a tall narrow writing desk with drawers. **2.** *U.S. & Canad.* a large sofa, esp. one convertible into a bed. [C19: sense 1 supposedly after Captain *Davenport,* who commissioned the first ones]

davit (ˈdævɪt, ˈdeɪ-) *n.* a cranelike device, usually one of a pair, fitted with a tackle for suspending or lowering equipment, esp. a lifeboat. [C14: < Anglo-F *daviot,* dim. of *Davi* David]

Davy Jones *n.* **1.** Also called: **Davy Jones's locker.** the ocean's bottom, esp. when regarded as the grave of those lost or buried at sea. **2.** the spirit of the sea. [C18: <?]

Davy lamp *n.* See **safety lamp.** [C19: after Sir Humphrey *Davy,* (1778-1829), E chemist]

daw (dɔː) *n.* an archaic, dialect, or poetic name for a **jackdaw.** [C15: rel. to OHG *taha*]

dawdle (ˈdɔːdᵊl) *vb.* **1.** (*intr.*) to be slow or lag behind. **2.** (when *tr.,* often foll. by *away*) to waste (time); trifle. [C17: <?] —**ˈdawdler** *n.*

dawn (dɔːn) *n.* **1.** daybreak. Related adj.: **auroral. 2.** the sky when light first appears in the morning. **3.** the beginning of something. ~*vb.* (*intr.*) **4.** to begin to grow light after the night. **5.** to begin to develop or appear. **6.** (usually foll. by *on* or *upon*) to begin to become apparent (to). [OE *dagian* to dawn] —**ˈdawnˌlike** *adj.*

dawn chorus *n.* the singing of large numbers of birds at dawn.

day (deɪ) *n.* **1.** Also called: **civil day.** the period of time, the **calendar day,** of 24 hours duration reckoned from one midnight to the next. **2. a.** the period of light between sunrise and sunset. **b.** (*as modifier*): *the day shift.* **3.** the part of a day occupied with regular activity, esp. work. **4.** (*sometimes pl.*) a period or point in time: *in days gone by; any day now.* **5.** the period of time, the **sidereal day,** during which the earth makes one complete revolution on its axis relative to a particular star. **6.** the period of time, the **solar day,** during which the earth makes one complete revolution on its axis relative to the sun. **7.** the period of time taken by a specified planet to make one complete rotation on its axis: *the Martian day.* **8.** (*often cap.*) a day designated for a special observance: *Christmas Day.* **9.** a time of success, recognition, etc.: *his day will come.* **10.** a struggle or issue at hand: *the day is lost.* **11. all in a day's work.** part of one's normal activity. **12. at the end of the day.** in the final reckoning. **13. call it a day.** to stop work or other activity. **14. day after day.** without respite; relentlessly. **15. day by day.** gradually or progressively. **16. day in, day out.** every day and all day long. **17. day of rest.** the Sabbath; Sunday. **18. every dog has his day.** one's luck will come. **19. in this day and age.** nowadays. **20. that will be the day. a.** that is most unlikely to happen. **b.** I look forward to that. ~Related adj.: **diurnal.** ~See also **days.** [OE *dæg*]

▷ **Usage.** Numerals are used for the day of the month: in formal written English, either cardinal or ordinal numbers may be used either preceding or following the month. In this dictionary the date is given in this manner: *May 15. 1974.*

Dayak (ˈdaɪæk) *n., pl.* **-aks** *or* **-ak.** a variant spelling of **Dyak.**

day bed *n.* a narrow bed intended for use as a seat and as a bed.

daybook (ˈdeɪˌbʊk) *n. Book-keeping.* a book in which the transactions of each day are recorded as they occur.

dayboy (ˈdeɪˌbɔɪ) *n. Brit.* a boy who attends a boarding school daily, but returns home each evening. —**ˈdaygirl** *n.*

daybreak (ˈdeɪˌbreɪk) *n.* the time in the morning when light first appears; dawn; sunrise.

daycare (ˈdeɪˌkɛə) *n. Brit. social welfare.* **1.** occupation, treatment, or supervision during the working day for people who might be at risk if left on their own. **2.** welfare services provided by a local authority, health service, etc., during the day.

daycentre (ˈdeɪˌsɛntə) *or* **day centre** *n. Social welfare.* (in Britain) **1.** a building used for daycare or other welfare services. **2.** the enterprise itself, including staff, users, and organization.

daydream (ˈdeɪˌdriːm) *n.* **1.** a pleasant dream-like fantasy indulged in while awake. **2.** a pleasant scheme or wish that is unlikely to be fulfilled. ~*vb.* **3.** (*intr.*) to indulge in idle fantasy. —ˈ**dayˌdreamer** *n.* —ˈ**dayˌdreamy** *adj.*

Day-Glo *n. Trademark.* **a.** a brand of fluorescent colouring materials, as of paint. **b.** (*as modifier*): *Day-Glo colours.*

day labourer *n.* an unskilled worker hired and paid by the day.

daylight (ˈdeɪˌlaɪt) *n.* **1.** light from the sun. **2.** daytime. **3.** daybreak. **4. see daylight. a.** to understand something previously obscure. **b.** to realize that the end of a difficult task is approaching.

daylight robbery *n. Inf.* blatant overcharging.

daylights (ˈdeɪˌlaɪts) *pl. n.* consciousness or wits (esp. in **scare, knock,** or **beat the (living) daylights out of someone).**

daylight-saving time *n.* time set usually one hour ahead of the local standard time, widely adopted in the summer to provide extra daylight in the evening.

daylong (ˈdeɪˌlɒŋ) *adj., adv.* lasting the entire day; all day.

day release *n. Brit.* a system whereby workers are released for part-time education without loss of pay.

day return *n.* a reduced fare for a journey (by train, etc.) travelling both ways in one day.

day room *n.* a communal living room in a residential institution such as a hospital.

days (deɪz) *adv. Inf.* during the day, esp. regularly: *he works days.*

day school *n.* **1.** a private school taking day students only. **2.** a school giving instruction during the daytime.

daytime (ˈdeɪˌtaɪm) *n.* the time between dawn and dusk.

day-to-day *adj.* routine; everyday.

day trip *n.* a journey made to and from a place within one day. —ˈ**day-ˌtripper** *n.*

daze (deɪz) *vb.* (*tr.*) **1.** to stun, esp. by a blow or shock. **2.** to bewilder or amaze. ~*n.* **3.** a state of stunned confusion or shock (esp. in **in a daze).** [C14: < ON *dasa-*, as in *dasast* to grow weary]

dazzle (ˈdæzᵊl) *vb.* **1.** (*usually tr.*) to blind or be blinded partially and temporarily by sudden excessive light. **2.** (*tr.*) to amaze, as with brilliance. ~*n.* **3.** bright light that dazzles. **4.** bewilderment caused by glamour, brilliance, etc.: *the dazzle of fame.* [C15: < DAZE] —ˈ**dazzler** *n.* —ˈ**dazzling** *adj.* —ˈ**dazzlingly** *adv.*

dB *or* **db** *symbol for* decibel *or* decibels.

DBE *abbrev. for* Dame Commander of the Order of the British Empire (a Brit. title).

DBS *abbrev. for* direct broadcasting by satellite.

DC *abbrev. for:* **1.** *Music.* da capo. **2.** direct current. Cf. **AC. 3.** Also: **D.C.** District of Columbia.

DCB *abbrev. for* Dame Commander of the Order of the Bath (a Brit. title).

DCM *Brit. mil. abbrev. for* Distinguished Conduct Medal.

dd *abbrev. for* delivered.

DD *abbrev. for:* **1.** Doctor of Divinity. **2.** direct debit.

D-day *n.* the day selected for the start of some operation, esp. of the Allied invasion of Europe on June 6, 1944. [C20: < *D(ay)-day*]

DDR *abbrev. for* Deutsche Demokratische Republik (East Germany; GDR).

DDS *or* **DDSc** *abbrev. for* Doctor of Dental Surgery *or* Science.

DDT *n.* dichlorodiphenyltrichloroethane; a colourless odourless substance used as an insecticide.

de- *prefix forming verbs and verbal derivatives.* **1.** removal of or from something: *deforest; dethrone.* **2.** reversal of something: *decode; desegregate.* **3.** departure from: *decamp.* [< L, < *dē* (prep.) from, away from, out of, etc. In compound words of Latin origin, *de-* also means away, away from (*decease*); down (*degrade*); reversal (*detect*); removal (*defoliate*); and is used intensively (*devote*) and pejoratively (*detest*)]

deacon (ˈdiːkən) *n. Christianity.* **1.** (in the Roman Catholic and other episcopal churches) an ordained minister ranking immediately below a priest. **2.** (in Protestant churches) a lay official who assists the minister, esp. in secular affairs. [OE, ult. < Gk *diakonos* servant] —ˈ**deaconate** *n.* —ˈ**deaconˌship** *n.*

deaconess (ˈdiːkənɪs) *n. Christianity.* (in the early church and in some modern Churches) a female member of the laity with duties similar to those of a deacon.

deactivate (diːˈæktɪˌveɪt) *vb.* **1.** (*tr.*) to make (a bomb, etc.) harmless or inoperative. **2.** (*intr.*) to become less radioactive. —**deˈactiˌvator** *n.*

dead (dɛd) *adj.* **1. a.** no longer alive. **b.** (*as collective n; preceded by the*): *the dead.* **2.** not endowed with life; inanimate. **3.** no longer in use, effective, or relevant: *a dead issue; a dead language.* **4.** unresponsive or unaware. **5.** lacking in freshness or vitality. **6.** devoid of physical sensation; numb. **7.** resembling death: a *dead sleep.* **8.** no longer burning or hot: *dead coals.* **9.** (of flowers or foliage) withered; faded. **10.** (*prenominal*) (intensifier): *a dead stop.* **11.** *Inf.* very tired. **12.** *Electronics.* **a.** drained of electric charge. **b.** not connected to a source of potential difference or electric charge. **13.** lacking acoustic reverberation: *a dead sound.* **14.** *Sport.* (of a ball, etc.) out of play. **15.** accurate; precise (esp. in **a dead shot).** **16.** lacking resilience or bounce: *a dead ball.* **17.** not yielding a return: *dead capital.* **18.** (of colours) not glossy or bright. **19.** stagnant: *dead air.* **20.** *Mil.* shielded from view, as by a geographic feature. **21. dead from the neck up.** *Inf.* stupid. **22. dead to the world.** *Inf.* unaware of one's surroundings, esp. asleep or drunk. ~*n.* **23.** a period during which coldness, darkness, etc. is at its most intense: *the dead of winter.* ~*adv.* **24.** (intensifier): *dead easy; stop dead.* **25. dead on.** exactly right. [OE *dēad*] —ˈ**deadness** *n.*

dead-and-alive *adj. Brit.* (of a place, activity, or person) dull; uninteresting.

dead-ball line *n. Rugby.* a line behind the goal line beyond which the ball is out of play.

deadbeat (ˈdɛdˌbiːt) *n.* **1.** *Inf., chiefly U.S. & Canad.* a lazy or socially undesirable person. **2.** a high grade escapement used in pendulum clocks. **3.** (*modifier*) without recoil.

dead beat *adj. Inf.* very tired; exhausted.

dead centre *n.* **1.** the exact top or bottom of the piston stroke in a reciprocating engine or pump. **2.** a rod mounted in the tailstock or headstock of a lathe to support a workpiece. ~Also called: **dead point.**

dead duck *n. Sl.* a person or thing doomed to death, failure, etc., esp. because of a mistake.

deaden (ˈdɛdᵊn) *vb.* **1.** to make or become less sensitive, intense, lively, etc. **2.** (*tr.*) to make acoustically less resonant. —ˈ**deadening** *adj.*

dead end *n.* **1.** a cul-de-sac. **2.** a situation in which further progress is impossible.

deadeye (ˈdɛdˌaɪ) *n.* **1.** *Naut.* either of a pair of disclike wooden blocks, supported by straps in grooves around them, between which a line is rove so as to draw them together to tighten a shroud. **2.** *Inf., chiefly U.S.* an expert marksman.

deadfall (ˈdɛdˌfɔːl) *n.* a trap in which a heavy weight falls to crush the prey.

dead finish *n. Austral.* **1.** *Inf.* the last straw; the extreme of tolerance. **2.** any of various trees or shrubs of Australia that form impenetrable thickets.

deadhead (ˈdɛdˌhɛd) *n. U.S. & Canad.* **1.** *Inf.* a person who uses a free ticket, as for the theatre, etc. **2.** *Inf.* a train, etc., travelling empty. **3.** *Sl.* a dull person. **4.** a log sticking out of the water as a snag to navigation. ~*vb.* **5.** *Inf.* (*intr.*) to drive an empty bus, train, etc. **6.** (*tr.*) to remove dead flower heads.

Dead Heart *n.* (usually preceded by *the*)

Austral. the remote interior of Australia. [C20: < *The Dead Heart of Australia* (1906) by J. W. Gregory]

dead heat *n.* **a.** a race or contest in which two or more participants tie for first place. **b.** a tie between two or more contestants in any position.

dead letter *n.* **1.** a law or ordinance that is no longer enforced. **2.** a letter that cannot be delivered or returned because it lacks adequate directions.

deadlight (ˈdɛdˌlaɪt) *n.* **1.** *Naut.* **a.** a bull's-eye to admit light to a cabin. **b.** a shutter for sealing off a porthole or cabin window. **2.** a skylight designed not to be opened.

deadline (ˈdɛdˌlaɪn) *n.* a time limit for any activity.

deadlock (ˈdɛdˌlɒk) *n.* **1.** a state of affairs in which further action between two opposing forces is impossible. **2.** a tie between opponents. **3.** a lock having a bolt that can be opened only with a key. ~*vb.* **4.** to bring or come to a deadlock.

dead loss *n.* **1.** a complete loss for which no compensation is paid. **2.** *Inf.* a useless person or thing.

deadly (ˈdɛdlɪ) *adj.* **-lier, -liest.** **1.** likely to cause death. **2.** *Inf.* extremely boring. ~*adv., adj.* **3.** like death in appearance or certainty.

deadly nightshade *n.* a poisonous Eurasian plant having purple bell-shaped flowers and black berries. Also called: **belladonna, dwale.**

deadly sins *pl. n.* the sins of pride, covetousness, lust, envy, gluttony, anger, and sloth.

dead man's handle *or* **pedal** *n.* a safety switch on a piece of machinery that allows operation only while depressed by the operator.

dead march *n.* a piece of solemn funeral music played to accompany a procession.

dead marine *n. Austral. & N.Z. inf.* an empty beer bottle.

dead-nettle *n.* any of several Eurasian plants having leaves resembling nettles but lacking stinging hairs.

deadpan (ˈdɛdˌpæn) *adj., adv.* with a deliberately emotionless face or manner.

dead reckoning *n.* a method of establishing one's position using the distance and direction travelled rather than astronomical observations.

dead set *adv.* **1.** absolutely: *he is dead set against going to Spain.* ~*n.* **2.** the motionless position of a dog when pointing towards game. ~*adj.* **3.** (of a hunting dog) in this position.

dead time *n. Electronics.* the time immediately following a stimulus, during which an electrical device, component, etc. is insensitive to a further stimulus.

dead weight *n.* **1.** a heavy weight or load. **2.** an oppressive burden. **3.** the difference between the loaded and the unloaded weights of a ship. **4.** the intrinsic invariable weight of a structure, such as a bridge.

dead wood *n.* **1.** dead trees or branches. **2.** *Inf.* a useless person; encumbrance.

deaf (dɛf) *adj.* **1. a.** partially or totally unable to hear. **b.** (*as collective n.; preceded by the*): *the deaf.* **2.** refusing to heed. [OE *dēaf*] —ˈ**deafness** *n.*

deaf-and-dumb *Offens.* ~*adj.* **1.** unable to hear or speak. ~*n.* **2.** a deaf-mute person.

deafen (ˈdɛfᵊn) *vb.* (*tr.*) to make deaf, esp. momentarily, as by a loud noise. —ˈ**deafeningly** *adv.*

deaf-mute *n.* **1.** a person who is unable to hear or speak. See also **mute** (sense 7). ~*adj.* **2.** unable to hear or speak. [C19: translation of F *sourd-muet*]

deal[1] (diːl) *vb.* **dealing, dealt.** **1.** (*intr.;* foll. by *in*) to engage in commercially: *to deal in upholstery.* **2.** (often foll. by *out*) to apportion or distribute. **3.** (*tr.*) to give (a blow, etc.) to (someone); inflict. **4.** (*intr.*) *Sl.* to sell any illegal drug. ~*n.* **5.** *Inf.* a bargain, transaction, or agreement. **6.** a particular type of treatment received, esp. as the result of an agreement: *a fair deal.* **7.** an indefinite amount (esp. in **good** *or* **great deal**). **8.** *Cards.* **a.** the process of distributing the cards. **b.** a player's turn to do this. **c.** a single round in a card game. **9. big deal.** *Sl.* an important person, event, or matter: often used sarcastically. ~See also **deal with.** [OE *dǣlan,* < *dǣl* a part; cf. OHG *teil* a part, ON *deild* a share]

deal[2] (diːl) *n.* **1.** a plank of softwood timber, such as fir or pine, or such planks collectively. **2.** the sawn wood of various coniferous trees. ~*adj.* **3.** of fir or pine. [C14: < MLow G *dele* plank]

dealer (ˈdiːlə) *n.* **1.** a person or firm engaged in commercial purchase and sale; trader: *a car dealer.* **2.** *Cards.* the person who distributes the cards. **3.** *Sl.* a person who sells illegal drugs.

dealings (ˈdiːlɪŋz) *pl. n.* (*sometimes sing.*) transactions or business relations.

dealt (dɛlt) *vb.* the past tense and past participle of **deal**[1].

deal with *vb.* (*tr., adv.*) **1.** to take action on: *to deal with each problem in turn.* **2.** to punish: *the headmaster will deal with the culprit.* **3.** to treat or be concerned with: *the book deals with architecture.* **4.** to conduct onself (towards others), esp. with regard to fairness. **5.** to do business with.

dean (diːn) *n.* **1.** the chief administrative official of a college or university faculty. **2.** (at Oxford and Cambridge universities) a college fellow with responsibility for undergraduate discipline. **3.** *Chiefly Church of England.* the head of a chapter of canons and administrator of a cathedral or collegiate church. **4.** *R.C. Church.* the cardinal bishop senior by consecration and head of the college of cardinals. ~ Related adj.: **decanal.** See also **rural dean.** [C14: < OF *deien,* < LL *decānus* one set over ten persons, < L *decem* ten]

deanery (ˈdiːnərɪ) *n., pl.* **-eries.** **1.** the office or residence of dean. **2.** the group of parishes presided over by a rural dean.

dear (dɪə) *adj.* **1.** beloved; precious. **2.** used in conventional forms of address, as in *Dear Sir.* **3.** (*postpositive;* foll. by *to*) important; close. **4. a.** highly priced. **b.** charging high prices. **5.** appealing. **6. for dear life.** with extreme vigour or desperation. ~*interj.* **7.** used in exclamations of surprise or dismay, such as *Oh dear!* ~*n.* **8.** Also: **dearest.** (*often used in direct address*) someone regarded with affection and tenderness. ~*adv.* **9.** dearly. [OE *dēore*] —ˈ**dearness** *n.*

dearly (ˈdɪəlɪ) *adv.* **1.** very much. **2.** affectionately. **3.** at a great cost.

dearth (dɜːθ) *n.* an inadequate amount, esp. of food; scarcity. [C13 *derthe,* < *dēr* DEAR]

deary *or* **dearie** (ˈdɪərɪ) *n.* **1.** (*pl.* **dearies**) *Inf.* a term of affection: now often sarcastic or facetious. **2. deary** *or* **dearie me!** an exclamation of surprise or dismay.

death (dɛθ) *n.* **1.** the permanent end of all functions of life in an organism. **2.** an instance of this: *his death ended an era.* **3.** a murder or killing. **4.** termination or destruction. **5.** a state of affairs or an experience considered as terrible as death. **6.** a cause or source of death. **7.** (*usually cap.*) a personification of death, usually a skeleton or an old man holding a scythe. **8. at death's door.** likely to die soon. **9. catch one's death (of cold).** *Inf.* to contract a severe cold. **10. do to death. a.** to kill. **b.** to overuse. **11. in at the death. a.** present when a hunted animal is killed. **b.** present at the finish or climax. **12. like death warmed up.** *Inf.* very ill. **13. like grim death.** as if afraid of one's life. **14. put to death.** to kill deliberately or execute. **15. to death. a.** until dead. **b.** very much. ~Related adjs.: **fatal, lethal, mortal.** [OE *dēath*]

death adder *n.* a venomous thick-bodied Australian snake.

deathbed (ˈdɛθˌbɛd) *n.* the bed in which a person is about to die.

deathblow (ˈdɛθˌbləʊ) *n.* a thing or event that destroys life or hope, esp. suddenly.

death cap *or* **angel** *n.* a poisonous woodland fungus with white gills and a cuplike structure at the base of the stalk.

death certificate *n.* a legal document issued by a qualified medical practitioner certifying the death of a person and stating the cause if known.

death duty *n.* a tax on property inheritances, in Britain replaced by capital transfer tax since 1975. Also called: **estate duty.**

death knell *or* **bell** *n.* **1.** something that heralds death or destruction. **2.** a bell rung to announce a death.

deathless (ˈdɛθlɪs) *adj.* immortal, esp. because of greatness; everlasting. —ˈ**deathlessness** *n.*

deathly (ˈdɛθlɪ) *adj.* **1.** deadly. **2.** resembling death: *a deathly quiet.*

death mask *n.* a cast of a dead person's face.

death rate *n.* the ratio of deaths in a specified area, group, etc., to the population of that area, group, etc. Also called: **mortality rate.**

death rattle *n.* a low-pitched gurgling sound sometimes made by a dying person.

death's-head *n.* a human skull or a representation of one.

death's-head moth *n.* a European hawk moth having markings resembling a human skull on its upper thorax.

deathtrap (ˈdɛθˌtræp) *n.* a building, vehicle, etc., that is considered very unsafe.

death warrant *n.* **1.** the official authorization for carrying out a sentence of death. **2. sign one's (own) death warrant.** to cause one's own destruction.

deathwatch (ˈdɛθˌwɒtʃ) *n.* **1.** a vigil held beside a dying or dead person. **2. deathwatch beetle.** a beetle whose woodboring larvae are a serious pest. The adult produces a tapping sound that was once supposed to presage death.

death wish *n.* (in Freudian psychology) the desire for self-annihilation.

deb (dɛb) *n. Inf.* short for **debutante.**

debacle (deɪˈbɑːkᵊl, dɪ-) *n.* **1.** a sudden disastrous collapse or defeat; rout. **2.** the breaking up of ice in a river, often causing flooding. **3.** a violent rush of water carrying along debris. [C19: < F, < OF *desbacler* to unbolt]

debag (diːˈbæg) *vb.* **-bagging, -bagged.** (*tr.*) *Brit. sl.* to remove the trousers from (someone) by force.

debar (dɪˈbɑː) *vb.* **-barring, -barred.** (*tr.;* usually foll. by *from*) to exclude from a place, a right, etc.; bar. —**deˈbarment** *n.*

debark[1] (dɪˈbɑːk) *vb.* another word for **disembark.** [C17: < F *débarquer,* < *dé-* DIS-[1] + *barque* BARQUE] —**debarkation** (ˌdiːbɑːˈkeɪʃən) *n.*

debark[2] (diːˈbɑːk) *vb.* (*tr.*) to remove the bark from (a tree). [C18: < DE- + BARK[2]]

debase (dɪˈbeɪs) *vb.* (*tr.*) to lower in quality, character, or value; adulterate. [C16: see DE-, BASE[2]] —**deˈbasement** *n.* —**deˈbaser** *n.*

debate (dɪˈbeɪt) *n.* **1.** a formal discussion, as in a legislative body, in which opposing arguments are put forward. **2.** discussion or dispute. **3.** the formal presentation and opposition of a specific motion, followed by a vote. ~*vb.* **4.** to discuss (a motion, etc.), esp. in a formal assembly. **5.** to deliberate upon (something). [C13: < OF *debatre* to discuss, argue, < L *battuere*] —**deˈbatable** *adj.* —**deˈbater** *n.*

debauch (dɪˈbɔːtʃ) *vb.* **1.** (when *tr., usually passive*) to lead into a life of depraved self-indulgence. **2.** (*tr.*) to seduce (a woman). ~*n.* **3.** an instance or period of extreme dissipation. [C16: < OF *desbaucher* to corrupt, lit.: to shape (timber) roughly, < *bauch* beam, of Gmc origin] —**deˈbaucher** *n.* —**deˈbauchery** *n.*

debauchee (ˌdɛbɔːˈtʃiː) *n.* a man who leads a life of promiscuity and self-indulgence.

debenture (dɪˈbɛntʃə) *n.* **1.** a long-term bond, bearing fixed interest and usually unsecured, issued by a company or governmental agency. **2.** a certificate acknowledging a debt. **3.** a customs certificate providing for a refund of excise or import duty. [C15: < L *dēbentur mihi* there are owed to me, < *dēbēre*] —**deˈbentured** *adj.*

debenture stock *n.* shares issued by a company, which guarantee a fixed return at regular intervals.

debilitate (dɪˈbɪlɪˌteɪt) *vb.* (*tr.*) to make feeble; weaken. [C16: < L, < *dēbilis* weak] —**deˌbiliˈtation** *n.* —**deˈbilitative** *adj.*

debility (dɪˈbɪlɪtɪ) *n., pl.* **-ties.** weakness or infirmity.

debit (ˈdɛbɪt) *n.* **1. a.** acknowledgment of a sum owing by entry on the left side of an account. **b.** the left side of an account. **c.** an entry on this side. **d.** the total of such entries. **e.** (*as modifier*): *a debit balance.* ~*vb.* **2.** (*tr.*) **a.** to record (an item) as a debit in an account. **b.** to charge (a person or his account) with a debt. [C15: < L *dēbitum* DEBT]

debit card *n.* (in cashless shopping developments) a card that would enable customers to pay for goods and services by immediate debit from their current account without using a cheque or cash.

debonair *or* **debonnaire** (ˌdɛbəˈnɛə) *adj.* **1.** suave and refined. **2.** carefree; gay. **3.** courteous and cheerful. [C13: < OF, < *de bon aire* having a good disposition] —ˌ**deboˈnairly** *adv.* —ˌ**deboˈnairness** *n.*

debouch (dɪˈbaʊtʃ) *vb.* (*intr.*) **1.** (esp. of troops) to move into a more open space. **2.** (of a river, glacier, etc.) to flow into a larger area or body. [C18: < F *déboucher,* < *dé-* DIS-[1] + *bouche* mouth] —**deˈbouchment** *n.*

Debrett (dəˈbrɛt) *n.* a list, considered exclusive, of the British aristocracy. In full: **Debrett's Peerage.** [C19: after J. *Debrett* (c 1750-1822), London publisher who first issued it]

debrief (diːˈbriːf) *vb.* (of a soldier, diplomat, etc.) to make or (of his superiors) to elicit a report after a mission or event. —**deˈbriefing** *n.*

debris *or* **débris** (ˈdeɪbrɪ, ˈdɛbrɪ) *n.* **1.** fragments of something destroyed or broken; rubble. **2.** a collection of loose material derived from rocks, or an accumulation of animal or vegetable matter. [C18: < F, < obs. *debrisier* to break into pieces, of Celtic origin]

debt (dɛt) *n.* **1.** something owed, such as money, goods, or services. **2. bad debt.** a debt that has little prospect of being paid. **3.** an obligation to pay or perform something. **4.** the state of owing something, or of being under an obligation (esp. in **in debt, in (someone's) debt**). [C13: < OF *dette,* < L *dēbitum,* < *dēbēre* to owe, < DE- + *habēre* to have]

debt collector *n.* a person employed to collect debts for creditors.

debt of honour *n.* a debt that is morally but not legally binding.

debtor (ˈdɛtə) *n.* a person or commercial enterprise that owes a financial obligation.

debug (diːˈbʌg) *vb.* **-bugging, -bugged.** (*tr.*) *Inf.* **1.** to locate and remove concealed microphones from (a room, etc.). **2.** to locate and remove defects in (a device, system, plan, etc.). **3.** to remove insects from. [C20: < DE- + BUG]

debunk (diːˈbʌŋk) *vb.* (*tr.*) *Inf.* to expose the pretensions or falseness of, esp. by ridicule. [C20: < DE- + BUNK[2]] —**deˈbunker** *n.*

debus (diːˈbʌs) *vb.* **debusing, debused** *or* **debussing, debussed.** to unload (goods, etc.) or (esp. of troops) to alight from a bus.

debut (ˈdeɪbjuː, ˈdɛbjuː) *n.* **1. a.** the first public appearance of an actor, musician, etc. **b.** (*as modifier*): *debut album.* **2.** the presentation of a debutante. [C18: < F, < OF *desbuter* to play first, < *des-* DE- + *but* goal, target]

debutante (ˈdɛbjʊˌtɑːnt, -ˌtænt) *n.* **1.** a young upper-class woman who is formally presented to society. **2.** a young woman regarded as being upper-class, wealthy, and frivolous. [C19: < F, < *débuter* to lead off in a game, make one's first appearance; see DEBUT]

dec. *abbrev. for:* **1.** deceased. **2.** decimal. **3.** decimetre. **4.** declaration. **5.** declension. **6.** declination. **7.** decrease. **8.** *Music.* decrescendo.

Dec. *abbrev. for* December.

deca-, deka- *or before a vowel* **dec-, dek-** *prefix.* denoting ten: *decagon.* In conjunction with scientific units the symbol **da** is used. [< Gk *deka*]

decade (ˈdɛkeɪd, dɪˈkeɪd) *n.* **1.** a period of ten years. **2.** a group of ten. [C15: < OF, < LL, < Gk, < *deka* ten] —**deˈcadal** *adj.*

▷ **Usage.** Specific decades are referred to as follows: *the 1660s: the 1970s.* Where ambiguity does not arise contractions are allowable though it is preferable to write out the contracted forms in words rather than numerals: *the sixties* rather than *the 60s* or *the '60s.*

decadence (ˈdɛkədəns) *or* **decadency** *n.* **1.** deterioration, esp. of morality or culture. **2.** the state reached through such a process. [C16: < F, < Med. L *dēcadentia,* lit.: a falling away; see DECAY]

decadent (ˈdɛkədənt) *adj.* **1.** characterized by decline, as in being self-indulgent or morally corrupt. **2.** belonging to a period of decline in artistic standards. ~*n.* **3.** a decadent person.

decaffeinate (dɪˈkæfɪˌneɪt) *vb.* (*tr.*) to remove all or part of the caffeine from (coffee, etc.).

decagon (ˈdɛkəˌgɒn) *n.* a polygon having ten sides. —**decagonal** (dɪˈkægənˀl) *adj.*

decahedron (ˌdɛkəˈhiːdrən) *n.* a solid figure having ten plane faces. —ˌ**decaˈhedral** *adj.*

decal (dɪˈkæl, ˈdiːkæl) *n.* **1.** short for **decalcomania.** ~*vb.* **2.** to transfer (a design, etc.) by decalcomania.

decalcify (diːˈkælsɪˌfaɪ) *vb.* **-fying, -fied.** (*tr.*) to remove calcium or lime from (bones, etc.). —**deˈcalciˌfier** *n.*

decalcomania (dɪˌkælkəˈmeɪnɪə) *n.* **1.** the process of transferring a design from prepared paper onto another surface, such as glass or paper. **2.** a design so transferred. [C19: < F, < *décalquer,* < *de-* DE- + *calquer* to trace + *-manie* -MANIA]

decalitre *or U.S.* **decaliter** (ˈdɛkəˌliːtə) *n.* a metric measure of volume equivalent to 10 litres.

Decalogue (ˈdɛkəˌlɒg) *n.* another name for the **Ten Commandments.** [C14: < Church L *decalogus,* < Gk, < *deka* ten + *logos* word]

decametre *or U.S.* **decameter** (ˈdɛkəˌmiːtə) *n.* a metric measure of length equivalent to 10 metres.

decamp (dɪˈkæmp) *vb.* (*intr.*) **1.** to leave a camp; break camp. **2.** to depart secretly or suddenly; abscond. —**deˈcampment** *n.*

decanal (dɪˈkeɪnˀl) *adj.* **1.** of a dean or deanery. **2.** on the same side of a cathedral, etc., as the dean; on the S side of the choir. [C18: < Med. L *decānālis, decānus* DEAN]

decani (dɪˈkeɪnaɪ) *adj., adv. Music.* to be sung by the decanal side of a choir. Cf. **cantoris.** [L: genitive of *decānus*]

decant (dɪˈkænt) *vb.* **1.** to pour (a liquid, such as wine) from one container to another, esp. without disturbing any sediment. **2.** (*tr.*) to rehouse (people) while their homes are being rebuilt or refurbished. [C17: < Med. L *dēcanthāre,* < *canthus* spout, rim]

decanter (dɪˈkæntə) *n.* a stoppered bottle, into which a drink is poured for serving.

decapitate (dɪˈkæpɪˌteɪt) *vb.* (*tr.*) to behead. [C17: < LL *dēcapitāre,* < L DE- + *caput* head] —**deˌcapiˈtation** *n.* —**deˈcapiˌtator** *n.*

decapod (ˈdɛkəˌpɒd) *n.* **1.** any crustacean having five pairs of walking limbs, as a crab, lobster, shrimp, etc. **2.** any cephalopod mollusc having eight short tentacles and two longer ones, as a squid or cuttlefish. —**decapodal** (dɪˈkæpədˀl), **deˈcapodan,** *or* **deˈcapodous** *adj.*

decarbonate (diːˈkɑːbəˌneɪt) *vb.* (*tr.*) to remove carbon dioxide from. —**deˌcarbonˈation** *n.* —**deˈcarbonˌator** *n.*

decarbonize *or* **-ise** (diːˈkɑːbəˌnaɪz) *vb.* (*tr.*) to remove carbon from (an internal-combustion engine, etc.). Also: **decoke, decarburize.** —**deˌcarboniˈzation** *or* **-iˈsation** *n.* —**deˈcarbonˌizer** *or* **-ˌiser** *n.*

decastyle (ˈdɛkəˌstaɪl) *n. Archit.* a portico consisting of ten columns.

decasyllable (ˈdɛkəˌsɪləbˀl) *n.* a word or line of verse consisting of ten syllables. —**decasyllabic** (ˌdɛkəsɪˈlæbɪk) *adj.*

decathlon (dɪˈkæθlɒn) *n.* an athletic contest in which each athlete competes in ten different events. [C20: < DECA- + Gk *athlon* contest, prize; see ATHLETE] —**deˈcathlete** *n.*

decay (dɪˈkeɪ) *vb.* **1.** to decline or cause to decline gradually in health, prosperity, excellence, etc.; deteriorate. **2.** to rot or cause to rot; decompose. **3.** (*intr.*) Also: **disintegrate.** *Physics.* **a.** (of an atomic nucleus) to undergo radioactive disintegration. **b.** (of an elementary particle) to transform into two or more different elementary particles. **4.** (*intr.*) *Physics.* (of a stored charge, magnetic flux, etc.) to decrease gradually when the source of energy has been removed. ~*n.* **5.** the process of decline, as in health, mentality, etc. **6.** the state brought about by this process. **7.** decomposition. **8.** rotten or decayed matter. **9.** *Physics.* **a.** See **radioactive decay. b.** a spontaneous transformation of an elementary particle into two or more different particles. **10.** *Physics.* a gradual decrease of a stored charge, current, etc., when the source of energy has been removed. [C15: < OF *decaïr,* < LL *dēcadere,* lit.: to fall away, < L *cadere* to fall] —**deˈcayable** *adj.*

decease (dɪˈsiːs) *n.* **1.** a more formal word for **death.** ~*vb.* **2.** (*intr.*) a more formal word for **die**[1]. [C14 (n.): < OF, < L *dēcēdere* to depart]

deceased (dɪˈsiːst) *adj.* **a.** a more formal word for **dead** (sense 1). **b.** (*as n.; preceded by the*): *the deceased.*

deceit (dɪˈsiːt) *n.* **1.** the act or practice of deceiving. **2.** a statement, act, or device intended to mislead; fraud; trick. **3.** a tendency to deceive. [C13: < OF, < *deceivre* to DECEIVE]

deceitful (dɪˈsiːtfʊl) *adj.* full of deceit.

deceive (dɪˈsiːv) *vb.* (*tr.*) **1.** to mislead by deliberate misrepresentation or lies. **2.** to delude (oneself). **3.** to be unfaithful to (one's sexual partner). **4.** *Arch.* to disappoint. [C13: < OF *deceivre,* < L *dēcipere* to ensnare, cheat, < *capere* to take] —**deˈceivable** *adj.* —**deˈceiver** *n.*

decelerate (diːˈsɛləˌreɪt) *vb.* to slow down or cause to slow down. [C19: < DE- + (AC)CELERATE] —**deˌcelerˈation** *n.* —**deˈcelerˌator** *n.*

December (dɪˈsɛmbə) *n.* the twelfth month of the year, consisting of 31 days. [C13: < OF, < L: the tenth month (the Roman year began with March), < *decem* ten]

decemvir (dɪˈsɛmvə) *n., pl.* **-virs** *or* **-viri** (-vɪˌriː). (in ancient Rome) a member of a board of ten magistrates. [C17: < L, < *decem* ten + *virī* men] —**deˈcemviral** *adj.* —**deˈcemvirate** *n.*

decencies (ˈdiːsˀnsɪz) *pl. n.* **1. the.** those things that are considered necessary for a decent life. **2.** another word for **proprieties.**

decency (ˈdiːsˀnsɪ) *n., pl.* **-cies. 1.** conformity to the prevailing standards of propriety, morality, modesty, etc. **2.** the quality of being decent.

decennial (dɪˈsɛnɪəl) *adj.* **1.** lasting for ten years. **2.** occurring every ten years. ~*n.* **3.** a tenth anniversary. —**deˈcennially** *adv.*

decent (ˈdiːsˀnt) *adj.* **1.** polite or respectable. **2.** proper and suitable; fitting. **3.** conforming to conventions of sexual behaviour; not indecent. **4.** free of oaths, blasphemy, etc. **5.** good or adequate: *a decent wage.* **6.** *Inf.* kind; generous. **7.** *Inf.* sufficiently clothed to be seen by other people: *are you decent?* [C16: < L *decēns* suitable, < *decēre* to be fitting] —ˈ**decently** *adv.*

decentralize *or* **-ise** (diːˈsɛntrəˌlaɪz) *vb.* **1.** to reorganize into smaller more autonomous units. **2.** to disperse (a concentration, as of industry or population). —**deˈcentralist** *n., adj.* —**deˌcentraliˈzation** *or* **-iˈsation** *n.*

deception (dɪˈsɛpʃən) *n.* **1.** the act of deceiving or the state of being deceived. **2.** something that deceives; trick.

deceptive (dɪˈsɛptɪv) *adj.* likely or designed to deceive; misleading. —**deˈceptively** *adv.* —**deˈceptiveness** *n.*

deci- *prefix.* denoting one tenth: *decimetre.* Symbol: d [< F *déci-,* < L *decimus* tenth]

decibel (ˈdɛsɪˌbɛl) *n.* **1.** a unit for comparing two currents, voltages, or power levels, equal to one tenth of a bel. **2.** a similar unit for measuring the intensity of a sound. Abbrev.: **dB.**

decide (dɪˈsaɪd) *vb.* **1.** (*may take a clause or an infinitive as object;* when *intr.,* sometimes foll. by *on* or *about*) to reach a decision: *decide what you want; he decided to go.* **2.** (*tr.*) to cause to reach a decision. **3.** (*tr.*) to determine or settle (a contest or question). **4.** (*tr.*) to influence decisively the outcome of (a contest or question). **5.** (*intr.; foll.* by *for* or *against*) to pronounce a formal verdict. [C14: < OF, < L *dēcīdere*, lit.: to cut off, < *caedere* to cut] **—deˈcidable** *adj.* **—deˈcider** *n.*

decided (dɪˈsaɪdɪd) *adj.* (*prenominal*) **1.** unmistakable. **2.** determined; resolute: *a girl of decided character.* **—deˈcidedly** *adv.*

deciduous (dɪˈsɪdjʊəs) *adj.* **1.** (of trees and shrubs) shedding all leaves annually at the end of the growing season. Cf. **evergreen. 2.** (of antlers, teeth, etc.) being shed at the end of a period of growth. [C17: < L: falling off, < *dēcidere* to fall down, < *cadere* to fall] **—deˈciduousness** *n.*

decilitre *or U.S.* **deciliter** (ˈdɛsɪˌliːtə) *n.* a metric measure of volume equivalent to one-tenth of a litre.

decillion (dɪˈsɪljən) *n.* **1.** (in Britain, France, and Germany) the number represented as one followed by 60 zeros (10^{60}). **2.** (in the U.S. and Canada) the number represented as one followed by 33 zeros (10^{33}). [C19: < L *decem* ten + *-illion* as in *million*] **—deˈcillionth** *adj.*

decimal (ˈdɛsɪməl) *n.* **1.** Also called: **decimal fraction.** a fraction that has an unwritten denominator of a power of ten. It is indicated by a decimal point to the left of the numerator: *.2=2/10.* **2.** any number used in the decimal system. ~*adj.* **3. a.** relating to or using powers of ten. **b.** of the base ten. **4.** (*prenominal*) expressed as a decimal. [C17: < Med. L *decimālis* of tithes, < L *decima* a tenth] **—ˈdecimally** *adv.*

decimal classification *n.* another term for **Dewey Decimal System.**

decimal currency *n.* a system of currency in which the monetary units are parts or powers of ten.

decimalize *or* **-ise** (ˈdɛsɪməˌlaɪz) *vb.* to change (a system, number, etc.) to the decimal system. **—ˌdecimaliˈzation** *or* **-iˈsation** *n.*

decimal place *n.* **1.** the position of a digit after the decimal point. **2.** the number of digits to the right of the decimal point.

decimal point *n.* a full stop or a raised full stop placed between the integral and fractional parts of a number in the decimal system.

▷ **Usage.** Conventions relating to the use of the decimal point are confused. The IX General Conference on Weights and Measures resolved in 1948 that the decimal point should be a point on the line or a comma, but not a centre dot. It also resolved that figures could be grouped in threes about the decimal point, but that no point or comma should be used for this purpose. These conventions are adopted in this dictionary. However, the Decimal Currency Board recommended that for sums of money the centre dot should be used as the decimal point and that the comma should be used as the thousand marker. Moreover, in some countries the position is reversed, the comma being used as the decimal point and the dot as the thousand marker.

decimal system *n.* **1.** the number system in general use, having a base of ten, in which numbers are expressed by combinations of the ten digits 0 to 9. **2.** a system of measurement in which the multiple and submultiple units are related to a basic unit by powers of ten.

decimate (ˈdɛsɪˌmeɪt) *vb.* (*tr.*) **1.** to destroy or kill a large proportion of. **2.** (esp. in the ancient Roman army) to kill every tenth man of (a mutinous section). [C17: < L *decimāre*, < *decem* ten] **—ˌdeciˈmation** *n.* **—ˈdeciˌmator** *n.*

▷ **Usage.** The use of *decimate* as in definition 1 was formerly regarded as unacceptable by many careful users of English, but is now by far the more common sense of the word, as in *myxomatosis decimated the rabbit population.*

decimetre *or U.S.* **decimeter** (ˈdɛsɪˌmiːtə) *n.* one tenth of a metre. Symbol: **dm**

decipher (dɪˈsaɪfə) *vb.* (*tr.*) **1.** to determine the meaning of (something obscure or illegible). **2.** to convert from code into plain text; decode. **—deˈcipherable** *adj.* **—deˈcipherment** *n.*

decision (dɪˈsɪʒən) *n.* **1.** a judgment, conclusion, or resolution reached or given; verdict. **2.** the act of making up one's mind. **3.** firmness of purpose or character; determination. [C15: < OF, < L *dēcīsiō*, lit.: a cutting off; see DECIDE]

decisive (dɪˈsaɪsɪv) *adj.* **1.** influential; conclusive. **2.** characterized by the ability to make decisions, esp. quickly; resolute. **—deˈcisively** *adv.* **—deˈcisiveness** *n.*

deck (dɛk) *n.* **1.** *Naut.* any of various platforms built into a vessel. **2.** a similar platform, as in a bus. **3. a.** the horizontal platform that supports the turntable and pick-up of a record player. **b.** See **tape deck. 4.** *Chiefly U.S.* a pack of playing cards. **5.** *Computers.* a collection of punched cards relevant to a particular program. **6. clear the decks.** *Inf.* to prepare for action, as by removing obstacles. **7. hit the deck.** *Inf.* **a.** to fall to the ground, esp. to avoid injury. **b.** to prepare for action. **c.** to get out of bed. ~*vb.* (*tr.*) **8.** (often foll. by *out*) to dress or decorate. **9.** to build a deck on (a vessel). [C15: < MDu. *dec* a covering]

deck-access *adj.* (of a block of flats) having a continuous balcony at each level onto which the front door of each flat opens.

deck chair *n.* a folding chair consisting of a wooden frame suspending a length of canvas.

-decker *adj.* (*in combination*): having a certain specified number of levels or layers: *a double-decker bus.*

deck hand *n.* **1.** a seaman assigned duties on the deck of a ship. **2.** (in Britain) a seaman who has seen sea duty for at least one year. **3.** a helper aboard a yacht.

deckle *or* **deckel** (ˈdɛkᵊl) *n.* **1.** a frame used to contain pulp on the mould in the making of handmade paper. **2.** a strap on a paper-making machine that fixes the width of the paper. [C19: < G *Deckel* lid, < *decken* to cover]

deckle edge *n.* **1.** the rough edge of paper made using a deckle, often left as ornamentation. **2.** an imitation of this. **—ˈdeckle-ˈedged** *adj.*

declaim (dɪˈkleɪm) *vb.* **1.** to make (a speech, etc.) loudly and in a rhetorical manner. **2.** to speak lines from (a play, poem, etc.) with studied eloquence. **3.** (*intr.; foll.* by *against*) to protest (against) loudly and publicly. [C14: < L *dēclāmāre*, < *clāmāre* to call out] **—deˈclaimer** *n.* **—declamatory** (dɪˈklæmətərɪ) *adj.*

declamation (ˌdɛkləˈmeɪʃən) *n.* **1.** a rhetorical or emotional speech, made esp. in order to protest; tirade. **2.** a speech, verse, etc., that is or can be spoken. **3.** the act or art of declaiming.

declaration (ˌdɛkləˈreɪʃən) *n.* **1.** an explicit or emphatic statement. **2.** a formal statement or announcement. **3.** the act of declaring. **4.** the ruling of a judge or court on a question of law. **5.** *Law.* an unsworn statement of a witness admissible in evidence under certain conditions. **6.** *Cricket.* the voluntary closure of an innings before all ten wickets have fallen. **7.** *Contract bridge.* the final contract. **8.** a statement or inventory of goods, etc., submitted for tax assessment. **—deˈclarer** *n.*

declarative (dɪˈklærətɪv) *adj.* making or having the nature of a declaration. **—deˈclaratively** *adv.*

declare (dɪˈklɛə) *vb.* (*mainly tr.*) **1.** (*may take a clause as object*) to make clearly known or announce officially: *war was declared.* **2.** to state officially that (a person, fact, etc.) is as specified: *he declared him fit.* **3.** (*may take a clause as object*) to state emphatically; assert. **4.** to show, reveal, or manifest. **5.** (*intr.;* often foll. by *for* or *against*) to make known one's choice or opinion. **6.** to make a statement of (dutiable goods, etc.). **7.** (*also intr.*) *Cards.* **a.** to display (cards) on the table so as to add to one's score. **b.** to decide (the trump suit) by making the winning bid. **8.** (*intr.*) *Cricket.* to close an innings voluntarily before all ten wickets have fallen. **9.** to authorize payment of (a dividend). [C14: < L *dēclārāre* to make clear, < *clārus* clear] **—deˈclarable** *adj.*

declassify (diːˈklæsɪˌfaɪ) *vb.* **-fying, -fied.** (*tr.*) to release (a document or information) from the security list. —**deˌclassifiˈcation** *n.*

declension (dɪˈklɛnʃən) *n.* **1.** *Grammar.* **a.** inflection of nouns, pronouns, or adjectives for case, number, and gender. **b.** the complete set of the inflections of such a word. **2.** a decline or deviation. **3.** a downward slope. [C15: < L *dēclīnātiō*, lit.: a bending aside, hence variation; see DECLINE] —**deˈclensional** *adj.*

declination (ˌdɛklɪˈneɪʃən) *n.* **1.** *Astron.* the angular distance of a star, planet, etc., north or south from the celestial equator. Symbol: δ. **2.** the angle made by a compass needle with the direction of the geographical north pole. **3.** a refusal, esp. a courteous or formal one. —ˌ**decliˈnational** *adj.*

decline (dɪˈklaɪn) *vb.* **1.** to refuse to do or accept (something), esp. politely. **2.** (*intr.*) to grow smaller; diminish. **3.** to slope or cause to slope downwards. **4.** (*intr.*) to deteriorate gradually. **5.** *Grammar.* to list the inflections of (a noun, adjective, or pronoun), or (of a noun, adjective, or pronoun) to be inflected for number, case, or gender. ~*n.* **6.** gradual deterioration or loss. **7.** a movement downward; diminution. **8.** a downward slope. **9.** *Arch.* any slowly progressive disease, such as tuberculosis. [C14: < OF *decliner*, < L *dēclīnāre* to bend away, inflect grammatically] —**deˈclinable** *adj.* —**deˈcliner** *n.*

declivity (dɪˈklɪvɪtɪ) *n.*, *pl.* **-ties.** a downward slope, esp. of the ground. [C17: < L *dēclīvitās*, < DE- + *clīvus* a slope, hill] —**deˈclivitous** *adj.*

declutch (dɪˈklʌtʃ) *vb.* (*intr.*) to disengage the clutch of a motor vehicle.

decoct (dɪˈkɒkt) *vb.* to extract (the essence or active principle) from (a medicinal or similar substance) by boiling. [C15: see DECOCTION]

decoction (dɪˈkɒkʃən) *n.* **1.** *Pharmacol.* the extraction of the water-soluble substances of a drug or medicinal plants by boiling. **2.** the liquor resulting from this. [C14: < OF, < LL, < *dēcoquere* to boil down, < *coquere* to cook]

decode (diːˈkəʊd) *vb.* to convert from code into ordinary language. —**deˈcoder** *n.*

decoke (diːˈkəʊk) *vb.* (*tr.*) another word for **decarbonize.**

décolletage (ˌdeɪkɒlˈtɑːʒ) *n.* a low-cut dress or neckline. [C19: < F; see DÉCOLLETÉ]

décolleté (deɪˈkɒlteɪ) *adj.* **1.** (of a woman's garment) low-cut. **2.** wearing a low-cut garment. [C19: < *décolleter* to cut out the neck (of a dress), < *collet* collar]

decolonize *or* **-ise** (diːˈkɒləˌnaɪz) *vb.* (*tr.*) to grant independence to (a colony). —**deˌcoloniˈzation** *or* **-iˈsation** *n.*

decolour, *U.S.* **decolor** (diːˈkʌlə) *or* **decolorize, -ise** *vb.* (*tr.*) to deprive of colour. —**deˌcoloriˈzation** *or* **-iˈsation** *n.*

decommission (ˌdiːkəˈmɪʃən) *vb.* (*tr.*) to dismantle (an industrial plant or nuclear reactor which is no longer required for use), to an extent such that it can be safely abandoned.

decompose (ˌdiːkəmˈpəʊz) *vb.* **1.** to break down or be broken down into constituent elements by bacterial or fungal action; rot. **2.** *Chem.* to break down or cause to break down into simpler chemical compounds. **3.** to break up or separate into constituent parts. —**decomposition** (ˌdiːkɒmpəˈzɪʃən) *n.*

decompress (ˌdiːkəmˈprɛs) *vb.* **1.** to relieve or be relieved of pressure. **2.** to return (a diver, etc.) to a condition of normal atmospheric pressure or to be returned to such a condition. —ˌ**decomˈpression** *n.*

decompression chamber *n.* a chamber in which the pressure of air can be varied slowly for returning people safely from abnormal pressures to atmospheric pressure.

decompression sickness *or* **illness** *n.* a disorder characterized by severe pain, cramp, and difficulty in breathing, caused by a sudden and substantial change in atmospheric pressure.

decongestant (ˌdiːkənˈdʒɛstənt) *adj.* **1.** relieving congestion, esp. nasal congestion. ~*n.* **2.** a decongestant drug.

deconsecrate (diːˈkɒnsɪˌkreɪt) *vb.* (*tr.*) to transfer (a church, etc.) to secular use. —**deˌconseˈcration** *n.*

deconstruct (ˌdiːkənˈstrʌkt) *vb.* (*tr.*) **1.** to apply the theories of deconstruction to (a text, film, etc.). **2.** to expose or dismantle the existing structure in (a system, organization, etc.).

deconstruction (ˌdiːkənˈstrʌkʃən) *n.* a development in the theory of criticism (esp. literary and film criticism) that seeks to expose the latent contradictions in a work of art arising from the rhetorical elements embedded in the very structure of language itself.

decontaminate (ˌdiːkənˈtæmɪˌneɪt) *vb.* (*tr.*) to render harmless by the removal or neutralization of poisons, radioactivity, etc. —ˌ**deconˌtamiˈnation** *n.*

decontrol (ˌdiːkənˈtrəʊl) *vb.* **-trolling, -trolled.** (*tr.*) to free of restraints or controls, esp. government controls: *to decontrol prices.*

décor *or* **decor** (ˈdeɪkɔː) *n.* **1.** a style or scheme of interior decoration, furnishings, etc., as in a room or house. **2.** stage decoration; scenery. [C19: < F, < *décorer* to DECORATE]

decorate (ˈdɛkəˌreɪt) *vb.* **1.** (*tr.*) to ornament; adorn. **2.** to paint or wallpaper. **3.** (*tr.*) to confer a mark of distinction, esp. a medal, upon. [C16: < L *decorāre*, < *decus* adornment] —ˈ**decorative** *adj.*

Decorated style *n.* a 14th-century style of English architecture characterized by geometrical tracery and floral decoration.

decoration (ˌdɛkəˈreɪʃən) *n.* **1.** an addition that renders something more attractive or ornate. **2.** the act or art of decorating. **3.** a medal, etc., conferred as a mark of honour.

decorator (ˈdɛkəˌreɪtə) *n.* **1.** *Brit.* a person whose profession is the painting and wallpapering of buildings or their interiors. **2.** a person who decorates.

decorous (ˈdɛkərəs) *adj.* characterized by propriety in manners, conduct, etc. [C17: < L, < *decor* elegance] —ˈ**decorously** *adv.* —ˈ**decorousness** *n.*

decorum (dɪˈkɔːrəm) *n.* **1.** propriety, esp. in behaviour or conduct. **2.** a requirement of correct behaviour in polite society. [C16: < L: propriety]

decoupage (ˌdeɪkuːˈpɑːʒ) *n.* the decoration of a surface with cutout shapes or illustrations. [C20: < F, < *découper*, < DE- + *couper* to cut]

decoy *n.* (ˈdiːkɔɪ, dɪˈkɔɪ). **1.** a person or thing used to lure someone into danger. **2.** *Mil.* something designed to deceive an enemy. **3.** a bird or animal, or an image of one, used to lure game into a trap or within shooting range. **4.** a place into which game can be lured for capture. ~*vb.* (dɪˈkɔɪ). **5.** to lure or be lured by or as if by means of a decoy. **6.** (*tr.*) *Canad.* another word for **deke.** [C17: prob. < Du. *de kooi*, lit.: the cage, < L *cavea* CAGE]

decrease *vb.* (dɪˈkriːs). **1.** to diminish or cause to diminish in size, strength, etc. ~*n.* (ˈdiːkriːs, dɪˈkriːs). **2.** a diminution; reduction. **3.** the amount by which something has been diminished. [C14: < OF, < L *dēcrescere* to grow less, < DE- + *crescere* to grow] —**deˈcreasingly** *adv.*

decree (dɪˈkriː) *n.* **1.** an edict, law, etc., made by someone in authority. **2.** an order or judgment of a court. ~*vb.* **decreeing, decreed. 3.** to order, adjudge, or ordain by decree. [C14: < OF, < L *dēcrētum* ordinance, < *dēcrētus* decided, p.p. of *dēcernere*]

decree absolute *n.* the final decree in divorce proceedings, which leaves the parties free to remarry. Cf. **decree nisi.**

decree nisi (ˈnaɪsaɪ) *n.* a provisional decree, esp. in divorce proceedings, which will later be made absolute unless cause is shown why it should not. Cf. **decree absolute.**

decrement (ˈdɛkrɪmənt) *n.* **1.** the act of decreasing; diminution. **2.** *Maths.* a negative increment. **3.** *Physics.* a measure of the damping of an oscillator, expressed by the ratio of amplitudes in successive cycles. [C17: < L *dēcrēmentum*, < *dēcrescere* to DECREASE]

decrepit (dɪˈkrɛpɪt) *adj.* **1.** enfeebled by old age; infirm. **2.** broken down or worn out by hard or long use; dilapidated. [C15: < L *dēcrepitus*, < *crepāre* to creak] —**deˈcrepiˌtude** *n.*

decrescendo (ˌdiːkrɪˈʃɛndəʊ) *n., adj.* another word for **diminuendo.** [It., < *decrescere* to DECREASE]

decrescent (dɪˈkrɛsənt) *adj.* (esp. of the moon) decreasing; waning. [C17: < L *dēcrescēns* growing less; see DECREASE] —**deˈcrescence** *n.*

decretal (dɪˈkriːtᵊl) *n.* **1.** *R.C. Church.* a papal decree; edict on doctrine or church law. ~*adj.* **2.** of or relating to a decree. [C15: < OF, < LL *dēcrētālis*; see DECREE]

decriminalize *or* **-ise** (diːˈkrɪmɪnᵊˌlaɪz) *vb.* (*tr.*) to remove (an action) from the legal category of criminal offence: *to decriminalize the possession of marijuana.*

decry (dɪˈkraɪ) *vb.* **-crying, -cried.** (*tr.*) **1.** to express open disapproval of; disparage. **2.** to depreciate by proclamation: *to decry obsolete coinage.* [C17: < OF *descrier*, < *des-* DIS-[1] + *crier* to CRY]

decumbent (dɪˈkʌmbənt) *adj.* **1.** lying down. **2.** *Bot.* (of stems) lying flat with the tip growing upwards. [C17: < L, present participle of *dēcumbere* to lie down] —**deˈcumbency** *n.*

dedicate (ˈdɛdɪˌkeɪt) *vb.* (*tr.*) **1.** (often foll. by *to*) to devote (oneself, one's time, etc.) wholly to a special purpose or cause. **2.** (foll. by *to*) to address a book, performance, etc. to a person, cause, etc. as a token of affection or respect. **3.** (foll. by *to*) to request or play (a record) on radio for another person as a greeting. **4.** to assign or allocate to a particular project, function, etc. **5.** to set apart for a deity or for sacred uses. [C15: < L *dēdicāre* to announce, < *dicāre* to make known] —**ˈdediˌcator** *n.* —**dedicatory** (ˈdɛdɪˌkeɪtərɪ, ˈdɛdɪkətərɪ) *or* **ˈdediˌcative** *adj.*

dedicated (ˈdɛdɪˌkeɪtɪd) *adj.* **1.** devoted to a particular purpose or cause. **2.** assigned or allocated to a particular project, function, etc.: *a dedicated transmission line.* **3.** *Computers.* designed to fulfil one function.

dedication (ˌdɛdɪˈkeɪʃən) *n.* **1.** the act of dedicating or being dedicated. **2.** an inscription prefixed to a book, etc., dedicating it to a person or thing. **3.** wholehearted devotion, esp. to a career, ideal, etc. —ˌ**dediˈcational** *adj.*

deduce (dɪˈdjuːs) *vb.* (*tr.*) **1.** (*may take a clause as object*) to reach (a conclusion) by reasoning; conclude (that); infer. **2.** *Arch.* to trace the origin or derivation of. [C15: < L *dēdūcere* to lead away, derive, < DE- + *dūcere* to lead] —**deˈducible** *adj.*

deduct (dɪˈdʌkt) *vb.* (*tr.*) to take away or subtract (a number, quantity, part, etc.). [C15: < L *dēductus*, p.p. of *dēdūcere* to DEDUCE]

deductible (dɪˈdʌktɪbᵊl) *adj.* **1.** capable of being deducted. **2.** *U.S.* short for **tax-deductible.** ~*n.* **3.** *Insurance.* the U.S. name for **excess** (sense 5).

deduction (dɪˈdʌkʃən) *n.* **1.** the act or process of deducting or subtracting. **2.** something that is or may be deducted. **3.** *Logic.* **a.** a process of reasoning by which a specific conclusion necessarily follows from a set of general premises. **b.** a logical conclusion reached by this process. —**deˈductive** *adj.*

deed (diːd) *n.* **1.** something that is done or performed; act. **2.** a notable achievement. **3.** action as opposed to words. **4.** *Law.* a legal document signed, sealed, and delivered to effect a conveyance or transfer of property or to create a legal contract. ~*vb.* **5.** (*tr.*) *U.S.* to convey or transfer (property) by deed. [OE *dēd*]

deed box *n.* a strong box in which deeds and other documents are kept.

deed poll *n. Law.* a deed made by one party only, esp. one by which a person changes his name.

deejay (ˈdiːˌdʒeɪ) *n.* an informal name for **disc jockey.** [C20: < the initials DJ (disc jockey)]

deem (diːm) *vb.* (*tr.*) to judge or consider. [OE *dēman*]

de-emphasize *or* **-ise** (diːˈɛmfəˌsaɪz) *vb.* (*tr.*) to remove emphasis from.

deemster (ˈdiːmstə) *n.* the title of one of the two justices in the Isle of Man. Also called: **dempster.**

deep (diːp) *adj.* **1.** extending or situated far down from a surface: *a deep pool.* **2.** extending or situated far inwards, backwards, or sideways. **3.** *Cricket.* far from the pitch: *the deep field.* **4.** (*postpositive*) of a specified dimension downwards, inwards, or backwards: *six feet deep.* **5.** coming from or penetrating to a great depth. **6.** difficult to understand; abstruse. **7.** intellectually demanding: *a deep discussion.* **8.** of great intensity: *deep trouble.* **9.** (*postpositive*; foll. by *in*) absorbed (by); immersed (in): *deep in study.* **10.** very cunning; devious. **11.** mysterious: *a deep secret.* **12.** (of a colour) having an intense or dark hue. **13.** low in pitch: *a deep voice.* **14. go off the deep end.** *Inf.* **a.** to lose one's temper; react angrily. **b.** *Chiefly U.S.* to act rashly. **15. in deep water.** *Inf.* in a tricky position or in trouble. ~*n.* **16.** any deep place on land or under water. **17. the deep. a.** a poetic term for the **ocean. b.** *Cricket.* the area of the field relatively far from the pitch. **18.** the most profound, intense, or central part: *the deep of winter.* **19.** a vast extent, as of space or time. ~*adv.* **20.** far on in time; late: *they worked deep into the night.* **21.** profoundly or intensely. **22. deep down.** *Inf.* in reality, esp. as opposed to appearance. [OE *dēop*] —**ˈdeeply** *adv.* —**ˈdeepness** *n.*

deepen (ˈdiːpᵊn) *vb.* to make or become deep, deeper, or more intense. —**ˈdeepener** *n.*

deepfreeze (ˌdiːpˈfriːz) *n.* **1.** a refrigerator in which food, etc., is stored for long periods at temperatures below freezing. **2.** storage in a deepfreeze. **3.** *Inf.* a state of suspended activity. ~*vb.* **deep-freeze, -froze** *or* **-freezed, -frozen** *or* **-freezed. 4.** (*tr.*) to freeze or keep in a deepfreeze.

deep-fry *vb.* **-frying, -fried.** to cook (fish, etc.) in sufficient hot fat to cover the food.

deep-laid *adj.* (of a plot or plan) carefully worked out and kept secret.

deep-rooted *or* **deep-seated** *adj.* (of ideas, beliefs, etc.) firmly fixed or held; ingrained.

deep-sea *n.* (*modifier*) of, found in, or characteristic of the deep parts of the sea.

deep-set *adj.* (esp. of eyes) deeply set.

deep space *n.* any region of outer space beyond the system of the earth and moon.

deep structure *n. Generative grammar.* a representation of a sentence at a level where logical or grammatical relations are made explicit. Cf. **surface structure.**

deer (dɪə) *n., pl.* **deer** *or* **deers.** any of a family of hoofed, ruminant mammals including reindeer, elk, and roe deer, typically having antlers in the male. Related adj.: **cervine.** [OE *dēor* beast]

deer lick *n.* a naturally or artificially salty area of ground where deer come to lick the salt.

deerskin (ˈdɪəˌskɪn) *n.* **a.** the hide of a deer. **b.** (*as modifier*): *a deerskin jacket.*

deerstalker (ˈdɪəˌstɔːkə) *n.* **1.** a person who stalks deer, esp. in order to shoot them. **2.** a hat, peaked in front and behind, with earflaps usually tied together on the top. —**ˈdeerˌstalking** *adj., n.*

de-escalate (diːˈɛskəˌleɪt) *vb.* to reduce the level or intensity of. —**de-ˌescaˈlation** *n.*

def (dɛf) *adj. Sl.* (esp. of hip-hop) very good. [C20: ? < *definitive*]

def. *abbrev. for:* **1.** defective. **2.** defence. **3.** defendant. **4.** deferred. **5.** definite. **6.** definition.

deface (dɪˈfeɪs) *vb.* (*tr.*) to spoil or mar the surface or appearance of; disfigure. —**deˈfaceable** *adj.* —**deˈfacement** *n.* —**deˈfacer** *n.*

de facto (deɪ ˈfæktəʊ) *adv.* **1.** in fact. ~*adj.* **2.** existing in fact, whether legally recognized or not: *a de facto regime.* Cf. **de jure.** ~*n., pl.* **-tos. 3.** *Austral. & N.Z.* a de facto wife or husband. [C17: L]

defalcate (ˈdiːfælˌkeɪt) *vb.* (*intr.*) *Law.* to misuse or misappropriate property or funds entrusted to one. [C15: < Med. L *dēfalcāre* to cut off, < L DE- + *falx* sickle] —**ˈdefalˌcator** *n.*

defame (dɪˈfeɪm) *vb.* (*tr.*) to attack the good name or reputation of; slander; libel. [C14: < OF, < L, < *diffāmāre* to spread by unfavourable report, < *fāma* FAME] —**defamation** (ˌdɛfəˈmeɪʃən) *n.* —**defamatory** (dɪˈfæmətərɪ) *adj.*

default (dɪˈfɔːlt) *n.* **1.** a failure to act, esp. a failure to meet a financial obligation or to appear in a court of law at a time specified. **2.** absence. **3. in default of.** through or in the lack or absence of. **4. judgment by default.** *Law.* a judgment in the plaintiff's favour when the defendant fails to plead or to appear. **5.** lack, want, or need. ~*vb.* **6.** (*intr.*; often foll. by *on* or *in*) to fail to make payment when due. **7.** (*intr.*) to fail to fulfil an obligation. **8.** *Law.* to lose (a case) by failure to appear in court. [C13: < OF *defaute*, < *defaillir* to fail, < Vulgar L *dēfallīre* (unattested) to be lacking]

defaulter (dɪˈfɔːltə) *n.* **1.** a person who defaults. **2.** *Chiefly Brit.* a person, esp. a soldier, who has broken the disciplinary code of his service.

defeat (dɪˈfiːt) *vb.* (*tr.*) **1.** to overcome; win a victory over. **2.** to thwart or frustrate. **3.** *Law.* to render null and void. ~*n.* **4.** a defeating or being defeated. [C14: < OF, < *desfaire* to undo, ruin, < *des-* DIS-[1] + *faire* to do, < L *facere*]

defeatism (dɪˈfiːtɪzəm) *n.* a ready acceptance or expectation of defeat. —**deˈfeatist** *n., adj.*

defecate (ˈdɛfɪˌkeɪt) *vb.* **1.** (*intr.*) to discharge waste from the body through the anus. **2.** (*tr.*) to remove impurities from. [C16: < L *dēfaecāre* to cleanse from dregs, < DE- + *faex* dregs] —ˌ**defeˈcation** *n.* —ˈ**defeˌcator** *n.*

defect *n.* (dɪˈfɛkt, ˈdiːfɛkt). **1.** a lack of something necessary for completeness; deficiency. **2.** an imperfection or blemish. ~*vb.* (dɪˈfɛkt). **3.** (*intr.*) to desert one's country, cause, etc., esp. in order to join the opposing forces. [C15: < L, < *dēficere* to forsake, fail] —**deˈfector** *n.*

defection (dɪˈfɛkʃən) *n.* **1.** abandonment of duty, allegiance, principles, etc. **2.** a shortcoming.

defective (dɪˈfɛktɪv) *adj.* **1.** having a defect or flaw; imperfect. **2.** (of a person) below the usual standard or level, esp. in intelligence. **3.** *Grammar.* lacking the full range of inflections characteristic of its form class. —**deˈfectiveness** *n.*

defence *or U.S.* **defense** (dɪˈfɛns) *n.* **1.** resistance against danger or attack. **2.** a person or thing that provides such resistance. **3.** a plea, essay, etc., in support of something. **4.** a country's military measures or resources. **5.** *Law.* a defendant's denial of the truth of the allegations or charge against him. **6.** *Law.* the defendant and his legal advisers collectively. **7.** *Sport.* **a.** the action of protecting oneself or part of the playing area against an opponent's attacks. **b.** (usually preceded by *the*) the players in a team whose function is to do this. **8.** (*pl.*) fortifications. [C13: < OF, < LL *dēfensum*, p.p. of *dēfendere* to DEFEND] —**deˈfenceless** *or U.S.* **deˈfenseless** *adj.*

defence mechanism *n.* **1.** *Psychoanalysis.* an unconscious mental process designed to reduce anxiety or shame. **2.** *Physiol.* the protective response of the body against disease.

defend (dɪˈfɛnd) *vb.* **1.** to protect from harm or danger. **2.** (*tr.*) to support in the face of criticism, esp. by argument. **3.** to represent (a defendant) in court. **4.** *Sport.* to guard (one's goal, etc.) against attack. **5.** (*tr.*) to protect (a title, etc.) against a challenge. [C13: < OF, < L *dēfendere* to ward off, < DE- + *-fendere* to strike] —**deˈfender** *n.*

defendant (dɪˈfɛndənt) *n.* **1.** a person against whom an action or claim is brought in a court of law. Cf. **plaintiff.** ~*adj.* **2.** defending.

defenestration (diːˌfɛnɪˈstreɪʃən) *n.* the act of throwing someone out of a window. [C17: < NL *dēfenestrātiō*, < L DE- + *fenestra* window]

defensible (dɪˈfɛnsɪbᵊl) *adj.* capable of being defended, as in war, an argument, etc. —**deˌfensiˈbility** *or* **deˈfensibleness** *n.*

defensive (dɪˈfɛnsɪv) *adj.* **1.** intended for defence. **2.** rejecting criticisms of oneself. ~*n.* **3.** a position of defence. **4. on the defensive.** in a position of defence, as in being ready to reject criticism. —**deˈfensively** *adv.*

defer[1] (dɪˈfɜː) *vb.* **-ferring, -ferred.** (*tr.*) to delay until a future time; postpone. [C14: < OF *differer* to be different, postpone; see DIFFER] —**deˈferment** *or* **deˈferral** *n.* —**deˈferrer** *n.*

defer[2] (dɪˈfɜː) *vb.* **-ferring, -ferred.** (*intr.*; foll. by *to*) to yield (to) or comply (with) the wishes or judgments of another. [C15: < L *dēferre*, lit.: to bear down, < DE- + *ferre* to bear]

deference (ˈdɛfərəns) *n.* **1.** compliance with the wishes of another. **2.** courteous regard; respect. [C17: < F *déférence*; see DEFER[2]]

deferent[1] (ˈdɛfərənt) *adj.* another word for **deferential.**

deferent[2] (ˈdɛfərənt) *adj.* (esp. of a nerve or duct) conveying an impulse, fluid, etc., down or away; efferent. [C17: < L *dēferre*; see DEFER[2]]

deferential (ˌdɛfəˈrɛnʃəl) *adj.* showing deference; respectful. —ˌ**deferˈentially** *adv.*

defiance (dɪˈfaɪəns) *n.* **1.** open or bold resistance to authority, opposition, or power. **2.** a challenge. —**deˈfiant** *adj.*

defibrillation (dɪˌfaɪbrɪˈleɪʃən) *n. Med.* the application of an electric current to the heart to restore normal contractions after a heart attack caused by fibrillation.

defibrillator (dɪˈfaɪbrɪˌleɪtə) *n. Med.* an apparatus for stopping fibrillation of the heart by application of an electric current.

deficiency (dɪˈfɪʃənsɪ) *n., pl.* **-cies. 1.** the state or quality of being deficient. **2.** a lack or insufficiency; shortage. **3.** a deficit.

deficiency disease *n.* any condition, such as pellagra, beriberi, or scurvy, produced by a lack of vitamins or other essential substances.

deficient (dɪˈfɪʃənt) *adj.* **1.** lacking some essential; incomplete; defective. **2.** inadequate in quantity or supply; insufficient. [C16: < L *dēficiēns* lacking, < *dēficere* to fall short] —**deˈficiently** *adv.*

deficit (ˈdɛfɪsɪt, dɪˈfɪsɪt) *n.* **1.** the amount by which an actual sum is lower than that expected or required. **2. a.** an excess of liabilities over assets. **b.** an excess of expenditures over revenues. [C18: < L, lit.: there is lacking, < *dēficere*]

deficit financing *n.* government spending in excess of revenues so that a budget deficit is incurred, which is financed by borrowing: recommended by some economists as a remedy for economic depression and unemployment.

defile[1] (dɪˈfaɪl) *vb.* (*tr.*) **1.** to make foul or dirty; pollute. **2.** to taint; corrupt. **3.** to damage or sully (someone's reputation, etc.). **4.** to make unfit for ceremonial use. **5.** to violate the chastity of. [C14: < earlier *defoilen*, < OF *defouler* to trample underfoot, abuse, < DE- + *fouler* to tread upon; see FULL[2]] —**deˈfilement** *n.*

defile[2] (ˈdiːfaɪl, dɪˈfaɪl) *n.* **1.** a narrow pass or gorge. **2.** a single file of soldiers, etc. ~*vb.* **3.** to march in single file. [C17: < F, < *défiler* to file off, < *filer* to march in a column, < OF, < L *fīlum* thread]

define (dɪˈfaɪn) *vb.* (*tr.*) **1.** to state precisely the meaning of. **2.** to describe the nature of. **3.** to determine the boundary or extent of. **4.** (*often passive*) to delineate the form or outline of. **5.** to fix with precision; specify. [C14: < OF: to determine, < L *dēfīnīre* to set bounds to, < *fīnīre* to FINISH] —**deˈfinable** *adj.* —**deˈfiner** *n.*

definite (ˈdɛfɪnɪt) *adj.* **1.** clearly defined; exact. **2.** having precise limits or boundaries. **3.** known for certain. [C15: < L *dēfīnītus* limited, distinct; see DEFINE] —ˈ**definiteness** *n.*

▷ **Usage.** *Definite* and *definitive* should be carefully distinguished. *Definite* indicates precision and firmness, as in *a definite decision. Definitive* includes these senses but also indicates conclusiveness. *A definite answer* indicates a clear and firm answer to a particular question; a *definitive answer* implies an authoritative resolution of a complex question.

definite article *n. Grammar.* a determiner that expresses specificity of reference, such as *the* in English. Cf. **indefinite article.**

definite integral *n.* See **integral.**

definitely (ˈdɛfɪnɪtlɪ) *adv.* **1.** in a definite manner. **2.** (*sentence modifier*) certainly: *he said he was coming, definitely.* ~*sentence substitute.* **3.** unquestionably.

definition (ˌdɛfɪˈnɪʃən) *n.* **1.** a formal and concise statement of the meaning of a word, phrase, etc. **2.** the act of defining. **3.** specification of the essential properties of something. **4.** the act of making clear or definite. **5.** the state of being clearly defined. **6.** a measure of the clarity of an optical, photographic, or television image as characterized by its sharpness and contrast.

definitive (dɪˈfɪnɪtɪv) *adj.* **1.** serving to decide or settle finally. **2.** most reliable or authoritative. **3.** serving to define or outline. **4.** *Zool.* fully developed. **5.** (of postage stamps) permanently on sale. ~*n.* **6.** *Grammar.* a word indicating specificity of reference. —**deˈfinitively** *adv.*

▷ **Usage.** See at **definite.**

deflagrate (ˈdɛfləˌgreɪt, ˈdiː-) *vb.* to burn with great heat and light. [C18: < L *dēflagrāre,* < DE- + *flagrāre* to burn] —ˌ**deflaˈgration** *n.*

deflate (diːˈfleɪt) *vb.* **1.** to collapse through the release of gas. **2.** (*tr.*) to take away the self-esteem or conceit from. **3.** *Econ.* to cause deflation of (an economy, the money supply, etc.). [C19: < DE- + (IN)FLATE] —**deˈflator** *n.*

deflation (diːˈfleɪʃən) *n.* **1.** a deflating or being deflated. **2.** *Econ.* a reduction in spending and economic activity resulting in lower levels of output, employment, investment, trade, profits, and prices. **3.** the removal of loose rock material, etc., by wind. —**deˈflationary** *adj.* —**deˈflationist** *n., adj.*

deflect (dɪˈflɛkt) *vb.* to turn or cause to turn aside from a course; swerve. [C17: < L *dēflectere,* < *flectere* to bend] —**deˈflector** *n.*

deflection *or* **deflexion** (dɪˈflɛkʃən) *n.* **1.** a deflecting or being deflected. **2.** the amount of deviation. **3.** the change in direction of a light beam as it crosses a boundary between two media with different refractive indexes. **4.** a deviation of the indicator of a measuring instrument from its zero position. —**deˈflective** *adj.*

deflower (diːˈflaʊə) *vb.* (*tr.*) **1.** to deprive (esp. a woman) of virginity. **2.** to despoil of beauty, innocence, etc. **3.** to rob or despoil of flowers. —ˌ**defloˈration** *n.*

defoliant (diːˈfəʊlɪənt) *n.* a chemical sprayed or dusted onto trees to cause their leaves to fall, esp. to remove cover from an enemy in warfare.

defoliate (diːˈfəʊlɪˌeɪt) *vb.* to deprive (a plant) of its leaves. [C18: < Med. L *dēfoliāre,* < L DE- + *folium* leaf] —**deˌfoliˈation** *n.*

deforest (diːˈfɒrɪst) *vb.* (*tr.*) to clear of trees. Also: **disforest.** —**deˌforesˈtation** *n.*

deform (dɪˈfɔːm) *vb.* **1.** to make or become misshapen or distorted. **2.** (*tr.*) to mar the beauty of; disfigure. **3.** (*tr.*) to subject or be subjected to a stress that causes a change of dimensions. [C15: < L *dēformāre,* < DE- + *forma* shape, beauty] —**deˈformable** *adj.* —ˌ**deforˈmation** *n.*

deformed (dɪˈfɔːmd) *adj.* **1.** disfigured or misshapen. **2.** morally perverted; warped.

deformity (dɪˈfɔːmɪtɪ) *n., pl.* **-ties. 1.** a deformed condition. **2.** *Pathol.* a distortion of an organ or part. **3.** a deformed person or thing. **4.** a defect, esp. of the mind or morals; depravity.

defraud (dɪˈfrɔːd) *vb.* (*tr.*) to take away or withhold money, rights, property, etc., from (a person) by fraud; swindle. —**deˈfrauder** *n.*

defray (dɪˈfreɪ) *vb.* (*tr.*) to provide money for (costs, expenses, etc.); pay. [C16: < OF *deffroier* to pay expenses, < *de-* DIS-[1] + *frai* expenditure] —**deˈfrayable** *adj.* —**deˈfrayal** *or* **deˈfrayment** *n.*

defrock (diːˈfrɒk) *vb.* (*tr.*) to deprive (a person in holy orders) of ecclesiastical status; unfrock.

defrost (diːˈfrɒst) *vb.* **1.** to make or become free of frost or ice. **2.** to thaw, esp. through removal from a deepfreeze.

defroster (diːˈfrɒstə) *n.* a device by which a de-icing process, as of a refrigerator, is accelerated.

deft (dɛft) *adj.* quick and neat in movement; nimble; dexterous. [C13 (in the sense: gentle): see DAFT] —ˈ**deftly** *adv.* —ˈ**deftness** *n.*

defunct (dɪˈfʌŋkt) *adj.* **1.** no longer living; dead or extinct. **2.** no longer operative or valid. [C16: < L *dēfungī* to discharge (one's obligations), die; see DE-, FUNCTION] —**deˈfunctness** *n.*

defuse *or U.S.* (*sometimes*) **defuze** (diːˈfjuːz) *vb.* (*tr.*) **1.** to remove the triggering device of (a bomb, etc.). **2.** to remove the cause of tension from (a crisis, etc.).

defy (dɪˈfaɪ) *vb.* **-fying, -fied.** (*tr.*) **1.** to resist openly and boldly. **2.** to elude, esp. in a baffling way. **3.** *Formal.* to challenge (someone to do something); dare. **4.** *Arch.* to invite to do battle or combat. [C14: < OF *desfier,* < *des-* DE- + *fier* to trust, < L *fīdere*] —**deˈfier** *n.*

deg. *abbrev. for* degree.

degauss (diːˈgaʊs) *vb.* (*tr.*) to neutralize by producing an opposing magnetic field. —**deˈgausser** *n.*

degeneracy (dɪˈdʒɛnərəsɪ) *n., pl.* **-cies. 1.** the act or state of being degenerate. **2.** the process of becoming degenerate.

degenerate *vb.* (dɪˈdʒɛnəˌreɪt). (*intr.*) **1.** to become degenerate. **2.** *Biol.* (of organisms or their parts) to become less specialized or functionally useless. ~*adj.* (dɪˈdʒɛnərɪt). **3.** having declined or deteriorated to a lower mental, moral, or physical level; degraded; corrupt. ~*n.* (dɪˈdʒɛnərɪt). **4.** a degenerate person. [C15: < L, < *dēgener* departing from its kind, ignoble, < DE- + *genus* race] —**deˈgenerately** *adv.* —**deˈgenerateness** *n.* —**deˈgenerative** *adj.*

degenerate matter *n. Astrophysics.* the highly compressed state of a star's matter when its atoms virtually touch in the final stage of its evolution into a white dwarf.

degeneration (dɪˌdʒɛnəˈreɪʃən) *n.* **1.** the process of degenerating. **2.** the state of being degenerate. **3.** *Biol.* the loss of specialization, function, or structure by organisms and their parts. **4.** impairment or loss of the function and structure of cells or tissues, as by disease or injury. **5.** *Electronics.* negative feedback of a signal.

degradable (dɪˈgreɪdəbᵊl) *adj.* **1.** capable of being decomposed chemically or biologically. **2.** capable of being degraded.

degradation (ˌdɛgrəˈdeɪʃən) *n.* **1.** a degrading or being degraded. **2.** a state of degeneration or squalor. **3.** some act, constraint, etc., that is degrading. **4.** the wearing down of the surface of rocks, cliffs, etc., by erosion. **5.** *Chem.* a breakdown of a molecule into atoms or smaller molecules. **6.** *Physics.* an irreversible process in which the energy available to do work is decreased. **7.** *R.C. Church.* the permanent unfrocking of a priest.

degrade (dɪˈgreɪd) *vb.* **1.** (*tr.*) to reduce in worth, character, etc.; disgrace. **2.** (diːˈgreɪd) (*tr.*) to reduce in rank or status; demote. **3.** (*tr.*) to reduce in strength, quality, etc. **4.** to reduce or be reduced by erosion or down-cutting, as a land surface or bed of a river. **5.** *Chem.* to decompose into atoms or smaller molecules. [C14: < LL *dēgradāre,* < L DE- + *gradus* rank, degree] —**deˈgrader** *n.*

degrading (dɪˈgreɪdɪŋ) *adj.* causing humiliation; debasing. —**deˈgradingly** *adv.*

degree (dɪˈgriː) *n.* **1.** a stage in a scale of relative amount or intensity: *a high degree of competence.* **2.** an academic award conferred by a university or college on successful completion of a course or as an honorary distinction (**honorary degree**). **3.** any of three categories of seriousness of a burn. **4.** (in the U.S.) any of the categories into which a crime is divided according to its seriousness. **5.** *Genealogy.* a step in a line of descent. **6.** *Grammar.* any of the forms of an adjective used to indicate relative amount or intensity: in English they are *positive, comparative,* and *superlative.* **7.** *Music.* any note of a diatonic scale relative to the other notes in that scale. **8.** a unit of temperature on a specified scale. Symbol: °. See also **Celsius scale, Fahrenheit scale. 9.** a measure of angle equal to one three-hundred-and-sixtieth of the angle traced by one complete revolution of a line about one of its ends. Symbol: °. **10.** a unit of latitude or longitude used to define points on the earth's surface. Symbol: °. **11.** a unit on any of several scales of measurement, as for specific gravity. Symbol: °. **12.** *Maths.* **a.** the highest power or the sum of the powers of any term in a polynomial or by itself: $x^4 + x + 3$ *and* xyz^2 *are of the fourth degree.* **b.** the greatest power of the highest order derivative in a differential equation. **13.** *Obs.* a step; rung. **14.** *Arch.* a stage in social status or rank. **15. by degrees.** little by little; gradually. **16. one degree under.** *Inf.* off colour; ill. **17. to a degree.** somewhat; rather. [C13: < OF *degre,* < L DE- + *gradus* step]

degree of freedom *n.* **1.** *Chem.* the least number of independently variable properties needed to determine the state of a system. See also **phase rule. 2.** one of the independent components of motion (translation, vibration, and rotation) of an atom or molecule.

dehisce (dɪˈhɪs) *vb.* (*intr.*) (of fruits, anthers, etc.) to burst open spontaneously, releasing seeds, pollen, etc. [C17: < L *dēhiscere* to split open, < DE- + *hiscere* to yawn, gape] **—deˈhiscent** *adj.*

dehorn (diːˈhɔːn) *vb.* (*tr.*) to remove the horns of (cattle, sheep, or goats).

dehumanize *or* **-ise** (diːˈhjuːməˌnaɪz) *vb.* (*tr.*) **1.** to deprive of human qualities. **2.** to render mechanical, artificial, or routine. **—deˌhumaniˈzation** *or* **-iˈsation** *n.*

dehumidify (ˌdiːhjuːˈmɪdɪˌfaɪ) *vb.* **-fying, -fied.** (*tr.*) to remove water from (the air, etc.) **—ˌdehuˌmidifiˈcation** *n.* **—ˌdehuˈmidiˌfier** *n.*

dehydrate (diːˈhaɪdreɪt, ˌdiːhaɪˈdreɪt) *vb.* **1.** to lose or cause to lose water. **2.** to lose or deprive of water, as the body or tissues. **—ˌdehyˈdration** *n.* **—deˈhydrator** *n.*

dehydrogenate (diːˈhaɪdrədʒəˌneɪt), **dehydrogenize,** *or* **-ise** (diːˈhaɪdrədʒəˌnaɪz) *vb.* (*tr.*) to remove hydrogen from. **—deˌhydrogeˈnation, deˌhydrogeniˈzation,** *or* **-iˈsation** *n.*

de-ice (diːˈaɪs) *vb.* to free or be freed of ice.

de-icer (diːˈaɪsə) *n.* **1.** a mechanical or thermal device designed to melt or stop the formation of ice on an aircraft. **2.** a substance used for this purpose, esp. an aerosol that can be sprayed on car windscreens to remove ice or frost.

deictic (ˈdaɪktɪk) *adj.* **1.** *Logic.* proving by direct argument. Cf. **elenctic** (see **elenchus**). **2.** *Grammar.* **a.** denoting a word whose reference is determined by the context of its utterance. **b.** (*as n.*)*: the word "here" is a deictic.* [C17: < Gk *deiktikos* concerning proof, < *deiknunai* to show]

deify (ˈdiːɪˌfaɪ, ˈdeɪ-) *vb.* **-fying, -fied.** (*tr.*) **1.** to exalt to the position of a god or personify as a god. **2.** to accord divine honour or worship to. [C14: < OF, < LL *deificāre,* < L *deus* god + *facere* to make] **—ˌdeifiˈcation** *n.* **—ˈdeiˌfier** *n.*

deign (deɪn) *vb.* **1.** (*intr.*) to think it fit or worthy of oneself (to do something); condescend. **2.** (*tr.*) *Arch.* to vouchsafe. [C13: < OF, < L *dignārī* to consider worthy, < *dignus*]

deism (ˈdiːɪzəm, ˈdeɪ-) *n.* belief in the existence of God based solely on natural reason, without reference to revelation. Cf. **theism.** [C17: < F *déisme,* < L *deus* god] **—ˈdeist** *n., adj.* **—deˈistic** *or* **deˈistical** *adj.* **—deˈistically** *adv.*

deity (ˈdiːɪtɪ, ˈdeɪ-) *n., pl.* **-ties. 1.** a god or goddess. **2.** the state of being divine; godhead. **3.** the rank of a god. **4.** the nature or character of God. [C14: < OF, < LL *deitās,* < L *deus* god]

Deity (ˈdiːɪtɪ, ˈdeɪ-) *n.* **the.** God.

déjà vu (ˈdeɪʒæ ˈvuː) *n.* the experience of perceiving a new situation as if it had occurred before. [< F, lit.: already seen]

deject (dɪˈdʒɛkt) *vb.* (*tr.*) to have a depressing effect on; dispirit; dishearten. [C15: < L *dēicere* to cast down, < DE- + *iacere* to throw]

dejected (dɪˈdʒɛktɪd) *adj.* miserable; despondent; downhearted. **—deˈjectedly** *adv.*

dejection (dɪˈdʒɛkʃən) *n.* **1.** lowness of spirits; depression. **2. a.** faecal matter. **b.** defecation.

de jure (deɪ ˈdʒʊəreɪ) *adv.* according to law; by right; legally. Cf. **de facto.** [L]

deka- *or* **dek-** *combining form.* variants of **deca-.**

deke (diːk) *Canad. sl.* ~*vb.* **1.** (*tr.*) (in ice hockey or box lacrosse) to draw a defending player out of position by faking a shot or movement. ~*n.* **2.** such a shot or movement.

dekko (ˈdɛkəʊ) *n., pl.* **-kos.** *Brit. sl.* a look; glance (esp. in **take a dekko (at)**). [C19: < Hindi *dekho!* look! < *dekhnā* to see]

del. *abbrev. for* delegate.

Delaware (ˈdɛləˌwɛə) *n.* **1.** (*pl.* **-wares** *or* **-ware**) a member of a North American Indian people formerly living near the Delaware River **2.** the language of this people.

delay (dɪˈleɪ) *vb.* **1.** (*tr.*) to put off to a later time; defer. **2.** (*tr.*) to slow up or cause to be late. **3.** (*intr.*) to be irresolute or put off doing something. **4.** (*intr.*) to linger; dawdle. ~*n.* **5.** a delaying or being delayed. **6.** the interval between one event and another. [C13: < OF, < *des-* off + *laier* to leave, < L *laxāre* to loosen] **—deˈlayer** *n.*

delayed action *or* **delay action** *n.* a device for operating a mechanism, such as a camera shutter, a short time after setting.

dele (ˈdiːlɪ) *n., pl.* **deles. 1.** a sign (₰) indicating that typeset matter is to be deleted. ~*vb.* **deleing, deled. 2.** (*tr.*) to mark (matter to be deleted) with a dele. [C18: < L: delete (imperative), < *dēlēre* to destroy, obliterate]

delectable (dɪˈlɛktəbᵊl) *adj.* highly enjoyable, esp. pleasing to the taste; delightful. [C14: < L *dēlectābilis,* < *dēlectāre* to DELIGHT] **—deˈlectableness** *or* **deˌlectaˈbility** *n.*

delectation (ˌdiːlɛkˈteɪʃən) *n.* pleasure; enjoyment.

delegate *n.* (ˈdɛlɪˌgeɪt, -gɪt). **1.** a person chosen to act for another or others, esp. at a conference or meeting. ~*vb.* (ˈdɛlɪˌgeɪt). **2.** to give (duties, powers, etc.) to another as representative; depute. **3.** (*tr.*) to authorize (a person) as representative. [C14: < L *dēlēgāre* to send on a mission, < *lēgāre* to send, depute] **—delegable** (ˈdɛlɪgəbᵊl) *adj.*

delegation (ˌdɛlɪˈgeɪʃən) *n.* **1.** a person or group chosen to represent another or others. **2.** a delegating or being delegated.

delete (dɪˈliːt) *vb.* (*tr.*) to remove (something printed or written); erase; strike out. [C17: < L *dēlēre* to destroy, obliterate] **—deˈletion** *n.*

deleterious (ˌdɛlɪˈtɪərɪəs) *adj.* harmful; injurious; hurtful. [C17: < NL, < Gk *dēlētērios,* < *dēleisthai* to hurt] **—ˌdeleˈteriousness** *n.*

Delft (dɛlft) *n.* tin-glazed earthenware which originated in Delft, a town in the SW Netherlands, typically having blue decoration on a white ground. Also called: **delftware.**

deli (ˈdɛlɪ) *n., pl.* **delis.** an informal word for **delicatessen.**

deliberate *adj.* (dɪˈlɪbərɪt). **1.** carefully thought out in advance; intentional. **2.** careful or unhurried: *a deliberate pace.* ~*vb.* (dɪˈlɪbəˌreɪt). **3.** to consider (something) deeply; think over. [C15: < L *dēlīberāre,* < *lībrāre* to weigh, < *lībra* scales] **—deˈliberately** *adv.* **—deˈliberateness** *n.* **—deˈliberˌator** *n.*

deliberation (dɪˌlɪbəˈreɪʃən) *n.* **1.** careful consideration. **2.** (*often pl.*) formal discussion, as of a committee. **3.** care or absence of hurry.

deliberative (dɪˈlɪbərətɪv) *adj.* **1.** of or for deliberating: *a deliberative assembly.* **2.** characterized by deliberation. **—deˈliberatively** *adv.* **—deˈliberativeness** *n.*

delicacy (ˈdɛlɪkəsɪ) *n., pl.* **-cies. 1.** fine or subtle quality, character, construction, etc. **2.** fragile or graceful beauty. **3.** something that is considered choice to eat, such as caviar. **4.** fragile construction or constitution. **5.** refinement of feeling, manner, or appreciation. **6.** fussy or squeamish refinement, esp. in matters of taste, propriety, etc. **7.** need for tactful or sensitive handling. **8.** sensitivity of response, as of an instrument.

delicate (ˈdɛlɪkɪt) *adj.* **1.** fine or subtle in quality, character, construction, etc. **2.** having a soft or fragile beauty. **3.** (of colour, tone, taste, etc.) pleasantly subtle. **4.** easily damaged or injured; fragile. **5.** precise or sensitive in action: *a delicate mechanism.* **6.** requiring tact. **7.** showing regard for the feelings of others. **8.** excessively refined; squeamish. [C14: < L *dēlicātus* affording pleasure, < *dēliciae* (pl.) delight, pleasure] —ˈ**delicately** *adv.* —ˈ**delicateness** *n.*

delicatessen (ˌdɛlɪkəˈtɛsᵊn) *n.* **1.** various foods, esp. unusual or imported foods, already cooked or prepared. **2.** a shop selling these foods. [C19: < G *Delikatessen,* lit.: delicacies, < F *délicatesse*]

delicious (dɪˈlɪʃəs) *adj.* **1.** very appealing, esp. to taste or smell. **2.** extremely enjoyable. [C13: < OF, < LL *dēliciōsus,* < L *dēliciae* delights, < *dēlicere* to entice; see DELIGHT] —**deˈliciously** *adv.* —**deˈliciousness** *n.*

delight (dɪˈlaɪt) *vb.* **1.** (*tr.*) to please greatly. **2.** (*intr.;* foll. by *in*) to take great pleasure (in). ~*n.* **3.** extreme pleasure. **4.** something that causes this. [C13: < OF, < *deleitier* to please, < L *dēlectāre,* < *dēlicere* to allure, < DE- + *lacere* to entice] —**deˈlighted** *adj.* —**deˈlightedly** *adv.*

delightful (dɪˈlaɪtfʊl) *adj.* giving great delight; very pleasing, beautiful, charming, etc. —**deˈlightfully** *adv.* —**deˈlightfulness** *n.*

Delilah (dɪˈlaɪlə) *n.* **1.** Samson's Philistine mistress, who betrayed him (Judges 16). **2.** a voluptuous and treacherous woman; temptress.

delimit (diːˈlɪmɪt) *or* **delimitate** *vb.* (*tr.*) to mark or prescribe the limits or boundaries of. —**deˌlimiˈtation** *n.* —**deˈlimitative** *adj.*

delineate (dɪˈlɪnɪˌeɪt) *vb.* (*tr.*) **1.** to trace the outline of. **2.** to represent pictorially; depict. **3.** to portray in words; describe. [C16: < L *dēlīneāre* to sketch out, < *līnea* LINE[1]] —**deˌlineˈation** *n.* —**deˈlineative** *adj.*

delinquency (dɪˈlɪŋkwənsɪ) *n., pl.* **-cies.** **1.** an offence or misdeed, esp. one committed by a young person. See **juvenile delinquency.** **2.** failure or negligence in duty or obligation. **3.** a delinquent nature or delinquent behaviour. [C17: < LL *dēlinquentia* fault, offence, < L *dēlinquere* to transgress, < DE- + *linquere* to forsake]

delinquent (dɪˈlɪŋkwənt) *n.* **1.** someone, esp. a young person, guilty of delinquency. ~*adj.* **2.** guilty of an offence or misdeed. **3.** failing in or neglectful of duty or obligation. [C17: < L *dēlinquēns* offending; see DELINQUENCY]

deliquesce (ˌdɛlɪˈkwɛs) *vb.* (*intr.*) (esp. of certain salts) to dissolve gradually in water absorbed from the air. [C18: < L *dēliquēscere,* < DE- + *liquēscere* to melt, < *liquēre* to be liquid] —ˌ**deliˈquescence** *n.* —ˌ**deliˈquescent** *adj.*

delirious (dɪˈlɪrɪəs) *adj.* **1.** affected with delirium. **2.** wildly excited, esp. with joy or enthusiasm. —**deˈliriously** *adv.*

delirium (dɪˈlɪrɪəm) *n., pl.* **-liriums** *or* **-liria** (-ˈlɪrɪə). **1.** a state of excitement and mental confusion, often accompanied by hallucinations, caused by high fever, poisoning, brain injury, etc. **2.** violent excitement or emotion; frenzy. [C16: < L: madness, < *dēlīrāre,* lit.: to swerve from a furrow, hence be crazy, < DE- + *līra* furrow]

delirium tremens (ˈtrɛmɛnz, ˈtriː-) *n.* a severe psychotic condition occurring in some persons with chronic alcoholism, characterized by delirium, tremor, anxiety, and vivid hallucinations. Abbrevs.: **DT's** (informal), **dt.** [C19: NL, lit.: trembling delirium]

deliver (dɪˈlɪvə) *vb.* (*mainly tr.*) **1.** to carry to a destination, esp. to distribute (goods, mail, etc.) to several places. **2.** (often foll. by *over* or *up*) to hand over or transfer. **3.** (often foll. by *from*) to release or rescue (from captivity, harm, etc.). **4.** (*also intr.*) **a.** to aid in the birth of (offspring). **b.** to give birth to (offspring). **c.** (usually foll. by *of*) to aid (a female) in the birth (of offspring). **d.** (*passive;* foll. by *of*) to give birth (to offspring). **5.** to present (a speech, idea, etc.). **6.** to utter: *to deliver a cry of exultation.* **7.** to discharge or release (something, such as a blow or shot) suddenly. **8.** (*intr.*) *Inf.* Also: **deliver the goods.** to produce something promised or expected. **9.** *Chiefly U.S.* to cause (voters, etc.) to support a given candidate, cause, etc. **10. deliver oneself of.** to speak with deliberation or at length. [C13: < OF, < LL *dēlīberāre* to set free, < L DE- + *līberāre* to free] —**deˈliverable** *adj.* —**deˈliverer** *n.*

deliverance (dɪˈlɪvərəns) *n.* **1.** a formal expression of opinion. **2.** rescue from moral corruption or evil; salvation.

delivery (dɪˈlɪvərɪ) *n., pl.* **-eries.** **1. a.** the act of delivering or distributing goods, mail, etc. **b.** something that is delivered. **2.** the act of giving birth to a child. **3.** manner or style of utterance, esp. in public speaking: *the chairman had a clear delivery.* **4.** the act of giving or transferring or the state of being given or transferred. **5.** a rescuing or being rescued; liberation. **6.** *Sport.* the act or manner of bowling or throwing a ball. **7.** the handing over of property, a deed, etc.

dell (dɛl) *n.* a small, esp. wooded hollow. [OE]

delouse (diːˈlaʊs, -ˈlaʊz) *vb.* (*tr.*) to rid (a person or animal) of lice as a sanitary measure.

Delphic (ˈdɛlfɪk) *or* **Delphian** *adj.* **1.** of or relating to the ancient Greek city of Delphi or its oracle or temple. **2.** obscure or ambiguous.

delphinium (dɛlˈfɪnɪəm) *n., pl.* **-iums** *or* **-ia** (-ɪə). a plant with spikes of blue, pink, or white spurred flowers. See also **larkspur.** [C17: NL, < Gk *delphinion* larkspur, < *delphis* dolphin, referring to the shape of the nectary]

delta (ˈdɛltə) *n.* **1.** the fourth letter in the Greek alphabet (Δ or δ). **2.** (*cap. when part of name*) the flat alluvial area at the mouth of some rivers where the mainstream splits up into several distributaries. **3.** *Maths.* a finite increment in a variable. [C16: via L < Gk, of Semitic origin] —**deltaic** (dɛlˈteɪɪk) *or* ˈ**deltic** *adj.*

delta connection *n.* a connection used in a three-phase electrical system in which three elements in series form a triangle, the supply being input and output at the three junctions.

delta ray *n.* a particle, esp. an electron, ejected from matter by ionizing radiation.

delta rhythm *or* **wave** *n. Physiol.* the normal electrical activity of the cerebral cortex during deep sleep. See also **brain wave.**

delta wing *n.* a triangular swept-back aircraft wing.

deltiology (ˌdɛltɪˈɒlədʒɪ) *n.* the collection and study of postcards. [C20: < Gk *deltion,* dim. of *deltos* a writing tablet + -LOGY] —ˌ**deltiˈologist** *n.*

deltoid (ˈdɛltɔɪd) *n.* a thick muscle of the shoulder that acts to raise the arm. [C18: < Gk *deltoeidēs* triangular, < DELTA]

delude (dɪˈluːd) *vb.* (*tr.*) to deceive; mislead; beguile. [C15: < L *dēlūdere* to mock, play false, < DE- + *lūdere* to play] —**deˈludable** *adj.* —**deˈluder** *n.*

deluge (ˈdɛljuːdʒ) *n.* **1.** a great flood of water. **2.** torrential rain. **3.** an overwhelming rush or number. ~*vb.* (*tr.*) **4.** to flood. **5.** to overwhelm; inundate. [C14: < OF, < L *dīluvium,* < *dīluere* to wash away, drench, < *di-* DIS-[1] + *-luere,* < *lavere* to wash]

Deluge (ˈdɛljuːdʒ) *n.* **the.** another name for the **Flood.**

delusion (dɪˈluːʒən) *n.* **1.** a mistaken idea, belief, etc. **2.** *Psychiatry.* a belief held in the face of evidence to the contrary, that is resistant to all reason. **3.** a deluding or being deluded. —**deˈlusional** *adj.* —**deˈlusive** *adj.* —**delusory** (dɪˈluːsərɪ) *adj.*

de luxe (də ˈlʌks, ˈlʊks) *adj.* **1.** rich or sumptuous; superior in quality: *the de luxe model of a car.* ~*adv.* **2.** *Chiefly U.S.* in a luxurious manner. [C19: < F, lit.: of luxury]

delve (dɛlv) *vb.* (*mainly intr.;* often foll. by *in* or *into*) **1.** to research deeply or intensively (for information, etc.). **2.** to search or rummage. **3.** to dig or burrow deeply. **4.** (*also tr.*) *Arch. or Brit. dialect.* to dig. [OE *delfan*] —ˈ**delver** *n.*

Dem. (in the U.S.) *abbrev. for* Democrat(ic).

demagnetize *or* **-ise** (diːˈmægnəˌtaɪz) *vb.* to remove or lose magnetic properties. Also:

degauss. —**deˌmagnetiˈzation** *or* **-iˈsation** *n.* —**deˈmagnetˌizer** *or* **-ˌiser** *n.*

demagogue *or U.S. (sometimes)* **demagog** (ˈdɛməˌgɒg) *n.* **1.** a political agitator who appeals with crude oratory to the prejudice and passions of the mob. **2.** (esp. in the ancient world) any popular political leader or orator. [C17: < Gk *dēmagōgos* people's leader, < *dēmos* people + *agein* to lead] —ˌ**demaˈgogic** *adj.* —ˌ**demaˈgoguery** *n.*

demagogy (ˈdɛməˌgɒgɪ) *n., pl.* **-gogies. 1.** demagoguery. **2.** rule by a demagogue or by demagogues. **3.** a group of demagogues.

demand (dɪˈmɑːnd) *vb.* (*tr.; may take a clause as object or an infinitive*) **1.** to request peremptorily or urgently. **2.** to require as just, urgent, etc.: *the situation demands attention.* **3.** to claim as a right; exact. **4.** *Law.* to make a formal legal claim to (property). ~*n.* **5.** an urgent or peremptory requirement or request. **6.** something that requires special effort or sacrifice. **7.** the act of demanding something or the thing demanded. **8.** an insistent question. **9.** *Econ.* **a.** willingness and ability to purchase goods and services. **b.** the amount of a commodity that consumers are willing and able to purchase at a specified price. Cf. **supply**[1]. **10.** *Law.* a formal legal claim, esp. to real property. **11. in demand.** sought after. **12. on demand.** as soon as requested. [C13: < Anglo-F, < Med. L *dēmandāre*, < L: to commit to, < DE- + *mandāre* to command, entrust] —**deˈmandable** *adj.* —**deˈmander** *n.*

demanding (dɪˈmɑːndɪŋ) *adj.* requiring great patience, skill, etc.: *a demanding job.*

demarcate (ˈdiːmɑːˌkeɪt) *vb.* (*tr.*) **1.** to mark the boundaries, limits, etc., of. **2.** to separate; distinguish. —ˈ**demarˌcator** *n.*

demarcation *or* **demarkation** (ˌdiːmɑːˈkeɪʃən) *n.* **1.** the act of establishing limits or boundaries. **2.** a limit or boundary. **3. a.** a strict separation of the kinds of work performed by members of different trade unions. **b.** (*as modifier*): *demarcation dispute.* **4.** separation or distinction (as in **line of demarcation**). [C18: < Sp. *demarcar* to appoint the boundaries of, < *marcar* to mark, < It., of Gmc origin]

démarche *French.* (demarʃ) *n.* a move, step, or manoeuvre, esp. in diplomatic affairs. [C17: lit.: walk, gait, < OF *demarcher* to tread, trample]

dematerialize *or* **-ise** (diːməˈtɪərɪəˌlaɪz) *vb.* (*intr.*) **1.** to cease to have material existence, as in science fiction or spiritualism. **2.** to vanish. —**demaˌterialiˈzation** *or* **-iˈsation** *n.*

deme (diːm) *n.* **1.** (in ancient Attica) a geographical unit of local government. **2.** *Biol.* a group of individuals within a species that possess particular characteristics of cytology, genetics, etc. [C19: < Gk *dēmos* district in local government, the populace]

demean[1] (dɪˈmiːn) *vb.* (*tr.*) to lower (oneself) in dignity, status, or character; humble; debase. [C17: see DE-, MEAN[2]]

demean[2] (dɪˈmiːn) *vb.* (*tr.*) *Rare.* to behave or conduct (oneself). [C13: < OF, < DE- + *mener* to lead, < L *mināre* to drive (animals), < *minārī* to use threats]

demeanour *or U.S.* **demeanor** (dɪˈmiːnə) *n.* **1.** the way a person behaves towards others. **2.** bearing or mien. [C15: see DEMEAN[2]]

dement (dɪˈmɛnt) *vb.* **1.** (*intr.*) to deteriorate mentally, esp. because of old age. **2.** (*tr.*) *Rare.* to drive mad; make insane. [C16: < LL *dēmentāre* to drive mad, < L DE- + *mēns* mind]

demented (dɪˈmɛntɪd) *adj.* mad; insane. —**deˈmentedly** *adv.* —**deˈmentedness** *n.*

dementia (dɪˈmɛnʃə, -ʃɪə) *n.* a state of serious mental deterioration, of organic or functional origin. [C19: < L: madness; see DEMENT]

dementia praecox (ˈpriːkɒks) *n.* a former name for **schizophrenia.** [C19: NL, lit.: premature dementia]

demerara (ˌdɛməˈrɛərə, -ˈrɑːrə) *n.* brown crystallized cane sugar from the West Indies. [C19: after *Demerara*, a region of Guyana]

demerit (diːˈmɛrɪt) *n.* **1.** something that deserves censure. **2.** *U.S. & Canad.* a mark given against a student, etc., for failure or misconduct. **3.** a fault. [C14 (orig.: worth, desert, ult.: something worthy of blame): < L *dēmerērī* to deserve] —**deˌmeriˈtorious** *adj.*

demersal (dɪˈmɜːsᵊl) *adj.* living or occurring in deep water or on the bottom of a sea or lake. [C19: < L *dēmersus* submerged (< *mergere* to dip) + -AL[1]]

demesne (dɪˈmeɪn, -ˈmiːn) *n.* **1.** land surrounding a house or manor. **2.** *Property law.* the possession and use of one's own property or land. **3.** realm; domain. **4.** a region or district. [C14: < OF *demeine;* see DOMAIN]

demi- *prefix.* **1.** half: *demirelief.* **2.** of less than full size, status, or rank: *demigod.* [via F < Med. L, < L *dīmīdius* half, < *dis-* apart + *medius* middle]

demigod (ˈdɛmɪˌgɒd) *n.* **1. a.** a being who is part mortal, part god. **b.** a lesser deity. **2.** a person with godlike attributes. [C16: translation of L *sēmideus*] —ˈ**demiˌgoddess** *fem. n.*

demijohn (ˈdɛmɪˌdʒɒn) *n.* a large bottle with a short narrow neck, often encased in wickerwork. [C18: prob. < F *dame-jeanne,* < *dame* lady + *Jeanne* Jane]

demilitarize *or* **-ise** (diːˈmɪlɪtəˌraɪz) *vb.* (*tr.*) **1.** to remove and prohibit any military presence or function in (an area): *demilitarized zone.* **2.** to free of military character, purpose, etc. —**deˌmilitariˈzation** *or* **-iˈsation** *n.*

demimondaine (ˌdɛmɪˈmɒndeɪn) *n.* a woman of the demimonde. [C19: < F]

demimonde (ˌdɛmɪˈmɒnd) *n.* **1.** (esp. in the 19th century) those women considered to be outside respectable society, esp. on account of sexual promiscuity. **2.** any group considered to be not wholly respectable. [C19: < F, lit.: half-world]

demise (dɪˈmaɪz) *n.* **1.** failure or termination. **2.** a euphemistic or formal word for **death. 3.** *Property law.* a transfer of an estate by lease or on the death of the owner. **4.** the transfer of sovereignty to a successor upon the death, abdication, etc., of a ruler (esp. in **demise of the crown**). ~*vb.* **5.** to transfer or be transferred by inheritance, will, or succession. **6.** (*tr.*) *Property law.* to transfer for a limited period; lease. **7.** (*tr.*) to transfer (sovereignty, a title, etc.) [C16: < OF, fem. of *demis* dismissed, < *demettre* to send away, < L *dīmittere*] —**deˈmisable** *adj.*

demisemiquaver (ˈdɛmɪˌsɛmɪˌkweɪvə) *n. Music.* a note having the time value of one thirty-second of a semibreve. Usual U.S. and Canad. name: **thirty-second note.**

demist (diːˈmɪst) *vb.* to free or become free of condensation. —**deˈmister** *n.*

demitasse (ˈdɛmɪˌtæs) *n.* **1.** a small cup for serving black coffee, as after dinner. **2.** the coffee itself. [C19: F, lit.: half-cup]

demiurge (ˈdɛmɪˌɜːdʒ) *n.* **1.** (in the philosophy of Plato) the creator of the universe. **2.** (in Gnostic philosophy) the creator of the universe, supernatural but subordinate to the Supreme Being. [C17: < Church L, < Gk *dēmiourgos* skilled workman, lit.: one who works for the people, < *dēmos* people + *ergon* work] —ˌ**demiˈurgic** *or* ˌ**demiˈurgical** *adj.*

demo (ˈdɛməʊ) *n., pl.* **-os.** *Inf.* **1.** short for **demonstration** (sense 5). **2.** a demonstration record or tape.

demo- *or before a vowel* **dem-** *combining form.* indicating people or population: *demography.* [< Gk *dēmos*]

demob (diːˈmɒb) *Brit. inf.* ~*vb.* **-mobbing, -mobbed. 1.** to demobilize. ~*n.* **2.** demobilization.

demobilize *or* **-ise** (diːˈməʊbɪˌlaɪz) *vb.* to disband, as troops, etc. —**deˌmobiliˈzation** *or* **-iˈsation** *n.*

democracy (dɪˈmɒkrəsɪ) *n., pl.* **-cies. 1.** government by the people or their elected representatives. **2.** a political or social unit governed ultimately by all its members. **3.** the practice or spirit of social equality. **4.** a social condition of classlessness and equality. [C16: < F, < LL, < Gk *dēmokratia* government by the people]

democrat (ˈdɛməˌkræt) *n.* **1.** an advocate of democracy. **2.** a member or supporter of a democratic party or movement.

Democrat (ˈdɛməˌkræt) *n. U.S. politics.* a member or supporter of the Democratic Party. —ˌ**Demoˈcratic** *adj.*

democratic (ˌdɛməˈkrætɪk) *adj.* **1.** of or relating to the principles of democracy. **2.** upholding democracy or the interests of the common people. **3.** popular with or for the benefit of all. —ˌ**demoˈcratically** *adv.*

democratize *or* **-ise** (dɪˈmɒkrəˌtaɪz) *vb.* (*tr.*) to make democratic. —**deˌmocratiˈzation** *or* **-iˈsation** *n.*

démodé *French.* (demɔde) *adj.* outmoded. [F, < *dé-* out of + *mode* fashion]

demodulate (diːˈmɒdjʊˌleɪt) *vb.* to carry out demodulation on. —**deˈmoduˌlator** *n.*

demodulation (ˌdiːmɒdjʊˈleɪʃən) *n. Electronics.* the act or process by which an output wave or signal is obtained having the characteristics of the original modulating wave or signal; the reverse of modulation.

demography (dɪˈmɒgrəfɪ) *n.* the scientific study of human populations, esp. with references to their size, distribution, etc. [C19: < F, < Gk *dēmos* the populace; see -GRAPHY] —**deˈmographer** *n.* —**demographic** (ˌdiːməˈgræfɪk, ˌdɛmə-) *adj.*

demoiselle (dəmwɑːˈzɛl) *n.* **1.** a small crane of central Asia, N Africa, and SE Europe, having a grey plumage with black breast feathers and white ear tufts. **2.** a less common name for a **damselfly. 3.** a literary word for **damsel.** [C16: < F: young woman; see DAMSEL]

demolish (dɪˈmɒlɪʃ) *vb.* (*tr.*) **1.** to tear down or break up (buildings, etc.). **2.** to put an end to (an argument, etc.). **3.** *Facetious.* to eat up. [C16: < F, < L *dēmōlīrī* to throw down, < DE- + *mōlīrī* to construct, < *mōles* mass] —**deˈmolisher** *n.*

demolition (ˌdɛməˈlɪʃən, ˌdiː-) *n.* **1.** a demolishing or being demolished. **2.** *Chiefly mil.* destruction by explosives. —ˌ**demoˈlitionist** *n., adj.*

demon (ˈdiːmən) *n.* **1.** an evil spirit or devil. **2.** a person, obsession, etc., thought of as evil or cruel. **3.** Also called: **daemon, daimon.** an attendant or ministering spirit; genius: *the demon of inspiration.* **4. a.** a person extremely skilful in or devoted to a given activity, esp. a sport: *a demon at cycling.* **b.** (*as modifier*): *a demon cyclist.* **5.** a variant spelling of **daemon** (sense 1). **6.** *Austral. & N.Z. sl.* a detective or policeman, esp. one in plain clothes. [C15: < L *daemōn* (evil) spirit, < Gk *daimōn* spirit, deity, fate] —**demonic** (dɪˈmɒnɪk) *adj.*

demonetize *or* **-ise** (diːˈmʌnɪˌtaɪz) *vb.* (*tr.*) **1.** to deprive (a metal) of its capacity as a monetary standard. **2.** to withdraw from use as currency. —**deˌmonetiˈzation** *or* **-iˈsation** *n.*

demoniac (dɪˈməʊnɪˌæk) *adj. also* **demoniacal** (ˌdiːməˈnaɪək°l). **1.** of or like a demon. **2.** suggesting inner possession or inspiration: *the demoniac fire of genius.* **3.** frantic; frenzied. ~*n.* **4.** a person possessed by a demon. —ˌ**demoˈniacally** *adv.*

demonism (ˈdiːməˌnɪzəm) *n.* belief in the existence and power of demons. —ˈ**demonist** *n.*

demonolatry (ˌdiːməˈnɒlətrɪ) *n.* the worship of demons. [C17: see DEMON, -LATRY]

demonology (ˌdiːməˈnɒlədʒɪ) *n.* the study of demons or demonic beliefs. Also called: **demonism.** —ˌ**demonˈologist** *n.*

demonstrable (ˈdɛmənstrəb°l, dɪˈmɒn-) *adj.* able to be demonstrated or proved. —ˌ**demonstraˈbility** *n.* —ˈ**demonstrably** *adv.*

demonstrate (ˈdɛmənˌstreɪt) *vb.* **1.** (*tr.*) to show or prove, esp. by reasoning, evidence, etc. **2.** (*tr.*) to evince; reveal the existence of. **3.** (*tr.*) to explain by experiment, example, etc. **4.** (*tr.*) to display and explain the workings of (a machine, product, etc.). **5.** (*intr.*) to manifest support, protest, etc., by public parades or rallies. **6.** (*intr.*) to be employed as a demonstrator of machinery, etc. **7.** (*intr.*) *Mil.* to make a show of force. [C16: < L *dēmonstrāre* to point out, < *monstrāre* to show]

demonstration (ˌdɛmənˈstreɪʃən) *n.* **1.** the act of demonstrating. **2.** proof or evidence leading to proof. **3.** an explanation, illustration, or experiment showing how something works. **4.** a manifestation of support or protest by public rallies, parades, etc. **5.** a manifestation of emotion. **6.** a show of military force. —ˌ**demonˈstrational** *adj.* —ˌ**demonˈstrationist** *n.*

demonstrative (dɪˈmɒnstrətɪv) *adj.* **1.** tending to express one's feelings easily or unreservedly. **2.** (*postpositive;* foll. by *of*) serving as proof; indicative. **3.** involving or characterized by demonstration. **4.** conclusive. **5.** *Grammar.* denoting or belonging to a class of determiners used to point out the individual referent or referents intended, such as *this* and *those.* Cf. **interrogative, relative.** ~*n.* **6.** *Grammar.* a demonstrative word. —**deˈmonstratively** *adv.* —**deˈmonstrativeness** *n.*

demonstrator (ˈdɛmənˌstreɪtə) *n.* **1.** a person who demonstrates equipment, machines, products, etc. **2.** a person who takes part in a public demonstration.

demoralize *or* **-ise** (dɪˈmɒrəˌlaɪz) *vb.* (*tr.*) **1.** to undermine the morale of; dishearten. **2.** to corrupt. **3.** to throw into confusion. —**deˌmoraliˈzation** *or* **-iˈsation** *n.*

demote (dɪˈməʊt) *vb.* (*tr.*) to lower in rank or position; relegate. [C19: < DE- + (PRO)MOTE] —**deˈmotion** *n.*

demotic (dɪˈmɒtɪk) *adj.* **1.** of or relating to the common people; popular. **2.** of or relating to a simplified form of hieroglyphics used in ancient Egypt. Cf. **hieratic.** ~*n.* **3.** the demotic script of ancient Egypt. [C19: < Gk *dēmotikos* of the people, < *dēmotēs* a man of the people, commoner] —**deˈmotist** *n.*

dempster (ˈdɛmpstə) *n.* a variant spelling of **deemster.**

demulcent (dɪˈmʌls°nt) *adj.* **1.** soothing. ~*n.* **2.** a drug or agent that soothes irritation. [C18: < L *dēmulcēre,* < DE- + *mulcēre* to stroke]

demur (dɪˈmɜː) *vb.* **-murring, -murred.** (*intr.*) **1.** to show reluctance; object. **2.** *Law.* to raise an objection by entering a demurrer. ~*n. also* **demurral** (dɪˈmʌrəl). **3.** the act of demurring. **4.** an objection raised. [C13: < OF, < L *dēmorārī,* < *morārī* to delay] —**deˈmurrable** *adj.*

demure (dɪˈmjʊə) *adj.* **1.** sedate; decorous; reserved. **2.** affectedly modest or prim; coy. [C14: ? < OF *demorer* to delay, linger; ? infl. by *meur* ripe, MATURE] —**deˈmurely** *adv.* —**deˈmureness** *n.*

demurrage (dɪˈmʌrɪdʒ) *n.* **1.** the delaying of a ship, etc., caused by the charterer's failure to load, unload, etc., before the time of scheduled departure. **2.** the extra charge required for such delay. [C14: < OF *demorage, demourage;* see DEMUR]

demurrer (dɪˈmʌrə) *n.* **1.** *Law.* a pleading that admits an opponent's point but denies that it is relevant or valid. **2.** any objection raised.

demy (dɪˈmaɪ) *n., pl.* **-mies. 1.** a size of printing paper, 17½ by 22½ inches (444.5 × 571.5 mm). **2.** a size of writing paper, 15½ by 20 inches (Brit.) (393.7 × 508 mm) or 16 by 21 inches (U.S.) (406.4 × 533.4 mm). [C16: see DEMI-]

demystify (diːˈmɪstɪˌfaɪ) *vb.* **-fying, -fied.** (*tr.*) to remove the mystery from; make clear. —**deˌmystifiˈcation** *n.*

demythologize *or* **-ise** (ˌdiːmɪˈθɒləˌdʒaɪz) *vb.* (*tr.*) **1.** to eliminate mythical elements from (a piece of writing, esp. the Bible). **2.** to restate (a religious message) in rational terms.

den (dɛn) *n.* **1.** the habitat or retreat of a wild animal; lair. **2.** a small or secluded room in a home, often used for carrying on a hobby. **3.** a squalid room or retreat. **4.** a site or haunt: *a den of vice.* **5.** *Scot.* a small wooded valley. ~*vb.* **denning, denned. 6.** (*intr.*) to live in or as if in a den. [OE *denn*]

Den. *abbrev. for* Denmark.

denarius (dɪˈnɛərɪəs) *n., pl.* **-narii** (-ˈnɛərɪˌaɪ). **1.**

a silver coin of ancient Rome, often called a penny in translation. **2.** a gold coin worth 25 silver denarii. [C16: < L: coin orig. equal to ten asses, < *dēnārius* (adj.) containing ten, < *decem* ten]

denary (ˈdiːnərɪ) *adj.* **1.** calculated by tens; decimal. **2.** containing ten parts; tenfold. [C16: < L *dēnārius;* see DENARIUS]

denationalize *or* **-ise** (diːˈnæʃənᵊˌlaɪz) *vb.* **1.** to transfer (an industry, etc.) from public to private ownership. **2.** to deprive of national character or nationality. —**deˌnationaliˈzation** *or* **-iˈsation** *n.*

denaturalize *or* **-ise** (diːˈnætʃrəˌlaɪz) *vb.* (*tr.*) **1.** to deprive of nationality. **2.** to make unnatural. —**deˌnaturaliˈzation** *or* **-iˈsation** *n.*

denature (diːˈneɪtʃə) *or* **denaturize, -ise** (diːˈneɪtʃəˌraɪz) *vb.* (*tr.*) **1.** to change the nature of. **2.** to change the properties of (a protein), as by the action of acid or heat. **3.** to render (something, such as alcohol) unfit for consumption by adding nauseous substances. **4.** to render (fissile material) unfit for use in nuclear weapons by addition of an isotope. —**deˈnaturant** *n.* —**deˌnaturˈation** *n.*

dendrite (ˈdɛndraɪt) *n.* **1.** any of the branched extensions of a nerve cell, which conduct impulses towards the cell body. **2.** a branching mosslike crystalline structure in some rocks and minerals. **3.** a crystal that has branched during growth. [C18: < Gk *dendritēs* relating to a tree] —**dendritic** (dɛnˈdrɪtɪk) *adj.*

dendro-, dendri-, *or before a vowel* **dendr-** *combining form.* tree: *dendrochronology.* [NL, < Gk, < *dendron* tree]

dendrochronology (ˌdɛndrəʊkrəˈnɒlədʒɪ) *n.* the study of the annual rings of trees, used esp. to date past events.

dendrology (dɛnˈdrɒlədʒɪ) *n.* the branch of botany that is concerned with the natural history of trees. —**dendrological** (ˌdɛndrəˈlɒdʒɪkᵊl) *or* **ˌdendroˈlogic** *adj.* —**denˈdrologist** *n.*

dene[1] *or* **dean** (diːn) *n. Brit.* a narrow wooded valley. [OE *denu* valley]

dene[2] *or* **dean** (diːn) *n. Dialect, chiefly southern English.* a sandy stretch of land or dune near the sea. [C13: prob. rel. to OE *dūn* hill]

dengue (ˈdɛŋgɪ) *or* **dandy** (ˈdændɪ) *n.* an acute viral disease transmitted by mosquitoes, characterized by headache, fever, pains in the joints, and skin rash. [C19: < Sp., prob. of African origin]

deniable (dɪˈnaɪəbᵊl) *adj.* able to be denied; questionable. —**deˈniably** *adv.*

denial (dɪˈnaɪəl) *n.* **1.** a refusal to agree or comply with a statement. **2.** the rejection of the truth of a proposition, doctrine, etc. **3.** a rejection of a request. **4.** a refusal to acknowledge; disavowal. **5.** abstinence; self-denial.

denier[1] *n.* **1.** (ˈdɛnɪˌeɪ, ˈdɛnjə). a unit of weight used to measure the fineness of silk and man-made fibres, esp. when woven into women's tights, etc. **2.** (dəˈnjeɪ, -ˈnɪə). any of several former European coins of various denominations. [C15: < OF: coin, < L *dēnārius* DENARIUS]

denier[2] (dɪˈnaɪə) *n.* a person who denies.

denigrate (ˈdɛnɪˌgreɪt) *vb.* (*tr.*) to belittle or disparage the character of; defame. [C16: < L *dēnigrāre* to make very black, < *nigrāre,* < *niger* black] —ˌ**deniˈgration** *n.* —ˈ**deniˌgrator** *n.*

denim (ˈdɛnɪm) *n.* **1.** a hard-wearing twill-weave cotton fabric used for trousers, work clothes, etc. **2.** a similar lighter fabric used in upholstery. [C17: < F (*serge*) *de Nîmes* (serge) of Nîmes, in S France]

denims (ˈdɛnɪmz) *pl. n.* jeans or overalls made of denim.

denizen (ˈdɛnɪzən) *n.* **1.** an inhabitant; resident. **2.** *Brit.* an individual permanently resident in a foreign country where he enjoys certain rights of citizenship. **3.** a plant or animal established in a place to which it is not native. **4.** a naturalized foreign word. [C15: < Anglo-F *denisein,* < OF *denzein,* < *denz* within, < L *de intus* from within]

denominate *vb.* (dɪˈnɒmɪˌneɪt). **1.** (*tr.*) to give a specific name to; designate. ~*adj.* (dɪˈnɒmɪnɪt, -ˌneɪt). **2.** *Maths.* (of a number) representing a multiple of a unit of measurement: *4 is the denominate number in 4 miles.* [C16: < L *dēnōminare* < DE- (intensive) + *nōminare* to name]

denomination (dɪˌnɒmɪˈneɪʃən) *n.* **1.** a group having a distinctive interpretation of a religious faith and usually its own organization. **2.** a grade or unit in a series of designations of value, weight, measure, etc. **3.** a name given to a class or group; classification. **4.** the act of giving a name. **5.** a name; designation. —**deˌnomiˈnational** *adj.*

denominative (dɪˈnɒmɪnətɪv) *adj.* **1.** giving or constituting a name. **2.** *Grammar.* **a.** formed from or having the same form as a noun. **b.** (*as n.*): *the verb "to mushroom" is a denominative.*

denominator (dɪˈnɒmɪˌneɪtə) *n.* the divisor of a fraction, as 8 in ⅞. Cf. **numerator.**

denotation (ˌdiːnəʊˈteɪʃən) *n.* **1.** a denoting; indication. **2.** a particular meaning given by a sign or symbol. **3.** specific meaning as distinguished from suggestive meaning and associations. **4.** *Logic.* another word for **extension** (sense 10).

denote (dɪˈnəʊt) *vb.* (*tr.; may take a clause as object*) **1.** to be a sign of; designate. **2.** (of words, phrases, etc.) to have as a literal or obvious meaning. [C16: < L *dēnotāre* to mark, < *notāre* to mark, NOTE] —**deˈnotative** *adj.*

denouement (deɪˈnuːmɒn) *or* **dénouement** (*French* denumɑ̃) *n.* **1.** the clarification or resolution of a plot in a play or other work. **2.** final outcome; solution. [C18: < F, lit.: an untying, < OF *desnoer,* < *des-* DE- + *noer* to tie, < L *nōdus* a knot]

denounce (dɪˈnaʊns) *vb.* (*tr.*) **1.** to condemn openly or vehemently. **2.** to give information against; accuse. **3.** to announce formally the termination of (a treaty, etc.). [C13: < OF *denoncier,* < L *dēnuntiāre* to make an official proclamation, threaten, < DE- + *nuntiāre* to announce] —**deˈnouncement** *n.* —**deˈnouncer** *n.*

de novo *Latin.* (diː ˈnəʊvəʊ) *adv.* from the beginning; anew.

dense (dɛns) *adj.* **1.** thickly crowded or closely set. **2.** thick; impenetrable. **3.** *Physics.* having a high density. **4.** stupid; dull. **5.** (of a photographic negative) having many dark or exposed areas. [C15: < L *densus* thick] —ˈ**densely** *adv.* —ˈ**denseness** *n.*

densimeter (dɛnˈsɪmɪtə) *n. Physics.* any instrument for measuring density. —**densimetric** (ˌdɛnsɪˈmɛtrɪk) *adj.* —**denˈsimetry** *n.*

density (ˈdɛnsɪtɪ) *n., pl.* **-ties.** **1.** the degree to which something is filled or occupied: *high density of building in towns.* **2.** stupidity. **3.** a measure of the compactness of a substance, expressed as its mass per unit volume. Symbol: ρ. See also **relative density.** **4.** a measure of a physical quantity per unit of length, area, or volume. **5.** *Physics, photog.* a measure of the extent to which a substance or surface transmits or reflects light.

dent (dɛnt) *n.* **1.** a hollow in a surface, as one made by pressure or a blow. **2.** an appreciable effect, esp. of lessening: *a dent in our resources.* ~*vb.* **3.** to make a dent in. [C13 (in the sense: a stroke, blow): var. of DINT]

dental (ˈdɛntᵊl) *adj.* **1.** of or relating to the teeth or dentistry. **2.** *Phonetics.* pronounced with the tip of the tongue touching the backs of the upper teeth, as for *t* in French *tout.* ~*n.* **3.** *Phonetics.* a dental consonant. [C16: < Med. L *dentālis,* < L *dēns* tooth]

dental floss *n.* a waxed thread used to remove food particles from between the teeth.

dental plaque *n.* a filmy deposit on the surface of a tooth consisting of a mixture of mucus, bacteria, food, etc.

dental surgeon *n.* another name for **dentist.**

dentate (ˈdɛnteɪt) *adj.* **1.** having teeth or toothlike processes. **2.** (of leaves) having a toothed margin. [C19: < L *dentātus*] —ˈ**dentately** *adv.*

denti- *or before a vowel* **dent-** *combining form.* indicating a tooth: *dentine.* [< L *dēns, dent-*]

denticulate (dɛnˈtɪkjʊlɪt, -ˌleɪt) *adj.* **1.** *Biol.* very finely toothed: *denticulate leaves.* **2.** *Arch.* having dentils. [C17: < L *denticulātus* having small teeth]

dentifrice (ˈdɛntɪfrɪs) *n.* any substance, esp. paste or powder, for use in cleaning the teeth. [C16: < L *dentifricium,* < *dent-, dens* tooth + *fricāre* to rub]

dentil (ˈdɛntɪl) *n.* one of a set of small square or rectangular blocks evenly spaced to form an ornamental row. [C17: < F, < obs. *dentille* a little tooth, < *dent* tooth]

dentine (ˈdɛntiːn) *or* **dentin** (ˈdɛntɪn) *n.* the calcified tissue comprising the bulk of a tooth. [C19: < DENTI- + -IN] —**ˈdentinal** *adj.*

dentist (ˈdɛntɪst) *n.* a person qualified to practise dentistry. [C18: < F *dentiste,* < *dent* tooth]

dentistry (ˈdɛntɪstrɪ) *n.* the branch of medical science concerned with the diagnosis and treatment of disorders of the teeth and gums.

dentition (dɛnˈtɪʃən) *n.* **1.** the arrangement, type, and number of the teeth in a particular species. **2.** the time or process of teething. [C17: < L *dentītiō* a teething]

denture (ˈdɛntʃə) *n.* (*usually pl.*) **1.** a partial or full set of artificial teeth. **2.** *Rare.* a set of natural teeth. [C19: < F, < *dent* tooth + -URE]

denuclearize *or* **-ise** (dɪˈnjuːklɪəˌraɪz) *vb.* (*tr.*) to deprive (a state, etc.) of nuclear weapons. —**deˌnucleariˈzation** *or* **-iˈsation** *n.*

denudate (ˈdɛnjʊˌdeɪt, dɪˈnjuːdeɪt) *vb.* **1.** a less common word for **denude.** ~*adj.* **2.** denuded.

denude (dɪˈnjuːd) *vb.* (*tr.*) **1.** to make bare; strip. **2.** to expose (rock) by the erosion of the layers above. —**denudation** (ˌdɛnjʊˈdeɪʃən) *n.*

denumerable (dɪˈnjuːmərəbᵊl) *adj. Maths.* capable of being put into a one-to-one correspondence with the positive integers; countable. —**deˈnumerably** *adv.*

denunciate (dɪˈnʌnsɪˌeɪt) *vb.* (*tr.*) to condemn; denounce. [C16: < L *dēnuntiāre;* see DENOUNCE] —**deˈnunciˌator** *n.* —**deˈnunciatory** *adj.*

denunciation (dɪˌnʌnsɪˈeɪʃən) *n.* **1.** open condemnation; denouncing. **2.** *Law, obsolete.* a charge or accusation of crime made before a public prosecutor or tribunal. **3.** a formal announcement of the termination of a treaty.

deny (dɪˈnaɪ) *vb.* **-nying, -nied.** (*tr.*) **1.** to declare (a statement, etc.) to be untrue. **2.** to reject as false. **3.** to withhold. **4.** to refuse to fulfil the expectations of: *it is hard to deny a child.* **5.** to refuse to acknowledge; disown. **6.** to refuse (oneself) things desired. [C13: < OF *denier,* < L *dēnegāre,* < *negāre*]

deodar (ˈdiːəʊˌdɑː) *n.* **1.** a Himalayan cedar with drooping branches. **2.** the durable fragrant highly valued wood of this tree. [C19: < Hindi, < Sansk. *devadāru,* lit.: wood of the gods]

deodorant (diːˈəʊdərənt) *n.* **1.** a substance applied to the body to suppress or mask the odour of perspiration. **2.** any substance for destroying or masking odours.

deodorize *or* **-ise** (diːˈəʊdəˌraɪz) *vb.* (*tr.*) to remove, disguise, or absorb the odour of, esp. when unpleasant. —**deˌodoriˈzation** *or* **-iˈsation** *n.* —**deˈodorˌizer** *or* **-ˌiser** *n.*

deontic (diːˈɒntɪk) *adj. Logic.* **a.** of such ethical concepts as obligation and permissibility. **b.** designating the branch of logic that deals with the formalization of these concepts. [C19: < Gk *deon* duty, < impersonal *dei* it behoves, it is binding] —ˌ**deonˈtology** *n.*

deoxidize *or* **-ise** (diːˈɒksɪˌdaɪz) *vb.* **1.** (*tr.*) to remove oxygen atoms from (a compound, molecule, etc.). **2.** another word for **reduce** (sense 11). —**deˌoxidiˈzation** *or* **-iˈsation** *n.* —**deˈoxiˌdizer** *or* **-iser** *n.*

deoxycorticosterone (diːˌɒksɪˌkɔːtɪkəʊˈstɪərəʊn) *or* **deoxycortone** (diːˌɒksɪˈkɔːtəʊn) *n.* a corticosteroid hormone important in maintaining sodium and water balance in the body.

deoxygenate (diːˈɒksɪdʒɪˌneɪt) *or* **deoxygenize, -ise** (diːˈɒksɪdʒɪˌnaɪz) *vb.* (*tr.*) to remove oxygen from. —**deˌoxygenˈation** *n.*

deoxyribonucleic acid (diːˌɒksɪˌraɪbəʊnjuːˈkleɪɪk) *or* **desoxyribonucleic acid** *n.* the full name for **DNA.**

dep. *abbrev. for:* **1.** department. **2.** departure. **3.** deposed. **4.** deposit. **5.** depot. **6.** deputy.

depart (dɪˈpɑːt) *vb.* (*mainly intr.*) **1.** to leave. **2.** to set forth. **3.** (usually foll. by *from*) to differ; vary: *to depart from normal procedure.* **4.** (*tr.*) to quit (arch., except in **depart this life**). [C13: < OF *departir,* < DE- + *partir* to go away, divide, < L *partīrī* to divide, distribute, < *pars* a part]

departed (dɪˈpɑːtɪd) *adj. Euphemistic.* **a.** dead. **b.** (*as sing. or collective n.;* preceded by *the*): *the departed.*

department (dɪˈpɑːtmənt) *n.* **1.** a specialized division of a large concern, such as a business, store, or university. **2.** a major subdivision of the administration of a government. **3.** a branch of learning. **4.** an administrative division in several countries, such as France. **5.** *Inf.* a specialized sphere of skill or activity: *wine-making is my wife's department.* [C18: < F *département,* < *départir* to divide; see DEPART] —**departmental** (ˌdiːpɑːtˈmɛntᵊl) *adj.*

departmentalize *or* **-ise** (ˌdiːpɑːtˈmɛntᵊˌlaɪz) *vb.* (*tr.*) to organize into departments, esp. excessively. —ˌ**departˌmentaliˈzation** *or* **-iˈsation** *n.*

department store *n.* a large shop divided into departments selling a great many kinds of goods.

departure (dɪˈpɑːtʃə) *n.* **1.** the act or an instance of departing. **2.** a variation from previous custom. **3.** a course of action, venture, etc.: *selling is a new departure for him.* **4.** *Naut.* the net distance travelled due east or west by a vessel. **5.** a euphemistic word for **death.**

depend (dɪˈpɛnd) *vb.* (*intr.*) **1.** (foll. by *on* or *upon*) to put trust (in); rely (on). **2.** (usually foll. by *on* or *upon*) to be influenced or determined (by): *it all depends on you.* **3.** (foll. by *on* or *upon*) to rely (on) for income, support, etc. **4.** (foll. by *from*) *Rare.* to hang down. **5.** to be undecided. [C15: < OF, < L *dēpendēre* to hang from, < DE- + *pendēre*]

dependable (dɪˈpɛndəbᵊl) *adj.* able to be depended on; reliable. —**deˌpendaˈbility** *or* **deˈpendableness** *n.* —**deˈpendably** *adv.*

dependant (dɪˈpɛndənt) *n.* a person who depends on another person, organization, etc., for support, aid, or sustenance, esp. financial support.

dependence *or U.S.* (*sometimes*) **dependance** (dɪˈpɛndəns) *n.* **1.** the state or fact of being dependent, esp. for support or help. **2.** reliance; trust; confidence.

dependency *or U.S.* (*sometimes*) **dependancy** (dɪˈpɛndənsɪ) *n., pl.* **-cies. 1.** a territory subject to a state on which it does not border. **2.** a dependent or subordinate person or thing. **3.** *Psychol.* overreliance on another person or on a drug, etc. **4.** another word for **dependence.**

dependent *or U.S.* (*sometimes*) **dependant** (dɪˈpɛndənt) *adj.* **1.** depending on a person or thing for aid, support, etc. **2.** (*postpositive;* foll. by *on* or *upon*) influenced or conditioned (by). **3.** subordinate; subject. **4.** *Obs.* hanging down. ~*n.* **5.** a variant spelling (esp. U.S.) of **dependant.** —**deˈpendently** *adv.*

dependent clause *n. Grammar.* another term for **subordinate clause.**

dependent variable *n.* a variable in a mathematical equation or statement whose value depends on that taken on by the independent variable.

depersonalize *or* **-ise** (dɪˈpɜːsnᵊˌlaɪz) *vb.* (*tr.*) **1.** to deprive (a person, organization, etc.) of individual or personal qualities. **2.** to cause (someone) to lose his sense of identity. —**deˌpersonaliˈzation** *or* **-iˈsation** *n.*

depict (dɪˈpɪkt) *vb.* (*tr.*) **1.** to represent by drawing, sculpture, painting, etc. **2.** to represent in words; describe. [C17: < L *dēpingere,* < *pingere* to paint] —**deˈpicter** *or* **deˈpictor** *n.* —**deˈpiction** *n.* —**deˈpictive** *adj.*

depilate (ˈdɛpɪˌleɪt) *vb.* (*tr.*) to remove the hair from. [C16: < L *dēpilāre,* < *pilāre* to make bald, < *pilus* hair] —ˌ**depiˈlation** *n.* —ˈ**depiˌlator** *n.*

depilatory (dɪˈpɪlətərɪ, -trɪ) *adj.* **1.** able or serving to remove hair. ~*n., pl.* **-ries. 2.** a chemical used to remove hair from the body.

deplane (diːˈpleɪn) *vb.* (*intr.*) *Chiefly U.S. & Canad.* to disembark from an aeroplane. [C20: < DE- + PLANE[1]]

deplete (dɪˈpliːt) *vb.* (*tr.*) **1.** to use up (supplies, money, etc.); exhaust. **2.** to empty entirely or partially. [C19: < L *dēplēre* to empty out, < DE- + *plēre* to fill] **—deˈpletion** *n.*

deplorable (dɪˈplɔːrəbᵊl) *adj.* **1.** lamentable. **2.** worthy of censure or reproach; very bad. **—deˈplorably** *adv.*

deplore (dɪˈplɔː) *vb.* (*tr.*) **1.** to express or feel sorrow about. **2.** to express or feel strong disapproval of; censure. [C16: < OF, < L *dēplōrāre* to weep bitterly, < *plōrāre* to weep] **—deˈploringly** *adv.*

deploy (dɪˈplɔɪ) *vb. Chiefly mil.* **1.** to adopt or cause to adopt a battle formation. **2.** (*tr.*) to redistribute (forces) to or within a given area. [C18: < F, < L *displicāre* to unfold; see DISPLAY] **—deˈployment** *n.*

depolarize *or* **-ise** (diːˈpəʊləˌraɪz) *vb.* to undergo or cause to undergo a loss of polarity or polarization. **—deˌpolariˈzation** *or* **-iˈsation** *n.*

deponent (dɪˈpəʊnənt) *adj.* **1.** *Grammar.* (of a verb, esp. in Latin) having the inflectional endings of a passive verb but the meaning of an active verb. ~*n.* **2.** *Grammar.* a deponent verb. **3.** *Law.* a person who makes an affidavit or a deposition. [C16: < L *dēpōnēns* putting aside, putting down, < *dēpōnere*]

depopulate (dɪˈpɒpjʊˌleɪt) *vb.* to be or cause to be reduced in population. **—deˌpopuˈlation** *n.*

deport (dɪˈpɔːt) *vb.* (*tr.*) **1.** to remove forcibly from a country; expel. **2.** to conduct, hold, or behave (oneself) in a specified manner. [C15: < F, < L *dēportāre* to carry away, banish, < DE- + *portāre* to carry] **—deˈportable** *adj.*

deportation (ˌdiːpɔːˈteɪʃən) *n.* the act of expelling someone from a country.

deportee (ˌdiːpɔːˈtiː) *n.* a person deported or awaiting deportation.

deportment (dɪˈpɔːtmənt) *n.* the manner in which a person behaves, esp. in physical bearing: *military deportment.* [C17: < F, < OF *deporter* to conduct (oneself); see DEPORT]

depose (dɪˈpəʊz) *vb.* **1.** (*tr.*) to remove from an office or position of power. **2.** *Law.* to testify or give (evidence, etc.) on oath. [C13: < OF: to put away, put down, < LL *dēpōnere* to depose from office, < L: to put aside]

deposit (dɪˈpɒzɪt) *vb.* (*tr.*) **1.** to put or set down, esp. carefully; place. **2.** to entrust for safekeeping. **3.** to place (money) in a bank or similar institution to earn interest or for safekeeping. **4.** to give (money) in part payment or as security. **5.** to lay down naturally: *the river deposits silt.* ~*n.* **6. a.** an instance of entrusting money or valuables to a bank or similar institution. **b.** the money or valuables so entrusted. **7.** money given in part payment or as security. **8.** an accumulation of sediments, minerals, coal, etc. **9.** any deposited material, such as a sediment. **10.** a depository or storehouse. **11. on deposit.** payable as the first instalment, as when buying on hire-purchase. [C17: < Med. L *dēpositāre*, < L *dēpositus* put down]

deposit account *n. Brit.* a bank account that earns interest and usually requires notice of withdrawal.

depositary (dɪˈpɒzɪtərɪ, -trɪ) *n., pl.* **-taries. 1.** a person or group to whom something is entrusted for safety. **2.** a variant spelling of **depository.**

deposition (ˌdɛpəˈzɪʃən) *n.* **1.** *Law.* **a.** the giving of testimony on oath. **b.** the testimony given. **c.** the sworn statement of a witness used in court in his absence. **2.** the act or instance of deposing. **3.** the act or an instance of depositing. **4.** something deposited. [C14: < LL *dēpositiō* a laying down, disposal, burying, testimony]

depositor (dɪˈpɒzɪtə) *n.* a person who places or has money on deposit, esp. in a bank.

depository (dɪˈpɒzɪtərɪ, -trɪ) *n., pl.* **-ries. 1.** a store for furniture, valuables, etc.; repository. **2.** a variant spelling of **depositary.** [C17 (in the sense: place of a deposit): < Med. L *dēpositōrium;* C18 (in the sense: depositary): see DEPOSIT, -ORY[1]]

depot (ˈdɛpəʊ) *n.* **1.** a storehouse or warehouse. **2.** *Mil.* **a.** a store for supplies. **b.** a training and holding centre for recruits and replacements. **3.** *Chiefly Brit.* a building used for the storage and servicing of buses or railway engines. **4.** *U.S. & Canad.* a bus or railway station. [C18: < F *dépôt*, < L *dēpositum* a deposit, trust]

deprave (dɪˈpreɪv) *vb.* (*tr.*) to make morally bad; corrupt. [C14: < L *dēprāvāre* to distort, corrupt, < DE- + *prāvus* crooked] **—depravation** (ˌdɛprəˈveɪʃən) *n.* **—deˈpraved** *adj.*

depravity (dɪˈprævɪtɪ) *n., pl.* **-ties.** the state or an instance of moral corruption.

deprecate (ˈdɛprɪˌkeɪt) *vb.* (*tr.*) **1.** to express disapproval of; protest against. **2.** to depreciate; belittle. [C17: < L *dēprecārī* to avert, ward off by entreaty, < DE- + *precārī* to PRAY] **—ˈdepreˌcating** *adj.* **—ˈdepreˌcatingly** *adv.* **—ˌdepreˈcation** *n.* **—ˈdeprecative** *adj.* **—ˈdepreˌcator** *n.*

deprecatory (ˈdɛprɪkətərɪ) *adj.* **1.** expressing disapproval; protesting. **2.** expressing apology; apologetic. **—ˈdeprecatorily** *adv.*

depreciate (dɪˈpriːʃɪˌeɪt) *vb.* **1.** to reduce or decline in value or price. **2.** (*tr.*) to lessen the value of by derision, criticism, etc. [C15: < LL *dēpretiāre* to lower the price of, < L DE- + *pretium* PRICE] **—deˈpreciˌatingly** *adv.* **—depreciatory** (dɪˈpriːʃɪətərɪ) *or* **deˈpreciative** *adj.*

depreciation (dɪˌpriːʃɪˈeɪʃən) *n.* **1.** *Accounting.* **a.** the reduction in value of a fixed asset due to use, obsolescence, etc. **b.** the amount deducted from gross profit to allow for this. **2.** the act or an instance of depreciating or belittling. **3.** a decrease in the exchange value of a currency brought about by excess supply of that currency under conditions of fluctuating exchange rates.

depredation (ˌdɛprɪˈdeɪʃən) *n.* the act or an instance of plundering; robbery; pillage.

depress (dɪˈprɛs) *vb.* (*tr.*) **1.** to lower in spirits; make gloomy. **2.** to weaken the force, or energy of. **3.** to lower prices of. **4.** to press or push down. [C14: < OF *depresser*, < L *dēprimere* < DE- + *premere* to PRESS[1]] **—deˈpressing** *adj.* **—deˈpressingly** *adv.*

depressant (dɪˈprɛsᵊnt) *adj.* **1.** *Med.* able to reduce nervous or functional activity. **2.** causing gloom; depressing. ~*n.* **3.** a depressant drug.

depressed (dɪˈprɛst) *adj.* **1.** low in spirits; downcast. **2.** lower than the surrounding surface. **3.** pressed down or flattened. **4.** Also: **distressed.** characterized by economic hardship, such as unemployment: *a depressed area.* **5.** lowered in force, intensity, or amount. **6.** *Bot., zool.* flattened.

depression (dɪˈprɛʃən) *n.* **1.** a depressing or being depressed. **2.** a depressed or sunken place. **3.** a mental disorder characterized by feelings of gloom and inadequacy. **4.** *Pathol.* an abnormal lowering of the rate of any physiological activity or function. **5.** an economic condition characterized by substantial unemployment, low output and investment, etc.; slump. **6.** Also called: **cyclone, low.** *Meteorol.* a body of moving air below normal atmospheric pressure, which often brings rain. **7.** (esp. in surveying and astronomy) the angular distance of an object below the horizontal plane.

Depression (dɪˈprɛʃən) *n.* (usually preceded by *the*) the worldwide economic depression of the early 1930s, when there was mass unemployment.

depressive (dɪˈprɛsɪv) *adj.* **1.** tending to depress. **2.** *Psychol.* tending to be subject to periods of depression. **—deˈpressively** *adv.*

depressor (dɪˈprɛsə) *n.* **1.** a person or thing that depresses. **2.** any muscle that draws down a part. **3.** any medical instrument used to press down or aside an organ or part.

depressurize *or* **-ise** (dɪˈprɛʃəˌraɪz) *vb.* (*tr.*) to reduce the pressure of a gas inside (a container or enclosed space), as in an aircraft cabin. **—deˌpressuriˈzation** *or* **-iˈsation** *n.*

deprive (dɪˈpraɪv) *vb.* (*tr.*) **1.** (foll. by *of*) to prevent from possessing or enjoying; dispossess (of). **2.** *Arch.* to depose; demote. [C14: < OF, < Med. L *dēprīvāre*, < L DE- + *prīvāre* to deprive of] —**de'prival** *n.* —**deprivation** (ˌdɛprɪ'veɪʃən) *n.*

deprived (dɪ'praɪvd) *adj.* lacking adequate food, shelter, education, etc.: *deprived inner-city areas.*

dept *abbrev. for* department.

depth (dɛpθ) *n.* **1.** the distance downwards, backwards, or inwards. **2.** the quality of being deep; deepness. **3.** intensity of emotion. **4.** profundity of moral character; sagacity; integrity. **5.** complexity or abstruseness, as of thought. **6.** intensity, as of silence, colour, etc. **7.** lowness of pitch. **8.** (*often pl.*) a deep, inner, or remote part, such as an inaccessible region of a country. **9.** (*often pl.*) the most intense or severe part: *the depths of winter.* **10.** (*usually pl.*) a low moral state. **11.** (*often pl.*) a vast space or abyss. **12.** **beyond** *or* **out of one's depth. a.** in water deeper than one is tall. **b.** beyond the range of one's competence or understanding. [C14: < *dep* DEEP + -TH[1]]

depth charge *or* **bomb** *n.* a bomb used to attack submarines that explodes at a preset depth of water.

depth of field *n.* the range of distance in front of and behind an object focused by an optical instrument, such as a camera or microscope, within which other objects will also appear clear and sharply defined in the resulting image.

depth psychology *n. Psychol.* the study of unconscious motives and attitudes.

depuration (ˌdɛpjʊ'reɪʃən) *n.* the act or process of eliminating impurities; self-purification. [C17: < F or Med. L, ult. < L *pūrus* pure]

deputation (ˌdɛpjʊ'teɪʃən) *n.* **1.** the act of appointing a person or body of people to represent others. **2.** a person or body of people so appointed; delegation.

depute *vb.* (dɪ'pjuːt). (*tr.*) **1.** to appoint as an agent. **2.** to assign (authority, duties, etc.) to a deputy. ~*n.* ('dɛpjuːt). **3.** *Scot.* **a.** a deputy. **b.** (*as modifier, usually postpositive*): *a sheriff-depute.* [C15: < OF, < LL *dēputāre* to assign, allot, < L DE- + *putāre* to think, consider]

deputize *or* **-ise** ('dɛpjʊˌtaɪz) *vb.* to appoint or act as deputy.

deputy ('dɛpjʊtɪ) *n., pl.* **-ties. 1. a.** a person appointed to act on behalf of or represent another. **b.** (*as modifier*): *the deputy chairman.* **2.** a member of a legislative assembly in various countries, such as France. [C16: < OF, < *deputer* to appoint; see DEPUTE]

der. *abbrev. for:* **1.** derivation. **2.** derivative.

deracinate (dɪ'ræsɪˌneɪt) *vb.* (*tr.*) to pull up by or as if by the roots; uproot. [C16: < OF *desraciner*, < *des-* DIS-[1] + *racine* root, < LL, < L *rādīx* a root] —**deˌraci'nation** *n.*

derail (dɪ'reɪl) *vb.* to go or cause to go off the rails, as a train, tram, etc. —**de'railment** *n.*

derange (dɪ'reɪndʒ) *vb.* (*tr.*) **1.** to throw into disorder; disarrange. **2.** to disturb the action of. **3.** to make insane. [C18: < OF *desrengier*, < des- DIS-[1] + *reng* row, order] —**de'rangement** *n.*

derby ('dɜːrbɪ) *n., pl.* **-bies.** the U.S. and Canad. name for **bowler**[2].

Derby ('dɑːbɪ; *U.S.* 'dɜːrbɪ) *n., pl.* **-bies. 1. the.** an annual horse race run at Epsom Downs, Surrey, since 1780. **2.** any of various other horse races. **3.** **local Derby.** a football match between two teams from the same area. [C18: after the twelfth Earl of *Derby* (died 1834), who founded the race in 1780]

deregulate (diː'rɛgjʊˌleɪt) *vb.* (*tr.*) to remove regulations or controls from. —**deˌregu'lation** *n.*

derelict ('dɛrɪlɪkt) *adj.* **1.** deserted or abandoned, as by an owner, occupant, etc. **2.** falling into ruins. **3.** neglectful of duty; remiss. ~*n.* **4.** a social outcast or vagrant. **5.** property deserted or abandoned by an owner, occupant, etc. **6.** a vessel abandoned at sea. **7.** a person who is neglectful of duty. [C17: < L, < *dērelinquere* to abandon, < DE- + *relinquere* to leave]

dereliction (ˌdɛrɪ'lɪkʃən) *n.* **1.** conscious or wilful neglect (esp. in **dereliction of duty**). **2.** an abandoning or being abandoned. **3.** *Law.* accretion of dry land gained by the gradual receding of the sea.

derestrict (ˌdiːrɪ'strɪkt) *vb.* (*tr.*) to render or leave free from restriction, esp. a road from speed limits. —ˌ**dere'striction** *n.*

deride (dɪ'raɪd) *vb.* (*tr.*) to speak of or treat with contempt or ridicule; scoff at. [C16: < L *dērīdēre* to laugh to scorn, < DE- + *rīdēre* to laugh, smile] —**de'rider** *n.* —**de'ridingly** *adv.*

de rigueur *French.* (də rigœr) *adj.* required by etiquette or fashion. [lit.: of strictness]

derision (dɪ'rɪʒən) *n.* the act of deriding; mockery; scorn. [C15: < LL *dērīsiō*, < L *dērīsus*; see DERIDE] —**de'risible** *adj.*

derisive (dɪ'raɪsɪv) *adj.* characterized by derision; mocking; scornful. —**de'risively** *adv.* —**de'risiveness** *n.*

derisory (dɪ'raɪsərɪ) *adj.* **1.** subject to or worthy of derision. **2.** another word for **derisive.**

deriv. *abbrev. for:* **1.** derivation. **2.** derivative. **3.** derived.

derivation (ˌdɛrɪ'veɪʃən) *n.* **1.** a deriving or being derived. **2.** the origin or descent of something, such as a word. **3.** something derived; a derivative. **4. a.** the process of deducing a mathematical theorem, formula, etc., as a necessary consequence of a set of accepted statements. **b.** this sequence of statements. —ˌ**deri'vational** *adj.*

derivative (dɪ'rɪvətɪv) *adj.* **1.** derived. **2.** based on other sources; not original. ~*n.* **3.** a term, idea, etc., that is based on or derived from another in the same class. **4.** a word derived from another word. **5.** *Chem.* a compound that is formed from, or can be regarded as formed from, a structurally related compound. **6.** *Maths.* **a.** Also called: **differential coefficient, first derivative.** the change of a function, f(x), with respect to an infinitesimally small change in the independent variable, x. **b.** the rate of change of one quantity with respect to another. —**de'rivatively** *adv.*

derive (dɪ'raɪv) *vb.* **1.** (usually foll. by *from*) to draw or be drawn (from) in source or origin. **2.** (*tr.*) to obtain by reasoning; deduce; infer. **3.** (*tr.*) to trace the source or development of. **4.** (usually foll. by *from*) to produce or be produced (from) by a chemical reaction. [C14: < OF: to spring from, < L *dērīvāre* to draw off, < DE- + *rīvus* a stream] —**de'rivable** *adj.* —**de'river** *n.*

derived unit *n.* a unit of measurement obtained by multiplication or division of the base units of a system without the introduction of numerical factors.

-derm *n. combining form.* indicating skin: *endoderm.* [via F < Gk *derma* skin]

derma ('dɜːmə) *n.* another name for **corium.** Also: **derm.** [C18: NL, < Gk: skin]

dermatitis (ˌdɜːmə'taɪtɪs) *n.* inflammation of the skin.

dermato-, derma- *or before a vowel* **dermat-, derm-** *combining form.* indicating skin: *dermatitis.* [< Gk *derma* skin]

dermatology (ˌdɜːmə'tɒlədʒɪ) *n.* the branch of medicine concerned with the skin and its diseases. —**dermatological** (ˌdɜːmətə'lɒdʒɪk°l) *adj.* —ˌ**derma'tologist** *n.*

dermis ('dɜːmɪs) *n.* another name for **corium.** [C19: NL, < EPIDERMIS] —'**dermic** *adj.*

dernier cri *French.* (dɛrnje kri) *n.* **le** (lə). the latest fashion; the last word. [lit.: last cry]

derogate ('dɛrəˌgeɪt) *vb.* **1.** (*intr.;* foll. by *from*) to cause to seem inferior; detract. **2.** (*intr.;* foll. by *from*) to deviate in standard or quality. **3.** (*tr.*) to cause to seem inferior, etc.; disparage. **4.** (*tr.*) to curtail the application of (a law or regulation). [C15: < L *dērogāre* to repeal some part of a law, modify it, < DE- + *rogāre* to ask, propose a law] —ˌ**dero'gation** *n.* —**derogative** (dɪ'rɒgətɪv) *adj.*

derogatory (dɪ'rɒgətərɪ) *adj.* tending or intended to detract, disparage, or belittle; intentionally offensive. —**de'rogatorily** *adv.*

derrick ('dɛrɪk) *n.* **1.** a simple crane having lifting tackle slung from a boom. **2.** the framework erected over an oil well to enable drill tubes to be raised and lowered. [C17 (in the sense: gallows): < *Derrick,* celebrated hangman at Tyburn, London]

derrière (ˌdɛrɪˈɛə) *n.* a euphemistic word for **buttocks.** [C18: lit.: behind (prep.), < OF *deriere,* < L *dē retrō* from the back]

derring-do (ˈdɛrɪŋˈduː) *n. Arch. or literary.* boldness or bold action. [C16: < ME *durring don* daring to do, < *durren* to dare + *don* to do]

derringer *or* **deringer** (ˈdɛrɪndʒə) *n.* a short-barrelled pocket pistol of large calibre. [C19: after Henry *Deringer,* American gunsmith, who invented it]

derris (ˈdɛrɪs) *n.* **1.** an East Indian woody climbing plant. **2.** an insecticide made from its powdered roots. [C19: NL, < Gk: covering, leather, < *deros* skin, hide, < *derein* to skin]

derv (dɜːv) *n.* a Brit. name for **diesel oil** when used for road transport. [C20: < *d(iesel) e(ngine) r(oad) v(ehicle)*]

dervish (ˈdɜːvɪʃ) *n.* a member of any of various Muslim orders of ascetics, some of which (**whirling dervishes**) are noted for a frenzied, ecstatic, whirling dance. [C16: < Turkish: beggar, < Persian *darvīsh* mendicant monk]

DES (in Britain) *abbrev. for* Department of Education and Science.

desalination (diːˌsælɪˈneɪʃən) *or* **desalinization, -isation** *n.* the process of removing salt, esp. from sea water.

descant (ˈdɛskænt) *n.* **1.** Also called: **discant.** a decorative counterpoint added above a basic melody. **2.** a comment or discourse. ~*adj.* **3.** Also: **discant.** of the highest member in common use in a family of musical instruments: *a descant recorder.* ~*vb.* (*intr.*) **4.** Also: **discant.** (often foll. by *on* or *upon*) to perform a descant. **5.** (often foll. by *on* or *upon*) to discourse or make comments. **6.** *Arch.* to sing sweetly. [C14: < OF, < Med. L *discanthus,* < L DIS-[1] + *cantus* song] —**desˈcanter** *n.*

descend (dɪˈsɛnd) *vb.* (*mainly intr.*) **1.** (*also tr.*) to move down (a slope, staircase, etc.) **2.** to lead or extend down; slope. **3.** to move to a lower level, pitch, etc.; fall. **4.** (often foll. by *from*) to be connected by a blood relationship (to a dead or extinct individual, species, etc.). **5.** to be inherited. **6.** to sink or come down in morals or behaviour. **7.** (often foll. by *on* or *upon*) to arrive or attack in a sudden or overwhelming way. **8.** (of the sun, moon, etc.) to move towards the horizon. [C13: < OF, < L *dēscendere,* < DE- + *scandere* to climb] —**desˈcendable** *or* **desˈcendible** *adj.*

descendant (dɪˈsɛndənt) *n.* **1.** a person, animal, or plant when described as descended from an individual, race, species, etc. **2.** something that derives from an earlier form. ~*adj.* **3.** a variant spelling of **descendent.**

descendent (dɪˈsɛndənt) *adj.* descending.

descender (dɪˈsɛndə) *n.* **1.** a person or thing that descends. **2.** *Printing.* the portion of a letter, such as j, p, or y, below the level of the line.

descent (dɪˈsɛnt) *n.* **1.** the act of descending. **2.** a downward slope. **3.** a path or way leading downwards. **4.** derivation from an ancestor; lineage. **5.** a generation in a particular lineage. **6.** a decline or degeneration. **7.** a movement or passage in degree or state from higher to lower. **8.** (often foll. by *on*) a sudden and overwhelming arrival or attack. **9.** *Property law.* (formerly) the transmission of real property to the heir.

deschool (ˌdiːˈskuːl) *vb.* (*tr.*) to separate education from the institution of school and operate through the pupil's life experience as opposed to a set curriculum.

describe (dɪˈskraɪb) *vb.* (*tr.*) **1.** to give an account or representation of in words. **2.** to pronounce or label. **3.** to draw a line or figure, such as a circle. [C15: < L *dēscrībere* to copy off, write out, < DE- + *scrībere* to write] —**deˈscribable** *adj.* —**deˈscriber** *n.*

description (dɪˈskrɪpʃən) *n.* **1.** a statement or account that describes. **2.** the act, process, or technique of describing. **3.** sort or variety: *reptiles of every description.*

descriptive (dɪˈskrɪptɪv) *adj.* **1.** characterized by or containing description. **2.** *Grammar.* (of an adjective) serving to describe the referent of the noun modified, as for example the adjective *brown* as contrasted with *my.* **3.** relating to description or classification rather than explanation or prescription. —**deˈscriptively** *adv.* —**deˈscriptiveness** *n.*

descry (dɪˈskraɪ) *vb.* **-scrying, -scried.** (*tr.*) **1.** to catch sight of. **2.** to discover by looking carefully. [C14: < OF *descrier* to proclaim, DECRY]

desecrate (ˈdɛsɪˌkreɪt) *vb.* (*tr.*) **1.** to violate the sacred character of (an object or place) by destructive, blasphemous, or sacrilegious action. **2.** to deconsecrate. [C17: < DE- + CONSECRATE] —**ˈdeseˌcrator** *or* **ˈdeseˌcrater** *n.* —**ˌdeseˈcration** *n.*

desegregate (diːˈsɛgrɪˌgeɪt) *vb.* to end racial segregation in (a school or other public institution). —**ˌdesegreˈgation** *n.*

deselect (ˌdiːsɪˈlɛkt) *vb.* (*tr.*) *Brit. politics.* (of a constituency organization) to refuse to select (an existing MP) for re-election. —**ˌdeseˈlection** *n.*

desensitize *or* **-tise** (diːˈsɛnsɪˌtaɪz) *vb.* (*tr.*) to render less sensitive or insensitive: *the patient was desensitized to the allergen.* —**deˌsensitiˈzation** *or* **-tiˈsation** *n.* —**deˈsensiˌtizer** *or* **-ˌtiser** *n.*

desert[1] (ˈdɛzət) *n.* **1.** a region that is devoid or almost devoid of vegetation, esp. because of low rainfall. **2.** an uncultivated uninhabited region. **3.** a place which lacks some desirable feature or quality: *a cultural desert.* **4.** (*modifier*) of, relating to, or like a desert. [C13: < OF, < Church L *dēsertum,* < L *dēserere* to abandon, lit.: to sever one's links with, < DE- + *serere* to bind together]

desert[2] (dɪˈzɜːt) *vb.* **1.** (*tr.*) to abandon (a person, place, etc.) without intending to return, esp. in violation of a promise or obligation. **2.** *Mil.* to abscond from (a post or duty) with no intention of returning. **3.** (*tr.*) to fail (someone) in time of need. [C15: < F *déserter,* < LL *dēsertāre,* < L *dēserere* to forsake; see DESERT[1]] —**deˈserter** *n.*

desert[3] (dɪˈzɜːt) *n.* **1.** (*often pl.*) just reward or punishment. **2.** the state of deserving a reward or punishment. [C13: < OF *deserte,* < *deservir* to DESERVE]

desert boots *pl. n.* ankle-high boots, often of suede, with laces and soft soles.

desertion (dɪˈzɜːʃən) *n.* **1.** a deserting or being deserted. **2.** *Law.* wilful abandonment, esp. of one's spouse or children.

desert island *n.* a small remote tropical island.

desert pea *n.* an Australian trailing leguminous plant with scarlet flowers.

desert rat *n.* **1.** a jerboa inhabiting the deserts of N Africa. **2.** *Brit. inf.* a soldier who served in North Africa with the British 7th Armoured Division in 1941–42.

deserve (dɪˈzɜːv) *vb.* **1.** (*tr.*) to be entitled to or worthy of; merit. **2.** (*intr.;* foll. by *of*) *Obs.* to be worthy. [C13: < OF *deservir,* < L *dēservīre* to serve devotedly, < DE- + *servīre* to SERVE]

deserved (dɪˈzɜːvd) *adj.* rightfully earned; justified; warranted. —**deservedly** (dɪˈzɜːvɪdlɪ) *adv.* —**deservedness** (dɪˈzɜːvɪdnɪs) *n.*

deserving (dɪˈzɜːvɪŋ) *adj.* (often *postpositive* and foll. by *of*) worthy, esp. of praise or reward. —**deˈservingly** *adv.* —**deˈservingness** *n.*

deshabille (ˌdeɪzæˈbiːl) *n.* a variant of **dishabille.**

desiccant (ˈdɛsɪkənt) *adj.* **1.** drying. ~*n.* **2.** a substance that absorbs water and is used to remove moisture. [C17: < L *dēsiccāns* drying up; see DESICCATE]

desiccate (ˈdɛsɪˌkeɪt) *vb.* **1.** (*tr.*) to remove most of the water from; dehydrate. **2.** (*tr.*) to preserve (food) by removing moisture; dry. **3.** (*intr.*) to become dried up. [C16: < L *dēsiccāre* to dry up, < DE- + *siccāre,* < *siccus* dry] —**ˈdesicˌcated** *adj.* —**ˌdesicˈcation** *n.*

desiderate (dɪˈzɪdəˌreɪt) *vb.* (*tr.*) to feel the lack of or need for; miss. [C17: < L *dēsīderāre,* < DE- + *sīdus* star; see DESIRE] —**deˌsiderˈation** *n.*

desideratum (dɪˌzɪdəˈrɑːtəm) *n., pl.* **-ta** (-tə). something lacked and wanted. [C17: < L; see DESIDERATE]

design (dɪˈzaɪn) *vb.* **1.** to work out the structure or form of (something), as by making a sketch or plans. **2.** to plan and make (something) artistically or skilfully. **3.** (*tr.*) to invent. **4.** (*tr.*) to intend, as for a specific purpose; plan. ~*n.* **5.** a plan or preliminary drawing. **6.** the arrangement, elements, or features of an artistic or decorative work: *the design of the desk is Chippendale.* **7.** a finished artistic or decorative creation. **8.** the art of designing. **9.** a plan or project. **10.** an intention; purpose. **11.** (*often pl.;* often foll. by *on* or *against*) a plot, often to gain possession of (something) by illegitimate means. [C16: < L *dēsignāre* to mark out, describe, < DE- + *signāre,* < *signum* a mark] —**deˈsignable** *adj.*

designate *vb.* (ˈdɛzɪgˌneɪt). (*tr.*) **1.** to indicate or specify. **2.** to give a name to; style; entitle. **3.** to select or name for an office or duty; appoint. ~*adj.* (ˈdɛzɪgnɪt, -ˌneɪt). **4.** (*immediately postpositive*) appointed, but not yet in office: *a minister designate.* [C15: < L *dēsignātus* marked out, defined; see DESIGN] —**ˈdesigˌnator** *n.*

designation (ˌdɛzɪgˈneɪʃən) *n.* **1.** something that designates, such as a name. **2.** the act of designating or the fact of being designated.

designedly (dɪˈzaɪnɪdlɪ) *adv.* by intention or design; on purpose.

designer (dɪˈzaɪnə) *n.* **1.** a person who devises and executes designs, as for clothes, machines, etc. **2.** (*modifier*) designed by and bearing the label of a well-known fashion designer: *designer jeans.* **3.** (*modifier*) (of things, ideas, etc.) having an appearance of fashionable trendiness: *designer pop songs; designer diplomacy.* **4.** a person who devises plots; intriguer.

designer drug *n.* **1.** *Med.* a synthetic antibiotic designed to be effective against a particular bacterium. **2.** any of various narcotic or hallucinogenic substances manufactured illegally from a range of chemicals.

designing (dɪˈzaɪnɪŋ) *adj.* artful and scheming.

desirable (dɪˈzaɪərəbᵊl) *adj.* **1.** worthy of desire: *a desirable residence.* **2.** arousing desire, esp. sexual desire; attractive. —**deˌsiraˈbility** *or* **deˈsirableness** *n.* —**deˈsirably** *adv.*

desire (dɪˈzaɪə) *vb.* (*tr.*) **1.** to wish or long for; crave. **2.** to request; ask for. ~*n.* **3.** a wish or longing. **4.** an expressed wish; request. **5.** sexual appetite. **6.** a person or thing that is desired. [C13: < OF, < L *dēsīderāre* to desire earnestly; see DESIDERATE] —**deˈsirer** *n.*

desirous (dɪˈzaɪərəs) *adj.* (usually *postpositive* and foll. by *of*) having or expressing desire (for).

desist (dɪˈzɪst) *vb.* (*intr.;* often foll. by *from*) to cease, as from an action; stop or abstain. [C15: < OF, < L *dēsistere* to leave off, stand apart, < DE- + *sistere* to stand, halt]

desk (dɛsk) *n.* **1.** a piece of furniture with a writing surface and usually drawers or other compartments. **2.** a service counter or table in a public building, such as a hotel. **3.** a support for the book from which services are read in a church. **4.** the editorial section of a newspaper, etc., responsible for a particular subject: *the news desk.* **5.** a music stand shared by two orchestral players. [C14: < Med. L *desca* table, < L *discus* disc, dish]

desk-bound *adj.* obliged by one's occupation to work sitting at a desk.

desk editor *n.* (in a publishing house) an editor responsible for the preparation and checking of manuscripts for printing.

desktop (ˈdɛskˌtɒp) *n.* (*modifier*) denoting a computer system, esp. for word processing, that is small enough to use at a desk but sophisticated enough to produce print-quality documents: *desktop publishing.*

desman (ˈdɛsmən) *n., pl.* **-mans.** either of two molelike amphibious mammals, the Russian desman or the Pyrenean desman, with dense fur and webbed feet. [C18: < Swedish *desmansråtta,* < *desman* musk + *råtta* rat]

desolate *adj.* (ˈdɛsəlɪt). **1.** uninhabited; deserted. **2.** made uninhabitable; laid waste; devastated. **3.** without friends, hope, or encouragement. **4.** dismal; depressing. ~*vb.* (ˈdɛsəˌleɪt). (*tr.*) **5.** to deprive of inhabitants; depopulate. **6.** to lay waste; devastate. **7.** to make wretched or forlorn. **8.** to forsake or abandon. [C14: < L *dēsōlāre* to leave alone, < DE- + *sōlāre* to make lonely, lay waste, < *sōlus* alone] —**ˈdesoˌlater** *or* **ˈdesoˌlator** *n.* —**ˈdesolately** *adv.* —**ˈdesolateness** *n.*

desolation (ˌdɛsəˈleɪʃən) *n.* **1.** a desolating or being desolated; ruin or devastation. **2.** solitary misery; wretchedness. **3.** a desolate region.

despair (dɪˈspɛə) *vb.* **1.** (*intr.;* often foll. by *of*) to lose or give up hope: *I despair of his coming.* ~*n.* **2.** total loss of hope. **3.** a person or thing that causes hopelessness or for which there is no hope. [C14: < OF *despoir* hopelessness, < *desperer* to despair, < L *dēspērāre,* < DE- + *spērāre* to hope]

despairing (dɪˈspɛərɪŋ) *adj.* hopeless, despondent; feeling or showing despair. —**deˈspairingly** *adv.*

despatch (dɪˈspætʃ) *vb.* (*tr.*) a less common spelling of **dispatch.** —**desˈpatcher** *n.*

desperado (ˌdɛspəˈrɑːdəʊ) *n., pl.* **-does** *or* **-dos.** a reckless or desperate person, esp. one ready to commit any violent illegal act. [C17: prob. pseudo-Spanish var. of obs. *desperate* (n.)]

desperate (ˈdɛspərɪt, -prɪt) *adj.* **1.** careless of danger, as from despair. **2.** (of an act) reckless; risky. **3.** used or undertaken as a last resort. **4.** critical; very grave: *in desperate need.* **5.** (often *postpositive* and foll. by *for*) in distress and having a great need or desire. **6.** moved by or showing despair. [C15: < L *dēspērāre* to have no hope; see DESPAIR] —**ˈdesperately** *adv.* —**ˈdesperateness** *n.*

desperation (ˌdɛspəˈreɪʃən) *n.* **1.** desperate recklessness. **2.** the state of being desperate.

despicable (ˈdɛspɪkəbᵊl, dɪˈspɪk-) *adj.* worthy of being despised; contemptible; mean. [C16: < LL *dēspicābilis,* < *dēspicārī* to disdain; cf. DESPISE] —**ˈdespicably** *adv.*

despise (dɪˈspaɪz) *vb.* (*tr.*) to look down on with contempt; scorn: *he despises flattery.* [C13: < OF *despire,* < L *dēspicere* to look down, < DE- + *specere* to look] —**deˈspiser** *n.*

despite (dɪˈspaɪt) *prep.* **1.** in spite of; undeterred by. ~*n.* **2.** *Arch.* contempt; insult. **3. in despite of.** (*prep.*) *Rare.* in spite of. [C13: < OF *despit,* < L *dēspectus* contempt; see DESPISE]

despoil (dɪˈspɔɪl) *vb.* (*tr.*) to deprive by force; plunder; loot. [C13: < OF, < L *dēspoliāre,* < DE- + *spoliāre* to rob (esp. of clothing)] —**deˈspoiler** *n.* —**deˈspoilment** *n.*

despoliation (dɪˌspəʊlɪˈeɪʃən) *n.* **1.** plunder or pillage. **2.** the state of being despoiled.

despond *vb.* (dɪˈspɒnd) (*intr.*) **1.** to become disheartened; despair. ~*n.* (ˈdɛspɒnd, dɪˈspɒnd). **2.** *Arch.* despondency. [C17: < L *dēspondēre* to promise, make over to, yield, lose heart, < DE- + *spondēre* to promise] —**deˈspondingly** *adv.*

despondent (dɪˈspɒndənt) *adj.* downcast or disheartened; dejected. —**deˈspondence** *or* **deˈspondency** *n.* —**deˈspondently** *adv.*

despot (ˈdɛspɒt) *n.* **1.** an absolute or tyrannical ruler. **2.** any person in power who acts tyrannically. [C16: < Med. L *despota,* < Gk *despotēs* lord, master] —**despotic** (dɛsˈpɒtɪk) *or* **desˈpotical** *adj.* —**desˈpotically** *adv.*

despotism (ˈdɛspəˌtɪzəm) *n.* **1.** the rule of a despot; absolute or tyrannical government. **2.** arbitrary or tyrannical authority or behaviour.

des res (dɛz rɛz) *n.* (in estate agents' jargon) a desirable residence.

dessert (dɪˈzɜːt) *n.* **1.** the sweet, usually last course of a meal. **2.** *Chiefly Brit.* (esp. formerly) fruit, dates, nuts, etc., served at the end of a meal. [C17: < F, < *desservir* to clear a table, < *des-* DIS-¹ + *servir* to SERVE]

dessertspoon (dɪˈzɜːtˌspuːn) *n.* a spoon intermediate in size between a tablespoon and a teaspoon.

destination (ˌdɛstɪˈneɪʃən) *n.* **1.** the predetermined end of a journey. **2.** the end or purpose for which something is created or a person is destined.

destine ('dɛstɪn) *vb.* (*tr.*) to set apart (for a certain purpose or person); intend; design. [C14: < OF, < L *dēstināre* to appoint, < DE- + *-stināre*, < *stāre* to stand]

destined ('dɛstɪnd) *adj.* (*postpositive*) **1.** foreordained; meant. **2.** (usually foll. by *for*) heading (towards a specific destination).

destiny ('dɛstɪnɪ) *n., pl.* **-nies. 1.** the future destined for a person or thing. **2.** the predetermined or inevitable course of events. **3.** the power that predetermines the course of events. [C14: < OF, < *destiner* to DESTINE]

destitute ('dɛstɪˌtju:t) *adj.* **1.** lacking the means of subsistence; totally impoverished. **2.** (*postpositive;* foll. by *of*) completely lacking: *destitute of words.* [C14: < L, < *dēstituere* to leave alone, < *statuere* to place]

destitution (ˌdɛstɪ'tju:ʃən) *n.* the state of being destitute; utter poverty.

destrier ('dɛstrɪə) *n. Arch.* a warhorse. [C13: < OF, < *destre* right hand, < L *dextra;* from the fact that a squire led a knight's horse with his right hand]

destroy (dɪ'strɔɪ) *vb.* (*mainly tr.*) **1.** to ruin; spoil. **2.** to tear down or demolish. **3.** to put an end to. **4.** to kill or annihilate. **5.** to crush or defeat. **6.** (*intr.*) to be destructive or cause destruction. [C13: < OF, < L *dēstruere* to pull down, < DE- + *struere* to pile up, build]

destroyer (dɪ'strɔɪə) *n.* **1.** a small fast lightly armoured but heavily armed warship. **2.** a person or thing that destroys.

destruct (dɪ'strʌkt) *vb.* **1.** to destroy (one's own missile, etc.) for safety. **2.** (*intr.*) (of a missile, etc.) to be destroyed, for safety, by those controlling it. ~*n.* **3.** the act of destructing. ~*adj.* **4.** designed to be capable of destroying itself or the object containing it: *destruct mechanism.*

destructible (dɪ'strʌktɪbᵊl) *adj.* capable of being or liable to be destroyed.

destruction (dɪ'strʌkʃən) *n.* **1.** the act of destroying or state of being destroyed; demolition. **2.** a cause of ruin or means of destroying. [C14: < L *dēstructiō* a pulling down; see DESTROY]

destructive (dɪ'strʌktɪv) *adj.* **1.** (often *postpositive* and foll. by *of* or *to*) causing or tending to cause the destruction (of). **2.** intended to discredit, esp. without positive suggestions or help; negative: *destructive criticism.* **—de'structively** *adv.* **—de'structiveness** *n.*

destructive distillation *n.* the decomposition of a complex substance, such as wood or coal, by heating it in the absence of air and collecting the volatile products.

destructor (dɪ'strʌktə) *n.* **1.** a furnace or incinerator for the disposal of refuse. **2.** a device used to blow up a defective missile.

desuetude (dɪ'sju:ɪˌtju:d, 'dɛswɪtju:d) *n.* the condition of not being in use or practice; disuse. [C15: < L, < *dēsuescere* to lay aside a habit, < DE- + *suescere* to grow accustomed]

desulphurize *or* **-ise** (di:'sʌlfjʊˌraɪz) *vb.* to free or become free from sulphur.

desultory ('dɛsəltərɪ, -trɪ) *adj.* **1.** passing from one thing to another, esp. in a fitful way; unmethodical; disconnected. **2.** random or incidental: *a desultory thought.* [C16: < L: relating to one who vaults or jumps, hence superficial, < *dēsilīre* to jump down, < DE- + *salīre*] **—'desultorily** *adv.* **—'desultoriness** *n.*

Det. *abbrev. for* Detective.

detach (dɪ'tætʃ) *vb.* (*tr.*) **1.** to disengage and separate or remove; unfasten; disconnect. **2.** *Mil.* to separate (a small unit) from a larger, esp. for a special assignment. [C17: < OF *destachier*, < *des-* DIS-[1] + *atachier* to ATTACH] **—de'tachable** *adj.* **—deˌtacha'bility** *n.*

detached (dɪ'tætʃt) *adj.* **1.** disconnected or standing apart; not attached: *a detached house.* **2.** showing no bias or emotional involvement.

detachment (dɪ'tætʃmənt) *n.* **1.** indifference; aloofness. **2.** freedom from self-interest or bias; disinterest. **3.** the act of detaching something. **4.** the condition of being detached; disconnection. **5.** *Mil.* **a.** the separation of a small unit from its main body. **b.** the unit so detached.

detail ('di:teɪl) *n.* **1.** an item that is considered separately; particular. **2.** an item that is unimportant: *passengers' comfort was regarded as a detail.* **3.** treatment of particulars: *this essay includes too much detail.* **4.** items collectively; particulars. **5.** a small section or element in a painting, building, statue, etc., esp. when considered in isolation. **6.** *Mil.* **a.** the act of assigning personnel for a specific duty. **b.** the personnel selected. **c.** the duty. **7. in detail.** including all or most particulars or items thoroughly. ~*vb.* (*tr.*) **8.** to list or relate fully. **9.** *Mil.* to select (personnel) for a specific duty. [C17: < F, < OF *detailler* to cut in pieces, < *de-* DIS-[1] + *tailler* to cut]

detailed ('di:teɪld) *adj.* having many details or giving careful attention to details.

detain (dɪ'teɪn) *vb.* (*tr.*) **1.** to delay; hold back. **2.** to confine or hold in custody. [C15: < OF, < L *dētinēre* to hold off, keep back, < DE- + *tenēre* to hold] **—de'tainable** *adj.* **—detainee** (ˌdi:teɪ'ni:) *n.* **—de'tainment** *n.*

detect (dɪ'tɛkt) *vb.* (*tr.*) **1.** to perceive or notice. **2.** to discover the existence or presence of (esp. something likely to elude observation). **3.** *Obs.* to discover, or reveal (a crime, criminal, etc.). **4.** to extract information from (an electromagnetic wave). [C15: < L *dētectus*, < *dētegere* to uncover, < DE- + *tegere* to cover] **—de'tectable** *or* **de'tectible** *adj.*

detection (dɪ'tɛkʃən) *n.* **1.** the act of discovering or the fact of being discovered. **2.** the act or process of extracting information, esp. at audio or video frequencies, from an electromagnetic wave; demodulation.

detective (dɪ'tɛktɪv) *n.* **1. a.** a police officer who investigates crimes. **b.** See **private detective. c.** (*as modifier*): *a detective story.* ~*adj.* **2.** of or for detection.

detector (dɪ'tɛktə) *n.* **1.** a person or thing that detects. **2.** any mechanical sensing device. **3.** *Electronics.* a device used in the detection of radio signals.

detent (dɪ'tɛnt) *n.* the locking piece of a mechanism, often spring-loaded to check the movement of a wheel in only one direction. [C17: < OF *destente* a loosening, trigger; see DÉTENTE]

détente (deɪ'tɑ:nt; *French* detɑ̃t) *n.* the relaxing or easing of tension, esp. between nations. [F, lit.: a loosening, < OF *destendre* to release, < *tendre* to stretch]

detention (dɪ'tɛnʃən) *n.* **1.** a detaining or being detained. **2. a.** custody or confinement, esp. of a suspect awaiting trial. **b.** (*as modifier*): *a detention order.* **3.** a form of punishment in which a pupil is detained after school. [C16: < L *dētentiō* a keeping back; see DETAIN]

detention centre *n.* a place where young persons may be detained for short periods by order of a court.

deter (dɪ'tɜ:) *vb.* **-terring, -terred.** (*tr.*) to discourage (from acting) or prevent (from occurring), usually by instilling fear, doubt, or anxiety. [C16: < L *dēterrēre*, < DE- + *terrēre* to frighten] **—de'terment** *n.*

deterge (dɪ'tɜ:dʒ) *vb.* (*tr.*) to cleanse: *to deterge a wound.* [C17: < L *dētergēre* to wipe away, < DE- + *tergēre* to wipe]

detergent (dɪ'tɜ:dʒənt) *n.* **1.** a cleansing agent, esp. a chemical such as an alkyl sulphonate, widely used in industry, laundering, etc. ~*adj.* **2.** having cleansing power. [C17: < L *dētergēns* wiping off; see DETERGE]

deteriorate (dɪ'tɪərɪəˌreɪt) *vb.* **1.** to make or become worse; depreciate. **2.** (*intr.*) to wear away or disintegrate. [C16: < LL *dēteriōrāre*, < L *dēterior* worse] **—deˌterio'ration** *n.* **—de'teriorative** *adj.*

determinacy (dɪ'tɜ:mɪnəsɪ) *n.* **1.** the quality of being defined or fixed. **2.** the condition of being predicted or deduced.

determinant (dɪˈtɜːmɪnənt) *adj.* **1.** serving to determine. *~n.* **2.** a factor that influences or determines. **3.** *Maths.* a square array of elements that represents the sum of certain products of these elements, used to solve simultaneous equations, in vector studies, etc.

determinate (dɪˈtɜːmɪnɪt) *adj.* **1.** definitely limited, defined, or fixed. **2.** determined. **3.** able to be predicted or deduced. **4.** *Bot.* having the main and branch stems ending in flowers. **—deˈterminateness** *n.*

determination (dɪˌtɜːmɪˈneɪʃən) *n.* **1.** the act of making a decision. **2.** the condition of being determined; resoluteness. **3.** an ending of an argument by the decision of an authority. **4.** the act of fixing the quality, limit, position, etc., of something. **5.** a decision or opinion reached. **6.** a resolute movement towards some object or end. **7.** *Law.* the termination of an estate or interest. **8.** *Law.* the decision reached by a court of justice on a disputed matter.

determinative (dɪˈtɜːmɪnətɪv) *adj.* **1.** serving to settle or determine; deciding. *~n.* **2.** a factor, circumstance, etc., that settles or determines. **—deˈterminatively** *adv.* **—deˈterminativeness** *n.*

determine (dɪˈtɜːmɪn) *vb.* **1.** to settle or decide (an argument, question, etc.) conclusively. **2.** (*tr.*) to conclude, esp. after observation or consideration. **3.** (*tr.*) to influence; give direction to. **4.** (*tr.*) to fix in scope, variety, etc.: *the river determined the edge of the property.* **5.** to make or cause to make a decision. **6.** (*tr.*) *Logic.* to define or limit (a notion) by adding or requiring certain features or characteristics. **7.** (*tr.*) *Geom.* to fix or specify the position or form of. **8.** *Chiefly law.* to come or bring to an end, as an estate. [C14: < OF, < L *dētermināre* to set boundaries to, < DE- + *termināre* to limit] **—deˈterminable** *adj.*

determined (dɪˈtɜːmɪnd) *adj.* of unwavering mind; resolute; firm. **—deˈterminedly** *adv.*

determiner (dɪˈtɜːmɪnə) *n.* **1.** a word, such as a number, an article, or *all,* that determines the referent or referents of a noun phrase. **2.** a person or thing that determines.

determinism (dɪˈtɜːmɪˌnɪzəm) *n.* the philosophical doctrine that all events, including human actions, are fully determined by preceding events, and so freedom of choice is illusory. Cf. **free will.** **—deˈterminist** *n., adj.* **—deˌterminˈistic** *adj.*

deterrent (dɪˈtɛrənt) *n.* **1.** something that deters. **2.** a weapon, esp. nuclear, held by one state, etc., to deter attack by another. *~adj.* **3.** tending or used to deter. [C19: < L *dēterrēns* hindering; see DETER] **—deˈterrence** *n.*

detest (dɪˈtɛst) *vb.* (*tr.*) to dislike intensely; loathe. [C16: < L *dētestārī* to curse (while invoking a god as witness), < DE- + *testārī,* < *testis* a witness] **—deˈtester** *n.*

detestable (dɪˈtɛstəbᵊl) *adj.* being or deserving to be abhorred or detested. **—deˌtestaˈbility** *or* **deˈtestableness** *n.* **—deˈtestably** *adv.*

detestation (ˌdiːtɛsˈteɪʃən) *n.* **1.** intense hatred; abhorrence. **2.** a person or thing that is detested.

dethrone (dɪˈθrəʊn) *vb.* (*tr.*) to remove from a throne or deprive of any high position or title. **—deˈthronement** *n.* **—deˈthroner** *n.*

detonate (ˈdɛtəˌneɪt) *vb.* to cause (a bomb, mine, etc.) to explode or (of a bomb, mine, etc.) to explode. [C18: < L *dētonāre* to thunder down, < DE- + *tonāre* to THUNDER] **—ˌdetoˈnation** *n.*

detonator (ˈdɛtəˌneɪtə) *n.* **1.** a small amount of explosive, as in a percussion cap, used to initiate a larger explosion. **2.** a device, such as an electrical generator, used to set off an explosion from a distance. **3.** an explosive.

detour (ˈdiːtʊə) *n.* **1.** a deviation from a direct route or course of action. *~vb.* **2.** to deviate or cause to deviate from a direct route or course of action. [C18: < F, < OF *destorner* to divert, turn away, < *des-* DE- + *torner* to TURN]

detoxify (diːˈtɒksɪˌfaɪ) *vb.* **-fying, -fied.** (*tr.*) to remove poison from. **—deˌtoxifiˈcation** *n.*

detract (dɪˈtrækt) *vb.* **1.** (when *intr.,* usually foll. by *from*) to take away a part (of); diminish: *her anger detracts from her beauty.* **2.** (*tr.*) to distract or divert. **3.** (*tr.*) *Obs.* to belittle or disparage. [C15: < L *dētractus,* < *dētrahere* to pull away, disparage, < DE- + *trahere* to drag] **—deˈtractive** *adj.* **—deˈtractor** *n.* **—deˈtraction** *n.*

detrain (diːˈtreɪn) *vb.* to leave or cause to leave a railway train. **—deˈtrainment** *n.*

detriment (ˈdɛtrɪmənt) *n.* **1.** disadvantage or damage. **2.** a cause of disadvantage or damage. [C15: < L *dētrīmentum,* a rubbing off, hence damage, < *dēterere,* < DE- + *terere* to rub]

detrimental (ˌdɛtrɪˈmɛntᵊl) *adj.* (when *postpositive,* foll. by *to*) harmful; injurious.

detritus (dɪˈtraɪtəs) *n.* **1.** a loose mass of stones, silt, etc., worn away from rocks. **2.** debris. [C18: < F, < L: a rubbing away; see DETRIMENT] **—deˈtrital** *adj.*

de trop *French.* (də tro) *adj.* (*postpositive*) not wanted; in the way. [lit.: of too much]

detumescence (ˌdiːtjʊˈmɛsəns) *n.* the subsidence of a swelling. [C17: < L *dētumescere* to cease swelling, < DE- + *tumescere,* < *tumēre* to swell]

deuce[1] (djuːs) *n.* **1. a.** a playing card or dice with two spots. **b.** a throw of two in dice. **2.** *Tennis, etc.* a tied score that requires one player to gain two successive points to win the game. [C15: < OF *deus* two, < L *duos,* < *duo* two]

deuce[2] (djuːs) *Inf.* *~interj.* **1.** an expression of annoyance or frustration. *~n.* **2. the deuce.** (intensifier) used in such phrases as **what the deuce, where the deuce,** etc. [C17: prob. special use of DEUCE[1] (in the sense: lowest throw at dice)]

deuced (ˈdjuːsɪd, djuːst) *Brit. inf.* *~adj.* **1.** (intensifier) confounded: *he's a deuced idiot.* *~adv.* **2.** (intensifier): *deuced good luck.*

Deus *Latin.* (ˈdeɪʊs) *n.* God. [rel. to Gk *Zeus*]

deus ex machina *Latin.* (ˈdeɪʊs ɛks ˈmækɪnə) *n.* **1.** (in ancient Greek and Roman drama) a god introduced into a play to resolve the plot. **2.** any unlikely device serving this purpose. [lit.: god out of a machine]

Deut. *Bible. abbrev. for* Deuteronomy.

deuterium (djuːˈtɪərɪəm) *n.* a stable isotope of hydrogen, occurring in natural hydrogen and in heavy water. Symbol: D or ^{2}H; atomic no.: 1; atomic wt.: 2.014. [C20: NL; see DEUTERO-, -IUM; from the fact that it is the second heaviest hydrogen isotope]

deuterium oxide *n.* another name for **heavy water.**

deutero-, deuto- *or before a vowel* **deuter-, deut-** *combining form.* second or secondary: *deuterium.* [< Gk *deuteros* second]

deuteron (ˈdjuːtəˌrɒn) *n.* the nucleus of a deuterium atom.

Deutschmark (ˈdɔɪtʃˌmɑːk) *or* **Deutsche Mark** (ˈdɔɪtʃə) *n.* the standard monetary unit of West Germany.

deutzia (ˈdjuːtsɪə, ˈdɔɪtsɪə) *n.* any of various shrubs with white, pink, or purplish flowers in early summer. [C19: NL, after J. *Deutz,* 18th-cent. Du. patron of botany]

devalue (diːˈvæljuː) *or* **devaluate** (diːˈvæljuːˌeɪt) *vb.* **-valuing, -valued** *or* **-valuating, -valuated.** **1.** to reduce (a currency) or (of a currency) be reduced in exchange value. **2.** (*tr.*) to reduce the value of. **—deˌvaluˈation** *n.*

Devanagari (ˌdeɪvəˈnɑːgərɪ) *n.* a syllabic script in which Sanskrit, Hindi, and other modern languages of India are written. [C18: < Sansk.: alphabet of the gods]

devastate (ˈdɛvəˌsteɪt) *vb.* (*tr.*) **1.** to lay waste or make desolate; ravage; destroy. **2.** to confound or overwhelm. [C17: < L *dēvastāre,* < DE- + *vastāre* to ravage; rel. to *vastus* waste, empty] **—ˌdevasˈtation** *n.* **—ˈdevasˌtator** *n.*

develop (dɪˈvɛləp) *vb.* **1.** to come or bring to a later or more advanced or expanded stage; grow or cause to grow gradually. **2.** (*tr.*) to work out in detail. **3.** to disclose or unfold (thoughts, a plot, etc.) gradually or (of thoughts, etc.) to be gradually disclosed or unfolded. **4.** to come or bring into existence: *he developed a new faith in God.* **5.** (*intr.*) to follow as a result of; ensue; a *row developed after her remarks.* **6.** (*tr.*) to contract (a disease or illness). **7.** (*tr.*) to improve the value or change the use of (land). **8.** to exploit or make available the natural resources of (a country or region). **9.** (*tr.*) *Photog.* to treat (exposed film, plate, or paper) with chemical solutions in order to produce a visible image. **10.** *Biol.* to progress or cause to progress from simple to complex stages in the growth of an individual or the evolution of a species. **11.** (*tr.*) to elaborate upon (a musical theme) by varying the melody, key, etc. **12.** (*tr.*) *Maths.* to expand (a function or expression) in the form of a series. **13.** (*tr.*) *Geom.* to project or roll out (a surface) onto a plane without stretching or shrinking any element. **14.** *Chess.* to bring (a piece) into play from its initial position on the back rank. [C19: < OF *desveloper* to unwrap, < *des-* DIS-[1] + *veloper* to wrap; see ENVELOP] —**deˈvelopable** *adj.*

developer (dɪˈvɛləpə) *n.* **1.** a person or thing that develops something, esp. a person who develops property. **2.** *Photog.* a chemical used to convert the latent image recorded in the emulsion of a film or paper into a visible image.

developing country *n.* a poor or non-industrial country that is seeking to develop its resources by industrialization.

development (dɪˈvɛləpmənt) *n.* **1.** the act or process of growing or developing. **2.** the product of developing. **3.** a fact or event, esp. one that changes a situation. **4.** an area of land that has been developed. **5.** the section of a movement, usually in sonata form, in which the basic musical themes are developed. **6.** *Chess.* the process of developing pieces. —**deˌvelopˈmental** *adj.*

development area *n.* (in Britain) an area which has experienced economic depression because of the decline of its main industry or industries, and which is given government assistance to establish new industry.

deviant (ˈdiːvɪənt) *adj.* **1.** deviating, as from what is considered acceptable behaviour. ~*n.* **2.** a person whose behaviour, esp. sexual behaviour, deviates from what is considered to be acceptable. —**ˈdeviance** *or* **ˈdeviancy** *n.*

deviate *vb.* (ˈdiːvɪˌeɪt). **1.** (*usually intr.*) to differ or cause to differ, as in belief or thought. **2.** (*usually intr.*) to turn aside or cause to turn aside. **3.** (*intr.*) *Psychol.* to depart from an accepted standard. ~*n., adj.* (ˈdiːvɪɪt). **4.** another word for **deviant.** [C17: < LL *dēviāre* to turn aside from the direct road, < DE- + *via* road] —**ˈdeviˌator** *n.* —**ˈdeviatory** *adj.*

deviation (ˌdiːvɪˈeɪʃən) *n.* **1.** an act or result of deviating. **2.** *Statistics.* the difference between an observed value in a series of such values and their arithmetic mean. **3.** the error of a compass due to local magnetic disturbances.

device (dɪˈvaɪs) *n.* **1.** a machine or tool used for a specific task. **2.** *Euphemistic.* a bomb. **3.** a plan, esp. a clever or evil one; trick. **4.** any ornamental pattern or picture, as in embroidery. **5.** computer hardware designed for a specific function. **6.** a design or figure, used as a heraldic sign, emblem, etc. **7.** a particular pattern of words, figures of speech, etc., used in literature to produce an effect on the reader. **8. leave (someone) to his own devices.** to leave (someone) alone to do as he wishes. [C13: < OF *devis* purpose, contrivance & *devise* difference, intention, < *deviser* to divide, control; see DEVISE]

devil (ˈdɛvᵊl) *n.* **1.** *Theol.* (*often cap.*) the chief spirit of evil and enemy of God, often depicted as a human figure with horns, cloven hoofs, and tail. **2.** any subordinate evil spirit. **3.** a person or animal regarded as wicked or ill-natured. **4.** a person or animal regarded as unfortunate or wretched. **5.** a person or animal regarded as daring, mischievous, or energetic. **6.** *Inf.* something difficult or annoying. **7.** *Christian Science.* an error, lie, or false belief. **8.** (in Malaysia) a ghost. **9.** a portable furnace or brazier. **10.** any of various mechanical devices, such as a machine for making wooden screws or a rag-tearing machine. **11.** See **printer's devil. 12.** *Law.* (in England) a junior barrister who does work for another in order to gain experience, usually for a half fee. **13. between the devil and the deep blue sea.** between equally undesirable alternatives. **14. devil of a.** *Inf.* (intensifier): *a devil of a fine horse.* **15. give the devil his due.** to acknowledge the talent or success of an unpleasant person. **16. go to the devil. a.** to fail or become dissipated. **b.** (*interj.*) used to express annoyance with the person causing it. **17. (let) the devil take the hindmost.** look after oneself and leave others to their fate. **18. talk** (*or* **speak**) **of the devil!** (*interj.*) used when an absent person who has been the subject of conversation appears. **19. the devil!** (intensifier): **a.** used in **what the devil, where the devil,** etc. **b.** an exclamation of anger, surprise, disgust, etc. **20. the devil to pay.** trouble to be faced as a consequence of an action. ~*vb.* **-illing, -illed** *or U.S.* **-iling, -iled. 21.** (*tr.*) to prepare (food) by coating with a highly flavoured spiced paste or mixture of condiments before cooking. **22.** (*tr.*) to tear (rags) with a devil. **23.** (*intr.*) to serve as a printer's devil. **24.** (*intr.*) *Chiefly Brit.* to do hackwork, esp. for a lawyer or author. **25.** (*tr.*) *U.S. inf.* to harass, vex, etc. [OE *dēofol,* < L *diabolus,* < Gk *diabolos* enemy, accuser, slanderer]

devilfish (ˈdɛvᵊlˌfɪʃ) *n., pl.* **-fish** *or* **-fishes. 1.** Also called: **devil ray.** another name for **manta** (the fish). **2.** another name for **octopus.**

devilish (ˈdɛvəlɪʃ) *adj.* **1.** of, resembling, or befitting a devil; diabolic; fiendish. ~*adv., adj.* **2.** *Inf.* (intensifier): *devilish good food.* —**ˈdevilishly** *adv.* —**ˈdevilishness** *n.*

devil-may-care *adj.* careless or reckless; happy-go-lucky: *a devil-may-care attitude.*

devilment (ˈdɛvᵊlmənt) *n.* devilish or mischievous conduct.

devilry (ˈdɛvᵊlrɪ) *or* **deviltry** *n., pl.* **-ries** *or* **-tries. 1.** reckless or malicious fun or mischief. **2.** wickedness. **3.** black magic or other forms of diabolism. [C18: < F *diablerie,* < *diable* DEVIL]

devil's advocate *n.* **1.** a person who advocates an opposing or unpopular view, often for the sake of argument. **2.** *R.C. Church.* the official appointed to put the case against the beatification or canonization of a candidate. [translation of NL *advocātus diabolī*]

devil's coach-horse *n.* a large black beetle with large jaws and ferocious habits.

devil's food cake *n. Chiefly U.S. & Canad.* a rich chocolate cake.

devious (ˈdiːvɪəs) *adj.* **1.** not sincere or candid; deceitful. **2.** (of a route or course of action) rambling; indirect. **3.** going astray; erring. [C16: < L *dēvius* lying to one side of the road, < DE- + *via* road] —**ˈdeviously** *adv.* —**ˈdeviousness** *n.*

devise (dɪˈvaɪz) *vb.* **1.** to work out or plan (something) in one's mind. **2.** (*tr.*) *Law.* to dispose of (real property) by will. ~*n. Law.* **3.** a disposition of property by will. **4.** a will or clause in a will disposing of real property. [C15: < OF *deviser* to divide, apportion, intend, < L *dīvidere* to DIVIDE] —**deˈviser** *n.*

devitalize *or* **-ise** (diːˈvaɪtəˌlaɪz) *vb.* (*tr.*) to lower or destroy the vitality of; make weak or lifeless. —**deˌvitaliˈzation** *or* **-iˈsation** *n.*

devoid (dɪˈvɔɪd) *adj.* (*postpositive;* foll. by *of*) destitute or void (of); free (from). [C15: orig. p.p. of *devoid* (*vb.*) to remove, < OF *devoider* < DE- + *voider* to void]

devoirs (dəˈvwɑː) *pl. n.* (*sometimes sing.*) compliments or respects. [C13: < OF: duty, < *devoir* to be obliged to, owe, < L *dēbēre*]

devolution (ˌdiːvəˈluːʃən) *n.* **1.** a devolving. **2.** a passing onwards or downwards from one stage to another. **3.** a transfer of authority from a central government to regional governments. [C16: < Med. L *dēvolūtiō* a rolling down, < L *dēvolvere;* see DEVOLVE] —**ˌdevoˈlutionary** *adj.* —**ˌdevoˈlutionist** *n., adj.*

devolve (dɪˈvɒlv) *vb.* **1.** (foll. by *on, upon, to,* etc.) to pass or cause to pass to a successor or substitute, as duties, power, etc. **2.** (*intr.* foll. by *on* or *upon*) *Law.* (of an estate, etc.) to pass to another by operation of law. [C15: < L *dēvolvere* to roll down, fall into, < DE- + *volvere* to roll] —**de'volvement** *n.*

Devonian (də'vəʊnɪən) *adj.* 1. of, denoting, or formed in the fourth period of the Palaeozoic era, between the Silurian and Carboniferous periods. 2. of or relating to Devon. ~*n.* 3. **the.** the Devonian period or rock system.

Devonshire split ('dɛvᵊnˌʃə) *n.* a kind of yeast bun split open and served with cream or jam.

devote (dɪ'vəʊt) *vb.* (*tr.*) to apply or dedicate (oneself, money, etc.) to some pursuit, cause, etc. [C16: < L *dēvōtus* devoted, solemnly promised, < *dēvovēre* to vow; see DE-, VOW]

devoted (dɪ'vəʊtɪd) *adj.* 1. feeling or demonstrating loyalty or devotion; devout. 2. (*postpositive;* foll. by *to*) dedicated or consecrated. —**de'votedly** *adv.* —**de'votedness** *n.*

devotee (ˌdɛvə'tiː) *n.* 1. a person ardently enthusiastic about something, such as a sport or pastime. 2. a zealous follower of a religion.

devotion (dɪ'vəʊʃən) *n.* 1. (often foll. by *to*) strong attachment (to) or affection (for a cause, person, etc.) marked by dedicated loyalty. 2. religious zeal; piety. 3. (*often pl.*) religious observance or prayers. —**de'votional** *adj.*

devour (dɪ'vaʊə) *vb.* (*tr.*) 1. to eat up greedily or voraciously. 2. to waste or destroy; consume. 3. to consume greedily or avidly with the senses or mind. 4. to engulf or absorb. [C14: < OF, < L *dēvorāre* to gulp down, < DE- + *vorāre;* see VORACIOUS] —**de'vourer** *n.* —**de'vouring** *adj.*

devout (dɪ'vaʊt) *adj.* 1. deeply religious; reverent. 2. sincere; earnest; heartfelt. [C13: < OF *devot,* < LL *dēvōtus,* < L: faithful; see DEVOTE] —**de'voutly** *adv.* —**de'voutness** *n.*

dew (djuː) *n.* 1. drops of water condensed on a cool surface, esp. at night, from vapour in the air. 2. something like this, esp. in freshness: *the dew of youth.* 3. small drops of moisture, such as tears. ~*vb.* 4. (*tr.*) to moisten with or as with dew. [OE *dēaw*]

dewberry ('djuːbərɪ, -brɪ) *n., pl.* **-ries.** 1. any trailing bramble having blue-black fruits. 2. the fruit of any such plant.

dewclaw ('djuːˌklɔː) *n.* 1. a nonfunctional claw in dogs. 2. an analogous rudimentary hoof in deer, goats, etc. —**'dewˌclawed** *adj.*

dewdrop ('djuːˌdrɒp) *n.* a drop of dew.

Dewey Decimal System ('djuːɪ) *n.* a system of library book classification with ten main subject classes. Also called: **decimal classification.** [C19: after Melvil *Dewey* (1851–1931), U.S. educator]

dewlap ('djuːˌlæp) *n.* 1. a loose fold of skin hanging from beneath the throat in cattle, dogs, etc. 2. loose skin on an elderly person's throat. [C14 *dewlappe,* < DEW (prob. < an earlier form of different meaning) + LAP[1] (< OE *læppa* hanging flap), ? < ON]

DEW line (djuː) *n. acronym for* distant early warning line, a network of radar stations situated mainly in Arctic regions of North America.

dew point *n.* the temperature at which dew begins to form.

dew pond *n.* a shallow pond, formerly thought to be kept full by dew and mist.

dewy ('djuːɪ) *adj.* **dewier, dewiest.** 1. moist with or as with dew. 2. of or resembling dew. 3. *Poetic.* suggesting, falling, or refreshing like dew: *dewy sleep.* —**'dewily** *adv.* —**'dewiness** *n.*

dexter ('dɛkstə) *adj.* 1. *Arch.* of or located on the right side. 2. (*usually postpositive*) *Heraldry.* of, on, or starting from the right side of a shield from the bearer's point of view and therefore on the spectator's left. ~Cf. **sinister.** [C16: < L; cf. Gk *dexios* on the right hand]

dexterity (dɛk'stɛrɪtɪ) *n.* 1. physical, esp. manual, skill or nimbleness. 2. mental skill or adroitness. [C16: < L *dexteritās* aptness, readiness; see DEXTER]

dexterous ('dɛkstrəs) *adj.* possessing or done with dexterity. —**'dexterously** *adv.* —**'dexterousness** *n.*

dextral ('dɛkstrəl) *adj.* 1. of or located on the right side, esp. of the body. 2. of a person who prefers to use his right foot, hand, or eye; right-handed. 3. (of shells) coiling in an anticlockwise direction from the apex. —**dextrality** (dɛk'strælɪtɪ) *n.* —**'dextrally** *adv.*

dextran ('dɛkstrən) *n. Biochem.* a chainlike polymer of glucose produced by the action of bacteria on sucrose: used as a substitute for plasma in blood transfusions. [C19: < DEXTRO- + -AN]

dextrin ('dɛkstrɪn) *or* **dextrine** ('dɛkstrɪn, -triːn) *n.* any of a group of sticky substances obtained from starch: used as thickening agents in foods and as gums. [C19: < F *dextrine;* see DEXTRO-, -IN]

dextro- *or before a vowel* **dextr-** *combining form.* on or towards the right: *dextrorotation.* [< L, < *dexter* on the right side]

dextrorotation (ˌdɛkstrəʊrəʊ'teɪʃən) *n.* a rotation to the right; clockwise rotation, esp. of the plane of polarization of plane-polarized light. Cf. **laevorotation.** —**dextrorotatory** (ˌdɛkstrəʊ'rəʊtəˌtərɪ, -trɪ) *or* ˌ**dextro'rotary** *adj.*

dextrorse ('dɛkstrɔːs) *or* **dextrorsal** (dɛk'strɔːsᵊl) *adj.* (of some climbing plants) growing upwards in a spiral from left to right or anticlockwise. [C19: < L *dextrorsum* towards the right, < DEXTRO- + *vorsus,* var. of *versus,* < *vertere* to turn] —**'dextrorsely** *adv.*

dextrose ('dɛkstrəʊz, -trəʊs) *n.* a glucose occurring widely in fruit, honey, and in the blood and tissue of animals. Formula: $C_6H_{12}O_6$. Also called: **grape sugar, dextroglucose.**

dextrous ('dɛkstrəs) *adj.* a variant spelling of **dexterous.** —**'dextrously** *adv.* —**'dextrousness** *n.*

DF *abbrev. for* Defender of the Faith.

D/F *or* **DF** *Telecomm. abbrev. for:* 1. direction finder. 2. direction finding.

DFC *abbrev. for* Distinguished Flying Cross.

DFM *abbrev. for* Distinguished Flying Medal.

dg *symbol for* decigram.

dhal, dal, *or* **dholl** (dɑːl) *n.* 1. a tropical African and Asian shrub cultivated for its nutritious pealike seeds. 2. the seed of this shrub. [C17: < Hindi, < Sansk. *dal* to split]

dharma ('dɑːmə) *n.* 1. *Hinduism.* social custom regarded as a religious and moral duty. 2. *Hinduism.* a. the essential principle of the cosmos; natural law. b. conduct that conforms with this. 3. *Buddhism.* ideal truth. [Sansk.: habit, usage, law]

dhobi ('dəʊbɪ) *n., pl.* **-bis.** (in India, E Africa, etc.) a washerman. [C19: < Hindi, < *dhōb* washing]

dhoti ('dəʊtɪ), **dhooti, dhootie,** *or* **dhuti** ('duːtɪ) *n., pl.* **-tis.** a long loincloth worn by men in India. [C17: < Hindi]

dhow (daʊ) *n.* a lateen-rigged coastal Arab sailing vessel. [C19: < Ar.]

DHSS (in Britain) *abbrev. for* Department of Health and Social Security.

di. *or* **dia.** *abbrev. for* diameter.

di-[1] *prefix.* 1. twice; two; double: *dicotyledon.* 2. a. containing two specified atoms or groups of atoms: *carbon dioxide.* b. a nontechnical equivalent of **bi-** (sense 5). [via L < Gk, < *dis* twice, double, rel. to *duo* two. Cf. BI-]

di-[2] *combining form.* a variant of **dia-** before a vowel: *diopter.*

dia- *or* **di-** *prefix.* 1. through or during: *diachronic.* 2. across: *diactinic.* 3. apart: *diacritic.* [< Gk *dia* through, between, across, by]

diabetes (ˌdaɪə'biːtɪs, -tiːz) *n.* any of various disorders, esp. diabetes mellitus, characterized by excretion of an abnormally large amount of urine. [C16: < L: siphon, < Gk, lit.: a passing through]

diabetes mellitus (mə'laɪtəs) *n.* a disorder of carbohydrate metabolism characterized by excessive thirst and excretion of abnormally large quantities of urine containing an excess of sugar, caused by a deficiency of insulin. [C18: NL, lit.: honey-sweet diabetes]

diabetic (ˌdaɪə'bɛtɪk) *adj.* 1. of, relating to, or having diabetes. 2. for the use of diabetics. ~*n.* 3. a person who has diabetes.

diablerie (dɪ'ɑːblərɪ) *n.* 1. magic or witchcraft connected with devils. 2. esoteric knowledge of devils. 3. devilry; mischief. [C18: < OF, < *diable* devil, < L *diabolus;* see DEVIL]

diabolic (ˌdaɪəˈbɒlɪk) *adj.* 1. of the devil; satanic. 2. extremely cruel or wicked; fiendish. 3. very difficult or unpleasant. [C14: < LL, < Gk *diabolikos,* < *diabolos* DEVIL] —ˌ**diaˈbolically** *adv.* —ˌ**diaˈbolicalness** *n.*

diabolical (ˌdaɪəˈbɒlɪkᵊl) *adj. Inf.* 1. excruciatingly bad. 2. (intensifier): *a diabolical liberty.* —ˌ**diaˈbolically** *adv.* —ˌ**diaˈbolicalness** *n.*

diabolism (daɪˈæbəˌlɪzəm) *n.* 1. a. witchcraft or sorcery. b. worship of devils or beliefs concerning them. 2. character or conduct that is devilish. —**diˈabolist** *n.*

diabolo (dɪˈæbəˌləʊ) *n., pl.* **-los.** 1. a game in which one throws and catches a top on a cord fastened to two sticks. 2. the top used in this. [C20: < It., lit.: devil]

diachronic (ˌdaɪəˈkrɒnɪk) *adj.* of the study of the development of a phenomenon through time; historical. Cf. **synchronic.** [C19: < DIA- + Gk *khronos* time]

diacidic (ˌdaɪəˈsɪdɪk) *adj.* (of a base) capable of neutralizing two protons with one of its molecules. Also: **diacid.**

diaconal (daɪˈækənᵊl) *adj.* of or associated with a deacon or the diaconate. [C17: < LL *diāconālis,* < *diāconus* DEACON]

diaconate (daɪˈækənɪt, -ˌneɪt) *n.* the office, sacramental status, or period of office of a deacon. [C17: < LL *diāconātus;* see DEACON]

diacritic (ˌdaɪəˈkrɪtɪk) *n.* 1. a sign placed above or below a character or letter to indicate that it has a different phonetic value, is stressed, or for some other reason. ~*adj.* 2. another word for **diacritical.** [C17: < Gk *diakritikos* serving to distinguish, < *diakrinein,* < DIA- + *krinein* to separate]

diacritical (ˌdaɪəˈkrɪtɪkᵊl) *adj.* 1. of or relating to a diacritic. 2. showing up a distinction.

diadem (ˈdaɪəˌdɛm) *n.* 1. a royal crown, esp. a light jewelled circlet. 2. royal dignity or power. [C13: < L, < Gk: fillet, royal headdress, < *diadein,* < DIA- + *dein* to bind]

diaeresis *or esp. U.S.* **dieresis** (daɪˈɛrɪsɪs) *n., pl.* **-ses** (-ˌsiːz). 1. the mark ¨ placed over the second of two adjacent vowels to indicate that it is to be pronounced separately, as in some spellings of *coöperate, naïve,* etc. 2. this mark used for any other purpose, such as to indicate a special pronunciation for a particular vowel. 3. a pause in a line of verse when the end of a foot coincides with the end of a word. [C17: < L, < Gk: a division, < *diairein,* < DIA- + *hairein* to take; cf. HERESY] —**diˈaeretic** *or esp. U.S.* **dieretic** (ˌdaɪəˈrɛtɪk) *adj.*

diag. *abbrev. for* diagram.

diagnose (ˈdaɪəgˌnəʊz) *vb.* 1. to determine by diagnosis. 2. (*tr.*) to examine (a person or thing), as for a disease. —ˌ**diagˈnosable** *adj.*

diagnosis (ˌdaɪəgˈnəʊsɪs) *n., pl.* **-ses** (-siːz). 1. a. the identification of diseases from the examination of symptoms. b. an opinion so reached. 2. a. thorough analysis of facts or problems in order to gain understanding. b. an opinion reached through such analysis. [C17: NL, < Gk: a distinguishing, < *diagignōskein,* < *gignōskein* to perceive, KNOW] —**diagnostic** (ˌdaɪəgˈnɒstɪk) *adj.*

diagonal (daɪˈægənᵊl) *adj.* 1. *Maths.* connecting any two vertices that in a polygon are not adjacent and in a polyhedron are not in the same face. 2. slanting; oblique. 3. marked with slanting lines or patterns. ~*n.* 4. a diagonal line, plane, or pattern. 5. something put, set, or drawn obliquely. [C16: < L, < Gk *diagōnios,* < DIA- + *gōnia* angle] —**diˈagonally** *adv.*

diagram (ˈdaɪəˌgræm) *n.* 1. a sketch or plan demonstrating the form or workings of something. 2. *Maths.* a pictorial representation of a quantity or of a relationship. ~*vb.* **-gramming, -grammed** *or U.S.* **-graming, -gramed.** 3. to show in or as if in a diagram. [C17: < L, < Gk, < *diagraphein,* < *graphein* to write] —**diagrammatic** (ˌdaɪəgrəˈmætɪk) *adj.*

dial (ˈdaɪəl) *n.* 1. the face of a watch, clock, etc., marked with divisions representing units of time. 2. the graduated disc of various measuring instruments. 3. a. the control on a radio or television set used to change the station or channel. b. the panel on a radio on which the frequency, wavelength, or station is indicated. 4. a numbered disc on a telephone that is rotated a set distance for each digit of a number being called. 5. *Brit.* a slang word for **face.** ~*vb.* **dialling, dialled** *or U.S.* **dialing, dialed.** 6. to try to establish a telephone connection with (a subscriber) by operating the dial or buttons on a telephone. 7. (*tr.*) to indicate, measure, or operate with a dial. [C14: < Med. L *diālis* daily, < L *diēs* day] —ˈ**dialler** *n.*

dial. *abbrev. for* dialect(al).

dialect (ˈdaɪəˌlɛkt) *n.* a. a form of a language spoken in a particular geographical area or by members of a particular social class or occupational group, distinguished by its vocabulary, grammar, and pronunciation. b. a form of a language that is considered inferior. [C16: < L, < Gk *dialektos* speech, dialect, discourse, < *dialegesthai* to converse, < *legein* to talk, speak] —ˌ**diaˈlectal** *adj.*

dialectic (ˌdaɪəˈlɛktɪk) *n.* 1. disputation or debate, esp. when intended to resolve differences between two views. 2. logical argumentation. 3. a variant of **dialectics** (sense 1). 4. *Philosophy.* an interpretive method used by Hegel in which contradictions are resolved at a higher level of truth (synthesis). ~*adj.* 5. of or relating to logical disputation. [C17: < L, < Gk *dialektikē* (*tekhnē*) (the art) of argument; see DIALECT] —ˌ**dialecˈtician** *n.*

dialectical (ˌdaɪəˈlɛktɪkᵊl) *adj.* of or relating to dialectic or dialectics. —ˌ**diaˈlectically** *adv.*

dialectical materialism *n.* the economic, political, and philosophical system of Marx and Engels that combines traditional materialism and Hegelian dialectic.

dialectics (ˌdaɪəˈlɛktɪks) *n.* (*functioning as pl. or* (*sometimes*) *sing.*) 1. the study of reasoning. 2. a particular methodology or system. 3. the application of the Hegelian dialectic or the rationale of dialectical materialism.

dialling code *n.* a sequence of numbers which is dialled for connection with another exchange before an individual subscriber's telephone number is dialled.

dialling tone *or U.S. & Canad.* **dial tone** *n.* a continuous sound, either purring or high-pitched, heard over a telephone indicating that a number can be dialled.

dialogue *or U.S.* (*often*) **dialog** (ˈdaɪəˌlɒg) *n.* 1. conversation between two or more people. 2. an exchange of opinions; discussion. 3. the lines spoken by characters in drama or fiction. 4. a passage of conversation in a literary or dramatic work. 5. a literary composition in the form of a dialogue. 6. a political discussion between representatives of two nations or groups. [C13: < OF, < L, < Gk, < *dialegesthai;* see DIALECT]

dialyse *or U.S.* **-lyze** (ˈdaɪəˌlaɪz) *vb.* (*tr.*) to separate by dialysis. —ˌ**dialyˈsation** *or U.S.* **-lyˈzation** *n.*

dialysis (daɪˈælɪsɪs) *n., pl.* **-ses** (-ˌsiːz). 1. the separation of the crystalloids from a solution containing crystalloids and colloids by osmosis of the crystalloids. 2. *Med.* the filtering of blood through a semipermeable membrane to remove waste products. [C16: < LL: a separation, < Gk *dialusis,* < *dialuein* to tear apart, dissolve, < *luein* to loosen] —**dialytic** (ˌdaɪəˈlɪtɪk) *adj.*

diam. *abbrev. for* diameter.

diamagnetic (ˌdaɪəmægˈnɛtɪk) *adj.* of, exhibiting, or concerned with diamagnetism.

diamagnetism (ˌdaɪəˈmægnɪˌtɪzəm) *n.* the phenomenon exhibited by substances that are repelled by both poles of a magnet and thus lie across the magnet's line of influence.

diamanté (ˌdaɪəˈmæntɪ) *adj.* 1. decorated with glittering ornaments, such as sequins. ~*n.* 2. a fabric so covered. [C20: < F, < *diamanter* to adorn with diamonds]

diameter (daɪˈæmɪtə) *n.* **1. a.** a straight line connecting the centre of a circle, sphere, etc. with two points on the perimeter or surface. **b.** the length of such a line. **2.** the thickness of something, esp. with circular cross section. [C14: < Med. L, < Gk: diameter, diagonal, < DIA- + *metron* measure]

diametric (ˌdaɪəˈmɛtrɪk) *or* **diametrical** *adj.* **1.** Also: **diametral.** of, related to, or along a diameter. **2.** completely opposed.

diametrically (ˌdaɪəˈmɛtrɪkəlɪ) *adv.* completely; utterly (esp. in **diametrically opposed**).

diamond (ˈdaɪəmənd) *n.* **1. a.** a usually colourless exceptionally hard form of carbon in cubic crystalline form. It is used as a precious stone and for industrial cutting or abrading. **b.** (*as modifier*): *a diamond ring.* **2.** *Geom.* a figure having four sides of equal length forming two acute angles and two obtuse angles; rhombus. **3. a.** a red lozenge-shaped symbol on a playing card. **b.** a card with one or more of these symbols or (*when pl.*) the suit of cards so marked. **4.** *Baseball.* **a.** the whole playing field. **b.** the square formed by the four bases. ~*vb.* **5.** (*tr.*) to decorate with or as with diamonds. [C13: < OF *diamant,* < Med. L *diamas,* < L *adamas* the hardest iron or steel, diamond; see ADAMANT] —**diamantine** (ˌdaɪəˈmæntaɪn) *adj.*

diamond anniversary *n.* a 60th, or occasionally 75th, anniversary.

diamondback (ˈdaɪəməndˌbæk) *n.* **1.** Also called: **diamondback terrapin** *or* **turtle.** any edible North American terrapin having diamond-shaped markings on the shell. **2.** a large North American rattlesnake having diamond-shaped markings.

diamond wedding *n.* the 60th, or occasionally the 75th, anniversary of a marriage.

dianthus (daɪˈænθəs) *n., pl.* **-thuses.** any Eurasian plant of the widely cultivated genus *Dianthus,* such as the carnation, pink, and sweet william. [C19: NL, < Gk DI-[1] + *anthos* flower]

diapason (ˌdaɪəˈpeɪzᵊn) *n. Music.* **1.** either of two stops (**open** and **stopped diapason**) found throughout the compass of a pipe organ that give it its characteristic tone colour. **2.** the compass of an instrument or voice. **3. a.** a standard pitch used for tuning. **b.** a tuning fork or pitch pipe. **4.** (in classical Greece) an octave. [C14: < L: the whole octave, < Gk: (*hē*) *dia pasōn* (*khordōn sumphōnia*) (concord) through all (the notes)]

diapause (ˈdaɪəˌpɔːz) *n.* a period of suspended development and growth accompanied by decreased metabolism in insects and some other animals. [C19: < Gk *diapausis* pause, < *diapauein* to pause, bring to an end, < DIA- + *pauein* to stop]

diaper (ˈdaɪəpə) *n.* **1.** the U.S. and Canad. word for **nappy**[1]. **2. a.** a fabric having a pattern of a small repeating design, esp. diamonds. **b.** such a pattern, used as decoration. ~*vb.* **3.** (*tr.*) to decorate with such a pattern. [C14: < OF *diaspre,* < Med. L *diasprus* made of diaper, < Med. Gk *diaspros* pure white, < DIA- + *aspros* white, shining]

diaphanous (daɪˈæfənəs) *adj.* (usually of fabrics) fine and translucent. [C17: < Med. L, < Gk *diaphanēs* transparent, < DIA- + *phainein* to show] —**diˈaphanously** *adv.*

diaphoresis (ˌdaɪəfəˈriːsɪs) *n.* perspiration, esp. when perceptible and excessive. [C17: via LL < Gk, < *diaphorein* to disperse by perspiration, < DIA- + *phorein* to carry]

diaphoretic (ˌdaɪəfəˈrɛtɪk) *adj.* **1.** relating to or causing perspiration. ~*n.* **2.** a diaphoretic drug.

diaphragm (ˈdaɪəˌfræm) *n.* **1.** *Anat.* any separating membrane, esp. the muscular partition that separates the abdominal and thoracic cavities in mammals. **2.** another name for **cap** (sense 11). **3.** any thin dividing membrane. **4.** Also called: **stop.** a device to control the amount of light entering an optical instrument, such as a camera. **5.** a thin vibrating disc used to convert sound signals to electrical signals or vice versa in telephones, etc. [C17: < LL, < Gk, < DIA- + *phragma* fence] —**diaphragmatic** (ˌdaɪəfrægˈmætɪk) *adj.*

diapositive (ˌdaɪəˈpɒzɪtɪv) *n.* a positive transparency; slide.

diarist (ˈdaɪərɪst) *n.* a person who writes a diary, esp. one that is subsequently published.

diarrhoea *or esp. U.S.* **diarrhea** (ˌdaɪəˈrɪə) *n.* frequent and copious discharge of abnormally liquid faeces. [C16: < LL, < Gk, < *diarrhein,* < DIA- + *rhein* to flow] —ˌ**diarˈrhoeal,** ˌ**diarˈrhoeic** *or esp. U.S.* ˌ**diarˈrheal,** ˌ**diarˈrheic** *adj.*

diary (ˈdaɪərɪ) *n., pl.* **-ries. 1.** a personal record of daily events, appointments, observations, etc. **2.** a book for this. [C16: < L *diārium* daily allocation of food or money, journal, < *diēs* day]

Diaspora (daɪˈæspərə) *n.* **1. a.** the dispersion of the Jews after the Babylonian and Roman conquests of Palestine. **b.** the Jewish people and communities outside Israel. **2.** (*often not cap.*) a dispersion, as of people originally belonging to one nation. [C19: < Gk: a scattering, < *diaspeirein,* < DIA- + *speirein* to scatter, sow]

diastalsis (ˌdaɪəˈstælsɪs) *n., pl.* **-ses** (-siːz). *Physiol.* a downward wave of contraction occurring in the intestine during digestion. [C20: NL, < DIA- + (PERI)STALSIS] —ˌ**diaˈstaltic** *adj.*

diastase (ˈdaɪəˌsteɪs, -ˌsteɪz) *n.* any of a group of enzymes that hydrolyse starch to maltose. They are present in germinated barley and in the pancreas. [C19: < F, < Gk *diastasis* a separation] —ˌ**diaˈstasic** *adj.*

diastole (daɪˈæstəlɪ) *n.* the dilation of the chambers of the heart that follows each contraction, during which they refill with blood. Cf. **systole.** [C16: via LL < Gk, < *diastellein* to expand, < DIA- + *stellein* to place, bring together, make ready] —**diastolic** (ˌdaɪəˈstɒlɪk) *adj.*

diastrophism (daɪˈæstrəˌfɪzəm) *n.* the process of movement of the earth's crust that gives rise to mountains, continents, and other large-scale features. [C19: < Gk *diastrophē* a twisting; see DIA-, STROPHE] —**diastrophic** (ˌdaɪəˈstrɒfɪk) *adj.*

diathermancy (ˌdaɪəˈθɜːmənsɪ) *n., pl.* **-cies.** the property of transmitting infrared radiation. [C19: < F, < DIA- + Gk *thermansis* heating, < *thermos* hot] —ˌ**diaˈthermanous** *adj.*

diathermy (ˈdaɪəˌθɜːmɪ) *or* **diathermia** (ˌdaɪəˈθɜːmɪə) *n.* local heating of the body tissues with an electric current for medical purposes. [C20: < NL, < DIA- + Gk *thermē* heat]

diatom (ˈdaɪətəm) *n.* a microscopic unicellular alga having a cell wall impregnated with silica. [C19: < NL, < Gk *diatomos* cut in two, < DIA- + *temnein* to cut]

diatomaceous (ˌdaɪətəˈmeɪʃəs) *adj.* of or containing diatoms or their fossil remains.

diatomic (ˌdaɪəˈtɒmɪk) *adj.* (of a compound or molecule) **a.** containing two atoms. **b.** containing two characteristic groups or atoms.

diatomite (daɪˈætəˌmaɪt) *n.* a soft whitish rock consisting of the siliceous remains of diatoms.

diatonic (ˌdaɪəˈtɒnɪk) *adj.* **1.** of, relating to, or based upon any scale of five tones and two semitones produced by playing the white keys of a keyboard instrument. **2.** not involving the sharpening or flattening of the notes of the major or minor scale nor the use of such notes as modified by accidentals. [C16: < LL, < Gk, < *diatonos* extending, < DIA- + *teinein* to stretch]

diatonic scale *n. Music.* the major and minor scales, made up of both tones and semitones.

diatribe (ˈdaɪəˌtraɪb) *n.* a bitter or violent criticism or attack. [C16: < L *diatriba* learned debate, < Gk *diatribē* discourse, pastime, < *diatribein* to while away, < DIA- + *tribein* to rub]

diazepam (daɪˈeɪzəˌpæm) *n.* a chemical compound used as a tranquillizer and muscle relaxant. [C20: < DI-[1] + *azo-* + *ep*(*oxide*) + *-am*]

diazo (daɪˈeɪzəʊ) *adj.* **1.** of, consisting of, or containing the divalent group, =N:N, or the divalent group, -N:N-. **2.** of the reproduction of documents using the bleaching action of ultraviolet radiation on diazonium salts. ~*n., pl.* **-os** *or* **-oes. 3.** a document produced by this method.

dibasic (daɪˈbeɪsɪk) *adj.* **1.** (of an acid) containing two acidic hydrogen atoms. **2.** (of a salt) derived by replacing two acidic hydrogen atoms. —**dibasicity** (ˌdaɪbeɪˈsɪsɪtɪ) *n.*

dibble (ˈdɪbᵊl) *n.* **1.** Also: **dibber.** a small hand tool used to make holes in the ground for bulbs, seeds, or roots. ~*vb.* **2.** to make a hole in (the ground) with a dibble. **3.** to plant (seeds, etc.) with a dibble. [C15: <?]

dibs (dɪbz) *pl. n.* **1.** another word for **jacks.** **2.** *Sl.* money. **3.** (foll. by *on*) *Inf.* rights (to) or claims (on): used mainly by children. [C18: < *dibstones* game played with knucklebones or pebbles, prob. < *dib* to tap]

dice (daɪs) *pl. n.* **1.** cubes of wood, plastic, etc., each of whose sides has a different number of spots (1 to 6), used in games of chance. **2.** (*functioning as sing.*) Also called: **die.** one of these cubes. **3.** small cubes as of vegetables, meat, etc. **4. no dice.** *Sl., chiefly U.S. & Canad.* an expression of refusal. ~*vb.* **5.** to cut (food, etc.) into small cubes. **6.** (*intr.*) to gamble or play with dice. **7.** (*intr.*) to take a chance or risk (esp. in **dice with death**). **8.** (*tr.*) *Austral. inf.* to abandon or reject. [C14: pl. of DIE[2]] —ˈ**dicer** *n.*

dicey (ˈdaɪsɪ) *adj.* **dicier, diciest.** *Inf., chiefly Brit.* difficult or dangerous; risky; tricky.

dichloride (daɪˈklɔːraɪd) *n.* a compound in which two atoms of chlorine are combined with another atom or group. Also called: **bichloride.**

dichlorodiphenyltrichloroethane (daɪˌklɔːrəʊ-daɪˌfiːnaɪltraɪˌklɔːrəʊˈiːθeɪn) *n.* the full name for **DDT.**

dichotomy (daɪˈkɒtəmɪ) *n., pl.* **-mies. 1.** division into two parts or classifications, esp. when they are sharply distinguished or opposed. **2.** *Bot.* a simple method of branching by repeated division into two equal parts. —**diˈchotomous** *adj.*

dichroism (ˈdaɪkrəʊˌɪzəm) *n.* a property of a uniaxial crystal of showing a difference in colour when viewed along two different axes (in transmitted white light). Also called: **dichromaticism.** See also **pleochromism.** —**diˈchroic** *adj.*

dichromate (daɪˈkrəʊmeɪt) *n.* any salt or ester of dichromic acid. Also called: **bichromate.**

dichromatic (ˌdaɪkrəʊˈmætɪk) *adj.* **1.** Also: **dichroic.** having two colours. **2.** (of animal species) having two different colour varieties. **3.** able to perceive only two colours (and mixes of them). —**dichromatism** (daɪˈkrəʊməˌtɪzəm) *n.*

dichromic (daɪˈkrəʊmɪk) *adj.* of or involving only two colours; dichromatic.

dick (dɪk) *n. Sl.* **1.** *Brit.* a fellow or person. **2. clever dick.** *Brit.* an opinionated person; know-all. **3.** a taboo word for **penis.** [C16 (meaning: fellow): < *Dick,* familiar form of *Richard,* applied to any fellow, lad, etc.; hence, C19: penis]

dickens (ˈdɪkɪnz) *n. Inf.* a euphemistic word for **devil** (used as intensifier in **what the dickens**). [C16: < the name *Dickens*]

Dickensian (dɪˈkɛnzɪən) *adj.* **1.** of Charles Dickens (1812–70), English novelist, or his novels. **2. a.** denoting poverty, distress, and exploitation as depicted in the novels of Dickens. **b.** grotesquely comic, as some of the characters of Dickens.

dicker (ˈdɪkə) *vb.* **1.** to trade (goods) by bargaining; barter. ~*n.* **2.** a petty bargain or barter. [C12: ult. < L *decuria* company of ten, < *decem* ten]

dicky[1] *or* **dickey** (ˈdɪkɪ) *n., pl.* **dickies** *or* **dickeys. 1.** a false blouse or shirt front. **2.** Also called: **dicky bow.** *Brit.* a bow tie. **3.** Also called: **dicky-bird, dickeybird.** a child's word for a bird. **4.** a folding outside seat at the rear of some early cars. [C18 (in the sense: shirt front): from *Dickey,* dim. of *Dick* (name)]

dicky[2] *or* **dickey** (ˈdɪkɪ) *adj.* **dickier, dickiest.** *Brit. inf.* shaky, unsteady, or unreliable: *I feel a bit dicky today.* [C18: ? < *as queer as Dick's hatband* feeling ill]

diclinous (ˈdaɪklɪnəs) *adj.* (of flowering plants) unisexual. Cf. **monoclinous** —ˈ**diclinism** *n.*

dicotyledon (ˌdaɪkɒtɪˈliːdᵊn) *n.* a flowering plant having two embryonic seed leaves. —ˌ**dicoty-ˈledonous** *adj.*

dict. *abbrev. for:* **1.** dictation. **2.** dictator. **3.** dictionary.

dicta (ˈdɪktə) *n.* a plural of **dictum.**

Dictaphone (ˈdɪktəˌfəʊn) *n. Trademark.* a tape recorder designed esp. for recording dictation for subsequent typing.

dictate *vb.* (dɪkˈteɪt). **1.** to say (letters, speeches, etc.) aloud for mechanical recording or verbatim transcription by another person. **2.** (*tr.*) to prescribe (commands, etc.) authoritatively. **3.** (*intr.*) to seek to impose one's will on others. ~*n.* (ˈdɪkteɪt). **4.** an authoritative command. **5.** a guiding principle: *the dictates of reason.* [C17: < L *dictāre* to say repeatedly, order, < *dīcere* to say]

dictation (dɪkˈteɪʃən) *n.* **1.** the act of dictating material to be recorded or taken down in writing. **2.** the material dictated. **3.** authoritative commands or the act of giving them.

dictator (dɪkˈteɪtə) *n.* **1. a.** a ruler who is not effectively restricted by a constitution, laws, etc. **b.** an absolute, esp. tyrannical, ruler. **2.** (in ancient Rome) a person appointed during a crisis to exercise supreme authority. **3.** a person who makes pronouncements, which are regarded as authoritative. **4.** a person who behaves in an authoritarian or tyrannical manner.

dictatorial (ˌdɪktəˈtɔːrɪəl) *adj.* **1.** of or characteristic of a dictator. **2.** tending to dictate; tyrannical; overbearing. —ˌ**dictaˈtorially** *adv.*

dictatorship (dɪkˈteɪtəˌʃɪp) *n.* **1.** the rank, office, or period of rule of a dictator. **2.** government by a dictator. **3.** a country ruled by a dictator. **4.** absolute power or authority.

diction (ˈdɪkʃən) *n.* **1.** the choice of words in writing or speech. **2.** the manner of enunciating words and sounds. [C15: < L *dictiō* a saying, mode of expression, < *dīcere* to speak, say]

dictionary (ˈdɪkʃənərɪ) *n., pl.* **-aries. 1. a.** a book that consists of an alphabetical list of words with their meanings, parts of speech, pronunciations, etymologies, etc. **b.** a similar book giving equivalent words in two or more languages. **2.** a reference book listing words or terms and giving information about a particular subject or activity. **3.** a collection of information or examples with the entries alphabetically arranged: *a dictionary of quotations.* [C16: < Med. L *dictiōnārium* collection of words, < LL *dictiō* word; see DICTION]

dictum (ˈdɪktəm) *n., pl.* **-tums** *or* **-ta. 1.** a formal or authoritative statement; pronouncement. **2.** a popular saying or maxim. **3.** *Law.* See **obiter dictum.** [C16: < L, < *dīcere* to say]

did (dɪd) *vb.* the past tense of **do**[1].

didactic (dɪˈdæktɪk) *adj.* **1.** intended to instruct, esp. excessively. **2.** morally instructive. **3.** (of works of art or literature) containing a political or moral message to which aesthetic considerations are subordinated. [C17: < Gk *didaktikos* skilled in teaching, < *didaskein*] —**diˈdactically** *adv.* —**diˈdacticism** *n.*

didactics (dɪˈdæktɪks) *n.* (*functioning as sing.*) the art or science of teaching.

diddle (ˈdɪdᵊl) *vb.* (*tr.*) *Inf.* to cheat or swindle. [C19: back formation < Jeremy *Diddler,* a scrounger in J. Kenney's farce *Raising the Wind* (1803)] —ˈ**diddler** *n.*

didgeridoo (ˌdɪdʒərɪˈduː) *n. Music.* a native deep-toned Australian wind instrument. [C20: imit.]

didn't (ˈdɪdᵊnt) *contraction of* did not.

dido (ˈdaɪdəʊ) *n., pl.* **-dos** *or* **-does.** (*usually pl.*) *Inf.* an antic; prank; trick. [C19: <?]

didst (dɪdst) *vb. Arch.* (used with *thou*) a form of the past tense of **do**[1].

didymium (daɪˈdɪmɪəm) *n.* a mixture of the metallic rare earths neodymium and praseodymium, once thought to be an element. [C19: < NL, < Gk *didumos* twin + -IUM]

die[1] (daɪ) *vb.* **dying, died.** (*mainly intr.*) **1.** (of an organism, organs, etc.) to cease all biological activity permanently. **2.** (of something inanimate) to cease to exist. **3.** (often foll. by *away, down,* or *out*) to lose strength, power, or energy, esp. by degrees. **4.** (often foll. by *away* or *down*) to become calm; subside. **5.** to stop functioning: *the engine died.* **6.** to languish, as with love, longing, etc. **7.** (usually foll. by *of*) *Inf.* to be nearly overcome (with laughter, boredom, etc.). **8.** *Christianity.* to lack spiritual life within the soul. **9.** (*tr.*) to suffer (a death of a specified kind): *he died a saintly death.* **10. be dying.** (foll. by *for* or an infinitive) to be eager or desperate (for something or to do something). **11. die hard.** to cease to exist after a struggle: *old habits die hard.* **12. die in harness.** to die while still working or active. **13. never say die.** *Inf.* never give up. ~See also **die down, die out.** [OE *dīegan,* prob. of Scand. origin]

die[2] (daɪ) *n.* **1. a.** a shaped block used to cut or form metal in a drop forge, press, etc. **b.** a tool with a conical hole through which wires, etc. are drawn to reduce their diameter. **2.** an internally-threaded tool for cutting external threads. **3.** a casting mould. **4.** *Archit.* the dado of a pedestal, usually cubic. **5.** another name for **dice** (sense 2). **6. the die is cast.** the irrevocable decision has been taken. [C13 *dee,* < OF *de,* ? < Vulgar L *datum* (unattested) a piece in games, < L *dare* to give, play]

die-cast *vb.* **-casting, -cast.** (*tr.*) to shape or form (an object) by introducing molten metal or plastic into a reusable mould, esp. under pressure. —**ˈdie-ˌcasting** *n.*

die down *vb.* (*intr., adv.*) **1.** (of plants) to wither above ground, leaving only the root alive during the winter. **2.** to lose strength or power, esp. by degrees. **3.** to become calm.

die-hard *n.* **1.** a person who resists change or who holds onto an untenable position. **2.** (*modifier*) obstinately resistant to change.

dieldrin (ˈdiːldrɪn) *n.* a crystalline substance, consisting of a chlorinated derivative of naphthalene: a contact insecticide. [C20: < *Diel(s-Al)d(e)r* (*reaction*) + -IN; Diels & Alder were G chemists]

dielectric (ˌdaɪɪˈlɛktrɪk) *n.* **1.** a substance that can sustain an electric field. **2.** a substance of very low electrical conductivity; insulator. ~*adj.* **3.** concerned with or having the properties of a dielectric. —ˌ**dieˈlectrically** *adv.*

-diene *n. combining form.* denoting an organic compound containing two double bonds between carbon atoms: *butadiene.* [< DI-[1] + -ENE]

die out *or* **off** *vb.* (*intr., adv.*) **1.** to die one after another until few or none are left. **2.** to become extinct, esp. after a period of gradual decline.

dieresis (daɪˈɛrɪsɪs) *n., pl.* **-ses** (-ˌsiːz). a variant spelling (esp. U.S.) of **diaeresis.**

diesel (ˈdiːzᵊl) *n.* **1.** See **diesel engine. 2.** a ship, locomotive, lorry, etc., driven by a diesel engine. **3.** *Inf.* short for **diesel oil** (*or* **fuel**). [after R. *Diesel* (1858–1913), G engineer]

diesel-electric *n.* **1.** a locomotive fitted with a diesel engine driving an electric generator that feeds electric traction motors. ~*adj.* **2.** of or relating to such a locomotive or system.

diesel engine *or* **motor** *n.* a type of internal-combustion engine in which atomized fuel oil is ignited by compression alone.

diesel oil *or* **fuel** *n.* a fuel obtained from petroleum distillation that is used in diesel engines. Also called (Brit.): **derv.**

Dies Irae *Latin.* (ˈdiːeɪz ˈɪəraɪ) *n.* **1.** a Latin hymn of the 13th century, describing the Last Judgment. It is used in the Mass for the dead. **2.** a musical setting of this. [lit.: day of wrath]

diesis (ˈdaɪɪsɪs) *n., pl.* **-ses** (-ˌsiːz). *Printing.* another name for **double dagger.** [C16: via L < Gk: a quarter tone, lit.: a sending through, < *diienai;* the double dagger was orig. used in musical notation]

diestock (ˈdaɪˌstɒk) *n.* the device holding the dies used to cut an external screw thread.

diet[1] (ˈdaɪət) *n.* **1.** a specific allowance or selection of food, esp. prescribed to control weight or for health reasons: *a salt-free diet.* **2.** the food and drink that a person or animal regularly consumes. **3.** regular activities or occupations. ~*vb.* **4.** (*usually intr.*) to follow or cause to follow a dietary regimen. [C13: < OF *diete,* < L *diaeta,* < Gk *diaita* mode of living, < *diaitan* to direct one's own life] —**ˈdieter** *n.*

diet[2] (ˈdaɪət) *n.* **1.** (*sometimes cap.*) a legislative assembly in various countries. **2.** (*sometimes cap.*) the assembly of the estates of the Holy Roman Empire. **3.** *Scots Law.* a single session of a court. [C15: < Med. L *diēta* public meeting, prob. < L *diaeta* DIET[1] but associated with L *diēs* day]

dietary (ˈdaɪətərɪ, -trɪ) *adj.* **1.** of or relating to a diet. ~*n., pl.* **-taries. 2.** a regulated diet. **3.** a system of dieting.

dietary fibre *n.* fibrous substances in fruits and vegetables, such as the structural polymers of cell walls, which aid digestion. Also called: **roughage.**

dietetic (ˌdaɪɪˈtɛtɪk) *or* **dietetical** *adj.* **1.** denoting or relating to diet. **2.** prepared for special dietary requirements. —ˌ**dieˈtetically** *adv.*

dietetics (ˌdaɪɪˈtɛtɪks) *n.* (*functioning as sing.*) the scientific study and regulation of food intake and preparation.

diethylene glycol *n.* a colourless soluble liquid used as an antifreeze and solvent.

dietitian *or* **dietician** (ˌdaɪɪˈtɪʃən) *n.* a person who specializes in dietetics.

differ (ˈdɪfə) *vb.* (*intr.*) **1.** (often foll. by *from*) to be dissimilar in quality, nature, or degree (to); vary (from). **2.** (often foll. by *from* or *with*) to disagree (with). **3.** *Dialect.* to quarrel or dispute. [C14: < L *differre,* to scatter, put off, be different, < *dis-* apart + *ferre* to bear]

difference (ˈdɪfərəns) *n.* **1.** the state or quality of being unlike. **2.** a specific instance of being unlike. **3.** a distinguishing mark or feature. **4.** a significant change. **5.** a disagreement or argument. **6.** a degree of distinctness, as between two people or things. **7.** the result of the subtraction of one number, quantity, etc., from another. **8.** *Maths.* (of two sets) the set of members of the first that are not members of the second. **9.** *Heraldry.* an addition to the arms of a family to represent a younger branch. **10. make a difference. a.** to have an effect. **b.** to treat differently. **11. split the difference. a.** to compromise. **b.** to divide a remainder equally. **12. with a difference.** with some distinguishing quality, good or bad.

different (ˈdɪfərənt) *adj.* **1.** partly or completely unlike. **2.** not identical or the same; other. **3.** unusual. —**ˈdifferently** *adv.* —**ˈdifferentness** *n.*

▷ **Usage.** The constructions *different from, different to,* and *different than* are all found in the works of writers of English during the past. Nowadays, however, the most widely acceptable preposition to use after *different* is *from.*

differentia (ˌdɪfəˈrɛnʃɪə) *n., pl.* **-tiae** (-ʃɪˌiː). *Logic.* a feature by which two subclasses of the same class of named objects can be distinguished. [C19: < L: diversity]

differential (ˌdɪfəˈrɛnʃəl) *adj.* **1.** of, relating to, or using a difference. **2.** constituting a difference; distinguishing. **3.** *Maths.* involving one or more derivatives or differentials. **4.** *Physics, engineering.* relating to, operating on, or based on the difference between two opposing effects, motions, forces, etc. ~*n.* **5.** a factor that differentiates between two comparable things. **6.** *Maths.* **a.** an increment in a given function, expressed as the product of the derivative of that function and the corresponding increment in the independent variable. **b.** an increment in a given function of two or more variables, $f(x_1, x_2, \ldots x_n)$, expressed as the sum of the products of each partial derivative and the increment in the corresponding variable. **7.** See **differential gear. 8.** *Chiefly Brit.* the difference between rates of pay for different types of labour, esp. when forming a pay structure within an industry. **9.** (in commerce) a difference in rates, esp. between comparable services. —ˌ**differˈentially** *adv.*

differential calculus *n.* the branch of calculus concerned with the study, evaluation, and use of derivatives and differentials.

differential equation *n.* an equation containing differentials or derivatives of a function of one independent variable.

differential gear *n.* the epicyclic gear mounted in the driving axle of a road vehicle that permits one driving wheel to rotate faster than the other, as when cornering.

differential operator *n.* a mathematical operator, ∇, used in vector analysis.

differentiate (ˌdɪfəˈrɛnʃɪˌeɪt) *vb.* **1.** (*tr.*) to serve to distinguish between. **2.** (when *intr.*, often foll. by *between*) to perceive, show, or make a difference (in or between); discriminate. **3.** (*intr.*) to become dissimilar or distinct. **4.** *Maths.* to perform a differentiation on (a quantity, expression, etc.). **5.** (*intr.*) (of unspecialized cells, etc.) to change during development to more specialized forms. —ˌ**differˈentiˌator** *n.*

differentiation (ˌdɪfəˌrɛnʃɪˈeɪʃən) *n.* **1.** the act, process, or result of differentiating. **2.** *Maths.* an operation used in calculus in which the derivative of a function or variable is determined.

difficult (ˈdɪfɪkᵊlt) *adj.* **1.** not easy to do; requiring effort. **2.** not easy to understand or solve. **3.** troublesome: *a difficult child.* **4.** not easily convinced, pleased, or satisfied. **5.** full of hardships or trials. [C14: back formation < DIFFICULTY] —ˈ**difficultly** *adv.*

difficulty (ˈdɪfɪkᵊltɪ) *n., pl.* **-ties.** **1.** the state or quality of being difficult. **2.** a task, problem, etc., that is hard to deal with. **3.** (*often pl.*) a troublesome or embarrassing situation, esp. a financial one. **4.** a disagreement. **5.** (*often pl.*) an objection or obstacle. **6.** a trouble or source of trouble; worry. **7.** lack of ease; awkwardness. [C14: < L *difficultās*, < *difficilis*, < *dis-* not + *facilis* easy]

diffident (ˈdɪfɪdənt) *adj.* lacking self-confidence; shy. [C15: < L *diffīdere*, < *dis-* not + *fīdere* to trust] —ˈ**diffidence** *n.* —ˈ**diffidently** *adv.*

diffract (dɪˈfrækt) *vb.* to undergo or cause to undergo diffraction. —**difˈfractive** *adj.* —**difˈfractively** *adv.* —**difˈfractiveness** *n.*

diffraction (dɪˈfrækʃən) *n.* **1.** *Physics.* a deviation in the direction of a wave at the edge of an obstacle in its path. **2.** any phenomenon caused by diffraction, such as the formation of light and dark fringes by the passage of light through a small aperture. [C17: < NL *diffractiō* a breaking to pieces, < L *diffringere* to shatter, < *dis-* apart + *frangere* to break]

diffraction grating *n.* a glass plate or a mirror marked with lines or grooves. It causes diffraction of light, ultraviolet radiation, or x-rays.

diffuse *vb.* (dɪˈfjuːz). **1.** to spread in all directions. **2.** to undergo or cause to undergo diffusion. **3.** to scatter; disperse. ~*adj.* (dɪˈfjuːs). **4.** spread out over a wide area. **5.** lacking conciseness. **6.** characterized by diffusion. [C15: < L *diffūsus* spread abroad, < *diffundere* to pour forth, < *dis-* away + *fundere* to pour] —**diffusely** (dɪˈfjuːslɪ) *adv.* —**difˈfuseness** *n.* —**diffusible** (dɪˈfjuːzɪbᵊl) *adj.*

diffuser *or* **diffusor** (dɪˈfjuːzə) *n.* **1.** a person or thing that diffuses. **2.** a part of a lighting fixture, as a translucent covering, used to scatter the light and prevent glare. **3.** a cone, wedge, or baffle placed in front of the diaphragm of a loudspeaker to diffuse the sound waves. **4.** a duct, esp. in a wind tunnel or jet engine, that reduces the speed and increases the pressure of the air or fluid. **5.** *Photog.* a light-scattering medium, such as a screen of fine fabric, used to reduce the sharpness of shadows and thus soften the lighting.

diffusion (dɪˈfjuːʒən) *n.* **1.** a diffusing or being diffused; dispersion. **2.** verbosity. **3.** *Physics.* **a.** the random thermal motion of atoms, molecules, etc., in gases, liquids, and some solids. **b.** the transfer of atoms or molecules by their random motion from one part of a medium to another. **4.** *Physics.* the transmission or reflection of electromagnetic radiation, esp. light, in which the radiation is scattered in many directions. **5.** *Anthropol.* the transmission of social institutions, skills, and myths from one culture to another.

diffusive (dɪˈfjuːsɪv) *adj.* characterized by diffusion. —**difˈfusively** *adv.* —**difˈfusiveness** *n.*

dig (dɪg) *vb.* **digging, dug.** **1.** (when *tr.*, often foll. by *up*) to cut into, break up, and turn over or remove (earth, etc.), esp. with a spade. **2.** to excavate (a hole, tunnel, etc.) by digging, usually with an implement or (of animals) with claws, etc. **3.** (often foll. by *through*) to make or force (one's way): *he dug his way through the crowd.* **4.** (*tr.*; often foll. by *out* or *up*) to obtain by digging. **5.** (*tr.*; often foll. by *out* or *up*) to find by effort or searching: *to dig out facts.* **6.** (*tr.*; foll. by *in* or *into*) to thrust or jab. **7.** (*tr.*; foll. by *in* or *into*) to mix (compost, etc.) with soil by digging. **8.** (*intr.*; foll. by *in* or *into*) *Inf.* to begin vigorously to do something. **9.** (*tr.*) *Inf.* to like, understand, or appreciate. **10.** (*intr.*) *U.S. sl.* to work hard, esp. for an examination. ~*n.* **11.** the act of digging. **12.** a thrust or poke. **13.** a cutting remark. **14.** *Inf.* an archaeological excavation. **15.** *Austral. & N.Z. inf.* short for **digger** (sense 4). ~See also **dig in.** [C13 *diggen*, <?]

digest *vb.* (dɪˈdʒɛst, daɪ-). **1.** to subject (food) to a process of digestion. **2.** (*tr.*) to assimilate mentally. **3.** *Chem.* to soften or disintegrate by the action of heat, moisture, or chemicals. **4.** (*tr.*) to arrange in a methodical order; classify. **5.** (*tr.*) to reduce to a summary. ~*n.* (ˈdaɪdʒɛst). **6.** a comprehensive and systematic compilation of information or material, often condensed. **7.** a magazine, periodical, etc., that summarizes news. **8.** a compilation of rules of law. [C14: < LL *dīgesta* writings grouped under various heads, < L *dīgerere* to divide, < *di-* apart + *gerere* to bear]

Digest (ˈdaɪdʒɛst) *n. Roman law.* the books of law compiled by order of Justinian in the sixth century A.D.

digestible (dɪˈdʒɛstɪbᵊl, daɪ-) *adj.* capable of being digested. —**diˌgestiˈbility** *n.*

digestion (dɪˈdʒɛstʃən, daɪ-) *n.* **1.** the act or process in living organisms of breaking down food into easily absorbed substances by the action of enzymes, etc. **2.** mental assimilation, esp. of ideas. **3.** the decomposition of sewage by bacteria. **4.** *Chem.* the treatment of material with heat, solvents, etc., to cause decomposition. [C14: < OF, < L *digestiō* a dissolving, digestion] —**diˈgestional** *adj.*

digestive (dɪˈdʒɛstɪv, daɪ-) *or* **digestant** (daɪˈdʒɛstənt) *adj.* **1.** relating to, aiding, or subjecting to digestion. ~*n.* **2.** any substance that aids digestion. —**diˈgestively** *adv.*

digestive biscuit *n.* a round semisweet biscuit made from wholemeal flour.

digger (ˈdɪgə) *n.* **1.** a person, animal, or machine that digs. **2.** a miner. **3.** a tool or machine used for excavation. **4.** (*sometimes cap.*) *Austral. & N.Z. inf.* an Australian or New Zealander, esp. a soldier: often used as a friendly term of address.

digger wasp *n.* a wasp that digs nest holes in the ground, rotten wood, etc. and stocks them with live insects for the larvae.

diggings (ˈdɪgɪŋz) *pl. n.* **1.** (*functioning as pl.*) material that has been dug out. **2.** (*functioning as sing. or pl.*) a place where mining has taken place. **3.** (*functioning as pl.*) *Brit. inf.* a less common name for **digs.**

dight (daɪt) *vb.* **dighting, dight** *or* **dighted.** (*tr.*) *Arch.* to adorn or equip, as for battle. [OE *dihtan* to compose, < L *dictāre* to DICTATE]

dig in *vb.* (*adv.*) **1.** *Mil.* to dig foxholes, trenches, etc. **2.** *Inf.* to entrench (oneself). **3.** (*intr.*) *Inf.* to defend a position firmly, as in an argument. **4.** (*intr.*) *Inf.* to begin to eat vigorously: *don't wait, just dig in.* **5. dig one's heels in.** *Inf.* to refuse to move or be persuaded.

digit (ˈdɪdʒɪt) *n.* **1.** a finger or toe. **2.** any of the ten Arabic numerals from 0 to 9. [C15: < L *digitus* toe, finger]

digital (ˈdɪdʒɪtᵊl) *adj.* **1.** of, resembling, or possessing a digit or digits. **2.** performed with the fingers. **3.** representing data as a series of numerical values. **4.** displaying information as numbers rather than by a pointer moving over a dial. ~*n.* **5.** *Music.* a key on a piano, harpsichord, etc. —ˈ**digitally** *adv.*

digital audio tape *n.* magnetic tape on which

sound is recorded digitally, giving high-fidelity reproduction. Abbrev.: **DAT.**

digital clock *or* **watch** *n.* a clock or watch in which the time is indicated by digits rather than by hands on a dial.

digital computer *n.* an electronic computer in which the input is discrete, consisting of numbers, letters, etc. that are represented internally in binary notation.

digitalin (ˌdɪdʒɪˈteɪlɪn) *n.* a poisonous glycoside extracted from digitalis and used in treating heart disease. [C19: < DIGITAL(IS) + -IN]

digitalis (ˌdɪdʒɪˈteɪlɪs) *n.* **1.** any of a genus of Eurasian plants such as the foxglove, having long spikes of bell-shaped flowers. **2.** a drug prepared from the dried leaves of the foxglove: used medicinally as a heart stimulant. [C17: < NL, < L: relating to a finger; based on G *Fingerhut* foxglove, lit.: finger-hat]

digitalize *or* **-ise** (ˈdɪdʒɪtəˌlaɪz) *vb.* (*tr.*) another word for **digitize.**

digital recording *n.* a sound recording process that converts audio or analogue signals into a series of pulses that correspond to the voltage level.

digitate (ˈdɪdʒɪˌteɪt) *or* **digitated** *adj.* **1.** (of leaves) having the leaflets in the form of a spread hand. **2.** (of animals) having digits. —ˈ**digiˌtately** *adv.* —ˌ**digiˈtation** *n.*

digitigrade (ˈdɪdʒɪtɪˌgreɪd) *adj.* **1.** (of dogs, cats, horses, etc.) walking so that only the toes touch the ground. ~*n.* **2.** a digitigrade animal.

digitize *or* **-ise** (ˈdɪdʒɪˌtaɪz) *vb.* (*tr.*) to transcribe (data) into a digital form for processing by a computer. —ˌ**digitiˈzation** *or* **-iˈsation** *n.* —ˈ**digiˌtizer** *or* **-iser** *n.*

dignified (ˈdɪgnɪˌfaɪd) *adj.* characterized by dignity of manner or appearance; stately; noble. —ˈ**digniˌfiedly** *adv.* —ˈ**digniˌfiedness** *n.*

dignify (ˈdɪgnɪˌfaɪ) *vb.* **-fying, -fied.** (*tr.*) **1.** to invest with honour or dignity. **2.** to add distinction to. **3.** to add a semblance of dignity to, esp. by the use of a pretentious name or title. [C15: < OF *dignifier,* < LL *dignificāre,* < L *dignus* worthy + *facere* to make]

dignitary (ˈdɪgnɪtərɪ) *n., pl.* **-taries.** a person of high official position or rank.

dignity (ˈdɪgnɪtɪ) *n., pl.* **-ties. 1.** a formal, stately, or grave bearing. **2.** the state or quality of being worthy of honour. **3.** relative importance; rank. **4.** sense of self-importance (often in **stand** (*or* **be**) **on one's dignity, beneath one's dignity**). **5.** high rank, esp. in government or the church. [C13: < OF *dignite,* < L *dignitās* merit, < *dignus* worthy]

digraph (ˈdaɪgrɑːf) *n.* a combination of two letters used to represent a single sound such as *gh* in *tough.* —**digraphic** (daɪˈgræfɪk) *adj.*

digress (daɪˈgrɛs) *vb.* (*intr.*) **1.** to depart from the main subject in speech or writing. **2.** to wander from one's path. [C16: < L *dīgressus* turned aside, < *dīgredī,* < *dis-* apart + *gradī* to go] —**diˈgresser** *n.* —**diˈgression** *n.*

digressive (daɪˈgrɛsɪv) *adj.* characterized by digression or tending to digress. —**diˈgressively** *adv.* —**diˈgressiveness** *n.*

digs (dɪgz) *pl. n. Brit. inf.* lodgings. [C19: < DIGGINGS, ? referring to where one *digs* or works, but see also DIG IN]

dihedral (daɪˈhiːdrəl) *adj.* **1.** having or formed by two intersecting planes. ~*n.* **2.** Also called: **dihedron, dihedral angle.** the figure formed by two intersecting planes. **3.** the upward inclination of an aircraft wing in relation to the lateral axis.

dik-dik (ˈdɪkˌdɪk) *n.* any of several small antelopes inhabiting semiarid regions of Africa. [C19: E African, prob. imit.]

dike (daɪk) *n.* **1.** *Inf., chiefly Austral.* a lavatory. ~*n.,vb.* **2.** a variant spelling of **dyke.**

diktat (ˈdɪktɑːt) *n.* **1.** a decree or settlement imposed, esp. by a ruler or a victorious nation. **2.** a dogmatic statement. [< G: dictation, < L *dictātum,* < *dictāre* to DICTATE]

dilapidate (dɪˈlæpɪˌdeɪt) *vb.* to fall or cause to fall into ruin. [C16: < L *dīlapidāre* to waste, < *dis-* apart + *lapidāre* to stone, < *lapis* stone] —**diˌlapiˈdation** *n.*

dilapidated (dɪˈlæpɪˌdeɪtɪd) *adj.* falling to pieces or in a state of disrepair; shabby.

dilate (daɪˈleɪt, dɪ-) *vb.* **1.** to make or become wider or larger. **2.** (*intr.;* often foll. by *on* or *upon*) to speak or write at length. [C14: < L *dīlātāre* to spread out, < *dis-* apart + *lātus* wide] —**diˈlatable** *adj.* —**diˌlataˈbility** *n.* —**diˈlation** *or* **dilatation** (ˌdaɪləˈteɪʃən) *n.* —**dilative** (daɪˈleɪtɪv) *adj.*

dilatory (ˈdɪlətərɪ, -trɪ) *adj.* **1.** tending to delay or waste time. **2.** intended to waste time or defer action. [C15: < LL *dīlātōrius* inclined to delay, < *differre* to postpone; see DIFFER] —ˈ**dilatorily** *adv.* —ˈ**dilatoriness** *n.*

dildo *or* **dildoe** (ˈdɪldəʊ) *n., pl.* **-dos** *or* **-does.** an object used as a substitute for an erect penis. [C17: <?]

dilemma (dɪˈlɛmə, daɪ-) *n.* **1.** a situation necessitating a choice between two equally undesirable alternatives. **2.** a problem that seems incapable of a solution. **3.** *Logic.* a type of argument which forces the maintainer of a proposition to accept one of two conclusions each of which contradicts the original assertion. **4. on the horns of a dilemma. a.** faced with the choice between two equally unpalatable alternatives. **b.** in an awkward situation. [C16: via L < Gk, < DI-[1] + *lēmma* proposition, < *lambanein* to grasp] —**dilemmatic** (ˌdɪlɪˈmætɪk) *adj.*

dilettante (ˌdɪlɪˈtɑːntɪ) *n., pl.* **-tantes** *or* **-tanti** (-ˈtɑːntɪ). **1.** a person whose interest in a subject is superficial rather than professional. **2.** a person who loves the arts. ~*adj.* **3.** of or characteristic of a dilettante. [C18: < It., < *dilettare* to delight, < L *dēlectāre*] —ˌ**diletˈtantish** *or* ˌ**diletˈtanteish** *adj.* —ˌ**diletˈtantism** *or* ˌ**diletˈtanteism** *n.*

diligence[1] (ˈdɪlɪdʒəns) *n.* **1.** steady and careful application. **2.** proper attention or care. [C14: < L *dīligentia* care]

diligence[2] (ˈdɪlɪdʒəns) *n. History.* a stagecoach. [C18: < F, shortened < *carosse de diligence,* lit.: coach of speed]

diligent (ˈdɪlɪdʒənt) *adj.* **1.** careful and persevering in carrying out tasks or duties. **2.** carried out with care and perseverance: *diligent work.* [C14: < OF, < L *dīligere* to value, < *dis-* apart + *legere* to read] —ˈ**diligently** *adv.*

dill[1] (dɪl) *n.* **1.** an aromatic Eurasian plant with umbrella-shaped clusters of yellow flowers. **2.** the leaves or fruits of this plant, used for flavouring and in medicine. [OE *dile*]

dill[2] (dɪl) *n. Austral. & N.Z. sl.* a fool. [C20: < DILLY[2]]

dill pickle *n.* a pickled cucumber flavoured with dill.

dilly[1] (ˈdɪlɪ) *n., pl.* **-lies.** *Sl., chiefly U.S. & Canad.* a person or thing that is remarkable. [C20: ? < girl's name *Dilly*]

dilly[2] (ˈdɪlɪ) *adj.* **-lier, -liest.** *Austral. sl.* silly. [C20: < E dialect, ? < SILLY]

dilly bag *n. Austral.* a small bag, esp., formerly, one made of plaited grass, etc., often used for carrying food. [< Abor. *dilly* small bag or basket]

dilly-dally (ˌdɪlɪˈdælɪ) *vb.* **-lying, -lied.** (*intr.*) *Inf.* to loiter or vacillate. [C17: by reduplication < DALLY]

dilute (daɪˈluːt) *vb.* **1.** to make or become less concentrated, esp. by adding water or a thinner. **2.** to make or become weaker in force, effect, etc. ~*adj.* **3.** *Chem.* **a.** (of a solution, etc.) having a low concentration. **b.** (of a substance) present in solution, esp. a weak solution in water: *dilute acetic acid.* [C16: < L *dīluere,* < *dis-* apart + *-luere,* < *lavāre* to wash] —**diˈluter** *n.*

dilution (daɪˈluːʃən) *n.* **1.** the act of diluting or state of being diluted. **2.** a diluted solution.

diluvial (daɪˈluːvɪəl, dɪ-) *or* **diluvian** *adj.* of or connected with a deluge, esp. with the great Flood described in Genesis. [C17: < LL *dīluviālis,* < L *dīluere* to wash away; see DILUTE]

dim (dɪm) *adj.* **dimmer, dimmest. 1.** badly illuminated. **2.** not clearly seen; faint. **3.** having weak or indistinct vision. **4.** mentally dull. **5.** not clear in the mind; obscure: *a dim memory.* **6.** lacking in brightness or lustre. **7.** unfavourable, gloomy or disapproving (esp. in **take a dim view**). ~*vb.* **dimming, dimmed. 8.** to become or cause to become dim. **9.** (*tr.*) to cause to seem less bright. **10.** the U.S. and Canad. word for **dip** (sense 5). [OE *dimm*] —ˈ**dimly** *adv.* —ˈ**dimness** *n.*

dim. *abbrev. for:* **1.** dimension. **2.** Also: **dimin.** *Music.* diminuendo. **3.** Also: **dimin.** diminutive.

dime (daɪm) *n.* **1.** a coin of the U.S. and Canada, worth one tenth of a dollar or ten cents. **2. a dime a dozen.** very cheap or common. [C14: < OF *disme,* < L *decimus* tenth, < *decem* ten]

dimenhydrinate (ˌdaɪmɛnˈhaɪdrɪˌneɪt) *n.* a crystalline substance, used as an antihistamine and for the prevention of nausea, esp. in travel sickness. [< DI-[1] + ME(THYL) + (AMI)N(E) + (*diphen*)*hydr*(*a-m*)*in*(*e*) + -ATE[1]]

dime novel *n. U.S.* (formerly) a cheap melodramatic novel, usually in paperback.

dimension (dɪˈmɛnʃən) *n.* **1.** (*often pl.*) a measurement of the size of something in a particular direction, such as the length, width, height, or diameter. **2.** (*often pl.*) scope; size; extent. **3.** aspect: *a new dimension to politics.* **4.** *Maths.* the number of coordinates required to locate a point in space. ~*vb.* **5.** (*tr.*) *Chiefly U.S.* to cut to or mark with specified dimensions. [C14: < OF, < L *dīmensiō* an extent, < *dīmētīrī* to measure out, < *mētīrī*] —**diˈmensional** *adj.* —**diˈmensionless** *adj.*

dimer (ˈdaɪmə) *n. Chem.* a compound the molecule of which is formed by the linking of two identical molecules. [C20: < DI-[1] + -MER] —**dimeric** (daɪˈmɛrɪk) *adj.*

dimerize *or* **-ise** (ˈdaɪməˌraɪz) *vb.* to react or cause to react to form a dimer. —**dimeriˈzation** *or* **-iˈsation** *n.*

dimeter (ˈdɪmɪtə) *n. Prosody.* a line of verse consisting of two metrical feet or a verse written in this metre.

dimethylsulphoxide (daɪˌmiːθaɪlsʌlˈfɒksaɪd) *n.* a liquid used as a solvent and in medicine to improve the penetration of drugs applied to the skin. Abbrev.: **DMSO.**

diminish (dɪˈmɪnɪʃ) *vb.* **1.** to make or become smaller, fewer, or less. **2.** (*tr.*) *Archit.* to cause to taper. **3.** (*tr.*) *Music.* to decrease (a minor or perfect interval) by a semitone. **4.** to reduce in authority, status, etc. [C15: blend of *diminuen* to lessen (< L *dēminuere,* < *minuere*) + archaic *minish* to lessen] —**diˈminishable** *adj.*

diminished (dɪˈmɪnɪʃt) *adj.* **1.** reduced or lessened; made smaller. **2.** *Music.* denoting any minor or perfect interval reduced by a semitone.

diminished responsibility *n. Law.* a plea under which mental derangement is submitted as demonstrating lack of criminal responsibility.

diminishing returns *pl. n. Econ.* progressively smaller increases in output resulting from equal increases in production.

diminuendo (dɪˌmɪnjʊˈɛndəʊ) *Music.* ~*n., pl.* **-dos. 1. a.** a gradual decrease in loudness. Symbol: >. **b.** a musical passage affected by a diminuendo. ~*adj.* **2.** gradually decreasing in loudness. **3.** with a diminuendo. [C18: < It., < *diminuire* to DIMINISH]

diminution (ˌdɪmɪˈnjuːʃən) *n.* **1.** reduction; decrease. **2.** *Music.* the presentation of the subject of a fugue, etc., in which the note values are reduced in length. [C14: < L *dēminūtiō*; see DIMINISH]

diminutive (dɪˈmɪnjʊtɪv) *adj.* **1.** very small; tiny. **2.** *Grammar.* **a.** denoting an affix added to a word to convey the meaning *small* or *unimportant* or to express affection. **b.** denoting a word formed by the addition of a diminutive affix. ~*n.* **3.** *Grammar.* a diminutive word or affix. **4.** a tiny person or thing. —**diˈminutively** *adv.* —**diˈminutiveness** *n.*

dimissory (dɪˈmɪsərɪ) *adj.* **1.** granting permission to be ordained: *a bishop's dimissory letter.* **2.** granting permission to depart.

dimity (ˈdɪmɪtɪ) *n., pl.* **-ties.** a light strong cotton fabric with woven stripes or squares. [C15: < Med. L *dimitum,* < Gk *dimiton,* < DI-[1] + *mitos* thread of the warp]

dimmer (ˈdɪmə) *n.* **1.** a device for dimming an electric light. **2.** (*often pl.*) *U.S.* **a.** a dipped headlight on a road vehicle. **b.** a parking light on a car.

dimorphism (daɪˈmɔːfɪzəm) *n.* **1.** the occurrence within a plant of two distinct forms of any part. **2.** the occurrence in an animal species of two distinct types of individual. **3.** a property of certain substances that enables them to exist in two distinct crystalline forms. —**diˈmorphic** *or* **diˈmorphous** *adj.*

dimple (ˈdɪmpᵊl) *n.* **1.** a small natural dent, esp. on the cheeks or chin. **2.** any slight depression in a surface. ~*vb.* **3.** to make or become dimpled. **4.** (*intr.*) to produce dimples by smiling. [C13 *dympull*] —ˈ**dimply** *adj.*

dim sum (dɪm sʌm) *n.* a Chinese appetizer of steamed dumplings containing various fillings. [Cantonese]

dimwit (ˈdɪmˌwɪt) *n. Inf.* a stupid or silly person. —ˌ**dim-ˈwitted** *adj.* —ˌ**dim-ˈwittedness** *n.*

din (dɪn) *n.* **1.** a loud discordant confused noise. ~*vb.* **dinning, dinned. 2.** (*tr.*; usually foll. by *into*) to instil by constant repetition. **3.** (*tr.*) to subject to a din. **4.** (*intr.*) to make a din. [OE *dynn*]

DIN *n.* **1.** a logarithmic expression of the speed of a photographic film, plate, etc.; high-speed films have high numbers. **2.** a system of standard plugs, sockets, etc. used for interconnecting domestic audio and video equipment. [C20: < G *D*(*eutsche*) *I*(*ndustrie*) *N*(*orm*) German Industry Standard]

dinar (ˈdiːnɑː) *n.* **1.** the standard monetary unit of Algeria, Iraq, Jordan, Kuwait, Libya, South Yemen, Tunisia, and Yugoslavia. **2.** an Iranian monetary unit. [C17: < Ar., < LGk *dēnarion,* < L *dēnārius* DENARIUS]

Dincs *or* **DINKS** (dɪŋks) *pl. n. acronym for* double income no children (*or* kids): used of couples.

dine (daɪn) *vb.* **1.** (*intr.*) to eat dinner. **2.** (*intr.*; often foll. by *on, off,* or *upon*) to make one's meal (of): *the guests dined upon roast beef.* **3.** (*tr.*) *Inf.* to entertain to dinner (esp. in **wine and dine someone**). [C13: < OF *disner,* < Vulgar L *disjējūnāre* (unattested), < *dis-* not + LL *jējūnāre* to fast]

dine out *vb.* (*intr., adv.*) **1.** to dine away from home. **2.** (foll. by *on*) to have dinner at the expense of someone else mainly for the sake of one's conversation about (a subject or story).

diner (ˈdaɪnə) *n.* **1.** a person eating a meal, esp. in a restaurant. **2.** *Chiefly U.S. & Canad.* a small cheap restaurant. **3.** short for **dining car.**

dinette (daɪˈnɛt) *n.* an alcove or small area for use as a dining room.

ding (dɪŋ) *vb.* **1.** to ring, esp. with tedious repetition. **2.** (*tr.*) another word for **din** (sense 2). ~*n.* **3.** an imitation of the sound of a bell. [C13: prob. imit., but infl. by DIN + RING[2]]

dingbat (ˈdɪŋˌbæt) *n. Austral. sl.* a crazy or stupid person.

dingbats (ˈdɪŋˌbæts) *pl. n. Austral. & N.Z. sl.* an attack of nervousness, irritation, or loathing: *he gives me the dingbats.*

ding-dong *n.* **1.** the sound of a bell or bells. **2.** an imitation of the sound of a bell. **3. a.** a violent exchange of blows or words. **b.** (*as modifier*): *a ding-dong battle.* ~*adj.* **4.** sounding or ringing repeatedly. [C16: imit.; see DING]

dinges (ˈdɪŋəs) *n. S. African inf.* a jocular word for something whose name is unknown or forgotten; thingumabob. [< Afrik., < Du. *dinges* thing]

dinghy (ˈdɪŋɪ) *n., pl.* **-ghies.** any small boat, powered by sail, oars, or outboard motor. Also (esp. formerly): **dingy, dingey.** [C19: < Hindi or Bengali *dingi*]

dingle (ˈdɪŋgᵊl) *n.* a small wooded dell. [C13: <?]

dingo (ˈdɪŋgəʊ) *n., pl.* **-goes.** a wild dog of Australia, having a yellowish-brown coat and resembling a wolf. [C18: < Abor.]

dingy (ˈdɪndʒɪ) *adj.* **-gier, -giest.** **1.** lacking light or brightness; drab. **2.** dirty; discoloured. [C18: perhaps < an earlier dialect word rel. to OE *dynge* dung] —ˈ**dingily** *adv.* —ˈ**dinginess** *n.*

dining car *n.* a railway coach in which meals are served at tables. Also called: **restaurant car.**

dining room *n.* a room where meals are eaten.

DINKS (dɪŋks) *pl. n.* a variant of **Dincs.**

dinkum (ˈdɪŋkəm) *adj. Austral. & N.Z. inf.* **1.** genuine or right: *a fair dinkum offer.* **2. dinkum oil.** the truth. [C19: < E dialect: work, <?]

dinky (ˈdɪŋkɪ) *adj.* **dinkier, dinkiest.** *Inf.* **1.** *Brit.* small and neat; dainty. **2.** *U.S.* inconsequential; insignificant. [C18: < Scot. & N English dialect *dink* neat, neatly dressed]

dinky-di (ˈdɪŋkɪˈdaɪ) *adj. Austral. inf.* typical: *dinky-di Pom idleness.* [C20: var. of DINKUM]

dinner (ˈdɪnə) *n.* **1.** a meal taken in the evening. **2.** a meal taken at midday, esp. when it is the main meal of the day; lunch. **3.** a formal meal or banquet in honour of someone or something. **4.** (*as modifier*): *dinner table; dinner hour.* [C13: < OF *disner;* see DINE]

dinner dance *n.* a formal dinner followed by dancing.

dinner jacket *n.* a man's semiformal evening jacket without tails, usually black. U.S. and Canad. name: **tuxedo.**

dinner service *n.* a set of matching plates, dishes, etc., suitable for serving a meal.

dinosaur (ˈdaɪnəˌsɔː) *n.* any of a large order of extinct reptiles many of which were of gigantic size and abundant in the Mesozoic era. [C19: < NL *dinosaurus,* < Gk *deinos* fearful + *sauros* lizard] —ˌ**dinoˈsaurian** *adj.*

dint (dɪnt) *n.* **1. by dint of.** by means or use of: *by dint of hard work.* **2.** *Arch.* a blow or a mark made by a blow. ~*vb.* **3.** (*tr.*) to mark with dints. [OE *dynt*]

dioc. *abbrev. for:* **1.** diocesan. **2.** diocese.

diocesan (daɪˈɒsɪsᵊn) *adj.* **1.** of or relating to a diocese. ~*n.* **2.** the bishop of a diocese.

diocese (ˈdaɪəsɪs) *n.* the district under the jurisdiction of a bishop. [C14: < OF, < LL *diocēsis,* < Gk *dioikēsis* administration, < *dioikein* to manage a household, < *oikos* house]

diode (ˈdaɪəʊd) *n.* **1.** a semiconductor device used in circuits for converting alternating current to direct current. **2.** the earliest type of electronic valve having two electrodes between which a current can flow only in one direction. [C20: < DI-[1] + -ODE[2]]

dioecious (daɪˈiːʃəs) *adj.* (of plants) having the male and female reproductive organs on separate plants. [C18: < NL *Dioecia* name of class, < DI-[1] + Gk *oikia* house]

Dionysian (ˌdaɪəˈnɪzɪən) *adj.* **1.** of or relating to Dionysus, the Greek god of wine and revelry. **2.** (*often not cap.*) wild or orgiastic.

Diophantine equation (ˌdaɪəʊˈfæntaɪn) *n.* (in number theory) an equation in more than one variable, for which integral solutions are sought.

dioptre *or U.S.* **diopter** (daɪˈɒptə) *n.* a unit for measuring the refractive power of a lens: the reciprocal of the focal length of the lens expressed in metres. [C16: < L *dioptra* optical instrument, < Gk, < *dia-* through + *opsesthai* to see] —**diˈoptral** *adj.*

dioptrics (daɪˈɒptrɪks) *n.* (*functioning as sing.*) the branch of geometrical optics concerned with the formation of images by lenses. [C20: < DIOPTRE + -ICS]

diorama (ˌdaɪəˈrɑːmə) *n.* **1.** a miniature three-dimensional scene, in which models of figures are seen against a background. **2.** a picture made up of illuminated translucent curtains, viewed through an aperture. **3.** a museum display, as of an animal, of a specimen in its natural setting. [C19: < F, < Gk *dia-* through + *horama* view, < *horan* to see] —**dioramic** (ˌdaɪəˈræmɪk) *adj.*

dioxide (daɪˈɒksaɪd) *n.* any oxide containing two oxygen atoms per molecule, both of which are bonded to an atom of another element.

dioxin (daɪˈɒksɪn) *n.* any of various chemical by-products of the manufacture of certain herbicides and bactericides, esp. the extremely toxic tetrachlorodibenzoparadioxin (TCDD).

dip (dɪp) *vb.* **dipping, dipped.** **1.** to plunge or be plunged quickly or briefly into a liquid, esp. to wet or coat. **2.** (*intr.*) to undergo a slight decline, esp. temporarily: *sales dipped in November.* **3.** (*intr.*) to slope downwards. **4.** (*intr.*) to sink quickly. **5.** (*tr.*) to switch (car headlights) from the main to the lower beam. U.S. and Canad. word: **dim.** **6.** (*tr.*) **a.** to immerse (sheep, etc.) briefly in a chemical to rid them of or prevent infestation by insects, etc. **b.** to immerse (grain, vegetables, or wood) in a preservative liquid. **7.** (*tr.*) to dye by immersing in a liquid. **8.** (*tr.*) to baptize (someone) by immersion. **9.** (*tr.*) to plate or galvanize (a metal, etc.) by immersion in an electrolyte or electrolytic cell. **10.** (*tr.*) to scoop up a liquid or something from a liquid in the hands or in a container. **11.** to lower or be lowered briefly. **12.** (*tr.*) to make (a candle) by plunging the wick into melted wax. **13.** (*intr.*) to plunge a container, the hands, etc., into something, esp. to obtain an object. **14.** (*intr.*) (of an aircraft) to drop suddenly and then regain height. ~*n.* **15.** the act of dipping or state of being dipped. **16.** a brief swim in water. **17. a.** any liquid chemical in which sheep, etc. are dipped. **b.** any liquid preservative into which objects are dipped. **18.** a dye into which fabric is immersed. **19.** a depression, esp. in a landscape. **20.** something taken up by dipping. **21.** a container used for dipping; dipper. **22.** a momentary sinking down. **23.** the angle of slope of rock strata, etc., from the horizontal plane. **24.** the angle between the direction of the earth's magnetic field and the plane of the horizon; the angle that a magnetic needle free to swing in a vertical plane makes with the horizontal. **25.** a creamy savoury mixture into which pieces of food are dipped before being eaten. **26.** *Surveying.* the angular distance of the horizon below the plane of observation. **27.** a candle made by plunging a wick into wax. **28.** a momentary loss of altitude when flying. ~See also **dip into.** [OE *dyppan*]

dip. *or* **Dip.** *abbrev. for* diploma.

DipAD *abbrev. for* Diploma in Art and Design.

DipEd (in Britain) *abbrev. for* Diploma in Education.

diphtheria (dɪpˈθɪərɪə) *n.* an acute contagious disease caused by a bacillus, producing fever, severe prostration, and difficulty in breathing and swallowing as the result of swelling of the throat and formation of a false membrane. [C19: NL, < F *diphthérie,* < Gk *diphthera* leather; from the nature of the membrane] —**diphˈtherial, diphtheritic** (ˌdɪpθəˈrɪtɪk), *or* **diphtheric** (dɪpˈθɛrɪk) *adj.*

diphthong (ˈdɪfθɒŋ) *n.* **1.** a vowel sound, occupying a single syllable, during the articulation of which the tongue moves continuously from one position to another, as in the pronunciation of *a* in *late.* **2.** a digraph or ligature representing a composite vowel such as this, as *ae* in *Caesar.* [C15: < LL *diphthongus,* < Gk *diphthongos,* < DI-[1] + *phthongos* sound] —**diphˈthongal** *adj.*

diphthongize *or* **-ise** (ˈdɪfθɒŋˌaɪz) *vb.* (*often passive*) to make (a simple vowel) into a diphthong. —ˌ**diphthongiˈzation** *or* **-iˈsation** *n.*

dip into *vb.* (*intr., prep.*) **1.** to draw upon: *he dipped into his savings.* **2.** to dabble (in); play at. **3.** to read passages at random from (a book, newspaper, etc.).

diplodocus (ˌdɪpləʊˈdəʊkəs, dɪˈplɒdəkəs) *n., pl.* **-cuses.** a herbivorous dinosaur characterized by a very long neck and tail and a total body length of 27 metres. [C19: < NL, < Gk *diplo-,* (< *diploos,* < DI-[1] + *-ploos* -fold) + *dokos* beam]

diploid (ˈdɪplɔɪd) *adj.* **1.** *Biol.* (of cells or organisms) having paired homologous chromosomes so that twice the haploid number is present. **2.** double or twofold. ~*n.* **3.** a diploid cell or organism. —**dipˈloidic** *adj.*

diploma (dɪˈpləʊmə) *n.* **1.** a document conferring a qualification, recording success in examinations or successful completion of a course of study. **2.**

an official document that confers an honour or privilege. [C17: < L: official letter or document, lit.: letter folded double, < Gk]

diplomacy (dɪˈpləʊməsɪ) *n., pl.* **-cies. 1.** the conduct of the relations of one state with another by peaceful means. **2.** skill in the management of international relations. **3.** tact, skill, or cunning in dealing with people. [C18: < F *diplomatie,* < *diplomatique* DIPLOMATIC]

diplomat (ˈdɪpləˌmæt) *n.* **1.** an official such as an ambassador, engaged in diplomacy. **2.** a person who deals with people tactfully or skilfully. ~Also called: **diplomatist** (dɪˈpləʊmətɪst).

diplomatic (ˌdɪpləˈmætɪk) *adj.* **1.** of or relating to diplomacy or diplomats. **2.** skilled in negotiating, esp. between states or people. **3.** tactful in dealing with people. [C18: < F *diplomatique* concerning the documents of diplomacy, < NL *diplōmaticus;* see DIPLOMA] —ˌ**diploˈmatically** *adv.*

diplomatic bag *n.* a container or bag in which official mail is sent, free from customs inspection, to and from an embassy or consulate.

diplomatic corps *or* **body** *n.* the entire body of diplomats accredited to a given state.

diplomatic immunity *n.* the immunity from local jurisdiction and exemption from taxation in the country to which they are accredited afforded to diplomats.

Diplomatic Service *n.* **1.** (in Britain) the division of the Civil Service which provides diplomats to represent the UK abroad. **2.** (*not caps.*) the equivalent institution of any other country.

dipole (ˈdaɪˌpəʊl) *n.* **1.** two equal but opposite electric charges or magnetic poles separated by a small distance. **2.** a molecule in which the centre of positive charge does not coincide with the centre of negative charge. **3.** a directional aerial consisting of two metal rods with a connecting wire fixed between them in the form of a T. —**diˈpolar** *adj.*

dipper (ˈdɪpə) *n.* **1.** a ladle used for dipping. **2.** Also called: **water ouzel.** any of a genus of aquatic songbirds that inhabit fast-flowing streams. **3.** a person or thing that dips. **4.** *Arch.* an Anabaptist. ~See also **big dipper.**

dippy (ˈdɪpɪ) *adj.* **-pier, -piest.** *Sl.* odd, eccentric, or crazy. [C20: <?]

dipsomania (ˌdɪpsəʊˈmeɪnɪə) *n.* a compulsive desire to drink alcoholic beverages. [C19: NL, < Gk *dipsa* thirst + -MANIA] —ˌ**dipsoˈmaniac** *n., adj.*

dipstick (ˈdɪpˌstɪk) *n.* a graduated rod or strip dipped into a container to indicate the fluid level.

dip switch *n.* a device for dipping car headlights.

dipteran (ˈdɪptərən) *or* **dipteron** (ˈdɪptəˌrɒn) *n.* **1.** any dipterous insect. ~*adj.* **2.** another word for **dipterous** (sense 1).

dipterous (ˈdɪptərəs) *adj.* **1.** Also: **dipteran.** of a large order of insects having a single pair of wings and sucking or piercing mouthparts. The group includes flies, mosquitoes, and midges. **2.** *Bot.* having two winglike parts. [C18: < Gk *dipteros* two-winged]

diptych (ˈdɪptɪk) *n.* **1.** a pair of hinged wooden tablets with waxed surfaces for writing. **2.** a painting or carving on two hinged panels.

dire (ˈdaɪə) *adj.* (*usually prenominal*) **1.** Also: **direful.** disastrous; fearful. **2.** desperate; urgent: *a dire need.* **3.** foreboding disaster; ominous. [C16: < L *dīrus* ominous] —ˈ**direly** *adv.* —ˈ**direness** *n.*

direct (dɪˈrɛkt, daɪ-) *vb.* (*mainly tr.*) **1.** to conduct or control the affairs of. **2.** (*also intr.*) to give commands or orders with authority to (a person or group). **3.** to tell or show (someone) the way to a place. **4.** to aim, point, or cause to move towards a goal. **5.** to address (a letter, etc.). **6.** to address (remarks, etc.). **7.** (*also intr.*) to provide guidance to (actors, cameramen, etc.) in a play or film. **8.** (*also intr.*) to conduct (a piece of music or musicians), usually while performing oneself. ~*adj.* **9.** without delay or evasion; straightforward. **10.** without turning aside; shortest; straight: *a direct route.* **11.** without intervening persons or agencies: *a direct link.* **12.** honest; frank. **13.** (*usually prenominal*) precise; exact: *a direct quotation.* **14.** diametrical: *the direct opposite.* **15.** in an unbroken line of descent: *a direct descendant.* **16.** (of government, decisions, etc.) by or from the electorate rather than through representatives. **17.** *Logic, maths.* (of a proof) progressing from the premises to the conclusion, rather than eliminating the possibility of the falsehood of the conclusion. Cf. **indirect proof. 18.** *Astron.* moving from west to east. Cf. **retrograde. 19.** of or relating to direct current. **20.** *Music.* (of an interval or chord) in root position; not inverted. ~*adv.* **21.** directly; straight. [C14: < L *dīrectus,* < *dīrigere* to guide, < *dis-* apart + *regere* to rule] —**diˈrectness** *n.*

direct access *n.* a method of reading data from a computer file without reading through the file from the beginning.

direct action *n.* action such as strikes or civil disobedience employed to obtain demands from an employer, government, etc.

direct current *n.* a continuous electric current that flows in one direction only.

direct-grant school *n.* (in Britain, formerly) a school financed by endowment, fees, and a state grant conditional upon admittance of a percentage of nonpaying pupils.

direction (dɪˈrɛkʃən, daɪ-) *n.* **1.** the act of directing or the state of being directed. **2.** management, control, or guidance. **3.** the work of a stage or film director. **4.** the course or line along which a person or thing moves, points, or lies. **5.** the place towards which a person or thing is directed. **6.** a line of action; course. **7.** the name and address on a letter, parcel, etc. **8.** *Music.* the process of conducting an orchestra, choir, etc. **9.** *Music.* an instruction to indicate tempo, dynamics, mood, etc.

directional (dɪˈrɛkʃənᵊl, daɪ-) *adj.* **1.** of or relating to a spatial direction. **2.** *Electronics.* **a.** having or relating to an increased sensitivity to radio waves, nuclear particles, etc., coming from a particular direction. **b.** (of an aerial) transmitting or receiving radio waves more effectively in some directions than in others. **3.** *Physics, electronics.* concentrated in, following, or producing motion in a particular direction. —**diˌrectionˈality** *n.*

directional drilling *n.* a method of drilling for oil in which the well is not drilled vertically, as when a number of wells are to be drilled from a single platform. Also called: **deviated drilling.**

direction finder *n.* a device to determine the direction of incoming radio signals, used esp. as a navigation aid.

directions (dɪˈrɛkʃənz, daɪ-) *pl. n.* (*sometimes sing.*) instructions for doing something or for reaching a place.

directive (dɪˈrɛktɪv, daɪ-) *n.* **1.** an instruction; order. ~*adj.* **2.** tending to direct; directing. **3.** indicating direction.

directly (dɪˈrɛktlɪ, daɪ-) *adv.* **1.** in a direct manner. **2.** at once; without delay. **3.** (foll. by *before* or *after*) immediately; just. ~*conj.* **4.** (*subordinating*) as soon as.

direct object *n. Grammar.* a noun, pronoun, or noun phrase whose referent receives the direct action of a verb. For example, *a book* in *They bought Anne a book.*

directoire (dɪˈrɛktwɑː) *adj.* (of ladies' knickers) knee-length, with elastic at waist and knees. [C19: after fashions of the period of the French *Directoire* Directorate (1795-99)]

director (dɪˈrɛktə, daɪ-) *n.* **1.** a person or thing that directs, controls, or regulates. **2.** a member of the governing board of a business concern. **3.** a person who directs the affairs of an institution, trust, etc. **4.** the person responsible for the artistic and technical aspects of the making of a film or television programme. Compare **producer** (sense 3). **5.** *Music.* another word (esp. U.S.) for **conductor.** —ˌ**direcˈtorial** *adj.* —ˌ**diˈrectorˌship** *n.* —**diˈrectress** *fem. n.*

directorate (dɪˈrɛktərɪt, daɪ-) *n.* **1.** a board of directors. **2.** Also: **directorship.** the position of director.

director-general *n., pl.* **directors-general.** the head of a large organization such as the CBI or BBC.

directory (dɪˈrɛktərɪ, -trɪ; daɪ-) *n., pl.* **-ries. 1.** a book listing names, addresses, telephone numbers, etc., of individuals or firms. **2.** a book giving directions. **3.** a book containing the rules to be observed in the forms of worship used in churches. **4.** a directorate. *~adj.* **5.** directing.

Directory (dɪˈrɛktərɪ; daɪ-) *n.* **the.** *History.* the body of five directors in power in France from 1795 until their overthrow by Napoleon in 1799. Also called: **French Directory.**

direct primary *n. U.S. government.* a primary in which voters directly select the candidates who will run for office.

direct speech *or esp. U.S.* **direct discourse** *n.* the reporting of what someone has said or written by quoting his exact words.

direct tax *n.* a tax paid by the person or organization on which it is levied.

dirge (dɜːdʒ) *n.* **1.** a chant of lamentation for the dead. **2.** the funeral service in its solemn or sung forms. **3.** any mourning song or melody. [C13: < L *dīrige* direct (imperative), opening word of antiphon used in the office of the dead] —**ˈdirgeful** *adj.*

dirham (ˈdɪəræm) *n.* **1.** the standard monetary unit of Morocco. **2.** a monetary unit of Kuwait, Tunisia, and Qatar. **3.** any of various N African coins. [C18: < Ar., < L: DRACHMA]

dirigible (ˈdɪrɪdʒɪbᵊl) *adj.* **1.** able to be steered or directed. *~n.* **2.** another name for **airship.** [C16: < L *dīrigere* to DIRECT] —**ˌdirigiˈbility** *n.*

dirigisme (diːriːˈʒiːzəm) *n.* control by the state of economic and social matters. [C20: < F] —**diriˈgiste** *adj.*

dirk (dɜːk) *n.* **1.** a dagger, esp. as formerly worn by Scottish Highlanders. *~vb.* **2.** (*tr.*) to stab with a dirk. [C16: < Scot. *durk*, ? < G *Dolch* dagger]

dirndl (ˈdɜːndᵊl) *n.* **1.** a woman's dress with a full gathered skirt and fitted bodice; originating from Tyrolean peasant wear. **2.** a gathered skirt of this kind. [G (Bavarian and Austrian): < *Dirndlkleid*, < *Dirndl* little girl + *Kleid* dress]

dirt (dɜːt) *n.* **1.** any unclean substance, such as mud, etc.; filth. **2.** loose earth; soil. **3. a.** packed earth, gravel, cinders, etc., used to make a racetrack. **b.** (*as modifier*): *a dirt track.* **4.** *Mining.* the gravel or soil from which minerals are extracted. **5.** a person or thing regarded as worthless. **6.** obscene or indecent speech or writing. **7.** moral corruption. **8. do (someone) dirt.** *Sl.* to do something vicious to (someone). **9. eat dirt.** *Sl.* to accept insult without complaining. [C13: < ON *drit* excrement]

dirt-cheap *adj., adv. Inf.* at an extremely low price.

dirty (ˈdɜːtɪ) *adj.* **dirtier, dirtiest. 1.** covered or marked with dirt; filthy. **2. a.** obscene: *dirty books.* **b.** sexually clandestine: *a dirty weekend.* **3.** causing one to become grimy: *a dirty job.* **4.** (of a colour) not clear and bright. **5.** unfair; dishonest. **6.** mean; nasty: *a dirty cheat.* **7.** scandalous; unkind. **8.** revealing dislike or anger. **9.** (of weather) rainy or squally; stormy. **10.** (of a nuclear weapon) producing a large quantity of radioactive fallout. **11. dirty linen.** *Inf.* intimate secrets, esp. those that might give rise to gossip. **12. dirty work.** unpleasant or illicit activity. *~n.* **13. do the dirty on.** *Inf.* to behave meanly towards. *~vb.* **dirtying, dirtied. 14.** to make or become dirty; stain; soil. —**ˈdirtily** *adv.* —**ˈdirtiness** *n.*

dis-[1] *prefix.* **1.** indicating reversal: *disconnect.* **2.** indicating negation, lack, or deprivation: *dissimilar; disgrace.* **3.** indicating removal or release: *disembowel.* **4.** expressing intensive force: *dissever.* [< L *dis-* apart; in some cases, via OF *des-*. In compound words of L origin, *dis-* becomes *dif-* before *f*, and *di-* before some consonants]

dis-[2] *combining form.* a variant of **di-**[1] before *s*: *dissyllable.*

disability (ˌdɪsəˈbɪlɪtɪ) *n., pl.* **-ties. 1.** the condition of being physically or mentally impaired. **2.** something that disables; handicap. **3.** lack of necessary intelligence, strength, etc. **4.** an incapacity in the eyes of the law to enter into certain transactions.

disable (dɪsˈeɪbᵊl) *vb.* (*tr.*) **1.** to make ineffective, unfit, or incapable, as by crippling. **2.** to make or pronounce legally incapable. —**disˈablement** *n.*

disabled (dɪˈseɪbᵊld) *adj.* **a.** lacking one or more physical powers, such as the ability to walk or to coordinate one's movements. **b.** (*as collective n.; preceded by the*): *the disabled.*

disabuse (ˌdɪsəˈbjuːz) *vb.* (*tr.;* usually foll. by *of*) to rid of a mistaken idea; set right.

disadvantage (ˌdɪsədˈvɑːntɪdʒ) *n.* **1.** an unfavourable circumstance, thing, person, etc. **2.** injury, loss, or detriment. **3.** an unfavourable situation (esp. in **at a disadvantage**). *~vb.* **4.** (*tr.*) to put at a disadvantage; handicap.

disadvantaged (ˌdɪsədˈvɑːntɪdʒd) *adj.* socially or economically deprived or discriminated against.

disadvantageous (dɪsˌædvɑːnˈteɪdʒəs, ˌdɪsæd-) *adj.* unfavourable to one's interests: detrimental. —**disˌadvanˈtageously** *adv.* —**disˌadvanˈtageousness** *n.*

disaffect (ˌdɪsəˈfɛkt) *vb.* (*tr.; often passive*) to cause to lose loyalty or affection; alienate. —**ˌdisafˈfectedly** *adv.* —**ˌdisafˈfection** *n.*

disaffiliate (ˌdɪsəˈfɪlɪˌeɪt) *vb.* to sever an affiliation (with). —**ˌdisafˌfiliˈation** *n.*

disafforest (ˌdɪsəˈfɒrɪst) *vb.* (*tr.*) *Law.* to reduce (land) from the status of a forest to the state of ordinary ground. —**ˌdisafˌforesˈtation** *n.*

disagree (ˌdɪsəˈgriː) *vb.* **-greeing, -greed.** (*intr.;* often foll. by *with*) **1.** to dissent in opinion or dispute (about an idea, fact, etc.). **2.** to fail to correspond; conflict. **3.** to be unacceptable (to) or unfavourable (for): *curry disagrees with me.* **4.** to be opposed (to).

disagreeable (ˌdɪsəˈgrɪəbᵊl) *adj.* **1.** not likable; bad-tempered, esp. disobliging, etc. **2.** not to one's liking; unpleasant. —**ˌdisaˈgreeableness** *n.* —**ˌdisaˈgreeably** *adv.*

disagreement (ˌdɪsəˈgriːmənt) *n.* **1.** refusal or failure to agree. **2.** a failure to correspond. **3.** an argument or dispute.

disallow (ˌdɪsəˈlaʊ) *vb.* (*tr.*) **1.** to reject as untrue or invalid. **2.** to cancel. —**ˌdisalˈlowable** *adj.* —**ˌdisalˈlowance** *n.*

disappear (ˌdɪsəˈpɪə) *vb.* (*intr.*) **1.** to cease to be visible; vanish. **2.** to go away or become lost, esp. without explanation. **3.** to cease to exist; become extinct or lost. —**ˌdisapˈpearance** *n.*

disappoint (ˌdɪsəˈpɔɪnt) *vb.* (*tr.*) **1.** to fail to meet the expectations, hopes, etc. of; let down. **2.** to prevent the fulfilment of (a plan, etc.); frustrate. [C15 (orig. meaning: to remove from office): < OF *desapointier;* see DIS-[1], APPOINT] —**ˌdisapˈpointed** *adj.* —**ˌdisapˈpointing** *adj.* —**ˌdisapˈpointingly** *adv.*

disappointment (ˌdɪsəˈpɔɪntmənt) *n.* **1.** a disappointing or being disappointed. **2.** a person or thing that disappoints.

disapprobation (ˌdɪsæprəʊˈbeɪʃən) *n.* moral or social disapproval.

disapproval (ˌdɪsəˈpruːvᵊl) *n.* the act or a state or feeling of disapproving; censure.

disapprove (ˌdɪsəˈpruːv) *vb.* **1.** (*intr.;* often foll. by *of*) to consider wrong, bad, etc. **2.** (*tr.*) to withhold approval from. —**ˌdisapˈproving** *adj.* —**ˌdisapˈprovingly** *adv.*

disarm (dɪsˈɑːm) *vb.* **1.** (*tr.*) to remove defensive or offensive capability from (a country, army, etc.). **2.** (*tr.*) to deprive of weapons. **3.** (*tr.*) to win the confidence or affection of. **4.** (*intr.*) (of a nation, etc.) to decrease the size and capability of one's armed forces. **5.** (*intr.*) to lay down weapons. —**disˈarmer** *n.*

disarmament (dɪsˈɑːməmənt) *n.* **1.** the reduction of fighting capability, as by a nation. **2.** a disarming or being disarmed.

disarming (dɪsˈɑːmɪŋ) *adj.* tending to neutralize hostility, suspicion, etc. —**disˈarmingly** *adv.*

disarrange (ˌdɪsəˈreɪndʒ) *vb.* (*tr.*) to throw into disorder. —ˌ**disarˈrangement** *n.*

disarray (ˌdɪsəˈreɪ) *n.* 1. confusion, dismay, and lack of discipline. 2. (esp. of clothing) disorderliness; untidiness. ~*vb.* (*tr.*) 3. to throw into confusion. 4. *Arch.* to undress.

disassemble (ˌdɪsəˈsɛmbᵊl) *vb.* (*tr.*) to take apart (a piece of machinery, etc.); dismantle.

disassociate (ˌdɪsəˈsəʊʃɪˌeɪt, -sɪ-) *vb.* a less common word for **dissociate.** —ˌ**disasˌsociˈation** *n.*

▷ **Usage.** While *disassociate* is sometimes encountered in both written and spoken English, the word *dissociate* is generally regarded as being the only acceptable term.

disaster (dɪˈzɑːstə) *n.* 1. an occurrence that causes great distress or destruction. 2. a thing, project, etc., that fails or has been ruined. [C16 (orig. in the sense: malevolent astral influence): < It. *disastro,* < *dis-* (pejorative) + *astro* star, ult. < Gk *astron*] —**disˈastrous** *adj.*

disavow (ˌdɪsəˈvaʊ) *vb.* (*tr.*) to deny knowledge of, connection with, or responsibility for. —ˌ**disaˈvowal** *n.* —**disavowedly** (ˌdɪsəˈvaʊɪdlɪ) *adv.*

disband (dɪsˈbænd) *vb.* to cease to function or cause to stop functioning, as a unit, group, etc. —**disˈbandment** *n.*

disbar (dɪsˈbɑː) *vb.* **-barring, -barred.** (*tr.*) *Law.* to deprive of the status of barrister; expel from the Bar. —**disˈbarment** *n.*

disbelief (ˌdɪsbɪˈliːf) *n.* refusal or reluctance to believe.

disbelieve (ˌdɪsbɪˈliːv) *vb.* 1. (*tr.*) to reject as false or lying. 2. (*intr.;* usually foll. by *in*) to have no faith (in). —ˌ**disbeˈliever** *n.* —ˌ**disbeˈlieving** *adj.*

disbud (dɪsˈbʌd) *vb.* **-budding, -budded.** to remove superfluous buds from (a plant).

disburden (dɪsˈbɜːdᵊn) *vb.* 1. to remove a load from. 2. (*tr.*) to relieve (one's mind, etc.) of a distressing worry.

disburse (dɪsˈbɜːs) *vb.* (*tr.*) to pay out. [C16: < OF *desborser,* < *des-* DIS-[1] + *borser* to obtain money, < *borse* bag, < LL *bursa*] —**disˈbursable** *adj.* —**disˈbursement** *n.* —**disˈburser** *n.*

disc (dɪsk) *n.* 1. a flat circular plate. 2. something resembling this. 3. a gramophone record. 4. *Anat.* any approximately circular flat structure in the body, esp. an intervertebral disc. 5. the flat receptacle of composite flowers, such as the daisy. 6. a. Also called: **parking disc.** a marker or device for display in a parked vehicle showing the time of arrival or the latest permitted time of departure or both. b. (*as modifier*): *disc parking.* 7. *Computers.* a variant spelling of **disk.** [C18: < L *discus* DISCUS]

disc. *abbrev. for:* 1. discount. 2. discovered.

discard *vb.* (dɪsˈkɑːd). 1. (*tr.*) to get rid of as useless or undesirable. 2. *Cards.* to throw out (a card or cards) from one's hand. 3. *Cards.* to play (a card not of the suit led nor a trump) when unable to follow suit. ~*n.* (ˈdɪskɑːd). 4. a person or thing that has been cast aside. 5. *Cards.* a discarded card. 6. the act of discarding.

disc brake *n.* a type of brake in which two pads rub against a flat disc attached to the wheel hub when the brake is applied.

disc camera *n.* a type of small compact camera in which the film is on a disc (**disc film**) instead of a spool.

discern (dɪˈsɜːn) *vb.* 1. (*tr.*) to recognize or perceive clearly. 2. to recognize or perceive (differences). [C14: < OF *discerner,* < L *discernere* to divide, < DIS-[1] apart + *cernere* to separate] —**disˈcernible** *adj.* —**disˈcernibly** *adv.*

discerning (dɪˈsɜːnɪŋ) *adj.* having or showing good taste or judgment; discriminating.

discernment (dɪˈsɜːnmənt) *n.* keen perception or judgment.

disc flower *or* **floret** *n.* any of the small tubular flowers at the centre of the flower head of certain composite plants, such as the daisy.

discharge *vb.* (dɪsˈtʃɑːdʒ). 1. (*tr.*) to release or allow to go. 2. (*tr.*) to dismiss from or relieve of duty, employment, etc. 3. to fire or be fired, as a gun. 4. to pour forth or cause to pour forth: *the boil discharges pus.* 5. (*tr.*) to remove (the cargo) from (a boat, etc.); unload. 6. (*tr.*) to perform the duties of or meet the demands of (an office, obligation, etc.). 7. (*tr.*) to relieve (oneself) of (a responsibility, debt, etc.). 8. (*intr.*) *Physics.* a. to lose or remove electric charge. b. to form an arc, spark, or corona in a gas. c. to take or supply electrical current from a cell or battery. 9. (*tr.*) *Law.* to release (a prisoner from custody, etc.). ~*n.* (ˈdɪstʃɑːdʒ, dɪsˈtʃɑːdʒ). 10. a person or thing that is discharged. 11. a. dismissal or release from an office, job, institution, etc. b. the document certifying such release. 12. the fulfilment of an obligation or release from a responsibility or liability. 13. the act of removing a load, as of cargo. 14. a pouring forth of a fluid; emission. 15. a. the act of firing a projectile. b. the volley, bullet, etc., fired. 16. *Law.* a. a release, as of a person held under legal restraint. b. an annulment, as of a court order. 17. *Physics.* a. the act or process of removing or losing charge. b. a conduction of electricity through a gas by the formation and movement of electrons and ions in an applied electric field. —**disˈchargeable** *adj.* —**disˈcharger** *n.*

disc harrow *n.* a harrow with sharp-edged discs used to cut clods on the surface of the soil or to cover seed after planting.

disciple (dɪˈsaɪpᵊl) *n.* 1. a follower of the doctrines of a teacher or a school of thought. 2. one of the personal followers of Christ (including his 12 apostles) during his earthly life. [OE *discipul,* < L *discipulus* pupil, < *discere* to learn] —**disˈcipleˌship** *n.* —**discipular** (dɪˈsɪpjʊlə) *adj.*

disciplinarian (ˌdɪsɪplɪˈnɛərɪən) *n.* a person who imposes or advocates strict discipline.

disciplinary (ˈdɪsɪˌplɪnərɪ) *adj.* 1. of, promoting, or used for discipline; corrective. 2. relating to a branch of learning.

discipline (ˈdɪsɪplɪn) *n.* 1. training or conditions imposed for the improvement of physical powers, self-control, etc. 2. systematic training in obedience. 3. the state of improved behaviour, etc., resulting from such training. 4. punishment or chastisement. 5. a system of rules for behaviour, etc. 6. a branch of learning or instruction. 7. the laws governing members of a Church. ~*vb.* (*tr.*) 8. to improve or attempt to improve the behaviour, orderliness, etc., of by training, conditions, or rules. 9. to punish or correct. [C13: < L *disciplīna* teaching, < *discipulus* DISCIPLE] —ˈ**disciˌplinable** *adj.* —**disciplinal** (ˌdɪsɪˈplaɪnᵊl) *adj.* —ˈ**disciˌpliner** *n.*

disc jockey *n.* a person who announces and plays recorded music, esp. pop music, on a radio programme, etc.

disclaim (dɪsˈkleɪm) *vb.* 1. (*tr.*) to deny or renounce (any claim, connection, etc.). 2. (*tr.*) to deny the validity or authority of. 3. *Law.* to renounce or repudiate (a legal claim or right).

disclaimer (dɪsˈkleɪmə) *n.* a repudiation or denial.

disclose (dɪsˈkləʊz) *vb.* (*tr.*) 1. to make known. 2. to allow to be seen. —**disˈcloser** *n.*

disclosure (dɪsˈkləʊʒə) *n.* 1. something that is disclosed. 2. the act of disclosing; revelation.

disco (ˈdɪskəʊ) *n., pl.* **-cos.** 1. a. an occasion at which people dance to pop records. b. (*as modifier*): *disco music.* 2. a nightclub or other public place where such dances are held. 3. mobile equipment for providing music for a disco.

discobolus (dɪsˈkɒbələs) *n., pl.* **-li** (-ˌlaɪ). a discus thrower. [C18: < L, < Gk, < *diskos* DISCUS + *-bolos,* < *ballein* to throw]

discography (dɪsˈkɒgrəfɪ) *n.* a classified list of gramophone records. —**disˈcographer** *n.*

discoid (ˈdɪskɔɪd) *adj. also* **discoidal.** 1. like a disc. ~*n.* 2. a disclike object.

discolour *or U.S.* **discolor** (dɪsˈkʌlə) *vb.* to change in colour; fade or stain. —**disˌcolorˈation** *or* **disˌcolourˈation** *n.*

discombobulate (ˌdɪskəmˈbɒbjʊˌleɪt) *vb.* (*tr.*) *Inf., chiefly U.S. & Canad.* to throw into confusion.

[C20: prob. a whimsical alteration of DISCOMPOSE or DISCOMFIT]

discomfit (dɪsˈkʌmfɪt) *vb.* (*tr.*) **1.** to make uneasy or confused. **2.** to frustrate the plans or purpose of. **3.** *Arch.* to defeat. [C14: < OF *desconfire* to destroy, < *des-* (indicating reversal) + *confire* to make, < L *conficere* to produce] —**disˈcomfiture** *n.*

discomfort (dɪsˈkʌmfət) *n.* **1.** an inconvenience, distress, or mild pain. **2.** something that disturbs or deprives of ease. ~*vb.* **3.** (*tr.*) to make uncomfortable or uneasy.

discommode (ˌdɪskəˈməʊd) *vb.* (*tr.*) to cause inconvenience to; disturb. —ˌ**discomˈmodious** *adj.*

discompose (ˌdɪskəmˈpəʊz) *vb.* (*tr.*) **1.** to disturb the composure of; disconcert. **2.** *Now rare.* to disarrange. —ˌ**discomˈposure** *n.*

disconcert (ˌdɪskənˈsɜːt) *vb.* (*tr.*) **1.** to disturb the composure of. **2.** to frustrate or upset. —ˌ**disconˈcerted** *adj.* —ˌ**disconˈcerting** *adj.* —ˌ**disconˈcertion** *n.*

disconformity (ˌdɪskənˈfɔːmɪtɪ) *n., pl.* **-ties. 1.** lack of conformity; discrepancy. **2.** the junction between two parallel series of stratified rocks.

disconnect (ˌdɪskəˈnɛkt) *vb.* (*tr.*) to undo or break the connection of or between (something, as a plug and a socket). —ˌ**disconˈnection** *n.*

disconnected (ˌdɪskəˈnɛktɪd) *adj.* **1.** not rationally connected; confused or incoherent. **2.** not connected or joined.

disconsolate (dɪsˈkɒnsəlɪt) *adj.* **1.** sad beyond comfort; inconsolable. **2.** disappointed; dejected. [C14: < Med. L *disconsōlātus,* < DIS-[1] + *consōlātus* comforted] —**disˈconsolately** *adv.* —**disˈconsolateness** *or* **disˌconsoˈlation** *n.*

discontent (ˌdɪskənˈtɛnt) *n.* **1.** Also called: **discontentment.** lack of contentment, as with one's condition or lot in life. ~*vb.* **2.** (*tr.*) to make dissatisfied. —ˌ**disconˈtented** *adj.* —ˌ**disconˈtentedness** *n.*

discontinue (ˌdɪskənˈtɪnjuː) *vb.* **-uing, -ued. 1.** to come or bring to an end; interrupt or be interrupted; stop. **2.** (*tr.*) *Law.* to terminate or abandon (an action, suit, etc.). —ˌ**disconˈtinuance** *n.* —ˌ**disconˌtinuˈation** *n.*

discontinuity (dɪsˌkɒntɪˈnjuːɪtɪ) *n., pl.* **-ties. 1.** lack of rational connection or cohesion. **2.** a break or interruption.

discontinuous (ˌdɪskənˈtɪnjʊəs) *adj.* characterized by interruptions or breaks; intermittent. —ˌ**disconˈtinuously** *adv.* —ˌ**disconˈtinuousness** *n.*

discord *n.* (ˈdɪskɔːd). **1.** lack of agreement or harmony. **2.** harsh confused mingling of sounds. **3.** a combination of musical notes, esp. one containing one or more dissonant intervals. ~*vb.* (dɪsˈkɔːd). **4.** (*intr.*) to disagree; clash. [C13: < OF *descort,* < *descorder* to disagree, < L *discordāre,* < *discors* at variance, < DIS-[1] + *cor* heart]

discordant (dɪsˈkɔːdᵊnt) *adj.* **1.** at variance; disagreeing. **2.** harsh in sound; inharmonious. —**disˈcordance** *n.* —**disˈcordantly** *adv.*

discotheque (ˈdɪskəˌtɛk) *n.* the full term for **disco.** [C20: < F *discothèque,* < Gk *diskos* disc + *-o-* + Gk *thēkē* case]

discount *vb.* (dɪsˈkaʊnt, ˈdɪskaʊnt). (*mainly tr.*) **1.** to leave out of account as being unreliable, prejudiced, or irrelevant. **2.** to anticipate and make allowance for. **3. a.** to deduct (an amount or percentage) from the price, cost, etc. **b.** to reduce (the regular price, etc.) by a percentage or amount. **4.** to sell or offer for sale at a reduced price. **5.** to buy or sell (a bill of exchange, etc.) before maturity, with a deduction for interest. **6.** (*also intr.*) to loan money on (a negotiable instrument) with a deduction for interest. ~*n.* (ˈdɪskaʊnt). **7.** a deduction from the full amount of a price or debt. See also **cash discount, trade discount. 8.** Also called: **discount rate. a.** the amount of interest deducted in the purchase or sale of or the loan of money on unmatured negotiable instruments. **b.** the rate of interest deducted. **9.** (in the issue of shares) a percentage deducted from the par value to give a reduced amount payable by subscribers. **10.** a discounting. **11. at a discount. a.** below the regular price. **b.** held in low regard. **12.** (*modifier*) offering or selling at reduced prices: *a discount shop.* —**disˈcountable** *adj.* —ˈ**discounter** *n.*

discountenance (dɪsˈkaʊntɪnəns) *vb.* (*tr.*) **1.** to make ashamed or confused. **2.** to disapprove of. ~*n.* **3.** disapproval.

discount house *n.* **1.** *Chiefly Brit.* a financial organization engaged in discounting bills of exchange, etc., on a large scale. **2.** Also called: **discount store.** *Chiefly U.S.* a shop offering for sale most of its merchandise at prices below the recommended prices.

discourage (dɪsˈkʌrɪdʒ) *vb.* (*tr.*) **1.** to deprive of the will to persist in something. **2.** to inhibit; prevent: *this solution discourages rust.* **3.** to oppose by expressing disapproval. —**disˈcouragement** *n.* —**disˈcouragingly** *adv.*

discourse *n.* (ˈdɪskɔːs, dɪsˈkɔːs). **1.** verbal communication; talk; conversation. **2.** a formal treatment of a subject in speech or writing. **3.** a unit of text used by linguists for the analysis of linguistic phenomena that range over more than one sentence. **4.** *Arch.* the ability to reason. ~*vb.* (dɪsˈkɔːs). **5.** (*intr.; often foll. by* on *or* upon) to speak or write (about) formally. **6.** (*intr.*) to hold a discussion. **7.** (*tr.*) *Arch.* to give forth (music). [C14: < Med. L *discursus* argument, < L: a running to and fro, < *discurrere,* < DIS-[1] + *currere* to run]

discourteous (dɪsˈkɜːtɪəs) *adj.* showing bad manners; impolite; rude. —**disˈcourteously** *adv.* —**disˈcourteousness** *n.*

discourtesy (dɪsˈkɜːtɪsɪ) *n., pl.* **-sies. 1.** bad manners; rudeness. **2.** a rude remark or act.

discover (dɪˈskʌvə) *vb.* (*tr.; may take a clause as object*) **1.** to be the first to find or find out about. **2.** to learn about for the first time; realize. **3.** to find after study or search. **4.** to reveal or make known. —**disˈcoverable** *adj.* —**disˈcoverer** *n.*

discovery (dɪˈskʌvərɪ) *n., pl.* **-eries. 1.** the act, process, or an instance of discovering. **2.** a person, place, or thing that has been discovered. **3.** *Law.* the compulsory disclosure by a party to an action of relevant documents in his possession.

discredit (dɪsˈkrɛdɪt) *vb.* (*tr.*) **1.** to damage the reputation of. **2.** to cause to be disbelieved or distrusted. **3.** to reject as untrue. ~*n.* **4.** something that causes disgrace. **5.** damage to a reputation. **6.** lack of belief or confidence.

discreditable (dɪsˈkrɛdɪtəbᵊl) *adj.* tending to bring discredit; shameful or unworthy.

discreet (dɪˈskriːt) *adj.* **1.** careful to avoid embarrassment, esp. by keeping confidences secret; tactful. **2.** unobtrusive. [C14: < OF *discret,* < Med. L *discrētus,* < L *discernere* to DISCERN] —**disˈcreetly** *adv.* —**disˈcreetness** *n.*

discrepancy (dɪˈskrɛpənsɪ) *n., pl.* **-cies.** a conflict or variation, as between facts, figures, or claims. [C15: < L *discrepāns,* < *discrepāre* to differ in sound, < DIS-[1] + *crepāre* to be noisy] —**disˈcrepant** *adj.*

discrete (dɪsˈkriːt) *adj.* **1.** separate or distinct. **2.** consisting of distinct or separate parts. [C14: < L *discrētus* separated; see DISCREET] —**disˈcretely** *adv.* —**disˈcreteness** *n.*

discretion (dɪˈskrɛʃən) *n.* **1.** the quality of behaving so as to avoid social embarrassment or distress. **2.** freedom or authority to make judgments and to act as one sees fit (esp. in **at one's own discretion, at the discretion of**). **3. age** *or* **years of discretion.** the age at which a person is thought able to manage his own affairs.

discretionary (dɪˈskrɛʃənərɪ, -ənrɪ) *or* **discretional** *adj.* having or using the ability to decide at one's own discretion: *discretionary powers.*

discriminate *vb.* (dɪˈskrɪmɪˌneɪt). **1.** (*intr.; usu. foll. by* in favour of *or* against) to single out a particular person, group, etc., for special favour or, esp., disfavour. **2.** (when *intr.,* foll. by *between* or *among*) to recognize or understand the difference (between); distinguish. **3.** (*intr.*) to constitute or mark a difference. **4.** (*intr.*) to be discerning in matters of taste. ~*adj.*

(dɪˈskrɪmɪnɪt). **5.** showing or marked by discrimination. [C17: < L *discrīmināre* to divide, < *discrīmen* a separation, < *discernere* to DISCERN] —**disˈcriminately** *adv.*

discriminating (dɪˈskrɪmɪˌneɪtɪŋ) *adj.* **1.** able to see fine distinctions and differences. **2.** discerning in matters of taste. **3.** (of a tariff, import duty, etc.) levied at differential rates.

discrimination (dɪˌskrɪmɪˈneɪʃən) *n.* **1.** unfair treatment of a person, racial group, minority, etc.; action based on prejudice. **2.** subtle appreciation in matters of taste. **3.** the ability to see fine distinctions and differences.

discriminatory (dɪˈskrɪmɪnətərɪ, -trɪ) *or* **discriminative** (dɪˈskrɪmɪnətɪv) *adj.* **1.** based on or showing prejudice; biased. **2.** capable of making fine distinctions.

discursive (dɪˈskɜːsɪv) *adj.* **1.** passing from one topic to another; digressive. **2.** *Philosophy.* of or relating to knowledge obtained by reason and argument rather than intuition. [C16: < Med. L *discursīvus,* < LL *discursus* DISCOURSE] —**disˈcursively** *adv.* —**disˈcursiveness** *n.*

discus (ˈdɪskəs) *n., pl.* **discuses** *or* **disci** (ˈdɪskaɪ). **1.** (originally) a circular stone or plate used in throwing competitions by the ancient Greeks. **2.** *Field sports.* a similar disc-shaped object with a heavy middle, thrown by athletes. **3.** (preceded by *the*) the event or sport of throwing the discus. [C17: < L, < Gk *diskos,* < *dikein* to throw]

discuss (dɪˈskʌs) *vb.* (*tr.*) **1.** to have a conversation about; consider by talking over. **2.** to treat (a subject) in speech or writing. [C14: < LL *discussus* examined, < *discutere,* < L: to dash to pieces, < DIS-[1] + *quatere* to shake] —**disˈcussant** *or* **disˈcusser** *n.* —**disˈcussible** *or* **disˈcussable** *adj.*

discussion (dɪˈskʌʃən) *n.* the examination or consideration of a matter in speech or writing.

disdain (dɪsˈdeɪn) *n.* **1.** a feeling or show of superiority and dislike; contempt; scorn. ~*vb.* **2.** (*tr.; may take an infinitive*) to refuse or reject with disdain. [C13 *dedeyne,* < OF *desdeign,* < *desdeigner* to reject as unworthy, < L *dēdignārī;* see DIS-[1], DEIGN] —**disˈdainful** *adj.*

disease (dɪˈziːz) *n.* **1.** any impairment of normal physiological function affecting an organism, esp. a change caused by infection, stress, etc., producing characteristic symptoms; illness or sickness in general. **2.** a corresponding condition in plants. **3.** any condition likened to this. [C14: < OF *desaise;* see DIS-[1], EASE] —**disˈeased** *adj.*

diseconomy (ˌdɪsɪˈkɒnəmɪ) *n. Econ.* disadvantage, such as lower efficiency or higher costs, resulting from the scale on which an enterprise operates.

disembark (ˌdɪsɪmˈbɑːk) *vb.* to land or cause to land from a ship, aircraft, etc. —**disembarkation** (dɪsˌɛmbɑːˈkeɪʃən) *n.*

disembarrass (ˌdɪsɪmˈbærəs) *vb.* (*tr.*) **1.** to free from embarrassment, entanglement, etc. **2.** to relieve or rid of something burdensome.

disembodied (ˌdɪsɪmˈbɒdɪd) *adj.* **1.** lacking a body or freed from the body. **2.** lacking in substance or any firm relation to reality.

disembody (ˌdɪsɪmˈbɒdɪ) *vb.* **-bodying, -bodied.** (*tr.*) to free from the body or from physical form. —ˌ**disemˈbodiment** *n.*

disembogue (ˌdɪsɪmˈbəʊg) *vb.* **-boguing, -bogued.** **1.** (of a river, stream, etc.) to discharge (water) at the mouth. **2.** (*intr.*) to flow out. [C16: < Sp. *desembocar,* < *des-* DIS-[1] + *embocar* to put into the mouth] —ˌ**disemˈboguement** *n.*

disembowel (ˌdɪsɪmˈbaʊəl) *vb.* **-elling, -elled** *or U.S.* **-eling, -eled.** (*tr.*) to remove the entrails of. —ˌ**disemˈbowelment** *n.*

disenchant (ˌdɪsɪnˈtʃɑːnt) *vb.* (*tr.*) to free from or as if from an enchantment; disillusion. —ˌ**disenˈchantingly** *adv.* —ˌ**disenˈchantment** *n.*

disencumber (ˌdɪsɪnˈkʌmbə) *vb.* (*tr.*) to free from encumbrances. —ˌ**disenˈcumberment** *n.*

disenfranchise (ˌdɪsɪnˈfræntʃaɪz) *vb.* another word for **disfranchise.** —**disenfranchisement** (ˌdɪsɪnˈfræntʃɪzmənt) *n.*

disengage (ˌdɪsɪnˈgeɪdʒ) *vb.* **1.** to release or become released from a connection, obligation, etc. **2.** *Mil.* to withdraw (forces) from close action. **3.** *Fencing.* to move (one's blade) from one side of an opponent's blade to another in a circular motion. —ˌ**disenˈgaged** *adj.* —ˌ**disenˈgagement** *n.*

disentangle (ˌdɪsɪnˈtæŋgᵊl) *vb.* **1.** to release or become free from entanglement or confusion. **2.** (*tr.*) to unravel or work out. —ˌ**disenˈtanglement** *n.*

disequilibrium (ˌdɪsiːkwɪˈlɪbrɪəm) *n.* a loss or absence of equilibrium, esp. in an economy.

disestablish (ˌdɪsɪˈstæblɪʃ) *vb.* (*tr.*) to deprive (a church, custom, institution, etc.) of established status. —ˌ**disesˈtablishment** *n.*

disesteem (ˌdɪsɪˈstiːm) *vb.* **1.** (*tr.*) to think little of. ~*n.* **2.** lack of esteem.

disfavour *or U.S.* **disfavor** (dɪsˈfeɪvə) *n.* **1.** disapproval or dislike. **2.** the state of being disapproved of or disliked. **3.** an unkind act. ~*vb.* **4.** (*tr.*) to treat with disapproval or dislike.

disfigure (dɪsˈfɪgə) *vb.* (*tr.*) **1.** to spoil the appearance or shape of; deface. **2.** to mar the effect or quality of. —**disˈfigurement** *n.*

disforest (dɪsˈfɒrɪst) *vb.* (*tr.*) **1.** another word for **deforest. 2.** *English law.* a less common word for **disafforest.** —**disˌforesˈtation** *n.*

disfranchise (dɪsˈfræntʃaɪz) *or* **disenfranchise** *vb.* (*tr.*) **1.** to deprive (a person) of the right to vote or other rights of citizenship. **2.** to deprive (a place) of the right to send representatives to an elected body. **3.** to deprive (a person, place, etc.) of any franchise or right. —**disfranchisement** (dɪsˈfræntʃɪzmənt) *or* ˌ**disenˈfranchisement** *n.*

disgorge (dɪsˈgɔːdʒ) *vb.* **1.** to throw out (food, etc.) from the throat or stomach; vomit. **2.** to discharge or empty of (contents). **3.** (*tr.*) to yield up unwillingly. —**disˈgorgement** *n.*

disgrace (dɪsˈgreɪs) *n.* **1.** a condition of shame, loss of reputation, or dishonour. **2.** a shameful person or thing. **3.** exclusion from confidence or trust: *he is in disgrace with his father.* ~*vb.* (*tr.*) **4.** to bring shame upon. **5.** to treat or cause to be treated with disfavour.

disgraceful (dɪsˈgreɪsfʊl) *adj.* shameful; scandalous. —**disˈgracefully** *adv.*

disgruntle (dɪsˈgrʌntᵊl) *vb.* (*tr.*) to make sulky or discontented. [C17: DIS-[1] + obs. *gruntle* to complain] —**disˈgruntlement** *n.*

disguise (dɪsˈgaɪz) *vb.* **1.** to modify the appearance or manner in order to conceal the identity of (someone or something). **2.** (*tr.*) to misrepresent in order to obscure the actual nature or meaning. ~*n.* **3.** a mask, costume, or manner that disguises. **4.** a disguising or being disguised. [C14: < OF *desguisier,* < *des-* DIS-[1] + *guise* manner] —**disˈguised** *adj.*

disgust (dɪsˈgʌst) *vb.* (*tr.*) **1.** to sicken or fill with loathing. **2.** to offend the moral sense of. ~*n.* **3.** a great loathing or distaste. **4. in disgust.** as a result of disgust. [C16: < OF *desgouster,* < *des-* DIS-[1] + *gouster* to taste, < L *gustus* taste] —**disˈgustedly** *adv.* —**disˈgustedness** *n.*

dish (dɪʃ) *n.* **1.** a container used for holding or serving food, esp. an open shallow container. **2.** the food in a dish. **3.** a particular kind of food. **4.** Also called: **dishful.** the amount contained in a dish. **5.** something resembling a dish. **6.** a concavity. **7.** short for **dish aerial. 8.** *Inf.* an attractive person. ~*vb.* (*tr.*) **9.** to put into a dish. **10.** to make concave. **11.** *Brit. inf.* to ruin or spoil. ~See also **dish out, dish up.** [OE *disc,* < L *discus* quoit] —ˈ**dishˌlike** *adj.*

dishabille (ˌdɪsæˈbiːl) *or* **deshabille** *n.* the state of being partly or carelessly dressed. [C17: < F *déshabillé,* < *dés-* DIS-[1] + *habiller* to dress]

dish aerial *n.* a microwave aerial, used esp. in radar, radio telescopes, and satellite broadcasting, consisting of a parabolic reflector.

disharmony (dɪsˈhɑːmənɪ) *n., pl.* **-nies. 1.** lack of accord or harmony. **2.** a situation, circumstance, etc., that is inharmonious. —**disharmonious** (ˌdɪshɑːˈməʊnɪəs) *adj.*

dishcloth (ˈdɪʃˌklɒθ) *n.* a cloth or rag for washing or drying dishes.

dishearten (dɪsˈhɑːtᵊn) *vb.* (*tr.*) to weaken or destroy the hope, courage, enthusiasm, etc., of. —**disˈhearteningly** *adv.* —**disˈheartenment** *n.*

dished (dɪʃt) *adj.* **1.** shaped like a dish. **2.** (of wheels) closer to one another at the bottom than at the top. **3.** *Inf.* exhausted or defeated.

dishevel (dɪˈʃɛvᵊl) *vb.* **-elling, -elled** *or U.S.* **-eling, -eled.** to disarrange (the hair or clothes) of (someone). [C15: back formation < DISHEVELLED] —**diˈshevelment** *n.*

dishevelled *or U.S.* **-eled** (dɪˈʃɛvᵊld) *adj.* **1.** (esp. of hair) hanging loosely. **2.** unkempt; untidy. [C15 *dischevelee,* < OF *deschevelé,* < *des-* DIS-[1] + *chevel* hair, < L *capillus*]

dishonest (dɪsˈɒnɪst) *adj.* not honest or fair; deceiving or fraudulent. —**disˈhonestly** *adv.*

dishonesty (dɪsˈɒnɪstɪ) *n., pl.* **-ties. 1.** lack of honesty. **2.** a deceiving act or statement.

dishonour *or U.S.* **dishonor** (dɪsˈɒnə) *vb.* (*tr.*) **1.** to treat with disrespect. **2.** to fail or refuse to pay (a cheque, etc.). **3.** to cause the disgrace of (a woman) by seduction or rape. ~*n.* **4.** a lack of honour or respect. **5.** a state of shame or disgrace. **6.** a person or thing that causes a loss of honour. **7.** an insult; affront. **8.** refusal or failure to accept or pay a commercial paper.

dishonourable *or U.S.* **dishonorable** (dɪsˈɒnərəbᵊl) *adj.* **1.** characterized by or causing dishonour or discredit. **2.** having little or no integrity; unprincipled. —**disˈhonourableness** *or U.S.* **disˈhonorableness** *n.* —**disˈhonourably** *or U.S.* **disˈhonorably** *adv.*

dish out *vb.* **1.** (*tr., adv.*) *Inf.* to distribute. **2.** **dish it out.** to inflict punishment.

dishtowel (ˈdɪʃˌtaʊəl) *n.* another name (esp. U.S. and Canad.) for a **tea towel.**

dish up *vb.* (*adv.*) **1.** to serve (a meal, food, etc.). **2.** (*tr.*) *Inf.* to prepare or present, esp. in an attractive manner.

dishwasher (ˈdɪʃˌwɒʃə) *n.* **1.** a machine for washing dishes, etc. **2.** a person who washes dishes, etc.

dishwater (ˈdɪʃˌwɔːtə) *n.* **1.** water in which dishes have been washed. **2.** something resembling this.

dishy (ˈdɪʃɪ) *adj.* **dishier, dishiest.** *Inf., chiefly Brit.* good-looking or attractive.

disillusion (ˌdɪsɪˈluːʒən) *vb.* **1.** (*tr.*) to destroy the ideals, illusions, or false ideas of. ~*n. also* **disillusionment. 2.** the act of disillusioning or the state of being disillusioned.

disincentive (ˌdɪsɪnˈsɛntɪv) *n.* **1.** something that acts as a deterrent. ~*adj.* **2.** acting as a deterrent: *a disincentive effect on productivity.*

disincline (ˌdɪsɪnˈklaɪn) *vb.* to make or be unwilling, reluctant, or averse. —**disinclination** (ˌdɪsɪnklɪˈneɪʃən) *n.*

disinfect (ˌdɪsɪnˈfɛkt) *vb.* (*tr.*) to rid of microorganisms potentially harmful to man, esp. by chemical means. —ˌ**disinˈfection** *n.*

disinfectant (ˌdɪsɪnˈfɛktənt) *n.* an agent that destroys or inhibits the activity of microorganisms that cause disease.

disinfest (ˌdɪsɪnˈfɛst) *vb.* (*tr.*) to rid of vermin. —ˌ**disinfesˈtation** *n.*

disinflation (ˌdɪsɪnˈfleɪʃən) *n. Econ.* a reduction or stabilization of the general price level intended to improve the balance of payments without incurring reductions in output, employment, etc.

disinformation (ˌdɪsɪnfəˈmeɪʃən) *n.* false information intended to deceive or mislead.

disingenuous (ˌdɪsɪnˈdʒenjʊəs) *adj.* not sincere; lacking candour. —ˌ**disinˈgenuously** *adv.* —ˌ**disinˈgenuousness** *n.*

disinherit (ˌdɪsɪnˈhɛrɪt) *vb.* (*tr.*) **1.** *Law.* to deprive (an heir or next of kin) of inheritance or right to inherit. **2.** to deprive of a right or heritage. —ˌ**disinˈheritance** *n.*

disintegrate (dɪsˈɪntɪˌgreɪt) *vb.* **1.** to break or be broken into fragments or parts; shatter. **2.** to lose or cause to lose cohesion. **3.** (*intr.*) to lose judgment or control. **4.** *Physics.* **a.** to induce or undergo nuclear fission. **b.** another word for **decay** (sense 3). —**disˌinteˈgration** *n.* —**disˈinteˌgrator** *n.*

disinter (ˌdɪsɪnˈtɜː) *vb.* **-terring, -terred.** (*tr.*) **1.** to remove or dig up; exhume. **2.** to bring to light; expose. —ˌ**disinˈterment** *n.*

disinterest (dɪsˈɪntrɪst, -tərɪst) *n.* **1.** freedom from bias or involvement. **2.** lack of interest.

disinterested (dɪsˈɪntrɪstɪd, -tərɪs-) *adj.* free from bias or partiality; objective. —**disˈinterestedly** *adv.* —**disˈinterestedness** *n.*

▷ **Usage.** In spoken and sometimes written English, *disinterested* (impartial) is used where *uninterested* (showing or feeling lack of interest) is meant. Careful writers and speakers avoid this confusion: *a disinterested judge; he was uninterested in public reaction.*

disinvest (dɪsɪnˈvɛst) *vb. Econ.* **1.** (usually foll. by *in*) to remove investment (from). **2.** (*intr.*) to reduce the capital stock of an economy or enterprise, as by not replacing obsolete machinery. —ˌ**disinˈvestment** *n.*

disjoin (dɪsˈdʒɔɪn) *vb.* to disconnect or become disconnected; separate. —**disˈjoinable** *adj.*

disjoint (dɪsˈdʒɔɪnt) *vb.* **1.** to take apart or come apart at the joints. **2.** (*tr.*) to disunite or disjoin. **3.** to dislocate or become dislocated. **4.** (*tr.; usually passive*) to end the unity, sequence, or coherence of.

disjointed (dɪsˈdʒɔɪntɪd) *adj.* **1.** having no coherence; disconnected. **2.** separated at the joint. **3.** dislocated. —**disˈjointedly** *adv.*

disjunct (ˈdɪsdʒʌŋkt) *n. Logic.* one of the propositions in a disjunction.

disjunction (dɪsˈdʒʌŋkʃən) *n.* **1.** Also called: **disjuncture.** a disconnecting or being disconnected; separation. **2.** *Logic.* **a.** the operator that forms a compound sentence from two given sentences and corresponds to the English *or.* **b.** the relation between such sentences.

disjunctive (dɪsˈdʒʌŋktɪv) *adj.* **1.** serving to disconnect or separate. **2.** *Grammar.* denoting a word, esp. a conjunction, that serves to express opposition or contrast: *but* in *She was poor but she was honest.* **3.** *Logic.* relating to, characterized by, or containing disjunction. ~*n.* **4.** *Grammar.* a disjunctive word, esp. a conjunction. **5.** *Logic.* a disjunctive proposition. —**disˈjunctively** *adv.*

disk (dɪsk) *n.* **1.** a variant spelling (esp. U.S. and Canad.) of **disc. 2.** Also called: **disk pack, magnetic disk.** *Computers.* a direct-access storage device consisting of a stack of plates coated with a magnetic layer, the whole assembly rotating rapidly as a single unit.

disk drive *n. Computers.* the unit that controls the mechanism for handling a floppy disk.

disk pack *n. Computers.* another name for **disk** (sense 2).

dislike (dɪsˈlaɪk) *vb.* **1.** (*tr.*) to consider unpleasant or disagreeable. ~*n.* **2.** a feeling of aversion or antipathy. —**disˈlikable** *or* **disˈlikeable** *adj.*

dislocate (ˈdɪsləˌkeɪt) *vb.* (*tr.*) **1.** to disrupt or shift out of place. **2.** to displace from its normal position, esp. a bone from its joint.

dislocation (ˌdɪsləˈkeɪʃən) *n.* **1.** a displacing or being displaced. **2.** the state or condition of being dislocated.

dislodge (dɪsˈlɒdʒ) *vb.* to remove from or leave a lodging place, hiding place, or previously fixed position. —**disˈlodgment** *or* **disˈlodgement** *n.*

disloyal (dɪsˈlɔɪəl) *adj.* not loyal or faithful; deserting one's allegiance. —**disˈloyally** *adv.*

disloyalty (dɪsˈlɔɪəltɪ) *n., pl.* **-ties.** the condition or an instance of being unfaithful or disloyal.

dismal (ˈdɪzməl) *adj.* **1.** causing gloom or depression. **2.** causing dismay or terror. [C13: < *dismal* (n.) list of 24 unlucky days in the year, < Med. L *diēs malī,* < L *diēs* day + *malus* bad] —ˈ**dismally** *adv.* —ˈ**dismalness** *n.*

dismantle (dɪsˈmæntᵊl) *vb.* (*tr.*) **1.** to take apart. **2.** to demolish or raze. **3.** to strip of covering. [C17: < OF *desmanteler* to remove a cloak from] —**disˈmantlement** *n.*

dismast (dɪsˈmɑːst) *vb.* (*tr.*) to break off the mast or masts of (a sailing vessel).

dismay (dɪsˈmeɪ) *vb.* (*tr.*) **1.** to fill with apprehension or alarm. **2.** to fill with depression or discouragement. ~*n.* **3.** consternation or agitation. [C13: < OF *desmaiier* (unattested), < *des-* DIS-[1] + *esmayer* to frighten, ult. of Gmc origin] —**dis'maying** *adj.*

dismember (dɪs'mɛmbə) *vb.* (*tr.*) **1.** to remove the limbs or members of. **2.** to cut to pieces. **3.** to divide or partition (something, such as an empire). —**dis'memberment** *n.*

dismiss (dɪs'mɪs) *vb.* (*tr.*) **1.** to remove or discharge from employment or service. **2.** to send away or allow to go. **3.** to dispel from one's mind; discard. **4.** to cease to consider (a subject). **5.** to decline further hearing to (a claim or action). **6.** *Cricket.* to bowl out a side for a particular number of runs. [C15: < Med. L *dismissus* sent away, < *dīmittere,* < *dī-* DIS-[1] + *mittere* to send] —**dis'missal** *n.* —**dis'missible** *adj.* —**dis'missive** *adj.*

dismount (dɪs'maʊnt) *vb.* **1.** to get off a horse, bicycle, etc. **2.** (*tr.*) to disassemble or remove from a mounting. ~*n.* **3.** the act of dismounting.

disobedience (ˌdɪsə'biːdɪəns) *n.* lack of obedience.

disobedient (ˌdɪsə'biːdɪənt) *adj.* not obedient; neglecting or refusing to obey. —ˌ**diso'bediently** *adv.*

disobey (ˌdɪsə'beɪ) *vb.* to neglect or refuse to obey (someone, an order, etc.). —ˌ**diso'beyer** *n.*

disoblige (ˌdɪsə'blaɪdʒ) *vb.* (*tr.*) **1.** to disregard the desires of. **2.** to slight; insult. **3.** *Inf.* to cause trouble or inconvenience to. —ˌ**diso'bliging** *adj.*

disorder (dɪs'ɔːdə) *n.* **1.** a lack of order; confusion. **2.** a disturbance of public order. **3.** an upset of health; ailment. **4.** a deviation from the normal system or order. ~*vb.* (*tr.*) **5.** to upset the order of. **6.** to disturb the health or mind of.

disorderly (dɪs'ɔːdəlɪ) *adj.* **1.** untidy; irregular. **2.** uncontrolled; unruly. **3.** *Law.* violating public peace or order. —**dis'orderliness** *n.*

disorderly house *n. Law.* an establishment in which unruly behaviour habitually occurs, esp. a brothel or a gaming house.

disorganize *or* **-ise** (dɪs'ɔːgəˌnaɪz) *vb.* (*tr.*) to disrupt the arrangement, system, or unity of. —**disˌorgani'zation** *or* **-i'sation** *n.*

disorientate (dɪs'ɔːrɪɛnˌteɪt) *or* **disorient** *vb.* (*tr.*) **1.** to cause (someone) to lose his bearings. **2.** to perplex; confuse. —**disˌorien'tation** *n.*

disown (dɪs'əʊn) *vb.* (*tr.*) to deny any connection with; refuse to acknowledge. —**dis'owner** *n.*

disparage (dɪ'spærɪdʒ) *vb.* (*tr.*) **1.** to speak contemptuously of; belittle. **2.** to damage the reputation of. [C14: < OF *desparagier,* < *des-* DIS-[1] + *parage* equality, < L *par* equal] —**dis'paragement** *n.* —**dis'paraging** *adj.*

disparate ('dɪspərɪt) *adj.* **1.** utterly different or distinct in kind. ~*n.* **2.** (*pl.*) unlike things or people. [C16: < L *disparāre* to divide, < DIS-[1] + *parāre* to prepare; also infl. by L *dispar* unequal] —'**disparately** *adv.* —'**disparateness** *n.*

disparity (dɪ'spærɪtɪ) *n., pl.* **-ties.** **1.** inequality or difference, as in age, rank, wages, etc. **2.** dissimilarity.

dispassionate (dɪs'pæʃənɪt) *adj.* devoid of or uninfluenced by emotion or prejudice; objective; impartial. —**dis'passionately** *adv.*

dispatch *or* **despatch** (dɪ'spætʃ) *vb.* (*tr.*) **1.** to send off promptly, as to a destination or to perform a task. **2.** to discharge or complete (a duty, etc.) promptly. **3.** *Inf.* to eat up quickly. **4.** to murder or execute. ~*n.* **5.** the act of sending off a letter, messenger, etc. **6.** prompt action or speed (often in **with dispatch**). **7.** an official communication or report, sent in haste. **8.** a report sent to a newspaper, etc., by a correspondent. **9.** murder or execution. [C16: < It. *dispacciare,* < Provençal *despachar,* < OF *despeechier* to set free, < *des-* DIS-[1] + *-peechier,* ult. < L *pedica* a fetter] —**dis'patcher** *n.*

dispatch case *n.* a case used for carrying papers, documents, books, etc.

dispatch rider *n.* a horseman or motorcyclist who carries dispatches.

dispel (dɪ'spɛl) *vb.* **-pelling, -pelled.** (*tr.*) to disperse or drive away. [C17: < L *dispellere,* < DIS-[1] + *pellere* to drive] —**dis'peller** *n.*

dispensable (dɪ'spɛnsəbᵊl) *adj.* **1.** not essential; expendable. **2.** (of a law, vow, etc.) able to be relaxed. —**disˌpensa'bility** *n.*

dispensary (dɪ'spɛnsərɪ) *n., pl.* **-ries.** a place where medicine, etc., is dispensed.

dispensation (ˌdɪspɛn'seɪʃən) *n.* **1.** the act of distributing or dispensing. **2.** something distributed or dispensed. **3.** a system or plan of administering or dispensing. **4.** *Chiefly R.C. Church.* permission to dispense with an obligation of church law. **5.** any exemption from an obligation. **6. a.** the ordering of life and events by God. **b.** a religious system or code of prescriptions for life and conduct regarded as of divine origin. —ˌ**dispen'sational** *adj.*

dispensatory (dɪ'spɛnsətərɪ, -trɪ) *n., pl.* **-ries.** a book listing the composition, preparation, and application of various drugs.

dispense (dɪ'spɛns) *vb.* **1.** (*tr.*) to give out or distribute in portions. **2.** (*tr.*) to prepare and distribute (medicine), esp. on prescription. **3.** (*tr.*) to administer (the law, etc.). **4.** (*intr.;* foll. by *with*) to do away (with) or manage (without). **5.** to grant a dispensation to. **6.** to exempt or excuse from a rule or obligation. [C14: < Med. L *dispensāre* to pardon, < L *dispendere* to weigh out, < DIS-[1] + *pendere*]

dispenser (dɪ'spɛnsə) *n.* **1.** a device that automatically dispenses a single item or a measured quantity. **2.** a person or thing that dispenses.

dispensing optician *n.* See **optician.**

dispersal (dɪ'spɜːsᵊl) *n.* **1.** another word for **dispersion** (sense 1). **2.** the spread of animals, plants, or seeds to new areas.

dispersant (dɪs'pɜːsənt) *n.* a liquid or gas used to disperse small particles or droplets, as in an aerosol.

disperse (dɪ'spɜːs) *vb.* **1.** to scatter; distribute over a wide area. **2.** to dissipate. **3.** to leave or cause to leave a gathering. **4.** to separate or be separated by dispersion. **5.** (*tr.*) to spread (news, etc.). **6.** to separate (particles) throughout a solid, liquid, or gas. ~*adj.* **7.** of or consisting of the particles in a colloid or suspension: *disperse phase.* [C14: < L *dispĕrsus,* < *dispergere* to scatter widely, < DI-[2] + *spargere* to strew] —**dis'perser** *n.*

dispersion (dɪ'spɜːʃən) *n.* **1.** a dispersing or being dispersed. **2.** *Physics.* **a.** the separation of electromagnetic radiation into constituents of different wavelengths. **b.** a measure of the ability of a substance to separate by refraction. **3.** *Statistics.* the degree to which values of a frequency distribution are scattered around some central point, usually the arithmetic mean or median. **4.** *Chem.* a system containing particles dispersed in a solid, liquid, or gas.

dispirit (dɪ'spɪrɪt) *vb.* (*tr.*) to lower the spirit of; make downhearted; discourage. —**dis'pirited** *adj.* —**dis'piritedness** *n.* —**dis'piriting** *adj.*

displace (dɪs'pleɪs) *vb.* (*tr.*) **1.** to move from the usual or correct location. **2.** to remove from office or employment. **3.** to occupy the place of; replace; supplant.

displaced person *n.* a person forced from his or her home or country, esp. by war or revolution.

displacement (dɪs'pleɪsmənt) *n.* **1.** a displacing or being displaced. **2.** the weight or volume displaced by a body in a fluid. **3.** *Psychoanal.* the transferring of emotional feelings from their original object to one that disguises their real nature.

displacement activity *n. Psychol.* behaviour that occurs typically when there is a conflict of motives and that has no relevance to either motive: e.g. head scratching.

display (dɪ'spleɪ) *vb.* **1.** (*tr.*) to show or make visible. **2.** (*tr.*) to put out to be seen; exhibit. **3.** (*tr.*) to disclose; reveal. **4.** (*tr.*) to flaunt in an ostentatious way. **5.** (*tr.*) to spread out; unfold. **6.** (*tr.*) to give prominence to. **7.** (*intr.*) *Zool.* to engage in a display. ~*n.* **8.** an exhibiting or displaying; show. **9.** something exhibited or displayed. **10.** an ostentatious exhibition. **11.** an arrangement of certain typefaces to give prominence to headings, etc. **12.** *Electronics.* **a.** a device capable of representing information visually, as on a cathode-ray tube screen. **b.** the information so presented. **13.** *Zool.* a pattern of behaviour by which the animal attracts attention while it is courting the female, defending its territory, etc. **14.** (*modifier*) designating typefaces that give prominence to the words they are used to set. [C14: < Anglo-F *despleier* to unfold, < LL *displicāre* to scatter, < DIS-¹ + *plicāre* to fold] **—dis'player** *n.*

displease (dɪs'pliːz) *vb.* to annoy, offend, or cause displeasure to (someone). **—dis'pleasing** *adj.* **—dis'pleasingly** *adv.*

displeasure (dɪs'plɛʒə) *n.* **1.** the condition of being displeased. **2.** *Arch.* **a.** pain. **b.** an act or cause of offence.

disport (dɪ'spɔːt) *vb.* **1.** (*tr.*) to indulge (oneself) in pleasure. **2.** (*intr.*) to frolic or gambol. ~*n.* **3.** *Arch.* amusement. [C14: < Anglo-F *desporter*, < *des-* DIS-¹ + *porter* to carry]

disposable (dɪ'spəʊzəbᵊl) *adj.* **1.** designed for disposal after use: *disposable cups.* **2.** available for use if needed: *disposable assets.* ~*n.* **3.** something, such as a baby's nappy, that is designed for disposal. **—dis,posa'bility** *n.*

disposal (dɪ'spəʊzᵊl) *n.* **1.** the act or means of getting rid of something. **2.** arrangement in a particular order. **3.** a specific method of tending to matters, as in business. **4.** the act or process of transferring something to or providing something for another. **5.** the power or opportunity to make use of someone or something (esp. in **at one's disposal**).

dispose (dɪ'spəʊz) *vb.* **1.** (*intr.*; foll. by *of*) **a.** to deal with or settle. **b.** to give, sell, or transfer to another. **c.** to throw out or away. **d.** to consume, esp. hurriedly. **e.** to kill. **2.** to arrange or settle (matters). **3.** (*tr.*) to make willing or receptive. **4.** (*tr.*) to place in a certain order. **5.** (*tr.*; often foll. by *to*) to accustom or condition. [C14: < OF *disposer*, < L *dispōnere* to set in different places, < DIS-¹ + *pōnere* to place] **—dis'poser** *n.*

disposed (dɪ'spəʊzd) *adj.* **a.** having an inclination as specified (towards something). **b.** (*in combination*): *well-disposed.*

disposition (,dɪspə'zɪʃən) *n.* **1.** a person's usual temperament or frame of mind. **2.** a tendency, inclination, or habit. **3.** another word for **disposal** (senses 2–5). **4.** *Arch.* manner of placing or arranging.

dispossess (,dɪspə'zɛs) *vb.* (*tr.*) to take away possession of something, esp. property; expel. **—,dispos'session** *n.* **—,dispos'sessor** *n.*

dispraise (dɪs'preɪz) *vb.* **1.** (*tr.*) to express disapproval or condemnation of. ~*n.* **2.** the disapproval, etc., expressed. **—dis'praiser** *n.*

disproof (dɪs'pruːf) *n.* **1.** facts that disprove something. **2.** the act of disproving.

disproportion (,dɪsprə'pɔːʃən) *n.* **1.** lack of proportion or equality. **2.** an instance of disparity or inequality. ~*vb.* **3.** (*tr.*) to cause to become exaggerated or unequal. **—,dispro'portional** *adj.*

disproportionate (,dɪsprə'pɔːʃənɪt) *adj.* out of proportion; unequal. **—,dispro'portionately** *adv.* **—,dispro'portionateness** *n.*

disprove (dɪs'pruːv) *vb.* (*tr.*) to show (an assertion, claim, etc.) to be incorrect. **—dis'provable** *adj.* **—dis'proval** *n.*

disputable (dɪ'spjuːtəbᵊl, 'dɪspjʊtə-) *adj.* capable of being argued; debatable. **—dis,puta'bility** *or* **dis'putableness** *n.* **—dis'putably** *adv.*

disputant (dɪ'spjuːtᵊnt, 'dɪspjʊtənt) *n.* **1.** a person who argues; contestant. ~*adj.* **2.** engaged in argument.

disputation (,dɪspjʊ'teɪʃən) *n.* **1.** the act or an instance of arguing. **2.** a formal academic debate on a thesis. **3.** an obsolete word for **conversation.**

disputatious (,dɪspjʊ'teɪʃəs) *or* **disputative** (dɪ'spjuːtətɪv) *adj.* inclined to argument. **—,dispu'tatiousness** *or* **dis'putativeness** *n.*

dispute *vb.* (dɪ'spjuːt). **1.** to argue, debate, or quarrel about (something). **2.** (*tr.*; *may take a clause as object*) to doubt the validity, etc., of. **3.** (*tr.*) to seek to win; contest for. **4.** (*tr.*) to struggle against; resist. ~*n.* (dɪ'spjuːt, 'dɪspjuːt). **5.** an argument or quarrel. **6.** *Rare.* a fight. [C13: < LL *disputāre* to contend verbally, < L: to discuss, < DIS-¹ + *putāre* to think] **—dis'puter** *n.*

disqualify (dɪs'kwɒlɪ,faɪ) *vb.* **-fying, -fied.** (*tr.*) **1.** to make unfit or unqualified. **2.** to make ineligible, as for entry to an examination. **3.** to debar from a contest. **4.** to deprive of rights, powers, or privileges. **—dis,qualifi'cation** *n.*

disquiet (dɪs'kwaɪət) *n.* **1.** a feeling or condition of anxiety or uneasiness. ~*vb.* **2.** (*tr.*) to make anxious or upset. **—dis'quieting** *adj.*

disquietude (dɪs'kwaɪɪ,tjuːd) *n.* a feeling or state of anxiety or uneasiness.

disquisition (,dɪskwɪ'zɪʃən) *n.* a formal examination of a subject. [C17: < L *disquīsītiō*, < *disquīrere* to make an investigation, < DIS-¹ + *quaerere* to seek] **—,disqui'sitional** *adj.*

disregard (,dɪsrɪ'gɑːd) *vb.* (*tr.*) **1.** to give little or no attention to; ignore. **2.** to treat as unworthy of consideration or respect. ~*n.* **3.** lack of attention or respect. **—,disre'gardful** *adj.*

disremember (,dɪsrɪ'mɛmbə) *vb. Inf., chiefly U.S.* to fail to recall.

disrepair (,dɪsrɪ'pɛə) *n.* the condition of being worn out or in poor working order; a condition requiring repairs.

disreputable (dɪs'rɛpjʊtəbᵊl) *adj.* **1.** having or causing a lack of repute. **2.** disordered in appearance. **—dis'reputably** *adv.*

disrepute (,dɪsrɪ'pjuːt) *n.* a loss or lack of credit or repute.

disrespect (,dɪsrɪ'spɛkt) *n.* contempt; rudeness; lack of respect. **—,disre'spectful** *adj.*

disrobe (dɪs'rəʊb) *vb.* **1.** to undress. **2.** (*tr.*) to divest of authority, etc. **—dis'robement** *n.*

disrupt (dɪs'rʌpt) *vb.* **1.** (*tr.*) to throw into turmoil or disorder. **2.** (*tr.*) to interrupt the progress of. **3.** to break or split apart. [C17: < L *disruptus* burst asunder, < *dīrumpere* to dash to pieces, < DIS-¹ + *rumpere* to burst] **—dis'rupter** *or* **dis'ruptor** *n.* **—dis'ruption** *n.*

disruptive (dɪs'rʌptɪv) *adj.* involving, causing, or tending to cause disruption.

dissatisfy (dɪs'sætɪs,faɪ) *vb.* **-fying, -fied.** (*tr.*) to fail to satisfy; disappoint. **—,dissatis'faction** *n.* **—,dissatis'factory** *adj.*

dissect (dɪ'sɛkt, daɪ-) *vb.* **1.** to cut open and examine the structure of (a dead animal or plant). **2.** (*tr.*) to examine critically and minutely. [C17: < L *dissecāre*, < DIS-¹ + *secāre* to cut] **—dis'section** *n.* **—dis'sector** *n.*

dissected (dɪ'sɛktɪd, daɪ-) *adj.* **1.** *Bot.* in the form of narrow lobes or segments. **2.** *Geol.* cut by erosion into hills and valleys.

disselboom ('dɪsᵊl,buːm) *n. S. African.* the single shaft of a wagon, esp. an ox wagon. [< Du. *dissel* shaft + *boom* beam]

dissemble (dɪ'sɛmbᵊl) *vb.* **1.** to conceal (one's real motives, emotions, etc.) by pretence. **2.** (*tr.*) to pretend; simulate. [C15: < earlier *dissimulen*, < L *dissimulāre*; prob. infl. by obs. *semble* to resemble] **—dis'semblance** *n.* **—dis'sembler** *n.*

disseminate (dɪ'sɛmɪ,neɪt) *vb.* (*tr.*) to distribute or scatter about; diffuse. [C17: < L *dissēmināre*, < DIS-¹ + *sēmināre* to sow, < *sēmen* seed] **—dis,semi'nation** *n.* **—dis'semi,nator** *n.*

disseminated sclerosis *n.* another name for **multiple sclerosis.**

dissension (dɪ'sɛnʃən) *n.* disagreement, esp. when leading to a quarrel. [C13: < L *dissēnsiō*, < *dissentīre* to DISSENT]

dissent (dɪ'sɛnt) *vb.* (*intr.*) **1.** to have a disagreement or withhold assent. **2.** *Christianity.* to reject the doctrines, beliefs, or practices of an established church, and to adhere to a different system of beliefs. ~*n.* **3.** a difference of opinion. **4.** *Christianity.* separation from an established church; Nonconformism. **5.** the voicing of a minority opinion in the decision on a case at law. [C16: < L *dissentīre* to disagree, < DIS-¹ + *sentīre* to feel] **—dis'senter** *n.* **—dis'senting** *adj.*

Dissenter (dɪˈsɛntə) *n. Christianity, chiefly Brit.* a Nonconformist or a person who refuses to conform to the established church.

dissentient (dɪˈsɛnʃənt) *adj.* **1.** dissenting, esp. from the opinion of the majority. ~*n.* **2.** a dissenter. —**disˈsentience** *or* **disˈsentiency** *n.*

dissertation (ˌdɪsəˈteɪʃən) *n.* **1.** a written thesis, often based on original research, usually required for a higher degree. **2.** a formal discourse. [C17: < L *dissertāre* to debate, < *disserere* to examine, < DIS-¹ + *serere* to arrange] —ˌ**disserˈtational** *adj.*

disserve (dɪsˈsɜːv) *vb.* (*tr.*) *Arch.* to do a disservice to.

disservice (dɪsˈsɜːvɪs) *n.* an ill turn; wrong; injury, esp. when trying to help.

dissever (dɪˈsɛvə) *vb.* **1.** to break off or become broken off. **2.** (*tr.*) to divide up into parts. [C13: < OF *dessevrer,* < LL DIS-¹ + *sēparāre* to SEPARATE] —**disˈseverance** *or* **disˈseverment** *n.*

dissident (ˈdɪsɪdənt) *adj.* **1.** disagreeing; dissenting. ~*n.* **2.** a person who disagrees, esp. one who disagrees with the government. [C16: < L *dissidēre* to be remote from, < DIS-¹ + *sedēre* to sit] —ˈ**dissidence** *n.* —ˈ**dissidently** *adv.*

dissimilar (dɪˈsɪmɪlə) *adj.* not alike; not similar; different. —**disˈsimilarly** *adv.* —ˌ**dissimiˈlarity** *n.*

dissimilate (dɪˈsɪmɪˌleɪt) *vb.* **1.** to make or become dissimilar. **2.** (usually foll. by *to*) *Phonetics.* to change or displace (a consonant) or (of a consonant) to be changed to or displaced by (another consonant) so that its manner of articulation becomes less similar to a speech sound in the same word. Thus (r) in the final syllable of French *marbre* is dissimilated to (l) in its English form *marble.* [C19: < DIS-¹ + ASSIMILATE]

dissimilation (ˌdɪsɪmɪˈleɪʃən) *n.* **1.** the act or an instance of making dissimilar. **2.** *Phonetics.* the alteration or omission of a consonant as a result of being dissimilated.

dissimilitude (ˌdɪsɪˈmɪlɪˌtjuːd) *n.* **1.** dissimilarity; difference. **2.** a point of difference.

dissimulate (dɪˈsɪmjʊˌleɪt) *vb.* to conceal (one's real feelings) by pretence. —**disˌsimuˈlation** *n.* —**disˈsimuˌlator** *n.*

dissipate (ˈdɪsɪˌpeɪt) *vb.* **1.** to exhaust or be exhausted by dispersion. **2.** (*tr.*) to scatter or break up. **3.** (*intr.*) to indulge in the pursuit of pleasure. [C15: < L *dissipāre* to disperse, < DIS-¹ + *supāre* to throw] —ˈ**dissiˌpater** *or* ˈ**dissiˌpator** *n.* —ˈ**dissiˌpative** *adj.*

dissipated (ˈdɪsɪˌpeɪtɪd) *adj.* **1.** indulging without restraint in the pursuit of pleasure; debauched. **2.** wasted, scattered, or exhausted.

dissipation (ˌdɪsɪˈpeɪʃən) *n.* **1.** a dissipating or being dissipated. **2.** unrestrained indulgence in physical pleasures. **3.** excessive expenditure; wastefulness.

dissociate (dɪˈsəʊʃɪˌeɪt, -sɪ-) *vb.* **1.** to break or cause to break the association between (people, organizations, etc.). **2.** (*tr.*) to regard or treat as separate or unconnected. **3.** to undergo or subject to dissociation. —**disˈsociative** *adj.*

▷ **Usage.** See at **disassociate.**

dissociation (dɪˌsəʊsɪˈeɪʃən, -ʃɪ-) *n.* **1.** a dissociating or being dissociated. **2.** *Chem.* the decomposition of the molecules of a single compound into two or more other compounds, atoms, ions, or radicals. **3.** *Psychiatry.* the separation of a group of mental processes or ideas from the rest of the personality, so that they lead an independent existence, as in cases of multiple personality.

dissoluble (dɪˈsɒljʊbᵊl) *adj.* a less common word for **soluble.** [C16: < L *dissolūbilis,* < *dissolvere* to DISSOLVE] —**disˌsoluˈbility** *n.*

dissolute (ˈdɪsəˌluːt) *adj.* given to dissipation; debauched. [C14: < L *dissolūtus* loose, < *dissolvere* to DISSOLVE] —ˈ**dissoˌlutely** *adv.* —ˈ**dissoˌluteness** *n.*

dissolution (ˌdɪsəˈluːʃən) *n.* **1.** separation into component parts; disintegration. **2.** destruction by breaking up and dispersing. **3.** the termination of a meeting or assembly, such as Parliament. **4.** the termination of a formal or legal relationship, such as a business, marriage, etc. **5.** the act or process of dissolving.

dissolve (dɪˈzɒlv) *vb.* **1.** to go or cause to go into solution. **2.** to become or cause to become liquid; melt. **3.** to disintegrate or disperse. **4.** to come or bring to an end. **5.** to dismiss (a meeting, Parliament, etc.) or (of a meeting, etc.) to be dismissed. **6.** to collapse or cause to collapse emotionally: *to dissolve into tears.* **7.** to lose or cause to lose distinctness. **8.** (*tr.*) to terminate legally, as a marriage, etc. **9.** (*intr.*) *Films, television.* to fade out one scene and replace with another to make two scenes merge imperceptibly or slowly overlap. ~*n.* **10.** *Films, television.* a scene filmed or televised by dissolving. [C14: < L *dissolvere* to make loose, < DIS-¹ + *solvere* to release] —**disˈsolvable** *adj.*

dissonance (ˈdɪsənəns) *or* **dissonancy** *n.* **1.** a discordant combination of sounds. **2.** lack of agreement or consistency. **3.** *Music.* **a.** a sensation of harshness and incompleteness associated with certain intervals and chords. **b.** an interval or chord of this kind.

dissonant (ˈdɪsənənt) *adj.* **1.** discordant. **2.** incongruous or discrepant. **3.** *Music.* characterized by dissonance. [C15: < L *dissonāre* to be discordant, < DIS-¹ + *sonāre* to sound]

dissuade (dɪˈsweɪd) *vb.* (*tr.*) **1.** (often foll. by *from*) to deter (someone) by persuasion from a course of action, policy, etc. **2.** to advise against (an action, etc.). [C15: < L *dissuādēre,* < DIS-¹ + *suādēre* to persuade] —**disˈsuader** *n.* —**disˈsuasion** *n.* —**disˈsuasive** *adj.*

dissyllable (dɪˈsɪləbᵊl) *or* **disyllable** *n.* a word of two syllables. —**dissyllabic** (ˌdɪsɪˈlæbɪk) *or* **disyllabic** (ˌdaɪsɪˈlæbɪk) *adj.*

dissymmetry (dɪˈsɪmɪtrɪ, dɪsˈsɪm-) *n., pl.* **-tries.** **1.** lack of symmetry. **2.** the relationship between two objects when one is the mirror image of the other. —**dissymmetric** (ˌdɪsɪˈmɛtrɪk, ˌdɪssɪ-) *or* ˌ**dissymˈmetrical** *adj.*

dist. *abbrev. for:* **1.** distant. **2.** distinguish(ed). **3.** district.

distaff (ˈdɪstɑːf) *n.* **1.** the rod on which wool, flax, etc., is wound preparatory to spinning. **2.** *Figurative.* women's work. [OE *distæf,* < *dis-* bunch of flax + *stæf* STAFF¹]

distaff side *n.* the female side of a family.

distal (ˈdɪstᵊl) *adj. Anat.* situated farthest from the centre or point of attachment or origin. [C19: < DISTANT + -AL¹] —ˈ**distally** *adv.*

distance (ˈdɪstəns) *n.* **1.** the space between two points. **2.** the length of this gap. **3.** the state of being apart in space; remoteness. **4.** an interval between two points in time. **5.** the extent of progress. **6.** a distant place or time. **7.** a separation or remoteness in relationship. **8.** (preceded by *the*) the most distant or a faraway part of the visible scene. **9.** *Horse racing.* **a.** *Brit.* a point on a racecourse 240 yards from the winning post. **b.** *U.S.* the part of a racecourse that a horse must reach before the winner passes the finishing line in order to qualify for later heats. **10. go the distance. a.** *Boxing.* to complete a bout without being knocked out. **b.** to be able to complete an assigned task or responsibility. **11. keep one's distance.** to maintain a reserve in respect of another person. **12. middle distance.** halfway between the foreground or the observer and the horizon. ~*vb.* (*tr.*) **13.** to hold or place at a distance. **14.** to separate (oneself) mentally from something. **15.** to outdo; outstrip.

distant (ˈdɪstənt) *adj.* **1.** far apart in space or time. **2.** (*postpositive*) separated in space or time by a specified distance. **3.** apart in relationship: a *distant cousin.* **4.** coming from or going to a faraway place. **5.** remote in manner; aloof. **6.** abstracted; absent: *a distant look.* [C14: < L *distāre* to be distant, < DIS-¹ + *stāre* to stand] —ˈ**distantly** *adv.* —ˈ**distantness** *n.*

distaste (dɪsˈteɪst) *n.* (often foll. by *for*) a dislike (of); aversion (to).

distasteful (dɪsˈteɪstfʊl) *adj.* unpleasant or offensive. **—disˈtastefulness** *n.*

distemper[1] (dɪsˈtɛmpə) *n.* **1.** any of various infectious diseases of animals, esp. **canine distemper,** a highly contagious viral disease of dogs. **2.** *Arch.* **a.** a disorder. **b.** disturbance. **c.** discontent. [C14: < LL *distemperāre* to derange the health of, < L DIS-[1] + *temperāre* to mix in correct proportions]

distemper[2] (dɪsˈtɛmpə) *n.* **1.** a technique of painting in which the pigments are mixed with water, glue, size, etc.: used for poster, mural, and scene painting. **2.** the paint used in this technique or any of various water-based paints. ~*vb.* **3.** to paint (something) with distemper. [C14: < Med. L *distemperāre* to soak, < L DIS-[1] + *temperāre* to mingle]

distend (dɪˈstɛnd) *vb.* **1.** to expand by or as if by pressure from within; swell; inflate. **2.** (*tr.*) to stretch out or extend. [C14: < L *distendere,* < DIS-[1] + *tendere* to stretch] **—disˈtensible** *adj.* **—disˈtension** *or* **disˈtention** *n.*

distich (ˈdɪstɪk) *n. Prosody.* a unit of two verse lines, usually a couplet. [C16: < Gk *distikhos* having two lines, < DI-[1] + *stikhos* row, line]

distil *or U.S.* **distill** (dɪsˈtɪl) *vb.* **-tilling, -tilled. 1.** to subject to or undergo distillation. **2.** (sometimes foll. by *out* or *off*) to purify, separate, or concentrate, or be purified, separated, or concentrated by distillation. **3.** to obtain or be obtained by distillation. **4.** to exude or give off (a substance) in drops. **5.** (*tr.*) to extract the essence of. [C14: < L *dēstillāre* to distil, < DE- + *stillāre* to drip]

distillate (ˈdɪstɪlɪt) *n.* **1.** the product of distillation. **2.** a concentrated essence.

distillation (ˌdɪstɪˈleɪʃən) *n.* **1.** a distilling. **2.** the process of evaporating or boiling a liquid and condensing its vapour. **3.** purification or separation of mixtures by using different evaporation rates or boiling points of their components. **4.** the process of obtaining the essence or an extract of a substance, usually by heating it in a solvent. **5.** a distillate. **6.** a concentrated essence. **—disˈtillatory** *adj.*

distiller (dɪˈstɪlə) *n.* a person or organization that distils, esp. a company that makes spirits.

distillery (dɪˈstɪlərɪ) *n., pl.* **-eries.** a place where alcoholic drinks, etc., are made by distillation.

distinct (dɪˈstɪŋkt) *adj.* **1.** easily sensed or understood; clear. **2.** (when postpositive, foll. by *from*) not the same (as); separate (from). **3.** not alike; different. **4.** sharp; clear. **5.** recognizable; definite. **6.** explicit; unequivocal. [C14: < L *distinctus,* < *distinguere* to DISTINGUISH] **—disˈtinctly** *adv.* **—disˈtinctness** *n.*

distinction (dɪˈstɪŋkʃən) *n.* **1.** the act or an instance of distinguishing or differentiating. **2.** a distinguishing feature. **3.** the state of being different or distinguishable. **4.** special honour, recognition, or fame. **5.** excellence of character; distinctive qualities. **6.** distinguished appearance. **7.** a symbol of honour or rank.

distinctive (dɪˈstɪŋktɪv) *adj.* serving or tending to distinguish; characteristic. **—disˈtinctively** *adv.* **—disˈtinctiveness** *n.*

distingué *French.* (distɛ̃ge) *adj.* distinguished or noble.

distinguish (dɪˈstɪŋgwɪʃ) *vb.* (*mainly tr.*) **1.** (when *intr.,* foll. by *between* or *among*) to make, show, or recognize a difference (between or among); differentiate (between). **2.** to be a distinctive feature of; characterize. **3.** to make out; perceive. **4.** to mark for a special honour. **5.** to make (oneself) noteworthy. **6.** to classify. [C16: < L *distinguere* to separate] **—disˈtinguishable** *adj.* **—disˈtinguishing** *adj.*

distinguished (dɪˈstɪŋgwɪʃt) *adj.* **1.** noble or dignified in appearance or behaviour. **2.** eminent; famous; celebrated.

distort (dɪˈstɔːt) *vb.* (*tr.*) **1.** (*often passive*) to twist or pull out of shape; contort; deform. **2.** to alter or misrepresent (facts, etc.). **3.** *Electronics.* to reproduce or amplify (a signal) inaccurately. [C16: < L *distortus,* < *distorquēre* to turn different ways, < DIS-[1] + *torquēre* to twist] **—disˈtorted** *adj.*

distortion (dɪˈstɔːʃən) *n.* **1.** a distorting or being distorted. **2.** something that is distorted. **3.** *Electronics.* an undesired change in the shape of an electrical wave or signal resulting in a loss of clarity in radio reception or sound reproduction. **—disˈtortional** *adj.*

distr. *abbrev. for:* **1.** distribution. **2.** distributor.

distract (dɪˈstrækt) *vb.* (*tr.*) **1.** (*often passive*) to draw the attention of (a person) away from something. **2.** to divide or confuse the attention of (a person). **3.** to amuse or entertain. **4.** to trouble greatly. **5.** to make mad. [C14: < L *distractus* perplexed, < *distrahere* to pull in different directions, < DIS-[1] + *trahere* to drag]

distracted (dɪˈstræktɪd) *adj.* **1.** bewildered; confused. **2.** mad. **—disˈtractedly** *adv.*

distraction (dɪˈstrækʃən) *n.* **1.** a distracting or being distracted. **2.** something that serves as a diversion or entertainment. **3.** an interruption; obstacle to concentration. **4.** mental turmoil or madness.

distrain (dɪˈstreɪn) *vb. Law.* to seize (personal property) as security or indemnity for a debt. [C13: < OF *destreindre,* < L *distringere* to impede, < DIS-[1] + *stringere* to draw tight] **—disˈtrainment** *n.* **—disˈtrainor** *or* **disˈtrainer** *n.*

distraint (dɪˈstreɪnt) *n. Law.* the act or process of distraining; distress.

distrait (dɪˈstreɪ; *French* distrɛ) *adj.* absent-minded; abstracted. [C18: < F, < *distraire* to DISTRACT]

distraught (dɪˈstrɔːt) *adj.* **1.** distracted or agitated. **2.** *Rare.* mad. [C14: changed from obs. *distract* through influence of obs. *straught,* p.p. of STRETCH]

distress (dɪˈstrɛs) *vb.* (*tr.*) **1.** to cause mental pain to; upset badly. **2.** (*usually passive*) to subject to financial or other trouble. **3.** to treat (something, esp. furniture) in order to make it appear older than it is. **4.** *Law.* a less common word for **distrain.** ~*n.* **5.** mental pain; anguish. **6.** a distressing or being distressed. **7.** physical or financial trouble. **8. in distress.** (of a ship, etc.) in dire need of help. **9.** *Law.* **a.** the seizure of property as security for or in satisfaction of a debt, claim, etc.; distraint. **b.** the property thus seized. **c.** (*as modifier*) *U.S.: distress merchandise.* [C13: < OF *destresse,* via Vulgar L, < L *districtus* divided in mind] **—disˈtressful** *adj.* **—disˈtressing** *adj.* **—disˈtressingly** *adv.*

distressed (dɪˈstrɛst) *adj.* **1.** much troubled; upset; afflicted. **2.** in financial straits; poor. **3.** (of furniture, fabric, etc.) having signs of ageing artificially applied. **4.** *Econ.* another word for **depressed.**

distress signal *n.* a signal by radio, Very light, etc., from a ship in need of immediate assistance.

distribute (dɪˈstrɪbjuːt) *vb.* (*tr.*) **1.** to give out in shares; dispense. **2.** to hand out or deliver. **3.** (*often passive*) to spread throughout an area. **4.** (*often passive*) to divide into classes or categories. **5.** *Printing.* to return (used type) to the correct positions in the typecase. **6.** *Logic.* to incorporate in a distributed term of a categorical proposition. [C15: < L *distribuere,* < DIS-[1] + *tribuere* to give] **—disˈtributable** *adj.*

distributed term *n. Logic.* a term referring to every member of the class it designates, as *men* in *all men are mortal.*

distribution (ˌdɪstrɪˈbjuːʃən) *n.* **1.** the act of distributing or the state or manner of being distributed. **2.** a thing or portion distributed. **3.** arrangement or location. **4.** the process of physically satisfying the demand for goods and services. **5.** *Econ.* the division of the total income of a community among its members. **6.** *Statistics.* the set of possible values of a random variable, considered in terms of theoretical or observed frequency. **7.** *Law.* the apportioning of the estate of a deceased intestate. **—ˌdistriˈbutional** *adj.*

distributive (dɪˈstrɪbjʊtɪv) *adj.* **1.** characterized by or relating to distribution. **2.** *Grammar.*

referring separately to the individual people or items in a group, as the words *each* and *every*. **3.** *Maths, logic.* obeying the distributive law for a specified pair of operators, enabling one to be validly distributed over the other. See **distribute** (sense 6). *~n.* **4.** *Grammar.* a distributive word. —**dis'tributively** *adv.* —**dis'tributiveness** *n.*

distributor (dɪ'strɪbjʊtə) *n.* **1.** a person or thing that distributes. **2.** a wholesaler or middleman engaged in the distribution of a category of goods, esp. to retailers in a specific area. **3.** the device in a petrol engine that distributes the high-tension voltage to the sparking plugs.

district ('dɪstrɪkt) *n.* **1. a.** an area of land marked off for administrative or other purposes. **b.** (*as modifier*): *district nurse.* **2.** a locality separated by geographical attributes; region. **3.** any subdivision of a territory, region, etc. **4.** a political subdivision of a county, region, etc., that elects a council responsible for certain local services. *~vb.* **5.** (*tr.*) to divide into districts. [C17: < Med. L *districtus* area of jurisdiction, < L *distringere* to stretch out]

district attorney *n.* (in the U.S.) the state prosecuting officer in a specified judicial district.

District Court *n.* **1.** (in Scotland) a court of summary jurisdiction which deals with minor criminal offences. **2.** (in the U.S.) **a.** a Federal trial court in each U.S. district. **b.** in some states, a court of general jurisdiction. **3.** (in New Zealand) a court lower than a High Court. Formerly called: **magistrates' court.**

district high school *n.* (in New Zealand) a school in a rural area providing both primary and secondary education.

district nurse *n.* (in Britain) a nurse appointed to attend patients within a particular district, usually in the patients' homes.

distrust (dɪs'trʌst) *vb.* **1.** to regard as untrustworthy or dishonest. *~n.* **2.** suspicion; doubt. —**dis'truster** *n.* —**dis'trustful** *adj.*

disturb (dɪ'stɜːb) *vb.* (*tr.*) **1.** to intrude on; interrupt. **2.** to destroy the quietness or peace of. **3.** to disarrange; muddle. **4.** (*often passive*) to upset; trouble. **5.** to inconvenience; put out. [C13: < L *disturbāre,* < DIS-[1] + *turbāre* to confuse] —**dis'turber** *n.* —**dis'turbing** *adj.* —**dis'turbingly** *adv.*

disturbance (dɪ'stɜːbəns) *n.* **1.** a disturbing or being disturbed. **2.** an interruption or intrusion. **3.** an unruly outburst or tumult. **4.** *Law.* an interference with another's rights. **5.** *Geol.* a minor movement of the earth causing a small earthquake. **6.** *Meteorol.* a small depression. **7.** *Psychiatry.* a mental or emotional disorder.

disturbed (dɪ'stɜːbd) *adj. Psychiatry.* emotionally upset, troubled, or maladjusted.

disulphide (daɪ'sʌlfaɪd) *n.* any chemical compound containing two sulphur atoms per molecule.

disunite (ˌdɪsjʊ'naɪt) *vb.* **1.** to separate; disrupt. **2.** (*tr.*) to set at variance; estrange. —**dis'union** *n.* —**dis'unity** *n.*

disuse (dɪs'juːs) *n.* the condition of being unused; neglect (often in **in** *or* **into disuse**).

disyllable ('daɪˌsɪləbᵊl) *n.* a variant of **dissyllable.**

ditch (dɪtʃ) *n.* **1.** a narrow channel dug in the earth, usually used for drainage, irrigation, or as a boundary marker. *~vb.* **2.** to make a ditch in. **3.** (*intr.*) to edge with a ditch. **4.** *Sl.* to crash, esp. deliberately, as to avoid more unpleasant circumstances: *he had to ditch the car.* **5.** (*tr.*) *Sl.* to abandon. **6.** *Sl.* to land (an aircraft) on water in an emergency. **7.** (*tr.*) *U.S. sl.* to evade. [OE *dīc*] —'**ditcher** *n.*

ditchwater ('dɪtʃˌwɔːtə) *n.* **1.** stagnant water, esp. found in ditches. **2. as dull as ditchwater.** very dull; very uninteresting.

dither ('dɪðə) *vb.* (*intr.*) **1.** *Chiefly Brit.* to be uncertain or indecisive. **2.** *Chiefly U.S.* to be in an agitated state. **3.** to tremble, as with cold. *~n.* **4.** *Chiefly Brit.* a state of indecision. **5.** a state of agitation. [C17: var. of C14 (N English dialect) *didder,* <?] —'**ditherer** *n.* —'**dithery** *adj.*

dithyramb ('dɪθɪˌræm, -ˌræmb) *n.* **1.** (in ancient Greece) a passionate choral hymn in honour of Dionysus. **2.** any utterance or a piece of writing that resembles this. [C17: < L *dīthyrambus,* < Gk *dithurambos*] —ˌ**dithy'rambic** *adj.*

dittany ('dɪtənɪ) *n., pl.* **-nies.** **1.** an aromatic Cretan plant with pink flowers: formerly credited with medicinal properties. **2.** a North American plant with purplish flowers. [C14: < OF *ditan,* < L *dictamnus,* < Gk *diktamnon,* ? < *Diktē,* mountain in Crete]

ditto ('dɪtəʊ) *n., pl.* **-tos.** **1.** the aforementioned; the above; the same. Used in accounts, lists, etc., to avoid repetition, and symbolized by two small marks („) known as **ditto marks,** placed under the thing repeated. **2.** *Inf.* a duplicate. *~adv.* **3.** in the same way. *~sentence substitute.* **4.** *Inf.* used to avoid repeating or to confirm agreement with an immediately preceding sentence. *~vb.* **-toing, -toed.** **5.** (*tr.*) to copy; repeat. [C17: < It. (dialect): var. of *detto* said, < *dicere* to say, < L]

ditty ('dɪtɪ) *n., pl.* **-ties.** a short simple song or poem. [C13: < OF *ditie* poem, < *ditier* to compose, < L *dictāre* to DICTATE]

ditty bag *or* **box** *n.* a sailor's bag or box for personal belongings or tools. [C19: ? < obs. *dutty* calico, < Hindi *dhōtī* loincloth]

diuretic (ˌdaɪjʊ'rɛtɪk) *adj.* **1.** acting to increase the flow of urine. *~n.* **2.** a drug or agent that increases the flow of urine. [ME, < LL, < Gk, < *dia-* through + *ourein* to urinate] —**diuresis** (ˌdaɪjʊ'riːsɪs) *n.*

diurnal (daɪ'ɜːnᵊl) *adj.* **1.** happening during the day or daily. **2.** (of flowers) open during the day and closed at night. **3.** (of animals) active during the day. ~Cf. **nocturnal.** [C15: < LL *diurnālis,* < L *diurnus,* < *diēs* day] —**di'urnally** *adv.*

div. *abbrev. for:* **1.** divide(d). **2.** dividend. **3.** division. **4.** divorce(d).

diva ('diːvə) *n., pl.* **-vas** *or* **-ve** (-vɪ). a highly distinguished female singer; prima donna. [C19: via It. < L: a goddess, < *dīvus* DIVINE]

divagate ('daɪvəˌgeɪt) *vb.* (*intr.*) *Rare.* to digress or wander. [C16: < L DI-[2] + *vagārī* to wander] —ˌ**diva'gation** *n.*

divalent (daɪ'veɪlənt, 'daɪˌveɪ-) *adj. Chem.* **1.** having a valency of two. **2.** having two valencies. ~Also: **bivalent.** —**di'valency** *n.*

divan (dɪ'væn) *n.* **1. a.** a backless sofa or couch. **b.** a bed resembling such a couch. **2.** (esp. formerly) a smoking room. **3. a.** a Muslim law court, council chamber, or counting house. **b.** a Muslim council of state. [C16: < Turkish *dīvān,* < Persian *dīwān*]

dive (daɪv) *vb.* **diving, dived** *or U.S.* **dove** (dəʊv), **dived.** (*mainly intr.*) **1.** to plunge headfirst into water. **2.** (of a submarine, etc.) to submerge under water. **3.** (*also tr.*) to fly in a steep nose-down descending path. **4.** to rush, go, or reach quickly, as in a headlong plunge: *he dived for the ball.* **5.** (*also tr.;* foll. by *in* or *into*) to dip or put (one's hand) quickly or forcefully (into). **6.** (usually foll. by *in* or *into*) to involve oneself (in something), as in eating food. *~n.* **7.** a headlong plunge into water. **8.** an act or instance of diving. **9.** a steep nose-down descent of an aircraft. **10.** *Sl.* a disreputable bar or club. **11.** *Boxing sl.* the act of a boxer pretending to be knocked down or out. [OE *dӯfan*]

dive bomber *n.* a military aircraft designed to release its bombs on a target during a steep dive. —'**dive-bomb** *vb.* (*tr.*)

diver ('daɪvə) *n.* **1.** a person or thing that dives. **2.** a person who works or explores underwater. **3.** any of various aquatic birds of northern oceans: noted for skill in diving. U.S. and Canad. name: **loon. 4.** any of various other diving birds.

diverge (daɪ'vɜːdʒ) *vb.* **1.** to separate or cause to separate and go in different directions from a point. **2.** (*intr.*) to be at variance; differ. **3.** (*intr.*) to deviate from a prescribed course. **4.** (*intr.*) *Maths.* (of a series) to have no limit. [C17: < Med. L *dīvergere,* < L DI-[2] + *vergere* to turn]

divergence (daɪ'vɜːdʒəns) *or* **divergency** *n.* **1.** the act or result of diverging or the amount by which something diverges. **2.** the condition of being divergent.

divergent (daɪˈvɜːdʒənt) *adj.* **1.** diverging or causing divergence. **2.** *Maths.* (of a series) having no limit. —**diˈvergently** *adv.*

divergent thinking *n. Psychol.* thinking in an unusual and unstereotyped way, for instance to generate several possible solutions to a problem.

divers (ˈdaɪvəz) *determiner. Arch. or literary.* various; sundry; some. [C13: < OF, < L *dīversus* turned in different directions]

▷ **Usage.** In spite of the frequency with which *divers* (several) and *diverse* (disparate, set apart by marked differences) are treated as synonyms, and although they were originally the same word, careful writers and speakers always distinguish between these two words: *there were divers persons in the room; the personalities of those present were extremely diverse.*

diverse (daɪˈvɜːs, ˈdaɪvɜːs) *adj.* **1.** having variety; assorted. **2.** distinct in kind. [C13: < L *dīversus;* see DIVERS] —**diˈversely** *adv.*

diversify (daɪˈvɜːsɪˌfaɪ) *vb.* **-fying, -fied. 1.** (*tr.*) to create different forms of; variegate; vary. **2.** (of an enterprise) to vary (products, operations, etc.) in order to spread risk, expand, etc. **3.** to distribute (investments) among several securities in order to spread risk. [C15: < OF *diversifier,* < Med. L *dīversificāre,* < L *dīversus* DIVERSE + *facere* to make] —**diˌversifiˈcation** *n.*

diversion (daɪˈvɜːʃən) *n.* **1.** the act of diverting from a specified course. **2.** *Chiefly Brit.* an official detour used by traffic when a main route is closed. **3.** something that distracts from business, etc.; amusement. **4.** *Mil.* a feint attack designed to draw an enemy away from the main attack. —**diˈversional** *or* **diˈversionary** *adj.*

diversity (daɪˈvɜːsɪtɪ) *n.* **1.** the state or quality of being different or varied. **2.** a point of difference.

divert (daɪˈvɜːt) *vb.* **1.** to turn aside; deflect. **2.** (*tr.*) to entertain; amuse. **3.** (*tr.*) to distract the attention of. [C15: < F *divertir,* < L *dīvertere* to turn aside, < DI-[2] + *vertere* to turn] —**diˈverting** *adj.* —**diˈvertingly** *adv.*

diverticulitis (ˌdaɪvəˌtɪkjʊˈlaɪtɪs) *n.* inflammation of one or more diverticula, esp. of the colon.

diverticulum (ˌdaɪvəˈtɪkjʊləm) *n., pl.* **-la** (-lə). any sac or pouch formed by herniation of the wall of a tubular organ or part, esp. the intestines. [C16: < NL, < L *dēverticulum* by-path, < *dēvertere* to turn aside, < *vertere* to turn]

divertimento (dɪˌvɜːtɪˈmɛntəʊ) *n., pl.* **-ti** (-tɪ). **1.** a piece of entertaining music, often scored for a mixed ensemble and having no fixed form. **2.** an episode in a fugue. [C18: < It.]

divertissement (dɪˈvɜːtɪsmənt) *n.* a brief entertainment or diversion, usually between the acts of a play. [C18: < F: entertainment]

Dives (ˈdaɪviːz) *n.* **1.** a rich man in the parable in Luke 16:19–31. **2.** a very rich man.

divest (daɪˈvɛst) *vb.* (*tr.;* usually foll. by *of*) **1.** to strip (of clothes). **2.** to deprive or dispossess. [C17: changed < earlier *devest*] —**divestiture** (daɪˈvɛstɪtʃə), **divesture** (daɪˈvɛstʃə), *or* **diˈvestment** *n.*

divi (ˈdɪvɪ) *n.* an alternative spelling of **divvy.**

divide (dɪˈvaɪd) *vb.* **1.** to separate into parts; split up. **2.** to share or be shared out in parts; distribute. **3.** to diverge or cause to diverge in opinion or aim. **4.** (*tr.*) to keep apart or be a boundary between. **5.** (*intr.*) to vote by separating into two groups. **6.** to categorize; classify. **7.** to calculate the quotient of (one number or quantity) and (another number or quantity) by division. **8.** (*intr.*) to diverge: *the roads divide.* **9.** (*tr.*) to mark increments of (length, angle, etc.). ~*n.* **10.** *Chiefly U.S. & Canad.* an area of relatively high ground separating drainage basins; watershed. **11.** a division; split. [C14: < L *dīvidere* to force apart, < DI-[2] + *vid-* separate, from the source of *viduus* bereaved]

divided (dɪˈvaɪdɪd) *adj.* **1.** *Bot.* another word for **dissected** (sense 1). **2.** split; not united.

dividend (ˈdɪvɪˌdɛnd) *n.* **1. a.** a distribution from the net profits of a company to its shareholders. **b.** a portion of this distribution received by a shareholder. **2.** the share of a cooperative society's surplus allocated to members. **3.** *Insurance.* a sum of money distributed from a company's net profits to the holders of certain policies. **4.** something extra; a bonus. **5.** a number or quantity to be divided by another number or quantity. **6.** *Law.* the proportion of an insolvent estate payable to the creditors. [C15: < L *dīvidendum* what is to be divided]

divider (dɪˈvaɪdə) *n.* **1.** Also called: **room divider.** a screen or piece of furniture placed so as to divide a room into separate areas. **2.** a person or thing that divides.

dividers (dɪˈvaɪdəz) *pl. n.* a type of compass with two pointed arms, used for measuring lines or dividing them.

divination (ˌdɪvɪˈneɪʃən) *n.* **1.** the art or practice of discovering future events or unknown things, as though by supernatural powers. **2.** a prophecy. **3.** a guess. —**divinatory** (dɪˈvɪnətərɪ, -trɪ) *adj.*

divine (dɪˈvaɪn) *adj.* **1.** of God or a deity. **2.** godlike. **3.** of or associated with religion or worship. **4.** of supreme excellence or worth. **5.** *Inf.* splendid; perfect. ~*n.* **6.** (*often cap.;* preceded by *the*) another term for **God. 7.** a priest, esp. one learned in theology. ~*vb.* **8.** to perceive (something) by intuition. **9.** to conjecture (something); guess. **10.** to discern (a hidden or future reality) as though by supernatural power. **11.** (*tr.*) to search for (water, metal, etc.) using a divining rod. [C14: < L *dīvīnus,* < *dīvus* a god] —**diˈvinely** *adv.* —**diˈviner** *n.*

divine office *n.* (*sometimes cap.*) the canonical prayers recited daily by priests, etc. Also called: **Liturgy of the Hours.**

divine right of kings *n. History.* the concept that the right to rule derives from God and that kings are answerable for their actions to God alone.

diving bell *n.* an early diving submersible having an open bottom and being supplied with compressed air.

diving board *n.* a platform or springboard from which swimmers may dive.

diving suit *or* **dress** *n.* a waterproof suit used by divers, having a heavy detachable helmet and an air supply.

divining rod *n.* a forked twig said to move when held over ground in which water, metal, etc., is to be found. Also called: **dowsing rod.**

divinity (dɪˈvɪnɪtɪ) *n., pl.* **-ties. 1.** the nature of a deity or the state of being divine. **2.** a god. **3.** (*often cap.;* preceded by *the*) another term for **God. 4.** another word for **theology.**

divisible (dɪˈvɪzɪbəl) *adj.* capable of being divided, usually with no remainder. —**diˌvisiˈbility** *or* **diˈvisibleness** *n.* —**diˈvisibly** *adv.*

division (dɪˈvɪʒən) *n.* **1.** a dividing or being divided. **2.** the act of sharing out; distribution. **3.** something that divides; boundary. **4.** one of the parts, groups, etc., into which something is divided. **5.** a part of a government, business, etc., that has been made into a unit for administrative or other reasons. **6.** a formal vote in Parliament or a similar legislative body. **7.** a difference of opinion. **8.** (in sports) a section or class organized according to age, weight, skill, etc. **9.** a mathematical operation in which the quotient of two numbers or quantities is calculated. Usually written: $a \div b$, a/b, $\frac{a}{b}$. **10.** *Army.* a major formation, larger than a brigade but smaller than a corps, containing the necessary arms to sustain independent combat. **11.** *Biol.* a major taxonomic division that corresponds to a phylum. [C14: < L *dīvīsiō,* < *dīvidere* to DIVIDE] —**diˈvisional** *or* **diˈvisionary** *adj.* —**diˈvisionally** *adv.*

division sign *n.* the symbol ÷, placed between the dividend and the divisor to indicate division, as in $12 \div 6 = 2$.

divisive (dɪˈvaɪsɪv) *adj.* tending to cause disagreement or dissension. —**diˈvisively** *adv.* —**diˈvisiveness** *n.*

divisor (dɪˈvaɪzə) *n.* **1.** a number or quantity to be divided into another number or quantity (the dividend). **2.** a number that is a factor of another number.

divorce (dɪˈvɔːs) *n.* **1.** the legal dissolution of a marriage. **2.** a judicial decree declaring a marriage to be dissolved. **3.** a separation, esp. one that is total or complete. ~*vb.* **4.** to separate or be separated by divorce; give or obtain a divorce. **5.** (*tr.*) to remove or separate, esp. completely. [C14: < OF, < L *dīvortium*, < *dīvertere* to separate] —**diˈvorceable** *adj.*

divorcée (dɪvɔːˈsiː) *or* (*masc.*) **divorcé** (dɪˈvɔːseɪ) *n.* a person who has been divorced.

divot (ˈdɪvət) *n.* a piece of turf dug out of a grass surface, esp. by a golf club or by horses' hooves. [C16: < Scot., <?]

divulge (daɪˈvʌldʒ) *vb.* (*tr.; may take a clause as object*) to make known; disclose. [C15: < L *dīvulgāre*, < DI-² + *vulgāre* to spread among the people, < *vulgus* the common people] —**diˈvulgence** *or* **diˈvulgement** *n.* —**diˈvulger** *n.*

divvy (ˈdɪvɪ) *Inf.* ~*n., pl.* **-vies. 1.** *Brit.* short for **dividend,** esp. (formerly) one paid by a cooperative society. **2.** *U.S. & Canad.* a share; portion. ~*vb.* **-vying, -vied. 3.** (*tr.;* usually foll. by *up*) to divide and share.

dixie (ˈdɪksɪ) *n.* **1.** *Chiefly mil.* a large metal pot for cooking, brewing tea, etc. **2.** a mess tin. [C19: < Hindi *degcī*, dim. of *degcā* pot]

Dixie (ˈdɪksɪ) *n.* **1.** Also called: **Dixieland.** the southern states of the U.S. ~*adj.* **2.** of the southern states of the U.S. [C19: ? < the nickname of New Orleans, < *dixie* a ten-dollar bill printed there, < F *dix* ten]

Dixieland (ˈdɪksɪˌlænd) *n.* **1.** a kind of jazz derived from the New Orleans tradition of playing, but with more emphasis on melody, regular rhythms, etc. **2.** See **Dixie.**

DIY *or* **d.i.y.** (in Britain) *abbrev. for* do-it-yourself.

dizzy (ˈdɪzɪ) *adj.* **-zier, -ziest. 1.** affected with a whirling or reeling sensation; giddy. **2.** mentally confused or bewildered. **3.** causing or tending to cause vertigo or bewilderment. **4.** *Inf.* foolish or flighty. ~*vb.* **-zying, -zied. 5.** (*tr.*) to make dizzy. [OE *dysig* silly] —ˈ**dizzily** *adv.* —ˈ**dizziness** *n.*

DJ *or* **dj** (ˈdiːˌdʒeɪ) *n.* **1.** a variant of **deejay. 2.** an informal term for **dinner jacket.**

djinni *or* **djinny** (dʒɪˈniː, ˈdʒɪnɪ) *n., pl.* **djinn** (dʒɪn). variant spellings of **jinni.**

dl *symbol for* decilitre.

D/L *abbrev. for* demand loan.

DLitt *or* **DLit** *abbrev. for:* **1.** Doctor of Letters. **2.** Doctor of Literature. [L *Doctor Litterarum*]

dm *symbol for* decimetre.

DM *abbrev. for* Deutsche Mark.

DMA *Computers. abbrev. for* direct memory access.

DMus *abbrev. for* Doctor of Music.

DMZ *abbrev. for* demilitarized zone.

DNA *n.* deoxyribonucleic acid, the main constituent of the chromosomes of all organisms in the form of a double helix. DNA is self-replicating and is responsible for the transmission of hereditary characteristics.

D-notice *n. Brit.* an official notice sent to newspapers prohibiting the publication of certain security information. [C20: < their administrative classification letter]

do¹ (duː; *unstressed* dʊ, də) *vb.* **does, doing, did, done. 1.** to perform or complete (a deed or action): *to do a portrait.* **2.** (often *intr.;* foll. by *for*) to serve the needs of; be suitable for; suffice. **3.** (*tr.*) to arrange or fix. **4.** (*tr.*) to prepare or provide; serve: *this restaurant doesn't do lunch on Sundays.* **5.** (*tr.*) to make tidy, elegant, ready, etc.: *to do one's hair.* **6.** (*tr.*) to improve (esp. in **do something to** *or* **for**). **7.** (*tr.*) to find an answer to (a problem or puzzle). **8.** (*tr.*) to translate or adapt the form or language of: *the book was done into a play.* **9.** (*intr.*) to conduct oneself: *do as you please.* **10.** (*intr.*) to fare or manage. **11.** (*tr.*) to cause or produce: *complaints do nothing to help.* **12.** (*tr.*) to give or render: *do me a favour.* **13.** (*tr.*) to work at, esp. as a course of study or a profession. **14.** (*tr.*) to perform (a play, etc.); act. **15.** (*tr.*) to travel at a specified speed, esp. as a maximum. **16.** (*tr.*) to travel or traverse (a distance). **17.** (takes an infinitive without *to*) used as an auxiliary **a.** before the subject of an interrogative sentence as a way of forming a question: *do you agree?* **b.** to intensify positive statements and commands: *I do like your new house; do hurry!* **c.** before a negative adverb to form negative statements or commands: *do not leave me here alone!* **d.** in inverted constructions: *little did he realize that.* **18.** used as an auxiliary to replace an earlier verb or verb phrase: *he likes you as much as I do.* **19.** (*tr.*) *Inf.* to visit as a sightseer or tourist. **20.** (*tr.*) to wear out; exhaust. **21.** (*intr.*) to happen (esp. in **nothing doing**). **22.** (*tr.*) *Sl.* to serve (a period of time) as a prison sentence. **23.** (*tr.*) *Inf.* to cheat or swindle. **24.** (*tr.*) *Sl.* to rob. **25.** (*tr.*) *Sl.* **a.** to arrest. **b.** to convict of a crime. **26.** (*tr.*) *Austral. sl.* to spend (money). **27.** (*tr.*) *Sl., chiefly Brit.* to treat violently; assault. **28.** *U.S. sl.* to take or use (a drug). **29.** (*tr.*) *Taboo sl.* (of a male) to have sexual intercourse with. **30. do or die.** to make a final or supreme effort. **31. make do.** to manage with whatever is available. ~*n., pl.* **dos** *or* **do's. 32.** *Sl.* an act or instance of cheating or swindling. **33.** *Inf., chiefly Brit. & N.Z.* a formal or festive gathering; party. **34. do's and don'ts.** *Inf.* rules. ~See also **do away with, do by,** etc. [OE *dōn*]

do² (dəʊ) *n., pl.* **dos.** a variant spelling of **doh.**

do. *abbrev. for* ditto.

DOA *abbrev. for* dead on arrival.

doable (ˈduːəbᵊl) *adj.* capable of being done.

do away with *vb.* (*intr., adv. + prep.*) **1.** to kill or destroy. **2.** to discard or abolish.

dobbin (ˈdɒbɪn) *n.* a name for a horse, esp. a workhorse. [C16: < *Robin*, pet form of *Robert*]

Doberman pinscher (ˈdəʊbəmən ˈpɪnʃə) *or* **Doberman** *n.* a breed of large dog with a glossy black-and-tan coat. [C19: after L. *Dobermann* (19th-cent. G dog breeder) who bred it + *Pinscher*, ? after *Pinzgau*, district in Austria]

dob in *vb.* **dobbing, dobbed.** (*adv.*) *Austral. sl.* **1.** (*tr.*) to inform against, esp. to the police. **2.** to contribute to a fund.

do by *vb.* (*intr., prep.*) to treat in the manner specified.

doc (dɒk) *n. Inf.* short for **doctor.**

DOCG *abbrev. for* Denominazione di Origine Controllata Garantita: used of wines. [It., lit: name of origin guaranteed controlled]

docile (ˈdəʊsaɪl) *adj.* **1.** easy to manage or discipline; submissive. **2.** *Rare.* easy to teach. [C15: < L *docilis* easily taught, < *docēre* to teach] —ˈ**docilely** *adv.* —**docility** (dəʊˈsɪlɪtɪ) *n.*

dock¹ (dɒk) *n.* **1.** a wharf or pier. **2.** a space between two wharves or piers for the mooring of ships. **3.** an area of water that can accommodate a ship and can be closed off to allow regulation of the water level. **4.** short for **dry dock. 5. in** *or* **into dock.** *Brit. inf.* **a.** (of people) in hospital. **b.** (of cars, etc.) in a repair shop. **6.** *Chiefly U.S. & Canad.* a platform from which lorries, goods trains, etc., are loaded and unloaded. ~*vb.* **7.** to moor or be moored at a dock. **8.** to put (a vessel) into, or (of a vessel) to come into a dry dock. **9.** (of two spacecraft) to link together in space or link together (two spacecraft) in space. [C14: < MDu. *docke;* ? rel. to L *ducere* to lead]

dock² (dɒk) *n.* **1.** the bony part of the tail of an animal. **2.** the part of an animal's tail left after the major part of it has been cut off. ~*vb.* (*tr.*) **3.** to remove (the tail or part of the tail) of (an animal) by cutting through the bone. **4.** to deduct (an amount) from (a person's wages, pension, etc.). [C14: *dok* <?]

dock³ (dɒk) *n.* an enclosed space in a court of law where the accused sits or stands during his trial. [C16: < Flemish *dok* sty]

dock⁴ (dɒk) *n.* any of various weedy plants having greenish or reddish flowers and broad leaves. [OE *docce*]

dockage (ˈdɒkɪdʒ) *n.* **1.** a charge levied upon a

vessel for using a dock. 2. facilities for docking vessels. 3. the practice of docking vessels.
docker (ˈdɒkə) *n. Brit.* a man employed in the loading or unloading of ships. U.S. and Canad. equivalent: **longshoreman.** See also **stevedore.**
docket (ˈdɒkɪt) *n.* 1. *Chiefly Brit.* a piece of paper accompanying or referring to a package or other delivery, stating contents, delivery instructions, etc., sometimes serving as a receipt. 2. *Law.* a. a summary of the proceedings in a court. b. a register containing this. 3. *Brit.* a. a customs certificate declaring that duty has been paid. b. a certificate giving particulars of a shipment. 4. a summary of contents, as in a document. 5. *U.S.* a list of things to be done. 6. *U.S. law.* a list of cases awaiting trial. ~*vb.* (*tr.*) 7. to fix a docket to (a package, etc.). 8. *Law.* a. to make a summary of (a judgment, etc.). b. to abstract and enter in a register. 9. to endorse (a document, etc.) with a summary. [C15: <?]
dockland (ˈdɒkˌlænd) *n.* the area around the docks.
dockside (ˈdɒkˌsaɪd) *n.* an area beside a dock.
dockyard (ˈdɒkˌjɑːd) *n.* a naval establishment with docks, workshops, etc., for the building, fitting out, and repair of vessels.
Doc Martens (dɒk ˈmɑːtənz) *pl. n. Trademark.* a brand of lace-up boots with thick lightweight resistant soles. In full: **Doctor Martens.**
doctor (ˈdɒktə) *n.* 1. a person licensed to practise medicine. 2. a person who has been awarded a higher academic degree in any field of knowledge. 3. *Chiefly U.S. & Canad.* a person licensed to practise dentistry or veterinary medicine. 4. (*often cap.*) Also called: **Doctor of the Church.** a title given to any of several of the early Fathers of the Christian Church. 5. *Angling.* any of various artificial flies. 6. *Inf.* a person who mends or repairs things. 7. *Sl.* a cook on a ship or at a camp. 8. *Arch.* a man, esp. a teacher, of learning. 9. **go for the doctor.** *Austral. sl.* to make a great effort or move very fast. 10. **what the doctor ordered.** something needed or desired. ~*vb.* 11. (*tr.*) to give medical treatment to. 12. (*intr.*) *Inf.* to practise medicine. 13. (*tr.*) to repair or mend. 14. (*tr.*) to make different in order to deceive. 15. (*tr.*) to adapt. 16. (*tr.*) *Inf.* to castrate (a cat, dog, etc.). [C14: < L: teacher, < *docēre* to teach] —ˈ**doctoral** *or* **doctorial** (dɒkˈtɔːrɪəl) *adj.*
doctorate (ˈdɒktərɪt, -trɪt) *n.* the highest academic degree in any field of knowledge.
Doctor of Philosophy *n.* a doctorate awarded for original research in any subject except law, medicine, or theology.
doctrinaire (ˌdɒktrɪˈnɛə) *adj.* 1. stubbornly insistent on the observation of the niceties of a theory, esp. without regard to practicality, suitability, etc. 2. theoretical; impractical. ~*n.* 3. a person who stubbornly attempts to apply a theory without regard to practical difficulties. —ˌ**doctriˈnairism** *n.* —ˌ**doctriˈnarian** *n.*
doctrine (ˈdɒktrɪn) *n.* 1. a creed or body of teachings of a religious, political, or philosophical group presented for acceptance or belief; dogma. 2. a principle or body of principles that is taught or advocated. [C14: < OF, < L *doctrīna* teaching, < *doctor;* see DOCTOR] —**doctrinal** (dɒkˈtraɪnᵊl) *adj.* —**docˈtrinally** *adv.*
docudrama (ˈdɒkjʊˌdrɑːmə) *n.* a film or television programme based on true events, presented in a dramatized form.
document *n.* (ˈdɒkjʊmənt). 1. a piece of paper, booklet, etc., providing information, esp. of an official nature. 2. *Arch.* proof. ~*vb.* (ˈdɒkjʊˌmɛnt). (*tr.*) 3. to record or report in detail, as in the press, on television, etc. 4. to support (statements in a book) with references, etc. 5. to support (a claim, etc.) with evidence. 6. to furnish (a vessel) with documents specifying its registration, dimensions, etc. [C15: < L *documentum* a lesson, < *docēre* to teach]
documentary (ˌdɒkjʊˈmɛntərɪ) *adj.* 1. Also: **documental.** consisting of or relating to documents. 2. presenting factual material with few or no fictional additions. ~*n., pl.* **-ries.** 3. a factual film or television programme about an event, person, etc., presenting the facts with little or no fiction. —ˌ**docuˈmentarily** *adv.*
documentation (ˌdɒkjʊmɛnˈteɪʃən) *n.* 1. the act of supplying with or using documents or references. 2. the documents or references supplied.
dodder[1] (ˈdɒdə) *vb.* (*intr.*) 1. to move unsteadily; totter. 2. to shake or tremble, as from age. [C17: var. of earlier *dadder*] —ˈ**dodderer** *n.* —ˈ**doddery** *adj.*
dodder[2] (ˈdɒdə) *n.* any of a genus of rootless parasitic plants lacking chlorophyll and having suckers for drawing nourishment from the host plant. [C13: of Gmc origin]
doddle (ˈdɒdᵊl) *n. Brit. inf.* something easily accomplished. [C20: ? < *doddle* (*vb.*) to totter]
dodeca- *combining form.* indicating twelve: *dodecaphonic.* [< Gk *dōdeka* twelve]
dodecagon (dəʊˈdɛkəˌgɒn) *n.* a polygon having twelve sides.
dodecahedron (ˌdəʊdɛkəˈhiːdrən) *n.* a solid figure having twelve plane faces. —ˌ**dodecaˈhedral** *adj.*
dodecaphonic (ˌdəʊdɛkəˈfɒnɪk) *adj.* of or relating to the twelve-tone system of serial music.
dodge (dɒdʒ) *vb.* 1. to avoid or attempt to avoid (a blow, discovery, etc.), as by moving suddenly. 2. to evade by cleverness or trickery. 3. (*intr.*) *Change-ringing.* to make a bell change places with its neighbour when sounding in successive changes. 4. (*tr.*) *Photog.* to lighten or darken (selected areas on a print). ~*n.* 5. a plan contrived to deceive. 6. a sudden evasive movement. 7. a clever contrivance. 8. *Change-ringing.* the act of dodging. [C16: <?]
Dodgem (ˈdɒdʒəm) *n. Trademark.* an electrically propelled vehicle driven and bumped against similar cars in a rink at a funfair.
dodger (ˈdɒdʒə) *n.* 1. a person who evades or shirks. 2. a shifty dishonest person. 3. a canvas shelter on a ship's bridge, etc., to protect the helmsman from bad weather. 4. *Dialect & Austral.* food, esp. bread.
dodgy (ˈdɒdʒɪ) *adj.* **dodgier, dodgiest.** *Brit., Austral. & N.Z. inf.* 1. risky, difficult, or dangerous. 2. uncertain or unreliable; tricky.
dodo (ˈdəʊdəʊ) *n., pl.* **dodos** *or* **dodoes.** 1. any of a now extinct family of flightless birds formerly found on Mauritius. They had a hooked bill and short stout legs. 2. *Inf.* an intensely conservative person who is unaware of changing fashions, ideas, etc. 3. **(as) dead as a dodo.** irretrievably defunct or out of date. [C17: < Port. *doudo,* < *duodo* stupid]
do down *vb.* (*tr., adv.*) 1. to belittle or humiliate. 2. to deceive or cheat.
doe (dəʊ) *n., pl.* **does** *or* **doe.** the female of the deer, hare, rabbit, and certain other animals. [OE *dā*]
Doe (dəʊ) *n. Law.* (formerly) the name of the fictitious plaintiff in an action of ejectment.
DOE (in Britain) *abbrev. for* Department of the Environment.
doek (dʊk) *n. S. African inf.* a square of cloth worn mainly by African women to cover the head. [C18: < Afrik.: cloth]
doer (ˈduːə) *n.* 1. a person or thing that does something. 2. an active or energetic person. 3. *N.Z.* a thriving farm animal.
does (dʌz) *vb.* (used with a singular noun or the pronouns *he, she,* or *it*) a form of the present tense (indicative mood) of **do**[1].
doeskin (ˈdəʊˌskɪn) *n.* 1. the skin of a deer, lamb, or sheep. 2. a very supple leather made from this. 3. a heavy smooth cloth.
doff (dɒf) *vb.* (*tr.*) 1. to take off or lift (one's hat) in salutation. 2. to remove (clothing). [OE *dōn of;* see DO[1], OFF; cf. DON[1]] —ˈ**doffer** *n.*
do for *vb.* (*prep.*) *Inf.* 1. (*tr.*) to convict of a crime or offence. 2. (*intr.*) to cause the ruin, death, or defeat of. 3. (*intr.*) to do housework for. 4. **do well for oneself.** to thrive or succeed.
dog (dɒg) *n.* 1. a domesticated canine mammal

occurring in many breeds that show a great variety in size and form. **2.** any other carnivore of the dog family, such as the dingo and coyote. **3.** the male of animals of the dog family. **4.** (*modifier*) spurious, inferior, or useless. **5.** a mechanical device for gripping or holding. **6.** *Inf.* a fellow; chap. **7.** *Inf.* a man or boy regarded as unpleasant or wretched. **8.** *U.S. sl.* an unattractive girl or woman. **9.** *U.S. & Canad. inf.* something unsatisfactory or inferior. **10.** short for **firedog. 11. a dog's chance.** no chance at all. **12. a dog's dinner** *or* **breakfast.** *Inf.* something messy or bungled. **13. a dog's life.** a wretched existence. **14. dog eat dog.** ruthless competition. **15. like a dog's dinner.** dressed smartly or ostentatiously. **16. put on the dog.** *U.S. & Canad. inf.* to behave pretentiously. ~*vb.* **dogging, dogged.** (*tr.*) **17.** to pursue or follow after like a dog. **18.** to trouble; plague. **19.** to chase with a dog. **20.** to grip or secure by a mechanical device. ~*adv.* **21.** (*usually in combination*) thoroughly; utterly: *dog-tired.* ~See also **dogs.** [OE *docga,* <?]

dog biscuit *n.* a hard biscuit for dogs.

dog box *n. N.Z. inf.* disgrace; disfavour: *in the dog box.*

dogcart (ˈdɒɡˌkɑːt) *n.* a light horse-drawn two-wheeled vehicle.

dog-catcher *n. Now chiefly U.S. & Canad.* a local official whose job is to impound and dispose of stray dogs.

dog collar *n.* **1.** a collar for a dog. **2.** *Inf.* a clerical collar. **3.** *Inf.* a tight-fitting necklace.

dog days *pl. n.* the hot period of the summer reckoned in ancient times from the heliacal rising of Sirius (the Dog Star). [C16: translation of LL *diēs caniculārēs,* translation of Gk *hēmerai kunades*]

doge (dəʊdʒ) *n.* (formerly) the chief magistrate in the republics of Venice and Genoa. [C16: via F < It. (Venetian dialect), < L *dux* leader]

dog-ear *vb.* **1.** (*tr.*) to fold down the corner of (a page). ~*n. also* **dog's-ear. 2.** a folded-down corner of a page.

dog-eared *adj.* **1.** having dog-ears. **2.** shabby or worn.

dog-end *n. Inf.* a cigarette end.

dogfight (ˈdɒɡˌfaɪt) *n.* **1.** close-quarters combat between fighter aircraft. **2.** any rough fight.

dogfish (ˈdɒɡˌfɪʃ) *n., pl.* **-fish** *or* **-fishes. 1.** any of several small sharks. **2.** a less common name for the **bowfin.**

dogged (ˈdɒɡɪd) *adj.* obstinately determined; wilful or tenacious. —**ˈdoggedly** *adv.* —**ˈdoggedness** *n.*

doggerel (ˈdɒɡərəl) *or* **dogrel** (ˈdɒɡrəl) *n.* **1. a.** comic verse, usually irregular in measure. **b.** (*as modifier*): *a doggerel rhythm.* **2.** nonsense. [C14 *dogerel* worthless, ? < *dogge* DOG]

doggish (ˈdɒɡɪʃ) *adj.* **1.** of or like a dog. **2.** surly; snappish.

doggo (ˈdɒɡəʊ) *adv. Brit. inf.* in hiding and keeping quiet (esp. in **lie doggo**). [C19: prob. < DOG]

doggone (ˈdɒɡɒn) *U.S. & Canad.* ~*interj.* **1.** an exclamation of annoyance, etc. ~*adj.* (*prenominal*), *adv.* **2.** Also: **doggoned.** another word for **damn.** [C19: euphemism for *God damn*]

doggy *or* **doggie** (ˈdɒɡɪ) *n., pl.* **-gies. 1.** a child's word for a **dog.** ~*adj.* **-gier, -giest. 2.** of, like, or relating to a dog. **3.** fond of dogs.

doggy bag *n.* a bag in which leftovers from a meal may be taken away for the diner's dog.

doghouse (ˈdɒɡˌhaʊs) *n.* **1.** the U.S. and Canad. name for **kennel. 2.** *Inf.* disfavour (in **in the doghouse**).

dogie, dogy, *or* **dogey** (ˈdəʊɡɪ) *n., pl.* **-gies** *or* **-geys.** *U.S. & Canad.* a motherless calf. [C19: < *dough-guts,* because they were fed on flour-and-water paste]

dog in the manger *n.* a person who prevents others from using something he has no use for.

dog Latin *n.* spurious or incorrect Latin.

dogleg (ˈdɒɡˌlɛɡ) *n.* **1.** a sharp bend or angle. ~*vb.* **-legging, -legged. 2.** (*intr.*) to go off at an angle. ~*adj.* **3.** of or with the shape of a dogleg. —**doglegged** (ˌdɒɡˈlɛɡɪd, ˈdɒɡˌlɛɡd) *adj.*

dogma (ˈdɒɡmə) *n., pl.* **-mas** *or* **-mata** (-mətə). **1.** a religious doctrine or system of doctrines proclaimed by ecclesiastical authority as true. **2.** a belief, principle, or doctrine or a code of beliefs, principles, or doctrines. [C17: via L < Gk: opinion, < *dokein* to seem good]

dogman (ˈdɒɡmən) *n., pl.* **-men.** *Austral.* a person who directs the operation of a crane whilst riding on an object being lifted by it.

dogmatic (dɒɡˈmætɪk) *or* **dogmatical** *adj.* **1. a.** (of a statement, opinion, etc.) forcibly asserted as if authoritative and unchallengeable. **b.** (of a person) prone to making such statements. **2.** of or constituting dogma. **3.** based on assumption rather than observation. —**dogˈmatically** *adv.*

dogmatics (dɒɡˈmætɪks) *n.* (*functioning as sing.*) the study of religious dogmas and doctrines. Also called: **dogmatic** (*or* **doctrinal**) **theology.**

dogmatize *or* **-ise** (ˈdɒɡməˌtaɪz) *vb.* to say or state (something) in a dogmatic manner. —**ˈdogmatism** *n.* —**ˈdogmatist** *n.*

do-gooder *n. Inf.* a well-intentioned person, esp. a naive or impractical one. —**ˌdo-ˈgooding** *n., adj.*

dog paddle *n.* **1.** a swimming stroke in which the swimmer paddles his hands in imitation of a swimming dog. ~*vb.* **dog-paddle. 2.** (*intr.*) to swim using the dog paddle.

dog rose *n.* a prickly wild European rose that has pink or white scentless flowers. [< belief that its root was effective against the bite of a mad dog]

dogs (dɒɡz) *pl. n.* **1.** *Sl.* the feet. **2. go to the dogs.** *Inf.* to go to ruin physically or morally. **3. let sleeping dogs lie.** to leave things undisturbed. **4. the dogs.** *Brit. inf.* greyhound racing.

dogsbody (ˈdɒɡzˌbɒdɪ) *Inf.* ~*n., pl.* **-bodies. 1.** a person who carries out menial tasks for others. ~*vb.* (*intr.*) **-bodying, -bodied. 2.** to act as a dogsbody.

dog's disease *n. Austral. inf.* influenza.

dogsled (ˈdɒɡˌslɛd) *n. Chiefly U.S. & Canad.* a sleigh drawn by dogs. Also called (Brit.): **dog sledge.**

Dog Star *n.* **the.** another name for **Sirius.**

dog-tired *adj.* (*usually postpositive*) *Inf.* exhausted.

dogtooth (ˈdɒɡˌtuːθ) *n., pl.* **-teeth.** *Archit.* a carved ornament in the form of a series of four-cornered pyramids set diagonally and often decorated with leaf shapes along each edge, used in England in the 13th century.

dogtooth violet *n.* any of a genus of plants, esp. a North American plant with yellow flowers, or a European plant with purple flowers.

dogtrot (ˈdɒɡˌtrɒt) *n.* a gently paced trot.

dog violet *n.* any of three wild violets found in Britain and northern Europe.

dogwatch (ˈdɒɡˌwɒtʃ) *n.* either of two two-hour watches aboard ship, from four to six p.m. or from six to eight p.m.

dogwood (ˈdɒɡˌwʊd) *n.* any of various trees or shrubs, esp. a European shrub with small white flowers and black berries.

dogy (ˈdəʊɡɪ) *n., pl.* **-gies.** a variant of **dogie.**

doh (dəʊ) *n. Music.* (in tonic sol-fa) the first degree of any major scale. [C18: < It.; see GAMUT]

doily *or* **doyley** (ˈdɔɪlɪ) *n., pl.* **-lies** *or* **-leys.** a decorative mat of lace or lacelike paper, etc., laid on plates. [C18: after *Doily,* a London draper]

do in *vb.* (*tr., adv.*) *Sl.* **1.** to kill. **2.** to exhaust.

doing (ˈduːɪŋ) *n.* **1.** an action or the performance of an action: *whose doing is this?* **2.** *Inf.* a beating or castigation.

doings (ˈduːɪŋz) *n.* **1.** (*functioning as pl.*) deeds, actions, or events. **2.** (*functioning as sing.*) *Inf.* anything of which the name is not known, or euphemistically left unsaid, etc.

do-it-yourself *n.* **a.** the hobby or process of constructing and repairing things oneself. **b.** (*as modifier*): *a do-it-yourself kit.*

dol. *abbrev. for:* **1.** *Music.* dolce. **2.** (*pl.* **dols.**) dollar.

Dolby (ˈdɒlbɪ) *n. Trademark.* any of various specialized electronic circuits, esp. those used in tape recorders for noise reduction in high-frequency signals. [after R. *Dolby* (born 1933), U.S. inventor]

dolce (ˈdɒltʃɪ) *adj., adv. Music.* (to be performed) gently and sweetly. [It.]

dolce vita (ˈdɒltʃɪ ˈviːtə) *n.* a life of luxury. [It., lit.: sweet life]

doldrums (ˈdɒldrəmz) *n.* **the.** **1.** a depressed or bored state of mind. **2.** a state of inactivity or stagnation. **3.** a belt of light winds or calms along the equator. [C19: prob. < OE *dol* DULL, infl. by TANTRUM]

dole[1] (dəʊl) *n.* **1.** (usually preceded by *the*) *Brit. inf.* money received from the state while out of work. **2. on the dole.** *Brit. inf.* receiving such money. **3.** a small portion of money or food given to a poor person. **4.** the act of distributing such portions. **5.** *Arch.* fate. ~*vb.* **6.** (*tr.;* usually foll. by *out*) to distribute, esp. in small portions. [OE *dāl* share]

dole[2] (dəʊl) *n. Arch.* grief or mourning. [C13: < OF, < LL *dolus,* < L *dolēre* to lament]

dole-bludger *n. Austral. sl.* a person who draws unemployment benefit without making any attempt to get work.

doleful (ˈdəʊlfʊl) *adj.* dreary; mournful. —ˈ**dolefully** *adv.* —ˈ**dolefulness** *n.*

dolerite (ˈdɒləˌraɪt) *n.* **1.** a dark basic igneous rock; a coarse-grained basalt. **2.** any dark igneous rock whose composition cannot be determined with the naked eye. [C19: < F *dolérite,* < Gk *doleros* deceitful; from the difficulty in determining its composition]

dolichocephalic (ˌdɒlɪkəʊsɪˈfælɪk) *or* **dolichocephalous** (ˌdɒlɪkəʊˈsɛfələs) *adj.* having a head much longer than it is broad. [C19: < Gk *dolichos* long + -CEPHALIC]

doll (dɒl) *n.* **1.** a small model or dummy of a human being, used as a toy. **2.** *Sl.* a pretty girl or woman of little intelligence. [C16: prob. < *Doll,* pet name for *Dorothy*]

dollar (ˈdɒlə) *n.* **1.** the standard monetary unit of the U.S., divided into 100 cents. **2.** the standard monetary unit, comprising 100 cents, of various other countries including: Australia, the Bahamas, Canada, Hong Kong, Jamaica, Malaysia, Singapore, Taiwan, New Zealand, and Zimbabwe. [C16: < Low G *daler,* < G *Taler, Thaler,* short for *Joachimsthaler,* coin made from metal mined in *Joachimsthal* Jachymov, town in Czechoslovakia]

dollarbird (ˈdɒləˌbɜːd) *n.* a bird of S and SE Asia and Australia with a round white spot on each wing.

dollar diplomacy *n. Chiefly U.S.* **1.** a foreign policy that encourages and protects commercial and financial involvement abroad. **2.** use of financial power as a diplomatic weapon.

dollop (ˈdɒləp) *Inf.* ~*n.* **1.** a semisolid lump. **2.** a measure or serving. ~*vb.* **3.** (*tr.;* foll. by *out*) to serve out (food). [C16: <?]

doll up *vb.* (*tr., adv.*) *Sl.* to dress in a stylish or showy manner.

dolly (ˈdɒlɪ) *n., pl.* **-lies.** **1.** a child's word for a **doll.** **2.** *Films, etc.* a wheeled support on which a camera may be mounted. **3.** a cup-shaped anvil used to hold a rivet. **4.** *Cricket.* **a.** a simple catch. **b.** a full toss bowled in a slow high arc. **5.** Also called: **dolly bird.** *Sl., chiefly Brit.* an attractive and fashionable girl. ~*vb.* **-lying, -lied.** **6.** *Films, etc.* to wheel (a camera) backwards or forwards on a dolly.

dolly mixture *n.* **1.** a mixture of tiny coloured sweets. **2.** one such sweet.

dolman sleeve (ˈdɒlmən) *n.* a sleeve that is very wide at the armhole and tapers to a tight wrist. [C19: < *dolman,* a type of Turkish robe, ult. < Turkish *dolamak* to wind]

dolmen (ˈdɒlmɛn) *n.* a Neolithic stone formation, consisting of a horizontal stone supported by several vertical stones, and thought to be a tomb. [C19: < F, prob. < OBreton *tol* table, < L *tabula* board + Breton *mēn* stone, of Celtic origin]

dolomite (ˈdɒləˌmaɪt) *n.* **1.** a mineral consisting of calcium magnesium carbonate. **2.** a rock resembling limestone but consisting principally of the mineral dolomite. [C18: after Déodat de *Dolomieu* (1750–1801), F mineralogist] —**dolomitic** (ˌdɒləˈmɪtɪk) *adj.*

doloroso (ˌdɒləˈrəʊsəʊ) *adj., adv. Music.* (to be performed) in a sorrowful manner. [It.]

dolorous (ˈdɒlərəs) *adj.* causing or involving pain or sorrow. —ˈ**dolorously** *adv.*

dolos (ˈdɒlɒs) *n., pl.* **dolosse.** *S. African.* a knucklebone of a sheep, buck, etc., used esp. by diviners. [<?]

dolour *or U.S.* **dolor** (ˈdɒlə) *n. Poetic.* grief or sorrow. [C14: < L, < *dolēre* to grieve]

dolphin (ˈdɒlfɪn) *n.* **1.** any of various marine mammals that are typically smaller than whales and larger than porpoises and have a beaklike snout. **2. river dolphin.** any of various freshwater mammals inhabiting rivers of North and South America and S Asia. **3.** Also called **dorado.** either of two large marine fishes that have an iridescent coloration. **4.** *Naut.* a post or buoy for mooring a vessel. [C13: < OF *dauphin,* via L, < Gk *delphin-, delphis*]

dolphinarium (ˌdɒlfɪˈnɛərɪəm) *n., pl.* **-iums** *or* **-ia** (-ɪə). a pool or aquarium for dolphins, esp. one in which they give public displays.

dolt (dəʊlt) *n.* a slow-witted or stupid person. [C16: prob. rel. to OE *dol* stupid] —ˈ**doltish** *adj.* —ˈ**doltishness** *n.*

dom. *abbrev. for:* **1.** domain. **2.** domestic.

-dom *suffix forming nouns.* **1.** state or condition: *freedom.* **2.** rank, office, or domain of: *earldom.* **3.** a collection of persons: *officialdom.* [OE *-dōm*]

domain (dəˈmeɪn) *n.* **1.** land governed by a ruler or government. **2.** land owned by one person or family. **3.** a field or scope of knowledge or activity. **4.** a region having specific characteristics. **5.** *Austral. & N.Z.* a park or recreation reserve maintained by a public authority, often the government. **6.** *Law.* the absolute ownership and right to dispose of land. **7.** *Maths.* the set of values of the independent variable of a function for which the functional value exists. **8.** *Logic.* another term for **universe of discourse.** **9.** *Philosophy.* range of significance. **10.** *Physics.* one of the regions in a ferromagnetic solid in which all the atoms have their magnetic moments aligned in the same direction. [C17: < F *domaine,* < L *dominium* property, < *dominus* lord]

dome (dəʊm) *n.* **1.** a hemispherical roof or vault. **2.** something shaped like this. **3.** a slang word for the **head.** ~*vb.* (*tr.*) **4.** to cover with or as if with a dome. **5.** to shape like a dome. [C16: < F, < It. *duomo* cathedral, < L *domus* house] —ˈ**domeˌlike** *adj.* —**domical** (ˈdəʊmɪkᵊl, ˈdɒm-) *adj.*

Domesday Book *or* **Doomsday Book** (ˈduːmzˌdeɪ) *n. History.* the record of a survey of the land of England carried out by the commissioners of William I in 1086.

domestic (dəˈmɛstɪk) *adj.* **1.** of the home or family. **2.** enjoying or accustomed to home or family life. **3.** (of an animal) bred or kept by man as a pet or for purposes such as the supply of food. **4.** of one's own country or a specific country: *domestic and foreign affairs.* ~*n.* **5.** a household servant. [C16: < OF *domestique,* < L *domesticus* belonging to the house, < *domus* house] —**doˈmestically** *adv.*

domesticate (dəˈmɛstɪˌkeɪt) *or U.S.* (*sometimes*) **domesticize** (dəˈmɛstɪˌsaɪz) *vb.* (*tr.*) **1.** to bring or keep (wild animals or plants) under control or cultivation. **2.** to accustom to home life. **3.** to adapt to an environment. —**doˈmesticable** *adj.* —**doˌmestiˈcation** *n.*

domesticity (ˌdəʊmɛˈstɪsɪtɪ) *n., pl.* **-ties.** **1.** home life. **2.** devotion to or familiarity with home life. **3.** (*usually pl.*) a domestic duty or matter.

domestic science *n.* the study of cooking, needlework, and other subjects concerned with household skills.

domicile (ˈdɒmɪˌsaɪl) *or* **domicil** (ˈdɒmɪsɪl) *n.* **1.** a dwelling place. **2.** a permanent legal residence. **3.** *Commerce, Brit.* the place where a bill of exchange is to be paid. ~*vb. also* **domiciliate**

(ˌdɒmɪˈsɪlɪˌeɪt). **4.** to establish or be established in a dwelling place. [C15: < L *domicilium*, < *domus* house] —**domiciliary** (ˌdɒmɪˈsɪlɪərɪ) *adj.*

dominance (ˈdɒmɪnəns) *n.* control; ascendancy.

dominant (ˈdɒmɪnənt) *adj.* **1.** having primary authority or influence; governing; ruling. **2.** predominant or primary: *the dominant topic of the day.* **3.** occupying a commanding position. **4.** *Genetics.* (of a gene) producing the same phenotype in the organism whether its allele is identical or dissimilar. Cf. **recessive. 5.** *Music.* of or relating to the fifth degree of a scale. **6.** *Ecology.* (of a plant or animal species) more prevalent than any other species and determining the appearance and composition of the community. ~*n.* **7.** *Genetics.* a dominant gene. **8.** *Music.* **a.** the fifth degree of a scale. **b.** a key or chord based on this. **9.** *Ecology.* a dominant plant or animal in a community. —ˈ**dominantly** *adv.*

dominant seventh chord *n. Music.* a chord consisting of the dominant and the major third, perfect fifth, and minor seventh above it.

dominate (ˈdɒmɪˌneɪt) *vb.* **1.** to control, rule, or govern. **2.** to tower above (surroundings, etc.). **3.** (*tr.; usually passive*) to predominate in. [C17: < L *dominārī* to be lord over, < *dominus* lord] —ˈ**domiˌnating** *adj.* —ˌ**domiˈnation** *n.*

dominee (ˈduːmɪnɪ, ˈdʊə-) *n.* (in South Africa) a minister in any of the Afrikaner Churches. [< Afrik., < Du.; cf. DOMINIE]

domineer (ˌdɒmɪˈnɪə) *vb.* (*intr.;* often foll. by *over*) to act with arrogance or tyranny; behave imperiously. [C16: < Du. *domineren,* < F *dominer* to DOMINATE] —ˌ**domiˈneering** *adj.*

dominical (dəˈmɪnɪkᵊl) *adj.* **1.** of Jesus Christ as Lord. **2.** of Sunday as the Lord's Day. [C15: < LL *dominicālis,* < L *dominus* lord]

Dominican[1] (dəˈmɪnɪkən) *n.* **1. a.** a member of an order of preaching friars founded by Saint Dominic in 1215; a Blackfriar. **b.** a nun of one of the orders founded under his patronage. ~*adj.* **2.** of Saint Dominic or the Dominican order.

Dominican[2] (dəˈmɪnɪkən) *adj.* **1.** of or relating to the Dominican Republic or Dominica. ~*n.* **2.** a native or inhabitant of the Dominican Republic or Dominica.

dominie (ˈdɒmɪnɪ) *n.* **1.** a Scots word for **schoolmaster. 2.** a minister or clergyman. [C17: < L *dominē,* vocative case of *dominus* lord]

dominion (dəˈmɪnjən) *n.* **1.** rule; authority. **2.** the land governed by one ruler or government. **3.** sphere of influence; area of control. **4.** a name formerly applied to self-governing divisions of the British Empire. **5. the Dominion.** New Zealand. [C15: < OF, < L *dominium* ownership, < *dominus* master]

Dominion Day *n.* the former name for **Canada Day.**

domino[1] (ˈdɒmɪˌnəʊ) *n., pl.* **-noes.** a small rectangular block marked with dots, used in dominoes. [C19: < F, < It., ? < *domino!* master!, said by the winner]

domino[2] (ˈdɒmɪˌnəʊ) *n., pl.* **-noes** *or* **-nos. 1.** a large hooded cloak worn with an eye mask at a masquerade. **2.** the eye mask worn with such a cloak. [C18: < F or It., prob. < L *dominus* lord, master]

domino effect *n.* a series of similar or related events occurring as a direct and inevitable result of one initial event. [C20: alluding to a row of dominoes, each standing on end, all of which fall when one is pushed]

dominoes (ˈdɒmɪˌnəʊz) *n.* (*functioning as sing.*) any of several games in which dominoes with matching halves are laid together.

domkop (ˈdɒmˌkɒp) *n. S. African sl.* an idiot; thickhead. [Afrik.]

don[1] (dɒn) *vb.* **donning, donned.** (*tr.*) to put on (clothing). [C14: < DO[1] + ON; cf. DOFF]

don[2] (dɒn) *n.* **1.** *Brit.* a member of the teaching staff at a university or college, esp. at Oxford or Cambridge. **2.** the head of a student dormitory at certain Canadian universities and colleges. **3.** a Spanish gentleman or nobleman. **4.** *Arch.* a person of rank. **5.** *Austral. & N.Z. inf.* an expert. [C17: ult. < L *dominus* lord]

Don (dɒn) *n.* a Spanish title equivalent to *Mr.* [C16: via Sp., < L *dominus* lord]

Doña (ˈdɒnjə) *n.* a Spanish title of address equivalent to *Mrs* or *Madam.* [C17: via Sp., < L *domina*]

donate (dəʊˈneɪt) *vb.* to give (money, time, etc.), esp. to a charity. —**doˈnator** *n.*

donation (dəʊˈneɪʃən) *n.* **1.** the act of donating. **2.** a contribution. [C15: < L *dōnātiō* a presenting, < *dōnāre* to give, < *dōnum* gift]

donative (ˈdəʊnətɪv) *n.* **1.** a gift or donation. **2.** a benefice capable of being conferred as a gift. ~*adj.* **3.** of or like a donation. **4.** being or relating to a benefice. [C15: < L *dōnātīvum* a donation made to soldiers by a Roman emperor, < *dōnāre* to present]

donder (ˈdɒnə) *S. African sl.* ~*vb.* **1.** (*tr.*) to beat someone up. ~*n.* **2.** a wretch; swine. [< Afrik., < Du. *donderen* to swear, bully]

done (dʌn) *vb.* **1.** the past participle of **do**[1]. **2. be** *or* **have done with.** to end relations with. **3. have done.** to be completely finished: *have you done?* ~*interj.* **4.** an expression of agreement, as on the settlement of a bargain. ~*adj.* **5.** completed. **6.** cooked enough. **7.** used up. **8.** socially acceptable. **9.** *Inf.* cheated; tricked. **10. done for.** *Inf.* **a.** dead or almost dead. **b.** in serious difficulty. **11. done in** *or* **up.** *Inf.* exhausted.

donee (dəʊˈniː) *n.* a person who receives a gift. [C16: < DON(OR) + -EE]

dong (dɒŋ) *n.* **1.** an imitation of the sound of a bell. **2.** *Austral. & N.Z. inf.* a heavy blow. ~*vb.* **3.** (*intr.*) to make such a sound. **4.** *Austral. & N.Z. inf.* to strike or punch. [C19: imit.]

donga (ˈdɒŋgə) *n. S. African, Austral. & N.Z.* a steep-sided gully created by soil erosion. [C19: < Afrik., < Zulu]

donjon (ˈdʌndʒən, ˈdɒn-) *n.* the heavily fortified central tower or keep of a medieval castle. Also: **dungeon.** [C14: arch. var. of *dungeon*]

Don Juan (ˈdɒn ˈdʒuːən) *n.* **1.** a legendary Spanish nobleman and philanderer: hero of many poems, plays, and operas. **2.** a successful seducer of women.

donkey (ˈdɒŋkɪ) *n.* **1.** a long-eared member of the horse family. **2.** a person who is considered to be stupid or stubborn. **3.** (*modifier*) auxiliary: *a donkey engine.* **4. talk the hind leg(s) off a donkey.** to talk endlessly. [C18: ? < *dun* dark + *-key,* as in *monkey*]

donkey jacket *n.* a thick hip-length jacket, usually navy blue, with a waterproof panel across the shoulders.

donkey's years *pl., n. Inf.* a long time.

donkey vote *n. Austral.* a vote in which the voter's order of preference follows the order in which the candidates are listed.

donkey-work *n.* **1.** groundwork. **2.** drudgery.

Donna (ˈdɒnə) *n.* an Italian title of address equivalent to *Madam.* [C17: < It., < L *domina* lady]

donnish (ˈdɒnɪʃ) *adj.* of or resembling a university don, esp. denoting pedantry or fussiness. —ˈ**donnishness** *n.*

donnybrook (ˈdɒnɪˌbrʊk) *n.* a rowdy brawl. [C19: after *Donnybrook Fair,* an annual event until 1855 near Dublin]

donor (ˈdəʊnə) *n.* **1.** a person who makes a donation. **2.** *Med.* any person who gives blood, organs, etc., for use in the treatment of another person. **3.** the atom supplying both electrons in a coordinate bond. [C15: < OF *doneur,* < L *dōnātor,* < *dōnāre* to give]

donor card *n.* a card carried to show that the bodily organs specified on it may be used for transplants after the carrier's death.

Don Quixote (ˈdɒn kiːˈhəʊtiː, ˈkwɪksət) *n.* an impractical idealist. [after the hero of Cervantes' *Don Quixote de la Mancha* (1605)]

don't (dəʊnt) *contraction of* do not.

▷ **Usage.** The use of *don't* for *doesn't* (*he don't care*) is not generally acceptable in either written or spoken English.

don't know *n.* a person who has no definite opinion, esp. as a response to a questionnaire.

doodah (ˈduːdɑː) *or U.S. & Canad.* **doodad** (ˈduːdæd) *n. Inf.* an unnamed thing, esp. an object the name of which is unknown or forgotten. [C20: <?]

doodle (ˈduːdᵊl) *Inf.* ~*vb.* **1.** to scribble or draw aimlessly. **2.** to play or improvise idly. **3.** (*intr.; often foll. by away*) *U.S.* to dawdle or waste time. ~*n.* **4.** a shape, picture, etc., drawn aimlessly. [C20: ? < C17: a foolish person, but infl. in meaning by DAWDLE] —ˈ**doodler** *n.*

doodlebug (ˈduːdᵊlˌbʌg) *n.* **1.** another name for the **V-1.** **2.** a diviner's rod. **3.** a U.S. name for an **antlion** (the larva). [C20: prob. < DOODLE + BUG]

doom (duːm) *n.* **1.** death or a terrible fate. **2.** a judgment. **3.** (*sometimes cap.*) another term for the **Last Judgment.** ~*vb.* **4.** (*tr.*) to destine or condemn to death or a terrible fate. [OE *dōm*]

doomsday *or* **domesday** (ˈduːmzˌdeɪ) *n.* **1.** (*sometimes cap.*) the day on which the Last Judgment will occur. **2.** any day of reckoning. **3.** (*modifier*) characterized by predictions of disaster: *doomsday scenario* [OE *dōmes dæg* Judgment Day]

doona (ˈduːnə) *n.* the Austral. name for **continental quilt.** [< a trademark]

door (dɔː) *n.* **1.** a hinged or sliding panel for closing the entrance to a room, cupboard, etc. **2.** a doorway or entrance. **3.** a means of access or escape: *a door to success.* **4. lay at someone's door.** to lay (the blame or responsibility) on someone. **5. out of doors.** in or into the open air. **6. show someone the door.** to order someone to leave. [OE *duru*]

do-or-die *adj.* (*prenominal*) of a determined and sometimes reckless effort to succeed.

doorjamb (ˈdɔːˌdʒæm) *n.* one of the two vertical members forming the sides of a doorframe. Also called: **doorpost.**

doorkeeper (ˈdɔːˌkiːpə) *n.* a person attending or guarding a door or gateway.

doorman (ˈdɔːˌmæn, -mən) *n., pl.* **-men.** a man employed to attend the doors of certain buildings.

doormat (ˈdɔːˌmæt) *n.* **1.** a mat, placed at an entrance, for wiping dirt from shoes. **2.** *Inf.* a person who offers little resistance to ill-treatment.

doornail (ˈdɔːˌneɪl) *n.* **(as) dead as a doornail.** dead beyond any doubt.

doorsill (ˈdɔːˌsɪl) *n.* a horizontal member of wood, stone, etc., forming the bottom of a doorframe.

doorstep (ˈdɔːˌstɛp) *n.* **1.** a step in front of a door. **2.** *Inf.* a thick slice of bread. ~*vb.* **-stepping, -stepped.** (*tr.*) **3.** to canvass or interview by or in the course of door-to-door visiting.

doorstop (ˈdɔːˌstɒp) *n.* **1.** any device which prevents an open door from moving. **2.** a piece of rubber, etc., fixed to the floor to stop a door striking a wall.

door to door *adj.* (**door-to-door** *when prenominal*), *adv.* **1.** (of selling, etc.) from one house to the next. **2.** (of journeys, etc.) direct.

doorway (ˈdɔːˌweɪ) *n.* **1.** an opening into a building, room, etc., esp. one that has a door. **2.** a means of access or escape: *a doorway to freedom.*

do over *vb.* (*tr., adv.*) **1.** *Inf.* to redecorate. **2.** *Brit., Austral. & N.Z. sl.* to beat up; thrash.

doo-wop (ˈduːˌwɒp) *n.* vocalizing based on rhythm-and-blues harmony. [C20: imit.]

dop (dɒp) *n. S. African sl.* **1.** Cape brandy. **2.** a tot of this. [< Afrik., <?]

dope (dəʊp) *n.* **1.** any of a number of preparations applied to fabric in order to improve strength, tautness, etc. **2.** an additive, such as an antiknock compound added to petrol. **3.** a thick liquid, such as a lubricant, applied to a surface. **4.** a combustible absorbent material used to hold the nitroglycerin in dynamite. **5.** *Sl.* an illegal drug, usually cannabis. **6.** a drug administered to a racehorse or greyhound to affect its performance. **7.** *Inf.* a stupid or slow-witted person. **8.** *Inf.* news or facts, esp. confidential information. ~*vb.* (*tr.*) **9.** *Electronics.* to add impurities to (a semiconductor) in order to produce or modify its properties. **10.** to apply or add dope to. **11.** to administer a drug to (oneself or another). [C19: < Du. *doop* sauce, < *doopen* to dip]

dopey *or* **dopy** (ˈdəʊpɪ) *adj.* **dopier, dopiest. 1.** *Sl.* silly. **2.** *Inf.* half-asleep or semiconscious, as when under the influence of a drug.

doppelgänger (ˈdɒpᵊlˌgɛŋə) *n. Legend.* a ghostly duplicate of a living person. [< G *Doppelgänger,* lit.: double-goer]

Doppler effect (ˈdɒplə) *n.* a change in the apparent frequency of a sound or light wave, etc., as a result of relative motion between the observer and the source. Also called: **Doppler shift.** [C19: after C. J. *Doppler* (1803–53), Austrian physicist]

Doric (ˈdɒrɪk) *adj.* **1.** of the inhabitants of Doris in ancient Greece or their dialect. **2.** of or denoting one of the five classical orders of architecture: characterized by a heavy fluted column and a simple capital. **3.** (*sometimes not cap.*) rustic. ~*n.* **4.** one of four chief dialects of Ancient Greek. **5.** any rural dialect of English, esp. a Scots one.

dorm (dɔːm) *n. Inf.* short for **dormitory.**

dormant (ˈdɔːmənt) *adj.* **1.** quiet and inactive, as during sleep. **2.** latent or inoperative. **3.** (of a volcano) neither extinct nor erupting. **4.** *Biol.* alive but in a resting condition with reduced metabolism. **5.** (*usually postpositive*) *Heraldry.* (of a beast) in a sleeping position. [C14: < OF *dormant,* < *dormir* to sleep, < L *dormīre*] —ˈ**dormancy** *n.*

dormer (ˈdɔːmə) *n.* a construction with a gable roof and a window that projects from a sloping roof. Also called: **dormer window.** [C16: < OF *dormoir,* < L *dormītōrium* DORMITORY]

dormie *or* **dormy** (ˈdɔːmɪ) *adj. Golf.* as many holes ahead of an opponent as there are still to play: *dormie three.* [C19: <?]

dormitory (ˈdɔːmɪtərɪ, -trɪ) *n., pl.* **-ries. 1.** a large room, esp. at a school, containing several beds. **2.** *U.S.* a building, esp. at a college or camp, providing living and sleeping accommodation. **3.** (*modifier*) *Brit.* denoting or relating to an area from which most of the residents commute to work (esp. in **dormitory suburb**). [C15: < L *dormītōrium,* < *dormīre* to sleep]

Dormobile (ˈdɔːməʊˌbiːl) *n. Trademark.* a vanlike vehicle specially equipped for living in while travelling.

dormouse (ˈdɔːˌmaʊs) *n., pl.* **-mice.** a small Eurasian rodent resembling a mouse with a furry tail. [C15: *dor-,* ? < OF *dormir* to sleep, (< L *dormīre*) + MOUSE]

doronicum (dəˈrɒnɪkəm) *n.* any of a genus of plants, such as leopard's-bane, with yellow daisy-like flowers. [C17: NL, < Ar.]

dorp (dɔːp) *n. S. African.* a small town or village. [C16: < Du.]

dorsal (ˈdɔːsᵊl) *adj. Anat., zool.* relating to the back or spinal part of the body. [C15: < Med. L *dorsālis,* < L *dorsum* back] —ˈ**dorsally** *adv.*

dorsal fin *n.* an unpaired fin on the back of a fish that maintains balance during locomotion.

dory[1] (ˈdɔːrɪ) *n., pl.* **-ries.** any of various spiny-finned food fishes, esp. the John Dory. [C14: < F *dorée* gilded, < LL *deaurāre* to gild, ult. < L *aurum* gold]

dory[2] (ˈdɔːrɪ) *n., pl.* **-ries.** *U.S. & Canad.* a flat-bottomed boat with a high bow and stern. [C18: < Amerind *dóri* dugout]

dosage (ˈdəʊsɪdʒ) *n.* **1.** the administration of a drug or agent in prescribed amounts. **2.** the optimum therapeutic dose and interval between doses. **3.** another name for **dose** (senses 3, 4).

dose (dəʊs) *n.* **1.** *Med.* a specific quantity of a therapeutic drug or agent taken at any one time or at specified intervals. **2.** *Inf.* something unpleasant to experience: *a dose of influenza.* **3.** Also called: **dosage.** the total energy of ionizing radiation absorbed by unit mass of material, esp. of living tissue; usually measured in grays (SI unit) or rads. **4.** Also called: **dosage.** a small amount of syrup added to wine during bottling. **5.** *Sl.* a venereal infection. ~*vb.* (*tr.*) **6.** to administer a dose to (someone). **7.** *Med.* to prescribe (a drug) in appropriate quantities. **8.** to add syrup to (wine) during bottling. [C15: < F, < LL *dosis,* < Gk: a giving, < *didonai* to give]

dosimeter (dəʊˈsɪmɪtə) *n.* an instrument for measuring the dose of radiation absorbed by matter or the intensity of a source of radiation. —**dosimetric** (ˌdəʊsɪˈmɛtrɪk) *adj.*

dosing strip *n.* (in New Zealand) an area set aside for treating dogs suspected of having hydatid disease.

doss (dɒs) *Brit. sl.* ~*vb.* **1.** (*intr.;* often foll. by *down*) to sleep, esp. in a dosshouse. ~*n.* **2.** a bed, esp. in a dosshouse. **3.** another word for **sleep. 4.** short for **dosshouse.** [C18: <?]

dosser (ˈdɒsə) *n.* **1.** *Brit. sl.* a person who sleeps in dosshouses. **2.** *Brit. sl.* another word for **dosshouse. 3.** *Dublin dialect.* a lazy person.

dosshouse (ˈdɒsˌhaʊs) *n. Brit. sl.* a cheap lodging house, esp. one used by tramps. U.S. name: **flophouse.**

dossier (ˈdɒsɪˌeɪ) *n.* a collection of papers about a subject or person. [C19: < F: a file with a label on the back, < *dos* back, < L *dorsum*]

dost (dʌst) *vb. Arch. or dialect.* (used with *thou*) a singular form of the present tense (indicative mood) of **do**[1].

dot[1] (dɒt) *n.* **1.** a small round mark; spot; point. **2.** anything resembling a dot; a small amount. **3.** the mark (˙) above the letters *i, j.* **4.** *Music.* **a.** the symbol (·) placed after a note or rest to increase its time value by half. **b.** this symbol written above or below a note indicating staccato. **5.** *Maths, logic.* **a.** the symbol (.) indicating multiplication or logical conjunction. **b.** a decimal point. **6.** the symbol (·) used, in combination with the symbol for *dash* (—), in Morse and other codes. **7. on the dot.** at exactly the arranged time. ~*vb.* **dotting, dotted. 8.** (*tr.*) to mark or form with a dot. **9.** (*tr.*) to scatter or intersperse (as with dots): *bushes dotting the plain.* **10.** (*intr.*) to make a dot or dots. **11. dot one's i's and cross one's t's.** *Inf.* to pay meticulous attention to detail. [OE *dott* head of a boil] —ˈ**dotter** *n.*

dot[2] (dɒt) *n.* a woman's dowry. [C19: < F < L *dōs;* rel. to *dōtāre* to endow, *dāre* to give]

dotage (ˈdəʊtɪdʒ) *n.* **1.** feebleness of mind, esp. as a result of old age. **2.** foolish infatuation. [C14: < DOTE + -AGE]

dotard (ˈdəʊtəd) *n.* a person who is weak-minded, esp. through senility. [C14: < DOTE + -ARD] —ˈ**dotardly** *adj.*

dote (dəʊt) *vb.* (*intr.*) **1.** (foll. by *on* or *upon*) to love to an excessive or foolish degree. **2.** to be foolish or weak-minded, esp. as a result of old age. [C13: rel. to MDu. *doten* to be silly] —ˈ**doter** *n.*

doth (dʌθ) *vb. Arch. or dialect.* (used with *he, she,* or *it*) a singular form of the present tense of **do**[1].

dot matrix printer *n. Computers.* a printer in which each character is produced by a subset of an array of needles.

dotterel *or* **dottrel** (ˈdɒtrəl) *n.* **1.** a rare Eurasian plover with white bands around the head and neck. **2.** *Dialect.* a person who is foolish or easily duped. [C15 *dotrelle;* see DOTE]

dottle (ˈdɒtᵊl) *n.* the plug of tobacco left in a pipe after smoking. [C15: dim. of *dot* lump]

dotty (ˈdɒtɪ) *adj.* **-tier, -tiest. 1.** *Sl., chiefly Brit.* feeble-minded; slightly crazy. **2.** *Brit. sl.* (foll. by *about*) extremely fond (of). **3.** marked with dots. [C19: < DOT[1]] —ˈ**dottily** *adv.* —ˈ**dottiness** *n.*

Douay Bible *or* **Version** (ˈduːeɪ) *n.* an English translation of the Bible from the Latin Vulgate text completed by Roman Catholic scholars at Douai, N France in 1610.

double (ˈdʌbᵊl) *adj.* (*usually prenominal*) **1.** as much again in size, strength, number, etc.: *a double portion.* **2.** composed of two equal or similar parts. **3.** designed for two users: *a double room.* **4.** folded in two; composed of two layers. **5.** stooping; bent over. **6.** having two aspects; ambiguous: *a double meaning.* **7.** false, deceitful, or hypocritical: *a double life.* **8.** (of flowers) having more than the normal number of petals. **9.** *Music.* **a.** (of an instrument) sounding an octave lower: *a double bass.* **b.** (of time) duple. ~*adv.* **10.** twice over; twofold. **11.** two together; two at a time (esp. in **see double**). ~*n.* **12.** twice the number, amount, size, etc. **13.** a double measure of spirits. **14.** a duplicate or counterpart, esp. a person who closely resembles another; understudy. **15.** a ghostly apparition of a living person; doppelgänger. **16.** a sharp turn, esp. a return on one's own tracks. **17.** *Bridge.* a call that increases certain scoring points if the last preceding bid becomes the contract. **18.** *Billiards, etc.* a strike in which the object ball is struck so as to make it rebound against the cushion to an opposite pocket. **19.** a bet on two horses in different races in which any winnings from the first race are placed on the horse in the later race. **20. a.** the narrow outermost ring on a dartboard. **b.** a hit on this ring. **21. at** *or* **on the double. a.** at twice normal marching speed. **b.** quickly or immediately. ~*vb.* **22.** to make or become twice as much. **23.** to bend or fold (material, etc.). **24.** (*tr.;* sometimes foll. by *up*) to clench (a fist). **25.** (*tr.;* often foll. by *together* or *up*) to join or couple. **26.** (*tr.*) to repeat exactly; copy. **27.** (*intr.*) to play two parts or serve two roles. **28.** (*intr.*) to turn sharply; follow a winding course. **29.** *Naut.* to sail around (a headland or other point). **30.** *Music.* **a.** to duplicate (a part) either in unison or at the octave above or below it. **b.** (*intr.;* usually foll. by *on*) to be capable of performing (upon an additional instrument). **31.** *Bridge.* to make a call that will double certain scoring points if the preceding bid becomes the contract. **32.** *Billiards, etc.* to cause (a ball) to rebound or (of a ball) to rebound from a cushion. **33.** (*intr.;* foll. by *for*) to act as substitute. **34.** (*intr.*) to go or march at twice the normal speed. ~See also **double back, doubles, double up.** [C13: < OF, < L *duplus* twofold, < *duo* two + *-plus* -FOLD] —ˈ**doubler** *n.*

double agent *n.* a spy employed by two mutually antagonistic countries, companies, etc.

double back *vb.* (*intr., adv.*) to go back in the opposite direction (esp. in **double back on one's tracks**).

double-bank *vb. Austral. & N.Z. inf.* to carry (a second person) on (a horse, bicycle, etc.). Also: **dub.**

double bar *n. Music.* a symbol, consisting of two ordinary bar lines or a single heavy one, that marks the end of a composition or section.

double-barrelled *or U.S.* **-barreled** *adj.* **1.** (of a gun) having two barrels. **2.** extremely forceful. **3.** *Brit.* (of surnames) having hyphenated parts. **4.** serving two purposes; ambiguous: *a double-barrelled remark.*

double bass (beɪs) *n.* **1.** Also called (U.S.): **bass viol.** a stringed instrument, the largest and lowest member of the violin family with a range of almost three octaves. Inf. name: **bass fiddle.** ~*adj.* **double-bass. 2.** of an instrument whose pitch lies below the bass; contrabass.

double bassoon *n. Music.* the lowest and largest instrument in the oboe class; contrabassoon.

double boiler *n.* the U.S. and Canad. name for **double saucepan.**

double-breasted *adj.* (of a garment) having overlapping fronts.

double-check *vb.* **1.** to check again; verify. ~*n.* **double check. 2.** a second examination or verification. **3.** *Chess.* a simultaneous check from two pieces.

double chin *n.* a fold of fat under the chin. —ˌ**double-**ˈ**chinned** *adj.*

double concerto *n.* a concerto for two solo instruments.

double cream *n.* thick cream with a high fat content.

double-cross *vb.* **1.** (*tr.*) to cheat or betray. ~*n.* **2.** the act or an instance of double-crossing; betrayal. —ˌ**double-**ˈ**crosser** *n.*

double dagger *n.* a character (‡) used in printing to indicate a cross-reference.

double-dealing *n.* **a.** action characterized by

treachery or deceit. **b.** (*as modifier*): *double-dealing treachery.* —ˌ**double-ˈdealer** *n.*

double-decker *n.* **1.** *Chiefly Brit.* a bus with two passenger decks. **2.** *Inf.* **a.** a thing or structure having two decks, layers, etc. **b.** (*as modifier*): *a double-decker sandwich.*

double-declutch *vb.* (*intr.*) *Brit.* to change to a lower gear in a motor vehicle by first placing the gear lever into neutral before engaging the desired gear. U.S. term: **double-clutch.**

double Dutch *n. Brit. inf.* incomprehensible talk; gibberish.

double-edged *adj.* **1.** acting in two ways. **2.** (of a remark, etc.) having two possible interpretations, esp. applicable both for and against, or being malicious though apparently innocuous. **3.** (of a knife, etc.) having a cutting edge on either side of the blade.

double entendre (ɑːnˈtɑːndrə) *n.* **1.** a word, phrase, etc., that can be interpreted in two ways, esp. one having one meaning that is indelicate. **2.** the type of humour that depends upon this. [C17: < obs. F: double meaning]

double entry *n.* **a.** a book-keeping system in which any commercial transaction is entered as a debit in one account and as a credit in another. **b.** (*as modifier*): *double-entry book-keeping.*

double exposure *n.* **1.** the act or process of recording two superimposed images on a photographic medium. **2.** the photograph resulting from such an act.

double-faced *adj.* **1.** (of textiles) having a finished nap on each side; reversible. **2.** insincere or deceitful.

double feature *n. Films.* a programme showing two full-length films. Inf. name (U.S.): **twin bill.**

double first *n. Brit.* a first-class honours degree in two subjects.

double glazing *n.* **1.** two panes of glass in a window, fitted to reduce heat loss, etc. **2.** the fitting of glass in such a manner.

double-header *n.* **1.** a train drawn by two locomotives coupled together. **2.** Also called: **twin bill.** *Sport, U.S. & Canad.* two games played consecutively. **3.** *Austral. & N.Z. inf.* a coin with the impression of a head on each side. **4.** *Austral. inf.* a double ice-cream cone.

double helix *n.* the form of the molecular structure of DNA, consisting of two helical chains coiled around the same axis.

double-jointed *adj.* having unusually flexible joints permitting an abnormal degree of motion.

double knitting *n.* a widely used medium thickness of knitting wool.

double negative *n.* a construction, often considered ungrammatical, in which two negatives are used where one is needed, as in *I wouldn't never have believed it.*

▷ **Usage.** There are two contexts where double negatives are found. An adjective with negative force is often used with a negative in order to express a nuance of meaning somewhere between the positive and the negative: *it is not an uncommon sight.* Two negatives are also found together where they reinforce each other rather than conflict: *he never went back, not even to collect his belongings.* These two uses of a double negative are acceptable. A third case, illustrated by *I shouldn't wonder if it didn't rain today,* has the force of a weak positive statement (*I expect it to rain today*) and is common in informal English.

double-park *vb.* to park (a vehicle) alongside or opposite another already parked by the roadside, thereby causing an obstruction.

double pneumonia *n.* pneumonia affecting both lungs.

double-quick *adj.* **1.** very quick; rapid. ~*adv.* **2.** in a very quick or rapid manner.

double-reed *adj.* relating to or denoting a wind instrument having two reeds that vibrate against each other.

double refraction *n.* the splitting of a ray of unpolarized light into two unequally refracted rays polarized in mutually perpendicular planes. Also called: **birefringence.**

doubles (ˈdʌbᵊlz) *n.* (*functioning as pl.*) **a.** a game between two pairs of players. **b.** (*as modifier*): *a doubles match.*

double saucepan *n. Brit.* a cooking utensil consisting of two saucepans: the lower pan is used to boil water to heat food in the upper pan. U.S. and Canad. name: **double boiler.**

double-space *vb.* to type (copy) with a full space between lines.

double standard *n.* a set of principles that allows greater freedom to one person or group than to another.

double-stop *vb.* **-stopping, -stopped.** to play (two notes or parts) simultaneously on a violin or related instrument.

doublet (ˈdʌblɪt) *n.* **1.** (formerly) a man's close-fitting jacket, with or without sleeves (esp. in **doublet and hose**). **2. a.** a pair of similar things, esp. two words deriving ultimately from the same source. **b.** one of such a pair. **3.** *Jewellery.* a false gem made by welding or fusing stones together. **4.** *Physics.* a closely spaced pair of related spectral lines. **5.** (*pl.*) two dice each showing the same number of spots on one throw. [C14: < OF, < DOUBLE]

double take *n.* (esp. in comedy) a delayed reaction by a person to a remark, situation, etc.

double talk *n.* **1.** rapid speech with a mixture of nonsense syllables and real words; gibberish. **2.** empty, deceptive, or ambiguous talk.

doublethink (ˈdʌbᵊlˌθɪŋk) *n.* deliberate, perverse, or unconscious acceptance or promulgation of conflicting facts, principles, etc.

double time *n.* **1.** a doubled wage rate, paid for working on public holidays, etc. **2.** *Music.* two beats per bar. **3.** *U.S. Army.* **a.** a fast march. **b.** a slow running pace, keeping in step.

doubletree (ˈdʌbᵊlˌtriː) *n.* a horizontal pivoted bar on a vehicle to the ends of which swingletrees are attached for harnessing two horses.

double up *vb.* (*adv.*) **1.** to bend or cause to bend in two. **2.** (*intr.*) to share a room or bed designed for one person, family, etc. **3.** (*intr.*) *Brit.* to use the winnings from one bet as the stake for another. U.S. and Canad. term: **parlay.**

doubloon (dʌˈbluːn) *n.* **1.** a former Spanish gold coin. **2.** (*pl.*) *Sl.* money. [C17: < Sp. *doblón,* < *dobla,* < L *dupla,* fem. of *duplus* twofold]

doubly (ˈdʌblɪ) *adv.* **1.** to or in a double degree, quantity, or measure. **2.** in two ways.

doubt (daʊt) *n.* **1.** uncertainty about the truth, fact, or existence of something (esp. in **in doubt, without doubt,** etc.). **2.** (*often pl.*) lack of belief in or conviction about something. **3.** an unresolved difficulty, point, etc. **4.** *Obs.* fear. **5. give (someone) the benefit of the doubt.** to presume (someone suspected of guilt) innocent. **6. no doubt.** almost certainly. ~*vb.* **7.** (*tr.; may take a clause as object*) to be inclined to disbelieve. **8.** (*tr.*) to distrust or be suspicious of. **9.** (*intr.*) to feel uncertainty or be undecided. **10.** (*tr.*) *Arch.* to fear. [C13: < OF *douter,* < L *dubitāre*] —ˈ**doubtable** *adj.* —ˈ**doubter** *n.* —ˈ**doubtingly** *adv.*

▷ **Usage.** Where a clause follows *doubt* in a positive statement, the conjunction may be *whether, that,* or *if. Whether* (*I doubt whether he is there*) is universally accepted; *that* (*I doubt that he is there*) is less widely accepted and *if* (*I doubt if he is there*) is usually restricted to informal contexts. In negative statements, *doubt* is followed by *that: I do not doubt that he is telling the truth.* In such sentences, *but* (*I do not doubt but that he is telling the truth*) is redundant.

doubtful (ˈdaʊtfʊl) *adj.* **1.** unlikely; improbable. **2.** uncertain: *a doubtful answer.* **3.** unsettled; unresolved. **4.** of questionable reputation or morality. **5.** having reservations or misgivings. —ˈ**doubtfully** *adv.* —ˈ**doubtfulness** *n.*

doubting Thomas (ˈtɒməs) *n.* a person who insists on proof before he will believe anything. [after *Thomas* (the apostle), who did not believe that Jesus had been resurrected until he had proof]

doubtless (ˈdaʊtlɪs) *adv. also* **doubtlessly** (*sen-*

tence modifier), *sentence substitute.* **1.** certainly. **2.** probably. *~adj.* **3.** certain; assured. —ˈ**doubtlessness** *n.*

douche (duːʃ) *n.* **1.** a stream of water directed onto or into the body for cleansing or medical purposes. **2.** the application of such a stream of water. **3.** an instrument for applying a douche. *~vb.* **4.** to cleanse or treat or be cleansed or treated by means of a douche. [C18: < F, < It. *doccia* pipe]

dough (dəʊ) *n.* **1.** a thick mixture of flour or meal and water or milk, used for making bread, pastry, etc. **2.** any similar pasty mass. **3.** a slang word for **money.** [OE *dāg*]

doughboy (ˈdəʊˌbɔɪ) *n.* **1.** *U.S. inf.* an infantryman, esp. in World War I. **2.** dough that is boiled or steamed as a dumpling.

doughnut (ˈdəʊnʌt) *n.* **1.** a small cake of sweetened dough, often ring-shaped, cooked in hot fat. **2.** anything shaped like a ring, such as the reaction vessel of a thermonuclear reactor.

doughty (ˈdaʊtɪ) *adj.* **-tier, -tiest.** hardy; resolute. [OE *dohtig*] —ˈ**doughtily** *adv.* —ˈ**doughtiness** *n.*

doughy (ˈdəʊɪ) *adj.* **doughier, doughiest.** resembling dough; soft, pallid, or flabby.

Douglas fir, spruce, *or* **hemlock** (ˈdʌgləs) *n.* a North American pyramidal coniferous tree, widely planted for ornament and for timber. [C19: after David *Douglas* (1798–1834), Scot. botanist]

Doukhobor *or* **Dukhobor** (ˈduːkəʊˌbɔː) *n.* a member of a Russian sect of Christians that originated in the 18th century. In the late 19th century a large number emigrated to W Canada, where most Doukhobors now live. [C19: < Russian *dukhoborets* spirit wrestlers]

do up *vb.* (*adv.; mainly tr.*) **1.** to wrap and make into a bundle: *to do up a parcel.* **2.** to beautify or adorn. **3.** (*also intr.*) to fasten or be fastened. **4.** *Inf.* to renovate or redecorate. **5.** *Sl.* to assault. **6.** (*Inf.*) to cause the downfall of (a person).

dour (dʊə) *adj.* **1.** sullen. **2.** hard or obstinate. [C14: prob. < L *dūrus* hard] —ˈ**dourly** *adv.* —ˈ**dourness** *n.*

douroucouli (ˌduːruːˈkuːlɪ) *n.* a nocturnal New World monkey of Central and South America with thick fur and large eyes. [< Amerind]

douse *or* **dowse** (daʊs) *vb.* **1.** to plunge or be plunged into liquid; duck. **2.** (*tr.*) to drench with water. **3.** (*tr.*) to put out (a light, candle, etc.). *~n.* **4.** an immersion. [C16: ? rel. to obs. *douse* to strike, <?]

dove (dʌv) *n.* **1.** any of a family of birds having a heavy body, small head, short legs, and long pointed wings. **2.** *Politics.* a person opposed to war. **3.** a gentle or innocent person: used as a term of endearment. **4. a.** a greyish-brown colour. **b.** (*as adj.*): *dove walls.* [OE *dūfe* (unattested except as a fem. proper name)] —ˈ**doveˌlike** *adj.*

Dove (dʌv) *n.* **the.** *Christianity.* a manifestation of the Holy Ghost (John 1:32).

dovecote (ˈdʌvˌkəʊt) *or* **dovecot** (ˈdʌvˌkɒt) *n.* a structure for housing pigeons.

dovetail (ˈdʌvˌteɪl) *n.* **1.** a wedge-shaped tenon. **2.** Also called: **dovetail joint.** a joint containing such tenons. *~vb.* **3.** (*tr.*) to join by means of dovetails. **4.** to fit or cause to fit together closely or neatly.

dowager (ˈdaʊədʒə) *n.* **1. a.** a widow possessing property or a title obtained from her husband. **b.** (*as modifier*): *the dowager duchess.* **2.** a wealthy or dignified elderly woman. [C16: < OF *douagiere*, < *douage* DOWER]

dowdy (ˈdaʊdɪ) *adj.* **-dier, -diest.** **1.** (esp. of a woman or a woman's dress) shabby or old-fashioned. *~n., pl.* **-dies.** **2.** a dowdy woman. [C14: *dowd* slut, <?] —ˈ**dowdily** *adv.* —ˈ**dowdiness** *n.* —ˈ**dowdyish** *adj.*

dowel (ˈdaʊəl) *n.* a wooden or metal peg that fits into two corresponding holes to join two adjacent parts. [C14: < MLow G *dövel* plug, < OHG *tubili*]

dower (ˈdaʊə) *n.* **1.** the life interest in a part of her husband's estate allotted to a widow by law. **2.** an archaic word for **dowry** (sense 1). **3.** a natural gift. *~vb.* **4.** (*tr.*) to endow. [C14: < OF *douaire*, < Med. L *dōtārium*, < L *dōs* gift]

dower house *n.* a house for the use of a widow, often on her deceased husband's estate.

dowitcher (ˈdaʊɪtʃə) *n.* either of two snipelike shore birds of arctic and subarctic North America. [C19: < Amerind]

do with *vb.* **1. could** *or* **can do with.** to find useful; benefit from. **2. have to do with.** to be involved in or connected with. **3. to do with.** concerning; related to. **4. what...do with. a.** to put or place: *what did you do with my coat?* **b.** to handle or treat. **c.** to fill one's time usefully: *she didn't know what to do with herself when the project was finished.*

do without *vb.* (*intr.*) **1.** to forgo; manage without. **2.** (*prep.*) not to require (uncalled-for comments): *we can do without your criticisms.*

Dow-Jones average (ˈdaʊˈdʒəʊnz) *n. U.S.* a daily index of stock-exchange prices based on the average price of a selected number of securities. [C20: after Charles H. *Dow* (died 1902) & Edward D. *Jones* (died 1920), American financial statisticians]

down[1] (daʊn) *prep.* **1.** used to indicate movement from a higher to a lower position. **2.** at a lower or further level or position on, in, or along: *he ran down the street.* *~adv.* **3.** downwards; at or to a lower level or position. **4.** (*particle*) used with many verbs when the result of the verb's action is to lower or destroy its object: *knock down.* **5.** (*particle*) used with several verbs to indicate intensity or completion: *calm down.* **6.** immediately: *cash down.* **7.** on paper: *write this down.* **8.** arranged; scheduled. **9.** in a helpless position. **10. a.** away from a more important place. **b.** away from a more northerly place. **c.** (of a member of some British universities) away from the university. **d.** in a particular part of a country: *down south.* **11.** *Naut.* (of a helm) having the rudder to windward. **12.** reduced to a state of lack or want: *down to the last pound.* **13.** lacking a specified amount. **14.** lower in price. **15.** including all intermediate grades. **16.** from an earlier to a later time. **17.** to a finer or more concentrated state: *to grind down.* **18.** *Sport.* being a specified number of points, goals, etc., behind another competitor, team, etc. **19.** (of a person) being inactive, owing to illness: *down with flu.* **20.** (*functioning as imperative*) (to dogs): *down, Rover!* **21.** (*functioning as imperative*) **down with.** wanting the end of somebody or something: *down with the king!* *~adj.* **22.** (*postpositive*) depressed. **23.** (*prenominal*) of or relating to a train or trains from a more important place or one regarded as higher: *the down line.* **24.** made in cash: *a down payment.* *~vb.* (*tr.*) **25.** to knock, push, or pull down. **26.** to cause to go or come down. **27.** *Inf.* to drink, esp. quickly. **28.** to bring (someone) down, esp. by tackling. *~n.* **29.** a descent; downward movement. **30.** a lowering or a poor period (esp. in **ups and downs**). **31.** (in Canadian football) any of a series of three attempts to advance the ball ten yards. **32. have a down on.** *Inf.* to bear ill will towards. [OE *dūne*, short for *adūne*, var. of *of dūne*, lit.: from the hill]

down[2] (daʊn) *n.* **1.** soft fine feathers. **2.** another name for **eiderdown** (sense 1). **3.** *Bot.* a fine coating of soft hairs, as on certain leaves, fruits, and seeds. **4.** any growth or coating of soft fine hair. [C14: < ON]

down[3] (daʊn) *n. Arch.* a hill, esp. a sand dune. See also **downs.** [OE *dūn*]

down-and-out *adj.* **1.** without any means of livelihood; poor and, often, socially outcast. *~n.* **2.** a person who is destitute and, often, homeless.

downbeat (ˈdaʊnˌbiːt) *n.* **1.** *Music.* the first beat of a bar or the downward gesture of a conductor's baton indicating this. *~adj. Inf.* **2.** depressed; gloomy. **3.** relaxed.

downcast (ˈdaʊnˌkɑːst) *adj.* **1.** dejected. **2.** (esp. of the eyes) directed downwards. *~n.* **3.** *Mining.* a ventilation shaft.

downer (ˈdaʊnə) *n. Sl.* **1.** a barbiturate, tranquillizer, or narcotic. **2.** a depressing experience. **3.** a state of depression.

downfall ('daʊnˌfɔːl) *n.* **1.** a sudden loss of position, health, or reputation. **2.** a fall of rain, snow, etc., esp. a sudden heavy one.

downgrade ('daʊnˌgreɪd) *vb.* (*tr.*) **1.** to reduce in importance or value, esp. to demote (a person) to a poorer job. **2.** to speak of disparagingly. ~*n.* **3.** *Chiefly U.S. & Canad.* a downward slope. **4. on the downgrade.** waning in importance, health, etc.

downhearted (ˌdaʊn'hɑːtɪd) *adj.* discouraged; dejected. —ˌ**down'heartedly** *adv.*

downhill ('daʊn'hɪl) *adj.* **1.** going or sloping down. ~*adv.* **2.** towards the bottom of a hill; downwards. **3. go downhill.** *Inf.* to decline; deteriorate. ~*n.* **4.** the downward slope of a hill; a descent. **5.** a skiing race downhill.

downhole ('daʊnˌhəʊl) *adj.* (in the oil industry) denoting any piece of equipment which is used in the well itself.

Downing Street ('daʊnɪŋ) *n.* **1.** a street in W central London: official residences of the prime minister of Great Britain and the chancellor of the exchequer. **2.** *Inf.* the prime minister or the British Government. [after Sir George *Downing* (1623–84), E statesman]

download ('daʊnˌləʊd) *vb.* (*tr.*) to copy or transfer (data or a program) from one computer's memory to that of another, esp. in a network of computers.

down-market *adj.* relating to commercial products, services, etc., that are cheap, have little prestige, or are poor in quality.

down payment *n.* the deposit paid on an item purchased on hire-purchase, mortgage, etc.

downpipe ('daʊnˌpaɪp) *n. Brit. and N.Z.* a pipe for carrying rainwater from a roof gutter to ground level. Usual U.S. & Canad. name: **downspout.**

downpour ('daʊnˌpɔː) *n.* a heavy continuous fall of rain.

downrange ('daʊn'reɪndʒ) *adj., adv.* in the direction of the intended flight path of a rocket or missile.

downright ('daʊnˌraɪt) *adj.* **1.** frank or straightforward; blunt. ~*adv., adj.* (*prenominal*) **2.** (intensifier): *downright rude.* —'**downˌrightly** *adv.* —'**downˌrightness** *n.*

downs (daʊnz) *pl. n.* **1.** rolling upland, esp. in the chalk areas of S Britain, characterized by lack of trees and used mainly as pasture. **2.** *Austral. & N.Z.* a flat grassy area, not necessarily of uplands.

Down's syndrome (daʊnz) *n.* **a.** *Pathol.* a chromosomal abnormality resulting in a flat face and nose, a vertical fold of skin at the inner edge of the eye, and mental retardation. Former name: **mongolism. b.** (*as modifier*): *a Down's syndrome baby.* [C19: after John *Langdon-Down* (1828–96), E physician]

downstage ('daʊn'steɪdʒ) *Theatre.* ~*adv.* **1.** at or towards the front of the stage. ~*adj.* **2.** of or relating to the front of the stage.

downstairs ('daʊn'stɛəz) *adv.* **1.** down the stairs; to or on a lower floor. ~*n.* **2. a.** a lower or ground floor. **b.** (*as modifier*): *a downstairs room.* **3.** *Brit. inf.* the servants of a household collectively.

downstream ('daʊn'striːm) *adv., adj.* in or towards the lower part of a stream; with the current.

downswing ('daʊnˌswɪŋ) *n.* a statistical downward trend in business activity, the death rate, etc.

downtime ('daʊnˌtaɪm) *n. Commerce.* time during which a computer or machine is not working, as when under repair.

down-to-earth *adj.* sensible; practical; realistic.

downtown ('daʊn'taʊn) *Chiefly U.S., Canad., & N.Z.* ~*n.* **1.** the central or lower part of a city, esp. the main commercial area. ~*adv.* **2.** towards, to, or into this area. ~*adj.* **3.** of, relating to, or situated in the downtown area: *a downtown cinema.*

downtrodden ('daʊnˌtrɒdᵊn) *adj.* **1.** subjugated; oppressed. **2.** trodden down.

downturn ('daʊnˌtɜːn) *n.* another term for **downswing.**

down under *Inf.* ~*n.* **1.** Australia or New Zealand. ~*adv.* **2.** in or to Australia or New Zealand.

downward ('daʊnwəd) *adj.* **1.** descending from a higher to a lower level, condition, position, etc. **2.** descending from a beginning. ~*adv.* **3.** a variant of **downwards.** —'**downwardly** *adv.*

downwards ('daʊnwədz) *or* **downward** *adv.* **1.** from a higher to a lower place, level, etc. **2.** from an earlier time or source to a later.

downwind ('daʊn'wɪnd) *adv., adj.* in the same direction towards which the wind is blowing; with the wind from behind.

downy ('daʊnɪ) *adj.* **downier, downiest. 1.** covered with soft fine hair or feathers. **2.** light, soft, and fluffy. **3.** made from or filled with down. **4.** *Brit. sl.* sharp-witted. —'**downiness** *n.*

dowry ('daʊərɪ) *n., pl.* **-ries. 1.** the property brought by a woman to her husband at marriage. **2.** a natural talent or gift. [C14: < Anglo-F *douarie,* < Med. L *dōtārium;* see DOWER]

dowse (daʊz) *vb.* (*intr.*) to search for underground water, minerals, etc., using a divining rod; divine. [C17: <?] —'**dowser** *n.*

doxology (dɒk'sɒlədʒɪ) *n., pl.* **-gies.** a hymn, verse, or form of words in Christian liturgy glorifying God. [C17: < Med. L *doxologia,* < Gk, < *doxologos* uttering praise, < *doxa* praise; see -LOGY] —**doxological** (ˌdɒksə'lɒdʒɪkᵊl) *adj.*

doxy ('dɒksɪ) *n., pl.* **doxies.** *Arch. sl.* a prostitute or mistress. [C16: prob. < MFlemish *docke* doll]

doyen ('dɔɪən) *n.* the senior member of a group, profession, or society. [C17: < F, < LL *decānus* leader of a group of ten] —**doyenne** (dɔɪ'ɛn) *fem. n.*

doyley ('dɔɪlɪ) *n.* a variant spelling of **doily.**

doz. *abbrev. for* dozen.

doze (dəʊz) *vb.* (*intr.*) **1.** to sleep lightly or intermittently. **2.** (often foll. by *off*) to fall into a light sleep. ~*n.* **3.** a short sleep. [C17: prob. < ON *dūs* lull] —'**dozer** *n.*

dozen ('dʌzᵊn) *determiner.* **1.** (preceded by a or a numeral) twelve or a group of twelve: *two dozen oranges.* ~*n., pl.* **dozens** *or* **dozen. 2. by the dozen.** in large quantities. **3. daily dozen.** *Brit.* regular physical exercises. **4. talk nineteen to the dozen.** to talk without stopping. [C13: < OF *douzaine,* < *douze* twelve, < L *duodecim,* < *duo* two + *decem* ten] —'**dozenth** *adj.*

dozy ('dəʊzɪ) *adj.* **dozier, doziest. 1.** drowsy. **2.** *Brit. inf.* stupid. —'**dozily** *adv.* —'**doziness** *n.*

DP *abbrev. for:* **1.** data processing. **2.** displaced person.

DPhil *or* **DPh** *abbrev. for* Doctor of Philosophy. Also: **PhD.**

DPP (in Britain) *abbrev. for* Director of Public Prosecutions.

dpt *abbrev. for:* **1.** department. **2.** depot.

dr *abbrev. for:* **1.** Also: **dr.** dram. **2.** debtor.

Dr *abbrev. for:* **1.** Doctor. **2.** Drive.

DR *abbrev. for* dry riser.

dr. *abbrev. for:* **1.** debit. **2.** drachma.

drab[1] (dræb) *adj.* **drabber, drabbest. 1.** dull; dingy. **2.** cheerless; dreary. **3.** of the colour drab. ~*n.* **4.** a light olive-brown colour. [C16: < OF *drap* cloth, < LL *drappus,* ? of Celtic origin] —'**drably** *adv.* —'**drabness** *n.*

drab[2] (dræb) *Arch.* ~*n.* **1.** a slatternly woman. **2.** a whore. ~*vb.* **drabbing, drabbed. 3.** (*intr.*) to consort with prostitutes. [C16: of Celtic origin]

drachm (dræm) *n.* **1.** Also called: **fluid dram.** *Brit.* one eighth of a fluid ounce. **2.** *U.S.* another name for **dram** (sense 2). **3.** another name for **drachma.** [C14: learned var. of DRAM]

drachma ('drækmə) *n., pl.* **-mas** *or* **-mae** (-miː). **1.** the standard monetary unit of Greece. **2.** *U.S.* another name for **dram** (sense 2). **3.** a silver coin of ancient Greece. [C16: < L, < Gk *drakhmē* a handful, < *drassesthai* to seize]

drack *or* **drac** (dræk) *adj. Austral. sl.* (of a woman) unattractive. [C20: ? < *Dracula's* daughter]

Draconian (dreɪ'kəʊnɪən) *or* **Draconic** (dreɪ-

ˈkɒnɪk) *adj.* (*sometimes not cap.*) **1.** of or relating to Draco (Athenian statesman, 7th century B.C.), or his code of laws. **2.** harsh.

draff (dræf) *n.* the residue of husks after fermentation of the grain in brewing, used as cattle fodder. [C13: < ON *draf*]

draft (drɑːft) *n.* **1.** a plan, sketch, or drawing of something. **2.** a preliminary outline of a book, speech, etc. **3.** another word for **bill of exchange.** **4.** a demand or drain on something. **5.** *U.S. & Austral.* selection for compulsory military service. **6.** detachment of military personnel from one unit to another. **7.** *Austral. & N.Z.* a group of livestock separated from the rest of the herd or flock. ~*vb.* (*tr.*) **8.** to draw up an outline or sketch for. **9.** to prepare a plan or design of. **10.** to detach (military personnel) from one unit to another. **11.** *U.S.* to select for compulsory military service. **12.** *Austral. & N.Z.* **a.** to select (cattle or sheep) from a herd or flock. **b.** to select (farm stock) for sale. ~*n., vb.* **13.** the usual U.S. spelling of **draught.** [C16: var. of DRAUGHT] —**ˈdrafter** *n.*

draftee (drɑːfˈtiː) *n. U.S.* a conscript.

drafty (ˈdrɑːftɪ) *adj.* **draftier, draftiest.** the usual U.S. spelling of **draughty.**

drag (dræg) *vb.* **dragging, dragged.** **1.** to pull or be pulled with force, esp. along the ground. **2.** (*tr.*; often foll. by *away* or *from*) to persuade to come away. **3.** to trail or cause to trail on the ground. **4.** (*tr.*) to move with effort or difficulty. **5.** to linger behind. **6.** (often foll. by *on* or *out*) to prolong or be prolonged unnecessarily or tediously: *his talk dragged on for hours.* **7.** (when *intr.*, usually foll. by *for*) to search (the bed of a river, etc.) with a dragnet or hook. **8.** (*tr.*; foll. by *out* or *from*) to crush (clods) or level (a soil surface) by use of a drag. **9.** (of hounds) to follow (a fox or its trail). **10.** (*intr.*) *Sl.* to draw (on a cigarette, etc.). **11. drag anchor.** (of a vessel) to move away from its mooring because the anchor has failed to hold. **12. drag one's feet** *or* **heels.** *Inf.* to act with deliberate slowness. ~*n.* **13.** the act of dragging or the state of being dragged. **14.** an implement, such as a dragnet, dredge, etc., used for dragging. **15.** a type of harrow used to crush clods, level soil, etc. **16.** a coach with seats inside and out, usually drawn by four horses. **17.** a braking device. **18.** a person or thing that slows up progress. **19.** slow progress or movement. **20.** *Aeronautics.* the resistance to the motion of a body passing through a fluid, esp. through air. **21.** the trail of scent left by a fox, etc. **22.** an artificial trail of scent drawn over the ground for hounds to follow. **23.** See **drag hunt.** **24.** *Inf.* a person or thing that is very tedious. **25.** *Sl.* a car. **26.** short for **drag race.** **27.** *Sl.* **a.** women's clothes worn by a man (esp. in **in drag**). **b.** (*as modifier*): *a drag show.* **c.** clothes collectively. **28.** *Inf.* a draw on a cigarette, etc. **29.** *U.S. sl.* influence. **30.** *Chiefly U.S. sl.* a street (esp. in **main drag**). ~See also **drag out of, drag up.** [OE *dragan* to DRAW]

dragée (dræˈʒeɪ) *n.* **1.** a sweet coated with a hard sugar icing. **2.** a tiny beadlike sweet used for decorating cakes, etc. **3.** a medicinal pill coated with sugar. [C19: < F; see DREDGE[2]]

draggle (ˈdrægˀl) *vb.* **1.** to make or become wet or dirty by trailing on the ground; bedraggle. **2.** (*intr.*) to lag; dawdle. [ME, prob. frequentative of DRAG]

drag hunt *n.* **1.** a hunt in which hounds follow an artificial trail of scent. **2.** a club that organizes such hunts. —**ˈdrag-ˌhunt** *vb.*

dragnet (ˈdrægˌnɛt) *n.* **1.** a net used to scour the bottom of a pond, river, etc., as when searching for something. **2.** any system of coordinated efforts to track down wanted persons.

dragoman (ˈdrægəʊmən) *n., pl.* **-mans** *or* **-men.** (in some Middle Eastern countries, esp. formerly) a professional interpreter or guide. [C14: < F, < It., < Med. Gk *dragoumanos,* < Ar. *targumān,* ult. < Akkadian]

dragon (ˈdrægən) *n.* **1.** a mythical monster usually represented as breathing fire and having a scaly reptilian body, wings, claws, and a long tail. **2.** *Inf.* a fierce person, esp. a woman. **3.** any of various very large lizards, esp. the Komodo dragon. **4. chase the dragon.** *Sl.* to smoke opium or heroin. [C13: < OF, < L *dracō,* < Gk *drakōn*]

dragonet (ˈdrægənɪt) *n.* a small fish with spiny fins, a flat head, and a tapering brighty coloured body. [C14 (meaning: small dragon): < F; applied to fish C18]

dragonfly (ˈdrægənˌflaɪ) *n., pl.* **-flies.** a predatory insect having a long slender body and two pairs of iridescent wings that are outspread at rest.

dragonnade (ˌdrægəˈneɪd) *n.* **1.** *History.* the persecution of French Huguenots during the reign of Louis XIV by dragoons quartered in their villages and homes. **2.** subjection by military force. ~*vb.* **3.** (*tr.*) to subject to persecution by military troops. [C18: < F, < *dragon* DRAGOON]

dragoon (drəˈguːn) *n.* **1.** (originally) a mounted infantryman armed with a carbine. **2.** (*sometimes cap.*) a domestic fancy pigeon. **3. a.** a type of cavalryman. **b.** (*pl.; cap. when part of a name*): *the Royal Dragoons.* ~*vb.* (*tr.*) **4.** to coerce; force. **5.** to persecute by military force. [C17: < F *dragon* (special use of DRAGON), soldier armed with a carbine]

drag out of *vb.* (*tr., adv. + prep.*) to obtain or extract (a confession, statement, etc.), esp. by force. Also: **drag from.**

drag race *n.* a type of motor race in which specially built or modified cars or motorcycles are timed over a measured course. —**drag racing** *n.*

dragster (ˈdrægstə) *n.* a car specially built or modified for drag racing.

drag up *vb.* (*tr., adv.*) *Inf.* **1.** to rear (a child) poorly and in an undisciplined manner. **2.** to introduce or revive (an unpleasant fact or story).

drain (dreɪn) *n.* **1.** a pipe or channel that carries off water, sewage, etc. **2.** an instance or cause of continuous diminution in resources or energy; depletion. **3.** *Surgery.* a device, such as a tube, to drain off pus, etc. **4. down the drain.** wasted. ~*vb.* **5.** (*tr.*; often foll. by *off*) to draw off or remove (liquid) from. **6.** (*intr.*; often foll. by *away*) to flow (away) or filter (off). **7.** (*intr.*) to dry or be emptied as a result of liquid running off or flowing away. **8.** (*tr.*) to drink the entire contents of (a glass, etc.). **9.** (*tr.*) to consume or make constant demands on (resources, energy, etc.); exhaust. **10.** (*intr.*) to disappear or leave, esp. gradually. **11.** (*tr.*) (of a river, etc.) to carry off the surface water from an area. **12.** (*intr.*) (of an area) to discharge its surface water into rivers, streams, etc. [OE *drēahnian*] —**ˈdrainer** *n.*

drainage (ˈdreɪnɪdʒ) *n.* **1.** the process or a method of draining. **2.** a system of watercourses or drains. **3.** liquid, sewage, etc., that is drained away.

drainage basin *or* **area** *n.* another name for **catchment area.**

draining board *n.* a sloping grooved surface at the side of a sink, used for draining washed dishes, etc. Also called: **drainer.**

drainpipe (ˈdreɪnˌpaɪp) *n.* a pipe for carrying off rainwater, sewage, etc.; downpipe.

drake (dreɪk) *n.* the male of any duck. [C13: ? < Low G]

Dralon (ˈdreɪlɒn) *n. Trademark.* an acrylic fibre fabric used esp. for upholstery.

dram (dræm) *n.* **1.** one sixteenth of an ounce (avoirdupois). 1 dram is equivalent to 0.0018 kilogram. **2.** *U.S.* one eighth of an apothecaries' ounce; 60 grains. 1 dram is equivalent to 0.0039 kilogram. **3.** a small amount of an alcoholic drink, esp. a spirit; tot. [C15: < OF *dragme,* < LL *dragma,* < Gk *drakhmē;* see DRACHMA]

drama (ˈdrɑːmə) *n.* **1.** a work to be performed by actors; play. **2.** the genre of literature represented by works intended for the stage. **3.** the art of the writing and production of plays. **4.** a situation that is highly emotional, tragic, or turbulent. [C17: < LL: a play, < Gk: something performed, < *drān* to do]

Dramamine (ˈdræməˌmiːn) *n.* a trademark for **dimenhydrinate.**

dramatic (drəˈmætɪk) *adj.* **1.** of drama. **2.** like a drama in suddenness, emotional impact, etc. **3.** striking; effective. **4.** acting or performed in a flamboyant way. —**dra'matically** *adv.*

dramatic irony *n. Theatre.* the irony occurring when the implications of a situation, speech, etc., are understood by the audience but not by the characters in the play.

dramatics (drəˈmætɪks) *n.* **1.** (*functioning as sing. or pl.*) **a.** the art of acting or producing plays. **b.** dramatic productions. **2.** (*usually functioning as pl.*) histrionic behaviour.

dramatis personae (ˈdrɑːmətɪs pəˈsəʊnaɪ) *pl. n.* (*often functioning as sing.*) the characters in a play. [C18: < NL]

dramatist (ˈdræmətɪst) *n.* a playwright.

dramatize *or* **-tise** (ˈdræməˌtaɪz) *vb.* **1.** (*tr.*) to put into dramatic form. **2.** to express (something) in a dramatic or exaggerated way. —ˌ**dramatiˈzation** *or* **-tiˈsation** *n.*

dramaturge (ˈdræməˌtɜːdʒ) *n.* **1.** Also called: **dramaturgist.** a dramatist. **2.** Also called: **dramaturg.** a literary adviser on the staff of a theatre, film company, etc. [C19: prob. < F, < Gk *dramatourgos* playwright, < DRAMA + *ergon* work]

dramaturgy (ˈdræməˌtɜːdʒɪ) *n.* the art and technique of the theatre; dramatics. —ˌ**dramaˈturgic** *or* ˌ**dramaˈturgical** *adj.*

drank (dræŋk) *vb.* the past tense of **drink.**

drape (dreɪp) *vb.* **1.** (*tr.*) to hang or cover with material or fabric, usually in folds. **2.** to hang or arrange or be hung or arranged, esp. in folds. **3.** (*tr.*) to place casually and loosely. ~*n.* **4.** (*often pl.*) a cloth or hanging that covers something in folds. **5.** the way in which fabric hangs. [C15: < OF *draper,* < *drap* piece of cloth; see DRAB[1]]

draper (ˈdreɪpə) *n.* **1.** *Brit.* a dealer in fabrics and sewing materials. **2.** *Arch.* a maker of cloth.

drapery (ˈdreɪpərɪ) *n., pl.* **-peries.** **1.** fabric or clothing arranged and draped. **2.** (*often pl.*) curtains or hangings that drape. **3.** *Brit.* the occupation or shop of a draper. **4.** fabrics and cloth collectively. —ˈ**draperied** *adj.*

drapes (dreɪps) *or* **draperies** (ˈdreɪpərɪz) *pl. n. Chiefly U.S. & Canad.* curtains, esp. ones of heavy fabric.

drastic (ˈdræstɪk) *adj.* extreme or forceful; severe. [C17: < Gk *drastikos,* < *drān* to do, act] —ˈ**drastically** *adv.*

drat (dræt) *interj. Sl.* an exclamation of annoyance. [C19: prob. alteration of *God rot*]

draught *or U.S.* **draft** (drɑːft) *n.* **1.** a current of air, esp. in an enclosed space. **2. a.** the act of pulling a load, as by a vehicle or animal. **b.** (*as modifier*): *a draught horse.* **3.** the load or quantity drawn. **4.** a portion of liquid to be drunk, esp. a dose of medicine. **5.** the act or an instance of drinking; a gulp or swallow. **6.** the act or process of drawing air, etc., into the lungs. **7.** the amount of air, etc., inhaled. **8. a.** beer, wine, etc., stored in bulk, esp. in a cask. **b.** (*as modifier*): *draught beer.* **c. on draught.** drawn from a cask or keg. **9.** any one of the flat discs used in the game of draughts. U.S. and Canad. equivalent: **checker.** **10.** the depth of a loaded vessel in the water. **11. feel the draught.** to be short of money. [C14: prob. < ON *drahtr,* of Gmc origin]

draughtboard (ˈdrɑːftˌbɔːd) *n.* a square board divided into 64 squares of alternating colours, used for playing draughts or chess.

draughts (drɑːfts) *n.* (*functioning as sing.*) a game for two players using a draughtboard and 12 draughtsmen each. U.S. and Canad. name: **checkers.** [C14: pl. of DRAUGHT (in obs. sense: a chess move)]

draughtsman *or U.S.* **draftsman** (ˈdrɑːftsmən) *n., pl.* **-men.** **1.** a person employed to prepare detailed scale drawings of machinery, buildings, etc. **2.** a person skilled in drawing. **3.** *Brit.* any of the flat discs used in the game of draughts. U.S. and Canad. equivalent: **checker.** —ˈ**draughtsmanˌship** *or U.S.* ˈ**draftsmanˌship** *n.*

draughty *or U.S.* **drafty** (ˈdrɑːftɪ) *adj.* **draughtier, draughtiest** *or U.S.* **draftier, draftiest.** characterized by or exposed to draughts of air. —ˈ**draughtily** *or U.S.* ˈ**draftily** *adv.* —ˈ**draughtiness** *or U.S.* ˈ**draftiness** *n.*

Dravidian (drəˈvɪdɪən) *n.* **1.** a family of languages spoken in S and central India and Sri Lanka, including Tamil, Malayalam, etc. **2.** a member of one of the aboriginal races of India, pushed south by the Indo-Europeans and now mixed with them. ~*adj.* **3.** of or denoting this family of languages or these peoples.

draw (drɔː) *vb.* **drawing, drew, drawn.** **1.** to cause (a person or thing) to move towards or away by pulling. **2.** to bring, take, or pull (something) out, as from a drawer, holster, etc. **3.** (*tr.*) to extract or pull or take out: *to draw teeth.* **4.** (*tr.;* often foll. by *off*) to take (liquid) out of a cask, etc., by means of a tap. **5.** (*intr.*) to move, esp. in a specified direction: *to draw alongside.* **6.** (*tr.*) to attract: *to draw attention.* **7.** (*tr.*) to cause to flow: *to draw blood.* **8.** to depict or sketch (a figure, picture, etc.) in lines, as with a pencil or pen. **9.** (*tr.*) to make, formulate, or derive: *to draw conclusions.* **10.** (*tr.*) to write (a legal document) in proper form. **11.** (*tr.;* sometimes foll. by *in*) to suck or take in (air, etc.). **12.** (*intr.*) to induce or allow a draught to carry off air, smoke, etc. **13.** (*tr.*) to take or receive from a source: *to draw money from the bank.* **14.** (*tr.*) to earn: *draw interest.* **15.** (*tr.*) to write out (a bill of exchange, etc.): *to draw a cheque.* **16.** (*tr.*) to choose at random. **17.** (*tr.*) to reduce the diameter of (a wire) by pulling it through a die. **18.** (*tr.*) to shape (metal or glass) by rolling, by pulling through a die, or by stretching. **19.** *Archery.* to bend (a bow) by pulling the string. **20.** to steep (tea) or (of tea) to steep in boiling water. **21.** (*tr.*) to disembowel. **22.** (*tr.*) to cause (pus, etc.) to discharge from an abscess or wound. **23.** (*intr.*) (of two teams, etc.) to finish a game with an equal number of points, goals, etc.; tie. **24.** (*tr.*) *Bridge, whist.* to keep leading a suit in order to force out (all outstanding cards). **25. draw trumps.** *Bridge, whist.* to play the trump suit until the opponents have none left. **26.** (*tr.*) *Billiards.* to cause (the cue ball) to spin back after a direct impact with another ball. **27.** (*tr.*) to search (a place) in order to find wild animals, etc., for hunting. **28.** *Golf.* to drive (the ball) too far to the left. **29.** (*tr.*) *Naut.* (of a vessel) to require (a certain depth) in which to float. **30. draw and quarter.** to disembowel and dismember (a person) after hanging. **31. draw stumps.** *Cricket.* to close play. **32. draw the shot.** *Bowls.* to deliver the bowl in such a way that it approaches the jack. ~*n.* **33.** the act of drawing. **34.** *U.S.* a sum of money advanced to finance anticipated expenses. **35.** *Inf.* an event, act, etc., that attracts a large audience. **36.** a raffle or lottery. **37.** something taken at random, as a ticket in a lottery. **38.** a contest or game ending in a tie. **39.** *U.S. & Canad.* a small natural drainage way or gully. ~See also **drawback, draw in,** etc. [OE *dragan*]

drawback (ˈdrɔːˌbæk) *n.* **1.** a disadvantage or hindrance. **2.** a refund of customs or excise paid on goods that are being exported or used in making goods for export. ~*vb.* **draw back.** (*intr., adv.;* often foll. by *from*) **3.** to retreat; move backwards. **4.** to turn aside from an undertaking.

drawbridge (ˈdrɔːˌbrɪdʒ) *n.* a bridge that may be raised to prevent access or to enable vessels to pass.

drawee (drɔːˈiː) *n.* the person or organization on which an order for payment is drawn.

drawer (ˈdrɔːə) *n.* **1.** a person or thing that draws, esp. a draughtsman. **2.** a person who draws a cheque. **3.** a person who draws up a commercial paper. **4.** *Arch.* a person who draws beer, etc., in a bar. **5.** (drɔː). a boxlike container in a chest, table, etc., made for sliding in and out.

drawers (drɔːz) *pl. n.* a legged undergarment for either sex, worn below the waist.

draw in *vb.* (*intr., adv.*) **1.** (of hours of daylight) to become shorter. **2.** (of a train) to arrive at a station.

drawing (ˈdrɔːɪŋ) *n.* **1.** a picture or plan made by

means of lines on a surface, esp. one made with a pencil or pen. **2.** a sketch or outline. **3.** the art of making drawings; draughtsmanship.

drawing pin *n. Brit.* a short tack with a broad smooth head for fastening papers to a drawing board, etc. U.S. and Canad. names: **thumbtack, pushpin.**

drawing room *n.* **1.** a room where visitors are received and entertained; living room; sitting room. **2.** *Arch.* a formal reception.

drawknife (ˈdrɔːˌnaɪf) *or* **drawshave** *n., pl.* **-knives** *or* **-shaves.** a tool with two handles, used to shave wood. U.S. name: **spokeshave.**

drawl (drɔːl) *vb.* **1.** to speak or utter (words) slowly, esp. prolonging the vowel sounds. ~*n.* **2.** the way of speech of someone who drawls. [C16: prob. frequentative of DRAW] —ˈ**drawling** *adj.*

drawn (drɔːn) *adj.* haggard, tired, or tense in appearance.

drawn work *n.* ornamental needlework done by drawing threads out of the fabric and using the remaining threads to form lacelike patterns. Also called: **drawn-thread work.**

draw off *vb.* (*adv.*) **1.** (*tr.*) to cause (a liquid) to flow from something. **2.** to withdraw (troops).

draw on *vb.* **1.** (*intr., prep.*) to use or exploit (a source, fund, etc.). **2.** (*intr., adv.*) to come near. **3.** (*tr., prep.*) to withdraw (money) from (an account). **4.** (*tr., adv.*) to put on (clothes). **5.** (*tr., adv.*) to lead further; entice.

draw out *vb.* (*adv.*) **1.** to extend. **2.** (*tr.*) to cause (a person) to talk freely. **3.** (*tr.;* foll. by *of*) Also: **draw from.** to elicit (information) (from). **4.** (*tr.*) to withdraw (money) as from a bank account. **5.** (*intr.*) (of hours of daylight) to become longer. **6.** (*intr.*) (of a train) to leave a station. **7.** (*tr.*) to extend (troops) in line. **8.** (*intr.*) (of troops) to proceed from camp.

drawstring (ˈdrɔːˌstrɪŋ) *n.* a cord, etc., run through a hem around an opening, so that when it is pulled tighter, the opening closes.

draw up *vb.* (*adv.*) **1.** to come or cause to come to a halt. **2.** (*tr.*) **a.** to prepare a draft of (a document, etc.). **b.** to formulate and write out: *to draw up a contract.* **3.** (*used reflexively*) to straighten oneself. **4.** to form or arrange (a body of soldiers, etc.) in order or formation.

dray[1] (dreɪ) *n.* **a.** a low cart used for carrying heavy loads. **b.** (*in combination*): *a drayman.* [OE *dræge* dragnet]

dray[2] (dreɪ) *n.* a variant spelling of **drey.**

dread (drɛd) *vb.* (*tr.*) **1.** to anticipate with apprehension or terror. **2.** to fear greatly. **3.** *Arch.* to be in awe of. ~*n.* **4.** great fear. **5.** an object of terror. **6.** *Sl.* a Rastafarian. **7.** *Arch.* deep reverence. [OE *ondrǣdan*]

dreadful (ˈdrɛdfʊl) *adj.* **1.** extremely disagreeable, shocking, or bad. **2.** (intensifier): *a dreadful waste of time.* **3.** causing dread; terrifying. **4.** *Arch.* inspiring awe.

dreadfully (ˈdrɛdfʊlɪ) *adv.* **1.** in a shocking or disagreeable manner. **2.** (intensifier): *you're dreadfully kind.*

dreadlocks (ˈdrɛdˌlɒks) *pl. n. Inf.* hair worn in the Rastafarian style of long tightly-curled strands.

dreadnought (ˈdrɛdˌnɔːt) *n.* **1.** a battleship armed with heavy guns of uniform calibre. **2.** an overcoat made of heavy cloth.

dream (driːm) *n.* **1. a.** mental activity, usually an imagined series of events, occurring during sleep. **b.** (*as modifier*): *a dream sequence.* **c.** (*in combination*): *dreamland.* **2. a.** a sequence of imaginative thoughts indulged in while awake; daydream; fantasy. **b.** (*as modifier*): *a dream world.* **3.** a person or thing seen or occurring in a dream. **4.** a cherished hope; aspiration. **5.** a vain hope. **6.** a person or thing that is as pleasant or seemingly unreal as a dream. **7. go like a dream.** to move, develop, or work very well. ~*vb.* **dreaming, dreamt** *or* **dreamed.** **8.** (*may take a clause as object*) to undergo or experience (a dream or dreams). **9.** (*intr.*) to indulge in daydreams. **10.** (*intr.*) to suffer delusions; be unrealistic. **11.** (when *intr.*, foll. by *of* or *about*) to have an image (of) or fantasy (about) in or as if in a dream. **12.** (*intr.;* foll. by *of*) to consider the possibility (of). ~*adj.* **13.** too good to be true; ideal: *dream kitchen.* [OE *drēam* song] —ˈ**dreamer** *n.*

dreamboat (ˈdriːmˌbəʊt) *n. Sl.* an ideal or desirable person, esp. one of the opposite sex.

dreamt (drɛmt) *vb.* a past tense and past participle of **dream.**

dream time *n.* **1.** another name for **alcheringa.** **2.** *Austral. inf.* any remote period, out of touch with the realities of the present.

dream up *vb.* (*tr., adv.*) to invent by ingenuity and imagination: *to dream up an excuse.*

dreamy (ˈdriːmɪ) *adj.* **dreamier, dreamiest.** **1.** vague or impractical. **2.** resembling a dream. **3.** relaxing; gentle: *dreamy music.* **4.** *Inf.* wonderful. **5.** having dreams, esp. daydreams. —ˈ**dreamily** *adv.* —ˈ**dreaminess** *n.*

dreary (ˈdrɪərɪ) *adj.* **drearier, dreariest.** **1.** sad or dull; dismal. **2.** wearying; boring. ~Also (literary): **drear.** [OE *drēorig* gory] —ˈ**drearily** *adv.* —ˈ**dreariness** *n.*

dredge[1] (drɛdʒ) *n.* **1.** a machine used to scoop or suck up material from a riverbed, channel, etc. **2.** another name for **dredger.** ~*vb.* **3.** to remove (material) from a riverbed, etc., by means of a dredge. **4.** (*tr.*) to search for (a submerged object) with or as if with a dredge; drag. [C16: ? ult. < OE *dragan* to DRAW]

dredge[2] (drɛdʒ) *vb.* to sprinkle or coat (food) with flour, etc. [C16: < OF *dragie,* ? < L *tragēmata* spices, < Gk] —ˈ**dredger** *n.*

dredger (ˈdrɛdʒə) *n.* **1.** a vessel used for dredging. **2.** another name for **dredge**[1].

dredge up *vb.* (*tr., adv.*) **1.** *Inf.* to bring to notice, esp. with effort and from an obscure source. **2.** to raise, as with a dredge.

dree (driː) *Scot., literary.* ~*vb.* **dreeing, dreed.** **1.** (*tr.*) to endure. ~*adj.* **2.** dreary. [OE *drēogan*]

D region *or* **layer** *n.* the lowest region of the ionosphere, extending from a height of about 60 kilometres to about 90 kilometres.

dregs (drɛgz) *pl. n.* **1.** solid particles that settle at the bottom of some liquids. **2.** residue or remains. **3.** *Brit. sl.* a despicable person. [C14 *dreg,* < ON *dregg*]

dreich *or* **dreigh** (driːx) *adj. Scot. dialect.* dreary. [ME *dreig, drih* enduring, < OE *drēog* (unattested)]

drench (drɛntʃ) *vb.* (*tr.*) **1.** to make completely wet; soak. **2.** to give liquid medicine to (an animal). ~*n.* **3.** a drenching. **4.** a dose of liquid medicine given to an animal. [OE *drencan* to cause to drink] —ˈ**drenching** *n., adj.*

Dresden (ˈdrɛzdᵊn) *n.* **1.** Also called: **Dresden china.** delicate and decorative porcelain ware made near Dresden, a city in East Germany. ~*adj.* **2.** designating or of Dresden china.

dress (drɛs) *vb.* **1.** to put clothes on; attire. **2.** (*intr.*) to put on more formal attire. **3.** (*tr.*) to provide (someone) with clothing; clothe. **4.** (*tr.*) to arrange merchandise in (a shop window). **5.** (*tr.*) to arrange (the hair). **6.** (*tr.*) to apply protective or therapeutic covering to (a wound, sore, etc.). **7.** (*tr.*) to prepare (food, esp. fowl and fish) by cleaning, gutting, etc. **8.** (*tr.*) to put a finish on (stone, metal, etc.). **9.** (*tr.*) to cultivate (land), esp. by applying fertilizer. **10.** (*tr.*) to trim (trees, etc.). **11.** (*tr.*) to groom (a horse). **12.** (*tr.*) to convert (tanned hides) into leather. **13.** *Mil.* to bring (troops) into line or (of troops) to come into line (esp. in **dress ranks**). **14. dress ship.** *Naut.* to decorate a vessel by displaying signal flags on lines. ~*n.* **15.** a one-piece garment for a woman, consisting of a skirt and bodice. **16.** complete style of clothing; costume: *military dress.* **17.** (*modifier*) suitable for a formal occasion: *a dress shirt.* **18.** outer covering or appearance. ~See also **dress down, dress up.** [C14: < OF *drecier,* ult. < L *dīrigere* to DIRECT]

dressage (ˈdrɛsɑːʒ) *n.* **a.** the training of a horse to perform manoeuvres in response to the rider's body signals. **b.** the manoeuvres performed. [F: preparation, < OF *dresser* to prepare; see DRESS]

dress circle *n.* a tier of seats in a theatre or other auditorium, usually the first gallery.

dress down *vb.* (*tr., adv.*) *Inf.* to reprimand severely or scold (a person).

dresser[1] (ˈdrɛsə) *n.* **1.** a set of shelves, usually also with cupboards, for storing or displaying dishes, etc. **2.** *U.S.* a chest of drawers for storing clothing, often having a mirror on top. [C14 *dressour,* < OF *dreceore,* < *drecier* to arrange; see DRESS]

dresser[2] (ˈdrɛsə) *n.* **1.** a person who dresses in a specified way: *a fashionable dresser.* **2.** *Theatre.* a person employed to assist actors with their costumes. **3.** a tool used for dressing stone, etc. **4.** *Brit.* a person who assists a surgeon during operations. **5.** *Brit.* See **window-dresser.**

dressing (ˈdrɛsɪŋ) *n.* **1.** a sauce for food, esp. for salad. **2.** the U.S. and Canad. name for **stuffing** (sense 2). **3.** a covering for a wound, etc. **4.** fertilizer spread on land. **5.** size used for stiffening textiles. **6.** the processes in the conversion of hides into leather.

dressing-down *n. Inf.* a severe scolding.

dressing gown *n.* a full robe worn before dressing or for lounging.

dressing room *n.* **1.** *Theatre.* a room backstage for an actor to change clothing and to make up. **2.** any room used for changing clothes.

dressing station *n. Mil.* a first-aid post close to a combat area.

dressing table *n.* a piece of bedroom furniture with a mirror and a set of drawers for clothes, cosmetics, etc.

dressmaker (ˈdrɛsˌmeɪkə) *n.* a person whose occupation is making clothes, esp. for women. —ˈ**dressˌmaking** *n.*

dress parade *n. Mil.* a formal parade in dress uniform.

dress rehearsal *n.* **1.** the last rehearsal of a play, etc., using costumes, lighting, etc., as for the first night. **2.** any full-scale practice.

dress shirt *n.* a man's evening shirt, worn as part of formal evening dress.

dress suit *n.* a man's evening suit, esp. tails.

dress uniform *n. Mil.* formal ceremonial uniform.

dress up *vb.* (*adv.*) **1.** to attire (oneself or another) in one's best clothes. **2.** to put fancy dress, etc., on. **3.** (*tr.*) to improve the appearance or impression of: *to dress up the facts.*

dressy (ˈdrɛsɪ) *adj.* **dressier, dressiest. 1.** (of clothes) elegant. **2.** (of persons) dressing stylishly. **3.** overelegant. —ˈ**dressiness** *n.*

drew (druː) *vb.* the past tense of **draw.**

drey *or* **dray** (dreɪ) *n.* a squirrel's nest. [C17: <?]

dribble (ˈdrɪbᵊl) *vb.* **1.** (*usually intr.*) to flow or allow to flow in a thin stream or drops; trickle. **2.** (*intr.*) to allow saliva to trickle from the mouth. **3.** (in soccer, basketball, hockey, etc.) to propel (the ball) by repeatedly tapping it with the hand, foot, or a stick. ~*n.* **4.** a small quantity of liquid falling in drops or flowing in a thin stream. **5.** a small quantity or supply. **6.** an act or instance of dribbling. [C16: frequentative of *drib,* var. of DRIP] —ˈ**dribbler** *n.* —ˈ**dribbly** *adj.*

driblet *or* **dribblet** (ˈdrɪblɪt) *n.* a small amount. [C17: < obs. *drib* to fall bit by bit + -LET]

dribs and drabs (drɪbz) *pl. n. Inf.* small sporadic amounts.

dried (draɪd) *vb.* the past tense and past participle of **dry.**

drier[1] (ˈdraɪə) *adj.* a comparative of **dry.**

drier[2] (ˈdraɪə) *n.* a variant spelling of **dryer**[1].

driest (ˈdraɪɪst) *adj.* a superlative of **dry.**

drift (drɪft) *vb.* (*mainly intr.*) **1.** (*also tr.*) to be carried along as by currents of air or water or (of a current) to carry (a vessel, etc.) along. **2.** to move aimlessly from one place or activity to another. **3.** to wander away from a fixed course or point; stray. **4.** (*also tr.*) (of snow, etc.) to accumulate in heaps or to drive (snow, etc.) into heaps. ~*n.* **5.** something piled up by the wind or current, as a snowdrift. **6.** tendency or meaning: *the drift of the argument.* **7.** a state of indecision or inaction. **8.** the extent to which a vessel, aircraft, etc., is driven off course by winds, etc. **9.** a general tendency of surface ocean water to flow in the direction of the prevailing winds. **10.** a driving movement, force, or influence; impulse. **11.** a controlled four-wheel skid used to take bends at high speed. **12.** a deposit of sand, gravel, etc., esp. one transported and deposited by a glacier. **13.** a horizontal passage in a mine that follows the mineral vein. **14.** something, esp. a group of animals, driven along. **15.** a steel tool driven into holes to enlarge or align them. **16.** an uncontrolled slow change in some operating characteristic of a piece of equipment. **17.** *S. African.* a ford. [C13: < ON: snowdrift]

driftage (ˈdrɪftɪdʒ) *n.* **1.** the act of drifting. **2.** matter carried along by drifting. **3.** the amount by which an aircraft or vessel has drifted.

drifter (ˈdrɪftə) *n.* **1.** a person or thing that drifts. **2.** a person who moves aimlessly from place to place. **3.** a boat used for drift-net fishing.

drift ice *n.* masses of ice floating in the sea.

drift net *n.* a large fishing net that is allowed to drift with the tide or current.

driftwood (ˈdrɪftˌwʊd) *n.* wood floating on or washed ashore by the sea or other body of water.

drill[1] (drɪl) *n.* **1.** a machine or tool for boring holes. **2.** *Mil.* **a.** training in procedures or movements, as for parades or the use of weapons. **b.** (*as modifier*): *drill hall.* **3.** strict and often repetitious training or exercises used in teaching. **4.** *Inf.* correct procedure. **5.** a marine mollusc that preys on oysters. ~*vb.* **6.** to pierce, bore, or cut (a hole) in (material) with or as if with a drill. **7.** to instruct or be instructed in military procedures or movements. **8.** (*tr.*) to teach by rigorous exercises or training. **9.** (*tr.*) *Inf.* to riddle with bullets. [C17: < MDu. *drillen*] —ˈ**driller** *n.*

drill[2] (drɪl) *n.* **1.** a machine for planting seeds in rows. **2.** a furrow in which seeds are sown. **3.** a row of seeds planted by means of a drill. ~*vb.* **4.** to plant (seeds) by means of a drill. [C18: <?; cf. G *Rille* furrow] —ˈ**driller** *n.*

drill[3] (drɪl) *n.* a hard-wearing twill-weave cotton cloth, used for uniforms, etc. [C18: var. of G *Drillich,* < L *trilīx,* < TRI- + *līcium* thread]

drill[4] (drɪl) *n.* an Old World monkey of W Africa, related to the mandrill. [C17: < a West African word]

drilling fluid *n.* a fluid, usually consisting of a suspension of clay in water, pumped down when an oil well is being drilled. Also called: **mud.**

drilling platform *n.* a structure, either fixed to the sea bed or mobile, which supports the machinery and equipment (**drilling rig**), together with the stores, etc., required for drilling an offshore oil well.

drilling rig *n.* **1.** the complete machinery, equipment, and structures needed to drill an oil well. **2.** a mobile drilling platform used for exploratory offshore drilling.

drillmaster (ˈdrɪlˌmɑːstə) *n.* **1.** Also called: **drill sergeant.** a military drill instructor. **2.** a person who instructs in a strict manner.

drill press *n.* a machine tool for boring holes.

drily (ˈdraɪlɪ) *adv.* a variant spelling of **dryly.**

drink (drɪŋk) *vb.* **drinking, drank, drunk. 1.** to swallow (a liquid). **2.** (*tr.*) to soak up (liquid); absorb. **3.** (*tr.; usually foll. by in*) to pay close attention to. **4.** (*tr.*) to bring (oneself) into a certain condition by consuming alcohol. **5.** (*tr.; often foll. by away*) to dispose of or ruin by excessive expenditure on alcohol. **6.** (*intr.*) to consume alcohol, esp. to excess. **7.** (when *intr.,* foll. by *to*) to drink (a toast). **8. drink the health of.** to salute or celebrate with a toast. **9. drink with the flies.** *Austral. inf.* to drink alone. ~*n.* **10.** liquid suitable for drinking. **11.** alcohol or its habitual or excessive consumption. **12.** a portion of liquid for drinking; draught. **13. the drink.** *Inf.* the sea. [OE *drincan*] —ˈ**drinkable** *adj.* —ˈ**drinker** *n.*

drink-driving *n.* (*modifier*) of or relating to driving a car after drinking alcohol: *drink-driving offences; drink-driving campaign.*

drinking fountain *n.* a device for providing a flow or jet of drinking water, esp. in public places.

drinking-up time *n.* (in Britain) a short time allowed for finishing drinks before closing time in a public house.

drinking water *n.* water reserved or suitable for drinking.

drip (drɪp) *vb.* **dripping, dripped.** **1.** to fall or let fall in drops. ~*n.* **2.** the formation and falling of drops of liquid. **3.** the sound made by falling drops. **4.** a projection at the edge of a sill or cornice designed to throw water clear of the wall. **5.** *Inf.* an inane, insipid person. **6.** *Med.* the usually intravenous drop-by-drop administration of a solution. [OE *dryppan,* < *dropa* DROP]

drip-dry *adj.* **1.** designating clothing or a fabric that will dry relatively free of creases if hung up when wet. ~*vb.* **-drying, -dried.** **2.** to dry or become dry thus.

drip feed *vb.* (*tr.*) **1.** to feed someone a liquid drop by drop, esp. intravenously. ~*n.* **drip-feed.** **2.** another term for **drip** (sense 6).

dripping (ˈdrɪpɪŋ) *n.* **1.** the fat that exudes from meat while it is being roasted or fried. **2.** (*often pl.*) liquid that falls in drops. ~*adv.* **3.** (intensifier): *dripping wet.*

drippy (ˈdrɪpɪ) *adj.* **-pier, -piest.** **1.** *Inf.* mawkish, insipid, or inane. **2.** tending to drip.

drive (draɪv) *vb.* **driving, drove, driven.** **1.** to push, propel, or be pushed or propelled. **2.** to guide the movement of (a vehicle, animal, etc.). **3.** (*tr.*) to compel or urge to work or act, esp. excessively. **4.** (*tr.*) to goad into a specified attitude or state: *work drove him to despair.* **5.** (*tr.*) to cause (an object) to make (a hole, crack, etc.). **6.** to move rapidly by striking or throwing with force. **7.** *Sport.* to hit (a ball) very hard and straight. **8.** *Golf.* to strike (the ball) with a driver. **9.** (*tr.*) to chase (game) from cover. **10.** to transport or be transported in a vehicle. **11.** (*intr.*) to rush or dash violently, esp. against an obstacle. **12.** (*tr.*) to transact with vigour (esp. in **drive a hard bargain**). **13.** (*tr.*) to force (a component) into or out of its location by means of blows or a press. **14.** (*tr.*) *Mining.* to excavate horizontally. **15.** **drive home. a.** to cause to penetrate to the fullest extent. **b.** to make clear by special emphasis. ~*n.* **16.** the act of driving. **17.** a journey in a driven vehicle. **18.** a road for vehicles, esp. a private road leading to a house. **19.** vigorous pressure, as in business. **20.** a united effort, esp. towards a common goal. **21.** *Brit.* a large gathering of persons to play cards, etc. **22.** energy, ambition, or initiative. **23.** *Psychol.* a motive or interest, such as sex, hunger, or ambition. **24.** a sustained and powerful military offensive. **25. a.** the means by which force, motion, etc., is transmitted in a mechanism: *fluid drive.* **b.** (*as modifier*): *a drive shaft.* **26.** *Sport.* a hard straight shot or stroke. **27.** a search for and chasing of game towards waiting guns. [OE *drīfan*] —ˈ**drivable** *or* ˈ**driveable** *adj.*

drive at *vb.* (*intr., prep.*) *Inf.* to intend or mean: *what are you driving at?*

drive-in *adj.* **1.** denoting a public facility or service designed to be used by patrons seated in their cars: *a drive-in bank.* ~*n.* **2.** *Chiefly U.S. & Canad.* a cinema designed to be used in such a manner.

drivel (ˈdrɪvᵊl) *vb.* **-elling, -elled** *or U.S.* **-eling, -eled.** **1.** to allow (saliva) to flow from the mouth; dribble. **2.** (*intr.*) to speak foolishly. ~*n.* **3.** foolish or senseless talk. **4.** saliva flowing from the mouth; slaver. [OE *dreflian* to slaver] —ˈ**driveller** *n.*

driven (ˈdrɪvᵊn) *vb.* the past participle of **drive.**

driver (ˈdraɪvə) *n.* **1.** a person who drives a vehicle. **2.** **in the driver's seat.** in a position of control. **3.** a person who drives animals. **4.** a mechanical component that exerts a force on another to produce motion. **5.** *Golf.* a club, a No. 1 wood, used for tee shots. **6.** *Electronics.* a circuit whose output provides the input of another circuit. —ˈ**driverless** *adj.*

driveway (ˈdraɪvˌweɪ) *n.* a path for vehicles, often connecting a house with a public road.

driving licence *n.* an official document authorizing a person to drive a motor vehicle.

drizzle (ˈdrɪzᵊl) *n.* **1.** very light rain. ~*vb.* **2.** (*intr.*) to rain lightly. [OE *drēosan* to fall] —ˈ**drizzly** *adj.*

drogue (drəʊg) *n.* **1.** any funnel-like device used as a sea anchor. **2. a.** a small parachute released behind an aircraft to reduce its landing speed. **b.** a small parachute released during the landing of a spacecraft. **3.** a device towed behind an aircraft as a target for firing practice. **4.** a device on the end of the hose of a tanker aircraft, to assist location of the probe of the receiving aircraft. **5.** a windsock. [C18: prob. based ult. on OE *dragan* to DRAW]

droll (drəʊl) *adj.* amusing in a quaint or odd manner; comical. [C17: < F *drôle* scamp, < MDu.: imp] —ˈ**drollness** *n.* —ˈ**drolly** *adv.*

drollery (ˈdrəʊlərɪ) *n., pl.* **-eries.** **1.** humour; comedy. **2.** *Rare.* a droll act, story, or remark.

-drome *n. combining form.* **1.** a course or race-course: *hippodrome.* **2.** a large place for a special purpose: *aerodrome.* [via L < Gk *dromos* race, course]

dromedary (ˈdrʌmədərɪ) *n., pl.* **-daries.** a type of Arabian camel bred for racing and riding, having a single hump. [C14: < LL *dromedārius* (*camēlus*), < Gk *dromas* running]

-dromous *adj. combining form.* moving or running: *anadromous; catadromous.* [via NL < Gk *-dromos,* < *dromos* a running]

drone[1] (drəʊn) *n.* **1.** a male honeybee whose sole function is to mate with the queen. **2.** a person who lives off the work of others. **3.** a pilotless radio-controlled aircraft. [OE *drān;* see DRONE[2]]

drone[2] (drəʊn) *vb.* **1.** (*intr.*) to make a monotonous low dull sound. **2.** (when *intr.,* often foll. by *on*) to utter (words) in a monotonous tone, esp. to talk without stopping. ~*n.* **3.** a monotonous low dull sound. **4.** *Music.* a sustained bass note or chord. **5.** one of the single-reed pipes in a set of bagpipes. **6.** a person who speaks in a low monotonous tone. [C16: rel. to DRONE[1] & MDu. *drōnen,* G *dröhnen*] —ˈ**droning** *adj.*

drongo (ˈdrɒŋgəʊ) *n., pl.* **-gos.** **1.** any of various songbirds of the Old World tropics, having a glossy black plumage. **2.** *Austral. & N.Z. sl.* a slow-witted person. [C19: < Malagasy]

drool (druːl) *vb.* **1.** (*intr.;* often foll. by *over*) to show excessive enthusiasm (for) or pleasure (in); gloat (over). ~*vb., n.* **2.** another word for **drivel** (senses 1, 2, 4). [C19: prob. alteration of DRIVEL]

droop (druːp) *vb.* **1.** to sag or allow to sag, as from weakness. **2.** (*intr.*) to be overcome by weariness. **3.** (*intr.*) to lose courage. ~*n.* **4.** the act or state of drooping. [C13: < ON *drūpa*] —ˈ**drooping** *adj.* —ˈ**droopy** *adj.*

drop (drɒp) *n.* **1.** a small quantity of liquid that forms or falls in a spherical mass. **2.** a very small quantity of liquid. **3.** a very small quantity of anything. **4.** something resembling a drop in shape or size. **5.** the act or an instance of falling; descent. **6.** a decrease in amount or value. **7.** the vertical distance that anything may fall. **8.** a steep incline or slope. **9.** the act of unloading troops, etc., by parachute. **10.** *Theatre.* See **drop curtain.** **11.** another word for **trap door** or **gallows.** **12.** *Chiefly U.S. & Canad.* a slot through which an object can be dropped into a receptacle. **13.** *Austral. cricket sl.* a fall of the wicket. **14.** See **drop shot.** **15.** **at the drop of a hat.** without hesitation or delay. **16.** **have the drop on (someone).** *U.S. & N.Z.* to have the advantage over (someone). ~*vb.* **dropping, dropped.** **17.** (of liquids) to fall or allow to fall in globules. **18.** to fall or allow to fall vertically. **19.** (*tr.*) to allow to fall by letting go of. **20.** to sink or fall or cause to sink to the ground, as from a blow, weariness, etc. **21.** (*intr.;* foll. by *back, behind,* etc.) to move in a specified manner, direction, etc. **22.** (*intr.;* foll. by *in, by,* etc.) *Inf.* to pay a casual visit (to). **23.** to decrease in amount or value. **24.** to sink or cause to sink to a lower position. **25.** to make or become less in strength, volume, etc. **26.** (*intr.*) to decline in health or condition. **27.** (*intr.; sometimes* foll. by *into*) to pass easily into a condition: *to drop into a habit.* **28.** (*intr.*) to move gently as with a current of air. **29.** (*tr.*) to mention casually: *to drop a hint.* **30.** (*tr.*) to leave out (a word or letter). **31.** (*tr.*) to set down (passengers or goods). **32.** (*tr.*) to send or post: *drop me a line.* **33.** (*tr.*) to discontinue: *let's drop the matter.* **34.** (*tr.*) to cease to associate with. **35.** (*tr.*) *Sl., chiefly U.S.* to cease to employ. **36.** (*tr.;* sometimes foll. by *in, off,* etc.) *Inf.* to leave or deposit. **37.** (of animals) to give birth to (offspring). **38.** *Sl., chiefly U.S. & Canad.* to lose (money). **39.** (*tr.*) to lengthen (a hem, etc.). **40.** (*tr.*) to unload (troops, etc.) by parachute. **41.** (*tr.*) *Naut.* to sail out of sight of. **42.** (*tr.*) *Sport.* to omit (a player) from a team. **43.** (*tr.*) to lose (a game, etc.). **44.** (*tr.*) *Golf, basketball, etc.* to hit or throw (a ball) into a goal. **45.** (*tr.*) to hit (a ball) with a drop shot. ~*n., vb.* **46.** *Rugby.* short for **drop kick** or **drop-kick.** ~See also **drop off, dropout, drops.** [OE *dropian*]

drop curtain *n. Theatre.* a curtain that can be raised and lowered onto the stage.

drop forge *n.* a device for forging metal between two dies, one of which is fixed, the other acting by gravity or by pressure. —**'drop-forge** *vb.* (*tr.*)

drop goal *n. Rugby.* a goal scored with a drop kick during the run of play.

drop hammer *n.* another name for **drop forge.**

drop-in *n.* (*modifier*) denoting a social service or meeting place provided where people may attend if and when they please.

drop kick *n.* **1.** a kick in which the ball is dropped and kicked as it bounces from the ground. **2.** a wrestling attack in which a wrestler leaps in the air and kicks his opponent. ~*vb.* **drop-kick. 3.** to kick (a ball, a wrestling opponent, etc.) by the use of a drop kick.

drop leaf *n.* **a.** a hinged flap on a table that can be raised to extend the surface. **b.** (*as modifier*): *a drop-leaf table.*

droplet ('drɒplɪt) *n.* a tiny drop.

drop off *vb.* (*adv.*) **1.** (*intr.*) to grow smaller or less. **2.** (*tr.*) to set down. **3.** (*intr.*) *Inf.* to fall asleep. ~*n.* **drop-off. 4.** a steep descent. **5.** a sharp decrease.

dropout ('drɒpˌaʊt) *n.* **1.** a student who fails to complete a course. **2.** a person who rejects conventional society. **3. drop-out.** *Rugby.* a drop kick taken to restart play. ~*vb.* **drop out.** (*intr., adv.;* often foll. by *of*) **4.** to abandon or withdraw from (a school, job, etc.).

dropper ('drɒpə) *n.* **1.** a small tube having a rubber bulb at one end for dispensing drops of liquid. **2.** a person or thing that drops.

droppings ('drɒpɪŋz) *pl. n.* the dung of certain animals, such as rabbits, sheep, and birds.

drops (drɒps) *pl. n.* any liquid medication applied by means of a dropper.

drop scone *n.* a flat spongy cake made by dropping a spoonful of batter on a hot griddle.

drop shot *n. Tennis, etc.* a softly played return that drops abruptly after clearing the net.

dropsy ('drɒpsɪ) *n.* **1.** *Pathol.* a condition characterized by an accumulation of watery fluid in the tissues or in a body cavity. **2.** *Sl.* a tip or bribe. [C13: < *ydropesie,* < L *hydrōpisis,* < Gk *hudrōps,* < *hudōr* water] —**dropsical** ('drɒpsɪkᵊl) *adj.*

droshky ('drɒʃkɪ) *or* **drosky** ('drɒskɪ) *n., pl.* **-kies.** an open four-wheeled carriage, formerly used in Russia. [C19: < Russian, dim. of *drogi* wagon]

drosophila (drɒ'sɒfɪlə) *n., pl.* **-las** *or* **-lae** (-ˌliː). any of a genus of small flies that are widely used in laboratory genetics studies. Also called: **fruit fly.** [C19: NL, < Gk *drosos* dew + *-phila* -PHILE]

dross (drɒs) *n.* **1.** the scum formed on the surfaces of molten metals. **2.** worthless matter; waste. [OE *drōs* dregs] —**'drossy** *adj.* —**'drossiness** *n.*

drought (draʊt) *n.* **1.** a prolonged period of scanty rainfall. **2.** a prolonged shortage. [OE *drūgoth*] —**'droughty** *adj.*

drove[1] (drəʊv) *vb.* the past tense of **drive.**

drove[2] (drəʊv) *n.* **1.** a herd of livestock being driven together. **2.** (*often pl.*) a moving crowd of people. ~*vb.* (*tr.*) **3.** to drive (livestock), usually for a considerable distance. [OE *drāf* herd]

drover ('drəʊvə) *n.* a person who drives sheep or cattle, esp. to and from market.

drown (draʊn) *vb.* **1.** to die or kill by immersion in liquid. **2.** (*tr.*) to get rid of: *he drowned his sorrows in drink.* **3.** (*tr.*) to drench thoroughly. **4.** (*tr.;* sometimes foll. by *out*) to render (a sound) inaudible by making a loud noise. [C13: prob. < OE *druncnian*]

drowse (draʊz) *vb.* **1.** to be or cause to be sleepy, dull, or sluggish. ~*n.* **2.** the state of being drowsy. [C16: prob. < OE *drūsian* to sink]

drowsy ('draʊzɪ) *adj.* **drowsier, drowsiest. 1.** heavy with sleepiness; sleepy. **2.** inducing sleep; soporific. **3.** sluggish or lethargic; dull. —**'drowsily** *adv.* —**'drowsiness** *n.*

drub (drʌb) *vb.* **drubbing, drubbed.** (*tr.*) **1.** to beat as with a stick. **2.** to defeat utterly, as in a contest. **3.** to drum or stamp (the feet). **4.** to instil with force or repetition. ~*n.* **5.** a blow, as from a stick. [C17: prob. < Ar. *dáraba* to beat]

drudge (drʌdʒ) *n.* **1.** a person who works hard at wearisome menial tasks. ~*vb.* **2.** (*intr.*) to toil at such tasks. [C16: ? < *druggen* to toil] —**'drudger** *n.* —**'drudgingly** *adv.*

drudgery ('drʌdʒərɪ) *n., pl.* **-eries.** hard, menial, and monotonous work.

drug (drʌg) *n.* **1.** any substance used in the treatment, prevention, or diagnosis of disease. Related adj.: **pharmaceutical. 2.** a chemical substance, esp. a narcotic, taken for the effects it produces. **3. drug on the market.** a commodity available in excess of demand. ~*vb.* **drugging, drugged.** (*tr.*) **4.** to mix a drug with (food, etc.). **5.** to administer a drug to. **6.** to stupefy or poison with or as if with a drug. [C14: < OF *drogue,* prob. of Gmc origin]

drug addict *n.* any person who is abnormally dependent on narcotic drugs.

drugget ('drʌgɪt) *n.* a coarse fabric used as a protective floor covering, etc. [C16: < F *droguet* useless fabric, < *drogue* trash]

druggist ('drʌgɪst) *n.* a U.S. and Canad. term for **pharmacist.**

drugstore ('drʌgˌstɔː) *n. U.S. & Canad.* a shop where medical prescriptions are made up and a wide variety of goods and usually light meals are sold.

druid ('druːɪd) *n.* (*sometimes cap.*) **1.** a member of an ancient order of priests in Gaul, Britain, and Ireland in the pre-Christian era. **2.** a member of any of several modern movements attempting to revive druidism. [C16: < L *druides* of Gaulish origin] —**druidess** ('druːɪdɪs) *fem. n.* —**dru'idic** *or* **dru'idical** *adj.* —**'druidˌism** *n.*

drum (drʌm) *n.* **1.** a percussion instrument sounded by striking a membrane stretched across the opening of a hollow cylinder or hemisphere. **2.** the sound produced by a drum or any similar sound. **3.** an object that resembles a drum in shape, such as a large spool or a cylindrical container. **4.** *Archit.* a cylindrical block of stone used to construct the shaft of a column. **5.** short for **eardrum. 6.** any of various North American fishes that utter a drumming sound. **7.** a type of hollow rotor for steam turbines or axial compressors. **8.** *Arch.* a drummer. **9.** *Austral. sl.* a brothel. **10. beat the drum for.** *Inf.* to attempt to arouse interest in. **11. the drum.** *Austral. inf.* the necessary information (esp. in **give (someone) the drum**). ~*vb.* **drumming, drummed. 12.** to play (music) on or as if on a drum. **13.** to tap rhythmically or regularly. **14.** (*tr.;* sometimes foll. by *up*) to summon or call by drumming. **15.** (*tr.*) to instil by constant repetition. ~See also **drum up.** [C16: prob. < MDu. *tromme,* imit.]

drumbeat ('drʌmˌbiːt) *n.* the sound made by beating a drum.

drum brake *n.* a type of brake used on the

wheels of vehicles, consisting of two shoes that rub against the brake drum when the brake is applied.

drumfish (ˈdrʌmˌfɪʃ) *n., pl.* **-fish** *or* **-fishes.** another name for **drum** (sense 6).

drumhead (ˈdrʌmˌhɛd) *n.* **1.** the part of a drum that is actually struck. **2.** the head of a capstan. **3.** another name for **eardrum.**

drumlin (ˈdrʌmlɪn) *n.* a streamlined mound of glacial drift. [C19: < Irish Gaelic *druim* ridge + *-lin* -LING[1]]

drum machine *n.* a synthesizer specially programmed to reproduce the sound of drums and other percussion instruments in variable rhythms and combinations selected by the musician; the resulting beat is produced continually until stopped or changed.

drum major *n.* the noncommissioned officer, usually of warrant officer's rank, who commands the corps of drums of a military band and who is in command of both the drums and the band when paraded together.

drum majorette *n.* a girl who marches at the head of a procession, twirling a baton.

drummer (ˈdrʌmə) *n.* **1.** a drum player. **2.** *Chiefly U.S.* a travelling salesman.

drumstick (ˈdrʌmˌstɪk) *n.* **1.** a stick used for playing a drum. **2.** the lower joint of the leg of a cooked fowl.

drum up *vb. (tr., adv.)* to obtain (support, business, etc.) by solicitation or canvassing.

drunk (drʌŋk) *adj.* **1.** intoxicated with alcohol to the extent of losing control over normal functions. **2.** overwhelmed by strong influence or emotion. ~*n.* **3.** a person who is drunk. **4.** *Inf.* a drinking bout.

drunkard (ˈdrʌŋkəd) *n.* a person who is frequently or habitually drunk.

drunken (ˈdrʌŋkən) *adj.* **1.** intoxicated. **2.** habitually drunk. **3.** (*prenominal*) caused by or relating to alcoholic intoxication: *a drunken brawl.* —ˈ**drunkenly** *adv.* —ˈ**drunkenness** *n.*

drupe (druːp) *n.* any fruit that has a fleshy or fibrous part around a stone that encloses a seed, as the peach, plum, and cherry. [C18: < L *druppa* wrinkled overripe olive, < Gk: olive] —**drupaceous** (druːˈpeɪʃəs) *adj.*

drupelet (ˈdruːplɪt) *or* **drupel** (ˈdruːpᵊl) *n.* a small drupe, usually one of a number forming a compound fruit.

dry (draɪ) *adj.* **drier, driest** *or* **dryer, dryest. 1.** lacking moisture; not damp or wet. **2.** having little or no rainfall. **3.** not in or under water. **4.** having the water drained away or evaporated: *a dry river.* **5.** not providing milk: *a dry cow.* **6.** (of the eyes) free from tears. **7. a.** *Inf.* thirsty. **b.** causing thirst. **8.** eaten without butter, jam, etc.: *dry toast.* **9.** (of wine, etc.) not sweet. **10.** not producing a mucous or watery discharge: *a dry cough.* **11.** consisting of solid as opposed to liquid substances. **12.** without adornment; plain: *dry facts.* **13.** lacking interest: *a dry book.* **14.** lacking warmth: *a dry greeting.* **15.** (of humour) shrewd and keen in an impersonal, sarcastic, or laconic way. **16.** *Inf.* opposed to or prohibiting the sale of alcoholic liquor: *a dry country.* ~*vb.* **drying, dried. 17.** (when *intr.*, often foll. by *off*) to make or become dry. **18.** (*tr.*) to preserve (fruit, etc.) by removing the moisture. ~*n., pl.* **drys** *or* **dries. 19.** *Brit. inf.* a Conservative politician who is a hardliner. **20. the dry.** (*sometimes cap.*) *Austral. inf.* the dry season. ~See also **dry out, dry up.** [OE *drȳge*] —ˈ**dryness** *n.*

dryad (ˈdraɪəd, -æd) *n., pl.* **-ads** *or* **-ades** (-əˌdiːz). *Greek myth.* a nymph or divinity of the woods. [C14: < L *Dryas*, < Gk *Druas*, < *drus* tree]

dry battery *n.* an electric battery consisting of two or more dry cells.

dry cell *n.* a primary cell in which the electrolyte is in the form of a paste or is treated in some way to prevent it from spilling.

dry-clean *vb. (tr.)* to clean (fabrics, etc.) with a solvent other than water. —ˌ**dry-**ˈ**cleaner** *n.* —ˌ**dry-**ˈ**cleaning** *n.*

dry dock *n.* a dock that can be pumped dry for work on a ship's bottom.

dryer[1] (ˈdraɪə) *n.* **1.** a person or thing that dries. **2.** an apparatus for removing moisture by forced draught, heating, or centrifuging. **3.** any of certain chemicals added to oils to accelerate their drying when used in paints, etc.

dryer[2] (ˈdraɪə) *adj.* a variant spelling of **drier**[1].

dry farming *n.* a system of growing crops in semiarid regions without irrigation, by reducing evaporation, etc. —**dry farmer** *n.*

dry fly *n. Angling.* **a.** an artificial fly designed to be floated on the surface of the water. **b.** (*as modifier*): *dry-fly fishing.*

dry hole *n.* (in the oil industry) a well which proves unsuccessful.

dry ice *n.* solid carbon dioxide used as a refrigerant. Also called: **carbon dioxide snow.**

drying (ˈdraɪɪŋ) *n.* the processing of timber until it has a moisture content suitable for the purposes for which it is to be used.

dryly *or* **drily** (ˈdraɪlɪ) *adv.* in a dry manner.

dry measure *n.* a unit or system of units for measuring dry goods, such as fruit, grains, etc.

dry out *vb. (adv.)* **1.** to make or become dry. **2.** to undergo or cause to undergo treatment for alcoholism or drug addiction.

dry point *n.* **1.** a technique of intaglio engraving with a hard steel needle, without acid, on a copper plate. **2.** the sharp steel needle used. **3.** the engraving or print produced.

dry riser *n.* a vertical pipe, not containing water, having connections on different floors of a building for a fireman's hose to be attached. A fire tender can be connected at the lowest level to make water rise under pressure within the pipe. Abbrev.: **DR.**

dry rot *n.* **1.** crumbling and drying of timber, bulbs, potatoes, or fruit, caused by certain fungi. **2.** any fungus causing this decay. **3.** moral degeneration or corrupt practices.

dry run *n.* **1.** *Mil.* practice in firing without live ammunition. **2.** *Inf.* a rehearsal.

drysalter (ˈdraɪˌsɔːltə) *n. Obs.* a dealer in dyestuffs and gums, and in dried, tinned, or salted foods and edible oils.

dry-stone *adj.* (of a wall) made without mortar.

dry up *vb. (adv.)* **1.** (*intr.*) to become barren or unproductive; fail. **2.** to dry (dishes, cutlery, etc.) with a tea towel after they have been washed. **3.** (*intr.*) *Inf.* to stop talking or speaking.

DS *or* **ds** *Music. abbrev. for* dal segno.

DSc *abbrev. for* Doctor of Science.

DSC *Mil. abbrev. for* Distinguished Service Cross.

DSM *Mil. abbrev. for* Distinguished Service Medal.

DSO *Brit. mil. abbrev. for* Distinguished Service Order.

DST *abbrev. for* Daylight Saving Time.

DSW (in New Zealand) *abbrev. for* Department of Social Welfare.

DTI (in Britain) *abbrev. for* Department of Trade and Industry.

DT's *Inf. abbrev. for* delirium tremens.

Du. *abbrev. for* Dutch.

dual (ˈdjuːəl) *adj.* **1.** relating to or denoting two. **2.** twofold; double. **3.** (in the grammar of some languages) denoting a form of a word indicating that exactly two referents are being referred to. **4.** *Maths, logic.* (of a pair of operators) convertible into one another by the distribution of negation over either. ~*n.* **5.** *Grammar.* **a.** the dual number. **b.** a dual form of a word. [C17: < L *duālis* concerning two, < *duo* two] —ˈ**dually** *adv.* —**duality** (djuːˈælɪtɪ) *n.*

dual carriageway *n. Brit.* a road on which traffic travelling in opposite directions is separated by a central strip of turf, etc. U.S. and Canad. name: **divided highway.**

dualism (ˈdjuːəˌlɪzəm) *n.* **1.** the state of being twofold or double. **2.** *Philosophy.* the doctrine that reality consists of two basic types of substance, usually taken to be mind and matter or mental and physical entities. **3. a.** the theory that the universe has been ruled from its origins by two conflicting powers, one good and one evil. **b.** the theory that there are two personalities, one human and one divine, in Christ. —ˈ**dualist** *n.* —**dualˈistic** *adj.*

dub[1] (dʌb) *vb.* **dubbing, dubbed.** **1.** (*tr.*) to invest (a person) with knighthood by tapping on the shoulder with a sword. **2.** (*tr.*) to invest with a title, name, or nickname. **3.** (*tr.*) to dress (leather) by rubbing. **4.** *Angling.* to dress (a fly). [OE *dubbian*]

dub[2] (dʌb) *vb.* **dubbing, dubbed.** **1.** to alter the soundtrack of (a film, etc.). **2.** (*tr.*) to provide (a film) with a new soundtrack, esp. in a different language. **3.** (*tr.*) to provide (a film or tape) with a soundtrack. ~*n.* **4.** the new sounds added. **5.** *Music.* a style of record production associated with reggae, involving exaggeration of instrumental parts, the use of echo, etc. [C20: shortened < DOUBLE]

dub[3] (dʌb) *vb.* **dubbing, dubbed.** *Austral. & N.Z. inf.* short for **double-bank.**

dubbin (ˈdʌbɪn) *n. Brit.* a greasy preparation applied to leather to soften it and make it waterproof. [C18: < *dub* to dress leather]

dubbing[1] (ˈdʌbɪŋ) *n. Films.* **1.** the replacement of a soundtrack, esp. by one in another language. **2.** the combination of several soundtracks. **3.** the addition of a soundtrack to a film, etc.

dubbing[2] (ˈdʌbɪŋ) *n.* **1.** *Angling.* fibrous material used for the body of an artificial fly. **2.** a variant of **dubbin.**

dubiety (djuːˈbaɪɪtɪ) *n., pl.* **-ties.** **1.** the state of being doubtful. **2.** a doubtful matter. [C18: < LL *dubietās,* < L *dubius* DUBIOUS]

dub in *or* **up** *vb.* (*adv.*) *Sl.* to contribute to the cost of something: *we'll all dub in a fiver for the trip.*

dubious (ˈdjuːbɪəs) *adj.* **1.** marked by or causing doubt. **2.** uncertain; doubtful. **3.** of doubtful quality; untrustworthy. **4.** not certain in outcome. [C16: < L *dubius* wavering] —ˈ**dubiously** *adv.* —ˈ**dubiousness** *n.*

Dublin Bay prawn (ˈdʌblɪn) *n.* a large prawn usually used in a dish of scampi.

ducal (ˈdjuːkᵊl) *adj.* of a duke or duchy. [C16: < F, < LL *ducālis* of a leader, < L *dux* leader]

ducat (ˈdʌkət) *n.* **1.** any of various former European gold or silver coins. **2.** (*often pl.*) money. [C14: < OF, < OIt. *ducato* coin stamped with the doge's image]

duce (ˈduːtʃɪ) *n.* leader. [C20: < It., < L *dux*]

Duce (*Italian* ˈduːtʃe) *n.* **Il** (il). the title assumed by Mussolini as leader of Fascist Italy (1922–43).

duchess (ˈdʌtʃɪs) *n.* **1.** the wife or widow of a duke. **2.** a woman who holds the rank of duke in her own right. ~*vb.* **3.** (*tr.*) *Austral. inf.* to overwhelm with flattering attention. [C14: < OF *duchesse*]

duchy (ˈdʌtʃɪ) *n., pl.* **duchies.** the territory of a duke or duchess; dukedom. [C14: < OF *duche,* < *duc* DUKE]

duck[1] (dʌk) *n., pl.* **ducks** *or* **duck.** **1.** any of a family of aquatic birds, esp. those having short legs, webbed feet, and a broad blunt bill. **2.** the flesh of this bird, used as food. **3.** the female of such a bird, as opposed to the male (drake). **4.** Also: **ducks.** *Brit. inf.* dear or darling: used as a term of address. See also **ducky.** **5.** *Cricket.* a score of nothing by a batsman. **6. like water off a duck's back.** *Inf.* without effect. [OE *dūce* duck, diver; rel. to DUCK[2]]

duck[2] (dʌk) *vb.* **1.** to move (the head or body) quickly downwards or away, esp. to escape observation or evade a blow. **2.** to plunge suddenly under water. **3.** (when *intr.,* often foll. by *out*) *Inf.* to dodge or escape (a person, duty, etc.). **4.** (*intr.*) *Bridge.* to play a low card rather than try to win a trick. ~*n.* **5.** the act or an instance of ducking. [C14: rel. to OHG *tūhhan* to dive, MDu. *dūken*] —ˈ**ducker** *n.*

duck[3] (dʌk) *n.* a heavy cotton fabric of plain weave, used for clothing, tents, etc. [C17: < MDu. *doek*]

duck[4] (dʌk) *n.* an amphibious vehicle used in World War II. [C20: < code name DUKW]

duck-billed platypus *n.* an amphibious egg-laying mammal of E Australia having dense fur, a broad bill and tail, and webbed feet.

duckboard (ˈdʌkˌbɔːd) *n.* a board or boards laid so as to form a path over wet or muddy ground.

ducking stool *n. History.* a chair used for punishing offenders by plunging them into water.

duckling (ˈdʌklɪŋ) *n.* a young duck.

ducks and drakes *n.* (*functioning as sing.*) **1.** a game in which a flat stone is bounced across the surface of water. **2. make ducks and drakes of** *or* **play (at) ducks and drakes with.** *Inf.* to use recklessly; squander.

duck soup *n. U.S. sl.* something that is easy to do.

duckweed (ˈdʌkˌwiːd) *n.* any of various small stemless aquatic plants that occur floating on still water in temperate regions.

ducky *or* **duckie** (ˈdʌkɪ) *Inf.* ~*n., pl.* **duckies.** **1.** *Brit.* darling or dear: a term of endearment. ~*adj.* **duckier, duckiest.** **2.** delightful; fine.

duct (dʌkt) *n.* **1.** a tube, pipe, or canal by means of which a substance, esp. a fluid or gas, is conveyed. **2.** any bodily passage, esp. one conveying secretions or excretions. **3.** a narrow tubular cavity in plants. **4.** a channel or pipe carrying electric wires. **5.** a passage through which air can flow, as in air conditioning. [C17: < L *ductus* a leading (in Med. L: aqueduct), < *dūcere* to lead] —ˈ**ductless** *adj.*

ductile (ˈdʌktaɪl) *adj.* **1.** (of a metal) able to sustain large deformations without fracture and able to be hammered into sheets or drawn out into wires. **2.** able to be moulded. **3.** easily led or influenced. [C14: < OF, < L *ductilis,* < *dūcere* to lead] —**ductility** (dʌkˈtɪlɪtɪ) *n.*

ductless gland *n. Anat.* See **endocrine gland.**

dud (dʌd) *Inf.* ~*n.* **1.** a person or thing that proves ineffectual. **2.** a shell, etc., that fails to explode. **3.** (*pl.*) *Old-fashioned.* clothes or other belongings. ~*adj.* **4.** failing in its purpose or function. [C15 (in the sense: an article of clothing, a thing, used disparagingly): <?]

dude (djuːd) *n. Inf.* **1.** *Western U.S. & Canad.* a city dweller, esp. one holidaying on a ranch. **2.** *U.S. & Canad.* a dandy. **3.** *U.S. & Canad.* any person. [C19: <?] —ˈ**dudish** *adj.* —ˈ**dudishly** *adv.*

dude ranch *n. U.S. & Canad.* a ranch used as a holiday resort.

dudgeon (ˈdʌdʒən) *n.* anger or resentment (arch., except in **in high dudgeon**). [C16: <?]

due (djuː) *adj.* **1.** (*postpositive*) immediately payable. **2.** (*postpositive*) owed as a debt. **3.** fitting; proper. **4.** (*prenominal*) adequate or sufficient. **5.** (*postpositive*) expected or appointed to be present or arrive. **6. due to.** attributable to or caused by. ~*n.* **7.** something that is owed, required, or due. **8. give (a person) his due.** to give or allow what is deserved or right. ~*adv.* **9.** directly or exactly. [C13: < OF *deu,* < *devoir* to owe, < L *debēre*]

▷ **Usage.** There is considerable controversy over the use of *due to* as a compound preposition equivalent to *because of.* Careful users of English prefer *because of* or *owing to.* There is no dispute about the postpositive adjectival use of *due to* to mean *caused by* (*the error was due to carelessness*), but *owing to* is not ordinarily used in this way.

duel (ˈdjuːəl) *n.* **1.** a formal prearranged combat with deadly weapons between two people in the presence of seconds, usually to settle a quarrel. **2.** a contest or conflict between two persons or parties. ~*vb.* **duelling, duelled** *or U.S.* **dueling, dueled.** (*intr.*) **3.** to fight in a duel. **4.** to contest closely. [C15: < Med. L *duellum,* < L, poetical var. of *bellum* war; associated with L *duo* two] —ˈ**dueller** *or* ˈ**duellist** *n.*

duenna (djuːˈɛnə) *n.* (in Spain and Portugal, etc.) an elderly woman retained by a family to act as governess and chaperon to girls. [C17: < Sp. *dueña,* < L *domina* lady]

due process of law *n.* the administration of justice in accordance with established rules and principles.

dues (dju:z) *pl. n.* (*sometimes sing.*) charges, as for membership of a club or organization; fees.

duet (dju:ˈɛt) *n.* **1.** a musical composition for two performers or voices. **2.** a pair of closely connected individuals; duo. [C18: < It. *duetto* a little duet, < *duo* duet, < L: two] —**duˈettist** *n.*

duff[1] (dʌf) *n.* **1.** a thick flour pudding boiled in a cloth bag. **2. up the duff.** *Sl., chiefly Austral.* pregnant. [C19: N English var. of DOUGH]

duff[2] (dʌf) *vb.* (*tr.*) **1.** *Sl.* to give a false appearance to (old or stolen goods); fake. **2.** (foll. by *up*) *Brit. sl.* to beat (a person) severely. **3.** *Austral. sl.* to steal (cattle), altering the brand. **4.** *Golf. inf.* to bungle a shot by hitting the ground behind the ball. ~*adj.* **5.** *Brit. inf.* bad or useless: *a duff engine.* [C19: prob. back formation < DUFFER]

duffel *or* **duffle** (ˈdʌfᵊl) *n.* **1.** a heavy woollen cloth. **2.** *Chiefly U.S. & Canad.* equipment or supplies. [C17: after *Duffel,* Belgian town]

duffel coat *n.* a usually knee-length wool coat, usually with a hood and fastened with toggles.

duffer (ˈdʌfə) *n.* **1.** *Inf.* a dull or incompetent person. **2.** *Sl.* something worthless. **3.** *Austral. sl.* **a.** a mine that proves unproductive. **b.** a person who steals cattle. [C19: <?]

dug[1] (dʌg) *vb.* the past tense and past participle of **dig.**

dug[2] (dʌg) *n.* a nipple, teat, udder, or breast. [C16: of Scand. origin]

dugong (ˈdu:gɒŋ) *n.* a whalelike mammal occurring in shallow tropical waters from E Africa to Australia. [C19: < Malay *duyong*]

dugout (ˈdʌgˌaʊt) *n.* **1.** a canoe made by hollowing out a log. **2.** *Mil.* a covered excavation dug to provide shelter. **3.** (at a sports ground) the covered bench where managers, substitutes, etc. sit. **4.** (in the Canadian prairies) a reservoir dug on a farm in which water from rain and snow is collected for use in irrigation, watering livestock, etc.

duiker *or* **duyker** (ˈdaɪkə) *n., pl.* **-kers** *or* **-ker. 1.** Also: **duikerbok.** any of various small African antelopes. **2.** *S. African.* any of several cormorants, esp. the long-tailed shag. [C18: via Afrik., < Du. *duiker* diver, < *duiken* to dive]

duke (dju:k) *n.* **1.** a nobleman of high rank: in the British Isles standing above the other grades of the nobility. **2.** the prince or ruler of a small principality or duchy. [C12: < OF *duc,* < L *dux* leader] —**ˈdukedom** *n.*

dukes (dju:ks) *pl. n. Sl.* the fists. [C19: < *Duke of Yorks* rhyming sl. for *forks* (fingers)]

dulcet (ˈdʌlsɪt) *adj.* (of a sound) soothing or pleasant; sweet. [C14: < L *dulcis* sweet]

dulcimer (ˈdʌlsɪmə) *n.* **1.** a tuned percussion instrument consisting of a set of strings stretched over a sounding board and struck with hammers. **2.** an instrument used in U.S. folk music, with an elliptical body and usually three strings plucked with a goose quill. [C15: < OF *doulcemer,* < OIt. *dolcimelo,* < *dolce* (< L *dulcis* sweet) + *-melo,* ? < Gk *melos* song]

dull (dʌl) *adj.* **1.** slow to think or understand; stupid. **2.** lacking in interest. **3.** lacking in perception; insensitive. **4.** lacking sharpness. **5.** not acute, intense, or piercing. **6.** (of weather) not bright or clear. **7.** not active, busy, or brisk. **8.** lacking in spirit; listless. **9.** (of colour) lacking brilliance; sombre. **10.** not loud or clear; muffled. ~*vb.* **11.** to make or become dull. [OE *dol*] —**ˈdullish** *adj.* —**ˈdullness** *or* **ˈdulness** *n.* —**ˈdully** *adv.*

dullard (ˈdʌləd) *n.* a dull or stupid person.

dulse (dʌls) *n.* any of several seaweeds that occur on rocks and have large red edible fronds. [C17: < OIrish *duilesc* seaweed]

duly (ˈdju:lɪ) *adv.* **1.** in a proper manner. **2.** at the proper time. [C14: see DUE, -LY[2]]

duma *Russian.* (ˈdu:mə) *n. Russian history.* **1.** (*usually cap.*) the elective legislative assembly established by Tsar Nicholas II in 1905: overthrown in 1917. **2.** (before 1917) any official assembly or council. [C20: < *duma* thought, of Gmc origin]

dumb (dʌm) *adj.* **1.** lacking the power to speak; mute. **2.** lacking the power of human speech: *dumb animals.* **3.** temporarily bereft of the power to speak: *struck dumb.* **4.** refraining from speech; uncommunicative. **5.** producing no sound: *a dumb piano.* **6.** made, done, or performed without speech. **7.** *Inf.* **a.** dim-witted. **b.** foolish. [OE] —**ˈdumbly** *adv.* —**ˈdumbness** *n.*

dumbbell (ˈdʌmˌbɛl) *n.* **1.** an exercising weight consisting of a single bar with a heavy ball or disc at either end. **2.** *Sl., chiefly U.S. & Canad.* a fool.

dumbfound *or* **dumfound** (dʌmˈfaʊnd) *vb.* (*tr.*) to strike dumb with astonishment; amaze. [C17: < DUMB + (CON)FOUND]

dumb show *n.* **1.** formerly, a part of a play acted in pantomime. **2.** meaningful gestures.

dumbstruck (ˈdʌmˌstrʌk) *adj.* temporarily deprived of speech through shock or surprise.

dumbwaiter (ˈdʌmˌweɪtə) *n.* **1.** *Brit.* **a.** a stand placed near a dining table to hold food. **b.** a revolving circular tray placed on a table to hold food. U.S. and Canad. name: **lazy Susan. 2.** a lift for carrying food, rubbish, etc., between floors.

dumdum (ˈdʌmˌdʌm) *n.* a soft-nosed bullet that expands on impact and inflicts extensive laceration. [C19: after *Dum-Dum,* town near Calcutta where orig. made]

dummy (ˈdʌmɪ) *n., pl.* **-mies. 1.** a figure representing the human form, used for displaying clothes, as a target, etc. **2. a.** a copy of an object, often lacking some essential feature of the original. **b.** (*as modifier*): *a dummy drawer.* **3.** *Sl.* a stupid person. **4.** *Derog., sl.* a person without the power of speech. **5.** *Inf.* a person who says or does nothing. **6. a.** a person who appears to act for himself while acting on behalf of another. **b.** (*as modifier*): *a dummy buyer.* **7.** *Mil.* a weighted round without explosives. **8.** *Bridge.* **a.** the hand exposed on the table by the declarer's partner and played by the declarer. **b.** the declarer's partner. **9. a.** a prototype of a book, indicating the appearance of the finished product. **b.** a designer's layout of a page. **10.** *Sport.* a feigned pass or move. **11.** *Brit.* a rubber teat for babies to suck or bite on. U.S. and Canad. equivalent: **pacifier. 12.** (*modifier*) counterfeit; sham. **13.** (*modifier*) (of a card game) played with one hand exposed or unplayed. **14. sell (someone) a dummy.** *Sport.* to trick (an opponent) with a dummy pass. [C16: see DUMB, -Y[3]]

dummy run *n.* an experimental run; practice; rehearsal.

dump (dʌmp) *vb.* **1.** to drop, fall, or let fall heavily or in a mass. **2.** (*tr.*) to empty (objects or material) out of a container. **3.** to unload or empty (a container), as by overturning. **4.** (*tr.*) **a.** *Inf.* to dispose of without subtlety or proper care. **b.** to dispose of (nuclear waste). **5.** *Commerce.* to market (goods) in bulk and at low prices, esp. abroad, in order to maintain a high price in the home market and obtain a share of the foreign markets. **6.** (*tr.*) to store (supplies, etc.) temporarily. **7.** (*tr.*) *Surfing.* (of a wave) to hurl a swimmer or surfer down. **8.** (*tr.*) *Austral. & N.Z.* to compact (bales of wool) by hydraulic pressure. **9.** (*tr.*) *Computers.* to record (the contents of the memory) on a storage device at a series of points during a computer run. ~*n.* **10.** a place or area where waste materials are dumped. **11.** a pile or accumulation of rubbish. **12.** the act of dumping. **13.** *Inf.* a dirty or unkempt place. **14.** *Mil.* a place where weapons, supplies, etc., are stored. [C14: prob. < ON]

dumper (ˈdʌmpə) *n.* **1.** a person or thing that dumps. **2.** *Surfing.* a wave that hurls a swimmer or surfer down.

dumpling (ˈdʌmplɪŋ) *n.* **1.** a small ball of dough cooked and served with stew. **2.** a pudding consisting of a round pastry case filled with fruit: *apple dumpling.* **3.** *Inf.* a short plump person. [C16: *dump-,* ? var. of LUMP[1] + -LING[1]]

dumps (dʌmps) *pl. n. Inf.* a state of melancholy or depression (esp. in **down in the dumps**). [C16: prob. < MDu. *domp* haze]

dump truck *or* **dumper-truck** *n.* a small truck

used on building sites, having a load-bearing container at the front that can be tipped up to dump the contents.

dumpy (ˈdʌmpɪ) *adj.* **dumpier, dumpiest.** short and plump; squat. [C18: ? rel. to DUMPLING] —**ˈdumpily** *adv.* —**ˈdumpiness** *n.*

dun[1] (dʌn) *vb.* **dunning, dunned.** **1.** (*tr.*) to press (a debtor) for payment. ~*n.* **2.** a person, esp. a hired agent, who importunes another for the payment of a debt. **3.** a demand for payment. [C17: <?]

dun[2] (dʌn) *n.* **1.** a brownish-grey colour. **2.** a horse of this colour. **3.** *Angling.* **a.** an immature adult mayfly. **b.** an artificial fly resembling this. ~*adj.* **dunner, dunnest.** **4.** of a dun colour. **5.** dark and gloomy. [OE *dunn*]

dunce (dʌns) *n.* a person who is stupid or slow to learn. [C16: < *Dunses* or *Dunsmen,* term of ridicule applied to the followers of John *Duns Scotus* (?1265–1308), Scot. scholastic theologian, esp. by 16th-cent. humanists]

dunce cap *or* **dunce's cap** *n.* a conical paper hat, formerly placed on the head of a dull child at school.

Dundee cake (dʌnˈdiː) *n. Chiefly Brit.* a fairly rich fruit cake decorated with almonds.

dunderhead (ˈdʌndəˌhɛd) *n.* a slow-witted person. [C17: prob. < Du. *donder* thunder + HEAD] —**ˈdunderˌheaded** *adj.*

dune (djuːn) *n.* a mound or ridge of drifted sand. [C18: via OF < MDu. *dūne*]

dung (dʌŋ) *n.* **1.** excrement, esp. of animals; manure. **2.** something filthy. ~*vb.* **3.** (*tr.*) to cover with manure. [OE: prison; rel. to OHG *tunc* cellar roofed with dung, ON *dyngja* manure heap]

dungaree (ˌdʌŋgəˈriː) *n.* **1.** a coarse cotton fabric used chiefly for work clothes, etc. **2.** (*pl.*) **a.** a suit of workman's overalls made of this material, consisting of trousers with a bib attached. **b.** a casual garment resembling this, usually worn by women or children. **3.** *U.S.* trousers. [C17: < Hindi, after *Dungrī,* district of Bombay, where this fabric originated]

dungeon (ˈdʌndʒən) *n.* **1.** a prison cell, often underground. **2.** a variant spelling of **donjon.** [C14: < OF *donjon*]

dunghill (ˈdʌŋˌhɪl) *n.* **1.** a heap of dung. **2.** a foul place, condition, or person.

dunk (dʌŋk) *vb.* **1.** to dip (bread, etc.) in tea, soup, etc., before eating. **2.** to submerge or be submerged. [C20: < Pennsylvania Du., < MHG *dunken,* < OHG *dunkōn*] —**ˈdunker** *n.*

dunlin (ˈdʌnlɪn) *n.* a small sandpiper of northern and arctic regions, having a brown back and black breast in summer. [C16: DUN[2] + -LING[1]]

dunnage (ˈdʌnɪdʒ) *n.* loose material used for packing cargo. [C14: <?]

dunno (dʌˈnəʊ, dʊ-, də-) *Sl. contraction of* (I) do not know.

dunnock (ˈdʌnək) *n.* another name for a **hedge sparrow.** [C15: < DUN[2] + -OCK]

dunny (ˈdʌnɪ) *n., pl.* **-nies.** **1.** *Scot. dialect.* a cellar or basement. **2.** *Austral. & N.Z. inf.* a lavatory, esp. one which is outside. [C20: <?]

duo (ˈdjuːəʊ) *n., pl.* **duos** *or* **dui** (ˈdjuːiː). **1.** *Music.* **a.** a pair of performers. **b.** a duet. **2.** a pair of actors, etc. **3.** *Inf.* a pair of closely connected individuals. [C16: via It. < L: two]

duo- *combining form.* indicating two. [< L]

duodecimal (ˌdjuːəʊˈdɛsɪməl) *adj.* **1.** relating to twelve or twelfths. ~*n.* **2.** a twelfth. **3.** one of the numbers used in a duodecimal number system. —**ˌduoˈdecimally** *adv.*

duodecimo (ˌdjuːəʊˈdɛsɪˌməʊ) *n., pl.* **-mos.** **1.** Also called: **twelvemo.** a book size resulting from folding a sheet of paper into twelve leaves. **2.** a book of this size. [C17: < L *in duodecimō* in twelfth]

duodenum (ˌdjuːəʊˈdiːnəm) *n., pl.* **-na** (-nə) *or* **-nums.** the first part of the small intestine, between the stomach and the jejunum. [C14: < Med. L, < *intestinum duodenum digitorum* intestine of twelve fingers' length] —**ˌduoˈdenal** *adj.*

duologue *or U.S. (sometimes)* **duolog** (ˈdjuːəˌlɒg) *n.* **1.** a part or all of a play in which the speaking roles are limited to two actors. **2.** a less common word for **dialogue.**

dup. *abbrev. for* duplicate.

dupe (djuːp) *n.* **1.** a person who is easily deceived. ~*vb.* **2.** (*tr.*) to deceive; cheat; fool. [C17: < F, < OF *duppe,* contraction of *de huppe* of (a) hoopoe; from the bird's reputation for extreme stupidity] —**ˈdupable** *adj.* —**ˈduper** *n.* —**ˈdupery** *n.*

duple (ˈdjuːpᵊl) *adj.* **1.** a less common word for **double.** **2.** *Music.* (of time or music) having two beats in a bar. [C16: < L *duplus* twofold, double]

duplex (ˈdjuːplɛks) *n.* **1.** *U.S. & Canad.* a duplex apartment or house. ~*adj.* **2.** having two parts. **3.** having pairs of components of independent but identical function. **4.** permitting the transmission of simultaneous signals in both directions. [C19: < L: twofold, < *duo* two + *-plex* -FOLD] —**duˈplexity** *n.*

duplex apartment *n. U.S. & Canad.* an apartment on two floors.

duplex house *n. U.S. & Canad.* a semidetached house.

duplicate *adj.* (ˈdjuːplɪkɪt). **1.** copied exactly from an original. **2.** identical. **3.** existing as a pair or in pairs. ~*n.* (ˈdjuːplɪkɪt). **4.** an exact copy. **5.** something additional of the same kind. **6.** two exact copies (esp. in **in duplicate**). ~*vb.* (ˈdjuːplɪˌkeɪt). (*tr.*) **7.** to make a replica of. **8.** to do or make again. **9.** to make in a pair; make double. [C15: < L *duplicāre* to double, < *duo* two + *plicāre* to fold] —**ˈduplicable** *adj.* —**ˌdupliˈcation** *n.*

duplicator (ˈdjuːplɪˌkeɪtə) *n.* an apparatus for making replicas of an original, such as a machine using a stencil wrapped on an ink-loaded drum.

duplicity (djuːˈplɪsɪtɪ) *n., pl.* **-ties.** deception; double-dealing. [C15: < OF *duplicite,* < LL *duplicitās* a being double, < L DUPLEX]

durable (ˈdjʊərəbᵊl) *adj.* long-lasting; enduring. [C14: < OF, < L *dūrābilis,* < *dūrāre* to last] —**ˌduraˈbility** *n.* —**ˈdurably** *adv.*

durable goods *pl. n.* goods that require infrequent replacement. Also called: **durables.**

Duralumin (djʊˈræljʊmɪn) *n. Trademark.* a light strong aluminium alloy containing copper, silicon, magnesium, and manganese.

dura mater (ˈdjʊərə ˈmeɪtə) *n.* the outermost and toughest of the three membranes covering the brain and spinal cord. Often shortened to **dura.** [C15: < Med. L: hard mother]

duramen (djʊˈreɪmɛn) *n.* another name for **heartwood.** [C19: < L: hardness, < *dūrāre* to harden]

durance (ˈdjʊərəns) *n. Arch. or literary.* **1.** imprisonment. **2.** duration. [C15: < OF, < *durer* to last, < L *dūrāre*]

duration (djʊˈreɪʃən) *n.* the length of time that something lasts or continues. [C14: < Med. L *dūrātiō,* < L *dūrāre* to last] —**duˈrational** *adj.*

durative (ˈdjʊərətɪv) *Grammar.* ~*adj.* **1.** denoting an aspect of verbs that includes the imperfective and the progressive. ~*n.* **2. a.** the durative aspect of a verb. **b.** a verb in this aspect.

durbar (ˈdɜːbɑː, ˌdɜːˈbɑː) *n.* **a.** (formerly) the court of a native ruler or a governor in India. **b.** a levee at such a court. [C17: < Hindi *darbār,* < Persian, < *dar* door + *bār* entry, audience]

duress (djʊˈrɛs, djʊə-) *n.* **1.** compulsion by use of force or threat; coercion (often in **under duress**). **2.** imprisonment. [C14: < OF *duresse,* < L *dūritia* hardness, < *dūrus* hard]

during (ˈdjʊərɪŋ) *prep.* **1.** concurrently with (some other activity). **2.** within the limit of (a period of time). [C14: < *duren* to last, ult. < L *dūrare* to last]

durmast *or* **durmast oak** (ˈdɜːˌmɑːst) *n.* a large Eurasian oak tree with lobed leaves and sessile acorns. Also called: **sessile oak.** [C18: prob. < DUN[2] + MAST[2]]

durra (ˈdʌrə) *n.* an Old World variety of sorghum, cultivated for grain and fodder. [C18: < Ar. *dhurah* grain]

durry (ˈdʌrɪ) *n., pl.* **-ries.** *Austral. sl.* a cigarette. [< *durrie* a type of Indian carpet]

durst (dɜːst) *vb.* an archaic past tense of **dare.**

durum *or* **durum wheat** (ˈdjʊərəm) *n.* a variety of wheat with a high gluten content, used chiefly to make pastas. [C20: < NL *trīticum dūrum,* lit.: hard wheat]

dusk (dʌsk) *n.* **1.** the darker part of twilight. **2.** *Poetic.* gloom; shade. ~*adj.* **3.** *Poetic.* shady; gloomy. ~*vb.* **4.** *Poetic.* to make or become dark. [OE *dox*]

dusky (ˈdʌskɪ) *adj.* **duskier, duskiest. 1.** dark in colour; swarthy or dark-skinned. **2.** dim. —ˈ**duskily** *adv.* —ˈ**duskiness** *n.*

dust (dʌst) *n.* **1.** dry fine powdery material, such as particles of dirt, earth, or pollen. **2.** a cloud of such fine particles. **3. a.** the mortal body of man. **b.** the corpse of a dead person. **4.** the earth; ground. **5.** *Inf.* a disturbance; fuss (esp. in **kick up a dust, raise a dust**). **6.** something of little worth. **7.** short for **gold dust. 8.** ashes or household refuse. **9. dust and ashes.** something that is very disappointing. **10. shake the dust off** (*or* **from**) **one's feet.** to depart angrily or contemptuously. **11. throw dust in the eyes of.** to confuse or mislead. ~*vb.* **12.** (*tr.*) to sprinkle or cover (something) with (dust or some other powdery substance). **13.** to remove dust (from) by wiping, sweeping, or brushing. **14.** *Arch.* to make or become dirty with dust. ~See also **dust down, dust-up.** [OE *dūst*] —ˈ**dustless** *adj.*

dustbin (ˈdʌstˌbɪn) *n.* a large, usually cylindrical container for rubbish, esp. one used by a household. U.S. and Canad. names: **garbage can, trash can.**

dust bowl *n.* a semiarid area in which the surface soil is exposed to wind erosion.

dustcart (ˈdʌstˌkɑːt) *n.* a road vehicle for collecting refuse. U.S. and Canad. name: **garbage truck.**

dust cover *n.* **1.** another name for **dustsheet. 2.** another name for **dust jacket. 3.** a perspex cover for the turntable of a record player.

dust devil *n.* a strong miniature whirlwind that whips up dust, litter, leaves, etc., into the air.

dust down *vb.* (*tr., adv.*). **1.** to remove dust from by brushing or wiping. **2.** to reprimand severely. —**dusting down** *n.*

duster (ˈdʌstə) *n.* **1.** a cloth used for dusting. U.S. name: **dust cloth. 2.** a machine for blowing out dust. **3.** a person or thing that dusts.

dusting-powder *n.* fine powder (such as talcum powder) used to absorb moisture, etc.

dust jacket *or* **cover** *n.* a removable paper cover used to protect a bound book.

dustman (ˈdʌstmən) *n., pl.* **-men.** *Brit.* a man whose job is to collect domestic refuse.

dustpan (ˈdʌstˌpæn) *n.* a short-handled hooded shovel into which dust is swept from floors, etc.

dustsheet (ˈdʌstˌʃiːt) *n. Brit.* a large cloth used to protect furniture from dust.

dust storm *n.* a windstorm that whips up clouds of dust.

dust-up *Inf.* ~*n.* **1.** a fight or argument. ~*vb.* **dust up. 2.** (*tr., adv.*) to attack (someone).

dusty (ˈdʌstɪ) *adj.* **dustier, dustiest. 1.** covered with or involving dust. **2.** like dust. **3.** (of a colour) tinged with grey; pale. **4. give** (*or* **get**) **a dusty answer.** to give (*or* get) an unhelpful or bad-tempered reply. —ˈ**dustily** *adv.* —ˈ**dustiness** *n.*

Dutch (dʌtʃ) *n.* **1.** the language of the Netherlands. **2. the Dutch.** (*functioning as pl.*) the natives, citizens, or inhabitants of the Netherlands. **3.** See **double Dutch. 4. in Dutch.** *Sl.* in trouble. ~*adj.* **5.** of the Netherlands, its inhabitants, or their language. ~*adv.* **6. go Dutch.** *Inf.* to share expenses equally.

Dutch auction *n.* an auction in which the price is lowered by stages until a buyer is found.

Dutch barn *n. Brit.* a farm building consisting of a steel frame and a curved roof.

Dutch courage *n.* **1.** false courage gained from drinking alcohol. **2.** alcoholic drink.

Dutch door *n.* the U.S. and Canad. name for **stable door.**

Dutch elm disease *n.* a fungal disease of elm trees characterized by withering of the foliage and stems and eventual death of the tree.

Dutchman (ˈdʌtʃmən) *n., pl.* **-men. 1.** a native, citizen, or inhabitant of the Netherlands. **2.** *S. African derog.* an Afrikaner.

Dutch medicine *n. S. African.* patent medicine, esp. made of herbs.

Dutch oven *n.* **1.** an iron or earthenware container with a cover, used for stews, etc. **2.** a metal box, open in front, for cooking in front of an open fire.

Dutch treat *n. Inf.* an entertainment, meal, etc., where each person pays for himself.

Dutch uncle *n. Inf.* a person who criticizes or reproves frankly and severely.

duteous (ˈdjuːtɪəs) *adj. Formal or arch.* dutiful; obedient. —ˈ**duteously** *adv.*

dutiable (ˈdjuːtɪəbᵊl) *adj.* (of goods) liable to duty. —ˌ**dutiaˈbility** *n.*

dutiful (ˈdjuːtɪfʊl) *adj.* **1.** exhibiting or having a sense of duty. **2.** characterized by or resulting from a sense of duty: *a dutiful answer.*

duty (ˈdjuːtɪ) *n., pl.* **-ties. 1.** a task or action that a person is bound to perform for moral or legal reasons. **2.** respect or obedience due to a superior, older persons, etc. **3.** the force that binds one morally or legally to one's obligations. **4.** a government tax, esp. on imports. **5.** *Brit.* **a.** the quantity of work for which a machine is designed. **b.** a measure of the efficiency of a machine. **6. a.** a job or service allocated. **b.** (*as modifier*): *duty rota.* **7. do duty for.** to act as a substitute for. **8. on** (*or* **off**) **duty.** at (*or* not at) work. [C13: < Anglo-F *dueté,* < OF *deu* DUE]

duty-bound *adj.* morally obliged.

duty-free *adj., adv.* with exemption from customs or excise duties.

duty-free shop *n.* a shop, esp. one at a port or on board a ship, that sells perfume, tobacco, etc., at duty-free prices.

duumvir (djuːˈʌmvə) *n., pl.* **-virs** *or* **-viri** (-vɪˌriː). **1.** *Roman history.* one of two coequal magistrates. **2.** either of two men who exercise a joint authority. [C16: < L, < *duo* two + *vir* man] —**duumvirate** (djuːˈʌmvɪrɪt) *n.*

duvet (ˈduːveɪ) *n.* **1.** another name for **continental quilt. 2.** Also called: **duvet jacket.** a down-filled jacket. [C18: < F, < earlier *dumet,* < OF *dum* DOWN²]

dux (dʌks) *n.* (esp. in Scottish schools) the top pupil in a class or school. [L: leader]

DV *abbrev. for:* **1.** Deo volente. [L: God willing] **2.** Douay Version (of the Bible).

dwaal (dwɑːl) *n. S. African.* a state of befuddlement; daze. [< Afrik. *dwaal* wander]

dwale (dweɪl) *n.* another name for **deadly nightshade.** [C14: ? < ON]

dwarf (dwɔːf) *n., pl.* **dwarfs** *or* **dwarves** (dwɔːvz). **1.** an abnormally undersized person. **2. a.** an animal or plant much below the average height for the species. **b.** (*as modifier*): *a dwarf tree.* **3.** (in folklore) a small ugly manlike creature, often possessing magical powers. **4.** *Astron.* short for **dwarf star.** ~*vb.* **5.** to become or cause to become small in size, importance, etc. **6.** (*tr.*) to stunt the growth of. [OE *dweorg*] —ˈ**dwarfish** *adj.*

dwarf star *n.* any of a class of faint stars having a very high density and small diameter compared to the much brighter **giant stars.**

dwell (dwɛl) *vb.* **dwelling, dwelt** *or* **dwelled.** (*intr.*) **1.** *Formal, literary.* to live as a permanent resident. **2.** to live (in a specified state): *to dwell in poverty.* ~*n.* **3.** a regular pause in the operation of a machine. [OE *dwellan* to seduce, get lost] —ˈ**dweller** *n.*

dwelling (ˈdwɛlɪŋ) *n. Formal, literary.* a place of residence.

dwell on *or* **upon** *vb.* (*intr., prep.*) to think, speak, or write at length.

dwelt (dwɛlt) *vb.* a past tense and past participle of **dwell.**

dwindle (ˈdwɪndᵊl) *vb.* to grow or cause to grow less in size, intensity, or number. [C16: < OE *dwīnan* to waste away]

Dy *the chemical symbol for* dysprosium.

dyad (ˈdaɪæd) *n.* **1.** *Maths.* an operator that is the unspecified product of two vectors. **2.** an atom or group that has a valency of two. **3.** a group of two; couple. [C17: < LL *dyas,* < Gk *duas* two] —**dyˈadic** *adj.*

Dyak *or* **Dayak** (ˈdaɪæk) *n., pl.* **-aks** *or* **-ak.** a member of a Malaysian people of Borneo. [< Malay: upcountry, < *darat* land]

dybbuk (ˈdɪbək) *n., pl.* **-buks** *or* **-bukkim.** *Judaism.* (in folklore) the soul of a dead sinner that has transmigrated into the body of a living person. [< Yiddish: devil, < Heb.]

dye (daɪ) *n.* **1.** a staining or colouring substance. **2.** a liquid that contains a colouring material and can be used to stain fabrics, skins, etc. **3.** the colour produced by dyeing. ~*vb.* **dyeing, dyed. 4.** (*tr.*) to impart a colour or stain to (fabric, hair, etc.) by or as if by the application of a dye. [OE *dēagian,* < *dēag* a dye] —ˈ**dyable** *or* ˈ**dyeable** *adj.* —ˈ**dyer** *n.*

dyed-in-the-wool *adj.* **1.** uncompromising or unchanging in attitude, opinion, etc. **2.** (of a fabric) made of dyed yarn.

dyeing (ˈdaɪɪŋ) *n.* the process or industry of colouring yarns, fabric, etc.

dyestuff (ˈdaɪˌstʌf) *n.* a substance that can be used as a dye or which yields a dye.

dying (ˈdaɪɪŋ) *vb.* **1.** the present participle of **die**[1]. ~*adj.* **2.** relating to or occurring at the moment of death: *a dying wish.*

dyke[1] *or esp. U.S.* **dike** (daɪk) *n.* **1.** an embankment constructed to prevent flooding or keep out the sea. **2.** a ditch or watercourse. **3.** a bank made of earth alongside a ditch. **4.** *Scot.* a wall, esp. a dry-stone wall. **5.** a barrier or obstruction. **6.** a wall-like mass of igneous rock in older sedimentary rock. **7.** *Austral. inf.* a lavatory. ~*vb.* **8.** (*tr.*) to protect, enclose, or drain (land) with a dyke. [C13: < OE *dic* ditch]

dyke[2] *or* **dike** (daɪk) *n. Sl.* a lesbian. [C20: <?]

dynamic (daɪˈnæmɪk) *adj.* **1.** of or concerned with energy or forces that produce motion, as opposed to *static.* **2.** of or concerned with dynamics. **3.** Also: **dynamical.** characterized by force of personality, ambition, energy, etc. **4.** *Computers.* (of a memory) needing its contents refreshed periodically. [C19: < F *dynamique,* < Gk *dunamikos* powerful, < *dunamis* power, < *dunasthai* to be able] —**dyˈnamically** *adv.*

dynamics (daɪˈnæmɪks) *n.* **1.** (*functioning as sing.*) the branch of mechanics concerned with the forces that change or produce the motions of bodies. **2.** (*functioning as sing.*) the branch of mechanics that includes statics and kinetics. **3.** (*functioning as sing.*) the branch of any science concerned with forces. **4.** (*functioning as pl.*) those forces that produce change in any field or system. **5.** (*functioning as pl.*) *Music.* **a.** the various degrees of loudness called for in performance. **b.** directions and symbols used to indicate degrees of loudness.

dynamism (ˈdaɪnəˌmɪzəm) *n.* **1.** *Philosophy.* any of several theories that attempt to explain phenomena in terms of an immanent force or energy. **2.** the forcefulness of an energetic personality. —ˈ**dynamist** *n.* —ˌ**dynaˈmistic** *adj.*

dynamite (ˈdaɪnəˌmaɪt) *n.* **1.** an explosive consisting of nitroglycerin mixed with an absorbent. **2.** *Inf.* a spectacular or potentially dangerous person or thing. ~*vb.* **3.** (*tr.*) to mine or blow up with dynamite. [C19 (coined by Alfred Nobel): < DYNAMO- + -ITE[1]] —ˈ**dynaˌmiter** *n.*

dynamo (ˈdaɪnəˌməʊ) *n., pl.* **-mos. 1.** a device for converting mechanical energy into electrical energy. **2.** *Inf.* an energetic hard-working person. [C19: short for *dynamoelectric machine*]

dynamo- *or sometimes before a vowel* **dynam-** *combining form.* indicating power: *dynamite.* [< Gk, < *dunamis* power]

dynamoelectric (ˌdaɪnəməʊɪˈlɛktrɪk) *or* **dynamoelectrical** *adj.* of or concerned with the interconversion of mechanical and electrical energy.

dynamometer (ˌdaɪnəˈmɒmɪtə) *n.* an instrument for measuring power or force.

dynamotor (ˈdaɪnəˌməʊtə) *n.* an electrical machine having two independent armature windings of which one acts as a motor and the other a generator: used to convert direct current into alternating current.

dynast (ˈdɪnəst, -æst) *n.* a ruler, esp. a hereditary one. [C17: < L *dynastēs,* < Gk, < *dunasthai* to be powerful]

dynasty (ˈdɪnəstɪ) *n., pl.* **-ties. 1.** a sequence of hereditary rulers. **2.** any sequence of powerful leaders of the same family. [C15: via LL < Gk, < *dunastēs* DYNAST] —**dynastic** (dɪˈnæstɪk) *adj.*

dyne (daɪn) *n.* the cgs unit of force; the force that imparts an acceleration of 1 centimetre per second per second to a mass of 1 gram. 1 dyne is equivalent to 10^{-5} newton or 7.233×10^{-5} poundal. [C19: < F, < Gk *dunamis* power, force]

dys- *prefix.* **1.** diseased, abnormal, or faulty. **2.** difficult or painful. **3.** unfavourable or bad. [via L < Gk *dus-*]

dysentery (ˈdɪsᵊntrɪ) *n.* infection of the intestine marked by severe diarrhoea with the passage of mucus and blood. [C14: via L < Gk, < *dusentera,* lit.: bad bowels, < DYS- + *enteron* intestine] —**dysenteric** (ˌdɪsᵊnˈtɛrɪk) *adj.*

dysfunction (dɪsˈfʌŋkʃən) *n. Med.* any disturbance or abnormality in the function of an organ or part. —ˌ**dysˈfunctional** *adj.*

dyslexia (dɪsˈlɛksɪə) *n.* impaired ability to read, not caused by low intelligence. [C19: NL, < DYS- + *-lexia,* < *legein* to speak] —**dyslectic** (dɪsˈlɛktɪk) *adj., n.* —**dysˈlexic** *adj.*

dysmenorrhoea *or esp. U.S.* **dysmenorrhea** (ˌdɪsmɛnəˈrɪə) *n.* abnormally difficult or painful menstruation. [C19: < DYS- + Gk *mēn* month + *rhoiā* a flowing]

dyspepsia (dɪsˈpɛpsɪə) *n.* indigestion or upset stomach. [C18: < L, < Gk *duspepsia,* < DYS- + *pepsis* digestion]

dyspeptic (dɪsˈpɛptɪk) *adj.* **1.** relating to or suffering from dyspepsia. **2.** irritable. ~*n.* **3.** a person suffering from dyspepsia.

dysphasia (dɪsˈfeɪzɪə) *n.* impaired coordination of speech. —**dysˈphasic** *adj., n.*

dysphoria (dɪsˈfɔːrɪə) *n.* a feeling of being ill at ease. [C20: NL, < Gk DYS- + *-phoria,* < *pherein* to bear]

dyspnoea *or U.S.* **dyspnea** (dɪspˈniːə) *n.* difficulty in breathing or in catching the breath. [C17: via L < Gk *duspnoia,* < DYS- + *pnoē* breath, < *pnein* to breathe] —**dyspˈnoeal, dyspˈnoeic** *or U.S.* **dyspˈneal, dyspˈneic** *adj.*

dysprosium (dɪsˈprəʊsɪəm) *n.* a metallic element of the lanthanide series: used in laser materials and as a neutron absorber in nuclear control rods. Symbol: Dy; atomic no.: 66; atomic wt.: 162.50. [C20: NL, < Gk *dusprositos* difficult to get near + -IUM]

dysthymia (dɪsˈθaɪmɪə) *n. Psychiatry.* the characteristics of the neurotic and introverted, including anxiety, depression, and compulsive behaviour. [C19: NL, < Gk *dusthumia,* < DYS- + *thumos* mind] —**dysˈthymic** *adj.*

dystrophy (ˈdɪstrəfɪ) *n.* any of various bodily disorders, characterized by wasting of tissues. See also **muscular dystrophy.** [C19: NL *dystrophia,* < DYS- + Gk *trophē* food] —**dystrophic** (dɪsˈtrɒfɪk) *adj.*

dz. *abbrev. for* dozen.

dzo (zəʊ) *n., pl.* **dzos** *or* **dzo.** a variant spelling of **zo.**

E

e *or* **E** (iː) *n., pl.* **e's, E's,** *or* **Es. 1.** the fifth letter and second vowel of the English alphabet. **2.** any of several speech sounds represented by this letter, as in *he, bet,* or *below.*

e *symbol for:* **1.** *Maths.* a transcendental number used as the base of natural logarithms. Approximate value: 2.718 282... **2.** electron.

E *symbol for:* **1.** *Music.* **a.** the third note of the scale of C major. **b.** the major or minor key having this note as its tonic. **2.** earth. **3.** East. **4.** English. **5.** Egypt(ian). **6.** *Physics.* **a.** energy. **b.** electromotive force. **7.** exa-.

e. *abbrev. for* engineer(ing).

E. *abbrev. for* Earl.

E- *prefix.* used with numbers indicating a standardized system within the European Economic Community, as of food additives. See also **E number.**

ea. *abbrev. for* each.

each (iːtʃ) *determiner.* **1. a.** every (one) of two or more considered individually: *each day; each person.* **b.** (*as pron.*): *each gave according to his ability.* ~*adv.* **2.** for, to, or from each one; apiece: *four apples each.* [OE *ǣlc*]

eager (ˈiːgə) *adj.* **1.** (*postpositive;* often foll. by *to* or *for*) impatiently desirous (of); anxious or avid (for). **2.** characterized by or feeling expectancy or great desire: *an eager look.* **3.** *Arch.* biting; sharp. [C13: < OF *egre,* < L *acer* sharp, keen] —ˈ**eagerly** *adv.* —ˈ**eagerness** *n.*

eager beaver *n. Inf.* a person who displays conspicuous diligence.

eagle (ˈiːgᵊl) *n.* **1.** any of various birds of prey having large broad wings and strong soaring flight. Related adj.: **aquiline. 2.** a representation of an eagle used as an emblem, etc., esp. representing power: *the Roman eagle.* **3.** a standard, seal, etc., bearing the figure of an eagle. **4.** *Golf.* a score of two strokes under par for a hole. **5.** a former U.S. gold coin worth ten dollars. [C14: < OF *aigle,* < OProvençal *aigla,* < L *aquila*]

eagle-eyed *adj.* having keen or piercing eyesight.

eagle-hawk *n.* a large brown Australian eagle. Also called: **wedge-tailed eagle.**

eagle owl *n.* a large Eurasian owl with brownish speckled plumage and large ear tufts.

eaglet (ˈiːglɪt) *n.* a young eagle.

ealdorman (ˈɔːldəmən) *n., pl.* **-men.** an official of Anglo-Saxon England, appointed by the king, and responsible for law and order in his shire and for leading local militia. [OE *ealdor* lord + MAN]

-ean *suffix forming adjectives and nouns.* a variant of **-an:** *Caesarean.*

ear[1] (ɪə) *n.* **1.** the organ of hearing and balance in higher vertebrates (see **middle ear**). Related adj.: **aural. 2.** the outermost cartilaginous part of the ear in mammals, esp. man. **3.** the sense of hearing. **4.** sensitivity to musical sounds, poetic diction, etc.: *he has an ear for music.* **5.** attention; consideration (esp. in **give ear to, lend an ear**). **6.** an object resembling the external ear. **7. all ears.** very attentive; listening carefully. **8. a thick ear.** *Inf.* a blow on the ear. **9. fall on deaf ears.** to be ignored or pass unnoticed. **10. in one ear and out the other.** heard but unheeded. **11. keep** (*or* **have**) **one's ear to the ground.** to be or try to be well informed about current trends and opinions. **12. out on one's ear.** *Inf.* dismissed unceremoniously. **13. play by ear. a.** *Inf.* to act according to the demands of a situation; improvise. **b.** to perform a musical piece on an instrument without written music. **14. turn a deaf ear.** to be deliberately unresponsive. **15. up to one's ears.** *Inf.* deeply involved, as in work or debt. [OE *ēare*] —**eared** *adj.* —ˈ**earless** *adj.*

ear[2] (ɪə) *n.* **1.** the part of a cereal plant, such as wheat or barley, that contains the seeds, grains, or kernels. ~*vb.* **2.** (*intr.*) (of cereal plants) to develop such parts. [OE *ēar*]

earache (ˈɪərˌeɪk) *n.* pain in the ear.

eardrum (ˈɪəˌdrʌm) *n.* the nontechnical name for **tympanic membrane.**

earful (ˈɪəfʊl) *n. Inf.* **1.** something heard or overheard. **2.** a rebuke or scolding.

earl (ɜːl) *n.* (in Britain) a nobleman ranking below a marquess and above a viscount. Female equivalent: **countess.** [OE *eorl*] —ˈ**earldom** *n.*

Earl Marshal *n.* an officer of the English peerage who presides over the College of Heralds and organizes royal processions and other important ceremonies.

early (ˈɜːlɪ) *adj., adv.* **-lier, -liest. 1.** before the expected or usual time. **2.** occurring in or characteristic of the first part of a period or sequence. **3.** occurring in or characteristic of a period far back in time. **4.** occurring in the near future. **5. in the early days. a.** during the first years of any enterprise, such as marriage. **b.** *Austral. & N.Z.* during the 19th-century pioneering period in Australia and New Zealand. [OE *ǣrlīce,* < *ǣr* ERE + *-līce* -LY[2]] —ˈ**earliness** *n.*

early closing *n. Brit.* the shutting of shops in a town one afternoon each week.

Early English *n.* a style of architecture used in England in the 12th and 13th centuries, characterized by lancet arches and plate tracery.

early warning *n.* advance notice of some impending event.

earmark (ˈɪəˌmɑːk) *vb.* (*tr.*) **1.** to set aside or mark out for a specific purpose. **2.** to make an identification mark on the ear of (a domestic animal). ~*n.* **3.** such a mark of identification. **4.** any distinguishing mark or characteristic.

earmuff (ˈɪəˌmʌf) *n.* one of a joined pair of pads of fur or cloth for keeping the ears warm.

earn (ɜːn) *vb.* **1.** to gain or be paid (money or other payment) in return for work or service. **2.** (*tr.*) to acquire or deserve through behaviour or action. **3.** (*tr.*) (of securities, investments, etc.) to gain (interest, profit, etc.). [OE *earnian*] —ˈ**earner** *n.*

earned income *n.* income derived from paid employment.

earnest[1] (ˈɜːnɪst) *adj.* **1.** serious in mind or intention. **2.** characterized by sincerity of intention. **3.** demanding or receiving serious attention. ~*n.* **4. in earnest.** with serious or sincere intentions. [OE *eornost*] —ˈ**earnestly** *adv.* —ˈ**earnestness** *n.*

earnest[2] (ˈɜːnɪst) *n.* **1.** a part of something given in advance as a guarantee of the remainder. **2.** Also called: **earnest money.** *Contract law.* something given, usually a nominal sum of money, to confirm a contract. **3.** any token of something to follow. [C13: < OF *erres* pledges, pl. of *erre* earnest money, < L *arrha,* < *arrabō* pledge, < Gk *arrabon,* < Heb. *'ērābhōn* pledge]

earnings (ˈɜːnɪŋz) *pl. n.* **1.** money or other payment earned. **2. a.** the profits of an enterprise. **b.** an individual's investment income.

EAROM (ˈɪərɒm) *n. Computers. acronym for* electrically alterable read only memory.

earphone (ˈɪəˌfəʊn) *n.* a device for converting electric currents into sound waves, held close to or inserted into the ear.

ear piercing *n.* **1.** the making of a hole in the lobe of an ear, using a sterilized needle, so that earrings may be worn fastened in the hole. ~*adj.* **ear-piercing. 2.** so loud or shrill as to hurt the ears.

earplug (ˈɪəˌplʌg) *n.* a piece of soft material placed in the ear to keep out noise or water.

earring (ˈɪəˌrɪŋ) *n.* an ornament for the ear, usually clipped onto the lobe or fastened through a hole pierced in the lobe.

earshot (ˈɪəˌʃɒt) *n.* the range or distance within

which sound may be heard (esp. in **out of earshot,** etc.)

ear-splitting *adj.* so loud or shrill as to hurt the ears.

earth (ɜːθ) *n.* **1.** (*sometimes cap.*) the third planet from the sun, the only planet on which life is known to exist. Related adjs.: **terrestrial, telluric. 2.** the inhabitants of this planet: *the whole earth rejoiced.* **3.** the dry surface of this planet; land; ground. **4.** the loose soft material on the surface of the ground that consists of disintegrated rock particles, mould, clay, etc.; soil. **5.** worldly or temporal matters as opposed to the concerns of the spirit. **6.** the hole in which a burrowing animal, esp. a fox, lives. **7.** *Chem.* See **rare earth, alkaline earth. 8. a.** a connection between an electric circuit or device and the earth, which is at zero potential. **b.** a terminal to which this connection is made. **9.** (*modifier*) *Astrol.* of or relating to a group of three signs of the zodiac: Taurus, Virgo, and Capricorn. **10. come back** *or* **down to earth.** to return to reality from a fantasy or daydream. **11. on earth.** used as an intensifier in **what on earth, who on earth,** etc. **12. run to earth. a.** to hunt (an animal, esp. a fox) to its earth and trap it there. **b.** to find (someone) after hunting. ~*vb.* **13.** (*tr.*) to connect (a circuit, device, etc.) to earth. ~See also **earth up.** [OE *eorthe*]

earthbound (ˈɜːθˌbaʊnd) *adj.* **1.** confined to the earth. **2.** heading towards the earth.

earth closet *n.* a type of lavatory in which earth is used to cover excreta.

earthen (ˈɜːθən) *adj.* (*prenominal*) **1.** made of baked clay: *an earthen pot.* **2.** made of earth.

earthenware (ˈɜːθənˌwɛə) *n.* **a.** vessels, etc., made of baked clay. **b.** (*as adj.*): *an earthenware pot.*

earthly (ˈɜːθlɪ) *adj.* **-lier, -liest. 1.** of or characteristic of the earth as opposed to heaven; materialistic; worldly. **2.** (*usually with a negative*) *Inf.* conceivable or possible (in **not an earthly (chance),** etc.). —ˈ**earthliness** *n.*

earthman (ˈɜːθˌmæn) *n., pl.* **-men.** (esp. in science fiction) an inhabitant or native of the earth. Also called: **earthling.**

earthnut (ˈɜːθˌnʌt) *n.* **1.** a perennial umbelliferous plant of Europe and Asia, having edible dark brown tubers. **2.** any of various plants having an edible root, tuber, or underground pod, such as the peanut or truffle.

earthquake (ˈɜːθˌkweɪk) *n.* a series of vibrations at the earth's surface caused by movement along a fault plane, volcanic activity, etc. Related adj.: **seismic.**

earth science *n.* any of various sciences, such as geology and geography, that are concerned with the structure, age, etc., of the earth.

earth up *vb.* (*tr., adv.*) to cover (part of a plant) with soil to protect from frost, light, etc.

earthward (ˈɜːθwəd) *adj.* **1.** directed towards the earth. ~*adv.* **2.** a variant of **earthwards.**

earthwards (ˈɜːθwədz) *or* **earthward** *adv.* towards the earth.

earthwork (ˈɜːθˌwɜːk) *n.* **1.** excavation of earth, as in engineering construction. **2.** a fortification made of earth.

earthworm (ˈɜːθˌwɜːm) *n.* any of numerous worms which burrow in the soil and help aerate and break up the ground.

earthy (ˈɜːθɪ) *adj.* **earthier, earthiest. 1.** of, composed of, or characteristic of earth. **2.** unrefined, coarse, or crude. —ˈ**earthily** *adv.* —ˈ**earthiness** *n.*

ear trumpet *n.* a trumpet-shaped instrument held to the ear: an old form of hearing aid.

earwax (ˈɪəˌwæks) *n.* the nontechnical name for **cerumen.**

earwig (ˈɪəˌwɪg) *n.* **1.** any of various insects that typically have an elongated body with small leathery forewings, semicircular membranous hindwings, and curved forceps at the tip of the abdomen. ~*vb.* **-wigging, -wigged. 2.** (*tr.*) *Arch.* to attempt to influence (a person) by private insinuation. [OE *ēarwicga,* < *ēare* ear + *wicga* beetle, insect; prob. < superstition that the insect crept into human ears]

ease (iːz) *n.* **1.** freedom from discomfort, worry, or anxiety. **2.** lack of difficulty, labour, or awkwardness. **3.** rest, leisure, or relaxation. **4.** freedom from poverty; affluence: *a life of ease.* **5.** lack of restraint, embarrassment, or stiffness: *ease of manner.* **6. at ease. a.** *Mil.* (of a standing soldier, etc.) in a relaxed position with the feet apart, rather than at attention. **b.** a command to adopt such a position. **c.** in a relaxed attitude or frame of mind. ~*vb.* **7.** to make or become less burdensome. **8.** (*tr.*) to relieve (a person) of worry or care; comfort. **9.** (*tr.*) to make comfortable or give rest to. **10.** (*tr.*) to make less difficult; facilitate. **11.** to move or cause to move into, out of, etc., with careful manipulation. **12.** (when *intr.*, often foll. by *off* or *up*) to lessen or cause to lessen in severity, pressure, tension, or strain. **13. ease oneself** *or* **ease nature.** *Arch., euphemistic.* to urinate or defecate. [C13: < OF *aise* ease, opportunity, < L *adjacēns* neighbouring (area); see ADJACENT] —ˈ**easer** *n.* —ˈ**easeful** *adj.*

easel (ˈiːzᵊl) *n.* a frame, usually an upright tripod, for supporting or displaying an artist's canvas, a blackboard, etc. [C17: < Du. *ezel*; ult. < L *asinus* ass]

easement (ˈiːzmənt) *n.* **1.** *Property law.* the right enjoyed by a landowner of making limited use of his neighbour's land, as by crossing it to reach his own property. **2.** the act of easing or something that brings ease.

easily (ˈiːzɪlɪ) *adv.* **1.** with ease; without difficulty or exertion. **2.** by far; undoubtedly: *easily the best.* **3.** probably; almost certainly.

▷ **Usage.** See at **easy.**

easiness (ˈiːzɪnɪs) *n.* **1.** the quality or condition of being easy to accomplish, do, obtain, etc. **2.** ease or relaxation of manner; nonchalance.

east (iːst) *n.* **1.** the direction along a parallel towards the sunrise, at 90° to north; the direction of the earth's rotation. **2. the east.** (*often cap.*) any area lying in or towards the east. Related adj.: **oriental. 3.** (*usually cap.*) *Cards.* the player or position at the table corresponding to east on the compass. ~*adj.* **4.** situated in, moving towards, or facing the east. **5.** (esp. of the wind) from the east. ~*adv.* **6.** in, to, or towards the east. **7. back East.** *Canad.* in or to E Canada, esp. east of Quebec. [OE *ēast*]

East (iːst) *n.* **the. 1.** the continent of Asia regarded as culturally distinct from Europe and the West; the Orient. **2.** the countries under Communist rule, lying mainly in the E hemisphere. ~*adj.* **3.** of or denoting the eastern part of a specified country, area, etc.

eastbound (ˈiːstˌbaʊnd) *adj.* going or leading towards the east.

east by north *n.* one point on the compass north of east.

east by south *n.* one point on the compass south of east.

Easter (ˈiːstə) *n.* **1.** a festival of the Christian Church commemorating the Resurrection of Christ: falls on the Sunday following the first full moon after the vernal equinox. **2.** Also called: **Easter Sunday, Easter Day.** the day on which this festival is celebrated. **3.** the period between Good Friday and Easter Monday. Related adj.: **Paschal.** [OE *ēastre*]

Easter egg *n.* an egg given to children at Easter, usually a chocolate egg or a hen's egg with its shell painted.

easterly (ˈiːstəlɪ) *adj.* **1.** of or in the east. ~*adv., adj.* **2.** towards the east. **3.** from the east: *an easterly wind.* ~*n., pl.* **-lies. 4.** a wind from the east.

eastern (ˈiːstən) *adj.* **1.** situated in or towards the east. **2.** facing or moving towards the east.

Eastern Church *n.* **1.** any of the Christian Churches of the former Byzantine Empire. **2.** any Church owing allegiance to the Orthodox Church. **3.** any Church having Eastern forms of liturgy and institutions.

Easterner (ˈiːstənə) *n.* (*sometimes not cap.*) a native or inhabitant of the east of any specified region.

eastern hemisphere *n.* (*often caps.*) **1.** that half of the globe containing Europe, Asia, Africa, and Australia, lying east of the Greenwich meridian. **2.** the lands in this, esp. Asia.

Eastern Orthodox Church *n.* another name for the **Orthodox Church.**

Eastertide (ˈiːstəˌtaɪd) *n.* the Easter season.

easting (ˈiːstɪŋ) *n.* **1.** *Naut.* the net distance eastwards made by a vessel moving towards the east. **2.** *Cartography.* the distance eastwards of a point from a given meridian indicated by the first half of a map grid reference.

east-northeast *n.* **1.** the point on the compass or the direction midway between northeast and east. ~*adj., adv.* **2.** in, from, or towards this direction.

east-southeast *n.* **1.** the point on the compass or the direction midway between east and southeast. ~*adj., adv.* **2.** in, from, or towards this direction.

eastward (ˈiːstwəd) *adj.* **1.** situated or directed towards the east. ~*adv.* **2.** a variant of **eastwards.** ~*n.* **3.** the eastward part, direction, etc. —ˈ**eastwardly** *adv., adj.*

eastwards (ˈiːstwədz) *or* **eastward** *adv.* towards the east.

easy (ˈiːzɪ) *adj.* **easier, easiest. 1.** not requiring much labour or effort; not difficult. **2.** free from pain, care, or anxiety. **3.** not restricting; lenient: *easy laws.* **4.** tolerant and undemanding; easygoing: *an easy disposition.* **5.** readily influenced; pliant: *an easy victim.* **6.** not constricting; loose: *an easy fit.* **7.** not strained or extreme; moderate: *an easy pace.* **8.** *Inf.* ready to fall in with any suggestion made; not predisposed: *he is easy about what to do.* **9.** *Sl.* sexually available. ~*adv.* **10.** *Inf.* in an easy or relaxed manner. **11. easy does it.** *Inf.* go slowly and carefully; be careful. **12. go easy.** (*usually imperative;* often foll. by *on*) to exercise moderation. **13. stand easy.** *Mil.* a command to soldiers standing at ease that they may relax further. **14. take it easy. a.** to avoid stress or undue hurry. **b.** to remain calm. [C12: < OF *aisié*, p.p. of *aisier* to relieve, EASE]

▷ **Usage.** *Easy* is not used as an adverb by careful speakers and writers except in certain set phrases: *to take it easy; easy does it.* Where a fixed expression is not involved, the usual adverbial form of *easy* is preferred: *this polish goes on more easily* (not *easier*) *than the other.*

easy-care *adj.* (esp. of a fabric or garment) hard-wearing and requiring no special treatment during washing, etc.

easy chair *n.* a comfortable upholstered armchair.

easy-going (ˈiːzɪˈgəʊɪŋ) *adj.* **1.** relaxed in manner or attitude; excessively tolerant. **2.** moving at a comfortable pace: *an easy-going horse.*

easy meat *n. Inf.* **1.** someone easily seduced or deceived. **2.** something easy.

easy money *n.* **1.** money made with little effort, sometimes dishonestly. **2.** *Commerce.* money that can be borrowed at a low interest rate.

Easy Street *n.* (*sometimes not caps.*) *Inf.* a state of financial security.

eat (iːt) *vb.* **eating, ate, eaten. 1.** to take into the mouth and swallow (food, etc.), esp. after biting and chewing. **2.** (*tr.;* often foll. by *away* or *up*) to destroy as if by eating: *the damp had eaten away the woodwork.* **3.** (often foll. by *into*) to use up or waste: *taxes ate into his inheritance.* **4.** (often foll. by *into* or *through*) to make (a hole, passage, etc.) by eating or gnawing: *rats ate through the floor.* **5.** to take or have (a meal or meals): *we eat at six.* **6.** (*tr.*) to include as part of one's diet: *he doesn't eat fish.* **7.** (*tr.*) *Inf.* to cause to worry; make anxious: *what's eating you?* ~See also **eat out, eats, eat up.** [OE *etan*] —ˈ**eater** *n.*

eatable (ˈiːtəbᵊl) *adj.* fit or suitable for eating; edible.

eatables (ˈiːtəbᵊlz) *pl. n.* (*sometimes sing.*) food.

eating (ˈiːtɪŋ) *n.* **1.** food, esp. in relation to quality or taste: *this fruit makes excellent eating.* ~*adj.* **2.** suitable for eating uncooked: *eating apples.* **3.** relating to or for eating: *an eating house.*

eat out *vb.* (*intr., adv.*) to eat away from home, esp. in a restaurant.

eats (iːts) *pl. n. Inf.* articles of food; provisions.

eat up *vb.* (*adv., mainly tr.*) **1.** (*also intr.*) to eat or consume entirely. **2.** *Inf.* to listen to with enthusiasm or appreciation: *the audience ate up his every word.* **3.** (*often passive*) *Inf.* to affect grossly: *she was eaten up by jealousy.* **4.** *Inf.* to travel (a distance) quickly: *we just ate up the miles.*

eau de Cologne (əʊ də kəˈləʊn) *n.* See **cologne.** [F, lit.: water of Cologne]

eau de nil (əʊ də niːl) *n., adj.* (of) a pale yellowish-green colour. [F, lit.: water of (the) Nile]

eau de vie (əʊ də viː) *n.* brandy or other spirits. [F, lit.: water of life]

eaves (iːvz) *pl. n.* the edge of a roof that projects beyond the wall. [OE *efes*]

eavesdrop (ˈiːvzˌdrɒp) *vb.* **-dropping, -dropped.** (*intr.*) to listen secretly to the private conversation of others. [C17: back formation < *evesdropper*, < OE *yfesdrype* water dripping from the eaves] —ˈ**eavesˌdropper** *n.*

ebb (ɛb) *vb.* (*intr.*) **1.** (of tide water) to flow back or recede. Cf. **flow** (sense 8). **2.** to fall away or decline. ~*n.* **3. a.** the flowing back of the tide from high to low water or the period in which this takes place. **b.** (*as modifier*): *the ebb tide.* Cf. **flood** (sense 3). **4. at a low ebb.** in a state of weakness or decline. [OE *ebba*]

EBCDIC (ˈɛpsɪˌdɪk) *n. acronym for* extended binary-coded decimal-interchange code: a computer code for representing alphanumeric characters.

ebon (ˈɛbᵊn) *adj., n.* a poetic word for **ebony.** [C14: < L *hebenus;* see EBONY]

ebonite (ˈɛbəˌnaɪt) *n.* another name for **vulcanite.**

ebonize *or* **-ise** (ˈɛbəˌnaɪz) *vb.* (*tr.*) to stain or otherwise finish in imitation of ebony.

ebony (ˈɛbənɪ) *n., pl.* **-onies. 1.** any of various tropical and subtropical trees that have hard dark wood. **2.** the wood of such a tree. **3. a.** a black colour. **b.** (*as adj.*): *an ebony skin.* [C16 *hebeny*, < LL, < Gk, < *ebenos* ebony, < Egyptian]

ebullient (ɪˈbʌljənt, ɪˈbʊl-) *adj.* **1.** overflowing with enthusiasm or excitement. **2.** boiling. [C16: < L *ēbullīre* to bubble forth, be boisterous, < *bullīre* to BOIL[1]] —**eˈbullience** *or* **eˈbulliency** *n.*

ebullition (ˌɛbəˈlɪʃən) *n.* **1.** the process of boiling. **2.** a sudden outburst, as of intense emotion. [C16: < LL *ēbullītiō;* see EBULLIENT]

EC *abbrev. for:* **1.** East Central. **2.** European Community.

ec- *combining form.* out from; away from: *eccentric; ecdysis.* [< Gk *ek* (before a vowel *ex*) out of, away from; see EX-[1]]

eccentric (ɪkˈsɛntrɪk) *adj.* **1.** deviating or departing from convention; irregular or odd. **2.** situated away from the centre or the axis. **3.** not having a common centre: *eccentric circles.* **4.** not precisely circular. ~*n.* **5.** a person who deviates from normal forms of behaviour. **6.** a device for converting rotary motion to reciprocating motion. [C16: < Med. L *eccentricus*, < Gk *ekkentros*, < *ek-* EX-[1] + *kentron* centre] —**ecˈcentrically** *adv.*

eccentricity (ˌɛksɛnˈtrɪsɪtɪ) *n., pl.* **-ties. 1.** unconventional or irregular behaviour. **2.** the state of being eccentric. **3.** deviation from a circular path or orbit. **4.** *Geom.* a number that expresses the shape of a conic section. **5.** the degree of displacement of the geometric centre of a part from the true centre, esp. of the axis of rotation of a wheel.

eccl. *or* **eccles.** *abbrev. for* ecclesiastic(al).

Eccles. *or* **Eccl.** *Bible. abbrev. for* Ecclesiastes.

ecclesiastic (ɪˌkliːzɪˈæstɪk) *n.* **1.** a clergyman or other person in holy orders. ~*adj.* **2.** of or associated with the Christian Church or clergy.

ecclesiastical (ɪˌkliːzɪˈæstɪkᵊl) *adj.* of or relating

to the Christian Church. —**ec͵clesi'astically** *adv.*

ecclesiasticism (ɪ͵kli:zɪ'æstɪ͵sɪzəm) *n.* exaggerated attachment to the practices or principles of the Christian Church.

ecclesiology (ɪ͵kli:zɪ'ɒlədʒɪ) *n.* **1.** the study of the Christian Church. **2.** the study of Church architecture and decoration. —**ecclesiological** (ɪ͵kli:zɪə'lɒdʒɪk'l) *adj.*

eccrine ('ɛkrɪn) *adj.* of or denoting glands that secrete externally, esp. the sweat glands. Cf. **apocrine.** [< Gk *ekkrinein,* < *ek-* EC- + *krinein* to separate] —**eccrinology** (͵ɛkrɪ'nɒlədʒɪ) *n.*

ecdysis ('ɛkdɪsɪs) *n., pl.* **-ses** (-͵si:z). the periodic shedding of the cuticle in insects and other arthropods or the outer epidermal layer in reptiles. [C19: NL, < Gk *ekdusis,* < *ekduein* to strip, < *ek-* EX-[1] + *duein* to put on]

ECG *abbrev. for:* **1.** electrocardiogram. **2.** electrocardiograph.

echelon ('ɛʃə͵lɒn) *n.* **1.** a level of command, responsibility, etc. (esp. in **the upper echelons**). **2.** *Mil.* **a.** a formation in which units follow one another but are offset sufficiently to allow each unit a line of fire ahead. **b.** a group formed in this way. ~*vb.* **3.** to assemble in echelon. [C18: < F *échelon,* lit.: rung of a ladder, < OF *eschiele* ladder, < L *scāla*]

echidna (ɪ'kɪdnə) *n., pl.* **-nas** *or* **-nae** (-ni:). a spine-covered monotreme mammal of Australia and New Guinea, having a long snout and claws. Also called: **spiny anteater.** [C19: < NL, < L: viper, < Gk *ekhidna*]

echinoderm (ɪ'kaɪnəʊ͵dɜ:m) *n.* any of various marine invertebrates characterized by tube feet, a calcite body-covering, and a five-part symmetrical body. The group includes the starfish, sea urchins, and sea cucumbers.

echinus (ɪ'kaɪnəs) *n., pl.* **-ni** (-naɪ). **1.** *Archit.* a moulding between the shaft and the abacus of a Doric column. **2.** any sea urchin of the genus *Echinus,* such as the Mediterranean edible sea urchin. [C14: < L, < Gk *ekhinos*]

echo ('ɛkəʊ) *n., pl.* **-oes. 1. a.** the reflection of sound or other radiation by a reflecting medium, esp. a solid object. **b.** the sound so reflected. **2.** a repetition or imitation, esp. an unoriginal reproduction of another's opinions. **3.** something that evokes memories. **4.** (*sometimes pl.*) an effect that continues after the original cause has disappeared: *echoes of the French Revolution.* **5.** a person who copies another, esp. one who obsequiously agrees with another's opinions. **6. a.** the signal reflected by a radar target. **b.** the trace produced by such a signal on a radar screen. ~*vb.* **-oing, -oed. 7.** to resound or cause to resound with an echo. **8.** (*intr.*) (of sounds) to repeat or resound by echoes; reverberate. **9.** (*tr.*) (of persons) to repeat (words, opinions, etc.) in imitation, agreement, or flattery. **10.** (*tr.*) (of things) to resemble or imitate (another style, an earlier model, etc.). [C14: via L < Gk *ēkhō;* rel. to Gk *ēkhē* sound] —'**echoing** *adj.* —'**echoless** *adj.* —'**echo-**͵**like** *adj.*

echo chamber *n.* a room with walls that reflect sound. It is used to make acoustic measurements and as a recording studio when echo effects are required. Also called: **reverberation chamber.**

echoic (ɛ'kəʊɪk) *adj.* **1.** characteristic of or resembling an echo. **2.** onomatopoeic; imitative.

echolalia (͵ɛkəʊ'leɪlɪə) *n. Psychiatry.* the tendency to repeat mechanically words just spoken by another person. [C19: < NL, < ECHO + Gk *lalia* talk, chatter]

echolocation (͵ɛkəʊləʊ'keɪʃən) *n.* determination of the position of an object by measuring the time taken for an echo to return from it and its direction.

echo sounder *n.* a navigation device that determines depth by measuring the time taken for a pulse of sound to reach the sea bed or a submerged object and for the echo to return. —**echo sounding** *n.*

echovirus *or* **ECHO virus** ('ɛkəʊ͵vaɪrəs) *n.* any of a group of viruses that can cause symptoms of mild meningitis, the common cold, or infections of the intestinal and respiratory tracts. [C20: < initials of *Enteric Cytopathic Human Orphan* ("orphan" because orig. believed to be unrelated to any disease) + VIRUS]

éclair (eɪ'klɛə, ɪ'klɛə) *n.* a finger-shaped cake of choux pastry, usually filled with cream and covered with chocolate. [C19: < F, lit.: lightning (prob. because it does not last long)]

eclampsia (ɪ'klæmpsɪə) *n. Pathol.* a toxic condition that sometimes develops in the last three months of pregnancy, characterized by high blood pressure, weight gain, and convulsions. [C19: < NL, < Gk *eklampsis* a shining forth]

éclat (eɪ'klɑ:) *n.* **1.** brilliant or conspicuous success, effect, etc. **2.** showy display; ostentation. **3.** social distinction. **4.** approval; acclaim; applause. [C17: < F, < *éclater* to burst]

eclectic (ɪ'klɛktɪk, ɛ'klɛk-) *adj.* **1.** selecting from various styles, ideas, methods, etc. **2.** composed of elements drawn from a variety of sources, styles, etc. ~*n.* **3.** a person who favours an eclectic approach. [C17: < Gk *eklektikos,* < *eklegein* to select, < *legein* to gather] —**e'clectically** *adv.* —**e'clecticism** *n.*

eclipse (ɪ'klɪps) *n.* **1.** the total or partial obscuring of one celestial body by another (**total eclipse** *or* **partial eclipse**). A **solar eclipse** occurs when the moon passes between the sun and the earth; a **lunar eclipse** when the earth passes between the sun and the moon. **2.** the period of time during which such a phenomenon occurs. **3.** any dimming or obstruction of light. **4.** a loss of importance, power, fame, etc., esp. through overshadowing by another. ~*vb.* (*tr.*) **5.** to cause an eclipse of. **6.** to cast a shadow upon; obscure. **7.** to overshadow or surpass. [C13: back formation < OE *eclypsis,* < L, < Gk *ekleipsis* a forsaking, < *ekleipein* to abandon] —**e'clipser** *n.*

eclipsing binary *n.* a binary star whose orbital plane lies in or near the line of sight so that one component is regularly eclipsed by its companion.

ecliptic (ɪ'klɪptɪk) *n.* **1.** *Astron.* **a.** the great circle on the celestial sphere representing the apparent annual path of the sun relative to the stars. **b.** (*as modifier*): *the ecliptic plane.* **2.** an equivalent great circle on the terrestrial globe. ~*adj.* **3.** of or relating to an eclipse. —**e'cliptically** *adv.*

eclogue ('ɛklɒg) *n.* a pastoral or idyllic poem, usually in the form of a conversation. [C15: < L *ecloga* short poem, collection of extracts, < Gk *eklogē* selection, < *eklegein* to select]

eclosion (ɪ'kləʊʒən) *n.* the emergence of an insect larva from the egg or an adult from the pupal case. [C19: < F, < *éclore* to hatch, ult. < L *exclūdere* to shut out]

eco- *combining form.* denoting ecology or ecological: *ecocide; ecosphere.*

ecol. *abbrev. for:* **1.** ecological. **2.** ecology.

ecology (ɪ'kɒlədʒɪ) *n.* **1.** the study of the relationships between living organisms and their environment. **2.** the set of relationships of a particular organism with its environment. [C19: < G *Ökologie,* < Gk *oikos* house (hence, environment)] —**ecological** (͵i:kə'lɒdʒɪk'l) *adj.* —**e'cologist** *n.*

econ. *abbrev. for:* **1.** economical. **2.** economics. **3.** economy.

econometrics (ɪ͵kɒnə'mɛtrɪks) *n.* (*functioning as sing.*) the application of mathematical and statistical techniques to economic theories. —**e͵cono'metric** *or* **e͵cono'metrical** *adj.* —**econometrician** (ɪ͵kɒnəmə'trɪʃən) *or* **e͵cono'metrist** *n.*

economic (͵i:kə'nɒmɪk, ͵ɛkə-) *adj.* **1.** of or relating to an economy, economics, or finance. **2.** *Brit.* capable of being produced, operated, etc., for profit; profitable. **3.** concerning or affecting material resources or welfare: *economic pests.* **4.** concerned with or relating to the necessities of life; utilitarian. **5.** a variant of **economical. 6.** *Inf.* inexpensive; cheap.

economical (͵i:kə'nɒmɪk'l, ͵ɛkə-) *adj.* **1.** using the minimum required; not wasteful. **2.** frugal; thrifty. **3.** a variant of **economic** (senses 1–4). —͵**eco'nomically** *adv.*

economics (ˌiːkəˈnɒmɪks, ˌɛkə-) *n.* **1.** (*functioning as sing.*) the social science concerned with the production and consumption of goods and services and the analysis of the commercial activities of a society. **2.** (*functioning as pl.*) financial aspects.

economist (ɪˈkɒnəmɪst) *n.* a specialist in economics.

economize *or* **-ise** (ɪˈkɒnəˌmaɪz) *vb.* (often foll. by *on*) to limit or reduce (expense, waste, etc.). —**eˌconomiˈzation** *or* **-iˈsation** *n.*

economy (ɪˈkɒnəmɪ) *n., pl.* **-mies.** **1.** careful management of resources to avoid unnecessary expenditure or waste; thrift. **2.** a means or instance of this; saving. **3.** sparing, restrained, or efficient use. **4. a.** the complex of activities concerned with the production, distribution, and consumption of goods and services. **b.** a particular type or branch of this: *a socialist economy.* **5.** the management of the resources, finances, income, and expenditure of a community, business enterprise, etc. **6. a.** a class of travel in aircraft, cheaper and less luxurious than first class. **b.** (*as modifier*): *economy class.* **7.** (*modifier*) purporting to offer a larger quantity for a lower price: *economy pack.* **8.** the orderly interplay between the parts of a system or structure. [C16: via L < Gk *oikonomia* domestic management, < *oikos* house + *-nomia,* < *nemein* to manage]

ecosphere (ˈiːkəʊˌsfɪə, ˈɛkəʊ-) *n.* the parts of the universe, esp. on earth, where life can exist.

écossaise (ˌeɪkɒˈseɪz) *n.* **1.** a lively dance in two-four time. **2.** the tune for such a dance. [C19: F, lit.: Scottish (dance)]

ecosystem (ˈiːkəʊˌsɪstəm, ˈɛkəʊ-) *n. Ecology.* a system involving the interactions between a community and its non-living environment. [C20: < ECO(LOGY) + SYSTEM]

ecru (ˈɛkruː, ˈeɪkruː) *n., adj.* (of) a greyish-yellow to a light greyish colour. [C19: < F, < *é-* (intensive) + *cru* raw, < L *crūdus;* see CRUDE]

ecstasy (ˈɛkstəsɪ) *n., pl.* **-sies.** **1.** (*often pl.*) a state of exalted delight, joy, etc.; rapture. **2.** intense emotion of any kind: *an ecstasy of rage.* **3.** *Psychol.* overpowering emotion sometimes involving temporary loss of consciousness: often associated with mysticism. [C14: < OF via Med. L < Gk *ekstasis* displacement, trance, < *ex-* out + *histanai* to cause to stand]

ecstatic (ɛkˈstætɪk) *adj.* **1.** in a trancelike state of rapture or delight. **2.** showing or feeling great enthusiasm. ~*n.* **3.** a person who has periods of intense trancelike joy. —**ecˈstatically** *adv.*

ECT *abbrev. for* electroconvulsive therapy.

ecto- *combining form.* indicating outer, outside. [< Gk *ektos* outside, < *ek, ex* out]

ectoblast (ˈɛktəʊˌblæst) *n.* another name for **ectoderm.** —ˌ**ectoˈblastic** *adj.*

ectoderm (ˈɛktəʊˌdɜːm) *or* **exoderm** *n.* the outer germ layer of an animal embryo, which gives rise to epidermis and nervous tissue. —ˌ**ectoˈdermal** *or* ˌ**ectoˈdermic** *adj.*

ectomorph (ˈɛktəʊˌmɔːf) *n.* a type of person having a body build characterized by thinness, weakness, and a lack of weight. —ˌ**ectoˈmorphic** *adj.* —ˈ**ectoˌmorphy** *n.*

-ectomy *n. combining form.* indicating surgical excision of a part: *appendectomy.* [< NL *-ectomia,* < Gk *ek-* out + -TOMY]

ectopic pregnancy (ɛkˈtɒpɪk) *n. Pathol.* the abnormal development of a fertilized egg outside the uterus, usually within a Fallopian tube.

ectoplasm (ˈɛktəʊˌplæzəm) *n.* **1.** *Cytology.* the outer layer of cytoplasm. **2.** *Spiritualism.* the substance supposedly emanating from the body of a medium during trances. —ˌ**ectoˈplasmic** *adj.*

ecumenical, oecumenical (ˌiːkjʊˈmɛnɪkᵊl, ˌɛk-) *or* **ecumenic, oecumenic** *adj.* **1.** of or relating to the Christian Church throughout the world, esp. with regard to its unity. **2.** tending to promote unity among Churches. [C16: via LL < Gk *oikoumenikos,* < *oikein* to inhabit, < *oikos* house] —ˌ**ecuˈmenically** *or* ˌ**oecuˈmenically** *adv.*

ecumenicalism (ˌiːkjʊˈmɛnɪkəˌlɪzəm, ˌɛk-), **ecumenicism** *or* **ecumenism** *n.* the aim of unity among all Christian churches throughout the world.

eczema (ˈɛksɪmə) *n. Pathol.* a skin inflammation with lesions that scale, crust, or ooze a serous fluid, often accompanied by intense itching. [C18: < NL, < Gk *ekzema,* < *ek-* out + *zein* to boil] —**eczematous** (ɛkˈsɛmətəs) *adj.*

ed. *abbrev. for:* **1.** edited. **2.** (*pl.* **eds.**) edition. **3.** (*pl.* **eds.**) editor. **4.** education.

-ed[1] *suffix.* forming the past tense of most English verbs. [OE *-de, -ede, -ode, -ade*]

-ed[2] *suffix.* forming the past participle of most English verbs. [OE *-ed, -od, -ad*]

-ed[3] *suffix forming adjectives from nouns.* possessing or having the characteristics of: *salaried; red-blooded.* [OE *-ede*]

Edam (ˈiːdæm) *n.* a round yellow cheese with a red outside covering. [after *Edam,* in Holland]

Edda (ˈɛdə) *n.* **1.** Also called: **Elder Edda, Poetic Edda.** a 12th-century collection of mythological Old Norse poems. **2.** Also called: **Younger Edda, Prose Edda.** a treatise on versification together with a collection of Scandinavian myths, legends, and poems (?1222). [C18: ON] —**Eddaic** (ɛˈdeɪɪk) *adj.*

eddy (ˈɛdɪ) *n., pl.* **-dies.** **1.** a movement in air, water, or other fluid in which the current doubles back on itself causing a miniature whirlwind or whirlpool. **2.** a deviation from or disturbance in the main trend of thought, life, etc. ~*vb.* **-dying, -died.** **3.** to move or cause to move against the main current. [C15: prob. < ON]

eddy current *n.* an electric current induced in a massive conductor by an alternating magnetic field.

edelweiss (ˈeɪdᵊlˌvaɪs) *n.* a small alpine flowering plant having white woolly oblong leaves and a tuft of floral leaves surrounding the flowers. [C19: G, lit.: noble white]

edema (ɪˈdiːmə) *n., pl.* **-mata** (-mətə). the usual U.S. spelling of **oedema.**

Eden (ˈiːdᵊn) *n.* **1.** Also called: **Garden of Eden.** *Bible.* the garden in which Adam and Eve were placed at the Creation. **2.** a place or state of great delight or contentment. [C14: < LL, < Heb. *'ēdhen* place of pleasure] —**Edenic** (iːˈdɛnɪk) *adj.*

edentate (iːˈdɛnteɪt) *n.* **1.** any mammal of the order *Edentata,* of tropical Central and South America, which have few or no teeth. The order includes anteaters, sloths, and armadillos. ~*adj.* **2.** of or relating to the order *Edentata.* [C19: < L *ēdentātus* lacking teeth, < *ēdentāre* to render toothless, < *e-* out + *dēns* tooth]

edge (ɛdʒ) *n.* **1.** a border, brim, or margin. **2.** a brink or verge. **3.** a line along which two faces or surfaces of a solid meet. **4.** the sharp cutting side of a blade. **5.** keenness, sharpness, or urgency. **6.** force, effectiveness, or incisiveness: *the performance lacked edge.* **7.** a ridge. **8. have the edge on** *or* **over.** to have a slight advantage or superiority over. **9. on edge. a.** nervously irritable; tense. **b.** nervously excited or eager. **10. set (someone's) teeth on edge.** to make (someone) acutely irritated or uncomfortable. ~*vb.* **11.** (*tr.*) to provide an edge or border for. **12.** (*tr.*) to shape or trim the edge or border of (something). **13.** to push (one's way, someone, something, etc.) gradually, esp. edgeways. **14.** (*tr.*) *Cricket.* to hit (a bowled ball) with the edge of the bat. **15.** (*tr.*) to sharpen (a knife, etc.). [OE *ecg*] —ˈ**edger** *n.*

edgeways (ˈɛdʒˌweɪz) *or esp. U.S. & Canad.* **edgewise** (ˈɛdʒˌwaɪz) *adv.* **1.** with the edge forwards or uppermost. **2.** on, by, with, or towards the edge. **3. get a word in edgeways.** (*usually with a negative*) to interrupt a conversation in which someone else is talking incessantly.

edging (ˈɛdʒɪŋ) *n.* **1.** anything placed along an edge to finish it, esp. as an ornament. **2.** the act of making an edge. ~*adj.* **3.** relating to or used for making an edge: *edging shears.*

edgy (ˈɛdʒɪ) *adj.* **edgier, edgiest.** (*usually*

postpositive) nervous, irritable, tense, or anxious. —ˈ**edgily** *adv.* —ˈ**edginess** *n.*

edh (ɛð) *or* **eth** (ɛθ, ɛð) *n.* a character of the runic alphabet (ð) used to represent the voiced dental fricative as in *then, mother, bathe.*

edible (ˈɛdɪbᵊl) *adj.* fit to be eaten; eatable. [C17: < LL *edibilis,* < L *edere* to eat] —ˌ**ediˈbility** *or* ˈ**edibleness** *n.*

edibles (ˈɛdɪbᵊlz) *pl. n.* articles fit to eat; food.

edict (ˈiːdɪkt) *n.* **1.** a decree or order issued by any authority. **2.** any formal or authoritative command, proclamation, etc. [C15: < L *ēdictum,* < *ēdīcere* to declare] —**eˈdictal** *adj.*

edifice (ˈɛdɪfɪs) *n.* **1.** a building, esp. a large or imposing one. **2.** a complex or elaborate institution or organization. [C14: < OF, < L *aedificium,* < *aedificāre* to build; see EDIFY]

edify (ˈɛdɪˌfaɪ) *vb.* **-fying, -fied.** (*tr.*) to improve the morality, intellect, etc., of, esp. by instruction. [C14: < OF, < L *aedificāre* to construct, < *aedēs* a dwelling, temple + *facere* to make] —ˌ**edifiˈcation** *n.* —ˈ**ediˌfier** *n.* —ˈ**ediˌfying** *adj.*

edit (ˈɛdɪt) *vb.* (*tr.*) **1.** to prepare (text) for publication by checking and improving its accuracy, clarity, etc. **2.** to be in charge of (a publication, esp. a periodical). **3.** to prepare (a film, tape, etc.) by rearrangement or selection of material. **4.** (often foll. by *out*) to remove, as from a manuscript or film. [C18: back formation < EDITOR]

edit. *abbrev. for:* **1.** edited. **2.** edition. **3.** editor.

edition (ɪˈdɪʃən) *n.* **1.** *Printing.* **a.** the entire number of copies of a book or other publication printed at one time. **b.** a copy from this number: *a first edition.* **2.** one of a number of printings of a book or other publication, issued at separate times with alterations, amendments, etc. **3. a.** an issue of a work identified by its format: *a leather-bound edition.* **b.** an issue of a work identified by its editor or publisher: *the Oxford edition.* [C16: < L *ēditiō* a bringing forth, publishing, < *ēdere* to give out; see EDITOR]

editor (ˈɛdɪtə) *n.* **1.** a person who edits written material for publication. **2.** a person in overall charge of a newspaper or periodical. **3.** a person in charge of one section of a newspaper or periodical: *the sports editor.* **4.** *Films.* a person who makes a selection and arrangement of shots. **5.** a person in overall control of a television or radio programme that consists of various items. [C17: < LL: producer, exhibitor, < *ēdere* to give out, publish, < *ē-* out + *dāre* to give] —ˈ**editorˌship** *n.*

editorial (ˌɛdɪˈtɔːrɪəl) *adj.* **1.** of or relating to editing or editors. **2.** of, relating to, or expressed in an editorial. **3.** of or relating to the content of a publication. ~*n.* **4.** an article in a newspaper, etc., expressing the opinion of the editor or the publishers. —ˌ**ediˈtorially** *adv.*

editorialize *or* **-ise** (ˌɛdɪˈtɔːrɪəˌlaɪz) *vb.* (*intr.*) to express an opinion as in an editorial. —ˌ**ediˌtorialiˈzation** *or* **-iˈsation** *n.* —ˌ**ediˈtorialˌizer** *or* **-iser** *n.*

EDP *abbrev. for* electronic data processing.

EDT (in the U.S. and Canada) *abbrev. for* Eastern Daylight Time.

educate (ˈɛdjʊˌkeɪt) *vb.* (*mainly tr.*) **1.** (*also intr.*) to impart knowledge by formal instruction to (a pupil); teach. **2.** to provide schooling for. **3.** to improve or develop (a person, taste, skills, etc.). **4.** to train for some particular purpose or occupation. [C15: < L *ēducāre* to rear, educate, < *dūcere* to lead] —ˈ**educable** *or* ˈ**eduˌcatable** *adj.* —ˌ**educaˈbility** *or* ˌ**eduˌcataˈbility** *n.* —ˈ**educative** *adj.*

educated (ˈɛdjʊˌkeɪtɪd) *adj.* **1.** having an education, esp. a good one. **2.** displaying culture, taste, and knowledge; cultivated. **3.** (*prenominal*) based on experience or information (esp. in **an educated guess**).

education (ˌɛdjʊˈkeɪʃən) *n.* **1.** the act or process of acquiring knowledge. **2.** the knowledge or training acquired by this process. **3.** the act or process of imparting knowledge, esp. at a school, college, or university. **4.** the theory of teaching and learning. **5.** a particular kind of instruction or training: *a university education.* —ˌ**eduˈcational** *adj.* —ˌ**eduˈcationalist** *or* ˌ**eduˈcationist** *n.*

educator (ˈɛdjʊˌkeɪtə) *n.* **1.** a person who educates; teacher. **2.** a specialist in education.

educe (ɪˈdjuːs) *vb.* (*tr.*) *Rare.* **1.** to evolve or develop. **2.** to draw out or elicit (information, solutions, etc.). [C15: < L *ēdūcere,* < *ē-* out + *dūcere* to lead] —**eˈducible** *adj.* —**eductive** (ɪˈdʌktɪv) *adj.*

Edwardian (ɛdˈwɔːdɪən) *adj.* of or characteristic of the reign of Edward VII, king of Great Britain and Ireland (1901–10). —**Edˈwardianism** *n.*

-ee *suffix forming nouns.* **1.** indicating a recipient of an action (as opposed, esp. in legal terminology, to the agent): *assignee; lessee.* **2.** indicating a person in a specified state or condition: *absentee.* **3.** indicating a diminutive form of something: *bootee.* [via OF *-é, -ée,* p.p. endings, < L *-ātus, -āta* -ATE[1]]

EEC *abbrev. for* European Economic Community (the Common Market).

EEG *abbrev. for:* **1.** electroencephalogram. **2.** electroencephalograph.

eel (iːl) *n.* **1.** any teleost fish such as the European freshwater eel, having a long snakelike body, a smooth slimy skin, and reduced fins. **2.** any of various similar animals, such as the mud eel and the electric eel. **3.** an evasive or untrustworthy person. [OE *ǣl*] —ˈ**eel-ˌlike** *adj.* —ˈ**eely** *adj.*

eelgrass (ˈiːlˌgrɑːs) *n.* any of several perennial submerged marine plants having grasslike leaves.

eelpout (ˈiːlˌpaʊt) *n.* **1.** a marine eel-like fish. **2.** another name for **burbot.** [OE *ǣlepūte*]

eelworm (ˈiːlˌwɜːm) *n.* any of various nematode worms, esp. the wheatworm and the vinegar eel.

e'en (iːn) *adv., n. Poetic or arch.* contraction of **even**[2] or **evening.**

e'er (ɛə) *adv. Poetic or arch.* contraction of **ever.**

-eer *or* **-ier** *suffix.* **1.** (*forming nouns*) indicating a person who is concerned with or who does something specified: *auctioneer; engineer; profiteer; mutineer.* **2.** (*forming verbs*) to be concerned with something specified: *electioneer.* [< OF *-ier,* < L *-arius* -ARY]

eerie (ˈɪərɪ) *adj.* **eerier, eeriest.** uncannily frightening or disturbing; weird. [C13: orig. Scot. & N English, prob. < OE *earg* cowardly] —ˈ**eerily** *adv.* —ˈ**eeriness** *n.*

EETPU (in Britain) *abbrev. for* Electrical, Electronic, Telecommunications, and Plumbing Union.

eff (ɛf) *vb.* **1.** euphemism for **fuck** (esp. in **eff off**). **2. eff and blind.** *Sl.* to use obscene language. —ˈ**effing** *n., adj., adv.*

efface (ɪˈfeɪs) *vb.* (*tr.*) **1.** to obliterate or make dim. **2.** to make (oneself) inconspicuous or humble. **3.** to rub out; erase. [C15: < F *effacer,* lit.: to obliterate the face; see FACE] —**efˈfaceable** *adj.* —**efˈfacement** *n.* —**efˈfacer** *n.*

effect (ɪˈfɛkt) *n.* **1.** something produced by a cause or agent; result. **2.** power to influence or produce a result. **3.** the condition of being operative (esp. in **in** *or* **into effect**). **4. take effect.** to become operative or begin to produce results. **5.** basic meaning or purpose (esp. in **to that effect**). **6.** an impression, usually contrived (esp. in **for effect**). **7.** a scientific phenomenon: *the Doppler effect.* **8. in effect. a.** in fact; actually. **b.** for all practical purposes. **9.** the overall impression or result. ~*vb.* **10.** (*tr.*) to cause to occur; accomplish. [C14: < L *effectus* a performing, tendency, < *efficere* to accomplish, < *facere* to do] —**efˈfecter** *n.* —**efˈfectible** *adj.*

effective (ɪˈfɛktɪv) *adj.* **1.** productive of or capable of producing a result. **2.** in effect; operative. **3.** impressive: *an effective entrance.* **4.** (*prenominal*) actual rather than theoretical. **5.** (of a military force, etc.) equipped and prepared for action. ~*n.* **6.** a serviceman equipped and prepared for action. —**efˈfectively** *adv.* —**efˈfectiveness** *n.*

effects (ɪˈfɛkts) *pl. n.* **1.** Also called: **personal effects.** personal belongings. **2.** lighting, sounds, etc., to accompany a stage, film, or broadcast production.

effectual (ɪˈfɛktjʊəl) *adj.* **1.** capable of or successful in producing an intended result; effective. **2.** (of documents, etc.) having legal force. —**efˌfectuˈality** *or* **efˈfectualness** *n.*

effectually (ɪˈfɛktjʊəlɪ) *adv.* **1.** with the intended effect. **2.** in effect.

effectuate (ɪˈfɛktjʊˌeɪt) *vb.* (*tr.*) to cause to happen; effect; accomplish. —**efˌfectuˈation** *n.*

effeminate (ɪˈfɛmɪnɪt) *adj.* (of a man or boy) displaying characteristics regarded as typical of a woman; not manly. [C14: < L *effēmināre* to make into a woman, < *fēmina* woman] —**efˈfeminacy** *or* **efˈfeminateness** *n.*

effendi (ɛˈfɛndɪ) *n., pl.* **-dis. 1.** (in the Ottoman Empire) a title of respect. **2.** (in Turkey since 1934) the oral title of address equivalent to *Mr.* [C17: < Turkish *efendi* master, < Mod. Gk *aphentēs,* < Gk *authentēs* lord, doer]

efferent (ˈɛfərənt) *adj. Physiol.* carrying or conducting outwards, esp. from the brain or spinal cord. Cf. **afferent.** [C19: < L *efferre* to bear off, < *ferre* to bear] —ˈ**efference** *n.*

effervesce (ˌɛfəˈvɛs) *vb.* (*intr.*) **1.** (of a liquid) to give off bubbles of gas. **2.** (of a gas) to issue in bubbles from a liquid. **3.** to exhibit great excitement, vivacity, etc. [C18: < L *effervescere* to foam up, ult. < *fervēre* to boil, ferment] —ˌ**efferˈvescingly** *adv.*

effervescent (ˌɛfəˈvɛsᵊnt) *adj.* **1.** (of a liquid) giving off bubbles of gas. **2.** high-spirited; vivacious. —ˌ**efferˈvescence** *n.*

effete (ɪˈfiːt) *adj.* **1.** weak or decadent. **2.** exhausted; spent. **3.** (of animals or plants) no longer capable of reproduction. [C17: < L *effētus* exhausted by bearing, < *fētus* having brought forth; see FETUS] —**efˈfeteness** *n.*

efficacious (ˌɛfɪˈkeɪʃəs) *adj.* capable of or successful in producing an intended result; effective. [C16: < L *efficāx* powerful, efficient, < *efficere* to achieve] —**efficacy** (ˈɛfɪkəsɪ) *or* ˌ**effiˈcaciousness** *n.*

efficiency (ɪˈfɪʃənsɪ) *n., pl.* **-cies. 1.** the quality or state of being efficient. **2.** the ratio of the useful work done by a machine, etc., to the energy input, often expressed as a percentage.

efficient (ɪˈfɪʃənt) *adj.* **1.** functioning or producing effectively and with the least waste of effort; competent. **2.** *Philosophy.* producing a direct effect. [C14: < L *efficiēns* effecting]

effigy (ˈɛfɪdʒɪ) *n., pl.* **-gies. 1.** a portrait, esp. as a monument. **2.** a crude representation of someone, used as a focus for contempt or ridicule (often in **burn** *or* **hang in effigy**). [C18: < L *effigiēs,* < *effingere* to form, portray, < *fingere* to shape]

effloresce (ˌɛflɔːˈrɛs) *vb.* (*intr.*) **1.** to burst forth as into flower; bloom. **2.** to become powdery by loss of water or crystallization. **3.** to become encrusted with powder or crystals as a result of chemical change or evaporation. [C18: < L *efflōrēscere* to blossom, < *flōrēscere,* < *flōs* flower]

efflorescence (ˌɛflɔːˈrɛsᵊns) *n.* **1.** a bursting forth or flowering. **2.** *Chem., geol.* **a.** the process of efflorescing. **b.** the powdery substance formed as a result of this process. **3.** any skin rash or eruption. —ˌ**effloˈrescent** *adj.*

effluence (ˈɛflʊəns) *or* **efflux** (ˈɛflʌks) *n.* **1.** the act or process of flowing out. **2.** something that flows out.

effluent (ˈɛflʊənt) *n.* **1.** liquid discharged as waste, as from an industrial plant or sewage works. **2.** radioactive waste released from a nuclear power station. **3.** a stream that flows out of another body of water. **4.** something that flows out or forth. ~*adj.* **5.** flowing out or forth. [C18: < L *effluere* to run forth, < *fluere* to flow]

effluvium (ɛˈfluːvɪəm) *n., pl.* **-via** (-vɪə) *or* **-viums.** an unpleasant smell or exhalation, as of gaseous waste or decaying matter. [C17: < L: a flowing out; see EFFLUENT] —**efˈfluvial** *adj.*

effort (ˈɛfət) *n.* **1.** physical or mental exertion. **2.** a determined attempt. **3.** achievement; creation. [C15: < OF *esfort,* < *esforcier* to force, ult. < L *fortis* strong] —ˈ**effortful** *adj.* —ˈ**effortless** *adj.*

effrontery (ɪˈfrʌntərɪ) *n., pl.* **-eries.** shameless or insolent boldness. [C18: < F, < OF *esfront* barefaced, shameless, < LL *effrons,* lit.: putting forth one's forehead]

effulgent (ɪˈfʌldʒənt) *adj.* radiant; brilliant. [C18: < L *effulgēre* to shine forth, < *fulgēre* to shine] —**efˈfulgence** *n.* —**efˈfulgently** *adv.*

effuse *vb.* (ɪˈfjuːz). **1.** to pour or flow out. **2.** to spread out; diffuse. ~*adj.* (ɪˈfjuːs). **3.** *Bot.* (esp. of an inflorescence) spreading out loosely. [C16: < L *effūsus* poured out, < *effundere* to shed]

effusion (ɪˈfjuːʒən) *n.* **1.** an unrestrained outpouring in speech or words. **2.** the act or process of being poured out. **3.** something that is poured out.

effusive (ɪˈfjuːsɪv) *adj.* **1.** extravagantly demonstrative of emotion; gushing. **2.** (of rock) formed by the solidification of magma. —**efˈfusively** *adv.* —**efˈfusiveness** *n.*

EFL *abbrev. for* English as a Foreign Language.

eft (ɛft) *n.* a dialect or archaic name for a **newt.** [OE *efeta*]

EFTA (ˈɛftə) *n. acronym for* European Free Trade Association; established in 1960 to eliminate trade tariffs on industrial products; originally comprised Britain, Denmark, Norway, Sweden, Switzerland, Austria, and Portugal.

Eftpos *or* **EFTPOS** (ˈɛftpɒs) *n. acronym for* electronic funds transfer at point of sale.

EFTS *abbrev. for* electronic funds transfer system.

eftsoons (ɛftˈsuːnz) *adv. Arch.* **1.** soon afterwards. **2.** repeatedly. [OE *eft sōna*]

Eg. *abbrev. for:* **1.** Egypt(ian). **2.** Egyptology.

e.g., eg, *or* **eg.** *abbrev. for* exempli gratia. [L: for example]

egad (ɪˈgæd, iːˈgæd) *interj. Arch.* a mild oath. [C17: prob. var. of *Ah God!*]

egalitarian (ɪˌgælɪˈtɛərɪən) *adj.* **1.** of or upholding the doctrine of the equality of mankind. ~*n.* **2.** an adherent of egalitarian principles. [C19: alteration of *equalitarian,* through infl. of F *égal* equal] —**eˌgaliˈtarianˌism** *n.*

egg[1] (ɛg) *n.* **1.** the oval or round reproductive body laid by the females of birds, reptiles, fishes, insects, and some other animals, consisting of a developing embryo, its food store, and sometimes jelly or albumen, all surrounded by an outer shell or membrane. **2.** Also called: **egg cell.** any female gamete; ovum. **3.** the egg of the domestic hen used as food. **4.** something resembling an egg, esp. in shape. **5. good** (*or* **bad**) **egg.** *Old-fashioned inf.* a good (or bad) person. **6. put** *or* **have all one's eggs in one basket.** to stake everything on a single venture. **7. teach one's grandmother to suck eggs.** *Inf.* to presume to teach someone something that he knows already. **8. with egg on one's face.** *Inf.* made to look ridiculous. [C14: < ON *egg;* rel. to OE *ǣg*]

egg[2] (ɛg) *vb.* (*tr.;* usually foll. by *on*) to urge or incite, esp. to daring or foolish acts. [OE *eggian*]

egg-and-spoon race *n.* a race in which runners carry an egg balanced in a spoon.

eggbeater (ˈɛgˌbiːtə) *n.* **1.** Also called: **eggwhisk.** a utensil for beating eggs; whisk. **2.** *Chiefly U.S. & Canad.* an informal name for **helicopter.**

egger *or* **eggar** (ˈɛgə) *n.* any of various European moths having brown bodies and wings. [C18: < EGG[1], < the egg-shaped cocoon]

egghead (ˈɛgˌhɛd) *n. Inf.* an intellectual.

eggnog (ˌɛgˈnɒg) *n.* a drink made of eggs, milk, sugar, spice, and brandy, rum, or other spirit. Also called: **egg flip.** [C19: < EGG[1] + NOG]

eggplant (ˈɛgˌplɑːnt) *n.* another name (esp. U.S. and Canad.) for **aubergine.**

eggshell (ˈɛgˌʃɛl) *n.* **1.** the hard porous outer layer of a bird's egg. **2.** (*modifier*) (of paint) having a very slight sheen.

eggshell porcelain *or* **china** *n.* a very thin translucent porcelain originally from China.

egg tooth *n.* (in embryo reptiles) a temporary

tooth or (in birds) projection of the beak used for piercing the eggshell.

eglantine (ˈɛɡlənˌtaɪn) *n.* another name for **sweetbrier.** [C14: < OF *aiglent,* ult. < L *acus* needle, < *acer* sharp, keen]

ego (ˈiːɡəʊ, ˈɛɡəʊ) *n., pl.* **egos.** **1.** the self of an individual person; the conscious subject. **2.** *Psychoanalysis.* the conscious mind, based on perception of the environment: responsible for modifying the antisocial instincts of the id and itself modified by the conscience (superego). **3.** one's image of oneself; morale. **4.** egotism; conceit. [C19: < L: I]

egocentric (ˌiːɡəʊˈsɛntrɪk, ˌɛɡ-) *adj.* **1.** regarding everything only in relation to oneself; self-centred. ~*n.* **2.** a self-centred person; egotist. —ˌ**egocenˈtricity** *n.* —ˌ**egoˈcentrism** *n.*

egoism (ˈiːɡəʊˌɪzəm, ˈɛɡ-) *n.* **1.** concern for one's own interests and welfare. **2.** *Ethics.* the theory that the pursuit of one's own welfare is the highest good. **3.** self-centredness; egotism. —ˈ**egoist** *n.*

egomania (ˌiːɡəʊˈmeɪnɪə, ˌɛɡ-) *n. Psychiatry.* obsessive love for oneself. —ˌ**egoˈmaniˌac** *n.* —**egomaniacal** (ˌiːɡəʊməˈnaɪək°l, ˌɛɡ-) *adj.*

egotism (ˈiːɡəˌtɪzəm, ˈɛɡə-) *n.* **1.** an inflated sense of self-importance or superiority; self-centredness. **2.** excessive reference to oneself. [C18: < L *ego* I + -ISM] —ˈ**egotist** *n.*

ego trip *n. Inf.* something undertaken to boost or draw attention to a person's own image or appraisal of himself.

egregious (ɪˈɡriːdʒəs, -dʒɪəs) *adj.* **1.** outstandingly bad; flagrant. **2.** *Arch.* distinguished; eminent. [C16: < L *ēgregius* outstanding (lit.: standing out from the herd), < *ē-* out + *grex* flock, herd] —eˈ**gregiousness** *n.*

egress (ˈiːɡrɛs) *n.* **1.** Also: **egression.** the act of going or coming out; emergence. **2.** a way out; exit. **3.** the right to go out or depart. [C16: < L *ēgredī* to come forth, depart, < *gradī* to move, step]

egret (ˈiːɡrɪt) *n.* any of various wading birds similar to herons but usually having white plumage and, in the breeding season, long feathery plumes. [C15: < OF *aigrette,* < OProvençal *aigreta,* < *aigron* heron, of Gmc origin]

Egyptian (ɪˈdʒɪpʃən) *adj.* **1.** of or relating to Egypt, a republic in NE Africa, its inhabitants, or their dialect of Arabic. **2.** of or characteristic of the ancient Egyptians, their language, or culture. ~*n.* **3.** a native or inhabitant of Egypt. **4.** a member of a people who established an advanced civilization in Egypt that flourished from the late fourth millennium B.C. **5.** the extinct language of the ancient Egyptians.

Egyptology (ˌiːdʒɪpˈtɒlədʒɪ) *n.* the study of the archaeology and language of ancient Egypt. —ˌ**Egypˈtologist** *n.*

eh (eɪ) *interj.* an exclamation used to express questioning surprise or to seek the repetition or confirmation of a statement or question.

EHF *abbrev. for* extremely high frequency.

eider *or* **eider duck** (ˈaɪdə) *n.* any of several sea ducks of the N hemisphere. See **eiderdown.** [C18: < ON *æthr*]

eiderdown (ˈaɪdəˌdaʊn) *n.* **1.** the breast down of the female eider duck, used for stuffing pillows, quilts, etc. **2.** a thick, warm cover for a bed, enclosing a soft filling.

eidetic (aɪˈdɛtɪk) *adj. Psychol.* **1.** (of visual, or sometimes auditory, images) very vivid and allowing detailed recall of something previously perceived: thought to be common in children. **2.** relating to or subject to such imagery. [C20: < Gk *eidētikos,* < *eidos* shape, form] —eiˈ**detically** *adv.*

eight (eɪt) *n.* **1.** the cardinal number that is the sum of one and seven and the product of two and four. **2.** a numeral, 8, VIII, etc., representing this number. **3.** the amount or quantity that is one greater than seven. **4.** something representing, represented by, or consisting of eight units. **5.** *Rowing.* **a.** a racing shell propelled by eight oarsmen. **b.** the crew of such a shell. **6.** Also called: **eight o'clock.** eight hours after noon or midnight. **7. have one over the eight.** *Sl.* to be drunk. ~*determiner.* **8. a.** amounting to eight. **b.** (*as pron.*): *I could only find eight.* [OE *eahta*]

eighteen (ˈeɪˈtiːn) *n.* **1.** the cardinal number that is the sum of ten and eight and the product of two and nine. **2.** a numeral, 18, XVIII, etc., representing this number. **3.** the amount or quantity that is eight more than ten. **4.** something represented by, representing, or consisting of 18 units. ~*determiner.* **5. a.** amounting to eighteen: *eighteen weeks.* **b.** (*as pron.*): *eighteen of them knew.* [OE *eahtatēne*] —ˈ**eighˈteenth** *adj., n.*

eightfold (ˈeɪtˌfəʊld) *adj.* **1.** equal to or having eight times as many or as much. **2.** composed of eight parts. ~*adv.* **3.** by eight times as much.

eighth (eɪtθ) *adj.* **1.** (*usually prenominal*) **a.** coming after the seventh and before the ninth in numbering, position, etc.; being the ordinal number of *eight:* often written 8th. **b.** (*as n.*): *the eighth in line.* ~*n.* **2. a.** one of eight equal parts of something. **b.** (*as modifier*): *an eighth part.* **3.** the fraction one divided by eight (1/8). **4.** another word for **octave.** ~*adv.* **5.** Also: **eighthly.** after the seventh person, position, event, etc.

eighth note *n. Music.* the usual U.S. and Canad. name for **quaver.**

eightsome reel (ˈeɪtsəm) *n.* a Scottish dance for eight people.

eighty (ˈeɪtɪ) *n., pl.* **eighties.** **1.** the cardinal number that is the product of ten and eight. **2.** a numeral, 80, LXXX, etc., representing this number. **3.** (*pl.*) the numbers 80-89, esp. the 80th to the 89th year of a person's life or of a century. **4.** the amount or quantity that is eight times ten. **5.** something represented by, representing, or consisting of 80 units. ~*determiner.* **6. a.** amounting to eighty: *eighty pages of nonsense.* **b.** (*as pron.*): *eighty are expected.* [OE *eahtatig*] —ˈ**eightieth** *adj., n.*

einsteinium (aɪnˈstaɪnɪəm) *n.* a radioactive metallic transuranic element artificially produced from plutonium. Symbol: Es; atomic no.: 99; half-life of most stable isotope, ^{254}Es: 276 days. [C20: NL, after Albert *Einstein* (1879–1955), German-born U.S. physicist & mathematician]

EIS *abbrev. for* Educational Institute of Scotland.

eisteddfod (aɪˈstɛdfəd) *n., pl.* **-fods** *or* **eisteddfodau** (*Welsh* aɪˌstɛðˈvɒdaɪ). any of a number of annual festivals in Wales in which competitions are held in music, poetry, drama, and the fine arts. [C19: < Welsh, lit.: session, < *eistedd* to sit + *-fod,* < *bod* to be] —ˌ**eisteddˈfodic** *adj.*

either (ˈaɪðə, ˈiːðə) *determiner.* **1. a.** one or the other (of two). **b.** (*as pron.*): *either is acceptable.* **2.** both one and the other: *at either end of the table.* ~*conj.* **3.** (*coordinating*) used preceding two or more possibilities joined by "*or*". ~*adv.* (*sentence modifier*) **4.** (*with a negative*) used to indicate that the clause immediately preceding is a partial reiteration of a previous clause: *John isn't a liar, but he isn't exactly honest either.* [OE *ǣgther,* short for *ǣghwæther* each of two; see WHETHER]

▷ **Usage.** *Either* is followed by a singular verb in good usage: *either of these books is useful.* Careful writers and speakers are cautious in using *either* to mean *both* or *each* because of possible ambiguity, as in: *a ship could be moored on either side of the channel.* Agreement between verb and subject in *either...or...* constructions follows the pattern for *neither...nor...* See at **neither.**

ejaculate *vb.* (ɪˈdʒækjʊˌleɪt). **1.** to eject or discharge (semen) in orgasm. **2.** (*tr.*) to utter abruptly; blurt out. ~*n.* (ɪˈdʒækjʊlɪt). **3.** another word for **semen.** [C16: < L *ējaculārī* to hurl out, < *jaculum* javelin, < *jacere* to throw] —eˌ**jacuˈlation** *n.* —eˈ**jaculatory** *or* eˈ**jaculative** *adj.* —eˈ**jacuˌlator** *n.*

eject (ɪˈdʒɛkt) *vb.* **1.** (*tr.*) to force out; expel or emit. **2.** (*tr.*) to compel (a person) to leave; evict. **3.** (*tr.*) to dismiss, as from office. **4.** (*intr.*) to leave an aircraft rapidly, using an ejection seat or capsule. [C15: < L *ējicere,* < *jacere* to throw] —eˈ**jection** *n.* —eˈ**jective** *adj.* —eˈ**jector** *n.*

ejection seat *or* **ejector seat** *n.* a seat, esp. in military aircraft, fired by a cartridge or rocket to eject the occupant in an emergency.

eke (iːk) *sentence connector. Arch.* also; moreover. [OE *eac*]

eke out (iːk) *vb.* (*tr., adv.*) **1.** to make (a supply) last, esp. by frugal use. **2.** to support (existence) with difficulty and effort. **3.** to add to (something insufficient), esp. with effort. [< obs. *eke* to enlarge]

elaborate *adj.* (ɪˈlæbərɪt). **1.** planned with care and exactness. **2.** marked by complexity or detail. ~*vb.* (ɪˈlæbəˌreɪt). **3.** (*intr.;* usually foll. by *on* or *upon*) to add detail (to an account); expand (upon). **4.** (*tr.*) to work out in detail; develop. **5.** (*tr.*) to produce by careful labour. **6.** (*tr.*) *Physiol.* to change (food or simple substances) into more complex substances for use in the body. [C16: < L *ēlabōrāre* to take pains, < *labōrāre* to toil] —**eˈlaborateness** *n.* —**eˌlaboˈration** *n.* —**elaborative** (ɪˈlæbərətɪv) *adj.* —**eˈlaboˌrator** *n.*

élan (eɪˈlɑːn) *n.* a combination of style and vigour. [C19: < F, < *élancer* to throw forth, ult. < L *lancea* LANCE]

eland (ˈiːlənd) *n.* **1.** a large spiral-horned antelope inhabiting bushland in eastern and southern Africa. **2. giant eland.** a similar but larger animal of central and W Africa. [C18: via Afrik., < Du. *eland* elk]

elapse (ɪˈlæps) *vb.* (*intr.*) (of time) to pass by. [C17: < L *ēlābī* to slip away, < *lābī* to slip, glide]

elasmobranch (ɪˈlæsməˌbræŋk) *n.* **1.** any cartilaginous fish of the subclass Elasmobranchii, which includes sharks, rays, and skates. ~*adj.* **2.** of or relating to the Elasmobranchii. [C19: < NL *elasmobranchii,* < Gk *elasmos* metal plate + *brankhia* gills]

elastic (ɪˈlæstɪk) *adj.* **1.** (of a body or material) capable of returning to its original shape after compression, stretching, or other deformation. **2.** capable of adapting to change. **3.** quick to recover from fatigue, dejection, etc. **4.** springy or resilient. **5.** made of elastic. ~*n.* **6.** tape, cord, or fabric containing flexible rubber or similar substance allowing it to stretch and return to its original shape. [C17: < NL *elasticus* impulsive, < Gk *elastikos,* < *elaunein* to beat, drive] —**eˈlastically** *adv.* —**elasˈticity** *n.*

elasticate (ɪˈlæstɪˌkeɪt) *vb.* (*tr.*) to insert elastic into (a fabric or garment). —**eˌlastiˈcation** *n.*

elastic band *n.* another name for **rubber band.**

elasticize *or* **-ise** (ɪˈlæstɪˌsaɪz) *vb.* **1.** to make elastic. **2.** another word for **elasticate.**

elastomer (ɪˈlæstəmə) *n.* any material, such as rubber, able to resume its original shape when a deforming force is removed. [C20: < ELASTIC + -MER] —**elastomeric** (ɪˌlæstəˈmɛrɪk) *adj.*

Elastoplast (ɪˈlæstəˌplɑːst) *n. Trademark.* a gauze surgical dressing backed by adhesive tape.

elate (ɪˈleɪt) *vb.* (*tr.*) to fill with high spirits, exhilaration, pride, or optimism. [C16: < p.p. of L *efferre* to bear away, < *ferre* to carry] —**eˈlated** *adj.* —**eˈlatedly** *adv.* —**eˈlatedness** *n.*

elation (ɪˈleɪʃən) *n.* joyfulness or exaltation of spirit, as from success, pleasure, or relief.

E layer *n.* another name for **E region.**

elbow (ˈɛlbəʊ) *n.* **1.** the joint between the upper arm and the forearm. **2.** the corresponding joint of birds or mammals. **3.** the part of a garment that covers the elbow. **4.** something resembling an elbow, such as a sharp bend in a road. **5. at one's elbow.** within easy reach. **6. out at elbow(s).** ragged or impoverished. ~*vb.* **7.** to make (one's way) by shoving, jostling, etc. **8.** (*tr.*) to knock or shove as with the elbow. **9.** (*tr.*) to reject; dismiss (esp. in **give** or **get the elbow**). [OE *elnboga*]

elbow grease *n. Facetious.* vigorous physical labour, esp. hard rubbing.

elbowroom (ˈɛlbəʊˌruːm, -ˌrʊm) *n.* sufficient scope to move or function.

elder[1] (ˈɛldə) *adj.* **1.** born earlier; senior. Cf. **older.** **2.** (in certain card games) denoting or relating to the nondealer (the **elder hand**), who has certain advantages in the play. **3.** *Arch.* **a.** prior in rank or office. **b.** of a previous time. ~*n.* **4.** an older person; one's senior. **5.** *Anthropol.* a senior member of a tribe who has authority. **6.** (in certain Protestant Churches) a lay office. **7.** another word for **presbyter.** [OE *eldra,* comp. of *eald* OLD] —**ˈelderˌship** *n.*

elder[2] (ˈɛldə) *n.* any of various shrubs or small trees having clusters of small white flowers and red, purple, or black berry-like fruits. Also called: **elderberry.** [OE *ellern*]

elderberry (ˈɛldəˌbɛrɪ) *n., pl.* **-ries. 1.** the fruit of the elder. **2.** another name for **elder**[2].

elder brother *n.* one of the senior members of Trinity House.

elderly (ˈɛldəlɪ) *adj.* (of people) quite old; past middle age. —**ˈelderliness** *n.*

eldest (ˈɛldɪst) *adj.* being the oldest, esp. the oldest surviving child of the same parents. [OE *eldesta,* sup. of *eald* OLD]

El Dorado (ɛl dɒˈrɑːdəʊ) *n.* **1.** a fabled city in South America, rich in treasure. **2.** Also: **eldorado.** any place of great riches or fabulous opportunity. [C16: < Sp., lit.: the gilded (place)]

eldritch *or* **eldrich** (ˈɛldrɪtʃ) *adj. Poetic, Scot.* unearthly; weird. [C16: ? < OE *ælf* elf + *rīce* realm]

elect (ɪˈlɛkt) *vb.* **1.** (*tr.*) to choose (someone) to be (a representative or official) by voting. **2.** to select; choose. **3.** (*tr.*) (of God) to predestine for the grace of salvation. ~*adj.* **4.** (*immediately postpositive*) voted into office but not yet installed: *president elect.* **5. a.** chosen; elite. **b.** (*as collective n.;* preceded by *the*): *the elect.* **6.** *Christian theol.* **a.** predestined by God to receive salvation. **b.** (*as collective n.;* preceded by *the*): *the elect.* [C15: < L *ēligere* to select, < *legere* to choose]

elect. *or* **elec.** *abbrev. for:* **1.** electric(al). **2.** electricity.

election (ɪˈlɛkʃən) *n.* **1.** the selection by vote of a person or persons for a position, esp. a political office. **2.** a public vote. **3.** the act or an instance of choosing. **4.** *Christian theol.* **a.** the doctrine that God chooses individuals for salvation without reference to faith or works. **b.** the doctrine that God chooses for salvation those who, by grace, persevere in faith and works.

electioneer (ɪˌlɛkʃəˈnɪə) *vb.* (*intr.*) **1.** to be active in a political election or campaign. ~*n.* **2.** a person who engages in this activity. —**eˌlectionˈeering** *n., adj.*

elective (ɪˈlɛktɪv) *adj.* **1.** of or based on selection by vote. **2.** selected by vote. **3.** having the power to elect. **4.** open to choice; optional. —**electivity** (ˌiːlɛkˈtɪvɪtɪ) *or* **eˈlectiveness** *n.*

elector (ɪˈlɛktə) *n.* **1.** someone who is eligible to vote in the election of a government. **2.** (*often cap.*) a member of the U.S. electoral college. **3.** (*often cap.*) (in the Holy Roman Empire) any of the German princes entitled to take part in the election of a new emperor. —**eˈlectoral** *adj.* —**eˈlectorˌship** *n.* —**eˈlectress** *fem. n.*

electoral college *n.* (*often cap.*) **1.** *U.S.* a body of electors chosen by the voters who formally elect the president and vice president. **2.** any body of electors.

electorate (ɪˈlɛktərɪt) *n.* **1.** the body of all qualified voters. **2.** the rank, position, or territory of an elector of the Holy Roman Empire. **3.** *Austral. & N.Z.* the area represented by a Member of Parliament. **4.** *Austral. & N.Z.* the voters in a constituency.

electret (ɪˈlɛktrət) *n.* a permanently polarized dielectric material; its field is similar to that of a permanent magnet. [C20: < *electr(icity* + *magn)et*]

electric (ɪˈlɛktrɪk) *adj.* **1.** of, derived from, produced by, producing, transmitting, or powered by electricity. **2.** (of a musical instrument) amplified electronically. **3.** very tense or exciting; emotionally charged. ~*n.* **4.** *Inf.* an electric train, car, etc. **5.** (*pl.*) an electric circuit or electric appliances. [C17: < NL *electricus* amber-like (because friction causes amber to become charged), < L *ēlectrum* amber, < Gk ēlektron, <?]

▷ **Usage.** See at **electronic.**

electrical (ɪˈlɛktrɪkᵊl) *adj.* of, relating to, or concerned with electricity. —eˈ**lectrically** *adv.*

▷ **Usage.** See at **electronic.**

electrical engineering *n.* the branch of engineering concerned with practical applications of electricity. —**electrical engineer** *n.*

electric blanket *n.* a blanket that contains an electric heating element, used to warm a bed.

electric chair *n.* (in the U.S.) **a.** an electrified chair for executing criminals. **b.** (usually preceded by *the*) execution by this method.

electric constant *n.* the permittivity of free space, which has the value 8.854 185 × 10^{-12} farad per metre.

electric eel *n.* an eel-like freshwater fish of N South America, having electric organs in the body.

electric eye *n.* another name for **photocell.**

electric field *n.* a field of force surrounding a charged particle within which another charged particle experiences a force.

electric guitar *n.* an electrically amplified guitar, used mainly in pop music.

electrician (ɪlɛkˈtrɪʃən, ˌiːlɛk-) *n.* a person whose occupation is the installation, maintenance, and repair of electrical devices.

electricity (ɪlɛkˈtrɪsɪtɪ, ˌiːlɛk-) *n.* **1.** any phenomenon associated with stationary or moving electrons, ions, or other charged particles. **2.** the science of electricity. **3.** an electric current or charge. **4.** emotional tension or excitement.

electric organ *n.* **1.** *Music.* **a.** a pipe organ operated by electrical means. **b.** another name for **electronic organ. 2.** a group of cells on certain fishes, such as the electric eel, that gives an electric shock to any animal touching them.

electric potential *n.* **a.** the work required to transfer a unit positive electric charge from an infinite distance to a given point. **b.** the potential difference between the point and some other point. Sometimes shortened to **potential.**

electric ray *n.* any ray of tropical and temperate seas, having a flat rounded body with an electric organ in each fin.

electrify (ɪˈlɛktrɪˌfaɪ) *vb.* **-fying, -fied.** (*tr.*) **1.** to adapt or equip (a system, device, etc.) for operation by electrical power. **2.** to charge with or subject to electricity. **3.** to startle or excite intensely. —**eˈlectriˌfiable** *adj.* —**eˌlectrifiˈcation** *n.* —**eˈlectriˌfier** *n.*

electro (ɪˈlɛktrəʊ) *n., pl.* **-tros.** short for **electroplate** or **electrotype.**

electro- *or sometimes before a vowel* **electr-** *combining form.* **1.** electric or electrically: *electrodynamic.* **2.** electrolytic: *electrodialysis.* [< NL, < L *ēlectrum* amber, < Gk *ēlektron*]

electrocardiograph (ɪˌlɛktrəʊˈkɑːdɪəʊˌgrɑːf) *n.* an instrument for making tracings (**electrocardiograms**) recording the electrical activity of the heart. —**eˌlectroˌcardioˈgraphic** *or* **eˌlectroˌcardioˈgraphical** *adj.* —**electrocardiography** (ɪˌlɛktrəʊˌkɑːdɪˈɒgrəfɪ) *n.*

electrochemistry (ɪˌlɛktrəʊˈkɛmɪstrɪ) *n.* the branch of chemistry concerned with electric cells and electrolysis. —**electrochemical** (ɪˌlɛktrəʊˈkɛmɪkᵊl) *adj.* —**eˌlectroˈchemist** *n.*

electroconvulsive therapy (ɪˌlɛktrəʊkənˈvʌlsɪv) *n. Med.* the treatment of certain psychotic conditions by passing an electric current through the brain to induce coma or convulsions. See also **shock therapy.**

electrocute (ɪˈlɛktrəˌkjuːt) *vb.* (*tr.*) **1.** to kill as a result of an electric shock. **2.** *U.S.* to execute in the electric chair. [C19: < ELECTRO- + (EXE)CUTE] —**eˌlectroˈcution** *n.*

electrode (ɪˈlɛktrəʊd) *n.* **1.** a conductor through which an electric current enters or leaves an electrolyte, an electric arc, or an electronic valve or tube. **2.** an element in a semiconducting device that emits, collects, or controls the movement of electrons or holes.

electrodeposit (ɪˌlɛktrəʊdɪˈpɒzɪt) *vb.* **1.** (*tr.*) to deposit (a metal) by electrolysis. ~*n.* **2.** the deposit so formed. —**electrodeposition** (ɪˌlɛktrəʊˌdɛpəˈzɪʃən) *n.*

electrodynamics (ɪˌlɛktrəʊdaɪˈnæmɪks) *n.* (*functioning as sing.*) the branch of physics concerned with the interactions between electrical and mechanical forces.

electroencephalograph (ɪˌlɛktrəʊɛnˈsɛfələˌgrɑːf) *n.* an instrument for making tracings (**electroencephalograms**) recording the electrical activity of the brain, usually by means of electrodes placed on the scalp. See also **brain wave.** —**eˌlectroenˌcephaloˈgraphic** *adj.* —**electroencephalography** (ɪˌlɛktrəʊɛnˌsɛfəˈlɒgrəfɪ) *n.*

electrolyse *or U.S.* **-lyze** (ɪˈlɛktrəʊˌlaɪz) *vb.* (*tr.*) **1.** to decompose (a chemical compound) by electrolysis. **2.** to destroy (living tissue, such as hair roots) by electrolysis. —**eˌlectrolyˈsation** *or U.S.* **-lyˈzation** *n.* —**eˈlectroˌlyser** *or U.S.* **-ˌlyzer** *n.*

electrolysis (ɪlɛkˈtrɒlɪsɪs) *n.* **1.** the conduction of electricity by an electrolyte, esp. the use of this process to induce chemical changes. **2.** the destruction of living tissue, such as hair roots, by an electric current, usually for cosmetic reasons.

electrolyte (ɪˈlɛktrəʊˌlaɪt) *n.* a solution or molten substance that conducts electricity.

electrolytic (ɪˌlɛktrəʊˈlɪtɪk) *adj.* **1.** *Physics.* **a.** of, concerned with, or produced by electrolysis or electrodeposition. **b.** of, relating to, or containing an electrolyte. ~*n.* **2.** *Electronics.* Also called: **electrolytic capacitor.** a small capacitor consisting of two electrodes separated by an electrolyte. —**eˌlectroˈlytically** *adv.*

electromagnet (ɪˌlɛktrəʊˈmægnɪt) *n.* a magnet consisting of an iron or steel core wound with a coil of wire, through which a current is passed.

electromagnetic (ɪˌlɛktrəʊmægˈnɛtɪk) *adj.* **1.** of, containing, or operated by an electromagnet. **2.** of, relating to, or consisting of electromagnetism. **3.** of or relating to electromagnetic radiation. —**eˌlectromagˈnetically** *adv.*

electromagnetic radiation *n.* radiation consisting of an electric and magnetic field at right angles to each other and to the direction of propagation.

electromagnetic spectrum *n.* the complete range of electromagnetic radiation from the longest radio waves to the shortest gamma radiation.

electromagnetic unit *n.* any unit of a system of electrical cgs units in which the magnetic constant is given the value of unity.

electromagnetic wave *n.* a wave of energy propagated in an electromagnetic field.

electromagnetism (ɪˌlɛktrəʊˈmægnɪˌtɪzəm) *n.* **1.** magnetism produced by electric current. **2.** the branch of physics concerned with this magnetism and with the interaction of electric and magnetic fields.

electrometer (ɪlɛkˈtrɒmɪtə, ˌiːlɛk-) *n.* an instrument for detecting or measuring a potential difference or charge by the electrostatic forces between charged bodies. —**electrometric** (ɪˌlɛktrəʊˈmɛtrɪk) *or* **eˌlectroˈmetrical** *adj.* —**elecˈtrometry** *n.*

electromotive (ɪˌlɛktrəʊˈməʊtɪv) *adj.* of, concerned with, or producing an electric current.

electromotive force *n. Physics.* **a.** a source of energy that can cause current to flow in an electrical circuit. **b.** the rate at which energy is drawn from this source when unit current flows through the circuit, measured in volts.

electron (ɪˈlɛktrɒn) *n.* an elementary particle in all atoms, orbiting the nucleus in numbers equal to the atomic number of the element. [C19: < ELECTRO- + -ON]

electronegative (ɪˌlɛktrəʊˈnɛgətɪv) *adj.* **1.** having a negative electric charge. **2.** (of an atom, molecule, etc.) tending to attract electrons and form negative ions or polarized bonds.

electron gun *n.* a heated cathode for producing and focusing a beam of electrons, used esp. in cathode-ray tubes.

electronic (ɪlɛkˈtrɒnɪk, ˌiːlɛk-) *adj.* **1.** of,

concerned with, using, or operated by devices, such as transistors, in which electrons are conducted through a semiconductor, free space, or gas. **2.** of or concerned with electronics. **3.** of or concerned with electrons. **4.** making use of electronic systems, such as computerized banking transactions: *electronic shopping.* —**elec'tronically** *adv.*

▷ **Usage.** *Electronic* is used to refer to equipment, such as television sets, computers, etc., in which current is controlled by transistors, valves, etc., and also to these components themselves. *Electrical* is used in a more general sense, often to refer to the use of electricity as opposed to other forms of energy: *an electrical appliance. Electric,* in many cases used interchangeably with *electrical,* is often restricted to the description of devices or to concepts relating to the flow of current: *electric fire.*

electronic data processing *n.* data processing largely performed by electronic equipment, such as computers.

electronic flash *n. Photog.* an electronic device for producing a very bright flash of light by means of an electric discharge in a gas-filled tube.

electronic funds transfer system *n.* a system of conducting financial transactions by a network of computers, without using cheques or cash: debits and credits are recorded when a card is inserted in an electronic machine as, for instance, when a person buys something in a shop.

electronic keyboard *n.* a typewriter keyboard used to operate an electronic device such as a computer.

electronic mail *n.* the transmission of information, facsimiles, etc., from one computer terminal to another.

electronic music *n.* music consisting of sounds produced by electric currents either controlled from an instrument panel or keyboard or prerecorded on magnetic tape.

electronic organ *n. Music.* an instrument played by means of a keyboard, in which sounds are produced by electronic or electrical means.

electronics (ɪlɛk'trɒnɪks, ˌiːlɛk-) *n.* **1.** (*functioning as sing.*) the science and technology concerned with the development, behaviour, and applications of electronic devices and circuits. **2.** (*functioning as pl.*) the circuits and devices of a piece of electronic equipment.

electron lens *n.* a system, such as an arrangement of electrodes or magnets, that produces a field for focusing a beam of electrons.

electron microscope *n.* a powerful microscope that uses electrons, rather than light, and electron lenses to produce a magnified image.

electron tube *n.* an electrical device, such as a valve, in which a flow of electrons between electrodes takes place.

electronvolt (ɪˌlɛktrɒn'vəʊlt) *n.* a unit of energy equal to the work done on an electron accelerated through a potential difference of 1 volt.

electrophoresis (ɪˌlɛktrəʊfə'riːsɪs) *n.* the motion of charged particles in a colloid under the influence of an applied electric field. —**electrophoretic** (ɪˌlɛktrəʊfə'rɛtɪk) *adj.*

electrophorus (ɪlɛk'trɒfərəs, ˌiːlɛk-) *n.* an apparatus for generating static electricity by induction. [C18: < ELECTRO- + *-phorus,* < Gk, < *pherein* to bear]

electroplate (ɪ'lɛktrəʊˌpleɪt) *vb.* **1.** (*tr.*) to plate (an object) by electrolysis. ~*n.* **2.** electroplated articles collectively, esp. when plated with silver. —**e'lectroˌplater** *n.*

electropositive (ɪˌlɛktrəʊ'pɒzɪtɪv) *adj.* **1.** having a positive electric charge. **2.** (of an atom, molecule, etc.) tending to release electrons and form positive ions or polarized bonds.

electroscope (ɪ'lɛktrəʊˌskəʊp) *n.* an apparatus for detecting an electric charge, typically consisting of a rod holding two gold foils that separate when a charge is applied. —**electroscopic** (ɪˌlɛktrəʊ'skɒpɪk) *adj.*

electroshock therapy (ɪ'lɛktrəʊˌʃɒk) *n.* another name for **electroconvulsive therapy.**

electrostatics (ɪˌlɛktrəʊ'stætɪks) *n.* (*functioning as sing.*) the branch of physics concerned with static electricity. —**eˌlectro'static** *adj.*

electrostatic unit *n.* any unit of a system of electrical cgs units in which the electric constant is given the value of unity.

electrotherapeutics (ɪˌlɛktrəʊˌθɛrə'pjuːtɪks) *n.* (*functioning as sing.*) the branch of medical science concerned with the use of electricity (**electrotherapy**) in treating disease. —**eˌlectroˌthera'peutic** *or* **eˌlectroˌthera'peutical** *adj.* —**eˌlectro'therapist** *n.*

electrotype (ɪ'lɛktrəʊˌtaɪp) *n.* **1.** a duplicate printing plate made by electrolytically depositing a layer of copper or nickel onto a mould of the original. ~*vb.* **2.** (*tr.*) to make an electrotype of (printed matter, etc.). —**e'lectroˌtyper** *n.*

electrovalent bond (ɪˌlɛktrəʊ'veɪlənt) *n.* a type of chemical bond in which one atom loses an electron to form a positive ion and the other atom gains the electron to form a negative ion. The resulting ions are held together by electrostatic attraction. —**eˌlectro'valency** *n.*

electrum (ɪ'lɛktrəm) *n.* an alloy of gold and silver. [C14: < L, < Gk *ēlektron* amber]

electuary (ɪ'lɛktjʊərɪ) *n., pl.* **-aries.** *Med.* a paste taken orally, containing a drug mixed with syrup or honey. [C14: < LL *ēlēctuārium,* prob. < Gk *ekleikton,* < *leikhein* to lick]

eleemosynary (ˌɛliː'mɒsɪnərɪ) *adj.* **1.** of or dependent on charity. **2.** given as an act of charity. [C17: < Church L *eleēmosyna* ALMS]

elegance ('ɛlɪgəns) *or* **elegancy** *n., pl.* **-gances** *or* **-gancies. 1.** dignified grace. **2.** good taste in design, style, arrangement, etc. **3.** something elegant; a refinement.

elegant ('ɛlɪgənt) *adj.* **1.** tasteful in dress, style, or design. **2.** dignified and graceful. **3.** cleverly simple; ingenious: *an elegant solution.* [C16: < L *ēlegāns* tasteful; see ELECT]

elegiac (ˌɛlɪ'dʒaɪək) *adj.* **1.** resembling, characteristic of, relating to, or appropriate to an elegy. **2.** lamenting; mournful. **3.** denoting or written in elegiac couplets (which consist of a dactylic hexameter followed by a dactylic pentameter) or elegiac stanzas (which consist of a quatrain in iambic pentameters with alternate lines rhyming). ~*n.* **4.** (*often pl.*) an elegiac couplet or stanza. —ˌ**ele'giacally** *adv.*

elegize *or* **-gise** ('ɛlɪˌdʒaɪz) *vb.* **1.** to compose an elegy (in memory of). **2.** (*intr.*) to write elegiacally. —'**elegist** *n.*

elegy ('ɛlɪdʒɪ) *n., pl.* **-gies. 1.** a mournful poem or song, esp. a lament for the dead. **2.** poetry written in elegiac couplets or stanzas. [C16: via F & L < Gk, < *elegos* lament sung to flute accompaniment]

elem. *abbrev. for:* **1.** element(s). **2.** elementary.

element ('ɛlɪmənt) *n.* **1.** any of the 105 known substances that consist of atoms with the same number of protons in their nuclei. **2.** one of the fundamental or irreducible components making up a whole. **3.** any group that is part of a larger unit, such as a military formation. **4.** a small amount; hint. **5.** a distinguishable section of a social group. **6.** the most favourable environment for an animal or plant. **7.** the situation in which a person is happiest or most effective (esp. in **in** *or* **out of one's element**). **8.** the resistance wire that constitutes the electrical heater in a cooker, heater, etc. **9.** one of the four substances thought in ancient and medieval cosmology to constitute the universe (earth, air, water, or fire). **10.** (*pl.*) atmospheric conditions, esp. wind, rain, and cold. **11.** (*pl.*) the basic principles. **12.** *Christianity.* the bread or wine consecrated in the Eucharist. [C13: < L *elementum* a first principle, element]

elemental (ˌɛlɪ'mɛntᵊl) *adj.* **1.** fundamental; basic. **2.** motivated by or symbolic of primitive powerful natural forces or passions. **3.** of or relating to earth, air, water, and fire considered as elements. **4.** of or relating to atmospheric forces, esp. wind, rain, and cold. **5.** of or relating to a chemical element. ~*n.* **6.** *Rare.* a disembodied spirit. —ˌ**ele'mentalˌism** *n.*

elementary (ˌɛlɪˈmɛntərɪ) *adj.* **1.** not difficult; rudimentary. **2.** of or concerned with the first principles of a subject; introductory or fundamental. **3.** *Chem.* another word for **elemental** (sense 5). —ˌ**eleˈmentariness** *n.*

elementary particle *n.* any of several entities, such as electrons, neutrons, or protons, that are less complex than atoms.

elementary school *n.* **1.** *Brit.* a former name for **primary school.** **2.** *U.S. & Canad.* a state school for the first six to eight years of a child's education.

elenchus (ɪˈlɛŋkəs) *n., pl.* **-chi** (-kaɪ). *Logic.* refutation of an argument by proving the contrary of its conclusion, esp. syllogistically. [C17: < L, < Gk, < *elenkhein* to refute] —**eˈlenctic** *adj.*

elephant (ˈɛlɪfənt) *n., pl.* **-phants** *or* **-phant.** either of two proboscidean mammals. The **African elephant** is the larger species, with large flapping ears and a less humped back than the **Indian elephant,** of S and SE Asia. [C13: < L, < Gk *elephas* elephant, ivory] —**ˈelephanˌtoid** *adj.*

elephantiasis (ˌɛlɪfənˈtaɪəsɪs) *n. Pathol.* a complication of chronic filariasis, in which nematode worms block the lymphatic vessels, usually in the legs or scrotum, causing extreme enlargement of the affected area. [C16: via L < Gk, < *elephas* ELEPHANT + -IASIS]

elephantine (ˌɛlɪˈfæntaɪn) *adj.* **1.** denoting, relating to, or characteristic of an elephant or elephants. **2.** huge, clumsy, or ponderous.

elephant seal *n.* either of two large earless seals, of southern oceans or of the N Atlantic, the males of which have a trunklike snout.

Eleusinian mysteries (ˌɛljʊˈsɪnɪən) *pl. n.* a mystical religious festival, held at Eleusis in SE Greece in classical times, to celebrate the gods Persephone, Demeter, and Dionysus.

elev. *or* **el.** *abbrev. for* elevation.

elevate (ˈɛlɪˌveɪt) *vb.* (*tr.*) **1.** to move to a higher place. **2.** to raise in rank or status. **3.** to put in a cheerful mood; elate. **4.** to put on a higher cultural plane; uplift. **5.** to raise the axis of a gun. **6.** to raise the intensity or pitch of (the voice). [C15: < L *ēlevāre,* < *levāre* to raise, < *levis* (adj.) light] —**ˈeleˌvatory** *adj.*

elevated (ˈɛlɪˌveɪtɪd) *adj.* **1.** raised to or being at a higher level. **2.** inflated or lofty; exalted. **3.** in a cheerful mood. **4.** *Inf.* slightly drunk.

elevation (ˌɛlɪˈveɪʃən) *n.* **1.** the act of elevating or the state of being elevated. **2.** the height of something above a given place, esp. above sea level. **3.** a raised area; height. **4.** nobleness or grandeur. **5.** a drawing to scale of the external face of a building or structure. **6.** a ballet dancer's ability to leap high. **7.** *Astron.* another name for **altitude** (sense 3). **8.** the angle formed between the muzzle of a gun and the horizontal. —ˌ**eleˈvational** *adj.*

elevator (ˈɛlɪˌveɪtə) *n.* **1.** a person or thing that elevates. **2.** a mechanical hoist, often consisting of a chain of scoops linked together on a conveyor belt. **3.** the U.S. and Canad. name for **lift** (sense 14a). **4.** *Chiefly U.S. & Canad.* a granary equipped with an elevator and, usually, facilities for cleaning and grading the grain. **5.** a control surface on the tailplane of an aircraft, for making it climb or descend. **6.** any muscle that raises a part of the body.

eleven (ɪˈlɛvᵊn) *n.* **1.** the cardinal number that is the sum of ten and one. **2.** a numeral, 11, XI, etc., representing this number. **3.** something representing, represented by, or consisting of 11 units. **4.** (*functioning as sing. or pl.*) a team of 11 players in football, cricket, etc. **5.** Also called: **eleven o'clock.** eleven hours after noon or midnight. ~*determiner.* **6. a.** amounting to eleven. **b.** (*as pron.*): *another eleven.* [OE *endleofan*] —**eˈleventh** *adj., n.*

eleven-plus *n.* (in Britain, esp. formerly) an examination taken by children aged 11 or 12 that determines the type of secondary education a child will be given.

elevenses (ɪˈlɛvᵊnzɪz) *pl. n.* (*sometimes functioning as sing.*) *Brit. inf.* a light snack, usually with tea or coffee, taken in mid-morning.

eleventh hour *n.* the latest possible time; last minute.

elf (ɛlf) *n., pl.* **elves. 1.** (in folklore) one of a kind of legendary beings, usually characterized as small, manlike, and mischievous. **2.** a mischievous or whimsical child or girl. [OE *ælf*] —**ˈelfish** *or* **ˈelvish** *adj.*

elfin (ˈɛlfɪn) *adj.* **1.** of or like an elf or elves. **2.** small, delicate, and charming.

elflock (ˈɛlfˌlɒk) *n.* a lock of hair, fancifully regarded as having been tangled by the elves.

elicit (ɪˈlɪsɪt) *vb.* (*tr.*) **1.** to give rise to; evoke. **2.** to bring to light. [C17: < L *ēlicere,* < *licere* to entice] —**eˈlicitable** *adj.* —**eˌliciˈtation** *n.* —**eˈlicitor** *n.*

elide (ɪˈlaɪd) *vb.* to undergo or cause to undergo elision. [C16: < L *ēlīdere* to knock, < *laedere* to hit, wound] —**eˈlidible** *adj.*

eligible (ˈɛlɪdʒəbᵊl) *adj.* **1.** fit, worthy, or qualified, as for office. **2.** desirable, esp. as a spouse. [C15: < LL *ēligere* to ELECT] —ˌ**eligiˈbility** *n.* —**ˈeligibly** *adv.*

eliminate (ɪˈlɪmɪˌneɪt) *vb.* (*tr.*) **1.** to remove or take out. **2.** to reject; omit from consideration. **3.** to remove (a competitor, team, etc.) from a contest, usually by defeat. **4.** *Sl.* to murder in cold blood. **5.** *Physiol.* to expel (waste) from the body. **6.** *Maths.* to remove (an unknown variable) from simultaneous equations. [C16: < L *ēlīmināre* to turn out of the house, < *e-* out + *līmen* threshold] —**eˈliminable** *adj.* —**eˌlimiˈnation** *n.* —**eˈliminative** *adj.* —**eˈlimiˌnator** *n.*

elision (ɪˈlɪʒən) *n.* **1.** omission of a syllable or vowel at the beginning or end of a word. **2.** omission of parts of a book, etc. [C16: < L *ēlīdere* to ELIDE]

elite *or* **élite** (ɪˈliːt, eɪ-) *n.* **1.** (*sometimes functioning as pl.*) the most powerful, rich, or gifted members of a group, community, etc. **2.** a typewriter type size having 12 characters to the inch. ~*adj.* **3.** of or suitable for an elite. [C18: < F, < OF *eslit* chosen, < L *ēligere* to ELECT]

elitism (ɪˈliːtɪzəm, eɪ-) *n.* **1. a.** the belief that society should be governed by an elite. **b.** such government. **2.** pride in or awareness of being one of an elite group. —**eˈlitist** *n.*

elixir (ɪˈlɪksə) *n.* **1.** an alchemical preparation supposed to be capable of prolonging life (**elixir of life**) or of transmuting base metals into gold. **2.** anything that purports to be a sovereign remedy. **3.** a quintessence. **4.** a liquid containing a medicine with syrup, glycerin, or alcohol added to mask its unpleasant taste. [C14: < Med. L, < Ar., prob. < Gk *xērion* powder used for drying wounds]

Eliz. *abbrev. for* Elizabethan.

Elizabethan (ɪˌlɪzəˈbiːθən) *adj.* **1.** of, characteristic of, or relating to the reigns of Elizabeth I (queen of England, 1558–1603) or Elizabeth II (queen of Great Britain and N Ireland since 1952). **2.** of, relating to, or designating a style of architecture used in England during the reign of Elizabeth I. ~*n.* **3.** a person who lived in England during the reign of Elizabeth I.

Elizabethan sonnet *n.* another term for **Shakespearean sonnet.**

elk (ɛlk) *n., pl.* **elks** *or* **elk. 1.** a large deer of N Europe and Asia: also occurs in N America, where it is called a moose. **2. American elk.** another name for **wapiti.** [OE *eolh*]

ell (ɛl) *n.* an obsolete unit of length, approximately 45 inches. [OE *eln* forearm (the measure orig. being from elbow to fingertips)]

ellipse (ɪˈlɪps) *n.* a closed conic section shaped like a flattened circle and formed by an inclined plane that does not cut the base of the cone. [C18: back formation < ELLIPSIS]

ellipsis (ɪˈlɪpsɪs) *n., pl.* **-ses** (-siːz). **1.** omission of parts of a word or sentence. **2.** *Printing.* a sequence of three dots (...) indicating an omission in text. [C16: < L, < Gk, < *en* in + *leipein* to leave]

ellipsoid (ɪˈlɪpsɔɪd) *n.* **a.** a geometric surface,

symmetrical about the three coordinate axes, whose plane sections are ellipses or circles. **b.** a solid having this shape. —**ellipsoidal** (ɪlɪpˈsɔɪdᵊl, ˌɛl-) *adj.*

ellipsoid of revolution *n.* a geometric surface produced by rotating an ellipse about one of its two axes and having circular plane sections perpendicular to the axis of revolution.

elliptical (ɪˈlɪptɪkᵊl) *adj.* **1.** relating to or having the shape of an ellipse. **2.** relating to or resulting from ellipsis. **3.** (of speech, literary style, etc.) **a.** very concise, often so as to be obscure or ambiguous. **b.** circumlocutory. ~Also (for senses 1 and 2): **elliptic.** —**elˈlipticalness** *n.*

▷ **Usage.** The use of *elliptical* to mean *circumlocutory* is avoided by many careful speakers and writers.

elm (ɛlm) *n.* **1.** any tree of the genus *Ulmus*, occurring in the N hemisphere, having serrated leaves and winged fruits (samaras). **2.** the hard heavy wood of this tree. [OE *elm*]

elocution (ˌɛləˈkjuːʃən) *n.* the art of public speaking. [C15: < L *ēloquī*, < *loquī* to speak] —ˌ**eloˈcutionary** *adj.* —ˌ**eloˈcutionist** *n.*

Elohist (ɛˈləʊhɪst) *n. Bible.* the supposed author or authors of the Pentateuch, identified chiefly by the use of the word *Elohim* for God.

elongate (ˈiːlɒŋgeɪt) *vb.* **1.** to make or become longer; stretch. ~*adj.* **2.** long and narrow. **3.** lengthened or tapered. [C16: < LL *ēlongāre* to keep at a distance, < *ē-* away + L *longē* (adv.) far] —ˌ**elonˈgation** *n.*

elope (ɪˈləʊp) *vb.* (*intr.*) to run away secretly with a lover, esp. in order to marry. [C16: < Anglo-F *aloper*, ? < MDu. *lōpen* to run; see LOPE] —**eˈlopement** *n.* —**eˈloper** *n.*

eloquence (ˈɛləkwəns) *n.* **1.** ease in using language. **2.** powerful and effective language. **3.** the quality of being persuasive or moving.

eloquent (ˈɛləkwənt) *adj.* **1.** (of speech, writing, etc.) fluent and persuasive. **2.** visibly or vividly expressive: *an eloquent yawn.* [C14: < L *ēloquēns*, < *loquī* to speak] —ˈ**eloquentness** *n.*

Elsan (ˈɛlsæn) *n. Trademark.* a type of portable chemical lavatory. [C20: < initials of *E. L.* Jackson, manufacturer + SAN(ITATION)]

else (ɛls) *determiner.* (*postpositive; used after an indefinite pronoun or an interrogative*) **1.** in addition; more: *there is nobody else here.* **2.** other; different: *where else could he be?* ~*adv.* **3. or else. a.** if not, then: *go away or else I won't finish my work today.* **b.** or something terrible will result: used as a threat: *sit down, or else!* [OE *elles*, genitive of *el-* strange, foreign]

▷ **Usage.** The possessive of the expressions *anybody else, everybody else*, etc., is formed by adding *'s* to *else: somebody else's letter. Who else* is an exception in that *whose else* is an acceptable alternative to *who else's: whose else can it be?* or *who else's can it be?*

elsewhere (ˌɛlsˈwɛə) *adv.* in or to another place; somewhere else. [OE *elles hwǣr*; see ELSE, WHERE]

ELT *abbrev. for* English Language Teaching.

elucidate (ɪˈluːsɪˌdeɪt) *vb.* to make clear (something obscure or difficult); clarify. [C16: < LL *ēlūcidāre* to enlighten; see LUCID] —**eˌluciˈdation** *n.* —**eˈluciˌdative** *or* **eˈluciˌdatory** *adj.* —**eˈluciˌdator** *n.*

elude (ɪˈluːd) *vb.* (*tr.*) **1.** to escape from or avoid, esp. by cunning. **2.** to avoid fulfilment of (a responsibility, obligation, etc.); evade. **3.** to escape discovery or understanding by; baffle. [C16: < L *ēlūdere* to deceive, < *lūdere* to play] —**eˈluder** *n.* —**elusion** (ɪˈluːʒən) *n.*

eluent *or* **eluant** (ˈɛljuːənt) *n.* a solvent used for eluting.

elusive (ɪˈluːsɪv) *adj.* **1.** difficult to catch. **2.** preferring or living in solitude and anonymity. **3.** difficult to remember. —**eˈlusiveness** *n.*

elute (iːˈluːt, ɪˈluːt) *vb.* (*tr.*) to wash out (a substance) by the action of a solvent, as in chromatography. [C18: < L *ēlūtus* rinsed out, < *luere* to wash, LAVE] —**eˈlution** *n.*

elutriate (ɪˈluːtrɪˌeɪt) *vb.* (*tr.*) to purify or separate (a substance or mixture) by washing and straining or decanting. [C18: < L *ēluere*, < *ē-* out + *lavere* to wash] —**eˌlutriˈation** *n.*

elver (ˈɛlvə) *n.* a young eel, esp. one migrating up a river. [C17: var. of *eelfare*, lit.: eel-journey; see EEL, FARE]

elves (ɛlvz) *n.* the plural of **elf.**

elvish (ˈɛlvɪʃ) *adj.* a variant of **elfish:** see **elf.**

Elysium (ɪˈlɪzɪəm) *n.* **1.** Also called: **Elysian fields.** *Greek myth.* the dwelling place of the blessed after death. **2.** a state or place of perfect bliss. [C16: < L, < Gk *Ēlusion pedion* Elysian (that is, blessed) fields]

elytron (ˈɛlɪˌtrɒn) *or* **elytrum** (ˈɛlɪtrəm) *n., pl.* **-tra** (-trə). either of the horny front wings of beetles and some other insects. [C18: < Gk *elutron* sheath]

em (ɛm) *n. Printing.* **1.** the square of a body of any size of type, used as a unit of measurement. **2.** Also called: **pica em, pica.** a unit of measurement in printing, equal to twelve points or one sixth of an inch. [C19: < the name of the letter *M*]

em- *prefix.* a variant of **en-**[1] and **en-**[2] before *b, m,* and *p.*

'em (əm) *pron.* an informal variant of **them.**

emaciate (ɪˈmeɪsɪˌeɪt) *vb.* (*usually tr.*) to become or cause to become abnormally thin. [C17: < L, < *macer* thin] —**eˈmaciˌated** *adj.* —**eˌmaciˈation** *n.*

emanate (ˈɛməˌneɪt) *vb.* **1.** (*intr.*; often foll. by *from*) to issue or proceed from or as from a source. **2.** (*tr.*) to send forth; emit. [C18: < L *ēmānāre* to flow out, < *mānāre* to flow] —**emanative** (ˈɛmənətɪv) *adj.* —ˈ**emaˌnator** *n.* —ˈ**emaˌnatory** *adj.*

emanation (ˌɛməˈneɪʃən) *n.* **1.** an act or instance of emanating. **2.** something that emanates or is produced. **3.** a gaseous product of radioactive decay. —ˌ**emaˈnational** *adj.*

emancipate (ɪˈmænsɪˌpeɪt) *vb.* (*tr.*) **1.** to free from restriction or restraint, esp. social or legal restraint. **2.** (*often passive*) to free from the inhibitions of conventional morality. **3.** to liberate (a slave) from bondage. [C17: < L *ēmancipāre* to give independence (to a son), < *mancipāre* to transfer property; see MANCIPLE] —**eˈmanciˌpated** *adj.* —**eˌmanciˈpation** *n.* —**eˈmanciˌpator** *n.* —**emancipatory** (ɪˈmænsɪpətərɪ, -trɪ) *adj.*

emasculate *vb.* (ɪˈmæskjʊˌleɪt). (*tr.*) **1.** to remove the testicles of; castrate; geld. **2.** to deprive of vigour, effectiveness, etc. ~*adj.* (ɪˈmæskjʊlɪt, -ˌleɪt). **3.** castrated; gelded. **4.** Also: **emasculated.** deprived of strength, effectiveness, etc. [C17: < L *ēmasculāre*, < *masculus* male; see MASCULINE] —**eˌmascuˈlation** *n.* —**eˈmascuˌlator** *n.* —**eˈmasculatory** *adj.*

embalm (ɪmˈbɑːm) *vb.* (*tr.*) **1.** to treat (a dead body) with preservatives to retard putrefaction. **2.** to preserve or cherish the memory of. **3.** *Poetic.* to give a sweet fragrance to. [C13: < OF *embaumer*; see BALM] —**emˈbalmer** *n.* —**emˈbalmment** *n.*

embank (ɪmˈbæŋk) *vb.* (*tr.*) to protect, enclose, or confine with an embankment.

embankment (ɪmˈbæŋkmənt) *n.* a man-made ridge of earth or stone that carries a road or railway or confines a waterway.

embargo (ɛmˈbɑːgəʊ) *n., pl.* **-goes.** **1.** a government order prohibiting the departure or arrival of merchant ships in its ports. **2.** any legal stoppage of commerce. **3.** a restraint or prohibition. ~*vb.* **-going, -goed.** (*tr.*) **4.** to lay an embargo upon. **5.** to seize for use by the state. [C16: < Sp., < *embargar*, < L IM- + *barra* BAR[1]]

embark (ɛmˈbɑːk) *vb.* **1.** to board (a ship or aircraft). **2.** (*intr.*; usually foll. by *on* or *upon*) to commence or engage (in) a new project, venture, etc. [C16: via F < OF, < EM- + *barca* boat, BARQUE] —ˌ**embarˈkation** *n.* —**emˈbarkment** *n.*

embarrass (ɪmˈbærəs) *vb.* (*mainly tr.*) **1.** to cause to feel confusion or self-consciousness; disconcert. **2.** (*usually passive*) to involve in financial difficulties. **3.** *Arch.* to complicate. **4.** *Arch.* to impede or hamper. [C17 (in the sense: to impede): via F & Sp. < It., < *imbarrare* to confine within bars] —**emˈbarrassed** *adj.* —**emˈbarrassing** *adj.* —**emˈbarrassment** *n.*

embassy (ˈɛmbəsɪ) *n., pl.* **-sies.** **1.** the residence or place of business of an ambassador. **2.** an ambassador and his entourage collectively. **3.** the position, business, or mission of an ambassador. **4.** any important or official mission. [C16: < OF *ambaisada*; see AMBASSADOR]

embattle (ɪmˈbætᵊl) *vb.* (*tr.*) **1.** to deploy (troops) for battle. **2.** to fortify (a position, town, etc.). **3.** to provide with battlements. [C14: < OF *embataillier;* see EN-[1] BATTLE]

embay (ɪmˈbeɪ) *vb.* (*tr.*) (*usually passive*) **1.** to form into a bay. **2.** to enclose in or as if in a bay.

embed (ɪmˈbɛd) *vb.* **-bedding, -bedded.** **1.** (usually foll. by *in*) to fix or become fixed firmly and deeply in a surrounding solid mass. **2.** (*tr.*) to surround closely. **3.** (*tr.*) to fix or retain (a thought, idea, etc.) in the mind. ~Also: **imbed.** —**emˈbedment** *n.*

embellish (ɪmˈbɛlɪʃ) *vb.* (*tr.*) **1.** to beautify; adorn. **2.** to make (a story, etc.) more interesting by adding detail. [C14: < OF *embelir,* < *bel* beautiful, < L *bellus*] —**emˈbellisher** *n.* —**emˈbellishment** *n.*

ember (ˈɛmbə) *n.* **1.** a glowing or smouldering piece of coal or wood, as in a dying fire. **2.** the remains of a past emotion. [OE *ǣmyrge*]

Ember days *pl. n. R.C. & Anglican Church.* any of four groups in the year of three days (always Wednesday, Friday, and Saturday) of prayer and fasting. [OE *ymbrendǣg,* < *ymb* around + *ryne* a course + *dǣg* day]

embezzle (ɪmˈbɛzᵊl) *vb.* to convert (money or property entrusted to one) fraudulently to one's own use. [C15: < Anglo-F *embeseiller* to destroy, < OF *beseiller* to make away with, <?] —**emˈbezzlement** *n.* —**emˈbezzler** *n.*

embitter (ɪmˈbɪtə) *vb.* (*tr.*) **1.** to make (a person) bitter. **2.** to aggravate (a hostile feeling, difficult situation, etc.). —**emˈbittered** *adj.* —**emˈbitterment** *n.*

emblazon (ɪmˈbleɪzᵊn) *vb.* (*tr.*) **1.** to portray heraldic arms on (a shield, one's notepaper, etc.). **2.** to make bright or splendid, as with colours, flowers, etc. **3.** to glorify, praise, or extol. —**emˈblazonment** *n.*

emblem (ˈɛmbləm) *n.* a visible object or representation that symbolizes a quality, type, group, etc. [C15: < L *emblēma,* < Gk, < *emballein* to insert, < *en* in + *ballein* to throw] —ˌ**emblemˈatic** *or* ˌ**emblemˈatical** *adj.* —ˌ**emblemˈatically** *adv.*

embody (ɪmˈbɒdɪ) *vb.* **-bodying, -bodied.** (*tr.*) **1.** to give a tangible, bodily, or concrete form to (an abstract concept). **2.** to be an example of or express (an idea, principle, etc.). **3.** (often foll. by *in*) to collect or unite in a comprehensive whole. **4.** to invest (a spiritual entity) with bodily form. —**emˈbodiment** *n.*

embolden (ɪmˈbəʊldᵊn) *vb.* (*tr.*) to encourage; make bold.

embolism (ˈɛmbəˌlɪzəm) *n.* the occlusion of a blood vessel by an embolus. [C14: < Med. L, < LGk *embolismos;* see EMBOLUS] —**embolic** (ɛmˈbɒlɪk) *adj.*

embolus (ˈɛmbələs) *n., pl.* **-li** (-ˌlaɪ). material, such as part of a blood clot or an air bubble, that becomes lodged within a small blood vessel and impedes the circulation. [C17: via L < Gk *embolos* stopper; see EMBLEM]

embonpoint *French.* (ɑ̃bɔ̃pwɛ̃) *n.* **1.** plumpness or stoutness. ~*adj.* **2.** plump; stout. [C18: < *en bon point* in good condition]

embosom (ɪmˈbʊzəm) *vb.* (*tr.*) *Arch.* **1.** to enclose or envelop, esp. protectively. **2.** to clasp to the bosom; hug. **3.** to cherish.

emboss (ɪmˈbɒs) *vb.* **1.** to mould or carve (a decoration) on (a surface) so that it is raised above the surface in low relief. **2.** to cause to bulge; make protrude. [C14: < OF *embocer,* < EM- + *boce* BOSS[2]] —**emˈbossed** *adj.* —**emˈbosser** *n.* —**emˈbossment** *n.*

embouchure (ˌɒmbʊˈʃʊə) *n.* **1.** the mouth of a river or valley. **2.** *Music.* **a.** the correct application of the lips and tongue in playing a wind instrument. **b.** the mouthpiece of a wind instrument. [C18: < F, < OF, < *bouche* mouth, < L *bucca* cheek]

embower (ɪmˈbaʊə) *vb.* (*tr.*) *Arch.* to enclose in or as in a bower.

embrace (ɪmˈbreɪs) *vb.* (*mainly tr.*) **1.** (*also intr.*) (of a person) to take or clasp (another person) in the arms, or (of two people) to clasp each other, as in affection, greeting, etc.; hug. **2.** to accept willingly or eagerly. **3.** to take up (a new idea, faith, etc.); adopt. **4.** to comprise or include as an integral part. **5.** to encircle or enclose. **6.** *Rare.* to perceive or understand. ~*n.* **7.** the act of embracing. [C14: < OF, < EM- + *brace* a pair of arms, < L *bracchia* arms] —**emˈbraceable** *adj.* —**emˈbracement** *n.* —**emˈbracer** *n.*

embrasure (ɪmˈbreɪʒə) *n.* **1.** *Fortifications.* an opening or indentation, as in a battlement, for shooting through. **2.** a door or window having splayed sides that increase the width of the opening in the interior. [C18: < F, < obs. *embraser* to widen] —**emˈbrasured** *adj.*

embrocate (ˈɛmbrəʊˌkeɪt) *vb.* (*tr.*) to apply a liniment or lotion to (a part of the body). [C17: < Med. L *embrocha* poultice, < Gk, < *brokhē* a moistening]

embrocation (ˌɛmbrəʊˈkeɪʃən) *n.* a drug or agent for rubbing into the skin; liniment.

embroider (ɪmˈbrɔɪdə) *vb.* **1.** to do decorative needlework (upon). **2.** to add fictitious or exaggerated detail to (a story, account, etc.). [C15: < OF *embroder*] —**emˈbroiderer** *n.*

embroidery (ɪmˈbrɔɪdərɪ) *n., pl.* **-deries.** **1.** decorative needlework done usually on loosely woven cloth or canvas, often being a picture or pattern. **2.** elaboration or exaggeration, esp. in writing or reporting; embellishment.

embroil (ɪmˈbrɔɪl) *vb.* (*tr.*) **1.** to involve (a person, oneself, etc.) in trouble, conflict, or argument. **2.** to throw (affairs, etc.) into a state of confusion or disorder; complicate; entangle. [C17: < F *embrouiller,* < *brouiller* to mingle, confuse] —**emˈbroiler** *n.* —**emˈbroilment** *n.*

embryo (ˈɛmbrɪˌəʊ) *n., pl.* **-bryos.** **1.** an animal in the early stages of development up to birth or hatching. **2.** the human product of conception up to approximately the end of the second month of pregnancy. Cf. **fetus.** **3.** a plant in the early stages of development. **4.** an undeveloped or rudimentary state (esp. in **in embryo**). **5.** something in an early stage of development. [C16: < LL, < Gk *embruon,* < *bruein* to swell]

embryology (ˌɛmbrɪˈɒlədʒɪ) *n.* **1.** the scientific study of embryos. **2.** the structure and development of the embryo of a particular organism. —**embryological** (ˌɛmbrɪəˈlɒdʒɪkᵊl) *or* ˌ**embryoˈlogic** *adj.* —ˌ**embryˈologist** *n.*

embryonic (ˌɛmbrɪˈɒnɪk) *or* **embryonal** (ˈɛmbrɪənᵊl) *adj.* **1.** of or relating to an embryo. **2.** in an early stage; rudimentary; undeveloped. —ˌ**embryˈonically** *adv.*

emcee (ˌɛmˈsiː) *Inf.* ~*n.* **1.** a master of ceremonies. ~*vb.* **-ceeing, -ceed.** **2.** to act as master of ceremonies (for or at). [C20: < MC]

-eme *suffix forming nouns. Linguistics.* indicating a minimal distinctive unit of a specified type in a language: *morpheme; phoneme.* [C20: via F, abstracted from PHONEME]

emend (ɪˈmɛnd) *vb.* (*tr.*) to make corrections or improvements in (a text) by critical editing. [C15: < L, < *ē-* out + *mendum* a mistake] —**eˈmendable** *adj.*

▷ **Usage.** See at **amend.**

emendation (ˌiːmɛnˈdeɪʃən) *n.* **1.** a correction or improvement in a text. **2.** the act or process of emending. —ˈ**emenˌdator** *n.* —**emendatory** (ɪˈmɛndətərɪ, -trɪ) *adj.*

emerald (ˈɛmərəld, ˈɛmrəld) *n.* **1.** a green transparent variety of beryl: highly valued as a gem. **2. a.** its clear green colour. **b.** (*as adj.*): *an emerald carpet.* [C13: < OF *esmeraude,* < L *smaragdus,* < Gk *smaragdos*]

Emerald Isle *n.* a poetic name for Ireland.

emerge (ɪˈmɜːdʒ) *vb.* (*intr.;* often foll. by *from*) **1.** to come up to the surface of or rise from water or other liquid. **2.** to come into view, as from concealment or obscurity. **3.** (foll. by *from*) to come out (of) or live (through (a difficult experience, etc.)). **4.** to become apparent. [C17: < L *ēmergere* to rise up from, < *mergere* to dip] —**eˈmergence** *n.* —**eˈmerging** *adj.*

emergency (ɪˈmɜːdʒənsɪ) *n., pl.* **-cies. 1. a.** an unforeseen or sudden occurrence, esp. of danger demanding immediate action. **b.** (*as modifier*): *an emergency exit.* **2. a.** a patient requiring urgent treatment. **b.** (*as modifier*): *an emergency ward.* **3.** *N.Z.* a player selected to stand by to replace an injured member of a team; reserve. **4. state of emergency.** a condition, declared by a government, in which martial law applies, usually because of civil unrest or natural disaster.

emergent (ɪˈmɜːdʒənt) *adj.* **1.** coming into being or notice. **2.** (of a nation) recently independent. —**eˈmergently** *adv.*

emeritus (ɪˈmɛrɪtəs) *adj.* (*usually postpositive*) retired or honourably discharged from full-time work, but retaining one's title on an honorary basis: *a professor emeritus.* [C19: < L, < *merēre* to deserve; see MERIT]

emersion (ɪˈmɜːʃən) *n.* **1.** the act or an instance of emerging. **2.** *Astron.* the reappearance of a celestial body after an eclipse or occultation. [C17: < L *ēmersus;* see EMERGE]

emery (ˈɛmərɪ) *n.* **a.** a hard greyish-black mineral consisting of corundum with either magnetite or haematite: used as an abrasive and polishing agent. **b.** (*as modifier*): *emery paper.* [C15: < OF *esmeril,* ult. < Gk *smuris* powder for rubbing]

emery board *n.* a strip of cardboard or wood with a rough surface of crushed emery, for filing one's nails.

emetic (ɪˈmɛtɪk) *adj.* **1.** causing vomiting. ~*n.* **2.** an emetic agent or drug. [C17: < LL, < Gk *emetikos,* < *emein* to vomit]

emf *or* **EMF** *abbrev. for* electromotive force.

-emia *n. combining form.* a U.S. variant of **-aemia.**

emigrant (ˈɛmɪgrənt) *n.* **a.** a person who leaves one place, esp. his native country, to settle in another. **b.** (*as modifier*): *an emigrant worker.*

emigrate (ˈɛmɪˌgreɪt) *vb.* (*intr.*) to leave one place, esp. one's native country, to settle in another. [C18: < L *ēmīgrāre,* < *mīgrāre* to depart, MIGRATE] —ˌ**emiˈgration** *n.* —ˈ**emiˌgratory** *adj.*

émigré (ˈɛmɪˌgreɪ) *n.* an emigrant, esp. one forced to leave his native country for political reasons. [C18: < F, < *émigrer* to EMIGRATE]

eminence (ˈɛmɪnəns) *n.* **1.** a position of superiority or fame. **2.** a high or raised piece of ground. ~Also: **eminency.** [C17: < F, < L *ēminentia* a standing out; see EMINENT]

Eminence (ˈɛmɪnəns) *or* **Eminency** *n., pl.* **-nences** *or* **-nencies.** (preceded by *Your* or *His*) a title used to address or refer to a cardinal.

éminence grise *French.* (eminɑ̃s griz) *n., pl.* **éminences grises** (eminɑ̃s griz). a person who wields power and influence unofficially or behind the scenes. [lit.: grey eminence, orig. applied to Père Joseph, F monk, secretary of Cardinal Richelieu (1585–1642), F statesman]

eminent (ˈɛmɪnənt) *adj:* **1.** above others in rank, merit, or reputation; distinguished. **2.** (*prenominal*) noteworthy or outstanding. **3.** projecting or protruding; prominent. [C15: < L *ēminēre* to project, stand out, < *minēre* to stand]

eminent domain *n. Law.* the right of a state to confiscate private property for public use, payment usually being made in compensation.

emir (ɛˈmɪə) *n.* (in the Islamic world) **1.** an independent ruler or chieftain. **2.** a military commander or governor. **3.** a descendant of Mohammed. [C17: via F < Sp., < Ar. *'amīr* commander] —**eˈmirate** *n.*

emissary (ˈɛmɪsərɪ, -ɪsrɪ) *n., pl.* **-saries. 1. a.** an agent sent on a mission, esp. one who represents a government or head of state. **b.** (*as modifier*): *an emissary delegation.* **2.** an agent sent on a secret mission, as a spy. [C17: < L *ēmissārius,* < *ēmittere* to send out; see EMIT]

emission (ɪˈmɪʃən) *n.* **1.** the act of emitting or sending forth. **2.** energy, in the form of heat, light, radio waves, etc., emitted from a source. **3.** a substance, fluid, etc., that is emitted; discharge. **4.** *Physiol.* any bodily discharge, esp. of semen. [C17: < L *ēmissiō,* < *ēmittere* to send forth, EMIT] —**eˈmissive** *adj.*

emission spectrum *n.* the spectrum or pattern of bright lines or bands seen when the electromagnetic radiation emitted by a substance is passed into a spectrometer.

emit (ɪˈmɪt) *vb.* **emitting, emitted.** (*tr.*) **1.** to give or send forth; discharge. **2.** to give voice to; utter. **3.** *Physics.* to give off (radiation or particles). [C17: < L *ēmittere* to send out, < *mittere* to send]

emitter (ɪˈmɪtə) *n.* **1.** a person or thing that emits. **2.** a substance that emits radiation. **3.** the region in a transistor in which the charge-carrying holes or electrons originate.

Emmenthal, Emmental (ˈɛmənˌtɑːl), *or* **Emmenthaler** *n.* a hard Swiss cheese with holes in it. [C20: after *Emmenthal,* valley in Switzerland]

Emmy (ˈɛmɪ) *n., pl.* **-mys** *or* **-mies.** (in the U.S.) one of the statuettes awarded annually for outstanding television performances and productions. [C20: < *Immy,* short for *image orthicon tube*]

emollient (ɪˈmɒljənt) *adj.* **1.** softening or soothing, esp. to the skin. ~*n.* **2.** any preparation or substance that has this effect. [C17: < L *ēmollīre* to soften, < *mollis* soft] —**eˈmollience** *n.*

emolument (ɪˈmɒljʊmənt) *n.* the profit arising from an office or employment; fees or wages. [C15: < L *ēmolumentum* benefit; orig., fee paid to a miller, < *molere* to grind]

emote (ɪˈməʊt) *vb.* (*intr.*) to display exaggerated emotion, as in acting. [C20: back formation < EMOTION] —**eˈmoter** *n.*

emotion (ɪˈməʊʃən) *n.* any strong feeling, as of joy, sorrow, or fear. [C16: < F, < OF, < L *ēmovēre* to disturb, < *movēre* to MOVE]

emotional (ɪˈməʊʃənᵊl) *adj.* **1.** of, characteristic of, or expressive of emotion. **2.** readily or excessively affected by emotion. **3.** appealing to or arousing emotion. **4.** caused or determined by emotion rather than reason: *an emotional argument.* —**eˌmotionˈality** *n.*

emotionalism (ɪˈməʊʃənəˌlɪzəm) *n.* **1.** emotional nature or quality. **2.** a tendency to yield readily to the emotions. **3.** an appeal to the emotions, esp. as to an audience. —**eˈmotionalist** *n.* —**eˌmotionalˈistic** *adj.*

emotionalize *or* **-ise** (ɪˈməʊʃənəˌlaɪz) *vb.* (*tr.*) to make emotional; subject to emotional treatment. —**eˌmotionaliˈzation** *or* **-iˈsation** *n.*

emotive (ɪˈməʊtɪv) *adj.* **1.** tending or designed to arouse emotion. **2.** of or characterized by emotion. —**eˈmotiveness** *or* ˌ**emoˈtivity** *n.*

Emp. *abbrev. for:* **1.** Emperor. **2.** Empire. **3.** Empress.

empanel *or* **impanel** (ɪmˈpænᵊl) *vb.* **-elling, -elled** *or U.S.* **-eling, -eled.** (*tr.*) *Law.* **1.** to enter on a list (names of persons to be summoned for jury service). **2.** to select (a jury) from such a list. —**emˈpanelment** *or* **imˈpanelment** *n.*

empathize *or* **-ise** (ˈɛmpəˌθaɪz) *vb.* (*intr.*) to engage in or feel empathy.

empathy (ˈɛmpəθɪ) *n.* **1.** the power of understanding and imaginatively entering into another person's feelings. **2.** the attribution to an object, such as a work of art, of one's own feelings about it. [C20: < Gk *empatheia* affection, passion] —**emˈpathic** *or* ˌ**empaˈthetic** *adj.* —ˈ**empathist** *n.*

emperor (ˈɛmpərə) *n.* a monarch who rules or reigns over an empire. [C13: < OF, < L *imperāre* to command, < IM- + *parāre* to make ready] —ˈ**emperorˌship** *n.*

emperor penguin *n.* an Antarctic penguin with orange-yellow patches on the neck: the largest penguin, reaching a height of 1.3 m (4 ft.).

emphasis (ˈɛmfəsɪs) *n., pl.* **-ses** (-siːz). **1.** special importance or significance. **2.** an object, idea, etc., that is given special importance or significance. **3.** stress on a particular syllable, word, or phrase in speaking. **4.** force or intensity of expression. **5.** sharpness or clarity of form or outline. [C16: via L < Gk: meaning, (in rhetoric) significant stress; see EMPHATIC]

emphasize *or* **-ise** (ˈɛmfəˌsaɪz) *vb.* (*tr.*) to give emphasis or prominence to; stress.

emphatic (ɪmˈfætɪk) *adj.* **1.** expressed, spoken, or done with emphasis. **2.** forceful and positive; definite; direct. **3.** sharp or clear in form, contour, or outline. **4.** important or significant; stressed. [C18: < Gk, < *emphainein* to display, < *phainein* to show] —**emˈphatically** *adv.*

emphysema (ˌɛmfɪˈsiːmə) *n. Pathol.* **1.** a condition in which the air sacs of the lungs are grossly enlarged, causing breathlessness and wheezing. **2.** the abnormal presence of air in a tissue or part. [C17: < NL, < Gk *emphusēma* a swelling up, < *phusan* to blow]

empire (ˈɛmpaɪə) *n.* **1.** an aggregate of peoples and territories under the rule of a single person, oligarchy, or sovereign state. **2.** any monarchy that has an emperor as head of state. **3.** the period during which a particular empire exists. **4.** supreme power; sovereignty. **5.** a large industrial organization with many ramifications. [C13: < OF, < L, < *imperāre* to command, < *parāre* to prepare]

Empire (ˈɛmpaɪə) *n.* **the. 1.** the British Empire. **2.** *French history.* **a.** the period of imperial rule in France from 1804 to 1815 under Napoleon Bonaparte. **b.** Also called: **Second Empire.** the period from 1852 to 1870 when Napoleon III ruled as emperor. ~*adj.* **3.** denoting, characteristic of, or relating to the British Empire. **4.** denoting, characteristic of, or relating to either French Empire, esp. the first.

empire-builder *n. Inf.* a person who seeks extra power, esp. by increasing the number of his staff. —**ˈempire-ˌbuilding** *n., adj.*

Empire Day *n.* the former name of **Commonwealth Day.**

empiric (ɛmˈpɪrɪk) *n.* **1.** a person who relies on empirical methods. **2.** a medical quack. ~*adj.* **3.** a variant of **empirical.** [C16: < L, < Gk *empeirikos* practised, < *peiran* to attempt]

empirical (ɛmˈpɪrɪkᵊl) *adj.* **1.** derived from or relating to experiment and observation rather than theory. **2.** (of medical treatment) based on practical experience rather than scientific proof. **3.** *Philosophy.* (of knowledge) derived from experience rather than by logic from first principles. **4.** of or relating to medical quackery. —**emˈpiricalness** *n.*

empiricism (ɛmˈpɪrɪˌsɪzəm) *n.* **1.** *Philosophy.* the doctrine that all knowledge derives from experience. **2.** the use of empirical methods. **3.** medical quackery. —**emˈpiricist** *n., adj.*

emplace (ɪmˈpleɪs) *vb.* (*tr.*) to put in position.

emplacement (ɪmˈpleɪsmənt) *n.* **1.** a prepared position for a gun or other weapon. **2.** the act of putting or state of being put in place. [C19: < F, < obs. *emplacer* to put in position, < PLACE]

emplane (ɪmˈpleɪn) *vb.* to board or put on board an aeroplane.

employ (ɪmˈplɔɪ) *vb.* (*tr.*) **1.** to engage or make use of the services of (a person) in return for money; hire. **2.** to provide work or occupation for; keep busy. **3.** to use as a means. ~*n.* **4.** the state of being employed (esp. in **in someone's employ**). [C15: < OF *emploier,* < L *implicāre* to entangle, engage, < *plicāre* to fold] —**emˈployable** *adj.* —**emˌployaˈbility** *n.*

employee *or U.S.* **employe** (ɛmˈplɔɪiː, ˌɛmplɔɪˈiː) *n.* a person who is hired to work for another or for a business, firm, etc., in return for payment.

employer (ɪmˈplɔɪə) *n.* **1.** a person, firm, etc., that employs workers. **2.** a person who employs.

employment (ɪmˈplɔɪmənt) *n.* **1.** the act of employing or state of being employed. **2.** a person's work or occupation.

employment exchange *n. Brit.* a former name for **employment office.**

employment office *n. Brit.* any government office established to collect and supply to the unemployed information about job vacancies and to employers information about availability of prospective workers. See also **Jobcentre.**

emporium (ɛmˈpɔːrɪəm) *n., pl.* **-riums** *or* **-ria** (-rɪə). a large retail shop offering for sale a wide variety of merchandise. [C16: < L, < Gk, < *emporos* merchant, < *poros* a journey]

empower (ɪmˈpaʊə) *vb.* (*tr.*) **1.** to give power or authority to; authorize. **2.** to give ability to; enable or permit. —**emˈpowerment** *n.*

empress (ˈɛmprɪs) *n.* **1.** the wife or widow of an emperor. **2.** a woman who holds the rank of emperor in her own right. [C12: < OF *empereriz,* < L *imperātrix;* see EMPEROR]

empty (ˈɛmptɪ) *adj.* **-tier, -tiest. 1.** containing nothing. **2.** without inhabitants; vacant or unoccupied. **3.** carrying no load, passengers, etc. **4.** without purpose, substance, or value: *an empty life.* **5.** insincere or trivial: *empty words.* **6.** not expressive or vital; vacant: *an empty look.* **7.** *Inf.* hungry. **8.** (*postpositive;* foll. by *of*) devoid; destitute. **9.** *Inf.* drained of energy or emotion. **10.** *Maths, logic.* (of a set or class) containing no members. ~*vb.* **-tying, -tied. 11.** to make or become empty. **12.** (when *intr.,* foll. by *into*) to discharge (contents). **13.** (*tr.;* often foll. by *of*) to unburden or rid (oneself). ~*n., pl.* **-ties. 14.** an empty container, esp. a bottle. [OE *ǣmtig*] —**ˈemptiable** *adj.* —**ˈemptier** *n.* —**ˈemptily** *adv.* —**ˈemptiness** *n.*

empty-handed *adj.* **1.** carrying nothing in the hands. **2.** having gained nothing.

empty-headed *adj.* lacking sense; frivolous.

empyema (ˌɛmpaɪˈiːmə) *n., pl.* **-emata** (-ˈiːmətə) *or* **-emas.** a collection of pus in a body cavity, esp. in the chest. [C17: < Med. L, < Gk *empuēma* abscess, < *empuein* to suppurate, < *puon* pus] —**ˌempyˈemic** *adj.*

empyrean (ˌɛmpaɪˈriːən) *n.* **1.** *Arch.* the highest part of the heavens, thought in ancient times to contain the pure element of fire and by early Christians to be the abode of God. **2.** *Poetic.* the heavens or sky. ~*adj. also* **empyreal. 3.** of or relating to the sky. **4.** heavenly or sublime. [C17: < LL, < Gk *empurios* fiery]

empyreuma (ˌɛmpɪˈruːmə) *n., pl.* **-mata** (-mətə). the smell and taste associated with burning vegetable and animal matter. [C17: < Gk, < *empureuein* to set on fire]

EMS *abbrev. for* European monetary system: a system designed to limit the fluctuation of exchange rates of member countries in relation to one another.

emu (ˈiːmjuː) *n.* a large Australian flightless bird, similar to the ostrich. [C17: changed < Port. *ema* ostrich]

e.m.u. *or* **EMU** *abbrev. for* electromagnetic unit.

emu-bob *Austral. inf.* ~*vb.* **-bobbing, -bobbed. 1.** (*intr.*) to bend over to collect litter or small pieces of wood. ~*n.* **2.** Also called: **emu parade.** a parade of soldiers or schoolchildren for litter collection. —**ˈemu-ˌbobbing** *n.*

emulate (ˈɛmjʊˌleɪt) *vb.* (*tr.*) **1.** to attempt to equal or surpass, esp. by imitation. **2.** to rival or compete with. [C16: < L *aemulus* competing with] —**ˈemulative** *adj.* —**ˌemuˈlation** *n.* —**ˈemuˌlator** *n.*

emulous (ˈɛmjʊləs) *adj.* **1.** desiring or aiming to equal or surpass another. **2.** characterized by or arising from emulation. [C14: < L; see EMULATE] —**ˈemulousness** *n.*

emulsifier (ɪˈmʌlsɪˌfaɪə) *n.* an agent that forms an emulsion, esp. a food additive that prevents separation of processed foods.

emulsify (ɪˈmʌlsɪˌfaɪ) *vb.* **-fying, -fied.** to make or form into an emulsion. —**eˌmulsiˈfiable** *or* **eˈmulsible** *adj.* —**eˌmulsifiˈcation** *n.*

emulsion (ɪˈmʌlʃən) *n.* **1.** *Photog.* a light-sensitive coating on a base, such as paper or film, consisting of silver bromide suspended in gelatin. **2.** *Chem.* a colloid in which both phases are liquids. **3.** a type of paint in which the pigment is suspended in a vehicle that is dispersed in water as an emulsion. **4.** *Pharmacol.* a mixture in which an oily medicine is dispersed in another liquid. **5.** any liquid resembling milk. [C17: < NL *ēmulsiō*, < L, < *ēmulgēre* to milk out, < *mulgēre* to milk] —**e'mulsive** *adj.*

emu-wren *n.* an Australian wren having long plumy tail feathers.

en (ɛn) *n. Printing.* a unit of measurement, half the width of an em.

en-[1] *or* **em-** *prefix forming verbs.* **1.** (*from nouns*) **a.** put in or on: *entomb; enthrone.* **b.** go on or into: *enplane.* **c.** surround or cover with: *enmesh.* **d.** furnish with: *empower.* **2.** (*from adjectives and nouns*) cause to be in a certain condition: *enable; enslave.* [via OF < L *in-* IN-[2]]

en-[2] *or* **em-** *prefix forming nouns and adjectives.* in; into; inside: *endemic.* [< Gk (often via L); cf. IN-[1], IN-[2]]

-en[1] *suffix forming verbs from adjectives and nouns.* cause to be; become; cause to have: *blacken; heighten.* [OE *-n-*, as in *fæst-n-ian* to fasten, of Gmc origin]

-en[2] *suffix forming adjectives from nouns.* of; made of; resembling: *ashen; wooden.* [OE *-en*]

enable (ɪn'eɪbᵊl) *vb.* (*tr.*) **1.** to provide (someone) with adequate power, means, opportunity, or authority (to do something). **2.** to make possible or easy. —**en'abler** *n.*

enabling act *n.* a legislative act conferring certain specified powers on a person or organization.

enact (ɪn'ækt) *vb.* (*tr.*) **1.** to make into an act or statute. **2.** to establish by law; decree. **3.** to represent or perform as in a play. —**en'actable** *adj.* —**en'active** *or* **en'actory** *adj.* —**en'actment** *or* **en'action** *n.* —**en'actor** *n.*

enamel (ɪ'næməl) *n.* **1.** a coloured glassy substance, translucent or opaque, fused to the surface of articles made of metal, glass, etc., for ornament or protection. **2.** an article or articles ornamented with enamel. **3.** an enamel-like paint or varnish. **4.** any coating resembling enamel. **5.** the hard white substance that covers the crown of each tooth. **6.** (*modifier*) decorated or covered with enamel. ~*vb.* **-elling, -elled** *or U.S.* **-eling, -eled.** (*tr.*) **7.** to decorate with enamel. **8.** to ornament with glossy variegated colours, as if with enamel. **9.** to portray in enamel. [C15: < OF *esmail*, of Gmc origin] —**e'nameller, e'namellist** *or U.S.* **e'nameler, e'namelist** *n.* —**e'namel,work** *n.*

enamour *or U.S.* **enamor** (ɪn'æmə) *vb.* (*tr.; usually passive* and foll. by *of*) to inspire with love; captivate. [C14: < OF, < *amour* love, < L *amor*] —**en'amoured** *or U.S.* **en'amored** *adj.*

en bloc *French.* (ɑ̃ blɔk) *adv.* in a lump or block; as a body or whole; all together.

en brosse *French.* (ɑ̃ brɔs) *adj., adv.* (of the hair) cut very short so that the hair stands up stiffly. [lit.: in the style of a brush]

enc. *abbrev. for:* **1.** enclosed. **2.** enclosure.

encamp (ɪn'kæmp) *vb.* to lodge or cause to lodge in a camp.

encampment (ɪn'kæmpmənt) *n.* **1.** the act of setting up a camp. **2.** the place where a camp, esp. a military camp, is set up.

encapsulate *or* **incapsulate** (ɪn'kæpsjʊ,leɪt) *vb.* **1.** to enclose or be enclosed as in a capsule. **2.** (*tr.*) to put in a short or concise form. —**en,capsu'lation** *or* **in,capsu'lation** *n.*

encase *or* **incase** (ɪn'keɪs) *vb.* (*tr.*) to place or enclose as in a case. —**en'casement** *or* **in'casement** *n.*

encash (ɪn'kæʃ) *vb.* (*tr.*) *Brit., formal.* to exchange (a cheque) for cash. —**en'cashable** *adj.* —**en'cashment** *n.*

encaustic (ɪn'kɒstɪk) *Ceramics, etc.* ~*adj.* **1.** decorated by any process involving burning in colours, esp. by inlaying coloured clays and baking or by fusing wax colours to the surface. ~*n.* **2.** the process of burning in colours. **3.** a product of such a process. [C17: < L *encausticus*, < Gk, < *enkaiein* to burn in, < *kaiein* to burn] —**en'caustically** *adv.*

-ence *or* **-ency** *suffix forming nouns.* indicating an action, state, condition, or quality: *benevolence; residence; patience.* [via OF < L *-entia*, < *-ēns*, present participial ending]

enceinte (ɒn'sænt) *adj.* another word for **pregnant.** [C17: < F, < L *inciēns* pregnant]

encephalic (,ɛnsɪ'fælɪk) *adj.* of or relating to the brain.

encephalin (ɛn'sɛfəlɪn) *n.* a variant of **enkephalin.**

encephalitis (,ɛnsɛfə'laɪtɪs) *n.* inflammation of the brain. —**encephalitic** (,ɛnsɛfə'lɪtɪk) *adj.*

encephalitis lethargica (lɪ'θɑːdʒɪkə) *n.* a technical name for **sleeping sickness** (sense 2).

encephalo- *or before a vowel* **encephal-** *combining form.* indicating the brain: *encephalogram; encephalitis.* [< NL, < Gk *enkephalos*, < *en-* in + *kephalē* head]

encephalogram (ɛn'sɛfələ,græm) *n.* **1.** an x-ray photograph of the brain, esp. one (a **pneumoencephalogram**) taken after replacing some of the cerebrospinal fluid with air or oxygen. **2.** short for **electroencephalogram;** see **electroencephalograph.**

encephalon (ɛn'sɛfə,lɒn) *n., pl.* **-la** (-lə). a technical name for **brain.** [C18: < NL, < Gk *enkephalos* brain, < EN-[2] + *kephalē* head] —**en'cephalous** *adj.*

enchain (ɪn'tʃeɪn) *vb.* (*tr.*) **1.** to bind with chains. **2.** to hold fast or captivate (the attention, etc.). —**en'chainment** *n.*

enchant (ɪn'tʃɑːnt) *vb.* (*tr.*) **1.** to cast a spell on; bewitch. **2.** to delight or captivate utterly. [C14: < OF, < L *incantāre*, < *cantāre* to chant, < *canere* to sing] —**en'chanted** *adj.* —**en'chanter** *n.* —**en'chantress** *fem. n.*

enchanting (ɪn'tʃɑːntɪŋ) *adj.* pleasant; delightful. —**en'chantingly** *adv.*

enchantment (ɪn'tʃɑːntmənt) *n.* **1.** the act of enchanting or state of being enchanted. **2.** a magic spell. **3.** great charm or fascination.

enchase (ɪn'tʃeɪs) *vb.* (*tr.*) a less common word for **chase**[3]. [C15: < OF *enchasser* to enclose, set, < EN-[1] + *casse* CASE[2]] —**en'chaser** *n.*

enchilada (,ɛntʃɪ'lɑːdə) *n.* a Mexican dish of a tortilla filled with meat, served with a chilli sauce. [American Sp., < *enchilado*, < *enchilar* to spice with chilli, < *chile* CHILLI]

-enchyma *n. combining form.* denoting cellular tissue. [C20: abstracted < PARENCHYMA]

encipher (ɪn'saɪfə) *vb.* (*tr.*) to convert (a message, etc.) into code or cipher. —**en'cipherer** *n.* —**en'cipherment** *n.*

encircle (ɪn'sɜːkᵊl) *vb.* (*tr.*) to form a circle around; enclose within a circle; surround. —**en'circlement** *n.* —**en'circling** *adj.*

enclave ('ɛnkleɪv) *n.* a part of a country entirely surrounded by foreign territory: viewed from the position of the surrounding territories. [C19: < F, < OF *enclaver* to enclose, < Vulgar L *inclāvāre* (unattested) to lock up, < L IN-[2] + *clavis* key]

enclitic (ɪn'klɪtɪk) *adj.* **1.** denoting or relating to a monosyllabic word or form that is treated as a suffix of the preceding word. ~*n.* **2.** an enclitic word or form. [C17: < LL, < Gk, < *enklinein* to cause to lean, < EN-[2] + *klinein* to lean] —**en'clitically** *adv.*

enclose *or* **inclose** (ɪn'kləʊz) *vb.* (*tr.*) **1.** to close; hem in; surround. **2.** to surround (land) with or as if with a fence. **3.** to put in an envelope or wrapper, esp. together with a letter. **4.** to contain or hold. —**en'closable** *or* **in'closable** *adj.* —**en'closer** *or* **in'closer** *n.*

enclosed order *n.* a Christian religious order that does not permit its members to go into the outside world.

enclosure *or* **inclosure** (ɪn'kləʊʒə) *n.* **1.** the act of enclosing or state of being enclosed. **2.** an area enclosed as by a fence. **3.** the act of appropriating land by setting up a fence, hedge, etc., around it. **4.** a fence, wall, etc., that encloses. **5.** something enclosed within an envelope or wrapper, esp. together with a letter. **6.** *Brit.* a section of a sports ground, racecourse, etc., allotted to certain spectators.

encode (ɪnˈkəʊd) *vb.* (*tr.*) to convert (a message) into code. —**enˈcodement** *n.* —**enˈcoder** *n.*

encomiast (ɛnˈkəʊmɪˌæst) *n.* a person who speaks or writes an encomium. [C17: < Gk, < *enkōmiazein* to utter an ENCOMIUM] —**enˌcomiˈastic** *or* **enˌcomiˈastical** *adj.*

encomium (ɛnˈkəʊmɪəm) *n., pl.* **-miums** *or* **-mia** (-mɪə). a formal expression of praise; eulogy. [C16: < L, < Gk, < EN-[2] + *kōmos* festivity]

encompass (ɪnˈkʌmpəs) *vb.* (*tr.*) **1.** to enclose within a circle; surround. **2.** to bring about: *he encompassed the enemy's ruin.* **3.** to include entirely or comprehensively. —**enˈcompassment** *n.*

encore (ˈɒŋkɔː) *sentence substitute.* **1.** again: used by an audience to demand an extra or repeated performance. ~*n.* **2.** an extra or repeated performance given in response to enthusiastic demand. ~*vb.* **3.** (*tr.*) to demand an extra or repeated performance of (a work, piece of music, etc.) by (a performer). [C18: < F: still, again, ? < L *in hanc hōram* until this hour]

encounter (ɪnˈkaʊntə) *vb.* **1.** to come upon or meet casually or unexpectedly. **2.** to meet (an enemy, army, etc.) in battle or contest. **3.** (*tr.*) to be faced with; contend with. ~*n.* **4.** a casual or unexpected meeting. **5.** a hostile meeting; contest. [C13: < OF, < Vulgar L *incontrāre* (unattested), < L IN-[2] + *contrā* against, opposite] —**enˈcounterer** *n.*

encounter group *n.* a group of people who meet in order to develop self-awareness and mutual understanding by openly expressing their feelings, by confrontation, etc.

encourage (ɪnˈkʌrɪdʒ) *vb.* (*tr.*) **1.** to inspire (someone) with the courage or confidence (to do something). **2.** to stimulate (something or someone) by approval or help. —**enˈcouragement** *n.* —**enˈcourager** *n.* —**enˈcouraging** *adj.* —**enˈcouragingly** *adv.*

encroach (ɪnˈkrəʊtʃ) *vb.* (*intr.*) **1.** (often foll. by *on* or *upon*) to intrude gradually or stealthily upon the rights, property, etc., of another. **2.** to advance beyond certain limits. [C14: < OF *encrochier* to seize, lit.: fasten upon with hooks, of Gmc origin] —**enˈcroacher** *n.* —**enˈcroachment** *n.*

encrust *or* **incrust** (ɪnˈkrʌst) *vb.* **1.** (*tr.*) to cover or overlay with or as with a crust or hard coating. **2.** to form or cause to form a crust or hard coating. **3.** (*tr.*) to decorate lavishly, as with jewels. —ˌ**encrusˈtation** *or* ˌ**incrusˈtation** *n.*

encumber *or* **incumber** (ɪnˈkʌmbə) *vb.* (*tr.*) **1.** to hinder or impede; hamper. **2.** to fill with superfluous or useless matter. **3.** to burden with debts, obligations, etc. [C14: < OF, < EN-[1] + *combre* a barrier, < LL *combrus,* <?]

encumbrance *or* **incumbrance** (ɪnˈkʌmbrəns) *n.* **1.** a thing that impedes or is burdensome; hindrance. **2.** *Law.* a burden or charge upon property, such as a mortgage or lien.

ency., encyc., *or* **encycl.** *abbrev. for* encyclopedia.

-ency *suffix forming nouns.* a variant of **-ence:** *fluency; permanency.*

encyclical (ɛnˈsɪklɪkᵊl) *n.* **1.** a letter sent by the pope to all Roman Catholic bishops. ~*adj. also* **encyclic. 2.** (of letters) intended for general circulation. [C17: < LL, < Gk, < *kuklos* circle]

encyclopedia *or* **encyclopaedia** (ɛnˌsaɪkləʊˈpiːdɪə) *n.* a book, often in many volumes, containing articles, often arranged in alphabetical order, dealing either with the whole range of human knowledge or with one particular subject. [C16: < NL, erroneously for Gk *enkuklios paideia* general education, < *enkuklios* general + *paideia* education] —**enˌcycloˈpedic** *or* **enˌcycloˈpaedic** *adj.*

encyclopedist *or* **encyclopaedist** (ɛnˌsaɪkləʊˈpiːdɪst) *n.* a person who compiles or contributes to an encyclopedia. —**enˌcycloˈpedism** *or* **enˌcycloˈpaedism** *n.*

encyst (ɛnˈsɪst) *vb. Biol.* to enclose or become enclosed by a cyst, thick membrane, or shell. —**enˈcystment** *or* ˌ**encysˈtation** *n.*

end (ɛnd) *n.* **1.** the extremity of the length of something, such as a road, line, etc. **2.** the surface at either extremity of an object. **3.** the extreme extent, limit, or degree of something. **4.** the most distant place or time that can be imagined: *the ends of the earth.* **5.** the time at which something is concluded. **6.** the last section or part. **7.** a share or part. **8.** (*often pl.*) a remnant or fragment (esp. in **odds and ends**). **9.** a final state, esp. death; destruction. **10.** the purpose of an action or existence. **11.** *Sport.* either of the two defended areas of a playing field, rink, etc. **12.** *Bowls.* a section of play from one side of the green to the other. **13. at an end.** exhausted or completed. **14. come to an end.** to become completed or exhausted. **15. have one's end away.** *Sl.* to have sexual intercourse. **16. in the end.** finally. **17. make (both) ends meet.** to spend no more than the money one has. **18. no end (of).** *Inf.* (intensifier): *I had no end of work.* **19. on end.** *Inf.* without pause or interruption. **20. the end.** *Sl.* the worst, esp. something that goes beyond the limits of endurance. ~*vb.* **21.** to bring or come to a finish; conclude. **22.** to die or cause to die. **23.** (*tr.*) to surpass or outdo: *a novel to end all novels.* **24. end it all.** *Inf.* to commit suicide. ~See also **end up.** [OE *ende*] —ˈ**ender** *n.*

end- *combining form.* a variant of **endo-** before a vowel.

-end *suffix forming nouns.* See **-and.**

endamoeba *or U.S.* **endameba** (ˌɛndəˈmiːbə) *n.* variant spellings of **entamoeba.**

endanger (ɪnˈdeɪndʒə) *vb.* (*tr.*) to put in danger or peril; imperil. —**enˈdangerment** *n.*

endangered (ɪnˈdeɪndʒəd) *adj.* in danger, esp. of extinction: *an endangered species.*

endear (ɪnˈdɪə) *vb.* (*tr.*) to cause to be beloved or esteemed. —**enˈdearing** *adj.*

endearment (ɪnˈdɪəmənt) *n.* something that endears, such as an affectionate utterance.

endeavour *or U.S.* **endeavor** (ɪnˈdɛvə) *vb.* **1.** to try (to do something). ~*n.* **2.** an effort to do or attain something. [C14 *endeveren,* < EN-[1] + *-deveren* < *dever* duty, < OF *deveir;* see DEVOIRS] —**enˈdeavourer** *or U.S.* **enˈdeavorer** *n.*

endemic (ɛnˈdɛmɪk) *adj. also* **endemial** (ɛnˈdɛmɪəl) *or* **endemical. 1.** present within a localized area or peculiar to persons in such an area. ~*n.* **2.** an endemic disease or plant. [C18: < NL *endēmicus,* < Gk *endēmos* native, < EN-[2] + *dēmos* the people] —**enˈdemically** *adv.* —ˈ**endemism** *or* ˌ**endeˈmicity** *n.*

endermic (ɛnˈdɜːmɪk) *adj.* (of a medicine, etc.) acting by absorption through the skin. [C19: < EN-[2] + Gk *derma* skin]

endgame (ˈɛndˌgeɪm) *n.* the closing stage of any of certain games, esp. chess, when there are only a few pieces left in play.

ending (ˈɛndɪŋ) *n.* **1.** the act of bringing to or reaching an end. **2.** the last part of something. **3.** the final part of a word, esp. a suffix.

endive (ˈɛndaɪv) *n.* a plant cultivated for its crisp curly leaves, which are used in salads. Cf. **chicory.** [C15: < OF, < Med. L, < var. of L *intubus, entubus*]

endless (ˈɛndlɪs) *adj.* **1.** having or seeming to have no end; eternal or infinite. **2.** continuing too long or continually recurring. **3.** formed with the ends joined. —ˈ**endlessness** *n.*

endmost (ˈɛndˌməʊst) *adj.* nearest the end; most distant.

endo- *or before a vowel* **end-** *combining form.* inside; within: *endocrine.* [< Gk, < *endon* within]

endoblast (ˈɛndəʊˌblæst) *n.* **1.** *Embryol.* a less common name for **endoderm. 2.** another name for **hypoblast.** —ˌ**endoˈblastic** *adj.*

endocarditis (ˌɛndəʊkɑːˈdaɪtɪs) *n.* inflammation of the lining of the heart. [C19: < NL, < ENDO- + Gk *kardia* heart + -ITIS] —**endocarditic** (ˌɛndəʊkɑːˈdɪtɪk) *adj.*

endocarp (ˈɛndəˌkɑːp) *n.* the inner layer of the pericarp of a fruit, such as the stone of a peach. —ˌ**endoˈcarpal** *or* ˌ**endoˈcarpic** *adj.*

endocrine (ˈɛndəʊˌkraɪn) *adj. also* **endocrinal** (ˌɛndəʊˈkraɪnᵊl), **endocrinic** (ˌɛndəʊˈkrɪnɪk). **1.** of or denoting endocrine glands or their secretions. ~*n.* **2.** an endocrine gland. [C20: < ENDO- + -*crine*, < Gk *krinein* to separate]

endocrine gland *n.* any of the glands that secrete hormones directly into the bloodstream, e.g. the pituitary, pineal, and thyroid.

endocrinology (ˌɛndəʊkraɪˈnɒlədʒɪ, -krɪ-) *n.* the branch of medical science concerned with the endocrine glands and their secretions. —ˌ**endocriˈnologist** *n.*

endoderm (ˈɛndəʊˌdɜːm) *or* **entoderm** *n.* the inner germ layer of an animal embryo, which gives rise to the lining of the digestive and respiratory tracts. —ˌ**endoˈdermal,** ˌ**endoˈdermic** *or* ˌ**entoˈdermal,** ˌ**entoˈdermic** *adj.*

end of steel *n. Canad.* **1.** a point up to which railway tracks have been laid. **2.** a town located at such a point.

endogamy (ɛnˈdɒgəmɪ) *n.* **1.** *Anthropol.* marriage within one's own tribe or similar unit. **2.** pollination between two flowers on the same plant. —**enˈdogamous** *or* **endogamic** (ˌɛndəʊˈgæmɪk) *adj.*

endogenous (ɛnˈdɒdʒɪnəs) *adj. Biol.* developing or originating within an organism or part of an organism. —**enˈdogeny** *n.*

endomorph (ˈɛndəʊˌmɔːf) *n.* **1.** a type of person having a body build characterized by fatness and heaviness. **2.** a mineral that naturally occurs enclosed within another mineral. —ˌ**endoˈmorphic** *adj.* —ˈ**endoˌmorphy** *n.*

endomorphism (ˌɛndəʊˈmɔːˌfɪzəm) *n. Geol.* metamorphism in which changes are induced in cooling molten rock by contact with older rocks.

endophyte (ˈɛndəʊˌfaɪt) *n.* any plant that lives within another plant. —**endophytic** (ˌɛndəʊˈfɪtɪk) *adj.*

endoplasm (ˈɛndəʊˌplæzəm) *n. Cytology.* the inner cytoplasm of a cell. —ˌ**endoˈplasmic** *adj.*

end organ *n. Anat.* the expanded end of a peripheral motor or sensory nerve.

endorphin (ɛnˈdɔːfɪn) *n.* any of a class of chemicals occurring in the brain, including enkephalin, which have a similar effect to morphine.

endorsation (ˌɛndɔːˈseɪʃən) *n. Canad.* approval or support.

endorse *or* **indorse** (ɪnˈdɔːs) *vb.* (*tr.*) **1.** to give approval or sanction to. **2.** to sign (one's name) on the back of (a cheque, etc.) to specify oneself as payee. **3.** *Commerce.* **a.** to sign the back of (a document) to transfer ownership of the rights to a specified payee. **b.** to specify (a sum) as transferable to another as payee. **4.** to write (a qualifying comment, etc.) on the back of a document. **5.** to sign a document, as when confirming receipt of payment. **6.** *Chiefly Brit.* to record a conviction on (a driving licence). [C16: < OF *endosser* to put on the back, < EN-[1] + *dos* back] —**enˈdorsable** *or* **inˈdorsable** *adj.* —**enˈdorser, enˈdorsor** *or* **inˈdorser, inˈdorsor** *n.* —**enˌdorˈsee** *or* **inˌdorˈsee** *n.*

endorsement *or* **indorsement** (ɪnˈdɔːsmənt) *n.* **1.** the act or an instance of endorsing. **2.** something that endorses, such as a signature. **3.** approval or support. **4.** a record of a motoring offence on a driving licence.

endoscope (ˈɛndəʊˌskəʊp) *n.* a medical instrument for examining the interior of hollow organs such as the stomach or bowel. —**endoscopic** (ˌɛndəʊˈskɒpɪk) *adj.*

endoskeleton (ˌɛndəʊˈskɛlɪtᵊn) *n.* an internal skeleton, esp. the bony or cartilaginous skeleton of vertebrates. —ˌ**endoˈskeletal** *adj.*

endosperm (ˈɛndəʊˌspɜːm) *n.* the tissue within the seed of a flowering plant that surrounds and nourishes the embryo. —ˌ**endoˈspermic** *adj.*

endothermic (ˌɛndəʊˈθɜːmɪk) *or* **endothermal** *adj.* (of a chemical reaction or compound) occurring or formed with the absorption of heat. —ˌ**endoˈthermically** *adv.* —ˌ**endoˈthermism** *n.*

endow (ɪnˈdaʊ) *vb.* (*tr.*) **1.** to provide with or bequeath a source of permanent income. **2.** (usually foll. by *with*) to provide (with qualities, characteristics, etc.). [C14: < OF, < EN-[1] + *douer* < L *dōtāre*, < *dōs* dowry] —**enˈdower** *n.*

endowment (ɪnˈdaʊmənt) *n.* **1.** the income with which an institution, etc., is endowed. **2.** the act or process of endowing. **3.** (*usually pl.*) natural talents or qualities. **4.** *Austral.* Also: **child endowment.** a social-security payment for dependent children.

endowment assurance *or* **insurance** *n.* a form of life insurance that provides for the payment of a specified sum directly to the policyholder at a designated date or to his beneficiary should he die before this date.

endpaper (ˈɛndˌpeɪpə) *n.* either of two leaves at the front and back of a book pasted to the inside of the board covers and the first leaf of the book.

end point *n.* **1.** *Chem.* the point at which a titration is complete. **2.** the point at which anything is complete.

end product *n.* the final result of a process, series, etc., esp. in manufacturing.

endue *or* **indue** (ɪnˈdjuː) *vb.* **-duing, -dued.** (*tr.*) (usually foll. by *with*) to invest or provide, as with some quality or trait. [C15: < OF, < L *indūcere*, < *dūcere* to lead]

end up *vb.* (*adv.*) **1.** (*copula*) to become eventually; turn out to be. **2.** (*intr.*) to arrive, esp. by a circuitous or lengthy route or process.

endurance (ɪnˈdjʊərəns) *n.* **1.** the capacity, state, or an instance of enduring. **2.** something endured; a hardship, strain, or privation.

endure (ɪnˈdjʊə) *vb.* **1.** to undergo (hardship, strain, etc.) without yielding; bear. **2.** (*tr.*) to permit or tolerate. **3.** (*intr.*) to last or continue to exist. [C14: < OF, < L *indūrāre* to harden, < *dūrus* hard] —**enˈdurable** *adj.* —**enˌduraˈbility** *or* **enˈdurableness** *n.*

enduring (ɪnˈdjʊərɪŋ) *adj.* **1.** permanent; lasting. **2.** having forbearance; long-suffering. —**enˈduringly** *adv.* —**enˈduringness** *n.*

end user *n.* **1.** (in international trading) the person, organization, or nation that will be the ultimate recipient of goods such as arms. **2.** *Computers.* the ultimate destination of information that is being transferred within a system.

endways (ˈɛndˌweɪz) *or esp. U.S. & Canad.* **endwise** (ˈɛndˌwaɪz) *adv.* **1.** having the end forwards or upwards. ~*adj.* **2.** vertical or upright. **3.** lengthways. **4.** standing or lying end to end.

ENE *symbol for* east-northeast.

-ene *n. combining form.* (in chemistry) indicating an unsaturated compound containing double bonds: *benzene; ethylene.* [< Gk *-ēnē*, fem. patronymic suffix]

enema (ˈɛnɪmə) *n., pl.* **-mas** *or* **-mata** (-mətə). *Med.* **1.** the introduction of liquid into the rectum to evacuate the bowels, medicate, or nourish. **2.** the liquid so introduced. [C15: < NL, < Gk: injection, < *enienai* to send in, < *hienai* to send]

enemy (ˈɛnəmɪ) *n., pl.* **-mies.** **1.** a person hostile or opposed to a policy, cause, person, or group. **2. a.** an armed adversary; opposing military force. **b.** (*as modifier*): *enemy aircraft.* **3. a.** a hostile nation or people. **b.** (*as modifier*): *an enemy alien.* **4.** something that harms or opposes. ~Related adj.: **inimical.** [C13: < OF, < L *inimīcus* hostile, < IN-[1] + *amīcus* friend]

energetic (ˌɛnəˈdʒɛtɪk) *adj.* having or showing energy; vigorous. —ˌ**enerˈgetically** *adv.*

energize *or* **-ise** (ˈɛnəˌdʒaɪz) *vb.* **1.** to have or cause to have energy; invigorate. **2.** (*tr.*) to apply electric current or electromotive force to (a circuit, etc.). —ˈ**enerˌgizer** *or* **-iser** *n.*

energy (ˈɛnədʒɪ) *n., pl.* **-gies.** **1.** intensity or vitality of action or expression; forcefulness. **2.** capacity or tendency for intense activity; vigour. **3.** *Physics.* **a.** the capacity of a body or system to do work. **b.** a measure of this capacity, measured in joules (SI units). [C16: < LL, < Gk *energeia* activity, < EN-[2] + *ergon* work]

energy band *n. Physics.* a range of energies associated with the quantum states of electrons in a crystalline solid.

enervate *vb.* (ˈɛnəˌveɪt). **1.** (*tr.*) to deprive of strength or vitality. ~*adj.* (ɪˈnɜːvɪt). **2.** deprived of strength or vitality. [C17: < L *ēnervāre* to remove the nerves from, < *nervus* nerve] —ˈ**ener,vating** *adj.* —,**enerˈvation** *n.*

en famille *French.* (ɑ̃ famij) *adv.* **1.** with one's family; at home. **2.** in a casual way; informally.

enfant terrible *French.* (ɑ̃fɑ̃ tɛriblə) *n., pl.* ***enfants terribles*** (ɑ̃fɑ̃ tɛriblə). a person given to unconventional conduct or indiscreet remarks. [C19: lit.: terrible child]

enfeeble (ɪnˈfiːbᵊl) *vb.* (*tr.*) to make weak. —**enˈfeeblement** *n.* —**enˈfeebler** *n.*

en fête *French.* (ɑ̃ fɛt) *adv.* dressed for or engaged in a festivity. [C19: lit.: in festival]

enfilade (,ɛnfɪˈleɪd) *Mil.* ~*n.* **1.** gunfire directed along the length of a position or formation. **2.** a position or formation subject to such fire. ~*vb.* (*tr.*) **3.** to attack (a position or formation) with enfilade. [C18: < F: suite, < *enfiler* to thread on string, < *fil* thread]

enfold *or* **infold** (ɪnˈfəʊld) *vb.* (*tr.*) **1.** to cover by enclosing. **2.** to embrace. —**enˈfolder** *or* **inˈfolder** *n.* —**enˈfoldment** *or* **inˈfoldment** *n.*

enforce (ɪnˈfɔːs) *vb.* (*tr.*) **1.** to ensure obedience to (a law, decision, etc.). **2.** to impose (obedience, etc.) as by force. **3.** to emphasize or reinforce (an argument, etc.). —**enˈforceable** *adj.* —**en,forceaˈbility** *n.* —**enforcedly** (ɪnˈfɔːsɪdlɪ) *adv.* —**enˈforcement** *n.* —**enˈforcer** *n.*

enfranchise (ɪnˈfræntʃaɪz) *vb.* (*tr.*) **1.** to grant the power of voting to. **2.** to liberate, as from servitude. **3.** (in England) to invest (a town, city, etc.) with the right to be represented in Parliament. —**enˈfranchisement** *n.* —**enˈfranchiser** *n.*

Eng. *abbrev. for:* **1.** England. **2.** English.

engage (ɪnˈgeɪdʒ) *vb.* (*mainly tr.*) **1.** to secure the services of. **2.** to secure for use; reserve. **3.** to involve (a person or his attention) intensely. **4.** to attract (the affection) of (a person). **5.** to draw (somebody) into conversation. **6.** (*intr.*) to take part; participate. **7.** to promise (to do something). **8.** (*also intr.*) *Mil.* to begin an action with (an enemy). **9.** to bring (a mechanism) into operation. **10.** (*also intr.*) to undergo or cause to undergo interlocking, as of the components of a driving mechanism. **11.** *Machinery.* to locate (a locking device) in its operative position or to advance (a tool) into a workpiece to commence cutting. [C15: < OF, < EN-[1] + *gage* a pledge; see GAGE[1]] —**enˈgager** *n.*

engagé *or* (*fem.*) ***engagée*** *French.* (ɑ̃gaʒe) *adj.* (of an artist) committed to some ideology.

engaged (ɪnˈgeɪdʒd) *adj.* **1.** pledged to be married; betrothed. **2.** occupied or busy. **3.** *Archit.* built against or attached to a wall or similar structure. **4.** (of a telephone line) in use.

engaged tone *n. Brit.* a repeated single note heard on a telephone when the number called is already in use.

engagement (ɪnˈgeɪdʒmənt) *n.* **1.** a pledge of marriage; betrothal. **2.** an appointment or arrangement, esp. for business or social purposes. **3.** the act of engaging or condition of being engaged. **4.** a promise, obligation, or other condition that binds. **5.** a period of employment, esp. a limited period. **6.** an action; battle.

engagement ring *n.* a ring given by a man to a woman as a token of their betrothal.

engaging (ɪnˈgeɪdʒɪŋ) *adj.* pleasing, charming, or winning. —**enˈgagingness** *n.*

en garde *French.* (ɑ̃ gard) *sentence substitute.* **1.** on guard; a call to a fencer to adopt a defensive stance in readiness for an attack or bout. ~*adj.* **2.** (of a fencer) in such a stance.

engender (ɪnˈdʒɛndə) *vb.* (*tr.*) to bring about or give rise to; cause to be born. [C14: < OF, < L *ingenerāre*, < *generāre* to beget]

engin. *abbrev. for* engineering.

engine (ˈɛndʒɪn) *n.* **1.** any machine designed to convert energy into mechanical work. **2.** a railway locomotive. **3.** *Mil.* any piece of equipment formerly used in warfare, such as a battering ram. **4.** any instrument or device. [C13: < OF, < L *ingenium* nature, talent, ingenious contrivance, < IN-[2] + *-genium*, rel. to *gignere* to beget, produce]

engine driver *n. Chiefly Brit.* a man who drives a railway locomotive; train driver.

engineer (,ɛndʒɪˈnɪə) *n.* **1.** a person trained in any branch of engineering. **2.** the originator or manager of a situation, system, etc. **3.** *U.S. & Canad.* the driver of a railway locomotive. **4.** an officer responsible for a ship's engines. **5.** a member of the armed forces trained in engineering and construction work. ~*vb.* (*tr.*) **6.** to originate, cause, or plan in a clever or devious manner. **7.** to design, plan, or construct as a professional engineer. [C14 *enginer*, < OF, < *engignier* to contrive, ult. < L *ingenium* skill, talent; see ENGINE]

engineering (,ɛndʒɪˈnɪərɪŋ) *n.* the profession of applying scientific principles to the design, construction, and maintenance of engines, cars, machines, etc. (**mechanical engineering**), buildings, bridges, roads, etc. (**civil engineering**), electrical machines and communication systems (**electrical engineering**), chemical plant and machinery (**chemical engineering**), or aircraft (**aeronautical engineering**).

English (ˈɪŋglɪʃ) *n.* **1.** the official language of Britain, the U.S., most of the Commonwealth, and certain other countries. **2. the English.** (*functioning as pl.*) the natives or inhabitants of England collectively. **3.** (*often not cap.*) the usual U.S. & Canad. term for **side** (in billiards). ~*adj.* **4.** of or relating to the English language. **5.** relating to or characteristic of England or the English. ~*vb.* (*tr.*) **6.** *Arch.* to translate or adapt into English. —ˈ**Englishness** *n.*

▷ **Usage.** The United Kingdom consists of England, Scotland, Wales, and Northern Ireland. Careful writers and speakers avoid the use of *England* to mean *Britain* or *English* to mean *British* as these usages are considered offensive by Scottish, Welsh, and Irish people.

English horn *n. Music.* another name for **cor anglais.**

Englishman (ˈɪŋglɪʃmən) *or* (*fem.*) **Englishwoman** *n., pl.* **-men** *or* **-women.** a native or inhabitant of England.

engorge (ɪnˈgɔːdʒ) *vb.* (*tr.*) **1.** *Pathol.* to congest with blood. **2.** to eat (food) greedily. **3.** to gorge (oneself); glut. —**enˈgorgement** *n.*

engr *abbrev. for:* **1.** engineer. **2.** engraver.

engr. *abbrev. for* engraved.

engraft *or* **ingraft** (ɪnˈgrɑːft) *vb.* (*tr.*) **1.** to graft (a shoot, bud, etc.) onto a stock. **2.** to incorporate in a firm or permanent way; implant. —,**engrafˈtation**, ,**ingrafˈtation** *or* **enˈgraftment, inˈgraftment** *n.*

engrain (ɪnˈgreɪn) *vb.* a variant spelling of **ingrain.**

engrave (ɪnˈgreɪv) *vb.* (*tr.*) **1.** to inscribe (a design, writing, etc.) onto (a block, plate, or other printing surface) by carving, etching, or other process. **2.** to print (designs or characters) from a plate so made. **3.** to fix deeply or permanently in the mind. [C16: < EN-[1] + GRAVE[3], on the model of F *engraver*] —**enˈgraver** *n.*

engraving (ɪnˈgreɪvɪŋ) *n.* **1.** the art of a person who engraves. **2.** a printing surface that has been engraved. **3.** a print made from this.

engross (ɪnˈgrəʊs) *vb.* (*tr.*) **1.** to occupy one's attention completely; absorb. **2.** to write or copy (manuscript) in large legible handwriting. **3.** *Law.* to write or type out formally (a document) preparatory to execution. [C14 (in the sense: to buy up wholesale); C15 (in the sense: to write in large letters): < L *grossus* thick, GROSS] —**enˈgrossed** *adj.* —**engrossedly** (ɪnˈgrəʊsɪdlɪ) *adv.* —**enˈgrossing** *adj.* —**enˈgrossment** *n.*

engulf *or* **ingulf** (ɪnˈgʌlf) *vb.* (*tr.*) **1.** to immerse, plunge, bury, or swallow up. **2.** (*often passive*) to overwhelm. —**enˈgulfment** *n.*

enhance (ɪnˈhɑːns) *vb.* (*tr.*) to intensify or increase in quality, value, power, etc.; improve; augment. [C14: < OF, < EN-[1] + *haucier* to raise, < Vulgar L *altiāre* (unattested), < L *altus* high] —**enˈhancement** *n.* —**enˈhancer** *n.*

enharmonic (ˌɛnhɑːˈmɒnɪk) *adj. Music.* **1.** denoting or relating to a small difference in pitch between two notes such as A flat and G sharp: not present in instruments of equal temperament such as the piano, but significant in the intonation of stringed and wind instruments. **2.** denoting or relating to enharmonic modulation. [C17: < L, < Gk, < EN-[2] + *harmonia;* see HARMONY] —ˌ**enharˈmonically** *adv.*

enigma (ɪˈnɪgmə) *n.* a person, thing, or situation that is mysterious, puzzling, or ambiguous. [C16: < L, < Gk, < *ainissesthai* to speak in riddles, < *ainos* fable, story] —**enigmatic** (ˌɛnɪgˈmætɪk) *or* ˌ**enigˈmatical** *adj.* —ˌ**enigˈmatically** *adv.*

enjambment *or* **enjambement** (ɪnˈdʒæmmənt) *n. Prosody.* the running over of a sentence from one line of verse into the next. [C19: < F, lit.: a straddling, < EN-[1] + *jambe* leg; see JAMB] —**enˈjambed** *adj.*

enjoin (ɪnˈdʒɔɪn) *vb.* (*tr.*) **1.** to order (someone) to do something. **2.** to impose or prescribe (a mode of behaviour, etc.). **3.** *Law.* to require (a person) to do or refrain from some act, esp. by an injunction. [C13: < OF *enjoindre,* < L *injungere* to fasten to, < IN-[2] + *jungere* to JOIN] —**enˈjoiner** *n.* —**enˈjoinment** *n.*

enjoy (ɪnˈdʒɔɪ) *vb.* (*tr.*) **1.** to receive pleasure from; take joy in. **2.** to have the benefit of; use. **3.** to have as a condition; experience. **4. enjoy oneself.** to have a good time. [C14: < OF, < EN-[1] + *joir* to find pleasure in, < L *gaudēre* to rejoice] —**enˈjoyable** *adj.* —**enˈjoyableness** *n.* —**enˈjoyably** *adv.* —**enˈjoyer** *n.*

enjoyment (ɪnˈdʒɔɪmənt) *n.* **1.** the act or condition of receiving pleasure from something. **2.** the use or possession of something that is satisfying. **3.** something that provides joy or satisfaction.

enkephalin (ɛnˈkɛfəlɪn) *or* **encephalin** (ɛnˈsɛfəlɪn) *n.* a chemical occurring in the brain, having effects similar to those of morphine.

enkindle (ɪnˈkɪndᵊl) *vb.* (*tr.*) **1.** to set on fire; kindle. **2.** to excite to activity or ardour; arouse.

enlace (ɪnˈleɪs) *vb.* (*tr.*) **1.** to bind or encircle with or as with laces. **2.** to entangle; intertwine. —**enˈlacement** *n.*

enlarge (ɪnˈlɑːdʒ) *vb.* **1.** to make or grow larger; increase or expand. **2.** (*tr.*) to make (a photographic print) of a larger size than the negative. **3.** (*intr.;* foll. by *on* or *upon*) to speak or write (about) in greater detail. —**enˈlargeable** *adj.* —**enˈlargement** *n.* —**enˈlarger** *n.*

enlighten (ɪnˈlaɪtᵊn) *vb.* (*tr.*) **1.** to give information or understanding to; instruct. **2.** to free from prejudice, superstition, etc. **3.** to give spiritual or religious revelation to. **4.** *Poetic.* to shed light on. —**enˈlightener** *n.* —**enˈlightening** *adj.*

enlightened (ɪnˈlaɪtᵊnd) *adj.* **1.** well-informed, tolerant, and guided by rational thought: *an enlightened administration.* **2.** privy to or claiming a spiritual revelation of truth.

enlightenment (ɪnˈlaɪtᵊnmənt) *n.* the act or means of enlightening or the state of being enlightened.

Enlightenment (ɪnˈlaɪtᵊnmənt) *n.* **the.** an 18th-century philosophical movement stressing the importance of reason.

enlist (ɪnˈlɪst) *vb.* **1.** to enter or persuade to enter the armed forces. **2.** (*tr.*) to engage or secure (a person or his support) for a venture, cause, etc. **3.** (*intr.;* foll. by *in*) to enter into or join an enterprise, cause, etc. —**enˈlister** *n.* —**enˈlistment** *n.*

enlisted man *n. U.S.* a serviceman who holds neither a commission nor a warrant.

enliven (ɪnˈlaɪvᵊn) *vb.* (*tr.*) **1.** to make active, vivacious, or spirited. **2.** to make cheerful or bright; gladden. —**enˈlivening** *adj.* —**enˈlivenment** *n.*

en masse (*French* ɑ̃ mas) *adv.* in a group or mass; as a whole; all together. [C19: < F]

enmesh, inmesh (ɪnˈmɛʃ), *or* **immesh** *vb.* (*tr.*) to catch or involve in or as if in a net or snare; entangle. —**enˈmeshment** *n.*

enmity (ˈɛnmɪtɪ) *n., pl.* **-ties.** a feeling of hostility or ill will, as between enemies. [C13: < OF; see ENEMY]

ennoble (ɪˈnəʊbᵊl) *vb.* (*tr.*) **1.** to make noble, honourable, or excellent; dignify; exalt. **2.** to raise to a noble rank. —**enˈnoblement** *n.* —**enˈnobler** *n.* —**enˈnobling** *adj.*

ennui (ˈɒnwiː) *n.* a feeling of listlessness and general dissatisfaction resulting from lack of activity or excitement. [C18: < F: apathy, < OF *enui* annoyance, vexation; see ANNOY]

enology (iːˈnɒlədʒɪ) *n.* the usual U.S. spelling of **oenology.**

enormity (ɪˈnɔːmɪtɪ) *n., pl.* **-ties. 1.** the quality or character of extreme wickedness. **2.** an act of great wickedness; atrocity. **3.** *Inf.* vastness of size or extent. [C15: < OF, < LL *ēnormitās* hugeness; see ENORMOUS]

▷ **Usage.** In careful usage, the noun *enormity* is not employed to convey the idea of great size.

enormous (ɪˈnɔːməs) *adj.* **1.** unusually large in size, extent, or degree; immense; vast. **2.** *Arch.* extremely wicked; heinous. [C16: < L, < *ē-* out of, away from + *norma* rule, pattern] —**eˈnormously** *adv.* —**eˈnormousness** *n.*

enosis (ˈɛnəʊsɪs) *n.* the union of Greece and Cyprus: the aim of a group of Greek Cypriots. [C20: Mod. Gk: < Gk *henoun* to unite, < *heis* one]

enough (ɪˈnʌf) *determiner.* **1. a.** sufficient to answer a need, demand or supposition. **b.** (*as pron.*): *enough is now known.* **2. that's enough!** that will do: used to put an end to an action, speech, performance, etc. ~*adv.* **3.** so as to be sufficient; as much as necessary. **4.** (*not used with a negative*) very or quite; rather. **5.** (intensifier): *oddly enough.* **6.** just adequately; tolerably. [OE *genōh*]

enow (ɪˈnaʊ) *adj., adv.* an archaic word for **enough.**

en passant (ɒn pæˈsɑːnt) *adv.* in passing: in chess, said of capturing a pawn that has made an initial move of two squares. The capture is made as if the captured pawn had moved one square instead of two. [C17: < F]

enquire (ɪnˈkwaɪə) *vb.* a variant of **inquire.** —**enˈquirer** *n.* —**enˈquiry** *n.*

enrage (ɪnˈreɪdʒ) *vb.* (*tr.*) to provoke to fury; put into a rage. —**enˈraged** *adj.* —**enˈragement** *n.*

en rapport *French.* (ɑ̃ rapɔr) *adj.* (*postpositive*), *adv.* in sympathy, harmony, or accord.

enrapture (ɪnˈræptʃə) *vb.* (*tr.*) to fill with delight; enchant.

enrich (ɪnˈrɪtʃ) *vb.* (*tr.*) **1.** to increase the wealth of. **2.** to endow with fine or desirable qualities. **3.** to make more beautiful; adorn; decorate. **4.** to improve in quality, colour, flavour, etc. **5.** to increase the food value of by adding nutrients. **6.** to fertilize (soil). **7.** *Physics.* to increase the concentration or abundance of one component or isotope in (a solution or mixture). —**enˈriched** *adj.* —**enˈrichment** *n.*

enrol *or U.S.* **enroll** (ɪnˈrəʊl) *vb.* **-rolling, -rolled.** (*mainly tr.*) **1.** to record or note in a roll or list. **2.** (*also intr.*) to become or cause to become a member; enlist; register. **3.** to put on record. —ˌ**enrolˈlee** *n.* —**enˈroller** *n.*

enrolment *or U.S.* **enrollment** (ɪnˈrəʊlmənt) *n.* **1.** the act of enrolling or state of being enrolled. **2.** a list of people enrolled. **3.** the total number of people enrolled.

en route (ɒn ˈruːt) *adv.* on or along the way. [C18: < F]

Ens. *abbrev. for* Ensign.

ENSA (ˈɛnsə) *n. acronym for* Entertainments National Service Association.

ensconce (ɪnˈskɒns) *vb.* (*tr.; often passive*) **1.** to establish or settle firmly or comfortably. **2.** to place in safety; hide. [C16: see EN-[1], SCONCE[2]]

ensemble (ɒnˈsɒmbᵊl) *n.* **1.** all the parts of something considered together. **2.** a person's complete costume; outfit. **3.** the cast of a play other than the principals. **4.** *Music.* a group of soloists singing or playing together. **5.** *Music.* the degree of precision and unity exhibited by a group of instrumentalists or singers performing together. 6. the general effect of something made up of individual parts. ~*adv.* 7. all together or at once. [C15: < F: together, < L, < IN-² + *simul* at the same time]

enshrine *or* **inshrine** (ɪnˈʃraɪn) *vb.* (*tr.*) 1. to place or enclose as in a shrine. 2. to hold as sacred; cherish; treasure. —**enˈshrinement** *n.*

enshroud (ɪnˈʃraʊd) *vb.* (*tr.*) to cover or hide as with a shroud.

ensign (ˈɛnsaɪn) *n.* 1. (*also* ˈɛnsən). a flag flown by a ship, branch of the armed forces, etc., to indicate nationality, allegiance, etc. See also **Red Ensign, White Ensign.** 2. any flag, standard, or banner. 3. a standard-bearer. 4. a symbol, token, or emblem; sign. 5. (in the U.S. Navy) a commissioned officer of the lowest rank. 6. (in the British infantry) a colours bearer. 7. (formerly in the British infantry) a commissioned officer of the lowest rank. [C14: < OF *enseigne*, < L INSIGNIA] —**ˈensignˌship** *or* **ˈensigncy** *n.*

ensilage (ˈɛnsɪlɪdʒ) *n.* 1. the process of ensiling green fodder. 2. a less common name for **silage.**

ensile (ɛnˈsaɪl, ˈɛnsaɪl) *vb.* (*tr.*) 1. to store and preserve (green fodder) in a silo. 2. to turn (green fodder) into silage by causing it to ferment in a silo. [C19: < F, < Sp., < EN-¹ + *silo* SILO]

enslave (ɪnˈsleɪv) *vb.* (*tr.*) to make a slave of; subjugate. —**enˈslavement** *n.* —**enˈslaver** *n.*

ensnare *or* **insnare** (ɪnˈsnɛə) *vb.* (*tr.*) to catch or trap as in a snare. —**enˈsnarement** *n.* —**enˈsnarer** *n.*

ensue (ɪnˈsjuː) *vb.* **-suing, -sued.** 1. (*intr.*) to come next or afterwards. 2. (*intr.*) to occur as a consequence; result. 3. (*tr.*) *Obs.* to pursue. [C14: < Anglo-F, < OF, < EN-¹ + *suivre* to follow, < L *sequī*] —**enˈsuing** *adj.*

en suite *French.* (ɑ̃ sɥit) *adv.* forming a unit: *a room with bathroom en suite.* [lit.: in sequence]

ensure (ɛnˈʃʊə, -ˈʃɔː) *or esp. U.S.* **insure** *vb.* (*tr.*) 1. (*may take a clause as object*) to make certain or sure; guarantee. 2. to make safe or secure; protect. —**enˈsurer** *n.*

ENT *Med. abbrev. for* ear, nose, and throat.

-ent *suffix forming adjectives and nouns.* causing or performing an action or existing in a certain condition; the agent that performs an action: *astringent; dependent.* [< L *-ent-, -ens*, present participial ending]

entablature (ɛnˈtæblətʃə) *n. Archit.* 1. the part of a classical temple above the columns, having an architrave, a frieze, and a cornice. 2. any similar construction. [C17: < F, < It. *intavolatura* something put on a table, hence, something laid flat, < *tavola* table, < L *tabula* TABLE]

entablement (ɪnˈteɪbᵊlmənt) *n.* the platform of a pedestal, above the dado, that supports a statue. [C17: < OF]

entail (ɪnˈteɪl) *vb.* (*tr.*) 1. to bring about or impose inevitably: *this task entails careful thought.* 2. *Property law.* to restrict (the descent of an estate) to designated heirs. 3. *Logic.* to have as a necessary consequence. ~*n.* 4. *Property law.* a. such a limitation. b. an entailed estate. [C14 *entaillen*, < EN-¹ + *taille* limitation, TAIL²] —**enˈtailer** *n.* —**enˈtailment** *n.*

entamoeba (ˌɛntəˈmiːbə), **endamoeba** *or U.S.* **entameba, endameba** *n., pl.* **-bae** (-biː) *or* **-bas.** any parasitic amoeba of the genus *Entamoeba* (or *Endamoeba*) which lives in the intestines of man and causes amoebic dysentery.

entangle (ɪnˈtæŋgᵊl) *vb.* (*tr.*) 1. to catch or involve in or as if in a tangle; ensnare or enmesh. 2. to make tangled or twisted; snarl. 3. to make complicated; confuse. 4. to involve in difficulties. —**enˈtanglement** *n.* —**enˈtangler** *n.*

entasis (ˈɛntəsɪs) *n., pl.* **-ses** (-siːz). a slightly convex curve given to the shaft of a column, or similar structure, to correct the illusion of concavity produced by a straight shaft. [C18: < Gk, < *enteinein* to stretch tight, < *teinein* to stretch]

entellus (ɛnˈtɛləs) *n.* an Old World monkey of S Asia. [C19: NL, apparently after a character in Virgil's *Aeneid*]

entente (*French* ɑ̃tɑ̃t) *n.* 1. short for **entente cordiale.** 2. the parties to an entente cordiale collectively. [C19: F: understanding]

entente cordiale (*French* ɑ̃tɑ̃t kɔrdjal) *n.* 1. a friendly understanding between political powers. 2. (*often caps.*) the understanding reached by France and Britain in April 1904, over colonial disputes. [C19: F: cordial understanding]

enter (ˈɛntə) *vb.* 1. to come or go into (a place, house, etc.). 2. to penetrate or pierce. 3. (*tr.*) to introduce or insert. 4. to join (a party, organization, etc.). 5. (when *intr.*, foll. by *into*) to become involved or take part (in). 6. (*tr.*) to record (an item) in a journal, account, etc. 7. (*tr.*) to record (a name, etc.) on a list. 8. (*tr.*) to present or submit: *to enter a proposal.* 9. (*intr.*) *Theatre.* to come on stage: used as a stage direction: *enter Juliet.* 10. (when *intr.*, often foll. by *into, on,* or *upon*) to begin; start: *to enter upon a new career.* 11. (*intr.;* often foll. by *upon*) to come into possession (of). 12. (*tr.*) to place (evidence, etc.) before a court of law. [C13: < OF, < L *intrāre*, < *intrā* within] —**ˈenterable** *adj.* —**ˈenterer** *n.*

enteric (ɛnˈtɛrɪk) *or* **enteral** (ˈɛntərəl) *adj.* intestinal. [C19: < Gk, < *enteron* intestine]

enter into *vb.* (*intr., prep.*) 1. to be considered as a necessary part of (one's plans, calculations, etc.). 2. to be in sympathy with.

enteritis (ˌɛntəˈraɪtɪs) *n.* inflammation of the intestine.

entero- *or before a vowel* **enter-** *combining form.* indicating an intestine: *enterovirus; enteritis.* [< NL, < Gk *enteron* intestine]

enterprise (ˈɛntəˌpraɪz) *n.* 1. a project or undertaking, esp. one that requires boldness or effort. 2. participation in such projects. 3. readiness to embark on new ventures; boldness and energy. 4. a company or firm. [C15: < OF *entreprise* (n.), < *entreprendre* < *entre-* between (< L: INTER-) + *prendre* to take, < L *prehendere* to grasp] —**ˈenterˌpriser** *n.*

enterprising (ˈɛntəˌpraɪzɪŋ) *adj.* ready to embark on new ventures; full of boldness and initiative. —**ˈenterˌprisingly** *adv.*

entertain (ˌɛntəˈteɪn) *vb.* 1. to provide amusement for (a person or audience). 2. to show hospitality to (guests). 3. (*tr.*) to hold in the mind. [C15: < OF, < *entre-* mutually + *tenir* to hold]

entertainer (ˌɛntəˈteɪnə) *n.* 1. a professional performer in public entertainments. 2. any person who entertains.

entertaining (ˌɛntəˈteɪnɪŋ) *adj.* serving to entertain or give pleasure; diverting; amusing.

entertainment (ˌɛntəˈteɪnmənt) *n.* 1. the act or art of entertaining or state of being entertained. 2. an act, production, etc., that entertains; diversion; amusement.

enthral *or U.S.* **enthrall** (ɪnˈθrɔːl) *vb.* **-thralling, -thralled.** (*tr.*) 1. to hold spellbound; enchant; captivate. 2. *Obs.* to hold as thrall; enslave. —**enˈthraller** *n.* —**enˈthralling** *adj.* —**enˈthralment** *or U.S.* **enˈthrallment** *n.*

enthrone (ɛnˈθrəʊn) *vb.* (*tr.*) 1. to place on a throne. 2. to honour or exalt. 3. to assign authority to. —**enˈthronement** *n.*

enthuse (ɪnˈθjuːz) *vb.* to feel or show or cause to feel or show enthusiasm.

enthusiasm (ɪnˈθjuːzɪˌæzəm) *n.* 1. ardent and lively interest or eagerness. 2. an object of keen interest. 3. *Arch.* extravagant religious fervour. [C17: < LL, < Gk, < *enthousiazein* to be possessed by a god, < EN-² + *theos* god]

enthusiast (ɪnˈθjuːzɪˌæst) *n.* 1. a person motivated by enthusiasm; fanatic. 2. *Arch.* one whose zeal for religion is extravagant. —**enˌthusiˈastic** *adj.* —**enˌthusiˈastically** *adv.*

enthymeme (ˈɛnθɪˌmiːm) *n. Logic.* a syllogism in which one or more premises are unexpressed. [C16: via L < Gk *enthumeisthai* to infer, < EN-² + *thumos* mind]

entice (ɪnˈtaɪs) *vb.* (*tr.*) to attract by exciting hope or desire; tempt; allure. [C13: < OF, < Vulgar L *intitiāre* (unattested) to incite] —**enˈticement** *n.* —**enˈticer** *n.* —**enˈticing** *adj.* —**enˈticingly** *adv.*

entire (ɪnˈtaɪə) *adj.* 1. (*prenominal*) whole;

complete. **2.** (*prenominal*) without reservation or exception. **3.** not broken or damaged. **4.** undivided; continuous. **5.** (of leaves, petals, etc.) having a smooth margin not broken up into teeth or lobes. **6.** not castrated: *an entire horse.* **7.** *Obs.* unmixed; pure. ~*n.* **8.** an uncastrated horse. [C14: < OF, < L *integer* whole, < IN-[1] + *tangere* to touch] —**en'tireness** *n.*

entirely (ɪn'taɪəlɪ) *adv.* **1.** wholly; completely. **2.** solely or exclusively.

entirety (ɪn'taɪərɪtɪ) *n., pl.* **-ties.** **1.** the state of being entire or whole; completeness. **2.** a thing, sum, amount, etc., that is entire; whole; total.

entitle (ɪn'taɪt'l) *vb.* (*tr.*) **1.** to give (a person) the right to do or have something; qualify; allow. **2.** to give a name or title to. **3.** to confer a title of rank or honour upon. [C14: < OF *entituler,* < LL, < L *titulus* TITLE] —**en'titlement** *n.*

entity ('ɛntɪtɪ) *n., pl.* **-ties.** **1.** something having real or distinct existence. **2.** existence or being. [C16: < Med. L, < *ēns* being, < L *esse* to be] —**entitative** ('ɛntɪtətɪv) *adj.*

ento- *combining form.* inside; within: *entoderm.* [NL, < Gk *entos* within]

entomb (ɪn'tuːm) *vb.* (*tr.*) **1.** to place in or as if in a tomb; bury; inter. **2.** to serve as a tomb for. —**en'tombment** *n.*

entomo- *combining form.* indicating an insect: *entomology.* [< Gk *entomon* insect]

entomol. *or* **entom.** *abbrev. for* entomology.

entomology (ˌɛntə'mɒlədʒɪ) *n.* the branch of science concerned with the study of insects. —**entomological** (ˌɛntəmə'lɒdʒɪk'l) *or* ˌ**entomo'logic** *adj.* —ˌ**ento'mologist** *n.*

entophyte ('ɛntəʊˌfaɪt) *n. Bot.* a variant spelling of **endophyte.** —**entophytic** (ˌɛntəʊ'fɪtɪk) *adj.*

entourage (ɒntʊ'rɑːʒ) *n.* **1.** a group of attendants or retainers; retinue. **2.** surroundings. [C19: < F, < *entourer* to surround, < *tour* circuit; see TOUR, TURN]

entr'acte (ɒn'trækt) *n.* **1.** an interval between two acts of a play or opera. **2.** (esp. formerly) an entertainment during such an interval. [C19: F, lit.: between-act]

entrails ('ɛntreɪlz) *pl. n.* **1.** the internal organs of a person or animal; intestines; guts. **2.** the innermost parts of anything. [C13: < OF, < Med. L *intrālia,* changed < L *interānea* intestines]

entrain (ɪn'treɪn) *vb.* to board or put aboard a train. —**en'trainment** *n.*

entrance[1] ('ɛntrəns) *n.* **1.** the act or an instance of entering; entry. **2.** a place for entering, such as a door. **3. a.** the power, liberty, or right of entering. **b.** (*as modifier*): *an entrance fee.* **4.** the coming of an actor or other performer onto a stage. [C16: < F, < *entrer* to ENTER]

entrance[2] (ɪn'trɑːns) *vb.* (*tr.*) **1.** to fill with wonder and delight; enchant. **2.** to put into a trance; hypnotize. —**en'trancement** *n.* —**en'trancing** *adj.*

entrant ('ɛntrənt) *n.* a person who enters. [C17: < F, lit.: entering, < *entrer* to ENTER]

entrap (ɪn'træp) *vb.* **-trapping, -trapped.** (*tr.*) **1.** to catch or snare as in a trap. **2.** to trick into danger, difficulty, or embarrassment. —**en'trapment** *n.* —**en'trapper** *n.*

entreat *or* **intreat** (ɪn'triːt) *vb.* **1.** to ask (a person) earnestly; beg or plead with; implore. **2.** to make an earnest request or petition for (something). **3.** an archaic word for **treat** (sense 4). [C15: < OF, < EN-[1] + *traiter* to TREAT] —**en'treatment** *or* **in'treatment** *n.*

entreaty (ɪn'triːtɪ) *n., pl.* **-treaties.** an earnest request or petition; supplication; plea.

entrechat (*French* ɑ̃trəʃa) *n.* a leap in ballet during which the dancer repeatedly crosses his feet or beats them together. [C18: < F *entrechase,* changed by folk etymology < It. (*capriola*) *intrecciata,* lit.: entwined (caper)]

entrecôte (*French* ɑ̃trəkot) *n.* a beefsteak cut from between the ribs. [F, < *entre-* INTER- + *côte* rib, < L *costa*]

entrée ('ɒntreɪ) *n.* **1.** a dish served before a main course. **2.** *Chiefly U.S.* the main course of a meal. **3.** the power or right of entry. [C18: < F, < *entrer* to ENTER; in cookery, so called because formerly the course was served after an intermediate course called the *relevé* (remove)]

entremets (*French* ɑ̃trəmɛ) *n., pl.* **-mets** (*French* -mɛ). **1.** a dessert. **2.** a light dish formerly served between the main course and the dessert. [C18: < F, < OF, < *entre-* between + *mes* dish]

entrench *or* **intrench** (ɪn'trɛntʃ) *vb.* **1.** (*tr.*) to construct a defensive position by digging trenches around it. **2.** (*tr.*) to fix or establish firmly. **3.** (*intr.;* foll. by *on* or *upon*) to trespass or encroach. —**en'trenched** *or* **in'trenched** *adj.* —**en'trenchment** *or* **in'trenchment** *n.*

entrepôt (*French* ɑ̃trəpo) *n.* **1.** a warehouse for commercial goods. **2.** a trading centre or port at which goods are imported and re-exported without incurring duty. [C18: F, < *entreposer,* < *entre* between + *poser* to place; formed on the model of DEPOT]

entrepreneur (ˌɒntrəprə'nɜː) *n.* **1.** the owner or manager of a business enterprise who, by risk and initiative, attempts to make profits. **2.** a middleman or commercial intermediary. [C19: < F, < *entreprendre* to undertake; see ENTERPRISE] —ˌ**entrepre'neurial** *adj.* —ˌ**entrepre'neurship** *n.*

entropy ('ɛntrəpɪ) *n., pl.* **-pies.** **1.** a thermodynamic quantity that changes in a reversible process by an amount equal to the heat absorbed or emitted divided by the thermodynamic temperature. It is measured in joules per kelvin. **2.** lack of pattern or organization; disorder. [C19: < EN-[2] + -TROPE]

entrust *or* **intrust** (ɪn'trʌst) *vb.* (*tr.*) **1.** (usually foll. by *with*) to invest or charge (with a duty, responsibility, etc.). **2.** (often foll. by *to*) to put into the care or protection of someone. —**en'trustment** *or* **in'trustment** *n.*

entry ('ɛntrɪ) *n., pl.* **-tries.** **1.** the act or an instance of entering; entrance. **2.** a point or place for entering, such as a door, etc. **3. a.** the right or liberty of entering. **b.** (*as modifier*): *an entry permit.* **4.** the act of recording an item in a journal, account, etc. **5.** an item recorded, as in a diary, dictionary, or account. **6.** a person, horse, car, etc., entering a competition or contest. **7.** the competitors entering a contest considered collectively. **8.** the action of an actor in going on stage. **9.** *Property law.* the act of going upon land with the intention of asserting the right to possession. **10.** any point in a piece of music at which a performer commences or resumes singing or playing. **11.** *Bridge, etc.* a card that enables one to transfer the lead from one's own hand to that of one's partner or to the dummy hand. **12.** *Dialect.* a passage between the backs of two rows of houses. [C13: < OF *entree,* p.p. of *entrer* to ENTER]

entryism ('ɛntrɪɪzəm) *n.* the policy or practice of joining an existing political party with the intention of changing it instead of forming a new party. —'**entryist** *n., adj.*

entwine *or* **intwine** (ɪn'twaɪn) *vb.* (of two or more things) to twine together or (of one or more things) to twine around (something else). —**en'twinement** *or* **in'twinement** *n.*

E number *n.* any of a series of numbers with the prefix E indicating a specific food additive recognized by the European Economic Community.

enumerate (ɪ'njuːməˌreɪt) *vb.* (*tr.*) **1.** to name one by one; list. **2.** to determine the number of; count. [C17: < L, < *numerāre* to count, reckon; see NUMBER] —**e'numerable** *adj.* —**eˌnumer'ation** *n.* —**e'numerative** *adj.*

enumerator (ɪ'njuːməˌreɪtə) *n.* **1.** a person or thing that enumerates. **2.** *Brit.* a person who issues and retrieves census forms.

enunciable (ɪ'nʌnsɪəb'l) *adj.* capable of being enunciated.

enunciate (ɪ'nʌnsɪˌeɪt) *vb.* **1.** to articulate or pronounce (words), esp. clearly and distinctly. **2.** (*tr.*) to state precisely or formally. [C17: < L *ēnuntiāre* to declare, < *nuntiāre* to announce] —**eˌnunci'ation** *n.* —**e'nunciative** *or* **e'nunciatory** *adj.* —**e'nunciˌator** *n.*

enuresis (ˌɛnjʊˈriːsɪs) *n.* involuntary discharge of urine, esp. during sleep. [C19: < NL, < Gk EN-[2] + *ouron* urine] —**enuretic** (ˌɛnjʊˈrɛtɪk) *adj.*

envelop (ɪnˈvɛləp) *vb.* (*tr.*) **1.** to wrap or enclose as in a covering. **2.** to conceal or obscure. **3.** to surround (an enemy force). [C14: < OF *envoluper,* < EN-[1] + *voluper, voloper,* <?] —**enˈvelopment** *n.*

envelope (ˈɛnvəˌləʊp, ˈɒn-) *n.* **1.** a flat covering of paper, usually rectangular and with a flap that can be sealed, used to enclose a letter, etc. **2.** any covering or wrapper. **3.** *Biol.* any enclosing structure, such as a membrane, shell, or skin. **4.** the bag enclosing gas in a balloon. **5.** *Maths.* a curve or surface that is tangential to each one of a group of curves or surfaces. [C18: < F, < *envelopper* to wrap around; see ENVELOP]

envenom (ɪnˈvɛnəm) *vb.* (*tr.*) **1.** to fill or impregnate with venom; make poisonous. **2.** to fill with bitterness or malice.

enviable (ˈɛnvɪəbᵊl) *adj.* exciting envy; fortunate or privileged. —ˈ**enviableness** *n.*

envious (ˈɛnvɪəs) *adj.* feeling, showing, or resulting from envy. [C13: < Anglo-Norman, ult. < L *invidiōsus* full of envy, INVIDIOUS; see ENVY] —ˈ**enviously** *adv.* —ˈ**enviousness** *n.*

environ (ɪnˈvaɪrən) *vb.* (*tr.*) to encircle or surround. [C14: < OF *environner* to surround, < EN-[1] + *viron* a circle, < *virer* to turn, VEER]

environment (ɪnˈvaɪrənmənt) *n.* **1.** external conditions or surroundings. **2.** *Ecology.* the external surroundings in which a plant or animal lives, which influence its development and behaviour. **3.** the state of being environed. —**enˌvironˈmental** *adj.*

environmentalist (ɪnˌvaɪrənˈmɛntəlɪst) *n.* **1.** a specialist in the maintenance of ecological balance and the conservation of the environment. **2.** a person concerned with issues that affect the environment, such as pollution.

environs (ɪnˈvaɪrənz) *pl. n.* a surrounding area or region, esp. the suburbs or outskirts of a city.

envisage (ɪnˈvɪzɪdʒ) *vb.* (*tr.*) **1.** to form a mental image of; visualize. **2.** to conceive of as a possibility in the future. **3.** *Arch.* to look in the face of. [C19: < F, < EN-[1] + *visage* face, VISAGE] —**enˈvisagement** *n.*

▷ **Usage.** In careful English, *envisage* is usually used with a direct object rather than a clause to refer to conceptions of future possibilities: *he envisaged great success for his project.*

envision (ɪnˈvɪʒən) *vb.* (*tr.*) to conceive of as a possibility, esp. in the future; foresee.

envoy[1] (ˈɛnvɔɪ) *n.* **1.** a diplomat ranking between an ambassador and a minister resident. **2.** an accredited agent or representative. [C17: < F, < *envoyer* to send, < Vulgar L *inviāre* (unattested) to send on a journey, < IN-[2] + *via* road] —ˈ**envoyship** *n.*

envoy[2] *or* **envoi** (ˈɛnvɔɪ) *n.* **1.** a brief concluding stanza, notably in ballades. **2.** a postscript in other forms of verse or prose. [C14: < OF, < *envoyer* to send; see ENVOY[1]]

envy (ˈɛnvɪ) *n., pl.* **-vies. 1.** a feeling of grudging or somewhat admiring discontent aroused by the possessions, achievements, or qualities of another. **2.** the desire to have something possessed by another; covetousness. **3.** an object of envy. ~*vb.* **-vying, -vied. 4.** to be envious of (a person or thing). [C13: via OF < L *invidia,* < *invidēre* to eye maliciously, < IN-[2] + *vidēre* to see] —ˈ**envier** *n.* —ˈ**envyingly** *adv.*

enwrap *or* **inwrap** (ɪnˈræp) *vb.* **-wrapping, -wrapped.** (*tr.*) **1.** to wrap or cover up; envelop. **2.** (*usually passive*) to engross or absorb.

enwreath (ɪnˈriːð) *vb.* (*tr.*) to surround or encircle with or as with a wreath or wreaths.

enzootic (ˌɛnzəʊˈɒtɪk) *adj.* **1.** (of diseases) affecting animals within a limited region. ~*n.* **2.** an enzootic disease. [C19: < EN-[2] + Gk *zōion* animal + -OTIC] —ˌ**enzoˈotically** *adv.*

enzyme (ˈɛnzaɪm) *n.* any of a group of complex proteins produced by living cells, that act as catalysts in specific biochemical reactions. [C19: < Med. Gk *enzumos* leavened, < Gk EN-[2] + *zumē* leaven] —**enzymatic** (ˌɛnzaɪˈmætɪk, -zɪ-) *or* **enzymic** (ɛnˈzaɪmɪk, -ˈzɪm-) *adj.*

eo- *combining form.* early or primeval: *Eocene; eohippus.* [< Gk, < *ēōs* dawn]

EOC *abbrev. for* Equal Opportunities Commission.

Eocene (ˈiːəʊˌsiːn) *adj.* **1.** of or denoting the second epoch of the Tertiary period, during which hooved mammals appeared. ~*n.* **2. the.** the Eocene epoch or rock series. [C19: < EO- + -CENE]

eohippus (ˌiːəʊˈhɪpəs) *n., pl.* **-puses.** the earliest horse: an extinct Eocene dog-sized animal. [C19: NL, < EO- + Gk *hippos* horse]

Eolithic (ˌiːəʊˈlɪθɪk) *adj.* denoting or relating to the early part of the Stone Age, characterized by the use of crude stone tools (**eoliths**).

eon (ˈiːən, ˈiːɒn) *n.* the usual U.S. spelling of **aeon.**

eosin (ˈiːəʊsɪn) *or* **eosine** (ˈiːəʊsɪn, -ˌsiːn) *n.* **1.** a red fluorescent crystalline water-insoluble compound. Its soluble salts are used as dyes. **2.** any of several similar dyes. [C19: < Gk *ēōs* dawn + -IN; referring to colour it gives to silk] —ˌ**eoˈsinic** *adj.*

-eous *suffix forming adjectives.* relating to or having the nature of: *gaseous.* [< L *-eus*]

EP *n.* **1.** Also called: **maxisingle.** an extended-play gramophone record, usually 7 inches (18 cm) in diameter: a longer recording than a single. ~*adj.* **2.** denoting such a record.

epact (ˈiːpækt) *n.* **1.** the difference in time, about 11 days, between the solar year and the lunar year. **2.** the number of days between the beginning of the calendar year and the new moon immediately preceding this. [C16: via LL < Gk *epaktē,* < *epagein* to bring in, intercalate]

eparch (ˈɛpɑːk) *n.* **1.** a bishop or metropolitan in the Orthodox Church. **2.** a governor of a subdivision of a province of modern Greece. [C17: < Gk *eparkhos,* < *epi-* over, on + -ARCH] —ˈ**eparchy** *n.*

epaulette *or U.S.* **epaulet** (ˈɛpəˌlɛt, -lɪt) *n.* a piece of ornamental material on the shoulder of a garment, esp. a military uniform. [C18: < F, < *épaule* shoulder, < L *spatula* shoulder blade]

épée (ˈɛpeɪ) *n.* a sword similar to the foil but with a heavier blade. [C19: < F: sword, < L *spatha,* < Gk *spathē* blade; see SPADE[1]] —ˈ**épéeist** *n.*

epeirogeny (ˌɛpaɪˈrɒdʒɪnɪ) *or* **epeirogenesis** (ɪˌpaɪrəʊˈdʒɛnɪsɪs) *n.* the formation of continents by relatively slow displacements of the earth's crust. [C19: < Gk *ēpeiros* continent + -GENY] —**epeirogenic** (ɪˌpaɪrəʊˈdʒɛnɪk) *or* **epeirogenetic** (ɪˌpaɪrəʊdʒɪˈnɛtɪk) *adj.*

epergne (ɪˈpɜːn) *n.* an ornamental centrepiece for a table, holding fruit, flowers, etc. [C18: prob. < F *épargne* a saving, < *épargner* to economize, of Gmc origin]

epexegesis (ɛˌpɛksɪˈdʒiːsɪs) *n., pl.* **-ses** (-ˌsiːz). *Rhetoric.* **1.** the addition of a phrase, clause, or sentence to a text to provide further explanation. **2.** the phrase, clause, or sentence added for this purpose. [C17: < Gk; see EPI-, EXEGESIS] —**epexegetic** (ɛˌpɛksɪˈdʒɛtɪk) *or* **epˌexeˈgetical** *adj.*

Eph. *or* **Ephes.** *Bible. abbrev. for* Ephesians.

ephah *or* **epha** (ˈiːfə) *n.* a Hebrew unit of measure equal to approximately one bushel or about 33 litres. [C16: < Heb., < Egyptian]

ephedrine *or* **ephedrin** (ɪˈfɛdrɪn, ˈɛfɪˌdriːn, -drɪn) *n.* a white crystalline alkaloid used for the treatment of asthma and hay fever. [C19: < NL < L < Gk, < EPI- + *hedra* seat + -INE[2]]

ephemera (ɪˈfɛmərə) *n., pl.* **-eras** *or* **-erae** (-əˌriː). **1.** a mayfly, esp. one of the genus *Ephemera.* **2.** something transitory or short-lived. **3.** (*functioning as pl.*) collectable items not originally intended to be long-lasting, such as tickets, posters, etc. **4.** a plural of **ephemeron.** [C16: see EPHEMERAL]

ephemeral (ɪˈfɛmərəl) *adj.* **1.** transitory; short-lived: *ephemeral pleasure.* ~*n.* **2.** a short-lived organism, such as the mayfly. [C16: < Gk *ephēmeros* lasting only a day, < *hēmera* day] —**eˌphemerˈality** *or* **eˈphemeralness** *n.*

ephemerid (ɪˈfɛmərɪd) *n.* any insect of the order *Ephemeroptera* (or *Ephemerida*), which comprises the mayflies. Also: **ephemeropteran.** [C19: < NL, < Gk *ephēmeros* short-lived + -ID[1]]

ephemeris (ɪˈfɛmərɪs) *n., pl.* **ephemerides** (ˌɛfɪˈmɛrɪˌdiːz). a table giving the future positions of a planet, comet, or satellite during a specified period. [C16: < L, < Gk: diary, journal; see EPHEMERAL]

ephemeron (ɪˈfɛməˌrɒn) *n., pl.* **-era** (-ərə) *or* **-erons.** (*usually pl.*). something transitory or short-lived. [C16: see EPHEMERAL]

ephod (ˈiːfɒd) *n. Bible.* an embroidered vestment worn by priests in ancient Israel. [C14: < Heb.]

ephor (ˈɛfɔː) *n., pl.* **-ors** *or* **-ori** (-əˌraɪ) (in ancient Greece) a senior magistrate, esp. one of the five Spartan ephors, who wielded effective power. [C16: < Gk, < *ephoran* to supervise, < EPI- + *horan* to look] —ˈ**ephoral** *adj.* —ˈ**ephorate** *n.*

epi-, eph-, *or before a vowel* **ep-** *prefix.* **1.** upon; above; over: *epidermis; epicentre.* **2.** in addition to: *epiphenomenon.* **3.** after: *epilogue.* **4.** near; close to: *epicalyx.* [< Gk, < *epi* (prep.)]

epic (ˈɛpɪk) *n.* **1.** a long narrative poem recounting in elevated style the deeds of a legendary hero. **2.** the genre of epic poetry. **3.** any work of literature, film, etc., having qualities associated with the epic. **4.** an episode in the lives of men in which heroic deeds are performed. *~adj.* **5.** denoting, relating to, or characteristic of an epic or epics. **6.** of heroic or impressive proportions. [C16: < L, < Gk *epikos*, < *epos* speech, word, song]

epicalyx (ˌɛpɪˈkeɪlɪks, -ˈkæl-) *n., pl.* **-lyxes** *or* **-lyces** (-lɪˌsiːz). *Bot.* a series of small sepal-like bracts forming an outer calyx beneath the true calyx in some flowers.

epicanthus (ˌɛpɪˈkænθəs) *n., pl.* **-thi** (-θaɪ). a fold of skin extending vertically over the inner angle of the eye: characteristic of Mongolian peoples. [C19: NL, < EPI- + L *canthus* corner of the eye, < Gk *kanthos*] —ˌ**epiˈcanthic** *adj.*

epicardium (ˌɛpɪˈkɑːdɪəm) *n., pl.* **-dia** (-dɪə). *Anat.* the innermost layer of the pericardium. [C19: NL, < EPI- + Gk *kardia* heart] —ˌ**epiˈcardiac** *or* ˌ**epiˈcardial** *adj.*

epicarp (ˈɛpɪˌkɑːp) *or* **exocarp** *n.* the outermost layer of the pericarp of fruits. [C19: < F, < EPI- + Gk *karpos* fruit]

epicene (ˈɛpɪˌsiːn) *adj.* **1.** having the characteristics of both sexes. **2.** of neither sex; sexless. **3.** effeminate. **4.** *Grammar.* **a.** denoting a noun that may refer to a male or a female. **b.** (in Latin, Greek, etc.) denoting a noun that retains the same gender regardless of the sex of the referent. [C15: < L *epicoenus* of both genders, < Gk *epikoinos* common to many, < *koinos* common] —ˌ**epiˈcenism** *n.*

epicentre *or U.S.* **epicenter** (ˈɛpɪˌsɛntə) *n.* the point on the earth's surface immediately above the origin of an earthquake. [C19: < NL, < Gk *epikentros* over the centre, < EPI- + CENTRE] —ˌ**epiˈcentral** *adj.*

epicure (ˈɛpɪˌkjʊə) *n.* **1.** a person who cultivates a discriminating palate for good food and drink. **2.** a person devoted to sensual pleasures. [C16: < Med. L *epicūrus*, after *Epicurus*; see EPICUREAN] —ˈ**epicurˌism** *n.*

epicurean (ˌɛpɪkjʊˈriːən) *adj.* **1.** devoted to sensual pleasures, esp. food and drink. **2.** suitable for an epicure. *~n.* **3.** an epicure; gourmet. —ˌ**epicuˈreanism** *n.*

Epicurean (ˌɛpɪkjʊˈriːən) *adj.* **1.** of or relating to the philosophy of Epicurus (341–270 B.C.), Greek philosopher, who held that the highest good is pleasure or freedom from pain. *~n.* **2.** a follower of the philosophy of Epicurus. —ˌ**Epicuˈreanism** *n.*

epicycle (ˈɛpɪˌsaɪkᵊl) *n.* a circle that rolls around the inside or outside of another circle. [C14: < LL, < Gk; see EPI-, CYCLE] —**epicyclic** (ˌɛpɪˈsaɪklɪk, -ˈsɪklɪk) *or* ˌ**epiˈcyclical** *adj.*

epicyclic train *n.* a cluster of gears consisting of a central gearwheel, a coaxial gearwheel of greater diameter, and one or more planetary gears engaging with both of them.

epicycloid (ˌɛpɪˈsaɪklɔɪd) *n.* the curve described by a point on the circumference of a circle as this circle rolls around the outside of another fixed circle. —ˌ**epicyˈcloidal** *adj.*

epideictic (ˌɛpɪˈdaɪktɪk) *adj.* designed to display something, esp. the skill of the speaker in rhetoric. Also: **epidictic** (ˌɛpɪˈdɪktɪk). [C18: < Gk, < *epideiknunai* to display, < *deiknunai* to show]

epidemic (ˌɛpɪˈdɛmɪk) *adj.* **1.** (esp. of a disease) attacking or affecting many persons simultaneously in a community or area. *~n.* **2.** a widespread occurrence of a disease. **3.** a rapid development, spread, or growth of something. [C17: < F, via LL < Gk *epidēmia*, lit.: among the people, < EPI- + *dēmos* people] —ˌ**epiˈdemically** *adv.*

epidemiology (ˌɛpɪˌdiːmɪˈɒlədʒɪ) *n.* the branch of medical science concerned with epidemic diseases. —**epidemiological** (ˌɛpɪˌdiːmɪəˈlɒdʒɪkᵊl) *adj.* —ˌ**epiˌdemiˈologist** *n.*

epidermis (ˌɛpɪˈdɜːmɪs) *n.* **1.** the thin protective outer layer of the skin. **2.** the outer layer of cells of an invertebrate. **3.** the outer protective layer of cells of a plant. [C17: via LL < Gk, < EPI- + *derma* skin] —ˌ**epiˈdermal,** ˌ**epiˈdermic,** *or* ˌ**epiˈdermoid** *adj.*

epidiascope (ˌɛpɪˈdaɪəˌskəʊp) *n.* an optical device for projecting a magnified image onto a screen.

epididymis (ˌɛpɪˈdɪdɪmɪs) *n., pl.* **-didymides** (-dɪˈdɪmɪˌdiːz). *Anat.* a convoluted tube behind each testis, in which spermatozoa are stored and conveyed to the vas deferens. [C17: < Gk *epididumis*, < EPI- + *didumos* twin, testicle]

epidural (ˌɛpɪˈdjʊərəl) *adj.* **1.** upon or outside the dura mater. *~n.* **2.** Also: **epidural anaesthesia. a.** injection of anaesthetic into the space outside the dura mater enveloping the spinal cord. **b.** anaesthesia induced by this method. [C19: < EPI- + DUR(A MATER) + -AL[1]]

epigeal (ˌɛpɪˈdʒiːəl), **epigean,** *or* **epigeous** *adj.* **1.** of or relating to seed germination in which the cotyledons appear above the ground. **2.** living or growing on or close to the surface of the ground. [C19: < Gk *epigeios* of the earth, < EPI- + *gē* earth]

epiglottis (ˌɛpɪˈglɒtɪs) *n., pl.* **-tises** *or* **-tides** (-tɪˌdiːz). a thin cartilaginous flap that covers the entrance to the larynx during swallowing, preventing food from entering the trachea. —ˌ**epiˈglottal** *or* ˌ**epiˈglottic** *adj.*

epigram (ˈɛpɪˌgræm) *n.* **1.** a witty, often paradoxical remark, concisely expressed. **2.** a short poem, esp. one having a witty and ingenious ending. [C15: < L *epigramma*, < Gk: inscription, < *graphein* to write] —ˌ**epigramˈmatic** *adj.* —ˌ**epigramˈmatically** *adv.*

epigrammatize *or* **-ise** (ˌɛpɪˈgræməˌtaɪz) *vb.* to make an epigram (about). —ˌ**epiˈgrammatism** *n.* —ˌ**epiˈgrammatist** *n.*

epigraph (ˈɛpɪˌgrɑːf) *n.* **1.** a quotation at the beginning of a book, chapter, etc. **2.** an inscription on a monument or building. [C17: < Gk; see EPIGRAM] —**epigraphic** (ˌɛpɪˈgræfɪk) or ˌ**epiˈgraphical** *adj.*

epigraphy (ɪˈpɪgrəfɪ) *n.* **1.** the study of ancient inscriptions. **2.** epigraphs collectively. —**eˈpigraphist** *or* **eˈpigrapher** *n.*

epilepsy (ˈɛpɪˌlɛpsɪ) *n.* a disorder of the central nervous system characterized by periodic loss of consciousness with or without convulsions. [C16: < LL *epilēpsia*, < Gk, < *epilambanein* to attack, seize, < *lambanein* to take]

epileptic (ˌɛpɪˈlɛptɪk) *adj.* **1.** of, relating to, or having epilepsy. *~n.* **2.** a person who has epilepsy. —ˌ**epiˈleptically** *adv.*

epilogue (ˈɛpɪˌlɒg) *n.* **1. a.** a speech addressed to the audience by an actor at the end of a play. **b.** the actor speaking this. **2.** a short postscript to any literary work. **3.** *Brit.* the concluding programme of the day on a radio or television station. [C15: < L, < Gk *epilogos*, < *logos* word, speech] —**epilogist** (ɪˈpɪlədʒɪst) *n.*

epinephrine (ˌɛpɪˈnɛfrɪn, -riːn) *or* **epinephrin** *n.* a U.S. name for **adrenaline.** [C19: < EPI- + *nephro-* + -INE[2]]

epiphany (ɪˈpɪfənɪ) *n., pl.* **-nies. 1.** the manifestation of a supernatural or divine reality. **2.** any moment of great or sudden revelation. **—epiphanic** (ˌɛpɪˈfænɪk) *adj.*

Epiphany (ɪˈpɪfənɪ) *n., pl.* **-nies.** a Christian festival held on Jan. 6, commemorating, in the Western Church, the manifestation of Christ to the Magi. [C17: via Church L < Gk *epiphaneia* an appearing, < EPI- + *phainein* to show]

epiphenomenon (ˌɛpɪfɪˈnɒmɪnən) *n., pl.* **-na** (-nə). **1.** a secondary or additional phenomenon. **2.** *Philosophy.* mind or consciousness regarded as a by-product of the biological activity of the human brain. **3.** *Pathol.* an unexpected symptom or occurrence during the course of a disease. **—ˌepipheˈnomenal** *adj.*

epiphyte (ˈɛpɪˌfaɪt) *n.* a plant that grows on another plant but is not parasitic on it. [C19: via NL < Gk, < EPI- + *phusis* growth] **—epiphytic** (ˌɛpɪˈfɪtɪk), **ˌepiˈphytal,** *or* **ˌepiˈphytical** *adj.*

Epis. *abbrev. for:* **1.** Also: **Episc.** Episcopal *or* Episcopalian. **2.** *Bible.* Also: **Epist.** Epistle.

episcopacy (ɪˈpɪskəpəsɪ) *n., pl.* **-cies. 1.** government of a Church by bishops. **2.** another word for **episcopate.**

episcopal (ɪˈpɪskəpᵊl) *adj.* of, denoting, governed by, or relating to a bishop or bishops. [C15: < Church L, < *episcopus* BISHOP]

Episcopal (ɪˈpɪskəpᵊl) *adj.* of or denoting the Episcopal Church, an autonomous church of Scotland and the U.S. which is in full communion with the Church of England.

episcopalian (ɪˌpɪskəˈpeɪlɪən) *adj. also* **episcopal. 1.** practising or advocating the principle of Church government by bishops. *~n.* **2.** an advocate of such Church government. **—eˌpiscoˈpalianism** *n.*

Episcopalian (ɪˌpɪskəˈpeɪlɪən) *adj.* **1.** belonging to or denoting the Episcopal Church. *~n.* **2.** a member or adherent of this Church.

episcopate (ɪˈpɪskəpɪt, -ˌpeɪt) *n.* **1.** the office, status, or term of office of a bishop. **2.** bishops collectively.

episiotomy (əˌpiːzɪˈɒtəmɪ) *n., pl.* **-mies.** surgical incision into the perineum during labour to prevent its laceration during childbirth. [C20: < Gk *epision* pubic region + -TOMY]

episode (ˈɛpɪˌsəʊd) *n.* **1.** an event or series of events. **2.** any of the sections into which a serialized novel or radio or television programme is divided. **3.** an incident or sequence that forms part of a narrative but may be a digression from the main story. **4.** (in ancient Greek tragedy) a section between two choric songs. **5.** *Music.* a contrasting section between statements of the subject, as in a fugue. [C17: < Gk *epeisodion* something added, < *epi-* (in addition) + *eisodios* coming in, < *eis-* in + *hodos* road]

episodic (ˌɛpɪˈsɒdɪk) *or* **episodical** *adj.* **1.** resembling or relating to an episode. **2.** divided into episodes. **3.** irregular or sporadic. **—ˌepiˈsodically** *adv.*

epistaxis (ˌɛpɪˈstæksɪs) *n.* the technical name for **nosebleed.** [C18: < Gk: a dropping, < *epistazein* to drop on, < *stazein* to drip]

epistemology (ɪˌpɪstɪˈmɒlədʒɪ) *n.* the theory of knowledge, esp. the critical study of its validity, methods, and scope. [C19: < Gk *epistēmē* knowledge] **—epistemological** (ɪˌpɪstɪməˈlɒdʒɪkᵊl) *adj.* **—eˌpisteˈmologist** *n.*

epistle (ɪˈpɪsᵊl) *n.* **1.** a letter, esp. one that is long, formal, or didactic. **2.** a literary work in letter form, esp. a verse letter. [OE *epistol,* via L < Gk *epistolē*]

Epistle (ɪˈpɪsᵊl) *n.* **1.** *Bible.* any of the letters of the apostles. **2.** a reading from one of the Epistles, part of the Eucharistic service in many Christian Churches.

epistolary (ɪˈpɪstələrɪ) *or* (*arch.*) **epistolatory** *adj.* **1.** relating to, denoting, conducted by, or contained in letters. **2.** (of a novel, etc.) in the form of a series of letters.

epistyle (ˈɛpɪˌstaɪl) *n.* another name for **architrave** (sense 1). [C17: via L < Gk, < EPI- + *stulos* column, STYLE]

epitaph (ˈɛpɪˌtɑːf) *n.* **1.** a commemorative inscription on a tombstone or monument. **2.** a commemorative speech or written passage. **3.** a final judgment on a person or thing. [C14: via L < Gk, < EPI- + *taphos* tomb] **—epitaphic** (ˌɛpɪˈtæfɪk) *adj.* **—ˈepiˌtaphist** *n.*

epithalamium (ˌɛpɪθəˈleɪmɪəm) *or* **epithalamion** *n., pl.* **-mia** (-mɪə). a poem or song written to celebrate a marriage. [C17: < L, < Gk *epithalamion* marriage song, < *thalamos* bridal chamber] **—epithalamic** (ˌɛpɪθəˈlæmɪk) *adj.*

epithelium (ˌɛpɪˈθiːlɪəm) *n., pl.* **-liums** *or* **-lia** (-lɪə). an animal cellular tissue covering the external and internal surfaces of the body. [C18: NL, < EPI- + Gk *thēlē* nipple] **—ˌepiˈthelial** *adj.*

epithet (ˈɛpɪˌθɛt) *n.* a descriptive word or phrase added to or substituted for a person's name. [C16: < L, < Gk, < *epitithenai* to add, < *tithenai* to put] **—ˌepiˈthetic** *or* **ˌepiˈthetical** *adj.*

epitome (ɪˈpɪtəmɪ) *n.* **1.** a typical example of a characteristic or class; embodiment; personification. **2.** a summary of a written work; abstract. [C16: via L < Gk, < *epitemnein* to abridge, < EPI- + *temnein* to cut] **—epitomical** (ˌɛpɪˈtɒmɪkᵊl) *or* **ˌepiˈtomic** *adj.*

epitomize *or* **-ise** (ɪˈpɪtəˌmaɪz) *vb.* (*tr.*) **1.** to be a personification of; typify. **2.** to make an epitome of. **—eˈpitomist** *n.* **—eˌpitomiˈzation** *or* **-iˈsation** *n.* **—eˈpitoˌmizer** *or* **-iser** *n.*

epizootic (ˌɛpɪzəʊˈɒtɪk) *adj.* **1.** (of a disease) suddenly and temporarily affecting a large number of animals. *~n.* **2.** an epizootic disease.

EPNS *abbrev. for* electroplated nickel silver.

epoch (ˈiːpɒk) *n.* **1.** a point in time beginning a new or distinctive period. **2.** a long period of time marked by some predominant characteristic; era. **3.** *Astron.* a precise date to which information relating to a celestial body is referred. **4.** a unit of geological time within a period during which a series of rocks is formed. [C17: < NL, < Gk *epokhē* cessation] **—epochal** (ˈɛpˌɒkᵊl) *adj.*

epode (ˈɛpəʊd) *n. Greek prosody.* **1.** the part of a lyric ode that follows the strophe and the antistrophe. **2.** a type of lyric poem composed of couplets in which a long line is followed by a shorter one. [C16: via L < Gk, < *epaidein* to sing after, < *aidein* to sing]

eponym (ˈɛpənɪm) *n.* **1.** a name, esp. a place name, derived from the name of a real or mythical person. **2.** the name of the person from which such a name is derived. [C19: < Gk *epōnumos* giving a significant name] **—eponymous** (ɪˈpɒnɪməs) *adj.* **—eˈponymously** *adv.* **—eˈponymy** *n.*

EPOS *abbrev. for* electronic point of sale.

epoxidize *or* **-ise** *vb.* (*tr.*) to convert into or treat with an epoxy resin.

epoxy (ɪˈpɒksɪ) *adj. Chem.* **1.** of, consisting of, or containing an oxygen atom joined to two different groups that are themselves joined to other groups: *epoxy group.* **2.** of, relating to, or consisting of an epoxy resin. *~n., pl.* **epoxies. 3.** short for **epoxy resin.** [C20: < EPI- + OXY-²]

epoxy *or* **epoxide resin** (ɪˈpɒksaɪd) *n.* any of various tough resistant thermosetting synthetic resins containing epoxy groups: used in surface coatings, laminates, and adhesives.

epsilon (ˈɛpsɪˌlɒn) *n.* the fifth letter of the Greek alphabet (Ε, ϵ). [Gk *e psilon,* lit.: simple *e*]

Epsom salts (ˈɛpsəm) *n.* (*functioning as sing. or pl.*) a medicinal preparation of hydrated magnesium sulphate, used as a purgative, etc. [C18: after *Epsom,* a town in England, where they occur in the water]

equable (ˈɛkwəbᵊl) *adj.* **1.** even-tempered; placid. **2.** unvarying; uniform: *an equable climate.* [C17: < L *aequābilis,* < *aequāre* to make equal] **—ˌequaˈbility** *or* **ˈequableness** *n.*

equal (ˈiːkwəl) *adj.* **1.** (often foll. by *to* or *with*) identical in size, quantity, degree, intensity, etc. **2.** having identical privileges, rights, status, etc. **3.** having uniform effect or application: *equal opportunities.* **4.** evenly balanced or proportioned. **5.** (usually foll. by *to*) having the necessary or adequate strength, ability, means, etc. (for). *~n.* **6.** a person or thing equal to another, esp. in merit, ability, etc. ~*vb.* **equalling, equalled** *or U.S.* **equaling, equaled.** **7.** (*tr.*) to be equal to; match. **8.** (*intr.;* usually foll. by *out*) to become equal. **9.** (*tr.*) to make or do something equal to. [C14: < L *aequālis,* < *aequus* level] —ˈ**equally** *adv.*

▷ **Usage.** *Equally* should not be followed by *as: the two were equally important* not *the two were equally as important.*

equalitarian (ɪˌkwɒlɪˈtɛərɪən) *adj., n.* a less common word for **egalitarian.** —**eˌqualiˈtarianism** *n.*

equality (ɪˈkwɒlɪtɪ) *n., pl.* **-ties.** the state of being equal.

equalize *or* **-ise** (ˈiːkwəˌlaɪz) *vb.* **1.** (*tr.*) to make equal or uniform. **2.** (*intr.*) (in sports) to reach the same score as one's opponent or opponents. —ˌ**equaliˈzation** *or* **-iˈsation** *n.*

equal opportunity *n.* **a.** the offering of employment, pay, or promotion without discrimination as to sex, race, etc. **b.** (*as modifier*): *an equal-opportunities employer.*

equal sign *or* **equals sign** *n.* the symbol =, used to indicate a mathematical equality.

equanimity (ˌiːkwəˈnɪmɪtɪ, ˌɛkwə-) *n.* calmness of mind or temper; composure. [C17: < L, < *aequus* even, EQUAL + *animus* mind, spirit] —**equanimous** (ɪˈkwænɪməs) *adj.*

equate (ɪˈkweɪt) *vb.* (*mainly tr.*) **1.** to make or regard as equivalent or similar. **2.** *Maths.* to indicate the equality of; form an equation from. **3.** (*intr.*) to be equal. [C15: < L *aequāre* to make EQUAL] —**eˈquatable** *adj.* —**eˌquataˈbility** *n.*

equation (ɪˈkweɪʒən, -ʃən) *n.* **1.** a mathematical statement that two expressions are equal. **2.** the act of equating. **3.** the state of being equal, equivalent, or equally balanced. **4.** a representation of a chemical reaction using symbols of the elements. —**eˈquational** *adj.* —**eˈquationally** *adv.*

equator (ɪˈkweɪtə) *n.* **1.** the great circle of the earth, equidistant from the poles, dividing the N and S hemispheres. **2.** a circle dividing a sphere into two equal parts. **3.** *Astron.* See **celestial equator.** [C14: < Med. L (*circulus*) *aequātor* (*diei et noctis*) (circle) that equalizes (the day and night), < L *aequāre* to make EQUAL]

equatorial (ˌɛkwəˈtɔːrɪəl) *adj.* **1.** of, like, or existing at or near the equator. **2.** (of a telescope) mounted on perpendicular axes, one of which is parallel to the earth's axis. ~*n.* **3.** an equatorial telescope or its mounting.

equerry (ˈɛkwərɪ; *at the British court* ɪˈkwɛrɪ) *n., pl.* **-ries.** **1.** an officer attendant upon the British sovereign. **2.** (formerly) an officer in a royal household responsible for the horses. [C16: alteration (through infl. of L *equus* horse) of earlier *escuirie,* < OF: stable]

equestrian (ɪˈkwɛstrɪən) *adj.* **1.** of or relating to horses and riding. **2.** on horseback; mounted. **3.** of, relating to, or composed of knights. ~*n.* **4.** a person skilled in riding and horsemanship. [C17: < L *equestris,* < *equus* horse] —**eˈquestrianˌism** *n.*

equi- *combining form.* equal or equally: *equidistant; equilateral.*

equiangular (ˌiːkwɪˈæŋgjʊlə) *adj.* having all angles equal.

equidistant (ˌiːkwɪˈdɪstənt) *adj.* equally distant. —ˌ**equiˈdistance** *n.* —ˌ**equiˈdistantly** *adv.*

equilateral (ˌiːkwɪˈlætərəl) *adj.* **1.** having all sides of equal length. ~*n.* **2.** a geometric figure having all sides of equal length. **3.** a side that is equal in length to other sides.

equilibrant (ɪˈkwɪlɪbrənt) *n.* a force capable of balancing another force.

equilibrate (ˌiːkwɪˈlaɪbreɪt, ɪˈkwɪlɪˌbreɪt) *vb.* to bring to or be in equilibrium; balance. [C17: < LL, < *aequilībris* in balance; see EQUILIBRIUM] —**equilibration** (ˌiːkwɪlaɪˈbreɪʃən, ɪˌkwɪlɪ-) *n.* —**equilibrator** (ɪˈkwɪlɪˌbreɪtə) *n.*

equilibrist (ɪˈkwɪlɪbrɪst) *n.* a person who performs balancing feats, esp. on a high wire. —**eˌquiliˈbristic** *adj.*

equilibrium (ˌiːkwɪˈlɪbrɪəm) *n., pl.* **-riums** *or* **-ria** (-rɪə). **1.** a stable condition in which forces cancel one another. **2.** any unchanging state of a body, system, etc., resulting from the balance of the influences to which it is subjected. **3.** *Physiol.* a state of bodily balance, maintained primarily by receptors in the inner ear. [C17: < L, < *aequi-* EQUI- + *lībra* pound, balance]

equine (ˈɛkwaɪn) *adj.* of, relating to, or resembling a horse. [C18: < L, < *equus* horse]

equinoctial (ˌiːkwɪˈnɒkʃəl) *adj.* **1.** relating to or occurring at either or both equinoxes. **2.** *Astron.* of or relating to the celestial equator. ~*n.* **3.** a storm or gale at or near an equinox. **4.** another name for **celestial equator.** [C14: < L: see EQUINOX]

equinoctial circle *or* **line** *n.* another name for **celestial equator.**

equinoctial point *n.* either of two points at which the celestial equator intersects the ecliptic.

equinoctial year *n.* another name for **solar year.** See **year** (sense 4).

equinox (ˈiːkwɪˌnɒks) *n.* **1.** either of the two occasions, six months apart, when day and night are of equal length. In the N hemisphere the **vernal equinox** occurs around March 21 (Sept. 23 in the S hemisphere). The **autumnal equinox** occurs around Sept. 23 in the N hemisphere (March 21 in the S hemisphere). **2.** another name for **equinoctial point.** [C14: < Med. L *equinoxium,* changed < L *aequinoctium,* < *aequi-* EQUI- + *nox* night]

equip (ɪˈkwɪp) *vb.* **equipping, equipped.** (*tr.*) **1.** to furnish (with necessary supplies, etc.). **2.** (*usually passive*) to provide with abilities, understanding, etc. **3.** to dress out; attire. [C16: < OF *eschiper* to embark, fit out (a ship), of Gmc origin] —**eˈquipper** *n.*

equipage (ˈɛkwɪpɪdʒ) *n.* **1.** a horse-drawn carriage, esp. one attended by liveried footmen. **2.** the stores and equipment of a military unit. **3.** *Arch.* a set of useful articles.

equipment (ɪˈkwɪpmənt) *n.* **1.** an act or instance of equipping. **2.** the items provided. **3.** a set of tools, kit, etc., assembled for a specific purpose.

equipoise (ˈɛkwɪˌpɔɪz) *n.* **1.** even balance of weight; equilibrium. **2.** a counterbalance; counterpoise. ~*vb.* **3.** (*tr.*) to offset or balance.

equipollent (ˌiːkwɪˈpɒlənt) *adj.* **1.** equal or equivalent in significance, power, or effect. ~*n.* **2.** something that is equipollent. [C15: < L *aequipollēns* of equal importance, < EQUI- + *pollēre* to be able, be strong] —ˌ**equiˈpollence** *or* ˌ**equiˈpollency** *n.*

equisetum (ˌɛkwɪˈsiːtəm) *n., pl.* **-tums** *or* **-ta** (-tə). any plant of the horsetail genus. [C19: NL, < L, < *equus* horse + *saeta* bristle]

equitable (ˈɛkwɪtəbᵊl) *adj.* **1.** fair; just. **2.** *Law.* relating to or valid in equity, as distinct from common law or statute law. [C17: < F, < *équité* EQUITY] —ˈ**equitableness** *n.*

equitation (ˌɛkwɪˈteɪʃən) *n.* the study and practice of riding and horsemanship. [C16: < L *equitātiō,* < *equitāre* to ride, < *equus* horse]

equities (ˈɛkwɪtɪz) *pl. n.* another name for **ordinary shares.**

equity (ˈɛkwɪtɪ) *n., pl.* **-ties.** **1.** the quality of being impartial; fairness. **2.** an impartial or fair act, decision, etc. **3.** *Law.* a system of jurisprudence founded on principles of natural justice and fair conduct. It supplements common law, as by providing a remedy where none exists at law. **4.** *Law.* an equitable right or claim. **5.** the interest of ordinary shareholders in a company. **6.** the value of a debtor's property in excess of debts to which it is liable. [C14: < OF, < L *aequitās,* < *aequus* level, EQUAL]

Equity (ˈɛkwɪtɪ) *n. Brit.* the actors' trade union.

equiv. *abbrev. for* equivalent.

equivalence (ɪˈkwɪvələns) *or* **equivalency** *n.* **1.** the state of being equivalent. **2.** *Logic, maths.* another term for **biconditional.**

equivalent (ɪˈkwɪvələnt) *adj.* **1.** equal in value, quantity, significance, etc. **2.** having the same or a similar effect or meaning. **3.** *Logic, maths.* (of two propositions) having a biconditional between them. ~*n.* **4.** something that is equivalent. **5.**

Also called: **equivalent weight.** the weight of a substance that will combine with or displace 8 grams of oxygen or 1.007 97 grams of hydrogen. [C15: < LL, < L *aequi-* EQUI- + *valēre* to be worth] —**eˈquivalently** *adv.*

equivocal (ɪˈkwɪvəkᵊl) *adj.* **1.** capable of varying interpretations; ambiguous. **2.** deliberately misleading or vague. **3.** of doubtful character or sincerity. [C17: < LL, < L EQUI- + *vōx* voice] —**eˌquivoˈcality** *or* —**eˈquivocalness** *n.*

equivocate (ɪˈkwɪvəˌkeɪt) *vb.* (*intr.*) to use equivocal language, esp. to avoid speaking directly or honestly. [C15: < Med. L, < LL *aequivocus* ambiguous, EQUIVOCAL] —**eˈquivoˌcatingly** *adv.* —**eˌquivoˈcation** *n.* —**eˈquivoˌcator** *n.* —**eˈquivocatory** *adj.*

er (ə, ɜː) *interj.* a sound made when hesitating in speech.

Er *the chemical symbol for* erbium.

ER *abbrev. for:* **1.** Elizabeth Regina. [L: Queen Elizabeth] **2.** Eduardus Rex. [L: King Edward]

-er[1] *suffix forming nouns.* **1.** a person or thing that performs a specified action: *reader; lighter.* **2.** a person engaged in a profession, occupation, etc.: *writer; baker.* **3.** a native or inhabitant of: *Londoner; villager.* **4.** a person or thing having a certain characteristic: *newcomer; fiver.* [OE *-ere*]

-er[2] *suffix.* forming the comparative degree of adjectives (*deeper, freer,* etc.) and adverbs (*faster, slower,* etc.). [OE *-rd, -re* (adj.), *-or* (adv.)]

era (ˈɪərə) *n.* **1.** a period of time considered as being of a distinctive character; epoch. **2.** an extended period of time the years of which are numbered from a fixed point: *the Christian era.* **3.** a point in time beginning a new or distinctive period. **4.** a major division of geological time, divided into periods. [C17: < L *aera* counters, pl. of *aes* brass, pieces of brass money]

eradicate (ɪˈrædɪˌkeɪt) *vb.* (*tr.*) **1.** to obliterate. **2.** to pull up by the roots. [C16: < L *ērādīcāre* to uproot, < EX-[1] + *rādīx* root] —**eˈradicable** *adj.* —**eˌradiˈcation** *n.* —**eˈradicative** *adj.* —**eˈradiˌcator** *n.*

erase (ɪˈreɪz) *vb.* **1.** to obliterate or rub out (something written, typed, etc.). **2.** (*tr.*) to destroy all traces of. **3.** to remove (a recording) from (magnetic tape). [C17: < L, < EX-[1] + *rādere* to scratch, scrape] —**eˈrasable** *adj.*

eraser (ɪˈreɪzə) *n.* an object, such as a piece of rubber, for erasing something written, typed, etc.

erasure (ɪˈreɪʒə) *n.* **1.** the act or an instance of erasing. **2.** the place or mark, as on a piece of paper, where something has been erased.

Erato (ˈɛrəˌtəʊ) *n. Greek myth.* the Muse of love poetry.

erbium (ˈɜːbɪəm) *n.* a soft malleable silvery-white element of the lanthanide series of metals. Symbol: Er; atomic no.: 68; atomic wt.: 167.26. [C19: < NL, < (*Ytt*)*erb*(*y*), Sweden, where it was first found + -IUM]

ere (ɛə) *conj., prep.* a poetic word for **before.** [OE *ǣr*]

erect (ɪˈrɛkt) *adj.* **1.** upright in posture or position. **2.** *Physiol.* (of the penis, clitoris, or nipples) firm or rigid after swelling with blood, esp. as a result of sexual excitement. **3.** (of plant parts) growing vertically or at right angles to the parts from which they arise. ~*vb.* (*mainly tr.*) **4.** to put up; build. **5.** to raise to an upright position. **6.** to found or form; set up. **7.** (*also intr.*) *Physiol.* to become or cause to become firm or rigid by filling with blood. **8.** to exalt. **9.** to draw or construct (a line, figure, etc.) on a given line or figure. [C14: < L *ērigere* to set up, < *regere* to control, govern] —**eˈrectable** *adj.* —**eˈrecter** *or* **eˈrector** *n.* —**eˈrectness** *n.*

erectile (ɪˈrɛktaɪl) *adj.* **1.** *Physiol.* (of tissues or organs, such as the penis or clitoris) capable of becoming erect. **2.** capable of being erected. —**erectility** (ɪrɛkˈtɪlɪtɪ, ˌiːrɛk-) *n.*

erection (ɪˈrɛkʃən) *n.* **1.** the act of erecting or the state of being erected. **2.** a building or construction. **3.** *Physiol.* the enlarged state of erectile tissues or organs, esp. the penis, when filled with blood. **4.** an erect penis.

E region *or* **layer** *n.* a region of the ionosphere, extending from a height of 90 to about 150 kilometres. It reflects radio waves of medium wavelength.

erelong (ɛəˈlɒŋ) *adv. Arch. or poetic.* before long; soon.

eremite (ˈɛrɪˌmaɪt) *n.* a Christian hermit or recluse. [C13: see HERMIT] —**eremitic** (ˌɛrɪˈmɪtɪk) *or* ˌ**ereˈmitical** *adj.* —ˈ**eremitˌism** *n.*

erepsin (ɪˈrɛpsɪn) *n.* a mixture of proteolytic enzymes secreted by the small intestine. [C20: *er-*, < L *ēripere* to snatch + (P)EPSIN]

erethism (ˈɛrɪˌθɪzəm) *n.* **1.** *Physiol.* an abnormal irritability or sensitivity in any part of the body. **2.** *Psychiatry.* an abnormal tendency to become aroused quickly, esp. sexually, as the result of a verbal or psychic stimulus. [C18: < F, < Gk, < *erethizein* to excite, irritate]

erf (ɜːf) *n., pl.* **erven** (ˈɜːvən). *S. African.* a plot of land, usually urban. [< Afrik., < Du.: inheritance, piece of land]

erg[1] (ɜːg) *n.* the cgs unit of work or energy. [C19: < Gk *ergon* work]

erg[2] (ɜːg) *n., pl.* **ergs** *or* **areg** (əˈrɛg). an area of shifting sand dunes, esp. in the Sahara Desert in N Africa. [C19: < Ar. *'irj*]

ergo (ˈɜːgəʊ) *sentence connector.* therefore; hence. [C14: < L: therefore]

ergonomics (ˌɜːgəˈnɒmɪks) *n.* (*functioning as sing.*) the study of the relationship between workers and their environment. [C20: < Gk *ergon* work + (ECO)NOMICS] —ˌ**ergoˈnomic** *adj.* —**ergonomist** (ɜːˈgɒnəmɪst) *n.*

ergosterol (ɜːˈgɒstəˌrɒl) *n.* a plant sterol that is converted into vitamin D by the action of ultraviolet radiation.

ergot (ˈɜːgət, -gɒt) *n.* **1.** a disease of cereals and other grasses caused by fungi of the genus *Claviceps.* **2.** any fungus causing this disease. **3.** the dried fungus, used as the source of certain alkaloids used in medicine. [C17: < F: spur (of a cock), <?]

ergotism (ˈɜːgəˌtɪzəm) *n.* ergot poisoning, producing either burning pains and eventually gangrene or itching skin and convulsions.

erica (ˈɛrɪkə) *n.* any shrub of the ericaceous genus *Erica,* including the heaths and some heathers. [C19: via L < Gk *ereikē* heath]

ericaceous (ˌɛrɪˈkeɪʃəs) *adj.* of or relating to the Ericaceae, a family of trees and shrubs with typically bell-shaped flowers: includes heather, rhododendron, azalea, and arbutus. [C19: < NL, < L *erīca* heath, < Gk *ereikē*]

erigeron (ɪˈrɪdʒərən, -ˈrɪg-) *n.* any plant of the genus *Erigeron,* whose flowers resemble asters. [C17: via L < Gk, < *ēri* early + *gerōn* old man; from the white down of some species]

Erin (ˈɪərɪn, ˈɛərɪn) *n.* an archaic or poetic name for Ireland. [< Irish Gaelic *Eirinn,* dative of *Erin* Ireland]

Erinyes (ɪˈrɪnɪˌiːz) *pl. n., sing.* **Erinys** (ɪˈrɪnɪs, ɪˈraɪ-). *Myth.* another name for the **Furies.** [Gk]

erk (ɜːk) *n. Brit. sl.* an aircraftman or naval rating. [C20: ? a corruption of *AC* (aircraftman)]

ermine (ˈɜːmɪn) *n., pl.* **-mines** *or* **-mine. 1.** the stoat in northern regions, where it has a white winter coat with a black-tipped tail. **2.** the fur of this animal. **3.** the dignity or office of a judge, noble, etc., whose state robes are trimmed with ermine. [C12: < OF, < Med. L *Armenius* (*mūs*) Armenian (mouse)]

erne *or* **ern** (ɜːn) *n.* a fish-eating sea eagle. [OE *earn*]

Ernie (ˈɜːnɪ) *n.* (in Britain) a computer that randomly selects winning numbers of Premium Bonds. [C20: acronym of *E*lectronic *R*andom *N*umber *I*ndicator *E*quipment]

erode (ɪˈrəʊd) *vb.* **1.** to grind or wear down or away or become ground or worn down or away. **2.** to deteriorate or cause to deteriorate. [C17: < L, < EX-[1] + *rōdere* to gnaw] —**eˈrodent** *adj., n.* —**eˈrodible** *adj.*

erogenous (ɪˈrɒdʒɪnəs) *or* **erogenic** (ˌɛrə-

ˈdʒɛnɪk) *adj.* **1.** sensitive to sexual stimulation. **2.** arousing sexual desire or giving sexual pleasure. [C19: < Gk *erōs* love, desire + -GENOUS] —**erogeneity** (ˌɛrədʒɪˈniːɪtɪ) *n.*

erosion (ɪˈrəʊʒən) *n.* **1.** the wearing away of rocks, soil, etc., by the action of water, ice, wind, etc. **2.** the act or process of eroding or the state of being eroded. —**eˈrosive** *or* **eˈrosional** *adj.*

erotic (ɪˈrɒtɪk) *adj.* **1.** of, concerning, or arousing sexual desire or giving sexual pleasure. **2.** marked by strong sexual desire or being especially sensitive to sexual stimulation. Also: **erotical.** [C17: < Gk *erōtikos*, < *erōs* love] —**eˈrotically** *adv.*

erotica (ɪˈrɒtɪkə) *pl. n.* explicitly sexual literature or art. [C19: < Gk: see EROTIC]

eroticism (ɪˈrɒtɪˌsɪzəm) *or* **erotism** (ˈɛrəˌtɪzəm) *n.* **1.** erotic quality or nature. **2.** the use of sexually arousing or pleasing symbolism in literature or art. **3.** sexual excitement or desire.

erotogenic (ɪˌrɒtəˈdʒɛnɪk) *adj.* originating from or causing sexual stimulation; erogenous.

err (ɜː) *vb.* (*intr.*) **1.** to make a mistake; be incorrect. **2.** to deviate from a moral standard. **3.** to act with bias, esp. favourable bias: *to err on the right side.* [C14 *erren* to wander, stray, < OF, < L *errāre*] —**ˈerrancy** *n.*

errand (ˈɛrənd) *n.* **1.** a short trip undertaken to perform a task or commission (esp. in **run errands**). **2.** the purpose or object of such a trip. [OE *ǣrende*]

errant (ˈɛrənt) *adj.* (*often postpositive*) **1.** *Arch. or literary.* wandering in search of adventure. **2.** erring or straying from the right course or accepted standards. [C14: < OF: journeying, < Vulgar L *iterāre* (unattested), < L *iter* journey; infl. by L *errāre* to err] —**ˈerrantry** *n.*

erratic (ɪˈrætɪk) *adj.* **1.** irregular in performance, behaviour, or attitude; unpredictable. **2.** having no fixed or regular course. ~*n.* **3.** a piece of rock that has been transported from its place of origin, esp. by glacial action. [C14: < L, < *errāre* to wander, err] —**erˈratically** *adv.*

erratum (ɪˈrɑːtəm) *n., pl.* **-ta** (-tə). **1.** an error in writing or printing. **2.** another name for **corrigendum.** [C16: < L: mistake, < *errāre* to err]

erroneous (ɪˈrəʊnɪəs) *adj.* based on or containing error; incorrect. [C14 (in the sense: deviating from what is right), < L, < *errāre* to wander] —**erˈroneousness** *n.*

error (ˈɛrə) *n.* **1.** a mistake or inaccuracy. **2.** an incorrect belief or wrong judgment. **3.** the condition of deviating from accuracy or correctness. **4.** deviation from a moral standard; wrongdoing. **5.** *Maths, statistics.* a measure of the difference between some quantity and an approximation of it, often expressed as a percentage. [C13: < L, < *errāre* to err] —**ˈerror-ˌfree** *adj.*

ersatz (ˈɛəzæts, ˈɜː-) *adj.* **1.** made in imitation; artificial. ~*n.* **2.** an ersatz substance or article. [C20: G, < *ersetzen* to substitute]

Erse (ɜːs) *n.* **1.** another name for **Gaelic.** ~*adj.* **2.** of or relating to the Gaelic language. [C14: < Lowland Scots *Erisch* Irish]

erst (ɜːst) *adv. Arch.* **1.** long ago; formerly. **2.** at first. [OE *ǣrest* earliest, sup. of *ǣr* early]

erstwhile (ˈɜːstˌwaɪl) *adj.* **1.** former; one-time. ~*adv.* **2.** *Arch.* long ago; formerly.

eruct (ɪˈrʌkt) *or* **eructate** *vb.* **1.** to belch. **2.** (of a volcano) to pour out (fumes or volcanic matter). [C17: < L, < *ructāre* to belch] —**eructation** (ɪˌrʌkˈteɪʃən, ˌiːrʌk-) *n.*

erudite (ˈɛrʊˌdaɪt) *adj.* having or showing extensive scholarship; learned. [C15: < L, < *ērudīre* to polish] —**erudition** (ˌɛrʊˈdɪʃən) *or* **ˈeruˌditeness** *n.*

erupt (ɪˈrʌpt) *vb.* **1.** to eject (steam, water, and volcanic material) violently or (of volcanic material, etc.) to be so ejected. **2.** (*intr.*) (of a blemish) to appear on the skin. **3.** (*intr.*) (of a tooth) to emerge through the gum during normal tooth development. **4.** (*intr.*) to burst forth suddenly and violently. [C17: < L *ēruptus* having burst forth, < *ērumpere*, < *rumpere* to burst] —**eˈruptive** *adj.* —**eˈruption** *n.*

-ery *or* **-ry** *suffix forming nouns.* **1.** indicating a place of business or activity: *bakery; refinery.* **2.** indicating a class or collection of things: *cutlery.* **3.** indicating qualities or actions: *snobbery; trickery.* **4.** indicating a practice or occupation: *husbandry.* **5.** indicating a state or condition: *slavery.* [< OF *-erie*; see -ER[1], -Y[3]]

erysipelas (ˌɛrɪˈsɪpɪləs) *n.* an acute streptococcal infectious disease of the skin, characterized by fever and purplish lesions. [C16: < L, < Gk, < *erusi-* red + *-pelas* skin]

erythro- *or before a vowel* **erythr-** *combining form.* red: *erythrocyte.* [< Gk *eruthros* red]

erythrocyte (ɪˈrɪθrəʊˌsaɪt) *n.* a blood cell of vertebrates that transports oxygen and carbon dioxide, combined with haemoglobin. —**erythrocytic** (ɪˌrɪθrəʊˈsɪtɪk) *adj.*

erythromycin (ɪˌrɪθrəʊˈmaɪsɪn) *n.* an antibiotic used in treating certain bacterial infections. [C20: < ERYTHRO- + Gk *mukēs* fungus + -IN]

Es *the chemical symbol for* einsteinium.

-es *suffix.* **1.** a variant of **-s**[1] for nouns ending in *ch, s, sh, z,* postconsonantal *y,* for some nouns ending in a vowel, and nouns in *f* with *v* in the plural: *ashes; heroes; calves.* **2.** a variant of **-s**[2] for verbs ending in *ch, s, sh, z,* postconsonantal *y,* or a vowel: *preaches; steadies; echoes.*

escadrille (ˌɛskəˈdrɪl) *n.* a French squadron of aircraft, esp. in World War I. [< F: flotilla, < Sp., < *escuadra* SQUADRON]

escalade (ˌɛskəˈleɪd) *n.* **1.** an assault using ladders, esp. on a fortification. ~*vb.* **2.** to gain access to (a place) by ladders. [C16: < F, < It., < *scalare* to mount, SCALE[3]]

escalate (ˈɛskəˌleɪt) *vb.* to increase or be increased in extent, intensity, or magnitude. [C20: back formation < ESCALATOR] —ˌ**escaˈlation** *n.*

▷ **Usage.** *Escalate* is very commonly used in journalistic contexts in the sense of gradually increasing the intensity or scope of a war, etc. This word is, however, not yet completely accepted as appropriate in formal English.

escalator (ˈɛskəˌleɪtə) *n.* **1.** a moving staircase consisting of stair treads fixed to a conveyor belt. **2.** short for **escalator clause.** [C20: orig. a trademark]

escalator clause *n.* a clause in a contract stipulating an adjustment in wages, prices, etc., in the event of specified changes in conditions, such as a large rise in the cost of living.

escallop (ɛˈskɒləp, ɛˈskæl-) *n., vb.* another word for **scallop.**

escalope (ˈɛskəˌlɒp) *n.* a thin slice of meat, usually veal. [C19: < OF: shell]

escapade (ˈɛskəˌpeɪd, ˌɛskəˈpeɪd) *n.* **1.** an adventure, esp. one that is mischievous or unlawful. **2.** a prank; romp. [C17: < F, < OIt., < Vulgar L *excappāre* (unattested) to ESCAPE]

escape (ɪˈskeɪp) *vb.* **1.** to get away or break free from (confinements, etc.). **2.** to manage to avoid (danger, etc.). **3.** (*intr.*; usually foll. by *from*) (of gases, liquids, etc.) to issue gradually, as from a crack; seep; leak. **4.** (*tr.*) to elude; be forgotten by: *the figure escapes me.* **5.** (*tr.*) to be articulated inadvertently or involuntarily from: *a roar escaped his lips.* ~*n.* **6.** the act of escaping or state of having escaped. **7.** avoidance of injury, harm, etc. **8. a.** a means or way of escape. **b.** (*as modifier*): *an escape route.* **9.** a means of distraction or relief. **10.** a gradual outflow; leakage; seepage. **11.** Also called: **escape valve, escape cock.** a valve that releases air, steam, etc., above a certain pressure. **12.** a plant originally cultivated but now growing wild. [C14: < OF, < Vulgar L *excappāre* (unattested) to escape (lit.: to slip out of one's cloak, hence free oneself), < EX-[1] + LL *cappa* cloak] —**esˈcapable** *adj.* —**esˈcaper** *n.*

escapee (ɪˌskeɪˈpiː) *n.* a person who has escaped, esp. an escaped prisoner.

escapement (ɪˈskeɪpmənt) *n.* **1.** a mechanism consisting of a toothed wheel (**escape wheel**) and anchor, used in timepieces to provide periodic impulses to the pendulum or balance. **2.** any similar mechanism that regulates movement. **3.** in pianos, the mechanism which allows the hammer to clear the string after striking, so the string can vibrate. **4.** *Rare.* an act or means of escaping.

escape road *n.* a road provided on a hill for a driver to drive into if his brakes fail or on a bend if he loses control of the turn.

escape velocity *n.* the minimum velocity necessary for a body to escape from the gravitational field of the earth or other celestial body.

escapism (ɪˈskeɪpɪzəm) *n.* an inclination to retreat from unpleasant reality, as through diversion or fantasy. —**esˈcapist** *n., adj.*

escapologist (ˌɛskəˈpɒlədʒɪst) *n.* an entertainer who specializes in freeing himself from confinement. —ˌ**escaˈpology** *n.*

escargot *French.* (ɛskargo) *n.* a variety of edible snail.

escarpment (ɪˈskɑːpmənt) *n.* **1.** the long continuous steep face of a ridge or plateau formed by erosion or faulting; scarp. **2.** a steep artificial slope made immediately in front of a fortified place. [C19: < F *escarpe;* see SCARP]

-escent *suffix forming adjectives.* beginning to be, do, show, etc.: *convalescent; luminescent.* [via OF < L *-ēscent-*, stem of present participial suffix of *-ēscere*, ending of inceptive verbs] —**-escence** *suffix forming nouns.*

eschatology (ˌɛskəˈtɒlədʒɪ) *n.* the branch of theology concerned with the end of the world. [C19: < Gk *eskhatos* last] —**eschatological** (ˌɛskətəˈlɒdʒɪkᵊl) *adj.* —ˌ**eschaˈtologist** *n.*

escheat (ɪsˈtʃiːt) *Law.* ~*n.* **1.** (in England before 1926) the reversion of property to the Crown in the absence of legal heirs. **2.** *Feudalism.* the reversion of property to the feudal lord in the absence of legal heirs. **3.** the property so reverting. ~*vb.* **4.** to take (land) by escheat or (of land) to revert by escheat. [C14: < OF, < *escheoir* to fall to the lot of, < LL *excadere* (unattested), < L *cadere* to fall] —**esˈcheatable** *adj.* —**esˈcheatage** *n.*

Escherichia (ˌɛʃəˈrɪkɪə) *n.* a genus of bacteria that form acid and gas on many carbohydrates and are found in the intestines of man and many animals. [C19: after Theodor *Escherich* (1857-1911), G paediatrician]

eschew (ɪsˈtʃuː) *vb.* (*tr.*) to keep clear of or abstain from (something disliked, injurious, etc.); shun; avoid. [C14: < OF *eschiver,* of Gmc origin; see SHY[1], SKEW] —**esˈchewal** *n.* —**esˈchewer** *n.*

eschscholzia (ɪsˈkɒlʃə) *n.* any of a genus of N American herbs having showy flowers. [C19: after J. F. von *Eschscholz* (1793–1831), G botanist]

escort *n.* (ˈɛskɔːt). **1.** one or more persons, soldiers, vehicles, etc., accompanying another or others for protection, as a mark of honour, etc. **2.** a man or youth who accompanies a woman or girl on a social occasion. ~*vb.* (ɪsˈkɔːt). **3.** (*tr.*) to accompany or attend as an escort. [C16: < F, < It., < *scorgere* to guide, < L *corrigere* to straighten; see CORRECT]

escritoire (ˌɛskrɪˈtwɑː) *n.* a writing desk with compartments and drawers. [C18: < F, < Med. L *scriptōrium* writing room in a monastery, < L *scrībere* to write]

escrow (ˈɛskrəʊ, ɛˈskrəʊ) *Law.* ~*n.* **1.** money, goods, or a written document, held by a third party pending fulfilment of some condition. **2.** the state or condition of being an escrow (esp. in **in escrow**). ~*vb.* (*tr.*) **3.** to place (money, a document, etc.) in escrow. [C16: < OF *escroe,* of Gmc origin; see SCREED, SHRED, SCROLL]

escudo (ɛˈskuːdəʊ) *n., pl.* **-dos. 1.** the standard monetary unit of Portugal. **2.** the standard monetary unit of Chile. **3.** an old Spanish silver coin. [C19: Sp., lit.: shield, < L *scūtum*]

esculent (ˈɛskjʊlənt) *n.* **1.** any edible substance. ~*adj.* **2.** edible. [C17: < L *ēsculentus* good to eat, < *ēsca* food, < *edere* to eat]

escutcheon (ɪˈskʌtʃən) *n.* **1.** a shield, esp. a heraldic one that displays a coat of arms. **2.** a plate or shield around a keyhole, door handle, etc. **3.** the place on the stern of a vessel where the name is shown. **4. blot on one's escutcheon.** a stain on one's honour. [C15: < OF *escuchon,* ult. < L *scūtum* shield] —**esˈcutcheoned** *adj.*

ESE *symbol for* east-southeast.

-ese *suffix forming adjectives and nouns.* indicating place of origin, language, or style: *Cantonese; Japanese; journalese.*

esker (ˈɛskə) *or* **eskar** (ˈɛskɑː, -kə) *n.* a long winding ridge of gravel, sand, etc., originally deposited by a meltwater stream running under a glacier. [C19: < OIrish *escir* ridge]

Eskimo (ˈɛskɪˌməʊ) *n.* **1.** (*pl.* **-mos** *or* **-mo**) a member of a group of peoples inhabiting N Canada, Greenland, Alaska, and E Siberia. The Eskimos are more properly referred to as the **Inuit. 2.** the language of these peoples. ~*adj.* **3.** of or relating to the Eskimos. [C18 *Esquimawes:* rel. to *esquimantsic* (< a native language) eaters of raw flesh]

Eskimo dog *n.* a large powerful breed of dog with a long thick coat and curled tail, developed for hauling sledges.

Esky (ˈɛskɪ) *n., pl.* **-kies.** (*sometimes not cap.*) *Austral. trademark.* a portable insulated container for keeping food and drink cool. [C20: < ESKIMO, alluding to the Eskimos' cold habitat]

ESN *abbrev. for* educationally subnormal.

esophagus (iːˈsɒfəgəs) *n.* the U.S. spelling of **oesophagus.**

esoteric (ˌɛsəʊˈtɛrɪk) *adj.* **1.** restricted to or intended for an enlightened or initiated minority. **2.** difficult to understand; abstruse. **3.** not openly admitted; private. [C17: < Gk, < *esōterō* inner] —ˌ**esoˈterically** *adv.* —ˌ**esoˈteriˌcism** *n.*

ESP *abbrev. for* extrasensory perception.

esp. *abbrev. for* especially.

espadrille (ˌɛspəˈdrɪl) *n.* a light shoe with a canvas upper, esp. with a braided cord sole. [C19: < F, < Provençal *espardilho,* dim. of *espart* ESPARTO; from use of esparto for the soles]

espalier (ɪˈspæljə) *n.* **1.** an ornamental shrub or fruit tree trained to grow flat, as against a wall. **2.** the trellis or framework on which such plants are trained. ~*vb.* **3.** (*tr.*) to train (a plant) on an espalier. [C17: < F: trellis, < OIt.: shoulder supports, < *spalla* shoulder, < LL SPATULA]

esparto *or* **esparto grass** (ɛˈspɑːtəʊ) *n., pl.* **-tos.** any of various grasses of S Europe and N Africa, used to make ropes, mats, etc. [C18: < Sp., via L < Gk *spartos* a kind of rush]

especial (ɪˈspɛʃəl) *adj.* (*prenominal*) **1.** unusual; notable. **2.** applying to one person or thing in particular; specific; peculiar: *he had an especial dislike of relatives.* [C14: < OF, < L *speciālis* individual; see SPECIAL] —**esˈpecially** *adv.*

▷ **Usage.** *Special* is always used in preference to *especial* when the sense is one of being out of the ordinary: *a special lesson. Special* is also used when something is referred to as being for a particular purpose: *the word was specially underlined for you.* Where an idea of preeminence or individuality is involved, either *especial* or *special* may be used: *he is my especial* (or *special*) *friend; he is especially* (or *specially*) *good at his job.* In informal English, however, *special* is usually preferred in all contexts.

Esperanto (ˌɛspəˈræntəʊ) *n.* an international artificial language based on words common to the chief European languages. [C19: lit.: the one who hopes, pseudonym of Dr L. L. Zamenhof (1859–1917), Polish inventor] —ˌ**EspeˈrantIst** *n., adj.*

espial (ɪˈspaɪəl) *n. Arch.* **1.** the act or fact of being seen or discovered. **2.** the act of noticing. **3.** the act of spying upon; secret observation.

espionage (ˈɛspɪəˌnɑːʒ) *n.* **1.** the use of spies to obtain secret information, esp. by governments. **2.** the act of spying. [C18: < F, < *espion* spy, < OIt. *spione,* of Gmc origin]

esplanade (ˌɛspləˈneɪd) *n.* **1.** a long open level stretch of ground for walking along, esp. beside the seashore. Cf. **promenade** (sense 1). **2.** an open area in front of a fortified place. [C17: < F,

< OIt. *spianata,* < *spianare* to make level, < L *explānāre;* see EXPLAIN]

espousal (ɪˈspaʊzᵊl) *n.* **1.** adoption or support: *an espousal of new beliefs.* **2.** (*sometimes pl.*) *Arch.* a marriage or betrothal ceremony.

espouse (ɪˈspaʊz) *vb.* (*tr.*) **1.** to adopt or give support to (a cause, ideal, etc.): *to espouse socialism.* **2.** *Arch.* (esp. of a man) to take as spouse; marry. [C15: < OF *espouser,* < L *spōnsāre* to affiance, espouse] **—esˈpouser** *n.*

espressivo (ɛsprɛˈsiːvəʊ) *adv. Music.* in an expressive manner. [It.]

espresso (ɛˈsprɛsəʊ) *n., pl.* **-sos. 1.** coffee made by forcing steam or boiling water through ground coffee beans. **2.** an apparatus for making coffee in this way. [C20: It., lit.: pressed]

esprit (ɛˈspriː) *n.* spirit and liveliness, esp. in wit. [C16: < F, < L *spīritus* a breathing, SPIRIT[1]]

esprit de corps (ɛˈspriː də ˈkɔː) *n.* consciousness of and pride in belonging to a particular group; the sense of shared purpose and fellowship.

espy (ɪˈspaɪ) *vb.* **espying, espied.** (*tr.*) to catch sight of or perceive; detect. [C14: < OF *espier* to SPY, of Gmc origin] **—esˈpier** *n.*

Esq. *abbrev. for* esquire.

-esque *suffix forming adjectives.* indicating a specified character, manner, style, or resemblance: *picturesque; Romanesque; statuesque.* [via F < It. *-esco,* of Gmc origin]

Esquimau (ˈɛskɪˌməʊ) *n., pl.* **-maus** *or* **-mau,** *adj.* a former spelling of **Eskimo.**

esquire (ɪˈskwaɪə) *n.* **1.** *Chiefly Brit.* a title of respect, usually abbreviated *Esq.,* placed after a man's name. **2.** (in medieval times) the attendant of a knight, subsequently often knighted himself. [C15: < OF *escuier,* < LL *scūtārius* shield bearer, < L *scūtum* shield]

ESRC (in Britain) *abbrev. for* Economic and Social Research Council.

ESRO (ˈɛzrəʊ) *n. acronym for* European Space Research Organization.

-ess *suffix forming nouns.* indicating a female: *waitress; lioness.* [via OF < LL *-issa,* < Gk]

▷ **Usage.** The suffix *-ess* in such words as *poetess, authoress* is now often regarded as disparaging; a sexually neutral term *poet, author* is preferred.

essay *n.* (ˈɛseɪ; *senses 2, 3 also* ɛˈseɪ). **1.** a short literary composition. **2.** an attempt; effort. **3.** a test or trial. *~vb.* (ɛˈseɪ). (*tr.*) **4.** to attempt or try. **5.** to test or try out. [C15: < OF *essai* an attempt, < LL *exagium* a weighing, < L *agere* to do, infl. by *exigere* to investigate]

essayist (ˈɛseɪɪst) *n.* a person who writes essays.

essence (ˈɛsᵊns) *n.* **1.** the characteristic or intrinsic feature of a thing, which determines its identity; fundamental nature. **2.** a perfect or complete form of something. **3.** *Philosophy.* the unchanging and unchangeable inward nature of something. **4. a.** the constituent of a plant, usually an oil, alkaloid, or glycoside, that determines its chemical properties. **b.** an alcoholic solution of such a substance. **5.** a rare word for **perfume. 6. in essence.** essentially; fundamentally. **7. of the essence.** indispensable; vitally important. [C14: < Med. L *essentia,* < L: the being (of something), < *esse* to be]

Essene (ˈɛsiːn, ɛˈsiːn) *n. Judaism.* a member of an ascetic sect that flourished in Palestine from the second century B.C. to the second century A.D.

essential (ɪˈsɛnʃəl) *adj.* **1.** vitally important; absolutely necessary. **2.** basic; fundamental. **3.** absolute; perfect. **4.** derived from or relating to an extract of a plant, drug, etc.: *an essential oil.* *~n.* **5.** something fundamental or indispensable. **—essentiality** (ɪˌsɛnʃɪˈælɪtɪ) *or* **esˈsentialness** *n.* **—esˈsentially** *adv.*

essentialism (ɪˈsɛnʃəˌlɪzəm) *n. Philosophy.* any doctrine that material objects have an essence distinguishable from their attributes and existence. **—esˈsentialist** *n.*

essential oil *n.* any of various volatile oils in plants, having the odour or flavour of the plant from which they are extracted.

EST *abbrev. for:* **1.** (in the U.S. and Canada) Eastern Standard Time. **2.** electric-shock treatment.

est. *abbrev. for:* **1.** established. **2.** estimate(d).

-est[1] *suffix.* forming the superlative degree of adjectives and adverbs: *fastest.* [OE *-est, -ost*]

-est[2] *or* **-st** *suffix.* forming the archaic second person singular present and past indicative tense of verbs: *thou goest; thou hadst.* [OE *-est, -ast*]

establish (ɪˈstæblɪʃ) *vb.* (*tr.*) **1.** to make secure or permanent in a certain place, condition, job, etc. **2.** to create or set up (an organization, etc.) as on a permanent basis. **3.** to prove correct; validate: *establish a fact.* **4.** to cause (a principle, theory, etc.) to be accepted: *establish a precedent.* **5.** to give (a Church) the status of a national institution. **6.** to cause (a person) to become recognized and accepted. **7.** (in works of imagination) to cause (a character, place, etc.) to be credible and recognized. [C14: < OF, < L *stabilis* STABLE[2]] **—esˈtablisher** *n.*

Established Church *n.* a Church that is officially recognized as a national institution, esp. the Church of England.

establishment (ɪˈstæblɪʃmənt) *n.* **1.** the act of establishing or state of being established. **2. a.** a business organization or other large institution. **b.** a place of business. **3.** the staff and equipment of an organization. **4.** any large organization or system. **5.** a household; residence. **6.** a body of employees or servants. **7.** (*modifier*) belonging to or characteristic of the Establishment.

Establishment (ɪˈstæblɪʃmənt) *n.* **the.** a group or class having institutional authority within a society: usually seen as conservative.

estate (ɪˈsteɪt) *n.* **1.** a large piece of landed property, esp. in the country. **2.** *Chiefly Brit.* a large area of property development, esp. of new houses or (**trading estate**) of factories. **3.** *Law.* **a.** property or possessions. **b.** the nature of interest that a person has in land or other property. **c.** the total extent of the property of a deceased person or bankrupt. **4.** Also called: **estate of the realm.** an order or class in a political community, regarded as a part of the body politic: the lords spiritual (**first estate**), lords temporal or peers (**second estate**), and commons (**third estate**). See also **fourth estate. 5.** state, period, or position in life: *youth's estate; a poor man's estate.* [C13: < OF *estat,* < L *status* condition, STATE]

estate agent *n.* **1.** *Brit.* an agent concerned with the valuation, management, lease, and sale of property. **2.** the administrator of a large landed property; estate manager.

estate car *n. Brit.* a car containing a large carrying space, reached through a rear door: usually the back seats fold forward to increase the carrying space.

estate duty *n.* another name for **death duty.**

esteem (ɪˈstiːm) *vb.* (*tr.*) **1.** to have great respect or high regard for. **2.** *Formal.* to judge or consider; deem. *~n.* **3.** high regard or respect; good opinion. **4.** *Arch.* judgment; opinion. [C15: < OF *estimer,* < L *aestimāre* ESTIMATE] **—esˈteemed** *adj.*

ester (ˈɛstə) *n. Chem.* any of a class of compounds produced by reaction between acids and alcohols with the elimination of water. [C19: < G, prob. a contraction of *Essigäther* acetic ether, < *Essig* vinegar (ult. < L *acētum*) + *Äther* ETHER]

Esth. *Bible. abbrev.for* Esther.

esthesia (iːsˈθiːzɪə) *n.* a U.S. spelling of **aesthesia.**

esthete (ˈiːsθiːt) *n.* a U.S. spelling of **aesthete.**

estimable (ˈɛstɪməbᵊl) *adj.* worthy of respect; deserving of admiration. **—ˈestimableness** *n.* **—ˈestimably** *adv.*

estimate *vb.* (ˈɛstɪˌmeɪt). **1.** to form an approximate idea of (size, cost, etc.); calculate roughly. **2.** (*tr.; may take a clause as object*) to form an opinion about; judge. **3.** to submit (an approximate price) for (a job) to a prospective client. *~n.* (ˈɛstɪmɪt). **4.** an approximate calculation. **5.** a statement of the likely charge for certain work. **6.** a judgment; appraisal. [C16: < L *aestimāre* to assess the worth of, < ?] **—ˈestiˌmator** *n.* **—ˈestimative** *adj.*

estimation (ˌɛstɪˈmeɪʃən) *n.* **1.** a considered opinion; judgment. **2.** esteem; respect. **3.** the act of estimating.

estival (iːˈstaɪvᵊl, ˈɛstɪ-) *adj.* the usual U.S. spelling of **aestival.**

estivate (ˈiːstɪˌveɪt, ˈɛs-) *vb.* (*intr.*) the usual U.S. spelling of **aestivate.**

Estonian (ɛˈstəʊnɪən) *adj.* **1.** of, relating to, or characteristic of Estonia, a Soviet Socialist Republic on the Gulf of Finland and the Baltic Sea. **2.** of or relating to the people of Estonia or their language. ~*n.* **3.** an official language of Estonia. **4.** a native or inhabitant of Estonia.

estop (ɪˈstɒp) *vb.* **-topping, -topped.** (*tr.*) **1.** *Law.* to preclude by estoppel. **2.** *Arch.* to stop. [C15: < OF *estoper* to plug, ult. < L *stuppa* tow; see STOP] —**esˈtoppage** *n.*

estoppel (ɪˈstɒpᵊl) *n. Law.* a rule of evidence whereby a person is precluded from denying the truth of a statement he has previously asserted. [C16: < OF *estoupail* plug; see ESTOP]

estovers (ɛˈstəʊvəz) *pl. n. Law.* necessaries allowed to tenant of land, esp. wood for fuel and repairs. [C15: < Anglo-F., pl. of *estover,* < OF *estovoir* to be necessary, < L *est opus* there is need]

estradiol (ˌɛstrəˈdaɪɒl, ˌiːstrə-) *n.* the usual U.S. spelling of **oestradiol.**

estrange (ɪˈstreɪndʒ) *vb.* (*tr.*) to antagonize or lose the affection of (someone previously friendly); alienate. [C15: < OF *estranger,* < LL *extrāneāre* to treat as a stranger, < L *extrāneus* foreign; see STRANGE] —**esˈtranged** *adj.* —**esˈtrangement** *n.*

estrogen (ˈɛstrədʒən, ˈiːstrə-) *n.* the usual U.S. spelling of **oestrogen.**

estrus (ˈɛstrəs, ˈiːstrəs) *n.* the usual U.S. spelling of **oestrus.**

estuary (ˈɛstjʊərɪ) *n., pl.* **-aries.** the widening channel of a river where it nears the sea. [C16: < L *aestuārium* marsh, channel, < *aestus* tide] —**estuarial** (ˌɛstjʊˈɛərɪəl) *adj.* —**ˈestuarine** *adj.*

e.s.u. *or* **ESU** *abbrev. for* electrostatic unit.

-et *suffix of nouns.* small or lesser: *islet; baronet.* [< OF *-et, -ete*]

eta (ˈiːtə) *n.* the seventh letter in the Greek alphabet (Η, η). [Gk, < Phoenician]

ETA *abbrev. for* estimated time of arrival.

et al. *abbrev. for:* **1.** et alibi. [L: and elsewhere] **2.** et alii. [L: and others]

etalon (ˈɛtəˌlɒn) *n. Physics.* a device used in spectroscopy to measure wavelengths by interference effects produced by multiple reflections between parallel half-silvered glass plates. [C20: F *étalon* a standard of weights & measures]

etc. *abbrev. for* et cetera.

et cetera *or* **etcetera** (ɪt ˈsɛtrə) *n. and vb. substitute.* **1.** and the rest; and others; and so forth. **2.** or the like; or something similar. [< L *et* and + *cetera* the other (things)]

▷ **Usage.** Since *et cetera* (or *etc.*) means *and other things,* careful writers do not use the expression *and etc.* The repetition of *etc.,* as in *notebooks, etc., etc.,* is avoided in formal contexts.

etceteras (ɪtˈsɛtrəz) *pl. n.* miscellaneous extra things or persons.

etch (ɛtʃ) *vb.* **1.** (*tr.*) to wear away the surface of (a metal, glass, etc.) by the action of an acid. **2.** to cut or corrode (a design, etc.) on (a metal or other printing plate) by the action of acid on parts not covered by an acid-resistant coating. **3.** (*tr.*) to cut as with a sharp implement. **4.** (*tr.; usually passive*) to imprint vividly. [C17: < Du. *etsen,* < OHG *azzen* to feed, bite] —**ˈetcher** *n.*

etching (ˈɛtʃɪŋ) *n.* **1.** the art, act, or process of preparing etched surfaces or of printing designs from them. **2.** an etched plate. **3.** an impression made from an etched plate.

ETD *abbrev. for* estimated time of departure.

eternal (ɪˈtɜːnᵊl)) *adj.* **1. a.** without beginning or end; lasting for ever. **b.** (*as n.*): *the eternal.* **2.** (*often cap.*) a name applied to God. **3.** unchanged by time; immutable: *eternal truths.* **4.** seemingly unceasing. [C14: < LL, < L *aeternus;* rel. to L *aevum* age] —ˌ**eterˈnality** *or* **eˈternalness** *n.*

eternalize (ɪˈtɜːnəˌlaɪz) *or* **eternize** (ɪˈtɜːnaɪz), **-ise** *vb.* (*tr.*) **1.** to make eternal. **2.** to make famous for ever; immortalize. —**eˌternaliˈzation** *or* **eˌterniˈzation, -iˈsation** *n.*

eternal triangle *n.* an emotional relationship in which there are conflicts involving a man and two women or a woman and two men.

eternity (ɪˈtɜːnɪtɪ) *n., pl.* **-ties. 1.** endless or infinite time. **2.** the quality, state, or condition of being eternal. **3.** (*usually pl.*) any aspect of life and thought considered timeless. **4.** the timeless existence, believed by some to characterize the afterlife. **5.** a seemingly endless period of time.

eternity ring *n.* a ring given as a token of lasting affection, esp. one set all around with stones to symbolize continuity.

etesian (ɪˈtiːʒɪən) *adj.* (of NW winds) recurring annually in the summer in the E Mediterranean. [C17: < L *etēsius* yearly, < Gk *etos* year]

Eth. *abbrev. for:* **1.** Ethiopia(n). **2.** Ethiopic.

-eth[1] *suffix.* forming the archaic third person singular present indicative tense of verbs: *goeth; taketh.* [OE *-eth, -th*]

-eth[2] *suffix forming ordinal numbers.* a variant of **-th**[2]: *twentieth.*

ethane (ˈiːθeɪn, ˈɛθ-) *n.* a colourless odourless flammable gaseous alkane obtained from natural gas and petroleum: used as a fuel. Formula: C_2H_6. [C19: < ETH(YL) + -ANE]

ethanediol (ˈiːθeɪnˌdaɪɒl, ˈɛθ-) *n.* a colourless soluble liquid used as an antifreeze and solvent. [C20: < ETHANE + DI-[1] + -OL[1]]

ethanoic acid (ˌɛθəˈnəʊɪk, ˌiːθə-) *n.* the modern name for **acetic acid.**

ethanol (ˈɛθəˌnɒl, ˈiːθə-) *n.* the technical name for **alcohol** (sense 1).

ethene (ˈɛθiːn) *n.* the technical name for **ethylene.**

ether (ˈiːθə) *n.* **1.** Also called: **diethyl ether, ethyl ether, ethoxyethane.** a colourless volatile highly flammable liquid: used as a solvent and anaesthetic. Formula: $C_2H_5OC_2H_5$. **2.** any of a class of organic compounds with the general formula ROR′, as in diethyl ether $C_2H_5OC_2H_5$. **3.** the medium formerly believed to fill all space and to support the propagation of electromagnetic waves. **4.** *Greek myth.* the upper regions of the atmosphere; clear sky or heaven. ~Also (for senses 3 and 4): **aether.** [C17: < L, < Gk *aithein* to burn] —**etheric** (iːˈθɛrɪk) *adj.*

ethereal (ɪˈθɪərɪəl) *adj.* **1.** extremely delicate or refined. **2.** almost as light as air; airy. **3.** celestial or spiritual. **4.** of, containing, or dissolved in an ether, esp. diethyl ether. **5.** of or relating to the ether. [C16: < L, < Gk *aithēr* ETHER] —**eˌthereˈality** *or* **eˈtherealness** *n.*

etherealize *or* **-ise** (ɪˈθɪərɪəˌlaɪz) *vb.* (*tr.*) **1.** to make or regard as being ethereal. **2.** to add ether to or make into ether. —**eˌtherealiˈzation** *or* **-iˈsation** *n.*

etherize *or* **-ise** (ˈiːθəˌraɪz) *vb.* (*tr.*) *Obs.* to subject (a person) to the anaesthetic influence of ether fumes; anaesthetize. —ˌ**etheriˈzation** *or* **-iˈsation** *n.* —**ˈetherˌizer** *or* **-ˌiser** *n.*

ethic (ˈɛθɪk) *n.* **1.** a moral principle or set of moral values held by an individual or group. ~*adj.* **2.** another word for **ethical.** [C15: < L, < Gk *ēthos* custom]

ethical (ˈɛθɪkᵊl) *adj.* **1.** in accordance with principles of conduct that are considered correct, esp. those of a given profession or group. **2.** of or relating to ethics. **3.** (of a medicinal agent) available legally only with a doctor's prescription. —**ˈethicalness** *or* ˌ**ethiˈcality** *n.*

ethics (ˈɛθɪks) *n.* **1.** (*functioning as sing.*) the philosophical study of the moral value of human conduct and of the rules and principles that ought to govern it. **2.** (*functioning as pl.*) a code of behaviour considered correct, esp. that of a particular group, profession, or individual. **3.** (*functioning as pl.*) the moral fitness of a decision, course of action, etc. —**ethicist** (ˈɛθɪsɪst) *n.*

Ethiopian (ˌiːθɪˈəʊpɪən) *adj.* **1.** of or relating to Ethiopia (a state in NE Africa), its people, or any of their languages. ~*n.* **2.** a native or inhabitant of Ethiopia. **3.** any of the languages of Ethiopia, esp. Amharic. ~*n., adj.* **4.** an archaic word for **Negro.**

Ethiopic (ˌiːθɪˈɒpɪk, -ˈəʊpɪk) *n.* **1.** the ancient Semitic language of Ethiopia: a Christian liturgical language. **2.** the group of languages developed from this language, including Amharic. ~*adj.* **3.** denoting or relating to this language or group of languages. **4.** a less common word for **Ethiopian.**

ethnic (ˈɛθnɪk) *or* **ethnical** *adj.* **1.** of or relating to a human group having racial, religious, linguistic, and other traits in common. **2.** relating to the classification of mankind into groups, esp. on the basis of racial characteristics. **3.** denoting or deriving from the cultural traditions of a group of people. **4.** characteristic of another culture, esp. a peasant one. ~*n.* **5.** *Chiefly U.S.* a member of an ethnic group, esp. a minority one. [C14 (in the senses: heathen, Gentile): < LL *ethnicus,* < Gk *ethnos* race] —**ethnicity** (ɛθˈnɪsɪtɪ) *n.*

ethno- *combining form.* indicating race, people, or culture. [via F < Gk *ethnos* race]

ethnocentrism (ˌɛθnəʊˈsɛnˌtrɪzəm) *n.* belief in the intrinsic superiority of the nation, culture, or group to which one belongs. —ˌ**ethnoˈcentric** *adj.* —ˌ**ethnoˈcentrically** *adv.* —ˌ**ethnocenˈtricity** *n.*

ethnography (ɛθˈnɒgrəfɪ) *n.* the branch of anthropology that deals with the scientific description of individual human societies. —ˌ**ethˈnographer** *n.* —**ethnographic** (ˌɛθnəʊˈgræfɪk) *or* ˌ**ethnoˈgraphical** *adj.*

ethnology (ɛθˈnɒlədʒɪ) *n.* the branch of anthropology that deals with races and peoples, their origins, characteristics, etc. —**ethnologic** (ˌɛθnəˈlɒdʒɪk) *or* ˌ**ethnoˈlogical** *adj.* —**ethˈnologist** *n.*

ethology (ɪˈθɒlədʒɪ) *n.* the study of the behaviour of animals in their normal environment. [C17 (in the obs. sense: mimicry): via L < Gk *ēthos* character; current sense, C19] —**ethological** (ˌɛθəˈlɒdʒɪkᵊl) *adj.* —**eˈthologist** *n.*

ethos (ˈiːθɒs) *n.* the distinctive character, spirit, and attitudes of a people, culture, era, etc.: *the revolutionary ethos.* [C19: < LL: habit, < Gk]

ethyl (ˈiːθaɪl, ˈɛθɪl) *n.* (*modifier*) of, consisting of, or containing the monovalent group C_2H_5–. [C19: < ETH(ER) + -YL] —**ethylic** (ɪˈθɪlɪk) *adj.*

ethyl acetate *n.* a colourless volatile flammable liquid ester: used in perfumes and flavourings and as a solvent. Formula: $CH_3COOC_2H_5$.

ethyl alcohol *n.* another name for **alcohol** (sense 1).

ethylene (ˈɛθɪˌliːn) *or* **ethene** (ˈɛθiːn) *n.* a colourless flammable gaseous alkene used in the manufacture of polythene and other chemicals. Formula: $CH_2{:}CH_2$. —**ethylenic** (ˌɛθɪˈliːnɪk) *adj.*

ethylene glycol *n.* another name for **ethanediol.**

ethylene group *or* **radical** *n. Chem.* the divalent group, $-CH_2CH_2-$, derived from ethylene.

ethylene series *n. Chem.* the homologous series of unsaturated hydrocarbons that contain one double bond and have the general formula, C_nH_{2n}; alkene series.

etiolate (ˈiːtɪəʊˌleɪt) *vb.* **1.** *Bot.* to whiten (a green plant) through lack of sunlight. **2.** to become or cause to become pale and weak. [C18: < F *étioler* to make pale, prob. < OF *estuble* straw, < L *stipula*] —ˌ**etioˈlation** *n.*

etiology *or* **aetiology** (ˌiːtɪˈɒlədʒɪ) *n., pl.* **-gies.** **1.** the philosophy or study of causation. **2.** the study of the causes of diseases. **3.** the cause of a disease. [C16: < LL *aetiologia,* < Gk *aitiologia* < *aitia* cause] —**etiological** *or* **aetiological** (ˌiːtɪəˈlɒdʒɪkᵊl) *adj.* —ˌ**etiˈologist** *or* ˌ**aetiˈologist** *n.*

etiquette (ˈɛtɪˌkɛt, ˌɛtɪˈkɛt) *n.* **1.** the customs or rules governing behaviour regarded as correct in social life. **2.** a conventional code of practice followed in certain professions or groups. [C18: < F, < OF *estiquette* label, < *estiquier* to attach; see STICK[2]]

Eton collar (ˈiːtᵊn) *n.* a broad stiff white collar worn outside a Eton jacket.

Eton crop *n.* a very short mannish hairstyle worn by women in the 1920s.

Eton jacket *n.* a waist-length jacket, open in front, formerly worn by pupils of Eton College, a public school for boys in S England.

Etruscan (ɪˈtrʌskən) *or* **Etrurian** (ɪˈtrʊərɪən) *n.* **1.** a member of an ancient people of Etruria in central Italy whose civilization greatly influenced the Romans. **2.** the language of the ancient Etruscans. ~*adj.* **3.** of or relating to Etruria, the Etruscans, their culture, or their language.

et seq. *abbrev. for:* **1.** et sequens [L: and the following] **2.** Also: **et seqq.** et sequentia [L: and those that follow]

-ette *suffix of nouns.* **1.** small: *cigarette.* **2.** female: *majorette.* **3.** (esp. in trade names) imitation: *Leatherette.* [< F, fem. of -ET]

étude (ˈeɪtjuːd) *n.* a short musical composition for a solo instrument, esp. one designed as an exercise or exploiting virtuosity. [C19: < F: STUDY]

ety., etym., *or* **etymol.** *abbrev. for:* **1.** etymological. **2.** etymology.

etymology (ˌɛtɪˈmɒlədʒɪ) *n., pl.* **-gies.** **1.** the study of the sources and development of words. **2.** an account of the source and development of a word. [C14: via L < Gk; see ETYMON, -LOGY] —**etymological** (ˌɛtɪməˈlɒdʒɪkᵊl) *adj.* —ˌ**etyˈmologist** *n.* —ˌ**etyˈmologize** *or* **-gise** *vb.*

etymon (ˈɛtɪˌmɒn) *n., pl.* **-mons** *or* **-ma** (-mə). a form of a word, usually the earliest recorded form or a reconstructed form, from which another word is derived. [C16: via L < Gk *etumon* basic meaning, < *etumos* true, actual]

Eu *the chemical symbol for* europium.

eu- *prefix.* well, pleasant, or good: *eupeptic; euphony.* [via L < Gk, < *eus* good]

eucalyptus (ˌjuːkəˈlɪptəs) *or* **eucalypt** (ˈjuːkəˌlɪpt) *n., pl.* **-lyptuses, -lypti** (-ˈlɪptaɪ), *or* **-lypts.** any tree of the mostly Australian genus *Eucalyptus,* widely cultivated for timber and gum, as ornament, and for the medicinal oil in their leaves (**eucalyptus oil**). [C19: NL, < EU- + Gk *kaluptos* covered, < *kaluptein* to cover, hide]

Eucharist (ˈjuːkərɪst) *n.* **1.** the Christian sacrament in which Christ's Last Supper is commemorated by the consecration of bread and wine. **2.** the consecrated elements of bread and wine offered in the sacrament. [C14: via Church L < Gk *eukharistos* thankful, < EU- + *kharis* favour] —ˌ**Euchaˈristic** *or* ˌ**Euchaˈristical** *adj.*

euchre (ˈjuːkə) *n.* **1.** a U.S. and Canad. card game for two, three, or four players, using a poker pack. **2.** an instance of euchring another player. ~*vb.* (*tr.*) **3.** to prevent (a player) from making his contracted tricks. **4.** (usually foll. by *out*) *U.S., Canad., Austral., & N.Z. inf.* to outwit or cheat. [C19: <?]

Euclidean *or* **Euclidian** (juːˈklɪdɪən) *adj.* denoting a system of geometry based on the axioms of Euclid, 3rd-century B.C. Greek mathematician, esp. upon the axiom that parallel lines meet at infinity.

eucryphia (juːˈkrɪfɪə) *n.* any of various mostly evergreen trees and shrubs of S America and Australia. [NL, < EU- + Gk *kryphios* covered]

eudiometer (ˌjuːdɪˈɒmɪtə) *n.* a graduated glass tube used in the study and volumetric analysis of gas reactions. [C18: < Gk *eudios,* lit.: clear-skied + -METER]

eugenics (juːˈdʒɛnɪks) *n.* (*functioning as sing.*) the study of methods of improving the quality of the human race, esp. by selective breeding. [C19: < Gk *eugenēs* well-born, < EU- + *-genēs* born; see -GEN] —**euˈgenic** *adj.* —**euˈgenically** *adv.* —**euˈgenicist** *n.* —**eugenist** (ˈjuːdʒənɪst) *n., adj.*

eukaryote *or* **eucaryote** (juːˈkærɪɒt) *n.* an organism having cells each with a nucleus in which the genetic material is carried on chromosomes. Cf. **prokaryote.** [< EU- + KARYO- + *-ote* as in *zygote*]

eulogize *or* **-gise** (ˈjuːləˌdʒaɪz) *vb.* to praise (a person or thing) highly in speech or writing. —ˈ**eulogist,** ˈ**euloˌgizer,** *or* -ˌ**giser** *n.* —ˌ**euloˈgistic** *or* ˌ**euloˈgistical** *adj.*

eulogy (ˈjuːlədʒɪ) *n., pl.* **-gies.** **1.** a speech or piece of writing praising a person or thing, esp. a person who has recently died. **2.** high praise or commendation. ~Also called (archaic): **eulogium** (juːˈləʊdʒɪəm). [C16: < LL, < Gk: praise, < EU- + -LOGY]

Eumenides (juːˈmɛnɪˌdiːz) *pl. n.* another name for the **Furies,** used by the Greeks as a euphemism. [< Gk, lit.: the benevolent ones, < *eumenēs* benevolent, < EU- + *menos* spirit]

eunuch (ˈjuːnək) *n.* **1.** a man who has been castrated, esp. (formerly) for some office such as a guard in a harem. **2.** *Inf.* an ineffective man. [C15: via L < Gk *eunoukhos* bedchamber attendant, < *eunē* bed + *ekhein* to have, keep]

euonymus (juːˈɒnɪməs) *or* **evonymus** (ɛˈvɒnɪməs) *n.* any tree or shrub of the N temperate genus *Euonymus,* such as the spindle tree. [C18: < L: spindle tree, < Gk *euōnumos* fortunately named, < EU- + *onoma* NAME]

eupepsia (juːˈpɛpsɪə) *or* **eupepsy** (juːˈpɛpsɪ) *n. Physiol.* good digestion. [C18: < NL, < Gk, < EU- + *pepsis* digestion] —**eupeptic** (juːˈpɛptɪk) *adj.*

euphemism (ˈjuːfɪˌmɪzəm) *n.* **1.** an inoffensive word or phrase substituted for one considered offensive or hurtful. **2.** the use of such inoffensive words or phrases. [C17: < Gk, < EU- + *phēmē* speech] —ˌ**eupheˈmistic** *adj.* —ˌ**eupheˈmistically** *adv.*

euphemize *or* **-mise** (ˈjuːfɪˌmaɪz) *vb.* to speak in euphemisms or refer to by means of a euphemism. —ˈ**eupheˌmizer** *or* **-ˌmiser** *n.*

euphonic (juːˈfɒnɪk) *or* **euphonious** (juːˈfəʊnɪəs) *adj.* **1.** denoting or relating to euphony; pleasing to the ear. **2.** (of speech sounds) altered for ease of pronunciation. —**euˈphonically** *or* **euˈphoniously** *adv.* —**euˈphoniousness** *n.*

euphonium (juːˈfəʊnɪəm) *n.* a brass musical instrument with four valves. [C19: NL, < EUPH(ONY + HARM)ONIUM]

euphonize *or* **-nise** (ˈjuːfəˌnaɪz) *vb.* **1.** to make pleasant to hear. **2.** to change (speech sounds) so as to facilitate pronunciation.

euphony (ˈjuːfənɪ) *n., pl.* **-nies.** **1.** the alteration of speech sounds, esp. by assimilation, so as to make them easier to pronounce. **2.** a pleasing sound, esp. in speech. [C17: < LL, < Gk, < EU- + *phōnē* voice]

euphorbia (juːˈfɔːbɪə) *n.* any plant of the genus *Euphorbia,* such as the spurges. [C14 *euforbia,* < L *euphorbea* African plant, after *Euphorbus,* first-cent. A.D. Gk physician]

euphoria (juːˈfɔːrɪə) *n.* a feeling of great elation, esp. when exaggerated. [C19: < Gk: good ability to endure, < EU- + *pherein* to bear] —**euphoric** (juːˈfɒrɪk) *adj.*

euphoriant (juːˈfɔːrɪənt) *adj.* **1.** able to produce euphoria. ~*n.* **2.** a euphoriant drug or agent.

euphotic (juːˈfəʊtɪk, -ˈfɒt-) *adj.* denoting or relating to the uppermost part of a sea or lake, which receives enough light for photosynthesis to take place. [C20: < EU- + PHOTIC]

euphrasy (ˈjuːfrəsɪ) *n., pl.* **-sies.** another name for **eyebright.** [C15: *eufrasie,* < Med. L, < Gk *euphrasia* gladness, < EU- + *phrēn* mind]

euphuism (ˈjuːfjuːˌɪzəm) *n.* **1.** an artificial prose style of the Elizabethan period, marked by extreme use of antithesis, alliteration, and extended similes and allusions. **2.** any stylish affectation in speech or writing. [C16: after *Euphues,* prose romance by John Lyly] —ˈ**euphuist** *n.* —ˌ**euphuˈistic** *or* ˌ**euphuˈistical** *adj.* —ˌ**euphuˈistically** *adv.*

Eur. *abbrev. for* Europe(an).

Eur- *combining form.* a variant of **Euro-** before a vowel.

Eurasian (jʊəˈreɪʃən, -ʒən) *adj.* **1.** of or relating to Europe and Asia considered as a whole. **2.** of mixed European and Asian descent. ~*n.* **3.** a person of mixed European and Asian descent.

Euratom (jʊəˈrætəm) *n.* short for **European Atomic Energy Community;** an authority established by the Common Market to develop peaceful uses of nuclear energy.

eureka (jʊˈriːkə) *interj.* an exclamation of triumph on discovering or solving something. [C17: < Gk *heurēka* I have found (it), < *heuriskein* to find; traditionally the exclamation of Archimedes when he realized, during bathing, that the volume of an irregular solid could be calculated by measuring the water displaced when it was immersed]

eurhythmic (juːˈrɪðmɪk), **eurhythmical,** *or esp. U.S.* **eurythmic, eurythmical** *adj.* **1.** having a pleasing and harmonious rhythm, order, or structure. **2.** of or relating to eurhythmics. [C19: < L, < Gk, < EU- + *rhuthmos* proportion, RHYTHM]

eurhythmics *or esp. U.S.* **eurythmics** (juːˈrɪðmɪks) *n.* (*functioning as sing.*) **1.** a system of training through physical movement to music. **2.** dancing of this style. [C20: < EURHYTHMIC] —**euˈrhythmy** *or* **euˈrythmy** *n.*

Euro- (ˈjʊərəʊ) *or before a vowel* **Eur-** *combining form.* Europe *or* European.

Eurobond (ˈjʊərəʊˌbɒnd) *n.* a bond sold in countries other than the country in the currency of which it is issued.

Eurocommunism (ˌjʊərəʊˈkɒmjʊˌnɪzəm) *n.* the policies, doctrines, and practices of Communist Parties in Western Europe, esp. insofar as these favour nonalignment with Russia or China. —ˌ**Euroˈcommunist** *n., adj.*

Eurocrat (ˈjʊərəˌkræt) *n.* a member of the administration of the Common Market.

Eurocurrency (ˈjuːrəʊˌkʌrənsɪ) *n.* the currency of any country held on deposit in Europe outside its home market: used as a source of short- or medium-term finance because of easy convertibility.

European (ˌjʊərəˈpɪən) *adj.* **1.** of or relating to Europe or its inhabitants. **2.** native to or derived from Europe. ~*n.* **3.** a native or inhabitant of Europe. **4.** a person of European descent. **5.** *S. African.* any White person. —ˌ**Euroˈpeanˌism** *n.*

European Economic Community *n.* the official name for the **Common Market.**

Europeanize *or* **-ise** (ˌjʊərəˈpɪəˌnaɪz) *vb.* (*tr.*) **1.** to make European. **2.** to integrate (a country, economy, etc.) into the Common Market. —ˌ**EuroˌpeaniˈzatIon** *or* **-iˈsation** *n.*

European Parliament *n.* the assembly of the European Economic Community in Strasbourg.

europium (jʊˈrəʊpɪəm) *n.* a silvery-white element of the lanthanide series of metals. Symbol: Eu; atomic no.: 63; atomic wt.: 151.96. [C20: after *Europe* + -IUM]

eurythmics (juːˈrɪðmɪks) *n.* a variant spelling (esp. U.S.) of **eurhythmics.**

Eustachian tube (juːˈsteɪʃən) *n.* a tube that connects the middle ear with the pharynx and equalizes the pressure between the two sides of the eardrum. [C18: after Bartolomeo *Eustachio,* 16th-cent. It. anatomist]

eustatic (juːˈstætɪk) *adj.* denoting or relating to worldwide changes in sea level, caused by the melting of ice sheets, sedimentation, etc. [C20: < Gk, < EU- + STATIC] —**eustasy** (ˈjuːstəsɪ) *n.*

eutectic (juːˈtɛktɪk) *adj.* **1.** (of a mixture of substances) having the lowest freezing point of all possible mixtures of the substances. **2.** concerned with or suitable for the formation of eutectic mixtures. ~*n.* **3.** a eutectic mixture. **4.** the temperature at which a eutectic mixture forms. [C19: < Gk *eutēktos* melting readily, < EU- + *tēkein* to melt]

Euterpe (juːˈtɜːpɪ) *n. Greek myth.* the Muse of lyric poetry and music. —**Euˈterpean** *adj.*

euthanasia (ˌjuːθəˈneɪzɪə) *n.* the act of killing someone painlessly, esp. to relieve suffering from an incurable illness. [C17: via NL < Gk: easy death, < EU- + *thanatos* death]

euthenics (juːˈθɛnɪks) *n.* (*functioning as sing.*) the study of the control of the environment, esp. with a view to improving the health and living standards of the human race. [C20: < Gk *euthēnein* to thrive] —**euˈthenist** *n.*

eutrophic (juːˈtrɒfɪk, -ˈtrəʊ-) *adj.* (of lakes, etc.) rich in organic and mineral nutrients and supporting an abundant plant life. [C18: prob. <

eutrophy, < Gk, < *eutrophos* well-fed, < EU- + *trephein* to nourish] —ˈ**eutrophy** *n.*

eV *abbrev. for* electronvolt.

EVA *Astronautics. abbrev. for* extravehicular activity.

evacuate (ɪˈvækjʊˌeɪt) *vb.* (*mainly tr.*) **1.** (*also intr.*) to withdraw or cause to withdraw (from a place of danger) to a place of safety. **2.** to make empty. **3.** (*also intr.*) *Physiol.* **a.** to eliminate or excrete (faeces). **b.** to discharge (any waste) from (the body). **4.** (*tr.*) to create a vacuum in (a bulb, flask, etc.). [C16: < L *ēvacuāre* to void, < *vacuus* empty] —eˌ**vacuˈation** *n.* —eˈ**vacuative** *adj.* —eˈ**vacuˌator** *n.* —eˌ**vacuˈee** *n.*

evade (ɪˈveɪd) *vb.* (*mainly tr.*) **1.** to get away from or avoid (imprisonment, captors, etc.). **2.** to get around, shirk, or dodge (the law, a duty, etc.). **3.** (*also intr.*) to avoid answering (a question). [C16: < F, < L *ēvādere* to go forth] —eˈ**vadable** *adj.* —eˈ**vader** *n.* —eˈ**vadingly** *adv.*

evaginate (ɪˈvædʒɪˌneɪt) *vb.* (*tr.*) *Med.* to turn (an organ or part) inside out. [C17: < LL *ēvāgīnare* to unsheathe, < L *vāgīna* sheath]

evaluate (ɪˈvæljʊˌeɪt) *vb.* (*tr.*) **1.** to ascertain or set the amount or value of. **2.** to judge or assess the worth of. [C19: back formation < *evaluation*, < F, < *évaluer*; see VALUE] —eˌ**valuˈation** *n.* —eˈ**valuative** *adj.* —eˈ**valuˌator** *n.*

evanesce (ˌɛvəˈnɛs) *vb.* (*intr.*) (of smoke, mist, etc.) to fade gradually from sight; vanish. [C19: < L *ēvānēscere* to disappear; see VANISH]

evanescent (ˌɛvəˈnɛsᵊnt) *adj.* **1.** passing out of sight; fading away; vanishing. **2.** ephemeral or transitory. —ˌ**evaˈnescence** *n.*

evangel (ɪˈvændʒəl) *n.* **1.** *Arch.* the gospel of Christianity. **2.** (*often cap.*) any of the four Gospels of the New Testament. **3.** any body of teachings regarded as basic. [C14: < Church L, < Gk *evangelion* good news, < EU- + *angelos* messenger; see ANGEL]

evangelical (ˌiːvænˈdʒɛlɪkᵊl) *Christianity.* ~*adj.* **1.** of or following from the Gospels. **2.** denoting or relating to any of certain Protestant sects, which emphasize personal conversion and faith in atonement through the death of Christ as a means of salvation. **3.** denoting or relating to an evangelist. ~*n.* **4.** a member of an evangelical sect. —ˌ**evanˈgelicalism** *n.*

evangelism (ɪˈvændʒɪˌlɪzəm) *n.* **1.** the practice of spreading the Christian gospel. **2.** ardent or missionary zeal for a cause.

evangelist (ɪˈvændʒɪlɪst) *n.* **1.** an occasional preacher, sometimes itinerant. **2.** a preacher of the Christian gospel. —eˌ**vangeˈlistic** *adj.*

Evangelist (ɪˈvændʒɪlɪst) *n.* any of the writers of the New Testament Gospels: Matthew, Mark, Luke, or John.

evangelize *or* **-lise** (ɪˈvændʒɪˌlaɪz) *vb.* **1.** to preach the Christian gospel (to). **2.** (*intr.*) to advocate a cause with the object of making converts. —eˌ**vangeliˈzation** *or* **-liˈsation** *n.* —eˈ**vangeˌlizer** *or* **-ˌliser** *n.*

evaporate (ɪˈvæpəˌreɪt) *vb.* **1.** to change or cause to change from a liquid or solid state to a vapour. **2.** to lose or cause to lose liquid by vaporization leaving a more concentrated residue. **3.** to disappear or cause to disappear. [C16: < LL, < L *vapor* steam; see VAPOUR] —eˈ**vaporable** *adj.* —eˌ**vapoˈration** *n.* —eˈ**vaporative** *adj.* —eˈ**vapoˌrator** *n.*

evaporated milk *n.* thick unsweetened tinned milk from which some of the water has been evaporated.

evasion (ɪˈveɪʒən) *n.* **1.** the act of evading, esp. a distasteful duty, responsibility, etc., by cunning or by illegal means: *tax evasion.* **2.** cunning or deception used to dodge a question, duty, etc.; means of evading. [C15: < LL *ēvāsio*; see EVADE]

evasive (ɪˈveɪsɪv) *adj.* **1.** tending or seeking to evade; not straightforward. **2.** avoiding or seeking to avoid trouble or difficulties. **3.** hard to catch or obtain; elusive. —eˈ**vasively** *adv.* —eˈ**vasiveness** *n.*

eve (iːv) *n.* **1.** the evening or day before some special event. **2.** the period immediately before an event: *the eve of war.* **3.** an archaic word for **evening.** [C13: var. of EVEN²]

even¹ (ˈiːvᵊn) *adj.* **1.** level and regular; flat. **2.** (*postpositive*; foll. by *with*) on the same level or in the same plane (as). **3.** without variation or fluctuation; regular; constant. **4.** not readily moved or excited; calm: *an even temper.* **5.** equally balanced between two sides: *an even game.* **6.** equal or identical in number, quantity, etc. **7. a.** (of a number) divisible by two. **b.** characterized or indicated by such a number: *the even pages.* **8.** relating to or denoting two or either of two alternatives, events, etc., that have an equal probability: *an even chance of missing or catching a train.* **9.** having no balance of debt; neither owing nor being owed. **10.** just and impartial; fair. **11.** exact in number, amount, or extent: *an even pound.* **12.** equal, as in score; level. **13. even money. a.** a bet that wins an identical sum if it succeeds. **b.** (*as modifier*): *the even-money favourite.* **14. get even (with).** *Inf.* to exact revenge (on); settle accounts (with). ~*adv.* **15.** (intensifier; used to suggest that the content of a statement is unexpected or paradoxical): *even an idiot can do that.* **16.** (intensifier; used with comparative forms): *even better.* **17.** notwithstanding; in spite of. **18.** used to introduce a more precise version of a word, phrase, or statement: *he is base, even depraved.* **19.** used preceding a clause of supposition or hypothesis to emphasize that whether or not the condition in it is fulfilled, the statement in the main clause remains valid: *even if she died he wouldn't care.* **20.** *Arch.* all the way; fully: *I love thee even unto death.* **21. even as.** (*conj.*) at the very same moment or in the very same way that. **22. even so.** in spite of any assertion to the contrary: nevertheless. ~See also **even out, evens, even up.** [OE *efen*] —ˈ**evener** *n.* —ˈ**evenly** *adv.* —ˈ**evenness** *n.*

even² (ˈiːvᵊn) *n.* an archaic word for **eve** or **evening.** [OE *ǣfen*]

even-handed *adj.* fair; impartial. —ˌ**evenˈhandedly** *adv.* —ˌ**even-ˈhandedness** *n.*

evening (ˈiːvnɪŋ) *n.* **1.** the latter part of the day, esp. from late afternoon until nightfall. **2.** the latter or concluding period: *the evening of one's life.* **3.** the early part of the night spent in a specified way: *an evening at the theatre.* **4.** (*modifier*) of, used in, or occurring in the evening: *the evening papers.* [OE *ǣfnung*]

evening dress *n.* attire for a formal occasion during the evening.

evening primrose *n.* any plant of the genus *Oenothera*, typically having yellow flowers that open in the evening.

evenings (ˈiːvnɪŋz) *adv. Inf.* in the evening, esp. regularly.

evening star *n.* a planet, usually Venus, seen shining brightly in the west just after sunset.

even out *vb.* (*adv.*) to make or become even, as by the removal of bumps, inequalities, etc.

evens (ˈiːvənz) *adj., adv.* **1.** (of a bet) winning an identical sum if successful. **2.** (of a runner) offered at such odds.

evensong (ˈiːvᵊnˌsɒŋ) *n.* **1.** Also called: **Evening Prayer, vespers.** *Church of England.* the daily evening service. **2.** *R.C. Church, arch.* another name for **vespers.**

event (ɪˈvɛnt) *n.* **1.** anything that takes place, esp. something important; an incident. **2.** the actual or final outcome (esp. in **in the event, after the event**). **3.** any one contest in a programme of sporting or other contests. **4. at all events** *or* **in any event.** regardless of circumstances; in any case. **5. in the event of.** in case of; if (such a thing) happens. **6. in the event that.** if it should happen that. [C16: < L *ēvenīre* to come forth, happen, < *venīre* to come]

even-tempered *adj.* not easily angered or excited; calm.

eventful (ɪˈvɛntfʊl) *adj.* full of events. —eˈ**ventfully** *adv.* —eˈ**ventfulness** *n.*

event horizon *n. Astron.* the spherical boundary of a black hole: objects passing through it would disappear completely and for ever, as no information can escape across the event horizon from the interior.

eventide (ˈiːvᵊnˌtaɪd) *n. Arch. or poetic.* another word for **evening.**

eventide home *n. Euphemistic.* an old people's home.

eventing (ɪˈvɛntɪŋ) *n. Chiefly Brit.* the sport of taking part in equestrian competitions (esp. **three-day events**), usually involving cross-country riding, jumping, and dressage.

eventual (ɪˈvɛntʃʊəl) *adj.* **1.** (*prenominal*) happening in due course of time; ultimate. **2.** *Arch.* contingent or possible.

eventuality (ɪˌvɛntʃʊˈælɪtɪ) *n., pl.* **-ties.** a possible event, occurrence, or result; contingency.

eventually (ɪˈvɛntʃʊəlɪ) *adv.* **1.** at the very end; finally. **2.** (*sentence modifier*) after a long time or long delay: *eventually, he arrived.*

eventuate (ɪˈvɛntʃʊˌeɪt) *vb.* (*intr.*) **1.** (often foll. by *in*) to result ultimately (in). **2.** to come about as a result. **—eˌventuˈation** *n.*

even up *vb.* (*adv.*) to make or become equal, esp. in respect of claims or debts.

ever (ˈɛvə) *adv.* **1.** at any time. **2.** by any chance; in any case: *how did you ever find out?* **3.** at all times; always. **4.** in any possible way or manner: *come as fast as ever you can.* **5.** *Inf., chiefly Brit.* (intensifier, in **ever so, ever such,** and **ever such a**). **6. is he** *or* **she ever!** *U.S. & Canad. sl.* he *or* she displays the quality concerned in abundance. ~See also **for ever.** [OE *ǣfre,* <?]

evergreen (ˈɛvəˌgriːn) *adj.* **1.** (of certain trees and shrubs) bearing foliage throughout the year. Cf. **deciduous. 2.** remaining fresh and vital. *~n.* **3.** an evergreen tree or shrub.

everlasting (ˌɛvəˈlɑːstɪŋ) *adj.* **1.** never coming to an end; eternal. **2.** lasting for an indefinitely long period. **3.** lasting so long or occurring so often as to become tedious. *~n.* **4.** eternity. **5.** Also called: **everlasting flower.** another name for **immortelle. —ˌeverˈlastingly** *adv.*

evermore (ˌɛvəˈmɔː) *adv.* (often preceded by *for*) all time to come.

evert (ɪˈvɜːt) *vb.* (*tr.*) to turn (an eyelid or other bodily part) outwards or inside out. [C16: < L *ēvertere* to overthrow, < *vertere* to turn] **—eˈversible** *adj.* **—eˈversion** *n.*

every (ˈɛvrɪ) *determiner.* **1.** each one (of the class specified), without exception. **2.** (*not used with a negative*) the greatest or best possible: *every hope.* **3.** each: used before a noun phrase to indicate the recurrent, intermittent, or serial nature of a thing: *every third day.* **4. every bit.** (used in comparisons with *as*) quite; just; equally. **5. every other.** each alternate; every second. **6. every which way.** *U.S. & Canad.* **a.** in all directions; everywhere. **b.** from all sides. [C15 *everich,* < OE *ǣfre ǣlc,* < *ǣfre* EVER + *ǣlc* EACH]

everybody (ˈɛvrɪˌbɒdɪ) *pron.* every person; everyone.

▷ **Usage.** See at **everyone.**

everyday (ˈɛvrɪˌdeɪ) *adj.* **1.** happening each day. **2.** commonplace or usual. **3.** suitable for or used on ordinary days.

Everyman (ˈɛvrɪˌmæn) *n.* **1.** a medieval English morality play in which the central figure represents mankind. **2.** (*often not cap.*) the ordinary person; common man.

everyone (ˈɛvrɪˌwʌn, -wən) *pron.* every person; everybody.

▷ **Usage.** *Anybody, anyone, everybody, everyone, none, no-one, nobody, somebody, someone,* and *each* function as singular in careful English: *everyone nodded his head* (not *their heads*). The use of *their* in such constructions is, however, common in informal English.

every one *pron.* each person or thing in a group, without exception.

everything (ˈɛvrɪˌθɪŋ) *pron.* **1.** the entirety of a specified or implied class. **2.** a great deal, esp. of something very important.

everywhere (ˈɛvrɪˌwɛə) *adv.* to or in all parts or places.

evict (ɪˈvɪkt) *vb.* (*tr.*) **1.** to expel (a tenant) from property by process of law; turn out. **2.** to recover (property or the title to property) by judicial process or by virtue of a superior title. [C15: < LL *ēvincere,* < L: to vanquish utterly, < *vincere* to conquer] **—eˈviction** *n.* **—eˈvictor** *n.*

evidence (ˈɛvɪdəns) *n.* **1.** ground for belief or disbelief; data on which to base proof or to establish truth or falsehood. **2.** a mark or sign that makes evident. **3.** *Law.* matter produced before a court of law in an attempt to prove or disprove a point in issue. **4. in evidence.** on display; apparent. *~vb.* (*tr.*) **5.** to make evident; show clearly. **6.** to give proof of or evidence for.

evident (ˈɛvɪdənt) *adj.* easy to see or understand; apparent. [C14: < L *ēvidēns,* < *vidēre* to see]

evidential (ˌɛvɪˈdɛnʃəl) *adj.* relating to, serving as, or based on evidence. **—ˌeviˈdentially** *adv.*

evidently (ˈɛvɪdəntlɪ) *adv.* **1.** without question; clearly. **2.** to all appearances; apparently.

evil (ˈiːvᵊl) *adj.* **1.** morally wrong or bad; wicked. **2.** causing harm or injury. **3.** marked or accompanied by misfortune: *an evil fate.* **4.** (of temper, disposition, etc.) characterized by anger or spite. **5.** infamous: *an evil reputation.* **6.** offensive or unpleasant: *an evil smell. ~n.* **7.** the quality or an instance of being morally wrong; wickedness. **8.** (*sometimes cap.*) a force or power that brings about wickedness or harm. *~adv.* **9.** (*now usually in combination*) in an evil manner; badly: *evil-smelling.* [OE *yfel*] **—ˈevilly** *adv.* **—ˈevilness** *n.*

evildoer (ˈiːvᵊlˌduːə) *n.* a person who does evil. **—ˈevilˌdoing** *n.*

evil eye *n.* **the. 1.** a look or glance superstitiously supposed to have the power of inflicting harm or injury. **2.** the power to inflict harm, etc., by such a look. **—ˌevil-ˈeyed** *adj.*

evil-minded *adj.* inclined to evil thoughts; malicious or spiteful. **—ˌevil-ˈmindedly** *adv.* **—ˌevil-ˈmindedness** *n.*

evince (ɪˈvɪns) *vb.* (*tr.*) to make evident; show (something) clearly. [C17: < L *ēvincere* to overcome; see EVICT] **—eˈvincible** *adj.* **—eˈvincive** *adj.*

eviscerate (ɪˈvɪsəˌreɪt) *vb.* (*tr.*) **1.** to remove the internal organs of; disembowel. **2.** to deprive of meaning or significance. [C17: < L *ēviscerāre,* < *viscera* entrails] **—eˌviscerˈation** *n.* **—eˈviscerˌator** *n.*

evocation (ˌɛvəˈkeɪʃən) *n.* the act or an instance of evoking. [C17: < L: see EVOKE] **—evocative** (ɪˈvɒkətɪv) *adj.*

evoke (ɪˈvəʊk) *vb.* (*tr.*) **1.** to call or summon up (a memory, feeling, etc.), esp. from the past. **2.** to provoke; elicit. **3.** to cause (spirits) to appear; conjure up. [C17: < L *ēvocāre* to call forth, < *vocāre* to call] **—evocable** (ˈɛvəkəbᵊl) *adj.* **—eˈvoker** *n.*

evolute (ˈɛvəˌluːt) *n.* a geometric curve that describes the locus of the centres of curvature of another curve (the **involute**). [C19: < L *ēvolūtus* unrolled, < *ēvolvere* to roll out, EVOLVE]

evolution (ˌiːvəˈluːʃən) *n.* **1.** *Biol.* a gradual change in the characteristics of a population of animals or plants over successive generations. **2.** a gradual development, esp. to a more complex form: *the evolution of modern art.* **3.** the act of throwing off, as heat, gas, vapour, etc. **4.** a pattern formed by a series of movements or something similar. **5.** an algebraic operation in which the root of a number, expression, etc., is extracted. **6.** *Mil.* an exercise carried out in accordance with a set procedure or plan. [C17: < L *ēvolūtiō* an unrolling, < *ēvolvere* to EVOLVE] **—ˌevoˈlutionary** *or* **ˌevoˈlutional** *adj.*

evolutionist (ˌiːvəˈluːʃənɪst) *n.* **1.** a person who believes in a theory of evolution. *~adj.* **2.** of or relating to a theory of evolution. **—ˌevoˈlutionism** *n.* **—ˌevolutionˈistic** *adj.*

evolve (ɪˈvɒlv) *vb.* **1.** to develop or cause to develop gradually. **2.** (of animal or plant species) to undergo evolution of (organs or parts). **3.** (*tr.*) to yield, emit, or give off (heat, gas, vapour, etc.). [C17: < L *ēvolvere* to unfold, < *volvere* to roll] **—eˈvolvable** *adj.* **—eˈvolvement** *n.*

evzone (ˈɛvzəʊn) *n.* a soldier in an elite Greek

infantry regiment. [C19: < Mod. Gk, < Gk *euzōnos*, lit.: well-girt, < EU- + *zōne* girdle]

ewe (juː) *n.* **a.** a female sheep. **b.** (*as modifier*): *a ewe lamb.* [OE *ēowu*]

ewer (ˈjuːə) *n.* a large jug or pitcher with a wide mouth. [C14: < OF *evier*, < L *aquārius* water carrier, < *aqua* water]

ex[1] (ɛks) *prep.* **1.** *Finance.* excluding; without: *ex dividend.* **2.** *Commerce.* without charge to the buyer until removed from: *ex warehouse.* [C19: < L: out of, from]

ex[2] (ɛks) *n. Inf.* (a person's) former wife, husband, etc.

ex-[1] *prefix.* **1.** out of; outside of; from: *exclosure; exurbia.* **2.** former: *ex-wife.* [< L, < *ex* (prep.), identical with Gk *ex, ek;* see EC-]

ex-[2] *combining form.* a variant of **exo-** before a vowel: *exergonic.*

Ex. *Bible. abbrev. for* Exodus.

exa- *prefix.* denoting 10^{18}: *exametres.* Symbol: E

exacerbate (ɪgˈzæsəˌbeɪt, ɪkˈsæs-) *vb.* (*tr.*) **1.** to make (pain, disease, etc.) more intense; aggravate. **2.** to irritate (a person). [C17: < L *exacerbāre* to irritate, < *acerbus* bitter] **—exˌacerˈbation** *n.*

exact (ɪgˈzækt) *adj.* **1.** correct in every detail; strictly accurate. **2.** precise, as opposed to approximate. **3.** (*prenominal*) specific; particular. **4.** operating with very great precision. **5.** allowing no deviation from a standard; rigorous; strict. **6.** based on measurement and the formulation of laws, as opposed to description and classification: *an exact science.* ~*vb.* (*tr.*) **7.** to force or compel (payment, etc.); extort: *to exact tribute.* **8.** to demand as a right; insist upon. **9.** to call for or require. [C16: < L *exactus* driven out, < *exigere* to drive forth, < *agere* to drive] **—exˈactable** *adj.* **—exˈactness** *n.* **—exˈactor** *or* **exˈacter** *n.*

exacting (ɪgˈzæktɪŋ) *adj.* making rigorous or excessive demands. **—exˈactingness** *n.*

exaction (ɪgˈzækʃən) *n.* **1.** the act or an instance of exacting. **2.** an excessive or harsh demand, esp. for money. **3.** a sum or payment exacted.

exactitude (ɪgˈzæktɪˌtjuːd) *n.* the quality of being exact; precision; accuracy.

exactly (ɪgˈzæktlɪ) *adv.* **1.** in an exact manner; accurately or precisely. **2.** in every respect; just. ~*sentence substitute.* **3.** just so!, precisely! **4. not exactly.** *Ironical.* not at all; by no means.

exacum (ˈɛksəkəm) *n.* any of various Asian flowering herbs. [NL, < EX-[1] + Gk *ago* to arrive]

exaggerate (ɪgˈzædʒəˌreɪt) *vb.* **1.** to regard or represent as larger or greater, more important or more successful, etc., than is true. **2.** (*tr.*) to make greater, more noticeable, etc. [C16: < L *exaggerāre* to magnify, < *aggerāre* to heap, < *agger* heap] **—exˈaggerˌated** *adj.* **—exˈaggerˌatingly** *adv.* **—exˌaggerˈation** *n.* **—exˈaggerative** *or* **exˈaggeratory** *adj.* **—exˈaggerˌator** *n.*

exalt (ɪgˈzɔːlt) *vb.* (*tr.*) **1.** to elevate in rank, dignity, etc. **2.** to praise highly; extol. **3.** to stimulate; excite. **4.** to fill with joy or delight; elate. [C15: < L *exaltāre* to raise, < *altus* high] **—exˈalted** *adj.* **—exˈalter** *n.*

exaltation (ˌɛgzɔːlˈteɪʃən) *n.* **1.** the act of exalting or state of being exalted. **2.** exhilaration; elation; rapture.

exam (ɪgˈzæm) *n.* short for **examination.**

examination (ɪgˌzæmɪˈneɪʃən) *n.* **1.** the act of examining or state of being examined. **2.** *Education.* **a.** written exercises, oral questions, etc., set to test a candidate's knowledge and skill. **b.** (*as modifier*): *an examination paper.* **3.** *Med.* **a.** physical inspection of a patient. **b.** laboratory study of secretory or excretory products, tissue samples, etc. **4.** *Law.* the formal interrogation of a person on oath. **—exˌamiˈnational** *adj.*

examine (ɪgˈzæmɪn) *vb.* (*tr.*) **1.** to inspect or scrutinize carefully or in detail; investigate. **2.** *Education.* to test the knowledge or skill of (a candidate) in (a subject or activity) by written or oral questions, etc. **3.** *Law.* to interrogate (a person) formally on oath. **4.** *Med.* to investigate the state of health of (a patient). [C14: < OF, < L *exāmināre* to weigh, < *exāmen* means of weighing] **—exˈaminable** *adj.* **—exˌamiˈnee** *n.* **—exˈaminer** *n.* **—exˈamining** *adj.*

example (ɪgˈzɑːmpᵊl) *n.* **1.** a specimen or instance that is typical of its group or set; sample. **2.** a person, action, thing, etc., that is worthy of imitation; pattern. **3.** a precedent, illustration of a principle, or model. **4.** a punishment or the recipient of a punishment intended to serve as a warning. **5. for example.** as an illustration; for instance. ~*vb.* **6.** (*tr.; now usually passive*) to present an example of; exemplify. [C14: < OF, < L *exemplum* pattern, < *eximere* to take out]

exanthema (ˌɛksænˈθiːmə) *n., pl.* **-themata** (-ˈθiːmətə) *or* **-themas.** a skin rash occurring in a disease such as measles. [C17: via LL < Gk, < *exanthein* to burst forth, < *anthein* to blossom]

exasperate (ɪgˈzɑːspəˌreɪt) *vb.* (*tr.*) **1.** to cause great irritation or anger to. **2.** to cause (something unpleasant) to worsen; aggravate. [C16: < L *exasperāre* to make rough, < *asper* rough] **—exˈasperˌatedly** *adv.* **—exˈasperˌater** *n.* **—exˈasperˌatingly** *adv.* **—exˌasperˈation** *n.*

ex cathedra (ɛks kəˈθiːdrə) *adj., adv.* **1.** with authority. **2.** *R.C. Church.* (of doctrines of faith or morals) defined by the pope as infallibly true, to be accepted by all Catholics. [L, lit.: from the chair]

excavate (ˈɛkskəˌveɪt) *vb.* **1.** to remove (soil, earth, etc.) by digging; dig out. **2.** to make (a hole or tunnel) in (solid matter) by hollowing. **3.** to unearth (buried objects) methodically to discover information about the past. [C16: < L *cavāre* to make hollow, < *cavus* hollow] **—ˌexcaˈvation** *n.* **—ˈexcaˌvator** *n.*

exceed (ɪkˈsiːd) *vb.* **1.** to be superior (to); excel. **2.** (*tr.*) to go beyond the limit or bounds of. **3.** (*tr.*) to be greater in degree or quantity than. [C14: < L *excēdere* to go beyond, < *cēdere* to go] **—exˈceedable** *adj.* **—exˈceeder** *n.*

exceeding (ɪkˈsiːdɪŋ) *adj.* **1.** very great; exceptional or excessive. ~*adv.* **2.** *Arch.* to a great or unusual degree. **—exˈceedingly** *adv.*

excel (ɪkˈsɛl) *vb.* **-celling, -celled. 1.** to be superior to (another or others); surpass. **2.** (*intr.; foll. by in or at*) to be outstandingly good or proficient. [C15: < L *excellere* to rise up]

excellence (ˈɛksələns) *n.* **1.** the state or quality of excelling or being exceptionally good; extreme merit. **2.** an action, feature, etc., in which a person excels. **—ˈexcellent** *adj.* **—ˈexcellently** *adv.*

Excellency (ˈɛksələnsɪ) *or* **Excellence** *n., pl.* **-lencies** *or* **-lences. 1.** (usually preceded by *Your, His,* or *Her*) a title used to address or refer to a high-ranking official, such as an ambassador. **2.** *R.C. Church.* a title of bishops and archbishops in many non-English-speaking countries.

excelsior (ɪkˈsɛlsɪˌɔː) *interj., n.* **1.** excellent: used as a motto and as a trademark for various products. **2.** upward. [C19: < L: higher]

except (ɪkˈsɛpt) *prep.* **1.** Also: **except for.** other than; apart from. **2. except that.** (*conj.*) but for the fact that; were it not true that. ~*conj.* **3.** an archaic word for **unless. 4.** *Inf. (not standard in the U.S.)* except that; but for the fact that. ~*vb.* **5.** (*tr.*) to leave out; omit; exclude. **6.** (*intr.; often foll. by to*) *Rare.* to take exception; object. [C14: < OF *excepter* to leave out, < L *excipere* to take out, < *capere* to take]

excepting (ɪkˈsɛptɪŋ) *prep.* **1.** except; except for (esp. in **not excepting**). ~*conj.* **2.** an archaic word for **unless.**

exception (ɪkˈsɛpʃən) *n.* **1.** the act of excepting or fact of being excepted; omission. **2.** anything excluded from or not in conformance with a general rule, principle, class, etc. **3.** criticism, esp. adverse; objection. **4.** *Law.* (formerly) a formal objection in legal proceedings. **5. take exception. a.** (usually foll. by *to*) to make objections (to); demur (at). **b.** (often foll. by *at*) to be offended (by); be resentful (at).

exceptionable (ɪkˈsɛpʃənəbᵊl) *adj.* open to or subject to objection; objectionable. **—exˈceptionableness** *n.* **—exˈceptionably** *adv.*

exceptional (ɪkˈsɛpʃənᵊl) *adj.* **1.** forming an exception; not ordinary. **2.** having much more than average intelligence, ability, or skill.

excerpt *n.* (ˈɛksɜːpt). **1.** a part or passage taken from a book, speech, etc.; extract. ~*vb.* (ɛkˈsɜːpt). **2.** (*tr.*) to take (a part or passage) from a book, speech, etc. [C17: < L *excerptum,* lit.: (something) picked out, < *excerpere* to select, < *carpere* to pluck] —**exˈcerptible** *adj.* —**exˈcerption** *n.* —**exˈcerptor** *n.*

excess *n.* (ɪkˈsɛs, ˈɛksɛs). **1.** the state or act of going beyond normal, sufficient, or permitted limits. **2.** an immoderate or abnormal amount. **3.** the amount, number, etc., by which one thing exceeds another. **4.** overindulgence or intemperance. **5.** *Insurance, chiefly Brit.* a specified contribution towards the cost of a claim, payable by the policyholder. **6. in excess of.** of more than; over. **7. to excess.** to an inordinate extent; immoderately. ~*adj.* (ˈɛksɛs, ɪkˈsɛs). (*usually prenominal*) **8.** more than normal, necessary, or permitted; surplus: *excess weight.* **9.** payable as a result of previous underpayment: *excess postage.* [C14: < L *excēdere* to go beyond; see EXCEED]

excessive (ɪkˈsɛsɪv) *adj.* exceeding the normal or permitted limits; immoderate; inordinate. —**exˈcessively** *adv.* —**exˈcessiveness** *n.*

excess luggage *or* **baggage** *n.* luggage that is more in weight or number of pieces than an airline, etc., will carry free.

exchange (ɪksˈtʃeɪndʒ) *vb.* **1.** (*tr.*) to give up or transfer (one thing) for an equivalent. **2.** (*tr.*) to give and receive (information, ideas, etc.); interchange. **3.** (*tr.*) to replace (one thing) with another, esp. to replace unsatisfactory goods. **4.** to hand over (goods) in return for the equivalent value in kind; barter; trade. ~*n.* **5.** the act or process of exchanging. **6. a.** anything given or received as an equivalent or substitute for something else. **b.** (*as modifier*): *an exchange student.* **7.** an argument or quarrel. **8.** Also called: **telephone exchange.** a switching centre in which telephone lines are interconnected. **9.** a place where securities or commodities are sold, bought, or traded, esp. by brokers or merchants. **10. a.** the system by which commercial debts are settled by commercial documents, esp. bills of exchange, instead of by direct payment of money. **b.** the percentage or fee charged for accepting payment in this manner. **11.** a transfer or interchange of sums of money of equivalent value, as between different currencies. **12. win** (*or* **lose**) **the exchange.** *Chess.* to win (*or* lose) a rook in return for a bishop or knight. ~See also **bill of exchange, exchange rate, labour exchange.** [C14: < Anglo-French *eschaungier,* < Vulgar L *excambiāre* (unattested), < L *cambīre* to barter] —**exˈchangeable** *adj.* —**exˌchangeaˈbility** *n.* —**exˈchangeably** *adv.* —**exˈchanger** *n.*

exchange rate *n.* the rate at which the currency unit of one country may be exchanged for that of another.

exchequer (ɪksˈtʃɛkə) *n.* **1.** (*often cap.*) *Government.* (in Britain and certain other countries) the accounting department of the Treasury. **2.** *Inf.* personal funds; finances. [C13 (in the sense: chessboard, counting table): < OF *eschequier,* < *eschec* CHECK]

excisable (ɪkˈsaɪzəbᵊl) *adj.* **1.** liable to an excise tax. **2.** suitable for deletion.

excise[1] *n.* (ˈɛksaɪz, ɛkˈsaɪz). **1.** Also called: **excise tax.** a tax on goods, such as spirits, produced for the home market. **2.** a tax paid for a licence to carry out various trades, sports, etc. **3.** *Brit.* that section of the government service responsible for the collection of excise, now the Board of Customs and Excise. ~*vb.* (ɪkˈsaɪz). **4.** (*tr.*) *Rare.* to compel (a person) to pay excise. [C15: prob. < MDu. *excijs,* prob. < OF *assise* a sitting, assessment, < L *assidēre* to sit beside, assist in judging] —**exˈcisable** *adj.*

excise[2] (ɪkˈsaɪz) *vb.* (*tr.*) **1.** to delete (a passage, sentence, etc.). **2.** to remove (an organ or part) surgically. [C16: < L *excīdere* to cut down] —**excision** (ɪkˈsɪʒən) *n.*

exciseman (ˈɛksaɪzˌmæn) *n., pl.* **-men.** *Brit.* (formerly) a government agent whose function was to collect excise and prevent smuggling.

excitable (ɪkˈsaɪtəbᵊl) *adj.* **1.** easily excited; volatile. **2.** (esp. of a nerve) ready to respond to a stimulus. —**exˌcitaˈbility** *or* **exˈcitableness** *n.*

excitation (ˌɛksɪˈteɪʃən) *n.* **1.** the act or process of exciting or state of being excited. **2.** a means of exciting or cause of excitement. **3.** the current in a field coil of a generator, motor, etc., or the magnetizing current in a transformer. **4.** the action of a stimulus on an animal or plant organ, inducing it to respond.

excite (ɪkˈsaɪt) *vb.* (*tr.*) **1.** to arouse (a person), esp. to pleasurable anticipation or nervous agitation. **2.** to arouse or elicit (an emotion, response, etc.); evoke. **3.** to cause or bring about; stir up. **4.** to arouse sexually. **5.** *Physiol.* to cause a response in or increase the activity of (an organ, tissue, or part); stimulate. **6.** to raise (an atom, molecule, etc.) from the ground state to a higher energy level. **7.** to supply electricity to (the coils of a generator or motor) in order to create a magnetic field. [C14: < L *exciēre* to stimulate, < *ciēre* to set in motion, rouse] —**exˈcitant** *n.* —**exˈcitative** *or* **exˈcitatory** *adj.* —**exˈciter** *or* **exˈcitor** *n.*

excited (ɪkˈsaɪtɪd) *adj.* **1.** emotionally aroused, esp. to pleasure or agitation. **2.** characterized by excitement. **3.** sexually aroused. **4.** (of an atom, molecule, etc.) having an energy level above the ground state. —**exˈcitedness** *n.*

excitement (ɪkˈsaɪtmənt) *n.* **1.** the state of being excited. **2.** a person or thing that excites.

exciting (ɪkˈsaɪtɪŋ) *adj.* causing excitement; stirring; stimulating. —**exˈcitingly** *adv.*

exclaim (ɪkˈskleɪm) *vb.* to cry out or speak suddenly or excitedly, as from surprise, delight, horror, etc. [C16: < L *exclāmāre,* < *clāmāre* to shout] —**exˈclaimer** *n.*

exclamation (ˌɛkskləˈmeɪʃən) *n.* **1.** an abrupt or excited cry or utterance; ejaculation. **2.** the act of exclaiming. —ˌ**exclaˈmational** *adj.* —**exˈclamatory** *adj.*

exclamation mark *or U.S.* **point** *n.* **1.** the punctuation mark ! used after exclamations and vehement commands. **2.** this mark used for any other purpose, as to draw attention to an obvious mistake, in road warning signs, etc.

exclave (ˈɛkskleɪv) *n.* a part of a country entirely surrounded by foreign territory: viewed from the position of the home country. [C20: < EX-[1] + *-clave,* on the model of ENCLAVE]

exclosure (ɪkˈskləʊʒə) *n.* an area of land fenced round to keep out unwanted animals.

exclude (ɪkˈskluːd) *vb.* (*tr.*) **1.** to keep out; prevent from entering. **2.** to reject or not consider; leave out. **3.** to expel forcibly; eject. [C14: < L *exclūdere,* < *claudere* to shut] —**exˈcludable** *or* **exˈcludible** *adj.* —**exˈcluder** *n.*

exclusion (ɪkˈskluːʒən) *n.* the act or an instance of excluding or the state of being excluded. —**exˈclusionary** *adj.*

exclusion principle *n.* See **Pauli exclusion principle.**

exclusive (ɪkˈskluːsɪv) *adj.* **1.** excluding all else; rejecting other considerations, events, etc. **2.** belonging to a particular individual or group and to no other; not shared. **3.** belonging to or catering for a privileged minority, esp. a fashionable clique. **4.** (*postpositive;* foll. by *to*) limited (to); found only (in). **5.** single; unique; only. **6.** separate and incompatible. **7.** (*immediately postpositive*) not including the numbers, dates, letters, etc., mentioned. **8.** (*postpositive;* foll. by *of*) except (for); not taking account (of). **9.** *Logic.* (of a disjunction) true if only one rather than both of its component propositions is true. ~*n.* **10.** an exclusive story; a story reported in only one newspaper. —**exˈclusiveness** *or* **exclusivity** (ˌɛkskluːˈsɪvɪtɪ) *n.*

exclusive OR circuit *or* **gate** *n. Electronics.* a computer logic circuit having two or more input wires and one output wire and giving a high-voltage output signal if a low-voltage signal is fed to one or more, but not all, of the input wires. Cf. **OR circuit.**

excommunicate *R.C. Church.* ~*vb.* (ˌɛkskəˈmjuːnɪˌkeɪt). 1. (*tr.*) to sentence (a member of the Church) to exclusion from the communion of believers and from the privileges and public prayers of the Church. ~*adj.* (ˌɛkskəˈmjuːnɪkɪt, -ˌkeɪt). 2. having incurred such a sentence. ~*n.* (ˌɛkskəˈmjuːnɪkɪt, -ˌkeɪt). 3. an excommunicated person. [C15: < LL *excommūnicāre*, lit.: to exclude from the community, < L *commūnis* COMMON] —ˌ**excomˌmuniˈcation** *n.* —ˌ**excomˈmunicative** *or* ˌ**excomˈmunicatory** *adj.* —ˌ**exˈcomˈmuniˌcator** *n.*

excoriate (ɪkˈskɔːrɪˌeɪt) *vb.* (*tr.*) 1. to strip the skin from (a person or animal). 2. to denounce vehemently. [C15: < LL *excoriāre* to strip, flay, < L *corium* skin, hide] —**exˌcoriˈation** *n.*

excrement (ˈɛkskrɪmənt) *n.* waste matter discharged from the body, esp. faeces; excreta. [C16: < L *excernere* to sift, EXCRETE] —**excremental** (ˌɛkskrɪˈmɛntᵊl) *or* **excrementitious** (ˌɛkskrɪmɛnˈtɪʃəs) *adj.*

excrescence (ɪkˈskrɛsᵊns) *n.* a projection or protuberance, esp. an outgrowth from an organ or part of the body. —**exˈcrescent** *adj.* —**excrescential** (ˌɛkskrɪˈsɛnʃəl) *adj.*

excrescency (ɪkˈskrɛsənsɪ) *n., pl.* **-cies.** 1. the state or condition of being excrescent. 2. another word for **excrescence.**

excreta (ɪkˈskriːtə) *pl. n.* waste matter, such as urine, faeces, or sweat, discharged from the body. [C19: NL, < L: see EXCRETE] —**exˈcretal** *adj.*

excrete (ɪkˈskriːt) *vb.* 1. to discharge (waste matter, such as urine, sweat, or faeces) from the body. 2. (of plants) to eliminate (waste matter) through the leaves, roots, etc. [C17: < L *excernere* to separate, discharge, < *cernere* to sift] —**exˈcreter** *n.* —**exˈcretion** *n.* —**exˈcretive** *or* **exˈcretory** *adj.*

excruciate (ɪkˈskruːʃɪˌeɪt) *vb.* (*tr.*) to inflict mental suffering on; torment. [C16: < L *excruciāre*, < *cruciāre* to crucify, < *crux* cross] —**exˌcruciˈation** *n.*

excruciating (ɪkˈskruːʃɪˌeɪtɪŋ) *adj.* 1. unbearably painful; agonizing. 2. intense; extreme. 3. *Inf.* irritating; trying. 4. *Humorous.* very bad: *an excruciating pun.*

exculpate (ˈɛkskʌlˌpeɪt, ɪkˈskʌlpeɪt) *vb.* (*tr.*) to free from blame or guilt; vindicate or exonerate. [C17: < Med. L, < L EX-[1] + *culpa* fault, blame] —**exculpable** (ɪkˈskʌlpəbᵊl) *adj.* —ˌ**exculˈpation** *n.* —**exˈculpatory** *adj.*

excursion (ɪkˈskɜːʃən, -ʒən) *n.* 1. a short outward and return journey, esp. for sightseeing, etc.; outing. 2. a group going on such a journey. 3. (*modifier*) of or relating to reduced rates offered on certain journeys by rail: *an excursion ticket.* 4. a digression or deviation; diversion. 5. (formerly) a raid or attack. [C16: < L *excursiō* an attack, < *excurrere* to run out, < *currere* to run] —**exˈcursionist** *n.*

excursive (ɪkˈskɜːsɪv) *adj.* 1. tending to digress. 2. involving detours; rambling. [C17: < L *excursus*, < *excurrere* to run forth] —**exˈcursively** *adv.* —**exˈcursiveness** *n.*

excuse *vb.* (ɪkˈskjuːz). (*tr.*) 1. to pardon or forgive. 2. to seek pardon or exemption for (a person, esp. oneself). 3. to make allowances for: *to excuse someone's ignorance.* 4. to serve as an apology or explanation for; justify: *her age excuses her.* 5. to exempt from a task, obligation, etc. 6. to dismiss or allow to leave. 7. to seek permission for (someone, esp. oneself) to leave. 8. **be excused.** *Euphemistic.* to go to the lavatory. 9. **excuse me!** an expression used to catch someone's attention or to apologize for an interruption, disagreement, etc. ~*n.* (ɪkˈskjuːs). 10. an explanation offered in defence of some fault or as a reason for not fulfilling an obligation, etc. 11. *Inf.* an inferior example of something; makeshift substitute: *she is a poor excuse for a hostess.* 12. the act of excusing. [C13: < L, < EX-[1] + *causa* cause, accusation] —**exˈcusable** *adj.* —**exˈcusableness** *n.* —**exˈcusably** *adv.*

excuse-me *n.* a dance in which a person may take another's partner.

ex-directory *adj. Chiefly Brit.* not listed in a telephone directory, by request, and not disclosed to inquirers.

ex dividend *adj., adv.* without the right to the current dividend: *to quote shares ex dividend.*

exeat (ˈɛksɪət) *n. Brit.* 1. leave of absence from school or some other institution. 2. a bishop's permission for a priest to leave his diocese in order to take up an appointment elsewhere. [C18: L, lit.: he may go out, < *exīre*]

exec. *abbrev. for:* 1. executive. 2. executor.

execrable (ˈɛksɪkrəbᵊl) *adj.* 1. deserving to be execrated; abhorrent. 2. of very poor quality. [C14: < L: see EXECRATE] —**ˈexecrableness** *n.* —**ˈexecrably** *adv.*

execrate (ˈɛksɪˌkreɪt) *vb.* 1. (*tr.*) to loathe; detest; abhor. 2. (*tr.*) to denounce; deplore. 3. to curse (a person or thing); damn. [C16: < L *exsecrārī* to curse, < EX-[1] + *-secrārī* < *sacer* SACRED] —ˌ**exeˈcration** *n.* —**ˈexeˌcrative** *or* **ˈexeˌcratory** *adj.* —**ˈexeˌcratively** *adv.*

execute (ˈɛksɪˌkjuːt) *vb.* (*tr.*) 1. to put (a condemned person) to death; inflict capital punishment upon. 2. to carry out; complete. 3. to perform; accomplish; effect. 4. to make or produce: *to execute a drawing.* 5. to carry into effect (a judicial sentence, the law, etc.). 6. *Law.* to render (a deed, etc.) effective, as by signing, sealing, and delivering. 7. to carry out the terms of (a contract, will, etc.). [C14: < OF *executer*, back formation < *executeur* EXECUTOR] —**ˈexeˌcutable** *adj.* —**executant** (ɪgˈzɛkjʊtənt) *n.* —**ˈexeˌcuter** *n.*

execution (ˌɛksɪˈkjuːʃən) *n.* 1. the act or process of executing. 2. the carrying out or undergoing of a sentence of death. 3. the style or manner in which something is accomplished or performed; technique. 4. a. the enforcement of the judgment of a court of law. b. the writ ordering such enforcement.

executioner (ˌɛksɪˈkjuːʃənə) *n.* an official charged with carrying out the death sentence passed upon a condemned person.

executive (ɪgˈzɛkjʊtɪv) *n.* 1. a person or group responsible for the administration of a project, activity, or business. 2. a. the branch of government responsible for carrying out laws, decrees, etc. b. any administration. ~*adj.* 3. having the function of carrying plans, orders, laws, etc., into effect. 4. of or relating to an executive. 5. *Inf.* very expensive or exclusive: *executive housing.* —**exˈecutively** *adv.*

Executive Council *n.* (in Australia and New Zealand) a body of ministers of the Crown presided over by the governor or governor-general that formally approves cabinet decisions, etc.

executive officer *n.* the second-in-command of any of certain military units.

executor (ɪgˈzɛkjʊtə) *n.* 1. *Law.* a person appointed by a testator to carry out his will. 2. a person who executes. [C14: < Anglo-F *executour*, < L *execūtor*] —**exˌecuˈtorial** *adj.* —**exˈecutory** *adj.* —**exˈecutorˌship** *n.*

executrix (ɪgˈzɛkjʊtrɪks) *n., pl.* **executrices** (ɪgˌzɛkjʊˈtraɪsiːz) *or* **executrixes.** *Law.* a female executor.

exegesis (ˌɛksɪˈdʒiːsɪs) *n., pl.* **-ses** (-siːz). explanation or critical interpretation of a text, esp. of the Bible. [C17: < Gk, < *exēgeisthai* to interpret, < EX-[1] + *hēgeisthai* to guide] —**exegetic** (ˌɛksɪˈdʒɛtɪk) *adj.* —ˌ**exeˈgetics** *n.* (*functioning as sing.*)

exegete (ˈɛksɪˌdʒiːt) *or* **exegetist** (ˌɛksɪˈdʒiːtɪst, -ˈdʒɛt-) *n.* a person who practises exegesis. [C18: < Gk: see EXEGESIS]

exemplar (ɪgˈzɛmplə, -plɑː) *n.* 1. a person or thing to be copied or imitated; model. 2. a typical specimen or instance; example. [C14: < L, < *exemplum* EXAMPLE]

exemplary (ɪgˈzɛmplərɪ) *adj.* 1. fit for imitation; model. 2. serving as a warning; admonitory. 3.

representative; typical. —**ex'emplarily** *adv.* —**ex'emplariness** *n.*

exemplary damages *pl. n. Law.* damages awarded to a plaintiff above the value of actual loss sustained so that they serve also as a punishment to the defendant.

exemplify (ɪg'zɛmplɪˌfaɪ) *vb.* **-fying, -fied.** (*tr.*) **1.** to show by example. **2.** to serve as an example of. **3.** *Law.* to make an official copy of (a document) under seal. [C15: via OF < Med. L *exemplificāre*, < L *exemplum* EXAMPLE + *facere* to make] —**ex'empliˌfiable** *adj.* —**exˌemplifi'cation** *n.* —**ex'empliˌficative** *adj.* —**ex'empliˌfier** *n.*

exempt (ɪg'zɛmpt) *vb.* **1.** (*tr.*) to release from an obligation, tax, etc.; excuse. ~*adj.* (*postpositive*) **2.** freed from or not subject to an obligation, tax, etc.; excused. ~*n.* **3.** a person who is exempt. [C14: < L *exemptus* removed, < *eximere* to take out, < *emere* to buy, obtain] —**ex'emption** *n.*

exequies ('ɛksɪkwɪz) *pl. n., sing.* **-quy.** the rites and ceremonies used at funerals. [C14: < L *exequiae* (pl.) funeral procession, rites, < *exequī* to follow to the end, < *sequī* to follow]

exercise ('ɛksəˌsaɪz) *vb.* (*mainly tr.*) **1.** to put into use; employ. **2.** (*intr.*) to take exercise or perform exercises. **3.** to practise using in order to develop or train. **4.** to perform or make use of: *to exercise one's rights.* **5.** to bring to bear: *to exercise one's influence.* **6.** (*often passive*) to occupy the attentions of, esp. so as to worry or vex: *to be exercised about a decision.* **7.** *Mil.* to carry out or cause to carry out simulated combat, manoeuvres, etc. ~*n.* **8.** physical exertion, esp. for development, training, or keeping fit. **9.** mental or other activity or practice, esp. to develop a skill. **10.** a set of movements, tasks, etc., designed to train, improve, or test one's ability: *piano exercises.* **11.** a performance or work of art done as practice or to demonstrate a technique. **12.** the performance of a function: *the exercise of one's rights.* **13.** (*usually pl.*) *Mil.* a manoeuvre or simulated combat operation. **14.** *Gymnastics.* a particular event, such as the horizontal bar. [C14: < OF, < L, < *exercēre* to drill, < EX-¹ + *arcēre* to ward off] —**'exerˌcisable** *adj.* —**'exerˌciser** *n.*

exercise bike *or* **cycle** *n.* a stationary exercise machine that is pedalled like a bicycle as a method of increasing cardiovascular fitness.

exert (ɪg'zɜːt) *vb.* (*tr.*) to apply (oneself) diligently; make a strenuous effort. [C17 (in the sense: push forth, emit): < L *exserere* to thrust out, < EX-¹ + *serere* to bind together, entwine] —**ex'ertion** *n.* —**ex'ertive** *adj.*

exeunt ('ɛksɪˌʌnt) *Latin.* they go out: used as a stage direction.

exeunt omnes ('ɒmneɪz) *Latin.* they all go out: used as a stage direction.

exfoliate (ɛks'fəʊlɪˌeɪt) *vb.* (of bark, skin, minerals, etc.) to peel off in layers, flakes, or scales. [C17: < LL *exfoliāre* to strip off leaves, < L *folium* leaf] —**exˌfoli'ation** *n.* —**ex'foliative** *adj.*

ex gratia ('greɪʃə) *adj.* given as a favour or gratuitously where no legal obligation exists: *an ex gratia payment.* [NL, lit.: out of kindness]

exhale (ɛks'heɪl, ɪg'zeɪl) *vb.* **1.** to expel (breath, smoke, etc.) from the lungs; breathe out. **2.** to give off (air, fumes, etc.) or (of air, etc.) to be given off. [C14: < L *exhālāre*, < *hālāre* to breathe] —**ex'halable** *adj.* —**ˌexha'lation** *n.*

exhaust (ɪg'zɔːst) *vb.* (*mainly tr.*) **1.** to drain the energy of; tire out. **2.** to deprive of resources, etc. **3.** to deplete totally; consume. **4.** to empty (a container) by drawing off or pumping out (the contents). **5.** to develop or discuss thoroughly so that no further interest remains. **6.** to remove gas from (a vessel, etc.) in order to reduce pressure or create a vacuum. **7.** (*intr.*) (of steam or other gases) to be emitted or to escape from an engine after being expanded. ~*n.* **8.** gases ejected from an engine as waste products. **9.** the expulsion of expanded gas or steam from an engine. **10. a.** the parts of an engine through which exhausted gases or steam pass. **b.** (*as modifier*): *exhaust pipe.* [C16: < L *exhaustus* made empty, < *exhaurīre* to draw out, < *haurīre* to draw, drain] —**ex'hausted** *adj.* —**ex'haustible** *adj.* —**ex'hausting** *adj.*

exhaustion (ɪg'zɔːstʃən) *n.* **1.** extreme tiredness. **2.** the condition of being used up. **3.** the act of exhausting or the state of being exhausted.

exhaustive (ɪg'zɔːstɪv) *adj.* **1.** comprehensive; thorough. **2.** tending to exhaust. —**ex'haustively** *adv.* —**ex'haustiveness** *n.*

exhibit (ɪg'zɪbɪt) *vb.* (*mainly tr.*) **1.** (*also intr.*) to display (something) to the public. **2.** to manifest; display; show. **3.** *Law.* to produce (a document or object) in court as evidence. ~*n.* **4.** an object or collection exhibited to the public. **5.** *Law.* a document or object produced in court as evidence. [C15: < L *exhibēre* to hold forth, < *habēre* to have] —**ex'hibitor** *n.* —**ex'hibitory** *adj.*

exhibition (ˌɛksɪ'bɪʃən) *n.* **1.** a public display of art, skills, etc. **2.** the act of exhibiting or the state of being exhibited. **3. make an exhibition of oneself.** to behave so foolishly that one excites notice or ridicule. **4.** *Brit.* an allowance or scholarship awarded to a student at a university or school.

exhibitioner (ˌɛksɪ'bɪʃənə) *n. Brit.* a student who has been awarded an exhibition.

exhibitionism (ˌɛksɪ'bɪʃəˌnɪzəm) *n.* **1.** a compulsive desire to attract attention to oneself, esp. by exaggerated behaviour. **2.** a compulsive desire to expose one's genital organs publicly. —**ˌexhi'bitionist** *n.* —**ˌexhiˌbition'istic** *adj.*

exhibitive (ɪg'zɪbɪtɪv) *adj.* (*usually postpositive* and foll. by *of*) illustrative or demonstrative.

exhilarate (ɪg'zɪləˌreɪt) *vb.* (*tr.*) to make lively and cheerful; elate. [C16: < L *exhilarāre*, < *hilarāre* to cheer] —**ex'hilaˌrating** *adj.* —**exˌhila'ration** *n.* —**ex'hilarative** *adj.*

exhort (ɪg'zɔːt) *vb.* to urge or persuade (someone) earnestly; advise strongly. [C14: < L *exhortārī*, < *hortārī* to urge] —**ex'hortative** *or* **ex'hortatory** *adj.* —**ˌexhor'tation** *n.* —**ex'horter** *n.*

exhume (ɛks'hjuːm) *vb.* (*tr.*) **1.** to dig up (something buried, esp. a corpse); disinter. **2.** to reveal; disclose. [C18: < Med. L, < L EX-¹ + *humāre* to bury, < *humus* the ground] —**exhumation** (ˌɛkshjʊ'meɪʃən) *n.* —**ex'humer** *n.*

ex hypothesi (ɛks haɪ'pɒθəsɪ) *adv.* in accordance with the hypothesis stated. [C17: NL]

exigency ('ɛksɪdʒənsɪ, ɪg'zɪdʒənsɪ) *or* **exigence** ('ɛksɪdʒəns) *n., pl.* **-gencies** *or* **-gences. 1.** urgency. **2.** (*often pl.*) an urgent demand; pressing requirement. **3.** an emergency.

exigent ('ɛksɪdʒənt) *adj.* **1.** urgent; pressing. **2.** exacting; demanding. [C15: < L *exigere* to drive out, weigh out, < *agere* to drive, compel]

exiguous (ɪg'zɪgjʊəs, ɪk'sɪg-) *adj.* scanty or slender; meagre. [C17: < L *exiguus*, < *exigere* to weigh out; see EXIGENT] —**exiguity** (ˌɛksɪ'gjuːɪtɪ) *or* **ex'iguousness** *n.*

exile ('ɛgzaɪl, 'ɛksaɪl) *n.* **1.** a prolonged, usually enforced absence from one's home or country. **2.** the official expulsion of a person from his native land. **3.** a person banished or living away from his home or country; expatriate. ~*vb.* **4.** (*tr.*) to expel from home or country, esp. by official decree; banish. [C13: < L *exsilium* banishment, < *exsul* banished person] —**exilic** (ɛg'zɪlɪk, ɛk'sɪlɪk) *or* **ex'ilian** *adj.*

exist (ɪg'zɪst) *vb.* (*intr.*) **1.** to have being or reality; be. **2.** to eke out a living; stay alive. **3.** to be living; live. **4.** to be present under specified conditions or in a specified place. [C17: < L *exsistere* to step forth, < EX-¹ + *sistere* to stand] —**ex'istent** *adj.* —**ex'isting** *adj.*

existence (ɪg'zɪstəns) *n.* **1.** the fact or state of existing; being. **2.** the continuance or maintenance of life; living, esp. in adverse circumstances. **3.** something that exists; a being or entity. **4.** everything that exists.

existential (ˌɛgzɪ'stɛnʃəl) *adj.* **1.** of or relating to existence, esp. human existence. **2.** *Philosophy.* known by experience rather than reason. **3.** of a formula or proposition asserting the existence of at least one object fulfilling a given condition. **4.** of or relating to existentialism.

existentialism (ˌɛgzɪˈstɛnʃəˌlɪzəm) *n.* a modern philosophical movement stressing personal experience and responsibility and their demands on the individual, who is seen as a free agent in a deterministic and seemingly meaningless universe. —ˌ**exisˈtentialist** *adj., n.*

exit (ˈɛgzɪt, ˈɛksɪt) *n.* **1.** a way out. **2.** the act or an instance of going out. **3. a.** the act of leaving or right to leave a particular place. **b.** (*as modifier*): *an exit visa.* **4.** departure from life; death. **5.** *Theatre.* the act of going offstage. **6.** *Brit.* a point at which vehicles may leave or join a motorway. **7.** *Computers.* (in processing) an instruction to leave a routine. ~*vb.* (*intr.*) **8.** to go away or out; depart. **9.** *Theatre.* to go offstage: used as a stage direction: *exit Hamlet.* **10.** to leave; withdraw (from). [C17: < L *exitus* a departure, < *exīre* to go out, < EX-¹ + *īre* to go]

exit poll *n.* a poll taken by an organization by asking people how they voted in an election as they leave a polling station.

ex libris (ɛks ˈliːbrɪs) *prep.* **1.** from the collection or library of. ~*n.* **ex-libris,** *pl.* **ex-libris. 2.** a bookplate bearing the owner's name, coat of arms, etc. [C19: < L, lit.: from the books (of)]

exo- *combining form.* external, outside, or beyond: *exothermal.* [< Gk *exō* outside]

exobiology (ˌɛksəʊbaɪˈɒlədʒɪ) *n.* another name for **astrobiology.** —ˌ**exobiˈologist** *n.*

exocarp (ˈɛksəʊˌkɑːp) *n.* another name for **epicarp.**

exocrine (ˈɛksəʊˌkraɪn) *adj.* **1.** of or relating to exocrine glands or their secretions. ~*n.* **2.** an exocrine gland. [C20: EXO- + *-crine* < Gk *krinein* to separate]

exocrine gland *n.* any gland, such as a salivary or sweat gland, that secretes its products through a duct onto an epithelial surface.

Exod. *Bible. abbrev. for* Exodus.

exodus (ˈɛksədəs) *n.* the act or an instance of going out. [C17: via L < Gk *exodos,* < EX-¹ + *hodos* way]

Exodus (ˈɛksədəs) *n.* **1. the.** the departure of the Israelites from Egypt. **2.** the second book of the Old Testament, recounting the events connected with this.

ex officio (ˈɛks əˈfɪʃɪəʊ, əˈfɪsɪəʊ) *adv., adj.* by right of position or office. [L]

exogamy (ɛkˈsɒgəmɪ) *n. Anthropol., sociol.* marriage outside one's own tribe or similar unit. —**exˈogamous** *or* **exogamic** (ˌɛksəʊˈgæmɪk) *adj.*

exogenous (ɛkˈsɒdʒɪnəs) *adj.* **1.** having an external origin. **2.** *Biol.* **a.** originating outside an organism. **b.** of or relating to external factors, such as light, that influence an organism.

exon (ˈɛksɒn) *n. Brit.* one of the four officers who command the Yeomen of the Guard. [C17: a pronunciation spelling of F *exempt* EXEMPT]

exonerate (ɪgˈzɒnəˌreɪt) *vb.* (*tr.*) **1.** to absolve from blame or a criminal charge. **2.** to relieve from an obligation. [C16: < L *exonerāre* to free from a burden, < *onus* a burden] —**exˌonerˈation** *n.* —**exˈonerative** *adj.* —**exˈonerˌator** *n.*

exophthalmos (ˌɛksɒfˈθælmɒs), **exophthalmus** (ˌɛksɒfˈθælməs), *or* **exophthalmia** (ˌɛksɒfˈθælmɪə) *n.* abnormal protrusion of the eyeball, as caused by hyperthyroidism. [C19: via NL < Gk, < EX-¹ + *ophthalmos* eye] —ˌ**exophˈthalmic** *adj.*

exorbitant (ɪgˈzɔːbɪtᵊnt) *adj.* (of prices, demands, etc.) excessive; extravagant; immoderate. [C15: < LL *exorbitāre* to deviate, < L *orbita* track] —**exˈorbitance** *n.* —**exˈorbitantly** *adv.*

exorcise *or* **-cize** (ˈɛksɔːˌsaɪz) *vb.* (*tr.*) to expel (evil spirits) from (a person or place), by adjurations and religious rites. [C15: < LL, < Gk, < EX-¹ + *horkizein* to adjure] —ˈ**exorˌciser** *or* **-ˌcizer** *n.* —ˈ**exorcism** *n.* —ˈ**exorcist** *n.*

exordium (ɛkˈsɔːdɪəm) *n., pl.* **-diums** *or* **-dia** (-dɪə). an introductory part or beginning, esp. of an oration or discourse. [C16: < L, < *exōrdīrī* to begin, < *ōrdīrī* to begin] —**exˈordial** *adj.*

exoskeleton (ˌɛksəʊˈskɛlɪtᵊn) *n.* the protective or supporting structure covering the outside of the body of many animals, such as the thick cuticle of arthropods. —ˌ**exoˈskeletal** *adj.*

exosphere (ˈɛksəʊˌsfɪə) *n.* the outermost layer of the earth's atmosphere. It extends from about 400 kilometres above the earth's surface.

exothermic (ˌɛksəʊˈθɜːmɪk) *or* **exothermal** *adj.* (of a chemical reaction or compound) occurring or formed with the evolution of heat. —ˌ**exoˈthermically** *or* ˌ**exoˈthermally** *adv.*

exotic (ɪgˈzɒtɪk) *adj.* **1.** originating in a foreign country, esp. one in the tropics; not native: *an exotic plant.* **2.** having a strange or bizarre allure, beauty, or quality. ~*n.* **3.** an exotic person or thing. [C16: < L, < Gk *exōtikos* foreign, < *exō* outside] —**exˈotically** *adv.* —**exˈotiˌcism** *n.* —**exˈoticness** *n.*

exotica (ɪgˈzɒtɪkə) *pl. n.* exotic objects, esp. when forming a collection. [C19: L, neuter pl. of *exōticus;* see EXOTIC]

exotic dancer *n.* a striptease or belly dancer.

expand (ɪkˈspænd) *vb.* **1.** to make or become greater in extent, volume, size, or scope. **2.** to spread out; unfold; stretch out. **3.** (*intr.;* often foll. by *on*) to enlarge or expatiate (on a story, topic, etc.). **4.** (*intr.*) to become increasingly relaxed, friendly, or talkative. **5.** *Maths.* to express (a function or expression) as the sum or product of terms. [C15: < L *expandere* to spread out] —**exˈpandable** *adj.* —**exˈpander** *n.*

expanded (ɪkˈspændɪd) *adj.* (of a plastic) having been foamed during manufacture by a gas to make a light packaging material or heat insulator: *expanded polystyrene.*

expanded metal *n.* an open mesh of metal used for reinforcing brittle or friable materials and in fencing.

expander (ɪkˈspændə) *n.* **1.** a device for exercising and developing the muscles of the body. **2.** an electronic device for increasing the variations in signal amplitude in a transmission system according to a specified law.

expanse (ɪkˈspæns) *n.* **1.** an uninterrupted surface of something that extends, esp. over a wide area; stretch. **2.** expansion or extension. [C17: < NL *expansum* the heavens, < L *expansus* spread out, < *expandere* to expand]

expansible (ɪkˈspænsəbᵊl) *adj.* able to expand or be expanded. —**exˌpansiˈbility** *n.*

expansion (ɪkˈspænʃən) *n.* **1.** the act of expanding or the state of being expanded. **2.** something expanded. **3.** the degree or amount by which something expands. **4.** an increase or development, esp. in the activities of a company. **5.** the increase in the dimensions of a body or substance when subjected to an increase in temperature, internal pressure, etc. —**exˈpansionary** *adj.*

expansionism (ɪkˈspænʃəˌnɪzəm) *n.* the doctrine or practice of expanding the economy or territory of a country. —**exˈpansionist** *n., adj.* —**exˌpansionˈ istic** *adj.*

expansive (ɪkˈspænsɪv) *adj.* **1.** able or tending to expand or characterized by expansion. **2.** wide; extensive. **3.** friendly, open, or talkative. **4.** grand or extravagant. —**exˈpansiveness** *or* **expansivity** (ˌɛkspænˈsɪvɪtɪ) *n.*

ex parte (ɛks ˈpɑːtɪ) *adj. Law.* (of an application in a judicial proceeding) on behalf of one side or party only: *an ex parte injunction.*

expat (ˌɛksˈpæt) *n., adj. Inf.* short for **expatriate.**

expatiate (ɪkˈspeɪʃɪˌeɪt) *vb.* (*intr.*) **1.** (foll. by *on* or *upon*) to enlarge (on a theme, topic, etc.); elaborate (on). **2.** *Rare.* to wander about. [C16: < L *exspatiārī* to digress, < *spatiārī* to walk about] —**exˌpatiˈation** *n.* —**exˈpatiˌator** *n.*

expatriate *adj.* (ɛksˈpætrɪɪt, -ˌeɪt). **1.** resident outside one's native country. **2.** exiled or banished from one's native country. ~*n.* (ɛksˈpætrɪɪt, -ˌeɪt). **3.** a person living outside his native country **4.** an exile; expatriate person. ~*vb.* (ɛksˈpætrɪˌeɪt). (*tr.*) **5.** to exile (oneself) from one's native country or cause (another) to go into exile. [C18: < Med. L, < L EX-¹ + *patria* native land] —**exˌpatriˈation** *n.*

expect (ɪk'spɛkt) *vb.* (*tr.; may take a clause as object or an infinitive*) **1.** to regard as likely; anticipate. **2.** to look forward to or be waiting for. **3.** to decide that (something) is necessary; require: *the teacher expects us to work late.* ~See also **expecting.** [C16: < L *exspectāre* to watch for, < *spectāre* to look at] —**ex'pectable** *adj.*

expectancy (ɪk'spɛktənsɪ) *or* **expectance** *n.* **1.** something expected, esp. on the basis of a norm or average: *his life expectancy was 30 years.* **2.** anticipation; expectation. **3.** the prospect of a future interest or possession.

expectant (ɪk'spɛktənt) *adj.* **1.** expecting, anticipating, or hopeful. **2.** having expectations, esp. of possession of something. **3.** pregnant. ~*n.* **4.** a person who expects something.

expectation (ˌɛkspɛk'teɪʃən) *n.* **1.** the act or state of expecting or the state of being expected. **2.** (*usually pl.*) something looked forward to, whether feared or hoped for. **3.** an attitude of expectancy or hope. **4.** *Statistics.* **a.** the numerical probability that an event will occur. **b.** another term for **expected value.** —**expectative** (ɪk'spɛktətɪv) *adj.*

expected frequency *n. Statistics.* the number of occasions on which an event may be presumed to occur on average in a given number of trials.

expected value *n. Statistics.* the sum or integral of all possible values of a random variable, or any given function of it, multiplied by the respective probabilities of the values of the variable.

expecting (ɪk'spɛktɪŋ) *adj. Inf.* pregnant.

expectorant (ɪk'spɛktərənt) *Med.* ~*adj.* **1.** promoting the secretion, liquefaction, or expulsion of sputum from the respiratory passages. ~*n.* **2.** an expectorant drug or agent.

expectorate (ɪk'spɛktəˌreɪt) *vb.* to cough up and spit out (sputum from the respiratory passages). [C17: < L *expectorāre*, lit.: to drive from the breast, expel, < *pectus* breast] —**exˌpecto'ration** *n.* —**ex'pectoˌrator** *n.*

expediency (ɪk'spiːdɪənsɪ) *or* **expedience** *n., pl.* **-encies** *or* **-ences.** **1.** appropriateness; suitability. **2.** the use of or inclination towards methods that are advantageous rather than fair or just. **3.** another word for **expedient** (sense 3).

expedient (ɪk'spiːdɪənt) *adj.* **1.** suitable to the circumstances; appropriate. **2.** inclined towards methods that are advantageous rather than fair or just. ~*n. also* **expediency. 3.** something suitable or appropriate, esp. during an urgent situation. [C14: < L *expediēns* setting free; see EXPEDITE]

expedite ('ɛkspɪˌdaɪt) *vb.* (*tr.*) **1.** to facilitate the progress of; hasten or assist. **2.** to do or process with speed and efficiency. [C17: < L *expedīre*, lit.: to free the feet (as from a snare), hence, liberate, < EX-[1] + *pēs* foot] —**'expeˌditer** *or* **'expeˌditor** *n.*

expedition (ˌɛkspɪ'dɪʃən) *n.* **1.** an organized journey or voyage, esp. for exploration or for a scientific or military purpose. **2.** the people and equipment comprising an expedition. **3.** promptness; dispatch. [C15: < L *expedīre* to prepare, EXPEDITE] —ˌ**expe'ditionary** *adj.*

expeditious (ˌɛkspɪ'dɪʃəs) *adj.* characterized by or done with speed and efficiency; prompt; quick. —ˌ**expe'ditiously** *adv.* —ˌ**expe'ditiousness** *n.*

expel (ɪk'spɛl) *vb.* **-pelling, -pelled.** (*tr.*) **1.** to eject or drive out with force. **2.** to deprive of participation in or membership of a school, club, etc. [C14: < L *expellere* to drive out, < *pellere* to thrust, drive] —**ex'pellable** *adj.* —**expellee** (ˌɛkspɛ'liː) *n.* —**ex'peller** *n.*

expellant *or* **expellent** (ɪk'spɛlənt) *adj.* **1.** forcing out or able to force out. ~*n.* **2.** a medicine used to expel undesirable substances or organisms from the body.

expend (ɪk'spɛnd) *vb.* (*tr.*) **1.** to spend; disburse. **2.** to consume or use up. [C15: < L *expendere*, < *pendere* to weigh] —**ex'pender** *n.*

expendable (ɪk'spɛndəbᵊl) *adj.* **1.** that may be expended or used up. **2.** able to be sacrificed to achieve an objective, esp. a military one. ~*n.* **3.** something expendable. —**exˌpenda'bility** *n.*

expenditure (ɪk'spɛndɪtʃə) *n.* **1.** something expended, esp. money. **2.** the act of expending.

expense (ɪk'spɛns) *n.* **1.** a particular payment of money; expenditure. **2.** money needed for individual purchases; cost; charge. **3.** (*pl.*) money spent in the performance of a job, etc., usually reimbursed by an employer or allowable against tax. **4.** something requiring money for its purchase or upkeep. **5. at the expense of.** to the detriment of. [C14: < LL, < L *expēnsus* weighed out; see EXPEND]

expense account *n.* **1.** an arrangement by which an employee's expenses are refunded by his employer or deducted from his income for tax purposes. **2.** a record of such expenses.

expensive (ɪk'spɛnsɪv) *adj.* high-priced; costly; dear. —**ex'pensiveness** *n.*

experience (ɪk'spɪərɪəns) *n.* **1.** direct personal participation or observation. **2.** a particular incident, feeling, etc., that a person has undergone. **3.** accumulated knowledge, esp. of practical matters. ~*vb.* (*tr.*) **4.** to participate in or undergo. **5.** to be moved by; feel. [C14: < L *experīrī* to prove; rel. to L *perīculum* PERIL] —**ex'perienceable** *adj.*

experienced (ɪk'spɪərɪənst) *adj.* having become skilful or knowledgeable from extensive participation or observation.

experiential (ɪkˌspɪərɪ'ɛnʃəl) *adj. Philosophy.* relating to or derived from experience; empirical.

experiment *n.* (ɪk'spɛrɪmənt). **1.** a test or investigation, esp. one planned to provide evidence for or against a hypothesis. **2.** the act of conducting such an investigation or test; research. **3.** an attempt at something new or original. ~*vb.* (ɪk'spɛrɪˌmɛnt). **4.** (*intr.*) to make an experiment or experiments. [C14: < L *experīmentum* proof, trial, < *experīrī* to test; see EXPERIENCE] —**ex'periˌmenter** *n.*

experimental (ɪkˌspɛrɪ'mɛntᵊl) *adj.* **1.** relating to, based on, or having the nature of experiment. **2.** based on or derived from experience; empirical. **3.** tending to experiment. **4.** tentative or provisional. —**exˌperi'mentalism** *n.*

experimentation (ɪkˌspɛrɪmɛn'teɪʃən) *n.* the act, process, or practice of experimenting.

expert ('ɛkspɜːt) *n.* **1.** a person who has extensive skill or knowledge in a particular field. ~*adj.* **2.** skilful or knowledgeable. **3.** of, involving, or done by an expert: *an expert job.* [C14: < L *expertus* known by experience; see EXPERIENCE] —**'expertly** *adv.* —**'expertness** *n.*

expertise (ˌɛkspɜː'tiːz) *n.* special skill, knowledge, or judgment; expertness. [C19: < F: expert skill, < EXPERT]

expiate ('ɛkspɪˌeɪt) *vb.* (*tr.*) to atone for (sin or wrongdoing); make amends for. [C16: < L *expiāre*, < *pius* dutiful; see PIOUS] —**'expiable** *adj.* —ˌ**expi'ation** *n.* —**'expiˌator** *n.*

expiatory ('ɛkspɪətərɪ, -trɪ) *adj.* **1.** capable of making expiation. **2.** offered in expiation.

expiration (ˌɛkspɪ'reɪʃən) *n.* **1.** the finish of something; expiry. **2.** the act, process, or sound of breathing out. —**expiratory** (ɪk'spaɪərətərɪ, -trɪ) *adj.*

expire (ɪk'spaɪə) *vb.* **1.** (*intr.*) to finish or run out; come to an end. **2.** to breathe out (air). **3.** (*intr.*) to die. [C15: < OF, < L *exspīrāre* to breathe out, < *spīrāre* to breathe] —**ex'pirer** *n.*

expiry (ɪk'spaɪərɪ) *n., pl.* **-ries. 1. a.** a coming to an end, esp. of a contract period; termination. **b.** (*as modifier*): *the expiry date.* **2.** death.

explain (ɪk'spleɪn) *vb.* **1.** (when *tr., may take a clause as object*) to make (something) comprehensible, esp. by giving a clear and detailed account of it. **2.** (*tr.*) to justify or attempt to justify (oneself) by reasons for one's actions. [C15: < L *explānāre* to flatten, < *plānus* level] —**ex'plainable** *adj.* —**ex'plainer** *n.*

explain away *vb.* (*tr., adv.*) to offer excuses or reasons for (bad conduct, mistakes, etc.).

explanation (ˌɛksplə'neɪʃən) *n.* **1.** the act or process of explaining. **2.** something that explains. **3.** a clarification of disputed points.

explanatory (ɪk'splænətərɪ, -trɪ) *or* **explanative**

adj. serving or intended to serve as an explanation. —**ex'planatorily** *adv.*

expletive (ɪk'spliːtɪv) *n.* **1.** an exclamation or swearword; an oath or sound expressing emotion rather than meaning. **2.** any syllable, word, or phrase conveying no independent meaning, esp. one inserted in verse for the sake of metre. ~*adj.* *also* **expletory** (ɪk'spliːtərɪ, -trɪ). **3.** without particular meaning, esp. when filling out a line of verse. [C17: < LL *explētīvus* for filling out, < *explēre*, < *plēre* to fill]

explicable ('ɛksplɪkəbᵊl, ɪk'splɪk-) *adj.* capable of being explained.

explicate ('ɛksplɪˌkeɪt) *vb.* (*tr.*) *Formal.* **1.** to make clear or explicit; explain. **2.** to formulate or develop (a theory, hypothesis, etc.). [C16: < L *explicāre* to unfold, < *plicāre* to fold] —ˌ**expli'cation** *n.* —**explicative** (ɪk'splɪkətɪv) *or* **explicatory** (ɪk'splɪkətərɪ, -trɪ) *adj.* —'**expliˌcator** *n.*

explicit (ɪk'splɪsɪt) *adj.* **1.** precisely and clearly expressed, leaving nothing to implication; fully stated. **2.** leaving little to the imagination; graphically detailed. **3.** openly expressed without reservations; unreserved. [C17: < L *explicitus* unfolded; see EXPLICATE] —**ex'plicitly** *adv.* —**ex'plicitness** *n.*

explode (ɪk'spləʊd) *vb.* **1.** to burst or cause to burst with great violence, esp. through detonation of an explosive; blow up. **2.** to destroy or be destroyed in this manner. **3.** (of a gas) to undergo or cause (a gas) to undergo a sudden violent expansion, as a result of a fast exothermic chemical or nuclear reaction. **4.** (*intr.*) to react suddenly or violently with emotion, etc. **5.** (*intr.*) (esp. of a population) to increase rapidly. **6.** (*tr.*) to show (a theory, etc.) to be baseless. [C16: < L *explōdere* to drive off by clapping, < EX-[1] + *plaudere* to clap] —**ex'ploder** *n.*

exploded view *n.* a drawing or photograph of a mechanism that shows its parts separately, usually indicating their relative positions.

exploit *n.* ('ɛksplɔɪt). **1.** a notable deed or feat, esp. one that is heroic. ~*vb.* (ɪk'splɔɪt). (*tr.*) **2.** to take advantage of (a person, situation, etc.) for one's own ends. **3.** to make the best use of. [C14: < OF: accomplishment, < L *explicitum* (something) unfolded, < *explicāre* to EXPLICATE] —**ex'ploitable** *adj.* —ˌ**exploi'tation** *n.* —**ex'ploitive** *or* **ex'ploitative** *adj.*

exploration (ˌɛksplə'reɪʃən) *n.* **1.** the act or process of exploring. **2.** an organized trip into unfamiliar regions, esp. for scientific purposes. —**exploratory** (ɪk'splɒrətərɪ, -trɪ) *or* **ex'plorative** *adj.*

explore (ɪk'splɔː) *vb.* **1.** (*tr.*) to examine or investigate, esp. systematically. **2.** to travel into (unfamiliar regions), esp. for scientific purposes. **3.** (*tr.*) *Med.* to examine (an organ or part) for diagnostic purposes. [C16: < L, < EX-[1] + *plōrāre* to cry aloud; prob. < the shouts of hunters sighting prey] —**ex'plorer** *n.*

explosion (ɪk'spləʊʒən) *n.* **1.** the act or an instance of exploding. **2.** a violent release of energy resulting from a rapid chemical or nuclear reaction. **3.** a sudden or violent outburst of activity, noise, emotion, etc. **4.** a rapid increase, esp. in a population. [C17: < L *explōsiō*, < *explōdere* to EXPLODE]

explosive (ɪk'spləʊsɪv) *adj.* **1.** of, involving, or characterized by explosion. **2.** capable of exploding or tending to explode. **3.** potentially violent or hazardous: *an explosive situation.* ~*n.* **4.** a substance capable of exploding or tending to explode. —**ex'plosiveness** *n.*

expo ('ɛkspəʊ) *n., pl.* **-pos.** short for **exposition** (sense 3).

exponent (ɪk'spəʊnənt) *n.* **1.** (usually foll. by *of*) a person or thing that acts as an advocate (of an idea, cause, etc.). **2.** a person or thing that explains or interprets. **3.** a performer or artist. **4.** Also called: **power, index.** *Maths.* a number or variable placed as a superscript to another number or quantity indicating the number of times the number or quantity is to be multiplied by itself. ~*adj.* **5.** offering a declaration, explanation, or interpretation. [C16: < L *expōnere* to set out, expound]

exponential (ˌɛkspəʊ'nɛnʃəl) *adj.* **1.** *Maths.* (of a function, curve, etc.) of or involving numbers or quantities raised to an exponent, esp. e^x. **2.** *Maths.* raised to the power of e, the base of natural logarithms. **3.** of or involving an exponent or exponents. **4.** *Inf.* very rapid. ~*n.* **5.** *Maths.* an exponential function, etc.

exponential distribution *n. Statistics.* a continuous single-parameter distribution used esp. when making statements about the length of life of materials or times between random events.

export *n.* ('ɛkspɔːt). **1.** (*often pl.*) **a.** goods (**visible exports**) or services (**invisible exports**) sold to a foreign country or countries. **b.** (*as modifier*): *an export licence.* ~*vb.* (ɪk'spɔːt, 'ɛkspɔːt). **2.** to sell (goods or services) or ship (goods) to a foreign country. **3.** (*tr.*) to transmit or spread (an idea, institution, etc.) abroad. [C15: < L *exportāre* to carry away] —**ex'portable** *adj.* —**exˌporta'bility** *n.* —**ex'porter** *n.*

export reject *n.* an article that fails to meet a standard of quality required for export and that is sold on the home market.

expose (ɪk'spəʊz) *vb.* (*tr.*) **1.** to display for viewing; exhibit. **2.** to bring to public notice; disclose. **3.** to divulge the identity of; unmask. **4.** (foll. by *to*) to make subject or susceptible (to attack, criticism, etc.). **5.** to abandon (a child, etc.) in the open to die. **6.** (foll. by *to*) to introduce (to) or acquaint (with). **7.** *Photog.* to subject (a film or plate) to light, x-rays, etc. **8.** **expose oneself.** to display one's sexual organs in public. [C15: < OF *exposer*, < L *expōnere* to set out] —**ex'posable** *adj.* —**ex'posal** *n.* —**ex'poser** *n.*

exposé (ɛks'pəʊzeɪ) *n.* the act or an instance of bringing a scandal, crime, etc., to public notice.

exposed (ɪk'spəʊzd) *adj.* **1.** not concealed; displayed for viewing. **2.** without shelter from the elements. **3.** susceptible to attack or criticism; vulnerable. —**exposedness** (ɪk'spəʊzɪdnɪs) *n.*

exposition (ˌɛkspə'zɪʃən) *n.* **1.** a systematic, usually written statement about or explanation of a subject. **2.** the act of expounding or setting forth information or a viewpoint. **3.** a large public exhibition, esp. of industrial products or arts and crafts. **4.** the act of exposing or the state of being exposed. **5.** *Music.* the first statement of the subjects or themes of a movement in sonata form or a fugue. **6.** *R.C. Church.* the exhibiting of the consecrated Eucharistic Host or a relic for public veneration. [C14: < L *expositiō* a setting forth, < *expōnere* to display] —ˌ**expo'sitional** *adj.*

expositor (ɪk'spɒzɪtə) *n.* a person who expounds.

expository (ɪk'spɒzɪtərɪ, -trɪ) *or* **expositive** *adj.* of or involving exposition; explanatory. —**ex'positorily** *or* **ex'positively** *adv.*

ex post facto (ɛks pəʊst 'fæktəʊ) *adj.* having retrospective effect. [C17: < L *ex* from + *post* afterwards + *factus* done, < *facere* to do]

expostulate (ɪk'spɒstjʊˌleɪt) *vb.* (*intr.;* usually foll. by *with*) to argue or reason (with), esp. in order to dissuade. [C16: < L *expostulāre* to require, < *postulāre* to demand; see POSTULATE] —**exˌpostu'lation** *n.* —**ex'postuˌlator** *n.* —**ex'postulatory** *or* **ex'postulative** *adj.*

exposure (ɪk'spəʊʒə) *n.* **1.** the act of exposing or the condition of being exposed. **2.** the position or outlook of a house, building, etc.: *a southern exposure.* **3.** lack of shelter from the weather, esp. the cold. **4.** a surface that is exposed. **5.** *Photog.* **a.** the act of exposing a film or plate to light, x-rays, etc. **b.** an area on a film or plate that has been exposed. **6.** *Photog.* **a.** the intensity of light falling on a film or plate multiplied by the time for which it is exposed. **b.** a combination of lens aperture and shutter speed used in taking a photograph. **7.** appearance before the public, as in a theatre, on television, etc.

exposure meter *n. Photog.* an instrument for measuring the intensity of light so that suitable camera settings can be determined. Also called: **light meter.**

expound (ɪkˈspaʊnd) *vb.* (when *intr.*, foll. by *on* or *about*) to explain or set forth (an argument, theory, etc.) in detail. [C13: < OF, < L *expōnere* to set forth, < *pōnere* to put] —**exˈpounder** *n.*

express (ɪkˈsprɛs) *vb.* (*tr.*) **1.** to transform (ideas) into words; utter; verbalize. **2.** to show or reveal. **3.** to communicate (emotion, etc.) without words, as through music, painting, etc. **4.** to indicate through a symbol, formula, etc. **5.** to squeeze out: *to express the juice from an orange.* **6. express oneself.** to communicate one's thoughts or ideas. ~*adj.* (*prenominal*) **7.** clearly indicated; explicitly stated. **8.** done or planned for a definite reason; particular. **9.** of or designed for rapid transportation of people, mail, etc.: *express delivery.* ~*n.* **10. a.** a system for sending mail, money, etc., rapidly. **b.** mail, etc., conveyed by such a system. **c.** *Chiefly U.S. & Canad.* an enterprise operating such a system. **11.** Also: **express train.** a fast train stopping at no or only a few stations between its termini. ~*adv.* **12.** by means of express delivery. [C14: < L *expressus*, lit.: squeezed out, hence, prominent, < *exprimere* to force out, < EX-[1] + *premere* to press] —**exˈpresser** *n.* —**exˈpressible** *adj.*

expressage (ɪkˈsprɛsɪdʒ) *n.* **1.** the conveyance of merchandise by express. **2.** the fee for this.

expression (ɪkˈsprɛʃən) *n.* **1.** the act or an instance of transforming ideas into words. **2.** a manifestation of an emotion, feeling, etc., without words. **3.** communication of emotion through music, painting, etc. **4.** a look on the face that indicates mood or emotion. **5.** the choice of words, intonation, etc., in communicating. **6.** a particular phrase used conventionally to express something. **7.** the act or process of squeezing out a liquid. **8.** *Maths.* a variable, function, or some combination of these. —**exˈpressional** *adj.* —**exˈpressionless** *adj.*

expressionism (ɪkˈsprɛʃəˌnɪzəm) *n.* (*sometimes cap.*) an artistic and literary movement originating in the early 20th century, which sought to express emotions rather than to represent external reality: characterized by symbolism and distortion. —**exˈpressionist** *n., adj.* —**exˌpressionˈistic** *adj.*

expression mark *n.* one of a set of musical directions, usually in Italian, indicating how a piece or passage is to be performed.

expressive (ɪkˈsprɛsɪv) *adj.* **1.** of, involving, or full of expression. **2.** (*postpositive;* foll. by *of*) indicative or suggestive (of). **3.** having a particular meaning or force; significant. —**exˈpressiveness** *n.*

expressly (ɪkˈsprɛslɪ) *adv.* **1.** for an express purpose. **2.** plainly, exactly, or unmistakably.

expresso (ɪkˈsprɛsəʊ) *n., pl.* **-sos.** a variant of **espresso.**

expressway (ɪkˈsprɛsˌweɪ) *n.* a motorway.

expropriate (ɛksˈprəʊprɪˌeɪt) *vb.* (*tr.*) to deprive (an owner) of (property), esp. by taking it for public use. [C17: < Med. L *expropriāre* to deprive of possessions, < *proprius* own] —**exˌpropriˈation** *n.* —**exˈpropriˌator** *n.*

expulsion (ɪkˈspʌlʃən) *n.* the act of expelling or the fact or condition of being expelled. [C14: < L *expulsiō* a driving out, < *expellere* to EXPEL] —**exˈpulsive** *adj.*

expunge (ɪkˈspʌndʒ) *vb.* (*tr.*) to delete or erase; blot out; obliterate. [C17: < L *expungere* to blot out, < *pungere* to prick] —**expunction** (ɪkˈspʌŋkʃən) *n.* —**exˈpunger** *n.*

expurgate (ˈɛkspəˌgeɪt) *vb.* (*tr.*) to amend (a book, text, etc.) by removing (offensive sections). [C17: < L *expurgāre* to clean out, < *purgāre* to purify; see PURGE] —ˌ**expurˈgation** *n.* —ˈ**expurˌgator** *n.* —**expurgatory** (ɛksˈpɜːgətərɪ) *or* **expurgatorial** (ɛkˌspɜːgəˈtɔːrɪəl) *adj.*

exquisite (ɪkˈskwɪzɪt, ˈɛkskwɪzɪt) *adj.* **1.** possessing qualities of unusual delicacy and craftsmanship. **2.** extremely beautiful. **3.** outstanding or excellent. **4.** sensitive; discriminating. **5.** fastidious and refined. **6.** intense or sharp in feeling. ~*n.* **7.** *Obs.* a dandy. [C15: < L *exquīsītus* excellent, < *exquīrere* to search out, < *quaerere* to seek] —**exˈquisiteness** *n.*

ex-serviceman *or* (*fem.*) **ex-servicewoman** *n., pl.* **-men** *or* **-women.** a person who has served in the armed forces.

extant (ɛkˈstænt, ˈɛkstənt) *adj.* still in existence; surviving. [C16: < L *exstāns* standing out, < *exstāre*, < *stāre* to stand]

▷ **Usage.** Careful writers distinguish between *extant* and *existent.* Both are used of that which exists at the present time, but *extant* has a further connotation of survival.

extemporaneous (ɪkˌstɛmpəˈreɪnɪəs) *or* **extemporary** (ɪkˈstɛmpərərɪ) *adj.* **1.** spoken, performed, etc., without preparation; extempore. **2.** done in a temporary manner; improvised. —**exˌtempoˈraneously** *or* **exˈtemporarily** *adv.* —**exˌtempoˈraneousness** *or* **exˈtemporariness** *n.*

extempore (ɪkˈstɛmpərɪ) *adv., adj.* without planning or preparation. [C16: < L *ex tempore* instantaneously, < EX-[1] out of + *tempus* time]

extemporize *or* **-rise** (ɪkˈstɛmpəˌraɪz) *vb.* **1.** to perform, speak, or compose (an act, speech, music, etc.) without preparation. **2.** to use a temporary solution; improvise. —**exˌtemporiˈzation** *or* **-riˈsation** *n.* —**exˈtempoˌrizer** *or* **-ˌriser** *n.*

extend (ɪkˈstɛnd) *vb.* **1.** to draw out or be drawn out; stretch. **2.** to last or cause to last for a certain time. **3.** (*intr.*) to reach a certain point in time or distance. **4.** (*intr.*) to exist or occur. **5.** (*tr.*) to increase (a building, etc.) in size; add to or enlarge. **6.** (*tr.*) to broaden the meaning or scope of: *the law was extended.* **7.** (*tr.*) to present or offer. **8.** to stretch forth (an arm, etc.). **9.** (*tr.*) to lay out (a body) at full length. **10.** (*tr.*) to strain or exert (a person or animal) to the maximum. **11.** (*tr.*) to prolong (the time) for payment of (a debt or loan), completion of (a task), etc. [C14: < L *extendere* to stretch out, < *tendere* to stretch] —**exˈtendible** *or* **exˈtendable** *adj.* —**exˌtendiˈbility** *or* **exˌtendaˈbility** *n.*

extended family *n. Sociol., anthropol.* the nuclear family together with blood relatives, often spanning three or more generations.

extended-play *adj.* denoting an EP record.

extender (ɪkˈstɛndə) *n.* **1.** a person or thing that extends. **2.** a substance added to paints to give body and decrease their rate of settlement. **3.** a substance added to glues and resins to dilute them or to modify their viscosity.

extensible (ɪkˈstɛnsɪbᵊl) *or* **extensile** (ɪkˈstɛnsaɪl) *adj.* capable of being extended. —**exˌtensiˈbility** *or* **exˈtensibleness** *n.*

extension (ɪkˈstɛnʃən) *n.* **1.** the act of extending or the condition of being extended. **2.** something that can be extended or that extends another object. **3.** the length, range, etc., over which something is extended. **4.** an additional telephone set connected to the same telephone line as another set. **5.** a room or rooms added to an existing building. **6.** a delay in the date originally set for payment of a debt or completion of a contract. **7.** the property of matter by which it occupies space. **8. a.** the act of straightening or extending an arm or leg. **b.** its position after being straightened or extended. **9. a.** a service by which the facilities of an educational establishment, library, etc., are offered to outsiders. **b.** (*as modifier*): *a university extension course.* **10.** *Logic.* the class of entities to which a given word correctly applies. [C14: < LL *extensiō* a stretching out; see EXTEND] —**exˈtensional** *adj.* —**exˌtensionˈality** *or* **exˈtensionalˌism** *n.*

extensive (ɪkˈstɛnsɪv) *adj.* **1.** having a large extent, area, degree, etc. **2.** widespread. **3.** *Agriculture.* involving or farmed with minimum expenditure of capital or labour, esp. depending on a large extent of land. Cf. **intensive** (sense 3). **4.** of or relating to logical extension. —**exˈtensiveness** *n.*

extensor (ɪkˈstɛnsə, -sɔː) *n.* any muscle that stretches or extends an arm, leg, or other bodily part. Cf. **flexor.** [C18: < NL, < L *extensus* stretched out]

extent (ɪk'stɛnt) *n.* **1.** the range over which something extends; scope. **2.** an area or volume. [C14: < OF, < L *extentus* extensive, < *extendere* to EXTEND]

extenuate (ɪk'stɛnjʊ,eɪt) *vb.* (*tr.*) **1.** to represent (an offence, fault, etc.) as being less serious than it appears, as by showing mitigating circumstances. **2.** to cause to be or appear less serious; mitigate. **3.** *Arch.* **a.** to emaciate or weaken. **b.** to dilute or thin out. [C16: < L *extenuāre* to make thin, < *tenuis* thin, frail] —**ex'tenu,ating** *adj.* —**ex,tenu'ation** *n.* —**ex'tenu,ator** *n.* —**ex'tenuatory** *adj.*

exterior (ɪk'stɪərɪə) *n.* **1.** a part, surface, or region that is on the outside. **2.** the outward behaviour or appearance of a person. **3.** a film or scene shot outside a studio. ~*adj.* **4.** of, situated on, or suitable for the outside. **5.** coming or acting from without. [C16: < L, comp. of *exterus* on the outside, < *ex* out of] —**ex'teriorly** *adv.*

exterior angle *n.* **1.** an angle of a polygon contained between one side extended and the adjacent side. **2.** any of the four angles made by a transversal that are outside the region between the two intersected lines.

exteriorize *or* **-ise** (ɪk'stɪərɪə,raɪz) *vb.* (*tr.*) **1.** *Surgery.* to expose (an attached organ or part) outside the body. **2.** another word for **externalize.** —**ex,teriori'zation** *or* **-i'sation** *n.*

exterminate (ɪk'stɜːmɪ,neɪt) *vb.* (*tr.*) to destroy (living things, esp. pests or vermin) completely; annihilate; eliminate. [C16: < L *extermināre* to drive away, < *terminus* boundary] —**ex'terminable** *adj.* —**ex,termi'nation** *n.* —**ex'terminative** *or* **ex'terminatory** *adj.* —**ex'termi,nator** *n.*

external (ɪk'stɜːnᵊl) *adj.* **1.** of, situated on, or suitable for the outside; outer. **2.** coming or acting from without. **3.** of or involving foreign nations. **4.** of, relating to, or designating a medicine that is applied to the outside of the body. **5.** *Anat.* situated on or near the outside of the body. **6.** *Austral. & N.Z.* (of a student) studying a university subject extramurally. **7.** *Philosophy.* (of objects, etc.) taken to exist independently of a perceiving mind. ~*n.* **8.** (*often pl.*) an external circumstance or aspect, esp. one that is superficial. **9.** *Austral. & N.Z.* an extramural student. [C15: < L *externus* outward, < *exterus* on the outside, < *ex* out of] —**,exter'nality** *n.*

externalize *or* **-ise** (ɪk'stɜːnə,laɪz) *vb.* (*tr.*) **1.** to make external; give outward shape to. **2.** *Psychol.* to attribute (one's feelings) to one's surroundings. —**ex,ternali'zation** *or* **-i'sation** *n.*

extinct (ɪk'stɪŋkt) *adj.* **1.** (of an animal or plant species) having died out. **2.** quenched or extinguished. **3.** (of a volcano) no longer liable to erupt; inactive. [C15: < L *exstinctus* quenched, < *exstinguere* to EXTINGUISH]

extinction (ɪk'stɪŋkʃən) *n.* **1.** the act of making extinct or the state of being extinct. **2.** the act of extinguishing or the state of being extinguished. **3.** complete destruction; annihilation. **4.** *Physics.* reduction of the intensity of radiation as a result of absorption or scattering by matter.

extinguish (ɪk'stɪŋgwɪʃ) *vb.* (*tr.*) **1.** to put out or quench (a light, flames, etc.). **2.** to remove or destroy entirely; annihilate. **3.** *Arch.* to eclipse or obscure. [C16: < L *exstinguere*, < *stinguere* to quench] —**ex'tinguishable** *adj.* —**ex'tinguisher** *n.* —**ex'tinguishment** *n.*

extirpate ('ɛkstə,peɪt) *vb.* (*tr.*) **1.** to remove or destroy completely. **2.** to pull up or out; uproot. [C16: < L *exstirpāre* to root out, < *stirps* root, stock] —**,extir'pation** *n.* —**'extir,pative** *adj.* —**'extir,pator** *n.*

extol *or U.S.* **extoll** (ɪk'stəʊl) *vb.* **-tolling, -tolled.** (*tr.*) to praise lavishly; exalt. [C15: < L *extollere* to elevate, < *tollere* to raise] —**ex'toller** *n.* —**ex'tolment** *n.*

extort (ɪk'stɔːt) *vb.* (*tr.*) **1.** to secure (money, favours, etc.) by intimidation, violence, or the misuse of authority. **2.** to obtain by importunate demands. [C16: < L *extortus* wrenched out, < *extorquēre* to wrest away, < *torquēre* to twist, wrench] —**ex'tortion** *n.* —**ex'tortioner, ex'tortionist,** *or* **ex'torter** *n.* —**ex'tortive** *adj.*

extortionate (ɪk'stɔːʃənɪt) *adj.* **1.** (of prices, etc.) excessive; exorbitant. **2.** (of persons) using extortion. —**ex'tortionately** *adv.*

extra ('ɛkstrə) *adj.* **1.** being more than what is usual or expected; additional. ~*n.* **2.** a person or thing that is additional. **3.** something for which an additional charge is made. **4.** an additional edition of a newspaper, esp. to report a new development. **5.** *Films.* a person temporarily engaged, usually for crowd scenes. **6.** *Cricket.* a run not scored from the bat, such as a wide, no-ball, or bye. ~*adv.* **7.** unusually; exceptionally: *an extra fast car.* [C18: ? shortened < EXTRAORDINARY]

extra- *prefix.* outside or beyond an area or scope: *extrasensory; extraterritorial.* [< L *extrā* outside, beyond, < *extera*, < *exterus* outward]

extra cover *n. Cricket.* a fielding position between cover and mid-off.

extract *vb.* (ɪk'strækt). (*tr.*) **1.** to pull out or uproot by force. **2.** to remove or separate. **3.** to derive (pleasure, information, etc.) from some source. **4.** to deduce or develop (a doctrine, policy, etc.). **5.** *Inf.* to extort (money, etc.). **6.** to obtain (a substance) from a mixture or material by a process, such as digestion, distillation, mechanical separation, etc. **7.** to cut out or copy out (an article, passage, etc.) from a publication. **8.** to determine the value of (the root of a number). ~*n.* ('ɛkstrækt). **9.** something extracted, such as a passage from a book, etc. **10.** a preparation containing the active principle or concentrated essence of a material. [C15: < L *extractus* drawn forth, < *extrahere*, < *trahere* to drag] —**ex'tractable** *adj.* —**ex,tracta'bility** *n.* —**ex'tractive** *adj.* —**ex'tractor** *n.*

extraction (ɪk'strækʃən) *n.* **1.** the act of extracting or the condition of being extracted. **2.** something extracted. **3.** the act or an instance of extracting a tooth. **4.** origin or ancestry.

extracurricular (,ɛkstrəkə'rɪkjʊlə) *adj.* **1.** taking place outside the normal school timetable. **2.** beyond the regular duties, schedule, etc.

extradite ('ɛkstrə,daɪt) *vb.* (*tr.*) **1.** to surrender (an alleged offender) for trial to a foreign state. **2.** to procure the extradition of. [C19: back formation < EXTRADITION] —**'extra,ditable** *adj.*

extradition (,ɛkstrə'dɪʃən) *n.* the surrender of an alleged offender to the state where the alleged offence was committed. [C19: < F, < L *trāditiō* a handing over; see TRADITION]

extrados (ɛk'streɪdɒs) *n., pl.* **-dos** (-dəʊz) *or* **-doses.** *Archit.* the outer curve of an arch or vault. [C18: < F, < EXTRA- + *dos* back]

extragalactic (,ɛkstrəgə'læktɪk) *adj.* occurring or existing beyond the Galaxy.

extramarital (,ɛkstrə'mærɪtᵊl) *adj.* (esp. of sexual relations) occurring outside marriage.

extramural (,ɛkstrə'mjʊərəl) *adj.* **1.** connected with but outside the normal courses of a university, college, etc. **2.** beyond the boundaries or walls of a city, castle, etc.

extraneous (ɪk'streɪnɪəs) *adj.* **1.** not essential. **2.** not pertinent; irrelevant. **3.** coming from without. **4.** not belonging. [C17: < L *extrāneus* external, < *extrā* outside] —**ex'traneousness** *n.*

extraordinary (ɪk'strɔːdᵊnrɪ) *adj.* **1.** very unusual or surprising. **2.** not in an established manner or order. **3.** employed for particular purposes. **4.** (*usually postpositive*) (of an official, etc.) additional or subordinate. [C15: < L *extraordinārius* beyond what is usual; see ORDINARY] —**ex'traordinarily** *adv.* —**ex'traordinariness** *n.*

extrapolate (ɪk'stræpə,leɪt) *vb.* **1.** *Maths.* to estimate (a value of a function etc.) beyond the known values, by the extension of a curve. Cf. **interpolate** (sense 4). **2.** to infer (something) by using but not strictly deducing from known facts. [C19: EXTRA- + *-polate*, as in INTERPOLATE] —**ex,trapo'lation** *n.* —**ex'trapolative** *or* **ex'trapolatory** *adj.* —**ex'trapo,lator** *n.*

extrasensory (,ɛkstrə'sɛnsərɪ) *adj.* of or relating to extrasensory perception.

extrasensory perception *n.* the supposed

ability of certain individuals to obtain information about the environment without the use of normal sensory channels.

extraterritorial (ˌɛkstrəˌtɛrɪˈtɔːrɪəl) *or* **exterritorial** *adj.* 1. beyond the limits of a country's territory. 2. of, relating to, or possessing extraterritoriality.

extraterritoriality (ˌɛkstrəˌtɛrɪˌtɔːrɪˈælɪtɪ) *n.* 1. the privilege granted to some aliens, esp. diplomats, of being exempt from the jurisdiction of the state in which they reside. 2. the right of a state to exercise authority in certain circumstances beyond the limits of its territory.

extra time *n. Sport.* an additional period played at the end of a match, to compensate for time lost through injury or (in certain circumstances) to allow the teams to achieve a conclusive result.

extravagance (ɪkˈstrævɪgəns) *n.* 1. excessive outlay of money; wasteful spending. 2. immoderate or absurd speech or behaviour.

extravagant (ɪkˈstrævɪgənt) *adj.* 1. spending money excessively or immoderately. 2. going beyond usual bounds; unrestrained. 3. ostentatious; showy. 4. exorbitant in price; overpriced. [C14: < Med. L *extravagāns,* < L EXTRA- + *vagārī* to wander]

extravaganza (ɪkˌstrævəˈgænzə) *n.* 1. an elaborately staged light entertainment. 2. any lavish or fanciful display, literary composition, etc. [C18: < It.: extravagance]

extravasate (ɪkˈstrævəˌseɪt) *vb. Pathol.* to cause (blood or lymph) to escape or (of blood or lymph) to escape into the surrounding tissues from their proper vessels. [C17: < L EXTRA- + *vās* vessel] —**exˌtravaˈsation** *n.*

extravehicular (ˌɛkstrəvɪˈhɪkjʊlə) *adj.* occurring or used outside a spacecraft, either in space or on the surface of a planet.

extraversion (ˌɛkstrəˈvɜːʃən) *n.* a variant spelling of **extroversion.** —ˈ**extraˌvert** *n., adj.*

extreme (ɪkˈstriːm) *adj.* 1. being of a high or of the highest degree or intensity. 2. exceeding what is usual or reasonable; immoderate. 3. very strict or severe; drastic. 4. (*prenominal*) farthest or outermost. ~*n.* 5. the highest or furthest degree (often in **in the extreme, go to extremes**). 6. (*often pl.*) either of the two limits or ends of a scale or range. 7. *Maths.* the first or last term of a series or a proportion. [C15: < L *extrēmus* outermost, < *exterus* on the outside; see EXTERIOR] —**exˈtremely** *adv.* —**exˈtremeness** *n.*

extreme unction *n. R.C. Church.* a sacrament in which a person who is seriously ill or dying is anointed by a priest.

extremist (ɪkˈstriːmɪst) *n.* 1. a person who favours immoderate or fanatical methods, esp. in being politically radical. ~*adj.* 2. of or characterized by immoderate or excessive actions, opinions, etc. —**exˈtremism** *n.*

extremity (ɪkˈstrɛmɪtɪ) *n., pl.* **-ties.** 1. the farthest or outermost point or section. 2. the greatest degree. 3. an extreme condition or state, as of adversity. 4. a limb, such as a leg or wing, or the end of such a limb. 5. (*usually pl.*) *Arch.* a drastic or severe measure.

extricate (ˈɛkstrɪˌkeɪt) *vb.* (*tr.*) to remove or free from complication, hindrance, or difficulty; disentangle. [C17: < L *extrīcāre* to disentangle, < EX-[1] + *trīcae* vexations] —ˈ**extricable** *adj.* —ˌ**extriˈcation** *n.*

extrinsic (ɛkˈstrɪnsɪk) *adj.* 1. not contained or included within; extraneous. 2. originating or acting from outside. [C16: < LL *extrinsecus* (adj.) outward, < L (adv.), ult. < *exter* outward + *secus* alongside] —**exˈtrinsically** *adv.*

extroversion *or* **extraversion** (ˌɛkstrəˈvɜːʃən) *n. Psychol.* the directing of one's interest outwards, esp. towards social contacts. [C17: < *extro-* (var. of EXTRA-, contrasting with *intro-*) + *-version,* < L *vertere* to turn] —ˌ**extroˈversive** *or* ˌ**extraˈversive** *adj.*

extrovert *or* **extravert** (ˈɛkstrəˌvɜːt) *Psychol.* ~*n.* 1. a person concerned more with external reality than inner feelings. ~*adj.* 2. of or characterized by extroversion. [C20: < *extro-* (var. of EXTRA-, contrasting with *intro-*) + *-vert,* < L *vertere* to turn] —ˈ**extroˌverted** *or* ˈ**extraˌverted** *adj.*

extrude (ɪkˈstruːd) *vb.* (*tr.*) 1. to squeeze or force out. 2. to produce (moulded sections of plastic, metal, etc.) by ejection from a shaped nozzle or die. 3. to chop up or pulverize (an item of food) and re-form it to look like a whole. [C16: < L *extrūdere* to thrust out, < *trūdere* to push, thrust] —**exˈtruded** *adj.*

extrusion (ɪkˈstruːʒən) *n.* 1. the act or process of extruding. 2. a. the movement of magma through volcano craters and cracks in the earth's crust, forming igneous rock. b. any igneous rock formed in this way. 3. anything formed by the process of extruding. [C16: < Med. L *extrūsiō,* < *extrūdere* to EXTRUDE] —**exˈtrusive** *adj.*

exuberant (ɪgˈzjuːbərənt) *adj.* 1. abounding in vigour and high spirits. 2. lavish or effusive; excessively elaborate. 3. growing luxuriantly or in profusion. [C15: < L *exūberāns,* < *ūberāre* to be fruitful] —**exˈuberance** *n.*

exuberate (ɪgˈzjuːbəˌreɪt) *vb.* (*intr.*) *Rare.* 1. to be exuberant. 2. to abound. [C15: < L *exūberāre* to be abundant; see EXUBERANT]

exude (ɪgˈzjuːd) *vb.* 1. to release or be released through pores, incisions, etc., as sweat or sap. 2. (*tr.*) to make apparent by mood or behaviour. [C16: < L *exsūdāre,* < *sūdāre* to sweat] —**exudation** (ˌɛksjʊˈdeɪʃən) *n.*

exult (ɪgˈzʌlt) *vb.* (*intr.*) 1. to be joyful or jubilant, esp. because of triumph or success. 2. (often foll. by *over*) to triumph (over). [C16: < L *exsultāre* to jump or leap for joy, < *saltāre* to leap] —**exultation** (ˌɛgzʌlˈteɪʃən) *n.* —**exˈultingly** *adv.*

exultant (ɪgˈzʌltənt) *adj.* elated or jubilant; esp. because of triumph or success. —**exˈultantly** *adv.*

exurbia (ɛksˈɜːbɪə) *n. Chiefly U.S.* the region outside the suburbs of a city, consisting of residential areas (**exurbs**) occupied predominantly by rich commuters (**exurbanites**). [C20: < EX-[1] + L *urbs* city] —**exˈurban** *adj.*

exuviate (ɪgˈzjuːvɪˌeɪt) *vb.* to shed (a skin or similar outer covering). —**exˌuviˈation** *n.*

-ey *suffix.* a variant of **-y**[1] and **-y**[2].

eyas (ˈaɪəs) *n.* a nestling hawk or falcon, esp. one reared for falconry. [C15: mistaken division of earlier *a nyas,* < OF *niais* nestling, < L *nīdus* nest]

eye[1] (aɪ) *n.* 1. the organ of sight of animals. Related adjs.: **ocular, ophthalmic.** 2. (*often pl.*) the ability to see; sense of vision. 3. the external part of an eye, often including the area around it. 4. a look, glance, expression, or gaze. 5. a sexually inviting or provocative look (esp. in **give (someone) the (glad) eye, make eyes at**). 6. attention or observation (often in **catch someone's eye, keep an eye on, cast an eye over**). 7. ability to recognize, judge, or appreciate. 8. (*often pl.*) opinion, judgment, point of view, or authority: *in the eyes of the law.* 9. a structure or marking resembling an eye, such as the bud on a potato tuber or a spot on a butterfly wing. 10. a small loop or hole, as at one end of a needle. 11. a small area of low pressure and calm in the centre of a tornado. 12. **electric eye.** another name for **photocell.** 13. **all eyes.** *Inf.* acutely vigilant or observant. 14. **(all) my eye.** *Inf.* rubbish; nonsense. 15. **an eye for an eye.** retributive or vengeful justice; retaliation. 16. **get one's eye in.** *Chiefly sport.* to become accustomed to the conditions, light, etc., with a consequent improvement in one's performance. 17. **go eyes out.** *Austral. & N.Z.* to make every possible effort. 18. **half an eye.** a modicum of perceptiveness. 19. **have eyes for.** to be interested in. 20. **in one's mind's eye.** pictured within the mind; imagined or remembered vividly. 21. **in the public eye.** exposed to public curiosity or publicity. 22. **keep an eye open** *or* **out (for).** to watch with special attention (for). 23. **keep one's eyes skinned** (*or* **peeled**). to watch vigilantly (for). 24. **lay, clap,** *or* **set eyes on.** (*usually with a negative*) to see. 25. **look (someone) in the eye.** to look openly and without shame or embarrassment at (someone). **26. make sheep's eyes (at).** *Old-fashioned.* to ogle amorously. **27. more than meets the eye.** hidden motives, meaning, or facts. **28. see eye to eye (with).** to agree (with). **29. shut one's eyes (to)** *or* **turn a blind eye (to).** to pretend not to notice or to ignore deliberately. **30. up to one's eyes (in).** extremely busy (with). **31. with** *or* **having an eye to.** (*prep.*) **a.** regarding; with reference to. **b.** with the intention or purpose of. **32. with one's eyes open.** in the full knowledge of all relevant facts. **33. with one's eyes shut. a.** with great ease, esp. as a result of thorough familiarity. **b.** without being aware of all the facts. ~*vb.* **eyeing** *or* **eying, eyed.** (*tr.*) **34.** to look at carefully or warily. **35.** Also: **eye up.** to look at in a manner indicating sexual interest; ogle. [OE *ēage*] —**'eyeless** *adj.* —**'eye,like** *adj.*

eye² (aɪ) *n.* another word for **nye.**

eyeball ('aɪ,bɔːl) *n.* **1.** the entire ball-shaped part of the eye. **2. eyeball to eyeball.** in close confrontation. ~*vb.* **3.** (*tr.*) *Sl., chiefly U.S.* to stare at.

eyebath ('aɪ,bɑːθ) *n.* a small vessel for applying medicated or cleansing solutions to the eye. Also called (U.S. and Canad.) **eyecup.**

eyeblack ('aɪ,blæk) *n.* another name for **mascara.**

eyebright ('aɪ,braɪt) *n.* an annual plant having small white-and-purple flowers: formerly used in the treatment of eye disorders.

eyebrow ('aɪ,braʊ) *n.* **1.** the transverse bony ridge over each eye. **2.** the arch of hair that covers this ridge. **3. raise an eyebrow.** to give rise to doubt or disapproval.

eyebrow pencil *n.* a cosmetic in pencil form for applying colour and shape to the eyebrows.

eye-catching *adj.* tending to attract attention; striking. —**'eye-,catcher** *n.*

eye contact *n.* a direct look between two people; meeting of eyes.

eyed (aɪd) *adj.* **a.** having an eye or eyes (as specified). **b.** (*in combination*): *brown-eyed.*

eye dog *n. N.Z.* a dog trained to control sheep by staring fixedly at them. Also called: **strong-eye dog.**

eyeful ('aɪ,fʊl) *n. Inf.* **1.** a view, glance, or gaze. **2.** a beautiful or attractive sight, esp. a woman.

eyeglass ('aɪ,glɑːs) *n.* **1.** a lens for aiding or correcting defective vision, esp. a monocle. **2.** another word for **eyepiece** or **eyebath.**

eyeglasses ('aɪ,glɑːsɪz) *pl. n. Now chiefly U.S.* another word for **spectacles.**

eyehole ('aɪ,həʊl) *n.* **1.** a hole through which a rope, hook, etc., is passed. **2.** the cavity that contains the eyeball. **3.** another word for **peephole.**

eyelash ('aɪ,læʃ) *n.* **1.** any one of the short curved hairs that grow from the edge of the eyelids. **2.** a row or fringe of these hairs.

eyelet ('aɪlɪt) *n.* **1.** a small hole for a lace, cord, or hook to be passed through. **2.** a small metal ring or tube reinforcing an eyehole in fabric. **3.** a small opening, such as a peephole. **4.** *Embroidery.* a small hole with finely stitched edges. **5.** a small eye or eyelike marking. ~*vb.* **6.** (*tr.*) to supply with an eyelet or eyelets. [C14: < OF *oillet,* lit.: a little eye, < *oill* eye, < L *oculus* eye]

eyelevel ('aɪ,lɛvᵊl) *adj.* level with a person's eyes when looking straight ahead: *an eyelevel grill.*

eyelid ('aɪ,lɪd) *n.* either of the two muscular folds of skin that can be moved to cover the exposed portion of the eyeball.

eyeliner ('aɪ,laɪnə) *n.* a cosmetic used to outline the eyes.

eye-opener *n. Inf.* **1.** something startling or revealing. **2.** *U.S. & Canad.* an alcoholic drink taken early in the morning.

eyepiece ('aɪ,piːs) *n.* the lens or lenses in an optical instrument nearest the eye of the observer.

eye rhyme *n.* a rhyme involving words that are similar in spelling but not in sound, such as *stone* and *none.*

eye shadow *n.* a coloured cosmetic put around the eyes.

eyeshot ('aɪ,ʃɒt) *n.* range of vision; view.

eyesight ('aɪ,saɪt) *n.* the ability to see; faculty of sight.

eyesore ('aɪ,sɔː) *n.* something very ugly.

eyespot ('aɪ,spɒt) *n.* **1.** a small area of light-sensitive pigment in some simple organisms. **2.** an eyelike marking, as on a butterfly wing.

eyestrain ('aɪ,streɪn) *n.* fatigue or irritation of the eyes, resulting from excessive use or uncorrected defects of vision.

Eyetie ('aɪtaɪ) *n., adj. Brit. sl., offensive.* Italian. [C20: < jocular mispronunciation of *Italian*]

eyetooth (,aɪ'tuːθ) *n., pl.* **-teeth. 1.** either of the two canine teeth in the upper jaw. **2. give one's eyeteeth for.** to go to any lengths to achieve or obtain (something).

eyewash ('aɪ,wɒʃ) *n.* **1.** a lotion for the eyes. **2.** *Inf.* nonsense; rubbish.

eyewitness ('aɪ,wɪtnɪs) *n.* a person present at an event who can describe what happened.

eyrie ('ɪərɪ, 'ɛərɪ, 'aɪərɪ) *or* **aerie** *n.* **1.** the nest of an eagle or other bird of prey, built in a high inaccessible place. **2.** any high isolated position or place. [C16: < Med. L *airea,* < L *ārea* open field, hence, nest]

eyrir ('eɪrɪə) *n., pl.* **aurar** ('ɔɪrɑː). an Icelandic monetary unit worth one hundredth of a krona. [ON: ounce (of silver), money; rel. to L *aureus* golden]

Ez. *or* **Ezr.** *Bible. abbrev. for* Ezra.

Ezek. *Bible. abbrev. for* Ezekiel.

F

f *or* **F** (ɛf) *n., pl.* **f's, F's,** *or* **Fs. 1.** the sixth letter of the English alphabet. **2.** a speech sound represented by this letter, as in *fat.*

f *symbol for:* **1.** *Music.* forte: an instruction to play loudly. **2.** *Physics.* frequency. **3.** *Maths.* function (of). **4.** *Physics.* femto-.

f, f/, *or* **f:** *symbol for* f-number.

F *symbol for:* **1.** *Music.* **a.** the fourth note of the scale of C major. **b.** the major or minor key having this note as its tonic. **2.** Fahrenheit. **3.** farad(s). **4.** *Chem.* fluorine. **5.** *Physics.* force. **6.** franc(s). **7.** *Genetics.* a generation of filial offspring, F_1 being the first generation of offspring.

f. *or* **F.** *abbrev. for:* **1.** fathom(s). **2.** female. **3.** *Grammar.* feminine. **4.** (*pl.* **ff.** *or* **FF.**) folio. **5.** (*pl.* **ff.**) following (page).

F- (of U.S. military aircraft) *abbrev. for* fighter.

fa (fɑː) *n. Music.* a variant spelling of **fah.**

FA (in Britain) *abbrev. for* Football Association.

f.a. *or* **FA** *abbrev. for* fanny adams.

Fabian (ˈfeɪbɪən) *adj.* **1.** of or resembling the delaying tactics of Q. Fabius Maximus, Roman general who wore out the strength of Hannibal while avoiding a pitched battle; cautious. *~n.* **2.** a member of or sympathizer with the Fabian Society. [C19: < L *Fabiānus* of Fabius] —**ˈFabiaˌnism** *n.*

Fabian Society *n.* an association of British socialists advocating the establishment of socialism by gradual reforms.

fable (ˈfeɪbᵊl) *n.* **1.** a short moral story, esp. one with animals as characters. **2.** a false, fictitious, or improbable account. **3.** a story or legend about supernatural or mythical characters or events. **4.** legends or myths collectively. *~vb.* **5.** to relate or tell (fables). **6.** (*intr.*) to tell lies. **7.** (*tr.*) to talk about or describe in the manner of a fable. [C13: < L *fābula* story, narrative, < *fārī* to speak, say] —**ˈfabler** *n.*

fabled (ˈfeɪbᵊld) *adj.* **1.** made famous in fable. **2.** fictitious.

fabliau (ˈfæblɪˌəʊ) *n., pl.* **fabliaux** (ˈfæblɪˌəʊz). a comic usually ribald verse tale, popular in France in the 12th and 13th centuries. [C19: < F: a little tale, < *fable* tale]

Fablon (ˈfæblən, -lɒn) *n. Trademark.* a brand of adhesive-backed plastic material used to cover and decorate shelves, worktops, etc.

fabric (ˈfæbrɪk) *n.* **1.** any cloth made from yarn or fibres by weaving, knitting, felting, etc. **2.** the texture of a cloth. **3.** a structure or framework: *the fabric of society.* **4.** a style or method of construction. **5.** *Rare.* a building. [C15: < L *fabrica* workshop, < *faber* craftsman]

fabricate (ˈfæbrɪˌkeɪt) *vb.* (*tr.*) **1.** to make, build, or construct. **2.** to devise or concoct (a story, etc.). **3.** to fake or forge. [C15: < L, < *fabrica* workshop; see FABRIC] —**ˌfabriˈcation** *n.* —**ˈfabriˌcator** *n.*

fabulist (ˈfæbjʊlɪst) *n.* **1.** a person who invents or recounts fables. **2.** a person who lies.

fabulous (ˈfæbjʊləs) *adj.* **1.** almost unbelievable; astounding; legendary: *fabulous wealth.* **2.** *Inf.* extremely good: *a fabulous time at the party.* **3.** of, relating to, or based upon fable: *a fabulous beast.* [C15: < L *fābulōsus* celebrated in fable, < *fābula* FABLE] —**ˈfabulously** *adv.* —**ˈfabulousness** *n.*

Fac. *abbrev. for* Faculty.

façade *or* **facade** (fəˈsɑːd, fæ-) *n.* **1.** the face of a building, esp. the main front. **2.** a front or outer appearance, esp. a deceptive one. [C17: < F, < It., < *faccia* FACE]

face (feɪs) *n.* **1. a.** the front of the head from the forehead to the lower jaw. **b.** (*as modifier*): *face flannel.* **2. a.** the expression of the countenance: *a sad face.* **b.** a distorted expression, esp. to indicate disgust. **3.** *Inf.* make-up (esp. in **put one's face on**). **4.** outward appearance: *the face of the countryside is changing.* **5.** appearance or pretence (esp. in **put a bold, good, bad,** etc., **face on**). **6.** dignity (esp. in **lose** *or* **save face**). **7.** *Inf.* impudence or effrontery. **8.** the main side of an object, building, etc., or the front: *a cliff face.* **9.** the marked surface of an instrument, esp. the dial of a timepiece. **10.** the functional or working side of an object, as of a tool or playing card. **11. a.** the exposed area of a mine from which coal, ore, etc., may be mined. **b.** (*as modifier*): *face worker.* **12.** the uppermost part or surface: *the face of the earth.* **13.** Also called: **side.** any one of the plane surfaces of a crystal or other solid figure. **14.** Also called: **typeface.** *Printing.* **a.** the printing surface of any type character. **b.** the style or design of the character on the type. **15.** *N.Z.* the exposed slope of a hill. **16. in (the) face of.** despite. **17. on the face of it.** to all appearances. **18. set one's face against.** to oppose with determination. **19. show one's face.** to make an appearance. **20. to someone's face.** in someone's presence: *I told him the truth to his face.* *~vb.* **21.** (when *intr.*, often foll. by *to, towards,* or *on*) to look or be situated or placed (in a specified direction): *the house faces onto the square.* **22.** to be opposite: *facing page 9.* **23.** (*tr.*) to be confronted by: *he faces many problems.* **24.** (*tr.*) to provide with a surface of a different material. **25.** to dress the surface of (stone or other material). **26.** (*tr.*) to expose (a card) with the face uppermost. **27.** *Mil.* to order (a formation) to turn in a certain direction or (of a formation) to turn as required: *right face!* ~See also **face up to.** [C13: < OF, < Vulgar L *facia* (unattested), < L *faciēs* form]

face card *n.* the usual U.S. and Canad. term for **court card.**

face cloth *or* **face flannel** *n. Brit.* a small piece of cloth used to wash the face and hands. U.S. equivalent: **washcloth.**

faceless (ˈfeɪslɪs) *adj.* **1.** without a face. **2.** without identity; anonymous. —**ˈfacelessness** *n.*

face-lift *n.* **1.** cosmetic surgery for tightening sagging skin and smoothing wrinkles on the face. **2.** any improvement or renovation. *~vb.* (*tr.*) **3.** to improve the appearance of, as by a face-lift.

face-off *Ice hockey, etc.* *~n.* **1.** the method of starting a game, in which the referee drops the puck, etc. between two opposing players. *~vb.* **face off.** (*adv.*) **2.** to start play by (a face-off).

face powder *n.* a cosmetic powder worn to make the face look less shiny, softer, etc.

facer (ˈfeɪsə) *n.* **1.** a person or thing that faces. **2.** *Brit. inf.* a difficulty or problem.

face-saving *adj.* maintaining dignity or prestige. —**ˈface-ˌsaver** *n.*

facet (ˈfæsɪt) *n.* **1.** any of the surfaces of a cut gemstone. **2.** an aspect or phase, as of a subject or personality. *~vb.* **-eting, -eted** *or* **-etting, -etted. 3.** (*tr.*) to cut facets in (a gemstone). [C17: < F *facette* a little FACE]

facetiae (fəˈsiːʃɪˌiː) *pl. n.* **1.** humorous or witty sayings. **2.** obscene or coarsely witty books. [C17: < L: jests, pl. of *facētia* witticism, < *facētus* elegant]

facetious (fəˈsiːʃəs) *adj.* **1.** characterized by love of joking. **2.** jocular or amusing, esp. at inappropriate times: *facetious remarks.* [C16: < OF *facetieux,* < *facetie* witticism; see FACETIAE] —**faˈcetiously** *adv.* —**faˈcetiousness** *n.*

face to face *adv., adj.* (**face-to-face** *as adj.*) **1.** opposite one another. **2.** in confrontation.

face up to *vb.* (*intr., adv.* + *prep.*) to accept (an unpleasant fact, reality, etc.).

face value *n.* **1.** the value written or stamped on the face of a commercial paper or coin. **2.** apparent worth or value.

facia (ˈfeɪʃɪə) *n.* a variant spelling of **fascia.**

facial (ˈfeɪʃəl) *adj.* **1.** of or relating to the face.

~*n.* **2.** a beauty treatment for the face involving massage and cosmetic packs. —**'facially** *adv.*

facial eczema *n.* a disease of sheep and cattle characterized by impairment of liver function, itching, scab formation, and swelling of the skin, esp. on the face.

-facient *suffix forming adjectives and nouns.* indicating a state or quality: *absorbefacient.* [< L *facient-, faciēns,* present participle of *facere* to do]

facies ('feɪʃɪˌiːz) *n., pl.* **-cies.** **1.** the general form and appearance of an individual or a group. **2.** the characteristics of a rock or rocks reflecting their appearance and conditions of formation. **3.** *Med.* the general facial expression of a patient. [C17: < L: appearance, FACE]

facile ('fæsaɪl) *adj.* **1.** easy to perform or achieve. **2.** working or moving easily or smoothly. **3.** superficial: *a facile solution.* [C15: < L *facilis* easy, < *facere* to do] —**'facilely** *adv.* —**'facileness** *n.*

facilitate (fəˈsɪlɪˌteɪt) *vb.* (*tr.*) to assist the progress of. —**faˌciliˈtation** *n.*

facility (fəˈsɪlɪtɪ) *n., pl.* **-ties.** **1.** ease of action or performance. **2.** ready skill or ease deriving from practice or familiarity. **3.** (*often pl.*) the means or equipment facilitating the performance of an action. **4.** *Rare.* easy-going disposition. **5.** (*usually pl.*) a euphemistic word for **lavatory.** [C15: < L *facilitās,* < *facilis* easy; see FACILE]

facing ('feɪsɪŋ) *n.* **1.** a piece of material used esp. to conceal the seam of a garment and prevent fraying. **2.** (*usually pl.*) the collar, cuffs, etc., of the jacket of a military uniform. **3.** an outer layer or coat of material applied to the surface of a wall.

facsimile (fækˈsɪmɪlɪ) *n.* **1.** an exact copy or reproduction. **2.** a telegraphic system in which a written or pictorial document is scanned photoelectrically, the resulting signals being transmitted and reproduced photographically. ~*vb.* **-leing, -led.** **3.** (*tr.*) to make an exact copy of. [C17: < L *fac simile!* make something like it!, < *facere* to make + *similis* similar, like]

fact (fækt) *n.* **1.** an event or thing known to have happened or existed. **2.** a truth verifiable from experience or observation. **3.** a piece of information: *get me all the facts of this case.* **4.** (*often pl.*) *Law.* an actual event, happening, etc., as distinguished from its legal consequences. **5.** **after** (*or* **before**) **the fact.** *Criminal law.* after (or before) the commission of the offence. **6. as a matter of fact, in fact, in point of fact.** in reality or actuality. **7. fact of life.** an inescapable truth, esp. an unpleasant one. See also **facts of life.** [C16: < L *factum* something done, < *factus* made, < *facere* to do, make]

faction[1] ('fækʃən) *n.* **1.** a group of people forming a minority within a larger body, esp. a dissentious group. **2.** strife or dissension within a group. [C16: < L *factiō* a making, < *facere* to do, make] —**'factional** *adj.*

faction[2] ('fækʃən) *n.* a television programme, film, or literary work comprising a dramatized presentation of actual events. [C20: a blend of FACT & FICTION]

faction fight *n.* conflict between different groups within a larger body, esp. in S Africa a fight between Blacks of different tribes.

factious ('fækʃəs) *adj.* given to, producing, or characterized by faction. —**'factiously** *adv.*

factitious (fækˈtɪʃəs) *adj.* **1.** artificial rather than natural. **2.** not genuine; sham: *factitious enthusiasm.* [C17: < L *facticius,* < *facere* to do, make] —**facˈtitiously** *adv.* —**facˈtitiousness** *n.*

factitive ('fæktɪtɪv) *adj. Grammar.* denoting a verb taking a direct object as well as a noun in apposition, as for example *elect* in *They elected John president,* where *John* is the direct object and *president* is the complement. [C19: < NL, < L *factitāre* to do frequently, < *facere* to do, make]

factoid ('fæktɔɪd) *n.* a piece of unreliable information believed to be true because of the way it is presented or repeated in print. [C20: coined by Norman Mailer (born 1923), U.S. author, < FACT + -OID]

factor ('fæktə) *n.* **1.** an element or cause that contributes to a result. **2.** *Maths.* one of two or more integers or polynomials whose product is a given integer or polynomial: *2 and 3 are factors of 6.* **3.** a person who acts on another's behalf, esp. one who transacts business for another. **4.** former name for a **gene.** **5.** *Commercial law.* a person to whom goods are consigned for sale and who is paid a commission. **6.** (in Scotland) the manager of an estate. ~*vb.* **7.** (*intr.*) to engage in the business of a factor. [C15: < L: one who acts, < *facere* to do, make] —**'factorable** *adj.* —**'factorship** *n.*

factor 8 *n.* a protein that participates in the clotting of blood. It is extracted from donated serum and used in the treatment of haemophilia.

factorial (fækˈtɔːrɪəl) *Maths.* ~*n.* **1.** the product of all the positive integers from one up to and including a given integer: *factorial four is* $1 \times 2 \times 3 \times 4$. ~*adj.* **2.** of or involving factorials or factors. —**facˈtorially** *adv.*

factorize *or* **-rise** ('fæktəˌraɪz) *vb.* (*tr.*) *Maths.* to resolve (an integer or polynomial) into factors. —**ˌfactoriˈzation** *or* **-riˈsation** *n.*

factory ('fæktərɪ) *n., pl.* **-ries.** **a.** a building or group of buildings containing a plant assembly for the manufacture of goods. **b.** (*as modifier*): *a factory worker.* [C16: < LL *factorium*; see FACTOR] —**'factory-ˌlike** *adj.*

factory farm *n.* a farm in which animals are intensively reared using modern industrial methods. —**factory farming** *n.*

factory ship *n.* a vessel that processes fish supplied by a fleet.

factotum (fækˈtəʊtəm) *n.* a person employed to do all kinds of work. [C16: < Med. L, < L *fac!* do! + *tōtum,* < *tōtus* (adj.) all]

facts and figures *pl. n.* details.

facts of life *pl. n.* **the.** the details of sexual behaviour and reproduction.

factual ('fæktʃʊəl) *adj.* **1.** of, relating to, or characterized by facts. **2.** real; actual. —**'factually** *adv.* —**'factualness** *or* **ˌfactuˈality** *n.*

facula ('fækjʊlə) *n., pl.* **-lae** (-ˌliː). any of the bright areas on the sun's surface, usually appearing just before a sunspot. [C18: < L: little torch, < *fax* torch] —**'facular** *adj.*

facultative ('fækəltətɪv) *adj.* **1.** empowering but not compelling the doing of an act. **2.** that may or may not occur. **3.** *Biol.* able to exist under more than one set of environmental conditions. **4.** of or relating to a faculty. —**'facultatively** *adv.*

faculty ('fækəltɪ) *n., pl.* **-ties.** **1.** one of the inherent powers of the mind or body, such as memory, sight, or hearing. **2.** any ability or power, whether acquired or inherent. **3.** a conferred power or right. **4. a.** a department within a university or college devoted to a particular branch of knowledge. **b.** the staff of such a department. **c.** *Chiefly U.S. & Canad.* all administrative and teaching staff at a university, school, etc. **5.** all members of a learned profession. [C14 (in the sense: department of learning): < L *facultās* capability; rel. to L *facilis* easy]

FA Cup *n. Soccer.* (in England and Wales) **1.** an annual knockout competition among member teams of the Football Association. **2.** the trophy itself.

fad (fæd) *n. Inf.* **1.** an intense but short-lived fashion. **2.** a personal idiosyncrasy. [C19: <?] —**'faddish** *or* **'faddy** *adj.*

fade (feɪd) *vb.* **1.** to lose or cause to lose brightness, colour, or clarity. **2.** (*intr.*) to lose vigour or youth. **3.** (*intr.; usually foll. by* *away* or *out*) to vanish slowly. **4. a.** to decrease the brightness or volume of (a television or radio programme) or (of a television programme, etc.) to decrease in this way. **b.** to decrease the volume of (a sound) in a recording system or (of a sound) to be so reduced in volume. **5.** (*intr.*) (of the brakes of a vehicle) to lose power. **6.** to cause (a golf ball) to veer from a straight line or (of a golf ball) to veer from a straight flight. ~*n.* **7.** the act or an instance of fading. [C14: < *fade* (adj.)

dull, < OF, < Vulgar L *fatidus* (unattested), prob. blend of L *vapidus* VAPID + L *fatuus* FATUOUS] —ˈ**fadeless** *adj.* —ˈ**fadedness** *n.* —ˈ**fader** *n.*

fade-in *n.* **1.** *Films.* an optical effect in which a shot appears gradually out of darkness. ~*vb.* **fade in.** (*adv.*) **2.** to increase or cause to increase gradually, as vision or sound in a film or broadcast.

fade-out *n.* **1.** *Films.* an optical effect in which a shot slowly disappears into darkness. **2.** a gradual and temporary loss of a radio or television signal. **3.** a slow or gradual disappearance. ~*vb.* **fade out.** (*adv.*) **4.** to decrease or cause to decrease gradually, as vision or sound in a film or broadcast.

faeces *or esp. U.S.* **feces** (ˈfiːsiːz) *pl. n.* bodily waste matter discharged through the anus. [C15: < L *faecēs*, pl. of *faex* sediment, dregs] —**faecal** *or esp. U.S.* **fecal** (ˈfiːkᵊl) *adj.*

faerie *or* **faery** (ˈfeɪərɪ, ˈfɛərɪ) *n., pl.* **-ries.** *Arch. or poetic.* **1.** the land of fairies. ~*adj., n.* **2.** a variant spelling of **fairy.**

Faeroese *or* **Faroese** (ˌfɛərəʊˈiːz) *adj.* **1.** of or characteristic of the Faeroes, islands in the N Atlantic, their inhabitants, or their language. ~*n.* **2.** the language of the Faeroes, closely related to Icelandic. **3.** (*pl.* **-ese**) a native or inhabitant of the Faeroes.

faff (fæf) *vb.* (*intr.; often foll. by about*) *Brit. inf.* to dither or fuss.

fag[1] (fæg) *n.* **1.** *Inf.* a boring or wearisome task. **2.** *Brit.* (esp. formerly) a young public school boy who performs menial chores for an older boy or prefect. ~*vb.* **fagging, fagged.** **3.** (when *tr.*, often foll. by *out*) *Inf.* to become or cause to become exhausted by hard work **4.** (*usually intr.*) *Brit.* to do or cause to do menial chores in a public school. [C18: <?]

fag[2] (fæg) *n. Brit. sl.* a cigarette. [C16 (in the sense: something hanging loose, flap): <?]

fag[3] (fæg) *n. Sl., chiefly U.S. & Canad.* short for **faggot**[2].

fag end *n.* **1.** the last and worst part. **2.** *Brit. inf.* the stub of a cigarette. [C17: see FAG[2]]

faggot[1] *or esp. U.S.* **fagot** (ˈfægət) *n.* **1.** a bundle of sticks or twigs, esp. when used as fuel. **2.** a bundle of iron bars, esp. to be forged into wrought iron. **3.** a ball of chopped meat bound with herbs and bread and eaten fried. ~*vb.* (*tr.*) **4.** to collect into a bundle or bundles. **5.** *Needlework.* to do faggoting on (a garment, etc.). [C14: < OF, ? < Gk *phakelos* bundle]

faggot[2] (ˈfægət) *n. Sl., chiefly U.S. & Canad.* a male homosexual. [C20: special use of FAGGOT[1]]

faggoting *or esp. U.S.* **fagoting** (ˈfægətɪŋ) *n.* **1.** decorative needlework done by tying vertical threads together in bundles. **2.** a decorative way of joining two hems by crisscross stitches.

fah *or* **fa** (fɑː) *n. Music.* **1.** (in the fixed system of solmization) the note F. **2.** (in tonic sol-fa) the fourth degree of any major scale. [C14: see GAMUT]

Fah. *or* **Fahr.** *abbrev. for* Fahrenheit.

Fahrenheit (ˈfærənˌhaɪt) *adj.* of or measured according to the Fahrenheit scale of temperature. Symbol: F [C18: after Gabriel *Fahrenheit* (1686–1736), G physicist]

Fahrenheit scale *n.* a scale of temperatures in which 32° represents the melting point of ice and 212° represents the boiling point of pure water under standard atmospheric pressure. Cf. **Celsius scale.**

faïence (faɪˈɑːns, feɪ-) *n.* tin-glazed earthenware, usually that of French, German, Italian, or Scandinavian origin. [C18: < F, strictly: pottery < *Faenza*, N Italy, where made]

fail (feɪl) *vb.* **1.** to be unsuccessful in an attempt (at something or to do something). **2.** (*intr.*) to stop operating or working properly: *the steering failed suddenly.* **3.** to judge or be judged as being below the officially accepted standard required in (a course, examination, etc.). **4.** (*tr.*) to prove disappointing or useless to (someone). **5.** (*tr.*) to neglect or be unable (to do something). **6.** (*intr.*) to prove insufficient in quantity or extent. **7.** (*intr.*) to weaken. **8.** (*intr.*) to go bankrupt. ~*n.* **9.** a failure to attain the required standard. **10. without fail.** definitely. [C13: < OF *faillir*, ult. < L *fallere* to disappoint]

▷ **Usage.** *Fail* is often used to emphasize the fact that something did not occur: *the expected number of visitors failed to materialize; the car failed to stop at the lights.* Careful users of English, however, at least in formal contexts, restrict the use of the word to the sense of something that has been tried but did not succeed: *the England team failed to win a place in the finals; she failed in her attempt to swim to France.*

failing (ˈfeɪlɪŋ) *n.* **1.** a weak point. ~*prep.* **2.** (*used to express a condition*) in default of: *failing a solution, the problem will have to wait until Monday.*

fail-safe *adj.* **1.** designed to return to a safe condition in the event of a failure or malfunction. **2.** safe from failure; foolproof.

failure (ˈfeɪljə) *n.* **1.** the act or an instance of failing. **2.** a person or thing that is unsuccessful or disappointing. **3.** nonperformance of something required or expected: *failure to attend will be punished.* **4.** cessation of normal operation: *a power failure.* **5.** an insufficiency: *a crop failure.* **6.** a decline or loss, as in health. **7.** the fact of not reaching the required standard in an examination, test, etc. **8.** bankruptcy.

fain (feɪn) *adv.* **1.** (usually with *would*) *Arch.* gladly: *she would fain be dead.* ~*adj.* **2.** *Obs.* **a.** willing. **b.** compelled. [OE *fægen;* see FAWN[2]]

faint (feɪnt) *adj.* **1.** lacking clarity, brightness, volume, etc. **2.** lacking conviction or force: *faint praise.* **3.** feeling dizzy or weak as if about to lose consciousness. **4.** timid (esp. in **faint-hearted**). **5. not the faintest (idea** *or* **notion).** no idea whatsoever: *I haven't the faintest.* ~*vb.* (*intr.*) **6.** to lose consciousness, as through weakness. **7.** *Arch. or poetic.* to become weak, esp. in courage. ~*n.* **8.** a sudden spontaneous loss of consciousness caused by an insufficient supply of blood to the brain. [C13: < OF, < *faindre* to be idle] —ˈ**faintish** *adj.* —ˈ**faintly** *adv.* —ˈ**faintness** *n.*

fair[1] (fɛə) *adj.* **1.** free from discrimination, dishonesty, etc. **2.** in conformity with rules or standards: *a fair fight.* **3.** (of the hair or complexion) light in colour. **4.** beautiful to look at. **5.** quite good: *a fair piece of work.* **6.** unblemished; untainted. **7.** (of the tide or wind) favourable to the passage of a vessel. **8.** fine or cloudless. **9.** pleasant or courteous. **10.** apparently good or valuable: *fair words.* **11. fair and square.** in a correct or just way. ~*adv.* **12.** in a fair way: *act fair, now!* **13.** absolutely or squarely; quite. ~*vb.* **14.** (*intr.*) *Dialect.* (of the weather) to become fine. ~*n.* **15.** *Arch.* a person or thing that is beautiful or valuable. [OE *fæger*] —ˈ**fairish** *adj.* —ˈ**fairness** *n.*

fair[2] (fɛə) *n.* **1.** a travelling entertainment with sideshows, rides, etc. **2.** a gathering of producers of and dealers in a given class of products to facilitate business: *a world fair.* **3.** a regular assembly at a specific place for the sale of goods, esp. livestock. [C13: < OF *feire*, < LL *fēria* holiday, < L *fēriae* days of rest]

fair game *n.* a legitimate object for ridicule or attack.

fairground (ˈfɛəˌgraʊnd) *n.* an open space used for a fair or exhibition.

fairing[1] (ˈfɛərɪŋ) *n.* an external metal structure fitted around parts of an aircraft, car, etc., to reduce drag. [C20: < *fair* to streamline + -ING[1]]

fairing[2] (ˈfɛərɪŋ) *n. Arch.* a present, esp. from a fair.

Fair Isle *n.* an intricate multicoloured pattern knitted with Shetland wool into various garments, such as sweaters. [C19: after one of the Shetland Islands where this type of pattern originated]

fairly (ˈfɛəlɪ) *adv.* **1.** (*not used with a negative*) moderately. **2.** as deserved; justly. **3.** (*not used with a negative*) positively: *the hall fairly rang with applause.*

fair-minded *adj.* just or impartial. —ˌ**fair**ˈ**mindedness** *n.*

fair play *n.* **1.** an established standard of decency, etc. **2.** abidance by this standard.

fair sex *n.* **the.** women collectively.

fair-spoken *adj.* civil, courteous, or elegant in speech. —ˌ**fair-ˈspokenness** *n.*

fairway (ˈfɛəˌweɪ) *n.* **1.** (on a golf course) the avenue approaching a green bordered by rough. **2.** *Naut.* the navigable part of a river, harbour, etc.

fair-weather *adj.* **1.** suitable for use in fair weather only. **2.** not reliable in situations of difficulty: *fair-weather friend.*

fairy (ˈfɛərɪ) *n., pl.* **fairies. 1.** an imaginary supernatural being, usually represented in diminutive human form and characterized as having magical powers. **2.** *Sl.* a male homosexual. ~*adj.* (*prenominal*) **3.** of a fairy or fairies. **4.** resembling a fairy or fairies. [C14: < OF *faerie* fairyland, < *feie* fairy, < L *Fāta* the Fates; see FATE, FAY] —ˈ**fairy-ˌlike** *adj.*

fairy cycle *n.* a child's bicycle.

fairyfloss (ˈfɛərɪˌflɒs) *n.* the Australian word for **candyfloss.**

fairy godmother *n.* a benefactress, esp. an unknown one.

fairyland (ˈfɛərɪˌlænd) *n.* **1.** the imaginary domain of the fairies. **2.** a fantasy world, esp. one resulting from a person's wild imaginings.

fairy lights *pl. n.* small coloured electric bulbs strung together and used as decoration, esp. on a Christmas tree.

fairy penguin *n.* a small penguin with a bluish head and back, found on the Australian coast. Also called: **little** or **blue penguin.**

fairy ring *n.* a ring of dark luxuriant vegetation in grassy ground corresponding to the outer edge of an underground fungal mycelium.

fairy tale *or* **story** *n.* **1.** a story about fairies or other mythical or magical beings. **2.** a highly improbable account.

fairy-tale *adj.* **1.** of or relating to a fairy tale. **2.** resembling a fairy tale, esp. in being extremely happy or fortunate: *a fairy-tale ending.* **3.** highly improbable: *a fairy-tale account.*

fait accompli *French.* (fɛt akɔ̃pli) *n., pl.* ***faits accomplis*** (fɛz akɔ̃pli). something already done and beyond alteration. [lit.: accomplished fact]

faith (feɪθ) *n.* **1.** strong or unshakeable belief in something, esp. without proof. **2.** a specific system of religious beliefs: *the Jewish faith.* **3.** *Christianity.* trust in God and in his actions and promises. **4.** a conviction of the truth of certain doctrines of religion. **5.** complete confidence or trust in a person, remedy, etc. **6.** loyalty, as to a person or cause (esp. in **keep faith, break faith**). **7. bad faith.** dishonesty. **8. good faith.** honesty. **9.** (*modifier*) using or relating to the supposed ability to cure bodily ailments by means of religious faith: *a faith healer.* ~*interj.* **10.** *Arch.* indeed. [C12: < Anglo-F *feid,* < L *fidēs* trust, confidence]

faithful (ˈfeɪθfʊl) *adj.* **1.** remaining true or loyal. **2.** maintaining sexual loyalty to one's lover or spouse. **3.** consistently reliable: *a faithful worker.* **4.** reliable or truthful. **5.** accurate in detail: *a faithful translation.* ~*n.* **6. the faithful. a.** the believers in a religious faith, esp. Christianity. **b.** any group of loyal and steadfast followers. —ˈ**faithfully** *adv.* —ˈ**faithfulness** *n.*

faithless (ˈfeɪθlɪs) *adj.* **1.** unreliable or treacherous. **2.** dishonest or disloyal. **3.** lacking religious faith. —ˈ**faithlessness** *n.*

fake (feɪk) *vb.* **1.** (*tr.*) to cause (something inferior or not genuine) to appear more valuable or real by fraud or pretence. **2.** to pretend to have (an illness, emotion, etc.). ~*n.* **3.** an object, person, or act that is not genuine; sham. ~*adj.* **4.** not genuine. [C18: prob. ult. < It. *facciare* to make or do] —ˈ**faker** *n.* —ˈ**fakery** *n.*

fakir (ˈfeɪkɪə, fəˈkɪə) *n.* **1.** a member of any religious order of Islam. **2.** a Hindu ascetic mendicant. [C17: < Ar. *faqīr* poor]

Falange (ˈfælændʒ) *n.* the Fascist movement founded in Spain in 1933. [Sp.: PHALANX] —**Faˈlangist** *n., adj.*

falcate (ˈfælkeɪt) *or* **falciform** (ˈfælsɪˌfɔːm) *adj. Biol.* shaped like a sickle. [C19: < L *falcātus,* < *falx* sickle]

falchion (ˈfɔːltʃən, ˈfɔːlʃən) *n.* **1.** a short and slightly curved medieval sword. **2.** an archaic word for **sword.** [C14: < It., < *falce,* < L *falx* sickle]

falcon (ˈfɔːlkən, ˈfɔːkən) *n.* **1.** a diurnal bird of prey such as the gyrfalcon, peregrine falcon, etc., having pointed wings and a long tail. **2. a.** any of these or related birds, trained to hunt small game. **b.** the female of such a bird (cf. **tercel**). [C13: < OF, < LL *falcō* hawk, prob. of Gmc origin; ? rel. to L *falx* sickle]

falconet (ˈfɔːlkəˌnɛt, ˈfɔːkə-) *n.* **1.** any of various small falcons. **2.** a small light cannon used from the 15th to 17th centuries.

falconry (ˈfɔːlkənrɪ, ˈfɔːkən-) *n.* the art of keeping falcons and training them to return from flight to a lure or to hunt quarry. —ˈ**falconer** *n.*

falderal (ˈfældəˌræl) *or* **folderol** (ˈfɒldəˌrɒl) *n.* **1.** a showy but worthless trifle. **2.** foolish nonsense. **3.** a nonsensical refrain in old songs.

faldstool (ˈfɔːldˌstuːl) *n.* a backless seat, sometimes capable of being folded, used by bishops and certain other prelates. [C11 *fyldestol,* prob. a translation of Med. L *faldistolium* folding stool, of Gmc origin; cf. OHG *faldstuol*]

fall (fɔːl) *vb.* **falling, fell, fallen.** (*mainly intr.*) **1.** to descend by the force of gravity from a higher to a lower place. **2.** to drop suddenly from an erect position. **3.** to collapse to the ground, esp. in pieces. **4.** to become less or lower in number, quality, etc.: *prices fell.* **5.** to become lower in pitch. **6.** to extend downwards: *her hair fell to her waist.* **7.** to be badly wounded or killed. **8.** to slope in a downward direction. **9.** to yield to temptation or sin. **10.** to diminish in status, estimation, etc. **11.** to yield to attack: *the city fell under the assault.* **12.** to lose power: *the government fell after the riots.* **13.** to pass into or take on a specified condition: *to fall asleep.* **14.** to adopt a despondent expression: *her face fell.* **15.** to be averted: *her gaze fell.* **16.** to come by chance or presumption: *suspicion fell on the butler.* **17.** to occur; take place: *night fell.* **18.** (foll. by *back, behind,* etc.) to move in a specified direction. **19.** to occur at a specified place: *the accent falls on the last syllable.* **20.** (foll. by *to*) to be inherited (by): *the estate falls to the eldest son.* **21.** (often foll. by *into, under,* etc.) to be classified: *the subject falls into two main areas.* **22.** to issue forth: *a curse fell from her lips.* **23.** *Cricket.* (of a batsman's wicket) to be taken by the bowling side: *the sixth wicket fell for 96.* **24. fall short. a.** to prove inadequate. **b.** (often foll. by *of*) to fail to reach or measure up to (a standard). ~*n.* **25.** an act or instance of falling. **26.** something that falls: *a fall of snow.* **27.** *Chiefly U.S. & Canad.* autumn. **28.** the distance that something falls: *a hundred-foot fall.* **29.** a sudden drop from an upright position. **30.** (*often pl.*) **a.** a waterfall or cataract. **b.** (*cap. when part of a name*): *Niagara Falls.* **31.** a downward slope or decline. **32.** a decrease in value, number, etc. **33.** a decline in status or importance. **34.** a capture or overthrow: *the fall of the city.* **35.** *Machinery, naut.* the end of a tackle to which power is applied to hoist it. **36.** Also called: **pinfall.** *Wrestling.* a scoring move, pinning both shoulders of one's opponent to the floor for a specified period. **37. a.** the birth of an animal. **b.** the animals produced at a single birth. ~See also **fall about, fall away,** etc. [OE *feallan:* cf. FELL²]

Fall (fɔːl) *n.* **the.** *Theol.* Adam's sin of disobedience and the state of innate sinfulness ensuing from this for himself and all mankind.

fall about *vb.* (*intr., adv.*) to laugh in an uncontrolled manner: *we fell about at the sight.*

fallacious (fəˈleɪʃəs) *adj.* **1.** containing or involving a fallacy. **2.** tending to mislead. **3.** delusive or disappointing. —**falˈlaciously** *adv.*

fallacy (ˈfæləsɪ) *n., pl.* **-cies. 1.** an incorrect or misleading notion or opinion based on inaccurate facts or invalid reasoning. **2.** unsound reasoning. **3.** the tendency to mislead. **4.** *Logic.* an error in reasoning that renders an argument logically invalid. [C15: < L, < *fallax* deceitful, < *fallere* to deceive]

fall away *vb.* (*intr., adv.*) **1.** (of friendship, etc.) to be withdrawn. **2.** to slope down.

fall back *vb.* (*intr., adv.*) **1.** to recede or retreat. **2.** (foll. by *on* or *upon*) to have recourse (to). ~*n.* **fall-back. 3.** a retreat. **4.** a reserve, esp. money, that can be called upon in need.

fall behind *vb.* (*intr., adv.*) **1.** to drop back; fail to keep up. **2.** to be in arrears, as with a payment.

fall down *vb.* (*intr., adv.*) **1.** to drop suddenly or collapse. **2.** (often foll. by *on*) *Inf.* to fail.

fallen (ˈfɔːlən) *vb.* **1.** the past participle of **fall.** ~*adj.* **2.** having sunk in reputation or honour: *a fallen woman.* **3.** killed in battle with glory.

fallen arch *n.* collapse of the arch formed by the instep of the foot, resulting in flat feet.

fall for *vb.* (*intr., prep.*) **1.** to become infatuated with (a person). **2.** to allow oneself to be deceived by (a lie, trick, etc.).

fall guy *n. Inf.* **1.** a person who is the victim of a confidence trick. **2.** a scapegoat.

fallible (ˈfælɪbᵊl) *adj.* **1.** capable of being mistaken. **2.** liable to mislead. [C15: < Med. L *fallibilis,* < L *fallere* to deceive] —ˌ**falliˈbility** *n.*

fall in *vb.* (*intr., adv.*) **1.** to collapse. **2.** to adopt a military formation, esp. as a soldier taking his place in a line. **3.** (of a lease) to expire. **4.** (often foll. by *with*) **a.** to meet and join. **b.** to agree with or support a person, suggestion, etc.

falling sickness *or* **evil** *n.* a former name (nontechnical) for **epilepsy.**

falling star *n.* an informal name for **meteor.**

fall off *vb.* (*intr.*) **1.** to drop unintentionally to the ground from (a high object, bicycle, etc.), esp. after losing one's balance. **2.** (*adv.*) to diminish in size, intensity, etc. ~*n.* **fall-off. 3.** a decline or drop.

fall on *vb.* (*intr., prep.*) **1.** Also: **fall upon.** to attack or snatch (an army, booty, etc.). **2. fall on one's feet.** to emerge unexpectedly well from a difficult situation.

Fallopian tube (fəˈləʊpɪən) *n.* either of a pair of slender tubes through which ova pass from the ovaries to the uterus in female mammals. [C18: after Gabriello *Fallopio* (1523–62), It. anatomist who first described the tubes]

fallout (ˈfɔːlˌaʊt) *n.* **1.** the descent of radioactive material following a nuclear explosion. **2.** any particles that so descend. **3.** secondary consequences. ~*vb.* **fall out.** (*intr., adv.*) **4.** *Inf.* to disagree. **5.** (*intr.*) to occur. **6.** *Mil.* to leave a disciplinary formation.

fallow[1] (ˈfæləʊ) *adj.* **1.** (of land) left unseeded after being ploughed to regain fertility for a crop. **2.** (of an idea, etc.) undeveloped, but potentially useful. ~*n.* **3.** land treated in this way. ~*vb.* **4.** (*tr.*) to leave (land) unseeded after ploughing it. [OE *fealga*] —ˈ**fallowness** *n.*

fallow[2] (ˈfæləʊ) *n., adj.* (of) a light yellowish-brown colour. [OE *fealu*]

fallow deer *n.* either of two species of deer, one of which is native to the Mediterranean region and the other to Persia. The summer coat is reddish with white spots.

fall through *vb.* (*intr., adv.*) to fail.

fall to *vb.* (*intr.*) **1.** (*adv.*) to begin some activity, as eating, working, or fighting. **2.** (*prep.*) to devolve on (a person): *the task fell to me.*

false (fɔːls) *adj.* **1.** not in accordance with the truth or facts. **2.** irregular or invalid: *a false start.* **3.** untruthful or lying: *a false account.* **4.** artificial; fake: *false teeth.* **5.** being or intended to be misleading or deceptive: *a false rumour.* **6.** treacherous: *a false friend.* **7.** based on mistaken or irrelevant ideas or facts: *a false argument.* **8.** (*prenominal*) (esp. of plants) superficially resembling the species specified: *false hellebore.* **9.** serving to supplement or replace, often temporarily: *a false keel.* **10.** *Music.* (of a note, interval, etc.) out of tune. ~*adv.* **11.** in a false or dishonest manner (esp. in **play (someone) false**). [OE *fals*] —ˈ**falsely** *adv.* —ˈ**falseness** *n.*

false dawn *n.* light appearing just before sunrise.

falsehood (ˈfɔːlsˌhʊd) *n.* **1.** the quality of being untrue. **2.** an untrue statement; lie. **3.** the act of deceiving or lying.

false imprisonment *n. Law.* the restraint of a person's liberty without lawful authority.

false pretences *pl. n.* a misrepresentation used to obtain anything, such as trust or affection (esp. in **under false pretences**).

false ribs *pl. n.* any of the lower five pairs of ribs in man, not attached directly to the breastbone.

false step *n.* **1.** an unwise action. **2.** a stumble; slip.

falsetto (fɔːlˈsɛtəʊ) *n., pl.* **-tos.** a form of vocal production used by male singers to extend their range upwards by limiting the vibration of the vocal cords. [C18: < It., < *falso* false]

falsies (ˈfɔːlsɪz) *pl. n. Inf.* pads of soft material, such as foam rubber, worn to exaggerate the size of a woman's breasts.

falsify (ˈfɔːlsɪˌfaɪ) *vb.* **-fying, -fied.** (*tr.*) **1.** to make (a report, evidence, etc.) false or inaccurate by alteration, esp. in order to deceive. **2.** to prove false. [C15: < OF, < LL, < L *falsus* FALSE + *facere* to do, make] —ˈ**falsiˌfiable** *adj.* —**falsification** (ˌfɔːlsɪfɪˈkeɪʃən) *n.*

falsity (ˈfɔːlsɪtɪ) *n., pl.* **-ties. 1.** the state of being false or untrue. **2.** a lie or deception.

Falstaffian (fɔːlˈstɑːfɪən) *adj.* jovial, plump, and dissolute. [C19: after Sir John *Falstaff,* a character in Shakespeare's play *Henry IV*]

falter (ˈfɔːltə) *vb.* **1.** (*intr.*) to be hesitant, weak, or unsure. **2.** (*intr.*) to move unsteadily or hesitantly. **3.** to utter haltingly or hesitantly. ~*n.* **4.** hesitancy in speech or action. **5.** a quavering sound. [C14: prob. < ON] —ˈ**falterer** *n.* —ˈ**falteringly** *adv.*

fame (feɪm) *n.* **1.** the state of being widely known or recognized. **2.** *Arch.* rumour or public report. ~*vb.* **3.** (*tr.; now usually passive*) to make famous: *he was famed for his ruthlessness.* [C13: < L *fāma* report; rel. to *fārī* to say]

familial (fəˈmɪlɪəl) *adj.* **1.** of or relating to the family. **2.** occurring in the members of a family: *a familial disease.*

familiar (fəˈmɪlɪə) *adj.* **1.** well-known: *a familiar figure.* **2.** frequent or customary: *a familiar excuse.* **3.** (*postpositive;* foll. by *with*) acquainted. **4.** friendly; informal. **5.** close; intimate. **6.** more intimate than is acceptable; presumptuous. ~*n.* **7.** Also called: **familiar spirit.** a supernatural spirit supposed to attend and aid a witch, wizard, etc. **8.** a person attached to the household of the pope or a bishop, who renders service in return for support. **9.** a friend. [C14: < L *familiāris* domestic, < *familia* FAMILY] —**faˈmiliarly** *adv.* —**faˈmiliarness** *n.*

familiarity (fəˌmɪlɪˈærɪtɪ) *n., pl.* **-ties. 1.** knowledge, as of a subject or place. **2.** close acquaintanceship. **3.** undue intimacy. **4.** (*sometimes pl.*) an instance of unwarranted intimacy.

familiarize *or* **-rise** (fəˈmɪljəˌraɪz) *vb.* (*tr.*) **1.** to make (oneself or someone else) familiar, as with a particular subject. **2.** to make (something) generally known. —**faˌmiliariˈzation** *or* **-riˈsation** *n.*

famille *French.* (famij) *n.* a type of Chinese porcelain characterized either by a design on a background of yellow (***famille jaune***) or black (***famille noire***) or by a design in which the predominant colour is pink (***famille rose***) or green (***famille verte***). [C19: lit.: family]

family (ˈfæmɪlɪ, ˈfæmlɪ) *n., pl.* **-lies. 1. a.** a primary social group consisting of parents and their offspring. **b.** (*as modifier*): *a family unit.* **2.** one's wife or husband and one's children. **3.** one's children, as distinguished from one's husband or wife. **4.** a group descended from a common ancestor. **5.** all the persons living together in one household. **6.** any group of related things or beings, esp. when scientifically categorized. **7.** *Biol.* any of the taxonomic groups into which an order is divided and which contains one or more genera. **8.** a group of historically related languages assumed to derive from one original language. **9.** *Maths.* a group of curves or surfaces whose equations differ from a given equation only in the values assigned to one or more constants. **10. in the family way.** *Inf.* pregnant. [C15: < L *familia* a household, servants of the house, < *famulus* servant]

Family Allowance *n.* **1.** (in Britain) a former name for **child benefit.** **2.** (in Canada) an allowance paid by the Federal Government to the parents of dependent children.

family benefit *n. N.Z.* a child allowance paid to the mothers of children under 18 years of age. Also called: **child benefit.**

family Bible *n.* a large Bible in which births, marriages, and deaths of the members of a family are recorded.

Family Compact *n. Canad.* **1. the.** the ruling oligarchy in Upper Canada in the early 19th century. **2.** (*often not cap.*) any influential clique.

Family Credit *n.* (in Britain) a proposed system of paying benefit replacing Family Income Supplement.

Family Income Supplement *n.* (in Britain) a means-tested benefit for families whose earnings from full-time work are low. Abbrev.: **FIS.**

family man *n.* a man who is married and has children, esp. one who is devoted to his family.

family name *n.* a surname, esp. when regarded as representing the family honour.

family planning *n.* the control of the number of children in a family and of the intervals between them, esp. by the use of contraceptives.

family tree *n.* a chart showing the genealogical relationships and lines of descent of a family. Also called: **genealogical tree.**

famine (ˈfæmɪn) *n.* **1.** a severe shortage of food, as through crop failure or overpopulation. **2.** acute shortage of anything. **3.** violent hunger. [C14: < OF, via Vulgar L, < L *famēs* hunger]

famish (ˈfæmɪʃ) *vb.* (*now usually passive*) to be or make very hungry or weak. [C14: < OF, < L *famēs* FAMINE]

famous (ˈfeɪməs) *adj.* **1.** known to or recognized by many people. **2.** *Inf.* excellent; splendid. [C14: < L *fāmōsus;* see FAME] —**ˈfamously** *adv.* —**ˈfamousness** *n.*

fan[1] (fæn) *n.* **1.** any device for creating a current of air by movement of a surface or number of surfaces, esp. a rotating device consisting of a number of blades attached to a central hub. **2.** any of various hand-agitated devices for cooling oneself, esp. a collapsible semicircular series of flat segments of paper, ivory, etc. **3.** something shaped like such a fan, such as the tail of certain birds. **4.** *Agriculture.* a kind of basket formerly used for winnowing grain. ~*vb.* **fanning, fanned.** (*mainly tr.*) **5.** to cause a current of air to blow upon, as by means of a fan: *to fan one's face.* **6.** to agitate or move (air, etc.) with or as if with a fan. **7.** to make fiercer, more ardent, etc.: *fan one's passion.* **8.** (*also intr.;* often foll. by *out*) to spread out or cause to spread out in the shape of a fan. **9.** to winnow (grain) by blowing the chaff away from it. [OE *fann,* < L *vannus*] —**ˈfanlike** *adj.* —**ˈfanner** *n.*

fan[2] (fæn) *n.* **1.** an ardent admirer of a pop star, football team, etc. **2.** a devotee of a sport, hobby, etc. [C17, re-formed C19: < FAN(ATIC)]

Fanagalo (ˈfænəgələʊ) *or* **Fanakalo** *n.* (in South Africa) a Zulu-based pidgin with English and Afrikaans components. [C20: < Fanagalo *fana ga lo,* lit.: to be like this]

fanatic (fəˈnætɪk) *n.* **1.** a person whose enthusiasm or zeal for something is extreme or beyond normal limits. **2.** *Inf.* a person devoted to a particular hobby or pastime. ~*adj.* **3.** a variant of **fanatical.** [C16: < L *fānāticus* belonging to a temple, hence, inspired by a god, frenzied, < *fānum* temple]

fanatical (fəˈnætɪkᵊl) *adj.* surpassing what is normal or accepted in enthusiasm for or belief in something. —**faˈnatically** *adv.*

fanaticism (fəˈnætɪˌsɪzəm) *n.* wildly excessive or irrational devotion, dedication, or enthusiasm.

fan belt *n.* the belt that drives a cooling fan in a car engine.

fancied (ˈfænsɪd) *adj.* **1.** imaginary; unreal. **2.** thought likely to win or succeed: *a fancied runner.*

fancier (ˈfænsɪə) *n.* **1.** a person with a special interest in something. **2.** a person who breeds special varieties of plants or animals: *a pigeon fancier.*

fanciful (ˈfænsɪfʊl) *adj.* **1.** not based on fact: *fanciful notions.* **2.** made or designed in a curious, intricate, or imaginative way. **3.** indulging in or influenced by fancy. —**ˈfancifully** *adv.* —**ˈfancifulness** *n.*

fancy (ˈfænsɪ) *adj.* **-cier, -ciest. 1.** ornamented or decorative: *fancy clothes.* **2.** requiring skill to perform: *a fancy dance routine.* **3.** capricious or illusory. **4.** (often used ironically) superior in quality. **5.** higher than expected: *fancy prices.* **6.** (of a domestic animal) bred for particular qualities. ~*n., pl.* **-cies. 7.** a sudden capricious idea. **8.** a sudden or irrational liking for a person or thing. **9.** the power to conceive and represent decorative and novel imagery, esp. in poetry. **10.** an idea or thing produced by this. **11.** a mental image. **12.** *Music.* a composition for solo lute, keyboard, etc., current during the 16th and 17th centuries. **13. the fancy.** *Arch.* those who follow a particular sport, esp. prize fighting. ~*vb.* **-cying, -cied.** (*tr.*) **14.** to picture in the imagination. **15.** to imagine: *I fancy it will rain.* **16.** (*often used with a negative*) to like: *I don't fancy your chances!* **17.** (*reflexive*) to have a high or ill-founded opinion of oneself. **18.** *Inf.* to have a wish for: *she fancied some chocolate.* **19.** *Brit. inf.* to be physically attracted to (another person). **20.** to breed (animals) for particular characteristics. ~*interj.* **21.** Also: **fancy that!** an exclamation of surprise. [C15 *fantsy,* shortened < *fantasie;* see FANTASY] —**ˈfancily** *adv.* —**ˈfanciness** *n.*

fancy dress *n.* **a.** costume worn at masquerades, etc., representing an historical figure, etc. **b.** (*as modifier*): *a fancy-dress ball.*

fancy-free *adj.* having no commitments.

fancy goods *pl. n.* small decorative gifts.

fancy man *n. Sl.* **1.** a woman's lover. **2.** a pimp.

fancy woman *n. Sl.* a mistress or prostitute.

fancywork (ˈfænsɪˌwɜːk) *n.* any ornamental needlework, such as embroidery or crochet.

fan dance *n.* a dance in which large fans are manipulated in front of the body, partially revealing or suggesting nakedness.

fandangle (fænˈdæŋgᵊl) *n. Inf.* **1.** elaborate ornament. **2.** nonsense. [C19: ? < FANDANGO]

fandango (fænˈdæŋgəʊ) *n., pl.* **-gos. 1.** an old Spanish courtship dance in triple time. **2.** a piece of music composed for or in the rhythm of this dance. [C18: < Sp., <?]

fane (feɪn) *n. Arch. or poetic.* a temple or shrine. [C14: < L *fānum*]

fanfare (ˈfænfɛə) *n.* **1.** a flourish or short tune played on brass instruments. **2.** an ostentatious flourish or display. [C17: < F, back formation < *fanfarer,* < Sp, < *fanfarron* boaster, < Ar. *farfār* garrulous]

fang (fæŋ) *n.* **1.** the long pointed hollow or grooved tooth of a venomous snake through which venom is injected. **2.** any large pointed tooth, esp. the canine tooth of a carnivorous mammal. **3.** the root of a tooth. **4.** (*usually pl.*) *Brit. inf.* a tooth. [OE *fang* what is caught, prey] —**fanged** *adj.* —**ˈfangless** *adj.*

fan heater *n.* a space heater consisting of an electrically heated element with an electrically driven fan to disperse the heat.

fanjet (ˈfænˌdʒɛt) *n.* another name for **turbofan.**

fanlight (ˈfænˌlaɪt) *n.* **1.** a semicircular window over a door or window, often having sash bars like the ribs of a fan. **2.** a small rectangular window over a door. U.S name: **transom.**

fan mail *n.* mail sent to a famous person, such as a pop musician or film star, by admirers.

fanny (ˈfænɪ) *n., pl.* **-nies.** *Sl.* **1.** *Taboo, Brit.* the female pudendum. **2.** *Chiefly U.S. & Canad.* the buttocks. [C20: ? < *Fanny,* pet name < *Frances*]

fanny adams *n. Brit. sl.* **1.** (usually preceded by *sweet*) absolutely nothing at all. **2.** *Chiefly naut.* (formerly) tinned meat. [C19: < the name of a young murder victim whose body was cut up into small pieces. For sense 1: a euphemism for *fuck all*]

fantail (ˈfænˌteɪl) *n.* **1.** a breed of domestic pigeon having a large tail that can be opened like a fan. **2.** an Old World flycatcher of Australia, New Zealand, and SE Asia, having a broad fan-shaped tail. **3.** a tail shaped like an outspread fan. **4.** an auxiliary sail on the upper portion of a windmill. **5.** *U.S.* a part of the deck projecting aft of the sternpost of a ship. —ˈ**fan-ˌtailed** *adj.*

fan-tan *n.* **1.** a Chinese gambling game. **2.** a card game played in sequence, the winner being the first to use up all his cards. [C19: < Chinese (Cantonese) *fan t'an* repeated divisions, < *fan* times + *t'an* division]

fantasia (fænˈteɪzɪə) *n.* **1.** any musical composition of a free or improvisatory nature. **2.** a potpourri of popular tunes woven loosely together. [C18: < It.: fancy; see FANTASY]

fantasize *or* **-sise** (ˈfæntəˌsaɪz) *vb.* **1.** (when *tr.*, takes a clause as object) to conceive extravagant or whimsical ideas, images, etc. **2.** (*intr.*) to conceive pleasant mental images.

fantastic (fænˈtæstɪk) *adj. also* **fantastical.** **1.** strange or fanciful in appearance, conception, etc. **2.** created in the mind; illusory. **3.** unrealistic: *fantastic plans.* **4.** incredible or preposterous: *a fantastic verdict.* **5.** *Inf.* very large or extreme: *a fantastic fortune.* **6.** *Inf.* very good; excellent. **7.** of or characterized by fantasy. **8.** capricious; fitful. [C14 *fantastik* imaginary, via LL < Gk *phantastikos* capable of imagining, < *phantazein* to make visible] —**fanˌtastiˈcality** *or* **fanˈtasticalness** *n.* —**fanˈtastically** *adv.*

fantasy *or* **phantasy** (ˈfæntəsɪ) *n., pl.* **-sies.** **1. a.** imagination unrestricted by reality. **b.** (*as modifier*): *a fantasy world.* **2.** a creation of the imagination, esp. a weird or bizarre one. **3.** *Psychol.* a series of pleasing mental images, usually serving to fulfil a need not gratified in reality. **4.** a whimsical or far-fetched notion. **5.** an illusion or phantom. **6.** a highly elaborate imaginative design or creation. **7.** *Music.* another word for **fantasia.** **8.** literature, etc., having a large fantasy content. ~*vb.* **-sying, -sied.** **9.** a less common word for **fantasize.** [C14 *fantasie,* < L, < Gk *phantazein* to make visible]

fan vaulting *n. Archit.* vaulting having ribs that radiate like those of a fan and spring from the top of a capital. Also called: **palm vaulting.**

fanzine (ˈfænˌziːn) *n.* a magazine produced by amateurs for fans of a specific interest, pop group, etc. [C20: < FAN[1] + (MAGA)ZINE]

FAO *abbrev. for* Food and Agriculture Organization (of the United Nations).

far (fɑː) *adv., adj.* **farther** *or* **further, farthest** *or* **furthest.** *adv.* **1.** at, to, or from a great distance. **2.** at or to a remote time: *far in the future.* **3.** to a considerable degree: *a far better plan.* **4. as far as. a.** to the degree or extent that. **b.** to the distance or place of. **c.** *Inf.* with reference to; as for. **5. by far.** by a considerable margin. **6. far and away.** by a very great margin. **7. far and wide.** everywhere. **8. far be it from me.** on no account: *far be it from me to tell you what to do.* **9. go far. a.** to be successful: *your son will go far.* **b.** to be sufficient or last long: *the wine didn't go far.* **10. go too far.** to exceed reasonable limits. **11. so far. a.** up to the present moment. **b.** up to a certain point, extent, degree, etc. ~*adj.* (*prenominal*) **12.** remote in space or time: *in the far past.* **13.** extending a great distance. **14.** more distant: *the far end of the room.* **15. far from.** in a degree, state, etc. remote from: *he is far from happy.* [OE *feorr*] —ˈ**farness** *n.*

farad (ˈfærəd) *n. Physics.* the derived SI unit of electric capacitance; the capacitance of a capacitor between the plates of which a potential of 1 volt is created by a charge of 1 coulomb. Symbol: F [C19: see FARADAY]

faraday (ˈfærəˌdeɪ) *n.* a quantity of electricity, used in electrochemical calculations, equivalent to unit amount of substance of electrons. Symbol: *F* [C20: after Michael *Faraday,* (1791–1867), E physicist]

faradic (fəˈrædɪk) *adj.* of or concerned with an intermittent alternating current such as that induced in the secondary winding of an induction coil. [C19: < F *faradique;* see FARADAY]

farandole (ˈfærənˌdəʊl) *n.* **1.** a lively dance from Provence. **2.** a piece of music composed for or in the rhythm of this dance. [C19: < F, < Provençal *farandoulo,* <?]

faraway (ˈfɑːrəˌweɪ) *adj.* (**far away** *when postpositive*). **1.** very distant. **2.** absent-minded.

farce (fɑːs) *n.* **1.** a broadly humorous play based on the exploitation of improbable situations. **2.** the genre of comedy represented by works of this kind. **3.** a ludicrous situation or action. **4.** another name for **forcemeat.** [C14 (in the sense: stuffing): < OF, < L *farcīre* to stuff, interpolate passages (in the mass, in religious plays, etc.)]

farcical (ˈfɑːsɪkᵊl) *adj.* **1.** absurd. **2.** of or relating to farce. —ˌ**farciˈcality** *n.* —ˈ**farcically** *adv.*

fardel (ˈfɑːdᵊl) *n. Arch.* a bundle or burden. [C13: < OF *farde,* ult. < Ar. *fardah*]

fare (fɛə) *n.* **1.** the sum charged or paid for conveyance in a bus, train, etc. **2.** a paying passenger, esp. when carried by taxi. **3.** a range of food and drink. ~*vb.* (*intr.*) **4.** to get on (as specified): *he fared well.* **5.** (with *it* as a subject) to happen as specified: *it fared badly with him.* **6.** *Arch.* to eat: *we fared sumptuously.* **7.** (often foll. by *forth*) *Arch.* to travel. [OE *faran*] —ˈ**farer** *n.*

Far East *n.* **the.** the countries of E Asia, including China, Japan, North and South Korea, E Siberia, Indochina, and adjacent islands: sometimes extended to include all territories east of Afghanistan. —**Far Eastern** *adj.*

fare stage *n.* **1.** a section of a bus journey for which a set charge is made. **2.** the bus stop marking the end of such a section.

farewell (ˌfɛəˈwɛl) *sentence substitute.* **1.** goodbye; adieu. ~*n.* **2.** a parting salutation. **3.** an act of departure. **4.** (*modifier*) expressing leave-taking: *a farewell speech.*

far-fetched *adj.* unlikely.

far-flung *adj.* **1.** widely distributed. **2.** far distant; remote.

farina (fəˈriːnə) *n.* **1.** flour or meal made from any kind of cereal grain. **2.** *Chiefly Brit.* starch. [C18: < L *fār* spelt, coarse meal]

farinaceous (ˌfærɪˈneɪʃəs) *adj.* **1.** consisting or made of starch. **2.** having a mealy texture or appearance. **3.** containing starch: *farinaceous seeds.*

farm (fɑːm) *n.* **1. a.** a tract of land, usually with house and buildings, cultivated as a unit or used to rear livestock. **b.** (*as modifier*): *farm produce.* **c.** (*in combination*): *farmland.* **2.** a unit of land or water devoted to the growing or rearing of some particular type of vegetable, fruit, animal, or fish: *a fish farm.* **3.** an installation for storage or disposal: *a sewage farm.* ~*vb.* **4.** (*tr.*) **a.** to cultivate (land). **b.** to rear (stock, etc.) on a farm. **5.** (*intr.*) to engage in agricultural work, esp. as a way of life. **6.** (*tr.*) to look after a child for a fixed sum. **7.** to collect the moneys due and retain the profits from (a tax district, business, etc.) for a specified period. ~See also **farm out.** [C13: < OF *ferme* rented land, ult. < L *firmāre* to settle] —ˈ**farmable** *adj.*

farmer (ˈfɑːmə) *n.* **1.** a person who operates or manages a farm. **2.** a person who obtains the right to collect and retain a tax, rent, etc., on payment of a fee. **3.** a person who looks after a child for a fixed sum.

farm hand *n.* a person who is hired to work on a farm.

farmhouse (ˈfɑːmˌhaʊs) *n.* a house attached to a farm, esp. the dwelling from which the farm is managed.

farming (ˈfɑːmɪŋ) *n.* **a.** the business or skill of agriculture. **b.** (*as modifier*): *farming methods.*

farm out *vb.* (*tr., adv.*) **1.** to send (work) to be done by another person, firm, etc. **2.** to put (a child, etc.) into the care of a private individual. **3.** to lease to another for a fee the right to collect (taxes).

farmstead (ˈfɑːmˌstɛd) *n.* a farm or the part of a farm comprising its main buildings together with adjacent grounds.

farmyard (ˈfɑːmˌjɑːd) *n.* an area surrounded by or adjacent to farm buildings.

Far North *n.* **the.** the Arctic and sub-Arctic regions of the world.

faro (ˈfɛərəʊ) *n.* a gambling game in which players bet against the dealer on what cards he will turn up. [C18: prob. spelling var. of *Pharoah*]

far-off *adj.* (**far off** *when postpositive*). remote in space or time; distant.

farouche *French.* (faruʃ) *adj.* sullen or shy. [C18: < F, < OF, < LL *forasticus* from without, < L *foras* out of doors]

far-out *Sl.* ~*adj.* (**far out** *when postpositive*) **1.** bizarre or avant-garde. **2.** wonderful. ~*interj.* **far out. 3.** an expression of amazement or delight.

farrago (fəˈrɑːgəʊ) *n., pl.* **-gos** *or* **-goes.** a hotchpotch. [C17: < L: mash for cattle (hence, a mixture), < *fār* spelt] —**farraginous** (fəˈrædʒɪnəs) *adj.*

far-reaching *adj.* extensive in influence, effect, or range.

farrier (ˈfærɪə) *n. Chiefly Brit.* **1.** a person who shoes horses. **2.** another name for **veterinary surgeon.** [C16: < OF, < L *ferrārius* smith, < *ferrum* iron] —ˈ**farriery** *n.*

farrow (ˈfærəʊ) *n.* **1.** a litter of piglets. ~*vb.* **2.** (of a sow) to give birth to (a litter). [OE *fearh*]

far-seeing *adj.* having shrewd judgment.

Farsi (ˈfɑːsɪ) *n.* a language spoken in Iran.

far-sighted *adj.* **1.** possessing prudence and foresight. **2.** another word for **long-sighted.** —ˌ**far-**ˈ**sightedly** *adv.* —ˌ**far-**ˈ**sightedness** *n.*

fart (fɑːt) *Taboo.* ~*n.* **1.** an emission of intestinal gas from the anus. **2.** *Sl.* a contemptible person. ~*vb.* (*intr.*) **3.** to break wind. **4. fart about** *or* **around.** *Sl.* **a.** to behave foolishly. **b.** to waste time. [ME *farten*]

farther (ˈfɑːðə) *adv.* **1.** to or at a greater distance in space or time. **2.** in addition. ~*adj.* **3.** more distant or remote in space or time. **4.** additional. [C13: see FAR, FURTHER]

▷ **Usage.** In careful usage, *farther* and *farthest* are preferred when referring to literal distance: *the farthest planet. Further* and *furthest* are regarded as more correct for figurative senses: *nothing could be further from the truth.*

farthermost (ˈfɑːðəˌməʊst) *adj.* most distant or remote.

farthest (ˈfɑːðɪst) *adv.* **1.** to or at the greatest distance in space or time. ~*adj.* **2.** most distant in space or time. **3.** most extended. [C14 *ferthest,* < *ferther* FURTHER]

farthing (ˈfɑːðɪŋ) *n.* **1.** a former British bronze coin worth a quarter of an old penny: withdrawn in 1961. **2.** something of negligible value; jot. [OE *fēorthing* < *fēortha* FOURTH + -ING[1]]

farthingale (ˈfɑːðɪŋˌgeɪl) *n.* a hoop or framework worn under skirts, esp. in the Elizabethan period, to shape and spread them. [C16: < F *verdugale,* < OSp. *verdugado,* < *verdugo* rod]

fasces (ˈfæsiːz) *pl. n., sing.* **-cis** (-sɪs). **1.** (in ancient Rome) one or more bundles of rods containing an axe with its blade protruding; a symbol of a magistrate's power. **2.** (in modern Italy) such an object used as the symbol of Fascism. [C16: < L, pl. of *fascis* bundle]

fascia *or* **facia** (ˈfeɪʃɪə) *n., pl.* **-ciae** (-ʃɪˌiː). **1.** the flat surface above a shop window. **2.** *Archit.* a flat band or surface, esp. a part of an architrave. **3.** (ˈfæʃɪə). fibrous connective tissue occurring in sheets between muscles. **4.** *Biol.* a distinctive band of colour, as on an insect or plant. **5.** *Brit.* the outer panel which covers the dashboard of a motor vehicle. [C16: < L: band: rel. to *fascis* bundle] —ˈ**fascial** *or* ˈ**facial** *adj.*

fasciate (ˈfæʃɪˌeɪt) *or* **fasciated** *adj.* **1.** *Bot.* (of stems and branches) abnormally flattened due to coalescence. **2.** (of birds, insects, etc.) marked by bands of colour. [C17: prob. < NL *fasciātus* (unattested) having bands; see FASCIA]

fascicle (ˈfæsɪkᵊl) *n.* **1.** a bundle of branches, leaves, etc. **2.** Also called: **fasciculus.** *Anat.* a small bundle of fibres, esp. nerve fibres. [C15: < L *fasciculus* a small bundle, < *fascis* a bundle] —ˈ**fascicled** *adj.* —**fascicular** (fəˈsɪkjʊlə) *or* **fasciculate** (fəˈsɪkjʊˌleɪt) *adj.* —**fas**ˌ**cicu**ˈ**lation** *n.*

fascicule (ˈfæsɪˌkjuːl) *n.* one part of a printed work that is published in instalments. Also called: **fascicle, fasciculus.**

fascinate (ˈfæsɪˌneɪt) *vb.* (*mainly tr.*) **1.** to attract and delight by arousing interest: *his stories fascinated me for hours.* **2.** to render motionless, as by arousing terror or awe. **3.** *Arch.* to put under a spell. [C16: < L, < *fascinum* a bewitching] —ˌ**fasci**ˈ**nation** *n.*

fascinating (ˈfæsɪˌneɪtɪŋ) *adj.* **1.** arousing great interest. **2.** enchanting or alluring.

fascinator (ˈfæsɪˌneɪtə) *n. Rare.* a lace or crocheted head covering for women.

Fascism (ˈfæʃɪzəm) *n.* **1.** the authoritarian nationalistic political movement led by Benito Mussolini in Italy (1922–43). **2.** (*sometimes not cap.*) any ideology or movement modelled on or inspired by this. **3.** *Inf.* (*often not cap.*) any doctrine or system regarded as opposed to democracy and liberalism. [C20: < It. *fascismo,* < *fascio* political group, < L *fascis* bundle; see FASCES]

Fascist (ˈfæʃɪst) *n.* **1.** a supporter or member of a Fascist movement. **2.** (*sometimes not cap.*) any person regarded as having right-wing authoritarian views. ~*adj.* **3.** characteristic of or relating to Fascism.

fashion (ˈfæʃən) *n.* **1. a.** style in clothes, behaviour, etc., esp. the latest style. **b.** (*as modifier*): *a fashion magazine.* **2.** (*modifier*) designed to be in the current fashion. **3. a.** manner of performance: *in a striking fashion.* **b.** (*in combination*): *crab-fashion.* **4.** a way of life that revolves around the activities, dress, interests, etc., that are most fashionable. **5.** shape or form. **6.** sort; kind. **7. after** *or* **in a fashion.** in some manner, but not very well: *I mended it, after a fashion.* **8. of fashion.** of high social standing. ~*vb.* (*tr.*) **9.** to give a particular form to. **10.** to make suitable or fitting. **11.** *Obs.* to contrive. [C13 *facioun* form, manner, < OF *faceon,* < L, < *facere* to make] —ˈ**fashioner** *n.*

fashionable (ˈfæʃənəbᵊl) *adj.* **1.** conforming to fashion; in vogue. **2.** of or patronized by people of fashion: *a fashionable café.* **3.** (usually foll. by *with*) patronized (by). —ˈ**fashionableness** *n.* —ˈ**fashionably** *adv.*

fashion plate *n.* **1.** an illustration of the latest fashion in dress. **2.** a fashionably dressed person.

fast[1] (fɑːst) *adj.* **1.** acting or moving or capable of acting or moving quickly. **2.** accomplished in or lasting a short time: *a fast visit.* **3.** (*prenominal*) adapted to or facilitating rapid movement: *the fast lane of a motorway.* **4.** (of a clock, etc.) indicating a time in advance of the correct time. **5.** given to an active dissipated life. **6.** of or characteristic of such activity: *a fast life.* **7.** not easily moved; firmly fixed; secure. **8.** firmly fastened or shut. **9.** steadfast; constant (esp. in **fast friends**). **10.** *Sport.* (of a playing surface, running track, etc.) conducive to rapid speed, as of a ball used on it or of competitors racing on it. **11.** that will not fade or change colour readily. **12.** proof against fading. **13.** *Photog.* **a.** requiring a relatively short time of exposure to produce a given density: *a fast film.* **b.** permitting a short exposure time: *a fast shutter.* **14. a fast one.** *Inf.* a deceptive or unscrupulous trick (esp. in **pull a fast one**). **15. fast worker.** a person who achieves results quickly, esp. in seductions. ~*adv.* **16.** quickly; rapidly. **17.** soundly; deeply: *fast asleep.* **18.** firmly; tightly. **19.** in quick succession. **20.** in advance of the correct time: *my watch is running fast.* **21.** in a reckless or dissipated way. **22. fast by** *or* **beside.** *Arch.* close by. **23. play fast and loose.** *Inf.* to behave in an insincere or unreliable manner. [OE *fæst* strong, tight]

fast[2] (fɑːst) *vb.* **1.** (*intr.*) to abstain from eating all or certain foods or meals, esp. as a religious observance. ~*n.* **2. a.** an act or period of fasting. **b.** (*as modifier*): *a fast day.* [OE *fæstan*] —ˈ**faster** *n.*

fastback (ˈfɑːstˌbæk) *n.* a car having a back that forms one continuous slope from roof to rear.

fast-breeder reactor *n.* a nuclear reactor that uses little or no moderator and produces more fissionable material than it consumes.

fasten (ˈfɑːsᵊn) *vb.* **1.** to make or become fast or secure. **2.** to make or become attached or joined. **3.** to close or become closed by fixing firmly in place, locking, etc. **4.** (*tr.;* foll. by *in* or *up*) to enclose or imprison. **5.** (*tr.;* usually foll. by *on*) to cause (blame, a nickname, etc.) to be attached (to). **6.** (usually foll. by *on* or *upon*) to direct or be directed in a concentrated way. **7.** (*intr.;* usually foll. by *on*) to take a firm hold (of). [OE *fæstnian; see* FAST[1]] —ˈ**fastener** *n.*

fastening (ˈfɑːsᵊnɪŋ) *n.* something that fastens, such as a clasp or lock.

fast food *n.* **a.** food, esp. hamburgers, fried chicken, etc., that is prepared and served very quickly. **b.** (*as modifier*): *a fast-food restaurant.*

fast-forward *vb.* (*intr.*) to move on rapidly. [C20: < the fast-forward wind control on a tape deck]

fastidious (fæˈstɪdɪəs) *adj.* **1.** hard to please. **2.** excessively particular about details. **3.** exceedingly delicate. [C15: < L *fastīdiōsus* scornful, < *fastīdium* loathing, < *fastus* pride, + *taedium* weariness] —**fasˈtidiously** *adv.* —**fasˈtidiousness** *n.*

fastigiate (fæˈstɪdʒɪɪt) *or* **fastigiated** *adj. Biol.* (of parts or organs) united in a tapering group. [C17: < Med. L *fastīgiātus* lofty, < L *fastīgium* height]

fast lane *n.* **1.** the outside lane on a motorway for vehicles overtaking or travelling at high speed. **2.** *Inf.* the quickest but most competitive route to success.

fastness (ˈfɑːstnɪs) *n.* **1.** a stronghold; fortress. **2.** the state or quality of being firm or secure. [OE *fæstnes;* see FAST[1]]

fat (fæt) *n.* **1.** any of a class of naturally occurring soft greasy solids that are present in some plants and animals, and are used in making soap and paint and in the food industry. **2.** vegetable or animal tissue containing fat. **3.** corpulence, obesity, or plumpness. **4.** the best or richest part of something. **5. the fat is in the fire.** an irrevocable action has been taken from which dire consequences are expected. **6. the fat of the land.** the best that is obtainable. ~*adj.* **fatter, fattest. 7.** having much or too much flesh or fat. **8.** consisting of or containing fat; greasy. **9.** profitable; lucrative. **10.** affording great opportunities: *a fat part in the play.* **11.** fertile or productive: *a fat land.* **12.** thick, broad, or extended: *a fat log of wood.* **13.** *Sl.* very little or none (in **a fat chance, a fat lot of good,** etc.). ~*vb.* **fatting, fatted. 14.** to make or become fat; fatten. [OE *fǣtt,* p.p. of *fǣtan* to cram] —ˈ**fatless** *adj.* —ˈ**fatly** *adv.* —ˈ**fatness** *n.* —ˈ**fattish** *adj.*

fatal (ˈfeɪtᵊl) *adj.* **1.** resulting in death: *a fatal accident.* **2.** bringing ruin. **3.** decisively important. **4.** inevitable. [C14: < OF or L < L *fātum;* see FATE] —ˈ**fatally** *adv.*

fatalism (ˈfeɪtəˌlɪzəm) *n.* **1.** the philosophical doctrine that all events are predetermined so that man is powerless to alter his destiny. **2.** the acceptance of and submission to this doctrine. —ˈ**fatalist** *n.* —ˌ**fatalˈistic** *adj.*

fatality (fəˈtælɪtɪ) *n., pl.* **-ties. 1.** an accident or disaster resulting in death. **2.** a person killed in an accident or disaster. **3.** the power of causing death or disaster. **4.** the quality or condition of being fated. **5.** something caused by fate.

fate (feɪt) *n.* **1.** the ultimate agency that predetermines the course of events. **2.** the inevitable fortune that befalls a person or thing. **3.** the end or final result. **4.** death, destruction, or downfall. ~*vb.* **5.** (*tr.; usually passive*) to predetermine: *he was fated to lose.* [C14: < L *fātum* oracular utterance, < *fārī* to speak]

fated (ˈfeɪtɪd) *adj.* **1.** destined. **2.** doomed to death or destruction.

fateful (ˈfeɪtfʊl) *adj.* **1.** having important consequences. **2.** bringing death or disaster. **3.** controlled by or as if by fate. **4.** prophetic. —ˈ**fatefully** *adv.* —ˈ**fatefulness** *n.*

Fates (feɪts) *pl. n. Greek myth.* the three goddesses, Atropos, Clotho, and Lachesis, who control the destinies of the lives of man.

fathead (ˈfætˌhɛd) *n. Inf.* a stupid person; fool. —ˈ**fatˌheaded** *adj.*

father (ˈfɑːðə) *n.* **1.** a male parent. **2.** a person who founds a line or family; forefather. **3.** any male acting in a paternal capacity. **4.** (*often cap.*) a respectful term of address for an old man. **5.** a male who originates something: *the father of modern psychology.* **6.** a leader of an association, council, etc.: *a city father.* **7.** *Brit.* the eldest or most senior member in a union, profession, etc. **8.** (*often pl.*) a senator in ancient Rome. ~*vb.* (*tr.*) **9.** to procreate or generate (offspring). **10.** to create, found, etc. **11.** to act as a father to. **12.** to acknowledge oneself as father or originator of. **13.** (foll. by *on* or *upon*) to impose or foist upon. [OE *fæder*] —ˈ**fatherhood** *n.* —ˈ**fatherless** *adj.* —ˈ**father-ˌlike** *adj.*

Father (ˈfɑːðə) *n.* **1.** God, esp. when considered as the first person of the Christian Trinity. **2.** any of the early writers on Christian doctrine. **3.** a title used for Christian priests.

father confessor *n.* **1.** *Christianity.* a priest who hears confessions. **2.** any person to whom one tells private matters.

father-in-law *n., pl.* **fathers-in-law.** the father of one's wife or husband.

fatherland (ˈfɑːðəˌlænd) *n.* **1.** a person's native country. **2.** the country of a person's ancestors.

fatherly (ˈfɑːðəlɪ) *adj.* of, resembling, or suitable to a father, esp. in kindliness, encouragement, etc. —ˈ**fatherliness** *n.*

Father's Day *n.* the third Sunday in June, observed as a day in honour of fathers.

fathom (ˈfæðəm) *n.* **1.** a unit of length equal to six feet, used to measure depths of water. ~*vb.* (*tr.*) **2.** to measure the depth of, esp. with a sounding line. **3.** to penetrate (a mystery, problem, etc.). [OE *fæthm*] —ˈ**fathomable** *adj.*

Fathometer (fəˈðɒmɪtə) *n. Trademark.* a type of echo sounder used for measuring the depth of water.

fathomless (ˈfæðəmlɪs) *adj.* another word for **unfathomable.** —ˈ**fathomlessness** *n.*

fatigue (fəˈtiːg) *n.* **1.** physical or mental exhaustion due to exertion. **2.** a tiring activity or effort. **3.** *Physiol.* the temporary inability of an organ or part to respond to a stimulus because of overactivity. **4.** the weakening of a material subjected to alternating stresses, esp. vibrations. **5.** any of the mainly domestic duties performed by military personnel, esp. as a punishment. **6.** (*pl.*) special clothing worn by military personnel to carry out such duties. ~*vb.* **-tiguing, -tigued. 7.** to make or become weary or exhausted. [C17: < F, < *fatiguer* to tire, < L *fatīgāre*] —**fatigable** *or* **fatiguable** (ˈfætɪgəbᵊl) *adj.*

fatshedera (fætsˈhɛdərə) *n.* a hybrid plant with five-lobed leaves. [< NL, < *Fatsia japonica* + *Hedera hibernica*]

fatsia (ˈfætsɪə) *n.* an evergreen hardy shrub. Also known as the **false castor-oil plant.** [< NL]

fat-soluble *adj.* soluble in substances, such as ether, chloroform, and oils. Fat-soluble compounds are often insoluble in water.

fat stock *n.* livestock fattened and ready for market.

fatten (ˈfætᵊn) *vb.* **1.** to grow or cause to grow fat or fatter. **2.** (*tr.*) to cause (an animal or fowl) to become fat by feeding it. **3.** (*tr.*) to make fuller or richer. **4.** (*tr.*) to enrich (soil). —ˈ**fattening** *adj.*

fatty (ˈfætɪ) *adj.* **-tier, -tiest. 1.** containing or derived from fat. **2.** greasy; oily. **3.** (esp. of tissues, organs, etc.) characterized by the excessive accumulation of fat. ~*n.*, *pl.* **-ties. 4.** *Inf.* a fat person. —**'fattily** *adv.* —**'fattiness** *n.*

fatty acid *n.* any of a class of aliphatic carboxylic acids, such as palmitic acid, stearic acid, and oleic acid.

fatty degeneration *n. Pathol.* the abnormal formation of tiny globules of fat within the cytoplasm of a cell.

fatuity (fə'tjuːɪtɪ) *n.*, *pl.* **-ties. 1.** inanity. **2.** a fatuous remark, act, sentiment, etc. —**fa'tuitous** *adj.*

fatuous ('fætjʊəs) *adj.* complacently or inanely foolish. [C17: < L *fatuus*; rel. to *fatiscere* to gape] —**'fatuously** *adv.* —**'fatuousness** *n.*

fauces ('fɔːsiːz) *n.*, *pl.* **-ces.** *Anat.* the area between the cavity of the mouth and the pharynx. [C16: < L: throat] —**faucal** ('fɔːkᵊl) *or* **faucial** ('fɔːʃəl) *adj.*

faucet ('fɔːsɪt) *n.* **1.** a tap fitted to a barrel **2.** the U.S. and Canad. name for **tap**[2]. [C14: < OF < Provençal *falsar* to bore]

fault (fɔːlt) *n.* **1.** a failing or defect; flaw. **2.** a mistake or error. **3.** a misdeed. **4.** responsibility for a mistake or misdeed. **5.** *Electronics.* a defect in a circuit, component, or line, such as a short circuit. **6.** *Geol.* a fracture in the earth's crust resulting in the relative displacement of the rocks on either side of it. **7.** *Tennis, squash, etc.* an invalid serve. **8.** (in showjumping) a penalty mark given for failing to clear, or refusing, a fence, etc. **9. at fault.** guilty of error; culpable. **10. find fault (with).** to seek out minor imperfections or errors (in). **11. to a fault.** excessively. ~*vb.* **12.** *Geol.* to undergo or cause to undergo a fault. **13.** (*tr.*) to criticize or blame. **14.** (*intr.*) to commit a fault. [C13: < OF *faute* ult. < L *fallere* to fail]

fault-finding *n.* **1.** continual criticism. ~*adj.* **2.** given to finding fault. —**'fault-ˌfinder** *n.*

faultless ('fɔːltlɪs) *adj.* perfect or blameless. —**'faultlessly** *adv.* —**'faultlessness** *n.*

faulty ('fɔːltɪ) *adj.* **faultier, faultiest.** defective or imperfect. —**'faultily** *adv.* —**'faultiness** *n.*

faun (fɔːn) *n.* (in Roman legend) a rural deity represented as a man with a goat's ears, horns, tail, and hind legs. [C14: back formation < *Faunes* (pl.), < L *Faunus* deity of forests] —**'faunˌlike** *adj.*

fauna ('fɔːnə) *n.*, *pl.* **-nas** *or* **-nae** (-niː). **1.** all the animal life of a given place or time. **2.** a descriptive list of such animals. [C18: < NL, < LL *Fauna* a goddess of living things] —**'faunal** *adj.*

Fauvism ('fəʊvɪzəm) *n.* a form of expressionist painting characterized by the use of bright colours and simplified forms. [C20: < F, < *fauve* wild beast] —**Fauve** *n.*, *adj.* —**'Fauvist** *n.*, *adj.*

faux pas (fəʊ pɑː) *n.*, *pl.* **faux pas** (fəʊ pɑːz). a social blunder. [C17: < F: false step]

favour *or U.S.* **favor** ('feɪvə) *n.* **1.** an approving attitude; good will. **2.** an act performed out of good will or mercy. **3.** prejudice and partiality. **4.** a condition of being regarded with approval (esp. in **in favour, out of favour**). **5.** a token of love, goodwill, etc. **6.** a small gift or toy given to a guest at a party. **7.** *History.* a badge or ribbon worn or given to indicate loyalty. **8. find favour with.** to be approved of by someone. **9. in favour of. a.** approving. **b.** to the benefit of. **c.** (of a cheque, etc.) made out to. **d.** in order to show preference for. ~*vb.* (*tr.*) **10.** to regard with especial kindness. **11.** to treat with partiality. **12.** to support; advocate. **13.** to oblige. **14.** to help; facilitate. **15.** *Inf.* to resemble: *he favours his father.* **16.** to wear habitually: *she favours red.* **17.** to treat gingerly: *a footballer favouring an injured leg.* [C14: < L, < *favēre* to protect] —**'favourer** *or U.S.* **'favorer** *n.*

favourable *or U.S.* **favorable** ('feɪvərəbᵊl) *adj.* **1.** advantageous, encouraging or promising. **2.** giving consent. —**'favourably** *or U.S.* **'favorably** *adv.*

-favoured *adj.* (*in combination*) having an appearance (as specified): *ill-favoured.*

favourite *or U.S.* **favorite** ('feɪvərɪt) *adj.* **1.** (*prenominal*) most liked. ~*n.* **2.** a person or thing regarded with especial preference or liking. **3.** *Sport.* a competitor thought likely to win. [C16: < It., < *favorire* to favour, < L *favēre*]

favouritism *or U.S.* **favoritism** ('feɪvərɪˌtɪzəm) *n.* the practice of giving special treatment to a person or group.

fawn[1] (fɔːn) *n.* **1.** a young deer of either sex aged under one year. **2. a.** a light greyish-brown colour. **b.** (*as adj.*): *a fawn raincoat.* ~*vb.* **3.** (of deer) to bear (young). [C14: < OF, < L *fētus* offspring; see FETUS] —**'fawnˌlike** *adj.*

fawn[2] (fɔːn) *vb.* (*intr.*; often foll. by *on* or *upon*) **1.** to seek attention and admiration (from) by cringing and flattering. **2.** (of animals, esp. dogs) to try to please by a show of extreme friendliness. [OE *fægnian* to be glad, < *fægen* glad; see FAIN] —**'fawner** *n.* —**'fawning** *adj.*

fax (fæks) *n.* **1.** short for **facsimile** ~*vb.* **2.** (*tr.*) to send (a document) by a telegraphic facsimile system.

fay (feɪ) *n.* a fairy or sprite. [C14: < OF *feie*, ult. < L *fātum* FATE]

faze (feɪz) *vb.* (*tr.*) *Inf., chiefly U.S. & Canad.* to disconcert; worry; disturb. [C19: var. of arch. *feeze* to beat off]

FBA *abbrev. for* Fellow of the British Academy.

FBI (in the U.S.) *abbrev. for* Federal Bureau of Investigation; an agency responsible for investigating violations of Federal laws.

FC (in Britain) *abbrev. for:* **1.** Football Club. **2.** Free Church.

fcap *abbrev. for* foolscap.

F clef *n.* another name for **bass clef.**

FD *abbrev. for* Fidei Defensor. [L: Defender of the Faith]

Fe *the chemical symbol for* iron. [< NL *ferrum*]

fealty ('fiːəltɪ) *n.*, *pl.* **-ties.** (in feudal society) the loyalty sworn to one's lord on becoming his vassal. [C14: < OF, < L *fidēlitās* FIDELITY]

fear (fɪə) *n.* **1.** a feeling of distress, apprehension, or alarm caused by impending danger, pain, etc. **2.** a cause of this feeling. **3.** awe; reverence: *fear of God.* **4.** concern; anxiety. **5.** possibility; chance. **6. for fear of, that** *or* **lest.** to forestall or avoid. **7. no fear.** certainly not. ~*vb.* **8.** to be afraid (to do something) or of (a person or thing). **9.** (*tr.*) to revere; respect. **10.** (*tr.; takes a clause as object*) to be sorry: *I fear that you have not won.* **11.** (*intr.*; foll. by *for*) to feel anxiety about something. [OE *fǣr*] —**'fearless** *adj.* —**'fearlessly** *adv.* —**'fearlessness** *n.*

fearful ('fɪəfʊl) *adj.* **1.** afraid. **2.** causing fear. **3.** *Inf.* very unpleasant: *a fearful cold.* —**'fearfully** *adv.* —**'fearfulness** *n.*

fearsome ('fɪəsəm) *adj.* **1.** frightening. **2.** timorous; afraid. —**'fearsomely** *adv.*

feasibility study *n.* a study designed to determine the practicability of a system or plan.

feasible ('fiːzəbᵊl) *adj.* **1.** able to be done or put into effect; possible. **2.** likely; probable. [C15: < Anglo-F *faisible*, < *faire* to do, < L *facere*] —**ˌfeasi'bility** *n.* —**'feasibly** *adv.*

feast (fiːst) *n.* **1.** a large and sumptuous meal. **2.** a periodic religious celebration. **3.** something extremely pleasing: *a feast for the eyes.* **4. moveable feast.** a festival of variable date. ~*vb.* **5.** (*intr.*) **a.** to eat a feast. **b.** (usually foll. by *on*) to enjoy the eating (of): *to feast on cakes.* **6.** (*tr.*) to give a feast to. **7.** (*intr.*; foll. by *on*) to take great delight (in): *to feast on beautiful paintings.* **8.** (*tr.*) to regale or delight: *to feast one's eyes.* [C13: < OF, < L *festa*, neuter pl. (later assumed to be fem. sing.) of *festus* joyful; rel. to L *fānum* temple, *fēriae* festivals] —**'feaster** *n.*

feat (fiːt) *n.* a remarkable, skilful, or daring action. [C14: < Anglo-F *fait*, < L *factum* deed; see FACT]

feather ('fɛðə) *n.* **1.** any of the flat light waterproof structures forming the plumage of birds, each consisting of a hollow shaft having a vane of barbs on either side. **2.** something resembling a feather, such as a tuft of hair or grass. **3.** *Archery.* **a.** a bird's feather or artificial substitute fitted to an arrow to direct its flight. **b.** the feathered end of an arrow. **4.** *Rowing.* the position of an oar turned parallel to the water between strokes. **5.** condition of spirits; fettle: *in fine feather.* **6.** something of negligible value: *I don't care a feather.* **7. feather in one's cap.** a cause for pleasure at one's achievements. ~*vb.* **8.** (*tr.*) to fit, cover, or supply with feathers. **9.** *Rowing.* to turn (an oar) parallel to the water during recovery between strokes, in order to lessen wind resistance. **10.** to change the pitch of (an aircraft propeller) so that the chord lines of the blades are in line with the airflow. **11.** (*intr.*) (of a bird) to grow feathers. **12. feather one's nest.** to provide oneself with comforts. [OE *fether*] —**ˈfeathering** *n.* —**ˈfeather-ˌlike** *adj.* —**ˈfeathery** *adj.*

feather bed *n.* **1.** a mattress filled with feathers or down. ~*vb.* **featherbed, -bedding, -bedded. 2.** (*tr.*) to pamper; spoil.

featherbedding (ˈfɛðəˌbɛdɪŋ) *n.* the practice of limiting production or of overmanning in order to prevent redundancies or create jobs.

featherbrain (ˈfɛðəˌbreɪn) *or* **featherhead** *n.* a frivolous or forgetful person. —**ˈfeatherˌbrained** *or* **ˈfeatherˌheaded** *adj.*

featheredge (ˈfɛðərˌɛdʒ) *n.* a board or plank that tapers to a thin edge at one side.

featherstitch (ˈfɛðəˌstɪtʃ) *n.* **1.** a zigzag embroidery stitch. ~*vb.* **2.** to decorate (cloth) with featherstitch.

featherweight (ˈfɛðəˌweɪt) *n.* **1. a.** something very light or of little importance. **b.** (*as modifier*): *featherweight considerations.* **2. a.** a professional boxer weighing 118–126 pounds (53.5–57 kg). **b.** an amateur boxer weighing 54–57 kg (119–126 pounds). **3.** an amateur wrestler weighing usually 127–137 pounds (58–62 kg).

feature (ˈfiːtʃə) *n.* **1.** any one of the parts of the face, such as the nose, chin, or mouth. **2.** a prominent or distinctive part, as of a landscape, book, etc. **3.** the principal film in a programme at a cinema. **4.** an item or article appearing at intervals in a newspaper, magazine, etc.: *a gardening feature.* **5.** Also called: **feature story.** a prominent story in a newspaper, etc.: *a feature on prison reform.* **6.** a programme given special prominence on radio or television. **7.** *Arch.* general form. ~*vb.* **8.** (*tr.*) to have as a feature or make a feature of. **9.** to give prominence to (an actor, famous event, etc.) in a film or (of an actor, etc.) to have prominence in a film. **10.** (*tr.*) to draw the main features or parts of. [C14: < Anglo-F *feture,* < L *factūra* a making, < *facere* to make] —**ˈfeatureless** *adj.*

-featured *adj.* (*in combination*) having features as specified: *heavy-featured.*

Feb. *abbrev. for* February.

febri- *combining form.* indicating fever: *febrifuge.* [< L *febris* fever]

febrifuge (ˈfɛbrɪˌfjuːdʒ) *n.* **1.** any drug or agent for reducing fever. ~*adj.* **2.** serving to reduce fever. [C17: < Med. L *febrifugia* feverfew; see FEBRI-, -FUGE] —**febrifugal** (fɪˈbrɪfjʊgᵊl) *adj.*

febrile (ˈfiːbraɪl) *adj.* of or relating to fever; feverish. [C17: < Medical L *febrīlis,* < L *febris* fever] —**febrility** (fɪˈbrɪlɪtɪ) *n.*

February (ˈfɛbrʊərɪ) *n., pl.* **-aries.** the second month of the year, consisting of 28 or (in a leap year) 29 days. [C13: < L *Februārius mēnsis* month of expiation, < *februa* Roman festival of purification held on February 15, < pl. of *februum* a purgation]

feces (ˈfiːsiːz) *pl. n.* the usual U.S. spelling of **faeces.** —**fecal** (ˈfiːkᵊl) *adj.*

feckless (ˈfɛklɪs) *adj.* feeble; weak; ineffectual. [C16: < obs. *feck* value, effect + -LESS] —**ˈfecklessly** *adv.* —**ˈfecklessness** *n.*

feculent (ˈfɛkjʊlənt) *adj.* **1.** filthy or foul. **2.** of or containing waste matter. [C15: < L *faeculentus;* see FAECES] —**ˈfeculence** *n.*

fecund (ˈfiːkənd, ˈfɛk-) *adj.* **1.** fertile. **2.** intellectually productive. [C14: < L *fēcundus*] —**fecundity** (fɪˈkʌndɪtɪ) *n.*

fecundate (ˈfiːkənˌdeɪt, ˈfɛk-) *vb.* (*tr.*) **1.** to make fruitful. **2.** to fertilize. [C17: < L *fēcundāre* to fertilize] —**ˌfecunˈdation** *n.*

fed (fɛd) *vb.* **1.** the past tense and past participle of **feed. 2. fed to death** *or* **fed (up) to the (back) teeth.** *Inf.* bored or annoyed.

Fed. *or* **fed.** *abbrev. for:* **1.** Federal. **2.** Federation. **3.** Federated.

fedayee (fəˈdɑːjiː) *n., pl.* **-yeen** (-jiːn). **a.** (*sometimes cap.*) (in Arab states) a commando, esp. one fighting against Israel. **b.** (esp. in Iran and Afghanistan) a member of a guerrilla organization. [< Ar. *fidā'ī* one who risks his life in a cause, < *fidā'* redemption]

federal (ˈfɛdərəl) *adj.* **1.** of or relating to a form of government or a country in which power is divided between one central and several regional governments. **2.** of or relating to the central government of a federation. [C17: < L *foedus* league] —**ˈfederaˌlism** *n.* —**ˈfederalist** *n., adj.* —**ˈfederally** *adv.*

Federal (ˈfɛdərəl) *adj.* **1.** characteristic of or supporting the Union government during the American Civil War. ~*n.* **2.** a supporter of the Union government during the American Civil War.

Federal Government *n.* the national government of a federated state, such as the Canadian national government located in Ottawa.

federalize *or* **-lise** (ˈfɛdərəˌlaɪz) *vb.* (*tr.*) **1.** to unite in a federal union. **2.** to subject to federal control. —**ˌfederaliˈzation** *or* **-liˈsation** *n.*

Federal Reserve System *n.* (in the U.S.) a banking system consisting of twelve **Federal Reserve Banks** and their member banks. It performs functions similar to those of the Bank of England.

federate *vb.* (ˈfɛdəˌreɪt). **1.** to unite or cause to unite in a federal union. ~*adj.* (ˈfɛdərɪt). **2.** federal; federated. —**ˈfederative** *adj.*

federation (ˌfɛdəˈreɪʃən) *n.* **1.** the act of federating. **2.** the union of several provinces, states, etc., to form a federal union. **3.** a political unit formed in such a way. **4.** any league, alliance, or confederacy.

fedora (fɪˈdɔːrə) *n.* a soft felt brimmed hat, usually with a band. [C19: allegedly after *Fédora* (1882), play by Victorien Sardou (1831–1908)]

fed up *adj.* (*usually postpositive*) *Inf.* annoyed or bored: *I'm fed up with your conduct.*

fee (fiː) *n.* **1.** a payment asked by professional people or public servants for their services: *school fees.* **2.** a charge made for a privilege: *an entrance fee.* **3.** *Property law.* an interest in land capable of being inherited. The interest can be with unrestricted rights of disposal (**fee simple**) or with restricted rights to one class of heirs (**fee tail**). **4.** (in feudal Europe) the land granted by a lord to his vassal. **5. in fee.** *Law.* (of land) in absolute ownership. ~*vb.* **feeing, feed. 6.** *Rare.* to give a fee to. **7.** *Chiefly Scot.* to hire for a fee. [C14: < OF *fie,* of Gmc origin; see FIEF]

feeble (ˈfiːbᵊl) *adj.* **1.** lacking in physical or mental strength. **2.** unconvincing: *feeble excuses.* **3.** easily influenced. [C12: < OF *feble, fleible,* < L *flēbilis* to be lamented, < *flēre* to weep] —**ˈfeebleness** *n.* —**ˈfeebly** *adv.*

feeble-minded *adj.* **1.** lacking in intelligence. **2.** mentally defective.

feed (fiːd) *vb.* **feeding, fed.** (*mainly tr.*) **1.** to give food to: *to feed the cat.* **2.** to give as food: *to feed meat to the cat.* **3.** (*intr.*) to eat food: *the horses feed at noon.* **4.** to provide food for. **5.** to gratify; satisfy. **6.** (*also intr.*) to supply (a machine, furnace, etc.) with (the necessary materials or fuel) for its operation, or (of such materials) to flow or move forwards into a machine, etc. **7.** *Theatre, inf.* to cue (an actor, esp. a comedian) with lines. **8.** *Sport.* to pass a ball to (a teammate). **9.** (*also intr.;* foll. by *on* or *upon*) to eat or cause to eat. ~*n.* **10.** the act or an instance of feeding. **11.** food, esp. that of animals or babies. **12.** the process of supplying a machine or furnace with a material or fuel. **13.** the quantity of material or fuel so supplied. **14.** *Theatre, inf.* a performer, esp. a straight man, who provides cues. **15.** *Inf.* a meal. [OE *fēdan*] —'**feedable** *adj.*

feedback ('fiːdˌbæk) *n.* **1. a.** the return of part of the output of an electronic circuit, device, or mechanical system to its input. In **negative feedback** a rise in output energy reduces the input energy; in **positive feedback** an increase in output energy reinforces the input energy. **b.** that part of the output signal fed back into the input. **2.** the return of part of the sound output of a loudspeaker to the microphone or pick-up, so that a high-pitched whistle is produced. **3.** the whistling noise so produced. **4.** the effect of a product or action in a cyclic biological reaction on another stage in the same reaction. **5.** information in response to an inquiry, experiment, etc.

feeder ('fiːdə) *n.* **1.** a person or thing that feeds or is fed. **2.** a child's feeding bottle or bib. **3.** a person or device that feeds the working material into a system or machine. **4.** a tributary channel. **5.** a road, service, etc., that links secondary areas to the main traffic network. **6.** a power line for transmitting electrical power from a generating station to a distribution network.

feeding bottle *n.* a bottle fitted with a rubber teat from which infants suck liquids.

feel (fiːl) *vb.* **feeling, felt. 1.** to perceive (something) by touching. **2.** to have a physical or emotional sensation of (something): *to feel anger.* **3.** (*tr.*) to examine (something) by touch. **4.** (*tr.*) to find (one's way) by testing or cautious exploration. **5.** (*copula*) to seem in respect of the sensation given: *it feels warm.* **6.** to sense (esp. in **feel (it) in one's bones**). **7.** to consider; believe; think. **8.** (*intr.; foll. by for*) to show sympathy or compassion (towards): *I feel for you in your sorrow.* **9.** (*tr.; often foll. by up*) *Sl.* to pass one's hands over the sexual organs of. **10. feel like.** to have an inclination (for something or doing something): *I don't feel like going to the pictures.* **11. feel up to.** (*usually used with a negative or in a question*) to be fit enough for (something or doing something): *I don't feel up to going out.* ~*n.* **12.** the act or an instance of feeling. **13.** the quality of or an impression from something perceived through feeling: *a homely feel.* **14.** the sense of touch. **15.** an instinctive aptitude; knack: *she's got a feel for this sort of work.* [OE *fēlan*]

▷ **Usage.** The verbs *feel, look,* and *smell* can be followed by an adverb or an adjective according to the sense in which they are used. Where a quality of the subject is involved, an adjective is used: *I feel sick; he looks strong.* For other senses an adverb would be used: *she feels strongly about that; I must look closely at his record.*

feeler ('fiːlə) *n.* **1.** a person or thing that feels. **2.** an organ in certain animals, such as an antenna, that is sensitive to touch. **3.** a remark designed to probe the reactions or intentions of others.

feeler gauge *n.* a thin metal strip of known thickness used to measure a narrow gap or to set a gap between two parts.

feeling ('fiːlɪŋ) *n.* **1.** the sense of touch. **2. a.** the ability to experience physical sensations, such as heat, etc. **b.** the sensation so experienced. **3.** a state of mind. **4.** a physical or mental impression: *a feeling of warmth.* **5.** fondness; sympathy: *to have a great deal of feeling for someone.* **6.** a sentiment: *a feeling that the project is feasible.* **7.** an emotional disturbance, esp. anger or dislike: *a lot of bad feeling.* **8.** intuitive appreciation and understanding: *a feeling for words.* **9.** sensibility in the performance of something. **10.** (*pl.*) emotional or moral sensitivity (esp. in **hurt** *or* **injure the feelings of**). ~*adj.* **11.** sentient; sensitive. **12.** expressing or containing emotion. —'**feelingly** *adv.*

feet (fiːt) *n.* **1.** the plural of **foot. 2. at (someone's) feet.** as someone's disciple. **3. be run** *or* **rushed off one's feet.** to be very busy. **4. carry** *or* **sweep off one's feet.** to fill with enthusiasm. **5. feet of clay.** a weakness that is not widely known. **6. have** (*or* **keep**) **one's feet on the ground.** to be practical and reliable. **7. on one's** *or* **its feet. a.** standing up. **b.** in good health. **8. stand on one's own feet.** to be independent.

feign (feɪn) *vb.* **1.** to pretend: *to feign innocence.* **2.** (*tr.*) to invent: *to feign an excuse.* **3.** (*tr.*) to copy; imitate. [C13: < OF, < L *fingere* to form, shape, invent] —'**feigningly** *adv.*

feint[1] (feɪnt) *n.* **1.** a mock attack or movement designed to distract an adversary, as in boxing, fencing, etc. **2.** a misleading action or appearance. ~*vb.* **3.** (*intr.*) to make a feint. [C17: < F, < OF *feindre* to FEIGN]

feint[2] (feɪnt) *n. Printing.* a narrow rule used in the production of ruled paper. [C19: var. of FAINT]

feldspar ('fɛldˌspɑː, 'fɛlˌspɑː) *or* **felspar** *n.* any of a group of hard rock-forming minerals consisting of aluminium silicates of potassium, sodium, calcium, or barium: the principal constituents of igneous rocks. [C18: < G, < *Feld* field + *Spat(h)* SPAR[3]] —**feldspathic** (fɛld'spæθɪk, fɛl'spæθ-) *or* **fel'spathic** *adj.*

felicitate (fɪ'lɪsɪˌteɪt) *vb.* to congratulate. —**feˌlici'tation** *n.* —**fe'liciˌtator** *n.*

felicitous (fɪ'lɪsɪtəs) *adj.* **1.** well-chosen; apt. **2.** possessing an agreeable style. **3.** marked by happiness. —**fe'licitously** *adv.*

felicity (fɪ'lɪsɪtɪ) *n., pl.* **-ties. 1.** happiness. **2.** a cause of happiness. **3.** an appropriate expression or style. **4.** the display of such expressions or style. [C14: < L *fēlīcitās* happiness, < *fēlix* happy]

feline ('fiːlaɪn) *adj.* **1.** of, relating to, or belonging to a family of predatory mammals, including cats, lions, leopards, and cheetahs, having a round head and retractile claws. **2.** resembling or suggestive of a cat, esp. in stealth or grace. ~*n.* **3.** any member of the cat family; a cat. [C17: < L, < *fēlēs* cat] —'**felinely** *adv.* —**felinity** (fɪ'lɪnɪtɪ) *n.*

fell[1] (fɛl) *vb.* the past tense of **fall.**

fell[2] (fɛl) *vb.* (*tr.*) **1.** to cut or knock down: *to fell a tree.* **2.** *Needlework.* to fold under and sew flat (the edges of a seam). ~*n.* **3.** *U.S. & Canad.* the timber felled in one season. **4.** a seam finished by felling. [OE *fellan;* cf. FALL] —'**feller** *n.*

fell[3] (fɛl) *adj.* **1.** *Arch.* cruel or fierce. **2.** *Arch.* destructive or deadly. **3. one fell swoop.** a single hasty action or occurrence. [C13 *fel,* < OF: cruel, < Med. L *fellō* villain; see FELON[1]]

fell[4] (fɛl) *n.* an animal skin or hide. [OE]

fell[5] (fɛl) *n.* (*often pl.*) *Scot. & N English.* **a.** a mountain, hill, or moor. **b.** (*in combination*): *fell-walking.* [C13: < ON *fjall;* rel. to OHG *felis* rock]

fellah ('fɛlə) *n., pl.* **fellahs, fellahin,** *or* **fellaheen** (ˌfɛlə'hiːn). a peasant in Arab countries. [C18: < Ar., dialect var. of *fallāh,* < *falaha* to cultivate]

fellatio (fɪ'leɪʃɪəʊ) *n.* a sexual activity in which the penis is stimulated by the mouth. [C19: NL, < L *fellāre* to suck]

felloe ('fɛləʊ) *or* **felly** ('fɛlɪ) *n., pl.* **-loes** *or* **-lies.** a segment or the whole rim of a wooden wheel to which the spokes are attached. [OE *felge*]

fellow ('fɛləʊ) *n.* **1.** a man or boy. **2.** an informal word for **boyfriend. 3.** *Inf.* one or oneself: *a fellow has to eat.* **4.** a person considered to be of little worth. **5. a.** (*often pl.*) a companion; associate. **b.** (*as modifier*): *fellow travellers.* **6.** a member of the governing body at any of various universities or colleges. **7.** a postgraduate student employed, esp. for a fixed period, to undertake research. **8. a.** a person in the same group, class, or condition: *the surgeon asked his fellows.* **b.** (*as modifier*): *a fellow sufferer.* **9.** one of a pair; counterpart; mate. [OE *fēolaga*]

Fellow ('fɛləʊ) *n.* a member of any of various learned societies: *Fellow of the British Academy.*

fellow feeling *n.* **1.** mutual sympathy or friendship. **2.** an opinion held in common.

fellowship ('fɛləʊˌʃɪp) *n.* **1.** the state of sharing mutual interests, activities, etc. **2.** a society of people sharing mutual interests, activities, etc. **3.** companionship; friendship. **4.** the state or relationship of being a fellow. **5.** *Education.* **a.** a financed research post providing study facilities, privileges, etc., often in return for teaching services. **b.** an honorary title carrying certain privileges awarded to a postgraduate student.

fellow traveller *n.* **1.** a companion on a journey. **2.** a non-Communist who sympathizes with Communism.

felon[1] (ˈfɛlən) *n.* **1.** *Criminal law.* (formerly) a person who has committed a felony. ~*adj.* **2.** *Arch.* evil. [C13: < OF: villain, < Med. L *fellō*, <?]

felon[2] (ˈfɛlən) *n.* a purulent inflammation of the end joint of a finger. [C12: < Med. L *fellō*, ? < L *fel* poison]

felonious (fɪˈləʊnɪəs) *adj.* **1.** *Criminal law.* of, involving, or constituting a felony. **2.** *Obs.* wicked. —**feˈloniously** *adv.* —**feˈloniousness** *n.*

felony (ˈfɛlənɪ) *n., pl.* **-nies.** *Criminal law.* (formerly) a serious crime, such as murder or arson.

felspar (ˈfɛlˌspɑː) *n.* a variant spelling (esp. Brit.) of **feldspar.** —**felspathic** (fɛlˈspæθɪk) *adj.*

felt[1] (fɛlt) *vb.* the past tense and past participle of **feel.**

felt[2] (fɛlt) *n.* **1.** a matted fabric of wool, hair, etc., made by working the fibres together under pressure or by heat or chemical action. **2.** any material, such as asbestos, made by a similar process of matting. ~*vb.* **3.** (*tr.*) to make into or cover with felt. **4.** (*intr.*) to become matted. [OE]

felt-tip pen *n.* a pen whose writing point is made from pressed fibres. Also called: **fibre-tip pen.**

felucca (fɛˈlʌkə) *n.* a narrow lateen-rigged vessel of the Mediterranean. [C17: < It., prob. < obs. Sp. *faluca,* prob. < Ar. *fulūk* ships, < Gk, < *ephelkein* to tow]

fem. *abbrev. for:* **1.** female. **2.** feminine.

female (ˈfiːmeɪl) *adj.* **1.** of, relating to, or designating the sex producing gametes (ova) that can be fertilized by male gametes (spermatozoa). **2.** of or characteristic of a woman. **3.** for or composed of women or girls: *a female choir.* **4.** (of reproductive organs such as the ovary and carpel) capable of producing female gametes. **5.** (of flowers) lacking, or having nonfunctional, stamens. **6.** having an internal cavity into which a projecting male counterpart can be fitted: *a female thread.* ~*n.* **7.** a female animal or plant. [C14: < earlier *femelle* (infl. by *male*), < L *fēmella* a young woman, < *fēmina* a woman] —ˈ**femaleness** *n.*

female impersonator *n.* a male theatrical performer who acts as a woman.

feminine (ˈfɛmɪnɪn) *adj.* **1.** suitable to or characteristic of a woman. **2.** possessing qualities or characteristics considered typical of or appropriate to a woman. **3.** effeminate; womanish. **4.** *Grammar.* **a.** denoting or belonging to a gender of nouns that includes all kinds of referents as well as some female animate referents. **b.** (*as n.*): *German* Zeit *"time" and* Ehe *"marriage" are feminines.* [C14: < L, < *fēmina* woman] —ˈ**femininely** *adv.* —ˌ**femiˈninity** *or* ˈ**feminineness** *n.*

feminism (ˈfɛmɪˌnɪzəm) *n.* a doctrine or movement that advocates equal rights for women. —ˈ**feminist** *n., adj.*

feminize *or* **-ise** (ˈfɛmɪˌnaɪz) *vb.* **1.** to make or become feminine. **2.** to cause (a male animal) to develop female characteristics. —ˌ**feminiˈzation** *or* **-iˈsation** *n.*

femme fatale *French.* (fam fatal) *n., pl.* ***femmes fatales*** (fam fatal). an alluring or seductive woman, esp. one who causes men to love her to their own distress. [fatal woman]

femto- *prefix.* denoting 10^{-15}: *femtometer.* Symbol: f [< Danish or Norwegian *femten* fifteen]

femur (ˈfiːmə) *n., pl.* **femurs** *or* **femora** (ˈfɛmərə). **1.** the longest thickest bone of the human skeleton, with the pelvis above and the knee below. Nontechnical name: **thighbone. 2.** the corresponding bone in other vertebrates or the corresponding segment of an insect's leg. [C18: < L: thigh] —ˈ**femoral** *adj.*

fen (fɛn) *n.* low-lying flat land that is marshy or artificially drained. [OE *fenn*] —ˈ**fenny** *adj.*

fence (fɛns) *n.* **1.** a structure that serves to enclose an area such as a garden or field, usually made of posts of timber, concrete, or metal connected by wire netting, rails, or boards. **2.** *Sl.* a dealer in stolen property. **3.** an obstacle for a horse to jump in steeplechasing or showjumping. **4.** *Machinery.* a guard or guide, esp. in a circular saw or plane. **5. (sit) on the fence.** (to be) unable or unwilling to commit oneself. ~*vb.* **6.** (*tr.*) to construct a fence on or around (a piece of land, etc.). **7.** (*tr.;* foll. by *in* or *off*) to close (in) or separate (off) with or as if with a fence: *he fenced in the livestock.* **8.** (*intr.*) to fight using swords or foils. **9.** (*intr.*) to evade a question or argument. **10.** (*intr.*) *Sl.* to receive stolen property. [C14 *fens,* shortened < *defens* DEFENCE] —ˈ**fenceless** *adj.* —ˈ**fencer** *n.*

fencible (ˈfɛnsəbᵊl) *n.* (formerly) a person who undertook military service in immediate defence of his homeland only.

fencing (ˈfɛnsɪŋ) *n.* **1.** the practice, art, or sport of fighting with foils, épées, sabres, etc. **2. a.** wire, stakes, etc., used as fences. **b.** fences collectively.

fend (fɛnd) *vb.* **1.** (*intr.;* foll. by *for*) to give support (to someone, esp. oneself). **2.** (*tr.;* usually foll. by *off*) to ward off or turn aside (blows, questions, etc.). ~*n.* **3.** *Scot. & N English dialect.* a shift or effort. [C13 *fenden,* shortened < *defenden* to DEFEND]

fender (ˈfɛndə) *n.* **1.** a low metal frame which confines falling coals to the hearth. **2.** *Chiefly U.S.* a metal frame fitted to the front of locomotives to absorb shock, etc. **3.** a cushion-like device, such as a car tyre hung over the side of a vessel to reduce damage resulting from collision. **4.** the U.S. and Canad. name for the wing of a car.

fenestra (fɪˈnɛstrə) *n., pl.* **-trae** (-triː). **1.** *Biol.* a small opening, esp. either of two openings between the middle and inner ears. **2.** *Zool.* a transparent marking or spot, as on the wings of moths. [C19: via NL < L: wall opening, window]

fenestrated (fɪˈnɛstreɪtɪd, ˈfɛnɪˌstreɪtɪd) *or* **fenestrate** *adj.* **1.** *Archit.* having windows. **2.** *Biol.* perforated or having fenestrae.

fenestration (ˌfɛnɪˈstreɪʃən) *n.* **1.** the arrangement of windows in a building. **2.** an operation to restore hearing by making an artificial opening into the labyrinth of the ear.

Fenian (ˈfiːnɪən, ˈfiːnjən) *n.* **1.** (formerly) a member of an Irish revolutionary organization founded in the U.S. in the 19th century to fight for an independent Ireland. ~*adj.* **2.** of or relating to the Fenians. [C19: < Irish Gaelic *fēinne,* after *Fiann* Irish folk hero] —ˈ**Fenianism** *n.*

fennec (ˈfɛnɛk) *n.* a very small nocturnal fox inhabiting deserts of N Africa and Arabia, having enormous ears. [C18: < Ar. *fenek* fox]

fennel (ˈfɛnᵊl) *n.* a strong-smelling yellow-flowered umbelliferous plant whose seeds, feathery leaves, and bulbous aniseed-flavoured root are used in cookery. [OE *fenol*]

fenugreek (ˈfɛnjʊˌgriːk) *n.* an annual heavily scented Mediterranean leguminous plant with hairy stems and white flowers. [OE *fēnogrēcum*]

feoff (fiːf) *History.* ~*n.* **1.** a variant spelling of **fief.** ~*vb.* **2.** (*tr.*) to invest with a benefice or fief. [C13: < Anglo-F a FIEF] —ˈ**feoffee** *n.* —ˈ**feoffment** *n.* —ˈ**feoffor** *or* ˈ**feoffer** *n.*

-fer *n. combining form.* indicating a person or thing that bears something specified: *crucifer; conifer.* [< L, < *ferre* to bear]

feral (ˈfɪərəl) *adj.* **1.** (of animals and plants) existing in a wild or uncultivated state. **2.** savage; brutal. [C17: < Med. L, < L, < *ferus* savage]

fer-de-lance (ˌfɛədəˈlɑːns) *n.* a large highly venomous tropical American snake with a greyish-brown mottled coloration. [C19: < F, lit.: iron (head) of a lance]

feretory (ˈfɛrɪtərɪ, -trɪ) *n., pl.* **-ries.** *Chiefly R.C. Church.* **1.** a shrine, usually portable, for a saint's relics. **2.** the chapel in which a shrine is kept. [C14: < MF *fiertre,* < L *feretrum* a bier, < Gk, < *pherein* to bear]

feria (ˈfɪərɪə) *n., pl.* **-rias** *or* **-riae** (-rɪˌiː). *R.C. Church.* a weekday, other than Saturday, on which no feast occurs. [C19: < LL: day of the week (as in *prīma fēria* Sunday), sing. of L *fēriae* festivals] —ˈ**ferial** *adj.*

fermata (fəˈmɑːtə) *n., pl.* **-tas** *or* **-te** (-tɪ). *Music.* another word for **pause** (sense 5). [< It., < *fermare* to stop, < L *firmāre* to establish]

ferment *n.* (ˈfɜːmɛnt). **1.** any agent or substance, such as a bacterium, mould, yeast, or enzyme, that causes fermentation. **2.** another word for **fermentation. 3.** commotion; unrest. ~*vb.* (fəˈmɛnt). **4.** to undergo or cause to undergo fermentation. **5.** to stir up or seethe with excitement. [C15: < L *fermentum* yeast, < *fervēre* to seethe] —**ferˈmentable** *adj.*

fermentation (ˌfɜːmɛnˈteɪʃən) *n.* a chemical reaction in which an organic molecule splits into simpler substances, esp. the conversion of sugar to ethyl alcohol by yeast. —**ferˈmentative** *adj.*

fermentation lock *n.* a valve placed on the top of bottles of fermenting wine to allow bubbles to escape.

fermi (ˈfɜːmɪ) *n.* a unit of length used in nuclear physics equal to 10^{-15} metre. [C20: see FERMION]

fermion (ˈfɜːmɪˌɒn) *n.* any of a group of elementary particles, such as a nucleon, that has half-integral spin and obeys the Pauli exclusion principle. Cf. **boson.** [C20: after Enrico *Fermi* (1901–54), It. nuclear physicist; see -ON]

fermium (ˈfɜːmɪəm) *n.* a transuranic element artificially produced by neutron bombardment of plutonium. Symbol: Fm; atomic no.: 100; half-life of most stable isotope, ^{257}Fm: 80 days (approx.). [C20: after Enrico *Fermi*]

fern (fɜːn) *n.* **1.** a plant having roots, stems, and fronds and reproducing by spores formed in structures (sori) on the fronds. **2.** any of certain similar but unrelated plants, such as the sweet fern. [OE *fearn*] —ˈ**ferny** *adj.*

fernbird (ˈfɜːnˌbɜːd) *n.* a New Zealand swamp bird with a fern-like tail.

ferocious (fəˈrəʊʃəs) *adj.* savagely fierce or cruel: *a ferocious tiger.* [C17: < L *ferox* fierce, warlike] —**ferocity** (fəˈrɒsɪtɪ) *n.*

-ferous *adj. combining form.* bearing or producing: *coniferous.* [< -FER + -OUS]

ferrate (ˈfɛreɪt) *n.* a salt containing the divalent ion, FeO_4^{2-}. [C19: < L *ferrum* iron]

ferret (ˈfɛrɪt) *n.* **1.** a domesticated albino variety of the polecat bred for hunting rats, rabbits, etc. **2.** an assiduous searcher. ~*vb.* **3.** to hunt (rabbits, rats, etc.) with ferrets. **4.** (*tr.;* usually foll. by *out*) to drive from hiding: *to ferret out snipers.* **5.** (*tr.;* usually foll. by *out*) to find by persistent investigation. **6.** (*intr.*) to search around. [C14: < OF *furet,* < L *fur* thief] —ˈ**ferreter** *n.* —ˈ**ferrety** *adj.*

ferri- *combining form.* indicating the presence of iron, esp. in the trivalent state: *ferricyanide; ferriferous.* Cf. **ferro-.** [< L *ferrum* iron]

ferriage (ˈfɛrɪɪdʒ) *n.* **1.** transportation by ferry. **2.** the fee charged for passage on a ferry.

ferric (ˈfɛrɪk) *adj.* of or containing iron in the trivalent state: *ferric oxide.* [C18: < L *ferrum* iron]

ferric oxide *n.* a red crystalline insoluble oxide of iron that occurs as haematite and rust: used as a pigment and metal polish (**jeweller's rouge**), and as a sensitive coating on magnetic tape. Formula: Fe_2O_3.

ferrimagnetism (ˌfɛrɪˈmægnɪˌtɪzəm) *n.* a phenomenon exhibited by certain substances, such as ferrites, in which the magnetic moments of neighbouring ions are nonparallel and unequal in magnitude. —**ferrimagnetic** (ˌfɛrɪmægˈnɛtɪk) *adj.*

Ferris wheel (ˈfɛrɪs) *n.* a fairground wheel having seats freely suspended from its rim. [C19: after G.W.G. *Ferris* (1859–96), American engineer]

ferrite-rod aerial *n.* a type of aerial, normally used in radio reception, consisting of a small coil of wire mounted on a ferromagnetic ceramic core, the coil serving as a tuning inductance.

ferro- *combining form.* **1.** indicating a property of iron or the presence of iron: *ferromagnetism.* **2.** indicating the presence of iron in the divalent state: *ferrocyanide.* Cf. **ferri-.** [< L *ferrum* iron]

ferroconcrete (ˌfɛrəʊˈkɒŋkriːt) *n.* another name for **reinforced concrete.**

ferromagnetism (ˌfɛrəʊˈmægnɪˌtɪzəm) *n.* the phenomenon exhibited by substances, such as iron, that have relative permeabilities much greater than unity and increasing magnetization with applied magnetizing field. Certain of these substances retain their magnetization in the absence of the applied field. —**ferromagnetic** (ˌfɛrəʊmægˈnɛtɪk) *adj.*

ferromanganese (ˌfɛrəʊˈmæŋgəˌniːz) *n.* an alloy of iron and manganese, used in making additions of manganese to cast iron and steel.

ferrous (ˈfɛrəs) *adj.* of or containing iron in the divalent state. [C19: < FERRI- + -OUS]

ferrous sulphate *n.* an iron salt usually obtained as greenish crystals: used in inks, tanning, etc. Also called: **copperas.**

ferruginous (fɛˈruːdʒɪnəs) *adj.* **1.** (of minerals, rocks, etc.) containing iron: *a ferruginous clay.* **2.** rust-coloured. [C17: < L *ferrūgineus* of a rusty colour, < *ferrum* iron]

ferrule (ˈfɛruːl) *n.* **1.** a metal ring, tube, or cap placed over the end of a stick or post for added strength or to increase wear. **2.** a small length of tube, etc., esp. one used for making a joint. [C17: < ME *virole,* < OF, < L, < *viria* bracelet; infl. by L *ferrum* iron]

ferry (ˈfɛrɪ) *n., pl.* **-ries. 1.** Also called: **ferryboat.** a vessel for transporting passengers and usually vehicles across a body of water, esp. as a regular service. **2. a.** such a service. **b.** (*in combination*): *a ferryman.* **3.** the delivering of aircraft by flying them to their destination. ~*vb.* **-rying, -ried. 4.** to transport or go by ferry. **5.** to deliver (an aircraft) by flying it to its destination. **6.** (*tr.*) to convey (passengers, goods, etc.). [OE *ferian* to carry, bring]

fertile (ˈfɜːtaɪl) *adj.* **1.** capable of producing offspring. **2. a.** (of land) capable of sustaining an abundant growth of plants. **b.** (of farm animals) capable of breeding stock. **3.** *Biol.* capable of undergoing growth and development: *fertile seeds; fertile eggs.* **4.** producing many offspring; prolific. **5.** highly productive: *a fertile brain.* **6.** *Physics.* (of a substance) able to be transformed into fissile or fissionable material. [C15: < L *fertilis,* < *ferre* to bear] —ˈ**fertilely** *adv.* —ˈ**fertileness** *n.*

Fertile Crescent *n.* an area of fertile land in the Middle East, extending around the Rivers Tigris and Euphrates in a semicircle from Israel to the Persian Gulf.

fertility (fɜːˈtɪlɪtɪ) *n.* **1.** the ability to produce offspring. **2.** the state or quality of being fertile.

fertility drug *n.* any of a group of preparations used to stimulate ovulation in women hitherto infertile.

fertilize *or* **-lise** (ˈfɜːtɪˌlaɪz) *vb.* (*tr.*) **1.** to provide (an animal, plant, etc.) with sperm or pollen to bring about fertilization. **2.** to supply (soil or water) with nutrients to aid the growth of plants. **3.** to make fertile. —ˌ**fertiliˈzation** *or* **-liˈsation** *n.*

fertilizer *or* **-liser** (ˈfɜːtɪˌlaɪzə) *n.* **1.** any substance, such as manure, added to soil or water to increase its productivity. **2.** an object or organism that fertilizes an animal or plant.

ferula (ˈfɛrʊlə) *n., pl.* **-las** *or* **-lae** (-ˌliː). a large umbelliferous plant having thick stems and dissected leaves. [C14: < L: giant fennel]

ferule (ˈfɛruːl) *n.* **1.** a flat piece of wood, such as a ruler, used in some schools to cane children on the hand. ~*vb.* **2.** (*tr.*) to punish with a ferule. [C16: < L *ferula* giant fennel]

fervent (ˈfɜːvənt) *or* **fervid** (ˈfɜːvɪd) *adj.* **1.** intensely passionate; ardent. **2.** *Arch. or poetic.* burning or glowing. [C14: < L *fervēre* to boil, glow] —ˈ**fervency** *n.* —ˈ**fervently** *or* ˈ**fervidly** *adv.*

fervour *or U.S.* **fervor** (ˈfɜːvə) *n.* **1.** great intensity of feeling or belief. **2.** *Rare.* intense heat. [C14: < L: heat, < *fervēre* to glow, boil]

fescue (ˈfɛskjuː) *or* **fescue grass** *n.* a widely cultivated pasture and lawn grass, having stiff narrow leaves. [C14: < OF *festu*, ult. < L *festūca* stem, straw]

fesse *or* **fess** (fɛs) *n. Heraldry.* an ordinary consisting of a horizontal band across a shield. [C15: < Anglo-F, < L *fascia* band, fillet]

festal (ˈfɛstᵊl) *adj.* another word for **festive.** [C15: < L *festum* holiday] —ˈ**festally** *adv.*

fester (ˈfɛstə) *vb.* **1.** to form or cause to form pus. **2.** (*intr.*) to become rotten; decay. **3.** to become or cause to become bitter, irritated, etc., esp. over a long period of time. ~*n.* **4.** a small ulcer or sore containing pus. [C13: < OF *festre* suppurating sore, < L: FISTULA]

festival (ˈfɛstɪvᵊl) *n.* **1.** a day or period set aside for celebration or feasting, esp. one of religious significance. **2.** any occasion for celebration. **3.** an organized series of special events and performances: *a festival of drama.* **4.** *Arch.* a time of revelry. **5.** (*modifier*) relating to or characteristic of a festival. [C14: < Church L *fēstivālis* of a feast, < L *festīvus* FESTIVE]

festive (ˈfɛstɪv) *adj.* appropriate to or characteristic of a holiday, etc. [C17: < L *festīvus* joyful, < *festus* of a FEAST] —ˈ**festively** *adv.*

festivity (fɛsˈtɪvɪtɪ) *n., pl.* **-ties. 1.** merriment characteristic of a festival, etc. **2.** any festival or other celebration. **3.** (*pl.*) celebrations.

festoon (fɛˈstuːn) *n.* **1.** a decorative chain of flowers, ribbons, etc., suspended in loops. **2.** a carved or painted representation of this, as in architecture, furniture, or pottery. ~*vb.* (*tr.*) **3.** to decorate or join together with festoons. **4.** to form into festoons. [C17: < F, < It. *festone* ornament for a feast, < *festa* FEAST]

feta (ˈfɛtə) *n.* a white sheep or goat cheese popular in Greece. [Mod. Gk, < the phrase *turi pheta*, < *turi* cheese + *pheta*, < It. *fetta* a slice]

fetch[1] (fɛtʃ) *vb.* (*mainly tr.*) **1.** to go after and bring back: *to fetch help.* **2.** to cause to come; bring or draw forth. **3.** (*also intr.*) to cost or sell for (a certain price): *the table fetched six hundred pounds.* **4.** to utter (a sigh, groan, etc.). **5.** *Inf.* to deal (a blow, slap, etc.). **6.** (used esp. as a command to dogs) to retrieve (an object thrown, etc.). **7. fetch and carry.** to perform menial tasks or run errands. ~*n.* **8.** the reach, stretch, etc., of a mechanism. **9.** a trick or stratagem. [OE *feccan*] —ˈ**fetcher** *n.*

fetch[2] (fɛtʃ) *n.* the ghost or apparition of a living person. [C18: <?]

fetching (ˈfɛtʃɪŋ) *adj. Inf.* **1.** attractively befitting. **2.** charming.

fetch up *vb.* (*adv.*) **1.** (*intr.;* usually foll. by *at* or *in*) *Inf.* to arrive (at) or end up (in): *to fetch up in New York.* **2.** *Sl.* to vomit (food, etc.).

fête *or* **fete** (feɪt) *n.* **1.** a gala, bazaar, or similar entertainment, esp. one held outdoors in aid of charity. **2.** a feast day or holiday, esp. one of religious significance. ~*vb.* **3.** (*tr.*) to honour or entertain with or as if with a fête: *the author was fêted.* [C18: < F: FEAST]

fetid *or* **foetid** (ˈfɛtɪd, ˈfiː-) *adj.* having a stale nauseating smell, as of decay. [C16: < L, < *fētēre* to stink; rel. to *fūmus* smoke] —ˈ**fetidly** *or* ˈ**foetidly** *adv.* —ˈ**fetidness** *or* ˈ**foetidness** *n.*

fetish (ˈfɛtɪʃ, ˈfiːtɪʃ) *n.* **1.** something, esp. an inanimate object, that is believed to have magical powers. **2. a.** a form of behaviour involving fetishism. **b.** any object that is involved in fetishism. **3.** any object, activity, etc., to which one is excessively devoted. [C17: < F, < Port. *feitiço* (n.) sorcery, < adj.: artificial, < L *factīcius* made by art, FACTITIOUS]

fetishism (ˈfɛtɪˌʃɪzəm, ˈfiː-) *n.* **1.** a condition in which the handling of an inanimate object or a part of the body other than the sexual organs is a source of sexual satisfaction. **2.** belief in or recourse to a fetish for magical purposes. —ˈ**fetishist** *n.* —ˌ**fetishˈistic** *adj.*

fetlock (ˈfɛtˌlɒk) *n.* **1.** a projection behind and above a horse's hoof. **2.** Also called: **fetlock joint.** the joint at this part of the leg. **3.** the tuft of hair growing from this part. [C14 *fetlak*]

fetor *or* **foetor** (ˈfiːtə) *n.* an offensive stale or putrid odour. [C15: < L, < *fētēre* to stink]

fetter (ˈfɛtə) *n.* **1.** (*often pl.*) a chain or bond fastened round the ankle. **2.** (*usually pl.*) a check or restraint: *in fetters.* ~*vb.* (*tr.*) **3.** to restrict or confine. **4.** to bind in fetters. [OE *fetor*]

fettle (ˈfɛtᵊl) *vb.* (*tr.*) **1.** to line or repair (the walls of a furnace). **2.** *Brit. dialect.* **a.** to prepare or arrange (a thing, oneself, etc.). **b.** to repair or mend (something). ~*n.* **3.** state of health, spirits, etc. (esp. in **in fine fettle**). [C14 (in the sense: to put in order): back formation < *fetled* girded up, < OE *fetel* belt]

fettler (ˈfɛtlə) *n. Austral.* a person employed to maintain railway tracks.

fetus *or* **foetus** (ˈfiːtəs) *n., pl.* **-tuses.** the embryo of a mammal in the later stages of development, esp. a human embryo from the end of the second month of pregnancy until birth. [C14: < L offspring] —ˈ**fetal** *adj.*

feu (fjuː) *n.* **1.** *Scot. legal history.* **a.** a feudal tenure of land for which rent was paid in money or grain instead of by the performance of military service. **b.** the land so held. **2.** *Scots Law.* a right to the use of land in return for a fixed annual payment (**feu duty**). [C15: < OF; see FEE]

feud[1] (fjuːd) *n.* **1.** long and bitter hostility between two families, clans, or individuals. **2.** a quarrel or dispute. ~*vb.* **3.** (*intr.*) to take part in or carry on a feud. [C13 *fede*, < OF, < OHG *fēhida;* rel. to OE *fæhth* hostility; see FOE] —ˈ**feudal** *adj.* —ˈ**feudist** *n.*

feud[2] *or* **feod** (fjuːd) *n. Feudal law.* land held in return for service. [C17: < Med. L *feodum*, of Gmc origin; see FEE]

feudal (ˈfjuːdᵊl) *adj.* **1.** of or characteristic of feudalism or its institutions. **2.** of or relating to a fief. **3.** *Disparaging.* old-fashioned. [C17: < Med. L, < *feudum* FEUD[2]]

feudalism (ˈfjuːdəˌlɪzəm) *n.* the legal and social system that evolved in W Europe in the 8th and 9th centuries, in which vassals were protected and maintained by their lords, usually through the granting of fiefs, and were required to serve under them in war. Also called: **feudal system.** —ˈ**feudalist** *n.* —ˌ**feudalˈistic** *adj.*

feudality (fjuːˈdælɪtɪ) *n., pl.* **-ties. 1.** the state or quality of being feudal. **2.** a fief or fee.

feudalize *or* **-lise** (ˈfjuːdəˌlaɪz) *vb.* (*tr.*) to create feudal institutions in (a society, etc.). —ˌ**feudaliˈzation** *or* **-liˈsation** *n.*

feudatory (ˈfjuːdətərɪ) (in feudal Europe) ~*n.* **1.** a person holding a fief; vassal. ~*adj.* **2.** relating to or characteristic of the relationship between lord and vassal. [C16: < Med. L *feudātor*]

feuilleton (*French* fœjtɔ̃) *n.* **1.** the part of a European newspaper carrying reviews, serialized fiction, etc. **2.** such a review or article. [C19: < F, < *feuillet* sheet of paper, dim. of *feuille* leaf, < L *folium*]

fever (ˈfiːvə) *n.* **1.** an abnormally high body temperature, accompanied by a fast pulse rate, dry skin, etc. Related adj.: **febrile. 2.** any of various diseases, such as yellow fever or scarlet fever, characterized by a high temperature. **3.** intense nervous excitement. ~*vb.* **4.** (*tr.*) to affect with or as if with fever. [OE *fēfor*, < L *febris*] —ˈ**fevered** *adj.*

feverfew (ˈfiːvəˌfjuː) *n.* a bushy European strong-scented perennial plant with white flower heads, formerly used medicinally. [OE *feferfuge*, < LL, < L *febris* fever + *fugāre* to put to flight]

feverish (ˈfiːvərɪʃ) *or* **feverous** *adj.* **1.** suffering from fever. **2.** in a state of restless excitement. **3.** of, caused by, or causing fever. —ˈ**feverishly** *or* ˈ**feverously** *adv.*

fever pitch *n.* a state of intense excitement.

fever therapy *n.* a former method of treating disease by raising the body temperature.

few (fjuː) *determiner.* **1. a.** hardly any: *few men are so cruel.* **b.** (*as pronoun; functioning as pl.*): *many are called but few are chosen.* **2.** (preceded by a) **a.** a small number of: *a few drinks.* **b.** (*as pronoun; functioning as pl.*): *a few of you.* **3. a good few.** *Inf.* several. **4. few and far between. a.** widely spaced. **b.** scarce. **5. not** *or* **quite a few.**

Inf. several. ~*n.* **6. the few.** a small number of people considered as a class: *the few who fell at Thermopylae.* [OE *fēawa*] —**ˈfewness** *n.*

▷ **Usage.** See at **less.**

fey (feɪ) *adj.* **1.** interested in or believing in the supernatural. **2.** clairvoyant; visionary. **3.** *Chiefly Scot.* fated to die; doomed. **4.** *Chiefly Scot.* in a state of high spirits. [OE *fæge* marked out for death] —**ˈfeyness** *n.*

fez (fɛz) *n., pl.* **fezzes.** an originally Turkish brimless felt or wool cap, shaped like a truncated cone. [C19: via F < Turkish, < *Fès* city in Morocco]

ff *Music. symbol for* fortissimo.

ff. 1. *abbrev. for* folios. **2.** *symbol for* and the following (pages, lines, etc.).

fiacre (fɪˈɑːkrə) *n.* a small four-wheeled horse-drawn carriage. [C17: after the Hotel de St *Fiacre*, Paris, where these vehicles were first hired out]

fiancé *or* (*fem.*) **fiancée** (fɪˈɒnseɪ) *n.* a person who is engaged to be married. [C19: < F, < OF *fiancier* to promise, betroth, < *fiance* a vow, < *fier* to trust, < L *fidere*]

fiasco (fɪˈæskəʊ) *n., pl.* **-cos** *or* **-coes.** a complete failure, esp. one that is ignominious or humiliating. [C19: < It., lit.: FLASK; sense development obscure]

fiat (ˈfaɪət) *n.* **1.** official sanction. **2.** an arbitrary order or decree. [C17: < L, lit.: let it be done]

fib (fɪb) *n.* **1.** a trivial and harmless lie. ~*vb.* **fibbing, fibbed. 2.** (*intr.*) to tell such a lie. [C17: ? < *fibble-fable* an unlikely story; see FABLE] —**ˈfibber** *n.*

Fibonacci sequence *or* **series** (ˌfɪbəˈnɑːtʃɪ) *n.* the infinite sequence of numbers, 0, 1, 1, 2, 3, 5, 8, etc., in which each member (**Fibonacci number**) is the sum of the previous two. [after Leonardo *Fibonacci* (?1170–?1250), Florentine mathematician]

fibre *or U.S.* **fiber** (ˈfaɪbə) *n.* **1.** a natural or synthetic filament that may be spun into yarn, such as cotton or nylon. **2.** cloth or other material made from such yarn. **3.** a long fine continuous thread or filament. **4.** the texture of any material or substance. **5.** essential substance or nature. **6.** strength of character (esp. in **moral fibre**). **7.** *Bot.* **a.** a narrow elongated thick-walled cell. **b.** a very small root or twig. **8.** a fibrous substance, such as bran, as part of someone's diet: *dietary fibre.* [C14: < L *fibra* filament, entrails] —**ˈfibred** *or U.S.* **ˈfibered** *adj.*

fibreboard *or U.S.* **fiberboard** (ˈfaɪbəˌbɔːd) *n.* a building material made of compressed wood or other plant fibres.

fibreglass (ˈfaɪbəˌglɑːs) *n.* **1.** material consisting of matted fine glass fibres, used as insulation in buildings, etc. **2.** a light strong material made by bonding fibreglass with a synthetic resin; used for car bodies, etc.

fibre optics *n.* (*functioning as sing.*) the transmission of information modulated on light down very thin flexible fibres of glass. See also **optical fibres.** —**fibre optic** *adj.*

fibril (ˈfaɪbrɪl) *or* **fibrilla** (faɪˈbrɪlə) *n., pl.* **-brils** *or* **-brillae** (-ˈbrɪliː). **1.** a small fibre or part of a fibre. **2.** *Biol.* a root hair. [C17: < NL *fibrilla* a little FIBRE] —**fiˈbrillar** *or* **fiˈbrillose** *adj.*

fibrillation (ˌfaɪbrɪˈleɪʃən, ˌfɪb-) *n.* **1.** a local and uncontrollable twitching of muscle fibres. **2.** irregular twitchings of the muscular wall of the heart.

fibrin (ˈfɪbrɪn) *n.* a white insoluble elastic protein formed from fibrinogen when blood clots: forms a network that traps red cells and platelets.

fibrinogen (fɪˈbrɪnədʒən) *n.* a soluble protein in blood plasma, converted to fibrin by the action of the enzyme thrombin when blood clots.

fibro (ˈfaɪbrəʊ) *n. Austral. inf.* **a.** short for **fibrocement. b.** (*as modifier*): *a fibro shack.*

fibro- *combining form.* **1.** indicating fibrous tissue: *fibrosis.* **2.** indicating fibre: *fibrocement.* [< L *fibra* FIBRE]

fibrocement (ˌfaɪbrəʊsɪˈmɛnt) *n.* cement combined with asbestos fibre, used esp. in sheets for building.

fibroid (ˈfaɪbrɔɪd) *adj.* **1.** *Anat.* (of structures or tissues) containing or resembling fibres. ~*n.* **2.** another word for **fibroma.**

fibroin (ˈfaɪbrəʊɪn) *n.* a tough elastic protein that is the principal component of spiders' webs and raw silk.

fibroma (faɪˈbrəʊmə) *n., pl.* **-mata** (-mətə) *or* **-mas.** a benign tumour derived from fibrous connective tissue.

fibrosis (faɪˈbrəʊsɪs) *n.* the formation of an abnormal amount of fibrous tissue in an organ or part.

fibrositis (ˌfaɪbrəˈsaɪtɪs) *n.* inflammation of white fibrous tissue, esp. that of muscle sheaths.

fibrous (ˈfaɪbrəs) *adj.* consisting of or resembling fibres: *fibrous tissue.* —**ˈfibrously** *adv.*

fibula (ˈfɪbjʊlə) *n., pl.* **-lae** (-ˌliː) *or* **-las. 1.** the outer and thinner of the two bones between the knee and ankle of the human leg. Cf. **tibia. 2.** the corresponding bone in other vertebrates. **3.** a metal brooch resembling a safety pin. [C17: < L: clasp, prob. < *figere* to fasten] —**ˈfibular** *adj.*

-fic *suffix forming adjectives.* making or producing: *honorific.* [< L *-ficus,* < *facere* to do, make]

fiche (fiːʃ) *n.* See **microfiche, ultrafiche.**

fichu (ˈfiːʃuː) *n.* a woman's shawl worn esp. in the 18th century. [C19: < F: small shawl, < *ficher* to fix with a pin, < L *figere* to fasten, FIX]

fickle (ˈfɪkᵊl) *adj.* changeable in purpose, affections, etc. [OE *ficol* deceitful] —**ˈfickleness** *n.*

fictile (ˈfɪktaɪl) *adj.* **1.** moulded or capable of being moulded from clay. **2.** made of clay by a potter. [C17: < L *fictilis* that can be moulded, < *fingere* to shape]

fiction (ˈfɪkʃən) *n.* **1.** literary works invented by the imagination, such as novels or short stories. **2.** an invented story or explanation. **3.** the act of inventing a story. **4.** *Law.* something assumed to be true for the sake of convenience, though probably false. [C14: < L *fictiō* a fashioning, hence something imaginary, < *fingere* to shape] —**ˈfictional** *adj.* —**ˈfictionally** *adv.* —**ˈfictive** *adj.*

fictionalize *or* **-lise** (ˈfɪkʃənəˌlaɪz) *vb.* (*tr.*) to make into fiction. —**ˌfictionaliˈzation** *or* **-liˈsation** *n.*

fictitious (fɪkˈtɪʃəs) *adj.* **1.** not genuine or authentic: *to give a fictitious address.* **2.** of, related to, or characteristic of fiction. —**ficˈtitiously** *adv.* —**ficˈtitiousness** *n.*

fid (fɪd) *n. Naut.* **1.** a spike for separating strands of rope in splicing. **2.** a wooden or metal bar for supporting the topmast. [C17: <?]

-fid *adj. combining form.* divided into parts or lobes: *bifid.* [< L *-fidus,* < *findere* to split]

fiddle (ˈfɪdᵊl) *n.* **1.** *Inf. or disparaging.* the violin. **2.** a violin played as a folk instrument. **3.** *Naut.* a small railing around the top of a table to prevent objects from falling off it. **4.** *Brit. inf.* an illegal transaction or arrangement. **5.** *Brit. inf.* a manually delicate or tricky operation. **6. at** *or* **on the fiddle.** *Inf.* engaged in an illegal or fradulent undertaking. **7. fit as a fiddle.** *Inf.* in very good health. **8. play second fiddle.** *Inf.* to play a minor part. ~*vb.* **9.** to play (a tune) on the fiddle. **10.** (*intr.;* often foll. by *with*) to make aimless movements with the hands. **11.** (when *intr.,* often foll. by *about* or *around*) *Inf.* to waste (time). **12.** (often foll. by *with*) *Inf.* to interfere (with). **13.** *Inf.* to contrive to do (something) by illicit means or deception. **14.** (*tr.*) *Inf.* to falsify (accounts, etc.). [OE *fithele;* see VIOLA[1]]

fiddle-faddle (ˈfɪdᵊlˌfædᵊl) *n., interj.* **1.** trivial matter. ~*vb.* **2.** (*intr.*) to fuss or waste time. [C16: reduplication of FIDDLE] —**ˈfiddle-ˌfaddler** *n.*

fiddler (ˈfɪdlə) *n.* **1.** a person who plays the fiddle. **2.** See **fiddler crab. 3.** *Inf.* a petty rogue.

fiddler crab *n.* any of various burrowing crabs of American coastal regions, the males of which have one of their pincer-like claws enlarged. [C19: referring to the rapid fiddling movement of the enlarged anterior claw of the males, used to attract females]

fiddlestick ('fɪdᵊl,stɪk) *n.* **1.** *Inf.* a violin bow. **2.** any trifle. **3. fiddlesticks!** an expression of annoyance or disagreement.

fiddling ('fɪdlɪŋ) *adj.* **1.** trifling or insignificant. **2.** another word for **fiddly.**

fiddly ('fɪdlɪ) *adj.* **-dlier, -dliest.** small and awkward to do or handle.

Fidei Defensor *Latin.* ('faɪdɪ,aɪ dɪ'fɛnsɔː) *n.* defender of the faith; a title given to Henry VIII by Pope Leo X, and appearing on British coins as FID DEF (before decimalization) or FD (after decimalization).

fidelity (fɪ'dɛlɪtɪ) *n., pl.* **-ties.** **1.** devotion to duties, obligations, etc. **2.** loyalty or devotion, as to a person or cause. **3.** faithfulness to one's spouse, lover, etc. **4.** accuracy in reporting detail. **5.** *Electronics.* the degree to which an amplifier or radio accurately reproduces the characteristics of the input signal. [C15: < L, < *fidēs* faith, loyalty]

fidget ('fɪdʒɪt) *vb.* **1.** (*intr.*) to move about restlessly. **2.** (*intr.;* often foll. by *with*) to make restless or uneasy movements (with something). **3.** (*tr.*) to cause to fidget. ~*n.* **4.** (*often pl.*) a state of restlessness or unease: *he's got the fidgets.* **5.** a person who fidgets. [C17: < earlier *fidge,* prob. < ON *fikjast* to desire eagerly] —**'fidgety** *adj.*

fiducial (fɪ'djuːʃɪəl) *adj.* **1.** *Physics, etc.* used as a standard of reference or measurement: *a fiducial point.* **2.** of or based on trust or faith. [C17: < LL *fīdūciālis,* < L *fīdūcia* confidence, < *fīdere* to trust]

fiduciary (fɪ'duːʃɪərɪ) *Law.* ~*n.* **1.** a person bound to act for another's benefit, as a trustee. ~*adj.* **2. a.** having the nature of a trust. **b.** of or relating to a trust or trustee. [C17: < L *fīdūciārius* relating to something held in trust, < *fīdūcia* trust]

fiduciary issue *n.* an issue of banknotes not backed by gold.

fie (faɪ) *interj. Obs. or facetious.* an exclamation of distaste or mock dismay. [C13: < OF *fi,* < L *fī,* exclamation of disgust]

fief *or* **feoff** (fiːf) *n.* (in feudal Europe) the property or fee granted to a vassal for his maintenance by his lord in return for service. [C17: < OF *fie,* of Gmc origin; cf. OE *fēo* cattle, money, L *pecus* cattle, *pecūnia* money, Gk *pokos* fleece]

field (fiːld) *n.* **1.** an open tract of uncultivated grassland; meadow. **2.** a piece of land cleared of trees and undergrowth used for pasture or growing crops: *a field of barley.* **3.** a limited or marked off area on which any of various sports, athletic competitions, etc., are held: *a soccer field.* **4.** an area that is rich in minerals or other natural resources: *a coalfield.* **5.** short for **battlefield** or **airfield.** **6.** the mounted followers that hunt with a pack of hounds. **7. a.** all the runners in a race or competitors in a competition. **b.** the runners in a race or competitors in a competition excluding the favourite. **8.** *Cricket.* the fielders collectively, esp. with regard to their positions. **9.** a wide or open expanse: *a field of snow.* **10. a.** an area of human activity: *the field of human knowledge.* **b.** a sphere or division of knowledge, etc.: *his field is physics.* **11.** a place away from the laboratory, office, library, etc., where practical work is done. **12.** the surface or background, as of a flag, coin, or heraldic shield, on which a design is displayed. **13.** Also called: **field of view.** the area within which an object may be observed with a telescope, etc. **14.** *Physics.* See **field of force.** **15.** *Maths.* a set of entities, such as numbers, subject to two binary operations, addition and multiplication, such that the set is a commutative group under addition and the set, minus the zero, is a commutative group under multiplication. **16.** *Computers.* a set of one or more characters comprising a unit of information. **17. play the field.** *Inf.* to disperse one's interests or attentions among a number of activities, people, or objects. **18. take the field.** to begin or carry on activity, esp. in sport or military operations. **19.** (*modifier*) *Mil.* of or relating to equipment, personnel, etc., specifically trained for operations in the field: *a field gun.* ~*vb.* **20.** (*tr.*) *Sport.* to stop, catch, or return (the ball) as a fielder. **21.** (*tr.*) *Sport.* to send (a player or team) onto the field to play. **22.** (*intr.*) *Sport.* (of a player or team) to act or take turn as a fielder or fielders. **23.** (*tr.*) to enter (a person) in a competition: *each party fielded a candidate.* **24.** (*tr.*) *Inf.* to deal with or handle: *to field a question.* [OE *feld*]

field artillery *n.* artillery capable of deployment in support of front-line troops, due mainly to its mobility.

field day *n.* **1.** a day spent in some special outdoor activity, such as nature study. **2.** *Mil.* a day devoted to manoeuvres or exercises, esp. before an audience. **3.** *Inf.* a day or time of exciting activity: *the children had a field day with their new toys.*

field effect transistor *n.* a unipolar transistor in which the transverse application of an electric field produces amplification.

fielder ('fiːldə) *n. Cricket, etc.* **a.** a player in the field. **b.** a member of the fielding side.

field event *n.* a competition, such as the discus, etc., that takes place on a field or similar area as opposed to those on the running track.

fieldfare ('fiːld,fɛə) *n.* a large Old World thrush having a pale grey head, brown wings and back, and a blackish tail. [OE *feldefare;* see FIELD, FARE]

field glasses *pl. n.* another name for **binoculars.**

field hockey *n. U.S. & Canad.* hockey played on a field, as distinguished from ice hockey.

field hospital *n.* a temporary hospital set up near a battlefield for emergency treatment.

field magnet *n.* a permanent magnet or an electromagnet that produces the magnetic field in a generator, electric motor, or similar device.

field marshal *n.* an officer holding the highest rank in certain armies.

fieldmouse ('fiːld,maʊs) *n., pl.* **-mice.** a nocturnal mouse inhabiting woods, fields, and gardens of the Old World that has yellowish-brown fur.

field officer *n.* an officer holding the rank of major, lieutenant colonel, or colonel.

field of force *n.* the region of space surrounding a body, such as a charged particle or a magnet, within which it can exert a force on another similar body not in contact with it.

fieldsman ('fiːldzmən) *n., pl.* **-men.** *Cricket.* another name for **fielder.**

field sports *pl. n.* sports carried on in the countryside, such as hunting or fishing.

field tile *n. N.Z.* an earthenware drain used in farm drainage.

field trial *n.* (*often pl.*) a test to display performance, efficiency, or durability, as of a vehicle or invention.

field trip *n.* an expedition, as by a group of students, to study something at first hand.

field winding ('waɪndɪŋ) *n.* the current-carrying coils on a field magnet that produce the magnetic field intensity required to set up the electrical excitation in a generator or motor.

fieldwork ('fiːld,wɜːk) *n. Mil.* a temporary structure used in fortifying a place or position.

field work *n.* an investigation or search for material, data, etc., made in the field as opposed to the classroom or laboratory. —**field worker** *n.*

fiend (fiːnd) *n.* **1.** an evil spirit. **2.** a cruel, brutal, or spiteful person. **3.** *Inf.* **a.** a person who is intensely interested in or fond of something: *a fresh-air fiend.* **b.** an addict: *a drug fiend.* [OE *fēond*]

Fiend (fiːnd) *n.* **the.** the devil; Satan.

fiendish ('fiːndɪʃ) *adj.* **1.** of or like a fiend. **2.** diabolically wicked or cruel. **3.** *Inf.* extremely difficult or unpleasant: *a fiendish problem.*

fierce (fɪəs) *adj.* **1.** having a violent and unrestrained nature: *a fierce dog.* **2.** wild or turbulent in force, action, or intensity: *a fierce storm.* **3.** intense or strong: *fierce competition.* **4.** *Inf.* very unpleasant. [C13: < OF *fiers,* < L *ferus*] —**'fiercely** *adv.* —**'fierceness** *n.*

fiery (ˈfaɪərɪ) *adj.* **fierier, fieriest.** 1. of, containing, or composed of fire. 2. resembling fire in heat, colour, ardour, etc.: *a fiery speaker.* 3. easily angered or aroused: *a fiery temper.* 4. (of food) producing a burning sensation: *a fiery curry.* 5. (of the skin or a sore) inflamed. 6. flammable. —ˈ**fierily** *adv.* —ˈ**fieriness** *n.*

fiesta (fɪˈɛstə) *n.* (esp. in Spain and Latin America) 1. a religious festival or celebration. 2. a holiday or carnival. [Sp., < L *festa;* see FEAST]

FIFA (ˈfiːfə) *n. acronym for* Fédération Internationale de Football Association. [< F]

fife (faɪf) *n.* 1. a small high-pitched flute similar to the piccolo, used esp. in military bands. ~*vb.* 2. to play (music) on a fife. [C16: < OHG *pfīfa;* see PIPE[1]] —ˈ**fifer** *n.*

fifteen (ˈfɪfˈtiːn) *n.* 1. the cardinal number that is the sum of ten and five. 2. a numeral, 15, XV, etc., representing this number. 3. something represented by, representing, or consisting of 15 units. 4. a rugby football team. ~*determiner.* 5. a. amounting to fifteen: *fifteen jokes.* b. (*as pronoun*): *fifteen of us danced.* [OE *fiftēne*] —ˈ**fifˈteenth** *adj., n.*

fifth (fɪfθ) *adj.* (*usually prenominal*) 1. a. coming after the fourth in order, position, etc. Often written 5th. b. (*as n.*): *he came on the fifth.* ~*n.* 2. a. one of five equal parts of an object, quantity, etc. b. (*as modifier*): *a fifth part.* 3. the fraction equal to one divided by five (1/5). 4. *Music.* a. the interval between one note and another five notes away from it in a diatonic scale. b. one of two notes constituting such an interval in relation to the other. ~*adv.* 5. Also: **fifthly.** after the fourth person, position, event, etc. ~*sentence connector.* 6. Also: **fifthly.** as the fifth point. [OE *fifta*]

fifth column *n.* 1. (originally) a group of Falangist sympathizers in Madrid during the Spanish Civil War who were prepared to join the insurgents marching on the city. 2. any group of hostile infiltrators. —**fifth columnist** *n.*

fifth wheel *n.* 1. a spare wheel for a four-wheeled vehicle. 2. a superfluous or unnecessary person or thing.

fifty (ˈfɪftɪ) *n., pl.* **-ties.** 1. the cardinal number that is the product of ten and five. 2. a numeral, 50, L, etc., representing this number. 3. something represented by, representing, or consisting of 50 units. ~*determiner.* 4. a. amounting to fifty: *fifty people.* b. (*as pronoun*): *fifty should be sufficient.* [OE *fiftig*] —ˈ**fiftieth** *adj., n.*

fifty-fifty *adj., adv. Inf.* in equal parts.

fig (fɪg) *n.* 1. a tree or shrub that produces a closed pear-shaped receptacle which becomes fleshy and edible when mature. 2. the receptacle of any of these trees, having sweet flesh containing numerous seedlike fruits. 3. (*used with a negative*) something of negligible value: *I don't care a fig for your opinion.* [C13: < OF, < *figa,* < L *fīcus* fig tree]

fig. *abbrev. for:* 1. figurative(ly). 2. figure.

fight (faɪt) *vb.* **fighting, fought.** 1. to oppose or struggle against (an enemy) in battle. 2. to oppose or struggle against (a person, cause, etc.) in any manner. 3. (*tr.*) to engage in or carry on (a battle, contest, etc.). 4. (when *intr.,* often foll. by *for*) to uphold or maintain (a cause, etc.) by fighting or struggling: *to fight for freedom.* 5. (*tr.*) to make or achieve (a way) by fighting. 6. to engage (another or others) in combat. 7. **fight it out.** to contend until a decisive result is obtained. 8. **fight shy.** to keep aloof from. ~*n.* 9. a battle, struggle, or physical combat. 10. a quarrel, dispute, or contest. 11. resistance (esp. in **to put up a fight**). 12. a boxing match. ~See also **fight off.** [OE *feohtan*]

fighter (ˈfaɪtə) *n.* 1. a person who fights, esp. a professional boxer. 2. a person who has determination. 3. *Mil.* an armed aircraft designed for destroying other aircraft.

fighter-bomber *n.* an aircraft that combines the roles of fighter and bomber.

fighting chance *n.* a slight chance of success dependent on a struggle.

fighting cock *n.* 1. a gamecock. 2. a pugnacious person.

fighting fish *n.* any of various tropical fishes of the genus *Betta,* esp. the Siamese fighting fish.

fight off *vb.* (*tr., adv.*) 1. to repulse; repel. 2. to struggle to avoid or repress: *to fight off a cold.*

fight-or-flight *n.* (*modifier*) involving or relating to an involuntary response to stress in which the hormone adrenaline is secreted into the blood in readiness for physical action, such as fighting or running away.

fig leaf *n.* 1. a leaf from a fig tree. 2. a representation of a fig leaf used in sculpture, etc. to cover the genitals of nude figures. 3. a device to conceal something regarded as shameful.

figment (ˈfɪgmənt) *n.* a fantastic notion or fabrication: *a figment of the imagination.* [C15: < LL *figmentum* a fiction, < L *fingere* to shape]

figurant (ˈfɪgjʊrənt) *n.* a ballet dancer who does group work but no solo roles. [C18: < F, < *figurer* to represent, appear, FIGURE] —**figurante** (ˌfɪgjʊˈrɒnt) *fem. n.*

figuration (ˌfɪgəˈreɪʃən) *n.* 1. *Music.* a. the employment of characteristic patterns of notes, esp. in variations on a theme. b. florid ornamentation. 2. an instance of representing figuratively, as by means of allegory. 3. a figurative representation. 4. the act of decorating with a design.

figurative (ˈfɪgərətɪv) *adj.* 1. involving a figure of speech; not literal; metaphorical. 2. using or filled with figures of speech. 3. representing by means of an emblem, likeness, etc. —ˈ**figuratively** *adv.* —ˈ**figurativeness** *n.*

figure (ˈfɪgə) *n.* 1. any written symbol other than a letter, esp. a whole number. 2. another name for **digit** (sense 2). 3. an amount expressed numerically: *a figure of £1800 was suggested.* 4. (*pl.*) calculations with numbers: *he's good at figures.* 5. visible shape or form; outline. 6. the human form: *a girl with a slender figure.* 7. a slim bodily shape (esp. in **keep** *or* **lose one's figure**). 8. a character or personage: *a figure in politics.* 9. the impression created by a person through behaviour (esp. in **to cut a fine, bold,** etc., **figure**). 10. a. a person as impressed on the mind. b. (*in combination*): *father-figure.* 11. a representation in painting or sculpture, esp. of the human form. 12. an illustration or diagram in a text. 13. a representative object or symbol. 14. a pattern or design, as in wood. 15. a predetermined set of movements in dancing or skating. 16. *Geom.* any combination of points, lines, curves, or planes. 17. *Logic.* one of four possible arrangements of the terms in the major and minor premises of a syllogism that give the same conclusion. 18. *Music.* a. a numeral written above or below a note in a part. b. a characteristic short pattern of notes. ~*vb.* 19. (when *tr.,* often foll. by *up*) to calculate or compute (sums, amounts, etc.). 20. (*tr.; usually takes a clause as object*) *Inf., U.S., Canad., & N.Z.* to consider. 21. (*tr.*) to represent by a diagram or illustration. 22. (*tr.*) to pattern or mark with a design. 23. (*tr.*) to depict or portray in a painting, etc. 24. (*tr.*) to imagine. 25. (*tr.*) *Music.* to decorate (a melody line or part) with ornamentation. 26. (*intr.;* usually foll. by *in*) to be included: *his name figures in the article.* 27. (*intr.*) *Inf.* to accord with expectation: *it figures that he wouldn't come.* ~See also **figure out.** [C13: < L *figūra* a shape, < *fingere* to mould] —ˈ**figurer** *n.*

figured (ˈfɪgəd) *adj.* 1. depicted as a figure in painting or sculpture. 2. decorated with a design. 3. having a form. 4. *Music.* a. ornamental. b. (of a bass part) provided with numerals indicating accompanying harmonies.

figured bass (beɪs) *n.* a shorthand method of indicating a thorough-bass part in which each bass note is accompanied by figures indicating the intervals to be played in the chord above it.

figurehead (ˈfɪgəˌhɛd) *n.* 1. a person nominally having a prominent position, but no real authority. 2. a carved bust on the bow of some sailing vessels.

figure of speech *n.* an expression of language, such as metaphor, by which the literal meaning of a word is not employed.
figure out *vb.* (*tr., adv.; may take a clause as object*) *Inf.* **1.** to calculate. **2.** to understand.
figure skating *n.* **1.** ice skating in which the skater traces outlines of selected patterns. **2.** the whole art of skating, as distinct from skating at speed. —**figure skater** *n.*
figurine (ˌfɪgəˈriːn) *n.* a small carved or moulded figure; statuette. [C19: < F, < It. *figurina* a little FIGURE]
figwort (ˈfɪgˌwɜːt) *n.* a plant related to the foxglove having square stems and small greenish flowers.
Fijian (fiːˈdʒiːən) *n.* **1.** a member of the indigenous people inhabiting Fiji. **2.** the language of this people, belonging to the Malayo-Polynesian family. ~*adj.* **3.** of or characteristic of Fiji or its inhabitants. ~Also: **Fiji.**
filagree (ˈfɪləˌgriː) *n., adj.* a less common spelling of **filigree.**
filament (ˈfɪləmənt) *n.* **1.** the thin wire, usually tungsten, inside a light bulb that emits light when heated to incandescence by an electric current. **2.** *Electronics.* a high-resistance wire forming the cathode in some valves. **3.** a single strand of a natural or synthetic fibre. **4.** *Bot.* the stalk of a stamen. **5.** any slender structure or part. [C16: < NL, < Med. L *filāre* to spin, < L *filum* thread] —**filamentary** (ˌfɪləˈmɛntərɪ) *or* ˌ**filaˈmentous** *adj.*
filaria (fɪˈlɛərɪə) *n., pl.* **-iae** (-ɪˌiː). a parasitic nematode worm that lives in the blood of vertebrates and is transmitted by insects: the cause of filariasis. [C19: NL (former name of genus), < L *filum* thread] —**fiˈlarial** *adj.*
filariasis (ˌfɪləˈraɪəsɪs, fɪˌlɛərɪˈeɪsɪs) *n.* a disease common in tropical and subtropical countries resulting from infestation of the lymphatic system with nematode worms transmitted by mosquitoes: characterized by inflammation. See also **elephantiasis.** [C19: < NL; see FILARIA]
filbert (ˈfɪlbət) *n.* **1.** any of several N temperate shrubs that have edible rounded brown nuts. **2.** Also called: **hazelnut, cobnut.** the nut of any of these shrubs. [C14: after St *Philbert*, 7th-century Frankish abbot, because the nuts are ripe around his feast day, Aug. 22]
filch (fɪltʃ) *vb.* (*tr.*) to steal or take in small amounts. [C16 *filchen* to steal, attack, ? < OE *gefylce* band of men] —ˈ**filcher** *n.*
file[1] (faɪl) *n.* **1.** a folder, box, etc., used to keep documents or other items in order. **2.** the documents, etc., kept in this way. **3.** documents or information about a specific subject, person, etc. **4.** a line of people in marching formation, one behind another. **5.** any of the eight vertical rows of squares on a chessboard. **6.** Also called: **data set.** *Computers.* an organized collection of related records, accessible from a storage device via an assigned address. **7. on file.** recorded or catalogued for reference, as in a file. ~*vb.* **8.** to place (a document, etc.) in a file. **9.** (*tr.*) to place (a legal document) on public or official record. **10.** (*tr.*) to bring (a suit, esp. a divorce suit) in a court of law. **11.** (*tr.*) to submit (copy) to a newspaper. **12.** (*intr.*) to march or walk in a file or files: *the ants filed down the hill.* [C16 (in the sense: string on which documents are hung): < OF, < Med. L *filāre*; see FILAMENT] —ˈ**filer** *n.*
file[2] (faɪl) *n.* **1.** a hand tool consisting of a steel blade with small cutting teeth on some or all of its faces. It is used for shaping or smoothing. ~*vb.* **2.** (*tr.*) to shape or smooth (a surface) with a file. [OE *fīl*] —ˈ**filer** *n.*
filefish (ˈfaɪlˌfɪʃ) *n., pl.* **-fish** *or* **-fishes.** any tropical triggerfish having a narrow compressed body and a very long dorsal spine. [C18: referring to its file-like scales]
filet (ˈfɪlɪt, ˈfɪleɪ) *n.* a variant spelling of **fillet** (senses 1-3). [C20: < F: net, < OF, < *fil* thread, < L *filum*]
filet mignon (ˈfɪleɪ ˈmiːnjɒn) *n.* a small tender boneless cut of beef. [< F, lit.: dainty fillet]
filial (ˈfɪljəl) *adj.* **1.** of, resembling, or suitable to a son or daughter: *filial affection.* **2.** *Genetics.* designating any of the generations following the parental generation. [C15: < LL *filiālis*, < L *filius* son] —ˈ**filially** *adv.*
filibeg *or* **philibeg** (ˈfɪlɪˌbɛg) *n.* the kilt worn by Scottish Highlanders. [C18: < Scot. Gaelic *fēileadhbeag*, < *fēileadh* kilt + *beag* small]
filibuster (ˈfɪlɪˌbʌstə) *n.* **1.** the process of obstructing legislation by means of delaying tactics. **2.** Also called: **filibusterer.** a legislator who engages in such obstruction. **3.** a freebooter or military adventurer, esp. in a foreign country. ~*vb.* **4.** to obstruct (legislation) with delaying tactics. **5.** (*intr.*) to engage in unlawful military action. [C16: < Sp., < F *flibustier*, prob. < Du. *vrijbuiter* pirate, lit.: one plundering freely; see FREEBOOTER] —ˈ**filiˌbusterer** *n.*
filigree (ˈfɪlɪˌgriː) *or* **filagree** *n.* **1.** delicate ornamental work of twisted gold, silver, or other wire. **2.** any fanciful delicate ornamentation. ~*adj.* **3.** made of or as if with filigree. [C17: < earlier *filigreen*, < F *filigrane*, < L *filum* thread + *grānum* GRAIN] —ˈ**filiˌgreed** *adj.*
filings (ˈfaɪlɪŋz) *pl. n.* shavings or particles removed by a file: *iron filings.*
Filipino (ˌfɪlɪˈpiːnəʊ) *n., pl.* **-nos. 1.** a native or inhabitant of the Philippines. **2.** another name for **Tagalog.** ~*adj.* **3.** of or relating to the Philippines or their inhabitants.
fill (fɪl) *vb.* (*mainly tr.;* often foll. by *up*) **1.** (*also intr.*) to make or become full: *to fill up a bottle.* **2.** to occupy the whole of: *the party filled the house.* **3.** to plug (a gap, crevice, etc.). **4.** to meet (a requirement or need) satisfactorily. **5.** to cover (a page or blank space) with writing, drawing, etc. **6.** to hold and perform the duties of (an office or position). **7.** to appoint or elect an occupant to (an office or position). **8.** (*also intr.*) to swell or cause to swell with wind, as in manoeuvring the sails of a sailing vessel. **9.** *Chiefly U.S. & Canad.* to put together the necessary materials for (a prescription or order). **10. fill the bill.** *Inf.* to serve or perform adequately. ~*n.* **11.** material such as gravel, stones, etc., used to bring an area of ground up to a required level. **12. one's fill.** the quantity needed to satisfy one. ~See also **fill in, fill out,** etc. [OE *fyllan*]
filler (ˈfɪlə) *n.* **1.** a person or thing that fills. **2.** an object or substance used to add weight or size to something or to fill in a gap. **3.** a paste, used for filling in cracks, holes, etc., in a surface before painting. **4.** the inner portion of a cigar. **5.** *Journalism.* articles, photographs, etc., to fill space between more important articles in a newspaper or magazine.
fillet (ˈfɪlɪt) *n.* **1, a.** Also called: **fillet steak.** a strip of boneless meat. **b.** the boned side of a fish. **2.** a narrow strip of any material. **3.** a thin strip of ribbon, lace, etc., worn in the hair or around the neck. **4.** a narrow flat moulding, esp. one between other mouldings. **5.** a narrow band between flutings on the shaft of a column. **6.** *Heraldry.* a horizontal division of a shield. **7.** a narrow decorative line, impressed on the cover of a book. ~*vb.* (*tr.*) **8.** to cut or prepare (meat or fish) as a fillet. **9.** to cut fillets from (meat or fish). **10.** to bind or decorate with or as if with a fillet. ~Also (for senses 1-3): **filet.** [C14: < OF *filet*, < *fil* thread, < L *filum*]
fill in *vb.* (*adv.*) **1.** (*tr.*) to complete (a form, drawing, etc.). **2.** (*intr.*) to act as a substitute. **3.** (*tr.*) to put material into (a hole or cavity), esp. so as to make it level with a surface. **4.** (*tr.*) *Inf.* to inform with facts or news. ~*n.* **fill-in. 5.** a substitute.
filling (ˈfɪlɪŋ) *n.* **1.** the substance or thing used to fill a space or container: *pie filling.* **2.** *Dentistry.* any of various substances (metal, plastic, etc.) for inserting into the prepared cavity of a tooth. **3.** *Chiefly U.S.* the weft in weaving. ~*adj.* **4.** (of food or a meal) substantial and satisfying.
filling station *n.* a place where petrol and other supplies for motorists are sold.
fillip (ˈfɪlɪp) *n.* **1.** something that adds stimulation

or enjoyment. **2.** the action of holding a finger towards the palm with the thumb and suddenly releasing it outwards to produce a snapping sound. **3.** a quick blow or tap made by this. ~*vb.* **4.** (*tr.*) to stimulate or excite. **5.** (*tr.*) to strike or project sharply with a fillip. **6.** (*intr.*) to make a fillip. [C15 *philippe*, imit.]

fill out *vb.* (*adv.*) **1.** to make or become fuller, thicker, or rounder. **2.** to make more substantial. **3.** (*tr.*) *Chiefly U.S. & Canad.* to fill in (a form, etc.).

fill up *vb.* (*adv.*) **1.** (*tr.*) to complete (a form, application, etc.). **2.** to make or become full. ~*n.* **fill-up. 3.** the act of filling something completely, esp. the petrol tank of a car.

filly (ˈfɪlɪ) *n., pl.* **-lies.** a female horse or pony under the age of four. [C15: < ON *fylja;* see FOAL]

film (fɪlm) *n.* **1. a.** a sequence of images of moving objects photographed by a camera and providing the optical illusion of continuous movement when projected onto a screen. **b.** a form of entertainment, etc., composed of such a sequence of images. **c.** (*as modifier*): *film techniques.* **2.** a thin flexible strip of cellulose coated with a photographic emulsion, used to make negatives and transparencies. **3.** a thin coating or layer. **4.** a thin sheet of any material, as of plastic for packaging. **5.** a fine haze, mist, or blur. **6.** a gauzy web of filaments or fine threads. ~*vb.* **7. a.** to photograph with a cine camera. **b.** to make a film of (a screenplay, event, etc.). **8.** (often foll. by *over*) to cover or become covered or coated with a film. [OE *filmen* membrane] —ˈ**filmic** *adj.*

film noir (nwɑː) *n.* a gangster thriller, made esp. in the 1940s in Hollywood, characterized by contrasty lighting and often somewhat impenetrable plots. [C20: F, lit.: black film]

filmography (fɪlˈmɒgrəfɪ) *n.* **1.** a list of the films made by a particular director, actor, etc. **2.** any writing that deals with films or the cinema.

filmset (ˈfɪlmˌsɛt) *vb.* **-setting, -set.** (*tr.*) *Brit.* to set (type matter) by filmsetting. —ˈ**filmˌsetter** *n.*

filmsetting (ˈfɪlmˌsɛtɪŋ) *n. Brit., printing.* typesetting by exposing type characters onto photographic film from which printing plates are made.

film strip *n.* a strip of film composed of different images projected separately as slides.

filmy (ˈfɪlmɪ) *adj.* **filmier, filmiest. 1.** transparent or gauzy. **2.** hazy; blurred. —ˈ**filmily** *adv.* —ˈ**filminess** *n.*

Filofax (ˈfaɪləʊˌfæks) *n. Trademark.* a type of loose-leaf ring binder with sets of different-coloured paper, used as a portable personal filing system, including appointments, addresses, etc.

filter (ˈfɪltə) *n.* **1.** a porous substance, such as paper or sand, that allows fluid to pass but retains suspended solid particles. **2.** any device containing such a porous substance for separating suspensions from fluids. **3.** any of various porous substances built into the mouth end of a cigarette or cigar for absorbing impurities such as tar. **4.** any electronic, optical, or acoustic device that blocks signals or radiations of certain frequencies while allowing others to pass. **5.** any transparent disc of gelatin or glass used to eliminate or reduce the intensity of given frequencies from the light leaving a lamp, entering a camera, etc. **6.** *Brit.* a traffic signal at a road junction which permits vehicles to turn either left or right when the main signals are red. ~*vb.* **7.** (often foll. by *out*) to remove or separate (suspended particles, etc.) from (a liquid, gas, etc.) by the action of a filter. **8.** (*tr.*) to obtain by filtering. **9.** (*intr.;* foll. by *through*) to pass (through a filter or something like a filter). **10.** (*intr.*) to flow slowly; trickle. [C16 *filtre,* < Med. L *filtrum* piece of felt used as a filter, of Gmc origin]

filterable (ˈfɪltərəbᵊl) *or* **filtrable** (ˈfɪltrəbᵊl) *adj.* **1.** capable of being filtered. **2.** (of most viruses and certain bacteria) capable of passing through the pores of a fine filter.

filter bed *n.* a layer of sand or gravel in a tank or reservoir through which a liquid is passed so as to purify it.

filter out *or* **through** *vb.* (*intr., adv.*) to become known gradually; leak.

filter paper *n.* a porous paper used for filtering liquids.

filter tip *n.* **1.** an attachment to the mouth end of a cigarette for trapping impurities such as tar during smoking. **2.** a cigarette having such an attachment. —ˈ**filter-ˌtipped** *adj.*

filth (fɪlθ) *n.* **1.** foul or disgusting dirt; refuse. **2.** extreme physical or moral uncleanliness. **3.** vulgarity or obscenity. **4. the filth.** *Sl.* the police. [OE *fȳlth*]

filthy (ˈfɪlθɪ) *adj.* **filthier, filthiest. 1.** very dirty or obscene. **2.** offensive or vicious: *that was a filthy trick to play.* **3.** *Inf., chiefly Brit.* extremely unpleasant: *filthy weather.* ~*adv.* **4.** extremely; disgustingly (esp. in **filthy rich**). —ˈ**filthily** *adv.* —ˈ**filthiness** *n.*

filtrate (ˈfɪltreɪt) *n.* **1.** a liquid or gas that has been filtered. ~*vb.* **2.** to filter. [C17: < Med. L *filtrāre* to FILTER] —**filˈtration** *n.*

fin (fɪn) *n.* **1.** any of the firm appendages that are the organs of locomotion and balance in fishes and some other aquatic animals. **2.** a part or appendage that resembles a fin. **3. a.** *Brit.* a vertical surface to which the rudder is attached at the rear of an aeroplane. **b.** a tail surface fixed to a rocket or missile to give stability. **4.** *Naut.* a fixed or adjustable blade projecting under water from the hull of a vessel to give it stability or control. **5.** a projecting rib to dissipate heat from the surface of an engine cylinder or radiator. ~*vb.* **finning, finned. 6.** (*tr.*) to provide with fins. [OE *finn*] —ˈ**finless** *adj.* —**finned** *adj.*

fin. *abbrev. for:* **1.** finance. **2.** financial.

Fin. *abbrev. for:* **1.** Finland. **2.** Finnish.

finable *or* **fineable** (ˈfaɪnəbᵊl) *adj.* liable to a fine. —ˈ**finableness** *or* ˈ**fineableness** *n.*

finagle (fɪˈneɪgᵊl) *vb. Inf.* **1.** (*tr.*) to get or achieve by craftiness or persuasion. **2.** to use trickery on (a person). [C20: ?< dialect *fainaigue* cheat] —**fiˈnagler** *n.*

final (ˈfaɪnᵊl) *adj.* **1.** of or occurring at the end; last. **2.** having no possibility of further discussion, action, or change: *a final decree of judgment.* **3.** relating to or constituting an end or purpose: *a final clause may be introduced by "in order to".* **4.** *Music.* another word for **perfect** (sense 9b.). ~*n.* **5.** a last thing; end. **6.** a deciding contest between the winners of previous rounds in a competition. ~See also **finals.** [C14: < L *fīnālis,* < *finis* limit, boundary]

finale (fɪˈnɑːlɪ) *n.* **1.** the concluding part of any performance or presentation. **2.** the closing section or movement of a musical composition. [C18: < It., n. use of adj. *finale,* < L *fīnālis* FINAL]

finalist (ˈfaɪnəlɪst) *n.* a contestant who has reached the last stage of a competition.

finality (faɪˈnælɪtɪ) *n., pl.* **-ties. 1.** the condition or quality of being final or settled: *the finality of death.* **2.** a final or conclusive act.

finalize *or* **-lise** (ˈfaɪnəˌlaɪz) *vb.* **1.** (*tr.*) to put into final form; settle: *to finalize plans for the merger.* **2.** to reach agreement on a transaction. —ˌ**finaliˈzation** *or* **-liˈsation** *n.*

▷ **Usage.** Although *finalize* has been in widespread use for some time, it carries strong associations of bureaucratic or commercial jargon for many careful speakers and writers, who usually prefer *complete, conclude,* or *make final,* esp. in formal contexts.

finally (ˈfaɪnəlɪ) *adv.* **1.** at last; eventually. **2.** at the end or final point; lastly. **3.** completely; conclusively. ~*sentence connector.* **4.** in the end; lastly: *finally, he put his tie on.* **5.** as the last or final point.

finals (ˈfaɪnᵊlz) *pl. n.* **1.** the deciding part of a competition. **2.** *Education.* the last examinations in an academic or professional course.

finance (fɪˈnæns, ˈfaɪnæns) *n.* **1.** the system of money, credit, etc., esp. with respect to government revenues and expenditures. **2.** funds or the provision of funds. **3.** (*pl.*) financial condition. ~*vb.* **4.** (*tr.*) to provide or obtain funds or credit for. [C14: < OF, < *finer* to end, settle by payment]

finance company *or* **house** *n.* an enterprise engaged in the loan of money against collateral, esp. one specializing in the financing of hire-purchase contracts.

financial (fɪˈnænʃəl, faɪ-) *adj.* **1.** of or relating to finance or finances. **2.** of or relating to persons who manage money, capital, or credit. **3.** *Austral. & N.Z. inf.* having money; in funds. **4.** *Austral. & N.Z.* (of a club member) fully paid-up. —**fiˈnancially** *adv.*

financial year *n. Brit.* **1.** any annual period at the end of which a firm's accounts are made up. **2.** the annual period ending April 5, over which Budget estimates are made by the British Government. ~U.S. and Canad. equivalent: **fiscal year.**

financier (fɪˈnænsɪə, faɪ-) *n.* a person who is engaged in large-scale financial operations.

finback (ˈfɪnˌbæk) *n.* another name for **rorqual.**

finch (fɪntʃ) *n.* any of various songbirds having a short stout bill for feeding on seeds, such as the bullfinch, chaffinch, siskin, and canary. [OE *finc*]

find (faɪnd) *vb.* **finding, found.** (*mainly tr.*) **1.** to meet with or discover by chance. **2.** to discover or obtain, esp. by search or effort: *to find happiness.* **3.** (*may take a clause as object*) to realize: *he found that nobody knew.* **4.** (*may take a clause as object*) to consider: *I find this wine a little sour.* **5.** to look for and point out (something to be criticized). **6.** (*also intr.*) *Law.* to determine an issue and pronounce a verdict (upon): *the court found the accused guilty.* **7.** to regain (something lost or not functioning): *to find one's tongue.* **8.** to reach (a target): *the bullet found its mark.* **9.** to provide, esp. with difficulty: *we'll find room for you too.* **10.** to be able to pay: *I can't find that amount of money.* **11. find oneself.** to realize and accept one's true character; discover one's vocation. **12. find one's feet.** to become capable or confident. ~*n.* **13.** a person, thing, etc., that is found, esp. a valuable discovery. [OE *findan*]

finder (ˈfaɪndə) *n.* **1.** a person or thing that finds. **2.** *Physics.* a small telescope fitted to a more powerful larger telescope. **3.** *Photog.* short for **viewfinder.** **4. finders keepers.** *Inf.* whoever finds something has the right to keep it.

fin de siècle *French.* (fɛ̃ də sjɛklə) *n.* **1.** the end of the 19th century. ~*adj.* ***fin-de-siècle.*** **2.** of or relating to the close of the 19th century. **3.** decadent, esp. in artistic tastes.

finding (ˈfaɪndɪŋ) *n.* **1.** a thing that is found or discovered. **2.** *Law.* the conclusion reached after a judicial inquiry; verdict.

find out *vb.* (*adv.*) **1.** to gain knowledge of (something); learn. **2.** to detect the crime, deception, etc., of (someone).

fine[1] (faɪn) *adj.* **1.** very good of its kind: *a fine speech.* **2.** superior in skill or accomplishment: *a fine violinist.* **3.** (of weather) clear and dry. **4.** enjoyable or satisfying: *a fine time.* **5.** (*postpositive*) *Inf.* quite well: *I feel fine.* **6.** satisfactory; acceptable: *that's fine by me.* **7.** of delicate composition or careful workmanship: *fine crystal.* **8.** (of precious metals) pure or having a high degree of purity: *fine silver.* **9.** discriminating: *a fine eye for antique brasses.* **10.** abstruse or subtle: *a fine point.* **11.** very thin or slender: *fine hair.* **12.** very small: *fine print.* **13.** (of edges, blades, etc.) sharp; keen. **14.** ornate, showy, or smart. **15.** good-looking: *a fine young woman.* **16.** polished, elegant, or refined: *a fine gentleman.* **17.** *Cricket.* (of a fielding position) oblique to and behind the wicket: *fine leg.* **18.** (*prenominal*) *Inf.* disappointing or terrible: *a fine mess.* ~*adv.* **19.** *Inf.* all right: *that suits me fine.* **20.** finely. ~*vb.* **21.** to make or become finer; refine. **22.** (often foll. by *down* or *away*) to make or become smaller. [C13: < OF *fin*, < L *finis* end, boundary, as in *finis honōrum* the highest degree of honour] —ˈ**finely** *adv.* —ˈ**fineness** *n.*

fine[2] (faɪn) *n.* **1.** a certain amount of money exacted as a penalty: *a parking fine.* **2.** a payment made by a tenant at the start of his tenancy to reduce his subsequent rent; premium. **3. in fine. a.** in short. **b.** in conclusion. ~*vb.* **4.** (*tr.*) to impose a fine on. [C12 (in the sense: conclusion, settlement): < OF *fin*; see FINE[1]]

fine[3] (ˈfiːneɪ) *n. Music.* the point at which a piece is to end. [It., < L *finis* end]

fine art *n.* **1.** art produced chiefly for its aesthetic value. **2.** (*often pl.*) any of the fields in which such art is produced, such as painting, sculpture, and engraving.

fine-draw *vb.* **-drawing, -drew, -drawn.** (*tr.*) to sew together so finely that the join is scarcely noticeable.

fine-drawn *adj.* **1.** (of arguments, distinctions, etc.) precise or subtle. **2.** (of wire, etc.) drawn out until very fine.

fine-grained *adj.* (of wood, leather, etc.) having a fine smooth even grain.

finery[1] (ˈfaɪnərɪ) *n.* elaborate or showy decoration, esp. clothing and jewellery.

finery[2] (ˈfaɪnərɪ) *n., pl.* **-eries.** a hearth for converting cast iron into wrought iron. [C17: < OF *finerie*, < *finer* to refine; see FINE[1]]

fines herbes (*French* finz ɛrb) *pl. n.* a mixture of finely chopped herbs, used to flavour omelettes, salads, etc.

finespun (ˈfaɪnˈspʌn) *adj.* **1.** spun or drawn out to a fine thread. **2.** excessively subtle or refined.

finesse (fɪˈnɛs) *n.* **1.** elegant skill in style or performance. **2.** subtlety and tact in handling difficult situations. **3.** *Bridge, whist.* an attempt to win a trick when opponents hold a high card in the suit led by playing a lower card. **4.** a trick, artifice, or strategy. ~*vb.* **5.** to bring about with finesse. **6.** to play (a card) as a finesse. [C15: < OF, < *fin* fine, delicate; see FINE[1]]

fine-tooth comb *or* **fine-toothed comb** *n.* **1.** a comb with fine teeth set closely together. **2. go over** (*or* **through**) **with a fine-tooth(ed) comb.** to examine very thoroughly.

fine-tune *vb.* (*tr.*) to make fine adjustments to (something) in order to obtain optimum performance.

finger (ˈfɪŋgə) *n.* **1. a.** any of the digits of the hand, often excluding the thumb. **b.** (*as modifier*): *a finger bowl.* **c.** (*in combination*): *a fingernail.* Related adj.: **digital.** **2.** the part of a glove made to cover a finger. **3.** something that resembles a finger in shape or function: *a finger of land.* **4.** the length or width of a finger used as a unit of measurement. **5.** a quantity of liquid in a glass, etc., as deep as a finger is wide. **6. get** *or* **pull one's finger out.** *Brit. inf.* to begin or speed up activity, esp. after initial delay. **7. have a** (*or* **one's**) **finger in the pie. a.** to have an interest in or take part in some activity. **b.** to meddle or interfere. **8. lay** *or* **put one's finger on.** to indicate or locate accurately. **9. not lift** (*or* **raise**) **a finger.** (*foll. by an infinitive*) not to make any effort (to do something). **10. twist** *or* **wrap around one's little finger.** to have easy and complete control or influence over. **11. put the finger on.** *Inf., U.S. & N.Z.* to inform on or identify, esp. for the police. ~*vb.* **12.** (*tr.*) to touch or manipulate with the fingers; handle. **13.** to use one's fingers in playing (an instrument, such as a piano or clarinet). **14.** to indicate on (a composition or part) the fingering required by a pianist, etc. [OE] —ˈ**fingerless** *adj.*

fingerboard (ˈfɪŋgəˌbɔːd) *n.* the long strip of hard wood on a violin, guitar, etc. upon which the strings are stopped by the fingers.

finger bowl *n.* a small bowl filled with water for rinsing the fingers at the table after a meal.

finger buffet (ˈbʊfeɪ) *n.* a buffet meal at which food that may be picked up in the fingers (**finger food**), such as canapés or vol-au-vents, is served.

fingered (ˈfɪŋgəd) *adj.* **1.** marked or dirtied by handling. **2. a.** having a finger or fingers. **b.** (*in combination*): *red-fingered.* **3.** (of a musical part) having numerals indicating the fingering.

fingering (ˈfɪŋgərɪŋ) *n.* **1.** the technique or art of using one's fingers in playing a musical instrument, esp. the piano. **2.** the numerals in a musical part indicating this.

fingerling (ˈfɪŋɡəlɪŋ) *n.* a very young fish, esp. the parr of salmon or trout.

fingermark (ˈfɪŋɡəˌmɑːk) *n.* a mark left by dirty or greasy fingers on paintwork, walls, etc.

fingernail (ˈfɪŋɡəˌneɪl) *n.* a thin horny translucent plate covering part of the dorsal surface of the end joint of each finger.

finger painting *n.* the process or art of painting with **finger paints** of starch, glycerin, and pigments, using the fingers, hand, or arm.

finger post *n.* a signpost showing a pointing finger or hand.

fingerprint (ˈfɪŋɡəˌprɪnt) *n.* **1.** an impression of the pattern of ridges on the surface of the end joint of each finger and thumb. **2.** any unique identifying characteristic. ~*vb.* (*tr.*) **3.** to take an inked impression of the fingerprints of (a person). **4.** to take a sample of (a person's) DNA.

fingerstall (ˈfɪŋɡəˌstɔːl) *n.* a protective covering for a finger. Also called: **cot.**

fingertip (ˈfɪŋɡəˌtɪp) *n.* **1.** the end joint or tip of a finger. **2. at one's fingertips.** readily available.

finial (ˈfaɪnɪəl) *n.* **1.** an ornament on top of a spire, etc., esp. in the form of a fleur-de-lis. **2.** an ornament at the top of a piece of furniture, etc. [C14: < *finial* (adj.), var. of FINAL]

finicky (ˈfɪnɪkɪ) *or* **finicking** *adj.* **1.** excessively particular; fussy. **2.** overelaborate. [C19: < *finical*, < FINE[1]]

finis (ˈfɪnɪs) *n.* the end; finish: used at the end of books, films, etc. [C15: < L]

finish (ˈfɪnɪʃ) *vb.* (*mainly tr.*) **1.** to bring to an end; conclude or stop. **2.** (*intr.*; sometimes foll. by *up*) to be at or come to the end; use up. **3.** to bring to a desired or complete condition. **4.** to put a particular surface texture on (wood, cloth, etc.). **5.** (often foll. by *off*) to destroy or defeat completely. **6.** to train (a person) in social graces and talents. **7.** (*intr.*; foll. by *with*) to end a relationship or association. ~*n.* **8.** the final or last stage or part; end. **9.** the death or absolute defeat of a person or one side in a conflict: *a fight to the finish.* **10.** the surface texture or appearance of wood, cloth, etc.: *a rough finish.* **11.** a thing, event, etc., that completes. **12.** completeness and high quality of workmanship. **13.** *Sport.* ability to sprint at the end of a race. [C14: < OF, < L *fīnīre*; see FINE[1]] —ˈ**finished** *adj.* —ˈ**finisher** *n.*

finishing school *n.* a private school for girls that teaches social graces.

finite (ˈfaɪnaɪt) *adj.* **1.** bounded in magnitude or spatial or temporal extent. **2.** *Maths, logic.* having a countable number of elements. **3.** limited or restricted in nature: *human existence is finite.* **4.** denoting any form of a verb inflected for grammatical features such as person, number, and tense. [C15: < L *fīnītus* limited, < *fīnīre* to limit, end] —ˈ**finitely** *adv.* —ˈ**finiteness** *or* **finitude** (ˈfaɪnɪˌtjuːd) *n.*

fink (fɪŋk) *n. Sl., chiefly U.S. & Canad.* **1.** a strikebreaker. **2.** an unpleasant or contemptible person. [C20: <?]

Finn (fɪn) *n.* a native, inhabitant, or citizen of Finland. [OE *Finnas* (pl.)]

finnan haddock (ˈfɪnən) *or* **haddie** (ˈhædɪ) *n.* smoked haddock. [C18: *finnan* after *Findon*, a village in NE Scotland]

Finnic (ˈfɪnɪk) *n.* **1.** one of the two branches of the Finno-Ugric family of languages, including Finnish and several languages of the N Soviet Union in Europe. ~*adj.* **2.** of or relating to this group of languages or to the Finns.

Finnish (ˈfɪnɪʃ) *adj.* **1.** of or characteristic of Finland, the Finns, or their language. ~*n.* **2.** the official language of Finland, belonging to the Finno-Ugric family.

Finno-Ugric (ˈfɪnəʊˈuːɡrɪk, -ˈjuː-) *or* **Finno-Ugrian** *n.* **1.** a family of languages spoken in Scandinavia, Hungary, and the Soviet Union, including Finnish, Estonian, and Hungarian. ~*adj.* **2.** of, relating to, or belonging to this family of languages.

finny (ˈfɪnɪ) *adj.* **-nier, -niest. 1.** *Poetic.* relating to or containing many fishes. **2.** having or resembling a fin or fins.

fino (ˈfiːnəʊ) *n.* a very dry sherry. [Sp.: FINE[1]]

fiord (fjɔːd) *n.* a variant spelling of **fjord.**

fioriture (ˌfjɔːrɪˈtʊəreɪ) *pl. n. Music.* flourishes; embellishments. [C19: It., < *fiorire* to flower]

fipple (ˈfɪpᵊl) *n.* a wooden plug forming a flue in the end of a pipe, as the mouthpiece of a recorder. [C17: <?]

fipple flute *n.* an end-blown flute provided with a fipple, such as the recorder or flageolet.

fir (fɜː) *n.* **1.** any of a genus of pyramidal coniferous trees having single needle-like leaves and erect cones. **2.** any of various other related trees, such as the Douglas fir. **3.** the wood of any of these trees. [OE *furh*]

fire (ˈfaɪə) *n.* **1.** the state of combustion in which inflammable material burns, producing heat, flames, and often smoke. **2. a.** a mass of burning coal, wood, etc., used esp. in a hearth to heat a room. **b.** (*in combination*): *firelighter.* **3.** a destructive conflagration, as of a forest, building, etc. **4.** a device for heating a room, etc. **5.** something resembling a fire in light or brilliance: *a diamond's fire.* **6.** the act of discharging weapons, artillery, etc. **7.** a burst or rapid volley: *a fire of questions.* **8.** intense passion; ardour. **9.** liveliness, as of imagination, etc. **10.** fever and inflammation. **11.** a severe trial or torment (esp. in **go through fire and water**). **12. between two fires.** under attack from two sides. **13. catch fire.** to ignite. **14. on fire. a.** in a state of ignition. **b.** ardent or eager. **15. open fire.** to start firing a gun, artillery, etc. **16. play with fire.** to be involved in something risky. **17. set fire to** *or* **set on fire. a.** to ignite. **b.** to arouse or excite. **18. under fire.** being attacked, as by weapons or by harsh criticism. **19.** (*modifier*) *Astrol.* of or relating to a group of three signs of the zodiac, Aries, Leo, and Sagittarius. ~*vb.* **20.** to discharge (a firearm or projectile), or (of a firearm, etc.) to be discharged. **21.** to detonate (an explosive charge or device), or (of such a charge or device) to be detonated. **22.** (*tr.*) *Inf.* to dismiss from employment. **23.** (*tr.*) *Ceramics.* to bake in a kiln to harden the clay, etc. **24.** to kindle or be kindled. **25.** (*tr.*) to provide with fuel: *oil fires the heating system.* **26.** (*tr.*) to subject to heat. **27.** (*tr.*) to heat slowly so as to dry. **28.** (*tr.*) to arouse to strong emotion. **29.** to glow or cause to glow. ~*sentence substitute.* **30.** a cry to warn others of a fire. **31.** the order to begin firing a gun, artillery, etc. [OE *fȳr*] —ˈ**firer** *n.*

fire alarm *n.* a device to give warning of fire, esp. a bell, siren, or hooter.

firearm (ˈfaɪərˌɑːm) *n.* a weapon from which a projectile can be discharged by an explosion caused by igniting gunpowder, etc.

fireback (ˈfaɪəˌbæk) *n.* an ornamental iron slab against the back wall of a hearth.

fireball (ˈfaɪəˌbɔːl) *n.* **1.** a ball-shaped discharge of lightning. **2.** the region of hot ionized gas at the centre of a nuclear explosion. **3.** *Astron.* a large bright meteor. **4.** *Sl.* an energetic person.

fire blight *n.* a disease of apples, pears, and similar fruit trees, caused by a bacterium and characterized by blackening of the blossoms and leaves.

fireboat (ˈfaɪəˌbəʊt) *n.* a motor vessel equipped with fire-fighting apparatus.

firebomb (ˈfaɪəˌbɒm) *n.* another name for **incendiary** (sense 6).

firebox (ˈfaɪəˌbɒks) *n.* the furnace chamber of a boiler in a steam locomotive.

firebrand (ˈfaɪəˌbrænd) *n.* **1.** a piece of burning wood. **2.** a person who causes unrest.

firebreak (ˈfaɪəˌbreɪk) *n.* a strip of open land in forest or prairie, serving to arrest the advance of a fire.

firebrick (ˈfaɪəˌbrɪk) *n.* a refractory brick made of fire clay, used for lining furnaces, flues, etc.

fire brigade *n. Chiefly Brit.* an organized body of firemen.

firebug (ˈfaɪəˌbʌɡ) *n. Inf.* a person who deliberately sets fire to property.

fire clay *n.* a heat-resistant clay used in the making of firebricks, furnace linings, etc.

fire company *n.* 1. an insurance company selling policies relating to fire risk. 2. *U.S.* an organized body of firemen.

fire control *n. Mil.* the procedures by which weapons are brought to engage a target.

firecracker (ˈfaɪəˌkrækə) *n.* a small cardboard container filled with explosive powder.

firecrest (ˈfaɪəˌkrɛst) *n.* a small European warbler having a crown striped with yellow, black, and white.

firedamp (ˈfaɪəˌdæmp) *n.* an explosive of hydrocarbons, chiefly methane, formed in coal mines. See also **afterdamp.**

firedog (ˈfaɪəˌdɒg) *n.* either of a pair of metal stands used to support logs in an open fire.

fire door *n.* 1. a door made of noncombustible material that prevents a fire spreading within a building. 2. a similar door leading to the outside of a building that can be easily opened from inside; emergency exit.

fire-eater *n.* 1. a performer who simulates the swallowing of fire. 2. a belligerent person.

fire engine *n.* a vehicle that carries firemen and fire-fighting equipment to a fire.

fire escape *n.* a means of evacuating persons from a building in the event of fire.

fire-extinguisher *n.* a portable device for extinguishing fires, usually consisting of a canister with a directional nozzle used to direct a spray of water, etc., onto the fire.

firefly (ˈfaɪəˌflaɪ) *n., pl.* **-flies.** a nocturnal beetle common in warm and tropical regions, having luminescent abdominal organs.

fireguard (ˈfaɪəˌgɑːd) *n.* a meshed frame put before an open fire to protect against falling logs, sparks, etc.

fire hall *n. Canad.* a fire station.

fire hydrant *n.* a hydrant for use as an emergency supply for fighting fires.

fire insurance *n.* insurance covering damage or loss caused by fire or lightning.

fire irons *pl. n.* metal fireside implements, such as poker, shovel, and tongs.

firelock (ˈfaɪəˌlɒk) *n.* 1. an obsolete type of gunlock with a priming mechanism ignited by sparks. 2. a gun or musket having such a lock.

fireman (ˈfaɪəmən) *n., pl.* **-men.** 1. a person who fights fires, usually a trained volunteer or public employee. 2. a. (on steam locomotives) the man who stokes the fire. b. (on diesel and electric locomotives) the driver's assistant. 3. a man who tends furnaces; stoker.

fire opal *n.* an orange-red translucent variety of opal, valued as a gemstone.

fireplace (ˈfaɪəˌpleɪs) *n.* an open recess at the base of a chimney, etc., for a fire; hearth.

fireplug (ˈfaɪəˌplʌg) *n.* another name (esp. U.S. and N.Z.) for **fire hydrant.**

fire power *n. Mil.* 1. the amount of fire that can be delivered by a unit or weapon. 2. the capability of delivering fire.

fireproof (ˈfaɪəˌpruːf) *adj.* 1. capable of resisting damage by fire. ~*vb.* 2. (*tr.*) to make resistant to fire.

fire raiser *n.* a person who deliberately sets fire to property, etc. —**fire raising** *n.*

fire screen *n.* 1. a decorative screen placed in the hearth when there is no fire. 2. a screen placed before a fire to protect the face.

fire ship *n.* a vessel loaded with explosives and used, esp. formerly, as a bomb by igniting it and directing it to drift among an enemy's warships.

fireside (ˈfaɪəˌsaɪd) *n.* 1. the hearth. 2. family life; the home.

fire station *n.* a building where fire-fighting vehicles and equipment are stationed. Also called (U.S.): **firehouse, station house.**

firestorm (ˈfaɪəˌstɔːm) *n.* an uncontrollable blaze sustained by violent winds that are drawn into the column of rising hot air over the burning area: often the result of heavy bombing.

firetrap (ˈfaɪəˌtræp) *n.* a building that would burn easily or one without fire escapes.

firewater (ˈfaɪəˌwɔːtə) *n.* any strong spirit, esp. whisky.

fireweed (ˈfaɪəˌwiːd) *n.* any of various plants that appear as first vegetation in burnt-over areas.

firework (ˈfaɪəˌwɜːk) *n.* a device, such as a Catherine wheel or rocket, in which combustible materials are ignited and produce coloured flames, sparks, and smoke.

fireworks (ˈfaɪəˌwɜːks) *pl. n.* 1. a show in which large numbers of fireworks are let off. 2. *Inf.* an exciting exhibition, as of musical virtuosity or wit. 3. *Inf.* a burst of temper.

firing (ˈfaɪərɪŋ) *n.* 1. the process of baking ceramics, etc., in a kiln. 2. the act of stoking a fire or furnace. 3. a discharge of a firearm. 4. something used as fuel, such as coal or wood.

firing line *n.* 1. *Mil.* the positions from which fire is delivered. 2. the leading or most advanced position in an activity.

firkin (ˈfɜːkɪn) *n.* 1. a small wooden barrel. 2. *Brit.* a unit of capacity equal to nine gallons. [C14 *fir,* < MDu. *vierde* FOURTH + -KIN]

firm[1] (fɜːm) *adj.* 1. not soft or yielding to a touch or pressure. 2. securely in position; stable or stationary. 3. decided; settled. 4. enduring or steady. 5. having determination or strength. 6. (of prices, markets, etc.) tending to rise. ~*adv.* 7. in a secure or unyielding manner: *he stood firm.* ~*vb.* 8. (sometimes foll. by *up*) to make or become firm. [C14: < L *firmus*] —ˈ**firmly** *adv.* —ˈ**firmness** *n.*

firm[2] (fɜːm) *n.* 1. a business partnership. 2. any commercial enterprise. 3. a team of doctors and their assistants. [C16 (in the sense: signature): < Sp. *firma* signature, < *firmar* to sign, < L *firmāre* to confirm, < *firmus* firm]

firmament (ˈfɜːməmənt) *n.* the expanse of the sky; heavens. [C13: < LL *firmāmentum* sky (considered as fixed above the earth), < L: prop, support, < *firmāre* to make FIRM[1]]

first (fɜːst) *adj.* (*usually prenominal*) 1. a. coming before all others. b. (*as n.*): *I was the first to arrive.* 2. preceding all others in numbering or counting order; the ordinal number of *one.* Often written: 1st. 3. rated, graded, or ranked above all other levels. 4. denoting the lowest forward ratio of a gearbox in a motor vehicle. 5. *Music.* a. denoting the highest part assigned to one of the voice parts in a chorus or one of the sections of an orchestra: *the first violins.* b. denoting the principal player in a specific orchestral section: *he plays first horn.* 6. **first thing.** as the first action of the day: *I'll see you first thing tomorrow.* ~*n.* 7. the beginning; outset: *I couldn't see at first because of the mist.* 8. *Education, chiefly Brit.* an honours degree of the highest class. Full term: **first-class honours degree.** 9. the lowest forward ratio of a gearbox in a motor vehicle. ~*adv.* 10. Also: **firstly.** before anything else in order, time, importance, etc.: *do this first.* 11. **first and last.** on the whole. 12. **from first to last.** throughout. 13. for the first time: *I've loved you since I first saw you.* 14. (*sentence modifier*) in the first place or beginning of a series of actions. [OE *fyrest*]

first aid *n.* a. immediate medical assistance given in an emergency. b. (*as modifier*): *first-aid box.*

first-born *adj.* 1. eldest of the children in a family. ~*n.* 2. the eldest child in a family.

first class *n.* 1. the class or grade of the best or highest value, quality, etc. ~*adj.* (**first-class** *when prenominal*). 2. of the best or highest class or grade: *a first-class citizen.* 3. excellent. 4. of or denoting the most comfortable class of accommodation in a hotel, aircraft, train, etc. 5. (in Britain) of letters that are handled faster than second-class letters. ~*adv.* **first-class.** 6. by first-class mail, means of transportation, etc.

first-day cover *n. Philately.* an envelope postmarked on the first day of the issue of its stamps.

first-degree burn *n. Pathol.* the least severe type of burn, in which the skin surface is red and painful.

first-foot *Chiefly Scot.* ~*n. also* **first-footer.** 1.

the first person to enter a household in the New Year. ~*vb.* **2.** to enter (a house) as first-foot. —ˈ**first-**ˈ**footing** *n.*

first fruits *pl. n.* **1.** the first results or profits of an undertaking. **2.** fruit that ripens first.

first-hand *adj., adv.* **1.** from the original source: *he got the news first-hand.* **2. at first hand.** directly.

first lady *n.* (*often caps.*) (in the U.S.) the wife or official hostess of a state governor or a president.

firstling (ˈfɜːstlɪŋ) *n.* the first, esp. the first offspring.

firstly (ˈfɜːstlɪ) *adv.* another word for **first.**

first mate *n.* an officer second in command to the captain of a merchant ship.

first mortgage *n.* a mortgage that has priority over other mortgages on the same property.

first name *n.* another term for **Christian name.**

first night *n.* **a.** the first public performance of a play, etc. **b.** (*as modifier*): *first-night nerves.*

first offender *n.* a person convicted of a criminal offence for the first time.

first officer *n.* **1.** another name for **first mate.** **2.** the member of an aircraft crew who is second in command to the captain.

first-past-the-post *n.* (*modifier*) of a voting system in which a candidate may be elected by a simple majority.

first person *n.* a grammatical category of pronouns and verbs used by the speaker to refer to or talk about himself.

first-rate *adj.* **1.** of the best or highest rated class or quality. **2.** *Inf.* very good; excellent.

first reading *n.* the introduction of a bill into a legislative assembly.

first-strike *adj.* (of a nuclear missile) intended for use in an opening attack calculated to destroy the enemy's nuclear weapons.

first water *n.* **1.** the finest quality of diamond or other precious stone. **2.** the highest grade or best quality.

firth (fɜːθ) *or* **frith** *n.* a narrow inlet of the sea, esp. in Scotland. [C15: < ON *fjörthr* FJORD]

FIS (fɪs) *n. acronym for* Family Income Supplement.

fiscal (ˈfɪskᵊl) *adj.* **1.** of or relating to government finances, esp. tax revenues. **2.** of or involving financial matters. ~*n.* **3. a.** (in some countries) a public prosecutor. **b.** *Scot.* short for **procurator fiscal.** [C16: < L *fiscālis* concerning the state treasury, < *fiscus* public money] —ˈ**fiscally** *adv.*

fiscal year *n.* the U.S. and Canad. term for **financial year.**

fish (fɪʃ) *n., pl.* **fish** *or* **fishes. 1. a.** any of a large group of cold-blooded aquatic vertebrates having jaws, gills, and usually fins and a skin covered in scales: includes the sharks, rays, teleosts, lungfish, etc. **b.** (*in combination*): *fishpond.* Related adj.: **piscine. 2.** any of various similar but jawless vertebrates, such as the hagfish and lamprey. **3.** (*not in technical use*) any of various aquatic invertebrates, such as the cuttlefish and crayfish. **4.** the flesh of fish used as food. **5.** *Inf.* a person of little emotion or intelligence: *a poor fish.* **6. drink like a fish.** to drink to excess. **7. have other fish to fry.** to have other activities to do, esp. more important ones. **8. like a fish out of water.** out of one's usual place. **9. neither fish, flesh, nor fowl.** neither this nor that. ~*vb.* **10.** (*intr.*) to attempt to catch fish, as with a line and hook or with nets, traps, etc. **11.** (*tr.*) to fish in (a particular area of water). **12.** to search (a body of water) for something or to search for something, esp. in a body of water. **13.** (*intr.;* foll. by *for*) to seek something indirectly: *to fish for compliments.* ~See also **fish out.** [OE *fisc*] —ˈ**fish**ˌ**like** *adj.*

fish and chips *n.* fish fillets coated with batter and deep-fried, eaten with potato chips.

fish cake *n.* a fried flattened ball of flaked fish mixed with mashed potatoes.

fisher (ˈfɪʃə) *n.* **1.** a fisherman. **2.** Also called: **pekan. a.** a large North American marten having dark brown fur. **b.** the fur of this animal.

fisherman (ˈfɪʃəmən) *n., pl.* **-men. 1.** a person who fishes as a profession or for sport. **2.** a vessel used for fishing.

fishery (ˈfɪʃərɪ) *n., pl.* **-eries. 1. a.** the industry of catching, processing, and selling fish. **b.** a place where this is carried on. **2.** a place where fish are reared. **3.** a fishing ground.

Fishes (ˈfɪʃɪz) *n.* **the.** the constellation Pisces, the twelfth sign of the zodiac.

fish-eye lens *n. Photog.* a lens of small focal length, having a highly curved protruding front element that covers almost 180°.

fishfinger (ˈfɪʃˈfɪŋgə) *or U.S. & Canad.* **fish stick** *n.* an oblong piece of filleted or minced fish coated in breadcrumbs.

fish hawk *n.* another name for the **osprey.**

fish-hook *n.* a sharp hook used in angling, esp. one with a barb.

fishing (ˈfɪʃɪŋ) *n.* **a.** the occupation of catching fish. **b.** (*as modifier*): *a fishing match.*

fishing rod *n.* a long tapered flexible pole for use with a fishing line and, usually, a reel.

fish joint *n.* a connection formed by fishplates at the meeting point of two rails, beams, etc.

fish meal *n.* ground dried fish used as feed for farm animals, as a fertilizer, etc.

fishmonger (ˈfɪʃˌmʌŋgə) *n. Chiefly Brit.* a retailer of fish.

fishnet (ˈfɪʃˌnɛt) *n.* **a.** an open mesh fabric resembling netting. **b.** (*as modifier*): *fishnet tights.*

fish out *vb.* (*tr., adv.*) to find or extract (something): *to fish keys out of a pocket.*

fishplate (ˈfɪʃˌpleɪt) *n.* a flat piece of metal joining one rail or beam to the next, esp. on railway tracks.

fishtail (ˈfɪʃˌteɪl) *n.* **1.** an aeroplane manoeuvre in which the tail is moved from side to side to reduce speed. **2.** a nozzle having a long narrow slot at the top, placed over a Bunsen burner to produce a thin fanlike flame.

fishwife (ˈfɪʃˌwaɪf) *n., pl.* **-wives. 1.** a woman who sells fish. **2.** a coarse scolding woman.

fishy (ˈfɪʃɪ) *adj.* **fishier, fishiest. 1.** of, involving, or suggestive of fish. **2.** abounding in fish. **3.** *Inf.* suspicious, doubtful, or questionable. **4.** dull and lifeless: *a fishy look.* —ˈ**fishily** *adv.*

fissile (ˈfɪsaɪl) *adj.* **1.** *Brit.* capable of undergoing nuclear fission. **2.** fissionable. **3.** tending to split or capable of being split. [C17: < L, < *fissus* split]

fission (ˈfɪʃən) *n.* **1.** the act or process of splitting or breaking into parts. **2.** *Biol.* a form of asexual reproduction involving a division into two or more equal parts. **3.** short for **nuclear fission.** [C19: < L *fissiō* a cleaving] —ˈ**fissionable** *adj.*

fissiparous (fɪˈsɪpərəs) *adj. Biol.* reproducing by fission. —**fis**ˈ**siparously** *adv.*

fissure (ˈfɪʃə) *n.* **1.** any long narrow cleft or crack, esp. in a rock. **2.** a weakness or flaw. **3.** *Anat.* a narrow split or groove that divides an organ such as the brain, lung, or liver into lobes. ~*vb.* **4.** to crack or split apart. [C14: < Medical L *fissūra,* < L *fissus* split]

fist (fɪst) *n.* **1.** a hand with the fingers clenched into the palm, as for hitting. **2.** Also called: **fistful.** the quantity that can be held in a fist or hand. **3.** *Inf.* handwriting. **4.** an informal word for **index** (sense 9). ~*vb.* **5.** (*tr.*) to hit with the fist. [OE *fȳst*]

fisticuffs (ˈfɪstɪˌkʌfs) *pl. n.* combat with the fists. [C17: prob. < *fisty* with the fist + CUFF[2]]

fistula (ˈfɪstjʊlə) *n., pl.* **-las** *or* **-lae** (-ˌliː). *Pathol.* an abnormal opening between one hollow organ and another or between a hollow organ and the surface of the skin, caused by ulceration, malformation, etc. [C14: < L: pipe, tube, hollow reed, ulcer] —ˈ**fistulous** *or* ˈ**fistular** *adj.*

fit[1] (fɪt) *vb.* **fitting, fitted. 1.** to be appropriate or suitable for (a situation, etc.). **2.** to be of the correct size or shape for (a container, etc.). **3.** (*tr.*) to adjust in order to render appropriate. **4.** (*tr.*) to supply with that which is needed. **5.** (*tr.*) to try clothes on (someone) in order to make adjustments if necessary. **6.** (*tr.*) to make competent or ready. **7.** (*tr.*) to locate with care. **8.** (*intr.*) to correspond with the facts or circumstances. ~*adj.* **fitter, fittest.** **9.** appropriate. **10.** having the right qualifications; qualifying. **11.** in good health. **12.** worthy or deserving. **13.** (*foll. by an infinitive*) *Inf.* ready (to); strongly disposed (to): *she was fit to scream.* ~*n.* **14.** the manner in which something fits. **15.** the act or process of fitting. **16.** *Statistics.* the correspondence between observed and predicted characteristics of a distribution or model. ~See also **fit in, fit out.** [C14: prob. < MDu. *vitten;* rel. to ON *fitja* to knit] —**'fitly** *adv.* —**'fitness** *n.* —**'fittable** *adj.*

fit² (fɪt) *n.* **1.** *Pathol.* a sudden attack or convulsion, such as an epileptic seizure. **2.** a sudden spell of emotion: *a fit of anger.* **3.** an impulsive period of activity or lack of activity. **4. by** *or* **in fits (and starts).** in spasmodic spells. **5. have** *or* **throw a fit.** *Inf.* to become very angry. [OE *fitt* conflict]

fitch (fɪtʃ) *n.* **1.** a polecat. **2.** the fur of the polecat. [C16: prob. < *ficheux,* < OF, <?]

fitful ('fɪtfʊl) *adj.* characterized by or occurring in irregular spells. —**'fitfully** *adv.*

fit in *vb.* **1.** (*tr.*) to give a place or time to. **2.** (*intr., adv.*) to belong or conform, esp. after adjustment: *he didn't fit in with their plans.*

fitment ('fɪtmənt) *n.* **1.** *Machinery.* an accessory attached to an assembly of parts. **2.** *Chiefly Brit.* a detachable part of the furnishings of a room.

fit out *vb.* (*tr., adv.*) to equip.

fitted ('fɪtɪd) *adj.* **1.** designed for excellent fit: *a fitted suit.* **2.** (of a carpet) cut or sewn to cover a floor completely. **3. a.** (of furniture) built to fit a particular space: *a fitted cupboard.* **b.** (of a room) equipped with fitted furniture: *a fitted kitchen.* **4.** (of sheets) having ends that are elasticated and shaped to fit tightly over a mattress.

fitter ('fɪtə) *n.* **1.** a person who fits a garment, esp. when it is made for a particular person. **2.** a person who is skilled in the assembly and adjustment of machinery, esp. of a specified sort.

fitting ('fɪtɪŋ) *adj.* **1.** appropriate or proper. ~*n.* **2.** an accessory or part: *an electrical fitting.* **3.** (*pl.*) furnishings or accessories in a building. **4.** work carried out by a fitter. **5.** the act of trying on clothes so that they can be adjusted to fit. —**'fittingly** *adv.*

Fitzgerald-Lorentz contraction (fɪts'dʒɛrəld lɔː'rɛnts) *n.* the contraction that a moving body exhibits when its velocity approaches that of light. [C19: after G. F. *Fitzgerald* (1851–1901), Irish physicist & H. A. *Lorentz* (1853–1928), Du. physicist]

five (faɪv) *n.* **1.** the cardinal number that is the sum of four and one. **2.** a numeral, 5, V, etc., representing this number. **3.** the amount or quantity that is one greater than four. **4.** something representing, represented by, or consisting of five units, such as a playing card with five symbols on it. **5. five o'clock.** five hours after noon or midnight. ~*determiner.* **6. a.** amounting to five: *five nights.* **b.** (*as pronoun*): *choose any five you like.* ~See also **fives.** [OE *fīf*]

five-a-side *n.* a version of soccer with five players on each side.

five-eighth *n. Austral. & N.Z.* a rugby player positioned between the half-backs and three-quarters.

five-finger *n.* any of various plants having five-petalled flowers or five lobed leaves, such as cinquefoil and Virginia creeper.

fivefold ('faɪvˌfəʊld) *adj.* **1.** equal to or having five times as many or as much. **2.** composed of five parts. ~*adv.* **3.** by or up to five times as many or as much.

five-o'clock shadow *n.* beard growth visible late in the day on a man's shaven face.

fivepins ('faɪvˌpɪnz) *n.* (*functioning as sing.*) a bowling game using five pins, played esp. in Canada. —**'fiveˌpin** *adj.*

fiver ('faɪvə) *n. Brit. inf.* a five-pound note.

fives (faɪvz) *n.* (*functioning as sing.*) a ball game similar to squash but played with bats or the hands.

Five-Year Plan *n.* (in socialist economies) a government plan for economic development over a period of five years.

fix (fɪks) *vb.* (*mainly tr.*) **1.** (*also intr.*) to make or become firm, stable, or secure. **2.** to attach or place permanently. **3.** (often foll. by *up*) to settle definitely; decide. **4.** to hold or direct (eyes, etc.) steadily: *he fixed his gaze on the woman.* **5.** to call to attention or rivet. **6.** to make rigid: *to fix one's jaw.* **7.** to place or ascribe: *to fix the blame.* **8.** to mend or repair. **9.** *Inf.* to provide or be provided with: *how are you fixed for supplies?* **10.** *Inf.* to influence (a person, etc.) unfairly, as by bribery. **11.** *Sl.* to take revenge on. **12.** *Inf.* to give (someone) his just deserts: *that'll fix him.* **13.** *Inf., chiefly U.S. & Canad.* to prepare: *to fix a meal.* **14.** *Dialect or inf.* to spay or castrate (an animal). **15.** *Photog.* to treat (a film, plate, or paper) with fixer to make permanent the image rendered visible by developer. **16.** to convert (atmospheric nitrogen) into nitrogen compounds, as in the manufacture of fertilizers or the action of bacteria in the soil. **17.** to reduce (a substance) to a solid state or a less volatile state. **18.** (*intr.*) *Sl.* to inject a narcotic drug. ~*n.* **19.** *Inf.* a predicament; dilemma. **20.** the ascertaining of the navigational position, as of a ship, by radar, etc. **21.** *Sl.* an intravenous injection of a narcotic such as heroin. ~See also **fix up.** [C15: < Med. L *fixāre,* < L *fixus* fixed, < L *fīgere*] —**'fixable** *adj.*

fixate ('fɪkseɪt) *vb.* **1.** to become or cause to become fixed. **2.** *Psychol.* to engage in fixation. **3.** (*tr.; usually passive*) *Inf.* to obsess. [C19: < L *fixus* fixed + -ATE¹]

fixation (fɪk'seɪʃən) *n.* **1.** the act of fixing or the state of being fixed. **2.** a preoccupation or obsession. **3.** *Psychol.* **a.** the situation of being set in a certain way of thinking or acting. **b.** a strong attachment of a person to another person or an object in early life. **4.** *Chem.* the conversion of nitrogen in the air into a compound, esp. a fertilizer. **5.** the reduction of a substance to a nonvolatile or solid form.

fixative ('fɪksətɪv) *adj.* **1.** serving or tending to fix. ~*n.* **2.** a fluid sprayed over drawings to prevent smudging or one that fixes tissues and cells for microscopic study. **3.** a substance added to a liquid, such as a perfume, to make it less volatile.

fixed (fɪkst) *adj.* **1.** attached or placed so as to be immovable. **2.** stable: *fixed prices.* **3.** steadily directed: *a fixed expression.* **4.** established as to relative position: *a fixed point.* **5.** always at the same time: *a fixed holiday.* **6.** (of ideas, etc.) firmly maintained. **7.** (of an element) held in chemical combination: *fixed nitrogen.* **8.** (of a substance) nonvolatile. **9.** arranged. **10.** *Inf.* equipped or provided for, as with money, possessions, etc. **11.** *Inf.* illegally arranged: *a fixed trial.* —**fixedly** ('fɪksɪdlɪ) *adv.* —**'fixedness** *n.*

fixed assets *pl. n.* nontrading business assets of a relatively permanent nature, such as plant, fixtures, or goodwill. Also called: **capital assets.**

fixed oil *n.* a natural animal or vegetable oil that is not volatile: a mixture of esters of fatty acids.

fixed-point representation *n. Computers.* the representation of numbers by a single set of digits such that the radix point has a predetermined location. Cf. **floating-point representation.**

fixed satellite *n.* a satellite revolving in a stationary orbit so that it appears to remain over a fixed point on the earth's surface.

fixed star *n.* an extremely distant star whose position appears to be almost stationary over a long period of time.

fixer ('fɪksə) *n.* **1.** *Photog.* a solution used to dissolve unexposed silver halides after developing. **2.** *Sl.* a person who makes arrangements, esp. by underhand or illegal means.

fixity ('fɪksɪtɪ) *n., pl.* **-ties.** **1.** the state or quality of being fixed. **2.** a fixture.

fixture ('fɪkstʃə) *n.* **1.** an object firmly fixed in place, esp. a household appliance. **2.** a person or thing regarded as fixed in a particular place or position. **3.** *Property law.* an article attached to land and regarded as part of it. **4.** *Chiefly Brit.* **a.** a sports match or social occasion. **b.** the date of such an event. [C17: < LL *fixūra* a fastening (with *-t-* by analogy with *mixture*)]

fix up *vb.* (*tr., adv.*) **1.** to arrange: *let's fix up a date.* **2.** (often foll. by *with*) to provide: *I'm sure we can fix you up with a room.*

fizgig ('fɪzˌgɪg) *n.* **1.** a frivolous or flirtatious girl. **2.** a firework that fizzes as it moves. [C16: prob. < obs. *fise* a breaking of wind + *gig* girl]

fizz (fɪz) *vb.* (*intr.*) **1.** to make a hissing or bubbling sound. **2.** (of a drink) to produce bubbles of carbon dioxide. ~*n.* **3.** a hissing or bubbling sound. **4.** the bubbly quality of a drink; effervescence. **5.** any effervescent drink. [C17: imit.] —'**fizzy** *adj.* —'**fizziness** *n.*

fizzle ('fɪzᵊl) *vb.* (*intr.*) **1.** to make a hissing or bubbling sound. **2.** (often foll. by *out*) *Inf.* to fail or die out, esp. after a promising start. ~*n.* **3.** a hissing or bubbling sound. **4.** *Inf.* a failure. [C16: prob. < obs. *fist* to break wind]

fjord *or* **fiord** (fjɔːd) *n.* a long narrow inlet of the sea between high steep cliffs, common in Norway. [C17: < Norwegian, < ON *fjörthr;* see FIRTH, FORD]

FL *abbrev. for* Flight Lieutenant.

fl. *abbrev. for:* **1.** floor. **2.** floruit. **3.** fluid.

Fl. *abbrev. for:* **1.** Flanders. **2.** Flemish.

flab (flæb) *n.* unsightly or unwanted fat on the body. [C20: back formation < FLABBY]

flabbergast ('flæbəˌgɑːst) *vb.* (*tr.; usually passive*) *Inf.* to amaze utterly; astound. [C18: <?]

flabby ('flæbɪ) *adj.* **-bier, -biest.** **1.** loose or yielding: *flabby muscles.* **2.** having flabby flesh, esp. through being overweight. **3.** lacking vitality; weak. [C17: alteration of *flappy* < FLAP + -Y[1]; cf. Du. *flabbe* drooping lip] —'**flabbiness** *n.*

flaccid ('flæksɪd) *adj.* lacking firmness; soft and limp. [C17: < L *flaccidus,* < *flaccus*] —**flac'cidity** *n.*

flacon (*French* flakɔ̃) *n.* a small stoppered bottle, esp. used for perfume. [C19: < F; see FLAGON]

flag[1] (flæg) *n.* **1.** a piece of cloth, esp. bunting, often attached to a pole or staff, decorated with a design and used as an emblem, symbol, or standard or as a means of signalling. **2.** a small piece of paper, etc., sold on flag days. **3.** the conspicuously marked or shaped tail of a deer or of certain dogs. **4.** *Brit., Austral., & N.Z.* the part of a taximeter that is raised when a taxi is for hire. **5.** **show the flag. a.** to assert a claim by military presence. **b.** *Inf.* to make an appearance. ~*vb.* **flagging, flagged.** (*tr.*) **6.** to decorate or mark with a flag or flags. **7.** (often foll. by *down*) to warn or signal (a vehicle) to stop. **8.** to send or communicate (messages, information, etc.) by flag. [C16: <?] —'**flagger** *n.*

flag[2] (flæg) *n.* **1.** any of various plants that have long swordlike leaves, esp. an iris (**yellow flag**). **2.** the leaf of any such plant. [C14: prob. < ON]

flag[3] (flæg) *vb.* **flagging, flagged.** (*intr.*) **1.** to hang down; droop. **2.** to become weak or tired. [C16: <?]

flag[4] (flæg) *n.* **1.** short for **flagstone.** ~*vb.* **flagging, flagged. 2.** (*tr.*) to furnish (a floor, etc.) with flagstones.

flag day *n.* a day on which money is collected by a charity and small flags or emblems are given to contributors.

flagellant ('flædʒɪlənt, flə'dʒɛlənt) *or* **flagellator** ('flædʒɪˌleɪtə) *n.* a person who whips himself or others either as part of a religious penance or for sexual gratification. [C16: < L *flagellāre* to whip, < FLAGELLUM]

flagellate *vb.* ('flædʒɪˌleɪt). **1.** (*tr.*) to whip; flog. ~*adj.* ('flædʒɪlɪt), *also* **flagellated. 2.** possessing one or more flagella. **3.** whiplike. ~*n.* ('flædʒɪlɪt). **4.** a flagellate organism. —ˌ**flagel'lation** *n.*

flagellum (flə'dʒɛləm) *n., pl.* **-la** (-lə) *or* **-lums. 1.** *Biol.* a long whiplike outgrowth from a cell that acts as an organ of locomotion: occurs in some protozoans, gametes, etc. **2.** *Bot.* a long thin shoot or runner. [C19: < L: a little whip, < *flagrum* a whip, lash] —**fla'gellar** *adj.*

flageolet[1] (ˌflædʒə'lɛt) *n.* a high-pitched musical instrument of the recorder family. [C17: < F, modification of OF *flajolet* a little flute, < Vulgar L *flabeolum* (unattested), < L *flāre* to blow]

flageolet[2] (ˌflædʒə'lɛt) *n.* a type of kidney bean. [C19: < F, corruption of *fageolet,* dim. of *fageol,* < L *faseolus*]

flag fall *n. Austral.* the minimum charge for hiring a taxi.

flag of convenience *n.* a national flag flown by a ship registered in that country to gain financial or legal advantage.

flag of truce *n.* a white flag indicating an invitation to an enemy to negotiate.

flagon ('flægən) *n.* **1.** a large bottle of wine, cider, etc. **2.** a vessel having a handle, spout, and narrow neck. [C15: < OF *flascon,* < LL *flascō,* prob. of Gmc origin; see FLASK]

flagpole ('flægˌpəʊl) *or* **flagstaff** ('flægˌstɑːf) *n., pl.* **-poles, -staffs,** *or* **-staves** (-ˌsteɪvz). a pole or staff on which a flag is hoisted and displayed.

flagrant ('fleɪgrənt) *adj.* blatant; outrageous. [C15: < L *flagrāre* to blaze, burn] —'**flagrancy** *n.* —'**flagrantly** *adv.*

flagrante delicto (flə'græntɪ dɪ'lɪktəʊ) *adv.* See **in flagrante delicto.**

flagship ('flægˌʃɪp) *n.* **1.** a ship, esp. in a fleet, aboard which the commander of the fleet is quartered. **2.** the most important ship belonging to a shipping company. **3.** the item in a group considered most important esp. in establishing a public image: *costume drama is the flagship of the BBC.*

flagstone ('flægˌstəʊn) *n.* **1.** a hard fine-textured rock that can be split up into slabs for paving. **2.** a slab of such a rock. [C15 *flag* (in the sense: sod, turf), < ON *flaga* slab; cf. OE *flæcg* plaster, poultice]

flag-waving *n. Inf.* an emotional appeal intended to arouse patriotic feeling. —'**flag-ˌwaver** *n.*

flail (fleɪl) *n.* **1.** an implement used for threshing grain, consisting of a wooden handle with a free-swinging metal or wooden bar attached to it. ~*vb.* **2.** (*tr.*) to beat with or as if with a flail. **3.** to thresh about: *with arms flailing.* [C12 *fleil,* ult. < LL *flagellum* flail, < L: whip]

flair (flɛə) *n.* **1.** natural ability; talent. **2.** perceptiveness. **3.** *Inf.* stylishness or elegance: *to dress with flair.* [C19: < F, lit.: sense of smell, < OF: scent, ult. < L *frāgrāre* to smell sweet; see FRAGRANT]

flak (flæk) *n.* **1.** anti-aircraft fire or artillery. **2.** *Inf.* adverse criticism. [C20: < G *Fl(ieger)a(bwehr)k(anone),* lit.: aircraft defence gun]

flake[1] (fleɪk) *n.* **1.** a small thin piece or layer chipped off or detached from an object or substance. **2.** a small piece or particle: *a flake of snow.* **3.** *Archaeol.* a fragment removed by chipping from a larger stone used as a tool or weapon. ~*vb.* **4.** to peel or cause to peel off in flakes. **5.** to cover or become covered with or as with flakes. **6.** (*tr.*) to form into flakes. [C14: < ON]

flake[2] (fleɪk) *n.* a rack or platform for drying fish. [C14: < ON *flaki;* rel. to Du. *vlaak* hurdle]

flake out *vb.* (*intr., adv.*) *Inf.* to collapse or fall asleep as through extreme exhaustion.

flake white *n.* a pigment made from flakes of white lead.

flak jacket *n.* a reinforced jacket for protection against gunfire or shrapnel worn by soldiers, policemen, etc.

flaky ('fleɪkɪ) *adj.* **flakier, flakiest. 1.** like or made of flakes. **2.** tending to break easily into flakes. **3.** Also spelt: **flakey.** *U.S. sl.* eccentric; crazy. —'**flakily** *adv.* —'**flakiness** *n.*

flambé ('flɑːmbeɪ) *adj.* (of food, such as steak or pancakes) served in flaming brandy, etc. [F, p.p. of *flamber* to FLAME]

flambeau ('flæmbəʊ) *n., pl.* **-beaux** (-bəʊ, -bəʊz) *or* **-beaus.** a burning torch, as used in night processions, etc. [C17: < OF: torch, lit.: a little flame, < *flambe* FLAME]

flamboyant (flæm'bɔɪənt) *adj.* **1.** elaborate or extravagant; showy. **2.** rich or brilliant in colour.

3. exuberant or ostentatious. **4.** of the French Gothic style of architecture characterized by flamelike tracery and elaborate carving. [C19: < F: flaming, < *flamboyer* to FLAME] —**flam'boyance** *or* **flam'boyancy** *n.* —**flam'boyantly** *adv.*

flame (fleɪm) *n.* **1.** a hot usually luminous body of burning gas emanating in flickering streams from burning material or produced by a jet of ignited gas. **2.** (*often pl.*) the state or condition of burning with flames: *to burst into flames.* **3.** a brilliant light. **4. a.** a strong reddish-orange colour. **b.** (*as adj.*): *a flame carpet.* **5.** intense passion or ardour. **6.** *Inf.* a lover or sweetheart (esp. in **an old flame**). ~*vb.* **7.** to burn or cause to burn brightly. **8.** (*intr.*) to become red or fiery: *his face flamed with anger.* **9.** (*intr.*) to become angry or excited. **10.** (*tr.*) to apply a flame to (something). [C14: < Anglo-F, < OF *flambe,* < L *flammula* a little flame, < *flamma* flame] —'**flame,like** *adj.* —'**flamy** *adj.*

flame gun *n.* a type of flame-thrower for destroying garden weeds, etc.

flamen ('fleɪmɛn) *n., pl.* **flamens** *or* **flamines** ('flæmɪˌniːz). (in ancient Rome) any of 15 priests who each served a particular deity. [C14: < L; prob. rel. to OE *blōtan* to sacrifice, Gothic *blotan* to worship]

flamenco (flə'mɛŋkəʊ) *n., pl.* **-cos. 1.** a type of dance music for vocal soloist and guitar, characterized by sad mood. **2.** the dance performed to such music. [< Sp.: like a Gipsy, lit.: Fleming, < MDu. *Vlaminc* Fleming]

flameout ('fleɪmˌaʊt) *n.* the failure of an aircraft jet engine in flight due to extinction of the flame.

flame-thrower *n.* a weapon that ejects a stream or spray of burning fluid.

flame tree *n.* any of various tropical trees with red or orange flowers.

flaming ('fleɪmɪŋ) *adj.* **1.** burning with or emitting flames. **2.** glowing brightly. **3.** intense or ardent: *a flaming temper.* **4.** *Inf.* (intensifier): *you flaming idiot.*

flamingo (flə'mɪŋgəʊ) *n., pl.* **-gos** *or* **-goes.** a large wading bird having a pink-and-red plumage and downward-bent bill and inhabiting brackish lakes. [C16: < Port., < Provençal, < L *flamma* flame + Gmc suffix *-ing* denoting descent from; cf. -ING[3]]

flammable ('flæməbəl) *adj.* readily combustible; inflammable. —ˌ**flamma'bility** *n.*

▷ **Usage.** *Flammable* and *inflammable* are interchangeable when used of the properties of materials. *Flammable* is, however, often preferred for warning labels as there is less likelihood of misunderstanding (*inflammable* being sometimes taken to mean *not flammable*). The word that does mean *not flammable* is *nonflammable.*

flan (flæn) *n.* **1.** an open pastry or sponge tart filled with fruit or a savoury mixture. **2.** a piece of metal ready to receive the die or stamp in the production of coins. [C19: < F, < OF *flaon,* < LL *fladō* flat cake, of Gmc origin]

flange (flændʒ) *n.* **1.** a radially projecting collar or rim on an object for strengthening it or for attaching it to another object. **2.** a flat outer face of a rolled-steel joist. ~*vb.* **3.** (*tr.*) to provide (a component) with a flange. [C17: prob. changed < earlier *flaunche* curved segment at side of a heraldic field, < F *flanc* FLANK] —**flanged** *adj.* —'**flangeless** *adj.*

flank (flæŋk) *n.* **1.** the side of a man or animal between the ribs and the hip. **2.** a cut of beef from the flank. **3.** the side of anything, such as a mountain or building. **4.** the side of a naval or military formation. ~*vb.* **5.** (when *intr.*, often foll. by *on* or *upon*) to be located at the side of (an object, etc.). **6.** *Mil.* to position or guard on or beside the flank of (a formation, etc.). [C12: < OF *flanc,* of Gmc origin]

flanker ('flæŋkə) *n.* **1.** one of a detachment of soldiers detailed to guard the flanks. **2.** a fortification used to protect a flank. **3.** Also called: **flank forward.** *Rugby.* another name for **winger.**

flannel ('flænəl) *n.* **1.** a soft light woollen fabric with a slight nap, used for clothing, etc. **2.** (*pl.*) trousers or other garments made of flannel. **3.** *Brit.* a small piece of cloth used to wash the face and hands; face flannel. U.S. and Canad. equivalent: **washcloth. 4.** *Brit. inf.* indirect or evasive talk. ~*vb.* **-nelling, -nelled** *or U.S.* **-neling, -neled.** (*tr.*) **5.** to cover or wrap with flannel. **6.** to rub or polish with flannel. **7.** *Brit. inf.* to flatter. [C14: prob. var. of *flanen* sackcloth, < Welsh, < *gwlân* wool] —'**flannelly** *adj.*

flannelette (ˌflænə'lɛt) *n.* a cotton imitation of flannel.

flap (flæp) *vb.* **flapping, flapped. 1.** to move (wings or arms) up and down, esp. in or as if in flying, or (of wings or arms) to move in this way. **2.** to move or cause to move noisily back and forth or up and down: *the curtains flapped in the breeze.* **3.** (*intr.*) *Inf.* to become agitated or flustered. **4.** to deal (a person or thing) a blow with a broad flexible object. ~*n.* **5.** the action, motion, or noise made by flapping: *with one flap of its wings the bird was off.* **6.** a piece of material, etc., attached at one edge and usually used to cover an opening, as on a tent, envelope, or pocket. **7.** a blow dealt with a flat object. **8.** a movable surface fixed to an aircraft wing that increases lift during takeoff and drag during landing. **9.** *Inf.* a state of panic or agitation. [C14: prob. imit.]

flapdoodle ('flæpˌduːdəl) *n. Sl.* foolish talk; nonsense. [C19: <?]

flapjack ('flæpˌdʒæk) *n.* **1.** a chewy biscuit made with rolled oats. **2.** *Chiefly U.S. & Canad.* another word for **pancake.**

flapper ('flæpə) *n.* (in the 1920s) a young woman, esp. one flaunting her unconventional behaviour.

flare (flɛə) *vb.* **1.** to burn or cause to burn with an unsteady or sudden bright flame. **2.** to burn off excess gas or oil. **3.** to spread or cause to spread outwards from a narrow to a wider shape. ~*n.* **4.** an unsteady flame. **5.** a sudden burst of flame. **6. a.** a blaze of light or fire used to illuminate, signal distress, alert, etc. **b.** the device producing such a blaze. **7.** a spreading shape or anything with a spreading shape: *a skirt with a flare.* **8.** an open flame used to burn off unwanted gas at an oil well. **9.** *Astron.* short for **solar flare.** [C16 (to spread out): <?]

flare-up *n.* **1.** a sudden burst of fire or light. **2.** *Inf.* a sudden burst of emotion or violence. ~*vb.* **flare up.** (*intr., adv.*). **3.** to burst suddenly into fire or light. **4.** *Inf.* to burst into anger.

flash (flæʃ) *n.* **1.** a sudden short blaze of intense light or flame: *a flash of sunlight.* **2.** a sudden occurrence or display, esp. one suggestive of brilliance: *a flash of understanding.* **3.** a very brief space of time: *over in a flash.* **4.** Also called: **news flash.** a short news announcement concerning a new event. **5.** Also called: **patch.** *Chiefly Brit.* an insignia or emblem worn on a uniform, vehicle, etc., to identify its military formation. **6.** a sudden rush of water down a river or watercourse. **7.** *Photog., inf.* short for **flashlight** (sense 2). **8.** (*modifier*) involving, using, or produced by a flash of heat, light, etc.: *flash distillation.* **9. flash in the pan.** a project, person, etc., that enjoys only short-lived success. ~*adj.* **10.** *Inf.* ostentatious or vulgar. **11.** sham or counterfeit. **12.** *Inf.* relating to or characteristic of the criminal underworld. **13.** brief and rapid: *flash freezing.* ~*vb.* **14.** to burst or cause to burst suddenly or intermittently into flame. **15.** to emit or reflect or cause to emit or reflect light suddenly or intermittently. **16.** (*intr.*) to move very fast: *he flashed by on his bicycle.* **17.** (*intr.*) to come rapidly (into the mind or vision). **18.** (*intr.;* foll. by *out* or *up*) to appear like a sudden light. **19. a.** to signal or communicate very fast: *to flash a message.* **b.** to signal by use of a light, such as car headlights. **20.** (*tr.*) *Inf.* to display ostentatiously: *to flash money around.* **21.** (*tr.*) *Inf.* to show suddenly and briefly. **22.** (*intr.*) *Brit. sl.* to expose oneself indecently. **23.** to send a sudden rush of water down (a river, etc.), or to carry (a vessel) down by this method. [C14 (in the sense: to rush, as of water): <?] —ˈ**flasher** *n.*

flashback (ˈflæʃˌbæk) *n.* a transition in a novel, film, etc., to an earlier scene or event.

flashboard (ˈflæʃˌbɔːd) *n.* a board or boarding that is placed along the top of a dam to increase its height and capacity.

flashbulb (ˈflæʃˌbʌlb) *n. Photog.* a small expendable glass light bulb that is triggered, usually electrically, to produce a bright flash of light.

flash burn *n. Pathol.* a burn caused by momentary exposure to intense radiant heat.

flash card *n.* a card on which are written or printed words for children to look at briefly, used as an aid to learning.

flashcube (ˈflæʃˌkjuːb) *n.* a boxlike camera attachment, holding four flashbulbs, that turns so that each flashbulb can be used.

flash flood *n.* a sudden short-lived torrent, usually caused by a heavy storm, esp. in desert regions.

flash gun *n.* a device, sometimes incorporated in a camera, for holding and electrically firing a flashbulb as the shutter opens.

flashing (ˈflæʃɪŋ) *n.* a weatherproof material, esp. thin sheet metal, used to cover the valleys between the slopes of a roof, the junction between a chimney and a roof, etc.

flashlight (ˈflæʃˌlaɪt) *n.* **1.** another word (esp. U.S. and Canad.) for **torch. 2.** *Photog.* the brief bright light emitted by a flashbulb or electronic flash. Often shortened to **flash.**

flash point *n.* **1.** the lowest temperature at which the vapour above a liquid can be ignited in air. **2.** a critical time or place beyond which a situation will inevitably erupt into violence.

flashy (ˈflæʃɪ) *adj.* **flashier, flashiest. 1.** brilliant and dazzling, esp. for a short time or in a superficial way. **2.** cheap and ostentatious. —ˈ**flashily** *adv.* —ˈ**flashiness** *n.*

flask (flɑːsk) *n.* **1.** a bottle with a narrow neck, esp. used in a laboratory or for wine, oil, etc. **2.** Also called: **hip flask.** a small flattened container of glass or metal designed to be carried in a pocket, esp. for liquor. **3.** See **vacuum flask.** [C14: < OF, < Med. L *flasca, flasco,* ? of Gmc origin; cf. OE *flasce, flaxe*]

flat[1] (flæt) *adj.* **flatter, flattest. 1.** horizontal; level: *a flat roof.* **2.** even or smooth, without projections or depressions: *a flat surface.* **3.** lying stretched out at full length: *he lay flat on the ground.* **4.** having little depth or thickness: *a flat dish.* **5.** (*postpositive;* often foll. by *against*) having a surface or side in complete contact with another surface: *flat against the wall.* **6.** (of a tyre) deflated. **7.** (of shoes) having an unraised heel. **8.** *Chiefly Brit.* **a.** (of races, racetracks, or racecourses) not having obstacles to be jumped. **b.** of, relating to, or connected with flat racing as opposed to steeplechasing and hurdling. **9.** without qualification; total: *a flat denial.* **10.** fixed: *a flat rate.* **11.** (*prenominal or immediately postpositive*) neither more nor less; exact: *he did the journey in thirty minutes flat.* **12.** unexciting: *a flat joke.* **13.** without variation or resonance; monotonous: *a flat voice.* **14.** (of beer, sparkling wines, etc.) having lost effervescence, as by exposure to air. **15.** (of trade, business, etc.) commercially inactive. **16.** (of a battery) fully discharged. **17.** (of a print, photograph, or painting) lacking contrast. **18.** (of paint) without gloss or lustre. **19.** *Music.* **a.** (*immediately postpositive*) denoting a note of a given letter name (or the sound it represents) that has been lowered in pitch by one chromatic semitone: *B flat.* **b.** (of an instrument, voice, etc.) out of tune by being too low in pitch. Cf. **sharp** (sense 12). **20.** *Phonetics.* **flat a.** the vowel sound of *a* as in the usual U.S. or S Brit. pronunciation of *hand, cat.* ~*adv.* **21.** in or into a prostrate, level, or flat state or position: *he held his hand out flat.* **22.** completely or utterly; absolutely. **23.** exactly; precisely: *in three minutes flat.* **24.** *Music.* **a.** lower than a standard pitch. **b.** too low in pitch: *she sings flat.* Cf. **sharp** (sense 17). **25. fall flat (on one's face).** to fail to achieve a desired effect. **26. flat out.** *Inf.* **a.** with the maximum speed or effort. **b.** totally exhausted. ~*n.* **27.** a flat object, surface, or part. **28.** (*often pl.*) a low-lying tract of land, esp. a marsh or swamp. **29.** (*often pl.*) a mud bank exposed at low tide. **30.** *Music.* **a.** an accidental that lowers the pitch of a note by one chromatic semitone. Usual symbol: ♭ **b.** a note affected by this accidental. Cf. **sharp** (sense 18). **31.** *Theatre.* a wooden frame covered with painted canvas, etc., used to form part of a stage setting. **32.** a punctured car tyre. **33.** (*often cap.;* preceded by *the*) *Chiefly Brit.* **a.** flat racing, esp. as opposed to steeplechasing and hurdling. **b.** the season of flat racing. ~*vb.* **flatting, flatted. 34.** to make or become flat. [C14: < ON *flatr*] —ˈ**flatly** *adv.* —ˈ**flatness** *n.* —ˈ**flattish** *adj.*

flat[2] (flæt) *n.* a set of rooms comprising a residence entirely on one floor of a building. Usual U.S. and Canad. name: **apartment.** [OE *flett* floor, hall, house]

flatbed lorry (ˈflætˌbɛd) *n.* a lorry with a flat platform for its body.

flatboat (ˈflætˌbəʊt) *n.* any boat with a flat bottom, usually for transporting goods on a canal.

flatette (ˌflætˈɛt) *n. Austral.* a flat having only a few rooms.

flatfish (ˈflætˌfɪʃ) *n., pl.* **-fish** *or* **-fishes.** any of an order of marine spiny-finned fish including the halibut, plaice, turbot, and sole, all of which have a flat body which has both eyes on the uppermost side.

flatfoot (ˈflætˌfʊt) *n.* **1.** Also called: **splayfoot.** a condition in which the instep arch of the foot is flattened. **2.** (*pl.* **-foots** *or* **-feet**) a slang word (usually derogatory) for a **policeman.**

flat-footed (ˌflætˈfʊtɪd) *adj.* **1.** having flatfoot. **2.** *Inf.* **a.** awkward. **b.** downright. **3.** *Inf.* off guard (often in **catch flat-footed**). —ˌ**flat-**ˈ**footedly** *adv.* —ˌ**flat-**ˈ**footedness** *n.*

flathead (ˈflætˌhɛd) *n., pl.* **-head** *or* **-heads.** a Pacific food fish which resembles the gurnard.

flatiron (ˈflætˌaɪən) *n.* (formerly) an iron for pressing clothes that was heated by being placed on a stove, etc.

flatlet (ˈflætlɪt) *n.* a flat having only a few rooms.

flat racing *n.* **a.** the racing of horses on racecourses without jumps. **b.** (*as modifier*): *the flat-racing season.*

flat spin *n.* **1.** an aircraft spin in which the longitudinal axis is more nearly horizontal than vertical. **2.** *Inf.* a state of confusion; dither.

flatten (ˈflæt^{ə}n) *vb.* **1.** (sometimes foll. by *out*) to make or become flat or flatter. **2.** (*tr.*) *Inf.* **a.** to knock down or injure. **b.** to crush or subdue. **3.** (*tr.*) *Music.* to lower the pitch of (a note) by one chromatic semitone. —ˈ**flattener** *n.*

flatter (ˈflætə) *vb.* **1.** to praise insincerely, esp. in order to win favour or reward. **2.** to show to advantage: *that dress flatters her.* **3.** (*tr.*) to make to appear more attractive, etc., than in reality. **4.** to gratify the vanity of (a person). **5.** (*tr.*) to encourage, esp. falsely. **6.** (*tr.*) to deceive (oneself): *I flatter myself that I am the best.* [C13: prob. < OF *flater* to lick, fawn upon, of Frankish origin] —ˈ**flatterable** *adj.* —ˈ**flatterer** *n.*

flattery (ˈflætərɪ) *n., pl.* **-teries. 1.** the act of flattering. **2.** excessive or insincere praise.

flattie (ˈflætɪ) *n. N.Z. inf.* a flounder or other flatfish.

flatties (ˈflætɪz) *pl. n.* shoes with flat heels or no heels.

flat top *n.* a style of haircut in which the hair is cut shortest on the top of the head so that it stands up from the scalp and appears flat from the crown to the forehead.

flatulent (ˈflætjʊlənt) *adj.* **1.** suffering from or caused by an excessive amount of gas in the alimentary canal. **2.** generating excessive gas in the alimentary canal. **3.** pretentious. [C16: < NL *flātulentus,* < L *flatus,* < *flāre* to breathe, blow] —ˈ**flatulence** *or* ˈ**flatulency** *n.* —ˈ**flatulently** *adv.*

flatus (ˈfleɪtəs) *n., pl.* **-tuses.** gas generated in the alimentary canal. [C17: < L: a blowing, < *flāre* to breathe, blow]

flatworm (ˈflætˌwɜːm) *n.* any parasitic or free-living invertebrate of the phylum *Platyhelminthes,* including flukes and tapeworms, having a flattened body.

flaunt (flɔːnt) *vb.* **1.** to display (possessions, oneself, etc.) ostentatiously. **2.** to wave or cause to wave freely. ~*n.* **3.** the act of flaunting. [C16: ? of Scand. origin]

▷ **Usage.** See at **flout.**

flautist (ˈflɔːtɪst) *or U.S.* **flutist** (ˈfluːtɪst) *n.* a player of the flute. [C19: < It. *flautista,* < *flauto* FLUTE]

flavescent (fləˈvɛsᵊnt) *adj.* turning yellow; yellowish. [C19: < L *flāvēscere* to become yellow, < *flāvus* yellow]

flavin *or* **flavine** (ˈfleɪvɪn) *n.* **1.** a heterocyclic ketone that forms the nucleus of certain natural yellow pigments, such as riboflavin. **2.** any yellow pigment based on flavin. [C19: < L *flāvus* yellow]

flavine (ˈfleɪvɪn) *n.* another name for **acriflavine hydrochloride.**

flavone (ˈfleɪvəʊn) *n.* **1.** a crystalline compound occurring in plants. **2.** any of a class of yellow plant pigments derived from flavone. [C19: < G, < L *flāvus* yellow + -ONE]

flavoprotein (ˌfleɪvəʊˈprəʊtiːn) *n.* any of a group of enzymes that contain a derivative of riboflavin linked to a protein and catalyse oxidation in cells.

flavour *or U.S.* **flavor** (ˈfleɪvə) *n.* **1.** taste perceived in food or liquid in the mouth. **2.** a substance added to food, etc., to impart a specific taste. **3.** a distinctive quality or atmosphere. ~*vb.* **4.** (*tr.*) to impart a flavour or quality to. [C14: < OF *flaour,* < LL *flātor* (unattested) bad smell, breath, < L *flāre* to blow] —ˈ**flavourless** *or U.S.* ˈ**flavorless** *adj.* —ˈ**flavourful** *or U.S.* ˈ**flavorful** *adj.*

flavour enhancer *n.* another term for **monosodium glutamate.**

flavouring *or U.S.* **flavoring** (ˈfleɪvərɪŋ) *n.* a substance used to impart a particular flavour to food: *rum flavouring.*

flaw[1] (flɔː) *n.* **1.** an imperfection or blemish. **2.** a crack or rift. **3.** *Law.* an invalidating defect in a document or proceeding. ~*vb.* **4.** to make or become blemished or imperfect. [C14: prob. < ON *flaga* stone slab] —ˈ**flawless** *adj.*

flaw[2] (flɔː) *n.* a sudden short gust of wind; squall. [C16: of Scand. origin]

flax (flæks) *n.* **1.** a herbaceous plant or shrub that has blue flowers and is cultivated for its seeds (flaxseed) and for the fibres of its stems. **2.** the fibre of this plant, made into thread and woven into linen fabrics. **3.** any of various similar plants. **4.** *N.Z.* a swamp plant producing a fibre that is used by Maoris for decorative work, baskets, etc. [OE *fleax*]

flaxen (ˈflæksən) *adj.* **1.** of or resembling flax. **2.** of a soft yellow colour: *flaxen hair.*

flaxseed (ˈflæksˌsiːd) *n.* the seed of the flax plant, which yields linseed oil. Also called: **linseed.**

flay (fleɪ) *vb.* (*tr.*) **1.** to strip off the skin or outer covering of, esp. by whipping. **2.** to attack with savage criticism. [OE *flēan*] —ˈ**flayer** *n.*

flea (fliː) *n.* **1.** a small wingless parasitic blood-sucking jumping insect living on the skin of mammals and birds. **2. flea in one's ear.** *Inf.* a sharp rebuke. [OE *flēah*]

fleabane (ˈfliːˌbeɪn) *n.* any of several plants, including one having purplish tubular flower heads with orange centres and one having yellow daisy-like flower heads, that are reputed to ward off fleas.

fleabite (ˈfliːˌbaɪt) *n.* **1.** the bite of a flea. **2.** a slight or trifling annoyance or discomfort.

flea-bitten *adj.* **1.** bitten by or infested with fleas. **2.** *Inf.* shabby or decrepit.

flea market *n.* an open-air market selling cheap and often second-hand goods.

fleapit (ˈfliːˌpɪt) *n. Inf.* a shabby cinema or theatre.

fleawort (ˈfliːˌwɜːt) *n.* **1.** any of various plants with yellow daisy-like flowers and rosettes of downy leaves. **2.** a Eurasian plantain whose seeds were formerly used as a flea repellent.

flèche (fleɪʃ, flɛʃ) *n.* a slender spire, esp. over the intersection of the nave and transept ridges of a church roof. Also called: **spirelet.** [C18: < F: spire (lit.: arrow), prob. of Gmc origin]

fleck (flɛk) *n.* **1.** a small marking or streak. **2.** a speck: *a fleck of dust.* ~*vb.* **3.** (*tr.*) Also: **flecker.** to speckle. [C16: prob. < ON *flekkr* stain, spot]

fled (flɛd) *vb.* the past tense and past participle of **flee.**

fledge (flɛdʒ) *vb.* (*tr.*) **1.** to feed and care for (a young bird) until it is able to fly. **2.** Also called: **fletch.** to fit (something, esp. an arrow) with a feather or feathers. **3.** to cover or adorn with or as if with feathers. [OE *-flycge,* as in *unflycge* unfledged; see FLY[1]]

fledgling *or* **fledgeling** (ˈflɛdʒlɪŋ) *n.* **1.** a young bird that has grown feathers. **2.** a young and inexperienced person.

flee (fliː) *vb.* **fleeing, fled. 1.** to run away from (a place, danger, etc.). **2.** (*intr.*) to run or move quickly. [OE *flēon*] —ˈ**fleer** *n.*

fleece (fliːs) *n.* **1.** the coat of wool that covers the body of a sheep or similar animal. **2.** the wool removed from a single sheep. **3.** something resembling a fleece. **4.** sheepskin or a fabric with soft pile, used as a lining for coats, etc. ~*vb.* (*tr.*) **5.** to defraud or charge exorbitantly. **6.** another term for **shear** (sense 1). [OE *flēos*]

fleecie (ˈfliːsɪ) *n. N.Z.* a person who collects fleeces after shearing and prepares them for baling. Also called: **fleece-oh.**

fleecy (ˈfliːsɪ) *adj.* **fleecier, fleeciest.** of or resembling fleece. —ˈ**fleecily** *adv.*

fleer (flɪə) *Arch.* ~*vb.* **1.** to scoff; sneer. ~*n.* **2.** a derisory glance. [C14: < ON; cf. Norwegian *flire* to snigger]

fleet[1] (fliːt) *n.* **1.** a number of warships organized as a tactical unit. **2.** all the warships of a nation. **3.** a number of aircraft, ships, buses, etc., operating together or under the same ownership. [OE *flēot*]

fleet[2] (fliːt) *adj.* **1.** rapid in movement; swift. **2.** *Poetic.* fleeting. ~*vb.* **3.** (*intr.*) to move rapidly. **4.** (*tr.*) *Obs.* to cause (time) to pass rapidly. [prob. OE *flēotan* to float, glide rapidly] —ˈ**fleetly** *adv.* —ˈ**fleetness** *n.*

Fleet Air Arm *n.* the aviation branch of the Royal Navy.

fleet chief petty officer *n.* a noncommissioned officer in the Royal Navy comparable in rank to a warrant officer in the army or the Royal Air Force.

fleeting (ˈfliːtɪŋ) *adj.* rapid and transient: *a fleeting glimpse of the sea.* —ˈ**fleetingly** *adv.*

Fleet Street *n.* **1.** a street in central London in which many newspaper offices are situated. **2.** British journalism or journalists collectively.

Fleming (ˈflɛmɪŋ) *n.* a native or inhabitant of Flanders, a medieval principality in the Low Countries, or of Flemish-speaking Belgium.

Flemish (ˈflɛmɪʃ) *n.* **1.** one of the two official languages of Belgium. **2. the Flemish.** (*functioning as pl.*) the Flemings collectively. ~*adj.* **3.** of or characteristic of Flanders, the Flemings, or their language.

flense (flɛns), **flench** (flɛntʃ), *or* **flinch** (flɪntʃ) *vb.* (*tr.*) to strip (a whale, seal, etc.) of (its blubber or skin). [C19: < Danish *flense;* rel. to Du. *flensen*]

flesh (flɛʃ) *n.* **1.** the soft part of the body of an animal or human, esp. muscular tissue, as distinct from bone and viscera. **2.** *Inf.* excess weight; fat. **3.** *Arch.* the edible tissue of animals as opposed to that of fish or, sometimes, fowl. **4.** the thick soft part of a fruit or vegetable. **5.** the human body and its physical or sensual nature as opposed to the soul or spirit. Related adj.: **carnal. 6.** mankind in general. **7.** animate creatures in general. **8.** one's own family; kin (esp. in **one's own flesh and blood**). **9. a.** a yellowish-pink colour. **b.** (*as adj.*): *flesh tights.* **10. in the flesh.** in person; actually present. ~*vb.* **11.** (*tr.*) *Hunting.* to stimulate the hunting instinct of (hounds or falcons) by giving them small quantities of raw flesh. **12.** *Arch. or poetic.* to accustom or incite to bloodshed or battle by initial experience. **13.** to fatten; fill out. [OE *flǣsc*]

fleshings (ˈflɛʃɪŋz) *pl. n.* flesh-coloured tights.

fleshly (ˈflɛʃlɪ) *adj.* **-lier, -liest. 1.** relating to the body; carnal: *fleshly desire.* **2.** worldly as opposed to spiritual. **3.** fat. —ˈ**fleshliness** *n.*

flesh out *vb.* (*adv.*) **1.** (*tr.*) to give substance to (an argument, description, etc.). **2.** (*intr.*) to expand or become more substantial.

fleshpots (ˈflɛʃˌpɒts) *pl. n. Often facetious.* **1.** luxurious living. **2.** places where bodily desires are gratified. [C16: < the Biblical use as applied to Egypt (Exodus 16:3)]

flesh wound (wuːnd) *n.* a wound affecting superficial tissues.

fleshy (ˈflɛʃɪ) *adj.* **fleshier, fleshiest. 1.** plump. **2.** related to or resembling flesh. **3.** *Bot.* (of some fruits, etc.) thick and pulpy. —ˈ**fleshiness** *n.*

fletcher (ˈflɛtʃə) *n.* a person who makes arrows. [C14: < OF *flechier,* < *fleche* arrow; see FLÈCHE]

fleur-de-lis *or* **fleur-de-lys** (ˌflɜːdəˈliː) *n., pl.* **fleurs-de-lis** *or* **fleurs-de-lys** (ˌflɜːdəˈliːz). **1.** *Heraldry.* a charge representing a lily with three distinct petals. **2.** another name for **iris** (sense 2). [C19: < OF *flor de lis,* lit.: lily flower]

fleurette *or* **fleuret** (flʊəˈrɛt) *n.* an ornament or motif resembling a flower. [C19: F, lit.: a small flower, < *fleur* flower]

flew (fluː) *vb.* the past tense of **fly**[1].

flews (fluːz) *pl. n.* the fleshy hanging upper lip of a bloodhound or similar dog. [C16: <?]

flex (flɛks) *n.* **1.** *Brit.* a flexible insulated electric cable, used esp. to connect appliances to mains. U.S. and Canad. name: **cord.** ~*vb.* **2.** to bend or be bent: *he flexed his arm.* **3.** to contract (a muscle) or (of a muscle) to contract. **4.** (*intr.*) to work flexitime. [C16: < L *flexus* bent, winding, < *flectere* to bend, bow]

flexible (ˈflɛksɪbᵊl) *adj.* **1.** Also **flexile** (ˈflɛksaɪl). able to be bent easily without breaking. **2.** adaptable or variable: *flexible working hours.* **3.** able to be persuaded easily. —ˌ**flexiˈbility** *n.* —ˈ**flexibly** *adv.*

flexion (ˈflɛkʃən) *or* **flection** *n.* **1.** the act of bending a joint or limb. **2.** the condition of the joint or limb so bent. —ˈ**flexional** *adj.*

flexitime (ˈflɛksɪˌtaɪm) *n.* a system permitting flexibility of working hours at the beginning or end of the day, provided an agreed period (**core time**) is spent at work. Also called: **flextime.**

flexor (ˈflɛksə) *n.* any muscle whose contraction serves to bend a joint or limb. Cf. **extensor.** [C17: NL; see FLEX]

flexuous (ˈflɛksjʊəs) *adj.* full of bends or curves; winding. [C17: < L *flexuōsus* full of bends, tortuous, < *flexus* a bending; see FLEX] —ˈ**flexuously** *adv.*

flexure (ˈflɛkʃə) *n.* **1.** the act of flexing or the state of being flexed. **2.** a bend, turn, or fold.

flibbertigibbet (ˈflɪbətɪˌdʒɪbɪt) *n.* an irresponsible, silly, or gossipy person. [C15: <?]

flick[1] (flɪk) *vb.* **1.** (*tr.*) to touch with or as if with the finger or hand in a quick jerky movement. **2.** (*tr.*) to propel or remove by a quick jerky movement, usually of the fingers or hand. **3.** to move or cause to move quickly or jerkily. **4.** (*intr.*; foll. by *through*) to read or look at (a book, etc.) quickly or idly. ~*n.* **5.** a tap or quick stroke with the fingers, a whip, etc. **6.** the sound made by such a stroke. **7.** a fleck or particle. [C15: imit.; cf. F *flicflac*]

flick[2] (flɪk) *n. Sl.* **1.** a cinema film. **2. the flicks.** the cinema: *what's on at the flicks tonight?*

flicker[1] (ˈflɪkə) *vb.* **1.** (*intr.*) to shine with an unsteady or intermittent light. **2.** (*intr.*) to move quickly to and fro. **3.** (*tr.*) to cause to flicker. ~*n.* **4.** an unsteady or brief light or flame. **5.** a swift quivering or fluttering movement. [OE *flicorian*]

flicker[2] (ˈflɪkə) *n.* a North American woodpecker which has a yellow undersurface to the wings and tail. [C19: ? imit. of the bird's call]

flick knife *n.* a knife with a retractable blade that springs out when a button is pressed.

flier *or* **flyer** (ˈflaɪə) *n.* **1.** a person or thing that flies or moves very fast. **2.** an aviator or pilot. **3.** *Inf.* a long flying leap. **4.** a rectangular step in a straight flight of stairs. Cf. **winder** (sense 5). **5.** *Athletics. Inf.* a flying start. **6.** *Chiefly U.S.* a speculative business transaction.

flight[1] (flaɪt) *n.* **1.** the act, skill, or manner of flying. **2.** a journey made by a flying animal or object. **3.** a group of flying birds or aircraft: a *flight of swallows.* **4.** the basic tactical unit of a military air force. **5.** a journey through space, esp. of a spacecraft. **6.** an aircraft flying on a scheduled journey. **7.** a soaring mental journey above or beyond the normal everyday world: *a flight of fancy.* **8.** a single line of hurdles across a track in a race. **9.** a feather or plastic attachment fitted to an arrow or dart to give it stability in flight. **10.** a set of steps or stairs between one landing or floor and the next. ~*vb.* (*tr.*) **11.** *Sport.* to cause (a ball, dart, etc.) to float slowly towards its target. **12.** to shoot (a bird) in flight. **13.** to fledge (an arrow or dart). [OE *flyht*]

flight[2] (flaɪt) *n.* **1.** the act of fleeing or running away, as from danger. **2. put to flight.** to cause to run away. **3. take (to) flight.** to run away; flee. [OE *flyht* (unattested)]

flight deck *n.* **1.** the crew compartment in an airliner. **2.** the upper deck of an aircraft carrier from which aircraft take off.

flightless (ˈflaɪtlɪs) *adj.* (of certain birds and insects) unable to fly. See also **ratite.**

flight lieutenant *n.* an officer holding a commissioned rank senior to a flying officer and junior to a squadron leader in the Royal Air Force.

flight path *n.* the course through the air of an aircraft, rocket, or projectile.

flight recorder *n.* an electronic device fitted to an aircraft for collecting and storing information concerning its performance in flight. It is often used to determine the cause of a crash. Also called: **black box.**

flight sergeant *n.* a noncommissioned officer in the Royal Air Force, junior in rank to that of master aircrew.

flight simulator *n.* a ground-training device that reproduces exactly the conditions experienced on the flight deck of an aircraft.

flighty (ˈflaɪtɪ) *adj.* **flightier, flightiest. 1.** frivolous and irresponsible. **2.** mentally erratic or wandering. —ˈ**flightiness** *n.*

flimflam (ˈflɪmˌflæm) *Inf.* ~*n.* **1. a.** nonsense; rubbish; foolishness. **b.** (*as modifier*): *flimflam arguments.* **2.** a deception; trick; swindle. ~*vb.* **-flamming, -flammed. 3.** (*tr.*) to deceive; trick; swindle; cheat. [C16: prob. of Scand. origin] —ˈ**flimˌflammer** *n.*

flimsy (ˈflɪmzɪ) *adj.* **-sier, -siest. 1.** not strong or substantial: *a flimsy building.* **2.** light and thin: *a flimsy dress.* **3.** unconvincing; weak: *a flimsy excuse.* ~*n.* **4.** thin paper used for making carbon copies of a letter, etc. **5.** a copy made on such paper. [C17: <?] —ˈ**flimsiness** *n.*

flinch (flɪntʃ) *vb.* (*intr.*) **1.** to draw back suddenly, as from pain, shock, etc.; wince. **2.** (often foll. by *from*) to avoid contact (with): *he never flinched from his duty.* [C16: < OF *flenchir;* rel. to MHG *lenken* to bend, direct] —ˈ**flinchingly** *adv.*

flinders (ˈflɪndəz) *pl. n. Rare.* small fragments or splinters (esp. in **fly into flinders**). [C15: prob. < ON; cf. Norwegian *flindra* thin piece of stone]

fling (flɪŋ) *vb.* **flinging, flung.** (*mainly tr.*) **1.** to throw, esp. with force or abandon. **2.** to put or send without warning or preparation: *to fling someone into jail.* **3.** (*also intr.*) to move (oneself or a part of the body) with abandon or speed. **4.** (usually foll. by *into*) to apply (oneself) diligently and with vigour (to). **5.** to cast aside: *she flung away her scruples.* ~*n.* **6.** the act or an instance of flinging. **7.** a period or occasion of unrestrained or extravagant behaviour. **8.** any of various vigorous Scottish reels full of leaps and turns, such as the Highland fling. **9.** a trial; try: *to* *have a fling at something different.* [C13: < ON] —'**flinger** *n.*

flint (flɪnt) *n.* **1.** an impure greyish-black form of quartz that occurs in chalk. It produces sparks when struck with steel and is used in the manufacture of pottery and road-construction materials. Formula: SiO_2. **2.** any piece of flint, esp. one used as a primitive tool or for striking fire. **3.** a small cylindrical piece of an iron alloy, used in cigarette lighters. **4.** Also called: **flint glass.** colourless glass other than plate glass. [OE]

flintlock ('flɪnt,lɒk) *n.* **1.** an obsolete gunlock in which the charge is ignited by a spark produced by a flint in the hammer. **2.** a firearm having such a lock.

flinty ('flɪntɪ) *adj.* **flintier, flintiest. 1.** of or resembling flint. **2.** hard or cruel; unyielding. —'**flintily** *adv.* —'**flintiness** *n.*

flip (flɪp) *vb.* **flipping, flipped. 1.** to throw (something light or small) carelessly or briskly. **2.** to throw or flick (an object such as a coin) so that it turns or spins in the air. **3.** to flick: *to flip a crumb across the room.* **4.** (foll. by *through*) to read or look at (a book, etc.) quickly, idly, or incompletely. **5.** (*intr.*) to make a snapping movement or noise with the finger and thumb. **6.** (*intr.*) *Sl.* to fly into a rage or an emotional outburst (also in **flip one's lid, flip one's top**). ~*n.* **7.** a snap or tap, usually with the fingers. **8.** a rapid jerk. **9.** any alcoholic drink containing beaten egg. ~*adj.* **10.** *Inf.* flippant or pert. [C16: prob. imit.; see FILLIP]

flip-flop *n.* **1.** a backward handspring. **2.** an electronic device or circuit that can assume either of two states by the application of a suitable pulse. **3.** a complete change of opinion, policy, etc. **4.** a repeated flapping noise. **5.** Also called (esp. U.S., Austral., N.Z., and Canad.): **thong.** a rubber-soled sandal attached to the foot by a thong between the big toe and the next toe. ~*vb.* **-flopping, -flopped. 6.** (*intr.*) to move with repeated flaps. [C16: reduplication of FLIP]

flippant ('flɪpənt) *adj.* **1.** marked by inappropriate levity; frivolous. **2.** impertinent; saucy. [C17: ? < FLIP] —'**flippancy** *n.* —'**flippantly** *adv.*

flipper ('flɪpə) *n.* **1.** the flat broad limb of seals, whales, etc., specialized for swimming. **2.** (*often pl.*) either of a pair of rubber paddle-like devices worn on the feet as an aid in swimming.

flip side *n.* **1.** another term for **B-side. 2.** another, less familiar, aspect of a person or thing.

flirt (flɜːt) *vb.* **1.** (*intr.*) to behave or act amorously without emotional commitment. **2.** (*intr.;* usually foll. by *with*) to deal playfully or carelessly (with something dangerous or serious): *the motorcyclist flirted with death.* **3.** (*intr.;* usually foll. by *with*) to toy (with): *to flirt with the idea of leaving.* **4.** (*intr.*) to dart; flit. **5.** (*tr.*) to flick or toss. ~*n.* **6.** a person who acts flirtatiously. [C16: <?] —'**flirter** *n.*

flirtation (flɜː'teɪʃən) *n.* **1.** behaviour intended to arouse sexual feelings or advances without emotional commitment. **2.** any casual involvement.

flirtatious (flɜː'teɪʃəs) *adj.* **1.** given to flirtation. **2.** expressive of playful sexual invitation: *a flirtatious glance.* —**flir'tatiously** *adv.*

flirty ('flɜːtɪ) *adj.* **flirtier, flirtiest. 1.** flirtatious. **2.** (of a skirt) full, frilly, and often short.

flit (flɪt) *vb.* **flitting, flitted.** (*intr.*) **1.** to move along rapidly and lightly. **2.** to fly rapidly and lightly. **3.** to pass quickly: *a memory flitted into his mind.* **4.** *Scot. & N English dialect.* to move house. **5.** *Brit. inf.* to depart hurriedly and stealthily in order to avoid obligations. ~*n.* **6.** the act or an instance of flitting. **7.** *Brit. inf.* a hurried and stealthy departure in order to avoid obligations. [C12: < ON *flytja* to carry] —'**flitter** *n.*

flitch (flɪtʃ) *n.* **1.** a side of pork salted and cured. **2.** a piece of timber cut lengthways from a tree trunk. [OE *flicce;* cf. FLESH]

flitter ('flɪtə) *vb.* a less common word for **flutter.**

flittermouse ('flɪtə,maʊs) *n., pl.* **-mice.** a dialect name for **bat**[2]. [C16: translation of G *Fledermaus*]

float (fləʊt) *vb.* **1.** to rest or cause to rest on the surface of a fluid or in a fluid or space without sinking: *oil floats on water.* **2.** to move or cause to move buoyantly, lightly, or freely across a surface or through air, water, etc. **3.** to move about aimlessly, esp. in the mind: *thoughts floated before him.* **4.** (*tr.*) **a.** to launch or establish (a commercial enterprise, etc.). **b.** to offer for sale (stock or bond issues, etc.) on the stock market. **5.** (*tr.*) *Finance.* to allow (a currency) to fluctuate against other currencies in accordance with market forces. **6.** (*tr.*) to flood, inundate, or irrigate (land). ~*n.* **7.** something that floats. **8.** *Angling.* an indicator attached to a baited line that sits on the water and moves when a fish bites. **9.** a small hand tool with a rectangular blade used for smoothing plaster, etc. **10.** Also called: **paddle.** a blade of a paddle wheel. **11.** *Brit.* a buoyant garment or device to aid a person in staying afloat. **12.** a structure fitted to the underside of an aircraft to allow it to land on water. **13.** a motor vehicle used to carry a tableau or exhibit in a parade, esp. a civic parade. **14.** a small delivery vehicle, esp. one powered by batteries: *a milk float.* **15.** *Austral. & N.Z.* a vehicle for transporting horses. **16.** a sum of money used by shopkeepers to provide change at the start of the day's business. **17.** the hollow floating ball of a ballcock. [OE *flotian;* see FLEET[2]] —'**floatable** *adj.* —,**floata'bility** *n.* —'**floaty** *adj.*

floatage ('fləʊtɪdʒ) *n.* a variant spelling of **flotage.**

floatation (fləʊ'teɪʃən) *n.* a variant spelling of **flotation.**

floatel (fləʊ'tɛl) *n.* a variant spelling of **flotel.**

floater ('fləʊtə) *n.* **1.** a person or thing that floats. **2.** a dark spot that appears in one's vision as a result of dead cells or cell fragments in the eye. **3.** *U.S. & Canad.* a person of no fixed political opinion. **4.** *U.S. inf.* a person who often changes employment, residence, etc.

floating ('fləʊtɪŋ) *adj.* **1.** having little or no attachment. **2.** (of an organ or part) displaced from the normal position or abnormally movable: *a floating kidney.* **3.** uncommitted or unfixed: *floating voters.* **4.** *Finance.* **a.** (of capital) available for current use. **b.** (of debt) short-term and unfunded, usually raised to meet current expenses. **c.** (of a currency) free to fluctuate against other currencies in accordance with market forces. —'**floatingly** *adv.*

floating-point representation *n. Computers.* the representation of numbers by two sets of digits (*a, b*), the set *a* indicating the significant digits, the set *b* giving the position of the radix point. Also called: **floating decimal point representation.** Cf. **fixed-point representation.**

floating rib *n.* any rib of the lower two pairs of ribs in man, which are not attached to the breastbone.

floats (fləʊts) *pl. n. Theatre.* another word for **footlights.**

flocculate ('flɒkjʊ,leɪt) *vb.* to form or be formed into an aggregated flocculent mass. —,**floccu'lation** *n.*

flocculent ('flɒkjʊlənt) *adj.* **1.** like wool; fleecy. **2.** *Chem.* aggregated in woolly cloudlike masses: *a flocculent precipitate.* **3.** *Biol.* covered with tufts or flakes. [C19: < L *floccus* FLOCK[2] + -ULENT] —'**flocculence** *n.*

flocculus ('flɒkjʊləs) *n., pl.* **-li** (-,laɪ). **1.** a cloudy marking on the sun's surface. It consists of calcium when lighter than the surroundings and of hydrogen when darker. **2.** *Anat.* a tiny prominence on each side of the cerebellum.

flock[1] (flɒk) *n.* (*sometimes functioning as pl.*) **1.** a group of animals of one kind, esp. sheep or birds. **2.** a large number of people. **3.** a body of Christians regarded as the pastoral charge of a priest, bishop, etc. ~*vb.* (*intr.*) **4.** to gather together or move in a flock. **5.** to go in large numbers: *people flocked to the church.* [OE *flocc*]

flock[2] (flɒk) *n.* **1.** a tuft, as of wool, hair, cotton, etc. **2.** waste from fabrics such as cotton or wool used for stuffing mattresses, etc. **3.** Also called:

flocking. very small tufts of wool applied to fabrics, wallpaper, etc., to give a raised pattern. [C13: < OF *floc*, < L *floccus*] —'**flocky** *adj.*

floe (fləʊ) *n.* See **ice floe.** [C19: prob. < Norwegian *flo* slab, layer, < ON; see FLAW[1]]

flog (flɒg) *vb.* **flogging, flogged. 1.** (*tr.*) to beat harshly, esp. with a whip, strap, etc. **2.** *Brit. sl.* to sell. **3.** (*intr.*) to make progress by painful work. **4. flog a dead horse.** *Chiefly Brit.* **a.** to harp on some long discarded subject. **b.** to pursue the solution of a problem long realized to be insoluble. [C17: prob. < L *flagellāre;* see FLAGELLANT] —'**flogger** *n.*

flong (flɒŋ) *n.* *Printing.* a material used for making moulds in stereotyping. [C20: var. of FLAN]

flood (flʌd) *n.* **1. a.** the inundation of land that is normally dry through the overflowing of a body of water, esp. a river. **b.** the state of a river that is at an abnormally high level. Related adj.: **diluvial. 2.** a great outpouring or flow: *a flood of words.* **3. a.** the rising of the tide from low to high water. **b.** (*as modifier*): *the flood tide.* Cf. **ebb** (sense 3). **4.** *Theatre.* short for **floodlight.** ~*vb.* **5.** (of water) to inundate or submerge (land) or (of land) to be inundated or submerged. **6.** to fill or be filled to overflowing, as with a flood. **7.** (*intr.*) to flow; surge: *relief flooded through him.* **8.** to supply an excessive quantity of petrol to (a carburettor or petrol engine) or (of a carburettor, etc.) to be supplied with such an excess. **9.** (*intr.*) to overflow. **10.** (*intr.*) to bleed profusely from the uterus, as following childbirth. [OE *flōd;* see FLOW, FLOAT]

Flood (flʌd) *n.* *Old Testament.* **the.** the flood from which Noah and his family and livestock were saved in the ark (Genesis 7–8).

floodgate ('flʌd,geɪt) *n.* **1.** Also called: **head gate, water gate.** a gate in a sluice that is used to control the flow of water. **2.** (*often pl.*) a control or barrier against an outpouring or flow.

floodlight ('flʌd,laɪt) *n.* **1.** a broad intense beam of artificial light, esp. as used in the theatre or to illuminate the exterior of buildings. **2.** the lamp producing such light. ~*vb.* **-lighting, -lit. 3.** (*tr.*) to illuminate as by floodlight.

flood plain *n.* the flat area bordering a river, composed of sediment deposited during flooding.

floor (flɔː) *n.* **1.** Also called: **flooring.** the inner lower surface of a room. **2.** a storey of a building: *the second floor.* **3.** a flat bottom surface in or on any structure: *a dance floor.* **4.** the bottom surface of a tunnel, cave, sea, etc. **5.** that part of a legislative hall in which debate and other business is conducted. **6.** the right to speak in a legislative body (esp. in **get, have,** *or* **be given the floor**). **7.** the room in a stock exchange where trading takes place. **8.** the earth; ground. **9.** a minimum price charged or paid. **10. take the floor.** to begin dancing on a dance floor. ~*vb.* **11.** to cover with or construct a floor. **12.** (*tr.*) to knock to the floor or ground. **13.** (*tr.*) *Inf.* to disconcert, confound, or defeat. [OE *flōr*]

floorboard ('flɔː,bɔːd) *n.* one of the boards forming a floor.

flooring ('flɔːrɪŋ) *n.* **1.** the material used in making a floor. **2.** another word for **floor** (sense 1).

floor manager *n.* **1.** the stage manager of a television programme. **2.** a person in overall charge of one floor of a large shop.

floor plan *n.* a drawing to scale of the arrangement of rooms on one floor of a building.

floor show *n.* a series of entertainments, such as singing and dancing, performed in a nightclub.

floozy, floozie, *or* **floosie** ('fluːzɪ) *n., pl.* **-zies** *or* **-sies.** *Sl.* a disreputable woman. [C20: <?]

flop (flɒp) *vb.* **flopping, flopped. 1.** (*intr.*) to bend, fall, or collapse loosely or carelessly: *his head flopped backwards.* **2.** (when *intr.*, often foll. by *into, onto,* etc.) to fall, cause to fall, or move with a sudden noise. **3.** (*intr.*) *Inf.* to fail: *the scheme flopped.* **4.** (*intr.*) to fall flat onto the surface of water. **5.** (*intr.;* often foll. by *out*) *Sl.* to go to sleep. ~*n.* **6.** the act of flopping. **7.** *Inf.* a complete failure. [C17: var. of FLAP]

floppy ('flɒpɪ) *adj.* **-pier, -piest. 1.** limp or hanging loosely. ~*n.* **2.** short for **floppy disk.** —'**floppily** *adv.* —'**floppiness** *n.*

floppy disk *n.* a flexible magnetic disk that stores information and can be used to store data in the memory of a digital computer.

flora ('flɔːrə) *n., pl.* **-ras** *or* **-rae** (-riː). **1.** all the plant life of a given place or time. **2.** a descriptive list of such plants, often including a key for identification. [C18: < NL, *Flōra* goddess of flowers, < *flōs* FLOWER]

floral ('flɔːrəl) *adj.* **1.** decorated with or consisting of flowers or patterns of flowers. **2.** of or associated with flowers. —'**florally** *adv.*

Florentine ('flɒrən,taɪn) *adj.* **1.** of or relating to Florence, in Italy. ~*n.* **2.** a native or inhabitant of Florence.

florescence (flɔː'rɛsəns) *n.* the process, state, or period of flowering. [C18: < NL, < L *flōrēscere* to come into flower]

floret ('flɔːrɪt) *n.* a small flower, esp. one of many making up the head of a composite flower. [C17: < OF, < *flor* FLOWER]

floriated *or* **floreated** ('flɔːrɪ,eɪtɪd) *adj.* *Archit.* having ornamentation based on flowers and leaves. [C19: < L *flōs* FLOWER]

floribunda (,flɔːrɪ'bʌndə) *n.* any of several varieties of cultivated hybrid roses whose flowers grow in large sprays. [C19: < NL, fem. of *flōribundus* flowering freely]

floriculture ('flɔːrɪ,kʌltʃə) *n.* the cultivation of flowering plants. —,**flori'cultural** *adj.* —,**flori'culturist** *n.*

florid ('flɒrɪd) *adj.* **1.** having a red or flushed complexion. **2.** excessively ornate; flowery: *florid architecture.* [C17: < L *flōridus* blooming] —**flo'ridity** *n.* —'**floridly** *adv.*

floriferous (flɔː'rɪfərəs) *adj.* bearing or capable of bearing many flowers.

florin ('flɒrɪn) *n.* **1.** a former British coin, originally silver, equivalent to ten (new) pence. **2.** (formerly) another name for **guilder** (sense 1). [C14: < F, < OIt. *fiorino* Florentine coin, < *fiore* flower, < L *flōs*]

florist ('flɒrɪst) *n.* a person who grows or deals in flowers.

floristic (flɒ'rɪstɪk) *adj.* of or relating to flowers or a flora. —**flo'ristically** *adv.*

-florous *adj. combining form.* indicating number or type of flowers: *tubuliflorous.*

floruit *Latin.* ('flɒruːɪt) *vb.* (he or she) flourished: used to indicate the period when a figure, whose birth and death dates are unknown, was most active.

floss (flɒs) *n.* **1.** the mass of fine silky fibres obtained from cotton and similar plants. **2.** any similar fine silky material. **3.** untwisted silk thread used in embroidery, etc. **4.** See **dental floss.** [C18: ? < OF *flosche* down]

flossy ('flɒsɪ) *adj.* **flossier, flossiest.** consisting of or resembling floss.

flotage *or* **floatage** ('fləʊtɪdʒ) *n.* **1.** the act or state of floating. **2.** power or ability to float. **3.** flotsam.

flotation *or* **floatation** (fləʊ'teɪʃən) *n.* **1. a.** the launching or financing of a commercial enterprise by bond or share issues. **b.** the raising of a loan or new capital by bond or share issues. **2.** power or ability to float. **3.** Also called: **froth flotation.** a process to concentrate the valuable ore in low-grade ores by using induced differences in surface tension to carry the valuable fraction to the surface.

flotel *or* **floatel** (fləʊ'tɛl) *n.* a rig used for accommodation of workers in off-shore oil fields. [C20: FLO(ATING) + (HO)TEL]

flotilla (flə'tɪlə) *n.* a small fleet or a fleet of small vessels. [C18: < Sp., < F *flotte,* ult. < ON *floti*]

flotsam ('flɒtsəm) *n.* **1.** wreckage from a ship found floating. Cf. **jetsam. 2.** odds and ends (esp. in **flotsam and jetsam**). **3.** vagrants. [C16: < Anglo-F *floteson,* < *floter* to FLOAT]

flounce[1] (flaʊns) *vb.* **1.** (*intr.;* often foll. by *about,* *away, out,* etc.) to move or go with emphatic movements. *~n.* **2.** the act of flouncing. [C16: of Scand. origin]

flounce[2] (flaʊns) *n.* an ornamental gathered ruffle sewn to a garment by its top edge. [C18: < OF, < *froncir* to wrinkle, of Gmc origin]

flounder[1] (ˈflaʊndə) *vb.* (*intr.*) **1.** to move with difficulty, as in mud. **2.** to make mistakes. *~n.* **3.** the act of floundering. [C16: prob. a blend of FOUNDER[2] + BLUNDER; ? infl. by FLOUNDER[2]]

flounder[2] (ˈflaʊndə) *n., pl.* **-der** *or* **-ders.** a European flatfish having a greyish-brown body covered with prickly scales: an important food fish. [C14: < ON]

flour (ˈflaʊə) *n.* **1.** a powder, which may be either fine or coarse, prepared by grinding the meal of a grass, esp. wheat. **2.** any finely powdered substance. *~vb.* (*tr.*) **3.** to make (grain, etc.) into flour. **4.** to dredge or sprinkle (food or utensils) with flour. [C13 *flur* finer portion of meal, FLOWER] —ˈ**floury** *adj.*

flourish (ˈflʌrɪʃ) *vb.* **1.** (*intr.*) to thrive; prosper. **2.** (*intr.*) to be at the peak of condition. **3.** (*intr.*) to be healthy: *plants flourish in the light.* **4.** to wave or cause to wave in the air with sweeping strokes. **5.** to display or make a display. **6.** to play (a fanfare, etc.) on a musical intrument. *~n.* **7.** the act of waving or brandishing. **8.** a showy gesture: *he entered with a flourish.* **9.** an ornamental embellishment in writing. **10.** a display of ornamental language or speech. **11.** a grandiose passage of music. [C13: < OF, ult. < L *flōrēre* to flower, < *flōs* a flower] —ˈ**flourisher** *n.*

flout (flaʊt) *vb.* (when *intr.*, usually foll. by *at*) to show contempt (for). [C16: ? < ME *flouten* to play the flute, < OF *flauter*] —ˈ**floutingly** *adv.*

▷ **Usage.** Confusion sometimes arises between *flout* and *flaunt* although the meanings of the words are quite different. *Flout,* to defy or disregard, is typically used in relation to law or authority: *both the law and the party rules were flouted by this disregard of precedent; be prepared to flout convention — serve red wine with your fish course. Flaunt* implies a deliberate and ostentatious displaying of possessions, abilities, etc.: *she flaunted her large engagement ring; flaunting his indifference to the danger.*

flow (fləʊ) *vb.* (*mainly intr.*) **1.** (of liquids) to move or be conveyed as in a stream. **2.** (of blood) to circulate around the body. **3.** to move or progress freely as if in a stream: *the crowd flowed into the building.* **4.** to be produced continuously and effortlessly: *ideas flowed from her pen.* **5.** to be marked by smooth or easy movement. **6.** to hang freely or loosely: *her hair flowed down her back.* **7.** to be present in abundance: *wine flows at their parties.* **8.** (of tide water) to advance or rise. Cf. **ebb** (sense 1). **9.** (of rocks such as slate) to yield to pressure so that the structure and arrangement of the constituent minerals are altered. *~n.* **10.** the act, rate, or manner of flowing: *a fast flow.* **11.** a continuous stream or discharge. **12.** continuous progression. **13.** the advancing of the tide. **14.** *Scot.* **a.** a marsh or swamp. **b.** an inlet or basin of the sea. **c.** (*cap. when part of a name*): *Scapa Flow.* [OE *flōwan*]

flow chart *or* **sheet** *n.* a diagrammatic representation of the sequence of operations in an industrial process, computer program, etc.

flower (ˈflaʊə) *n.* **1. a.** a bloom or blossom on a plant. **b.** a plant that bears blooms or blossoms. **2.** the reproductive structure of angiosperm plants, consisting of stamens and carpels surrounded by petals and sepals. In some plants it is brightly coloured and attracts insects for pollination. Related adj.: **floral. 3.** any similar reproductive structure in other plants. **4.** the prime; peak: *in the flower of his youth.* **5.** the choice or finest product, part, or representative. **6.** a decoration or embellishment. **7.** (*pl.*) fine powder, usually produced by sublimation: *flowers of sulphur.* *~vb.* **8.** (*intr.*) to produce flowers; bloom. **9.** (*intr.*) to reach full growth or maturity. **10.** (*tr.*) to deck or decorate with flowers or floral designs. [C13: < OF *flor,* < L *flōs*] —ˈ**flowerless** *adj.* —ˈ**flower-ˌlike** *adj.*

flowered (ˈflaʊəd) *adj.* **1.** having flowers. **2.** decorated with flowers or a floral design.

floweret (ˈflaʊərɪt) *n.* another name for **floret.**

flower girl *n.* a girl or woman who sells flowers in the street.

flowering (ˈflaʊərɪŋ) *adj.* (of certain species of plants) capable of producing conspicuous flowers.

flowerpot (ˈflaʊəˌpɒt) *n.* a pot in which plants are grown.

flower power *n. Inf.* a youth cult of the late 1960s advocating peace and love; associated with drug-taking. Its adherents were known as **flower children** or **flower people.**

flowery (ˈflaʊərɪ) *adj.* **1.** abounding in flowers. **2.** decorated with flowers or floral patterns. **3.** like or suggestive of flowers. **4.** (of language or style) elaborate. —ˈ**floweriness** *n.*

flown (fləʊn) *vb.* the past participle of **fly**[1].

flow-on *n. Austral. & N.Z.* **a.** a wage or salary increase granted to one group of workers as a consequence of a similar increase granted to another group. **b.** (*as modifier*): *a flow-on effect.*

fl. oz. *abbrev. for* fluid ounce.

flu (fluː) *n. Inf.* **1.** (often preceded by *the*) short for **influenza. 2.** any of various viral infections, esp. a respiratory or intestinal infection.

fluctuate (ˈflʌktjʊˌeɪt) *vb.* **1.** to change or cause to change position constantly. **2.** (*intr.*) to rise and fall like a wave. [C17: < L, < *fluctus* a wave, < *fluere* to flow] —ˈ**fluctuant** *adj.* —ˌ**fluctuˈation** *n.*

flue (fluː) *n.* a shaft, tube, or pipe, esp. as used in a chimney, to carry off smoke, gas, etc. [C16: <?]

fluent (ˈfluːənt) *adj.* **1.** able to speak or write a specified foreign language with facility. **2.** spoken or written with facility. **3.** graceful in motion or shape. **4.** flowing or able to flow freely. [C16: < L: flowing, < *fluere* to flow] —ˈ**fluency** *n.* —ˈ**fluently** *adv.*

flue pipe *or* **flue** *n.* an organ pipe whose sound is produced by the passage of air across a fissure in the side, as distinguished from a **reed pipe.**

fluff (flʌf) *n.* **1.** soft light particles, such as the down or nap of cotton or wool. **2.** any light downy substance. **3.** *Inf.* a mistake, esp. in speaking or reading lines or performing music. **4.** *Inf.* a young woman (esp. in **a bit of fluff**). *~vb.* **5.** to make or become soft and puffy. **6.** *Inf.* to make a mistake in performing (an action, music, etc.). [C18: ? < *flue* downy matter]

fluffy (ˈflʌfɪ) *adj.* **fluffier, fluffiest. 1.** of, resembling, or covered with fluff. **2.** soft and light. —ˈ**fluffily** *adv.* —ˈ**fluffiness** *n.*

flugelhorn (ˈfluːgəlˌhɔːn) *n.* a type of valved brass instrument consisting of a tube of conical bore with a cup-shaped mouthpiece, used esp. in brass bands. [G, < *Flügel* wing + *Horn* HORN]

fluid (ˈfluːɪd) *n.* **1.** a substance, such as a liquid or gas, that can flow, has no fixed shape, and offers little resistance to an external stress. *~adj.* **2.** capable of flowing and easily changing shape. **3.** of or using a fluid or fluids. **4.** constantly changing or apt to change. **5.** flowing. [C15: < L, < *fluere* to flow] —ˈ**fluidal** *adj.* —**fluˈidity** *or* ˈ**fluidness** *n.*

fluidics (fluːˈɪdɪks) *n.* (*functioning as sing.*) the study and use of systems in which the flow of fluids in tubes simulates the flow of electricity in conductors. —**fluˈidic** *adj.*

fluidize *or* **-dise** (ˈfluːɪˌdaɪz) *vb.* (*tr.*) to make fluid, esp. to make (solids) fluid by pulverizing them so that they can be transported in gas as if they were liquids. —ˌ**fluidiˈzation** *or* **-diˈsation** *n.*

fluid mechanics *n.* (*functioning as sing.*) the study of the mechanical and flow properties of fluids, esp. as they apply to practical engineering. Also called: **hydraulics.**

fluid ounce *n.* **1.** *Brit.* a unit of capacity equal to one twentieth of an Imperial pint. **2.** *U.S.* a unit of capacity equal to one sixteenth of a U.S. pint.

fluke[1] (fluːk) *n.* **1.** a flat bladelike projection at the end of the arm of an anchor. **2.** either of the two lobes of the tail of a whale. **3.** the barb of a harpoon, arrow, etc. [C16: ? a special use of FLUKE[3] (in the sense: a flounder)]

fluke[2] (fluːk) *n.* **1.** an accidental stroke of luck. **2.** any chance happening. ~*vb.* **3.** (*tr.*) to gain, make, or hit by a fluke. [C19: <?]

fluke[3] (fluːk) *n.* any parasitic flatworm, such as the blood fluke and liver fluke. [OE *flōc;* rel. to ON *flōki* flounder]

fluky *or* **flukey** (ˈfluːkɪ) *adj.* **flukier, flukiest.** *Inf.* **1.** done or gained by an accident, esp. a lucky one. **2.** variable; uncertain. —ˈ**flukiness** *n.*

flume (fluːm) *n.* **1.** a ravine through which a stream flows. **2.** a narrow artificial channel made for providing water for power, floating logs, etc. ~*vb.* **3.** (*tr.*) to transport (logs) in a flume. [C12: < OF, ult. < L *flūmen* stream, < *fluere* to flow]

flummery (ˈflʌmərɪ) *n., pl.* **-meries. 1.** *Inf.* meaningless flattery. **2.** *Chiefly Brit.* a cold pudding of oatmeal, etc. [C17: < Welsh *llymru*]

flummox (ˈflʌməks) *vb.* (*tr.*) to perplex or bewilder. [C19: <?]

flung (flʌŋ) *vb.* the past tense and past participle of **fling.**

flunk (flʌŋk) *vb. Inf., U.S., Canad., & N.Z.* **1.** to fail or cause to fail to reach the required standard in (an examination, course, etc.). **2.** (*intr.;* foll. by *out*) to be dismissed from a school. [C19: ? < FLINCH + FUNK[1]]

flunky *or* **flunkey** (ˈflʌŋkɪ) *n., pl.* **flunkies** *or* **flunkeys. 1.** a servile person. **2.** a person who performs menial tasks. **3.** *Usually derog.* a manservant in livery. [C18: <?]

fluor (ˈfluːɔː) *n.* another name for **fluorspar.** [C17: < L: a flowing; so called from its use as a metallurgical flux]

fluor- *combining form.* a variant of **fluoro-** before a vowel: *fluorine.*

fluoresce (ˌflʊəˈrɛs) *vb.* (*intr.*) to exhibit fluorescence. [C19: back formation < FLUORESCENCE]

fluorescence (ˌflʊəˈrɛsəns) *n.* **1.** *Physics.* **a.** the emission of light or other radiation from atoms or molecules that are bombarded by particles, such as electrons, or by radiation from a separate source. **b.** such an emission of photons that ceases as soon as the bombarding radiation is discontinued. **2.** the radiation emitted as a result of fluorescence. Cf. **phosphorescence.** [C19: FLUOR + *-escence* (as in *opalescence*)] —ˌ**fluoˈrescent** *adj.*

fluorescent lamp *n.* a type of lamp in which ultraviolet radiation from an electrical gas discharge causes a thin layer of phosphor on a tube's inside surface to fluoresce.

fluoridate (ˈflʊərɪˌdeɪt) *vb.* to subject (water) to fluoridation.

fluoridation (ˌflʊərɪˈdeɪʃən) *n.* the addition of fluorides to the public water supply as a protection against tooth decay.

fluoride (ˈflʊəˌraɪd) *n.* **1.** any salt of hydrofluoric acid, containing the fluoride ion, F^-. **2.** any compound containing fluorine, such as methyl fluoride.

fluorinate (ˈflʊərɪˌneɪt) *vb.* to treat or combine with fluorine. —ˌ**fluoriˈnation** *n.*

fluorine (ˈflʊəriːn) *n.* a toxic pungent pale yellow gas of the halogen group that is the most electronegative and reactive of all the elements: used in the production of uranium, fluorocarbons, and other chemicals. Symbol: F; atomic no.: 9; atomic wt.: 18.998.

fluorite (ˈflʊəraɪt) *n.* the U.S. and Canad. name for **fluorspar.**

fluoro- *or before a vowel* **fluor-** *combining form.* **1.** indicating the presence of fluorine: *fluorocarbon.* **2.** indicating fluorescence: *fluoroscope.*

fluorocarbon (ˌflʊərəʊˈkɑːbᵊn) *n.* any compound derived by replacing all or some of the hydrogen atoms in hydrocarbons by fluorine atoms. Many of them are used as lubricants, solvents, and coatings.

fluorometer (ˌflʊəˈrɒmɪtə) *or* **fluorimeter** (ˌflʊəˈrɪmɪtə) *n.* a device for detecting and measuring ultraviolet radiation by determining the amount of fluorescence that it produces from a phosphor.

fluoroscope (ˈflʊərəˌskəʊp) *n.* a device consisting of a fluorescent screen and an x-ray source that enables an x-ray image of an object, person, or part to be observed directly.

fluoroscopy (flʊəˈrɒskəpɪ) *n.* examination of a person or object by means of a fluoroscope.

fluorosis (flʊəˈrəʊsɪs) *n.* fluoride poisoning, due to ingestion of too much fluoride.

fluorspar (ˈflʊəˌspɑː), **fluor,** *or U.S. & Canad.* **fluorite** *n.* a white or colourless soft mineral, sometimes fluorescent or tinted by impurities, consisting of calcium fluoride in crystalline form: the chief ore of fluorine.

flurry (ˈflʌrɪ) *n., pl.* **-ries. 1.** a sudden commotion. **2.** a light gust of wind or rain or fall of snow. ~*vb.* **-rying, -ried. 3.** to confuse or bewilder or be confused or bewildered. [C17: < obs. *flurr* to scatter, ? formed on analogy with HURRY]

flush[1] (flʌʃ) *vb.* **1.** to blush or cause to blush. **2.** to flow or flood or cause to flow or flood with or as if with water. **3.** to glow or shine or cause to glow or shine with a rosy colour. **4.** to send a volume of water quickly through (a pipe, etc.) or into (a toilet) for the purpose of cleansing, etc. **5.** (*tr.; usually passive*) to excite or elate. ~*n.* **6.** a rosy colour, esp. in the cheeks. **7.** a sudden flow or gush, as of water. **8.** a feeling of excitement or elation: *the flush of success.* **9.** freshness: *the flush of youth.* **10.** redness of the skin, as from the effects of a fever, alcohol, etc. [C16: (in the sense: to gush forth): ?< FLUSH[3]] —ˈ**flusher** *n.*

flush[2] (flʌʃ) *adj.* (*usually postpositive*) **1.** level or even with another surface. **2.** directly adjacent; continuous. **3.** *Inf.* having plenty of money. **4.** *Inf.* abundant or plentiful, as money. **5.** full to the brim. ~*adv.* **6.** so as to be level or even. **7.** directly or squarely. ~*vb.* (*tr.*) **8.** to cause (surfaces) to be on the same level or in the same plane. ~*n.* **9.** a period of fresh growth of leaves, shoots, etc. [C18: prob. < FLUSH[1] (in the sense: spring out)] —ˈ**flushness** *n.*

flush[3] (flʌʃ) *vb.* (*tr.*) to rouse (game, etc.) and put to flight. [C13 *flusshen,* ? imit.]

flush[4] (flʌʃ) *n.* (in poker and similar games) a hand containing only one suit. [C16: < OF, < L *fluxus* FLUX]

fluster (ˈflʌstə) *vb.* **1.** to make or become nervous or upset. ~*n.* **2.** a state of confusion or agitation. [C15: < ON]

flute (fluːt) *n.* **1.** a wind instrument consisting of an open cylindrical tube of wood or metal having holes in the side stopped either by the fingers or by pads controlled by keys. The breath is directed across a mouth hole cut in the side. **2.** *Archit.* a rounded shallow concave groove on the shaft of a column, pilaster, etc. ~*vb.* **3.** to produce or utter (sounds) in the manner or tone of a flute. **4.** (*tr.*) to make grooves or furrows in. [C14: < OF *flahute,* < Vulgar L *flabeolum* (unattested); ? also infl. by OF *laut* lute] —ˈ**fluteˌlike** *adj.* —ˈ**fluty** *adj.*

fluting (ˈfluːtɪŋ) *n.* a design or decoration of flutes on a column, pilaster, etc.

flutist (ˈfluːtɪst) *n. Now chiefly U.S.* a variant spelling of **flautist.**

flutter (ˈflʌtə) *vb.* **1.** to wave or cause to wave rapidly. **2.** (*intr.*) (of birds, butterflies, etc.) to flap the wings. **3.** (*intr.*) to move, esp. downwards, with an irregular motion. **4.** (*intr.*) *Pathol.* (of the heart) to beat abnormally rapidly, esp. in a regular rhythm. **5.** to be or make nervous or restless. **6.** (*intr.*) to move about restlessly. ~*n.* **7.** a quick flapping or vibrating motion. **8.** a state of nervous excitement or confusion. **9.** excited interest; stir. **10.** *Brit. inf.* a modest bet or wager. **11.** *Pathol.* an abnormally rapid beating of the heart, esp. in a regular rhythm. **12.** *Electronics.* a slow variation in pitch in a sound-reproducing system, similar to wow but occurring at higher frequencies. **13.** a potentially dangerous oscillation of an aircraft, or part of an aircraft. **14.** Also called: **flutter tonguing.** *Music.* a method of sounding a wind instrument, esp. the flute, with a rolling movement of the tongue. [OE *floterian* to float to and fro] —ˈ**flutterer** *n.* —ˈ**fluttery** *adj.*

fluvial (ˈfluːvɪəl) *adj.* of or occurring in a river: *fluvial deposits.* [C14: < L, < *fluvius* river, < *fluere* to flow]

flux (flʌks) *n.* **1.** a flow or discharge. **2.** continuous change; instability. **3.** a substance, such as borax or salt, that gives a low melting-point mixture with a metal oxide to assist in fusion. **4.** *Metallurgy.* a chemical used to increase the fluidity of refining slags. **5.** *Physics.* **a.** the rate of flow of particles, energy, or a fluid, such as that of neutrons (**neutron flux**) or of light energy (**luminous flux**). **b.** the strength of a field in a given area: *magnetic flux.* **6.** *Pathol.* an excessive discharge of fluid from the body, such as watery faeces in diarrhoea. ~*vb.* **7.** to make or become fluid. **8.** (*tr.*) to apply flux to (a metal, soldered joint, etc.). [C14: < L *fluxus* a flow, < *fluere* to flow]

flux density *n. Physics.* the amount of flux per unit of cross-sectional area.

fluxion (ˈflʌkʃən) *n. Maths., obs.* the rate of change of a function; derivative. [C16: < LL *fluxiō* a flowing]

fly[1] (flaɪ) *vb.* **flying, flew, flown. 1.** (*intr.*) (of birds, aircraft, etc.) to move through the air in a controlled manner using aerodynamic forces. **2.** to travel over (an area of land or sea) in an aircraft. **3.** to operate (an aircraft or spacecraft). **4.** to float, flutter, or be displayed in the air or cause to float, etc., in this way: *they flew the flag.* **5.** to transport or be transported by or through the air by aircraft, wind, etc. **6.** (*intr.*) to move or be moved very quickly, or suddenly: *the door flew open.* **7.** (*intr.*) to pass swiftly: *time flies.* **8.** to escape from (an enemy, place, etc.); flee. **9.** (*intr.*; may be foll. by *at* or *upon*) to attack a person. **10. fly a kite. a.** to procure money by an accommodation bill. **b.** to release information or take a step in order to test public opinion. **11. fly high.** *Inf.* **a.** to have a high aim. **b.** to prosper or flourish. **12. let fly.** *Inf.* **a.** to lose one's temper (with a person): *she really let fly at him.* **b.** to shoot or throw (an object). ~*n., pl.* **flies. 13.** (*often pl.*) Also called: **fly front.** a closure that conceals a zip, buttons, or other fastening, by having one side overlapping, as on trousers. **14. a.** a flap forming the entrance to a tent. **b.** a piece of canvas drawn over the ridgepole of a tent to form an outer roof. **15.** short for **flywheel. 16. a.** the outer edge of a flag. **b.** the distance from the outer edge of a flag to the staff. **17.** *Brit.* a light one-horse covered carriage formerly let out on hire. **18.** (*pl.*) *Theatre.* the space above the stage out of view of the audience, used for storing scenery, etc. **19.** *Rare.* the act of flying. [OE *flēogan*] —ˈ**flyable** *adj.*

fly[2] (flaɪ) *n., pl.* **flies. 1.** any dipterous insect, esp. the housefly, characterized by active flight. **2.** any of various similar but unrelated insects, such as the caddis fly, firefly, and dragonfly. **3.** *Angling.* a lure made from a fish-hook dressed with feathers, tinsel, etc., to resemble any of various flies or nymphs: used in fly-fishing. **4. fly in the ointment.** *Inf.* a slight flaw that detracts from value or enjoyment. **5. fly on the wall. a.** a person who watches others, while not being noticed himself. **b.** (*as modifier*): *a fly-on-the-wall documentary.* **6. there are no flies on him, her,** etc. *Inf.* he, she, etc., is no fool. [OE *flēoge*] —ˈ**flyless** *adj.*

fly[3] (flaɪ) *adj. Sl., chiefly Brit.* knowing and sharp; smart. [C19: <?]

fly agaric *n.* a woodland fungus having a scarlet cap with white warts and white gills: poisonous but rarely fatal. [so named from its use as a poison on flypaper]

fly ash *n.* fine solid particles of ash carried into the air during combustion.

flyaway (ˈflaɪəˌweɪ) *adj.* **1.** (of hair or clothing) loose and fluttering. **2.** frivolous or flighty; giddy.

flyblow (ˈflaɪˌbləʊ) *vb.* **-blowing, -blew, -blown. 1.** (*tr.*) to contaminate, esp. with the eggs or larvae of the blowfly; taint. ~*n.* **2.** (*usually pl.*) the eggs or young larva of a blowfly.

flyblown (ˈflaɪˌbləʊn) *adj.* **1.** covered with flyblows. **2.** contaminated; tainted.

flybook (ˈflaɪˌbʊk) *n.* a small case or wallet used by anglers for storing artificial flies.

flyby (ˈflaɪˌbaɪ) *n., pl.* **-bys.** a flight past a particular position or target, esp. the close approach of a spacecraft to a planet or satellite.

fly-by-night *Inf.* ~*adj.* **1.** unreliable or untrustworthy, esp. in finance. ~*n.* **2.** an untrustworthy person, esp. one who departs secretly or by night to avoid paying debts.

flycatcher (ˈflaɪˌkætʃə) *n.* **1.** a small insectivorous songbird of the Old World having a small slender bill fringed with bristles. **2.** an American passerine bird.

flyer (ˈflaɪə) *n.* a variant spelling of **flier.**

fly-fish *vb.* (*intr.*) *Angling.* to fish using artificial flies as lures. —ˈ**fly-ˌfishing** *n.*

fly half *n. Rugby.* another name for **stand-off half.**

flying (ˈflaɪɪŋ) *adj.* **1.** (*prenominal*) hurried; fleeting: *a flying visit.* **2.** (*prenominal*) designed for fast action. **3.** (*prenominal*) moving or passing quickly on or as if on wings: *flying hours.* **4.** hanging, waving, or floating freely: *flying hair.* ~*n.* **5.** the act of piloting, navigating, or travelling in an aircraft. **6.** (*modifier*) relating to, accustomed to, or adapted for flight: *a flying machine.*

flying boat *n.* a seaplane in which the fuselage consists of a hull that provides buoyancy.

flying bridge *n.* an auxiliary bridge of a vessel.

flying buttress *n.* a buttress supporting a wall or other structure by an arch that transmits the thrust outwards and downwards.

flying colours *pl. n.* conspicuous success; triumph: *he passed his test with flying colours.*

flying doctor *n.* (in areas of sparse or scattered population) a doctor who visits patients by aircraft.

flying fish *n.* a fish common in warm and tropical seas, having enlarged winglike pectoral fins used for gliding above the surface of the water.

flying fox *n.* **1.** any large fruit bat of tropical Africa and Asia. **2.** *Austral. & N.Z.* a cable mechanism used for transportation across a river, gorge, etc.

flying gurnard *n.* a marine spiny-finned gurnard-like fish having enlarged fan-shaped pectoral fins used to glide above the surface of the sea.

flying jib *n.* the jib set furthest forward or outboard on a vessel with two or more jibs.

flying lemur *n.* either of the two arboreal mammals of S and SE Asia that resemble lemurs but have a fold of skin between the limbs enabling movement by gliding leaps.

flying officer *n.* an officer holding commissioned rank senior to a pilot officer but junior to a flight lieutenant in the British and certain other air forces.

flying phalanger *n.* a nocturnal arboreal phalanger of E Australia and New Guinea, moving with gliding leaps using folds of skin between the hind limbs and forelimbs.

flying picket *n.* (in industrial disputes) a member of a group of pickets organized to be able to move quickly from place to place.

flying saucer *n.* any unidentified disc-shaped flying object alleged to come from outer space.

flying squad *n.* a small group of police, soldiers, etc., ready to move into action quickly.

flying squirrel *n.* a nocturnal rodent of Asia and North America, related to the squirrel. Furry folds of skin between the forelegs and hind legs enable these animals to move by gliding leaps.

flying start *n.* **1.** (in sprinting) a start by a competitor anticipating the starting signal. **2.** a start to a race in which the competitor is already travelling at speed as he passes the starting line.

3. any promising beginning. 4. an initial advantage.

flying wing *n.* 1. an aircraft consisting mainly of one large wing or tailplane and no fuselage. 2. (in Canadian football) the twelfth player, who has a variable position behind the scrimmage line.

flyleaf ('flaɪˌliːf) *n., pl.* **-leaves.** the inner leaf of the endpaper of a book, pasted to the first leaf.

flyover ('flaɪˌəʊvə) *n.* 1. *Brit.* an intersection of two roads at which one is carried over the other by a bridge. 2. the U.S. name for **fly-past.**

flypaper ('flaɪˌpeɪpə) *n.* paper with a sticky and poisonous coating, usually hung from the ceiling to trap flies.

fly-past *n.* a ceremonial flight of aircraft over a given area.

flyposting ('flaɪˌpəʊstɪŋ) *n.* the posting of advertising or political posters, etc., in unauthorized places.

flyscreen ('flaɪˌskriːn) *n.* a wire-mesh screen over a window to prevent flies entering a room.

fly sheet *n.* 1. another term for **fly**[1] (sense 14). 2. a short handbill.

flyspeck ('flaɪˌspɛk) *n.* 1. the small speck of the excrement of a fly. 2. a small spot or speck. ~*vb.* 3. (*tr.*) to mark with flyspecks.

fly spray *n.* a liquid used to destroy flies and other insects, sprayed from an aerosol.

fly-tipping *n.* the deliberate dumping of rubbish in an unauthorized place.

flytrap ('flaɪˌtræp) *n.* 1. any of various insectivorous plants. 2. a device for catching flies.

fly way *n.* the usual route used by birds when migrating.

flyweight ('flaɪˌweɪt) *n.* 1. a. a professional boxer weighing not more than 112 pounds (51 kg). b. an amateur boxer weighing 48–51 kg (106–112 pounds). 2. an amateur wrestler weighing 107–115 pounds (49–52 kg).

flywheel ('flaɪˌwiːl) *n.* a heavy wheel that stores kinetic energy and smooths the operation of a reciprocating engine by maintaining a constant speed of rotation over the whole cycle.

fm *abbrev. for:* 1. fathom. 2. from.

Fm *the chemical symbol for* fermium.

FM *abbrev. for:* 1. frequency modulation. 2. Field Marshal.

f-number *or* **f number** *n. Photog.* the numerical value of the relative aperture. If the relative aperture is f8, 8 is the f-number.

FO *abbrev. for:* 1. *Army.* Field Officer. 2. *Air Force.* Flying Officer. 3. Foreign Office.

fo. *abbrev. for* folio.

foal (fəʊl) *n.* 1. the young of a horse or related animal. ~*vb.* 2. to give birth to (a foal). [OE *fola*]

foam (fəʊm) *n.* 1. a mass of small bubbles of gas formed on the surface of a liquid, such as the froth produced by a solution of soap or detergent in water. 2. frothy saliva sometimes formed in and expelled from the mouth, as in rabies. 3. the frothy sweat of a horse or similar animal. 4. a. any of a number of light cellular solids made by creating bubbles of gas in the liquid material: used as insulation and packaging. b. (*as modifier*): *foam rubber; foam plastic.* ~*vb.* 5. to produce or cause to produce foam; froth. 6. (*intr.*) to be very angry (esp. in **foam at the mouth**). [OE *fām*] —'**foamless** *adj.*

foamy ('fəʊmɪ) *adj.* **foamier, foamiest.** of, resembling, consisting of, or covered with foam.

fob[1] (fɒb) *n.* 1. a chain or ribbon by which a pocket watch is attached to a waistcoat. 2. any ornament hung on such a chain. 3. a small pocket in a man's waistcoat, etc., for holding a watch. [C17: prob. of Gmc origin]

fob[2] (fɒb) *vb.* **fobbing, fobbed.** (*tr.*) *Arch.* to cheat. [C15: prob. < G *foppen* to trick]

f.o.b. *or* **FOB** *Commerce. abbrev. for* free on board.

fob off *vb.* (*tr., adv.*) 1. to trick (a person) with lies or excuses. 2. to dispose of (goods) by trickery.

focal ('fəʊkᵊl) *adj.* 1. of or relating to a focus. 2. situated at or measured from the focus.

focalize *or* **-lise** ('fəʊkəˌlaɪz) *vb.* a less common word for **focus.** —ˌ**focali'zation** *or* **-li'sation** *n.*

focal length *or* **distance** *n.* the distance from the focal point of a lens or mirror to the reflecting surface of the mirror or the centre point of the lens.

focal plane *n.* the plane that is perpendicular to the axis of a lens or mirror and passes through the focal point.

focal point *n.* the point on the axis of a lens or mirror to which parallel rays of light converge or from which they appear to diverge after refraction or reflection. Also called: **focus.**

fo'c's'le *or* **fo'c'sle** ('fəʊksᵊl) *n.* a variant spelling of **forecastle.**

focus ('fəʊkəs) *n., pl.* **-cuses** *or* **-ci** (-saɪ). 1. a point of convergence of light or sound waves, etc., or a point from which they appear to diverge. 2. another name for **focal point** or **focal length.** 3. *Optics.* the state of an optical image when it is distinct and clearly defined or the state of an instrument producing this image: *the telescope is out of focus.* 4. a point upon which attention, activity, etc., is concentrated. 5. *Geom.* a fixed reference point on the concave side of a conic section, used when defining its eccentricity. 6. the point beneath the earth's surface at which an earthquake originates. 7. *Pathol.* the main site of an infection. ~*vb.* **-cusing, -cused** *or* **-cussing, -cussed.** 8. to bring or come to a focus or into focus. 9. (*tr.*; often foll. by *on*) to concentrate. [C17: via NL < L: hearth, fireplace] —'**focuser** *n.*

fodder ('fɒdə) *n.* 1. bulk feed for livestock, esp. hay, straw, etc. ~*vb.* 2. (*tr.*) to supply (livestock) with fodder. [OE *fōdor*]

foe (fəʊ) *n. Formal or literary.* another word for **enemy.** [OE *fāh* hostile]

FoE *or* **FOE** *abbrev. for* Friends of the Earth.

foehn (fɜːn; *German* føːn) *n. Meteorol.* a variant spelling of **föhn.**

foeman ('fəʊmən) *n., pl.* **-men.** *Arch. & poetic.* an enemy in war; foe.

foetid ('fɛtɪd, 'fiː-) *adj.* a variant spelling of **fetid.** —'**foetidly** *adv.* —'**foetidness** *n.*

foetus ('fiːtəs) *n., pl.* **-tuses.** a variant spelling of **fetus.** —'**foetal** *adj.*

fog[1] (fɒg) *n.* 1. a mass of droplets of condensed water vapour suspended in the air, often greatly reducing visibility. 2. a cloud of any substance in the atmosphere reducing visibility. 3. a state of mental uncertainty. 4. *Photog.* a blurred area on a developed negative, print, or transparency. ~*vb.* **fogging, fogged.** 5. to envelop or become enveloped with or as if with fog. 6. to confuse or become confused. 7. *Photog.* to produce fog on (a negative, print, or transparency) or (of a negative, print, or transparency) to be affected by fog. [C16: ? back formation < *foggy* damp, boggy, < FOG[2]]

fog[2] (fɒg) *n.* a second growth of grass after the first mowing. [C14: prob. < ON]

fog bank *n.* a distinct mass of fog, esp. at sea.

fogbound ('fɒgˌbaʊnd) *adj.* prevented from operation by fog: *the airport was fogbound.*

fogbow ('fɒgˌbəʊ) *n.* a faint arc of light sometimes seen in a fog bank.

foggy ('fɒgɪ) *adj.* **-gier, -giest.** 1. thick with fog. 2. obscure or confused. 3. **not the foggiest (idea** *or* **notion**). no idea whatsoever: *I haven't the foggiest.* —'**fogginess** *n.*

foghorn ('fɒgˌhɔːn) *n.* 1. a mechanical instrument sounded at intervals to serve as a warning to vessels in fog. 2. *Inf.* a loud deep resounding voice.

fog signal *n.* a signal used to warn railway engine drivers in fog, consisting of a detonator placed on the line.

fogy *or* **fogey** ('fəʊgɪ) *n., pl.* **-gies** *or* **-geys.** an extremely fussy or conservative person (esp. in **old fogy**). [C18: <?] —'**fogyish** *or* '**fogeyish** *adj.*

föhn *or* **foehn** (fɜːn; *German* føːn) *n.* a warm dry wind blowing down the northern slopes of the

Alps. [G, < OHG, < L *favōnius;* rel. to *fovēre* to warm]

foible (ˈfɔɪbᵊl) *n.* **1.** a slight peculiarity or minor weakness; idiosyncrasy. **2.** the most vulnerable part of a sword's blade, from the middle to the tip. [C17: < obs. F, < obs. adj.: FEEBLE]

foie gras (*French* fwa grɑ) *n.* See **pâté de foie gras.**

foil[1] (fɔɪl) *vb.* (*tr.*) **1.** to baffle or frustrate (a person, attempt, etc.). **2.** *Hunting.* (of hounds, hunters, etc.) to obliterate the scent left by a hunted animal or (of a hunted animal) to run back over its own trail. ~*n.* **3.** *Arch.* a setback or defeat. [C13 *foilen* to trample, < OF, *fuler* tread down] —ˈ**foilable** *adj.*

foil[2] (fɔɪl) *n.* **1.** metal in the form of very thin sheets: *tin foil.* **2.** the thin metallic sheet forming the backing of a mirror. **3.** a thin leaf of shiny metal set under a gemstone to add brightness or colour. **4.** a person or thing that gives contrast to another. **5.** *Archit.* a small arc between cusps. **6.** short for **hydrofoil.** ~*vb.* (*tr.*) **7.** Also: **foliate.** *Archit.* to ornament (windows, etc.) with foils. [C14: < OF, < L *folia* leaves]

foil[3] (fɔɪl) *n.* a light slender flexible sword tipped by a button. [C16: <?]

foist (fɔɪst) *vb.* (*tr.*) **1.** (often foll. by *off* or *on*) to sell or pass off (something, esp. an inferior article) as genuine, valuable, etc. **2.** (usually foll. by *in* or *into*) to insert surreptitiously or wrongfully. [C16: prob. < obs. Du. *vuisten* to enclose in one's hand, < MDu. *vuist* fist]

FOL (in New Zealand) *abbrev. for* Federation of Labour.

fol. *abbrev. for:* **1.** folio. **2.** following.

fold[1] (fəʊld) *vb.* **1.** to bend or be bent double so that one part covers another. **2.** (*tr.*) to bring together and intertwine (the arms, legs, etc.). **3.** (*tr.*) (of birds, insects, etc.) to close (the wings) together from an extended position. **4.** (*tr.;* often foll. by *up* or *in*) to enclose in or as if in a surrounding material. **5.** (*tr.;* foll. by *in*) to clasp (a person) in the arms. **6.** (*tr.;* usually foll. by *round, about,* etc.) to wind (around); entwine. **7.** Also: **fold in.** (*tr.*) to mix (a whisked mixture) with other ingredients by gently turning one part over the other with a spoon. **8.** (*intr.;* often foll. by *up*) *Inf.* to collapse; fail: *the business folded.* ~*n.* **9.** a piece or section that has been folded: *a fold of cloth.* **10.** a mark, crease, or hollow made by folding. **11.** a hollow in undulating terrain. **12.** a bend in stratified rocks that results from movements within the earth's crust. **13.** a coil, as in a rope, etc. [OE *fealdan*] —ˈ**foldable** *adj.*

fold[2] (fəʊld) *n.* **1. a.** a small enclosure or pen for sheep or other livestock, where they can be gathered. **b.** a flock of sheep. **2.** a church or the members of it. ~*vb.* **3.** (*tr.*) to gather or confine (sheep, etc.) in a fold. [OE *falod*]

-fold *suffix forming adjectives and adverbs.* having so many parts or being so many times as much or as many: *three-hundredfold.* [OE *-fald, -feald*]

foldaway (ˈfəʊldəˌweɪ) *adj.* (*prenominal*) (of a bed, etc.) able to be folded away when not in use.

folded dipole *n.* a type of aerial consisting of two parallel dipoles connected together at their outer ends and fed at the centre of one of them. The length is usually half the operating wavelength.

folder (ˈfəʊldə) *n.* **1.** a binder or file for holding loose papers, etc. **2.** a folded circular. **3.** a person or thing that folds.

folderol (ˈfɒldəˌrɒl) *n.* a variant spelling of **falderal.**

folding door *n.* a door in the form of two or more vertical hinged leaves that can be folded one against another.

foliaceous (ˌfəʊlɪˈeɪʃəs) *adj.* **1.** having the appearance of the leaf of a plant. **2.** bearing leaves or leaflike structures. **3.** *Geol.* consisting of thin layers. [C17: < L *foliāceus*]

foliage (ˈfəʊlɪɪdʒ) *n.* **1.** the green leaves of a plant. **2.** sprays of leaves used for decoration. **3.** an ornamental leaflike design. [C15: < OF *fuellage,* < *fuelle* leaf; infl. in form by L *folium*]

foliar (ˈfəʊlɪə) *adj.* of or relating to a leaf or leaves. [C19: < F, < L *folium* leaf]

foliate *adj.* (ˈfəʊlɪɪt, -ˌeɪt). **1. a.** relating to, possessing, or resembling leaves. **b.** (*in combination*): *trifoliate.* ~*vb.* (ˈfəʊlɪˌeɪt). **2.** (*tr.*) to ornament with foliage or with leaf forms such as foils. **3.** to hammer or cut (metal) into thin plates or foil. **4.** (*tr.*) to number the leaves of (a book, etc.). Cf. **paginate. 5.** (*intr.*) (of plants) to grow leaves. [C17: < L *foliātus* leaved, leafy]

foliation (ˌfəʊlɪˈeɪʃən) *n.* **1.** *Bot.* **a.** the process of producing leaves. **b.** the state of being in leaf. **c.** the arrangement of leaves in a leaf bud. **2.** *Archit.* ornamentation consisting of cusps and foils. **3.** the consecutive numbering of the leaves of a book. **4.** *Geol.* the arrangement of the constituents of a rock in leaflike layers, as in schists.

folic acid (ˈfəʊlɪk) *n.* any of a group of vitamins of the B complex, used in the treatment of anaemia. Also called: **folacin.** [C20: < L *folium* leaf; so called because it may be obtained from green leaves]

folio (ˈfəʊlɪəʊ) *n., pl.* **-lios. 1.** a sheet of paper folded in half to make two leaves for a book. **2.** a book of the largest common size made up of such sheets. **3. a.** a leaf of paper numbered on the front side only. **b.** the page number of a book. **4.** *Law.* a unit of measurement of the length of legal documents, determined by the number of words, generally 72 or 90 in Britain and 100 in the U.S. ~*adj.* **5.** relating to or having the format of a folio: *a folio edition.* [C16: < L phrase *in foliō* in a leaf, < *folium* leaf]

folk (fəʊk) *n., pl.* **folk** *or* **folks. 1.** (*functioning as pl.; often pl. in form*) people in general, esp. those of a particular group or class: *country folk.* **2.** (*functioning as pl.; usually pl. in form*) *Inf.* members of a family. **3.** (*functioning as sing.*) *Inf.* short for **folk music. 4.** a people or tribe. **5.** (*modifier*) originating from or traditional to the common people of a country: *a folk song.* [OE *folc*] —ˈ**folkish** *adj.*

folk dance *n.* **1.** any of various traditional rustic dances. **2.** a piece of music composed for or in the rhythm of this dance. —**folk dancing** *n.*

folk etymology *n.* the gradual change in the form of a word through the influence of a more familiar word or phrase with which it becomes associated, as for example *sparrow-grass* for *asparagus.*

folkie *or* **folky** (ˈfəʊkɪ) *n., pl.* **folkies.** *Inf.* a devotee of folk music.

folklore (ˈfəʊkˌlɔː) *n.* **1.** the unwritten literature of a people as expressed in folk tales, songs, etc. **2.** the body of stories and legends attached to a particular place, group, etc.: *rugby folklore.* **3.** study of folkloric materials. —ˈ**folkˌloric** *adj.* —ˈ**folkˌlorist** *n., adj.*

folk medicine *n.* medicine as practised among rustic communities and primitive peoples, consisting typically of the use of herbal remedies.

folk music *n.* **1.** music that is passed on from generation to generation. **2.** any music composed in this idiom.

folk-rock *n.* a combination of folk-oriented lyrics with a pop accompaniment.

folk song *n.* **1.** a song which has been handed down among the common people. **2.** a modern song which reflects the folk idiom.

folksy (ˈfəʊksɪ) *adj.* **-sier, -siest.** *Inf., chiefly U.S. & Canad.* **1.** of or like ordinary people. **2.** friendly; affable.

folk tale *or* **story** *n.* a tale or legend originating among a people and becoming part of an oral tradition.

folk weave *n.* a type of fabric with a loose weave.

follicle (ˈfɒlɪkᵊl) *n.* **1.** any small sac or cavity in the body having an excretory, secretory, or protective function: *a hair follicle.* **2.** *Bot.* a dry fruit that splits along one side only to release its seeds. [C17: < L *folliculus* small bag, < *follis* pair of bellows, leather money-bag] —**follicular** (fɒˈlɪkjʊlə), **folliculate** (fɒˈlɪkjʊˌleɪt), *or* **folˈlicuˌlated** *adj.*

follow (ˈfɒləʊ) *vb.* **1.** to go or come after in the same direction. **2.** (*tr.*) to accompany: *she followed her sister everywhere.* **3.** to come after as a logical or natural consequence. **4.** (*tr.*) to keep to the course or track of: *she followed the towpath.* **5.** (*tr.*) to act in accordance with: *to follow instructions.* **6.** (*tr.*) to accept the ideas or beliefs of (a previous authority, etc.): *he followed Donne in most of his teachings.* **7.** to understand (an explanation, etc.): *the lesson was difficult to follow.* **8.** to watch closely or continuously: *she followed his progress.* **9.** (*tr.*) to have a keen interest in: *to follow athletics.* **10.** (*tr.*) to help in the cause of: *the men who followed Napoleon.* [OE *folgian*]

follower (ˈfɒləʊə) *n.* **1.** a person who accepts the teachings of another: *a follower of Marx.* **2.** an attendant. **3.** a supporter, as of a sport or team. **4.** (esp. formerly) a male admirer.

following (ˈfɒləʊɪŋ) *adj.* **1. a.** (*prenominal*) about to be mentioned, specified, etc.: *the following items.* **b.** (*as n.*): *will the following please raise their hands?* **2.** (of winds, currents, etc.) moving in the same direction as a vessel. ~*n.* **3.** a group of supporters or enthusiasts: *he attracted a large following.*

follow-on *Cricket.* ~*n.* **1.** an immediate second innings forced on a team scoring a prescribed number of runs fewer than its opponents in the first innings. ~*vb.* **follow on. 2.** (*intr., adv.*) (of a team) to play a follow-on.

follow out *vb.* (*tr., adv.*) to implement (an idea or action) to a conclusion.

follow through *vb.* (*adv.*) **1.** *Sport.* to complete (a stroke or shot) by continuing the movement to the end of its arc. **2.** (*tr.*) to pursue (an aim) to a conclusion. ~*n.* **follow-through. 3.** the act of following through.

follow up *vb.* (*tr., adv.*) **1.** to pursue or investigate (a person, etc.) closely. **2.** to continue (action) after a beginning, esp. to increase its effect. ~*n.* **follow-up. 3. a.** something done to reinforce an initial action. **b.** (*as modifier*): *a follow-up letter.* **4.** *Med.* an examination of a patient at intervals after treatment.

folly (ˈfɒlɪ) *n., pl.* **-lies. 1.** the state or quality of being foolish. **2.** a foolish action, idea, etc. **3.** a building in the form of a castle, temple, etc., built to satisfy a fancy or conceit. **4.** (*pl.*) *Theatre.* an elaborately costumed review. [C13: < OF *folie* madness, < *fou* mad; see FOOL[1]]

foment (fəˈmɛnt) *vb.* (*tr.*) **1.** to encourage or instigate (trouble, discord, etc.). **2.** *Med.* to apply heat and moisture to (a part of the body) to relieve pain. [C15: < LL, < L *fōmentum* a poultice, ult. < *fovēre* to foster] —**fomentation** (ˌfəʊmɛnˈteɪʃən) *n.* —**foˈmenter** *n.*

fond (fɒnd) *adj.* **1.** (*postpositive;* foll. by *of*) having a liking (for). **2.** loving; tender. **3.** indulgent: *a fond mother.* **4.** (of hopes, wishes, etc.) cherished but unlikely to be realized: *he had fond hopes of starting his own firm.* **5.** *Arch. or dialect.* **a.** foolish. **b.** credulous. [C14 *fonned,* < *fonne* a fool] —**ˈfondly** *adv.* —**ˈfondness** *n.*

fondant (ˈfɒndənt) *n.* **1.** a thick flavoured paste of sugar and water, used in sweets and icings. **2.** a sweet made of this mixture. ~*adj.* **3.** (of a colour) soft, pastel. [C19: < F, lit.: melting, < *fondre* to melt, < L *fundere;* see FOUND[3]]

fondle (ˈfɒndᵊl) *vb.* (*tr.*) to touch or stroke tenderly. [C17: < (obs.) vb. *fond* to fondle; see FOND] —**ˈfondler** *n.*

fondue (ˈfɒndjuː; *French* fɔ̃dy) *n.* a Swiss dish, consisting of melted cheese into which small pieces of bread are dipped. [C19: < F, fem. of *fondu* melted; see FONDANT]

font[1] (fɒnt) *n.* **1. a.** a large bowl for baptismal water. **b.** a receptacle for holy water. **2.** the reservoir for oil in an oil lamp. **3.** *Arch. or poetic.* a fountain or well. [OE, < Church L *fons* < L: fountain]

font[2] (fɒnt) *n. Printing.* another name (esp. U.S. and Canad.) for **fount**[2].

fontanelle *or chiefly U.S.* **fontanel** (ˌfɒntəˈnɛl) *n. Anat.* any of the soft membranous gaps between the bones of the skull in a fetus or infant. [C16 (in the sense: hollow between muscles): < OF *fontanele,* lit.: a little spring, < *fontaine* FOUNTAIN]

food (fuːd) *n.* **1.** any substance that can be ingested by a living organism and metabolized into energy and body tissue. Related adj.: **alimentary. 2.** nourishment in more or less solid form: *food and drink.* **3.** anything that provides mental nourishment or stimulus. [OE *fōda*]

food additive *n.* any of various natural or synthetic substances, such as salt or citric acid, used in the commercial processing of food as preservatives, antioxidants, emulsifiers, etc.

food chain *n. Ecology.* a series of organisms in a community, each member of which feeds on another in the chain and is in turn eaten.

foodie *or* **foody** (ˈfuːdɪ) *n., pl.* **foodies.** a person having an enthusiastic interest in the preparation and consumption of good food.

food poisoning *n.* an acute illness caused by food that is either naturally poisonous or contaminated by bacteria.

food processor *n. Cookery.* an electric domestic appliance for automatic chopping, grating, blending, etc.

foodstuff (ˈfuːdˌstʌf) *n.* any material, substance, etc., that can be used as food.

food value *n.* the relative degree of nourishment obtained from different foods.

fool[1] (fuːl) *n.* **1.** a person who lacks sense or judgement. **2.** a person who is made to appear ridiculous. **3.** (formerly) a professional jester living in a royal or noble household. **4.** *Obs.* an idiot or imbecile: *the village fool.* **5. act** *or* **play the fool.** to deliberately act foolishly. ~*vb.* **6.** (*tr.*) to deceive (someone), esp. in order to make him look ridiculous. **7.** (*intr.;* foll. by *with, around with,* or *about with*) *Inf.* to act or play (with) irresponsibly or aimlessly. **8.** (*intr.*) to speak or act in a playful or jesting manner. **9.** (*tr.;* foll. by *away*) to squander; fritter. ~*adj.* **10.** *U.S. inf.* short for **foolish.** [C13: < OF *fol* mad person, < LL *follis* empty-headed fellow, < L: bellows]

fool[2] (fuːl) *n. Chiefly Brit.* a dessert made from a purée of fruit with cream. [C16: ?< FOOL[1]]

foolery (ˈfuːlərɪ) *n., pl.* **-eries. 1.** foolish behaviour. **2.** an instance of this.

foolhardy (ˈfuːlˌhɑːdɪ) *adj.* **-hardier, -hardiest.** heedlessly rash or adventurous. [C13: < OF, < *fol* foolish + *hardi* bold] —**ˈfoolˌhardily** *adv.* —**ˈfoolˌhardiness** *n.*

foolish (ˈfuːlɪʃ) *adj.* **1.** unwise; silly. **2.** resulting from folly or stupidity. **3.** ridiculous or absurd. **4.** weak-minded; simple. —**ˈfoolishly** *adv.* —**ˈfoolishness** *n.*

foolproof (ˈfuːlˌpruːf) *adj. Inf.* **1.** proof against failure. **2.** (esp. of machines, etc.) proof against human misuse, error, etc.

fool's cap *n.* **1.** a hood or cap with bells or tassels, worn by court jesters. **2.** a dunce's cap.

foolscap (ˈfuːlzˌkæp) *n. Chiefly Brit.* a size of writing or printing paper, 13½ by 17 inches. [C17: see FOOL[1], CAP; so called from the watermark formerly used on this kind of paper]

fool's errand *n.* a fruitless undertaking.

fool's gold *n.* any of various yellow minerals, esp. pyrite, that can be mistaken for gold.

fool's paradise *n.* illusory happiness.

fool's-parsley *n.* an evil-smelling Eurasian umbelliferous plant with small white flowers.

foot (fʊt) *n., pl.* **feet. 1.** the part of the vertebrate leg below the ankle joint that is in contact with the ground during standing and walking. Related adj.: **pedal. 2.** the part of a garment covering a foot. **3.** any of various organs of locomotion or attachment in invertebrates, including molluscs. **4.** *Bot.* the lower part of some plants or plant structures. **5.** a unit of length equal to one third of a yard or 12 inches. 1 foot is equivalent to 0.3048 metre. **6.** any part resembling a foot in form or function: *the foot of a chair.* **7.** the lower part of something; bottom: *the foot of a hill.* **8.** the end of a series or group: *the foot of the list.* **9.** manner of walking or moving: *a heavy foot.* **10. a.** infantry, esp. in the British army. **b.** (*as modifier*): *a foot soldier.* **11.** any of various attachments on a sewing machine that hold the fabric in position. **12.** *Prosody.* a group of two or more syllables in which one syllable has the major stress, forming the basic unit of poetic rhythm. **13. my foot!** an expression of disbelief, often of the speaker's own preceding statement. **14. of foot.** *Arch.* in manner of movement: *fleet of foot.* **15. one foot in the grave.** *Inf.* near to death. **16. on foot. a.** walking or running. **b.** astir; afoot. **17. put a foot wrong.** to make a mistake. **18. put one's best foot forward. a.** to try to do one's best. **b.** to hurry. **19. put one's foot down.** *Inf.* to act firmly. **20. put one's foot in it.** *Inf.* to blunder. **21. under foot.** on the ground; beneath one's feet. ~*vb.* **22.** to dance to music (esp. in **foot it**). **23.** (*tr.*) to walk over or set foot on (esp. in **foot it**). **24.** (*tr.*) to pay the entire cost of (esp. in **foot the bill**). ~See also **feet.** [OE *fōt*] —**'footless** *adj.*

footage ('fʊtɪdʒ) *n.* **1.** a length or distance measured in feet. **2.** the extent of film material shot and exposed.

foot-and-mouth disease *n.* an acute highly infectious viral disease of cattle, pigs, sheep, and goats, characterized by the formation of vesicular eruptions in the mouth and on the feet.

football ('fʊt,bɔːl) *n.* **1. a.** any of various games played with a round or oval ball and usually based on two teams competing to kick, head, carry, or otherwise propel the ball into each other's goal, territory, etc. **b.** (*as modifier*): *a football supporter.* **2.** the ball used in any of these games or their variants. **3.** a problem, issue, etc., that is continually passed from one group or person to another as a pretext for argument. —**'foot,baller** *n.*

footboard ('fʊt,bɔːd) *n.* **1.** a board for a person to stand or rest his feet on. **2.** a treadle or foot-operated lever on a machine. **3.** a vertical board at the foot of a bed.

footbridge ('fʊt,brɪdʒ) *n.* a narrow bridge for the use of pedestrians.

-footed *adj.* **1.** having a foot or feet as specified: *four-footed.* **2.** having a tread as specified: *heavy-footed.*

footer[1] ('fʊtə) *n.* (*in combination*) a person or thing of a specified length or height in feet: *a six-footer.*

footer[2] ('fʊtə) *n. Brit. inf.* short for **football** (the game).

footfall ('fʊt,fɔːl) *n.* the sound of a footstep.

foot fault *n. Tennis.* a fault that occurs when the server fails to keep both feet behind the baseline until he has served.

foothill ('fʊt,hɪl) *n.* (*often pl.*) a relatively low hill at the foot of a mountain.

foothold ('fʊt,həʊld) *n.* **1.** a ledge or other place affording a secure grip, as during climbing. **2.** a secure position from which further progress may be made.

footing ('fʊtɪŋ) *n.* **1.** the basis or foundation on which something is established: *the business was on a secure footing.* **2.** the relationship or status existing between two persons, groups, etc. **3.** a secure grip by or for the feet. **4.** the lower part of a foundation of a column, wall, building, etc.

footle ('fuːtᵊl) *vb.* (*intr.*; often foll. by *around* or *about*) *Inf.* to loiter aimlessly. [C19: prob. < F *foutre* to copulate with, < L *futuere*] —**'footling** *adj.*

footlights ('fʊt,laɪts) *pl. n. Theatre.* lights set in a row along the front of the stage floor.

footloose ('fʊt,luːs) *adj.* **1.** free to go or do as one wishes. **2.** restless: *to feel footloose.*

footman ('fʊtmən) *n., pl.* **-men. 1.** a male servant, esp. one in livery. **2.** (formerly) a foot soldier.

footnote ('fʊt,nəʊt) *n.* **1.** a note printed at the bottom of a page, to which attention is drawn by means of a mark in the text. ~*vb.* **2.** (*tr.*) to supply (a page, etc.) with footnotes.

footpad ('fʊt,pæd) *n. Arch.* a robber or highwayman, on foot rather than horseback.

footpath ('fʊt,pɑːθ) *n.* a narrow path for walkers only.

footplate ('fʊt,pleɪt) *n. Chiefly Brit.* a platform in the cab of a locomotive on which the crew stand to operate the controls.

foot-pound-second *n.* See **fps units.**

footprint ('fʊt,prɪnt) *n.* an indentation or outline of the foot of a person or animal on a surface.

footrest ('fʊt,rɛst) *n.* something that provides a support for the feet, such as a low stool, rail, etc.

foot rot *n. Vet. science.* See **rot** (sense 10).

footsie ('fʊtsɪ) *n. Inf.* flirtation involving the touching together of feet, etc.

foot soldier *n.* an infantryman.

footsore ('fʊt,sɔː) *adj.* having sore or tired feet, esp. from much walking. —**'foot,soreness** *n.*

footstep ('fʊt,stɛp) *n.* **1.** the action of taking a step in walking. **2.** the sound made by walking. **3.** the distance covered with a step. **4.** a footmark. **5.** a single stair. **6. follow in someone's footsteps.** to continue the example of another.

footstool ('fʊt,stuːl) *n.* a low stool used for supporting or resting the feet of a seated person.

footwear ('fʊt,wɛə) *n.* anything worn to cover the feet.

footwork ('fʊt,wɜːk) *n.* skilful use of the feet, as in sports, dancing, etc.

fop (fɒp) *n.* a man who is excessively concerned with fashion and elegance. [C15: rel. to G *foppen* to trick] —**'foppery** *n.* —**'foppish** *adj.*

for (fɔː; *unstressed* fə) *prep.* **1.** directed or belonging to: *there's a phone call for you.* **2.** to the advantage of: *I only did it for you.* **3.** in the direction of: *heading for the border.* **4.** over a span of (time or distance): *working for six days.* **5.** in favour of: *vote for me.* **6.** in order to get or achieve: *I do it for money.* **7.** designed to meet the needs of: *these kennels are for puppies.* **8.** at a cost of: *I got it for hardly any money.* **9.** such as explains or results in: *his reason for changing his job was not given.* **10.** in place of: *a substitute for the injured player.* **11.** because of: *she wept for pure relief.* **12.** with regard or consideration to the usual characteristics of: *it's cool for this time of year.* **13.** concerning: *desire for money.* **14.** as being: *I know that for a fact.* **15.** at a specified time: *a date for the next evening.* **16.** to do or partake of: *an appointment for supper.* **17.** in the duty or task of: *that's for him to say.* **18.** to allow of: *too big a job for us to handle.* **19.** despite: *she's a good wife, for all her nagging.* **20.** in order to preserve, retain, etc.: *to fight for survival.* **21.** as a direct equivalent to: *word for word.* **22.** in order to become or enter: *to train for the priesthood.* **23.** in recompense for: *I paid for it last week.* **24. for it.** *Brit. inf.* liable for punishment or blame: *you'll be for it if she catches you.* ~*conj.* **25.** (*coordinating*) because; seeing that: *I couldn't stay, for the area was violent.* [OE]

for- *prefix.* **1.** indicating rejection or prohibition: *forbid.* **2.** indicating falsity: *forswear.* **3.** used to give intensive force: *forlorn.* [OE *for-*]

▷ **Usage.** The difference in meaning between the prefixes *for-* and *fore-* helps to distinguish between pairs of similar words like *forbear, forebear* and *forgo, forego. For-* implies negation or prohibition, so that *forbear* means "not to do something" and *forgo* means "to deny oneself something". *Fore-* has the sense "before, earlier", hence *forebear* means "one who has gone before, i.e., an ancestor", and *forego* means "to go or have happened before", as in *a foregone conclusion.* In practice, the above words are used interchangeably with or without the *e,* but careful writers of English may prefer to maintain the distinction between them.

forage ('fɒrɪdʒ) *n.* **1.** food for horses or cattle, esp. hay or straw. **2.** the act of searching for food or provisions. ~*vb.* **3.** to search (the countryside or a town) for food, etc. **4.** (*intr.*) *Mil.* to carry out a raid. **5.** (*tr.*) to obtain by searching about. **6.** (*tr.*) to give food or other provisions to. **7.** (*tr.*) to feed (cattle or horses) with such food. [C14: < OF *fourrage*, prob. of Gmc origin] —'**forager** *n.*

forage cap *n.* a soldier's undress cap.

foramen (fɒ'reɪmɛn) *n., pl.* **-ramina** (-'ræmɪnə) *or* **-ramens.** a natural hole, esp. one in a bone. [C17: < L, < *forāre* to bore, pierce]

foraminifer (ˌfɒrə'mɪnɪfə) *n.* a protozoan of the order *Foraminifera*, having a shell with numerous openings through which the pseudopodia protrude. [C19: < NL, < FORAMEN + -FER]

forasmuch as (fərəz'mʌtʃ) *conj.* (*subordinating*) *Arch. or legal.* seeing that.

foray ('fɒreɪ) *n.* **1.** a short raid or incursion. ~*vb.* **2.** to raid or ravage (a town, district, etc.). [C14: < *forrayen* to pillage, < OF, < *fuerre* fodder]

forbade (fə'bæd, -'beɪd) *or* **forbad** (fə'bæd) *vb.* the past tense of **forbid.**

forbear[1] (fɔː'bɛə) *vb.* **-bearing, -bore, -borne.** **1.** (when *intr.*, often foll. by *from* or an infinitive) to cease or refrain (from doing something). **2.** *Arch.* to tolerate (misbehaviour, etc.). [OE *forberan*]

▷ **Usage.** See at **for-.**

forbear[2] ('fɔːˌbɛə) *n.* a variant spelling of **forebear.**

forbearance (fɔː'bɛərəns) *n.* **1.** the act of forbearing. **2.** self-control; patience.

forbid (fə'bɪd) *vb.* **-bidding, -bade** *or* **-bad, -bidden** *or* **-bid.** (*tr.*) **1.** to prohibit (a person) in a forceful or authoritative manner (from doing or having something). **2.** to make impossible. **3.** to shut out or exclude. [OE *forbēodan;* see FOR-, BID] —**for'bidder** *n.*

forbidden (fə'bɪdᵊn) *adj.* **1.** not permitted by order or law. **2.** *Physics.* involving a change in quantum numbers that is not permitted by certain rules derived from quantum mechanics.

forbidden fruit *n.* any pleasure or enjoyment regarded as illicit, esp. sexual indulgence.

forbidding (fə'bɪdɪŋ) *adj.* **1.** hostile or unfriendly. **2.** dangerous or ominous.

forbore (fɔː'bɔː) *vb.* the past tense of **forbear**[1].

forborne (fɔː'bɔːn) *vb.* the past participle of **forbear**[1].

force[1] (fɔːs) *n.* **1.** strength or energy; power: *the force of the blow.* **2.** exertion or the use of exertion against a person or thing that resists. **3.** *Physics.* **a.** a dynamic influence that changes a body from a state of rest to one of motion or changes its rate of motion. **b.** a static influence that produces a strain in a body or system. Symbol: *F* **4. a.** intellectual, political, or moral influence or strength: *the force of his argument.* **b.** a person or thing with such influence: *he was a force in the land.* **5.** vehemence or intensity: *she spoke with great force.* **6.** a group of persons organized for military or police functions: *armed forces.* **7.** (*sometimes cap.;* preceded by *the*) *Inf.* the police force. **8.** a group of persons organized for particular duties or tasks: *a workforce.* **9.** *Criminal law.* violence unlawfully committed or threatened. **10. in force. a.** (of a law) having legal validity. **b.** in great strength or numbers. ~*vb.* (*tr.*) **11.** to compel or cause (a person, group, etc.) to do something through effort, superior strength, etc. **12.** to acquire or produce through effort, superior strength, etc.: *to force a confession.* **13.** to propel or drive despite resistance. **14.** to break down or open (a lock, door, etc.). **15.** to impose or inflict: *he forced his views on them.* **16.** to cause (plants or farm animals) to grow or fatten artificially at an increased rate. **17.** to strain to the utmost: *to force the voice.* **18.** to rape. **19.** *Cards.* **a.** to compel a player by the lead of a particular suit to play (a certain card). **b.** (in bridge) to induce (a bid) from one's partner. [C13: < OF, < Vulgar L *fortia* (unattested), < L *fortis* strong] —'**forceable** *adj.* —'**forceless** *adj.* —'**forcer** *n.*

force[2] (fɔːs) *n.* (in N England) a waterfall. [C17: < ON *fors*]

forced (fɔːst) *adj.* **1.** done because of force: *forced labour.* **2.** false or unnatural: *a forced smile.* **3.** due to an emergency or necessity: *a forced landing.*

force-feed *vb.* **-feeding, -fed.** (*tr.*) to force (a person or animal) to eat or swallow food.

forceful ('fɔːsfʊl) *adj.* **1.** powerful. **2.** persuasive or effective. —'**forcefully** *adv.* —'**forcefulness** *n.*

forcemeat ('fɔːsˌmiːt) *n.* a mixture of chopped ingredients used for stuffing. Also called: **farce.** [C17: < *force* (see FARCE) + MEAT]

forceps ('fɔːsɪps) *n., pl.* **-ceps.** **1. a.** a surgical instrument in the form of a pair of pincers, used esp. in the delivery of babies. **b.** (*as modifier*): *a forceps baby.* **2.** any part of an organism shaped like a forceps. [C17: < L, < *formus* hot + *capere* to seize]

force pump *n.* a pump that ejects fluid under pressure. Cf. **lift pump.**

Forces ('fɔːsɪz) *pl. n.* (usually preceded by *the*) the armed services of a nation.

forcible ('fɔːsəbᵊl) *adj.* **1.** done by, involving, or having force. **2.** convincing or effective: *a forcible argument.* —'**forcibly** *adv.*

ford (fɔːd) *n.* **1.** a shallow area in a river that can be crossed by car, on horseback, etc. ~*vb.* **2.** (*tr.*) to cross (a river, brook, etc.) over a shallow area. [OE] —'**fordable** *adj.*

fore[1] (fɔː) *adj.* **1.** (*usually in combination*) located at, in, or towards the front: *the forelegs of a horse.* ~*n.* **2.** the front part. **3.** something located at, or towards the front. **4. fore and aft.** located at both ends of a vessel: *a fore-and-aft rig.* **5. to the fore.** to the front or conspicuous position. ~*adv.* **6.** at or towards a ship's bow. **7.** *Obs.* before. ~*prep., conj.* **8.** a less common word for **before.** [OE]

fore[2] (fɔː) *sentence substitute.* (in golf) a warning shout made by a player about to make a shot. [C19: prob. short for BEFORE]

fore- *prefix.* **1.** before in time or rank: *forefather.* **2.** at or near the front: *forecourt.* [OE, < *fore* (adv.)]

▷ **Usage.** See at **for-.**

fore-and-after *n. Naut.* **1.** any vessel with a fore-and-aft rig. **2.** a double-ended vessel.

forearm[1] ('fɔːrˌɑːm) *n.* the part of the arm from the elbow to the wrist. [C18: < FORE- + ARM[1]]

forearm[2] (fɔːr'ɑːm) *vb.* (*tr.*) to prepare or arm (someone) in advance. [C16: < FORE- + ARM[2]]

forebear *or* **forbear** ('fɔːˌbɛə) *n.* an ancestor.

▷ **Usage.** See at **for-.**

forebode (fɔː'bəʊd) *vb.* **1.** to warn of or indicate (an event, result, etc.) in advance. **2.** to have a premonition of (an event).

foreboding (fɔː'bəʊdɪŋ) *n.* **1.** a feeling of impending evil, disaster, etc. **2.** an omen or portent. ~*adj.* **3.** presaging something.

forebrain ('fɔːˌbreɪn) *n.* the nontechnical name for **prosencephalon.**

forecast ('fɔːˌkɑːst) *vb.* **-casting, -cast** *or* **-casted.** **1.** to predict or calculate (weather, events, etc.), in advance. **2.** (*tr.*) to serve as an early indication of. ~*n.* **3.** a statement of probable future weather calculated from meteorological data. **4.** a prediction. **5.** the practice or power of forecasting. —'**foreˌcaster** *n.*

forecastle, fo'c's'le, *or* **fo'c'sle** ('fəʊksᵊl) *n.* the part of a vessel at the bow where the crew is quartered.

foreclose (fɔː'kləʊz) *vb.* **1.** *Law.* to deprive (a mortgagor, etc.) of the right to redeem (a mortgage or pledge). **2.** (*tr.*) to shut out; bar. **3.** (*tr.*) to prevent or hinder. [C15: < OF, < *for-* out + *clore* to close, < L *claudere*] —**fore'closable** *adj.* —**foreclosure** (fɔː'kləʊʒə) *n.*

forecourt ('fɔːˌkɔːt) *n.* **1.** a courtyard in front of a building, as one in a filling station. **2.** the section of the court in tennis, badminton, etc., between the service line and the net.

foredoom (fɔː'duːm) *vb.* (*tr.*) to doom or condemn beforehand.

forefather ('fɔːˌfɑːðə) *n.* an ancestor, esp. a male. —'**foreˌfatherly** *adj.*

forefinger ('fɔːˌfɪŋgə) *n.* the finger next to the thumb. Also called: **index finger.**

forefoot ('fɔːˌfʊt) *n., pl.* **-feet.** either of the front feet of a quadruped.

forefront (ˈfɔːˌfrʌnt) *n.* **1.** the extreme front. **2.** the position of most prominence or action.

foregather (fɔːˈgæðə) *vb.* a variant spelling of **forgather.**

forego[1] (fɔːˈgəʊ) *vb.* **-going, -went, -gone.** to precede in time, place, etc. [OE *foregān*]

forego[2] (fɔːˈgəʊ) *vb.* **-going, -went, -gone.** (*tr.*) a variant spelling of **forgo.**

▷ **Usage.** See at **for-.**

foregoing (fɔːˈgəʊɪŋ) *adj.* (*prenominal*) (esp. of writing or speech) going before; preceding.

foregone (fɔːˈgɒn, ˈfɔːˌgɒn) *adj.* gone or completed; past. —**foreˈgoneness** *n.*

foregone conclusion *n.* an inevitable result or conclusion.

foreground (ˈfɔːˌgraʊnd) *n.* **1.** the part of a scene situated towards the front or nearest to the viewer. **2.** a conspicuous position.

forehand (ˈfɔːˌhænd) *adj.* (*prenominal*) **1.** *Tennis, squash, etc.* (of a stroke) made with the palm of the hand facing the direction of the stroke. ~*n.* **2.** *Tennis, squash, etc.* **a.** a forehand stroke. **b.** the side on which such strokes are made. **3.** the part of a horse in front of the saddle.

forehead (ˈfɒrɪd, ˈfɔːˌhɛd) *n.* the part of the face between the natural hairline and the eyes. Related adj.: **frontal.** [OE *forhēafod*]

foreign (ˈfɒrɪn) *adj.* **1.** of, located in, or coming from another country, area, people, etc.: *a foreign resident.* **2.** dealing or concerned with another country, area, people, etc.: *a foreign office.* **3.** not pertinent or related: *a matter foreign to the discussion.* **4.** not familiar; strange. **5.** in an abnormal place or position: *foreign matter.* [C13: < OF, < Vulgar L *forānus* (unattested) on the outside, < L *foris* outside] —**ˈforeignness** *n.*

foreign affairs *pl. n.* matters abroad that involve the homeland, such as relations with another country.

foreigner (ˈfɒrɪnə) *n.* **1.** a person from a foreign country. **2.** an outsider. **3.** something from a foreign country, such as a ship or product.

foreign minister *or* **secretary** *n.* (*often caps.*) a cabinet minister who is responsible for a country's dealings with other countries. U.S. equivalent: **secretary of state.**

foreign office *n.* the ministry of a country or state that is concerned with dealings with other states. U.S. equivalent: **State Department.**

foreknowledge (fɔːˈnɒlɪdʒ) *n.* knowledge of a thing before it exists or occurs; prescience. —**foreˈknow** *vb.* —**foreˈknowable** *adj.*

foreland (ˈfɔːlənd) *n.* **1.** a headland, cape, or promontory. **2.** land lying in front of something, such as water.

foreleg (ˈfɔːˌlɛg) *n.* either of the front legs of a horse, sheep, or other quadruped.

forelimb (ˈfɔːˌlɪm) *n.* either of the front or anterior limbs of a four-limbed vertebrate.

forelock (ˈfɔːˌlɒk) *n.* a lock of hair growing or falling over the forehead.

foreman (ˈfɔːmən) *n., pl.* **-men. 1.** a person, often experienced, who supervises other workmen. **2.** *Law.* the principal juror, who presides at the deliberations of a jury.

foremast (ˈfɔːˌmɑːst; *Naut.* ˈfɔːməst) *n.* the mast nearest the bow on vessels with two or more masts.

foremost (ˈfɔːˌməʊst) *adj., adv.* first in time, place, rank, etc. [OE, < *forma* first]

forename (ˈfɔːˌneɪm) *n.* another term for **Christian name.**

forenamed (ˈfɔːˌneɪmd) *adj.* (*prenominal*) named or mentioned previously; aforesaid.

forenoon (ˈfɔːˌnuːn) *n.* the daylight hours before or just before noon.

forensic (fəˈrɛnsɪk) *adj.* used in, or connected with a court of law: *forensic science.* [C17: < L *forēnsis* public, < FORUM] —**foˈrensically** *adv.*

forensic medicine *n.* the use of medical knowledge, esp. pathology, to the purposes of the law, as in determining the cause of death. Also called: **medical jurisprudence.**

foreordain (ˌfɔːrɔːˈdeɪn) *vb.* (*tr.; may take a clause as object*) to determine (events, etc.) in the future. —**foreordination** (ˌfɔːrɔːdɪˈneɪʃən) *n.*

forepaw (ˈfɔːˌpɔː) *n.* either of the front feet of most land mammals that do not have hoofs.

foreplay (ˈfɔːˌpleɪ) *n.* mutual sexual stimulation preceding sexual intercourse.

forequarter (ˈfɔːˌkwɔːtə) *n.* the front portion, including the leg, of half of a carcass, as of beef.

forequarters (ˈfɔːˌkwɔːtəz) *pl. n.* the part of the body of a horse, etc. that consists of the forelegs, shoulders, and adjoining parts.

forerun (fɔːˈrʌn) *vb.* **-running, -ran, -run.** (*tr.*) **1.** to serve as a herald for. **2.** to precede. **3.** to forestall.

forerunner (ˈfɔːˌrʌnə) *n.* **1.** a person or thing that precedes another. **2.** a person or thing coming in advance to herald the arrival of someone or something. **3.** an omen; portent.

foresail (ˈfɔːˌseɪl; *Naut.* ˈfɔːsᵊl) *n. Naut.* **1.** the aftermost headsail of a fore-and-aft rigged vessel. **2.** the lowest sail set on the foremast of a square-rigged vessel.

foresee (fɔːˈsiː) *vb.* **-seeing, -saw, -seen.** (*tr.; may take a clause as object*) to see or know beforehand: *he did not foresee that.* —**foreˈseeable** *adj.* —**foreˈseer** *n.*

foreshadow (fɔːˈʃædəʊ) *vb.* (*tr.*) to show, indicate, or suggest in advance; presage.

foreshank (ˈfɔːˌʃænk) *n.* **1.** the top of the front leg of an animal. **2.** a cut of meat from this part.

foresheet (ˈfɔːˌʃiːt) *n.* **1.** the sheet of a foresail. **2.** (*pl.*) the part forward of the foremost thwart of a boat.

foreshock (ˈfɔːˌʃɒk) *n. Chiefly U.S.* a relatively small earthquake heralding the arrival of a much larger one.

foreshore (ˈfɔːˌʃɔː) *n.* **1.** the part of the shore that lies between the limits for high and low tides. **2.** the part of the shore that lies just above the high water mark.

foreshorten (fɔːˈʃɔːtᵊn) *vb.* (*tr.*) to represent (a line, form, object, etc.) as shorter than actual length in order to give an illusion of recession or projection.

foreshow (fɔːˈʃəʊ) *vb.* **-showing, -showed, -shown.** (*tr.*) *Arch.* to indicate in advance.

foresight (ˈfɔːˌsaɪt) *n.* **1.** provision for or insight into future problems, needs, etc. **2.** the act or ability of foreseeing. **3.** the act of looking forward. **4.** *Surveying.* a reading taken looking forwards. **5.** the front sight on a firearm. —ˌ**foreˈsighted** *adj.* —ˌ**foreˈsightedly** *adv.* —ˌ**foreˈsightedness** *n.*

foreskin (ˈfɔːˌskɪn) *n. Anat.* the nontechnical name for **prepuce.**

forest (ˈfɒrɪst) *n.* **1.** a large wooded area having a thick growth of trees and plants. **2.** the trees of such an area. **3.** *N.Z.* an area planted with pines or similar trees, not native trees. Cf. **bush** (sense 4). **4.** something resembling a large wooded area, esp. in density: *a forest of telegraph poles.* **5.** *Law.* (formerly) an area of woodland, esp. one owned by the sovereign and set apart as a hunting ground. **6.** (*modifier*) of, involving, or living in a forest or forests: *a forest glade.* ~*vb.* **7.** (*tr.*) to create a forest. [C13: < OF, < Med. L *forestis* unfenced woodland, < L *foris* outside] —**ˈforested** *adj.*

forestall (fɔːˈstɔːl) *vb.* (*tr.*) **1.** to delay, stop, or guard against beforehand. **2.** to anticipate. **3.** to buy up merchandise for profitable resale. [C14 *forestallen* to waylay, < OE, < *fore-* in front of + *steall* place] —**foreˈstaller** *n.* —**foreˈstalment** *n.*

forestation (ˌfɒrɪˈsteɪʃən) *n.* the planting of trees over a wide area.

forestay (ˈfɔːˌsteɪ) *n. Naut.* an adjustable stay leading from the truck of the foremast to the deck, for controlling the bending of the mast.

forester (ˈfɒrɪstə) *n.* **1.** a person skilled in forestry or in charge of a forest. **2.** a person or animal that lives in a forest. **3.** (*cap.*) a member of the Ancient Order of Foresters, a friendly society.

forest park *n. N.Z.* a recreational reserve which may include bush and exotic trees.

forestry (ˈfɒrɪstrɪ) *n.* **1.** the science of planting and caring for trees. **2.** the planting and management of forests. **3.** *Rare.* forest land.

foretaste (ˈfɔːˌteɪst) *n.* an early but limited experience of something to come.

foretell (fɔːˈtɛl) *vb.* **-telling, -told.** (*tr.; may take a clause as object*) to tell or indicate (an event, a result, etc.) beforehand.

forethought (ˈfɔːˌθɔːt) *n.* **1.** advance consideration or deliberation. **2.** thoughtful anticipation of future events.

foretoken *n.* (ˈfɔːˌtəʊkən). **1.** a sign of a future event. ~*vb.* (fɔːˈtəʊkən). **2.** (*tr.*) to foreshadow.

foretop (ˈfɔːˌtɒp; *Naut.* ˈfɔːtəp) *n. Naut.* a platform at the top of the foremast.

fore-topgallant (ˌfɔːtɒpˈgælənt; *Naut.* ˌfɔːtəˈgælənt) *adj. Naut.* of, relating to, or being the topmost portion of a foremast.

fore-topmast (fɔːˈtɒpˌmɑːst; *Naut.* fɔːˈtɒpməst) *n. Naut.* a mast stepped above a foremast.

fore-topsail (fɔːˈtɒpˌseɪl; *Naut.* fɔːˈtɒpsᵊl) *n. Naut.* a sail set on a fore-topmast.

for ever *or* **forever** (fɔːˈrɛvə, fə-) *adv.* **1.** without end; everlastingly. **2.** at all times. **3.** *Inf.* for a very long time: *he went on speaking for ever.* ~*n.* **forever. 4.** (*as object*) *Inf.* a very long time: *it took him forever to reply.*

for evermore *or* **forevermore** (fɔːˌrɛvəˈmɔː, fə-) *adv.* a more emphatic or emotive term for **for ever.**

forewarn (fɔːˈwɔːn) *vb.* (*tr.*) to warn beforehand. —**foreˈwarner** *n.*

forewent (fɔːˈwɛnt) *vb.* the past tense of **forego.**

forewing (ˈfɔːˌwɪŋ) *n.* either wing of the anterior pair of an insect's two pairs of wings.

foreword (ˈfɔːˌwɜːd) *n.* an introductory statement to a book. [C19: literal translation of G *Vorwort*]

forfeit (ˈfɔːfɪt) *n.* **1.** something lost or given up as a penalty for a fault, mistake, etc. **2.** the act of losing or surrendering something in this manner. **3.** *Law.* something confiscated as a penalty for an offence, etc. **4.** (*sometimes pl.*) **a.** a game in which a player has to give up an object, perform a specified action, etc., if he commits a fault. **b.** an object so given up. ~*vb.* (*tr.*) **5.** to lose or be liable to lose in consequence of a mistake, fault, etc. **6.** *Law.* to confiscate as punishment. ~*adj.* **7.** surrendered or liable to be surrendered as a penalty. [C13: < OF *forfet* offence, < *forfaire* to commit a crime, < Med. L, < L *foris* outside + *facere* to do] —**ˈforfeiter** *n.*

forfeiture (ˈfɔːfɪtʃə) *n.* **1.** something forfeited. **2.** the act of forfeiting or paying a penalty.

forfend *or* **forefend** (fɔːˈfɛnd) *vb.* (*tr.*) **1.** *U.S.* to protect or secure. **2.** *Obs.* to prevent.

forgather *or* **foregather** (fɔːˈgæðə) *vb.* (*intr.*) **1.** to gather together. **2.** (foll. by *with*) to socialize.

forgave (fəˈgeɪv) *vb.* the past tense of **forgive.**

forge[1] (fɔːdʒ) *n.* **1.** a place in which metal is worked by heating and hammering; smithy. **2.** a hearth or furnace used for heating metal. ~*vb.* **3.** (*tr.*) to shape (metal) by heating and hammering. **4.** (*tr.*) to form, make, or fashion (objects, etc.). **5.** (*tr.*) to invent or devise (an agreement, etc.). **6.** to make a fraudulent imitation of (a signature, etc.) or to commit forgery. [C14: < OF *forgier* to construct, < L *fabricāre*, < *faber* craftsman] —**ˈforger** *n.*

forge[2] (fɔːdʒ) *vb.* (*intr.*) **1.** to move at a steady pace. **2. forge ahead.** to increase speed. [C17: <?]

forgery (ˈfɔːdʒərɪ) *n., pl.* **-geries. 1.** the act of reproducing something for a fraudulent purpose. **2.** something forged, such as an antique. **3.** *Criminal law.* **a.** the false making or altering of a document, such as a cheque, etc., or any tape or disc storing information, with intent to defraud. **b.** something forged.

forget (fəˈgɛt) *vb.* **-getting, -got, -gotten** *or* (*Arch. or dialect*) **-got. 1.** (when *tr., may take a clause as object or an infinitive*) to fail to recall (someone or something once known). **2.** (*tr.; may take a clause as object or an infinitive*) to neglect, either as the result of an unintentional error or intentionally. **3.** (*tr.*) to leave behind by mistake. **4. forget oneself. a.** to act in an improper manner. **b.** to be unselfish. **c.** to be deep in thought. [OE *forgietan*] —**forˈgettable** *adj.* —**forˈgetter** *n.*

forgetful (fəˈgɛtfʊl) *adj.* **1.** tending to forget. **2.** (*often postpositive;* foll. by *of*) inattentive (to) or neglectful (of). —**forˈgetfully** *adv.*

forget-me-not *n.* a temperate low-growing plant having clusters of small blue flowers.

forgive (fəˈgɪv) *vb.* **-giving, -gave, -given. 1.** to cease to blame (someone or something). **2.** to grant pardon for (a mistake, etc.). **3.** (*tr.*) to free (someone) from penalty. **4.** (*tr.*) to free from the obligation of (a debt, etc.). [OE *forgiefan*] —**forˈgivable** *adj.* —**forˈgiver** *n.*

forgiveness (fəˈgɪvnɪs) *n.* **1.** the act of forgiving or the state of being forgiven. **2.** willingness to forgive.

forgiving (fəˈgɪvɪŋ) *adj.* willing to forgive.

forgo *or* **forego** (fɔːˈgəʊ) *vb.* **-going, -went, -gone.** (*tr.*) to give up or do without. [OE *forgān*]
▷ **Usage.** See at **for-.**

forgot (fəˈgɒt) *vb.* **1.** the past tense of **forget. 2.** *Arch. or dialect.* a past participle of **forget.**

forgotten (fəˈgɒtᵊn) *vb.* a past participle of **forget.**

forint (*Hungarian* ˈforint) *n.* the standard monetary unit of Hungary. [< Hungarian, < It. *fiorino* FLORIN]

fork (fɔːk) *n.* **1.** a small usually metal implement consisting of two, three, or four long thin prongs on the end of a handle, used for lifting food to the mouth, etc. **2.** a similar-shaped agricultural tool, used for lifting, digging, etc. **3.** a pronged part of any machine, device, etc. **4.** (of a road, river, etc.) **a.** a division into two or more branches. **b.** the point where the division begins. **c.** such a branch. ~*vb.* **5.** (*tr.*) to pick up, dig, etc., with a fork. **6.** (*tr.*) *Chess.* to place (two enemy pieces) under attack with one of one's own pieces. **7.** (*intr.*) to be divided into two or more branches. **8.** to take one or other branch at a fork in a road, etc. [OE *forca*, < L *furca*]

forked (fɔːkt) *adj.* **1. a.** having a fork or forklike parts. **b.** (*in combination*): *two-forked.* **2.** zigzag: *forked lightning.* —**forkedly** (ˈfɔːkɪdlɪ) *adv.*

fork-lift truck *n.* a vehicle having two power-operated horizontal prongs that can be raised and lowered for transporting and unloading goods. Sometimes shortened to **fork-lift.**

fork out, over, *or* **up** *vb.* (*adv.*) *Sl.* to pay (money, goods, etc.), esp. with reluctance.

forlorn (fəˈlɔːn) *adj.* **1.** miserable or cheerless. **2.** forsaken. **3.** (*postpositive;* foll. by *of*) bereft: *forlorn of hope.* **4.** desperate: *the last forlorn attempt.* [OE *forloren* lost, < *forlēosan* to lose] —**forˈlornness** *n.*

forlorn hope *n.* **1.** a hopeless enterprise. **2.** a faint hope. **3.** *Obs.* a group of soldiers assigned to an extremely dangerous duty. [C16 (in the obs. sense): changed (by folk etymology) < Du. *verloren hoop* lost troop, < *verloren,* p.p. of *verliezen* to lose + *hoop* troop (lit.: heap)]

form (fɔːm) *n.* **1.** the shape or configuration of something as distinct from its colour, texture, etc. **2.** the particular mode, appearance, etc., in which a thing or person manifests itself: *water in the form of ice.* **3.** a type or kind: *imprisonment is a form of punishment.* **4.** a printed document, esp. one with spaces in which to insert facts or answers: *an application form.* **5.** physical or mental condition, esp. good condition, with reference to ability to perform: *off form.* **6.** the previous record of a horse, athlete, etc., esp. with regard to fitness. **7.** *Brit. sl.* a criminal record. **8.** a fixed mode of artistic expression or representation in literary, musical, or other artistic works: *sonata form.* **9.** a mould, frame, etc., that gives shape to something. **10.** *Education, chiefly Brit.* a group of children who are taught together. **11.** behaviour or procedure, esp. as governed by custom or etiquette: *good form.* **12.** formality or ceremony. **13.** a prescribed set or order of words, terms, etc., as in a religious ceremony or legal document. **14.** *Philosophy.* **a.** the structure of anything as opposed to its content. **b.** essence as opposed to matter. **15.** See **logical form.** **16.** *Brit.* a bench, esp. one that is long, low, and backless. **17.** a hare's nest. **18.** any of the various ways in which a word may be spelt or inflected. ~*vb.* **19.** to give shape or form to or to take shape or form, esp. a particular shape. **20.** to come or bring into existence: *a scum formed.* **21.** to make or construct or be made or constructed. **22.** to construct or develop in the mind: *to form an opinion.* **23.** (*tr.*) to train or mould by instruction or example. **24.** (*tr.*) to acquire or develop: *to form a habit.* **25.** (*tr.*) to be an element of or constitute: *this plank will form a bridge.* **26.** (*tr.*) to organize: *to form a club.* [C13: < OF, < L *forma* shape, model]

-form *adj. combining form.* having the shape or form of or resembling: *cruciform; vermiform.* [< NL *-formis*, < L, < *fōrma* FORM]

formal (ˈfɔːməl) *adj.* **1.** of or following established forms, conventions, etc.: *a formal document.* **2.** characterized by observation of conventional forms of ceremony, behaviour, etc.: *a formal dinner.* **3.** methodical or stiff. **4.** suitable for occasions organized according to conventional ceremony: *formal dress.* **5.** denoting idiom, vocabulary, etc., used by educated speakers and writers of a language. **6.** acquired by study in academic institutions. **7.** symmetrical in form: *a formal garden.* **8.** of or relating to the appearance, form, etc., of something as distinguished from its substance. **9.** logically deductive: *formal proof.* **10.** denoting a second-person pronoun in some languages: *in French the pronoun "vous" is formal, while "tu" is informal.* [C14: < L *formālis*] —ˈ**formally** *adv.* —ˈ**formalness** *n.*

formaldehyde (fɔːˈmældɪˌhaɪd) *n.* a colourless poisonous irritating gas with a pungent characteristic odour, used as formalin and in the manufacture of synthetic resins. [C19: FORM(IC) + ALDEHYDE; on the model of G *Formaldehyd*]

formalin (ˈfɔːməlɪn) *n.* a solution of formaldehyde in water, used as a disinfectant, preservative for biological specimens, etc.

formalism (ˈfɔːməˌlɪzəm) *n.* **1.** scrupulous or excessive adherence to outward form at the expense of content. **2.** the mathematical or logical structure of a scientific argument as distinguished from its subject matter. **3.** *Theatre.* a stylized mode of production. **4.** (in Marxist criticism, etc.) excessive concern with artistic technique at the expense of social values, etc. —ˈ**formalist** *n.* —ˌ**formalˈistic** *adj.*

formality (fɔːˈmælɪtɪ) *n., pl.* **-ties.** **1.** a requirement of custom, etiquette, etc. **2.** the quality of being formal or conventional. **3.** strict or excessive observance of ceremony, etc.

formalize *or* **-lise** (ˈfɔːməˌlaɪz) *vb.* **1.** to be or make formal. **2.** (*tr.*) to make official or valid. **3.** (*tr.*) to give a definite shape or form to. —ˌ**formaliˈzation** *or* **-liˈsation** *n.*

formal language *n.* any of various languages designed for use in fields such as mathematics, logic, or computer programming, the symbols and formulas of which stand in precisely specified syntactic and semantic relations to one another.

formal logic *n.* the study of systems of deductive argument in which symbols are used to represent precisely defined categories of expressions.

formant (ˈfɔːmənt) *n. Acoustics, phonetics.* any of the constituents of a sound, esp. a vowel sound, that impart to the sound its own special quality, tone colour, or timbre.

format (ˈfɔːmæt) *n.* **1.** the general appearance of a publication, including type style, paper, binding, etc. **2.** style, plan, or arrangement, as of a television programme. **3.** *Computers.* the arrangement of data on magnetic tape, etc., to comply with a computer's input device. ~*vb.* **-matting, -matted.** (*tr.*) **4.** to arrange (a book, page, etc.) into a specified format. [C19: via F < G, < L *liber formātus* volume formed]

formation (fɔːˈmeɪʃən) *n.* **1.** the act of giving or taking form or existence. **2.** something that is formed. **3.** the manner in which something is arranged. **4. a.** a formal arrangement of a number of persons or things acting as a unit, such as a troop of soldiers or a football team. **b.** (*as modifier*): *formation dancing.* **5.** a series of rocks with certain characteristics in common.

formative (ˈfɔːmətɪv) *adj.* **1.** of or relating to formation, development, or growth: *formative years.* **2.** shaping; moulding: *a formative experience.* **3.** functioning in the formation of derived, inflected, or compound words. ~*n.* **4.** an inflectional or derivational affix. —ˈ**formatively** *adv.* —ˈ**formativeness** *n.*

form class *n.* **1.** another term for **part of speech.** **2.** a group of words distinguished by common inflections, such as the weak verbs of English.

forme *or U.S.* **form** (fɔːm) *n. Printing.* type matter, blocks, etc., assembled in a chase and ready for printing. [C15: < F: FORM]

former[1] (ˈfɔːmə) *adj.* (*prenominal*) **1.** belonging to or occurring in an earlier time: *former glory.* **2.** having been at a previous time: *a former colleague.* **3.** denoting the first or first mentioned of two. ~*n.* **4. the former.** the first or first mentioned of two: distinguished from *latter.*

former[2] (ˈfɔːmə) *n.* **1.** a person or thing that forms or shapes. **2.** *Electrical engineering.* a tool for giving a coil or winding the required shape.

formerly (ˈfɔːməlɪ) *adv.* at or in a former time; in the past.

formic (ˈfɔːmɪk) *adj.* **1.** of, relating to, or derived from ants. **2.** of, containing, or derived from formic acid. [C18: < L *formīca* ant; the acid occurs naturally in ants]

Formica (fɔːˈmaɪkə) *n. Trademark.* any of various laminated plastic sheets used esp. for heat-resistant surfaces.

formic acid *n.* a colourless corrosive liquid carboxylic acid found in some insects, esp. ants, and many plants: used in the manufacture of insecticides. Formula: HCOOH.

formidable (ˈfɔːmɪdəbᵊl) *adj.* **1.** arousing or likely to inspire fear or dread. **2.** extremely difficult to defeat, overcome, manage, etc. **3.** tending to inspire awe or admiration because of great size, excellence, etc. [C15: < L, < *formīdāre* to dread, < *formīdō* fear] —ˈ**formidably** *adv.*

formless (ˈfɔːmlɪs) *adj.* without a definite shape or form; amorphous. —ˈ**formlessly** *adv.*

form letter *n.* a single copy of a letter that has been mechanically reproduced in large numbers for circulation.

formula (ˈfɔːmjʊlə) *n., pl.* **-las** *or* **-lae** (-ˌliː). **1.** an established form or set of words, as used in religious ceremonies, legal proceedings, etc. **2.** *Maths, physics.* a general relationship, principle, or rule stated, often as an equation, in the form of symbols. **3.** *Chem.* a representation of molecules, radicals, ions, etc., expressed in the symbols of the atoms of their constituent elements. **4. a.** a method, pattern, or rule for doing or producing something, often one proved to be successful. **b.** (*as modifier*): *formula fiction.* **5.** *U.S. & Canad.* a prescription for making up a medicine, baby's food, etc. **6.** *Motor racing.* the category in which a type of car competes, judged according to engine size, weight, and fuel capacity. [C17: < L: dim. of *forma* FORM] —**formulaic** (ˌfɔːmjʊˈleɪɪk) *adj.*

formularize *or* **-ise** (ˈfɔːmjʊləˌraɪz) *vb.* a less common word for **formulate** (sense 1).

formulary (ˈfɔːmjʊlərɪ) *n., pl.* **-laries.** **1.** a book of prescribed formulas, esp. relating to religious procedure or doctrine. **2.** a formula. **3.** *Pharmacol.* a book containing a list of pharmaceutical products with their formulas. ~*adj.* **4.** of or relating to a formula.

formulate (ˈfɔːmjʊˌleɪt) *vb.* (*tr.*) **1.** to put into or express in systematic terms; express in or as if in a formula. **2.** to devise. —ˌ**formuˈlation** *n.*

formwork (ˈfɔːmˌwɜːk) *n.* an arrangement of wooden boards, etc., used to shape concrete while it is setting.

fornicate (ˈfɔːnɪˌkeɪt) *vb.* (*intr.*) to commit fornication. [C16: < LL *fornicārī*, < L *fornix* vault, brothel situated therein] —**ˈforniˌcator** *n.*

fornication (ˌfɔːnɪˈkeɪʃən) *n.* **1.** voluntary sexual intercourse outside marriage. **2.** *Bible.* sexual immorality in general, esp. adultery.

forsake (fəˈseɪk) *vb.* **-saking, -sook, -saken.** (*tr.*) **1.** to abandon. **2.** to give up (something valued or enjoyed). [OE *forsacan*] —**forˈsaker** *n.*

forsaken (fəˈseɪkən) *vb.* **1.** the past participle of **forsake.** ~*adj.* **2.** completely deserted or helpless. —**forˈsakenly** *adv.* —**forˈsakenness** *n.*

forsook (fəˈsʊk) *vb.* the past tense of **forsake.**

forsooth (fəˈsuːθ) *adv. Arch.* in truth; indeed. [OE *forsōth*]

forswear (fɔːˈswɛə) *vb.* **-swearing, -swore, -sworn.** **1.** (*tr.*) to reject or renounce with determination or as upon oath. **2.** (*tr.*) to deny or disavow absolutely or upon oath. **3.** to perjure (oneself). [OE *forswearian*] —**forˈswearer** *n.*

forsworn (fɔːˈswɔːn) *vb.* the past participle of **forswear.** —**forˈswornness** *n.*

forsythia (fɔːˈsaɪθɪə) *n.* a shrub native to China, Japan, and SE Europe but widely cultivated for its showy yellow bell-shaped flowers, which appear in spring before the foliage. [C19: NL, after William *Forsyth* (1737–1804), E botanist]

fort (fɔːt) *n.* **1.** a fortified enclosure, building, or position able to be defended against an enemy. **2.** **hold the fort.** *Inf.* to guard something temporarily. [C15: < OF, < *fort* (adj.) strong, < L *fortis*]

fort. *abbrev. for:* **1.** fortification. **2.** fortified.

forte[1] (fɔːt, ˈfɔːteɪ) *n.* **1.** something at which a person excels: *cooking is my forte.* **2.** *Fencing.* the stronger section of a sword, between the hilt and the middle. [C17: < F, < *fort* (adj.) strong, < L *fortis*]

forte[2] (ˈfɔːtɪ) *Music.* ~*adj., adv.* **1.** loud or loudly. Symbol: f ~*n.* **2.** a loud passage in music. [C18: < It., < L *fortis* strong]

forte-piano (ˌfɔːtɪˈpjɑːnəʊ) *Music.* ~*adj., adv.* **1.** loud and then immediately soft. Symbol: fp ~*n.* **2.** a note played in this way.

forth (fɔːθ) *adv.* **1.** forward in place, time, order, or degree. **2.** out, as from concealment or inaction. **3.** away, as from a place or country. **4.** **and so forth.** and so on. ~*prep.* **5.** *Arch.* out of. [OE]

forthcoming (ˌfɔːθˈkʌmɪŋ) *adj.* **1.** approaching in time: *the forthcoming debate.* **2.** about to appear: *his forthcoming book.* **3.** available or ready. **4.** open or sociable.

forthright *adj.* (ˈfɔːθˌraɪt). **1.** direct and outspoken. ~*adv.* (ˌfɔːθˈraɪt, ˈfɔːθˌraɪt), *also* **forthrightly.** **2.** in a direct manner; frankly. **3.** at once. —**ˈforthˌrightness** *n.*

forthwith (ˌfɔːθˈwɪθ) *adv.* at once.

fortification (ˌfɔːtɪfɪˈkeɪʃən) *n.* **1.** the act, art, or science of fortifying or strengthening. **2.** **a.** a wall, mound, etc., used to fortify a place. **b.** such works collectively.

fortify (ˈfɔːtɪˌfaɪ) *vb.* **-fying, -fied.** (*mainly tr.*) **1.** (*also intr.*) to make (a place) defensible, as by building walls, etc. **2.** to strengthen physically, mentally, or morally. **3.** to add alcohol to (wine), in order to produce sherry, port, etc. **4.** to increase the nutritious value of (a food), as by adding vitamins. **5.** to confirm: *to fortify an argument.* [C15: < OF, < LL, < L *fortis* strong + *facere* to make] —**ˈfortiˌfiable** *adj.* —**ˈfortiˌfier** *n.*

fortissimo (fɔːˈtɪsɪˌməʊ) *Music.* ~*adj., adv.* **1.** very loud. Symbol: ff ~*n.* **2.** a very loud passage in music. [C18: < It., < L, < *fortis* strong]

fortitude (ˈfɔːtɪˌtjuːd) *n.* strength and firmness of mind. [C15: < L *fortitūdō* courage]

fortnight (ˈfɔːtˌnaɪt) *n.* a period of 14 consecutive days; two weeks. [OE *fēowertīene niht* fourteen nights]

fortnightly (ˈfɔːtˌnaɪtlɪ) *Chiefly Brit.* ~*adj.* **1.** occurring or appearing once each fortnight. ~*adv.* **2.** once a fortnight. ~*n., pl.* **-lies.** **3.** a publication issued at intervals of two weeks.

FORTRAN (ˈfɔːtræn) *n.* a high-level computer programming language for mathematical and scientific purposes. [C20: < *for*(*mula*) *tran*(*slation*)]

fortress (ˈfɔːtrɪs) *n.* **1.** a large fort or fortified town. **2.** a place or source of refuge or support. ~*vb.* **3.** (*tr.*) to protect. [C13: < OF, < Med. L *fortalitia*, < L *fortis* strong]

fortuitous (fɔːˈtjuːɪtəs) *adj.* happening by chance, esp. by a lucky chance. [C17: < L *fortuitus* happening by chance, < *fors* chance, luck] —**forˈtuitously** *adv.*

fortuity (fɔːˈtjuːɪtɪ) *n., pl.* **-ties.** **1.** a chance or accidental occurrence. **2.** chance or accident.

fortunate (ˈfɔːtʃənɪt) *adj.* **1.** having good luck. **2.** occurring by or bringing good fortune or luck. —**ˈfortunately** *adv.*

fortune (ˈfɔːtʃən) *n.* **1.** an amount of wealth or material prosperity, esp. a great amount. **2.** **small fortune.** a large sum of money. **3.** a power or force, often personalized, regarded as being responsible for human affairs. **4.** luck, esp. when favourable. **5.** (*often pl.*) a person's destiny. ~*vb.* **6.** (*intr.*) *Arch.* to happen by chance. [C13: < OF, < L, < *fors* chance]

fortune-hunter *n.* a person who seeks to secure a fortune, esp. through marriage.

fortune-teller *n.* a person who makes predictions about the future as by looking into a crystal ball, etc. —**ˈfortune-ˌtelling** *adj., n.*

forty (ˈfɔːtɪ) *n., pl.* **-ties.** **1.** the cardinal number that is the product of ten and four. **2.** a numeral, 40, XL, etc., representing this number. **3.** something representing, represented by, or consisting of 40 units. ~*determiner.* **4.** **a.** amounting to forty: *forty thieves.* **b.** (*as pronoun*): *there were forty in the herd.* [OE *fēowertig*] —**ˈfortieth** *adj., n.*

forty-five *n.* a gramophone record played at 45 revolutions per minute.

Forty-Five *n.* **the.** *British history.* another name for the **Jacobite Rebellion** of 1745-46, led by Charles Edward Stuart. See **Young Pretender.**

forty-niner *n.* (*sometimes cap.*) *U.S. history.* a prospector who took part in the California gold rush of 1849.

forty winks *n.* (*functioning as sing. or pl.*) *Inf.* a short light sleep; nap.

forum (ˈfɔːrəm) *n., pl.* **-rums** *or* **-ra** (-rə). **1.** a meeting for the open discussion of subjects of public interest. **2.** a medium for open discussion, such as a magazine. **3.** a public meeting place for open discussion. **4.** a court; tribunal. **5.** (in ancient Italy) an open space serving as a city's marketplace and centre of public business. [C15: < L: public place]

Forum *or* **Forum Romanum** (rəʊˈmɑːnəm) *n.* **the.** the main forum of ancient Rome.

forward (ˈfɔːwəd) *adj.* **1.** directed or moving ahead. **2.** lying or situated in or near the front part of something. **3.** presumptuous, pert, or impudent. **4.** well developed or advanced, esp. in physical or intellectual development. **5.** **a.** of or relating to the future or favouring change. **b.** (*in combination*): *forward-looking.* **6.** (*often postpositive*) *Arch.* ready, eager, or willing. **7.** *Commerce.* relating to fulfilment at a future date. ~*n.* **8.** an attacking player in any of various sports, such as soccer. ~*adv.* **9.** a variant of **forwards.** **10.** (ˈfɔːwəd; *Naut.* ˈfɒrəd). towards the front or bow of an aircraft or ship. **11.** into a position of being subject to public scrutiny: *the witness came forward.* ~*vb.* (*tr.*) **12.** to send forward or pass on to an ultimate destination: *the letter was forwarded.* **13.** to advance or promote: *to forward one's career.* [OE *foreweard*] —**ˈforwarder** *n.* —**ˈforwardly** *adv.* —**ˈforwardness** *n.*

forwards (ˈfɔːwədz) *or* **forward** *adv.* **1.** towards or at a place ahead or in advance, esp. in space but also in time. **2.** towards the front.

forwent (fɔːˈwɛnt) *vb.* the past tense of **forgo.**

forza (ˈfɔːtsə) *n. Music.* force. [C19: It., lit.: force]

fossa (ˈfɒsə) *n., pl.* **-sae** (-siː). an anatomical depression or hollow area. [C19: < L: ditch, < *fossus* dug up, < *fodere* to dig up]

fosse *or* **foss** (fɒs) *n.* a ditch or moat, esp. one dug as a fortification. [C14: < OF, < L *fossa;* see FOSSA]

fossick (ˈfɒsɪk) *vb. Austral. & N.Z.* **1.** (*intr.*) to search for gold or precious stones in abandoned workings, rivers, etc. **2.** to rummage or search for (something): *to fossick around for.* [C19: Austral., prob. < E dialect *fussock* to bustle about, < FUSS] —**ˈfossicker** *n.*

fossil (ˈfɒsᵊl) *n.* **1. a.** a relic or representation of a plant or animal that existed in a past geological age, occurring in the form of mineralized bones, shells, etc. **b.** (*as modifier*): *fossil insects.* **2.** *Inf., derog.* a person, idea, thing, etc., that is outdated or incapable of change. **3.** *Linguistics.* a form once current but now appearing only in one or two special contexts. [C17: < L *fossilis* dug up, < *fodere* to dig]

fossil fuel *n.* any naturally occurring fuel, such as coal, and natural gas, formed by the decomposition of prehistoric organisms.

fossiliferous (ˌfɒsɪˈlɪfərəs) *adj.* (of sedimentary rocks) containing fossils.

fossilize *or* **-lise** (ˈfɒsɪˌlaɪz) *vb.* **1.** to convert or be converted into a fossil. **2.** to become or cause to become antiquated or inflexible. —ˌ**fossiliˈzation** *or* **-liˈsation** *n.*

fossorial (fɒˈsɔːrɪəl) *adj.* (of the forelimbs and skeleton of burrowing animals) adapted for digging. [C19: < Med. L, < L *fossor* digger, < *fodere* to dig]

foster (ˈfɒstə) *vb.* (*tr.*) **1.** to promote the growth or development of. **2.** to bring up (a child, etc.). **3.** to cherish (a plan, hope, etc.) in one's mind. **4.** *Chiefly Brit.* **a.** to place (a child) in the care of foster parents. **b.** to bring up under fosterage. ~*adj.* **5.** (*in combination*) of or involved in the rearing of a child by persons other than his natural parents: *foster home.* [OE *fōstrian* to feed, < *fōstor* FOOD] —**ˈfosterer** *n.* —**ˈfostering** *n.*

fosterage (ˈfɒstərɪdʒ) *n.* **1.** the act of caring for a foster child. **2.** the state of being a foster child. **3.** the act of encouraging.

fought (fɔːt) *vb.* the past tense and past participle of **fight.**

foul (faʊl) *adj.* **1.** offensive to the senses; revolting. **2.** stinking. **3.** charged with or full of dirt or offensive matter. **4.** (of food) putrid; rotten. **5.** morally or spiritually offensive. **6.** obscene; vulgar: *foul language.* **7.** unfair: *to resort to foul means.* **8.** (esp. of weather) unpleasant or adverse. **9.** blocked or obstructed with dirt or foreign matter: *a foul drain.* **10.** (of the bottom of a vessel) covered with barnacles that slow forward motion. **11.** *Inf.* unsatisfactory; bad: *a foul book.* ~*n.* **12.** *Sport.* **a.** a violation of the rules. **b.** (*as modifier*): *a foul blow.* **13.** an entanglement or collision, esp. in sailing or fishing. ~*vb.* **14.** to make or become polluted. **15.** to become or cause to become entangled. **16.** (*tr.*) to disgrace. **17.** to become or cause to become clogged. **18.** (*tr.*) *Naut.* (of underwater growth) to cling to (the bottom of a vessel) so as to slow its motion. **19.** (*tr.*) *Sport.* to commit a foul against (an opponent). **20.** (*intr.*) *Sport.* to infringe the rules. **21.** to collide (with a boat, etc.). ~*adv.* **22.** in a foul manner. **23. fall foul of. a.** come into conflict with. **b.** *Naut.* to come into collision with. [OE *fūl*] —**ˈfoully** *adv.* —**ˈfoulness** *n.*

foulard (fuːˈlɑːd) *n.* a soft light fabric of plain-weave or twill-weave silk or rayon, usually with a printed design. [C19: < F, <?]

foul play *n.* **1.** unfair conduct esp. with violence. **2.** a violation of the rules in a game or sport.

foul up *vb.* (*adv.*) **1.** (*tr.*) to bungle. **2.** (*tr.*) to contaminate. **3.** to be or cause to be blocked, choked, or entangled.

found[1] (faʊnd) *vb.* **1.** the past tense and past participle of **find.** ~*adj.* **2.** furnished or fitted out. **3.** *Brit.* with meals, heating, etc., provided without extra charge.

found[2] (faʊnd) *vb.* **1.** (*tr.*) to bring into being or establish (something, such as an institution, etc.). **2.** (*tr.*) to build or establish the foundation of. **3.** (*also intr.;* foll. by *on* or *upon*) to have a basis (in). [C13: < OF, < L, < *fundus* bottom]

found[3] (faʊnd) *vb.* (*tr.*) **1.** to cast (a material, such as metal or glass) by melting and pouring into a mould. **2.** to make (articles) in this way. [C14: < OF, < L *fundere* to melt]

foundation (faʊnˈdeɪʃən) *n.* **1.** that on which something is founded. **2.** (*often pl.*) a construction below the ground that distributes the load of a building, wall, etc. **3.** the base on which something stands. **4.** the act of founding or establishing or the state of being founded or established. **5.** an endowment for the support of an institution such as a school. **6.** an institution supported by an endowment, often one that provides funds for charities, research, etc. **7.** a cosmetic used as a base for make-up. —**founˈdational** *adj.*

foundation garment *n.* a woman's undergarment worn to shape and support the figure. Also called: **foundation.**

foundation stone *n.* a stone laid at a ceremony to mark the foundation of a new building.

founder[1] (ˈfaʊndə) *n.* a person who establishes an institution, society, etc. [C14: see FOUND[2]]

founder[2] (ˈfaʊndə) *vb.* (*intr.*) **1.** (of a ship, etc.) to sink. **2.** to break down or fail: *the project foundered.* **3.** to sink into or become stuck in soft ground. **4.** to collapse. **5.** (of a horse) to stumble or go lame. [C13: < OF *fondrer* to submerge, < L *fundus* bottom]

founder[3] (ˈfaʊndə) *n.* **a.** a person who makes metal castings. **b.** (*in combination*): *an iron founder.* [C15: see FOUND[3]]

foundling (ˈfaʊndlɪŋ) *n.* an abandoned infant whose parents are not known. [C13 *foundeling;* see FIND]

foundry (ˈfaʊndrɪ) *n., pl.* **-ries.** a place in which metal castings are produced. [C17: < OF, < *fondre;* see FOUND[3]]

fount[1] (faʊnt) *n.* **1.** *Poetic.* a spring or fountain. **2.** source. [C16: back formation < FOUNTAIN]

fount[2] (faʊnt, fɒnt) *n. Printing.* a complete set of type of one style and size. Also called (esp. U.S. and Canad.): **font.** [C16: < OF *fonte* a founding, casting, < Vulgar L *funditus* (unattested) a casting, < L *fundere* to melt]

fountain (ˈfaʊntɪn) *n.* **1.** a jet or spray of water or some other liquid. **2.** a structure from which such a jet or a number of such jets spurt. **3.** a natural spring of water, esp. the source of a stream. **4.** a stream, jet, or cascade of sparks, lava, etc. **5.** a principal source. **6.** a reservoir, as for oil in a lamp. [C15: < OF, < LL, < L *fons* spring, source] —**ˈfountained** *adj.*

fountainhead (ˈfaʊntɪnˌhɛd) *n.* **1.** a spring that is the source of a stream. **2.** a principal or original source.

fountain pen *n.* a pen the nib of which is supplied with ink from a cartridge or a reservoir in its barrel.

four (fɔː) *n.* **1.** the cardinal number that is the sum of three and one. **2.** a numeral, 4, IV, etc., representing this number. **3.** something representing, represented by, or consisting of four units, such as a playing card with four symbols on it. **4.** Also called: **four o'clock.** four hours after noon or midnight. **5.** *Cricket.* **a.** a shot that crosses the boundary after hitting the ground. **b.** the four runs scored for such a shot. **6.** *Rowing.* **a.** a racing shell propelled by four oarsmen. **b.** the crew of such a shell. ~*determiner.* **7. a.** amounting to four: *four times.* **b.** (*as pronoun*): *four are ready.* [OE *fēower*]

four flush *n.* a useless poker hand, containing four of a suit and one odd card.

fourfold (ˈfɔːˌfəʊld) *adj.* **1.** equal to or having four times as many or as much. **2.** composed of four parts. ~*adv.* **3.** by or up to four times as many or as much.

four-in-hand *n.* **1.** a road vehicle drawn by four horses and driven by one driver. **2.** a four-horse team. **3.** *U.S.* a long narrow tie tied in a flat slipknot with the ends dangling.

four-leaf clover *or* **four-leaved clover** *n.* a

clover with four leaves rather than three, supposed to bring good luck.

four-letter word *n.* any of several short English words referring to sex or excrement: regarded generally as offensive or obscene.

four-o'clock *n.* a tropical American plant, cultivated for its tubular yellow, red, or white flowers that open in late afternoon. Also called: **marvel-of-Peru.**

four-poster *n.* a bed with posts at each corner supporting a canopy and curtains.

fourscore (ˌfɔːˈskɔː) *determiner.* an archaic word for **eighty.**

foursome (ˈfɔːsəm) *n.* **1.** a set or company of four. **2.** Also called: **four-ball.** *Golf.* a game between two pairs of players.

foursquare (ˌfɔːˈskwɛə) *adv.* **1.** squarely; firmly. *~adj.* **2.** solid and strong. **3.** forthright. **4.** a rare word for **square.**

four-stroke *adj.* designating an internal-combustion engine in which the piston makes four strokes for every explosion.

fourteen (ˈfɔːˈtiːn) *n.* **1.** the cardinal number that is the sum of ten and four. **2.** a numeral, 14, XIV, etc., representing this number. **3.** something represented by or consisting of 14 units. *~determiner.* **4. a.** amounting to fourteen: *fourteen cats.* **b.** (*as pronoun*)*: the fourteen who remained.* [OE *fēowertīene*] —ˈ**four**ˈ**teenth** *adj., n.*

fourth (fɔːθ) *adj.* (*usually prenominal*) **1. a.** coming after the third in order, position, time, etc. Often written: 4th. **b.** (*as n.*)*: the fourth in succession.* **2.** denoting the highest forward ratio of a gearbox in most motor vehicles. *~n.* **3.** *Music.* **a.** the interval between one note and another four notes away from it in a diatonic scale. **b.** one of two notes constituting such an interval in relation to the other. **4.** the fourth forward ratio of a gearbox in a motor vehicle, usually the highest gear in cars. **5.** a less common word for **quarter** (sense 2). *~adv. also:* **fourthly.** **6.** after the third person, position, event, etc. *~sentence connector. also:* **fourthly.** **7.** as the fourth point.

fourth dimension *n.* **1.** the dimension of time, which in addition to three spatial dimensions specifies the position of a point or particle. **2.** the concept in science fiction of a dimension in addition to three spatial dimensions. —ˌ**fourth-di**ˈ**mensional** *adj.*

fourth estate *n.* (*sometimes caps.*) journalists or their profession; the press.

fovea (ˈfəʊvɪə) *n., pl.* **-veae** (-vɪˌiː). *Anat.* any small pit or depression in the surface of a bodily organ or part. [C19: < L: a small pit]

fowl (faʊl) *n.* **1.** Also called: **domestic fowl.** a domesticated gallinaceous bird occurring in many varieties. **2.** any other bird that is used as food or hunted as game. **3.** the flesh or meat of fowl, esp. of chicken. **4.** an archaic word for any **bird.** *~vb.* **5.** (*intr.*) to hunt or snare wildfowl. [OE *fugol*] —ˈ**fowler** *n.* —ˈ**fowling** *n., adj.*

fowl pest *n.* an acute and usually fatal viral disease of domestic fowl, characterized by discoloration of the comb and wattles.

fox (fɒks) *n., pl.* **foxes** *or* **fox.** **1.** any canine mammal of the genus *Vulpes* and related genera. They are mostly predators and have a pointed muzzle and a bushy tail. **2.** the fur of any of these animals, usually reddish-brown or grey in colour. **3.** a person who is cunning and sly. *~vb.* **4.** (*tr.*) *Inf.* to perplex: *to fox a person with a problem.* **5.** to cause (paper, wood, etc.) to become discoloured with spots, or (of paper, etc.) to become discoloured. **6.** (*tr.*) to trick; deceive. **7.** (*intr.*) to act deceitfully or craftily. [OE] —ˈ**fox**ˌ**like** *adj.*

foxfire (ˈfɒksˌfaɪə) *n.* a luminescent glow emitted by certain fungi on rotting wood.

foxglove (ˈfɒksˌglʌv) *n.* a plant having spikes of purple or white thimble-like flowers. The soft wrinkled leaves are a source of digitalis. [OE]

foxhole (ˈfɒksˌhəʊl) *n. Mil.* a small pit dug to provide shelter against hostile fire.

foxhound (ˈfɒksˌhaʊnd) *n.* a breed of short-haired hound, usually kept for hunting foxes.

fox hunt *n.* **1. a.** the hunting of foxes with hounds. **b.** an instance of this. **2.** an organization for fox hunting within a particular area. —ˈ**fox**ˌ**hunter** *n.* —ˈ**fox-**ˌ**hunting** *n.*

foxtail (ˈfɒksˌteɪl) *n.* any grass of Europe, Asia, and South America, having soft cylindrical spikes of flowers: cultivated as a pasture grass.

fox terrier *n.* either of two breeds of small tan-black-and-white terrier, the wire-haired and the smooth.

foxtrot (ˈfɒksˌtrɒt) *n.* **1.** a ballroom dance in quadruple time, combining short and long steps in various sequences. *~vb.* **-trotting, -trotted.** **2.** (*intr.*) to perform this dance.

foxy (ˈfɒksɪ) *adj.* **foxier, foxiest.** **1.** of or resembling a fox, esp. in craftiness. **2.** of a reddish-brown colour. **3.** (of paper, etc.) spotted, esp. by mildew. —ˈ**foxily** *adv.* —ˈ**foxiness** *n.*

foyer (ˈfɔɪeɪ, ˈfɔɪə) *n.* a hall, lobby, or anteroom, as in a hotel, theatre, cinema, etc. [C19: < F: fireplace, < Med. L, < L *focus* fire]

fp *Music. abbrev. for* forte-piano.

FP *abbrev. for:* **1.** fire plug. **2.** former pupil. **3.** Also: **fp.** freezing point.

FPA *abbrev. for* Family Planning Association.

fps *abbrev. for:* **1.** feet per second. **2.** foot-pound-second. **3.** *Photog.* frames per second.

fps units *pl. n.* an Imperial system of units based on the foot, pound, and second as the units of length, mass, and time.

Fr *abbrev. for:* **1.** *Christianity.* **a.** Father. **b.** Frater. [L: brother] **2.** *the chemical symbol for* francium.

fr. *abbrev. for:* **1.** fragment. **2.** franc. **3.** from.

Fr. *abbrev. for:* **1.** France. **2.** French.

Fra (frɑː) *n.* brother: a title given to an Italian monk or friar. [It., short for *frate* brother, < L *frāter* BROTHER]

fracas (ˈfrækɑː) *n.* a noisy quarrel; brawl. [C18: < F, < *fracasser* to shatter, < L *frangere* to break, infl. by *quassāre* to shatter]

fractal (ˈfræktəl) *n.* any of various irregular and fragmented shapes or surfaces that are not normally represented in geometry. [C20: < L *frāctus,* p.p. of *frangere* to break]

fraction (ˈfrækʃən) *n.* **1.** *Maths.* a ratio of two expressions or numbers other than zero. **2.** any part or subdivision. **3.** a small piece; fragment. **4.** *Chem.* a component of a mixture separated by fractional distillation. **5.** *Christianity.* the formal breaking of the bread in Communion. [C14: < LL, < L *fractus* broken, < *frangere* to break] —ˈ**fractional** *adj.* —ˈ**fraction**ˌ**ize** *or* **-**ˌ**ise** *vb.*

fractional distillation *n.* the process of separating the constituents of a liquid mixture by heating it and condensing separately the components according to their different boiling points. Sometimes shortened to **distillation.**

fractionate (ˈfrækʃəˌneɪt) *vb.* **1.** to separate or cause to separate into constituents. **2.** (*tr.*) *Chem.* to obtain (a constituent of a mixture) by a fractional process. —ˌ**fraction**ˈ**ation** *n.*

fractious (ˈfrækʃəs) *adj.* **1.** irritable. **2.** unruly. [C18: < (obs.) *fraction* discord + -OUS] —ˈ**fractiously** *adv.* —ˈ**fractiousness** *n.*

fracture (ˈfræktʃə) *n.* **1.** the act of breaking or the state of being broken. **2. a.** the breaking or cracking of a bone or the tearing of a cartilage. **b.** the resulting condition. **3.** a division, split, or breach. **4.** *Mineralogy.* **a.** the characteristic appearance of the surface of a freshly broken mineral or rock. **b.** the way in which a mineral or rock naturally breaks. *~vb.* **5.** to break or cause to break. **6.** to break or crack (a bone) or (of a bone) to become broken or cracked. [C15: < OF, < L, < *frangere* to break] —ˈ**fractural** *adj.*

fraenum *or* **frenum** (ˈfriːnəm) *n., pl.* **-na** (-nə). a fold of membrane or skin, such as the fold beneath the tongue. [C18: < L: bridle]

fragile (ˈfrædʒaɪl) *adj.* **1.** able to be broken easily. **2.** in a weakened physical state. **3.** delicate; light: *a fragile touch.* **4.** slight; tenuous. [C17: < L *fragilis,* < *frangere* to break] —ˈ**fragilely** *adv.* —**fragility** (frəˈdʒɪlɪtɪ) *n.*

fragment *n.* (ˈfrægmənt). **1.** a piece broken off or detached. **2.** an incomplete piece: *fragments of a novel.* **3.** a scrap; bit. ~*vb.* (frægˈmɛnt). **4.** to break or cause to break into fragments. [C15: < L *fragmentum,* < *frangere* to break] —ˌ**fragmenˈtation** *n.*

fragmentary (ˈfrægməntərı) *adj.* made up of fragments; disconnected. Also: **fragmental.**

fragrance (ˈfreıgrəns) *or* **fragrancy** *n., pl.* **-grances** *or* **-grancies. 1.** a pleasant or sweet odour. **2.** the state of being fragrant.

fragrant (ˈfreıgrənt) *adj.* having a pleasant or sweet smell. [C15: < L, < *frāgrāre* to emit a smell] —ˈ**fragrantly** *adv.*

frail[1] (freıl) *adj.* **1.** physically weak and delicate. **2.** fragile: *a frail craft.* **3.** easily corrupted or tempted. [C13: < OF *frele,* < L *fragilis,* FRAGILE]

frail[2] (freıl) *n.* **1.** a rush basket for figs or raisins. **2.** a quantity of raisins or figs equal to between 50 and 75 pounds. [C13: < OF *fraiel,* <?]

frailty (ˈfreıltı) *n., pl.* **-ties. 1.** physical or moral weakness. **2.** (*often pl.*) a fault symptomatic of moral weakness.

framboesia *or U.S.* **frambesia** (fræmˈbi:zıə) *n. Pathol.* another name for **yaws.** [C19: < NL, < F *framboise* raspberry; from its raspberry-like excrescences]

frame (freım) *n.* **1.** an open structure that gives shape and support to something, such as the ribs of a ship's hull or an aircraft's fuselage or the beams of a building. **2.** an enclosing case or border into which something is fitted: *the frame of a picture.* **3.** the system around which something is built up: *the frame of government.* **4.** the structure of the human body. **5.** a condition; state (esp. in **frame of mind**). **6. a.** one of a series of exposures on film used in making motion pictures. **b.** an exposure on a film used in still photography. **7.** a television picture scanned by one or more electron beams at a particular frequency. **8.** *Snooker, etc.* **a.** the wooden triangle used to set up the balls. **b.** the balls when set up. **c.** a single game finished when all the balls have been potted. **9.** short for **cold frame. 10.** one of the sections of which a beehive is composed, esp. one designed to hold a honeycomb. **11.** *Statistics.* an enumeration of a population for the purposes of sampling. **12.** *Sl.* another word for **frame-up. 13.** *Obs.* shape; form. ~*vb.* (*mainly tr.*) **14.** to construct by fitting parts together. **15.** to draw up the plans or basic details for: *to frame a policy.* **16.** to compose or conceive: *to frame a reply.* **17.** to provide, support, or enclose with a frame: *to frame a picture.* **18.** to form (words) with the lips, esp. silently. **19.** *Sl.* to conspire to incriminate (someone) on a false charge. [OE *framiae* to avail] —ˈ**frameless** *adj.* —ˈ**framer** *n.*

frame house *n.* a house that has a timber framework and cladding.

frame of reference *n.* **1.** *Sociol.* a set of standards that determines and sanctions behaviour. **2.** any set of planes or curves, such as the three coordinate axes, used to locate a point in space.

frame-up *n. Sl.* **1.** a conspiracy to incriminate someone on a false charge. **2.** a plot to bring about a dishonest result, as in a contest.

framework (ˈfreımˌwɜ:k) *n.* **1.** a structural plan or basis of a project. **2.** a structure or frame supporting or containing something.

franc (fræŋk; *French* frɑ̃) *n.* **1.** the standard monetary unit of France, French dependencies, and Monaco, divided into 100 centimes. **2.** the standard monetary and currency unit, comprising 100 centimes, of various countries including Belgium, the Central African Republic, Gabon, Guinea, Liechtenstein, Luxembourg, Mauritania, Niger, the Republic of Congo, Senegal, Switzerland, Togo, etc. **3.** a Moroccan monetary unit worth one hundredth of a dirham. [C14: < OF; < L *Rex Francōrum* King of the Franks, inscribed on 14th-century francs]

franchise (ˈfræntʃaız) *n.* **1.** (usually preceded by *the*) the right to vote, esp. for representatives in a legislative body. **2.** any exemption, privilege, or right granted to an individual or group by a public authority. **3.** *Commerce.* authorization granted by a manufacturing enterprise to a distributor to market the manufacturer's products. **4.** the full rights of citizenship. ~*vb.* **5.** (*tr.*) *Commerce, chiefly U.S. & Canad.* to grant (a person, firm, etc.) a franchise. [C13: < OF, < *franchir* to set free, < *franc* free] —**franchisement** (ˈfræntʃızmənt) *n.*

Franciscan (frænˈsıskən) *n.* **a.** a member of a Christian religious order of friars or nuns tracing their origins back to Saint Francis of Assisi. **b.** (*as modifier*): *a Franciscan friary.*

francium (ˈfrænsıəm) *n.* an unstable radioactive element of the alkali-metal group, occurring in minute amounts in uranium ores. Symbol: Fr; atomic no.: 87; half-life of most stable isotope, ^{223}Fr: 22 minutes. [C20: < NL, < *France* + -IUM; because first found in France]

Franco- (ˈfræŋkəʊ-) *combining form.* indicating France or French: *Franco-Prussian.* [< Med. L *Francus,* < LL: FRANK]

francolin (ˈfræŋkəʊlın) *n.* an African or Asian partridge. [C17: < F, < OIt. *francolino,* <?]

Francophone (ˈfræŋkəʊˌfəʊn) (*often not cap.*) ~*n.* **1.** a person who speaks French, esp. a native speaker. ~*adj.* **2.** speaking French as a native language. **3.** using French as a lingua franca.

frangible (ˈfrændʒıbᵊl) *adj.* breakable or fragile. [C15: < OF, ult. < L *frangere* to break] —ˌ**frangiˈbility** *or* ˈ**frangibleness** *n.*

frangipane (ˈfrændʒıˌpeın) *n.* **1.** a pastry filled with cream and flavoured with almonds. **2.** a variant of **frangipani** (the perfume).

frangipani (ˌfrændʒıˈpɑ:nı) *n., pl.* **-panis** *or* **-pani. 1.** a tropical American shrub cultivated for its waxy white or pink flowers, which have a sweet overpowering scent. **2.** a perfume prepared from this plant or resembling the odour of its flowers. **3. native frangipani.** *Austral.* an Australian evergreen tree with large fragrant yellow flowers. [C17: via F < It.: perfume for scenting gloves, after the Marquis Muzio *Frangipani,* 16th-century Roman nobleman who invented it]

Franglais (*French* frɑ̃glɛ) *n.* informal French containing a high proportion of English. [C20: < F *français* French + *anglais* English]

frank (fræŋk) *adj.* **1.** honest and straightforward in speech or attitude: *a frank person.* **2.** outspoken or blunt. **3.** open and avowed: *frank interest.* ~*vb.* (*tr.*) **4.** *Chiefly Brit.* to put a mark on (a letter, etc.), either cancelling the postage stamp or in place of a stamp, ensuring free carriage. **5.** to mark (a letter, etc.) with an official mark or signature, indicating the right of free delivery. **6.** to facilitate or assist (a person) to enter easily. **7.** to obtain immunity for (a person). ~*n.* **8.** an official mark or signature affixed to a letter, etc., ensuring free delivery or delivery without stamps. [C13: < OF, < Med. L *francus* free; identical with FRANK (in Frankish Gaul only members of this people enjoyed full freedom)] —ˈ**frankable** *adj.* —ˈ**franker** *n.* —ˈ**frankness** *n.*

Frank (fræŋk) *n.* a member of a group of West Germanic peoples who spread from the east in the late 4th century A.D., gradually conquering most of Gaul and Germany. [OE *Franca;* ? < the name of a Frankish weapon (cf. OE *franca* javelin)]

Frankenstein (ˈfræŋkınˌstaın) *n.* a thing that destroys its creator. Also called: **Frankenstein's monster.** [C19: after Baron *Frankenstein,* who created a destructive monster from parts of corpses in the novel by Mary Shelley (1818)]

frankfurter (ˈfræŋkˌfɜ:tə) *n.* a smoked sausage, made of finely minced pork or beef. [C20: short for G *Frankfurter Wurst* sausage from *Frankfurt,* in W Germany]

frankincense (ˈfræŋkınˌsɛns) *n.* an aromatic gum resin obtained from trees of the genus *Boswellia,* which occur in Asia and Africa. [C14: < OF *franc* free, pure + *encens* INCENSE; see FRANK]

Frankish (ˈfræŋkıʃ) *n.* **1.** the ancient West

Germanic language of the Franks. *~adj.* **2.** of or relating to the Franks or their language.

franklin (ˈfræŋklɪn) *n.* (in 14th- and 15th-century England) a substantial landholder of free but not noble birth. [C13: < Anglo-F, < OF *franc* free, on the model of CHAMBERLAIN]

frankly (ˈfræŋklɪ) *adv.* **1.** (*sentence modifier*) to be honest. **2.** in a frank manner.

frantic (ˈfræntɪk) *adj.* **1.** distracted with fear, pain, joy, etc. **2.** marked by or showing frenzy: *frantic efforts.* [C14: < OF, < L *phrenēticus* mad] —**ˈfrantically** *or* **ˈfranticly** *adv.*

frappé (ˈfræpeɪ) *n.* **1.** a drink consisting of a liqueur, etc., poured over crushed ice. *~adj.* **2.** (*postpositive*) (esp. of drinks) chilled. [C19: < F, < *frapper* to strike, hence, chill]

frater (ˈfreɪtə) *n. Arch.* a refectory. [C13: < OF *fraiteur,* < *refreitor,* < LL *rēfectōrium* REFECTORY]

fraternal (frəˈtɜːnᵊl) *adj.* **1.** of or suitable to a brother; brotherly. **2.** of a fraternity. **3.** designating twins of the same or opposite sex that developed from two separate fertilized ova. Cf. **identical** (sense 3). [C15: < L, < *frāter* brother] —**fraˈternalism** *n.*

fraternity (frəˈtɜːnɪtɪ) *n., pl.* **-ties.** **1.** a body of people united in interests, aims, etc.: *the teaching fraternity.* **2.** brotherhood. **3.** *U.S. & Canad.* a secret society joined by male students, functioning as a social club.

fraternize *or* **-nise** (ˈfrætəˌnaɪz) *vb.* (*intr.;* often foll. by *with*) to associate on friendly terms. —ˌ**fraterniˈzation** *or* **-ˌniˈsation** *n.* —**ˈfraterˌnizer** *or* **-ˌniser** *n.*

fratricide (ˈfrætrɪˌsaɪd, ˈfreɪ-) *n.* **1.** the act of killing one's brother. **2.** a person who kills his brother. [C15: < L, < *frater* brother + -CIDE] —ˌ**fratriˈcidal** *adj.*

Frau (fraʊ) *n., pl.* **Frauen** (ˈfraʊən) *or* **Fraus.** a married German woman: usually used as a title equivalent to *Mrs.* [< OHG *frouwa*]

fraud (frɔːd) *n.* **1.** deliberate deception, trickery, or cheating intended to gain an advantage. **2.** an act or instance of such deception. **3.** *Inf.* a person who acts in a false or deceitful way. [C14: < OF, < L *fraus* deception] —**ˈfraudster** *n.*

fraudulent (ˈfrɔːdjʊlənt) *adj.* **1.** acting with or having the intent to deceive. **2.** relating to or proceeding from fraud. [C15: < L *fraudulentus* deceitful] —**ˈfraudulence** *n.* —**ˈfraudulently** *adv.*

fraught (frɔːt) *adj.* **1.** (*usually postpositive* and foll. by *with*) filled or charged: *a venture fraught with peril.* **2.** *Inf.* showing or producing tension or anxiety. [C14: < MDu. *vrachten,* < *vracht* FREIGHT]

Fräulein (*German* ˈfrɔylaɪn) *n., pl.* **-lein** *or English* **-leins.** an unmarried German woman: often used as a title equivalent to *Miss.* [< MHG *vrouwelīn,* dim. of *vrouwe* lady]

Fraunhofer lines (*German* ˈfraunhoːfə) *pl. n.* a set of dark lines appearing in the continuous emission spectrum of the sun. [C19: after Joseph von *Fraunhofer* (1787–1826), G physicist]

fraxinella (ˌfræksɪˈnɛlə) *n.* another name for **gas plant.** [C17: < NL: a little ash tree, < L *frāxinus* ash]

fray[1] (freɪ) *n.* **1.** a noisy quarrel. **2.** a fight or brawl. [C14: short for AFFRAY]

fray[2] (freɪ) *vb.* **1.** to wear or cause to wear away into loose threads, esp. at an edge or end. **2.** to make or become strained or irritated. **3.** to rub or chafe (another object). [C14: < F *frayer* to rub, < L *fricāre* to rub]

frazil (ˈfreɪzɪl) *n.* small pieces of ice that form in water moving turbulently enough to prevent the formation of a sheet of ice. [C19: < Canad. F, < F *fraisil* cinders, ult. < L *fax* torch]

frazzle (ˈfræzᵊl) *Inf.* *~vb.* **1.** to make or become exhausted or weary. *~n.* **2.** the state of being frazzled or exhausted. **3. to a frazzle.** completely (esp. in **burnt to a frazzle**). [C19: prob. < ME *faselen* to fray, < *fasel* fringe; infl. by FRAY[2]]

freak (friːk) *n.* **1.** a person, animal, or plant that is abnormal or deformed. **2. a.** an object, event, etc., that is abnormal. **b.** (*as modifier*): *a freak storm.* **3.** a personal whim or caprice. **4.** *Inf.* a person who acts or dresses in a markedly unconventional way. **5.** *Inf.* a person who is ardently fond of something specified: *a jazz freak.* *~vb.* **6.** See **freak out.** [C16: <?] —**ˈfreakish** *adj.* —**ˈfreaky** *adj.*

freak out *vb.* (*adv.*) *Inf.* to be or cause to be in a heightened emotional state.

freckle (ˈfrɛkᵊl) *n.* **1.** a small brownish spot on the skin developed by exposure to sunlight. Technical name: **lentigo.** **2.** any small area of discoloration. *~vb.* **3.** to mark or become marked with freckles or spots. [C14: < ON *freknur*] —**ˈfreckled** *or* **ˈfreckly** *adj.*

free (friː) *adj.* **freer, freest.** **1.** able to act at will; not under compulsion or restraint. **2. a.** not enslaved or confined. **b.** (*as n.*)*: land of the free.* **3.** (*often postpositive* and foll. by *from*) not subject (to) or restricted (by some regulation, constraint, etc.): *free from pain.* **4.** (of a country, etc.) autonomous or independent. **5.** exempt from external direction: *free will.* **6.** not subject to conventional constraints: *free verse.* **7.** not exact or literal: *a free translation.* **8.** provided without charge: *free entertainment.* **9.** *Law.* (of property) **a.** not subject to payment of rent or performance of services; freehold. **b.** not subject to any burden or charge; unencumbered. **10.** (*postpositive;* often foll. by *of* or *with*) ready or generous in using or giving: *free with advice.* **11.** not occupied or in use; available: *a free cubicle.* **12.** (of a person) not busy. **13.** open or available to all. **14.** without charge to the subscriber or user: *freepost; freephone.* **15.** not fixed or joined; loose: *the free end of a chain.* **16.** without obstruction or impediment: *free passage.* **17.** *Chem.* chemically uncombined: *free nitrogen.* **18.** *Logic.* denoting an occurrence of a variable not bound by a quantifier. Cf. **bound**[1] (sense 8). **19.** (of routines in figure-skating competitions) chosen by the competitor. **20. for free.** *Nonstandard.* without charge or cost. **21. free and easy.** casual or tolerant; easy-going. **22. make free with.** to behave too familiarly towards. *~adv.* **23.** in a free manner; freely. **24.** without charge or cost. **25.** *Naut.* with the wind blowing from the quarter. *~vb.* **freeing, freed.** (*tr.*) **26.** to set at liberty; release. **27.** to remove obstructions or impediments from. **28.** (often foll. by *of* or *from*) to relieve or rid (of obstacles, pain, etc.). [OE *frēo*] —**ˈfreely** *adv.* —**ˈfreeness** *n.*

-free *adj. combining form.* free from: *trouble-free; lead-free petrol.*

free alongside ship *adj.* (of a shipment of goods) delivered to the dock without charge to the buyer, but excluding the cost of loading onto the vessel. Cf. **free on board.**

free association *n. Psychoanal.* a method of exploring a person's unconscious by eliciting words and thoughts that are associated with key words provided by a psychoanalyst.

freebase (ˈfriːˌbeɪs) *vb. Sl.* to refine (cocaine) for smoking.

freebie (ˈfriːbɪ) *n. Sl.* something provided without charge.

freeboard (ˈfriːˌbɔːd) *n.* the space or distance between the deck of a vessel and the waterline.

freebooter (ˈfriːˌbuːtə) *n.* a person, such as a pirate, living from plunder. [C16: < Du., < *vrijbuit* booty; see FILIBUSTER] —**ˈfreeboot** *vb.* (*intr.*)

freeborn (ˈfriːˌbɔːn) *adj.* **1.** not born in slavery. **2.** of or suitable for people not born in slavery.

Free Church *n. Chiefly Brit.* any Protestant Church, esp. the Presbyterian, other than the Established Church.

free city *n.* a sovereign or autonomous city.

freedman (ˈfriːdˌmæn) *n., pl.* **-men.** a man who has been freed from slavery.

freedom (ˈfriːdəm) *n.* **1.** personal liberty, as from slavery, serfdom, etc. **2.** liberation, as from confinement or bondage. **3.** the quality or state of being free, esp. to enjoy political and civil liberties. **4.** (usually foll. by *from*) exemption or immunity: *freedom from taxation.* **5.** the right or privilege of unrestricted use or access: *the freedom of a city.* **6.** autonomy, self-government, or independence. **7.** the power or liberty to order one's own actions. **8.** *Philosophy.* the quality, esp. of the will or the individual, of not being totally constrained. **9.** ease or frankness of manner: *she talked with complete freedom.* **10.** excessive familiarity of manner. **11.** ease and grace, as of movement. [OE *frēodōm*]

freedom fighter *n.* a militant revolutionary.

free energy *n.* a thermodynamic property that expresses the capacity of a system to perform work under certain conditions.

free enterprise *n.* an economic system in which commercial organizations compete for profit with little state control.

free fall *n.* **1.** free descent of a body in which the gravitational force is the only force acting on it. **2.** the part of a parachute descent before the parachute opens.

free flight *n.* the flight of a rocket, missile, etc., when its engine has ceased to produce thrust.

free-for-all *n. Inf.* a disorganized brawl or argument, usually involving all those present.

free-form *adj. Arts.* freely flowing, spontaneous.

free hand *n.* **1.** unrestricted freedom to act (esp. in **give (someone) a free hand**). ~*adj., adv.* **freehand. 2.** (done) by hand without the use of guiding instruments: *a freehand drawing.*

free-handed *adj.* generous or liberal; unstinting. —ˌ**free-ˈhandedly** *adv.*

freehold (ˈfriːˌhəʊld) *Property law.* ~*n.* **1. a.** tenure by which land is held in fee simple, fee tail, or for life. **b.** an estate held by such tenure. ~*adj.* **2.** relating to or having the nature of freehold. —ˈ**freeˌholder** *n.*

free house *n. Brit.* a public house not bound to sell only one brewer's products.

free kick *n. Soccer.* a place kick awarded for a foul or infringement.

freelance (ˈfriːˌlɑːns) *n.* **1. a.** Also called: **freelancer.** a self-employed person, esp. a writer or artist, who is hired to do specific assignments. **b.** (*as modifier*): *a freelance journalist.* **2.** (in medieval Europe) a mercenary soldier or adventurer. ~*vb.* **3.** to work as a freelance on (an assignment, etc.). ~*adv.* **4.** as a freelance. [C19 (in sense 2): later applied to politicians, writers, etc.]

free-living *adj.* **1.** given to ready indulgence of the appetites. **2.** (of animals and plants) not parasitic. —ˌ**free-ˈliver** *n.*

freeloader (ˈfriːˌləʊdə) *n. Sl.* a person who habitually depends on others for food, shelter, etc.

free love *n.* the practice of sexual relationships without fidelity to a single partner.

freeman (ˈfriːmən) *n., pl.* **-men. 1.** a person who is not a slave. **2.** a person who enjoys political and civil liberties. **3.** a person who enjoys a privilege, such as the freedom of a city.

free market economy *n.* an economic system which allows supply and demand to regulate prices, wages, etc. rather than government policy.

freemartin (ˈfriːˌmɑːtɪn) *n.* the female of a pair of twin calves of unlike sex that is imperfectly developed and sterile. [C17: <?]

Freemason (ˈfriːˌmeɪsᵊn) *n.* a member of the widespread secret order, constituted in London in 1717, of **Free and Accepted Masons,** pledged to brotherliness and mutual aid. Sometimes shortened to **Mason.**

freemasonry (ˈfriːˌmeɪsᵊnrɪ) *n.* natural or tacit sympathy and understanding.

Freemasonry (ˈfriːˌmeɪsᵊnrɪ) *n.* **1.** the institutions, rites, practices, etc., of Freemasons. **2.** Freemasons collectively.

free on board *adj.* (of a shipment of goods) delivered on board ship or other carrier without charge to the buyer. Cf. **free alongside ship.**

free port *n.* **1.** a port open to all commercial vessels on equal terms. **2.** a port that permits the duty-free entry of foreign goods intended for re-export.

free radical *n.* an atom or group of atoms containing at least one unpaired electron and existing for a brief period of time before reacting to produce a stable molecule.

free-range *adj. Chiefly Brit.* kept or produced in natural conditions: *free-range eggs.*

free-select *vb.* (*tr.*) *Austral. history.* to select (areas of crown land) and acquire the freehold by a series of annual payments. —ˈ**free-seˈlection** *n.* —ˈ**free-seˈlector** *n.*

freesia (ˈfriːzɪə) *n.* a plant of Southern Africa, cultivated for its white, yellow, or pink tubular fragrant flowers. [C19: NL, after F. H. T. *Freese* (died 1876), G physician]

free skating *n.* either of two parts in a figure-skating competition in which the skater chooses the sequence of figures and the music and which are judged on technique and artistic presentation. The short programme consists of specified movements and the long programme is entirely the skater's own choice.

free space *n.* a region that has no gravitational and electromagnetic fields. It is used as an absolute standard and was formerly referred to as a vacuum.

free-spoken *adj.* speaking frankly or without restraint. —ˌ**free-ˈspokenly** *adv.*

freestanding (ˌfriːˈstændɪŋ) *adj.* not attached to or supported by another object.

freestone (ˈfriːˌstəʊn) *n.* **1.** any fine-grained stone, esp. sandstone or limestone, that can be worked in any direction without breaking. **2.** *Bot.* a fruit, such as a peach, in which the flesh separates readily from the stone.

freestyle (ˈfriːˌstaɪl) *n.* **1.** a competition or race, as in swimming, in which each participant may use a style of his or her choice instead of a specified style. **2. a. International freestyle.** an amateur style of wrestling with an agreed set of rules. **b.** Also called: **all-in wrestling.** a style of professional wrestling with no internationally agreed set of rules.

freethinker (ˌfriːˈθɪŋkə) *n.* a person who forms his ideas and opinions independently of authority or accepted views, esp. in matters of religion. —**free thought** *n.*

free trade *n.* **1.** international trade that is free of such government interference as protective tariffs. **2.** *Arch.* smuggling.

free verse *n.* unrhymed verse without a metrical pattern.

freeway (ˈfriːˌweɪ) *n. U.S.* **1.** an expressway. **2.** a major road that can be used without paying a toll.

freewheel (ˌfriːˈwiːl) *n.* **1.** a ratchet device in the rear hub of a bicycle wheel that permits the wheel to rotate freely while the pedals are stationary. ~*vb.* **2.** (*intr.*) to coast on a bicycle using the freewheel.

free will *n.* **1. a.** the apparent human ability to make choices that are not externally determined. **b.** the doctrine that such human freedom of choice is not illusory. Cf. **determinism. 2.** the ability to make a choice without outside coercion: *he left of his own free will.*

Free World *n.* **the.** the non-Communist countries collectively.

freeze (friːz) *vb.* **freezing, froze, frozen. 1.** to change (a liquid) into a solid as a result of a reduction in temperature, or (of a liquid) to solidify in this way. **2.** (when *intr.,* sometimes foll. by *over* or *up*) to cover, clog, or harden with ice, or become so covered, clogged, or hardened. **3.** to fix fast or become fixed (to something) because of the action of frost. **4.** (*tr.*) to preserve (food) by subjection to extreme cold, as in a freezer. **5.** to feel or cause to feel the sensation or effects of extreme cold. **6.** to die or cause to die of extreme cold. **7.** to become or cause to become paralysed, fixed, or motionless, esp. through fear, shock, etc. **8.** (*tr.*) to cause (moving film) to stop at a particular frame. **9.** to make or become formal, haughty, etc., in manner. **10.** (*tr.*) to fix (prices, incomes, etc.) at a particular level. **11.** (*tr.*) to forbid by law the exchange, liquidation, or collection of (loans, assets, etc.). **12.** (*tr.*) to stop (a process) at a particular stage of development.

13. (*intr.*; foll. by *onto*) *Inf., chiefly U.S.* to cling. ~*n.* **14.** the act of freezing or state of being frozen. **15.** *Meteorol.* a spell of temperatures below freezing point, usually over a wide area. **16.** the fixing of incomes, prices, etc., by legislation. ~*sentence substitute.* **17.** *Chiefly U.S.* a command to stop instantly or risk being shot. [OE *frēosan*] —ˈ**freezable** *adj.*

freeze-dry *vb.* **-drying, -dried.** (*tr.*) to preserve (a substance) by rapid freezing and subsequently drying in a vacuum.

freeze-frame *n.* **1.** *Films, television.* a single frame of a film repeated to give an effect like a still photograph. **2.** *Video.* a single frame of a video recording viewed as a still by stopping the tape.

freeze out *vb.* (*tr., adv.*) *Inf.* to exclude, as by unfriendly behaviour, etc.

freezer (ˈfriːzə) *n.* an insulated cold-storage cabinet for long-term storage of perishable foodstuffs. Also called: **deepfreeze.**

freezing point *n.* the temperature below which a liquid turns into a solid.

freezing works *n. Austral. & N.Z.* a slaughterhouse at which animal carcasses are frozen for export.

freight (freɪt) *n.* **1. a.** commercial transport that is slower and cheaper than express. **b.** the price charged for such transport. **c.** goods transported by this means. **d.** (*as modifier*): *freight transport.* **2.** *Chiefly Brit.* a ship's cargo or part of it. ~*vb.* (*tr.*) **3.** to load with goods for transport. [C16: < MDu *vrecht*, var. of *vracht*]

freightage (ˈfreɪtɪdʒ) *n.* **1.** the commercial conveyance of goods. **2.** the goods so transported. **3.** the price charged for such conveyance.

freighter (ˈfreɪtə) *n.* **1.** a ship or aircraft designed for transporting cargo. **2.** a person concerned with the loading of a ship.

Freightliner (ˈfreɪtˌlaɪnə) *n. Trademark.* a type of goods train carrying containers that can be transferred onto lorries or ships.

French (frɛntʃ) *n.* **1.** the official language of France: also an official language of Switzerland, Belgium, Canada, and certain other countries. Historically, French is an Indo-European language belonging to the Romance group. **2. the French.** (*functioning as pl.*) the natives, citizens, or inhabitants of France collectively. ~*adj.* **3.** relating to, denoting, or characteristic of France, the French, or their language. **4.** (in Canada) of French Canadians. [OE *Frencisc* French, Frankish] —ˈ**Frenchness** *n.*

French bread *n.* white bread in a long slender loaf that has a crisp brown crust.

French Canadian *n.* **1.** a Canadian citizen whose native language is French. ~*adj.* **French-Canadian. 2.** of or relating to French Canadians or their language.

French chalk *n.* a variety of talc used to mark cloth, remove grease stains, or as a dry lubricant.

French doors *pl. n.* the U.S. and Canad. name for **French windows.**

French dressing *n.* a salad dressing made from oil and vinegar with seasonings; vinaigrette.

French fried potatoes *pl. n.* a more formal name for **chips.** Also called (U.S. and Canad.): **French fries.**

French horn *n. Music.* a valved brass instrument with a funnel-shaped mouthpiece and a tube of conical bore coiled into a spiral.

Frenchify (ˈfrɛntʃɪˌfaɪ) *vb.* **-fying, -fied.** *Inf.* to make or become French in appearance, etc.

French kiss *n.* a kiss involving insertion of the tongue into the partner's mouth.

French knickers *pl. n.* women's wide-legged underpants.

French leave *n.* an unauthorized absence or departure. [C18: alluding to a custom in France of leaving without saying goodbye to one's host]

French letter *n. Brit.* a slang term for **condom.**

Frenchman (ˈfrɛntʃmən) *n., pl.* **-men.** a native, citizen, or inhabitant of France. —ˈ**Frenchˌwoman** *fem. n.*

French mustard *n.* a mild mustard paste made with vinegar rather than water.

French polish *n.* **1.** a varnish for wood consisting of shellac dissolved in alcohol. **2.** the gloss finish produced by this polish.

French-polish *vb.* to treat with French polish or give a French polish (to).

French seam *n.* a seam in which the edges are not visible.

French toast *n.* **1.** *Brit.* toast cooked on one side only. **2.** bread dipped in beaten egg and lightly fried.

French windows *pl. n.* (*sometimes sing.*) *Brit.* a pair of casement windows extending to floor level and opening onto a balcony, garden, etc.

frenetic (frɪˈnɛtɪk) *adj.* distracted or frantic. [C14: via OF, < L, < Gk, < *phrenitis* insanity, < *phrēn* mind] —**freˈnetically** *adv.*

frenum (ˈfriːnəm) *n., pl.* **-na** (-nə). a variant spelling (esp. U.S.) of **fraenum.**

frenzy (ˈfrɛnzɪ) *n., pl.* **-zies. 1.** violent mental derangement. **2.** wild excitement or agitation. **3.** a bout of wild or agitated activity: *a frenzy of preparations.* ~*vb.* **-zying, -zied. 4.** (*tr.*) to drive into a frenzy. [C14: < OF, < LL *phrēnēsis* madness, < LGk, ult. < Gk *phrēn* mind] —ˈ**frenzied** *adj.*

freq. *abbrev. for:* **1.** frequent(ly). **2.** frequentative.

frequency (ˈfriːkwənsɪ) *n., pl.* **-cies. 1.** the state of being frequent. **2.** the number of times that an event occurs within a given period. **3.** *Physics.* the number of times that a periodic function or vibration repeats itself in a specified time, often 1 second. It is usually measured in hertz. **4.** *Statistics.* **a.** the number of individuals in a class (**absolute frequency**). **b.** the ratio of this number to the total number of individuals under survey (**relative frequency**). [C16: < L, < *frequēns* crowded]

frequency distribution *n. Statistics.* the function of the distribution of a sample corresponding to the probability density function of the underlying population and tending to it as the sample size increases.

frequency modulation *n.* a method of transmitting information using a radio-frequency carrier wave. The frequency of the carrier wave is varied in accordance with the amplitude of the input signal, the amplitude of the carrier remaining unchanged. Cf. **amplitude modulation.**

frequent *adj.* (ˈfriːkwənt). **1.** recurring at short intervals. **2.** habitual. ~*vb.* (frɪˈkwɛnt). **3.** (*tr.*) to visit repeatedly or habitually. [C16: < L *frequēns* numerous] —ˌ**frequenˈtation** *n.* —**freˈquenter** *n.* —ˈ**frequently** *adv.*

frequentative (frɪˈkwɛntətɪv) *Grammar.* ~*adj.* **1.** denoting an aspect of verbs in some languages used to express repeated or habitual action. **2.** (in English) denoting a verb or an affix meaning repeated action, such as the verb *wrestle*, from *wrest.* ~*n.* **3.** a frequentative verb or affix.

fresco (ˈfrɛskəʊ) *n., pl.* **-coes** *or* **-cos. 1.** a very durable method of wall-painting using watercolours on wet plaster. **2.** a painting done in this way. [C16: < It.: fresh plaster, < *fresco* (adj.) fresh, cool, of Gmc origin]

fresh (frɛʃ) *adj.* **1.** newly made, harvested, etc.: *fresh bread; fresh strawberries.* **2.** newly acquired, found, etc.: *fresh publications.* **3.** novel; original: *a fresh outlook.* **4.** most recent: *fresh developments.* **5.** further; additional: *fresh supplies.* **6.** not canned, frozen, or otherwise preserved: *fresh fruit.* **7.** (of water) not salt. **8.** bright or clear: *a fresh morning.* **9.** chilly or invigorating: *a fresh breeze.* **10.** not tired; alert. **11.** not worn or faded: *fresh colours.* **12.** having a healthy or ruddy appearance. **13.** newly or just arrived: *fresh from the presses.* **14.** youthful or inexperienced. **15.** *Inf.* presumptuous or disrespectful; forward. ~*n.* **16.** the fresh part or time of something. **17.** another name for **freshet.** ~*adv.* **18.** in a fresh manner. [OE *fersc* fresh, unsalted] —ˈ**freshly** *adv.* —ˈ**freshness** *n.*

fresh breeze *n.* a wind of force 5 on the Beaufort scale, blowing at speeds between 19 and 24 mph.

freshen (ˈfrɛʃən) *vb.* **1.** to make or become fresh or fresher. **2.** (often foll. by *up*) to refresh (oneself), esp. by washing. **3.** (*intr.*) (of the wind) to increase.

fresher (ˈfrɛʃə) *or* **freshman** (ˈfrɛʃmən) *n., pl.* **-ers** *or* **-men.** a first-year student at college or university.

freshet (ˈfrɛʃɪt) *n.* **1.** the sudden overflowing of a river caused by heavy rain or melting snow. **2.** a stream of fresh water emptying into the sea.

freshwater (ˈfrɛʃˌwɔːtə) *n.* (*modifier*) **1.** of or living in fresh water. **2.** (esp. of a sailor who has not sailed on the sea) inexperienced. **3.** *U.S.* little known: *a freshwater school.*

fresnel (ˈfreɪnɛl) *n.* a unit of frequency equivalent to 10^{12} hertz. [C20: after A. J. *Fresnel* (1788–1827), F physicist]

fret[1] (frɛt) *vb.* **fretting, fretted.** **1.** to distress or be distressed. **2.** to rub or wear away. **3.** to feel or give annoyance or vexation. **4.** to eat away or be eaten away, as by chemical action. **5.** (*tr.*) to make by wearing away; erode. ~*n.* **6.** a state of irritation or anxiety. [OE *fretan* to eat]

fret[2] (frɛt) *n.* **1.** a repetitive geometrical figure, esp. one used as an ornamental border. **2.** such a pattern made in relief; fretwork. ~*vb.* **fretting, fretted.** **3.** (*tr.*) to ornament with fret or fretwork. [C14: < OF *frete* interlaced design used on a shield, prob. of Gmc origin] —ˈ**fretless** *adj.*

fret[3] (frɛt) *n.* any of several small metal bars set across the fingerboard of a musical instrument of the lute, guitar, or viol family at various points along its length so as to produce the desired notes. [C16: <?] —ˈ**fretless** *adj.*

fretful (ˈfrɛtfʊl) *adj.* peevish, irritable, or upset. —ˈ**fretfully** *adv.* —ˈ**fretfulness** *n.*

fret saw *n.* a fine-toothed saw with a long thin narrow blade, used for cutting designs in thin wood or metal.

fretwork (ˈfrɛtˌwɜːk) *n.* decorative geometrical carving or openwork.

Freudian (ˈfrɔɪdɪən) *adj.* **1.** of or relating to Sigmund Freud (1856–1939), Austrian psychiatrist, or his ideas. ~*n.* **2.** a person who follows or believes in the basic ideas of Sigmund Freud. —ˈ**Freudianˌism** *n.*

Freudian slip *n.* any action, such as a slip of the tongue, that may reveal an unconscious thought.

Fri. *abbrev. for* Friday.

friable (ˈfraɪəbᵊl) *adj.* easily broken up; crumbly. [C16: < L, < *friāre* to crumble] —ˌ**friaˈbility** *or* ˈ**friableness** *n.*

friar (ˈfraɪə) *n.* a member of any of various chiefly mendicant religious orders of the Roman Catholic Church. [C13 *frere,* < OF: brother, < L *frāter* BROTHER]

friar's balsam *n.* a compound containing benzoin, mixed with hot water and used as an inhalant to relieve colds and sore throats.

friary (ˈfraɪərɪ) *n., pl.* **-aries.** *Christianity.* a convent or house of friars.

fricandeau (ˈfrɪkənˌdəʊ) *n., pl.* **-deaus** *or* **-deaux** (-ˌdəʊz). a larded and braised veal fillet. [C18: < OF, prob. based on FRICASSEE]

fricassee (ˌfrɪkəˈsiː, ˈfrɪkəsɪ) *n.* **1.** stewed meat, esp. chicken or veal, served in a thick white sauce. ~*vb.* **-seeing, -seed.** **2.** (*tr.*) to prepare (meat, etc.) as a fricassee. [C16: < OF, < *fricasser* to fricassee]

fricative (ˈfrɪkətɪv) *n.* **1.** a consonant produced by partial occlusion of the airstream, such as (f) or (z). ~*adj.* **2.** relating to or denoting a fricative. [C19: < NL, < L *fricāre* to rub]

friction (ˈfrɪkʃən) *n.* **1.** a resistance encountered when one body moves relative to another body with which it is in contact. **2.** the act, effect, or an instance of rubbing one object against another. **3.** disagreement or conflict. [C16: < F, < L *frictiō* a rubbing, < *fricāre* to rub] —ˈ**frictional** *adj.* —ˈ**frictionless** *adj.*

Friday (ˈfraɪdɪ) *n.* **1.** the sixth day of the week; fifth day of the working week. **2.** See **man Friday.** [OE *Frigedæg*]

fridge (frɪdʒ) *n.* short for **refrigerator.**

fried (fraɪd) *vb.* the past tense and past participle of **fry**[1].

friend (frɛnd) *n.* **1.** a person known well to another and regarded with liking, affection, and loyalty. **2.** an acquaintance or associate. **3.** an ally in a fight or cause. **4.** a fellow member of a party, society, etc. **5.** a patron or supporter. **6. be friends (with).** to be friendly (with). **7. make friends (with).** to become friendly (with). ~*vb.* **8.** (*tr.*) an archaic word for **befriend.** [OE *frēond*] —ˈ**friendless** *adj.* —ˈ**friendship** *n.*

Friend (frɛnd) *n.* a member of the Society of Friends; Quaker.

friend at court *n.* an influential acquaintance who can promote one's interests.

friendly (ˈfrɛndlɪ) *adj.* **-lier, -liest.** **1.** showing or expressing liking, goodwill, or trust. **2.** on the same side; not hostile. **3.** tending or disposed to help or support: *a friendly breeze helped them escape.* ~*n., pl.* **-lies.** **4.** Also: **friendly match.** *Sport.* a match played for its own sake. —ˈ**friendlily** *adv.* —ˈ**friendliness** *n.*

friendly society *n. Brit.* an association of people who pay regular dues or other sums in return for old-age pensions, sickness benefits, etc.

Friends of the Earth *n.* an organization of environmentalists and conservationists.

frier (ˈfraɪə) *n.* a variant spelling of **fryer.** See **fry**[1].

Friesian (ˈfriːʒən) *n.* **1.** *Brit.* any of several breeds of black-and-white dairy cattle having a high milk yield. **2.** see **Frisian.**

frieze[1] (friːz) *n.* **1.** *Archit.* **a.** the horizontal band between the architrave and cornice of a classical entablature. **b.** the upper part of the wall of a room, below the cornice. **2.** any ornamental band on a wall. [C16: < F *frise,* ? < Med. L *frisium,* changed < L *Phrygium* Phrygian (work), < Phrygia, famous for embroidery in gold]

frieze[2] (friːz) *n.* a heavy woollen fabric used for coats, etc. [C15: < OF, < MDu. ? < *Vriese* Frisian]

frigate (ˈfrɪgɪt) *n.* **1.** a medium-sized square-rigged warship of the 18th and 19th centuries. **2. a.** *Brit.* a warship smaller than a destroyer. **b.** *U.S.* (formerly) a warship larger than a destroyer. **c.** *U.S.* a small escort vessel. [C16: < F *frégate,* < It. *fregata,* <?]

frigate bird *n.* a bird of tropical and subtropical seas, having a long bill, a wide wingspan, and a forked tail.

fright (fraɪt) *n.* **1.** sudden fear or alarm. **2.** a sudden alarming shock. **3.** *Inf.* a horrifying or ludicrous person or thing: *she looks a fright.* **4. take fright.** to become frightened. ~*vb.* **5.** a poetic word for **frighten.** [OE *fryhto*]

frighten (ˈfraɪtᵊn) *vb.* (*tr.*) **1.** to terrify; scare. **2.** to drive or force to go (away, off, out, in, etc.) by making afraid. —ˈ**frightener** *n.* —ˈ**frighteningly** *adv.*

frightful (ˈfraɪtfʊl) *adj.* **1.** very alarming or horrifying. **2.** unpleasant, annoying, or extreme: *a frightful hurry.* —ˈ**frightfully** *adv.* —ˈ**frightfulness** *n.*

frigid (ˈfrɪdʒɪd) *adj.* **1.** formal or stiff in behaviour or temperament. **2.** (esp. of women) lacking sexual responsiveness. **3.** characterized by physical coldness: *a frigid zone.* [C15: < L *frigidus* cold, < *frīgēre* to be cold] —**friˈgidity** *or* ˈ**frigidness** *n.* —ˈ**frigidly** *adv.*

Frigid Zone *n.* the cold region inside the Arctic or Antarctic Circle where the sun's rays are very oblique.

frijol (*Spanish* friˈxol) *n., pl.* **-joles** (*Spanish* -ˈxoles). a variety of bean extensively cultivated for food in Mexico. [C16: < Sp., ult. < L *phaseolus,* < Gk *phasēlos* bean with edible pod]

frill (frɪl) *n.* **1.** a gathered, ruched, or pleated strip of cloth sewn on at one edge only, as on garments, as ornament, or to give extra body. **2.** a ruff of hair or feathers around the neck of a dog or bird or a fold of skin around the neck of a reptile or amphibian. **3.** (*often pl.*) *Inf.* a superfluous or pretentious thing or manner;

affectation: *he made a plain speech with no frills.* ~*vb.* **4.** (*tr.*) to adorn or fit with a frill or frills. **5.** to form into a frill or frills. [C14: ? of Flemish origin] —**'frilliness** *n.* —**'frilly** *adj.*

frilled lizard *n.* a large arboreal insectivorous Australian lizard having an erectile fold of skin around the neck.

fringe (frɪndʒ) *n.* **1.** an edging consisting of hanging threads, tassels, etc. **2. a.** an outer edge; periphery. **b.** (*as modifier*): *a fringe area.* **3.** (*modifier*) unofficial; not conventional in form: *fringe theatre.* **4.** *Chiefly Brit.* a section of the front hair cut short over the forehead. **5.** an ornamental border. **6.** *Physics.* any of the light and dark bands produced by diffraction or interference of light. ~*vb.* (*tr.*) **7.** to adorn with a fringe or fringes. **8.** to be a fringe for. [C14: < OF *frenge,* ult. < L *fimbria* fringe, border] —**'fringeless** *adj.*

fringe benefit *n.* an additional advantage, esp. a benefit provided by an employer to supplement an employee's regular pay.

fringing reef *n.* a coral reef close to the shore to which it is attached, having a steep seaward edge.

frippery ('frɪpərɪ) *n., pl.* **-peries. 1.** ornate or showy clothing or adornment. **2.** ostentation. **3.** trifles; trivia. [C16: < OF, < *frepe* frill, rag, < Med. L *faluppa* a straw, splinter, <?]

Frisbee ('frɪzbiː) *n. Trademark.* a light plastic disc thrown with a spinning motion for recreation or in competition.

Frisian ('frɪʒən) *or* **Friesian** *n.* **1.** a language spoken in the NW Netherlands and adjacent islands. **2.** a speaker of this language. ~*adj.* **3.** of or relating to this language or its speakers. [C16: < L *Frīsiī* people of northern Germany]

frisk (frɪsk) *vb.* **1.** (*intr.*) to leap, move about, or act in a playful manner. **2.** (*tr.*) (esp. of animals) to whisk or wave briskly: *the dog frisked its tail.* **3.** (*tr.*) *Inf.* to search (someone) by feeling for concealed weapons, etc. ~*n.* **4.** a playful antic or movement. **5.** *Inf.* an instance of frisking a person. [C16: < OF *frisque,* of Gmc origin] —**'frisker** *n.*

frisky ('frɪskɪ) *adj.* **friskier, friskiest.** lively, high-spirited, or playful. —**'friskily** *adv.*

frisson *French.* (frisɔ̃) *n.* a shiver; thrill. [C18 (but in common use only from C20): lit.: shiver]

frit (frɪt) *n.* **1. a.** the basic materials, partially or wholly fused, for making glass, glazes for pottery, enamel, etc. **b.** a glassy substance used in some soft-paste porcelain. ~*vb.* **fritting, fritted. 2.** (*tr.*) to fuse (materials) in making frit. [C17: < It. *fritta,* lit.: fried, < *friggere* to fry, < L *frīgere*]

fritillary (frɪ'tɪlərɪ) *n., pl.* **-laries. 1.** a liliaceous plant having purple or white drooping bell-shaped flowers, typically marked in a chequered pattern. **2.** any of various butterflies having brownish wings chequered with black and silver. [C17: < NL *fritillāria,* < L *fritillus* dice box; prob. with reference to the markings]

fritter[1] ('frɪtə) *vb.* (*tr.*) **1.** (usually foll. by *away*) to waste: *to fritter away time.* **2.** to break into small pieces. [C18: prob. < obs. *fitter* to break into small pieces, ult. < OE *fitt* a piece]

fritter[2] ('frɪtə) *n.* a piece of food, such as apple, that is dipped in batter and fried in deep fat. [C14: < OF, < L *frictus* fried, < *frīgere* to fry]

frivolous ('frɪvələs) *adj.* **1.** not serious or sensible in content, attitude, or behaviour. **2.** unworthy of serious or sensible treatment: *frivolous details.* [C15: < L *frīvolus*] —**'frivolously** *adv.* —**'frivolousness** *or* **frivolity** (frɪ'vɒlɪtɪ) *n.*

frizz (frɪz) *vb.* **1.** (of the hair, nap, etc.) to form or cause (the hair, etc.) to form tight curls or crisp tufts. ~*n.* **2.** hair that has been frizzed. **3.** the state of being frizzed. [C19: < F *friser* to curl]

frizzle[1] ('frɪzᵊl) *vb.* **1.** to form (the hair) into tight crisp curls. ~*n.* **2.** a tight curl. [C16: prob. rel. to OE *frīs* curly]

frizzle[2] ('frɪzᵊl) *vb.* **1.** to scorch or be scorched, esp. with a sizzling noise. **2.** (*tr.*) to fry (bacon, etc.) until crisp. [C16: prob. blend of FRY[1] + SIZZLE]

frizzy ('frɪzɪ) *or* **frizzly** ('frɪzlɪ) *adj.* **-zier, -ziest** *or* **-zlier, -zliest.** (of the hair) in tight crisp wiry curls. —**'frizziness** *or* **'frizzliness** *n.*

fro (frəʊ) *adv.* back or from. [C12: < ON *frā*]

frock (frɒk) *n.* **1.** a girl's or woman's dress. **2.** a loose garment of several types, such as a peasant's smock. **3.** a wide-sleeved outer garment worn by members of some religious orders. ~*vb.* **4.** (*tr.*) to invest (a person) with the office of a cleric. [C14: < OF *froc*]

frock coat *n.* a man's single- or double-breasted skirted coat, as worn in the 19th century.

Froebel ('frəʊbᵊl) *adj.* of, denoting, or relating to a system of kindergarten education developed by Friedrich Froebel (1782-1852), German educator, or to the training and qualification of teachers to use this system.

frog[1] (frɒg) *n.* **1.** an insectivorous amphibian, having a short squat tailless body with a moist smooth skin and very long hind legs specialized for hopping. **2.** any of various similar amphibians, such as the tree frog. **3.** any spiked object used to support plant stems in a flower arrangement. **4. a frog in one's throat.** phlegm on the vocal cords that affects one's speech. [OE *frogga*] —**'froggy** *adj.*

frog[2] (frɒg) *n.* **1.** (*often pl.*) a decorative fastening of looped braid or cord, as on a military uniform. **2.** an attachment on a belt to hold the scabbard of a sword, etc. [C18: ? ult. < L *floccus* tuft of hair] —**frogged** *adj.* —**'frogging** *n.*

frog[3] (frɒg) *n.* a tough elastic horny material in the centre of the sole of a horse's foot. [C17: <?]

frog[4] (frɒg) *n.* a plate of iron or steel to guide train wheels over an intersection of railway lines. [C19: <?; ? a special use of FROG[1]]

Frog (frɒg) *or* **Froggy** ('frɒgɪ) *n., pl.* **Frogs** *or* **Froggies.** *Brit. sl.* a derogatory word for a French person.

froghopper ('frɒg,hɒpə) *n.* any small leaping insect whose larvae secrete a protective spittle-like substance around themselves.

frogman ('frɒgmən) *n., pl.* **-men.** a swimmer equipped with a rubber suit, flippers, and breathing equipment for working underwater.

frogmarch ('frɒg,mɑːtʃ) *Chiefly Brit.* ~*n.* **1.** a method of carrying a resisting person in which each limb is held and the victim is carried horizontally and face downwards. **2.** any method of making a person move against his will. ~*vb.* **3.** (*tr.*) to carry in a frogmarch or cause to move forward unwillingly.

frogmouth ('frɒg,maʊθ) *n.* a nocturnal insectivorous bird of SE Asia and Australia, similar to the nightjars.

frogspawn ('frɒg,spɔːn) *n.* a mass of fertilized frogs' eggs surrounded by a protective nutrient jelly.

frog spit *or* **spittle** *n.* **1.** another name for **cuckoo spit. 2.** a foamy mass of threadlike green algae floating on ponds.

frolic ('frɒlɪk) *n.* **1.** a light-hearted entertainment or occasion. **2.** light-hearted activity; gaiety. ~*vb.* **-icking, -icked. 3.** (*intr.*) to caper about. ~*adj.* **4.** *Arch.* full of fun; gay. [C16: < Du. *vrolijk,* < MDu. *vro* happy] —**'frolicker** *n.*

frolicsome ('frɒlɪksəm) *adj.* merry and playful. —**'frolicsomely** *adv.*

from (frɒm; *unstressed* frəm) *prep.* **1.** used to indicate the original location, situation, etc.: *from behind the bushes.* **2.** in a period of time starting at: *he lived from 1910 to 1970.* **3.** used to indicate the distance between two things or places: *a hundred miles from here.* **4.** used to indicate a lower amount: *from five to fifty pounds.* **5.** showing the model of: *painted from life.* **6.** used with the gerund to mark prohibition, etc.: *nothing prevents him from leaving.* **7.** because of: *exhausted from his walk.* [OE *fram*]

▷ **Usage.** See at **off.**

frond (frɒnd) *n.* **1.** the compound leaf of a fern. **2.** the leaf of a palm. [C18: < *frōns*]

front (frʌnt) *n.* **1.** that part or side that is forward, or most often seen or used. **2.** a position or place directly before or ahead: *a fountain stood at the* *front of the building.* **3.** the beginning, opening, or first part. **4.** the position of leadership: *in the front of scientific knowledge.* **5.** land bordering a lake, street, etc. **6.** land along a seashore or large lake, esp. a promenade. **7.** *Mil.* **a.** the total area in which opposing armies face each other. **b.** the space in which a military unit is operating: *to advance on a broad front.* **8.** *Meteorol.* the dividing line or plane between two air masses of different origins. **9.** outward aspect or bearing, as when dealing with a situation: *a bold front.* **10.** *Inf.* a business or other activity serving as a respectable cover for another, usually criminal, organization. **11.** Also called: **front man.** a nominal leader of an organization etc.; figurehead. **12.** *Inf.* outward appearance of rank or wealth. **13.** a particular field of activity: *on the wages front.* **14.** a group of people with a common goal: *a national liberation front.* **15.** a false shirt front; a dicky. **16.** *Arch.* the forehead or the face. ~*adj.* (*prenominal*) **17.** of, at, or in the front: *a front seat.* **18.** *Phonetics.* of or denoting a vowel articulated with the tongue brought forward, as for the sound of *ee* in English *see* or *a* in English *hat.* ~*vb.* **19.** (when *intr.,* foll. by *on* or *onto*) to face (onto): *this house fronts the river.* **20.** (*tr.*) to be a front of or for. **21.** (*tr.*) to appear as a presenter in a television show. **22.** (*tr.*) to confront. **23.** to supply a front for. **24.** (*intr.;* often foll. by *up*) *Austral. inf.* to appear (at): *to front up at the police station.* [C13 (in the sense: forehead, face): < L *frōns* forehead, foremost part] —ˈ**frontless** *adj.*

frontage (ˈfrʌntɪdʒ) *n.* **1.** the façade of a building or the front of a plot of ground. **2.** the extent of the front of a shop, plot of land, etc. **3.** the direction in which a building faces.

frontal (ˈfrʌntəl) *adj.* **1.** of, at, or in the front. **2.** of or relating to the forehead: *frontal artery.* ~*n.* **3.** a decorative hanging for the front of an altar. [C14 (in the sense: adornment for forehead, altarcloth): via OF *frontel,* < L *frōns* forehead] —ˈ**frontally** *adv.*

frontal lobe *n. Anat.* the anterior portion of each cerebral hemisphere.

front bench *n.* **1.** *Brit.* **a.** the foremost bench of either the Government or Opposition in the House of Commons. **b.** the leadership (**frontbenchers**) of either group, who occupy this bench. **2.** the leadership of the government or opposition in various legislative assemblies.

front-end *adj.* (of money, costs, etc.) required or incurred in advance of a project in order to get it under way.

frontier (ˈfrʌntɪə, frʌnˈtɪə) *n.* **1. a.** the region of a country bordering on another or a line, barrier, etc., marking such a boundary. **b.** (*as modifier*): *a frontier post.* **2.** *U.S.* the edge of the settled area of a country. **3.** (*often pl.*) the limit of knowledge in a particular field: *the frontiers of physics have been pushed back.* [C14: < OF, < *front* (in the sense: part which is opposite)]

frontiersman (ˈfrʌntɪəzmən, frʌnˈtɪəz-) *n., pl.* **-men.** (formerly) a man living on a frontier, esp. in a newly pioneered territory of the U.S.

frontispiece (ˈfrʌntɪsˌpiːs) *n.* **1.** an illustration facing the title page of a book. **2.** the principal façade of a building. **3.** a pediment over a door, window, etc. [C16 *frontispice,* < F, < LL *frontispicium* façade, < L *frōns* forehead + *specere* to look at; infl. by PIECE]

frontlet (ˈfrʌntlɪt) *n. Judaism.* a phylactery attached to the forehead. [C15: < OF *frontelet* a little FRONTAL]

front line *n.* **1.** *Military.* **a.** the most advanced military units in a battle. **b.** (*modifier*): of, relating to, or suitable for the military front line: *frontline troops.* **2.** (*modifier*) close to a hostile country or scene of armed conflict: *the frontline states.*

front loader *n.* a washing machine with a door at the front which opens one side of the drum into which washing is placed.

front-page *n.* (*modifier*) important enough to be put on the front page of a newspaper.

frontrunner (ˈfrʌntˌrʌnə) *n. Inf.* the leader or a favoured contestant in a race, election, etc.

frost (frɒst) *n.* **1.** a white deposit of ice particles, esp. one formed on objects out of doors at night. **2.** an atmospheric temperature of below freezing point, characterized by the production of this deposit. **3. degrees of frost.** degrees below freezing point. **4.** *Inf.* something given a cold reception; failure. **5.** *Inf.* coolness of manner. **6.** the act of freezing. ~*vb.* **7.** to cover or be covered with frost. **8.** (*tr.*) to give a frostlike appearance to (glass, etc.), as by means of a fine-grained surface. **9.** (*tr.*) *Chiefly U.S. & Canad.* to decorate (cakes, etc.) with icing or frosting. **10.** (*tr.*) to kill or damage (crops, etc.) with frost. [OE *frost*]

frostbite (ˈfrɒstˌbaɪt) *n.* destruction of tissues, esp. those of the fingers, ears, toes, and nose, by freezing. —ˈ**frostˌbitten** *adj.*

frosted (ˈfrɒstɪd) *adj.* **1.** covered or injured by frost. **2.** covered with icing, as a cake. **3.** (of glass, etc.) having a surface roughened to prevent clear vision through it.

frosting (ˈfrɒstɪŋ) *n.* **1.** another word (esp. U.S. and Canad.) for **icing.** **2.** a rough or matt finish on glass, silver, etc.

frosty (ˈfrɒstɪ) *adj.* **frostier, frostiest.** **1.** characterized by frost: *a frosty night.* **2.** covered by or decorated with frost. **3.** lacking warmth or enthusiasm: *the new plan had a frosty reception.* —ˈ**frostily** *adv.* —ˈ**frostiness** *n.*

froth (frɒθ) *n.* **1.** a mass of small bubbles of air or a gas in a liquid, produced by fermentation, etc. **2.** a mixture of saliva and air bubbles formed at the lips in certain diseases, such as rabies. **3.** trivial ideas or entertainment. ~*vb.* **4.** to produce or cause to produce froth. **5.** (*tr.*) to give out in the form of froth. [C14: < ON *frotha* or *frauth*] —ˈ**frothy** *adj.* —ˈ**frothily** *adv.*

froufrou (ˈfruːˌfruː) *n.* a swishing sound, as made by a long silk dress. [C19: < F, imit.]

froward (ˈfrəʊəd) *adj. Arch.* obstinate; contrary. [C14: see FRO, -WARD] —ˈ**frowardly** *adv.* —ˈ**frowardness** *n.*

frown (fraʊn) *vb.* **1.** (*intr.*) to draw the brows together and wrinkle the forehead, esp. in worry, anger, or concentration. **2.** (*intr.;* foll. by *on* or *upon*) to look disapprovingly (upon). **3.** (*tr.*) to express (worry, etc.) by frowning. ~*n.* **4.** the act of frowning. **5.** a show of dislike or displeasure. [C14: < OF *froigner,* of Celtic origin] —ˈ**frowner** *n.* —ˈ**frowningly** *adv.*

frowst (fraʊst) *n. Brit. inf.* a hot and stale atmosphere; fug. [C19: back formation < *frowsty* musty, stuffy, var. of FROWZY]

frowsty (ˈfraʊstɪ) *adj.* ill-smelling; stale; musty. —ˈ**frowstiness** *n.*

frowzy *or* **frowsy** (ˈfraʊzɪ) *adj.* **frowzier, frowziest,** *or* **frowsier, frowsiest.** **1.** untidy or unkempt in appearance. **2.** ill-smelling; frowsty. [C17: <?] —ˈ**frowziness** *or* ˈ**frowsiness** *n.*

froze (frəʊz) *vb.* the past tense of **freeze.**

frozen (ˈfrəʊzən) *vb.* **1.** the past participle of **freeze.** ~*adj.* **2.** turned into or covered with ice. **3.** killed or stiffened by extreme cold. **4.** (of a region or climate) icy or snowy. **5.** (of food) preserved by a freezing process. **6. a.** (of prices, wages, etc.) arbitrarily pegged at a certain level. **b.** (of business assets) not convertible into cash. **7.** frigid or disdainful in manner. **8.** motionless or unyielding: *he was frozen with horror.* —ˈ**frozenly** *adv.*

frozen shoulder *n. Pathol.* painful stiffness in a shoulder joint.

FRS (in Britain) *abbrev. for* Fellow of the Royal Society.

FRSNZ *abbrev. for* Fellow of the Royal Society of New Zealand.

fructify (ˈfrʌktɪˌfaɪ) *vb.* **-fying, -fied.** **1.** to bear or cause to bear fruit. **2.** to make or become fruitful. [C14: < OF, < LL *frūctificāre,* < L *frūctus* fruit + *facere* to produce] —ˌ**fructifiˈcation** *n.* —**frucˈtiferous** *adj.* —ˈ**fructiˌfier** *n.*

fructose (ˈfrʌktəʊs) *n.* a white crystalline sugar

occurring in many fruits. Formula: $C_6H_{12}O_6$. [C19: < L *frūctus* fruit + -OSE[2]]

frugal (ˈfruːgᵊl) *adj.* **1.** practising economy; thrifty. **2.** not costly; meagre. [C16: < L, < *frūgī* useful, temperate, < *frux* fruit] —**fruˈgality** *n.* —**ˈfrugally** *adv.*

frugivorous (fruːˈdʒɪvərəs) *adj.* fruit-eating. [C18: < *frugi-* (as in FRUGAL) + -VOROUS]

fruit (fruːt) *n.* **1.** *Bot.* the ripened ovary of a flowering plant, containing one or more seeds. It may be dry, as in the poppy, or fleshy, as in the peach. **2.** any fleshy part of a plant that supports the seeds and is edible, such as the strawberry. **3.** any plant product useful to man, including grain, vegetables, etc. **4.** (*often pl.*) the result or consequence of an action or effort. **5.** *Arch.* offspring of man or animals. ~*vb.* **6.** to bear or cause to bear fruit. [C12: < OF, < L *frūctus* enjoyment, fruit, < *frūī* to enjoy] —**ˈfruitˌlike** *adj.*

fruit bat *n.* a large Old World bat occurring in tropical and subtropical regions and feeding on fruit.

fruitcake (ˈfruːtˌkeɪk) *n.* a rich cake containing mixed dried fruit, lemon peel, etc.

fruiterer (ˈfruːtərə) *n. Chiefly Brit.* a fruit dealer or seller.

fruit fly *n.* **1.** a small dipterous fly which feeds on and lays its eggs in plant tissues. **2.** any dipterous fly of the genus *Drosophila.* See **drosophila.**

fruitful (ˈfruːtfʊl) *adj.* **1.** bearing fruit in abundance. **2.** productive or prolific. **3.** producing results or profits: *a fruitful discussion.* —**ˈfruitfully** *adv.* —**ˈfruitfulness** *n.*

fruition (fruːˈɪʃən) *n.* **1.** the attainment of something worked for or desired. **2.** enjoyment of this. **3.** the act or condition of bearing fruit. [C15: < LL, < L *fruī* to enjoy]

fruitless (ˈfruːtlɪs) *adj.* **1.** yielding nothing or nothing of value; unproductive. **2.** without fruit. —**ˈfruitlessly** *adv.* —**ˈfruitlessness** *n.*

fruit machine *n. Brit.* a gambling machine that pays out when certain combinations of diagrams, usually of fruit, appear on a dial.

fruit salad *n.* a dessert consisting of sweet fruits cut up and served in a syrup.

fruit sugar *n.* another name for **fructose.**

fruit tree *n.* any tree that bears edible fruit.

fruity (ˈfruːtɪ) *adj.* **fruitier, fruitiest. 1.** of or resembling fruit. **2.** (of a voice) mellow or rich. **3.** *Inf., chiefly Brit.* erotically stimulating; salacious. —**ˈfruitiness** *n.*

frumenty (ˈfruːməntɪ) *or* **furmenty** *n. Brit.* a kind of porridge made from hulled wheat boiled with milk, sweetened, and spiced. [C14: < OF, < *frument* grain, < L *frūmentum*]

frump (frʌmp) *n.* a woman who is dowdy, drab, or unattractive. [C16 (in the sense: to be sullen; C19: dowdy woman): < MDu. *verrompelen* to wrinkle] —**ˈfrumpish** *or* **ˈfrumpy** *adj.*

frustrate (frʌˈstreɪt) *vb.* (*tr.*) **1.** to hinder or prevent (the efforts, plans, or desires) of. **2.** to upset, agitate, or tire. ~*adj.* **3.** *Arch.* frustrated or thwarted. [C15: < L *frustrāre* to cheat, < *frustrā* in error] —**frusˈtration** *n.*

frustrated (frʌˈstreɪtɪd) *adj.* having feelings of dissatisfaction or lack of fulfilment.

frustum (ˈfrʌstəm) *n., pl.* **-tums** *or* **-ta** (-tə). *Geom.* **a.** the part of a solid, such as a cone or pyramid, contained between the base and a plane parallel to the base that intersects the solid. **b.** the part of such a solid contained between two parallel planes intersecting the solid. [C17: < L: piece]

fry[1] (fraɪ) *vb.* **frying, fried. 1.** (when *tr.*, sometimes foll. by *up*) to cook or be cooked in fat, oil, etc., usually over direct heat. **2.** *Sl., chiefly U.S.* to kill or be killed by electrocution. ~*n., pl.* **fries. 3.** a dish of something fried, esp. the offal of a specified animal: *pig's fry.* **4. fry-up.** *Brit. inf.* the act of preparing a mixed fried dish or the dish itself. [C13: < OF *frire*, < L *frīgere* to fry] —**ˈfryer** *or* **ˈfrier** *n.*

fry[2] (fraɪ) *pl. n.* **1.** the young of various species of fish. **2.** the young of certain other animals, such as frogs. [C14 (in the sense: young, offspring): < OF *freier* to spawn, < L *fricāre* to rub]

frying pan *n.* **1.** a long-handled shallow pan used for frying. **2. out of the frying pan into the fire.** from a bad situation to a worse one.

f-stop (ˈɛfˌstɒp) *n.* any of the settings for the f-number of a camera.

ft. *abbrev. for* foot *or* feet.

fth. *or* **fthm.** *abbrev. for* fathom.

FT Index *abbrev. for* Financial Times Industrial Ordinary Share Index. A listing designed to show the general trend in share prices, produced daily by the Financial Times newspaper.

fuchsia (ˈfjuːʃə) *n.* **1.** a shrub widely cultivated for its showy drooping purple, red, or white flowers. **2. a.** a reddish-purple to purplish-pink colour. **b.** (*as adj.*): *a fuchsia dress.* [C18: < NL, after Leonhard *Fuchs* (1501–66), G botanist]

fuchsin (ˈfuːksɪn) *or* **fuchsine** (ˈfuːksiːn, -sɪn) *n.* an aniline dye forming a red solution in water: used as a textile dye and a biological stain. [C19: < FUCHS(IA) + -IN; from its similarity in colour to the flower]

fuck (fʌk) *Taboo.* ~*vb.* **1.** to have sexual intercourse with (someone). ~*n.* **2.** an act of sexual intercourse. **3.** *Sl.* a partner in sexual intercourse. **4. not care** *or* **give a fuck.** not to care at all. ~*interj.* **5.** *Offens.* an expression of strong disgust or anger. [C16: of Gmc origin]

fucus (ˈfjuːkəs) *n., pl.* **-ci** (-saɪ) *or* **-cuses.** a seaweed of the genus *Fucus*, having greenish-brown slimy fronds. [C16: < L: rock lichen, < Gk *phukos* seaweed, of Semitic origin]

fuddle (ˈfʌdᵊl) *vb.* **1.** (*tr.; often passive*) to cause to be confused or intoxicated. ~*n.* **2.** a muddled or confused state. [C16: <?]

fuddy-duddy (ˈfʌdɪˌdʌdɪ) *n., pl.* **-dies.** *Inf.* a person, esp. an elderly one, who is extremely conservative or dull. [C20: <?]

fudge[1] (fʌdʒ) *n.* a soft variously flavoured sweet made from sugar, butter, etc. [C19: <?]

fudge[2] (fʌdʒ) *n.* **1.** foolishness; nonsense. ~*interj.* **2.** a mild exclamation of annoyance. [C18: <?]

fudge[3] (fʌdʒ) *n.* **1.** a small section of type matter in a box in a newspaper allowing late news to be included without the whole page having to be remade. **2.** the late news so inserted. ~*vb.* **3.** (*tr.*) to make or adjust in a false or clumsy way. **4.** (*tr.*) to misrepresent; falsify. **5.** to evade (a problem, issue, etc.). [C19: ? rel. to arch. *fadge* to agree, succeed]

fuel (fjʊəl) *n.* **1.** any substance burned as a source of heat or power, such as coal or petrol. **2.** the material, containing a fissile substance such as uranium-235, that produces energy in a nuclear reactor. **3.** something that nourishes or builds up emotion, action, etc. ~*vb.* **fuelling, fuelled** *or U.S.* **fueling, fueled. 4.** to supply with or receive fuel. [C14: < OF, < *feu* fire, ult. < L *focus* hearth]

fuel cell *n.* a cell in which chemical energy is converted directly into electrical energy.

fuel injection *n.* a system for introducing fuel directly into the combustion chambers of an internal-combustion engine without the use of a carburettor.

fuel oil *n.* a liquid petroleum product used as a substitute for coal in industrial furnaces, ships, and locomotives.

fug (fʌg) *n. Chiefly Brit.* a hot, stale, or suffocating atmosphere. [C19: ? var. of FOG[1]] —**ˈfuggy** *adj.*

fugacity (fjuːˈgæsɪtɪ) *n. Thermodynamics.* a property of a gas that expresses its tendency to escape or expand.

-fuge *n. combining form.* indicating an agent or substance that expels or drives away: *vermifuge.* [< L *fugāre* to expel]

fugitive (ˈfjuːdʒɪtɪv) *n.* **1.** a person who flees. **2.** a thing that is elusive or fleeting. ~*adj.* **3.** fleeing, esp. from arrest or pursuit. **4.** not permanent; fleeting. [C14: < L, < *fugere* to take flight] —**ˈfugitively** *adv.*

fugleman (ˈfjuːgᵊlmən) *n., pl.* **-men. 1.** (formerly) a soldier used as an example for those learning drill. **2.** a leader or example. [C19: < G *Flügelmann,* < *Flügel* wing + *Mann* MAN]

fugue (fjuːg) *n.* **1.** a musical form consisting of a theme repeated a fifth above or a fourth below the continuing first statement. **2.** *Psychiatry.* a dreamlike altered state of consciousness, during which a person may lose his memory and wander away. [C16: < F, < It. *fuga,* < L: a running away] —**ˈfugal** *adj.*

Führer *or* **Fuehrer** *German.* (ˈfyːrər) *n.* a leader: applied esp. to Adolf Hitler while he was Chancellor. [G, < *führen* to lead]

-ful *suffix.* **1.** (*forming adjectives*) full of or characterized by: *painful; restful.* **2.** (*forming adjectives*) able or tending to: *useful.* **3.** (*forming nouns*) indicating as much as will fill the thing specified: *mouthful.* [OE *-ful, -full,* < FULL[1]]

▷ **Usage.** Where the amount held by a spoon, etc., is used as a rough unit of measurement, the correct form is *spoonful,* etc.: *take a spoonful of this medicine every day.* The plural of a word like spoonful is *spoonfuls* and not *spoonsful.*

fulcrum (ˈfʊlkrəm, ˈfʌl-) *n., pl.* **-crums** *or* **-cra** (-krə). **1.** the pivot about which a lever turns. **2.** something that supports or sustains; prop. [C17: < L: foot of a couch, < *fulcire* to prop up]

fulfil *or U.S.* **fulfill** (fʊlˈfɪl) *vb.* **-filling, -filled.** (*tr.*) **1.** to bring about the completion or achievement of (a desire, promise, etc.). **2.** to carry out or execute (a request, etc.). **3.** to conform with or satisfy (regulations, etc.). **4.** to finish or reach the end of. **5. fulfil oneself.** to achieve one's potentials or desires. [OE *fulfyllan*] —**fulˈfilment** *or U.S.* **fulˈfillment** *n.*

fulgent (ˈfʌldʒənt) *adj. Poetic.* shining brilliantly; gleaming. [C15: < L *fulgēre* to shine]

fulgurate (ˈfʌlgjʊˌreɪt) *vb.* (*intr.*) *Rare.* to flash like lightning. [C17: < L, < *fulgur* lightning]

fulgurite (ˈfʌlgjʊˌraɪt) *n.* glassy mineral matter found in sand and rock, formed by the action of lightning. [C19: < L *fulgur* lightning]

fuliginous (fjuːˈlɪdʒɪnəs) *adj.* **1.** sooty or smoky. **2.** of the colour of soot. [C16: < LL *fūlīginōsus* full of soot, < L *fūlīgō* soot]

full[1] (fʊl) *adj.* **1.** holding or containing as much as possible. **2.** abundant in supply, quantity, number, etc.: *full of energy.* **3.** having consumed enough food or drink. **4.** (esp. of the face or figure) rounded or plump. **5.** (*prenominal*) complete: *a full dozen.* **6.** (*prenominal*) with all privileges, rights, etc.: *a full member.* **7.** (*prenominal*) having the same parents: *a full brother.* **8.** filled with emotion or sentiment: *a full heart.* **9.** (*postpositive;* foll. by *of*) occupied or engrossed (with): *full of his own projects.* **10.** *Music.* **a.** powerful or rich in volume and sound. **b.** completing a piece or section; concluding: *a full close.* **11.** (of a garment, esp. a skirt) containing a large amount of fabric. **12.** (of sails, etc.) distended by wind. **13.** (of wine, such as a burgundy) having a heavy body. **14.** (of a colour) rich; saturated. **15.** *Inf.* drunk. **16. full of oneself.** full of pride or conceit. **17. full up.** filled to capacity. **18. in full swing.** at the height of activity: *the party was in full swing.* ~*adv.* **19. a.** completely; entirely. **b.** (*in combination*): *full-fledged.* **20.** directly; right: *he hit him full in the stomach.* **21.** very; extremely (esp. in **full well**). ~*n.* **22.** the greatest degree, extent, etc. **23. in full.** without omitting or shortening: *we paid in full for our mistake.* **24. to the full.** thoroughly; fully. ~*vb.* **25.** (*tr.*) *Needlework.* to gather or tuck. **26.** (*intr.*) (of the moon) to be fully illuminated. [OE] —**ˈfullness** *or esp. U.S.* **ˈfulness** *n.*

full[2] (fʊl) *vb.* (of cloth, yarn, etc.) to become or to make (cloth, yarn, etc.) more compact during manufacture through shrinking and pressing. [C14: < OF *fouler,* ult. < L *fullō* a FULLER]

fullback (ˈfʊlˌbæk) *n. Soccer, hockey, rugby.* **a.** a defensive player. **b.** the position held by this player.

full-blooded *adj.* **1.** (esp. of horses) of unmixed ancestry. **2.** having great vigour or health; hearty. —**ˌfull-ˈbloodedness** *n.*

full-blown *adj.* **1.** characterized by the fullest, strongest, or best development. **2.** in full bloom.

full-bodied *adj.* having a full rich flavour or quality.

full dress *n.* **a.** a formal style of dress, such as white tie and tails for a man. **b.** (*as modifier*): *full-dress uniform.*

fuller (ˈfʊlə) *n.* a person who fulls cloth for his living. [OE *fullere*]

fuller's earth *n.* a natural absorbent clay used, after heating, for clarifying oils and fats, fulling cloth, etc.

full face *adj.* facing towards the viewer, with the entire face visible.

full-fledged *adj.* See **fully fledged.**

full-frontal *adj. Inf.* **1.** (of a nude person or a photograph of a nude person) exposing the genitals to full view. **2.** all-out; unrestrained.

full house *n.* **1.** *Poker.* a hand with three cards of the same value and another pair. **2.** a theatre, etc., filled to capacity. **3.** (in bingo, etc.) the set of numbers needed to win.

full-length *n.* (*modifier*) **1.** showing the complete length. **2.** not abridged.

full moon *n.* one of the four phases of the moon when the moon is visible as a fully illuminated disc.

full nelson *n.* a wrestling hold in which a wrestler places both arms under his opponent's arms from behind and exerts pressure on the back of the neck.

full pitch *or* **full toss** *n. Cricket.* a bowled ball that reaches the batsman without bouncing.

full sail *adv.* **1.** at top speed. ~*adj.* (*postpositive*), *adv.* **2.** with all sails set.

full-scale *n.* (*modifier*) **1.** (of a plan, etc.) of actual size. **2.** using all resources; all-out.

full stop *or* **full point** *n.* the punctuation mark (.) used at the end of a sentence that is not a question or exclamation, after abbreviations, etc. Also called (esp. U.S. and Canad.): **period.**

full time *n.* the end of a football or other match.

full-time *adj.* **1.** for the entire time appropriate to an activity: *a full-time job.* ~*adv.* **full time. 2.** on a full-time basis: *he works full time.* ~Cf. **part-time.** —**ˌfull-ˈtimer** *n.*

fully (ˈfʊlɪ) *adv.* **1.** to the greatest degree or extent. **2.** amply; adequately: *they were fully fed.* **3.** at least: *it was fully an hour before she came.*

fully fashioned *adj.* (of stockings, knitwear, etc.) shaped and seamed so as to fit closely.

fully fledged *or* **full-fledged** *adj.* **1.** (of a young bird) having acquired its adult feathers and thus able to fly. **2.** developed or matured to the fullest degree. **3.** of full rank or status.

fulmar (ˈfʊlmə) *n.* a heavily built short-tailed oceanic bird of polar regions. [C17: of Scand. origin]

fulminate (ˈfʌlmɪˌneɪt) *vb.* **1.** (*intr.;* often foll. by *against*) to make severe criticisms or denunciations; rail. **2.** to explode with noise and violence. ~*n.* **3.** any salt or ester of **fulminic acid,** an isomer of cyanic acid, which is used as a detonator. [C15: < Med. L, < L, < *fulmen* lightning that strikes] —**ˈfulminant** *adj.* —**ˌfulmiˈnation** *n.* —**ˈfulmiˌnatory** *adj.*

fulsome (ˈfʊlsəm) *adj.* excessive or insincere, esp. in an offensive or distasteful way: *fulsome compliments.* —**ˈfulsomely** *adv.* —**ˈfulsomeness** *n.*

fulvous (ˈfʌlvəs) *adj.* of a dull brownish-yellow colour. [C17: < L *fulvus* reddish yellow]

fumarole (ˈfjuːməˌrəʊl) *n.* a vent in or near a volcano from which hot gases, esp. steam, are emitted. [C19: < F, < LL *fūmāriolum* smoke hole, < L *fūmus* smoke]

fumble (ˈfʌmbᵊl) *vb.* **1.** (*intr.;* often foll. by *for* or *with*) to grope about clumsily or blindly, esp. in searching. **2.** (*intr.;* foll. by *at* or *with*) to finger or play with, esp. in an absent-minded way. **3.** to say or do awkwardly: *he fumbled the introduction badly.* **4.** to fail to catch or grasp (a ball, etc.) cleanly. ~*n.* **5.** the act of fumbling. [C16: prob. of Scand. origin] —**ˈfumbler** *n.* —**ˈfumblingly** *adv.*

fume (fju:m) *vb.* **1.** (*intr.*) to be overcome with anger or fury. **2.** to give off (fumes) or (of fumes) to be given off, esp. during a chemical reaction. **3.** (*tr.*) to fumigate. ~*n.* **4.** (*often pl.*) a pungent or toxic vapour, gas, or smoke. **5.** a sharp or pungent odour. [C14: < OF *fum,* < L *fūmus* smoke, vapour] —ˈ**fumeless** *adj.* —ˈ**fumingly** *adv.* —ˈ**fumy** *adj.*

fumed (fju:md) *adj.* (of wood, esp. oak) having a dark colour and distinctive grain from exposure to ammonia fumes.

fumigant (ˈfju:mɪgənt) *n.* a substance used for fumigating.

fumigate (ˈfju:mɪˌgeɪt) *vb.* to treat (something contaminated or infected) with fumes or smoke. [C16: < L, < *fūmus* smoke + *agere* to drive] —ˌ**fumiˈgation** *n.* —ˈ**fumiˌgator** *n.*

fuming sulphuric acid *n.* a mixture of acids, made by dissolving sulphur trioxide in concentrated sulphuric acid. Also called: **oleum.**

fumitory (ˈfju:mɪtərɪ) *n., pl.* **-ries.** any plant of the genus *Fumaria* having spurred flowers and formerly used medicinally. [C14: < OF, < Med. L *fūmus terrae,* lit.: smoke of the earth]

fun (fʌn) *n.* **1.** a source of enjoyment, amusement, diversion, etc. **2.** pleasure, gaiety, or merriment. **3.** jest or sport (esp. in **in** *or* **for fun**). **4. fun and games.** *Ironic or facetious.* frivolous or hetic activity. **5. make fun of** *or* **poke fun at.** to ridicule or deride. **6.** (*modifier*) full of amusement, diversion, gaiety, etc.: *a fun sport.* [C17: ? < obs. *fon* to make a fool of; see FOND]

funambulist (fju:ˈnæmbjʊlɪst) *n.* a tightrope walker. [C18: < L, < *fūnis* rope + *ambulāre* to walk] —**fuˈnambulism** *n.*

function (ˈfʌŋkʃən) *n.* **1.** the natural action of a person or thing: *the function of the kidneys is to filter waste products from the blood.* **2.** the intended purpose of a person or thing in a specific role: *the function of a hammer is to hit nails into wood.* **3.** an official or formal social gathering or ceremony. **4.** a factor dependent upon another or other factors. **5.** *Maths, logic.* a relation between two sets that associates a unique element (the value) of the second (the range) with each element (the argument) of the first (the domain). Symbol: $f(x)$. The value of $f(x)$ for $x=2$ is $f(2)$. Also called: **map, mapping.** ~*vb.* (*intr.*) **6.** to operate or perform as specified. **7.** (foll. by *as*) to perform the action or role (of something or someone else): *a coin may function as a screwdriver.* [C16: < L *functiō,* < *fungī* to perform]

functional (ˈfʌŋkʃənᵊl) *adj.* **1.** of, involving, or containing a function or functions. **2.** practical rather than decorative; utilitarian. **3.** capable of functioning; working. **4.** *Med.* affecting a function of an organ without structural change. —ˈ**functionally** *adv.*

functionalism (ˈfʌŋkʃənəˌlɪzəm) *n.* **1.** the theory of design that the form of a thing should be determined by its use. **2.** any doctrine that stresses purpose. —ˈ**functionalist** *n., adj.*

functionary (ˈfʌŋkʃənərɪ) *n., pl.* **-aries.** a person acting in an official capacity, as for a government; an official.

fund (fʌnd) *n.* **1.** a reserve of money, etc., set aside for a certain purpose. **2.** a supply or store of something; stock: *it exhausted his fund of wisdom.* ~*vb.* (*tr.*) **3.** to furnish money to in the form of a fund. **4.** to place or store up in a fund. **5.** to convert (short-term floating debt) into long-term debt bearing fixed interest and represented by bonds. **6.** to accumulate a fund for the discharge of (a recurrent liability): *to fund a pension plan.* ~See also **funds.** [C17: < L *fundus* the bottom, piece of land]

fundament (ˈfʌndəmənt) *n. Euphemistic or facetious.* the buttocks. [C13: < L, < *fundāre* to FOUND[2]]

fundamental (ˌfʌndəˈmɛntᵊl) *adj.* **1.** of, involving, or comprising a foundation; basic. **2.** of, involving, or comprising a source; primary. **3.** *Music.* denoting or relating to the principal or lowest note of a harmonic series. ~*n.* **4.** a principle, law, etc., that serves as the basis of an idea or system. **5. a.** the principal or lowest note of a harmonic series. **b.** the bass note of a chord in root position. —ˌ**fundamenˈtality** *n.* —ˌ**fundaˈmentally** *adv.*

fundamentalism (ˌfʌndəˈmɛntəˌlɪzəm) *n.* **1.** *Christianity.* the view that the Bible is divinely inspired and is therefore literally true. **2.** *Islam.* a movement favouring strict observance of the teachings of the Koran and Islamic law. —ˌ**fundaˈmentalist** *n., adj.*

fundamental particle *n.* another name for **elementary particle.**

fundamental unit *n.* one of a set of unrelated units that form the basis of a system of units. For example, the metre, kilogram, and second are fundamental units of the SI system.

funded debt *n.* that part of the British national debt which the government is not obliged to repay by a fixed date.

funds (fʌndz) *pl. n.* **1.** money that is readily available. **2.** British government securities representing national debt.

fundus (ˈfʌndəs) *n., pl.* **-di** (-daɪ). *Anat.* the base of an organ or the part farthest away from its opening. [C18: < L, lit.: the bottom]

funeral (ˈfju:nərəl) *n.* **1. a.** a ceremony at which a dead person is buried or cremated. **b.** (*as modifier*): *a funeral service.* **2.** a procession of people escorting a corpse to burial. **3.** *Inf.* concern; affair: *that's your funeral.* [C14: < Med. L, < LL, < L *fūnus* funeral] —ˈ**funerary** *adj.*

funeral director *n.* an undertaker.

funeral parlour *n.* a place where the dead are prepared for burial or cremation. Usual U.S. name: **funeral home.**

funereal (fju:ˈnɪərɪəl) *adj.* suggestive of a funeral; gloomy or mournful. Also: **funebrial.** [C18: < L *fūnereus*] —**fuˈnereally** *adv.*

funfair (ˈfʌnˌfɛə) *n. Brit.* an amusement park or fairground.

fungible (ˈfʌndʒɪbᵊl) *n. Law.* (*often pl.*) moveable perishable goods of a sort that may be estimated by number or weight, such as grain, wine, etc. [C18: < Med. L *fungibilis,* < L *fungī* to perform] —ˌ**fungiˈbility** *n.*

fungicide (ˈfʌndʒɪˌsaɪd) *n.* a substance or agent that destroys or is capable of destroying fungi. —ˌ**fungiˈcidal** *adj.* —ˌ**fungiˈcidally** *adv.*

fungoid (ˈfʌŋgɔɪd) *adj.* resembling a fungus or fungi: *a fungoid growth.*

fungous (ˈfʌŋgəs) *adj.* appearing suddenly and spreading quickly like a fungus.

fungus (ˈfʌŋgəs) *n., pl.* **fungi** (ˈfʌŋgaɪ, ˈfʌndʒaɪ, ˈfʌndʒɪ) *or* **funguses.** **1.** any plant of the division *Fungi,* lacking chlorophyll, leaves, true stems, and roots, and reproducing by spores. The group includes moulds, yeasts, and mushrooms. **2.** something resembling a fungus, esp. in suddenly growing. **3.** *Pathol.* any soft tumorous growth. [C16: < L: mushroom, fungus] —ˈ**fungal** *adj.*

funicular (fju:ˈnɪkjʊlə) *n.* **1.** Also called: **funicular railway.** a railway up the side of a mountain, consisting of two cars at either end of a cable passing round a driving wheel at the summit. ~*adj.* **2.** relating to or operated by a rope, etc. [C17: < L, < *fūnis* rope]

funk[1] (fʌŋk) *Inf., chiefly Brit.* ~*n.* **1.** Also called: **blue funk.** a state of nervousness, fear, or depression. **2.** a coward. ~*vb.* **3.** to flinch from (responsibility, etc.) through fear. **4.** (*tr.; usually passive*) to make afraid. [C18: university sl., ? rel. to *funk* to smoke]

funk[2] (fʌŋk) *n. Inf.* a type of polyrhythmic Black dance music with heavy syncopation. [C20: back formation < FUNKY]

funky (ˈfʌŋkɪ) *adj.* **funkier, funkiest.** *Inf.* (of jazz, pop, etc.) passionate; soulful. [C20: < *funk* to smoke (tobacco), ? alluding to music that was smelly, that is, earthy]

funnel (ˈfʌnᵊl) *n.* **1.** a hollow utensil with a wide mouth tapering to a small hole, used for pouring liquids, etc., into a narrow-necked vessel. **2.** something resembling this in shape or function. **3.** a smokestack for smoke and exhaust gases, as on a steam locomotive. ~*vb.* **-nelling, -nelled** *or*

U.S. **-neling, -neled.** **4.** to move or cause to move or pour through or as if through a funnel. [C15: < OProvençal *fonilh,* ult. < L *infundibulum,* < *infundere* to pour in] —ˈ**funnel-ˌlike** *adj.*

funnel-web *n. Austral.* a large poisonous black spider that constructs funnel-shaped webs.

funny (ˈfʌnɪ) *adj.* **-nier, -niest.** **1.** causing amusement or laughter; humorous. **2.** peculiar; odd. **3.** suspicious or dubious (esp. in **funny business**). **4.** *Inf.* faint or ill. ~*n., pl.* **-nies.** **5.** *Inf.* a joke or witticism. —ˈ**funnily** *adv.* —ˈ**funniness** *n.*

funny bone *n.* the area near the elbow where the ulnar nerve is close to the surface of the skin: when it is struck, a sharp tingling sensation is experienced.

fun run *n.* a long run or part-marathon run for exercise and pleasure, often by large numbers of people.

fuoco (fuːˈəʊkəʊ) *Music.* ~*n.* **1.** fire. ~*adv., adj.* **2. con fuoco.** in a fiery manner. [C19: It., lit.: fire]

fur (fɜː) *n.* **1.** the dense coat of fine silky hairs on such mammals as the cat and mink. **2. a.** the dressed skin of certain fur-bearing animals, with the hair left on. **b.** (*as modifier*): *a fur coat.* **3.** a garment made of fur, such as a stole. **4.** a pile fabric made in imitation of animal fur. **5.** *Heraldry.* any of various stylized representations of animal pelts used in coats of arms. **6. make the fur fly.** to cause a scene or disturbance. **7.** *Inf.* a whitish coating on the tongue, caused by excessive smoking, an upset stomach, etc. **8.** *Brit.* a whitish-grey deposit precipitated from hard water onto the insides of pipes, kettles, etc. ~*vb.* **furring, furred.** **9.** (*tr.*) to line or trim a garment, etc., with fur. **10.** (often foll. by *up*) to cover or become covered with a furlike lining or deposit. [C14: < OF *forrer* to line a garment, < *fuerre* sheath, of Gmc origin] —ˈ**furless** *adj.*

fur. *abbrev. for* furlong.

furbelow (ˈfɜːbɪˌləʊ) *n.* **1.** a flounce, ruffle, or other ornamental trim. **2.** (*often pl.*) showy ornamentation. ~*vb.* **3.** (*tr.*) to put a furbelow on (a garment, etc.). [C18: by folk etymology < F dialect *farbella* a frill]

furbish (ˈfɜːbɪʃ) *vb.* (*tr.*) **1.** to make bright by polishing. **2.** (often foll. by *up*) to renovate; restore. [C14: < OF *fourbir* to polish, of Gmc origin] —ˈ**furbisher** *n.*

furcate (ˈfɜːkeɪt) *vb.* **1.** to divide into two parts. ~*adj.* **2.** forked: *furcate branches.* [C19: < LL, < L *furca* a fork] —**furˈcation** *n.*

furfuraceous (ˌfɜːfjʊˈreɪʃəs) *adj.* **1.** relating to or resembling bran. **2.** *Med.* resembling dandruff. [C17: < L *furfur* bran, scurf + -ACEOUS]

Furies (ˈfjʊərɪz) *pl. n., sing.* **Fury.** *Classical myth.* the snake-haired goddesses of vengeance, usually three in number, who pursued unpunished criminals. Also called: **Erinyes, Eumenides.**

furioso (ˌfjʊərɪˈəʊsəʊ) *Music.* ~*adj., adv.* **1.** in a frantically rushing manner. ~*n.* **2.** a passage or piece to be performed in this way. [C19: It., lit.: furious]

furious (ˈfjʊərɪəs) *adj.* **1.** extremely angry or annoyed. **2.** violent or unrestrained, as in speed, energy, etc. —ˈ**furiously** *adv.* —ˈ**furiousness** *n.*

furl (fɜːl) *vb.* **1.** to roll up (an umbrella, flag, etc.) neatly and securely or (of an umbrella, flag, etc.) to be rolled up in this way. ~*n.* **2.** the act or an instance of furling. **3.** a single rolled-up section. [C16: < OF, < *ferm* tight (< L *firmus* FIRM[1]) + *lier* to bind, < L *ligāre*] —ˈ**furlable** *adj.*

furlong (ˈfɜːˌlɒŋ) *n.* a unit of length equal to 220 yards (201.168 metres). [OE *furlang,* < *furh* furrow + *lang* long]

furlough (ˈfɜːləʊ) *n.* **1.** leave of absence from military duty. ~*vb.* (*tr.*) **2.** to grant a furlough to. [C17: < Du. *verlof,* < *ver-* FOR- + *lof* leave, permission]

furnace (ˈfɜːnɪs) *n.* **1.** an enclosed chamber in which heat is produced to destroy refuse, smelt or refine ores, etc. **2.** a very hot place. [C13: < OF, < L *fornax* oven, furnace]

furnish (ˈfɜːnɪʃ) *vb.* (*tr.*) **1.** to provide (a house, room, etc.) with furniture, etc. **2.** to equip with what is necessary. **3.** to supply: *the records furnished the information.* [C15: < OF *fournir,* of Gmc origin] —ˈ**furnisher** *n.*

furnishings (ˈfɜːnɪʃɪŋz) *pl. n.* furniture, carpets, etc., with which a room or house is furnished.

furniture (ˈfɜːnɪtʃə) *n.* **1.** the movable articles that equip a room, house, etc. **2.** the equipment necessary for a ship, factory, etc. **3.** *Printing.* lengths of wood, plastic, or metal, used in assembling formes to surround the type. **4.** Also called: **door furniture.** locks, handles, etc., designed for use on doors. [C16: < F, < *fournir* to equip]

furore (fjʊˈrɔːrɪ) *or esp. U.S.* **furor** (ˈfjʊərɔː) *n.* **1.** a public outburst; uproar. **2.** a sudden widespread enthusiasm; craze. **3.** frenzy; rage. [C15: < L: frenzy, < *furere* to rave]

furphy (ˈfɜːfɪ) *n., pl.* **-phies.** *Austral. sl.* a rumour or fictitious story. [C20: < *Furphy* carts (used for water or sewage in World War I), made at a foundry established by the Furphy family]

furred (fɜːd) *adj.* **1.** made of, lined with, or covered in fur. **2.** wearing fur. **3.** (of animals) having fur. **4.** another word for **furry** (sense 3). **5.** provided with furring strips. **6.** (of a pipe, kettle, etc.) lined with hard lime.

furrier (ˈfʌrɪə) *n.* a person whose occupation is selling, making, or repairing fur garments. [C14: *furour,* < OF *fourrer* to trim with FUR] —ˈ**furriery** *n.*

furring (ˈfɜːrɪŋ) *n.* **1.** short for **furring strip.** **2.** the formation of fur on the tongue. **3.** trimming of animal fur, as on a coat.

furring strip *n.* a strip of wood or metal fixed to a wall, floor, or ceiling to provide a surface for the fixing of plasterboard, floorboards, etc.

furrow (ˈfʌrəʊ) *n.* **1.** a long narrow trench made in the ground by a plough. **2.** any long deep groove, esp. a deep wrinkle on the forehead. ~*vb.* **3.** to develop or cause to develop furrows or wrinkles. **4.** to make a furrow or furrows in (land). [OE *furh*] —ˈ**furrower** *n.* —ˈ**furrowless** *adj.* —ˈ**furrowy** *adj.*

furry (ˈfɜːrɪ) *adj.* **-rier, -riest.** **1.** covered with fur or something furlike. **2.** of, relating to, or resembling fur. **3.** Also: **furred.** (of the tongue) coated with whitish cellular debris. —ˈ**furrily** *adv.* —ˈ**furriness** *n.*

further (ˈfɜːðə) *adv.* **1.** in addition; furthermore. **2.** to a greater degree or extent. **3.** to or at a more advanced point. **4.** to or at a greater distance in time or space. ~*adj.* **5.** additional; more. **6.** more distant or remote in time or space. ~*vb.* **7.** (*tr.*) to assist the progress of. ~See also **far, furthest.** [OE *furthor*]

▷ **Usage.** See at **farther.**

furtherance (ˈfɜːðərəns) *n.* **1.** the act of furthering. **2.** something that furthers.

further education *n.* (in Britain) formal education beyond school other than at a university or polytechnic.

furthermore (ˈfɜːðəˌmɔː) *adv.* in addition; moreover.

furthermost (ˈfɜːðəˌməʊst) *adj.* most distant; furthest.

furthest (ˈfɜːðɪst) *adv.* **1.** to the greatest degree or extent. **2.** to or at the greatest distance in time or space; farthest. ~*adj.* **3.** most distant or remote in time or space; farthest.

furtive (ˈfɜːtɪv) *adj.* characterized by stealth; sly and secretive. [C15: < L *furtīvus* stolen, < *furtum* a theft, < *fūr* a thief] —ˈ**furtively** *adv.* —ˈ**furtiveness** *n.*

furuncle (ˈfjʊərʌŋkᵊl) *n. Pathol.* the technical name for **boil**[2]. [C17: < L *fūrunculus* pilferer, sore, < *fūr* thief] —**furuncular** (fjʊˈrʌŋkjʊlə) *or* **fuˈrunculous** *adj.*

furunculosis (fjʊˌrʌŋkjʊˈləʊsɪs) *n.* **1.** a skin condition characterized by the presence of multiple boils. **2.** a disease of salmon and trout caused by a bacterium.

fury (ˈfjʊərɪ) *n., pl.* **-ries.** **1.** violent or uncontrolled anger. **2.** an outburst of such anger. **3.** uncontrolled violence: *the fury of the storm.* **4.** a person, esp. a woman, with a violent temper. **5.**

See **Furies.** **6. like fury.** *Inf.* violently; furiously. [C14: < L, < *furere* to be furious]

furze (fɜːz) *n.* another name for **gorse.** [OE *fyrs*] —ˈ**furzy** *adj.*

fuscous (ˈfʌskəs) *adj.* of a brownish-grey colour. [C17: < L *fuscus* dark, swarthy, tawny]

fuse[1] *or U.S.* **fuze** (fjuːz) *n.* **1.** a lead of combustible black powder (**safety fuse**), or a lead containing an explosive (**detonating fuse**), used to fire an explosive charge. **2.** any device by which an explosive charge is ignited. ~*vb.* **3.** (*tr.*) to equip with such a fuse. [C17: < It. *fuso* spindle, < L *fūsus*] —ˈ**fuseless** *adj.*

fuse[2] (fjuːz) *vb.* **1.** to unite or become united by melting, esp. by the action of heat. **2.** to become or cause to become liquid, esp. by the action of heat. **3.** to join or become combined. **4.** (*tr.*) to equip (a plug, etc.) with a fuse. **5.** *Brit.* to fail or cause to fail as a result of the blowing of a fuse: *the lights fused.* ~*n.* **6.** a protective device for safeguarding electric circuits, etc., containing a wire that melts and breaks the circuit when the current exceeds a certain value. [C17: < L *fūsus* melted, cast, < *fundere* to pour out; sense 5 infl. by FUSE[1]]

fusee *or* **fuzee** (fjuːˈziː) *n.* **1.** (in early clocks and watches) a spirally grooved spindle, functioning as an equalizing force on the unwinding of the mainspring. **2.** a friction match with a large head. [C16: < F *fusée* spindleful of thread, < OF *fus* spindle, < L *fūsus*]

fuselage (ˈfjuːzɪˌlɑːʒ) *n.* the main body of an aircraft. [C20: < F, < *fuseler* to shape like a spindle, < OF *fusel* spindle]

fusel oil *or* **fusel** (ˈfjuːzᵊl) *n.* a poisonous by-product formed in the distillation of fermented liquors and used as a source of amyl alcohols. [C19: < G *Fusel* bad spirits]

fusible (ˈfjuːzəbᵊl) *adj.* capable of being fused or melted. —ˌ**fusiˈbility** *n.* —ˈ**fusibly** *adv.*

fusiform (ˈfjuːzɪˌfɔːm) *adj.* elongated and tapering at both ends. [C18: < L *fūsus* spindle]

fusil (ˈfjuːzɪl) *n.* a light flintlock musket. [C16 (in the sense: steel for a tinderbox): < OF, < Vulgar L *focīlis* (unattested), < L *focus* fire]

fusilier (ˌfjuːzɪˈlɪə) *n.* **1.** (formerly) an infantryman armed with a light musket. **2.** Also: **fusileer.** **a.** a soldier, esp. a private, serving in any of certain British or other infantry regiments. **b.** (*pl.; cap. when part of a name*): *the Royal Welsh Fusiliers.* [C17: < F; see FUSIL]

fusillade (ˌfjuːzɪˈleɪd) *n.* **1.** a rapid continual discharge of firearms. **2.** a sudden outburst, as of criticism. ~*vb.* **3.** (*tr.*) to attack with a fusillade. [C19: < F, < *fusiller* to shoot; see FUSIL]

fusion (ˈfjuːʒən) *n.* **1.** the act or process of fusing or melting together. **2.** the state of being fused. **3.** something produced by fusing. **4.** See **nuclear fusion.** **5.** a coalition of political parties. [C16: < L *fūsiō* a pouring out, melting, < *fundere* to pour out, FOUND[3]]

fusion bomb *n.* a type of bomb in which most of the energy is provided by nuclear fusion. Also called: **thermonuclear bomb, fission-fusion bomb.**

fuss (fʌs) *n.* **1.** nervous activity or agitation, esp. when unnecessary. **2.** complaint or objection: *he made a fuss over the bill.* **3.** an exhibition of affection or admiration: *they made a great fuss over the new baby.* **4.** a quarrel. ~*vb.* **5.** (*intr.*) to worry unnecessarily. **6.** (*intr.*) to be excessively concerned over trifles. **7.** (when *intr.*, usually foll. by *over*) to show great or excessive concern, affection, etc. (for). **8.** (*tr.*) to bother (a person). [C18: <?] —ˈ**fusser** *n.*

fusspot (ˈfʌsˌpɒt) *n. Brit. inf.* a person who fusses unnecessarily.

fussy (ˈfʌsɪ) *adj.* **fussier, fussiest.** **1.** inclined to fuss over minor points. **2.** very particular about detail. **3.** characterized by overelaborate detail. —ˈ**fussily** *adv.* —ˈ**fussiness** *n.*

fustanella (ˌfʌstəˈnɛlə) *n.* a white knee-length pleated skirt worn by men in Greece and Albania. [C19: < It., < Mod. Gk *phoustani,* prob. < It. *fustagno* FUSTIAN]

fustian (ˈfʌstɪən) *n.* **1. a.** a hard-wearing fabric of cotton mixed with flax or wool. **b.** (*as modifier*): *a fustian jacket.* **2.** pompous talk or writing. ~*adj.* **3.** cheap; worthless. **4.** bombastic. [C12: < OF, < Med. L *fustāneum,* < L *fustis* cudgel]

fustic (ˈfʌstɪk) *n.* **1.** Also called: **old fustic.** a large tropical American tree. **2.** the yellow dye obtained from the wood of this tree. **3.** any of various trees or shrubs that yield a similar dye, esp. a European sumach (**young fustic**). [C15: < F *fustoc,* < Sp., < Ar. *fustuq,* < Gk *pistakē* pistachio tree]

fusty (ˈfʌstɪ) *adj.* **-tier, -tiest.** **1.** smelling of damp or mould. **2.** old-fashioned in attitude. [C14: < *fust* wine cask, < OF: cask, < L *fūstis* cudgel] —ˈ**fustily** *adv.* —ˈ**fustiness** *n.*

fut. *abbrev. for* future.

futhark (ˈfuːθɑːk) *or* **futhorc, futhork** (ˈfuːθɔːk) *n.* a phonetic alphabet consisting of runes. [C19: from the first six letters: *f, u, th, a, r, k*]

futile (ˈfjuːtaɪl) *adj.* **1.** having no effective result; unsuccessful. **2.** pointless; trifling. **3.** inane or foolish. [C16: < L *futtilis* pouring out easily, < *fundere* to pour out] —ˈ**futilely** *adv.* —**futility** (fjuːˈtɪlɪtɪ) *n.*

futon (ˈfuːtɒn) *n.* a Japanese padded quilt, laid on the floor as a bed. [C19: < Japanese]

futtock (ˈfʌtək) *n. Naut.* one of the ribs in the frame of a wooden vessel. [C13: ? var. of *foothook*]

future (ˈfjuːtʃə) *n.* **1.** the time yet to come. **2.** undetermined events that will occur in that time. **3.** the condition of a person or thing at a later date: *the future of the school is undecided.* **4.** likelihood of later improvement: *he has a future as a singer.* **5.** *Grammar.* **a.** a tense of verbs used when the action or event described is to occur after the time of utterance. **b.** a verb in this tense. **6. in future.** from now on. ~*adj.* **7.** that is yet to come or be. **8.** of or expressing time yet to come. **9.** (*prenominal*) destined to become. **10.** *Grammar.* in or denoting the future as a tense of verbs. ~See also **futures.** [C14: < L *fūtūrus* about to be, < *esse* to be] —ˈ**futureless** *adj.*

future perfect *Grammar.* ~*adj.* **1.** denoting a tense of verbs describing an action that will have been performed by a certain time. ~*n.* **2. a.** the future perfect tense. **b.** a verb in this tense.

futures (ˈfjuːtʃəz) *pl. n.* commodities bought or sold at an agreed price for delivery at a specified future date.

futurism (ˈfjuːtʃəˌrɪzəm) *n.* an artistic movement that arose in Italy in 1909 to replace traditional aesthetic values with the characteristics of the machine age. —ˈ**futurist** *n., adj.*

futuristic (ˌfjuːtʃəˈrɪstɪk) *adj.* **1.** denoting or relating to design, etc., that is thought likely to be fashionable at some future time. **2.** of or relating to futurism. —ˌ**futurˈistically** *adv.*

futurity (fjuːˈtjʊərɪtɪ) *n., pl.* **-ties.** **1.** a less common word for **future.** **2.** the quality of being in the future. **3.** a future event.

futurology (ˌfjuːtʃəˈrɒlədʒɪ) *n.* the study or prediction of the future of mankind. —ˌ**futurˈologist** *n.*

fuze (fjuːz) *n. U.S.* a variant spelling of **fuse**[1].

fuzee (fjuːˈziː) *n.* a variant spelling of **fusee.**

fuzz[1] (fʌz) *n.* **1.** a mass or covering of fine or curly hairs, fibres, etc. **2.** a blur. ~*vb.* **3.** to make or become fuzzy. **4.** to make or become indistinct. [C17: ? < Low G *fussig* loose]

fuzz[2] (fʌz) *n.* a slang word for **police** or **policeman.** [C20: <?]

fuzzy (ˈfʌzɪ) *adj.* **fuzzier, fuzziest.** **1.** of, resembling, or covered with fuzz. **2.** unclear or distorted. **3.** (of the hair) tightly curled or very wavy. —ˈ**fuzzily** *adv.* —ˈ**fuzziness** *n.*

fwd *abbrev. for* forward.

-fy *suffix forming verbs.* to make or become: *beautify.* [< OF *-fier,* < L *-ficāre,* < *-ficus* -FIC]

fylfot (ˈfaɪlfɒt) *n.* a rare word for **swastika.** [C16 (apparently meaning: a sign or device for the lower part or foot of a painted window): < *fillen* to fill + *fot* foot]

G

g *or* **G** (dʒiː) *n., pl.* **g's, G's,** *or* **Gs.** **1.** the seventh letter of the English alphabet. **2.** a speech sound represented by this letter, usually either as in *grass,* or as in *page.*

g *symbol for:* **1.** gallon(s). **2.** gram(s). **3.** grav. **4.** acceleration of free fall (due to gravity).

G *symbol for:* **1.** *Music.* **a.** the fifth note of the scale of C major. **b.** the major or minor key having this note as its tonic. **2.** gauss. **3.** gravitational constant. **4.** *Physics.* conductance. **5.** German. **6.** giga. **7.** good. **8.** *Sl., chiefly U.S.* grand (a thousand dollars or pounds).

G. *or* **g.** *abbrev. for:* **1.** gauges. **2.** gelding. **3.** guilder(s). **4.** guinea(s). **5.** Gulf.

Ga *the chemical symbol for* gallium.

gab (gæb) *Inf.* ~*vb.* **gabbing, gabbed. 1.** (*intr.*) to talk excessively or idly; gossip; chatter. ~*n.* **2.** idle or trivial talk. **3. gift of the gab.** ability to speak glibly or persuasively. [C18: prob. < Irish Gaelic *gob* mouth] —ˈ**gabber** *n.*

gabble (ˈgæbᵊl) *vb.* **1.** to utter (words, etc.) rapidly and indistinctly; jabber. **2.** (*intr.*) (of geese, etc.) to utter rapid cackling noises. ~*n.* **3.** rapid and indistinct speech or noises. [C17: < MDu. *gabbelen,* imit.] —ˈ**gabbler** *n.*

gabbro (ˈgæbrəʊ) *n., pl.* **-bros.** a dark coarse-grained igneous rock consisting of feldspar, pyroxene, and often olivine. [C19: < It., prob. < L *glaber* smooth, bald]

gabby (ˈgæbɪ) *adj.* **-bier, -biest.** *Inf.* inclined to chatter; talkative.

gaberdine (ˈgæbəˌdiːn, ˌgæbəˈdiːn) *n.* **1.** a twill-weave worsted, cotton, or spun-rayon fabric. **2.** Also called: **gabardine.** an ankle-length loose coat or frock worn by men, esp. by Jews, in the Middle Ages. **3.** any of various other garments made of gaberdine, esp. a child's raincoat. [C16: < OF *gauvardine* pilgrim's garment, < MHG *wallewart* pilgrimage]

gabfest (ˈgæbˌfɛst) *n. Inf., chiefly U.S. & Canad.* **1.** prolonged gossiping or conversation. **2.** an informal gathering for conversation. [C19: < GAB + G *Fest* festival]

gabion (ˈgeɪbɪən) *n.* **1.** a cylindrical metal container filled with stones, used in the construction of underwater foundations. **2.** a wickerwork basket filled with stones or earth, used (esp. formerly) as part of a fortification. [C16: < F: basket, < It., < *gabbia* cage, < L *cavea;* see CAGE]

gable (ˈgeɪbᵊl) *n.* **1.** the triangular upper part of a wall between the sloping ends of a pitched roof (**gable roof**). **2.** a triangular ornamental feature, esp. as used over a door or window. [C14: OF, prob. < ON *gafl*] —ˈ**gabled** *adj.*

gable end *n.* the end wall of a building on the side which is topped by a gable.

gaby (ˈgeɪbɪ) *n., pl.* **-bies.** *Arch. or dialect.* a simpleton. [C18: <?]

gad (gæd) *vb.* **gadding, gadded. 1.** (*intr.;* often foll. by *about* or *around*) to go out in search of pleasure; gallivant. ~*n.* **2.** carefree adventure (esp. in **on the gad**). [C15: back formation < obs. *gadling* companion, < OE, < *gæd* fellowship] —ˈ**gadder** *n.*

gadabout (ˈgædəˌbaʊt) *n. Inf.* a person who restlessly seeks amusement, etc.

Gadarene (ˈgædəˌriːn) *adj.* relating to or engaged in a headlong rush. [C19: via LL < Gk *Gadarēnos,* of Gadara (Palestine), alluding to the Gadarene swine (Matthew 8:28ff.)]

gadfly (ˈgædˌflaɪ) *n., pl.* **-flies. 1.** any of various large dipterous flies, esp. the horsefly, that annoy livestock by sucking their blood. **2.** a constantly irritating person. [C16: < *gad* sting + FLY[2]]

gadget (ˈgædʒɪt) *n.* **1.** a small mechanical device or appliance. **2.** any object that is interesting for its ingenuity. [C19: <?]

gadgetry (ˈgædʒɪtrɪ) *n.* **1.** gadgets collectively. **2.** use of or preoccupation with gadgets.

gadoid (ˈgeɪdɔɪd) *adj.* **1.** of or belonging to an order of marine soft-finned fishes typically having the pectoral and pelvic fins close together and small cycloid scales. The group includes cod and hake. ~*n.* **2.** any gadoid fish. [C19: < NL *Gadidae,* < *gadus* cod; see -OID]

gadolinium (ˌgædəˈlɪnɪəm) *n.* a ductile malleable silvery-white ferromagnetic element of the lanthanide series of metals. Symbol: Gd; atomic no.: 64; atomic wt.: 157.25. [C19: NL, after Johan *Gadolin* (1760–1852), Finnish mineralogist]

gadroon *or* **godroon** (gəˈdruːn) *n.* a decorative moulding composed of a series of convex flutes and curves, used esp. as an edge to silver articles. [C18: < F *godron,* ?< OF *godet* cup, goblet]

gadwall (ˈgædˌwɔːl) *n., pl.* **-walls** *or* **-wall.** a duck related to the mallard. The male has a grey body and black tail. [C17: <?]

gadzooks (gædˈzuːks) *interj. Arch.* a mild oath. [C17: ?< *God's hooks* (the nails of the cross) < *Gad* arch. euphemism for God]

Gael (geɪl) *n.* a person who speaks a Gaelic language, esp. a Highland Scot or an Irishman. [C19: < Gaelic *Gaidheal*] —ˈ**Gaeldom** *n.*

Gaelic (ˈgeɪlɪk, ˈgæ-) *n.* **1.** any of the closely related languages of the Celts in Ireland, Scotland, or the Isle of Man. ~*adj.* **2.** of, denoting, or relating to the Celtic people of Ireland, Scotland, or the Isle of Man or their language or customs.

Gaelic coffee *n.* another name for **Irish coffee.**

Gaeltacht (ˈgeːltəxt) *n.* any of the regions in Ireland in which Irish Gaelic is the vernacular speech. [C20: < Irish Gaelic]

gaff[1] (gæf) *n.* **1.** *Angling.* a stiff pole with a stout prong or hook attached for landing large fish. **2.** *Naut.* a boom hoisted aft of a mast to support a fore-and-aft sail. **3.** a metal spur fixed to the leg of a gamecock. ~*vb.* **4.** (*tr.*) *Angling.* to hook or land (a fish) with a gaff. [C13: < F *gaffe,* < Provençal *gaf* boat hook]

gaff[2] (gæf) *n.* **1.** *Sl.* nonsense. **2. blow the gaff.** *Brit. sl.* to divulge a secret. [C19: <?]

gaffe (gæf) *n.* a social blunder, esp. a tactless remark. [C19: < F]

gaffer (ˈgæfə) *n.* **1.** an old man: often used affectionately or patronizingly. **2.** *Inf., chiefly Brit.* a boss, foreman, or owner of a factory, etc. **3.** *Inf.* the senior electrician on a television or film set. [C16: < GODFATHER]

gag[1] (gæg) *vb.* **gagging, gagged. 1.** (*tr.*) to stop up (a person's mouth), esp. with a piece of cloth, etc., to prevent him from speaking or crying out. **2.** (*tr.*) to suppress or censor (free expression, information, etc.). **3.** to retch or cause to retch. **4.** (*intr.*) to struggle for breath; choke. ~*n.* **5.** a piece of cloth, rope, etc., stuffed into or tied across the mouth. **6.** any restraint on or suppression of information, free speech, etc. **7.** *Parliamentary procedure.* another word for **closure** (sense 4). [C15 *gaggen;* ? imit. of a gasping sound]

gag[2] (gæg) *Inf.* ~*n.* **1.** a joke or humorous story, esp. one told by a professional comedian. **2.** a hoax, practical joke, etc. ~*vb.* **gagging, gagged. 3.** (*intr.*) to tell jokes or funny stories, as comedians in nightclubs, etc. [C19: ? special use of GAG[1]]

gaga (ˈgɑːgɑː) *adj. Inf.* **1.** senile; doting. **2.** slightly crazy. [C20: < F, imit.]

gage[1] (geɪdʒ) *n.* **1.** something deposited as security against the fulfilment of an obligation; pledge. **2.** (formerly) a glove or other object thrown down to indicate a challenge to combat. ~*vb.* **3.** (*tr.*) *Arch.* to stake, pledge, or wager. [C14: < OF, of Gmc origin]

gage[2] (geɪdʒ) *n.* short for **greengage.**

gage[3] (geɪdʒ) *n., vb. U.S.* a variant spelling (esp. in technical senses) of **gauge.**

gaggle (ˈgægᵊl) *vb.* **1.** (*intr.*) (of geese) to cackle. ~*n.* **2.** a flock of geese. **3.** *Inf.* a disorderly group of people. [C14: of Gmc origin; imit.]

gaiety (ˈgeɪətɪ) *n., pl.* **-ties. 1.** the state or condition of being gay. **2.** festivity; merrymaking. **3.** colourful bright appearance.

gaillardia (geɪˈlɑːdɪə) *n.* a plant of the composite family having ornamental flower heads with yellow or red rays and purple discs. [C19: < NL, after *Gaillard* de Marentonneau, 18th-cent. F amateur botanist]

gaily (ˈgeɪlɪ) *adv.* **1.** in a gay manner; merrily. **2.** with bright colours; showily.

gain (geɪn) *vb.* **1.** (*tr.*) to acquire (something desirable); obtain. **2.** (*tr.*) to win in competition: *to gain the victory.* **3.** to increase, improve, or advance: *the car gained speed.* **4.** (*tr.*) to earn (a wage, living, etc.). **5.** (*intr.;* usually foll. by *on* or *upon*) **a.** to get nearer (to) or catch up (on). **b.** to get farther away (from). **6.** (*tr.*) (esp. of ships) to get to; reach: *the steamer gained port.* **7.** (of a timepiece) to operate too fast, so as to indicate a time ahead of the true time. ~*n.* **8.** something won, acquired, earned, etc.; profit; advantage. **9.** an increase in size, amount, etc. **10.** the act of gaining; attainment; acquisition. **11.** Also called: **amplification.** *Electronics.* the ratio of the output signal of an amplifier to the input signal, usually measured in decibels. [C15: < OF *gaaignier,* of Gmc origin]

gainer (ˈgeɪnə) *n.* **1.** a person or thing that gains. **2.** a type of dive in which the diver leaves the board facing forward and completes a full backward somersault to enter the water feet first with his back to the diving board.

gainful (ˈgeɪnfʊl) *adj.* profitable; lucrative. —ˈ**gainfully** *adv.* —ˈ**gainfulness** *n.*

gainsay (geɪnˈseɪ) *vb.* **-saying, -said.** (*tr.*) *Arch. or literary.* to deny (an allegation, statement, etc.); contradict. [C13 *gainsaien,* < *gain-* AGAINST + *saien* to SAY] —**gainˈsayer** *n.*

'gainst *or* **gainst** (gɛnst, geɪnst) *prep. Poetic.* short for **against.**

gait (geɪt) *n.* **1.** manner of walking or running. **2.** (used esp. of horses and dogs) the pattern of footsteps at a particular speed, as the walk, canter, etc. ~*vb.* **3.** (*tr.*) to teach (a horse) a particular gait. [C16: var. of GATE]

gaiter (ˈgeɪtə) *n.* (*often pl.*) **1.** a cloth or leather covering for the leg or ankle. **2.** Also called: **spat.** a similar covering extending from the ankle to the instep. [C18: < F *guêtre,* prob. of Gmc origin]

gal (gæl) *n. Sl.* a girl.

gal. *or* **gall.** *abbrev. for* gallon.

Gal. *Bible. abbrev. for* Galatians.

gala (ˈgɑːlə, ˈgeɪlə) *n.* **1. a.** a celebration; festive occasion. **b.** (*as modifier*): *a gala occasion.* **2.** *Chiefly Brit.* a sporting occasion involving competitions in several events: *a swimming gala.* [C17: < F or It., < OF *gale,* < *galer* to make merry, prob. of Gmc origin]

galactic (gəˈlæktɪk) *adj.* **1.** *Astron.* of or relating to a galaxy, esp. the Galaxy. **2. galactic plane.** the plane passing through the spiral arms of the Galaxy, contained by the great circle of the celestial sphere (**galactic equator**) and perpendicular to an imaginary line joining opposite points (**galactic poles**) on the celestial sphere. **3.** *Med.* of or relating to milk. [C19: < Gk *galaktikos;* see GALAXY]

galago (gəˈlɑːgəʊ) *n., pl.* **-gos.** another name for **bushbaby.** [C19: < NL, ?< Wolof *golokh* monkey]

galah (gəˈlɑː) *n.* **1.** an Australian cockatoo, having grey wings, back, and crest, and a pink body. **2.** *Austral. sl.* a fool or simpleton. [C19: < Abor.]

Galahad (ˈgæləˌhæd) *n.* **1. Sir.** (in Arthurian legend) the most virtuous knight of the Round Table. **2.** a pure or noble man.

galantine (ˈgælənˌtiːn) *n.* a cold dish of meat or poultry, which is boned, cooked, then pressed and glazed. [C14: < OF, < Med. L *galatina,* prob. < L *gelātus* frozen, set]

galaxy (ˈgæləksɪ) *n., pl.* **-axies. 1.** any of a vast number of star systems held together by gravitational attraction. **2.** a splendid gathering, esp. one of famous or distinguished people. [C14 (in the sense: the Milky Way): < Med. L *galaxia,* < L, < Gk, < *gala* milk]

Galaxy (ˈgæləksɪ) *n.* **the.** the spiral galaxy that contains the solar system about three fifths of the distance from its centre. Also called: the **Milky Way System.**

galbanum (ˈgælbənəm) *n.* a bitter aromatic gum resin extracted from any of several Asian umbelliferous plants. [C14: < L, < Gk, < Heb. *helbenāh*]

gale (geɪl) *n.* **1.** a strong wind, specifically one of force 8 on the Beaufort scale or from 39-46 mph. **2.** (*often pl.*) a loud outburst, esp. of laughter. **3.** *Arch. & poetic.* a gentle breeze. [C16: <?]

galea (ˈgeɪlɪə) *n., pl.* **-leae** (-lɪˌiː). a part shaped like a helmet, such as the petals of certain flowers. [C18: < L: helmet] —ˈ**galeˌate** *or* ˈ**galeˌated** *adj.*

galena (gəˈliːnə) *or* **galenite** (gəˈliːnaɪt) *n.* a soft heavy bluish-grey or black mineral consisting of lead sulphide: the chief source of lead. Formula: PbS. [C17: < L: lead ore]

Galenic (geɪˈlɛnɪk, gə-) *adj.* of or relating to Galen, 2nd-century Greek physician, or his teachings or methods.

Galilean[1] (ˌgælɪˈliːən) *n.* **1.** a native or inhabitant of Galilee. **2. the.** an epithet of Jesus Christ. ~*adj.* **3.** of Galilee.

Galilean[2] (ˌgælɪˈleɪən) *adj.* of or relating to Galileo (1564–1642), Italian astronomer and physicist.

galingale (ˈgælɪŋˌgeɪl) *or* **galangal** (gəˈlæŋgᵊl) *n.* a European plant with rough-edged leaves, reddish spikelets of flowers, and aromatic roots. [C13: < OF, < Ar., < Chinese]

galiot *or* **galliot** (ˈgælɪət) *n.* **1.** a small swift galley formerly sailed on the Mediterranean. **2.** a ketch formerly used along the coasts of Germany and the Netherlands. [C14: < OF, < It., < Med. L *galea* GALLEY]

galipot (ˈgælɪˌpɒt) *n.* a resin obtained from several species of pine. [C18: < F, <?]

gall[1] (gɔːl) *n.* **1.** *Inf.* impudence. **2.** bitterness; rancour. **3.** something bitter or disagreeable. **4.** *Physiol.* an obsolete term for **bile.** See also **gall bladder.** [< ON, replacing OE *gealla*]

gall[2] (gɔːl) *n.* **1.** a sore on the skin caused by chafing. **2.** something that causes vexation or annoyance. **3.** irritation; exasperation. ~*vb.* **4.** to abrade (the skin, etc.) as by rubbing. **5.** (*tr.*) to irritate or annoy; vex. [C14: of Gmc origin; rel. to OE *gealla* sore on a horse, &? to GALL[1]]

gall[3] (gɔːl) *n.* an abnormal outgrowth in plant tissue caused by certain parasitic insects, fungi, or bacteria. [C14: < OF, < L *galla*]

gall. *or* **gal.** *abbrev. for* gallon.

gallant *adj.* (ˈgælənt). **1.** brave and high-spirited; courageous and honourable: *a gallant warrior.* **2.** (gəˈlænt, ˈgælənt). (of a man) attentive to women; chivalrous. **3.** imposing; dignified; stately: *a gallant ship.* **4.** *Arch.* showy in dress. ~*n.* (ˈgælənt, gəˈlænt). **5.** a woman's lover or suitor. **6.** a dashing or fashionable young man, esp. one who pursues women. **7.** a brave, high-spirited, or adventurous man. ~*vb.* (gəˈlænt, ˈgælənt). *Rare.* **8.** (when *intr.,* usually foll. by *with*) to court or flirt (with). [C15: < OF, < *galer* to make merry, < *gale* enjoyment, of Gmc origin] —ˈ**gallantly** *adv.*

gallantry (ˈgæləntrɪ) *n., pl.* **-ries. 1.** conspicuous courage, esp. in war. **2.** polite attentiveness to women. **3.** a gallant action, speech, etc.

gall bladder *n.* a muscular sac, attached to the right lobe of the liver, that stores bile.

galleass (ˈgælɪˌæs) *n.* a three-masted galley used as a warship in the Mediterranean from the 15th to the 18th centuries. [C16: < F, < It., < Med. L *galea* GALLEY]

galleon (ˈgælɪən) *n.* a large sailing ship having three or more masts, used as a warship or trader from the 15th to the 18th centuries. [C16: < Sp. *galeón,* < F, < OF *galie* GALLEY]

gallery (ˈgælərɪ) *n., pl.* **-leries. 1.** a covered

passageway open on one side or on both sides. **2.** a balcony running along or around the inside wall of a church, hall, etc. **3.** *Theatre.* **a.** an upper floor that projects from the rear and contains the cheapest seats. **b.** the seats there. **c.** the audience seated there. **4.** a glass-fronted soundproof room overlooking a television studio, used for lighting, etc. **5.** a long narrow room, esp. one used for a specific purpose: *a shooting gallery.* **6.** a room or building for exhibiting works of art. **7.** an underground passage, as in a mine, etc. **8.** a small ornamental railing, esp. one surrounding the top of a desk, table, etc. **9.** any group of spectators, as at a golf match. **10. play to the gallery.** to try to gain popular favour, esp. by crude appeals. [C15: < OF, < Med. L, prob. < *galilea* galilee, porch or chapel at entrance to medieval church] —**'galleried** *adj.*

galley ('gælɪ) *n.* **1.** any of various kinds of ship propelled by oars or sails used in ancient or medieval times. **2.** the kitchen of a ship, boat, or aircraft. **3.** any of various long rowing boats. **4.** *Printing.* **a.** a tray for holding composed type. **b.** short for **galley proof.** [C13: < OF *galie,* < Med. L *galea,* < Gk *galaia,* <?]

galley proof *n.* a printer's proof, esp. one taken from type in a galley, used to make corrections before the matter has been split into pages. Often shortened to **galley.**

galley slave *n.* **1.** a criminal or slave condemned to row in a galley. **2.** *Inf.* a drudge.

gallfly ('gɔːlˌflaɪ) *n., pl.* **-flies.** any of several small insects that produce galls in plant tissues.

galliard ('gæljəd) *n.* **1.** a spirited dance in triple time for two persons, popular in the 16th and 17th centuries. **2.** a piece of music composed for or in the rhythm of this dance. [C14: < OF *gaillard* valiant, ? of Celtic origin]

Gallic ('gælɪk) *adj.* **1.** of or relating to France. **2.** of or relating to ancient Gaul or the Gauls.

gallic acid ('gælɪk) *n.* a colourless crystalline compound obtained from tannin: used as a tanning agent and in making inks and paper. [C18: < F *gallique;* see GALL[3]]

Gallicism ('gælɪˌsɪzəm) *n.* a word or idiom borrowed from French.

Gallicize *or* **-cise** ('gælɪˌsaɪz) *vb.* to make or become French in attitude, language, etc.

galligaskins (ˌgælɪ'gæskɪnz) *pl. n.* **1.** loose wide breeches or hose, esp. as worn by men in the 17th century. **2.** leather leggings, as worn in the 19th century. [C16: < obs. F, < It. *grechesco* Greek, < L *Graecus*]

gallimaufry (ˌgælɪ'mɔːfrɪ) *n., pl.* **-fries.** a jumble; hotchpotch. [C16: < F *galimafrée* ragout, hash, <?]

gallinacean (ˌgælɪ'neɪʃən) *n.* any gallinaceous bird.

gallinaceous (ˌgælɪ'neɪʃəs) *adj.* of, relating to, or belonging to an order of birds, including domestic fowl, pheasants, grouse, etc., having a heavy rounded body, short bill, and strong legs. [C18: < L, < *gallīna* hen]

galling ('gɔːlɪŋ) *adj.* irritating, exasperating, or bitterly humiliating. —**'gallingly** *adv.*

gallinule ('gælɪˌnjuːl) *n.* any of various aquatic birds, typically having a dark plumage, red bill, and a red shield above the bill. [C18: < NL *Gallīnula,* < LL, < L *gallīna* hen]

galliot ('gælɪət) *n.* a variant spelling of **galiot.**

gallipot ('gælɪˌpɒt) *n.* a small earthenware pot used by pharmacists as a container for ointments, etc. [C16: prob. < GALLEY + POT[1]; because imported in galleys]

gallium ('gælɪəm) *n.* a silvery metallic element that is liquid for a wide temperature range. It is used in high-temperature thermometers, semiconductors, and low-melting alloys. Symbol: Ga; atomic no.: 31; atomic wt.: 69.72. [C19: < NL, < L *gallus* cock, translation of F *coq* in the name of its discoverer, *Lecoq* de Boisbaudran, 19th-cent. F chemist]

gallivant ('gælɪˌvænt) *vb.* (*intr.*) to go about in search of pleasure, etc.; gad about. [C19: ? whimsical < GALLANT]

galliwasp ('gælɪˌwɒsp) *n.* a lizard of the West Indies. [C18: <?]

gallnut ('gɔːlˌnʌt) *or* **gall-apple** *n.* a type of plant gall that resembles a nut.

Gallo- ('gæləʊ) *combining form.* denoting Gaul or France: *Gallo-Roman.* [< L *Gallus* a Gaul]

gallon ('gælən) *n.* **1.** Also called: **imperial gallon.** *Brit.* a unit of capacity equal to 277.42 cubic inches. 1 Brit. gallon is equivalent to 1.20 U.S. gallons or 4.55 litres. **2.** *U.S.* a unit of capacity equal to 231 cubic inches. 1 U.S. gallon is equivalent to 0.83 imperial gallon or 3.79 litres. **3.** (*pl.*) *Inf.* great quantities. [C13: < ONorthern F *galon* (OF *jalon*), ? of Celtic origin]

gallonage ('gælənɪdʒ) *n.* a capacity measured in gallons.

galloon (gə'luːn) *n.* a narrow band of cord, embroidery, silver or gold braid, etc., used on clothes and furniture. [C17: < F, < OF *galonner* to trim with braid, <?]

gallop ('gæləp) *vb.* **1.** (*intr.*) (of a horse or other quadruped) to run fast with a two-beat stride in which all four legs are off the ground at once. **2.** to ride (a horse, etc.) at a gallop. **3.** (*intr.*) to move, read, progress, etc., rapidly. ~*n.* **4.** the fast two-beat gait of horses. **5.** an instance of galloping. [C16: < OF *galoper,* <?] —**'galloper** *n.*

Galloway ('gæləˌweɪ) *n.* a breed of hardy black cattle originally bred in Galloway, SW Scotland.

gallows ('gæləʊz) *n., pl.* **-lowses** *or* **-lows.** **1.** a wooden structure usually consisting of two upright posts with a crossbeam, used for hanging criminals. **2.** any timber structure resembling this. **3. the gallows.** execution by hanging. [C13: < ON *galgi,* replacing OE *gealga*]

gallows bird *n. Inf.* a person considered deserving of hanging.

gallows humour *n.* sinister and ironic humour.

gallows tree *or* **gallow tree** *n.* another name for **gallows** (sense 1).

gallstone ('gɔːlˌstəʊn) *n.* a small hard concretion formed in the gall bladder or its ducts.

Gallup Poll ('gæləp) *n.* a sampling of the views of a representative cross section of the population, used esp. as a means of forecasting voting. [C20: after G.H. *Gallup* (1901–84), U.S. statistician]

galluses ('gæləsɪz) *pl. n. Dialect.* braces for trousers. [C18: var. of *gallowses,* < GALLOWS (in the obs. sense: braces)]

gall wasp *n.* any small solitary wasp that produces galls in plant tissue.

galoot *or* **galloot** (gə'luːt) *n. Sl., chiefly U.S.* a clumsy or uncouth person. [C19: <?]

galop ('gæləp) *n.* **1.** a 19th-century dance in quick duple time. **2.** a piece of music for this dance. [C19: < F; see GALLOP]

galore (gə'lɔː) *determiner.* (*immediately postpositive*) in great numbers or quantity: *there were daffodils galore in the park.* [C17: < Irish Gaelic *go leór* to sufficiency]

galoshes *or* **goloshes** (gə'lɒʃɪz) *pl. n.* (*sometimes sing.*) a pair of waterproof overshoes. [C14 (in the sense: wooden shoe): < OF, < LL *gallicula* Gallic shoe]

galumph (gə'lʌmpf, -'lʌmf) *vb.* (*intr.*) *Inf.* to leap or move about clumsily or joyfully. [C19 (coined by Lewis Carroll): prob. a blend of GALLOP + TRIUMPH]

galvanic (gæl'vænɪk) *adj.* **1.** of, producing, or concerned with an electric current, esp. a direct current produced chemically. **2.** *Inf.* resembling the effect of an electric shock; convulsive, startling, or energetic. —**gal'vanically** *adv.*

galvanism ('gælvəˌnɪzəm) *n.* **1.** *Obs.* electricity, esp. when produced by chemical means as in a cell or battery. **2.** *Med.* treatment involving the application of electric currents to tissues. [C18: via F < It. *galvanismo,* after *Galvani* (1737–98), It. physiologist]

galvanize *or* **-ise** ('gælvəˌnaɪz) *vb.* (*tr.*) **1.** to stimulate to action; excite; startle. **2.** to cover (iron, steel, etc.) with a protective zinc coating. **3.** to stimulate by application of an electric current. —ˌ**galvani'zation** *or* **-i'sation** *n.*

galvano- *combining form.* indicating a galvanic current: *galvanometer.*

galvanometer (ˌgælvəˈnɒmɪtə) *n.* any sensitive instrument for detecting or measuring small electric currents. —**galvanometric** (ˌgælvənəʊˈmɛtrɪk, gælˌvænəʊ-) *adj.* —ˌ**galvaˈnometry** *n.*

gam (gæm) *n. Sl.* a leg. [C18: < F *jambe* leg]

gambier *or* **gambir** (ˈgæmbɪə) *n.* an astringent resinous substance obtained from a tropical Asian plant: used as an astringent and tonic and in tanning. [C19: < Malay]

gambit (ˈgæmbɪt) *n.* **1.** *Chess.* an opening move in which a chessman, usually a pawn, is sacrificed to secure an advantageous position. **2.** an opening comment, manoeuvre, etc., intended to secure an advantage. [C17: < F, < It. *gambetto* a tripping up, < *gamba* leg]

gamble (ˈgæmbᵊl) *vb.* **1.** (*intr.*) to play games of chance to win money, etc. **2.** to risk or bet (money, etc.) on the outcome of an event, sport, etc. **3.** (*intr.;* often foll. by *on*) to act with the expectation of: *to gamble on its being a sunny day.* **4.** (often foll. by *away*) to lose by or as if by betting; squander. ~*n.* **5.** a risky act or venture. **6.** a bet or wager. [C18: prob. var. of GAME[1]] —ˈ**gambler** *n.* —ˈ**gambling** *n.*

gamboge (gæmˈbəʊdʒ, -ˈbuːʒ) *n.* **1. a.** a gum resin used as the source of a yellow pigment and as a purgative. **b.** the pigment made from this resin. **2. gamboge tree.** any of several tropical Asian trees that yield this resin. [C18: < NL *gambaugium,* < *Cambodia* (now Kampuchea), where first found]

gambol (ˈgæmbᵊl) *vb.* **-bolling, -bolled** *or U.S.* **-boling, -boled. 1.** (*intr.*) to skip or jump about in a playful manner; frolic. ~*n.* **2.** a playful antic; frolic. [C16: < F *gambade;* see JAMB]

gambrel (ˈgæmbrəl) *n.* **1.** the hock of a horse or similar animal. **2.** short for **gambrel roof.** [C16: < OF, < *gambe* leg]

gambrel roof *n.* **1.** *Chiefly Brit.* a hipped roof having a small gable at both ends. **2.** *Chiefly U.S. & Canad.* a roof having two slopes on both sides, the lower slopes being steeper than the upper.

game[1] (geɪm) *n.* **1.** an amusement or pastime; diversion. **2.** a contest with rules, the result being determined by skill, strength, or chance. **3.** a single period of play in such a contest, sport, etc. **4.** the score needed to win a contest. **5.** a single contest in a series; match. **6.** (*pl.; often cap.*) an event consisting of various sporting contests, esp. in athletics: *Olympic Games.* **7.** equipment needed for playing certain games. **8.** style or ability in playing a game. **9.** a scheme, proceeding, etc., practised like a game: *the game of politics.* **10.** an activity undertaken in a spirit of levity; joke: *marriage is just a game to him.* **11. a.** wild animals, including birds and fish, hunted for sport, food, or profit. **b.** (*as modifier*): *game laws.* **12.** the flesh of such animals, used as food. **13.** an object of pursuit; quarry; prey (esp. in **fair game**). **14.** *Inf.* work or occupation. **15.** *Inf.* a trick, strategy, or device: *I can see through your little game.* **16.** *Sl., chiefly Brit.* prostitution (esp. in **on the game**). **17. give the game away.** to reveal one's intentions or a secret. **18. make (a) game of.** to make fun of; ridicule; mock. **19. play the game.** to behave fairly or in accordance with the rules. **20. the game is up.** there is no longer a chance of success. ~*adj.* **21.** *Inf.* full of fighting spirit; plucky; brave. **22.** (usually foll. by *for*) *Inf.* prepared or ready; willing: *I'm game for a try.* ~*vb.* **23.** (*intr.*) to play games of chance for money, stakes, etc.; gamble. [OE *gamen*] —ˈ**gamely** *adv.* —ˈ**gameness** *n.*

game[2] (geɪm) *adj.* a less common word for **lame** (esp. in **game leg**). [C18: prob. < Irish *cam* crooked]

gamecock (ˈgeɪmˌkɒk) *n.* a cock bred and trained for fighting. Also called: **fighting cock.**

game fish *n.* any fish providing sport for the angler.

gamekeeper (ˈgeɪmˌkiːpə) *n.* a person employed to take care of game, as on an estate.

gamelan (ˈgæmɪˌlæn) *n.* a type of percussion orchestra common in the East Indies. [< Javanese]

game laws *pl. n.* laws governing the hunting and preservation of game.

game point *n. Tennis, etc.* a stage at which winning one further point would enable one player or side to win a game.

gamesmanship (ˈgeɪmzmənˌʃɪp) *n. Inf.* the art of winning games or defeating opponents by cunning practices without actually cheating.

gamesome (ˈgeɪmsəm) *adj.* full of merriment; sportive. —ˈ**gamesomeness** *n.*

gamester (ˈgeɪmstə) *n.* a person who habitually plays games for money; gambler.

gametangium (ˌgæmɪˈtændʒɪəm) *n., pl.* **-gia** (-dʒɪə). *Bot.* an organ or cell in which gametes are produced, esp. in algae and fungi. [C19: NL, < GAMETO- + Gk *angeion* vessel]

gamete (ˈgæmiːt, gəˈmiːt) *n.* a haploid germ cell that fuses with another during fertilization. [C19: < NL, < Gk *gametē* wife, < *gamos* marriage] —**gametic** (gəˈmɛtɪk) *adj.*

game theory *n.* mathematical theory concerned with the optimum choice of strategy in situations involving a conflict of interest.

gameto- *or sometimes before a vowel* **gamet-** *combining form.* gamete: *gametophyte.*

gametophyte (gəˈmiːtəʊˌfaɪt) *n.* the plant body, in species showing alternation of generations, that produces the gametes. —**gametophytic** (ˌgæmɪtəʊˈfɪtɪk) *adj.*

gamin (ˈgæmɪn) *n.* a street urchin. [< F]

gamine (ˈgæmiːn) *n.* a slim and boyish girl or young woman; an elfish tomboy. [< F]

gaming (ˈgeɪmɪŋ) *n.* **a.** gambling on games of chance. **b.** (*as modifier*): *gaming house.*

gamma (ˈgæmə) *n.* **1.** the third letter in the Greek alphabet (Γ, γ). **2.** the third in a group or series. [C14: < Gk]

gamma distribution *n. Statistics.* a continuous two-parameter distribution from which the chi-square and exponential distributions are derived.

gamma globulin *n.* any of a group of proteins in blood plasma that includes most known antibodies.

gamma radiation *n.* electromagnetic radiation of shorter wavelength and higher energy than x-rays.

gamma rays *pl. n.* streams of gamma radiation.

gammer (ˈgæmə) *n. Rare, chiefly Brit.* a dialect word for an old woman: now chiefly humorous or contemptuous. [C16: prob. < GODMOTHER or GRANDMOTHER]

gammon[1] (ˈgæmən) *n.* **1.** a cured or smoked ham. **2.** the hindquarter of a side of bacon, cooked either whole or in rashers. [C15: < OF *gambon,* < *gambe* leg]

gammon[2] (ˈgæmən) *n.* **1.** a double victory in backgammon in which one player throws off all his pieces before his opponent throws any. ~*vb.* **2.** (*tr.*) to score such a victory over. [C18: prob. special use of ME *gamen* GAME[1]]

gammon[3] (ˈgæmən) *Brit. inf.* ~*n.* **1.** deceitful nonsense; humbug. ~*vb.* **2.** to deceive (a person). [C18: ? special use of GAMMON[1]]

gammy (ˈgæmɪ) *adj.* **-mier, -miest.** *Brit. sl.* (esp. of the leg) malfunctioning, injured, or lame; game. [C19: dialect var. of GAME[2]]

gamo- *or before a vowel* **gam-** *combining form.* **1.** indicating sexual union or reproduction: *gamogenesis.* **2.** united or fused: *gamopetalous.* [< Gk *gamos* marriage]

gamopetalous (ˌgæməʊˈpɛtələs) *adj.* (of flowers) having petals that are united or partly united, as the primrose.

gamp (gæmp) *n. Brit. inf.* an umbrella. [C19: after Mrs Sarah *Gamp,* a nurse in Dickens' *Martin Chuzzlewit,* who carried a faded cotton umbrella]

gamut (ˈgæmət) *n.* **1.** entire range or scale, as of emotions. **2.** *Music.* **a.** a scale, esp. (in medieval theory) one starting on the G on the bottom line of the bass staff. **b.** the whole range of notes. [C15: < Med. L, < *gamma,* the lowest note of the hexachord as established by Guido d'Arezzo + *ut* (now, *doh*), the first of the notes of the scale *ut, re, mi, fa, sol, la, si*]

gamy *or* **gamey** ('geɪmɪ) *adj.* **gamier, gamiest.** **1.** having the smell or flavour of game, esp. high game. **2.** *Inf.* spirited; plucky; brave. —'**gamily** *adv.* —'**gaminess** *n.*

-gamy *n. combining form.* denoting marriage or sexual union: *bigamy.* [< Gk, < *gamos* marriage] —**-gamous** *adj. combining form.*

gander ('gændə) *n.* **1.** a male goose. **2.** *Inf.* a quick look (esp. in **take** (*or* **have**) **a gander**). **3.** *Inf.* a simpleton. [OE *gandra, ganra*]

gang[1] (gæŋ) *n.* **1.** a group of people who associate together or act as an organized body, esp. for criminal or illegal purposes. **2.** an organized group of workmen. **3.** a series of similar tools arranged to work simultaneously in parallel. ~*vb.* **4.** to form into, become part of, or act as a gang. ~See also **gang up.** [OE: journey]

gang[2] (gæŋ) *n.* a variant spelling of **gangue.**

gang[3] (gæŋ) *vb.* (*intr.*) *Scot.* to go or walk. [OE *gangan*]

gangbang ('gæŋˌbæŋ) *n. Sl.* an instance of sexual intercourse between one woman and several men one after the other, esp. against her will.

ganger ('gæŋə) *n. Chiefly Brit.* the foreman of a gang of labourers.

gangland ('gæŋˌlænd, -lənd) *n.* the criminal underworld.

gangling ('gæŋglɪŋ) *or* **gangly** *adj.* tall, lanky, and awkward in movement. [see GANG[3]]

ganglion ('gæŋglɪən) *n., pl.* **-glia** (-glɪə) *or* **-glions.** **1.** an encapsulated collection of nerve-cell bodies, usually located outside the brain and spinal cord. **2.** any concentration or centre of energy, activity, or strength. **3.** a cystic tumour on a tendon sheath. [C17: < LL: swelling, < Gk: cystic tumour] —'**gangliar** *adj.* —ˌ**gangli'onic** *or* '**gangliˌated** *adj.*

gangplank ('gæŋˌplæŋk) *or* **gangway** *n. Naut.* a portable bridge for boarding and leaving a vessel at dockside.

gangrene ('gæŋgriːn) *n.* **1.** death and decay of tissue as the result of interrupted blood supply, disease, or injury. ~*vb.* **2.** to become or cause to become affected with gangrene. [C16: < L, < Gk *gangraina* an eating sore] —**gangrenous** ('gæŋgrɪnəs) *adj.*

gang-saw *n.* a multiple saw used in a timber mill to cut planks from logs.

gangster ('gæŋstə) *n.* a member of an organized gang of criminals.

gangue *or* **gang** (gæŋ) *n.* valueless and undesirable material in an ore. [C19: < F, < G *Gang* vein of metal, course]

gang up *vb.* (*intr., adv.;* often foll. by *on* or *against*) *Inf.* to combine in a group (against).

gangway ('gæŋˌweɪ) *n.* **1.** another word for **gangplank.** **2.** an opening in a ship's side to take a gangplank. **3.** *Brit.* an aisle between rows of seats. **4.** temporary planks over mud or earth, as on a building site. ~*sentence substitute.* **5.** clear a path!

ganister *or* **gannister** ('gænɪstə) *n.* a refractory siliceous sedimentary rock occurring beneath coal seams: used for lining furnaces.

gannet ('gænɪt) *n.* **1.** any of several heavily built marine birds having a long stout bill and typically white plumage with dark markings. **2.** *Sl.* a greedy person. [OE *ganot*]

ganoid ('gænɔɪd) *adj.* **1.** (of the scales of certain fishes) consisting of an inner bony layer and an outer layer of an enamel-like substance (**ganoin**). **2.** denoting fishes, including the sturgeon and bowfin, having such scales. ~*n.* **3.** a ganoid fish. [C19: < F, < Gk *ganos* brightness + -OID]

gantry ('gæntrɪ) *n., pl.* **-tries.** **1.** a bridgelike framework used to support a travelling crane, signals over a railway track, etc. **2.** Also called: **gantry scaffold.** the framework tower used to attend to a large rocket on its launching pad. **3.** a supporting framework for a barrel. **4. a.** the area behind a bar where bottles, esp. spirit bottles mounted in optics, are kept. **b.** the range or quality of the spirits on display there. [C16 (in the sense: wooden platform for barrels): < OF *chantier,* < Med. L, < L *canthērius* supporting frame, pack ass]

gaol (dʒeɪl) *n., vb. Brit.* a variant spelling of **jail.** —'**gaoler** *n.*

gap (gæp) *n.* **1.** a break or opening in a wall, fence, etc. **2.** a break in continuity; interruption; hiatus. **3.** a break in a line of hills or mountains affording a route through. **4.** *Chiefly U.S.* a gorge or ravine. **5.** a divergence or difference; disparity: *the generation gap.* **6.** *Electronics.* **a.** a break in a magnetic circuit that increases the inductance and saturation point of the circuit. **b.** See **spark gap.** **7. bridge, close, fill,** *or* **stop a gap.** to remedy a deficiency. ~*vb.* **gapping, gapped.** **8.** (*tr.*) to make a breach or opening in. [C14: < ON *gap* chasm] —'**gappy** *adj.*

gape (geɪp) *vb.* (*intr.*) **1.** to stare in wonder, esp. with the mouth open. **2.** to open the mouth wide, esp. involuntarily, as in yawning. **3.** to be or become wide open: *the crater gaped under his feet.* ~*n.* **4.** the act of gaping. **5.** a wide opening. **6.** the width of the widely opened mouth of a vertebrate. **7.** a stare of astonishment. [C13: < ON *gapa*] —'**gaper** *n.* —'**gaping** *adj.*

gapes (geɪps) *n.* (*functioning as sing.*) **1.** a disease of young domestic fowl, characterized by gaping and caused by parasitic worms (**gapeworms**). **2.** *Inf.* a fit of yawning.

gar (gɑː) *n., pl.* **gar** *or* **gars.** short for **garpike.**

garage ('gærɑːʒ, -rɪdʒ) *n.* **1.** a building used to house a motor vehicle. **2.** a commercial establishment in which motor vehicles are repaired, serviced, bought, and sold, and which usually also sells motor fuels. ~*vb.* **3.** (*tr.*) to put into or keep in a garage. [C20: < F, < OF: to protect, < OHG *warōn*]

garage band *n.* a rough-and-ready amateurish rock group. [? < the practice of such bands rehearsing in a garage]

garage sale *n.* a sale of personal belongings or household effects held at a person's home, usually in the garage.

garb (gɑːb) *n.* **1.** clothes, esp. the distinctive attire of an occupation: *clerical garb.* **2.** style of dress; fashion. **3.** external appearance, covering, or attire. ~*vb.* **4.** (*tr.*) to clothe; attire. [C16: < OF: graceful contour, < OIt. *garbo* grace, prob. of Gmc origin]

garbage ('gɑːbɪdʒ) *n.* **1.** worthless, useless, or unwanted matter. **2.** another word (esp. U.S. and Canad.) for **rubbish.** **3.** *Computers.* invalid data. [C15: prob. < Anglo-F *garbelage* removal of discarded matter, <?]

garble ('gɑːbᵊl) *vb.* (*tr.*) **1.** to jumble (a story, quotation, etc.), esp. unintentionally. **2.** to distort the meaning of (an account, text, etc.), as by making misleading omissions; corrupt. ~*n.* **3. a.** the act of garbling. **b.** garbled matter. [C15: < OIt. *garbellare* to strain, sift, < Ar., < LL *crībellum* small sieve] —'**garbler** *n.*

garboard ('gɑːˌbɔːd) *n. Naut.* the bottommost plank of a vessel's hull. Also called: **garboard strake.** [C17: < Du. *gaarboord,* prob. < MDu. *gaderen* to GATHER + *boord* BOARD]

garçon (*French* garsɔ̃) *n.* a waiter or male servant, esp. if French. [C19: < OF *gars* lad, prob. of Gmc origin]

garda ('gɑːrdə) *n., pl.* **gardaí** ('gɑːrdɪ). a member of the **Garda Síochána,** the police force of the Republic of Ireland.

garden ('gɑːdᵊn) *n.* **1.** *Brit.* **a.** an area of land, usually planted with grass, trees, flowerbeds, etc., adjoining a house. U.S. and Canad. word: **yard.** **b.** (*as modifier*): *a garden chair.* **2. a.** an area of land used for the cultivation of ornamental plants, herbs, fruit, vegetables, trees, etc. **b.** (*as modifier*): *garden tools.* Related adj.: **horticultural.** **3.** (*often pl.*) such an area of land that is open to the public, sometimes part of a park: *botanical gardens.* **4.** a fertile and beautiful region. **5. lead (a person) up the garden path.** *Inf.* to mislead or deceive. ~*vb.* **6.** to work in, cultivate, or take care of (a garden, plot of land, etc.). [C14: < OF gardin, of Gmc origin] —ˈ**gardener** *n.* —ˈ**gardening** *n.*

garden centre *n.* a place where gardening tools and equipment, plants, seeds, etc., are sold.

garden city *n. Brit.* a planned town of limited size surrounded by a rural belt.

gardenia (gɑːˈdiːnɪə) *n.* **1.** any evergreen shrub or tree of the Old World tropical genus *Gardenia*, cultivated for their large fragrant waxlike typically white flowers. **2.** the flower of any of these shrubs. [C18: NL, after Dr Alexander *Garden* (1730–91), American botanist]

garderobe (ˈgɑːdˌrəʊb) *n. Arch.* **1.** a wardrobe or its contents. **2.** a private room. **3.** a privy. [C14: < F, < *garder* to keep + *robe* dress, clothing; see WARDROBE]

garfish (ˈgɑːˌfɪʃ) *n., pl.* **-fish** *or* **-fishes. 1.** another name for **garpike** (sense 1). **2.** an elongated marine teleost fish with long toothed jaws: related to the flying fishes. [OE *gār* spear + FISH]

garganey (ˈgɑːgənɪ) *n.* a small Eurasian duck closely related to the mallard. The male has a white stripe over each eye. [C17: < It. dialect *garganei*, imit.]

gargantuan (gɑːˈgæntjʊən) *adj.* (*sometimes cap.*) huge; enormous. [after *Gargantua*, a giant in Rabelais' satire *Gargantua and Pantagruel* (1534)]

gargle (ˈgɑːgᵊl) *vb.* **1.** to rinse the mouth and throat with (a liquid, esp. a medicinal fluid) by slowly breathing through the liquid. ~*n.* **2.** the liquid used for gargling. **3.** the sound produced by gargling. [C16: < OF, < *gargouille* throat, ? imit.]

gargoyle (ˈgɑːgɔɪl) *n.* **1.** a waterspout carved in the form of a grotesque face or creature and projecting from a roof gutter. **2.** a person with a grotesque appearance. [C15: < OF *gargouille* gargoyle, throat; see GARGLE]

garibaldi (ˌgærɪˈbɔːldɪ) *n. Brit.* a type of biscuit having a layer of currants in the centre.

garish (ˈgɛərɪʃ) *adj.* gay or colourful in a crude manner; gaudy. [C16: < earlier *gaure* to stare + -ISH] —ˈ**garishly** *adv.* —ˈ**garishness** *n.*

garland (ˈgɑːlənd) *n.* **1.** a wreath of flowers, leaves, etc., worn round the head or neck or hung up. **2.** a collection of short literary pieces, such as poems; anthology. ~*vb.* **3.** (*tr.*) to adorn with a garland or garlands. [C14: < OF *garlande*, ? of Gmc origin]

garlic (ˈgɑːlɪk) *n.* **1.** a hardy widely cultivated Asian alliaceous plant having whitish flowers. **2.** the bulb of this plant, made up of small segments (cloves) that have a strong odour and pungent taste and are used in cooking. [OE *gārlēac*, < *gār* spear + *lēac* LEEK] —ˈ**garlicky** *adj.*

garment (ˈgɑːmənt) *n.* **1.** (*often pl.*) an article of clothing. **2.** outer covering. ~*vb.* **3.** (*tr.; usually passive*) to cover or clothe. [C14: < OF *garniment*, < *garnir* to equip; see GARNISH]

garner (ˈgɑːnə) *vb.* (*tr.*) **1.** to gather or store as in a granary. ~*n.* **2.** an archaic word for **granary. 3.** a place for storage. [C12: < OF: granary, < L *grānārium*, < *grānum* grain]

garnet (ˈgɑːnɪt) *n.* any of a group of hard glassy red, yellow, or green minerals consisting of silicates in cubic crystalline form: used as a gemstone and abrasive. [C13: < OF, < *grenat* (adj.) red, < *pome grenate* POMEGRANATE]

garnish (ˈgɑːnɪʃ) *vb.* (*tr.*) **1.** to decorate; trim. **2.** to add something to (food) in order to improve its appearance or flavour. **3.** *Law.* **a.** to serve with notice of proceedings; warn. **b.** to attach (a debt). ~*n.* **4.** a decoration; trimming. **5.** something, such as parsley, added to a dish for its flavour or decorative effect. [C14: < OF *garnir* to adorn, equip, of Gmc origin] —ˈ**garnisher** *n.*

garnishee (ˌgɑːnɪˈʃiː) *Law.* ~*n.* **1.** a person upon whom a garnishment has been served. ~*vb.* **-nisheeing, -nisheed.** (*tr.*) **2.** to attach (a debt or other property) by garnishment. **3.** to serve (a person) with a garnishment.

garnishment (ˈgɑːnɪʃmənt) *n.* **1.** decoration or embellishment. **2.** *Law.* **a.** a notice or warning. **b.** *Obs.* a summons to court proceedings already in progress. **c.** a notice warning a person holding money or property belonging to a debtor whose debt has been attached to hold such property until directed by the court to apply it.

garniture (ˈgɑːnɪtʃə) *n.* decoration or embellishment. [C16: < F, < *garnir* to GARNISH]

garpike (ˈgɑːˌpaɪk) *n.* **1.** Also called: **garfish, gar.** any primitive freshwater elongated bony fish of North and Central America, having very long toothed jaws and a body covering of thick scales. **2.** another name for **garfish** (sense 2).

garret (ˈgærɪt) *n.* another word for **attic** (sense 1). [C14: < OF: watchtower, < *garir* to protect, of Gmc origin]

garrison (ˈgærɪsᵊn) *n.* **1.** the troops who maintain and guard a base or fortified place. **2.** the place itself. ~*vb.* **3.** (*tr.*) to station (troops) in (a fort, etc.). [C13: < OF, < *garir* to defend, of Gmc origin]

garrotte *or* **garotte** (gəˈrɒt) *n.* **1.** a Spanish method of execution by strangulation. **2.** the device, usually an iron collar, used in such executions. **3.** *Obs.* strangulation of one's victim while committing robbery. ~*vb.* (*tr.*) **4.** to execute by means of the garrotte. **5.** to strangle, esp. in order to commit robbery. [C17: < Sp. *garrote*, ? < OF *garrot* cudgel; <?] —**garˈrotter** *or* **gaˈrotter** *n.*

garrulous (ˈgærʊləs) *adj.* **1.** given to constant chatter; talkative. **2.** wordy or diffuse. [C17: < L, < *garrīre* to chatter] —ˈ**garrulously** *adv.* —ˈ**garrulousness** *or* **garrulity** (gæˈruːlɪtɪ) *n.*

garryowen (ˌgærɪˈəʊɪn) *n.* (in rugby union) another term for **up-and-under.** [< *Garryowen* RFC, Ireland]

garter (ˈgɑːtə) *n.* **1.** a band, usually of elastic, worn round the leg to hold up a sock or stocking. **2.** the U.S. and Canad. word for **suspender.** ~*vb.* **3.** (*tr.*) to fasten or secure as with a garter. [C14: < OF *gartier*, < *garet* bend of the knee, prob. of Celtic origin]

Garter (ˈgɑːtə) *n.* **the. 1. Order of the Garter.** the highest order of British knighthood. **2.** (*sometimes not cap.*) **a.** the badge of this Order. **b.** membership of this Order.

garter snake *n.* a nonvenomous North American snake, typically marked with longitudinal stripes.

garter stitch *n.* knitting in which all the rows are knitted in plain stitch.

garth (gɑːθ) *n.* **1.** a courtyard surrounded by a cloister. **2.** *Arch.* a yard or garden. [C14: < ON *garthr*]

gas (gæs) *n., pl.* **gases** *or* **gasses. 1.** a substance in a physical state in which it does not resist change of shape and will expand indefinitely to fill any container. **2.** any substance that is gaseous at room temperature and atmospheric pressure. **3.** any gaseous substance that is above its critical temperature and therefore not liquefiable by pressure alone. Cf. **vapour** (sense 2). **4. a.** a fossil fuel in the form of a gas, used as a source of domestic and industrial heat. **b.** (*as modifier*): *a gas cooker; gas fire.* **5.** a gaseous anaesthetic, such as nitrous oxide. **6.** *Mining.* firedamp or the explosive mixture of firedamp and air. **7.** the usual U.S., Canad., Austral., and N.Z. word for **petrol. 8. step on the gas.** *Inf.* **a.** to accelerate a motor vehicle. **b.** to hurry. **9.** a toxic, etc., substance in suspension in air used against an enemy, etc. **10.** *Inf.* idle talk or boasting. **11.** *Sl.* a delightful or successful person or thing: *his latest record is a gas.* ~*vb.* **gases** *or* **gasses, gassing, gassed. 12.** (*tr.*) to provide or fill with gas. **13.** (*tr.*) to subject to gas fumes, esp. so as to asphyxiate or render unconscious. **14.** (*intr.; foll. by to*) *Inf.* to talk in an idle or boastful way (to a person). [C17 (coined by J. B. van Helmont (1577–1644), Flemish chemist): < Gk *khaos* atmosphere]

gasbag (ˈgæsˌbæg) *n. Inf.* a person who talks in a vapid or empty way.

gas chamber *or* **oven** *n.* an airtight room into which poison gas is introduced to kill people or animals.

gas chromatography *n.* a technique for analysing a mixture of volatile substances in which the mixture is carried by an inert gas through a column packed with a selective adsorbent and a detector records on a moving strip the conductivity of the gas leaving the tube.

Gascon (ˈgæskən) *n.* **1.** a native or inhabitant of Gascony. **2.** the dialect of French spoken in Gascony. ~*adj.* **3.** of or relating to Gascony, its inhabitants, or their dialect of French.

gasconade (ˌgæskəˈneɪd) *Rare.* ~*n.* **1.** boastful talk or bluster. ~*vb.* **2.** (*intr.*) to boast, brag, or bluster. [C18: < F, < *gasconner* to chatter, boast like a GASCON]

gas-cooled reactor *n.* a nuclear reactor using a gas as the coolant.

gaseous (ˈgæsɪəs, -ʃəs, -ʃɪəs, ˈgeɪ-) *adj.* of, concerned with, or having the characteristics of a gas. —ˈ**gaseousness** *n.*

gas equation *n.* an equation relating the product of the pressure and the volume of an ideal gas to the product of its thermodynamic temperature and the gas constant.

gas gangrene *n.* gangrene resulting from infection of a wound by anaerobic bacteria that cause gas bubbles in the surrounding tissues.

gash (gæʃ) *vb.* **1.** (*tr.*) to make a long deep cut in; slash. ~*n.* **2.** a long deep cut. [C16: < OF *garser* to scratch, wound, < Vulgar L, < Gk *kharassein*]

gasholder (ˈgæsˌhəʊldə) *n.* **1.** Also called: **gasometer.** a large tank for storing coal gas or natural gas prior to distribution to users. **2.** any vessel for storing or measuring a gas.

gasify (ˈgæsɪˌfaɪ) *vb.* **-fying, -fied.** to make into or become a gas. —ˌ**gasifiˈcation** *n.*

gasket (ˈgæskɪt) *n.* **1.** a compressible packing piece of paper, rubber, asbestos, etc., sandwiched between the faces of a metal joint to provide a seal. **2.** *Naut.* a piece of line used as a sail stop. [C17 (in the sense: rope lashing a furled sail): prob. < F *garcette* rope's end, lit.: little girl, < OF]

gaslight (ˈgæsˌlaɪt) *n.* **1.** a type of lamp in which the illumination is produced by an incandescent mantle heated by a jet of gas. **2.** the light produced by such a lamp.

gasman (ˈgæsˌmæn) *n., pl.* **-men.** a man employed to read household gas meters, supervise gas fittings, etc.

gas mantle *n.* a mantle for use in a gaslight. See **mantle** (sense 3).

gas mask *n.* a mask fitted with a chemical filter to enable the wearer to breathe air free of poisonous or corrosive gases.

gas meter *n.* an apparatus for measuring and recording the amount of gas passed through it.

gasoline *or* **gasolene** (ˈgæsəˌliːn) *n.* a U.S. and Canad. name for **petrol.**

gasometer (gæsˈɒmɪtə) *n.* a nontechnical name for **gasholder.**

gasp (gɑːsp) *vb.* **1.** (*intr.*) to draw in the breath sharply or with effort, esp. in expressing awe, horror, etc. **2.** (*intr.;* foll. by *after* or *for*) to crave. **3.** (*tr.;* often foll. by *out*) to utter breathlessly. ~*n.* **4.** a short convulsive intake of breath. **5. at the last gasp. a.** at the point of death. **b.** at the last moment. [C14: < ON *geispa* to yawn]

gasper (ˈgɑːspə) *n.* **1.** a person who gasps. **2.** *Brit. sl.* a cheap cigarette.

gas plant *n.* an aromatic white-flowered Eurasian plant that emits vapour capable of being ignited. Also called: **burning bush, dittany, fraxinella.**

gas ring *n.* a circular assembly of gas jets, used esp. for cooking.

gassy (ˈgæsɪ) *adj.* **-sier, -siest. 1.** filled with, containing, or resembling gas. **2.** *Inf.* full of idle or vapid talk. —ˈ**gassiness** *n.*

gasteropod (ˈgæstərəˌpɒd) *n., adj.* a variant spelling of **gastropod.**

gas thermometer *n.* a device for measuring temperature by observing the pressure of gas at a constant volume or the volume of a gas kept at a constant pressure.

gastric (ˈgæstrɪk) *adj.* of, relating to, near, or involving the stomach.

gastric juice *n.* a digestive fluid secreted by the stomach, containing hydrochloric acid, pepsin, rennin, etc.

gastric ulcer *n.* an ulcer of the mucous membrane lining the stomach.

gastritis (gæsˈtraɪtɪs) *n.* inflammation of the stomach.

gastro- *or often before a vowel* **gastr-** *combining form.* stomach: *gastroenteritis; gastritis.* [< Gk *gastēr*]

gastroenteritis (ˌgæstrəʊˌɛntəˈraɪtɪs) *n.* inflammation of the stomach and intestines.

gastrointestinal (ˌgæstrəʊɪnˈtɛstɪnᵊl) *adj.* of or relating to the stomach and intestinal tract.

gastronome (ˈgæstrəˌnəʊm), **gastronomer** (gæsˈtrɒnəmə), *or* **gastronomist** *n.* less common words for **gourmet.**

gastronomy (gæsˈtrɒnəmɪ) *n.* the art of good eating. [C19: < F, < Gk, < *gastēr* stomach; see -NOMY] —**gastronomic** (ˌgæstrəˈnɒmɪk) *or* ˌ**gastroˈnomical** *adj.* —ˌ**gastroˈnomically** *adv.*

gastropod (ˈgæstrəˌpɒd) *or* **gasteropod** *n.* any of a class of molluscs typically having a flattened muscular foot for locomotion and a head that bears stalked eyes. The class includes the snails, whelks and slugs. —**gastropodous** (gæsˈtrɒpədəs) *adj.*

gastroscope (ˈgæstrəˌskəʊp) *n.* a medical instrument for examining the interior of the stomach.

gastrula (ˈgæstrʊlə) *n., pl.* **-las** *or* **-lae** (-ˌliː). a saclike animal embryo consisting of three layers of cells surrounding a central cavity with a small opening to the exterior. [C19: NL: little stomach, < Gk *gastēr* belly]

gas turbine *n.* an internal-combustion engine in which the expanding gases emerging from one or more combustion chambers drive a turbine.

gasworks (ˈgæsˌwɜːks) *n.* (*functioning as sing.*) a plant in which gas, esp. coal gas, is made.

gate (geɪt) *n.* **1.** a movable barrier, usually hinged, for closing an opening in a wall, fence, etc. **2.** an opening to allow passage into or out of an enclosed place. **3.** any means of entrance or access. **4.** a mountain pass or gap, esp. one providing entry into another country or region. **5. a.** the number of people admitted to a sporting event or entertainment. **b.** the total entrance money received from them. **6.** *Electronics.* a logic circuit having one or more input terminals and one output terminal, the output being switched between two voltage levels determined by the combination of input signals. **7.** a component in a motion-picture camera or projector that holds each frame flat and momentarily stationary behind the lens. **8.** a slotted metal frame that controls the positions of the gear lever in a motor vehicle. ~*vb.* **9.** (*tr.*) *Brit.* to restrict (a student) to the school or college grounds as a punishment. [OE *geat*]

-gate *n. combining form.* indicating a person or thing associated with a public scandal. [C20: < *Watergate*]

gâteau (ˈgætəʊ) *n., pl.* **-teaux** (-təʊz). a rich cake usually elaborately decorated. [F: cake]

gate-crash *vb. Inf.* to gain entry to (a party, concert, etc.) without invitation or payment. —ˈ**gate-ˌcrasher** *n.*

gatefold (ˈgeɪtˌfəʊld) *n.* an oversize page in a book or magazine that is folded in.

gatehouse (ˈgeɪtˌhaʊs) *n.* **1.** a building at or above a gateway, used by a porter or guard, or, formerly, as a fortification. **2.** a small house at the entrance to the grounds of a country mansion.

gatekeeper (ˈgeɪtˌkiːpə) *n.* **1.** a person who has charge of a gate and controls who may pass through it. **2.** any of several Eurasian butterflies having brown-bordered orange wings.

gate-leg table *or* **gate-legged table** *n.* a table with one or two leaves supported by a hinged leg swung out from the frame.

gatepost (ˈgeɪtˌpəʊst) *n.* **1. a.** the post on which a gate is hung. **b.** the post to which a gate is fastened when closed. **2. between you, me, and the gatepost.** confidentially.

gateway (ˈgeɪtˌweɪ) *n.* **1.** an entrance that may be closed by or as by a gate. **2.** a means of entry or access: *Bombay, gateway to India.*

gather ('gæðə) *vb.* **1.** to assemble or cause to assemble. **2.** to collect or be collected gradually; muster. **3.** (*tr.*) to learn from information given; conclude or assume. **4.** (*tr.*) to pick or harvest (flowers, fruit, etc.). **5.** (*tr.*) to bring close (to). **6.** to increase or cause to increase gradually, as in force, speed, intensity, etc. **7.** to contract (the brow) or (of the brow) to become contracted into wrinkles; knit. **8.** (*tr.*) to assemble (sections of a book) in the correct sequence for binding. **9.** (*tr.*) to prepare or make ready: *to gather one's wits.* **10.** to draw (material) into a series of small tucks or folds. **11.** (*intr.*) (of a boil or other sore) to come to a head; form pus. ~*n.* **12. a.** the act of gathering. **b.** the amount gathered. **13.** a small fold in material, as made by a tightly pulled stitch; tuck. [OE *gadrian*] —'**gatherer** *n.*

gathering ('gæðərɪŋ) *n.* **1.** a group of people, things, etc., that are gathered together; assembly. **2.** *Sewing.* a series of gathers in material. **3.** *Inf.* **a.** the formation of pus in a boil. **b.** the pus so formed. **4.** *Printing.* an informal name for **section** (sense 16).

Gatling gun ('gætlɪŋ) *n.* a machine gun equipped with a rotating cluster of barrels that are fired in succession. [C19: after R. J. *Gatling* (1818–1903), its U.S. inventor]

GATT (gæt) *n. acronym for* General Agreement on Tariffs and Trade: a multilateral international treaty signed in 1947 to promote trade.

gauche (gəʊʃ) *adj.* lacking ease of manner; tactless. [C18: F: awkward, left, < OF *gauchir* to swerve, ult. of Gmc origin] —'**gauchely** *adv.* —'**gaucheness** *n.*

gaucherie (ˌgəʊʃə'riː, 'gəʊʃərɪ) *n.* **1.** the quality of being gauche. **2.** a gauche act.

gaucho ('gaʊtʃəʊ) *n., pl.* **-chos.** a cowboy of the South American pampas, usually one of mixed Spanish and Indian descent. [C19: < American Sp., prob. < Quechuan *wáhcha* orphan, vagabond]

gaud (gɔːd) *n.* an article of cheap finery. [C14: prob. < OF *gaudir* to be joyful, < L *gaudēre*]

gaudy[1] ('gɔːdɪ) *adj.* **gaudier, gaudiest.** bright or colourful in a crude or vulgar manner. [C16: < GAUD] —'**gaudily** *adv.* —'**gaudiness** *n.*

gaudy[2] ('gɔːdɪ) *n., pl.* **gaudies.** *Brit.* a celebratory feast held at some schools and colleges. [C16: < L *gaudium* joy, < *gaudēre* to rejoice]

gauge *or* **gage** (geɪdʒ) *vb.* (*tr.*) **1.** to measure or determine the amount, quantity, size, condition, etc., of. **2.** to estimate or appraise; judge. **3.** to check for conformity or bring into conformity with a standard measurement, etc. ~*n.* **4.** a standard measurement, dimension, capacity, or quantity. **5.** any of various instruments for measuring a quantity: *a pressure gauge.* **6.** any of various devices used to check for conformity with a standard measurement. **7.** a standard or means for assessing; test; criterion. **8.** scope, capacity, or extent. **9.** the diameter of the barrel of a gun, esp. a shotgun. **10.** the thickness of sheet metal or the diameter of wire. **11.** the distance between the rails of a railway track. **12.** the distance between two wheels on the same axle of a vehicle, truck, etc. **13.** *Naut.* the position of a vessel in relation to the wind and another vessel. **14.** a measure of the fineness of woven or knitted fabric. ~*adj.* **15.** (of a pressure measurement) measured on a pressure gauge that registers zero at atmospheric pressure. [C15: < OF, prob. of Gmc origin] —'**gaugeable** *or* '**gageable** *adj.*

Gaul (gɔːl) *n.* **1.** a native of ancient Gaul, a region in Roman times stretching from what is now N Italy to the S Netherlands. **2.** a Frenchman.

Gauleiter ('gaʊˌlaɪtə) *n.* **1.** a provincial governor in Germany under Hitler. **2.** (*sometimes not cap.*) a person in a position of petty authority who behaves in an overbearing manner. [G, < *Gau* district + *Leiter* leader]

Gaulish ('gɔːlɪʃ) *n.* **1.** the extinct Celtic language of the pre-Roman Gauls. ~*adj.* **2.** of ancient Gaul, the Gauls, or their language.

gaunt (gɔːnt) *adj.* **1.** bony and emaciated in appearance. **2.** (of places) bleak or desolate. [C15: ? < ON] —'**gauntly** *adv.* —'**gauntness** *n.*

gauntlet[1] ('gɔːntlɪt) *n.* **1.** a medieval armoured leather glove. **2.** a heavy glove with a long cuff. **3. take up** (*or* **throw down**) **the gauntlet.** to accept (*or* offer) a challenge. [C15: < OF *gantelet*, dim. of *gant* glove, of Gmc origin]

gauntlet[2] ('gɔːntlɪt) *n.* **1.** a punishment in which the victim is forced to run between two rows of men who strike at him as he passes: formerly a military punishment. **2. run the gauntlet. a.** to suffer this punishment. **b.** to endure an onslaught, as of criticism. **3.** a testing ordeal. [C15: changed (through infl. of GAUNTLET[1]) < earlier *gantlope*, < Swedish *gatlopp* passageway]

gaur ('gaʊə) *n.* a large wild ox of mountainous regions of S Asia. [C19: < Hindi, < Sansk. *gāura*]

gauss (gaʊs) *n., pl.* **gauss.** the cgs unit of magnetic flux density. 1 gauss is equivalent to 10^{-4} tesla. [after K. F. *Gauss*, G mathematician (1777–1855)]

Gaussian distribution ('gaʊsɪən) *n.* another name for **normal distribution.**

gauze (gɔːz) *n.* **1.** a transparent cloth of loose weave. **2.** a surgical dressing of muslin or similar material. **3.** any thin openwork material, such as wire. **4.** a fine mist or haze. [C16: < F *gaze*, ? < *Gaza*, Israel, where it was believed to originate]

gauzy ('gɔːzɪ) *adj.* **gauzier, gauziest.** resembling gauze; thin and transparent. —'**gauzily** *adv.* —'**gauziness** *n.*

gave (geɪv) *vb.* the past tense of **give.**

gavel ('gævᵊl) *n.* a small hammer used by a chairman, auctioneer, etc., to call for order or attention. [C19: <?]

gavial ('geɪvɪəl), **gharial,** *or* **garial** ('gærɪəl) *n.* a large fish-eating Indian crocodile with a very long slender snout. [C19: < F, < Hindi]

gavotte *or* **gavot** (gə'vɒt) *n.* **1.** an old formal dance in quadruple time. **2.** a piece of music composed for or in the rhythm of this dance. [C17: < F, < Provençal, < *gavot* mountaineer, dweller in the Alps (where the dance originated)]

gawk (gɔːk) *n.* **1.** a clumsy stupid person; lout. ~*vb.* **2.** (*intr.*) to stare in a stupid way; gape. [C18: < ODanish *gaukr*; prob. rel. to GAPE]

gawky ('gɔːkɪ) *adj.* **gawkier, gawkiest.** clumsy or ungainly; awkward. Also: **gawkish.** —'**gawkily** *adv.* —'**gawkiness** *n.*

gawp *or* **gaup** (gɔːp) *vb.* (*intr.*; often foll. by *at*) *Brit. sl.* to stare stupidly; gape. [C14 *galpen*; prob. rel. to OE *gielpan* to boast, YELP]

gay (geɪ) *adj.* **1. a.** homosexual. **b.** (*as n.*): *a group of gays.* **2.** carefree and merry: *a gay temperament.* **3.** brightly coloured; brilliant: *a gay hat.* **4.** given to pleasure, esp. in social entertainment: *a gay life.* [C13: < OF *gai*, < OProvençal, of Gmc origin] —'**gayness** *n.*

gazania (gə'zeɪnɪə) *n.* any of a genus of S. African plants of the composite family having large showy flowers. [? after Theodore of *Gaza* (1398–1478), who translated the botanical works of Theophrastus into Latin]

gaze (geɪz) *vb.* **1.** (*intr.*) to look long and fixedly, esp. in wonder. ~*n.* **2.** a fixed look. [C14: < Swedish dialect *gasa* to gape at] —'**gazer** *n.*

gazebo (gə'ziːbəʊ) *n., pl.* **-bos** *or* **-boes.** a summerhouse, garden pavilion, or belvedere, sited to command a view. [C18: ? a pseudo-Latin coinage based on GAZE]

gazelle (gə'zɛl) *n., pl.* **-zelles** *or* **-zelle.** any small graceful usually fawn-coloured antelope of Africa and Asia. [C17: < OF, < Ar. *ghazāl*]

gazette (gə'zɛt) *n.* **1.** a newspaper or official journal. **2.** *Brit.* an official document containing public notices, appointments, etc. ~*vb.* **3.** (*tr.*) *Brit.* to announce or report (facts or an event) in a gazette. [C17: < F, < It., < Venetian dialect *gazeta* news-sheet costing one *gazet*, small copper coin]

gazetteer (ˌgæzɪ'tɪə) *n.* **1.** a book or section of a book that lists and describes places. **2.** *Arch.* a writer for a gazette.

gazpacho (gəz'pɑːtʃəʊ, gæs-) *n.* a Spanish soup made from tomatoes, peppers, etc., and served cold. [< Sp.]

gazump (gə'zʌmp) *Brit.* ~*vb.* **1.** to raise the

price of something, esp. a house, after agreeing a price verbally with (an intending buyer). **2.** (*tr.*) to swindle or overcharge. ~*n.* **3.** an instance of gazumping. [C20: <?] **—ga'zumper** *n.*

GB *abbrev. for* Great Britain.

GBE *abbrev. for* (Knight or Dame) Grand Cross of the British Empire (a Brit. title).

GBH *abbrev. for* grievous bodily harm.

GC *abbrev. for* George Cross (a Brit. award for bravery).

GCB *abbrev. for* (Knight) Grand Cross of the Bath (a Brit. title).

gcd *or* **GCD** *abbrev. for* greatest common divisor.

GCE (in Britain) **1.** *abbrev. for* General Certificate of Education: either of two public examinations in specified subjects taken as school-leaving qualifications or as qualifying examinations for entry into a university, college, etc. See also **O level, A level.** ~*n.* **2.** *Inf.* any subject taken for one of these examinations.

GCHQ (in Britain) *abbrev. for* Government Communications Headquarters.

G clef *n.* another name for **treble clef.**

GCMG *abbrev. for* (Knight or Dame) Grand Cross of the Order of St Michael and St George (a Brit. title).

GCSE (in Britain) *abbrev. for* General Certificate of Secondary Education.

GCVO *abbrev. for* (Knight or Dame) Grand Cross of the Royal Victorian Order (a Brit. title).

Gd *the chemical symbol for* gadolinium.

Gdns *abbrev. for* Gardens.

Ge *the chemical symbol for* germanium.

gean (giːn) *n.* a white-flowered tree of the rose family of Europe, W Asia, and N Africa; the ancestor of the cultivated sweet cherries.

gear (gɪə) *n.* **1.** a toothed wheel that engages with another toothed wheel or with a rack in order to change the speed or direction of transmitted motion. **2.** a mechanism for transmitting motion by gears. **3.** the engagement or specific ratio of a system of gears: *in gear; high gear.* **4.** personal belongings. **5.** equipment and supplies for a particular operation, sport, etc. **6.** *Naut.* all equipment or appurtenances belonging to a certain vessel, sailor, etc. **7.** short for **landing gear. 8.** *Inf.* up-to-date clothes and accessories. **9.** *Sl.* drugs of any type. **10.** a less common word for **harness** (sense 1). **11. out of gear.** out of order; not functioning properly. ~*vb.* **12.** (*tr.*) to adjust or adapt (one thing) so as to fit in or work with another: *to gear our output to current demand.* **13.** (*tr.*) to equip with or connect by gears. **14.** (*intr.*) to be in or come into gear. **15.** (*tr.*) to equip with a harness. [C13: < ON *gervi*]

gearbox ('gɪəˌbɒks) *n.* **1.** the metal casing within which a train of gears is sealed. **2.** this metal casing and its contents, esp. in a motor vehicle.

gearing ('gɪərɪŋ) *n.* **1.** an assembly of gears designed to transmit motion. **2.** the act or technique of providing gears to transmit motion. **3.** *Accounting, Brit.* the ratio of a company's debt capital to its equity capital.

gear lever *or U.S. & Canad.* **gearshift** ('gɪəˌʃɪft) *n.* a lever used to move gearwheels relative to each other, esp. in a motor vehicle.

gearwheel ('gɪəˌwiːl) *n.* another name for **gear** (sense 1).

gecko ('gɛkəʊ) *n., pl.* **geckos** *or* **geckoes.** a small insectivorous terrestrial lizard of warm regions. [C18: < Malay *ge'kok*, imit.]

gee[1] (dʒiː) *interj.* **1.** Also: **gee up!** an exclamation, as to a horse or draught animal, to encourage it to turn to the right, go on, or go faster. ~*vb.* **geeing, geed. 2.** (usually foll. by *up*) to move (an animal, esp. a horse) ahead; urge on. [C17: <?]

gee[2] (dʒiː) *interj. U.S. & Canad. inf.* a mild exclamation. Also: **gee whiz.** [C20: euphemism for JESUS]

geebung ('dʒiːbʌŋ) *n.* **1.** any of several Australian trees or shrubs with edible but tasteless fruit. **2.** the fruit of these trees. [< Abor.]

geek (giːk) *n. Sl.* a degenerate.

geelbek ('xiːlˌbɛk) *n. S. African.* an edible marine fish with yellow jaws. Also called: **Cape salmon.** [< Afrik. *geel* yellow + *bek* mouth]

geese (giːs) *n.* the plural of **goose**[1].

geezer ('giːzə) *n. Inf.* a man, esp. an old one regarded as eccentric. [C19: prob. < dialect pronunciation of GUISER]

Gehenna (gɪ'hɛnə) *n.* **1.** *Old Testament.* the valley below Jerusalem, where children were sacrificed and, later, unclean things were burnt. **2.** *New Testament, Judaism.* a place where the wicked are punished after death. **3.** a place or state of pain and torment. [C16: < LL, < Gk, < Heb. *Gê' Hinnōm*, lit.: valley of Hinnom, symbolic of hell]

Geiger counter ('gaɪgə) *or* **Geiger-Müller counter** ('mʊlə) *n.* an instrument for detecting and measuring the intensity of ionizing radiation. [C20: after Hans *Geiger* and W. *Müller*, 20th-cent. G physicists]

geisha ('geɪʃə) *n., pl.* **-sha** *or* **-shas.** a professional female companion for men in Japan, trained in music, dancing, and the art of conversation. [C19: < Japanese, < Ancient Chinese]

Geissler tube ('gaɪslə) *n.* a glass or quartz vessel for maintaining an electric discharge in a low-pressure gas as a source of visible or ultraviolet light for spectroscopy, etc. [C19: after Heinrich *Geissler* (1814–79), G mechanic]

gel (dʒɛl) *n.* **1.** a semirigid jelly-like colloid in which a liquid is dispersed in a solid: *nondrip paint is a gel.* **2.** a jelly-like substance applied to the hair before styling in order to retain the style. ~*vb.* **gelling, gelled. 3.** to become or cause to become a gel. **4.** a variant spelling of **jell.** [C19: < GELATIN]

gelatin ('dʒɛlətɪn) *or* **gelatine** ('dʒɛləˌtiːn) *n.* **1.** a colourless or yellowish water-soluble protein prepared by boiling animal hides and bones: used in foods, glue, photographic emulsions, etc. **2.** an edible jelly made of this substance. [C19: < F *gélatine*, < Med. L, < L *gelāre* to freeze]

gelatinize *or* **-ise** (dʒɪ'lætɪˌnaɪz) *vb.* **1.** to make or become gelatinous. **2.** (*tr.*) *Photog.* to coat (glass, paper, etc.) with gelatin. **—geˌlatini'zation** *or* **-i'sation** *n.*

gelatinous (dʒɪ'lætɪnəs) *adj.* **1.** consisting of or resembling jelly; viscous. **2.** of, containing, or resembling gelatin. **—ge'latinously** *adv.* **—ge'latinousness** *n.*

gelation[1] (dʒɪ'leɪʃən) *n.* the act or process of freezing a liquid. [C19: < L *gelātiō* a freezing; see GELATIN]

gelation[2] (dʒɪ'leɪʃən) *n.* the act or process of forming into a gel. [C20: < GEL]

geld (gɛld) *vb.* **gelding, gelded** *or* **gelt** (gɛlt). (*tr.*) **1.** to castrate (a horse or other animal). **2.** to deprive of virility or vitality; emasculate; weaken. [C13: < ON, < *geldr* barren]

gelding ('gɛldɪŋ) *n.* a castrated male horse. [C14: < ON *geldingr;* see GELD, -ING[1]]

gelid ('dʒɛlɪd) *adj.* very cold, icy, or frosty. [C17: < L *gelidus*, < *gelu* frost] **—ge'lidity** *n.*

gelignite ('dʒɛlɪgˌnaɪt) *n.* a type of dynamite in which the nitrogelatin is absorbed in a base of wood pulp and potassium or sodium nitrate. Also called (informal): **gelly.** [C19: < GEL(ATIN) + L *ignis* fire + -ITE[1]]

gem (dʒɛm) *n.* **1.** a precious or semiprecious stone used in jewellery as a decoration; jewel. **2.** a person or thing held to be a perfect example; treasure. ~*vb.* **gemming, gemmed. 3.** (*tr.*) to set or ornament with gems. [C14: < OF, < L *gemma* bud, precious stone] **—'gemˌlike** *adj.* **—'gemmy** *adj.*

Gemara (gɛ'mɑːrə; *Hebrew* gɛma'ra) *n. Judaism.* the later main part of the Talmud, being a commentary on the Mishnah: the primary source of Jewish religious law. [C17: < Aramaic *gemārā* completion]

geminate *adj.* ('dʒɛmɪnɪt, -ˌneɪt) *also* **geminated. 1.** combined in pairs; doubled: *a geminate leaf.* ~*vb.* ('dʒɛmɪˌneɪt). **2.** to arrange or be arranged in pairs: *the "t"s in Italian "gatto" are geminated.* [C17: < L *gemināre* to double, < *geminus* twin] **—'geminately** *adv.* **—ˌgemi'nation** *n.*

Gemini (ˈdʒɛmɪˌnaɪ, -ˌniː) *n.* **1.** *Astron.* a zodiacal constellation in the N hemisphere containing the stars Castor and Pollux. **2.** *Astrol.* Also called: the **Twins.** the third sign of the zodiac. The sun is in this sign between about May 21 and June 20.

gemma (ˈdʒɛmə) *n., pl.* **-mae** (-miː). **1.** a small asexual reproductive structure in mosses, etc., that becomes detached from the parent and develops into a new individual. **2.** *Zool.* another name for **gemmule.** [C18: < L: bud, GEM]

gemmate (ˈdʒɛmeɪt) *adj.* **1.** (of some plants and animals) having or reproducing by gemmae. ~*vb.* **2.** (*intr.*) to produce or reproduce by gemmae. —**gemˈmation** *n.*

gemmiparous (dʒɛˈmɪpərəs) *adj.* (of plants and animals) reproducing by gemmae or buds.

gemmule (ˈdʒɛmjuːl) *n.* **1.** *Zool.* a cell or mass of cells produced asexually by sponges and developing into a new individual; bud. **2.** *Bot.* a small gemma. [C19: < F, < L *gemmula* a little bud; see GEM]

gemology *or* **gemmology** (dʒɛˈmɒlədʒɪ) *n.* the branch of mineralogy concerned with gems and gemstones. —**gemˈologist** *or* **gemˈmologist** *n.*

gemsbok *or* **gemsbuck** (ˈgɛmzˌbʌk) *n., pl.* **-bok, -boks** *or* **-buck, -bucks.** an oryx of southern Africa, marked with a broad black band along its flanks. [C18: < Afrik., < G *Gemsbock,* < *Gemse* chamois + *Bock* BUCK[1]]

gemstone (ˈdʒɛmˌstəʊn) *n.* a precious or semiprecious stone, esp. one cut and polished.

gen (dʒɛn) *n. Brit. inf.* information: *give me the gen on your latest project.* See also **gen up.** [C20: < *gen*(*eral information*)]

gen. *abbrev. for:* **1.** gender. **2.** general(ly). **3.** generic. **4.** genitive. **5.** genus.

Gen. *abbrev. for:* **1.** General. **2.** *Bible.* Genesis.

-gen *suffix forming nouns.* **1.** producing or that which produces: *hydrogen.* **2.** something produced: *carcinogen.* [via F *-gène,* < Gk *-genēs* born]

gendarme (ˈʒɒndɑːm) *n.* **1.** a member of the police force in France or in countries influenced or controlled by France. **2.** a sharp pinnacle of rock on a mountain ridge. [C16: < F, < *gens d'armes* people of arms]

gendarmerie *or* **gendarmery** (ʒɒnˈdɑːmərɪ) *n.* **1.** the whole corps of gendarmes. **2.** the headquarters of a body of gendarmes.

gender (ˈdʒɛndə) *n.* **1.** a set of two or more grammatical categories into which the nouns of certain languages are divided. **2.** any of the categories, such as masculine, feminine, neuter, or common, within such a set. **3.** *Inf.* the state of being male, female, or neuter. **4.** *Inf.* all the members of one sex: *the female gender.* [C14: < OF, < L *genus* kind]

gender-bender *n. Inf.* a person who adopts an androgynous style of dress, hair, etc.

gene (dʒiːn) *n.* a unit of heredity composed of DNA occupying a fixed position on a chromosome and transmitted from parent to offspring during reproduction. [C20: < G *Gen,* shortened < *Pangen;* see PAN-, -GEN]

-gene *suffix forming nouns.* a variant of **-gen.**

genealogy (ˌdʒiːnɪˈælədʒɪ) *n., pl.* **-gies. 1.** the direct descent of an individual or group from an ancestor. **2.** the study of the evolutionary development of animals and plants from earlier forms. **3.** a chart showing the relationships and descent of an individual, group, etc. [C13: < OF, < LL, < Gk, < *genea* race] —**genealogical** (ˌdʒiːnɪəˈlɒdʒɪkᵊl) *adj.* —ˌ**geneaˈlogically** *adv.* —ˌ**geneˈalogist** *n.*

genera (ˈdʒɛnərə) *n.* a plural of **genus.**

general (ˈdʒɛnərəl, ˈdʒɛnrəl) *adj.* **1.** common; widespread. **2.** of, applying to, or participated in by all or most of the members of a group, category, or community. **3.** relating to various branches of an activity, profession, etc.; not specialized: *general office work.* **4.** including various or miscellaneous items: *general knowledge; a general store.* **5.** not specific as to detail; overall: *a general description.* **6.** not definite; vague: *the general idea.* **7.** applicable or true in most cases; usual. **8.** (*prenominal or immediately postpositive*) having superior or extended authority or rank: *general manager; consul general.* ~*n.* **9.** an officer of a rank senior to lieutenant general, esp. one who commands a large military formation. **10.** any person acting as a leader and applying strategy or tactics. **11.** a general condition or principle: opposed to *particular.* **12.** a title for the head of a religious order, congregation, etc. **13.** *Arch.* the people; public. **14. in general.** generally; mostly or usually. [C13: < L *generālis* of a particular kind, < *genus* kind] —ˈ**generalness** *n.*

general anaesthetic *n.* See **anaesthesia.**

General Assembly *n.* **1.** the deliberative assembly of the United Nations. Abbrev.: **GA. 2.** *N.Z.* an older name for **parliament. 3.** the supreme governing body of certain religious denominations, esp. of the Presbyterian Church.

General Certificate of Education *n.* See **GCE.**

general election *n.* **1.** an election in which representatives are chosen in all constituencies of a state. **2.** *U.S.* a final election from which successful candidates are sent to a legislative body. **3.** *U.S. & Canad.* a national, state, or provincial election.

generalissimo (ˌdʒɛnərəˈlɪsɪˌməʊ, ˌdʒɛnrə-) *n., pl.* **-mos.** a supreme commander of combined military, naval, and air forces. [C17: < It., sup. of *generale* GENERAL]

generality (ˌdʒɛnəˈrælɪtɪ) *n., pl.* **-ties. 1.** a principle or observation having general application. **2.** the state or quality of being general. **3.** *Arch.* the majority.

generalization *or* **-isation** (ˌdʒɛnrəlaɪˈzeɪʃən) *n.* **1.** a principle, theory, etc., with general application. **2.** the act or an instance of generalizing. **3.** *Logic.* **a.** the derivation of a universal statement from a particular one by replacing its subject term with a bound variable and prefixing the universal quantifier. **b.** the analogous derivation of any general statement from a particular one.

generalize *or* **-ise** (ˈdʒɛnrəˌlaɪz) *vb.* **1.** to form (general principles or conclusions) from (detailed facts, experience, etc.); infer. **2.** (*intr.*) to think or speak in generalities, esp. in a prejudiced way. **3.** (*tr.; usually passive*) to cause to become widely used or known.

generally (ˈdʒɛnrəlɪ) *adv.* **1.** usually; as a rule. **2.** commonly or widely. **3.** without reference to specific details or facts; broadly.

general practitioner *n.* a physician who does not specialize but has a medical practice (**general practice**) in which he treats all illnesses. Informal name: **family doctor.** Abbrev.: **GP.**

general-purpose *adj.* having a range of uses; not restricted to one function.

generalship (ˈdʒɛnrəlˌʃɪp) *n.* **1.** the art or duties of exercising command of a major military formation or formations. **2.** tactical or administrative skill.

general staff *n.* officers assigned to advise commanders in the planning and execution of military operations.

general strike *n.* a strike by all or most of the workers of a country, province, city, etc.

generate (ˈdʒɛnəˌreɪt) *vb.* (*mainly tr.*) **1.** to produce or bring into being; create. **2.** (*also intr.*) to produce (electricity). **3.** to produce (a substance) by a chemical process. **4.** *Maths, linguistics.* to provide a precise criterion for membership in (a set): *these rules will generate all the noun phrases in English.* **5.** *Geom.* to trace or form by moving a point, line, or plane in a specific way: *circular motion of a line generates a cylinder.* [C16: < L *generāre* to beget, < *genus* kind] —**generable** (ˈdʒɛnərəbᵊl) *adj.*

generation (ˌdʒɛnəˈreɪʃən) *n.* **1.** the act or process of bringing into being; production or reproduction, esp. of offspring. **2.** a successive stage in natural descent of people or animals or the individuals produced at each stage. **3.** the average time between two such generations of a species: about 35 years for humans. **4.** all the people of approximately the same age, esp. when considered as sharing certain attitudes, etc. **5.** production of electricity, heat, etc. **6.** (*modifier, in combination*) **a.** belonging to a generation specified as having been born in or as having parents, grandparents, etc., born in a given country: *a third-generation American.* **b.** belonging to a specified stage of development in manufacture: *a second-generation computer.*

generation gap *n.* the years separating one generation from the next, esp. when regarded as representing the difference in outlook and the lack of understanding between them.

generative (ˈdʒɛnərətɪv) *adj.* **1.** of or relating to the production of offspring, parts, etc. **2.** capable of producing or originating.

generative grammar *n.* a description of a language in terms of explicit rules that ideally generate all and only the grammatical sentences of the language.

generator (ˈdʒɛnəˌreɪtə) *n.* **1.** *Physics.* **a.** any device for converting mechanical energy into electrical energy. **b.** a device for producing a voltage electrostatically. **2.** an apparatus for producing a gas. **3.** a person or thing that generates.

generatrix (ˈdʒɛnəˌreɪtrɪks) *n., pl.* **generatrices** (ˈdʒɛnəˌreɪtrɪˌsiːz). a point, line, or plane moved in a specific way to produce a geometric figure.

generic (dʒɪˈnɛrɪk) *adj.* **1.** applicable or referring to a whole class or group; general. **2.** *Biol.* of, relating to, or belonging to a genus: *the generic name.* **3.** (of a drug, food product, etc.) not having a trademark. [C17: < F; see GENUS] —**geˈnerically** *adv.*

generosity (ˌdʒɛnəˈrɒsɪtɪ) *n., pl.* **-ties.** **1.** willingness and liberality in giving away one's money, time, etc.; magnanimity. **2.** freedom from pettiness in character and mind. **3.** a generous act. **4.** abundance; plenty.

generous (ˈdʒɛnərəs, ˈdʒɛnrəs) *adj.* **1.** willing and liberal in giving away one's money, time, etc.; munificent. **2.** free from pettiness in character and mind. **3.** full or plentiful: *a generous portion.* **4.** (of wine) rich in alcohol. [C16: via OF < L *generōsus* nobly born, < *genus* race] —ˈ**generously** *adv.* —ˈ**generousness** *n.*

genesis (ˈdʒɛnɪsɪs) *n., pl.* **-ses** (-ˌsiːz). a beginning or origin of anything. [OE: via L < Gk; rel. to Gk *gignesthai* to be born]

Genesis (ˈdʒɛnɪsɪs) *n.* the first book of the Old Testament recounting the Creation of the world.

-genesis *n. combining form.* indicating genesis, development, or generation: *biogenesis; parthenogenesis.* [NL, < L: GENESIS] —**-genetic** *or* **-genic** *adj. combining form.*

genet[1] (ˈdʒɛnɪt) *or* **genette** (dʒɪˈnɛt) *n.* **1.** an agile catlike mammal of Africa and S Europe, having thick spotted fur and a very long tail. **2.** the fur of such an animal. [C15: < OF, < Ar. *jarnayt*]

genet[2] (ˈdʒɛnɪt) *n.* an obsolete spelling of **jennet.**

genetic (dʒɪˈnɛtɪk) *or* **genetical** *adj.* of or relating to genetics, genes, or the origin of something. [C19: < GENESIS] —**geˈnetically** *adv.*

genetic code *n. Biochem.* the order in which the four nitrogenous bases of DNA are arranged in the molecule, which determines the type and amount of protein synthesized in the cell.

genetic engineering *n.* alteration of the DNA of a cell as a means of manufacturing animal proteins, making improvements to plants and animals bred by man, etc.

genetic fingerprinting *n.* the pattern of DNA unique to each individual which can be analysed in a sample of blood, saliva, or tissue: used as a means of identification.

genetics (dʒɪˈnɛtɪks) *n.* **1.** (*functioning as sing.*) the study of heredity and variation in organisms. **2.** (*functioning as pl.*) the genetic features and constitution of a single organism, species, or group. —**geˈneticist** *n.*

Geneva bands (dʒɪˈniːvə) *pl. n.* a pair of white linen strips hanging from the front of the collar of some ecclesiastical robes. [C19: after *Geneva,* Switzerland, where orig. worn by Swiss Calvinist clergy]

Geneva Convention *n.* the international agreement, first formulated in 1864 at Geneva, establishing a code for wartime treatment of the sick or wounded: revised and extended to cover maritime warfare and prisoners of war.

Geneva gown *n.* a long loose black gown with very wide sleeves worn by Protestant clerics. [C19: after *Geneva;* see GENEVA BANDS]

genial[1] (ˈdʒiːnjəl, -nɪəl) *adj.* **1.** cheerful, easy-going, and warm in manner. **2.** pleasantly warm, so as to give life, growth, or health. [C16: < L *geniālis* relating to birth or marriage, < *genius* tutelary deity; see GENIUS] —**geniality** (ˌdʒiːnɪˈælɪtɪ) *n.* —ˈ**genially** *adv.*

genial[2] (dʒɪˈniːəl) *adj. Anat.* of or relating to the chin. [C19: < Gk, < *genus* jaw]

genic (ˈdʒɛnɪk) *adj.* of or relating to a gene or genes.

-genic *adj. combining form.* **1.** relating to production or generation: *carcinogenic.* **2.** suited to or suitable for: *photogenic.* [< -GEN + -IC]

genie (ˈdʒiːnɪ) *n., pl.* **-nies** *or* **-nii** (-nɪˌaɪ). **1.** (in fairy tales and stories) a servant who appears by magic and fulfils a person's wishes. **2.** another word for **jinni.** [C18: < F, < Ar. *jinni* demon, infl. by L *genius* attendant spirit; see GENIUS]

genista (dʒɪˈnɪstə) *n.* any of a genus of leguminous deciduous shrubs, usually having yellow, often fragrant, flowers; broom. [C17: < L]

genital (ˈdʒɛnɪtᵊl) *adj.* **1.** of or relating to the sexual organs or to reproduction. **2.** *Psychoanal.* relating to the mature stage of psychosexual development. [C14: < L *genitālis* concerning birth, < *gignere* to beget]

genitals (ˈdʒɛnɪtᵊlz) *or* **genitalia** (ˌdʒɛnɪˈteɪlɪə, -ˈteɪljə) *pl. n.* the external sexual organs.

genitive (ˈdʒɛnɪtɪv) *Grammar.* ~*adj.* **1.** denoting a case of nouns, pronouns, and adjectives in inflected languages used to indicate a relation of ownership or association. ~*n.* **2. a.** the genitive case. **b.** a word or speech element in this case. [C14: < L *genetīvus* relating to birth, < *gignere* to produce] —**genitival** (ˌdʒɛnɪˈtaɪvᵊl) *adj.* —ˌ**geniˈtivally** *adv.*

genitourinary (ˌdʒɛnɪtəʊˈjʊərɪnərɪ) *adj.* another name for **urogenital.**

genius (ˈdʒiːnɪəs, -njəs) *n., pl.* **-uses** *or* (*for senses 5, 6*) **genii** (ˈdʒiːnɪˌaɪ). **1.** a person with exceptional ability, esp. of a highly original kind. **2.** such ability. **3.** the distinctive spirit of a nation, era, language, etc. **4.** a person considered as exerting influence of a certain sort: *an evil genius.* **5.** *Roman myth.* **a.** the guiding spirit who attends a person from birth to death. **b.** the guardian spirit of a place. **6.** (*usually pl.*) *Arabic myth.* a demon; jinn. [C16: < L, < *gignere* to beget]

genizah (gɛˈniːzə) *n. Judaism.* a repository for sacred objects which can no longer be used but which may not be destroyed. [C19: < Heb., lit.: a hiding place]

genoa (ˈdʒɛnəʊə) *n. Yachting.* a large jib sail.

genocide (ˈdʒɛnəʊˌsaɪd) *n.* the policy of deliberately killing a nationality or ethnic group. [C20: < Gk *genos* race + -CIDE] —ˌ**genoˈcidal** *adj.*

genotype (ˈdʒɛnəʊˌtaɪp) *n.* **1.** the genetic constitution of an organism. **2.** a group of organisms with the same genetic constitution. —**genotypic** (ˌdʒɛnəʊˈtɪpɪk) *adj.*

-genous *adj. combining form.* **1.** yielding or generating: *erogenous.* **2.** generated by or issuing from: *endogenous.* [< -GEN + -OUS]

genre (ˈʒɑːnrə) *n.* **1.** kind, category, or sort, esp. of literary or artistic work. **2. a.** a category of painting in which incidents from everyday life are depicted. **b.** (*as modifier*): *genre painting.* [C19: < F, < OF *gendre;* see GENDER]

gens (dʒɛnz) *n., pl.* **gentes** (ˈdʒɛntiːz). **1.** (in ancient Rome) any of a group of families, having a common name and claiming descent from a common ancestor in the male line. **2.** *Anthropol.* a group based on descent in the male line. [C19: < L: race]

gent (dʒɛnt) *n. Inf.* short for **gentleman.**

genteel (dʒɛnˈtiːl) *adj.* **1.** affectedly proper or refined; excessively polite. **2.** respectable, polite, and well-bred. **3.** appropriate to polite or fashionable society. [C16: < F *gentil* well-born; see GENTLE] —**genˈteelly** *adv.* —**genˈteelness** *n.*

gentian (ˈdʒɛnʃən) *n.* **1.** any plant of the genus *Gentiana,* having blue, yellow, white, or red showy flowers. **2.** the bitter-tasting roots of the yellow gentian, which can be used as a tonic. [C14: < L *gentiāna;* ? after *Gentius,* a second-century B.C. Illyrian king, reputedly the first to use it medicinally]

gentian violet *n.* a greenish crystalline substance that forms a violet solution in water, used as an indicator, antiseptic, and in the treatment of burns.

Gentile (ˈdʒɛntaɪl) *n.* **1.** a person, esp. a Christian, who is not a Jew. **2.** a Christian, as contrasted with a Jew. **3.** a person who is not a member of one's own church: used esp. by Mormons. **4.** a heathen or pagan. ~*adj.* **5.** of or relating to a race or religion that is not Jewish. **6.** Christian, as contrasted with Jewish. **7.** not being a member of one's own church: used esp. by Mormons. **8.** pagan or heathen. [C15 *gentil,* < LL *gentīlis,* < L: one belonging to the same tribe]

gentility (dʒɛnˈtɪlɪtɪ) *n., pl.* **-ties. 1.** respectability and polite good breeding. **2.** affected politeness. **3.** noble birth or ancestry. **4.** people of noble birth. [C14: < OF, < L *gentīlitās* relationship of those belonging to the same tribe or family; see GENS]

gentle (ˈdʒɛntᵊl) *adj.* **1.** having a mild or kindly nature or character. **2.** soft or temperate; mild; moderate. **3.** gradual: *a gentle slope.* **4.** easily controlled; tame. **5.** *Arch.* of good breeding; noble: *gentle blood.* **6.** *Arch.* gallant; chivalrous. ~*vb.* (*tr.*) **7.** to tame or subdue (a horse, etc.). **8.** to appease or mollify. ~*n.* **9.** a maggot, esp. when used as bait in fishing. [C13: < OF *gentil* noble, < L *gentīlis* belonging to the same family; see GENS] —**ˈgentleness** *n.* —**ˈgently** *adv.*

gentle breeze *n.* a wind of force 3 on the Beaufort scale, blowing at 8-12 mph.

gentlefolk (ˈdʒɛntᵊlˌfəʊk) *or* **gentlefolks** *pl. n.* persons regarded as being of good breeding.

gentleman (ˈdʒɛntᵊlmən) *n., pl.* **-men. 1.** a man regarded as having qualities of refinement associated with a good family. **2.** a man who is cultured, courteous, and well-educated. **3.** a polite name for a man. **4.** the personal servant of a gentleman (esp. in **gentleman's gentleman**). —**ˈgentlemanly** *adj.* —**ˈgentlemanliness** *n.*

gentleman-farmer *n., pl.* **gentlemen-farmers. 1.** a person who engages in farming but does not depend on it for his living. **2.** a person who owns farmland but does not farm it personally.

gentlemen's agreement *or* **gentleman's agreement** *n.* an understanding or arrangement based on honour and not legally binding.

gentlewoman (ˈdʒɛntᵊlˌwʊmən) *n., pl.* **-women. 1.** *Arch.* a woman regarded as being of good family or breeding; lady. **2.** (formerly) a woman in personal attendance on a high-ranking lady.

gentrification (ˌdʒɛntrɪfɪˈkeɪʃən) *n. Brit.* a process by which middle-class people take up residence in a traditionally working-class area, changing its character. —**ˈgentriˌfy** *vb.* (*tr.*)

gentry (ˈdʒɛntrɪ) *n.* **1.** *Brit.* persons just below the nobility in social rank. **2.** people of a particular class, esp. one considered to be inferior. [C14: < OF *genterie,* < *gentil* GENTLE]

gents (dʒɛnts) *n.* (*functioning as sing.*) *Brit. inf.* a men's public lavatory.

genuflect (ˈdʒɛnjʊˌflɛkt) *vb.* (*intr.*) **1.** to act in a servile or deferential manner. **2.** *R.C. Church.* to bend one or both knees as a sign of reverence. [C17: < Med. L, < L *genu* knee + *flectere* to bend] —ˌ**genuˈflection** *or* (*esp. Brit.*) ˌ**genuˈflexion** *n.* —**ˈgenuˌflector** *n.*

genuine (ˈdʒɛnjʊɪn) *adj.* **1.** not fake or counterfeit; original; real; authentic. **2.** not pretending; frank; sincere. **3.** being of authentic or original stock. [C16: < L *genuīnus* inborn, hence (in LL) authentic] —**ˈgenuinely** *adv.* —**ˈgenuineness** *n.*

gen up *vb.* **genning, genned.** (*adv.; often passive;* when *intr.,* usually foll. by *on*) *Brit. inf.* to make or become fully conversant (with).

genus (ˈdʒiːnəs) *n., pl.* **genera** *or* **genuses. 1.** *Biol.* any of the taxonomic groups into which a family is divided and which contains one or more species. **2.** *Logic.* a class of objects or individuals that can be divided into two or more groups or species. **3.** a class, group, etc., with common characteristics. [C16: < L: race]

-geny *n. combining form.* origin or manner of development: *phylogeny.* [< Gk, < *-genēs* born] —**-genic** *adj. combining form.*

geo- *combining form.* indicating earth: *geomorphology.* [< Gk, < *gē* earth]

geocentric (ˌdʒiːəʊˈsɛntrɪk) *adj.* **1.** having the earth at its centre. **2.** measured as from the centre of the earth. —ˌ**geoˈcentrically** *adv.*

geochronology (ˌdʒiːəʊkrəˈnɒlədʒɪ) *n.* the branch of geology concerned with ordering and dating events in the earth's history. —**geochronological** (ˌdʒiːəʊˌkrɒnᵊˈlɒdʒɪkᵊl) *adj.*

geode (ˈdʒiːəʊd) *n.* a cavity, usually lined with crystals, within a rock mass or nodule. [C17: < L *geōdēs* a precious stone, < Gk: earthlike; see GEO-, -ODE[1]] —**geodic** (dʒɪˈɒdɪk) *adj.*

geodesic (ˌdʒiːəʊˈdɛsɪk, -ˈdiː-) *adj.* **1.** Also: **geodetic.** relating to the geometry of curved surfaces. ~*n.* **2.** Also called: **geodesic line.** the shortest line between two points on a curved surface.

geodesic dome *n.* a light structural framework arranged as a set of polygons in the form of a shell.

geodesy (dʒɪˈɒdɪsɪ) *n.* the branch of science concerned with determining the exact position of geographical points and the shape and size of the earth. [C16: < F, < Gk *geōdaisia,* < GEO- + *daiein* to divide] —**geˈodesist** *n.*

geodetic (ˌdʒiːəʊˈdɛtɪk) *adj.* **1.** of or relating to geodesy. **2.** another word for **geodesic.** —ˌ**geoˈdetically** *adv.*

geog. *abbrev. for:* **1.** geographer. **2.** geographic(al). **3.** geography.

geographical mile *n.* another name for **nautical mile.**

geography (dʒɪˈɒgrəfɪ) *n., pl.* **-phies. 1.** the study of the natural features of the earth's surface, including topography, climate, soil, vegetation, etc., and man's response to them. **2.** the natural features of a region. —**geˈographer** *n.* —**geographical** (ˌdʒɪəˈgræfɪkᵊl) *or* ˌ**geoˈgraphic** *adj.* —ˌ**geoˈgraphically** *adv.*

geoid (ˈdʒiːɔɪd) *n.* **1.** a hypothetical surface that corresponds to mean sea level and extends under the continents. **2.** the shape of the earth.

geol. *abbrev. for:* **1.** geologic(al). **2.** geologist. **3.** geology.

geology (dʒɪˈɒlədʒɪ) *n.* **1.** the scientific study of the origin, structure, and composition of the earth. **2.** the geological features of a district or country. —**geological** (ˌdʒɪəˈlɒdʒɪkᵊl) *or* ˌ**geoˈlogic** *adj.* —ˌ**geoˈlogically** *adv.* —**geˈologist** *n.*

geom. *abbrev. for:* **1.** geometric(al). **2.** geometry.

geomagnetism (ˌdʒiːəʊˈmægnɪˌtɪzəm) *n.* **1.** the magnetic field of the earth. **2.** the branch of physics concerned with this. —**geomagnetic** (ˌdʒiːəʊmægˈnɛtɪk) *adj.*

geometric (ˌdʒɪəˈmɛtrɪk) *or* **geometrical** *adj.* **1.** of, relating to, or following the methods and principles of geometry. **2.** consisting of, formed by, or characterized by points, lines, curves, or surfaces. **3.** (of design or ornamentation) composed predominantly of simple geometric forms, such as circles, triangles, etc. —ˌ**geoˈmetrically** *adv.*

geometric mean *n.* the average value of a set of *n* integers, terms, or quantities, expressed as the *n*th root of their product.

geometric progression *n.* **1.** a sequence of numbers, each of which differs from the succeeding one by a constant ratio, as 1, 2, 4, 8, ...

Cf. **arithmetic progression.** **2. geometric series.** such numbers written as a sum.

geometrid (dʒɪˈɒmɪtrɪd) *n.* any of a family of moths, the larvae of which are called measuring worms, inchworms, or loopers. [C19: < NL, < L, < Gk *geometrēs* land measurer, < the looping gait of the larvae]

geometry (dʒɪˈɒmɪtrɪ) *n.* **1.** the branch of mathematics concerned with the properties, relationships, and measurement of points, lines, curves, and surfaces. **2.** a shape, configuration, or arrangement. [C14: < L, < Gk, < *geōmetrein* to measure the land] **—geˌomeˈtrician** *n.*

geomorphology (ˌdʒiːəʊmɔːˈfɒlədʒɪ) *n.* the branch of geology that is concerned with the structure, origin, and development of the topographical features of the earth's crust. **—geomorphological** (ˌdʒiːəʊˌmɔːfəˈlɒdʒɪkᵊl) *or* **ˌgeoˌmorphoˈlogic** *adj.*

geophysics (ˌdʒiːəʊˈfɪzɪks) *n.* (*functioning as sing.*) the study of the earth's physical properties and of the physical processes acting upon, above, and within the earth. It includes seismology, meteorology, and oceanography. **—ˌgeoˈphysical** *adj.* **—ˌgeoˈphysicist** *n.*

geopolitics (ˌdʒiːəʊˈpɒlɪtɪks) *n.* **1.** (*functioning as sing.*) the study of the effect of geographical factors on politics. **2.** (*functioning as pl.*) the combination of geographical and political factors affecting a country or area. **3.** (*functioning as pl.*) politics as they affect the whole world; global politics. **—geopolitical** (ˌdʒiːəʊpəˈlɪtɪkᵊl) *adj.* **—ˌgeoˌpoliˈtician** *n.*

George Cross (dʒɔːdʒ) *n.* a British award for bravery, esp. of civilians. Abbrev.: **GC.**

georgette *or* **georgette crepe** (dʒɔːˈdʒɛt) *n.* a thin silk or cotton crepe fabric. [C20: < Mme *Georgette*, a F modiste]

Georgian (ˈdʒɔːdʒjən) *adj.* **1.** of or relating to any or all of the four kings who ruled Great Britain from 1714 to 1830, or to their reigns: *Georgian architecture.* **2.** of or relating to George V of Great Britain or his reign (1910–36): *the Georgian poets.* **3.** of or relating to the Georgian SSR, its people, or their language. **4.** of or relating to the American State of Georgia or its inhabitants. **5.** (of furniture, furnishings, etc.) in or imitative of the style prevalent in England during the 18th century. *~n.* **6.** the official language of the Georgian SSR, belonging to the South Caucasian family. **7.** a native or inhabitant of the Georgian SSR. **8.** a native or inhabitant of the American State of Georgia.

geostatics (ˌdʒiːəʊˈstætɪks) *n.* (*functioning as sing.*) the branch of physics concerned with the statics of rigid bodies, esp. the balance of forces within the earth.

geostationary (ˌdʒiːəʊˈsteɪʃənərɪ) *adj.* (of a satellite, etc.) orbiting at such speed that it appears to remain stationary with respect to the earth's surface.

geostrophic (ˌdʒiːəʊˈstrɒfɪk) *adj.* of, relating to, or caused by the force produced by the rotation of the earth: *geostrophic wind.*

geosyncline (ˌdʒiːəʊˈsɪŋklaɪn) *n.* a broad elongated depression in the earth's crust.

geothermal (ˌdʒiːəʊˈθɜːməl) *or* **geothermic** *adj.* of or relating to the heat in the interior of the earth.

geotropism (dʒɪˈɒtrəˌpɪzəm) *n.* the response of a plant part to the stimulus of gravity. Plant stems, which grow upwards irrespective of the position in which they are placed, show **negative geotropism.** **—geotropic** (ˌdʒiːəʊˈtrɒpɪk) *adj.*

ger. *abbrev. for:* **1.** gerund. **2.** gerundive.

Ger. *abbrev. for:* **1.** German. **2.** Germany.

geranium (dʒɪˈreɪnɪəm) *n.* **1.** a cultivated plant of the genus *Pelargonium* having scarlet, pink, or white showy flowers. See also **pelargonium.** **2.** any plant such as cranesbill and herb Robert, having divided leaves and pink or purplish flowers. [C16: < L: cranesbill, < Gk, < *geranos* CRANE]

gerbera (ˈdʒɜːbərə) *n.* a genus of African or Asian plants belonging to the composite family, esp. the Transvaal daisy. [C19: < NL, after T. *Gerber* (died 1743), G naturalist]

gerbil *or* **gerbille** (ˈdʒɜːbɪl) *n.* a burrowing rodent inhabiting hot dry regions of Asia and Africa. [C19: < F, < NL *gerbillus* a little JERBOA]

gerfalcon (ˈdʒɜːˌfɔːlkən, -ˌfɔːkən) *n.* a variant spelling of **gyrfalcon.**

geriatric (ˌdʒɛrɪˈætrɪk) *adj.* **1.** of or relating to geriatrics or to elderly people. **2.** *Inf.* old, decrepit, or useless. *~n.* **3.** an elderly person. [C20: < Gk *gēras* old age + -IATRIC]

geriatrics (ˌdʒɛrɪˈætrɪks) *n.* (*functioning as sing.*) the branch of medical science concerned with the diagnosis and treatment of diseases affecting elderly people. **—ˌgeriaˈtrician** *n.*

germ (dʒɜːm) *n.* **1.** a microorganism, esp. one that produces disease. **2.** (*often pl.*) the rudimentary or initial form of something: *the germs of revolution.* **3.** a simple structure that is capable of developing into a complete organism. [C17: < F, < L *germen* sprout, seed]

german (ˈdʒɜːmən) *adj.* **1.** (used in combination) **a.** having the same parents as oneself: *a brother-german.* **b.** having a parent that is a brother or sister of either of one's own parents: *cousin-german.* **2.** a less common word for **germane.** [C14: via OF, < L *germānus* of the same race, < *germen* sprout, offshoot]

German (ˈdʒɜːmən) *n.* **1.** the official language of East and West Germany and Austria and one of the official languages of Switzerland. **2.** a native, inhabitant, or citizen of East or West Germany. **3.** a person whose native language is German. *~adj.* **4.** denoting, relating to, or using the German language. **5.** relating to, denoting, or characteristic of any German state or its people.

germander (dʒɜːˈmændə) *n.* any of several plants of Europe, having two-lipped flowers with a very small upper lip. [C15: < Med. L, ult. < Gk *khamai* on the ground + *drus* oak tree]

germane (dʒɜːˈmeɪn) *adj.* (*postpositive; usually foll. by to*) related (to the topic being considered); akin; relevant. [var. of GERMAN] **—gerˈmanely** *adv.* **—gerˈmaneness** *n.*

Germanic (dʒɜːˈmænɪk) *n.* **1.** a branch of the Indo-European family of languages that includes English, Dutch, German, the Scandinavian languages, and Gothic. Abbrev.: **Gmc.** **2.** Also called: **Proto-Germanic.** the unrecorded language from which all of these languages developed. *~adj.* **3.** of, denoting, or relating to this group of languages. **4.** of, relating to, or characteristic of the German language or any people that speaks a Germanic language. **5.** (formerly) of the German people.

germanium (dʒɜːˈmeɪnɪəm) *n.* a brittle crystalline grey element that is a semiconducting metalloid: used in transistors, and to strengthen alloys. Symbol: Ge; atomic no.: 32; atomic wt.: 72.59. [C19: NL, after *Germany*]

German measles *n.* (*functioning as sing.*) a nontechnical name for **rubella.**

German shepherd dog *n.* another name for **Alsatian.**

German silver *n.* another name for **nickel silver.**

germ cell *n.* a sexual reproductive cell.

germicide (ˈdʒɜːmɪˌsaɪd) *n.* any substance that kills germs. **—ˌgermiˈcidal** *adj.*

germinal (ˈdʒɜːmɪnᵊl) *adj.* **1.** of, relating to, or like germs or a germ cell. **2.** of or in the earliest stage of development. [C19: < NL, < L *germen* bud; see GERM] **—ˈgerminally** *adv.*

germinate (ˈdʒɜːmɪˌneɪt) *vb.* **1.** to cause (seeds or spores) to sprout or (of seeds or spores) to sprout. **2.** to grow or cause to grow; develop. **3.** to come or bring into existence; originate: *the idea germinated with me.* [C17: < L *germināre* to sprout; see GERM] **—ˈgerminative** *adj.* **—ˌgermiˈnation** *n.* **—ˈgermiˌnator** *n.*

germ plasm *n.* **a.** the part of a germ cell that contains hereditary material. **b.** the germ cells collectively.

germ warfare *n.* the military use of disease-spreading bacteria against an enemy.

gerontology (ˌdʒɛrɒnˈtɒlədʒɪ) *n.* the scientific study of ageing and the problems associated with elderly people. —**gerontological** (ˌdʒɛrɒntəˈlɒdʒɪkᵊl) *adj.* —ˌ**geronˈtologist** *n.*

-gerous *adj. combining form.* bearing or producing: *armigerous.* [< L *-ger* bearing + -OUS]

gerrymander (ˈdʒɛrɪˌmændə) *vb.* **1.** to divide the constituencies of (a voting area) so as to give one party an unfair advantage. **2.** to manipulate or adapt to one's advantage. ~*n.* **3.** an act or result of gerrymandering. [C19: from Elbridge *Gerry,* U.S. politician + (SALA)MANDER; < the salamander-like outline of an electoral district reshaped (1812) for political purposes while Gerry was governor of Massachusetts]

gerund (ˈdʒɛrənd) *n.* a noun formed from a verb, ending in *-ing,* denoting an action or state: *the living is easy.* [C16: < LL, < L *gerundum* something to be carried on, < *gerere* to wage] —**gerundial** (dʒɪˈrʌndɪəl) *adj.*

gerundive (dʒɪˈrʌndɪv) *n.* **1.** (in Latin grammar) an adjective formed from a verb, expressing the desirability, etc., of the activity denoted by the verb. ~*adj.* **2.** of or relating to the gerund or gerundive. [C17: < LL, < *gerundium* GERUND] —**gerundival** (ˌdʒɛrənˈdaɪvᵊl) *adj.*

gesso (ˈdʒɛsəʊ) *n.* **1.** a white ground of plaster and size, used to prepare panels or canvas for painting or gilding. **2.** any white substance, esp. plaster of Paris, that forms a ground when mixed with water. [C16: < It.: chalk, GYPSUM]

gest *or* **geste** (dʒɛst) *n. Arch.* **1.** a notable deed or exploit. **2.** a tale of adventure or romance, esp. in verse. [C14: < OF, < L *gesta* deeds, < *gerere* to carry out]

Gestalt psychology (gəˈʃtælt) *n.* a system of thought that regards all mental phenomena as being arranged in patterns or structures (**gestalts**) perceived as a whole and not merely as the sum of their parts. [C20: < G *Gestalt* form]

Gestapo (gɛˈstɑːpəʊ) *n.* the secret state police in Nazi Germany. [< G *Ge(heime) Sta(ats)po(lizei)* lit.: secret state police]

gestate (ˈdʒɛsteɪt) *vb.* **1.** (*tr.*) to carry (developing young) in the uterus during pregnancy. **2.** (*tr.*) to develop (a plan or idea) in the mind. **3.** (*intr.*) to be in the process of gestating. [C19: < L p.p. of *gestare,* < *gerere* to bear] —**gesˈtation** *n.*

gesticulate (dʒɛˈstɪkjʊˌleɪt) *vb.* to express by or make gestures. [C17: < L, < *gesticulus* (unattested except in LL) gesture, < *gerere* to bear, conduct] —**gesˌticuˈlation** *n.* —**gesˈticulative** *adj.* —**gesˈticuˌlator** *n.* —**gesˈticulatory** *adj.*

gesture (ˈdʒɛstʃə) *n.* **1.** a motion of the hands, head, or body to express or emphasize an idea or emotion. **2.** something said or done as a formality or as an indication of intention. ~*vb.* **3.** to express by or make gestures; gesticulate. [C15: < Med. L *gestūra* bearing, < L *gestus,* p.p. of *gerere* to bear] —ˈ**gestural** *adj.* —ˈ**gesturer** *n.*

get (gɛt) *vb.* **getting, got.** (*mainly tr.*) **1.** to come into possession of; receive or earn. **2.** to bring or fetch. **3.** to contract or be affected by: *he got a chill.* **4.** to capture or seize: *the police got him.* **5.** (*also intr.*) to become or cause to become or act as specified: *to get one's hair cut; get wet.* **6.** (*intr.;* foll. by a preposition or adverbial particle) to succeed in going, coming, leaving, etc.: *get off the bus.* **7.** (*takes an infinitive*) to manage or contrive: *how did you get to be captain?* **8.** to make ready or prepare: *to get a meal.* **9.** to hear, notice, or understand: *I didn't get your meaning.* **10.** to learn or master by study. **11.** (*intr.;* often foll. by *to*) to come (to) or arrive (at): *we got home safely; to get to London.* **12.** to catch or enter: *to get a train.* **13.** to induce or persuade: *get him to leave.* **14.** to reach by calculation: *add 2 and 2 and you will get 4.* **15.** to receive (a broadcast signal). **16.** to communicate with (a person or place), as by telephone. **17.** (*also intr.;* foll. by *to*) *Inf.* to have an emotional effect (on): *that music really gets me.* **18.** *Inf.* to annoy or irritate: *her voice gets me.* **19.** *Inf.* to bring a person into a difficult position from which he cannot escape. **20.** *Inf.* to puzzle; baffle. **21.** *Inf.* to hit: *the blow got him in the back.* **22.** *Inf.* to be revenged on, esp. by killing. **23.** *Inf.* to have the better of: *your extravagant habits will get you in the end.* **24.** (*intr.;* foll. by present participle) *Inf.* to begin: *get moving.* **25.** (used as a command) *Inf.* go! leave now! **26.** *Arch.* to beget or conceive. **27. get with child.** *Arch.* to make pregnant. ~*n.* **28.** *Rare.* the act of begetting. **29.** *Rare.* something begotten; offspring. **30.** *Brit. sl.* a variant of **git.** ~See also **get about, get across,** etc. [OE *gietan*] —ˈ**getable** *or* ˈ**gettable** *adj.* —ˈ**getter** *n.*

get about *or* **around** *vb.* (*intr., adv.*) **1.** to move around, as when recovering from an illness. **2.** to be socially active. **3.** (of news, rumour, etc.) to become known; spread.

get across *vb.* **1.** to cross or cause to cross. **2.** (*adv.*) to be or cause to be understood.

get at *vb.* (*intr., prep.*) **1.** to gain access to. **2.** to mean or intend: *what are you getting at?* **3.** to irritate or annoy persistently; criticize: *she is always getting at him.* **4.** to influence or seek to influence, esp. illegally by bribery, intimidation, etc.: *someone had got at the witness before the trial.*

get away *vb.* (*adv., mainly intr.*) **1.** to make an escape; leave. **2.** to make a start. **3. get away with. a.** to steal and escape with (money, goods, etc.). **b.** to do (something wrong, illegal, etc.) without being discovered or punished. ~*interj.* **4.** an exclamation indicating mild disbelief. ~*n.* **getaway. 5.** the act of escaping, esp. by criminals. **6.** a start or acceleration. **7.** (*modifier*) used for escaping: *a getaway car.*

get back *vb.* (*adv.*) **1.** (*tr.*) to recover or retrieve. **2.** (*intr.;* often foll. by *to*) to return, esp. to a former position or activity. **3.** (*intr.;* foll. by *at*) to retaliate (against); wreak vengeance (on). **4. get one's own back.** *Inf.* to obtain one's revenge.

get by *vb.* **1.** to pass; go past or overtake. **2.** (*intr., adv.*) *Inf.* to manage, esp. in spite of difficulties. **3.** (*intr.*) to be accepted or permitted: *that book will never get by the authorities.*

get in *vb.* (*mainly adv.*) **1.** (*intr.*) to enter a car, train, etc. **2.** (*intr.*) to arrive, esp. at one's home or place of work. **3.** (*tr.*) to bring in or inside: *get the milk in.* **4.** (*tr.*) to insert or slip in: *he got his suggestion in before anyone else.* **5.** (*tr.*) to gather or collect (crops, debts, etc.). **6.** to be elected or cause to be elected. **7.** (*intr.*) to obtain a place at university, college, etc. **8.** (foll. by *on*) to join or cause to join (an activity or organization).

get off *vb.* **1.** (*intr., adv.*) to escape the consequences of an action: *he got off very lightly.* **2.** (*adv.*) to be or cause to be acquitted: *a good lawyer got him off.* **3.** (*adv.*) to depart or cause to depart: *to get the children off to school.* **4.** (*intr.*) to descend (from a bus, train, etc.); dismount: *she got off at the terminus.* **5.** to move or cause to move to a distance (from): *get off the field.* **6.** (*tr., adv.*) to remove; take off: *get your coat off.* **7.** (*adv.*) to go or send to sleep. **8.** (*adv.*) to send (letters) or (of letters) to be sent. **9. get off with.** *Brit. inf.* to establish an amorous or sexual relationship (with).

get on *vb.* (*mainly adv.*) **1.** Also (*when prep.*): **get onto.** to board or cause or help to board (a bus, train, etc.). **2.** (*tr.*) to dress in (clothes as specified). **3.** (*intr.*) to grow late or (of time) to elapse: *it's getting on and I must go.* **4.** (*intr.*) (of a person) to grow old. **5.** (*intr.;* foll. by *for*) to approach (a time, age, amount, etc.): *she is getting on for seventy.* **6.** (*intr.*) to make progress, manage, or fare: *how did you get on in your exam?* **7.** (*intr.;* often foll. by *with*) to establish a friendly relationship: *he gets on well with other people.* **8.** (*intr.;* foll. by *with*) to continue to do: *get on with your homework!*

get out *vb.* (*adv.*) **1.** to leave or escape or cause to leave or escape: used in the imperative when dismissing a person. **2.** to make or become known; publish or be published. **3.** (*tr.*) to express with difficulty. **4.** (*tr.;* often foll. by *of*) to extract (information or money) (from a person): *to get a confession out of a criminal.* **5.** (*tr.*) to gain or receive something, esp. something of significance or value. **6.** (foll. by *of*) to avoid or cause to avoid: *she always gets out of swimming.* **7.** *Cricket.* to dismiss or be dismissed.

get over *vb.* **1.** to cross or surmount (something). **2.** (*intr., prep.*) to recover from (an illness, shock, etc.). **3.** (*intr., prep.*) to overcome or master (a problem). **4.** (*intr., prep.*) to appreciate fully: *I just can't get over seeing you again.* **5.** (*tr., adv.*) to communicate effectively. **6.** (*tr., adv.;* sometimes foll. by *with*) to bring (something necessary but unpleasant) to an end: *let's get this job over with quickly.*

get round *or* **around** *vb.* (*intr.*) **1.** (*prep.*) to circumvent or overcome. **2.** (*prep.*) *Inf.* to have one's way with; cajole: *that girl can get round anyone.* **3.** (*prep.*) to evade (a law or rules). **4.** (*adv.;* foll. by *to*) to reach or come to at length: *I'll get round to that job in an hour.*

get through *vb.* **1.** to succeed or cause or help to succeed in an examination, test, etc. **2.** to bring or come to a destination, esp. after overcoming problems: *we got through the blizzards to the survivors.* **3.** (*intr., adv.*) to contact, as by telephone. **4.** (*intr., prep.*) to use, spend, or consume (money, supplies, etc.). **5.** to complete or cause to complete (a task, process, etc.): *to get a bill through Parliament.* **6.** (*adv.;* foll. by *to*) to reach the awareness and understanding (of a person): *I just can't get the message through to him.*

get-together *n.* **1.** *Inf.* a small informal meeting or social gathering. *~vb.* **get together.** (*adv.*) **2.** (*tr.*) to gather or collect. **3.** (*intr.*) (of people) to meet socially. **4.** (*intr.*) to discuss, esp. in order to reach an agreement.

get up *vb.* (*mainly adv.*) **1.** to wake and rise from one's bed or cause to wake and rise from bed. **2.** (*intr.*) to rise to one's feet; stand up. **3.** (*also prep.*) to ascend or cause to ascend. **4.** to increase or cause to increase in strength: *the wind got up at noon.* **5.** (*tr.*) *Inf.* to dress (oneself) in a particular way, esp. elaborately. **6.** (*tr.*) *Inf.* to devise or create: *to get up an entertainment for Christmas.* **7.** (*tr.*) *Inf.* to study or improve one's knowledge of: *I must get up my history.* **8.** (*intr.;* foll. by *to*) *Inf.* to be involved in: *he's always getting up to mischief.* *~n.* **get-up.** *Inf.* **9.** a costume or outfit. **10.** the arrangement or production of a book, etc.

get-up-and-go *n. Inf.* energy or drive.

geum ('dʒiːəm) *n.* any herbaceous plant of the rose type, having compound leaves and red, orange, yellow, or white flowers. [C19: NL, < L: herb bennet, avens]

gewgaw ('gjuːgɔː, 'guː-) *n.* a showy but valueless trinket. [C15: <?]

geyser ('giːzə; *U.S.* 'gaɪzər) *n.* **1.** a spring that discharges steam and hot water. **2.** *Brit.* a domestic gas water heater. [C18: < Icelandic *Geysir,* < ON *geysa* to gush]

G-force *n.* the force of gravity.

gharry *or* **gharri** ('gærɪ) *n., pl.* **-ries.** a horse-drawn vehicle used in India. [C19: < Hindi *gāṛī*]

ghastly ('gɑːstlɪ) *adj.* **-lier, -liest. 1.** *Inf.* very bad or unpleasant. **2.** deathly pale; wan. **3.** *Inf.* extremely unwell; ill. **4.** terrifying; horrible. *~adv.* **5.** unhealthily; sickly: *ghastly pale.* [OE *gāstlīc* spiritual] —'**ghastliness** *n.*

ghat (gɔːt) *n.* (in India) **1.** stairs or a passage leading down to a river. **2.** a mountain pass. [C17: < Hindi, < Sansk.]

ghazi ('gɑːzɪ) *n., pl.* **-zis. 1.** a Muslim fighter against infidels. **2.** (*often cap.*) a Turkish warrior of high rank. [C18: < Ar., < *ghazā* he made war]

ghee (giː) *n.* a clarified butter used in Indian cookery. [C17: < Hindi *ghī,* < Sansk. *ghri* sprinkle]

gherkin ('gɜːkɪn) *n.* **1.** the small immature fruit of any of various cucumbers, used for pickling. **2. a.** a tropical American climbing plant. **b.** its small spiny edible fruit. [C17: < Du., dim. of *gurk,* ult. < Gk *angourion*]

ghetto ('gɛtəʊ) *n., pl.* **-tos** *or* **-toes. 1.** a densely populated slum area of a city inhabited by a socially and economically deprived minority. **2.** an area or community that is segregated or isolated. **3.** an area in a European city in which Jews were formerly required to live. [C17: < It., ? < *borghetto,* dim. of *borgo* settlement outside a walled city, or < *ghetto* foundry, because one occupied the site of the later Venetian ghetto]

ghetto blaster *n. Inf.* a portable cassette recorder with built-in speakers.

ghillie ('gɪlɪ) *n.* a variant spelling of **gillie.**

ghost (gəʊst) *n.* **1.** the disembodied spirit of a dead person, supposed to haunt the living as a pale or shadowy vision; phantom. Related adj.: **spectral. 2.** a haunting memory: *the ghost of his former life rose up before him.* **3.** a faint trace or possibility of something; glimmer: *a ghost of a smile.* **4.** the spirit; soul (archaic, except in **the Holy Ghost**). **5.** *Physics.* **a.** a faint secondary image produced by an optical system. **b.** a similar image on a television screen. **6. give up the ghost.** to die. *~vb.* **7.** See **ghostwrite. 8.** (*tr.*) to haunt. [OE *gāst*] —'**ghost,like** *adj.* —'**ghostly** *adj.*

ghost town *n.* a deserted town, esp. one in the western U.S. that was formerly a boom town.

ghost word *n.* a word that has entered the language through the perpetuation, in dictionaries, etc., of an error.

ghostwrite ('gəʊst,raɪt) *vb.* **-writing, -wrote, -written.** to write (an article, etc.) on behalf of a person who is then credited as author. Often shortened to **ghost.** —'**ghost,writer** *n.*

ghoul (guːl) *n.* **1.** a malevolent spirit or ghost. **2.** a person interested in morbid or disgusting things. **3.** a person who robs graves. **4.** (in Muslim legend) an evil demon thought to eat corpses. [C18: < Ar. *ghūl,* < *ghāla* he seized] —'**ghoulish** *adj.* —'**ghoulishly** *adv.* —'**ghoulishness** *n.*

GHQ *Mil. abbrev. for* General Headquarters.

ghyll (gɪl) *n.* a variant spelling of **gill**[3].

GI *n. U.S. inf.* **1.** (*pl.* **GIs** *or* **GI's**) a soldier in the U.S. Army, esp. an enlisted man. *~adj.* **2.** conforming to U.S. Army regulations. [C20: abbrev. of *government issue*]

gi. *abbrev. for* gill (unit of measure).

giant ('dʒaɪənt) *n.* **1.** Also (fem.): **giantess** ('dʒaɪəntɪs). a mythical figure of superhuman size and strength, esp. in folklore or fairy tales. **2.** a person or thing of exceptional size, reputation, etc. *~adj.* **3.** remarkably or supernaturally large. [C13: < OF *geant,* < L *gigant-, gigās,* < Gk]

giant hogweed *n.* a species of cow parsley that grows up to 3½ metres (10 ft.) and whose irritant hairs and sap can cause a severe reaction.

giantism ('dʒaɪən,tɪzəm) *n.* another term for **gigantism** (sense 1).

giant panda *n.* See **panda.**

giant star *n.* any of a class of very bright stars having a diameter up to 100 times that of the sun.

giaour ('dʒaʊə) *n.* a derogatory term for a non-Muslim, esp. a Christian. [C16: < Turkish: unbeliever, < Persian *gaur*]

gib (gɪb) *n.* **1.** a metal wedge, pad, or thrust bearing, esp. a brass plate let into a steam engine crosshead. *~vb.* **gibbing, gibbed. 2.** (*tr.*) to fasten or supply with a gib. [C18: <?]

Gib (dʒɪb) *n.* an informal name for Gibraltar.

gibber[1] ('dʒɪbə) *vb.* **1.** to utter rapidly and unintelligibly; prattle. **2.** (*intr.*) (of monkeys and related animals) to make characteristic chattering sounds. [C17: imit.]

gibber[2] ('dʒɪbə) *n. Austral.* **1.** a stone or boulder. **2.** (*modifier*) of or relating to a dry flat area of land covered with wind-polished stones: *gibber plains.* [C19: < Abor.]

gibberellin (,dʒɪbə'rɛlɪn) *n.* any of several plant hormones whose main action is to cause elongation of the stem. [C20: < NL *Gibberella,* lit.: a little hump, < L *gibber* hump + -IN]

gibberish ('dʒɪbərɪʃ) *n.* **1.** rapid chatter. **2.** incomprehensible talk; nonsense.

gibbet ('dʒɪbɪt) *n.* **1. a.** a wooden structure resembling a gallows, from which the bodies of executed criminals were formerly hung to public view. **b.** a gallows. ~*vb.* (*tr.*) **2.** to put to death by hanging on a gibbet. **3.** to hang (a corpse) on a gibbet. **4.** to expose to public ridicule. [C13: < OF: gallows, lit.: little cudgel, < *gibe* cudgel; <?]

gibbon (ˈgɪbᵊn) *n.* a small agile arboreal anthropoid ape inhabiting forests in S Asia. [C18: < F, prob. < an Indian dialect word]

gibbous (ˈgɪbəs) *or* **gibbose** (ˈgɪbəʊs) *adj.* **1.** (of the moon or a planet) more than half but less than fully illuminated. **2.** hunchbacked. **3.** bulging. [C17: < LL *gibbōsus* humpbacked, < L *gibba* hump] —ˈ**gibbously** *adv.* —ˈ**gibbousness** *or* **gibbosity** (gɪˈbɒsɪtɪ) *n.*

gibe[1] *or* **jibe** (dʒaɪb) *vb.* **1.** to make jeering or scoffing remarks (at); taunt. ~*n.* **2.** a derisive or provoking remark. [C16: ? < OF *giber* to treat roughly, <?] —ˈ**giber** *or* ˈ**jiber** *n.*

gibe[2] (dʒaɪb) *vb., n. Naut.* a variant spelling of **gybe.**

giblets (ˈdʒɪblɪts) *pl. n.* (*sometimes sing.*) the gizzard, liver, heart, and neck of a fowl. [C14: < OF *gibelet* stew of game birds, prob. < *gibier* game, of Gmc origin]

gidday (gəˈdaɪ) *sentence substitute.* an Austral. and N.Z. informal variant of **good day.**

giddy (ˈgɪdɪ) *adj.* **-dier, -diest.** **1.** affected with a reeling sensation and feeling as if about to fall; dizzy. **2.** causing or tending to cause vertigo. **3.** impulsive; scatterbrained. ~*vb.* **giddying, giddied.** **4.** to make or become giddy. [OE *gydig* mad, frenzied, possessed by God; rel. to GOD] —ˈ**giddily** *adv.* —ˈ**giddiness** *n.*

gidgee *or* **gidjee** (ˈgɪdʒiː) *n. Austral.* **1.** a small acacia tree yielding useful timber. **2.** a spear made of this. [C19: < Abor.]

gie (giː) *vb.* a Scot. word for **give.**

gift (gɪft) *n.* **1.** something given; a present. **2.** a special aptitude, ability, or power; talent. **3.** the power or right to give or bestow (esp. in **in the gift of, in (someone's) gift**). **4.** the act or process of giving. **5. look a gift-horse in the mouth.** (*usually negative*) to find fault with a free gift or chance benefit. ~*vb.* (*tr.*) **6.** to present (something) as a gift to (a person). [OE *gift* payment for a wife, dowry; see GIVE]

gifted (ˈgɪftɪd) *adj.* having or showing natural talent or aptitude: *a gifted musician.* —ˈ**giftedly** *adv.* —ˈ**giftedness** *n.*

gift of tongues *n.* an utterance, partly or wholly unintelligible, produced under the influence of ecstatic religious emotion. Also called: **glossolalia.**

giftwrap (ˈgɪftˌræp) *vb.* **-wrapping, -wrapped.** to wrap (a gift) attractively.

gig[1] (gɪg) *n.* **1.** a light two-wheeled one-horse carriage without a hood. **2.** *Naut.* a light tender for a vessel. **3.** a long light rowing boat, used esp. for racing. ~*vb.* **gigging, gigged.** **4.** (*intr.*) to travel in a gig. [C13 (in the sense: flighty girl, spinning top): ? < ON]

gig[2] (gɪg) *n.* **1.** a cluster of barbless hooks drawn through a shoal of fish to try to impale them. ~*vb.* **gigging, gigged.** **2.** to catch (fish) with a gig. [C18: ? shortened from obs. *fishgig* or *fizgig* kind of harpoon]

gig[3] (gɪg) *n.* **1.** a job, esp. a single booking for jazz or pop musicians. **2.** the performance itself. ~*vb.* **gigging, gigged.** **3.** (*intr.*) to perform a gig. [C20: <?]

giga- (ˈgɪgə-, ˈgaɪgə) *combining form.* **1.** denoting 10^9: *gigavolt.* **2.** *Computers.* denoting 2^{30}: *gigabyte.* Symbol: G [< Gk *gigas* GIANT]

gigahertz (ˈgaɪgəˌhɜːts, ˈdʒɪg-) *n., pl.* **-hertz.** a unit of frequency equal to 10^9 hertz. Symbol: GHz

gigantic (dʒaɪˈgæntɪk) *adj.* **1.** very large; enormous. **2.** Also: **gigantesque** (ˌdʒaɪgænˈtɛsk). of or suitable for giants. [C17: < Gk *gigantikos,* < *gigas* GIANT] —**giˈgantically** *adv.*

gigantism (ˈdʒaɪgænˌtɪzəm, dʒaɪˈgæntɪzəm) *n.* **1.** Also called: **giantism.** excessive growth of the entire body, caused by overproduction of growth hormone by the pituitary gland. **2.** the state or quality of being gigantic.

giggle (ˈgɪgᵊl) *vb.* **1.** (*intr.*) to laugh nervously or foolishly. ~*n.* **2.** such a laugh. **3.** *Inf.* something or someone that causes amusement. [C16: imit.] —ˈ**giggler** *n.* —ˈ**giggling** *adj., n.* —ˈ**giggly** *adj.*

gigolo (ˈʒɪgəˌləʊ) *n., pl.* **-los.** **1.** a man who is kept by a woman, esp. an older woman. **2.** a man who is paid to dance with or escort women. [C20: < F, back formation < *gigolette* girl for hire as a dancing partner, prostitute, ult. < *gigue* a fiddle]

gigot (ˈdʒɪgət) *n.* **1.** a leg of lamb or mutton. **2.** a leg-of-mutton sleeve. [C16: < OF: leg, a small fiddle, < *gigue* a fiddle, of Gmc origin]

gigue (ʒiːg) *n.* a piece of music, usually in six-eight time, incorporated into the classical suite. [C17: < F, < It. *giga,* lit.: a fiddle; see GIGOT]

Gila monster (ˈhiːlə) *n.* a large venomous brightly coloured lizard inhabiting deserts of the southwestern U.S. and Mexico.

gilbert (ˈgɪlbət) *n.* the cgs unit of magnetomotive force. Symbol: Gb, Gi [C19: after William *Gilbert* (1540-1603), E scientist]

gild[1] (gɪld) *vb.* **gilding, gilded** *or* **gilt.** (*tr.*) **1.** to cover with or as if with gold. **2. gild the lily. a.** to adorn unnecessarily something already beautiful. **b.** to praise someone inordinately. **3.** to give a falsely attractive or valuable appearance to. [OE *gyldan,* < *gold* GOLD] —ˈ**gilder** *n.*

gild[2] (gɪld) *n.* a variant spelling of **guild.**

gilding (ˈgɪldɪŋ) *n.* **1.** the act or art of applying gilt to a surface. **2.** the surface so produced. **3.** another word for **gilt**[1] (sense 2).

gilet (dʒɪˈleɪ) *n.* a garment resembling a waistcoat. [C20: F, lit.: waistcoat]

gill[1] (gɪl) *n.* **1.** the respiratory organ in many aquatic animals. **2.** any of the radiating leaflike spore-producing structures on the undersurface of the cap of a mushroom. [C14: < ON] —**gilled** *adj.*

gill[2] (dʒɪl) *n.* a unit of liquid measure equal to one quarter of a pint. [C14: < OF *gille* vat, tub, < LL *gillō,* <?]

gill[3] *or* **ghyll** (gɪl) *n. Dialect.* **1.** a narrow stream; rivulet. **2.** a wooded ravine. [C11: < ON *gil* steep-sided valley]

gillie, ghillie, *or* **gilly** (ˈgɪlɪ) *n., pl.* **-lies.** *Scot.* **1.** an attendant or guide for hunting or fishing. **2.** (formerly) a Highland chieftain's male attendant. [C17: < Scot. Gaelic *gille* boy, servant]

gills (gɪlz) *pl. n.* **1.** (*sometimes sing.*) the wattle of birds such as domestic fowl. **2.** the cheeks and jowls of a person. **3. green about the gills.** *Inf.* looking or feeling nauseated.

gillyflower *or* **gilliflower** (ˈdʒɪlɪˌflaʊə) *n.* **1.** any of several plants having fragrant flowers, such as the stock and wallflower. **2.** an archaic name for **carnation.** [C14: < *gilofre,* < OF *girofle,* < Med. L, < Gk: clove tree, < *karuon* nut + *phullon* leaf]

gilt[1] (gɪlt) *vb.* **1.** a past tense and past participle of **gild**[1]. ~*n.* **2.** gold or a substance simulating it, applied in gilding. **3.** another word for **gilding** (senses 1, 2). **4.** superficial or false appearance of excellence. **5.** a gilt-edged security. **6. take the gilt off the gingerbread.** to destroy the part of something that gives it its appeal. ~*adj.* **7.** covered with or as if with gold or gilt; gilded.

gilt[2] (gɪlt) *n.* a young female pig, esp. one that has not had a litter. [C15: < ON *gyltr*]

gilt-edged *adj.* **1.** denoting government securities on which interest payments will certainly be met and that will certainly be repaid at par on the due date. **2.** (of books, papers, etc.) having gilded edges.

gimbals (ˈdʒɪmbᵊlz, ˈgɪm-) *pl. n.* a device, consisting of two or three pivoted rings at right angles to each other, that provides free suspension in all planes for a compass, chronometer, etc. Also called: **gimbal ring.** [C16: var. of earlier *gimmal,* < OF *gemel* double finger ring, < L *gemellus,* dim. of *geminus* twin]

gimcrack (ˈdʒɪmˌkræk) *adj.* **1.** cheap; shoddy. ~*n.* **2.** a cheap showy trifle or gadget. [C18: < C14 *gibecrake* little ornament, <?] —ˈ**gimˌcrackery** *n.*

gimlet (ˈgɪmlɪt) *n.* **1.** a small hand tool consisting of a pointed spiral tip attached at right angles to a handle, used for boring small holes in wood. **2.** *U.S.* a cocktail consisting of half gin or vodka and half lime juice. ~*vb.* **3.** (*tr.*) to make holes in (wood) using a gimlet. ~*adj.* **4.** penetrating; piercing (esp. in **gimlet-eyed**). [C15: < OF *guimbelet*, of Gmc origin, see WIMBLE]

gimmick (ˈgɪmɪk) *n. Inf.* **1.** something designed to attract extra attention, interest, or publicity. **2.** any clever device, gadget, or stratagem, esp. one used to deceive. [C20: orig. U.S. sl., <?] —ˈ**gimmickry** *n.* —ˈ**gimmicky** *adj.*

gimp *or* **guimpe** (gɪmp) *n.* a tapelike trimming. [C17: prob. < Du. *gimp*, <?]

gin[1] (dʒɪn) *n.* an alcoholic drink obtained by distillation of the grain of malted barley, rye, or maize, flavoured with juniper berries. [C18: < Du. *genever*, via OF < L *jūniperus* JUNIPER]

gin[2] (dʒɪn) *n.* **1.** a primitive engine in which a vertical shaft is turned by horses driving a horizontal beam in a circle. **2.** Also called: **cotton gin.** a machine of this type used for separating seeds from raw cotton. **3.** a trap for catching small mammals, consisting of a noose of thin strong wire. ~*vb.* **ginning, ginned.** (*tr.*) **4.** to free (cotton) of seeds with a gin. **5.** to trap or snare (game) with a gin. [C13 *gyn*, < ENGINE]

gin[3] (gɪn) *vb.* **ginning, gan** (gæn), **gun** (gʌn). an archaic word for **begin.**

gin[4] (dʒɪn) *n. Austral. derog. sl.* an Aboriginal woman. [C19: < Abor.]

ginger (ˈdʒɪndʒə) *n.* **1.** any of several plants of the East Indies, cultivated throughout the tropics for their spicy hot-tasting underground stems. **2.** the underground stem of this plant, which is powdered and used as a seasoning or sugared and eaten as a sweetmeat. **3. a.** a reddish-brown or yellowish-brown colour. **b.** (*as adj.*): *ginger hair.* **4.** *Inf.* liveliness; vigour. [C13: < OF *gingivre*, ult. < Sansk. *śṛñgaveram*, < *śṛñga-* horn + *vera-* body, referring to its shape] —ˈ**gingery** *adj.*

ginger ale *n.* a sweetened effervescent nonalcoholic drink flavoured with ginger extract.

ginger beer *n.* a slightly alcoholic drink made by fermenting a mixture of syrup and root ginger.

gingerbread (ˈdʒɪndʒəˌbrɛd) *n.* **1.** a moist brown cake, flavoured with ginger and treacle. **2. a.** a biscuit, similarly flavoured, cut into various shapes. **b.** (*as modifier*): *gingerbread man.* **3.** an elaborate but unsubstantial ornamentation.

ginger group *n. Chiefly Brit.* a group within a party, association, etc., that enlivens or radicalizes its parent body.

gingerly (ˈdʒɪndʒəlɪ) *adv.* **1.** in a cautious, reluctant, or timid manner. ~*adj.* **2.** cautious, reluctant, or timid. [C16: ? < OF *gensor* dainty, < *gent* of noble birth; see GENTLE]

ginger snap *or* **nut** *n.* a crisp biscuit flavoured with ginger.

gingham (ˈgɪŋəm) *n.* a cotton fabric, usually woven of two coloured yarns in a checked or striped design. [C17: < F, < Malay *ginggang* striped cloth]

gingili (ˈdʒɪndʒɪlɪ) *n.* **1.** the oil obtained from sesame seeds. **2.** another name for **sesame.** [C18: < Hindi *jingalī*]

gingiva (ˈdʒɪndʒɪvə, dʒɪnˈdʒaɪvə) *n., pl.* **-givae** (-dʒɪˌviː, -ˈdʒaɪviː). *Anat.* the technical name for the **gum**[2]. [< L] —ˈ**gingival** *adj.*

gingivitis (ˌdʒɪndʒɪˈvaɪtɪs) *n.* inflammation of the gums.

ginglymus (ˈdʒɪŋglɪməs, ˈgɪŋ-) *n., pl.* **-mi** (-ˌmaɪ). *Anat.* a hinge joint. [C17: NL, < Gk *ginglumos* hinge]

gink (gɪŋk) *n. Sl.* a man or boy, esp. one considered to be odd. [C20: <?]

ginkgo (ˈgɪŋkgəʊ) *or* **gingko** (ˈgɪŋkəʊ) *n., pl.* **-goes** *or* **-koes.** a widely planted ornamental Chinese tree with fan-shaped deciduous leaves and fleshy yellow fruit. Also called: **maidenhair tree.** [C18: < Japanese, < Ancient Chinese: silver + apricot]

ginormous (dʒaɪˈnɔːməs) *adj. Inf.* very large. [C20: blend of *giant* or *gigantic* & *enormous*]

gin palace (dʒɪn) *n.* (formerly) a gaudy drinking house.

gin rummy (dʒɪn) *n.* a version of rummy in which a player may go out if the odd cards outside his sequences total less than ten points. [C20: < GIN[1] + RUMMY]

ginseng (ˈdʒɪnsɛŋ) *n.* **1.** either of two plants of China or of North America, whose forked aromatic roots are used medicinally in China. **2.** the root of either of these plants or a substance obtained from the roots, believed to possess tonic and energy-giving properties. [C17: < Mandarin Chinese *jen shen*]

Gioconda (*Italian* dʒoˈkonda) *n.* **1. La.** Also called: **Mona Lisa.** the portrait by Leonardo da Vinci of a young woman with an enigmatic smile. ~*adj.* **2.** mysterious or enigmatic. [It.: the smiling (lady)]

giocoso (dʒəˈkəʊzəʊ) *adj. Music.* jocose. [It.]

gip (dʒɪp) *vb.* **gipping, gipped.** **1.** a variant spelling of **gyp**[1]. ~*n.* **2.** a variant spelling of **gyp**[2].

Gipsy (ˈdʒɪpsɪ) *n., pl.* **-sies.** (*sometimes not cap.*) a variant spelling of **Gypsy.**

gipsy moth *n.* a variant spelling of **gypsy moth.**

giraffe (dʒɪˈrɑːf, -ˈræf) *n., pl.* **-raffes** *or* **-raffe.** a large ruminant mammal inhabiting savannas of tropical Africa: the tallest mammal, with very long legs and neck. [C17: < It. *giraffa*, < Ar. *zarāfah*, prob. of African origin]

girandole (ˈdʒɪrənˌdəʊl) *n.* **1.** a branched wall candleholder. **2.** an earring or pendant having a central gem surrounded by smaller ones. **3.** a revolving firework. **4.** *Artillery.* a group of connected mines. [C17: < F, < It. *girandola*, < L *gȳrāre* to GYRATE]

girasol *or* **girasole** (ˈdʒɪrəˌsɒl, -ˌsəʊl) *n.* a type of opal that has a red or pink glow; fire opal. [C16: < It., < *girare* to revolve (see GYRATE) + *sole* the sun]

gird[1] (gɜːd) *vb.* **girding, girded** *or* **girt.** (*tr.*) **1.** to put a belt, girdle, etc., around (the waist or hips). **2.** to bind or secure with or as if with a belt: *to gird on one's armour.* **3.** to surround; encircle. **4.** to prepare (oneself) for action (esp. in **gird (up) one's loins**). [OE *gyrdan*, of Gmc origin]

gird[2] (gɜːd) *N English dialect.* ~*vb.* **1.** (when *intr.*, foll. by *at*) to jeer (at someone); mock. ~*n.* **2.** a taunt; gibe. [C13 *girden* to strike, cut, <?]

girder (ˈgɜːdə) *n.* a large beam, esp. one made of steel, used in the construction of bridges, buildings, etc.

girdle[1] (ˈgɜːdᵊl) *n.* **1.** a woman's elastic corset covering the waist to the thigh. **2.** anything that surrounds or encircles. **3.** a belt or sash. **4.** *Jewellery.* the outer edge of a gem. **5.** *Anat.* any encircling structure or part. **6.** the mark left on a tree trunk after the removal of a ring of bark. ~*vb.* (*tr.*) **7.** to put a girdle on or around. **8.** to surround or encircle. **9.** to remove a ring of bark from (a tree). [OE *gyrdel*, of Gmc origin; see GIRD[1]] —ˈ**girdle-**ˌ**like** *adj.*

girdle[2] (ˈgɜːdᵊl) *n. Scot. & N English dialect.* another word for **griddle.**

girl (gɜːl) *n.* **1.** a female child from birth to young womanhood. **2.** a young unmarried woman; lass; maid. **3.** *Inf.* a sweetheart or girlfriend. **4.** *Inf.* a woman of any age. **5.** a female employee, esp. a female servant. **6.** *S. African derog.* a Black female servant. [C13: <?; ? rel. to Low G *Göre* boy, girl] —ˈ**girlish** *adj.*

girlfriend (ˈgɜːlˌfrɛnd) *n.* **1.** a female friend with whom a person is romantically or sexually involved. **2.** any female friend.

Girl Guide *n.* See **Guide.**

girlhood (ˈgɜːlˌhʊd) *n.* the state or time of being a girl.

girlie (ˈgɜːlɪ) *n.* (*modifier*) *Inf.* featuring nude or scantily dressed women: *a girlie magazine.*

giro (ˈdʒaɪrəʊ) *n., pl.* **-ros.** **1.** a system of transferring money within a financial organization, such as a bank or post office, directly from the account of one person into that of another. **2.** *Brit. inf.* an unemployment or supplementary benefit payment by giro cheque. [C20: ult. < Gk *guros* circuit]

girt[1] (gɜːt) *vb.* a past tense and past participle of **gird**[1].

girt[2] (gɜːt) *vb.* **1.** (*tr.*) to bind or encircle; gird. **2.** to measure the girth of (something).

girth (gɜːθ) *n.* **1.** the distance around something; circumference. **2.** a band around a horse's belly to keep the saddle in position. ~*vb.* **3.** (usually foll. by *up*) to fasten a girth on (a horse). **4.** (*tr.*) to encircle or surround. [C14: < ON *gjörth* belt; see GIRD[1]]

gismo *or* **gizmo** (ˈgɪzməʊ) *n., pl.* **-mos.** *Sl., chiefly U.S. & Canad.* a device; gadget [C20: <?]

gist (dʒɪst) *n.* the point or substance of an argument, speech, etc. [C18: < Anglo-F, as in *cest action gist en* this action consists in, lit.: lies in, < OF *gésir*, < L *jacēre*]

git (gɪt) *n. Brit. sl.* **1.** a contemptible person, often a fool. **2.** a bastard. [C20: < GET (in the sense: *to beget*, hence a bastard, fool)]

gittern (ˈgɪtɜːn) *n.* an obsolete medieval stringed instrument resembling the guitar. [C14: < OF, ult. < OSp. *guitarra* GUITAR; see CITTERN]

giusto (ˈdʒuːstəʊ) *adj. Music.* (of tempo) exact; strict. [It.]

give (gɪv) *vb.* **giving, gave, given.** (*mainly tr.*) **1.** (*also intr.*) to present or deliver voluntarily (something that is one's own) to another. **2.** (often foll. by *for*) to transfer (something that is one's own, esp. money) to the possession of another as part of an exchange: *to give fifty pounds for a painting.* **3.** to place in the temporary possession of another: *I gave him my watch while I went swimming.* **4.** (when *intr.*, foll. by *of*) to grant, provide, or bestow: *give me some advice.* **5.** to administer: *to give a reprimand.* **6.** to award or attribute: *to give blame, praise,* etc. **7.** to be a source of: *he gives no trouble.* **8.** to impart or communicate: *to give news.* **9.** to utter or emit: *to give a shout.* **10.** to perform, make, or do: *the car gave a jolt.* **11.** to sacrifice or devote: *he gave his life for his country.* **12.** to surrender: *to give place to others.* **13.** to concede or yield: *I will give you this game.* **14.** (*intr.*) *Inf.* to happen: *what gives?* **15.** (often foll. by *to*) to cause; lead: *she gave me to believe that she would come.* **16.** to perform or present as an entertainment: *to give a play.* **17.** to act as a host of (a party, etc.). **18.** (*intr.*) to yield or break under force or pressure: *this surface will give if you sit on it.* **19. give as good as one gets.** to respond to verbal or bodily blows to at least an equal extent as those received. **20. give or take.** plus or minus: *three thousand people came, give or take a few hundred.* ~*n.* **21.** tendency to yield under pressure; resilience. ~See also **give away, give in,** etc. [OE *giefan*] —ˈ**givable** *or* ˈ**giveable** *adj.* —ˈ**giver** *n.*

give-and-take *n.* **1.** mutual concessions, shared benefits, and cooperation. **2.** a smoothly flowing exchange of ideas and talk. ~*vb.* **give and take.** (*intr.*) **3.** to make mutual concessions.

give away *vb.* (*tr., adv.*) **1.** to donate or bestow as a gift, prize, etc. **2.** to sell very cheaply. **3.** to reveal or betray. **4.** to fail to use (an opportunity) through folly or neglect. **5.** to present (a bride) formally to her husband in a marriage ceremony. ~*n.* **giveaway. 6.** a betrayal or disclosure esp. when unintentional. **7.** (*modifier*) **a.** very cheap (esp. in **giveaway prices**). **b.** free of charge: *a giveaway property magazine.*

give in *vb.* (*adv.*) **1.** (*intr.*) to yield; admit defeat. **2.** (*tr.*) to submit or deliver (a document).

given (ˈgɪvᵊn) *vb.* **1.** the past participle of **give.** ~*adj.* **2.** (*postpositive;* foll. by *to*) tending (to); inclined or addicted (to). **3.** specific or previously stated. **4.** assumed as a premise. **5.** *Maths.* known or determined independently: *a given volume.* **6.** (on official documents) issued or executed, as on a stated date.

given name *n.* another term (esp. U.S.) for **Christian name.**

give off *vb.* (*tr., adv.*) to emit or discharge: *the mothballs gave off an acrid odour.*

give out *vb.* (*adv.*) **1.** (*tr.*) to emit or discharge. **2.** (*tr.*) to publish or make known: *the chairman gave out that he would resign.* **3.** (*tr.*) to hand out or distribute: *they gave out free chewing gum.* **4.** (*intr.*) to become exhausted; fail: *the supply of candles gave out.*

give over *vb.* (*adv.*) **1.** (*tr.*) to transfer, esp. to the care or custody of another. **2.** (*tr.*) to assign or resign to a specific purpose or function: *the day was given over to pleasure.* **3.** *Inf.* to cease (an activity): *give over fighting, will you!*

give up *vb.* (*adv.*) **1.** to abandon hope (for). **2.** (*tr.*) to renounce (an activity, belief, etc.): *I have given up smoking.* **3.** (*tr.*) to relinquish or resign from: *he gave up the presidency.* **4.** (*tr.; usually reflexive*) to surrender: *the escaped convict gave himself up.* **5.** (*intr.*) to admit one's defeat or inability to do something. **6.** (*tr.; often passive or reflexive*) to devote completely (to): *she gave herself up to caring for the sick.*

gizzard (ˈgɪzəd) *n.* **1.** the thick-walled part of a bird's stomach, in which hard food is broken up. **2.** *Inf.* the stomach and entrails generally. [C14: < OF *guisier* fowl's liver, < L *gigēria* entrails of poultry when cooked, <?]

Gk *abbrev. for* Greek.

glabella (gləˈbɛlə) *n., pl.* **-lae** (-liː). *Anat.* a smooth elevation of the frontal bone just above the bridge of the nose. [C19: NL, < L, < *glaber* bald, smooth] —**glaˈbellar** *adj.*

glabrous (ˈgleɪbrəs) *adj. Biol.* without hair or a similar growth; smooth. [C17 *glabrous,* < L *glaber*] —ˈ**glabrousness** *n.*

glacé (ˈglæsɪ) *adj.* **1.** crystallized or candied: *glacé cherries.* **2.** covered in icing. **3.** (of leather, silk, etc.) having a glossy finish. ~*vb.* **-céing, -céed. 4.** (*tr.*) to ice or candy (cakes, fruits, etc.). [C19: < F *glacé*, lit.: iced, < *glacer* to freeze, < L *glaciēs* ice]

glacial (ˈgleɪsɪəl, -ʃəl) *adj.* **1.** characterized by the presence of masses of ice. **2.** relating to, caused by, or deposited by a glacier. **3.** extremely cold; icy. **4.** cold or hostile in manner. **5.** (of a chemical compound) of or tending to form crystals that resemble ice. **6.** very slow in progress: *a glacial pace.* —ˈ**glacially** *adv.*

glacial acetic acid *n.* pure acetic acid.

glacial period *n.* **1.** any period of time during which a large part of the earth's surface was covered with ice, due to the advance of glaciers. **2.** (*often caps.*) the Pleistocene epoch. ~Also called: **glacial epoch, ice age.**

glaciate (ˈgleɪsɪˌeɪt) *vb.* **1.** to cover or become covered with glaciers or masses of ice. **2.** (*tr.*) to subject to the effects of glaciers, such as denudation and erosion. —ˌ**glaciˈation** *n.*

glacier (ˈglæsɪə, ˈgleɪs-) *n.* a slowly moving mass of ice originating from an accumulation of snow. [C18: < F (dialect), < OF *glace* ice, < LL, < L *glaciēs* ice]

glaciology (ˌglæsɪˈɒlədʒɪ, ˌgleɪ-) *n.* the study of the distribution, character, and effects of glaciers. —**glaciological** (ˌglæsɪəˈlɒdʒɪkᵊl, ˌgleɪ-) *adj.* —ˌ**glaciˈologist** *n.*

glacis (ˈglæsɪs, ˈglæsɪ, ˈgleɪ-) *n., pl.* **-ises** *or* **-is** (-iːz, -ɪz). **1.** a slight incline; slope. **2.** an open slope in front of a fortified place. [C17: < F, < OF *glacier* to freeze, slip, < L, < *glaciēs* ice]

glad[1] (glæd) *adj.* **gladder, gladdest. 1.** happy and pleased; contented. **2.** causing happiness or contentment. **3.** (*postpositive;* foll. by *to*) very willing: *he was glad to help.* ~*vb.* **gladding, gladded. 4.** (*tr.*) an archaic word for **gladden.** [OE *glæ̅d*] —ˈ**gladly** *adv.* —ˈ**gladness** *n.*

glad[2] (glæd) *n. Inf.* short for **gladiolus.**

gladden (ˈglædᵊn) *vb.* to make or become glad and joyful. —ˈ**gladdener** *n.*

glade (gleɪd) *n.* an open place in a forest; clearing. [C16: <?; ? rel. to GLAD[1] (in obs. sense: bright); see GLEAM]

glad eye *n. Inf.* an inviting or seductive glance (esp. in **give (someone) the glad eye**).

gladiator (ˈglædɪˌeɪtə) *n.* **1.** (in ancient Rome) a man trained to fight in arenas to provide entertainment. **2.** a person who supports and fights publicly for a cause. [C16: < L: swordsman, < *gladius* sword] —**gladiatorial** (ˌglædɪəˈtɔːrɪəl) *adj.*

gladiolus (ˌglædɪˈəʊləs) *n., pl.* **-lus, -li** (-laɪ), *or*

-luses. any plant of a widely cultivated genus having sword-shaped leaves and spikes of funnel-shaped brightly coloured flowers. Also called: **gladiola.** [C16: < L: a small sword, sword lily, < *gladius* a sword]

glad rags *pl. n. Inf.* best clothes or clothes used on special occasions.

gladsome (ˈglædsəm) *adj.* an archaic word for **glad**[1]. —ˈ**gladsomely** *adv.* —ˈ**gladsomeness** *n.*

Gladstone bag (ˈglædstən) *n.* a piece of hand luggage consisting of two equal-sized hinged compartments. [C19: after W. E. *Gladstone* (1809–98), Brit. statesman]

Glagolitic (ˌglægəˈlɪtɪk) *adj.* of, relating to, or denoting a Slavic alphabet whose invention is attributed to Saint Cyril. [C19: < NL, < Serbo-Croatian *glagolica* the Glagolitic alphabet]

glair (glɛə) *n.* **1.** white of egg, esp. when used as a size, glaze, or adhesive. **2.** any substance resembling this. ~*vb.* **3.** (*tr.*) to apply glair to (something). [C14: < OF *glaire*, < Vulgar L *clāria* (unattested) CLEAR, < L *clārus*] —ˈ**glairy** *or* ˈ**glaireous** *adj.*

glamorize, -ise, *or U.S.* (*sometimes*) **glamourize** (ˈglæməˌraɪz) *vb.* (*tr.*) to cause to be or seem glamorous; romanticize or beautify. —ˌ**glamoriˈzation** *or* **-iˈsation** *n.*

glamorous (ˈglæmərəs) *adj.* **1.** possessing glamour; alluring and fascinating. **2.** beautiful and smart, esp. in a showy way: *a glamorous woman.* —ˈ**glamorously** *adv.*

glamour *or U.S.* (*sometimes*) **glamor** (ˈglæmə) *n.* **1.** charm and allure; fascination. **2. a.** fascinating or voluptuous beauty. **b.** (*as modifier*): *a glamour girl.* **3.** *Arch.* a magic spell; charm. [C18: Scot. var. of GRAMMAR (hence a magic spell, because occult practices were popularly associated with learning)]

glance[1] (glɑːns) *vb.* **1.** (*intr.*) to look hastily or briefly. **2.** (*intr.*; foll. by *over, through,* etc.) to look over briefly: *to glance through a report.* **3.** (*intr.*) to reflect, glint, or gleam: *the sun glanced on the water.* **4.** (*intr.*; usually foll. by *off*) to depart (from an object struck) at an oblique angle: *the arrow glanced off the tree.* ~*n.* **5.** a hasty or brief look; peep. **6.** a flash or glint of light; gleam. **7.** the act or an instance of an object glancing off another. **8.** a brief allusion. [C15: < *glacen* to strike obliquely, < OF *glacier* to slide (see GLACIS)] —ˈ**glancingly** *adv.*

glance[2] (glɑːns) *n.* any mineral having a metallic lustre. [C19: < G *Glanz* brightness, lustre]

gland[1] (glænd) *n.* **1.** a cell or organ in man and other animals that synthesizes chemical substances and secretes them for the body to use or eliminate, either through a duct (exocrine gland) or directly into the bloodstream (endocrine gland). **2.** a structure, such as a lymph node, that resembles a gland in form. **3.** a cell or organ in plants that synthesizes and secretes a particular substance. [C17: < L *glāns* acorn]

gland[2] (glænd) *n.* a device that prevents leakage of fluid along a rotating shaft or reciprocating rod passing between areas of high and low pressure. It often consists of a flanged metal sleeve bedding into a stuffing box. [C19: <?]

glanders (ˈglændəz) *n.* (*functioning as sing.*) a highly infectious bacterial disease of horses, sometimes communicated to man, characterized by inflammation and ulceration of the mucous membranes of the air passages, skin and lymph glands. [C16: < OF *glandres,* < L *glandulae,* lit.: little acorns, < *glāns* acorn; see GLAND[1]]

glandular (ˈglændjʊlə) *or* **glandulous** (ˈglændjʊləs) *adj.* of, relating to, containing, functioning as, or affecting a gland. [C18: < L *glandula,* lit.: a little acorn; see GLANDERS] —ˈ**glandularly** *or* ˈ**glandulously** *adv.*

glandular fever *n.* another name for **infectious mononucleosis.**

glandule (ˈglændjuːl) *n.* a small gland.

glans (glænz) *n., pl.* **glandes** (ˈglændiːz). *Anat.* any small rounded body or glandlike mass, such as the head of the penis (**glans penis**). [C17: < L: acorn; see GLAND[1]]

glare (glɛə) *vb.* **1.** (*intr.*) to stare angrily; glower. **2.** (*tr.*) to express by glowering. **3.** (*intr.*) (of light, colour, etc.) to be very bright and intense. **4.** (*intr.*) to be dazzlingly ornamented or garish. ~*n.* **5.** an angry stare. **6.** a dazzling light or brilliance. **7.** garish ornamentation or appearance. [C13: prob. < MLow G, MDu. *glaren* to gleam]

glaring (ˈglɛərɪŋ) *adj.* **1.** conspicuous: *a glaring omission.* **2.** dazzling or garish. —ˈ**glaringly** *adv.* —ˈ**glaringness** *n.*

glasnost (ˈglæsˌnɒst) *n.* the policy of public frankness and accountability developed in Russia under the leadership of Mikhail Gorbachov. [C20: Russian, lit.: openness]

glass (glɑːs) *n.* **1. a.** a hard brittle transparent or translucent noncrystalline solid, consisting of metal silicates or similar compounds. It is made from a fused mixture of oxides, such as lime, silicon dioxide, phosphorus pentoxide, etc. **b.** (*as modifier*): *a glass bottle.* Related adj.: **vitreous.** **2.** something made of glass, esp. a drinking vessel, a barometer, or a mirror. **3.** Also called: **glassful.** the amount or volume contained in a drinking glass: *he drank a glass of wine.* **4.** glassware collectively. **5.** See **fibreglass.** ~*vb.* **6.** (*tr.*) to cover with, enclose in, or fit with glass. [OE *glæs*] —ˈ**glassless** *adj.* —ˈ**glassˌlike** *adj.*

glass-blowing *n.* the process of shaping a mass of molten glass by blowing air into it through a tube. —ˈ**glass-ˌblower** *n.*

glasses (ˈglɑːsɪz) *pl. n.* a pair of lenses for correcting faulty vision, in a frame that rests on the bridge of the nose and hooks behind the ears. Also called: **spectacles, eyeglasses.**

glass harmonica *n.* a musical instrument of the 18th century consisting of a set of glass bowls of graduated pitches, played by rubbing the fingers over the moistened rims or by a keyboard mechanism. Sometimes shortened to **harmonica.** Also called: **musical glasses.**

glasshouse (ˈglɑːsˌhaʊs) *n.* **1.** *Brit.* a glass building, esp. a greenhouse, used for growing plants in protected or controlled conditions. **2.** *Inf., chiefly Brit.* a military detention centre.

glassine (glæˈsiːn) *n.* a glazed translucent paper.

glass snake *n.* any snakelike lizard of Europe, Asia, or North America, with vestigial hind limbs and a tail that breaks off easily.

glassware (ˈglɑːsˌwɛə) *n.* articles made of glass, esp. drinking glasses.

glass wool *n.* fine spun glass massed into a wool-like bulk, used in insulation, filtering, etc.

glasswort (ˈglɑːsˌwɜːt) *n.* **1.** any plant of salt marshes having fleshy stems and scalelike leaves: formerly used as a source of soda for glass-making. **2.** another name for **saltwort.**

glassy (ˈglɑːsɪ) *adj.* **glassier, glassiest.** **1.** resembling glass, esp. in smoothness or transparency. **2.** void of expression, life, or warmth: *a glassy stare.* —ˈ**glassily** *adv.* —ˈ**glassiness** *n.*

Glaswegian (glæzˈwiːdʒən) *adj.* **1.** of or relating to Glasgow, a city in Scotland, or its inhabitants. ~*n.* **2.** a native or inhabitant of Glasgow. [C19: infl. by NORWEGIAN]

Glauber's salt (ˈglaʊbəz) *or* **Glauber salt** *n.* the crystalline decahydrate of sodium sulphate: used in making glass, detergents and pulp. [C18: after J. R. *Glauber* (1604–68), G chemist]

glaucoma (glɔːˈkəʊmə) *n.* a disease of the eye in which increased pressure within the eyeball causes impaired vision, sometimes progressing to blindness. [C17: < L, < Gk, < *glaukos;* see GLAUCOUS] —**glauˈcomatous** *adj.*

glaucous (ˈglɔːkəs) *adj.* **1.** *Bot.* covered with a waxy or powdery bloom. **2.** bluish-green. [C17: < L *glaucus* silvery, bluish-green, < Gk *glaukos*]

glaze (gleɪz) *vb.* **1.** (*tr.*) to fit or cover with glass. **2.** (*tr.*) *Ceramics.* to cover with a vitreous solution, rendering impervious to liquid. **3.** (*tr.*) to cover (foods) with a shiny coating by applying beaten egg, sugar, etc. **4.** (*tr.*) to make glossy or shiny. **5.** (when *intr.*, often foll. by *over*) to become or cause to become glassy: *his eyes were glazing over.* ~*n.* **6.** *Ceramics.* **a.** a vitreous coating. **b.** the substance used to produce such a coating. **7.**

a smooth lustrous finish on a fabric produced by applying various chemicals. **8.** something used to give a glossy surface to foods: *a syrup glaze.* [C14 *glasen*, < *glas* GLASS] —**glazed** *adj.* —**'glazer** *n.*

glaze ice *n. Brit.* a thin clear layer of ice caused by the freezing of rain in the air or by refreezing after a thaw.

glazier ('gleɪzɪə) *n.* a person who fits windows, doors, etc., with glass. —**'glaziery** *n.*

glazing ('gleɪzɪŋ) *n.* **1.** the surface of a glazed object. **2.** glass fitted, or to be fitted, in a door, frame, etc.

GLC *abbrev. for* Greater London Council.

gleam (gliːm) *n.* **1.** a small beam or glow of light, esp. reflected light. **2.** a brief or dim indication: *a gleam of hope.* ~*vb.* (*intr.*) **3.** to send forth or reflect a beam of light. **4.** to appear, esp. briefly. [OE *glǣm*] —**'gleaming** *adj.* —**'gleamingly** *adv.* —**'gleamy** *adj.*

glean (gliːn) *vb.* **1.** to gather (something) slowly and carefully in small pieces: *to glean information.* **2.** to gather (the useful remnants of a crop) from the field after harvesting. [C14: < OF *glener*, < LL *glennāre*, prob. of Celtic origin] —**'gleaner** *n.*

gleanings ('gliːnɪŋz) *pl. n.* the useful remnants of a crop that can be gathered from the field after harvesting.

glebe (gliːb) *n.* **1.** *Brit.* land granted to a clergyman as part of his benefice. **2.** *Poetic.* land, esp. for growing things. [C14: < L *glaeba*]

glee (gliː) *n.* **1.** great merriment; joy. **2.** a type of song originating in 18th-century England, sung by three or more unaccompanied voices. [OE *glēo*]

glee club *n. Now chiefly U.S. & Canad.* a society organized for the singing of choral music.

gleeful ('gliːfʊl) *adj.* full of glee; merry. —**'gleefully** *adv.* —**'gleefulness** *n.*

gleeman ('gliːmən) *n., pl.* **-men.** *Obs.* a minstrel.

glen (glɛn) *n.* a narrow and deep mountain valley, esp. in Scotland or Ireland. [C15: < Scot. Gaelic *gleann*, < OIrish *glend*]

glengarry (glɛn'gærɪ) *n., pl.* **-ries.** a brimless Scottish cap with a crease down the crown, often with ribbons at the back. Also called: **glengarry bonnet.** [C19: after *Glengarry*, Scotland]

glib (glɪb) *adj.* **glibber, glibbest.** fluent and easy, often in an insincere or deceptive way. [C16: prob. < MLow G *glibberich* slippery] —**'glibly** *adv.* —**'glibness** *n.*

glide (glaɪd) *vb.* **1.** to move or cause to move easily without jerks or hesitations. **2.** (*intr.*) to pass slowly or without perceptible change: *to glide into sleep.* **3.** to cause (an aircraft) to come into land without engine power, or (of an aircraft) to land in this way. **4.** (*intr.*) to fly a glider. **5.** (*intr.*) *Music.* to execute a portamento from one note to another. **6.** (*intr.*) *Phonetics.* to produce a glide. ~*n.* **7.** a smooth easy movement. **8. a.** any of various dances featuring gliding steps. **b.** a step in such a dance. **9.** a manoeuvre in which an aircraft makes a gentle descent without engine power. **10.** the act or process of gliding. **11.** *Music.* a portamento or slur. **12.** *Phonetics.* a transitional sound as the speech organs pass from the articulatory position of one speech sound to that of the next. [OE *glīdan*] —**'glidingly** *adv.*

glider ('glaɪdə) *n.* **1.** an aircraft capable of gliding and soaring in air currents without the use of an engine. **2.** a person or thing that glides.

glide time *n.* the N.Z. term for **flexitime.**

glimmer ('glɪmə) *vb.* (*intr.*) **1.** (of a light) to glow faintly or flickeringly. **2.** to be indicated faintly: *hope glimmered in his face.* ~*n.* **3.** a glow or twinkle of light. **4.** a faint indication. [C14: cf. MHG *glimmern*] —**'glimmeringly** *adv.*

glimpse (glɪmps) *n.* **1.** a brief or incomplete view: *to catch a glimpse of the sea.* **2.** a vague indication. **3.** *Arch.* a glimmer of light. ~*vb.* **4.** (*tr.*) to catch sight of momentarily. [C14: of Gmc origin; cf. MHG *glimsen* to glimmer] —**'glimpser** *n.*

glint (glɪnt) *vb.* **1.** to gleam or cause to gleam brightly. ~*n.* **2.** a bright gleam or flash. **3.** brightness or gloss. **4.** a brief indication. [C15: prob. < ON]

glioma (glaɪ'əʊmə) *n., pl.* **-mata** (-mətə) *or* **-mas.** a tumour of the brain and spinal cord, composed of neuroglia cells and fibres. [C19: < NL, < Gk *glia* glue + -OMA]

glissade (glɪ'sɑːd, -'seɪd) *n.* **1.** a gliding step in ballet. **2.** a controlled slide down a snow slope. ~*vb.* **3.** (*intr.*) to perform a glissade. [C19: < F, < *glisser* to slip, < OF *glicier*, of Frankish origin]

glissando (glɪ'sændəʊ) *n., pl.* **-di** (-diː) *or* **-dos.** a rapidly executed series of notes, each of which is discretely audible. [C19: prob. It. var. of GLISSADE]

glisten ('glɪsᵊn) *vb.* (*intr.*) **1.** (of a wet or glossy surface) to gleam by reflecting light. **2.** (of light) to reflect with brightness: *the sunlight glistens on wet leaves.* ~*n.* **3.** *Rare.* a gleam or gloss. [OE *glisnian*]

glister ('glɪstə) *vb., n.* an archaic word for **glitter.** [C14: prob. < MDu. *glisteren*]

glitch (glɪtʃ) *n.* a sudden instance of malfunctioning in an electronic system. [C20: <?]

glitter ('glɪtə) *vb.* (*intr.*) **1.** (of a hard, wet, or polished surface) to reflect light in bright flashes. **2.** (of light) to be reflected in bright flashes. **3.** (usually foll. by *with*) to be decorated or enhanced by the glamour (of): *the show glitters with famous actors.* ~*n.* **4.** sparkle or brilliance. **5.** show and glamour. **6.** tiny pieces of shiny decorative material. **7.** *Canad.* Also called: **silver thaw.** ice formed from freezing rain. [C14: < ON *glitra*] —**'glitteringly** *adv.* —**'glittery** *adj.*

glitterati (ˌglɪtə'rɑːtiː) *pl. n. Inf.* the leaders of society, esp. the rich and beautiful. [C20: < GLITTER + *-ati* as in LITERATI]

glitzy ('glɪtsɪ) *adj.* **glitzier, glitziest.** *Sl.* showily attractive; flashy or glittery. [C20: prob. via Yiddish < G *glitzern* to glitter]

gloaming ('gləʊmɪŋ) *n. Scot. or poetic.* twilight or dusk. [OE *glōmung*, < *glōm*]

gloat (gləʊt) *vb.* **1.** (*intr.*; often foll. by *over*) to dwell (on) with malevolent smugness or exultation. ~*n.* **2.** the act of gloating. [C16: prob. of Scand. origin; cf. ON *glotta* to grin, MHG *glotzen* to stare] —**'gloater** *n.*

glob (glɒb) *n. Inf.* a rounded mass of some thick fluid substance. [C20: prob. < GLOBE, infl. by BLOB]

global ('gləʊbᵊl) *adj.* **1.** covering or relating to the whole world. **2.** comprehensive; total. —**'globally** *adv.*

globe (gləʊb) *n.* **1.** a sphere on which a map of the world is drawn. **2. the globe.** the world; the earth. **3.** a planet or some other astronomical body. **4.** an object shaped like a sphere, such as a glass lampshade or fishbowl. **5.** an orb, usually of gold, symbolic of sovereignty. ~*vb.* **6.** to form or cause to form into a globe. [C16: < OF, < L *globus*] —**'globeˌlike** *adj.*

globefish ('gləʊbˌfɪʃ) *n., pl.* **-fish** *or* **-fishes.** another name for **puffer.**

globeflower ('gləʊbˌflaʊə) *n.* a plant having pale yellow, white, or orange globe-shaped flowers.

globetrotter ('gləʊbˌtrɒtə) *n.* a habitual worldwide traveller, esp. a tourist. —**'globeˌtrotting** *n., adj.*

globigerina (gləʊˌbɪdʒə'raɪnə) *n., pl.* **-nas** *or* **-nae** (-niː). **1.** a marine protozoan having a rounded shell with spiny processes. **2. globigerina ooze.** a deposit on the ocean floor consisting of the shells of these protozoans. [C19: < NL, < L *globus* GLOBE + *gerere* to bear]

globoid ('gləʊbɔɪd) *adj.* **1.** shaped like a globe. ~*n.* **2.** a globoid body.

globose ('gləʊbəʊs, gləʊ'bəʊs) *or* **globous** ('gləʊbəs) *adj.* spherical or approximately spherical. [C15: < L *globōsus*; see GLOBE] —**'globosely** *adv.*

globular ('glɒbjʊlə) *or* **globulous** *adj.* **1.** shaped like a globe or globule. **2.** having or consisting of globules. —**'globularly** *adv.*

globule ('glɒbjuːl) *n.* a small globe, esp. a drop of liquid. [C17: < L *globulus*, dim. of *globus* GLOBE]

globulin ('glɒbjʊlɪn) *n.* any of a group of simple proteins that are generally insoluble in water but soluble in salt solutions.

glockenspiel (ˈglɒkənˌspiːl, -ˌʃpiːl) *n.* a percussion instrument consisting of a set of tuned metal plates played with a pair of small hammers. [C19: G, < *Glocken* bells + *Spiel* play]

glomerate (ˈglɒmərɪt) *adj.* **1.** gathered into a compact rounded mass. **2.** *Anat.* (esp. of glands) conglomerate in structure. [C18: < L *glomerāre*, < *glomus* ball] —ˌ**glomeˈration** *n.*

glomerule (ˈglɒməˌruːl) *n. Bot.* an inflorescence in the form of a ball-like cluster of flowers. [C18: < NL *glomerulus*]

gloom (gluːm) *n.* **1.** partial or total darkness. **2.** a state of depression or melancholy. **3.** an appearance or expression of despondency or melancholy. **4.** *Poetic.* a dim or dark place. ~*vb.* **5.** (*intr.*) to look sullen or depressed. **6.** to make or become dark or gloomy. [C14 *gloumben* to look sullen]

gloomy (ˈgluːmɪ) *adj.* **gloomier, gloomiest. 1.** dark or dismal. **2.** causing depression, dejection, or gloom: *gloomy news.* **3.** despairing; sad. —ˈ**gloomily** *adv.* —ˈ**gloominess** *n.*

gloria (ˈglɔːrɪə) *n.* a halo or nimbus, esp. as represented in art. [C16: < L: GLORY]

Gloria (ˈglɔːrɪə, -ˌɑː) *n.* **1.** any of several doxologies beginning with the word *Gloria.* **2.** a musical setting of one of these.

glorify (ˈglɔːrɪˌfaɪ) *vb.* **-fying, -fied.** (*tr.*) **1.** to make glorious. **2.** to make more splendid; adorn. **3.** to worship, exalt, or adore. **4.** to extol. **5.** to cause to seem more splendid or imposing than reality. —ˌ**glorifiˈcation** *n.* —ˈ**gloriˌfier** *n.*

gloriole (ˈglɔːrɪˌəʊl) *n.* another name for a **halo.** [C19: < L *glōriola*, lit.: a small GLORY]

glorious (ˈglɔːrɪəs) *adj.* **1.** having or full of glory; illustrious. **2.** conferring glory or renown: *a glorious victory.* **3.** brilliantly beautiful. **4.** delightful or enjoyable. —ˈ**gloriously** *adv.* —ˈ**gloriousness** *n.*

glory (ˈglɔːrɪ) *n., pl.* **-ries. 1.** exaltation, praise, or honour. **2.** something that brings or is worthy of praise (esp. in **crowning glory**). **3.** thanksgiving, adoration, or worship: *glory be to God.* **4.** pomp; splendour: *the glory of the king's reign.* **5.** radiant beauty; resplendence: *the glory of the sunset.* **6.** the beauty and bliss of heaven. **7.** a state of extreme happiness or prosperity. **8.** another word for **halo** or **nimbus.** ~*vb.* **-rying, -ried. 9.** (*intr.;* often foll. by *in*) to triumph or exalt. ~*interj.* **10.** *Inf.* a mild interjection to express pleasure or surprise (often **glory be!**). [C13: < OF *glorie*, < L *glōria*, <?]

glory box *n. Austral. & N.Z.* (esp. formerly) a box in which a young woman stores clothes, etc., in preparation for marriage.

glory hole *n.* **1.** a cupboard or storeroom, esp. one which is very untidy. **2.** *Naut.* another term for **lazaretto** (sense 1).

Glos *abbrev. for* Gloucestershire.

gloss[1] (glɒs) *n.* **1. a.** lustre or sheen, as of a smooth surface. **b.** (*as modifier*): *gloss paint.* **2.** a superficially attractive appearance. **3.** a cosmetic used to give a sheen. ~*vb.* **4.** to give a gloss to or obtain a gloss. **5.** (*tr.;* often foll. by *over*) to hide under a deceptively attractive surface or appearance. [C16: prob. of Scand. origin] —ˈ**glosser** *n.*

gloss[2] (glɒs) *n.* **1.** a short or expanded explanation or interpretation of a word, expression, or foreign phrase in the margin or text of a manuscript, etc. **2.** an intentionally misleading explanation. **3.** short for **glossary.** ~*vb.* (*tr.*) **4.** to add glosses to. **5.** (often foll. by *over*) to give a false or misleading interpretation of. [C16: < L *glōssa* unusual word requiring explanatory note, < Ionic Gk] —ˈ**glosser** *n.*

glossary (ˈglɒsərɪ) *n., pl.* **-ries.** an alphabetical list of terms peculiar to a field of knowledge with explanations. [C14: < LL *glossārium;* see GLOSS[2]] —**glossarial** (glɒˈsɛərɪəl) *adj.* —ˈ**glossarist** *n.*

glosseme (ˈglɒsiːm) *n.* the smallest meaningful unit of a language, such as stress, form, etc. [C20: < Gk; see GLOSS[2], -EME]

glossitis (glɒˈsaɪtɪs) *n.* inflammation of the tongue. —**glossitic** (glɒˈsɪtɪk) *adj.*

glosso- *or before a vowel* **gloss-** *combining form.* indicating a tongue or language: *glossolaryngeal.* [< Gk *glossa* tongue]

glossolalia (ˌglɒsəˈleɪlɪə) *n.* another term for **gift of tongues.** [C19: NL, < GLOSSO- + Gk *lalein* to babble]

glossy (ˈglɒsɪ) *adj.* **glossier, glossiest. 1.** smooth and shiny; lustrous. **2.** superficially attractive; plausible. **3.** (of a magazine) lavishly produced on shiny paper. ~*n., pl.* **glossies. 4.** Also called (U.S.): **slick.** an expensively produced magazine, printed on shiny paper and containing high-quality colour photography. **5.** a photograph printed on paper that has a smooth shiny surface. —ˈ**glossily** *adv.* —ˈ**glossiness** *n.*

glottal (ˈglɒtᵊl) *adj.* **1.** of or relating to the glottis. **2.** *Phonetics.* articulated or pronounced at or with the glottis.

glottal stop *n.* a plosive speech sound produced by tightly closing the glottis and allowing the air pressure to build up before opening the glottis, causing the air to escape with force.

glottis (ˈglɒtɪs) *n., pl.* **-tises** *or* **-tides** (-tɪˌdiːz). the vocal apparatus of the larynx, consisting of the two true vocal cords and the opening between them. [C16: < NL, < Gk, < Attic form of Ionic *glōssa* tongue; see GLOSS[2]]

glove (glʌv) *n.* **1.** (*often pl.*) a shaped covering for the hand with individual sheaths for the fingers and thumb, made of leather, fabric, etc. **2.** any of various large protective hand covers worn in sports, such as a boxing glove. ~*vb.* **3.** (*tr.*) to cover or provide with or as if with gloves. [OE *glōfe*]

glove box *n.* a closed box in which toxic or radioactive substances can be handled by an operator who places his hands through protective gloves sealed to the box.

glove compartment *n.* a small compartment in a car dashboard for the storage of miscellaneous articles.

glover (ˈglʌvə) *n.* a person who makes or sells gloves.

glow (gləʊ) *n.* **1.** light emitted by a substance or object at a high temperature. **2.** a steady even light without flames. **3.** brilliance of colour. **4.** brightness of complexion. **5.** a feeling of wellbeing or satisfaction. **6.** intensity of emotion. ~*vb.* (*intr.*) **7.** to emit a steady even light without flames. **8.** to shine intensely, as if from great heat. **9.** to be exuberant, as from excellent health or intense emotion. **10.** to experience a feeling of wellbeing or satisfaction: *to glow with pride.* **11.** (esp. of the complexion) to show a strong bright colour, esp. red. **12.** to be very hot. [OE *glōwan*]

glow discharge *n.* a silent luminous discharge of electricity through a low-pressure gas.

glower (ˈglaʊə) *vb.* **1.** (*intr.*) to stare hard and angrily. ~*n.* **2.** a sullen or angry stare. [C16: prob. of Scand. origin] —ˈ**gloweringly** *adv.*

glowing (ˈgləʊɪŋ) *adj.* **1.** emitting light without flames: *glowing embers.* **2.** warm and rich in colour: *glowing shades of gold and orange.* **3.** flushed and rosy: *glowing cheeks.* **4.** displaying or indicative of extreme pride or emotion: *a glowing account of his son's achievements.*

glow-worm *n.* a European beetle, the females and larvae of which bear luminescent organs producing a soft greenish light.

gloxinia (glɒkˈsɪnɪə) *n.* any of several tropical plants cultivated for their large white, red, or purple bell-shaped flowers. [C19: after Benjamin P. *Gloxin*, 18th-cent. G physician & botanist]

gloze (gləʊz) *vb. Arch.* **1.** (*tr.;* often foll. by *over*) to explain away; minimize the effect or importance of. **2.** to make explanatory notes or glosses on (a text). **3.** to use flattery (on). [C13: < OF *glosser* to comment; see GLOSS[2]]

glucose (ˈgluːkəʊz, -kəʊs) *n.* **1.** a white crystalline sugar, the most abundant form being dextrose. Formula: $C_6H_{12}O_6$. **2.** a yellowish syrup obtained by incomplete hydrolysis of starch: used in confectionery, fermentation, etc. [C19: < F, < Gk *gleukos* sweet wine; rel. to Gk *glukus* sweet]

glucoside (ˈgluːkəʊˌsaɪd) *n. Biochem.* any of a

large group of glycosides that yield glucose on hydrolysis. —**glucosidic** (ˌgluːkəʊˈsɪdɪk) *adj.*

glue (gluː) *n.* **1.** any natural or synthetic adhesive, esp. a sticky gelatinous substance prepared by boiling animal products such as bones, skin, and horns. **2.** any other sticky or adhesive substance. ~*vb.* **gluing** *or* **glueing, glued. 3.** (*tr.*) to join or stick together as with glue. [C14: < OF *glu,* < LL *glūs*] —ˈ**glueˌlike** *adj.* —ˈ**gluer** *n.* —ˈ**gluey** *adj.*

glue-sniffing *n.* the practice of inhaling the fumes of certain types of glue to produce intoxicating or hallucinatory effects. —ˈ**glue-ˌsniffer** *n.*

gluhwein (ˈgluːˌvaɪn) *n.* mulled wine. [G]

glum (glʌm) *adj.* **glummer, glummest.** silent or sullen, as from gloom. [C16: var. of GLOOM] —ˈ**glumly** *adv.* —ˈ**glumness** *n.*

glume (gluːm) *n. Bot.* one of a pair of dry membranous bracts at the base of the spikelet of grasses. [C18: < L *glūma* husk of corn] —**gluˈmaceous** *adj.*

gluon (ˈgluːɒn) *n.* a hypothetical particle believed to be exchanged between quarks in order to bind them together to form particles. [C20: coined < GLUE + -ON]

glut (glʌt) *n.* **1.** an excessive amount, as in the production of a crop. **2.** the act of glutting or state of being glutted. ~*vb.* **glutting, glutted.** (*tr.*) **3.** to feed or supply beyond capacity. **4.** to supply (a market, etc.) with a commodity in excess of the demand for it. [C14: prob. < OF *gloutir,* < L *gluttīre;* see GLUTTON[1]]

glutamic acid (gluːˈtæmɪk) *n.* an amino acid, occurring in proteins.

gluten (ˈgluːtᵊn) *n.* a protein present in cereal grains, esp. wheat. [C16: < L: GLUE] —ˈ**glutenous** *adj.*

gluteus (glʊˈtiːəs) *n., pl.* **-tei** (-ˈtiːaɪ). any one of the three large muscles that form the human buttock. [C17: < NL, < Gk *gloutos* buttock, rump] —**gluˈteal** *adj.*

glutinous (ˈgluːtɪnəs) *adj.* resembling glue in texture; sticky. —ˈ**glutinously** *adv.*

glutton[1] (ˈglʌtᵊn) *n.* **1.** a person devoted to eating and drinking to excess; greedy person. **2.** a person who has or appears to have a voracious appetite for something: *a glutton for punishment.* [C13: < OF *glouton,* < L < *gluttīre* to swallow] —ˈ**gluttonous** *adj.* —ˈ**gluttonously** *adv.*

glutton[2] (ˈglʌtᵊn) *n.* another name for **wolverine.** [C17: < GLUTTON[1], apparently translating G *Vielfrass* great eater]

gluttony (ˈglʌtənɪ) *n., pl.* **-tonies.** the act or practice of eating to excess.

glyceride (ˈglɪsəˌraɪd) *n.* any fatty-acid ester of glycerol.

glycerin (ˈglɪsərɪn) *or* **glycerine** (ˈglɪsəriːn, ˌglɪsəˈriːn) *n.* another name (not in technical usage) for **glycerol.** [C19: < F, < Gk *glukeros* sweet + *-ine* -IN; rel. to Gk *glukus* sweet]

glycerol (ˈglɪsəˌrɒl) *n.* a colourless odourless syrupy liquid: a by-product of soap manufacture, used as a solvent, antifreeze, plasticizer, and sweetener (**E422**). [C19: < GLYCER(IN) + -OL[1]]

glycine (ˈglaɪsiːn, glaɪˈsiːn) *n.* a white sweet crystalline amino acid occurring in most proteins. [C19: GLYCO- + -INE[2]]

glyco- *or before a vowel* **glyc-** *combining form.* sugar: *glycogen.* [< Gk *glukus* sweet]

glycogen (ˈglaɪkəʊdʒən) *n.* a polysaccharide consisting of glucose units: the form in which carbohydrate is stored in animals. —**glycogenic** (ˌglaɪkəʊˈdʒɛnɪk) *adj.* —ˌ**glycoˈgenesis** *n.*

glycol (ˈglaɪkɒl) *n.* another name (not in technical usage) for **ethanediol.**

glycolic acid (glaɪˈkɒlɪk) *n.* a colourless crystalline compound found in sugar cane and sugar beet: used in the manufacture of pharmaceuticals, pesticides, and plasticizers.

glycolysis (glaɪˈkɒlɪsɪs) *n. Biochem.* the breakdown of glucose by enzymes with the liberation of energy.

glycoside (ˈglaɪkəʊˌsaɪd) *n.* any of a group of substances derived from simple sugars by replacing the hydroxyl group by another group. —**glycosidic** (ˌglaɪkəʊˈsɪdɪk) *adj.*

glycosuria (ˌglaɪkəʊˈsjʊərɪə) *n.* the presence of excess sugar in the urine, as in diabetes. [C19: < NL, < F *glycose* GLUCOSE + -URIA]

glyph (glɪf) *n.* **1.** a carved channel or groove, esp. a vertical one. **2.** *Now rare.* another word for **hieroglyphic.** [C18: < F, < Gk, < *gluphein* to carve] —ˈ**glyphic** *adj.*

glyptic (ˈglɪptɪk) *adj.* of or relating to engraving or carving, esp. on precious stones. [C19: < F, < Gk, < *gluphein* to carve]

glyptodont (ˈglɪptəˌdɒnt) *n.* an extinct mammal of South America which resembled the giant armadillo. [C19: < Gk *gluptos* carved + -ODONT]

GM *abbrev. for:* **1.** general manager. **2.** (in Britain) George Medal. **3.** Grand Master.

G-man *n., pl.* **G-men. 1.** *U.S. sl.* an FBI agent. **2.** *Irish.* a political detective.

Gmc *abbrev. for* Germanic.

GMT *abbrev. for* Greenwich Mean Time.

GMWU (in Britain) *abbrev. for* National Union of General and Municipal Workers.

gnarl (nɑːl) *n.* **1.** any knotty swelling on a tree. ~*vb.* **2.** (*tr.*) to knot or cause to knot. [C19: back formation < *gnarled*]

gnarled (nɑːld) *or* **gnarly** *adj.* **1.** having gnarls: *the gnarled trunk of the old tree.* **2.** (esp. of hands) rough, twisted, and weather-beaten.

gnash (næʃ) *vb.* **1.** to grind (the teeth) together, as in pain or anger. **2.** (*tr.*) to bite or chew as by grinding the teeth. ~*n.* **3.** the act of gnashing the teeth. [C15: prob. < ON; cf. *gnastan* gnashing of teeth]

gnat (næt) *n.* any of various small fragile biting two-winged insects. [OE *gnætt*]

gnathic (ˈnæθɪk) *adj. Anat.* of or relating to the jaw. [C19: < Gk *gnathos* jaw]

-gnathous *adj. combining form.* indicating or having a jaw of a specified kind: *prognathous.* [< NL, < Gk *gnathos* jaw]

gnaw (nɔː) *vb.* **gnawing, gnawed; gnawed** *or* **gnawn. 1.** (when *intr.,* often foll. by *at* or *upon*) to bite (at) or chew (upon) constantly so as to wear away little by little. **2.** (*tr.*) to form by gnawing: *to gnaw a hole.* **3.** to cause erosion of (something). **4.** (when *intr.,* often foll. by *at*) to cause constant distress or anxiety (to). ~*n.* **5.** the act or an instance of gnawing. [OE *gnagan*]

gnawing (ˈnɔːɪŋ) *n.* a dull persistent pang or pain, esp. of hunger.

gneiss (naɪs) *n.* any coarse-grained metamorphic rock that is banded or foliated. [C18: < G *Gneis,* prob. < MHG *ganeist* spark] —ˈ**gneissic,** ˈ**gneissoid,** *or* ˈ**gneissose** *adj.*

gnocchi (ˈnɒkɪ) *pl. n.* dumplings made of pieces of semolina pasta, or sometimes potato, served with cheese sauce. [It., pl. of *gnocco* lump, prob. of Gmc origin]

gnome (nəʊm) *n.* **1.** one of a species of legendary creatures, usually resembling small misshapen old men, said to live in the depths of the earth and guard buried treasure. **2.** the statue of a gnome, esp. in a garden. **3.** a very small or ugly person. **4.** *Facetious or derog.* an international banker or financier (esp. in **gnomes of Zürich**). [C18: < F, < NL *gnomus,* coined by Paracelsus (1493-1541), Swiss alchemist, <?] —ˈ**gnomish** *adj.*

gnomic (ˈnəʊmɪk, ˈnɒm-) *adj.* of or relating to aphorisms; pithy. —ˈ**gnomically** *adv.*

gnomon (ˈnəʊmɒn) *n.* **1.** the stationary arm that projects the shadow on a sundial. **2.** a geometric figure remaining after a parallelogram has been removed from one corner of a larger parallelogram. [C16: < L, < Gk: interpreter, < *gignōskein* to know] —**gnoˈmonic** *adj.*

-gnosis *n. combining form.* (esp. in medicine) recognition or knowledge: *diagnosis.* [via L < Gk: knowledge] —**-gnostic** *adj. combining form.*

gnostic (ˈnɒstɪk) *adj.* of, relating to, or possessing knowledge, esp. spiritual knowledge.

Gnostic (ˈnɒstɪk) *n.* **1.** an adherent of Gnosticism. ~*adj.* **2.** of or relating to Gnostics or to Gnosticism. [C16: < LL, < Gk *gnōstikos* relating to knowledge]

Gnosticism (ˈnɒstɪˌsɪzəm) *n.* a religious movement characterized by a belief in intuitive spiritual knowledge: regarded as a heresy by the Christian Church.

GNP *abbrev. for* gross national product.

gnu (nuː) *n., pl.* **gnus** *or* **gnu.** either of two sturdy antelopes inhabiting the savannas of Africa, having an oxlike head and a long tufted tail. Also called: **wildebeest.** [C18: < Xhosa *nqu*]

go (gəʊ) *vb.* **going, went, gone.** (*mainly intr.*) **1.** to move or proceed, esp. to or from a point or in a certain direction: *go home.* **2.** (*tr.; takes an infinitive,* often with *to* omitted or replaced by *and*) to proceed towards a particular person or place with some specified purpose: *I must go and get that book.* **3.** to depart: *we'll have to go at eleven.* **4.** to start, as in a race: often used in commands. **5.** to make regular journeys: *this train service goes to the east coast.* **6.** to operate or function effectively: *the radio won't go.* **7.** (*copula*) to become: *his face went red.* **8.** to make a noise as specified: *the gun went bang.* **9.** to enter into a specified state or condition: *to go into hysterics.* **10.** to be or continue to be in a specified state or condition: *to go in rags; to go in poverty.* **11.** to lead, extend, or afford access: *this route goes to the north.* **12.** to proceed towards an activity: *to go to sleep.* **13.** (*tr.; takes an infinitive*) to serve or contribute: *this letter goes to prove my point.* **14.** to follow a course as specified; fare: *the lecture went badly.* **15.** to be applied or allotted to a particular purpose or recipient: *his money went on drink.* **16.** to be sold: *the necklace went for three thousand pounds.* **17.** to be ranked; compare: *this meal is good as my meals go.* **18.** to blend or harmonize: *these chairs won't go with the rest of your furniture.* **19.** (foll. by *by* or *under*) to be known (by a name or disguise). **20.** to have a usual or proper place: *those books go on this shelf.* **21.** (of music, poetry, etc.) to be sounded; expressed, etc.: *how does that song go?* **22.** to fail or give way: *my eyesight is going.* **23.** to break down or collapse abruptly: *the ladder went at the critical moment.* **24.** to die: *the old man went at 2 a.m.* **25.** (often foll. by *by*) **a.** (of time, etc.) to elapse: *the hours go by so slowly.* **b.** to travel past: *the train goes by her house.* **c.** to be guided (by). **26.** to occur: *happiness does not always go with riches.* **27.** to be eliminated, abolished, or given up: *this entry must go to save space.* **28.** to be spent or finished: *all his money has gone.* **29.** to attend: *go to school.* **30.** to join a stated profession: *go on the stage.* **31.** (foll. by *to*) to have recourse (to); turn: *to go to arbitration.* **32.** (foll. by *to*) to subject or put oneself (to): *she goes to great pains to please him.* **33.** to proceed, esp. up to or beyond certain limits: *you will go too far one day and then you will be punished.* **34.** to be acceptable or tolerated: *anything goes.* **35.** to carry the weight of final authority: *what the boss says goes.* **36.** (*tr.*) *Nonstandard.* to say: *Then she goes, "Give it to me!" and she just snatched it.* **37.** (foll. by *into*) to be contained in: *four goes into twelve three times.* **38.** (often foll. by *for*) to endure or last out: *we can't go for much longer without water.* **39.** (*tr.*) *Cards.* to bet or bid: *I go two hearts.* **40. be going.** to intend or be about to start (to do or be doing something): often used as an alternative future construction: *what's going to happen to us?* **41. go and.** *Inf.* to be so foolish or unlucky as to: *then she had to go and lose her hat.* **42. go it.** *Sl.* to do something or move energetically. **43. go it alone.** *Inf.* to act or proceed without allies or help. **44. go one better.** *Inf.* to surpass or outdo (someone). **45. let go. a.** to relax one's hold (on); release. **b.** to discuss or consider no further. **46. let oneself go. a.** to act in an uninhibited manner. **b.** to lose interest in one's appearance, manners, etc. **47. to go. a.** remaining. **b.** *U.S. & Canad. inf.* (of food served by a restaurant) for taking away. ~*n., pl.* **goes. 48.** the act of going. **49. a.** an attempt or try: *he had a go at the stamp business.* **b.** an attempt at stopping a person suspected of a crime: *the police are not always in favour of the public having a go.* **c.** an attack, esp. verbal: *she had a real go at them.* **50.** a turn: *it's my go next.* **51.** *Inf.* the quality of being active and energetic: *she has much more go than I.* **52.** *Inf.* hard or energetic work: *it's all go.* **53.** *Inf.* a successful venture or achievement: *he made a go of it.* **54.** *Inf.* a bargain or agreement. **55. from the word go.** *Inf.* from the very beginning. **56. no go.** *Inf.* impossible; abortive or futile: *it's no go, I'm afraid.* **57. on the go.** *Inf.* active and energetic. ~*adj.* **58.** (*postpositive*) *Inf.* functioning properly and ready for action: esp. used in astronautics: *all systems are go.* ~See also **go about, go against,** etc. [OE *gān*]

go about *vb.* (*intr.*) **1.** (*prep.*) to busy oneself with: *to go about one's duties.* **2.** (*prep.*) to tackle (a problem or task). **3.** to circulate (in): *there's a lot of flu going about.* **4.** (*adv.*) (of a sailing ship) to change from one tack to another.

goad (gəʊd) *n.* **1.** a sharp pointed stick for urging on cattle, etc. **2.** anything that acts as a spur or incitement. ~*vb.* **3.** (*tr.*) to drive as if with a goad; spur; incite. [OE *gād*, of Gmc origin]

go against *vb.* (*intr., prep.*) **1.** to be contrary to (principles or beliefs). **2.** to be unfavourable to (a person): *the case went against him.*

go-ahead *n.* **1.** (usually preceded by *the*) *Inf.* permission to proceed. ~*adj.* **2.** enterprising or ambitious.

goal (gəʊl) *n.* **1.** the aim or object towards which an endeavour is directed. **2.** the terminal point of a journey or race. **3.** (in various sports) the net, basket, etc., into or over which players try to propel the ball, puck, etc., to score. **4.** *Sport.* **a.** a successful attempt at scoring. **b.** the score so made. **5.** (in soccer, hockey, etc.) the position of goalkeeper. [C16: ? rel. to ME *gol* boundary, OE *gǣlan* to hinder] —ˈ**goalless** *adj.*

goalie (ˈgəʊlɪ) *n. Inf.* short for **goalkeeper.**

goalkeeper (ˈgəʊlˌkiːpə) *n. Sport.* a player in the goal whose duty is to prevent the ball, puck, etc., from entering or crossing it.

goal kick *n. Soccer.* a kick taken from the six-yard line by the defending team after the ball has been put out of play by an opposing player.

goal line *n. Sport.* the line marking each end of the pitch, on which the goals stand.

go along *vb.* (*intr., adv.;* often foll. by *with*) to refrain from disagreement; assent.

goal post *n.* **1.** either of two upright posts supporting the crossbar of a goal. **2. move the goal posts.** to change the target required during negotiations, etc.

goanna (gəʊˈænə) *n.* any of various Australian monitor lizards. [C19: < IGUANA]

goat (gəʊt) *n.* **1.** any sure-footed agile ruminant mammal with hollow horns, naturally inhabiting rough stony ground in Europe, Asia, and N Africa. **2.** *Inf.* a lecherous man. **3.** a foolish person. **4. get (someone's) goat.** *Sl.* to cause annoyance to (someone). [OE *gāt*] —ˈ**goatish** *adj.*

Goat (gəʊt) *n.* **the.** the constellation Capricorn, the tenth sign of the zodiac.

go at *vb.* (*intr., prep.*) **1.** to make an energetic attempt at (something). **2.** to attack vehemently.

goatee (gəʊˈtiː) *n.* a pointed tuftlike beard on the chin. [C19: < GOAT + *-ee* (see -Y[2])]

goatherd (ˈgəʊtˌhɜːd) *n.* a person employed to tend or herd goats.

goatsbeard *or* **goat's-beard** (ˈgəʊtsˌbɪəd) *n.* **1.** Also called: **Jack-go-to-bed-at-noon.** a Eurasian plant of the composite family, with woolly stems and large heads of yellow rayed flowers. **2.** an American plant with long spikes of small white flowers.

goatskin (ˈgəʊtˌskɪn) *n.* **1.** the hide of a goat. **2.** something made from the hide of a goat, such as leather or a container for wine.

goatsucker (ˈgəʊtˌsʌkə) *n.* the U.S. and Canad. name for **nightjar.**

gob[1] (gɒb) *n.* **1.** a lump or chunk, esp. of a soft substance. **2.** (*often pl.*) *Inf.* a great quantity or amount. **3.** *Inf.* a globule of spittle or saliva. ~*vb.* **gobbing, gobbed. 4.** (*intr.*) *Brit. inf.* to spit. [C14: < OF *gobe* lump, < *gober;* see GOBBET]

gob[2] (gɒb) *n.* a slang word (esp. Brit.) for the **mouth.** [C16: ? < Gaelic *gob*]

go back *vb.* (*intr., adv.*) **1.** to return. **2.** (often foll. by *to*) to originate (in): *the links with France go back to the Norman Conquest.* **3.** (foll. by *on*) to change one's mind about; repudiate (esp. in **go back on one's word**).

gobbet (ˈgɒbɪt) *n.* a chunk, lump, or fragment, esp. of raw meat. [C14: < OF *gobet,* < *gober* to gulp down]

gobble[1] (ˈgɒbᵊl) *vb.* **1.** (when *tr.,* often foll. by *up*) to eat or swallow (food) hastily and in large mouthfuls. **2.** (*tr.;* often foll. by *up*) *Inf.* to snatch. [C17: prob. < GOB[1]]

gobble[2] (ˈgɒbᵊl) *n.* **1.** the loud rapid gurgling sound made by male turkeys. ~*vb.* **2.** (*intr.*) (of a turkey) to make this sound. [C17: prob. imit.]

gobbledegook *or* **gobbledygook** (ˈgɒbᵊl dɪˌguːk) *n.* pretentious language, esp. as characterized by obscure phraseology. [C20: whimsical formation < GOBBLE[2]]

gobbler (ˈgɒblə) *n. Inf.* a male turkey.

Gobelin (ˈgəʊbəlɪn; *French* gɔblɛ̃) *adj.* **1.** of or resembling tapestry made at the Gobelins' factory in Paris, having vivid pictorial scenes. ~*n.* **2.** a tapestry of this kind. [C19: < the *Gobelin* family, who founded the factory]

go-between *n.* a person who acts as agent or intermediary for two people or groups in a transaction or dealing.

goblet (ˈgɒblɪt) *n.* **1.** a vessel for drinking, with a base and stem but without handles. **2.** *Arch.* a large drinking cup. [C14: < OF *gobelet* a little cup, < *gobel,* ult. of Celtic origin]

goblin (ˈgɒblɪn) *n.* (in folklore) a small grotesque supernatural creature, regarded as malevolent towards human beings. [C14: < OF, < MHG *kobolt;* cf. COBALT]

gobo (ˈgəʊbəʊ) *n., pl.* **-bos** *or* **-boes.** a shield placed round a microphone to exclude unwanted sounds, or round a camera lens, etc., to reduce the incident light. [C20: <?]

goby (ˈgəʊbɪ) *n., pl.* **-by** *or* **-bies.** a small spiny-finned fish of coastal or brackish waters, having a large head, an elongated tapering body, and the ventral fins modified as a sucker. [C18: < L *gōbius* gudgeon < Gk *kōbios*]

go-by *n. Sl.* a deliberate snub or slight (esp. in **give (a person) the go-by**).

go by *vb.* (*intr.*) **1.** to pass: *as the years go by.* **2.** (*prep.*) to be guided by: *in the darkness we could only go by the stars.* **3.** (*prep.*) to use as a basis for forming an opinion or judgment: *it's wise not to go only by appearances.*

go-cart *n.* See **kart.**

god (gɒd) *n.* **1.** a supernatural being, who is worshipped as the controller of some part of the universe or some aspect of life in the world or is the personification of some force. **2.** an image, idol, or symbolic representation of such a deity. **3.** any person or thing to which excessive attention is given: *money was his god.* **4.** a man who has qualities regarded as making him superior to other men. **5.** (*pl.*) the gallery of a theatre. [OE *god*]

God (gɒd) *n.* **1.** the sole Supreme Being, eternal, spiritual, and transcendent, who is the Creator and ruler of all and is infinite in all attributes; the object of worship in monotheistic religions. ~*interj.* **2.** an oath or exclamation used to indicate surprise, annoyance, etc. (and in such expressions as **My God!** or **God Almighty!**).

godchild (ˈgɒdˌtʃaɪld) *n., pl.* **-children.** a person who is sponsored by adults at baptism.

goddaughter (ˈgɒdˌdɔːtə) *n.* a female godchild.

goddess (ˈgɒdɪs) *n.* **1.** a female divinity. **2.** a woman who is adored or idealized, esp. by a man.

godetia (gəˈdiːʃə) *n.* any plant of the American genus *Godetia,* esp. one grown as a showy-flowered annual garden plant. [C19: after C. H. *Godet* (died 1879), Swiss botanist]

godfather (ˈgɒdˌfɑːðə) *n.* **1.** a male godparent. **2.** the head of a Mafia family or other criminal ring.

God-fearing *adj.* pious; devout.

godforsaken (ˈgɒdfəˌseɪkən) *adj.* (*sometimes cap.*) **1.** (*usually prenominal*) desolate; dreary; forlorn. **2.** wicked.

Godhead (ˈgɒdˌhɛd) *n.* (*sometimes not cap.*) **1.** the essential nature and condition of being God. **2. the Godhead.** God.

godhood (ˈgɒdˌhʊd) *n.* the state of being divine.

godless (ˈgɒdlɪs) *adj.* **1.** wicked or unprincipled. **2.** lacking a god. **3.** refusing to acknowledge God. —ˈ**godlessly** *adv.* —ˈ**godlessness** *n.*

godlike (ˈgɒdˌlaɪk) *adj.* resembling or befitting a god or God; divine.

godly (ˈgɒdlɪ) *adj.* **-lier, -liest.** having a religious character; pious; devout. —ˈ**godliness** *n.*

godmother (ˈgɒdˌmʌðə) *n.* a female godparent.

godown (ˈgəʊˌdaʊn) *n.* (in the East, esp. in India) a warehouse. [C16: < Malay *godong*]

go down *vb.* (*intr., mainly adv.*) **1.** (*also prep.*) to move or lead to or as if to a lower place or level; sink, decline, decrease, etc. **2.** to be defeated; lose. **3.** to be remembered or recorded (esp. in **go down in history**). **4.** to be received: *his speech went down well.* **5.** (of food) to be swallowed. **6.** *Brit.* to leave a college or university at the end of a term. **7.** (usually foll. by *with*) to fall ill; be infected. **8.** (of a celestial body) to sink or set.

godparent (ˈgɒdˌpɛərənt) *n.* a person who stands sponsor to another at baptism.

God's acre *n. Literary.* a churchyard or burial ground. [C17: translation of G *Gottesacker*]

godsend (ˈgɒdˌsɛnd) *n.* a person or thing that comes unexpectedly but is particularly welcome. [C19: < C17 *God's send,* alteration of *goddes sand* God's message, < OE *sand;* see SEND]

godson (ˈgɒdˌsʌn) *n.* a male godchild.

Godspeed (ˈgɒdˈspiːd) *sentence substitute, n.* an expression of good wishes for a person's success and safety. [C15: < *God spede* may God prosper (you)]

godwit (ˈgɒdwɪt) *n.* a large shore bird of the sandpiper family having long legs and a long upturned bill. [C16: <?]

goer (ˈgəʊə) *n.* **1. a.** a person who attends something regularly. **b.** (*in combination*): *filmgoer.* **2.** a person or thing that goes, esp. one that goes very fast. **3.** an energetic person. **4.** *Austral. inf.* an acceptable or feasible idea, proposal, etc.

goffer (ˈgəʊfə) *vb.* (*tr.*) **1.** to press pleats into (a frill). **2.** to decorate (the edges of a book). ~*n.* **3.** an ornamental frill made by pressing pleats. **4.** the decoration formed by goffering books. **5.** the iron or tool used in making goffers. [C18: < F *gaufrer* to impress a pattern, < *gaufre,* < MLow G *wāfel;* see WAFFLE[1], WAFER]

go for *vb.* (*intr., prep.*) **1.** to go somewhere in order to have or fetch: *he went for a drink.* **2.** to seek to obtain: *I'd go for that job if I were you.* **3.** to prefer or choose; like: *I really go for that new idea of yours.* **4.** to make a physical or verbal attack on. **5.** to be considered to be of a stated importance or value: *his twenty years went for nothing when he was made redundant.*

go-getter *n. Inf.* an ambitious enterprising person. —ˌ**go-**ˈ**getting** *adj.*

gogga (ˈxɒxə) *n. S. African inf.* any small animal that crawls or flies, esp. an insect. [C20: < Hottentot *xoxon* insects collectively]

goggle (ˈgɒgᵊl) *vb.* **1.** (*intr.*) to stare fixedly, as in astonishment. **2.** to cause (the eyes) to roll or bulge or (of the eyes) to roll or bulge. ~*n.* **3.** a bulging stare. **4.** (*pl.*) spectacles, often of coloured glass or covered with gauze: used to protect the eyes. [C14: < *gogelen* to look aside, <?; see AGOG] —ˈ**goggle-**ˌ**eyed** *adj.*

gogglebox (ˈgɒgᵊlˌbɒks) *n. Brit. sl.* a television set.

Go-Go *n.* a form of soul music originating in Washington, DC, characterized by the use of funk rhythms and a brass section.

go-go dancer *n.* a dancer, usually scantily dressed, who performs rhythmic and often erotic modern dance routines, esp. in a nightclub.

Goidelic (gɔɪˈdɛlɪk) *n.* **1.** the N group of Celtic

languages, consisting of Irish Gaelic, Scottish Gaelic, and Manx. ~*adj.* **2.** of, relating to, or characteristic of this group of languages. [C19: < OIrish *Goidel* a Celt, < OWelsh, < *gwydd* savage]

go in *vb.* (*intr., adv.*) **1.** to enter. **2.** (*prep.*) See **go into.** **3.** (of the sun) to become hidden behind a cloud. **4. go in for. a.** to enter as a competitor or contestant. **b.** to adopt as an activity, interest, or guiding principle: *she went in for nursing.*

going (ˈgəʊɪŋ) *n.* **1.** a departure or farewell. **2.** the condition of a surface such as a road or field with regard to walking, riding, etc.: *muddy going.* **3.** *Inf.* speed, progress, etc.: *we made good going on the trip.* ~*adj.* **4.** thriving (esp. in **a going concern**). **5.** current or accepted: *the going rate.* **6.** (*postpositive*) available: *the best going.*

going-over *n., pl.* **goings-over.** *Inf.* **1.** a check, examination, or investigation. **2.** a castigation or thrashing.

goings-on *pl. n. Inf.* **1.** actions or conduct, esp. when regarded with disapproval. **2.** happenings or events, esp. when mysterious or suspicious.

go into *vb.* (*intr., prep.*) **1.** to enter. **2.** to start a career in: *to go into publishing.* **3.** to investigate or examine. **4.** to discuss: *we won't go into that now.* **5.** to be admitted to, esp. temporarily: *she went into hospital.* **6.** to enter a specified state: *she went into fits of laughter.*

goitre *or U.S.* **goiter** (ˈgɔɪtə) *n. Pathol.* a swelling of the thyroid gland, in some cases nearly doubling the size of the neck. [C17: < F, < OF *goitron* ult. < L *guttur* throat] —**ˈgoitred** *or U.S.* **ˈgoitered** *adj.* —**ˈgoitrous** *adj.*

go-kart *or* **go-cart** *n.* See **kart.**

Golconda (gɒlˈkɒndə) *n.* (*sometimes not cap.*) a source of wealth or riches, esp. a mine. [C18: < former city in India, renowned for its diamond mines]

gold (gəʊld) *n.* **1. a.** a dense inert bright yellow element that is the most malleable and ductile metal, occurring in rocks and alluvial deposits: used as a monetary standard and in jewellery, dentistry, and plating. Symbol: Au; atomic no.: 79; atomic wt.: 196.97. Related adj.: **auric. b.** (*as modifier*): *a gold mine.* **2.** a coin or coins made of this metal. **3.** money; wealth. **4.** something precious, beautiful, etc., such as a noble nature (esp. in **heart of gold**). **5. a.** a deep yellow colour, sometimes with a brownish tinge. **b.** (*as adj.*): *a gold carpet.* **6.** short for **gold medal.** [OE *gold*]

goldcrest (ˈgəʊldˌkrɛst) *n.* a small Old World warbler having a greenish plumage and a bright yellow-and-black crown.

gold-digger *n.* **1.** a person who prospects or digs for gold. **2.** *Inf.* a woman who uses her sexual attractions to accumulate gifts and wealth.

gold dust *n.* gold in the form of small particles or powder.

golden (ˈgəʊldən) *adj.* **1.** of the yellowish colour of gold: *golden hair.* **2.** made from or largely consisting of gold: *a golden statue.* **3.** happy or prosperous: *golden days.* **4.** (*sometimes cap.*) (of anniversaries) the 50th in a series: *Golden Jubilee; golden wedding.* **5.** *Inf.* very successful or destined for success: *the golden girl of tennis.* **6.** extremely valuable or advantageous: *a golden opportunity.* —**ˈgoldenly** *adv.* —**ˈgoldenness** *n.*

golden age *n.* **1.** *Classical myth.* the first and best age of mankind, when existence was happy, prosperous, and innocent. **2.** the most flourishing and outstanding period, esp. in the history of an art or nation: *the golden age of poetry.*

golden eagle *n.* a large eagle of mountainous regions of the N hemisphere, having a plumage that is golden brown on the back.

goldeneye (ˈgəʊldənˌaɪ) *n., pl.* **-eyes** *or* **-eye.** either of two black-and-white diving ducks of northern regions.

Golden Fleece *n. Greek myth.* the fleece of a winged ram stolen by Jason and the Argonauts.

golden goose *n.* a goose in folklore that laid a golden egg every day until its greedy owner killed it in an attempt to get all the gold at once.

golden handcuffs *pl. n.* payments deferred over a number of years that induce a person to stay with a particular company or in a particular job.

golden handshake *n. Inf.* a sum of money given to an employee, either on retirement or as compensation for loss of employment.

golden hello *n.* a payment made to a sought-after recruit on signing a contract of employment with a company.

golden mean *n.* **1.** the middle course between extremes. **2.** another term for **golden section.**

golden number *n.* a number between 1 and 19, used to indicate the position of any year in the Metonic cycle: so called from its importance in fixing the date of Easter.

golden retriever *n.* a breed of retriever with a silky wavy coat of a golden colour.

goldenrod (ˌgəʊldənˈrɒd) *n.* a plant of the composite family of North America, Europe, and Asia, having spikes of small yellow flowers.

golden rule *n.* **1.** the rule of conduct formulated by Christ: *Whatsoever ye would that men should do to you, do ye even so to them* (Matthew 7:12). **2.** any important principle: *a golden rule of sailing is to wear a life jacket.* **3.** another name for **rule of three.**

golden section *or* **mean** *n.* the proportion of the two divisions of a straight line such that the smaller is to the larger as the larger is to the sum of the two.

golden syrup *n. Brit.* a light golden-coloured treacle produced by the evaporation of cane sugar juice, used to flavour cakes, puddings, etc.

golden wattle *n.* **1.** an Australian yellow-flowered plant that yields a useful gum and bark. **2.** any of several similar and related Australian plants.

goldfinch (ˈgəʊldˌfɪntʃ) *n.* a common European finch, the male of which has a red-and-white face and yellow-and-black wings.

goldfish (ˈgəʊldˌfɪʃ) *n., pl.* **-fish** *or* **-fishes.** a freshwater fish of E Europe and Asia, esp. China, widely introduced as a pond or aquarium fish. It resembles the carp and has a typically golden or orange-red coloration.

gold foil *n.* thin gold sheet that is thicker than gold leaf.

gold leaf *n.* very thin gold sheet produced by rolling or hammering gold and used for gilding woodwork, etc.

gold medal *n.* a medal of gold, awarded to the winner of a competition or race.

gold plate *n.* **1.** a thin coating of gold, usually produced by electroplating. **2.** vessels or utensils made of gold. —**ˌgold-ˈplate** *vb.* (*tr.*)

gold reserve *n.* the gold reserved by a central bank to support domestic credit expansion, to cover balance of payments deficits, and to protect currency.

gold rush *n.* a large-scale migration of people to a territory where gold has been found.

goldsmith (ˈgəʊldˌsmɪθ) *n.* **1.** a dealer in articles made of gold. **2.** an artisan who makes such articles.

gold standard *n.* a monetary system in which the unit of currency is defined with reference to gold.

golf (gɒlf) *n.* **1.** a game played on a large open course, the object of which is to hit a ball using clubs, with as few strokes as possible, into each of usually 18 holes. ~*vb.* **2.** (*intr.*) to play golf. [C15: ? < MDu. *colf* CLUB] —**ˈgolfer** *n.*

golf ball *n.* **1.** a small resilient white ball of strands of rubber wound at high tension around a core with a cover made of gutta-percha, etc., used in golf. **2.** (in some electric typewriters) a small detachable metal sphere, around the surface of which type characters are arranged.

golf club *n.* **1.** any of various long-shafted clubs with wood or metal heads used to strike a golf ball. **2. a.** an association of golf players, usually having its own course and facilities. **b.** the premises of such an association.

golf course *or* **links** *n.* an area of ground laid out for the playing of golf.

Goliath (gəˈlaɪəθ) *n. Bible.* a Philistine giant who

was killed by David with a stone from his sling (I Samuel 17).

golliwog (ˈgɒlɪˌwɒg) *n.* a soft doll with a black face, usually made of cloth or rags. [C19: < a doll in a series of American children's books]

gollop (ˈgɒləp) *vb.* to eat or drink (something) quickly or greedily. [dialect var. of GULP]

golly (ˈgɒlɪ) *interj.* an exclamation of mild surprise. [C19: orig. a euphemism for GOD]

goloshes (gəˈlɒʃɪz) *pl. n.* a less common spelling of **galoshes.**

-gon *n. combining form.* indicating a figure having a specified number of angles: *pentagon.* [< Gk *-gōnon,* < *gōnia* angle]

gonad (ˈgɒnæd) *n.* an animal organ in which gametes are produced, such as a testis or an ovary. [C19: < NL *gonas,* < Gk *gonos* seed] —ˈ**gonadal** *or* **gonadial** (gɒˈneɪdɪəl) *adj.*

gondola (ˈgɒndələ) *n.* **1.** a long narrow flat-bottomed boat with a high ornamented stem: traditionally used on the canals of Venice. **2. a.** a car or cabin suspended from an airship or balloon. **b.** a moving cabin suspended from a cable across a valley, etc. **3.** a flat-bottomed barge used on canals and rivers of the U.S. **4.** *U.S. & Canad.* a low open flat-bottomed railway goods wagon. **5.** a set of island shelves in a self-service shop: used for displaying goods. **6.** *Canad.* a broadcasting booth built close to the roof of an ice-hockey stadium. [C16: < It. (dialect), < Med. L, ? ult. < Gk *kondu* drinking vessel]

gondolier (ˌgɒndəˈlɪə) *n.* a man who propels a gondola.

Gondwanaland (gɒndˈwɑːnəˌlænd) *n.* one of the two ancient supercontinents comprising chiefly what are now Africa, South America, Australia, Antarctica, and the Indian subcontinent. [C19: < *Gondwana,* region in central north India, where the rock series was orig. found]

gone (gɒn) *vb.* **1.** the past participle of **go.** ~*adj.* (*usually postpositive*) **2.** ended; past. **3.** lost; ruined. **4.** dead. **5.** spent; consumed; used up. **6.** *Inf.* faint or weak. **7.** *Inf.* having been pregnant (for a specified time): *six months gone.* **8.** (usually foll. by *on*) *Sl.* in love (with).

goner (ˈgɒnə) *n. Sl.* a person or thing beyond help or recovery, esp. a person who is about to die.

gonfalon (ˈgɒnfələn) *n.* **1.** a banner hanging from a crossbar, used esp. by certain medieval Italian republics. **2.** a battle flag suspended crosswise on a staff, usually having a serrated edge. [C16: < OIt., < OF, of Gmc origin]

gong (gɒŋ) *n.* **1.** a percussion instrument consisting of a metal platelike disc struck with a soft-headed drumstick. **2.** a rimmed metal disc, hollow metal hemisphere, or metal strip, tube, or wire that produces a note when struck. **3.** a fixed saucer-shaped bell, as on an alarm clock, struck by a mechanically operated hammer. **4.** *Brit. sl.* a medal, esp. a military one. ~*vb.* **5.** (*intr.*) to sound a gong. **6.** (*tr.*) (of traffic police) to summon (a driver) to stop by sounding a gong. [C17: < Malay, imit.]

goniometer (ˌgəʊnɪˈɒmɪtə) *n.* **1.** an instrument for measuring the angles between the faces of a crystal. **2.** an instrument used to determine the bearing of a distant radio station. [C18: via F < Gk *gōnia* angle] —**goniometric** (ˌgəʊnɪəˈmɛtrɪk) *adj.* —ˌ**goniˈometry** *n.*

-gonium *n. combining form.* indicating a seed or reproductive cell: *archegonium.* [< NL, < Gk *gonos* seed]

gonococcus (ˌgɒnəʊˈkɒkəs) *n., pl.* **-cocci** (-ˈkɒksaɪ). a spherical bacterium that causes gonorrhoea.

gonorrhoea *or esp. U.S.* **gonorrhea** (ˌgɒnəˈrɪə) *n.* an infectious venereal disease characterized by a discharge of mucus and pus from the urethra or vagina. [C16: < L, < Gk *gonos* semen + *rhoia* flux] —ˌ**gonorˈrhoeal** *or esp. U.S.* ˌ**gonorˈrheal** *adj.*

-gony *n. combining form.* genesis, origin, or production: *cosmogony.* [< L, < Gk, < *gonos* seed, procreation]

goo (guː) *n. Inf.* **1.** a sticky substance. **2.** coy or sentimental language or ideas. [C20: <?]

good (gʊd) *adj.* **better, best. 1.** having admirable, pleasing, superior, or positive qualities; not negative, bad, or mediocre: *a good teacher.* **2. a.** morally excellent or admirable; virtuous; righteous: *a good man.* **b.** (*as collective n.;* preceded by *the*): *the good.* **3.** suitable or efficient for a purpose: *a good winter coat.* **4.** beneficial or advantageous: *vegetables are good for you.* **5.** not ruined or decayed: *the meat is still good.* **6.** kindly or generous: *you are good to him.* **7.** valid or genuine: *I would not do this without good reason.* **8.** honourable or held in high esteem: *a good family.* **9.** financially secure, sound, or safe: *a good investment.* **10.** (of a draft, etc.) drawn for a stated sum. **11.** (of debts) expected to be fully paid. **12.** clever, competent, or talented: *he's good at science.* **13.** obedient or well-behaved: *a good dog.* **14.** reliable, safe, or recommended: *a good make of clothes.* **15.** affording material pleasure: *the good life.* **16.** having a well-proportioned or generally fine appearance: *a good figure.* **17.** complete; full: *I took a good look round the house.* **18.** propitious; opportune: *a good time to ask for a rise.* **19.** satisfying or gratifying: *a good rest.* **20.** comfortable: *did you have a good night?* **21.** newest or of the best quality: *keep the good plates for guests.* **22.** fairly large, extensive, or long: *a good distance away.* **23.** sufficient; ample: *we have a good supply of food.* **24. a good one. a.** an unbelievable assertion. **b.** a very funny joke. **25. as good as.** virtually; practically: *it's as good as finished.* **26. good and.** *Inf.* (intensifier): *good and mad.* ~*interj.* **27.** an exclamation of approval, agreement, pleasure, etc. ~*n.* **28.** moral or material advantage or use; benefit or profit: *for the good of our workers; what is the good of worrying?* **29.** positive moral qualities; goodness; virtue; righteousness; piety. **30.** (*sometimes cap.*) moral qualities seen as an abstract entity: *we must pursue the Good.* **31.** a good thing. **32. for good (and all).** forever; permanently: *I have left them for good.* **33. good for** *or* **on you.** well done, well said, etc.: a term of congratulation. **34. make good. a.** to recompense or repair damage or injury. **b.** to be successful. **c.** to prove the truth of (a statement or accusation). **d.** to secure and retain (a position). **e.** to effect or fulfil (something intended or promised). ~See also **goods.** [OE *gōd*] —ˈ**goodish** *adj.*

▷ **Usage.** Careful speakers and writers of English do not use *good* and *bad* as adverbs: *she dances well* (not *good*); *he sings really badly* (not *really bad*).

Good Book *n.* a name for the **Bible.**

goodbye (ˌgʊdˈbaɪ) *sentence substitute.* **1.** farewell: a conventional expression used at leave-taking or parting with people. ~*n.* **2.** a leave-taking; parting: *they prolonged their goodbyes.* **3.** a farewell: *they said goodbyes to each other.* [C16: < *God be with ye*]

good day *sentence substitute.* a conventional expression of greeting or farewell used during the day.

good-for-nothing *n.* **1.** an irresponsible or worthless person. ~*adj.* **2.** irresponsible; worthless.

Good Friday *n.* the Friday before Easter, observed as a commemoration of the Crucifixion of Jesus.

good-humoured *adj.* being in or expressing a pleasant, tolerant, and kindly state of mind. —ˌ**good-ˈhumouredly** *adv.*

goodies (ˈgʊdɪz) *pl. n.* any objects, rewards, etc., considered particularly desirable.

good-looking *adj.* handsome or pretty.

goodly (ˈgʊdlɪ) *adj.* **-lier, -liest. 1.** considerable: *a goodly amount of money.* **2.** *Obs.* attractive, pleasing, or fine. —ˈ**goodliness** *n.*

goodman (ˈgʊdmən) *n., pl.* **-men.** *Arch.* **1.** a husband. **2.** a man not of gentle birth: used as a title. **3.** a master of a household.

good morning *sentence substitute.* a conventional expression of greeting or farewell used in the morning.

good-natured *adj.* of a tolerant and kindly disposition. —ˌ**good-ˈnaturedly** *adv.*

goodness (ˈgʊdnɪs) *n.* **1.** the state or quality of being good. **2.** generosity; kindness. **3.** moral excellence; piety; virtue. **4.** what is good in something; essence. ~*interj.* **5.** a euphemism for **God:** used as an exclamation of surprise.

goodness of fit *n. Statistics.* the extent to which observed sample values of a variable approximate to values derived from a theoretical density.

good night *sentence substitute.* a conventional expression of farewell, used in the evening or at night, esp. when departing to bed.

good-oh *or* **good-o** (ˌgʊdˈəʊ) *interj. Brit. & Austral. inf.* an exclamation of pleasure, agreement, etc.

good oil *n.* (usually preceded by *the*) *Austral. sl.* true or reliable facts, information, etc.

goods (gʊdz) *pl. n.* **1.** possessions and personal property. **2.** (*sometimes sing.*) *Econ.* commodities that are tangible, usually movable, and generally not consumed at the same time as they are produced. **3.** articles of commerce; merchandise. **4.** *Chiefly Brit.* **a.** merchandise when transported, esp. by rail; freight. **b.** (*as modifier*): *a goods train.* **5. the goods. a.** *Inf.* that which is expected or promised: *to deliver the goods.* **b.** *Sl.* the real thing. **c.** *U.S. & Canad. sl.* incriminating evidence (esp. in **have the goods on someone**).

Good Samaritan *n.* **1.** *New Testament.* a figure in one of Christ's parables (Luke 10:30–37) who is an example of compassion towards those in distress. **2.** a kindly person who helps another in difficulty or distress.

Good Shepherd *n. New Testament.* a title given to Jesus Christ in John 10:11–12.

good-sized *adj.* quite large.

good-tempered *adj.* of a kindly and generous disposition.

good turn *n.* a helpful and friendly act; favour.

goodwife (ˈgʊdˌwaɪf) *n., pl.* **-wives.** *Arch.* **1.** the mistress of a household. **2.** a woman not of gentle birth: used as a title.

goodwill (ˌgʊdˈwɪl) *n.* **1.** benevolence, approval, and kindly interest. **2.** willingness or acquiescence. **3.** an intangible asset of an enterprise reflecting its commercial reputation, customer connections, etc.

goody[1] (ˈgʊdɪ) *interj.* **1.** a child's exclamation of pleasure. ~*n., pl.* **goodies. 2.** short for **goody-goody. 3.** *Inf.* the hero in a film, book, etc. **4.** See **goodies.**

goody[2] (ˈgʊdɪ) *n., pl.* **goodies.** *Arch. or literary.* a married woman of low rank: used as a title: *Goody Two-Shoes.* [C16: < GOODWIFE]

goody-goody *n., pl.* **-goodies. 1.** *Inf.* a smugly virtuous or sanctimonious person. ~*adj.* **2.** smug and sanctimonious.

gooey (ˈguːɪ) *adj.* **gooier, gooiest.** *Inf.* **1.** sticky, soft, and often sweet. **2.** oversweet and sentimental. —ˈ**gooily** *adv.*

goof (guːf) *Inf.* ~*n.* **1.** a foolish error. **2.** a stupid person. ~*vb.* **3.** to bungle (something); botch. **4.** (*intr.;* often foll. by *about* or *around*) to fool (around); mess (about). [C20: prob. < (dialect) *goff* simpleton, < OF *goffe* clumsy, < It. *goffo,* <?]

go off *vb.* (*intr.*) **1.** (*adv.*) (of power, a water supply, etc.) to cease to be available or functioning: *the lights suddenly went off.* **2.** (*adv.*) to explode. **3.** (*adv.*) to occur as specified: *the meeting went off well.* **4.** to leave (a place): *the actors went off stage.* **5.** (*adv.*) (of a sensation) to gradually cease to be felt. **6.** (*adv.*) to fall asleep. **7.** (*adv.*) (of concrete, mortar, etc.) to harden. **8.** (*adv.*) *Brit. inf.* (of food, etc.) to become stale or rotten. **9.** (*prep.*) *Brit. inf.* to cease to like.

goofy (ˈguːfɪ) *adj.* **goofier, goofiest.** *Inf.* foolish; silly. —ˈ**goofily** *adv.* —ˈ**goofiness** *n.*

goog (gʊg) *n. Austral. sl.* an egg. [? < Du. *oog*]

googly (ˈguːglɪ) *n., pl.* **-lies.** *Cricket.* an off break bowled with a leg break action. [C20: Austral.]

goolie *or* **gooly** (ˈguːlɪ) *n., pl.* **goolies. 1.** (*usually pl.*) *Taboo sl.* a testicle. **2.** *Austral. sl.* a stone or pebble. [< Hindi *golī* ball]

goon (guːn) *n.* **1.** a stupid or deliberately foolish person. **2.** *U.S. inf.* a thug hired to commit acts of violence or intimidation, esp. in an industrial dispute. [C20: partly < dialect *gooney* fool, partly after the character Alice the *Goon,* created by E. C. Segar (1894–1938), American cartoonist]

go on *vb.* (*intr., mostly adv.*) **1.** to continue or proceed. **2.** to happen: *there's something peculiar going on here.* **3.** (*prep.*) to ride on, esp. as a treat: *children love to go on donkeys at the seaside.* **4.** *Theatre.* to make an entrance on stage. **5.** to talk excessively; chatter. **6.** to continue talking, esp. after a short pause. **7.** to criticize or nag: *stop going on at me all the time!* ~*sentence substitute.* **8.** I don't believe what you're saying.

gooney bird (ˈguːnɪ) *n.* an informal name for **albatross,** esp. the black-footed albatross. [C19 *gony* (orig. sailors' sl.), prob. < dialect *gooney* fool, <?]

goop (guːp) *n. U.S. & Canad. sl.* a rude or ill-mannered person. [C20: coined by G. Burgess (1866–1951), American humorist] —ˈ**goopy** *adj.*

goorie *or* **goory** (ˈguːrɪ) *n., pl.* **goories.** *N.Z. inf.* a mongrel dog. [< Maori *kurī*]

goosander (guːˈsændə) *n.* a common merganser (a duck) of Europe and North America, having a dark head and white body in the male. [C17: prob. < GOOSE[1] + ON *önd* (genitive *andar*) duck]

goose[1] (guːs) *n., pl.* **geese. 1.** any of various web-footed long-necked birds typically larger and less aquatic than ducks. They are gregarious and migratory. **2.** the female of such a bird, as opposed to the male (gander). **3.** *Inf.* a silly person. **4.** (*pl.* **gooses**) a pressing iron with a long curving handle, used esp. by tailors. **5.** the flesh of the goose, used as food. **6. cook someone's goose.** *Inf.* **a.** to spoil someone's chances or plans completely. **b.** to bring about someone's downfall. **7. kill the goose that lays the golden eggs.** See **golden goose.** [OE *gōs*]

goose[2] (guːs) *Sl.* ~*vb.* **1.** (*tr.*) to prod (a person) playfully in the bottom. ~*n., pl.* **gooses. 2.** such a prod. [C19: < GOOSE[1], prob. < a comparison with the jabbing of a goose's bill]

gooseberry (ˈgʊzbərɪ, -brɪ) *n., pl.* **-ries. 1.** a Eurasian shrub having ovoid yellow-green or red-purple berries. **2. a.** the berry of this plant. **b.** (*as modifier*): *gooseberry jam.* **3.** *Brit. inf.* an unwanted single person, esp. a third person with a couple (often in **play gooseberry**).

goose flesh *n.* the bumpy condition of the skin induced by cold, fear, etc., caused by contraction of the muscles at the base of the hair follicles with consequent erection of papillae. Also called: **goose bumps, goose pimples, goose skin.**

goosefoot (ˈguːsˌfʊt) *n., pl.* **-foots.** any typically weedy plant having small greenish flowers and leaves shaped like a goose's foot.

goosegog (ˈgʊzgɒg) *n. Brit.* a dialect or informal word for **gooseberry.** [< *goose* in GOOSEBERRY + *gog,* var. of GOB[1]]

goosegrass (ˈguːsˌgrɑːs) *n.* another name for **cleavers.**

gooseneck (ˈguːsˌnɛk) *n.* something, such as a jointed pipe, in the form of the neck of a goose.

goose step *n.* **1.** a military march step in which the leg is swung rigidly to an exaggerated height. ~*vb.* **goose-step, -stepping, -stepped. 2.** (*intr.*) to march in goose step.

go out *vb.* (*intr., adv.*) **1.** to depart from a room, house, country, etc. **2.** to cease to illuminate, burn, or function: *the fire has gone out.* **3.** to cease to be fashionable or popular: *that style went out ages ago!* **4.** (of a broadcast) to be transmitted. **5.** to go to entertainments, social functions, etc. **6.** (usually foll. by *with* or *together*) to associate (with a person of the opposite sex) regularly. **7.** (of workers) to begin to strike. **8.** *Card games, etc.* to get rid of the last card, token, etc., in one's hand.

go over *vb.* (*intr.*) **1.** to be received in a specified manner: *the concert went over very* *well.* **2.** (*prep.*) Also: **go through.** to examine and revise as necessary: *he went over the accounts.* **3.** (*prep.*) to check and repair: *can you go over my car, please?* **4.** (*prep.*) Also: **go through.** to rehearse: *I'll go over my lines before the play.*

gopak (ˈgəʊˌpæk) *n.* a spectacular high-leaping Russian peasant dance for men. [< Russian]

gopher (ˈgəʊfə) *n.* **1.** Also called: **pocket gopher.** a burrowing rodent of North and Central America, having a thickset body, short legs, and cheek pouches. **2.** another name for **ground squirrel. 3.** a burrowing tortoise of SE North America. [C19: < earlier *megopher* or *magopher,* <?]

goral (ˈgɔːrəl) *n.* a small goat antelope inhabiting mountainous regions of S Asia. [C19: < Hindi, prob. < Sansk.]

Gordian knot (ˈgɔːdɪən) *n.* **1.** (in Greek legend) a complicated knot, tied by King Gordius of Phrygia, that Alexander the Great cut with a sword. **2.** a complicated and intricate problem (esp. in **cut the Gordian knot**).

gore[1] (gɔː) *n.* **1.** blood shed from a wound, esp. when coagulated. **2.** *Inf.* killing, fighting, etc. [OE *gor* dirt]

gore[2] (gɔː) *vb.* (*tr.*) (of an animal, such as a bull) to pierce or stab (a person or another animal) with a horn or tusk. [C16: prob. < OE *gār* spear]

gore[3] (gɔː) *n.* **1.** a tapering or triangular piece of material used in making a shaped skirt, umbrella, etc. ~*vb.* **2.** (*tr.*) to make into or with a gore or gores. [OE *gāra*] —**gored** *adj.*

gorge (gɔːdʒ) *n.* **1.** a deep ravine, esp. one through which a river runs. **2.** the contents of the stomach. **3.** feelings of disgust or resentment (esp. in **one's gorge rises**). **4.** an obstructing mass: *an ice gorge.* **5.** *Fortifications.* a narrow rear entrance to a work. **6.** *Arch.* the throat or gullet. ~*vb.* **7.** to swallow (food) ravenously. **8.** (*tr.*) to stuff (oneself) with food. [C14: < OF *gorger* to stuff, < *gorge* throat, < LL *gurga,* < L *gurges* whirlpool]

gorgeous (ˈgɔːdʒəs) *adj.* **1.** strikingly beautiful or magnificent: *a gorgeous array; a gorgeous girl.* **2.** *Inf.* extremely pleasing, fine, or good: *gorgeous weather.* [C15: < OF *gorgias* elegant, < *gorge;* see GORGE] —ˈ**gorgeously** *adv.* —ˈ**gorgeousness** *n.*

gorget (ˈgɔːdʒɪt) *n.* **1.** a collar-like piece of armour worn to protect the throat. **2.** a part of a wimple worn by women to cover the throat and chest, esp. in the 14th century. **3.** a band of distinctive colour on the throat of an animal, esp. a bird. [C15: < OF, < *gorge;* see GORGE]

Gorgio (ˈgɔːdʒɪəʊ) *n., pl.* **-gios.** the Gypsy name for a non-Gypsy. [C19: < Romany]

Gorgon (ˈgɔːgən) *n.* **1.** *Greek myth.* any of three winged monstrous sisters who had live snakes for hair, huge teeth, and brazen claws. **2.** (*often not cap.*) *Inf.* a fierce or unpleasant woman. [via L *Gorgō* < Gk, < *gorgos* terrible]

gorgonian (gɔːˈgəʊnɪən) *n.* any of various corals having a horny or calcareous branching skeleton, such as the sea fans and red corals.

Gorgonzola (ˌgɔːgənˈzəʊlə) *n.* a semihard blue-veined cheese of sharp flavour, made from pressed milk. [C19: after *Gorgonzola,* It. town where it originated]

gorilla (gəˈrɪlə) *n.* **1.** the largest anthropoid ape, inhabiting the forests of central W Africa. It is stocky with a short muzzle and coarse dark hair. **2.** *Inf.* a large, strong, and brutal-looking man. [C19: NL, < Gk *Gorillai,* an African tribe renowned for their hirsute appearance]

gormand (ˈgɔːmənd) *n.* a less common spelling of **gourmand.**

gormandize *or* **-ise** (ˈgɔːmənˌdaɪz) *vb.* to eat (food) greedily and voraciously. —ˈ**gormandˌizer** *or* **-ˌiser** *n.*

gormless (ˈgɔːmlɪs) *adj. Brit. inf.* stupid; dull. [C19: var. of C18 *gaumless,* < dialect *gome,* < OE *gom, gome,* < ON *gaumr* heed]

go round *vb.* (*intr.*) **1.** (*adv.*) to be sufficient: *are there enough sweets to go round?* **2.** to circulate (in): *measles is going round the school.* **3.** to be long enough to encircle: *will that belt go round you?*

gorse (gɔːs) *n.* an evergreen shrub which has yellow flowers and thick green spines instead of leaves. Also called: **furze, whin.** [OE *gors*] —ˈ**gorsy** *adj.*

gory (ˈgɔːrɪ) *adj.* **gorier, goriest. 1.** horrific or bloodthirsty: *a gory story.* **2.** involving bloodshed and killing: *a gory battle.* **3.** covered in gore. —ˈ**gorily** *adv.* —ˈ**goriness** *n.*

gosh (gɒʃ) *interj.* an exclamation of mild surprise or wonder. [C18: euphemistic for GOD]

goshawk (ˈgɒsˌhɔːk) *n.* a large hawk of Europe, Asia, and North America, having a bluish-grey back and wings and paler underparts: used in falconry. [OE *gōshafoc;* see GOOSE[1], HAWK[1]]

gosling (ˈgɒzlɪŋ) *n.* **1.** a young goose. **2.** an inexperienced or youthful person. [C15: < ON *gæslingr;* rel. to Danish *gäsling;* see GOOSE[1], -LING[1]]

go-slow *n.* **1.** *Brit.* a deliberate slackening of the rate of production by organized labour as a tactic in industrial conflict. U.S. and Canad. equivalent: **slowdown.** ~*vb.* **go slow. 2.** (*intr.*) to work deliberately slowly as a tactic in industrial conflict.

gospel (ˈgɒspᵊl) *n.* **1.** Also called: **gospel truth.** an unquestionable truth: *to take someone's word as gospel.* **2.** a doctrine maintained to be of great importance. **3.** Black religious music originating in the churches of the Southern states of the United States. **4.** the message or doctrine of a religious teacher. **5. a.** the story of Christ's life and teachings as narrated in the Gospels. **b.** the good news of salvation in Jesus Christ. **c.** (*as modifier*): *the gospel story.* [OE *gōdspell,* < *gōd* GOOD + *spell* message; see SPELL[2]]

Gospel (ˈgɒspᵊl) *n.* **1.** any of the first four books of the New Testament, namely Matthew, Mark, Luke, and John. **2.** a reading from one of these in a religious service.

gossamer (ˈgɒsəmə) *n.* **1.** a gauze or silk fabric of the very finest texture. **2.** a filmy cobweb often seen on foliage or floating in the air. **3.** anything resembling gossamer in fineness or filminess. [C14 (in sense 2): prob. < *gos* GOOSE[1] + *somer* SUMMER; the phrase refers to *St Martin's summer,* a period in November when goose was traditionally eaten; from the prevalence of the cobweb in the autumn] —ˈ**gossamery** *adj.*

gossip (ˈgɒsɪp) *n.* **1.** casual and idle chat. **2.** a conversation involving malicious chatter or rumours about other people. **3.** Also called: **gossipmonger.** a person who habitually talks about others, esp. maliciously. **4.** light easy communication: *to write a letter full of gossip.* **5.** *Arch.* a close woman friend. ~*vb.* **6.** (*intr.;* often foll. by *about*) to talk casually or maliciously (about other people). [OE *godsibb* godparent, < GOD + SIB; came to be applied esp. to a woman's female friends at the birth of a child, hence a woman fond of light talk] —ˈ**gossiper** *n.* —ˈ**gossipy** *adj.*

gossypol (ˈgɒsɪˌpɒl) *n.* a toxic crystalline pigment that is a constituent of cottonseed oil: discovered to have medical applications and currently the subject of research as a male contraceptive. [C19: < Mod. L *gossypium* cotton plant + -OL[1]]

got (gɒt) *vb.* **1.** the past tense and past participle of **get. 2. have got. a.** to possess. **b.** (*takes an infinitive*) used as an auxiliary to express compulsion: *I've got to get a new coat.*

Goth (gɒθ) *n.* **1.** a member of an East Germanic people from Scandinavia who invaded many parts of the Roman Empire from the 3rd to the 5th century. **2.** a rude or barbaric person. **3.** another name for **Gothic** (sense 10). ~*adj.* **4.** another word for **Gothic** (sense 6). [C14: < LL (pl.) *Gothī* < Gk *Gothoi*]

Gothic (ˈgɒθɪk) *adj.* **1.** denoting, relating to, or resembling the style of architecture that was used in W Europe from the 12th to the 16th centuries, characterized by the lancet arch, the ribbed vault, and the flying buttress. **2.** (*sometimes not cap.*) of or relating to a literary style characterized by gloom, the grotesque, and the supernatural, popular esp. in the late 18th century. **3.** of, relating to, or characteristic of the Goths or their language. **4.** (*sometimes not cap.*) primitive and barbarous in style, behaviour, etc. **5.** of or relating to the Middle Ages. **6.** (*sometimes not cap.*) Also: **Goth. a.** (of music) in a style halfway between heavy metal and punk. **b.** (of fashion) characterized by black clothes and deathly white make-up. ~*n.* **7.** Gothic architecture or art. **8.** the extinct language of the ancient Goths; East Germanic. **9.** Also called (esp. Brit): **black letter.** the family of heavy script typefaces in use from about the 15th to 18th centuries. **10.** (*sometimes not cap.*) Also called: **Goth.** an aficionado of the Gothic style in music and fashion. —**'Gothically** *adv.* —**'Gothi,cism** *n.*

go through *vb.* (*intr.*) **1.** (*adv.*) to be approved or accepted: *the amendment went through.* **2.** (*prep.*) to consume; exhaust: *we went through our supplies in a day.* **3.** (*prep.*) Also: **go over.** to examine: *he went through the figures.* **4.** (*prep.*) to suffer: *she went through tremendous pain.* **5.** (*prep.*) Also: **go over.** to rehearse: *let's just go through the details again.* **6.** (*prep.*) to search: *she went through the cupboards.* **7.** (*adv.*; foll. by *with*) to come or bring to a successful conclusion, often by persistence.

go together *vb.* (*intr., adv.*) **1.** to be mutually suited; harmonize: *the colours go well together.* **2.** *Inf.* (of two people of opposite sex) to associate frequently with each other: *they had been going together for two years.*

gotten ('gɒtᵊn) *vb. U.S.* a past participle of **get.**

Götterdämmerung (,gɒtə'dɛmə,rʊŋ) *n. German myth.* the twilight of the gods; their ultimate destruction in a battle with the forces of evil.

gouache (gʊ'ɑːʃ) *n.* **1.** Also called: **body colour.** a painting technique using opaque watercolour in which the pigments are bound with glue. **2.** the paint used in this technique. **3.** a painting done by this method. [C19: < F, < It. *guazzo* puddle, < L, < *aqua* water]

Gouda ('gaʊdə) *n.* a large flat round mild Dutch cheese, orig. made in the town of Gouda.

gouge (gaʊdʒ) *vb.* (*mainly tr.*) **1.** (usually foll. by *out*) to scoop or force (something) out of its position. **2.** (sometimes foll. by *out*) to cut (a hole or groove) in (something) with a sharp instrument or tool. **3.** *U.S. & Canad. inf.* to extort from. **4.** (*also intr.*) *Austral.* to dig for (opal). ~*n.* **5.** a type of chisel with a blade that has a concavo-convex section. **6.** a mark or groove made as with a gouge. **7.** *U.S. & Canad. inf.* extortion; swindling. [C15: < F, < LL *gulbia* a chisel, of Celtic origin] —**'gouger** *n.*

goulash ('guːlæʃ) *n.* **1.** Also called: **Hungarian goulash.** a rich stew, originating in Hungary, made of beef, lamb, or veal highly seasoned with paprika. **2.** *Bridge.* a method of dealing in threes and fours without first shuffling the cards, to produce freak hands. [C19: < Hungarian *gulyás hus* herdsman's meat]

go under *vb.* (*intr., mainly adv.*) **1.** (*also prep.*) to sink below (a surface). **2.** to be overwhelmed: *the firm went under in the economic crisis.*

go up *vb.* (*intr., mainly adv.*) **1.** (*also prep.*) to move or lead as to a higher place or level; rise; increase: *prices are always going up.* **2.** to be destroyed: *the house went up in flames.* **3.** *Brit.* to go or return (to college or university).

gourami ('gʊərəmɪ) *n., pl.* **-mi** *or* **-mis. 1.** a large SE Asian labyrinth fish used for food. **2.** any of various other labyrinth fishes, many of which are brightly coloured and popular aquarium fishes. [< Malay *gurami*]

gourd (gʊəd) *n.* **1.** the fruit of any of various plants of the cucumber family, esp. the bottle gourd and some squashes, whose dried shells are used for ornament, drinking cups, etc. **2.** any plant that bears this fruit. **3.** a bottle or flask made from the dried shell of the bottle gourd. [C14: < OF *gourde*, ult. < L *cucurbita*]

gourmand ('gʊəmənd) *or* **gormand** *n.* a person devoted to eating and drinking, esp. to excess. [C15: < OF *gourmant*, <?] —**'gourmand,ism** *n.*

gourmet ('gʊəmeɪ) *n.* a person who cultivates a discriminating palate for the enjoyment of good food and drink. [C19: < F, < OF *gromet* serving boy]

gout (gaʊt) *n.* **1.** a metabolic disease characterized by painful inflammation of certain joints, esp. of the big toe, caused by deposits of sodium urate. **2.** *Arch.* a drop or splash, esp. of blood. [C13: < OF, < L *gutta* a drop] —**'gouty** *adj.* —**'goutily** *adv.* —**'goutiness** *n.*

Gov. *or* **gov.** *abbrev. for:* **1.** government. **2.** governor.

govern ('gʌvᵊn) *vb.* (*mainly tr.*) **1.** (*also intr.*) to direct and control the actions, affairs, policies, functions, etc., of (an organization, nation, etc.); rule. **2.** to exercise restraint over; regulate or direct: *to govern one's temper.* **3.** to decide or determine (something): *his injury governed his decision to avoid sports.* **4.** to control the speed of (an engine, machine, etc.) using a governor. **5.** (of a word) to determine the inflection of (another word): *Latin nouns govern adjectives that modify them.* [C13: < OF, < L *gubernāre* to steer, < Gk *kubernan*] —**'governable** *adj.*

governance ('gʌvənəns) *n.* **1.** government, control, or authority. **2.** the action, manner, or system of governing.

governess ('gʌvənɪs) *n.* a woman teacher employed in a private household to teach and train the children.

government ('gʌvənmənt, 'gʌvəmənt) *n.* **1.** the exercise of political authority over the actions, affairs, etc., of a political unit, people, etc.; the action of governing; political rule and administration. **2.** the system or form by which a community, etc., is ruled: *tyrannical government.* **3. a.** the executive policy-making body of a political unit, community, etc.; ministry or administration. **b.** (*cap. when of a specific country*): *the British Government.* **4. a.** the state and its administration: *blame it on the government.* **b.** (*as modifier*): *a government agency.* **5.** regulation; direction. **6.** *Grammar.* the determination of the form of one word by another word. —**governmental** (,gʌvən'mɛntᵊl, ,gʌvə'mɛntᵊl) *adj.* —**,govern'mentally** *adv.*

governor ('gʌvənə) *n.* **1.** a person who governs. **2.** the ruler or chief magistrate of a colony, province, etc. **3.** the representative of the Crown in a British colony. **4.** *Brit.* the senior administrator of a society, prison, etc. **5.** the chief executive of any state in the U.S. **6.** a device that controls the speed of an engine, esp. by regulating the supply of fuel. **7.** *Brit. inf.* a name or title of respect for a father, employer, etc. —**'governor,ship** *n.*

governor general *n., pl.* **governors general** *or* **governor generals. 1.** the representative of the Crown in a dominion of the Commonwealth or a British colony; vicegerent. **2.** *Brit.* a governor with jurisdiction or precedence over other governors. —**,governor-'general,ship** *n.*

Govt *or* **govt** *abbrev. for* government.

go with *vb.* (*intr., prep.*) **1.** to accompany. **2.** to blend or harmonize: *that new wallpaper goes well with the furniture.* **3.** to be a normal part of: *three acres of land go with the house.* **4.** (of two people of the opposite sex) to associate frequently with each other.

go without *vb.* (*intr.*) *Chiefly Brit.* to be denied or deprived of (something, esp. food): *if you don't like your tea you can go without.*

gowk (gaʊk) *n. Scot. & N English dialect.* **1.** a fool. **2.** a cuckoo. [< ON *gaukr* cuckoo]

gown (gaʊn) *n.* **1.** any of various outer garments, such as a woman's elegant or formal dress, a dressing robe, or a protective garment, esp. one worn by surgeons during operations. **2.** a loose wide garment indicating status, such as worn by academics. **3.** the members of a university as opposed to the other residents of the university town. ~*vb.* **4.** (*tr.*) to supply with or dress in a gown. [C14: < OF, < LL *gunna* garment made of leather or fur, of Celtic origin]

goy (gɔɪ) *n., pl.* **goyim** ('gɔɪɪm) *or* **goys.** *Sl.* a

Jewish word for a **Gentile.** [< Yiddish, < Heb. *goi* people] —**ˈgoyish** *adj.*

GP *abbrev. for:* **1.** Gallup Poll. **2.** *Music.* general pause. **3.** general practitioner. **4.** (in Britain) graduated pension. **5.** Grand Prix.

GPO *abbrev. for* general post office.

Gr. *abbrev. for:* **1.** Grecian. **2.** Greece. **3.** Greek.

Graafian follicle (ˈgrɑːfɪən) *n.* a fluid-filled vesicle in the mammalian ovary containing a developing egg cell. [C17: after R. de *Graaf* (1641–73), Du. anatomist]

grab (græb) *vb.* **grabbing, grabbed. 1.** to seize hold of (something). **2.** (*tr.*) to seize illegally or unscrupulously. **3.** (*tr.*) to arrest; catch. **4.** (*tr.*) *Inf.* to catch the attention or interest of; impress. ~*n.* **5.** the act or an instance of grabbing. **6.** a mechanical device for gripping objects, esp. the hinged jaws of a mechanical excavator. **7.** something that is grabbed. [C16: prob. < MLow G or MDu. *grabben*] —**ˈgrabber** *n.*

grace (greɪs) *n.* **1.** elegance and beauty of movement, form, expression, or proportion. **2.** a pleasing or charming quality. **3.** goodwill or favour. **4.** a delay granted for the completion of a task or payment of a debt. **5.** a sense of propriety and consideration for others. **6.** (*pl.*) **a.** affectation of manner (esp. in **airs and graces**). **b. in (someone's) good graces.** regarded favourably and with kindness by (someone). **7.** mercy; clemency. **8.** *Christian theol.* **a.** the free and unmerited favour of God shown towards man. **b.** the divine assistance given to man in spiritual rebirth. **c.** the condition of being favoured or sanctified by God. **d.** an unmerited gift, favour, etc., granted by God. **9.** a short prayer recited before or after a meal to give thanks for it. **10.** *Music.* a melodic ornament or decoration. **11. with (a) bad grace.** unwillingly or grudgingly. **12. with (a) good grace.** willingly or cheerfully. ~*vb.* **13.** (*tr.*) to add elegance and beauty to: *flowers graced the room.* **14.** (*tr.*) to honour or favour: *to grace a party with one's presence.* **15.** to ornament or decorate (a melody, part, etc.) with nonessential notes. [C12: < OF, < L *grātia*, < *grātus* pleasing]

Grace (greɪs) *n.* (preceded by *your, his,* or *her*) a title used to address or refer to a duke, duchess, or archbishop.

grace-and-favour *n.* (*modifier*) *Brit.* (of a house, flat, etc.) owned by the sovereign and granted free of rent to a person to whom the sovereign wishes to express gratitude.

graceful (ˈgreɪsfʊl) *adj.* characterized by beauty of movement, style, form, etc. —**ˈgracefully** *adv.* —**ˈgracefulness** *n.*

graceless (ˈgreɪslɪs) *adj.* **1.** lacking manners. **2.** lacking elegance. —**ˈgracelessly** *adv.* —**ˈgracelessness** *n.*

grace note *n. Music.* a note printed in small type to indicate that it is melodically and harmonically nonessential.

Graces (ˈgreɪsɪz) *pl. n. Greek myth.* three sister goddesses, givers of charm and beauty.

gracious (ˈgreɪʃəs) *adj.* **1.** characterized by or showing kindness and courtesy. **2.** condescendingly courteous, benevolent, or indulgent. **3.** characterized by or suitable for a life of elegance, ease, and indulgence: *gracious living.* **4.** merciful or compassionate. ~*interj.* **5.** an expression of mild surprise or wonder. —**ˈgraciously** *adv.* —**ˈgraciousness** *n.*

grackle (ˈgræk^{ə}l) *n.* **1.** an American songbird of the oriole family, having a dark iridescent plumage. **2.** any of various starlings, such as the Indian grackle or hill myna. [C18: < NL, < L *grāculus* jackdaw]

grad. *abbrev. for:* **1.** *Maths.* gradient. **2.** *Education.* graduate(d).

gradate (grəˈdeɪt) *vb.* **1.** to change or cause to change imperceptibly, as from one colour, tone, or degree to another. **2.** (*tr.*) to arrange in grades or ranks.

gradation (grəˈdeɪʃən) *n.* **1.** a series of systematic stages; gradual progression. **2.** (*often pl.*) a stage or degree in such a series or progression. **3.** the act or process of arranging or forming in stages, grades, etc., or of progressing evenly. **4.** (in painting, drawing, or sculpture) transition from one colour, tone, or surface to another through a series of very slight changes. **5.** *Linguistics.* any change in the quality or length of a vowel within a word indicating certain distinctions, such as inflectional or tense differentiations. See **ablaut.** —**graˈdational** *adj.*

grade (greɪd) *n.* **1.** a position or degree in a scale, as of quality, rank, size, or progression: *high-grade timber.* **2.** a group of people or things of the same category. **3.** *Chiefly U.S.* a military or other rank. **4.** a stage in a course of progression. **5.** a mark or rating indicating achievement or the worth of work done, as at school. **6.** *U.S. & Canad.* a unit of pupils of similar age or ability taught together at school. **7. make the grade.** *Inf.* **a.** to reach the required standard. **b.** to succeed. ~*vb.* **8.** (*tr.*) to arrange according to quality, rank, etc. **9.** (*tr.*) to determine the grade of or assign a grade to. **10.** (*intr.*) to achieve or deserve a grade or rank. **11.** to change or blend (something) gradually; merge. **12.** (*tr.*) to level (ground, a road, etc.) to a suitable gradient. [C16: < F, < L *gradus* step, < *gradī* to step]

-grade *adj. combining form.* indicating a kind or manner of movement or progression: *plantigrade; retrograde.* [via F < L *-gradus*, < *gradus* a step, < *gradī* to walk]

gradely (ˈgreɪdlɪ) *adj.* **-lier, -liest.** *Midland English dialect.* fine; excellent. [C13: < ON *greidhligr*, < *greidhr* ready]

grader (ˈgreɪdə) *n.* **1.** a person or thing that grades. **2.** a machine that levels earth, rubble, etc., as in road construction.

gradient (ˈgreɪdɪənt) *n.* **1.** Also called (esp. U.S.): **grade.** a part of a railway, road, etc., that slopes upwards or downwards; inclination. **2.** Also called (esp. U.S. and Canad.): **grade.** a measure of such a slope, esp. the ratio of the vertical distance between two points on the slope to the horizontal distance between them. **3.** *Physics.* a measure of the change of some physical quantity, such as temperature or electric potential, over a specified distance. **4.** *Maths.* (of a curve) the slope of the tangent at any point on a curve with respect to the horizontal axis. ~*adj.* **5.** sloping uniformly. [C19: < L *gradiēns* stepping, < *gradī* to go]

gradin (ˈgreɪdɪn) *or* **gradine** (grəˈdiːn) *n.* **1.** a ledge above or behind an altar for candles, etc., to stand on. **2.** one of a set of steps or seats arranged on a slope, as in an amphitheatre. [C19: < F, < It. *gradino*, dim. of *grado* a step]

gradual (ˈgrædjʊəl) *adj.* **1.** occurring, developing, moving, etc., in small stages: *a gradual improvement in health.* **2.** not steep or abrupt: *a gradual slope.* ~*n.* **3.** (*often cap.*) *Christianity.* **a.** an antiphon usually from the Psalms, sung or recited immediately after the epistle at Mass. **b.** a book of plainsong containing the words and music of the parts of the Mass that are sung by the cantors and choir. [C16: < Med. L: relating to steps, < L *gradus* a step] —**ˈgradually** *adv.* —**ˈgradualness** *n.*

gradualism (ˈgrædjʊəˌlɪzəm) *n.* **1.** the policy of seeking to change something gradually, esp. in politics. **2.** the theory that explains major changes in fossils, rock strata, etc., in terms of gradual evolutionary processes rather than sudden violent catastrophes. —**ˈgradualist** *n., adj.* —**ˌgradualˈistic** *adj.*

graduand (ˈgrædjʊˌænd) *n. Chiefly Brit.* a person who is about to graduate. [C19: < Med. L gerundive of *graduārī* to GRADUATE]

graduate *n.* (ˈgrædjʊɪt). **1.** a person who has been awarded a first degree from a university or college. **2.** *U.S. & Canad.* a student who has completed a course of studies at a high school and received a diploma. ~*vb.* (ˈgrædjʊˌeɪt). **3.** to receive or cause to receive a degree or diploma. **4.** *Chiefly U.S. & Canad.* to confer a degree, diploma, etc., upon. **5.** (*tr.*) to mark (a thermometer, flask, etc.) with units of measurement; calibrate. **6.** (*tr.*) to arrange or sort into groups according to type, quality, etc. **7.** (*intr.*; often foll. by *to*) to change by degrees (from something to something else). [C15: < Med. L *graduārī* to take a degree, < L *gradus* a step] —ˈ**graduˌator** *n.*

graduated pension *n.* (in Britain) a national pension scheme in which employees' contributions are scaled in accordance with their wage rate.

graduation (ˌgrædjʊˈeɪʃən) *n.* **1.** the act of graduating or the state of being graduated. **2.** the ceremony at which school or college degrees and diplomas are conferred. **3.** a mark or division or all the marks or divisions that indicate measure on an instrument or vessel.

Graecism *or esp. U.S.* **Grecism** (ˈgriːsɪzəm) *n.* **1.** Greek characteristics or style. **2.** admiration for or imitation of these, as in sculpture or architecture. **3.** a form of words characteristic or imitative of the idiom of the Greek language.

Graeco- *or esp. U.S.* **Greco-** (ˈgriːkəʊ, ˈgrɛkəʊ) *combining form.* Greek: *Graeco-Roman.*

Graeco-Roman *or esp. U.S.* **Greco-Roman** *adj.* of, characteristic of, or relating to Greek and Roman influences.

graffiti (græˈfiːtɪ) *pl. n.* (*sometimes functioning as sing.*) drawings, messages, etc., often obscene, scribbled on the walls of public lavatories, advertising posters, etc. [C19: see GRAFFITO]

graffito (græˈfiːtəʊ) *n., pl.* **-ti** (-tɪ). **1.** *Archaeol.* any inscription or drawing scratched onto a surface, esp. rock or pottery. **2.** See **graffiti.** [C19: < It.: a little scratch, < L *graphium* stylus, < Gk *grapheion;* see GRAFT[1]]

graft[1] (grɑːft) *n.* **1.** *Horticulture.* **a.** a small piece of plant tissue (the scion) that is made to unite with an established plant (the stock), which supports and nourishes it. **b.** the plant resulting from the union of scion and stock. **c.** the point of union between the scion and the stock. **2.** *Surgery.* a piece of tissue transplanted from a donor or from the patient's own body to an area of the body in need of the tissue. **3.** the act of joining one thing to another as by grafting. ~*vb.* **4.** *Horticulture.* **a.** to induce (a plant or part of a plant) to unite with another part or (of a plant or part of a plant) to unite in this way. **b.** to produce (fruit, flowers, etc.) by this means or (of fruit, etc.) to grow by this means. **5.** to transplant (tissue) or (of tissue) to be transplanted. **6.** to attach or incorporate or become attached or incorporated: *to graft a happy ending onto a sad tale.* [C15: < OF *graffe,* < Med. L *graphium,* < L: stylus, < Gk *grapheion,* < *graphein* to write] —ˈ**grafter** *n.* —ˈ**grafting** *n.*

graft[2] (grɑːft) *n.* **1.** *Inf.* work (esp. in **hard graft**). **2. a.** the acquisition of money, power, etc., by dishonest or unfair means, esp. by taking advantage of a position of trust. **b.** something gained in this way. **c.** a payment made to a person profiting by such a practice. ~*vb.* **3.** (*intr.*) *Inf.* to work, esp. hard. **4.** to acquire by or practise graft. [C19: <?] —ˈ**grafter** *n.*

Grail (greɪl) *n.* See **Holy Grail.**

grain (greɪn) *n.* **1.** the small hard seedlike fruit of a grass, esp. a cereal plant. **2.** a mass of such fruits, esp. when gathered for food. **3.** the plants, collectively, from which such fruits are harvested. **4.** a small hard particle: *a grain of sand.* **5. a.** the general direction or arrangement of the fibres, layers, or particles in wood, leather, stone, etc. **b.** the pattern or texture resulting from such an arrangement. **6.** the relative size of the particles of a substance: *sugar of fine grain.* **7.** the granular texture of a rock, mineral, etc. **8.** the outer layer of a hide or skin from which the hair or wool has been removed. **9.** the smallest unit of weight in the avoirdupois, Troy, and apothecaries' systems: equal to 0.0648 gram. **10.** the threads or direction of threads in a woven fabric. **11.** *Photog.* any of a large number of particles in a photographic emulsion. **12.** cleavage lines in crystalline material. **13.** *Chem.* any of a large number of small crystals forming a solid. **14.** a very small amount: *a grain of truth.* **15.** natural disposition, inclination, or character (esp. in **go against the grain**). **16.** *Astronautics.* a homogenous mass of solid propellant in a form designed to give the required combustion characteristics for a particular rocket. **17.** (not in technical usage) kermes or a red dye made from this insect. ~*vb.* (*mainly tr.*) **18.** (*also intr.*) to form grains or cause to form into grains; granulate; crystallize. **19.** to give a granular or roughened appearance or texture to. **20.** to paint, stain, etc., in imitation of the grain of wood or leather. **21. a.** to remove the hair or wool from (a hide or skin) before tanning. **b.** to raise the grain pattern on (leather). [C13: < OF, < L *grānum*]

grain alcohol *n.* ethanol containing about 10 per cent of water, made by the fermentation of grain.

grain elevator *n.* a machine for raising grain to a higher level, esp. one having an endless belt fitted with scoops.

graining (ˈgreɪnɪŋ) *n.* **1.** the pattern or texture of the grain of wood, leather, etc. **2.** the process of painting, printing, staining, etc., a surface in imitation of a grain. **3.** a surface produced by such a process.

grainy (ˈgreɪnɪ) *adj.* **grainier, grainiest. 1.** resembling, full of, or composed of grain; granular. **2.** resembling the grain of wood, leather, etc. **3.** *Photog.* having poor definition because of large grain size. —ˈ**graininess** *n.*

grallatorial (ˌgrælәˈtɔːrɪәl) *adj.* of or relating to long-legged wading birds. [C19: < NL, < L *grallātor* one who walks on stilts, < *grallae* stilts]

gram[1] *or* **gramme** (græm) *n.* a metric unit of mass equal to one thousandth of a kilogram. Symbol: g [C18: < F *gramme,* < LL *gramma,* < Gk: small weight, < *graphein* to write]

gram[2] (græm) *n.* **1.** any of several leguminous plants whose seeds are used as food in India. **2.** the seed of any of these plants. [C18: < Port. *gram* (modern spelling: *grão*), < L *grānum* GRAIN]

gram. *abbrev. for:* **1.** grammar. **2.** grammatical.

-gram *n. combining form.* indicating a drawing or something written or recorded: *hexagram; telegram.* [< L *-gramma,* < Gk, < *gramma* letter & *grammē* line]

gram atom *or* **gram-atomic weight** *n.* an amount of an element equal to its atomic weight expressed in grams: now replaced by the mole.

gramineous (grәˈmɪnɪәs) *adj.* **1.** of, relating to, or belonging to the grass family. **2.** resembling a grass; grasslike. ~Also: **graminaceous** (ˌgræmɪˈneɪʃәs). [C17: < L, < *grāmen* grass]

graminivorous (ˌgræmɪˈnɪvәrәs) *adj.* (of animals) feeding on grass. [C18: < L *grāmen* grass + -VOROUS]

grammar (ˈgræmә) *n.* **1.** the branch of linguistics that deals with syntax and morphology, sometimes also phonology and semantics. **2.** the abstract system of rules in terms of which a person's mastery of his native language can be explained. **3.** a systematic description of the grammatical facts of a language. **4.** a book containing an account of the grammatical facts of a language or recommendations as to rules for the proper use of a language. **5.** the use of language with regard to its correctness or social propriety, esp. in syntax: *the teacher told him to watch his grammar.* [C14: < OF, < L, < Gk *grammatikē* (*tekhnē*) the grammatical (art), < *grammatikos* concerning letters, < *gramma* letter]

grammarian (grәˈmɛәrɪәn) *n.* **1.** a person whose occupation is the study of grammar. **2.** the author of a grammar.

grammar school *n.* **1.** *Brit.* (esp. formerly) a state-maintained secondary school providing an education with an academic bias. **2.** *U.S.* another term for **elementary school. 3.** *Austral.* a private school, esp. one controlled by a church. **4.** *N.Z.* a secondary school forming part of the public education system.

grammatical (grәˈmætɪkәl) *adj.* **1.** of or relating to grammar. **2.** (of a sentence) well formed;

regarded as correct. —**gram'matically** *adv.* —**gram'maticalness** *n.*

gramme (græm) *n.* a variant spelling of **gram**[1].

gram molecule *or* **gram-molecular weight** *n.* an amount of a compound equal to its molecular weight expressed in grams: now replaced by the mole. See **mole**[3].

Grammy ('græmɪ) *n., pl.* **-mys** *or* **-mies.** (in the U.S.) one of the gold-plated discs awarded annually for outstanding achievement in the record industry. [C20: < GRAM(OPHONE) + *-my* as in EMMY]

gramophone ('græməˌfəʊn) *n.* **1. a.** Also called: **record player.** a device for reproducing the sounds stored on a record: now usually applied to the early type that uses an acoustic horn. U.S. and Canad. word: **phonograph. b.** (*as modifier*): *a gramophone record.* **2.** the technique of recording sound on disc: *the gramophone has made music widely available.* [C19: orig. a trademark, ? based on an inversion of *phonogram;* see PHONO-, -GRAM]

grampus ('græmpəs) *n., pl.* **-puses. 1.** a widely distributed slaty-grey dolphin with a blunt snout. **2.** another name for **killer whale.** [C16: < OF *graspois,* < *gras* fat (< L *crassus*) + *pois* fish (< L *piscis*)]

Gram's method (græmz) *n. Bacteriol.* **1.** a technique used to classify bacteria by staining them with a violet iodine solution. **2. Gram-positive** (*or* **Gram-negative**). *adj.* denoting bacteria that do (*or* do not) retain this stain. [C19: after H. C. J. *Gram* (1853–1938), Danish physician]

granadilla (ˌgrænə'dɪlə) *n.* **1.** any of various passionflowers that have edible egg-shaped fleshy fruit. **2.** Also called: **passion fruit.** the fruit of such a plant. [C18: < Sp., dim. of *granada* pomegranate, < LL *grānātum*]

granary ('grænərɪ; *U.S.* 'greɪnərɪ) *n., pl.* **-ries. 1.** a building for storing threshed grain. **2.** a region that produces a large amount of grain. [C16: < L *grānārium,* < *grānum* GRAIN]

grand (grænd) *adj.* **1.** large or impressive in size, extent, or consequence: *grand mountain scenery.* **2.** characterized by or attended with magnificence or display; sumptuous: *a grand feast.* **3.** of great distinction or pretension; dignified or haughty. **4.** designed to impress: *grand gestures.* **5.** very good; wonderful. **6.** comprehensive; complete: *a grand total.* **7.** worthy of respect; fine: *a grand old man.* **8.** large or impressive in conception or execution: *grand ideas.* **9.** most important; chief: *the grand arena.* ~*n.* **10.** See **grand piano. 11.** (*pl.* **grand**) *Sl.* a thousand pounds or dollars. [C16: < OF, < L *grandis*] —'**grandly** *adv.* —'**grandness** *n.*

grand- *prefix.* (in designations of kinship) one generation removed in ascent or descent: *grandson; grandfather.* [< F *grand-*, on the model of L *magnus* in such phrases as *avunculus magnus* great-uncle]

grandam ('grændəm, -dæm) *or* **grandame** ('grændeɪm, -dəm) *n.* an archaic word for **grandmother.** [C13: < Anglo-F *grandame,* < OF GRAND- + *dame* lady, mother]

grandaunt ('grændˌɑːnt) *n.* another name for **great-aunt.**

grandchild ('grænˌtʃaɪld) *n., pl.* **-children.** the son or daughter of one's child.

granddad ('grænˌdæd) *or* **granddaddy** *n., pl.* **-dads** *or* **-daddies.** informal words for **grandfather.**

granddaughter ('grænˌdɔːtə) *n.* a daughter of one's son or daughter.

grand duchess *n.* **1.** the wife or widow of a grand duke. **2.** a woman who holds the rank of grand duke in her own right.

grand duchy *n.* the territory, state, or principality of a grand duke or grand duchess.

grand duke *n.* **1.** a prince or nobleman who rules a territory, state, or principality. **2.** a son or a male descendant in the male line of a Russian tsar. **3.** a medieval Russian prince who ruled over other princes.

grande dame *French.* (grɑ̃d dam) *n.* a woman regarded as the most experienced, prominent, or venerable member of her profession, etc.

grandee (græn'diː) *n.* **1.** a Spanish or Portuguese prince or nobleman of the highest rank. **2.** a person of high station. [C16: < Sp. *grande*]

grandeur ('grændʒə) *n.* **1.** personal greatness, esp. when based on dignity, character, or accomplishments. **2.** magnificence; splendour. **3.** pretentious or bombastic behaviour.

grandfather ('grænˌfɑːðə, 'grænd-) *n.* **1.** the father of one's father or mother. **2.** (*often pl.*) a male ancestor. **3.** (*often cap.*) a familiar term of address for an old man. —'**grandˌfatherly** *adj.*

grandfather clock *n.* a long-pendulum clock in a tall standing wooden case.

Grand Guignol *French.* (grɑ̃ giɲɔl) *n.* **a.** a brief sensational play intended to horrify. **b.** (*modifier*) of or like plays of this kind. [C20: after *Le Grand Guignol,* a small theatre in Montmartre, Paris]

grandiloquent (græn'dɪləkwənt) *adj.* inflated, pompous, or bombastic in style or expression. [C16: < L *grandiloquus,* < *grandis* great + *loquī* to speak] —**gran'diloquence** *n.* —**gran'diloquently** *adv.*

grandiose ('grændɪˌəʊs) *adj.* **1.** pretentiously grand or stately. **2.** imposing in conception or execution. [C19: < F, < It., < *grande* great; see GRAND] —'**grandiˌosely** *adv.* —**grandiosity** (ˌgrændɪ'ɒsɪtɪ) *n.*

grand jury *n. Law.* (esp. in the U.S. and, now rarely, in Canada) a jury summoned to inquire into accusations of crime and ascertain whether the evidence is adequate to found an indictment. Abolished in England in 1948.

grand larceny *n.* **1.** (formerly, in England) the theft of property valued at over 12 pence. Abolished in 1827. **2.** (in some states of the U.S.) the theft of property of which the value is above a specified figure.

grandma ('grænˌmɑː), **grandmama,** *or* **grandmamma** ('grænməˌmɑː) *n.* informal words for **grandmother.**

grand mal (grɒn mæl) *n.* a form of epilepsy characterized by loss of consciousness for up to five minutes and violent convulsions. Cf. **petit mal.** [F: great illness]

grandmaster ('grændˌmɑːstə) *n.* **1.** *Chess.* one of the top chess players of a particular country. **2.** a leading exponent of any of various arts.

Grand Master *n.* the title borne by the head of any of various societies, orders, and other organizations, such as the Templars, Freemasons, or the various martial arts.

grandmother ('grænˌmʌðə, 'grænd-) *n.* **1.** the mother of one's father or mother. **2.** (*often pl.*) a female ancestor. —'**grandˌmotherly** *adj.*

Grand National *n.* **the.** an annual steeplechase run at Aintree, Liverpool, since 1839.

grandnephew ('grænˌnɛvjuː, -ˌnɛfjuː, 'grænd-) *n.* another name for **great-nephew.**

grandniece ('grænˌniːs, 'grænd-) *n.* another name for **great-niece.**

grand opera *n.* an opera that has a serious plot and is entirely in musical form, with no spoken dialogue.

grandpa ('grænˌpɑː) *or* **grandpapa** ('grænpəˌpɑː) *n.* informal words for **grandfather.**

grandparent ('grænˌpɛərənt, 'grænd-) *n.* the father or mother of either of one's parents.

grand piano *n.* a form of piano in which the strings are arranged horizontally.

Grand Prix (*French* grɑ̃ pri) *n.* any of a series of formula motor races to determine the annual Driver's World Championship. [F: great prize]

grandsire ('grænˌsaɪə, 'grænd-) *n.* an archaic word for **grandfather.**

grand slam *n.* **1.** *Bridge, etc.* the winning of 13 tricks by one player or side or the contract to do so. **2.** the winning of all major competitions in a season, esp. in tennis and golf.

grandson ('grænsʌn, 'grænd-) *n.* a son of one's son or daughter.

grandstand ('grænˌstænd, 'grænd-) *n.* **1.** a terraced block of seats commanding the best view at racecourses, football pitches, etc. **2.** the spectators in a grandstand.

grand tour *n.* **1.** (formerly) an extended tour through the major cities of Europe, esp. one undertaken by a rich or aristocratic Englishman to complete his education. **2.** *Inf.* an extended sightseeing trip, tour of inspection, etc.

granduncle (ˈgrændˌʌŋkᵊl) *n.* another name for **great-uncle.**

grange (greɪndʒ) *n.* **1.** *Chiefly Brit.* a farm, esp. a farmhouse or country house with its various outbuildings. **2.** *Arch.* a granary or barn. [C13: < Anglo-F *graunge,* < Med. L *grānica,* < L *grānum* GRAIN]

granite (ˈgrænɪt) *n.* **1.** a light-coloured coarse-grained acid plutonic igneous rock consisting of quartz and feldspars: widely used for building. **2.** great hardness, endurance, or resolution. [C17: < It. *granito* grained, < *grano* grain, < L *grānum*] **—granitic** (grəˈnɪtɪk) *adj.*

graniteware (ˈgrænɪtˌwɛə) *n.* **1.** iron vessels coated with enamel of a granite-like appearance. **2.** a type of pottery with a speckled glaze.

granivorous (græˈnɪvərəs) *adj.* (of animals) feeding on seeds and grain. **—granivore** (ˈgrænɪˌvɔː) *n.*

granny *or* **grannie** (ˈgrænɪ) *n., pl.* **-nies. 1.** informal words for **grandmother.** Often shortened to **gran. 2.** *Inf.* an irritatingly fussy person. **3.** See **granny knot.**

granny bond *n. Brit. inf.* a savings scheme available originally only to people over retirement age.

granny flat *n.* self-contained accommodation within or built onto a house, suitable for an elderly parent.

granny knot *or* **granny's knot** *n.* a reef knot with the ends crossed the wrong way, making it liable to slip or jam.

grant (grɑːnt) *vb.* (*tr.*) **1.** to consent to perform or fulfil: *to grant a wish.* **2.** (*may take a clause as object*) to permit as a favour, indulgence, etc.: *to grant an interview.* **3.** (*may take a clause as object*) to acknowledge the validity of; concede: *I grant what you say is true.* **4.** to bestow, esp. in a formal manner. **5.** to transfer (property) to another, esp. by deed; convey. **6. take for granted. a.** to accept (something) as true and not requiring verification. **b.** to take advantage of the benefits of (something) without due appreciation. *~n.* **7.** a sum of money provided by a government or public fund to finance educational study, overseas aid, etc. **8.** a privilege, right, etc., that has been granted. **9.** the act of granting. **10.** a transfer of property by deed; conveyance. [C13: < OF *graunter,* < Vulgar L *credentāre* (unattested), < L *crēdere* to believe] **—ˈgrantable** *adj.* **—ˈgranter** *or* (*Law*) **ˈgrantor** *n.*

grantee (grɑːnˈtiː) *n. Law.* a person to whom a grant is made.

Granth (grʌnt) *n.* the sacred scripture of the Sikhs. [< Hindi, < Sansk. *grantha* a book]

grant-in-aid *n., pl.* **grants-in-aid.** a sum of money granted by one government to a lower level of government for a programme, etc.

gran turismo (ˈgræn tʊəˈrɪzməʊ) *n., pl.* **gran turismos.** See **GT.** [C20: < It.]

granular (ˈgrænjʊlə) *adj.* **1.** of, like, or containing granules. **2.** having a grainy surface. **—granularity** (ˌgrænjʊˈlærɪtɪ) *n.* **—ˈgranularly** *adv.*

granulate (ˈgrænjʊˌleɪt) *vb.* **1.** (*tr.*) to make into grains: *granulated sugar.* **2.** to make or become roughened in surface texture. **—ˌgranuˈlation** *n.* **—ˈgranulative** *adj.* **—ˈgranuˌlator** *or* **ˈgranuˌlater** *n.*

granule (ˈgrænjuːl) *n.* a small grain. [C17: < LL *grānulum* a small GRAIN]

granulocyte (ˈgrænjʊləˌsaɪt) *n.* any of a group of unpigmented blood cells having cytoplasmic granules that take up various dyes.

grape (greɪp) *n.* **1.** the fruit of the grapevine, which has a purple or green skin and sweet flesh: eaten raw, dried to make raisins, currants, or sultanas, or used for making wine. **2.** See **grapevine** (sense 1). **3. the grape.** *Inf.* wine. **4.** See **grapeshot.** [C13: < OF *grape* bunch of grapes, of Gmc origin; rel. to CRAMP², GRAPPLE] **—ˈgrapey** *or* **ˈgrapy** *adj.*

grapefruit (ˈgreɪpˌfruːt) *n., pl.* **-fruit** *or* **-fruits. 1.** a tropical or subtropical evergreen tree. **2.** the large round edible fruit of this tree, which has yellow rind and juicy slightly bitter pulp.

grape hyacinth *n.* any of various Eurasian bulbous plants of the lily family with clusters of rounded blue flowers resembling tiny grapes.

grapeshot (ˈgreɪpˌʃɒt) *n.* ammunition for cannons consisting of a cluster of iron balls that scatter after firing.

grape sugar *n.* another name for **dextrose.**

grapevine (ˈgreɪpˌvaɪn) *n.* **1.** any of several vines of E Asia, widely cultivated for its fruit (grapes). **2.** *Inf.* an unofficial means of relaying information, esp. from person to person.

graph (grɑːf) *n.* **1.** Also called: **chart.** a drawing depicting the relation between certain sets of numbers or quantities by means of a series of dots, lines, etc., plotted with reference to a set of axes. **2.** *Maths.* a drawing depicting a functional relation between two or three variables by means of a curve or surface containing only those points whose coordinates satisfy the relation. **3.** *Linguistics.* a symbol in a writing system not further subdivisible into other such symbols. *~vb.* **4.** (*tr.*) to draw or represent in a graph. [C19: short for *graphic formula*]

-graph *n. combining form.* **1.** an instrument that writes or records: *telegraph.* **2.** a writing, record, or drawing: *autograph; lithograph.* [via L < Gk, < *graphein* to write] **—-graphic** *or* **-graphical** *adj. combining form.* **—-graphically** *adv. combining form.*

grapheme (ˈgræfiːm) *n. Linguistics.* the complete class of letters or combinations of letters that represent one speech sound: for instance, the *f* in *full,* the *gh* in *cough,* and the *ph* in *photo* are members of the same grapheme. [C20: < Gk *graphēma* a letter] **—graˈphemically** *adv.*

-grapher *n. combining form.* **1.** indicating a person skilled in a subject: *geographer; photographer.* **2.** indicating a person who writes or draws in a specified way: *stenographer; lithographer.*

graphic (ˈgræfɪk) *or* **graphical** *adj.* **1.** vividly or clearly described: *a graphic account of the disaster.* **2.** of or relating to writing: *graphic symbols.* **3.** *Maths.* using, relating to, or determined by a graph: *a graphic representation of the figures.* **4.** of or relating to the graphic arts. **5.** *Geol.* having or denoting a texture resembling writing: *graphic granite.* [C17: < L *graphicus,* < Gk *graphikos,* < *graphein* to write] **—ˈgraphically** *adv.* **—ˈgraphicness** *n.*

graphicacy (ˈgræfɪkəsɪ) *n.* the ability to understand and use maps, symbols, etc. [C20: formed on the model of *literacy*]

graphic arts *pl. n.* any of the fine or applied visual arts based on drawing or the use of line, esp. illustration and printmaking of all kinds.

graphic equalizer *n.* an electronic device for cutting or boosting selected frequencies, using small linear faders.

graphics (ˈgræfɪks) *n.* **1.** (*functioning as sing.*) the process or art of drawing in accordance with mathematical principles. **2.** (*functioning as sing.*) the study of writing systems. **3.** (*functioning as pl.*) the drawings, photographs, etc., in a magazine or book, or in a television or film production. **4.** (*functioning as pl.*) *Computers.* information displayed in the form of diagrams, graphs, etc.

graphite (ˈgræfaɪt) *n.* a blackish soft form of carbon used in pencils, electrodes, as a lubricant, as a moderator in nuclear reactors, and, in carbon fibre form, for tough lightweight sports equipment. [C18: < G *Graphit,* < Gk *graphein* to write + -ITE¹] **—graphitic** (grəˈfɪtɪk) *adj.*

graphology (græˈfɒlədʒɪ) *n.* **1.** the study of handwriting, esp. to analyse the writer's character. **2.** *Linguistics.* the study of writing systems. **—ˌgraphoˈlogical** *adj.* **—graˈphologist** *n.*

graph paper *n.* paper printed with intersecting lines for drawing graphs, diagrams, etc.

-graphy *n. combining form.* **1.** indicating a form of writing, representing, etc.: *calligraphy; photography.* **2.** indicating an art or descriptive science: *choreography; oceanography.* [via L < Gk, < *graphein* to write]

grapnel (ˈgræpnᵊl) *n.* **1.** a device with a multiple hook at one end and attached to a rope, which is thrown or hooked over a firm mooring to secure an object attached to the other end of the rope. **2.** a light anchor for small boats. [C14: < OF *grapin*, < *grape* a hook; see GRAPE]

grappa (ˈgræpə) *n.* a spirit distilled from the fermented remains of grapes after pressing. [It.: grape stalk, of Gmc origin; see GRAPE]

grapple (ˈgræpᵊl) *vb.* **1.** to come to grips with (one or more persons), esp. to struggle in hand-to-hand combat. **2.** (*intr.;* foll. by *with*) to cope or contend: *to grapple with a financial problem.* **3.** (*tr.*) to secure with a grapple. ~*n.* **4.** any form of hook or metal instrument by which something is secured, such as a grapnel. **5. a.** the act of gripping or seizing, as in wrestling. **b.** a grip or hold. [C16: < OF *grappelle* a little hook, < *grape* hook; see GRAPNEL] —ˈ**grappler** *n.*

grappling iron *or* **hook** *n.* a grapnel, esp. one used for securing ships.

graptolite (ˈgræptəˌlaɪt) *n.* an extinct Palaeozoic colonial animal: a common fossil. [C19: < Gk *graptos* written, < *graphein* to write + -LITE]

grasp (grɑːsp) *vb.* **1.** to grip (something) firmly as with the hands. **2.** (when *intr.*, often foll. by *at*) to struggle, snatch, or grope (for). **3.** (*tr.*) to understand, esp. with effort. ~*n.* **4.** the act of grasping. **5.** a grip or clasp, as of a hand. **6.** total rule or possession. **7.** understanding; comprehension. [C14: < Low G *grapsen;* rel. to OE *græppian* to seize] —ˈ**graspable** *adj.* —ˈ**grasper** *n.*

grasping (ˈgrɑːspɪŋ) *adj.* greedy; avaricious. —ˈ**graspingly** *adv.* —ˈ**graspingness** *n.*

grass (grɑːs) *n.* **1.** any of a family of plants having jointed stems sheathed by long narrow leaves, flowers in spikes, and seedlike fruits. The family includes cereals, bamboo, etc. **2.** such plants collectively, in a lawn, meadow, etc. Related adj.: **verdant. 3.** ground on which such plants grow; a lawn, field, etc. **4.** ground on which animals are grazed; pasture. **5.** a slang word for **marijuana. 6.** *Brit. sl.* a person who informs, esp. on criminals. **7. let the grass grow under one's feet.** to squander time or opportunity. ~*vb.* **8.** to cover or become covered with grass. **9.** to feed or be fed with grass. **10.** (*tr.*) to spread (cloth, etc.) out on grass for drying or bleaching in the sun. **11.** (*intr.;* usually foll. by *on*) *Brit. sl.* to inform, esp. to the police. [OE *græs*] —ˈ**grassˌlike** *adj.*

grass hockey *n.* in W Canada, field hockey, as contrasted with ice hockey.

grasshopper (ˈgrɑːsˌhɒpə) *n.* an insect having hind legs adapted for leaping: typically terrestrial, feeding on plants, and producing a ticking sound by rubbing the hind legs against the leathery forewings.

grassland (ˈgrɑːsˌlænd) *n.* **1.** land, such as a prairie, on which grass predominates. **2.** land reserved for natural grass pasture.

grass roots *pl. n.* **1.** ordinary people as distinct from the active leadership of a group or organization, esp. a political party. **2.** the essentials.

grass snake *n.* **1.** a harmless nonvenomous European snake having a brownish-green body with variable markings. **2.** any of several similar related European snakes.

grass tree *n.* **1.** Also called: **blackboy.** an Australian plant of the lily family, having a woody stem, stiff grasslike leaves, and a spike of small white flowers. **2.** any of several similar Australasian plants.

grass widow *or* (*masc.*) **grass widower** *n.* a person whose spouse is regularly away for a short period. [C16: ? an allusion to a grass bed as representing an illicit relationship]

grassy (ˈgrɑːsɪ) *adj.* **grassier, grassiest.** covered with, containing, or resembling grass. —ˈ**grassiness** *n.*

grate[1] (greɪt) *vb.* **1.** (*tr.*) to reduce to small shreds by rubbing against a rough or sharp perforated surface: *to grate carrots.* **2.** to scrape (an object) against something or (objects) together, producing a harsh rasping sound, or (of objects) to scrape with such a sound. **3.** (*intr.;* foll. by *on* or *upon*) to annoy. [C15: < OF *grater* to scrape, of Gmc origin] —ˈ**grater** *n.*

grate[2] (greɪt) *n.* **1.** a framework of metal bars for holding fuel in a fireplace, stove, or furnace. **2.** a less common word for **fireplace. 3.** another name for **grating**[1] (sense 1). ~*vb.* **4.** (*tr.*) to provide with a grate or grates. [C14: < OF, < L *crātis* hurdle]

grateful (ˈgreɪtfʊl) *adj.* **1.** thankful for gifts, favours, etc.; appreciative. **2.** showing gratitude: *a grateful letter.* **3.** favourable or pleasant: *a grateful rest.* [C16: < obs. *grate,* < L *grātus* + -FUL] —ˈ**gratefully** *adv.* —ˈ**gratefulness** *n.*

graticule (ˈgrætɪˌkjuːl) *n.* **1.** the grid of intersecting lines of latitude and longitude on which a map is drawn. **2.** another name for **reticle.** [C19: < F, < L *crāticula,* < *crātis* wickerwork]

gratify (ˈgrætɪˌfaɪ) *vb.* **-fying, -fied.** (*tr.*) **1.** to satisfy or please. **2.** to yield to or indulge (a desire, whim, etc.). [C16: < L *grātificārī,* < *grātus* grateful + *facere* to make] —ˌ**gratifiˈcation** *n.* —ˈ**gratiˌfier** *n.* —ˈ**gratiˌfying** *adj.* —ˈ**gratiˌfyingly** *adv.*

grating[1] (ˈgreɪtɪŋ) *n.* **1.** Also called: **grate.** a framework of metal bars in the form of a grille set into a wall, pavement, etc., serving as a cover or guard but admitting air and sometimes light. **2.** short for **diffraction grating.**

grating[2] (ˈgreɪtɪŋ) *adj.* **1.** (of sounds) harsh and rasping. **2.** annoying; irritating. ~*n.* **3.** (*often pl.*) something produced by grating. —ˈ**gratingly** *adv.*

gratis (ˈgreɪtɪs, ˈgrætɪs, ˈgrɑːtɪs) *adv., adj.* (*postpositive*) without payment; free of charge. [C15: < L: out of kindness, < *grātiīs,* ablative pl. of *grātia* favour]

gratitude (ˈgrætɪˌtjuːd) *n.* a feeling of thankfulness, as for gifts or favours. [C16: < Med. L *grātitūdō,* < L *grātus* GRATEFUL]

gratuitous (grəˈtjuːɪtəs) *adj.* **1.** given or received without payment or obligation. **2.** without cause; unjustified. [C17: < L *grātuītus* < *grātia* favour] —**graˈtuitously** *adv.* —**graˈtuitousness** *n.*

gratuity (grəˈtjuːɪtɪ) *n., pl.* **-ties. 1.** a gift or reward, usually of money, for services rendered; tip. **2.** *Mil.* a financial award granted for long or meritorious service.

gratulatory (ˈgrætjʊlətərɪ) *adj.* expressing congratulation. [C16: < L *grātulārī* to congratulate]

grav (græv) *n.* a unit of acceleration equal to the standard acceleration of free fall. 1 grav is equivalent to 9.806 65 metres per second per second. Symbol: g

gravamen (grəˈveɪmɛn) *n., pl.* **-vamina** (-ˈvæmɪnə). **1.** *Law.* that part of an accusation weighing most heavily against an accused. **2.** *Law.* the substance or material grounds of a complaint. **3.** a rare word for **grievance.** [C17: < LL: trouble, < L *gravāre* to load, < *gravis* heavy]

grave[1] (greɪv) *n.* **1.** a place for the burial of a corpse, esp. beneath the ground and usually marked by a tombstone. Related adj.: **sepulchral. 2.** something resembling a grave or resting place: *the ship went to its grave.* **3.** (often preceded by *the*) a poetic term for **death. 4. make (someone) turn in his grave.** to do something that would have shocked or distressed a person now dead. [OE *græf*]

grave[2] (greɪv) *adj.* **1.** serious and solemn: *a grave look.* **2.** full of or suggesting danger: *a grave situation.* **3.** important; crucial: *grave matters of state.* **4.** (of colours) sober or dull. **5.** (grɑːv). *Phonetics.* of or relating to an accent (`) over vowels, denoting a pronunciation with lower or falling musical pitch (as in ancient Greek), with certain special quality (as in French), or in a manner that gives the vowel status as a syllable (as in English *agèd*). ~*n.* **6.** (*also* grɑːv). a grave accent. [C16: < OF, < L *gravis*] —ˈ**gravely** *adv.* —ˈ**graveness** *n.*

grave[3] (greɪv) *vb.* **graving, graved; graved** *or* **graven.** (*tr.*) *Arch.* **1.** to carve or engrave. **2.** to fix firmly in the mind. [OE *grafan*]

grave[4] (ˈgrɑːveɪ) *adj. Music.* solemn. [It.]

grave clothes (greɪv) *pl. n.* the wrappings in which a dead body is interred.

gravel (ˈgrævəl) *n.* **1.** a mixture of rock fragments and pebbles that is coarser than sand. **2.** *Pathol.* small rough calculi in the kidneys or bladder. ~*vb.* **-elling, -elled** *or U.S.* **-eling, -eled.** (*tr.*) **3.** to cover with gravel. **4.** to confound or confuse. **5.** *U.S. inf.* to annoy or disturb. [C13: < OF *gravele*, dim. of *grave*, ? of Celtic origin]

gravel-blind *adj. Literary.* almost completely blind. [C16: < GRAVEL + BLIND]

gravelly (ˈgrævəlɪ) *adj.* **1.** consisting of or abounding in gravel. **2.** of or like gravel. **3.** (esp. of a voice) harsh and grating.

graven (ˈgreɪvən) *vb.* **1.** a past participle of **grave**[3]. ~*adj.* **2.** strongly fixed.

graven image *n. Chiefly Bible.* a carved image used as an idol.

graver (ˈgreɪvə) *n.* any of various engraving or sculpting tools, such as a burin.

Graves (grɑːv) *n.* (*functioning as sing.*) **1.** (*sometimes not cap.*) a white or red wine from the district around Bordeaux, France. **2.** a dry or medium sweet white wine from any country: *Spanish Graves.*

gravestone (ˈgreɪvˌstəʊn) *n.* a stone marking a grave.

graveyard (ˈgreɪvˌjɑːd) *n.* a place for graves; a burial ground, esp. a small one or one in a churchyard.

gravid (ˈgrævɪd) *adj.* the technical word for **pregnant.** [C16: < L *gravidus*, < *gravis* heavy]

gravimeter (grəˈvɪmɪtə) *n.* **1.** an instrument for measuring the earth's gravitational field at points on its surface. **2.** an instrument for measuring relative density. [C18: < F *gravimètre*, < L *gravis* heavy] —**graˈvimetry** *n.*

gravimetric (ˌgrævɪˈmɛtrɪk) *adj.* **1.** of, concerned with, or using measurement by weight. **2.** *Chem.* of analysis of quantities by weight.

graving dock *n.* another term for **dry dock.**

gravitate (ˈgrævɪˌteɪt) *vb.* (*intr.*) **1.** *Physics.* to move under the influence of gravity. **2.** (usually foll. by *to* or *towards*) to be influenced or drawn, as by strong impulses. **3.** to sink or settle. —ˈ**graviˌtater** *n.* —ˈ**graviˌtative** *adj.*

gravitation (ˌgrævɪˈteɪʃən) *n.* **1.** the force of attraction that bodies exert on one another as a result of their mass. **2.** any process or result caused by this interaction. ~Also called: **gravity.** —ˌ**graviˈtational** *adj.* —ˌ**graviˈtationally** *adv.*

gravitational constant *n.* the factor relating force to mass and distance in Newton's law of gravitation. Symbol: *G*

gravitational field *n.* the field of force surrounding a body of finite mass in which another body would experience an attractive force that is proportional to the product of the masses and inversely proportional to the square of the distance between them.

graviton (ˈgrævɪˌtɒn) *n.* a postulated quantum of gravitational energy, usually considered to be a particle with zero charge and rest mass and a spin of 2.

gravity (ˈgrævɪtɪ) *n., pl.* **-ties.** **1.** the force of attraction that moves or tends to move bodies towards the centre of a celestial body, such as the earth or moon. **2.** the property of being heavy or having weight. **3.** another name for **gravitation.** **4.** seriousness or importance, esp. as a consequence of an action or opinion. **5.** manner or conduct that is solemn or dignified. **6.** lowness in pitch. **7.** (*modifier*) of or relating to gravity or gravitation or their effects: *gravity feed.* [C16: < L *gravitās* weight, < *gravis* heavy]

gravlax (ˈgrævˌlæks) *n.* dry-cured salmon, marinated in salt, sugar, and spices, as served in Scandinavia. [C20: < Norwegian, < *grav* grave (because the salmon is left to ferment) + *laks* or Swedish *lax* salmon]

gravure (grəˈvjʊə) *n.* **1.** a method of intaglio printing using a plate with many small etched recesses. See also **rotogravure.** **2.** See **photogravure.** **3.** matter printed by this process. [C19: < F, < *graver* to engrave, of Gmc origin]

gravy (ˈgreɪvɪ) *n., pl.* **-vies.** **1. a.** the juices that exude from meat during cooking. **b.** the sauce made by thickening and flavouring such juices. **2.** *Sl.* money or gain acquired with little effort, esp. above that needed for ordinary living. [C14: < OF *gravé*, <?]

gravy boat *n.* a small often boat-shaped vessel for serving gravy or other sauces.

gray[1] (greɪ) *adj., n., vb.* a variant spelling (now esp. U.S.) of **grey.**

gray[2] (greɪ) *n.* the derived SI unit of the absorbed dose of ionizing radiation: equal to 1 joule per kilogram. Symbol: Gy [C20: after L. H. *Gray*, Brit. radiobiologist]

grayling (ˈgreɪlɪŋ) *n., pl.* **-ling** *or* **-lings.** **1.** a freshwater food fish of the salmon family of the N hemisphere, having a long spiny dorsal fin, a silvery back, and greyish-green sides. **2.** any of various European butterflies having grey or greyish-brown wings.

graze[1] (greɪz) *vb.* **1.** to allow (animals) to consume the vegetation on (an area of land), or (of animals) to feed thus. **2.** (*tr.*) to tend (livestock) while at pasture. [OE *grasian*, < *græs* GRASS]

graze[2] (greɪz) *vb.* **1.** (when *intr.*, often foll. by *against* or *along*) to brush or scrape (against) gently, esp. in passing. **2.** (*tr.*) to break the skin of (a part of the body) by scraping. ~*n.* **3.** the act of grazing. **4.** a scrape or abrasion made by grazing. [C17: prob. special use of GRAZE[1]]

grazier (ˈgreɪzɪə) *n.* a rancher or farmer who rears or fattens cattle or sheep on grazing land.

grazing (ˈgreɪzɪŋ) *n.* **1.** the vegetation on pastures that is available for livestock to feed upon. **2.** the land on which this is growing.

grazioso (ˌgrɑːtsɪˈəʊsəʊ) *adj. Music.* graceful. [It.]

grease (griːs, griːz) *n.* **1.** animal fat in a soft or melted condition. **2.** any thick fatty oil, esp. one used as a lubricant for machinery, etc. ~*vb.* (*tr.*) **3.** to soil, coat, or lubricate with grease. **4.** **grease the palm** (*or* **hand**) **of.** *Sl.* to bribe; influence by giving money to. [C13: < OF *craisse*, < L *crassus* thick] —ˈ**greaser** *n.*

grease gun *n.* a device for forcing grease through nipples into bearings.

grease monkey *n. Inf.* a mechanic, esp. one who works on cars or aircraft.

greasepaint (ˈgriːsˌpeɪnt) *n.* **1.** a waxy or greasy substance used as make-up by actors. **2.** theatrical make-up.

greasy (ˈgriːsɪ, -zɪ) *adj.* **greasier, greasiest.** **1.** coated or soiled with or as if with grease. **2.** composed of or full of grease. **3.** resembling grease. **4.** unctuous or oily in manner. —ˈ**greasily** *adv.* —ˈ**greasiness** *n.*

greasy wool *n.* untreated wool still retaining the lanolin; used for waterproof clothing.

great (greɪt) *adj.* **1.** relatively large in size or extent; big. **2.** relatively large in number; having many parts or members: *a great assembly.* **3.** of relatively long duration: *a great wait.* **4.** of larger size or more importance than others of its kind: *the great auk.* **5.** extreme or more than usual: *great worry.* **6.** of significant importance or consequence: *a great decision.* **7. a.** of exceptional talents or achievements; remarkable: *a great writer.* **b.** (*as n.*): *the great; one of the greats.* **8.** doing or exemplifying (something) on a large scale: *she's a great reader.* **9.** arising from or possessing idealism in thought, action, etc.; heroic: *great deeds.* **10.** illustrious or eminent: *a great history.* **11.** impressive or striking: *a great show of wealth.* **12.** active or enthusiastic: *a great walker.* **13.** (often foll. by *at*) skilful or adroit: *a great carpenter; you are great at singing.* **14.** *Inf.*

excellent; fantastic. ~*n.* **15.** Also called: **great organ.** the principal manual on an organ. [OE *grēat*] —'**greatly** *adv.* —'**greatness** *n.*

great- *prefix.* **1.** being the parent of a person's grandparent (in the combinations **great-grandfather, great-grandmother, great-grandparent**). **2.** being the child of a person's grandchild (in the combinations **great-grandson, great-granddaughter, great-grandchild**).

great auk *n.* a large flightless auk, extinct since the middle of the 19th century.

great-aunt *or* **grandaunt** *n.* an aunt of one's father or mother; sister of one's grandfather or grandmother.

Great Bear *n.* **the.** the English name for **Ursa Major.**

Great Britain *n.* the largest island in Europe and in the British Isles: consists of England, Scotland, and Wales; forms, with Northern Ireland, the United Kingdom of Great Britain and Northern Ireland.

great circle *n.* a circular section of a sphere that has a radius equal to that of the sphere.

greatcoat ('greɪtˌkəʊt) *n.* a heavy overcoat.

Great Dane *n.* one of a very large breed of dog with a short smooth coat.

great gross *n.* a unit of quantity equal to one dozen gross (or 1728).

great-hearted *adj.* benevolent or noble; magnanimous. —ˌ**great-'heartedness** *n.*

great-nephew *or* **grandnephew** *n.* a son of one's nephew or niece; grandson of one's brother or sister. —ˌ**great-'niece** *or* '**grandˌniece** *fem. n.*

Great Russian *n.* **1.** *Linguistics.* the technical name for **Russian. 2.** a member of the chief East Slavonic people of Russia. ~*adj.* **3.** of or relating to this people or their language.

Greats (greɪts) *pl. n.* (at Oxford University) **1.** the Honour School of Literae Humaniores, involving the study of Greek and Roman history and literature and philosophy. **2.** the final examinations at the end of this course.

great seal *n.* (*often caps.*) the principal seal of a nation, sovereign, etc., used to authenticate documents of the highest importance.

great tit *n.* a Eurasian tit with yellow-and-black underparts and a black-and-white head.

great-uncle *or* **granduncle** *n.* an uncle of one's father or mother; brother of one's grandfather or grandmother.

Great War *n.* another name for **World War I.**

greave (griːv) *n.* (*often pl.*) a piece of armour worn to protect the shin. [C14: < OF *greve*, ? < *graver* to part the hair, of Gmc origin]

grebe (griːb) *n.* an aquatic bird, such as the great crested grebe and little grebe, similar to the divers but with lobate rather than webbed toes and a vestigial tail. [C18: < F *grèbe*, <?]

Grecian ('griːʃən) *adj.* **1.** (esp. of beauty or architecture) conforming to Greek ideals. ~*n.* **2.** a scholar of Greek. ~*adj., n.* **3.** another word for **Greek.**

Grecism ('griːˌsɪzəm) *n.* a variant spelling (esp. U.S.) of **Graecism.**

Greco- ('griːkəʊ, 'grɛkəʊ) *combining form.* a variant (esp. U.S.) of **Graeco-.**

greed (griːd) *n.* **1.** excessive consumption of or desire for food. **2.** excessive desire, as for wealth or power. [C17: back formation < GREEDY]

greedy ('griːdɪ) *adj.* **greedier, greediest. 1.** excessively desirous of food or wealth, esp. in large amounts; voracious. **2.** (*postpositive;* foll. by *for*) eager (for): *a man greedy for success.* [OE *grǣdig*] —'**greedily** *adv.* —'**greediness** *n.*

greegree ('griːgriː) *n.* a variant spelling of **grigri.**

Greek (griːk) *n.* **1.** the official language of Greece, constituting the Hellenic branch of the Indo-European family of languages. **2.** a native or inhabitant of Greece or a descendant of such a native. **3.** a member of the Greek Orthodox Church. **4.** *Inf.* anything incomprehensible (esp. in **it's (all) Greek to me**). ~*adj.* **5.** denoting, relating to, or characteristic of Greece, the Greeks, or the Greek language; Hellenic. **6.** of, relating to, or designating the Greek Orthodox Church. —'**Greekness** *n.*

Greek cross *n.* a cross with each of the four arms of the same length.

Greek fire *n.* a Byzantine weapon consisting of an unknown mixture that caught fire when wetted.

Greek gift *n.* a gift given with the intention of tricking and causing harm to the recipient. [C19: in allusion to Virgil's *Aeneid* ii 49; see also TROJAN HORSE]

Greek Orthodox Church *n.* **1.** Also called: **Greek Church.** the established Church of Greece, governed by the holy synod of Greece, in which the Metropolitan of Athens has primacy of honour. **2.** another name for **Orthodox Church.**

green (griːn) *n.* **1.** any of a group of colours, such as that of fresh grass, that lie between yellow and blue in the visible spectrum. Related adj.: **verdant. 2.** a dye or pigment of or producing these colours. **3.** something of the colour green. **4.** a small area of grassland, esp. in the centre of a village. **5.** an area of smooth turf kept for a special purpose: *a putting green.* **6.** (*pl.*) **a.** the edible leaves and stems of certain plants, eaten as a vegetable. **b.** freshly cut branches of ornamental trees, shrubs, etc., used as a decoration. **7.** (*sometimes cap.*) a person, esp. a politician, who supports environmentalist issues. ~*adj.* **8.** of the colour green. **9.** greenish in colour or having parts or marks that are greenish. **10.** vigorous; not faded: *a green old age.* **11.** envious or jealous. **12.** immature, unsophisticated, or gullible. **13.** characterized by foliage or green plants: *a green wood; a green salad.* **14.** denoting a unit of account that is adjusted in accordance with fluctuations between the currencies of the EEC nations and is used to make payments to agricultural producers within the EEC: *green pound.* **15.** (*sometimes cap.*) of or concerned with conservation of natural resources and improvement of the environment: used esp. in a political context. **16.** fresh, raw, or unripe: *green bananas.* **17.** unhealthily pale in appearance: *he was green after his boat trip.* **18.** (of meat) not smoked or cured: *green bacon.* **19.** (of timber) freshly felled; not dried or seasoned. ~*vb.* **20.** to make or become green. [OE *grēne*] —'**greenish** *or* '**greeny** *adj.* —'**greenly** *adv.* —'**greenness** *n.*

greenback ('griːnˌbæk) *n. U.S.* **1.** *Inf.* a legal-tender U.S. currency note. **2.** *Sl.* a dollar bill.

green bean *n.* any bean plant, such as the French bean, having narrow green edible pods.

green belt *n.* a zone of farmland, parks, and open country surrounding a town or city.

Green Cross Code *n. Brit.* a code for children giving rules for road safety.

greenery ('griːnərɪ) *n., pl.* **-eries.** green foliage, esp. when used for decoration.

green-eyed *adj.* **1.** jealous or envious. **2. the green-eyed monster.** jealousy or envy.

greenfield ('griːnˌfiːld) *n.* (*modifier*) denoting or located in a rural area which has not previously been built on.

greenfinch ('griːnˌfɪntʃ) *n.* a European finch the male of which has a dull green plumage with yellow patches on the wings and tail.

green fingers *pl. n.* considerable talent or ability to grow plants.

greenfly ('griːnˌflaɪ) *n., pl.* **-flies.** a greenish aphid commonly occurring as a pest on garden and crop plants.

greengage ('griːnˌgeɪdʒ) *n.* **1.** a cultivated variety of plum tree with edible green plumlike fruits. **2.** the fruit of this tree. [C18: GREEN + *-gage*, after Sir W. *Gage* (1777–1864), E botanist who brought it from France]

greengrocer ('griːnˌgrəʊsə) *n. Chiefly Brit.* a retail trader in fruit and vegetables. —'**green-ˌgrocery** *n.*

greenheart ('griːnˌhɑːt) *n.* **1.** Also called: **bebeeru.** a tropical American tree that has dark green durable wood. **2.** any of various similar trees. **3.** the wood of any of these trees.

greenhorn (ˈgriːnˌhɔːn) *n.* **1.** an inexperienced person, esp. one who is extremely gullible. **2.** *Chiefly U.S.* a newcomer. [C17: orig. an animal with *green* (that is, young) horns]

greenhouse (ˈgriːnˌhaʊs) *n.* a building with glass walls and roof for the cultivation of plants under controlled conditions.

greenhouse effect *n.* **1.** an effect occurring in greenhouses, etc., in which radiant heat from the sun passes through the glass warming the contents, the radiant heat from inside being trapped by the glass. **2.** the application of this effect to a planet's atmosphere, esp. the warming up of the earth's surface as man-made carbon dioxide in the atmosphere traps the sun's heat.

greenkeeper (ˈgriːnˌkiːpə) *n.* a person responsible for maintaining a golf course or bowling green.

green leek *n.* any of several Australian parrots with a green or mostly green plumage.

green light *n.* **1.** a signal to go, esp. a green traffic light. **2.** permission to proceed with a project, etc.

greenmail (ˈgriːnˌmeɪl) *n.* (esp. in the U.S.) the practice of a company buying sufficient shares in another company to threaten takeover and making a quick profit as a result of the threatened company buying back its shares at a higher price.

green paper *n.* (*often caps.*) (in Britain) a government document containing policy proposals to be discussed, esp. by Parliament.

Green Party *n.* (esp. in West Germany and now in Britain) a political party whose policies are based on concern for the environment.

green pepper *n.* the green unripe fruit of the sweet pepper, eaten raw or cooked.

green pound *n.* a unit of account used in calculating Britain's contributions to and payments from the Community Agricultural Fund of the EEC. See also **green** (sense 14).

greenroom (ˈgriːnˌruːm, -ˌrʊm) *n.* (esp. formerly) a backstage room in a theatre where performers may rest or receive visitors. [C18: prob. < its original colour]

greensand (ˈgriːnˌsænd) *n.* an olive-green sandstone consisting mainly of quartz and glauconite.

greenshank (ˈgriːnˌʃæŋk) *n.* a large European sandpiper with greenish legs and a slightly upturned bill.

greensickness (ˈgriːnˌsɪknɪs) *n.* an informal name for **chlorosis.**

greenstick fracture (ˈgriːnˌstɪk) *n.* a fracture in children in which the bone is partly bent and splinters only on the convex side of the bend. [C20: alluding to the similar way in which a green stick splinters]

greenstone (ˈgriːnˌstəʊn) *n.* **1.** any basic dark green igneous rock. **2.** a variety of jade formerly used in New Zealand by Maoris for ornaments and tools, now used for jewellery.

greensward (ˈgriːnˌswɔːd) *n. Arch. or literary.* fresh green turf or an area of such turf.

green tea *n.* a sharp tea made from tea leaves that have been dried quickly without fermenting.

green turtle *n.* a mainly tropical edible turtle, with greenish flesh.

green-wellie *n.* (*modifier*) characterizing or belonging to the upper-class set devoted to hunting, shooting, and fishing: *the green-wellie brigade.*

Greenwich Mean Time *or* **Greenwich Time** (ˈgrɪnɪdʒ) *n.* the local time of the 0° meridian passing through Greenwich, England: a standard time for Britain and a basis for calculating times throughout most of the world. Abbrev.: **GMT.**

greenwood (ˈgriːnˌwʊd) *n.* a forest or wood when the leaves are green.

greet[1] (griːt) *vb.* (*tr.*) **1.** to meet or receive with expressions of gladness or welcome. **2.** to send a message of friendship to. **3.** to receive in a specified manner: *her remarks were greeted by silence.* **4.** to become apparent to: *the smell of bread greeted him.* [OE *grētan*] —ˈ**greeter** *n.*

greet[2] (griːt) *Scot. or dialect.* ~*vb.* **1.** (*intr.*) to weep; lament. ~*n.* **2.** weeping; lamentation. [< OE *grētan,* N dialect var. of *grætan*]

greeting (ˈgriːtɪŋ) *n.* **1.** the act or an instance of welcoming or saluting on meeting. **2.** (*often pl.*) **a.** an expression of friendly salutation. **b.** (*as modifier*): *a greetings card.*

gregarious (grɪˈgɛərɪəs) *adj.* **1.** enjoying the company of others. **2.** (of animals) living together in herds or flocks. **3.** (of plants) growing close together. **4.** of or characteristic of crowds or communities. [C17: < L, < *grex* flock] —**greˈgariously** *adv.* —**greˈgariousness** *n.*

Gregorian calendar (grɪˈgɔːrɪən) *n.* the revision of the Julian calendar introduced in 1582 by Pope Gregory XIII and still in force, whereby the ordinary year is made to consist of 365 days.

Gregorian chant *n.* another name for **plainsong.**

Gregorian telescope *n.* a type of reflecting astronomical telescope with a concave secondary mirror and the eyepiece set in the centre of the parabolic primary mirror. [C18: after J. *Gregory* (died 1675), Scot. mathematician]

gremial (ˈgriːmɪəl) *n. R.C. Church.* a cloth spread upon the lap of a bishop when seated during a solemn High Mass. [C17: < L *gremium* lap]

gremlin (ˈgrɛmlɪn) *n.* **1.** an imaginary imp jokingly said to be responsible for mechanical troubles in aircraft, esp. in World War II. **2.** any mischievous troublemaker. [C20: <?]

grenade (grɪˈneɪd) *n.* **1.** a small container filled with explosive thrown by hand or fired from a rifle. **2.** a sealed glass vessel that is thrown and shatters to release chemicals, such as tear gas. [C16: < F, < Sp.: pomegranate, < LL, < L *grānātus* seedy; see GRAIN]

grenadier (ˌgrɛnəˈdɪə) *n.* **1.** *Mil.* **a.** (in the British Army) a member of the senior regiment of infantry in the Household Brigade. **b.** (formerly) a member of a special formation, usually selected for strength and height. **c.** (formerly) a soldier trained to throw grenades. **2.** any of various deep-sea fish, typically having a large head and a long tapering tail. [C17: < F; see GRENADE]

grenadine[1] (ˌgrɛnəˈdiːn) *n.* a light thin fabric of silk, wool, rayon, or nylon, used for dresses, etc. [C19: < F]

grenadine[2] (ˌgrɛnəˈdiːn, ˈgrɛnəˌdiːn) *n.* a syrup made from pomegranate juice, used as a sweetening and colouring agent in various drinks. [C19: < F: a little pomegranate; see GRENADE]

Gresham's law (ˈgrɛʃəmz) *n.* the economic hypothesis that bad money drives good money out of circulation; the superior currency will tend to be hoarded and the inferior will thus dominate the circulation. [C16: after Sir T. *Gresham* (?1519-79), E financier]

gressorial (grɛˈsɔːrɪəl) *or* **gressorious** *adj.* **1.** (of the feet of certain birds) specialized for walking. **2.** (of birds, such as the ostrich) having such feet. [C19: < NL, < *gressus* having walked, < *gradī* to step]

grew (gruː) *vb.* the past tense of **grow.**

grey *or U.S.* **gray** (greɪ) *adj.* **1.** of a neutral tone, intermediate between black and white, that has no hue and reflects and transmits only a little light. **2.** greyish in colour or having greyish marks. **3.** dismal or dark, esp. from lack of light; gloomy. **4.** neutral or dull, esp. in character or opinion. **5.** having grey hair. **6.** of or characteristic of old age; wise. **7.** ancient; venerable. ~*n.* **8.** any of a group of grey tones. **9.** grey cloth or clothing. **10.** an animal, esp. a horse, that is grey or whitish. ~*vb.* **11.** to become or make grey. [OE *grǣg*] —ˈ**greyish** *or U.S.* ˈ**grayish** *adj.* —ˈ**greyly** *or U.S.* ˈ**grayly** *adv.* —ˈ**greyness** *or U.S.* ˈ**grayness** *n.*

grey area *n.* **1.** an area or part of something existing between two extremes and having mixed characteristics of both. **2.** an area, situation, etc., lacking clearly defined characteristics.

greybeard *or U.S.* **graybeard** (ˈgreɪˌbɪəd) *n.* **1.** an old man, esp. a sage. **2.** a large stoneware or earthenware jar or jug for spirits.

grey eminence *n.* the English equivalent of *éminence grise.*

Grey Friar *n.* a Franciscan friar.

greyhen (ˈgreɪˌhɛn) *n.* the female of the black grouse.

greyhound (ˈgreɪˌhaʊnd) *n.* a tall slender fast-moving breed of dog.

greylag *or* **greylag goose** (ˈgreɪˌlæg) *n.* a large grey Eurasian goose: the ancestor of many domestic breeds of goose. U.S. spelling: **graylag.** [C18: < GREY + LAG¹, < its migrating later than other species]

grey matter *n.* **1.** the greyish tissue of the brain and spinal cord, containing nerve cell bodies and fibres. **2.** *Inf.* brains or intellect.

grey squirrel *n.* a grey-furred squirrel, native to E North America but now widely established.

greywacke (ˈgreɪˌwækə) *n.* any dark sandstone or grit having a matrix of clay minerals. [C19: partial translation of G *Grauwacke;* see WACKE]

grey wolf *n.* another name for **timber wolf.**

grid (grɪd) *n.* **1.** See **gridiron. 2.** a network of horizontal and vertical lines superimposed over a map, building plan, etc., for locating points. **3. the grid.** the national network of transmission lines, pipes, etc., by which electricity, gas, or water is distributed. **4.** Also called: **control grid.** *Electronics.* an electrode usually consisting of a cylindrical mesh of wires, that controls the flow of electrons between the cathode and anode of a valve. **5.** any interconnecting system of links: *the bus service formed a grid across the country.* [C19: back formation < GRIDIRON]

grid bias *n.* the fixed voltage applied between the control grid and cathode of a valve.

griddle (ˈgrɪdᵊl) *n.* **1.** Also called: **girdle.** *Brit.* a thick round iron plate with a half hoop handle over the top, for making scones, etc. **2.** any flat heated surface, esp. on the top of a stove, for cooking food. ~*vb.* **3.** (*tr.*) to cook (food) on a griddle. [C13: < OF *gridil,* < LL *crāticulum* (unattested) fine wickerwork; see GRILL]

griddlecake (ˈgrɪdᵊlˌkeɪk) *n.* another name for **drop scone.**

gridiron (ˈgrɪdˌaɪən) *n.* **1.** a utensil of parallel metal bars, used to grill meat, fish, etc. **2.** any framework resembling this utensil. **3.** a framework above the stage in a theatre from which suspended scenery, lights, etc., are manipulated. **4.** the field of play in American football. ~Often shortened to **grid.** [C13 *gredire,* ? a var. (through influence of *ire* IRON) of *gredile* GRIDDLE]

grief (griːf) *n.* **1.** deep or intense sorrow, esp. at the death of someone. **2.** something that causes keen distress. **3. come to grief.** *Inf.* to end unsuccessfully or disastrously. [C13: < Anglo-F *gref,* < *grever* to GRIEVE]

grievance (ˈgriːvᵊns) *n.* **1.** a real or imaginary wrong causing resentment and regarded as grounds for complaint. **2.** a feeling of resentment or injustice at having been unfairly treated. [C15 *grevance,* < OF, < *grever* to GRIEVE]

grieve (griːv) *vb.* to feel or cause to feel great sorrow or distress, esp. at the death of someone. [C13: < OF *grever,* < L *gravāre* to burden, < *gravis* heavy] —ˈ**griever** *n.* —ˈ**grieving** *n., adj.*

grievous (ˈgriːvəs) *adj.* **1.** very severe or painful: *a grievous injury.* **2.** very serious; heinous: *a grievous sin.* **3.** showing or marked by grief. **4.** causing great pain or suffering. —ˈ**grievously** *adv.* —ˈ**grievousness** *n.*

grievous bodily harm *n. Criminal law.* serious injury caused by one person to another.

griffin (ˈgrɪfɪn), **griffon,** *or* **gryphon** *n.* a winged monster with an eagle-like head and the body of a lion. [C14: < OF *grifon,* < L *grȳphus,* < Gk *grups,* < *grupos* hooked]

griffon (ˈgrɪfᵊn) *n.* **1.** any of various small wire-haired breeds of dog, originally from Belgium. **2.** a large vulture of Africa, S Europe, and SW Asia, having a pale plumage with black wings. [C19: < F: GRIFFIN]

grigri, gris-gris, *or* **greegree** (ˈgriːgriː) *n., pl.* **-gris** (-griːz) *or* **-grees.** an African talisman, amulet, or charm. [of African origin]

grill (grɪl) *vb.* **1.** to cook (meat, etc.) by direct heat, as under a grill or over a hot fire, or (of meat, etc.) to be cooked in this way. Usual U.S. and Canad. word: **broil. 2.** (*tr.; usually passive*) to torment with or as if with extreme heat: *the travellers were grilled by the scorching sun.* **3.** (*tr.*) *Inf.* to subject to insistent or prolonged questioning. ~*n.* **4.** a device with parallel bars of thin metal on which meat, etc., may be cooked by a fire; gridiron. **5.** a device on a cooker that radiates heat downwards for grilling meat, etc. **6.** food cooked by grilling. **7.** See **grillroom.** [C17: < F *gril* gridiron, < L *crāticula* fine wickerwork; see GRILLE] —**grilled** *adj.* —ˈ**griller** *n.*

grillage (ˈgrɪlɪdʒ) *n.* an arrangement of beams and crossbeams used as a foundation on soft ground. [C18: < F, < *griller* to furnish with a grille]

grille *or* **grill** (grɪl) *n.* **1.** a framework, esp. of metal bars arranged to form an ornamental pattern, used as a screen or partition. **2.** Also called: **radiator grille.** a grating that admits cooling air to the radiator of a motor vehicle. **3.** a metal or wooden openwork grating used as a screen or divider. **4.** a protective screen, usually plastic or metal, in front of the loudspeaker in a radio, record player, etc. [C17: < OF, < L *crāticula* fine hurdlework, < *crātis* a hurdle]

grillroom (ˈgrɪlˌruːm, -ˌrʊm) *n.* a restaurant where grilled steaks and other meat are served.

grilse (grɪls) *n., pl.* **grilses** *or* **grilse.** a salmon at the stage when it returns for the first time from the sea to fresh water. [C15 *grilles* (pl.), <?]

grim (grɪm) *adj.* **grimmer, grimmest. 1.** stern; resolute: *grim determination.* **2.** harsh or formidable in manner or appearance. **3.** harshly ironic or sinister: *grim laughter.* **4.** cruel, severe, or ghastly: *a grim accident.* **5.** *Arch. or poetic.* fierce: *a grim warrior.* **6.** *Inf.* unpleasant; disagreeable. [OE *grimm*] —ˈ**grimly** *adv.* —ˈ**grimness** *n.*

grimace (grɪˈmeɪs) *n.* **1.** an ugly or distorted facial expression, as of wry humour, disgust, etc. ~*vb.* **2.** (*intr.*) to contort the face. [C17: < F, of Gmc origin; rel. to Sp. *grimazo* caricature] —**griˈmacer** *n.*

grimalkin (grɪˈmælkɪn, -ˈmɔːl-) *n.* **1.** an old cat, esp. an old female cat. **2.** a crotchety or shrewish old woman. [C17: < GREY + *malkin,* dim. of female name *Maud*]

grime (graɪm) *n.* **1.** dirt, soot, or filth, esp. when ingrained. ~*vb.* **2.** (*tr.*) to make dirty or coat with filth. [C15: < MDu. *grime*] —ˈ**grimy** *adj.* —ˈ**griminess** *n.*

grin (grɪn) *vb.* **grinning, grinned. 1.** to smile with the lips drawn back revealing the teeth or express (something) by such a smile: *to grin a welcome.* **2.** (*intr.*) to draw back the lips revealing the teeth, as in a snarl or grimace. **3. grin and bear it.** *Inf.* to suffer trouble or hardship without complaint. ~*n.* **4.** a broad smile. **5.** a snarl or grimace. [OE *grennian*] —ˈ**grinning** *adj., n.*

grind (graɪnd) *vb.* **grinding, ground. 1.** to reduce or be reduced to small particles by pounding or abrading: *to grind corn.* **2.** (*tr.*) to smooth, sharpen, or polish by friction or abrasion: *to grind a knife.* **3.** to scrape or grate together (two things, esp. the teeth) with a harsh rasping sound or (of such objects) to be scraped together. **4.** (*tr.; foll. by out*) to speak or say something in a rough voice. **5.** (*tr.; often foll. by down*) to hold down; oppress; tyrannize. **6.** (*tr.*) to operate (a machine) by turning a handle. **7.** (*tr.; foll. by out*) to produce in a routine or uninspired manner: *he ground out his weekly article for the paper.* **8.** (*intr.*) *Inf.* to study or work laboriously. ~*n.* **9.** *Inf.* laborious or routine work or study. **10.** a specific grade of pulverization, as of coffee beans: *coarse grind.* **11.** the act or sound of grinding. [OE *grindan*] —ˈ**grindingly** *adv.*

grinder (ˈgraɪndə) *n.* **1.** a person who grinds, esp. one who grinds cutting tools. **2.** a machine for grinding. **3.** a molar tooth.

grindstone (ˈgraɪndˌstəʊn) *n.* **1. a.** a machine having a circular block of stone rotated for sharpening tools or grinding metal. **b.** the stone used in this machine. **c.** any stone used for sharpening; whetstone. **2. keep** *or* **have one's nose to the grindstone.** to work hard and perseveringly.

gringo ('grɪŋgəʊ) *n., pl.* **-gos.** a person from an English-speaking country: used as a derogatory term by Latin Americans. [C19: < Sp.: foreigner, prob. < *griego* Greek, hence an alien]

grip (grɪp) *n.* **1.** the act or an instance of grasping and holding firmly: *he lost his grip on the slope.* **2.** Also called: **handgrip.** the strength or pressure of such a grasp, as in a handshake. **3.** the style or manner of grasping an object, such as a tennis racket. **4.** understanding, control, or mastery of a subject, problem, etc. **5. come** *or* **get to grips.** (often foll. by *with*) **a.** to deal with (a problem or subject). **b.** to tackle (an assailant). **6.** Also called: **handgrip.** a part by which an object is grasped; handle. **7.** Also called: **handgrip.** a travelling bag or holdall. **8.** See **hairgrip. 9.** any device that holds by friction, such as certain types of brake. ~*vb.* **gripping, gripped. 10.** to take hold of firmly or tightly, as by a clutch. **11.** to hold the interest or attention of: *to grip an audience.* [OE *gripe* grasp] —'**gripper** *n.* —'**gripping** *adj.*

gripe (graɪp) *vb.* **1.** (*intr.*) *Inf.* to complain, esp. in a persistent nagging manner. **2.** to cause sudden intense pain in the intestines of (a person) or (of a person) to experience this pain. **3.** *Arch.* to clutch; grasp. **4.** (*tr.*) *Arch.* to afflict. ~*n.* **5.** (*usually pl.*) a sudden intense pain in the intestines; colic. **6.** *Inf.* a complaint or grievance. **7.** *Now rare.* **a.** the act of gripping. **b.** a firm grip. **c.** a device that grips. [OE *grīpan*] —'**griper** *n.*

Gripe Water *n. Trademark. Brit.* a solution given to infants to relieve colic.

grippe *or* **grip** (grɪp) *n.* a former name for **influenza.** [C18: < F *grippe,* < *gripper* to seize, of Gmc origin; see GRIP]

Grips (grɪps) *n.* (*functioning as sing.*) *Films.* the member of the film crew who carries heavy camera equipment from place to place.

grisaille (grɪ'zeɪl) *n.* **1.** a technique of monochrome painting in shades of grey, imitating the effect of relief. **2.** a painting, stained-glass window, etc., in this manner. [C19: < F, < *gris* grey]

griseofulvin (ˌgrɪzɪəʊ'fʊlvɪn) *n.* an antibiotic used to treat fungal infections of the skin and hair. [C20: < NL, ult. < Med. L *griseus* grey + L *fulvus* reddish-yellow]

grisette (grɪ'zɛt) *n.* (esp. formerly) a French working girl. [C18: < F, < grey fabric used for dresses, < *gris* grey]

gris-gris ('griːgriː) *n., pl.* **-gris** (-griːz). a variant spelling of **grigri.**

grisly ('grɪzlɪ) *adj.* **-lier, -liest.** causing horror or dread; gruesome. [OE *grislic*] —'**grisliness** *n.*

grist (grɪst) *n.* **1. a.** grain intended to be or that has been ground. **b.** the quantity of such grain processed in one grinding. **2.** *Brewing.* malt grains that have been cleaned and cracked. **3. grist to** (*or* **for**) **the** (*or* **one's**) **mill.** anything that can be turned to profit or advantage. [OE *grist*]

gristle ('grɪsᵊl) *n.* cartilage, esp. when in meat. [OE *gristle*] —'**gristly** *adj.* —'**gristliness** *n.*

grit (grɪt) *n.* **1.** small hard particles of sand, earth, stone, etc. **2.** Also called: **gritstone.** any coarse sandstone that can be used as a grindstone or millstone. **3.** indomitable courage, toughness, or resolution. ~*vb.* **gritting, gritted. 4.** to clench or grind together (two objects, esp. the teeth). **5.** to cover (a surface, such as icy roads) with grit. [OE *grēot*] —'**gritter** *n.*

Grit (grɪt) *n., adj. Canad.* an informal word for **Liberal.**

grits (grɪts) *pl. n.* **1.** hulled or coarsely ground grain. **2.** *U.S.* See **hominy grits.** [OE *grytt*]

gritty ('grɪtɪ) *adj.* **-tier, -tiest. 1.** courageous; hardy; resolute. **2.** of, like, or containing grit. —'**grittily** *adv.* —'**grittiness** *n.*

grizzle[1] ('grɪzᵊl) *vb.* **1.** to make or become grey. ~*n.* **2.** a grey colour. **3.** grey hair. [C15: < OF *grisel,* < *gris,* of Gmc origin]

grizzle[2] ('grɪzᵊl) *vb.* (*intr.*) *Inf., chiefly Brit.* (esp. of a child) to fret; whine. [C18: of Gmc origin] —'**grizzler** *n.*

grizzled ('grɪzᵊld) *adj.* **1.** streaked or mixed with grey; grizzly. **2.** having grey hair.

grizzly ('grɪzlɪ) *adj.* **-zlier, -zliest. 1.** somewhat grey; grizzled. ~*n., pl.* **-zlies. 2.** See **grizzly bear.**

grizzly bear *n.* a variety of the brown bear, formerly widespread in W North America; its brown fur has cream or white tips on the back, giving a grizzled appearance. Often shortened to **grizzly.**

groan (grəʊn) *n.* **1.** a prolonged stressed dull cry expressive of agony, pain, or disapproval. **2.** a loud harsh creaking sound, as of a tree bending in the wind. **3.** *Inf.* a grumble or complaint, esp. a persistent one. ~*vb.* **4.** to utter (low inarticulate sounds) expressive of pain, grief, disapproval, etc. **5.** (*intr.*) to make a sound like a groan. **6.** (*intr.*; usually foll. by *beneath* or *under*) to be weighed down (by) or suffer greatly (under). **7.** (*intr.*) *Inf.* to complain or grumble. [OE *grānian*] —'**groaner** *n.* —'**groaning** *adj., n.* —'**groaningly** *adv.*

groat (grəʊt) *n.* an obsolete English silver coin worth four pennies. [C14: < MDu. *groot,* < MLow G *gros,* < Med. L (*denarius*) *grossus* thick (coin); see GROSCHEN]

groats (grəʊts) *pl. n.* the hulled and crushed grain of oats, wheat, or certain other cereals. [OE *grot* particle]

grocer ('grəʊsə) *n.* a dealer in foodstuffs and other household supplies. [C15: < OF *grossier,* < *gros* large; see GROSS]

groceries ('grəʊsərɪz) *pl. n.* merchandise, esp. foodstuffs, sold by a grocer.

grocery ('grəʊsərɪ) *n., pl.* **-ceries.** the business or premises of a grocer.

grog (grɒg) *n.* **1.** diluted spirit, usually rum, as an alcoholic drink. **2.** *Austral. & N.Z. inf.* alcoholic drink in general, esp. spirits. [C18: < Old *Grog,* nickname of Edward Vernon (1684–1757), British admiral, who in 1740 issued naval rum diluted with water; his nickname arose from his grogram cloak]

groggy ('grɒgɪ) *adj.* **-gier, -giest.** *Inf.* **1.** dazed or staggering, as from exhaustion, blows, or drunkenness. **2.** faint or weak. —'**groggily** *adv.* —'**grogginess** *n.*

grogram ('grɒgrəm) *n.* a coarse fabric of silk, wool, or silk mixed with wool or mohair, often stiffened with gum, formerly used for clothing. [C16: < F *gros grain* coarse grain; see GROSGRAIN]

groin (grɔɪn) *n.* **1.** the depression or fold where the legs join the abdomen. **2.** *Euphemistic.* the genitals, esp. the testicles. **3.** a variant spelling (esp. U.S.) of **groyne. 4.** *Archit.* a curved arris formed where two intersecting vaults meet. ~*vb.* **5.** (*tr.*) *Archit.* to provide or construct with groins. [C15: ? < E *grynde* abyss]

grommet ('grɒmɪt) *or* **grummet** *n.* a ring of rubber or plastic or a metal eyelet designed to line a hole to prevent a cable or pipe passed through it from chafing. [C15: < obs. F *gourmette* chain linking the ends of a bit, < *gourmer* bridle, <?]

groom (gruːm, grʊm) *n.* **1.** a person employed to clean and look after horses. **2.** See **bridegroom. 3.** any of various officers of a royal or noble household. **4.** *Arch.* a male servant. ~*vb.* (*tr.*) **5.** to make or keep (clothes, appearance, etc.) clean and tidy. **6.** to rub down, clean, and smarten (a horse, dog, etc.). **7.** to train or prepare for a particular task, occupation, etc.: *to groom someone for the Presidency.* [C13 *grom* manservant; ? rel. to OE *grōwan* to GROW]

groomsman ('gruːmzmən, 'grʊmz-) *n., pl.* **-men.** a man who attends the bridegroom at a wedding, usually the best man.

groove (gruːv) *n.* **1.** a long narrow channel or furrow, esp. one cut into wood by a tool. **2.** the spiral channel in a gramophone record. **3.** a settled existence, routine, etc., to which one is suited or accustomed. **4.** *Dated sl.* an experience, event, etc., that is groovy. **5. in the groove. a.** *Jazz.* playing well and apparently effortlessly, with a good beat, etc. **b.** *U.S.* fashionable. ~*vb.* **6.** (*tr.*) to form or cut a groove in. **7.** (*intr.*) *Dated sl.* to enjoy oneself or feel in rapport with one's surroundings. **8.** (*intr.*) *Jazz.* to play well, with a good beat, etc. [C15: < obs. Du. *groeve*, of Gmc origin]

groovy (ˈgruːvɪ) *adj.* **groovier, grooviest.** *Dated sl.* attractive, fashionable, or exciting.

grope (grəʊp) *vb.* **1.** (*intr.*; usually foll. by *for*) to feel or search about uncertainly (for something) with the hands. **2.** (*intr.*; usually foll. by *for* or *after*) to search uncertainly or with difficulty (for a solution, answer, etc.). **3.** (*tr.*) to find (one's way) by groping. **4.** (*tr.*) *Sl.* to fondle the body of (someone) for sexual gratification. ~*n.* **5.** the act of groping. [OE *grāpian*] —ˈ**gropingly** *adv.*

groper (ˈgrəʊpə) *or* **grouper** *n., pl.* **-er** *or* **-ers.** a large marine fish of warm and tropical seas. [C17: < Port. *garupa*, prob. < a South American Indian word]

grosbeak (ˈgrəʊsˌbiːk, ˈgrɒs-) *n.* any of various finches that have a massive powerful bill. [C17: < F *grosbec*, < OF *gros* large, thick + *bec* BEAK[1]]

groschen (ˈgrəʊʃən) *n., pl.* **-schen. 1.** an Austrian monetary unit worth one hundredth of a schilling. **2.** a German coin worth ten pfennigs. **3.** a former German silver coin. [C17: < G: alteration of MHG *grosse*, < Med. L (*denarius*) *grossus* thick (penny); see GROSS, GROAT]

grosgrain (ˈgrəʊˌgreɪn) *n.* a heavy ribbed silk or rayon fabric or tape for trimming clothes, etc. [C19: < F *gros grain* coarse grain; see GROSS, GRAIN]

gros point (grəʊ) *n.* **1.** a needlepoint stitch covering two horizontal and two vertical threads. **2.** work done in this stitch.

gross (grəʊs) *adj.* **1.** repellently or excessively fat or bulky. **2.** with no deductions for expenses, tax, etc.; total: *gross sales.* Cf. **net**[2]. **3.** (of personal qualities, tastes, etc.) conspicuously coarse or vulgar. **4.** obviously or exceptionally culpable or wrong; flagrant: *gross inefficiency.* **5.** lacking in perception, sensitivity, or discrimination: *gross judgments.* **6.** (esp. of vegetation) dense; thick; luxuriant. ~*n.* **7.** (*pl.* **gross**). a unit of quantity equal to 12 dozen. **8.** (*pl.* **grosses**). **a.** the entire amount. **b.** the great majority. ~*vb.* (*tr.*) **9.** to earn as total revenue, before deductions for expenses, tax, etc. [C14: < OF *gros* large, < LL *grossus* thick] —ˈ**grossly** *adv.* —ˈ**grossness** *n.*

gross domestic product *n.* the total value of all goods and services produced domestically by a nation during a year. It is equivalent to gross national product minus net investment incomes from foreign nations. Abbrev.: **GDP.**

gross national product *n.* the total value of all final goods and services produced annually by a nation. Abbrev.: **GNP.**

gross profit *n. Accounting.* the difference between total revenue from sales and the total cost of purchases or materials, with an adjustment for stock.

gross weight *n.* total weight of an article inclusive of the weight of the container and packaging.

grotesque (grəʊˈtɛsk) *adj.* **1.** strangely or fantastically distorted; bizarre. **2.** of or characteristic of the grotesque in art. **3.** absurdly incongruous; in a ludicrous context. ~*n.* **4.** a 16th-century decorative style in which parts of human, animal, and plant forms are distorted and mixed. **5.** a decorative device, as in painting or sculpture, in this style. **6.** *Printing.* the family of 19th-century sans serif display types. **7.** any grotesque person or thing. [C16: < F, < OIt. (*pittura*) *grottesca* cave painting, < *grotta* cave; see GROTTO] —**groˈtesquely** *adv.* —**groˈtesqueness** *n.* —**groˈtesquery** *or* **groˈtesquerie** *n.*

grotto (ˈgrɒtəʊ) *n., pl.* **-toes** *or* **-tos. 1.** a small cave, esp. one with attractive features. **2.** a construction in the form of a cave, esp. as in landscaped gardens during the 18th century. [C17: < OIt. *grotta*, < LL *crypta* vault; see CRYPT]

grotty (ˈgrɒtɪ) *adj.* **-tier, -tiest.** *Brit. sl.* **1.** nasty or unattractive. **2.** of poor quality or in bad condition. [C20: < GROTESQUE]

grouch (graʊtʃ) *Inf.* ~*vb.* (*intr.*) **1.** to complain; grumble. ~*n.* **2.** a complaint, esp. a persistent one. **3.** a person who is always grumbling. [C20: < obs. *grutch*, < OF *grouchier* to complain; see GRUDGE] —ˈ**grouchy** *adj.* —ˈ**grouchily** *adv.* —ˈ**grouchiness** *n.*

ground[1] (graʊnd) *n.* **1.** the land surface. **2.** earth or soil. **3.** (*pl.*) the land around a dwelling house or other building. **4.** (*sometimes pl.*) an area of land given over to a purpose: *football ground.* **5.** land having a particular characteristic: *high ground.* **6.** matter for consideration or debate; field of research or inquiry: *the report covered a lot of ground.* **7.** a position or viewpoint, as in an argument or controversy (esp. in **give ground, hold, stand,** *or* **shift one's ground**). **8.** position or advantage, as in a subject or competition (esp. in **gain ground, lose ground,** etc.). **9.** (*often pl.*) reason; justification: *grounds for complaint.* **10.** *Arts.* **a.** the prepared surface applied to a wall, canvas, etc., to prevent it reacting with or absorbing the paint. **b.** the background of a painting against which the other parts of a work of art appear superimposed. **11. a.** the first coat of paint applied to a surface. **b.** (*as modifier*): *ground colour.* **12.** the bottom of a river or the sea. **13.** (*pl.*) sediment or dregs, esp. from coffee. **14.** *Chiefly Brit.* the floor of a room. **15.** *Cricket.* the area from the popping crease back past the stumps, in which a batsman may legally stand. **16.** *Electrical.* the usual U.S. and Canad. word for **earth** (sense 8). **17. break new ground.** to do something that has not been done before. **18. common ground.** an agreed basis for identifying issues in an argument. **19. cut the ground from under someone's feet.** to anticipate someone's action or argument and thus make it irrelevant or meaningless. **20. (down) to the ground.** *Brit. inf.* completely; absolutely: *it suited him down to the ground.* **21. home ground.** a familiar area or topic. **22. into the ground.** beyond what is requisite or can be endured; to exhaustion. **23.** (*modifier*) on or concerned with the ground: *ground frost; ground forces.* ~*vb.* **24.** (*tr.*) to put or place on the ground. **25.** (*tr.*) to instruct in fundamentals. **26.** (*tr.*) to provide a basis or foundation for; establish. **27.** (*tr.*) to confine (an aircraft, pilot, etc.) to the ground. **28.** the usual U.S. and Canad. word for **earth** (sense 13). **29.** (*tr.*) *Naut.* to run (a vessel) aground. **30.** (*intr.*) to hit or reach the ground. [OE *grund*]

ground[2] (graʊnd) *vb.* **1.** the past tense and past participle of **grind.** ~*adj.* **2.** having the surface finished, thickness reduced, or an edge sharpened by grinding. **3.** reduced to fine particles by grinding.

groundage (ˈgraʊndɪdʒ) *n. Brit.* a fee levied on a vessel entering a port or anchored off a shore.

groundbait (ˈgraʊndˌbeɪt) *n. Angling.* bait, such as bread or maggots, thrown into an area of water to attract fish.

ground bass (beɪs) *n. Music.* a short melodic bass line that is repeated over and over again.

ground control *n.* **1.** the personnel, radar, computers, etc., on the ground that monitor the progress of aircraft or spacecraft. **2.** a system for feeding continuous radio messages to an aircraft pilot to enable him to make a blind landing.

ground cover *n.* dense low herbaceous plants and shrubs that grow over the surface of the ground.

ground elder *n.* a widely naturalized Eurasian umbelliferous plant with white flowers and creeping underground stems. Also called: **bishop's weed, goutweed.**

ground floor *n.* **1.** the floor of a building level or almost level with the ground. **2. get in on the ground floor.** *Inf.* to be in a project, undertaking, etc., from its inception.

ground glass *n.* **1.** glass that has a rough surface produced by grinding, used for diffusing light. **2.** glass in the form of fine particles produced by grinding, used as an abrasive.

groundhog (ˈgraʊndˌhɒg) *n.* another name for **woodchuck.**

grounding (ˈgraʊndɪŋ) *n.* a foundation, esp. the basic general knowledge of a subject.

ground ivy *n.* a creeping or trailing Eurasian aromatic herbaceous plant with scalloped leaves and purplish-blue flowers.

groundless (ˈgraʊndlɪs) *adj.* without reason or justification: *his suspicions were groundless.* —ˈ**groundlessly** *adv.* —ˈ**groundlessness** *n.*

groundling (ˈgraʊndlɪŋ) *n.* **1.** any animal or plant that lives close to the ground or at the bottom of a lake, river, etc. **2.** (in Elizabethan theatre) a spectator standing in the yard in front of the stage and paying least. **3.** a person on the ground as distinguished from one in an aircraft.

groundnut (ˈgraʊndˌnʌt) *n.* **1.** a North American climbing leguminous plant with small edible underground tubers. **2.** the tuber of this plant. **3.** *Brit.* another name for **peanut.**

ground plan *n.* **1.** a drawing of the ground floor of a building, esp. one to scale. **2.** a preliminary or basic outline.

ground rule *n.* a procedural or fundamental principle.

groundsel (ˈgraʊnsəl) *n.* any of certain plants of the composite family, esp. a Eurasian weed with heads of small yellow flowers. [OE, < *gundeswilge,* < *gund* pus + *swelgan* to swallow; after its use in poultices]

groundsheet (ˈgraʊndˌʃiːt) *n.* a waterproof rubber, plastic, or polythene sheet placed on the ground in a tent, etc., to keep out damp.

groundsill (ˈgraʊndˌsɪl) *n.* a joist forming the lowest member of a timber frame. Also called: **ground plate.**

groundsman (ˈgraʊndzmən) *n., pl.* **-men.** a person employed to maintain a sports ground, park, etc.

groundspeed (ˈgraʊndˌspiːd) *n.* the speed of an aircraft relative to the ground.

ground squirrel *n.* a burrowing rodent resembling a chipmunk and occurring in North America, E Europe, and Asia. Also called: **gopher.**

ground swell *n.* **1.** a considerable swell of the sea, often caused by a distant storm or earthquake. **2.** a rapidly developing general feeling or opinion.

ground water *n.* underground water that is held in the soil and in pervious rocks.

groundwork (ˈgraʊndˌwɜːk) *n.* **1.** preliminary work as a foundation or basis. **2.** the ground or background of a painting, etc.

ground zero *n.* a point on the ground directly below the centre of a nuclear explosion.

group (gruːp) *n.* **1.** a number of persons or things considered as a collective unit. **2. a.** a number of persons bound together by common social standards, interests, etc. **b.** (*as modifier*): *group behaviour.* **3.** a small band of players or singers, esp. of pop music. **4.** a number of animals or plants considered as a unit because of common characteristics, habits, etc. **5.** an association of companies under a single ownership and control. **6.** two or more figures or objects forming a design in a painting or sculpture. **7.** a military formation comprising complementary arms and services: *a brigade group.* **8.** an air force organization of higher level than a squadron. **9.** Also called: **radical.** *Chem.* two or more atoms that are bound together in a molecule and behave as a single unit: *a methyl group* $-CH_3$. **10.** a vertical column of elements in the periodic table that all have similar electronic structures, properties, and valencies: *the halogen group.* **11.** *Maths.* a set under an operation involving any two members of the set such that the set is closed, associative, and contains both an identity and the inverse of each member. **12.** See **blood group.** ~*vb.* **13.** to arrange or place (things, people, etc.) in or into a group, or (of things, etc.) to form into a group. [C17: < F *groupe,* of Gmc origin; cf. It. *gruppo;* see CROP]

group captain *n.* an officer holding commissioned rank senior to a wing commander but junior to an air commodore in the RAF and certain other air forces.

group dynamics *n.* (*functioning as sing.*) *Psychol.* a field of social psychology concerned with the nature of human groups, their development, and their interactions.

grouper (ˈgruːpə) *n.* a variant spelling of **groper.**

groupie (ˈgruːpɪ) *n. Sl.* an ardent fan of a celebrity, esp. a girl who follows the members of a pop group on tour in order to have sexual relations with them.

group therapy *n. Psychol.* the simultaneous treatment of a number of individuals who are brought together to share their problems in group discussion.

grouse[1] (graʊs) *n., pl.* **grouse** *or* **grouses.** a game bird occurring mainly in the N hemisphere, having a stocky body and feathered legs and feet. [C16: <?]

grouse[2] (graʊs) *vb.* **1.** (*intr.*) to grumble; complain. ~*n.* **2.** a persistent complaint. [C19: <?] —ˈ**grouser** *n.*

grouse[3] (graʊs) *adj. Austral. & N.Z. sl.* fine; excellent. [<?]

grout (graʊt) *n.* **1.** a thin mortar for filling joints between tiles, masonry, etc. **2.** a fine plaster used as a finishing coat. **3.** (*pl.*) sediment or dregs. ~*vb.* **4.** (*tr.*) to fill (joints) or finish (walls, etc.) with grout. [OE *grūt*] —ˈ**grouter** *n.*

grove (grəʊv) *n.* **1.** a small wooded area or plantation. **2.** a road lined with houses and often trees, esp. in a suburban area. [OE *grāf*]

grovel (ˈgrɒvᵊl) *vb.* **-elling, -elled** *or U.S.* **-eling, -eled.** (*intr.*) **1.** to humble or abase oneself, as in making apologies or showing respect. **2.** to lie or crawl face downwards, as in fear or humility. **3.** (often foll. by *in*) to indulge or take pleasure (in sensuality or vice). [C16: back formation < obs. *groveling* (adv.), < ME *on grufe* on the face, of Scand. origin; see -LING[2]] —ˈ**groveller** *n.*

grow (grəʊ) *vb.* **growing, grew, grown.** **1.** (of an organism or part of an organism) to increase in size or develop (hair, leaves, or other structures). **2.** (*intr.;* usually foll. by *out of* or *from*) to originate, as from an initial cause or source: *the federation grew out of the Empire.* **3.** (*intr.*) to increase in size, number, degree, etc.: *the population is growing rapidly.* **4.** (*intr.*) to change in length or amount in a specified direction: *some plants grow downwards.* **5.** (*copula; may take an infinitive*) (esp. of emotions, physical states, etc.) to develop or come into existence or being gradually: *to grow cold; he grew to like her.* **6.** (*intr.;* foll. by *together*) to be joined gradually by or as by growth: *the branches on the tree grew together.* **7.** (when *intr.,* foll. by *with*) to become covered with a growth: *the path grew with weeds.* **8.** to produce (plants) by controlling or encouraging their growth, esp. for home consumption or on a commercial basis. ~See also **grow into, grow on,** etc. [OE *grōwan*] —ˈ**growable** *adj.* —ˈ**grower** *n.*

grow bag *n.* a plastic bag containing a sterile growing medium that enables a plant to be grown to full size in it, usually for one season only. [C20: < *Gro-bag,* trademark for the first ones marketed]

growing pains *pl. n.* **1.** pains in muscles or joints sometimes experienced by growing children. **2.** difficulties besetting a new enterprise in its early stages.

grow into *vb.* (*intr., prep.*) to become big or mature enough for: *his clothes were always big enough for him to grow into.*

growl (graʊl) *vb.* **1.** (of animals, esp. when hostile) to utter (sounds) in a low inarticulate manner: *the dog growled.* **2.** to utter (words) in a gruff or angry manner. **3.** (*intr.*) to make sounds suggestive of an animal growling: *the thunder growled.* ~*n.* **4.** the act or sound of growling.

[C18: < earlier *grolle,* < OF *grouller* to grumble] —ˈ**growler** *n.* —ˈ**growlingly** *adv.*

grown (grəʊn) *adj.* **a.** developed or advanced: *fully grown.* **b.** (*in combination*): *half-grown.*

grown-up *adj.* **1.** having reached maturity; adult. **2.** suitable for or characteristic of an adult. ~*n.* **3.** an adult.

grow on *vb.* (*intr., prep.*) to become progressively more acceptable or pleasant to.

grow out of *vb.* (*intr., adv.* + *prep.*) to become too big or mature for: *she soon grew out of her girlish ways.*

growth (grəʊθ) *n.* **1.** the process or act of growing. **2.** an increase in size, number, significance, etc. **3.** something grown or growing: *a new growth of hair.* **4.** a stage of development: *a full growth.* **5.** any abnormal tissue, such as a tumour. **6.** (*modifier*) of, relating to, or characterized by growth: *a growth industry.*

grow up *vb.* (*intr., adv.*) **1.** to reach maturity; become adult. **2.** to come into existence; develop.

groyne *or esp. U.S.* **groin** (grɔɪn) *n.* a wall or jetty built out from a riverbank or seashore to control erosion. Also called: **spur, breakwater.** [C16: ? < OF *groign* snout, promontory]

grub (grʌb) *vb.* **grubbing, grubbed. 1.** (when *tr.,* often foll. by *up* or *out*) to search for and pull up (roots, stumps, etc.) by digging in the ground. **2.** to dig up the surface of (ground, soil, etc.), esp. to clear away roots, stumps, etc. **3.** (*intr.;* often foll. by *in* or *among*) to search carefully. **4.** (*intr.*) to work unceasingly, esp. at a dull task. ~*n.* **5.** the short legless larva of certain insects, esp. beetles. **6.** *Sl.* food; victuals. **7.** a person who works hard, esp. in a dull plodding way. [C13: of Gmc origin; cf. OHG *grubilōn* to dig] —ˈ**grubber** *n.*

grubby (ˈgrʌbɪ) *adj.* **-bier, -biest. 1.** dirty; slovenly. **2.** mean; beggarly. **3.** infested with grubs. —ˈ**grubbily** *adv.* —ˈ**grubbiness** *n.*

grub screw *n.* a small headless screw used to secure a sliding component in position.

grubstake (ˈgrʌbˌsteɪk) *n. U.S. & Canad. inf.* ~**1.** supplies provided for a prospector on the condition that the donor has a stake in any finds. ~*vb.* (*tr.*) **2.** to furnish with such supplies. **3.** *Chiefly U.S. & Canad.* to supply (a person) with a stake in a gambling game. —ˈ**grubˌstaker** *n.*

Grub Street *n.* **1.** a former street in London frequented by literary hacks and needy authors. **2.** the world or class of literary hacks, etc. ~*adj. also* **Grubstreet. 3.** (*sometimes not cap.*) relating to or characteristic of hack literature.

grudge (grʌdʒ) *n.* **1.** a persistent feeling of resentment, esp. one due to an insult or injury. ~*vb.* **2.** (*tr.*) to give unwillingly. **3.** to feel resentful or envious about (someone else's success, possessions, etc.). [C15: < OF *grouchier* to grumble, prob. of Gmc origin] —ˈ**grudging** *adj.* —ˈ**grudgingly** *adv.*

gruel (ˈgruːəl) *n.* a drink or thin porridge made by boiling meal, esp. oatmeal, in water or milk. [C14: < OF, of Gmc origin]

gruelling *or U.S.* **grueling** (ˈgruːəlɪŋ) *adj.* **1.** extremely severe or tiring. ~*n.* **2.** *Inf.* a severe or tiring experience, esp. punishment. [C19: < obs. *gruel* (vb.) to punish]

gruesome (ˈgruːsəm) *adj.* inspiring repugnance and horror; ghastly. [C16: orig. Northern E and Scot., of Scand. origin] —ˈ**gruesomely** *adv.* —ˈ**gruesomeness** *n.*

gruff (grʌf) *adj.* **1.** rough or surly in manner, speech, etc. **2.** (of a voice, bark, etc.) low and throaty. [C16: orig. Scot., < Du. *grof,* of Gmc origin; rel. to OE *hrēof*] —ˈ**gruffly** *adv.* —ˈ**gruffness** *n.*

grumble (ˈgrʌmbᵊl) *vb.* **1.** to utter (complaints) in a nagging way. **2.** (*intr.*) to make low dull rumbling sounds. ~*n.* **3.** a complaint; grouse. **4.** a low rumbling sound. [C16: < MLow G *grommelen,* of Gmc origin] —ˈ**grumbler** *n.* —ˈ**grumblingly** *adv.* —ˈ**grumbly** *adj.*

grumbling appendix *n. Inf.* a condition in which the appendix causes intermittent pain or discomfort but appendicitis has not developed.

grummet (ˈgrʌmɪt) *n.* a variant of **grommet.**

grump (grʌmp) *Inf.* ~*n.* **1.** a surly or bad-tempered person. **2.** (*pl.*) a sulky or morose mood (esp. in **have the grumps**). ~*vb.* **3.** (*intr.*) to complain or grumble. [C18: dialect: surly remark, prob. imit.]

grumpy (ˈgrʌmpɪ) *or* **grumpish** *adj.* **grumpier, grumpiest.** peevish; sulky. [C18: < GRUMP + -Y[1]] —ˈ**grumpily** *or* ˈ**grumpishly** *adv.* —ˈ**grumpiness** *or* ˈ**grumpishness** *n.*

Grundy (ˈgrʌndɪ) *n.* a narrow-minded person who keeps critical watch on the propriety of others. [C18: after Mrs *Grundy,* the character in T. Morton's play *Speed the Plough* (1798)]

grungy (ˈgrʌndʒɪ) *adj.* **-gier, -giest.** *Sl., chiefly U.S. & Canad.* squalid, seedy, grotty. [< ?]

grunion (ˈgrʌnjən) *n.* a Californian marine fish that spawns on beaches. [C20: prob. < Sp. *gruñón* a grunter]

grunt (grʌnt) *vb.* **1.** (*intr.*) (esp. of pigs and some other animals) to emit a low short gruff noise. **2.** (when *tr., may take a clause as object*) to express something gruffly: *he grunted his answer.* ~*n.* **3.** the characteristic low short gruff noise of pigs, etc., or a similar sound, as of disgust. **4.** any of various mainly tropical marine fishes that utter a grunting sound when caught. [OE *grunnettan,* prob. imit.; cf. OHG *grunnizōn, grunni* moaning] —ˈ**grunter** *n.*

Gruyère *or* **Gruyère cheese** (ˈgruːjɛə) *n.* a hard flat whole-milk cheese, pale yellow in colour and with holes. [C19: after *Gruyère,* Switzerland, where it originated]

gr. wt. *abbrev. for* gross weight.

gryphon (ˈgrɪfᵊn) *n.* a variant spelling of **griffin.**

grysbok (ˈgraɪsˌbɒk) *n.* either of two small antelopes of central and southern Africa, having small straight horns. [C18: Afrik., < Du. *grijs* grey + *bok* BUCK[1]]

GS *abbrev. for:* **1.** General Secretary. **2.** General Staff.

G-string *n.* **1.** a piece of cloth worn by striptease artistes covering the pubic area only and attached to a very narrow waistband. **2.** a strip of cloth attached to the front and back of a waistband and covering the loins. **3.** *Music.* a string tuned to G.

G-suit *n.* a close-fitting garment that is worn by the crew of high-speed aircraft and can be pressurized to prevent blackout during certain manoeuvres. [C20: < *g(ravity) suit*]

GT *abbrev. for* gran turismo: a touring car; usually a fast sports car with a hard fixed roof.

gtd *abbrev. for* guaranteed.

guaiacum (ˈgwaɪəkəm) *n.* **1.** any of a family of tropical American evergreen trees such as the lignum vitae. **2.** the hard heavy wood of any of these trees. **3.** a brownish resin obtained from the lignum vitae, used medicinally and in making varnishes. [C16: NL, < Sp. *guayaco,* of Amerind origin]

guanaco (gwɑːˈnɑːkəʊ) *n., pl.* **-cos.** a cud-chewing South American mammal closely related to the domesticated llama. [C17: < Sp., < Quechuan *huanacu*]

guanine (ˈgwɑːniːn, ˈguːəˌniːn) *n.* a white almost insoluble compound: one of the purine bases in nucleic acids. [C19: < GUANO + -INE[2]]

guano (ˈgwɑːnəʊ) *n., pl.* **-nos. 1.** the dried excrement of fish-eating sea birds, deposited in rocky coastal regions of South America: used as a fertilizer. **2.** any similar but artificially produced fertilizer. [C17: < Sp., < Quechuan *huano* dung]

Guarani (ˌgwɑːrəˈniː) *n.* **1.** (*pl.* **-ni** *or* **-nis**) a member of a South American Indian people of Paraguay, S Brazil, and Bolivia. **2.** the language of this people.

guarantee (ˌgærənˈtiː) *n.* **1.** a formal assurance, esp. in writing, that a product, service, etc., will meet certain standards or specifications. **2.** *Law.* a promise, esp. a collateral agreement, to answer for the debt, default, or miscarriage of another. **3. a.** a person, company, etc., to whom a guarantee is made. **b.** a person, company, etc., who gives a guarantee. **4.** a person who acts as a guarantor. **5.** something that makes a specified condition or outcome certain. **6.** a variant spelling of **guaranty.** ~*vb.* **-teeing, -teed.** (*mainly tr.*) **7.** (*also intr.*) to take responsibility for (someone else's debts, obligations, etc.). **8.** to serve as a guarantee for. **9.** to secure or furnish security for: *a small deposit will guarantee any dress.* **10.** (usually foll. by *from* or *against*) to undertake to protect or keep secure, as against injury, loss, etc. **11.** to ensure: *good planning will guarantee success.* **12.** (*may take a clause as object or an infinitive*) to promise or make certain. [C17: ? < Sp. *garante* or F *garant,* of Gmc origin; cf. WARRANT]

guarantor (ˌgærənˈtɔː) *n.* a person who gives or is bound by a guarantee or guaranty; surety.

guaranty (ˈgærəntɪ) *n., pl.* **-ties. 1.** a pledge of responsibility for fulfilling another person's obligations in case of that person's default. **2.** a thing given or taken as security for a guaranty. **3.** the act of providing security. **4.** a person who acts as a guarantor. ~*vb.* **-tying, -tied. 5.** a variant spelling of **guarantee.** [C16: < OF *garantie,* var. of *warantie,* of Gmc origin; see WARRANTY]

guard (gɑːd) *vb.* **1.** to watch over or shield (a person or thing) from danger or harm; protect. **2.** to keep watch over (a prisoner or other potentially dangerous person or thing), as to prevent escape. **3.** (*tr.*) to control: *to guard one's tongue.* **4.** (*intr.;* usually foll. by *against*) to take precautions. **5.** to control entrance and exit through (a gate, door, etc.). **6.** (*tr.*) to provide (machinery, etc.) with a device to protect the operator. **7.** (*tr.*) **a.** *Chess, cards.* to protect or cover (a chessman or card) with another. **b.** *Curling, bowling.* to protect or cover (a stone or bowl) by placing one's own stone or bowl between it and another player. ~*n.* **8.** a person or group who keeps a protecting, supervising, or restraining watch or control over people, such as prisoners, things, etc. Related adj.: **custodial. 9.** a person or group of people, such as soldiers, who form a ceremonial escort. **10.** *Brit.* the official in charge of a train. **11. a.** the act or duty of protecting, restraining, or supervising. **b.** (*as modifier*): *guard duty.* **12.** a device, part, or attachment on an object, such as a weapon or machine tool, designed to protect the user against injury. **13.** anything that provides or is intended to provide protection: *a guard against infection.* **14.** *Sport.* an article of light tough material worn to protect any of various parts of the body. **15.** the posture of defence or readiness in fencing, boxing, cricket, etc. **16. mount guard. a.** (of a sentry, etc.) to begin to keep watch. **b.** (with *over*) to take a protective or defensive stance (towards something). **17. off (one's) guard.** having one's defences down; unprepared. **18. on (one's) guard.** prepared to face danger, difficulties, etc. **19. stand guard.** (of a sentry, etc.) to keep watch. [C15: < OF, < *garder* to protect, of Gmc origin; see WARD] —ˈ**guarder** *n.*

guarded (ˈgɑːdɪd) *adj.* **1.** protected or kept under surveillance. **2.** prudent, restrained, or noncommittal: *a guarded reply.* —ˈ**guardedly** *adv.* —ˈ**guardedness** *n.*

guard hair *n.* any of the coarse hairs that form the outer fur in certain mammals.

guardhouse (ˈgɑːdˌhaʊs) *n. Mil.* a building serving as headquarters for military police and in which military prisoners are detained.

guardian (ˈgɑːdɪən) *n.* **1.** one who looks after, protects, or defends: *the guardian of public morals.* **2.** *Law.* someone legally appointed to manage the affairs of a person incapable of acting for himself, as a minor or person of unsound mind. ~*adj.* **3.** protecting or safeguarding. —ˈ**guardian**ˌ**ship** *n.*

guard ring *n.* **1.** Also called: **keeper ring.** a ring worn to prevent another from slipping off the finger. **2.** an electrode used to counteract distortion of the electric fields at the edges of other electrodes.

Guards (gɑːdz) *pl. n.* (esp. in European armies) any of various regiments responsible for ceremonial duties and, formerly, the protection of the head of state: *the Life Guards.*

guardsman (ˈgɑːdzmən) *n., pl.* **-men. 1.** (in Britain) a member of a Guards battalion or regiment. **2.** (in the U.S.) a member of the National Guard. **3.** a guard.

guard's van *n. Railways, Brit. & N.Z.* the van in which the guard travels, usually attached to the rear of a train. U.S. and Canad. equivalent: **caboose.**

guava (ˈgwɑːvə) *n.* **1.** any of various tropical American trees, grown esp. for their edible fruit. **2.** the fruit of such a tree, having yellow skin and pink pulp. [C16: < Sp. *guayaba,* < a South American Indian word]

guayule (gwəˈjuːlɪ) *n.* **1.** a bushy shrub of the southwestern U.S. **2.** rubber derived from the sap of this plant. [< American Sp., < Nahuatl *cuauhuli,* < *cuahuitl* tree + *uli* gum]

gubbins (ˈgʌbɪnz) *n.* **1.** (*functioning as sing.*) an object of little value. **2.** (*functioning as sing.*) a small gadget. **3.** (*functioning as pl.*) odds and ends; rubbish. **4.** (*functioning as sing.*) a silly person. [C16 (meaning: fragments): < obs. *gobbon*]

gubernatorial (ˌgjuːbənəˈtɔːrɪəl, ˌguː-) *adj. Chiefly U.S.* of or relating to a governor. [C18: < L *gubernātor* governor]

guddle (ˈgʌdᵊl) *Scot.* ~*vb.* **1.** to catch (fish) by groping with the hands under the banks or stones of a stream. ~*n.* **2.** a muddle; confusion. [C19: <?]

gudgeon[1] (ˈgʌdʒən) *n.* **1.** a small slender European freshwater fish with a barbel on each side of the mouth: used as bait by anglers. **2.** any of various other fishes, such as the goby. **3.** *Sl.* a person who is easy to trick or cheat. ~*vb.* **4.** (*tr.*) *Sl.* to trick or cheat. [C15: < OF *gougon,* prob. < L *gōbius;* see GOBY]

gudgeon[2] (ˈgʌdʒən) *n.* **1.** the female or socket portion of a pinned hinge. **2.** *Naut.* one of two or more looplike sockets, fixed to the transom of a boat, into which the pintles of a rudder are fitted. [C14: < OF *goujon,* ? < LL *gulbia* chisel]

gudgeon pin *n. Brit.* the pin through the skirt of a piston in an internal-combustion engine, to which the little end of the connecting rod is attached. U.S. and Canad. name: **wrist pin.**

guelder-rose (ˈgɛldəˌrəʊz) *n.* a Eurasian shrub with clusters of white flowers and small red fruits. [C16: < Du. *geldersche roos,* < *Gelderland* or *Gelders,* province of Holland]

guenon (gəˈnɒn) *n.* a slender agile Old World monkey inhabiting wooded regions of Africa and having long hind limbs and tail and long hair surrounding the face. [C19: < F, <?]

guerdon (ˈgɜːdᵊn) *Poetic.* ~*n.* **1.** a reward or payment. ~*vb.* **2.** (*tr.*) to give a guerdon to. [C14: < OF *gueredon,* of Gmc origin; final element infl. by L *dōnum* gift]

Guernsey (ˈgɜːnzɪ) *n.* **1.** a breed of dairy cattle producing rich creamy milk, originating from the island of Guernsey, one of the Channel Islands. **2. Guernsey lily.** See **nerine. 3.** (*sometimes not cap.*) a seaman's knitted woollen sweater. **4.** (*not cap.*) *Austral.* a sleeveless woollen shirt or jumper worn by an Australian Rules football player. **5. get a guernsey.** *Austral.* to be selected for a team or gain recognition for something.

guerrilla *or* **guerilla** (gəˈrɪlə) *n.* **a.** a member of an irregular usually politically motivated armed force that combats stronger regular forces. **b.** (*as modifier*): *guerrilla warfare.* [C19: < Sp., dim. of *guerra* WAR]

guess (gɛs) *vb.* (when *tr., may take a clause as object*) **1.** (when *intr.,* often foll. by *at* or *about*) to form or express an uncertain estimate or conclusion (about something), based on insufficient information: *guess what we're having for dinner.* **2.** to arrive at a correct estimate of (something) by guessing: *he guessed my age.* **3.** *Inf., chiefly U.S. & Canad.* to believe, think, or suppose (something): *I guess I'll go now.* ~*n.* **4.** an estimate or conclusion arrived at by guessing:

a bad guess. **5.** the act of guessing. [C13: prob. < ON] —**ˈguesser** *n.*

guesstimate *or* **guestimate** *Inf.* ~*n.* (ˈɡɛstɪmɪt). **1.** an estimate calculated mainly or only by guesswork. ~*vb.* (ˈɡɛstɪˌmeɪt). (*tr.*) **2.** to form a guesstimate of.

guesswork (ˈɡɛsˌwɜːk) *n.* **1.** a set of conclusions, estimates, etc., arrived at by guessing. **2.** the process of making guesses.

guest (ɡɛst) *n.* **1.** a person who is entertained, taken out to eat, etc., and paid for by another. **2. a.** a person who receives hospitality at the home of another. **b.** (*as modifier*): *the guest room.* **3. a.** a person who receives the hospitality of a government, establishment, or organization. **b.** (*as modifier*): *a guest speaker.* **4. a.** an actor, contestant, entertainer, etc., taking part as a visitor in a programme in which there are also regular participants. **b.** (*as modifier*): *a guest appearance.* **5.** a patron of a hotel, boarding house, restaurant, etc. ~*vb.* **6.** (*intr.*) (in theatre and broadcasting) to be a guest: *to guest on a show.* [OE *giest* guest, stranger, enemy]

guesthouse (ˈɡɛstˌhaʊs) *n.* a private home or boarding house offering accommodation.

guest rope *n. Naut.* any line trailed over the side of a vessel as a convenience for boats drawing alongside, as an aid in towing, etc.

guff (ɡʌf) *n. Sl.* ridiculous or insolent talk. [C19: imit. of empty talk]

guffaw (ɡʌˈfɔː) *n.* **1.** a crude and boisterous laugh. ~*vb.* **2.** to laugh or express (something) in this way. [C18: imit.]

guidance (ˈɡaɪdᵊns) *n.* **1.** leadership, instruction, or direction. **2. a.** counselling or advice on educational, vocational, or psychological matters. **b.** (*as modifier*): *the marriage-guidance counsellor.* **3.** something that guides. **4.** any process by which the flight path of a missile is controlled in flight.

guide (ɡaɪd) *vb.* **1.** to lead the way for (a person). **2.** to control the movement or course of (an animal, vehicle, etc.) by physical action; steer. **3.** to supervise or instruct (a person). **4.** (*tr.*) to direct the affairs of (a person, company, nation, etc.). **5.** (*tr.*) to advise or influence (a person) in his standards or opinions: *let truth guide you.* ~*n.* **6. a.** a person, animal, or thing that guides. **b.** (*as modifier*): *a guide dog.* **7.** a person, usually paid, who conducts tour expeditions, etc. **8.** a model or criterion, as in moral standards or accuracy. **9.** Also called: **guidebook.** a handbook with information for visitors to a place. **10.** a book that instructs or explains the fundamentals of a subject or skill. **11.** any device that directs the motion of a tool or machine part. **12.** a mark, sign, etc., that points the way. **13. a.** *Naval.* a ship in a formation used as a reference for manoeuvres. **b.** *Mil.* a soldier stationed to one side of a column or line to regulate alignment, show the way, etc. [C14: < (O)F *guider,* of Gmc origin] —**ˈguidable** *adj.* —**ˈguider** *n.*

Guide (ɡaɪd) *n.* (*sometimes not cap.*) a member of the organization for girls equivalent to the Scouts. U.S. equivalent: **Girl Scout.**

guided missile *n.* a missile, esp. one that is rocket-propelled, having a flight path controlled either by radio signals or by internal preset or self-actuating homing devices.

guide dog *n.* a dog that has been specially trained to accompany someone who is blind, enabling the blind person to move about safely.

guideline (ˈɡaɪdˌlaɪn) *n.* a principle put forward to set standards or determine a course of action.

guidepost (ˈɡaɪdˌpəʊst) *n.* **1.** a sign on a post by a road indicating directions. **2.** a principle or guideline.

Guider (ˈɡaɪdə) *n.* (*sometimes not cap.*) a woman leader of a company of Guides or of a pack of Brownie Guides.

guidon (ˈɡaɪdᵊn) *n.* **1.** a small pennant, used as a marker or standard, esp. by cavalry regiments. **2.** the man or vehicle that carries this. [C16: < F, < OProvençal *guidoo,* < *guida* GUIDE]

guild *or* **gild** (ɡɪld) *n.* **1.** an organization, club, or fellowship. **2.** (esp. in medieval Europe) an association of men sharing the same interests, such as merchants or artisans: formed for mutual aid and protection and to maintain craft standards. [C14: < ON; cf. *gjald* payment, *gildi* guild; rel. to OE *gield* offering, OHG *gelt* money] —**ˈguildsman, ˈgildsman** *or* (*fem.*) **ˈguildswoman, ˈgildswoman** *n.*

guilder (ˈɡɪldə) *or* **gulden** *n., pl.* **-ders, -der** *or* **-dens, -den. 1.** Also: **gilder.** the standard monetary unit of the Netherlands, divided into 100 cents. **2.** any of various former gold or silver coins of Germany, Austria, or the Netherlands. [C15: < MDu. *gulden,* lit.: GOLDEN]

guildhall (ˈɡɪldˌhɔːl) *n. Brit.* **a.** the hall of a guild or corporation. **b.** a town hall.

guile (ɡaɪl) *n.* clever or crafty character or behaviour. [C18: < OF *guile,* of Gmc origin; see WILE] —**ˈguileful** *adj.* —**ˈguilefully** *adv.* —**ˈguilefulness** *n.* —**ˈguileless** *adj.* —**ˈguilelessly** *adv.* —**ˈguilelessness** *n.*

guillemot (ˈɡɪlɪˌmɒt) *n.* a northern oceanic diving bird having a black-and-white plumage and long narrow bill. [C17: < F, dim. of *Guillaume* William]

guilloche (ɡɪˈlɒʃ) *n.* an ornamental border with a repeating pattern of two or more interwoven wavy lines, as in architecture. [C19: < F: tool used in ornamental work, ? < *Guillaume* William]

guillotine *n.* (ˈɡɪləˌtiːn). **1. a.** a device for beheading persons, consisting of a weighted blade set between two upright posts. **b. the guillotine.** execution by this instrument. **2.** a device for cutting or trimming sheet material, such as paper or sheet metal, consisting of a slightly inclined blade that descends onto the sheet. **3.** a surgical instrument for removing tonsils, growths in the throat, etc. **4.** (in Parliament, etc.) a form of closure under which a bill is divided into compartments, groups of which must be completely dealt with each day. ~*vb.* (ˌɡɪləˈtiːn). (*tr.*) **5.** to behead (a person) by guillotine. **6.** (in Parliament, etc.) to limit debate on (a bill, motion, etc.) by the guillotine. [C18: < F, after Joseph Ignace *Guillotin* (1738–1814), F physician, who advocated its use in 1789] —**ˌguilloˈtiner** *n.*

guilt (ɡɪlt) *n.* **1.** the fact or state of having done wrong or committed an offence. **2.** responsibility for a criminal or moral offence deserving punishment or a penalty. **3.** remorse or self-reproach caused by feeling that one is responsible for a wrong or offence. **4.** *Arch.* sin or crime. [OE *gylt,* <?]

guiltless (ˈɡɪltlɪs) *adj.* free of all responsibility for wrongdoing or crime; innocent. —**ˈguiltlessly** *adv.* —**ˈguiltlessness** *n.*

guilty (ˈɡɪltɪ) *adj.* **guiltier, guiltiest. 1.** responsible for an offence or misdeed. **2.** *Law.* having committed an offence or adjudged to have done so: *the accused was found guilty.* **3.** of, showing, or characterized by guilt. —**ˈguiltily** *adv.* —**ˈguiltiness** *n.*

guimpe (ɡɪmp) *n.* a variant spelling of **gimp.**

guinea (ˈɡɪnɪ) *n.* **1. a.** a British gold coin taken out of circulation in 1813, worth 21 shillings. **b.** the sum of 21 shillings (£1.05), still used in quoting professional fees. **2.** See **guinea fowl.** [C16: the coin was orig. made of gold from Guinea]

guinea fowl *or* **guinea** *n.* a domestic fowl of Africa and SW Asia, having a dark plumage mottled with white, a naked head and neck, and a heavy rounded body.

guinea hen *n.* a guinea fowl, esp. a female.

guinea pig *n.* **1.** a domesticated cavy, commonly kept as a pet and used in scientific experiments. **2.** a person or thing used for experimentation. [C17: < ?]

guipure (ɡɪˈpjʊə) *n.* **1.** Also called: **guipure lace.** any of many types of heavy lace that have their pattern connected by threads, rather than supported on a net mesh. **2.** a heavy corded trimming; gimp. [C19: < OF, < *guiper* to cover with cloth, of Gmc origin]

guise (ɡaɪz) *n.* **1.** semblance or pretence: *under the guise of friendship.* **2.** external appearance in general. **3.** *Arch.* manner or style of dress. [C13: < OF *guise,* of Gmc origin]

guising (ˈgaɪzɪŋ) *n.* (in Scotland and N England) the practice or custom of disguising oneself in fancy dress, often with mask, and visiting people's houses, esp. at Hallowe'en. —ˈ**guiser** *n.*

guitar (gɪˈtɑː) *n.* a plucked stringed instrument originating in Spain, usually having six strings, a flat sounding board with a circular sound hole in the centre, a flat back, and a fretted fingerboard. [C17: < Sp. *guitarra,* < Ar. *qītār,* < Gk: CITHARA] —**guiˈtarist** *n.*

Gulag (ˈguːlæg) *n.* **1.** the central administrative department of the Soviet security service, responsible for maintaining prisons and labour camps. **2.** (*not cap.*) any system used to silence dissidents. [C20: < Russian *G(lavnoye) U(pravleniye Ispravitelno-Trudovykh) Lag(erei)* Main Administration for Corrective Labour Camps]

gulch (gʌltʃ) *n. U.S. & Canad.* a narrow ravine cut by a fast stream. [C19: <?]

gulden (ˈgʊldᵊn) *n., pl.* **-dens** *or* **-den.** a variant spelling of **guilder.**

gules (gjuːlz) *adj.* (*usually postpositive*), *n. Heraldry.* red. [C14: < OF *gueules* red fur worn around the neck, < *gole* throat, < L *gula* GULLET]

gulf (gʌlf) *n.* **1.** a large deep bay. **2.** a deep chasm. **3.** something that divides or separates, such as a lack of understanding. **4.** something that engulfs, such as a whirlpool. ~*vb.* **5.** (*tr.*) to swallow up; engulf. [C14: < OF *golfe,* < It. *golfo,* < Gk *kolpos*]

Gulf States *pl. n.* **the. 1.** the oil-producing states around the Persian Gulf: Iran, Iraq, Kuwait, Saudi Arabia, Bahrain, Qatar, the United Arab Emirates, and Oman. **2.** the states of the U.S. that border on the Gulf of Mexico: Alabama, Florida, Louisiana, Mississippi, and Texas.

Gulf Stream *n.* a relatively warm ocean current flowing northeastwards from the Gulf of Mexico towards NW Europe. Also called: **North Atlantic Drift.**

gulfweed (ˈgʌlfˌwiːd) *n.* a brown seaweed having air bladders and forming dense floating masses in tropical Atlantic waters, esp. the Gulf Stream. Also called: **sargasso, sargasso weed.**

gull[1] (gʌl) *n.* an aquatic bird such as the common gull or mew having long pointed wings, short legs, and a mostly white plumage. [C15: of Celtic origin]

gull[2] (gʌl) *Arch.* ~*n.* **1.** a person who is easily fooled or cheated. ~*vb.* **2.** (*tr.*) to fool, cheat, or hoax. [C16: ? < dialect *gull* unfledged bird, prob. < *gul,* < ON *gulr* yellow]

gullet (ˈgʌlɪt) *n.* **1.** a less formal name for the **oesophagus. 2.** the throat or pharynx. [C14: < OF *goulet,* dim. of *goule,* < L *gula* throat]

gullible (ˈgʌlɪbᵊl) *adj.* easily taken in or tricked. —ˌ**gulliˈbility** *n.* —ˈ**gullibly** *adv.*

gully *or* **gulley** (ˈgʌlɪ) *n., pl.* **-lies** *or* **-leys. 1.** a channel or small valley, esp. one cut by heavy rainwater. **2.** *N.Z.* a bush-clad small valley. **3.** *Cricket.* **a.** a fielding position between the slips and point. **b.** a fielder in this position. ~*vb.* **-lying, -lied. 4.** (*tr.*) to make channels in (the ground, sand, etc.). [C16: < F *goulet* neck of a bottle; see GULLET]

gulp (gʌlp) *vb.* **1.** (*tr.;* often foll. by *down*) to swallow rapidly, esp. in large mouthfuls. **2.** (*tr.;* often foll. by *back*) to stifle or choke: *to gulp back sobs.* **3.** (*intr.*) to swallow air convulsively because of nervousness, surprise, etc. **4.** (*intr.*) to make a noise, as when swallowing too quickly. ~*n.* **5.** the act of gulping. **6.** the quantity taken in a gulp. [C15: < MDu. *gulpen,* imit.] —ˈ**gulper** *n.* —ˈ**gulpingly** *adv.* —ˈ**gulpy** *adj.*

gum[1] (gʌm) *n.* **1.** any of various sticky substances that exude from certain plants, hardening on exposure to air and dissolving or forming viscous masses in water. **2.** any of various products, such as adhesives, that are made from such substances. **3.** any sticky substance used as an adhesive; mucilage; glue. **4.** See **chewing gum, bubble gum,** and **gumtree. 5.** *N.Z.* See **kauri gum. 6.** *Chiefly Brit.* a gumdrop. ~*vb.* **gumming, gummed. 7.** to cover or become covered, clogged, or stiffened as with gum. **8.** (*tr.*) to stick together or in place with gum. **9.** (*intr.*) to emit or form gum. ~See also **gum up.** [C14: < OF *gomme,* < L *gummi,* < Gk *kommi,* < Egyptian *kemai*]

gum[2] (gʌm) *n.* the fleshy tissue that covers the jawbones around the bases of the teeth. Technical name: **gingiva.** Related adj.: **gingival.** [OE *gōma* jaw]

gum ammoniac *n.* another name for **ammoniac.**

gum arabic *n.* a gum exuded by certain acacia trees, used in the manufacture of ink, food thickeners, pills, emulsifiers, etc.

gumbo (ˈgʌmbəʊ) *n., pl.* **-bos.** *U.S.* **1.** the mucilaginous pods of okra. **2.** another name for **okra. 3.** a soup or stew thickened with okra pods. **4.** a fine soil in the W prairies that becomes muddy when wet. [C19: < Louisiana F *gombo,* of Bantu origin]

gumboil (ˈgʌmˌbɔɪl) *n.* an abscess on the gums.

gumboots (ˈgʌmˌbuːts) *pl. n.* another name for **Wellington boots** (sense 1).

gum-digger *n. N.Z.* a person who digs for fossilized kauri gum in a **gum-field,** an area where it is found buried.

gumdrop (ˈgʌmˌdrɒp) *n.* a small jelly-like sweet containing gum arabic and various colourings and flavourings. Also called (esp. Brit.): **gum.**

gummy[1] (ˈgʌmɪ) *adj.* **-mier, -miest. 1.** sticky or tacky. **2.** consisting of, coated with, or clogged by gum or a similar substance. **3.** producing gum. [C14: < GUM[1] + -Y[1]] —ˈ**gumminess** *n.*

gummy[2] (ˈgʌmɪ) *adj.* **-mier, -miest. 1.** toothless. ~*n., pl.* **-mies. 2.** Also called: **gummy shark.** *Austral.* a small crustacean-eating shark with flat crushing teeth. [C20: < GUM[2] + -Y[1]]

gum nut *n. Austral.* the hardened seed container of the gumtree *Eucalyptus gummifera.*

gumption (ˈgʌmpʃən) *n. Inf.* **1.** *Brit.* common sense or resourcefulness. **2.** initiative or courage. [C18: orig. Scot., <?]

gum resin *n.* a mixture of resin and gum obtained from various plants and trees.

gumtree (ˈgʌmˌtriː) *n.* **1.** any of various trees that yield gum, such as the eucalyptus, sweet gum, and sour gum. Sometimes shortened to **gum. 2. up a gumtree.** *Inf.* in a very awkward position; in difficulties.

gum up *vb.* (*tr., adv.*) **1.** to cover, dab, or stiffen with gum. **2.** *Inf.* to make a mess of; bungle (often in **gum up the works**).

gun (gʌn) *n.* **1. a.** a weapon with a metallic tube or barrel from which a missile is discharged, usually by force of an explosion. It may be portable or mounted. **b.** (*as modifier*): *a gun barrel.* **2.** the firing of a gun as a salute or signal, as in military ceremonial. **3.** a member of or a place in a shooting party or syndicate. **4.** any device used to project something under pressure: *a spray gun.* **5.** *U.S. sl.* an armed criminal; gunman. **6.** *Austral. & N.Z. sl.* **a.** an expert. **b.** (*as modifier*): *a gun shearer.* **7. give it the gun.** *Sl.* to increase speed, effort, etc., to a considerable or maximum degree. **8. go great guns.** *Sl.* to act or function with great speed, intensity, etc. **9. jump** *or* **beat the gun. a.** (of a runner, etc.) to set off before the starting signal is given. **b.** *Inf.* to act prematurely. **10. stick to one's guns.** *Inf.* to maintain one's opinions or intentions in spite of opposition. ~*vb.* **gunning, gunned. 11.** (when *tr.,* often foll. by *down*) to shoot (someone) with a gun. **12.** (*tr.*) to press hard on the accelerator of (an engine): *to gun the engine of a car.* **13.** (*intr.*) to hunt with a gun. ~See also **gun for.** [C14: prob. < a female pet name, < the Scand. name *Gunnhildr* (< ON *gunnr* war + *hildr* war)]

gunboat (ˈgʌnˌbəʊt) *n.* a small shallow-draft vessel carrying mounted guns and used by coastal patrols, etc.

gunboat diplomacy *n.* diplomacy conducted by threats of military intervention.

guncotton (ˈgʌnˌkɒtᵊn) *n.* cellulose nitrate

containing a relatively large amount of nitrogen: used as an explosive.

gun dog *n.* **1.** a dog trained to work with a hunter or gamekeeper, esp. in retrieving, pointing at, or flushing game. **2.** a dog belonging to any breed adapted to these activities.

gunfight (ˈgʌnˌfaɪt) *n. Chiefly U.S.* a fight between persons using firearms. —ˈ**gunˌfighter** *n.*

gunfire (ˈgʌnˌfaɪə) *n.* **1.** the firing of one or more guns, esp. when done repeatedly. **2.** the use of firearms, as contrasted with other military tactics.

gun for *vb.* (*intr., prep.*) **1.** to search for in order to reprimand, punish, or kill. **2.** to try earnestly for: *he was gunning for promotion.*

gunge (gʌndʒ) *Inf.* ~*n.* **1.** sticky, rubbery, or congealed matter. ~*vb.* **2.** (*tr.; usually passive;* foll. by *up*) to block or encrust with gunge; clog. [C20: imit., ? infl. by GOO & SPONGE] —ˈ**gungy** *adj.*

gunk (gʌŋk) *n. Inf.* slimy, oily, or filthy matter. [C20: ? imit.]

gunlock (ˈgʌnˌlɒk) *n.* the mechanism in some firearms that causes the charge to be exploded.

gunman (ˈgʌnmən) *n., pl.* **-men. 1.** a man who is armed with a gun, esp. unlawfully. **2.** a man who is skilled with a gun.

gunmetal (ˈgʌnˌmɛtᵊl) *n.* **1.** a type of bronze containing copper, tin, and zinc. **2. a.** a dark grey colour. **b.** (*as adj.*): *gunmetal chiffon.*

gunnel[1] (ˈgʌnᵊl) *n.* any eel-like fish occurring in coastal regions of northern seas. [C17: <?]

gunnel[2] (ˈgʌnᵊl) *n.* a variant spelling of **gunwale.**

gunner (ˈgʌnə) *n.* **1.** a serviceman who works with, uses, or specializes in guns. **2.** *Naval.* (formerly) a warrant officer responsible for the training of gun crews, their performance in action, and accounting for ammunition. **3.** (in the British Army) an artilleryman, esp. a private. **4.** a person who hunts with a rifle or shotgun.

gunnery (ˈgʌnərɪ) *n.* **1.** the art and science of the efficient design and use of ordnance, esp. artillery. **2.** guns collectively. **3.** the use and firing of guns.

gunny (ˈgʌnɪ) *n., pl.* **-nies.** *Chiefly U.S.* **1.** a coarse hard-wearing fabric usually made from jute and used for sacks, etc. **2.** Also called: **gunny sack.** a sack made from this fabric. [C18: < Hindi, < Sansk. *gōnī* sack, prob. of Dravidian origin]

gunplay (ˈgʌnˌpleɪ) *n. Chiefly U.S.* the use of firearms, as by criminals, etc.

gunpoint (ˈgʌnˌpɔɪnt) *n.* **1.** the muzzle of a gun. **2. at gunpoint.** being under or using the threat of being shot.

gunpowder (ˈgʌnˌpaʊdə) *n.* an explosive mixture of potassium nitrate, charcoal, and sulphur: used in time fuses and in fireworks.

gun room *n.* **1.** (esp. in the Royal Navy) the mess allocated to junior officers. **2.** a room where guns are stored.

gunrunning (ˈgʌnˌrʌnɪŋ) *n.* the smuggling of guns and ammunition or other weapons of war into a country. —ˈ**gunˌrunner** *n.*

gunshot (ˈgʌnˌʃɒt) *n.* **1. a.** shot fired from a gun. **b.** (*as modifier*): *gunshot wounds.* **2.** the range of a gun. **3.** the shooting of a gun.

gunslinger (ˈgʌnˌslɪŋə) *n. Sl.* a gunfighter or gunman, esp. in the Old West.

gunsmith (ˈgʌnˌsmɪθ) *n.* a person who makes or repairs firearms, esp. portable guns.

gunstock (ˈgʌnˌstɒk) *n.* the wooden handle or support to which is attached the barrel of a rifle.

Gunter's chain (ˈgʌntəz) *n. Surveying.* a measuring chain 22 yards in length, or this length as a unit. [C17: after E. *Gunter* (1581–1626), E mathematician]

gunwale *or* **gunnel** (ˈgʌnᵊl) *n. Naut.* the top of the side of a boat or ship. [C15: < GUN + WALE < its use to support guns]

gunyah (ˈgʌnjɑː) *n. Austral.* a bush hut or shelter. [C19: < Abor.]

guppy (ˈgʌpɪ) *n., pl.* **-pies.** a small brightly coloured freshwater fish of N South America and the West Indies: a popular aquarium fish. [C20: after R. J. L. *Guppy,* 19th-cent. clergyman of Trinidad who first presented specimens to the British Museum]

gurdwara (ˈgɜːdwɑːrə) *n.* a Sikh place of worship. [C20: < Punjabi *gurduārā,* < Sansk. *guru* teacher + *dvārā* door]

gurgle (ˈgɜːgᵊl) *vb.* (*intr.*) **1.** (of liquids, esp. of streams, etc.) to make low bubbling noises when flowing. **2.** to utter low throaty bubbling noises, esp. as a sign of contentment: *the baby gurgled with delight.* ~*n.* **3.** the act or sound of gurgling. [C16: ? < Vulgar L *gurgulāre,* < L *gurguliō* gullet]

gurnard (ˈgɜːnəd) *or* **gurnet** (ˈgɜːnɪt) *n., pl.* **-nard, -nards** *or* **-net, -nets.** a European marine fish having a heavily armoured head and finger-like pectoral fins. [C14: < OF *gornard,* < *grognier* to grunt, < L *grunnīre*]

guru (ˈgʊruː, ˈguːruː) *n.* **1.** a Hindu or Sikh religious teacher or leader, giving personal spiritual guidance to his disciples. **2.** *Often derog.* a leader or chief theoretician of a movement, esp. a spiritual or religious cult. [C17: < Hindi *gurū,* < Sansk. *guruh* weighty]

gush (gʌʃ) *vb.* **1.** to pour out or cause to pour out suddenly and profusely, usually with a rushing sound. **2.** to act or utter in an overeffusive, affected, or sentimental manner. ~*n.* **3.** a sudden copious flow or emission, esp. of liquid. **4.** something that flows out or is emitted. **5.** an extravagant and insincere expression of admiration, sentiment, etc. [C14: prob. imit.; cf. ON *gjósa*] —ˈ**gushing** *adj.* —ˈ**gushingly** *adv.*

gusher (ˈgʌʃə) *n.* **1.** a person who gushes, as in being effusive or sentimental. **2.** something, such as a spurting oil well, that gushes.

gushy (ˈgʌʃɪ) *adj.* **gushier, gushiest.** *Inf.* displaying excessive admiration or sentimentality. —ˈ**gushily** *adv.* —ˈ**gushiness** *n.*

gusset (ˈgʌsɪt) *n.* **1.** an inset piece of material used esp. to strengthen or enlarge a garment. **2.** a triangular metal plate for strengthening a corner joist. ~*vb.* **3.** (*tr.*) to put a gusset in (a garment). [C15: < OF *gousset* a piece of mail, dim. of *gousse* pod, <?] —ˈ**gusseted** *adj.*

gust (gʌst) *n.* **1.** a sudden blast of wind. **2.** a sudden rush of smoke, sound, etc. **3.** an outburst of emotion. ~*vb.* **4.** (*intr.*) to blow in gusts. [C16: < ON *gustr;* rel. to *gjōsa* to GUSH; see GEYSER]

gustation (gʌˈsteɪʃən) *n.* the act of tasting or the faculty of taste. [C16: < L *gustātiō,* < *gustāre* to taste] —**gustatory** (ˈgʌstətərɪ) *adj.*

gusto (ˈgʌstəʊ) *n.* vigorous enjoyment, zest, or relish: *the aria was sung with great gusto.* [C17: < Sp.: taste, < L *gustus* a tasting]

gusty (ˈgʌstɪ) *adj.* **gustier, gustiest. 1.** blowing in gusts or characterized by blustery weather: *a gusty wind.* **2.** given to sudden outbursts, as of emotion. —ˈ**gustily** *adv.* —ˈ**gustiness** *n.*

gut (gʌt) *n.* **1. a.** the lower part of the alimentary canal; intestine. **b.** the entire alimentary canal. Related adj.: **visceral. 2.** (*often pl.*) the bowels or entrails, esp. of an animal. **3.** *Sl.* the belly; paunch. **4.** See **catgut. 5.** a silky fibrous substance extracted from silkworms, used in the manufacture of fishing tackle. **6.** a narrow channel or passage. **7.** (*pl.*) *Inf.* courage, willpower, or daring; forcefulness. **8.** (*pl.*) *Inf.* the essential part: *the guts of a problem.* ~*vb.* **gutting, gutted.** (*tr.*) **9.** to remove the entrails from (fish, etc.). **10.** (esp. of fire) to destroy the inside of (a building). **11.** to take out the central points of (an article, etc.), esp. in summary form. ~*adj.* **12.** *Inf.* arising from or characterized by what is basic, essential, or natural: *a gut problem; a gut reaction.* [OE *gutt;* rel. to *gēotan* to flow]

gutless (ˈgʌtlɪs) *adj. Inf.* lacking courage or determination.

gutsy (ˈgʌtsɪ) *adj.* **gutsier, gutsiest.** *Sl.* **1.** gluttonous; greedy. **2.** full of courage or boldness. **3.** passionate; lusty.

gutta-percha (ˈgʌtəˈpɜːtʃə) *n.* **1.** any of several tropical trees with leathery leaves. **2.** a whitish rubber substance derived from the coagulated milky latex of any of these trees: used in electrical insulation and dentistry. [C19: < Malay *getah* gum + *percha* tree that produces it]

guttate (ˈgʌteɪt) *adj. Biol.* (esp. of plants) covered with small drops or droplike markings. [C19: < L *guttātus* dappled, < *gutta* a drop]

gutter (ˈgʌtə) *n.* **1.** a channel along the eaves or on the roof of a building, used to collect and carry away rainwater. **2.** a channel running along the kerb or the centre of a road to collect and carry away rainwater. **3.** either of the two channels running parallel to a tenpin bowling lane. **4.** *Printing.* the white space between the facing pages of an open book. **5.** *Surfing.* a dangerous deep channel formed by currents and waves. **6.** **the gutter.** a poverty-stricken, degraded, or criminal environment. ~*vb.* **7.** (*tr.*) to make gutters in. **8.** (*intr.*) to flow in a stream. **9.** (*intr.*) (of a candle) to melt away as the wax forms channels and runs down in drops. **10.** (*intr.*) (of a flame) to flicker and be about to go out. [C13: < Anglo-F *goutiere,* < OF *goute* a drop, < L *gutta*] —ˈ**guttering** *n.*

gutter press *n.* the section of the popular press that seeks sensationalism in its coverage.

guttersnipe (ˈgʌtəˌsnaɪp) *n.* a child who spends most of his time in the streets, esp. in a slum area.

guttural (ˈgʌtərəl) *adj.* **1.** *Anat.* of or relating to the throat. **2.** *Phonetics.* pronounced in the throat or the back of the mouth. **3.** raucous. ~*n.* **4.** *Phonetics.* a guttural consonant. [C16: < NL *gutturālis,* < L *guttur* gullet] —ˈ**gutturally** *adv.*

guy[1] (gaɪ) *n.* **1.** *Inf.* a man or youth. **2.** *Brit.* a crude effigy of Guy Fawkes, usually made of old clothes stuffed with straw or rags, that is burnt on top of a bonfire on Guy Fawkes Day (November 5). **3.** *Brit.* a person in shabby or ludicrously odd clothes. ~*vb.* **4.** (*tr.*) to make fun of; ridicule. [C19: short for *Guy* Fawkes, who plotted to blow up King James I and the Houses of Parliament (1605)]

guy[2] (gaɪ) *n.* **1.** a rope, chain, wire, etc., for anchoring an object in position or for steadying or guiding it. ~*vb.* **2.** (*tr.*) to anchor, steady, or guide with a guy or guys. [C14: prob. < Low G; cf. OF *guie* guide, < *guier* to GUIDE]

guzzle (ˈgʌzᵊl) *vb.* to consume (food or drink) excessively or greedily. [C16: <?] —ˈ**guzzler** *n.*

gwyniad (ˈgwɪnɪˌæd) *n.* a freshwater white fish occurring in Lake Bala in Wales. [Welsh, < *gwyn* white]

gybe *or* **jibe** (dʒaɪb) *Naut.* ~*vb.* **1.** (*intr.*) (of a fore-and-aft sail) to shift suddenly from one side of the vessel to the other when running before the wind. **2.** to cause (a sailing vessel) to gybe or (of a sailing vessel) to undergo gybing. ~*n.* **3.** an instance of gybing. [C17: < obs. Du. *gijben* (now *gijpen*), <?]

gym (dʒɪm) *n, adj.* short for **gymnasium, gymnastics, gymnastic.**

gymkhana (dʒɪmˈkɑːnə) *n.* **1.** *Chiefly Brit.* an event in which horses and riders display skill and aptitude in various races and contests. **2.** (in Anglo-India) a place providing sporting and athletic facilities. [C19: < Hindi *gend-khānā,* lit.: ball house]

gymnasium (dʒɪmˈneɪzɪəm) *n., pl.* **-siums** *or* **-sia** (-zɪə). **1.** a large room or hall equipped with bars, weights, ropes, etc., for physical training. **2.** (in various European countries) a secondary school that prepares pupils for university. [C16: < L: school for gymnastics, < Gk *gumnasion,* < *gumnazein* to exercise naked]

gymnast (ˈdʒɪmnæst) *n.* a person who is skilled or trained in gymnastics.

gymnastic (dʒɪmˈnæstɪk) *adj.* of, like, or involving gymnastics. —**gym**ˈ**nastically** *adv.*

gymnastics (dʒɪmˈnæstɪks) *n.* **1.** (*functioning as sing.*) practice or training in exercises that develop physical strength and agility or mental capacity. **2.** (*functioning as pl.*) gymnastic exercises.

gymno- *combining form.* naked, bare, or exposed: *gymnosperm.* [< Gk *gumnos* naked]

gymnosperm (ˈdʒɪmnəʊˌspɜːm, ˈgɪm-) *n.* any seed-bearing plant in which the ovules are borne naked on open scales, which are often arranged in cones; any conifer or related plant. Cf. **angiosperm.** —ˌ**gymno**ˈ**spermous** *adj.*

gympie (ˈgɪmpɪ) *n.* a tall Australian tree with stinging hairs on its leaves. Also: **nettle tree.**

gym shoe *n.* another name for **plimsoll.**

gymslip (ˈdʒɪmˌslɪp) *n.* a tunic or pinafore dress worn by schoolgirls, often part of a school uniform.

gyn- *combining form.* a variant of **gyno-** before a vowel.

gynaeco- *or U.S.* **gyneco-** *combining form.* relating to women; female: *gynaecology.* [< Gk, < *gunē, gunaik-* woman, female]

gynaecology *or U.S.* **gynecology** (ˌgaɪnɪˈkɒlədʒɪ) *n.* the branch of medicine concerned with diseases in women. —**gynaecological** (ˌgaɪnɪkəˈlɒdʒɪkᵊl), ˌ**gynaeco**ˈ**logic** *or U.S.* ˌ**gyneco**ˈ**logical,** ˌ**gyneco**ˈ**logic** *adj.* —ˌ**gynae**ˈ**cologist** *or U.S.* ˌ**gyne**ˈ**cologist** *n.*

gynandromorph (dʒɪˈnændrəʊˌmɔːf, gaɪ-) *n.* an abnormal organism, esp. an insect, that has both male and female physical characteristics.

gynandrous (dʒaɪˈnændrəs, gaɪ-) *adj.* (of flowers such as the orchid) having the stamens and styles united in a column. [C19: < Gk *gunandros* of uncertain sex, < *gunē* woman + *anēr* man]

gyno- *or before a vowel* **gyn-** *combining form.* **1.** relating to women; female: *gynarchy.* **2.** denoting a female reproductive organ: *gynophore.* [< Gk, < *gunē* woman]

gynoecium, gynaeceum, *or esp. U.S.* **gynecium** (dʒaɪˈniːsɪəm, gaɪ-) *n., pl.* **-cia** *or* **-cea** (-sɪə). the carpels of a flowering plant collectively. [C18: NL, < Gk *gunaikeion* women's quarters, < *gunaik-, gunē* woman + *-eion,* suffix indicating place]

gynophore (ˈdʒaɪnəʊˌfɔː, ˈgaɪ-) *n.* a stalk in some plants that bears the gynoecium above the level of the other flower parts.

-gynous *adj. combining form.* **1.** of or relating to women or females: *androgynous; misogynous.* **2.** relating to female organs: *epigynous.* [< NL, < Gk, < *gunē* woman] —**-gyny** *n. combining form.*

gyp[1] *or* **gip** (dʒɪp) *Sl.* ~*vb.* **gypping, gypped** *or* **gipping, gipped.** **1.** (*tr.*) to swindle, cheat, or defraud. ~*n.* **2.** an act of cheating. **3.** a person who gyps. [C18: back formation < GYPSY]

gyp[2] *or* **gip** (dʒɪp) *n. Brit. & N.Z. sl.* severe pain; torture: *his arthritis gave him gyp.* [C19: prob. a contraction of *gee up!;* see GEE[1]]

gyp[3] (dʒɪp) *n.* a college servant at the universities of Cambridge or Durham. [C18: ? < obs. *gippo* scullion]

gypsophila (dʒɪpˈsɒfɪlə) *n.* any of a Mediterranean genus of plants, having small white or pink fragrant flowers. [C18: NL, < Gk *gupsos* chalk + *philos* loving]

gypsum (ˈdʒɪpsəm) *n.* a mineral consisting of hydrated calcium sulphate that occurs in sedimentary rocks and clay and is used principally in making plasters and cements, esp. plaster of Paris. Formula: $CaSO_4.2H_2O$. [C17: < L, < Gk *gupsos* chalk, plaster, cement, of Semitic origin] —**gypseous** (ˈdʒɪpsɪəs) *adj.*

Gypsy *or* **Gipsy** (ˈdʒɪpsɪ) *n., pl.* **-sies.** (*sometimes not cap.*) **1. a.** a member of a people scattered throughout Europe and North America, who maintain a nomadic way of life in industrialized societies. They migrated from NW India about the 9th century onwards. **b.** (*as modifier*): *a Gypsy fortune-teller.* **2.** the language of the Gypsies; Romany. **3.** a person who looks or behaves like a Gypsy. [C16: < EGYPTIAN, since they were thought to have come orig. from Egypt] —ˈ**Gypsyish** *or* ˈ**Gipsyish** *adj.*

gypsy moth *or* **gipsy moth** *n.* a European moth whose caterpillars are pests on deciduous trees.

gyrate *vb.* (dʒaɪˈreɪt). **1.** (*intr.*) to rotate or spiral, esp. about a fixed point or axis. ~*adj.* (ˈdʒaɪrɪt). **2.** *Biol.* curved or coiled into a circle. [C19: < LL *gȳrāre,* < L *gȳrus* circle, < Gk *guros*] —**gy**ˈ**ration** *n.* —**gy**ˈ**rator** *n.* —**gyratory** (ˈdʒaɪrətərɪ) *adj.*

gyre (ˈdʒaɪə) *Chiefly literary.* ~*n.* **1.** a circular or spiral movement or path. **2.** a ring, circle, or spiral. ~*vb.* **3.** (*intr.*) to whirl. [C16: < L *gȳrus* circle, < Gk *guros*]

gyrfalcon *or* **gerfalcon** (ˈdʒɜːˌfɔːlkən, -ˌfɔːkən) *n.* a very large rare falcon of northern and arctic regions. [C14: < OF *gerfaucon*, ? < ON *geirfalki*, < *geirr* spear + *falki* falcon]

gyro (ˈdʒaɪrəʊ) *n., pl.* **-ros. 1.** See **gyrocompass. 2.** See **gyroscope.**

gyro- *or before a vowel* **gyr-** *combining form.* **1.** indicating rotating or gyrating motion: *gyroscope.* **2.** indicating a gyroscope: *gyrocompass.* [via L < Gk, < *guros* circle]

gyrocompass (ˈdʒaɪrəʊˌkʌmpəs) *n.* a nonmagnetic compass that uses a motor-driven gyroscope to indicate true north.

gyromagnetic (ˌdʒaɪrəʊmægˈnɛtɪk) *adj.* of or caused by magnetic properties resulting from the spin of a charged particle, such as an electron.

gyroscope (ˈdʒaɪrəˌskəʊp) *n.* a device containing a disc rotating on an axis that can turn freely in any direction so that the disc maintains the same orientation irrespective of the movement of the surrounding structure. —**gyroscopic** (ˌdʒaɪrəˈskɒpɪk) *adj.* —ˌ**gyro**ˈ**scopically** *adv.*

gyrostabilizer *or* **-liser** (ˌdʒaɪrəʊˈsteɪbɪˌlaɪzə) *n.* a gyroscopic device used to stabilize the rolling motion of a ship.

gyve (dʒaɪv) *Arch.* ~*vb.* **1.** (*tr.*) to shackle or fetter. ~*n.* **2.** (*usually pl.*) fetter. [C13: <?]

h *or* **H** (eɪtʃ) *n., pl.* **h's, H's,** *or* **Hs. 1.** the eighth letter of the English alphabet. **2.** a speech sound represented by this letter. **3. a.** something shaped like an H. **b.** (*in combination*): *an H-beam.*

h *symbol for:* **1.** *Physics.* Planck constant. **2.** hecto-. **3.** hour.

H *symbol for:* **1.** *Chem.* hydrogen. **2.** *Physics.* magnetic field strength. **3.** *Electronics.* henry. **4.** (on Brit. pencils, signifying degree of hardness of lead) hard.

h. *or* **H.** *abbrev. for:* **1.** harbour. **2.** height. **3.** high. **4.** hour. **5.** hundred. **6.** husband.

ha[1] *or* **hah** (hɑː) *interj.* **1.** an exclamation expressing derision, triumph, surprise, etc. **2.** (*reiterated*) a representation of the sound of laughter.

ha[2] *symbol for* hectare.

haar (hɑː) *n. Eastern Brit.* a cold sea mist or fog off the North Sea. [C17: rel. to Du. dialect *harig* damp]

Hab. *Bible. abbrev. for* Habakkuk.

habanera (ˌhæbəˈnɛərə) *n.* **1.** a slow Cuban dance in duple time. **2.** a piece of music for this dance. [< Sp. *danza habanera* Havanan dance]

habeas corpus (ˈheɪbɪəs ˈkɔːpəs) *n. Law.* a writ ordering a person to be brought before a court or judge, esp. so that the court may ascertain whether his detention is lawful. [C15: < the opening of the L writ, lit.: you may have the body]

haberdasher (ˈhæbəˌdæʃə) *n.* **1.** *Brit.* a dealer in small articles for sewing, such as buttons and ribbons. **2.** *U.S.* a men's outfitter. [C14: < Anglo-F *hapertas* small items of merchandise, <?]

haberdashery (ˈhæbəˌdæʃərɪ) *n., pl.* **-eries.** the goods or business kept by a haberdasher.

habergeon (ˈhæbədʒən) *n.* a light sleeveless coat of mail worn in the 14th century under the plated hauberk. [C14: < OF *haubergeon* a little HAUBERK]

habiliment (həˈbɪlɪmənt) *n.* (*often pl.*) dress or attire. [C15: < OF *habillement,* < *habiller* to dress]

habilitate (həˈbɪlɪˌteɪt) *vb.* **1.** (*tr.*) *U.S.* to equip and finance (a mine). **2.** (*intr.*) to qualify for office. [C17: < Med. L *habilitāre* to make fit, < L *habilitās* aptness] **—haˌbiliˈtation** *n.*

habit (ˈhæbɪt) *n.* **1.** a tendency or disposition to act in a particular way. **2.** established custom, usual practice, etc. **3.** *Psychol.* a learned behavioural response to a particular situation. **4.** mental disposition or attitude: *a good working habit of mind.* **5. a.** a practice or substance to which a person is addicted: *drink has become a habit with him.* **b.** the state of being dependent on something, esp. a drug. **6.** *Bot., zool.* method of growth, type of existence, or general appearance: *a burrowing habit.* **7.** the customary apparel of a particular occupation, rank, etc., now esp. the costume of a nun or monk. **8.** Also called: **riding habit.** a woman's riding dress. *~vb.* (*tr.*) **9.** to clothe. **10.** an archaic word for **inhabit.** [C13: < L *habitus* custom, < *habēre* to have]

habitable (ˈhæbɪtəbəl) *adj.* able to be lived in. **—ˌhabitaˈbility** *or* **ˈhabitableness** *n.* **—ˈhabitably** *adv.*

habitant (ˈhæbɪtənt) *n.* **1.** a less common word for **inhabitant. 2. a.** an early French settler in Canada or Louisiana. **b.** a descendant of these settlers, esp. a farmer.

habitat (ˈhæbɪˌtæt) *n.* **1.** the natural home of an animal or plant. **2.** the place in which a person, group, class, etc., is normally found. [C18: < L: it inhabits, < *habitāre* to dwell, < *habēre* to have]

habitation (ˌhæbɪˈteɪʃən) *n.* **1.** a dwelling place. **2.** occupation of a dwelling place.

habit-forming *adj.* tending to become a habit or addiction.

habitual (həˈbɪtjʊəl) *adj.* **1.** (*usually prenominal*) done or experienced regularly and repeatedly: *the habitual Sunday walk.* **2.** (*usually prenominal*) by habit: *a habitual drinker.* **3.** customary; usual. **—haˈbitually** *adv.* **—haˈbitualness** *n.*

habituate (həˈbɪtjʊˌeɪt) *vb.* **1.** to accustom; make used to. **2.** *U.S. arch. & Canad.* to frequent. **—haˌbituˈation** *n.*

habitude (ˈhæbɪˌtjuːd) *n. Rare.* habit; tendency.

habitué (həˈbɪtjʊˌeɪ) *n.* a frequent visitor to a place. [C19: < F, < *habituer* to frequent]

HAC *abbrev. for* Honourable Artillery Company.

hachure (hæˈʃjʊə) *n.* shading of short lines drawn on a relief map to indicate gradients. [C19: < F, < *hacher* to chop up]

hacienda (ˌhæsɪˈɛndə) *n.* (in Spain or Spanish-speaking countries) **1. a.** a ranch or large estate. **b.** any substantial manufacturing establishment in the country. **2.** the main house on such a ranch or establishment. [C18: < Sp., < L *facienda* things to be done, < *facere* to do]

hack[1] (hæk) *vb.* **1.** (when *intr.*, usually foll. by *at* or *away*) to chop (at) roughly or violently. **2.** to cut and clear (a way), as through undergrowth. **3.** (in sport, esp. rugby) to foul (an opposing player) by kicking his shins. **4.** (*intr.*) to cough in short dry bursts. **5.** (*tr.*) to cut (a story, article, etc.) in a damaging way. *~n.* **6.** a cut or gash. **7.** any tool used for shallow digging, such as a mattock or pick. **8.** a chopping blow. **9.** a dry spasmodic cough. **10.** a kick on the shins, as in rugby. [OE *haccian*]

hack[2] (hæk) *n.* **1.** a horse kept for riding. **2.** an old or overworked horse. **3.** a horse kept for hire. **4.** *Brit.* a country ride on horseback. **5.** a drudge. **6.** a person who produces mediocre literary work. **7.** *U.S. inf.* **a.** a cab driver. **b.** a taxi. *~vb.* **8.** *Brit.* to ride (a horse) cross-country for pleasure. **9.** (*tr.*) *Inf.* to write (an article, etc.) in the manner of a hack. *~adj.* **10.** (*prenominal*) banal, mediocre, or unoriginal: *hack writing.* [C17: short for HACKNEY]

hack[3] (hæk) *n.* **1.** a rack used for fodder for livestock. **2.** a board on which meat is placed for a hawk. **3.** a pile or row of unfired bricks stacked to dry. [C16: var. of HATCH[2]]

hackamore (ˈhækəˌmɔː) *n. U.S. & N.Z.* a rope or rawhide halter used for unbroken foals. [C19: < Sp. *jáquima* headstall, ult. < Ar. *shaqīmah*]

hackberry (ˈhækˌbɛrɪ) *n., pl.* **-ries. 1.** an American tree having edible cherry-like fruits. **2.** the fruit. [C18: var. of C16 *hagberry,* of Scand. origin]

hacker (ˈhækə) *n.* **1.** a person that hacks. **2.** *Sl.* a computer fanatic, esp. one who through a personal computer breaks into the computer system of a company, government, etc.

hackery (ˈhækərɪ) *n.* **1.** *Ironic.* journalism; hackwork. **2.** *Inf.* the practice of gaining illegal access to a computer system.

hacking (ˈhækɪŋ) *adj.* (of a cough) harsh, dry, and spasmodic.

hackle (ˈhækəl) *n.* **1.** any of the long slender feathers on the neck of poultry and other birds. **2.** *Angling.* parts of an artificial fly made from hackle feathers, representing the legs and sometimes the wings of a real fly. **3.** a feathered ornament worn in the headdress of some Highland regiments. **4.** a steel flax comb. *~vb.* (*tr.*) **5.** to comb (flax) using a hackle. [C15: *hakell* prob. < OE]

hackles (ˈhækəlz) *pl. n.* **1.** the hairs on the back of the neck and the back of a dog, cat, etc., which rise when the animal is angry or afraid. **2.** anger or resentment: *to make one's hackles rise.*

hackney (ˈhæknɪ) *n.* **1.** a compact breed of harness horse with a high-stepping trot. **2.** a coach or carriage that is for hire. **3.** a popular term for **hack**[2] (sense 1). *~vb.* **4.** (*tr.; usually passive*) to make commonplace and banal by too frequent use. [C14: prob. after *Hackney*, London, where horses were formerly raised]

hackneyed ('hæknɪd) *adj.* used so often as to be trite, dull, and stereotyped.

hacksaw ('hækˌsɔː) *n.* a handsaw for cutting metal, with a blade in a frame under tension.

hackwork ('hækˌwɜːk) *n.* undistinguished literary work produced to order.

had (hæd) *vb.* the past tense and past participle of **have.**

haddock ('hædək) *n., pl.* **-docks** *or* **-dock.** a North Atlantic gadoid food fish similar to but smaller than the cod. [C14: <?]

hade (heɪd) *Geol.* ~*n.* **1.** the angle made to the vertical by the plane of a fault or vein. ~*vb.* **2.** (*intr.*) to incline from the vertical. [C18: <?]

hadedah ('hɑːdɪˌdɑː) *n.* a large grey-green S. African ibis. [imit.]

Hades ('heɪdiːz) *n.* **1.** *Greek myth.* **a.** the underworld abode of the souls of the dead. **b.** Pluto, the god of the underworld. **2.** (*often not cap.*) hell.

Hadith ('hædɪθ, hɑː'diːθ) *n.* the body of tradition about Mohammed and his followers. [Ar.]

hadj (hædʒ) *n.* a variant spelling of **hajj.**

hadji ('hædʒɪ) *n., pl.* **hadjis.** a variant spelling of **hajji.**

hadn't ('hædᵊnt) *contraction of* had not.

hadron ('hædrɒn) *n.* an elementary particle capable of taking part in a strong nuclear interaction. [C20: < Gk *hadros* heavy, < *hadēn* enough + -ON] —**had'ronic** *adj.*

hadst (hædst) *vb. Arch. or dialect.* (used with the pronoun *thou*) a singular form of the past tense (indicative mood) of **have.**

haecceity (hɛk'siːɪtɪ, hiːk-) *n., pl.* **-ties.** *Philosophy.* the property that uniquely identifies an object. [C17: < Med. L *haecceitas*, lit.: thisness, < *haec*, fem. of *hic* this]

haem *or U.S.* **heme** (hiːm) *n. Biochem.* a complex red organic pigment containing ferrous iron, present in haemoglobin. [C20: < HAEMATIN]

haem- *combining form.* a variant of **haemo-** before a vowel. Also (U.S.): **hem-.**

haemal *or U.S.* **hemal** ('hiːməl) *adj.* **1.** of the blood. **2.** denoting or relating to the region of the body containing the heart.

haematemesis *or U.S.* **hematemesis** (ˌhiːmə'tɛmɪsɪs) *n.* vomiting of blood, esp. as the result of a bleeding ulcer. [C19: < HAEMATO- + Gk *emesis* vomiting]

haematic *or U.S.* **hematic** (hiː'mætɪk) *adj.* relating to, acting on, having the colour of, or containing blood. Also: **haemic.**

haematin *or U.S.* **hematin** ('hɛmətɪn, 'hiː-) *n. Biochem.* a dark bluish or brownish pigment obtained by the oxidation of haem.

haematite ('hiːməˌtaɪt, 'hɛm-) *n.* a variant spelling of **hematite.**

haemato- *or before a vowel* **haemat-** *combining form.* indicating blood: *haematology.* Also: **haemo-** or (U.S.) **hemato-, hemat-.** [< Gk *haima, haimat-* blood]

haematocrit *or U.S.* **hematocrit** ('hɛmətəʊkrɪt, 'hiː-) *n.* **1.** a centrifuge for separating blood cells from plasma. **2.** the ratio of the volume occupied by these cells, esp. the red cells, to the total volume of blood, expressed as a percentage. [C20: < HAEMATO- + *-crit*, < Gk *kritēs* judge, < *krinein* to separate]

haematology *or U.S.* **hematology** (ˌhiːmə'tɒlədʒɪ) *n.* the branch of medical science concerned with diseases of the blood. —**haematologic** (ˌhiːmətə'lɒdʒɪk), **ˌhaemato'logical** *or U.S.* **ˌhemato'logic, ˌhemato'logical** *adj.*

haematoma *or U.S.* **hematoma** (ˌhiːmə'təʊmə) *n., pl.* **-mas** *or* **-mata** (-mətə). *Pathol.* a tumour of clotted blood.

haematuria *or U.S.* **hematuria** (ˌhiːmə'tjʊərɪə) *n. Pathol.* the presence of blood or red blood cells in the urine.

-haemia *or esp. U.S.* **-hemia** *n. combining form.* variants of **-aemia.**

haemo-, haema-, *or before a vowel* **haem-** *combining form.* denoting blood. Also: (U.S.) **hemo-, hema-,** or **hem-.** [< Gk *haima* blood]

haemocyanin *or U.S.* **hemocyanin** (ˌhiːməʊ'saɪənɪn) *n.* a blue copper-containing respiratory pigment in crustaceans and molluscs that functions as haemoglobin.

haemocytometer *or U.S.* **hemocytometer** (ˌhiːməʊsaɪ'tɒmɪtə) *n. Med.* an apparatus for counting the number of cells in a quantity of blood.

haemodialysis *or U.S.* **hemodialysis** (ˌhiːməʊdaɪ'ælɪsɪs) *n., pl.* **-ses** (-ˌsiːz). *Med.* the filtering of circulating blood through a membrane in an apparatus (**haemodialyser** or **artificial kidney**) to remove waste products: performed in cases of kidney failure. [C20: < HAEMO- + DIALYSIS]

haemoglobin *or U.S.* **hemoglobin** (ˌhiːməʊ'gləʊbɪn) *n.* a protein that gives red blood cells their characteristic colour. It combines reversibly with oxygen and is thus very important in the transportation of oxygen to tissues. [C19: shortened < *haematoglobulin:* see HAEMATIN + GLOBULIN]

haemolysis (hɪ'mɒlɪsɪs), **haematolysis** (ˌhiːmə'tɒlɪsɪs) *or U.S.* **hemolysis, hematolysis** *n., pl.* **-ses** (-ˌsiːz). the disintegration of red blood cells, with the release of haemoglobin. —**haemolytic** *or U.S.* **hemolytic** (ˌhiːməʊ'lɪtɪk) *adj.*

haemophilia *or U.S.* **hemophilia** (ˌhiːməʊ'fɪlɪə) *n.* an inheritable disease, usually affecting only males, characterized by loss or impairment of the normal clotting ability of blood. —**ˌhaemo'philiac** *or U.S.* **ˌhemo'philiac** *n.* —**ˌhaemo'philic** *or U.S.* **ˌhemo'philic** *adj.*

haemoptysis *or U.S.* **hemoptysis** (hɪ'mɒptɪsɪs) *n., pl.* **-ses** (-ˌsiːz). spitting or coughing up of blood, as in tuberculosis. [C17: < HAEMO- + *-ptysis*, < Gk *ptyein* to spit]

haemorrhage *or U.S.* **hemorrhage** ('hɛmərɪdʒ) *n.* **1.** profuse bleeding from ruptured blood vessels. ~*vb.* **2.** (*intr.*) to bleed profusely. [C17: < L *haemorrhagia;* see HAEMO-, -RRHAGIA]

haemorrhoids *or U.S.* **hemorrhoids** ('hɛməˌrɔɪdz) *pl. n. Pathol.* swollen and twisted veins in the region of the anus. Nontechnical name: **piles.** [C14: < L *haemorrhoidae* (pl.), < Gk, < *haimorrhoos* discharging blood, < *haimo-* HAEMO- + *rhein* to flow] —**ˌhaemor'rhoidal** *or U.S.* **ˌhemor'rhoidal** *adj.*

haemostasis *or U.S.* **hemostasis** (ˌhiːməʊ'steɪsɪs) *n.* the stopping of bleeding or of blood circulation, as during a surgical operation. [C18: < NL, < HAEMO- + Gk *stasis* a standing still] —**ˌhaemo'static** *or U.S.* **ˌhemo'static** *adj.*

haemostat *or U.S.* **hemostat** ('hiːməʊˌstæt) *n.* a surgical instrument or chemical agent that retards or stops bleeding.

haeremai ('haɪrəˌmaɪ) *N.Z.* ~*sentence substitute.* **1.** an expression of greeting or welcome. ~*n.* **2.** the act of saying "haeremai". [C18: Maori, lit.: come hither]

hafiz ('hɑːfɪz) *n. Islam.* a title for a person who knows the Koran by heart. [< Persian, < Ar., < *hafiza* to guard]

hafnium ('hæfnɪəm) *n.* a bright metallic element found in zirconium ores. Symbol: Hf; atomic no.: 72; atomic wt.: 178.49. [C20: NL, after *Hafnia*, L name of Copenhagen + -IUM]

haft (hɑːft) *n.* **1.** the handle of an axe, knife, etc. ~*vb.* **2.** (*tr.*) to provide with a haft. [OE *hæft*]

hag[1] (hæg) *n.* **1.** an unpleasant or ugly old woman. **2.** a witch. **3.** short for **hagfish.** [OE *hægtesse* witch] —**'haggish** *adj.*

hag[2] (hæg) *n. Scot. & N English dialect.* **1.** a firm spot in a bog. **2.** a soft place in a moor. [C13: < ON]

Hag. *Bible. abbrev. for* Haggai.

hagfish ('hægˌfɪʃ) *n., pl.* **-fish** *or* **-fishes.** an eel-like marine vertebrate having a round sucking mouth and feeding on the tissues of other animals and on dead organic material.

Haggadah *or* **Haggodoh** (hə'gɑːdə) *n., pl.* **Haggadahs, Haggadas** *or* **Haggadoth** (hægə'dəʊt). *Judaism.* **a.** a book containing the order of service of the traditional Passover meal. **b.** the narrative of the Exodus from Egypt that constitutes the main part of that service. ~See also **Seder.** [C19: < Heb.: story, < *hagged* to tell] —**haggadic** (həˈgædɪk, -ˈgɑː-) *adj.*

haggard (ˈhægəd) *adj.* **1.** careworn or gaunt, as from anxiety or starvation. **2.** wild or unruly. **3.** (of a hawk) having reached maturity in the wild before being caught. ~*n.* **4.** *Falconry.* a haggard hawk. [C16: < OF *hagard,* ? rel. to HEDGE] —ˈ**haggardly** *adv.* —ˈ**haggardness** *n.*

haggis (ˈhægɪs) *n.* a Scottish dish made from sheep's or calf's offal, oatmeal, suet, and seasonings boiled in a skin made from the animal's stomach. [C15: ? < *haggen* to HACK[1]]

haggle (ˈhægᵊl) *vb.* (*intr.;* often foll. by *over*) to bargain or wrangle (over a price, terms of an agreement, etc.); barter. [C16: of Scand. origin] —ˈ**haggler** *n.*

hagio- *or before a vowel* **hagi-** *combining form.* indicating a saint, saints, or holiness: *hagiography.* [via LL < Gk, < *hagios* holy]

Hagiographa (ˌhægɪˈɒgrəfə) *n.* the third of the three main parts into which the books of the Old Testament are divided in Jewish tradition (the other two parts being the Law and the Prophets).

hagiographer (ˌhægɪˈɒgrəfə) *or* **hagiographist** *n.* **1.** a person who writes about the lives of the saints. **2.** one of the writers of the Hagiographa.

hagiography (ˌhægɪˈɒgrəfɪ) *n., pl.* **-phies. 1.** the writing of the lives of the saints. **2.** a biography that idealizes or idolizes its subject. —**hagiographic** (ˌhægɪəˈgræfɪk) *or* ˌ**hagioˈgraphical** *adj.*

hagiolatry (ˌhægɪˈɒlətrɪ) *n.* worship or veneration of saints.

hagiology (ˌhægɪˈɒlədʒɪ) *n., pl.* **-gies.** literature concerned with the lives and legends of saints. —**hagiological** (ˌhægɪəˈlɒdʒɪkᵊl) *adj.* —ˌ**hagiˈologist** *n.*

hag-ridden *adj.* tormented or worried, as if by a witch.

hah (hɑː) *interj.* a variant spelling of **ha**[1].

ha-ha[1] (ˈhɑːˈhɑː) *or* **haw-haw** (ˈhɔːˈhɔː) *interj.* **1.** a representation of the sound of laughter. **2.** an exclamation expressing derision, mockery, etc.

ha-ha[2] (ˈhɑːhɑː) *or* **haw-haw** (ˈhɔːhɔː) *n.* a sunk fence bordering a garden or park, that allows uninterrupted views from within. [C18: < F *haha,* prob. based on *ha!* ejaculation denoting surprise]

hahnium (ˈhɑːnɪəm) *n.* a transuranic element artificially produced from californium. Symbol: Ha; atomic no.: 105; half-life of most stable isotope, ^{262}Ha: 40 seconds. [C20: after Otto *Hahn* (1879–1968), G physicist]

haik *or* **haick** (haɪk, heɪk) *n.* an Arab's outer garment for the head and body. [C18: < Ar.]

haiku (ˈhaɪkuː) *or* **hokku** (ˈhɒkuː) *n., pl.* **-ku.** an epigrammatic Japanese verse form in 17 syllables. [< Japanese, < *hai* amusement + *ku* verse]

hail[1] (heɪl) *n.* **1.** small pellets of ice falling from cumulonimbus clouds when there are strong rising air currents. **2.** a storm of such pellets. **3.** words, ideas, missiles, etc., directed with force and in great quantity: *a hail of abuse.* ~*vb.* **4.** (*intr.;* with *it* as subject) to be the case that hail is falling. **5.** (often with *it* as subject) to fall or cause to fall as or like hail. [OE *hægl*]

hail[2] (heɪl) *vb.* (*mainly tr.*) **1.** to greet, esp. enthusiastically: *the crowd hailed the actress with joy.* **2.** to acclaim or acknowledge: *they hailed him as their hero.* **3.** to attract the attention of by shouting or gesturing: *to hail a taxi.* **4.** (*intr.;* foll. by *from*) to be a native of: *she hails from India.* ~*n.* **5.** the act or an instance of hailing. **6.** a distance across which one can attract attention (esp. in **within hail**). ~*sentence substitute.* **7.** *Poetic.* an exclamation of greeting. [C12: < ON *heill* WHOLE]

hail-fellow-well-met *adj.* genial and familiar, esp. in an offensive or ingratiating way.

Hail Mary *n. R.C. Church.* a prayer to the Virgin Mary, based on the salutations of the angel Gabriel (Luke 1:28) and Elizabeth (Luke 1:42) to her. Also called: **Ave Maria.**

hailstone (ˈheɪlˌstəʊn) *n.* a pellet of hail.

hailstorm (ˈheɪlˌstɔːm) *n.* a storm during which hail falls.

hair (hɛə) *n.* **1.** any of the threadlike structures that grow from follicles beneath the skin of mammals. **2.** a growth of such structures, as on an animal's body, which helps prevent heat loss. **3.** *Bot.* any threadlike outgrowth, such as a root hair. **4.** a fabric made from the hair of some animals. **5.** another word for **hair's-breadth:** *to lose by a hair.* **6. get in someone's hair.** *Inf.* to annoy someone persistently. **7. hair of the dog (that bit one).** an alcoholic drink taken as an antidote to a hangover. **8. keep your hair on!** *Brit. inf.* keep calm. **9. let one's hair down.** to behave without reserve. **10. not turn a hair.** to show no surprise, anger, fear, etc. **11. split hairs.** to make petty and unnecessary distinctions. [OE *hær*] —ˈ**hairless** *adj.* —ˈ**hairˌlike** *adj.*

haircloth (ˈhɛəˌklɒθ) *n.* a cloth woven from horsehair, used (esp. formerly) in upholstery, etc.

haircut (ˈhɛəˌkʌt) *n.* **1.** the act of cutting the hair. **2.** the style in which hair has been cut.

hairdo (ˈhɛəˌduː) *n., pl.* **-dos.** the arrangement of a person's hair, esp. after styling and setting.

hairdresser (ˈhɛəˌdrɛsə) *n.* **1.** a person whose business is cutting, colouring and arranging hair. **2.** a hairdresser's establishment. ~Related adj.: **tonsorial.** —ˈ**hairˌdressing** *n.*

-haired *adj.* having hair as specified: *long-haired.*

hairgrip (ˈhɛəˌgrɪp) *n. Chiefly Brit.* a small tightly bent metal hair clip. Also called (U.S., Canad., and N.Z.): **bobby pin.**

hairline (ˈhɛəˌlaɪn) *n.* **1.** the natural margin formed by hair on the head. **2. a.** a very narrow line. **b.** (*as modifier*): *a hairline crack.*

hairnet (ˈhɛəˌnɛt) *n.* any of several kinds of light netting worn over the hair to keep it in place.

hairpiece (ˈhɛəˌpiːs) *n.* **1.** a wig or toupee. **2.** a section of extra hair attached to a woman's real hair to give it greater bulk or length.

hairpin (ˈhɛəˌpɪn) *n.* **1.** a thin double-pronged pin used to fasten the hair. **2.** (*modifier*) (esp. of a bend in a road) curving very sharply.

hair-raising *adj.* inspiring horror; terrifying.

hair's-breadth *n.* **a.** a very short or imperceptible margin or distance. **b.** (*as modifier*): *a hair's-breadth escape.*

hair shirt *n.* **1.** a shirt made of haircloth worn next to the skin as a penance. **2.** a secret trouble or affliction.

hair slide *n.* a hinged clip with a tortoiseshell, bone, or similar back, used to fasten a girl's hair.

hairsplitting (ˈhɛəˌsplɪtɪŋ) *n.* **1.** the making of petty distinctions. ~*adj.* **2.** occupied with or based on petty distinctions. —ˈ**hairˌsplitter** *n.*

hairspring (ˈhɛəˌsprɪŋ) *n.* a fine spiral spring in some timepieces which, in combination with the balance wheel, controls the timekeeping.

hairstreak (ˈhɛəˌstriːk) *n.* a small butterfly having fringed wings with narrow white streaks.

hairstyle (ˈhɛəˌstaɪl) *n.* a particular mode of arranging the hair. —ˈ**hairˌstylist** *n.*

hair trigger *n.* **1.** a trigger of a firearm that responds to very slight pressure. **2.** *Inf.* any mechanism, reaction, etc., set in operation by slight provocation.

hairy (ˈhɛərɪ) *adj.* **hairier, hairiest. 1.** covered with hair. **2.** *Sl.* **a.** difficult or problematic. **b.** dangerous or exciting. —ˈ**hairiness** *n.*

hajj *or* **hadj** (hædʒ) *n.* the pilgrimage to Mecca that every Muslim is required to make at least once in his life. [< Ar.]

hajji, hadji, *or* **haji** (ˈhædʒɪ) *n., pl.* **hajjis, hadjis,** *or* **hajis. 1.** a Muslim who has made a pilgrimage to Mecca: also used as a title. **2.** a Christian who has visited Jerusalem.

haka (ˈhɑːkə) *n. N.Z.* **1.** a Maori war chant accompanied by gestures. **2.** a similar performance by, for instance, a football team.

hake (heɪk) *n., pl.* **hake** *or* **hakes. 1.** a gadoid food fish of the N hemisphere, having an elongated body with a large head and two dorsal fins. **2.** a similar North American fish. [C15: ? < ON *haki* hook]

hakea (ˈhɑːkɪə, ˈheɪkɪə) *n.* any shrub or tree of the

Australian genus *Hakea*, having a hard woody fruit and often yielding a useful wood. [C19: NL, after C. L. von *Hake* (died 1818), G botanist]

hakim *or* **hakeem** (hɑːˈkiːm) *n.* **1.** a Muslim judge, ruler, or administrator. **2.** a Muslim physician. [C17: < Ar., < *hakama* to rule]

Halakah *or* **Halacha** (ˌhɑːləˈkɑː, həˈlɑːkə) *n.* that part of traditional Jewish literature concerned with the law, as contrasted with Haggadah. [C19: < Heb.: way, < *hālakh* to go] —**Halakic** *or* **Halachic** (həˈlækɪk) *adj.*

halal *or* **hallal** (hɑːˈlɑːl) *n.* **1. a.** meat from animals that have been killed according to Muslim law. **b.** (*as modifier*): *a halal butcher.* ~*vb.* **-alling, -alled** (*tr.*) **2.** to kill (animals) in this way. [< Ar.: lawful]

halation (həˈleɪʃən) *n. Photog.* fogging usually seen as a bright ring surrounding a source of light. [C19: < HALO + -ATION]

halberd (ˈhælbəd) *or* **halbert** (ˈhælbət) *n.* a weapon consisting of a long shaft with an axe blade and a pick, topped by a spearhead: used in 15th- and 16th-century warfare. [C15: < OF *hallebarde,* < MHG *helm* handle + *barde* axe] —ˌ**halberˈdier** *n.*

halcyon (ˈhælsɪən) *adj.* **1.** peaceful, gentle, and calm. **2. halcyon days. a.** a fortnight of calm weather during the winter solstice. **b.** a period of peace and happiness. ~*n.* **3.** *Greek myth.* a fabulous bird associated with the winter solstice. **4.** a poetic name for the **kingfisher.** [C14: < L *alcyon,* < Gk *alkuōn* kingfisher, <?]

hale[1] (heɪl) *adj.* healthy and robust (esp. in **hale and hearty**). [OE *hæl* WHOLE] —ˈ**haleness** *n.*

hale[2] (heɪl) *vb.* (*tr.*) to pull or drag. [C13: < OF *haler,* of Gmc origin] —ˈ**haler** *n.*

half (hɑːf) *n., pl.* **halves** (hɑːvz). **1. a.** either of two equal or corresponding parts that together comprise a whole. **b.** a quantity equalling such a part: *half a dozen.* **2.** half a pint, esp. of beer. **3.** *Scot.* a small drink of spirits, esp. whisky. **4.** *Football, hockey, etc.* the half of the pitch regarded as belonging to one team. **5.** *Golf.* an equal score with an opponent. **6.** (in various games) either of two periods of play separated by an interval. **7.** a half-price ticket on a bus, etc. **8.** short for **half-hour. 9.** *Sport.* short for **halfback. 10.** *Obs.* a half-year period. **11. by halves.** (*used with a negative*) without being thorough: *we don't do things by halves.* **12. go halves.** (often foll. by *on, in,* etc.) **a.** to share expenses. **b.** to share the whole amount (of something): *to go halves on an orange.* ~*determiner.* **13. a.** being a half or approximately a half: *half the kingdom.* **b.** (*as pron.; functioning as sing. or pl.*): *half of them came.* ~*adj.* **14.** not perfect or complete: *he only did a half job on it.* ~*adv.* **15.** to the amount or extent of a half. **16.** to a great amount or extent. **17.** partially; to an extent. **18. by half.** to an excessive degree: *he's too arrogant by half.* **19. half two,** etc. *Inf.* 30 minutes after two o'clock, etc. **20. have half a mind to.** to have a vague intention to. **21. not half.** *Inf.* **a.** not in any way: *he's not half clever enough.* **b.** *Brit.* very; indeed: *he isn't half stupid.* **c.** yes, indeed. [OE *healf*]

half- *prefix.* **1.** one of two equal parts: *half-moon.* **2.** related through one parent only: *half-brother.* **3.** not completely, partly: *half-hardy.*

half-and-half *n.* **1.** a mixture of half one thing and half another thing. **2.** a drink consisting of equal parts of beer (or ale) and porter.

halfback (ˈhɑːfˌbæk) *n.* **1.** *Soccer.* any of three players positioned behind the line of forwards and in front of the fullbacks. **2.** *Rugby.* either the scrum half or the stand-off half. **3.** any of certain similar players in other team sports.

half-baked *adj.* **1.** insufficiently baked. **2.** *Inf.* foolish; stupid. **3.** *Inf.* poorly planned.

halfbeak (ˈhɑːfˌbiːk) *n.* a marine and freshwater teleost fish having an elongated body with a short upper jaw and a long protruding lower jaw.

half-binding *n.* a type of bookbinding in which the backs are bound in one material and the sides in another.

half-blood *n.* **1. a.** the relationship between individuals having only one parent in common. **b.** an individual having such a relationship. **2.** a less common name for a **half-breed.** —ˌ**half-ˈblooded** *adj.*

half board *n.* the daily provision by a hotel of bed, breakfast, and one main meal. Also called: **demi-pension.**

half-boot *n.* a boot reaching to the midcalf.

half-breed *n.* **1.** a person whose parents are of different races, esp. the offspring of a White person and an American Indian. ~*adj. also* **half-bred. 2.** of, relating to, or designating offspring of people or animals of different races or breeds.

half-brother *n.* the son of either of one's parents by another partner.

half-butt *n.* a cue that is longer than an ordinary cue.

half-caste *n.* **1.** a person having parents of different races, esp. the offspring of a European and an Indian. ~*adj.* **2.** of, relating to, or designating such a person.

half-cock *n.* **1.** the halfway position of a firearm's hammer when the trigger is cocked by the hammer and the hammer cannot reach the primer to fire the weapon. **2. go off at half-cock** *or* **half-cocked.** to fail as a result of inadequate preparation or premature starting.

half-crown *n.* a former British coin worth two shillings and sixpence (12½p). Also called: **half-a-crown.**

half gainer *n.* a type of dive in which the diver completes a half backward somersault to enter the water headfirst facing the diving board.

half-hardy *adj.* (of a cultivated plant) able to survive out of doors except during severe frost.

half-hearted *adj.* without enthusiasm or determination. —ˌ**half-ˈheartedly** *adv.*

half-hitch *n.* a knot made by passing the end of a piece of rope around itself and through the loop thus made.

half-hour *n.* **1.** a period of 30 minutes. **2.** the point of time 30 minutes after the beginning of an hour. —ˌ**half-ˈhourly** *adv., adj.*

half-hunter *n.* a watch with a hinged lid in which a small circular opening or crystal allows the approximate time to be read.

half landing *n.* a landing halfway up a flight of stairs.

ˌ**half-aˈfraid** *adj.*
ˌ**half-aˈlive** *adj.*
ˌ**half-aˈshamed** *adj.*
ˌ**half-aˈsleep** *adj.*
ˌ**half-aˈwake** *adj.*
ˌ**half-ˈbarrel** *n.*
ˌ**half-beˈgun** *adj.*
ˌ**half-ˈblind** *adj.*
ˌ**half-ˈbottle** *n.*
ˌ**half-ˈburied** *adj.*
ˌ**half-ˈcentury** *n.*
ˌ**half-ˈcivilˌized** *or* **-ˌised** *adj.*
ˌ**half-ˈclad** *adj.*
ˌ**half-ˈclosed** *adj.*
ˌ**half-ˈclothed** *adj.*
ˌ**half-comˈpleted** *adj.*
ˌ**half-conˈcealed** *adj.*
ˌ**half-ˈconscious** *adj.*
ˌ**half-conˈsumed** *adj.*
ˌ**half-conˈvinced** *adj.*
ˌ**half-ˈcooked** *adj.*
ˌ**half-ˈcovered** *adj.*
ˌ**half-ˈcrazy** *adj.*
ˌ**half-ˈday** *n.*
ˌ**half-ˈdazed** *adj.*
ˌ**half-ˈdeaf** *adj.*
ˌ**half-deˈveloped** *adj.*
ˌ**half-diˈgested** *adj.*
ˌ**half-ˈdone** *adj.*
ˌ**half-ˈdozen** *n.*
ˌ**half-ˈdressed** *adj.*
ˌ**half-ˈdrowned** *adj.*
ˌ**half-ˈdrunk** *adj.*
ˌ**half-ˈeaten** *adj.*
ˌ**half-ˈeduˌcated** *adj.*
ˌ**half-ˈfilled** *adj.*
ˌ**half-ˈfinished** *adj.*
ˌ**half-forˈgotten** *adj.*
ˌ**half-ˈformed** *adj.*
ˌ**half-ˈfrozen** *adj.*
ˌ**half-ˈfull** *adj.*
ˌ**half-ˈgrown** *adj.*
ˌ**half-ˈheard** *adj.*
ˌ**half-ˈhuman** *adj.*
ˌ**half-inˈclined** *adj.*
ˌ**half-inˈformed** *adj.*
ˌ**half-inˈstinctive** *adj.*
ˌ**half-ˈjoking** *adj.*

half-life *n.* the time taken for half of the atoms in a radioactive material to undergo decay.

half-light *n.* a dim light, as at dawn or dusk.

half-mast *n.* the lower than normal position to which a flag is lowered on a mast as a sign of mourning.

half measure *n.* (*often pl.*) an inadequate measure or action; compromise.

half-moon *n.* **1.** the moon at first or last quarter when half its face is illuminated. **2.** the time at which a half-moon occurs. **3.** something shaped like a half-moon.

half-nelson *n.* a wrestling hold in which a wrestler places an arm under one of his opponent's arms from behind and exerts pressure with his palm on the back of his opponent's neck.

half-note *n.* the usual U.S. name for **minim.**

halfpenny *or* **ha'penny** (ˈheɪpnɪ, *for sense 1* ˈhɑːfˌpɛnɪ) *n.* **1.** (*pl.* **-pennies**) a small British coin worth half a new penny (withdrawn 1985). **2.** (*pl.* **-pennies**) an old British coin worth half an old penny. **3.** (*pl.* **-pence**) something of negligible value. —**halfpennyworth** *or* **ha'p'orth** (ˈheɪpəθ) *n.*

half-pie *adj. N.Z. inf.* ill planned; not properly thought out: *a half-pie scheme.* [< Maori *pai* good]

half-pint *n. Sl.* a small or insignificant person.

half-plate *or* **half-print** *n. Photog.* a size of plate measuring 16.5 cm by 10.8 cm.

half seas over *adj. Brit. inf.* drunk.

half-sister *n.* the daughter of either of one's parents by another partner.

half-size *n.* any size, esp. in clothing, that is halfway between two sizes.

half-sole *n.* a sole from the shank of a shoe to the toe.

half term *n. Brit. education.* a short holiday midway through an academic term.

half-timbered *or* **half-timber** *adj.* (of a building) having an exposed timber framework filled with brick, stone, or plastered laths, as in Tudor architecture. —ˌ**half-ˈtimbering** *n.*

half-time *n. Sport.* **a.** a rest period between the two halves of a game. **b.** (*as modifier*): *the half-time score.*

half-title *n.* **1.** the short title of a book as printed on the right-hand page preceding the title page. **2.** a title on a separate page preceding a section of a book.

halftone (ˈhɑːfˌtəʊn) *n.* **1.** a process used to reproduce an illustration by photographing it through a fine screen to break it up into dots. **2.** the print obtained.

half-track *n.* a vehicle with caterpillar tracks on the wheels that supply motive power only.

half-truth *n.* a partially true statement intended to mislead. —ˌ**half-ˈtrue** *adj.*

half volley *n. Sport.* a stroke or shot in which the ball is hit immediately after it bounces.

halfway (ˌhɑːfˈweɪ) *adv., adj.* **1.** at or to half the distance. **2.** in or of an incomplete manner. **3.** **meet halfway.** to compromise with.

halfway house *n.* **1.** a place to rest midway on a journey. **2.** the halfway point in any progression. **3.** a centre or hostel designed to facilitate the readjustment to private life of released prisoners, mental patients, etc.

halfwit (ˈhɑːfˌwɪt) *n.* **1.** a feeble-minded person. **2.** a foolish or inane person. —ˌ**halfˈwitted** *adj.*

halibut (ˈhælɪbət) *n., pl.* **-buts** *or* **-but.** the largest flatfish: a dark green North Atlantic species that is a very important food fish. [C15: < *hali* HOLY (because it was eaten on holy days) + *butte* flatfish, < MDu.]

halide (ˈhælaɪd) *or* **halid** (ˈhælɪd) *n.* any binary salt of a halogen acid; a chloride, bromide, iodide, or fluoride.

halite (ˈhælaɪt) *n.* a mineral consisting of sodium chloride in cubic crystalline form, occurring in sedimentary beds and dried salt lakes: an important source of table salt. Also called: **rock salt.** [C19: < NL *halītes*, < Gk *hals* salt + -ITE[2]]

halitosis (ˌhælɪˈtəʊsɪs) *n.* the state or condition of having bad breath. [C19: NL, < L *hālitus* breath, < *hālāre* to breathe]

hall (hɔːl) *n.* **1.** a room serving as an entry area. **2.** (*sometimes cap.*) a building for public meetings. **3.** (*often cap.*) the great house of an estate; manor. **4.** a large building or room used for assemblies, dances, etc. **5.** a residential building in a university. **6. a.** a large room, esp. for dining, in a college or university. **b.** a meal eaten in this room. **7.** the large room of a house, castle, etc. **8.** *U.S. & Canad.* a corridor into which rooms open. **9.** (*often pl.*) *Inf.* short for **music hall.** [OE *heall*]

hallelujah, halleluiah (ˌhælɪˈluːjə), *or* **alleluia** (ˌælɪˈluːjə) *interj.* **1.** an exclamation of praise to God. ~*n.* **2.** an exclamation of "Hallelujah". **3.** a musical composition that uses the word *Hallelujah* as its text. [C16: < Heb. *hallēl* to praise + *yāh* the Lord]

halliard (ˈhæljəd) *n.* a variant spelling of **halyard.**

hallmark (ˈhɔːlˌmɑːk) *n.* **1.** *Brit.* an official series of marks stamped by the London Guild of Goldsmiths on gold, silver, or platinum articles to guarantee purity, date of manufacture, etc. **2.** a mark of authenticity or excellence. **3.** an outstanding feature. ~*vb.* **4.** (*tr.*) to stamp with or as if with a hallmark. [C18: after Goldsmiths' *Hall* in London, where items were graded and stamped]

hallo (həˈləʊ) *sentence substitute, n.* **1.** a variant spelling of **hello.** ~*sentence substitute, n., vb.* **2.** a variant spelling of **halloo.**

halloo (həˈluː), **hallo,** *or* **halloa** (həˈləʊ) *sentence substitute.* **1.** a shout to attract attention, esp. to call hounds at a hunt. ~*n., pl.* **-loos, -los,** *or* **-loas. 2.** a shout of "halloo". ~*vb.* **-looing, -looed; -loing, -loed,** *or* **-loaing, -loaed. 3.** to shout. **4.** (*tr.*) to urge on (dogs) with shouts. [C16: ? var. of *hallow* to encourage hounds by shouting]

hallow (ˈhæləʊ) *vb.* (*tr.*) **1.** to consecrate or set apart as being holy. **2.** to venerate as being holy. [OE *hālgian*, < *hālig* HOLY] —ˈ**hallower** *n.*

hallowed (ˈhæləʊd; *liturgical* ˈhæləʊɪd) *adj.* **1.** set apart as sacred. **2.** consecrated or holy.

Hallowe'en *or* **Halloween** (ˌhæləʊˈiːn) *n.* the eve of All Saints' Day celebrated on Oct. 31; Allhallows Eve. [C18: see ALLHALLOWS, EVEN[2]]

hall stand *or esp. U.S.* **hall tree** *n.* a piece of furniture for hanging coats, hats, etc., on.

Hallstatt (ˈhælstæt) *adj.* of a late Bronze Age culture extending from central Europe to Britain and lasting from the 9th to the 5th century B.C. [C19: after *Hallstatt*, Austrian village where remains were found]

hallucinate (həˈluːsɪˌneɪt) *vb.* (*intr.*) to experience hallucinations. [C17: < L *ālūcinārī* to wander in mind] —**halˈluciˌnator** *n.*

hallucination (həˌluːsɪˈneɪʃən) *n.* the alleged perception of an object when no object is present, occurring under hypnosis, in some mental disorders, etc. —**halˈlucinatory** *adj.*

hallucinogen (həˈluːsɪnəˌdʒɛn) *n.* any drug that induces hallucinations. —**hallucinogenic** (həˌluːsɪnəˈdʒɛnɪk) *adj.*

hallux (ˈhæləks) *n.* the first digit on the hind foot of a mammal, bird, reptile, or amphibian; the big toe of man. [C19: NL, < LL *allex* big toe]

hallway (ˈhɔːlˌweɪ) *n.* a hall or corridor.

halm (hɔːm) *n.* a variant spelling of **haulm.**

ˌ**half-ˈmile** *n.*
ˌ**half-ˈnaked** *adj.*
ˌ**half-ˈopen** *adj.*
ˌ**half-proˈtesting** *adj.*
ˌ**half-ˈraw** *adj.*
ˌ**half-reˈluctantly** *adv.*
ˌ**half-reˈmembered** *adj.*
ˌ**half-ˈrotten** *adj.*
ˌ**half-ˈseriously** *adv.*
ˌ**half-ˈshut** *adj.*
ˌ**half-ˈstarved** *adj.*
ˌ**half-subˈmerged** *adj.*
ˌ**half-ˈtrained** *adj.*
ˌ**half-underˈstood** *adj.*
ˌ**half-ˈused** *adj.*
ˌ**half-ˈwild** *adj.*
ˌ**half-ˈwrong** *adj.*

halma (ˈhælmə) *n.* a board game in which players attempt to transfer their pieces from their own to their opponents' bases. [C19: < Gk *halma* leap]

halo (ˈheɪləʊ) *n., pl.* **-loes** *or* **-los.** **1.** a disc or ring of light around the head of an angel, saint, etc., as in painting. **2.** the aura surrounding a famous or admired person, thing, or event. **3.** a circle of light around the sun or moon, caused by the refraction of light by particles of ice. ~*vb.* **-loes** *or* **-los, -loing, -loed.** **4.** to surround with or form a halo. [C16: < Med. L, < L *halōs* circular threshing floor, < Gk]

halogen (ˈhæləˌdʒɛn) *n.* any of the chemical elements fluorine, chlorine, bromine, iodine, and astatine. They are all monovalent and readily form negative ions. [C19: < Swedish, < Gk *hals* salt + -GEN] —**halogenous** (həˈlɒdʒɪnəs) *adj.*

halogenate (ˈhælədʒəˌneɪt) *vb. Chem.* to treat or combine with a halogen. —ˌ**halogenˈation** *n.*

haloid (ˈhælɔɪd) *Chem.* ~*adj.* **1.** derived from a halogen: *a haloid salt.* ~*n.* **2.** a compound containing halogen atoms in its molecules.

halt[1] (hɔːlt) *n.* **1.** an interruption or end to movement or progress. **2.** *Chiefly Brit.* a minor railway station, without permanent buildings. **3.** **call a halt (to).** to put an end (to); stop. ~*n., sentence substitute.* **4.** a command to halt, esp. as an order when marching. ~*vb.* **5.** to come or bring to a halt. [C17: < *to make halt,* translation of G *halt machen,* < *halten* to stop]

halt[2] (hɔːlt) *vb.* (*intr.*) **1.** (esp. of verse) to falter or be defective. **2.** to be unsure. **3.** *Arch.* to be lame. ~*adj.* **4.** *Arch.* **a.** lame. **b.** (*as collective n.; preceded by the*): *the halt.* [OE *healt* lame]

halter (ˈhɔːltə) *n.* **1.** headgear for a horse, usually with a rope for leading. **2.** a style of woman's top fastened behind the neck and waist, leaving the back and arms bare. **3.** a rope having a noose for hanging a person. **4.** death by hanging. ~*vb.* (*tr.*) **5.** to put on a halter. **6.** to hang (someone). [OE *hælfter*]

haltere (ˈhæltɪə) *n., pl.* **halteres** (hælˈtɪəriːz). one of a pair of short projections in dipterous insects that are modified hind wings, used for maintaining equilibrium during flight. [C18: < Gk *haltēres* (pl.) hand-held weights used as balancers or to give impetus in leaping, < *hallesthai* to leap]

halting (ˈhɔːltɪŋ) *adj.* **1.** hesitant: *halting speech.* **2.** lame. —ˈ**haltingly** *adv.*

halvah, halva (ˈhælvɑː), *or* **halavah** (ˈhæləvɑː) *n.* an Eastern sweetmeat made of honey and containing sesame seeds, nuts, etc. [< Yiddish *halva,* ult. < Ar. *halwā*]

halve (hɑːv) *vb.* (*tr.*) **1.** to divide into two approximately equal parts. **2.** to share equally. **3.** to reduce by half, as by cutting. **4.** *Golf.* to take the same number of strokes on (a hole or round) as one's opponent. [OE *hielfan*]

halyard *or* **halliard** (ˈhæljəd) *n. Naut.* a line for hoisting or lowering a sail, flag, or spar. [C14 *halier,* infl. by YARD[1]; see HALE[2]]

ham[1] (hæm) *n.* **1.** the part of the hindquarters of a pig between the hock and the hip. **2.** the meat of this part. **3.** *Inf.* the back of the leg above the knee. [OE *hamm*]

ham[2] (hæm) *n.* **1.** *Theatre, inf.* **a.** an actor who overacts or relies on stock gestures. **b.** overacting or clumsy acting. **c.** (*as modifier*): *a ham actor.* **2.** *Inf.* a licensed amateur radio operator. ~*vb.* **hamming, hammed.** **3.** *Inf.* to overact. [C19: special use of HAM[1]; in some senses prob. infl. by AMATEUR]

hamadryad (ˌhæməˈdraɪəd) *n.* **1.** *Classical myth.* a nymph who inhabits a tree and dies with it. **2.** another name for **king cobra.** [C14: < L *Hamādryas,* < Gk *Hamadruas,* < *hama* together with + *drus* tree]

hamadryas (ˌhæməˈdraɪəs) *n.* a baboon of Arabia and NE Africa, having long silvery hair on the head, neck, and chest. [C19: via NL < L; see HAMADRYAD]

hamba (ˈhæmbə) *sentence substitute. S. African, usually offens.* go away; be off. [< a Bantu language, < *ukuttamba* to go]

hamburger (ˈhæmˌbɜːgə) *n.* a cake of minced beef, often served in a bread roll. Also called: **beefburger.** [C20: < *Hamburger steak* (steak in the fashion of *Hamburg,* Germany)]

hame (heɪm) *n.* either of the two curved bars holding the traces of the harness, attached to the collar of a draught animal. [C14: < MDu. *hame*]

ham-handed *or* **ham-fisted** *adj. Inf.* lacking dexterity or elegance; clumsy.

Hamitic (hæˈmɪtɪk, hə-) *n.* **1.** a group of N African languages related to Semitic. ~*adj.* **2.** denoting or belonging to this group of languages. **3.** denoting or characteristic of the Hamites, a group of peoples of N Africa, including the ancient Egyptians, supposedly descended from Noah's son Ham.

hamlet (ˈhæmlɪt) *n.* a small village, esp. (in Britain) one without its own church. [C14: < OF *hamelet,* dim. of *hamel,* < *ham,* of Gmc origin]

hammer (ˈhæmə) *n.* **1.** a hand tool consisting of a heavy usually steel head held transversely on the end of a handle, used for driving in nails, etc. **2.** any tool or device with a similar function, such as the striking head on a bell. **3.** a power-driven striking tool, esp. one used in forging. **4.** a part of a gunlock that strikes the primer or percussion cap when the trigger is pulled. **5.** *Field sports.* **a.** a heavy metal ball attached to a flexible wire: thrown in competitions. **b.** the sport of throwing the hammer. **6.** an auctioneer's gavel. **7.** a device on a piano that is made to strike a string or group of strings causing them to vibrate. **8.** *Anat.* the nontechnical name for **malleus.** **9.** **go under the hammer.** to be offered for sale by an auctioneer. **10.** **hammer and tongs.** with great effort or energy. **11.** **on someone's hammer.** *Austral. & N.Z. sl.* in hot pursuit of someone. ~*vb.* **12.** to strike or beat with or as if with a hammer. **13.** (*tr.*) to shape with or as if with a hammer. **14.** (*tr.; foll. by in or into*) to force (facts, ideas, etc.) into (someone) through constant repetition. **15.** (*intr.*) to feel or sound like hammering. **16.** (*intr.; often foll. by away*) to work at constantly. **17.** (*tr.*) *Brit.* to criticize severely. **18.** (*tr.*) *Inf.* to defeat. **19.** (*tr.*) *Stock Exchange.* **a.** to announce the default of (a member). **b.** to cause prices of (securities, the market, etc.) to fall by bearish selling. [OE *hamor*] —ˈ**hammer-**ˌ**like** *adj.*

hammer and sickle *n.* the emblem on the flag of the Soviet Union, representing the industrial workers and the peasants respectively.

hammer beam *n.* either of a pair of short horizontal beams that project from opposite walls to support arched braces and struts.

hammerhead (ˈhæməˌhɛd) *n.* **1.** a ferocious shark having a flattened hammer-shaped head. **2.** a tropical African wading bird having a dark plumage and a long backward-pointing crest. **3.** a large African fruit bat with a hammer-shaped muzzle. —ˈ**hammer**ˌ**headed** *adj.*

hammerlock (ˈhæməˌlɒk) *n.* a wrestling hold in which a wrestler twists his opponent's arm upwards behind his back.

hammer out *vb.* (*tr., adv.*) **1.** to shape or remove with or as if with a hammer. **2.** to settle or reconcile (differences, problems, etc.).

hammertoe (ˈhæməˌtəʊ) *n.* a deformity causing the toe to be bent in a clawlike arch.

hammock (ˈhæmək) *n.* a length of canvas, net, etc., suspended at the ends and used as a bed. [C16: < Sp. *hamaca,* < Amerind]

hammy (ˈhæmɪ) *adj.* **-mier, -miest.** *Inf.* **1.** (of an actor) tending to overact. **2.** (of a play, performance, etc.) overacted or exaggerated.

hamper[1] (ˈhæmpə) *vb.* **1.** (*tr.*) to prevent the progress or free movement of. ~*n.* **2.** *Naut.* gear aboard a vessel that, though essential, is often in the way. [C14: <?; ? rel. to OE *hamm* enclosure, *hemm* HEM[1]]

hamper[2] (ˈhæmpə) *n.* **1.** a large basket, usually with a cover. **2.** *Brit.* a selection of food and drink packed in a hamper or other container. [C14: var. of earlier *hanaper* a small basket, < OF, of Gmc origin]

hamster (ˈhæmstə) *n.* a Eurasian burrowing rodent having a stocky body, short tail, and cheek pouches: a popular pet. [C17: < G, < OHG *hamustro*, of Slavic origin]

hamstring (ˈhæmˌstrɪŋ) *n.* **1.** one of the tendons at the back of the knee. **2.** the large tendon at the back of the hind leg of a horse, etc. ~*vb.* **-stringing, -strung.** (*tr.*) **3.** to cripple by cutting the hamstring of. **4.** to thwart. [C16: HAM[1] + STRING]

hamulus (ˈhæmjʊləs) *n., pl.* **-li** (-ˌlaɪ). *Biol.* a hook or hooklike process, between the fore and hind wings of a bee. [C18: < L: a little hook, < *hāmus* hook]

hand (hænd) *n.* **1.** the prehensile part of the body at the end of the arm, consisting of a thumb, four fingers, and a palm. Related adj.: **manual.** **2.** the corresponding part in animals. **3.** something resembling this in shape or function. **4. a.** the cards dealt in one round of a card game. **b.** a player holding such cards. **c.** one round of a card game. **5.** agency or influence: *the hand of God.* **6.** a part in something done: *he had a hand in the victory.* **7.** assistance: *to give someone a hand.* **8.** a pointer on a dial, indicator, or gauge, esp. on a clock. **9.** acceptance or pledge of partnership, as in marriage. **10.** a position indicated by its location to the side of an object or the observer: *on the right hand.* **11.** a contrastive aspect, condition, etc.: *on the other hand.* **12.** source or origin: *a story heard at third hand.* **13.** a person, esp. one who creates something: *a good hand at painting.* **14.** a manual worker. **15.** a member of a ship's crew: *all hands on deck.* **16.** a person's handwriting: *the letter was in his own hand.* **17.** a round of applause: *give him a hand.* **18.** a characteristic way of doing something: *the hand of a master.* **19.** a unit of length equalling four inches, used for measuring the height of horses. **20.** a cluster of bananas. **21. a free hand.** freedom to do as desired. **22.** (*modifier*) **a.** of or involving the hand: *a hand grenade.* **b.** carried in or worn on the hand: *hand luggage.* **c.** operated by hand: *a hand drill.* **23.** (*in combination*) made by hand rather than machine: *hand-sewn.* **24. a heavy hand.** tyranny or oppression: *he ruled with a heavy hand.* **25. a high hand.** a dictatorial manner. **26. by hand. a.** by manual rather than mechanical means. **b.** by messenger or personally: *the letter was delivered by hand.* **27. force someone's hand.** to force someone to act. **28. from hand to mouth. a.** in poverty: *living from hand to mouth.* **b.** without preparation or planning. **29. hand and foot.** in all ways possible; completely: *they waited on him hand and foot.* **30. hand in glove.** in close association. **31. hand over fist.** steadily and quickly: *he makes money hand over fist.* **32. hold one's hand.** to stop or postpone a planned action or punishment. **33. hold someone's hand.** to support, help, or guide someone, esp. by giving sympathy. **34. in hand. a.** under control. **b.** receiving attention. **c.** available in reserve. **d.** with deferred payment: *he works a week in hand.* **35. keep one's hand in.** to continue or practise. **36. (near) at hand.** very close, esp. in time. **37. on hand.** close by; present. **38. out of hand. a.** beyond control. **b.** without reservation or deeper examination: *he condemned him out of hand.* **39. show one's hand.** to reveal one's stand, opinion, or plans. **40. take in hand.** to discipline; control. **41. throw one's hand in.** to give up a venture, game, etc. **42. to hand.** accessible. **43. try one's hand.** to attempt to do something. ~*vb.* (*tr.*) **44.** to transmit or offer by the hand or hands. **45.** to help or lead with the hand. **46.** *Naut.* to furl (a sail). **47. hand it to someone.** to give credit to someone. ~See also **hand down, hand in,** etc., **hands.** [OE *hand*] —ˈ**handless** *adj.*

handbag (ˈhændˌbæg) *n.* **1.** Also called: **bag, purse** (U.S. and Canad.), **pocketbook** (chiefly U.S.). a woman's small bag carried to contain personal articles. **2.** a small suitcase that can be carried by hand.

handball (ˈhændˌbɔːl) *n.* **1.** a game in which two or four people strike a ball against a wall with the hand. **2.** the small hard rubber ball used. ~*vb.* **3.** *Australian Rules football.* to pass (the ball) with a blow of the fist.

handbarrow (ˈhændˌbærəʊ) *n.* a flat tray for transporting loads, usually carried by two men.

handbill (ˈhændˌbɪl) *n.* a small printed notice for distribution by hand.

handbook (ˈhændˌbʊk) *n.* a reference book listing brief facts on a subject or place or directions for maintenance or repair, as of a car.

handbrake (ˈhændˌbreɪk) *n.* **1.** a brake operated by a hand lever. **2.** the lever that operates the handbrake.

handbreadth (ˈhændˌbrɛtθ, -ˌbrɛdθ) *or* **hand's-breadth** *n.* the width of a hand used as an indication of length.

h and c *abbrev. for* hot and cold (water).

handcart (ˈhændˌkɑːt) *n.* a simple cart, usually with one or two wheels, pushed or drawn by hand.

handcraft (ˈhændˌkrɑːft) *n.* **1.** another word for **handicraft.** ~*vb.* **2.** (*tr.*) to make by handicraft. —ˈ**handˌcrafted** *adj.*

handcuff (ˈhændˌkʌf) *vb.* **1.** (*tr.*) to put handcuffs on (a person); manacle. ~*n.* **2.** (*pl.*) a pair of locking metal rings joined by a short bar or chain for securing prisoners, etc.

hand down *vb.* (*tr., adv.*) **1.** to bequeath. **2.** to pass (an outgrown garment) on from one member of a family to a younger one. **3.** *U.S. & Canad. law.* to announce (a verdict).

-handed *adj.* of, for, or using a hand or hands as specified: *left-handed; a four-handed game of cards.*

handful (ˈhændfʊl) *n., pl.* **-fuls.** **1.** the amount or number that can be held in the hand. **2.** a small number or quantity. **3.** *Inf.* a person or thing difficult to manage or control.

handgun (ˈhændˌgʌn) *n. U.S. & Canad.* a firearm that can be fired with one hand, such as a pistol.

handicap (ˈhændɪˌkæp) *n.* **1.** something that hampers or hinders. **2. a.** a contest, esp. a race, in which competitors are given advantages or disadvantages of weight, distance, etc., in an attempt to equalize their chances. **b.** the advantage or disadvantage prescribed. **3.** *Golf.* the number of strokes by which a player's averaged score exceeds par for the course. **4.** any disability or disadvantage resulting from physical, mental, or social impairment or abnormality. ~*vb.* **-capping, -capped.** (*tr.*) **5.** to be a hindrance or disadvantage to. **6.** to assign a handicap to. **7.** to organize (a contest) by handicapping. [C17: prob. < *hand in cap,* a lottery game in which players drew forfeits from a cap or deposited money in it] —ˈ**handiˌcapper** *n.*

handicapped (ˈhændɪˌkæpt) *adj.* **1. a.** physically or mentally disabled. **b.** (*as collective n.;* preceded by *the*): *the handicapped.* **2.** (of a competitor) assigned a handicap.

handicraft (ˈhændɪˌkrɑːft) *n.* **1.** skill in working with the hands. **2.** a particular skill performed with the hands, such as weaving. **3.** the work so produced. ~Also called: **handcraft.** [C15: changed < HANDCRAFT through infl. of HANDIWORK]

hand in *vb.* (*tr., adv.*) to return or submit (something, such as an examination paper).

handiwork (ˈhændɪˌwɜːk) *n.* **1.** work produced by hand. **2.** the result of the action or endeavours of a person or thing. [OE *handgeweorc,* < HAND + *ge-* (collective prefix) + *weorc* WORK]

handkerchief (ˈhæŋkətʃɪf, -tʃiːf) *n.* a small square of soft absorbent material carried and used to wipe the nose, etc.

handle (ˈhændᵊl) *n.* **1.** the part of a utensil, drawer, etc., designed to be held in order to move, use, or pick up the object. **2.** *N.Z.* a glass beer mug with a handle. **3.** *Sl.* a title put before a person's name. **4.** *CB radio.* a slang name for **call sign.** **5.** an excuse for doing something: *his background served as a handle for their mockery.* **6.** the quality, as of textiles, perceived by feeling. **7. fly off the handle.** *Inf.* to become suddenly extremely angry. ~*vb.* (*mainly tr.*) **8.** to hold, move, or touch with the hands. **9.** to operate using the hands: *the boy handled the reins well.*

10. to control: *my wife handles my investments.* **11.** to manage successfully: *a secretary must be able to handle clients.* **12.** to discuss (a theme, subject, etc.). **13.** to deal with in a specified way: *I was handled with great tact.* **14.** to trade or deal in (specified merchandise). **15.** (*intr.*) to react in a specified way to operation: *the car handles well on bends.* [OE] —**ˈhandled** *adj.* —**ˈhandling** *n.*

handlebar moustache (ˈhændəlˌbɑː) *n.* a bushy extended moustache with curled ends.

handlebars (ˈhændəlˌbɑːz) *pl. n.* (*sometimes sing.*) a metal bar having its ends curved to form handles, used for steering a bicycle, etc.

handler (ˈhændlə) *n.* **1.** a person who trains and controls an animal, esp. a police dog. **2.** the trainer or second of a boxer.

handmade (ˌhændˈmeɪd) *adj.* made by hand, not by machine, esp. with care or craftsmanship.

handmaiden (ˈhændˌmeɪdən) *or* **handmaid** *n.* **1.** a person or thing that serves a useful but subordinate purpose. **2.** *Arch.* a female servant.

hand-me-down *n. Inf.* **1.** something, esp. an outgrown garment, passed down from one person to another. **2.** anything that has already been used by another.

hand-off *Rugby.* ~*n.* **1.** the act of warding off an opposing player with the open hand. ~*vb.* **hand off. 2.** (*tr., adv.*) to ward off thus.

hand on *vb.* (*tr., adv.*) to pass to the next in a succession.

hand organ *n.* another name for **barrel organ.**

hand-out *n.* **1.** clothing, food, or money given to a needy person. **2.** a leaflet, free sample, etc., given out to publicize something. **3.** a statement distributed to the press or an audience to confirm or replace an oral presentation. ~*vb.* **hand out. 4.** (*tr., adv.*) to distribute.

hand over *vb.* **1.** (*tr., adv.*) to surrender possession of; transfer. ~*n.* **handover. 2.** a transfer; surrender.

hand-pick *vb.* (*tr.*) to select with great care, as for a special job. —ˌ**hand-ˈpicked** *adj.*

handrail (ˈhændˌreɪl) *n.* a rail alongside a stairway, etc., to provide support.

hands (hændz) *pl. n.* **1.** power or keeping: *your welfare is in his hands.* **2.** Also called: **handling.** *Soccer.* the infringement of touching the ball with the hand or arm. **3. change hands.** to pass from the possession of one person to another. **4. hands down.** without effort; easily. **5. have one's hands full. a.** to be completely occupied. **b.** to be beset with problems. **6. have one's hands tied.** to be unable to act. **7. lay hands on** *or* **upon. a.** to get possession of. **b.** to beat up; assault. **c.** to find. **d.** *Christianity.* to confirm or ordain by the imposition of hands. **8. off one's hands.** for which one is no longer responsible. **9. on one's hands. a.** for which one is responsible: *I've got too much on my hands to help.* **b.** to spare: *time on my hands.* **10. wash one's hands of.** to have nothing more to do with; refuse to accept responsibility for.

handsaw (ˈhændˌsɔː) *n.* any saw for use in one hand only.

hand's-breadth *n.* another name for **hand-breadth.**

handsel *or* **hansel** (ˈhænsəl) *Arch. or dialect.* ~*n.* **1.** a gift for good luck at the beginning of a new year, new venture, etc. ~*vb.* **-selling, -selled** *or U.S.* **-seling, -seled.** (*tr.*) **2.** to give a handsel to (a person). **3.** to inaugurate. [OE *handselen* delivery into the hand]

handset (ˈhændˌsɛt) *n.* a telephone mouthpiece and earpiece mounted as a single unit.

handshake (ˈhændˌʃeɪk) *n.* the act of grasping and shaking a person's hand, as when being introduced or agreeing on a deal.

handsome (ˈhændsəm) *adj.* **1.** (of a man) good-looking. **2.** (of a woman) fine-looking in a dignified way. **3.** well-proportioned; stately: *a handsome room.* **4.** liberal: *a handsome allowance.* **5.** gracious or generous: *a handsome action.* [C15 *handsom* easily handled] —**ˈhandsomely** *adv.* —**ˈhandsomeness** *n.*

hands-on *adj.* involving practical experience of equipment, etc.: *hands-on training in computers.*

handspring (ˈhændˌsprɪŋ) *n.* a gymnastic feat in which a person starts from a standing position and leaps forwards or backwards into a handstand and then onto his feet.

handstand (ˈhændˌstænd) *n.* the act of supporting the body on the hands in an upside-down position.

hand-to-hand *adj., adv.* at close quarters.

hand-to-mouth *adj., adv.* with barely enough money or food to satisfy immediate needs.

handwork (ˈhændˌwɜːk) *n.* work done by hand rather than by machine. —**ˈhandˌworked** *adj.*

handwriting (ˈhændˌraɪtɪŋ) *n.* **1.** writing by hand rather than by typing or printing. **2.** a person's characteristic writing style: *that is in my handwriting.* —**ˈhandˌwritten** *adj.*

handy (ˈhændɪ) *adj.* **handier, handiest. 1.** conveniently within reach. **2.** easy to handle or use. **3.** skilful with one's hands. —**ˈhandily** *adv.* —**ˈhandiness** *n.*

handyman (ˈhændɪˌmæn) *n., pl.* **-men.** a man employed to do or skilled in odd jobs, etc.

hanepoot (ˈhɑːnəˌpɔːt) *n. S. African.* a kind of grape for eating or wine making. [< Du.]

hang (hæŋ) *vb.* **hanging, hung. 1.** to fasten or be fastened from above, esp. by a cord, chain, etc. **2.** to place or be placed in position as by a hinge so as to allow free movement: *to hang a door.* **3.** (*intr.;* sometimes foll. by *over*) to be suspended; hover: *a pall of smoke hung over the city.* **4.** (*intr.;* sometimes foll. by *over*) to threaten. **5.** (*intr.*) to be or remain doubtful (esp. in **hang in the balance**). **6.** (*p.t. & p.p.* **hanged**) to suspend or be suspended by the neck until dead. **7.** (*tr.*) to decorate, furnish, or cover with something suspended. **8.** (*tr.*) to fasten to a wall: *to hang wallpaper.* **9.** to exhibit or be exhibited in an art gallery, etc. **10.** to droop or allow to droop: *to hang one's head.* **11.** (of cloth, clothing, etc.) to drape, fall, or flow: *her skirt hangs well.* **12.** (*tr.*) to suspend (game such as pheasant) so that it becomes slightly decomposed and therefore more tasty. **13.** (of a jury) to prevent or be prevented from reaching a verdict. **14.** (*p.t. & p.p.* **hanged**) *Sl.* to damn or be damned: used in mild curses or interjections. **15.** (*intr.*) to pass slowly (esp. in **time hangs heavily**). **16. hang fire.** to be delayed or to procrastinate. ~*n.* **17.** the way in which something hangs. **18.** (*usually used with a negative*) *Sl.* a damn: *I don't care a hang.* **19. get the hang of.** *Inf.* **a.** to understand the technique of doing something. **b.** to perceive the meaning of. ~See also **hang about, hang back,** etc. [OE *hangian*]

hang about *or* **around** *vb.* (*intr.*) **1.** to waste time; loiter. **2.** (*adv.;* foll. by *with*) to frequent the company (of someone).

hangar (ˈhæŋə) *n.* a large building for storing and maintaining aircraft. [C19: < F: shed, ? < Med. L *angārium* shed used as a smithy, <?]

hang back *vb.* (*intr., adv.;* often foll. by *from*) to be reluctant to go forward or carry on.

hangdog (ˈhæŋˌdɒg) *adj.* downcast, furtive, or guilty in appearance or manner.

hanger (ˈhæŋə) *n.* **1. a.** any support, such as a peg or loop, on or by which something may be hung. **b.** See **coat hanger. 2. a.** a person who hangs something. **b.** (*in combination*): *paper-hanger.* **3.** a type of dagger worn on a sword belt. **4.** *Brit.* a wood on a steep hillside.

hanger-on *n., pl.* **hangers-on.** a sycophantic follower or dependant.

hang-glider *n.* an unpowered aircraft consisting of a large cloth wing stretched over a light framework from which the pilot hangs in a harness. —**ˈhang-ˌgliding** *n.*

hangi (ˈhʌŋiː) *n. N.Z.* **1.** an open-air cooking pit. **2.** the food cooked in it. **3.** the social gathering at the resultant meal. [< Maori]

hang in *vb.* (*intr., prep.*) *Inf., chiefly U.S. & Canad.* to persist: *just hang in there for a bit longer.*

hanging (ˈhæŋɪŋ) *n.* **1. a.** the putting of a person to death by suspending the body by the neck. **b.** (*as modifier*): *a hanging offence.* **2.** (*often pl.*) a decorative drapery hung on a wall or over a window. ~*adj.* **3.** not supported from below; suspended. **4.** undecided; still under discussion. **5.** projecting downwards; overhanging. **6.** situated on a steep slope. **7.** (*prenominal*) given to issuing death sentences: *a hanging judge.*

hanging valley *n. Geog.* a tributary valley entering a main valley at a much higher level because of overdeepening of the main valley, esp. by glacial erosion.

hangman (ˈhæŋmən) *n., pl.* **-men.** an official who carries out a sentence of hanging.

hangnail (ˈhæŋˌneɪl) *n.* a piece of skin torn away from, but still attached to, the base or side of a fingernail. [C17: < OE *angnægl,* < *enge* tight + *nægl* nail; infl. by HANG]

hang on *vb.* (*intr.*) **1.** (*adv.*) to continue or persist, esp. with effort or difficulty. **2.** (*adv.*) to grasp or hold. **3.** (*prep.*) to depend on: *everything hangs on this deal.* **4.** (*prep.*) Also: **hang onto, hang upon.** to listen attentively to. **5.** (*adv.*) *Inf.* to wait: *hang on for a few minutes.*

hang out *vb.* (*adv.*) **1.** to suspend, be suspended, or lean. **2.** (*intr.*) *Inf.* to frequent a place. **3. let it all hang out.** *Inf., chiefly U.S.* **a.** to relax completely in an unassuming way. **b.** to act or speak freely. ~*n.* **hang-out. 4.** *Inf.* a place that one frequents.

hangover (ˈhæŋˌəʊvə) *n.* **1.** the delayed aftereffects of drinking too much alcohol. **2.** a person or thing left over from or influenced by a past age.

hang together *vb.* (*intr., adv.*) **1.** to be cohesive or united. **2.** to be consistent: *your statements don't quite hang together.*

hang up *vb.* (*adv.*) **1.** (*tr.*) to put on a hook, hanger, etc. **2.** to replace (a telephone receiver) on its cradle at the end of a conversation. **3.** (*tr.; usually passive;* usually foll. by *on*) *Inf.* to cause to have an emotional or psychological preoccupation or problem: *he's really hung up on his mother.* ~*n.* **hang-up.** *Inf.* **4.** an emotional or psychological preoccupation or problem. **5.** a persistent cause of annoyance.

hank (hæŋk) *n.* **1.** a loop, coil, or skein, as of rope. **2.** *Naut.* a ringlike fitting that can be opened to admit a stay for attaching the luff of a sail. **3.** a unit of measurement of cloth, yarn, etc., such as a length of 840 yards (767 m) of cotton or 560 yards (512 m) of worsted yarn. [C13: < ON]

hanker (ˈhæŋkə) *vb.* (foll. by *for, after,* or an infinitive) to have a yearning. [C17: prob. < Du. dialect *hankeren*] —ˈ**hankering** *n.*

hanky *or* **hankie** (ˈhæŋkɪ) *n., pl.* **hankies.** *Inf.* short for **handkerchief.**

hanky-panky (ˈhæŋkɪˈpæŋkɪ) *n. Inf.* **1.** dubious or foolish behaviour. **2.** illicit sexual relations. [C19: var. of HOCUS-POCUS]

Hanoverian (ˌhænəˈvɪərɪən) *adj.* of or relating to the British royal house ruling from 1714 to 1901. [< the princely House of *Hanover,* former province of Germany]

Hansard (ˈhænsɑːd) *n.* **1.** the official verbatim report of the proceedings of the British Parliament. **2.** a similar report kept by the Canadian House of Commons and other legislative bodies. [C19: after L. *Hansard* (1752–1828) and his descendants, who compiled the reports until 1889]

Hanse (hæns) *n.* **1.** a medieval guild of merchants. **2.** a fee paid by the new members of a medieval trading guild. **3.** another name for the **Hanseatic League.** [C12: of Gmc origin] —**Hanseatic** (ˌhænsɪˈætɪk) *adj.*

Hanseatic League *n.* a commercial organization of towns in N Germany formed in the mid-14th century to protect and control trade.

hansel (ˈhænsᵊl) *n., vb.* a variant spelling of **handsel.**

hansom (ˈhænsəm) *n.* (*sometimes cap.*) a two-wheeled one-horse carriage with a fixed hood. The driver sits on a high outside seat at the rear. Also called: **hansom cab.** [C19: after its designer J. A. *Hansom* (1803–82)]

Hants (hænts) *abbrev. for* Hampshire.

Hanukkah (ˈhɑːnəkə, -nʊˌkɑː) *n.* a variant of **Chanukah.**

Hanuman (ˌhʌnʊˈmɑːn) *n.* **1.** (*pl.* **mans**) another word for **entellus** (the monkey). **2.** the monkey chief of Hindu mythology. [< Hindi, < Sansk. *hanumant* having (conspicuous) jaws, < *hanu* jaw]

hap (hæp) *Arch.* ~*n.* **1.** luck; chance. **2.** an occurrence. ~*vb.* **happing, happed. 3.** (*intr.*) to happen. [C13: < ON *happ* good luck]

ha'penny (ˈheɪpnɪ) *n., pl.* **-nies.** *Brit.* a variant spelling of **halfpenny.**

haphazard (hæpˈhæzəd) *adv., adj.* **1.** at random. ~*adj.* **2.** careless; slipshod. —**hapˈhazardly** *adv.* —**hapˈhazardness** *n.*

hapless (ˈhæplɪs) *adj.* unfortunate; wretched. —ˈ**haplessly** *adv.* —ˈ**haplessness** *n.*

haplography (hæpˈlɒgrəfɪ) *n., pl.* **-phies.** the accidental omission of a letter or syllable which recurs, as in spelling *endodontics* as *endontics.* [C19: < Gk, < *haplous* single + -GRAPHY]

haploid (ˈhæplɔɪd) *Biol.* ~*adj.* **1.** (esp. of gametes) having a single set of unpaired chromosomes. ~*n.* **2.** a haploid cell or organism. [C20: < Gk *haploeidēs,* < *haplous* single]

haplology (hæpˈlɒlədʒɪ) *n.* omission of a repeated occurrence of a sound or syllable in fluent speech, as for example in the pronunciation of *library* as (ˈlaɪbrɪ).

haply (ˈhæplɪ) *adv.* (*sentence modifier*) an archaic word for **perhaps.**

happen (ˈhæpᵊn) *vb.* **1.** (*intr.*) to take place; occur. **2.** (*intr.;* foll. by *to*) (of some unforeseen event, esp. death) to fall to the lot (of): *if anything happens to me it'll be your fault.* **3.** (*tr.*) to chance (to be or do something): *I happen to know him.* **4.** (*tr.; takes a clause as object*) to be the case, esp. by chance: *it happens that I know him.* ~*adv., sentence substitute.* **5.** *N English dialect.* another word for **perhaps.** [C14: see HAP, -EN[1]]

▷ **Usage.** See at **occur.**

happening (ˈhæpənɪŋ, ˈhæpnɪŋ) *n.* **1.** an event. **2.** an improvised or spontaneous performance consisting of bizarre events.

happen on *or* **upon** *vb.* (*intr.; prep.*) to find by chance.

happy (ˈhæpɪ) *adj.* **-pier, -piest. 1.** feeling or expressing joy; pleased. **2.** causing joy or gladness. **3.** fortunate: *the happy position of not having to work.* **4.** aptly expressed; appropriate: *a happy turn of phrase.* **5.** (*postpositive*) *Inf.* slightly intoxicated. [C14: see HAP, -Y[1]] —ˈ**happily** *adv.* —ˈ**happiness** *n.*

happy event *n. Inf.* the birth of a child.

happy-go-lucky *adj.* carefree or easy-going.

happy hour *n.* a time when some pubs or bars sell drinks at reduced prices.

happy hunting ground *n.* **1.** (in Amerind legend) the paradise to which a person passes after death. **2.** a productive or profitable area to explore: *jumble sales can be happy hunting grounds.*

happy medium *n.* a course or state that avoids extremes.

haptic (ˈhæptɪk) *adj.* relating to or based on the sense of touch. [C19: < Gk, < *haptein* to touch]

hapuka *or* **hapuku** (həˈpuːkə, ˈhɑːpʊkə) *n. N.Z.* another name for **groper.** [< Maori]

hara-kiri (ˌhærəˈkɪrɪ) *or* **hari-kari** (ˌhærɪˈkɑːrɪ) *n.* (formerly, in Japan) ritual suicide by disembowelment when disgraced or under sentence of death. [C19: < Japanese taboo sl., < *hara* belly + *kiri* cut]

harangue (həˈræŋ) *vb.* **1.** to address (a person or crowd) in an angry, vehement, or forcefully persuasive way. ~*n.* **2.** a loud, forceful, or angry speech. [C15: < OF, < OIt. *aringa* public speech, prob. of Gmc origin] —**haˈranguer** *n.*

harass (ˈhærəs, həˈræs) *vb.* (*tr.*) to trouble, torment, or confuse by continual persistent attacks, questions, etc. [C17: < F *harasser,* var. of OF *harer* to set a dog on, of Gmc origin] —ˈ**harassed** *adj.* —ˈ**harassment** *n.*

harbinger (ˈhɑːbɪndʒə) *n.* **1.** a person or thing that announces or indicates the approach of something; forerunner. ~*vb.* **2.** (*tr.*) to announce the approach or arrival of. [C12: < OF *herbergere*, < *herberge* lodging, < OSaxon]

harbour *or U.S.* **harbor** (ˈhɑːbə) *n.* **1.** a sheltered port. **2.** a place of refuge or safety. ~*vb.* **3.** (*tr.*) to give shelter to: *to harbour a criminal.* **4.** (*tr.*) to maintain secretly: *to harbour a grudge.* **5.** to shelter (a vessel) in a harbour or (of a vessel) to seek shelter. [OE *herebeorg*, < *here* army + *beorg* shelter]

harbourage *or U.S.* **harborage** (ˈhɑːbərɪdʒ) *n.* shelter or refuge, as for a ship.

harbour master *n.* an official in charge of a harbour.

hard (hɑːd) *adj.* **1.** firm or rigid. **2.** toughened; not soft or smooth: *hard skin.* **3.** difficult to do or accomplish: *a hard task.* **4.** difficult to understand: *a hard question.* **5.** showing or requiring considerable effort or application: *hard work.* **6.** demanding: *a hard master.* **7.** harsh; cruel: *a hard fate.* **8.** inflicting pain, sorrow, or hardship: *hard times.* **9.** tough or violent: *a hard man.* **10.** forceful: *a hard knock.* **11.** cool or uncompromising: *we took a long hard look at our profit factor.* **12.** indisputable; real: *hard facts.* **13.** *Chem.* (of water) impairing the formation of a lather by soap. **14.** practical, shrewd, or calculating: *he is a hard man in business.* **15.** harsh: *hard light.* **16. a.** (of currency) high and stable in exchange value. **b.** (of credit) difficult to obtain; tight. **17.** (of alcoholic drink) being a spirit rather than a wine, beer, etc. **18.** (of a drug) highly addictive. **19.** *Physics.* (of radiation) having high energy and the ability to penetrate solids. **20.** *Chiefly U.S.* (of goods) durable. **21.** short for **hard-core.** **22.** *Phonetics.* (not in technical usage) denoting the consonants *c* and *g* when they are pronounced as in *cat* and *got.* **23. a.** heavily fortified. **b.** (of nuclear missiles) located underground. **24.** politically extreme: *the hard left.* **25.** *Brit. & N.Z. inf.* incorrigible or disreputable (esp. in **a hard case**). **26. a hard nut to crack. a.** a person not easily won over. **b.** a thing not easily done or understood. **27. hard by.** close by. **28. hard of hearing.** slightly deaf. **29. hard up.** *Inf.* **a.** in need of money. **b.** (foll. by *for*) in great need (of): *hard up for suggestions.* ~*adv.* **30.** with great energy, force, or vigour: *the team always played hard.* **31.** as far as possible: *hard left.* **32.** earnestly or intently: *she thought hard about the formula.* **33.** with great intensity: *his son's death hit him hard.* **34.** (foll. by *on, upon, by,* or *after*) close; near: *hard on his heels.* **35.** (foll. by *at*) assiduously; devotedly. **36. a.** with effort or difficulty: *their victory was hard won.* **b.** (*in combination*): *hard-earned.* **37.** slowly: *prejudice dies hard.* **38. go hard with.** to cause pain or difficulty to (someone). **39. hard put (to it).** scarcely having the capacity (to do something). ~*n.* **40.** *Brit.* a roadway across a foreshore. **41.** *Sl.* hard labour. **42.** *Taboo sl.* an erection of the penis (esp. in **get** or **have a hard on**). [OE *heard*] —ˈ**hardness** *n.*

hard and fast *adj.* (**hard-and-fast** *when prenominal*). (of rules, etc.) invariable or strict.

hardback (ˈhɑːdˌbæk) *n.* **1.** a book with covers of cloth, cardboard, or leather. ~*adj.* **2.** Also: **casebound, hardbound, hardcover.** of or denoting a hardback or the publication of hardbacks.

hard-bitten *adj. Inf.* tough and realistic.

hardboard (ˈhɑːdˌbɔːd) *n.* a thin stiff sheet made of compressed sawdust and woodchips bound together under heat and pressure.

hard-boiled *adj.* **1.** (of an egg) boiled until solid. **2.** *Inf.* **a.** tough, realistic. **b.** cynical.

hard cash *n.* money or payment in money, as opposed to payment by cheque, credit, etc.

hard coal *n.* another name for **anthracite.**

hard copy *n.* computer output printed on paper, as contrasted with machine-readable output such as magnetic tape.

hard core *n.* **1.** the members of a group who form an intransigent nucleus resisting change. **2.** material, such as broken stones, used to form a foundation for a road, etc. ~*adj.* **hard-core. 3.** (of pornography) describing or depicting sexual acts in explicit detail. **4.** completely established in a belief, etc.: *hard-core Communists.*

hard disk *n. Computers.* an inflexible disk in a sealed container, usually with a storage capacity of several megabytes.

harden (ˈhɑːdᵊn) *vb.* **1.** to make or become hard or harder; freeze, stiffen, or set. **2.** to make or become tough or unfeeling. **3.** to make or become stronger or firmer. **4.** (*intr.*) *Commerce.* **a.** (of prices, a market, etc.) to cease to fluctuate. **b.** (of price) to rise higher. —ˈ**hardener** *n.*

hardened (ˈhɑːdᵊnd) *adj.* **1.** rigidly set, as in a mode of behaviour. **2.** toughened; seasoned.

harden off *vb.* (*tr., adv.*) to cause (plants) to become resistant to cold, frost, etc., by gradually exposing them to such conditions.

hard feeling *n.* (*often pl.; often used with a negative*) resentment; ill will: *no hard feelings?*

hard hat *n.* **1.** a hat made of a hard material for protection, worn esp. by construction workers. **2.** *Inf., chiefly U.S.* a construction worker.

hard-headed *adj.* tough, realistic, or shrewd; not moved by sentiment.

hardhearted (ˌhɑːdˈhɑːtɪd) *adj.* unkind or intolerant. —ˌ**hard**ˈ**heartedness** *n.*

hardihood (ˈhɑːdɪˌhʊd) *n.* courage or daring.

hard labour *n. Criminal law.* (formerly) the penalty of compulsory physical labour imposed in addition to a sentence of imprisonment.

hard landing *n.* a landing by a rocket or spacecraft in which the vehicle is destroyed on impact.

hard line *n.* an uncompromising course or policy. —ˌ**hard**ˈ**liner** *n.*

hardly (ˈhɑːdlɪ) *adv.* **1.** scarcely; barely: *we hardly knew the family.* **2.** only just: *he could hardly hold the cup.* **3.** *Often used ironically.* not at all: *he will hardly incriminate himself.* **4.** with difficulty. **5.** *Rare.* harshly or cruelly.

▷ **Usage.** Since *hardly, scarcely,* and *barely* already have negative force, it is redundant to use another negative in the same clause: *he had hardly had* (not *he hadn't hardly had*) *time to think.*

hard-nosed *adj. Inf.* tough, shrewd, and practical.

hard pad *n.* (in dogs) an abnormal increase in the thickness of the foot pads: one of the clinical signs of canine distemper. See **distemper**[1].

hard palate *n.* the anterior bony portion of the roof of the mouth.

hardpan (ˈhɑːdˌpæn) *n.* a hard impervious layer of clay below the soil.

hard paste *n.* **a.** porcelain made with kaolin and petuntse, of Chinese origin and made in Europe from the early 18th century. **b.** (*as modifier*): *hard-paste porcelain.*

hard-pressed *adj.* **1.** in difficulties. **2.** subject to severe competition or attack. **3.** closely pursued.

hard sauce *n.* butter and sugar creamed together with rum or brandy.

hard science *n.* one of the natural or physical sciences, such as physics, chemistry, biology, geology, or astronomy. —**hard scientist** *n.*

hard sell *n.* an aggressive insistent technique of selling or advertising.

hard-shell *adj.* also **hard-shelled. 1.** *Zool.* having a shell or carapace that is thick, heavy, or hard. **2.** *U.S.* strictly orthodox.

hardship (ˈhɑːdʃɪp) *n.* **1.** conditions of life difficult to endure. **2.** something that causes suffering or privation.

hard shoulder *n. Brit.* a surfaced verge running along the edge of a motorway for emergency stops.

hardtack (ˈhɑːdˌtæk) *n.* a kind of hard saltless biscuit, formerly eaten esp. by sailors as a staple aboard ship. Also called: **ship's biscuit, sea biscuit.**

hardtop (ˈhɑːdˌtɒp) *n.* a car with a metal or plastic roof that is sometimes detachable.

hardware (ˈhɑːdˌwɛə) *n.* **1.** metal tools, implements, etc., esp. cutlery or cooking utensils. **2.** *Computers.* the physical equipment used in a computer system, such as the central processing unit, peripheral devices, and memory. Cf. **software.** **3.** mechanical equipment, components, etc. **4.** heavy military equipment, such as tanks and missiles. **5.** *Inf.* a gun.

hard-wired *adj.* (of a circuit or instruction) permanently wired into a computer, replacing separate software.

hardwood (ˈhɑːdˌwʊd) *n.* **1.** the wood of any of numerous broad-leaved trees, such as oak, beech, ash, etc., as distinguished from the wood of a conifer. **2.** any tree from which this wood is obtained.

hardy (ˈhɑːdɪ) *adj.* **-dier, -diest.** **1.** having or demanding a tough constitution; robust. **2.** bold; courageous. **3.** foolhardy; rash. **4.** (of plants) able to live out of doors throughout the winter. [C13: < OF *hardi*, p.p. of *hardir* to become bold, of Gmc origin; cf. OE *hierdan* to HARDEN, ON *hertha*, OHG *herten*] —ˈ**hardily** *adv.* —ˈ**hardiness** *n.*

hare (hɛə) *n., pl.* **hares** *or* **hare.** **1.** a solitary mammal which is larger than a rabbit, has longer ears and legs, and lives in a shallow nest (form). **2. run with the hare and hunt with the hounds.** to be on good terms with both sides. **3. start a hare.** to raise a topic for conversation. ~*vb.* **4.** (*intr.; often foll. by off, after*, etc.) *Brit. inf.* to run fast or wildly. [OE *hara*] —ˈ**hareˌlike** *adj.*

hare and hounds *n.* (*functioning as sing.*) a game in which certain players (**hares**) run across country scattering pieces of paper that the other players (**hounds**) follow in an attempt to catch the hares.

harebell (ˈhɛəˌbɛl) *n.* a N temperate plant having slender stems and leaves, and bell-shaped blue flowers.

harebrained *or* **hairbrained** (ˈhɛəˌbreɪnd) *adj.* rash, foolish, or badly thought out.

harelip (ˈhɛəˌlɪp) *n.* a congenital cleft or fissure in the midline of the upper lip, often occurring with cleft palate. —ˈ**hareˌlipped** *adj.*

harem (ˈhɛərəm, hɑːˈriːm) *or* **hareem** (hɑːˈriːm) *n.* **1.** the part of an Oriental house reserved strictly for wives, concubines, etc. **2.** a Muslim's wives and concubines collectively. **3.** a group of female animals that are the mates of a single male. [C17: < Ar. *harīm* forbidden (place)]

hare's-foot *n.* a plant that grows on sandy soils in Europe and NW Asia and has downy heads of white or pink flowers.

haricot (ˈhærɪkəʊ) *n.* a variety of French bean with light-coloured edible seeds, which can be dried and stored. [C17: < F, ? < Amerind]

Harijan (ˈhʌrɪdʒən) *n.* a member of certain classes in India, formerly considered inferior and untouchable. [Hindi, lit.: man of God (so called by Mahatma Gandhi)]

hari-kari (ˌhærɪˈkɑːrɪ) *n.* a non-Japanese variant spelling of **hara-kiri.**

hark (hɑːk) *vb.* (*intr.; usually imperative*) to listen; pay attention. [OE *heorcnian* to HEARKEN]

hark back *vb.* (*intr., adv.*) to return to an earlier subject in speech or thought.

harken (ˈhɑːkən) *vb.* a variant spelling (esp. U.S.) of **hearken.** —ˈ**harkener** *n.*

harl (hɑːl) *n. Angling.* a variant of **herl.**

harlequin (ˈhɑːlɪkwɪn) *n.* **1.** (*sometimes cap.*) *Theatre.* a stock comic character originating in the commedia dell'arte; the foppish lover of Columbine in the English harlequinade. He is usually represented in diamond-patterned multi-coloured tights, wearing a black mask. **2.** a clown or buffoon. ~*adj.* **3.** varied in colour or decoration. [C16: < OF *Herlequin, Hellequin* leader of band of demon horsemen]

harlequinade (ˌhɑːlɪkwɪˈneɪd) *n.* **1.** (*sometimes cap.*) *Theatre.* a play in which harlequin has a leading role. **2.** buffoonery.

Harley Street (ˈhɑːlɪ) *n.* a street in central London famous for its large number of medical specialists' consulting rooms.

harlot (ˈhɑːlət) *n.* a prostitute. [C13: < OF *herlot* rascal, <?] —ˈ**harlotry** *n.*

harm (hɑːm) *n.* **1.** physical or mental injury. **2.** moral wrongdoing. ~*vb.* **3.** (*tr.*) to injure physically, morally, or mentally. [OE *hearm*]

harmattan (hɑːˈmætᵊn) *n.* a dry dusty wind from the Sahara blowing towards the W African coast. [C17: < native African language *haramata*, ? < Ar. *harām* forbidden thing; see HAREM]

harmful (ˈhɑːmfʊl) *adj.* causing or tending to cause harm; injurious. —ˈ**harmfully** *adv.*

harmless (ˈhɑːmlɪs) *adj.* not causing or tending to cause harm. —ˈ**harmlessly** *adv.*

harmonic (hɑːˈmɒnɪk) *adj.* **1.** of, producing, or characterized by harmony; harmonious. **2.** *Music.* of or belonging to harmony. **3.** *Maths.* **a.** capable of expression in the form of sine and cosine functions. **b.** of or relating to numbers whose reciprocals form an arithmetic progression. **4.** *Physics.* of or concerned with a harmonic or harmonics. ~*n.* **5.** *Physics, music.* a component of a periodic quantity, such as a musical tone, with a frequency that is an integral multiple of the fundamental frequency. **6.** *Music.* (not in technical use) overtone. ~See also **harmonics.** [C16: < L *harmonicus* relating to HARMONY] —**harˈmonically** *adv.*

harmonica (hɑːˈmɒnɪkə) *n.* **1.** a small wind instrument in which reeds of graduated lengths set into a metal plate enclosed in a narrow oblong box are made to vibrate by blowing and suction. **2.** See **glass harmonica.** [C18: < L *harmonicus* relating to HARMONY]

harmonic analysis *n.* the representation of a periodic function by means of the summation and integration of simple trigonometric functions.

harmonic mean *n.* the reciprocal of the arithmetic mean of the reciprocals of a set of specified numbers: the harmonic mean of 2, 3, and 4 is $3/(\frac{1}{2} + \frac{1}{3} + \frac{1}{4}) = \frac{36}{13}$.

harmonic minor scale *n. Music.* a minor scale modified from the natural by the sharpening of the seventh degree.

harmonic motion *n.* a periodic motion in which the displacement is symmetrical about a point or a periodic motion that is composed of such motions.

harmonic progression *n.* a sequence of numbers whose reciprocals form an arithmetic progression, as $1, \frac{1}{2}, \frac{1}{3}, \ldots$.

harmonics (hɑːˈmɒnɪks) *n.* **1.** (*functioning as sing.*) the science of musical sounds and their acoustic properties. **2.** (*functioning as pl.*) the overtones of a fundamental note, as produced by lightly touching the string of a stringed instrument at one of its node points while playing.

harmonic series *n.* **1.** *Maths.* a series whose terms are in harmonic progression, as in $1 + \frac{1}{4} + \frac{1}{7} + \frac{1}{10} + \ldots$ **2.** *Acoustics.* the series of tones with frequencies strictly related to one another and to the fundamental tone, as obtained by touching lightly the node points of a string while playing it.

harmonious (hɑːˈməʊnɪəs) *adj.* **1.** (esp. of colours or sounds) fitting together well. **2.** having agreement. **3.** tuneful or melodious.

harmonist (ˈhɑːmənɪst) *n.* **1.** a person skilled in the art and techniques of harmony. **2.** a person who combines and collates parallel narratives.

harmonium (hɑːˈməʊnɪəm) *n.* a musical keyboard instrument in which air from pedal-operated bellows causes the reeds to vibrate. [C19: < F, < *harmonie* HARMONY]

harmonize *or* **-nise** (ˈhɑːməˌnaɪz) *vb.* **1.** to make or become harmonious. **2.** (*tr.*) *Music.* to provide a harmony for (a tune, etc.). **3.** (*intr.*) to sing in harmony, as with other singers. **4.** to collate parallel narratives. —ˌ**harmoniˈzation** *or* **-niˈsation** *n.*

harmony (ˈhɑːmənɪ) *n., pl.* **-nies.** **1.** agreement in action, opinion, feeling, etc. **2.** order or congruity of parts to their whole or to one another. **3.** agreeable sounds. **4.** *Music.* **a.** any combination of notes sounded simultaneously. **b.** the vertically represented structure of a piece of music. Cf. **melody** (sense 1b). **c.** the art or science concerned with combinations of chords. **5.** a collation of parallel narratives, esp. of the four

Gospels. [C14: < L *harmonia* concord of sounds, < Gk: harmony, < *harmos* a joint]

harness (ˈhɑːnɪs) *n.* **1.** an arrangement of straps fitted to a draught animal in order that the animal can be attached to and pull a cart. **2.** something resembling this, esp. for attaching something to the body: *a parachute harness.* **3.** *Weaving.* the part of a loom that raises and lowers the warp threads. **4.** *Arch.* armour. **5. in harness.** at one's routine work. ~*vb.* (*tr.*) **6.** to put a harness on (a horse). **7.** (usually foll. by *to*) to attach (a draught animal) to (a cart, etc.). **8.** to control so as to employ the energy or potential power of: *to harness the atom.* **9.** to equip with armour. [C13: < OF *harneis* baggage, prob. < ON *hernest* (unattested), < *herr* army + *nest* provisions] —ˈ**harnesser** *n.*

harness race *n. Horse racing.* a trotting or pacing race for horses pulling sulkies.

harp (hɑːp) *n.* **1.** a large triangular plucked stringed instrument consisting of a soundboard connected to an upright pillar by means of a curved crossbar from which the strings extend downwards. ~*vb.* (*intr.*) **2.** to play the harp. **3.** (foll. by *on* or *upon*) to speak or write in a persistent and tedious manner. [OE *hearpe*] —ˈ**harper** *or* ˈ**harpist** *n.*

harpoon (hɑːˈpuːn) *n.* **1. a.** a barbed missile attached to a long cord and hurled or fired from a gun when hunting whales, etc. **b.** (*as modifier*): *a harpoon gun.* ~*vb.* **2.** (*tr.*) to spear with or as if with a harpoon. [C17: prob. < Du. *harpoen,* < OF *harpon* clasp, ? of Scand. origin] —**harˈpooner** *or* ˌ**harpoonˈeer** *n.*

harp seal *n.* a brownish-grey North Atlantic and Arctic seal, having a dark mark on its back.

harpsichord (ˈhɑːpsɪˌkɔːd) *n.* a horizontally strung stringed keyboard instrument, triangular in shape, with strings plucked by plectra mounted on pivoted jacks. [C17: < NL *harpichordium,* < LL *harpa* HARP + L *chorda* CHORD[1]] —ˈ**harpsiˌchordist** *n.*

harpy (ˈhɑːpɪ) *n., pl.* **-pies.** a cruel grasping person. [C16: < L *Harpyia,* < Gk *Harpuiai* the Harpies, lit.: snatchers, < *harpazein* to seize]

Harpy (ˈhɑːpɪ) *n., pl.* **-pies.** *Greek myth.* a ravenous creature with a woman's head and trunk and a bird's wings and claws.

harquebus (ˈhɑːkwɪbəs) *n., pl.* **-buses.** a variant spelling of **arquebus.**

harridan (ˈhærɪdᵊn) *n.* a scolding old woman; nag. [C17: <?; ? rel. to F *haridelle,* lit.: broken-down horse]

harrier[1] (ˈhærɪə) *n.* **1.** a person or thing that harries. **2.** a diurnal bird of prey having broad wings and long legs and tail.

harrier[2] (ˈhærɪə) *n.* **1.** a smallish breed of hound used originally for hare-hunting. **2.** a cross-country runner. [C16: < HARE + -ER[1]; infl. by HARRIER[1]]

Harris Tweed (ˈhærɪs) *n. Trademark.* a loose-woven tweed made in the Outer Hebrides.

harrow (ˈhærəʊ) *n.* **1.** any of various implements used to level the ground, stir the soil, break up clods, destroy weeds, etc., in soil. ~*vb.* (*tr.*) **2.** to draw a harrow over (land). **3.** to distress; vex. [C13: < ON] —ˈ**harrower** *n.* —ˈ**harrowing** *adj.*

harrumph (həˈrʌmf) *vb.* (*intr.*) *Chiefly U.S. & Canad.* to clear or make the noise of clearing the throat.

harry (ˈhærɪ) *vb.* **-rying, -ried.** **1.** (*tr.*) to harass; worry. **2.** to ravage (a town, etc.), esp. in war. [OE *hergian;* rel. to *here* army, ON *herja* to lay waste]

harsh (hɑːʃ) *adj.* **1.** rough or grating to the senses. **2.** stern, severe, or cruel. [C16: prob. of Scand. origin] —ˈ**harshly** *adv.* —ˈ**harshness** *n.*

hart (hɑːt) *n., pl.* **harts** *or* **hart.** the male of the deer, esp. the red deer aged five years or more. [OE *heorot*]

hartal (hɑːˈtɑːl) *n.* (in India) the act of closing shops or suspending work, esp. in political protest. [C20: < Hindi *hartāl,* < *hāt* shop + *tālā* bolt for a door, < Sansk.]

hartebeest (ˈhɑːtɪˌbiːst) *or* **hartbeest** (ˈhɑːtˌbiːst) *n.* either of two large African antelopes having an elongated muzzle, lyre-shaped horns, and a fawn-coloured coat. [C18: via Afrik. < Du.; see HART, BEAST]

hartshorn (ˈhɑːtsˌhɔːn) *n.* an obsolete name for **sal volatile.** [OE *heortes horn* hart's horn (formerly a chief source of ammonia)]

hart's-tongue *n.* an evergreen Eurasian fern with narrow undivided fronds.

harum-scarum (ˈhɛərəmˈskɛərəm) *adj., adv.* **1.** in a reckless way or of a reckless nature. ~*n.* **2.** a person who is impetuous or rash. [C17: ? < *hare* (in obs. sense: harass) + *scare,* var. of STARE]

haruspex (həˈrʌspɛks) *n., pl.* **haruspices** (həˈrʌspɪˌsiːz). (in ancient Rome) a priest who practised divination, esp. by examining the entrails of animals. [C16: < L, prob. < *hīra* gut + *specere* to look] —**haruspicy** (həˈrʌspɪsɪ) *n.*

harvest (ˈhɑːvɪst) *n.* **1.** the gathering of a ripened crop. **2.** the crop itself. **3.** the season for gathering crops. **4.** the product of an effort, action, etc.: *a harvest of love.* ~*vb.* **5.** to gather (a ripened crop) from (the place where it has been growing). **6.** (*tr.*) to receive (consequences). [OE *hærfest*] —ˈ**harvesting** *n.*

harvester (ˈhɑːvɪstə) *n.* **1.** a person who harvests. **2.** a harvesting machine, esp. a combine harvester.

harvest home *n.* **1.** the bringing in of the harvest. **2.** *Chiefly Brit.* a harvest supper.

harvestman (ˈhɑːvɪstmən) *n., pl.* **-men.** **1.** a person engaged in harvesting. **2.** Also called (U.S. and Canad.): **daddy-longlegs.** an arachnid having a small rounded body and very long thin legs.

harvest moon *n.* the full moon occurring nearest to the autumnal equinox.

harvest mouse *n.* a very small reddish-brown Eurasian mouse inhabiting cornfields, hedgerows, etc.

has (hæz) *vb.* (used with *he, she, it,* or a singular noun) a form of the present tense (indicative mood) of **have.**

has-been *n. Inf.* a person or thing that is no longer popular, successful, effective, etc.

hash[1] (hæʃ) *n.* **1.** a dish of diced cooked meat, vegetables, etc., reheated in a sauce. **2.** a reuse or rework of old material. **3. make a hash of.** *Inf.* to mess up or destroy. **4. settle someone's hash.** *Inf.* to subdue or silence someone. ~*vb.* (*tr.*) **5.** to chop into small pieces. **6.** to mess up. [C17: < OF *hacher* to chop up, < *hache* HATCHET]

hash[2] (hæʃ) *n. Sl.* short for **hashish.**

hashish (ˈhæʃiːʃ, -ɪʃ) *or* **hasheesh** *n.* a resinous extract of the dried flower tops of the female hemp plant, used as a hallucinogenic. See also **cannabis.** [C16: < Ar. *hashīsh* hemp]

haslet (ˈhæzlɪt) *or* **harslet** *n.* a loaf of cooked minced pig's offal, eaten cold. [C14: < OF *hastelet* piece of spit-roasted meat, < *haste* spit, of Gmc origin]

hasn't (ˈhæzᵊnt) *contraction of* has not.

hasp (hɑːsp) *n.* **1.** a metal fastening consisting of a hinged strap with a slot that fits over a staple and is secured by a pin, bolt, or padlock. ~*vb.* **2.** (*tr.*) to secure (a door, window, etc.) with a hasp. [OE *hæpse*]

Hassid (ˈhæsɪd) *n.* a variant spelling of **Chassid.**

hassle (ˈhæsᵊl) *Inf.* ~*n.* **1.** a prolonged argument. **2.** a great deal of trouble. ~*vb.* **3.** (*intr.*) to quarrel or wrangle. **4.** (*tr.*) to cause annoyance or trouble to (someone); harass. [C20: <?]

hassock (ˈhæsək) *n.* **1.** a firm upholstered cushion used for kneeling on, esp. in church. **2.** a thick clump of grass. [OE *hassuc* matted grass]

hast (hæst) *vb. Arch. or dialect.* (used with the pronoun *thou*) a singular form of the present tense (indicative mood) of **have.**

hastate (ˈhæsteɪt) *adj.* (of a leaf) having a pointed tip and two outward-pointing lobes at the base. [C18: < L *hastātus,* < *hasta* spear]

haste (heɪst) *n.* **1.** speed, esp. in an action. **2.** the act of hurrying in a careless manner. **3.** a necessity for hurrying; urgency. **4. make haste.** to hurry; rush. ~*vb.* **5.** a poetic word for **hasten.** [C14: < OF *haste,* of Gmc origin]

hasten (ˈheɪsᵊn) *vb.* **1.** (*may take an infinitive*) to hurry or cause to hurry; rush. **2.** (*tr.*) to be anxious (to say something). —ˈ**hastener** *n.*

hasty (ˈheɪstɪ) *adj.* **-tier, -tiest. 1.** rapid; swift; quick. **2.** excessively or rashly quick. **3.** short-tempered. **4.** showing irritation or anger: *hasty words.* —ˈ**hastily** *adv.* —ˈ**hastiness** *n.*

hat (hæt) *n.* **1.** a head covering, esp. one with a brim and a shaped crown. **2.** *Inf.* a role or capacity. **3. I'll eat my hat.** *Inf.* I will be greatly surprised if (something that proves me wrong) happens. **4. keep (something) under one's hat.** to keep (something) secret. **5. pass** (*or* **send**) **the hat round.** to collect money, as for a cause. **6. take off one's hat to.** to admire or congratulate. **7. talk through one's hat. a.** to talk foolishly. **b.** to deceive or bluff. ~*vb.* **hatting, hatted. 8.** (*tr.*) to supply (a person, etc.) with a hat or put a hat on (someone). [OE *hætt*] —ˈ**hatless** *adj.*

hatband (ˈhætˌbænd) *n.* a band or ribbon around the base of the crown of a hat.

hatbox (ˈhætˌbɒks) *n.* a box or case for a hat.

hatch[1] (hætʃ) *vb.* **1.** to cause (the young of various animals, esp. birds) to emerge from the egg or (of young birds, etc.) to emerge from the egg. **2.** to cause (eggs) to break and release the fully developed young or (of eggs) to break and release the young animal within. **3.** (*tr.*) to contrive or devise (a scheme, plot, etc.). ~*n.* **4.** the act or process of hatching. **5.** a group of newly hatched animals. [C13: of Gmc origin]

hatch[2] (hætʃ) *n.* **1.** a covering for a hatchway. **2. a.** short for **hatchway. b.** a door in an aircraft or spacecraft. **3.** Also called: **serving hatch.** an opening in a wall separating a kitchen from a dining area. **4.** the lower half of a divided door. **5.** a sluice in a dam, dyke, or weir. **6. down the hatch.** *Sl.* (used as a toast) drink up! **7. under hatches. a.** below decks. **b.** out of sight. **c.** dead. [OE *hæcc*]

hatch[3] (hætʃ) *vb. Drawing, engraving, etc.* to mark (a figure, etc.) with fine parallel or crossed lines to indicate shading. [C15: < OF *hacher* to chop, < *hache* HATCHET] —ˈ**hatching** *n.*

hatchback (ˈhætʃˌbæk) *n.* **1.** a sloping rear end of a car having a single door that is lifted to open. **2.** a car having such a rear end.

hatchery (ˈhætʃərɪ) *n., pl.* **-eries.** a place where eggs are hatched under artificial conditions.

hatchet (ˈhætʃɪt) *n.* **1.** a short axe used for chopping wood, etc. **2.** a tomahawk. **3.** (*modifier*) of narrow dimensions and sharp features: *a hatchet face.* **4. bury the hatchet.** to cease hostilities and become reconciled. [C14: < OF *hachette*, < *hache* axe, of Gmc origin]

hatchet job *n. Inf.* a malicious or devastating verbal or written attack.

hatchet man *n. Inf.* **1.** a person carrying out unpleasant assignments for an employer or superior. **2.** a severe or malicious critic.

hatchment (ˈhætʃmənt) *n. Heraldry.* a diamond-shaped tablet displaying the coat of arms of a dead person. [C16: changed < earlier use of *achievement* in this sense]

hatchway (ˈhætʃˌweɪ) *n.* **1.** an opening in the deck of a vessel to provide access below. **2.** a similar opening in a wall, floor, ceiling, or roof.

hate (heɪt) *vb.* **1.** to dislike (something) intensely; detest. **2.** (*intr.*) to be unwilling (to be or do something). ~*n.* **3.** intense dislike. **4.** *Inf.* a person or thing that is hated (esp. in **pet hate**). [OE *hatian*] —ˈ**hateable** *or* ˈ**hatable** *adj.*

hateful (ˈheɪtfʊl) *adj.* **1.** causing or deserving hate; loathsome; detestable. **2.** *Arch.* full of hate. —ˈ**hatefully** *adv.* —ˈ**hatefulness** *n.*

hath (hæθ) *vb. Arch. or dialect.* (used with the pronouns *he, she,* or *it* or a singular noun) a form of the present tense (indicative mood) of **have.**

hatred (ˈheɪtrɪd) *n.* intense dislike; enmity.

hat stand *or esp. U.S.* **hat tree** *n.* a pole equipped with hooks for hanging up hats, etc.

hatter (ˈhætə) *n.* **1.** a person who makes and sells hats. **2. mad as a hatter.** eccentric.

hat trick *n.* **1.** *Cricket.* the achievement of a bowler in taking three wickets with three successive balls. **2.** any achievement of three successive points, victories, etc.

hauberk (ˈhɔːbɜːk) *n.* a long coat of mail, often sleeveless. [C13: < OF *hauberc*, of Gmc origin; cf. OHG *halsberc*, OE *healsbeorg*, < *heals* neck + *beorg* protection]

haughty (ˈhɔːtɪ) *adj.* **-tier, -tiest.** having or showing arrogance. [C16: < OF *haut* lofty, < L *altus* high] —ˈ**haughtily** *adv.* —ˈ**haughtiness** *n.*

haul (hɔːl) *vb.* **1.** to drag (something) with effort. **2.** (*tr.*) to transport, as in a lorry. **3.** *Naut.* to alter the course of (a vessel), esp. so as to sail closer to the wind. **4.** (*intr.*) *Naut.* (of the wind) to blow from a direction nearer the bow. ~*n.* **5.** the act of dragging with effort. **6.** (esp. of fish) the amount caught at a single time. **7.** something that is hauled. **8.** a distance of hauling or travelling. [C16: < OF *haler*, of Gmc origin] —ˈ**hauler** *n.*

haulage (ˈhɔːlɪdʒ) *n.* **1.** the act or labour of hauling. **2.** a rate or charge levied for the transportation of goods, esp. by rail.

haulier (ˈhɔːljə) *n.* **1.** *Brit.* a person or firm that transports goods by road. **2.** a mine worker who conveys coal from the workings to the foot of the shaft.

haulm *or* **halm** (hɔːm) *n.* **1.** the stalks of beans, peas, potatoes, grasses, etc., collectively. **2.** a single stem of such a plant. [OE *healm*]

haul up *vb.* (*adv.*) **1.** (*tr.*) *Inf.* to call to account or criticize. **2.** *Naut.* to sail (a vessel) closer to the wind.

haunch (hɔːntʃ) *n.* **1.** the human hip or fleshy hindquarter of an animal. **2.** the leg and loin of an animal, used for food. **3.** *Archit.* the part of an arch between the impost and apex. [C13: < OF *hanche*; rel. to Sp., It. *anca*, of Gmc origin]

haunt (hɔːnt) *vb.* **1.** to visit (a person or place) in the form of a ghost. **2.** (*tr.*) to recur to (the memory, thoughts, etc.): *he was haunted by the fear of insanity.* **3.** to visit (a place) frequently. **4.** to associate with (someone) frequently. ~*n.* **5.** (*often pl.*) a place visited frequently. **6.** a place to which animals habitually resort for food, drink, shelter, etc. [C13: < OF *hanter*, of Gmc origin]

haunted (ˈhɔːntɪd) *adj.* **1.** frequented or visited by ghosts. **2.** (*postpositive*) obsessed or worried.

haunting (ˈhɔːntɪŋ) *adj.* **1.** (of memories) poignant or persistent. **2.** poignantly sentimental; eerily evocative. —ˈ**hauntingly** *adv.*

Hausa (ˈhaʊsə) *n.* **1.** (*pl.* **-sas** *or* **-sa**) a member of a Negroid people of W Africa, living chiefly in N Nigeria. **2.** the language of this people, widely used as a trading language throughout W Africa.

hausfrau (ˈhaʊsˌfraʊ) *n.* a German housewife. [G, < *Haus* house + *Frau* woman, wife]

hautboy (ˈəʊbɔɪ) *n.* **1.** a strawberry with large fruit. **2.** an archaic word for **oboe.** [C16: < F *hautbois*, < *haut* high + *bois* wood, of Gmc origin]

haute couture *French.* (ot kutyr) *n.* high fashion. [lit.: high dressmaking]

haute cuisine *French.* (ot kwizin) *n.* high-class cooking. [lit.: high cookery]

haute école *French.* (ot ekɔl) *n.* the classical art of riding. [lit.: high school]

hauteur (əʊˈtɜː) *n.* pride; haughtiness. [C17: < F, < *haut* high; see HAUGHTY]

haut monde *French.* (o mɔ̃d) *n.* high society. [lit.: high world]

Havana cigar (həˈvænə) *n.* any of various cigars manufactured in Cuba, known esp. for their high quality. Also: **Havana.**

have (hæv) *vb.* **has, having, had.** (*mainly tr.*) **1.** to be in possession of; own: *he has two cars.* **2.** to possess as a quality or attribute: *he has dark hair.* **3.** to receive, take, or obtain: *she had a present; have a look.* **4.** to hold in the mind: *to have an idea.* **5.** to possess a knowledge of: *I have no German.* **6.** to experience: *to have a shock.* **7.** to suffer from: *to have a cold.* **8.** to gain control of or advantage over: *you have me on that point.* **9.** (*usually passive*) *Sl.* to cheat or outwit: *he was had by that dishonest salesman.* **10.** (foll. by *on*) to exhibit (mercy, etc., towards). **11.** to take part in: *to have a conversation.* **12.** to arrange or hold: *to have a party.* **13.** to cause, compel, or require to (be, do, or be done): *have my shoes mended.* **14.** (takes an infinitive with *to*) used as an auxiliary to express compulsion or necessity: *I had to run quickly to escape him.* **15.** to eat, drink, or partake of. **16.** *Taboo sl.* to have sexual intercourse with. **17.** (*used with a negative*) to tolerate or allow: *I won't have all this noise.* **18.** to state or assert: *rumour has it that they will marry.* **19.** to place: *I'll have the sofa in this room.* **20.** to receive as a guest: *to have people to stay.* **21.** to be pregnant with or bear (offspring). **22.** (*takes a past participle*) used as an auxiliary to form compound tenses expressing completed action: *I have gone; I had gone.* **23. had rather** *or* **sooner.** to consider preferable that: *I had rather you left at once.* **24. have had it.** *Inf.* **a.** to be exhausted, defeated, or killed. **b.** to have lost one's last chance. **c.** to become unfashionable. **25. have it away** (*or* **off**). *Taboo, Brit. sl.* to have sexual intercourse. **26. have it so good.** to have so many material benefits. **27. have to do with. a.** to have dealings with. **b.** to be of relevance to. **28. let (someone) have it.** *Sl.* to launch an attack on (someone). ~*n.* **29.** (*usually pl.*) *Inf.* a person or group in possession of wealth, security, etc.: *the haves and the have-nots.* ~See also **have at, have on,** etc. [OE *habban*]

have at *vb.* (*intr., prep.*) *Arch.* to make an opening attack on, esp. in fencing.

havelock (ˈhævlɒk) *n.* a light-coloured cover for a service cap with a flap extending over the back of the neck to protect the head and neck from the sun. [C19: after Sir H. *Havelock* (1795–1857), E general in India]

haven (ˈheɪvᵊn) *n.* **1.** a harbour or other sheltered place for shipping. **2.** a place of safety; shelter. ~*vb.* **3.** (*tr.*) to shelter as in a haven. [OE *hæfen,* < ON *hǒfn*]

have-not *n.* (*usually pl.*) a person or group in possession of relatively little material wealth.

haven't (ˈhævᵊnt) *contraction of* have not.

have on *vb.* (*tr.*) **1.** (*usually adv.*) to wear. **2.** (*usually adv.*) to have a commitment: *what does your boss have on this afternoon*? **3.** (*adv.*) *Inf.* to trick or tease (a person). **4.** (*prep.*) to have available (information, esp. when incriminating) about (a person).

have out *vb.* (*tr., adv.*) **1.** to settle (a matter) or come to (a final decision), esp. by fighting or by frank discussion (often in **have it out**). **2.** to have extracted or removed.

haver (ˈheɪvə) *vb.* (*intr.*) **1.** *Scot. & N English dialect.* to babble; talk nonsense. **2.** to dither. ~*n.* **3.** (*usually pl.*) *Scot.* nonsense. [C18: <?]

haversack (ˈhævəˌsæk) *n.* a canvas bag for provisions or equipment, carried on the back or shoulder. [C18: < F *havresac,* < G *Habersack* oat bag, < OHG *habaro* oats + *Sack* SACK[1]]

haversine (ˈhævəˌsaɪn) *n.* half the value of the versed sine. [C19: combination of *half* + *versed* + *sine*[1]]

have up *vb.* (*tr., adv.; usually passive*) to cause to appear for trial: *he was had up for breaking and entering.*

havildar (ˈhævɪlˌdɑː) *n.* a noncommissioned officer in the Indian army, equivalent in rank to sergeant. [C17: < Hindi, < Persian *hawāldār* one in charge]

havoc (ˈhævək) *n.* **1.** destruction; devastation; ruin. **2.** *Inf.* confusion; chaos. **3. cry havoc.** *Arch.* to give the signal for pillage and destruction. **4. play havoc.** (often foll. by *with*) to cause a great deal of damage, distress, or confusion (to). [C15: < OF *havot* pillage, prob. of Gmc origin]

haw[1] (hɔː) *n.* **1.** the fruit of the hawthorn. **2.** another name for **hawthorn.** [OE *haga,* identical with *haga* hedge]

haw[2] (hɔː) *n., interj.* **1.** an inarticulate utterance, as of hesitation, embarrassment, etc.; hem. ~*vb.* **2.** (*intr.*) to make this sound. [C17: imit.]

haw[3] (hɔː) *n.* the nictitating membrane of a horse or other domestic animal. [C15: <?]

Hawaiian (həˈwaɪən) *adj.* **1.** of or relating to Hawaii, its people, or their language. ~*n.* **2.** a native or inhabitant of Hawaii. **3.** a language of Hawaii belonging to the Malayo-Polynesian family.

hawfinch (ˈhɔːˌfɪntʃ) *n.* an uncommon European finch having a very stout bill.

hawk[1] (hɔːk) *n.* **1.** any of various diurnal birds of prey of the family Accipitridae, typically having short rounded wings and a long tail. **2.** a person who advocates or supports war or warlike policies. **3.** a ruthless or rapacious person. ~*vb.* **4.** (*intr.*) to hunt with falcons, hawks, etc. **5.** (*intr.*) (of falcons or hawks) to fly in quest of prey. **6.** to pursue or attack on the wing, as a hawk. [OE *hafoc*] —ˈ**hawking** *n.* —ˈ**hawkish** *adj.* —ˈ**hawkˌlike** *adj.*

hawk[2] (hɔːk) *vb.* **1.** to offer (goods) for sale, as in the street. **2.** (*tr.;* often foll. by *about*) to spread (news, gossip, etc.). [C16: back formation < HAWKER[1]]

hawk[3] (hɔːk) *vb.* **1.** (*intr.*) to clear the throat noisily. **2.** (*tr.*) to force (phlegm, etc.) up from the throat. [C16: imit.]

hawk[4] (hɔːk) *n.* a small square board with a handle underneath, for carrying wet mortar. Also called: **mortarboard.** [<?]

hawker[1] (ˈhɔːkə) *n.* a person who travels from place to place selling goods. [C16: prob. < MLow G *hōker,* < *hōken* to peddle; see HUCKSTER]

hawker[2] (ˈhɔːkə) *n.* a person who hunts with hawks, falcons, etc. [OE *hafecere*]

hawk-eyed *adj.* **1.** having extremely keen sight. **2.** vigilant, watchful, or observant.

hawk moth *n.* any of various moths having long narrow wings and powerful flight, with the ability to hover over flowers when feeding from the nectar.

hawksbill turtle *or* **hawksbill** (ˈhɔːksˌbɪl) *n.* a small tropical turtle with a hooked beaklike mouth: a source of tortoiseshell.

hawkweed (ˈhɔːkˌwiːd) *n.* a hairy plant with clusters of dandelion-like flowers.

hawse (hɔːz) *n. Naut.* **1.** the part of the bows of a vessel where the hawseholes are. **2.** short for **hawsehole** or **hawsepipe.** **3.** the distance from the bow of an anchored vessel to the anchor. **4.** the arrangement of port and starboard anchor ropes when a vessel is riding on both anchors. [C14: < earlier *halse,* prob. < ON *háls* neck, ship's bow]

hawsehole (ˈhɔːzˌhəʊl) *n. Naut.* one of the holes in the upper part of the bows of a vessel through which the anchor ropes pass.

hawsepipe (ˈhɔːzˌpaɪp) *n. Naut.* a strong metal pipe through which an anchor rope passes.

hawser (ˈhɔːzə) *n. Naut.* a large heavy rope. [C14: < Anglo-F *hauceour,* < OF *haucier* to hoist, ult. < L *altus* high]

hawthorn (ˈhɔːˌθɔːn) *n.* any of various thorny trees or shrubs of a N temperate genus, having white or pink flowers and reddish fruits (haws). Also called (in Britain): **may, may tree, mayflower.** [OE *haguthorn,* < *haga* hedge + *thorn* thorn]

hay (heɪ) *n.* **1. a.** grass, clover, etc., cut and dried as fodder. **b.** (*in combination*): *a hayfield.* **2. hit the hay.** *Sl.* to go to bed. **3. make hay of.** to throw into confusion. **4. make hay while the sun shines.** to take full advantage of an opportunity. **5. roll in the hay.** *Inf.* sexual intercourse or heavy petting. ~*vb.* **6.** to cut, dry, and store (grass, etc.) as fodder. [OE *hieg*]

haybox (ˈheɪˌbɒks) *n.* an airtight box full of hay used for cooking preheated food by retained heat.

haycock (ˈheɪˌkɒk) *n.* a small cone-shaped pile of hay left in the field until dry.

hay fever *n.* an allergic reaction to pollen, dust, etc., characterized by sneezing, runny nose, and watery eyes due to inflammation of the mucous membranes of the eyes and nose.

haymaker (ˈheɪˌmeɪkə) *n.* **1.** a person who helps to cut, turn, or carry hay. **2.** either of two machines, one designed to crush stems of hay, the other to break and bend them, in order to cause more rapid and even drying. **3.** *Boxing sl.* a wild swinging punch. —ˈ**hayˌmaking** *adj., n.*

haymow (ˈheɪˌmaʊ) *n.* **1.** a part of a barn where hay is stored. **2.** a quantity of hay stored.
hayseed (ˈheɪˌsiːd) *n.* **1.** seeds or fragments of grass or straw. **2.** *U.S. & Canad. inf., derog.* a yokel.
haystack (ˈheɪˌstæk) *or* **hayrick** *n.* a large pile of hay, esp. one built in the open air and covered with thatch.
haywire (ˈheɪˌwaɪə) *adj.* (*postpositive*) *Inf.* **1.** (of things) not functioning properly. **2.** (of people) erratic or crazy. [C20: < the disorderly tangle of wire removed from bales of hay]
hazard (ˈhæzəd) *n.* **1.** exposure or vulnerability to injury, loss, etc. **2. at hazard.** at risk; in danger. **3.** a thing likely to cause injury, etc. **4.** *Golf.* an obstacle such as a bunker, a sand pit, etc. **5.** chance; accident. **6.** a gambling game played with two dice. **7.** *Real Tennis.* **a.** the receiver's side of the court. **b.** one of the winning openings. **8.** *Billiards.* a scoring stroke made either when a ball other than the striker's is pocketed (**winning hazard**) or the striker's cue ball itself (**losing hazard**). ~*vb.* (*tr.*) **9.** to risk. **10.** to venture (an opinion, guess, etc.). **11.** to expose to danger. [C13: < OF *hasard,* < Ar. *az-zahr* the die]
hazardous (ˈhæzədəs) *adj.* **1.** involving great risk. **2.** depending on chance. —ˈ**hazardously** *adv.* —ˈ**hazardousness** *n.*
hazard warning device *n.* a mechanism in a motor vehicle which enables both indicators to flash simultaneously: used as a warning signal, as after an accident or breakdown.
haze[1] (heɪz) *n.* **1.** *Meteorol.* reduced visibility in the air as a result of condensed water vapour, dust, etc., in the atmosphere. **2.** obscurity of perception, feeling, etc. ~*vb.* **3.** (when *intr.,* often foll. by *over*) to make or become hazy. [C18: back formation < HAZY]
haze[2] (heɪz) *vb.* (*tr.*) **1.** *Chiefly U.S. & Canad.* to subject (fellow students) to ridicule or abuse. **2.** *Naut.* to harass with humiliating tasks. [C17: <?]
hazel (ˈheɪzᵊl) *n.* **1.** Also called: **cob.** any of several shrubs of a N temperate genus, having edible rounded nuts. **2.** the wood of any of these trees. **3.** short for **hazelnut. 4. a.** a light yellowish-brown colour. **b.** (*as adj.*): *hazel eyes.* [OE *hæsel*]
hazelhen (ˈheɪzᵊlˌhɛn) *n.* a European woodland gallinaceous bird with a speckled brown plumage and slightly crested crown.
hazelnut (ˈheɪzᵊlˌnʌt) *n.* the nut of a hazel shrub, having a smooth shiny hard shell. Also called: **filbert,** (Brit.) **cobnut, cob.**
hazy (ˈheɪzɪ) *adj.* **-zier, -ziest.** misty; indistinct; vague. [C17: <?] —ˈ**hazily** *adv.* —ˈ**haziness** *n.*
Hb *symbol for* haemoglobin.
HB (on Brit. pencils) *symbol for* hard-black: denoting a medium-hard lead.
HBC *abbrev. for* Hudson's Bay Company.
HBM (in Britain) *abbrev. for* His (*or* Her) Britannic Majesty.
H-bomb *n.* short for **hydrogen bomb.**
HC *abbrev. for:* **1.** Holy Communion. **2.** (in Britain) House of Commons.
HCF *or* **hcf** *abbrev. for* highest common factor.
hcp *abbrev. for* handicap.
HD *abbrev. for* heavy duty.
hdqrs *abbrev. for* headquarters.
he (hiː; *unstressed* iː) *pron.* (*subjective*) **1.** refers to a male person or animal. **2.** refers to an indefinite antecedent such as *whoever* or *anybody: everybody can do as he likes.* **3.** refers to a person or animal of unknown or unspecified sex: *a member may vote as he sees fit.* ~*n.* **4. a.** a male person or animal. **b.** (*in combination*): *he-goat.* **5.** (in children's play) another name for **tag**[2] (sense 1), **it** (sense 7). [OE *hē*]
He *the chemical symbol for* helium.
HE *abbrev. for:* **1.** high explosive. **2.** His Eminence. **3.** His (*or* Her) Excellency.
head (hɛd) *n.* **1.** the upper or front part of the body in vertebrates, including man, that contains and protects the brain, eyes, mouth, nose, and ears. Related adj.: **cephalic. 2.** the corresponding part of an invertebrate animal. **3.** something resembling a head in form or function, such as the top of a tool. **4. a.** the person commanding most authority within a group, organization, etc. **b.** (*as modifier*): *head buyer.* **c.** (*in combination*): *headmaster.* **5.** the position of leadership or command. **6.** the most forward part of a thing; front: *the head of a queue.* **7.** the highest part of a thing; upper end: *the head of the pass.* **8.** the froth on the top of a glass of beer. **9.** aptitude, intelligence, and emotions (esp. in **over one's head, lose one's head,** etc.): *she has a good head for figures.* **10.** (*pl.* **head**) a person or animal considered as a unit: *the show was two pounds per head; six hundred head of cattle.* **11.** the head considered as a measure: *he's a head taller than his mother.* **12.** *Bot.* **a.** a dense inflorescence such as that of the daisy. **b.** any other compact terminal part of a plant, such as the leaves of a cabbage. **13.** a culmination or crisis (esp. in **bring** or **come to a head**). **14.** the pus-filled tip or central part of a pimple, boil, etc. **15.** the source of a river or stream. **16.** (*cap. when part of a name*) a headland or promontory. **17.** the obverse of a coin, usually bearing a portrait of the head of a monarch, etc. **18.** a main point of an argument, discourse, etc. **19.** (*often pl.*) a headline or heading. **20.** (*often pl.*) *Naut.* a lavatory. **21.** the taut membrane of a drum, tambourine, etc. **22. a.** the height of the surface of liquid above a specific point, esp. as a measure of the pressure at that point: *a head of four feet.* **b.** pressure of water, caused by height or velocity, measured in terms of a vertical column of water. **c.** any pressure: *a head of steam in the boiler.* **23.** *Sl.* **a.** a person who regularly takes drugs, esp. LSD or cannabis. **b.** (*in combination*): *an acidhead.* **24.** *Mining.* a road driven into the coalface. **25. a.** the terminal point of a route. **b.** (*in combination*): *railhead.* **26.** a device on a turning or boring machine equipped with one or more cutting tools held to the work by this device. **27. cylinder head.** See **cylinder** (sense 4). **28.** an electromagnet that can read, write, or erase information on a magnetic medium, used in computers, tape recorders, etc. **29.** *Inf.* short for **headmaster** *or* **headmistress. 30.** a narrow margin of victory (esp. in **(win) by a head**). **31.** *Inf.* short for **headache. 32. bite** *or* **snap someone's head off.** to speak sharply to someone. **33. give someone** (*or* **something**) **his** (*or* **its**) **head. a.** to allow a person greater freedom or responsibility. **b.** to allow a horse to gallop by lengthening the reins. **34. go to one's head. a.** to make one dizzy or confused, as might an alcoholic drink. **b.** to make one conceited: *his success has gone to his head.* **35. head and shoulders above.** greatly superior to. **36. head over heels. a.** turning a complete somersault. **b.** completely; utterly (esp. in **head over heels in love**). **37. hold up one's head.** to be unashamed. **38. keep one's head.** to remain calm. **39. keep one's head above water.** to manage to survive difficulties, esp. financial ones. **40. make head or tail of.** (*used with a negative*) to attempt to understand (a problem, etc.). **41. off** (*or* **out of**) **one's head.** *Sl.* insane or delirious. **42. on one's (own) head.** at a one's (own) risk or responsibility. **43. over someone's head. a.** without a person in the obvious position being considered: *the graduate was promoted over the heads of several of his seniors.* **b.** without consulting a person in the obvious position but referring to a higher authority: *he went straight to the director, over the head of his immediate boss.* **c.** beyond a person's comprehension. **44. put (our, their,** etc.) **heads together.** *Inf.* to consult together. **45. take it into one's head.** to conceive a notion (to do something). **46. turn someone's head.** to make someone vain, conceited, etc. ~*vb.* **47.** (*tr.*) to be at the front or top of: *to head the field.* **48.** (*tr.;* often foll. by *up*) to be in the commanding or most important position. **49.** (often foll. by *for*) to go or cause to go (towards): *where are you heading?* **50.** to turn or steer (a vessel) as specified: *to head into the wind.* **51.** *Soccer.* to propel (the ball) by striking it with the head. **52.** (*tr.*) to provide with or be a head or heading for. **53.** (*tr.*) to cut the top

branches or shoots off a tree or plant. **54.** (*intr.*) to form a head, as a plant. **55.** (*intr.; often foll. by in*) (of streams, rivers, etc.) to originate or rise. ~See also **head off, heads.** [OE *hēafod*] —ˈ**headless** *adj.* —ˈ**head**ˌ**like** *adj.*

headache (ˈhɛdˌeɪk) *n.* **1.** a continuous pain in the head. **2.** *Inf.* any cause of worry, difficulty, or annoyance. —ˈ**head**ˌ**achy** *adj.*

headband (ˈhɛdˌbænd) *n.* **1.** a ribbon or band worn around the head. **2.** a narrow cloth band attached to the top of the spine of a book for protection or decoration.

head-banger *n. Sl.* **1.** a person, esp. a teenager, who shakes his head violently to the beat of loud music. **2.** a crazy or stupid person.

headboard (ˈhɛdˌbɔːd) *n.* a vertical board or terminal at the head of a bed.

headdress (ˈhɛdˌdrɛs) *n.* any head covering, esp. an ornate one or one denoting a rank.

headed (ˈhɛdɪd) *adj.* **1. a.** having a head or heads. **b.** (*in combination*): *two-headed; bullet-headed.* **2.** having a heading: *headed notepaper.*

header (ˈhɛdə) *n.* **1.** a machine that trims the heads from castings, forgings, etc., or one that forms heads, as in wire, to make nails. **2.** a person who operates such a machine. **3.** Also called: **header tank.** a reservoir that maintains a gravity feed or a static fluid pressure in an apparatus. **4.** a brick or stone laid across a wall so that its end is flush with the outer surface. **5.** the action of striking a ball with the head. **6.** *Inf.* a headlong fall or dive.

headfirst (ˈhɛdˈfɜːst) *adj., adv.* **1.** with the head foremost; headlong. ~*adv.* **2.** rashly.

headgear (ˈhɛdˌgɪə) *n.* **1.** a hat. **2.** any part of a horse's harness that is worn on the head. **3.** the hoisting mechanism at the pithead of a mine.

headguard (ˈhɛdˌgɑːd) *n.* a lightweight helmet-like piece of equipment worn to protect the head in various sports.

head-hunting *n.* **1.** the practice among certain peoples of removing the heads of slain enemies and preserving them as trophies. **2.** *U.S. sl.* the destruction or neutralization of political opponents. **3.** (of a company or corporation) the recruitment of, or a drive to recruit, new high-level personnel, esp. in management or in specialist fields. —ˈ**head-**ˌ**hunter** *n.*

heading (ˈhɛdɪŋ) *n.* **1.** a title for a page, chapter, etc. **2.** a main division, as of a speech. **3.** *Mining.* **a.** a horizontal tunnel. **b.** the end of such a tunnel. **4.** the angle between the direction of an aircraft and a specified meridian, often due north. **5.** the compass direction parallel to the keel of a vessel. **6.** the act of heading.

headland *n.* **1.** (ˈhɛdlənd). a narrow area of land jutting out into a sea, lake, etc. **2.** (ˈhɛdˌlænd). a strip of land along the edge of an arable field left unploughed to allow space for machines.

headlight (ˈhɛdˌlaɪt) *or* **headlamp** *n.* a powerful light, equipped with a reflector and attached to the front of a motor vehicle, etc.

headline (ˈhɛdˌlaɪn) *n.* **1. a.** a phrase at the top of a newspaper or magazine article indicating the subject of the article, usually in larger and heavier type. **b.** a line at the top of a page indicating the title, page number, etc. **2. hit the headlines.** to become prominent in the news. **3.** (*usually pl.*) the main points of a television or radio news broadcast, read out before the full broadcast.

headlong (ˈhɛdˌlɒŋ) *adv., adj.* **1.** with the head foremost; headfirst. **2.** with great haste. ~*adj.* **3.** *Arch.* (of slopes, etc.) very steep; precipitous.

headman (ˈhɛdmən) *n., pl.* **-men.** **1.** *Anthropol.* a chief or leader. **2.** a foreman or overseer.

headmaster (ˌhɛdˈmɑːstə) *or* (*fem.*) **headmistress** *n.* the principal of a school.

headmost (ˈhɛdˌməʊst) *adj.* foremost.

head off *vb.* (*tr., adv.*) **1.** to intercept and force to change direction: *to head off the stampede.* **2.** to prevent or forestall.

head-on *adv., adj.* **1.** front foremost: *a head-on collision.* **2.** with directness or without compromise: *in his usual head-on fashion.*

headphones (ˈhɛdˌfəʊnz) *pl. n.* an electrical device consisting of two earphones held in position by a flexible metallic strap passing over the head. Informal name: **cans.**

headpiece (ˈhɛdˌpiːs) *n.* **1.** *Printing.* a decorative band at the top of a page, chapter, etc. **2.** a helmet. **3.** *Arch.* the intellect.

headpin (ˈhɛdˌpɪn) *n. Tenpin bowling.* another word for **kingpin** (sense 2).

headquarters (ˌhɛdˈkwɔːtəz) *pl. n.* (*sometimes functioning as sing.*) **1.** any centre from which operations are directed, as in the police. **2.** a military formation comprising the commander and his staff. ~Abbrev.: **HQ, h.q.**

headrace (ˈhɛdˌreɪs) *n.* a channel that carries water to a water wheel, turbine, etc.

headrest (ˈhɛdˌrɛst) *n.* a support for the head, as on a dentist's chair or car seat.

head restraint *n.* an adjustable support for the head, attached to a car seat, to prevent the neck from being jolted backwards sharply in the event of a crash or sudden stop.

headroom (ˈhɛdˌrʊm, -ˌruːm) *or* **headway** *n.* the height of a bridge, room, etc.; clearance.

heads (hɛdz) *interj., adv.* with the obverse side of a coin uppermost, esp. if it has a head on it: used as a call before tossing a coin.

headscarf (ˈhɛdˌskɑːf) *n., pl.* **-scarves.** a scarf for the head, often worn tied under the chin.

headset (ˈhɛdˌsɛt) *n.* a pair of headphones, esp. with a microphone attached.

headship (ˈhɛdʃɪp) *n.* **1.** the position or state of being a leader; command. **2.** *Brit.* the position of headmaster or headmistress of a school.

headshrinker (ˈhɛdˌʃrɪŋkə) *n.* **1.** a slang name for **psychiatrist.** Often shortened to **shrink.** **2.** a head-hunter who shrinks the heads of his victims.

headsman (ˈhɛdzmən) *n., pl.* **-men.** (formerly) an executioner who beheaded condemned persons.

headstall (ˈhɛdˌstɔːl) *n.* the part of a bridle that fits round a horse's head.

head start *n.* an initial advantage in a competitive situation.

headstock (ˈhɛdˌstɒk) *n.* the part of a machine that supports and transmits the drive.

headstone (ˈhɛdˌstəʊn) *n.* **1.** a memorial stone at the head of a grave. **2.** *Archit.* another name for **keystone.**

headstream (ˈhɛdˌstriːm) *n.* a stream that is the source or a source of a river.

headstrong (ˈhɛdˌstrɒŋ) *adj.* **1.** self-willed; obstinate. **2.** (of an action) heedless; rash.

head-up display *n.* a projection of readings from instruments onto a windscreen, enabling a pilot or driver to see them without moving his eyes.

head voice *or* **register** *n.* the high register of the human voice, in which the vibrations of sung notes are felt in the head.

headwaters (ˈhɛdˌwɔːtəz) *pl. n.* the tributary streams of a river in the area in which it rises.

headway (ˈhɛdˌweɪ) *n.* **1.** motion forward: *the vessel made no headway.* **2.** progress: *he made no headway with the problem.* **3.** another name for **headroom.** **4.** the interval between consecutive trains, buses, etc., on the same route.

headwind (ˈhɛdˌwɪnd) *n.* a wind blowing directly against the course of an aircraft or ship.

headword (ˈhɛdˌwɜːd) *n.* a key word placed at the beginning of a line, paragraph, etc., as in a dictionary entry.

headwork (ˈhɛdˌwɜːk) *n.* **1.** mental work. **2.** the ornamentation of the keystone of an arch.

heady (ˈhɛdɪ) *adj.* **headier, headiest.** **1.** (of alcoholic drink) intoxicating. **2.** strongly affecting the senses; extremely exciting. **3.** rash; impetuous. —ˈ**headily** *adv.* —ˈ**headiness** *n.*

heal (hiːl) *vb.* **1.** to restore or be restored to health. **2.** (*intr.; often foll. by over or up*) (of a wound) to repair by natural processes, as by scar formation. **3.** (*tr.*) to cure (a disease or disorder). **4.** to restore or be restored to friendly relations, harmony, etc. [OE *hælan;* see HALE[1], WHOLE] —ˈ**healer** *n.* —ˈ**healing** *n., adj.*

health (hɛlθ) *n.* **1.** the state of being bodily and mentally vigorous and free from disease. **2.** the general condition of body and mind: *in poor health.* **3.** the condition of any unit, society, etc.: *the economic health of a nation.* **4.** a toast to a person. **5.** (*modifier*) of or relating to food or other goods reputed to be beneficial to the health: *health food.* **6.** (*modifier*) of or relating to health: *health service.* [OE *hǣlth;* rel. to *hāl* HALE[1]]

health centre *n.* the surgery and offices of a group medical practice.

health food *n.* vegetarian food organically grown and with no additives, eaten for its benefit to health. **b.** (*as modifier*): *a health-food shop.*

healthful (ˈhɛlθfʊl) *adj.* a less common word for **healthy** (senses 1-3).

health salts *pl. n.* magnesium sulphate or similar salts taken as a mild laxative.

health visitor *n.* (in Britain) a nurse employed to visit esp. mothers of babies, the handicapped, or elderly people in their homes to give help and advice on health and social welfare.

healthy (ˈhɛlθɪ) *adj.* **healthier, healthiest. 1.** enjoying good health. **2.** sound: *the company's finances are not very healthy.* **3.** conducive to health. **4.** indicating soundness of body or mind: *a healthy appetite.* **5.** *Inf.* considerable: *a healthy sum.* —ˈ**healthily** *adv.* —ˈ**healthiness** *n.*

heap (hiːp) *n.* **1.** a collection of articles or mass of material gathered in a pile. **2.** (*often pl.;* usually foll. by *of*) *Inf.* a large number or quantity. **3.** *Inf.* a thing that is very old, unreliable, etc.: *the car was a heap.* ~*adv.* **4. heaps.** (intensifier): *he was heaps better.* ~*vb.* **5.** (often foll. by *up* or *together*) to collect or be collected into or as if into a pile. **6.** (*tr.;* often foll. by *with, on,* or *upon*) to load (with) abundantly: *to heap with riches.* [OE *héap*]

hear (hɪə) *vb.* **hearing, heard** (hɜːd). **1.** (*tr.*) to perceive (a sound) with the sense of hearing. **2.** (*tr.; may take a clause as object*) to listen to: *did you hear what I said?* **3.** (when *intr.*, sometimes foll. by *of* or *about;* when *tr., may take a clause as object*) to be informed (of); receive information (about). **4.** *Law.* to give a hearing to (a case). **5.** (when *intr.*, usually foll. by *of* and used with a negative) to listen (to) with favour, assent, etc.: *she wouldn't hear of it.* **6.** (*intr.;* foll. by *from*) to receive a letter (from). **7. hear! hear!** an exclamation of approval. **8. hear tell (of).** *Dialect.* to be told (about). [OE *hieran*] —ˈ**hearer** *n.*

hearing (ˈhɪərɪŋ) *n.* **1.** the sense by which sound is perceived. **2.** an opportunity to be listened to. **3.** the range within which sound can be heard; earshot. **4.** the investigation of a matter by a court of law, esp. the preliminary inquiry into an indictable crime by magistrates.

hearing aid *n.* a device for assisting the hearing of partially deaf persons, typically a small battery-powered amplifier worn in or behind the ear.

hearken *or U.S.* (*sometimes*) **harken** (ˈhɑːkən) *vb. Arch.* to listen to (something). [OE *heorcnian*]

hear out *vb.* (*tr., adv.*) to listen in regard to every detail and give a proper or full hearing to.

hearsay (ˈhɪəˌseɪ) *n.* gossip; rumour.

hearsay evidence *n. Law.* evidence based on what has been reported to a witness by others rather than what he has himself observed.

hearse (hɜːs) *n.* a vehicle, such as a car or carriage, used to carry a coffin to the grave. [C14: < OF *herce,* < L *hirpex* harrow]

heart (hɑːt) *n.* **1.** the hollow muscular organ in vertebrates whose contractions propel the blood through the circulatory system. Related adj.: **cardiac. 2.** the corresponding organ in invertebrates. **3.** this organ considered as the seat of emotions, esp. love. **4.** emotional mood: *a change of heart.* **5.** tenderness or pity: *you have no heart.* **6.** courage or spirit. **7.** the most central part: *the heart of the city.* **8.** the most important part: *the heart of the matter.* **9.** (of vegetables, such as cabbage) the inner compact part. **10.** the breast: *she held him to her heart.* **11.** a dearly loved person: *dearest heart.* **12.** a conventionalized representation of the heart, having two rounded lobes at the top meeting in a point at the bottom. **13. a.** a red heart-shaped symbol on a playing card. **b.** a card with one or more of these symbols or (*when pl.*) the suit of cards so marked. **14.** a fertile condition in land (esp. in **in good heart**). **15. after one's own heart.** appealing to one's own disposition or taste. **16. break one's** (*or* **someone's**) **heart.** to grieve (or cause to grieve) very deeply, esp. through love. **17. by heart.** by committing to memory. **18. eat one's heart out.** to brood or pine with grief or longing. **19. from (the bottom of) one's heart.** very sincerely or deeply. **20. have a change of heart.** to experience a profound change of outlook, attitude, etc. **21. have one's heart in one's mouth** (*or* **throat**). to be full of apprehension, excitement, or fear. **22. have one's heart in the right place.** to be kind, thoughtful, or generous. **23. have the heart.** (*usually used with a negative*) to have the necessary will, callousness, etc. (to do something): *I didn't have the heart to tell him.* **24. heart of hearts.** the depths of one's conscience or emotions. **25. heart of oak.** a brave person. **26. lose heart.** to become despondent or disillusioned (over something). **27. lose one's heart to.** to fall in love with. **28. set one's heart on.** to have as one's ambition to obtain; covet. **29. take heart.** to become encouraged. **30. take to heart.** to take seriously or be upset about. **31. wear one's heart on one's sleeve.** to show one's feelings openly. **32. with all one's heart.** very willingly. ~*vb.* (*intr.*) **33.** (of vegetables) to form a heart. ~See also **hearts.** [OE *heorte*]

heartache (ˈhɑːtˌeɪk) *n.* intense anguish or mental suffering.

heart attack *n.* any sudden severe instance of abnormal heart functioning, esp. coronary thrombosis.

heartbeat (ˈhɑːtˌbiːt) *n.* one complete pulsation of the heart.

heart block *n.* impaired conduction of the impulse that regulates the heartbeat, resulting in a lack of coordination between the beating of the atria and the ventricles.

heartbreak (ˈhɑːtˌbreɪk) *n.* intense and overwhelming grief, esp. through disappointment in love. —ˈ**heartˌbreaker** *n.* —ˈ**heartˌbreaking** *adj.*

heartburn (ˈhɑːtˌbɜːn) *n.* a burning sensation beneath the breastbone caused by irritation of the oesophagus. Technical names: **cardialgia, pyrosis.**

-hearted *adj.* having a heart or disposition as specified: *cold-hearted; heavy-hearted.*

hearten (ˈhɑːtᵊn) *vb.* to make or become cheerful. —ˈ**heartening** *adj.*

heart failure *n.* **1.** a condition in which the heart is unable to pump an adequate amount of blood to the tissues. **2.** sudden cessation of the heartbeat, resulting in death.

heartfelt (ˈhɑːtˌfɛlt) *adj.* sincerely and strongly felt.

hearth (hɑːθ) *n.* **1. a.** the floor of a fireplace, esp. one that extends outwards into the room. **b.** (*as modifier*): *hearth rug.* **2.** this as a symbol of the home, etc. **3.** the bottom part of a metallurgical furnace in which the molten metal is produced or contained. [OE *heorth*]

hearthstone (ˈhɑːθˌstəʊn) *n.* **1.** a stone that forms a hearth. **2.** soft stone used (esp. formerly) to clean and whiten floors, steps, etc.

heartily (ˈhɑːtɪlɪ) *adv.* **1.** thoroughly or vigorously. **2.** in a sincere manner.

heartland (ˈhɑːtˌlænd) *n.* the central or most important region of a country or continent.

heartless (ˈhɑːtlɪs) *adj.* unkind or cruel. —ˈ**heartlessly** *adv.* —ˈ**heartlessness** *n.*

heart-lung machine *n.* a machine used to maintain the circulation and oxygenation of the blood during heart surgery.

heart-rending *adj.* causing great mental pain and sorrow. —ˈ**heart-ˌrendingly** *adv.*

hearts (hɑːts) *n.* (*functioning as sing.*) a card game in which players must avoid winning tricks containing hearts or the queen of spades. Also called: **Black Maria.**

heart-searching *n.* examination of one's feelings or conscience.

heartsease *or* **heart's-ease** (ˈhɑːtsˌiːz) *n.* **1.** another name for the **wild pansy.** **2.** peace of mind.

heartsick (ˈhɑːtˌsɪk) *adj.* deeply despondent. —ˈ**heartˌsickness** *n.*

heartstrings (ˈhɑːtˌstrɪŋz) *pl. n. Often facetious.* deep emotions. [C15: orig. referring to the tendons supposed to support the heart]

heart-throb *n.* **1.** *Brit.* an object of infatuation. **2.** a heartbeat.

heart-to-heart *adj.* **1.** (esp. of a conversation) concerned with personal problems or intimate feelings. ~*n.* **2.** an intimate conversation.

heart-warming *adj.* **1.** pleasing; gratifying. **2.** emotionally moving.

heartwood (ˈhɑːtˌwʊd) *n.* the central core of dark hard wood in tree trunks, consisting of nonfunctioning xylem tissue that has become blocked with resins, tannins, and oils.

hearty (ˈhɑːtɪ) *adj.* **heartier, heartiest.** **1.** warm and unreserved in manner. **2.** vigorous and heartfelt: *hearty dislike.* **3.** healthy and strong (esp. in **hale and hearty**). **4.** substantial and nourishing. ~*n., pl.* **hearties.** *Inf.* **5.** a comrade, esp. a sailor. **6.** a vigorous sporting man: *a rugby hearty.* —ˈ**heartily** *adv.* —ˈ**heartiness** *n.*

heat (hiːt) *n.* **1.** the energy transferred as a result of a difference in temperature. Related adjs.: **thermal, calorific.** **2.** the sensation caused by heat energy; warmth. **3.** the state of being hot. **4.** hot weather: *the heat of summer.* **5.** intensity of feeling: *the heat of rage.* **6.** the most intense part: *the heat of the battle.* **7.** a period of sexual excitement in female mammals that occurs at oestrus. **8.** *Sport.* **a.** a preliminary eliminating contest in a competition. **b.** a single section of a contest. **9.** *Sl.* police activity after a crime: *the heat is off.* **10.** *Sl., chiefly U.S.* criticism or abuse: *he took a lot of heat for that mistake.* **11. in** *or* **on heat. a.** Also: **in season.** of some female mammals) sexually receptive. **b.** in a state of sexual excitement. **12. in the heat of the moment.** without pausing to think. ~*vb.* **13.** to make or become hot or warm. **14.** to make or become excited or intense. [OE *hǣtu*]

heat barrier *n.* another name for **thermal barrier.**

heat capacity *n.* the heat required to raise the temperature of a substance by unit temperature interval under specified conditions.

heat death *n. Thermodynamics.* the condition of any closed system when its total entropy is a maximum and it has no available energy. If the universe is a closed system it should eventually reach this state.

heated (ˈhiːtɪd) *adj.* **1.** made hot. **2.** impassioned or highly emotional. —ˈ**heatedly** *adv.*

heat engine *n.* an engine that does work when heat is supplied to it.

heater (ˈhiːtə) *n.* **1.** any device for supplying heat, such as a convector. **2.** *U.S. sl.* a pistol. **3.** *Electronics.* a conductor carrying a current that indirectly heats the cathode in some types of valve.

heat exchanger *n.* a device for transferring heat from one fluid to another without allowing them to mix.

heat exhaustion *n.* a condition resulting from exposure to intense heat, characterized by dizziness, abdominal cramp, and prostration.

heath (hiːθ) *n.* **1.** *Brit.* a large open area, usually with sandy soil and scrubby vegetation, esp. heather. **2.** Also called: **heather.** a low-growing evergreen shrub having small bell-shaped typically pink or purple flowers. **3.** any of several heathlike plants, such as sea heath. [OE *hǣth*] —ˈ**heathˌlike** *adj.* —ˈ**heathy** *adj.*

heathen (ˈhiːðən) *n., pl.* **-thens** *or* **-then.** **1.** a person who does not acknowledge the God of Christianity, Judaism, or Islam; pagan. **2.** an uncivilized or barbaric person. ~*adj.* **3.** irreligious; pagan. **4.** uncivilized; barbaric. **5.** of or relating to heathen peoples or their customs and beliefs. [OE *hǣthen*] —ˈ**heathendom** *n.* —ˈ**heathenism** *or* ˈ**heathenry** *n.*

heathenize *or* **-nise** (ˈhiːðəˌnaɪz) *vb.* to render or become heathen.

heather (ˈhɛðə) *n.* **1.** Also called: **ling, heath.** a low-growing evergreen Eurasian shrub that grows in dense masses on open ground and has clusters of small bell-shaped typically pinkish-purple flowers. **2.** a purplish-red to pinkish-purple colour. ~*adj.* **3.** of a heather colour. **4.** of or relating to interwoven yarns of mixed colours: *heather mixture.* [C14: orig. Scot. & N English, prob. < HEATH] —ˈ**heathery** *adj.*

Heath Robinson (hiːθ ˈrɒbɪnsᵊn) *adj.* (of a mechanical device) absurdly complicated in design and having a simple function. [C20: after William *Heath Robinson* (1872–1944), E cartoonist who drew such contrivances]

heating (ˈhiːtɪŋ) *n.* **1.** a device or system for supplying heat, esp. central heating, to a building. **2.** the heat supplied.

heat pump *n.* a device for extracting heat from a source and delivering it elsewhere at a much higher temperature.

heat rash *n.* a nontechnical name for **miliaria.**

heat shield *n.* a coating or barrier for shielding from excessive heat, such as that experienced by a spacecraft on re-entry into the earth's atmosphere.

heat sink *n.* **1.** a metal plate designed to conduct and radiate heat from an electrical component. **2.** a layer within the outer skin of high-speed aircraft to absorb heat.

heatstroke (ˈhiːtˌstrəʊk) *n.* a condition resulting from prolonged exposure to intense heat, characterized by high fever.

heat-treat *vb.* (*tr.*) to apply heat to (a metal or alloy) in one or more temperature cycles to give it desirable properties. —**heat treatment** *n.*

heat wave *n.* **1.** a continuous spell of abnormally hot weather. **2.** an extensive slow-moving air mass at a relatively high temperature.

heave (hiːv) *vb.* **heaving, heaved** *or* **hove.** **1.** (*tr.*) to lift or move with a great effort. **2.** (*tr.*) to throw (something heavy) with effort. **3.** to utter (sounds) noisily or unhappily: *to heave a sigh.* **4.** to rise and fall or cause to rise and fall heavily. **5.** (*p.t. & p.p.* **hove**) *Naut.* **a.** to move or cause to move in a specified direction: *to heave in sight.* **b.** (*intr.*) (of a vessel) to pitch or roll. **6.** (*tr.*) to displace (rock strata, etc.) in a horizontal direction. **7.** (*intr.*) to retch. ~*n.* **8.** the act of heaving. **9.** a horizontal displacement of rock strata at a fault. ~See also **heave to, heaves.** [OE *hebban*] —ˈ**heaver** *n.*

heave-ho *interj.* a sailors' cry, as when hoisting anchor.

heaven (ˈhɛvᵊn) *n.* **1.** (*sometimes cap.*) *Christianity.* **a.** the abode of God and the angels. **b.** a state of communion with God after death. **2.** (*usually pl.*) the firmament surrounding the earth. **3.** (in various mythologies) a place, such as Elysium or Valhalla, to which those who have died in the gods' favour are brought to dwell in happiness. **4.** a place or state of happiness. **5.** (*sing.* or *pl.; sometimes cap.*) God or the gods, used in exclamatory phrases: *for heaven's sake.* **6. move heaven and earth.** to do everything possible (to achieve something). [OE *heofon*]

heavenly (ˈhɛvᵊnlɪ) *adj.* **1.** *Inf.* wonderful. **2.** of or occurring in space: *a heavenly body.* **3.** holy. —ˈ**heavenliness** *n.*

heavenward (ˈhɛvᵊnwəd) *adj.* **1.** directed towards heaven or the sky. ~*adv.* **2.** Also **heavenwards.** towards heaven or the sky.

heaves (hiːvz) *n.* a chronic respiratory disorder of animals of the horse family, of unknown cause. Also called: **broken wind.**

heave to *vb.* (*adv.*) to stop (a vessel) or (of a vessel) to stop, as by trimming the sails, etc.

Heaviside layer (ˈhɛvɪˌsaɪd) *n.* another name for **E region** (of the ionosphere). [C20: after O. *Heaviside* (1850–1925), E physicist who predicted its existence (1902)]

heavy (ˈhɛvɪ) *adj.* **heavier, heaviest.** **1.** of

comparatively great weight. **2.** having a relatively high density: *lead is a heavy metal.* **3.** great in yield, quality, or quantity: *heavy traffic.* **4.** considerable: *heavy emphasis.* **5.** hard to bear or fulfil: *heavy demands.* **6.** sad or dejected: *heavy at heart.* **7.** coarse or broad: *heavy features.* **8.** (of soil) having a high clay content; cloggy. **9.** solid or fat: *heavy legs.* **10.** (of an industry) engaged in the large-scale complex manufacture of capital goods or extraction of raw materials. **11.** serious; grave. **12.** *Mil.* **a.** equipped with large weapons, armour, etc. **b.** (of guns, etc.) of a large and powerful type. **13.** (of a syllable) having stress or accentuation. **14.** dull and uninteresting: *a heavy style.* **15.** prodigious: *a heavy drinker.* **16.** (of cakes, etc.) insufficiently leavened. **17.** deep and loud: *a heavy thud.* **18.** (of music, literature, etc.) **a.** dramatic and powerful. **b.** not immediately comprehensible or appealing. **19.** *Sl.* (of rock music) having a powerful beat; hard. **20.** burdened: *heavy with child.* **21. heavy on.** *Inf.* using large quantities of: *this car is very heavy on petrol.* **22.** clumsy and slow: *heavy going.* **23.** cloudy or overcast: *heavy skies.* **24.** not easily digestible: *a heavy meal.* **25.** (of an element or compound) being or containing an isotope with greater atomic weight than that of the naturally occurring element: *heavy water.* **26.** (of the going on a racecourse) soft and muddy. **27.** *Sl.* using, or prepared to use, violence or brutality. *~n., pl.* **heavies. 28. a.** a villainous role. **b.** an actor who plays such a part. **29.** *Mil.* **a.** a large fleet unit, esp. an aircraft carrier or battleship. **b.** a large piece of artillery. **30.** *Inf.* (*usually pl.;* often preceded by *the*) a serious newspaper: *the Sunday heavies.* **31.** *Inf.* a heavyweight boxer, wrestler, etc. **32.** *Sl.* a man hired to threaten violence or deter others by his presence. *~adv.* **33. a.** in a heavy manner; heavily: *time hangs heavy.* **b.** (*in combination*): *heavy-laden.* [OE *hefig*] —**ˈheavily** *adv.* —**ˈheaviness** *n.*

heavy-duty *n.* (*modifier*) made to withstand hard wear, bad weather, etc.

heavy-handed *adj.* **1.** clumsy. **2.** harsh and oppressive. —ˌ**heavy-ˈhandedly** *adv.*

heavy-hearted *adj.* sad; melancholy.

heavy hydrogen *n.* another name for **deuterium.**

heavy metal *n.* a type of rock music characterized by a strong beat and amplified instrumental effects.

heavy middleweight *n.* a professional wrestler weighing 177–187 pounds (81–85 kg).

heavy spar *n.* another name for **barytes.**

heavy water *n.* water that has been electrically decomposed until the hydrogen isotope has disappeared leaving deuterium. Also called: **deuterium oxide.**

heavyweight (ˈhɛvɪˌweɪt) *n.* **1.** a person or thing that is heavier than average. **2. a.** a professional boxer weighing more than 175 pounds (79 kg). **b.** an amateur boxer weighing more than 81 kg (179 pounds). **3. a.** a professional wrestler weighing over 209 pounds (95 kg). **b.** an amateur wrestler weighing over 220 pounds (100kg). **4.** *Inf.* an important or highly influential person.

Heb. *or* **Hebr.** *abbrev. for:* **1.** Hebrew (language). **2.** *Bible.* Hebrews.

hebdomadal (hɛbˈdɒmədᵊl) *adj.* weekly. [C18: < L, < Gk *hebdomas* seven (days), < *hepta* seven]

hebetate (ˈhɛbɪˌteɪt) *adj.* **1.** (of plant parts) having a blunt or soft point. *~vb.* **2.** *Rare.* to make or become blunted. [C16: < L *hebetāre* to make blunt, < *hebes* blunt] —ˌ**hebeˈtation** *n.*

Hebraic (hɪˈbreɪɪk) *or* **Hebraical** *adj.* of, relating to, or characteristic of the Hebrews or their language or culture. —**Heˈbraically** *adv.*

Hebraism (ˈhiːbreɪˌɪzəm) *n.* a linguistic usage, custom, or other feature borrowed from or particular to the Hebrew language, or to the Jewish people or their culture. —**ˈHebraist** *n.* —**ˈHebraˌize** *or* **-ˌise** *vb.*

Hebrew (ˈhiːbruː) *n.* **1.** the ancient language of the Hebrews, revived as the official language of Israel. **2.** a member of an ancient Semitic people claiming descent from Abraham; an Israelite. **3.** *Arch. or offens.* a Jew. *~adj.* **4.** of or relating to the Hebrews or their language. **5.** *Arch. or offens.* Jewish. [C13: < OF *Ebreu,* ult. < Heb. *ʿibhrī* one from beyond (the river)]

hecatomb (ˈhɛkəˌtəʊm, -ˌtuːm) *n.* **1.** (in ancient Greece or Rome) any great public sacrifice and feast, originally one in which 100 oxen were sacrificed. **2.** a great sacrifice. [C16: < L *hecatombē,* < Gk, < *hekaton* hundred + *bous* ox]

heck (hɛk) *interj.* a mild exclamation of surprise, irritation, etc. [C19: euphemistic for *hell*]

heckelphone (ˈhɛkəlˌfəʊn) *n. Music.* a type of bass oboe. [C20: after W. *Heckel* (1856-1909), G inventor]

heckle (ˈhɛkᵊl) *vb.* **1.** to interrupt (a public speaker, etc.) by comments, questions, or taunts. **2.** (*tr.*) Also: **hackle, hatchel.** to comb (hemp or flax). *~n.* **3.** an instrument for combing flax or hemp. [C15: N English & East Anglian form of HACKLE] —**ˈheckler** *n.*

hectare (ˈhɛktɑː) *n.* one hundred ares (10 000 square metres or 2.471 acres). Symbol: ha [C19: < F; see HECTO-, ARE[2]]

hectic (ˈhɛktɪk) *adj.* **1.** characterized by extreme activity or excitement. **2.** associated with or symptomatic of tuberculosis (esp. in **hectic fever, hectic flush**). *~n.* **3.** a hectic fever or flush. **4.** *Rare.* a person who is consumptive. [C14: < LL *hecticus,* < Gk *hektikos* habitual, < *hexis* state, < *ekhein* to have] —**ˈhectically** *adv.*

hecto- *or before a vowel* **hect-** *prefix.* denoting 100: *hectogram.* Symbol: h [via F < Gk *hekaton* hundred]

hectog *abbrev. for* hectogram.

hectogram *or* **hectogramme** (ˈhɛktəʊˌgræm) *n.* one hundred grams (3.527 ounces). Symbol: hg

hectograph (ˈhɛktəʊˌgrɑːf) *n.* **1.** a process for copying type or manuscript from a glycerin-coated gelatin master to which the original has been transferred. **2.** a machine using this process.

hector (ˈhɛktə) *vb.* **1.** to bully or torment by teasing. *~n.* **2.** a blustering bully. [C17: after *Hector* (son of Priam), in the sense: a bully]

he'd (hiːd; *unstressed* iːd, hɪd, ɪd) *contraction of* he had *or* he would.

heddle (ˈhɛdᵊl) *n.* one of a set of frames of vertical wires on a loom, each wire having an eye through which a warp thread can be passed. [OE *hefeld* chain]

hedera (ˈhɛdərə) *n.* the genus name of **ivy** (sense 1). [L]

hedge (hɛdʒ) *n.* **1.** a row of shrubs or bushes forming a boundary. **2.** a barrier or protection against something. **3.** the act or a method of reducing the risk of loss on an investment, etc. **4.** a cautious or evasive statement. **5.** (*as modifier*) low, inferior, or illiterate: *hedge priest.* *~vb.* **6.** (*tr.*) to enclose or separate with or as if with a hedge. **7.** (*intr.*) to make or maintain a hedge. **8.** (*tr.*) to hinder or restrict. **9.** (*intr.*) to evade decision, esp. by making noncommittal statements. **10.** (*tr.*) to guard against the risk of loss in (a bet, etc.), esp. by laying bets with other bookmakers. **11.** (*intr.*) to protect against loss through future price fluctuations, as by investing in futures. [OE *hecg*] —**ˈhedger** *n.* —**ˈhedging** *n.*

hedgehog (ˈhɛdʒˌhɒg) *n.* a small nocturnal Old World mammal having a protective covering of spines on the back.

hedgehop (ˈhɛdʒˌhɒp) *vb.* **-hopping, -hopped.** (*intr.*) (of an aircraft) to fly close to the ground, as in crop spraying. —**ˈhedgeˌhopping** *n., adj.*

hedgerow (ˈhɛdʒˌrəʊ) *n.* a hedge of shrubs or low trees, esp. one bordering a field.

hedge sparrow *n.* a small brownish European songbird. Also called: **dunnock.**

hedonics (hiːˈdɒnɪks) *n.* (*functioning as sing.*) **1.** the branch of psychology concerned with the study of pleasant and unpleasant sensations. **2.** (in philosophy) the study of pleasure.

hedonism (ˈhiːdᵊˌnɪzəm, ˈhɛd-) *n.* **1.** *Ethics.* **a.** the doctrine that moral value can be defined in terms of pleasure. **b.** the doctrine that the pursuit of pleasure is the highest good. **2.** indulgence in sensual pleasures. [C19: < Gk *hēdonē* pleasure] —ˌ**hedon'istic** *adj.* —'**hedonist** *n.*

-hedron *n. combining form.* indicating a solid having a specified number of surfaces: *tetrahedron.* [< Gk *-edron* -sided, < *hedra* seat, base] —**-hedral** *adj. combining form.*

heebie-jeebies ('hiːbɪ'dʒiːbɪz) *pl. n.* **the.** *Sl.* apprehension and nervousness. [C20: coined by W. De Beck (1890–1942), American cartoonist]

heed (hiːd) *n.* **1.** careful attention; notice: *to take heed.* ~*vb.* **2.** to pay close attention to (someone or something. [OE *hēdan*] —'**heedful** *adj.* —'**heedfully** *adv.* —'**heedfulness** *n.*

heedless ('hiːdlɪs) *adj.* taking no notice; careless or thoughtless. —'**heedlessly** *adv.* —'**heedlessness** *n.*

heehaw (ˌhiː'hɔː) *interj.* an imitation or representation of the braying sound of a donkey.

heel[1] (hiːl) *n.* **1.** the back part of the human foot. **2.** the corresponding part in other vertebrates. **3.** the part of a stocking, etc., designed to fit the heel. **4.** the outer part of a shoe underneath the heel. **5.** the end or back section of something: *the heel of a loaf.* **6.** *Horticulture.* the small part of the parent plant that remains attached to a young shoot cut for propagation. **7.** the back part of a golf club head where it bends to join the shaft. **8.** *Sl.* a contemptible person. **9. at** (*or* **on**) **one's heels.** following closely. **10. cool** (*or* **kick**) **one's heels.** to wait or be kept waiting. **11. down at heel. a.** shabby or worn. **b.** slovenly. **12. take to one's heels.** to run off. **13. to heel.** under control, as a dog walking by a person's heel. ~*vb.* **14.** (*tr.*) to repair or replace the heel of (a shoe, etc.). **15.** (*tr.*) *Golf.* to strike (the ball) with the heel of the club. **16.** to follow at the heels of (a person). [OE *hēla*] —'**heelless** *adj.*

heel[2] (hiːl) *vb.* **1.** (of a vessel) to lean over; list. ~*n.* **2.** inclined position from the vertical. [OE *hieldan*]

heelball ('hiːlˌbɔːl) *n.* **a.** a mixture of beeswax and lampblack used by shoemakers to blacken the edges of heels and soles. **b.** a similar substance used to take rubbings, esp. brass rubbings.

heeler ('hiːlə) *n.* **1.** *U.S.* See **ward heeler. 2.** a person or thing that heels. **3.** *Austral. & N.Z.* a dog that herds cattle, etc., by biting at their heels.

heel in *vb.* (*tr., adv.*) to insert (cuttings, shoots, etc.) into the soil before planting to keep them moist.

heeltap ('hiːlˌtæp) *n.* **1.** a layer of leather, etc., in the heel of a shoe. **2.** a small amount of alcoholic drink left at the bottom of a glass.

heft (hɛft) *vb.* (*tr.*) *Brit. dialect. & U.S. inf.* **1.** to assess the weight of (something) by lifting. **2.** to lift. ~*n.* **3.** weight. **4.** *U.S.* the main part. [C19: prob. < HEAVE, by analogy with *thieve, theft, cleave, cleft*]

hefty ('hɛftɪ) *adj.* **heftier, heftiest.** *Inf.* **1.** big and strong. **2.** characterized by vigour or force: *a hefty blow.* **3.** bulky or heavy. **4.** sizable; involving a large amount of money: *a hefty bill.* —'**heftily** *adv.*

Hegelian (hɪ'geɪlɪən, heɪ'giː-) *adj.* relating to G. W. F. Hegel (1770-1831), German philosopher, or his system of thought, esp. his concept of dialectic, in which the contradiction between a proposition (thesis) and its antithesis is resolved at a higher level of truth (synthesis).

hegemony (hɪ'gɛmənɪ) *n., pl.* **-nies.** ascendancy or domination of one power or state within a league, confederation, etc. [C16: < Gk *hēgemonia*, < *hēgemōn* leader, < *hēgeisthai* to lead] —**hegemonic** (ˌhɛgə'mɒnɪk) *adj.*

Hegira *or* **Hejira** ('hɛdʒɪrə) *n.* **1.** the flight of Mohammed from Mecca to Medina in 622 A.D.; the starting point of the Muslim era. **2.** the Muslim era itself. **3.** (*often not cap.*) an escape or flight. [C16: < Med. L, < Ar. *hijrah* flight]

heifer ('hɛfə) *n.* a young cow. [OE *heahfore*]

heigh-ho ('heɪ'həʊ) *interj.* an exclamation of weariness, surprise, or happiness.

height (haɪt) *n.* **1.** the vertical distance from the bottom of something to the top. **2.** the vertical distance of a place above sea level. **3.** relatively great altitude. **4.** the topmost point; summit. **5.** *Astron.* the angular distance of a celestial body above the horizon. **6.** the period of greatest intensity: *the height of the battle.* **7.** an extreme example: *the height of rudeness.* **8.** (*often pl.*) an area of high ground. [OE *hīehthu*; see HIGH]

heighten ('haɪtᵊn) *vb.* to make or become higher or more intense. —'**heightened** *adj.*

height of land *n. U.S. & Canad.* a watershed.

heinous ('heɪnəs, 'hiː-) *adj.* evil; atrocious. [C14: < OF *haineus*, < *haine* hatred, of Gmc origin] —'**heinously** *adv.*

heir (ɛə) *n.* **1.** the person legally succeeding to all property of a deceased person. **2.** any person or thing that carries on some tradition, circumstance, etc., from a forerunner. [C13: < OF, < L *hērēs*] —'**heirdom** *or* '**heirship** *n.*

heir apparent *n., pl.* **heirs apparent.** a person whose right to succeed to certain property cannot be defeated, provided such person survives his ancestor.

heiress ('ɛərɪs) *n.* **1.** a woman who inherits or expects to inherit great wealth. **2.** a female heir.

heirloom ('ɛəˌluːm) *n.* **1.** an object that has been in a family for generations. **2.** an item of personal property inherited in accordance with the terms of a will. [C15: < HEIR + *lome* tool; see LOOM[1]]

heir presumptive *n. Property law.* a person who expects to succeed to an estate but whose right may be defeated by the birth of one nearer in blood to the ancestor.

heist (haɪst) *Sl., chiefly U.S. & Canad.* ~*n.* **1.** a robbery. ~*vb.* **2.** (*tr.*) to steal. [var. of HOIST]

Hejira ('hɛdʒɪrə) *n.* a variant spelling of **Hegira.**

held (hɛld) *vb.* the past tense and past participle of **hold**[1].

helenium (hɛ'liːnɪəm) *n.* a perennial garden plant with yellow, bronze, or crimson flowers. [< Gk *helenion* name of a plant]

heliacal rising (hɪ'laɪəkᵊl) *n.* **1.** the rising of a celestial object at the same time as the sun. **2.** the date at which such a celestial object first becomes visible. [C17: < LL *hēliacus* relating to the sun, < Gk, < *hēlios* sun]

helianthemum (hiːlɪ'ænθəməm) *n.* any of a genus of dwarf shrubs with brightly coloured flowers: often grown in rockeries. [< Gk *helios* sun + *anthemon* flower]

helianthus (ˌhiːlɪ'ænθəs) *n., pl.* **-thuses.** a plant of the composite family having large yellow daisy-like flowers with yellow, brown, or purple centres. [C18: NL, < Gk *hēlios* sun + *anthos* flower]

helical ('hɛlɪkᵊl) *adj.* of or like a helix; spiral.

helical gear *n.* a gearwheel having the tooth form generated on a helical path about the axis of the wheel.

helices ('hɛlɪˌsiːz) *n.* a plural of **helix.**

helichrysum (ˌhɛlɪ'kraɪzəm) *n.* any plant of the genus *Helichrysum*, whose flowers retain their shape and colour when dried. [C16: < L, < Gk, < *helix* spiral + *khrusos* gold]

helicoid ('hɛlɪˌkɔɪd) *adj.* **1.** *Biol.* shaped like a spiral: *a helicoid shell.* ~*n.* **2.** *Geom.* any surface resembling that of a screw thread.

helicon ('hɛlɪkən) *n.* a bass tuba made to coil over the shoulder of a band musician. [C19: prob. < *Helicon*, Gk mountain, believed to be source of poetic inspiration; associated with Gk *helix* spiral]

helicopter ('hɛlɪˌkɒptə) *n.* an aircraft capable of hover, vertical flight, and horizontal flight in any direction. Most get all of their lift and propulsion from the rotation of overhead blades. [C19: < F, < Gk *helix* spiral + *pteron* wing]

helicopter gunship *n.* a large heavily armed helicopter used for ground attack.

helio- *or before a vowel* **heli-** *combining form.* indicating the sun: *heliocentric.* [< Gk, < *hēlios* sun]

heliocentric (ˌhiːlɪəʊ'sɛntrɪk) *adj.* **1.** having the sun at its centre. **2.** measured from or in relation to the sun. —ˌ**helio'centrically** *adv.*

heliograph ('hiːlɪəʊˌgrɑːf) *n.* **1.** an instrument with mirrors and a shutter used for sending messages in Morse code by reflecting the sun's rays. **2.** a device used to photograph the sun. —ˌ**heli'ography** *n.*

heliometer (ˌhiːlɪ'ɒmɪtə) *n.* a refracting telescope used to determine angular distances between celestial bodies. —ˌ**heli'ometry** *n.*

heliopsis (ˌhɛlɪ'ɒpsɪs) *n.* a perennial plant with yellow daisy-like flowers.

heliostat ('hiːlɪəʊˌstæt) *n.* an astronomical instrument used to reflect the light of the sun in a constant direction. —ˌ**helio'static** *adj.*

heliotrope ('hiːlɪəˌtrəʊp, 'hɛljə-) *n.* **1.** any plant of the genus *Heliotropium,* esp. the South American variety, cultivated for its small fragrant purple flowers. **2. a.** a bluish-violet to purple colour. **b.** (*as adj.*): *a heliotrope dress.* **3.** another name for **bloodstone.** [C17: < L *hēliotropium,* < Gk, < *hēlios* sun + *trepein* to turn]

heliotropism (ˌhiːlɪ'ɒtrəˌpɪzəm) *n.* the growth of a plant in response to the stimulus of sunlight. —**heliotropic** (ˌhiːlɪəʊ'trɒpɪk) *adj.*

heliport ('hɛlɪˌpɔːt) *n.* an airport for helicopters. [C20: < HELI(COPTER) + PORT¹]

helium ('hiːlɪəm) *n.* a very light nonflammable colourless odourless element that is an inert gas, occurring in certain natural gases. Symbol: He; atomic no.: 2; atomic wt.: 4.0026. [C19: NL, < HELIO- + -IUM; because first detected in the solar spectrum]

helix ('hiːlɪks) *n., pl.* **helices** *or* **helixes. 1.** a spiral. **2.** the incurving fold that forms the margin of the external ear. **3.** another name for **volute** (sense 2). **4.** any terrestrial mollusc of the genus *Helix,* which includes the garden snail. [C16: < L, < Gk: spiral; prob. rel. to Gk *helissein* to twist]

hell (hɛl) *n.* **1.** (*sometimes cap.*) *Christianity.* **a.** the place or state of eternal punishment of the wicked after death. **b.** forces of evil regarded as residing there. **2.** (*sometimes cap.*) (in various religions and cultures) the abode of the spirits of the dead. **3.** pain, extreme difficulty, etc. **4.** *Inf.* a cause of such suffering: *war is hell.* **5.** *U.S. & Canad.* high spirits or mischievousness. **6.** *Now rare.* a gambling house. **7. (come) hell or high water.** *Inf.* whatever difficulties may arise. **8. for the hell of it.** *Inf.* for the fun of it. **9. give someone hell.** *Inf.* **a.** to give someone a severe reprimand or punishment. **b.** to be a source of torment to someone. **10. hell for leather.** at great speed. **11. hell to pay.** *Inf.* serious consequences, as of a foolish action. **12. the hell.** *Inf.* **a.** (intensifier): used in such phrases as **what the hell. b.** an expression of strong disagreement: *the hell I will.* ~*interj.* **13.** *Inf.* an exclamation of anger, surprise, etc. [OE *hell*]

he'll (hiːl; *unstressed* iːl, hɪl, ɪl) *contraction of* he will *or* he shall.

Helladic (hɛ'lædɪk) *adj.* of or relating to the Bronze Age civilization that flourished about 2900 to 1100 B.C. on the Greek mainland and islands.

Hellas ('hɛləs) *n.* transliteration of the ancient Greek name for Greece.

hellbent (ˌhɛl'bɛnt) *adj.* (*postpositive;* foll. by *on*) *Inf.* strongly or rashly intent.

hellcat ('hɛlˌkæt) *n.* a spiteful fierce-tempered woman.

hellebore ('hɛlɪˌbɔː) *n.* **1.** any plant of the Eurasian genus *Helleborus,* typically having showy flowers and poisonous parts. See also **Christmas rose. 2.** any of various plants which yield alkaloids used in the treatment of heart disease. [C14: < Gk *helleboros,* <?]

Hellene ('hɛliːn) *or* **Hellenian** (hɛ'liːnɪən) *n.* another name for a **Greek.**

Hellenic (hɛ'lɛnɪk, -'liː-) *adj.* **1.** of or relating to the ancient or modern Greeks or their language. **2.** of or relating to ancient Greece or the Greeks of the classical period (776–323 B.C.). Cf. **Hellenistic.** ~*n.* **3.** the Greek language in its various ancient and modern dialects.

Hellenism ('hɛlɪˌnɪzəm) *n.* **1.** the principles, ideals, and pursuits associated with classical Greek civilization. **2.** the spirit or national character of the Greeks. **3.** imitation of or devotion to the culture of ancient Greece. —'**Hellenist** *n.*

Hellenistic (ˌhɛlɪ'nɪstɪk) *or* **Hellenistical** *adj.* characteristic of or relating to Greek civilization in the Mediterranean world, esp. from the death of Alexander the Great (323 B.C.) to the defeat of Antony and Cleopatra (30 B.C.).

Hellenize *or* **-nise** ('hɛlɪˌnaɪz) *vb.* to make or become like the ancient Greeks. —ˌ**Helleni'zation** *or* **-ni'sation** *n.*

hellfire ('hɛlˌfaɪə) *n.* **1.** the torment of hell, envisaged as eternal fire. **2.** (*modifier*) characterizing sermons that emphasize this.

hellion ('hɛljən) *n. Chiefly U.S. inf.* a rowdy person, esp. a child; troublemaker. [C19: prob. < dialect *hallion* rogue, <?]

hellish ('hɛlɪʃ) *adj.* **1.** of or resembling hell. **2.** wicked; cruel. **3.** *Inf.* very unpleasant. ~*adv.* **4.** *Brit. inf.* (intensifier): *a hellish good idea.*

hello, hallo, *or* **hullo** (hɛ'ləʊ, hə-; 'hɛləʊ) *sentence substitute.* **1.** an expression of greeting. **2.** a call used to attract attention. **3.** an expression of surprise. ~*n., pl.* **-los. 4.** the act of saying or calling "hello". [C19: see HOLLO]

Hell's Angel *n.* a member of a motorcycle gang who typically dress in Nazi-style paraphernalia and are noted for their lawless behaviour.

helm¹ (hɛlm) *n.* **1.** *Naut.* **a.** the wheel or entire apparatus by which a vessel is steered. **b.** the position of the helm: that is, on the side of the keel opposite from that of the rudder. **2.** a position of leadership or control (esp. in **at the helm).** ~*vb.* **3.** (*tr.*) to steer. [OE *helma*] —'**helmsman** *n.*

helm² (hɛlm) *n.* an archaic or poetic word for **helmet.** [OE *helm*]

helmet ('hɛlmɪt) *n.* **1.** a piece of protective or defensive armour for the head worn by soldiers, policemen, firemen, divers, etc. **2.** *Biol.* a part or structure resembling a helmet, esp. the upper part of the calyx of certain flowers. [C15: < OF, dim. of *helme,* of Gmc origin] —'**helmeted** *adj.*

helminth ('hɛlmɪnθ) *n.* any parasitic worm, esp. a nematode or fluke. [C19: < Gk *helmins* parasitic worm] —**hel'minthic** *or* **helminthoid** ('hɛlmɪnˌθɔɪd, hɛl'mɪnθɔɪd) *adj.*

helminthiasis (ˌhɛlmɪn'θaɪəsɪs) *n.* infestation of the body with parasitic worms. [C19: < NL, < Gk *helminthian* to be infested with worms]

helot ('hɛlət, 'hiː-) *n.* **1.** (*cap.*) (in ancient Sparta) a member of the class of serfs owned by the state. **2.** a serf or slave. [C16: < L *Hēlōtēs,* < Gk *Heilōtes,* alleged to have meant orig.: inhabitants of Helos, who, after its conquest, were serfs of the Spartans] —'**helotism** *n.* —'**helotry** *n.*

help (hɛlp) *vb.* **1.** to assist (someone to do something), esp. by sharing the work, cost, or burden of something. **2.** to alleviate the burden of (someone else) by giving assistance. **3.** (*tr.*) to assist (a person) to go in a specified direction: *help the old lady up.* **4.** to contribute to: *to help the relief operations.* **5.** to improve (a situation, etc.): *crying won't help.* **6.** (*tr.;* preceded by *can, could,* etc.; *usually used with a negative*) **a.** to refrain from: *we can't help wondering who he is.* **b.** (usually foll. by *it*) to be responsible for: *I can't help it if it rains.* **7.** to alleviate (an illness, etc.). **8.** (*tr.*) to serve (a customer). **9.** (*tr.;* foll. by *to*) **a.** to serve (someone with food, etc.) (usually in **help oneself**). **b.** to provide (oneself with) without permission. **10. cannot help but.** to be unable to do anything else except: *I cannot help but laugh.* **11. so help me. a.** on my honour. **b.** no matter what: *so help me, I'll get revenge.* ~*n.* **12.** the act of helping or being helped, or a person or thing that helps. **13. a.** a person hired for a job, esp. a farm worker or domestic servant. **b.** (*functioning as sing.*) several employees collectively. **14.** a remedy: *there's no help for it.* ~*sentence substitute.* **15.** used to ask for assistance. ~See also **help out.** [OE *helpan*] —'**helper** *n.*

helpful ('hɛlpfʊl) *adj.* giving help. —'**helpfully** *adv.* —'**helpfulness** *n.*

helping ('hɛlpɪŋ) *n.* a single portion of food.

helping hand *n.* assistance: *many people lent a helping hand in making arrangements.*

helpless (ˈhɛlplɪs) *adj.* **1.** unable to manage independently. **2.** made weak: *they were helpless from giggling.* —ˈ**helplessly** *adv.* —ˈ**helplessness** *n.*

helpline (ˈhɛlpˌlaɪn) *n.* a telephone line specially set aside to enable callers to contact an agency or organization for help with a particular problem.

helpmate (ˈhɛlpˌmeɪt) *n.* a companion and helper, esp. a wife.

helpmeet (ˈhɛlpˌmiːt) *n.* a less common word for **helpmate.** [C17: < *an helpe meet* (suitable) *for him* Genesis 2:18]

help out *vb.* (*adv.*) to assist, esp. by sharing the burden or cost of something with (another person).

helter-skelter (ˈhɛltəˈskɛltə) *adj.* **1.** haphazard or careless. ~*adv.* **2.** in a helter-skelter manner. ~*n.* **3.** *Brit.* a high spiral slide, as at a fairground. **4.** disorder. [C16: prob. imit.]

helve (hɛlv) *n.* the handle of a hand tool such as an axe or pick. [OE *hielfe*]

Helvetian (hɛlˈviːʃən) *adj.* **1.** Swiss. ~*n.* **2.** a native or citizen of Switzerland. [< L *Helvetia* Switzerland]

hem[1] (hɛm) *n.* **1.** an edge to a piece of cloth, made by folding the raw edge under and stitching it down. **2.** short for **hemline.** ~*vb.* **hemming, hemmed.** (*tr.*) **3.** to provide with a hem. **4.** (usually foll. by *in, around,* or *about*) to enclose or confine. [OE *hemm*] —ˈ**hemmer** *n.*

hem[2] (hɛm) *n., interj.* **1.** a representation of the sound of clearing the throat, used to gain attention, etc. ~*vb.* **hemming, hemmed. 2.** (*intr.*) to utter this sound. **3. hem** (*or* **hum**) **and haw.** to hesitate in speaking.

he-man *n., pl.* **-men.** *Inf.* a strongly built muscular man.

hematite *or* **haematite** (ˈhɛməˌtaɪt, ˈhiːm-) *n.* a red, grey, or black mineral, found as massive beds and in veins and igneous rocks. It is the chief source of iron. Composition: iron (ferric) oxide. Crystal structure: hexagonal (rhombohedral). [C16: via L < Gk *haimatitēs* resembling blood, < *haima* blood] —**hematitic** *or* **haematitic** (ˌhɛməˈtɪtɪk, ˌhiː-) *adj.*

hemato- *or before a vowel* **hemat-** *combining form.* U.S. variants of **haemato-.**

hemeralopia (ˌhɛmərəˈləʊpɪə) *n.* inability to see clearly in bright light. Nontechnical name: **day blindness.** [C18: NL, < Gk, < *hēmera* day + *alaos* blind + *ōps* eye]

hemerocallis (hɛmərˈɒkælɪs) *n.* a N temperate plant with large funnel-shaped orange flowers: each single flower lasts for only one day. Also called: **day lily.** [C17: < Gk *hēmera* day + *kallos* beauty]

hemi- *prefix.* half: *hemicycle; hemisphere.* [< L, < Gk *hēmi-*]

-hemia *n. combining form.* a U.S. variant of **-aemia.**

hemidemisemiquaver (ˌhɛmɪˌdɛmɪˈsɛmɪˌkweɪvə) *n. Music.* a note having the time value of one sixty-fourth of a semibreve. Usual U.S. & Canad. name: **sixty-fourth note.**

hemiplegia (ˌhɛmɪˈpliːdʒɪə) *n.* paralysis of one side of the body. —ˌ**hemiˈplegic** *adj.*

hemipode (ˈhɛmɪˌpəʊd) *n.* a small quail-like bird occurring in tropical and subtropical regions of the Old World. Also called: **button quail.**

hemipteran (hɪˈmɪptərən) *n.* any hemipterous insect. [C19: < HEMI- + Gk *pteron* wing]

hemipterous (hɪˈmɪptərəs) *adj.* of or belonging to a large order of insects having sucking or piercing mouthparts.

hemisphere (ˈhɛmɪˌsfɪə) *n.* **1.** one half of a sphere. **2. a.** half of the terrestrial globe, divided into **northern** and **southern hemispheres** by the equator or into **eastern** and **western hemispheres** by some meridians, usually 0° and 180°. **b.** a map or projection of one of the hemispheres. **3.** *Anat.* short for **cerebral hemisphere,** a half of the cerebrum. —**hemispheric** (ˌhɛmɪˈsfɛrɪk) *or* ˌ**hemiˈspherical** *adj.*

hemistich (ˈhɛmɪˌstɪk) *n. Prosody.* a half line of verse.

hemline (ˈhɛmˌlaɪn) *n.* the level to which the hem of a skirt or dress hangs.

hemlock (ˈhɛmˌlɒk) *n.* **1.** an umbelliferous poisonous Eurasian plant having finely divided leaves, spotted stems, and small white flowers. **2.** a poisonous drug derived from this plant. **3.** Also called: **hemlock spruce.** a coniferous tree of North America and Asia. [OE *hymlic*]

hemo- *combining form.* a U.S. variant of **haemo-.**

hemp (hɛmp) *n.* **1.** Also called: **cannabis, marijuana.** an Asian plant having tough fibres, deeply lobed leaves, and small greenish flowers. See also **Indian hemp. 2.** the fibre of this plant, used to make canvas, rope, etc. **3.** any of several narcotic drugs obtained from some varieties of this plant, esp. from Indian hemp. [OE *hænep*] —ˈ**hempen** *or* ˈ**hempˌlike** *adj.*

hemstitch (ˈhɛmˌstɪtʃ) *n.* **1.** a decorative edging stitch, usually for a hem, in which the cross threads are stitched in groups. ~*vb.* **2.** to decorate (a hem, etc.) with hemstitches.

hen (hɛn) *n.* **1.** the female of any bird, esp. of the domestic fowl. **2.** the female of certain other animals, such as the lobster. **3.** *Scot. dialect.* a term of address used to women. [OE *henn*]

henbane (ˈhɛnˌbeɪn) *n.* a poisonous Mediterranean plant with sticky hairy leaves: yields the drug hyoscyamine.

hence (hɛns) *sentence connector.* **1.** for this reason; therefore. ~*adv.* **2.** from this time: *a year hence.* **3.** *Arch.* from here; away. ~*sentence substitute.* **4.** *Arch.* begone! away! [OE *hionane*]

henceforth (ˈhɛnsˈfɔːθ), **henceforwards,** *or* **henceforward** *adv.* from now on.

henchman (ˈhɛntʃmən) *n., pl.* **-men. 1.** a faithful attendant or supporter. **2.** *Arch.* a squire; page. [C14 *hengestman,* < OE *hengest* stallion + MAN]

hendeca- *combining form.* eleven: *hendecagon; hendecasyllable.* [< Gk *hendeka,* < *hen,* neuter of *heis* one + *deka* ten]

hendecagon (hɛnˈdɛkəgən) *n.* a polygon having 11 sides. —**hendecagonal** (ˌhɛndɪˈkægənˀl) *adj.*

hendecasyllable (ˈhɛndɛkəˌsɪləbˀl) *n. Prosody.* a verse line of 11 syllables. [C18: < Gk]

hendiadys (hɛnˈdaɪədɪs) *n.* a rhetorical device by which two nouns joined by a conjunction are used instead of a noun and a modifier, as in *to run with fear and haste* instead of *to run with fearful haste.* [C16: < Med. L, < Gk *hen dia duoin,* lit.: one through two]

henequen, henequin, *or* **heniquen** (ˈhɛnɪkɪn) *n.* **1.** an agave plant that is native to Mexico. **2.** the fibre of this plant, used in making rope, twine, and coarse fabrics. [C19: < American Sp. *henequén,* prob. of Amerind origin]

henge (hɛndʒ) *n.* a circular monument, often containing a circle of stones, dating from the Neolithic and Bronze Ages. [back formation < *Stonehenge,* site of important megalithic ruins on Salisbury Plain, S England]

hen harrier *n.* a common harrier that nests in marshes and open land.

henhouse (ˈhɛnˌhaʊs) *n.* a coop for hens.

henna (ˈhɛnə) *n.* **1.** a shrub or tree of Asia and N Africa. **2.** a reddish dye obtained from the powdered leaves of this plant, used as a cosmetic and industrial dye. **3. a.** a reddish-brown colour. **b.** (*as adj.*): *henna tresses.* ~*vb.* **4.** (*tr.*) to dye with henna. [C16: < Ar. *hinnā'*; see ALKANET]

henotheism (ˈhɛnəʊθiːˌɪzəm) *n.* the worship of one deity (of several) as the special god of one's family, clan, or tribe. [C19: < Gk *heis* one + *theos* god] —ˌ**henotheˈistic** *adj.*

hen party *n. Inf.* a party at which only women are present.

henpeck (ˈhɛnˌpɛk) *vb.* (*tr.*) (of a woman) to harass or torment (a man, esp. her husband) by persistent nagging. —ˈ**henˌpecked** *adj.*

henry (ˈhɛnrɪ) *n., pl.* **-ry, -ries,** *or* **-rys.** the derived SI unit of electric inductance; the inductance of a closed circuit in which an emf of 1 volt is produced when the current varies uniformly at the rate of 1 ampere per second. Symbol: H [C19: after Joseph *Henry* (1797–1878), U.S. physicist]

hep (hɛp) *adj.* **hepper, heppest.** *Sl.* an earlier word for **hip**[4].

heparin (ˈhɛpərɪn) *n.* a polysaccharide, containing sulphate groups, present in most body tissues: an anticoagulant used in the treatment of thrombosis. [C20: < Gk *hēpar* the liver + -IN]

hepatic (hɪˈpætɪk) *adj.* **1.** of the liver. **2.** having the colour of liver. ~*n.* **3.** any of various drugs for use in treating diseases of the liver. [C15: < L *hēpaticus*, < Gk *hēpar* liver]

hepatica (hɪˈpætɪkə) *n.* a woodland plant of a N temperate genus, having three-lobed leaves and white, mauve, or pink flowers. [C16: < Med. L: liverwort, < L *hēpaticus* of the liver]

hepatitis (ˌhɛpəˈtaɪtɪs) *n.* inflammation of the liver.

Hepplewhite (ˈhɛpᵊlˌwaɪt) *adj.* of or in a style of ornamental and carved 18th-century English furniture, of which oval or shield-shaped open chairbacks are characteristic. [C18: after George *Hepplewhite* (died 1786), E cabinetmaker]

hepta- *or before a vowel* **hept-** *combining form.* seven: *heptameter.* [< Gk]

heptad (ˈhɛptæd) *n.* a group or series of seven. [C17: < Gk *heptas* seven]

heptagon (ˈhɛptəgən) *n.* a polygon having seven sides. —**heptagonal** (hɛpˈtægənᵊl) *adj.*

heptahedron (ˌhɛptəˈhiːdrən) *n.* a solid figure having seven plane faces. —ˌ**heptaˈhedral** *adj.*

heptameter (hɛpˈtæmɪtə) *n. Prosody.* a verse line of seven metrical feet. —**heptametrical** (ˌhɛptəˈmɛtrɪkᵊl) *adj.*

heptane (ˈhɛpteɪn) *n.* an alkane which is found in petroleum and used as an anaesthetic. [C19: < HEPTA- + -ANE, because it has seven carbon atoms]

heptarchy (ˈhɛptɑːkɪ) *n., pl.* **-chies. 1.** government by seven rulers. **2.** the seven kingdoms into which Anglo-Saxon England is thought to have been divided from about the 7th to the 9th centuries A.D. —ˈ**heptarch** *n.* —**hepˈtarchic** *or* **hepˈtarchal** *adj.*

heptathlon (hɛpˈtæθlɒn) *n.* an athletic contest for women in which each athlete competes in seven different events. [C20: < HEPTA- + Gk *athlon* contest] —**hepˈtathlete** *n.*

heptavalent (hɛpˈtævələnt, ˌhɛptəˈveɪlənt) *adj. Chem.* having a valency of seven.

her (hɜː; *unstressed* hə, ə) *pron.* (*objective*) **1.** refers to a female person or animal: *he loves her.* **2.** refers to things personified as feminine or traditionally to ships and nations. ~*determiner.* **3.** of, belonging to, or associated with her: *her hair.* [OE *hire*, genitive & dative of *hēo* SHE, fem. of *hē* HE]

▷ **Usage.** See at **me.**

herald (ˈhɛrəld) *n.* **1.** a person who announces important news. **2.** *Often literary.* a forerunner; harbinger. **3.** the intermediate rank of heraldic officer, between king-of-arms and pursuivant. **4.** (in the Middle Ages) an official at a tournament. ~*vb.* (*tr.*) **5.** to announce publicly. **6.** to precede or usher in. [C14: < OF *herault*, of Gmc origin]

heraldic (hɛˈrældɪk) *adj.* of or relating to heraldry or heralds. —**heˈraldically** *adv.*

heraldry (ˈhɛrəldrɪ) *n., pl.* **-ries. 1.** the study concerned with the classification of armorial bearings, the tracing of genealogies, etc. **2.** armorial bearings, insignia, etc. **3.** the show and ceremony of heraldry. —ˈ**heraldist** *n.*

herb (hɜːb; *U.S.* ɜːrb) *n.* **1.** a plant whose aerial parts do not persist above ground at the end of the growing season; herbaceous plant. **2.** any of various usually aromatic plants, such as parsley and rosemary, that are used in cookery and medicine. [C13: < OF *herbe*, < L *herba* grass, green plants] —ˈ**herbˌlike** *adj.* —ˈ**herby** *adj.*

herbaceous (hɜːˈbeɪʃəs) *adj.* **1.** designating or relating to plants that are fleshy as opposed to woody: *a herbaceous plant.* **2.** (of petals and sepals) green and leaflike.

herbaceous border *n.* a flower bed that contains perennials rather than annuals.

herbage (ˈhɜːbɪdʒ) *n.* **1.** herbaceous plants collectively, esp. the edible parts on which cattle, sheep, etc., graze. **2.** the vegetation of pasture land; pasturage.

herbal (ˈhɜːbᵊl) *adj.* **1.** of herbs. ~*n.* **2.** a book describing the properties of plants.

herbalist (ˈhɜːbᵊlɪst) *n.* **1.** a person who grows or specializes in the use of herbs, esp. medicinal herbs. **2.** (formerly) a descriptive botanist.

herbarium (hɜːˈbɛərɪəm) *n., pl.* **-iums** *or* **-ia** (-ɪə). **1.** a collection of dried plants that are mounted and classified systematically. **2.** a room, etc., in which such a collection is kept.

herb bennet (ˈbɛnɪt) *n.* a Eurasian and N African plant with yellow flowers. Also called: **wood avens, bennet.** [< OF *herbe benoite*, lit.: blessed herb, < Med. L *herba benedicta*]

herbicide (ˈhɜːbɪˌsaɪd) *n.* a chemical that destroys plants, esp. one used to control weeds.

herbivore (ˈhɜːbɪˌvɔː) *n.* an animal that feeds on grass and other plants. [C19: < NL *herbivora* grass-eaters] —**herbivorous** (hɜːˈbɪvərəs) *adj.*

herb Paris (ˈpærɪs) *n., pl.* **herbs Paris.** a Eurasian woodland plant with a whorl of four leaves and a solitary yellow flower. [C16: < Med. L *herba paris*, lit.: herb of a pair: because the four leaves on the stalk look like a true lovers' knot]

herb Robert (ˈrɒbət) *n., pl.* **herbs Robert.** a low-growing N temperate plant with strongly scented divided leaves and small purplish flowers. [C13: < Med. L *herba Roberti* herb of Robert, prob. after St *Robert*, 11th-cent. F ecclesiastic]

herculean (ˌhɜːkjʊˈliːən) *adj.* **1.** requiring tremendous effort, strength, etc. **2.** (*sometimes cap.*) resembling Hercules, hero of classical myth, in strength, courage, etc.

herd[1] (hɜːd) *n.* **1.** a large group of mammals living and feeding together, esp. cattle. **2.** *Often disparaging.* a large group of people. ~*vb.* **3.** to collect or be collected into or as if into a herd. [OE *heord*]

herd[2] (hɜːd) *n.* **1. a.** *Arch. or dialect.* a man who tends livestock; herdsman. **b.** (*in combination*): *goatherd.* ~*vb.* (*tr.*) **2.** to drive forwards in a large group. **3.** to look after (livestock). [OE *hirde*: see HERD[1]]

herd instinct *n. Psychol.* the inborn tendency to associate with others and follow the group's behaviour.

herdsman (ˈhɜːdzmən) *n., pl.* **-men.** *Chiefly Brit.* a person who breeds or cares for cattle or (rarely) other livestock. U.S. equivalent: **herder.**

here (hɪə) *adv.* **1.** in, at, or to this place, point, case, or respect: *we come here every summer; here comes Roy.* **2. here and there.** at several places in or throughout an area. **3. here's to.** a formula used in proposing a toast to someone or something. **4. neither here nor there.** of no relevance or importance. ~*n.* **5.** this place or point: *they leave here tonight.* [OE *hēr*]

hereabouts (ˈhɪərəˌbaʊts) *or* **hereabout** *adv.* in this region or neighbourhood.

hereafter (ˌhɪərˈɑːftə) *adv.* **1.** *Formal or law.* in a subsequent part of this document, matter, case, etc. **2.** a less common word for **henceforth. 3.** at some time in the future. **4.** in a future life after death. ~*n.* (usually preceded by *the*) **5.** life after death. **6.** the future.

hereat (ˌhɪərˈæt) *adv. Arch.* because of this.

hereby (ˌhɪəˈbaɪ) *adv.* (used in official statements, etc.) by means of or as a result of this.

hereditable (hɪˈrɛdɪtəbᵊl) *adj.* a less common word for **heritable.** —**heˌreditaˈbility** *n.*

hereditament (ˌhɛrɪˈdɪtəmənt) *n. Property law.* any kind of property capable of being inherited.

hereditary (hɪˈrɛdɪtərɪ, -trɪ) *adj.* **1.** of or denoting factors that can be transmitted genetically from one generation to another. **2.** *Law.* **a.** descending to succeeding generations by inheritance. **b.** transmitted according to established rules of descent. **3.** derived from one's ancestors; traditional: *hereditary feuds.* —**heˈreditarily** *adv.* —**heˈreditariness** *n.*

heredity (hɪˈrɛdɪtɪ) *n., pl.* **-ties.** **1.** the transmission from one generation to another of genetic factors that determine individual characteristics. **2.** the sum total of the inherited factors in an organism. [C16: < OF *heredite,* < L *hērēditās* inheritance; see HEIR]

herein (ˌhɪərˈɪn) *adv.* **1.** *Formal or law.* in or into this place, thing, document, etc. **2.** *Rare.* in this respect, circumstance, etc.

hereinafter (ˌhɪərɪnˈɑːftə) *adv. Formal or law.* from this point on in this document, etc.

hereinto (ˌhɪərˈɪntuː) *adv. Formal or law.* into this place, circumstance, etc.

hereof (ˌhɪərˈɒv) *adv. Formal or law.* of or concerning this.

hereon (ˌhɪərˈɒn) *adv.* an archaic word for **hereupon.**

heresiarch (hɪˈriːzɪˌɑːk) *n.* the leader or originator of a heretical movement or sect.

heresy (ˈhɛrəsɪ) *n., pl.* **-sies.** **1. a.** an opinion contrary to the orthodox tenets of a religious body. **b.** the act of maintaining such an opinion. **2.** any belief that is or is thought to be contrary to official or established theory. **3.** adherence to unorthodox opinion. [C13: < OF *eresie,* < LL, < L: sect, < Gk, < *hairein* to choose]

heretic (ˈhɛrətɪk) *n.* **1.** *Now chiefly R.C. Church.* a person who maintains beliefs contrary to the established teachings of his Church. **2.** a person who holds unorthodox opinions in any field. —**heretical** (hɪˈrɛtɪkᵊl) *adj.* —**heˈretically** *adv.*

hereto (ˌhɪəˈtuː) *adv. Formal or law.* to this place, thing, matter, document, etc.

heretofore (ˌhɪətʊˈfɔː) *adv. Formal or law.* until now; before this time.

hereunder (ˌhɪərˈʌndə) *adv. Formal or law.* **1.** (in documents, etc.) below this; subsequently; hereafter. **2.** under the terms or authority of this.

hereupon (ˌhɪərəˈpɒn) *adv.* **1.** following immediately after this; at this stage. **2.** *Formal or law.* upon this thing, point, subject, etc.

herewith (ˌhɪəˈwɪð, -ˈwɪθ) *adv. Formal.* together with this: *we send you herewith your statement of account.*

heriot (ˈhɛrɪət) *n.* (in medieval England) a death duty paid by villeins and free tenants to their lord, often consisting of the dead man's best beast or chattel. [OE *heregeatwa,* < *here* army + *geatwa* equipment]

heritable (ˈhɛrɪtəbᵊl) *adj.* **1.** capable of being inherited; inheritable. **2.** *Chiefly law.* capable of inheriting. [C14: < OF, < *heriter* to INHERIT] —ˌ**heritaˈbility** *n.* —ˈ**heritably** *adv.*

heritage (ˈhɛrɪtɪdʒ) *n.* **1.** something inherited at birth. **2.** anything that has been transmitted from the past or handed down by tradition. **3.** the evidence of the past, such as historical sites, and the unspoilt natural environment, considered as the inheritance of present-day society. **4.** *Law.* any property, esp. land, that by law has descended or may descend to an heir. [C13: < OF; see HEIR]

herl (hɜːl) *or* **harl** *n. Angling.* **1.** the barb or barbs of a feather, used to dress fishing flies. **2.** an artificial fly dressed with such barbs. [C15: < MLow G *herle,* <?]

hermaphrodite (hɜːˈmæfrəˌdaɪt) *n.* **1.** *Biol.* an animal or flower that has both male and female reproductive organs. **2.** a person having both male and female sexual characteristics. **3.** a person or thing in which two opposite qualities are combined. ~*adj.* **4.** having the characteristics of a hermaphrodite. [C15: < L *hermaphrodītus,* < Gk, after *Hermaphroditus,* a son of Hermes and Aphrodite, who merged with the nymph Salmacis to form one body] —**herˌmaphroˈditic** *or* **herˌmaphroˈditical** *adj.* —**herˈmaphroditˌism** *n.*

hermaphrodite brig *n.* a sailing vessel with two masts, rigged square on the foremast and fore-and-aft on the aftermast.

hermeneutic (ˌhɜːmɪˈnjuːtɪk) *or* **hermeneutical** *adj.* **1.** of or relating to the interpretation of Scripture. **2.** interpretive. —ˌ**hermeˈneutically** *adv.*

hermeneutics (ˌhɜːmɪˈnjuːtɪks) *n.* (*functioning as sing.*) **1.** the science of interpretation, esp. of Scripture. **2.** *Philosophy.* the study and interpretation of human behaviour and social institutions. [C18: < Gk *hermēneutikos* expert in interpretation, < *hermēneuein* to interpret, <?]

hermetic (hɜːˈmɛtɪk) *or* **hermetical** *adj.* sealed so as to be airtight. [C17: < Med. L *hermēticus* belonging to *Hermes Trismegistus* (Gk, lit.: Hermes thrice-greatest), traditionally the inventor of a magic seal] —**herˈmetically** *adv.*

hermit (ˈhɜːmɪt) *n.* **1.** one of the early Christian recluses. **2.** any person living in solitude. [C13: < OF *hermite,* < LL, < Gk *erēmitēs* living in the desert, < *erēmos* lonely] —**herˈmitic** *or* **herˈmitical** *adj.*

hermitage (ˈhɜːmɪtɪdʒ) *n.* **1.** the abode of a hermit. **2.** any retreat.

hermit crab *n.* a small soft-bodied crustacean living in and carrying about the empty shells of whelks or similar molluscs.

hernia (ˈhɜːnɪə) *n., pl.* **-nias** *or* **-niae** (-nɪˌiː). the projection of an organ or part through the lining of the cavity in which it is normally situated, esp. the intestine through the front wall of the abdominal cavity. Also called: **rupture.** [C14: < L] —ˈ**hernial** *adj.* —ˈ**herniˌated** *adj.*

hero (ˈhɪərəʊ) *n., pl.* **-roes.** **1.** a man distinguished by exceptional courage, nobility, etc. **2.** a man who is idealized for possessing superior qualities in any field. **3.** *Classical myth.* a being of extraordinary strength and courage, often the offspring of a mortal and a god. **4.** the principal male character in a novel, play, etc. [C14: < L *hērōs,* < Gk]

heroic (hɪˈrəʊɪk) *or* **heroical** *adj.* **1.** of, like, or befitting a hero. **2.** courageous but desperate. **3.** treating of heroes and their deeds. **4.** of or resembling the heroes of classical mythology. **5.** (of language, manner, etc.) extravagant. **6.** *Prosody.* of or resembling heroic verse. **7.** (of the arts, esp. sculpture) larger than life-size; smaller than colossal. —**heˈroically** *adv.*

heroic age *n.* the period in an ancient culture, when legendary heroes are said to have lived.

heroic couplet *n. Prosody.* a verse form consisting of two rhyming lines in iambic pentameter.

heroics (hɪˈrəʊɪks) *pl. n.* **1.** *Prosody.* short for **heroic verse.** **2.** extravagant or melodramatic language, behaviour, etc.

heroic verse *n. Prosody.* a type of verse suitable for epic or heroic subjects, such as the classical hexameter or the French Alexandrine.

heroin (ˈhɛrəʊɪn) *n.* a white bitter-tasting crystalline powder derived from morphine: a highly addictive narcotic. [C19: coined in G as a trademark, prob. < HERO, referring to its aggrandizing effect on the personality]

heroine (ˈhɛrəʊɪn) *n.* **1.** a woman possessing heroic qualities. **2.** a woman idealized for possessing superior qualities. **3.** the main female character in a novel, play, film, etc.

heroism (ˈhɛrəʊˌɪzəm) *n.* the state or quality of being a hero.

heron (ˈhɛrən) *n.* any of various wading birds having a long neck, slim body, and a plumage that is commonly grey or white. [C14: < OF *hairon,* of Gmc origin]

heronry (ˈhɛrənrɪ) *n., pl.* **-ries.** a colony of breeding herons.

hero worship *n.* **1.** admiration for heroes or idealized persons. **2.** worship by the ancient Greeks and Romans of heroes. ~*vb.* **hero-worship, -shipping, -shipped** *or U.S.* **-shiping, -shiped.** **3.** (*tr.*) to feel admiration or adulation for. —ˈ**hero-ˌworshipper** *n.*

herpes (ˈhɜːpiːz) *n.* any of several inflammatory diseases of the skin, esp. herpes simplex. [C17: via L < Gk, < *herpein* to creep] —**herpetic** (hɜːˈpɛtɪk) *adj., n.*

herpes simplex (ˈsɪmplɛks) *n.* an acute viral disease characterized by formation of clusters of watery blisters. [NL: simple herpes]

herpes zoster (ˈzɒstə) *n.* a technical name for

shingles. [NL: girdle herpes, < HERPES + Gk *zōstēr* girdle]

herpetology (ˌhɜːpɪˈtɒlədʒɪ) *n.* the study of reptiles and amphibians. [C19: < Gk *herpeton* creeping animal] —**herpetologic** (ˌhɜːpɪtəˈlɒdʒɪk) *or* ˌ**herpetoˈlogical** *adj.*

Herr (*German* hɛr) *n., pl.* **Herren** (ˈhɛrən). a German man: used before a name as a title equivalent to *Mr.* [G, < OHG *herro* lord]

Herrenvolk *German.* (ˈhɛrənfɔlk) *n.* a race, nation, or group, such as the Germans or Nazis as viewed by Hitler, believed by themselves to be superior to other races. Also called: **master race.** [lit.: master race, < *Herren,* pl. of HERR + *Volk* folk]

herring (ˈhɛrɪŋ) *n., pl.* **-rings** *or* **-ring.** an important food fish of northern seas, having an elongated body covered with large silvery scales. [OE *hǣring*]

herringbone (ˈhɛrɪŋˌbəʊn) *n.* **1. a.** a pattern consisting of two or more rows of short parallel strokes slanting in alternate directions to form a series of zigzags. **b.** (*as modifier*): *a herringbone pattern.* **2.** *Skiing.* a method of ascending a slope by walking with the skis pointing outwards and one's weight on the inside edges. *~vb.* **3.** to decorate (textiles, brickwork, etc.) with herringbone. **4.** (*intr.*) *Skiing.* to ascend a slope in herringbone fashion.

herring gull *n.* a common gull that has a white plumage with black-tipped wings.

hers (hɜːz) *pron.* **1.** something or someone belonging to her: *hers is the nicest dress; that cat is hers.* **2. of hers.** belonging to her. [C14 *hires;* see HER]

herself (həˈsɛlf) *pron.* **1. a.** the reflexive form of *she* or *her.* **b.** (intensifier): *the queen herself signed.* **2.** (*preceded by a copula*) her normal self: *she looks herself again after the operation.*

▷ **Usage.** See at **myself.**

hertz (hɜːts) *n., pl.* **hertz.** the derived SI unit of frequency; the frequency of a periodic phenomenon that has a periodic time of 1 second; 1 cycle per second. Symbol: Hz [C20: after H. R. *Hertz* (1857–94), G physicist]

Hertzian wave (ˈhɜːtsɪən) *n.* an electromagnetic wave with a frequency in the range from about 3×10^{10} hertz to about 1.5×10^{5} hertz. [C19: after H. R. *Hertz*]

he's (hiːz) *contraction of* he is *or* he has.

hesitant (ˈhɛzɪtᵊnt) *adj.* wavering, hesitating, or irresolute. —ˈ**hesitantly** *adv.*

hesitate (ˈhɛzɪˌteɪt) *vb.* (*intr.*) **1.** to be slow in acting; be uncertain. **2.** to be reluctant (to do something). **3.** to stammer or pause in speaking. [C17: < L *haesitāre,* < *haerēre* to cling to] —**hesitancy** (ˈhɛzɪtᵊnsɪ) *or* ˌ**hesiˈtation** *n.* —ˈ**hesiˌtatingly** *adv.*

Hesperian (hɛˈspɪərɪən) *adj.* **1.** *Poetic.* western. **2.** of or relating to the Hesperides or Islands of the Blessed where, in Greek mythology, the souls of the good went after death.

hesperidium (ˌhɛspəˈrɪdɪəm) *n. Bot.* the fruit of citrus plants, in which the flesh consists of fluid-filled hairs and is protected by a tough rind. [C19: NL; alluding to the fruit in the garden of the *Hesperides,* nymphs in Gk myth (daughters of Hesperus)]

Hesperus (ˈhɛspərəs) *n.* an evening star, esp. Venus. [< L, < Gk, < *hesperos* western]

hessian (ˈhɛsɪən) *n.* a coarse jute fabric similar to sacking. [C18: < HESSIAN]

Hessian (ˈhɛsɪən) *n.* **1.** a native or inhabitant of Hesse, a state of West Germany. **2.** a Hessian soldier in any of the mercenary units of the British Army in the War of American Independence or the Napoleonic Wars. *~adj.* **3.** of Hesse or its inhabitants.

Hessian fly *n.* a small dipterous fly whose larvae damage wheat, barley, and rye. [C18: thought to have been introduced into America by Hessian soldiers]

hest (hɛst) *n.* an archaic word for **behest.** [OE *hǣs*]

hetaera (hɪˈtɪərə) *or* **hetaira** (hɪˈtaɪrə) *n., pl.* **-taerae** (-ˈtɪəriː) *or* **-tairai** (-ˈtaɪraɪ). (esp. in ancient Greece) a prostitute, esp. an educated courtesan. [C19: < Gk *hetaira* concubine]

hetaerism (hɪˈtɪərɪzəm) *or* **hetairism** (hɪˈtaɪrɪzəm) *n.* **1.** the state of being a concubine. **2.** *Sociol., anthropol.* a social system attributed to some primitive societies, in which women are communally shared.

hetero- *combining form.* other, another, or different: *heterosexual.* [< Gk *heteros* other]

heteroclite (ˈhɛtərəˌklaɪt) *adj. also* **heteroclitic** (ˌhɛtərəˈklɪtɪk). **1.** (esp. of the form of a word) irregular or unusual. *~n.* **2.** an irregularly formed word. [C16: < LL *heteroclitus* declining irregularly, < Gk, < HETERO- + *klinein* to inflect]

heterocyclic (ˌhɛtərəʊˈsaɪklɪk, -ˈsɪk-) *adj.* (of an organic compound) containing a closed ring of atoms, at least one of which is not a carbon atom.

heterodox (ˈhɛtərəʊˌdɒks) *adj.* **1.** at variance with established or accepted doctrines or beliefs. **2.** holding unorthodox opinions. [C17: < Gk *heterodoxos,* < HETERO- + *doxa* opinion] —ˈ**heteroˌdoxy** *n.*

heterodyne (ˈhɛtərəʊˌdaɪn) *vb.* **1.** *Electronics.* to combine by modulation (two alternating signals) to produce two signals having frequencies corresponding to the sum and the difference of the original frequencies. *~adj.* **2.** produced by, operating by, or involved in heterodyning two signals.

heteroecious (ˌhɛtəˈriːʃəs) *adj.* (of parasites) undergoing different stages of the life cycle on different host species. [< HETERO- + *-oecious,* < Gk *oikia* house] —**heteroecism** (ˌhɛtəˈriːˌsɪzəm) *n.*

heterogamete (ˌhɛtərəʊgæˈmiːt) *n.* a gamete that differs in size and form from the one with which it unites in fertilization.

heterogamy (ˌhɛtəˈrɒgəmɪ) *n.* **1.** a type of sexual reproduction in which the gametes differ in both size and form. **2.** a condition in which different types of reproduction occur in successive generations of an organism. **3.** the presence of both male and female flowers in one inflorescence. —ˌ**heterˈogamous** *adj.*

heterogeneous (ˌhɛtərəʊˈdʒiːnɪəs) *adj.* **1.** composed of unrelated parts. **2.** not of the same type. [C17: < Med. L *heterogeneus,* < Gk, < HETERO- + *genos* sort] —**heterogeneity** (ˌhɛtərəʊdʒɪˈniːɪtɪ) *or* ˌ**heteroˈgeneousness** *n.*

heterogony (ˌhɛtəˈrɒgənɪ) *n.* **1.** *Biol.* the alternation of parthenogenetic and sexual generations in rotifers and similar animals. **2.** the condition in plants, such as the primrose, of having flowers that differ from each other in the length of their stamens and styles. —ˌ**heterˈogonous** *adj.*

heterologous (ˌhɛtəˈrɒləgəs) *adj.* **1.** *Pathol.* designating cells or tissues not normally present in a particular part of the body. **2.** differing in structure or origin. —ˌ**heterˈology** *n.*

heteromerous (ˌhɛtəˈrɒmərəs) *adj. Biol.* having parts that differ, esp. in number.

heteromorphic (ˌhɛtərəʊˈmɔːfɪk) *or* **heteromorphous** *adj. Biol.* **1.** differing from the normal form. **2.** (esp. of insects) having different forms at different stages of the life cycle. —ˌ**heteroˈmorphism** *n.*

heteronomous (ˌhɛtəˈrɒnɪməs) *adj.* **1.** subject to an external law. **2.** (of parts of an organism), differing in the manner of growth, development, or specialization. —ˌ**heterˈonomy** *n.*

heteronym (ˈhɛtərəʊˌnɪm) *n.* one of two or more words pronounced differently but spelt alike: *the two English words spelt "bow" are heteronyms.* Cf. **homograph.** [C17: < LGk *heteronumos,* < Gk HETERO- + *onoma* name]

heterophyllous (ˌhɛtərəʊˈfɪləs, ˌhɛtəˈrɒfɪləs) *adj.* having more than one type of leaf on the same plant. —ˈ**heteroˌphylly** *n.*

heteropterous (ˌhɛtəˈrɒptərəs) *or* **heteropteran** *adj.* of or belonging to a suborder of hemipterous insects, including bedbugs, water bugs, etc., in which the forewings are membranous but have leathery tips. [C19: < NL *Heteroptera,* < HETERO- + Gk *pteron* wing]

heterosexual (ˌhɛtərəʊˈsɛksjʊəl) *n.* **1.** a person who is sexually attracted to the opposite sex. ~*adj.* **2.** of or relating to heterosexuality. —ˌ**heteroˌsexuˈality** *n.*

heterotaxis (ˌhɛtərəʊˈtæksɪs) *or* **heterotaxy** *n.* an abnormal or asymmetrical arrangement of parts, as of the organs of the body.

heterotrophic (ˌhɛtərəʊˈtrɒfɪk) *adj.* (of animals and some plants) using complex organic compounds to manufacture their own organic constituents. [C20: < HETERO- + Gk *trophikos* concerning food, < *trophē* nourishment]

heterozygote (ˌhɛtərəʊˈzaɪgəʊt) *n.* an animal or plant that is heterozygous; a hybrid.

heterozygous (ˌhɛtərəʊˈzaɪgəs) *adj. Genetics.* (of an organism) having dissimilar alleles for any one gene: *heterozygous for eye colour.*

hetman (ˈhɛtmən) *n., pl.* **-mans.** an elected leader of the Cossacks. Also called: **ataman.** [C18: < Polish, < G *Hauptmann* headman]

het up *adj. Inf.* angry; excited: *don't get het up.* [C19: < dialect p.p. of HEAT]

heuchera (ˈhɔɪkərə) *n.* a North American shrub with red or pink flowers and ornamental foliage. [after J. H. *Heucher* (1677–1747), G botanist]

heuristic (hjʊəˈrɪstɪk) *adj.* **1.** helping to learn; guiding in investigation. **2.** (of a method of teaching) allowing pupils to learn things for themselves. **3. a.** *Maths, science, philosophy.* using or obtained by exploration of possibilities rather than by following set rules. **b.** *Computers.* denoting a rule of thumb for solving a problem without the exhaustive application of an algorithm. ~*n.* **4.** (*pl.*) the science of heuristic procedure. [C19: < NL *heuristicus,* < Gk *heuriskein* to discover] —**heuˈristically** *adv.*

hew (hjuː) *vb.* **hewing, hewed, hewed** *or* **hewn. 1.** to strike (something, esp. wood) with cutting blows, as with an axe. **2.** (*tr.;* often foll. by *out*) to carve from a substance. **3.** (*tr.;* often foll. by *away, off,* etc.) to sever from a larger portion. **4.** (*intr.;* often foll. by *to*) *U.S. & Canad.* to conform. [OE *hēawan*] —ˈ**hewer** *n.*

hex[1] (hɛks) *n.* **a.** short for **hexadecimal (notation). b.** (*as modifier*): *hex code.*

hex[2] (hɛks) *U.S. & Canad. inf.* ~*vb.* **1.** (*tr.*) to bewitch. ~*n.* **2.** an evil spell. **3.** a witch. [C19: via Pennsylvania Du. < G *Hexe* witch, < MHG *hecse,* ? < OHG *hagzissa*]

hex. *abbrev. for:* **1.** hexachord. **2.** hexagon(al).

hexa- *or before a vowel* **hex-** *combining form.* six: *hexachord; hexameter.* [< Gk, < *hex* SIX]

hexachlorophene (ˌhɛksəˈklɔːrəfiːn) *n.* an insoluble white bactericidal substance used in antiseptic soaps, deodorants, etc. Formula: $(C_6HCl_3OH)_2CH_2$.

hexachord (ˈhɛksəˌkɔːd) *n.* (in medieval musical theory) any of three diatonic scales based upon C, F, and G, each consisting of six notes, from which solmization was developed.

hexad (ˈhɛksæd) *n.* a group or series of six. [C17: < Gk *hexas,* < *hex* six]

hexadecimal notation *or* **hexadecimal** (ˌhɛksəˈdɛsɪməl) *n.* a number system having a base 16; the symbols for the numbers 0 - 9 are the same as those used in the decimal system, and the numbers 10 - 15 are usually represented by the letters A - F. The system is used as a convenient way of representing the internal binary code of a computer.

hexagon (ˈhɛksəgən) *n.* a polygon having six sides. —**hexˈagonal** *adj.*

hexagram (ˈhɛksəˌgræm) *n.* a star-shaped figure formed by extending the sides of a regular hexagon to meet at six points.

hexahedron (ˌhɛksəˈhiːdrən) *n.* a solid figure having six plane faces. —ˌ**hexaˈhedral** *adj.*

hexameter (hɛkˈsæmɪtə) *n. Prosody.* **1.** a verse line consisting of six metrical feet. **2.** (in Greek and Latin epic poetry) a verse line of six metrical feet, of which the first four are usually dactyls or spondees, the fifth almost always a dactyl, and the sixth a spondee or trochee. —**hexametric** (ˌhɛksəˈmɛtrɪk) *or* ˌ**hexaˈmetrical** *adj.*

hexane (ˈhɛkseɪn) *n.* a liquid alkane existing in five isomeric forms that are found in petroleum and used as solvents. Formula: $CH_3(CH_2)_4CH_3$ (*n*-). [C19: < HEXA- + -ANE]

hexapla (ˈhɛksəplə) *n.* an edition of the Old Testament compiled by Origen (?185–?254 A.D.), Christian theologian, containing six versions of the text. [C17: < Gk *hexaploos* sixfold] —ˈ**hexaplar** *adj.*

hexapod (ˈhɛksəˌpɒd) *n.* an insect.

hexavalent (hɛkˈsævələnt, ˌhɛksəˈveɪlənt) *adj. Chem.* having a valency of six. Also: **sexivalent.**

hexose (ˈhɛksəʊs, -əʊz) *n.* a monosaccharide, such as glucose, that contains six carbon atoms per molecule.

hey (heɪ) *interj.* **1.** an expression indicating surprise, dismay, discovery, etc. **2. hey presto.** an exclamation used by conjurers to herald the climax of a trick. [C13: imit.]

heyday (ˈheɪˌdeɪ) *n.* the time of most power, popularity, vigour, etc. [C16: prob. based on HEY]

hf *abbrev. for* half.

Hf *the chemical symbol for* hafnium.

HF *or* **h.f.** *abbrev. for* high frequency.

hg *abbrev. for* hectogram.

Hg *the chemical symbol for* mercury. [< NL *hydrargyrum*]

HG *abbrev. for* His (*or* Her) Grace.

hgt *abbrev. for* height.

HGV (in Britain) *abbrev. for* heavy goods vehicle.

HH *abbrev. for:* **1.** His (*or* Her) Highness. **2.** His Holiness (title of the Pope). ~**3.** (on British pencils) *symbol for* double hard.

hi (haɪ) *sentence substitute.* an informal word for **hello.** [C20: prob. < *how are you*?]

hiatus (haɪˈeɪtəs) *n., pl.* **-tuses** *or* **-tus. 1.** (esp. in manuscripts) a break or interruption in continuity. **2.** a break between adjacent vowels in the pronunciation of a word. [C16: < L: gap, cleft, < *hiāre* to gape]

hiatus hernia *n.* protrusion of part of the stomach through the diaphragm at the oesophageal opening.

hibachi (hɪˈbɑːtʃɪ) *n.* a portable brazier for heating and cooking food. [< Japanese, < *hi* fire + *bachi* bowl]

hibernal (haɪˈbɜːnˀl) *adj.* of or occurring in winter. [C17: < L *hībernālis,* < *hiems* winter]

hibernate (ˈhaɪbəˌneɪt) *vb.* (*intr.*) **1.** (of some animals) to pass the winter in a dormant condition with metabolism greatly slowed down. **2.** to cease from activity. [C19: < L *hībernāre* to spend the winter, < *hībernus* of winter] —ˌ**hiberˈnation** *n.* —ˈ**hiberˌnator** *n.*

Hibernia (haɪˈbɜːnɪə) *n.* the Roman name for Ireland: used poetically in later times. —**Hiˈbernian** *adj., n.*

Hibernicism (haɪˈbɜːnɪˌsɪzəm) *n.* an Irish expression, idiom, trait, custom, etc.

hibiscus (hɪˈbɪskəs) *n., pl.* **-cuses.** any plant of the chiefly tropical and subtropical genus *Hibiscus,* cultivated for its large brightly coloured flowers. [C18: < L, < Gk *hibiskos* marsh mallow]

hiccup (ˈhɪkʌp) *n.* **1.** a spasm of the diaphragm producing a sudden breathing in of air resulting in a characteristic sharp sound. **2.** the state of having such spasms. **3.** *Inf.* a minor difficulty. ~*vb.* **-cuping, -cuped** *or* **-cupping, -cupped. 4.** (*intr.*) to make a hiccup or hiccups. **5.** (*tr.*) to utter with a hiccup. ~Also: **hiccough** (ˈhɪkʌp). [C16: imit.]

hic jacet *Latin.* (hɪk ˈjækɛt) (on gravestones, etc.) here lies.

hick (hɪk) *n. Inf., chiefly U.S. & Canad.* a country bumpkin. [C16: after *Hick,* familiar form of *Richard*]

hickory (ˈhɪkərɪ) *n., pl.* **-ries. 1.** a tree of a chiefly North American genus having nuts with edible kernels and hard smooth shells. **2.** the hard tough wood of this tree. [C17: ult. < Algonquian *pawcohiccora* food made from ground hickory nuts]

hid (hɪd) *vb.* the past tense and a past participle of **hide**[1].

hidalgo (hɪˈdælgəʊ) *n., pl.* **-gos.** a member of the lower nobility in Spain. [C16: < Sp., < OSp. *fijo dalgo* nobleman, < L *filius* son + *dē* of + *aliquid* something]

hidden (ˈhɪdᵊn) *vb.* **1.** a past participle of **hide**[1]. ~*adj.* **2.** concealed or obscured: *a hidden cave; a hidden meaning.*

hide[1] (haɪd) *vb.* **hiding, hid, hidden** *or* **hid. 1.** to conceal (oneself or an object) from view or discovery: *to hide a pencil; to hide from the police.* **2.** (*tr.*) to obscure: *clouds hid the sun.* **3.** (*tr.*) to keep secret. **4.** (*tr.*) to turn (one's eyes, etc.) away. ~*n.* **5.** *Brit.* a place of concealment, usually disguised to appear as part of the natural environment, used by hunters, birdwatchers, etc. U.S. and Canad. equivalent: **blind.** [OE *hȳdan*] —ˈ**hider** *n.*

hide[2] (haɪd) *n.* **1.** the skin of an animal, either tanned or raw. **2.** *Inf.* the human skin. ~*vb.* **hiding, hided. 3.** (*tr.*) *Inf.* to flog. [OE *hȳd*]

hide[3] (haɪd) *n.* an obsolete Brit. land measure, varying from about 60 to 120 acres. [OE *hīgid*]

hide-and-seek *or U.S. & Canad.* **hide-and-go-seek** *n.* a game in which one player covers his eyes while the others hide, and he then tries to find them.

hideaway (ˈhaɪdəˌweɪ) *n.* a hiding place or secluded spot.

hidebound (ˈhaɪdˌbaʊnd) *adj.* **1.** restricted by petty rules, a conservative attitude, etc. **2.** (of cattle, etc.) having the skin closely attached to the flesh as a result of poor feeding.

hideous (ˈhɪdɪəs) *adj.* **1.** extremely ugly; repulsive. **2.** terrifying and horrific. [C13: < OF *hisdos,* < *hisde* fear; <?] —ˈ**hideously** *adv.* —ˈ**hideousness** *n.*

hide-out *n.* a hiding place, esp. a remote place used by outlaws, etc.; hideaway.

hiding[1] (ˈhaɪdɪŋ) *n.* **1.** the state of concealment: *in hiding.* **2. hiding place.** a place of concealment.

hiding[2] (ˈhaɪdɪŋ) *n. Inf.* a flogging; beating.

hidrosis (hɪˈdrəʊsɪs) *n.* a technical word for **perspiration** or **sweat.** [C18: via NL < Gk, < *hidrōs* sweat] —**hidrotic** (hɪˈdrɒtɪk) *adj.*

hidy-hole *or* **hidey-hole** *n. Inf.* a hiding place.

hie (haɪ) *vb.* **hieing** *or* **hying, hied.** *Arch. or poetic.* to hurry; speed. [OE *hīgian* to strive]

hierarch (ˈhaɪəˌrɑːk) *n.* **1.** a high priest. **2.** a person at a high level in a hierarchy. —ˌ**hierˈarchal** *adj.*

hierarchy (ˈhaɪəˌrɑːkɪ) *n., pl.* **-chies. 1.** a system of persons or things arranged in a graded order. **2.** a body of persons in holy orders organized into graded ranks. **3.** the collective body of those so organized. **4.** a series of ordered groupings within a system, such as the arrangement of plants into classes, orders, etc. **5.** government by a priesthood. [C14: < Med. L *hierarchia,* < LGk, < *hierarkhēs* high priest; see HIERO-, -ARCHY] —ˌ**hierˈarchical** *or* ˌ**hierˈarchic** *adj.* —ˈ**hierˌarchism** *n.*

hieratic (ˌhaɪəˈrætɪk) *adj.* **1.** of priests. **2.** of a cursive form of hieroglyphics used by priests in ancient Egypt. **3.** of styles in art that adhere to certain fixed types, as in ancient Egypt. ~*n.* **4.** the hieratic script of ancient Egypt. [C17: < L *hierāticus,* < Gk, < *hiereus* priest] —ˌ**hierˈatically** *adv.*

hiero- *or before a vowel* **hier-** *combining form.* holy or divine: *hierarchy.* [< Gk, < *hieros* holy]

hieroglyphic (ˌhaɪərəˈglɪfɪk) *adj. also* **hieroglyphical. 1.** of or relating to a form of writing using picture symbols, esp. as used in ancient Egypt. **2.** difficult to decipher. ~*n. also* **hieroglyph. 3.** a picture or symbol representing an object, concept, or sound. **4.** a symbol that is difficult to decipher. [C16: < LL *hieroglyphicus,* < Gk, < HIERO- + *gluphē,* < *gluphein* to carve] —ˌ**hieroˈglyphically** *adv.*

hieroglyphics (ˌhaɪərəˈglɪfɪks) *n.* (*functioning as sing. or pl.*) **1.** a form of writing, esp. as used in ancient Egypt, in which pictures or symbols are used to represent objects, concepts, or sounds. **2.** difficult or undecipherable writing.

hierophant (ˈhaɪərəˌfænt) *n.* **1.** (in ancient Greece) a high priest of religious mysteries. **2.** a person who interprets esoteric mysteries. [C17: < LL *hierophanta,* < Gk, < HIERO- + *phainein* to reveal] —ˌ**hieroˈphantic** *adj.*

hi-fi (ˈhaɪˌfaɪ) *n. Inf.* **1. a.** short for **high fidelity. b.** (*as modifier*): *hi-fi equipment.* **2.** a set of high-quality sound-reproducing equipment.

higgledy-piggledy (ˈhɪgᵊldɪˈpɪgᵊldɪ) *Inf.* ~*adj., adv.* **1.** in a jumble. ~*n.* **2.** a muddle.

high (haɪ) *adj.* **1.** being a relatively great distance from top to bottom; tall: *a high building.* **2.** situated at a relatively great distance above sea level: *a high plateau.* **3.** (*postpositive*) being a specified distance from top to bottom: *three feet high.* **4.** extending from or performed at an elevation: *a high dive.* **5.** (*in combination*) coming up to a specified level: *knee-high.* **6.** being at its peak: *high noon.* **7.** of greater than average height: *a high collar.* **8.** greater than normal in intensity or amount: *a high wind; high mileage.* **9.** (of sound) acute in pitch. **10.** (of latitudes) relatively far north or south from the equator. **11.** (of meat) slightly decomposed, regarded as enhancing the flavour of game. **12.** very important: *the high priestess.* **13.** exalted in style or character: *high drama.* **14.** expressing contempt or arrogance: *high words.* **15.** elated; cheerful: *high spirits.* **16.** *Inf.* being in a state of altered consciousness induced by alcohol, narcotics, etc. **17.** *Inf.* overexcited: *by Christmas the children are high.* **18.** luxurious or extravagant: *high life.* **19.** advanced in complexity: *high finance.* **20.** (of a gear) providing a relatively great forward speed for a given engine speed. **21.** *Phonetics.* denoting a vowel whose articulation is produced by raising the tongue, such as for the *ee* in *see* or *oo* in *moon.* **22.** (*cap. when part of a name*) formal and elaborate: *High Mass.* **23.** (*usually cap.*) relating to the High Church. **24.** *Cards.* having a relatively great value in a suit. **25. high and dry.** stranded; destitute. **26. high and mighty.** *Inf.* arrogant. **27. high opinion.** a favourable opinion. ~*adv.* **28.** at or to a height: *he jumped high.* **29.** in a high manner. **30.** *Naut.* close to the wind with sails full. ~*n.* **31.** a high place or level. **32.** *Inf.* a state of altered consciousness induced by alcohol, narcotics, etc. **33.** another word for **anticyclone. 34. on high. a.** at a height. **b.** in heaven. [OE *hēah*]

High Arctic *n.* the regions of Canada, esp. the northern islands, within the Arctic Circle.

highball (ˈhaɪˌbɔːl) *n. Chiefly U.S.* a long iced drink consisting of spirits with soda water, etc.

highborn (ˈhaɪˌbɔːn) *adj.* of noble birth.

highboy (ˈhaɪˌbɔɪ) *n. U.S. & Canad.* a tallboy.

highbrow (ˈhaɪˌbraʊ) *Often disparaging.* ~*n.* **1.** a person of scholarly and erudite tastes. ~*adj. also* **highbrowed. 2.** appealing to highbrows.

highchair (ˈhaɪˌtʃɛə) *n.* a long-legged chair for a child, esp. one with a table-like tray.

High Church *n.* **1.** the party or movement within the Church of England stressing continuity with Catholic Christendom, the authority of bishops, and the importance of sacraments. ~*adj.* **High-Church. 2.** of or relating to this party or movement. —ˈ**High-ˈChurchman** *n.*

high-class *adj.* **1.** of very good quality: *a high-class grocer.* **2.** belonging to or exhibiting the characteristics of an upper social class.

high-coloured *adj.* (of the complexion) deep red or purplish; florid.

high comedy *n.* comedy set largely among cultured and articulate people and featuring witty dialogue.

high commissioner *n.* the senior diplomatic representative sent by one Commonwealth country to another instead of an ambassador.

high country *n.* (often preceded by *the*) *N.Z.* sheep pastures in the foothills of the Southern Alps, New Zealand.

High Court *n.* **1.** Also called: **High Court of Justice.** (in England) the supreme court dealing with civil law cases. **2.** (in Australia) the highest court of appeal, deciding esp. constitutional issues. **3.** (in New Zealand) a court of law that is superior to a District Court. Former name: **Supreme Court.**

higher (ˈhaɪə) *adj.* **1.** the comparative of **high.** ~*n.* (*usually cap.*) (in Scotland) **2. a.** the advanced level of the Scottish Certificate of Education. **b.** (*as modifier*): *Higher Latin.* **3.** a pass in a subject at Higher level: *she has four Highers.*

higher education *n.* education and training at colleges, universities, etc.

higher mathematics *n.* (*functioning as sing.*) mathematics that is more abstract than normal arithmetic, algebra, geometry, and trigonometry.

higher-up *n. Inf.* a person of higher rank or in a superior position.

highest common factor *n.* the largest number or quantity that is a factor of each member of a group of numbers or quantities.

high explosive *n.* an extremely powerful chemical explosive, such as TNT or gelignite.

highfalutin (ˌhaɪfəˈluːtɪn) *or* **highfaluting** *adj. Inf.* pompous or pretentious. [C19: < HIGH + *-falutin,* ? var. of *fluting,* < FLUTE]

high fidelity *n.* **a.** the reproduction of sound using electronic equipment that gives faithful reproduction with little or no distortion. **b.** (*as modifier*): *a high-fidelity amplifier.* ~Often shortened to **hi-fi.**

high-flier *or* **high-flyer** *n.* **1.** a person who is extreme in aims, ambition, etc. **2.** a person of great ability, esp. in a career. —**ˈhigh-ˌflying** *adj., n.*

high-flown *adj.* extravagant or pretentious in conception or intention: *high-flown ideas.*

high frequency *n.* a radio frequency lying between 30 and 3 megahertz. Abbrev.: **HF.**

High German *n.* the standard German language, historically developed from the form of West Germanic spoken in S Germany.

high-handed *adj.* tactlessly overbearing and inconsiderate. —ˌ**high-ˈhandedness** *n.*

high-hat *adj.* **1.** *Inf.* snobbish and arrogant. ~*vb.* **-hatting, -hatted.** (*tr.*) **2.** *Inf. chiefly U.S. & Canad.* to treat in a snobbish or offhand way. ~*n.* **3.** *Inf.* a snobbish person.

highjack (ˈhaɪˌdʒæk) *vb., n.* a less common spelling of **hijack.** —**ˈhighˌjacker** *n.*

high jump *n.* **1.** (usually preceded by *the*) an athletic event in which a competitor has to jump over a high bar. **2. the high jump.** *Brit. inf.* a severe reprimand or punishment. —**high jumper** *n.* —**high jumping** *n.*

high-key *adj.* (of a painting, etc.) having a predominance of light tones or colours.

highland (ˈhaɪlənd) *n.* **1.** relatively high ground. **2.** (*modifier*) of or relating to a highland. —**ˈhighlander** *n.*

Highland (ˈhaɪlənd) *n.* (*modifier*) of or denoting the Highlands of Scotland. —**ˈHighlander** *n.*

Highland cattle *n.* a breed of cattle with shaggy reddish-brown hair and long horns.

Highland dress *n.* **1.** the historical costume including the plaid and kilt, of Highland clansmen and soldiers. **2.** a modern version of this worn for formal occasions.

Highland fling *n.* a vigorous Scottish solo dance.

Highlands (ˈhaɪləndz) *n.* **the. 1. a.** the part of Scotland that lies to the northwest of the great fault that runs from Dumbarton to Stonehaven. **b.** a mountainous region of NW Scotland: distinguished by Gaelic culture. **2.** (*often not cap.*) the highland region of any country.

high-level language *n.* a computer-programming language that is closer to human language or mathematical notation than to machine language.

highlight (ˈhaɪˌlaɪt) *n.* **1.** an area of the lightest tone in a painting, photograph, etc. **2.** Also called: **high spot.** the most exciting or memorable part or time. **3.** (*pl.*) a lightened or brightened effect produced in the hair by bleaching selected strands. ~*vb.* (*tr.*) **4.** *Painting, photog., etc.* to mark with light tone. **5.** to bring emphasis to. **6.** to produce highlights in (the hair).

highly (ˈhaɪlɪ) *adv.* **1.** (intensifier): *highly disappointed.* **2.** with great approbation: *we spoke highly of it.* **3.** in a high position: *placed highly in class.* **4.** at or for a high cost.

highly strung *or U.S. & Canad.* **high-strung** *adj.* tense and easily upset; excitable; nervous.

High Mass *n.* a solemn and elaborate sung Mass.

high-minded *adj.* **1.** having or characterized by high moral principles. **2.** *Arch.* arrogant; haughty. —ˌ**high-ˈmindedness** *n.*

highness (ˈhaɪnɪs) *n.* the condition of being high.

Highness (ˈhaɪnɪs) *n.* (preceded by *Your, His,* or *Her*) a title used to address or refer to a royal person.

high-octane *adj.* (of petrol) having a high octane number.

high-pass filter *n. Electronics.* a filter that transmits all frequencies above a specified value, attenuating frequencies below this value.

high-pitched *adj.* **1.** pitched high in tone. **2.** (of a roof) having steeply sloping sides. **3.** (of an argument, style, etc.) lofty or intense.

high-powered *adj.* **1.** (of an optical instrument or lens) having a high magnification. **2.** dynamic and energetic; highly capable.

high-pressure *adj.* **1.** having, using, or designed to withstand pressure above normal. **2.** *Inf.* (of selling) persuasive in an aggressive and persistent manner.

high priest *n.* **1.** *Judaism.* the priest of highest rank who alone was permitted to enter the holy of holies of the Temple. **2.** Also (*fem.*): **high priestess.** the head of a cult. —**high priesthood** *n.*

high-rise *adj.* (*prenominal*) of or relating to a building that has many storeys, esp. one used for flats or offices: *a high-rise block.*

high-risk *adj.* denoting a group, part, etc., that is particularly subject to a danger.

highroad (ˈhaɪˌrəʊd) *n.* **1.** a main road; highway. **2.** (usually preceded by *the*) the sure way: *the highroad to fame.*

high school *n.* **1.** *Brit.* another term for **grammar school. 2.** *U.S., Canad., & N.Z.* a secondary school.

high seas *pl. n.* (*sometimes sing.*) the open seas, outside the jurisdiction of any one nation.

high season *n.* the most popular time of year at a holiday resort, etc.

high-sounding *adj.* another term for **high-flown.**

high-spirited *adj.* vivacious, bold, or lively. —ˌ**high-ˈspiritedness** *n.*

High Street *n.* (*often not cap.;* usually preceded by *the*) *Brit.* the main street of a town, usually where the principal shops are situated.

high table *n.* (*sometimes cap.*) the table in the dining hall of a school, college, etc., at which the principal teachers, fellows, etc., sit.

hightail (ˈhaɪˌteɪl) *vb.* (*intr.*) *Inf., chiefly U.S. & Canad.* to go or move in a great hurry.

high tea *n. Brit.* a substantial early evening meal consisting of a cooked dish, cakes, etc., and usually accompanied by tea.

high tech (tɛk) *n.* **1.** short for **high technology.** ~*adj.* **high-tech. 2.** of or relating to a style of interior decoration using features of industrial equipment.

high technology *n.* any type of sophisticated industrial process, esp. electronic.

high-tension *n.* (*modifier*) carrying or operating at a relatively high voltage.

high tide *n.* **1.** the tide at its highest level. **2.** a culminating point.

high time *Inf.* ~*adv.* **1.** the latest possible time: *it's high time you left.* ~*n.* **2.** Also: **high old time.** an enjoyable and exciting time.

high-toned *adj.* **1.** having a superior social, moral, or intellectual quality. **2.** affectedly superior. **3.** high in tone.

high treason *n.* an act of treason directly affecting a sovereign or state.

high-up *n. Inf.* a person who holds an important or influential position.

highveld (ˈhaɪˌfɛlt) *n.* **the.** the high grassland region of the Transvaal, South Africa.

high water *n.* **1.** another name for **high tide. 2.** the state of any stretch of water at its highest level, as during a flood. ~Abbrev.: **HW.**

high-water mark *n.* **1.** the level reached by sea water at high tide or by other stretches of water in flood. **2.** the highest point.

highway (ˈhaɪˌweɪ) *n.* **1.** a public road that all may use. **2.** *Now chiefly U.S. & Canad. except in legal contexts.* a main road, esp. one that connects towns. **3.** a direct path or course.

Highway Code *n.* (in Britain) a booklet compiled by the Department of Transport for the guidance of users of public roads.

highwayman (ˈhaɪweɪmən) *n., pl.* **-men.** (formerly) a robber, usually on horseback, who held up travellers on public roads.

high wire *n.* a tightrope stretched high in the air for balancing acts.

HIH *abbrev. for* His (*or* Her) Imperial Highness.

hijack *or* **highjack** (ˈhaɪˌdʒæk) *vb.* **1.** (*tr.*) to seize or divert (a vehicle or the goods it carries) while in transit: *to hijack an aircraft.* ~*n.* **2.** the act or an instance of hijacking. [C20: <?] —**ˈhiˌjacker** *or* **ˈhighˌjacker** *n.*

hike (haɪk) *vb.* **1.** (*intr.*) to walk a long way, usually for pleasure, esp. in the country. **2.** (usually foll. by *up*) to pull or be pulled; hitch. **3.** (*tr.;* usually foll. by *up*) to raise (prices). ~*n.* **4.** a long walk. **5.** a rise in price. [C18: <?] —**ˈhiker** *n.*

hilarious (hɪˈlɛərɪəs) *adj.* very funny. [C19: < L *hilaris* glad, < Gk *hilaros*] —**hiˈlariously** *adv.* —**hiˈlariousness** *n.*

hilarity (hɪˈlærɪtɪ) *n.* mirth and merriment.

Hilary term (ˈhɪlərɪ) *n.* the spring term at Oxford University and some other educational establishments. [C16: after Saint *Hilary* of Poitiers (?315–?367), F bishop]

hill (hɪl) *n.* **1. a.** a natural elevation of the earth's surface, less high or craggy than a mountain. **b.** (*in combination*): *a hillside.* **2. a.** a heap or mound. **b.** (*in combination*): *a dunghill.* **3.** an incline; slope. **4. hill and dale.** (of gramophone records) having vertical groove undulations. **5. over the hill. a.** *Inf.* beyond one's prime. **b.** *Mil. sl.* absent without leave or deserting. ~*vb.* (*tr.*) **6.** to form into a hill. **7.** to cover or surround with a heap of earth. [OE *hyll*] —**ˈhilly** *adj.*

hillbilly (ˈhɪlˌbɪlɪ) *n., pl.* **-lies. 1.** *Usually disparaging.* an unsophisticated person, esp. from the mountainous areas in the southeastern U.S. **2.** another name for **country and western.** [C20: < HILL + *Billy* (the nickname)]

hillock (ˈhɪlək) *n.* a small hill or mound. [C14 *hilloc*] —**ˈhillocked** *or* **ˈhillocky** *adj.*

hills (hɪlz) *pl. n.* **1. as old as the hills.** very old. **2. the.** a hilly and often remote region.

hill station *n.* (in northern India, etc.) a settlement or resort at a high altitude.

hilt (hɪlt) *n.* **1.** the handle or shaft of a sword, dagger, etc. **2. to the hilt.** to the full. [OE]

hilum (ˈhaɪləm) *n., pl.* **-la** (-lə). *Bot.* a scar on a seed marking its point of attachment to the seed stalk. [C17: < L: trifle]

him (hɪm; *unstressed* ɪm) *pron.* (*objective*) refers to a male person or animal: *they needed him; she baked him a cake; not him again!* [OE *him,* dative of *hē* HE]

▷ **Usage.** See at **me.**

HIM *abbrev. for* His (*or* Her) Imperial Majesty.

himation (hɪˈmætɪˌɒn) *n., pl.* **-ia** (-ɪə). (in ancient Greece) a cloak draped around the body. [C19: < Gk, < *heima* dress, < *hennunai* to clothe]

himself (hɪmˈsɛlf; *medially often* ɪmˈsɛlf) *pron.* **1. a.** the reflexive form of *he* or *him.* **b.** (intensifier): *the king himself waved to me.* **2.** (*preceded by a copula*) his normal self: *he seems himself once more.* [OE *him selfum,* dative sing. of *hē self;* see HE, SELF]

▷ **Usage.** See at **myself.**

Hinayana (ˌhiːnəˈjɑːnə) *n.* any of various early forms of Buddhism. [< Sansk., < *hīna* lesser + *yāna* vehicle]

hind[1] (haɪnd) *adj.* **hinder, hindmost** *or* **hindermost.** (*prenominal*) (esp. of parts of the body) situated at the back: *a hind leg.* [OE *hindan* at the back, rel. to G *hinten*]

hind[2] (haɪnd) *n., pl.* **hinds** *or* **hind. 1.** the female of the deer, esp. the red deer when aged three years or more. **2.** any of several marine fishes related to the groper. [OE *hind*]

hind[3] (haɪnd) *n.* (formerly) **1.** a simple peasant. **2.** (in Scotland and N England) a skilled farm worker. **3.** a steward. [OE *hīne,* < *hīgna,* genitive pl. of *hīgan* servants]

hinder[1] (ˈhɪndə) *vb.* **1.** to be or get in the way of (someone or something); hamper. **2.** (*tr.*) to prevent. [OE *hindrian*]

hinder[2] (ˈhaɪndə) *adj.* (*prenominal*) situated at or further towards the back; posterior. [OE]

Hindi (ˈhɪndɪ) *n.* **1.** a language or group of dialects of N central India. See also **Hindustani. 2.** a formal literary dialect of this language, the official language of India. **3.** a person whose native language is Hindi. [C18: < Hindi, < *Hind* India, < OPersian *Hindu* the river Indus]

hindmost (ˈhaɪndˌməʊst) *or* **hindermost** (ˈhaɪndəˌməʊst) *adj.* furthest back; last.

Hindoo (ˈhɪnduː, hɪnˈduː) *n., pl.* **-doos,** *adj.* an older spelling of **Hindu.** —**ˈHindooˌism** *n.*

hindquarter (ˈhaɪndˌkwɔːtə) *n.* **1.** one of the two back quarters of a carcass of beef, lamb, etc. **2.** (*pl.*) the rear, esp. of a four-legged animal.

hindrance (ˈhɪndrəns) *n.* **1.** an obstruction or snag; impediment. **2.** the act of hindering.

hindsight (ˈhaɪndˌsaɪt) *n.* **1.** the ability to understand, after something has happened, what should have been done. **2.** a firearm's rear sight.

Hindu (ˈhɪnduː, hɪnˈduː) *n., pl.* **-dus. 1.** a person who adheres to Hinduism. **2.** an inhabitant or native of Hindustan or India. ~*adj.* **3.** relating to Hinduism, Hindus, or India. [C17: < Persian *Hindū,* < *Hind* India; see HINDI]

Hinduism (ˈhɪndʊˌɪzəm) *n.* the complex of beliefs and customs comprising the dominant religion of India, characterized by the worship of many gods, a caste system, belief in reincarnation, etc.

Hindustani (ˌhɪndʊˈstɑːnɪ) *n.* **1.** the dialect of Hindi spoken in Delhi: used as a lingua franca throughout India. **2.** all the spoken forms of Hindi and Urdu considered together. ~*adj.* **3.** of or relating to these languages or Hindustan.

hinge (hɪndʒ) *n.* **1.** a device for holding together two parts such that one can swing relative to the other. **2.** a natural joint, such as the knee joint, that functions in only one plane. **3.** something on which events, opinions, etc., turn. **4.** Also called: **mount.** *Philately.* a small transparent strip of gummed paper for affixing a stamp to a page. ~*vb.* **5.** (*tr.*) to fit a hinge to (something). **6.** (*intr.;* usually foll. by *on* or *upon*) to depend (on). **7.** (*intr.*) to hang or turn on or as if on a hinge. [C13: prob. of Gmc origin] —**hinged** *adj.*

hinny[1] (ˈhɪnɪ) *n., pl.* **-nies.** the sterile hybrid offspring of a male horse and a female donkey. [C19: < L *hinnus,* < Gk *hinnos*]

hinny[2] (ˈhɪnɪ) *n. Scot. & N English dialect.* a term of endearment, esp. for a woman. [var. of HONEY]

hint (hɪnt) *n.* **1.** a suggestion given in an indirect or subtle manner. **2.** a helpful piece of advice. **3.** a small amount; trace. ~*vb.* **4.** (when *intr.,* often foll. by *at;* when *tr., takes a clause as object*) to suggest indirectly. [C17: <?]

hinterland (ˈhɪntəˌlænd) *n.* **1.** land lying behind something, esp. a coast or the shore of a river. **2.** remote or undeveloped areas. **3.** an area near and dependent on a large city, esp. a port. [C19: < G, < *hinter* behind + *land* LAND]

hip[1] (hɪp) *n.* **1.** (*often pl.*) either side of the body below the waist and above the thigh. **2.** another name for **pelvis** (sense 1). **3.** short for **hip joint. 4.** the angle formed where two sloping sides of a roof meet. [OE *hype*] —**ˈhipless** *adj.*

hip[2] (hɪp) *n.* the berry-like brightly coloured fruit of a rose plant. Also called: **rosehip.** [OE *héopa*]

hip[3] (hɪp) *interj.* an exclamation used to introduce cheers (in **hip, hip, hurrah**). [C18: <?]

hip[4] (hɪp) *adj.* **hipper, hippest.** *Sl.* **1.** aware of or following the latest trends. **2.** (*often postpositive;* foll. by *to*) informed (about). [var. of earlier *hep*]

hip bath *n.* a portable bath in which the bather sits.

hipbone (ˈhɪpˌbəʊn) *n.* the nontechnical name for **innominate bone.**

hip flask *n.* a small metal flask for spirits, etc.

hip-hop (ˈhɪpˌhɒp) *n.* a U.S. pop culture movement of the 1980s comprising rap music, graffiti, and break dancing.

hip joint *n.* the ball-and-socket joint that connects each leg to the trunk of the body.

hippeastrum (ˌhɪpɪˈæstrəm) *n.* any plant of a South American genus cultivated for their large funnel-shaped typically red flowers. [C19: NL, < Gk *hippeus* knight + *astron* star]

hipped[1] (hɪpt) *adj.* **1. a.** having a hip or hips. **b.** (*in combination*): *broad-hipped.* **2.** (esp. of cows, sheep, etc.) having an injury to the hip, such as a dislocation. **3.** *Archit.* having a hip or hips: *hipped roof.*

hipped[2] (hɪpt) *adj.* (*often postpositive;* foll. by *on*) *U.S. & Canad. dated sl.* very enthusiastic. [C20: < HIP[4]]

hippie *or* **hippy** (ˈhɪpɪ) *n., pl.* **-pies.** (esp. during the 1960s) a person whose behaviour, dress, use of drugs, etc., implies a rejection of conventional values. [C20: see HIP[4]]

hippo (ˈhɪpəʊ) *n., pl.* **-pos.** *Inf.* short for **hippopotamus.**

hippocampus (ˌhɪpəʊˈkæmpəs) *n., pl.* **-pi** (-paɪ). **1.** a mythological sea creature with the forelegs of a horse and the tail of a fish. **2.** any of various small sea fishes with a horselike head; sea horse. **3.** a structure in the floor of the brain, which in cross section has the shape of a sea horse. [C16: < L, < Gk *hippos* horse + *kampos* a sea monster]

hippocras (ˈhɪpəʊˌkræs) *n.* an old English drink of wine flavoured with spices. [C14 *ypocras,* < OF: *Hippocrates,* prob. referring to a filter called *Hippocrates' sleeve,* Hippocrates being regarded as the father of medicine]

Hippocratic oath (ˌhɪpəʊˈkrætɪk) *n.* an oath taken by a doctor to observe a code of medical ethics derived from that of Hippocrates (?460–?377 B.C.), Greek physician.

hippodrome (ˈhɪpəˌdrəʊm) *n.* **1.** a music hall, variety theatre, or circus. **2.** (in ancient Greece or Rome) an open-air course for horse and chariot races. [C16: < L *hippodromos,* < Gk *hippos* horse + *dromos* race]

hippogriff *or* **hippogryph** (ˈhɪpəʊˌgrɪf) *n.* a monster with a griffin's head, wings, and claws and a horse's body. [C17: < It. *ippogrifo,* < *ippo-* horse (< Gk) + *grifo* GRIFFIN]

hippopotamus (ˌhɪpəˈpɒtəməs) *n., pl.* **-muses** *or* **-mi** (-ˌmaɪ). a very large gregarious mammal living in or around the rivers of tropical Africa. [C16: < L, < Gk: river horse, < *hippos* horse + *potamos* river]

hippy[1] (ˈhɪpɪ) *adj.* **-pier, -piest.** *Inf.* (esp. of a woman) having large hips.

hippy[2] (ˈhɪpɪ) *n., pl.* **-pies.** a variant spelling of **hippie.**

hip roof *n.* a roof having sloping ends and sides.

hipster (ˈhɪpstə) *n.* **1.** *Sl., now rare.* **a.** an enthusiast of modern jazz. **b.** an outmoded word for **hippie. 2.** (*modifier*) (of trousers) cut so that the top encircles the hips.

hipsters (ˈhɪpstəz) *pl. n. Brit.* trousers cut so that the top encircles the hips. Usual U.S. word: **hip-huggers.**

hircine (ˈhɜːsaɪn, -sɪn) *adj.* **1.** *Arch.* of or like a goat. **2.** *Literary.* lascivious. [C17: < L *hircīnus,* < *hircus* goat]

hire (ˈhaɪə) *vb.* (*tr.*) **1.** to acquire the temporary use of (a thing) or the services of (a person) in exchange for payment. **2.** to employ (a person) for wages. **3.** (often foll. by *out*) to provide (something) or the services of (oneself or others) for payment, usually for an agreed period. **4.** (*tr.;* foll. by *out*) *Chiefly Brit.* to pay independent contractors for (work to be done). ~*n.* **5. a.** the act of hiring or the state of being hired. **b.** (*as modifier*): *a hire car.* **6.** the price for a person's services or the temporary use of something. **7. for** *or* **on hire.** available for hire. [OE *hӯrian*] —ˈ**hirable** *or* ˈ**hireable** *adj.* —ˈ**hirer** *n.*

hireling (ˈhaɪəlɪŋ) *n. Derog.* a person who works only for money. [OE *hӯrling*]

hire-purchase *n. Brit.* a system in which a buyer takes possession of merchandise on payment of a deposit and completes the purchase by paying a series of instalments while the seller retains ownership until the final instalment is paid. Abbrev.: **HP, h.p.** U.S. and Canad. equivalents: **installment plan, instalment plan.**

hirsute (ˈhɜːsjuːt) *adj.* **1.** covered with hair. **2.** (of plants) covered with long but not stiff hairs. **3.** (of a person) having long, thick, or untrimmed hair. [C17: < L *hirsūtus* shaggy] —ˈ**hirsuteness** *n.*

his (hɪz; *unstressed* ɪz) *determiner.* **1. a.** of, belonging to, or associated with him: *his knee; I don't like his being out so late.* **b.** (*as pron.*): *his is on the left; that book is his.* **2. his and hers.** for a man and woman respectively. ~*pron.* **3. of his.** belonging to him. [OE *his,* genitive of *hē* HE & of *hit* IT]

Hispanic (hɪˈspænɪk) *adj.* of or derived from Spain or the Spanish. —**Hisˈpanicism** *n.*

hispid (ˈhɪspɪd) *adj. Biol.* covered with stiff hairs or bristles. [C17: < L *hispidus* bristly]

hiss (hɪs) *n.* **1.** a sound like that of a prolonged *s.* **2.** such a sound as an exclamation of derision, contempt, etc. ~*vb.* **3.** (*intr.*) to produce or utter a hiss. **4.** (*tr.*) to express with a hiss. **5.** (*tr.*) to show derision or anger towards (a speaker, performer, etc.) by hissing. [C14: imit.]

hist (hɪst) *interj.* an exclamation used to attract attention or as a warning to be silent.

histamine (ˈhɪstəˌmiːn) *n.* an amine released by the body tissues in allergic reactions, causing irritation. Formula: $C_5H_9N_3$. [C20: < HIST- + AMINE] —**histaminic** (ˌhɪstəˈmɪnɪk) *adj.*

histo- *or before a vowel* **hist-** *combining form.* indicating animal or plant tissue: *histology; histamine.* [< Gk, < *histos* web]

histogenesis (ˌhɪstəʊˈdʒɛnɪsɪs) *n.* the formation of tissues and organs from undifferentiated cells. —**histogenetic** (ˌhɪstəʊdʒəˈnɛtɪk) *or* ˌ**histoˈgenic** *adj.*

histogram (ˈhɪstəˌgræm) *n.* a figure that represents a frequency distribution, consisting of contiguous rectangles whose width is in proportion to the class interval under consideration and whose area represents relative frequency of the phenomenon in question. [C20: < HISTO(RY) + -GRAM]

histology (hɪˈstɒlədʒɪ) *n.* the study of the tissues of an animal or plant. —**histological** (ˌhɪstəˈlɒdʒɪkᵊl) *or* ˌ**histoˈlogic** *adj.*

histolysis (hɪˈstɒlɪsɪs) *n.* the disintegration of organic tissues. —**histolytic** (ˌhɪstəˈlɪtɪk) *adj.*

historian (hɪˈstɔːrɪən) *n.* a person who writes or studies history, esp. one who is an authority on it.

historic (hɪˈstɒrɪk) *adj.* **1.** famous in history; significant. **2.** *Linguistics.* (of Latin, Greek, or Sanskrit verb tenses) referring to past time.

▷ **Usage.** A distinction is made between *historic* (important, significant) and *historical* (pertaining to history): *a historic decision; a historical perspective.*

historical (hɪˈstɒrɪkᵊl) *adj.* **1.** belonging to or typical of the study of history: *historical methods.* **2.** concerned with events of the past: *historical accounts.* **3.** based on or constituting factual material as distinct from legend or supposition. **4.** based on history: *a historical novel.* **5.** occurring in history. —**hisˈtorically** *adv.*

▷ **Usage.** See at **historic.**

historical linguistics *n.* (*functioning as sing.*) the study of language as it changes in the course of time.

historical present *n.* the present tense used to narrate past events, employed for effect or in informal use, as in *a week ago I see this accident.*

historicism (hɪˈstɒrɪˌsɪzəm) *n.* **1.** the belief that natural laws govern historical events. **2.** the doctrine that each period of history has its own beliefs and values inapplicable to any other. **3.** excessive emphasis on history, past styles, etc. —**his'toricist** *n., adj.*

historicity (ˌhɪstəˈrɪsɪtɪ) *n.* historical authenticity.

historiographer (hɪˌstɔːrɪˈɒgrəfə) *n.* **1.** a historian, esp. one concerned with historical method. **2.** a historian employed to write the history of a group or public institution. —**hiˌstori'ography** *n.*

history (ˈhɪstərɪ) *n., pl.* **-ries. 1.** a record or account of past events, developments, etc. **2.** all that is preserved of the past, esp. in written form. **3.** the discipline of recording and interpreting past events. **4.** past events, esp. when considered as an aggregate. **5.** an event in the past, esp. one that has been reduced in importance: *their quarrel was just history.* **6.** the past, previous experiences, etc., of a thing or person: *the house had a strange history.* **7.** a play that depicts historical events. **8.** a narrative relating the events of a character's life: *the history of Joseph Andrews.* [C15: < L *historia,* < Gk: inquiry, < *historein* to narrate, < *histōr* judge]

histrionic (ˌhɪstrɪˈɒnɪk) *adj.* **1.** excessively dramatic or artificial: *histrionic gestures.* **2.** *Now rare.* dramatic. ~*n.* **3.** (*pl.*) melodramatic displays of temperament. **4.** *Rare.* (*pl.; functioning as sing.*) dramatics. [C17: < LL *histriōnicus,* < L *histriō* actor] —ˌ**histri'onically** *adv.*

hit (hɪt) *vb.* **hitting, hit.** (*mainly tr.*) **1.** (*also intr.*) to deal (a blow) to (a person or thing); strike. **2.** to come into violent contact with: *the car hit the tree.* **3.** to strike with a missile: *to hit a target.* **4.** to knock or bump: *I hit my arm on the table.* **5.** to propel by striking: *to hit a ball.* **6.** *Cricket.* to score (runs). **7.** to affect (a person, place, or thing), esp. suddenly or adversely: *his illness hit his wife very hard.* **8.** to reach: *unemployment hit a new high.* **9.** to experience: *I've hit a slight snag here.* **10.** *Sl.* to murder (a rival criminal) in fulfilment of an underworld vendetta. **11.** *Inf.* to set out on: *let's hit the road.* **12.** *Inf.* to arrive: *he will hit town tomorrow.* **13.** *Inf., chiefly U.S. & Canad.* to demand or request from: *he hit me for a pound.* **14. hit the bottle.** *Sl.* to drink an excessive amount of alcohol. ~*n.* **15.** an impact or collision. **16.** a shot, blow, etc., that reaches its object. **17.** an apt, witty, or telling remark. **18.** *Inf.* **a.** a person or thing that gains wide appeal: *she's a hit with everyone.* **b.** (*as modifier*): *a hit record.* **19.** *Inf.* a stroke of luck. **20.** *Sl.* **a.** a murder carried out as the result of an underworld vendetta. **b.** (*as modifier*): *a hit squad.* **21. make a hit with.** *Inf.* to make a favourable impression on. ~See also **hit off, hit on, hit out.** [OE *hittan,* < ON *hitta*] —'**hitter** *n.*

hit-and-run *adj.* (*prenominal*) **1.** denoting a motor-vehicle accident in which the driver leaves the scene without stopping to give assistance, inform the police, etc. **2.** (of an attack, raid, etc.) relying on surprise allied to a rapid departure from the scene of operations: *hit-and-run tactics.*

hitch (hɪtʃ) *vb.* **1.** to fasten or become fastened with a knot or tie. **2.** (*tr.;* often foll. by *up*) to pull up (the trousers, etc.) with a quick jerk. **3.** (*intr.*) *Chiefly U.S.* to move in a halting manner. **4.** (*tr.; passive*) *Sl.* to marry (esp. in **get hitched**). **5.** *Inf.* to obtain (a ride) by hitchhiking. ~*n.* **6.** an impediment or obstacle, esp. one that is temporary or minor. **7.** a knot that can be undone by pulling against the direction of the strain that holds it. **8.** a sudden jerk: *he gave it a hitch and it came loose.* **9.** *Inf.* a ride obtained by hitchhiking. [C15: <?] —'**hitcher** *n.*

hitchhike (ˈhɪtʃˌhaɪk) *vb.* (*intr.*) to travel by obtaining free lifts in motor vehicles. —'**hitchˌhiker** *n.*

hither (ˈhɪðə) *adv.* **1.** to or towards this place (esp. in **come hither**). **2. hither and thither.** this way and that, as in confusion. ~*adj.* **3.** *Arch. or dialect.* (of a side or part) nearer; closer. [OE *hider*]

hithermost (ˈhɪðəˌməʊst) *adj. Now rare.* nearest to this place or in this direction.

hitherto (ˌhɪðəˈtuː) *adv.* until this time: *hitherto, there have been no problems.*

Hitlerism (ˈhɪtləˌrɪzəm) *n.* the policies, principles, and methods of the Nazi party as developed by Adolf Hitler.

hit list *n. Inf.* **1.** a list of people to be murdered: *a terrorist hit list.* **2.** a list of targets to be eliminated in some way: *a hit list of pits to be closed.*

hit man *n.* a hired assassin.

hit off *vb.* **1.** (*tr., adv.*) to represent or mimic accurately. **2. hit it off with.** *Inf.* to have a good relationship with.

hit on *vb.* (*intr., prep.*) to discover unexpectedly or guess correctly. Also: **hit upon.**

hit or miss *adj.* (**hit-or-miss** *when prenominal*) *Inf.* random; haphazard. Also: **hit and miss.**

hit out *vb.* (*intr., adv.;* often foll. by *at*) **1.** to direct blows forcefully and vigorously. **2.** to make a verbal attack (upon someone).

Hittite (ˈhɪtaɪt) *n.* **1.** a member of an ancient people of Anatolia, who built a great empire in N Syria and Asia Minor in the second millennium B.C. **2.** the extinct language of this people. ~*adj.* **3.** of or relating to this people, their civilization, or their language.

HIV *abbrev. for* human immunodeficiency virus.

hive (haɪv) *n.* **1.** a structure in which social bees live. **2.** a colony of social bees. **3.** a place showing signs of great industry (esp. in **a hive of activity**). **4.** a teeming multitude. ~*vb.* **5.** to cause (bees) to collect or (of bees) to collect inside a hive. **6.** to live or cause to live in or as if in a hive. **7.** (*tr.;* often foll. by *up* or *away*) to store, esp. for future use. [OE *hȳf*]

hive off *vb.* (*adv.*) **1.** to transfer or be transferred from a larger group or unit. **2.** (*usually tr.*) to transfer (profitable activities of a nationalized industry) back to private ownership.

hives (haɪvz) *n.* (*functioning as sing. or pl.*) *Pathol.* a nontechnical name for **urticaria.** [C16: <?]

hiya (ˈhaɪjə, ˌhaɪˈjɑː) *sentence substitute.* an informal term of greeting. [C20: shortened < *how are you?*]

hl *abbrev. for* hectolitre.

HL (in Britain) *abbrev. for* House of Lords.

hm *symbol for* hectometre.

HM *abbrev. for:* **1.** His (*or* Her) Majesty. **2.** headmaster; headmistress.

h'm (*spelling pron.* hmmm) *interj.* used to indicate hesitation, doubt, assent, pleasure, etc.

HMAS *abbrev. for* His (*or* Her) Majesty's Australian Ship.

HMCS *abbrev. for* His (*or* Her) Majesty's Canadian Ship.

HMI (in Britain) *abbrev. for* Her Majesty's Inspector; a government official who examines and supervises schools.

H.M.S. *or* **HMS** *abbrev. for:* **1.** His (*or* Her) Majesty's Service. **2.** His (*or* Her) Majesty's Ship.

HMSO (in Britain) *abbrev. for* His (*or* Her) Majesty's Stationery Office.

HNC (in Britain) *abbrev. for* Higher National Certificate; a qualification recognized by many national technical and professional institutions.

HND (in Britain) *abbrev. for* Higher National Diploma; a qualification in technical subjects equivalent to an ordinary degree.

ho (həʊ) *interj.* **1.** Also: **ho-ho.** an imitation or representation of a deep laugh. **2.** an exclamation used to attract attention, etc. [C13: imit.]

Ho *the chemical symbol for* holmium.

hoar (hɔː) *n.* **1.** short for **hoarfrost.** ~*adj.* **2.** *Rare.* covered with hoarfrost. **3.** *Arch.* a poetic variant of **hoary.** [OE *hār*]

hoard (hɔːd) *n.* **1.** an accumulated store hidden away for future use. **2.** a cache of ancient coins, treasure, etc. ~*vb.* **3.** to gather or accumulate (a hoard). [OE *hord*] —'**hoarder** *n.*

hoarding (ˈhɔːdɪŋ) *n.* **1.** Also called (esp. U.S. and Canad.): **billboard.** a large board used for displaying advertising posters, as by a road. **2.** a temporary wooden fence erected round a building or demolition site. [C19: < C15 *hoard* fence, < OF *hourd* palisade, of Gmc origin]

hoarfrost (ˈhɔːˌfrɒst) *n.* a deposit of needle-like ice crystals formed on the ground by direct condensation at temperatures below freezing point. Also called: **white frost.**

hoarhound (ˈhɔːˌhaʊnd) *n.* a variant spelling of **horehound.**

hoarse (hɔːs) *adj.* **1.** gratingly harsh in tone. **2.** having a husky voice, as through illness, shouting, etc. [C14: < ON] —ˈ**hoarsely** *adv.* —ˈ**hoarseness** *n.*

hoarsen (ˈhɔːsᵊn) *vb.* to make or become hoarse.

hoary (ˈhɔːrɪ) *adj.* **hoarier, hoariest. 1.** having grey or white hair. **2.** white or whitish-grey in colour. **3.** ancient or venerable. —ˈ**hoariness** *n.*

hoatzin (həʊˈætsɪn) *n.* a unique South American bird with clawed wing digits in the young. [C17: < American Sp., < Nahuatl *uatzin* pheasant]

hoax (həʊks) *n.* **1.** a deception, esp. a practical joke. ~*vb.* **2.** (*tr.*) to deceive or play a joke on (someone). [C18: prob. < HOCUS] —ˈ**hoaxer** *n.*

hob[1] (hɒb) *n.* **1.** the flat top part of a cooking stove, or a separate flat surface, containing hotplates or burners. **2.** a shelf beside an open fire, for keeping kettles, etc., hot. **3.** a steel pattern used in forming a mould or die in cold metal. [C16: var. of obs. *hubbe;* ? rel. to HUB]

hob[2] (hɒb) *n.* **1.** a hobgoblin or elf. **2. raise** *or* **play hob.** *U.S. inf.* to cause mischief. **3.** a male ferret. [C14: var. of *Rob,* short for *Robin* or *Robert*]

hobble (ˈhɒbᵊl) *vb.* **1.** (*intr.*) to walk with a lame awkward movement. **2.** (*tr.*) to fetter the legs of (a horse) in order to restrict movement. **3.** (*intr.*) to progress with difficulty. ~*n.* **4.** a strap, rope, etc., used to hobble a horse. **5.** a limping gait. ~Also (for senses 2, 4): **hopple.** [C14: prob. < Low G] —ˈ**hobbler** *n.*

hobbledehoy (ˌhɒbᵊldɪˈhɔɪ) *n.* a clumsy or bad-mannered youth. [C16: < earlier *hobbard de hoy,* <?]

hobby[1] (ˈhɒbɪ) *n., pl.* **-bies. 1.** an activity pursued in spare time for pleasure or relaxation. **2.** *Arch.* a small horse. **3.** short for **hobbyhorse** (sense 1). **4.** an early form of bicycle, without pedals. [C14 *hobyn,* prob. var. of name *Robin*] —ˈ**hobbyist** *n.*

hobby[2] (ˈhɒbɪ) *n., pl.* **-bies.** any of several small Old World falcons. [C15: < OF *hobet,* < *hobe* falcon]

hobbyhorse (ˈhɒbɪˌhɔːs) *n.* **1.** a toy consisting of a stick with a figure of a horse's head at one end. **2.** a rocking horse. **3.** a figure of a horse attached to a performer's waist in a morris dance, etc. **4.** a favourite topic (esp. in **on one's hobbyhorse**). [C16: < HOBBY[1], orig. a small horse; then generalized to apply to any pastime]

hobgoblin (ˌhɒbˈgɒblɪn) *n.* **1.** a mischievous goblin. **2.** a bogey; bugbear. [C16: < HOB[2] + GOBLIN]

hobnail (ˈhɒbˌneɪl) *n.* **a.** a short nail with a large head for protecting the soles of heavy footwear. **b.** (*as modifier*): *hobnail boots.* [C16: < HOB[1] (in archaic sense: peg) + NAIL] —ˈ**hobˌnailed** *adj.*

hobnob (ˈhɒbˌnɒb) *vb.* **-nobbing, -nobbed.** (*intr.;* often foll. by *with*) **1.** to socialize or talk informally. **2.** *Obs.* to drink (with). [C18: < *hob or nob* to drink to one another in turns, ult. < OE *habban* to HAVE + *nabban* not to have]

hobo (ˈhəʊbəʊ) *n., pl.* **-boes** *or* **-bos.** *Chiefly U.S. & Canad.* **1.** a tramp; vagrant. **2.** a migratory worker. [C19 (U.S.): <?] —ˈ**hoboism** *n.*

Hobson's choice (ˈhɒbsᵊnz) *n.* the choice of taking what is offered or nothing at all. [C16: after Thomas *Hobson* (1544–1631), E liveryman who gave his customers no choice but had them take the nearest horse]

hock[1] (hɒk) *n.* **1.** the joint at the tarsus of a horse or similar animal, corresponding to the human ankle. ~*vb.* **2.** another word for **hamstring.** [C16: short for *hockshin,* < OE *hōhsinu* heel sinew]

hock[2] (hɒk) *n.* any of several white wines from the German Rhine. [C17: short for obs. *hockamore* < G *Hochheimer*]

hock[3] (hɒk) *Inf., chiefly U.S. & Canad.* ~*vb.* **1.** (*tr.*) to pawn or pledge. ~*n.* **2.** the state of being in pawn. **3. in hock. a.** in prison. **b.** in debt. **c.** in pawn. [C19: < Du. *hok* prison, debt]

hockey (ˈhɒkɪ) *n.* **1.** Also called (esp. U.S. and Canad.): **field hockey.** a game played on a field by two opposing teams of 11 players each, who try to hit a ball into their opponents' goal using long sticks curved at the end. **2.** See **ice hockey.** [C19: < earlier *hawkey,* <?]

hocus (ˈhəʊkəs) *vb.* **-cusing, -cused** *or* **-cussing, -cussed.** (*tr.*) *Now rare.* **1.** to trick. **2.** to stupefy, esp. with a drug. **3.** to drug (a drink).

hocus-pocus (ˈhəʊkəsˈpəʊkəs) *n.* **1.** trickery or chicanery. **2.** an incantation used by conjurers or magicians. **3.** conjuring skill. ~*vb.* **-cusing, -cused** *or* **-cussing, -cussed. 4.** to deceive or trick (someone). [C17: ? dog Latin invented by jugglers]

hod (hɒd) *n.* **1.** an open wooden box attached to a pole, for carrying bricks, mortar, etc. **2.** a tall narrow coal scuttle. [C14: ?< C13 dialect *hot,* < OF *hotte* pannier, prob. of Gmc origin]

hodgepodge (ˈhɒdʒˌpɒdʒ) *n.* a variant spelling (esp. U.S. and Canad.) of **hotchpotch.**

Hodgkin's disease (ˈhɒdʒkɪnz) *n.* a malignant disease characterized by enlargement of the lymph nodes, spleen, and liver. [C19: after Thomas *Hodgkin* (1798–1866), London physician, who first described it]

hodograph (ˈhɒdəˌgrɑːf) *n.* a curve of which the radius vector represents the velocity of a moving particle. [C19: < Gk *hodos* way + -GRAPH]

hodometer (hɒˈdɒmɪtə) *n.* another name for **odometer.** —**hoˈdometry** *n.*

hoe (həʊ) *n.* **1.** any of several kinds of long-handled hand implement used to till the soil, weed, etc. ~*vb.* **hoeing, hoed. 2.** to dig, scrape, weed, or till (surface soil) with or as if with a hoe. [C14: via OF *houe,* of Gmc origin] —ˈ**hoer** *n.*

hoedown (ˈhəʊˌdaʊn) *n. U.S. & Canad.* **1.** a boisterous square dance. **2.** a party at which hoedowns are danced.

hog (hɒg) *n.* **1.** a domesticated pig, esp. a castrated male. **2.** *U.S. & Canad.* any mammal of the family Suidae; pig. **3.** Also: **hogget** (ˈhɒgɪt), **hogg.** *Dialect. Austral. & N.Z.* a young sheep that has yet to be sheared. **4.** *Inf.* a greedy person. **5. go the whole hog.** *Sl.* to do something thoroughly or unreservedly. ~*vb.* **hogging, hogged.** (*tr.*) **6.** *Sl.* to take more than one's share of. **7.** to arch (the back) like a hog. **8.** to cut (the mane) of (a horse) very short. [OE *hogg,* of Celtic origin] —ˈ**hogger** *n.* —ˈ**hogˌlike** *adj.*

hogan (ˈhəʊgən) *n.* a wooden dwelling covered with earth, typical of the Navaho Indians of North America. [of Amerind origin]

hogback (ˈhɒgˌbæk) *n.* **1.** Also called: **hog's back.** a narrow ridge with steep sides. **2.** *Archaeol.* a tomb with sloping sides.

hogfish (ˈhɒgˌfɪʃ) *n., pl.* **-fish** *or* **-fishes.** a wrasse that occurs in the Atlantic. The head of the male resembles a pig's snout.

hoggish (ˈhɒgɪʃ) *adj.* selfish, gluttonous, or dirty.

Hogmanay (ˌhɒgməˈneɪ) *n.* (*sometimes not cap.*) New Year's Eve in Scotland. [C17: ? < Norman F *hoguinane,* < OF *aguillanneuf* a New Year's Eve gift]

hognose snake (ˈhɒgˌnəʊz) *n.* a North American nonvenomous snake that has a trowel-shaped snout and inflates its body when alarmed. Also called: **puff adder.**

hogshead (ˈhɒgzˌhɛd) *n.* **1.** a unit of capacity, used esp. for alcoholic beverages. It has several values. **2.** a large cask. [C14: <?]

hogtie (ˈhɒgˌtaɪ) *vb.* **-tying, -tied.** (*tr.*) *Chiefly U.S.* **1.** to tie together the legs or the arms and legs of. **2.** to impede, hamper, or thwart.

hogwash (ˈhɒgˌwɒʃ) *n.* **1.** nonsense. **2.** pigswill.

hogweed (ˈhɒgˌwiːd) *n.* any of several coarse weedy plants.

hoick (hɔɪk) *vb.* to rise or raise abruptly and sharply. [C20: <?]

hoi polloi (ˈhɔɪ pəˈlɔɪ) *n.* **the.** *Often derog.* the masses; common people. [Gk, lit.: the many]

hoist (hɔɪst) *vb.* **1.** (*tr.*) to raise or lift up, esp. by mechanical means. ~*n.* 2. any apparatus or device for hoisting. 3. the act of hoisting. 4. *Naut.* a group of signal flags. 5. the inner edge of a flag next to the staff. [C16: var. of *hoise*, prob. < Low G] —'**hoister** *n.*

hoity-toity (ˌhɔɪtɪˈtɔɪtɪ) *adj. Inf.* arrogant or haughty. [C17: rhyming compound based on C16 *hoit* to romp, <?]

hokonui (ˌhəʊkəˈnuːiː) *n. N.Z.* illicit whisky. [< *Hokonui*, district of Southland Province, N.Z.]

hokum (ˈhəʊkəm) *n. Sl., chiefly U.S. & Canad.* 1. claptrap; bunk. 2. obvious or hackneyed material of a sentimental nature in a play, film, etc. [C20: prob. a blend of HOCUS-POCUS & BUNKUM]

Holarctic (həʊˈlɑːktɪk) *adj.* of or denoting a zoogeographical region consisting of the entire arctic regions. [C19: < HOLO- + ARCTIC]

hold[1] (həʊld) *vb.* **holding, held.** 1. to have or keep (an object) with or within the hands, arms, etc.; clasp. 2. (*tr.*) to support: *to hold a drowning man's head above water.* 3. to maintain or be maintained in a specified state: *to hold firm.* 4. (*tr.*) to set aside or reserve: *they will hold our tickets until tomorrow.* 5. (when *intr., usually used in commands*) to restrain or be restrained from motion, action, departure, etc.: *hold that man until the police come.* 6. (*intr.*) to remain fast or unbroken: *that cable won't hold much longer.* 7. (*intr.*) (of the weather) to remain dry and bright. 8. (*tr.*) to keep the attention of. 9. (*tr.*) to engage in or carry on: *to hold a meeting.* 10. (*tr.*) to have the ownership, possession, etc., of: *he holds a law degree; who's holding the ace?* 11. (*tr.*) to have the use of or responsibility for: *to hold office.* 12. (*tr.*) to have the capacity for: *the carton will hold eight books.* 13. (*tr.*) to be able to control the outward effects of drinking beer, spirits, etc. 14. (often foll. by *to* or *by*) to remain or cause to remain committed (to): *hold him to his promise.* 15. (*tr.; takes a clause as object*) to claim: *he holds that the theory is incorrect.* 16. (*intr.*) to remain relevant, valid, or true: *the old philosophies don't hold nowadays.* 17. (*tr.*) to consider in a specified manner: *I hold him very dear.* 18. (*tr.*) to defend successfully: *hold the fort against the attack.* 19. (sometimes foll. by *on*) *Music.* to sustain the sound of (a note) throughout its specified duration. 20. (*tr.*) *Computers.* to retain (data) in a storage device after copying onto another storage device or location. 21. **hold (good) for.** to apply or be relevant to: *the same rules hold for everyone.* 22. **there is no holding him.** he is so spirited that he cannot be restrained. ~*n.* 23. the act or method of holding fast or grasping. 24. something to hold onto, as for support or control. 25. an object or device that holds fast or grips something else. 26. controlling influence: *she has a hold on him.* 27. a short pause. 28. a prison or a cell in a prison. 29. *Wrestling.* a way of seizing one's opponent. 30. *Music.* a pause or fermata. 31. a. a tenure, esp. of land. b. (*in combination*): *freehold.* 32. *Arch.* a fortified place. 33. **no holds barred.** all limitations removed. ~See also **hold back, hold down,** etc. [OE *healdan*] —'**holdable** *adj.*

hold[2] (həʊld) *n.* the space in a ship or aircraft for storing cargo. [C16: var. of HOLE]

holdall (ˈhəʊldˌɔːl) *n. Brit.* a large strong bag or basket. Usual U.S. and Canad. name: **carryall.**

hold back *vb.* (*adv.*) 1. to restrain or be restrained. 2. (*tr.*) to withhold: *he held back part of the payment.*

hold down *vb.* (*tr., adv.*) 1. to restrain or control. 2. *Inf.* to manage to retain or keep possession of: *to hold down two jobs at once.*

holder (ˈhəʊldə) *n.* 1. a person or thing that holds. 2. a. a person who has possession or control of something. b. (*in combination*): *householder.* 3. *Law.* a person who has possession of a bill of exchange, cheque, or promissory note that he is legally entitled to enforce.

holdfast (ˈhəʊldˌfɑːst) *n.* 1. the act of gripping strongly. 2. any device used to secure an object, such as a hook, clamp, etc. 3. the organ of attachment of a seaweed or related plant.

hold forth *vb.* (*adv.*) 1. (*intr.*) to speak for a long time or in public. 2. (*tr.*) to offer (an attraction or enticement).

hold in *vb.* (*tr., adv.*) 1. to curb, control, or keep in check. 2. to conceal (feelings).

holding (ˈhəʊldɪŋ) *n.* 1. land held under a lease. 2. (*often pl.*) property to which the holder has legal title, such as land, stocks, shares, and other investments. 3. *Sport.* the obstruction of an opponent with the hands or arms, esp. in boxing.

holding company *n.* a company with controlling shareholdings in one or more other companies.

holding operation *n.* a plan or procedure devised to prolong the existing situation.

holding paddock *n. Austral. & N.Z.* a paddock in which cattle or sheep are kept temporarily, as before shearing, etc.

holding pattern *n.* the oval or circular path of an aircraft flying around an airport awaiting permission to land.

hold off *vb.* (*adv.*) 1. (*tr.*) to keep apart or at a distance. 2. (*intr.;* often foll. by *from*) to refrain (from doing something).

hold on *vb.* (*intr., adv.*) 1. to maintain a firm grasp. 2. to continue or persist. 3. (foll. by *to*) to keep or retain: *hold on to those stamps as they'll soon be valuable.* 4. *Inf.* to keep a telephone line open. ~*sentence substitute.* 5. *Inf.* stop! wait!

hold out *vb.* (*adv.*) 1. (*tr.*) to offer. 2. (*intr.*) to last or endure. 3. (*intr.*) to continue to stand firm, as a person refusing to succumb to persuasion. 4. *Chiefly U.S.* to withhold (something due). 5. **hold out for.** to wait patiently for (the fulfilment of one's demands). 6. **hold out on.** *Inf.* to keep from telling (a person) some important information.

hold over *vb.* (*tr., mainly adv.*) 1. to defer or postpone. 2. (*prep.*) to intimidate (a person) with (a threat).

hold-up *n.* 1. a robbery, esp. an armed one. 2. a delay; stoppage. ~*vb.* **hold up.** (*tr., adv.*) 3. to delay; hinder. 4. to support. 5. to waylay in order to rob, esp. using a weapon. 6. to exhibit or present.

hold with *vb.* (*intr., prep.*) to support; approve of.

hole (həʊl) *n.* 1. an area hollowed out in a solid. 2. an opening in or through something. 3. an animal's burrow. 4. *Inf.* an unattractive place, such as a town. 5. a fault (esp. in **pick holes in**). 6. *Sl.* a difficult and embarrassing situation. 7. the cavity in various games into which the ball must be thrust. 8. (on a golf course) a. each of the divisions of a course (usually 18) represented by the distance between the tee and a green. b. the score made in striking the ball from the tee into the hole. 9. *Physics.* a vacancy in a nearly full band of quantum states of electrons in a semiconductor or an insulator. Under the action of an electric field holes behave as carriers of positive charge. 10. **hole in the wall.** *Inf.* a small dingy place, esp. one difficult to find. 11. **in holes.** so worn as to be full of holes. 12. **make a hole in.** to consume or use a great amount of (food, drink, money, etc.). ~*vb.* 13. to make a hole or holes in (something). 14. (when *intr.*, often foll. by *out*) *Golf.* to hit (the ball) into the hole. [OE *hol*] —'**holey** *adj.*

hole-and-corner *adj.* (*usually prenominal*) *Inf.* furtive or secretive.

hole in one *n. Golf.* a shot from the tee that finishes in the hole. Also (esp. U.S.): **ace.**

hole in the heart *n.* a defect of the heart in which there is an abnormal opening in any of the walls dividing the four heart chambers.

hole up *vb.* (*intr., adv.*) 1. (of an animal) to hibernate. 2. *Inf.* to hide or remain secluded.

-holic *suffix forming noun* indicating desire for or dependence on; *workaholic; chocoholic.* [C20: abstracted < (*alco*)*holic*]

holiday (ˈhɒlɪˌdeɪ) *n.* 1. (*often pl.*) *Chiefly Brit.* a period in which a break is taken from work or studies for rest, travel, or recreation. U.S. and

Canad. word: **vacation.** **2.** a day on which work is suspended by law or custom, such as a religious festival, bank holiday, etc. Related adj.: **ferial.** ~*vb.* **3.** (*intr.*) *Chiefly Brit.* to spend a holiday. [OE *hāligdæg*, lit.: holy day]

holiday camp *n. Brit.* a place, esp. one at the seaside, providing accommodation, recreational facilities, etc., for holiday-makers.

holiday-maker *n. Brit.* a person who goes on holiday. U.S. and Canad. equivalents: **vacationer, vacationist.**

holily (ˈhəʊlɪlɪ) *adv.* in a holy, devout, or sacred manner.

holiness (ˈhəʊlɪnɪs) *n.* the state or quality of being holy.

Holiness (ˈhəʊlɪnɪs) *n.* (preceded by *His* or *Your*) a title reserved for the pope.

holism (ˈhəʊlɪzəm) *n.* **1.** *Philosophy.* the idea that the whole is greater than the sum of its parts. **2.** (in medicine) the consideration of the complete person in the treatment of disease. [C20: < HOLO- + -ISM] —**hoˈlistic** *adj.*

holland (ˈhɒlənd) *n.* a coarse linen cloth. [C15: after *Holland*, where it was made]

hollandaise sauce (ˌhɒlənˈdeɪz, ˈhɒlənˌdeɪz) *n.* a rich sauce of egg yolks, butter, vinegar, etc. [C19: < F *sauce hollandaise* Dutch sauce]

Hollands (ˈhɒləndz) *n.* (*functioning as sing.*) Dutch gin, often sold in stone bottles. [C18: < Du. *hollandsch genever*]

holler (ˈhɒlə) *Inf.* ~*vb.* **1.** to shout or yell (something). ~*n.* **2.** a shout; call. [var. of C16 *hollow*, < *holla*, < F *holà* stop! (lit.: ho there!)]

hollo (ˈhɒləʊ) *or* **holla** (ˈhɒlə) *n., pl.* **-los** *or* **-las,** *interj.* **1.** a cry for attention, or of encouragement. ~*vb.* **2.** (*intr.*) to shout. [C16: < F *holà* ho there!]

hollow (ˈhɒləʊ) *adj.* **1.** having a hole or space within; not solid. **2.** having a sunken area; concave. **3.** deeply set: *hollow cheeks.* **4.** (of sounds) as if resounding in a hollow place. **5.** without substance or validity. **6.** hungry or empty. **7.** insincere; cynical. ~*adv.* **8. beat (someone) hollow.** *Brit. inf.* to defeat thoroughly. ~*n.* **9.** a cavity, opening, or space in or within something. **10.** a depression in the land. ~*vb.* (often foll. by *out*, usually when *tr.*) **11.** to make or become hollow. **12.** to form (a hole, cavity, etc.) or (of a hole, etc.) to be formed. [C12: < *holu*, inflected form of OE *holh* cave] —**ˈhollowly** *adv.* —**ˈhollowness** *n.*

hollow-eyed *adj.* with the eyes appearing to be sunk into the face, as from excessive fatigue.

holly (ˈhɒlɪ) *n., pl.* **-lies.** **1.** a tree or shrub having bright red berries and shiny evergreen leaves with prickly edges. **2.** its branches, used for Christmas decorations. **3. holly oak.** another name for **holm oak.** [OE *holegn*]

hollyhock (ˈhɒlɪˌhɒk) *n.* a tall plant with stout hairy stems and spikes of white, yellow, red, or purple flowers. Also called (U.S.): **rose mallow.** [C16: < HOLY + *hock*, < OE *hoc* mallow]

Hollywood (ˈhɒlɪˌwʊd) *n.* **1.** a NW suburb of Los Angeles, California: centre of the American film industry. **2.** the American film industry.

holm[1] (həʊm) *n. Dialect, chiefly northwestern English.* **1.** an island in a river or lake. **2.** low flat land near a river. [OE *holm* sea, island]

holm[2] (həʊm) *n.* **1.** short for **holm oak.** **2.** *Chiefly Brit.* a dialect word for **holly.** [C14: var. of obs. *holin*, < OE *holegn* holly]

holmium (ˈhɒlmɪəm) *n.* a malleable silver-white metallic element of the lanthanide series. Symbol: Ho; atomic no.: 67; atomic wt.: 164.93. [C19: < NL *Holmia* Stockholm]

holm oak *n.* an evergreen Mediterranean oak tree with prickly leaves resembling holly. Also called: **holm, holly oak, ilex.**

holo- *or before a vowel* **hol-** *combining form.* whole or wholly: *holograph.* [< Gk *holos*]

holocaust (ˈhɒləˌkɔːst) *n.* **1.** great destruction or loss of life or the source of such destruction, esp. fire. **2.** (*usually cap.*) **the.** the mass murder of Jews in Nazi Germany. **3.** a rare word for **burnt offering.** [C13: < LL *holocaustum* whole burnt offering, < Gk, < HOLO- + *kaiein* to burn]

Holocene (ˈhɒləˌsiːn) *adj.* **1.** of, denoting, or formed in the second and most recent epoch of the Quaternary period, which began 10 000 years ago. ~*n.* **2. the.** the Holocene epoch or rock series. ~Also: **Recent.**

hologram (ˈhɒləˌgræm) *n.* a photographic record produced by illuminating the object with coherent light (as from a laser) and, without using lenses, exposing a film to light reflected from this object and to a direct beam of coherent light. When interference patterns on the film are illuminated by the coherent light a three-dimensional image is produced.

holograph (ˈhɒləˌgrɑːf) *n.* a book or document handwritten by its author; original manuscript; autograph.

holography (hɒˈlɒgrəfɪ) *n.* the science or practice of producing holograms. —**holographic** (ˌhɒləˈgræfɪk) *adj.* —ˌ**holoˈgraphically** *adv.*

holohedral (ˌhɒləˈhiːdrəl) *adj.* (of a crystal) exhibiting all the planes required for the symmetry of the crystal system.

holophytic (ˌhɒləˈfɪtɪk) *adj.* (of plants) capable of synthesizing their food from inorganic molecules, esp. by photosynthesis.

holothurian (ˌhɒləˈθjʊərɪən) *n.* **1.** an echinoderm of the class *Holothuroidea*, having a leathery elongated body with a ring of tentacles around the mouth. ~*adj.* **2.** of the *Holothuroidea*. [C19: < NL *Holothūria*, name of type genus, < L: water polyp, < Gk, <?]

hols (hɒlz) *pl. n. Brit. school sl.* holidays.

holster (ˈhəʊlstə) *n.* a sheathlike leather case for a pistol, attached to a belt or saddle. [C17: via Du., of Gmc origin]

holt[1] (həʊlt) *n. Arch. or poetic.* a wood or wooded hill. [OE *holt*]

holt[2] (həʊlt) *n.* the lair of an animal, esp. an otter. [C16: < HOLD[1]]

holy (ˈhəʊlɪ) *adj.* **-lier, -liest.** **1.** of or associated with God or a deity; sacred. **2.** endowed or invested with extreme purity. **3.** devout or virtuous. **4. holier-than-thou.** offensively sanctimonious or self-righteous. ~*n., pl.* **-lies.** **5.** a sacred place. [OE *hālig, hǣlig*]

Holy Communion *n.* **1.** the celebration of the Eucharist. **2.** the consecrated elements.

holy day *n.* a day on which a religious festival is observed.

Holy Father *n. R.C. Church.* the pope.

Holy Ghost *n.* another name for the **Holy Spirit.**

Holy Grail *n.* (in medieval legend) the bowl used by Jesus at the Last Supper. It was brought to Britain by Joseph of Arimathea, where it became the quest of many knights. Also called: **Grail, Sangraal.** [C14: *grail* < OF *graal*, < Med. L *gradālis* bowl, <?]

Holy Land *n.* **the.** another name for Palestine.

holy of holies *n.* **1.** any place of special sanctity. **2.** (*cap.*) the innermost compartment of the Jewish tabernacle, where the Ark was enshrined.

holy orders *pl. n.* **1.** the sacrament whereby a person is admitted to the Christian ministry. **2.** the grades of the Christian ministry. **3.** the status of an ordained Christian minister.

Holy Roman Empire *n.* the complex of European territories under the rule of the Frankish or German king who bore the title of Roman emperor, beginning with the coronation of Charlemagne in 800 A.D.

Holy Scripture *n.* another term for the **Scriptures.**

Holy See *n. R.C. Church.* **1.** the see of the pope as bishop of Rome. **2.** the Roman curia.

Holy Spirit *n. Christianity.* the third person of the Trinity. Also called: **Holy Ghost.**

holystone (ˈhəʊlɪˌstəʊn) *n.* **1.** a soft sandstone used for scrubbing the decks of a vessel. ~*vb.* **2.** (*tr.*) to scrub (a vessel's decks) with a holystone. [C19: ? < its being used in a kneeling position]

holy synod *n.* the governing body of any of the Orthodox Churches.

holy water *n.* water that has been blessed by a priest for use in symbolic rituals of purification.

Holy Week *n.* the week preceding Easter Sunday.

Holy Writ *n.* another term for the **Scriptures.**

homage (ˈhɒmɪdʒ) *n.* **1.** a public show of respect or honour towards someone or something (esp. in **pay** *or* **do homage to**). **2.** (in feudal society) the act of respect and allegiance made by a vassal to his lord. [C13: < OF, < *home* man, < L *homo*]

homburg (ˈhɒmbɜːg) *n.* a man's hat of soft felt with a dented crown and a stiff upturned brim. [C20: after *Homburg,* in West Germany, where orig. made]

home (həʊm) *n.* **1.** the place where one lives. **2.** a house or other dwelling. **3.** a family or other group living in a house. **4.** a person's country, city, etc., esp. viewed as a birthplace or a place dear to one. **5.** the habitat of an animal. **6.** the place where something is invented, founded, or developed. **7.** a building or organization set up to care for people in a certain category, such as orphans, the aged, etc. **8.** *Sport.* one's own ground: *the match is at home.* **9. a.** the objective towards which a player strives in certain sports. **b.** an area where a player is safe from attack. **10. a home from home.** a place other than one's own home where one can be at ease. **11. at home. a.** in one's own home or country. **b.** at ease. **c.** giving an informal party at one's own home. **12. at home in, on,** *or* **with.** familiar with. **13. home and dry.** *Brit. sl.* definitely safe or successful. Austral. and N.Z. equivalent: **home and hosed. 14. near home.** concerning one deeply. ~*adj.* (*usually prenominal*) **15.** of one's home, country, etc.; domestic. **16.** (of an activity) done in one's house: *home taping.* **17.** *Sport.* relating to one's own ground: *a home game.* **18.** *U.S.* central; principal: *the company's home office.* ~*adv.* **19.** to or at home: *I'll be home tomorrow.* **20.** to or on the point. **21.** to the fullest extent: *hammer the nail home.* **22. bring home to. a.** to make clear to. **b.** to place the blame on. **23. nothing to write home about.** *Inf.* to be of no particular interest: *the film was nothing to write home about.* ~*vb.* **24.** (*intr.*) (of birds and other animals) to return home accurately from a distance. **25.** (often foll. by *in on* or *onto*) to direct or be directed onto a point or target, esp. by automatic navigational aids. **26.** to send or go home. **27.** (*tr.*) to furnish with a home. **28.** (*intr.;* often foll. by *in* or *in on*) to be directed towards a goal, target, etc. [OE *hām*] —ˈ**homeless** *adj., n.* —ˈ**homelessness** *n.*

home banking *n.* a system whereby a person at home or in an office can use a computer with a modem to call up information from a bank or to transfer funds electronically.

home-brew *n.* **1.** a beer or other alcoholic drink brewed at home rather than commercially. **2.** *Canad. inf.* a professional football player who was born in Canada and is not an import. —ˌ**home-**ˈ**brewed** *adj.*

homecoming (ˈhəʊmˌkʌmɪŋ) *n.* the act of coming home.

Home Counties *pl. n.* the counties surrounding London.

home economics *n.* (*functioning as sing. or pl.*) the study of diet, budgeting, child care, and other subjects concerned with running a home.

home farm *n. Brit.* (esp. formerly) a farm attached to and providing food for a large country house.

Home Guard *n.* a volunteer part-time military force recruited for the defence of the United Kingdom in World War II.

home help *n. Brit.* a woman employed, esp. by a local authority, to do housework in a person's home. N.Z equivalent: **home aid.**

homeland (ˈhəʊmˌlænd) *n.* **1.** the country in which one lives or was born. **2.** the official name for a **Bantustan.**

homely (ˈhəʊmlɪ) *adj.* **-lier, -liest. 1.** characteristic of or suited to the ordinary home; unpretentious. **2.** (of a person) **a.** *Brit.* warm and domesticated. **b.** *Chiefly U.S. & Canad.* plain. —ˈ**homeliness** *n.*

home-made *adj.* **1.** (esp. of foods) made at home or on the premises, esp. of high-quality ingredients. **2.** crudely fashioned.

homeo-, homoeo-, *or* **homoio-** *combining form.* like or similar: *homeomorphism.* [< L *homoeo-,* < Gk *homoio-,* < *homos* same]

Home Office *n. Brit. government.* the department responsible for the maintenance of law and order, and all other domestic affairs not specifically assigned to another department.

homeopathy *or* **homoeopathy** (ˌhəʊmɪˈɒpəθɪ) *n.* a method of treating disease by the use of small amounts of a drug that, in healthy persons, produces symptoms similar to those of the disease being treated. —**homeopathic** *or* **homoeopathic** (ˌhəʊmɪəˈpæθɪk) *adj.* —**homeopathist, homoeopathist** (ˌhəʊmɪˈɒpəθɪst) *or* **homeopath, homoeopath** (ˈhəʊmɪəˌpæθ) *n.*

homeostasis *or* **homoeostasis** (ˌhəʊmɪəʊˈsteɪsɪs) *n.* **1.** the maintenance of metabolic equilibrium within an animal by a tendency to compensate for disrupting changes. **2.** the maintenance of equilibrium within a social group, person, etc.

homer (ˈhəʊmə) *n.* a homing pigeon.

Homeric (həʊˈmɛrɪk) *adj.* **1.** of, relating to, or resembling Homer, Greek poet (circa 800 B.C.), to whom are attributed the *Iliad* and the *Odyssey,* or his poems. **2.** imposing or heroic.

home rule *n.* **1.** self-government, esp. in domestic affairs. **2.** the partial autonomy sometimes granted to a national minority or a colony.

Home Secretary *n. Brit. government.* the head of the Home Office.

homesick (ˈhəʊmˌsɪk) *adj.* depressed or melancholy at being away from home and family. —ˈ**home**ˌ**sickness** *n.*

homespun (ˈhəʊmˌspʌn) *adj.* **1.** having plain or unsophisticated character. **2.** woven or spun at home. ~*n.* **3.** cloth made at home or made of yarn spun at home.

homestead (ˈhəʊmˌstɛd, -stɪd) *n.* **1.** a house or estate and the adjoining land, buildings, etc., esp. a farm. **2.** (in the U.S.) a house and adjoining land designated by the owner as his fixed residence and exempt under the homestead laws from seizure and forced sale for debts. **3.** (in western Canada) a piece of land granted to a settler by the federal government. **4.** *Austral. & N.Z.* (on a sheep or cattle station) the owner's or manager's residence; in New Zealand, the term includes all outbuildings.

Homestead Act *n.* **1.** an act passed by the U.S. Congress in 1862 making available to settlers 160-acre tracts of public land for cultivation. **2.** (in Canada) a similar act passed by the Canadian Parliament in 1872.

homesteader (ˈhəʊmˌstɛdə) *n. U.S. & Canad.* a person who possesses land under a homestead law.

homestead law *n.* (in the U.S. & Canada) any of various laws conferring privileges on homesteaders.

home straight *n.* **1.** *Horse racing.* the section of a racecourse forming the approach to the finish. **2.** the final stage of an undertaking. ~Also (chiefly U.S.): **home stretch.**

home truth *n.* (*often pl.*) an unpleasant fact told to a person about himself.

home unit *n. Austral. & N.Z.* a self-contained residence which is part of a series of similar residences. Often shortened to **unit.**

homeward (ˈhəʊmwəd) *adj.* **1.** going home. **2.** (of a voyage, etc.) returning to the home port. ~*adv.* *also* **homewards. 3.** towards home.

homework (ˈhəʊmˌwɜːk) *n.* **1.** school work done at home. **2.** any preparatory study. **3.** work done at home for pay.

homey (ˈhəʊmɪ) *adj.* **homier, homiest.** a variant spelling (esp. U.S.) of **homy.** —ˈ**homeyness** *n.*

homicide (ˈhɒmɪˌsaɪd) *n.* **1.** the killing of a human being by another person. **2.** a person who kills another. [C14: < OF, < L *homo* man + *caedere* to slay] —ˌ**homiˈcidal** *adj.*

homiletics (ˌhɒmɪˈlɛtɪks) *n.* (*functioning as sing.*) the art of preaching or writing sermons. [C17: < Gk *homilētikos* cordial, < *homilein;* see HOMILY]

homily (ˈhɒmɪlɪ) *n., pl.* **-lies. 1.** a sermon. **2.** moralizing talk or writing. [C14: < Church L *homīlia,* < Gk: discourse, < *homilein* to converse with, < *homilos* crowd, < *homou* together + *ilē* crowd] —ˌ**homiˈletic** *adj.* —ˈ**homilist** *n.*

homing (ˈhəʊmɪŋ) *n.* (*modifier*) **1.** *Zool.* relating to the ability to return home after travelling great distances. **2.** (of an aircraft, missile, etc.) capable of guiding itself onto a target.

homing pigeon *n.* any breed of pigeon developed for its homing instinct, used for racing. Also called: **homer.**

hominid (ˈhɒmɪnɪd) *n.* **1.** any primate of the family Hominidae, which includes modern man (*Homo sapiens*) and the extinct precursors of man. ~*adj.* **2.** of or belonging to the Hominidae. [C19: via NL < L *homo* man + -ID[1]]

hominoid (ˈhɒmɪˌnɔɪd) *adj.* **1.** of or like man; manlike. **2.** of or belonging to the primate family, which includes the anthropoid apes and man. ~*n.* **3.** a hominoid animal. [C20: < L *homin-, homo* man + -OID]

hominy (ˈhɒmɪnɪ) *n. Chiefly U.S.* coarsely ground maize prepared as a food by boiling in milk or water. [C17: prob. of Algonquian origin]

hominy grits *pl. n. U.S.* finely ground hominy.

homo (ˈhəʊməʊ) *n., pl.* **-mos.** *Inf.* short for **homosexual.**

Homo (ˈhəʊməʊ) *n.* any primate of the hominid genus *Homo,* including modern man (see **Homo sapiens**). [L: man]

homo- *combining form.* same or like: *homologous; homosexual.* [via L < Gk *homos* same]

homocyclic (ˌhəʊməʊˈsaɪklɪk) *adj.* (of an organic compound) containing a closed ring of atoms of the same kind, esp. carbon atoms.

homoeo- *combining form.* a variant of **homeo-.**

homogamy (hɒˈmɒgəmɪ) *n.* **1.** a condition in which all the flowers of an inflorescence are either of the same sex or hermaphrodite. **2.** the maturation of the anthers and stigmas at the same time, ensuring self-pollination. —**hoˈmogamous** *adj.*

homogeneous (ˌhəʊməˈdʒiːnɪəs, ˌhɒm-) *adj.* **1.** composed of similar or identical parts or elements. **2.** of uniform nature. **3.** similar in kind or nature. **4.** *Maths.* containing terms of the same degree with respect to all the variables, as in $x^2 + 2xy + y^2$. —**homogeneity** (ˌhəʊməʊdʒɪˈniːɪtɪ, ˌhɒm-) *n.* —ˌ**homoˈgeneousness** *n.*

homogenize *or* **-nise** (hɒˈmɒdʒɪˌnaɪz) *vb.* **1.** (*tr.*) to break up the fat globules in (milk or cream) so that they are evenly distributed. **2.** to make or become homogeneous. —**hoˌmogeniˈzation** *or* **-niˈsation** *n.* —**hoˈmogeˌnizer** *or* **-ˌniser** *n.*

homogenous (həˈmɒdʒɪnəs) *adj.* of, relating to, or exhibiting homogeny.

homogeny (hɒˈmɒdʒɪnɪ) *n. Biol.* similarity in structure because of common ancestry. [C19: < Gk *homogeneia* community of origin, < *homogenēs* of the same kind]

homograph (ˈhɒməˌgrɑːf) *n.* one of a group of words spelt in the same way but having different meanings. —ˌ**homoˈgraphic** *adj.*

homoiothermic (həʊˌmɔɪəˈθɜːmɪk) *or* **homothermal** *adj.* having a constant body temperature, usually higher than the temperature of the surroundings; warm-blooded.

homologize *or* **-gise** (hɒˈmɒləˌdʒaɪz) *vb.* to be, show to be, or make homologous.

homologous (həʊˈmɒləgəs, hɒ-), **homological** (ˌhəʊməˈlɒdʒɪkᵊl, ˌhɒm-), *or* **homologic** *adj.* **1.** having a related or similar position, structure, etc. **2.** *Biol.* (of organs and parts) having the same evolutionary origin but different functions: *the wing of a bat and the paddle of a whale are homologous.* —ˌ**homoˈlogically** *adv.* —ˈ**homoˌlogue** *or U.S.* (*sometimes*) ˈ**homolog** *n.*

homology (həʊˈmɒlədʒɪ) *n., pl.* **-gies.** the condition of being homologous. [C17: < Gk *homologia* agreement, < *homologos* agreeing, < HOMO- + *legein* to speak]

homolosine projection (hɒˈmɒləˌsaɪn) *n.* a map projection of the world on which the oceans are distorted to allow for greater accuracy in representing the continents. [C20: < Gk *homologos* agreeing + SINE[1]]

homomorphism (ˌhəʊməʊˈmɔːfɪzəm, ˌhɒm-) *or* **homomorphy** *n. Biol.* similarity in form. —ˌ**homoˈmorphic** *or* ˌ**homoˈmorphous** *adj.*

homonym (ˈhɒmənɪm) *n.* **1.** one of a group of words pronounced or spelt in the same way but having different meanings. Cf. **homograph, homophone. 2.** *Biol.* a specific or generic name that has been used for two or more different organisms. [C17: < L *homōnymum,* < Gk, < *homōnumos* of the same name; see HOMO-, -ONYM] —ˌ**homoˈnymic** *or* **hoˈmonymous** *adj.*

homophobia (ˌhəʊməʊˈfəʊbɪə) *n.* intense hatred or fear of homosexuals or homosexuality. [C20: < HOMO(SEXUAL) + -PHOBIA] —ˈ**homoˌphobe** *n.*

homophone (ˈhɒməˌfəʊn) *n.* **1.** one of a group of words pronounced in the same way but differing in meaning or spelling or both, as *bear* and *bare.* **2.** a written letter or combination of letters that represents the same speech sound as another: *"ph" is a homophone of "f".*

homophonic (ˌhɒməˈfɒnɪk) *adj.* of or relating to music in which the parts move together rather than exhibit individual rhythmic independence.

homopterous (həʊˈmɒptərəs) *or* **homopteran** *adj.* of or belonging to a suborder of hemipterous insects having wings of a uniform texture held over the back at rest. [C19: < Gk *homopteros,* < HOMO- + *pteron* wing]

Homo sapiens (ˈsæpɪˌɛnz) *n.* the specific name of modern man; the only extant species of the genus *Homo.* This species also includes extinct types of primitive man such as Cro-Magnon man. [NL, < L *homo* man + *sapiens* wise]

homosexual (ˌhəʊməʊˈsɛksjʊəl, ˌhɒm-) *n.* **1.** a person who is sexually attracted to members of the same sex. ~*adj.* **2.** of or relating to homosexuals or homosexuality. **3.** of or relating to the same sex.

homosexuality (ˌhəʊməʊˌsɛksjʊˈælɪtɪ, ˌhɒm-) *n.* sexual attraction to or sexual relations with members of the same sex.

homozygote (ˌhəʊməʊˈzaɪgəʊt) *n.* an animal or plant that is homozygous and breeds true to type. —**homozygotic** (ˌhəʊməʊzaɪˈgɒtɪk) *adj.*

homozygous (ˌhəʊməʊˈzaɪgəs) *adj. Genetics.* (of an organism) having identical alleles for any one gene: *these two fruit flies are homozygous for red eye colour.*

homunculus (hɒˈmʌŋkjʊləs) *n., pl.* **-li** (-ˌlaɪ). a miniature man; midget. Also called: **homuncule** (həʊˈmʌŋkjuːl). [C17: < L, dim. of *homo* man] —**hoˈmuncular** *adj.*

homy *or esp. U.S.* **homey** (ˈhəʊmɪ) *adj.* **homier, homiest.** like a home; cosy. —ˈ**hominess** *or esp. U.S.* ˈ**homeyness** *n.*

hon. *abbrev. for:* **1.** honorary. **2.** honourable.

Hon. *abbrev. for* Honourable (title).

hone (həʊn) *n.* **1.** a fine whetstone for sharpening. ~*vb.* **2.** (*tr.*) to sharpen or polish with or as if with a hone. [OE *hān* stone]

honest (ˈɒnɪst) *adj.* **1.** not given to lying, cheating, stealing, etc.; trustworthy. **2.** not false or misleading; genuine. **3.** just or fair: *honest wages.* **4.** characterized by sincerity: *an honest appraisal.* **5.** without pretensions: *honest farmers.* **6.** *Arch.* (of a woman) respectable. **7. honest broker.** a mediator in disputes, esp. international ones. **8. make an honest woman of.** to marry (a woman, esp. one who is pregnant) to prevent scandal. [C13: < OF *honeste,* < L *honestus* distinguished, < *honōs* HONOUR]

honestly (ˈɒnɪstlɪ) *adv.* **1.** in an honest manner. **2.** (intensifier): *I honestly don't believe it.*

honesty (ˈɒnɪstɪ) *n., pl.* **-ties. 1.** the condition of being honest. **2.** *Arch.* virtue or respect. **3.** Also called: **moonwort, satinpod.** a purple-flowered

European plant cultivated for its flattened silvery pods, which are used for indoor decoration.

honey (ˈhʌnɪ) *n.* **1.** a sweet viscid substance made by bees from nectar and stored in their nests or hives as food. **2.** anything that is sweet or delightful. **3.** (*often cap.*) *Chiefly U.S. & Canad.* a term of endearment. **4.** *Inf., chiefly U.S. & Canad.* something very good of its kind. ~*vb.* **honeying, honeyed. 5.** (*tr.*) to sweeten with or as if with honey. **6.** (often foll. by *up*) to talk to (someone) in a flattering way. [OE *huneg*] —ˈ**honey**-ˌ**like** *adj.*

honey badger *n.* another name for **ratel.**

honeybee (ˈhʌnɪˌbiː) *n.* any of various social bees widely domesticated as a source of honey and beeswax. Also called: **hive bee.**

honey buzzard *n.* a common European bird of prey having broad wings and a typically dull brown plumage with white-streaked underparts.

honeycomb (ˈhʌnɪˌkəʊm) *n.* **1.** a waxy structure, constructed by bees in a hive, that consists of adjacent hexagonal cells in which honey is stored, eggs are laid, and larvae develop. **2.** something resembling this in structure. **3.** *Zool.* another name for **reticulum** (sense 2). ~*vb.* (*tr.*) **4.** to pierce with holes, cavities, etc. **5.** to permeate: *honeycombed with spies.*

honey creeper *n.* a small tropical American songbird having a slender downward-curving bill and feeding on nectar.

honeydew (ˈhʌnɪˌdjuː) *n.* **1.** a sugary substance excreted by aphids and similar insects. **2.** a similar substance exuded by certain plants.

honeydew melon *n.* a variety of muskmelon with a smooth greenish-white rind and sweet greenish flesh.

honey-eater (ˈhʌnɪˌiːtə) *n.* a small Australasian songbird having a downward-curving bill and a brushlike tongue specialized for extracting nectar from flowers.

honeyed *or* **honied** (ˈhʌnɪd) *adj. Poetic.* **1.** flattering or soothing. **2.** made sweet or agreeable: *honeyed words.* **3.** full of honey.

honey guide *n.* a small bird inhabiting tropical forests of Africa and Asia and feeding on beeswax, honey, and insects.

honeymoon (ˈhʌnɪˌmuːn) *n.* **1.** a holiday taken by a newly married couple. **2.** a holiday considered to resemble a honeymoon: *a second honeymoon.* **3.** the early, usually calm period of a relationship or enterprise. ~*vb.* **4.** (*intr.*) to take a honeymoon. [C16: traditionally explained as an allusion to the feelings of married couples as changing with the phases of the moon] —ˈ**honey**ˌ**mooner** *n.*

honeysuckle (ˈhʌnɪˌsʌkᵊl) *n.* **1.** a temperate climbing shrub with fragrant white, yellow, or pink tubular flowers. **2.** any of various Australian trees or shrubs of the genus *Banksia,* having flowers in dense spikes. [OE *hunigsūce,* < HONEY + SUCK]

honk (hɒŋk) *n.* **1.** a representation of the sound made by a goose. **2.** any sound resembling this, esp. a motor horn. ~*vb.* **3.** to make or cause (something) to make such a sound. **4.** (*intr.*) *Brit. sl.* to vomit.

honky (ˈhɒnkɪ) *n., pl.* **honkies.** *Derog. sl., chiefly U.S.* a White man or White men collectively. [C20: <?]

honky-tonk (ˈhɒŋkɪˌtɒŋk) *n.* **1.** *U.S. & Canad. sl.* a cheap disreputable nightclub, bar, etc. **2. a.** a style of ragtime piano-playing, esp. on a tinny-sounding piano. **b.** (*as modifier*): *honky-tonk music.* [C19: rhyming compound based on HONK]

honorarium (ˌɒnəˈrɛərɪəm) *n., pl.* **-iums** *or* **-ia** (-ɪə). a fee paid for a nominally free service. [C17: < L: something presented on being admitted to a post of HONOUR]

honorary (ˈɒnərərɪ) *adj.* (*usually prenominal*) **1. a.** held or given only as an honour, without the normal privileges or duties: *an honorary degree.* **b.** (of a secretary, treasurer, etc.) unpaid. **2.** having such a position or title. **3.** depending on honour rather than legal agreement.

honorific (ˌɒnəˈrɪfɪk) *adj.* **1.** showing respect. **2. a.** (of a pronoun, verb inflection, etc.) indicating the speaker's respect for the addressee. **b.** (*as n.*): *a Japanese honorific.* —ˌ**honor**ˈ**ifically** *adv.*

honour *or U.S.* **honor** (ˈɒnə) *n.* **1.** personal integrity; allegiance to moral principles. **2. a.** fame or glory. **b.** a person who wins this for his country, school, etc. **3.** (*often pl.*) great respect, esteem, etc., or an outward sign of this. **4.** (*often pl.*) high or noble rank. **5.** a privilege or pleasure: *it is an honour to serve you.* **6.** a woman's chastity. **7. a.** *Bridge, etc.* any of the top five cards in a suit or any of the four aces at no trumps. **b.** *Whist.* any of the top four cards. **8.** *Golf.* the right to tee off first. **9. do the honours. a.** to serve as host or hostess. **b.** to perform a social act, such as carving meat, etc. **10. in honour bound.** under a moral obligation. **11. in honour of.** out of respect for. **12. on one's honour.** on the pledge of one's word or good name. ~*vb.* (*tr.*) **13.** to hold in respect. **14.** to show courteous behaviour towards. **15.** to worship. **16.** to confer a distinction upon. **17.** to accept and then pay when due (a cheque, draft, etc.). **18.** to keep (one's promise); fulfil (a previous agreement). **19.** to bow or curtsy to (one's dancing partner). [C12: < OF *onor,* < L *honor* esteem]

Honour (ˈɒnə) *n.* (preceded by *Your, His,* or *Her*) a title used to or of certain judges.

honourable *or U.S.* **honorable** (ˈɒnərəbᵊl) *adj.* **1.** possessing or characterized by high principles. **2.** worthy of honour or esteem. **3.** consistent with or bestowing honour. —ˈ**honourably** *or U.S.* ˈ**honorably** *adv.*

Honourable *or U.S.* **Honorable** (ˈɒnərəbᵊl) *adj.* (*prenominal*) **the.** a title of respect placed before a name: used of various officials in the English-speaking world, as a courtesy title in Britain for the children of certain peers, and in Parliament by one member speaking of another. Abbrev.: **Hon.**

honours *or U.S.* **honors** (ˈɒnəz) *pl. n.* **1.** observances of respect. **2.** (*often cap.*) **a.** (in a university degree course) a rank of the highest academic standard. **b.** (*as modifier*): *an honours degree.* Abbrev.: **Hons. 3.** a high mark awarded for an examination; distinction. **4. last** (*or* **funeral**) **honours.** observances of respect at a funeral. **5. military honours.** ceremonies performed by troops in honour of royalty, at the burial of an officer, etc.

honours of war *pl. n. Mil.* the honours granted by the victorious to the defeated, esp. as of marching out with all arms and flags flying.

hooch *or* **hootch** (huːtʃ) *n. Inf., chiefly U.S. & Canad.* alcoholic drink, esp. illicitly distilled spirits. [C20: of Amerind origin, *Hootchinoo,* name of a tribe that distilled a type of liquor]

hood[1] (hʊd) *n.* **1.** a loose head covering either attached to a cloak or coat or made as a separate garment. **2.** something resembling this in shape or use. **3.** the U.S. and Canad. name for **bonnet** (of a car). **4.** the folding roof of a convertible car. **5.** a hoodlike garment worn over an academic gown, indicating its wearer's degree and university. **6.** *Biol.* a hoodlike structure, such as the fold of skin on the head of a cobra ~*vb.* **7.** (*tr.*) to cover with or as if with a hood. [OE *hōd*] —ˈ**hooded** *adj.* —ˈ**hood**ˌ**like** *adj.*

hood[2] (hʊd) *n. Sl.* short for **hoodlum.**

-hood *suffix forming nouns.* **1.** indicating state or condition: *manhood.* **2.** indicating a body of persons: *knighthood; priesthood.* [OE *-hād*]

hooded crow *n.* a crow that has a grey body and black head, wings, and tail. Also called (Scot.): **hoodie** (ˈhʊdɪ), **hoodie crow.**

hoodlum (ˈhuːdləm) *n.* **1.** a petty gangster. **2.** a lawless youth. [C19: ? < Southern G *Haderlump* ragged good-for-nothing]

hoodman-blind (ˌhʊdmənˈblaɪnd) *n. Brit., arch.* blind man's buff.

hoodoo (ˈhuːduː) *n., pl.* **-doos. 1.** a variant of **voodoo. 2.** *Inf.* a person or thing that brings bad luck. **3.** *Inf.* bad luck. ~*vb.* **-dooing, -dooed. 4.** (*tr.*) *Inf.* to bring bad luck to.

hoodwink (ˈhʊdˌwɪŋk) *vb.* (*tr.*) **1.** to dupe; trick.

2. *Obs.* to cover or hide. [C16: orig., to cover the eyes with a hood, blindfold]

hooey (ˈhuːɪ) *n., interj. Sl.* nonsense. [C20: <?]

hoof (huːf) *n., pl.* **hooves** *or* **hoofs. 1. a.** the horny covering of the end of the foot in the horse, deer, and all other ungulate mammals. **b.** (*in combination*): *a hoofbeat.* Related adj.: **ungular. 2.** the foot of an ungulate mammal. **3.** a hoofed animal. **4.** *Facetious.* a person's foot. **5. on the hoof.** (of livestock) alive. *~vb.* **6. hoof it.** *Sl.* **a.** to walk. **b.** to dance. [OE *hōf*] **—hoofed** *adj.*

hoo-ha (ˈhuːˌhɑː) *n.* a noisy commotion or fuss. [C20: <?]

hook (hʊk) *n.* **1.** a curved piece of material, usually metal, used to suspend, hold, or pull something. **2.** short for **fish-hook. 3.** a trap or snare. **4.** something resembling a hook in design or use. **5. a.** a sharp bend, esp. in a river. **b.** a sharply curved spit of land. **6.** *Boxing.* a short swinging blow delivered with the elbow bent. **7.** *Cricket.* a shot in which the ball is hit square on the leg side with the bat held horizontally. **8.** *Golf.* a shot that causes the ball to go to the player's left. **9.** a hook-shaped stroke used in writing, such as a part of a letter extending above or below the line. **10.** *Music.* a stroke added to the stem of a note to indicate time values shorter than a crotchet. **11.** a sickle. **12.** *Naut.* an anchor. **13. by hook or (by) crook.** by any means. **14. hook, line, and sinker.** *Inf.* completely: *he fell for it hook, line, and sinker.* **15. off the hook.** *Sl.* free from obligation or guilt. **16. sling one's hook.** *Brit. sl.* to leave. *~vb.* **17.** (often foll. by *up*) to fasten or be fastened with or as if with a hook or hooks. **18.** (*tr.*) to catch (something, such as a fish) on a hook. **19.** to curve like or into the shape of a hook. **20.** (*tr.*) to make (a rug) by hooking yarn through a stiff fabric backing with a special instrument. **21.** *Boxing.* to hit (an opponent) with a hook. **22.** *Cricket, etc.* to play (a ball) with a hook. **23.** *Rugby.* to obtain and pass (the ball) backwards from a scrum, using the feet. **24.** (*tr.*) *Sl.* to steal. [OE *hōc*] **—ˈhookˌlike** *adj.*

hookah *or* **hooka** (ˈhʊkə) *n.* an oriental pipe for smoking marijuana, tobacco, etc., consisting of one or more long flexible stems connected to a container of water or other liquid through which smoke is drawn and cooled. Also called: **hubble-bubble, water pipe.** [C18: < Ar. *huqqah*]

hooked (hʊkt) *adj.* **1.** bent like a hook. **2.** having a hook or hooks. **3.** caught or trapped. **4.** a slang word for **married. 5.** *Sl.* addicted to a drug. **6.** (often foll. by *on*) obsessed (with).

hooker (ˈhʊkə) *n.* **1.** a person or thing that hooks. **2.** *U.S. & Canad. sl.* a prostitute. **3.** *Rugby.* the central forward in the front row of a scrum whose main job is to hook the ball.

Hooke's law (hʊks) *n.* the principle that the stress imposed on a solid is directly proportional to the strain produced, within the elastic limit. [C18: after R. *Hooke* (1635-1703), E scientist]

hook-up *n.* **1.** the contact of an aircraft in flight with the refuelling hose of a tanker aircraft. **2.** an alliance or relationship. **3.** the linking of broadcasting equipment or stations to transmit a special programme. *~vb.* **hook up** (*adv.*). **4.** to connect (two or more people or things).

hookworm (ˈhʊkˌwɜːm) *n.* any of various parasitic bloodsucking worms which cause disease. They have hooked mouthparts and enter their hosts by boring through the skin. Cf. **ancylostomiasis.**

hooky *or* **hookey** (ˈhʊkɪ) *n. Inf., chiefly U.S., Canad., & N.Z.* truancy, usually from school (esp. in **play hooky**). [C20: ? < *hook it* to escape]

hooligan (ˈhuːlɪgən) *n. Sl.* a rough lawless young person. [C19: ? var. of *Houlihan*, Irish surname] **—ˈhooliganism** *n.*

hoop[1] (huːp) *n.* **1.** a rigid circular band of metal or wood. **2.** something resembling this. **3.** a band of iron that holds the staves of a barrel together. **4.** a child's toy shaped like a hoop and rolled on the ground or whirled around the body. **5.** *Croquet.* any of the iron arches through which the ball is driven. **6. a.** a light curved frame to spread out a skirt. **b.** (*as modifier*): *a hoop skirt.* **7.** *Basketball.* the round metal frame to which the net is attached to form the basket. **8.** a large ring often with paper stretched over it through which performers or animals jump. **9. go** *or* **be put through the hoop.** to be subjected to an ordeal. *~vb.* **10.** (*tr.*) to surround with or as if with a hoop. [OE *hōp*] **—hooped** *adj.*

hoop[2] (huːp) *n., vb.* a variant spelling of **whoop.**

hoopla (ˈhuːplɑː) *n.* **1.** *Brit.* a fairground game in which a player tries to throw a hoop over an object and so win it. **2.** *U.S. & Canad. sl.* **a.** noise; bustle. **b.** nonsense; ballyhoo. [C20: see WHOOP, LA[2]]

hoopoe (ˈhuːpuː) *n.* an Old World bird having a pinkish-brown plumage with black-and-white wings and an erectile crest. [C17: < earlier *hoopoop*, imit.]

hoop pine *n.* a fast-growing timber tree of Australia having rough bark with hooplike cracks around the trunk and branches.

hooray (huːˈreɪ) *or* **hoorah** (huːˈrɑː) *interj., n., vb.* **1.** variant spellings of **hurrah.** *~sentence substitute.* **2.** Also: **hooroo** (huːˈruː). *Austral. & N.Z.* cheerio.

Hooray Henry (ˈhuːˌreɪ ˈhɛnrɪ) *n., pl.* **Hooray Henries** *or* **-rys.** a young upper-class man, often with affectedly hearty voice and manners. Sometimes shortened to **Hooray.**

hoosegow *or* **hoosgow** (ˈhuːsgaʊ) *n. U.S.* a slang word for **jail.** [C20: < Mexican Sp. *jusgado* prison, < Sp.: court of justice, ult. < L *judex* a JUDGE]

hoot[1] (huːt) *n.* **1.** the mournful wavering cry of some owls. **2.** a similar sound, such as that of a train whistle. **3.** a jeer of derision. **4.** *Inf.* an amusing person or thing. *~vb.* **5.** (often foll. by *at*) to jeer or yell (something) contemptuously (at someone). **6.** (*tr.*) to drive (speakers, actors on stage, etc.) off by hooting. **7.** (*intr.*) to make a hoot. **8.** (*intr.*) *Brit.* to blow a horn. [C13 *hoten*, imit.]

hoot[2] (huːt) *n. Austral. & N.Z.* a slang word for **money.** [< Maori *utu* price]

hootenanny (ˈhuːtᵊˌnænɪ) *or* **hootnanny** (ˈhuːtˌnænɪ) *n., pl.* **-nies.** *U.S. & Canad.* an informal performance by folk singers. [C20: <?]

hooter (ˈhuːtə) *n. Chiefly Brit.* **1.** a person or thing that hoots, esp. a car horn. **2.** *Sl.* a nose.

Hoover (ˈhuːvə) *n.* **1.** *Trademark.* a type of vacuum cleaner. *~vb.* **2.** (*usually not cap.*) to vacuum-clean (a carpet, etc.).

hooves (huːvz) *n.* a plural of **hoof.**

hop[1] (hɒp) *vb.* **hopping, hopped. 1.** (*intr.*) to jump forwards or upwards on one foot. **2.** (*intr.*) (esp. of frogs, birds, etc.) to move forwards in short jumps. **3.** (*tr.*) to jump over. **4.** (*intr.*) *Inf.* to move quickly (in, on, out of, etc.): *hop on a bus.* **5.** (*tr.*) *Inf.* to cross (an ocean) in an aircraft. **6.** (*tr.*) *U.S. & Canad. inf.* to travel by means of: *he hopped a train to Chicago.* **7.** (*intr.*) another word for **limp**[1]. **8. hop it** (*or* **off**). *Brit. sl.* to go away. *~n.* **9.** the act or an instance of hopping. **10.** *Inf.* an informal dance. **11.** *Inf.* a trip, esp. in an aircraft. **12. on the hop.** *Inf.* **a.** active or busy. **b.** *Brit.* unawares or unprepared. [OE *hoppian*]

hop[2] (hɒp) *n.* **1.** a climbing plant which has green conelike female flowers and clusters of small male flowers. **2. hop garden.** a field of hops. **3.** *Obs. sl.* opium or any other narcotic drug. *~See also* **hops.** [C15: < MDu. *hoppe*] **—ˈhopˌpicker** *n.*

hope (həʊp) *n.* **1.** (*sometimes pl.*) a feeling of desire for something and confidence in the possibility of its fulfilment: *his hope for peace was justified.* **2.** a reasonable ground for this feeling: *there is still hope.* **3.** a person or thing that gives cause for hope. **4.** a thing, situation, or event that is desired: *my hope is that prices will fall.* **5. not a hope** *or* **some hope.** used ironically to express little confidence that expectations will be fulfilled. *~vb.* **6.** (*tr.; takes a clause as object or an infinitive*) to desire (something) with some possibility of fulfilment: *I hope to tell you.* **7.** (*intr.;* often foll. by *for*) to have a wish. **8.** (*tr.;*

takes a clause as object) to trust or believe: *we hope that this is satisfactory.* [OE *hopa*]

hope chest *n.* the U.S., Canad., and N.Z. name for **bottom drawer.**

hopeful (ˈhəʊpfʊl) *adj.* **1.** having or expressing hope. **2.** inspiring hope; promising. ~*n.* **3.** a person considered to be on the brink of success (esp. in **a young hopeful**). —ˈ**hopefulness** *n.*

hopefully (ˈhəʊpfʊlɪ) *adv.* **1.** in a hopeful manner. **2.** *Inf.* it is hoped: *hopefully they will be married soon.*

▷ **Usage.** The use of *hopefully* to mean 'it is hoped that' is not universally accepted as standard. It does, however, represent a construction well-established in colloquial English, as in the use of *happily* in *the two vehicles crashed, but happily no one was injured.*

hopeless (ˈhəʊplɪs) *adj.* **1.** having or offering no hope. **2.** impossible to solve. **3.** unable to learn, function, etc. **4.** *Inf.* without skill or ability. —ˈ**hopelessly** *adv.* —ˈ**hopelessness** *n.*

Hopi (ˈhəʊpɪ) *n.* **1.** (*pl.* **-pis** *or* **-pi**) a member of a North American Indian people of NE Arizona. **2.** the language of this people. [< Hopi *Hópi* peaceful]

hoplite (ˈhɒplaɪt) *n.* (in ancient Greece) a heavily armed infantryman. [C18: < Gk *hoplitēs,* < *hoplon* weapon, < *hepein* to prepare]

hopper (ˈhɒpə) *n.* **1.** a person or thing that hops. **2.** a funnel-shaped reservoir from which solid materials can be discharged into a receptacle below, esp. for feeding fuel to a furnace, loading a truck, etc. **3.** a machine used for picking hops. **4.** any of various long-legged hopping insects. **5.** an open-topped railway truck for loose minerals, etc., unloaded through doors on the underside. **6.** *S. African.* another name for **cocopan. 7.** *Computers.* a device for holding punched cards and feeding them to a card reader.

hopping (ˈhɒpɪŋ) *adv.* **hopping mad.** in a terrible rage.

hops (hɒps) *pl. n.* the dried flowers of the hop plant, used to give a bitter taste to beer.

hopsack (ˈhɒpˌsæk) *n.* **1.** a roughly woven fabric of wool, cotton, etc., used for clothing. **2.** Also called: **hopsacking.** a coarse fabric used for bags, etc., made generally of hemp or jute.

hopscotch (ˈhɒpˌskɒtʃ) *n.* a children's game in which a player throws a small stone or other object to land in one of a pattern of squares marked on the ground and then hops over to it to pick it up. [C19: HOP[1] + SCOTCH[1]]

horary (ˈhɔːrərɪ) *adj. Arch.* **1.** relating to the hours. **2.** hourly. [C17: < Med. L *hōrārius,* < L *hora*]

horde (hɔːd) *n.* **1.** a vast crowd; throng; mob. **2.** a nomadic group of people, esp. an Asiatic group. **3.** a large moving mass of animals, esp. insects. [C16: < Polish *horda,* < Turkish *ordū* camp]

horehound *or* **hoarhound** (ˈhɔːˌhaʊnd) *n.* a downy herbaceous Old World plant with small white flowers that contain a bitter juice formerly used as a cough medicine and flavouring. [OE *hārhūne,* < *hār* grey + *hūne* horehound, <?]

horizon (həˈraɪzᵊn) *n.* **1.** Also called: **visible horizon, apparent horizon.** the apparent line that divides the earth and the sky. **2.** *Astron.* **a.** Also called: **sensible horizon.** the circular intersection with the celestial sphere of the plane tangential to the earth at the position of the observer. **b.** Also called: **celestial horizon.** the great circle on the celestial sphere, the plane of which passes through the centre of the earth and is parallel to the sensible horizon. **3.** the range or limit of scope, interest, knowledge, etc. **4.** a layer of rock within a stratum that has a particular composition by which the stratum may be dated. [C14: < L, < Gk *horizōn kuklos* limiting circle, < *horizein* to limit]

horizontal (ˌhɒrɪˈzɒntᵊl) *adj.* **1.** parallel to the plane of the horizon; level; flat. **2.** of or relating to the horizon. **3.** in a plane parallel to that of the horizon. **4.** applied uniformly to all members of a group. **5.** *Econ.* relating to identical stages of commercial activity: *horizontal integration.* ~*n.* **6.** a horizontal plane, position, line, etc. —ˌ**horizonˈtality** *n.* —ˌ**horiˈzontally** *adv.*

horizontal bar *n. Gymnastics.* a raised bar on which swinging exercises are performed.

hormone (ˈhɔːməʊn) *n.* **1.** a chemical substance produced in an endocrine gland and transported in the blood to a certain tissue, on which it exerts a specific effect. **2.** an organic compound produced by a plant that is essential for growth. **3.** any synthetic substance having the same effects. [C20: < Gk *hormōn,* < *horman* to stir up, < *hormē* impulse] —**horˈmonal** *adj.*

horn (hɔːn) *n.* **1.** either of a pair of permanent bony outgrowths on the heads of cattle, antelopes, etc. **2.** the outgrowth from the nasal bone of a rhinoceros, consisting of a mass of fused hairs. **3.** any hornlike projection, such as the eyestalk of a snail. **4.** the antler of a deer. **5. a.** the constituent substance, mainly keratin, of horns, hooves, etc. **b.** (*in combination*): *horn-rimmed spectacles.* **6.** a container or device made from this substance or an artificial substitute: *a drinking horn.* **7.** an object resembling a horn in shape, such as a cornucopia. **8.** a primitive musical wind instrument made from horn. **9.** any musical instrument consisting of a pipe or tube of brass fitted with a mouthpiece. See **French horn, cor anglais. 10.** *Jazz sl.* any wind instrument. **11. a.** a device for producing a warning or signalling noise. **b.** (*in combination*): *a foghorn.* **12.** (*usually pl.*) the imaginary hornlike parts formerly supposed to appear on the forehead of a cuckold. **13. a.** a hollow conical device coupled to a gramophone to control the direction and quality of the sound. **b.** a similar device attached to an electrical loudspeaker, esp. in a public-address system. **14.** a stretch of land or water shaped like a horn. **15.** *Brit. taboo sl.* an erection of the penis. ~*vb.* (*tr.*) **16.** to provide with a horn or horns. **17.** to gore or butt with a horn. **18.** to remove or shorten the horns of (cattle, etc.). ~See also **horn in.** [OE] —**horned** *adj.* —ˈ**hornless** *adj.*

hornbeam (ˈhɔːnˌbiːm) *n.* **1.** a tree of Europe and Asia having smooth grey bark and hard white wood. **2.** its wood. ~Also called: **ironwood.** [C14: < HORN + BEAM, referring to its tough wood]

hornbill (ˈhɔːnˌbɪl) *n.* a bird of tropical Africa and Asia, having a very large bill with a basal bony protuberance.

hornblende (ˈhɔːnˌblɛnd) *n.* a mineral of the amphibole group consisting of the aluminium silicates of calcium, sodium, magnesium, and iron: varies in colour from green to black. [C18: < G *Horn* horn + BLENDE]

hornbook (ˈhɔːnˌbʊk) *n.* a page bearing a religious text or the alphabet, held in a frame with a thin window of horn over it.

horned toad *or* **lizard** *n.* a small insectivorous burrowing lizard inhabiting desert regions of America, having a flattened toadlike body covered with spines.

horned viper *n.* a venomous snake that occurs in desert regions of N Africa and SW Asia and has a small horny spine above each eye.

hornet (ˈhɔːnɪt) *n.* **1.** any of various large social wasps that can inflict a severe sting. **2. hornet's nest.** a strongly unfavourable reaction (often in **stir up a hornet's nest**). [OE *hyrnetu*]

horn in *vb.* (*intr., adv.;* often foll. by *on*) *Sl.* to interrupt or intrude.

horn of plenty *n.* another term for **cornucopia.**

hornpipe (ˈhɔːnˌpaɪp) *n.* **1.** an obsolete reed instrument with a mouthpiece made of horn. **2.** an old British solo dance to a hornpipe accompaniment, traditionally performed by sailors. **3.** a piece of music for such a dance.

hornswoggle (ˈhɔːnˌswɒgᵊl) *vb.* (*tr.*) *Sl.* to cheat or trick; bamboozle. [C19: <?]

horny (ˈhɔːnɪ) *adj.* **hornier, horniest. 1.** of, like, or hard as horn. **2.** having a horn or horns. **3.** *Sl.* aroused sexually. —ˈ**horniness** *n.*

horologe (ˈhɒrəˌlɒdʒ) *n.* a rare word for **timepiece.** [C14: < L *hōrologium,* < Gk *hōrologion,* < *hōra* HOUR + *-logos* < *legein* to tell]

horologist (hɒˈrɒlədʒɪst) *or* **horologer** *n.* a person skilled in horology.

horology (hɒˈrɒlədʒɪ) *n.* the art or science of making timepieces or of measuring time. —**horologic** (ˌhɒrəˈlɒdʒɪk) *or* ˌ**horoˈlogical** *adj.*

horoscope (ˈhɒrəˌskəʊp) *n.* **1.** the prediction of a person's future based on zodiacal data for the time of birth. **2.** the configuration of the planets, sun, and moon in the sky at a particular moment. **3.** a diagram showing the positions of the planets, sun, moon, etc., at a particular time and place. [OE *horoscopus,* < L, < Gk *hōroskopos,* < *hōra* HOUR + -SCOPE] —**horoscopic** (ˌhɒrəˈskɒpɪk) *adj.* —**horoscopy** (hɒˈrɒskəpɪ) *n.*

horrendous (hɒˈrɛndəs) *adj.* another word for **horrific.** [C17: < L *horrendus* fearful, < *horrēre* to bristle, shudder, tremble; see HORROR] —**horˈrendously** *adv.*

horrible (ˈhɒrɪbᵊl) *adj.* **1.** causing horror; dreadful. **2.** disagreeable. **3.** *Inf.* cruel or unkind. [C14: via OF < L *horribilis,* < *horrēre* to tremble] —ˈ**horribleness** *n.* —ˈ**horribly** *adv.*

horrid (ˈhɒrɪd) *adj.* **1.** disagreeable; unpleasant: *a horrid meal.* **2.** repulsive or frightening. **3.** *Inf.* unkind. [C16 (in the sense: bristling, shaggy): < L *horridus* prickly, < *horrēre* to bristle] —ˈ**horridly** *adv.* —ˈ**horridness** *n.*

horrific (hɒˈrɪfɪk, hə-) *adj.* provoking horror; horrible. —**horˈrifically** *adv.*

horrify (ˈhɒrɪˌfaɪ) *vb.* **-fying, -fied.** (*tr.*) **1.** to cause feelings of horror in; terrify. **2.** to shock greatly. —ˌ**horrifiˈcation** *n.* —ˈ**horriˌfied** *adj.* —ˈ**horriˌfying** *adj.* —ˈ**horriˌfyingly** *adv.*

horripilation (hɒˌrɪpɪˈleɪʃən) *n. Physiol.* a technical name for **goose flesh.** [C17: < LL *horripilātiō* a bristling, < L *horrēre* to stand on end + *pilus* hair]

horror (ˈhɒrə) *n.* **1.** extreme fear; terror; dread. **2.** intense hatred. **3.** (*often pl.*) a thing or person causing fear, loathing, etc. **4.** (*modifier*) having a frightening subject: *a horror film.* [C14: < L: a trembling with fear]

horrors (ˈhɒrəz) *pl. n.* **1.** *Sl.* a fit of depression or anxiety. **2.** *Inf.* See **delirium tremens.** ~*interj.* **3.** an expression of dismay, sometimes facetious.

hors de combat *French.* (ɔr də kɔ̃ba) *adj.* (*postpositive*), *adv.* disabled or injured. [lit.: out of (the) fight]

hors d'oeuvre (ɔː ˈdɜːvr) *n., pl.* **hors d'oeuvre** *or* **hors d'oeuvres** (ˈdɜːvr). an appetizer, usually served before the main meal. [C18: < F, lit.: outside the work]

horse (hɔːs) *n.* **1.** a solid-hoofed, herbivorous, domesticated mammal used for draught work and riding. Related adj.: **equine.** **2.** the adult male of this species; stallion. **3. wild horse.** another name for **Przewalski's horse.** **4.** (*functioning as pl.*) horsemen, esp. cavalry: *a regiment of horse.* **5.** Also called: **buck.** *Gymnastics.* a padded apparatus on legs, used for vaulting, etc. **6.** a narrow board supported by a pair of legs at each end, used as a frame for sawing or as a trestle, barrier, etc. **7.** a contrivance on which a person may ride and exercise. **8.** a slang word for **heroin.** **9.** *Mining.* a mass of rock within a vein of ore. **10.** *Naut.* a rod, rope, or cable, fixed at the ends, along which something may slide; traveller. **11.** *Inf.* short for **horsepower.** **12.** (*modifier*) drawn by a horse or horses: *a horse cart.* **13. a horse of another** *or* **a different colour.** a completely different topic, argument, etc. **14. be** (*or* **get**) **on one's high horse.** *Inf.* to act disdainfully aloof. **15. hold one's horses.** to restrain oneself. **16. horses for courses.** a policy, course of action, etc. modified slightly to take account of special circumstances without departing in essentials from the original. **17. the horse's mouth.** the most reliable source. ~*vb.* **18.** (*tr.*) to provide with a horse or horses. **19.** to put or be put on horseback. [OE *hors*] —ˈ**horseˌlike** *adj.*

horse around *or* **about** *vb.* (*intr., adv.*) *Inf.* to indulge in horseplay.

horseback (ˈhɔːsˌbæk) *n.* **a.** a horse's back (esp. in **on horseback**). **b.** *Chiefly U.S.* (*as modifier*): *horseback riding.*

horsebox (ˈhɔːsˌbɒks) *n. Brit.* a van or trailer used for carrying horses.

horse brass *n.* a decorative brass ornament, originally attached to a horse's harness.

horse chestnut *n.* **1.** a tree having palmate leaves, erect clusters of white, pink, or red flowers, and brown shiny inedible nuts enclosed in a spiky bur. **2.** Also called: **conker.** the nut of this tree. [C16: < its having been used in the treatment of respiratory disease in horses]

horseflesh (ˈhɔːsˌflɛʃ) *n.* **1.** horses collectively. **2.** the flesh of a horse, esp. edible horse meat.

horsefly (ˈhɔːsˌflaɪ) *n., pl.* **-flies.** a large stout-bodied dipterous fly, the female of which sucks the blood of mammals, esp. horses, cattle, and man. Also called: **gadfly, cleg.**

horsehair (ˈhɔːsˌhɛə) *n.* hair taken chiefly from the tail or mane of a horse, used in upholstery and for fabric, etc.

horsehide (ˈhɔːsˌhaɪd) *n.* **1.** the hide of a horse. **2.** leather made from this hide.

horse latitudes *pl. n. Naut.* the latitudes near 30°N or 30°S at sea, characterized by baffling winds, calms, and high barometric pressure. [C18: referring either to the high mortality of horses on board ship in these latitudes or to *dead horse* (nautical slang: advance pay), which sailors expected to work off by this stage of a voyage]

horse laugh *n.* a coarse or raucous laugh.

horseleech (ˈhɔːsˌliːtʃ) *n.* **1.** any of several large carnivorous freshwater leeches. **2.** an archaic name for a **veterinary surgeon.**

horse mackerel *n.* **1.** Also called: **scad.** a mackerel-like fish of European Atlantic waters, with a row of bony scales along the lateral line. Sometimes called (U.S.): **saurel.** **2.** any of various large tunnies or related fishes.

horseman (ˈhɔːsmən) *n., pl.* **-men.** **1.** a person skilled in riding. **2.** a person who rides a horse. —ˈ**horsemanˌship** *n.* —ˈ**horseˌwoman** *fem. n.*

horse mushroom *n.* a large edible mushroom, with a white cap and greyish gills.

horse pistol *n.* a large holstered pistol formerly carried by horsemen.

horseplay (ˈhɔːsˌpleɪ) *n.* rough or rowdy play.

horsepower (ˈhɔːsˌpaʊə) *n.* an fps unit of power, equal to 550 foot-pounds per second (equivalent to 745.7 watts). Abbrev.: **HP, h.p.**

horseradish (ˈhɔːsˌrædɪʃ) *n.* a coarse Eurasian plant cultivated for its thick white pungent root, which is ground and combined with vinegar, etc., to make a sauce.

horse sense *n.* another term for **common sense.**

horseshoe (ˈhɔːsˌʃuː) *n.* **1.** a piece of iron shaped like a U nailed to the underside of the hoof of a horse to protect the soft part of the foot: commonly thought to be a token of good luck. **2.** an object of similar shape.

horseshoe bat *n.* any of numerous large-eared Old World bats with a fleshy growth around the nostrils, used in echolocation.

horseshoe crab *n.* a marine arthropod of North America and Asia, having a rounded heavily armoured body with a long pointed tail. Also called: **king crab.**

horsetail (ˈhɔːsˌteɪl) *n.* **1.** a plant having jointed stems with whorls of small dark toothlike leaves. **2.** a stylized horse's tail formerly used as the emblem of a pasha.

horse trading *n.* shrewd bargaining.

horsewhip (ˈhɔːsˌwɪp) *n.* **1.** a whip, usually with a long thong, used for managing horses. ~*vb.* **-whipping, -whipped.** **2.** (*tr.*) to flog with such a whip. —ˈ**horseˌwhipper** *n.*

horst (hɔːst) *n.* a ridge of land that has been forced upwards between two faults. [C20: < G *Horst* thicket]

horsy *or* **horsey** (ˈhɔːsɪ) *adj.* **horsier, horsiest.** **1.** of or relating to horses: *a horsy smell.* **2.** dealing with or devoted to horses. **3.** like a horse: *a horsy face.* —ˈ**horsily** *adv.* —ˈ**horsiness** *n.*

hortatory (ˈhɔːtətərɪ) *or* **hortative** (ˈhɔːtətɪv) *adj.* tending to exhort; encouraging. [C16: < LL *hortātōrius,* < L *hortārī* to EXHORT] —**horˈtation** *n.* —ˈ**hortatorily** *or* ˈ**hortatively** *adv.*

iculture (ˈhɔːtɪˌkʌltʃə) *n.* the art or science of cultivating gardens. [C17: < L *hortus* garden + CULTURE; cf. AGRICULTURE] —ˌ**hortiˈcultural** *adj.* —ˌ**hortiˈculturist** *n.*

Hos. *Bible. abbrev. for* Hosea.

hosanna (həʊˈzænə) *interj.* an exclamation of praise, esp. one to God. [OE *osanna*, via LL < Gk, < Heb. *hōshi 'āh nnā* save now, we pray]

hose[1] (həʊz) *n.* **1.** a flexible pipe, for conveying a liquid or gas. ~*vb.* **2.** (sometimes foll. by *down*) to wash, water, or sprinkle (a person or thing) with or as if with a hose. [C15: later use of HOSE[2]]

hose[2] (həʊz) *n., pl.* **hose** *or* **hosen. 1.** stockings, socks, and tights collectively. **2.** *History.* a man's garment covering the legs and reaching up to the waist. **3. half-hose.** socks. [OE *hosa*]

hosier (ˈhəʊzɪə) *n.* a person who sells stockings, etc.

hosiery (ˈhəʊzɪərɪ) *n.* stockings, socks, and knitted underclothing collectively.

hospice (ˈhɒspɪs) *n.* **1.** a nursing home that specializes in caring for the terminally ill. **2.** *Arch.* a place of shelter for travellers, esp. one kept by a monastic order. [C19: < F, < L *hospitium* hospitality, < *hospes* guest]

hospitable (ˈhɒspɪtəbᵊl, hɒˈspɪt-) *adj.* **1.** welcoming to guests or strangers. **2.** fond of entertaining. [C16: < Med. L *hospitāre* to receive as a guest, < L *hospes* guest] —ˈ**hospitableness** *n.* —ˈ**hospitably** *adv.*

hospital (ˈhɒspɪtᵊl) *n.* **1.** an institution for the medical or psychiatric care and treatment of patients. **2.** (*modifier*) having the function of a hospital: *a hospital ship.* **3.** a repair shop for something specified: *a dolls' hospital.* **4.** *Arch.* a charitable home, hospice, or school. [C13: < Med. L *hospitāle* hospice, < L, < *hospes* guest]

hospitality (ˌhɒspɪˈtælɪtɪ) *n., pl.* **-ties.** kindness in welcoming strangers or guests.

hospitality suite *n.* a room or suite, as at a conference, where free drinks are offered.

hospitalize *or* **-lise** (ˈhɒspɪtəˌlaɪz) *vb.* (*tr.*) to admit or send (a person) into a hospital. —ˌ**hospitaliˈzation** *or* **-liˈsation** *n.*

hospitaller *or U.S.* **hospitaler** (ˈhɒspɪtələ) *n.* a person, esp. a member of certain religious orders, dedicated to hospital work, ambulance services, etc. [C14: < OF *hospitalier*, < Med. L, < *hospitāle* hospice; see HOSPITAL]

Hospitaller *or U.S.* **Hospitaler** (ˈhɒspɪtələ) *n.* a member of the order of the Knights Hospitallers.

host[1] (həʊst) *n.* **1.** a person who receives or entertains guests, esp. in his own home. **2.** the compere of a show or television programme. **3.** *Biol.* **a.** an animal or plant that supports a parasite. **b.** an animal into which tissue is experimentally grafted. **4.** the owner or manager of an inn. ~*vb.* **5.** to be the host of (a party, programme, etc.): *to host one's own show.* [C13: < F *hoste*, < L *hospes* guest]

host[2] (həʊst) *n.* **1.** a great number; multitude. **2.** an archaic word for **army.** [C13: < OF *hoste*, < L *hostis* stranger]

Host (həʊst) *n. Christianity.* the wafer of unleavened bread consecrated in the Eucharist. [C14: < OF *oiste*, < L *hostia* victim]

hosta (ˈhɒstə) *n.* a plant cultivated esp. for its ornamental foliage. [C19: NL, after N. T. *Host* (1761–1834), Austrian physician]

hostage (ˈhɒstɪdʒ) *n.* **1.** a person given to or held by another as a security or pledge. **2.** the state of being held as a hostage. **3.** any security or pledge. **4. give hostages to fortune.** to place oneself in a position in which misfortune may strike through the loss of what one values most. [C13: < OF, < *hoste* guest]

hostel (ˈhɒstᵊl) *n.* **1.** a building providing overnight accommodation, as for homeless people. **2.** See **youth hostel. 3.** *Brit.* a supervised lodging house for nurses, workers, etc. **4.** *Arch.* another word for **hostelry.** [C13: < OF, < Med. L *hospitāle* hospice; see HOSPITAL]

hosteller *or U.S.* **hosteler** (ˈhɒstələ) *n.* **1.** a person who stays at youth hostels. **2.** an archaic word for **innkeeper.**

hostelling *or U.S.* **hosteling** (ˈhɒstəlɪŋ) *n.* the practice of staying at youth hostels when travelling.

hostelry (ˈhɒstəlrɪ) *n., pl.* **-ries.** *Arch. or facetious.* an inn.

hostess (ˈhəʊstɪs) *n.* **1.** a woman acting as host. **2.** a woman who receives and entertains patrons of a club, restaurant, etc. **3.** See **air hostess.**

hostile (ˈhɒstaɪl) *adj.* **1.** antagonistic; opposed. **2.** of or relating to an enemy. **3.** unfriendly. [C16: < L *hostīlis*, < *hostis* enemy] —ˈ**hostilely** *adv.*

hostility (hɒˈstɪlɪtɪ) *n., pl.* **-ties. 1.** enmity. **2.** an act expressing enmity. **3.** (*pl.*) fighting; warfare.

hostler (ˈɒslə) *n.* a variant (esp. Brit.) of **ostler.**

hot (hɒt) *adj.* **hotter, hottest. 1.** having a relatively high temperature. **2.** having a temperature higher than desirable. **3.** causing a sensation of bodily heat. **4.** causing a burning sensation on the tongue: *a hot curry.* **5.** expressing or feeling intense emotion, such as anger or lust. **6.** intense or vehement. **7.** recent; new: *hot from the press.* **8.** *Ball games.* (of a ball) thrown or struck hard, and so difficult to respond to. **9.** much favoured: *a hot favourite.* **10.** *Inf.* having a dangerously high level of radioactivity. **11.** *Sl.* stolen or otherwise illegally obtained. **12.** *Sl.* (of people) being sought by the police. **13.** (of a colour) intense; striking: *hot pink.* **14.** following closely: *hot on the scent.* **15.** *Inf.* at a dangerously high electric potential. **16.** *Sl.* good (esp. in **not so hot**). **17.** *Jazz sl.* arousing great excitement by inspired improvisation, strong rhythms, etc. **18.** *Inf.* dangerous or unpleasant (esp. in **make it hot for someone**). **19.** (in various games) very near the answer. **20.** *Metallurgy.* (of a process) at a sufficiently high temperature for metal to be in a soft workable state. **21.** *Austral. & N.Z. inf.* (of a price, etc.) excessive. **22. hot on.** *Inf.* **a.** very severe: *the police are hot on drunk drivers.* **b.** particularly knowledgeable about. **23. hot under the collar.** *Inf.* aroused with anger, annoyance, etc. **24. in hot water.** *Inf.* in trouble. ~*adv.* **25.** in a hot manner; hotly. ~See also **hot up.** [OE *hāt*] —ˈ**hotly** *adv.* —ˈ**hotness** *n.* —ˈ**hottish** *adj.*

hot air *n. Inf.* empty and usually boastful talk.

hotbed (ˈhɒtˌbɛd) *n.* **1.** a glass-covered bed of soil, usually heated, for propagating plants, forcing early vegetables, etc. **2.** a place offering ideal conditions for the growth of an idea, activity, etc., esp. one considered bad.

hot-blooded *adj.* **1.** passionate or excitable. **2.** (of a horse) being of thoroughbred stock.

hotchpotch (ˈhɒtʃˌpɒtʃ) *or esp. U.S. & Canad.* **hodgepodge** *n.* **1.** a jumbled mixture. **2.** a thick soup or stew. [C15: var. of hotchpot < OF, < *hocher* to shake + POT[1]]

hot cross bun *n.* a yeast bun marked with a cross and traditionally eaten on Good Friday.

hot dog *n.* a sausage, esp. a frankfurter, usually served hot in a long roll split lengthways.

hotel (həʊˈtɛl) *n.* **1.** a commercially run establishment providing lodging and usually meals for guests. **2.** *Austral. & N.Z.* a public house. [C17: < F *hôtel*, < OF *hostel*; see HOSTEL]

hotelier (hɒˈtɛljeɪ) *n.* an owner or manager of one or more hotels.

hotel ship *n.* an accommodation barge anchored near an oil production rig.

hotfoot (ˈhɒtˌfʊt) *adv.* with all possible speed.

hot-gospeller *n. Inf.* a revivalist preacher with a highly enthusiastic style of addressing his audience. —ˈ**hot-ˈgospel** *adj.*

hothead (ˈhɒtˌhɛd) *n.* an excitable person.

hot-headed *adj.* impetuous, rash, or hot-tempered. —ˌ**hot-ˈheadedness** *n.*

hothouse (ˈhɒtˌhaʊs) *n.* **1. a.** a greenhouse in which the temperature is maintained at a fixed level. **b.** (*as modifier*): *a hothouse plant.* **2. a.** an environment that encourages rapid development. **b.** (*as modifier*): *a hothouse atmosphere.* **3.** (*modifier*) *Inf., often disparaging.* sensitive or delicate: *a hothouse temperament.*

hot line *n.* **1.** a direct telephone or teletype link between heads of government, etc., for emergency use. **2.** any such direct line kept for urgent use.

hot money *n.* capital that is transferred from one financial centre to another seeking the best opportunity for short-term gain.

hotplate ('hɒt,pleɪt) *n.* **1.** an electrically heated plate on a cooker or one set into a working surface. **2.** a portable device on which food can be kept warm.

hotpot ('hɒt,pɒt) *n. Brit.* a casserole covered with a layer of potatoes.

hot potato *n. Inf.* a delicate or awkward matter.

hot-press *n.* **1.** a machine for applying a combination of heat and pressure to give a smooth surface to paper, to express oil from it, etc. ~*vb.* **2.** (*tr.*) to subject (paper, cloth, etc.) to such a process.

hot rod *n.* a car with an engine that has been radically modified to produce increased power.

hot seat *n.* **1.** *Inf.* a difficult or dangerous position. **2.** *U.S.* a slang term for **electric chair.**

hot spot *n.* **1.** an area of potential violence. **2.** a lively nightclub. **3.** any local area of high temperature in a part of an engine, etc. **4.** a small area of exceptionally high radioactivity or of some chemical or mineral considered harmful.

hot spring *n.* a natural spring of mineral water at 21°C (70°F) or above, found in areas of volcanic activity. Also called: **thermal spring.**

hotspur ('hɒt,spɜː) *n.* an impetuous or fiery person. [C15: < *Hotspur,* nickname of Sir Henry Percy (1364-1403), E rebel, killed leading an army against Henry IV]

hot stuff *n. Inf.* **1.** a person, object, etc., considered important, attractive, etc. **2.** a pornographic or erotic book, play, film, etc.

Hottentot ('hɒtᵊn,tɒt) *n.* **1.** (*pl.* **-tot** *or* **-tots**) a member of a race of people of southern Africa, who formerly occupied the region near the Cape of Good Hope and are now almost extinct. **2.** any of the languages of this people. [C17: < Afrik., <?]

hot up *vb.* **hotting, hotted.** (*adv.*) *Inf.* **1.** to make or become more exciting, active, or intense. **2.** (*tr.*) another term for **soup up.**

hot-water bottle *n.* a receptacle now usually made of rubber, designed to be filled with hot water and used for warming a bed.

hot-wire *vb.* (*tr.*) *Sl.* to start the engine of (a motor vehicle) by short-circuiting the ignition.

hough (hɒk) *Brit.* ~*n.* **1.** a variant of **hock**[1]. ~*vb.* (*tr.*) **2.** to hamstring (cattle, horses, etc.). [C14: < OE *hōh* heel]

hound (haʊnd) *n.* **1. a.** any of several breeds of dog used for hunting. **b.** (*in combination*): *a deerhound.* **2.** a dog, esp. one regarded as annoying. **3.** a despicable person. **4.** (in hare and hounds) a runner who pursues a hare. **5.** *Sl., chiefly U.S. & Canad.* an enthusiast: *an autograph hound.* **6. ride to hounds** *or* **follow the hounds.** to take part in a fox hunt. **7. the hounds.** a pack of foxhounds, etc. ~*vb.* (*tr.*) **8.** to pursue relentlessly. **9.** to urge on. [OE *hund*] —'**hounder** *n.*

hound's-tongue *n.* a plant which has small reddish-purple flowers and spiny fruits. Also called: **dog's-tongue.** [OE *hundestunge,* translation of L *cynoglōssos,* < Gk, < *kuōn* dog + *glōssa* tongue; referring to the shape of its leaves]

hound's-tooth check *n.* a pattern of broken or jagged checks, esp. on cloth. Also called: **dog's-tooth check, dogtooth check.**

hour ('aʊə) *n.* **1.** a period of time equal to 3600 seconds; 1/24th of a calendar day. Related adj.: **horary.** **2.** any of the points on the face of a timepiece that indicate intervals of 60 minutes. **3.** the time. **4.** the time allowed for or used for something: *the lunch hour.* **5.** a special moment: *our finest hour.* **6.** the distance covered in an hour: *we live an hour from the city.* **7.** *Astron.* an angular measurement of right ascension equal to 15° or a 24th part of the celestial equator. **8. one's last hour.** the time of one's death. **9. the hour.** an exact number of complete hours: *the bus leaves on the hour.* ~See also **hours.** [C13: < OF *hore,* < L *hōra,* < Gk: season]

hour circle *n.* a great circle on the celestial sphere passing through the celestial poles and a specified point, such as a star.

hourglass ('aʊə,glɑːs) *n.* **1.** a device consisting of two transparent chambers linked by a narrow channel, containing a quantity of sand that takes a specified time to trickle from one chamber to the other. **2.** (*modifier*) well-proportioned with a small waist: *an hourglass figure.*

hour hand *n.* the pointer on a timepiece that indicates the hour.

houri ('hʊərɪ) *n., pl.* **-ris.** **1.** (in Muslim belief) any of the nymphs of Paradise. **2.** any alluring woman. [C18: < F, < Persian, < Ar. *hūr,* pl. of *haurā'* woman with dark eyes]

hourly ('aʊəlɪ) *adj.* **1.** of, occurring, or done every hour. **2.** done in or measured by the hour: *an hourly rate.* **3.** continual or frequent. ~*adv.* **4.** every hour. **5.** at any moment.

hours ('aʊəz) *pl. n.* **1.** a period regularly appointed for work, etc. **2.** one's times of rising and going to bed: *he keeps late hours.* **3. till all hours.** until very late. **4.** an indefinite time. **5.** *R.C. Church.* Also called: **canonical hours. a.** the seven times of the day laid down for the recitation of the prayers of the divine office. **b.** the prayers recited at these times.

house *n.* (haʊs), *pl.* **houses** ('haʊzɪz). **1. a.** a building used as a home; dwelling. **b.** (*as modifier*): *house dog.* **2.** the people present in a house. **3. a.** a building for some specific purpose. **b.** (*in combination*): *a schoolhouse.* **4.** (*often cap.*) a family or dynasty: *the House of York.* **5. a.** a commercial company: *a publishing house.* **b.** (*as modifier*): *a house journal.* **6.** a legislative body. **7.** a quorum in such a body (esp. in **make a house**). **8.** a dwelling for a religious community. **9.** *Astrol.* any of the 12 divisions of the zodiac. **10.** any of several divisions of a large school. **11.** a hotel, restaurant, club, etc., or the management of such an establishment. **12.** the audience in a theatre or cinema. **13.** an informal word for **brothel.** **14.** a hall in which a legislative body meets. **15.** See **full house.** **16.** *Naut.* any structure or shelter on the weather deck of a vessel. **17. bring the house down.** *Theatre.* to win great applause. **18. like a house on fire.** *Inf.* very well. **19. on the house.** (usually of drinks) paid for by the management of the hotel, bar, etc. **20. put one's house in order.** to settle or organize one's affairs. **21. safe as houses.** *Brit.* very secure. ~*vb.* (haʊz). **22.** (*tr.*) to provide with or serve as accommodation. **23.** to give or receive lodging. **24.** (*tr.*) to contain or cover; protect. **25.** (*tr.*) to fit (a piece of wood) into a mortise, joint, etc. [OE *hūs*] —'**houseless** *adj.*

house agent *n. Brit.* another name for **estate agent.**

house arrest *n.* confinement to one's own home rather than in prison.

houseboat ('haʊs,bəʊt) *n.* a stationary boat or barge used as a home.

housebound ('haʊs,baʊnd) *adj.* unable to leave one's house because of illness, injury, etc.

housebreaking ('haʊs,breɪkɪŋ) *n. Criminal law.* the act of entering a building as a trespasser for an unlawful purpose. Assimilated with burglary (1968). —'**house,breaker** *n.*

housecoat ('haʊs,kəʊt) *n.* a woman's loose robelike informal garment.

house-craft *n.* skill in domestic management.

housefather ('haʊs,fɑːðə) *n.* a man in charge of the welfare of a particular group of children in an institution. —'**house,mother** *fem. n.*

housefly ('haʊs,flaɪ) *n., pl.* **-flies.** a common dipterous fly that frequents human habitations, spreads disease, and lays its eggs in carrion, decaying vegetables, etc.

household ('haʊs,həʊld) *n.* **1.** the people living together in one house. **2.** (*modifier*) relating to the running of a household: *household management.*

householder ('haʊs,həʊldə) *n.* a person who owns or rents a house. —'**house,holder,ship** *n.*

household name *or* **word** *n.* a person or thing that is very well known.

housekeeper (ˈhausˌkiːpə) *n.* a person, esp. a woman, employed to run a household.

housekeeping (ˈhausˌkiːpɪŋ) *n.* **1.** the running of a household. **2.** money allotted for this. **3.** general maintenance as of records, data, etc., in an organization.

houseleek (ˈhausˌliːk) *n.* an Old World plant which has a rosette of succulent leaves and pinkish flowers: grows on walls.

house lights *pl. n.* the lights in the auditorium of a theatre, cinema, etc.

housemaid (ˈhausˌmeɪd) *n.* a girl or woman employed to do housework, esp. one who is resident in the household.

housemaid's knee *n.* inflammation and swelling of the bursa in front of the kneecap, caused esp. by constant kneeling on a hard surface. Technical name: **prepatellar bursitis.**

houseman (ˈhausmən) *n., pl.* **-men.** *Med.* a junior doctor who is a member of the medical staff of a hospital. U.S. and Canad. equivalent: **intern.**

house martin *n.* a Eurasian swallow with a slightly forked tail.

house mouse *n.* any of various greyish mice, a common household pest in most parts of the world.

House of Assembly *n.* a legislative assembly or the lower chamber of such an assembly.

house of cards *n.* an unstable situation, etc.

House of Commons *n.* (in Britain, Canada, etc.) the lower chamber of Parliament.

house of correction *n.* (formerly) a place of confinement for persons convicted of minor offences.

house of ill repute *or* **ill fame** *n.* a euphemistic name for **brothel.**

House of Keys *n.* the lower chamber of the legislature of the Isle of Man.

House of Lords *n.* (in Britain) the upper chamber of Parliament, composed of the peers of the realm.

House of Representatives *n.* **1.** (in the U.S.) the lower chamber of Congress, or of many state legislatures. **2.** (in Australia) the lower chamber of Parliament. **3.** the sole chamber of New Zealand's Parliament.

house party *n.* **1.** a party, usually in a country house, at which guests are invited to stay for several days. **2.** the guests who are invited.

house plant *n.* a plant that can be grown indoors.

house-proud *adj.* proud of the appearance, cleanliness, etc., of one's house, sometimes excessively so.

houseroom (ˈhausˌrum, -ˌruːm) *n.* **1.** room for storage or lodging. **2. give (something) houseroom.** (*used with a negative*) to have or keep (something) in one's house.

house sparrow *n.* a small Eurasian bird, now established in North America and Australia. It has a brown plumage with grey underparts. Also called (U.S.): **English sparrow.**

housetop (ˈhausˌtɒp) *n.* **1.** the roof of a house. **2. proclaim from the housetops.** to announce (something) publicly.

house-train *vb.* (*tr.*) *Brit.* to train (pets) to urinate and defecate outside the house.

house-warming *n.* a party given after moving into a new home.

housewife *n., pl.* **-wives. 1.** (ˈhausˌwaɪf). a woman who keeps house. **2.** (ˈhʌzɪf). Also called: **hussy, huswife.** *Chiefly Brit.* a small sewing kit. —**housewifery** (ˈhausˌwɪfərɪ) *n.* —ˈ**housewifely** *adj.*

housework (ˈhausˌwɜːk) *n.* the work of running a home, such as cleaning, cooking, etc.

housey-housey (ˈhauzɪˈhauzɪ) *n.* another name for **bingo** or **lotto.** [C20: < the cry of "house!" shouted by the winner, prob. < FULL HOUSE]

housing[1] (ˈhauzɪŋ) *n.* **1. a.** houses collectively. **b.** (*as modifier*): *a housing problem.* **2.** the act of providing with accommodation. **3.** a hole or slot made in one wooden member to receive another. **4.** a part designed to contain or support a component or mechanism: *a wheel housing.*

housing[2] (ˈhauzɪŋ) *n.* (*often pl.*) *Arch.* another word for **trappings** (sense 2). [C14: < OF *houce* covering, of Gmc origin]

housing estate *n.* a planned area of housing, often with its own shops and other amenities.

housing scheme *n.* a local-authority housing estate. Often shortened to **scheme.**

hove (həuv) *vb. Chiefly naut.* a past tense and past participle of **heave.**

hovel (ˈhɒvᵊl) *n.* **1.** a ramshackle dwelling place. **2.** an open shed for livestock, carts, etc. **3.** the conical building enclosing a kiln. [C15: <?]

hover (ˈhɒvə) *vb.* (*intr.*) **1.** to remain suspended in one place. **2.** (of certain birds, esp. hawks) to remain in one place in the air by rapidly beating the wings. **3.** to linger uncertainly. **4.** to be in a state of indecision. ~*n.* **5.** the act of hovering. [C14 *hoveren*, var. of *hoven*, <?] —ˈ**hoverer** *n.*

hovercraft (ˈhɒvəˌkrɑːft) *n.* a vehicle that is able to travel across both land and water on a cushion of air.

hover fly *n.* a dipterous fly with a hovering flight.

hoverport (ˈhɒvəˌpɔːt) *n.* a port for hovercraft.

hovertrain (ˈhɒvəˌtreɪn) *n.* a train that moves over a concrete track and is supported by a cushion of air supplied by powerful fans.

how (hau) *adv.* **1.** in what way? by what means?: *how did it happen?* Also used in indirect questions: *tell me how he did it.* **2.** to what extent?: *how tall is he?* **3.** how good? how well? what...like?: *how did she sing? how was the holiday?* **4. and how!** (intensifier) very much so! **5. how about?** used to suggest something: *how about a cup of tea?* **6. how are you?** what is your state of health? **7. how come?** *Inf.* what is the reason (that)?: *how come you told him?* **8. how's that? a.** what is your opinion? **b.** *Cricket.* Also written: **howzat** (hauˈzæt). (an appeal to the umpire) is the batsman out? **9. how now?** *or* **how so?** *Arch.* what is the meaning of this? **10.** in whatever way: *do it how you wish.* ~*n.* **11.** the way a thing is done: *the how of it.* [OE *hu*]

howbeit (hauˈbiːɪt) *Arch.* ~*sentence connector.* **1.** however. ~*conj.* **2.** (*subordinating*) though; although.

howdah (ˈhaudə) *n.* a seat for riding on an elephant's back, esp. one with a canopy. [C18: < Hindi *haudah,* < Ar. *haudaj* load carried by elephant or camel]

how do you do *sentence substitute.* **1.** a formal greeting said by people who are being introduced to each other. ~*n.* **how-do-you-do. 2.** *Inf.* a difficult situation.

howdy (ˈhaudɪ) *sentence substitute. Chiefly U.S.* an informal word for **hello.** [C16: < *how d'ye do*]

however (hauˈɛvə) *sentence connector.* **1.** still; nevertheless. **2.** on the other hand; yet. ~*adv.* **3.** by whatever means. **4.** (*used with adjectives of quantity or degree*) no matter how: *however long it takes, finish it.* **5.** an emphatic form of **how** (sense 1).

howitzer (ˈhauɪtsə) *n.* a cannon having a short barrel with a low muzzle velocity and a steep angle of fire. [C16: < Du. *houwitser,* < G, < Czech *houfnice* stone-sling]

howl (haul) *n.* **1.** a long plaintive cry characteristic of a wolf or hound. **2.** a similar cry of pain or sorrow. **3.** a prolonged outburst of laughter. **4.** *Electronics.* an unwanted high-pitched sound produced by a sound-producing system as a result of feedback. ~*vb.* **5.** to express in a howl or utter such cries. **6.** (*intr.*) (of the wind, etc.) to make a wailing noise. **7.** (*intr.*) *Inf.* to shout or laugh. [C14 *houlen*]

howl down *vb.* (*tr., adv.*) to prevent (a speaker) from being heard by shouting disapprovingly.

howler (ˈhaulə) *n.* **1.** Also called: **howler monkey.** a large New World monkey inhabiting tropical forests in South America and having a loud howling cry. **2.** *Inf.* a glaring mistake. **3.** a person or thing that howls.

howling (ˈhaʊlɪŋ) *adj.* (*prenominal*) *Inf.* (intensifier): *a howling success; a howling error.*

howsoever (ˌhaʊsəʊˈɛvə) *sentence connector, adv.* a less common word for **however.**

hoy[1] (hɔɪ) *n. Naut.* **1.** a freight barge. **2.** a coastal fishing and trading vessel used during the 17th and 18th centuries. [C15: < MDu. *hoei*]

hoy[2] (hɔɪ) *interj.* a cry used to attract attention or drive animals. [C14: var. of HEY]

hoya (ˈhɔɪə) *n.* any plant of the genus *Hoya,* of E Asia and Australia, esp. the waxplant. [C19: after Thomas *Hoy* (died 1821), E gardener]

hoyden *or* **hoiden** (ˈhɔɪdᵊn) *n.* a wild boisterous girl; tomboy. [C16: ? < MDu. *heidijn* heathen] —ˈ**hoydenish** *or* ˈ**hoidenish** *adj.*

Hoyle (hɔɪl) *n.* an authoritative book of rules for card games. [after Sir Edmund *Hoyle,* 18th-cent. E authority on games, its compiler]

HP *abbrev. for:* **1.** *Brit.* hire-purchase. **2.** horsepower. **3.** high pressure. **4.** (in Britain) Houses of Parliament. ~Also (for senses 1-3): **h.p.**

HQ *or* **h.q.** *abbrev. for* headquarters.

hr *abbrev. for* hour.

HRH *abbrev. for* His (*or* Her) Royal Highness.

HRT *abbrev. for* hormone replacement therapy.

HS (in Britain) *abbrev. for* Home Secretary.

HSH *abbrev. for* His (*or* Her) Serene Highness.

ht *abbrev. for* height.

HT *Physics. abbrev. for* high tension.

HTLV *abbrev. for* human T-cell lymphotrophic virus: any one of a small family of viruses that cause certain rare diseases in the T-cells of human beings.

hub (hʌb) *n.* **1.** the central portion of a wheel, propeller, fan, etc., through which the axle passes. **2.** the focal point. [C17: prob. var. of HOB[1]]

hubble-bubble (ˈhʌbᵊlˈbʌbᵊl) *n.* **1.** another name for **hookah. 2.** turmoil. **3.** a gargling sound. [C17: rhyming jingle based on BUBBLE]

hubbub (ˈhʌbʌb) *n.* **1.** a confused noise of many voices. **2.** tumult; uproar. [C16: prob. < Irish *hooboobbes*]

hubby (ˈhʌbɪ) *n., pl.* **-bies.** an informal word for **husband.** [C17: by shortening and altering]

hubcap (ˈhʌbˌkæp) *n.* a metal cap fitting over the hub of a wheel.

hubris (ˈhjuːbrɪs) *n.* **1.** pride or arrogance. **2.** (in Greek tragedy) an excess of ambition, pride, etc., ultimately causing the transgressor's ruin. [C19: < Gk] —**huˈbristic** *adj.*

huckaback (ˈhʌkəˌbæk) *n.* a coarse absorbent linen or cotton fabric used for towels, etc. Also: **huck** (hʌk). [C17: <?]

huckleberry (ˈhʌkᵊlˌbɛrɪ) *n., pl.* **-ries. 1.** an American shrub having edible dark blue berries. **2.** the fruit of this shrub. **3.** a Brit. name for **whortleberry** (senses 1, 2). [C17: prob. var. of *hurtleberry,* <?]

huckster (ˈhʌkstə) *n.* **1.** a person who uses aggressive or questionable methods of selling. **2.** *Now rare.* a person who sells small articles or fruit in the street. **3.** *U.S.* a person who writes for radio or television advertisements. ~*vb.* **4.** (*tr.*) to peddle. **5.** (*tr.*) to sell or advertise aggressively or questionably. **6.** to haggle (over). [C12: ? < MDu. *hoekster,* < *hoeken* to carry on the back]

huddle (ˈhʌdᵊl) *n.* **1.** a heaped or crowded mass of people or things. **2.** *Inf.* a private or impromptu conference (esp. in **go into a huddle**). ~*vb.* **3.** to crowd or nestle closely together. **4.** (often foll. by *up*) to hunch (oneself), as through cold. **5.** (*intr.*) *Inf.* to confer privately. **6.** (*tr.*) *Chiefly Brit.* to do (something) in a careless way. **7.** (*tr.*) *Rare.* to put on (clothes) hurriedly. [C16: <?; cf. ME *hoderen* to wrap up] —ˈ**huddler** *n.*

hue (hjuː) *n.* **1.** the attribute of colour that enables an observer to classify it as red, blue, etc., and excludes white, black, and grey. **2.** a shade of a colour. **3.** aspect: *a different hue on matters.* [OE *hīw* beauty] —**hued** *adj.*

hue and cry *n.* **1.** (formerly) the pursuit of a suspected criminal with loud cries in order to raise the alarm. **2.** any loud public outcry. [C16: < Anglo-F *hu et cri,* < OF *hue* outcry, < *hu!* shout of warning + *cri* CRY]

huff (hʌf) *n.* **1.** a passing mood of anger or pique (esp. in **in a huff**). ~*vb.* **2.** to make or become angry or resentful. **3.** (*intr.*) to blow or puff heavily. **4.** Also: **blow.** *Draughts.* to remove (an opponent's draught) from the board for failure to make a capture. **5.** (*tr.*) *Obs.* to bully. **6. huffing and puffing.** empty threats or objections: bluster. [C16: imit.; cf. PUFF] —ˈ**huffish** *or* ˈ**huffy** *adj.* —ˈ**huffily** *or* ˈ**huffishly** *adv.*

hug (hʌg) *vb.* **hugging, hugged.** (*mainly tr.*) **1.** (*also intr.*) to clasp tightly, usually with affection; embrace. **2.** to keep close to a shore, kerb, etc. **3.** to cling to (beliefs, etc.); cherish. **4.** to congratulate (oneself). ~*n.* **5.** a tight or fond embrace. [C16: prob. of Scand. origin] —ˈ**huggable** *adj.*

huge (hjuːdʒ) *adj.* extremely large. [C13: < OF *ahuge,* <?] —ˈ**hugely** *adv.* —ˈ**hugeness** *n.*

huggermugger (ˈhʌgəˌmʌgə) *n.* **1.** confusion. **2.** *Rare.* secrecy. ~*adj., adv. Arch.* **3.** with secrecy. **4.** in confusion. ~*vb. Obs.* **5.** (*tr.*) to keep secret. **6.** (*intr.*) to act secretly. [C16: <?]

Huguenot (ˈhjuːgəˌnəʊ, -ˌnɒt) *n.* **1.** a French Calvinist, esp. of the 16th or 17th centuries. ~*adj.* **2.** designating the French Protestant Church. [C16: < F, < Genevan dialect *eyguenot* one who opposed annexation by Savoy, ult. < Swiss G *Eidgenoss* confederate]

huh (*spelling pron.* hʌ) *interj.* an exclamation of derision, bewilderment, inquiry, etc.

huhu (ˈhuːhuː) *n.* a New Zealand beetle with a hairy body. [< Maori]

hui (ˈhuːɪ) *n. N.Z.* **1.** a Maori social gathering. **2.** *Inf.* any party. [< Maori]

huia (ˈhʊɪjə) *n.* an extinct New Zealand bird, prized by early Maoris for its distinctive tail feathers. [< Maori]

hula (ˈhuːlə) *or* **hula-hula** *n.* a Hawaiian dance performed by a woman. [< Hawaiian]

Hula-Hoop *n. Trademark.* a light hoop that is whirled around the body by movements of the waist and hips.

hulk (hʌlk) *n.* **1.** the body of an abandoned vessel. **2.** *Disparaging.* a large or unwieldy vessel. **3.** *Disparaging.* a large ungainly person or thing. **4.** (*often pl.*) the hull of a ship, used as a storehouse, etc., or (esp. in 19th-century Britain) as a prison. [OE *hulc,* < Med. L *hulca,* < Gk *holkas* barge, < *helkein* to tow]

hulking (ˈhʌlkɪŋ) *adj.* big and ungainly.

hull (hʌl) *n.* **1.** the main body of a vessel, tank, etc. **2.** the outer covering of a fruit or seed. **3.** the calyx at the base of a strawberry, raspberry, or similar fruit. **4.** the outer casing of a missile, rocket, etc. ~*vb.* **5.** to remove the hulls from (fruit or seeds). **6.** (*tr.*) to pierce the hull of (a vessel, tank, etc.). [OE *hulu*]

hullabaloo *or* **hullaballoo** (ˌhʌləbəˈluː) *n., pl.* **-loos.** loud confused noise; commotion. [C18: ? < HALLO + Scot. *baloo* lullaby]

hullo (hʌˈləʊ) *sentence substitute, n.* a variant spelling of **hello.**

hum (hʌm) *vb.* **humming, hummed.** (*intr.*) **1.** to make a low continuous vibrating sound. **2.** (of a person) to sing with the lips closed. **3.** to utter an indistinct sound, as in hesitation; hem. **4.** *Sl.* to be in a state of feverish activity. **5.** *Sl.* to smell unpleasant. **6. hum and haw.** See **hem**[2] (sense 3). ~*n.* **7.** a low continuous murmuring sound. **8.** *Electronics.* an undesired low-frequency noise in the output of an amplifier or receiver. ~*interj., n.* **9.** an indistinct sound of hesitation, embarrassment, etc.; hem. [C14: imit.]

human (ˈhjuːmən) *adj.* **1.** of or relating to mankind: *human nature.* **2.** consisting of people: *a human chain.* **3.** having the attributes of man as opposed to animals, divine beings, or machines: *human failings.* **4. a.** kind or considerate. **b.** natural. ~*n.* **5.** a human being; person. [C14: < L *hūmānus;* rel. to L *homō* man] —ˈ**humanness** *n.*

human being *n.* a member of any of the races of *Homo sapiens;* person; man, woman, or child.

humane (hjuːˈmeɪn) *adj.* **1.** characterized by

kindness, sympathy, etc. **2.** inflicting as little pain as possible: *a humane killing.* **3.** civilizing or liberal: *humane studies.* [C16: var. of HUMAN] —**huˈmanely** *adv.* —**huˈmaneness** *n.*

human interest *n.* (in a newspaper story, etc.) reference to individuals and their emotions, sometimes from exploitative motives.

humanism (ˈhjuːməˌnɪzəm) *n.* **1.** the rejection of religion in favour of a belief in the advancement of humanity by its own efforts. **2.** (*often cap.*) a cultural movement of the Renaissance, based on classical studies. **3.** interest in the welfare of people. —**ˈhumanist** *n.* —ˌ**humanˈistic** *adj.*

humanitarian (hjuːˌmænɪˈtɛərɪən) *adj.* **1.** having the interests of mankind at heart. ~*n.* **2.** a philanthropist. —**huˌmaniˈtarianism** *n.*

humanity (hjuːˈmænɪtɪ) *n., pl.* **-ties. 1.** the human race. **2.** the quality of being human. **3.** kindness or mercy. **4.** (*pl.; usually preceded by the*) the study of literature, philosophy, and the arts, esp. study of Ancient Greece and Rome.

humanize *or* **-nise** (ˈhjuːməˌnaɪz) *vb.* **1.** to make or become human. **2.** to make or become humane. —ˌ**humaniˈzation** *or* **-niˈsation** *n.*

humankind (ˌhjuːmənˈkaɪnd) *n.* the human race; humanity.

humanly (ˈhjuːmənlɪ) *adv.* **1.** by human powers or means. **2.** in a human or humane manner.

human nature *n.* the qualities common to humanity, esp. with reference to human weakness.

humanoid (ˈhjuːməˌnɔɪd) *adj.* **1.** like a human being in appearance. ~*n.* **2.** a being with human rather than anthropoid characteristics. **3.** (in science fiction) a robot or creature resembling a human being.

human rights *pl. n.* the rights of individuals to liberty, justice, etc.

humble (ˈhʌmbᵊl) *adj.* **1.** conscious of one's failings. **2.** unpretentious; lowly: *a humble cottage; my humble opinion.* **3.** deferential or servile. ~*vb.* (*tr.*) **4.** to cause to become humble; humiliate. **5.** to lower in status. [C13: < OF, < L *humilis* low, < *humus* the ground] —**ˈhumbleness** *n.* —**ˈhumbly** *adv.*

humblebee (ˈhʌmbᵊlˌbiː) *n.* another name for the **bumblebee.** [C15: rel. to MDu. *hommel* bumblebee, OHG *humbal*]

humble pie *n.* **1.** (formerly) a pie made from the heart, entrails, etc., of a deer. **2. eat humble pie.** to be forced to behave humbly; be humiliated. [C17: earlier *an umble pie,* by mistaken word division < *a numble pie,* < *numbles* offal of a deer, ult. < L *lumbulus* a little loin]

humbug (ˈhʌmˌbʌg) *n.* **1.** a person or thing that deceives. **2.** nonsense. **3.** *Brit.* a hard boiled sweet, usually having a striped pattern. ~*vb.* **-bugging, -bugged. 4.** to cheat or deceive (someone). [C18: <?] —**ˈhumˌbugger** *n.* —**ˈhumˌbuggery** *n.*

humdinger (ˈhʌmˌdɪŋə) *n. Sl.* an excellent person or thing. [C20: <?]

humdrum (ˈhʌmˌdrʌm) *adj.* **1.** ordinary; dull. ~*n.* **2.** a monotonous routine, task, or person. [C16: rhyming compound, prob. based on HUM]

humectant (hjuːˈmɛktənt) *adj.* **1.** producing moisture. ~*n.* **2.** a substance added to another to keep it moist. [C17: < L *ūmectāre* to wet, < *ūmēre* to be moist]

humerus (ˈhjuːmərəs) *n., pl.* **-meri** (-məˌraɪ). **1.** the bone that extends from the shoulder to the elbow in man. **2.** the corresponding bone in other vertebrates. [C17: < L *umerus;* rel. to Gothic *ams* shoulder, Gk *ōmos*] —**ˈhumeral** *adj.*

humid (ˈhjuːmɪd) *adj.* moist; damp. [C16: < L *ūmidus,* < *ūmēre* to be wet] —**ˈhumidly** *adv.* —**ˈhumidness** *n.*

humidex (ˈhjuːmɪˌdɛks) *n. Canad.* an index of discomfort showing the combined effect of humidity and temperature.

humidify (hjuːˈmɪdɪˌfaɪ) *vb.* **-fying, -fied.** (*tr.*) to make (air, etc.) humid or damp. —**huˌmidifiˈcation** *n.* —**huˈmidiˌfier** *n.*

humidity (hjuːˈmɪdɪtɪ) *n.* **1.** dampness. **2.** a measure of the amount of moisture in the air.

humidor (ˈhjuːmɪˌdɔː) *n.* a humid place or container for storing cigars, tobacco, etc.

humiliate (hjuːˈmɪlɪˌeɪt) *vb.* (*tr.*) to lower or hurt the dignity or pride of. [C16: < LL *humiliāre,* < L *humilis* HUMBLE] —**huˈmiliˌatingly** *adv.* —**huˌmiliˈation** *n.* —**huˈmiliˌator** *n.*

humility (hjuːˈmɪlɪtɪ) *n., pl.* **-ties.** the state or quality of being humble.

hummingbird (ˈhʌmɪŋˌbɜːd) *n.* a very small American bird having a brilliant iridescent plumage, long slender bill, and wings specialized for very powerful vibrating flight.

hummock (ˈhʌmək) *n.* **1.** a hillock; knoll. **2.** a ridge or mound of ice in an ice field. **3.** *Chiefly southern U.S.* a wooded area lying above the level of an adjacent marsh. [C16: <?; cf. HUMP] —**ˈhummocky** *adj.*

hummus *or* **houmous** (ˈhʊməs) *n.* a creamy dip originating in the Middle East, made from purĕed chickpeas. [< Turkish *humus*]

humoral (ˈhjuːmərəl) *adj. Obs.* of or relating to the four bodily fluids (humours).

humoresque (ˌhjuːməˈrɛsk) *n.* a short lively piece of music. [C19: < G *Humoreske,* ult. < E HUMOUR]

humorist (ˈhjuːmərɪst) *n.* a person who acts, speaks, or writes in a humorous way.

humorous (ˈhjuːmərəs) *adj.* **1.** funny; comical; amusing. **2.** displaying or creating humour. —**ˈhumorously** *adv.* —**ˈhumorousness** *n.*

humour *or U.S.* **humor** (ˈhjuːmə) *n.* **1.** the quality of being funny. **2.** Also called: **sense of humour.** the ability to appreciate or express that which is humorous. **3.** situations, speech, or writings that are humorous. **4. a.** a state of mind; mood. **b.** (*in combination*): *good humour.* **5.** temperament or disposition. **6.** a caprice or whim. **7.** any of various fluids in the body: *aqueous humour.* **8.** Also called: **cardinal humour.** *Arch.* any of the four bodily fluids (blood, phlegm, choler or yellow bile, melancholy or black bile) formerly thought to determine emotional and physical disposition. **9. out of humour.** in a bad mood. ~*vb.* (*tr.*) **10.** to gratify; indulge: *he humoured the boy's whims.* **11.** to adapt oneself to: *to humour someone's fantasies.* [C14: < L: liquid; rel. to L *ūmēre* to be wet] —**ˈhumourless** *or U.S.* **ˈhumorless** *adj.*

hump (hʌmp) *n.* **1.** a rounded protuberance or projection. **2.** a rounded deformity of the back, consisting of a spinal curvature. **3.** a rounded protuberance on the back of a camel or related animal. **4. the hump.** *Brit. inf.* a fit of sulking. ~*vb.* **5.** to form or become a hump; hunch; arch. **6.** (*tr.*) *Sl.* to carry or heave. **7.** *Taboo sl.* to have sexual intercourse with (someone). [C18: prob. < earlier *humpbacked*] —**ˈhumpy** *adj.*

humpback (ˈhʌmpˌbæk) *n.* **1.** another word for **hunchback. 2.** Also called: **humpback whale.** a large whalebone whale with a humped back and long flippers. **3.** a Pacific salmon, the male of which has a humped back. **4.** Also: **humpback bridge.** *Brit.* a road bridge having a sharp incline and decline and usually a narrow roadway. [C17: alteration of earlier *crumpbacked,* ? infl. by HUNCHBACK] —**ˈhumpˌbacked** *adj.*

humph (*spelling pron.* hʌmf) *interj.* an exclamation of annoyance, indecision, etc.

humpty dumpty (ˈhʌmptɪ ˈdʌmptɪ) *n., pl.* **dumpties.** *Chiefly Brit.* **1.** a short fat person. **2.** a person or thing that once broken cannot be mended. [C18: < the nursery rhyme *Humpty Dumpty*]

humpy (ˈhʌmpɪ) *n., pl.* **humpies.** *Austral.* a primitive hut. [C19: < Abor.]

humus (ˈhjuːməs) *n.* a dark brown or black colloidal mass of partially decomposed organic matter in the soil. It improves the fertility and water retention of the soil. [C18: < L: soil]

Hun (hʌn) *n., pl.* **Huns** *or* **Hun. 1.** a member of any of several Asiatic nomadic peoples who dominated much of Asia and E Europe from before 300 B.C., invading the Roman Empire in the 4th and 5th centuries A.D. **2.** *Inf.* (esp. in World War I) a derogatory name for a **German. 3.** *Inf.* a vandal. [OE *Hūnas,* < LL *Hūnī,* < Turkish *Hunyū*] —ˈ**Hunnish** *adj.* —ˈ**Hunˌlike** *adj.*

hunch (hʌntʃ) *n.* **1.** an intuitive guess or feeling. **2.** another word for **hump. 3.** a lump or large piece. ~*vb.* **4.** to draw (oneself or a part of the body) up or together. **5.** (*intr.;* usually foll. by *up*) to sit in a hunched position. [C16: <?]

hunchback (ˈhʌntʃˌbæk) *n.* **1.** a person having an abnormal curvature of the spine. **2.** such a curvature. ~Also called: **humpback.** [C18: < earlier *hunchbacked]* —ˈ**hunchˌbacked** *adj.*

hundred (ˈhʌndrəd) *n., pl.* **-dreds** *or* **-dred. 1.** the cardinal number that is the product of ten and ten; five score. **2.** a numeral, 100, C, etc., representing this number. **3.** (*often pl.*) a large but unspecified number, amount, or quantity. **4.** (*pl.*) the 100 years of a specified century: *in the sixteen hundreds.* **5.** something representing, represented by, or consisting of 100 units. **6.** *Maths.* the position containing a digit representing that number followed by two zeros: *in 4376, 3 is in the hundred's place.* **7.** an ancient division of a county. ~*determiner.* **8.** amounting to or approximately a hundred: *a hundred reasons for that.* [OE] —ˈ**hundredth** *adj., n.*

hundreds and thousands *pl. n.* tiny beads of coloured sugar, used in decorating cakes, etc.

hundredweight (ˈhʌndrədˌweɪt) *n., pl.* **-weights** *or* **-weight. 1.** Also called: **long hundredweight.** *Brit.* a unit of weight equal to 112 pounds (50.802 kg). **2.** Also called: **short hundredweight.** *U.S. & Canad.* a unit of weight equal to 100 pounds (45.359 kg). **3.** Also called: **metric hundredweight.** a metric unit of weight equal to 50 kilograms. ~Abbrev. (for senses 1, 2): **cwt.**

hung (hʌŋ) *vb.* **1.** the past tense and past participle of **hang** (except in the sense of *to execute*). ~*adj.* **2.** (of a political party, jury, etc.) not having a majority: *a hung parliament.* **3. hung over.** *Inf.* suffering from the effects of a hangover. **4. hung up.** *Sl.* **a.** impeded by some difficulty or delay. **b.** emotionally disturbed. **5. hung up on.** *Sl.* obsessively interested in.

Hungarian (hʌŋˈgɛərɪən) *n.* **1.** the official language of Hungary, also spoken in Romania and elsewhere, belonging to the Finno-Ugric family. **2.** a native, inhabitant, or citizen of Hungary. ~*adj.* **3.** of or relating to Hungary, its people, or their language. ~Cf. **Magyar.**

hunger (ˈhʌŋgə) *n.* **1.** a feeling of emptiness or weakness induced by lack of food. **2.** desire or craving: *hunger for a woman.* ~*vb.* **3.** (*intr.;* usually foll. by *for* or *after*) to have a great appetite or desire (for). [OE]

hunger march *n.* a procession of protest or demonstration, esp. by the unemployed.

hunger strike *n.* a voluntary fast undertaken, usually by a prisoner, as a means of protest. —**hunger striker** *n.*

hungry (ˈhʌŋgrɪ) *adj.* **-grier, -griest. 1.** desiring food. **2.** (*postpositive;* foll. by *for*) having a craving, desire, or need (for). **3.** expressing or appearing to express greed, craving, or desire. **4.** lacking fertility; poor. **5.** *Austral. & N.Z.* greedy; mean. **6.** *N.Z.* (of timber) dry and bare. —ˈ**hungrily** *adv.* —ˈ**hungriness** *n.*

hunk (hʌŋk) *n.* **1.** a large piece. **2.** *Sl.* a sexually attractive man. [C19: prob. rel. to Flemish *hunke*]

hunkers (ˈhʌŋkəz) *pl. n.* haunches. [C18: < ?]

hunky-dory (ˌhʌŋkɪˈdɔːrɪ) *adj. Inf.* very satisfactory; fine. [C20: <?]

hunt (hʌnt) *vb.* **1.** to seek out and kill (animals) for food or sport. **2.** (*intr.;* often foll. by *for*) to search (for): *to hunt for a book.* **3.** (*tr.*) to use (hounds, horses, etc.) in the pursuit of wild animals, game, etc.: *to hunt a pack of hounds.* **4.** (*tr.*) to search (country) to hunt game, etc.: *to hunt the parkland.* **5.** (*tr.;* often foll. by *down*) to track diligently so as to capture: *to hunt down a criminal.* **6.** (*tr.; usually passive*) to persecute; hound. **7.** (*intr.*) (of a gauge indicator, etc.) to oscillate about a mean value or position. **8.** (*intr.*) (of an aircraft, rocket, etc.) to oscillate about a flight path or its course axis. ~*n.* **9.** the act or an instance of hunting. **10.** chase or search, esp. of animals. **11.** the area of a hunt. **12.** a party or institution organized for the pursuit of wild animals, esp. for sport. **13.** the members of such a party or institution. [OE *huntian*]

huntaway (ˈhʌntəˌweɪ) *n. N.Z.* a dog trained to drive sheep at a long distance from the shepherd.

hunted (ˈhʌntɪd) *adj.* harassed: *a hunted look.*

hunter (ˈhʌntə) *n.* **1.** a person or animal that seeks out and kills or captures game. Fem.: **huntress** (ˈhʌntrɪs). **2. a.** a person who looks diligently for something. **b.** (*in combination*): *a fortune-hunter.* **3.** a specially bred horse used in hunting, characterized by strength and stamina. **4.** a watch with a hinged metal lid or case (**hunting case**) to protect the crystal.

hunter-killer *adj.* denoting a type of submarine designed and equipped to pursue and destroy enemy craft.

hunter's moon *n.* the full moon following the harvest moon.

hunting (ˈhʌntɪŋ) *n.* **a.** the pursuit and killing or capture of wild animals, regarded as a sport. **b.** (*as modifier*): *hunting lodge.*

hunting horn *n.* a long straight metal tube with a flared end, used in giving signals in hunting.

huntsman (ˈhʌntsmən) *n., pl.* **-men. 1.** a person who hunts. **2.** a person who trains hounds, beagles, etc., and manages them during a hunt.

Huon pine (ˈhjuːɒn) *n.* a tree of Australasia, SE Asia, and Chile, with scalelike leaves and cup-shaped berry-like fruits. [after the *Huon* River, Tasmania]

hurdle (ˈhɜːdᵊl) *n.* **1. a.** *Athletics.* one of a number of light barriers over which runners leap in certain events. **b.** a low barrier used in certain horse races. **2.** an obstacle: *the next hurdle in his career.* **3.** a light framework of interlaced osiers, etc., used as a temporary fence. **4.** a sledge on which criminals were dragged to their executions. ~*vb.* **5.** to jump (a hurdle). **6.** (*tr.*) to surround with hurdles. **7.** (*tr.*) to overcome. [OE *hyrdel*] —ˈ**hurdler** *n.*

hurdy-gurdy (ˈhɜːdɪˈgɜːdɪ) *n., pl.* **hurdy-gurdies.** any mechanical musical instrument, such as a barrel organ. [C18: rhyming compound, prob. imit.]

hurl (hɜːl) *vb.* (*tr.*) **1.** to throw with great force. **2.** to utter with force; yell: *to hurl insults.* ~*n.* **3.** the act of hurling. [C13: prob. imit.]

hurling (ˈhɜːlɪŋ) *or* **hurley** *n.* a traditional Irish game resembling hockey, played with sticks and a ball between two teams of 15 players.

hurly-burly (ˈhɜːlɪˈbɜːlɪ) *n., pl.* **hurly-burlies.** confusion or commotion. [C16: < earlier *hurling and burling,* rhyming phrase based on *hurling* in obs. sense of uproar]

Huron (ˈhjʊərən) *n.* **1.** (*pl.* **-rons** *or* **-ron**) a member of a North American Indian people formerly living in the region east of Lake Huron. **2.** the Iroquoian language of this people.

hurrah (hʊˈrɑː), **hooray** (huːˈreɪ), *or* **hoorah** (huːˈrɑː) *interj., n.* **1.** a cheer of joy, victory, etc. ~*vb.* **2.** to shout "hurrah". [C17: prob. < G *hurra;* cf. HUZZAH]

hurricane (ˈhʌrɪkᵊn) *n.* **1.** a severe, often destructive storm, esp. a tropical cyclone. **2.** a wind of force 12 on the Beaufort scale, with speeds over 72 mph. [C16: < Sp. *huracán,* of Amerind origin, < *hura* wind]

hurricane deck *n.* a ship's deck that is covered by a light deck as a sunshade.

hurricane lamp *n.* a paraffin lamp with a glass covering. Also called: **storm lantern.**

hurried (ˈhʌrɪd) *adj.* performed with great or excessive haste. —ˈ**hurriedly** *adv.* —ˈ**hurriedness** *n.*

hurry (ˈhʌrɪ) *vb.* **-rying, -ried. 1.** (*intr.;* often foll. by *up*) to hasten; rush. **2.** (*tr.;* often foll. by *along*) to speed up the completion, progress, etc., of. ~*n.* **3.** haste. **4.** urgency or eagerness. **5. in a hurry.** *Inf.* **a.** easily: *you won't beat him in a hurry.* **b.** willingly: *we won't go there again in a hurry.* [C16 *horyen,* prob. imit.]

hurst (hɜːst) *n. Arch.* **1.** a wood. **2.** a sandbank. [OE *hyrst*]

hurt (hɜːt) *vb.* **hurting, hurt.** **1.** (*tr.*) to cause physical or mental injury to. **2.** (*intr.*) to produce a painful sensation: *the bruise hurts.* **3.** (*intr.*) *Inf.* to feel pain. ~*n.* **4.** physical or mental pain or suffering. **5.** a wound, cut, or sore. **6.** damage or injury; harm. ~*adj.* **7.** injured or pained: *a hurt knee; a hurt look.* [C12 *hurten* to hit, < OF *hurter* to knock against, prob. of Gmc origin]

hurtful (ˈhɜːtfʊl) *adj.* causing distress or injury: *to say hurtful things.* —ˈ**hurtfully** *adv.*

hurtle (ˈhɜːtᵊl) *vb.* to project or be projected very quickly, noisily, or violently. [C13 *hurtlen*, < *hurten* to strike; see HURT]

husband (ˈhʌzbənd) *n.* **1.** a woman's partner in marriage. **2.** *Arch.* a manager of an estate. ~*vb.* **3.** to manage or use (resources, finances, etc.) thriftily. **4.** (*tr.*) *Arch.* to find a husband for. **5.** (*tr.*) *Obs.* to till (the soil). [OE *hūsbonda*, < ON *hūsbōndi*, < *hūs* house + *bōndi* one who has a household] —ˈ**husbander** *n.*

husbandman (ˈhʌzbəndmən) *n., pl.* **-men.** *Arch.* a farmer.

husbandry (ˈhʌzbəndrɪ) *n.* **1.** farming, esp. when regarded as a science, skill, or art. **2.** management of affairs and resources.

hush (hʌʃ) *vb.* **1.** to make or become silent; quieten; soothe. ~*n.* **2.** stillness; silence. ~*interj.* **3.** a plea or demand for silence. [C16: prob. < earlier *husht* quiet!, the *-t* being thought to indicate a past participle] —**hushed** *adj.*

hushaby (ˈhʌʃəˌbaɪ) *interj.* **1.** used in quietening a baby or child to sleep. ~*n., pl.* **-bies.** **2.** a lullaby. [C18: < HUSH + *by*, as in BYE-BYE]

hush-hush *adj. Inf.* (esp. of official work, documents, etc.) secret; confidential.

hush money *n. Sl.* money given to a person to ensure that something is kept secret.

hush up *vb.* (*tr., adv.*) to suppress information or rumours about.

husk (hʌsk) *n.* **1.** the external green or membranous covering of certain fruits and seeds. **2.** any worthless outer covering. ~*vb.* **3.** (*tr.*) to remove the husk from. [C14: prob. based on MDu. *huusken* little house, < *hūs* house]

husky[1] (ˈhʌskɪ) *adj.* **huskier, huskiest.** **1.** (of a voice, utterance, etc.) slightly hoarse or rasping. **2.** of or containing husks. **3.** *Inf.* big and strong. [C19: prob. < HUSK, from the toughness of a corn husk] —ˈ**huskily** *adv.* —ˈ**huskiness** *n.*

husky[2] (ˈhʌskɪ) *n., pl.* **huskies.** **1.** a breed of Arctic sled dog with a thick dense coat, pricked ears, and a curled tail. **2.** *Canad. sl.* **a.** a member of the Inuit people. **b.** their language. [C19: prob. based on ESKIMO]

hussar (hʊˈzɑː) *n.* **1.** a member of any of various light cavalry regiments, renowned for their elegant dress. **2.** a Hungarian horseman of the 15th century. [C15: < Hungarian *huszár* hussar, formerly freebooter, ult. < OIt. *corsaro* CORSAIR]

Hussite (ˈhʌsaɪt) *n.* **1.** an adherent of the ideas of John Huss, 14th-century Bohemian religious reformer, or a member of the movement initiated by him. ~*adj.* **2.** of or relating to John Huss, his teachings, followers, etc. —ˈ**Hussitism** *n.*

hussy (ˈhʌsɪ, -zɪ) *n., pl.* **-sies.** *Contemptuous.* a shameless or promiscuous woman. [C16 (in the sense: housewife): < *hussif* HOUSEWIFE]

hustings (ˈhʌstɪŋz) *n.* (*functioning as pl. or sing.*) **1.** *Brit.* (before 1872) the platform on which candidates were nominated for Parliament and from which they addressed the electors. **2.** the proceedings at a parliamentary election. [C11: < ON *hūsthing*, < *hūs* HOUSE + *thing* assembly]

hustle (ˈhʌsᵊl) *vb.* **1.** to shove or crowd (someone) roughly. **2.** to move hurriedly or furtively: *he hustled her out of sight.* **3.** (*tr.*) to deal with hurriedly: *to hustle legislation through.* **4.** *Sl.* to obtain (something) forcefully. **5.** *U.S. & Canad. sl.* (of procurers and prostitutes) to solicit. ~*n.* **6.** an instance of hustling. [C17: < Du. *husselen* to shake, < MDu. *hutsen*] —ˈ**hustler** *n.*

hut (hʌt) *n.* **1.** a small house or shelter. ~*vb.* **hutting, hutted.** **2.** to furnish with or live in a hut. [C17: < F *hutte*, of Gmc origin] —ˈ**hut**ˌ**like** *adj.*

hutch (hʌtʃ) *n.* **1.** a cage, usually of wood and wire mesh, for small animals. **2.** *Inf., derog.* a small house. **3.** a cart for carrying ore. [C14 *hucche*, < OF *huche*, < Med. L *hutica*, <?]

hutment (ˈhʌtmənt) *n. Chiefly mil.* a number or group of huts.

huzzah (həˈzɑː) *interj., n., vb.* an archaic word for **hurrah.** [C16: <?]

HV *or* **h.v.** *abbrev. for* high voltage.

HWM *abbrev. for* high-water mark.

hwyl (ˈhuːɪl) *n.* emotional fervour, as in the recitation of poetry. [C19: Welsh]

hyacinth (ˈhaɪəsɪnθ) *n.* **1.** any plant of the Mediterranean genus *Hyacinthus*, esp. a cultivated variety having a thick flower stalk bearing bell-shaped fragrant flowers. **2.** the flower or bulb of such a plant. **3.** any similar plant, such as the grape hyacinth. **4.** Also called: **jacinth.** a reddish transparent variety of the mineral zircon, used as a gemstone. **5. a.** a purplish-blue colour. **b.** (*as adj.*): *hyacinth eyes.* [C16: < L *hyacinthus*, < Gk *huakinthos*] —**hyacinthine** (ˌhaɪəˈsɪnθaɪn) *adj.*

Hyades (ˈhaɪəˌdiːz) *pl. n.* an open cluster of stars in the constellation Taurus, formerly believed to bring rain when they rose with the sun. [C16: via L < Gk *huades*, ? < *huein* to rain]

hyaena (haɪˈiːnə) *n.* a variant spelling of **hyena.**

hyaline (ˈhaɪəlɪn) *adj. Biol.* clear and translucent, as a common type of cartilage. [C17: < LL *hyalinus*, < Gk, < *hualos* glass]

hyalite (ˈhaɪəˌlaɪt) *n.* a clear and colourless variety of opal in globular form.

hyaloid (ˈhaɪəˌlɔɪd) *adj. Anat., zool.* clear and transparent; hyaline. [C19: < Gk *hualoeidēs*]

hyaloid membrane *n.* the delicate transparent membrane enclosing the vitreous humour of the eye.

hybrid (ˈhaɪbrɪd) *n.* **1.** an animal or plant resulting from a cross between genetically unlike individuals; usually sterile. **2.** anything of mixed ancestry. **3.** a word, part of which is derived from one language and part from another, such as *monolingual.* ~*adj.* **4.** denoting or being a hybrid; of mixed origin. [C17: < L *hibrida* offspring of a mixed union (human or animal)] —ˈ**hybridism** *n.* —**hy**ˈ**bridity** *n.*

hybrid computer *n.* a computer that uses both analogue and digital techniques.

hybridize *or* **-ise** (ˈhaɪbrɪˌdaɪz) *vb.* to produce or cause to produce hybrids; crossbreed. —ˌ**hybridi**ˈ**zation** *or* **-i**ˈ**sation** *n.*

hybridoma (ˌhaɪbrɪˈdəʊmə) *n.* a hybrid cell formed by the fusion of two different types of cell, esp. one capable of producing antibodies fused with an immortal tumour cell. [C20: < HYBRID + -OMA]

hybrid vigour *n. Biol.* the increased size, strength, etc., of a hybrid as compared to either of its parents. Also called: **heterosis.**

hydatid (ˈhaɪdətɪd) *n.* **1.** a large bladder containing encysted larvae of the tapeworm *Echinococcus:* causes serious disease in man. **2.** Also called: **hydatid cyst.** a sterile fluid-filled cyst produced in man and animals during infestation by *Echinococcus* larval forms. [C17: < Gk *hudatis* watery vesicle, < *hudōr, hudat-* water]

hydr- *combining form.* a variant of **hydro-** before a vowel.

hydra (ˈhaɪdrə) *n., pl.* **-dras** *or* **-drae** (-driː). **1.** a freshwater coelenterate in which the body is a slender polyp with tentacles around the mouth. **2.** a persistent trouble or evil. [C16: < L, < Gk *hudra* water serpent]

hydracid (haɪˈdræsɪd) *n.* an acid, such as hydrochloric acid, that does not contain oxygen.

hydrangea (haɪˈdreɪndʒə) *n.* a shrub or tree of an Asian and American genus cultivated for their large clusters of white, pink, or blue flowers. [C18: < NL, < Gk *hudōr* water + *angeion* vessel: prob. < the cup-shaped fruit]

hydrant (ˈhaɪdrənt) *n.* an outlet from a water main, usually an upright pipe with a valve attached, from which water can be tapped for fighting fires, etc. [C19: < HYDRO- + -ANT]

hydrate (ˈhaɪdreɪt) *n.* **1.** a chemical compound containing water that is chemically combined with a substance and can usually be expelled without changing the constitution of the substance. **2.** a chemical compound that can dissociate reversibly into water and another compound. ~*vb.* **3.** to undergo or cause to undergo treatment or impregnation with water. —**hy'dration** *n.* —**'hydrator** *n.*

hydrated ('haɪdreɪtɪd) *adj.* (of a compound) chemically bonded to water molecules.

hydraulic (haɪ'drɒlɪk) *adj.* **1.** operated by pressure transmitted through a pipe by a liquid, such as water or oil. **2.** of or employing liquids in motion. **3.** of hydraulics. **4.** hardening under water: *hydraulic cement.* [C17: < L *hydraulicus*, < Gk *hudraulikos*, < *hudraulos* water organ, < HYDRO- + *aulos* pipe] —**hy'draulically** *adv.*

hydraulic brake *n.* a type of brake, used in motor vehicles, in which the braking force is transmitted from the brake pedal to the brakes by a liquid under pressure.

hydraulic press *n.* a press that utilizes liquid pressure to enable a small force applied to a small piston to produce a large force on a larger piston.

hydraulic ram *n.* **1.** the larger or working piston of a hydraulic press. **2.** a form of water pump utilizing the kinetic energy of running water to provide static pressure to raise water to a reservoir higher than the source.

hydraulics (haɪ'drɒlɪks) *n.* (*functioning as sing.*) another name for **fluid mechanics.**

hydraulic suspension *n.* a system of motor-vehicle suspension using hydraulic members, often with hydraulic compensation between front and rear systems (**hydroelastic suspension**).

hydrazine ('haɪdrəˌziːn, -zɪn) *n.* a colourless liquid made from sodium hypochlorite and ammonia: used as a rocket fuel. Formula: N_2H_4. [C19: < HYDRO- + AZO + -INE[2]]

hydric ('haɪdrɪk) *adj.* **1.** of or containing hydrogen. **2.** containing or using moisture.

hydride ('haɪdraɪd) *n.* any compound of hydrogen with another element.

hydrilla (haɪ'drɪlə) *n.* a type of underwater aquatic weed that was introduced from Asia into the south U.S., where it has become a serious problem, choking fish and hindering navigation. [C20: NL, prob. < L *hydra*: see HYDRA]

hydriodic acid (ˌhaɪdrɪ'ɒdɪk) *n.* the solution of hydrogen iodide: a strong acid. [C19: < HYDRO- + IODIC]

hydro[1] ('haɪdrəʊ) *n., pl.* **-dros.** *Brit.* a hotel or resort, often near a spa, offering facilities (esp. formerly) for hydropathic treatment.

hydro[2] ('haɪdrəʊ) *adj.* **1.** short for **hydroelectric.** ~*n.* **2.** a Canadian name for **electricity.**

Hydro ('haɪdrəʊ) *n.* (esp. in Canada) a hydroelectric power company or board.

hydro- *or before a vowel* **hydr-** *combining form.* **1.** indicating water or fluid: *hydrodynamics.* **2.** indicating hydrogen in a chemical compound: *hydrochloric acid.* **3.** indicating a hydroid: *hydrozoan.* [< Gk *hudōr* water]

hydrobromic acid (ˌhaɪdrəʊ'brəʊmɪk) *n.* the solution of hydrogen bromide: a strong acid.

hydrocarbon (ˌhaɪdrəʊ'kɑːbᵊn) *n.* any organic compound containing only carbon and hydrogen.

hydrocele ('haɪdrəʊˌsiːl) *n.* an abnormal collection of fluid in any saclike space.

hydrocephalus (ˌhaɪdrəʊ'sɛfələs) *or* **hydrocephaly** (ˌhaɪdrəʊ'sɛfəlɪ) *n.* accumulation of cerebrospinal fluid within the ventricles of the brain because its normal outlet has been blocked by congenital malformation or disease. Nontechnical name: **water on the brain.** —**hydrocephalic** (ˌhaɪdrəʊsɛ'fælɪk) *or* **ˌhydro'cephalous** *adj.*

hydrochloric acid (ˌhaɪdrə'klɒrɪk) *n.* the aqueous solution of hydrogen chloride: a strong acid used in many industrial and laboratory processes.

hydrochloride (ˌhaɪdrə'klɔːraɪd) *n.* a quaternary salt formed by the addition of hydrochloric acid to an organic base.

hydrocyanic acid (ˌhaɪdrəʊsaɪ'ænɪk) *n.* another name for **hydrogen cyanide.**

hydrodynamics (ˌhaɪdrəʊdaɪ'næmɪks, -dɪ-) *n.* (*functioning as sing.*) the branch of science concerned with the mechanical properties of fluids, esp. liquids. Also called: **hydromechanics.**

hydroelastic suspension (ˌhaɪdrəʊɪ'læstɪk) *n.* See **hydraulic suspension.**

hydroelectric (ˌhaɪdrəʊɪ'lɛktrɪk) *adj.* **1.** generated by the pressure of falling water: *hydroelectric power.* **2.** of the generation of electricity by water pressure: *a hydroelectric scheme.* —**hydroelectricity** (ˌhaɪdrəʊɪlɛk'trɪsɪtɪ) *n.*

hydrofluoric acid (ˌhaɪdrəʊfluː'ɒrɪk) *n.* the colourless aqueous solution of hydrogen fluoride: a strong acid that attacks glass.

hydrofoil ('haɪdrəˌfɔɪl) *n.* **1.** a fast light vessel the hull of which is raised out of the water on one or more pairs of fixed vanes. **2.** any of these vanes.

hydrogen ('haɪdrɪdʒən) *n.* **a.** a flammable colourless gas that is the lightest and most abundant element in the universe. It occurs in water and in most organic compounds. Symbol: H; atomic no.: 1; atomic wt.: 1.007 97. **b.** (*as modifier*): *hydrogen bomb.* [C18: < F *hydrogène*, < HYDRO- + -GEN; because its combustion produces water] —**hydrogenous** (haɪ'drɒdʒɪnəs) *adj.*

hydrogenate ('haɪdrədʒɪˌneɪt, haɪ'drɒdʒɪˌneɪt) *vb.* to undergo or cause to undergo a reaction with hydrogen: *to hydrogenate ethylene.* —**ˌhydrogen'ation** *n.*

hydrogen bomb *n.* a type of bomb in which energy is released by fusion of hydrogen nuclei to give helium nuclei. The energy required to initiate the fusion is provided by the detonation of an atom bomb, which is surrounded by a hydrogen-containing substance. Also called: **H-bomb.**

hydrogen bond *n.* a weak chemical bond between an electronegative atom, such as fluorine, oxygen, or nitrogen, and a hydrogen atom bound to another electronegative atom.

hydrogen cyanide *n.* a colourless poisonous liquid with a faint odour of bitter almonds. It forms prussic acid in aqueous solution and is used for making plastics and as a war gas. Formula: HCN.

hydrogen ion *n.* an ionized hydrogen atom, occurring in aqueous solutions of acids; proton. Formula: H^+.

hydrogenize *or* **-nise** ('haɪdrədʒɪˌnaɪz, haɪ'drɒdʒɪˌnaɪz) *vb.* a variant of **hydrogenate.**

hydrogen peroxide *n.* a colourless oily unstable liquid used as a bleach and as an oxidizer in rocket fuels. Formula: H_2O_2.

hydrogen sulphide *n.* a colourless poisonous gas with an odour of rotten eggs. Formula: H_2S. Also called: **sulphuretted hydrogen.**

hydrography (haɪ'drɒgrəfɪ) *n.* the study, surveying, and mapping of the oceans, seas, and rivers. —**hy'drographer** *n.* —**hydrographic** (ˌhaɪdrə'græfɪk) *adj.*

hydroid ('haɪdrɔɪd) *adj.* **1.** of or relating to the *Hydroida*, an order of hydrozoan coelenterates that have the polyp phase dominant. **2.** having or consisting of hydra-like polyps. ~*n.* **3.** a hydroid colony or individual.

hydrokinetics (ˌhaɪdrəʊkɪ'nɛtɪks, -kaɪ-) *n.* (*functioning as sing.*) the branch of science concerned with the behaviour and properties of fluids in motion. Also called: **hydrodynamics.**

hydrology (haɪ'drɒlədʒɪ) *n.* the study of the distribution, conservation, use, etc., of the water of the earth and its atmosphere. —**hydrologic** (ˌhaɪdrə'lɒdʒɪk) *adj.* —**hy'drologist** *n.*

hydrolyse *or U.S.* **-lyze** ('haɪdrəˌlaɪz) *vb.* to subject to or undergo hydrolysis.

hydrolysis (haɪ'drɒlɪsɪs) *n.* a chemical reaction in which a compound reacts with water to produce other compounds. —**hydrolytic** (ˌhaɪdrə'lɪtɪk) *adj.*

hydrolyte ('haɪdrəˌlaɪt) *n.* a substance subjected to hydrolysis.

hydromel ('haɪdrəʊˌmɛl) *n. Arch.* another word for **mead** (the drink). [C15: < L, < Gk *hudromeli*, < HYDRO- + *meli* honey]

hydrometer (haɪ'drɒmɪtə) *n.* an instrument for

measuring the relative density of a liquid. —**hydrometric** (ˌhaɪdrəʊˈmɛtrɪk) *or* ˌ**hydroˈmetrical** *adj.*

hydronaut (ˈhaɪdrəʊˌnɔːt) *n. U.S. Navy.* a person trained to operate deep submergence vessels. [C20: < Gk, < HYDRO- + *-naut,* as in *astronaut*]

hydropathy (haɪˈdrɒpəθɪ) *n.* a pseudoscientific method of treating disease by the use of large quantities of water both internally and externally. —**hydropathic** (ˌhaɪdrəʊˈpæθɪk) *adj.*

hydrophilic (ˌhaɪdrəʊˈfɪlɪk) *adj. Chem.* tending to dissolve in, mix with, or be wetted by water: *a hydrophilic colloid.* —**hydrophile** (ˈhaɪdrəʊˌfaɪl) *n.*

hydrophobia (ˌhaɪdrəˈfəʊbɪə) *n.* **1.** another name for **rabies. 2.** a fear of drinking fluids, esp. that of a person with rabies, because of painful spasms when trying to swallow. —ˌ**hydroˈphobic** *adj.*

hydrophone (ˈhaɪdrəˌfəʊn) *n.* an electroacoustic transducer that converts sound travelling through water into electrical oscillations.

hydrophyte (ˈhaɪdrəʊˌfaɪt) *n.* a plant that grows only in water or very moist soil.

hydroplane (ˈhaɪdrəʊˌpleɪn) *n.* **1.** a motorboat equipped with hydrofoils or with a shaped bottom that raises its hull out of the water at high speeds. **2.** an attachment to an aircraft to enable it to glide along the surface of the water. **3.** another name for a **seaplane. 4.** a horizontal vane on the hull of a submarine for controlling its vertical motion. ~*vb.* **5.** (*intr.*) (of a boat) to rise out of the water in the manner of a hydroplane.

hydroponics (ˌhaɪdrəʊˈpɒnɪks) *n.* (*functioning as sing.*) a method of cultivating plants by growing them in gravel, etc., through which water containing dissolved inorganic nutrient salts is pumped. [C20: < HYDRO- + (*geo*)*ponics* science of agriculture] —ˌ**hydroˈponic** *adj.* —ˌ**hydroˈponically** *adv.*

hydropower (ˈhaɪdrəʊˌpaʊə) *n.* hydroelectric power.

hydroquinone (ˌhaɪdrəʊkwɪˈnəʊn) *or* **hydroquinol** (ˌhaɪdrəʊˈkwɪnɒl) *n.* a white crystalline soluble phenol used as a photographic developer.

hydrosphere (ˈhaɪdrəˌsfɪə) *n.* the watery part of the earth's surface, including oceans, lakes, water vapour in the atmosphere, etc.

hydrostatics (ˌhaɪdrəʊˈstætɪks) *n.* (*functioning as sing.*) the branch of science concerned with the mechanical properties and behaviour of fluids that are not in motion. —ˌ**hydroˈstatic** *adj.*

hydrotherapeutics (ˌhaɪdrəʊˌθɛrəˈpjuːtɪks) *n.* (*functioning as sing.*) the branch of medical science concerned with hydrotherapy.

hydrotherapy (ˌhaɪdrəʊˈθɛrəpɪ) *n. Med.* the treatment of certain diseases by the external application of water, as for mobilizing stiff joints or strengthening weakened muscles.

hydrothermal (ˌhaɪdrəʊˈθɜːməl) *adj.* of or relating to the action of water under conditions of high temperature, esp. in forming rocks.

hydrotropism (haɪˈdrɒtrəˌpɪzəm) *n.* the directional growth of plants in response to the stimulus of water.

hydrous (ˈhaɪdrəs) *adj.* containing water.

hydroxide (haɪˈdrɒksaɪd) *n.* **1.** a base or alkali containing the ion OH^-. **2.** any compound containing an -OH group.

hydroxy (haɪˈdrɒksɪ) *adj.* (of a chemical compound) containing one or more hydroxyl groups. [C19: HYDRO- + OXY(GEN)]

hydroxyl (haɪˈdrɒksɪl) *n.* (*modifier*) of, consisting of, or containing the monovalent group -OH or the ion OH^-: *a hydroxyl group or radical.*

hydrozoan (ˌhaɪdrəʊˈzəʊən) *n.* **1.** any coelenterate of the class *Hydrozoa,* which includes the hydra and the Portuguese man-of-war. ~*adj.* **2.** of the *Hydrozoa.*

hyena *or* **hyaena** (haɪˈiːnə) *n.* any of several long-legged carnivorous doglike mammals such as the spotted or laughing hyena, of Africa and S Asia. [C16: < Med. L, < L *hyaena,* < Gk, < *hus* hog] —**hyˈenic** *or* **hyˈaenic** *adj.*

hygiene (ˈhaɪdʒiːn) *n.* **1.** Also called: **hygienics.** the science concerned with the maintenance of health. **2.** clean or healthy practices or thinking: *personal hygiene.* [C18: < NL *hygiēna,* < Gk *hugieinē,* < *hugiēs* healthy]

hygienic (haɪˈdʒiːnɪk) *adj.* promoting health or cleanliness; sanitary. —**hyˈgienically** *adv.*

hygienics (haɪˈdʒiːnɪks) *n.* (*functioning as sing.*) another word for **hygiene** (sense 1).

hygienist (ˈhaɪdʒiːnɪst) *n.* a person skilled in the practice of hygiene.

hygro- *or before a vowel* **hygr-** *combining form.* indicating moisture: *hygrometer.* [< Gk *hugros* wet]

hygrometer (haɪˈgrɒmɪtə) *n.* any of various instruments for measuring humidity. —**hygrometric** (ˌhaɪgrəˈmɛtrɪk) *adj.*

hygroscope (ˈhaɪgrəˌskəʊp) *n.* any device that indicates the humidity of the air without necessarily measuring it.

hygroscopic (ˌhaɪgrəˈskɒpɪk) *adj.* (of a substance) tending to absorb water from the air. —ˌ**hygroˈscopically** *adv.*

hying (ˈhaɪɪŋ) *vb.* a present participle of **hie.**

hyla (ˈhaɪlə) *n.* a tree frog of tropical America. [C19: < NL, < Gk *hulē* forest]

hylomorphism (ˌhaɪləˈmɔːfɪzəm) *n.* the philosophical doctrine that identifies matter with the first cause of the universe.

hylozoism (ˌhaɪləˈzəʊɪzəm) *n.* the philosophical doctrine that life is one of the properties of matter. [C17: < Gk *hulē* wood, matter + *zōē* life]

hymen (ˈhaɪmɛn) *n. Anat.* a fold of mucous membrane that partly covers the entrance to the vagina and is usually ruptured when sexual intercourse takes place for the first time. [C17: < Gk: membrane] —ˈ**hymenal** *adj.*

hymeneal (ˌhaɪmɛˈniːəl) *adj.* **1.** *Chiefly poetic.* of or relating to marriage. ~*n.* **2.** a wedding song or poem.

hymenopteran (ˌhaɪmɪˈnɒptərən) *or* **hymenopteron** *n., pl.* **-terans, -tera** (-tərə), *or* **-terons.** any hymenopterous insect.

hymenopterous (ˌhaɪmɪˈnɒptərəs) *adj.* of or belonging to an order of insects, including bees, wasps, and ants, having two pairs of membranous wings. [C19: < Gk *humenopteros* membrane wing; see HYMEN, -PTEROUS]

hymn (hɪm) *n.* **1.** a Christian song of praise sung to God or a saint. **2.** a similar song praising other gods, a nation, etc. ~*vb.* **3.** to express (praises, thanks, etc.) by singing hymns. [C13: < L *hymnus,* < Gk *humnos*] —**hymnic** (ˈhɪmnɪk) *adj.*

hymnal (ˈhɪmnᵊl) *n.* **1.** Also: **hymn book.** a book of hymns. ~*adj.* **2.** of, relating to, or characteristic of hymns.

hymnody (ˈhɪmnədɪ) *n.* **1.** the composition or singing of hymns. **2.** hymns collectively. ~Also called: **hymnology.** [C18: < Med. L *hymnōdia,* < Gk, < *humnōidein,* < HYMN + *aeidein* to sing]

hymnology (hɪmˈnɒlədʒɪ) *n.* **1.** the study of hymn composition. **2.** another word for **hymnody.** —**hymˈnologist** *n.*

hyoid (ˈhaɪɔɪd) *adj.* of or relating to the **hyoid bone,** the horseshoe-shaped bone that lies at the base of the tongue. [C19: < NL *hyoïdes,* < Gk *huoeidēs* having the shape of the letter UPSILON, < *hu* upsilon + -OID]

hyoscine (ˈhaɪəˌsiːn) *n.* another name for **scopolamine.** [C19: < *huosc*(*yamus*) a medicinal plant + -INE[2]; see HYOSCYAMINE]

hyoscyamine (ˌhaɪəˈsaɪəˌmiːn) *n.* a poisonous alkaloid occurring in henbane and related plants: used in medicine. [C19: < NL, < Gk *huoskuamos* (< *hus* pig + *kuamos* bean) + AMINE]

hyp. *abbrev. for:* **1.** hypotenuse. **2.** hypothesis. **3.** hypothetical.

hypaethral *or U.S.* **hypethral** (hɪˈpiːθrəl, haɪ-) *adj.* (esp. of a classical temple) having no roof. [C18: < L *hypaethrus* uncovered, < Gk, < HYPO- + *aithros* clear sky]

hypallage (haɪˈpæləˌdʒiː) *n. Rhetoric.* a figure of speech in which the natural relations of two words in a statement are interchanged, as in *the fire spread the wind.* [C16: via LL < Gk *hupallagē,* < HYPO- + *allassein* to exchange]

hype[1] (haɪp) *Sl.* ~*n.* **1.** a hypodermic needle or injection. ~*vb.* **2.** (*intr.;* usually foll. by *up*) to inject oneself with a drug. **3.** (*tr.*) to stimulate artificially or excite. [C20: shortened < HYPODERMIC]

hype[2] (haɪp) *Sl.* ~*n.* **1.** a deception or racket. **2.** an intensive or exaggerated publicity or sales promotion. ~*vb.* **3.** (*tr.*) to market or promote (a product) using exaggerated or intensive publicity. [C20: <?]

hyped up *adj. Sl.* stimulated or excited by or as if by the effect of a stimulating drug.

hyper- *prefix.* **1.** above, over, or in excess: *hypercritical.* **2.** denoting an abnormal excess: *hyperacidity.* **3.** indicating that a chemical compound contains a greater than usual amount of an element: *hyperoxide.* [< Gk *huper* over]

hyperacidity (ˌhaɪpərəˈsɪdɪtɪ) *n.* excess acidity of the gastrointestinal tract, esp. the stomach, producing a burning sensation.

hyperactive (ˌhaɪpərˈæktɪv) *adj.* abnormally active. —ˌ**hyperacˈtivity** *n.*

hyperaemia *or U.S.* **hyperemia** (ˌhaɪpərˈiːmɪə) *n. Pathol.* an excessive amount of blood in an organ or part.

hyperaesthesia *or U.S.* **hyperesthesia** (ˌhaɪpəriːsˈθiːzɪə) *n. Pathol.* increased sensitivity of any of the sense organs. —**hyperaesthetic** *or U.S.* **hyperesthetic** (ˌhaɪpəriːsˈθɛtɪk) *adj.*

hyperbaton (haɪˈpɜːbəˌtɒn) *n. Rhetoric.* a figure of speech in which the normal order of words is reversed, as in *cheese I love.* [C16: via L < Gk, lit.: an overstepping, < HYPER- + *bainein* to step]

hyperbola (haɪˈpɜːbələ) *n., pl.* **-las** *or* **-le** (-ˌliː). a conic section formed by a plane that cuts a cone at a steeper angle to its base than its side. [C17: < Gk *huperbolē,* lit.: excess, extravagance, < HYPER- + *ballein* to throw]

hyperbole (haɪˈpɜːbəlɪ) *n.* a deliberate exaggeration used for effect: *he embraced her a thousand times.* [C16: < Gk, < HYPER- + *bolē,* < *ballein* to throw] —**hyˈperbolism** *n.*

hyperbolic (ˌhaɪpəˈbɒlɪk) *or* **hyperbolical** *adj.* **1.** of a hyperbola. **2.** *Rhetoric.* of a hyperbole. —ˌ**hyperˈbolically** *adv.*

hyperbolic function *n.* any of a group of functions of an angle expressed as a relationship between the distances of a point on a hyperbola to the origin and to the coordinate axes.

hyperbolize *or* **-lise** (haɪˈpɜːbəˌlaɪz) *vb.* to express (something) by means of hyperbole.

hyperboloid (haɪˈpɜːbəˌlɔɪd) *n.* a geometric surface consisting of one sheet, or of two sheets separated by a finite distance, whose sections parallel to the three coordinate planes are hyperbolas or ellipses.

Hyperborean (ˌhaɪpəˈbɔːrɪən) *n.* **1.** *Greek myth.* one of a people believed to have lived beyond the North Wind in a sunny land. **2.** an inhabitant of the extreme north. ~*adj.* **3.** (*sometimes not cap.*) of or relating to the extreme north. [C16: < L *hyperboreus,* < Gk, < HYPER- + *Boreas* the north wind]

hypercritical (ˌhaɪpəˈkrɪtɪkᵊl) *adj.* excessively or severely critical. —ˌ**hyperˈcritically** *adv.*

hyperfocal distance (ˌhaɪpəˈfəʊkᵊl) *n.* the distance from a camera lens to the point beyond which all objects appear sharp and clearly defined.

hyperglycaemia *or U.S.* **hyperglycemia** (ˌhaɪpəglaɪˈsiːmɪə) *n. Pathol.* an abnormally large amount of sugar in the blood. [C20: < HYPER- + GLYCO- + -AEMIA] —ˌ**hyperglyˈcaemic** *or U.S.* ˌ**hyperglyˈcemic** *adj.*

hypergolic (ˌhaɪpəˈgɒlɪk) *adj.* (of a rocket fuel) able to ignite spontaneously on contact with an oxidizer. [C20: < G *Hypergol* (? < HYP(ER-) + ERG[1] + -OL[2]) + -IC]

hypericum (haɪˈpɛrɪkəm) *n.* any herbaceous plant or shrub of the temperate genus *Hypericum.* See **rose of Sharon, Saint John's wort.** [C16: via L < Gk *hupereikon,* < HYPER- + *ereikē* heath]

hypermarket (ˈhaɪpəˌmɑːkɪt) *n. Brit.* a huge self-service store, usually built on the outskirts of a town. [C20: translation of F *hypermarché*]

hypermetropia (ˌhaɪpəmɪˈtrəʊpɪə) *or* **hypermetropy** (ˌhaɪpəˈmɛtrəpɪ) *n. Pathol.* a variant of **hyperopia.** [C19: < Gk *hupermetros* beyond measure (< HYPER- + *metron* measure) + -OPIA]

hyperon (ˈhaɪpəˌrɒn) *n. Physics.* any baryon that is not a nucleon. [C20: < HYPER- + -ON]

hyperopia (ˌhaɪpəˈrəʊpɪə) *n.* inability to see near objects clearly because the images received by the eye are focused behind the retina; long-sightedness. —**hyperopic** (ˌhaɪpəˈrɒpɪk) *adj.*

hyperphysical (ˌhaɪpəˈfɪzɪkᵊl) *adj.* beyond the physical; supernatural or immaterial.

hyperpyrexia (ˌhaɪpəpaɪˈrɛksɪə) *n. Pathol.* an extremely high fever, with a temperature of 41°C (106°F) or above.

hypersensitive (ˌhaɪpəˈsɛnsɪtɪv) *adj.* **1.** having unduly vulnerable feelings. **2.** abnormally sensitive to an allergen, a drug, or other agent. —ˌ**hyperˈsensitiveness** *or* ˌ**hyperˌsensiˈtivity** *n.*

hypersonic (ˌhaɪpəˈsɒnɪk) *adj.* concerned with or having a velocity of at least five times that of sound in the same medium under the same conditions. —ˌ**hyperˈsonics** *n.*

hyperspace (ˌhaɪpəˈspeɪs) *n.* **1.** *Maths.* space having more than three dimensions. **2.** (in science fiction) a theoretical dimension within which conventional space-time relationship does not apply.

hypersthene (ˈhaɪpəˌsθiːn) *n.* a green, brown, or black pyroxene mineral. [C19: < HYPER- + Gk *sthenos* strength]

hypertension (ˌhaɪpəˈtɛnʃən) *n. Pathol.* abnormally high blood pressure. —**hypertensive** (ˌhaɪpəˈtɛnsɪv) *adj., n.*

hyperthermia (ˌhaɪpəˈθɜːmɪə) *or* **hyperthermy** (ˌhaɪpəˈθɜːmɪ) *n. Pathol.* a variant of **hyperpyrexia.** —ˌ**hyperˈthermal** *adj.*

hyperthyroidism (ˌhaɪpəˈθaɪrɔɪˌdɪzəm) *n.* overproduction of thyroid hormone by the thyroid gland, causing nervousness, insomnia, and sensitivity to heat. —ˌ**hyperˈthyroid** *adj., n.*

hypertonic (ˌhaɪpəˈtɒnɪk) *adj.* **1.** (esp. of muscles) being in a state of abnormally high tension. **2.** (of a solution) having a higher osmotic pressure than that of a specified solution.

hypertrophy (haɪˈpɜːtrəfɪ) *n., pl.* **-phies. 1.** enlargement of an organ or part resulting from an increase in the size of the cells. ~*vb.* **-phying, -phied. 2.** to undergo or cause to undergo this condition.

hyperventilation (ˌhaɪpəˌvɛntɪˈleɪʃən) *n.* an increase in the rate of breathing, sometimes resulting in cramp and dizziness.

hypha (ˈhaɪfə) *n., pl.* **-phae** (-fiː). any of the filaments that constitute the body (mycelium) of a fungus. [C19: < NL, < Gk *huphē* web] —ˈ**hyphal** *adj.*.

hyphen (ˈhaɪfᵊn) *n.* **1.** the punctuation mark (-), used to separate parts of compound words, to link the words of a phrase, and between syllables of a word split between two consecutive lines. ~*vb.* **2.** (*tr.*) another word for **hyphenate.** [C17: < LL (meaning: the combining of two words), < Gk *huphen* (adv.) together, < HYPO- + *heis* one]

hyphenate (ˈhaɪfəˌneɪt) *vb.* (*tr.*) to separate (words, etc.) with a hyphen. —ˌ**hyphenˈation** *n.*

hyphenated (ˈhaɪfəˌneɪtɪd) *adj.* **1.** containing or linked with a hyphen. **2.** *Chiefly U.S.* having a nationality denoted by a hyphenated word: *Irish-American.*

hypno- *or before a vowel* **hypn-** *combining*

ˌ**hyperaˈcute** *adj.*
ˌ**hyperconˈformity** *n.*
ˌ**hyperˈconscious** *adj.*
ˌ**hyperconˈservative** *adj.*
ˌ**hypercorˈrect** *adj.*
ˌ**hypereˈmotional** *adj.*
ˌ**hyperˌenerˈgetic** *adj.*
ˌ**hyperenˈthusiasm** *n.*
ˌ**hyperˈfunctional** *adj.*
ˌ**hyperˌintelˈlectual** *adj.*
ˌ**hyperroˈmantic** *adj.*
ˌ**hyperˌsentiˈmental** *adj.*
ˌ**hypersoˈphistiˌcated** *adj.*
ˌ**hyperˈtechnical** *adj.*
ˌ**hyperˈtoxic** *adj.*

form. **1.** indicating sleep: *hypnopaedia.* **2.** relating to hypnosis: *hypnotherapy.* [< Gk *hupnos* sleep]

hypnoid (ˈhɪpˌnɔɪd) *or* **hypnoidal** (hɪpˈnɔɪdˀl) *adj. Psychol.* of or relating to a state resembling sleep or hypnosis.

hypnology (hɪpˈnɒlədʒɪ) *n. Psychol.* the study of sleep and hypnosis. —**hypˈnologist** *n.*

hypnopaedia (ˌhɪpnəʊˈpiːdɪə) *n.* the learning of lessons heard during sleep. [C20: < HYPNO- + Gk *paideia* education]

hypnopompic (ˌhɪpnəʊˈpɒmpɪk) *adj. Psychol.* relating to the state existing between sleep and full waking, characterized by the persistence of dreamlike imagery. [C20: < HYPNO- + Gk *pompē* a sending forth, escort + -IC]

hypnosis (hɪpˈnəʊsɪs) *n., pl.* **-ses** (-siːz). an artificially induced state of relaxation and concentration in which deeper parts of the mind become more accessible.

hypnotherapy (ˌhɪpnəʊˈθɛrəpɪ) *n.* the use of hypnosis in the treatment of emotional and psychogenic problems.

hypnotic (hɪpˈnɒtɪk) *adj.* **1.** of or producing hypnosis or sleep. **2.** (of a person) susceptible to hypnotism. ~*n.* **3.** a drug that induces sleep. **4.** a person susceptible to hypnosis. [C17: < LL *hypnōticus,* < Gk, < *hupnoun* to put to sleep, < *hupnos* sleep] —**hypˈnotically** *adv.*

hypnotism (ˈhɪpnəˌtɪzəm) *n.* **1.** the scientific study and practice of hypnosis. **2.** the process of inducing hypnosis. —ˈ**hypnotist** *n.*

hypnotize *or* **-tise** (ˈhɪpnəˌtaɪz) *vb.* (*tr.*) **1.** to induce hypnosis in (a person). **2.** to charm or beguile; fascinate. —ˌ**hypnotiˈzation** *or* **-tiˈsation** *n.* —ˈ**hypnoˌtizer** *or* **-ˌtiser** *n.*

hypo[1] (ˈhaɪpəʊ) *n.* short for **hyposulphite.** [C19]

hypo[2] (ˈhaɪpəʊ) *n., pl.* **-pos.** *Inf.* short for **hypodermic syringe.**

hypo- *or before a vowel* **hyp-** *prefix.* **1.** beneath or below: *hypodermic.* **2.** lower: *hypogastrium.* **3.** less than; denoting a deficiency: *hypothyroid.* **4.** indicating that a chemical compound contains an element in a lower oxidation state than usual: *hypochlorous acid.* [< Gk, < *hupo* under]

hypoallergenic (ˌhaɪpəʊˌæləˈdʒɛnɪk) *adj.* (of cosmetics) not likely to cause an allergic reaction.

hypoblast (ˈhaɪpəˌblæst) *n. Embryol.* the inner layer of an embryo at an early stage of development that becomes the endoderm.

hypocaust (ˈhaɪpəˌkɔːst) *n.* an ancient Roman heating system in which hot air circulated under the floor and between double walls. [C17: < L *hypocaustum,* < Gk, < *hupokaiein* to light a fire beneath, < HYPO- + *kaiein* to burn]

hypocentre (ˈhaɪpəʊˌsɛntə) *n.* the point immediately below the centre of explosion of a nuclear bomb. Also called: **ground zero.**

hypochlorite (ˌhaɪpəˈklɔːraɪt) *n.* any salt or ester of hypochlorous acid.

hypochlorous acid (ˌhaɪpəˈklɔːrəs) *n.* an unstable acid known only in solution and in the form of its salts: a strong oxidizing and bleaching agent. Formula: HOCl.

hypochondria (ˌhaɪpəˈkɒndrɪə) *n.* chronic abnormal anxiety concerning the state of one's health. Also called: **hypochondriasis** (ˌhaɪpəkɒnˈdraɪəsɪs). [C18: < LL: abdomen, supposedly the seat of melancholy, < Gk, < *hupokhondrios,* < HYPO- + *khondros* cartilage]

hypochondriac (ˌhaɪpəˈkɒndrɪˌæk) *n.* **1.** a person suffering from hypochondria. ~*adj. also* **hypochondriacal** (ˌhaɪpəkɒnˈdraɪəkˀl). **2.** relating to or suffering from hypochondria.

hypocorism (haɪˈpɒkəˌrɪzəm) *n.* a pet name, esp. one using a diminutive affix: *"Sally" is a hypocorism for "Sarah".* [C19: < Gk *hupokorisma,* < *hupokorizesthai* to use pet names, < *hypo-* beneath + *korizesthai,* < *korē* girl, *koros* boy] —**hypocoristic** (ˌhaɪpəkɔːˈrɪstɪk) *adj.*

hypocotyl (ˌhaɪpəˈkɒtɪl) *n.* the part of an embryo plant between the cotyledons and the radicle. [C19: < HYPO- + COTYL(EDON)]

hypocrisy (hɪˈpɒkrəsɪ) *n., pl.* **-sies.** **1.** the practice of professing standards, beliefs, etc., contrary to one's real character or actual behaviour. **2.** an act or instance of this.

hypocrite (ˈhɪpəkrɪt) *n.* a person who pretends to be what he is not. [C13: < OF *ipocrite,* via LL < Gk *hupokritēs* one who plays a part, < *hupokrinein* to feign, < *krinein* to judge] —ˌ**hypoˈcritical** *adj.* —ˌ**hypoˈcritically** *adv.*

hypocycloid (ˌhaɪpəˈsaɪklɔɪd) *n.* a curve described by a point on the circumference of a circle as the circle rolls around the inside of a fixed coplanar circle. —ˌ**hypocyˈcloidal** *adj.*

hypodermic (ˌhaɪpəˈdɜːmɪk) *adj.* **1.** of or relating to the region of the skin beneath the epidermis. **2.** injected beneath the skin. ~*n.* **3.** a hypodermic syringe or needle. **4.** a hypodermic injection. —ˌ**hypoˈdermically** *adv.*

hypodermic syringe *n. Med.* a type of syringe consisting of a hollow cylinder, usually of glass or plastic, a tightly fitting piston, and a hollow needle (**hypodermic needle**), used for withdrawing blood samples, etc.

hypodermis (ˌhaɪpəˈdɜːmɪs) *or* **hypoderm** *n.* **1.** *Bot.* a layer of thick-walled supportive or water-storing cells beneath the epidermis in some plants. **2.** *Zool.* the epidermis of arthropods, annelids, etc. [C19: < HYPO- + EPIDERMIS]

hypogastrium (ˌhaɪpəˈgæstrɪəm) *n., pl.* **-tria** (-trɪə). *Anat.* the lower front central region of the abdomen. [C17: < NL, < Gk *hupogastrion,* < HYPO- + *gastrion,* dim. of *gastēr* stomach]

hypogeal (ˌhaɪpəˈdʒiːəl) *or* **hypogeous** *adj.* occurring or living below the surface of the ground. [C19: < L *hypogēus,* < Gk, < HYPO- + *gē* earth]

hypogene (ˈhaɪpəˌdʒiːn) *adj.* formed or originating beneath the surface of the earth.

hypogeum (ˌhaɪpəˈdʒiːəm) *n., pl.* **-gea** (-ˈdʒiːə). an underground vault, esp. one used for burials. [C18: < L, < Gk *hupogeion;* see HYPOGEAL]

hypoid gear (ˈhaɪpɔɪd) *n.* a gear having a tooth form generated by a hypocycloidal curve. [C20: *hypoid,* shortened < HYPOCYCLOID]

hyponasty (ˈhaɪpəˌnæstɪ) *n.* increased growth of the lower surface of a plant part, resulting in an upward bending of the part. —ˌ**hypoˈnastic** *adj.*

hypophosphate (ˌhaɪpəˈfɒsfeɪt) *n.* any salt or ester of hypophosphoric acid.

hypophosphite (ˌhaɪpəˈfɒsfaɪt) *n.* any salt of hypophosphorous acid.

hypophosphoric acid (ˌhaɪpəfɒsˈfɒrɪk) *n.* a tetrabasic acid produced by the slow oxidation of phosphorus in moist air. Formula: $H_4P_2O_6$.

hypophosphorous acid (ˌhaɪpəˈfɒsfərəs) *n.* a monobasic acid and a reducing agent. Formula: H_3PO_2.

hypophysis (haɪˈpɒfɪsɪs) *n., pl.* **-ses** (-ˌsiːz). the technical name for **pituitary gland.** [C18: < Gk: outgrowth, < HYPO- + *phuein* to grow] —**hypophyseal** *or* **hypophysial** (ˌhaɪpəˈfɪzɪəl, haɪˌpɒfɪˈsɪəl) *adj.*

hypostasis (haɪˈpɒstəsɪs) *n., pl.* **-ses** (-ˌsiːz). **1.** *Metaphysics.* the essential nature of a substance. **2.** *Christianity.* **a.** any of the three persons of the Godhead. **b.** the one person of Christ in which the divine and human natures are united. **3.** the accumulation of blood in an organ or part as the result of poor circulation. [C16: < LL: substance, < Gk *hupostasis* foundation, < *huphistasthai,* < HYPO- + *histanai* to cause to stand] —**hypostatic** (ˌhaɪpəˈstætɪk) *or* ˌ**hypoˈstatical** *adj.*

hypostyle (ˈhaɪpəʊˌstaɪl) *adj.* **1.** having a roof supported by columns. ~*n.* **2.** a building constructed in this way.

hyposulphite (ˌhaɪpəˈsʌlfaɪt) *n.* another name for **sodium thiosulphate,** esp. when used as a photographic fixer. Often shortened to **hypo.**

hyposulphurous acid (ˌhaɪpəˈsʌlfərəs) *n.* an unstable acid known only in solution: a powerful reducing agent. Formula $H_2S_2O_4$.

hypotension (ˌhaɪpəʊˈtɛnʃən) *n. Pathol.* abnormally low blood pressure. —**hypotensive** (ˌhaɪpəʊˈtɛnsɪv) *adj.*

hypotenuse (haɪˈpɒtɪˌnjuːz) *n.* the side in a right-angled triangle that is opposite the right angle. Abbrev.: **hyp.** [C16: < L *hypotēnūsa,* < Gk *hupoteinousa grammē* subtending line, < HYPO- + *teinein* to stretch]

hypothalamus (ˌhaɪpəˈθæləməs) *n., pl.* **-mi** (-ˌmaɪ). a neural control centre at the base of the brain, concerned with hunger, thirst, satiety, and other autonomic functions. —**hypothalamic** (ˌhaɪpəθəˈlæmɪk) *adj.*

hypothec (haɪˈpɒθɪk) *n. Roman & Scots. Law.* a charge on property in favour of a creditor. [C16: < LL *hypotheca,* < Gk *hupothēkē* pledge, < *hupotithenai* to deposit as a security, < HYPO- + *tithenai* to place]

hypothecate (haɪˈpɒθɪˌkeɪt) *vb.* (*tr.*) *Law.* to pledge (personal property or a ship) as security for a debt without transferring possession or title. —**hyˌpotheˈcation** *n.* —**hyˈpotheˌcator** *n.*

hypothermia (ˌhaɪpəʊˈθɜːmɪə) *n.* **1.** *Pathol.* an abnormally low body temperature, as induced in the elderly by exposure to cold weather. **2.** *Med.* the intentional reduction of normal body temperature to reduce the patient's metabolic rate.

hypothesis (haɪˈpɒθɪsɪs) *n., pl.* **-ses** (-ˌsiːz). **1.** a suggested explanation for a group of facts or phenomena, either accepted as a basis for further verification (**working hypothesis**) or accepted as likely to be true. **2.** an assumption used in an argument; supposition. [C16: < Gk, < *hupotithenai* to propose, lit.: put under; see HYPO-, THESIS] —**hyˈpothesist** *n.*

hypothesize *or* **-ise** (haɪˈpɒθɪˌsaɪz) *vb.* to form or assume as a hypothesis. —**hyˈpotheˌsizer** *or* **-iser** *n.*

hypothetical (ˌhaɪpəˈθɛtɪkᵊl) *or* **hypothetic** *adj.* **1.** having the nature of a hypothesis. **2.** assumed or thought to exist. **3.** *Logic.* another word for **conditional** (sense 3). —ˌ**hypoˈthetically** *adv.*

hypothyroidism (ˌhaɪpəʊˈθaɪrɔɪˌdɪzəm) *n. Pathol.* **1.** insufficient production of thyroid hormones by the thyroid gland. **2.** any disorder, such as cretinism or myxoedema, resulting from this. —ˌ**hypoˈthyroid** *n., adj.*

hypotonic (ˌhaɪpəˈtɒnɪk) *adj.* **1.** *Pathol.* (of muscles) lacking normal tone or tension. **2.** (of a solution) having a lower osmotic pressure than that of a specified solution.

hypoxia (haɪˈpɒksɪə) *n.* deficiency in the amount of oxygen delivered to the body tissues. [C20: < HYPO- + OXY-² + -IA] —**hypoxic** (haɪˈpɒksɪk) *adj.*

hypso- *or before a vowel* **hyps-** *combining form.* indicating height: *hypsometry.* [< Gk *hupsos*]

hypsography (hɪpˈsɒgrəfɪ) *n.* the scientific study and mapping of the earth's topography above sea level.

hypsometer (hɪpˈsɒmɪtə) *n.* **1.** an instrument for measuring altitudes by determining the boiling point of water at a given altitude. **2.** any instrument used to calculate the heights of trees by triangulation.

hypsometry (hɪpˈsɒmɪtrɪ) *n.* (in mapping) the establishment of height above sea level.

hyrax (ˈhaɪræks) *n., pl.* **hyraxes** *or* **hyraces** (ˈhaɪrəˌsiːz). any of various agile herbivorous mammals of Africa and SW Asia. They resemble rodents but have feet with hooflike toes. Also called: **dassie.** [C19: < NL, < Gk *hurax* shrew-mouse]

hyssop (ˈhɪsəp) *n.* **1.** a widely cultivated Asian plant with spikes of small blue flowers and aromatic leaves, used as a condiment and in perfumery and folk medicine. **2.** a Biblical plant, used for sprinkling in the ritual practices of the Hebrews. [OE *ysope,* < L *hyssōpus,* < Gk *hussōpos,* of Semitic origin]

hysterectomy (ˌhɪstəˈrɛktəmɪ) *n., pl.* **-mies.** surgical removal of the uterus.

hysteresis (ˌhɪstəˈriːsɪs) *n. Physics.* the lag in a variable property of a system with respect to the effect producing it as this effect varies, esp. the phenomenon in which the magnetic induction of a ferromagnetic material lags behind the changing external field. [< Gk *husterēsis,* < *husteros* coming after] —**hysteretic** (ˌhɪstəˈrɛtɪk) *adj.*

hysteresis loop *n.* a closed curve showing the variation of the magnetic induction of a ferromagnetic material with the external magnetic field producing it, when this field is changed through a complete cycle.

hysteria (hɪˈstɪərɪə) *n.* **1.** a mental disorder characterized by emotional outbursts and, often, symptoms such as paralysis. **2.** any frenzied emotional state, esp. of laughter or crying. [C19: < NL, < L *hystericus* HYSTERIC]

hysteric (hɪˈstɛrɪk) *n.* **1.** a hysterical person. ~*adj.* **2.** hysterical. [C17: < L *hystericus,* lit.: of the womb, < Gk, < *hustera* womb; from the belief that hysteria in women originated in disorders of the womb]

hysterical (hɪˈstɛrɪkᵊl) *adj.* **1.** suggesting hysteria: *hysterical cries.* **2.** suffering from hysteria. **3.** *Inf.* wildly funny. —**hysˈterically** *adv.*

hysterics (hɪˈstɛrɪks) *n.* (*functioning as pl. or sing.*) **1.** an attack of hysteria. **2.** *Inf.* wild uncontrollable bursts of laughter.

hystero- *or before a vowel* **hyster-** *combining form.* the uterus: *hysterectomy.* [< Gk *hustera* womb]

hysteron proteron (ˈhɪstəˌrɒn ˈprɒtəˌrɒn) *n.* **1.** *Logic.* a fallacious argument in which the proposition to be proved is assumed as a premise. **2.** *Rhetoric.* a figure of speech in which the normal order of two sentences, clauses, etc., is reversed: *bred and born* (for *born and bred*). [C16: < LL, < Gk *husteron proteron* the latter (placed as) former]

hystricomorph (hɪˈstraɪkəʊˌmɔːf) *n.* **1.** any rodent of the suborder *Hystricomorpha,* which includes porcupines, cavies, agoutis, and chinchillas. ~*adj.* also: **hystricomorphic** (hɪˌstraɪkəʊˈmɔːfɪk). **2.** of the *Hystricomorpha.* [C19: < L *hystrix* porcupine, < Gk *hustrix*]

Hz *symbol for* hertz.

I

i *or* **I** (aɪ) *n., pl.* **i's, I's,** *or* **Is.** **1.** the ninth letter and third vowel of the English alphabet. **2.** any of several speech sounds represented by this letter. **3. a.** something shaped like an I. **b.** (*in combination*): *an I-beam.*

i *symbol for* the imaginary number $\sqrt{-1}$.

I[1] (aɪ) *pron.* (*subjective*) refers to the speaker or writer. [C12: < OE *ic;* cf. OSaxon *ik,* OHG *ih,* Sansk. *ahám*]

I[2] *symbol for:* **1.** *Chem.* iodine. **2.** *Physics.* current. **3.** *Physics.* isospin. ~ **4.** *the Roman numeral for* one. See **Roman numerals.**

I. *abbrev. for:* **1.** Independence. **2.** Independent. **3.** Institute. **4.** International. **5.** Island; Isle.

-ia *suffix forming nouns.* **1.** in place names: *Columbia.* **2.** in names of diseases: *pneumonia.* **3.** in words denoting condition or quality: *utopia.* **4.** in names of botanical genera and zoological classes: *Reptilia.* **5.** in collective nouns borrowed from Latin: *regalia.* [(for senses 1–4) NL, < L & Gk, suffix of fem. nouns; (for sense 5) < L, neuter pl. suffix]

IAEA *abbrev. for* International Atomic Energy Agency.

-ial *suffix forming adjectives.* of or relating to: *managerial.* [< L *-iālis,* adj. suffix; cf. -AL[1]]

iamb (ˈaɪæm, ˈaɪæmb) *or* **iambus** (aɪˈæmbəs) *n., pl.* **iambs, iambi** (aɪˈæmbaɪ), *or* **iambuses.** *Prosody.* **1.** a metrical foot of two syllables, a short one followed by a long one. **2.** a line of verse of such feet. [C19 *iamb,* < C16 *iambus,* < L, < Gk *iambos*]

iambic (aɪˈæmbɪk) *Prosody.* ~*adj.* **1.** of, relating to, or using an iamb. **2.** (in Greek literature) denoting a satirical verse written in iambs. ~*n.* **3.** a metrical foot, line, or stanza consisting of iambs. **4.** an ancient Greek satirical verse written in iambs.

-ian *suffix.* a variant of **-an:** *Etonian.* [< L *-iānus*]

-iana *suffix forming nouns.* a variant of **-ana.**

-iasis *or* **-asis** *n. combining form.* (in medicine) indicating a diseased condition: *psoriasis.* Cf. **-osis** (sense 2). [< NL, < Gk, suffix of action]

IATA (aɪˈɑːtə, iːˈɑːtə) *n. acronym for* International Air Transport Association.

-iatrics *n. combining form.* indicating medical care or treatment: *paediatrics.* [C19: < Gk, < *iasthai* to heal]

iatrogenic (aɪˌætrəʊˈdʒenɪk) *adj. Med.* (of an illness) induced in a patient as the result of a physician's action. —**iatrogenicity** (aɪˌætrəʊdʒɪˈnɪsɪtɪ) *n.*

-iatry *n. combining form.* indicating healing or medical treatment: *psychiatry.* Cf. **-iatrics.** [< NL *-iatria,* < Gk *iatreia* the healing art, < *iatros* healer, physician] —**-iatric** *adj. combining form.*

IBA (in Britain) *abbrev. for* Independent Broadcasting Authority.

Iberian (aɪˈbɪərɪən) *n.* **1.** a member of a group of ancient Caucasoid peoples who inhabited the Iberian Peninsula, in SW Europe, in classical times. **2.** a native or inhabitant of the Iberian Peninsula; a Spaniard or Portuguese. **3.** a native or inhabitant of ancient Iberia. ~*adj.* **4.** relating to the pre-Roman peoples of the Iberian Peninsula or of Caucasian Iberia. **5.** of or relating to the Iberian Peninsula, its inhabitants, or any of their languages.

iberis (aɪˈbɪərɪs) *n.* any of various Mediterranean plants with white, lilac, or purple flowers. Also called: **candytuft.** [< Gk *ibēris* pepperwort]

ibex (ˈaɪbɛks) *n., pl.* **ibexes, ibices** (ˈɪbɪˌsiːz, ˈaɪ-), *or* **ibex.** any of three species of wild goat of mountainous regions of Europe, Asia, and North Africa, having large backward-curving horns. [C17: < L: chamois]

ibid. *or* **ib.** (referring to a book, etc., previously cited) *abbrev. for* ibidem. [L: in the same place]

ibis (ˈaɪbɪs) *n., pl.* **ibises** *or* **ibis.** any of various wading birds such as the sacred ibis, that occur in warm regions and have a long thin down-curved bill. [C14: via L < Gk, < Egyptian *hby*]

-ible *suffix forming adjectives.* a variant of **-able.** —**-ibly** *suffix forming adverbs.* —**-ibility** *suffix forming nouns.*

Ibo *or* **Igbo** (ˈiːbəʊ) *n.* **1.** (*pl.* **-bos** *or* **-bo**) a member of a Negroid people of W Africa, living in S Nigeria. **2.** their language, belonging to the Niger-Congo family.

IBRD *abbrev. for* International Bank for Reconstruction and Development (the World Bank).

ibuprofen (ˌaɪbjuːˈprəʊfən) *n.* a drug that relieves pain and reduces inflammation: used to treat arthritis and muscular strains.

i/c *abbrev. for:* **1.** in charge (of). **2.** internal combustion.

-ic *suffix forming adjectives.* **1.** of, relating to, or resembling: *periodic.* See also **-ical.** **2.** (in chemistry) indicating that an element is chemically combined in the higher of two possible valence states: *ferric.* Cf. **-ous** (sense 2). [< L *-icus* or Gk *-ikos; -ic* also occurs in nouns that represent a substantive use of adjectives (*magic*) and in nouns borrowed directly from L or Gk (*critic, music*)]

ICA *abbrev. for:* **1.** (in Britain) Institute of Contemporary Arts. **2.** Institute of Chartered Accountants.

-ical *suffix forming adjectives.* a variant of **-ic,** but having a less literal application than corresponding adjectives ending in *-ic: economical.* [< L *-icālis*] —**-ically** *suffix forming adverbs.*

ICAO *abbrev. for* International Civil Aviation Organization.

ICBM *abbrev. for* intercontinental ballistic missile.

ice (aɪs) *n.* **1.** water in the solid state, formed by freezing liquid water. Related adj.: **glacial.** **2.** a portion of ice cream. **3.** *Sl.* a diamond or diamonds. **4. break the ice. a.** to relieve shyness, etc., esp. between strangers. **b.** to be the first of a group to do something. **5. on ice.** in abeyance; pending. **6. on thin ice.** unsafe; vulnerable. ~*vb.* **7.** (often foll. by *up, over,* etc.) to form ice; freeze. **8.** (*tr.*) to mix with ice or chill (a drink, etc.). **9.** (*tr.*) to cover (a cake, etc.) with icing. [OE *īs*] —**iced** *adj.*

ICE (in Britain) *abbrev. for* Institution of Civil Engineers.

Ice. *abbrev. for* Iceland(ic).

ice age *n.* another name for **glacial period.**

ice axe *n.* a light axe used by mountaineers for cutting footholds in ice.

ice bag *n.* a waterproof bag used as an ice pack.

iceberg (ˈaɪsbɜːg) *n.* **1.** a large mass of ice floating in the sea. **2. tip of the iceberg.** the small visible part of something, esp. a problem, that is much larger. **3.** *Sl., chiefly U.S.* a person considered to have a cold or reserved manner. **4.** *Austral. inf.* a person who swims or surfs in winter. [C18: prob. part translation of MDu. *ijsberg* ice mountain; cf. Norwegian *isberg*]

iceblink (ˈaɪsˌblɪŋk) *n.* a reflected glare in the sky over an ice field. Also called: **blink.**

icebound (ˈaɪsˌbaʊnd) *adj.* covered or made immobile by ice; frozen in: *an icebound ship.*

icebox (ˈaɪsˌbɒks) *n.* **1.** a compartment in a refrigerator for storing or making ice. **2.** an insulated cabinet packed with ice for storing food. **3.** a U.S. and Canad. name for **refrigerator.**

icebreaker (ˈaɪsˌbreɪkə) *n.* **1.** Also called: **iceboat.** a vessel with a reinforced bow for breaking up the ice in bodies of water. **2.** a device for breaking ice into smaller pieces. **3.** something intended to relieve shyness between strangers.

ice bucket *n.* a bucket-shaped container in which ice cubes are kept to be used for serving with drinks or into which a wine bottle is plunged to keep it cool at table.

icecap (ˈaɪsˌkæp) *n.* a thick mass of glacial ice that permanently covers an area, such as the polar regions or the peak of a mountain.

ice cream *n.* a sweetened frozen liquid, made from cream, milk, or a custard base, flavoured in various ways.

ice dance *n.* any of a number of dances, mostly based on ballroom dancing, performed by a couple skating on ice. —**ice dancer** *n.* —**ice dancing** *n.*

icefall (ˈaɪsˌfɔːl) *n.* a steep part of a glacier that resembles a frozen waterfall.

ice field *n.* **1.** a large ice floe. **2.** a large mass of ice permanently covering an extensive area of land.

ice floe *n.* a sheet of ice, of variable size, floating in the sea. See also **ice field** (sense 1).

ice hockey *n.* a game played on ice by two teams wearing skates, who try to propel a flat puck into their opponents' goal with long sticks.

ice house *n.* a building for storing ice.

Icelander (ˈaɪslændə, ˈaɪsləndə) *n.* a native or inhabitant of Iceland.

Icelandic (aɪsˈlændɪk) *adj.* **1.** of or relating to Iceland, its people, or their language. ~*n.* **2.** the official language of Iceland.

Iceland poppy (ˈaɪslənd) *n.* any of various arctic poppies with white or yellow nodding flowers.

Iceland spar *n.* a pure transparent variety of calcite with double-refracting crystals.

ice lolly *n. Brit. inf.* a water ice or an ice cream on a stick. Also called: **lolly.**

ice pack *n.* **1.** a bag or folded cloth containing ice, applied to a part of the body to reduce swelling, etc. **2.** another name for **pack ice. 3.** a sachet containing a gel that retains its temperature for an extended period of time, used esp. in cool bags.

ice pick *n.* a pointed tool used for breaking ice.

ice plant *n.* a low-growing plant of southern Africa, with fleshy leaves covered with icelike hairs and pink or white rayed flowers.

ice point *n.* the temperature at which a mixture of ice and water are in equilibrium at a pressure of one atmosphere. It is 0° on the Celsius scale and 32° on the Fahrenheit scale. Cf. **steam point.**

ice sheet *n.* a thick layer of ice covering a large area of land for a long time, esp. the layer that covered much of the N hemisphere during the last glacial period.

ice shelf *n.* a thick mass of ice that is permanently attached to the land but projects into and floats on the sea.

ice skate *n.* **1.** a boot having a steel blade fitted to the sole to enable the wearer to glide over ice. **2.** the steel blade on such a boot. ~*vb.* **ice-skate. 3.** (*intr.*) to glide over ice on ice skates. —ˈ**ice-**ˌ**skater** *n.*

ice station *n.* a scientific research station in polar regions, where ice movement, weather, and environmental conditions are monitored.

IChemE *abbrev. for* Institution of Chemical Engineers.

I Ching (ˈiː ˈtʃɪŋ) *n.* an ancient Chinese book of divination and a source of Confucian and Taoist philosophy.

ichneumon (ɪkˈnjuːmən) *n.* a mongoose of Africa and S Europe, having greyish-brown speckled fur. [C16: via L < Gk, lit.: tracker, hunter, < *ikhneuein* to track, < *ikhnos* a footprint; so named from the animal's alleged ability to locate the eggs of crocodiles]

ichneumon fly *or* **wasp** *n.* any hymenopterous insect whose larvae are parasitic in caterpillars and other insect larvae.

ichnography (ɪkˈnɒgrəfɪ) *n.* **1.** the art of drawing ground plans. **2.** the ground plan of a building. [C16: < L, < Gk, < *ikhnos* trace, track] —**ichnographic** (ˌɪknəˈgræfɪk) *or* ˌ**ichno**ˈ**graphical** *adj.*

ichor (ˈaɪkɔː) *n.* **1.** *Greek myth.* the fluid said to flow in the veins of the gods. **2.** *Pathol.* a foul-smelling watery discharge from a wound or ulcer. [C17: < Gk *ikhōr*, <?] —ˈ**ichorous** *adj.*

ichthyo- *or before a vowel* **ichthy-** *combining form.* indicating or relating to fishes: *ichthyology.* [< L, < Gk *ikhthus* fish]

ichthyoid (ˈɪkθɪˌɔɪd) *adj. also* **ichthyoidal. 1.** resembling a fish. ~*n.* **2.** a fishlike vertebrate.

ichthyology (ˌɪkθɪˈɒlədʒɪ) *n.* the study of fishes. —**ichthyologic** (ˌɪkθɪəˈlɒdʒɪk) *or* ˌ**ichthyo**ˈ**logical** *adj.* —ˌ**ichthy**ˈ**ologist** *n.*

ichthyosaur (ˈɪkθɪəˌsɔː) *or* **ichthyosaurus** (ˌɪkθɪəˈsɔːrəs) *n., pl.* **-saurs, -sauruses,** *or* **-sauri** (-ˈsɔːraɪ). an extinct marine Mesozoic reptile which had a porpoise-like body with dorsal and tail fins and paddle-like limbs. See also **plesiosaur.**

ichthyosis (ˌɪkθɪˈəʊsɪs) *n.* a congenital disease in which the skin is coarse, dry, and scaly. —**ichthyotic** (ˌɪkθɪˈɒtɪk) *adj.*

ICI *abbrev. for* Imperial Chemical Industries.

-ician *suffix forming nouns.* indicating a person skilled or involved in a subject or activity: *physician; beautician.* [< F *-icien;* see -IC, -IAN]

icicle (ˈaɪsɪkᵊl) *n.* a hanging spike of ice formed by the freezing of dripping water. [C14: < ICE + *ickel,* < OE *gicel* icicle, rel. to ON *jökull* glacier]

icing (ˈaɪsɪŋ) *n.* **1.** Also (esp. U.S. and Canad.): **frosting.** a sugar preparation, variously flavoured and coloured, for coating and decorating cakes, etc. **2.** any unexpected extra or bonus (esp. in **icing on the cake**). **3.** the formation of ice, as on a ship, due to the freezing of moisture in the atmosphere.

icing sugar *n. Brit.* a very finely ground sugar used for icings, confections, etc. U.S. term: **confectioners' sugar.**

icon *or* **ikon** (ˈaɪkɒn) *n.* **1.** a representation of Christ or a saint, esp. one painted in oil on a wooden panel in a traditional Byzantine style and venerated in the Eastern Church. **2.** an image, picture, etc. **3.** a symbol resembling or analogous to the thing it represents. [C16: < L, < Gk *eikōn* image, < *eikenai* to be like]

icono- *or before a vowel* **icon-** *combining form.* indicating an image or likeness: *iconology.*

iconoclast (aɪˈkɒnəˌklæst) *n.* **1.** a person who attacks established or traditional concepts, principles, etc. **2. a.** a destroyer of religious images or objects. **b.** an adherent of a heretical iconoclastic movement within the Greek Orthodox Church from 725 to 842 A.D. [C16: < LL, < LGk *eikonoklastes,* < *eikōn* icon + *klastes* breaker] —**i**ˌ**cono**ˈ**clastic** *adj.* —**i**ˈ**cono**ˌ**clasm** *n.*

iconography (ˌaɪkɒˈnɒgrəfɪ) *n., pl.* **-phies. 1. a.** the symbols used in a work of art. **b.** the conventional significance attached to such symbols. **2.** a collection of pictures of a particular subject. **3.** the representation of the subjects of icons or portraits, esp. on coins. —ˌ**ico**ˈ**nographer** *n.* —**iconographic** (aɪˌkɒnəˈgræfɪk) *or* **i**ˌ**cono**ˈ**graphical** *adj.*

iconolatry (ˌaɪkɒˈnɒlətrɪ) *n.* the worship of icons as idols. —ˌ**ico**ˈ**nolater** *n.* —ˌ**ico**ˈ**nolatrous** *adj.*

iconology (ˌaɪkɒˈnɒlədʒɪ) *n.* **1.** the study of icons. **2.** icons collectively. **3.** the symbolic representation of icons. —**iconological** (aɪˌkɒnəˈlɒdʒɪkᵊl) *adj.* —ˌ**ico**ˈ**nologist** *n.*

iconoscope (aɪˈkɒnəˌskəʊp) *n.* a television camera tube in which an electron beam scans a surface, converting an optical image into electrical pulses.

iconostasis (ˌaɪkəʊˈnɒstəsɪs) *or* **iconostas** (aɪˈkɒnəˌstæs) *n., pl.* **iconostases** (ˌaɪkəʊˈnɒstəˌsiːz). *Eastern Church.* screen with doors and icons set in tiers, which separates the sanctuary from the nave. [C19: Church L, < LGk *eikonostasion* shrine, lit.: area where images are placed, < *icono-* + *histanai* to stand]

icosahedron (ˌaɪkəsəˈhiːdrən) *n., pl.* **-drons** *or* **-dra** (-drə). a solid figure having 20 faces. [C16: < Gk, < *eikosi* twenty + *-edron* -HEDRON] —ˌ**icosa**ˈ**hedral** *adj.*

-ics *suffix forming nouns; functioning as sing.* **1.** indicating a science, art, or matters relating to a particular subject: *politics*. **2.** indicating certain activities: *acrobatics*. [pl. of *-ic*, representing L *-ica*, < Gk *-ika*]

ictus (ˈɪktəs) *n., pl.* **-tuses** *or* **-tus. 1.** *Prosody*. metrical or rhythmical stress in verse feet, as contrasted with the stress accent on words. **2.** *Med.* a sudden attack or stroke. [C18: < L *icere* to strike] —ˈ**ictal** *adj.*

ICU *abbrev. for* intensive care unit.

icy (ˈaɪsɪ) *adj.* **icier, iciest. 1.** made of, covered with, or containing ice. **2.** resembling ice. **3.** freezing or very cold. **4.** cold or reserved in manner; aloof. —ˈ**icily** *adv.* —ˈ**iciness** *n.*

id (ɪd) *n. Psychoanal.* the primitive instincts and energies in the unconscious mind that, modified by the ego and the superego, underlie all psychic activity. [C20: NL, < L: it; used to render G *Es*]

ID *abbrev. for* identification.

id. *abbrev. for* idem.

I'd (aɪd) *contraction of* I had *or* I would.

-id[1] *suffix forming nouns and adjectives.* indicating members of a zoological family: *cyprinid*. [< NL *-idae* or *-ida*, < Gk *-idēs* suffix indicating offspring]

-id[2] *suffix forming nouns.* a variant of **-ide.**

IDA *abbrev. for* International Development Association.

-idae *suffix forming plural proper nouns.* indicating names of zoological families: *Felidae*. [NL, < L, < Gk *-idai*, suffix indicating offspring]

-ide *or* **-id** *suffix forming nouns.* **1.** (*added to the combining form of the nonmetallic or electronegative elements*) indicating a binary compound: *sodium chloride*. **2.** indicating an organic compound derived from another: *acetanilide*. **3.** indicating one of a class of compounds or elements: *peptide*. [< G *-id*, < F *oxide* OXIDE, based on the suffix of *acide* ACID]

idea (aɪˈdɪə) *n.* **1.** any product of mental activity; thought. **2.** the thought of something: *the idea appals me*. **3.** a belief; opinion. **4.** a scheme, intention, plan, etc. **5.** a vague notion; inkling: *he had no idea of the truth*. **6.** a person's conception of something: *her idea of honesty is not the same as mine*. **7.** significance or purpose: *the idea of the game is to discover the murderer*. **8.** *Philosophy.* **a.** an immediate object of thought or perception. **b.** (*sometimes cap.*) (in Plato) the universal essence or archetype of any class of things or concepts. **9. get ideas.** to become ambitious, restless, etc. **10. not one's idea of.** not what one regards as (hard work, a holiday, etc.). **11. that's an idea.** that is worth considering. **12. the very idea!** that is preposterous, unreasonable, etc. [C16: via LL < Gk: model, notion, < *idein* to see]

ideal (aɪˈdɪəl) *n.* **1.** a conception of something that is perfect. **2.** a person or thing considered to represent perfection. **3.** something existing only as an idea. **4.** a pattern or model, esp. of ethical behaviour. ~*adj.* **5.** conforming to an ideal. **6.** of, involving, or existing in the form of an idea. **7.** *Philosophy.* **a.** of or relating to a highly desirable and possible state of affairs. **b.** of or relating to idealism. —iˈ**deally** *adv.* —iˈ**dealness** *n.*

ideal element *n.* any element added to a mathematical theory in order to eliminate special cases. The ideal element $i = \sqrt{-1}$ allows all algebraic equations to be solved.

ideal gas *n.* a hypothetical gas which obeys Boyle's law exactly at all temperatures and pressures, and which has internal energy that depends only upon the temperature.

idealism (aɪˈdɪəˌlɪzəm) *n.* **1.** belief in or pursuance of ideals. **2.** the tendency to represent things in their ideal forms, rather than as they are. **3.** *Philosophy.* the doctrine that material objects and the external world do not exist in reality, but are creations of the mind. Cf. **materialism.** —iˈ**dealist** *n.* —iˌ**dealˈistic** *adj.* —iˌ**dealˈistically** *adv.*

idealize *or* **-ise** (aɪˈdɪəˌlaɪz) *vb.* **1.** to consider or represent (something) as ideal. **2.** (*tr.*) to portray as ideal; glorify. **3.** (*intr.*) to form an ideal or ideals. —iˌ**dealiˈzation** *or* **-iˈsation** *n.* —iˈ**dealˌizer** *or* **-ˌiser** *n.*

idée fixe *French.* (ide fiks) *n., pl.* ***idées fixes*** (ide fiks). a fixed idea; obsession.

idem *Latin.* (ˈaɪdɛm, ˈɪdɛm) *pron., adj.* the same: used to refer to an article, chapter, etc., previously cited.

identic (aɪˈdɛntɪk) *adj. Diplomacy.* (esp. of opinions expressed by two or more governments) having the same wording or intention regarding another power.

identical (aɪˈdɛntɪkᵊl) *adj.* **1.** being the same: *we got the identical hotel room as last year*. **2.** exactly alike or equal. **3.** designating either or both of a pair of twins of the same sex who developed from a single fertilized ovum that split into two. Cf. **fraternal** (sense 3). [C17: < Med. L *identicus*, < L *idem* the same] —iˈ**dentically** *adv.*

identification (aɪˌdɛntɪfɪˈkeɪʃən) *n.* **1.** the act of identifying or the state of being identified. **2. a.** something that identifies a person or thing. **b.** (*as modifier*): *an identification card*. **3.** *Psychol.* **a.** the process of recognizing specific objects as the result of remembering. **b.** the process by which one incorporates aspects of another person's personality. **c.** the transferring of a response from one situation to another because the two bear similar features.

identification parade *n.* a group of persons, including one suspected of a crime, assembled for the purpose of discovering whether a witness can identify the suspect.

identify (aɪˈdɛntɪˌfaɪ) *vb.* **-fying, -fied.** (*mainly tr.*) **1.** to prove or recognize as being a certain person or thing; determine the identity of. **2.** to consider as the same or equivalent. **3.** (*also intr.*; often foll. by *with*) to consider (oneself) as similar to another. **4.** to determine the taxonomic classification of (a plant or animal). **5.** (*intr.*; usually foll. by *with*) *Psychol.* to engage in identification. —iˈ**dentiˌfiable** *adj.* —iˈ**dentiˌfier** *n.*

Identikit (aɪˈdɛntɪˌkɪt) *n. Trademark.* **a.** a set of transparencies of typical facial characteristics that can be superimposed on one another to build up a picture of a person sought by the police. **b.** (*as modifier*): *an Identikit picture*.

identity (aɪˈdɛntɪtɪ) *n., pl.* **-ties. 1. a.** the state of having unique identifying characteristics. **b.** (*as modifier*): *an identity card*. **2.** the individual characteristics by which a person or thing is recognized. **3.** the state of being the same in nature, quality, etc.: *linked by the identity of their tastes*. **4.** the state of being the same as a person or thing described or known: *the identity of the stolen goods was soon established*. **5.** *Maths.* **a.** an equation that is valid for all values of its variables, as in $(x - y)(x + y) = x^2 - y^2$. Often denoted by the symbol ≡. **b.** Also called: **identity element.** a member of a set that when operating on another member, *x*, produces that member *x*: the identity for multiplication of numbers is 1 since $x.1 = 1.x = x$. **6.** *Logic.* the relationship between an object and itself. **7.** *Austral. inf.* a well-known local person; figure: *a Barwidgee identity*. **8.** *Austral. & N.Z. inf.* an eccentric; character: *an old identity in the town*. [C16: < LL *identitās*, < L *idem* the same]

ideo- *combining form.* of or indicating idea or ideas: *ideology*. [< F *idéo-*, < Gk *idea* IDEA]

ideogram (ˈɪdɪəʊˌgræm) *or* **ideograph** (ˈɪdɪəʊˌgrɑːf) *n.* **1.** a sign or symbol, used in a writing system such as that of China, that directly represents a concept or thing, rather than a word for it. **2.** any graphic sign or symbol, such as % or &.

ideography (ˌɪdɪˈɒgrəfɪ) *n.* the use of ideograms to communicate ideas.

ideology (ˌaɪdɪˈɒlədʒɪ) *n., pl.* **-gies. 1.** a body of ideas that reflects the beliefs of a nation, political system, class, etc. **2.** speculation that is imaginary or visionary. **3.** the study of the nature and origin of ideas. —**ideological** (ˌaɪdɪəˈlɒdʒɪkᵊl) or ˌ**ideo'logic** *adj.* —ˌ**ideo'logically** *adv.* —ˌ**ide'ologist** *n.*

ides (aɪdz) *n.* (*functioning as sing.*) (in the Roman calendar) the 15th day in March, May, July, and October and the 13th day of each other month. [C15: < OF, < L *īdūs* (pl.), <?]

id est *Latin.* ('ɪd 'ɛst) the full form of **i.e.**

idiocy ('ɪdɪəsɪ) *n., pl.* **-cies. 1.** (*not in technical usage*) severe mental retardation. **2.** foolishness; stupidity. **3.** a foolish act or remark.

idiom ('ɪdɪəm) *n.* **1.** a group of words whose meaning cannot be predicted from the constituent words: (*It was raining*) *cats and dogs.* **2.** linguistic usage that is grammatical and natural to native speakers. **3.** the characteristic vocabulary or usage of a specific human group or subject. **4.** the characteristic artistic style of an individual, school, etc. [C16: < L *idiōma* peculiarity of language, < Gk *idios* private, separate] —**idiomatic** (ˌɪdɪə'mætɪk) *adj.* —ˌ**idio'matically** *adv.*

idiosyncrasy (ˌɪdɪəʊ'sɪŋkrəsɪ) *n., pl.* **-sies. 1.** a tendency, type of behaviour, etc., of a person; quirk. **2.** the composite physical or psychological make-up of a person. **3.** an abnormal reaction of an individual to specific foods, drugs, etc. [C17: < Gk, < *idios* private, separate + *sunkrasis* mixture, temperament] —**idiosyncratic** (ˌɪdɪəʊsɪŋ'krætɪk) *adj.* —ˌ**idiosyn'cratically** *adv.*

idiot ('ɪdɪət) *n.* **1.** a person with severe mental retardation. **2.** a foolish or senseless person. [C13: < L *idiōta* ignorant person, < Gk *idiōtēs* private person, ignoramus]

idiot board *n.* a slang name for **autocue.**

idiot box *n. Sl.* a television set.

idiotic (ˌɪdɪ'ɒtɪk) *adj.* of or resembling an idiot; foolish; senseless. —ˌ**idi'otically** *adv.*

idiot savant ('iːdjəʊ sæ'vɑ̃, 'ɪdɪət 'sævənt) *n., pl.* **idiots savants** ('iːdjəʊ sæ'vɑ̃) *or* **idiot savants.** a person of subnormal intelligence who performs brilliantly at some specialized intellectual task.

idiot tape *n. Computers.* a tape that prints out information in a continuous stream, with no line breaks.

idle ('aɪd'l) *adj.* **1.** unemployed or unoccupied; inactive. **2.** not operating or being used. **3.** (of money) not used to earn interest, etc. **4.** not wanting to work; lazy. **5.** (*usually prenominal*) frivolous or trivial: *idle pleasures.* **6.** ineffective or powerless; vain. **7.** without basis; unfounded. ~*vb.* **8.** (when *tr.*, often foll. by *away*) to waste or pass (time) fruitlessly or inactively. **9.** (*intr.*) (of a shaft, etc.) to turn without doing useful work. **10.** (*intr.*) (of an engine) to run at low speed with the transmission disengaged. [OE *īdel*] —'**idleness** *n.* —'**idly** *adv.*

idle pulley *or* **idler pulley** *n.* a freely rotating pulley used to control the tension or direction of a belt. Also called: **idler.**

idler ('aɪdlə) *n.* **1.** a person who idles. **2.** another name for **idle pulley** or **idle wheel.**

idle wheel *n.* a gearwheel interposed between two others to transmit torque without changing the direction of rotation or the velocity ratio. Also called: **idler.**

idol ('aɪd'l) *n.* **1.** a material object that is worshipped as a god. **2.** *Christianity, Judaism.* any being (other than the one God) to which divine honour is paid. **3.** a person who is revered, admired, or highly loved. [C13: < LL, < L: image, < Gk, < *eidos* shape, form]

idolatry (aɪ'dɒlətrɪ) *n.* **1.** the worship of idols. **2.** great devotion or reverence. —**i'dolater** *n. or* **i'dolatress** *fem. n.* —**i'dolatrous** *adj.*

idolize *or* **-ise** ('aɪdəˌlaɪz) *vb.* **1.** (*tr.*) to admire or revere greatly. **2.** (*tr.*) to worship as an idol. **3.** (*intr.*) to worship idols. —ˌ**idoli'zation** *or* **-i'sation** *n.* —'**idolˌizer** *or* **-ˌiser** *n.*

idolum (ɪ'dəʊləm) *n.* **1.** a mental picture; idea. **2.** a false idea; fallacy. [C17: < L: IDOL]

IDP *abbrev. for* integrated data processing.

idyll *or U.S.* (*sometimes*) **idyl** ('ɪdɪl) *n.* **1.** a poem or prose work describing an idealized rural life, pastoral scenes, etc. **2.** a charming or picturesque scene or event. **3.** a piece of music with a pastoral character. [C17: < L, < Gk *eidullion,* < *eidos* shape, (literary) form] —**i'dyllic** *adj.* —**i'dyllically** *adv.*

IE *abbrev. for* Indo-European (languages).

i.e. *abbrev. for* id est. [L: that is (to say); in other words]

-ie *suffix forming nouns.* a variant of **-y**[2]: *groupie.*

IEE *abbrev. for* Institution of Electrical Engineers.

-ier *suffix forming nouns.* a variant of **-eer:** *brigadier.* [< OE *-ere* -ER[1] or (in some words) < OF *-ier,* < L *-ārius* -ARY]

if (ɪf) *conj.* (*subordinating*) **1.** in case that, or on condition that: *if you try hard it might work.* **2.** used to introduce an indirect question. In this sense, *if* approaches the meaning of *whether.* **3.** even though: *an attractive if awkward girl.* **4. a.** used to introduce expressions of desire, with *only: if I had only known.* **b.** used to introduce exclamations of surprise, dismay, etc.: *if this doesn't top everything!* ~*n.* **5.** an uncertainty or doubt: *the big if is whether our plan will work.* **6.** a condition or stipulation: *I won't have any ifs or buts.* [OE *gif*]

IF *or* **i.f.** *Electronics. abbrev. for* intermediate frequency.

IFC *abbrev. for* International Finance Corporation.

-iferous *suffix forming adjectives.* containing or yielding: *carboniferous.*

iffy ('ɪfɪ) *adj.* **-fier, -fiest.** *Inf.* uncertain or subject to contingency. [C20: < IF + -Y[1]]

-ify *suffix forming verbs.* a variant of **-fy:** *intensify.* **—-ification** *suffix forming nouns.*

igloo *or* **iglu** ('ɪgluː) *n., pl.* **-loos** *or* **-lus. 1.** a dome-shaped Eskimo house, built of blocks of solid snow. **2.** a hollow made by a seal in the snow over its breathing hole in the ice. [C19: < Eskimo *igdlu* house]

igneous ('ɪgnɪəs) *adj.* **1.** (of rocks) derived from magma or lava that has solidified on or below the earth's surface. **2.** of or relating to fire. [C17: < L *igneus* fiery, < *ignis* fire]

ignis fatuus ('ɪgnɪs 'fætjʊəs) *n., pl.* **ignes fatui** ('ɪgniːz 'fætjʊˌaɪ). another name for **will-o'-the-wisp.** [C16: < Med. L, lit.: foolish fire]

ignite (ɪg'naɪt) *vb.* **1.** to catch fire or set fire to; burn or cause to burn. **2.** (*tr.*) *Chem.* to heat strongly. [C17: < L, < *ignis* fire] —**ig'nitable** *or* **ig'nitible** *adj.* —**igˌnita'bility** *or* **igˌniti'bility** *n.* —**ig'niter** *n.*

ignition (ɪg'nɪʃən) *n.* **1.** the act or process of initiating combustion. **2.** the process of igniting the fuel in an internal-combustion engine. **3.** (preceded by *the*) the devices used to ignite the fuel in an internal-combustion engine.

ignition key *n.* the key used in a motor vehicle to turn the switch that connects the battery to the ignition system.

ignitron (ɪg'naɪtrɒn, 'ɪgnɪˌtrɒn) *n.* a rectifier controlled by a subsidiary electrode, the igniter, partially immersed in a mercury cathode. A current passed between igniter and cathode forms a hot spot sufficient to strike an arc between cathode and anode. [C20: < *igniter* + ELECTRON]

ignoble (ɪg'nəʊb'l) *adj.* **1.** dishonourable; base; despicable. **2.** of low birth or origins; humble; common. **3.** of low quality; inferior. [C16: < L, < IN-[1] + OL *gnōbilis* NOBLE] —ˌ**igno'bility** *or* **ig'nobleness** *n.* —**ig'nobly** *adv.*

ignominy ('ɪgnəˌmɪnɪ) *n., pl.* **-minies. 1.** disgrace or public shame; dishonour. **2.** a cause of disgrace; a shameful act. [C16: < L *ignōminia* disgrace, < *ig-* (see IN-[2]) + *nōmen* name, reputation] —ˌ**igno'minious** *adj.* —ˌ**igno'miniously** *adv.* —ˌ**igno'miniousness** *n.*

ignoramus (ˌɪgnə'reɪməs) *n., pl.* **-muses.** an ignorant person; fool. [C16: < legal L, lit.: we have no knowledge of, < L *ignōrāre* to be ignorant of; see IGNORE; modern usage originated from use of *Ignoramus* as the name of an unlettered lawyer in a play by G. Ruggle, 17th-century E dramatist]

ignorance ('ɪgnərəns) *n.* lack of knowledge,

information, or education; the state of being ignorant.

ignorant (ˈɪgnərənt) *adj.* **1.** lacking in knowledge or education; unenlightened. **2.** (*postpositive;* often foll. by *of*) lacking in awareness or knowledge (of): *ignorant of the law.* **3.** resulting from or showing lack of knowledge or awareness: *an ignorant remark.* —ˈ**ignorantly** *adv.*

ignore (ɪgˈnɔː) *vb.* (*tr.*) to fail or refuse to notice; disregard. [C17: < L *ignōrāre* not to know, < *ignārus* ignorant of] —**igˈnorer** *n.*

iguana (ɪˈgwɑːnə) *n.* either of two large tropical American arboreal herbivorous lizards, esp. the common iguana, having a greyish-green body with a row of spines along the back. [C16: < Sp., < Amerind *iwana*] —**iˈguanian** *n., adj.*

iguanodon (ɪˈgwɑːnəˌdɒn) *n.* a massive herbivorous long-tailed bipedal dinosaur common in Europe and N Africa in Jurassic and Cretaceous times. [C19: NL, < IGUANA + Gk *odōn* tooth]

IHC (in New Zealand) *abbrev. for* intellectually handicapped child.

IHS the first three letters of the name Jesus in Greek (ΙΗΣΟΥΣ), often used as a Christian emblem.

ikebana (ˌiːkəˈbɑːnə) *n.* the Japanese decorative art of flower arrangement.

ikon (ˈaɪkɒn) *n.* a variant spelling of **icon.**

il- *prefix.* a variant of **in-**[1] and **in-**[2] before *l.*

-ile *or* **-il** *suffix forming adjectives and nouns.* indicating capability, liability, or a relationship with something: *agile; juvenile.* [via F < L or directly < L *-īlis*] —**-ility** *suffix forming nouns.*

ileitis (ˌɪlɪˈaɪtɪs) *n.* inflammation of the ileum.

ileostomy (ˌɪlɪˈɒstəmɪ) *n., pl.* **-mies.** the surgical formation of a permanent opening through the abdominal wall into the ileum.

ileum (ˈɪlɪəm) *n.* the part of the small intestine between the jejunum and the caecum. [C17: NL, < L *īlium, īleum* flank, groin, <?] —ˈ**ileˌac** *adj.*

ilex (ˈaɪlɛks) *n.* **1.** any of a genus of trees or shrubs such as the holly and inkberry. **2.** another name for the **holm oak.** [C16: < L]

ilium (ˈɪlɪəm) *n., pl.* **-ia** (-ɪə). the uppermost and widest of the three sections of the hipbone.

ilk (ɪlk) *n.* **1.** a type; class; sort (esp. in **of that, his,** etc., **ilk**): *people of that ilk should not be allowed here.* **2. of that ilk.** *Scot.* of the place of the same name: to indicate that the person is laird of the place named: *Moncrieff of that ilk.* [OE *ilca* the same family, same kind]

▷ **Usage.** Although the use of *ilk* in sense 1 is often condemned as being the result of a misunderstanding of the original Scottish expression, it is nevertheless well established and generally acceptable.

ill (ɪl) *adj.* **worse, worst. 1.** (*usually postpositive*) not in good health; sick. **2.** characterized by or intending harm, etc.; hostile: *ill deeds.* **3.** causing pain, harm, adversity, etc. **4.** ascribing or imputing evil to something referred to: *ill repute.* **5.** promising an unfavourable outcome; unpropitious: *an ill omen.* **6.** harsh; lacking kindness: *ill will.* **7.** not up to an acceptable standard; faulty: *ill manners.* **8. ill at ease.** unable to relax; uncomfortable. ~*n.* **9.** evil or harm; misfortune; trouble. **10.** a mild disease. ~*adv.* **11.** badly: *the title ill befits him.* **12.** with difficulty; hardly: *he can ill afford the money.* **13.** not rightly: *he ill deserves such good fortune.* [C11 (in the sense: evil): < ON *illr* bad]

ill. *abbrev. for:* **1.** illustrated. **2.** illustration.

I'll (aɪl) *contraction of* I will *or* I shall.

ill-advised *adj.* **1.** acting without reasonable care or thought: *you would be ill-advised to sell your house now.* **2.** badly thought out; not or insufficiently considered: *an ill-advised plan of action.* —**ill-advisedly** (ˌɪlədˈvaɪzɪdlɪ) *adv.*

ill-affected *adj.* (often foll. by *towards*) not well disposed; disaffected.

ill-assorted *adj.* badly matched; incompatible.

illative (ɪˈleɪtɪv) *adj.* **1.** relating to inference; inferential. **2.** *Grammar.* denoting a word or morpheme used to signal inference, for example *so* or *therefore.* **3.** (esp. in Finnish grammar) denoting a case of nouns expressing a relation of motion or direction, usually translated by *into* or *towards.* ~*n.* **4.** *Grammar.* **a.** the illative case. **b.** an illative word or speech element. [C16: < LL *illātīvus* inferring, concluding] —**ilˈlatively** *adv.*

ill-bred *adj.* badly brought up; lacking good manners. —ˌ**ill-ˈbreeding** *n.*

ill-considered *adj.* done without due consideration; not thought out: *an ill-considered decision.*

ill-defined *adj.* imperfectly defined; having no clear outline.

ill-disposed *adj.* (often foll. by *towards*) not kindly disposed.

illegal (ɪˈliːgᵊl) *adj.* **1.** forbidden by law; unlawful; illicit. **2.** unauthorized or prohibited by a code of official or accepted rules. —**ilˈlegally** *adv.* —ˌ**illeˈgality** *n.*

illegible (ɪˈlɛdʒɪbᵊl) *adj.* unable to be read or deciphered. —**ilˌlegiˈbility** *or* **ilˈlegibleness** *n.* —**ilˈlegibly** *adv.*

illegitimate (ˌɪlɪˈdʒɪtɪmɪt) *adj.* **1. a.** born of parents who were not married to each other at the time of birth; bastard. **b.** occurring outside marriage: *of illegitimate birth.* **2.** illegal; unlawful. **3.** contrary to logic; incorrectly reasoned. ~*n.* **4.** an illegitimate person; bastard. —ˌ**illeˈgitimacy** *or* ˌ**illeˈgitimateness** *n.* —ˌ**illeˈgitimately** *adv.*

ill-fated *adj.* doomed or unlucky.

ill-favoured *adj.* **1.** unattractive or repulsive in appearance; ugly. **2.** disagreeable or objectionable. —ˌ**ill-ˈfavouredly** *adv.* —ˌ**ill-ˈfavouredness** *n.*

ill feeling *n.* hostile feeling; animosity.

ill-founded *adj.* not founded on true or reliable premises; unsubstantiated.

ill-gotten *adj.* obtained dishonestly or illegally (esp. in **ill-gotten gains**).

ill humour *n.* a disagreeable or sullen mood; bad temper. —ˌ**ill-ˈhumoured** *adj.* —ˌ**ill-ˈhumouredly** *adv.*

illiberal (ɪˈlɪbərəl) *adj.* **1.** narrow-minded; prejudiced; intolerant. **2.** not generous; mean. **3.** lacking in culture or refinement. —**ilˌliberˈality** *n.* —**ilˈliberally** *adv.*

illicit (ɪˈlɪsɪt) *adj.* **1.** another word for **illegal. 2.** not allowed or approved by common custom, rule, or standard: *illicit sexual relations.* —**ilˈlicitly** *adv.* —**ilˈlicitness** *n.*

illimitable (ɪˈlɪmɪtəbᵊl) *adj.* limitless; boundless. —**ilˌlimitaˈbility** *or* **ilˈlimitableness** *n.*

illiterate (ɪˈlɪtərɪt) *adj.* **1.** unable to read and write. **2.** violating accepted standards in reading and writing: *an illiterate scrawl.* **3.** uneducated, ignorant, or uncultured: *scientifically illiterate.* ~*n.* **4.** an illiterate person. —**ilˈliteracy** *or* **ilˈliterateness** *n.* —**ilˈliterately** *adv.*

ill-judged *adj.* rash; ill-advised.

ill-mannered *adj.* having bad manners; rude; impolite. —ˌ**ill-ˈmanneredly** *adv.*

ill-natured *adj.* naturally unpleasant and mean. —ˌ**ill-ˈnaturedly** *adv.* —ˌ**ill-ˈnaturedness** *n.*

illness (ˈɪlnɪs) *n.* **1.** a disease or indisposition; sickness. **2.** a state of ill health.

illogical (ɪˈlɒdʒɪkᵊl) *adj.* **1.** characterized by lack of logic; senseless or unreasonable. **2.** disregarding logical principles. —**illogicality** (ɪˌlɒdʒɪˈkælɪtɪ) *or* **ilˈlogicalness** *n.* —**ilˈlogically** *adv.*

ill-starred *adj.* unlucky; unfortunate; ill-fated.

ill temper *n.* bad temper; irritability. —ˌ**ill-ˈtempered** *adj.* —ˌ**ill-ˈtemperedly** *adv.*

ill-timed *adj.* occurring at or planned for an unsuitable time.

ill-treat *vb.* (*tr.*) to behave cruelly or harshly towards; misuse; maltreat. —ˌ**ill-ˈtreatment** *n.*

illuminance (ɪˈluːmɪnəns) *n.* the luminous flux incident on unit area of a surface. Sometimes called: **illumination.** Cf. **irradiance.**

illuminant (ɪˈluːmɪnənt) *n.* **1.** something that provides or gives off light. ~*adj.* **2.** giving off light; illuminating.

illuminate *vb.* (ɪˈluːmɪˌneɪt). **1.** (*tr.*) to throw light in or into; light up. **2.** (*tr.*) to make easily understood; clarify. **3.** to adorn, decorate, or be decorated with lights. **4.** (*tr.*) to decorate (a letter, etc.) by the application of colours, gold, or silver. **5.** (*intr.*) to become lighted up. ~*adj.* (ɪˈluːmɪnɪt, -ˌneɪt). **6.** *Arch.* made clear or bright with light. ~*n.* (ɪˈluːmɪnɪt, -ˌneɪt). **7.** a person who claims to have special enlightenment. [C16: < L *illūmināre* to light up, < *lūmen* light] —**ilˈlumiˌnating** *adj.* —**ilˈluminative** *adj.* —**ilˈlumiˌnator** *n.*

illuminati (ɪˌluːmɪˈnɑːtiː) *pl. n., sing.* **-to** (-təʊ). **1.** a group of persons claiming exceptional enlightenment on some subject, esp. religion. **2.** (*cap.*) any of several groups of illuminati, esp. in 18th-century France and Bavaria or 16th-century Spain. [C16: < L, lit.: the enlightened ones, < *illūmināre* to ILLUMINATE]

illumination (ɪˌluːmɪˈneɪʃən) *n.* **1.** the act of illuminating or the state of being illuminated. **2.** a source of light. **3.** (*often pl.*) *Chiefly Brit.* a light or lights used as decoration in streets, parks, etc. **4.** spiritual or intellectual enlightenment; insight or understanding. **5.** the act of making understood; clarification. **6.** decoration in colours, gold, or silver used on some manuscripts. **7.** *Physics.* another name (not in technical usage) for **illuminance.**

illumine (ɪˈluːmɪn) *vb.* a literary word for **illuminate.** [C14: < L *illūmināre* to make light] —**ilˈluminable** *adj.*

ill-use *vb.* (ˈɪlˈjuːz). **1.** to use badly or cruelly; abuse; maltreat. ~*n.* (ˈɪlˈjuːs), *also* **ill-usage. 2.** harsh or cruel treatment; abuse.

illusion (ɪˈluːʒən) *n.* **1.** a false appearance or deceptive impression of reality: *the mirror gives an illusion of depth.* **2.** a false or misleading perception or belief; delusion. **3.** *Psychol.* a perception that is not true to reality, having been altered subjectively in the mind of the perceiver. See also **hallucination.** [C14: < L *illūsiō* deceit, < *illūdere* to sport with, < *ludus* game] —**ilˈlusionary** *or* **ilˈlusional** *adj.* —**ilˈlusioned** *adj.*

illusionism (ɪˈluːʒəˌnɪzəm) *n.* **1.** *Philosophy.* the doctrine that the external world exists only in illusory sense perceptions. **2.** the use of highly illusory effects in art.

illusionist (ɪˈluːʒənɪst) *n.* **1.** a person given to illusions; visionary; dreamer. **2.** *Philosophy.* a person who believes in illusionism. **3.** an artist who practises illusionism. **4.** a conjurer; magician. —**ilˌlusionˈistic** *adj.*

illusory (ɪˈluːsərɪ) *or* **illusive** (ɪˈluːsɪv) *adj.* producing or based on illusion; deceptive or unreal. —**ilˈlusorily** *adv.* —**ilˈlusoriness** *n.*

illust. *or* **illus.** *abbrev. for:* **1.** illustrated. **2.** illustration.

illustrate (ˈɪləˌstreɪt) *vb.* **1.** to clarify or explain by use of examples, analogy, etc. **2.** (*tr.*) to be an example of. **3.** (*tr.*) to explain or decorate (a book, text, etc.) with pictures. [C16: < L, < *lustrāre* to purify, brighten; see LUSTRUM] —ˈ**illusˌtrative** *adj.* —ˈ**illusˌtrator** *n.*

illustration (ˌɪləˈstreɪʃən) *n.* **1.** pictorial matter used to explain or decorate a text. **2.** an example: *an illustration of his ability.* **3.** the act of illustrating or the state of being illustrated. —ˌ**illusˈtrational** *adj.*

illustrious (ɪˈlʌstrɪəs) *adj.* **1.** of great renown; famous and distinguished. **2.** glorious or great: *illustrious deeds.* [C16: < L *illustris* bright, famous, < *illustrāre* to make light; see ILLUSTRATE] —**ilˈlustriously** *adv.* —**ilˈlustriousness** *n.*

ill will *n.* hostile feeling; enmity; antagonism.

ILO *abbrev. for* International Labour Organisation.

I'm (aɪm) *contraction of* I am.

im- *prefix.* a variant of **in-**[1] and **in-**[2] before *b, m,* and *p.*

image (ˈɪmɪdʒ) *n.* **1.** a representation or likeness of a person or thing, esp. in sculpture. **2.** an optically formed reproduction of an object, such as one formed by a lens or mirror. **3.** a person or thing that resembles another closely; double or copy. **4.** a mental picture; idea produced by the imagination. **5.** the personality presented to the public by a person, organization, etc.: *a politician's image.* **6.** the pattern of light that is focused onto the retina. **7.** *Psychol.* the mental experience of something that is not immediately present to the senses, often involving memory. See also **imagery. 8.** a personification of a specified quality; epitome: *the image of good breeding.* **9.** a mental picture or association of ideas evoked in a literary work. **10.** a figure of speech such as a simile or metaphor. ~*vb.* (*tr.*) **11.** to picture in the mind; imagine. **12.** to make or reflect an image of. **13.** to project or display on a screen, etc. **14.** to portray or describe. **15.** to be an example or epitome of; typify. [C13: < OF *imagene,* < L *imāgō* copy, representation; rel. to L *imitārī* to IMITATE] —ˈ**imageable** *adj.* —ˈ**imageless** *adj.*

image enhancement *n.* a method of improving the definition of a video picture by a computer program which reduces the lowest grey values to black and the highest to white: used for pictures from microscopes, surveillance cameras, and scanners.

image intensifier *n.* **1.** (in fluoroscopy) a device by which a smaller brighter image is produced by electrons from an x-ray beam released from one screen being focused onto a second fluorescent screen. **2.** a device that concentrates ambient light so as to allow the user to see objects at night.

image orthicon *n.* a television camera tube in which electrons, emitted from a surface in proportion to the intensity of the incident light, are focused onto the target causing secondary emission of electrons.

imagery (ˈɪmɪdʒrɪ, -dʒərɪ) *n., pl.* **-ries. 1.** figurative or descriptive language in a literary work. **2.** images collectively. **3.** *Psychol.* **a.** the materials or general processes of the imagination. **b.** the characteristic kind of mental images formed by a particular individual. See also **image** (sense 7), **imagination** (sense 1).

imaginary (ɪˈmædʒɪnərɪ, -dʒɪnrɪ) *adj.* **1.** existing in the imagination; unreal; illusory. **2.** *Maths.* involving or containing imaginary numbers. —**imˈaginarily** *adv.*

imaginary number *n.* any complex number of the form $a + bi$, where b is not zero and $i = \sqrt{-1}$.

imagination (ɪˌmædʒɪˈneɪʃən) *n.* **1.** the faculty or action of producing ideas, esp. mental images of what is not present or has not been experienced. **2.** mental creative ability. **3.** the ability to deal resourcefully with unexpected or unusual problems, circumstances, etc.

imaginative (ɪˈmædʒɪnətɪv) *adj.* **1.** produced by or indicative of a creative imagination. **2.** having a vivid imagination. —**imˈaginatively** *adv.* —**imˈaginativeness** *n.*

imagine (ɪˈmædʒɪn) *vb.* **1.** (when *tr., may take a clause as object*) to form a mental image of. **2.** (when *tr., may take a clause as object*) to think, believe, or guess. **3.** (*tr.; takes a clause as object*) to suppose; assume: *I imagine he'll come.* **4.** (*tr.; takes a clause as object*) to believe without foundation: *he imagines he knows the whole story.* [C14: < L *imāginārī* to fancy, picture mentally, < *imāgō* likeness; see IMAGE] —**imˈaginable** *adj.* —**imˈaginably** *adv.* —**imˈaginer** *n.*

imagism (ˈɪmɪˌdʒɪzəm) *n.* an early 20th-century poetic movement, advocating the use of ordinary speech and the precise presentation of images. —ˈ**imagist** *n., adj.* —ˌ**imagˈistic** *adj.*

imago (ɪˈmeɪgəʊ) *n., pl.* **imagoes** *or* **imagines** (ɪˈmædʒəˌniːz). **1.** an adult sexually mature insect. **2.** *Psychoanal.* an idealized image of another person, usually a parent, carried in the unconscious. [C18: NL, < L: likeness]

imam (ɪˈmɑːm) *or* **imaum** (ɪˈmɑːm, ɪˈmɔːm) *n.* *Islam.* **1.** a leader of congregational prayer in a mosque. **2.** a caliph, as leader of a Muslim community. **3.** any of a succession of Muslim religious leaders regarded by their followers as divinely inspired. [C17: < Ar.: leader.]

imamate (ɪˈmɑːmeɪt) *n.* *Islam.* **1.** the region or territory governed by an imam. **2.** the office, rank, or period of office of an imam.

imbalance (ɪmˈbæləns) *n.* a lack of balance, as in

emphasis, proportion, etc.: *the political imbalance of the programme.*

imbecile (ˈɪmbɪˌsiːl, -ˌsaɪl) *n.* **1.** *Psychol.* a person of very low intelligence (IQ of 25 to 50). **2.** *Inf.* an extremely stupid person; dolt. ~*adj.* also **imbecilic** (ˌɪmbɪˈsɪlɪk). **3.** of or like an imbecile; mentally deficient; feeble-minded. **4.** stupid or senseless: *an imbecile thing to do.* [C16: < L *imbēcillus* feeble (physically or mentally)] —**ˈimbeˌcilely** *or* **ˌimbeˈcilically** *adv.* —**ˌimbeˈcility** *n.*

imbed (ɪmˈbɛd) *vb.* **-bedding, -bedded.** a less common spelling of **embed.**

imbibe (ɪmˈbaɪb) *vb.* **1.** to drink (esp. alcoholic drinks). **2.** *Literary.* to take in or assimilate (ideas, etc.): *to imbibe the spirit of the Renaissance.* **3.** (*tr.*) to take in as if by drinking: *to imbibe fresh air.* **4.** to absorb or cause to absorb liquid or moisture; assimilate or saturate. [C14: < L *imbibere,* < *bibere* to drink] —**imˈbiber** *n.*

imbricate *adj.* (ˈɪmbrɪkɪt, -ˌkeɪt), *also* **imbricated.** **1.** *Archit.* relating to or having tiles, shingles, or slates that overlap. **2.** (of leaves, scales, etc.) overlapping each other. ~*vb.* (ˈɪmbrɪˌkeɪt). **3.** (*tr.*) to decorate with a repeating pattern resembling scales or overlapping tiles. [C17: < L *imbricāre* to cover with overlapping tiles, < *imbrex* pantile] —**ˈimbricately** *adv.* —**ˌimbriˈcation** *n.*

imbroglio (ɪmˈbrəʊlɪˌəʊ) *n., pl.* **-glios.** **1.** a confused or perplexing political or interpersonal situation. **2.** *Obs.* a confused heap; jumble. [C18: < It., < *imbrogliare* to confuse, EMBROIL]

imbrue (ɪmˈbruː) *vb.* **-bruing, -brued.** (*tr.*) *Rare.* **1.** to stain, esp. with blood. **2.** to permeate or impregnate. [C15: < OF *embreuver,* < L *imbibere* to IMBIBE] —**imˈbruement** *n.*

imbue (ɪmˈbjuː) *vb.* **-buing, -bued.** (*tr.;* usually foll. by *with*) **1.** to instil or inspire (with ideals, principles, etc.). **2.** *Rare.* to soak, esp. with dye, etc. [C16: < L *imbuere* to stain, accustom] —**imˈbuement** *n.*

IMechE *abbrev. for* Institution of Mechanical Engineers.

IMF *abbrev. for* International Monetary Fund.

imit. *abbrev. for:* **1.** imitation. **2.** imitative.

imitate (ˈɪmɪˌteɪt) *vb.* (*tr.*) **1.** to try to follow the manner, style, etc., of or take as a model: *many writers imitated the language of Shakespeare.* **2.** to pretend to be or to impersonate, esp. for humour; mimic. **3.** to make a copy or reproduction of; duplicate. [C16: < L *imitārī;* see IMAGE] —**imitable** (ˈɪmɪtəbᵊl) *adj.* —**ˌimitaˈbility** *n.* —**ˈimiˌtator** *n.*

imitation (ˌɪmɪˈteɪʃən) *n.* **1.** the act or practice of imitating; mimicry. **2.** an instance or product of imitating, such as a copy of the manner of a person; impression. **3. a.** a copy of a genuine article; counterfeit. **b.** (*as modifier*): *imitation jewellery.* **4.** *Music.* the repetition of a phrase or figure in one part after its appearance in another, as in a fugue. —**ˌimiˈtational** *adj.*

imitative (ˈɪmɪtətɪv) *adj.* **1.** imitating or tending to copy. **2.** characterized by imitation. **3.** copying or reproducing an original, esp. in an inferior manner: *imitative painting.* **4.** another word for **onomatopoeic.** —**ˈimitatively** *adv.* —**ˈimitativeness** *n.*

immaculate (ɪˈmækjʊlɪt) *adj.* **1.** completely clean; extremely tidy: *his clothes were immaculate.* **2.** completely flawless, etc.: *an immaculate rendering of the symphony.* **3.** morally pure; free from sin or corruption. **4.** *Biol.* with no spots or markings. [C15: < L, < IM- (not) + *macula* blemish] —**imˈmaculacy** *or* **imˈmaculateness** *n.* —**imˈmaculately** *adv.*

immanent (ˈɪmənənt) *adj.* **1.** existing, operating, or remaining within; inherent. **2.** (of God) present throughout the universe. [C16: < L *immanēre* to remain in] —**ˈimmanence** *or* **ˈimmanency** *n.* —**ˈimmanently** *adv.* —**ˈimmanenˌtism** *n.*

▷ **Usage.** See at **imminent.**

immaterial (ˌɪməˈtɪərɪəl) *adj.* **1.** of no real importance; inconsequential. **2.** not formed of matter; incorporeal; spiritual. —**ˌimmaˌteriˈality** *n.* —**ˌimmaˈterially** *adv.*

immaterialism (ˌɪməˈtɪərɪəˌlɪzəm) *n. Philosophy.* the doctrine that the material world exists only in the mind. —**ˌimmaˈterialist** *n.*

immature (ˌɪməˈtjʊə, -ˈtʃʊə) *adj.* **1.** not fully grown or developed. **2.** deficient in maturity; lacking wisdom, insight, emotional stability, etc. —**ˌimmaˈturely** *adv.* —**ˌimmaˈturity** *or* **ˌimmaˈtureness** *n.*

immeasurable (ɪˈmɛʒərəbᵊl) *adj.* incapable of being measured, esp. by virtue of great size; limitless. —**imˌmeasuraˈbility** *or* **imˈmeasurableness** *n.* —**imˈmeasurably** *adv.*

immediate (ɪˈmiːdɪət) *adj.* (*usually prenominal*) **1.** taking place or accomplished without delay: *an immediate reaction.* **2.** closest or most direct in effect or relationship: *the immediate cause of his downfall.* **3.** having no intervening medium; direct in effect: *an immediate influence.* **4.** contiguous in space, time, or relationship: *our immediate neighbour.* **5.** present; current: *the immediate problem is food.* **6.** *Philosophy.* of or relating to a concept that is directly known or intuited. [C16: < Med. L, < L IM- (not) + *mediāre* to be in the middle; see MEDIATE] —**imˈmediacy** *or* **imˈmediateness** *n.*

immediately (ɪˈmiːdɪətlɪ) *adv.* **1.** without delay or intervention; at once; instantly. **2.** very closely or directly: *this immediately concerns you.* **3.** near or close by: *somewhere immediately in this area.* ~*conj.* **4.** (*subordinating*) *Chiefly Brit.* as soon as: *immediately he opened the door, there was a gust of wind.*

immemorial (ˌɪmɪˈmɔːrɪəl) *adj.* originating in the distant past; ancient (postpositive in **time immemorial**). [C17: < Med. L, < L IM- (not) + *memoria* MEMORY] —**ˌimmeˈmorially** *adv.*

immense (ɪˈmɛns) *adj.* **1.** unusually large; huge; vast. **2.** without limits; immeasurable. **3.** *Inf.* very good; excellent. [C15: < L *immensus,* lit.: unmeasured, < IM- (not) + *mētīrī* to measure] —**imˈmensely** *adv.* —**imˈmenseness** *n.*

immensity (ɪˈmɛnsɪtɪ) *n., pl.* **-ties.** **1.** the state of being immense; vastness; enormity. **2.** enormous expanse, distance, or volume. **3.** *Inf.* a huge amount: *an immensity of wealth.*

immerse (ɪˈmɜːs) *vb.* (*tr.*) **1.** (often foll. by *in*) to plunge or dip into liquid. **2.** (*often passive;* often foll. by *in*) to involve deeply; engross: *to immerse oneself in a problem.* **3.** to baptize by dipping the whole body into water. [C17: < L *immergere,* < IM- (in) + *mergere* to dip] —**imˈmersible** *adj.* —**imˈmersion** *n.*

immerser (ɪˈmɜːsə) *n.* an informal term for **immersion heater.**

immersion heater *n.* an electrical device, usually thermostatically controlled, for heating the liquid in which it is immersed, esp. as a fixture in a domestic hot-water tank.

immigrant (ˈɪmɪgrənt) *n.* **1. a.** a person who immigrates. **b.** (*as modifier*): *an immigrant community.* **2.** *Brit.* a person who has been settled in a country of which he is not a native for less than ten years.

immigrate (ˈɪmɪˌgreɪt) *vb.* **1.** (*intr.*) to come to a place or country of which one is not a native in order to settle there. **2.** (*tr.*) to introduce or bring in as an immigrant. [C17: < L *immigrāre* to go into] —**ˌimmiˈgration** *n.* —**ˈimmiˌgrator** *n.* —**ˈimmiˌgratory** *adj.*

imminent (ˈɪmɪnənt) *adj.* **1.** liable to happen soon; impending. **2.** *Obs.* overhanging. [C16: < L *imminēre* to project over; rel. to *mons* mountain] —**ˈimminence** *n.* —**ˈimminently** *adv.*

▷ **Usage.** The spelling of *imminent* should not be confused with that of *immanent,* a word used chiefly in religious contexts, and in distinguishing the two it may be helpful to note the etymologies, which show why the spelling differs. *Imminent* means "likely to happen soon" and is generally used of something dangerous or unpleasant: *he believed that war was imminent.*

immiscible (ɪˈmɪsɪbᵊl) *adj.* (of liquids) incapable

of being mixed: *oil and water are immiscible.* **—im,misci'bility** *n.* **—im'miscibly** *adv.*

immitigable (ɪ'mɪtɪgəb^{ə}l) *adj. Rare.* unable to be mitigated. **—im,mitiga'bility** *n.* **—im'mitigably** *adv.*

immobile (ɪ'məʊbaɪl) *adj.* **1.** not moving; motionless. **2.** not able to move or be moved; fixed. **—immobility** (,ɪməʊ'bɪlɪtɪ) *n.*

immobilize *or* **-lise** (ɪ'məʊbɪ,laɪz) *vb.* (*tr.*) **1.** to make immobile: *to immobilize a car.* **2.** *Finance.* to convert (circulating capital) into fixed capital. **—im,mobili'zation** *or* **-li'sation** *n.* **—im'mobi,lizer** *or* **-,liser** *n.*

immoderate (ɪ'mɒdərɪt, ɪ'mɒdrɪt) *adj.* lacking in moderation; excessive: *immoderate demands.* **—im'moderately** *adv.* **—im,moder'ation** *or* **im'moderateness** *n.*

immodest (ɪ'mɒdɪst) *adj.* **1.** indecent, esp. with regard to sexual propriety; improper. **2.** bold, impudent, or shameless. **—im'modestly** *adv.* **—im'modesty** *n.*

immolate ('ɪməʊ,leɪt) *vb.* (*tr.*) **1.** to kill or offer as a sacrifice. **2.** *Literary.* to sacrifice (something highly valued). [C16: < L *immolāre* to sprinkle an offering with sacrificial meal, sacrifice; see MILL] **—,immo'lation** *n.* **—'immo,lator** *n.*

immoral (ɪ'mɒrəl) *adj.* **1.** transgressing accepted moral rules; corrupt. **2.** sexually dissolute; profligate or promiscuous. **3.** unscrupulous or unethical: *immoral trading.* **4.** tending to corrupt or resulting from corruption: *immoral earnings.* **—im'morally** *adv.*

▷ **Usage.** See at **amoral.**

immorality (,ɪmə'rælɪtɪ) *n., pl.* **-ties. 1.** the quality or state of being immoral. **2.** immoral behaviour, esp. in sexual matters; licentiousness; promiscuity. **3.** an immoral act.

immortal (ɪ'mɔːt^{ə}l) *adj.* **1.** not subject to death or decay; having perpetual life. **2.** having everlasting fame; remembered throughout time. **3.** everlasting; perpetual; constant. **4.** of or relating to immortal beings or concepts. ~*n.* **5.** an immortal being. **6.** (*often pl.*) a person who is remembered enduringly, esp. an author. **—,immor'tality** *n.* **—im'mortally** *adv.*

immortalize *or* **-ise** (ɪ'mɔːtə,laɪz) *vb.* (*tr.*) **1.** to give everlasting fame to, as by treating in a literary work: *Macbeth was immortalized by Shakespeare.* **2.** to give immortality to. **—im,mortali'zation** *or* **-i'sation** *n.* **—im'mortal,izer** *or* **-,iser** *n.*

immortelle (,ɪmɔː'tɛl) *n.* any of various composite plants that retain their colour when dried. Also called: **everlasting.** [C19: < F (*fleur*) *immortelle* everlasting (flower)]

immovable *or* **immoveable** (ɪ'muːvəb^{ə}l) *adj.* **1.** unable to move or be moved; immobile. **2.** unable to be diverted from one's intentions; steadfast. **3.** unaffected by feeling; impassive. **4.** unchanging; unalterable. **5.** (of feasts, etc.) on the same date every year. **6.** *Law.* **a.** (of property) not liable to be removed; fixed. **b.** of or relating to immovable property. **—im,mova'bility, im,movea'bility** *or* **im'movableness, im'moveableness** *n.* **—im'movably** *or* **im'moveably** *adv.*

immune (ɪ'mjuːn) *adj.* **1.** protected against a specific disease by inoculation or as the result of innate or acquired resistance. **2.** relating to or conferring immunity: *an immune body* (see **antibody**). **3.** (*usually postpositive;* foll. by *to*) unsusceptible (to) or secure (against): *immune to inflation.* **4.** exempt from obligation, penalty, etc. ~*n.* **5.** an immune person or animal. [C15: < L *immūnis* exempt from a public service]

immunity (ɪ'mjuːnɪtɪ) *n., pl.* **-ties. 1.** the ability of an organism to resist disease, as by producing its own antibodies or as a result of inoculation. **2.** freedom from obligation or duty, esp. exemption from tax, legal liability, etc.

immunize *or* **-nise** ('ɪmjʊ,naɪz) *vb.* (*tr.*) to make immune, esp. by inoculation. **—,immuni'zation** *or* **-ni'sation** *n.* **—'immu,nizer** *or* **-,niser** *n.*

immuno- *or before a vowel* **immun-** *combining form.* indicating immunity or immune: *immunology.*

immunodeficiency (,ɪmjʊnəʊdɪ'fɪʃənsɪ) *n.* a deficiency in or breakdown of a person's immune system.

immunoglobulin (,ɪmjʊnəʊ'glɒbjʊlɪn) *n.* any of five classes of proteins, all of which show antibody activity.

immunology (,ɪmjʊ'nɒlədʒɪ) *n.* the branch of biological science concerned with the study of immunity. **—immunologic** (,ɪmjʊnə'lɒdʒɪk) *or* **,immuno'logical** *adj.* **—,immuno'logically** *adv.* **—,immu'nologist** *n.*

immunoreaction (ɪ,mjuːnəʊrɪ'ækʃən) *n.* the reaction between an antigen and its antibody.

immunosuppressive (,ɪmjʊnəʊsə'prɛsɪv) *n.* **1.** any drug that lessens the body's rejection, esp. of a transplanted organ. ~*adj.* **2.** of or relating to such a drug **—,immunosup'pressant** *n., adj.*

immure (ɪ'mjʊə) *vb.* (*tr.*) **1.** *Arch. or literary.* to enclose within or as if within walls; imprison. **2.** to shut (oneself) away from society. [C16: < Med. L, < L IM- (in) + *mūrus* wall] **—im'murement** *n.*

immutable (ɪ'mjuːtəb^{ə}l) *adj.* unchanging through time; unalterable; ageless: *immutable laws.* **—im,muta'bility** *or* **im'mutableness** *n.*

imp (ɪmp) *n.* **1.** a small demon or devil; mischievous sprite. **2.** a mischievous child. ~*vb.* **3.** (*tr.*) *Falconry.* to insert new feathers in order to repair (the wing of a falcon). [OE *impa* bud, graft, hence offspring, child, < *impian* to graft]

imp. *abbrev. for:* **1.** imperative. **2.** imperfect. **3.** imperial. **4.** impersonal. **5.** import. **6.** importer.

impact *n.* ('ɪmpækt). **1.** the act of one body, etc., striking another; collision. **2.** the force with which one thing hits another. **3.** the impression made by an idea, social group, etc. ~*vb.* (ɪm'pækt). **4.** to drive or press (an object) firmly into (another object, thing, etc.) or (of two objects) to be driven or pressed firmly together. **5.** to have an impact or strong effect (on). [C18: < L *impactus* pushed against, fastened on, < *impingere* to thrust at, < *pangere* to drive in] **—im'paction** *n.*

impacted (ɪm'pæktɪd) *adj.* **1.** (of a tooth) unable to erupt, esp. because of being wedged against another tooth below the gum. **2.** (of a fracture) having the jagged broken ends wedged into each other.

impair (ɪm'pɛə) *vb.* (*tr.*) to reduce or weaken in strength, quality, etc.: *his hearing was impaired by an accident.* [C14: < OF *empeirer* to make worse, < LL, < L *pēior* worse; see PEJORATIVE] **—im'pairable** *adj.* **—im'pairer** *n.* **—im'pairment** *n.*

impala (ɪm'pɑːlə) *n., pl.* **-las** *or* **-la.** an antelope of southern and eastern Africa, having lyre-shaped horns and able to move with enormous leaps. [< Zulu]

impale *or* **empale** (ɪm'peɪl) *vb.* (*tr.*) **1.** (often foll. by *on, upon,* or *with*) to pierce with a sharp instrument: *they impaled his severed head on a spear.* **2.** *Heraldry.* to charge (a shield) with two coats of arms placed side by side. [C16: < Med. L, < L IM- (in) + *pālus* PALE[2]] **—im'palement** *or* **em'palement** *n.*

impalpable (ɪm'pælpəb^{ə}l) *adj.* **1.** imperceptible, esp. to the touch: *impalpable shadows.* **2.** difficult to understand; abstruse. **—im,palpa'bility** *n.* **—im'palpably** *adv.*

impanel (ɪm'pæn^{ə}l) *vb.* **-elling, -elled** *or U.S.* **-eling, -eled.** a variant spelling (esp. U.S.) of **empanel. —im'panelment** *n.*

impart (ɪm'pɑːt) *vb.* (*tr.*) **1.** to communicate (information, etc.); relate. **2.** to give or bestow (an abstract quality): *to impart wisdom.* [C15: < OF, < L, < IM- (in) + *partīre* to share, < *pars* part] **—im'partable** *adj.* **—,impar'tation** *or* **im'partment** *n.*

impartial (ɪm'pɑːʃəl) *adj.* not prejudiced towards or against any particular side; fair; unbiased. **—im,parti'ality** *or* **im'partialness** *n.* **—im'partially** *adv.*

impartible (ɪm'pɑːtəb^{ə}l) *adj. Law.* (of land, an estate, etc.) incapable of partition; indivisible. **—im,parti'bility** *n.* **—im'partibly** *adv.*

impassable (ɪmˈpɑːsəbᵊl) *adj.* (of terrain, roads, etc.) not able to be travelled through or over. —**imˌpassaˈbility** *or* **imˈpassableness** *n.* —**imˈpassably** *adv.*

impasse (æmˈpɑːs, ˈæmpɑːs) *n.* a situation in which progress is blocked; an insurmountable difficulty; stalemate. [C19: < F; see IM-, PASS]

impassible (ɪmˈpæsəbᵊl) *adj. Rare.* **1.** not susceptible to pain or injury. **2.** impassive or unmoved. —**imˌpassiˈbility** *or* **imˈpassibleness** *n.* —**imˈpassibly** *adv.*

impassion (ɪmˈpæʃən) *vb.* (*tr.*) to arouse the passions of; inflame.

impassioned (ɪmˈpæʃənd) *adj.* filled with passion; fiery; inflamed: *an impassioned appeal.* —**imˈpassionedly** *adv.* —**imˈpassionedness** *n.*

impassive (ɪmˈpæsɪv) *adj.* **1.** not revealing or affected by emotion; reserved. **2.** calm; serene; imperturbable. —**imˈpassively** *adv.* —**imˈpassiveness** *or* **impassivity** (ˌɪmpæˈsɪvɪtɪ) *n.*

impasto (ɪmˈpæstəʊ) *n.* **1.** paint applied thickly, so that brush marks are evident. **2.** the technique of painting in this way. [C18: < It., < *impastare,* < *pasta* PASTE]

impatience (ɪmˈpeɪʃəns) *n.* **1.** lack of patience; intolerance of or irritability with anything that impedes or delays. **2.** restless desire for change and excitement.

impatiens (ɪmˈpeɪʃɪˌɛnz) *n., pl.* **-ens.** a plant with explosive pods, such as balsam, touch-me-not, and busy Lizzie. [C18: NL < L: impatient; from the fact that the ripe pods burst open when touched]

impatient (ɪmˈpeɪʃənt) *adj.* **1.** lacking patience; easily irritated at delay, etc. **2.** exhibiting lack of patience. **3.** (*postpositive;* foll. by *of*) intolerant (of) or indignant (at): *impatient of indecision.* **4.** (*postpositive;* often foll. by *for*) restlessly eager (for *or* to do something). —**imˈpatiently** *adv.*

impeach (ɪmˈpiːtʃ) *vb.* (*tr.*) **1.** *Criminal law.* to bring a charge or accusation against. **2.** *Brit. criminal law.* to accuse of a crime against the state. **3.** *Chiefly U.S.* to charge (a public official) with an offence committed in office. **4.** to challenge or question (a person's honesty, etc.). [C14: < OF, < LL *impedicāre* to entangle, catch, < L IM- (in) + *pedica* a fetter, < *pēs* foot] —**imˈpeachable** *adj.* —**imˈpeachment** *n.*

impeccable (ɪmˈpɛkəbᵊl) *adj.* **1.** without flaw or error; faultless: *an impeccable record.* **2.** *Rare.* incapable of sinning. [C16: < LL *impeccābilis* sinless, < L IM- (not) + *peccāre* to sin] —**imˌpeccaˈbility** *n.* —**imˈpeccably** *adv.*

impecunious (ˌɪmpɪˈkjuːnɪəs) *adj.* without money; penniless. [C16: < IM- (not) + < L *pecūniōsus* wealthy, < *pecūnia* money] —ˌ**impeˈcuniously** *adv.* —ˌ**impeˈcuniousness** *or* **impecuniosity** (ˌɪmpɪkjuːnɪˈɒsɪtɪ) *n.*

impedance (ɪmˈpiːdᵊns) *n.* **1.** a measure of the opposition to the flow of an alternating current equal to the square root of the sum of the squares of the resistance and the reactance, expressed in ohms. **2.** the ratio of the sound pressure in a medium to the rate of alternating flow through a specified surface due to the sound wave. **3.** the ratio of the mechanical force to the velocity of the resulting vibration.

impede (ɪmˈpiːd) *vb.* (*tr.*) to restrict or retard in action, progress, etc.; obstruct. [C17: < L *impedīre* to hinder, lit.: shackle the feet, < *pēs* foot] —**imˈpeder** *n.* —**imˈpedingly** *adv.*

impediment (ɪmˈpɛdɪmənt) *n.* **1.** a hindrance or obstruction. **2.** a physical defect, esp. one of speech, such as a stammer. **3.** (*pl.* **-ments** *or* **-menta** (-ˈmɛntə)) *Law.* an obstruction to the making of a contract, esp. one of marriage. —**imˌpediˈmental** *or* **imˌpediˈmentary** *adj.*

impedimenta (ɪmˌpɛdɪˈmɛntə) *pl. n.* **1.** any objects that impede progress, esp. the baggage and equipment carried by an army. **2.** a plural of **impediment** (sense 3). [C16: < L, pl. of *impedīmentum* hindrance; see IMPEDE]

impel (ɪmˈpɛl) *vb.* **-pelling, -pelled.** (*tr.*) **1.** to urge or force (a person) to an action; constrain or motivate. **2.** to push, drive, or force into motion. [C15: < L *impellere* to push against, drive forward] —**imˈpellent** *n., adj.*

impeller (ɪmˈpɛlə) *n.* the vaned rotating disc of a centrifugal pump, compressor, etc.

impend (ɪmˈpɛnd) *vb.* (*intr.*) **1.** (esp. of something threatening) to be imminent. **2.** (foll. by *over*) *Rare.* to be suspended; hang. [C16: < L *impendēre* to overhang, < *pendēre* to hang] —**imˈpendence** *or* **imˈpendency** *n.* —**imˈpending** *adj.*

impenetrable (ɪmˈpɛnɪtrəbᵊl) *adj.* **1.** incapable of being pierced through or penetrated: *an impenetrable forest.* **2.** incapable of being understood; incomprehensible. **3.** incapable of being seen through: *impenetrable gloom.* **4.** not susceptible to ideas, influence, etc.: *impenetrable ignorance.* **5.** *Physics.* (of a body) incapable of occupying the same space as another body. —**imˌpenetraˈbility** *n.* —**imˈpenetrableness** *n.* —**imˈpenetrably** *adv.*

impenitent (ɪmˈpɛnɪtənt) *adj.* not sorry or penitent; unrepentant. —**imˈpenitence, imˈpenitency,** *or* **imˈpenitentness** *n.* —**imˈpenitently** *adv.*

imper. *abbrev. for* imperative.

imperative (ɪmˈpɛrətɪv) *adj.* **1.** extremely urgent or important; essential. **2.** peremptory or authoritative: *an imperative tone of voice.* **3.** Also: **imperatival** (ɪmˌpɛrəˈtaɪvᵊl). *Grammar.* denoting a mood of verbs used in giving orders, making requests, etc. ~*n.* **4.** something that is urgent or essential. **5.** an order or command. **6.** *Grammar.* **a.** the imperative mood. **b.** a verb in this mood. [C16: < LL, < L *imperāre* to command] —**imˈperatively** *adv.* —**imˈperativeness** *n.*

imperator (ˌɪmpəˈrɑːtɔː) *n.* (in ancient Rome) a title bestowed upon generals and, later, emperors. [C16: < L: commander, < *imperāre* to command] —**imperatorial** (ɪmˌpɛrəˈtɔːrɪəl) *adj.* —ˌ**impeˈratorˌship** *n.*

imperceptible (ˌɪmpəˈsɛptɪbᵊl) *adj.* too slight, subtle, gradual, etc., to be perceived. —ˌ**imperˌceptiˈbility** *or* ˌ**imperˈceptibleness** *n.* —ˌ**imperˈceptibly** *adv.*

imperceptive (ˌɪmpəˈsɛptɪv) *adj., also* **impercipient** (ˌɪmpəˈsɪpɪənt). lacking in perception; obtuse. —ˌ**imperˈception** *n.* —ˌ**imperˈceptively** *adv.* —ˌ**imperˈceptiveness** *or* ˌ**imperˈcipience** *n.*

imperf. *abbrev. for:* **1.** Also: **impf.** imperfect. **2.** (of stamps) imperforate.

imperfect (ɪmˈpɜːfɪkt) *adj.* **1.** exhibiting or characterized by faults, mistakes, etc.; defective. **2.** not complete or finished; deficient. **3.** *Grammar.* denoting a tense of verbs used most commonly in describing continuous or repeated past actions or events. **4.** *Law.* legally unenforceable. **5.** *Music.* **a.** proceeding to the dominant from the tonic, subdominant, or any chord other than the dominant. **b.** of or relating to all intervals other than the fourth, fifth, and octave. Cf. **perfect** (sense 9). ~*n.* **6.** *Grammar.* **a.** the imperfect tense. **b.** a verb in this tense. —**imˈperfectly** *adv.* —**imˈperfectness** *n.*

imperfection (ˌɪmpəˈfɛkʃən) *n.* **1.** the condition or quality of being imperfect. **2.** a fault or defect.

imperfective (ˌɪmpəˈfɛktɪv) *Grammar.* ~*adj.* **1.** denoting an aspect of the verb to indicate that the action is in progress without regard to its completion. Cf. **perfective.** ~*n.* **2. a.** the imperfective aspect of a verb. **b.** a verb in this aspect. —ˌ**imperˈfectively** *adv.*

imperforate (ɪmˈpɜːfərɪt, -ˌreɪt) *adj.* **1.** not perforated. **2.** (of a postage stamp) not provided with perforation or any other means of separation. **3.** *Anat.* without the normal opening. —**imˌperfoˈration** *n.*

imperial (ɪmˈpɪərɪəl) *adj.* **1.** of or relating to an empire, emperor, or empress. **2.** characteristic of an emperor; majestic; commanding. **3.** exercising supreme authority; imperious. **4.** (esp. of products) of a superior size or quality. **5.** (*usually prenominal*) (of weights, measures, etc.) conforming to standards legally established in Great Britain. ~*n.* **6.** a book size, esp. 7½ by 11 inches or 11 by 15 inches. **7.** a size of writing paper, 23 by 31 inches (U.S. and Canad.) or 22 by 30 inches (Brit.). **8.** *U.S.* **a.** the top of a carriage. **b.** a luggage case carried there. **9.** a small tufted beard popularized by the French emperor Napoleon III. [C14: < LL, < L *imperium* command, authority, empire] **—im'perially** *adv.* **—im'perialness** *n.*

imperialism (ɪm'pɪərɪəˌlɪzəm) *n.* **1.** the policy or practice of extending a state's rule over other territories. **2.** the extension or attempted extension of authority, influence, power, etc., by any person, country, institution, etc.: *cultural imperialism.* **3.** a system of imperial government or rule by an emperor. **4.** the spirit, character, authority, etc., of an empire. **—im'perialist** *adj., n.* **—imˌperial'istic** *adj.* **—imˌperial'istically** *adv.*

imperil (ɪm'perɪl) *vb.* **-illing, -illed** *or U.S.* **-iling, -iled.** (*tr.*) to place in danger or jeopardy; endanger. **—im'perilment** *n.*

imperious (ɪm'pɪərɪəs) *adj.* **1.** domineering; overbearing. **2.** *Rare.* urgent. [C16: < L, < *imperium* command, power] **—im'periously** *adv.* **—im'periousness** *n.*

imperishable (ɪm'perɪʃəb°l) *adj.* **1.** not subject to decay or deterioration. **2.** not likely to be forgotten: *imperishable truths.* **—imˌperisha'bility** *or* **im'perishableness** *n.* **—im'perishably** *adv.*

impermanent (ɪm'pɜːmənənt) *adj.* not permanent; fleeting. **—im'permanence** *or* **im'permanency** *n.* **—im'permanently** *adv.*

impermeable (ɪm'pɜːmɪəb°l) *adj.* (of a substance) not allowing the passage of a fluid through interstices; not permeable. **—imˌpermea'bility** *or* **im'permeableness** *n.* **—im'permeably** *adv.*

impermissible (ˌɪmpə'mɪsɪb°l) *adj.* not permissible; not allowed. **—ˌimperˌmissi'bility** *n.*

impersonal (ɪm'pɜːsən°l) *adj.* **1.** without reference to any individual person; objective: *an impersonal assessment.* **2.** devoid of human warmth or sympathy; cold: *an impersonal manner.* **3.** not having human characteristics: *an impersonal God.* **4.** *Grammar.* (of a verb) having no logical subject: *it is raining.* **5.** *Grammar.* (of a pronoun) not denoting a person. **—imˌperson'ality** *n.* **—im'personally** *adv.*

impersonalize *or* **-ise** (ɪm'pɜːsənəˌlaɪz) *vb.* (*tr.*) to make impersonal, esp. to rid of such human characteristics as sympathy, etc.; dehumanize. **—imˌpersonali'zation** *or* **-i'sation** *n.*

impersonate (ɪm'pɜːsəˌneɪt) *vb.* (*tr.*) **1.** to pretend to be (another person). **2.** to imitate the character, mannerisms, etc., of (another person). **3.** *Rare.* to play the part or character of. **4.** an archaic word for **personify.** **—imˌperson'ation** *n.* **—im'personˌator** *n.*

impertinence (ɪm'pɜːtɪnəns) *or* **impertinency** *n.* **1.** disrespectful behaviour or language; rudeness; insolence. **2.** an impertinent act, gesture, etc. **3.** *Rare.* lack of pertinence; irrelevance; inappropriateness.

impertinent (ɪm'pɜːtɪnənt) *adj.* **1.** rude; insolent; impudent. **2.** irrelevant or inappropriate. [C14: < L *impertinēns* not belonging, < L IM- (not) + *pertinēre* to be relevant; see PERTAIN] **—im'pertinently** *adv.*

imperturbable (ˌɪmpə'tɜːbəb°l) *adj.* not easily perturbed; calm; unruffled. **—ˌimperˌturba'bility** *or* **ˌimper'turbableness** *n.* **—ˌimper'turbably** *adv.*

impervious (ɪm'pɜːvɪəs) *or* **imperviable** *adj.* **1.** not able to be penetrated, as by water, light, etc.; impermeable. **2.** (*often postpositive;* foll. by *to*) not able to be influenced (by) or not receptive (to): *impervious to argument.* **—im'perviously** *adv.* **—im'perviousness** *n.*

impetigo (ˌɪmpɪ'taɪgəʊ) *n.* a contagious pustular skin disease. [C16: < L: scabby eruption, < *impetere* to assail; see IMPETUS; for form, cf. VERTIGO] **—impetiginous** (ˌɪmpɪ'tɪdʒɪnəs) *adj.*

impetuous (ɪm'petjʊəs) *adj.* **1.** liable to act without consideration; rash; impulsive. **2.** resulting from or characterized by rashness or haste. **3.** *Poetic.* moving with great force or violence; rushing: *the impetuous stream hurtled down the valley.* [C14: < LL *impetuōsus* violent; see IMPETUS] **—im'petuously** *adv.* **—im'petuousness** *or* **impetuosity** (ɪmˌpetjʊ'ɒsɪtɪ) *n.*

impetus ('ɪmpɪtəs) *n., pl.* **-tuses.** **1.** an impelling movement or force; incentive or impulse; stimulus. **2.** *Physics.* the force that sets a body in motion or that tends to resist changes in a body's motion. [C17: < L: attack, < *impetere* to assail, < IM- (in) + *petere* to make for, seek out]

impf. *or* **imperf.** *abbrev. for* imperfect.

impi ('ɪmpɪ) *n., pl.* **-pi** *or* **-pies.** a group of Bantu warriors. [C19: < Zulu]

impiety (ɪm'paɪɪtɪ) *n., pl.* **-ties.** **1.** lack of reverence or proper respect for a god. **2.** any lack of proper respect. **3.** an impious act.

impinge (ɪm'pɪndʒ) *vb.* **1.** (*intr.;* usually foll. by *on* or *upon*) to encroach or infringe; trespass: *to impinge on someone's time.* **2.** (*intr.;* usually foll. by *on, against,* or *upon*) to collide (with); strike. [C16: < L *impingere* to drive at, dash against, < *pangere* to fasten, drive in] **—im'pingement** *n.* **—im'pinger** *n.*

impious ('ɪmpɪəs) *adj.* **1.** lacking piety or reverence for a god. **2.** lacking respect; undutiful. **—'impiously** *adv.* **—'impiousness** *n.*

impish ('ɪmpɪʃ) *adj.* of or like an imp; mischievous. **—'impishly** *adv.* **—'impishness** *n.*

implacable (ɪm'plækəb°l) *adj.* **1.** incapable of being placated or pacified; unappeasable. **2.** inflexible; intractable. **—imˌplaca'bility** *n.* **—im'placably** *adv.*

implant *vb.* (ɪm'plɑːnt). (*tr.*) **1.** to inculcate; instil: *to implant sound moral principles.* **2.** to plant or embed; infix; entrench. **3.** *Surgery.* to graft or insert (a tissue, hormone, etc.) into the body. ~*n.* ('ɪmplɑːnt). **4.** anything implanted, esp. surgically, such as a tissue graft. **—ˌimplan'tation** *n.*

implausible (ɪm'plɔːzəb°l) *adj.* not plausible; provoking disbelief; unlikely. **—imˌplausi'bility** *or* **im'plausibleness** *n.* **—im'plausibly** *adv.*

implement *n.* ('ɪmplɪmənt). **1.** a piece of equipment; tool or utensil: *gardening implements.* **2.** a means to achieve a purpose; agent. ~*vb.* ('ɪmplɪˌment). (*tr.*) **3.** to carry out; put into action: *to implement a plan.* **4.** *Rare.* to supply with tools. [C17: < LL *implēmentum,* lit.: a filling up, < L *implēre* to fill up, satisfy, fulfil] **—ˌimple'mental** *adj.* **—ˌimplemen'tation** *n.*

implicate ('ɪmplɪˌkeɪt) *vb.* (*tr.*) **1.** to show to be involved, esp. in a crime. **2.** to imply: *his protest implicated censure by the authorities.* **3.** *Rare.* to entangle. [C16: < L *implicāre* to involve, < *plicāre* to fold] **—implicative** (ɪm'plɪkətɪv) *adj.* **—im'plicatively** *adv.*

implication (ˌɪmplɪ'keɪʃən) *n.* **1.** the act of implicating. **2.** something that is implied. **3.** *Logic.* a relation between two propositions, such that the second can be logically deduced from the first.

implicit (ɪm'plɪsɪt) *adj.* **1.** not explicit; implied; indirect. **2.** absolute and unreserved; unquestioning: *implicit trust.* **3.** (when *postpositive,* foll. by *in*) contained or inherent: *to bring out the anger implicit in the argument.* [C16: < L *implicitus,* var. of *implicātus* interwoven; see IMPLICATE] **—im'plicitly** *adv.* **—im'plicitness** *n.*

implied (ɪm'plaɪd) *adj.* hinted at or suggested; not directly expressed: *an implied criticism.*

implode (ɪm'pləʊd) *vb.* to collapse inwards. Cf. **explode.** [C19: < IM- + (EX)PLODE]

implore (ɪm'plɔː) *vb.* (*tr.*) to beg or ask (someone) earnestly (to do something); plead with; beseech; supplicate. [C16: < L *implōrāre,* < IM- + *plōrāre* to bewail] **—ˌimplo'ration** *n.* **—im'ploratory** *adj.* **—im'ploringly** *adv.*

imply (ɪm'plaɪ) *vb.* **-plying, -plied.** (*tr.; may take a clause as object*) **1.** to express or indicate by a hint; suggest. **2.** to suggest or involve as a necessary consequence. [C14: < OF *emplier,* < L; see IMPLICATE]

▷ **Usage.** See at **infer.**

impolder (ɪm'pəʊldə) *or* **empolder** *vb.* to make

into a polder; reclaim (land) from the sea. [C19: < Du. *inpolderen*, see IN-², POLDER]

impolite (ˌɪmpəˈlaɪt) *adj.* discourteous; rude. —ˌ**impoˈlitely** *adv.* —ˌ**impoˈliteness** *n.*

impolitic (ɪmˈpɒlɪtɪk) *adj.* not politic or expedient; unwise. —**imˈpoliticly** *adv.*

imponderable (ɪmˈpɒndərəbᵊl, -drəbᵊl) *adj.* **1.** unable to be weighed or assessed. ~*n.* **2.** something difficult or impossible to assess. —**imˌponderaˈbility** *or* **imˈponderableness** *n.* —**imˈponderably** *adv.*

import *vb.* (ɪmˈpɔːt, ˈɪmpɔːt). **1.** to buy or bring in (goods or services) from a foreign country. **2.** (*tr.*) to bring in from an outside source: *to import foreign words into the language.* **3.** *Rare.* to signify; mean: *to import doom.* ~*n.* (ˈɪmpɔːt). **4.** (*often pl.*) **a.** goods or services that are bought from foreign countries. **b.** (*as modifier*): *an import licence.* **5.** importance: *a man of great import.* **6.** meaning. **7.** *Canad. sl.* a sportsman who is not native to the area where he plays. [C15: < L *importāre* to carry in] —**imˈportable** *adj.* —**imˈporter** *n.*

importance (ɪmˈpɔːtᵊns) *n.* **1.** the state of being important; significance. **2.** social status; standing; esteem: *a man of importance.* **3.** *Obs.* **a.** meaning or signification. **b.** an important matter. **c.** importunity.

important (ɪmˈpɔːtᵊnt) *adj.* **1.** of great significance or value; outstanding. **2.** of social significance; notable; eminent; esteemed: *an important man in the town.* **3.** (when postpositive, usually foll. by *to*) of great concern (to); valued highly (by): *your wishes are important to me.* [C16: < OIt., < Med. L *importāre* to signify, be of consequence, < L: to carry in] —**imˈportantly** *adv.*

▷ **Usage.** In a sentence such as *he changed the financial structure of the parent company and, more important, he altered its social policy,* careful writers often prefer *more important* to *more importantly,* since the *-ly* ending of the adverb is unnecessary in parenthetical constructions. This is also true of *first, second, last,* etc., which are often preferred to *firstly, secondly, lastly,* etc.; *first, he introduced the sonnet to his homeland; second, he initiated influential poetic experiments; last and most important, he was able to create an atmosphere of sincerity in his poetry.*

importation (ˌɪmpɔːˈteɪʃən) *n.* **1.** the act, business, or process of importing goods or services. **2.** an imported product or service.

importunate (ɪmˈpɔːtjʊnɪt) *adj.* **1.** persistent or demanding; insistent. **2.** *Rare.* troublesome; annoying. —**imˈportunately** *adv.* —**imˈportunateness** *n.*

importune (ɪmˈpɔːtjuːn, ˌɪmpɔːˈtjuːn) *vb.* (*tr.*) **1.** to harass with persistent requests; demand of (someone) insistently. **2.** to beg for persistently; request with insistence. [C16: < L *importūnus* tiresome, < *im-* IN-¹ + *-portūnus* as in *opportūnus* OPPORTUNE] —**imˈportunely** *adv.* —**imˈportuner** *n.* —ˌ**imporˈtunity** *or* **imˈportunacy** *n.*

impose (ɪmˈpəʊz) *vb.* (usually foll. by *on* or *upon*) **1.** (*tr.*) to establish as something to be obeyed or complied with; enforce. **2.** to force (oneself, one's presence, etc.) on others; obtrude. **3.** (*intr.*) to take advantage, as of a person or quality: *to impose on someone's kindness.* **4.** (*tr.*) *Printing.* to arrange (pages, type, etc.) in a chase so that the pages will be in the correct order. **5.** (*tr.*) to pass off deceptively; foist. [C15: < OF, < L *impōnere* to place upon, < *pōnere* to place, set] —**imˈposable** *adj.* —**imˈposer** *n.*

imposing (ɪmˈpəʊzɪŋ) *adj.* grand or impressive: *an imposing building.* —**imˈposingly** *adv.* —**imˈposingness** *n.*

imposition (ˌɪmpəˈzɪʃən) *n.* **1.** the act of imposing. **2.** something imposed unfairly on someone. **3.** a task set as a school punishment. **4.** the arrangement of pages for printing.

impossibility (ɪmˌpɒsəˈbɪlɪtɪ, ˌɪmpɒs-) *n., pl.* **-ties.** **1.** the state or quality of being impossible. **2.** something that is impossible.

impossible (ɪmˈpɒsəbᵊl) *adj.* **1.** incapable of being done, undertaken, or experienced. **2.** incapable of occurring or happening. **3.** absurd or inconceivable; unreasonable. **4.** *Inf.* intolerable; outrageous: *those children are impossible.* —**imˈpossibleness** *n.* —**imˈpossibly** *adv.*

impossible figure *n.* a picture of an object that at first sight looks three-dimensional but cannot be a two-dimensional projection of a real three-dimensional object, for example a picture of a staircase that re-enters itself while appearing to ascend continuously.

impost¹ (ˈɪmpəʊst) *n.* **1.** a tax, esp. a customs duty. **2.** the weight that a horse must carry in a handicap race. ~*vb.* **3.** (*tr.*) *U.S.* to classify (imported goods) according to the duty payable on them. [C16: < Med. L *impostus* tax, < L *impositus* imposed; see IMPOSE] —ˈ**imposter** *n.*

impost² (ˈɪmpəʊst) *n. Archit.* a member at the top of a column that supports an arch. [C17: < F *imposte,* < L *impositus* placed upon; see IMPOSE]

impostor *or* **imposter** (ɪmˈpɒstə) *n.* a person who deceives others, esp. by assuming a false identity; charlatan. [C16: < LL: deceiver; see IMPOSE]

imposture (ɪmˈpɒstʃə) *n.* the act or an instance of deceiving others, esp. by assuming a false identity. [C16: < F, < LL, < L *impōnere;* see IMPOSE] —**impostrous** (ɪmˈpɒstrəs) *or* **impostorous** (ɪmˈpɒstərəs) *adj.*

impotent (ˈɪmpətənt) *adj.* **1.** (when *postpositive,* often takes an infinitive) lacking sufficient strength; powerless. **2.** (esp. of males) unable to perform sexual intercourse. —ˈ**impotence** *or* ˈ**impotency** *n.* —ˈ**impotently** *adv.*

impound (ɪmˈpaʊnd) *vb.* (*tr.*) **1.** to confine (animals, etc.) in a pound. **2.** to take legal possession of (a document, evidence, etc.). **3.** to collect (water) in a reservoir or dam. —**imˈpoundable** *adj.* —**imˈpoundage** *or* **imˈpoundment** *n.* —**imˈpounder** *n.*

impoverish (ɪmˈpɒvərɪʃ) *vb.* (*tr.*) **1.** to make poor or diminish the quality of: *to impoverish society by cutting the grant to the arts.* **2.** to deprive (soil, etc.) of fertility. [C15: < OF *empovrir,* < *povre* POOR] —**imˈpoverishment** *n.*

impracticable (ɪmˈpræktɪkəbᵊl) *adj.* **1.** incapable of being put into practice or accomplished; not feasible. **2.** unsuitable for a desired use; unfit. —**imˌpracticaˈbility** *or* **imˈpracticableness** *n.* —**imˈpracticably** *adv.*

impractical (ɪmˈpræktɪkᵊl) *adj.* **1.** not practical or workable: *an impractical solution.* **2.** not given to practical matters or gifted with practical skills. —**imˌpractiˈcality** *or* **imˈpracticalness** *n.* —**imˈpractically** *adv.*

imprecate (ˈɪmprɪˌkeɪt) *vb.* **1.** (*intr.*) to swear or curse. **2.** (*tr.*) to invoke or bring down (evil, a curse, etc.). [C17: < L *imprecārī* to invoke, < *im-* IN-² + *precārī* to PRAY] —ˌ**impreˈcation** *n.* —ˈ**impreˌcatory** *adj.*

imprecise (ˌɪmprɪˈsaɪs) *adj.* not precise; inexact or inaccurate. —ˌ**impreˈcisely** *adv.* —**imprecision** (ˌɪmprɪˈsɪʒən) *or* ˌ**impreˈciseness** *n.*

impregnable¹ (ɪmˈprɛgnəbᵊl) *adj.* **1.** unable to be broken into or taken by force: *an impregnable castle.* **2.** unshakable: *impregnable self-confidence.* **3.** incapable of being refuted: *an impregnable argument.* [C15 *imprenable,* < OF, < IM- (not) + *prenable* able to be taken, < *prendre* to take] —**imˌpregnaˈbility** *n.* —**imˈpregnably** *adv.*

impregnable² (ɪmˈprɛgnəbᵊl) *or* **impregnatable** (ˌɪmprɛgˈneɪtəbᵊl) *adj.* able to be impregnated; fertile.

impregnate *vb.* (ˈɪmprɛgˌneɪt). (*tr.*) **1.** to saturate, soak, or infuse. **2.** to imbue or permeate; pervade. **3.** to cause to conceive; make pregnant; fertilize. **4.** to make (land, soil, etc.) fruitful. ~*adj.* (ɪmˈprɛgnɪt, -ˌneɪt). **5.** pregnant or fertilized. [C17: < LL, < L *im-* IN-² + *praegnans* PREGNANT] —ˌ**impregˈnation** *n.* —**imˈpregnator** *n.*

impresario (ˌɪmprəˈsɑːrɪˌəʊ) *n., pl.* **-sarios.** the director or manager of an opera, ballet, etc. [C18: < It., lit.: one who undertakes]

imprescriptible (ˌɪmprɪˈskrɪptəbᵊl) *adj. Law.* immune or exempt from prescription. —ˌ**impreˌscriptiˈbility** *n.* —ˌ**impreˈscriptibly** *adv.*

impress[1] *vb.* (ɪmˈprɛs). (*tr.*) **1.** to make an impression on; have a strong, lasting, or favourable effect on: *I am impressed by your work.* **2.** to produce (an imprint, etc.) by pressure in or on (something): *to impress a seal in wax.* **3.** (often foll. by *on*) to stress (something to a person); urge; emphasize. **4.** to exert pressure on; press. ~*n.* (ˈɪmprɛs). **5.** the act or an instance of impressing. **6.** a mark, imprint, or effect produced by impressing. [C14: < L *imprimere* to press into, imprint] —**imˈpresser** *n.* —**imˈpressible** *adj.*

impress[2] *vb.* (ɪmˈprɛs). **1.** to commandeer or coerce (men or things) into government service; press-gang. ~*n.* (ˈɪmprɛs). **2.** the act of commandeering or coercing into government service. [C16: see *im-* IN-[2], PRESS[2]]

impression (ɪmˈprɛʃən) *n.* **1.** an effect produced in the mind by a stimulus; sensation: *he gave the impression of wanting to help.* **2.** an imprint or mark produced by pressing. **3.** a vague idea, consciousness, or belief: *I had the impression we had met before.* **4.** a strong, favourable, or remarkable effect. **5.** the act of impressing or the state of being impressed. **6.** *Printing.* **a.** the act, process, or result of printing from type, plates, etc. **b.** the total number of copies of a publication printed at one time. **7.** an imprint of the teeth and gums for preparing crowns, dentures, etc. **8.** an imitation or impersonation. —**imˈpressional** *adj.* —**imˈpressionally** *adv.*

impressionable (ɪmˈprɛʃənəbᵊl, -ˈprɛʃnə-) *adj.* easily influenced or characterized by susceptibility to influence: *an impressionable age.* —**imˌpressionaˈbility** *or* **imˈpressionableness** *n.*

impressionism (ɪmˈprɛʃəˌnɪzəm) *n.* (*often cap.*) a 19th-century movement in French painting, having the aim of objectively recording experience by a system of fleeting impressions, esp. of natural light effects. —**imˈpressionist** *n.*

impressive (ɪmˈprɛsɪv) *adj.* capable of impressing, esp. by size, magnificence, etc.; awe-inspiring; commanding. —**imˈpressively** *adv.* —**imˈpressiveness** *n.*

imprest (ɪmˈprɛst) *n.* **1.** a fund of cash from which a department, etc., pays incidental expenses, topped up periodically from central funds. **2.** *Chiefly Brit.* an advance from government funds for some public business or service. [C16: prob. < It. *imprestare* to lend, < L *in-* towards + *praestāre* to pay, < *praestō* at hand; see PRESTO]

imprimatur (ˌɪmprɪˈmeɪtə, -ˈmɑː-) *n.* **1.** sanction or approval for something to be printed. **2.** *R.C. Church.* a licence certifying the Church's approval. [C17: NL, lit.: let it be printed]

imprint *n.* (ˈɪmprɪnt). **1.** a mark or impression produced by pressure, printing, or stamping. **2.** a characteristic mark or indication; stamp: *the imprint of great sadness on his face.* **3. a.** the publisher's name and address, often with the date of publication, printed in a book, usually on the title page or the verso title page. **b.** the printer's name and address on any printed matter. ~*vb.* (ɪmˈprɪnt). (*tr.*) **4.** to produce (a mark, impression, etc.) on (a surface) by pressure, printing, or stamping: *to imprint a seal on wax.* **5.** to establish firmly; impress: *to imprint the details on one's mind.* **6.** to cause (a young animal) to undergo the process of imprinting: *chicks can be imprinted on human beings if the mother is absent.*

imprinting (ɪmˈprɪntɪŋ) *n.* the development in young animals of recognition of and attraction to members of their own species or surrogates.

imprison (ɪmˈprɪzən) *vb.* (*tr.*) to confine in or as if in prison. —**imˈprisonment** *n.*

improbable (ɪmˈprɒbəbᵊl) *adj.* not likely or probable; doubtful; unlikely. —**imˌprobaˈbility** *or* **imˈprobableness** *n.* —**imˈprobably** *adv.*

improbity (ɪmˈprəʊbɪtɪ) *n., pl.* **-ties.** dishonesty, wickedness, or unscrupulousness.

impromptu (ɪmˈprɒmptjuː) *adj.* **1.** unrehearsed; spontaneous; extempore. **2.** produced or done without care or planning; improvised. ~*adv.* **3.** in a spontaneous or improvised way: *he spoke impromptu.* ~*n.* **4.** something that is impromptu. **5.** a short piece of instrumental music, sometimes improvisatory in character. [C17: < F, < L *in promptū* in readiness, < *promptus* (adj.) ready, PROMPT]

improper (ɪmˈprɒpə) *adj.* **1.** lacking propriety; not seemly. **2.** unsuitable for a certain use or occasion; inappropriate. **3.** irregular or abnormal. —**imˈproperly** *adv.* —**imˈproperness** *n.*

improper fraction *n.* a fraction in which the numerator is greater than the denominator, as 7/6.

impropriate *vb.* (ɪmˈprəʊprɪˌeɪt). **1.** (*tr.*) to transfer (property, rights, etc.) from the Church into lay hands. ~*adj.* (ɪmˈprəʊprɪɪt, -ˌeɪt). **2.** transferred in this way. [C16: < Med. L *impropriāre* to make one's own, < L *im-* IN-[2] + *propriāre* to APPROPRIATE] —**imˌpropriˈation** *n.* —**imˈpropriˌator** *n.*

impropriety (ˌɪmprəˈpraɪɪtɪ) *n., pl.* **-ties.** **1.** lack of propriety; indecency; indecorum. **2.** an improper act or use. **3.** the state of being improper.

improve (ɪmˈpruːv) *vb.* **1.** to make or become better in quality; ameliorate. **2.** (*tr.*) to make (buildings, land, etc.) more valuable by additions or betterment. **3.** (*intr.;* usually foll. by *on* or *upon*) to achieve a better standard or quality in comparison (with): *to improve on last year's crop.* [C16: < Anglo-F *emprouer* to turn to profit, < LL *prōde* beneficial, < L *prōdesse* to be advantageous] —**imˈprovable** *adj.* —**imˌprovaˈbility** *or* **imˈprovableness** *n.* —**imˈprover** *n.*

improvement (ɪmˈpruːvmənt) *n.* **1.** the act of improving or the state of being improved. **2.** something that improves, esp. an addition or alteration. **3.** *Austral. & N.Z.* a building on a piece of land, adding to its value.

improvident (ɪmˈprɒvɪdənt) *adj.* **1.** not provident; thriftless, imprudent, or prodigal. **2.** heedless or incautious; rash. —**imˈprovidence** *n.* —**imˈprovidently** *adv.*

improvise (ˈɪmprəˌvaɪz) *vb.* **1.** to perform or make quickly from materials and sources available, without previous planning. **2.** to perform (a poem, play, piece of music, etc.), composing as one goes along. [C19: < F, < It., < L *imprōvīsus* unforeseen, < *prōvidēre* to foresee; see PROVIDE] —**ˈimproˌviser** *n.* —ˌ**improviˈsation** *n.* —**improvisatory** (ˌɪmprəˈvaɪzətərɪ, -ˈvɪz-, ˌɪmprəvaɪzˈeɪtərɪ) *adj.*

imprudent (ɪmˈpruːdᵊnt) *adj.* not prudent; rash, heedless, or indiscreet. —**imˈprudence** *n.* —**imˈprudently** *adv.*

impudence (ˈɪmpjʊdəns) *or* **impudency** *n.* **1.** the quality of being impudent. **2.** an impudent act or statement. [C14: < L *impudēns* shameless]

impudent (ˈɪmpjʊdənt) *adj.* **1.** mischievous, impertinent, or disrespectful. **2.** *Obs.* immodest. —**ˈimpudently** *adv.* —**ˈimpudentness** *n.*

impugn (ɪmˈpjuːn) *vb.* (*tr.*) to challenge or attack as false; criticize. [C14: < OF, < L *impugnāre* to fight against, attack] —**imˈpugnable** *adj.* —**imˈpugnment** *n.* —**imˈpugner** *n.*

impulse (ˈɪmpʌls) *n.* **1.** an impelling force or motion; thrust; impetus. **2.** a sudden desire, whim, or inclination. **3.** an instinctive drive; urge. **4.** tendency; current; trend. **5.** *Physics.* **a.** the product of the average magnitude of a force acting on a body and the time for which it acts. **b.** the change in the momentum of a body as a result of a force acting upon it. **6.** *Physiol.* See **nerve impulse.** **7. on impulse.** spontaneously or impulsively. [C17: < L *impulsus* a pushing against, incitement, < *impellere* to strike against; see IMPEL]

impulse buying *n.* the buying of merchandise prompted by a whim. —**impulse buyer** *n.*

impulsion (ɪmˈpʌlʃən) *n.* **1.** the act of impelling

or the state of being impelled. 2. motion produced by an impulse; propulsion. 3. a driving force; compulsion.

impulsive (ɪmˈpʌlsɪv) *adj.* 1. characterized by actions based on sudden desires, whims, or inclinations: *an impulsive man.* 2. based on emotional impulses or whims; spontaneous. 3. forceful, inciting, or impelling. 4. (of physical forces) acting for a short time; not continuous. —**imˈpulsively** *adv.* —**imˈpulsiveness** *n.*

impundulu (ˈɪmpʊnˌdʊlʊ) *n. S. African.* a mythical bird often associated with witchcraft. [< Bantu]

impunity (ɪmˈpjuːnɪtɪ) *n., pl.* **-ties.** 1. exemption or immunity from punishment, recrimination, or other unpleasant consequences. 2. **with impunity.** with no care or heed for such consequences. [C16: < L, < *impūnis* unpunished, < IM- (not) + *poena* punishment]

impure (ɪmˈpjʊə) *adj.* 1. not pure; combined with something else; tainted or sullied. 2. (in certain religions) ritually unclean. 3. (of a colour) mixed with another colour. 4. of more than one origin or style, as of architecture. —**imˈpurely** *adv.* —**imˈpureness** *n.*

impurity (ɪmˈpjʊərɪtɪ) *n., pl.* **-ties.** 1. the quality of being impure. 2. an impure thing, constituent, or element: *impurities in the water.* 3. *Electronics.* a small quantity of an element added to a pure semiconductor crystal to control its electrical conductivity.

impute (ɪmˈpjuːt) *vb.* (*tr.*) 1. to attribute or ascribe (something dishonest or dishonourable) to a person. 2. to attribute to a source or cause: *I impute your success to nepotism.* 3. *Commerce.* to give (a notional value) to goods, etc., when the real value is unknown. [C14: < L, < IM- + *putāre* to think, calculate] —ˌ**impuˈtation** *n.* —**imˈputative** *adj.* —**imˈputer** *n.* —**imˈputable** *adj.*

IMunE *abbrev. for* Institution of Municipal Engineers.

in (ɪn) *prep.* 1. inside; within: *no smoking in the auditorium.* 2. at a place where there is: *in the shade; in the rain.* 3. indicating a state, situation, or condition: *in silence.* 4. when (a period of time) has elapsed: *come back in one year.* 5. using: *written in code.* 6. concerned with, esp. as an occupation: *in journalism.* 7. while or by performing the action of: *in crossing the street he was run over.* 8. used to indicate purpose: *in honour of the president.* 9. (of certain animals) pregnant with: *in calf.* 10. a variant of **into:** *she fell in the water.* 11. **have it in one.** (often foll. by an infinitive) to have the ability (to do something). 12. **in that** *or* **in so far as.** (*conj.*) because or to the extent that: *I regret my remark in that it upset you.* 13. **nothing in it.** no difference or interval between two things. ~*adv.* (*particle*) 14. in or into a particular place; inward or indoors: *come in.* 15. so as to achieve office or power: *the Conservatives got in at the last election.* 16. so as to enclose: *block in.* 17. (in certain games) so as to take one's turn of the play: *you have to get the other side out before you go in.* 18. *N.Z.* competing: *you've got to be in to win.* 19. *Brit.* (of a fire) alight. 20. (*in combination*) indicating an activity or gathering: *teach-in; work-in.* 21. **in at.** present at (the beginning, end, etc.). 22. **in for.** about to be affected by (something, esp. something unpleasant): *you're in for a shock.* 23. **in on.** acquainted with or sharing in: *I was in on all his plans.* 24. **in with.** associated with; friendly with; regarded highly by. 25. **have (got) it in for.** to wish or intend harm towards. ~*adj.* 26. (*stressed*) fashionable; modish: *the in thing to do.* ~*n.* 27. **ins and outs.** intricacies or complications; details. [OE]

In *the chemical symbol for* indium.

in. *abbrev. for* inch(es).

in-[1], **il-, im-,** *or* **ir-** *prefix.* **a.** not; non-: *incredible; illegal; imperfect; irregular.* **b.** lack of: *inexperience.* Cf. **un-**[1]. [< L *in-;* rel. to *ne-, nōn* not]

in-[2], **il-, im-,** *or* **ir-** *prefix.* 1. in; into; towards; within; on: *infiltrate; immigrate.* 2. having an intensive or causative function: *inflame; imperil.* [< IN (prep., adv.)]

-in *suffix forming nouns.* 1. indicating a neutral organic compound, including proteins, glucosides, and glycerides: *insulin; tripalmitin.* 2. indicating an enzyme in certain nonsystematic names: *pepsin.* 3. indicating a pharmaceutical substance: *penicillin; aspirin.* 4. indicating a chemical substance in certain nonsystematic names: *coumarin.* [< NL *-ina;* cf. -INE[2]]

in absentia *Latin.* (ɪn æbˈsɛntɪə) *adv.* in the absence of (someone indicated).

inaccessible (ˌɪnækˈsɛsəbᵊl) *adj.* not accessible; unapproachable. —ˌ**inacˌcessiˈbility** *or* ˌ**inacˈcessibleness** *n.* —ˌ**inacˈcessibly** *adv.*

inaccuracy (ɪnˈækjʊrəsɪ) *n., pl.* **-cies.** 1. lack of accuracy; imprecision. 2. an error, mistake, or slip. —**inˈaccurate** *adj.*

inaction (ɪnˈækʃən) *n.* lack of action; idleness; inertia.

inactivate (ɪnˈæktɪˌveɪt) *vb.* (*tr.*) to render inactive. —**inˌactiˈvation** *n.*

inactive (ɪnˈæktɪv) *adj.* 1. idle or inert; not active. 2. sluggish or indolent. 3. *Mil.* of or relating to persons or equipment not in active service. 4. *Chem.* (of a substance) having little or no reactivity. —**inˈactively** *adv.* —ˌ**inacˈtivity** *n.*

inadequate (ɪnˈædɪkwɪt) *adj.* 1. not adequate; insufficient. 2. not capable; lacking. —**inˈadequacy** *n.* —**inˈadequately** *adv.*

inadvertence (ˌɪnədˈvɜːtᵊns) *or* **inadvertency** *n.* 1. lack of attention; heedlessness. 2. an oversight; slip.

inadvertent (ˌɪnədˈvɜːtᵊnt) *adj.* 1. failing to act carefully or considerately; inattentive. 2. resulting from heedless action; unintentional. —ˌ**inadˈvertently** *adv.*

-inae *suffix forming plural proper nouns.* occurring in names of zoological subfamilies: *Felinae.* [NL, < L, fem. pl. of *-īnus* -INE[1]]

inalienable (ɪnˈeɪljənəbᵊl) *adj.* not able to be transferred to another; not alienable: *the inalienable rights of the citizen.* —**inˌalienaˈbility** *or* **inˈalienableness** *n.* —**inˈalienably** *adv.*

inalterable (ɪnˈɔːltərəbᵊl) *adj.* not alterable; unalterable. —**inˌalteraˈbility** *or* **inˈalterableness** *n.* —**inˈalterably** *adv.*

inamorata (ɪnˌæməˈrɑːtə, ˌɪnæmə-) *or* (*masc.*) **inamorato** (ɪnˌæməˈrɑːtəʊ, ˌɪnæmə-) *n., pl.* **-tas** *or* (*masc.*) **-tos.** a person with whom one is in love; lover. [C17: < It., < *innamorare* to cause to fall in love, < *amore* love, < L *amor*]

inane (ɪˈneɪn) *adj.* 1. senseless, unimaginative, or empty; unintelligent: *inane remarks.* ~*n.* 2. *Arch.* something empty or vacant, esp. the void of space. [C17: < L *inānis* empty] —**inˈanely** *adv.*

inanimate (ɪnˈænɪmɪt) *adj.* 1. lacking the qualities of living beings; not animate: *inanimate objects.* 2. lacking any sign of life or consciousness; appearing dead. 3. lacking vitality; dull. —**inˈanimately** *adv.* —**inˈanimateness** *or* **inanimation** (ɪnˌænɪˈmeɪʃən) *n.*

inanition (ˌɪnəˈnɪʃən) *n.* 1. exhaustion resulting from lack of food. 2. mental, social, or spiritual weakness or lassitude. [C14: < LL *inānītio* emptiness, < L *inānis* empty; see INANE]

inanity (ɪˈnænɪtɪ) *n., pl.* **-ties.** 1. lack of intelligence or imagination; senselessness; silliness. 2. a senseless action, remark, etc. 3. an archaic word for **emptiness.**

inapposite (ɪnˈæpəzɪt) *adj.* not appropriate or pertinent; unsuitable. —**inˈappositely** *adv.* —**inˈappositeness** *n.*

inapt (ɪnˈæpt) *adj.* 1. not apt or fitting; inappropriate. 2. lacking skill; inept. —**inˈaptiˌtude** *or* **inˈaptness** *n.* —**inˈaptly** *adv.*

ˌ**inaˈbility** *n.*
ˌ**inadˈmissible** *adj.*
ˌ**inadˈvisable** *adj.*
inˈappetence *n.*
inˈapplicable *adj.*
ˌ**inapˈpreciable** *adj.*
ˌ**inapˈpreciative** *adj.*
ˌ**inapˈpropriate** *adj.*

inarch (ɪnˈɑːtʃ) *vb.* (*tr.*) to graft (a plant) by uniting stock and scion while both are still growing independently.

inasmuch as (ˌɪnəzˈmʌtʃ) *conj.* (*subordinating*) **1.** in view of the fact that; seeing that; since. **2.** to the extent or degree that; in so far as.

inaugural (ɪnˈɔːgjʊrəl) *adj.* **1.** characterizing or relating to an inauguration. *~n.* **2.** a speech made at an inauguration, esp. by a president of the U.S.

inaugurate (ɪnˈɔːgjʊˌreɪt) *vb.* (*tr.*) **1.** to commence officially or formally; initiate. **2.** to place in office formally and ceremonially; induct. **3.** to open ceremonially; dedicate formally: *to inaugurate a factory.* [C17: < L *inaugurāre*, lit.: to take omens, practise augury, hence to install in office after taking auguries; see IN-², AUGUR] **—inˌauguˈration** *n.* **—inˈauguˌrator** *n.* **—inauguratory** (ɪnˈɔːgjʊrətərɪ, -trɪ) *adj.*

in-between *adj.* intermediate: *he's at the in-between stage, neither a child nor an adult.*

inboard (ˈɪnˌbɔːd) *adj.* **1.** (esp. of a boat's motor or engine) situated within the hull. **2.** situated between the wing tip of an aircraft and its fuselage: *an inboard engine.* *~adv.* **3.** towards the centre line of or within a vessel, aircraft, etc.

inborn (ˈɪnˈbɔːn) *adj.* existing from birth; congenital; innate.

inbred (ˈɪnˈbrɛd) *adj.* **1.** produced as a result of inbreeding. **2.** deeply ingrained; innate: *inbred good manners.*

inbreed (ˈɪnˈbriːd) *vb.* **-breeding, -bred. 1.** to breed from unions between closely related individuals, esp. over several generations. **2.** (*tr.*) to develop within; engender. **—ˈinˈbreeding** *n., adj.*

in-built *adj.* built-in, integral.

inc. *abbrev. for:* **1.** including. **2.** inclusive. **3.** income. **4.** increase.

Inc. (esp. U.S.) *abbrev. for* incorporated.

incalculable (ɪnˈkælkjʊləbᵊl) *adj.* beyond calculation; unable to be predicted or determined. **—inˌcalculaˈbility** *n.* **—inˈcalculably** *adv.*

incandesce (ˌɪnkænˈdɛs) *vb.* (*intr.*) to make or become incandescent.

incandescent (ˌɪnkænˈdɛsᵊnt) *adj.* emitting light as a result of being heated; red-hot or white-hot. [C18: < L *incandescere* to become hot, glow, < *candēre* to be white; see CANDID] **—ˌincanˈdescently** *adv.* **—ˌincanˈdescence** *n.*

incandescent lamp *n.* a source of light that contains a heated solid, such as an electrically heated filament.

incantation (ˌɪnkænˈteɪʃən) *n.* **1.** ritual recitation of magic words or sounds. **2.** the formulaic words or sounds used; a magic spell. [C14: < LL *incantātiō* an enchanting, < *incantāre* to repeat magic formulas, < L, < IN-² + *cantāre* to sing; see ENCHANT] **—ˌincanˈtational** *or* **inˈcantatory** *adj.*

incapacitate (ˌɪnkəˈpæsɪˌteɪt) *vb.* (*tr.*) **1.** to deprive of power, strength, or capacity; disable. **2.** to deprive of legal capacity or eligibility. **—ˌincaˌpaciˈtation** *n.*

incapacity (ˌɪnkəˈpæsɪtɪ) *n., pl.* **-ties. 1.** lack of power, strength, or capacity; inability. **2.** *Law.* legal disqualification or ineligibility.

in-car *adj.* (of hi-fi equipment, etc.) installed inside a car.

incarcerate (ɪnˈkɑːsəˌreɪt) *vb.* (*tr.*) to confine or imprison. [C16: < Med. L, < L IN-² + *carcer* prison] **—inˌcarcerˈation** *n.* **—inˈcarcerˌator** *n.*

incarnadine (ɪnˈkɑːnəˌdaɪn) *Arch. or literary.* *~vb.* **1.** (*tr.*) to tinge or stain with red. *~adj.* **2.** of a pinkish or reddish colour similar to that of flesh or blood. [C16: < F *incarnadin* flesh-coloured, < It., < LL *incarnātus* made flesh, INCARNATE]

incarnate *adj.* (ɪnˈkɑːnɪt, -neɪt). (*usually immediately postpositive*) **1.** possessing bodily form, esp. the human form: *a devil incarnate.* **2.** personified or typified: *stupidity incarnate.* *~vb.* (ɪnˈkɑːneɪt). (*tr.*) **3.** to give a bodily or concrete form to. **4.** to be representative or typical of. [C14: < LL *incarnāre* to make flesh, < L IN-² + *carō* flesh]

incarnation (ˌɪnkɑːˈneɪʃən) *n.* **1.** the act of manifesting or state of being manifested in bodily form, esp. human form. **2.** a bodily form assumed by a god, etc. **3.** a person or thing that typifies or represents some quality, idea, etc.

Incarnation (ˌɪnkɑːˈneɪʃən) *n. Christian theol.* the assuming of a human body by the Son of God.

incarvillea (ˌɪnkɑːˈvɪlɪə) *n.* any of various perennials with pink flowers and pinnate leaves. Also called: **Chinese trumpet flower.** [C18: after Pierre d'*Incarville*, F missionary in China]

incase (ɪnˈkeɪs) *vb.* a variant spelling of **encase.** **—inˈcasement** *n.*

incautious (ɪnˈkɔːʃəs) *adj.* not careful or cautious. **—inˈcautiously** *adv.* **—inˈcautiousness** *or* **inˈcaution** *n.*

incendiary (ɪnˈsɛndɪərɪ) *adj.* **1.** of or relating to the illegal burning of property, goods, etc. **2.** tending to create strife, violence, etc. **3.** (of a substance) capable of catching fire or burning readily. *~n., pl.* **-aries. 4.** a person who illegally sets fire to property, goods, etc.; arsonist. **5.** (esp. formerly) a person who stirs up civil strife, violence, etc.; agitator. **6.** Also called: **incendiary bomb.** a bomb that is designed to start fires. **7.** an incendiary substance, such as phosphorus. [C17: < L, < *incendium* fire, < *incendere* to kindle] **—inˈcendiaˌrism** *n.*

incense[1] (ˈɪnsɛns) *n.* **1.** any of various aromatic substances burnt for their fragrant odour, esp. in religious ceremonies. **2.** the odour or smoke so produced. **3.** any pleasant fragrant odour; aroma. *~vb.* **4.** to burn incense in honour of (a deity). **5.** (*tr.*) to perfume or fumigate with incense. [C13: < OF *encens*, < Church L *incensum*, < L *incendere* to kindle]

incense[2] (ɪnˈsɛns) *vb.* (*tr.*) to enrage greatly. [C15: < L *incensus* set on fire, < *incendere* to kindle] **—inˈcensement** *n.*

incensory (ˈɪnsɛnsərɪ) *n., pl.* **-ries.** a less common name for **censer.** [C17: < Med. L *incensorium*]

incentive (ɪnˈsɛntɪv) *n.* **1.** a motivating influence; stimulus. **2. a.** an additional payment made to employees to increase production. **b.** (*as modifier*): *an incentive scheme.* *~adj.* **3.** serving to incite to action. [C15: < LL, < L: striking up, setting the tune, < *incinere* to sing]

incept (ɪnˈsɛpt) *vb.* (*tr.*) **1.** (of organisms) to ingest (food). **2.** *Brit.* (formerly) to take a master's or doctor's degree at a university. [C19: < L *inceptus* begun, attempted, < *incipere* to begin, take in hand] **—inˈceptor** *n.*

inception (ɪnˈsɛpʃən) *n.* the beginning, as of a project or undertaking.

inceptive (ɪnˈsɛptɪv) *adj.* **1.** beginning; incipient; initial. **2.** Also called: **inchoative.** *Grammar.* denoting a verb used to indicate the beginning of an action. *~n.* **3.** *Grammar.* an inceptive verb. **—inˈceptively** *adv.*

incertitude (ɪnˈsɜːtɪˌtjuːd) *n.* **1.** uncertainty; doubt. **2.** a state of mental or emotional insecurity.

incessant (ɪnˈsɛsᵊnt) *adj.* not ceasing; continual. [C16: < LL, < L IN-¹ + *cessāre* to CEASE] **—inˈcessancy** *n.* **—inˈcessantly** *adv.*

incest (ˈɪnsɛst) *n.* sexual intercourse between two persons who are too closely related to marry. [C13: < L, < IN-¹ + *castus* CHASTE]

incestuous (ɪnˈsɛstjʊəs) *adj.* **1.** relating to or involving incest: *an incestuous union.* **2.** guilty of incest. **3.** resembling incest in excessive or claustrophobic intimacy. **—inˈcestuously** *adv.* **—inˈcestuousness** *n.*

inch[1] (ɪntʃ) *n.* **1.** a unit of length equal to one twelfth of a foot or 0.0254 metre. **2.** *Meteorol.* **a.** an amount of precipitation that would cover a surface with water one inch deep. **b.** a unit of

---

ˌ**inarˈticulate** *adj.*
ˌ**inarˈtistic** *adj.*
ˌ**inatˈtentive** *adj.*
inˈaudible *adj.*
ˌ**inausˈpicious** *adj.*
inˈcapable *adj.*

pressure equal to a mercury column one inch high in a barometer. **3.** a very small distance, degree, or amount. **4. every inch.** in every way; completely: *every inch an aristocrat.* **5. inch by inch.** gradually; little by little. **6. within an inch of one's life.** almost to death. ~*vb.* **7.** to move or be moved very slowly or in very small steps: *the car inched forward.* [OE *ynce;* see OUNCE[1]]

inch[2] (ɪntʃ) *n. Scot. & Irish.* a small island. [C15: < Gaelic *innis* island; cf. Welsh *ynys*]

inchoate *adj.* (ɪnˈkəʊeɪt, -ˈkəʊɪt). **1.** just beginning; incipient. **2.** undeveloped; immature; rudimentary. ~*vb.* (ɪnˈkəʊeɪt). (*tr.*) **3.** to begin. [C16: < L *incohāre* to make a beginning, lit.: to hitch up, < IN-[2] + *cohum* yokestrap] —**inˈchoately** *adv.* —**inˈchoateness** *n.* —ˌ**inchoˈation** *n.* —**inchoative** (ɪnˈkəʊətɪv) *adj.*

inchworm (ˈɪntʃˌwɜːm) *n.* another name for **measuring worm.**

incidence (ˈɪnsɪdəns) *n.* **1.** degree, extent, or frequency of occurrence; amount: *a high incidence of death from pneumonia.* **2.** the act or manner of impinging on or affecting by proximity or influence. **3.** *Physics.* the arrival of a beam of light or particles at a surface. See also **angle of incidence. 4.** *Geom.* the partial coincidence of two configurations, such as a point on a circle.

incident (ˈɪnsɪdənt) *n.* **1.** a definite occurrence; event. **2.** a minor, subsidiary, or related event. **3.** a relatively insignificant event that might have serious consequences. **4.** a public disturbance. ~*adj.* **5.** (*postpositive;* foll. by *to*) related (to) or dependent (on). **6.** (when *postpositive,* often foll. by *to*) having a subsidiary or minor relationship (with). **7.** (esp. of a beam of light or particles) arriving at or striking a surface. [C15: < Med. L, < L *incidere,* lit.: to fall into, hence befall, happen]

incidental (ˌɪnsɪˈdɛntᵊl) *adj.* **1.** happening in connection with or resulting from something more important; casual or fortuitous. **2.** (*postpositive;* foll. by *to*) found in connection (with); related (to). **3.** (*postpositive;* foll. by *upon*) caused (by). **4.** occasional or minor: *incidental expenses.* ~*n.* **5.** (*often pl.*) a minor expense, event, or action. —ˌ**inciˈdentalness** *n.*

incidentally (ˌɪnsɪˈdɛntəlɪ) *adv.* **1.** as a subordinate or chance occurrence. **2.** (*sentence modifier*) by the way.

incidental music *n.* background music for a film, etc.

incinerate (ɪnˈsɪnəˌreɪt) *vb.* to burn up completely; reduce to ashes. [C16: < Med. L, < L IN-[2] + *cinis* ashes] —**inˌcinerˈation** *n.*

incinerator (ɪnˈsɪnəˌreɪtə) *n.* a furnace or apparatus for incinerating something, esp. refuse.

incipient (ɪnˈsɪpɪənt) *adj.* just starting to be or happen; beginning. [C17: < L, < *incipere* to begin, take in hand] —**inˈcipience** *or* **inˈcipiency** *n.* —**inˈcipiently** *adv.*

incise (ɪnˈsaɪz) *vb.* (*tr.*) to produce (lines, a design, etc.) by cutting into the surface of (something) with a sharp tool. [C16: < L *incīdere* to cut into]

incision (ɪnˈsɪʒən) *n.* **1.** the act of incising. **2.** a cut, gash, or notch. **3.** a cut made with a knife during a surgical operation.

incisive (ɪnˈsaɪsɪv) *adj.* **1.** keen, penetrating, or acute. **2.** biting or sarcastic; mordant: *an incisive remark.* **3.** having a sharp cutting edge: *incisive teeth.* —**inˈcisively** *adv.* —**inˈcisiveness** *n.*

incisor (ɪnˈsaɪzə) *n.* a chisel-edged tooth at the front of the mouth.

incite (ɪnˈsaɪt) *vb.* (*tr.*) to stir up or provoke to action. [C15: < L, < IN-[2] + *citāre* to excite] —ˌ**inciˈtation** *n.* —**inˈcitement** *n.* —**inˈciter** *n.* —**inˈcitingly** *adv.*

incivility (ˌɪnsɪˈvɪlɪtɪ) *n., pl.* **-ties. 1.** lack of civility or courtesy; rudeness. **2.** an impolite or uncivil act or remark.

incl. *abbrev. for:* **1.** including. **2.** inclusive.

inclement (ɪnˈklɛmənt) *adj.* **1.** (of weather) stormy, severe, or tempestuous. **2.** severe or merciless. —**inˈclemency** *n.* —**inˈclemently** *adv.*

inclination (ˌɪnklɪˈneɪʃən) *n.* **1.** (often foll. by *for, to, towards,* or an infinitive) a particular disposition, esp. a liking; tendency: *I've no inclination for such dull work.* **2.** the degree of deviation from a particular plane, esp. a horizontal or vertical plane. **3.** a sloping or slanting surface; incline. **4.** the act of inclining or the state of being inclined. **5.** the act of bowing or nodding the head. **6.** another name for **dip** (sense 24). —ˌ**incliˈnational** *adj.*

incline *vb.* (ɪnˈklaɪn). **1.** to deviate from a particular plane, esp. a vertical or horizontal plane; slope or slant. **2.** (when *tr.,* may take an infinitive) to be disposed or cause to be disposed (towards some attitude or to do something): *that does not incline me to think that you are right.* **3.** to bend or lower (part of the body, esp. the head), as in a bow or in order to listen. **4. incline one's ear.** to listen favourably (to). ~*n.* (ˈɪnklaɪn, ɪnˈklaɪn). **5.** an inclined surface or slope; gradient. [C13: < L *inclīnāre* to cause to lean, < *clīnāre* to bend; see LEAN[1]] —**inˈclined** *adj.* —**inˈcliner** *n.*

inclined plane *n.* a plane whose angle to the horizontal is less than a right angle.

inclinometer (ˌɪnklɪˈnɒmɪtə) *n.* an aircraft instrument for indicating the angle that an aircraft makes with the horizontal.

inclose (ɪnˈkləʊz) *vb.* a less common spelling of **enclose.** —**inˈclosure** *n.*

include (ɪnˈkluːd) *vb.* (*tr.*) **1.** to have as contents or part of the contents; be made up of or contain. **2.** to add as part of something else; put in as part of a set, group, or category. **3.** to contain as a secondary or minor ingredient or element. [C15 (in the sense: to enclose): < L, < IN-[2] + *claudere* to close] —**inˈcludable** *or* **inˈcludible** *adj.*

▷ **Usage.** See at **comprise.**

include out *vb.* (*tr., adv.*) *Inf.* to exclude: *you can include me out of that deal.*

inclusion (ɪnˈkluːʒən) *n.* **1.** the act of including or the state of being included. **2.** something included.

inclusion body *n. Pathol.* any of the small particles found in cells infected with certain viruses.

inclusive (ɪnˈkluːsɪv) *adj.* **1.** (*postpositive;* foll. by *of*) considered together (with): *capital inclusive of profit.* **2.** (*postpositive*) including the limits specified: *Monday to Friday inclusive.* **3.** comprehensive. **4.** *Logic.* (of a disjunction) true if at least one of its component propositions is true. —**inˈclusively** *adv.* —**inˈclusiveness** *n.*

incognito (ˌɪnkɒgˈniːtəʊ, ɪnˈkɒgnɪtəʊ) *or* (*fem.*) **incognita** *adv., adj.* (*postpositive*) **1.** under an assumed name or appearance; in disguise. ~*n., pl.* **-tos** *or* (*fem.*) **-tas. 2.** a person who is incognito. **3.** the assumed name or disguise of such a person. [C17: < It., < L *incognitus* unknown]

incognizant (ɪnˈkɒgnɪzənt) *adj.* (when *postpositive,* often foll. by *of*) unaware (of). —**inˈcognizance** *n.*

incoherent (ˌɪnkəʊˈhɪərənt) *adj.* **1.** lacking in clarity or organization; disordered. **2.** unable to express oneself clearly; inarticulate. —ˌ**incoˈherence** *or* ˌ**incoˈherency** *n.* —ˌ**incoˈherently** *adv.*

income (ˈɪnkʌm, ˈɪnkəm) *n.* **1.** the amount of monetary or other returns, either earned or unearned, accruing over a given period of time. **2.** receipts; revenue. [C13 (in the sense: arrival, entrance): < OE *incumen* a coming in]

incomer (ˈɪnkʌmə) *n.* a person who comes to live in a place in which he was not born.

income tax *n.* a personal tax levied on annual income subject to certain deductions.

incoming (ˈɪnˌkʌmɪŋ) *adj.* **1.** coming in; entering. **2.** about to come into office; succeeding. **3.** (of interest, dividends, etc.) being received; accruing.

ˌ**incomˈbustible** *adj.*

~*n.* **4.** the act of coming in; entrance. **5.** (*usually pl.*) income or revenue.

incommensurable (ˌɪnkəˈmɛnʃərəbᵊl) *adj.* **1.** incapable of being judged, measured, or considered comparatively. **2.** (*postpositive;* foll. by *with*) not in accordance; incommensurate. **3.** *Maths.* not having a common factor other than 1, such as 2 and √-5. ~*n.* **4.** something incommensurable. —ˌ**incomˌmensuraˈbility** *n.* —ˌ**incomˈmensurably** *adv.*

incommensurate (ˌɪnkəˈmɛnʃərɪt) *adj.* **1.** (when *postpositive,* often foll. by *with*) not commensurate; disproportionate. **2.** incommensurable. —ˌ**incomˈmensurately** *adv.* —ˌ**incomˈmensurateness** *n.*

incommode (ˌɪnkəˈməʊd) *vb.* (*tr.*) to bother, disturb, or inconvenience. [C16: < L *incommodāre* to be troublesome, < *incommodus* inconvenient; see COMMODE]

incommodious (ˌɪnkəˈməʊdɪəs) *adj.* **1.** insufficiently spacious; cramped. **2.** troublesome or inconvenient. —ˌ**incomˈmodiously** *adv.*

incommodity (ˌɪnkəˈmɒdɪtɪ) *n., pl.* **-ties.** anything that causes inconvenience.

incommunicado (ˌɪnkəˌmjuːnɪˈkɑːdəʊ) *adv., adj.* (*postpositive*) deprived of communication with other people, as while in solitary confinement. [C19: < Sp., < *incomunicar* to deprive of communication; see IN-[1], COMMUNICATE]

incomparable (ɪnˈkɒmpərəbᵊl, -prəbᵊl) *adj.* **1.** beyond or above comparison; matchless; unequalled. **2.** lacking a basis for comparison; not having qualities or features that can be compared. —**inˌcomparaˈbility** *or* **inˈcomparableness** *n.* —**inˈcomparably** *adv.*

incompatible (ˌɪnkəmˈpætəbᵊl) *adj.* **1.** incapable of living or existing together in harmony; conflicting or antagonistic. **2.** opposed in nature or quality; inconsistent. **3.** *Med.* (esp. of two drugs or two types of blood) incapable of being combined or used together; antagonistic. **4.** *Logic.* (of two propositions) unable to be both true at the same time. **5.** (of plants) incapable of self-fertilization. ~*n.* **6.** (*often pl.*) a person or thing that is incompatible with another. —ˌ**incomˌpatiˈbility** *or* ˌ**incomˈpatibleness** *n.* —ˌ**incomˈpatibly** *adv.*

incompetent (ɪnˈkɒmpɪtənt) *adj.* **1.** not possessing the necessary ability, skill, etc., to do or carry out a task; incapable. **2.** marked by lack of ability, skill, etc. **3.** *Law.* not legally qualified: *an incompetent witness.* ~*n.* **4.** an incompetent person. —**inˈcompetence** *or* **inˈcompetency** *n.* —**inˈcompetently** *adv.*

inconceivable (ˌɪnkənˈsiːvəbᵊl) *adj.* incapable of being conceived, imagined, or considered. —ˌ**inconˌceivaˈbility** *or* ˌ**inconˈceivableness** *n.* —ˌ**inconˈceivably** *adv.*

incongruous (ɪnˈkɒŋgrʊəs) *or* **incongruent** *adj.* **1.** (when *postpositive,* foll. by *with* or *to*) incompatible with (what is suitable); inappropriate. **2.** containing disparate or discordant elements or parts. —**inˈcongruously** *adv.* —**inˈcongruousness** *or* **incongruity** (ˌɪnkɒŋˈgruːɪtɪ) *n.*

inconnu (ˈɪnkənjuː, ˈɪnkənuː) *n. Canad.* a whitefish of Far Northern waters. [C19: < F, lit: unknown]

inconsequential (ˌɪnkɒnsɪˈkwɛnʃəl, ɪnˌkɒn-) *or* **inconsequent** (ɪnˈkɒnsɪkwənt) *adj.* **1.** not following logically as a consequence. **2.** trivial or insignificant. **3.** not in a logical sequence; haphazard. —ˌ**inconseˌquentiˈality,** ˌ**inconseˈquentialness,** *or* **inˈconsequence** *n.* —ˌ**inconseˈquentially** *or* **inˈconsequently** *adv.*

inconsiderable (ˌɪnkənˈsɪdərəbᵊl) *adj.* **1.** relatively small. **2.** not worthy of consideration; insignificant. —ˌ**inconˈsiderableness** *n.* —ˌ**inconˈsiderably** *adv.*

inconsiderate (ˌɪnkənˈsɪdərɪt) *adj.* lacking in care or thought for others; thoughtless. —ˌ**inconˈsiderately** *adv.* —ˌ**inconˈsiderateness** *or* ˌ**inconˌsiderˈation** *n.*

inconsistency (ˌɪnkənˈsɪstənsɪ) *n., pl.* **-cies. 1.** lack of consistency or agreement; incompatibility. **2.** an inconsistent feature or quality.

inconsistent (ˌɪnkənˈsɪstənt) *adj.* **1.** lacking in consistency, agreement, or compatibility; at variance. **2.** containing contradictory elements. **3.** irregular or fickle in behaviour or mood. **4.** *Logic.* (of a set of propositions) enabling an explicit contradiction to be validly derived. —ˌ**inconˈsistently** *adv.*

inconsolable (ˌɪnkənˈsəʊləbᵊl) *adj.* incapable of being consoled or comforted; disconsolate. —ˌ**inconˌsolaˈbility** *or* ˌ**inconˈsolableness** *n.* —ˌ**inconˈsolably** *adv.*

inconsonant (ɪnˈkɒnsənənt) *adj.* lacking in harmony or compatibility; discordant. —**inˈconsonance** *n.* —**inˈconsonantly** *adv.*

inconspicuous (ˌɪnkənˈspɪkjʊəs) *adj.* not easily noticed or seen; not prominent or striking. —ˌ**inconˈspicuously** *adv.* —ˌ**inconˈspicuousness** *n.*

incontinent[1] (ɪnˈkɒntɪnənt) *adj.* **1.** relating to or exhibiting involuntary urination or defecation. **2.** lacking in restraint or control, esp. sexually. **3.** (foll. by *of*) having little or no control (over). **4.** unrestrained; uncontrolled. [C14: < OF, < L, < IN-[1] + *continere* to hold, restrain] —**inˈcontinence** *n.* —**inˈcontinently** *adv.*

incontinent[2] (ɪnˈkɒntɪnənt) *or* **incontinently** *adv.* obsolete words for **immediately.** [C15: < LL *in continentī tempore,* lit.: in continuous time, that is, with no interval]

incontrovertible (ˌɪnkɒntrəˈvɜːtəbᵊl, ɪnˌkɒn-) *adj.* incapable of being contradicted or disputed; undeniable. —ˌ**incontroˌvertiˈbility** *n.* —ˌ**incontroˈvertibly** *adv.*

incorporate *vb.* (ɪnˈkɔːpəˌreɪt). **1.** to include or be included as a part or member of a united whole. **2.** to form a united whole or mass; merge or blend. **3.** to form into a corporation or other organization with a separate legal identity. ~*adj.* (ɪnˈkɔːpərɪt, -prɪt). **4.** combined into a whole; incorporated. **5.** formed into or constituted as a corporation. [C14 (in the sense: put into the body of something else): < LL *incorporāre* to embody, < L IN-[2] + *corpus* body] —**inˈcorpoˌrated** *adj.* —**inˌcorpoˈration** *n.* —**inˈcorporative** *adj.*

incorporeal (ˌɪnkɔːˈpɔːrɪəl) *adj.* **1.** without material form, body, or substance. **2.** spiritual or metaphysical. **3.** *Law.* having no material existence but existing by reason of its annexation of something material: *an incorporeal hereditament.* —ˌ**incorˈporeally** *adv.* —**incorporeity** (ɪnˌkɔːpəˈriːɪtɪ) *or* ˌ**incorporeˈality** *n.*

incorrigible (ɪnˈkɒrɪdʒəbᵊl) *adj.* **1.** beyond correction, reform, or alteration. **2.** firmly rooted; ineradicable. ~*n.* **3.** a person or animal that is incorrigible. —**inˌcorrigiˈbility** *or* **inˈcorrigibleness** *n.* —**inˈcorrigibly** *adv.*

incorruptible (ˌɪnkəˈrʌptəbᵊl) *adj.* **1.** incapable of being corrupted; honest; just. **2.** not subject to decay or decomposition. —ˌ**incorˌruptiˈbility** *n.* —ˌ**incorˈruptibly** *adv.*

incr. *abbrev. for:* **1.** increase. **2.** increased. **3.** increasing.

incrassate *adj.* (ɪnˈkræsɪt, -eɪt), *also* **incrassated. 1.** *Biol.* thickened or swollen. ~*vb.* (ɪnˈkræseɪt). **2.** *Obs.* to make or become thicker. [C17: < LL, < L *crassus* thick, dense] —ˌ**incrasˈsation** *n.*

increase *vb.* (ɪnˈkriːs). **1.** to make or become greater in size, degree, frequency, etc.; grow or expand. ~*n.* (ˈɪnkriːs). **2.** the act of increasing; augmentation. **3.** the amount by which something increases. **4. on the increase.** increasing, esp.

ˌ**incomˈmunicable** *adj.*
ˌ**incomˈmunicative** *adj.*
ˌ**incomˈmutable** *adj.*
ˌ**incomˈplete** *adj.*
ˌ**incompreˈhensible** *adj.*
ˌ**incomˈpressible** *adj.*
ˌ**inconˈclusive** *adj.*
inˈconstant *adj.*
ˌ**inconˈtestable** *adj.*
ˌ**inconˈvenience** *n., vb.*
ˌ**inconˈvenient** *adj.*
ˌ**inconˈvertible** *adj.*
ˌ**incoˌordiˈnation** *n.*
ˌ**incorˈrect** *adj.*
ˌ**incorˈrupt** *adj.*

becoming more frequent. [C14: < OF *encreistre*, < L, < IN-² + *crēscere* to grow] —**in'creasable** *adj.* —**increasedly** (ɪn'kriːsɪdlɪ) *or* **in'creasingly** *adv.* —**in'creaser** *n.*

incredible (ɪn'krɛdəbᵊl) *adj.* **1.** beyond belief or understanding; unbelievable. **2.** *Inf.* marvellous; amazing. —**in,credi'bility** *or* **in'credibleness** *n.* —**in'credibly** *adv.*

incredulity (,ɪnkrɪ'djuːlɪtɪ) *n.* lack of belief; scepticism.

incredulous (ɪn'krɛdjʊləs) *adj.* (often foll. by *of*) not prepared or willing to believe (something); unbelieving. —**in'credulously** *adv.* —**in'credulousness** *n.*

increment ('ɪnkrɪmənt) *n.* **1.** an increase or addition, esp. one of a series. **2.** the act of increasing; augmentation. **3.** *Maths.* a small positive or negative change in a variable or function. [C15: < L *incrēmentum* growth, INCREASE] —**incremental** (,ɪnkrɪ'mɛntᵊl) *adj.*

incremental plotter *n.* a device that plots graphs on paper from computer-generated instructions.

incriminate (ɪn'krɪmɪ,neɪt) *vb.* (*tr.*) **1.** to imply or suggest the guilt or error of (someone). **2.** to charge with a crime or fault. [C18: < LL *incrīmināre* to accuse, < L *crīmen* accusation; see CRIME] —**in,crimi'nation** *n.* —**in'crimi,nator** *n.* —**in'criminatory** *adj.*

incrust (ɪn'krʌst) *vb.* a variant spelling of **encrust.** —**in'crustant** *n., adj.* —**,incrus'tation** *n.*

incubate ('ɪnkjʊ,beɪt) *vb.* **1.** (of birds) to supply (eggs) with heat for their development, esp. by sitting on them. **2.** to cause (bacteria, etc.) to develop, esp. in an incubator or culture medium. **3.** (*intr.*) (of embryos, etc.) to develop in favourable conditions, esp. in an incubator. **4.** (*intr.*) (of disease germs) to remain inactive in an animal or human before causing disease. **5.** to develop gradually; foment or be fomented. [C18: < L *incubāre* to lie upon, hatch, < IN-² + *cubāre* to lie down] —**,incu'bation** *n.* —**,incu'bational** *adj.* —**'incu,bative** *or* **'incu,batory** *adj.*

incubation period *n. Med.* the time between exposure to an infectious disease and the appearance of the first signs or symptoms.

incubator ('ɪnkjʊ,beɪtə) *n.* **1.** *Med.* an apparatus for housing prematurely born babies until they are strong enough to survive. **2.** a container in which birds' eggs can be artificially hatched or bacterial cultures grown. **3.** a person, animal, or thing that incubates.

incubus ('ɪnkjʊbəs) *n., pl.* **-bi** (-,baɪ) *or* **-buses.** **1.** a demon believed in folklore to have sexual intercourse with sleeping women. Cf. **succubus.** **2.** something that oppresses or disturbs greatly, esp. a nightmare or obsession. [C14: < LL, < L *incubāre* to lie upon; see INCUBATE]

inculcate ('ɪnkʌl,keɪt, ɪn'kʌlkeɪt) *vb.* (*tr.*) to instil by insistent repetition. [C16: < L *inculcāre* to tread upon, ram down, < IN-² + *calcāre* to trample, < *calx* heel] —**,incul'cation** *n.* —**'incul,cator** *n.*

inculpate ('ɪnkʌl,peɪt, ɪn'kʌlpeɪt) *vb.* (*tr.*) to incriminate; cause blame to be imputed to. [C18: < LL, < L *culpāre* to blame, < *culpa* fault, blame] —**,incul'pation** *n.* —**inculpative** (ɪn'kʌlpətɪv) *or* **inculpatory** (ɪn'kʌlpətərɪ, -trɪ) *adj.*

incumbency (ɪn'kʌmbənsɪ) *n., pl.* **-cies.** **1.** the state or quality of being incumbent. **2.** the office, duty, or tenure of an incumbent.

incumbent (ɪn'kʌmbənt) *adj.* **1.** *Formal.* (often *postpositive* and foll. by *on* or *upon* and an infinitive) morally binding; obligatory: *it is incumbent on me to attend.* **2.** (usually *postpositive* and foll. by *on*) resting or lying (on). **3.** (usually *prenominal*) occupying or holding an office. ~*n.* **4.** a person who holds an office, esp. a clergyman holding a benefice. [C16: < L *incumbere* to lie upon, devote one's attention to]

incunabula (,ɪnkjʊ'næbjʊlə) *pl. n., sing.* **-lum** (-ləm). **1.** any book printed before 1500. **2.** the earliest stages of something; beginnings. [C19: < L, orig.: swaddling clothes, hence beginnings, < IN-² + *cūnābula* cradle] —**,incu'nabular** *adj.*

incur (ɪn'kɜː) *vb.* **-curring, -curred.** (*tr.*) **1.** to make oneself subject to (something undesirable); bring upon oneself. **2.** to run into or encounter. [C16: < L *incurrere* to run into, < *currere* to run] —**in'currable** *adj.*

incurable (ɪn'kjʊərəbᵊl) *adj.* **1.** (esp. of a disease) not curable; unresponsive to treatment. ~*n.* **2.** a person having an incurable disease. —**in,cura'bility** *or* **in'curableness** *n.* —**in'curably** *adv.*

incurious (ɪn'kjʊərɪəs) *adj.* not curious; indifferent or uninterested. —**incuriosity** (ɪn,kjʊərɪ'ɒsɪtɪ) *or* **in'curiousness** *n.* —**in'curiously** *adv.*

incursion (ɪn'kɜːʃən) *n.* **1.** a sudden invasion, attack, or raid. **2.** the act of running or leaking into; penetration. [C15: < L *incursiō* onset, attack, < *incurrere* to run into; see INCUR] —**incursive** (ɪn'kɜːsɪv) *adj.*

incus ('ɪŋkəs) *n., pl.* **incudes** (ɪn'kjuːdiːz). the central of the three small bones in the middle ear of mammals. Cf. **malleus, stapes.** [C17: < L: anvil, < *incūdere* to forge]

incuse (ɪn'kjuːz) *n.* **1.** a design stamped or hammered onto a coin. ~*vb.* **2.** to impress (a coin) with a design by hammering or stamping. ~*adj.* **3.** stamped or hammered onto a coin. [C19: < L *incūsus* hammered; see INCUS]

ind. *abbrev. for:* **1.** independence. **2.** independent. **3.** index. **4.** indicative. **5.** indirect. **6.** industrial. **7.** industry.

Ind. *abbrev. for:* **1.** Independent. **2.** India. **3.** Indian. **4.** Indies.

indaba (ɪn'dɑːbə) *n.* **1.** (among Bantu peoples of southern Africa) a meeting to discuss a serious topic. **2.** *S. African inf.* a matter of concern or for discussion. [C19: < Zulu: topic]

indebted (ɪn'dɛtɪd) *adj.* (*postpositive*) **1.** owing gratitude for help, favours, etc.; obligated. **2.** owing money.

indebtedness (ɪn'dɛtɪdnɪs) *n.* **1.** the state of being indebted. **2.** the total of a person's debts.

indecency (ɪn'diːsənsɪ) *n., pl.* **-cies.** **1.** the state or quality of being indecent. **2.** an indecent act, etc.

indecent (ɪn'diːsᵊnt) *adj.* **1.** offensive to standards of decency, esp. in sexual matters. **2.** unseemly or improper (esp. in **indecent haste**). —**in'decently** *adv.*

indecent exposure *n.* the offence of indecently exposing one's body in public, esp. the genitals.

indecisive (,ɪndɪ'saɪsɪv) *adj.* **1.** (of a person) vacillating; irresolute. **2.** not decisive or conclusive. —**,inde'cision** *or* **,inde'cisiveness** *n.* —**,inde'cisively** *adv.*

indecorum (,ɪndɪ'kɔːrəm) *n.* lack of decorum; unseemliness. —**in'decorous** *adj.*

indeed (ɪn'diːd) (*sentence connector*). **1.** certainly; actually: *indeed, it may never happen.* ~*adv.* **2.** (intensifier): *that is indeed amazing.* **3.** or rather; what is more: *a comfortable, indeed wealthy family.* ~*interj.* **4.** an expression of doubt, surprise, etc.

indef. *abbrev. for* indefinite.

indefatigable (,ɪndɪ'fætɪgəbᵊl) *adj.* unable to be tired out; unflagging. [C16: < L, < *fatīgāre* to tire] —**,inde,fatiga'bility** *n.* —**,inde'fatigably** *adv.*

indefeasible (,ɪndɪ'fiːzəbᵊl) *adj. Law.* not liable to be annulled or forfeited. —**,inde,feasi'bility** *n.* —**,inde'feasibly** *adv.*

indefensible (,ɪndɪ'fɛnsəbᵊl) *adj.* **1.** not justifiable or excusable. **2.** capable of being disagreed with; untenable. **3.** incapable of defence against attack. —**,inde,fensi'bility** *n.* —**,inde'fensibly** *adv.*

indefinite (ɪn'dɛfɪnɪt) *adj.* **1.** not certain or determined; unsettled. **2.** without exact limits; indeterminate: *an indefinite number.* **3.** vague or unclear. **4.** in traditional logic, a proposition in

---

,inde'cipherable *adj.* **,inde'clinable** *adj.* **,inde'finable** *adj.*

which it is not stated whether the subject is universal or particular, as in *men are mortal.* —**in'definitely** *adv.* —**in'definiteness** *n.*

indefinite article *n. Grammar.* a determiner that expresses nonspecificity of reference, such as *a, an,* or *some.*

indehiscent (ˌɪndɪ'hɪsᵊnt) *adj.* (of fruits, etc.) not dehiscent; not opening to release seeds, etc. —ˌ**inde'hiscence** *n.*

indelible (ɪn'dɛlɪbᵊl) *adj.* **1.** incapable of being erased or obliterated. **2.** making indelible marks: *indelible ink.* [C16: < L, < IN-[1] + *delēre* to destroy] —**inˌdeli'bility** *or* **in'delibleness** *n.* —**in'delibly** *adv.*

indelicate (ɪn'dɛlɪkɪt) *adj.* **1.** coarse, crude, or rough. **2.** offensive, embarrassing, or tasteless. —**in'delicacy** *or* **in'delicateness** *n.* —**in'delicately** *adv.*

indemnify (ɪn'dɛmnɪˌfaɪ) *vb.* **-fying, -fied.** (*tr.*) **1.** to secure against future loss, damage, or liability; give security for; insure. **2.** to compensate for loss, etc.; reimburse. —**inˌdemnifi'cation** *n.* —**in'demniˌfier** *n.*

indemnity (ɪn'dɛmnɪtɪ) *n., pl.* **-ties. 1.** compensation for loss or damage; reimbursement. **2.** protection or insurance against future loss or damage. **3.** legal exemption from penalties incurred through one's acts or defaults. **4.** *Canad.* the annual salary paid by the government to a member of Parliament or of a provincial legislature. [C15: < LL, < *indemnis* uninjured, < L IN-[1] + *damnum* damage]

indene ('ɪndiːn) *n.* a colourless liquid hydrocarbon obtained from coal tar and used in making synthetic resins. Formula: C_9H_8. [C20: < INDOLE + -ENE]

indent[1] *vb.* (ɪn'dɛnt). (*mainly tr.*) **1.** to place (written matter, etc.) in from the margin. **2.** to cut (a document in duplicate) so that the irregular lines may be matched. **3.** *Chiefly Brit.* (in foreign trade) to place an order for (foreign goods). **4.** (when *intr.*, foll. by *for, on,* or *upon*) *Chiefly Brit.* to make an order on (a source or supply) or for (something). **5.** to notch (an edge, border, etc.); make jagged. **6.** to bind (an apprentice, etc.) by indenture. ~*n.* ('ɪnˌdɛnt). *Chiefly Brit.* **7.** (in foreign trade) an order for foreign merchandise. **8.** an official order for goods. [C14: < OF *endenter,* < EN-[1] + *dent* tooth, < L *dēns*] —**in'denter** *or* **in'dentor** *n.*

indent[2] *vb.* (ɪn'dɛnt). **1.** (*tr.*) to make a dent or depression in. ~*n.* ('ɪnˌdɛnt). **2.** a dent or depression. [C15: < IN-[2] + DENT]

indentation (ˌɪndɛn'teɪʃən) *n.* **1.** a hollowed, notched, or cut place, as on an edge or on a coastline. **2.** a series of hollows, notches, or cuts. **3.** the act of indenting or the condition of being indented. **4.** Also: **indention, indent.** the leaving of space or the amount of space left between a margin and the start of an indented line.

indention (ɪn'dɛnʃən) *n.* another word for **indentation** (sense 4).

indenture (ɪn'dɛntʃə) *n.* **1.** any deed, contract, or sealed agreement between two or more parties. **2.** (formerly) a deed drawn up in duplicate, each part having correspondingly indented edges for identification and security. **3.** (*often pl.*) a contract between an apprentice and his master. **4.** a less common word for **indentation.** ~*vb.* **5.** (*intr.*) to enter into an agreement by indenture. **6.** (*tr.*) to bind (an apprentice, servant, etc.) by indenture. —**in'dentureˌship** *n.*

independence (ˌɪndɪ'pɛndəns) *n.* the state or quality of being independent. Also: **independency.**

independency (ˌɪndɪ'pɛndənsɪ) *n., pl.* **-cies. 1.** a territory or state free from the control of any other power. **2.** another word for **independence.**

independent (ˌɪndɪ'pɛndənt) *adj.* **1.** free from control in action, judgment, etc.; autonomous. **2.** not dependent on anything else for function, validity, etc.; separate. **3.** not reliant on the support, esp. financial support, of others. **4.** capable of acting for oneself or on one's own: *a very independent little girl.* **5.** providing a large unearned sum towards one's support (esp. in **independent income, independent means**). **6.** living on an unearned income. **7.** *Maths.* (of a system of equations) not linearly dependent. See also **independent variable. 8.** *Logic.* (of two or more propositions) unrelated. ~*n.* **9.** an independent person or thing. **10.** a person who is not affiliated to or who acts independently of a political party. —ˌ**inde'pendently** *adv.*

Independent (ˌɪndɪ'pɛndənt) *Christianity.* ~*n.* **1.** (in England) a member of the Congregational Church. ~*adj.* **2.** of or relating to the Congregational Church.

independent clause *n. Grammar.* a main or coordinate clause.

independent school *n.* (in Britain) a school that is neither financed nor controlled by the government or local authorities.

independent variable *n.* a variable in a mathematical equation or statement whose value determines that of the dependent variable: in $y = f(x)$, x is the independent variable.

in-depth *adj.* detailed and thorough: *an in-depth study.*

indescribable (ˌɪndɪ'skraɪbəbᵊl) *adj.* beyond description; too intense, extreme, etc., for words. —ˌ**indeˌscriba'bility** *n.* —ˌ**inde'scribably** *adv.*

indeterminate (ˌɪndɪ'tɜːmɪnɪt) *adj.* **1.** uncertain in extent, amount, or nature. **2.** not definite; inconclusive: *an indeterminate reply.* **3.** unable to be predicted, calculated, or deduced. **4.** *Maths.* **a.** having no numerical meaning, as 0/0. **b.** (of an equation) having more than one variable and an unlimited number of solutions. —ˌ**inde'terminacy** *or* ˌ**inde'terminateness** *n.* —ˌ**inde'terminately** *adv.*

indeterminism (ˌɪndɪ'tɜːmɪˌnɪzəm) *n.* the philosophical doctrine that behaviour is not entirely determined by motives. —ˌ**inde'terminist** *n., adj.* —ˌ**indeˌtermin'istic** *adj.*

index ('ɪndɛks) *n., pl.* **-dexes** *or* **-dices** (-dɪˌsiːz). **1.** an alphabetical list of persons, subjects, etc., mentioned in a printed work, usually at the back, and indicating where they are referred to. **2.** See **thumb index. 3.** *Library science.* a systematic list of book titles or authors' names, giving cross-references and the location of each book; catalogue. **4.** an indication, sign, or token. **5.** a pointer, needle, or other indicator, as on an instrument. **6.** *Maths.* **a.** another name for **exponent** (sense 4). **b.** a number or variable placed as a superscript to the left of a radical sign indicating the root to be extracted, as in $\sqrt[3]{8} = 2$. **7.** a numerical scale by means of which levels of the cost of living can be compared with some base number. **8.** a number or ratio indicating a specific characteristic, property, etc.: *refractive index.* **9.** Also called: **fist.** a printer's mark, ☞ used to indicate notes, paragraphs, etc. ~*vb.* (*tr.*) **10.** to put an index in (a book). **11.** to enter (a word, item, etc.) in an index. **12.** to point out; indicate. **13.** to make index-linked. **14.** to move (a machine, etc.) so that an operation will be repeated at certain defined intervals. [C16: < L: pointer, hence forefinger, title, index, < *indicāre* to disclose, show; see INDICATE] —'**indexer** *n.* —**in'dexical** *adj.*

indexation (ˌɪndɛk'seɪʃən) *or* **index-linking** *n.* the act of making wages, interest rates, etc., index-linked.

index finger *n.* the finger next to the thumb. Also called: **forefinger.**

Index Librorum Prohibitorum *Latin.* ('ɪndɛks laɪ'brɔːrʊm prəʊˌhɪbɪ'tɔːrʊm) *n. R.C. Church.* (formerly) an official list of proscribed books. Often called: **the Index.** [C17, lit.: list of forbidden books]

index-linked *adj.* (of wages, interest rates, etc.)

ˌ**inde'monstrable** *adj.* ˌ**inde'structible** *adj.* ˌ**inde'terminable** *adj.*

directly related to the cost-of-living index and rising or falling accordingly.

index number *n. Statistics.* a statistic indicating the relative change occurring in the price or value of a commodity or in a general economic variable, with reference to a previous base period conventionally given the number 100.

Indiaman ('ɪndɪəmən) *n., pl.* **-men.** (formerly) a merchant ship engaged in trade with India.

Indian ('ɪndɪən) *n.* **1.** a native or inhabitant of the Republic of India, in a subcontinent of Asia. **2.** an American Indian. **3.** (*not in scholarly usage*) any of the languages of the American Indians. ~*adj.* **4.** of or relating to India, its inhabitants, or any of their languages. **5.** of or relating to the American Indians or any of their languages.

Indian club *n.* a bottle-shaped club, usually used in pairs by gymnasts, jugglers, etc.

Indian corn *n.* another name for **maize** (sense 1).

Indian file *n.* another term for **single file.**

Indian hemp *n.* another name for **hemp,** esp. the variety *Cannabis indica,* from which several narcotic drugs are obtained.

Indian ink *or esp. U.S. & Canad.* **India ink** ('ɪndɪə) *n.* **1.** a black pigment made from a mixture of lampblack and a binding agent such as gelatin or glue: usually formed into solid cakes and sticks. **2.** a black liquid ink made from this pigment. ~Also called: **China ink, Chinese ink.**

Indian list *n. Inf.* (in Canada) a list of persons to whom spirits may not be sold.

Indian meal *n.* another name for **corn meal.**

Indian rope-trick *n.* the supposed Indian feat of climbing an unsupported rope.

Indian summer *n.* **1.** a period of unusually warm weather, esp. in the autumn. **2.** a period of tranquillity or of renewed productivity towards the end of something, esp. a person's life. [orig. U.S.: prob. so named because it was first noted in Amerind regions]

Indian tobacco *n.* a poisonous North American plant with small pale bell-shaped blue flowers and rounded inflated seed capsules.

India paper *n.* a thin soft opaque printing paper originally made in the Orient.

India rubber *n.* another name for **rubber**[1] (sense 1).

Indic ('ɪndɪk) *adj.* **1.** denoting, belonging to, or relating to a branch of Indo-European consisting of certain languages of India, including Sanskrit, Hindi and Urdu. ~*n.* **2.** this group of languages. ~Also: **Indo-Aryan.**

indicate ('ɪndɪˌkeɪt) *vb.* (*tr.*) **1.** (*may take a clause as object*) to be or give a sign or symptom of; imply: *cold hands indicate a warm heart.* **2.** to point out or show. **3.** (*may take a clause as object*) to state briefly; suggest. **4.** (of instruments) to show a reading of. **5.** (*usually passive*) to recommend or require: *surgery seems to be indicated for this patient.* [C17: < L *indicāre* to point out, < IN-[2] + *dicāre* to proclaim; cf. INDEX] —'**indiˌcatable** *adj.* —**indicatory** (ɪn'dɪkətərɪ, -trɪ) *adj.*

indication (ˌɪndɪ'keɪʃən) *n.* **1.** something that serves to indicate or suggest; sign: *an indication of foul play.* **2.** the degree or quantity represented on a measuring instrument or device. **3.** the action of indicating. **4.** something that is indicated as advisable, necessary, or expedient.

indicative (ɪn'dɪkətɪv) *adj.* **1.** (*usually postpositive;* foll. by *of*) serving as a sign; suggestive: *indicative of trouble ahead.* **2.** *Grammar.* denoting a mood of verbs used chiefly to make statements. ~*n.* **3.** *Grammar.* **a.** the indicative mood. **b.** a verb in the indicative mood. ~Abbrev.: **indic.** —**in'dicatively** *adv.*

indicator ('ɪndɪˌkeɪtə) *n.* **1.** a device to attract attention, such as the pointer of a gauge or a warning lamp. **2.** an instrument that displays certain operating conditions in a machine, such as a gauge showing temperature, etc. **3.** a device that registers something, such as the movements of a lift, or that shows information, such as train departure times. **4.** Also called: **blinkers.** a device for indicating that a motor vehicle is about to turn left or right, esp. two pairs of lights that flash. **5.** a delicate measuring instrument used to determine small differences in the height of mechanical components. **6.** *Chem.* a substance used to indicate the completion of a chemical reaction, usually by a change of colour.

indices ('ɪndɪˌsiːz) *n.* a plural of **index.**

indicia (ɪn'dɪʃɪə) *pl. n., sing.* **-cium** (-ʃɪəm). distinguishing markings or signs; indications. [C17: < L, pl. of *indicium* a notice, < INDEX] —**in'dicial** *adj.*

indict (ɪn'daɪt) *vb.* (*tr.*) to charge (a person) with crime, esp. formally in writing; accuse. [C14: alteration of *enditen* to INDITE] —ˌ**indict'ee** *n.* —**in'dicter** *or* **in'dictor** *n.* —**in'dictable** *adj.*

indictment (ɪn'daɪtmənt) *n. Criminal law.* **1.** a formal written charge of crime formerly referred to and presented on oath by a grand jury. **2.** any formal accusation of crime. **3.** the act of indicting or the state of being indicted.

indie ('ɪndɪ) *n. Inf.* **a.** an independent record company. **b.** (*as modifier*): *the indie charts.*

indifference (ɪn'dɪfrəns, -fərəns) *n.* **1.** the fact or state of being indifferent; lack of care or concern. **2.** lack of quality; mediocrity. **3.** lack of importance; insignificance.

indifferent (ɪn'dɪfrənt, -fərənt) *adj.* **1.** (often foll. by *to*) showing no care or concern; uninterested: *he was indifferent to my pleas.* **2.** unimportant; immaterial. **3. a.** of only average or moderate size, extent, quality, etc. **b.** not at all good; poor. **4.** showing or having no preferences; impartial. [C14: < L *indifferēns* making no distinction] —**in'differently** *adv.*

indifferentism (ɪn'dɪfrənˌtɪzəm, -fərən-) *n.* systematic indifference, esp. in matters of religion. —**in'differentist** *n.*

indigenous (ɪn'dɪdʒɪnəs) *adj.* (when *postpositive,* foll. by *to*) **1.** originating or occurring naturally (in a country, etc.); native. **2.** innate (to); inherent (in). [C17: < L *indigenus,* < *indi-* in + *gignere* to beget] —**in'digenously** *adv.* —**in'digenousness** *n.*

indigent ('ɪndɪdʒənt) *adj.* **1.** so poor as to lack even necessities; very needy. **2.** (usually foll. by *of*) *Arch.* lacking (in) or destitute (of). ~*n.* **3.** an impoverished person. [C14: < L *indigēre* to need, < *egēre* to lack] —'**indigence** *n.* —'**indigently** *adv.*

indigestible (ˌɪndɪ'dʒɛstəbᵊl) *adj.* **1.** incapable of being digested or difficult to digest. **2.** difficult to understand or absorb mentally: *an indigestible book.* —ˌ**indiˌgesti'bility** *n.* —ˌ**indi'gestibly** *adv.*

indigestion (ˌɪndɪ'dʒɛstʃən) *n.* difficulty in digesting food, accompanied by abdominal pain, heartburn, and belching.

indignant (ɪn'dɪgnənt) *adj.* feeling or showing indignation. [C16: < L *indignārī* to be displeased with] —**in'dignantly** *adv.*

indignation (ˌɪndɪg'neɪʃən) *n.* anger aroused by something felt to be unfair, unworthy, or wrong.

indignity (ɪn'dɪgnɪtɪ) *n., pl.* **-ties.** injury to one's self-esteem or dignity; humiliation.

indigo ('ɪndɪˌgəʊ) *n., pl.* **-gos** *or* **-goes. 1.** a blue vat dye originally obtained from plants but now made synthetically. **2.** any of various leguminous tropical plants, such as the anil, that yield this dye. **3. a.** any of a group of colours that have the same blue-violet hue; a spectral colour. **b.** (*as adj.*): *an indigo rug.* [C16: < Sp. *indico,* via L < Gk *Indikos* of India] —**indigotic** (ˌɪndɪ'gɒtɪk) *adj.*

indigo blue *n., adj.* (**indigo-blue** *when prenominal*). the full name for **indigo** (the colour and the dye).

indirect (ˌɪndɪ'rɛkt) *adj.* **1.** deviating from a direct course or line; roundabout; circuitous. **2.** not coming as a direct effect or consequence; secondary: *indirect benefits.* **3.** not straightforward, open, or fair; devious or evasive. —ˌ**indi'rectly** *adv.* —ˌ**indi'rectness** *n.*

indirect costs *pl. n.* another name for **overheads.**

indirection (ˌɪndɪ'rɛkʃən) *n.* **1.** indirect pro-

cedure, courses, or methods. **2.** lack of direction or purpose; aimlessness. **3.** indirect dealing; deceit.
indirect lighting *n.* reflected or diffused light from a concealed source.
indirect object *n. Grammar.* a noun, pronoun, or noun phrase indicating the recipient or beneficiary of the action of a verb and its direct object, as *John* in the sentence *I bought John a newspaper.*
indirect proof *n. Logic, maths.* proof of a conclusion by showing its negation to be self-contradictory. Cf. **direct** (sense 17).
indirect question *n.* a question reported in indirect speech, as in *She asked why you came.*
indirect speech *or esp. U.S.* **indirect discourse** *n.* the reporting of something said or written by conveying what was meant rather than repeating the exact words, as in the sentence *He asked me whether I would go* as opposed to *He asked me, "Will you go?"* Also called: **reported speech.**
indirect tax *n.* a tax levied on goods or services rather than on individuals or companies.
indiscreet (ˌɪndɪˈskriːt) *adj.* not discreet; imprudent or tactless. —ˌ**indisˈcreetly** *adv.* —ˌ**indisˈcreetness** *n.*
indiscrete (ˌɪndɪˈskriːt) *adj.* not divisible or divided into parts.
indiscretion (ˌɪndɪˈskrɛʃən) *n.* **1.** the characteristic or state of being indiscreet. **2.** an indiscreet act, remark, etc.
indiscriminate (ˌɪndɪˈskrɪmɪnɪt) *adj.* **1.** lacking discrimination or careful choice; random or promiscuous. **2.** jumbled; confused. —ˌ**indisˈcriminately** *adv.* —ˌ**indisˈcriminateness** *n.* —ˌ**indisˌcrimiˈnation** *n.*
indispensable (ˌɪndɪˈspɛnsəbᵊl) *adj.* **1.** absolutely necessary; essential. **2.** not to be disregarded or escaped: *an indispensable role.* ~*n.* **3.** an indispensable person or thing. —ˌ**indisˌpensaˈbility** *or* ˌ**indisˈpensableness** *n.* —ˌ**indisˈpensably** *adv.*
indispose (ˌɪndɪˈspəʊz) *vb.* (*tr.*) **1.** to make unwilling or opposed; disincline. **2.** to cause to feel ill. **3.** to make unfit (for something or to do something).
indisposed (ˌɪndɪˈspəʊzd) *adj.* **1.** sick or ill. **2.** unwilling. [C15: < L *indispositus* disordered] —**indisposition** (ˌɪndɪspəˈzɪʃən) *n.*
indissoluble (ˌɪndɪˈsɒljʊbᵊl) *adj.* incapable of being dissolved or broken; permanent. —ˌ**indisˈsolubly** *adv.*
indistinct (ˌɪndɪˈstɪŋkt) *adj.* incapable of being clearly distinguished, as by the eyes, ears, or mind; not distinct. —ˌ**indisˈtinctly** *adv.* —ˌ**indisˈtinctness** *n.*
indite (ɪnˈdaɪt) *vb.* (*tr.*) *Arch.* to write. [C14: < OF *enditer,* < L *indīcere* to declare, < IN-[2] + *dīcere* to say] —**inˈditement** *n.* —**inˈditer** *n.*
indium (ˈɪndɪəm) *n.* a rare soft silvery metallic element associated with zinc ores: used in alloys, electronics, and electroplating. Symbol: In; atomic no.: 49; atomic wt.: 114.82. [C19: NL, < INDIGO + -IUM]
individual (ˌɪndɪˈvɪdjʊəl) *adj.* **1.** of, relating to, characteristic of, or meant for a single person or thing. **2.** separate or distinct, esp. from others of its kind; particular: *please mark the individual pages.* **3.** characterized by unusual and striking qualities; distinctive. **4.** *Obs.* indivisible; inseparable. ~*n.* **5.** a single person, esp. when regarded as distinct from others. **6.** *Biol.* a single animal or plant, esp. as distinct from a species. **7.** *Inf.* a person: *a most obnoxious individual.* [C15: < Med. L, < L *indīviduus* indivisible, < IN-[1] + *dīvidere* to DIVIDE] —ˌ**indiˈvidually** *adv.*
▷ **Usage.** In careful speech and writing, the noun *individual* is not loosely used as a synonym of *person,* although it is appropriate in that sense when a single person is being considered in contrast to a group, as in *in mass democracy the rights of the individual must be protected.*
individualism (ˌɪndɪˈvɪdjʊəˌlɪzəm) *n.* **1.** the principle of asserting one's independence and individuality; egoism. **2.** an individual quirk. **3.** another word for **laissez faire** (sense 1). **4.** *Philosophy.* the doctrine that only individual things exist. —ˌ**indiˈvidualist** *n.*
individuality (ˌɪndɪˌvɪdjʊˈælɪtɪ) *n., pl.* **-ties. 1.** distinctive or unique character or personality: *a work of great individuality.* **2.** the qualities that distinguish one person or thing from another; identity. **3.** the state or quality of being a separate entity; discreteness.
individualize *or* **-ise** (ˌɪndɪˈvɪdjʊəˌlaɪz) *vb.* (*tr.*) **1.** to make or mark as individual or distinctive in character. **2.** to consider or treat individually; particularize. **3.** to make or modify so as to meet the special requirements of a person. —ˌ**indiˌvidualiˈzation** *or* **-iˈsation** *n.* —ˌ**indiˈvidualˌizer** *or* **-ˌiser** *n.*
individuate (ˌɪndɪˈvɪdjʊˌeɪt) *vb.* (*tr.*) **1.** to give individuality or an individual form to. **2.** to distinguish from others of the same species or group; individualize. —ˌ**indiˈviduˌator** *n.*
indivisible (ˌɪndɪˈvɪzəbᵊl) *adj.* **1.** unable to be divided. **2.** *Maths.* leaving a remainder when divided by a given number. —ˌ**indiˌvisiˈbility** *n.* —ˌ**indiˈvisibly** *adv.*
Indo- (ˈɪndəʊ) *combining form.* denoting India or Indian: *Indo-European.*
indoctrinate (ɪnˈdɒktrɪˌneɪt) *vb.* (*tr.*) **1.** to teach (a person or group of people) systematically to accept doctrines, esp. uncritically. **2.** *Rare.* to instruct. —**inˌdoctriˈnation** *n.* —**inˈdoctriˌnator** *n.*
Indo-European *adj.* **1.** denoting, belonging to, or relating to a family of languages that includes English: characteristically marked, esp. in the older languages, such as Latin, by inflection showing gender, number, and case. **2.** denoting or relating to the hypothetical parent language of this family, primitive Indo-European. **3.** denoting, belonging to, or relating to any of the peoples speaking these languages. ~*n.* **4.** the Indo-European family of languages. **5.** the reconstructed hypothetical parent language of this family. ~Also (*obs.*): **Indo-Germanic.**
Indo-Iranian *adj.* **1.** of or relating to the Indic and Iranian branches of the Indo-European family of languages. ~*n.* **2.** this group of languages, sometimes considered as forming a single branch of Indo-European.
indole (ˈɪndəʊl) *or* **indol** (ˈɪndəʊl, -dɒl) *n.* a white or yellowish crystalline heterocyclic compound extracted from coal tar and used in perfumery, medicine, and as a flavouring agent. [C19: < IND(IGO) + -OLE[1]]
indolent (ˈɪndələnt) *adj.* **1.** disliking work or effort; lazy; idle. **2.** *Pathol.* causing little pain: *an indolent tumour.* **3.** (esp. of a painless ulcer) slow to heal. [C17: < L *indolēns* not feeling pain, < IN-[1] + *dolēre* to grieve, cause distress] —ˈ**indolence** *n.* —ˈ**indolently** *adv.*
indomitable (ɪnˈdɒmɪtəbᵊl) *adj.* (of courage, pride, etc.) difficult or impossible to defeat or subdue. [C17: < LL, < L *indomitus* untameable, < *domāre* to tame] —**inˌdomitaˈbility** *or* **inˈdomitableness** *n.* —**inˈdomitably** *adv.*
Indonesian (ˌɪndəʊˈniːzɪən) *adj.* **1.** of or relating to Indonesia, a republic in SE Asia, its people, or their language. ~*n.* **2.** a native or inhabitant of Indonesia.
indoor (ˈɪnˌdɔː) *adj.* (*prenominal*) of, situated in, or appropriate to the inside of a house or other building: *an indoor pool; indoor amusements.*
indoors (ˌɪnˈdɔːz) *adv., adj.* (*postpositive*) inside or into a house or other building.
indorse (ɪnˈdɔːs) *vb.* a variant of **endorse.**
indraught *or U.S.* **indraft** (ˈɪnˌdrɑːft) *n.* **1.** the

ˌ**indisˈcernible** *adj.*
ˌ**indisˈputable** *adj.*
ˌ**indisˈtinctive** *adj.*
ˌ**indisˈtinguishable** *adj.*

act of drawing or pulling in. **2.** an inward flow, esp. of air.

indrawn (ˌɪnˈdrɔːn) *adj.* **1.** drawn or pulled in. **2.** inward-looking or introspective.

indris (ˈɪndrɪs) *or* **indri** (ˈɪndrɪ) *n., pl.* **-dris. 1.** a large Madagascan arboreal lemuroid primate with thick silky fur patterned in black, white, and fawn. **2. woolly indris.** a related nocturnal Madagascan animal with thick grey-brown fur and a long tail. [C19: < F: lemur, < native word *indry!* look! mistaken for the animal's name]

indubitable (ɪnˈdjuːbɪtəbᵊl) *adj.* incapable of being doubted; unquestionable. [C18: < L, < IN-[1] + *dubitāre* to doubt] **—inˈdubitably** *adv.*

induce (ɪnˈdjuːs) *vb. (tr.)* **1.** (often foll. by an infinitive) to persuade or use influence on. **2.** to cause or bring about. **3.** *Med.* to initiate or hasten (labour), as by administering a drug to stimulate uterine contractions. **4.** *Logic, obs.* to assert or establish (a general proposition, etc.) by induction. **5.** to produce (an electromotive force or electrical current) by induction. **6.** to transmit (magnetism) by induction. [C14: < L *indūcere* to lead in] **—inˈducer** *n.* **—inˈducible** *adj.*

inducement (ɪnˈdjuːsmənt) *n.* **1.** the act of inducing. **2.** a means of inducing; persuasion; incentive. **3.** *Law.* the introductory part that leads up to and explains the matter in dispute.

induct (ɪnˈdʌkt) *vb. (tr.)* **1.** to bring in formally or install in an office, place, etc.; invest. **2.** (foll. by *to* or *into*) to initiate in knowledge (of). **3.** *U.S.* to enlist for military service. **4.** *Physics.* another word for **induce** (senses 5, 6). [C14: < L *inductus* led in, p.p. of *indūcere* to introduce; see INDUCE]

inductance (ɪnˈdʌktəns) *n.* **1.** the property of an electric circuit as a result of which an electromotive force is created by a change of current in the same or in a neighbouring circuit. **2.** a component, such as a coil, in an electrical circuit, the main function of which is to produce inductance.

induction (ɪnˈdʌkʃən) *n.* **1.** the act of inducting or state of being inducted. **2.** the act of inducing. **3.** (in an internal-combustion engine) the drawing in of mixed air and fuel from the carburettor to the cylinder. **4.** *Logic.* **a.** a process of reasoning by which a general conclusion is drawn from a set of premises, based mainly on experience or experimental evidence. **b.** a conclusion reached by this process of reasoning. **5.** the process by which electrical or magnetic properties are transferred, without physical contact, from one circuit or body to another. See also **inductance. 6.** *Maths.* a method of proving a proposition $P(n)$ by showing that it is true for all preceding values of n and for $n + 1$. **7. a.** a formal introduction or entry into an office or position. **b.** (*as modifier*): *induction course.* **8.** *U.S.* the enlistment of a civilian into military service. **—inˈductional** *adj.*

induction coil *n.* a transformer for producing a high voltage from a low voltage. It consists of a cylindrical primary winding of few turns, a concentric secondary winding of many turns, and often a common soft-iron core.

induction heating *n.* the heating of a conducting material as a result of the electric currents induced in it by an externally applied alternating magnetic field.

induction motor *n.* a type of electric motor in which an alternating supply fed to the windings of the stator creates a magnetic field that induces a current in the windings of the rotor. Rotation of the rotor results from the interaction of the magnetic field created by the rotor current with the field of the stator.

inductive (ɪnˈdʌktɪv) *adj.* **1.** relating to or operated by electrical or magnetic induction: *an inductive reactance.* **2.** *Logic, maths.* of, relating to, or using induction: *inductive reasoning.* **3.** serving to induce or cause. **—inˈductively** *adv.* **—inˈductiveness** *n.*

inductor (ɪnˈdʌktə) *n.* **1.** a person or thing that inducts. **2.** another name for an **inductance** (sense 2).

indue (ɪnˈdjuː) *vb.* **-duing, -dued.** a variant spelling of **endue.**

indulge (ɪnˈdʌldʒ) *vb.* **1.** (when *intr.*, often foll. by *in*) to yield to or gratify (a whim or desire for): *to indulge in new clothes.* **2.** (*tr.*) to yield to the wishes of; pamper: *to indulge a child.* **3.** (*tr.*) to allow (oneself) the pleasure of something: *he indulged himself.* **4.** (*intr.*) *Inf.* to take alcoholic drink, esp. to excess. [C17: < L *indulgēre* to concede] **—inˈdulger** *n.* **—inˈdulgingly** *adv.*

indulgence (ɪnˈdʌldʒəns) *n.* **1.** the act of indulging or state of being indulgent. **2.** a pleasure, habit, etc., indulged in; extravagance. **3.** liberal or tolerant treatment. **4.** something granted as a favour or privilege. **5.** *R.C. Church.* a remission of the temporal punishment for sin after its guilt has been forgiven. **6.** Also called: **Declaration of Indulgence.** a royal grant during the reigns of Charles II and James II of England giving Nonconformists and Roman Catholics a measure of religious freedom.

indulgent (ɪnˈdʌldʒənt) *adj.* showing or characterized by indulgence. **—inˈdulgently** *adv.*

induna (ɪnˈduːnə) *n.* (in South Africa) a Black African overseer in a factory, mine, etc. [C20: < Zulu *nduna* an official]

indurate *vb.* (ˈɪndjʊˌreɪt). **1.** to make or become hard or callous. **2.** to make or become hardy. ~*adj.* (ˈɪndjʊrɪt). **3.** hardened, callous, or unfeeling. [C16: < L *indūrāre* to make hard; see ENDURE] **—ˌinduˈration** *n.* **—ˈinduˌrative** *adj.*

indusium (ɪnˈdjuːzɪəm) *n., pl.* **-sia** (-zɪə). **1.** a membranous outgrowth on the undersurface of fern leaves that protects the developing spores. **2.** an enveloping membrane, such as the amnion. [C18: NL, < L: tunic, < *induere* to put on] **—inˈdusial** *adj.*

industrial (ɪnˈdʌstrɪəl) *adj.* **1.** of, relating to, or derived from industry. **2.** employed in industry: *the industrial workforce.* **3.** relating to or concerned with workers in industry: *industrial conditions.* **4.** used in industry: *industrial chemicals.* **—inˈdustrially** *adv.*

industrial action *n. Brit.* any action, such as a strike or go-slow, taken by employees in industry to protest against working conditions, etc.

industrial archaeology *n.* the study of industrial machines, works, etc. of the past.

industrial design *n.* the art or practice of designing any object for manufacture. **—industrial designer** *n.*

industrial estate *n. Brit.* an area of land set aside for industry and business. U.S. equivalent: **industrial park.**

industrialism (ɪnˈdʌstrɪəˌlɪzəm) *n.* an organization of society characterized by large-scale mechanized manufacturing industry rather than trade, farming, etc.

industrialist (ɪnˈdʌstrɪəlɪst) *n.* a person who has a substantial interest in the ownership or control of industrial enterprise.

industrialize *or* **-lise** (ɪnˈdʌstrɪəˌlaɪz) *vb.* **1.** (*tr.*) to develop industry on an extensive scale in (a country, region, etc.). **2.** (*intr.*) (of a country, region, etc.) to undergo the development of industry on an extensive scale. **—inˌdustrialiˈzation** *or* **-liˈsation** *n.*

industrial relations *n.* **1.** (*functioning as pl.*) relations between the employers and employees in an industrial enterprise. **2.** (*functioning as sing.*) the management of such relations.

Industrial Revolution *n.* **the.** the transformation in the 18th and 19th centuries of Britain and other countries into industrial nations.

industrious (ɪnˈdʌstrɪəs) *adj.* hard-working, diligent, or assiduous. **—inˈdustriously** *adv.* **—inˈdustriousness** *n.*

industry (ˈɪndəstrɪ) *n., pl.* **-tries. 1.** organized economic activity concerned with manufacture, processing of raw materials, or construction. **2.** a

---

inˈductile *adj.*

branch of commercial enterprise concerned with the output of a specified product: *the steel industry.* **3. a.** industrial ownership and management interests collectively. **b.** manufacturing enterprise collectively, as opposed to agriculture. **4.** diligence; assiduity. [C15: < L *industria* diligence, < *industrius* active, <?]

indwell (ɪnˈdwɛl) *vb.* **-dwelling, -dwelt. 1.** (*tr.*) (of a spirit, principle, etc.) to inhabit; suffuse. **2.** (*intr.*) to dwell; exist. **—inˈdweller** *n.*

-ine[1] *suffix forming adjectives.* **1.** of, relating to, or belonging to: *saturnine.* **2.** consisting of or resembling: *crystalline.* [< L *-īnus,* < Gk *-inos*]

-ine[2] *suffix forming nouns.* **1.** indicating a halogen: *chlorine.* **2.** indicating a nitrogenous organic compound, including amino acids, alkaloids, and certain other bases: *nicotine.* **3.** Also: **-in.** indicating a chemical substance in certain nonsystematic names: *glycerine.* **4.** indicating a mixture of hydrocarbons: *benzine.* **5.** indicating feminine form: *heroine.* [via F < L *-ina* (< *-inus*) and Gk *-inē*]

inebriate *vb.* (ɪnˈiːbrɪˌeɪt). (*tr.*) **1.** to make drunk; intoxicate. **2.** to arouse emotionally; make excited. *~n.* (ɪnˈiːbrɪɪt). **3.** a person who is drunk, esp. habitually. *~adj.* (ɪnˈiːbrɪɪt), *also* **inebriated. 4.** drunk, esp. habitually. [C15: < L, < IN-[2] + *ēbriāre* to intoxicate, < *ēbrius* drunk] **—inˌebriˈation** *n.* **—inebriety** (ˌɪnɪˈbraɪɪtɪ) *n.*

inedible (ɪnˈɛdɪbᵊl) *adj.* not fit to be eaten. **—inˌediˈbility** *n.*

▷ **Usage.** In careful speech and writing, *inedible* is not synonymous with *uneatable. Inedible* implies that something is of a sort not suitable for eating, while *uneatable* implies that it is so disgusting as to be beyond eating.

ineducable (ɪnˈɛdjʊkəbᵊl) *adj.* incapable of being educated, esp. on account of mental retardation. **—inˌeducaˈbility** *n.*

ineffable (ɪnˈɛfəbᵊl) *adj.* **1.** too great or intense to be expressed in words; unutterable. **2.** too sacred to be uttered. **3.** indescribable; indefinable. [C15: < L, < IN-[1] + *effābilis,* < *fārī* to speak] **—inˌeffaˈbility** *or* **inˈeffableness** *n.* **—inˈeffably** *adv.*

ineffective (ˌɪnɪˈfɛktɪv) *adj.* **1.** having no effect. **2.** incompetent or inefficient. **—ˌinefˈfectively** *adv.* **—ˌinefˈfectiveness** *n.*

ineffectual (ˌɪnɪˈfɛktʃʊəl) *adj.* **1.** having no effect or an inadequate effect. **2.** lacking in power or forcefulness; impotent: *an ineffectual ruler.* **—ˌinefˌfectuˈality** *or* **ˌinefˈfectualness** *n.* **—ˌinefˈfectually** *adv.*

inefficacious (ˌɪnɛfɪˈkeɪʃəs) *adj.* failing to produce the desired effect. **—ˌineffiˈcaciously** *adv.* **—inefficacy** (ɪnˈɛfɪkəsɪ), **ˌineffiˈcaciousness,** *or* **inefficacity** (ˌɪnɛfɪˈkæsɪtɪ) *n.*

ineluctable (ˌɪnɪˈlʌktəbᵊl) *adj.* (esp. of fate) incapable of being avoided; inescapable. [C17: < L, < IN-[1] + *ēluctārī* to escape, < *luctārī* to struggle] **—ˌineˌluctaˈbility** *n.* **—ˌineˈluctably** *adv.*

inept (ɪnˈɛpt) *adj.* **1.** awkward, clumsy, or incompetent. **2.** not suitable, appropriate, or fitting; out of place. [C17: < L *ineptus,* < IN-[1] + *aptus* fitting] **—inˈeptiˌtude** *n.* **—inˈeptly** *adv.* **—inˈeptness** *n.*

inequable (ɪnˈɛkwəbᵊl) *adj.* **1.** uneven. **2.** not uniform. **3.** changeable.

inequality (ˌɪnɪˈkwɒlɪtɪ) *n., pl.* **-ties. 1.** the state or quality of being unequal; disparity. **2.** an instance of disparity. **3.** lack of smoothness or regularity. **4.** social or economic disparity. **5.** *Maths.* **a.** a statement indicating that the value of one quantity or expression is not equal to another. **b.** the relation of being unequal.

inert (ɪnˈɜːt) *adj.* **1.** having no inherent ability to move or to resist motion. **2.** inactive, lazy, or sluggish. **3.** having only a limited ability to react chemically; unreactive. [C17: < L *iners* unskilled, < IN-[1] + *ars* skill; see ART[1]] **—inˈertly** *adv.* **—inˈertness** *n.*

inert gas *n.* **1.** any of the unreactive gaseous elements helium, neon, argon, krypton, xenon, and radon. **2.** (loosely) any gas, such as carbon dioxide, that is nonoxidizing.

inertia (ɪnˈɜːʃə, -ʃɪə) *n.* **1.** the state of being inert; disinclination to move or act. **2.** *Physics.* **a.** the tendency of a body to preserve its state of rest or uniform motion unless acted upon by an external force. **b.** an analogous property of other physical quantities that resist change: *thermal inertia.* **—inˈertial** *adj.*

inertial guidance *or* **navigation** *n.* a method of controlling the flight path of a missile by instruments contained within it.

inertial mass *n.* the mass of a body as determined by its momentum, as opposed to the extent to which it responds to the force of gravity.

inertia-reel seat-belt *n.* a type of car seat-belt in which the belt is free to unwind from a metal drum except when the drum locks as a result of rapid deceleration.

inertia selling *n.* the illegal practice of sending unrequested goods to householders, followed by a bill for the goods if they do not return them.

inescapable (ˌɪnɪˈskeɪpəbᵊl) *adj.* incapable of being escaped or avoided. **—ˌinesˈcapably** *adv.*

inestimable (ɪnˈɛstɪməbᵊl) *adj.* **1.** not able to be estimated; immeasurable. **2.** of immeasurable value. **—inˌestimaˈbility** *or* **inˈestimableness** *n.* **—inˈestimably** *adv.*

inevitable (ɪnˈɛvɪtəbᵊl) *adj.* **1.** unavoidable. **2.** sure to happen; certain. *~n.* **3.** (often preceded by *the*) something that is unavoidable. [C15: < L, < IN-[1] + *ēvītāre* to shun, < *vītāre* to avoid] **—inˌevitaˈbility** *or* **inˈevitableness** *n.* **—inˈevitably** *adv.*

inexhaustible (ˌɪnɪgˈzɔːstəbᵊl) *adj.* **1.** incapable of being used up; endless. **2.** incapable or apparently incapable of becoming tired; tireless. **—ˌinexˌhaustiˈbility** *n.* **—ˌinexˈhaustibly** *adv.*

inexorable (ɪnˈɛksərəbᵊl) *adj.* **1.** not able to be moved by entreaty or persuasion. **2.** relentless. [C16: < L, < IN-[1] + *exōrāre* to prevail upon, < *ōrāre* to pray] **—inˌexoraˈbility** *n.* **—inˈexorably** *adv.*

inexpiable (ɪnˈɛkspɪəbᵊl) *adj.* **1.** incapable of being expiated; unpardonable. **2.** *Arch.* implacable. **—inˈexpiableness** *n.*

in extenso *Latin.* (ɪn ɪkˈstɛnsəʊ) *adv.* at full length.

in extremis *Latin.* (ɪn ɪkˈstriːmɪs) *adv.* **1.** in extremity; in dire straits. **2.** at the point of death. [lit.: in the furthest reaches]

inextricable (ˌɪnɛksˈtrɪkəbᵊl) *adj.* **1.** not able to be escaped from: *an inextricable dilemma.* **2.** not able to be disentangled, etc.: *an inextricable knot.* **3.** extremely involved or intricate. **—ˌinextricaˈbility** *or* **ˌinexˈtricableness** *n.* **—ˌinexˈtricably** *adv.*

inf. *abbrev. for:* **1.** Also: **Inf.** infantry. **2.** inferior. **3.** infinitive. **4.** informal. **5.** information.

infallible (ɪnˈfæləbᵊl) *adj.* **1.** not fallible; not liable to error. **2.** not liable to failure; certain; sure: *an infallible cure.* *~n.* **3.** a person or thing that is incapable of error or failure. **—inˌfalliˈbility** *or* **inˈfallibleness** *n.* **—inˈfallibly** *adv.*

infamous (ˈɪnfəməs) *adj.* **1.** having a bad reputation; notorious. **2.** causing or deserving a bad reputation; shocking: *infamous conduct.* **—ˈinfamously** *adv.* **—ˈinfamousness** *n.*

---

inˈedited *adj.*
ˌinefˈfaceable *adj.*
ˌinefˈficient *adj.*
ˌineˈlastic *adj.*
inˈelegant *adj.*
inˈeligible *adj.*
inˈequitable *adj.*
inˈequity *n.*
ˌineˈradicable *adj.*
ˌinesˈsential *adj., n.*
ˌinexˈact *adj.*
ˌinexˈcusable *adj.*
ˌinexˈpedient *adj.*
ˌinexˈpensive *adj.*
ˌinexˈperience *n.*
inˈexpert *adj.*
inˈexplicable *adj.*
ˌinexˈplicit *adj.*
ˌinexˈpressible *adj.*
ˌinexˈpressive *adj.*
ˌinexˈtinguishable *adj.*

infamy (ˈɪnfəmɪ) *n., pl.* **-mies.** **1.** the state or condition of being infamous. **2.** an infamous act or event. [C15: < L *infāmis* of evil repute, < IN-[1] + *fāma* FAME]

infancy (ˈɪnfənsɪ) *n., pl.* **-cies.** **1.** the state or period of being an infant; childhood. **2.** an early stage of growth or development. **3.** infants collectively. **4.** the period of life prior to attaining legal majority; minority nonage.

infant (ˈɪnfənt) *n.* **1.** a child at the earliest stage of its life; baby. **2.** *Law.* another word for **minor** (sense 9). **3.** *Brit.* a young schoolchild. **4.** a person who is beginning or inexperienced in an activity. **5.** (*modifier*) **a.** of or relating to young children or infancy. **b.** designed or intended for young children. ~*adj.* **6.** in an early stage of development; nascent: *an infant science.* **7.** *Law.* of or relating to the legal status of infancy. [C14: < L *infāns*, lit.: speechless, < IN-[1] + *fārī* to speak] —**ˈinfantˌhood** *n.*

infanta (ɪnˈfæntə) *n.* **1.** (formerly) a daughter of a king of Spain or Portugal. **2.** the wife of an infante. [C17: < Sp. or Port., fem. of INFANTE]

infante (ɪnˈfæntɪ) *n.* (formerly) a son of a king of Spain or Portugal, esp. one not heir to the throne. [C16: < Sp. or Port., lit.: INFANT]

infanticide (ɪnˈfæntɪˌsaɪd) *n.* **1.** the killing of an infant. **2.** the practice of killing newborn infants, still prevalent in some primitive tribes. **3.** a person who kills an infant. —**inˌfantiˈcidal** *adj.*

infantile (ˈɪnfənˌtaɪl) *adj.* **1.** like a child in action or behaviour; childishly immature; puerile. **2.** of, relating to, or characteristic of infants or infancy. **3.** in an early stage of development. —**infantility** (ˌɪnfənˈtɪlɪtɪ) *n.*

infantile paralysis *n.* a former name for **poliomyelitis.**

infantilism (ɪnˈfæntɪˌlɪzəm) *n.* **1.** *Psychol.* a condition in which an older child or adult is mentally or physically undeveloped. **2.** childish speech; baby talk.

infantry (ˈɪnfəntrɪ) *n., pl.* **-tries.** **a.** soldiers or units of soldiers who fight on foot with small arms. **b.** (*as modifier*): *an infantry unit.* [C16: < It. *infanteria*, < *infante* boy, foot soldier; see INFANT]

infantryman (ˈɪnfəntrɪmən) *n., pl.* **-men.** a soldier belonging to the infantry.

infant school *n. Brit.* a school for children aged between 5 and 7.

infarct (ɪnˈfɑːkt) *n.* a localized area of dead tissue resulting from obstruction of the blood supply to that part. Also called: **infarction.** [C19: via NL < L *infarctus* stuffed into, < *farcīre* to stuff] —**inˈfarcted** *adj.*

infatuate *vb.* (ɪnˈfætjʊˌeɪt). (*tr.*) **1.** to inspire or fill with foolish, shallow, or extravagant passion. **2.** to cause to act foolishly. ~*n.* (ɪnˈfætjʊɪt, -ˌeɪt). **3.** *Literary.* a person who is infatuated. [C16: < L *infatuāre*, < IN-[2] + *fatuus* FATUOUS] —**inˌfatuˈation** *n.*

infatuated (ɪnˈfætjʊˌeɪtɪd) *adj.* (often foll. by *with*) possessed by a foolish or extravagant passion, esp. for another person.

infect (ɪnˈfɛkt) *vb.* (*mainly tr.*) **1.** to cause infection in; contaminate (an organism, wound, etc.) with pathogenic microorganisms. **2.** (*also intr.*) to affect or become affected with a communicable disease. **3.** to taint, pollute, or contaminate. **4.** to affect, esp. adversely, as if by contagion. ~*adj.* **5.** *Arch.* contaminated or polluted with or as if with a disease; infected. [C14: < L *inficere* to dip into, stain, < *facere* to make] —**inˈfector** *or* **inˈfecter** *n.*

infection (ɪnˈfɛkʃən) *n.* **1.** invasion of the body by pathogenic microorganisms. **2.** the resulting condition in the tissues. **3.** an infectious disease. **4.** the act of infecting or state of being infected. **5.** an agent or influence that infects. **6.** persuasion or corruption, as by ideas, perverse influences, etc.

infectious (ɪnˈfɛkʃəs) *adj.* **1.** (of a disease) capable of being transmitted. **2.** (of a disease) caused by microorganisms, such as bacteria, viruses, or protozoa. **3.** causing or transmitting infection. **4.** tending or apt to spread, as from one person to another: *infectious mirth.* —**inˈfectiously** *adv.* —**inˈfectiousness** *n.*

infectious hepatitis *n.* an acute infectious viral disease characterized by inflammation of the liver, fever, and jaundice.

infectious mononucleosis *n.* an acute infectious disease, caused by a virus (**Epstein-Barr virus**), characterized by fever, sore throat, swollen and painful lymph nodes, and abnormal lymphocytes in the blood. Also called: **glandular fever.**

infective (ɪnˈfɛktɪv) *adj.* **1.** capable of causing infection. **2.** a less common word for **infectious.** —**inˈfectively** *adv.* —**inˈfectiveness** *n.*

infelicity (ˌɪnfɪˈlɪsɪtɪ) *n., pl.* **-ties.** **1.** unhappiness; misfortune. **2.** an instance of bad luck or mischance. **3.** something, esp. a remark or expression, that is inapt or inappropriate. —**ˌinfeˈlicitous** *adj.*

infer (ɪnˈfɜː) *vb.* **-ferring, -ferred.** (when *tr., may take a clause as object*) **1.** to conclude (a state of affairs, supposition, etc.) by reasoning from evidence; deduce. **2.** (*tr.*) to have or lead to as a necessary or logical consequence; indicate. **3.** (*tr.*) to hint or imply. [C16: < L *inferre* to bring into, < *ferre* to bear, carry] —**inˈferable** *or* **inˈferrable** *adj.* —**inˈferrer** *n.*

▷ **Usage.** The use of *infer* in the sense of *imply* often occurs in both speech and writing but is avoided by all careful speakers and writers of English.

inference (ˈɪnfərəns, -frəns) *n.* **1.** the act or process of inferring. **2.** an inferred conclusion, deduction, etc. **3.** any process of reasoning from premises to a conclusion. **4.** *Logic.* the specific mode of reasoning used.

inferential (ˌɪnfəˈrɛnʃəl) *adj.* of, relating to, or derived from inference. —**ˌinferˈentially** *adv.*

inferior (ɪnˈfɪərɪə) *adj.* **1.** lower in value or quality. **2.** lower in rank, position, or status; subordinate. **3.** not of the best; mediocre; commonplace. **4.** lower in position; situated beneath. **5.** (of a plant ovary) situated below the other floral parts. **6.** *Astron.* **a.** orbiting between the sun and the earth: *an inferior planet.* **b.** lying below the horizon. **7.** *Printing.* (of a character) printed at the foot of an ordinary character. ~*n.* **8.** an inferior person. **9.** *Printing.* an inferior character. [C15: < L: lower, < *inferus* low] —**inferiority** (ɪnˌfɪərɪˈɒrɪtɪ) *n.* —**inˈferiorly** *adv.*

inferiority complex *n. Psychiatry.* a disorder arising from the conflict between the desire to be noticed and the fear of being humiliated, characterized by aggressiveness or withdrawal into oneself.

infernal (ɪnˈfɜːnᵊl) *adj.* **1.** of or relating to an underworld of the dead. **2.** deserving or befitting hell; diabolic; fiendish. **3.** *Inf.* irritating; confounded. [C14: < LL, < *infernus* hell, < L (adj.): lower, hellish; rel. to L *inferus* low] —**ˌinferˈnality** *n.* —**inˈfernally** *adv.*

infernal machine *n. Arch.* an explosive device (usually disguised) or booby trap.

inferno (ɪnˈfɜːnəʊ) *n., pl.* **-nos.** **1.** (*sometimes cap.;* usually preceded by *the*) hell; the infernal region. **2.** any place or state resembling hell, esp. a conflagration. [C19: < It., < LL *infernus* hell]

infest (ɪnˈfɛst) *vb.* (*tr.*) **1.** to inhabit or overrun in unpleasantly large numbers. **2.** (of parasites such as lice) to invade and live on or in (a host). [C15: < L *infestāre* to molest, < *infestus* hostile] —**ˌinfesˈtation** *n.* —**inˈfester** *n.*

infeudation (ˌɪnfjuˈdeɪʃən) *n. History.* **1.** (in feudal society) the act of putting a vassal in possession of a fief. **2.** the granting of tithes to laymen.

infidel (ˈɪnfɪdᵊl) *n.* **1.** a person who has no religious belief; unbeliever. ~*adj.* **2.** rejecting a specific religion, esp. Christianity or Islam. **3.** of

---

inˈfeasible *adj.* **inˈfertile** *adj.* **ˌinferˈtility** *n.*

or relating to unbelievers or unbelief. [C15: < Med. L, < L (adj.): unfaithful, < IN-[1] + *fidēlis* faithful; see FEALTY]

infidelity (ˌɪnfɪˈdɛlɪtɪ) *n., pl.* **-ties.** **1.** lack of faith or constancy, esp. sexual faithfulness. **2.** lack of religious faith; disbelief. **3.** an act or instance of disloyalty.

infield (ˈɪnˌfiːld) *n.* **1.** *Cricket.* the area of the field near the pitch. **2.** *Baseball.* the area of the playing field enclosed by the base lines. **3.** *Agriculture.* the part of a farm nearest to the farm buildings. **—ˈinˌfielder** *n.*

infighting (ˈɪnˌfaɪtɪŋ) *n.* **1.** *Boxing.* combat at close quarters in which proper blows are inhibited. **2.** intense competition, as between members of an organization. **—ˈinˌfighter** *n.*

infill (ˈɪnfɪl) *or* **infilling** (ˈɪnfɪlɪŋ) *n.* **1.** the act of filling or closing gaps, etc., in something, such as a row of buildings. **2.** material used to fill a cavity, gap, hole, etc.

infiltrate (ˈɪnfɪlˌtreɪt) *vb.* **1.** to undergo the process in which a fluid passes into the pores or interstices of a solid; permeate. **2.** *Mil.* to pass undetected through (an enemy-held line or position). **3.** to gain or cause to gain entrance or access surreptitiously: *they infiltrated the party structure.* ~*n.* **4.** something that infiltrates. [C18: < IN-[2] + FILTRATE] **—ˌinfilˈtration** *n.* **—ˈinfilˌtrative** *adj.* **—ˈinfilˌtrator** *n.*

infin. *abbrev. for* infinitive.

infinite (ˈɪnfɪnɪt) *adj.* **1. a.** having no limits or boundaries in time, space, extent, or magnitude. **b.** (*as n.; preceded by the*): *the infinite.* **2.** extremely or immeasurably great or numerous: *infinite wealth.* **3.** all-embracing, absolute, or total: *God's infinite wisdom.* **4.** *Maths.* having an unlimited or uncountable number of digits, factors, terms, etc. **—ˈinfinitely** *adv.* **—ˈinfiniteness** *n.*

infinitesimal (ˌɪnfɪnɪˈtɛsɪməl) *adj.* **1.** infinitely or immeasurably small. **2.** *Maths.* of, relating to, or involving a small change in the value of a variable that approaches zero as a limit. ~*n.* **3.** *Maths.* an infinitesimal quantity. **—ˌinfiniˈtesimally** *adv.*

infinitesimal calculus *n.* another name for **calculus** (sense 1).

infinitive (ɪnˈfɪnɪtɪv) *n. Grammar.* a form of the verb not inflected for grammatical categories such as tense and person and used without an overt subject. In English, the infinitive usually consists of the word *to* followed by the verb. **—infinitival** (ˌɪnfɪnɪˈtaɪvᵊl) *adj.* **—inˈfinitively** *or* **ˌinfiniˈtivally** *adv.*

infinitude (ɪnˈfɪnɪˌtjuːd) *n.* **1.** the state or quality of being infinite. **2.** an infinite extent, quantity, degree, etc.

infinity (ɪnˈfɪnɪtɪ) *n., pl.* **-ties.** **1.** the state or quality of being infinite. **2.** endless time, space, or quantity. **3.** an infinitely or indefinitely great number or amount. **4.** *Maths.* **a.** the concept of a value greater than any finite numerical value. **b.** the reciprocal of zero. **c.** the limit of an infinite sequence of numbers.

infirm (ɪnˈfɜːm) *adj.* **1. a.** weak in health or body, esp. from old age. **b.** (*as collective n.; preceded by the*): *the infirm.* **2.** lacking moral certainty; indecisive or irresolute. **3.** not stable, sound, or secure: *an infirm structure.* **4.** *Law.* (of a law, etc.) lacking legal force; invalid. **—inˈfirmly** *adv.* **—inˈfirmness** *n.*

infirmary (ɪnˈfɜːmərɪ) *n., pl.* **-ries.** a place for the treatment of the sick or injured; hospital.

infirmity (ɪnˈfɜːmɪtɪ) *n., pl.* **-ties.** **1.** the state or quality of being infirm. **2.** physical weakness or debility; frailty. **3.** a moral flaw or failing.

infix *vb.* (ɪnˈfɪks, ˈɪnˌfɪks). **1.** (*tr.*) to fix firmly in. **2.** (*tr.*) to instil or inculcate. **3.** *Grammar.* to insert (an affix) into the middle of a word. ~*n.* (ˈɪnˌfɪks). **4.** *Grammar.* an affix inserted into the middle of a word. **—ˌinfixˈation** *or* **infixion** (ɪnˈfɪkʃən) *n.*

in flagrante delicto (ɪn fləˈgræntɪ dɪˈlɪktəʊ) *adv. Chiefly law.* while committing the offence; red-handed. Also: **flagrante delicto.** [L, lit.: with the crime still blazing]

inflame (ɪnˈfleɪm) *vb.* **1.** to arouse or become aroused to violent emotion. **2.** (*tr.*) to increase or intensify; aggravate. **3.** to produce inflammation in (a tissue, organ, or part) or (of a tissue, etc.) to become inflamed. **4.** to set or be set on fire. **5.** (*tr.*) to cause to redden. **—inˈflamer** *n.*

inflammable (ɪnˈflæməbᵊl) *adj.* **1.** liable to catch fire; flammable. **2.** readily aroused to anger or passion. ~*n.* **3.** something that is liable to catch fire. **—inˌflammaˈbility** *or* **inˈflammableness** *n.* **—inˈflammably** *adv.*

▷ **Usage.** See at **flammable.**

inflammation (ˌɪnfləˈmeɪʃən) *n.* **1.** the reaction of living tissue to injury or infection, characterized by heat, redness, swelling, and pain. **2.** the act of inflaming or the state of being inflamed.

inflammatory (ɪnˈflæmətərɪ, -trɪ) *adj.* **1.** characterized by or caused by inflammation. **2.** tending to arouse violence, strong emotion, etc. **—inˈflammatorily** *adv.*

inflatable (ɪnˈfleɪtəbᵊl) *n.* **1.** any of various large air-filled objects made of strong plastic or rubber. ~*adj.* **2.** capable of being inflated.

inflate (ɪnˈfleɪt) *vb.* **1.** to expand or cause to expand by filling with gas or air. **2.** (*tr.*) to cause to increase excessively; puff up; swell: *to inflate one's opinion of oneself.* **3.** (*tr.*) to cause inflation of (prices, money, etc.). **4.** (*tr.*) to raise in spirits; elate. **5.** (*intr.*) to undergo economic inflation. [C16: < L *inflāre* to blow into, < *flāre* to blow] **—inˈflatedly** *adv.* **—inˈflatedness** *n.* **—inˈflater** *or* **inˈflator** *n.*

inflation (ɪnˈfleɪʃən) *n.* **1.** the act of inflating or state of being inflated. **2.** *Econ.* a progressive increase in the general level of prices brought about by an expansion in demand or the money supply or by autonomous increases in costs. **3.** *Inf.* the rate of increase of prices. **—inˈflationary** *adj.*

inflationism (ɪnˈfleɪʃəˌnɪzəm) *n.* the policy of inflation through expansion of the supply of money and credit. **—inˈflationist** *n., adj.*

inflect (ɪnˈflɛkt) *vb.* **1.** *Grammar.* to change (the form of a word) by inflection. **2.** (*tr.*) to change (the voice) in tone or pitch; modulate. **3.** (*tr.*) to cause to deviate from a straight or normal line or course; bend. [C15: < L *inflectere* to curve round, alter, < *flectere* to bend] **—inˈflectedness** *n.* **—inˈflective** *adj.* **—inˈflector** *n.*

inflection *or* **inflexion** (ɪnˈflɛkʃən) *n.* **1.** modulation of the voice. **2.** *Grammar.* a change in the form of a word, signalling change in such grammatical functions as tense, person, gender, number, or case. **3.** an angle or bend. **4.** the act of inflecting or the state of being inflected. **5.** *Maths.* a change in curvature from concave to convex or vice versa. **—inˈflectional** *or* **inˈflexional** *adj.* **—inˈflectionally** *or* **inˈflexionally** *adv.* **—inˈflectionless** *or* **inˈflexionless** *adj.*

inflict (ɪnˈflɪkt) *vb.* (*tr.*) **1.** (often foll. by *on* or *upon*) to impose (something unwelcome, such as pain, oneself, etc.). **2.** to deal out (blows, lashes, etc.). [C16: < L *inflīgere* to strike (something) against, dash against, < *flīgere* to strike] **—inˈflictable** *adj.* **—inˈflicter** *or* **inˈflictor** *n.* **—inˈfliction** *n.*

in-flight *adj.* provided during flight in an aircraft: *in-flight meals.*

inflorescence (ˌɪnflɔːˈrɛsəns) *n.* **1.** the part of a plant that consists of the flower-bearing stalks. **2.** the arrangement of the flowers on the stalks. **3.** the process of flowering; blossoming. [C16: < NL, < LL, < *flōrescere* to bloom] **—ˌinfloˈrescent** *adj.*

inflow (ˈɪnˌfləʊ) *n.* **1.** something, such as a liquid or gas, that flows in. **2.** Also called: **inflowing.** the act of flowing in; influx.

influence (ˈɪnflʊəns) *n.* **1.** an effect of one person

---

inˈflexible *adj.*

or thing on another. **2.** the power of a person or thing to have such an effect. **3.** power or sway resulting from ability, wealth, position, etc. **4.** a person or thing having influence. **5.** *Astrol.* an ethereal fluid regarded as emanating from the stars and affecting a person's future. **6. under the influence.** *Inf.* drunk. ~*vb.* (*tr.*) **7.** to persuade or induce. **8.** to have an effect upon (actions, events, etc.); affect. [C14: < Med. L *influentia* emanation of power from the stars, < L *influere* to flow into, < *fluere* to flow] —**'influenceable** *adj.* —**'influencer** *n.*

influent ('ɪnflʊənt) *adj. also* **inflowing. 1.** flowing in. ~*n.* **2.** something flowing in, esp. a tributary. **3.** *Ecology.* an organism that has a major effect on the nature of its community.

influential (ˌɪnflʊ'ɛnʃəl) *adj.* having or exerting influence. —ˌ**influ'entially** *adv.*

influenza (ˌɪnflʊ'ɛnzə) *n.* a highly contagious viral disease characterized by fever, muscular aches and pains, and inflammation of the respiratory passages. [C18: < It., lit.: INFLUENCE, hence, incursion, epidemic (first applied to influenza in 1743)] —ˌ**influ'enzal** *adj.*

influx ('ɪnˌflʌks) *n.* **1.** the arrival or entry of many people or things. **2.** the act of flowing in; inflow. **3.** the mouth of a stream or river. [C17: < LL *influxus*, < *influere*; see INFLUENCE]

info ('ɪnfəʊ) *n. Inf.* short for **information.**

infold (ɪn'fəʊld) *vb.* (*tr.*) a variant of **enfold.**

inform (ɪn'fɔːm) *vb.* **1.** (*tr.*; often foll. by *of* or *about*) to give information to; tell. **2.** (*tr.*; often foll. by *of* or *about*) to make conversant (with). **3.** (*intr.*; often foll. by *against* or *on*) to give information regarding criminals, to the police, etc. **4.** (*tr.*) to give form to. **5.** (*tr.*) to impart some essential or formative characteristic to. **6.** (*tr.*) to animate or inspire. [C14: < L *informāre* to give form to, describe, < *formāre* to FORM] —**in'formable** *adj.*

informal (ɪn'fɔːməl) *adj.* **1.** not of a formal, official, or stiffly conventional nature. **2.** appropriate to everyday life or use: *informal clothes.* **3.** denoting or characterized by idiom, vocabulary, etc., appropriate to conversational language rather than to formal written language. **4.** denoting a second-person pronoun in some languages used when the addressee is regarded as a friend or social inferior. —**in'formally** *adv.*

informality (ˌɪnfɔː'mælɪtɪ) *n., pl.* **-ties. 1.** the condition or quality of being informal. **2.** an informal act.

informal vote *n. Austral. & N.Z.* an invalid vote or ballot.

informant (ɪn'fɔːmənt) *n.* a person who gives information.

information (ˌɪnfə'meɪʃən) *n.* **1.** knowledge acquired through experience or study. **2.** knowledge of specific and timely events or situations; news. **3.** the act of informing or the condition of being informed. **4. a.** an office, agency, etc., providing information. **b.** (*as modifier*): *information service.* **5.** a charge or complaint made before justices of the peace, usually on oath, to institute summary criminal proceedings. **6.** *Computers.* **a.** the meaning given to data by the way it is interpreted. **b.** another word for **data** (sense 2). —ˌ**infor'mational** *adj.*

information retrieval *n. Computers.* the process of recovering information from stored data.

information technology *n.* the production, storage, and communication of information using computers and microelectronics.

information theory *n.* a collection of mathematical theories concerned with coding, transmitting, storing, retrieving, and decoding information.

informative (ɪn'fɔːmətɪv) *or* **informatory** *adj.* providing information; instructive. —**in'formatively** *adv.* —**in'formativeness** *n.*

informed (ɪn'fɔːmd) *adj.* **1.** having much knowledge or education; learned or cultured. **2.** based on information: an informed judgment.

informer (ɪn'fɔːmə) *n.* **1.** a person who informs against someone, esp. a criminal. **2.** a person who provides information.

infra- *prefix.* below; beneath; after: *infrasonic.* [< L *infrā*]

infract (ɪn'frækt) *vb.* (*tr.*) to violate or break (a law, etc.). [C18: < L *infractus* broken off; see INFRINGE] —**in'fraction** *n.* —**in'fractor** *n.*

infra dig ('ɪnfrə 'dɪg) *adj.* (*postpositive*) *Inf.* beneath one's dignity. [C19: < L *infrā dignitātem*]

infrangible (ɪn'frændʒɪbᵊl) *adj.* **1.** incapable of being broken. **2.** not capable of being violated or infringed. [C16: < LL, < L IN-[1] + *frangere* to break] —**in**ˌ**frangi'bility** *or* **in'frangibleness** *n.* —**in'frangibly** *adv.*

infrared (ˌɪnfrə'rɛd) *n.* **1.** the part of the electromagnetic spectrum with a longer wavelength than light but a shorter wavelength than radio waves. ~*adj.* **2.** of, relating to, using, or consisting of radiation lying within the infrared.

infrared photography *n.* photography using film with an emulsion that is sensitive to infrared light, enabling it to be used in dark or misty conditions.

infrasonic (ˌɪnfrə'sɒnɪk) *adj.* having a frequency below the audible range, i.e. below about 16 Hz.

infrastructure ('ɪnfrəˌstrʌktʃə) *n.* **1.** the basic structure of an organization, system, etc. **2.** the stock of fixed capital equipment in a country, including factories, roads, schools, etc., considered as a determinant of economic growth.

infringe (ɪn'frɪndʒ) *vb.* **1.** (*tr.*) to violate or break (a law, agreement, etc.). **2.** (*intr.*; foll. by *on* or *upon*) to encroach or trespass. [C16: < L *infringere* to break off, < *frangere* to break] —**in'fringement** *n.* —**in'fringer** *n.*

infundibular (ˌɪnfʌn'dɪbjʊlə) *adj.* funnel-shaped. [C18: < L *infundibulum* funnel]

infuriate *vb.* (ɪn'fjʊərɪˌeɪt). **1.** (*tr.*) to anger; annoy. ~*adj.* (ɪn'fjʊərɪɪt). **2.** *Arch.* furious. [C17: < Med. L *infuriāre* (vb.); see IN-[2], FURY] —**in'furi**ˌ**ating** *adj.* —**in'furi**ˌ**atingly** *adv.*

infuse (ɪn'fjuːz) *vb.* **1.** (*tr.*; often foll. by *into*) to instil or inculcate. **2.** (*tr.*; foll. by *with*) to inspire; emotionally charge. **3.** to soak or be soaked in order to extract flavour or other properties. **4.** *Rare.* (foll. by *into*) to pour. [C15: < L *infundere* to pour into] —**in'fuser** *n.*

infusible[1] (ɪn'fjuːzəbᵊl) *adj.* not fusible; not easily melted; having a high melting point. [C16: < IN-[1] + FUSIBLE] —**in**ˌ**fusi'bility** *or* **in'fusibleness** *n.*

infusible[2] (ɪn'fjuːzəbᵊl) *adj.* capable of being infused. [C17: < INFUSE + -IBLE] —**in**ˌ**fusi'bility** *or* **in'fusibleness** *n.*

infusion (ɪn'fjuːʒən) *n.* **1.** the act of infusing. **2.** something infused. **3.** an extract obtained by soaking. —**infusive** (ɪn'fjuːsɪv) *adj.*

infusorian (ˌɪnfjʊ'zɔːrɪən) *Obs.* ~*n.* **1.** any of the microscopic organisms, such as protozoans, found in infusions of organic material. ~*adj.* **2.** of or relating to infusorians. [C18: < NL *Infusoria* former class name; see INFUSE] —ˌ**infu'sorial** *adj.*

-ing[1] *suffix forming nouns.* **1.** (*from verbs*) the action of, process of, result of, or something connected with the verb: *meeting; a wedding; winnings.* **2.** (*from other nouns*) something used in, consisting of, involving, etc.: *tubing; soldiering.* **3.** (*from other parts of speech*): *an outing.* [OE *-ing, -ung*]

-ing[2] *suffix.* **1.** forming the present participle of verbs: *walking; believing.* **2.** forming participial adjectives: *a growing boy; a sinking ship.* **3.** forming adjectives not derived from verbs: *swashbuckling.* [ME *-ing, -inde,* < OE *-ende*]

-ing[3] *suffix forming nouns.* a person or thing having a certain quality or being of a certain kind: *sweeting; whiting.* [OE *-ing;* rel. to ON *-ingr*]

ingather (ɪn'gæðə) *vb.* (*tr.*) to gather together or in (a harvest, etc.). —**in'gatherer** *n.*

---

in'frequent *adj.*

ingeminate (ɪnˈdʒɛmɪˌneɪt) *vb.* (*tr.*) *Rare.* to repeat; reiterate. [C16: < L *ingemināre* to redouble, < IN-^{2} + *gemināre* to GEMINATE]

ingenious (ɪnˈdʒiːnjəs, -nɪəs) *adj.* possessing or done with ingenuity; skilful or clever. [C15: < L, < *ingenium* natural ability; see ENGINE] —**inˈgeniously** *adv.* —**inˈgeniousness** *n.*

ingénue (ˌænʒeɪˈnjuː) *n.* an artless, innocent, or inexperienced girl or young woman. [C19: < F, fem. of *ingénu* INGENUOUS]

ingenuity (ˌɪndʒɪˈnjuːɪtɪ) *n., pl.* **-ties.** **1.** inventive talent; cleverness. **2.** an ingenious device, act, etc. **3.** *Arch.* frankness; candour. [C16: < L *ingenuitās* a freeborn condition, outlook consistent with such a condition, < *ingenuus* native, freeborn (see INGENUOUS); meaning infl. by INGENIOUS]

ingenuous (ɪnˈdʒɛnjʊəs) *adj.* **1.** naive, artless, or innocent. **2.** candid; frank; straightforward. [C16: < L *ingenuus* freeborn, virtuous, < IN-^{2} + *gignere* to beget] —**inˈgenuously** *adv.* —**inˈgenuousness** *n.*

ingest (ɪnˈdʒɛst) *vb.* (*tr.*) to take (food or liquid) into the body. [C17: < L *ingerere* to put into, < IN-^{2} + *gerere* to carry; see GEST] —**inˈgestible** *adj.* —**inˈgestion** *n.* —**inˈgestive** *adj.*

ingle (ˈɪŋgᵊl) *n. Arch. or dialect.* a fire in a room or a fireplace. [C16: prob. < Scot. Gaelic *aingeal* fire]

inglenook (ˈɪŋgᵊlˌnʊk) *n. Brit.* a corner by a fireplace; chimney corner.

ingoing (ˈɪnˌgəʊɪŋ) *adj.* going in; entering.

ingot (ˈɪŋgət) *n.* a piece of cast metal obtained from a mould in a form suitable for storage, etc. [C14: ? < IN-^{2} + OE *goten*, p.p. of *geotan* to pour]

ingraft (ɪnˈgrɑːft) *vb.* a variant spelling of **engraft.** —**inˈgraftment** *or* **ˌingrafˈtation** *n.*

ingrain *or* **engrain** *vb.* (ɪnˈgreɪn). (*tr.*) **1.** to impress deeply on the mind or nature; instil. **2.** *Arch.* to dye into the fibre of (a fabric). ~*adj.* (ˈɪnˌgreɪn). **3.** (of woven or knitted articles) made of dyed yarn or of fibre that is dyed before being spun into yarn. ~*n.* (ˈɪnˌgreɪn). **4.** a carpet made from ingrained yarn. [C18: < *dyed in grain* dyed with kermes through the fibre]

ingrained *or* **engrained** (ɪnˈgreɪnd) *adj.* **1.** deeply impressed or instilled. **2.** (*prenominal*) complete or inveterate; utter. **3.** (esp. of dirt) worked into or through the fibre, grain, pores, etc. —**ingrainedly** *or* **engrainedly** (ɪnˈgreɪnɪdlɪ) *adv.* —**inˈgrainedness** *or* **enˈgrainedness** *n.*

ingrate (ˈɪngreɪt, ɪnˈgreɪt) *Arch.* ~*n.* **1.** an ungrateful person. ~*adj.* **2.** ungrateful. [C14: < L *ingrātus* (adj.), < IN-^{1} + *grātus* GRATEFUL] —**ˈingrately** *adv.*

ingratiate (ɪnˈgreɪʃɪˌeɪt) *vb.* (*tr.; often foll. by with*) to place (oneself) purposely in the favour (of another). [C17: < L, < IN-^{2} + *grātia* grace, favour] —**inˈgratiˌating** *or* **inˈgratiatory** *adj.* —**inˈgratiˌatingly** *adv.* —**inˌgratiˈation** *n.*

ingredient (ɪnˈgriːdɪənt) *n.* a component of a mixture, compound, etc., esp. in cooking. [C15: < L *ingrediēns* going into, < *ingredī* to enter; see INGRESS]

ingress (ˈɪngrɛs) *n.* **1.** the act of going or coming in; an entering. **2.** a way in; entrance. **3.** the right or permission to enter. [C15: < L *ingressus*, < *ingredī* to go in, < *gradī* to step, go] —**ingression** (ɪnˈgrɛʃən) *n.*

in-group *n. Sociol.* a highly cohesive and relatively closed social group characterized by the preferential treatment reserved for its members.

ingrowing (ˈɪnˌgrəʊɪŋ) *adj.* **1.** (esp. of a toenail) growing abnormally into the flesh. **2.** growing within or into. —**ˈinˌgrowth** *n.*

ingrown (ˈɪnˌgrəʊn, ɪnˈgrəʊn) *adj.* **1.** (esp. of a toenail) grown abnormally into the flesh; covered by adjacent tissues. **2.** grown within; native; innate.

inguinal (ˈɪŋgwɪnᵊl) *adj. Anat.* of or relating to the groin. [C17: < L *inguinālis*, < *inguen* groin]

ingulf (ɪnˈgʌlf) *vb.* (*tr.*) a variant of **engulf.**

ingurgitate (ɪnˈgɜːdʒɪˌteɪt) *vb.* to swallow (food, etc.) greedily or in excess. [C16: < L *ingurgitāre* to flood, < IN-^{2} + *gurges* abyss] —**inˌgurgiˈtation** *n.*

inhabit (ɪnˈhæbɪt) *vb.* (*tr.*) to live or dwell in; occupy. [C14: < L *inhabitāre*, < *habitāre* to dwell] —**inˈhabitable** *adj.* —**inˌhabitaˈbility** *n.* —**inˌhabiˈtation** *n.*

inhabitant (ɪnˈhæbɪtənt) *n.* a person or animal that is a permanent resident of a particular place or region. —**inˈhabitancy** *or* **inˈhabitance** *n.*

inhalant (ɪnˈheɪlənt) *adj.* **1.** (esp. of a medicinal preparation) inhaled for its therapeutic effect. **2.** inhaling. ~*n.* **3.** an inhalant medicinal preparation.

inhale (ɪnˈheɪl) *vb.* to draw (breath, etc.) into the lungs; breathe in. [C18: < IN-^{2} + L *halāre* to breathe] —**ˌinhaˈlation** *n.*

inhaler (ɪnˈheɪlə) *n.* **1.** a device for breathing in therapeutic vapours, esp. one for relieving nasal congestion. **2.** a person who inhales.

inhere (ɪnˈhɪə) *vb.* (*intr.; foll. by in*) to be an inseparable part (of). [C16: < L *inhaerēre* to stick in, < *haerēre* to stick]

inherent (ɪnˈhɪərənt, -ˈhɛr-) *adj.* existing as an inseparable part; intrinsic. —**inˈherently** *adv.*

inherit (ɪnˈhɛrɪt) *vb.* **1.** to receive (property, etc.) by succession or under a will. **2.** (*intr.*) to succeed as heir. **3.** (*tr.*) to possess (a characteristic) through genetic transmission. **4.** (*tr.*) to receive (a position, etc.) from a predecessor. [C14: < OF *enheriter*, < LL *inhērēditāre* to appoint an heir, < L *hērēs* HEIR] —**inˈherited** *adj.* —**inˈheritor** *n.* —**inˈheritress** *or* **inˈheritrix** *fem. n.*

inheritable (ɪnˈhɛrɪtəbᵊl) *adj.* **1.** capable of being transmitted by heredity from one generation to a later one. **2.** capable of being inherited. **3.** *Rare.* having the right to inherit. —**inˌheritaˈbility** *or* **inˈheritableness** *n.* —**inˈheritably** *adv.*

inheritance (ɪnˈhɛrɪtəns) *n.* **1.** *Law.* **a.** hereditary succession to an estate, title, etc. **b.** the right of an heir to succeed on the death of an ancestor. **c.** something that may legally be transmitted to an heir. **2.** the act of inheriting. **3.** something inherited; heritage. **4.** the derivation of characteristics of one generation from an earlier one by heredity.

inhibit (ɪnˈhɪbɪt) *vb.* (*tr.*) **1.** to restrain or hinder (an impulse, desire, etc.). **2.** to prohibit, forbid, or prevent. **3.** to stop, prevent, or decrease the rate of (a chemical reaction). [C15: < L *inhibēre* to restrain, < IN-^{2} + *habēre* to have] —**inˈhibitable** *adj.* —**inˈhibiter** *or* **inˈhibitor** *n.* —**inˈhibitive** *or* **inˈhibitory** *adj.*

inhibition (ˌɪnɪˈbɪʃən, ˌɪnhɪ-) *n.* **1.** the act of inhibiting or the condition of being inhibited. **2.** *Psychol.* a mental state or condition in which the varieties of expression and behaviour of an individual become restricted. **3.** the process of stopping or retarding a chemical reaction. **4.** *Physiol.* the suppression of the function or action of an organ or part, as by stimulation of its nerve supply.

inhibitor (ɪnˈhɪbɪtə) *n.* a substance that retards or stops a chemical reaction.

in-house *adj., adv.* within an organization or group: *an in-house job; the job was done in-house.*

inhuman (ɪnˈhjuːmən) *adj.* **1.** Also: **inhumane** (ˌɪnhjuːˈmeɪn). lacking humane feelings, such as sympathy, understanding, etc.; cruel; brutal. **2.** not human. —**ˌinhuˈmanely** *adv.* —**inˈhumanly** *adv.* —**inˈhumanness** *n.*

inhumanity (ˌɪnhjuːˈmænɪtɪ) *n., pl.* **-ties.** **1.** lack of humane qualities. **2.** an inhumane act, decision, etc.

inhume (ɪnˈhjuːm) *vb.* (*tr.*) to inter; bury. [C17: < L, < IN-^{2} + *humus* ground] —**ˌinhuˈmation** *n.* —**inˈhumer** *n.*

---

inˈglorious *adj.*
inˈgratiˌtude *n.*
ˌinharˈmonious *adj.*
inˈhospitable *adj.*
ˌinhospiˈtality *n.*

inimical (ɪˈnɪmɪkᵊl) *adj.* **1.** adverse or unfavourable. **2.** not friendly; hostile. [C17: < LL, < *inimīcus*, < IN-[1] + *amīcus* friendly; see ENEMY] —**inˈimically** *adv.* —**inˈimicalness** *or* **inˌimiˈcality** *n.*

inimitable (ɪˈnɪmɪtəbᵊl) *adj.* incapable of being duplicated or imitated; unique. —**inˌimitaˈbility** *or* **inˈimitableness** *n.* —**inˈimitably** *adv.*

iniquity (ɪˈnɪkwɪtɪ) *n., pl.* **-ties. 1.** lack of justice or righteousness; wickedness; injustice. **2.** a wicked act; sin. [C14: < L, < *inīquus* unfair, < IN-[1] + *aequus* even, level; see EQUAL] —**inˈiquitous** *adj.* —**inˈiquitously** *adv.* —**inˈiquitousness** *n.*

initial (ɪˈnɪʃəl) *adj.* **1.** of, at, or concerning the beginning. ~*n.* **2.** the first letter of a word, esp. a person's name. **3.** *Printing.* a large letter set at the beginning of a chapter or work. **4.** *Bot.* a cell from which tissues and organs develop by division and differentiation. ~*vb.* **-tialling, -tialled** *or U.S.* **-tialing, -tialed. 5.** (*tr.*) to sign with one's initials, esp. to indicate approval; endorse. [C16: < L *initiālis* of the beginning, < *initium* beginning, lit.: an entering upon, < *inīre* to go in] —**inˈitialer** *or* **inˈitialler** *n.* —**inˈitially** *adv.*

initialize *or* **-ise** (ɪˈnɪʃəˌlaɪz) *vb.* (*tr.*) to assign an initial value to (a variable or storage location) in a computer program. —**inˌitialiˈzation** *or* **-iˈsation** *n.*

initiate *vb.* (ɪˈnɪʃɪˌeɪt). (*tr.*) **1.** to begin or originate. **2.** to accept (new members) into an organization such as a club, through often secret ceremonies. **3.** to teach fundamentals to. ~*adj.* (ɪˈnɪʃɪɪt, -ˌeɪt). **4.** initiated; begun. ~*n.* (ɪˈnɪʃɪɪt, -ˌeɪt). **5.** a person who has been initiated, esp. recently. **6.** a beginner; novice. [C17: < L *initiāre* (vb.), < *initium;* see INITIAL] —**inˈitiˌator** *n.* —**inˈitiatory** *adj.*

initiation (ɪˌnɪʃɪˈeɪʃən) *n.* **1.** the act of initiating or the condition of being initiated. **2.** the ceremony, often secret, initiating new members into an organization.

initiative (ɪˈnɪʃɪətɪv, -ˈnɪʃətɪv) *n.* **1.** the first step or action of a matter; commencing move: *a peace initiative.* **2.** the right or power to begin or initiate something: *he has the initiative.* **3.** the ability or attitude required to begin or initiate something. **4.** *Government.* the right of citizens to introduce legislation, etc., in a legislative body, as in Switzerland. **5. on one's own initiative.** without being prompted. ~*adj.* **6.** of or concerning initiation or serving to initiate; initiatory. —**inˈitiatively** *adv.*

inject (ɪnˈdʒɛkt) *vb.* (*tr.*) **1.** *Med.* to introduce (a fluid) into the body (of a person or animal) by means of a syringe. **2.** (foll. by *into*) to introduce (a new aspect or element): *to inject humour into a scene.* **3.** to interject (a comment, idea, etc.). [C17: < *injicere* to throw in, < *jacere* to throw] —**inˈjectable** *adj.* —**inˈjector** *n.*

injection (ɪnˈdʒɛkʃən) *n.* **1.** fluid injected into the body, esp. for medicinal purposes. **2.** something injected. **3.** the act of injecting. **4. a.** the act or process of introducing fluid under pressure, such as fuel into the combustion chamber of an engine. **b.** (*as modifier*): *injection moulding.* —**inˈjective** *adj.*

injunction (ɪnˈdʒʌŋkʃən) *n.* **1.** *Law.* an instruction or order issued by a court to a party to an action, esp. to refrain from some act. **2.** a command, admonition, etc. **3.** the act of enjoining. [C16: < LL, < L *injungere* to ENJOIN] —**inˈjunctive** *adj.* —**inˈjunctively** *adv.*

injure (ˈɪndʒə) *vb.* (*tr.*) **1.** to cause physical or mental harm or suffering to; hurt or wound. **2.** to offend, esp. by an injustice. [C16: back formation < INJURY] —**ˈinjurable** *adj.* —**ˈinjured** *adj.* —**ˈinjurer** *n.*

injurious (ɪnˈdʒʊərɪəs) *adj.* **1.** causing damage or harm; deleterious; hurtful. **2.** abusive, slanderous, or libellous. —**inˈjuriously** *adv.* —**inˈjuriousness** *n.*

injury (ˈɪndʒərɪ) *n., pl.* **-ries. 1.** physical damage or hurt. **2.** a specific instance of this: *a leg injury.* **3.** harm done to a reputation. **4.** *Law.* a violation or infringement of another person's rights that causes him harm and is actionable at law. [C14: < L *injūria* injustice, wrong, < *injūriōsus* acting unfairly, wrongful, < IN-[1] + *jūs* right]

injury time *n. Soccer, rugby, etc.* extra playing time added on to compensate for time spent attending to injured players during the match.

injustice (ɪnˈdʒʌstɪs) *n.* **1.** the condition or practice of being unjust or unfair. **2.** an unjust act.

ink (ɪŋk) *n.* **1.** a fluid or paste used for printing, writing, and drawing. **2.** a dark brown fluid ejected into the water for self-concealment by an octopus or related mollusc. ~*vb.* (*tr.*) **3.** to mark with ink. **4.** to coat (a printing surface) with ink. [C13: < OF *enque,* < LL *encaustum* a purplish-red ink, < Gk *enkauston* purple ink, < *enkaustos* burnt in, < *enkaiein* to burn in; see EN-[2], CAUSTIC] —**ˈinker** *n.*

inkblot (ˈɪŋkˌblɒt) *n.* a patch of ink accidentally or deliberately spilled. Ten such patches, of different shapes, are used in the Rorschach test.

ink-cap *n.* any of several saprophytic fungi whose caps disintegrate into a black inky fluid after the spores mature.

inkhorn (ˈɪŋkˌhɔːn) *n.* (formerly) a small portable container for ink, usually made from horn.

ink in *vb.* (*adv.*) **1.** (*tr.*) to use ink to go over pencil lines in (a drawing). **2.** to apply ink to (a printing surface) in preparing to print from it.

inkling (ˈɪŋklɪŋ) *n.* a slight intimation or suggestion; suspicion. [C14: prob. < *inclen* to hint at]

inkstand (ˈɪŋkˌstænd) *n.* a stand or tray on which are kept writing implements and containers for ink.

inkwell (ˈɪŋkˌwɛl) *n.* a small container for pen ink, often let into the surface of a desk.

inky (ˈɪŋkɪ) *adj.* **inkier, inkiest. 1.** resembling ink, esp. in colour; dark or black. **2.** of, containing, or stained with ink. —**ˈinkiness** *n.*

INLA *abbrev. for* Irish National Liberation Army.

inlaid (ˈɪnˌleɪd, ɪnˈleɪd) *adj.* **1.** set in the surface, as a design in wood. **2.** having such a design or inlay: *an inlaid table.*

inland *adj.* (ˈɪnlənd). **1.** of or located in the interior of a country or region away from a sea or border. **2.** *Chiefly Brit.* operating within a country or region; domestic; not foreign. ~*n.* (ˈɪnˌlænd, -lənd). **3.** the interior of a country or region. ~*adv.* (ˈɪnˌlænd, -lənd). **4.** towards or into the interior of a country or region. —**ˈinlander** *n.*

Inland Revenue *n.* (in Britain and New Zealand) a government board that administers and collects major direct taxes, such as income tax.

in-law *n.* **1.** a relative by marriage. ~*adj.* **2.** (*postpositive; in combination*) related by marriage: *a father-in-law.* [C19: back formation < *father-in-law,* etc.]

inlay *vb.* (ɪnˈleɪ), **-laying, -laid.** (*tr.*) **1.** to decorate (an article, esp. of furniture) by inserting pieces of wood, ivory, etc., into slots in the surface. ~*n.* (ˈɪnˌleɪ). **2.** *Dentistry.* a filling inserted into a cavity and held in position by cement. **3.** decoration made by inlaying. **4.** an inlaid article, surface, etc. —**ˈinˌlayer** *n.*

inlet *n.* (ˈɪnˌlɛt). **1.** a narrow inland opening of the coastline. **2.** an entrance or opening. **3.** the act of letting someone or something in. **4.** something let in or inserted. **5. a.** a passage or valve through which a substance, esp. a fluid, enters a machine. **b.** (*as modifier*): *an inlet valve.* ~*vb.* (ɪnˈlɛt), **-letting, -let. 6.** (*tr.*) to insert or inlay.

inlier (ˈɪnˌlaɪə) *n.* an outcrop of rocks that is entirely surrounded by younger rocks.

in loco parentis *Latin.* (ɪn ˈləʊkəʊ pəˈrɛntɪs) in

ˌinjuˈdicious *adj.*

place of a parent: said of a person acting in a parental capacity.

inly (ˈɪnlɪ) *adv. Poetic.* inwardly; intimately.

inmate (ˈɪnˌmeɪt) *n.* a person who is confined to an institution such as a prison or hospital.

in medias res *Latin.* (ɪn ˈmiːdɪˌæs ˈreɪs) in or into the middle of events or a narrative. [lit.: into the midst of things, taken from a passage in Horace's *Ars Poetica*]

in memoriam (ɪn mɪˈmɔːrɪəm) in memory of: used in obituaries, epitaphs, etc. [L]

inmost (ˈɪnˌməʊst) *adj.* another word for **innermost.**

inn (ɪn) *n.* a pub or small hotel providing food and accommodation. [OE] —**ˈinnless** *adj.*

innards (ˈɪnədz) *pl. n. Inf.* **1.** the internal organs of the body, esp. the viscera. **2.** the interior parts or components of anything, esp. the working parts. [C19: colloquial var. of *inwards*]

innate (ɪˈneɪt, ˈɪneɪt) *adj.* **1.** existing from birth; congenital; inborn. **2.** being an essential part of the character of a person or thing. **3.** instinctive; not learned: *innate capacities.* **4.** *Philosophy.* (of ideas) present in the mind before any experience and knowable by pure reason. [C15: < L, < *innascī* to be born in, < *nascī* to be born] —**inˈnately** *adv.* —**inˈnateness** *n.*

inner (ˈɪnə) *adj.* (*prenominal*) **1.** being or located further inside: *an inner room.* **2.** happening or occurring inside. **3.** relating to the soul, mind, spirit, etc. **4.** more profound or obscure; less apparent: *the inner meaning.* **5.** exclusive or private: *inner regions of the party.* ~*n.* **6.** *Archery.* **a.** the red innermost ring on a target. **b.** a shot which hits this ring. —**ˈinnerly** *adv.* —**ˈinnerness** *n.*

inner bar *n.* **the.** *Brit.* all Queen's or King's Counsel collectively.

inner city *n.* **a.** the parts of a city in or near its centre, esp. when associated with poverty, substandard housing, etc. **b.** (*as modifier*): *inner-city schools.*

inner man or (*fem.*) **inner woman** *n.* **1.** the mind or soul. **2.** *Jocular.* the stomach or appetite.

innermost (ˈɪnəˌməʊst) *adj.* **1.** being or located furthest within; central. **2.** intimate; private.

inner tube *n.* an inflatable rubber tube that fits inside a pneumatic tyre casing.

innervate (ˈɪnɜːˌveɪt) *vb.* (*tr.*) **1.** to supply nerves to (a bodily organ or part). **2.** to stimulate (a bodily organ or part) with nerve impulses. —ˌ**innerˈvation** *n.*

innings (ˈɪnɪŋz) *n.* **1.** (*functioning as sing.*) *Cricket, etc.* **a.** the batting turn of a player or team. **b.** the runs scored during such a turn. **2.** (*sometimes sing.*) a period of opportunity or action.

innkeeper (ˈɪnˌkiːpə) *n.* an owner or manager of an inn.

innocence (ˈɪnəsəns) *n.* the quality or state of being innocent. Archaic word: **innocency** (ˈɪnəsənsɪ). [C14: < L *innocentia* harmlessness, < *innocēns* blameless, < IN-[1] + *nocēre* to hurt]

innocent (ˈɪnəsənt) *adj.* **1.** not corrupted or tainted with evil; sinless; pure. **2.** not guilty of a particular crime; blameless. **3.** (*postpositive;* foll. by *of*) free (of); lacking: *innocent of all knowledge of history.* **4.** harmless or innocuous: *an innocent game.* **5.** credulous, naive, or artless. **6.** simple-minded; slow-witted. ~*n.* **7.** an innocent person, esp. a young child or an ingenuous adult. **8.** a simple-minded person; simpleton. —**ˈinnocently** *adv.*

innocuous (ɪˈnɒkjʊəs) *adj.* having little or no adverse or harmful effect; harmless. [C16: < L *innocuus* harmless, < IN-[1] + *nocēre* to harm] —**inˈnocuously** *adv.* —**inˈnocuousness** or **innocuity** (ˌɪnəˈkjuːɪtɪ) *n.*

innominate bone (ɪˈnɒmɪnɪt) *n.* either of the two bones that form the sides of the pelvis, consisting of the ilium, ischium, and pubis. Nontechnical name: **hipbone.**

innovate (ˈɪnəˌveɪt) *vb.* to invent or begin to apply (methods, ideas, etc.). [C16: < L *innovāre* to renew, < IN-[2] + *novāre* to make new, < *novus* new] —**ˈinnoˌvative** or **ˈinnoˌvatory** *adj.* —**ˈinnoˌvator** *n.*

innovation (ˌɪnəˈveɪʃən) *n.* **1.** something newly introduced, such as a new method or device. **2.** the act of innovating. —ˌ**innoˈvational** *adj.* —ˌ**innoˈvationist** *n.*

innuendo (ˌɪnjʊˈɛndəʊ) *n., pl.* **-dos** or **-does.** **1.** an indirect or subtle reference, esp. one made maliciously or indicating criticism or disapproval; insinuation. **2.** *Law.* (in an action for defamation) an explanation of the construction put upon words alleged to be defamatory where this meaning is not apparent. [C17: < L, lit.: by hinting, < *innuere* to convey by a nod, < IN-[2] + *nuere* to nod]

Innuit (ˈɪnjuːɪt) *n.* a variant spelling of **Inuit.**

innumerable (ɪˈnjuːmərəbəl, ɪˈnjuːmrəbəl) or **innumerous** *adj.* so many as to be uncountable; extremely numerous. —**inˌnumeraˈbility** or **inˈnumerableness** *n.* —**inˈnumerably** *adv.*

innumerate (ɪˈnjuːmərɪt) *adj.* **1.** having neither knowledge nor understanding of mathematics or science. ~*n.* **2.** an innumerate person. —**inˈnumeracy** *n.*

inoculate (ɪˈnɒkjʊˌleɪt) *vb.* **1.** to introduce (the causative agent of a disease) into the body in order to induce immunity. **2.** (*tr.*) to introduce (microorganisms, esp. bacteria) into (a culture medium). **3.** (*tr.*) to cause to be influenced or imbued, as with ideas. [C15: < L *inoculāre* to implant, < IN-[2] + *oculus* eye, bud] —**inˌocuˈlation** *n.* —**inˈoculative** *adj.* —**inˈocuˌlator** *n.*

inoculum (ɪˈnɒkjʊləm) or **inoculant** *n., pl.* **-la** (-lə) or **-lants.** *Med.* the substance used in giving an inoculation. [C20: NL; see INOCULATE]

in-off *n. Billiards.* a shot that goes into a pocket after striking another ball.

inoperable (ɪnˈɒpərəbəl, -ˈɒprə-) *adj.* **1.** incapable of being implemented or operated. **2.** *Surgery.* not suitable for operation without risk, esp. because of metastasis. —**inˌoperaˈbility** or **inˈoperableness** *n.* —**inˈoperably** *adv.*

inordinate (ɪnˈɔːdɪnɪt) *adj.* **1.** exceeding normal limits; immoderate. **2.** unrestrained, as in behaviour or emotion; intemperate. **3.** irregular or disordered. [C14: < L *inordinātus* disordered, < IN-[1] + *ordināre* to put in order] —**inˈordinacy** or **inˈordinateness** *n.* —**inˈordinately** *adv.*

inorganic (ˌɪnɔːˈgænɪk) *adj.* **1.** not having the structure or characteristics of living organisms; not organic. **2.** relating to or denoting chemical compounds that do not contain carbon. **3.** not having a system, structure, or ordered relation of parts; amorphous. **4.** not resulting from or produced by growth; artificial. —ˌ**inorˈganically** *adv.*

inorganic chemistry *n.* the branch of chemistry concerned with the elements and all their compounds except those containing carbon.

inosculate (ɪnˈɒskjʊˌleɪt) *vb.* **1.** *Physiol.* (of small blood vessels) to communicate by anastomosis. **2.** to unite or be united so as to be continuous; blend. **3.** to intertwine or cause to intertwine. [C17: < IN-[2] + L *ōsculāre* to equip with an opening, < *ōsculum*, dim. of *ōs* mouth] —**inˌoscuˈlation** *n.*

inositol (ɪˈnəʊsɪˌtɒl) *n.* a cyclic alcohol, one isomer of which (*i*-inositol) is present in yeast and is a growth factor for some organisms. [C19: < Gk *in-, is* sinew + -OSE[2] + -ITE[1] + -OL[1]]

inpatient (ˈɪnˌpeɪʃənt) *n.* a patient living in the hospital where he is being treated.

in perpetuum *Latin.* (ɪn pɜːˈpɛtjʊəm) for ever.

input (ˈɪnˌpʊt) *n.* **1.** the act of putting in. **2.** that which is put in. **3.** (*often pl.*) a resource required for industrial production, such as capital goods, etc. **4.** *Electronics.* the signal or current fed into a component or circuit. **5.** *Computers.* the data

---

ˌ**inofˈfensive** *adj.*
ˌ**inofˈficious** *adj.*
inˈoperative *adj.*
inˈopporˌtune *adj.*

fed into a computer from a peripheral device. **6.** (*modifier*) of or relating to electronic, computer, or other input: *input program.* ~*vb.* **7.** (*tr.*) to insert (data) into a computer.

input/output *n. Computers.* **1.** the data or information passed into or out of a computer. **2.** (*modifier*) concerned with or relating to such passage of data or information.

inquest (ˈɪnˌkwɛst) *n.* **1.** an inquiry, esp. into the cause of an unexplained, sudden, or violent death, held by a coroner, in certain cases with a jury. **2.** *Inf.* any inquiry or investigation. [C13: < Med. L, < L IN-² + *quaesītus* investigation, < *quaerere* to examine]

inquietude (ɪnˈkwaɪɪˌtjuːd) *n.* restlessness, uneasiness, or anxiety. —**inquiet** (ɪnˈkwaɪət) *adj.* —**inˈquietly** *adv.*

inquiline (ˈɪnkwɪˌlaɪn) *n.* **1.** an animal that lives in close association with another animal without harming it. See also **commensal** (sense 1). ~*adj.* **2.** of or living as an inquiline. [C17: < L *inquilīnus* lodger, < IN-² + *colere* to dwell] —**inquilinous** (ˌɪnkwɪˈlaɪnəs) *adj.*

inquire *or* **enquire** (ɪnˈkwaɪə) *vb.* **1. a.** to seek information (about); ask: *she inquired his age; she inquired about rates of pay.* **b.** (*intr.;* foll. by *of*) to ask (a person) for information: *I'll inquire of my aunt when she is coming.* **2.** (*intr.;* often foll. by *into*) to make a search or investigation. [C13: < L *inquīrere,* < IN-² + *quaerere* to seek] —**inˈquirer** *or* **enˈquirer** *n.* —**inˈquiry** *or* **enˈquiry** *n.*

inquisition (ˌɪnkwɪˈzɪʃən) *n.* **1.** the act of inquiring deeply or searchingly; investigation. **2.** a deep or searching inquiry, esp. a ruthless official investigation in order to suppress revolt or root out the unorthodox. **3.** an official inquiry, esp. one held by a jury before an officer of the Crown. [C14: < legal L *inquīsītiō,* < *inquīrere* to seek for; see INQUIRE] —ˌ**inquiˈsitional** *adj.* —ˌ**inquiˈsitionist** *n.*

Inquisition (ˌɪnkwɪˈzɪʃən) *n. History.* a judicial institution of the Roman Catholic Church (1232–1820) founded to suppress heresy.

inquisitive (ɪnˈkwɪzɪtɪv) *adj.* **1.** excessively curious, esp. about the affairs of others; prying. **2.** eager to learn; inquiring. —**inˈquisitively** *adv.* —**inˈquisitiveness** *n.*

inquisitor (ɪnˈkwɪzɪtə) *n.* **1.** a person who inquires, esp. deeply, searchingly, or ruthlessly. **2.** (*often cap.*) an official of the ecclesiastical court of the Inquisition.

inquisitorial (ɪnˌkwɪzɪˈtɔːrɪəl) *adj.* **1.** of, relating to, or resembling inquisition or an inquisitor. **2.** offensively curious; prying. **3.** *Law.* denoting criminal procedure in which one party is both prosecutor and judge, or in which the trial is held in secret. Cf. **accusatorial** (sense 2). —**inˌquisiˈtorially** *adv.* —**inˌquisiˈtorialness** *n.*

inquorate (ɪnˈkwɔːˌreɪt) *adj. Brit.* not consisting of or being a quorum: *this meeting is inquorate.*

in re (ɪn ˈreɪ) *prep.* in the matter of: used esp. in bankruptcy proceedings. [C17: < L]

INRI *abbrev. for* Iesus Nazarenus Rex Iudaeorum (the inscription placed over Christ's head during the Crucifixion). [L: Jesus of Nazareth, King of the Jews]

inro (ˈɪnrəʊ) *n., pl.* **inro.** a set of small lacquer boxes formerly worn hung from the belt by Japanese men and used to carry medicines, seals, etc.

inroad (ˈɪnˌrəʊd) *n.* **1.** an invasion or hostile attack; raid or incursion. **2.** an encroachment or intrusion.

inrush (ˈɪnˌrʌʃ) *n.* a sudden usually overwhelming inward flow or rush; influx. —ˈ**inˌrushing** *n., adj.*

ins. *abbrev. for:* **1.** inches. **2.** insulated. **3.** insurance.

insane (ɪnˈseɪn) *adj.* **1. a.** mentally deranged; crazy; of unsound mind. **b.** (*as collective n.;* preceded by *the*): *the insane.* **2.** characteristic of a person of unsound mind: *an insane stare.* **3.** irresponsible; very foolish; stupid. —**inˈsanely** *adv.* —**inˈsaneness** *n.*

insanitary (ɪnˈsænɪtərɪ, -trɪ) *adj.* not sanitary; dirty or infected.

insanity (ɪnˈsænɪtɪ) *n., pl.* **-ties.** **1.** relatively permanent disorder of the mind; state or condition of being insane. **2.** utter folly; stupidity.

insatiable (ɪnˈseɪʃəbᵊl, -ʃɪə-) *or* **insatiate** (ɪnˈseɪʃɪɪt) *adj.* not able to be satisfied; greedy or unappeasable. —**inˌsatiaˈbility** *or* **inˈsatiateness** *n.* —**inˈsatiably** *or* **inˈsatiately** *adv.*

inscape (ˈɪnskeɪp) *n.* the essential inner nature of a person, object, etc., as expressed in literary or artistic works. [C19: < IN-² + *-scape,* as in LANDSCAPE; coined by Gerard Manley Hopkins (1844-89), E poet]

inscribe (ɪnˈskraɪb) *vb.* (*tr.*) **1.** to make, carve, or engrave (writing, letters, etc.) on (a surface such as wood, stone, or paper). **2.** to enter (a name) on a list or in a register. **3.** to sign one's name on (a book, etc.) before presentation to another person. **4.** to draw (a geometric construction) inside another construction so that the two are in contact but do not intersect. [C16: < L *inscrībere;* see INSCRIPTION] —**inˈscribable** *adj.* —**inˈscribableness** *n.* —**inˈscriber** *n.*

inscription (ɪnˈskrɪpʃən) *n.* **1.** something inscribed, esp. words carved or engraved on a coin, tomb, etc. **2.** a signature or brief dedication in a book or on a work of art. **3.** the act of inscribing. [C14: < L *inscriptiō* a writing upon, < *inscrībere* to write upon, < IN-² + *scrībere* to write] —**inˈscriptional** *or* **inˈscriptive** *adj.* —**inˈscriptively** *adv.*

inscrutable (ɪnˈskruːtəbᵊl) *adj.* mysterious or enigmatic; incomprehensible. [C15: < LL, < L IN-¹ + *scrūtārī* to examine] —**inˌscrutaˈbility** *or* **inˈscrutableness** *n.* —**inˈscrutably** *adv.*

insect (ˈɪnsɛkt) *n.* **1.** any of a class of small air-breathing arthropods, having a body divided into head, thorax, and abdomen, three pairs of legs, and (in most species) two pairs of wings. **2.** (loosely) any similar invertebrate, such as a spider, tick, or centipede. **3.** a contemptible, loathsome, or insignificant person. [C17: < L *insectum* (animal that has been) cut into, insect, < *insecāre,* < IN-² + *secāre* to cut] —**inˈsectile** *adj.* —ˈ**insect-ˌlike** *adj.*

insectarium (ˌɪnsɛkˈtɛərɪəm) *or* **insectary** (ɪnˈsɛktərɪ) *n., pl.* **-tariums, -taria** (-ˈtɛərɪə), *or* **-taries.** a place where living insects are kept, bred, and studied.

insecticide (ɪnˈsɛktɪˌsaɪd) *n.* a substance used to destroy insect pests. —**inˌsectiˈcidal** *adj.*

insectivore (ɪnˈsɛktɪˌvɔː) *n.* **1.** any of an order of placental mammals, being typically small, with simple teeth, and feeding on invertebrates. The group includes shrews, moles, and hedgehogs. **2.** any animal or plant that derives nourishment from insects. —ˌ**insecˈtivorous** *adj.*

insecure (ˌɪnsɪˈkjʊə) *adj.* **1.** anxious or afraid; not confident or certain. **2.** not adequately protected: *an insecure fortress.* **3.** unstable or shaky. —ˌ**inseˈcurely** *adv.* —ˌ**inseˈcureness** *n.* —ˌ**inseˈcurity** *n.*

inselberg (ˈɪnzᵊlˌbɜːg) *n.* an isolated rocky hill rising abruptly from a flat plain. [< G, < *Insel* island + *Berg* mountain]

inseminate (ɪnˈsɛmɪˌneɪt) *vb.* (*tr.*) **1.** to impregnate (a female) with semen. **2.** to introduce (ideas or attitudes) into the mind of (a person or group). [C17: < L *insēmināre,* < IN-² + *sēmināre* to sow, < *sēmen* seed] —**inˌsemiˈnation** *n.* —**inˈsemiˌnator** *n.*

insensate (ɪnˈsɛnseɪt, -sɪt) *adj.* **1.** lacking sensation or consciousness. **2.** insensitive; unfeeling. **3.** foolish; senseless. —**inˈsensately** *adv.* —**inˈsensateness** *n.*

insensible (ɪnˈsɛnsəbᵊl) *adj.* **1.** lacking sensation or consciousness. **2.** (foll. by *of* or *to*) unaware (of) or indifferent (to): *insensible to suffering.* **3.** thoughtless or callous. **4.** a less common word for

ˌ**insaˈlubrious** *adj.* **inˈsensitive** *adj.*

imperceptible. —**in,sensi'bility** *or* **in'sensibleness** *n.* —**in'sensibly** *adv.*

insentient (ɪn'sɛnʃɪənt) *adj.* lacking consciousness or senses; inanimate. —**in'sentience** *n.*

insert *vb.* (ɪn'sɜːt). (*tr.*) **1.** to put in or between; introduce. **2.** to introduce into text, as in a newspaper; interpolate. ~*n.* ('ɪnsɜːt). **3.** something inserted. **4. a.** a folded section placed in another for binding in with a book. **b.** a printed sheet, esp. one bearing advertising, placed loose between the leaves of a book, periodical, etc. [C16: < L *inserere* to plant in, < IN-[2] + *serere* to join] —**in'sertable** *adj.* —**in'serter** *n.*

insertion (ɪn'sɜːʃən) *n.* **1.** the act of inserting or something that is inserted. **2.** a word, sentence, correction, etc., inserted into text, such as a newspaper. **3.** a strip of lace, embroidery, etc., between two pieces of material. **4.** *Anat.* the point or manner of attachment of a muscle to the bone that it moves. —**in'sertional** *adj.*

in-service *adj.* denoting training that is given to employees during the course of employment: *an in-service course.*

insessorial (,ɪnsɛ'sɔːrɪəl) *adj.* **1.** (of feet or claws) adapted for perching. **2.** (of birds) having insessorial feet. [C19: < NL *Insessōrēs* birds that perch, < L: perchers, < *insidēre* to sit upon]

inset *vb.* (ɪn'sɛt), **-setting, -set. 1.** (*tr.*) to set or place in or within; insert. ~*n.* ('ɪn,sɛt). **2.** something inserted. **3.** *Printing.* **a.** a small map or diagram set within the borders of a larger one. **b.** another name for **insert** (sense 4). **4.** a piece of fabric inserted into a garment, as to shape it or for decoration. —**'in,setter** *n.*

inshallah (ɪn'ʃæləl) *sentence substitute. Islam.* if Allah wills it. [C19: < Ar.]

inshore ('ɪn'ʃɔː) *adj.* **1.** in or on the water, but close to the shore: *inshore weather.* ~*adv., adj.* **2.** towards the shore from the water: *an inshore wind; we swam inshore.*

inside *n.* ('ɪn'saɪd). **1.** the interior; inner or enclosed part or surface. **2.** the side of a path away from the road or adjacent to a wall. **3.** (*also pl.*) *Inf.* the internal organs of the body, esp. the stomach and bowels. **4. inside of.** in a period of time less than; within. **5. inside out.** with the inside facing outwards. **6. know (something) inside out.** to know thoroughly or perfectly. ~*prep.* (,ɪn'saɪd). **7.** in or to the interior of; within or to within; on the inside of. ~*adj.* ('ɪn,saɪd). **8.** on or of an interior; on the inside: *an inside door.* **9.** (*prenominal*) arranged or provided by someone within an organization or building, esp. illicitly: *the raid was an inside job; inside information.* ~*adv.* (,ɪn'saɪd). **10.** within or to within a thing or place; indoors. **11.** *Sl.* in or into prison.

▷ **Usage.** See at **outside.**

inside job *n. Inf.* a crime committed with the assistance of someone associated with the victim.

inside lane *n. Athletics.* the inside and advantageous position in a race that uses the curved parts of the track.

insider (,ɪn'saɪdə) *n.* **1.** a member of a specified group. **2.** a person with access to exclusive information.

insider dealing *or* **trading** *n.* the illegal practice of a person on the Stock Exchange or in some branches of the Civil Service taking advantage of early confidential information in order to deal in shares for personal profit. —**insider dealer** *or* **trader** *n.*

insidious (ɪn'sɪdɪəs) *adj.* **1.** stealthy, subtle, cunning, or treacherous. **2.** working in a subtle or apparently innocuous way, but nevertheless deadly: *an insidious illness.* [C16: < L *insidiōsus* cunning, < *insidiae* an ambush, < *insidēre* to sit in] —**in'sidiously** *adv.* —**in'sidiousness** *n.*

insight ('ɪn,saɪt) *n.* **1.** the ability to perceive clearly or deeply; penetration. **2.** a penetrating and often sudden understanding, as of a complex situation or problem. **3.** *Psychol.* the capacity for understanding one's own or another's mental processes. **4.** *Psychiatry.* the ability to understand one's own problems. —**'in,sightful** *adj.*

insignia (ɪn'sɪgnɪə) *n., pl.* **-nias** *or* **-nia. 1.** a badge or emblem of membership, office, or dignity. **2.** a distinguishing sign or mark. [C17: < L: badges, < *insignis* distinguished by a mark, prominent, < IN-[2] + *signum* mark]

insignificant (,ɪnsɪg'nɪfɪkənt) *adj.* **1.** having little or no importance; trifling. **2.** almost or relatively meaningless. **3.** small or inadequate: *an insignificant wage.* **4.** not distinctive in character, etc. —**,insig'nificance** *or* **,insig'nificancy** *n.* —**,insig'nificantly** *adv.*

insincere (,ɪnsɪn'sɪə) *adj.* lacking sincerity; hypocritical. —**,insin'cerely** *adv.* —**insincerity** (,ɪnsɪn'sɛrɪtɪ) *n.*

insinuate (ɪn'sɪnjʊ,eɪt) *vb.* **1.** (*may take a clause as object*) to suggest by indirect allusion, hints, innuendo, etc. **2.** (*tr.*) to introduce subtly or deviously. **3.** (*tr.*) to cause (someone, esp. oneself) to be accepted by gradual approaches or manoeuvres. [C16: < L *insinuāre* to wind one's way into, < IN-[2] + *sinus* curve] —**in'sinuative** *or* **in'sinuatory** *adj.* —**in'sinu,ator** *n.*

insinuation (ɪn,sɪnjʊ'eɪʃən) *n.* **1.** an indirect or devious hint or suggestion. **2.** the act or practice of insinuating.

insipid (ɪn'sɪpɪd) *adj.* **1.** lacking spirit or interest; boring. **2.** lacking taste; unpalatable. [C17: < L, < IN-[1] + *sapidus* full of flavour, SAPID] —**,insi'pidity** *or* **in'sipidness** *n.* —**in'sipidly** *adv.*

insist (ɪn'sɪst) *vb.* (when *tr., takes a clause as object;* when *intr.,* usually foll. by *on* or *upon*) **1.** to make a determined demand (for): *he insisted on his rights.* **2.** to express a convinced belief (in) or assertion (of). [C16: < L *insistere* to stand upon, urge, < IN-[2] + *sistere* to stand] —**in'sister** *n.* —**in'sistingly** *adv.*

insistent (ɪn'sɪstənt) *adj.* **1.** making continual and persistent demands. **2.** demanding notice or attention; compelling: *the insistent cry of a bird.* —**in'sistence** *or* **in'sistency** *n.* —**in'sistently** *adv.*

in situ *Latin.* (ɪn 'sɪtjuː) *adv., adj.* (*postpositive*) in the natural, original, or appropriate position.

in so far *or U.S.* **insofar** (,ɪnsəʊ'fɑː) *adv.* (usually foll. by *as*) to the degree or extent (that).

insolation (,ɪnsəʊ'leɪʃən) *n.* **1.** the quantity of solar radiation falling upon a body or planet, esp. per unit area. **2.** exposure to the sun's rays. **3.** another name for **sunstroke.**

insole ('ɪn,səʊl) *n.* **1.** the inner sole of a shoe or boot. **2.** a loose additional inner sole used to give extra warmth or to make a shoe fit.

insolent ('ɪnsələnt) *adj.* impudent or disrespectful. [C14: < L, < IN-[1] + *solēre* to be accustomed] —**'insolence** *n.* —**'insolently** *adv.*

insoluble (ɪn'sɒljʊb°l) *adj.* **1.** incapable of being dissolved; incapable of forming a solution, esp. in water. **2.** incapable of being solved. —**in,solu'bility** *or* **in'solubleness** *n.* —**in'solubly** *adv.*

insolvent (ɪn'sɒlvənt) *adj.* **1.** having insufficient assets to meet debts and liabilities; bankrupt. **2.** of or relating to bankrupts or bankruptcy. ~*n.* **3.** a person who is insolvent; bankrupt. —**in'solvency** *n.*

insomnia (ɪn'sɒmnɪə) *n.* chronic inability to fall asleep or to enjoy uninterrupted sleep. [C18: < L, < *insomnis* sleepless, < *somnus* sleep] —**in'somni,ac** *n., adj.* —**in'somnious** *adj.*

insomuch (,ɪnsəʊ'mʌtʃ) *adv.* **1.** (foll. by *as* or *that*) to such an extent or degree. **2.** (foll. by *as*) because of the fact (that); inasmuch (as).

insouciant (ɪn'suːsɪənt) *adj.* carefree or unconcerned; light-hearted. [C19: < F, < IN-[1] + *souciant* worrying, < *soucier* to trouble, < L *sollicitāre*] —**in'souciance** *n.* —**in'souciantly** *adv.*

inspan (ɪn'spæn) *vb.* **-spanning, -spanned.** (*tr.*) *Chiefly S. African.* **1.** to harness (animals) to (a vehicle); yoke. **2.** to press (people) into service.

in'separable *adj.* **,inso'briety** *n.* **in'solvable** *adj.*

[C19: < Afrik., < MDu. *inspannen*, < *spannen* to stretch]

inspect (ɪnˈspɛkt) *vb.* (*tr.*) **1.** to examine closely, esp. for faults or errors. **2.** to scrutinize officially (a document, military personnel on ceremonial parade, etc.). [C17: < L *inspicere*, < *specere* to look] —**inˈspectable** *adj.* —**inˈspection** *n.* —**inˈspective** *adj.*

inspector (ɪnˈspɛktə) *n.* **1.** a person who inspects, esp. an official who examines for compliance with regulations, standards, etc. **2.** a police officer ranking below a superintendent and above a sergeant. —**inˈspectoral** *or* **inspectorial** (ˌɪnspɛkˈtɔːrɪəl) *adj.* —**inˈspectorˌship** *n.*

inspectorate (ɪnˈspɛktərɪt) *n.* **1.** the office, rank, or duties of an inspector. **2.** a body of inspectors. **3.** a district under an inspector.

inspiration (ˌɪnspɪˈreɪʃən) *n.* **1.** stimulation or arousal of the mind, feelings, etc., to special activity or creativity. **2.** the state or quality of being so stimulated or aroused. **3.** someone or something that causes this state. **4.** an idea or action resulting from such a state. **5.** the act or process of inhaling; breathing in.

inspiratory (ɪnˈspaɪərətərɪ, -trɪ) *adj.* of or relating to inhalation or the drawing in of air.

inspire (ɪnˈspaɪə) *vb.* **1.** to exert a stimulating or beneficial effect upon (a person, etc.); animate or invigorate. **2.** (*tr.; foll. by with or to; may take an infinitive*) to arouse (with a particular emotion or to a particular action); stir. **3.** (*tr.*) to prompt or instigate; give rise to. **4.** (*tr.; often passive*) to guide or arouse by divine influence or inspiration. **5.** to take or draw (air, gas, etc.) into the lungs; inhale. **6.** (*tr.*) *Arch.* to breathe into or upon. [C14 (in the sense: to breathe upon, blow into): < L *inspīrāre*, < *spīrāre* to breathe] —**inˈspirable** *adj.* —**inˈspirative** *adj.* —**inˈspirer** *n.* —**inˈspiringly** *adv.*

inspirit (ɪnˈspɪrɪt) *vb.* (*tr.*) to fill with vigour; inspire. —**inˈspiriter** *n.* —**inˈspiriting** *adj.* —**inˈspiritment** *n.*

inspissate (ɪnˈspɪseɪt) *vb. Arch.* to thicken, as by evaporation. [C17: < LL *inspissātus* thickened, < L, < *spissus* thick] —ˌ**inspisˈsation** *n.* —ˈ**inspisˌsator** *n.*

inst. *abbrev. for:* **1.** instant (this month). **2.** instantaneous. **3.** instrumental.

Inst. *abbrev. for:* **1.** Institute. **2.** Institution.

install *or* **instal** (ɪnˈstɔːl) *vb.* **-stalling, -stalled.** (*tr.*) **1.** to place (equipment) in position and connect and adjust for use. **2.** to put in a position, rank, etc. **3.** to settle (a person, esp. oneself) in a position or state: *she installed herself in an armchair.* [C16: < Med. L *installāre*, < IN-[2] + *stallum* STALL[1]] —**inˈstaller** *n.*

installation (ˌɪnstəˈleɪʃən) *n.* **1.** the act of installing or the state of being installed. **2.** a large device, system, or piece of equipment that has been installed.

installment plan *or esp. Canad.* **instalment plan** *n.* the U.S. and Canad. name for **hire-purchase.**

instalment *or U.S.* **installment** (ɪnˈstɔːlmənt) *n.* **1.** one of the portions into which a debt is divided for payment at specified intervals over a fixed period. **2.** a portion of something that is issued, broadcast, or published in parts. [C18: < obs. *estallment*, prob. < OF *estaler* to fix, < *estal* something fixed, < OHG *stal* STALL[1]]

instance (ˈɪnstəns) *n.* **1.** a case or particular example. **2. for instance.** for or as an example. **3.** a specified stage in proceedings; step (in **in the first, second,** etc., **instance**). **4.** urgent request or demand (esp. in **at the instance of**). ~*vb.* (*tr.*) **5.** to cite as an example. [C14 (in the sense: case, example): < Med. L *instantia* example, (in the sense: urgency) < L: a being close upon, < *instāns* urgent; see INSTANT]

instant (ˈɪnstənt) *n.* **1.** a very brief time; moment. **2.** a particular moment or point in time: *at the same instant.* **3. on the instant.** immediately; without delay. ~*adj.* **4.** immediate; instantaneous. **5.** (esp. of foods) prepared or designed for preparation with very little time and effort: *instant coffee.* **6.** urgent or imperative. **7.** (*postpositive*) of the present month: *a letter of the 7th instant.* Abbrev.: **inst.** [C15: < L *instāns*, < *instāre* to be present, press closely, < IN-[2] + *stāre* to stand]

instantaneous (ˌɪnstənˈteɪnɪəs) *adj.* **1.** occurring with almost no delay; immediate. **2.** happening or completed within a moment: *instantaneous death.* —ˌ**instanˈtaneously** *adv.* —ˌ**instanˈtaneousness** *or* **instantaneity** (ɪnˌstæntəˈniːɪtɪ) *n.*

instanter (ɪnˈstæntə) *adv. Law.* without delay; the same day or within 24 hours. [C17: < L: urgently, < *instans* INSTANT]

instantly (ˈɪnstəntlɪ) *adv.* **1.** immediately; at once. **2.** *Arch.* urgently or insistently.

instar (ˈɪnstɑː) *n.* the stage in the development of an insect between any two moults. [C19: NL < L: image]

instate (ɪnˈsteɪt) *vb.* (*tr.*) to place in a position or office; install. —**inˈstatement** *n.*

instead (ɪnˈstɛd) *adv.* **1.** as a replacement, substitute, or alternative. **2. instead of.** (*prep.*) in place of or as an alternative to. [C13: < *in stead* in place]

instep (ˈɪnˌstɛp) *n.* **1.** the middle section of the human foot, forming the arch between the ankle and toes. **2.** the part of a shoe, stocking, etc., covering this. [C16: prob. < IN-[2] + STEP]

instigate (ˈɪnstɪˌgeɪt) *vb.* (*tr.*) **1.** to bring about, as by incitement: *to instigate rebellion.* **2.** to urge on to some drastic or unadvisable action. [C16: < L *instīgāre* to incite] —ˌ**instiˈgation** *n.* —ˈ**instiˌgative** *adj.* —ˈ**instiˌgator** *n.*

instil *or* **instill** (ɪnˈstɪl) *vb.* **-stilling, -stilled.** (*tr.*) **1.** to introduce gradually; implant or infuse. **2.** *Rare.* to pour in or inject in drops. [C16: < L *instillāre* to pour in a drop at a time, < *stillāre* to drip] —**inˈstiller** *n.* —**inˈstilment, inˈstillment,** *or* ˌ**instilˈlation** *n.*

instinct *n.* (ˈɪnstɪŋkt). **1.** the innate capacity of an animal to respond to a given stimulus in a relatively fixed way. **2.** inborn intuitive power. ~*adj.* (ɪnˈstɪŋkt). **3.** *Rare.* (*postpositive;* often foll. by *with*) **a.** animated or impelled (by). **b.** imbued or infused (with). [C15: < L *instinctus* roused, < *instinguere* to incite]

instinctive (ɪnˈstɪŋktɪv) *or* **instinctual** *adj.* **1.** of, relating to, or resulting from instinct. **2.** conditioned so as to appear innate: *an instinctive movement in driving.* —**inˈstinctively** *or* **inˈstinctually** *adv.*

institute (ˈɪnstɪˌtjuːt) *vb.* (*tr.*) **1.** to organize; establish. **2.** to initiate: *to institute a practice.* **3.** to establish in a position or office; induct. ~*n.* **4.** an organization founded for particular work, such as education, promotion of the arts, or scientific research. **5.** the building where such an organization is situated. **6.** something instituted, esp. a rule, custom, or precedent. [C16: < L *instituere*, < *statuere* to place] —ˈ**instiˌtutor** *or* ˈ**instiˌtuter** *n.*

institutes (ˈɪnstɪˌtjuːts) *pl. n.* a digest or summary, esp. of laws.

institution (ˌɪnstɪˈtjuːʃən) *n.* **1.** the act of instituting. **2.** an organization or establishment founded for a specific purpose, such as a hospital or college. **3.** the building where such an organization is situated. **4.** an established custom, law, or relationship in a society or community. **5.** *Inf.* a constant feature or practice: *Jones's drink at the bar was an institution.* **6.** the appointment of an incumbent to an ecclesiastical office or pastoral charge. —ˌ**instiˈtutionary** *adj.*

institutional (ˌɪnstɪˈtjuːʃənᵊl) *adj.* **1.** of, relating to, or characteristic of institutions. **2.** dull, routine, and uniform: *institutional meals.* **3.** relating to principles or institutes, esp. of law. —ˌ**instiˈtutionally** *adv.* —ˌ**instiˈtutionaˌlism** *n.*

institutionalize *or* **-ise** (ˌɪnstɪˈtjuːʃənəˌlaɪz) *vb.*

ˌ**instaˈbility** *n.*

1. (*tr.; often passive*) to subject to the deleterious effects of confinement in an institution. 2. (*tr.*) to place in an institution. 3. to make or become an institution —ˌinstiˌtutionaliˈzation *or* -iˈsation *n.*

in-store *adj.* available within a department store: *in-store banking facilities.*

instruct (ɪnˈstrʌkt) *vb.* (*tr.*) 1. to direct to do something; order. 2. to teach (someone) how to do (something). 3. to furnish with information; apprise. 4. *Law, chiefly Brit.* (esp. of a client to his solicitor or a solicitor to a barrister) to give relevant facts or information to. [C15: < L *instruere* to construct, equip, teach, < *struere* to build] —**inˈstructible** *adj.*

instruction (ɪnˈstrʌkʃən) *n.* 1. a direction; order. 2. the process or act of imparting knowledge; teaching; education. 3. *Computers.* a part of a program consisting of a coded command to the computer to perform a specified function. —**inˈstructional** *adj.*

instructions (ɪnˈstrʌkʃənz) *pl. n.* 1. directions, orders, or recommended rules for guidance, use, etc. 2. *Law.* the facts and details relating to a case given by a client to his solicitor or by a solicitor to a barrister.

instructive (ɪnˈstrʌktɪv) *adj.* serving to instruct or enlighten; conveying information. —**inˈstructively** *adv.* —**inˈstructiveness** *n.*

instructor (ɪnˈstrʌktə) *n.* 1. someone who instructs; teacher. 2. *U.S. & Canad.* a university teacher ranking below assistant professor. —**inˈstructorship** *n.* —**instructress** (ɪnˈstrʌktrɪs) *fem. n.*

instrument *n.* (ˈɪnstrəmənt). 1. a mechanical implement or tool, esp. one used for precision work. 2. *Music.* any of various contrivances or mechanisms that can be played to produce musical tones or sounds. 3. an important factor or agency in something: *her evidence was an instrument in his arrest.* 4. *Inf.* a person used by another to gain an end; dupe. 5. a measuring device, such as a pressure gauge. 6. a. a device or system for use in navigation or control, esp. of aircraft. b. (*as modifier*): *instrument landing.* 7. a formal legal document. ~*vb.* (ˈɪnstrəˌmɛnt). (*tr.*) 8. another word for **orchestrate** (sense 1). 9. to equip with instruments. [C13: < L *instrūmentum* tool, < *instruere* to erect, furnish; see INSTRUCT]

instrumental (ˌɪnstrəˈmɛntᵊl) *adj.* 1. serving as a means or influence; helpful. 2. of, relating to, or characterized by an instrument. 3. played by or composed for musical instruments. 4. *Grammar.* denoting a case of nouns, etc. indicating the instrument used in performing an action, usually using the prepositions *with* or *by means of.* ~*n.* 5. a piece of music composed for instruments rather than for voices. 6. *Grammar.* the instrumental case. —ˌ**instrumenˈtality** *n.* —ˌ**instruˈmentally** *adv.*

instrumentalist (ˌɪnstrəˈmɛntəlɪst) *n.* a person who plays a musical instrument.

instrumentation (ˌɪnstrəmɛnˈteɪʃən) *n.* 1. the instruments specified in a musical score or arrangement. 2. another word for **orchestration.** 3. the study of the characteristics of musical instruments. 4. the use of instruments or tools.

instrument panel *or* **board** *n.* 1. a panel on which instruments are mounted, as on a car. See also **dashboard.** 2. an array of instruments, gauges, etc., mounted to display the condition or performance of a machine.

insubordinate (ˌɪnsəˈbɔːdɪnɪt) *adj.* 1. not submissive to authority; disobedient or rebellious. 2. not in a subordinate position or rank. ~*n.* 3. an insubordinate person. —ˌ**insubˈordinately** *adv.* —ˌ**insubˌordiˈnation** *n.*

insubstantial (ˌɪnsəbˈstænʃəl) *adj.* 1. not substantial; flimsy, tenuous, or slight. 2. imaginary; unreal. —ˌ**insubˌstantiˈality** *n.* —ˌ**insubˈstantially** *adv.*

insufferable (ɪnˈsʌfərəbᵊl) *adj.* intolerable; unendurable. —**inˈsufferableness** *n.* —**inˈsufferably** *adv.*

insufficiency (ˌɪnsəˈfɪʃənsɪ) *n.* 1. Also: ˌ**insufˈficience.** the state of being insufficient. 2. *Pathol.* failure in the functioning of an organ, tissue, etc.: *cardiac insufficiency.*

insufflate (ˈɪnsʌˌfleɪt) *vb.* 1. (*tr.*) to breathe or blow (something) into (a room, area, etc.). 2. *Med.* to blow (air, medicated powder, etc.) into a body cavity. 3. (*tr.*) to breathe or blow upon (someone or something) as a ritual or sacramental act. —ˌ**insufˈflation** *n.* —ˈ**insufˌflator** *n.*

insular (ˈɪnsjʊlə) *adj.* 1. of, relating to, or resembling an island. 2. remote, detached, or aloof. 3. illiberal or narrow-minded. 4. isolated or separated. [C17: < LL, < L *insula* island] —ˈ**insularism** *or* **insularity** (ˌɪnsjʊˈlærɪtɪ) *n.* —ˈ**insularly** *adv.*

insulate (ˈɪnsjʊˌleɪt) *vb.* (*tr.*) 1. to prevent the transmission of electricity, heat, or sound to or from (a body or device) by surrounding with a nonconducting material. 2. to isolate or detach. [C16: < LL *insulātus:* made into an island]

insulation (ˌɪnsjʊˈleɪʃən) *n.* 1. Also: **insulant.** material used to insulate a body or device. 2. the act or process of insulating.

insulator (ˈɪnsjʊˌleɪtə) *n.* any material or device that insulates, esp. a material with a very low electrical conductivity or thermal conductivity.

insulin (ˈɪnsjʊlɪn) *n.* a protein hormone, secreted in the pancreas by the islets of Langerhans, that controls the concentration of glucose in the blood. [C20: < NL *insula* islet (of the pancreas) + -IN]

insult *vb.* (ɪnˈsʌlt). (*tr.*) 1. to treat, mention, or speak to rudely; offend; affront. ~*n.* (ˈɪnsʌlt). 2. an offensive or contemptuous remark or action; affront; slight. 3. a person or thing producing the effect of an affront: *some television is an insult to intelligence.* 4. *Med.* an injury or trauma. [C16: < L *insultāre* to jump upon] —**inˈsulter** *n.*

insuperable (ɪnˈsuːpərəbᵊl, -prəbᵊl, -ˈsjuː-) *adj.* incapable of being overcome; insurmountable. —**inˌsuperaˈbility** *n.* —**inˈsuperably** *adv.*

insupportable (ˌɪnsəˈpɔːtəbᵊl) *adj.* 1. incapable of being endured; intolerable; insufferable. 2. incapable of being supported or justified; indefensible. —ˌ**insupˈportableness** *n.* —ˌ**insupˈportably** *adv.*

insurance (ɪnˈʃʊərəns, -ˈʃɔː-) *n.* 1. a. the act, system, or business of providing financial protection against specified contingencies, such as death, loss, or damage. b. the state of having such protection. c. Also called: **insurance policy.** the policy providing such protection. d. the pecuniary amount of such protection. e. the premium payable in return for such protection. f. (*as modifier*): *insurance agent; insurance company; insurance stamp.* 2. a means of protecting or safeguarding against risk or injury.

insure (ɪnˈʃʊə, -ˈʃɔː) *vb.* 1. (often foll. by *against*) to guarantee or protect (against risk, loss, etc.). 2. (often foll. by *against*) to issue (a person) with an insurance policy or take out an insurance policy (on): *his house was heavily insured against fire.* 3. a variant spelling (esp. U.S.) of **ensure.** ~Also (rare) (for senses 1, 2): **ensure.** —**inˈsurable** *adj.* —**inˌsuraˈbility** *n.*

insured (ɪnˈʃʊəd, -ˈʃɔːd) *adj.* 1. covered by insurance: *an insured risk.* ~*n.* 2. the person, persons, or organization covered by an insurance policy.

insurer (ɪnˈʃʊərə, -ˈʃɔː-) *n.* 1. a person or company offering insurance policies in return for premiums. 2. a person or thing that insures.

insurgence (ɪnˈsɜːdʒəns) *n.* rebellion, uprising, or riot.

insurgent (ɪnˈsɜːdʒənt) *adj.* 1. rebellious or in revolt, as against a government in power or the civil authorities. ~*n.* 2. a person who takes part in an uprising or rebellion; insurrectionist. [C18:

ˌ**insufˈficient** *adj.* ˌ**insurˈmountable** *adj.*

< L *insurgēns* rising upon or against, < *surgere* to rise] —**in'surgency** *n.*

insurrection (ˌɪnsəˈrɛkʃən) *n.* the act or an instance of rebelling against a government in power or the civil authorities; insurgency. [C15: < LL *insurrectiō*, < *insurgere* to rise up] —ˌ**insur'rectional** *adj.* —ˌ**insur'rectionary** *n., adj.* —ˌ**insur'rectionist** *n., adj.*

int. *abbrev. for:* **1.** interest. **2.** interior. **3.** internal. **4.** Also: **Int.** international.

intact (ɪnˈtækt) *adj.* untouched or unimpaired; left complete or perfect. [C15: < L *intactus* not touched, < *tangere* to touch] —**in'tactness** *n.*

intaglio (ɪnˈtɑːlɪˌəʊ) *n., pl.* **-lios** *or* **-li** (-ljiː). **1.** a seal, gem, etc., ornamented with a sunken or incised design. **2.** the art or process of incised carving. **3.** a design, figure, or ornamentation carved, engraved, or etched into the surface of the material used. **4.** any of various printing techniques using an etched or engraved plate. **5.** an incised die used to make a design in relief. [C17: < It., < *intagliare* to engrave, < *tagliare* to cut, < LL *tāliāre;* see TAILOR] —**intagliated** (ɪnˈtɑːlɪˌeɪtɪd) *adj.*

intake (ˈɪnˌteɪk) *n.* **1.** a thing or a quantity taken in: *an intake of students.* **2.** the act of taking in. **3.** the opening through which fluid enters a duct or channel, esp. the air inlet of a jet engine. **4.** a ventilation shaft in a mine. **5.** a contraction or narrowing: *an intake in a garment.*

intangible (ɪnˈtændʒɪbᵊl) *adj.* **1.** incapable of being perceived by touch; impalpable. **2.** imprecise or unclear to the mind: *intangible ideas.* **3.** (of property or a business asset) saleable though not possessing intrinsic productive value. ~*n.* **4.** something that is intangible. —**in**ˌ**tangi'bility** *n.* —**in'tangibly** *adv.*

intarsia (ɪnˈtɑːsɪə) *or* **tarsia** *n.* **1.** a decorative mosaic of inlaid wood of a style developed in the Italian Renaissance. **2.** (in knitting) an individually worked motif. [C19: changed < It. *intarsio*]

integer (ˈɪntɪdʒə) *n.* **1.** any rational number that can be expressed as the sum or difference of a finite number of units, as 1, 2, 3, etc. **2.** an individual entity or whole unit. [C16: < L: untouched, < *tangere* to touch]

integral (ˈɪntɪgrəl, ɪnˈtɛgrəl) *adj.* **1.** (often foll. by *to*) being an essential part (of); intrinsic (to). **2.** intact; entire. **3.** formed of constituent parts; united. **4.** *Maths.* **a.** of or involving an integral. **b.** involving or being an integer. ~*n.* **5.** *Maths.* the sum of a large number of infinitesimally small quantities, summed either between stated limits (**definite integral**) or in the absence of limits (**indefinite integral**). **6.** a complete thing; whole. —**integrality** (ˌɪntɪˈgrælɪtɪ) *n.* —**'integrally** *adv.*

integral calculus *n.* the branch of calculus concerned with the determination of integrals (**integration**) and their application to the solution of differential equations.

integrand (ˈɪntɪˌgrænd) *n.* a mathematical function to be integrated. [C19: < L: to be integrated]

integrant (ˈɪntəgrənt) *adj.* **1.** part of a whole; integral; constituent. ~*n.* **2.** an integrant part.

integrate *vb.* (ˈɪntɪˌgreɪt). **1.** to make or be made into a whole; incorporate or be incorporated. **2.** (*tr.*) to designate (a school, park, etc.) for use by all races or groups; desegregate. **3.** to amalgamate or mix (a racial or religious group) with an existing community. **4.** *Maths.* to determine the integral of a function or variable. ~*adj.* (ˈɪntɪgrɪt). **5.** made up of parts; integrated. [C17: < L *integrāre;* see INTEGER] —**integrable** (ˈɪntəgrəbᵊl) *adj.* —ˌ**integra'bility** *n.* —ˌ**inte'gration** *n.* —**'inte**ˌ**grative** *adj.*

integrated circuit *n.* a very small electronic circuit consisting of an assembly of elements made from a chip of semiconducting material.

integrity (ɪnˈtɛgrɪtɪ) *n.* **1.** adherence to moral principles; honesty. **2.** the quality of being unimpaired; soundness. **3.** unity; wholeness. [C15: < L *integritās;* see INTEGER]

integument (ɪnˈtɛgjʊmənt) *n.* any outer protective layer or covering, such as a cuticle, seed coat, rind, or shell. [C17: < L *integumentum*, < *tegere* to cover] —**in**ˌ**tegu'mental** *or* **in**ˌ**tegu'mentary** *adj.*

intellect (ˈɪntɪˌlɛkt) *n.* **1.** the capacity for understanding, thinking, and reasoning. **2.** a mind or intelligence, esp. a brilliant one: *his intellect is wasted on that job.* **3.** *Inf.* a person possessing a brilliant mind; brain. [C14: < L *intellectus* comprehension, < *intellegere* to understand; see INTELLIGENCE] —ˌ**intel'lective** *adj.* —ˌ**intel'lectively** *adv.*

intellection (ˌɪntɪˈlɛkʃən) *n.* **1.** mental activity; thought. **2.** an idea or thought.

intellectual (ˌɪntɪˈlɛktʃʊəl) *adj.* **1.** of or relating to the intellect. **2.** appealing to or characteristic of people with a developed intellect: *intellectual literature.* **3.** expressing or enjoying mental activity. ~*n.* **4.** a person who enjoys mental activity and has highly developed tastes in art, etc. **5.** a person who uses his intellect. **6.** a highly intelligent person. —ˌ**intel**ˌ**lectu'ality** *or* ˌ**intel'lectualness** *n.* —ˌ**intel'lectual**ˌ**ize** *or* **-**ˌ**ise** *vb.* —ˌ**intel'lectually** *adv.*

intellectualism (ˌɪntɪˈlɛktʃʊəˌlɪzəm) *n.* **1.** development and exercise of the intellect. **2.** *Philosophy.* the doctrine that reason is the ultimate criterion of knowledge. —ˌ**intel'lectualist** *n., adj.* —ˌ**intel**ˌ**lectual'istic** *adj.*

intelligence (ɪnˈtɛlɪdʒəns) *n.* **1.** the capacity for understanding; ability to perceive and comprehend meaning. **2.** *Old-fashioned.* news; information. **3.** military information about enemies, spies, etc. **4.** a group or department that gathers or deals with such information. **5.** (*often cap.*) an intelligent being, esp. one that is not embodied. **6.** (*modifier*) of or relating to intelligence: *an intelligence network.* [C14: < L *intellegentia*, < *intellegere* to discern, lit.: to choose between, < INTER- + *legere* to choose] —**in**ˌ**telli'gential** *adj.*

intelligence quotient *n.* a measure of the intelligence of an individual. The quotient is derived by dividing an individual's mental age by his chronological age and multiplying the result by 100. Abbrev.: **IQ.**

intelligence test *n.* any of a number of tests designed to measure a person's mental skills.

intelligent (ɪnˈtɛlɪdʒənt) *adj.* **1.** having or indicating intelligence; clever. **2.** indicating high intelligence; perceptive: *an intelligent guess.* **3.** (of computerized functions) able to modify action in the light of ongoing events. **4.** (*postpositive;* foll. by *of*) *Arch.* having knowledge or information. —**in'telligently** *adv.*

intelligent card *n.* a plastic card with a built-in microprocessor, used for processing transaction details.

intelligentsia (ɪnˌtɛlɪˈdʒɛntsɪə) *n.* (usually preceded by *the*) the educated or intellectual people in a society or community. [C20: < Russian *intelligentsiya*, < L *intellegentia* INTELLIGENCE]

intelligible (ɪnˈtɛlɪdʒəbᵊl) *adj.* **1.** able to be understood; comprehensible. **2.** *Philosophy.* capable of being apprehended by the mind or intellect alone. [C14: < L *intellegibilis;* see INTELLECT] —**in**ˌ**telligi'bility** *n.* —**in'telligibly** *adv.*

intemperate (ɪnˈtɛmpərɪt, -prɪt) *adj.* **1.** consuming alcoholic drink habitually or to excess; immoderate. **2.** unrestrained: *intemperate rage.* **3.** extreme or severe: *an intemperate climate.* —**in'temperance** *or* **in'temperateness** *n.* —**in'temperately** *adv.*

intend (ɪnˈtɛnd) *vb.* **1.** (*may take a clause as object*) to propose or plan (something or to do something); have in mind; mean. **2.** (*tr.;* often foll. by *for*) to design or destine (for a certain purpose, person, etc.). **3.** (*tr.*) to mean to express or indicate: *what do his words intend?* **4.** (*intr.*) to

ˌ**insus'ceptible** *adj.*

have a purpose as specified; mean: *he intends well.* [C14: < L *intendere* to stretch forth, give one's attention to, < *tendere* to stretch] —**inˈtender** *n.*

intendancy (ɪnˈtɛndənsɪ) *n.* **1.** the position or work of an intendant. **2.** intendants collectively.

intendant (ɪnˈtɛndənt) *n.* a senior administrator; superintendent or manager.

intended (ɪnˈtɛndɪd) *adj.* **1.** planned or future. ~*n.* **2.** *Inf.* a person whom one is to marry; fiancé or fiancée.

intense (ɪnˈtɛns) *adj.* **1.** of extreme force, strength, degree, or amount: *intense heat.* **2.** characterized by deep or forceful feelings: *an intense person.* [C14: < L *intensus* stretched, < *intendere* to stretch out] —**inˈtensely** *adv.* —**inˈtenseness** *n.*

intensifier (ɪnˈtɛnsɪˌfaɪə) *n.* **1.** a person or thing that intensifies. **2.** a word, esp. an adjective or adverb, that serves to intensify the meaning of the word or phrase that it modifies. **3.** a substance, esp. one containing silver or uranium, used to increase the density of a photographic film or plate.

intensify (ɪnˈtɛnsɪˌfaɪ) *vb.* **-fying, -fied.** **1.** to make or become intense or more intense. **2.** (*tr.*) to increase the density of (a photographic film or plate). —**inˌtensifiˈcation** *n.*

intension (ɪnˈtɛnʃən) *n.* *Logic.* the set of characteristics or properties that distinguish the referent or referents of a given word. —**inˈtensional** *adj.*

intensity (ɪnˈtɛnsɪtɪ) *n., pl.* **-ties.** **1.** the state or quality of being intense. **2.** extreme force, degree, or amount. **3.** *Physics.* **a.** a measure of field strength or of the energy transmitted by radiation. **b.** (of sound in a specified direction) the average rate of flow of sound energy for one period through unit area at right angles to the specified direction.

intensive (ɪnˈtɛnsɪv) *adj.* **1.** of, relating to, or characterized by intensity: *intensive training.* **2.** (*usually in combination*) using one factor of production proportionately more than others, as specified: *capital-intensive; labour-intensive.* **3.** *Agriculture.* involving or farmed using large amounts of capital or labour to increase production from a particular area. Cf. **extensive** (sense 3). **4.** denoting or relating to a grammatical intensifier. **5.** denoting or belonging to a class of pronouns used to emphasize a noun or personal pronoun. **6.** of or relating to intension. ~*n.* **7.** an intensifier or intensive pronoun or grammatical construction. —**inˈtensively** *adv.* —**inˈtensiveness** *n.*

intensive care *n.* extensive and continuous care provided for an acutely ill patient in a hospital.

intent (ɪnˈtɛnt) *n.* **1.** something that is intended; aim; purpose; design. **2.** the act of intending. **3.** *Law.* the will or purpose with which one does an act. **4.** implicit meaning; connotation. **5. to all intents and purposes.** for all practical purposes; virtually. ~*adj.* **6.** firmly fixed; determined; concentrated: *an intent look.* **7.** (*postpositive; usually foll. by on or upon*) having the fixed intention (of); directing one's mind or energy (to): *intent on committing a crime.* [C13 (in the sense: intention): < LL *intentus* aim, < L: a stretching out; see INTEND] —**inˈtently** *adv.* —**inˈtentness** *n.*

intention (ɪnˈtɛnʃən) *n.* **1.** a purpose or goal; aim: *it is his intention to reform.* **2.** *Med.* a natural healing process in which the edges of a wound cling together with no tissue between (**first intention**), or in which the edges adhere with tissue between (**second intention**). **3.** (*usually pl.*) design or purpose with respect to a proposal of marriage (esp. in **honourable intentions**).

intentional (ɪnˈtɛnʃənᵊl) *adj.* **1.** performed by or expressing intention; deliberate. **2.** of or relating to intention or purpose. —**inˌtentionˈality** *n.* —**inˈtentionally** *adv.*

inter (ɪnˈtɜː) *vb.* **-terring, -terred.** (*tr.*) to place (a body, etc.) in the earth; bury, esp. with funeral rites. [C14: < OF *enterrer,* < L IN-[2] + *terra* earth]

inter- *prefix.* **1.** between or among: *international.* **2.** together, mutually, or reciprocally: *interdependent; interchange.* [< L]

interact (ˌɪntərˈækt) *vb.* (*intr.*) to act on or in close relation with each other. —ˌ**interˈaction** *n.*

interactive (ˌɪntərˈæktɪv) *adj.* **1.** allowing or relating to continuous two-way transfer of information between a user and the central point of a communication system, such as a computer or television. **2.** (of two or more persons, forces, etc.) acting upon or in close relation with each other; interacting.

inter alia *Latin.* (ˈɪntər ˈeɪlɪə) *adv.* among other things.

interbreed (ˌɪntəˈbriːd) *vb.* **-breeding, -bred.** **1.** to breed within a single family or strain so as to produce particular characteristics in the offspring. **2.** another term for **crossbreed** (sense 1).

interbroker dealer (ˌɪntəˈbrəʊkə) *n.* *Stock Exchange.* a specialist who matches the needs of different market makers and facilitates dealings between them.

intercalary (ɪnˈtɜːkələrɪ) *adj.* **1.** (of a day, month, etc.) inserted in the calendar. **2.** (of a particular year) having one or more days inserted. **3.** inserted, introduced, or interpolated. [C17: < L *intercalārius;* see INTERCALATE]

intercalate (ɪnˈtɜːkəˌleɪt) *vb.* (*tr.*) **1.** to insert (one or more days) into the calendar. **2.** to interpolate or insert. [C17: < L *intercalāre* to insert, proclaim that a day has been inserted, < INTER- + *calāre* to proclaim] —**inˌtercaˈlation** *n.* —**inˈtercalative** *adj.*

intercede (ˌɪntəˈsiːd) *vb.* (*intr.;* often foll. by *in*) to come between parties or act as mediator or advocate: *to intercede in the strike.* [C16: < L *intercēdere,* < INTER- + *cēdere* to move] —ˌ**interˈceder** *n.*

intercensal (ˌɪntəˈsɛnsəl) *adj.* (of population figures, etc.) estimated at a time between official censuses. [C19: < INTER- + *censal,* irregularly formed < CENSUS]

intercept *vb.* (ˌɪntəˈsɛpt). (*tr.*) **1.** to stop, deflect, or seize on the way from one place to another; prevent from arriving or proceeding. **2.** *Sport.* to seize or cut off (a pass) on its way from one opponent to another. **3.** *Maths.* to cut off, mark off, or bound (some part of a line, curve, plane, or surface). ~*n.* (ˈɪntəˌsɛpt). **4.** *Maths.* **a.** a point at which two figures intersect. **b.** the distance from the origin to the point at which a line, curve, or surface cuts a coordinate axis. **5.** *Sport, U.S. & Canad.* the act of intercepting an opponent's pass. [C16: < L *intercipere* to seize before arrival, < INTER- + *capere* to take] —ˌ**interˈception** *n.* —ˌ**interˈceptive** *adj.*

interceptor *or* **intercepter** (ˌɪntəˈsɛptə) *n.* **1.** a person or thing that intercepts. **2.** a fast highly manoeuvrable fighter aircraft used to intercept enemy aircraft.

intercession (ˌɪntəˈsɛʃən) *n.* **1.** the act or an instance of interceding. **2.** the act of interceding or offering petitionary prayer to God on behalf of others. **3.** such petitionary prayer. [C16: < L *intercessio;* see INTERCEDE] —ˌ**interˈcessional** *or* ˌ**interˈcessory** *adj.* —ˌ**interˈcessor** *n.* —ˌ**intercesˈsorial** *adj.*

interchange *vb.* (ˌɪntəˈtʃeɪndʒ). **1.** to change places or cause to change places; alternate; exchange; switch. ~*n.* (ˈɪntəˌtʃeɪndʒ). **2.** the act of interchanging; exchange or alternation. **3.** a motorway junction of interconnecting roads and bridges designed to prevent streams of traffic crossing one another. —ˌ**interˈchangeable** *adj.*

ˌ**interˌacaˈdemic** *adj.*
ˌ**interalˈlied** *adj.*
ˌ**interaˈtomic** *adj.*
ˌ**interˈbank** *adj.*
ˌ**interˈblend** *vb.*
ˌ**interˈbranch** *adj.*
ˌ**interˈcaste** *adj.*
ˌ**interˈcellular** *adj.*

—ˌinterˌchangeaˈbility *or* ˌinterˈchangeableness *n.* —ˌinterˈchangeably *adv.*

inter-city *adj.* **1.** (in Britain) denoting a fast rail service between main towns. ~*n.* **2.** such a rail service.

intercom (ˈɪntəˌkɒm) *n. Inf.* an internal telephone system for communicating within a building, aircraft, etc. [C20: short for INTERCOMMUNICATION]

intercommunicate (ˌɪntəkəˈmjuːnɪˌkeɪt) *vb.* (*intr.*) **1.** to communicate mutually. **2.** to interconnect, as two rooms, etc. —ˌintercomˈmunicable *adj.* —ˌintercomˌmuniˈcation *n.* —ˌintercomˈmunicative *adj.*

intercommunion (ˌɪntəkəˈmjuːnjən) *n.* association between Churches, involving esp. mutual reception of Holy Communion.

intercostal (ˌɪntəˈkɒstᵊl) *adj. Anat.* between the ribs: *intercostal muscles.* [C16: via NL < L INTER- + *costa* rib]

intercourse (ˈɪntəˌkɔːs) *n.* **1.** See **sexual intercourse. 2.** communication or exchange between individuals; mutual dealings. [C15: < Med. L *intercursus* business, < L *intercurrere* to run between]

intercurrent (ˌɪntəˈkʌrənt) *adj.* **1.** occurring during or in between; intervening. **2.** *Pathol.* (of a disease) occurring during the course of another disease. —ˌinterˈcurrence *n.*

interdict *n.* (ˈɪntəˌdɪkt). **1.** *R.C. Church.* the exclusion of a person in a particular place from certain sacraments, although not from communion. **2.** *Civil law.* any order made by a court or official prohibiting an act. **3.** *Scots Law.* an order having the effect of an injunction. ~*vb.* (ˌɪntəˈdɪkt) (*tr.*) **4.** to place under legal or ecclesiastical sanction; prohibit; forbid. **5.** *Mil.* to destroy (an enemy's lines of communication) by firepower. [C13: < L *interdictum* prohibition, < *interdīcere* to forbid, < INTER- + *dīcere* to say] —ˌinterˈdiction *n.* —ˌinterˈdictive *or* ˌinterˈdictory *adj.* —ˌinterˈdictively *adv.* —ˌinterˈdictor *n.*

interdigitate (ˌɪntəˈdɪdʒɪˌteɪt) *vb.* (*intr.*) to interlock like the fingers of clasped hands. [C19: < INTER- + L *digitus* (see DIGIT) + -ATE[1]]

interdisciplinary (ˌɪntəˈdɪsɪˌplɪnərɪ) *adj.* involving two or more academic disciplines.

interest (ˈɪntrɪst, -tərɪst) *n.* **1.** the sense of curiosity about or concern with something or someone. **2.** the power of stimulating such a sense: *to have great interest.* **3.** the quality of such stimulation. **4.** something in which one is interested; a hobby or pursuit. **5.** (*often pl.*) benefit; advantage: *in one's own interest.* **6.** (*often pl.*) a right, share, or claim, esp. in a business or property. **7. a.** a charge for the use of credit or borrowed money. **b.** such a charge expressed as a percentage per time unit of the sum borrowed or used. **8.** (*often pl.*) a section of a community, etc., whose members have common aims: *the landed interest.* **9. declare an interest.** to make known one's connection, esp. a prejudicial connection, with an affair. ~*vb.* (*tr.*) **10.** to arouse or excite the curiosity or concern of. **11.** to cause to become involved in something; concern. [C15: < L: it concerns, < *interesse*, < INTER- + *esse* to be]

interested (ˈɪntrɪstɪd, -tərɪs-) *adj.* **1.** showing or having interest. **2.** (*usually prenominal*) personally involved or implicated: *the interested parties met to discuss the business.* —ˈinterestedly *adv.* —ˈinterestedness *n.*

interesting (ˈɪntrɪstɪŋ, -tərɪs-) *adj.* inspiring interest; absorbing. —ˈinterestingly *adv.* —ˈinterestingness *n.*

interface *n.* (ˈɪntəˌfeɪs). **1.** *Physical chem.* a surface that forms the boundary between two liquids or chemical phases. **2.** a common point or boundary between two things. **3.** an electrical circuit linking one device, esp. a computer, with another. ~*vb.* (ˌɪntəˈfeɪs). **4.** (*tr.*) to design or adapt the input and output configurations of (two electronic devices) so that they may work together compatibly. **5.** to be an interface (with). **6.** to be interactive (with). —**interfacial** (ˌɪntəˈfeɪʃəl) *adj.* —ˌinterˈfacially *adv.*

interfacing (ˈɪntəˌfeɪsɪŋ) *n.* **1.** a piece of fabric sewn beneath the facing of a garment, usually at the inside of the neck, armholes, etc., to give shape and firmness. **2.** another name for **interlining.**

interfere (ˌɪntəˈfɪə) *vb.* (*intr.*) **1.** (often foll. by *in*) to interpose, esp. meddlesomely or unwarrantedly; intervene. **2.** (often foll. by *with*) to come between or into opposition; hinder. **3.** (foll. by *with*) *Euphemistic.* to assault sexually. **4.** to strike one against the other, as a horse's legs. **5.** *Physics.* to cause or produce interference. [C16: < OF *s'entreferir* to collide, < *entre-* INTER- + *ferir* to strike, < L *ferīre*] —ˌinterˈfering *adj.*

interference (ˌɪntəˈfɪərəns) *n.* **1.** the act or an instance of interfering. **2.** *Physics.* the process in which two or more coherent waves combine to form a resultant wave in which the displacement at any point is the vector sum of the displacements of the individual waves. **3.** any undesired signal that tends to interfere with the reception of radio waves. —**interferential** (ˌɪntəfəˈrɛnʃəl) *adj.*

interferometer (ˌɪntəfəˈrɒmɪtə) *n. Physics.* any acoustic, optical, or microwave instrument that uses interference patterns to make accurate measurements of wavelength, distance, etc. —**interferometric** (ˌɪntəˌfɛrəˈmɛtrɪk) *adj.* —ˌinterˌferoˈmetrically *adv.* —ˌinterferˈometry *n.*

interferon (ˌɪntəˈfɪərɒn) *n. Biochem.* any of a family of proteins made by cells in response to virus infection that prevent the growth of the virus. [C20: < INTERFERE + -ON]

interfuse (ˌɪntəˈfjuːz) *vb.* **1.** to diffuse or mix throughout or become so diffused or mixed; intermingle. **2.** to blend or fuse or become blended or fused. —ˌinterˈfusion *n.*

interim (ˈɪntərɪm) *adj.* **1.** (*prenominal*) temporary, provisional, or intervening: *interim measures to deal with the emergency.* ~*n.* **2.** (usually preceded by *the*) the intervening time; the meantime (esp. in **in the interim**). ~*adv.* **3.** *Rare.* meantime. [C16: < L: meanwhile]

interior (ɪnˈtɪərɪə) *n.* **1.** a part, surface, or region that is inside or on the inside: *the interior of Africa.* **2.** inner character or nature. **3.** a film or scene shot inside a building, studio, etc. **4.** a picture of the inside of a room or building, as in a painting or stage design. **5.** the inside of a building or room, with respect to design and decoration. ~*adj.* **6.** of, situated on, or suitable for the inside; inner. **7.** coming or acting from within; internal. **8.** of or involving a nation's domestic affairs; internal. **9.** (esp. of one's spiritual or mental life) secret or private; not observable. [C15: < L (adj.), comp. of *inter* within] —inˈteriorly *adv.*

interior angle *n.* an angle of a polygon contained between two adjacent sides.

ˌinterˈclasp *vb.*
ˌinterˈclass *adj.*
ˌinterˈclub *adj.*
ˌintercolˈlegiate *adj.*
ˌintercoˈlonial *adj.*
ˌintercomˈmunity *adj.*
ˌinterˈcompany *adj.*
ˌinterconˈnect *vb.*
ˌinterconˈnection *n.*
ˌinterˌconsoˈnantal *adj.*
ˌinterˌcontiˈnental *adj.*
ˌinterˈcounty *adj.*
ˌinterdeˌnomiˈnational *adj.*
ˌinterˌdepartˈmental *adj.*
ˌinterˌdepartˈmentally *adv.*
ˌinterdeˈpend *vb.*
ˌinterdeˈpendence *n.*
ˌinterdeˈpendent *adj.*
ˌinterˈdigital *adj.*
ˌinterˈdigitally *adv.*
ˌinterˈfactional *adj.*
ˌinterˈfibrous *adj.*
ˌinterˈflow *vb.*
ˌinterˈfold *vb.*
ˌintergaˈlactic *adj.*
ˌinterˈglacial *adj.*
ˌinterˌgovernˈmental *adj.*
ˌinterˈgroup *adj.*
ˌinteriˈonic *adj.*

interior decoration *n.* **1.** the colours, furniture, etc., of the interior of a house, etc. **2.** Also called: **interior design.** the art or business of planning the interiors of houses, etc.

interiorize *or* **-ise** (ɪnˈtɪərɪəˌraɪz) *vb.* (*tr.*) another word for **internalize.**

interj. *abbrev. for* interjection.

interject (ˌɪntəˈdʒɛkt) *vb.* (*tr.*) to interpose abruptly or sharply; interrupt with; throw in: *she interjected clever remarks.* [C16: < L *interjicere* to place between, < *jacere* to throw] —ˌ**interˈjector** *n.*

interjection (ˌɪntəˈdʒɛkʃən) *n.* **1.** the act of interjecting. **2.** a word or phrase that is used in syntactic isolation and that expresses sudden emotion; expletive. Abbrev.: **interj.** —ˌ**interˈjectional** *or* ˌ**interˈjectory** *adj.* —ˌ**interˈjectionally** *adv.*

interlard (ˌɪntəˈlɑːd) *vb.* (*tr.*) **1.** to scatter thickly in or between; intersperse: *to interlard one's writing with foreign phrases.* **2.** to occur frequently in; be scattered in or through: *foreign phrases interlard his writings.*

interlay (ˌɪntəˈleɪ) *vb.* **-laying, -laid.** (*tr.*) to insert (layers) between; interpose: *to interlay gold among the silver; to interlay the silver with gold.*

interleaf (ˈɪntəˌliːf) *n., pl.* **-leaves.** a blank leaf inserted between the leaves of a book.

interleave (ˌɪntəˈliːv) *vb.* (*tr.*) **1.** (often foll. by *with*) to intersperse (with), esp. alternately, as the illustrations in a book (with protective leaves). **2.** to provide (a book) with blank leaves for notes, etc., or to protect illustrations.

interleukin (ˌɪntəˈluːkɪn) *n.* a substance extracted from white blood cells that stimulates their activity against infection and may be used to combat some forms of cancer.

interline[1] (ˌɪntəˈlaɪn) *or* **interlineate** (ˌɪntəˈlɪnɪˌeɪt) *vb.* (*tr.*) to write or print (matter) between the lines of (a text, book, etc.). —ˈ**interˌlining** *or* ˌ**interˌlineˈation** *n.*

interline[2] (ˌɪntəˈlaɪn) *vb.* (*tr.*) to provide (a part of a garment) with a second lining, esp. of stiffened material. —ˈ**interˌliner** *n.*

interlinear (ˌɪntəˈlɪnɪə) *or* **interlineal** *adj.* **1.** written or printed between lines of text. **2.** written or printed with the text in different languages or versions on alternate lines. —ˌ**interˈlinearly** *or* ˌ**interˈlineally** *adv.*

interlining (ˈɪntəˌlaɪnɪŋ) *n.* the material used to interline parts of garments, now often made of reinforced paper.

interlock *vb.* (ˌɪntəˈlɒk). **1.** to join or be joined firmly, as by a mutual interconnection of parts. ~*n.* (ˈɪntəˌlɒk). **2.** the act of interlocking or the state of being interlocked. **3.** a device, esp. one operated electromechanically, used in a logic circuit to prevent an activity being initiated unless preceded by certain events. **4.** a closely knitted fabric. ~*adj.* **5.** closely knitted. —ˈ**interˌlocker** *n.*

interlocutor (ˌɪntəˈlɒkjʊtə) *n.* **1.** a person who takes part in a conversation. **2.** the man in the centre of a troupe of minstrels who engages the others in talk or acts as announcer. **3.** *Scots Law.* a decree by a judge. —ˌ**interˈlocutress,** ˌ**interˈlocutrice,** *or* ˌ**interˈlocutrix** *fem. n.*

interlocutory (ˌɪntəˈlɒkjʊtərɪ, -trɪ) *adj.* **1.** *Law.* pronounced during the course of proceedings; provisional: *an interlocutory injunction.* **2.** interposed, as into a conversation, narrative, etc. **3.** of, relating to, or characteristic of dialogue. —ˌ**interˈlocutorily** *adv.*

interlope (ˌɪntəˈləʊp) *vb.* (*intr.*) **1.** to interfere; meddle; intrude. **2.** to intercept another's trade, esp. illegally. [C17: prob. back formation < *interloper,* < INTER- + *-loper,* < MDu. *loopen* to LEAP] —ˈ**interˌloper** *n.*

interlude (ˈɪntəˌluːd) *n.* **1.** a period of time or different activity between longer periods, processes, or events; episode or interval. **2.** *Theatre.* a short dramatic piece played separately or as part of a longer entertainment, common in 16th-century England. **3.** a brief piece of music, dance, etc., given between the sections of another performance. [C14: < Med. L, < L INTER- + *lūdus* play]

intermarry (ˌɪntəˈmærɪ) *vb.* **-rying, -ried.** (*intr.*) **1.** (of different races, religions, etc.) to become connected by marriage. **2.** to marry within one's own family, clan, group, etc. —ˌ**interˈmarriage** *n.*

intermediary (ˌɪntəˈmiːdɪərɪ) *n., pl.* **-aries. 1.** a person who acts as a mediator or agent between parties. **2.** something that acts as a medium or means. ~*adj.* **3.** acting as an intermediary. **4.** situated, acting, or coming between; intermediate.

intermediate *adj.* (ˌɪntəˈmiːdɪɪt). **1.** occurring or situated between two points, extremes, places, etc.; in between. ~*n.* (ˌɪntəˈmiːdɪɪt). **2.** something intermediate. **3.** a substance formed during one of the stages of a chemical process before the desired product is obtained. ~*vb.* (ˌɪntəˈmiːdɪˌeɪt). **4.** (*intr.*) to act as an intermediary or mediator. [C17: < Med. L *intermediāre* to intervene, < L INTER- + *medius* middle] —ˌ**interˈmediacy** *or* ˌ**interˈmediateness** *n.* —ˌ**interˈmediately** *adv.* —ˌ**interˌmediˈation** *n.* —ˌ**interˈmediˌator** *n.*

intermediate frequency *n. Electronics.* the frequency to which the signal carrier frequency is changed in a superheterodyne receiver and at which most of the amplification takes place.

interment (ɪnˈtɜːmənt) *n.* burial, esp. with ceremonial rites.

intermezzo (ˌɪntəˈmɛtsəʊ) *n., pl.* **-zos** *or* **-zi** (-tsiː). **1.** a short piece of instrumental music composed for performance between the acts or scenes of an opera, drama, etc. **2.** an instrumental piece either inserted between two longer movements in an extended composition or intended for independent performance. [C19: < It., < LL *intermedium* interval; see INTERMEDIATE]

interminable (ɪnˈtɜːmɪnəbᵊl) *adj.* endless or seemingly endless because of monotony or tiresome length. —**inˈterminableness** *n.* —**inˈterminably** *adv.*

intermission (ˌɪntəˈmɪʃən) *n.* **1.** an interval, as between parts of a film, etc. **2.** a period between events or activities; pause. **3.** the act of intermitting or the state of being intermitted. [C16: < L, < *intermittere* to INTERMIT] —ˌ**interˈmissive** *adj.*

intermit (ˌɪntəˈmɪt) *vb.* **-mitting, -mitted.** to suspend (activity) or (of activity) to be suspended temporarily or at intervals. [C16: < L *intermittere* to leave off, < INTER- + *mittere* to send] —ˌ**interˈmittor** *n.*

intermittent (ˌɪntəˈmɪtᵊnt) *adj.* occurring occasionally or at regular or irregular intervals; periodic. —ˌ**interˈmittence** *or* ˌ**interˈmittency** *n.* —ˌ**interˈmittently** *adv.*

intermixture (ˌɪntəˈmɪkstʃə) *n.* **1.** the act of intermixing or state of being intermixed. **2.** an additional constituent or ingredient.

intern *vb.* **1.** (ɪnˈtɜːn). (*tr.*) to detain or confine within a country or a limited area, esp. during wartime. **2.** (ˈɪntɜːn). (*intr.*) *Chiefly U.S.* to serve or train as an intern. ~*n.* (ˈɪntɜːn). **3.** another word for **internee. 4.** Also: **interne.** the approximate U.S. and Canad. equivalent of **houseman. 5.** Also: **interne.** *Chiefly U.S.* a student teacher. **6.** Also: **interne.** *Chiefly U.S* a student or recent graduate undergoing practical training in a working environment. [C19: < L *internus* internal] —**inˈternment** *n.* —ˈ**internship** *or* ˈ**interneship** *n.*

internal (ɪnˈtɜːnᵊl) *adj.* **1.** of, situated on, or suitable for the inside; inner. **2.** coming or acting from within; interior. **3.** involving the spiritual or mental life; subjective. **4.** of or involving a

---

ˌ**interˈknit** *vb.*
ˌ**interˈlace** *vb.*
ˌ**interˈlibrary** *adj.*
ˌ**interˈlink** *vb.*
ˌ**interˈmesh** *vb.*
ˌ**interˈmingle** *vb.*
ˌ**interˈmix** *vb.*
ˌ**interˈmixable** *adj.*
ˌ**interˈmuscular** *adj.*

nation's domestic as opposed to foreign affairs. **5.** situated within, affecting, or relating to the inside of the body. ~*n.* **6.** *Euphemistic.* a medical examination of the vagina or uterus. [C16: < Med. L, < LL *internus* inward] —ˌ**interˈnality** *or* **inˈternalness** *n.* —**inˈternally** *adv.*

internal-combustion engine *n.* a heat engine in which combustion occurs within the engine rather than in an external furnace.

internal energy *n.* the thermodynamic property of a system that changes by an amount equal to the work done on the system when it suffers an adiabatic change.

internalize *or* **-ise** (ɪnˈtɜːnəˌlaɪz) *vb.* (*tr.*) *Psychol., sociol.* to make internal, esp. to incorporate within oneself (values, attitudes, etc.) through learning or socialization. Also: **interiorize.** —**inˌternaliˈzation** *or* **-iˈsation** *n.*

internal medicine *n.* the branch of medical science concerned with the diagnosis and nonsurgical treatment of disorders of the internal structures of the body.

international (ˌɪntəˈnæʃənᵊl) *adj.* **1.** of, concerning, or involving two or more nations or nationalities. **2.** established by, controlling, or legislating for several nations: *an international court.* **3.** available for use by all nations: *international waters.* ~*n.* **4.** *Sport.* **a.** a contest between two national teams. **b.** a member of a national team. —ˌ**interˌnationˈality** *n.* —ˌ**interˈnationally** *adv.*

International (ˌɪntəˈnæʃənᵊl) *n.* **1.** any of several international socialist organizations, esp. **First International** (1864–76) and **Second International** (1889 until World War I). **2.** a member of any of these organizations.

International Court of Justice *n.* a court established in the Hague, in the Netherlands, to settle disputes brought by members of the United Nations. Also called: **World Court.**

International Date Line *n.* the line approximately following the 180° meridian from Greenwich on the east side of which the date is one day earlier than on the west.

internationalism (ˌɪntəˈnæʃənəˌlɪzəm) *n.* **1.** the ideal or practice of cooperation and understanding between nations. **2.** the state or quality of being international. —ˌ**interˈnationalist** *n.*

internationalize *or* **-ise** (ˌɪntəˈnæʃənəˌlaɪz) *vb.* (*tr.*) **1.** to make international. **2.** to put under international control. —ˌ**interˌnationaliˈzation** *or* **-iˈsation** *n.*

international law *n.* the body of rules generally recognized by civilized nations as governing their conduct towards each other.

International Phonetic Alphabet *n.* a series of signs and letters for the representation of human speech sounds. It is based on the Roman alphabet but supplemented by modified signs or symbols from other writing systems.

International Practical Temperature Scale *n.* a temperature scale adopted by international agreement in 1968 based on thermodynamic temperature and using experimental values to define 11 fixed points.

interne (ˈɪntɜːn) *n.* a variant spelling of **intern** (senses 4, 5, 6).

internecine (ˌɪntəˈniːsaɪn) *adj.* **1.** mutually destructive or ruinous; maiming both or all sides: *internecine war.* **2.** of or relating to slaughter or carnage; bloody. **3.** of or involving conflict within a group or organization. [C17: < L, < *internecāre* to destroy, < *necāre* to kill]

internee (ˌɪntɜːˈniː) *n.* a person who is interned, esp. an enemy citizen in wartime or a terrorism suspect.

internist (ˈɪntɜːnɪst, ɪnˈtɜːnɪst) *n.* a physician who specializes in internal medicine.

interpellate (ɪnˈtɜːpɛˌleɪt) *vb.* (*tr.*) *Parliamentary procedure.* (in European legislatures) to question (a member of the government) on a point of government policy, often interrupting the business of the day. [C16: < L *interpellāre* to disturb, < INTER- + *pellere* to push] —**inˌterpelˈlation** *n.* —**inˈterpelˌlator** *n.*

interpenetrate (ˌɪntəˈpɛnɪˌtreɪt) *vb.* **1.** to penetrate (something) thoroughly; pervade. **2.** to penetrate each other or one another mutually. —ˌ**interˈpenetrable** *adj.* —ˌ**interˈpenetrant** *adj.* —ˌ**interˌpeneˈtration** *n.* —ˌ**interˈpenetrative** *adj.* —ˌ**interˈpenetratively** *adv.*

interplay (ˈɪntəˌpleɪ) *n.* reciprocal and mutual action and reaction, as in circumstances, events, or personal relations.

interpleader (ˌɪntəˈpliːdə) *n. Law.* **1.** a process by which a person holding money claimed by two or more parties and having no interest in it himself can require the claimants to litigate with each other. **2.** a person who interpleads.

Interpol (ˈɪntəˌpɒl) *n. acronym for* International Criminal Police Organization, an association of over 100 national police forces, devoted chiefly to fighting international crime.

interpolate (ɪnˈtɜːpəˌleɪt) *vb.* **1.** to insert or introduce (a comment, passage, etc.) into (a conversation, text, etc.). **2.** to falsify or alter (a text, manuscript, etc.) by the later addition of (material, esp. spurious passages). **3.** (*intr.*) to make additions, interruptions, or insertions. **4.** *Maths.* to estimate (a value of a function) between the values already known or determined. Cf. **extrapolate** (sense 1). [C17: < L *interpolāre* to give a new appearance to] —**inˈterpoˌlater** *or* **inˈterpoˌlator** *n.* —**inˈterpolative** *adj.*

interpose (ˌɪntəˈpəʊz) *vb.* **1.** to put or place between or among other things. **2.** to introduce (comments, questions, etc.) into a speech or conversation; interject. **3.** to exert or use influence or action in order to alter or intervene in (a situation). [C16: < OF, < L *interpōnere,* < INTER- + *pōnere* to put] —ˌ**interˈposal** *n.* —ˌ**interˈposer** *n.* —ˌ**interpoˈsition** *n.*

interpret (ɪnˈtɜːprɪt) *vb.* **1.** (*tr.*) to clarify or explain the meaning of; elucidate. **2.** (*tr.*) to construe the significance or intention of. **3.** (*tr.*) to convey or represent the spirit or meaning of (a poem, song, etc.) in performance. **4.** (*intr.*) to act as an interpreter; translate orally. [C14: < L *interpretārī,* < *interpres* negotiator, one who explains] —**inˈterpretable** *adj.* —**inˌterpretaˈbility** *or* **inˈterpretableness** *n.* —**inˈterpretably** *adv.* —**inˈterpretive** *adj.*

interpretation (ɪnˌtɜːprɪˈteɪʃən) *n.* **1.** the act or process of interpreting or explaining; elucidation. **2.** the result of interpreting; an explanation. **3.** a particular view of an artistic work, esp. as expressed by stylistic individuality in its performance. **4.** explanation, as of a historical site, provided by the use of original objects, visual display material, etc. —**inˌterpreˈtational** *adj.*

interpreter (ɪnˈtɜːprɪtə) *n.* **1.** a person who translates orally from one language into another. **2.** a person who interprets the work of others. **3.** *Computers.* a program that translates a statement in a source program to machine code and executes it before translating and executing the next statement. —**inˈterpretership** *n.* —**inˈterpretress** *fem. n.*

interpretive centre *n.* (at a historical site, etc.) a building that provides interpretation of the site through a variety of media, such as video displays and exhibitions, and, often, includes facilities such as refreshment rooms.

interregnum (ˌɪntəˈrɛgnəm) *n., pl.* **-nums** *or* **-na** (-nə). **1.** an interval between two reigns, governments, etc. **2.** any period in which a state lacks a ruler, government, etc. **3.** a period of absence of some control, authority, etc. **4.** a gap in a continuity. [C16: < L, < INTER- + *regnum* REIGN] —ˌ**interˈregnal** *adj.*

ˌ**interˈnuclear** *adj.*
ˌ**interˈoffice** *adj.*
ˌ**interˈplait** *vb.*
ˌ**interˈplanetary** *adj.*
ˌ**interˈpolar** *adj.*
ˌ**interproˈfessional** *adj.*
ˌ**interproˈvincial** *adj.*
ˌ**interˈracial** *adj.*
ˌ**interˈregional** *adj.*

interrelate (ˌɪntərɪˈleɪt) *vb.* to place in or come into a mutual or reciprocal relationship. —ˌ**interreˈlation** *n.* —ˌ**interreˈlationˌship** *n.*

interrogate (ɪnˈtɛrəˌgeɪt) *vb.* to ask questions (of), esp. to question (a witness in court, spy, etc.) closely. [C15: < L *interrogāre,* < *rogāre* to ask] —**inˈterroˌgator** *n.*

interrogation (ɪnˌtɛrəˈgeɪʃən) *n.* **1.** the technique, practice, or an instance of interrogating. **2.** a question or query. **3.** *Telecomm.* the transmission of one or more triggering pulses to a transponder. —**inˌterroˈgational** *adj.*

interrogation mark *n.* a less common term for **question mark.**

interrogative (ˌɪntəˈrɒgətɪv) *adj.* **1.** asking or having the nature of a question. **2.** denoting a form or construction used in asking a question. **3.** denoting or belonging to a class of words, such as *which* and *whom,* that serve to question which individual referent is intended. ~*n.* **4.** an interrogative word, phrase, sentence, or construction. **5.** a question mark. —ˌ**interˈrogatively** *adv.*

interrogatory (ˌɪntəˈrɒgətərɪ, -trɪ) *adj.* **1.** expressing or involving a question. ~*n., pl.* **-tories. 2.** a question or interrogation.

interrupt (ˌɪntəˈrʌpt) *vb.* **1.** to break the continuity of (an action, event, etc.) or hinder (a person) by intrusion. **2.** (*tr.*) to cease to perform (some action). **3.** (*tr.*) to obstruct (a view, etc.). **4.** to prevent or disturb (a conversation, discussion, etc.) by questions, interjections, or comment. [C15: < L *interrumpere,* < INTER- + *rumpere* to break] —ˌ**interˈruptible** *adj.* —ˌ**interˈruptive** *adj.* —ˌ**interˈruptively** *adv.* —ˌ**interˈrupted** *adj.*

interrupted screw *n.* a screw with a slot cut into the thread, esp. one used in the breech of some guns permitting both engagement and release of the block by a partial turn of the screw.

interrupter *or* **interruptor** (ˌɪntəˈrʌptə) *n.* **1.** a person or thing that interrupts. **2.** an electromechanical device for opening and closing an electric circuit.

interruption (ˌɪntəˈrʌpʃən) *n.* **1.** something that interrupts, such as a comment, question, or action. **2.** an interval or intermission. **3.** the act of interrupting or the state of being interrupted.

interscholastic (ˌɪntəskəˈlæstɪk) *adj.* **1.** (of sports events, competitions, etc.) occurring between two or more schools. **2.** representative of various schools.

intersect (ˌɪntəˈsɛkt) *vb.* **1.** to divide, cut, or mark off by passing through or across. **2.** (esp. of roads) to cross (each other). **3.** *Maths.* (often foll. by *with*) to have one or more points in common (with another configuration). [C17: < L *intersecāre* to divide, < INTER- + *secāre* to cut]

intersection (ˌɪntəˈsɛkʃən, ˈɪntəˌsɛk-) *n.* **1.** a point at which things intersect, esp. a road junction. **2.** the act of intersecting or the state of being intersected. **3.** *Maths.* **a.** a point or set of points common to two or more geometric configurations. **b.** Also called: **product.** the set of elements that are common to two sets. **c.** the operation that yields that set from a pair of given sets. —ˌ**interˈsectional** *adj.*

intersex (ˈɪntəˌsɛks) *n. Zool.* an individual with characteristics intermediate between those of a male and a female.

intersexual (ˌɪntəˈsɛksjʊəl) *adj.* **1.** occurring or existing between the sexes. **2.** relating to or being an intersex. —ˌ**interˌsexuˈality** *n.* —ˌ**interˈ sexually** *adv.*

interspace *vb.* (ˌɪntəˈspeɪs). **1.** (*tr.*) to make or occupy a space between. ~*n.* (ˈɪntəˌspeɪs). **2.** space between or among things. —**interspatial** (ˌɪntəˈspeɪʃəl) *adj.* —ˌ**interˈspatially** *adv.*

intersperse (ˌɪntəˈspɜːs) *vb.* (*tr.*) **1.** to scatter or distribute among, between, or on. **2.** to diversify (something) with other things scattered here and there. [C16: < L *interspargere,* < INTER- + *spargere* to sprinkle] —**interspersedly** (ˌɪntəˈspɜːsɪdlɪ) *adv.* —**interspersion** (ˌɪntəˈspɜːʃən) *or* ˌ**interˈspersal** *n.*

interstice (ɪnˈtɜːstɪs) *n.* (*usually pl.*) **1.** a minute opening or crevice between things. **2.** *Physics.* the space between adjacent atoms in a crystal lattice. [C17: < L *interstitium* interval, < *intersistere,* < INTER- + *sistere* to stand]

interstitial (ˌɪntəˈstɪʃəl) *adj.* **1.** of or relating to an interstice or interstices. **2.** *Physics.* forming or occurring in an interstice: *an interstitial atom.* **3.** *Anat., zool.* occurring in the spaces between organs, tissues, etc.: *interstitial cells.* ~*n.* **4.** *Chem.* an atom or ion situated in the interstices of a crystal lattice. —ˌ**interˈstitially** *adv.*

intertrigo (ˌɪntəˈtraɪgəʊ) *n.* chafing between two skin surfaces, as at the armpit. [C18: < INTER- + *-trigo,* < L *terere* to rub]

interval (ˈɪntəvəl) *n.* **1.** the period of time between two events, instants, etc. **2.** the distance between two points, objects, etc. **3.** a pause or interlude, as between periods of intense activity. **4.** *Brit.* a short period between parts of a play, etc.; intermission. **5.** *Music.* the difference of pitch between two notes, either sounded simultaneously or in succession as in a musical part. **6.** the ratio of the frequencies of two sounds. **7. at intervals. a.** occasionally or intermittently. **b.** with spaces between. [C13: < L *intervallum,* lit.: space between two palisades, < INTER- + *vallum* palisade] —**intervallic** (ˌɪntəˈvælɪk) *adj.*

intervene (ˌɪntəˈviːn) *vb.* (*intr.*) **1.** (often foll. by *in*) to take a decisive or intrusive role (in) in order to determine events. **2.** (foll. by *in* or *between*) to come or be (among or between). **3.** (of a period of time) to occur between events or points in time. **4.** (of an event) to disturb or hinder a course of action. **5.** *Econ.* to take action to affect the market forces of an economy, esp. to maintain the stability of a currency. **6.** *Law.* to interpose and become a party to a legal action between others, esp. in order to protect one's interests. [C16: < L *intervenīre* to come between] —ˌ**interˈvener** *or* ˌ**interˈvenor** *n.*

intervention (ˌɪntəˈvɛnʃən) *n.* **1.** an act of intervening. **2.** any interference in the affairs of others, esp. by one state in the affairs of another. **3.** *Econ.* the action of a central bank in supporting the international value of a currency by buying large quantities of the currency to keep the price up. **4.** *Commerce.* the action of the EEC in buying up surplus produce when the market price drops to a certain value.

interventionist (ˌɪntəˈvɛnʃənɪst) *adj.* **1.** of, relating to, or advocating intervention, esp. in order to achieve a policy objective. ~*n.* **2.** a person or state that pursues a policy of intervention.

intervertebral disc (ˌɪntəˈvɜːtɪbrəl) *n.* any of the cartilaginous discs between individual vertebrae, acting as shock absorbers.

interview (ˈɪntəˌvjuː) *n.* **1.** a conversation with or questioning of a person, usually conducted for television or a newspaper. **2.** a formal discussion, esp. one in which an employer assesses a job applicant. ~*vb.* **3.** to conduct an interview with (someone). [C16: < OF *entrevue*] —ˌ**interviewˈee** *n.* —ˈ**interˌviewer** *n.*

intestate (ɪnˈtɛsteɪt, -tɪt) *adj.* **1. a.** (of a person) not having made a will. **b.** (of property) not disposed of by will. ~*n.* **2.** a person who dies

ˌ**interreˈligious** *adj.*
ˌ**interˈschool** *adj.*
ˌ**intersoˈcietal** *adj.*
ˌ**interˈspinal** *adj.*
ˌ**interˈstellar** *adj.*
ˌ**interˌterriˈtorial** *adj.*
ˌ**interˈtribal** *adj.*
ˌ**interˈtropical** *adj.*
ˌ**interˈtwine** *vb.*
ˌ**interˌuniˈversity** *adj.*
ˌ**interˈurban** *adj.*
ˌ**interˈvarsity** *adj.*
ˌ**interˈvertebral** *adj.*
ˌ**interˈwar** *adj.*
ˌ**interˈweave** *vb.*
ˌ**interˈwind** *vb.*
ˌ**interˈwrought** *adj.*

without having made a will. [C14: < L *intestātus*, < IN-[1] + *testārī* to bear witness, make a will, < *testis* a witness] —**in'testacy** *n.*

intestine (ɪn'tɛstɪn) *n.* the part of the alimentary canal between the stomach and the anus. See **large intestine, small intestine.** [C16: < L *intestīnum* gut, < *intestīnus* internal, < *intus* within] —**intestinal** (ɪn'tɛstɪn°l, ˌɪntɛs'taɪn°l) *adj.*

intimacy ('ɪntɪməsɪ) *n., pl.* **-cies.** **1.** close or warm friendship or understanding; personal relationship. **2.** (*often pl.*) *Euphemistic.* sexual relations.

intimate[1] ('ɪntɪmɪt) *adj.* **1.** characterized by a close or warm personal relationship: *an intimate friend.* **2.** deeply personal, private, or secret. **3.** (*often postpositive;* foll. by *with*) *Euphemistic.* having sexual relations (with). **4.** (*postpositive;* foll. by *with*) having a deep or unusual knowledge (of). **5.** having a friendly, warm, or informal atmosphere: *an intimate nightclub.* **6.** of or relating to the essential part or nature of something; intrinsic. ~*n.* **7.** a close friend. [C17: < L *intimus* very close friend, < (adj.): innermost, < *intus* within] —**'intimately** *adv.* —**'intimateness** *n.*

intimate[2] ('ɪntɪˌmeɪt) *vb.* (*tr.; may take a clause as object*) **1.** to hint; suggest. **2.** to proclaim; make known. [C16: < LL *intimāre* to proclaim, < L *intimus* innermost] —**'intiˌmater** *n.* —**ˌinti'mation** *n.*

intimidate (ɪn'tɪmɪˌdeɪt) *vb.* (*tr.*) **1.** to make timid or frightened; scare. **2.** to discourage, restrain, or silence unscrupulously, as by threats. [C17: < Med. L *intimidāre,* < L IN-[2] + *timidus* fearful, < *timor* fear] —**ˌin'timiˌdating** *adj.* —**inˌtimi'dation** *n.* —**in'timiˌdator** *n.*

intinction (ɪn'tɪŋkʃən) *n. Christianity.* the practice of dipping the Eucharistic bread into the wine at Holy Communion. [C16: < LL *intinctiō* a dipping in, < L *intingere,* < *tingere* to dip]

intitule (ɪn'tɪtjuːl) *vb.* (*tr.*) *Parliamentary procedure.* (in Britain) to entitle (an Act). [C15: < OF *intituler,* < L *titulus* TITLE]

intl *abbrev. for* international.

into ('ɪntuː; *unstressed* 'ɪntə) *prep.* **1.** to the interior or inner parts of: *to look into a case.* **2.** to the middle or midst of so as to be surrounded by: *into the bushes.* **3.** against; up against: *he drove into a wall.* **4.** used to indicate the result of a change: *he changed into a monster.* **5.** *Maths.* used to indicate a dividend: *three into six is two.* **6.** *Inf.* interested or enthusiastically involved in: *I'm really into Freud.*

intonation (ˌɪntəʊ'neɪʃən) *n.* **1.** the sound pattern of phrases and sentences produced by pitch variation in the voice. **2.** the act or manner of intoning. **3.** an intoned, chanted, or monotonous utterance; incantation. **4.** *Music.* the opening of a piece of plainsong, sung by a soloist. **5.** *Music.* the capacity to play or sing in tune. —**ˌinto'national** *adj.*

intone (ɪn'təʊn) *or* **intonate** *vb.* **1.** to utter, recite, or sing (a chant, prayer, etc.) in a monotonous or incantatory tone. **2.** (*intr.*) to speak with a particular or characteristic intonation or tone. **3.** to sing (the opening phrase of a psalm, etc.) in plainsong. [C15: < Med. L *intonare,* < IN-[2] + TONE] —**in'toner** *n.*

in toto *Latin.* (ɪn 'təʊtəʊ) *adv.* totally; entirely.

intoxicant (ɪn'tɒksɪkənt) *n.* **1.** anything that causes intoxication. ~*adj.* **2.** causing intoxication.

intoxicate (ɪn'tɒksɪˌkeɪt) *vb.* (*tr.*) **1.** (of an alcoholic drink) to produce in (a person) a state ranging from euphoria to stupor; make drunk; inebriate. **2.** to stimulate, excite, or elate so as to overwhelm. **3.** (of a drug, etc.) to poison. [C16: < Med. L, < *intoxicāre* to poison, < L *toxicum* poison; see TOXIC] —**in'toxicable** *adj.* —**in'toxiˌcating** *adj.* —**in'toxiˌcatingly** *adv.*

intoxication (ɪnˌtɒksɪ'keɪʃən) *n.* **1.** drunkenness; inebriation. **2.** great elation. **3.** the act of intoxicating. **4.** poisoning.

intr. *abbrev. for* intransitive.

intra- *prefix.* within; inside: *intrastate; intravenous.* [< L *intrā* within; see INTERIOR]

intractable (ɪn'træktəb°l) *adj.* **1.** difficult to influence or direct: *an intractable disposition.* **2.** (of a problem, illness, etc.) difficult to solve, alleviate, or cure. —**inˌtracta'bility** *or* **in'tractableness** *n.* —**in'tractably** *adv.*

intrados (ɪn'treɪdɒs) *n., pl.* **-dos** *or* **-doses.** *Archit.* the inner curve or surface of an arch. [C18: < F, < INTRA- + *dos* back, < L *dorsum*]

intramural (ˌɪntrə'mjʊərəl) *adj. Education, chiefly U.S. & Canad.* operating within or involving those in a single establishment. —**ˌintra'murally** *adv.*

intrans. *abbrev. for* intransitive.

intransigent (ɪn'trænsɪdʒənt) *adj.* **1.** not willing to compromise; obstinately maintaining an attitude. ~*n.* **2.** an intransigent person, esp. in politics. [C19: < Sp. *los intransigentes* the uncompromising (ones), a name adopted by certain political extremists, < IN-[1] + *transigir* to compromise, < L *transigere* to settle; see TRANSACT] —**in'transigence** *or* **in'transigency** *n.* —**in'transigently** *adv.*

intransitive (ɪn'trænsɪtɪv) *adj.* **1. a.** denoting a verb that does not require a direct object. **b.** (*as n.*) such a verb. **2.** denoting an adjective or noun that does not require any particular noun phrase as a referent. **3.** having the property that if it holds between one argument and a second, and between the second and a third, it must fail to hold between the first and third: *"being the mother of" is an intransitive relation.* ~Cf. **transitive.** —**in'transitively** *adv.* —**inˌtransi'tivity** *or* **in'transitiveness** *n.*

intrapreneur (ˌɪntrəprə'nɜː) *n.* a person who while remaining within a larger organization uses entrepreneurial skills to develop a new product or line of business as a subsidiary of the organization.

intrauterine (ˌɪntrə'juːtəraɪn) *adj.* within the womb.

intrauterine device *n.* a metal or plastic device, in the shape of a loop, coil, or ring, inserted into the uterus to prevent conception. Abbrev.: **IUD.**

intravenous (ˌɪntrə'viːnəs) *adj. Anat.* within a vein: *an intravenous injection.* Abbrev. (esp. of an injection): **IV, i.v.** —**ˌintra'venously** *adv.*

in-tray *n.* a tray for incoming papers, etc., requiring attention.

intrench (ɪn'trɛntʃ) *vb.* a less common spelling of **entrench.** —**in'trencher** *n.* —**in'trenchment** *n.*

intrepid (ɪn'trɛpɪd) *adj.* fearless; daring; bold. [C17: < L *intrepidus,* < IN-[1] + *trepidus* fearful] —**ˌintre'pidity** *n.* —**in'trepidly** *adv.*

intricate ('ɪntrɪkɪt) *adj.* **1.** difficult to understand; obscure; complex; puzzling. **2.** entangled or involved: *intricate patterns.* [C15: < L *intrīcāre* to entangle, perplex, < IN-[2] + *trīcae* trifles, perplexities] —**'intricacy** *or* **'intricateness** *n.* —**'intricately** *adv.*

intrigue *vb.* (ɪn'triːg), **-triguing, -trigued.** **1.** (*tr.*) to make interested or curious. **2.** (*intr.*) to make secret plots or employ underhand methods; conspire. **3.** (*intr.;* often foll. by *with*) to carry on a clandestine love affair. ~*n.* (ɪn'triːg, 'ɪntriːg). **4.** the act or an instance of secret plotting, etc. **5.** a clandestine love affair. **6.** the quality of arousing interest or curiosity; beguilement. [C17: < F *intriguer,* < It., < L *intrīcāre;* see INTRICATE] —**in'triguer** *n.* —**in'triguingly** *adv.*

intrinsic (ɪn'trɪnsɪk) *or* **intrinsical** *adj.* **1.** of or relating to the essential nature of a thing; inherent. **2.** *Anat.* situated within or peculiar to a part: *intrinsic muscles.* [C15: < LL *intrinsecus* < L, inwardly, < *intrā* within + *secus* alongside] —**in'trinsically** *adv.*

intro ('ɪntrəʊ) *n., pl.* **-tros.** *Inf.* short for **introduction.**

in'tolerable *adj.* **in'tolerance** *n.* **in'tolerant** *adj.*

intro. *or* **introd.** *abbrev. for:* **1.** introduction. **2.** introductory.

intro- *prefix.* in, into, or inward: *introvert.* [< L *intrō* inwardly, within]

introduce (ˌɪntrəˈdjuːs) *vb.* (*tr.*) **1.** (often foll. by *to*) to present (someone) by name (to another person). **2.** (foll. by *to*) to cause to experience for the first time: *to introduce a visitor to beer.* **3.** to present for consideration or approval, esp. before a legislative body: *to introduce a bill in parliament.* **4.** to bring in; establish: *to introduce decimal currency.* **5.** to present (a radio or television programme, etc.) verbally. **6.** (foll. by *with*) to start: *he introduced his talk with some music.* **7.** (often foll. by *into*) to insert or inject: *he introduced the needle into his arm.* **8.** to place (members of a plant or animal species) in a new environment with the intention of producing a resident breeding population. [C16: < L *intrōdūcere* to bring inside] —ˌ**introˈducer** *n.* —ˌ**introˈducible** *adj.*

introduction (ˌɪntrəˈdʌkʃən) *n.* **1.** the act of introducing or fact of being introduced. **2.** a presentation of one person to another or others. **3.** a means of presenting a person to another person, such as a letter of introduction or reference. **4.** a preliminary part, as of a book. **5.** *Music.* an opening passage in a movement or composition that precedes the main material. **6.** a basic or elementary work of instruction, reference, etc.

introductory (ˌɪntrəˈdʌktərɪ, -trɪ) *adj.* serving as an introduction; preliminary; prefatory.

introit (ˈɪntrɔɪt) *n. R.C. Church, Church of England.* a short prayer said or sung as the celebrant is entering the sanctuary to celebrate Mass or Holy Communion. [C15: < Church L *introitus* introit, < L: entrance, < *introīre* to go in] —**inˈtroital** *adj.*

intromit (ˌɪntrəˈmɪt) *vb.* **-mitting, -mitted.** (*tr.*) *Rare.* to enter or insert. [C15: < L *intrōmittere* to send in] —ˌ**introˈmissible** *adj.* —ˌ**introˈmission** *n.* —ˌ**introˈmittent** *adj.*

introspection (ˌɪntrəˈspɛkʃən) *n.* the examination of one's own thoughts, impressions, and feelings. [C17: < L *intrōspicere* to look within] —ˌ**introˈspective** *adj.* —ˌ**introˈspectively** *adv.*

introversion (ˌɪntrəˈvɜːʃən) *n. Psychol.* the directing of interest inwards towards one's own thoughts and feelings rather than towards the external world or making social contacts. —ˌ**introˈversive** *or* ˌ**introˈvertive** *adj.*

introvert *n.* (ˈɪntrəˌvɜːt). **1.** *Psychol.* a person prone to introversion. ~*adj.* (ˈɪntrəˌvɜːt). **2.** Also: **introverted.** characterized by introversion. ~*vb.* (ˌɪntrəˈvɜːt). **3.** (*tr.*) *Pathol.* to turn (a hollow organ or part) inside out. [C17: see INTRO-, INVERT]

intrude (ɪnˈtruːd) *vb.* **1.** (often foll. by *into, on,* or *upon*) to put forward or interpose (oneself, one's views, something) abruptly or without invitation. **2.** *Geol.* to force or thrust (molten magma) between solid rocks. [C16: < L *intrūdere* to thrust in] —**inˈtruder** *n.* —**inˈtrudingly** *adv.*

intrusion (ɪnˈtruːʒən) *n.* **1.** the act or an instance of intruding; an unwelcome visit, etc.: *an intrusion on one's privacy.* **2. a.** the movement of magma into spaces in the overlying strata to form igneous rock. **b.** any igneous rock formed in this way. **3.** *Property law.* an unlawful entry onto land by a stranger after determination of a particular estate of freehold. —**inˈtrusional** *adj.*

intrusive (ɪnˈtruːsɪv) *adj.* **1.** characterized by intrusion or tending to intrude. **2.** (of igneous rocks) formed by intrusion. **3.** *Phonetics.* relating to or denoting a speech sound that is introduced into a word or piece of connected speech for a phonetic reason. —**inˈtrusively** *adv.* —**inˈtrusiveness** *n.*

intrust (ɪnˈtrʌst) *vb.* a less common spelling of **entrust.**

intubate (ˈɪntjʊˌbeɪt) *vb.* (*tr.*) *Med.* to insert a tube into (a hollow organ). —ˌ**intuˈbation** *n.*

intuit (ɪnˈtjuːɪt) *vb.* to know or discover by intuition. —**inˈtuitable** *adj.*

intuition (ˌɪntjʊˈɪʃən) *n.* **1.** knowledge or belief obtained neither by reason nor perception. **2.** instinctive knowledge or belief. **3.** a hunch or unjustified belief. [C15: < LL *intuitiō* a contemplation, < L *intuērī* to gaze upon, < *tuērī* to look at] —ˌ**intuˈitional** *adj.* —ˌ**intuˈitionally** *adv.*

intuitionism (ˌɪntjʊˈɪʃəˌnɪzəm) *or* **intuitionalism** *n. Philosophy.* **1.** the doctrine that knowledge is acquired primarily by intuition. **2.** the theory that the solution to moral problems can be discovered by intuition. **3.** the doctrine that external objects are known to be real by intuition. —ˌ**intuˈitionist** *or* ˌ**intuˈitionalist** *n.*

intuitive (ɪnˈtjuːɪtɪv) *adj.* **1.** resulting from intuition: *an intuitive awareness.* **2.** of, characterized by, or involving intuition. —**inˈtuitively** *adv.* —**inˈtuitiveness** *n.*

intumesce (ˌɪntjʊˈmɛs) *vb.* (*intr.*) to swell. [C18: < L *intumescere,* < *tumescere* to begin to swell, < *tumēre* to swell] —ˌ**intuˈmescence** *n.*

intussusception (ˌɪntəssəˈsɛpʃən) *n.* **1.** *Pathol.* the telescoping of one section of the intestinal tract into a lower section. **2.** *Biol.* growth in the surface area of a cell by the deposition of new particles between the existing particles of the cell wall. [C18: < L *intus* within + *susceptiō* a taking up]

Inuit *or* **Innuit** (ˈɪnjuːɪt) *n., pl.* **-it** *or* **-its.** an Eskimo of North America or Greenland, as distinguished from one from Asia or the Aleuts. [< Eskimo *inuit* people, pl. of *inuk* a man]

Inuktitut (ɪˈnʊktəˌtʊt) *n. Canad.* the language of the Inuit; Eskimo. [< Eskimo *inuk* man + *titut* speech]

inunction (ɪnˈʌŋkʃən) *n.* **1.** the application of an ointment to the skin, esp. by rubbing. **2.** the ointment so used. **3.** the act of anointing; anointment. [C15: < L *inunguere* to anoint, < *unguere;* see UNCTION]

inundate (ˈɪnʌnˌdeɪt) *vb.* (*tr.*) **1.** to cover completely with water; overflow; flood; swamp. **2.** to overwhelm, as if with a flood: *to be inundated with requests.* [C17: < L *inundāre,* < *unda* wave] —ˈ**inundant** *or* **inˈundatory** *adj.* —ˌ**inunˈdation** *n.* —ˈ**inunˌdator** *n.*

inure *or* **enure** (ɪˈnjʊə) *vb.* **1.** (*tr.; often passive;* often foll. by *to*) to cause to accept or become hardened to; habituate. **2.** (*intr.*) (esp. of a law, etc.) to come into operation; take effect. [C15 *enuren* to accustom, < *ure* use, < OF *euvre* custom, work, < L *opera* works] —**inˈurement** *or* **enˈurement** *n.*

inv. *abbrev. for:* **1.** invented. **2.** inventor. **3.** invoice.

in vacuo *Latin.* (ɪn ˈvækjʊˌəʊ) *adv.* in a vacuum.

invade (ɪnˈveɪd) *vb.* **1.** to enter (a country, territory, etc.) by military force. **2.** (*tr.*) to occupy in large numbers; overrun; infest. **3.** (*tr.*) to trespass or encroach upon (privacy, etc.). **4.** (*tr.*) to enter and spread throughout, esp. harmfully; pervade. [C15: < L *invādere,* < *vādere* to go] —**inˈvadable** *adj.* —**inˈvader** *n.*

invaginate *vb.* (ɪnˈvædʒɪˌneɪt). **1.** *Pathol.* to push one section of (a tubular organ or part) back into itself so that it becomes ensheathed. **2.** (*intr.*) (of the outer layer of an organism or part) to undergo this process. ~*adj.* (ɪnˈvædʒɪnɪt, -ˌneɪt). **3.** (of an organ or part) folded back upon itself. [C19: < Med. L *invāgīnāre,* < L IN-[2] + *vāgīna* sheath] —**inˈvaginable** *adj.* —**inˌvagiˈnation** *n.*

invalid[1] (ˈɪnvəˌliːd, -lɪd) *n.* **1. a.** a person suffering from disablement or chronic ill health. **b.** (*as modifier*): *an invalid chair.* ~*adj.* **2.** suffering from or disabled by injury, sickness, etc. ~*vb.* (*tr.*) **3.** to cause to become an invalid; disable. **4.** (*often passive* usually foll. by *out*); *Chiefly Brit.* to require (a member of the armed forces) to retire from active service through wounds or illness. [C17: < L *invalidus* infirm, < IN-[1] + *validus* strong] —**invalidity** (ˌɪnvəˈlɪdɪtɪ) *n.*

invalid[2] (ɪnˈvælɪd) *adj.* **1.** not valid; having no cogency or legal force. **2.** *Logic.* (of an argument) having a conclusion that does not follow from the premises. [C16: < Med. L *invalidus* without legal force; see INVALID[1]] —ˌ**invaˈlidity** *or* **inˈvalidness** *n.* —**inˈvalidly** *adv.*

invalidate (ɪnˈvælɪˌdeɪt) *vb.* (*tr.*) **1.** to render weak or ineffective (an argument). **2.** to take away the legal force or effectiveness of; annul (a contract). —**inˌvaliˈdation** *n.* —**inˈvaliˌdator** *n.*

invaluable (ɪnˈvæljʊəbᵊl) *adj.* having great value that is impossible to calculate; priceless. —**inˈvaluableness** *n.* —**inˈvaluably** *adv.*

Invar (ɪnˈvɑː) *n. Trademark.* an alloy containing iron, nickel, and carbon. It has a very low coefficient of expansion and is used for the balance springs of watches, etc. [C20: shortened < INVARIABLE]

invariable (ɪnˈvɛərɪəbᵊl) *adj.* **1.** not subject to alteration; unchanging. ~*n.* **2.** a mathematical quantity having an unchanging value; a constant. —**inˌvariaˈbility** *or* **inˈvariableness** *n.* —**inˈvariably** *adv.*

invariant (ɪnˈvɛərɪənt) *Maths.* ~*n.* **1.** an entity, quantity, etc., that is unaltered by a particular transformation of coordinates. ~*adj.* **2.** (of a relationship or a property of a function, configuration, or equation) unaltered by a particular transformation of coordinates. —**inˈvariance** *or* **inˈvariancy** *n.*

invasion (ɪnˈveɪʒən) *n.* **1.** the act of invading with armed forces. **2.** any encroachment or intrusion: *an invasion of rats.* **3.** the onset or advent of something harmful, esp. of a disease. **4.** the movement of plants to an area to which they are not native. —**invasive** (ɪnˈveɪsɪv) *adj.*

invective (ɪnˈvɛktɪv) *n.* **1.** vehement accusation or denunciation, esp. of a bitterly abusive or sarcastic kind. ~*adj.* **2.** characterized by or using abusive language, bitter sarcasm, etc. [C15: < LL *invectīvus* reproachful, < L *invectus* carried in; see INVEIGH] —**inˈvectively** *adv.* —**inˈvectiveness** *n.*

inveigh (ɪnˈveɪ) *vb.* (*intr.*; foll. by *against*) to speak with violent or invective language; rail. [C15: < L *invehī*, lit.: to be carried in, hence, assail physically or verbally] —**inˈveigher** *n.*

inveigle (ɪnˈviːgᵊl, -ˈveɪ-) *vb.* (*tr.*; often foll. by *into* or an infinitive) to lead (someone into a situation) or persuade (to do something) by cleverness or trickery; cajole. [C15: < OF *avogler* to blind, deceive, < *avogle* blind, < Med. L *ab oculis* without eyes] —**inˈveiglement** *n.* —**inˈveigler** *n.*

invent (ɪnˈvɛnt) *vb.* **1.** to create or devise (new ideas, machines, etc.). **2.** to make up (falsehoods, etc.); fabricate. [C15: < L *invenīre* to find, come upon] —**inˈventable** *adj.*

invention (ɪnˈvɛnʃən) *n.* **1.** the act or process of inventing. **2.** something that is invented. **3.** *Patent law.* the discovery or production of some new or improved process or machine. **4.** creative power or ability; inventive skill. **5.** *Euphemistic.* a fabrication; lie. **6.** *Music.* a short piece consisting of two or three parts usually in imitative counterpoint. —**inˈventional** *adj.* —**inˈventionless** *adj.*

inventive (ɪnˈvɛntɪv) *adj.* **1.** skilled or quick at contriving; ingenious; resourceful. **2.** characterized by inventive skill: *an inventive programme of work.* **3.** of or relating to invention. —**inˈventively** *adv.* —**inˈventiveness** *n.*

inventor (ɪnˈvɛntə) *n.* a person who invents, esp. as a profession. —**inˈventress** *fem. n.*

inventory (ˈɪnvəntərɪ, -trɪ) *n., pl.* **-tories.** **1.** a detailed list of articles, goods, property, etc. **2.** (*often pl.*) *Accounting, chiefly U.S.* **a.** the amount or value of a firm's current assets that consist of raw materials, work in progress, and finished goods; stock. **b.** such assets individually. ~*vb.* **-torying, -toried.** **3.** (*tr.*) to enter (items) in an inventory; make a list of. [C16: < Med. L *inventōrium*; see INVENT] —ˈ**inventoriable** *adj.* —ˌ**invenˈtorial** *adj.* —ˌ**invenˈtorially** *adv.*

Inverness (ˌɪnvəˈnɛs) *n.* (*sometimes not cap.*) an overcoat with a removable cape. [C19: after *Inverness*, town in NE Scotland]

inverse (ɪnˈvɜːs, ˈɪnvɜːs) *adj.* **1.** opposite or contrary in effect, sequence, direction, etc. **2.** *Maths.* **a.** (of a relationship) containing two variables such that an increase in one results in a decrease in the other. **b.** (of an element) operating on a specified member of a set to produce the identity of the set: *the additive inverse element of x is -x.* **3.** (*usually prenominal*) upside-down; inverted: *in an inverse position.* ~*n.* **4.** *Maths.* an inverse element. [C17: < L *inversus*, < *invertere* to INVERT] —**inˈversely** *adv.*

inverse function *n.* a function whose independent variable is the dependent variable of a given trigonometric or hyperbolic function: *the inverse function of* sin *x is* arcsin *y* (*also written* $\sin^{-1}y$).

inversion (ɪnˈvɜːʃən) *n.* **1.** the act of inverting or state of being inverted. **2.** something inverted, esp. a reversal of order, mutual functions, etc.: *an inversion of their previous relationship.* **3.** Also: **anastrophe.** *Rhetoric.* the reversal of a normal order of words. **4.** *Chem.* **a.** the conversion of a dextrorotatory solution of sucrose into a laevorotatory solution of glucose and fructose by hydrolysis. **b.** any similar reaction in which the optical properties of the reactants are opposite to those of the products. **5.** *Music.* **a.** the process or result of transposing the notes of a chord such that the root, originally in the bass, is placed in an upper part. **b.** the modification of an interval in which the higher note becomes the lower or the lower one the higher. **6.** *Pathol.* abnormal positioning of an organ or part, as in being upside down or turned inside out. **7.** *Psychiatry.* **a.** the adoption of the role or characteristics of the opposite sex. **b.** another word for **homosexuality.** **8.** *Meteorol.* an abnormal condition in which the layer of air next to the earth's surface is cooler than an overlying layer. **9.** *Computers.* an operation by which each digit of a binary number is changed to the alternative digit, as *10110* to *01001.* —**inˈversive** *adj.*

invert *vb.* (ɪnˈvɜːt). **1.** to turn or cause to turn upside down or inside out. **2.** (*tr.*) to reverse in effect, sequence, direction, etc. **3.** (*tr.*) *Phonetics.* to turn (the tip of the tongue) up and back to pronounce (a speech sound). ~*n.* (ˈɪnvɜːt). **4.** *Psychiatry.* **a.** a person who adopts the role of the opposite sex. **b.** another word for **homosexual.** **5.** *Archit.* **a.** the lower inner surface of a drain, sewer, etc. **b.** an arch that is concave upwards, esp. one used in foundations. [C16: < L *invertere*, < IN-[2] + *vertere* to turn] —**inˈvertible** *adj.* —**inˌvertiˈbility** *n.*

invertase (ɪnˈvɜːteɪz) *n.* an enzyme, occurring in the intestinal juice of animals and in yeasts, that hydrolyses sucrose to glucose and fructose.

invertebrate (ɪnˈvɜːtɪbrɪt, -ˌbreɪt) *n.* **1.** any animal lacking a backbone, including all species not classified as vertebrates. ~*adj. also* **invertebral.** **2.** of, relating to, or designating invertebrates.

inverted comma *n.* another term for **quotation mark.**

inverted mordent *n. Music.* a melodic ornament consisting of the rapid alternation of a principal note with a note one degree higher.

inverter *or* **invertor** (ɪnˈvɜːtə) *n.* any device for converting a direct current into an alternating current.

invert sugar *n.* a mixture of fructose and glucose obtained by the inversion of sucrose.

invest (ɪnˈvɛst) *vb.* **1.** (often foll. by *in*) to lay out (money or capital in an enterprise) with the expectation of profit. **2.** (*tr.*; often foll. by *in*) to devote (effort, resources, etc., to a project). **3.** (*tr.*; often foll. by *in* or *with*) *Arch. or ceremonial.* to clothe or adorn (in some garment, esp. the robes of an office). **4.** (*tr.*; often foll. by *in*) to install formally or ceremoniously (in an official

---

ˌ**inveˈracity** *n.*

position, rank, etc.). **5.** (*tr.;* foll. by *in* or *with*) to place (power, authority, etc., in) or provide (with power or authority): *to invest new rights in the monarchy.* **6.** (*tr.; usually passive;* foll. by *in* or *with*) to provide or endow (a person with qualities, characteristics, etc.). **7.** (*tr.;* foll. by *with*) *Usually poetic.* to cover or adorn, as if with a coat or garment: *when spring invests the trees with leaves.* **8.** (*tr.*) *Rare.* to surround with military forces; besiege. **9.** (*intr.;* foll. by *in*) *Inf.* to purchase; buy. [C16: < Med. L *investīre* to clothe, < L, < *vestīre,* < *vestis* a garment] —**in'vestable** *or* **in'vestible** *adj.* —**in'vestor** *n.*

investigate (ɪn'vɛstɪˌgeɪt) *vb.* to inquire into (a situation or problem, esp. a crime or death) thoroughly; examine systematically, esp. in order to discover the truth. [C16: < L *investīgāre* to search after, < IN-[2] + *vestīgium* track; see VESTIGE] —**in'vestiˌgative** *or* **in'vestigatory** *adj.* —**in'vestiˌgator** *n.*

investigation (ɪnˌvɛstɪ'geɪʃən) *n.* the act or process of investigating; a careful search or examination in order to discover facts, etc.

investiture (ɪn'vɛstɪtʃə) *n.* **1.** the act of presenting with a title or with the robes and insignia of an office or rank. **2.** (in feudal society) the formal bestowal of the possessory right to a fief. —**in'vestitive** *adj.*

investment (ɪn'vɛstmənt) *n.* **1. a.** the act of investing money. **b.** the amount invested. **c.** an enterprise, asset, etc., in which money is or can be invested. **2. a.** the act of investing effort, resources, etc. **b.** the amount invested. **3.** *Biol.* the outer layer or covering of an organ, part, or organism. **4.** a less common word for **investiture** (sense 1). **5.** the act of investing or state of being invested, as with an official robe, specific quality, etc. **6.** *Rare.* the act of besieging with military forces, works, etc.

investment trust *n.* a financial enterprise that invests its subscribed capital in securities for its investors' benefit.

inveterate (ɪn'vɛtərɪt) *adj.* **1.** long established, esp. so as to be deep-rooted or ingrained: *an inveterate feeling of hostility.* **2.** (*prenominal*) confirmed in a habit or practice, esp. a bad one; hardened. [C16: < L *inveterātus* of long standing, < *inveterāre* to make old, < IN-[2] + *vetus* old] —**in'veteracy** *n.* —**in'veterately** *adv.*

invidious (ɪn'vɪdɪəs) *adj.* **1.** incurring or tending to arouse resentment, unpopularity, etc.: *an invidious task.* **2.** (of comparisons or distinctions) unfairly or offensively discriminating. [C17: < L *invidiōsus* full of envy, < *invidia* ENVY] —**in'vidiously** *adv.* —**in'vidiousness** *n.*

invigilate (ɪn'vɪdʒɪˌleɪt) *vb.* (*intr.*) **1.** *Brit.* to watch examination candidates, esp. to prevent cheating. U.S. word: **proctor. 2.** *Arch.* to keep watch. [C16: < L *invigilāre* to watch over; see VIGIL] —**inˌvigi'lation** *n.* —**in'vigiˌlator** *n.*

invigorate (ɪn'vɪgəˌreɪt) *vb.* (*tr.*) to give vitality and vigour to; animate; brace; refresh: *to be invigorated by fresh air.* [C17: < IN-[2] + L *vigor* VIGOUR] —**in'vigorˌating** *adj.* —**inˌvigor'ation** *n.* —**in'vigorative** *adj.* —**in'vigorˌator** *n.*

invincible (ɪn'vɪnsəb°l) *adj.* incapable of being defeated; unconquerable. [C15: < LL *invincibilis,* < L IN-[1] + *vincere* to conquer] —**inˌvinci'bility** *or* **in'vincibleness** *n.* —**in'vincibly** *adv.*

inviolable (ɪn'vaɪələb°l) *adj.* that must not or cannot be transgressed, dishonoured, or broken; to be kept sacred: *an inviolable oath.* —**inˌviola'bility** *n.* —**in'violably** *adv.*

inviolate (ɪn'vaɪəlɪt, -ˌleɪt) *adj.* **1.** free from violation, injury, disturbance, etc. **2.** a less common word for **inviolable.** —**in'violacy** *or* **in'violateness** *n.* —**in'violately** *adv.*

invisible (ɪn'vɪzəb°l) *adj.* **1.** not visible; not able to be perceived by the eye: *invisible rays.* **2.** concealed from sight; hidden. **3.** not easily seen or noticed: *invisible mending.* **4.** kept hidden from public view; secret. **5.** *Econ.* of or relating to services, such as insurance and freight, rather than goods: *invisible earnings.* ~*n.* **6.** *Econ.* an invisible item of trade; service. —**inˌvisi'bility** *or* **in'visibleness** *n.* —**in'visibly** *adv.*

invitation (ˌɪnvɪ'teɪʃən) *n.* **1. a.** the act of inviting, such as an offer of entertainment or hospitality. **b.** (*as modifier*): *an invitation race.* **2.** the act of enticing or attracting; allurement.

invite *vb.* (ɪn'vaɪt). (*tr.*) **1.** to ask (a person) in a friendly or polite way (to do something, attend an event, etc.). **2.** to make a request for, esp. publicly or formally: *to invite applications.* **3.** to bring on or provoke; give occasion for: *you invite disaster by your actions.* **4.** to welcome or tempt. ~*n.* ('ɪnvaɪt). **5.** *Inf.* an invitation. [C16: < L *invītāre* to invite, entertain] —**in'viter** *n.*

inviting (ɪn'vaɪtɪŋ) *adj.* tempting; alluring; attractive. —**in'vitingness** *n.*

in vitro (ɪn 'viːtrəʊ) *adv., adj.* (of biological processes or reactions) made to occur outside the body of the organism in an artificial environment. [NL, lit.: in glass]

in vivo (ɪn 'viːvəʊ) *adv., adj.* (of biological processes or experiments) occurring or carried out in the living organism. [NL, lit.: in a living (thing)]

invocation (ˌɪnvə'keɪʃən) *n.* **1.** the act of invoking or calling upon some agent for assistance. **2.** a prayer asking God for help, forgiveness, etc. **3.** an appeal for inspiration from a Muse or deity at the beginning of a poem. **4. a.** the act of summoning a spirit from another world by ritual incantation or magic. **b.** the incantation used in this act. —ˌ**invo'cational** *adj.* —**invocatory** (ɪn'vɒkətərɪ, -trɪ) *adj.*

invoice ('ɪnvɔɪs) *n.* **1.** a document issued by a seller to a buyer listing the goods or services supplied and stating the sum of money due. **2.** *Rare.* a consignment of invoiced merchandise. ~*vb.* **3.** (*tr.*) **a.** to present (a customer, etc.) with an invoice. **b.** to list (merchandise sold) on an invoice. [C16: < earlier *invoyes,* < OF *envois,* pl. of *envoi* message; see ENVOY[1]]

invoke (ɪn'vəʊk) *vb.* (*tr.*) **1.** to call upon (an agent, esp. God or another deity) for help, inspiration, etc. **2.** to put (a law, penalty, etc.) into use: *the union invoked the dispute procedure.* **3.** to appeal to (an outside authority) for confirmation, corroboration, etc. **4.** to implore or beg (help, etc.). **5.** to summon (a spirit, etc.); conjure up. [C15: < L *invocāre* to appeal to, < *vocāre* to call] —**in'vocable** *adj.* —**in'voker** *n.*

involucre ('ɪnvəˌluːkə) *or* **involucrum** (ˌɪnvə'luːkrəm) *n., pl.* **-cres** *or* **-cra** (-krə). a ring of bracts at the base of an inflorescence. [C16 (in the sense: envelope): < NL *involucrum,* < L: wrapper, < *involvere* to wrap] —ˌ**invo'lucral** *adj.* —ˌ**invo'lucrate** *adj.*

involuntary (ɪn'vɒləntərɪ, -trɪ) *adj.* **1.** carried out without one's conscious wishes; not voluntary; unintentional. **2.** *Physiol.* (esp. of a movement or muscle) performed or acting without conscious control. —**in'voluntarily** *adv.* —**in'voluntariness** *n.*

involute *adj.* ('ɪnvəˌluːt), *also* **involuted. 1.** complex, intricate, or involved. **2.** *Bot.* (esp. of petals, leaves, etc., in bud) having margins that are rolled inwards. **3.** (of certain shells) closely coiled so that the axis is obscured. ~*n.* ('ɪnvəˌluːt). **4.** *Geom.* the curve described by the free end of a thread as it is wound around another curve, the **evolute,** such that its normals are tangential to the evolute. ~*vb.* (ˌɪnvə'luːt). **5.** (*intr.*) to become involute. [C17: < L *involūtus,* < *involvere;* see INVOLVE] —'**invoˌlutely** *adv.* —ˌ**invo'lutedly** *adv.*

involution (ˌɪnvə'luːʃən) *n.* **1.** the act of involving or complicating or the state of being involved or complicated. **2.** something involved or complicated. **3.** *Zool.* degeneration or structural deformation. **4.** *Biol.* an involute formation or structure. **5.** *Physiol.* reduction in size of an organ or part, as of the uterus following childbirth or as a result of ageing. **6.** an algebraic operation in which a number, expression, etc., is raised to a specified power. —ˌ**invo'lutional** *adj.*

involve (ɪn'vɒlv) *vb.* (*tr.*) **1.** to include or contain as a necessary part. **2.** to have an effect on; spread to: *the investigation involved many innocent people.* **3.** (*often passive;* usually foll. by *in* or *with*) to concern or associate significantly: *many people were involved in the crime.* **4.** (*often passive*) to make complicated; tangle. **5.** *Rare, often poetic.* to wrap or surround. **6.** *Maths, obs.* to raise to a specified power. [C14: < L *involvere* to surround, < IN-² + *volvere* to roll] **—in'volvement** *n.* **—in'volver** *n.*

invulnerable (ɪn'vʌlnərəbᵊl, -'vʌlnrəbᵊl) *adj.* **1.** incapable of being wounded, hurt, damaged, etc. **2.** incapable of being damaged or captured: *an invulnerable fortress.* **—in,vulnera'bility** *or* **in'vulnerableness** *n.* **—in'vulnerably** *adv.*

inward ('ɪnwəd) *adj.* **1.** going or directed towards the middle of or into something. **2.** situated within; inside. **3.** of, relating to, or existing in the mind or spirit: *inward meditation.* ~*adv.* **4.** a variant of **inwards.** ~*n.* **5.** the inward part; inside. **—'inwardness** *n.*

inwardly ('ɪnwədlɪ) *adv.* **1.** within the private thoughts or feelings; secretly. **2.** not aloud: *to laugh inwardly.* **3.** with reference to the inside or inner part; internally.

inwards *adv.* ('ɪnwədz), *also* **inward.** **1.** towards the interior or middle of something. **2.** in, into, or towards the mind or spirit. ~*pl. n.* ('ɪnədz). **3.** a variant of **innards** (sense 1).

inweave (ɪn'wiːv) *vb.* **-weaving, -wove** *or* **-weaved; -woven** *or* **-weaved.** (*tr.*) to weave together into or as if into a design, fabric, etc.

inwrap (ɪn'ræp) *vb.* **-wrapping, -wrapped.** a less common spelling of **enwrap.**

inwrought (,ɪn'rɔːt) *adj.* **1.** worked or woven into material, esp. decoratively. **2.** *Rare.* blended with other things.

inyala (ɪn'jɑːlə) *n.* a spiral-horned southern African antelope with a fringe of white hairs along the back and neck. [< Zulu]

Io *the chemical symbol for* ionium.

iodic (aɪ'ɒdɪk) *adj.* of or containing iodine, esp. in the pentavalent state.

iodide ('aɪə,daɪd) *n.* **1.** a salt of hydriodic acid, containing the iodide ion, I^-. **2.** a compound containing an iodine atom, such as methyl iodide.

iodine ('aɪə,diːn) *n.* a bluish-black element of the halogen group that sublimates into a violet irritating gas. Its compounds are used in medicine and photography and in dyes. The radioisotope **iodine-131** is used in the treatment of thyroid disease. Symbol: I; atomic no.: 53; atomic wt.: 126.90. [C19: < F *iode,* < Gk *iōdēs* rust-coloured, but mistaken as violet-coloured, < *ion* violet]

iodize *or* **-dise** ('aɪə,daɪz) *vb.* (*tr.*) to treat or react with iodine or an iodine compound. Also: **iodate.** **—,iodi'zation** *or* **-di'sation** *n.* **—'io,dizer** *or* **-,diser** *n.*

iodoform (aɪ'ɒdə,fɔːm) *n.* a yellow crystalline solid made by heating alcohol with iodine and an alkali: used as an antiseptic. Formula: CHI_3.

iodopsin (,aɪə'dɒpsɪn) *n.* a violet light-sensitive pigment in the cones of the retina of the eye. See also **rhodopsin.**

IOM *abbrev. for* Isle of Man.

ion ('aɪən, -ɒn) *n.* an electrically charged atom or group of atoms formed by the loss or gain of one or more electrons. See also **cation, anion.** [C19: < Gk, lit.: going, < *ienai* to go]

-ion *suffix forming nouns.* indicating an action, process, or state: *creation; objection.* Cf. **-ation, -tion.** [< L *-iōn-, -io*]

ion exchange *n.* the process in which ions are exchanged between a solution and an insoluble solid, usually a resin. It is used to soften water.

ionic (aɪ'ɒnɪk) *adj.* of, relating to, or occurring in the form of ions.

Ionic (aɪ'ɒnɪk) *adj.* **1.** of, denoting, or relating to one of the five classical orders of architecture, characterized by fluted columns and capitals with scroll-like ornaments. **2.** of or relating to Ionia, on the coast of Asia Minor, its inhabitants or their dialect of Ancient Greek. ~*n.* **3.** one of four chief dialects of Ancient Greek; the dialect spoken in Ionia.

ionium (aɪ'əʊnɪəm) *n. Obs.* a naturally occurring radioisotope of thorium with a mass number of 230. Symbol: Io [C20: < NL]

ionization *or* **-isation** (,aɪənaɪ'zeɪʃən) *n.* **a.** the formation of ions as a result of a chemical reaction, high temperature, electrical discharge, or radiation. **b.** (*as modifier*): *ionization temperature.*

ionize *or* **-ise** ('aɪə,naɪz) *vb.* to change or become changed into ions. **—'ion,izable** *or* **-,isable** *adj.* **—'ion,izer** *or* **-,iser** *n.*

ionosphere (aɪ'ɒnə,sfɪə) *n.* a region of the earth's atmosphere, extending from about 60 to 1000 km above the earth's surface, in which there is a high concentration of free electrons formed as a result of ionizing radiation entering the atmosphere from space. **—ionospheric** (aɪ,ɒnə'sfɛrɪk) *adj.*

iota (aɪ'əʊtə) *n.* **1.** the ninth letter in the Greek alphabet (Ι, ι), a vowel or semivowel. **2.** (*usually used with a negative*) a very small amount; jot (esp. in **not one** *or* **an iota**). [C16: via L < Gk, of Semitic origin]

IOU *n.* a written promise or reminder to pay a debt. [C17: representing *I owe you*]

-ious *suffix forming adjectives from nouns.* characterized by or full of: *ambitious; suspicious.* [< L *-ius* & *-iōsus* full of]

IOW *abbrev. for* Isle of Wight.

IPA *abbrev. for* International Phonetic Alphabet.

ipecac ('ɪpɪ,kæk) *or* **ipecacuanha** (,ɪpɪ,kækjʊ'ænə) *n.* **1.** a low-growing South American shrub. **2.** a drug prepared from the dried roots of this plant, used as a purgative and emetic. [C18: < Port. *ipecacuanha,* < Amerind *ipekaaguéne,* < *ipeh* low + *kaa* leaves + *guéne* vomit]

ipomoea (,ɪpə'mɪə, ,aɪ-) *n.* **1.** any tropical or subtropical plant, such as the morning-glory, sweet potato, and jalap, having trumpet-shaped flowers. **2.** the dried root of a Mexican species which yields a cathartic resin. [C18: NL, < Gk *ips* worm + *homoios* like]

ipse dixit *Latin.* ('ɪpseɪ 'dɪksɪt) *n.* an arbitrary and unsupported assertion. [C16, lit.: he himself said it]

ipso facto ('ɪpsəʊ 'fæktəʊ) *adv.* by that very fact or act. [< L]

IQ *abbrev. for* intelligence quotient.

Ir *the chemical symbol for* iridium.

Ir. *abbrev. for:* **1.** Ireland. **2.** Irish.

ir- *prefix.* a variant of **in-**¹ and **in-**² before *r.*

IRA *abbrev. for* Irish Republican Army.

irade (ɪ'rɑːdɛ) *n.* a written edict of a Muslim ruler. [C19: < Turkish: will, < Ar. *irādah*]

Iranian (ɪ'reɪnɪən) *n.* **1.** a native or inhabitant of Iran, in SW Asia. **2.** a branch of the Indo-European family of languages, including Persian. **3.** the modern Persian language. ~*adj.* **4.** relating to or characteristic of Iran, its inhabitants, or their language; Persian. **5.** belonging to or relating to the Iranian branch of Indo-European.

Iraqi (ɪ'rɑːkɪ) *adj.* **1.** of or characteristic of Iraq, in SW Asia, its inhabitants, or their language. ~*n., pl.* **-qis.** **2.** a native or inhabitant of Iraq.

irascible (ɪ'ræsɪbᵊl) *adj.* **1.** easily angered; irritable. **2.** showing irritability: *an irascible action.* [C16: < LL *īrascibilis,* < L *īra* anger] **—i,rasci'bility** *or* **i'rascibleness** *n.* **—i'rascibly** *adv.*

irate (aɪ'reɪt) *adj.* **1.** incensed with anger; furious. **2.** marked by extreme anger: *an irate letter.* [C19: < L *īrātus* enraged, < *īrascī* to be angry] **—i'rately** *adv.*

IRBM *abbrev. for* intermediate range ballistic missile.

ire ('aɪə) *n. Literary.* anger; wrath. [C13: < OF, < L *īra*] **—'ireful** *adj.* **—'irefulness** *n.*

Ire. *abbrev. for* Ireland.

irenic, eirenic (aɪ'riːnɪk, -'rɛn-) *or* **irenical, eirenical** *adj.* tending to conciliate or promote peace. [C19: < Gk *eirēnikos,* < *eirēnē* peace] **—i'renically** *or* **ei'renically** *adv.*

iridaceous (,ɪrɪ'deɪʃəs, ,aɪ-) *adj.* of, relating to, or belonging to the family of monocotyledonous plants, including the iris, having swordlike leaves and showy flowers.

iridescent (ˌɪrɪˈdɛs^{ə}nt) *adj.* displaying a spectrum of colours that shimmer and change due to interference and scattering as the observer's position changes. [C18: < L *irid-* iris + -ESCENT] —ˌ**iriˈdescence** *n.* —ˌ**iriˈdescently** *adv.*

iridium (aɪˈrɪdɪəm, ɪˈrɪd-) *n.* a very hard yellowish-white transition element that is the most corrosion-resistant metal known. It occurs in platinum ores and is used as an alloy with platinum. Symbol: Ir; atomic no.: 77; atomic wt.: 192.2. [C19: NL, < L *irid-* iris + -IUM; from its colourful appearance when dissolving in certain acids]

iris (ˈaɪrɪs) *n., pl.* **irises** *or* **irides** (ˈaɪrɪˌdiːz, ˈɪrɪ-). **1.** the coloured muscular diaphragm that surrounds and controls the size of the pupil. **2.** Also called: **fleur-de-lis.** any iridaceous plant having brightly coloured flowers composed of three petals and three drooping sepals. **3.** a poetic word for **rainbow. 4.** short for **iris diaphragm.** [C14: < L: rainbow, iris (flower), crystal, < Gk]

iris diaphragm *n.* an adjustable diaphragm that regulates the amount of light entering an optical instrument, esp. a camera.

Irish (ˈaɪrɪʃ) *adj.* **1.** of, relating to, or characteristic of Ireland, its people, their Celtic language, or their dialect of English. **2.** *Offensive.* ludicrous or illogical. ~*n.* **3. the Irish.** (*functioning as pl.*) the natives or inhabitants of Ireland. **4.** another name for **Irish Gaelic. 5.** the dialect of English spoken in Ireland.

Irish coffee *n.* hot coffee mixed with Irish whiskey and topped with double cream.

Irish Gaelic *n.* the Goidelic language of the Celts of Ireland, now spoken mainly along the west coast; an official language of the Republic of Ireland since 1921.

Irishman (ˈaɪrɪʃmən) *or* (*fem.*) **Irishwoman** *n., pl.* **-men** *or* **-women.** a native or inhabitant of Ireland.

Irish stew *n.* a stew made of mutton, lamb, or beef, with potatoes, onions, etc.

Irish wolfhound *n.* a large breed of hound with a rough thick coat.

iritis (aɪˈraɪtɪs) *n.* inflammation of the iris of the eye. —**iritic** (aɪˈrɪtɪk) *adj.*

irk (ɜːk) *vb.* (*tr.*) to irritate, vex, or annoy. [C13 *irken* to grow weary]

irksome (ˈɜːksəm) *adj.* causing vexation, annoyance, or boredom; troublesome or tedious. —ˈ**irksomely** *adv.* —ˈ**irksomeness** *n.*

IRO *abbrev. for:* **1.** (in Britain) Inland Revenue Office. **2.** International Refugee Organization.

iron (ˈaɪən) *n.* **1. a.** a malleable ductile silvery-white ferromagnetic metallic element. It is widely used for structural and engineering purposes. Symbol: Fe; atomic no.: 26; atomic wt.: 55.847. Related adjs.: **ferric, ferrous.** Related prefix: **ferro-. b.** (*as modifier*): *iron railings.* **2.** any of certain tools or implements made of iron or steel, esp. for use when hot: *a grappling iron; a soldering iron.* **3.** an appliance for pressing fabrics using dry heat or steam, esp. a small electrically heated device with a handle and a weighted flat bottom. **4.** any of various golf clubs with metal heads, numbered from 2 to 10 according to the slant of the face. **5.** a splintlike support for a malformed leg. **6.** great hardness, strength, or resolve: *a will of iron.* **7. strike while the iron is hot.** to act at an opportune moment. ~*adj.* **8.** very hard, immovable, or implacable: *iron determination.* **9.** very strong; extremely robust: *an iron constitution.* **10.** cruel or unyielding: *he ruled with an iron hand.* ~*vb.* **11.** to smooth (clothes or fabric) by removing (creases or wrinkles) using a heated iron; press. **12.** (*tr.*) to furnish or clothe with iron. **13.** (*tr.*) *Rare.* to place (a prisoner) in irons. ~See also **iron out, irons.** [OE *irēn*] —ˈ**ironer** *n.* —ˈ**ironless** *adj.* —ˈ**ironˌlike** *adj.*

Iron Age *n.* **a.** the period following the Bronze Age characterized by the extremely rapid spread of iron tools and weapons. **b.** (*as modifier*) *an Iron-Age weapon.*

ironbark (ˈaɪənˌbɑːk) *n.* any of several Australian eucalyptus trees that have hard rough bark.

ironbound (ˈaɪənˌbaʊnd) *adj.* **1.** bound with iron. **2.** unyielding; inflexible. **3.** (of a coast) rocky; rugged.

ironclad *adj.* (ˌaɪənˈklæd). **1.** covered or protected with iron: *an ironclad warship.* **2.** inflexible; rigid: *an ironclad rule.* ~*n.* (ˈaɪənˌklæd). **3.** a large wooden 19th-century warship with armoured plating.

Iron Curtain *n.* **1. a.** the guarded border between the countries of the Soviet bloc and the rest of Europe. **b.** (*as modifier*): *Iron Curtain countries.* **2.** (*sometimes not caps.*) any barrier that separates communities or ideologies.

iron hand *n.* harsh or rigorous control; overbearing or autocratic force.

iron horse *n. Arch.* a steam-driven railway locomotive.

ironic (aɪˈrɒnɪk) *or* **ironical** *adj.* of, characterized by, or using irony. —**iˈronically** *adv.* —**iˈronicalness** *n.*

ironing (ˈaɪənɪŋ) *n.* **1.** the act of ironing washed clothes. **2.** clothes, etc., that are to be or that have been ironed.

ironing board *n.* a board, usually on legs, with a suitable covering on which to iron clothes.

iron lung *n.* an airtight metal cylinder enclosing the entire body up to the neck and providing artificial respiration.

iron maiden *n.* a medieval instrument of torture, consisting of a hinged case (often shaped in the form of a woman) lined with iron spikes, which was forcibly closed on the victim.

iron man *n. Austral.* an event at a surf carnival in which contestants compete at swimming, surfing, running, etc.

ironmaster (ˈaɪənˌmɑːstə) *n. Brit.* a manufacturer of iron.

ironmonger (ˈaɪənˌmʌŋgə) *n. Brit.* a dealer in metal utensils, hardware, locks, etc. U.S. and Canad. equivalent: **hardware dealer.** —ˈ**ironˌmongery** *n.*

iron out *vb.* (*tr., adv.*) **1.** to smooth, using a heated iron. **2.** to put right or settle (a problem or difficulty) as a result of negotiations or discussions. **3.** *Austral. inf.* to knock unconscious.

iron pyrites (ˈpaɪraɪts) *n.* another name for **pyrite.**

iron rations *pl. n.* emergency food supplies, esp. for military personnel in action.

irons (ˈaɪənz) *pl. n.* **1.** fetters or chains (often in **in** *or* **into irons**). **2. have several irons in the fire.** to be involved in many projects, etc.

ironsides (ˈaɪənˌsaɪdz) *n.* **1.** a person with great stamina or resistance. **2.** an ironclad ship. **3.** (*often cap.*) (in the English Civil War) **a.** the cavalry regiment trained and commanded by Oliver Cromwell. **b.** Cromwell's entire army.

ironstone (ˈaɪənˌstəʊn) *n.* **1.** any rock consisting mainly of an iron-bearing ore. **2.** a tough durable earthenware.

ironware (ˈaɪənˌwɛə) *n.* domestic articles made of iron.

ironwood (ˈaɪənˌwʊd) *n.* **1.** any of various trees, such as hornbeam, that have very hard wood. **2.** a Californian rosaceous tree with very hard wood. **3.** the wood of any of these trees.

ironwork (ˈaɪənˌwɜːk) *n.* **1.** work done in iron, esp. decorative work. **2.** the craft or practice of working in iron.

ironworks (ˈaɪənˌwɜːks) *n.* (*sometimes functioning as sing.*) a building in which iron is smelted, cast, or wrought.

irony[1] (ˈaɪrənɪ) *n., pl.* **-nies. 1.** the humorous or mildly sarcastic use of words to imply the opposite of what they normally mean. **2.** an instance of this, used to draw attention to some incongruity or irrationality. **3.** incongruity between what is expected to be and what actually is, or a situation or result showing such incongruity. **4.** See **dramatic irony. 5.** *Philoso-*

phy. See **Socratic irony.** [C16: < L, < Gk *eirōneia,* < *eirōn* dissembler, < *eirein* to speak]

irony[2] (ˈaɪənɪ) *adj.* of, resembling, or containing iron.

Iroquois (ˈɪrəˌkwɔɪ) *n.* **1.** (*pl.* **-quois**) a member of a confederacy of North American Indian tribes formerly living in and around New York State. **2.** any of the languages of these people. —ˌ**Iroˈquoian** *adj.*

irradiance (ɪˈreɪdɪəns) *n.* the radiant flux incident on unit area of a surface. Also called: **irradiation.** Cf. **illuminance.**

irradiate (ɪˈreɪdɪˌeɪt) *vb.* **1.** (*tr.*) *Physics.* to subject to or treat with light or other electromagnetic radiation or with beams of particles. **2.** (*tr.*) to subject to or treat with atomic radiation. **3.** (*tr.*) to make clear or bright intellectually or spiritually; illumine. **4.** a less common word for **radiate** (sense 1). **5.** (*intr.*) *Obs.* to become radiant. —**irˈradiˌation** *n.* —**irˈradiative** *adj.* —**irˈradiˌator** *n.*

irrational (ɪˈræʃən°l) *adj.* **1.** inconsistent with reason or logic; illogical; absurd. **2.** incapable of reasoning. **3. a.** *Maths.* (of an equation, etc.) containing one or more variables in irreducible radical form or raised to a fractional power: $\sqrt{(x^2 + 1)} = x^{5/3}$. **b.** (*as n.*): *an irrational.* —**irˌrationˈality** *n.* —**irˈrationally** *adv.*

irrational number *n.* any real number that cannot be expressed as the ratio of two integers, such as π.

irreclaimable (ˌɪrɪˈkleɪməb°l) *adj.* not able to be reclaimed. —**ˌirreˌclaimaˈbility** *or* **ˌirreˈclaimableness** *n.* —**ˌirreˈclaimably** *adv.*

irreconcilable (ɪˈrɛk°nˌsaɪləb°l, ɪˌrɛk°nˈsaɪ-) *adj.* **1.** not able to be reconciled; uncompromisingly conflicting; incompatible. ~*n.* **2.** a person or thing that is implacably hostile or uncompromisingly opposed. **3.** (*usually pl.*) one of various principles, ideas, etc., that are incapable of being brought into agreement. —**irˌreconˌcilaˈbility** *or* **irˈreconˌcilableness** *n.* —**irˈreconˌcilably** *adv.*

irrecoverable (ˌɪrɪˈkʌvərəb°l, -ˈkʌvrə-) *adj.* **1.** not able to be recovered or regained. **2.** not able to be remedied or rectified. —**ˌirreˈcoverableness** *n.* —**ˌirreˈcoverably** *adv.*

irrecusable (ˌɪrɪˈkjuːzəb°l) *adj.* not able to be rejected or challenged, as evidence, etc.

irredeemable (ˌɪrɪˈdiːməb°l) *adj.* **1.** (of bonds, shares, etc.) without a date of redemption of capital; incapable of being bought back directly or paid off. **2.** (of paper money) not convertible into specie. **3.** (of a loss) not able to be recovered; irretrievable. **4.** not able to be improved or rectified; irreparable. —**ˌirreˌdeemaˈbility** *or* **ˌirreˈdeemableness** *n.* —**ˌirreˈdeemably** *adv.*

irredentist (ˌɪrɪˈdɛntɪst) *n.* **1.** (*sometimes cap.*) a person, esp. a member of a 19th-century Italian association, who favours the acquisition of territory that was once part of his country or is considered to have been. ~*adj.* **2.** of or relating to irredentists or their policies. [C19: < It. *irredentista,* < *ir-* IN-[1] + *redento* redeemed, < L *redemptus* bought back; see REDEEM] —**ˌirreˈdentism** *n.*

irreducible (ˌɪrɪˈdjuːsɪb°l) *adj.* **1.** not able to be reduced or lessened. **2.** not able to be brought to a simpler or reduced form. **3.** *Maths.* (of a polynomial) unable to be factorized into polynomials of lower degree, as $(x^2 + 1)$. —**ˌirreˌduciˈbility** *n.* —**ˌirreˈducibly** *adv.*

irrefragable (ɪˈrɛfrəgəb°l) *adj.* not able to be denied or refuted. [C16: < LL *irrefrāgābilis,* < L *ir-* + *refrāgārī* to resist] —**irˌrefragaˈbility** *or* **irˈrefragableness** *n.* —**irˈrefragably** *adv.*

irrefrangible (ˌɪrɪˈfrændʒəb°l) *adj.* **1.** not to be broken or transgressed; inviolable. **2.** *Physics.* incapable of being refracted. —**ˌirreˌfrangiˈbility** *or* **ˌirreˈfrangibleness** *n.* —**ˌirreˈfrangibly** *adv.*

irrefutable (ɪˈrɛfjutəb°l, ˌɪrɪˈfjuːtəb°l) *adj.* impossible to deny or disprove; incontrovertible. —**irˌrefutaˈbility** *n.* —**irˈrefutably** *adv.*

irreg. *abbrev. for* irregular(ly).

irregular (ɪˈrɛgjulə) *adj.* **1.** lacking uniformity or symmetry; uneven in shape, position, arrangement, etc. **2.** not occurring at expected or equal intervals: *an irregular pulse.* **3.** differing from the normal or accepted practice or routine; unconventional. **4.** (of the formation, inflections, or derivations of a word) not following the usual pattern of formation in a language. **5.** of or relating to guerrillas or volunteers not belonging to regular forces: *irregular troops.* **6.** (of flowers) having any of their petals differing in size, shape, etc. **7.** *U.S.* (of merchandise) not up to the manufacturer's standards or specifications; imperfect. ~*n.* **8.** a soldier not in a regular army. **9.** (*often pl.*) *U.S.* imperfect or flawed merchandise. —**irˌreguˈlarity** *n.* —**irˈregularly** *adv.*

irrelevant (ɪˈrɛləvənt) *adj.* not relating or pertinent to the matter at hand. —**irˈrelevance** *or* **irˈrelevancy** *n.* —**irˈrelevantly** *adv.*

irreligion (ˌɪrɪˈlɪdʒən) *n.* **1.** lack of religious faith. **2.** indifference or opposition to religion. —**ˌirreˈligionist** *n.* —**ˌirreˈligious** *adj.* —**ˌirreˈligiously** *adv.* —**ˌirreˈligiousness** *n.*

irremediable (ˌɪrɪˈmiːdɪəb°l) *adj.* not able to be remedied; incurable or irreparable. —**ˌirreˈmediableness** *n.* —**ˌirreˈmediably** *adv.*

irremissible (ˌɪrɪˈmɪsəb°l) *adj.* **1.** unpardonable; inexcusable. **2.** that must be done, as through duty or obligation. —**ˌirreˌmissiˈbility** *or* **ˌirreˈmissibleness** *n.* —**ˌirreˈmissibly** *adv.*

irremovable (ˌɪrɪˈmuːvəb°l) *adj.* not able to be removed. —**ˌirreˌmovaˈbility** *n.* —**ˌirreˈmovably** *adv.*

irreparable (ɪˈrɛpərəb°l, ɪˈrɛprəb°l) *adj.* not able to be repaired or remedied; beyond repair. —**irˌreparaˈbility** *or* **irˈreparableness** *n.* —**irˈreparably** *adv.*

irreplaceable (ˌɪrɪˈpleɪsəb°l) *adj.* not able to be replaced: *an irreplaceable antique.* —**ˌirreˈplaceably** *adv.*

irrepressible (ˌɪrɪˈprɛsəb°l) *adj.* not capable of being repressed, controlled, or restrained. —**ˌirreˌpressiˈbility** *or* **ˌirreˈpressibleness** *n.* —**ˌirreˈpressibly** *adv.*

irreproachable (ˌɪrɪˈprəutʃəb°l) *adj.* not deserving reproach; blameless. —**ˌirreˌproachaˈbility** *or* **ˌirreˈproachableness** *n.* —**ˌirreˈproachably** *adv.*

irresistible (ˌɪrɪˈzɪstəb°l) *adj.* **1.** not able to be resisted or refused; overpowering: *an irresistible impulse.* **2.** very fascinating or alluring: *an irresistible woman.* —**ˌirreˌsistiˈbility** *or* **ˌirreˈsistibleness** *n.* —**ˌirreˈsistibly** *adv.*

irresolute (ɪˈrɛzəˌluːt) *adj.* lacking resolution; wavering; hesitating. —**irˈresoˌlutely** *adv.* —**irˈresoˌluteness** *or* **irˌresoˈlution** *n.*

irrespective (ˌɪrɪˈspɛktɪv) *adj.* **1. irrespective of.** without taking account of; regardless of. ~*adv.* **2.** *Inf.* regardless; without due consideration: *he carried on with his plan irrespective.* —**ˌirreˈspectively** *adv.*

irresponsible (ˌɪrɪˈspɒnsəb°l) *adj.* **1.** not showing or done with due care for the consequences of one's actions or attitudes; reckless. **2.** not capable of bearing responsibility. —**ˌirreˌsponsiˈbility** *or* **ˌirreˈsponsibleness** *n.* —**ˌirreˈsponsibly** *adv.*

irresponsive (ˌɪrɪˈspɒnsɪv) *adj.* not responsive. —**ˌirreˈsponsively** *adv.* —**ˌirreˈsponsiveness** *n.*

irretrievable (ˌɪrɪˈtriːvəb°l) *adj.* not able to be retrieved, recovered, or repaired. —**ˌirreˌtrievaˈbility** *n.* —**ˌirreˈtrievably** *adv.*

irreverence (ɪˈrɛvərəns, ɪˈrɛvrəns) *n.* **1.** lack of due respect or veneration; disrespect. **2.** a disrespectful remark or act. —**irˈreverent** *or* **irˌreveˈrential** *adj.* —**irˈreverently** *adv.*

irreversible (ˌɪrɪˈvɜːsəb°l) *adj.* **1.** not able to be reversed: *the irreversible flow of time.* **2.** not able to be revoked or repealed; irrevocable. **3.** *Chem., physics.* capable of changing or producing a change in one direction only: *an irreversible reaction.* —**ˌirreˌversiˈbility** *or* **ˌirreˈversibleness** *n.* —**ˌirreˈversibly** *adv.*

irrevocable (ɪˈrɛvəkəb°l) *adj.* not able to be revoked, changed, or undone. —**irˌrevocaˈbility** *or* **irˈrevocableness** *n.* —**irˈrevocably** *adv.*

irrigate (ˈɪrɪˌgeɪt) *vb.* **1.** to supply (land) with

water by means of artificial canals, etc., esp. to promote the growth of food crops. **2.** *Med.* to bathe or wash out (a bodily part, cavity, or wound). **3.** (*tr.*) to make fertile, fresh, or vital by or as if by watering. [C17: < L *irrigāre*, < *rigāre* to moisten, conduct water] —**'irrigable** *adj.* —**ˌirri'gation** *n.* —**'irriˌgative** *adj.* —**'irriˌgator** *n.*

irritable ('ɪrɪtəbᵊl) *adj.* **1.** quickly irritated; easily annoyed; peevish. **2.** (of all living organisms) capable of responding to such stimuli as heat, light, and touch. **3.** *Pathol.* abnormally sensitive. —**ˌirrita'bility** *n.* —**'irritableness** *n.* —**'irritably** *adv.*

irritant ('ɪrɪtənt) *adj.* **1.** causing irritation; irritating. ~*n.* **2.** something irritant. —**'irritancy** *n.*

irritate ('ɪrɪˌteɪt) *vb.* **1.** to annoy or anger (someone). **2.** (*tr.*) *Biol.* to stimulate (an organism or part) to respond in a characteristic manner. **3.** (*tr.*) *Pathol.* to cause (a bodily organ or part) to become excessively stimulated, resulting in inflammation, tenderness, etc. [C16: < L *irrītāre* to provoke] —**'irriˌtator** *n.*

irritation (ˌɪrɪ'teɪʃən) *n.* **1.** something that irritates. **2.** the act of irritating or the condition of being irritated. —**'irriˌtative** *adj.*

irrupt (ɪ'rʌpt) *vb.* (*intr.*) **1.** to enter forcibly or suddenly. **2.** (of a plant or animal population) to enter a region suddenly and in very large numbers. **3.** (of a population) to increase suddenly and greatly. [C19: < L *irrumpere* to rush into, invade, < *rumpere* to break, burst] —**ir'ruption** *n.* —**ir'ruptive** *adj.*

is (ɪz) *vb.* (used with *he, she, it,* and with singular nouns) a form of the present tense (indicative mood) of **be.** [OE]

Is. *abbrev. for:* **1.** Also: **Isa.** *Bible.* Isaiah. **2.** Island(s) or Isle(s).

is- *combining form.* a variant of **iso-** before a vowel: *isentropic.*

isagogics (ˌaɪsə'gɒdʒɪks) *n.* introductory studies, esp. in the history of the Bible. [C19: < L, < Gk, < *eisagein* to introduce, < *eis-* into + *agein* to lead]

isallobar (aɪ'sæləˌbɑː) *n.* a line on a map connecting places with equal pressure changes.

isatin ('aɪsətɪn) *or* **isatine** ('aɪsəˌtiːn) *n.* a yellowish-red crystalline compound soluble in hot water, used for the preparation of vat dyes. [C19: < L *isatis* woad + -IN] —**ˌisa'tinic** *adj.*

ISBN *abbrev. for* International Standard Book Number.

ischaemia *or* **ischemia** (ɪ'skiːmɪə) *n. Pathol.* an inadequate supply of blood to an organ or part, as from an obstructed blood flow. [C19: < Gk *iskhein* to restrict, + -AEMIA] —**ischaemic** *or* **ischemic** (ɪ'skɛmɪk) *adj.*

ischium ('ɪskɪəm) *n., pl.* **-chia** (-kɪə). one of the three sections of the hipbone, situated below the ilium. [C17: < L: hip joint, < Gk *iskhion*] —**'ischial** *adj.*

-ise *suffix forming verbs.* a variant of **-ize.**
▷ **Usage.** See at **-ize.**

isentropic (ˌaɪsɛn'trɒpɪk) *adj.* having or taking place at constant entropy.

-ish *suffix forming adjectives.* **1.** of or belonging to a nationality: *Scottish.* **2.** *Often derog.* having the manner or qualities of; resembling: *slavish; boyish.* **3.** somewhat; approximately: *yellowish; sevenish.* **4.** concerned or preoccupied with: *bookish.* [OE *-isc*]

isinglass ('aɪzɪŋˌglɑːs) *n.* **1.** a gelatin made from the air bladders of freshwater fish, used as a clarifying agent and adhesive. **2.** another name for **mica.** [C16: < MDu. *huysenblase,* lit.: sturgeon bladder; infl. by E GLASS]

Isl. *abbrev. for:* **1.** Island. **2.** Isle.

Islam ('ɪzlɑːm) *n.* **1.** Also called: **Islamism.** the religion of Muslims, teaching that there is only one God and that Mohammed is his prophet; Mohammedanism. **2. a.** Muslims collectively and their civilization. **b.** the countries where the Muslim religion is predominant. [C19: < Ar.: surrender (to God), < *aslama* to surrender] —**Is'lamic** *adj.*

Islamize *or* **-ise** ('ɪzləˌmaɪz) *vb.* (*tr.*) to convert or subject to the influence of Islam. —**ˌIslami'zation** *or* **-i'sation** *n.*

island ('aɪlənd) *n.* **1.** a mass of land that is surrounded by water and is smaller than a continent. **2.** something resembling this, esp. in being isolated, detached, or surrounded: *a traffic island.* **3.** *Anat.* a part, structure, or group of cells distinct in constitution from its immediate surroundings. ~Related adj.: **insular.** ~*vb.* (*tr.*) *Rare.* **4.** to cause to become an island. **5.** to intersperse with islands. **6.** to place on an island; insulate; isolate. [OE *īgland*] —**'island-ˌlike** *adj.*

islander ('aɪləndə) *n.* a native or inhabitant of an island.

island universe *n.* a former name for **galaxy.**

isle (aɪl) *n. Poetic except when cap. and part of place name.* an island, esp. a small one. [C13: < OF, < L *insula* island]

islet ('aɪlɪt) *n.* a small island. [C16: < OF *islette;* see ISLE]

islets *or* **islands of Langerhans** ('læŋəˌhæns) *pl. n.* small groups of endocrine cells in the pancreas that secrete insulin. [C19: after Paul *Langerhans* (1847–88), G physician]

ism ('ɪzəm) *n. Inf., often derog.* an unspecified doctrine, system, or practice.

-ism *suffix forming nouns.* **1.** indicating an action, process, or result: *criticism.* **2.** indicating a state or condition: *paganism.* **3.** indicating a doctrine, system, or body of principles and practices: *Leninism; spiritualism.* **4.** indicating behaviour or a characteristic quality: *heroism.* **5.** indicating a characteristic usage, esp. of a language: *Scotticism.* [< OF *-isme,* < L *-ismus,* < Gk *-ismos*]

Ismaili *or* **Isma'ili** (ˌɪzmɑː'iːlɪ) *n. Islam.* **1.** a Shiah sect whose adherents believe that Ismail, son of the sixth imam, was the rightful seventh imam. **2.** a member of this sect.

isn't ('ɪzᵊnt) *contraction of* is not.

ISO *abbrev. for:* **1.** International Standards Organization. **2.** Imperial Service Order (a Brit. decoration).

iso- *or before a vowel* **is-** *combining form.* **1.** equal or identical: *isomagnetic.* **2.** indicating that a chemical compound is an isomer of a specified compound: *isobutane.* [< Gk *isos* equal]

isobar ('aɪsəʊˌbɑː) *n.* **1.** a line on a map connecting places of equal atmospheric pressure, usually reduced to sea level for purposes of comparison, at a given time or period. **2.** *Physics.* any of two or more atoms that have the same mass number but different atomic numbers. Cf. **isotope.** [C19: < Gk *isobarēs* of equal weight] —**ˌiso'baric** *adj.* —**'isobarˌism** *n.*

isocheim *or* **isochime** ('aɪsəʊˌkaɪm) *n.* a line on a map connecting places with the same mean winter temperature. Cf. **isothere.** [C19: < ISO- + Gk *kheima* winter weather] —**ˌiso'cheimal** *or* **ˌiso'chimal** *adj.*

isochronal (aɪ'sɒkrənᵊl) *or* **isochronous** *adj.* **1.** having the same duration; equal in time. **2.** occurring at equal time intervals; having a uniform period of vibration. [C17: < NL, < Gk *isokhronos,* < ISO- + *khronos* time] —**i'sochronally** *or* **i'sochronously** *adv.* —**i'sochroˌnism** *n.*

isoclinal (ˌaɪsəʊ'klaɪnᵊl) *or* **isoclinic** (ˌaɪsəʊ'klɪnɪk) *adj.* **1.** sloping in the same direction and at the same angle. **2.** *Geol.* (of folds) having limbs that are parallel to each other. ~*n.* **3.** Also: **isocline, isoclinal line.** an imaginary line connecting points on the earth's surface having equal angles of magnetic dip.

isocline ('aɪsəʊˌklaɪn) *n.* **1.** a series of rock strata with isoclinal folds. **2.** another name for **isoclinal** (sense 3).

isodynamic (ˌaɪsəʊdaɪ'næmɪk) *adj. Physics.* **1.** having equal force or strength. **2.** of or relating to an imaginary line on the earth's surface connecting points of equal magnetic intensity.

isogeotherm (ˌaɪsəʊ'dʒiːəʊˌθɜːm) *n.* an imaginary line below the surface of the earth connecting points of equal temperature. —ˌ**isoˌgeo'thermal** *or* ˌ**isoˌgeo'thermic** *adj.*

isogloss ('aɪsəʊˌglɒs) *n.* a line drawn on a map around the area in which a linguistic feature is to be found. —ˌ**iso'glossal** *or* ˌ**iso'glottic** *adj.*

isogonic (ˌaɪsəʊ'gɒnɪk) *or* **isogonal** (aɪ'sɒgənᵊl) *adj.* 1. *Maths.* having, making, or involving equal angles. ~*n.* 2. Also called: **isogonic line, isogonal line, isogone.** *Physics.* an imaginary line connecting points on the earth's surface having equal magnetic declination.

isohel ('aɪsəʊˌhɛl) *n.* a line on a map connecting places with an equal period of sunshine. [C20: < ISO- + Gk *hēlios* sun]

isohyet (ˌaɪsəʊ'haɪɪt) *n.* a line on a map connecting places having equal rainfall. [C19: < ISO- + *-hyet,* < Gk *huetos* rain]

isolate *vb.* ('aɪsəˌleɪt). (*tr.*) 1. to place apart; cause to be alone. 2. *Med.* to quarantine (a person or animal) having a contagious disease. 3. to obtain (a compound) in an uncombined form. 4. to obtain pure cultures of (bacteria, esp. those causing a particular disease). 5. *Electronics.* to prevent interaction between (circuits, components, etc.); insulate. ~*n.* ('aɪsəlɪt). 6. an isolated person or group. [C19: back formation < *isolated,* via It. < L *insulātus,* lit.: made into an island] —'**isolable** *adj.* —ˌ**isola'bility** *n.* —'**isoˌlator** *n.* —ˌ**iso'lation** *n.*

isolationism (ˌaɪsə'leɪʃəˌnɪzəm) *n.* 1. a policy of nonparticipation in or withdrawal from international affairs. 2. an attitude favouring such a policy. —ˌ**iso'lationist** *n., adj.*

isomer ('aɪsəmə) *n.* 1. *Chem.* a compound that exhibits isomerism with one or more other compounds. 2. *Physics.* a nuclide that exhibits isomerism with one or more other nuclides. —**isomeric** (ˌaɪsə'mɛrɪk) *adj.*

isomerism (aɪ'sɒməˌrɪzəm) *n.* 1. the existence of two or more compounds having the same molecular formula but a different arrangement of atoms within the molecule. 2. the existence of two or more nuclides having the same atomic numbers and mass numbers but different energy states.

isomerous (aɪ'sɒmərəs) *adj.* (of flowers) having floral whorls with the same number of parts.

isometric (ˌaɪsəʊ'mɛtrɪk) *adj. also* **isometrical.** 1. having equal dimensions or measurements. 2. *Physiol.* of or relating to muscular contraction that does not produce shortening of the muscle. 3. (of a crystal or system of crystallization) having three mutually perpendicular equal axes. 4. (of a method of projecting a drawing in three dimensions) having the three axes equally inclined and all lines drawn to scale. ~*n.* 5. Also called: **isometric drawing.** a drawing made in this way. [C19: < Gk *isometria*] —ˌ**iso'metrically** *adv.*

isometrics (ˌaɪsəʊ'mɛtrɪks) *n.* (*functioning as sing.*) physical exercise involving isometric contraction of muscles.

isomorphism (ˌaɪsəʊ'mɔːˌfɪzəm) *n.* 1. *Biol.* similarity of form, as in different generations of the same life cycle. 2. *Chem.* the existence of two or more substances of different composition in a similar crystalline form. 3. *Maths.* a one-to-one correspondence between the elements of two or more sets, such as those of Arabic and Roman numerals. —'**isoˌmorph** *n.* —ˌ**iso'morphic** *or* ˌ**iso'morphous** *adj.*

isopleth ('aɪsəʊˌplɛθ) *n.* a line on a map connecting places registering the same amount or ratio of some geographical, etc. phenomenon. [C20: < Gk *isoplēthēs* equal in number, < ISO- + *plēthos* multitude]

isopod ('aɪsəʊˌpɒd) *n.* a crustacean, such as the woodlouse, in which the body is flattened. —**isopodan** (aɪ'sɒpədən) *or* **i'sopodous** *adj.*

isoprene ('aɪsəʊˌpriːn) *n.* a colourless volatile liquid with a penetrating odour: used in making synthetic rubbers. [C20: < ISO- + PR(OPYL) + -ENE]

isosceles (aɪ'sɒsɪˌliːz) *adj.* (of a triangle) having two sides of equal length. [C16: < LL, < Gk, < ISO- + *skelos* leg]

isoseismal (ˌaɪsəʊ'saɪzməl) *adj.* 1. of or relating to equal intensity of earthquake shock. ~*n.* 2. a line on a map connecting points at which earthquake shocks are of equal intensity. ~Also: **isoseismic.**

isostasy (aɪ'sɒstəsɪ) *n.* the state of balance which sections of the earth's lithosphere are thought ultimately to achieve when the vertical forces upon them remain unchanged. If a section is loaded as by ice, it slowly subsides. If a section is reduced in mass, as by erosion, it slowly rises. [C19: ISO- + *-stasy,* < Gk *stasis* a standing] —**isostatic** (ˌaɪsəʊ'stætɪk) *adj.*

isothere ('aɪsəʊˌθɪə) *n.* a line on a map linking places with the same mean summer temperature. Cf. **isocheim.** [C19: < ISO- + Gk *theros* summer] —**isotheral** (aɪ'sɒθərəl) *adj.*

isotherm ('aɪsəʊˌθɜːm) *n.* 1. a line on a map linking places of equal temperature. 2. *Physics.* a curve on a graph that connects points of equal temperature. ~Also called: **isothermal, isothermal line.**

isothermal (ˌaɪsəʊ'θɜːməl) *adj.* 1. (of a process or change) taking place at constant temperature. 2. of or relating to an isotherm. ~*n.* 3. another word for **isotherm.** —ˌ**iso'thermally** *adv.*

isotonic (ˌaɪsəʊ'tɒnɪk) *adj.* 1. *Physiol.* (of two or more muscles) having equal tension. 2. Also: **isosmotic.** (of two solutions) having the same osmotic pressure, commonly having physiological osmotic pressure. Cf. **hypertonic, hypotonic.** —**isotonicity** (ˌaɪsəʊtəʊ'nɪsɪtɪ) *n.*

isotope ('aɪsəˌtəʊp) *n.* one of two or more atoms with the same atomic number that contain different numbers of neutrons. [C20: < ISO- + Gk *topos* place] —**isotopic** (ˌaɪsə'tɒpɪk) *adj.* —ˌ**iso'topically** *adv.* —**isotopy** (aɪ'sɒtəpɪ) *n.*

isotropic (ˌaɪsəʊ'trɒpɪk) *or* **isotropous** (aɪ'sɒtrəpəs) *adj.* 1. having uniform physical properties in all directions. 2. *Biol.* not having predetermined axes: *isotropic eggs.* —ˌ**iso'tropically** *adv.* —**i'sotropy** *n.*

I-spy *n.* a game in which one player specifies the initial letter of the name of an object that he can see, which the other players then try to guess.

Israeli (ɪz'reɪlɪ) *n., pl.* **-lis** *or* **-li.** 1. a citizen or inhabitant of the state of Israel, in SW Asia. ~*adj.* 2. of or relating to the state of Israel or its inhabitants.

Israelite ('ɪzrɪəˌlaɪt, -rə-) *n.* 1. *Bible.* a member of the ethnic group claiming descent from Jacob; a Hebrew. 2. a member of any of various Christian sects who regard themselves as God's chosen people. 3. an archaic word for a **Jew.** [< *Israel,* the ancient kingdom of the Jews, at the SE end of the Mediterranean + -ITE[1]]

issuance ('ɪʃjʊəns) *n.* the act of issuing.

issue ('ɪʃjuː) *n.* 1. the act of sending or giving out something; supply; delivery. 2. something issued; an edition of stamps, a magazine, etc. 3. the act of emerging; outflow; discharge. 4. something flowing out, such as a river. 5. a place of outflow; outlet. 6. the descendants of a person; offspring; progeny. 7. a topic of interest or discussion. 8. an important subject requiring a decision. 9. an outcome or consequence; result. 10. *Pathol.* discharge from a wound. 11. *Law.* the matter remaining in dispute between the parties to an action after the pleadings. 12. the yield from or profits arising out of land or other property. 13. **at issue. a.** under discussion. **b.** in disagreement. 14. **force the issue.** to compel decision on some matter. 15. **join issue.** to join in controversy. 16. **take issue.** to disagree. ~*vb.* **-suing, -sued.** 17. to come forth or emerge or cause to come forth or emerge. 18. to publish or deliver (a newspaper, magazine, etc.). 19. (*tr.*) to make known or announce. 20. (*intr.*) to originate or proceed. 21. (*intr.*) to be a consequence; result. 22. (*intr.; foll. by in*) to end or terminate. 23. (*tr.*) (foll. by *with*) to supply officially (with). [C13: < OF *eissue* way out, < *eissir* to go out, < L *exīre*] —'**issuable** *adj.* —'**issuer** *n.*

-ist *suffix.* 1. (*forming nouns*) a person who performs a certain action or is concerned with something specified: *motorist; soloist.* **2.** (*forming nouns*) a person who practises in a specific field: *physicist.* **3.** (*forming nouns and adjectives*) a person who advocates a particular doctrine, system, etc., or relating to such a person or the doctrine advocated: *socialist.* **4.** (*forming nouns and adjectives*) a person characterized by a specified trait, tendency, etc., or relating to such a person or trait: *purist.* [via OF < L *-ista, -istēs,* < Gk *-istēs*]

isthmian (ˈɪsθmɪən) *adj.* relating to or situated in an isthmus.

isthmus (ˈɪsməs) *n., pl.* **-muses** *or* **-mi** (-maɪ). **1.** a narrow strip of land connecting two relatively large land areas. **2.** *Anat.* **a.** a narrow band of tissue connecting two larger parts of a structure. **b.** a narrow passage connecting two cavities. [C16: < L, < Gk *isthmos*] —ˈ**isthmoid** *adj.*

-istic *suffix forming adjectives.* equivalent to a combination of **-ist** and **-ic** but in some words having a less specific or literal application and sometimes a mildly pejorative force, as compared with corresponding adjectives ending in **-ist**: *communistic; impressionistic.* [< L *-isticus,* < Gk *istikos*]

istle (ˈɪstlɪ) *or* **ixtle** *n.* a fibre obtained from various tropical American agave and yucca trees used in making carpets, cord, etc. [C19: < Mexican Sp. *ixtle,* < Amerind *ichtli*]

it (ɪt) *pron.* (*subjective or objective*) **1.** refers to a nonhuman, animal, plant, or inanimate thing, or sometimes to a small baby: *it looks dangerous; give it a bone.* **2.** refers to an unspecified or implied antecedent or to a previous or understood clause, phrase, etc.: *it is impossible; I knew it.* **3.** used to represent human life or experience in respect of the present situation: *how's it going? I've had it; to brazen it out.* **4.** used as a formal subject (or object), referring to a following clause, phrase, or word: *it helps to know the truth; I consider it dangerous to go on.* **5.** used in the nominative as the formal grammatical subject of impersonal verbs: *it is raining; it hurts.* **6.** (used as complement with *be*) *Inf.* the crucial or ultimate point: *the steering failed and I thought that was it.* ~*n.* **7.** (in children's games) the player whose turn it is to try to touch another. **8.** *Inf.* **a.** sexual intercourse. **b.** sex appeal. [OE *hit*]

IT *abbrev. for* information technology.

It. *abbrev. for:* **1.** Italian. **2.** Italy.

i.t.a. *or* **ITA** *abbrev. for* initial teaching alphabet, a partly phonetic alphabet used to teach reading.

ital. *abbrev. for* italic.

Ital. *abbrev. for:* **1.** Italian. **2.** Italy.

Italian (ɪˈtæljən) *n.* **1.** the official language of Italy and one of the official languages of Switzerland. **2.** a native or inhabitant of Italy or a descendant of one. ~*adj.* **3.** relating to, denoting, or characteristic of Italy, its inhabitants, or their language.

Italianate (ɪˈtæljənɪt, -ˌneɪt) *or* **Italianesque** *adj.* Italian in style or character.

italic (ɪˈtælɪk) *adj.* **1.** Also: **Italian.** of, relating to, or denoting a style of handwriting with the letters slanting to the right. **2.** of, relating to, or denoting a style of printing type modelled on this, chiefly used to indicate emphasis, a foreign word, etc. Cf. **roman.** ~*n.* **3.** (*often pl.*) italic type or print. [C16 (after an edition of Virgil (1501) printed in Venice and dedicated to Italy): < L *Italicus* of Italy, < Gk *Italikos*]

Italic (ɪˈtælɪk) *n.* **1.** a branch of the Indo-European family of languages that includes many of the ancient languages of Italy. ~*adj.* **2.** denoting, relating to, or belonging to this group of languages, esp. the extinct ones.

italicize *or* **-ise** (ɪˈtælɪˌsaɪz) *vb.* **1.** to print (textual matter) in italic type. **2.** (*tr.*) to underline (words, etc.) with a single line to indicate italics. —**iˌtaliciˈzation** *or* **-iˈsation** *n.*

itch (ɪtʃ) *n.* **1.** an irritation or tickling sensation of the skin causing a desire to scratch. **2.** a restless desire. **3.** any skin disorder, such as scabies, characterized by intense itching. ~*vb.* (*intr.*) **4.** to feel or produce an irritating or tickling sensation. **5.** to have a restless desire (to do something). **6. have itchy feet.** to be restless; have a desire to travel. **7. itching palm.** a grasping nature; avarice. [OE *gīccean*] —ˈ**itchy** *adj.* —ˈ**itchiness** *n.*

-ite[1] *suffix forming nouns.* **1.** a native or inhabitant of: *Israelite.* **2.** a follower or advocate of; a supporter of a group: *Luddite; labourite.* **3.** (in biology) indicating a division of a body or organ: *somite.* **4.** indicating a mineral or rock: *nephrite; peridotite.* **5.** indicating a commercial product: *vulcanite.* [via L *-ita* < Gk *-itēs* or directly < Gk]

-ite[2] *suffix forming nouns.* indicating a salt or ester of an acid having a name ending in *-ous: a nitrite is a salt of nitrous acid.* [< F, arbitrary alteration of -ATE[1]]

item *n.* (ˈaɪtəm). **1.** a thing or unit, esp. included in a list or collection. **2.** *Book-keeping.* an entry in an account. **3.** a piece of information, detail, or note: *a news item.* ~*vb.* (ˈaɪtəm). **4.** (*tr.*) *Arch.* to itemize. ~*adv.* (ˈaɪtɛm). **5.** likewise; also. [C14 (adv.) < L: in like manner]

itemize *or* **-ise** (ˈaɪtəˌmaɪz) *vb.* (*tr.*) to put on a list or make a list of. —ˌ**itemiˈzation** *or* **-iˈsation** *n.* —ˈ**itemˌizer** *or* **-ˌiser** *n.*

iterate (ˈɪtəˌreɪt) *vb.* (*tr.*) to say or do again. [C16: < L *iterāre,* < *iterum* again] —ˈ**iterant** *adj.* —ˌ**iterˈation** *n.* —ˈ**iterative** *adj.*

itinerancy (ɪˈtɪnərənsɪ, aɪ-) *or* **itineracy** *n.* **1.** the act of itinerating. **2.** *Chiefly Methodist Church.* the system of appointing a minister to a circuit of churches or chapels. **3.** itinerants collectively.

itinerant (ɪˈtɪnərənt, aɪ-) *adj.* **1.** itinerating. **2.** working for a short time in various places, esp. as a casual labourer. ~*n.* **3.** an itinerant worker or other person. [C16: < LL *itinerārī* to travel, < L *iter* a journey] —**iˈtinerantly** *adv.*

itinerary (aɪˈtɪnərərɪ, ɪ-) *n., pl.* **-aries.** **1.** a plan or line of travel; route. **2.** a record of a journey. **3.** a guidebook for travellers. ~*adj.* **4.** of or relating to travel or routes of travel.

itinerate (aɪˈtɪnəˌreɪt, ɪ-) *vb.* (*intr.*) to travel from place to place. —**iˌtinerˈation** *n.*

-itis *suffix forming nouns.* **1.** indicating inflammation of a specified part: *tonsillitis.* **2.** *Inf.* indicating a preoccupation with or imaginery condition of illness caused by: *computeritis; telephonitis.* [NL, < Gk, fem. of *-itēs* belonging to]

it'll (ˈɪtᵊl) *contraction of* it will *or* it shall.

ITO *abbrev. for* International Trade Organization.

-itol *suffix forming nouns.* indicating that certain chemical compounds are alcohols containing two or more hydroxyl groups: *inisitol; sorbitol.* [< -ITE[2] + -OL[1]]

its (ɪts) *determiner.* **a.** of, belonging to, or associated in some way with it: *its left rear wheel; I can see its logical consequence.* **b.** (*as pronoun*)*: its is over there.*

▷ **Usage.** The possessive adjective and pronoun *its* is never written with an apostrophe: *the cat has hurt its ear.* The contraction of *it is* (*or* it has), *it's* always has an apostrophe: *it's a pity that the cat has hurt its ear.*

it's (ɪts) *contraction of* it is *or* it has.

itself (ɪtˈsɛlf) *pron.* **1. a.** the reflexive form of **it. b.** (intensifier)*: even the money itself won't convince me.* **2.** (*preceded by a copula*) its normal or usual self: *my cat doesn't seem itself these days.*

▷ **Usage.** See at **myself.**

itsy-bitsy (ˈɪtsɪˈbɪtsɪ) *or* **itty-bitty** (ˈɪtɪˈbɪtɪ) *adj.* *Inf.* very small; tiny. [C20: baby talk alteration of *little bit*]

ITU *abbrev. for:* **1.** Intensive Therapy Unit. **2.** International Telecommunications Union.

ITV (in Britain) *abbrev. for* Independent Television.

-ity *suffix forming nouns.* indicating state or condition: *technicality.* [< OF *-ite,* < L *-itās*]

IU *abbrev. for:* **1.** immunizing unit. **2.** international unit.

IU(C)D *abbrev. for* intrauterine (contraceptive) device.

-ium *or sometimes* **-um** *suffix forming nouns.* **1.** indicating a metallic element: *platinum; barium.* **2.** (in chemistry) indicating groups forming positive ions: *ammonium chloride; hydroxonium ion.* **3.** indicating a biological structure: *syncytium.* [NL, < L, < Gk *-ion,* dim. suffix]

i.v. *abbrev. for:* **1.** initial velocity. **2.** Also: **IV.** intravenous(ly).

I've (aɪv) *contraction of* I have.

-ive *suffix.* **1.** (*forming adjectives*) indicating a tendency, inclination, character, or quality: *divisive; festive; massive.* **2.** (*forming nouns of adjectival origin*): *detective; expletive.* [< L *-īvus*]

IVF *abbrev. for* in vitro fertilization.

ivied (ˈaɪvɪd) *adj.* covered with ivy.

ivories (ˈaɪvərɪz, -vrɪz) *pl. n. Sl.* **1.** the keys of a piano. **2.** billiard balls. **3.** another word for **teeth. 4.** another word for **dice.**

ivory (ˈaɪvərɪ, -vrɪ) *n., pl.* **-ries. 1. a.** a hard smooth creamy white variety of dentine that makes up a major part of the tusks of elephants and walruses. **b.** (*as modifier*): *ivory ornaments.* **2.** a tusk made of ivory. **3. a.** a yellowish-white colour; cream. **b.** (*as adj.*): *ivory shoes.* **4.** a substance resembling elephant tusk. **5.** an ornament, etc., made of ivory. **6. black ivory.** *Obs.* Negro slaves collectively. [C13: < OF, < L *evoreus* made of ivory, < *ebur* ivory] —ˈ**ivory-**ˌ**like** *adj.*

ivory black *n.* a black pigment obtained by grinding charred scraps of ivory in oil.

ivory nut *n.* **1.** the seed of the ivory palm, which contains an ivory-like substance used to make buttons, etc. **2.** any similar seed from other palms. ~Also called: **vegetable ivory.**

ivory tower (ˈtaʊə) *n.* **a.** seclusion or remoteness of attitude regarding problems, everyday life, etc. **b.** (*as modifier*): *ivory-tower aestheticism.* —ˌ**ivory-**ˈ**towered** *adj.*

IVR *abbrev. for* International Vehicle Registration.

ivy (ˈaɪvɪ) *n., pl.* **ivies. 1.** a woody climbing or trailing plant having lobed evergreen leaves and black berry-like fruits. **2.** any of various other climbing or creeping plants, such as poison ivy and ground ivy. [OE *īfig*] —ˈ**ivy-**ˌ**like** *adj.*

IWW *abbrev. for* Industrial Workers of the World.

ixia (ˈɪksɪə) *n.* an iridaceous plant of southern Africa, having showy ornamental funnel-shaped flowers. [C18: NL < Gk *ixos* mistletoe]

ixtle (ˈɪkstlɪ, ˈɪst-) *n.* a variant spelling of **istle.**

izard (ˈɪzəd) *n.* (esp. in the Pyrenees) another name for **chamois.**

-ize *or* **-ise** *suffix forming verbs.* **1.** to cause to become, resemble, or agree with: *legalize.* **2.** to become; change into: *crystallize.* **3.** to affect in a specified way; subject to: *hypnotize.* **4.** to act according to some practice, principle, policy, etc.: *economize.* [< OF *-iser,* < LL *-izāre,* < Gk *-izein*]

▷ **Usage.** In Britain and the U.S. *-ize* is the preferred ending for many verbs, but *-ise* is equally acceptable in British English. Certain words (chiefly those not formed by adding the suffix to an existing word) are, however always spelt with *-ise* in both Britain and the U.S.: *advertise, revise.*

J

j *or* **J** (dʒeɪ) *n., pl.* **j's, J's,** *or* **Js.** **1.** the tenth letter of the English alphabet. **2.** a speech sound represented by this letter.

j *symbol for:* **1.** *Maths.* the unit vector along the *y*-axis. **2.** the imaginary number $\sqrt{-1}$.

J *symbol for:* **1.** current density. **2.** *Cards.* jack. **3.** joule(s).

J. *abbrev. for:* **1.** Journal. **2.** (*pl.* **JJ.**) Judge. **3.** (*pl.* **JJ.**) Justice.

jab (dʒæb) *vb.* **jabbing, jabbed.** **1.** to poke or thrust sharply. **2.** to strike with a quick short blow or blows. ~*n.* **3.** a sharp poke or stab. **4.** a quick short blow. **5.** *Inf.* an injection: *polio jabs.* [C19: orig. Scot. var. of JOB] —ˈ**jabbing** *adj.*

jabber (ˈdʒæbə) *vb.* **1.** to speak or say rapidly, incoherently, and without making sense; chatter. ~*n.* **2.** such talk. [C15: imit.]

jabberwocky (ˈdʒæbəˌwɒkɪ) *n.* nonsense verse. [C19: coined by Lewis Carroll as the title of a poem in *Through the Looking Glass* (1871)]

jabiru (ˈdʒæbɪˌruː) *n.* **1.** a large white tropical American stork with a dark naked head and a dark bill. **2.** Also called: **black-necked stork, policeman bird.** a large Australian stork, having a white plumage, dark green back and tail, and red legs. **3.** another name for **saddlebill.** [C18: via Port., of Amerind origin]

jabot (ˈʒæbəʊ) *n.* a frill or ruffle on the breast or throat of a garment. [C19: < F: bird's crop, jabot]

jaçana (ˌʒɑːsəˈnɑː, ˌdʒæ-) *n.* a bird of tropical and subtropical marshy regions, having long legs and very long toes that enable walking on floating plants. [C18: < Port., of Amerind origin, < *jasaná*]

jacaranda (ˌdʒækəˈrændə) *n.* **1.** a tropical American tree having fernlike leaves and pale purple flowers. **2.** the fragrant ornamental wood of this tree. **3.** any of several related or similar trees or their wood. [C18: < Port., of Amerind origin, < *yacarandá*]

jacinth (ˈdʒæsɪnθ) *n.* another name for **hyacinth** (sense 4). [C13: < Med. L *jacinthus,* < L *hyacinthus* plant, precious stone; see HYACINTH]

jack (dʒæk) *n.* **1.** a man or fellow. **2.** a sailor. **3.** the male of certain animals, esp. of the ass or donkey. **4.** a mechanical or hydraulic device for exerting a large force, esp. to raise a heavy weight such as a motor vehicle. **5.** any of several mechanical devices that replace manpower, such as a contrivance for rotating meat on a spit. **6.** one of four playing cards in a pack, one for each suit; knave. **7.** *Bowls.* a small usually white bowl at which the players aim with their own bowls. **8.** *Electrical engineering.* a female socket designed to receive a male plug. **9.** a flag, esp. a small flag flown at the bow of a ship indicating the ship's nationality. **10.** a part of the action of a harpsichord, consisting of a fork-shaped device on the end of a pivoted lever on which a plectrum is mounted. **11. a.** any of various tropical and subtropical fishes. **b.** an immature pike. **12.** Also called: **jackstone.** one of the pieces used in the game of jacks. **13.** *U.S.* a slang word for **money. 14. every man jack.** everyone without exception. **15. the jack.** *Austral. sl.* syphilis. ~*adj.* **16.** *Austral. sl.* tired or fed up (esp. in **be jack of something**). ~*vb.* **17.** (*tr.*) to lift or push (an object) with a jack. ~See also **jack in, jack up.** [C16 *jakke,* var. of *Jankin,* dim. of *John*]

Jack (dʒæk) *n.* **I'm all right, Jack.** *Brit. inf.* a remark indicating smug and complacent selfishness.

jackal (ˈdʒækɔːl) *n.* **1.** any of several African or S Asian mammals closely related to the dog, having long legs and pointed ears and muzzle: they are predators and carrion-eaters. **2.** a person who does menial tasks for another. [C17: < Turkish, < Persian, < Sansk. *srgāla*]

jackanapes (ˈdʒækəˌneɪps) *n.* (*functioning as sing.*) **1.** a conceited impertinent person. **2.** a mischievous child. **3.** *Arch.* a monkey. [C16: var. of *Jakken-apes,* lit.: Jack of the ape, nickname of William de la Pole (1396–1450), first Duke of Suffolk, whose badge showed an ape's ball and chain]

jackass (ˈdʒækˌæs) *n.* **1.** a male donkey. **2.** a fool. [C18: < JACK (male) + ASS[1]]

jackboot (ˈdʒækˌbuːt) *n.* **1.** an all-leather military boot, extending up to or above the knee. **2.** authoritarian rule or behaviour. —ˈ**jackˌbooted** *adj.*

jackdaw (ˈdʒækˌdɔː) *n.* a large Eurasian bird, related to the crow, having a black and dark grey plumage: noted for its thieving habits. [C16: < JACK + *daw,* obs. name for jackdaw]

jackeroo *or* **jackaroo** (ˌdʒækəˈruː) *n., pl.* **-roos.** *Austral. inf.* a novice on a sheep or cattle station. [C19: < JACK + (KANG)AROO]

jacket (ˈdʒækɪt) *n.* **1.** a short coat, esp. one that is hip-length and has a front opening and sleeves. **2.** something that resembles this: *a life jacket.* **3.** any exterior covering or casing, such as the insulating cover of a boiler. **4.** See **dust jacket. 5. a.** the skin of a baked potato. **b.** (*as modifier*): *jacket potatoes.* **6.** *Oil industry.* the support structure, esp. the legs, of an oil platform. ~*vb.* **7.** (*tr.*) to put a jacket on (someone or something). [C15: < OF *jaquet* short jacket, < *jacque* peasant, < *Jacques* James] —ˈ**jacketed** *adj.*

Jack Frost *n.* a personification of frost.

jack in *vb.* (*tr., adv.*) *Sl.* to abandon or leave (an attempt or enterprise).

jack-in-office *n.* a self-important petty official.

jack-in-the-box *n., pl.* **jack-in-the-boxes** *or* **jacks-in-the-box.** a toy consisting of a figure on a tight spring in a box, which springs out when the lid is opened.

Jack Ketch (kɛtʃ) *n. Brit. arch.* a hangman. [C18: after *John Ketch* (died 1686), public executioner in England]

jackknife (ˈdʒækˌnaɪf) *n., pl.* **-knives.** **1.** a knife with the blade pivoted to fold into a recess in the handle. **2.** a former name for a type of dive in which the diver bends at the waist in midair; forward pike dive. ~*vb.* (*intr.*) **3.** (of an articulated lorry) to go out of control in such a way that the trailer swings round at an angle to the tractor.

jack of all trades *n., pl.* **jacks of all trades.** a person who undertakes many different kinds of work.

jack-o'-lantern *n.* **1.** a lantern made from a hollowed pumpkin, which has holes cut in it to represent a human face. **2.** a will-o'-the-wisp.

jack plane *n.* a carpenter's plane, usually with a wooden body, used for rough planing of timber.

jackpot (ˈdʒækˌpɒt) *n.* **1.** any large prize, kitty, or accumulated stake that may be won in gambling. **2. hit the jackpot. a.** to win a jackpot. **b.** *Inf.* to achieve great success, esp. through luck. [C20: prob. < JACK (playing card) + POT[1]]

jack rabbit *n.* any of various W North American hares having long hind legs and large ears. [C19: shortened < *jackass-rabbit,* referring to its long ears]

Jack Robinson (ˈrɒbɪnsən) *n.* **before you could** (*or* **can**) **say Jack Robinson.** extremely quickly or suddenly.

Jack Russell (ˈrʌsəl) *n.* a small short-legged terrier having a white coat with tan, black, or lemon markings. [after John *Russell* (1795-1883), E clergyman who developed the breed]

jacks (dʒæks) *n.* (*functioning as sing.*) a game in which bone or metal pieces (**jackstones**) are thrown and then picked up between bounces or throws of a small ball. [C19: shortened < *jackstones,* var. of *checkstones* pebbles]

jacksnipe (ˈdʒækˌsnaɪp) *n., pl.* **-snipe** *or* **-snipes.** a small Eurasian short-billed snipe.

jackstraws (ˈdʒækˌstrɔːz) *n.* (*functioning as sing.*) another name for **spillikins.**

Jack Tar *n. Now chiefly literary.* a sailor.

jack up *vb.* (*adv.*) **1.** (*tr.*) to increase (prices, salaries, etc.). **2.** (*tr.*) to raise an object, such as a car, with or as with a jack. **3.** (*intr.*) *Sl.* to inject oneself with a drug. **4.** (*intr.*) *Austral. inf.* to refuse to comply.

Jacobean (ˌdʒækəˈbɪən) *adj.* **1.** *History.* relating to James I of England or to the period of his rule (1603–25). **2.** of or relating to the style of furniture current at this time, characterized by the use of dark brown carved oak. **3.** relating to or having the style of architecture used in England during this period. [C18: < NL, < *Jacōbus* James]

Jacobin (ˈdʒækəbɪn) *n.* **1.** a member of the most radical club founded during the French Revolution, which instituted the Reign of Terror. **2.** an extreme political radical. **3.** a French Dominican friar. ~*adj.* **4.** of or relating to the Jacobins or their policies. [C14: < OF, < Med. L *Jacōbīnus,* < LL *Jacōbus* James; the political club orig. met in the convent near the church of *St Jacques* in 1789] —ˌ**Jacoˈbinic** *or* ˌ**Jacoˈbinical** *adj.* —ˈ**Jacobinism** *n.*

Jacobite (ˈdʒækəˌbaɪt) *n. Brit. history.* an adherent of James II after his overthrow in 1688, or of his descendants in their attempts to regain the throne. [C17: < LL *Jacōbus* James + -ITE[1]] —**Jacobitic** (ˌdʒækəˈbɪtɪk) *adj.*

Jacob's ladder (ˈdʒeɪkəbz) *n.* **1.** *Old Testament.* the ladder reaching up to heaven that Jacob saw in a dream (Genesis 28:12–17). **2.** a ladder made of wooden or metal steps supported by ropes or chains. **3.** a North American plant with blue flowers and a ladder-like arrangement of leaves.

Jacob's staff *n.* a medieval instrument for measuring heights and distances.

jaconet (ˈdʒækənɪt) *n.* a light cotton fabric used for clothing, etc. [C18: < Urdu *jagannāthī,* < *Jagannāthpūrī,* India, where orig. made]

Jacquard (ˈdʒækɑːd, dʒəˈkɑːd) *n.* **1.** Also called: **Jacquard weave.** a fabric in which the design is incorporated into the weave. **2.** Also called: **Jacquard loom.** the loom that produces this fabric. [C19: after Joseph M. *Jacquard* (1752–1834), F inventor]

jactation (dʒækˈteɪʃən) *n.* **1.** *Rare.* the act of boasting. **2.** *Pathol.* another word for **jactitation.** [C16: < L *jactātiō* bragging, < *jactāre* to flourish, < *jacere* to throw]

jactitation (ˌdʒæktɪˈteɪʃən) *n.* **1.** the act of boasting. **2.** a false assertion that one is married to another, formerly actionable at law. **3.** *Pathol.* restless tossing in bed, characteristic of severe fevers. [C17: < Med. L, < L *jacitāre* to utter publicly, < *jactitāre* to toss about; see JACTATION]

Jacuzzi (dʒəˈkuːzɪ) *n. Trademark.* **1.** a device which swirls water in a bath. **2.** a bath containing such a device.

jade[1] (dʒeɪd) *n.* **1.** a semiprecious stone which varies in colour from white to green and is used for making ornaments and jewellery. **2. a.** the green colour of jade. **b.** (*as adj.*): *a jade skirt.* [C18: < F, < It. *giada,* < obs. Sp. *piedra de ijada* colic stone (lit.: stone of the flank, because it was believed to cure renal colic)]

jade[2] (dʒeɪd) *n.* **1.** an old overworked horse. **2.** *Derog., facetious.* a woman considered to be disreputable. ~*vb.* **3.** to exhaust or make exhausted from work or use. [C14: <?] —ˈ**jadish** *adj.*

jaded (ˈdʒeɪdɪd) *adj.* **1.** exhausted or dissipated. **2.** satiated. —ˈ**jadedly** *adv.* —ˈ**jadedness** *n.*

jadeite (ˈdʒeɪdaɪt) *n.* a green or white mineral, a variety of jade, consisting of sodium aluminium silicate in monoclinic crystalline form.

j'adoube *French.* (ʒadub) *interj. Chess.* an expression of an intention to touch a piece in order to adjust its placement rather than to make a move. [lit.: I adjust]

Jaffa (ˈdʒæfə, ˈdʒɑː-) *n.* a large variety of orange having a thick skin. [after *Jaffa,* port in W Israel (now part of Tel Aviv) where orig. cultivated]

jag[1] (dʒæg) *vb.* **jagging, jagged.** **1.** (*tr.*) to cut unevenly. ~*n., vb.* **2.** an informal word for **jab.** ~*n.* **3.** a jagged notch or projection. [C14: <?]

jag[2] (dʒæg) *n. Sl.* **a.** intoxication from drugs or alcohol. **b.** a bout of drinking or drug taking. [C16: ? < OE *ceacga* broom]

jagged (ˈdʒægɪd) *adj.* having sharp projecting notches. —ˈ**jaggedly** *adv.*

jaggy (ˈdʒægɪ) *adj.* **-gier, -giest.** **1.** a less common word for **jagged.** **2.** *Scot.* prickly.

jaguar (ˈdʒægjʊə) *n.* a large feline mammal of S North America, Central America, and N South America, similar to the leopard but with larger spots on its coat. [C17: < Port., < Guarani *yaguara*]

jai alai (ˈhaɪ ˈlaɪ, ˈhaɪ əˌlaɪ) *n.* a version of pelota played by two or four players. [via Sp. < Basque, < *jai* game + *alai* merry]

jail *or* **gaol** (dʒeɪl) *n.* **1.** a place for the confinement of persons convicted and sentenced to imprisonment or of persons awaiting trial. ~*vb.* **2.** (*tr.*) to confine in prison. [C13: < OF *jaiole* cage, < Vulgar L *caveola* (unattested), < L *cavea* enclosure]

jailbird *or* **gaolbird** (ˈdʒeɪlˌbɜːd) *n.* a person who is or has been confined to jail, esp. repeatedly; convict.

jailbreak *or* **gaolbreak** (ˈdʒeɪlˌbreɪk) *n.* an escape from jail.

jailer, jailor, *or* **gaoler** (ˈdʒeɪlə) *n.* a person in charge of prisoners in a jail.

Jain (dʒaɪn) *or* **Jaina** (ˈdʒaɪnə) *n.* **1.** an adherent of Jainism. ~*adj.* **2.** of or relating to Jainism. [C19: < Hindi *jaina* saint, lit.: overcomer, < Sansk.]

Jainism (ˈdʒaɪˌnɪzəm) *n.* an ancient Hindu religion, characterized by the belief that the material world is progressing endlessly in a series of cycles. —ˈ**Jainist** *n., adj.*

jake (dʒeɪk) *adj. Austral. & N.Z. sl.* all right; fine: *she's jake.* [<?]

jalap *or* **jalop** (ˈdʒæləp) *n.* **1.** a Mexican climbing plant. **2.** the dried and powdered root of any of these plants, used as a purgative. [C17: < F, < Mexican Sp. *jalapa*] —**jalapic** (dʒəˈlæpɪk) *adj.*

jalapeño (ˌhɑːləˈpeɪnjəʊ) *n., pl.* **-ños.** a type of red capsicum with a hot taste used in Mexican cookery. [Mexican Sp.]

jalopy *or* **jaloppy** (dʒəˈlɒpɪ) *n., pl.* **-lopies** *or* **-loppies.** *Inf.* a dilapidated old car. [C20: <?]

jalousie (ˈʒæluˌziː) *n.* **1.** a window blind or shutter constructed from angled slats of wood, etc. **2.** a window made of angled slats of glass. [C19: < OF *gelosie* latticework screen]

jam[1] (dʒæm) *vb.* **jamming, jammed.** **1.** (*tr.*) to cram or wedge into or against something: *to jam paper into an incinerator.* **2.** (*tr.*) to crowd or pack: *cars jammed the roads.* **3.** to make or become stuck or locked. **4.** (*tr.;* often foll. by *on*) to activate suddenly (esp. in **jam on the brakes**). **5.** (*tr.*) to block; congest. **6.** (*tr.*) to crush or squeeze. **7.** *Radio.* to prevent the clear reception of (radio communications) by transmitting other signals on the same frequency. **8.** (*intr.*) *Sl.* to play in a jam session. ~*n.* **9.** a crowd or congestion in a confined space: *a traffic jam.* **10.** the act of jamming or the state of being jammed. **11.** *Inf.* a predicament: *to help a friend out of a jam.* **12.** See **jam session.** [C18: prob. imit.] —ˈ**jammer** *n.*

jam[2] (dʒæm) *n.* a preserve containing fruit, which has been boiled with sugar until the mixture sets. [C18: ? < JAM[1] (the act of squeezing)]

Jam. *Bible. abbrev. for* James.

jamb *or* **jambe** (dʒæm) *n.* a vertical side member of a doorframe, window frame, or lining. [C14: < OF *jambe* leg, jamb, < LL *gamba* hoof, < Gk *kampē* joint]

jamboree (ˌdʒæmbəˈriː) *n.* **1.** a large and often international gathering of Scouts. **2.** a party or spree. [C19: <?]

jammy (ˈdʒæmɪ) *adj.* **-mier, -miest.** *Brit. sl.* **1.** pleasant; desirable. **2.** lucky.

jam-packed *adj.* packed or filled to capacity.

jam session *n. Sl.* an unrehearsed or improvised performance by jazz or rock musicians. [C20: prob. < JAM[1]]

Jan. *abbrev. for* January.

Jandal (ˈdʒændᵊl) *n. N.Z. trademark.* a kind of sandal with a strip of material between the big toe and the other toes and over the foot.

jangle (ˈdʒæŋgᵊl) *vb.* **1.** to sound or cause to sound discordantly, harshly, or unpleasantly. **2.** (*tr.*) to produce a jarring effect on: *the accident jangled his nerves.* **3.** *Arch.* to wrangle. [C13: < OF *jangler*, of Gmc origin] —ˈ**jangler** *n.*

janissary (ˈdʒænɪsərɪ) *or* **janizary** (ˈdʒænɪzərɪ) *n., pl.* **-saries** *or* **-zaries.** an infantryman in the Turkish army, originally a member of the sovereign's guard, from the 14th to the 19th century. [C16: < F, < It., < Turkish *yeniçeri*, < *yeni* new + *çeri* soldiery]

janitor (ˈdʒænɪtə) *n.* **1.** *Scot.* the caretaker of a building, esp. a school. **2.** *Chiefly U.S. & Canad.* a person employed to clean and maintain a building. [C17: L: doorkeeper, < *jānua* door, < *jānus* covered way] —**janitorial** (ˌdʒænɪˈtɔːrɪəl) *adj.*

Jansenism (ˈdʒænsəˌnɪzəm) *n. R.C. Church.* the doctrine of Cornelis Jansen and his disciples, who believed in predestination and denied free will. —ˈ**Jansenist** *n., adj.* —ˌ**Jansen**ˈ**istic** *adj.*

Jansky (ˈdʒænskɪ) *n., pl.* **-skys.** (in radio astronomy) a unit used to measure the intensity of radio waves. Also called: **flux unit.** [C20: after Karl G. *Jansky* (1905-50), U.S. electrical engineer]

January (ˈdʒænjʊərɪ) *n., pl.* **-aries.** the first month of the year, consisting of 31 days. [C14: < L *Jānuārius*]

japan (dʒəˈpæn) *n.* **1.** a glossy black lacquer originally from the Orient, used on wood, metal, etc. **2.** work decorated and varnished in the Japanese manner. ~*vb.* **-panning, -panned. 3.** (*tr.*) to lacquer with japan or any similar varnish.

Japanese (ˌdʒæpəˈniːz) *adj.* **1.** of or characteristic of Japan, its people, or their language. ~*n.* **2.** (*pl.* **-nese**) a native or inhabitant of Japan. **3.** the official language of Japan.

Japanese stranglehold *n.* a wrestling hold in which an opponent's arms exert pressure on his own windpipe.

jape (dʒeɪp) *n.* **1.** a jest or joke. ~*vb.* **2.** to joke or jest (about). [C14: ? < OF *japper* to yap, imit.] —ˈ**japer** *n.* —ˈ**japery** *n.*

Japlish (ˈdʒæplɪʃ) *n.* the adoption and adaptation of English words into the Japanese language. [C20: < a blend of JAPANESE + ENGLISH]

japonica (dʒəˈpɒnɪkə) *n.* **1.** Also called: **Japanese quince.** a Japanese shrub cultivated for its red flowers and yellowish fruit. **2.** another name for the **camellia.** [C19: < NL, fem. of *japonicus* Japanese, < *Japonia* Japan]

jar[1] (dʒɑː) *n.* **1.** a wide-mouthed container that is usually cylindrical, made of glass or earthenware, and without handles. **2.** Also: **jarful.** the contents or quantity contained in a jar. **3.** *Brit. inf.* a glass of beer. [C16: < OF *jarre, jarra,* < Ar. *jarrah* large earthen vessel]

jar[2] (dʒɑː) *vb.* **jarring, jarred. 1.** to vibrate or cause to vibrate. **2.** to make or cause to make a harsh discordant sound. **3.** (often foll. by *on*) to have a disturbing or painful effect (on the nerves, mind, etc.). **4.** (*intr.*) to disagree; clash. ~*n.* **5.** a jolt or shock. **6.** a harsh discordant sound. [C16: prob. imit.] —ˈ**jarring** *adj.* —ˈ**jarringly** *adv.*

jar[3] (dʒɑː) *n.* **on a** (*or* **the**) **jar.** (of a door) slightly open; ajar. [C17 (in the sense: turn): < earlier *char,* < OE *cierran* to turn]

jardinière (ˌʒɑːdɪˈnjɛə) *n.* **1.** an ornamental pot or trough for plants. **2.** a garnish of fresh vegetables for a dish of meat. [C19: < F, fem. of *jardinier* gardener, < *jardin* GARDEN]

jargon (ˈdʒɑːgən) *n.* **1.** specialized language concerned with a particular subject, culture, or profession. **2.** language characterized by pretentious vocabulary or meaning. **3.** gibberish. [C14: < OF, ? imit.]

jarl (jɑːl) *n. Medieval history.* a Scandinavian chieftain or noble. [C19: < ON] —ˈ**jarldom** *n.*

jarrah (ˈdʒærə) *n.* an Australian eucalyptus tree that yields a valuable timber. [< Abor.]

jasmine (ˈdʒæsmɪn, ˈdʒæz-) *n.* **1.** Also called: **jessamine.** any tropical or subtropical oleaceous shrub or climbing plant widely cultivated for their white, yellow, or red fragrant flowers. **2.** any of several other shrubs with fragrant flowers, such as the Cape jasmine, yellow jasmine, and frangipani (**red jasmine**). [C16: < OF *jasmin,* < Ar., < Persian *yāsmīn*]

jaspé (ˈdʒæspeɪ) *adj.* resembling jasper; variegated. [C19: < F, < *jasper* to marble]

jasper (ˈdʒæspə) *n.* **1.** an opaque impure form of quartz, red, yellow, brown, or dark green in colour, used as a gemstone and for ornamental decoration. **2.** Also called: **jasper ware.** a dense hard stoneware. [C14: < OF *jaspe,* < L *jaspis,* < Gk *iaspis,* of Semitic origin]

jato (ˈdʒeɪtəʊ) *n., pl.* **-tos.** *Aeronautics.* jet-assisted takeoff. [C20: < *j(et-)a(ssisted) t(ake)-o(ff)*]

jaundice (ˈdʒɔːndɪs) *n.* **1.** Also called: **icterus.** yellowing of the skin due to the abnormal presence of bile pigments in the blood, as in hepatitis. **2.** jealousy, envy, and ill humour. ~*vb.* **3.** to distort (the judgment, etc.) adversely: *jealousy had jaundiced his mind.* **4.** (*tr.*) to affect with or as if with jaundice. [C14: < OF *jaunisse,* < *jaune* yellow, < L *galbinus* yellowish]

jaunt (dʒɔːnt) *n.* **1.** a short pleasurable excursion; outing. ~*vb.* **2.** (*intr.*) to go on such an excursion. [C16: <?]

jaunting car *n.* a light two-wheeled one-horse car, formerly widely used in Ireland.

jaunty (ˈdʒɔːntɪ) *adj.* **-tier, -tiest. 1.** sprightly and cheerful: *a jaunty step.* **2.** smart; trim: *a jaunty hat.* [C17: < F *gentil* noble; see GENTEEL] —ˈ**jauntily** *adv.* —ˈ**jauntiness** *n.*

Java man (ˈdʒɑːvə) *n.* a type of primitive man, *Homo erectus,* that lived in the middle Palaeolithic Age in Java.

Javanese (ˌdʒɑːvəˈniːz) *adj.* **1.** of or relating to the island of Java, in Indonesia. ~*n.* **2.** (*pl.* **-nese**) a native or inhabitant of Java. **3.** the Malayo-Polynesian language of Java.

javelin (ˈdʒævlɪn) *n.* **1.** a long pointed spear thrown as a weapon or in competitive field events. **2. the javelin.** the event or sport of throwing the javelin. [C16: < OF *javeline,* var. of *javelot,* of Celtic origin]

jaw (dʒɔː) *n.* **1.** the part of the skull of a vertebrate that frames the mouth and holds the teeth. **2.** the corresponding part of an invertebrate, esp. an insect. **3.** a pair or either of a pair of hinged or sliding components of a machine or tool designed to grip an object. **4.** *Sl.* **a.** impudent talk. **b.** idle conversation. **c.** a lecture. ~*vb.* **5.** (*intr.*) *Sl.* **a.** to chat; gossip. **b.** to lecture. [C14: prob. < OF *joue* cheek]

jawbone (ˈdʒɔːˌbəʊn) *n.* a nontechnical name for **mandible** or (less commonly) **maxilla.**

jawbreaker (ˈdʒɔːˌbreɪkə) *n.* **1.** a device having hinged jaws for crushing rocks and ores. **2.** *Inf.* a word that is hard to pronounce. —ˈ**jaw**ˌ**breaking** *adj.*

jaws (dʒɔːz) *pl. n.* **1.** the narrow opening of some confined place such as a gorge. **2. the jaws.** a dangerously close position: *the jaws of death.*

jay (dʒeɪ) *n.* **1.** a passerine bird related to the crow having a pinkish-brown body, blue-and-black wings, and a black-and-white crest. **2.** a foolish or gullible person. [C13: < OF *jai,* < LL *gāius,* ? < name *Gāius*]

Jaycee (ˈdʒeɪˈsiː) *n. U.S., Canad., Austral., & N.Z.* a young person who belongs to a junior chamber of commerce. [C20: < *J(unior) C(hamber)*]

jaywalk (ˈdʒeɪˌwɔːk) *vb.* (*intr.*) to cross or walk in a street recklessly or illegally. [C20: < JAY (sense 2)] —ˈ**jay**ˌ**walker** *n.* —ˈ**jay**ˌ**walking** *n.*

jazz (dʒæz) *n.* **1. a.** a kind of music of American Negro origin, characterized by syncopated rhythms, solo and group improvisation, and a variety of harmonic idioms and instrumental techniques. **b.** (*as modifier*): *a jazz band.* **c.** (*in combination*): *a jazzman.* **2.** *Sl.* rigmarole: *legal papers and all that jazz.* ~*vb.* **3.** (*intr.*) to play or dance to jazz music. [C20: <?] —ˈ**jazzy** *adj.* —ˈ**jazzily** *adv.* —ˈ**jazziness** *n.*

jazz up *vb.* (*tr., adv.*) *Inf.* **1.** to imbue (a piece of music) with jazz qualities, esp. by playing at a quicker tempo. **2.** to make more lively or appealing.

JCB *n. Trademark.* a type of construction machine with a hydraulically operated shovel on the front and an excavator arm on the back. [< the initials of *J*(oseph) *C*(yril) *B*(amford) (born 1916), its E manufacturer]

jealous (ˈdʒɛləs) *adj.* **1.** suspicious or fearful of being displaced by a rival. **2.** (often *postpositive* and foll. by *of*) resentful (of) or vindictive (towards). **3.** (often *postpositive* and foll. by *of*) possessive and watchful in the protection (of): *jealous of one's reputation.* **4.** characterized by or resulting from jealousy. **5.** *Obsolete except in Biblical use.* demanding exclusive loyalty: *a jealous God.* [C13: < OF *gelos,* < Med. L, < LL *zēlus* emulation, < Gk *zēlos* ZEAL] —ˈ**jealously** *adv.*

jealousy (ˈdʒɛləsɪ) *n., pl.* **-ousies.** the state or quality of being jealous.

jean (dʒiːn) *n.* a tough twill-weave cotton fabric used for hard-wearing trousers, overalls, etc. [C16: short for *jean fustian,* < *Gene* Genoa]

Jean Baptiste (*French* ʒɑ̃bɑtist) *n. Canad. sl.* a French Canadian. [F: John the Baptist, traditional patron saint of French Canada]

jeans (dʒiːnz) *pl. n.* trousers for casual wear, made esp. of denim or corduroy. [pl. of JEAN]

Jeep (dʒiːp) *n. Trademark.* a small road vehicle with four-wheel drive. [C20: ? < *GP,* for *general-purpose* (*vehicle*), infl. by Eugene the *Jeep,* creature in a comic strip by E. C. Segar]

jeepers *or* **jeepers creepers** (ˈdʒiːpəz ˈkriːpəz) *interj. U.S. sl.* a mild exclamation of surprise. [C20: euphemism for *Jesus*]

jeer (dʒɪə) *vb.* **1.** (often foll. by *at*) to laugh or scoff (at a person or thing). ~*n.* **2.** a remark or cry of derision. [C16: <?] —ˈ**jeerer** *n.* —ˈ**jeering** *adj., n.* —ˈ**jeeringly** *adv.*

jehad (dʒɪˈhæd) *n.* a variant spelling of **jihad.**

Jehovah (dʒɪˈhəʊvə) *n. Old Testament.* the personal name of God, revealed to Moses on Mount Horeb (Exodus 3). [C16: < Med. L, < Heb. YHVH YAHWEH]

Jehovah's Witness *n.* a member of a Christian Church of American origin, the followers of which believe that the end of the present world system of government is near.

Jehu (ˈdʒiːhjuː) *n.* **1.** *Old Testament.* the successor to Ahab as king of Israel. **2.** *Humorous.* a reckless driver.

jejune (dʒɪˈdʒuːn) *adj.* **1.** naive; unsophisticated. **2.** insipid; dull. **3.** lacking nourishment. [C17: < L *jējūnus* hungry, empty] —**je**ˈ**junely** *adv.* —**je**ˈ**juneness** *n.*

jejunum (dʒɪˈdʒuːnəm) *n.* the part of the small intestine between the duodenum and the ileum. [C16: < L, < *jējūnus* empty; from the belief that the jejunum is empty after death]

Jekyll and Hyde (ˈdʒɛkᵊl; haɪd) *n.* **a.** a person with two distinct personalities, one good, the other evil. **b.** (*as modifier*): *a Jekyll-and-Hyde personality.* [C19: after the principal character of Robert Louis Stevenson's novel *The Strange Case of Dr Jekyll and Mr Hyde* (1886)]

jell *or* **gel** (dʒɛl) *vb.* **1.** to make or become gelatinous; congeal. **2.** (*intr.*) to assume definite form: *his ideas have jelled.* [C19: back formation < JELLY¹]

jellaba *or* **jellabah** (ˈdʒɛləbə) *n.* a kind of loose cloak with a hood, worn esp. in N Africa. [< Ar. *jallabah, jallābīya*]

jellify (ˈdʒɛlɪˌfaɪ) *vb.* **-fying, -fied.** to make into or become jelly. —ˌ**jellifiˈcation** *n.*

jelly¹ (ˈdʒɛlɪ) *n., pl.* **-lies. 1.** a fruit-flavoured clear dessert set with gelatin. **2.** a preserve made from the juice of fruit boiled with sugar and used as jam. **3.** a savoury food preparation set with gelatin or with gelatinous stock: *calf's-foot jelly.* ~*vb.* **-lying, -lied. 4.** to jellify. [C14: < OF *gelee* frost, jelly, < *geler* to set hard, < L, < *gelu* frost] —ˈ**jellied** *adj.* —ˈ**jelly-**ˌ**like** *adj.*

jelly² (ˈdʒɛlɪ) *n. Brit.* a slang name for **gelignite.**

jelly baby *n. Brit.* a small sweet made from a gelatinous substance formed to resemble a baby.

jellyfish (ˈdʒɛlɪˌfɪʃ) *n., pl.* **-fish** *or* **-fishes. 1.** any marine coelenterate having a gelatinous umbrella-shaped body with trailing tentacles. **2.** *Inf.* a weak indecisive person.

jelly fungus *n.* a fungus that grows on trees and has a jelly-like consistency when wet.

jemmy (ˈdʒɛmɪ) *or U.S.* **jimmy** *n., pl.* **-mies. 1.** a short steel crowbar used, esp. by burglars, for forcing doors and windows. ~*vb.* **-mying, -mied. 2.** (*tr.*) to prise (something) open with a jemmy. [C19: < the pet name for *James*]

jennet, genet, *or* **gennet** (ˈdʒɛnɪt) *n.* a small Spanish riding horse. [C15: < OF *genet,* < Catalan *ginet,* horse used by the *Zenete,* < Ar. *Zanātah* the Zenete, a Moorish people renowned for their horsemanship]

jenny (ˈdʒɛnɪ) *n., pl.* **-nies. 1.** a machine for turning up the edge of a piece of sheet metal in preparation for making a joint. **2.** the female of certain animals or birds, esp. a donkey, ass, or wren. **3.** short for **spinning jenny. 4.** *Billiards, etc.* an in-off. [C17: < name *Jenny,* dim. of *Jane*]

jeopardize *or* **-ise** (ˈdʒɛpəˌdaɪz) *vb.* (*tr.*) **1.** to risk; hazard: *he jeopardized his job by being persistently unpunctual.* **2.** to put in danger.

jeopardy (ˈdʒɛpədɪ) *n.* (usually preceded by *in*) **1.** danger of injury, loss, death, etc.: *his health was in jeopardy.* **2.** *Law.* danger of being convicted and punished for a criminal offence. [C14: < OF *jeu parti,* lit.: divided game, hence uncertain issue, < *jeu* game, < L *jocus* joke, game + *partir* to divide]

jequirity (dʒɪˈkwɪrɪtɪ) *n., pl.* **-ties.** a tropical climbing plant with scarlet black-spotted seeds used as beads, and roots used as a substitute for liquorice. Also called: **Indian liquorice.** [C19: < Port. *jequirití,* of Amerind origin, < *jekiriti*]

Jer. *Bible. abbrev. for* Jeremiah.

jerbil (ˈdʒɜːbɪl) *n.* a variant spelling of **gerbil.**

jerboa (dʒɜːˈbəʊə) *n.* any small nocturnal burrowing rodent inhabiting dry regions of Asia and N Africa, having long hind legs specialized for jumping. [C17: < NL, < Ar. *yarbū'*]

jeremiad (ˌdʒɛrɪˈmaɪəd) *n.* a long mournful lamentation or complaint. [C18: < F *jérémiade,* referring to the Lamentations of Jeremiah in the Old Testament]

jerepigo (ˌdʒɛrɪˈpɪgəʊ) *n. S. African.* a sweet white or red sherry-type wine. [< Port. *cheripiga* an adulterant of port wine]

jerk¹ (dʒɜːk) *vb.* **1.** to move or cause to move with an irregular or spasmodic motion. **2.** to throw, twist, pull, or push (something) abruptly or spasmodically. **3.** (*tr.;* often foll. by *out*) to utter (words, etc.) in a spasmodic or breathless manner. ~*n.* **4.** an abrupt or spasmodic movement. **5.** an irregular jolting motion: *the car moved with a jerk.* **6.** (*pl.*) Also called: **physical jerks.** *Brit. inf.* physical exercises. **7.** *Sl., chiefly U.S. & Canad.* a stupid or ignorant person. [C16: prob. var. of *yerk* to pull stitches tight] —ˈ**jerker** *n.*

jerk² (dʒɜːk) *vb.* (*tr.*) **1.** to preserve beef, etc., by cutting into thin strips and drying in the sun. ~*n.* **2.** Also called: **jerky.** jerked meat. [C18: back formation < *jerky,* < Sp. *charqui,* < Quechuan]

jerkin (ˈdʒɜːkɪn) *n.* **1.** a sleeveless short jacket worn by men or women. **2.** a man's sleeveless fitted jacket, often made of leather, worn in the 16th and 17th centuries. [C16: <?]

jerky (ˈdʒɜːkɪ) *adj.* **jerkier, jerkiest.** characterized by jerks. —ˈ**jerkily** *adv.* —ˈ**jerkiness** *n.*

jeroboam (ˌdʒɛrəˈbəʊəm) *n.* a wine bottle holding the equivalent of four normal bottles. [C19: allusion to Jeroboam, a "mighty man of valour" (I Kings 11:28) who "made Israel to sin" (I Kings 14:16)]

jerry (ˈdʒɛrɪ) *n., pl.* **-ries.** *Brit.* an informal word for **chamber pot.**

Jerry (ˈdʒɛrɪ) *n., pl.* **-ries.** *Brit. sl.* **1.** a German, esp. a German soldier. **2.** the Germans collectively.

jerry-build *vb.* **-building, -built.** (*tr.*) to build (houses, flats, etc.) badly using cheap materials. —ˈ**jerry-ˌbuilder** *n.*

jerry can *n.* a flat-sided can with a capacity of between 4.5 and 5 gallons used for storing or transporting liquids, esp. motor fuel. [C20: < JERRY]

jersey (ˈdʒɜːzɪ) *n.* **1.** a knitted garment covering the upper part of the body. **2. a.** a machine-knitted slightly elastic cloth of wool, silk, nylon, etc., used for clothing. **b.** (*as modifier*): *a jersey suit.* **3.** *Austral. & N.Z.* a football strip. [C16: < *Jersey,* < the woollen sweaters worn by the fishermen]

Jersey (ˈdʒɜːzɪ) *n.* a breed of dairy cattle producing milk with a high butterfat content, originating from the island of Jersey. [after *Jersey,* island in the English Channel]

Jerusalem artichoke (dʒəˈruːsələm) *n.* **1.** a North American sunflower widely cultivated for its underground edible tubers. **2.** the tuber of this plant, which is eaten as a vegetable. [C17: by folk etymology < It. *girasole articiocco;* see GIRASOL]

jess (dʒɛs) *n. Falconry.* a short leather strap, one end of which is permanently attached to the leg of a hawk or falcon. [C14: < OF *ges,* < L *jactus* a throw, < *jacere* to throw] —**jessed** *adj.*

jessamine (ˈdʒɛsəmɪn) *n.* another name for **jasmine** (sense 1).

jest (dʒɛst) *n.* **1.** something done or said for amusement; joke. **2.** playfulness; fun: *to act in jest.* **3.** a jeer or taunt. **4.** an object of derision. ~*vb.* **5.** to act or speak in an amusing or frivolous way. **6.** to make fun of (a person or thing). [C13: var. of GEST] —ˈ**jesting** *adj., n.* —ˈ**jestingly** *adv.*

jester (ˈdʒɛstə) *n.* a professional clown employed by a king or nobleman during the Middle Ages.

Jesuit (ˈdʒɛzjʊɪt) *n.* **1.** a member of a Roman Catholic religious order (the **Society of Jesus**) founded by Ignatius Loyola in 1534 with the aim of defending Catholicism against the Reformation. **2.** (*sometimes not cap.*) *Inf., offens.* a person given to subtle and equivocating arguments. [C16: < NL *Jēsuita,* < LL *Jēsus* + *-ita* -ITE[1]] —ˌ**Jesuˈitical** *adj.*

Jesus (ˈdʒiːzəs) *n.* **1.** Also called: **Jesus Christ, Jesus of Nazareth.** ?4 B.C.–?29 A.D., founder of Christianity, born in Bethlehem and brought up as a Jew. He is believed by Christians to be the Son of God. ~*interj. also* **Jesus wept. 2.** used to express intense surprise, dismay, etc. [via L < Gk *Iēsous,* < Heb. *Yeshūaʻ,* shortened < *Yehōshūaʻ* God is help]

jet[1] (dʒɛt) *n.* **1.** a thin stream of liquid or gas forced out of a small aperture. **2.** an outlet or nozzle for emitting such a stream. **3.** a jet-propelled aircraft. ~*vb.* **jetting, jetted. 4.** to issue or cause to issue in a jet: *water jetted from the hose.* **5.** to transport or be transported by jet aircraft. [C16: < OF *jeter* to throw, < L *jactāre* to toss about]

jet[2] (dʒɛt) *n.* **a.** a hard black variety of lignite that takes a brilliant polish and is used for jewellery, etc. **b.** (*as modifier*): *jet earrings.* [C14: < OF *jaiet,* < L, < Gk *lithos gagatēs* stone of *Gagai,* a town in Lycia, Asia Minor]

jet black *n.* **a.** a deep black colour. **b.** (*as adj.*): *jet-black hair.*

jet condenser *n.* a steam condenser in which steam is condensed by jets of water.

jeté (ʒəˈteɪ) *n. Ballet.* a step in which the dancer springs from one leg and lands on the other. [F, lit.: thrown, < *jeter;* see JET[1]]

jet engine *n.* a gas turbine, esp. one fitted to an aircraft.

jet lag *n.* a general feeling of fatigue often experienced by travellers by jet aircraft who cross several time zones in relatively few hours.

jet-propelled *adj.* **1.** driven by jet propulsion. **2.** *Inf.* very fast.

jet propulsion *n.* **1.** propulsion by means of a jet of fluid. **2.** propulsion by means of a gas turbine, esp. when the exhaust gases provide the propulsive thrust.

jetsam (ˈdʒɛtsəm) *n.* **1.** that portion of the cargo of a vessel thrown overboard to lighten her, as during a storm. Cf. **flotsam** (sense 1). **2.** another word for **flotsam** (sense 2). [C16: shortened < JETTISON]

jet set *n.* **a.** a rich and fashionable social set, the members of which travel widely for pleasure. **b.** (*as modifier*): *jet-set travellers.* —ˈ**jetˌsetter** *n.* —ˈ**jet-ˌsetting** *n., adj.*

jet stream *n.* **1.** *Meteorol.* a narrow belt of high-altitude winds moving east at high speeds. **2.** the jet of exhaust gases produced by a gas turbine, etc.

jettison (ˈdʒɛtɪsᵊn, -zᵊn) *vb.* (*tr.*) **1.** to abandon: *to jettison old clothes.* **2.** to throw overboard. ~*n.* **3.** another word for **jetsam** (sense 1). [C15: < OF, ult. < L *jactātiō* a tossing about]

jetton (ˈdʒɛtᵊn) *n.* a counter or token, esp. a chip used in such gambling games as roulette. [C18: < F *jeton,* < *jeter* to cast up (accounts); see JET[1]]

jetty (ˈdʒɛtɪ) *n., pl.* **-ties.** a pier, dock, groyne, mole, or other structure extending into the water from the shore. [C15: < OF *jetee* projecting part, lit.: something thrown out, < *jeter* to throw]

jeu d'esprit (*French* ʒø dɛspri) *n., pl.* ***jeux d'esprit*** (ʒø dɛspri). a light-hearted display of wit or cleverness, esp. in literature. [lit.: play of spirit]

Jew (dʒuː) *n.* **1.** a member of the Semitic people who are descended from the ancient Israelites. **2.** a person whose religion is Judaism. **3.** (*modifier*) *Offens.* Jewish: *a Jew boy.* **4.** (*sometimes not cap.*) *Offens.* **a.** a person who drives a hard bargain. **b.** a miserly person. ~*vb.* **5.** (*tr.; often not cap.*) *Offens.* to drive a hard bargain with. [C12: < OF *juiu,* < L *jūdaeus,* < Gk *ioudaios,* < Heb., < *yehūdāh* Judah]

jewel (ˈdʒuːəl) *n.* **1.** a precious or semiprecious stone; gem. **2.** a person or thing resembling a jewel in preciousness, brilliance, etc. **3.** a gemstone used as a bearing in a watch. **4.** a piece of jewellery. ~*vb.* **-elling, -elled** *or U.S.* **-eling, -eled. 5.** (*tr.*) to fit or decorate with a jewel or jewels. [C13: < OF *jouel,* ? < *jeu* game, < L *jocus*]

jewelfish (ˈdʒuːəlˌfɪʃ) *n., pl.* **-fish** *or* **-fishes.** a beautifully coloured and popular aquarium fish native to Africa.

jeweller *or U.S.* **jeweler** (ˈdʒuːələ) *n.* a person whose business is the cutting or setting of gemstones or the making or selling of jewellery.

jeweller's rouge *n.* a finely powdered form of ferric oxide used as a metal polish.

jewellery *or U.S.* **jewelry** (ˈdʒuːəlrɪ) *n.* objects that are worn for personal adornment, such as rings, necklaces, etc., considered collectively.

Jewess (ˈdʒuːɪs) *n.* a Jewish girl or woman.

jewfish (ˈdʒuːˌfɪʃ) *n., pl.* **-fish** *or* **-fishes. 1.** any of various large dark fishes of warm or tropical seas. **2.** *Austral.* a freshwater catfish. [C17: <?]

Jewish (ˈdʒuːɪʃ) *adj.* **1.** of or characteristic of Jews. **2.** *Offens.* miserly. —ˈ**Jewishly** *adv.* —ˈ**Jewishness** *n.*

Jew lizard *n.* a large Australian lizard with spiny scales round its neck.

Jewry (ˈdʒʊərɪ) *n., pl.* **-ries. 1. a.** Jews collectively. **b.** the Jewish religion or culture. **2.** a quarter of a town inhabited by Jews.

jew's-ear *n.* a pinky-red fungus.

jew's-harp *n.* a musical instrument consisting of a small lyre-shaped metal frame held between the teeth, with a steel tongue plucked with the finger.

Jezebel (ˈdʒɛzəˌbɛl) *n.* **1.** *Old Testament.* the wife of Ahab, king of Israel. **2.** (*sometimes not cap.*) a shameless or scheming woman.

jib[1] (dʒɪb) *n.* **1.** *Naut.* any triangular sail set forward of the foremast of a vessel. **2. cut of someone's jib.** someone's manner, style, etc. [C17: <?]

jib[2] (dʒɪb) *vb.* **jibbing, jibbed.** (*intr.*) *Chiefly Brit.* **1.** (often foll. by *at*) to be reluctant (to). **2.** (of an animal) to stop short and refuse to go forwards. **3.** *Naut.* a variant of **gybe.** [C19: <?] —ˈ**jibber** *n.*

jib[3] (dʒɪb) *n.* the projecting arm of a crane or the boom of a derrick. [C18: prob. based on GIBBET]

jib boom *n. Naut.* a spar forming an extension of the bowsprit.

jibe[1] (dʒaɪb) *or* **jib** (dʒɪb) *vb., n. Naut.* a variant of **gybe.**

jibe[2] (dʒaɪb) *vb.* a variant spelling of **gibe**[1].

jibe[3] (dʒaɪb) *vb.* (*intr.*) *Inf.* to agree; accord; harmonize. [C19: <?]

jiffy (ˈdʒɪfɪ) *or* **jiff** *n., pl.* **jiffies** *or* **jiffs.** *Inf.* a very short time: *wait a jiffy.* [C18: <?]

Jiffy bag *n. Trademark.* a large padded envelope.

jig (dʒɪg) *n.* **1.** any of several old rustic kicking and leaping dances. **2.** a piece of music composed for or in the rhythm of this dance. **3.** a mechanical device designed to hold and locate a component during machining. **4.** *Angling.* any of various spinning lures that wobble when drawn through the water. **5.** Also called: **jigger.** *Mining.* a device for separating ore or coal from waste material by agitation in water. ~*vb.* **jigging, jigged. 6.** to dance (a jig). **7.** to jerk or cause to jerk up and down rapidly. **8.** (often foll. by *up*) to fit or be fitted in a jig. **9.** (*tr.*) to drill or cut (a workpiece) in a jig. **10.** (*tr.*) *Mining.* to separate ore or coal from waste material using a jig. [C16: <?]

jigger[1] (ˈdʒɪgə) *n.* **1.** a person or thing that jigs. **2.** *Golf.* (formerly) an iron club, usually No. 4. **3.** any of a number of mechanical devices having a vibratory motion. **4.** a light lifting tackle used on ships. **5.** a small glass, esp. for whisky. **6.** *Billiards.* another word for **bridge**[1]. **7.** *N.Z.* a light hand- or power-propelled vehicle used on railway lines.

jigger[2] *or* **jigger flea** (ˈdʒɪgə) *n.* another name for the **chigoe** (sense 1).

jiggered (ˈdʒɪgəd) *adj.* (*postpositive*) *Inf.* damned; blowed: *I'm jiggered if he'll get away with it.* [C19: prob. euphemism for *buggered;* see BUGGER]

jiggermast (ˈdʒɪgəˌmɑːst) *n. Naut.* any small mast on a sailing vessel.

jiggery-pokery (ˈdʒɪgərɪˈpəʊkərɪ) *n. Inf., chiefly Brit.* dishonest or deceitful behaviour. [C19: < Scot. dialect *joukery-pawkery*]

jiggle (ˈdʒɪgᵊl) *vb.* **1.** to move or cause to move up and down or to and fro with a short jerky motion. ~*n.* **2.** a short jerky motion. [C19: frequentative of JIG] —ˈ**jiggly** *adj.*

jigsaw (ˈdʒɪgˌsɔː) *n.* **1.** a mechanical saw with a fine steel blade for cutting intricate curves in sheets of material. **2.** See **jigsaw puzzle.** [C19: < JIG (to jerk up and down rapidly) + SAW[1]]

jigsaw puzzle *n.* a puzzle in which the player has to reassemble a picture that has been cut into irregularly shaped interlocking pieces.

jihad *or* **jehad** (dʒɪˈhæd) *n. Islam.* a holy war against infidels undertaken by Muslims. [C19: < Ar. *jihād* a conflict]

jilt (dʒɪlt) *vb.* **1.** (*tr.*) to leave or reject (a lover), esp. without previous warning. ~*n.* **2.** a woman who jilts a lover. [C17: < dialect *jillet* flighty girl, dim. of name *Gill*]

jim crow (ˈdʒɪm ˈkrəʊ) *n. (often caps.) U.S.* **1. a.** the policy or practice of segregating Negroes. **b.** (*as modifier*): *jim-crow laws.* **2.** a derogatory term for **Negro. 3.** an implement for bending iron bars or rails. [C19: < *Jim Crow,* name of song used as the basis of an act by Thomas Rice (1808–60), American entertainer] —ˈ**jim**-ˈ**crowism** *n.*

jimjams (ˈdʒɪmˌdʒæmz) *pl. n.* **1.** *Sl.* delirium tremens. **2.** a state of nervous tension or anxiety. [C19: whimsical formation based on JAM[1]]

jimmy (ˈdʒɪmɪ) *n., pl.* **-mies,** *vb.* **-mying, -mied.** a U.S. variant of **jemmy.**

jingle (ˈdʒɪŋgᵊl) *vb.* **1.** to ring or cause to ring lightly and repeatedly. **2.** (*intr.*) to sound in a manner suggestive of jingling: *a jingling verse.* ~*n.* **3.** a sound of metal jingling. **4.** a rhythmical verse, etc., esp. one used in advertising. [C16: prob. imit.] —ˈ**jingly** *adj.*

jingo (ˈdʒɪŋgəʊ) *n., pl.* **-goes. 1.** a loud and bellicose patriot. **2.** jingoism. **3. by jingo.** an exclamation of surprise. [C17: orig. ? euphemism for *Jesus;* applied to bellicose patriots after the use of *by Jingo!* in a 19th-cent. song]

jingoism (ˈdʒɪŋgəʊˌɪzəm) *n.* the belligerent spirit or foreign policy of jingoes. —ˈ**jingoist** *n., adj.* —ˌ**jingo**ˈ**istic** *adj.*

jink (dʒɪŋk) *vb.* **1.** (*intr.*) to move swiftly or turn in order to dodge. ~*n.* **2.** a jinking movement. [C18: of Scot. origin, imit. of swift movement]

jinker (ˈdʒɪŋkə) *n. Austral.* a vehicle for transporting timber, consisting of a tractor and two sets of wheels for supporting the logs. [<?]

jinks (dʒɪŋks) *pl. n.* boisterous or mischievous play (esp. in **high jinks**). [C18: <?]

jinn (dʒɪn) *n.* (*often functioning as sing.*) the plural of **jinni.**

jinni, jinnee, *or* **djinni** (dʒɪˈniː) *n., pl.* **jinn** *or* **djinn** (dʒɪn). a spirit in Muslim mythology who could assume human or animal form and influence man by supernatural powers. [C17: < Ar.]

jinrikisha, jinricksha, *or* **jinrickshaw** (dʒɪnˈrɪkʃɔː) *n.* another name for **rickshaw.** [C19: < Japanese, < *jin* man + *riki* power + *sha* carriage]

jinx (dʒɪŋks) *n.* **1.** an unlucky force, person, or thing. ~*vb.* **2.** (*tr.*) to be or put a jinx on. [C20: ? < NL *Jynx,* genus name of the wryneck, < Gk *iunx* wryneck, a bird used in magic]

jitter (ˈdʒɪtə) *Inf.* ~*vb.* **1.** (*intr.*) to be anxious or nervous. ~*n.* **2. the jitters.** nervousness and anxiety. [C20: <?] —ˈ**jittery** *adj.* —ˈ**jitteriness** *n.*

jitterbug (ˈdʒɪtəˌbʌg) *n.* **1.** a fast jerky American dance, usually to a jazz accompaniment, that was popular in the 1940s. **2.** a person who dances the jitterbug. ~*vb.* **-bugging, -bugged. 3.** (*intr.*) to perform such a dance.

jiujitsu *or* **jiujutsu** (dʒuːˈdʒɪtsuː) *n.* a variant spelling of **jujitsu.**

jive (dʒaɪv) *n.* **1.** a style of lively and jerky dance, popular esp. in the 1940s and 1950s. **2.** *Sl., chiefly U.S.* **a.** misleading or deceptive talk. **b.** (*as modifier*): *jive talk.* ~*vb.* **3.** (*intr.*) to dance the jive. **4.** *Sl., chiefly U.S.* to mislead; tell lies (to). [C20: <?] —ˈ**jiver** *n.*

job (dʒɒb) *n.* **1.** an individual piece of work or task. **2.** an occupation. **3.** an object worked on or a result produced from working. **4.** a duty or responsibility: *her job was to cook the dinner.* **5.** *Inf.* a difficult task or problem: *I had a job to contact him.* **6.** a state of affairs: *make the best of a bad job.* **7.** *Inf.* a particular type of something: *a four-wheel drive job.* **8.** *Inf.* a crime, esp. a robbery. **9.** *Computers.* a unit of work for a computer. **10. jobs for the boys.** jobs given to or created for allies or favourites. **11. just the job.** exactly what was required. **12. on the job.** actively engaged in one's employment. ~*vb.* **jobbing, jobbed. 13.** (*intr.*) to work by the piece or at casual jobs. **14.** to make a private profit out of (a public office, etc.). **15.** (*intr.; usually foll. by in*) **a.** to buy and sell (goods or services) as a middleman: *he jobs in government surplus.* **b.** *Brit.* to buy and sell stocks and shares as a stockjobber. **16.** *Austral. sl.* to punch. [C16: <?] —ˈ**jobless** *adj.*

jobber (ˈdʒɒbə) *n.* **1.** *Brit.* short for **stockjobber** (sense 1). See also **market maker. 2.** a person who jobs.

jobbery (ˈdʒɒbərɪ) *n.* the practice of making private profit out of a public office.

jobbing (ˈdʒɒbɪŋ) *adj.* working by the piece, not regularly employed: *a jobbing gardener.*

Jobcentre (ˈdʒɒbˌsɛntə) *or* **job centre** *n. Brit.* any of a number of government offices having premises situated in the main shopping area of a town in which people seeking jobs can consult displayed advertisements.

job lot *n.* **1.** a miscellaneous collection of articles sold as a lot. **2.** a collection of cheap or trivial items.

job satisfaction *n.* the extent to which the desires and hopes of a worker are fulfilled as a result of his work.

Job's comforter (dʒəʊbz) *n.* a person who, while purporting to give sympathy, succeeds only in adding to distress. [< *Job* in the Old Testament (Job 16: 1-5)]

job sharing *n.* the division of a job between two or more people such that each covers the same job for complementary parts of the day or week. —**job share** *n.*

jobsworth (ˈdʒɒbzˌwɜːθ) *n. Inf.* a person in a position of minor authority who invokes the letter of the law in order to avoid any action requiring initiative, cooperation, etc. [C20: < *it's more than my job's worth to...*]

jock (dʒɒk) *n. Inf.* short for **jockey** or **jockstrap.**

Jock (dʒɒk) *n.* a slang word or name for a **Scot.**

jockey (ˈdʒɒkɪ) *n.* **1.** a person who rides horses in races, esp. as a profession. ~*vb.* **2. a.** (*tr.*) to ride (a horse) in a race. **b.** (*intr.*) to ride as a jockey. **3.** (*intr.:* often foll. by *for*) to try to obtain an advantage by manoeuvring (esp. in **jockey for position**). **4.** to trick or cheat (a person). [C16 (in the sense: lad): < name *Jock* + -EY]

jockstrap (ˈdʒɒkˌstræp) *n.* an elasticated belt with a pouch worn by men, esp. athletes, to support the genitals. Also called: **athletic support.** [C20: < sl. *jock* penis + STRAP]

jocose (dʒəˈkəʊs) *adj.* characterized by humour. [C17: < L *jocōsus* given to jesting, < *jocus* joke] —**joˈcosely** *adv.* —**jocosity** (dʒəˈkɒsɪtɪ) *n.*

jocular (ˈdʒɒkjʊlə) *adj.* **1.** characterized by joking and good humour. **2.** meant lightly or humorously. [C17: < L *joculāris*, < *joculus* little JOKE] —**jocularity**(ˌdʒɒkjʊˈlærɪtɪ) *n.* —ˈ**jocularly** *adv.*

jocund (ˈdʒɒkənd) *adj.* of a humorous temperament; merry. [C14: < LL *jocundus*, < L *jūcundus* pleasant, < *juvāre* to please] —**jocundity** (dʒəʊˈkʌndɪtɪ) *n.* —ˈ**jocundly** *adv.*

jodhpurs (ˈdʒɒdpəz) *pl. n.* riding breeches, loose-fitting around the hips and tight-fitting from the thighs to the ankles. [C19: < *Jodhpur*, town in NW India]

Joe Blake (bleɪk) *n. Austral. sl.* **1.** a snake. **2. the Joe Blakes.** the DT's.

Joe Bloggs (blɒgz) *n. Brit. sl.* an average or typical man. U.S., Canad., and Austral. equivalent: **Joe Blow.**

Joe Public *n. Sl.* the general public.

joes (dʒəʊz) *pl. n.* **the.** *Austral. inf.* a fit of depression. [short for *the Joe Blakes*]

joey (ˈdʒəʊɪ) *n. Austral. inf.* **1.** a young kangaroo. **2.** a young animal or child. [C19: < Abor.]

jog (dʒɒg) *vb.* **jogging, jogged. 1.** (*intr.*) to run or move slowly or at a jog trot, esp. for physical exercise. **2.** (*intr.;* foll. by *on* or *along*) to continue in a plodding way. **3.** (*tr.*) to jar or nudge slightly. **4.** (*tr.*) to remind: *jog my memory.* ~*n.* **5.** the act of jogging. **6.** a slight jar or nudge. **7.** a jogging motion; trot. [C14: prob. var. of *shog* to shake]

jogger (ˈdʒɒgə) *n.* **1.** a person who runs at a jog trot over some distance for exercise. **2.** *N.Z.* a cart with rubber tyres used on farms.

jogging (ˈdʒɒgɪŋ) *n.* a slow run or trot, esp. as a keep-fit exercise.

joggle (ˈdʒɒgᵊl) *vb.* **1.** to shake or move (someone or something) with a slightly jolting motion. **2.** (*tr.*) to join or fasten (two pieces of building material) by means of a joggle. ~*n.* **3.** the act of joggling. **4.** a slight irregular shake. **5.** a joint between two pieces of building material by means of a projection on one piece that fits into a notch in the other. [C16: frequentative of JOG] —ˈ**joggler** *n.*

jog trot *n.* **1.** an easy bouncy gait, esp. of a horse, midway between a walk and a trot. **2.** a regular way of living or doing something.

john (dʒɒn) *n. Chiefly U.S. & Canad.* a slang word for **lavatory.** [C20: special use of the name]

John Barleycorn *n. Usually humorous.* the personification of alcoholic drink.

John Bull *n.* **1.** a personification of England or the English people. **2.** a typical Englishman. [C18: name of a character intended to be representative of the English nation in *The History of John Bull* (1712) by John Arbuthnot]

John Doe *n.* See **Doe.**

John Dory (ˈdɔːrɪ) *n.* a European dory (the fish), having a deep compressed body and massive mobile jaws. [C18: < name *John* + DORY[1]; on the model of DOE]

John Hop *n. Austral. sl.* a policeman. [rhyming sl. for COP[1]]

johnny (ˈdʒɒnɪ) *n., pl.* **-nies.** *Brit. inf.* (*often cap.*) a man or boy; chap.

Johnny Canuck (ˈdʒɒnɪ kəˈnʌk) *n. Canad.* **1.** an informal name for a **Canadian. 2.** a personification of Canada.

Johnny-come-lately *n., pl.* **Johnny-come-latelies** *or* **Johnnies-come-lately.** *Sl.* a brash newcomer, novice, or recruit.

Johnsonian (dʒɒnˈsəʊnɪən) *adj.* of, relating to, or characteristic of Samuel Johnson, 18th-cent. English lexicographer, his works, or his style of writing.

joie de vivre *French.* (ʒwa də vivrə) *n.* joy of living; enjoyment of life; ebullience.

join (dʒɔɪn) *vb.* **1.** to come or bring together. **2.** to become a member of (a club, etc.). **3.** (*intr.;* often foll. by *with*) to become associated or allied. **4.** (*intr.;* usually foll. by *in*) to take part. **5.** (*tr.*) to meet (someone) as a companion. **6.** (*tr.*) to become part of. **7.** (*tr.*) to unite (two people) in marriage. **8.** (*tr.*) *Geom.* to connect with a straight line or a curve. **9. join hands. a.** to hold one's own hands together. **b.** (of two people) to hold each other's hands. **c.** (usually foll. by *with*) to work together in an enterprise. ~*n.* **10.** a joint; seam. **11.** the act of joining. ~See also **join up.** [C13: < OF, < L *jungere* to yoke]

joinder (ˈdʒɔɪndə) *n.* **1.** the act of joining, esp. in legal contexts. **2.** *Law.* **a.** (in pleading) the stage at which the parties join issue (**joinder of issue**). **b.** the joining of two or more persons as coplaintiffs or codefendants (**joinder of parties**). [C17: < F *joindre* to JOIN]

joiner (ˈdʒɔɪnə) *n.* **1.** *Chiefly Brit.* a person skilled in making finished woodwork, such as windows and stairs. **2.** a person or thing that joins. **3.** *Inf.* a person who joins many clubs, etc.

joinery (ˈdʒɔɪnərɪ) *n.* **1.** the skill or craft of a joiner. **2.** work made by a joiner.

joint (dʒɔɪnt) *n.* **1.** a junction of two or more parts or objects. **2.** *Anat.* the junction between two or more bones. **3.** the point of connection between movable parts in invertebrates. **4.** the part of a plant stem from which a branch or leaf grows. **5.** one of the parts into which a carcass of meat is cut by the butcher, esp. for roasting. **6.** *Geol.* a crack in a rock along which no displacement has occurred. **7.** *Sl.* **a.** a bar or nightclub. **b.** *Often facetious.* a dwelling or meeting place. **8.** *Sl.* a cannabis cigarette. **9. out of joint. a.** dislocated. **b.** out of order. ~*adj.* **10.** shared by or belonging to two or more: *joint property.* **11.** created by combined effort. **12.** sharing with others or with one another: *joint rulers.* ~*vb.* (*tr.*) **13.** to provide with or fasten by a joint or joints. **14.** to plane the edge of (a board, etc.) into the correct shape for a joint. **15.** to cut or divide (meat, etc.) into joints. —ˈ**jointed** *adj.* —ˈ**jointly** *adv.*

joint account *n.* a bank account registered in the name of two or more persons, any of whom may make deposits and withdrawals.

joint stock *n.* capital funds held in common and usually divided into shares.

joint-stock company *n.* **1.** *Brit.* a business enterprise characterized by the sharing of ownership between shareholders, whose liability is limited. **2.** *U.S.* a business enterprise whose owners are issued shares of transferable stock but do not enjoy limited liability.

jointure (ˈdʒɔɪntʃə) *n. Law.* **a.** provision made by a husband for his wife by settling property upon her at marriage for her use after his death. **b.** the property so settled. [C14: < OF, < L *junctūra* a joining]

join up *vb.* (*adv.*) **1.** (*intr.*) to become a member of a military or other organization; enlist. **2.** (often foll. by *with*) to unite or connect.

joist (dʒɔɪst) *n.* a beam made of timber, steel, or

reinforced concrete, used in the construction of floors, roofs, etc. [C14: < OF *giste* beam supporting a bridge, < Vulgar L *jacitum* (unattested) support, < *jacēre* to lie]

jojoba (həʊˈhəʊbə) *n.* a shrub or small tree of SW North America that has edible seeds containing a valuable oil: used in cosmetics.

joke (dʒəʊk) *n.* **1.** a humorous anecdote. **2.** something that is said or done for fun. **3.** a ridiculous or humorous circumstance. **4.** a person or thing inspiring ridicule or amusement. **5. no joke.** something very serious. ~*vb.* **6.** (*intr.*) to tell jokes. **7.** (*intr.*) to speak or act facetiously. **8.** to make fun of (someone). **9. joking apart.** seriously: said after there has been joking in a discussion. [C17: < L *jocus* a jest] —ˈ**jokey** *or* ˈ**joky** *adj.* —ˈ**jokingly** *adv.*

joker (ˈdʒəʊkə) *n.* **1.** a person who jokes, esp. in an obnoxious manner. **2.** *Sl.* a person. **3.** an extra playing card in a pack, which in many card games can rank above any other card.

jollify (ˈdʒɒlɪˌfaɪ) *vb.* **-fying, -fied.** to be or cause to be jolly. —ˌ**jollifiˈcation** *n.*

jollity (ˈdʒɒlɪtɪ) *n., pl.* **-ties.** the condition of being jolly.

jolly (ˈdʒɒlɪ) *adj.* **-lier, -liest. 1.** full of good humour. **2.** having or provoking gaiety and merrymaking. **3.** pleasing. ~*adv.* **4.** *Brit.* (intensifier): *you're jolly nice.* ~*vb.* **-lying, -lied.** (*tr.*) *Inf.* **5.** (often foll. by *up* or *along*) to try to make or keep (someone) cheerful. **6.** to make good-natured fun of. [C14: < OF *jolif,* prob. < ON *jōl* YULE] —ˈ**jolliness** *n.*

jolly boat *n.* a small boat used as a utility tender for a vessel. [C18 *jolly* prob. < Danish *jolle* YAWL]

Jolly Roger *n.* the traditional pirate flag, consisting of a white skull and crossbones on a black field.

jolt (dʒəʊlt) *vb.* **1.** (*tr.*) to bump against with a jarring blow. **2.** to move in a jolting manner. **3.** (*tr.*) to surprise or shock. ~*n.* **4.** a sudden jar or blow. **5.** an emotional shock. [C16: prob. blend of dialect *jot* to jerk & dialect *joll* to bump]

Jon. *Bible. abbrev. for* Jonah.

Jonah (ˈdʒəʊnə) *or* **Jonas** (ˈdʒəʊnəs) *n.* **1.** *Old Testament.* a Hebrew prophet who, having been thrown overboard from a ship was swallowed by a great fish and vomited onto dry land. **2.** a person believed to bring bad luck to those around him.

jongleur (*French* ʒɔ̃glœr) *n.* (in medieval France) an itinerant minstrel. [C18: < OF *jogleour,* < L *joculātor* jester]

jonquil (ˈdʒɒŋkwɪl) *n.* a Eurasian variety of narcissus with long fragrant yellow or white short-tubed flowers. [C17: < F *jonquille,* < Sp. *junquillo,* dim. of *junco* reed]

jorum (ˈdʒɔːrəm) *n.* a large drinking bowl or vessel or its contents. [C18: prob. after *Jorum,* who brought vessels of silver, gold, and brass to King David (II Samuel 8:10)]

josh (dʒɒʃ) *Sl., chiefly U.S. & Canad.* ~*vb.* **1.** to tease (someone) in a bantering way. ~*n.* **2.** a teasing joke. [C19: ? < JOKE, infl. by BOSH] —ˈ**josher** *n.*

Josh. *Bible. abbrev. for* Joshua.

joss (dʒɒs) *n.* a Chinese deity worshipped in the form of an idol. [C18: < pidgin E, < Port. *deos* god, < L *deus*]

joss house *n.* a Chinese temple or shrine where an idol or idols are worshipped.

joss stick *n.* a stick of dried perfumed paste, giving off a fragrant odour when burnt as incense.

jostle (ˈdʒɒsᵊl) *vb.* **1.** to bump or push (someone) roughly. **2.** to come or bring into contact. **3.** to force (one's way) by pushing. ~*n.* **4.** the act of jostling. **5.** a rough bump or push. [C14: see JOUST]

jot (dʒɒt) *vb.* **jotting, jotted. 1.** (*tr.;* usually foll. by *down*) to write a brief note of. ~*n.* **2.** (*used with a negative*) a little bit (in **not care** (*or* **give**) **a jot**). [C16: < L *jota,* < Gk *iōta,* of Semitic origin]

jota (*Spanish* ˈxɔta) *n.* a Spanish dance in fast triple time. [Sp., prob. < OSp. *sota,* < *sotar* to dance, < L *saltāre*]

jotter (ˈdʒɒtə) *n.* a small notebook.

jotting (ˈdʒɒtɪŋ) *n.* something jotted down.

joual (ʒwɑːl) *n.* nonstandard Canadian French dialect, esp. as associated with ill-educated speakers. [from the pronunciation in this dialect of F *cheval* horse]

joule (dʒuːl) *n.* the derived SI unit of work or energy; the work done when the point of application of a force of 1 newton is displaced through a distance of 1 metre in the direction of the force. Symbol: J [C19: after J. P. *Joule* (1818-89), E physicist]

jounce (dʒaʊns) *vb.* **1.** to shake or jolt or cause to shake or jolt. ~*n.* **2.** a shake; bump. [C15: prob. < dialect *joll* to bump + BOUNCE]

journal (ˈdʒɜːnᵊl) *n.* **1.** a newspaper or periodical. **2.** a book in which a daily record of happenings, etc., is kept. **3.** an official record of the proceedings of a legislative body. **4.** *Book-keeping.* one of several books in which transactions are initially recorded to facilitate subsequent entry in the ledger. **5.** the part of a shaft or axle in contact with or enclosed by a bearing. [C14: < OF: daily, < L *diurnālis;* see DIURNAL]

journal box *n. Machinery.* a case enclosing or supporting a journal.

journalese (ˌdʒɜːnᵊˈliːz) *n. Derog.* a superficial style of writing regarded as typical of newspapers, etc.

journalism (ˈdʒɜːnᵊˌlɪzəm) *n.* **1.** the profession or practice of reporting about, photographing, or editing news stories for one of the mass media. **2.** newspapers and magazines collectively.

journalist (ˈdʒɜːnᵊlɪst) *n.* **1.** a person whose occupation is journalism. **2.** a person who keeps a journal. —ˌ**journaˈlistic** *adj.* —ˌ**journaˈlistically** *adv.*

journalize *or* **-lise** (ˈdʒɜːnᵊˌlaɪz) *vb.* to record (daily events) in a journal. —ˌ**journaliˈzation** *or* **-liˈsation** *n.*

journey (ˈdʒɜːnɪ) *n.* **1.** a travelling from one place to another. **2. a.** the distance travelled in a journey. **b.** the time taken to make a journey. ~*vb.* **3.** (*intr.*) to make a journey. [C13: < OF *journee* a day, a day's travelling, < L *diurnum* day's portion] —ˈ**journeyer** *n.*

journeyman (ˈdʒɜːnɪmən) *n., pl.* **-men. 1.** a craftsman, artisan, etc., who is qualified to work at his trade in the employment of another. **2.** a competent workman. [C15: < JOURNEY (in obs. sense: a day's work) + MAN]

joust (dʒaʊst) *History.* ~*n.* **1.** a combat between two mounted knights tilting against each other with lances. ~*vb.* **2.** (*intr.;* often foll. by *against* or *with*) to encounter or engage in such a tournament: *he jousted with five opponents.* [C13: < OF, < *jouster* to fight on horseback, < Vulgar L *juxtāre* (unattested) to come together, < L *juxtā* close] —ˈ**jouster** *n.*

Jove (dʒəʊv) *n.* **1.** another name for **Jupiter**[1]. **2. by Jove.** an exclamation of surprise or excitement. [C14: < OL *Jovis* Jupiter] —ˈ**Jovian** *n.*

jovial (ˈdʒəʊvɪəl) *adj.* having or expressing convivial humour. [C16: < L *joviālis* of (the planet) Jupiter, considered by astrologers to foster good humour] —**joviality** (ˌdʒəʊvɪˈælɪtɪ) *n.* —ˈ**jovially** *adv.*

jowl[1] (dʒaʊl) *n.* **1.** the jaw, esp. the lower one. **2.** (*often pl.*) a cheek. **3. cheek by jowl.** See **cheek.** [OE *ceafl* jaw] —**jowled** *adj.*

jowl[2] (dʒaʊl) *n.* **1.** fatty flesh hanging from the lower jaw. **2.** a similar fleshy part in animals, such as the dewlap of a bull. [OE *ceole* throat]

joy (dʒɔɪ) *n.* **1.** a deep feeling or condition of happiness or contentment. **2.** something causing such a feeling. **3.** an outward show of pleasure or delight. **4.** *Brit. inf.* success; satisfaction: *I went for a loan, but got no joy.* ~*vb. Chiefly poetic.* **5.** (*intr.*) to feel joy. **6.** (*tr.*) to gladden. [C13: < OF, < L *gaudium* joy, < *gaudēre* to be glad]

joyful (ˈdʒɔɪfʊl) *adj.* **1.** full of joy; elated. **2.** expressing or producing joy: *a joyful look; a joyful occasion.* —ˈ**joyfully** *adv.* —ˈ**joyfulness** *n.*

joyless (ˈdʒɔɪlɪs) *adj.* having or producing no joy or pleasure. —ˈ**joylessly** *adv.* —ˈ**joylessness** *n.*

joyous (ˈdʒɔɪəs) *adj.* **1.** having a happy nature or mood. **2.** joyful. —**ˈjoyously** *adv.*

joy ride *n.* **1.** a ride taken for pleasure in a car, esp. in a stolen car driven recklessly. ~*vb.* **joy-ride, -riding, -rode, -ridden.** **2.** (*intr.*) to take such a ride. —**ˈjoyˌrider** *n.* —**ˈjoyriding** *n.*

joystick (ˈdʒɔɪˌstɪk) *n.* **1.** *Inf.* the control stick of an aircraft, machine, etc. **2.** *Computers.* a lever for controlling the movement of a cursor on a screen.

JP *abbrev. for* Justice of the Peace.

Jr *or* **jr** *abbrev. for* junior.

jubbah (ˈdʒʊbə) *n.* a long loose outer garment with wide sleeves, worn by Muslim men and women, esp. in India. [C16: < Ar.]

jube (dʒuːb) *n. Austral. & N.Z. inf.* any jelly-like sweet. [C20: shortened < JUJUBE]

jubilant (ˈdʒuːbɪlənt) *adj.* feeling or expressing great joy. [C17: < L, < *jūbilāre* to give a joyful cry, < *jūbilum* a shout] —**ˈjubilance** *n.* —**ˈjubilantly** *adv.*

jubilate (ˈdʒuːbɪˌleɪt) *vb.* (*intr.*) **1.** to have or express great joy; rejoice. **2.** to celebrate a jubilee. [C17: < L *jūbilāre*; see JUBILANT]

jubilation (ˌdʒuːbɪˈleɪʃən) *n.* **1.** the act of rejoicing. **2.** a celebration or joyful occasion.

jubilee (ˈdʒuːbɪˌliː) *n.* **1.** a time or season for rejoicing. **2.** a special anniversary, esp. a 25th or 50th one. **3.** *R.C. Church.* a specially appointed period in which special indulgences are granted. **4.** *Old Testament.* a year that was to be observed every 50th year, during which Hebrew slaves were to be liberated, etc. **5.** a less common word for **jubilation.** [C14: < OF *jubile*, < LL *jubilaeus*, < LGk, < Heb. *yōbhēl* ram's horn, used for the proclamation of the year of jubilee]

Jud. *Bible.* ~*abbrev. for:* **1.** Also: **Judg.** Judges. **2.** Judith.

Judaic (dʒuːˈdeɪɪk) *adj.* of or relating to the Jews or Judaism. —**Juˈdaically** *adv.*

Judaism (ˈdʒuːdeɪˌɪzəm) *n.* **1.** the religion of the Jews, based on the Old Testament and the Talmud and having as its central point a belief in one God. **2.** the religious and cultural traditions of the Jews. —ˌ**Judaˈistic** *adj.*

Judaize *or* **-ise** (ˈdʒʊdeɪˌaɪz) *vb.* **1.** to conform or bring into conformity with Judaism. **2.** (*tr.*) to convert to Judaism. —ˌ**Judaiˈzation** *or* **-iˈsation** *n.*

Judas (ˈdʒuːdəs) *n.* **1.** *New Testament.* the apostle who betrayed Jesus to his enemies for 30 pieces of silver (Luke 22:3–6, 47–48). **2.** a person who betrays a friend; traitor.

Judas tree *n.* small Eurasian leguminous tree with pinkish-purple flowers that bloom before the leaves appear.

judder (ˈdʒʌdə) *Inf., chiefly Brit.* ~*vb.* **1.** (*intr.*) to shake or vibrate. ~*n.* **2.** abnormal vibration in a mechanical system. **3.** a juddering motion. [prob. blend of JAR² + SHUDDER]

judge (dʒʌdʒ) *n.* **1.** a public official with authority to hear cases in a court of law and pronounce judgment upon them. **2.** a person who is appointed to determine the result of contests or competitions. **3.** a person qualified to comment critically: *a good judge of antiques.* **4.** a leader of the peoples of Israel from Joshua's death to the accession of Saul. ~*vb.* **5.** to hear and decide upon (a case at law). **6.** (*tr.*) to pass judgment on. **7.** (when *tr., may take a clause as object or an infinitive*) to decide (something) after inquiry. **8.** to determine the result of (a contest or competition). **9.** to appraise (something) critically. **10.** (*tr.; takes a clause as object*) to believe something to be the case. [C14: < OF, < L *jūdicāre* to pass judgment, < *jūdex* a judge] —**ˈjudgeˌlike** *adj.* —**ˈjudger** *n.* —**ˈjudgeship** *n.*

judge advocate *n., pl.* **judge advocates.** an officer who superintends proceedings at a military court martial.

judges' rules *pl. n.* (in English law) a set of rules, not legally binding, governing the behaviour of police towards suspects.

judgment *or* **judgement** (ˈdʒʌdʒmənt) *n.* **1.** the faculty of being able to make critical distinctions and achieve a balanced viewpoint. **2. a.** the verdict pronounced by a court of law. **b.** an obligation arising as a result of such a verdict, such as a debt. **c.** (*as modifier*): *a judgment debtor.* **3.** the formal decision of one or more judges at a contest or competition. **4.** a particular decision formed in a case in dispute or doubt. **5.** an estimation: *a good judgment of distance.* **6.** criticism or censure. **7. against one's better judgment.** contrary to a preferred course of action. **8. sit in judgment. a.** to preside as judge. **b.** to assume the position of critic. —**judgmental** *or* **judgemental** (dʒʌdʒˈmɛntᵊl) *adj.*

Judgment (ˈdʒʌdʒmənt) *n.* **1.** the estimate by God of the ultimate worthiness or unworthiness of the individual or of all mankind. **2.** God's subsequent decision determining the final destinies of all individuals.

Judgment Day *n.* the occasion of the Last Judgment by God at the end of the world. Also called: **Day of Judgment.** See **Last Judgment.**

judicatory (ˈdʒuːdɪkətərɪ) *adj.* **1.** of or relating to the administration of justice. ~*n.* **2.** a court of law. **3.** the administration of justice.

judicature (ˈdʒuːdɪkətʃə) *n.* **1.** the administration of justice. **2.** the office, function, or power of a judge. **3.** the extent of authority of a court or judge. **4.** a body of judges; judiciary. **5.** a court of justice or such courts collectively.

judicial (dʒuːˈdɪʃəl) *adj.* **1.** of or relating to the administration of justice. **2.** of or relating to judgment in a court of law or to a judge exercising this function. **3.** allowed or enforced by a court of law: *judicial separation.* **4.** having qualities appropriate to a judge. **5.** giving or seeking judgment. [C14: < L *jūdiciālis* belonging to the law courts, < *jūdicium* judgment, < *jūdex* a judge] —**juˈdicially** *adv.*

judiciary (dʒuːˈdɪʃɪərɪ) *adj.* **1.** of or relating to courts of law, judgment, or judges. ~*n., pl.* **-aries.** **2.** the branch of the central authority in a state concerned with the administration of justice. **3.** the system of courts in a country. **4.** the judges collectively.

judicious (dʒuːˈdɪʃəs) *adj.* having or proceeding from good judgment. —**juˈdiciously** *adv.* —**juˈdiciousness** *n.*

judo (ˈdʒuːdəʊ) *n.* **a.** the modern sport derived from jujitsu, in which the object is to force an opponent to submit using the minimum of physical effort. **b.** (*as modifier*): *a judo throw.* [Japanese, < *jū* gentleness + *dō* art] —**ˈjudoist** *n.*

Judy (ˈdʒuːdɪ) *n., pl.* **-dies.** **1.** the wife of Punch in the children's puppet show *Punch and Judy.* See **Punch.** **2.** (*often not cap.*) *Brit. sl.* a girl.

jug (dʒʌg) *n.* **1.** a vessel for holding or pouring liquids, usually having a handle and a lip. U.S. equivalent: **pitcher.** **2.** *Austral. & N.Z.* a container in which water is boiled, esp. an electric kettle. **3.** *U.S.* a large vessel with a narrow mouth. **4.** Also called: **jugful.** the amount of liquid held by a jug. **5.** *Brit. inf.* a glass of beer. **6.** *Sl.* jail. ~*vb.* **jugging, jugged.** **7.** to stew or boil (meat, esp. hare) in an earthenware container. **8.** (*tr.*) *Sl.* to put in jail. [C16: prob. < *Jug*, nickname from name *Joan*]

jugate (ˈdʒuːgeɪt, -gɪt) *adj.* (esp. of compound leaves) having parts arranged in pairs. [C19: < NL *jugātus* (unattested), < L *jugum* a yoke]

juggernaut (ˈdʒʌgəˌnɔːt) *n.* **1.** any terrible force, esp. one that demands complete self-sacrifice. **2.** *Brit.* a very large heavy lorry. [C17: < Hindi, < Sansk. *Jagannātha* lord of the world: devotees formerly threw themselves under a cart carrying *Juggernaut*, an idol of Krishna]

juggins (ˈdʒʌgɪnz) *n.* (*functioning as sing.*) *Brit. inf.* a silly person. [C19: special use of the surname *Juggins*]

juggle (ˈdʒʌgᵊl) *vb.* **1.** to throw and catch (several objects) continuously so that most are in the air all the time. **2.** to manipulate (facts, etc.) so as to give a false picture. **3.** (*tr.*) to keep (several activities) in progress, esp. with difficulty. ~*n.* **4.** an act of juggling. [C14: < OF *jogler* to perform as a jester, < L, < *jocus* a jest] —ˈ**juggler** *n.*

Jugoslav (ˈjuːgəʊˌslɑːv) *n., adj.* a variant spelling of **Yugoslav.**

jugular (ˈdʒʌgjʊlə) *adj.* **1.** of, relating to, or situated near the throat or neck. ~*n.* **2.** Also called: **jugular vein.** any of the large veins in the neck carrying blood to the heart from the head. [C16: < LL, < L *jugulum* throat]

juice (dʒuːs) *n.* **1.** any liquid that occurs naturally in or is secreted by plant or animal tissue: *the juice of an orange.* **2.** *Inf.* **a.** petrol. **b.** electricity. **c.** alcoholic drink. **3.** vigour or vitality. [C13: < OF *jus,* < L] —ˈ**juiceless** *adj.*

juice up *vb. (tr., adv.) U.S. sl.* to make lively: *to juice up a party.*

juicy (ˈdʒuːsɪ) *adj.* **juicier, juiciest. 1.** full of juice. **2.** provocatively interesting; spicy: *juicy gossip.* **3.** profitable: *a juicy contract.* —ˈ**juicily** *adv.* —ˈ**juiciness** *n.*

jujitsu, jujutsu, *or* **jiujutsu** (dʒuːˈdʒɪtsuː) *n.* the traditional Japanese system of unarmed self-defence perfected by the samurai. See also **judo.** [C19: < Japanese, < *jū* gentleness + *jutsu* art]

juju (ˈdʒuːdʒuː) *n.* **1.** an object superstitiously revered by certain West African peoples and used as a charm or fetish. **2.** the power associated with a juju. [C19: prob. < Hausa *djudju* evil spirit, fetish]

jujube (ˈdʒuːdʒuːb) *n.* **1.** any of several Old World spiny trees that have small yellowish flowers and dark red edible fruits. **2.** the fruit of any of these trees. **3.** a chewy sweet made of flavoured gelatin and sometimes medicated to soothe sore throats. [C14: < Med. L *jujuba,* modification of L *zīzyphum,* < Gk *zizuphon*]

jukebox (ˈdʒuːkˌbɒks) *n.* an automatic record player, usually in a large case, in which records may be selected by inserting coins and pressing appropriate buttons. [C20: < Gullah (a Negro language) *juke* bawdy (as in *juke house* brothel) + BOX[1]]

jukskei (ˈjʊkˌskeɪ) *n.* a South African game in which a peg is thrown over a fixed distance at a stake driven into the ground. [< Afrik. *juk* yoke + *skei* pin]

julep (ˈdʒuːlɪp) *n.* **1.** a sweet drink, variously prepared and sometimes medicated. **2.** *Chiefly U.S.* short for **mint julep.** [C14: < OF, < Ar. *julāb,* < Persian, < *gul* rose + *āb* water]

Julian calendar (ˈdʒuːljən) *n.* the calendar introduced by Julius Caesar in 46 B.C., in which leap years occurred every fourth year and in every centenary year. Cf. **Gregorian calendar.**

julienne (ˌdʒuːlɪˈɛn) *adj.* **1.** (of vegetables) cut into thin shreds. ~*n.* **2.** a clear consommé to which such vegetables have been added.

July (dʒuːˈlaɪ) *n., pl.* **-lies.** the seventh month of the year, consisting of 31 days. [C13: < Anglo-F *julie,* < L *Jūlius,* after Gaius *Julius* Caesar, in whose honour it was named]

jumble (ˈdʒʌmbᵊl) *vb.* **1.** to mingle (objects, etc.) in a state of disorder. **2.** (*tr.; usually passive*) to remember in a confused form. ~*n.* **3.** a disordered mass, state, etc. **4.** *Brit.* articles donated for a jumble sale. [C16: <?] —ˈ**jumbly** *adj.*

jumble sale *n. Brit.* a sale of miscellaneous articles, usually second-hand, in aid of charity. U.S. and Canad. equivalent: **rummage sale.**

jumbo (ˈdʒʌmbəʊ) *n., pl.* **-bos. 1.** *Inf.* **a.** a very large person or thing. **b.** (*as modifier*): *a jumbo box of detergent.* **2.** See **jumbo jet.** [C19: after a famous elephant exhibited by P. T. Barnum, < Swahili *jumbe* chief]

jumbo jet *n. Inf.* a type of large jet-propelled airliner.

jumbo pack *n.* **1.** the promotion of bulk sales of small unit items, such as confectionery, by packing several in one wrapping, usually with a unit price reduction. **2.** such a package of items.

jumbuck (ˈdʒʌmˌbʌk) *n. Austral.* an informal word for **sheep.** [C19: < Abor.]

jump (dʒʌmp) *vb.* **1.** (*intr.*) to leap or spring clear of the ground or other surface by using the muscles in the legs and feet. **2.** (*tr.*) to leap over or clear (an obstacle): *to jump a gap.* **3.** (*tr.*) to cause to leap over an obstacle: *to jump a horse over a hedge.* **4.** (*intr.*) to move or proceed hastily (into, onto, out of, etc.): *she jumped into a taxi.* **5.** (*tr.*) *Inf.* to board so as to travel illegally on: *he jumped the train as it was leaving.* **6.** (*intr.*) to parachute from an aircraft. **7.** (*intr.*) to jerk or start, as with astonishment, surprise, etc. **8.** to rise or cause to rise suddenly or abruptly. **9.** to pass or skip over (intervening objects or matter): *she jumped a few lines and then continued reading.* **10.** (*intr.*) to change from one thing to another, esp. from one subject to another. **11.** *Draughts.* to capture (an opponent's piece) by moving one of one's own pieces over it to an unoccupied square. **12.** (*intr.*) *Bridge.* to bid in response to one's partner at a higher level than is necessary, to indicate a strong hand. **13.** (*tr.*) to come off (a track, etc.): *the locomotive jumped the rails.* **14.** (*intr.*) (of the stylus of a record player) to be jerked out of the groove. **15.** (*intr.*) *Sl.* to be lively: *the party was jumping.* **16.** (*tr.*) *Inf.* to attack without warning: *thieves jumped the old man.* **17.** (*tr.*) *Inf.* (of a driver or a motor vehicle) to pass through (a red traffic light) or move away from (traffic lights) before they change to green. **18. jump down someone's throat.** *Inf.* to address or reply to someone sharply. **19. jump ship.** to desert, esp. to leave a ship in which one is legally bound to serve. **20. jump the queue.** *Inf.* to obtain some advantage out of turn or unfairly. **21. jump to it.** *Inf.* to begin something quickly and efficiently. ~*n.* **22.** an act or instance of jumping. **23.** a space, distance, or obstacle to be jumped or that has been jumped. **24.** a descent by parachute from an aircraft. **25.** *Sport.* any of several contests involving a jump: *the high jump.* **26.** a sudden rise: *the jump in prices last month.* **27.** a sudden or abrupt transition. **28.** a sudden jerk or involuntary muscular spasm, esp. as a reaction of surprise. **29.** a step or degree: *one jump ahead.* **30.** *Draughts.* a move that captures an opponent's piece by jumping over it. **31.** *Films.* **a.** a break in continuity in the normal sequence of shots. **b.** (*as modifier*): *a jump cut.* **32. on the jump.** *Inf., chiefly U.S. & Canad.* **a.** in a hurry. **b.** busy. **33. take a running jump.** *Brit. inf.* a contemptuous expression of dismissal. ~See also **jump at, jump-off,** etc. [C16: prob. imit.]

jump at *vb. (intr., prep.)* to be glad to accept: *I would jump at the chance of going.*

jumped-up *adj. Inf.* suddenly risen in significance, esp. when appearing arrogant.

jumper[1] (ˈdʒʌmpə) *n.* **1.** *Chiefly Brit.* a knitted or crocheted garment covering the upper part of the body. **2.** the U.S. and Canad. term for **pinafore dress.** [C19: < obs. *jump* man's loose jacket, var. of *jupe,* < OF, < Ar. *jubbah* long cloth coat]

jumper[2] (ˈdʒʌmpə) *n.* **1.** a boring tool that works by repeated impact, such as a steel bit in a drill used in boring rock. **2.** Also called: **jumper cable, jumper lead.** a short length of wire used to make a connection, usually temporarily. **3.** a person or animal that jumps.

jumping bean *n.* a seed of any of several Mexican plants that contains a moth caterpillar whose movements cause it to jerk about.

jumping jack *n.* a toy figure of a man with jointed limbs that can be moved by pulling attached strings.

jump jet *n. Inf.* a fixed-wing jet aircraft that is capable of landing and taking off vertically.

jump jockey *n. Brit. inf.* a jockey riding in a steeplechase, as opposed to racing on the flat.

jump leads (liːdz) *pl. n.* two heavy cables fitted with crocodile clips used to start a motor vehicle with a discharged battery by connecting the battery to an external battery.

jump-off *n.* **1.** an extra round in a showjumping contest when two or more horses are equal first, deciding the winner. ~*vb.* **jump off. 2.** (*intr., adv.*) to engage in a jump-off.

jump on *vb. (intr., prep.) Inf.* to reprimand or attack suddenly and forcefully.
jump seat *n.* **1.** a folding seat on some aircraft for an additional crew member. **2.** *Brit.* a folding seat in a motor vehicle.
jump-start *vb.* **1.** to start the engine of (a car) by pushing or rolling it and then engaging the gears or (of a car) to start in this way. *~n.* **2.** the act of starting a car in this way. ~Also called (Brit.): **bump-start.**
jump suit *n.* a one-piece garment of combined trousers and jacket or shirt.
jumpy (ˈdʒʌmpɪ) *adj.* **jumpier, jumpiest. 1.** nervous or apprehensive. **2.** moving jerkily or fitfully. —ˈ**jumpily** *adv.* —ˈ**jumpiness** *n.*
Jun. *abbrev. for:* **1.** June. **2.** Also: **jun.** junior.
junco (ˈdʒʌŋkəʊ) *n., pl.* **-cos** *or* **-coes.** a North American bunting having a greyish plumage. [C18: < Sp.: a rush, < L *juncus* rush]
junction (ˈdʒʌŋkʃən) *n.* **1.** a place where several routes, lines, or roads meet, link, or cross each other: *a railway junction.* **2.** a point on a motorway where traffic may leave or join it. **3.** *Electronics.* **a.** a contact between two different metals or other materials: *a thermocouple junction.* **b.** a transition region in a semiconductor. **4.** the act of joining or the state of being joined. [C18: < L *junctiō* a joining, < *jungere* to join]
junction box *n.* an earthed enclosure within which wires or cables can be safely connected.
junction transistor *n.* a bipolar transistor consisting of two p-n junctions combined to form either an n-p-n or a p-n-p transistor.
juncture (ˈdʒʌŋktʃə) *n.* **1.** a point in time, esp. a critical one (often in **at this juncture**). **2.** *Linguistics.* the set of phonological features signalling a division between words, such as those that distinguish *a name* from *an aim.* **3.** a less common word for **junction.**
June (dʒuːn) *n.* the sixth month of the year, consisting of 30 days. [OE *iunius,* < L *junius,* prob. < *Junius* name of Roman gens]
jungle (ˈdʒʌŋgᵊl) *n.* **1.** an equatorial forest area with luxuriant vegetation. **2.** any dense or tangled thicket or growth. **3.** a place of intense or ruthless struggle for survival: *the concrete jungle.* [C18: < Hindi, < Sansk. *jāngala* wilderness] —ˈ**jungly** *adj.*
jungle fever *n.* a serious malarial fever occurring in the East Indies.
jungle fowl *n.* **1.** any small gallinaceous bird of S and SE Asia, the males of which (**junglecock**) have an arched tail and a combed and wattled head. **2.** *Austral.* any of several megapodes.
jungle juice *n. Sl.* alcoholic liquor.
junior (ˈdʒuːnjə) *adj.* **1.** lower in rank or length of service; subordinate. **2.** younger in years. **3.** of or relating to youth or childhood. **4.** *Brit.* of schoolchildren between the ages of 7 and 11 approximately. **5.** *U.S.* of or designating the third year of a four-year course at college or high school. *~n.* **6.** *Law.* (in England) any barrister below the rank of Queen's Counsel. **7.** a junior person. **8.** *Brit.* a junior schoolchild. **9.** *U.S.* a junior student. [C17: < L: younger, < *juvenis* young]
Junior (ˈdʒuːnjə) *adj. Chiefly U.S.* being the younger: usually used after a name to distinguish the son from the father: *Charles Parker, Junior.* Abbrev.: **Jnr, Jr, Jun., Junr.**
junior common room *n.* (in certain universities and colleges) a common room for the use of students.
junior lightweight *n.* **a.** a professional boxer weighing 126–130 pounds (57–59 kg). **b.** (*as modifier*): *a junior-lightweight bout.*
junior middleweight *n.* **a.** a professional boxer weighing 147–154 pounds (66.5–70 kg). **b.** (*as modifier*): *the junior-middleweight championship.*
junior school *n. Brit.* a school for children aged between 7 and 11.
junior technician *n.* a rank in the Royal Air Force comparable to that of private in the army.
junior welterweight *n.* **a.** a professional boxer weighing 135–140 pounds (61–63.5 kg). **b.** (*as modifier*): *a junior-welterweight fight.*
juniper (ˈdʒuːnɪpə) *n.* a coniferous shrub or small tree of the N hemisphere having purple berry-like cones. The cones of the **common** or **dwarf juniper** are used as a flavouring in making gin. [C14: < L *jūniperus,* <?]
junk[1] (dʒʌŋk) *n.* **1.** discarded objects, etc., collectively. **2.** *Inf.* **a.** rubbish generally. **b.** nonsense: *the play was absolute junk.* **3.** *Sl.* any narcotic drug, esp. heroin. *~vb.* **4.** (*tr.*) *Inf.* to discard as junk. [C15 *jonke* old useless rope]
junk[2] (dʒʌŋk) *n.* a sailing vessel used in Chinese waters and characterized by a very high poop, flat bottom, and square sails supported by battens. [C17: < Port. *junco,* < Javanese *jon*]
Junker (ˈjʊŋkə) *n.* **1.** *History.* any of the aristocratic landowners of Prussia who were devoted to maintaining their privileges. **2.** an arrogant and tyrannical German army officer or official. **3.** (formerly) a young German nobleman. [C16: < G, < OHG *junchērro* young lord] —ˈ**Junkerdom** *n.*
junket (ˈdʒʌŋkɪt) *n.* **1.** a sweet dessert made of flavoured milk set to a curd with rennet. **2.** a feast. **3.** *U.S. & Canad.* an excursion, esp. one made for pleasure at public expense. *~vb.* **4.** to have or entertain with a feast. **5.** (*intr.*) *U.S. & Canad.* (of a public official, etc.) to go on a junket. [C14 (in the sense: rush basket, hence custard served on rushes): < OF (dialect) *jonquette,* < *jonc* rush, < L *juncus* reed] —ˈ**junketing** *n.*
junk food *n.* food which is eaten in addition to or instead of regular meals, and which often has a low nutritional value.
junkie *or* **junky** (ˈdʒʌŋkɪ) *n., pl.* **junkies.** an informal word for **drug addict.**
junk shop *n.* a shop selling miscellaneous second-hand goods and sometimes antiques.
junta (ˈdʒʌntə, ˈhʊntə) *n.* (*functioning as sing. or pl.*) **1.** a group of military officers holding the power in a country, esp. after a coup d'état. **2.** Also called: **junto.** a small group of men. **3.** a legislative or executive council in some parts of Latin America. [C17: < Sp.: council, < L, < *jungere* to join]
junto (ˈdʒʊntəʊ) *n., pl.* **-tos.** a variant of **junta** (sense 2). [C17]
Jupiter[1] (ˈdʒuːpɪtə) *n.* (in Roman tradition) the king and ruler of the Olympian gods.
Jupiter[2] (ˈdʒuːpɪtə) *n.* the largest of the planets and the fifth from the sun.
Jurassic (dʒʊˈræsɪk) *adj.* **1.** of or formed in the second period of the Mesozoic era, during which dinosaurs and ammonites flourished. *~n.* **2. the.** the Jurassic period or rock system. [C19: < F *jurassique,* after the Jura (Mountains) in W central Europe]
jurat (ˈdʒʊəræt) *n.* **1.** *Law.* a statement at the foot of an affidavit, naming the parties, stating when, where, and before whom it was sworn, etc. **2.** (in England) a municipal officer of the Cinque Ports. **3.** (in France and the Channel Islands) a magistrate. [C16: < Med. L *jūrātus* one who has been sworn, < L *jūrāre* to swear]
juridical (dʒʊˈrɪdɪkᵊl) *adj.* of or relating to law or to the administration of justice; legal. [C16: < L, < *iūs* law + *dicere* to say] —**juˈridically** *adv.*
jurisdiction (ˌdʒʊərɪsˈdɪkʃən) *n.* **1.** the right or power to administer justice and to apply laws. **2.** the exercise or extent of such right or power. **3.** authority in general. [C13: < L *jūrisdictiō* administration of justice, < *jus* law + DICTION] —ˌ**jurisˈdictional** *adj.*
jurisprudence (ˌdʒʊərɪsˈpruːdᵊns) *n.* **1.** the science or philosophy of law. **2.** a system or body of law. **3.** a branch of law: *medical jurisprudence.* [C17: < L *jūris prūdentia,* < *jus* law + PRUDENCE] —**jurisprudential** (ˌdʒʊərɪspruːˈdenʃəl) *adj.*
jurist (ˈdʒʊərɪst) *n.* a person versed in the science of law, esp. Roman or civil law. [C15: < F *juriste,* < Med. L *jūrista*]
juristic (dʒʊˈrɪstɪk) *or* **juristical** *adj.* **1.** of or

relating to jurists. **2.** of or characteristic of the study of law or the legal profession.

juror ('dʒʊərə) *n.* **1.** a member of a jury. **2.** a person who takes an oath. [C14: < Anglo-F *jurour,* < OF *jurer* to take an oath, < L *jūrāre*]

jury[1] ('dʒʊərɪ) *n., pl.* **-ries. 1.** a group of, usually, twelve people sworn to deliver a true verdict according to the evidence upon a case presented in a court of law. **2.** a body of persons appointed to judge a competition and award prizes. [C14: < OF *juree,* < *jurer* to swear]

jury[2] ('dʒʊərɪ) *adj. Chiefly naut.* (*in combination*) makeshift: *jury-rigged.* [C17: <?]

jury box *n.* an enclosure where the jury sits in court.

juryman ('dʒʊərɪmən) *or* (*fem.*) **jurywoman** *n., pl.* **-men** *or* **-women.** a member of a jury.

jury-rigged *adj. Chiefly naut.* set up in a makeshift manner.

just *adj.* (dʒʌst). **1. a.** fair or impartial in action or judgment. **b.** (*as collective n.; preceded by the*): *the just.* **2.** conforming to high moral standards; honest. **3.** consistent with justice: *a just action.* **4.** rightly applied or given: *a just reward.* **5.** legally valid; lawful: *a just inheritance.* **6.** well-founded: *just criticism.* **7.** correct or true: *a just account.* ~*adv.* (dʒʌst; *unstressed* dʒəst). **8.** used with forms of *have* to indicate an action performed in the very recent past: *I have just closed the door.* **9.** at this very instant: *he's just coming in to land.* **10.** no more than; only: *just an ordinary car.* **11.** exactly: *that's just what I mean.* **12.** barely: *he just got there in time.* **13. just about. a.** at the point of starting (to do something). **b.** almost: *I've just about had enough.* **14. just a moment, second,** *or* **minute.** an expression requesting the hearer to wait or pause for a brief period of time. **15. just so.** arranged with precision. [C14: < L *jūstus* righteous, < *jūs* justice] —'**justly** *adv.* —'**justness** *n.*

justice ('dʒʌstɪs) *n.* **1.** the quality or fact of being just. **2.** *Ethics.* the principle of fairness that like cases should be treated alike. **3.** the administration of law according to prescribed and accepted principles. **4.** conformity to the law. **5.** a judge of the Supreme Court of Judicature. **6.** short for **justice of the peace. 7.** good reason (esp. in **with justice**). **8. bring to justice.** to capture, try, and usually punish (a criminal, etc.). **9. do justice to. a.** to show to full advantage. **b.** to show full appreciation of by action. **c.** to treat or judge fairly. **10. do oneself justice.** to make full use of one's abilities. [C12: < OF, < L *jūstitia,* < *justus* JUST] —'**justice,ship** *n.*

justice of the peace *n.* a lay magistrate whose function is to preserve the peace in his area and try summarily such cases as are within his jurisdiction.

justiciar (dʒʌ'stɪʃɪ,ɑː) *n. English legal history.* the chief political and legal officer from the time of William I to that of Henry III, who deputized for the king in his absence. Also called: **justiciary.** —**jus'ticiar,ship** *n.*

justiciary (dʒʌ'stɪʃɪərɪ) *adj.* **1.** of or relating to the administration of justice. ~*n., pl.* **-aries. 2.** an officer or administrator of justice; judge.

justifiable ('dʒʌstɪ,faɪəb°l) *adj.* capable of being justified. —,**justi,fia'bility** *n.* —'**justi,fiably** *adv.*

justifiable homicide *n.* lawful killing, as in the execution of a death sentence.

justification (,dʒʌstɪfɪ'keɪʃən) *n.* **1.** reasonable grounds for complaint, defence, etc. **2.** proof, vindication, or exculpation. **3.** *Christian theol.* **a.** the act of justifying. **b.** the process of being justified or the condition of having been justified. —'**justifi,catory** *adj.*

justify ('dʒʌstɪ,faɪ) *vb.* **-fying, -fied.** (*mainly tr.*) **1.** (*often passive*) to prove or see to be just or valid; vindicate. **2.** to show to be reasonable: *his behaviour justifies our suspicion.* **3.** to declare or show to be free from blame or guilt. **4.** *Law.* to show good reason in court for (some action taken). **5.** (*also intr.*) *Printing, computers.* to adjust the spaces between words in (a line of type or data) so that it is of the required length or (of a line of type or data) to fit exactly. **6. a.** *Protestant theol.* to declare righteous by the imputation of Christ's merits to the sinner. **b.** *R.C. theol.* to change from sinfulness to righteousness by the transforming effects of grace. **7.** (*also intr.*) *Law.* to prove (a person) to have sufficient means to act as surety, etc., or (of a person) to qualify to provide bail or surety. [C14: < OF *justifier,* < L *justificāre,* < *jūstus* JUST + *facere* to make] —'**justi,fier** *n.*

justle ('dʒʌs°l) *vb.* a less common word for **jostle.**

jut (dʒʌt) *vb.* **jutting, jutted. 1.** (*intr.; often foll. by out*) to stick out or overhang beyond the surface or main part. ~*n.* **2.** something that juts out. [C16: var. of JET[1]] —'**jutting** *adj.*

jute (dʒuːt) *n.* **1.** either of two Old World tropical yellow-flowered herbaceous plants, cultivated for their strong fibre. **2.** this fibre, used in making sacks, rope, etc. [C18: < Bengali *jhuto,* < Sansk. *jūta* braid of hair]

juv. *abbrev. for* juvenile.

juvenescence (,dʒuːvɪ'nɛsəns) *n.* **1.** youth or immaturity. **2.** the act or process of growing from childhood to youth. —,**juve'nescent** *adj.*

juvenile ('dʒuːvɪ,naɪl) *adj.* **1.** young, youthful, or immature. **2.** suitable or designed for young people: *juvenile pastimes.* ~*n.* **3.** a juvenile person, animal, or plant. **4.** an actor who performs youthful roles. **5.** a book intended for young readers. [C17: < L *juvenīlis* youthful, < *juvenis* young] —'**juve,nilely** *adv.*

juvenile court *n.* a court that deals with juvenile offenders and children beyond parental control or in need of care.

juvenile delinquency *n.* antisocial or criminal conduct by juvenile delinquents.

juvenile delinquent *n.* a child or young person guilty of some offence, act of vandalism, or antisocial behaviour and who may be brought before a juvenile court.

juvenilia (,dʒuːvɪ'nɪlɪə) *n.* works of art, literature, or music produced in youth, before the artist, author, or composer has formed a mature style. [C17: < L, lit.: youthful things]

juxtapose (,dʒʌkstə'pəʊz) *vb.* (*tr.*) to place close together or side by side. [C19: back formation < *juxtaposition,* < L *juxta* next to + POSITION] —,**juxtapo'sition** *n.* —,**juxtapo'sitional** *adj.*

K

k *or* **K** (keɪ) *n., pl.* **k's, K's,** *or* **Ks. 1.** the 11th letter and 8th consonant of the English alphabet. **2.** a speech sound represented by this letter, usually a voiceless velar stop, as in *kitten.*

k *symbol for:* **1.** kilo(s). **2.** *Maths.* the unit vector along the *z*-axis.

K *symbol for:* **1.** Kelvin(s). **2.** *Chess.* king. **3.** *Chem.* potassium. [< NL *kalium*] **4.** *Physics.* kaon. **5.** *Currency.* **a.** kina. **b.** kip. **c.** kopeck. **d.** kwacha. **e.** kyat. **6.** one thousand. [< KILO-] **7.** *Computers.* originally or strictly a unit of 1024 words, bits , or bytes.

K *or* **K.** *abbrev. for* Köchel: indicating the serial number in the catalogue of the works of Mozart made by Ludwig von Köchel, 1800–77.

k. *abbrev. for:* **1.** karat. **2.** Also: **K.** king.

Kaaba *or* **Caaba** (ˈkɑːbə) *n.* a cube-shaped building in Mecca, the most sacred Muslim pilgrim shrine, into which is built the black stone believed to have been given by Gabriel to Abraham. [< Ar. *ka'bah,* < *ka'b* cube]

kabbala *or* **kabala** (kəˈbɑːlə) *n.* variant spellings of **cabbala.**

kabuki (kæˈbuːkɪ) *n.* a form of Japanese drama based on legends and characterized by elaborate costumes and the use of male actors. [Japanese, < *ka* singing + *bu* dancing + *ki* art]

Kabyle (kəˈbaɪl) *n.* **1.** (*pl.* **-byles** *or* **-byle**) a member of a Berber people in Tunisia and Algeria. **2.** the dialect of Berber spoken by this people. [C19: < Ar. *qabā'il,* pl. of *qabīlah* tribe]

kadi (ˈkɑːdɪ, ˈkeɪdɪ) *n., pl.* **-dis.** a variant spelling of **cadi.**

Kaffir *or* **Kafir** (ˈkæfə) *n., pl.* **-firs** *or* **-fir. 1.** *Offens.* **a.** (in southern Africa) any Black African. **b.** (*as modifier*): *Kaffir farming.* **2.** a former name for the **Xhosa** language. [C19: < Ar. *kāfir* infidel, < *kafara* to deny]

kaffir beer *n. S. African.* beer made from sorghum (kaffir corn) or millet.

kaffirboom (ˈkæfəˌbuəm) *n.* a S. African deciduous flowering tree. [< KAFFIR + Afrik. *boom* tree]

kaffir corn *n.* a southern African variety of sorghum, cultivated in dry regions for its grain and as fodder. Sometimes shortened to **kaffir.**

Kafir (ˈkæfə) *n., pl.* **-irs** *or* **-ir. 1.** a member of a people inhabiting E Afghanistan. **2.** a variant spelling of **Kaffir.** [C19: < Ar.; see KAFFIR]

Kafkaesque (ˌkæfkəˈɛsk) *adj.* of or like the writings of Franz Kafka (1883-1924), Czech novelist, esp. in having a nightmarish and dehumanized quality.

kaftan *or* **caftan** (ˈkæftæn) *n.* **1.** a long coatlike garment, usually with a belt, worn in the East. **2.** an imitation of this, worn esp. by women, consisting of a loose dress with long wide sleeves. [C16: < Turkish *qaftān*]

kagoul (kəˈguːl) *n.* a variant spelling of **cagoule.**

kahawai (ˈkɑːhəwaɪ, ˈkɑːwaɪ) *n.* a New Zealand food and game fish. [< Maori]

kai (kaɪ) *n. N.Z. inf.* food. [< Maori]

kaiak (ˈkaɪæk) *n.* a variant spelling of **kayak.**

kail (keɪl) *n.* a variant spelling of **kale.**

kainite (ˈkaɪnaɪt) *n.* a white mineral consisting of potassium chloride and magnesium sulphate: a fertilizer and source of potassium salts. [C19: < G *Kainit,* < Gk *kainos* new + -ITE¹]

Kaiser (ˈkaɪzə) *n.* (*sometimes not cap.*) *History.* **1.** any of the three German emperors. **2.** *Obs.* any Austro-Hungarian emperor. [C16: < G, ult. < L *Caesar* emperor]

kaka (ˈkɑːkə) *n.* a green New Zealand parrot with a long compressed bill. [C18: < Maori, ? imit. of its call]

kaka beak *n.* a New Zealand shrub with beaklike red flowers. [< KAKA]

kakapo (ˈkɑːkəˌpəʊ) *n., pl.* **-pos.** a ground-living nocturnal parrot of New Zealand, resembling an owl. [C19: < Maori, lit.: night kaka]

kakemono (ˌkækɪˈməʊnəʊ) *n., pl.* **-nos.** a Japanese paper or silk wall hanging, usually long and narrow, with a picture or inscription on it. [C19: < Japanese, < *kake* hanging + *mono* thing]

kala-azar (ˌkɑːləəˈzɑː) *n.* a tropical infectious disease caused by a protozoan in the liver, spleen, etc. [C19: < Assamese *kālā* black + *āzār* disease]

kalashnikov (kəˈlæʃnɪˌkɒf) *n.* a Russian-made sub-machine-gun, used esp. by terrorists and guerrillas. [C20: < Russian]

kale *or* **kail** (keɪl) *n.* **1.** a cultivated variety of cabbage with crinkled leaves. **2.** *Scot.* a cabbage. ~Cf. **sea kale.** [OE *cāl*]

kaleidoscope (kəˈlaɪdəˌskəʊp) *n.* **1.** an optical toy for producing symmetrical patterns by multiple reflections in inclined mirrors enclosed in a tube. Loose pieces of coloured glass, paper, etc., are placed in the tube between the mirrors. **2.** any complex pattern of frequently changing shapes and colours. [C19: < Gk *kalos* beautiful + *eidos* form + -SCOPE] —**kaleidoscopic** (kəˌlaɪdəˈskɒpɪk) *adj.*

kalends (ˈkælɪndz) *pl. n.* a variant spelling of **calends.**

Kalevala (ˌkɑːləˈvɑːlə) *n. Finnish legend.* **1.** the land of the hero Kaleva, who performed legendary exploits. **2.** the Finnish national epic in which these exploits are recounted. [Finnish, < *kaleva* of a hero + *-la* home]

kaleyard *or* **kailyard** (ˈkeɪlˌjɑːd) *n. Scot.* a vegetable garden. [C19: lit.: cabbage garden]

kaleyard school *or* **kailyard school** *n.* a group of writers who depicted the homely aspects of life in the Scottish Lowlands. The best-known contributor was J. M. Barrie.

kalmia (ˈkælmɪə) *n.* an evergreen North American ericaceous shrub having showy clusters of white or pink flowers. [C18: after Peter *Kalm* (1715–79), Swedish botanist and pupil of Linnaeus]

Kalmuck (ˈkælmʌk) *or* **Kalmyk** (ˈkælmɪk) *n.* **1.** (*pl.* **-mucks, -muck** *or* **-myks, -myk**) a member of a Mongoloid people of Buddhist tradition, who migrated from NE China to the USSR in the 17th century. **2.** the language of this people.

kalong (ˈkɑːlɒŋ) *n.* a fruit bat of the Malay Archipelago; a flying fox. [Javanese]

kalpa (ˈkælpə) *n.* (in Hindu cosmology) a period in which the universe experiences a cycle of creation and destruction. [C18: Sansk.]

Kamasutra (ˌkɑːməˈsuːtrə) *n.* **the.** an ancient Hindu text on erotic pleasure. [Sansk.: book on love, < *kāma* love + *sūtra* thread]

kame (keɪm) *n.* an irregular mound or ridge of gravel, sand, etc., deposited by water derived from melting glaciers. [C19: Scot. & N English var. of COMB]

kamikaze (ˌkæmɪˈkɑːzɪ) *n.* **1.** (*often cap.*) (in World War II) one of a group of Japanese pilots who performed suicidal missions. **2.** (*modifier*) (of an action) undertaken or (of a person) undertaking an action in the knowledge that it will result in the death of the person performing it in order to inflict maximum damage on an enemy: *a kamikaze attack.* **3.** (*modifier*) extremely foolhardy and possibly self-defeating. [C20: < Japanese, < *kami* divine + *kaze* wind]

Kamloops trout (ˈkæmluːps) *n.* a variety of rainbow trout common in British Columbia.

kampong (ˈkæmpɒŋ) *n.* (in Malaysia) a village. [C19: < Malay]

Kampuchean (ˌkæmpʊˈtʃɪən) *n.* **1.** a native or inhabitant of Kampuchea, in SE Asia. ~*adj.* **2.** of or relating to the inhabitants of Kampuchea.

Kanaka (kəˈnækə) *n.* **1.** a native Hawaiian. **2.** (*often not cap.*) *Austral.* any native of the South Pacific islands, esp. (formerly) one abducted to work in Australia. [C19: < Hawaiian: man]

Kanarese *or* **Canarese** (ˌkænəˈriːz) *n.* **1.** (*pl.* **-rese**) a member of a people of S India living chiefly in Kanara. **2.** the language of this people.

kanga *or* **khanga** (ˈkæŋgə) *n.* a piece of gaily decorated thin cotton cloth used as a woman's garment, originally in E Africa. [< Swahili]

kangaroo (ˌkæŋgəˈruː) *n., pl.* **-roos.** a large herbivorous marsupial of Australia and New Guinea, having large powerful hind legs used for leaping, and a long thick tail. [C18: prob. < Abor.] —ˌ**kangaˈroo-ˌlike** *adj.*

kangaroo closure *n. Parliamentary procedure.* a form of closure in which the chairman or speaker selects certain amendments for discussion and excludes others.

kangaroo court *n.* an irregular court, esp. one set up by strikers to judge strikebreakers.

kangaroo paw *n.* any of various Australian plants having green-and-red hairy flowers.

kangaroo rat *n.* **1.** a small leaping rodent related to the squirrels and inhabiting desert regions of North America, having a stocky body and very long hind legs and tail. **2.** Also called: **kangaroo mouse.** any of several leaping Australian rodents.

kanji (ˈkændʒɪ) *n., pl.* **-ji** *or* **-jis.** a Japanese syllabary derived from Chinese orthography. [Japanese, < Chinese, < *han* Chinese + *tsû* word]

KANU (ˈkɑːnuː) *n. acronym for* Kenya African National Union.

kaolin (ˈkeɪəlɪn) *n.* a fine white clay used for the manufacture of hard-paste porcelain and bone china and in medicine as a poultice. Also called: **china clay.** [C18: < F, < Chinese *Kaoling* Chinese mountain where supplies for Europe were first obtained] —ˌ**kaoˈlinic** *adj.*

kaon (ˈkeɪɒn) *n.* a meson that has a rest mass of about 996 or 964 electron masses. Also called: **K-meson.** [C20 *ka* representing the letter *k* + (MES)ON]

kapellmeister (kæˈpɛlˌmaɪstə) *n.* a variant spelling of **capellmeister.**

kapok (ˈkeɪpɒk) *n.* a silky fibre obtained from the hairs covering the seeds of a tropical tree (**kapok tree**): used for stuffing pillows, etc. [C18: < Malay]

Kaposi's sarcoma (kæˈpəʊsɪz) *n.* a form of skin cancer found in Africans and more recently in victims of AIDS. [C20: after Moritz Kohn *Kaposi* (1837-1902), Austrian dermatologist who first described the sores that characterize the disease]

kappa (ˈkæpə) *n.* the tenth letter in the Greek alphabet (Κ, κ). [Gk, of Semitic origin]

kaput (kæˈpʊt) *adj.* (*postpositive*) *Inf.* ruined, broken, or not functioning. [C20: < G *kaputt* done for]

karabiner (ˌkærəˈbiːnə) *n. Mountaineering.* a metal clip with a spring for attaching to a piton, belay, etc. Also called: **snaplink, krab.** [shortened < G *Karabinerhaken,* lit.: carbine hook]

karakul *or* **caracul** (ˈkærəkᵊl) *n.* **1.** a breed of sheep of central Asia having coarse black, grey, or brown hair: the lambs have soft curled hair. **2.** the fur prepared from these lambs. ~See also **Persian lamb.** [C19: < Russian, < the name of a region in Bokhara where the sheep originated]

karat (ˈkærət) *n.* the usual U.S. and Canad. spelling of **carat** (sense 2).

karate (kəˈrɑːtɪ) *n.* **a.** a traditional Japanese system of unarmed combat, employing smashes, chops, kicks, etc., made with the hands, feet, elbows, or legs. **b.** (*as modifier*): *karate chop.* [Japanese, lit.: empty hand]

Karitane (ˌkærɪˈtɑːnɛ) *n. N.Z.* a nurse for babies; nanny. [< former child-care hospital at *Karitane,* New Zealand]

karma (ˈkɑːmə) *n.* **1.** *Hinduism, Buddhism.* the principle of retributive justice determining a person's state of life and the state of his reincarnations as the effect of his past deeds. **2.** destiny or fate. **3.** *Inf.* an aura or quality that a person, place, or thing is felt to have. [C19: < Sansk.: action, effect, < *karoti* he does] —ˈ**karmic** *adj.*

karoo *or* **karroo** (kəˈruː) *n., pl.* **-roos.** a dry tableland of southern Africa, with semidesert vegetation. [C18: < Afrik. *karo,* ? < Hottentot *garo* desert]

kaross (kəˈrɒs) *n.* a garment of skins worn by indigenous peoples in southern Africa. [C18: < Afrik. *karos,* ? < Du., < F *cuirasse* CUIRASS]

karri (ˈkɑːrɪ) *n., pl.* **-ris.** **1.** an Australian eucalyptus tree. **2.** the durable dark red wood of this tree, used for construction, etc. [< Abor.]

karst (kɑːst) *n.* (*modifier*) denoting the characteristic scenery of a limestone region, including underground streams, gorges, etc. [C19: G, < *Karst,* limestone plateau near Trieste]

kart (kɑːt) *n.* a light low-framed vehicle with small wheels and engine used for recreational racing (**karting**). Also called: **go-cart, go-kart.**

karyo- *or* **caryo-** *combining form.* indicating the nucleus of a cell. [< NL, < Gk *karuon* kernel]

kasbah *or* **casbah** (ˈkæzbɑː) *n.* (*sometimes cap.*) **1.** the citadel of various North African cities. **2.** the quarter in which a kasbah is located. [< Ar. *qaṣbạ* citadel]

kashruth *or* ***kashrut*** *Hebrew.* (kaʃˈruːt) *n.* **1.** the condition of being fit for ritual use in general. **2.** the system of dietary laws which require ritual slaughter, the removal of excess blood from meat, and the complete separation of milk and meat, and prohibit such foods as pork and shell fish. ~See also **kosher** (senses 1, 3). [lit.: appropriateness]

kata- *prefix.* a variant of **cata-.**

katabatic (ˌkætəˈbætɪk) *adj.* (of winds) blowing downhill through having become denser with cooling.

katydid (ˈkeɪtɪˌdɪd) *n.* a green long-horned grasshopper living among the foliage of trees in North America. [C18: imit.]

kauri (ˈkaʊrɪ) *n., pl.* **-ris.** a New Zealand coniferous tree with oval leaves and round cones, cultivated for wood and resin. [C19: < Maori]

kauri gum *n.* the fossil resin of the kauri tree.

kava (ˈkɑːvə) *n.* **1.** a Polynesian shrub. **2.** a drink prepared from the aromatic roots of this shrub. [C18: < Polynesian: bitter]

kayak *or* **kaiak** (ˈkaɪæk) *n.* **1.** a canoe-like boat used by Eskimos, consisting of a frame covered with animal skins. **2.** a fibreglass or canvas-covered canoe of similar design. [C18: < Eskimo]

kayo *or* **KO** (ˈkeɪˈəʊ) *n., pl.* **kayos,** *vb.* **kayoing, kayoed.** *Boxing, sl.* another term for **knockout** or **knock out.** [C20: < the initial letters of *knock out*]

kazoo (kəˈzuː) *n., pl.* **-zoos.** a cigar-shaped musical instrument of metal or plastic with a membranous diaphragm of thin paper that vibrates with a nasal sound when the player hums into it. [C20: prob. imit.]

KB (in Britain) *abbrev. for:* **1.** King's Bench. **2.** *Computers.* kilobyte.

KBE *abbrev. for* Knight (Commander of the Order) of the British Empire.

kbyte *Computers. abbrev. for* kilobyte.

kc *abbrev. for* kilocycle.

KC (in Britain) *abbrev. for:* **1.** King's Counsel. **2.** Kennel Club.

kcal *abbrev. for* kilocalorie.

KCB *abbrev. for* Knight Commander of the Bath (a Brit. title).

KCMG *abbrev. for* Knight Commander (of the Order) of St Michael and St George (a Brit. title).

KE *abbrev. for* kinetic energy.

kea (ˈkɛə) *n.* a large New Zealand parrot with brownish-green plumage. [C19: < Maori, imit. of its call]

kebab (kəˈbæb) *n.* a dish consisting of small pieces of meat, tomatoes, onions, etc., threaded onto skewers and grilled. Also called: **shish kebab.** [C17: via Urdu < Ar. *kabāb* roast meat]

kedge (kɛdʒ) *Naut.* ~*vb.* **1.** to draw (a vessel) along by hauling in on the cable of a light anchor, or (of a vessel) to be drawn in this fashion. ~*n.* **2.** a light anchor, used esp. for kedging. [C15: < *caggen* to fasten]

kedgeree (ˌkɛdʒəˈriː) *n. Chiefly Brit.* a dish

consisting of rice, cooked flaked fish, and hard-boiled eggs. [C17: < Hindi, < Sansk. *khiccā*]

keek (kiːk) *n., vb.* a Scot. word for **peep**[1]. [C18: prob. < MDu. *kīken* to look]

keel[1] (kiːl) *n.* **1.** one of the main longitudinal structural members of a vessel to which the frames are fastened. **2. on an even keel.** well-balanced; steady. **3.** any structure corresponding to or resembling the keel of a ship. **4.** *Biol.* a ridgelike part; carina. ~*vb.* **5.** to capsize. ~See also **keel over.** [C14: < ON *kjölr*]

keel[2] (kiːl) *n. Eastern English dialect.* **1.** a flat-bottomed vessel, esp. one used for carrying coal. **2.** a measure of coal. [C14 *kele*, < MDu. *kiel*]

keelhaul (ˈkiːlˌhɔːl) *vb.* (*tr.*) **1.** to drag (a person) by a rope from one side of a vessel to the other through the water under the keel. **2.** to rebuke harshly. [C17: < Du. *kielhalen;* see KEEL[1], HAUL]

keel over *vb.* (*adv.*) **1.** to turn upside down; capsize. **2.** (*intr.*) *Inf.* to collapse suddenly.

keelson (ˈkɛlsən, ˈkiːl-) *or* **kelson** *n.* a longitudinal beam fastened to the keel of a vessel for strength and stiffness. [C17: prob. < Low G *kielswin* keel swine, ult. of Scand. origin]

keen[1] (kiːn) *adj.* **1.** eager or enthusiastic. **2.** (*postpositive;* foll. by *on*) fond (of); devoted (to): *keen on golf.* **3.** intellectually acute: *a keen wit.* **4.** (of sight, smell, hearing, etc.) capable of recognizing fine distinctions. **5.** having a sharp cutting edge or point. **6.** extremely cold and penetrating: *a keen wind.* **7.** intense or strong: *a keen desire.* **8.** *Chiefly Brit.* extremely low so as to be competitive: *keen prices.* [OE *cēne*] —ˈ**keenly** *adv.* —ˈ**keenness** *n.*

keen[2] (kiːn) *vb.* (*intr.*) **1.** to lament the dead. ~*n.* **2.** a dirge or lament for the dead. [C19: < Irish Gaelic *caoine*, < OIrish *coīnim* I wail] —ˈ**keener** *n.*

keep (kiːp) *vb.* **keeping, kept. 1.** (*tr.*) to have or retain possession of. **2.** (*tr.*) to have temporary possession or charge of: *keep my watch for me.* **3.** (*tr.*) to store in a customary place: *I keep my books in the desk.* **4.** to remain or cause to remain in a specified state or condition: *keep ready.* **5.** to continue or cause to continue: *keep in step.* **6.** (*tr.*) to have or take charge or care of: *keep the shop for me till I return.* **7.** (*tr.*) to look after or maintain for use, pleasure, etc.: *to keep chickens.* **8.** (*tr.*) to provide for the upkeep or livelihood of. **9.** (*tr.*) to support financially, esp. in return for sexual favours. **10.** to confine or detain or be confined or detained. **11.** to withhold or reserve or admit of withholding or reserving: *your news will keep.* **12.** (*tr.*) to refrain from divulging or violating: *to keep a secret.* **13.** to preserve or admit of preservation. **14.** (*tr.;* sometimes foll. by *up*) to observe with due rites or ceremonies. **15.** (*tr.*) to maintain by writing regular records in: *to keep a diary.* **16.** (when *intr.*, foll. by *in, on, to,* etc.) to stay in, on, or at (a place or position): *keep to the path.* **17.** (*tr.*) to associate with (esp. in **keep bad company**). **18.** (*tr.*) to maintain in existence: *to keep court in the palace.* **19.** (*tr.*) *Chiefly Brit.* to have habitually in stock: *this shop keeps all kinds of wool.* **20. how are you keeping?** how are you? ~*n.* **21.** living or support. **22.** *Arch.* charge or care. **23.** Also called: **dungeon, donjon.** the main tower within the walls of a medieval castle or fortress. **24. for keeps.** *Inf.* **a.** permanently. **b.** for the winner or possessor to keep permanently. ~See also **keep at, keep away,** etc. [OE *cēpan* to observe]

keep at *vb.* (*prep.*) **1.** (*intr.*) to persist in. **2.** (*tr.*) to constrain (a person) to continue doing (a task).

keep away *vb.* (*adv.;* often foll. by *from*) to refrain or prevent from coming (near).

keep back *vb.* (*adv.;* often foll. by *from*) **1.** (*tr.*) to refuse to reveal or disclose. **2.** to prevent or be prevented from advancing, entering, etc.

keep down *vb.* (*adv., mainly tr.*) **1.** to repress. **2.** to restrain or control: *he had difficulty keeping his anger down.* **3.** to cause not to increase or rise. **4.** (*intr.*) to lie low. **5.** not to vomit.

keeper (ˈkiːpə) *n.* **1.** a person in charge of animals, esp. in a zoo. **2.** a person in charge of a museum, collection, or section of a museum. **3.** a person in charge of other people, such as a warder in a jail. **4.** See **goalkeeper, wicket-keeper, gamekeeper, park keeper. 5.** a person who keeps something. **6.** a bar placed across the poles of a permanent magnet to close the magnetic circuit when it is not in use.

keep fit *n.* exercises designed to promote physical fitness if performed regularly.

keep from *vb.* (*prep.*) **1.** (foll. by a gerund) to prevent or restrain (oneself or another); refrain or cause to refrain. **2.** (*tr.*) to preserve or protect.

keeping (ˈkiːpɪŋ) *n.* **1.** conformity or harmony (esp. in **in** *or* **out of keeping**). **2.** charge or care: *valuables in the keeping of a bank.*

keepnet (ˈkiːpˌnɛt) *n.* a net strung on wire hoops and sealed at one end, suspended in water by anglers to keep alive the fish they have caught.

keep off *vb.* **1.** to stay or cause to stay at a distance (from). **2.** (*prep.*) not to eat or drink or to prevent from eating or drinking. **3.** (*prep.*) to avoid or cause to avoid (a topic).

keep on *vb.* (*adv.*) **1.** to continue or persist in (doing something): *keep on running.* **2.** (*tr.*) to continue to wear. **3.** (*tr.*) to continue to employ: *the firm kept on only ten men.* **4.** (*intr.;* foll. by *about*) to persist in talking (about). **5.** (*intr.;* foll. by *at*) to nag (a person).

keep out *vb.* (*adv.*) **1.** to remain or cause to remain outside. **2. keep out of. a.** to remain or cause to remain unexposed to. **b.** to avoid or cause to avoid: *keep out of his way.*

keepsake (ˈkiːpˌseɪk) *n.* a gift that evokes memories of a person or event.

keep to *vb.* (*prep.*) **1.** to adhere to or stand by or cause to adhere to or stand by. **2.** to confine or be confined to. **3. keep oneself to oneself.** to avoid the society of others. **4. keep to oneself. a.** (*intr.*) to avoid the society of others. **b.** (*tr.*) to refrain from sharing or disclosing.

keep up *vb.* (*adv.*) **1.** (*tr.*) to maintain (prices, one's morale) at the present level. **2.** (*intr.;* often foll. by *with*) to maintain a pace or rate set by another. **3.** (*intr.;* often foll. by *with*) to remain informed: *to keep up with developments.* **4.** (*tr.*) to maintain in good condition. **5.** (*tr.*) to hinder (a person) from going to bed at night. **6. keep it up.** to continue a good performance. **7. keep up with.** to remain in contact with, esp. by letter. **8. keep up with (the Joneses).** *Inf.* to compete with (one's neighbours) in material possessions, etc.

kef (kɛf) *n.* a variant spelling of **kif.**

keffiyeh (kɛˈfiːjə), **kaffiyeh,** *or* **kufiyah** *n.* a cotton headdress worn by Arabs. [C19: < Ar., ? < LL *cofea* COIF]

keg (kɛg) *n.* **1.** a small barrel with a capacity of between five and ten gallons. **2.** *Brit.* an aluminium container in which beer is transported and stored. [C17: var. of ME *kag*, of Scand. origin]

keloid (ˈkiːlɔɪd) *n. Pathol.* a hard smooth pinkish raised growth of scar tissue at the site of an injury, tending to occur more frequently in dark-skinned races. [C19: < Gk *khēlē* claw]

kelp (kɛlp) *n.* **1.** any large brown seaweed. **2.** the ash of such seaweed, used as a source of iodine and potash. [C14: <?]

kelpie[1] *or* **kelpy** (ˈkɛlpɪ) *n., pl.* **-pies.** an Australian breed of sheepdog having a smooth coat of various colours and erect ears. [named after a particular specimen of the breed, c. 1870]

kelpie[2] (ˈkɛlpɪ) *n.* (in Scottish folklore) a water spirit in the form of a horse. [C18: prob. rel. to Scot. Gaelic *cailpeach* heifer, <?]

kelson (ˈkɛlsən) *n.* a variant spelling of **keelson.**

kelt (kɛlt) *n.* a salmon that has recently spawned. [C14: <?]

Kelt (kɛlt) *n.* a variant spelling of **Celt.**

kelter (ˈkɛltə) *n.* a variant of **kilter.**

kelvin (ˈkɛlvɪn) *n.* the basic SI unit of thermodynamic temperature; the fraction 1/273.16 of the thermodynamic temperature of the triple point of water. Symbol: K [C20: after William Thomson *Kelvin* 1st Baron Kelvin (1824-1907), Brit. physicist]

Kelvin scale *n.* a thermodynamic temperature

scale in which the zero is absolute zero. Originally the degree was equal to that on the Celsius scale but it is now defined so that the triple point of water is exactly 273.16 kelvins.

kempt (kɛmpt) *adj.* (of hair) tidy; combed. See also **unkempt.** [C20: back formation < *unkempt;* orig. p.p. of dialect *kemb* to COMB]

ken (kɛn) *n.* **1.** range of knowledge or perception (esp. in **beyond** *or* **in one's ken**). ~*vb.* **kenning, kenned** *or* **kent. 2.** *Scot. & northern English dialect.* to know. **3.** *Scot. & northern English dialect.* to understand. [OE *cennan*]

kendo (ˈkɛndəʊ) *n.* the Japanese art of fencing with pliable bamboo staves or, sometimes, real swords. [< Japanese]

kennel (ˈkɛnᵊl) *n.* **1.** a hutlike shelter for a dog. U.S. name: **doghouse. 2.** (*usually pl.*) an establishment where dogs are bred, trained, boarded, etc. **3.** a hovel. **4.** a pack of hounds. ~*vb.* **-nelling, -nelled** *or U.S.* **-neling, -neled. 5.** to keep or stay in a kennel. [C14: < OF, < Vulgar L *canīle* (unattested), < L *canis* dog]

kenning (ˈkɛnɪŋ) *n.* a conventional metaphoric name for something, esp. in Old Norse and Old English poetry. [C14: < ON, < *kenna;* see KEN]

kenspeckle (ˈkɛnˌspɛkᵊl) *adj. Scot.* easily seen or recognized. [C18: < dialect *kenspeck,* of Scand. origin]

kepi (ˈkeɪpiː) *n., pl.* **kepis.** a military cap with a circular top and a horizontal peak. [C19: < F *képi,* < G (Swiss dialect) *käppi* a little cap, < *kappe* CAP]

Kepler's laws (ˈkɛpləz) *pl. n.* three laws of planetary motion published by Johan Kepler (1571-1630), German astronomer, between 1609 and 1619. They deal with the shape of a planet's orbit, the constant velocity of the planet in orbit, and the relationship between the length of a planetary year and the distance from the sun.

kept (kɛpt) *vb.* **1.** the past tense and past participle of **keep. 2. kept woman.** *Censorious.* a woman maintained by a man as his mistress.

keratin (ˈkɛrətɪn) *n.* a fibrous sulphur-containing protein that occurs in the outer layer of the skin and in hair, nails, hooves, etc.

keratose (ˈkɛrəˌtəʊs, -ˌtəʊz) *adj.* (esp. of certain sponges) having a horny skeleton. [C19: < Gk *keras* horn + -OSE[1]]

kerb *or U.S. & Canad.* **curb** (kɜːb) *n.* a line of stone or concrete forming an edge between a pavement and a roadway. [C17: < OF *courbe* bent, < L *curvus;* see CURVE] —ˈ**kerbing** *n.*

kerb crawling *n.* the act of driving slowly beside the pavement seeking to entice someone into the car for sexual purposes. —**kerb crawler** *n.*

kerb drill *n.* a pedestrian's procedure for crossing a road safely, esp. as taught to children.

kerbstone *or U.S. & Canad.* **curbstone** (ˈkɜːbˌstəʊn) *n.* one of a series of stones that form a kerb.

kerchief (ˈkɜːtʃɪf) *n.* a piece of cloth worn over the head. [C13: < OF, < *covrir* to COVER + *chef* head] —ˈ**kerchiefed** *adj.*

kerel (ˈkɛərəl) *n. S. African.* a young man. [< Afrik. *kêrel;* cf. OE *ceorl*]

kerf (kɜːf) *n.* the cut made by a saw, an axe, etc. [OE *cyrf* a cutting]

kerfuffle (kəˈfʌfᵊl) *n. Inf., chiefly Brit.* commotion; disorder. [< Scot. *curfuffle, carfuffle,* < Scot. Gaelic *car* twist, turn + *fuffle* to disarrange]

kermes (ˈkɜːmɪz) *n.* **1.** the dried bodies of female scale insects used as a red dyestuff. **2.** a small evergreen Eurasian oak tree: the host plant of kermes scale insects. [C16: < F, < Ar. *qirmiz,* < Sansk. *krmija-* red dye, lit.: produced by a worm]

kermis *or* **kirmess** (ˈkɜːmɪs) *n.* **1.** (formerly, esp. in Holland and northern Germany) an annual country festival. **2.** *U.S. & Canad.* a similar event held to collect money for charity. [C16: < MDu., < *kerc* church + *misse* MASS; orig. a festival held to celebrate the dedication of a church]

kern[1] *or* **kerne** (kɜːn) *n.* the part of the character on a piece of printer's type that projects beyond the body. [C17: < F *carne* corner of type, ult. < L *cardō* hinge]

kern[2] (kɜːn) *n.* **1.** a lightly armed foot soldier in medieval Ireland or Scotland. **2.** *Arch.* a loutish peasant. [C14: < MIrish *cethern* band of foot soldiers, < *cath* battle]

kernel (ˈkɜːnᵊl) *n.* **1.** the edible seed of a nut or fruit within the shell or stone. **2.** the grain of a cereal, esp. wheat, consisting of the seed in a hard husk. **3.** the central or essential part of something. [OE *cyrnel* a little seed, < *corn* seed] —ˈ**kernel-less** *adj.*

kerosene *or* **kerosine** (ˈkɛrəˌsiːn) *n.* **1.** another name (esp. U.S. and Canad.) for **paraffin** (sense 1). **2.** the general name for paraffin as a fuel for jet aircraft. [C19: < Gk *kēros* wax + -ENE]

kersey (ˈkɜːzɪ) *n.* a twilled woollen cloth with a cotton warp. [C14: prob. < *Kersey,* village in Suffolk]

kerseymere (ˈkɜːzɪˌmɪə) *n.* a fine soft woollen cloth of twill weave. [C18: < KERSEY + (*cassi*)*mere,* var. of CASHMERE]

kestrel (ˈkɛstrəl) *n.* any of several small falcons that feed on small mammals and tend to hover against the wind. [C15: changed < OF *cresserele,* < *cressele* rattle, < Vulgar L *crepicella* (unattested), < L, < *crepāre* to rustle]

ketch (kɛtʃ) *n.* a two-masted sailing vessel, fore-and-aft rigged, with a tall mainmast. [C15 *cache,* prob. < *cacchen* to hunt; see CATCH]

ketchup (ˈkɛtʃəp), **catchup,** *or* **catsup** *n.* any of various sauces containing vinegar: *tomato ketchup.* [C18: < Chinese *kōetsiap* brine of pickled fish, < *kōe* seafood + *tsiap* sauce]

ketone (ˈkiːtəʊn) *n.* any of a class of compounds with the general formula R′COR, where R and R′ are usually alkyl or aryl groups. [C19: < G, < *Aketon* ACETONE] —**ketonic** (kɪˈtɒnɪk) *adj.*

ketone body *n. Biochem.* any of three compounds produced when fatty acids are broken down in the liver to provide a source of energy. Excess ketone bodies are present in the blood and urine of people unable to use glucose as an energy source, as in diabetes.

kettle (ˈkɛtᵊl) *n.* **1.** a metal container with a handle and spout for boiling water. **2.** any of various metal containers for heating liquids, cooking fish, etc. [C13: < ON *ketill,* ult. < L *catillus* a little pot, < *catīnus* pot]

kettledrum (ˈkɛtᵊlˌdrʌm) *n.* a percussion instrument of definite pitch, consisting of a hollow bowl-like hemisphere covered with a skin or membrane, supported on a tripod. The pitch may be adjusted by means of screws, which alter the tension of the skin. —ˈ**kettleˌdrummer** *n.*

kettle hole *n.* a round hollow formed by the melting of a mass of buried ice.

kettle of fish *n.* **1.** a situation; state of affairs (often used ironically in **a pretty** *or* **fine kettle of fish**). **2.** case; matter for consideration: *that's quite a different kettle of fish.*

key[1] (kiː) *n.* **1.** a metal instrument, usually of a specifically contoured shape, that is made to fit a lock and, when rotated, operates the lock's mechanism. **2.** any instrument that is rotated to operate a valve, clock winding mechanism, etc. **3.** a small metal peg or wedge inserted to prevent relative motion. **4.** any of a set of levers operating a typewriter, computer, etc. **5.** any of the visible parts of the lever mechanism of a musical keyboard instrument that when depressed cause the instrument to sound. **6. a.** Also called: **tonality.** any of the 24 major and minor diatonic scales considered as a corpus of notes upon which a piece of music draws for its tonal framework. **b.** the main tonal centre in an extended composition: *a symphony in the key of F major.* **7.** something that is crucial in providing an explanation or interpretation. **8.** a means of achieving a desired end: *the key to happiness.* **9.** a means of access or control: *Gibraltar is the key to the Mediterranean.* **10.** a list of explanations of symbols, codes, etc. **11.** a text that explains or gives information about a work of literature, art, or music. **12.** *Electrical engineering.* a hand-operated switch that is pressed to transmit coded signals, esp. Morse code. **13.** the grooving or scratching of a surface or the application of a rough coat of plaster, etc., to provide a bond for a subsequent finish. **14.** pitch: *he spoke in a low key.* **15.** a mood or style: *a poem in a melancholic key.* **16.** short for **keystone** (sense 1). **17.** *Bot.* any dry winged fruit, esp. that of the ash. **18.** (*modifier*) of great importance: *a key issue.* ~*vb.* (*mainly tr.*) **19.** (foll. by *to*) to harmonize (with): *to key one's actions to the prevailing mood.* **20.** to adjust or fasten with a key or some similar device. **21.** to provide with a key or keys. **22.** (*also intr.*) another word for **keyboard** (sense 2). **23.** to include a distinguishing device in (an advertisement, etc.), so that responses to it can be identified. ~See also **key in, key up.** [OE *cǣg*] —ˈ**keyless** *adj.*

key[2] (kiː) *n.* a variant spelling of **cay.**

keyboard (ˈkiːˌbɔːd) *n.* **1. a.** a set of keys, usually hand-operated, as on a piano, typewriter, or typesetting machine. **b.** (*as modifier*): *a keyboard instrument.* ~*vb.* **2.** (*tr.*) to set (a text) in type by using a keyboard machine. —ˈ**keyˌboarder** *n.*

key grip *n.* the person in charge of moving and setting up camera tracks and scenery in a film or television studio.

keyhole (ˈkiːˌhəʊl) *n.* an aperture in a door or a lock case through which a key may be passed to engage the lock mechanism.

key in *vb.* (*tr., adv.*) to enter (information or instructions) in a computer or other device by means of a keyboard or keypad.

key money *n.* a fee payment required from a new tenant of a house or flat before he moves in.

keynote (ˈkiːˌnəʊt) *n.* **1. a.** a central or determining principle in a speech, literary work, etc. **b.** (*as modifier*): *a keynote speech.* **2.** the note upon which a scale or key is based; tonic. ~*vb.* (*tr.*) **3.** to deliver a keynote address to (a political convention, etc.).

keypad (ˈkiːˌpæd) *n.* a small panel with a set of buttons for operating a teletext system, electronic calculator, etc.

key punch *n.* **1.** Also called: **card punch.** a device having a keyboard that is operated manually to transfer data onto punched cards, paper tape, etc. ~*vb.* **key-punch. 2.** to transfer (data) by using a key punch.

key signature *n. Music.* a group of sharps or flats appearing at the beginning of each stave line to indicate the key in which a piece, section, etc., is to be performed.

keystone (ˈkiːˌstəʊn) *n.* **1.** the central stone at the top of an arch or the top stone of a dome or vault. **2.** something that is necessary to connect other related things.

key up *vb.* (*tr., adv.*) to raise the intensity, excitement, tension, etc., of.

kg **1.** *abbrev. for* **keg.** ~**2.** *symbol for* **kilogram.**

KG *abbrev. for* Knight of the Order of the Garter (a Brit. title).

KGB *abbrev. for* the Soviet secret police since 1954. [< Russian *Komitet gosudarstvennoi bezopasnosti* State Security Committee]

khaddar (ˈkɑːdə) *or* **khadi** (ˈkɑːdɪ) *n.* a cotton cloth of plain weave, produced in India. [< Hindi *khādar*]

khaki (ˈkɑːkɪ) *n., pl.* **-kis. 1.** a dull yellowish-brown colour. **2. a.** a hard-wearing fabric of this colour, used esp. for military uniforms. **b.** (*as modifier*): *a khaki jacket.* [C19: < Urdu, < Persian: dusty, < *khāk* dust]

khalif (ˈkeɪlɪf) *n.* a variant spelling of **caliph.**

khan[1] (kɑːn) *n.* **1. a.** (formerly) a title borne by medieval Chinese emperors and Mongol and Turkic rulers. **b.** such a ruler. **2.** a title of respect borne by important personages in Afghanistan and central Asia. [C14: < OF, < Med. L, < Turkish *khān,* contraction of *khāqān* ruler] —ˈ**khanate** *n.*

khan[2] (kɑːn) *n.* an inn in Turkey, etc.; caravanserai. [C14: via Ar. < Persian]

khedive (kɪˈdiːv) *n.* the viceroy of Egypt under Ottoman suzerainty (1867–1914). [C19: < F, < Turkish, < Persian *khidīw* prince] —**kheˈdival** *or* **kheˈdivial** *adj.*

Khmer (kmɛə) *n.* **1.** a member of a people of Kampuchea (formerly Cambodia), noted for a civilization that flourished from about 800 A.D. to about 1370. **2.** the language of this people: the official language of Kampuchea. ~*adj.* **3.** of or relating to this people or their language. —ˈ**Khmerian** *adj.*

kHz *symbol for* kilohertz.

kiang (kɪˈæŋ) *n.* a variety of the wild ass that occurs in Tibet and surrounding regions. [C19: < Tibetan *rkyan*]

kia ora (ˌkɪə ˈɔːrə) *sentence substitute. N.Z.* greetings! good luck! [Maori, lit.: be well!]

kibble[1] (ˈkɪbᵊl) *n. Brit.* a bucket used in wells or in mining for hoisting. [C17: < G *Kübel,* ult. < Med. L *cuppa* CUP]

kibble[2] (ˈkɪbᵊl) *vb.* (*tr.*) to grind into small pieces. [C18: <?]

kibbutz (kɪˈbʊts) *n., pl.* **kibbutzim** (ˌkɪbʊtˈsiːm). a collective agricultural settlement in modern Israel, owned and administered communally by its members. [C20: < Mod. Heb. *qibbūs* gathering, < Heb. *qibbūtz*]

kibe (kaɪb) *n.* a chilblain, esp. an ulcerated one on the heel. [C14: prob. < Welsh *cibi,* <?]

kiblah (ˈkɪblɑː) *n. Islam.* the direction of Mecca, to which Muslims turn in prayer. [C18: < Ar. *qiblah* that which is placed opposite]

kibosh (ˈkaɪˌbɒʃ) *n. Sl.* **put the kibosh on.** to put a stop to; prevent from continuing; halt. [C19: <?]

kick (kɪk) *vb.* **1.** (*tr.*) to drive or impel with the foot. **2.** (*tr.*) to hit with the foot or feet. **3.** (*intr.*) to strike out or thrash about with the feet, as in fighting or swimming. **4.** (*intr.*) to raise a leg high, as in dancing. **5.** (of a gun, etc.) to recoil or strike in recoiling when fired. **6.** (*tr.*) *Rugby.* to make (a conversion or a drop goal) by means of a kick. **7.** (*tr.*) *Soccer.* to score (a goal) by a kick. **8.** (*intr.*) *Athletics.* to put on a sudden spurt. **9.** (*intr.*) to make a sudden violent movement. **10.** (*intr.;* sometimes foll. by *against*) *Inf.* to object or resist. **11.** (*intr.*) *Inf.* to be active and in good health (esp. in **alive and kicking**). **12.** *Inf.* to change gear in (a car): *he kicked into third.* **13.** (*tr.*) *Inf.* to free oneself of (an addiction, etc.): *to kick the habit.* **14. kick up one's heels.** *Inf.* to enjoy oneself without inhibition. ~*n.* **15.** a thrust or blow with the foot. **16.** any of certain rhythmic leg movements used in swimming. **17.** the recoil of a gun or other firearm. **18.** *Inf.* exciting quality or effect (esp. in **get a kick out of, for kicks**). **19.** *Athletics.* a sudden spurt, acceleration or boost. **20.** a sudden violent movement. **21.** *Inf.* the sudden stimulating effect of strong alcoholic drink or certain drugs. **22.** *Inf.* power or force. **23. kick in the teeth.** *Sl.* a humiliating rebuff. ~See also **kick about, kick in,** etc. [C14 *kiken,* ? < ON] —ˈ**kickable** *adj.*

kick about *or* **around** *vb.* (*mainly adv.*) *Inf.* **1.** (*tr.*) to treat harshly. **2.** (*tr.*) to discuss (ideas, etc.) informally. **3.** (*intr.*) to wander aimlessly. **4.** (*intr.*) to lie neglected or forgotten.

kickback (ˈkɪkˌbæk) *n.* **1.** a strong reaction. **2.** part of an income paid to a person having influence over the size or payment of the income, esp. by some illegal arrangement. ~*vb.* **kick back.** (*adv.*) **3.** (*intr.*) to have a strong reaction. **4.** (*intr.*) (esp. of a gun) to recoil. **5.** to pay a kickback to (someone).

kickdown (ˈkɪkˌdaʊn) *n.* a method of changing gear in a car with automatic transmission, by fully depressing the accelerator.

kicker (ˈkɪkə) *n.* **1.** a person or thing that kicks. **2.** *U.S. & Canad. sl.* a hidden and disadvantageous factor.

kick in *vb.* (*tr., adv.*) *Austral. inf.* to contribute.

kick off *vb.* (*intr., adv.*) **1.** to start play in a game of football by kicking the ball from the centre of the field. **2.** *Inf.* to commence (a discussion, job, etc.). ~*n.* **kickoff. 3. a.** a place kick from the centre of the field in a game of football. **b.** the time at which the first such kick is due to take place.

kick on *vb.* (*adv.*) *Austral. inf.* to continue.

kick out *vb.* (*tr., adv.*) *Inf.* to eject or dismiss.

kickshaw (ˈkɪkˌʃɔː) *or* **kickshaws** *n.* **1.** a valueless trinket. **2.** *Arch.* a small exotic delicacy. [C16: back formation < *kickshaws*, by folk etymology < F *quelque chose* something]

kickstand (ˈkɪkˌstænd) *n.* a short metal bar attached to the frame of a motorcycle or bicycle, which when kicked into a vertical position holds the stationary vehicle upright.

kick-start (ˈkɪkˌstɑːt) *vb.* (*tr.*) to start (an engine, esp. of a motorcycle) by means of a pedal that is kicked downwards. —ˈ**kick-**ˌ**starter** *n.*

kick up *vb.* (*adv.*) *Inf.* to cause (trouble, etc.).

kick upstairs *vb.* (*tr., adv.*) *Inf.* to promote to a higher but effectively powerless position.

kid[1] (kɪd) *n.* **1.** the young of a goat or of a related animal, such as an antelope. **2.** soft smooth leather made from the hide of a kid. **3.** *Inf.* **a.** a young person; child. **b.** (*modifier*) younger or being still a child: *kid brother.* ~*vb.* **kidding, kidded. 4.** (of a goat) to give birth to (young). [C12: < ON] —ˈ**kiddishness** *n.* —ˈ**kid**ˌ**like** *adj.*

kid[2] (kɪd) *vb.* **kidding, kidded.** *Inf.* (sometimes foll. by *on* or *along*) **1.** (*tr.*) to tease or deceive for fun. **2.** (*intr.*) to behave or speak deceptively for fun. **3.** (*tr.*) to fool (oneself) into believing (something): *don't kid yourself that no-one else knows.* [C19: prob. < KID[1]] —ˈ**kidder** *n.* —ˈ**kiddingly** *adv.*

Kidderminster (ˈkɪdəˌmɪnstə) *n.* a type of ingrain reversible carpet originally made at Kidderminster. [after *Kidderminster*, town in W central England]

kiddy *or* **kiddie** (ˈkɪdɪ) *n., pl.* **-dies.** *Inf.* an affectionate word for **child.**

kid glove *n.* **1.** a glove made of kidskin. **2. handle with kid gloves.** to treat with great tact or caution. ~*adj.* **kidglove. 3.** overdelicate. **4.** diplomatic; tactful: *a kidglove approach.*

kidnap (ˈkɪdnæp) *vb.* **-napping, -napped** *or U.S.* **-naping, -naped.** (*tr.*) to carry off and hold (a person), usually for ransom. [C17: KID[1] + obs. *nap* to steal; see NAB] —ˈ**kidnapper** *n.*

kidney (ˈkɪdnɪ) *n.* **1.** either of two bean-shaped organs at the back of the abdominal cavity in man. They filter waste products from the blood, which are excreted as urine. Related adj.: **renal. 2.** the corresponding organ in other animals. **3.** the kidneys of certain animals used as food. **4.** class, type, or disposition (esp. in **of the same** *or* **a different kidney**). [C14: <?]

kidney bean *n.* **1.** any of certain bean plants having kidney-shaped seeds, esp. the scarlet runner. **2.** the seed of any of these beans.

kidney machine *n.* a machine carrying out the functions of a kidney, esp. used in haemodialysis.

kidney stone *n. Pathol.* a hard mass formed in the kidney, usually composed of oxalates, phosphates, and carbonates.

kidology (kɪˈdɒlədʒɪ) *n. Brit. inf.* the practice of bluffing or deception. [C20: < KID[2] + *ology* a science]

kidskin (ˈkɪdˌskɪn) *n.* a soft smooth leather made from the hide of a young goat. Often shortened to **kid.**

kids' stuff *n. Sl.* **1.** something considered fit only for children. **2.** something considered easy.

kidstakes (ˈkɪdˌsteɪks) *Austral. inf.* ~*pl. n.* **1.** pretence; nonsense: *cut the kidstakes!* ~*interj.* **2.** an exclamation of annoyance or disagreement.

kie kie (ˈkiːɛ kiːɛ) *n.* a New Zealand climbing plant with edible bracts. [< Maori]

kieselguhr (ˈkiːzəlˌgʊə) *n.* an unconsolidated form of **diatomite.** [C19: < G *Kieselgur*, < *Kiesel* flint + *Gur* loose earthy deposit]

kif (kɪf, kiːf), **kef,** *or* **kief** (kiːf) *n.* **1.** another name for **marijuana. 2.** any drug that when smoked is capable of producing a euphoric condition. **3.** the euphoric condition produced by smoking marijuana. [C20: < Ar. *kayf* pleasure]

kike (kaɪk) *n. U.S. & Canad. sl.* an offensive word for **Jew.** [C20: prob. var. of *kiki*, reduplication of *-ki*, common name-ending among Jews from Slavic countries]

kilderkin (ˈkɪldəkɪn) *n.* **1.** an obsolete unit of liquid capacity equal to 16 or 18 Imperial gallons or of dry capacity equal to 16 or 18 wine gallons. **2.** a cask capable of holding a kilderkin. [C14: < MDu. *kindekijn*, < *kintal* hundredweight, < Med. L *quintale*]

kill (kɪl) *vb.* (*mainly tr.*) **1.** (*also intr.*; when *tr.*, sometimes foll. by *off*) to cause the death of (a person or animal). **2.** to put an end to: *to kill someone's interest.* **3.** to make (time) pass quickly, esp. while waiting for something. **4.** to deaden (sound). **5.** *Inf.* to tire out: *the effort killed him.* **6.** *Inf.* to cause to suffer pain or discomfort: *my shoes are killing me.* **7.** *Inf.* to quash or veto: *the bill was killed in the House of Lords.* **8.** *Inf.* to switch off; stop. **9.** (*also intr.*) *Inf.* to overcome with attraction, laughter, surprise, etc.: *she was dressed to kill.* **10.** *Tennis, squash, etc.* to hit (a ball) so hard or so accurately that the opponent cannot return it. **11.** *Soccer.* to bring (a moving ball) under control. **12. kill oneself.** *Inf.* to overexert oneself: *don't kill yourself.* **13. kill two birds with one stone.** to achieve two results with one action. ~*n.* **14.** the act of causing death, esp. at the end of a hunt, bullfight, etc. **15.** the animal or animals killed during a hunt. **16.** *N.Z.* a seasonal tally of the number of stock killed at a meatworks. **17.** the destruction of a battleship, tank, etc. **18. in at the kill.** present at the end of some undertaking. [C13 *cullen*; see QUELL]

killdeer (ˈkɪlˌdɪə) *n., pl.* **-deer** *or* **-deers.** a large brown-and-white North American plover with two black breast bands. [C18: imit.]

killer (ˈkɪlə) *n.* **1. a.** a person or animal that kills, esp. habitually. **b.** (*as modifier*): *a killer shark.* **2.** something, esp. a task or activity, that is particularly taxing or exhausting. **3.** *Austral. & N.Z.* a farm animal selected to be killed for food.

killer bee *n.* an African honeybee, or one of its hybrids originating in Brazil, that is extremely aggressive when disturbed.

killer whale *n.* a ferocious black-and-white toothed whale most common in cold seas.

killick (ˈkɪlɪk) *or* **killock** (ˈkɪlək) *n. Naut.* a small anchor, esp. one made of a heavy stone. [C17: <?]

killifish (ˈkɪlɪˌfɪʃ) *n., pl.* **-fish** *or* **-fishes.** any of various chiefly American minnow-like fishes of fresh and brackish waters: used to control mosquitoes and as anglers' bait. [C19: < MDu. *kille* river + FISH]

killing (ˈkɪlɪŋ) *Inf.* ~*adj.* **1.** very tiring: *a killing pace.* **2.** extremely funny. **3.** causing death; fatal. ~*n.* **4.** the act of causing death; slaying. **5.** a sudden stroke of success, usually financial, as in speculations on the stock market (esp. in **make a killing**).

killjoy (ˈkɪlˌdʒɔɪ) *n.* a person who spoils other people's pleasure.

kiln (kɪln) *n.* a large oven for burning, drying, or processing something, such as porcelain or bricks. [OE *cylen*, < LL *culīna* kitchen, < L *coquere* to COOK]

kilo (ˈkiːləʊ) *n., pl.* **kilos.** short for **kilogram** or **kilometre.**

kilo- *prefix.* **1.** denoting 10^3 (1000): *kilometre.* Symbol: k **2.** (in computers) denoting 2^{10} (1024): *kilobyte:* in computer usage, *kilo-* is restricted to sizes of storage (e.g. *kilobit*) when it means 1024; in other computer contexts it retains its usual meaning of 1000. [< F, < Gk *khilioi* thousand]

kilobyte (ˈkɪləˌbaɪt) *n. Computers.* 1024 bytes. Abbrev.: **KB, kbyte.** See also **kilo-** (sense 2).

kilocalorie (ˈkɪləʊˌkælərɪ) *n.* another name for **Calorie.**

kilocycle (ˈkɪləʊˌsaɪkəl) *n.* short for kilocycle per second: a former unit of frequency equal to 1 kilohertz.

kilogram *or* **kilogramme** (ˈkɪləʊˌgræm) *n.* **1.** one thousand grams. **2.** the basic SI unit of mass, equal to the mass of the international prototype held by the *Bureau International des Poids et Mesures.* Symbol: kg

kilohertz (ˈkɪləʊˌhɜːts) *n.* one thousand hertz; one thousand cycles per second. Symbol: kHz

kilolitre (ˈkɪləˌliːtə) *n.* one thousand litres. Symbol: kl

kilometre *or U.S.* **kilometer** (ˈkɪləˌmiːtə,

kɪˈlɒmɪtə) *n.* one thousand metres. Symbol: km —**kilometric** (ˌkɪləʊˈmɛtrɪk) *adj.*

kiloton (ˈkɪləʊˌtʌn) *n.* **1.** one thousand tons. **2.** an explosive power, esp. of a nuclear weapon, equal to the power of 1000 tons of TNT. Abbrev.: **kt.**

kilovolt (ˈkɪləʊˌvəʊlt) *n.* one thousand volts. Symbol: kV

kilowatt (ˈkɪləʊˌwɒt) *n.* one thousand watts. Symbol: kW

kilowatt-hour *n.* a unit of energy equal to the work done by a power of 1000 watts in one hour. Symbol: kWh

kilt (kɪlt) *n.* **1.** a knee-length pleated skirt, esp. one in tartan, as worn by men in Highland dress. ~*vb.* (*tr.*) **2.** to tuck (the skirt) up around one's body. **3.** to put pleats in (cloth, etc.). [C18: of Scand. origin] —ˈ**kilted** *adj.*

kilter (ˈkɪltə) *or* **kelter** *n.* working order (esp. in **out of kilter**). [C17: <?]

kimberlite (ˈkɪmbəˌlaɪt) *n.* an intrusive igneous rock consisting largely of peridotite and often containing diamonds. [C19: < *Kimberley,* city in South Africa + -ITE¹]

kimono (kɪˈməʊnəʊ) *n., pl.* **-nos.** a loose sashed ankle-length garment with wide sleeves, worn in Japan. [C19: < Japanese: clothing, < *ki* to wear + *mono* thing] —**kiˈmonoed** *adj.*

kin (kɪn) *n.* **1.** a person's relatives collectively. **2.** a class or group with similar characteristics. **3.** See **next of kin.** ~*adj.* **4.** (*postpositive*) related by blood. [OE *cyn*]

-kin *suffix forming nouns.* small: *lambkin.* [< MDu., of West Gmc origin]

kinaesthesia (ˌkɪnɪsˈθiːzɪə) *or U.S.* **kinesthesia** *n.* the sensation by which bodily position, weight, muscle tension, and movement are perceived. [C19: < NL, < Gk *kinein* to move + AESTHESIA] —**kinaesthetic** *or U.S.* **kinesthetic** (ˌkɪnɪsˈθɛtɪk) *adj.*

kincob (ˈkɪŋkɒb) *n.* a fine silk fabric embroidered with threads of gold or silver, of a kind made in India. [C18: < Urdu *kimkhāb*]

kind¹ (kaɪnd) *adj.* **1.** having a friendly nature or attitude. **2.** helpful to others or to another: *a kind deed.* **3.** considerate or humane. **4.** cordial; courteous (esp. in **kind regards**). **5.** pleasant; mild: *a kind climate.* **6.** *Inf.* beneficial or not harmful. [OE *gecynde* natural, native]

kind² (kaɪnd) *n.* **1.** a class or group having characteristics in common; sort; type: *two of a kind.* **2.** an instance or example of a class or group, esp. a rudimentary one: *heating of a kind.* **3.** essential nature or character: *the difference is one of kind rather than degree.* **4.** *Arch.* nature; the natural order. **5. in kind. a.** (of payment) in goods or produce rather than in money. **b.** with something of the same sort: *to return an insult in kind.* [OE *gecynd* nature]

▷ **Usage.** Careful users of English avoid the mixture of plural and singular constructions frequently used with *kind* and *sort,* as in *those kind* (instead of *kinds*) *of buildings seem badly designed* or *these sort* (instead of *sorts*) *of distinctions are becoming blurred.*

kindergarten (ˈkɪndəˌgɑːtᵊn) *n.* a class or small school for young children, usually between the ages of four and six. [C19: < G, lit.: children's garden]

kind-hearted *adj.* kindly, readily sympathetic. —ˌ**kind-ˈheartedly** *adv.* —ˌ**kind-ˈheartedness** *n.*

kindle (ˈkɪndᵊl) *vb.* **1.** to set alight or start to burn. **2.** to arouse or be aroused: *the project kindled his interest.* **3.** to make or become bright. [C12: < ON *kynda,* infl. by ON *kyndill* candle] —ˈ**kindler** *n.*

kindling (ˈkɪndlɪŋ) *n.* material for starting a fire, such as dry wood, straw, etc.

kindly (ˈkaɪndlɪ) *adj.* **-lier, -liest. 1.** having a sympathetic or warm-hearted nature. **2.** motivated by warm and sympathetic feelings. **3.** pleasant: *a kindly climate.* **4.** *Arch.* natural; normal. ~*adv.* **5.** in a considerate or humane way. **6.** with tolerance: *he kindly forgave my rudeness.* **7.** cordially: *he greeted us kindly.* **8.** please (often used to express impatience or formality): *will you kindly behave yourself!* **9.** *Arch.* appropriately. **10. take kindly.** to react favourably. —ˈ**kindliness** *n.*

kindness (ˈkaɪndnɪs) *n.* **1.** the practice or quality of being kind. **2.** a kind or helpful act.

kindred (ˈkɪndrɪd) *adj.* **1.** having similar or common qualities, origin, etc. **2.** related by blood or marriage. **3. kindred spirit.** a person with whom one has something in common. ~*n.* **4.** relationship by blood. **5.** similarity in character. **6.** a person's relatives collectively. [C12 *kinred,* < KIN + *-red,* < OE *rǣden* rule, < *rǣdan* to rule]

kine (kaɪn) *n.* (*functioning as pl.*) an archaic word for cows or cattle. [OE *cȳna* of cows, < *cū* cow¹]

kinematics (ˌkɪnɪˈmætɪks) *n.* (*functioning as sing.*) the study of the motion of bodies without reference to mass or force. [C19: < Gk *kinēma* movement; see CINEMA, -ICS] —ˌ**kineˈmatic** *adj.* —ˌ**kineˈmatically** *adv.*

kinematograph (ˌkɪnɪˈmætəˌgrɑːf) *n.* a variant spelling of **cinematograph.**

kinesics (kɪˈniːsɪks) *n.* (*functioning as sing.*) the study of the role of body movements, such as winking, shrugging, etc., in communication.

kinesthesia (ˌkɪnɪsˈθiːzɪə) *n.* the usual U.S. spelling of **kinaesthesia.**

kinetic (kɪˈnɛtɪk) *adj.* relating to or caused by motion. [C19: < Gk *kinētikos,* < *kinein* to move] —**kiˈnetically** *adv.*

kinetic art *n.* art, esp. sculpture, that moves or has moving parts.

kinetic energy *n.* the energy of motion of a body equal to the work it would do if it were brought to rest. It is equal to the product of the increase of mass caused by motion times the square of the speed of light.

kinetics (kɪˈnɛtɪks, kaɪ-) *n.* (*functioning as sing.*) **1.** another name for **dynamics** (sense 2). **2.** the branch of mechanics, including both dynamics and kinematics, concerned with the study of bodies in motion. **3.** the branch of dynamics that excludes the study of bodies at rest.

kinetic theory (of gases) *n.* **the.** a theory of gases postulating that they consist of particles moving at random and undergoing elastic collisions.

kinfolk (ˈkɪnˌfəʊk) *pl. n. Chiefly U.S. & Canad.* another word for **kinsfolk.**

king (kɪŋ) *n.* **1.** a male sovereign prince who is the official ruler of an independent state; monarch. Related adjs.: **royal, regal. 2. a.** a ruler or chief: *king of the fairies.* **b.** (*in combination*): *the pirate king.* **3.** a person, animal, or thing considered as the best or most important of its kind. **4.** any of four playing cards in a pack, one for each suit, bearing the picture of a king. **5.** the most important chess piece. **6.** *Draughts.* a piece that has moved entirely across the board and has been crowned, after which it may move backwards as well as forwards. **7. king of kings. a.** God. **b.** a title of any of various oriental monarchs. ~*vb.* (*tr.*) **8.** to make (someone) a king. **9. king it.** to act in a superior fashion. [OE *cyning*] —ˈ**kingˌhood** *n.* —ˈ**kingˌlike** *adj.*

kingbird (ˈkɪŋˌbɜːd) *n.* any of several large American flycatchers.

kingbolt (ˈkɪŋˌbəʊlt) *or* **king rod** *n.* **a.** the pivot bolt that connects the body of a horse-drawn carriage to the front axle and provides the steering joint. **b.** a similar bolt placed between a railway carriage and the bogies.

King Charles spaniel *n.* a toy breed of spaniel with a short turned-up nose and a domed skull. [C17: after *Charles* II of England, who popularized the breed]

king cobra *n.* a very large venomous tropical Asian snake that extends its neck into a hood when alarmed. Also called: **hamadryad.**

King Country *n.* an area in the centre of North Island, New Zealand. [< *The Maori King,* name given to Maori chief there]

king crab *n.* another name for the **horseshoe crab.**

kingcup (ˈkɪŋˌkʌp) *n. Brit.* any of several yellow-flowered plants, esp. the marsh marigold.

kingdom (ˈkɪŋdəm) *n.* **1.** a territory, state, people, or community ruled or reigned over by a king or queen. **2.** any of the three groups into which natural objects may be divided: the animal, plant, and mineral kingdoms. **3.** *Theol.* the eternal sovereignty of God. **4.** an area of activity: *the kingdom of the mind.*

kingdom come *n.* **1.** the next world. **2.** *Inf.* the end of the world (esp. in **until kingdom come**). **3.** *Inf.* unconsciousness.

kingfish (ˈkɪŋˌfɪʃ) *n., pl.* **-fish** *or* **-fishes. 1.** a marine food and game fish occurring in warm American Atlantic coastal waters. **2.** *Austral.* any of various types of trevally, mulloway, and barracouta. **3.** any of various other large food fishes, esp. the Spanish mackerel.

kingfisher (ˈkɪŋˌfɪʃə) *n.* a bird which has a greenish-blue and orange plumage, a large head, short tail, and long sharp bill, and feeds on fish. [C15: orig. *king's fisher*]

King James Version *or* **Bible** *n.* **the.** another name for the **Authorized Version.**

kingklip (ˈkɪŋˌklɪp) *n.* an edible eel-like marine fish. [< Afrik., < Du. *koning* king + *klip* rock]

kinglet (ˈkɪŋlɪt) *n.* **1.** *Often derog.* the king of a small or insignificant territory. **2.** *U.S. & Canad.* any of various small warblers having a black-edged yellow crown.

kingly (ˈkɪŋlɪ) *adj.* **-lier, -liest. 1.** appropriate to a king. **2.** royal. ~*adv.* **3.** *Poetic or arch.* in a manner appropriate to a king. —ˈ**kingliness** *n.*

kingmaker (ˈkɪŋˌmeɪkə) *n.* a person who has control over appointments to positions of authority.

king-of-arms *n., pl.* **kings-of-arms. 1.** the highest rank of heraldic officer. **2.** a person holding this rank.

king of the castle *n. Chiefly Brit.* a children's game in which each child attempts to stand alone on a mound by pushing other children off it.

king penguin *n.* a large New Zealand subantarctic penguin.

kingpin (ˈkɪŋˌpɪn) *n.* **1.** the most important person in an organization. **2.** Also called (Brit.): **swivel pin.** a pivot pin that provides a steering joint in a motor vehicle by securing the stub axle to the axle beam. **3.** *Tenpin bowling.* the front pin in the triangular arrangement of the ten pins. **4.** (in ninepins) the central pin in the diamond pattern of the nine pins.

king post *n.* a vertical post connecting the apex of a triangular roof truss to the tie beam.

King's Bench *n.* (when the sovereign is male) another name for **Queen's Bench Division.**

King's Counsel *n.* (when the sovereign is male) another name for **Queen's Counsel.**

King's English *n.* (esp. when the British sovereign is male) standard Southern British English.

king's evidence *n.* (when the sovereign is male) another name for **queen's evidence.**

king's evil *n.* **the.** *Pathol.* a former name for **scrofula.** [C14: < the belief that the king's touch would heal scrofula]

king's highway *n.* (in Britain, esp. when the sovereign is male) any public road or right of way.

kingship (ˈkɪŋʃɪp) *n.* **1.** the position or authority of a king. **2.** the skill of ruling as a king.

king-size *or* **king-sized** *adj.* larger or longer than a standard size.

kinin (ˈkaɪnɪn) *n.* **1.** any of a group of polypeptides in the blood that cause dilation of the blood vessels. **2.** a substance that promotes cell division and retards ageing in plants. [C20: < Gk *kin(ēma)* motion + -IN]

kink (kɪŋk) *n.* **1.** a sharp twist or bend in a wire, rope, hair, etc. **2.** a crick in the neck or similar muscular spasm. **3.** a flaw or minor difficulty in some undertaking. **4.** a flaw or idiosyncrasy of personality. [C17: < Du.: a curl in a rope]

kinkajou (ˈkɪŋkəˌdʒuː) *n.* an arboreal fruit-eating mammal of Central and South America, with a long prehensile tail. Also called: **honey bear.** [C18: < F *quincajou,* < Algonquian]

kinky (ˈkɪŋkɪ) *adj.* **kinkier, kinkiest. 1.** *Sl.* given to unusual, abnormal, or deviant sexual practices. **2.** *Inf.* exhibiting unusual idiosyncrasies of personality. **3.** *Inf.* attractive or provocative in a bizarre way: *kinky clothes.* **4.** tightly looped, as a wire or rope. **5.** tightly curled, as hair. —ˈ**kinkily** *adv.* —ˈ**kinkiness** *n.*

kino (ˈkiːnəʊ) *n.* a dark red resin obtained from various tropical plants, esp. an Indian leguminous tree, used as an astringent and in tanning. [C18: of West African origin]

kinsfolk (ˈkɪnzˌfəʊk) *pl. n.* one's family or relatives.

kinship (ˈkɪnʃɪp) *n.* **1.** blood relationship. **2.** the state of having common characteristics.

kinsman (ˈkɪnzmən) *n., pl.* **-men.** a blood relation or a relation by marriage. —ˈ**kinsˌwoman** *fem. n.*

kiosk (ˈkiːɒsk) *n.* **1.** a small sometimes movable booth from which cigarettes, newspapers, sweets, etc., are sold. **2.** *Chiefly Brit.* a telephone box. **3.** (in Turkey, Iran, etc.) a light open-sided pavilion. [C17: < F *kiosque* bandstand, < Turkish, < Persian *kūshk* pavilion]

kip[1] (kɪp) *Brit. sl.* ~*n.* **1.** sleep or slumber: *to get some kip.* **2.** a bed or lodging. ~*vb.* **kipping, kipped.** (*intr.*) **3.** to sleep or take a nap. **4.** (foll. by *down*) to prepare for sleep. [C18: <?]

kip[2] (kɪp) *or* **kipskin** *n.* the hide of a young animal, esp. a calf or lamb. [C16: < MDu. *kipp*]

kip[3] (kɪp) *n. Austral.* a small board used to spin the coins in two-up. [C19: < Brit. dialect *kep* to catch]

kipper (ˈkɪpə) *n.* **1.** a fish, esp. a herring, that has been cleaned, salted, and smoked. **2.** a male salmon during the spawning season. ~*vb.* **3.** (*tr.*) to cure (herrings, etc.) by salting and smoking. [OE *cypera,* ? < *coper* COPPER[1], referring to its colour]

kir (kɜː; *French* kir) *n.* a drink made from dry white wine and cassis. [after Canon F. *Kir* (1876-1968), mayor of Dijon, who is said to have invented it]

kirby grip (ˈkɜːbɪ) *n. Trademark.* a type of hairgrip with one straight and one wavy side.

kirk (kɜːk) *n.* **1.** a Scottish word for **church. 2.** a Scottish church. [C12: < ON *kirkja,* < OE *cirice* CHURCH]

kirk session *n.* the lowest court of the Presbyterian Church.

kirmess (ˈkɜːmɪs) *n.* a variant spelling of **kermis.**

Kirsch (kɪəʃ) *or* **Kirschwasser** (ˈkɪəʃˌvɑːsə) *n.* a brandy distilled from cherries, made chiefly in the Black Forest in Germany. [G *Kirschwasser* cherry water]

kirtle (ˈkɜːtˀl) *n. Arch.* **1.** a woman's skirt or dress. **2.** a man's coat. [OE *cyrtel,* prob. < *cyrtan* to shorten, ult. < L *curtus* cut short]

kismet (ˈkɪzmɛt, ˈkɪs-) *n.* **1.** *Islam.* the will of Allah. **2.** fate or destiny. [C19: < Turkish, < Persian *qismat,* < Ar. *qasama* he divided]

kiss (kɪs) *vb.* **1.** (*tr.*) to touch with the lips or press the lips against as an expression of love, greeting, respect, etc. **2.** (*intr.*) to join lips with another person in an act of love or desire. **3.** to touch (each other) lightly. **4.** *Billiards.* (of balls) to touch (each other) lightly while moving. ~*n.* **5.** a caress with the lips. **6.** a light touch. [OE *cyssan,* < *coss*] —ˈ**kissable** *adj.*

kissagram (ˈkɪsəˌgræm) *n.* a greetings service in which a person is employed to present greetings by kissing the person celebrating. [C20: blend of *kiss* and *telegram*]

kiss curl *n. Brit.* a circular curl of hair pressed flat against the cheek or forehead.

kisser (ˈkɪsə) *n.* **1.** a person who kisses, esp. in a way specified. **2.** a slang word for **mouth** or **face.**

kissing gate *n.* a gate set in a U- or V-shaped enclosure, allowing only one person to pass through at a time.

kiss of life *n.* **the.** mouth-to-mouth resuscitation in which a person blows gently into the mouth of an unconscious person, allowing the lungs to deflate after each blow.

kist (kɪst) *n. S. African.* a large wooden chest in which linen is stored, esp. one used to store a bride's trousseau. [< Afrik., < Du.: CHEST]

kit[1] (kɪt) *n.* **1.** a set of tools, supplies, etc., for use together or for a purpose: *a first-aid kit.* **2.** the case or container for such a set. **3.** a set of pieces of equipment sold ready to be assembled. **4.** clothing and other personal effects, esp. those of a traveller or soldier: *safari kit.* ~See also **kit out.** [C14: < MDu. *kitte* tankard]

kit[2] (kɪt) *n. N.Z.* a string bag for shopping. [< Maori *kete*]

kitbag (ˈkɪtˌbæg) *n.* a canvas or other bag for a serviceman's kit.

kitchen (ˈkɪtʃɪn) *n.* **a.** a room or part of a building equipped for preparing and cooking food. **b.** (*as modifier*): *a kitchen table.* [OE *cycene,* ult. < LL *coquīna,* < L *coquere* to COOK]

kitchen Dutch *n. S. African derog.* an impoverished form of Afrikaans often mixed with words from other languages, as English.

kitchenette (ˌkɪtʃɪˈnɛt) *n.* a small kitchen or part of a room equipped for use as a kitchen.

kitchen garden *n.* a garden where vegetables and sometimes also fruit are grown.

kitchen midden *n. Archaeol.* the site of a large mound of domestic refuse marking a prehistoric settlement.

kitchen sink *n.* **1.** a sink in a kitchen for washing dishes, vegetables, etc. **2.** (*modifier*) denoting a type of drama or painting of the 1950s depicting sordid reality.

kitchen tea *n. Austral. & N.Z.* a party held before a wedding to which guests bring items of kitchen equipment as wedding presents.

kitchenware (ˈkɪtʃɪnˌwɛə) *n.* pots and pans, knives, forks, spoons, etc., used in the kitchen.

kite (kaɪt) *n.* **1.** a light frame covered with a thin material flown in the wind at the end of a length of string. **2.** *Brit. sl.* an aeroplane. **3.** (*pl.*) *Naut.* any of various light sails set in addition to the working sails of a vessel. **4.** a bird of prey having a long forked tail and long broad wings and usually preying on small mammals and insects. **5.** *Arch.* a person who preys on others. **6.** *Commerce.* a negotiable paper drawn without any actual transaction or assets and designed to obtain money on credit. ~*vb.* **7.** to issue (fictitious papers) to obtain credit or money. **8.** (*intr.*) to soar and glide. [OE *cȳta*]

Kite mark *n. Brit.* the official mark of quality and reliability, in the form of a kite, on articles approved by the British Standards Institution.

kith (kɪθ) *n.* **kith and kin.** one's friends and relations. [OE *cȳthth,* < *cūth;* see UNCOUTH]

kit out *or* **up** *vb.* **kitting, kitted.** (*tr., adv.*) *Chiefly Brit.* to provide with (a kit of personal effects and necessities).

kitsch (kɪtʃ) *n.* tawdry, vulgarized, or pretentious art, literature, etc., usually with popular appeal. [C20: < G] —ˈ**kitschy** *adj.*

kitten (ˈkɪtᵊn) *n.* **1.** a young cat. **2. have kittens.** *Brit. inf.* to react with disapproval, anxiety, etc.: *she had kittens when she got the bill.* ~*vb.* **3.** (of cats) to give birth to (young). [C14: < OF *caton,* < CAT; prob. infl. by ME *kiteling*]

kittenish (ˈkɪtᵊnɪʃ) *adj.* **1.** like a kitten; lively. **2.** (of a woman) flirtatious, esp. coyly flirtatious.

kittiwake (ˈkɪtɪˌweɪk) *n.* either of two oceanic gulls having pale grey black-tipped wings and a square-cut tail. [C17: imit.]

kitty[1] (ˈkɪtɪ) *n., pl.* **-ties.** a diminutive or affectionate name for a **kitten** or **cat.** [C18]

kitty[2] (ˈkɪtɪ) *n., pl.* **-ties. 1.** the pool of bets in certain gambling games. **2.** any shared fund of money. **3.** (in bowls) the jack. [C19: see KIT[1]]

kiwi (ˈkiːwiː) *n., pl.* **kiwis. 1.** a nocturnal flightless New Zealand bird having a long beak, stout legs, and weakly barbed feathers. **2.** *Inf. except in N.Z.* a New Zealander. **3.** *N.Z. inf.* a lottery. [C19: < Maori, imit.: N.Z. sense from the *Golden Kiwi Lottery*]

kiwi fruit *n.* the fuzzy edible fruit of an Asian climbing plant. Also called: **Chinese gooseberry.**

KKK *abbrev. for* Ku Klux Klan.

kl. *symbol for* kilolitre.

Klan (klæn) *n.* (usually preceded by *the*) short for **Ku Klux Klan.** —ˈ**Klanism** *n.*

klaxon (ˈklæksᵊn) *n.* a type of loud horn formerly used on motor vehicles. [C20: former trademark]

Kleenex (ˈkliːnɛks) *n., pl.* **-ex** *or* **-exes.** *Trademark.* a kind of soft paper tissue, used esp. as a handkerchief.

Klein bottle (klaɪn) *n. Maths.* a three-dimensional surface that is formed by inserting the smaller end of an open tapered tube through the surface of the tube and making this end stretch to fit the other end. [after Felix *Klein* (1849–1925), G mathematician]

kleptomania (ˌklɛptəʊˈmeɪnɪə) *n. Psychol.* a strong impulse to steal, esp. when there is no obvious motivation. [C19: *klepto-* < Gk, < *kleptein* to steal + -MANIA] —ˌ**kleptoˈmaniˌac** *n.*

klieg light (kliːg) *n.* an intense carbon-arc light used in producing films. [C20: after John H. *Kliegl* (1869–1959) & his brother Anton (1872–1927), German-born American inventors]

klipspringer (ˈklɪpˌsprɪŋə) *n.* a small agile antelope inhabiting rocky regions of Africa south of the Sahara. [C18: < Afrik., < Du. *klip* rock + *springer,* < *springen* to SPRING]

kloof (kluːf) *n.* a mountain pass or gorge in southern Africa. [C18: < Afrik., < MDu. *clove* a cleft]

klystron (ˈklɪstrɒn) *n.* an electron tube for the amplification or generation of microwaves. [C20: *klys-,* < Gk *kluzein* to wash over + -TRON]

km *symbol for* kilometre.

K-meson *n.* another name for **kaon.**

knack (næk) *n.* **1.** a skilful, ingenious, or resourceful way of doing something. **2.** a particular talent or aptitude, esp. an intuitive one. [C14: prob. var. of *knak* sharp knock, imit.]

knacker (ˈnækə) *Brit.* ~*n.* **1.** a person who buys up old horses for slaughter. **2.** a person who buys up old buildings and breaks them up for scrap. ~*vb.* **3.** (*tr.; usually passive*) *Sl.* to tire. [C16: prob. < *nacker* saddler, prob. of Scand. origin] —ˈ**knackery** *n.*

knag (næg) *n.* **1.** a knot in wood. **2.** a wooden peg. [C15: ? < Low G *knagge*]

knap (næp) *vb.* **knapping, knapped.** (*tr.*) *Dialect.* to hit or chip. [C15 (in the sense: to strike with a sharp sound): imit.] —ˈ**knapper** *n.*

knapsack (ˈnæpˌsæk) *n.* a canvas or leather bag carried strapped on the back or shoulder. [C17: < Low G, prob. < *knappen* to bite + *sack* bag]

knapweed (ˈnæpˌwiːd) *n.* any of several plants having purplish thistle-like flowers. [C15 *knopwed,* < *knop* of Gmc origin + WEED]

knar (nɑː) *n.* a variant of **knur.** [C14 *knarre* rough stone, knot on a tree]

knave (neɪv) *n.* **1.** *Arch.* a dishonest man. **2.** another word for **jack** (the playing card). **3.** *Obs.* a male servant. [OE *cnafa*] —ˈ**knavish** *adj.*

knavery (ˈneɪvərɪ) *n., pl.* **-eries. 1.** a deceitful or dishonest act. **2.** dishonest conduct; trickery.

knead (niːd) *vb.* (*tr.*) **1.** to work and press (a soft substance, such as bread dough) into a uniform mixture with the hands. **2.** to squeeze or press with the hands. **3.** to make by kneading. [OE *cnedan*] —ˈ**kneader** *n.*

knee (niː) *n.* **1.** the joint of the human leg connecting the tibia and fibula with the femur and protected in front by the patella. Technical name: **genu. 2. a.** the area surrounding and above this joint. **b.** (*modifier*) reaching or covering the knee: *knee socks.* **3.** the upper surface of a sitting person's thigh: *the child sat on her mother's knee.* **4.** a corresponding or similar part in other vertebrates. **5.** the part of a garment that covers the knee. **6.** anything resembling a knee in action or shape. **7.** any of the hollow rounded protuberances that project upwards from the roots of the swamp cypress. **8. bend** *or* **bow the knee.** to kneel or submit. **9. bring someone to his knees.** to force someone into submission. ~*vb.* **kneeing, kneed. 10.** (*tr.*) to strike, nudge, or push with the knee. [OE *cnēow*]

kneecap (ˈniːˌkæp) *n.* **1.** *Anat.* a nontechnical name for **patella.** ~*vb.* **-capping, -capped.** (*tr.*) **2.** (esp. of certain terrorist groups) to shoot (a person) in the kneecap.

knee-deep *adj.* **1.** so deep as to reach or cover the knees. **2.** (*postpositive;* often foll. by *in*) **a.** sunk or covered to the knees: *knee-deep in sand.* **b.** deeply involved: *knee-deep in work.*

knee-high *adj.* another word for **knee-deep** (sense 1).

kneehole (ˈniːˌhəʊl) *n.* a space for the knees, esp. under a desk.

knee jerk *n.* **1.** *Physiol.* an outward reflex kick of the lower leg caused by a sharp tap on the tendon just below the kneecap. ~*modifier.* **kneejerk. 2.** made or occurring as a predictable and automatic response, without thought: *a kneejerk reaction.*

kneel (niːl) *vb.* **kneeling, knelt** *or* **kneeled. 1.** (*intr.*) to rest, fall, or support oneself on one's knees. ~*n.* **2.** the act or position of kneeling. [OE *cnēowlian;* see KNEE] —ˈ**kneeler** *n.*

knees-up *n., pl.* **knees-up.** *Brit. inf.* a lively party. [C20: after popular song *Knees-up, Mother Brown!*]

knell (nɛl) *n.* **1.** the sound of a bell rung to announce a death or a funeral. **2.** something that precipitates or indicates death or destruction. ~*vb.* **3.** (*intr.*) to ring a knell. **4.** (*tr.*) to proclaim by or as if by a tolling bell. [OE *cnyll*]

knelt (nɛlt) *vb.* a past tense and past participle of **kneel.**

knew (njuː) *vb.* the past tense of **know.**

knickerbocker glory (ˈnɪkəˌbɒkə) *n.* a rich confection consisting of layers of ice cream, jelly, cream, and fruit, served in a tall glass.

knickerbockers (ˈnɪkəˌbɒkəz) *pl. n.* baggy breeches fastened with a band at the knee or above the ankle. Also called (U.S.): **knickers.** [C19: regarded as the traditional dress of the Du. settlers in America; after Diedrich *Knickerbocker* fictitious author of Washington Irving's *History of New York* (1809)]

knickers (ˈnɪkəz) *pl. n.* an undergarment for women covering the lower trunk and sometimes the thighs and having separate legs or leg-holes. [C19: contraction of KNICKERBOCKERS]

knick-knack *or* **nick-nack** (ˈnɪkˌnæk) *n.* **1.** a cheap ornament. **2.** an ornamental article of furniture, dress, etc. [C17: by reduplication < *knack*, in obs. sense: toy]

knife (naɪf) *n., pl.* **knives** (naɪvz). **1.** a cutting instrument consisting of a sharp-edged blade of metal fitted into a handle or onto a machine. **2.** a similar instrument used as a weapon. **3. have one's knife in someone.** to have a grudge against someone. **4. under the knife.** undergoing a surgical operation. ~*vb.* (*tr.*) **5.** to stab or kill with a knife. **6.** to betray or depose in an underhand way. [OE *cnīf*] —ˈ**knife,like** *adj.*

knife edge *n.* **1.** the sharp cutting edge of a knife. **2.** any sharp edge, esp. an arête. **3.** a sharp-edged wedge of hard material on which the beam of a balance pivots. **4.** a critical point.

knight (naɪt) *n.* **1.** (in medieval Europe) **a.** (originally) a person who served his lord as a mounted and heavily armed soldier. **b.** (later) a gentleman with the military and social standing of this rank. **2.** (in modern times) a person invested by a sovereign with a nonhereditary rank and dignity usually in recognition of personal services, achievements, etc. **3.** a chess piece, usually shaped like a horse's head. **4.** a champion of a lady or of a cause or principle. **5.** a member of the Roman class below the senators. ~*vb.* **6.** (*tr.*) to make (a person) a knight. [OE *cniht* servant]

knight errant *n., pl.* **knights errant.** (esp. in medieval romance) a knight who wanders in search of deeds of courage, chivalry, etc. —**knight errantry** *n.*

knighthood (ˈnaɪthʊd) *n.* **1.** the order, dignity, or rank of a knight. **2.** the qualities of a knight.

knightly (ˈnaɪtlɪ) *adj.* of, relating to, resembling, or befitting a knight. —ˈ**knightliness** *n.*

knight of the road *n. Brit. inf. or facetious.* **1.** a tramp. **2.** a commercial traveller. **3.** a lorry driver.

Knights Hospitallers *pl. n.* a military Christian religious order founded about the time of the first crusade (1096-99).

Knight Templar *n., pl.* **Knights Templars** *or* **Knights Templar.** another term for **Templar.**

kniphofia (nɪfˈəʊfɪə) *n.* the Latin name for **red-hot poker.** [C19: after Johann Hieronymus *Kniphof* (1704-63), G professor of medicine]

knit (nɪt) *vb.* **knitting, knitted** *or* **knit. 1.** to make (a garment, etc.) by looping and entwining (wool) by hand by means of long eyeless needles (**knitting needles**) or by machine (**knitting machine**). **2.** to join or be joined together closely. **3.** to draw (the brows) together or (of the brows) to come together, as in frowning or concentrating. ~*n.* **4. a.** a fabric made by knitting. **b.** (*in combination*): *a heavy knit.* [OE *cnyttan* to tie in] —ˈ**knitter** *n.*

knitting (ˈnɪtɪŋ) *n.* knitted work or the process of producing it.

knitwear (ˈnɪtˌwɛə) *n.* knitted clothes, esp. sweaters.

knives (naɪvz) *n.* the plural of **knife.**

knob (nɒb) *n.* **1.** a rounded projection from a surface, such as a lump on a tree trunk. **2.** a handle of a door, drawer, etc., esp. one that is rounded. **3.** a round hill or knoll. ~*vb.* **knobbing, knobbed. 4.** (*tr.*) to supply or ornament with knobs. **5.** (*intr.*) to bulge. [C14: < MLow G *knobbe* knot in wood] —ˈ**knobbly** *adj.* —ˈ**knobby** *adj.* —ˈ**knob,like** *adj.*

knobkerrie (ˈnɒbˌkɛrɪ), **knobkierie,** *or* **knob-stick** *n.* a stick with a round knob at the end, used as a club or missile by South African tribesmen. [C19: < Afrik., < *knop* knob, < MDu. *cnoppe* + *kierie* stick, < Hottentot *kīrri*]

knock (nɒk) *vb.* **1.** (*tr.*) to give a blow or push to. **2.** (*intr.*) to rap sharply with the knuckles, a hard object, etc.: *to knock at the door.* **3.** (*tr.*) to make or force by striking: *to knock a hole in the wall.* **4.** (*intr.;* usually foll. by *against*) to collide (with). **5.** (*tr.*) to bring into a certain condition by hitting: *to knock someone unconscious.* **6.** (*tr.*) *Inf.* to criticize adversely. **7.** (*intr.*) Also: **pink.** (of an internal-combustion engine) to emit a metallic noise as a result of faulty combustion. **8.** (*intr.*) (of a bearing, esp. one in an engine) to emit a regular characteristic sound as a result of wear. **9.** *Brit. sl.* to have sexual intercourse with (a person). **10. knock (a person) into the middle of next week.** *Inf.* to hit (a person) with a very heavy blow. **11. knock on the head. a.** to daze or kill (a person) by striking on the head. **b.** to prevent the further development of (a plan). ~*n.* **12. a.** a blow, push, or rap: *he gave the table a knock.* **b.** the sound so caused. **13.** the sound of knocking in an engine or bearing. **14.** *Inf.* a misfortune, rebuff, or setback. **15.** *Inf.* criticism. ~See also **knock about, knock back,** etc. [OE *cnocian,* imit.]

knock about *or* **around** *vb.* **1.** (*intr., adv.*) to wander about aimlessly. **2.** (*intr., prep.*) to travel about, esp. as resulting in varied experience: *he's knocked about the world.* **3.** (*intr., adv.;* foll. by *with*) to associate. **4.** (*tr., adv.*) to treat brutally: *he knocks his wife about.* **5.** (*tr., adv.*) to consider or discuss informally. ~*adj.* **knockabout. 6.** tough; boisterous: *knockabout farce.*

knock back *vb.* (*tr., adv.*) *Inf.* **1.** to drink, esp. quickly. **2.** to cost. **3.** to reject or refuse. **4.** to shock; disconcert. ~*n.* **knockback. 5.** *Sl.* a refusal or rejection. **6.** *Prison sl.* failure to obtain parole.

knock down *vb.* (*tr., adv.*) **1.** to strike to the ground with a blow, as in boxing. **2.** (in auctions) to declare (an article) sold. **3.** to demolish. **4.** to dismantle for ease of transport. **5.** *Inf.* to reduce (a price, etc.). ~*adj.* **knockdown.** (*prenominal*) **6.** powerful: *a knockdown blow.* **7.** *Chiefly Brit.* cheap: *a knockdown price.* **8.** easily dismantled: *knockdown furniture.*

knocker (ˈnɒkə) *n.* **1.** an object, usually made of metal, attached to a door by a hinge and used for knocking. **2.** *Inf.* a person who finds fault or disparages. **3.** (*usually pl.*) *Sl.* a female breast. **4.** a person or thing that knocks. **5. on the knocker.** *Inf.* promptly: *you pay on the knocker here.*

knocking copy *n.* publicity material designed to denigrate a competing product.

knocking-shop *n. Brit.* a slang word for **brothel.**

knock-knee *n.* a condition in which the legs are bent inwards causing the knees to touch when standing. —ˌ**knock-ˈkneed** *adj.*

knock off *vb.* (*mainly adv.*) **1.** (*intr., also prep.*) *Inf.* to finish work: *we knocked off an hour early.* **2.** (*tr.*) *Inf.* to make or do hastily or easily: *to knock off a novel in a week.* **3.** (*tr.; also prep.*) *Inf.* to reduce the price of (an article). **4.** (*tr.*) *Sl.* to kill. **5.** (*tr.*) *Sl.* to rob or steal: *to knock off a bank.* **6.** (*tr.*) *Sl.* to stop doing something, used as a command: *knock it off!*

knock-on *Rugby.* ~*n.* **1.** the infringement of playing the ball forward with the hand or arm. ~*vb.* **knock on.** (*adv.*) **2.** to play (the ball) forward with the hand or arm.

knock-on effect *n.* the indirect result of an action: *the number of redundancies was not great but there were as many again from the knock-on effect.*

knockout (ˈnɒkˌaʊt) *n.* **1.** the act of rendering unconscious. **2.** a blow that renders an opponent unconscious. **3. a.** a competition in which competitors are eliminated progressively. **b.** (*as modifier*): *a knockout contest.* **4.** *Inf.* a person or thing that is overwhelmingly impressive or attractive: *she's a knockout.* ~*vb.* **knock out.** (*tr., adv.*) **5.** to render unconscious, esp. by a blow. **6.** *Boxing.* to defeat (an opponent) by a knockout. **7.** to destroy or injure badly. **8.** to eliminate, esp. in a knockout competition. **9.** *Inf.* to overwhelm or amaze: *I was knocked out by that new song.* **10. knock the bottom out of.** *Inf.* to invalidate (an argument).

knockout drops *pl. n. Sl.* a drug secretly put into someone's drink to cause stupefaction.

knock up *vb.* (*adv., mainly tr.*) **1.** Also: **knock together.** *Inf.* to assemble quickly: *to knock up a set of shelves.* **2.** *Brit. inf.* to waken; rouse: *to knock someone up early.* **3.** *Sl.* to make pregnant. **4.** *Brit. inf.* to exhaust. **5.** *Cricket.* to score (runs). **6.** (*intr.*) *Tennis, squash, etc.* to practise, esp. before a match. ~*n.* **knock-up. 7.** a practice session at tennis, squash, etc.

knoll (nəʊl) *n.* a small rounded hill. [OE *cnoll*]

knot[1] (nɒt) *n.* **1.** any of various fastenings formed by looping and tying a piece of rope, cord, etc., in upon itself or to another piece of rope. **2.** a prescribed method of tying a particular knot. **3.** a tangle, as in hair or string. **4.** a decorative bow, as of ribbon. **5.** a small cluster or huddled group. **6.** a tie or bond: *the marriage knot.* **7.** a difficult problem. **8. a.** a hard mass of wood where a branch joins the trunk of a tree. **b.** a cross section of this visible on a piece of timber. **9.** a sensation of constriction, caused by tension or nervousness: *his stomach was tying itself in knots.* **10.** *Pathol.* a lump of vessels or fibres formed in a part, as in a muscle. **11.** a unit of speed used by nautical vessels and aircraft, being one nautical mile (about 1.15 statute miles or 1.85km) per hour. **12.** another term (not in technical use) for **nautical mile. 13. at a rate of knots.** very fast. **14. tie (someone) in knots.** to completely perplex (someone). ~*vb.* **knotting, knotted. 15.** (*tr.*) to tie or fasten in a knot. **16.** to form or cause to form into a knot. **17.** (*tr.*) to entangle or become entangled. **18.** (*tr.*) to make (an article or design) by tying thread in ornamental knots. [OE *cnotta*] —ˈ**knotted** *adj.* —ˈ**knotter** *n.* —ˈ**knotless** *adj.*

knot[2] (nɒt) *n.* a small northern sandpiper with a short bill and grey plumage. [C15: <?]

knot garden *n.* (esp. formerly) a formal garden of intricate design.

knotgrass (ˈnɒtˌgrɑːs) *n.* **1.** Also called: **allseed.** a weed whose small green flowers produce numerous seeds. **2.** any of several related plants.

knothole (ˈnɒtˌhəʊl) *n.* a hole in a piece of wood where a knot has been.

knotty (ˈnɒtɪ) *adj.* **-tier, -tiest. 1.** (of wood, rope, etc.) full of or characterized by knots. **2.** extremely difficult or intricate.

knout (naʊt) *n.* a stout whip used formerly in Russia as an instrument of punishment. [C17: < Russian *knut,* of Scand. origin]

know (nəʊ) *vb.* **knowing, knew, known.** (*mainly tr.*) **1.** (*also intr.; may take a clause as object*) to be or feel certain of the truth or accuracy of (a fact, etc.). **2.** to be acquainted or familiar with: *she's known him five years.* **3.** to have a familiarity or grasp of: *he knows French.* **4.** (*also intr.; may take a clause as object*) to understand, be aware of, or perceive (facts, etc.): *he knows the answer now.* **5.** (foll. by *how*) to be sure or aware of (how to be or do something). **6.** to experience, esp. deeply: *to know poverty.* **7.** to be intelligent, informed, or sensible enough (to do something). **8.** (*may take a clause as object*) to be able to distinguish or discriminate. **9.** *Arch.* to have sexual intercourse with. **10. know what's what.** to know how one thing or things in general work. **11. you never know.** things are uncertain. ~*n.* **12. in the know.** *Inf.* aware or informed. [OE *gecnāwan*] —ˈ**knowable** *adj.* —ˈ**knower** *n.*

know-all *n. Inf., disparaging.* a person who pretends or appears to know a great deal.

know-how *n. Inf.* **1.** ingenuity, aptitude, or skill. **2.** commercial and saleable knowledge of how to do a particular thing.

knowing (ˈnəʊɪŋ) *adj.* **1.** suggesting secret knowledge. **2.** wise, shrewd, or clever. **3.** deliberate. ~*n.* **4. there is no knowing.** one cannot tell. —ˈ**knowingly** *adv.* —ˈ**knowingness** *n.*

knowledge (ˈnɒlɪdʒ) *n.* **1.** the facts or experiences known by a person or group of people. **2.** the state of knowing. **3.** consciousness or familiarity gained by experience or learning. **4.** erudition or informed learning. **5.** specific information about a subject. **6. to my knowledge. a.** as I understand it. **b.** as I know.

knowledgeable *or* **knowledgable** (ˈnɒlɪdʒəbᵊl) *adj.* possessing or indicating much knowledge. —ˈ**knowledgeably** *or* ˈ**knowledgably** *adv.*

known (nəʊn) *vb.* **1.** the past participle of **know.** ~*adj.* **2.** identified: *a known criminal.*

knuckle (ˈnʌkᵊl) *n.* **1.** a joint of a finger, esp. that connecting a finger to the hand. **2.** a joint of veal, pork, etc., consisting of the part of the leg below the knee joint. **3. near the knuckle.** *Inf.* approaching indecency. ~*vb.* **4.** (*tr.*) to rub or press with the knuckles. **5.** (*intr.*) to keep the knuckles on the ground while shooting a marble. ~See also **knuckle down, knuckle under.** [C14] —ˈ**knuckly** *adj.*

knucklebones (ˈnʌkᵊlˌbəʊnz) *n.* (*functioning as sing.*) a less common name for **jacks** (the game).

knuckle down *vb.* (*intr., adv.*) *Inf.* to apply oneself diligently: *to knuckle down to some work.*

knuckle-duster *n.* (*often pl.*) a metal bar fitted over the knuckles, often with holes for the fingers, for inflicting injury by a blow with the fist.

knucklehead (ˈnʌkᵊlˌhɛd) *n. Inf.* a fool; idiot. —ˈ**knuckleˌheaded** *adj.*

knuckle under *vb.* (*intr., adv.*) to give way under pressure or authority; yield.

knur, knurr (nɜː), *or* **knar** *n.* a knot or protuberance in a tree trunk or in wood. [C16 *knor;* cf. KNAR]

knurl *or* **nurl** (nɜːl) *vb.* (*tr.*) **1.** to impress with a series of fine ridges or serrations. ~*n.* **2.** a small ridge, esp. one of a series. [C17: prob. < KNUR]

KO *or* **k.o.** (ˈkeɪˈəʊ) *vb.* **KO'ing, KO'd; k.o.'ing, k.o.'d,** *n., pl.* **KO's** *or* **k.o.'s.** a slang term for **knock out** or **knockout.**

koala *or* **koala bear** (kəʊˈɑːlə) *n.* a slow-moving Australian arboreal marsupial, having dense greyish fur and feeding on eucalyptus leaves. Also called (Austral.): **native bear.** [< Abor.]

koan (ˈkəʊæn) *n.* (in Zen Buddhism) a problem that admits no logical solution. [< Japanese]

kobold (ˈkɒbəʊld) *n. German myth.* **1.** a mischievous household sprite. **2.** a spirit that haunts mines. [C19: < G; see COBALT]

kochia (ˈkɒˈʃiːə) *n.* an annual plant with ornamental foliage that turns purple-red in late summer. [C19: after W.D.J. *Koch,* G botanist]

Kodiak bear *or* **Kodiak** (ˈkəʊdɪˌæk) *n.* a large variety of the brown bear inhabiting the W coast of Alaska and neighbouring islands, esp. Kodiak.

koeksister (ˈkʊkˌsɪstə) *n. S. African.* a small cake

of sweetened dough, usually dipped in syrup. [< Afrik., < Du. *koek* cake + *sissen* to sizzle]

koel (ˈkəʊəl) *n.* any of several parasitic cuckoos of S and SE Asia and Australia. [C19: < Hindi, < Sansk. *kokila*]

kohl (kəʊl) *n.* a cosmetic powder used, originally esp. in Muslim and Asian countries, to darken the area around the eyes. [C18: < Ar. *kohl;* see ALCOHOL]

kohlrabi (kəʊlˈrɑːbɪ) *n., pl.* **-bies.** a cultivated variety of cabbage whose thickened stem is eaten as a vegetable. Also called: **turnip cabbage.** [C19: < G, < It. *cavoli rape* (pl.), < *cavolo* cabbage (< L *caulis*) + *rapa* turnip (< L)]

koine (ˈkɔɪniː) *n.* a common language among speakers of different languages; lingua franca. [< Gk *koinē dialektos* common language]

Koine (ˈkɔɪniː) *n.* (*sometimes not cap.*) **the.** the ancient Greek dialect that was the lingua franca of the empire of Alexander the Great and in Roman times.

kokanee (kəʊˈkænɪ) *n.* a landlocked salmon of lakes in W North America: a variety of sockeye. [prob. < *Kokanee* Creek, in SE British Columbia]

kola (ˈkəʊlə) *n.* a variant spelling of **cola.**

kola nut *n.* a variant spelling of **cola nut.**

kolinsky (kəˈlɪnskɪ) *n., pl.* **-skies.** **1.** any of various Asian minks. **2.** the rich tawny fur of this animal. [C19: < Russian *kolinski* of *Kola,* peninsula in the USSR]

kolkhoz (kɒlˈhɔːz) *n.* a Russian collective farm. [C20: < Russian, short for *kollektivnoe khozyaistvo* collective farm]

Kol Nidre (kɔːl ˈnɪdreɪ) *n. Judaism.* **1.** the evening service with which Yom Kippur begins. **2.** the opening prayer of that service. [Aramaic *kōl nidhrē* all the vows; the prayer's opening words]

komatik (ˈkəʊmætɪk) *n.* a sledge having wooden runners and crossbars bound with rawhide, used by Eskimos. [C20: < Eskimo]

koodoo (ˈkuːduː) *n.* a variant spelling of **kudu.**

kook (kuːk) *n. U.S. & Canad. inf.* an eccentric or foolish person. [C20: prob. < CUCKOO] —**ˈkooky** *or* **ˈkookie** *adj.*

kookaburra (ˈkʊkəˌbʌrə) *n.* a large Australian kingfisher with a cackling cry. Also called: **laughing jackass.** [C19: < Abor.]

kopeck *or* **copeck** (ˈkəʊpɛk) *n.* a Soviet monetary unit worth one hundredth of a rouble. [Russian *kopeika,* < *kopye* lance]

koppie *or* **kopje** (ˈkɒpɪ) *n.* (in southern Africa) a small hill. [C19: < Afrik., < Du. *kopje,* lit.: a little head, < *kop* head]

Koran (kɔːˈrɑːn) *n.* the sacred book of Islam, believed by Muslims to be the infallible word of God dictated to Mohammed. Also: **Qur'an.** [C17: < Ar. *qur'ān* reading, book] —**Koˈranic** *adj.*

Korean (kəˈriːən) *adj.* **1.** of or relating to Korea in SE Asia, its people, or their language. ~*n.* **2.** a native or inhabitant of Korea. **3.** the official language of North and South Korea.

korfball (ˈkɔːfˌbɔːl) *n.* a game similar to basketball, in which each team consists of six men and six women. [C20: < Du. *korfbal* basketball]

kosher (ˈkəʊʃə) *adj.* **1.** *Judaism.* conforming to religious law; fit for use: esp. (of food) prepared in accordance with the dietary laws. **2.** *Inf.* **a.** genuine or authentic. **b.** legitimate. ~*n.* **3.** kosher food. [C19: < Yiddish, < Heb. *kāshēr* proper]

koto (ˈkəʊtəʊ) *n., pl.* **kotos.** a Japanese stringed instrument. [Japanese]

kotuku (ˈkəʊtʊkuː) *n., pl.* **-ku.** *N.Z.* a white heron having brilliant white plumage, black legs and yellow eyes and bill. [Maori]

kowhai (ˈkoːwaɪ) *n., pl.* **-hais.** *N.Z.* a small leguminous tree of New Zealand and Chile with clusters of yellow flowers. [C19: < Maori]

kowtow (ˌkaʊˈtaʊ) *vb.* (*intr.*) **1.** to touch the forehead to the ground as a sign of deference: a former Chinese custom. **2.** (often foll. by *to*) to be servile (towards). ~*n.* **3.** the act of kowtowing. [C19: < Chinese, < *k'o* to strike, knock + *t'ou* head]

Kr **1.** *Currency. symbol for:* **a.** krona. **b.** krone. **2.** *the chemical symbol for* krypton.

kr. *abbrev. for:* **1.** krona. **2.** krone.

kraal (krɑːl) *n. S. African.* **1.** a hut village in southern Africa, esp. one surrounded by a stockade. **2.** an enclosure for livestock. [C18: < Afrik., < Port. *curral* pen]

kraft (krɑːft) *n.* strong wrapping paper. [G: force]

krait (kraɪt) *n.* any nonaggressive brightly coloured venomous snake of S and SE Asia. [C19: < Hindi *karait,* <?]

kraken (ˈkrɑːkən) *n.* a legendary sea monster of gigantic size believed to dwell off the coast of Norway. [C18: < Norwegian, <?]

krans (krɑːns) *n. S. African.* a sheer rock face; precipice. [C18: < Afrik.]

kremlin (ˈkrɛmlɪn) *n.* the citadel of any Russian city. [C17: < obs. G *Kremelin,* < Russian *kreml*]

Kremlin (ˈkrɛmlɪn) *n.* **1.** the 12th-century citadel in Moscow, containing the offices of the Soviet government. **2.** the central government of the Soviet Union.

krill (krɪl) *n., pl.* **krill.** any small shrimplike marine crustacean: the principal food of whalebone whales. [C20: < Norwegian *kril* young fish]

krimmer (ˈkrɪmə) *n.* a tightly curled light grey fur obtained from the skins of lambs from Crimea in the USSR. [C20: < G, < *Krim* Crimea]

kris (krɪs) *n.* a Malayan and Indonesian stabbing or slashing knife with a scalloped edge. Also called: **crease, creese.** [C16: < Malay]

krona (ˈkrəʊnə) *n., pl.* **-nor** (-nə). the standard monetary unit of Sweden.

króna (ˈkrəʊnə) *n., pl.* **-nur** (-nə). the standard monetary unit of Iceland.

krone (ˈkrəʊnə) *n., pl.* **-ner** (-nə). **1.** the standard monetary unit of Denmark. **2.** the standard monetary unit of Norway. [C19: < Danish or Norwegian, ult. < L *corōna* CROWN]

Krugerrand (ˈkruːgəˌrænd) *n.* a one-ounce gold coin minted in South Africa. [C20: < Paul *Kruger* (1825-1904), Boer statesman + RAND[1]]

krummhorn (ˈkrʌmˌhɔːn) *or* **crumhorn** *n.* a medieval wind instrument consisting of an upward-curving tube blown through a double reed.

krypton (ˈkrɪptɒn) *n.* an inert gaseous element occurring in trace amounts in air and used in fluorescent lights and lasers. Symbol: Kr; atomic no.: 36; atomic wt.: 83.80. [C19: < Gk, < *kruptos* hidden]

Kshatriya (ˈkʃætrɪə) *n.* a member of the second of the four main Hindu castes, the warrior caste. [C18: < Sansk., < *kshatra* rule]

kt *abbrev. for:* **1.** karat. **2.** *Naut.* knot.

Kt **1.** Also: **knt.** *abbrev. for* Knight. **2.** Also: **N.** *Chess. symbol for* knight.

kudos (ˈkjuːdɒs) *n.* (*functioning as sing.*) acclaim, glory, or prestige. [C18: < Gk]

kudu *or* **koodoo** (ˈkuːduː) *n.* either of two spiral-horned antelopes (**greater kudu** or **lesser kudu**), which inhabit the bush of Africa. [C18: < Afrik. *koedoe,* prob. < Xhosa *iqudu*]

Ku Klux Klan (ˌkuː klʌks ˈklæn) *n.* **1.** a secret organization of white Southerners formed after the U.S. Civil War to fight Black emancipation. **2.** a secret organization of White Protestant Americans, mainly in the South, who use violence against Blacks, Jews, etc. [C19 *Ku Klux,* prob. based on Gk *kuklos* CIRCLE + *Klan* CLAN] —**Ku Klux Klanner** (ˈklænə) *n.*

kukri (ˈkʊkrɪ) *n., pl.* **-ris.** a knife with a curved blade that broadens towards the point, esp. as used by Gurkhas. [< Hindi]

kulak (ˈkuːlæk) *n.* (in Russia after 1906) a member of the class of peasants who became proprietors of their own farms In 1929 Stalin initiated their liquidation. [C19: < Russian: fist, hence, tightfisted person]

kumera *or* **kumara** (ˈkuːmərə) *n. N.Z.* the sweet potato. [< Maori]

kumiss *or* **koumiss** (ˈkuːmɪs) *n.* a drink made from fermented mare's or other milk, drunk by certain Asian tribes. [C17: < Russian *kumys*]

kümmel (ˈkʊməl) *n.* a German liqueur flavoured

with aniseed and cumin. [C19: < G, < OHG *kumil*, prob. var. of *kumin* CUMIN]
kumquat *or* **cumquat** (ˈkʌmkwɒt) *n.* **1.** a small Chinese citrus tree. **2.** the small round orange fruit of such a tree, with a sweet rind, used in preserves and confections. [C17: < Mandarin Chinese *chin chü* golden orange]
kung fu (ˈkʌŋ ˈfuː) *n.* a Chinese martial art combining principles of karate and judo. [< Chinese: martial art]
kurchatovium (ˌkɜːtʃəˈtəʊvɪəm) *n.* another name for **rutherfordium**, esp. as used in the Soviet Union. [C20: < Russian, after I. V. *Kurchatov* (1903–60), Soviet physicist]
Kurd (kɜːd) *n.* a member of a largely nomadic Turkic people living chiefly in E Turkey, N Iraq, and W Iran.
Kurdish (ˈkɜːdɪʃ) *n.* **1.** the language of the Kurds. ~*adj.* **2.** of or relating to the Kurds or their language.
kuri (ˈkuːrɪ) *n., pl.* **-ris.** *N.Z.* a mongrel dog. Also called: **goorie.** [Maori]
kurrajong *or* **currajong** (ˈkʌrəˌdʒɒŋ) *n.* any of various Australian trees or shrubs, esp. one that yields a tough durable fibre. [C19: < Abor.]
kursaal (ˈkɜːzᵊl) *n.* a public room at a health resort. [< G, lit.: cure room]
kurtosis (kəˈtəʊsɪs) *n. Statistics.* a measure of the concentration of a distribution around its mean. [< Gk, < *kurtos* arched]
kvass (kvɑːs) *n.* an alcoholic drink of low strength made in the Soviet Union from cereals and stale bread. [C16: < Russian *kvas*]
kW *abbrev. for* kilowatt.
kwacha (ˈkwɑːtʃɑː) *n.* **1.** the standard monetary unit of Zambia. **2.** the standard monetary unit of Malawi. [< a native word in Zambia]
kwashiorkor (ˌkwæʃɪˈɔːkə) *n.* severe malnutrition of infants and young children, resulting from dietary deficiency of protein. [C20: < native word in Ghana]
kWh *abbrev. for* kilowatt-hour.
KWIC (kwɪk) *n. acronym for* keyword in context (esp. in **KWIC index**).
KWOC (kwɒk) *n. acronym for* key word out of context.
kyanite (ˈkaɪəˌnaɪt) *n.* a variant spelling of **cyanite.** —**kyanitic** (ˌkaɪəˈnɪtɪk) *adj.*
kyanize *or* **-ise** (ˈkaɪəˌnaɪz) *vb.* (*tr.*) to treat (timber) with corrosive sublimate to make it resistant to decay. [C19: after J. H. *Kyan* (died 1850), E inventor of the process] —ˌ**kyaniˈzation** *or* **-iˈsation** *n.*
kyle (kaɪl) *n. Scot.* (esp. in place names) a narrow strait or channel: *Kyle of Lochalsh.* [C16: < Gaelic *caol* narrow]
kylie *or* **kiley** (ˈkaɪlɪ) *n. Austral.* a boomerang that is flat on one side and convex on the other. [C19: < Abor.]
kyloe (ˈkaɪləʊ) *n.* a breed of small long-horned long-haired beef cattle from NW Scotland. [C19: <?]
kymograph (ˈkaɪməˌgrɑːf) *n.* a rotatable drum for holding paper on which a tracking stylus continuously records variations in sound waves, blood pressure, respiratory movements, etc. [C20: < Gk *kuma* wave + -GRAPH] —ˌ**kymoˈgraphic** *adj.*
Kymric (ˈkɪmrɪk) *n., adj.* a variant spelling of **Cymric.**
Kymry (ˈkɪmrɪ) *pl. n.* a variant spelling of **Cymry.**
kyphosis (kaɪˈfəʊsɪs) *n. Pathol.* backward curvature of the thoracic spine, of congenital origin or resulting from injury or disease. [C19: < NL, < Gk *kuphōsis*, < *kuphos* humpbacked] —**kyphotic** (kaɪˈfɒtɪk) *adj.*
Kyrie eleison (ˈkɪrɪɪ əˈleɪsᵊn) *n.* **1.** a formal invocation used in the liturgies of the Roman Catholic, Greek Orthodox, and Anglican Churches. **2.** a musical setting of this. Often shortened to **Kyrie.** [C14: via LL < LGk *kurie, eleēson* Lord, have mercy]
kyu (kjuː) *n. Judo.* one of the student grades for inexperienced competitors. [< Japanese]

L

l *or* **L** (ɛl) *n., pl.* **l's, L's,** *or* **Ls. 1.** the 12th letter of the English alphabet. **2.** a speech sound represented by this letter. **3. a.** something shaped like an L. **b.** (*in combination*): *an L-shaped room.*

l *symbol for* litre.

L *symbol for:* **1.** lambert(s). **2.** large. **3.** Latin. **4.** (on British motor vehicles) learner driver. **5.** *Physics.* length. **6.** live. **7.** Usually written: £ pound. [L *libra*]. **8.** lire. **9.** *Electronics.* inductor (in circuit diagrams). **10.** *Physics.* **a.** latent heat. **b.** self-inductance. ~**11.** the Roman numeral for 50. See **Roman numerals.**

L. *or* **l.** *abbrev. for:* **1.** lake. **2.** law. **3.** leaf. **4.** league. **5.** left. **6.** length. **7.** (*pl.* **LL** *or* **ll.**) line. **8.** link. **9.** low.

L. *abbrev. for:* **1.** *Politics.* Liberal. **2.** (in titles) Licentiate. **3.** Linnaeus.

la[1] (lɑː) *n. Music.* a variant spelling of **lah.**

la[2] (lɔː) *interj.* an exclamation of surprise or emphasis. [OE *lā* lo]

La *the chemical symbol for* lanthanum.

laager (ˈlɑːgə) *n.* **1.** (in Africa) a camp, esp. one defended by a circular formation of wagons. **2.** *Mil.* a place where armoured vehicles are parked. ~*vb.* **3.** to form (wagons) into a laager. **4.** (*tr.*) to park (armoured vehicles) in a laager. [C19: < Afrik. *lager,* via G < OHG *legar* bed, lair]

lab (læb) *n. Inf.* short for **laboratory.**

lab. *abbrev. for:* **1.** laboratory. **2.** labour.

Lab. *abbrev. for:* **1.** *Politics.* Labour. **2.** Labrador.

label (ˈleɪbᵊl) *n.* **1.** a piece of paper, card, or other material attached to an object to identify it or give instructions or details concerning its ownership, use, nature, destination, etc.; tag. **2.** a brief descriptive phrase or term given to a person, group, school of thought, etc.: *the label "Romantic" is applied to many different kinds of poetry.* **3.** a word or phrase heading a piece of text to indicate or summarize its contents. **4.** a trademark or company or brand name on certain goods, esp. on gramophone records. **5.** *Computers.* a group of characters appended to a statement in a program to allow it to be identified. **6.** *Chem.* a radioactive element used in a compound to trace the mechanism of a chemical reaction. ~*vb.* **-belling, -belled** *or U.S.* **-beling, -beled.** (*tr.*) **7.** to fasten a label to. **8.** to mark with a label. **9.** to describe or classify in a word or phrase: *to label someone a liar.* **10.** to make (one or more atoms in a compound) radioactive, for use in determining the mechanism of a reaction. [C14: < OF, < Gmc] —**ˈlabeller** *n.*

labia (ˈleɪbɪə) *n.* the plural of **labium.**

labial (ˈleɪbɪəl) *adj.* **1.** of, relating to, or near lips or labia. **2.** *Music.* producing sounds by the action of an air stream over a narrow liplike fissure, as in a flue pipe of an organ. **3.** *Phonetics.* relating to a speech sound whose articulation involves movement or use of the lips. ~*n.* **4.** Also called: **labial pipe.** *Music.* an organ pipe with a liplike fissure. **5.** *Phonetics.* a speech sound such as English *p* or *m,* whose articulation involves movement or use of the lips. [C16: < Med. L *labiālis,* < L *labium* lip] —**ˈlabially** *adv.*

labiate (ˈleɪbɪˌeɪt, -ɪt) *n.* **1.** any plant of the family *Labiatae,* having square stems, aromatic leaves, and a two-lipped corolla: includes mint, thyme, sage, rosemary, etc. ~*adj.* **2.** of, relating to, or belonging to the family *Labiatae.* [C18: < NL *labiātus,* < L *labium* lip]

labile (ˈleɪbɪl) *adj. Chem.* (of a compound) prone to chemical change. [C15: via LL *lābilis,* < L *lābī* to slide] —**lability** (ləˈbɪlɪtɪ) *n.*

labiodental (ˌleɪbɪəʊˈdɛntᵊl) *Phonetics.* ~*adj.* **1.** pronounced by bringing the bottom lip into contact with the upper teeth, as for *f* in *fat, puff.* ~*n.* **2.** a labiodental consonant. [C17: < L LABIUM + DENTAL]

labium (ˈleɪbɪəm) *n., pl.* **-bia** (-bɪə). **1.** a lip or liplike structure. **2.** any one of the four lip-shaped folds of the female vulva, comprising an outer pair (**labia majora**) and an inner pair (**labia minora**). [C16: NL, < L.: lip]

laboratory (ləˈbɒrətərɪ, -trɪ; *U.S.* ˈlæbrəˌtɔːrɪ) *n., pl.* **-ries. 1. a.** a building or room equipped for conducting scientific research or for teaching practical science. **b.** (*as modifier*): *laboratory equipment.* **2.** a place where chemicals or medicines are manufactured. ~Often shortened to **lab.** [C17: < Med. L *labōrātōrium* workshop, < L *labōrāre* to LABOUR]

Labor Day *n.* **1.** a public holiday in the U.S. and Canada in honour of labour, held on the first Monday in September. **2.** a public holiday in Australia, observed on different days in different states.

laborious (ləˈbɔːrɪəs) *adj.* **1.** involving great exertion or long effort. **2.** given to working hard. **3.** (of literary style, etc.) not fluent. —**laˈboriously** *adv.* —**laˈboriousness** *n.*

Labor Party *n.* one of the two chief political parties of Australia, generally supporting the interests of organized labour.

labour *or U.S.* **labor** (ˈleɪbə) *n.* **1.** productive work, esp. physical toil done for wages. **2. a.** the people, class, or workers involved in this, esp. as opposed to management, capital, etc. **b.** (*as modifier*): *labour relations.* **3. a.** difficult or arduous work or effort. **b.** (*in combination*): *labour-saving.* **4.** a particular job or task, esp. of a difficult nature. **5.** the pain or effort of childbirth or the time during which this takes place. ~*vb.* **6.** (*intr.*) to perform labour; work. **7.** (*intr.;* foll. by *for,* etc.) to strive or work hard (for something). **8.** (*intr.;* usually foll. by *under*) to be burdened (by) or be at a disadvantage (because of): *to labour under a misapprehension.* **9.** (*intr.*) to make one's way with difficulty. **10.** (*tr.*) to deal with too persistently: *to labour a point.* **11.** (*intr.*) (of a woman) to be in labour. **12.** (*intr.*) (of a ship) to pitch and toss. [C13: via OF < L *labor*]

labour camp *n.* **1.** a penal colony involving forced labour. **2.** a camp for migratory labourers.

Labour Day *n.* a public holiday in many countries in honour of labour, usually held on May 1.

laboured *or U.S.* **labored** (ˈleɪbəd) *adj.* **1.** (of breathing) performed with difficulty. **2.** showing effort.

labourer *or U.S.* **laborer** (ˈleɪbərə) *n.* a person engaged in physical work, esp. unskilled work.

labour exchange *n. Brit.* a former name for the **employment office.**

Labourite (ˈleɪbəˌraɪt) *n.* an adherent of the Labour Party.

Labour Party *n.* **1.** a British political party, formed in 1900 as an amalgam of various trade unions and socialist groups, generally supporting the interests of organized labour. **2.** any similar party in any of various other countries.

Labrador retriever (ˈlæbrəˌdɔː) *n.* a powerfully-built variety of retriever with a short dense black or golden-brown coat. Often shortened to **Labrador.**

labret (ˈleɪbrɛt) *n.* a piece of bone, shell, etc., inserted into the lip as an ornament by certain peoples. [C19: < L *labrum* lip]

labrum (ˈleɪbrəm, ˈlæb-) *n., pl.* **-bra** (-brə). a lip or liplike part, such as the cuticular plate forming the upper lip of insects. [C19: NL, < L]

laburnum (ləˈbɜːnəm) *n.* any tree or shrub of a Eurasian genus having clusters of yellow drooping flowers: all parts of the plant are poisonous. [C16: NL, < L]

labyrinth (ˈlæbərɪnθ) *n.* **1.** a mazelike network of tunnels, chambers, or paths, either natural or man-made. **2.** any complex or confusing system of streets, passages, etc. **3.** a complex or intricate situation. **4.** any system of interconnecting cavities, esp. those comprising the internal ear. **5.** *Electronics.* an enclosure behind a high-performance loudspeaker, consisting of a series of air chambers designed to absorb unwanted sound waves. [C16: via L < Gk *laburinthos,* <?]

labyrinthine (ˌlæbəˈrɪnθaɪn) *adj.* **1.** of or relating to a labyrinth. **2.** resembling a labyrinth in complexity.

lac[1] (læk) *n.* a resinous substance secreted by certain insects (**lac insects**), used in the manufacture of shellac. [C16: < Du. *lak* or F *laque,* < Hindi *lākh* resin, ult. < Sansk. *lākshā*]

lac[2] (lɑːk) *n.* a variant spelling of **lakh.**

laccolith (ˈlækəlɪθ) *or* **laccolite** (ˈlækəˌlaɪt) *n.* a dome of igneous rock between two layers of older sedimentary rock. [C19: < Gk *lakkos* cistern + -LITH]

lace (leɪs) *n.* **1.** a delicate decorative fabric made from cotton, silk, etc., woven in an open web of different symmetrical patterns and figures. **2.** a cord or string drawn through eyelets or around hooks to fasten a shoe or garment. **3.** ornamental braid often used on military uniforms, etc. ~*vb.* **4.** to fasten (shoes, etc.) with a lace. **5.** (*tr.*) to draw (a cord or thread) through holes, eyes, etc., as when tying shoes. **6.** (*tr.*) to compress the waist of (someone), as with a corset. **7.** (*tr.*) to add a dash of spirits to (a beverage). **8.** (*tr.; usually passive* and foll. by *with*) to streak or mark with lines or colours: *the sky was laced with red.* **9.** (*tr.*) to intertwine; interlace. **10.** (*tr.*) *Inf.* to give a sound beating to. [C13 *las,* < OF *laz,* < L *laqueus* noose]

lacebark (ˈleɪsbɑːk) *n.* another name for **ribbonwood.**

lacerate *vb.* (ˈlæsəˌreɪt). (*tr.*) **1.** to tear (the flesh, etc.) jaggedly. **2.** to hurt or harrow (the feelings, etc.). ~*adj.* (ˈlæsəˌreɪt, -rɪt). **3.** having edges that are jagged: *lacerate leaves.* [C16: < L *lacerāre* to tear, < *lacer* mangled]

lace up *vb.* **1.** (*tr., adv.*) to tighten or fasten (clothes or footwear) with laces. ~*adj.* **lace-up.** **2.** (of footwear) to be fastened with laces. ~*n.* **lace-up.** **3.** a lace-up shoe or boot.

lacewing (ˈleɪsˌwɪŋ) *n.* any of various insects, esp. the green lacewings and brown lacewings, having lacy wings and preying on aphids and similar pests.

laches (ˈlætʃɪz) *n. Law.* negligence or unreasonable delay in pursuing a legal remedy. [C14 *lachesse,* via OF *lasche* slack, < L *laxus* LAX]

Lachesis (ˈlækɪsɪs) *n. Greek myth.* one of the three Fates. [via L < Gk, < *lakhesis* destiny, < *lakhein* to befall by lot]

lachrymal (ˈlækrɪməl) *adj.* a variant spelling of **lacrimal.**

lachrymatory (ˈlækrɪmətərɪ, -trɪ) *n., pl.* **-ries.** **1.** a small vessel found in ancient tombs, formerly thought to hold the tears of mourners. ~*adj.* **2.** a variant spelling of **lacrimatory.**

lachrymose (ˈlækrɪˌməʊs) *adj.* **1.** given to weeping; tearful. **2.** mournful; sad. [C17: < L, < *lacrima* a tear] —ˈ**lachryˌmosely** *adv.*

lacing (ˈleɪsɪŋ) *n.* **1.** *Chiefly Brit.* a course of bricks, stone, etc., for strengthening a rubble or flint wall. **2.** another word for **lace** (senses 2, 3). **3.** *Inf.* a severe beating.

laciniate (ləˈsɪnɪˌeɪt, -ɪt) *or* **laciniated** *adj.* **1.** *Biol.* jagged: *a laciniate leaf.* **2.** having a fringe. [C17: < L *lacinia* flap] —**laˌciniˈation** *n.*

lack (læk) *n.* **1.** an insufficiency, shortage, or absence of something required or desired. **2.** something that is required but is absent or in short supply. ~*vb.* **3.** (when *intr.*, often foll. by *in* or *for*) to be deficient (in) or have need (of). [C12: rel. to MDu. *laken* to be wanting]

lackadaisical (ˌlækəˈdeɪzɪkᵊl) *adj.* **1.** lacking vitality and purpose. **2.** lazy, esp. in a dreamy way. [C18: < earlier *lackadaisy*] —ˌ**lackaˈdaisically** *adv.*

lackey (ˈlækɪ) *n.* **1.** a servile follower; hanger-on. **2.** a liveried male servant or valet. **3.** a person who is treated like a servant. ~*vb.* **4.** (when *intr.*, often foll. by *for*) to act as a lackey (to). [C16: via F *laquais,* < OF, ? < Catalan *lacayo, alacayo*]

lacklustre *or U.S.* **lackluster** (ˈlækˌlʌstə) *adj.* lacking force, brilliance, or vitality.

laconic (ləˈkɒnɪk) *adj.* (of a person's speech) using few words; terse. [C16: via L < Gk *Lakōnikos,* < *Lakōn* Laconian, Spartan; referring to the Spartans' terseness of speech] —**laˈconically** *adv.*

lacquer (ˈlækə) *n.* **1.** a hard glossy coating made by dissolving cellulose derivatives or natural resins in a volatile solvent. **2.** a black resinous substance, obtained from certain trees (**lacquer trees**), used to give a hard glossy finish to wooden furniture. **3.** Also called: **hair lacquer.** a mixture of shellac and alcohol for spraying onto the hair to hold a style in place. **4.** *Art.* decorative objects coated with such lacquer, often inlaid. ~*vb.* (*tr.*) **5.** to apply lacquer to. [C16: < obs. F *lacre* sealing wax, < Port. *laca* LAC[1]] —ˈ**lacquerer** *n.*

lacrimal, lachrymal, *or* **lacrymal** (ˈlækrɪməl) *adj.* of or relating to tears or to the glands that secrete tears. [C16: < Med. L, < L *lacrima* a tear]

lacrimation (ˌlækrɪˈmeɪʃən) *n.* the secretion of tears.

lacrimatory, lachrymatory, *or* **lacrymatory** (ˈlækrɪmətərɪ, -trɪ) *adj.* of, causing, or producing tears.

lacrosse (ləˈkrɒs) *n.* a ball game invented by American Indians, now played by two teams who try to propel a ball into each other's goal by means of long-handled pouched sticks (**lacrosse sticks**). [C19: Canad. F: the hooked stick, crosier]

lactate[1] (ˈlækteɪt) *n.* an ester or salt of lactic acid. [C18]

lactate[2] (ˈlækteɪt) *vb.* (*intr.*) (of mammals) to produce or secrete milk.

lactation (lækˈteɪʃən) *n.* **1.** the secretion of milk from the mammary glands after parturition. **2.** the period during which milk is secreted.

lacteal (ˈlæktɪəl) *adj.* **1.** of, relating to, or resembling milk. **2.** (of lymphatic vessels) conveying or containing chyle. ~*n.* **3.** any of the lymphatic vessels conveying chyle from the small intestine to the thoracic duct. [C17: < L *lacteus* of milk, < *lac* milk]

lactescent (lækˈtɛsᵊnt) *adj.* **1.** (of plants and certain insects) secreting a milky fluid. **2.** milky or becoming milky. [C18: < L, < *lactescēre* to become milky, < *lact-*, *lac* milk] —**lacˈtescence** *n.*

lactic (ˈlæktɪk) *adj.* relating to or derived from milk. [C18: < L *lact-*, *lac* milk]

lactic acid *n.* a colourless syrupy carboxylic acid found in sour milk and many fruits and used as a preservative (**E270**) for foodstuffs.

lactiferous (lækˈtɪfərəs) *adj.* producing, conveying, or secreting milk or a milky fluid. [C17: < L *lactifer,* < *lact-*, *lac* milk]

lacto- *or before a vowel* **lact-** *combining form.* indicating milk: *lactobacillus.* [< L *lact-*, *lac* milk]

lactose (ˈlæktəʊs, -təʊz) *n.* a white crystalline sugar occurring in milk and used in pharmaceuticals and baby foods. Formula: $C_{12}H_{22}O_{11}$.

lacuna (ləˈkjuːnə) *n., pl.* **-nae** (-niː) *or* **-nas.** **1.** a gap or space, esp. in a book or manuscript. **2.** *Biol.* a cavity or depression, such as any of the spaces in the matrix of bone. [C17: < L *lacūna* pool, cavity, < *lacus* lake] —**laˈcunose, laˈcunal, laˈcunar,** *or* **laˈcunary** *adj.*

lacustrine (ləˈkʌstraɪn) *adj.* **1.** of or relating to lakes. **2.** living or growing in or on the shores of a lake. [C19: < It. *lacustre,* < L *lacus* lake]

lacy (ˈleɪsɪ) *adj.* **lacier, laciest.** made of or resembling lace. —ˈ**lacily** *adv.* —ˈ**laciness** *n.*

lad (læd) *n.* **1.** a boy or young man. **2.** *Inf.* a familiar form of address for any male. **3.** a lively or dashing man or youth (esp. in **a bit of a lad**). **4.** *Brit.* a boy or man who looks after horses. [C13 *ladde;* ? < ON]

ladanum (ˈlædənəm) *n.* a dark resinous juice obtained from various rockroses: used in perfumery. [C16: L < Gk, < *lēdon* rockrose]

ladder (ˈlædə) *n.* **1.** a portable framework of

wood, metal, rope, etc., in the form of two long parallel members connected by rungs or steps fixed to them at right angles, for climbing up or down. **2.** any hierarchy conceived of as having a series of ascending stages, levels, etc.: *the social ladder.* **3.** Also called: **run.** *Chiefly Brit.* a line of connected stitches that have come undone in knitted material, esp. stockings. ~*vb.* **4.** *Chiefly Brit.* to cause a line of interconnected stitches in (stockings, etc.) to undo, as by snagging, or (of a stocking) to come undone in this way. [OE *hlǣdder*]

ladder back *n.* a type of chair in which the back is constructed of horizontal slats between two uprights.

laddie (ˈlædɪ) *n. Chiefly Scot.* a familiar term for a male, esp. a boy; lad.

lade (leɪd) *vb.* **lading, laded, laden** *or* **laded. 1.** to put cargo or freight on board (a ship, etc.) or (of a ship, etc.) to take on cargo or freight. **2.** (*tr.; usually passive* and foll. by *with*) to burden or oppress. **3.** (*tr.; usually passive* and foll. by *with*) to fill or load. **4.** to remove (liquid) with or as if with a ladle. [OE *hladen* to load]

laden (ˈleɪdᵊn) **1.** a past participle of **lade.** ~*adj.* **2.** weighed down with a load; loaded. **3.** encumbered; burdened.

la-di-da, lah-di-dah, *or* **la-de-da** (ˌlɑːdiːˈdɑː) *adj. Inf.* affecting exaggeratedly genteel manners or speech. [C19: mockingly imit. of affected speech]

ladies *or* **ladies' room** *n.* (*functioning as sing.*) *Inf.* a women's public lavatory.

lading (ˈleɪdɪŋ) *n.* a load; cargo; freight.

ladle (ˈleɪdᵊl) *n.* **1.** a long-handled spoon having a deep bowl for serving or transferring liquids. **2.** a large bucket-shaped container for transferring molten metal. ~*vb.* **3.** (*tr.*) to serve out as with a ladle. [OE *hlædel,* < *hladan* to draw out] —ˈ**ladleful** *n.*

ladle out *vb.* (*tr., adv.*) *Inf.* to distribute (money, gifts, etc.) generously.

lady (ˈleɪdɪ) *n., pl.* **-dies. 1.** a woman regarded as having the characteristics of a good family and high social position. **2. a.** a polite name for a woman. **b.** (*as modifier*)*: a lady doctor.* **3.** an informal name for **wife. 4. lady of the house.** the female head of the household. **5.** *History.* a woman with proprietary rights and authority, as over a manor. [OE *hlǣfdīge,* < *hlāf* bread + *dīge* kneader, rel. to *dāh* dough]

Lady (ˈleɪdɪ) *n., pl.* **-dies. 1.** (in Britain) a title of honour borne by various classes of women of the peerage. **2. my lady.** a term of address to holders of the title Lady. **3. Our Lady.** a title of the Virgin Mary.

ladybird (ˈleɪdɪˌbɜːd) *n.* any of various small brightly coloured beetles, esp. one having red elytra with black spots. [C18: after Our *Lady,* the Virgin Mary]

lady bountiful *n.* an ostentatiously charitable woman. [C19: after a character in George Farquhar's play *The Beaux' Stratagem* (1707)]

Lady Chapel *n.* a chapel within a church or cathedral, dedicated to the Virgin Mary.

Lady Day *n.* March 25, the feast of the Annunciation of the Virgin Mary. Also called: **Annunciation Day.**

lady-in-waiting *n., pl.* **ladies-in-waiting.** a lady who attends a queen or princess.

lady-killer *n. Inf.* a man who is, or believes he is, irresistibly fascinating to women.

ladylike (ˈleɪdɪˌlaɪk) *adj.* like or befitting a lady in manners and bearing; refined and fastidious.

ladylove (ˈleɪdɪˌlʌv) *n. Now rare.* a beloved woman.

lady's bedstraw *n.* a Eurasian plant with clusters of small yellow flowers.

lady's finger *n.* another name for **bhindi.**

Ladyship (ˈleɪdɪʃɪp) *n.* (preceded by *your* or *her*) a title used to address or refer to any peeress except a duchess.

lady's-slipper *n.* any of various orchids having reddish or purple flowers.

lady's-smock *n.* a N temperate plant with white or rose-pink flowers. Also called: **cuckooflower.**

laevo- *or U.S.* **levo-** *combining form.* **1.** on or towards the left: *laevorotatory.* **2.** (in chemistry) denoting a laevorotatory compound. [< L *laevus* left]

laevorotation (ˌliːvəʊrəʊˈteɪʃən) *n.* **1.** a rotation to the left. **2.** an anticlockwise rotation of the plane of polarization of plane-polarized light as a result of its passage through a crystal, liquid, or solution. ~Cf. **dextrorotation.** —**laevorotatory** (ˌliːvəʊˈrəʊtətərɪ) *adj.*

lag[1] (læg) *vb.* **lagging, lagged.** (*intr.*) **1.** (often foll. by *behind*) to hang (back) or fall (behind) in movement, progress, development, etc. **2.** to fall away in strength or intensity. ~*n.* **3.** the act or state of slowing down or falling behind. **4.** the interval of time between two events, esp. between an action and its effect. [C16: <?]

lag[2] (læg) *Sl.* ~*n.* **1.** a convict or ex-convict (esp. in **old lag**). **2.** a term of imprisonment. ~*vb.* **lagging, lagged. 3.** (*tr.*) to arrest or put in prison. [C19: <?]

lag[3] (læg) *vb.* **lagging, lagged. 1.** (*tr.*) to cover (a pipe, cylinder, etc.) with lagging to prevent loss of heat. ~*n.* **2.** the insulating casing of a steam cylinder, boiler, etc. **3.** a stave. [C17: of Scand. origin]

lagan (ˈlægᵊn) *n.* goods or wreckage on the sea bed, sometimes attached to a buoy to permit recovery. [C16: < OF *lagan,* prob. of Gmc origin]

lager (ˈlɑːgə) *n.* a light-bodied effervescent beer, stored for varying periods before use. [C19: < G *Lagerbier* beer for storing, < *Lager* storehouse]

laggard (ˈlægəd) *n.* **1.** a person who lags behind. ~*adj.* **2.** *Rare.* sluggish, slow, or dawdling. —ˈ**laggardly** *adj., adv.* —ˈ**laggardness** *n.*

lagging (ˈlægɪŋ) *n.* **1.** insulating material wrapped around pipes, boilers, etc., or laid in a roof loft, to prevent loss of heat. **2.** the act or process of applying lagging.

lagomorph (ˈlægəʊˌmɔːf) *n.* any placental mammal having two pairs of upper incisors specialized for gnawing, such as rabbits and hares. [C19: via NL < Gk *lagōs* hare; see -MORPH]

lagoon (ləˈguːn) *n.* **1.** a body of water cut off from the open sea by coral reefs or sand bars. **2.** any small body of water, esp. one adjoining a larger one. [C17: < It. *laguna,* < L *lacūna* pool; see LACUNA]

lah (lɑː) *n. Music.* (in tonic sol-fa) the sixth note of any major scale; submediant. [C14: see GAMUT]

lah-di-dah (ˌlɑːdiːˈdɑː) *adj., n. Inf.* a variant spelling of **la-di-da.**

laic (ˈleɪɪk) *adj. also* **laical. 1.** of or involving the laity; secular. ~*n.* **2.** a rare word for **layman.** [C15: < LL *lāicus* LAY[3]] —ˈ**laically** *adv.*

laicize *or* **-cise** (ˈleɪɪˌsaɪz) *vb.* (*tr.*) to withdraw clerical or ecclesiastical character or status from (an institution, building, etc.). —ˌ**laiciˈzation** *or* **-ciˈsation** *n.*

laid (leɪd) *vb.* the past tense and past participle of **lay**[1].

laid-back *adj.* relaxed in style or character; easy-going and unhurried.

laid paper *n.* paper with a regular mesh impressed upon it.

lain (leɪn) *vb.* the past participle of **lie**[2].

Laingian (ˈlæŋɪən) *adj.* of or relating to the theory propounded by R. D. Laing (born 1927), Scottish psychiatrist, that mental illnesses are understandable as natural responses to stress in family and social situations.

lair[1] (lɛə) *n.* **1.** the resting place of a wild animal. **2.** *Inf.* a place of seclusion or hiding. ~*vb.* **3.** (*intr.*) (esp. of a wild animal) to retreat to or rest in a lair. **4.** (*tr.*) to drive or place (an animal) in a lair. [OE *leger*]

lair[2] (lɛə) *Austral. sl.* ~*n.* **1.** a flashy man who shows off. ~*vb.* **2.** (*intr.;* foll. by *up* or *around*) to behave or dress like a lair. [? < LEER]

laird (lɛəd) *n. Scot.* a landowner, esp. of a large estate. [C15: Scot. var. of LORD]

laissez faire *or* ***laisser faire*** *French.* (ˌlɛseɪ ˈfɛə) *n.* **1. a.** Also called: **individualism.** the doctrine of unrestricted freedom in commerce, esp. for private interests. **b.** (*as modifier*): *a laissez-faire economy.* **2.** indifference or noninterference, esp. in the affairs of others. [F, lit.: let (them) act]

laity (ˈleɪɪtɪ) *n.* **1.** laymen, as distinguished from clergymen. **2.** all people not of a specific occupation. [C16: < LAY[3]]

lake[1] (leɪk) *n.* **1.** an expanse of water entirely surrounded by land and unconnected to the sea except by rivers or streams. Related adj.: **lacustrine.** **2.** anything resembling this. **3.** a surplus of a liquid commodity: *a wine lake.* [C13 *lac,* via OF < L *lacus* basin]

lake[2] (leɪk) *n.* **1.** a bright pigment produced by the combination of an organic colouring matter with an inorganic compound, usually a metallic salt, oxide, or hydroxide. **2.** a red dye obtained by combining a metallic compound with cochineal. [C17: var. of LAC[1]]

Lake District *n.* a region of lakes and mountains in NW England, in Cumbria. Also called: **Lakeland, the Lakes.**

lake dwelling *n.* a dwelling, esp. in prehistoric villages, constructed on platforms supported by wooden piles driven into the bottom of a lake. —**lake dweller** *n.*

Lakeland terrier (ˈleɪkˌlænd) *n.* a wire-haired breed of terrier, originally from the Lake District.

Lake Poets *pl. n.* the English poets Wordsworth, Coleridge, and Southey, who lived in and drew inspiration from the Lake District at the beginning of the 19th century.

lake trout *n.* a yellow-spotted char of the Great Lakes region of Canada.

lakh *or* **lac** (lɑːk) *n.* (in India) the number 100 000, esp. referring to this sum of rupees. [C17: < Hindi *lākh,* ult. < Sansk. *lakshā* a sign]

-lalia *n. combining form.* indicating a speech defect or abnormality: *echolalia.* [NL, < Gk *lalia* chatter, < *lalein* to babble]

Lallans (ˈlælənz) *or* **Lallan** (ˈlælən) *n.* **1.** a literary version of the variety of English spoken and written in the Lowlands of Scotland. **2.** (*modifier*) of or relating to the Lowlands of Scotland or their dialects. [Scot. var. of *Lowlands*]

lallation (læˈleɪʃən) *n. Phonetics.* a defect of speech consisting of the pronunciation of (r) as (l). [C17: < L *lallāre* to sing lullaby, imit.]

lam[1] (læm) *vb.* **lamming, lammed.** *Sl.* **1.** (*tr.*) to thrash or beat. **2.** (*intr.; usually foll. by into or out*) to make a sweeping stroke or blow. [C16: < Scand.]

lam[2] (læm) *n. U.S. & Canad. sl.* **1.** a sudden flight or escape, esp. to avoid arrest. **2. on the lam.** making an escape. [C19: ? < LAM[1]; (hence, to be off)]

Lam. *Bible. abbrev. for* Lamentations.

lama (ˈlɑːmə) *n.* a priest or monk of Lamaism. [C17: < Tibetan *blama*]

Lamaism (ˈlɑːməˌɪzəm) *n.* the Mahayana form of Buddhism of Tibet and Mongolia. —ˈ**Lamaist** *n., adj.* —ˌ**Lamaˈistic** *adj.*

Lamarckism (lɑːˈmɑːkɪzəm) *n.* the theory of organic evolution proposed by Lamarck (1744–1829), French naturalist, based on the principle that characteristics of an organism modified during its lifetime are inheritable.

lamasery (ˈlɑːməsərɪ) *n., pl.* **-series.** a monastery of lamas. [C19: < F *lamaserie,* < LAMA + F *-serie,* < Persian *serāī* palace]

lamb (læm) *n.* **1.** the young of a sheep. **2.** the meat of a young sheep. **3.** a person, esp. a child, who is innocent, meek, good, etc. **4.** a person easily deceived. ~*vb.* **5.** (*intr.*) (of a ewe) to give birth. **6.** (*intr.*) (of a shepherd) to tend the ewes and newborn lambs at lambing time. [OE *lamb,* < Gmc] —ˈ**lambˌlike** *adj.*

Lamb (læm) *n.* **the.** a title given to Christ in the New Testament.

lambaste (læmˈbeɪst) *or* **lambast** (læmˈbæst) *vb.* (*tr.*) **1.** to beat or whip severely. **2.** to reprimand or scold. [C17: ? < LAM[1] + BASTE[3]]

lambda (ˈlæmdə) *n.* the 11th letter of the Greek alphabet (Λ, λ). [C14: < Gk, < Semitic]

lambent (ˈlæmbənt) *adj.* **1.** (esp. of a flame) flickering softly over a surface. **2.** glowing with soft radiance. **3.** (of wit or humour) light or brilliant. [C17: < the present participle of L *lambere* to lick] —ˈ**lambency** *n.* —ˈ**lambently** *adv.*

lambert (ˈlæmbət) *n.* the cgs unit of illumination, equal to 1 lumen per square centimetre. Symbol: L [C20: after J. H. *Lambert* (1728–77), G mathematician & physicist]

lambing (ˈlæmɪŋ) *n.* **1.** the birth of lambs. **2.** the shepherd's work of tending the ewes and newborn lambs at this time.

lambkin (ˈlæmkɪn) *n.* **1.** a small lamb. **2.** a term of affection for a small endearing child.

lambrequin (ˈlæmbrɪkɪn, ˈlæmbə-) *n.* **1.** an ornamental hanging covering the edge of a shelf or the upper part of a window or door. **2.** (*often pl.*) a scarf worn over a helmet. [C18: < F, < Du. *lamperkin* (unattested), dim. of *lamper* veil]

lambskin (ˈlæmˌskɪn) *n.* **1.** the skin of a lamb, esp. with the wool still on. **2.** a material or garment prepared from this skin.

lamb's lettuce *n.* another name for **corn salad.**

lamb's tails *pl. n.* the pendulous catkins of the hazel tree.

lame (leɪm) *adj.* **1.** disabled or crippled in the legs or feet. **2.** painful or weak: *a lame back.* **3.** weak; unconvincing: *a lame excuse.* **4.** not effective or enthusiastic: *a lame try.* **5.** *U.S. sl.* conventional or uninspiring. ~*vb.* **6.** (*tr.*) to make lame. [OE *lama*] —ˈ**lamely** *adv.* —ˈ**lameness** *n.*

lamé (ˈlɑːmeɪ) *n.* a fabric of silk, cotton, or wool interwoven with threads of metal. [C20: < F, < OF *lame* gold or silver thread, thin plate, < L *lāmina* thin plate]

lame duck *n.* **1.** a person or thing that is disabled or ineffectual. **2.** *Stock Exchange.* a speculator who cannot discharge his liabilities. **3.** *U.S.* an elected official or body of officials remaining in office in the interval between the election and inauguration of a successor.

lamella (ləˈmɛlə) *n., pl.* **-lae** (-liː) *or* **-las.** a thin layer, plate, or membrane, esp. any of the calcified layers of which bone is formed. [C17: NL, < L, dim. of *lāmina* thin plate] —**laˈmellar, lamellate** (ˈlæmɪˌleɪt, -lɪt), *or* **lamellose** (ləˈmɛləʊs, ˈlæmɪˌləʊs) *adj.*

lamellibranch (ləˈmɛlɪˌbræŋk) *n., adj.* another word for **bivalve.** [C19: < NL *lamellibranchia* plate-gilled (animals)]

lamellicorn (ləˈmɛlɪˌkɔːn) *n.* **1.** any beetle having flattened terminal plates to the antennae, such as the scarabs and stag beetles. ~*adj.* **2.** designating antennae with platelike terminal segments. [C19: < NL *Lamellicornia* plate-horned (animals)]

lament (ləˈmɛnt) *vb.* **1.** to feel or express sorrow, remorse, or regret (for or over). ~*n.* **2.** an expression of sorrow. **3.** a poem or song in which a death is lamented. [C16: < L *lāmentum*] —**laˈmenter** *n.* —**laˈmentingly** *adv.*

lamentable (ˈlæməntəbᵊl) *adj.* **1.** wretched, deplorable, or distressing. **2.** an archaic word for **mournful.** —ˈ**lamentably** *adv.*

lamentation (ˌlæmɛnˈteɪʃən) *n.* **1.** a lament; expression of sorrow. **2.** the act of lamenting.

lamented (ləˈmɛntɪd) *adj.* grieved for or regretted (often in **late lamented**): *our late lamented employer.* —**laˈmentedly** *adv.*

lamina (ˈlæmɪnə) *n., pl.* **-nae** (-ˌniː) *or* **-nas.** **1.** a thin plate, esp. of bone or mineral. **2.** *Bot.* the flat blade of a leaf. [C17: NL, < L: thin plate] —ˈ**laminar** *or* **laminose** (ˈlæmɪˌnəʊs, -ˌnəʊz) *adj.*

laminar flow *n.* nonturbulent motion of a fluid in which parallel layers have different velocities relative to each other.

laminate *vb.* (ˈlæmɪˌneɪt). **1.** (*tr.*) to make (material in sheet form) by bonding together two or more thin sheets. **2.** to split or be split into thin sheets. **3.** (*tr.*) to beat, form, or press (material, esp. metal) into thin sheets. **4.** (*tr.*) to cover or overlay with a thin sheet of material. ~*n.* (ˈlæmɪˌneɪt, -nɪt). **5.** a material made by bonding together two or more sheets. ~*adj.* (ˈlæmɪˌneɪt,

-nɪt). **6.** having or composed of lamina; laminated. [C17: < NL *lāminātus* plated] —**laminable** (ˈlæmɪnəbᵊl) *adj.* —ˌ**lamiˈnation** *n.* —ˈ**lamiˌnator** *n.*

laminated (ˈlæmɪˌneɪtɪd) *adj.* **1.** composed of many layers of plastic, wood, etc., bonded together. **2.** covered with a thin protective layer of plastic, etc.

lamington (ˈlæmɪŋtən) *n. Austral. & N.Z.* a cube of sponge cake coated in chocolate and dried coconut. [C20 (in the earlier sense: a homburg hat): after Lady *Lamington,* wife of Baron Lamington, governor of Queensland (1896–1901)]

Lammas (ˈlæməs) *n.* **1.** *R.C. Church.* Aug. 1, held as a feast, commemorating St Peter's miraculous deliverance from prison. **2.** Also called: **Lammas Day.** the same day formerly observed in England as a harvest festival. [OE *hlāfmæsse* loaf mass]

lammergeier *or* **lammergeyer** (ˈlæməˌgaɪə) *n.* a rare vulture of S Europe, Africa, and Asia, with dark wings, a pale breast, and black feathers around the bill. [C19: < G *Lämmergeier,* < *Lämmer* lambs + *Geier* vulture]

lamp (læmp) *n.* **1. a.** any of a number of devices that produce illumination: *an electric lamp; a gas lamp; an oil lamp.* **b.** (*in combination*): *lampshade.* **2.** a device for holding one or more electric light bulbs: *a table lamp.* **3.** a vessel in which a liquid fuel is burned to supply illumination. **4.** any of a variety of devices that produce radiation, esp. for therapeutic purposes: *an ultraviolet lamp.* [C13 *lampe,* via OF < L *lampas,* < Gk, < *lampein* to shine]

lampblack (ˈlæmpˌblæk) *n.* a finely divided form of almost pure carbon produced by the incomplete combustion of organic compounds, such as natural gas, used in making carbon electrodes and dynamo brushes and as a pigment.

lamp chimney *n.* a glass tube that surrounds the wick in an oil lamp.

lamplight (ˈlæmpˌlaɪt) *n.* the light produced by a lamp or lamps.

lamplighter (ˈlæmpˌlaɪtə) *n.* **1.** (formerly) a person who lit and extinguished street lamps, esp. gas ones. **2.** *Chiefly U.S. & Canad.* any of various devices used to light lamps.

lampoon (læmˈpuːn) *n.* **1.** a satire in prose or verse ridiculing a person, literary work, etc. ~*vb.* **2.** (*tr.*) to attack or satirize in a lampoon. [C17: < F *lampon,* ? < *lampons* let us drink (frequently used as a refrain in poems)] —**lamˈpooner** *or* **lamˈpoonist** *n.* —**lamˈpoonery** *n.*

lamppost (ˈlæmpˌpəʊst) *n.* a post supporting a lamp, esp. in a street.

lamprey (ˈlæmprɪ) *n.* any eel-like vertebrate having a round sucking mouth for clinging to and feeding on the blood of other animals. Also called: **lamper eel.** [C13: < OF *lamproie,* < LL *lamprēda,* <?]

Lancashire (ˈlæŋkəˌʃɪə) *n.* a mild whitish-coloured cheese with a crumbly texture. [after *Lancashire,* a county in England]

Lancastrian (læŋˈkæstrɪən) *n.* **1.** a native or resident of Lancashire or Lancaster. **2.** an adherent of the house of Lancaster in the Wars of the Roses. ~*adj.* **3.** of or relating to Lancashire or Lancaster. **4.** of or relating to the house of Lancaster.

lance (lɑːns) *n.* **1.** a long weapon with a pointed head used by horsemen. **2.** a similar weapon used for hunting, whaling, etc. **3.** *Surgery.* another name for **lancet.** ~*vb.* (*tr.*) **4.** to pierce (an abscess or boil) with a lancet. **5.** to pierce with or as with a lance. [C13 *launce,* < OF *lance,* < L *lancea*]

lance corporal *n.* a noncommissioned officer of the lowest rank in the British Army.

lancelet (ˈlɑːnslɪt) *n.* any of several marine animals closely related to the vertebrates: they burrow in sand. Also called: **amphioxus.** [C19: referring to the slender shape]

lanceolate (ˈlɑːnsɪəˌleɪt, -lɪt) *adj.* narrow and tapering to a point at each end: *lanceolate leaves.* [C18: < LL *lanceolātus,* < *lanceola* small LANCE]

lancer (ˈlɑːnsə) *n.* **1.** (formerly) a cavalryman armed with a lance. **2.** a member of a regiment retaining such a title.

lancers (ˈlɑːnsəz) *n.* (*functioning as sing.*) **1.** a quadrille for eight or sixteen couples. **2.** a piece of music composed for or in the rhythm of this dance.

lancet (ˈlɑːnsɪt) *n.* **1.** Also called: **lance.** a pointed surgical knife with two sharp edges. **2.** short for **lancet arch** or **lancet window.** [C15 *lancette,* < OF: small LANCE]

lancet arch *n.* a narrow acutely pointed arch.

lancet window *n.* a narrow window having a lancet arch.

lancewood (ˈlɑːnsˌwʊd) *n.* a New Zealand tree with slender leaves showing different configurations in youth and maturity.

Lancs (læŋks) *abbrev. for* Lancashire.

land (lænd) *n.* **1.** the solid part of the surface of the earth as distinct from seas, lakes, etc. Related adj.: **terrestrial. 2.** ground, esp. with reference to its use, quality, etc. **3.** rural or agricultural areas as contrasted with urban ones. **4.** farming as an occupation or way of life. **5.** *Law.* any tract of ground capable of being owned as property. **6. a.** a country, region, or area. **b.** the people of a country, etc. **7.** *Econ.* the factor of production consisting of all natural resources. ~*vb.* **8.** to transfer (something) or go from a ship or boat to the shore: *land the cargo.* **9.** (*intr.*) to come to or touch shore. **10.** (*intr.*) (in Canada) to be legally admitted to the country, as an immigrant or **landed immigrant. 11.** to come down or bring (something) down to earth after a flight or jump. **12.** to come or bring to some point, condition, or state. **13.** (*tr.*) *Angling.* to retrieve (a hooked fish) from the water. **14.** (*tr.*) *Inf.* to win or obtain: *to land a job.* **15.** (*tr.*) *Inf.* to deliver (a blow). ~See also **land up.** [OE] —ˈ**landless** *adj.*

land agent *n.* **1.** a person who administers a landed estate and its tenancies. **2.** a person who acts as an agent for the sale of land. —**land agency** *n.*

landau (ˈlændɔː) *n.* a four-wheeled horse-drawn carriage with two folding hoods over the passenger compartment. [C18: after *Landau* (a town in Germany), where first made]

landaulet (ˌlændɔːˈlɛt) *n.* **1.** a small landau. **2.** *U.S.* an early type of car with a folding hood over the passenger seats.

landed (ˈlændɪd) *adj.* **1.** owning land: *landed gentry.* **2.** consisting of or including land: *a landed estate.*

landfall (ˈlændˌfɔːl) *n.* **1.** the act of sighting or nearing land, esp. from the sea. **2.** the land sighted or neared.

landfill (ˈlændˌfɪl) *adj.* of or denoting low-lying sites or tips being filled up with alternate layers of rubbish and earth.

landform (ˈlændˌfɔːm) *n. Geol.* any natural feature of the earth's surface.

land girl *n.* a girl or woman who does farm work, esp. in wartime.

landgrave (ˈlændˌgreɪv) *n. German history.* **1.** (from the 13th century to 1806) a count who ruled over a specified territory. **2.** (after 1806) the title of any of various sovereign princes. [C16: via G, < MHG *lantgrāve,* < *lant* land + *grāve* count]

land-holder *n.* a person who owns or occupies land. —ˈ**land-ˌholding** *adj., n.*

landing (ˈlændɪŋ) *n.* **1. a.** the act of coming to land, esp. after a sea voyage. **b.** (*as modifier*): *landing place.* **2.** a place of disembarkation. **3.** the floor area at the top of a flight of stairs.

landing craft *n. Mil.* any small vessel designed for the landing of troops and equipment on beaches.

landing field *n.* an area of land on which aircraft land and from which they take off.

landing gear *n.* another name for **undercarriage.**

landing net *n. Angling.* a loose long-handled net for lifting hooked fish from the water.

landing stage *n.* a platform used for landing goods and passengers from a vessel.

landing strip *n.* another name for **airstrip.**

landlady (ˈlændˌleɪdɪ) *n., pl.* **-dies. 1.** a woman who owns and leases property. **2.** a woman who owns or runs a lodging house, pub, etc.

ländler (*German* ˈlɛntlər) *n.* **1.** an Austrian country dance in which couples spin and clap. **2.** a piece of music composed for or in the rhythm of this dance, in three-four time. [G, < dialect *Landl* Upper Austria]

land line *n.* a telecommunications wire or cable laid over land.

landlocked (ˈlændˌlɒkt) *adj.* **1.** (esp. of lakes) completely surrounded by land. **2.** (esp. of certain salmon) living in fresh water that is permanently isolated from the sea.

landlord (ˈlændˌlɔːd) *n.* **1.** a man who owns and leases property. **2.** a man who owns or runs a lodging house, pub, etc.

landlubber (ˈlændˌlʌbə) *n. Naut.* any person having no experience at sea.

landmark (ˈlændˌmɑːk) *n.* **1.** a prominent or well-known object in or feature of a particular landscape. **2.** an important or unique decision, event, fact, discovery, etc. **3.** a boundary marker.

landmass (ˈlændˌmæs) *n.* a large continuous area of land, as opposed to seas or islands.

land mine *n. Mil.* an explosive charge placed in the ground, usually detonated by stepping or driving on it.

land of milk and honey *n.* **1.** *Old Testament.* the land of natural fertility promised to the Israelites by God. (Ezekiel 20:6) **2.** any fertile land, state, etc.

land of Nod *n.* **1.** *Old Testament.* a region to the east of Eden to which Cain went after he had killed Abel (Genesis 4:14). **2.** an imaginary land of sleep.

landowner (ˈlændˌəʊnə) *n.* a person who owns land. —**ˈlandˌownerˌship** *n.* —**ˈlandˌowning** *n., adj.*

land rail *n.* another name for **corncrake.**

land reform *n.* the redistributing of large agricultural holdings among the landless.

landscape (ˈlændˌskeɪp) *n.* **1.** an extensive area of scenery as viewed from a single aspect. **2.** a painting, drawing, photograph, etc., depicting natural scenery. **3.** the genre including such pictures. ~*vb.* **4.** (*tr.*) to improve the natural features of (a garden, park, etc.), as by creating contoured features and planting trees. **5.** (*intr.*) to work as a landscape gardener. [C16 *landskip* (orig. a term in painting), < MDu. *lantscap* region]

landscape gardening *n.* the art of laying out grounds in imitation of natural scenery. Also called: **landscape architecture.** —**landscape gardener** *n.*

landscapist (ˈlændˌskeɪpɪst) *n.* a painter of landscapes.

landslide (ˈlændˌslaɪd) *n.* **1.** Also called: **landslip. a.** the sliding of a large mass of rock material, soil, etc., down the side of a mountain or cliff. **b.** the material dislodged in this way. **2.** an overwhelming electoral victory.

landsman (ˈlændzmən) *n., pl.* **-men.** a person who works or lives on land, as distinguished from a seaman.

land up *vb.* (*adv., usually intr.*) to arrive or cause to arrive at a final point or condition.

landward (ˈlændwəd) *adj.* **1.** lying, facing, or moving towards land. **2.** in the direction of the land. ~*adv.* **3.** a variant of **landwards.**

landwards (ˈlændwədz) *or* **landward** *adv.* towards land.

lane (leɪn) *n.* **1.** a narrow road or way between buildings, hedges, fences, etc. **2.** any narrow well-defined track or course, as for lines of traffic in a road, or for ships or aircraft. **3.** one of the parallel strips into which a running track or swimming bath is divided for races. **4.** the long strip of wooden flooring down which balls are bowled in a bowling alley. [OE *lane, lanu*]

lang. *abbrev. for* language.

langlauf (ˈlɑːŋˌlaʊf) *n.* cross-country skiing. [G, lit.: long run] —**langläufer** (ˈlɑːŋˌlɔɪfə) *n.*

langouste (ˈlɒŋguːst, lɒŋˈguːst) *n.* another name for the **spiny lobster.** [F, < OProvençal *langosta,* ? < L *lōcusta* lobster, locust]

langoustine (ˌlɒŋguːsˈtiːn) *n.* a large prawn or small lobster. [< F, dim. of LANGOUSTE]

langsam (ˈlæŋzæm) *adj. Music.* slow. [G]

langsyne (ˌlæŋˈsaɪn) *Scot.* ~*adv.* **1.** long ago; long since. ~*n.* **2.** times long past, esp. those fondly remembered. [C16: Scot.: long since]

language (ˈlæŋgwɪdʒ) *n.* **1.** a system for the expression of thoughts, feelings, etc., by the use of spoken sounds or conventional symbols. **2.** the faculty for the use of such systems, which is a distinguishing characteristic of man as compared with other animals. **3.** the language of a particular nation or people. **4.** any other means of communicating, such as gesture or animal sounds: *the language of love.* **5.** the specialized vocabulary used by a particular group: *medical language.* **6.** a particular manner or style of verbal expression: *your language is disgusting.* **7.** *Computers.* See **programming language.** [C13: < OF *language,* ult. < L *lingua* tongue]

language laboratory *n.* a room equipped with tape recorders, etc., for learning foreign languages.

langue (lɑːŋg) *n. Linguistics.* language considered as an abstract system or a social institution, being the common possession of a speech community. [C19: < F: language]

langue d'oc *French.* (lɑ̃g dɔk) *n.* the group of medieval French dialects spoken in S France: often regarded as including Provençal. [lit.: language of *oc* (form for the Provençal *yes*), ult. < L *hoc* this]

langue d'oïl *French.* (lɑ̃g dɔj) *n.* the group of medieval French dialects spoken in France north of the Loire; the medieval basis of modern French. [lit.: language of *oïl* (the northern form for *yes*), ult. < L *hoc ille* (*fecit*) this he (did)]

languid (ˈlæŋgwɪd) *adj.* **1.** without energy or spirit. **2.** without interest or enthusiasm. **3.** sluggish; inactive. [C16: < L *languidus,* < *languēre* to languish] —**ˈlanguidly** *adv.* —**ˈlanguidness** *n.*

languish (ˈlæŋgwɪʃ) *vb.* (*intr.*) **1.** to lose or diminish in strength or energy. **2.** (often foll. by *for*) to be listless with desire; pine. **3.** to suffer deprivation, hardship, or neglect: *to languish in prison.* **4.** to put on a tender, nostalgic, or melancholic expression. [C14 *languishen,* < OF *languiss-,* stem of *languir,* ult. < L *languēre*] —**ˈlanguishing** *adj.* —**ˈlanguishingly** *adv.* —**ˈlanguishment** *n.*

languor (ˈlæŋgə) *n.* **1.** physical or mental laziness or weariness. **2.** a feeling of dreaminess and relaxation. **3.** oppressive silence or stillness. [C14 *langour,* via OF < L *languor,* < *languēre* to languish; the modern spelling is directly < L] —**ˈlanguorous** *adj.*

langur (lʌŋˈgʊə) *n.* any of various agile arboreal Old World monkeys of S and SE Asia having a long tail and long hair surrounding the face. [Hindi]

laniard (ˈlænjəd) *n.* a variant spelling of **lanyard.**

laniary (ˈlænɪərɪ) *adj.* **1.** (esp. of canine teeth) adapted for tearing. ~*n., pl.* **-aries. 2.** a tooth adapted for tearing. [C19: < L *lanius* butcher, < *laniāre* to tear]

laniferous (ləˈnɪfərəs) *or* **lanigerous** (ləˈnɪdʒərəs) *adj. Biol.* bearing wool or fleecy hairs resembling wool. [C17: < L *lānifer,* < *lāna* wool]

lank (læŋk) *adj.* **1.** long and limp. **2.** thin or gaunt. [OE *hlanc* loose] —**ˈlankly** *adv.* —**ˈlankness** *n.*

lanky (ˈlæŋkɪ) *adj.* **lankier, lankiest.** tall, thin, and loose-jointed. —**ˈlankily** *adv.* —**ˈlankiness** *n.*

lanner (ˈlænə) *n.* **1.** a large falcon of Mediterranean regions, N Africa, and S Asia. **2.** *Falconry.* the female of this falcon. The male is called **lanneret.** [C15: < OF (*faucon*) *lanier* cowardly (falcon), < L *lanārius* wool worker, coward; referring to its sluggish flight and timid nature]

lanolin (ˈlænəlɪn) *or* **lanoline** (ˈlænəlɪn, -ˌliːn) *n.* a yellowish viscous substance extracted from wool: used in some ointments. [C19: via G < L *lāna* wool + *oleum* oil; see -IN]

lantern (ˈlæntən) *n.* **1.** a light with a transparent protective case. **2.** a structure on top of a dome or roof having openings or windows to admit light or air. **3.** the upper part of a lighthouse that houses the light. [C13: < L *lanterna,* < Gk *lamptēr* lamp, < *lampein* to shine]

lantern jaw *n.* (when *pl.,* refers to upper and lower jaw; when *sing.,* usually to lower jaw) a long hollow jaw that gives the face a drawn appearance. —ˈ**lantern-**ˌ**jawed** *adj.*

lantern slide *n.* (formerly) a photographic slide for projection, used in a magic lantern.

lanthanide series (ˈlænθəˌnaɪd) *n.* a class of 15 chemically related elements (**lanthanides**) with atomic numbers from 57 (lanthanum) to 71 (lutecium).

lanthanum (ˈlænθənəm) *n.* a silvery-white ductile metallic element of the lanthanide series: used in pyrophoric alloys, electronic devices, and in glass manufacture. Symbol: La; atomic no.: 57; atomic wt.: 138.91. [C19: NL, < Gk *lanthanein* to lie unseen]

lanthorn (ˈlæntˌhɔːn, ˈlæntən) *n.* an archaic word for **lantern.**

lanugo (ləˈnjuːgəʊ) *n., pl.* **-gos.** a layer of fine hairs, esp. the covering of the human fetus before birth. [C17: < L: down, < *lāna* wool]

lanyard *or* **laniard** (ˈlænjəd) *n.* **1.** a cord, esp. one worn around the neck, to hold a whistle, knife, etc. **2.** a cord used in firing certain types of cannon. **3.** *Naut.* a line for extending or tightening standing rigging. [C15 *lanyer,* < F *lanière,* < *lasne* strap, prob. of Gmc origin]

laodicean (ˌleɪəʊdɪˈsɪən) *adj.* **1.** lukewarm and indifferent, esp. in religious matters. ~*n.* **2.** a person having a lukewarm attitude towards religious matters. [C17: referring to the early Christians of Laodicea (Revelation 3:14–16)]

lap[1] (læp) *n.* **1.** the area formed by the upper surface of the thighs of a seated person. **2.** Also called: **lapful.** the amount held in one's lap. **3.** a protected place or environment: *in the lap of luxury.* **4.** the part of one's clothing that covers the lap. **5. drop in someone's lap.** give someone the responsibility of. [OE *læppa* flap]

lap[2] (læp) *n.* **1.** one circuit of a racecourse or track. **2.** a stage or part of a journey, race, etc. **3. a.** an overlapping part or projection. **b.** the extent of overlap. **4.** the length of material needed to go around an object. **5.** a rotating disc coated with fine abrasive for polishing gemstones. ~*vb.* **lapping, lapped. 6.** (*tr.*) to wrap or fold (around or over): *he lapped a bandage around his wrist.* **7.** (*tr.*) to enclose or envelop in: *he lapped his wrist in a bandage.* **8.** to place or lie partly or completely over or project beyond. **9.** (*tr.; usually passive*) to envelop or surround with comfort, love, etc.: *lapped in luxury.* **10.** (*intr.*) to be folded. **11.** (*tr.*) to overtake (an opponent) in a race so as to be one or more circuits ahead. **12.** (*tr.*) to polish or cut (a workpiece, gemstone, etc.) with a fine abrasive. [C13 (in the sense: to wrap): prob. < LAP[1]] —ˈ**lapper** *n.*

lap[3] (læp) *vb.* **lapping, lapped. 1.** (of small waves) to wash against (a shore, boat, etc.), usually with light splashing sounds. **2.** (often foll. by *up*) (esp. of animals) to scoop (a liquid) into the mouth with the tongue. ~*n.* **3.** the act or sound of lapping. **4.** a thin food for dogs or other animals. ~See also **lap up.** [OE *lapian*] —ˈ**lapper** *n.*

laparoscope (ˈlæpərəˌskəʊp) *n.* a medical instrument consisting of a tube that is inserted through the abdominal wall and illuminated to enable a doctor to view the internal organs. [C19 (applied to various instruments used to examine the abdomen) and C20 (in the specific modern sense): < Gk *lapara* (see LAPAROTOMY) + -SCOPE] —ˌ**lapa**ˈ**roscopy** *n.*

laparotomy (ˌlæpəˈrɒtəmɪ) *n., pl.* **-mies.** surgical incision through the abdominal wall. [C19: < Gk *lapara* flank, < *laparos* soft + -TOMY]

lap dissolve *n. Films.* the transposing from one picture to another by reducing one picture in brightness and amplitude while increasing the other until it replaces the first.

lapdog (ˈlæpˌdɒg) *n.* a pet dog small and docile enough to be cuddled in the lap.

lapel (ləˈpɛl) *n.* the continuation of the turned or folded back collar on a suit, coat, jacket, etc. [C18: < LAP[1]] —**la**ˈ**pelled** *adj.*

lapheld (ˈlæpˌhɛld) *adj.* (esp. of a personal computer) small enough to be used on one's lap; portable.

lapidary (ˈlæpɪdərɪ) *n., pl.* **-daries. 1.** a person whose business is to cut, polish, set, or deal in gemstones. ~*adj.* **2.** of or relating to gemstones or the work of a lapidary. **3.** Also: **lapidarian** (ˌlæpɪˈdɛərɪən). engraved, cut, or inscribed in a stone or gemstone. **4.** of sufficiently high quality to be engraved on a stone: *a lapidary inscription.* [C14: < L *lapidārius,* < *lapid-, lapis* stone]

lapillus (ləˈpɪləs) *n., pl.* **-li** (-laɪ). a small piece of lava thrown from a volcano. [C18: L: little stone]

lapis lazuli (ˈlæpɪs ˈlæzjʊˌlaɪ) *n.* **1.** a brilliant blue mineral used as a gemstone. **2.** the deep blue colour of lapis lazuli. [C14: < L *lapis* stone + Med. L *lazulī,* < Ar. *lāzaward,* < Persian *lāzhuward,* <?]

lap joint *n.* a joint made by placing one member over another and fastening them together. Also called: **lapped joint.** —ˈ**lap-**ˌ**jointed** *adj.*

Laplace operator (*French* laplas) *n. Maths.* the operator $\partial^2/\partial x^2 + \partial^2/\partial y^2 + \partial^2/\partial z^2$, used in differential analysis. Symbol: ∇^2 [C19: Pierre Simon *Laplace* (1749–1827), F mathematician]

lap of honour *n.* a ceremonial circuit of a racing track, etc., by the winner of a race.

Lapp (læp) *n.* **1.** Also **Laplander.** a member of a nomadic people living chiefly in N Scandinavia and the Kola Peninsula of the Soviet Union. **2.** the language of this people. ~*adj.* **3.** of or relating to this people or their language. —ˈ**Lappish** *adj., n.*

lappet (ˈlæpɪt) *n.* **1.** a small hanging flap or piece of lace, etc. **2.** *Zool.* a lobelike hanging structure, such as the wattle on a bird's head. [C16: < LAP[1] + -ET]

lapse (læps) *n.* **1.** a drop in standard of an isolated or temporary nature: *a lapse of justice.* **2.** a break in occurrence, usage, etc.: *a lapse of five weeks between letters.* **3.** a gradual decline or a drop to a lower degree, condition, or state: *a lapse from high office.* **4.** a moral fall. **5.** *Law.* the termination of some right, interest, or privilege, as by neglecting to exercise it or through failure of some contingency. **6.** *Insurance.* the termination of coverage following a failure to pay the premiums. ~*vb.* (*intr.*) **7.** to drop in standard or fail to maintain a norm. **8.** to decline gradually or fall in status, condition, etc. **9.** to be discontinued, esp. through negligence or other failure. **10.** (usually foll. by *into*) to drift or slide (into a condition): *to lapse into sleep.* **11.** (often foll. by *from*) to turn away (from beliefs or norms). **12.** (of time) to slip away. [C15: < L *lāpsus* error, < *lābī* to glide] —ˈ**lapsable** *or* ˈ**lapsible** *adj.* —**lapsed** *adj.* —ˈ**lapser** *n.*

lapse rate *n.* the rate of change of any meteorological factor with altitude, esp. atmospheric temperature.

lap up *vb.* (*tr., adv.*) **1.** to eat or drink. **2.** to relish or delight in: *he laps up horror films.* **3.** to believe or accept eagerly and uncritically: *he laps up stories.*

lapwing (ˈlæpˌwɪŋ) *n.* any of several plovers, typically having a crested head, wattles, and spurs. Also called: **green plover, peewit.** [C17: altered form of OE *hlēapewince* plover]

larboard (ˈlɑːbəd) *n., adj. Naut.* a former word for **port**[2]. [C14 *laddeborde* (changed to *larboard* by association with *starboard*), < *laden* to load + *borde* BOARD]

larceny (ˈlɑːsɪnɪ) *n., pl.* **-nies.** *Law.* (formerly) a technical word for **theft.** [C15: < OF *larcin,* < L *lātrocinium* robbery, < *latrō* robber] —ˈ**larcenist** *or* ˈ**larcener** *n.* —ˈ**larcenous** *adj.*

larch (lɑːtʃ) *n.* **1.** any coniferous tree having deciduous needle-like leaves and egg-shaped cones. **2.** the wood of any of these trees. [C16: < G *Lärche*, ult. < L *larix*]

lard (lɑːd) *n.* **1.** the rendered fat from a pig, used in cooking. ~*vb.* (*tr.*) **2.** to prepare (lean meat, poultry, etc.) by inserting small strips of bacon or fat before cooking. **3.** to cover or smear (foods) with lard. **4.** to add extra material to (speech or writing); embellish. [C15: via OF < L *lāridum* bacon fat] —**'lardy** *adj.*

larder ('lɑːdə) *n.* a room or cupboard, used as a store for food. [C14: < OF *lardier*, < LARD]

lardon ('lɑːdᵊn) *or* **lardoon** (lɑː'duːn) *n.* a strip of fat used in larding meat. [C15: < OF, < LARD]

lardy cake ('lɑːdɪ) *n. Brit.* a rich sweet cake made of bread dough, lard, sugar, and dried fruit.

lares and penates ('lɛəriːz, 'lɑː-) *pl. n.* **1.** *Roman myth.* **a.** household gods. **b.** statues of these gods kept in the home. **2.** the valued possessions of a household. [< L]

large (lɑːdʒ) *adj.* **1.** having a relatively great size, quantity, extent, etc.; big. **2.** of wide or broad scope, capacity, or range; comprehensive. **3.** having or showing great breadth of understanding. ~*n.* **4. at large. a.** (esp. of a dangerous criminal or wild animal) free; not confined. **b.** roaming freely, as in a foreign country. **c.** as a whole; in general. **d.** in full detail; exhaustively. **e. ambassador at large.** See **ambassador** (sense 4). [C12 (orig.: generous): via OF < L *largus* ample] —**'largeness** *n.*

large intestine *n.* the part of the alimentary canal consisting of the caecum, colon, and rectum.

largely ('lɑːdʒlɪ) *adv.* **1.** principally; to a great extent. **2.** on a large scale or in a large manner.

larger-than-life *adj.* exceptionally striking or colourful.

large-scale *adj.* **1.** wide-ranging or extensive. **2.** (of maps and models) constructed or drawn to a big scale.

largess *or* **largesse** (lɑː'dʒɛs) *n.* **1.** the generous bestowal of gifts, favours, or money. **2.** the things so bestowed. **3.** generosity of spirit or attitude. [C13: < OF, < LARGE]

larghetto (lɑː'gɛtəʊ) *Music.* ~*adj., adv.* **1.** to be performed moderately slowly. ~*n., pl.* **-tos. 2.** a piece or passage to be performed in this way. [It.: dim. of LARGO]

largish ('lɑːdʒɪʃ) *adj.* fairly large.

largo ('lɑːgəʊ) *Music.* ~*adj., adv.* **1.** to be performed slowly and broadly. ~*n., pl.* **-gos. 2.** a piece or passage to be performed in this way. [C17: < It., < L *largus* large]

lariat ('lærɪət) *n. U.S. & Canad.* **1.** another word for **lasso. 2.** a rope for tethering animals. [C19: < Sp. *la reata* the lasso]

lark[1] (lɑːk) *n.* **1.** any brown bird of a predominantly Old World family of songbirds, esp. the skylark: noted for their singing. **2.** short for **titlark.** [OE *lāwerce*, *lǣwerce*, of Gmc origin]

lark[2] (lɑːk) *Inf.* ~*n.* **1.** a carefree adventure or frolic. **2.** a harmless piece of mischief. ~*vb.* (*intr.*) **3.** (often foll. by *about*) to have a good time by frolicking. **4.** to play a prank. [C19: orig. sl.] —**'larkish** *or* **'larky** *adj.*

larkspur ('lɑːkˌspɜː) *n.* any of various plants related to the delphinium, with spikes of blue, pink, or white irregular spurred flowers. [C16: LARK[1] + SPUR]

larn (lɑːn) *vb. Not standard.* **1.** *Facetious.* to learn. **2.** (*tr.*) to teach (someone) a lesson: *that'll larn you!* [C18: < a dialect form of LEARN]

larrigan ('lærɪgən) *n.* a knee-high oiled leather moccasin boot worn by trappers, etc. [C19: <?]

larrikin ('lærɪkɪn) *n. Austral. & N.Z. sl.* **a.** a hooligan. **b.** (*as modifier*): *a larrikin bloke.* [C19: < E dialect: a mischievous youth]

larrup ('lærəp) *vb.* (*tr.*) *Dialect.* to beat or flog. [C19: <?] —**'larruper** *n.*

Larry ('lærɪ) *n. Inf., chiefly Austral.* **happy as Larry.** very happy.

larva ('lɑːvə) *n., pl.* **-vae** (-viː). an immature free-living form of many animals that develops into a different adult form by metamorphosis. [C18: (C17 in the orig. L sense: ghost): NL] —**'larval** *adj.*

laryngeal (ˌlærɪn'dʒiːəl, lə'rɪndʒɪəl) *or* **laryngal** (lə'rɪŋgᵊl) *adj.* **1.** of or relating to the larynx. **2.** *Phonetics.* articulated at the larynx; glottal. [C18: < NL *laryngeus* of the LARYNX]

laryngitis (ˌlærɪn'dʒaɪtɪs) *n.* inflammation of the larynx. —**laryngitic** (ˌlærɪn'dʒɪtɪk) *adj.*

laryngo- *or before a vowel* **laryng-** *combining form.* indicating the larynx: *laryngoscope.*

laryngoscope (lə'rɪŋgəˌskəʊp) *n.* a medical instrument for examining the larynx. —**ˌlaryn'goscopy** *n.*

laryngotomy (ˌlærɪŋ'gɒtəmɪ) *n., pl.* **-mies.** surgical incision into the larynx to facilitate breathing.

larynx ('lærɪŋks) *n., pl.* **larynges** (lə'rɪndʒiːz) *or* **larynxes.** a cartilaginous and muscular hollow organ forming part of the air passage to the lungs: in higher vertebrates it contains the vocal cords. [C16: < NL, < Gk *larunx*]

lasagne *or* **lasagna** (lə'zænjə, -'sæn-) *n.* **1.** a form of pasta consisting of wide flat sheets. **2.** any of several dishes made from layers of lasagne and meat, cheese, etc. [< It. *lasagna*, < L *lasanum* cooking pot]

lascar ('læskə) *n.* a sailor from the East Indies. [C17: < Urdu *lashkar* soldier, < Persian: the army]

lascivious (lə'sɪvɪəs) *adj.* **1.** lustful; lecherous. **2.** exciting sexual desire. [C15: < LL *lascīviōsus*, < L *lascīvia* wantonness, < *lascīvus*] —**las'civiously** *adv.* —**las'civiousness** *n.*

lase (leɪz) *vb.* (*intr.*) (of a substance, such as carbon dioxide or ruby) to be capable of acting as a laser.

laser ('leɪzə) *n.* **1.** Also called: **optical maser.** a device for converting light of mixed frequencies into an intense narrow monochromatic beam of coherent light. **2.** any similar device for producing a beam of any electromagnetic radiation, such as infrared or microwave radiation. [C20: < *l*ight *a*mplification by *s*timulated *e*mission of *r*adiation]

lash[1] (læʃ) *n.* **1.** a sharp cutting blow from a whip or other flexible object. **2.** the flexible end or ends of a whip. **3.** a cutting or hurtful blow to the feelings, as one caused by ridicule or scolding. **4.** a forceful beating or impact, as of wind, rain, or waves against something. **5. have a lash at.** *Austral. & N.Z. inf.* to make an attempt at or take part in (something). **6.** See **eyelash.** ~*vb.* (*tr.*) **7.** to hit (a person or thing) sharply with a whip, rope, etc., esp., formerly, as punishment. **8.** (of rain, waves, etc.) to beat forcefully against. **9.** to attack with words, ridicule, etc. **10.** to flick or wave sharply to and fro: *the panther lashed his tail.* **11.** to urge or drive as with a whip: *to lash the audience into a violent mood.* ~See also **lash out.** [C14: ? imit.] —**'lasher** *n.*

lash[2] (læʃ) *vb.* (*tr.*) to bind or secure with rope, string, etc. [C15: < OF *lachier*, ult. < L *laqueāre* to ensnare, < *laqueus* noose]

-lashed *adj.* having eyelashes as specified: *long-lashed.*

lashing[1] ('læʃɪŋ) *n.* **1.** a whipping; flogging. **2.** a scolding. **3.** (*pl.*; usually foll. by *of*) *Brit. inf.* large amounts; lots.

lashing[2] ('læʃɪŋ) *n.* rope, cord, etc., used for binding or securing.

lash out *vb.* (*intr., adv.*) **1.** to burst into or resort to verbal or physical attack. **2.** *Inf.* to be extravagant, as in spending.

lash-up *n.* a temporary connection of equipment for experimental or emergency use.

lass (læs) *n.* a girl or young woman. [C13: <?]

Lassa fever ('læsə) *n.* a serious viral disease of Central West Africa, characterized by high fever and muscular pains. [< *Lassa*, the Nigerian village where it was first identified]

lassie ('læsɪ) *n. Inf.* a little lass; girl.

lassitude ('læsɪˌtjuːd) *n.* physical or mental weariness. [C16: < L *lassitūdō*, < *lassus* tired]

lasso (læ'suː, 'læsəʊ) *n., pl.* **-sos** *or* **-soes. 1.** a long rope or thong with a running noose at one end, used (esp. in America) for roping horses, cattle, etc.; lariat. ~*vb.* **-soing, -soed.** **2.** (*tr.*) to catch as with a lasso. [C19: < Sp. *lazo*, ult. < L *laqueus* noose] —**las'soer** *n.*

last[1] (lɑːst) *adj.* (*often prenominal*) **1.** being, happening, or coming at the end or after all others: *the last horse in the race.* **2.** being or occurring just before the present; most recent: *last Thursday.* **3.** only remaining: *one's last cigarette.* **4.** most extreme; utmost. **5.** least suitable, appropriate, or likely: *he was the last person I would have chosen.* **6.** (esp. relating to the end of a person's life or of the world) final or ultimate: *last rites.* ~*adv.* **7.** after all others; at or in the end: *he came last.* **8.** most recently: *he was last seen in the mountains.* **9.** (*sentence modifier*) as the last or latest item. ~*n.* **10. the last. a.** a person or thing that is last. **b.** the final moment; end. **11.** one's last moments before death. **12.** the final appearance, mention, or occurrence: *we've seen the last of him.* **13. at last.** in the end; finally. **14. at long last.** finally, after difficulty, delay, or irritation. [var. of OE *latest, lætest*, sup. of LATE]

last[2] (lɑːst) *vb.* **1.** (when *intr.*, often foll. by *for*) to remain in being (for a length of time); continue: *his hatred lasted for several years.* **2.** to be sufficient for the needs of (a person) for (a length of time): *it will last us until Friday.* **3.** (when *intr.*, often foll. by *for*) to remain fresh, uninjured, or unaltered (for a certain time). ~See also **last out.** [OE *lǣstan*] —**'laster** *n.*

last[3] (lɑːst) *n.* **1.** the wooden or metal form on which a shoe or boot is fashioned or repaired. ~*vb.* **2.** (*tr.*) to fit (a shoe or boot) on a last. [OE *lǣste*, < *lāst* footprint] —**'laster** *n.*

last-ditch *n.* **a.** a last resort or place of last defence. **b.** (*as modifier*): *a last-ditch effort.*

last-gasp *n.* (*modifier*) done in desperation at the last minute: *a last-gasp attempt to save the talks.*

lasting ('lɑːstɪŋ) *adj.* permanent or enduring. —**'lastingly** *adv.* —**'lastingness** *n.*

Last Judgment *n.* **the.** the occasion, after the resurrection of the dead at the end of the world, when, according to biblical tradition, God will decree the final destinies of all men according to the good and evil in their earthly lives. Also called: **the Last Day, Doomsday, Judgment Day.**

lastly ('lɑːstlɪ) *adv.* **1.** at the end or at the last point. ~*sentence connector.* **2.** finally.

last name *n.* another term for **surname.**

last out *vb.* (*intr., adv.*) **1.** to be sufficient for one's needs: *how long will our supplies last out?* **2.** to endure or survive: *some old people don't last out the winter.*

last post *n.* (in the British military services) **1.** a bugle call that orders men to retire for sleep. **2.** a similar call sounded at military funerals.

last rites *pl. n. Christianity.* religious rites prescribed for those close to death.

Last Supper *n.* **the.** the meal eaten by Christ with his disciples on the night before his Crucifixion.

lat. *abbrev. for* latitude.

Lat. *abbrev. for* Latin.

latch (lætʃ) *n.* **1.** a fastening for a gate or door that consists of a bar that may be slid or lowered into a groove, hole, etc. **2.** a spring-loaded door lock that can be opened by a key from outside. **3.** Also called: **latch circuit.** *Electronics.* a logic circuit that transfers the input states to the output states when signalled. ~*vb.* **4.** to fasten, fit, or be fitted as with a latch. [OE *læccan* to seize, of Gmc origin]

latchkey ('lætʃˌkiː) *n.* **1.** a key for an outside door or gate, esp. one that lifts a latch. **2.** a supposed freedom from restrictions.

latchkey child *n.* a child who has to let himself in at home on returning from school, as his parents are out at work.

latch on *vb.* (*intr., adv.*; often foll. by *to*) *Inf.* **1.** to attach oneself (to). **2.** to understand.

latchstring ('lætʃˌstrɪŋ) *n.* a length of string fastened to a latch and passed through a hole in the door so that it can be opened from the other side.

late (leɪt) *adj.* **1.** occurring or arriving after the correct or expected time: *the train was late.* **2.** (*prenominal*) occurring at, scheduled for, or being at a relatively advanced time: *a late marriage.* **3.** (*prenominal*) towards or near the end: *the late evening.* **4.** at an advanced time in the evening or at night: *it was late.* **5.** (*prenominal*) occurring or being just previous to the present time: *his late remarks on industry.* **6.** (*prenominal*) having died, esp. recently: *my late grandfather.* **7.** (*prenominal*) just preceding the present or existing person or thing; former: *the late manager of this firm.* **8. of late.** recently; lately. ~*adv.* **9.** after the correct or expected time: *he arrived late.* **10.** at a relatively advanced age: *she married late.* **11.** recently; lately: *as late as yesterday he was selling books.* **12. late in the day. a.** at a late or advanced stage. **b.** too late. [OE *læt*] —**'lateness** *n.*

lateen (lə'tiːn) *adj. Naut.* denoting a rig with a triangular sail (**lateen sail**) bent to a yard hoisted to the head of a low mast, used esp. in the Mediterranean. [C18: < F *voile latine* Latin sail]

Late Greek *n.* the Greek language from about the 3rd to the 8th centuries A.D.

Late Latin *n.* the form of written Latin used from the 3rd to the 7th centuries A.D.

lately ('leɪtlɪ) *adv.* in recent times; of late.

La Tène (læ 'tɛn) *adj.* of or relating to a Celtic culture in Europe from about the 5th to the 1st centuries B.C., characterized by a distinctive type of curvilinear decoration. [C20: < *La Tène*, a part of Lake Neuchâtel, Switzerland, where remains of this culture were first discovered]

latent ('leɪt'nt) *adj.* **1.** potential but not obvious or explicit. **2.** (of buds, spores, etc.) dormant. **3.** *Pathol.* (esp. of an infectious disease) not yet revealed or manifest. [C17: < L *latēnt-*, < *latēre* to lie hidden] —**'latency** *n.* —**'latently** *adv.*

latent heat *n.* (*no longer in technical usage*) the heat evolved or liberated when a substance changes phase without any change in its temperature.

latent image *n. Photog.* the invisible image produced by the action of light, etc., on silver halide crystals suspended in the emulsion of a photographic material. It becomes visible after development.

later ('leɪtə) *adj., adv.* **1.** the comparative of **late.** ~*adv.* **2.** afterwards; subsequently.

lateral ('lætərəl) *adj.* **1.** of or relating to the side or sides: *a lateral blow.* ~*n.* **2.** a lateral object, part, passage, or movement. [C17: < L *laterālis*, < *latus* side] —**'laterally** *adv.*

lateral thinking *n.* a way of solving problems by employing unorthodox and apparently illogical means.

laterite ('lætəˌraɪt) *n.* any of a group of residual insoluble deposits of ferric and aluminium oxides: formed by weathering of rocks in tropical regions. [C19: < L *later* brick]

latest ('leɪtɪst) *adj., adv.* **1.** the superlative of **late.** ~*adj.* **2.** most recent, modern, or new: *the latest fashions.* ~*n.* **3. at the latest.** no later than the time specified. **4. the latest.** *Inf.* the most recent fashion or development.

latex ('leɪtɛks) *n., pl.* **latexes** *or* **latices** ('lætɪˌsiːz). **1.** a whitish milky fluid containing protein, starch, alkaloids, etc., that is produced by many plants. Latex from the rubber tree is used in the manufacture of rubber. **2.** a suspension of synthetic rubber or plastic in water, used in the manufacture of synthetic rubber products, etc. [C19: NL, < L: liquid]

lath (lɑːθ) *n., pl.* **laths** (lɑːðz, lɑːθs). **1.** one of several thin narrow strips of wood used to provide a supporting framework for plaster, tiles, etc. **2.** expanded sheet metal, wire mesh, etc., used to provide backing for plaster or rendering. **3.** any thin strip of wood. ~*vb.* **4.** (*tr.*) to attach laths to (a ceiling, roof, floor, etc.). [OE *lætt*]

lathe (leɪð) *n.* **1.** a machine for shaping or boring metal, wood, etc., in which the workpiece is turned about a horizontal axis against a fixed tool. ~*vb.* **2.** (*tr.*) to shape or bore (a workpiece) on a lathe. [? C15 *lath* a support, < ON]

lather ('lɑːðə) *n.* **1.** foam formed by the action of soap or a detergent in water. **2.** foam formed by other liquid, such as the saliva of a horse. **3.** *Inf.* a state of agitation. ~*vb.* **4.** to coat or become coated with lather. **5.** (*intr.*) to form a lather. **6.** (*tr.*) *Inf.* to beat; flog. [OE *lēathor* soap] —'**lathery** *adj.*

lathi ('lɑːtɪ) *n., pl.* **-this.** a long heavy wooden stick used as a weapon in India, esp. by the police. [Hindi]

Latin ('lætɪn) *n.* **1.** the language of ancient Rome and the Roman Empire and of the educated in medieval Europe. Having originally been the language of Latium in W central Italy, belonging to the Italic branch of the Indo-European family, it later formed the basis of the Romance group. **2.** a member of any of those peoples whose languages are derived from Latin. **3.** an inhabitant of ancient Latium. ~*adj.* **4.** of or relating to the Latin language, the ancient Latins, or Latium. **5.** characteristic of or relating to those peoples whose languages are derived from Latin. **6.** of or relating to the Roman Catholic Church. [OE *latin* and *læden* Latin, language, < L *Latīnus* of Latium]

Latin America *n.* those areas of America whose official languages are Spanish and Portuguese, derived from Latin: South America, Central America, Mexico, and certain islands in the Caribbean. —**Latin American** *n., adj.*

Latinate ('lætɪˌneɪt) *adj.* (of writing, vocabulary, etc.) imitative of or derived from Latin.

Latinism ('lætɪˌnɪzəm) *n.* a word, idiom, or phrase borrowed from Latin.

Latinist ('lætɪnɪst) *n.* a person who studies or is proficient in Latin.

Latinize *or* **-ise** ('lætɪˌnaɪz) *vb.* (*tr.*) **1.** to translate into Latin or Latinisms. **2.** to cause to acquire Latin style or customs. **3.** to bring Roman Catholic influence to bear upon (the form of religious ceremonies, etc.). —ˌ**Latini'zation** *or* **-i'sation** *n.* —'**Latinˌizer** *or* **-ˌiser** *n.*

latish ('leɪtɪʃ) *adj., adv.* rather late.

latitude ('lætɪˌtjuːd) *n.* **1. a.** an angular distance measured in degrees north or south of the equator (latitude 0°). **b.** (*often pl.*) a region considered with regard to its distance from the equator. **2.** scope for freedom of action, thought, etc.; freedom from restriction: *his parents gave him a great deal of latitude.* [C14: < L *lātitūdō*, < *lātus* broad] —ˌ**lati'tudinal** *adj.* —ˌ**lati'tudinally** *adv.*

latitudinarian (ˌlætɪˌtjuːdɪ'nɛərɪən) *adj.* **1.** permitting or marked by freedom of attitude or behaviour, esp. in religious matters. ~*n.* **2.** a person with latitudinarian views. [C17: < L *lātitūdō* breadth, infl. in form by TRINITARIAN] —ˌ**latiˌtudi'narianism** *n.*

latria (lə'traɪə) *n. R.C. Church, theol.* the adoration that may be offered to God alone. [C16: via L < Gk *latreia* worship]

latrine (lə'triːn) *n.* a lavatory, as in a barracks, camp, etc. [C17: < F, < L *lātrīna*, shortened form of *lavātrīna* bath, < *lavāre* to wash]

-latry *n. combining form.* indicating worship of or excessive veneration of: *idolatry; Mariolatry.* [< Gk *-latria*, < *latreia* worship] —**-latrous** *adj. combining form.*

latter ('lætə) *adj.* (*prenominal*) **1. a.** denoting the second or second mentioned of two: distinguished from *former.* **b.** (*as n.; functioning as sing. or pl.*): *the latter is not important.* **2.** near or nearer the end: *the latter part of a film.* **3.** more advanced in time or sequence; later. [OE *lætra*]

▷ **Usage.** In careful usage, *latter* is used when only two items are in question: *he gave the money to Christopher and not to John, the latter being less in need of it. Last-named* is used to refer to the last-named of three or more items.

latter-day *adj.* present-day; modern.

Latter-day Saint *n.* a more formal name for a **Mormon.**

latterly ('lætəlɪ) *adv.* recently; lately.

lattice ('lætɪs) *n.* **1.** Also called: **latticework.** an open framework of strips of wood, metal, etc., arranged to form an ornamental pattern. **2. a.** a gate, screen, etc., formed of such a framework. **b.** (*as modifier*): *a lattice window.* **3.** something, such as a decorative or heraldic device, resembling such a framework. **4.** an array of objects or points in a periodic pattern in two or three dimensions, esp. an array of atoms, ions, etc., in a crystal or an array of points indicating their positions in space. ~*vb.* **5.** to make, adorn, or supply with a lattice or lattices. [C14: < OF *lattis*, < *latte* LATH] —'**latticed** *adj.*

Latvian ('lætvɪən) *adj.* **1.** of or relating to Latvia, a Soviet Socialist Republic on the Gulf of Riga and the Baltic Sea. **2.** of or relating to the people of Latvia or their language. ~*n.* **3.** Also called: **Lettish.** an official language of the Latvian SSR. **4.** a native or inhabitant of Latvia.

laud (lɔːd) *Literary.* ~*vb.* **1.** (*tr.*) to praise or glorify. ~*n.* **2.** praise or glorification. [C14: vb. < L *laudāre*; n. < *laudēs*, pl. of L *laus* praise]

laudable ('lɔːdəbᵊl) *adj.* deserving or worthy of praise; admirable; commendable. —'**laudableness** *or* ˌ**lauda'bility** *n.* —'**laudably** *adv.*

laudanum ('lɔːdᵊnəm) *n.* **1.** a tincture of opium. **2.** (formerly) any medicine of which opium was the main ingredient. [C16: NL, name chosen by Paracelsus (1493–1541), Swiss alchemist, for a preparation prob. containing opium]

laudation (lɔː'deɪʃən) *n.* a formal word for **praise.**

laudatory ('lɔːdətərɪ, -trɪ) *or* **laudative** *adj.* expressing or containing praise; eulogistic.

lauds (lɔːdz) *n.* (*functioning as sing. or pl.*) *Chiefly R.C. Church.* the traditional morning prayer, constituting with matins the first of the seven canonical hours. [C14: see LAUD]

laugh (lɑːf) *vb.* **1.** (*intr.*) to express or manifest emotion, esp. mirth or amusement, typically by expelling air from the lungs in short bursts to produce an inarticulate voiced noise, with the mouth open. **2.** (*intr.*) (esp. of certain mammals or birds) to make a noise resembling a laugh. **3.** (*tr.*) to utter or express with laughter: *he laughed his derision at the play.* **4.** (*tr.*) to bring or force (someone, esp. oneself) into a certain condition by laughter: *he laughed himself sick.* **5.** (*intr.*; foll. by *at*) to make fun (of); jeer (at). **6. laugh up one's sleeve.** to laugh or have grounds for amusement, self-satisfaction, etc., secretly. **7. laugh on the other side of one's face.** to show sudden disappointment or shame after appearing cheerful or confident. ~*n.* **8.** the act or an instance of laughing. **9.** a manner of laughter. **10.** *Inf.* a person or thing that causes laughter: *that holiday was a laugh.* **11. the last laugh.** the final success in an argument, situation, etc., after previous defeat. ~See also **laugh off.** [OE *læhan, hliehhen*] —'**laugher** *n.* —'**laughing** *n., adj.* —'**laughingly** *adv.*

laughable ('lɑːfəbᵊl) *adj.* **1.** producing scorn; ludicrous: *he offered me a laughable sum for the picture.* **2.** arousing laughter. —'**laughableness** *n.* —'**laughably** *adv.*

laughing gas *n.* another name for **nitrous oxide.**

laughing jackass *n.* another name for the **kookaburra.**

laughing stock *n.* an object of humiliating ridicule.

laugh off *vb.* (*tr., adv.*) to treat or dismiss lightly, esp. with stoicism.

laughter ('lɑːftə) *n.* **1.** the action of or noise produced by laughing. **2.** the experience or manifestation of mirth, amusement, scorn, or joy. [OE *hleahtor*]

launch[1] (lɔːntʃ) *vb.* **1.** to move (a vessel) into the water. **2.** to move (a newly built vessel) into the water for the first time. **3.** (*tr.*) **a.** to start off or set in motion: *to launch a scheme.* **b.** to put (a new product) on the market. **4.** (*tr.*) to propel with force. **5.** to involve (oneself) totally and enthusiastically: *to launch oneself into work.* **6.** (*tr.*) to set (a missile, spacecraft, etc.) into motion.

7. (*intr.;* foll. by *into*) to start talking or writing (about): *he launched into a story.* 8. (*intr.;* usually foll. by *out*) to start (out) on a fresh course. ~*n.* 9. an act or instance of launching. [C14: < Anglo-F *lancher,* < LL *lanceāre* to use a lance, hence, to set in motion. See LANCE] —ˈ**launcher** *n.*

launch[2] (lɔːntʃ) *n.* 1. a motor driven boat used chiefly as a transport boat. 2. the largest of the boats of a man-of-war. [C17: via Sp. *lancha* and Port. < Malay *lancharan* boat, < *lanchar* speed]

launching pad *or* **launch pad** *n.* a platform from which a spacecraft, rocket, etc., is launched.

launch window *n.* the limited period during which a spacecraft can be launched on a particular mission.

launder (ˈlɔːndə) *vb.* 1. to wash and often also iron (clothes, linen, etc.). 2. (*intr.*) to be capable of being laundered without shrinking, fading, etc. 3. (*tr.*) to make (money illegally obtained) appear to be legally gained by passing it through foreign banks or legitimate enterprises. [C14 (n., meaning: a person who washes linen): changed < *lavender* washerwoman, < OF *lavandiere,* ult. < L *lavāre* to wash] —ˈ**launderer** *n.*

Launderette (ˌlɔːndəˈrɛt, lɔːnˈdrɛt) *Brit. & N.Z. trademark.* a commercial establishment where clothes can be washed and dried, using coin-operated machines. Also called (U.S., Canad., and N.Z.): **Laundromat.**

laundress (ˈlɔːndrɪs) *n.* a woman who launders clothes, sheets, etc., for a living.

laundry (ˈlɔːndrɪ) *n., pl.* **-dries.** 1. a place where clothes and linen are washed and ironed. 2. the clothes or linen washed and ironed. 3. the act of laundering. [C16: changed < C14 *lavendry;* see LAUNDER]

laundryman (ˈlɔːndrɪmən) *or* (*fem.*) **laundry-woman** *n., pl.* **-men** *or* **-women.** 1. a person who collects or delivers laundry. 2. a person who works in a laundry.

Laurasia (lɔːˈreɪʃə) *n.* one of the two ancient supercontinents comprising what are now North America, Greenland, Europe, and Asia (excluding India). [C20: < NL *Laur(entia)* (referring to the ancient N American landmass, < *Laurentian* strata of the Canadian Shield) + *(Eur)asia*]

laureate (ˈlɔːrɪɪt) *adj.* (*usually immediately postpositive*) 1. *Literary.* crowned with laurel leaves as a sign of honour. ~*n.* 2. short for **poet laureate.** 3. a person honoured with an award for art or science: *a Nobel laureate.* 4. *Rare.* a person honoured with the laurel crown or wreath. [C14: < L *laureātus,* < *laurea* LAUREL] —ˈ**laureateˌship** *n.*

laurel (ˈlɒrəl) *n.* 1. Also called: **bay, bay laurel, sweet bay, true laurel.** a small Mediterranean evergreen tree with glossy aromatic leaves, used for flavouring in cooking, and small blackish berries. 2. a similar and related tree of the Canary Islands and Azores. 3. short for **mountain laurel.** 4. **spurge laurel.** a European evergreen shrub, *Daphne laureola,* with glossy leaves and small green flowers. 5. (*pl.*) a wreath of true laurel, worn on the head as an emblem of victory or honour in classical times. 6. (*pl.*) honour, distinction, or fame. 7. **look to one's laurels.** to be on guard against one's rivals. 8. **rest on one's laurels.** to be satisfied with distinction won by past achievements and cease to strive for further achievements. ~*vb.* **-relling, -relled** *or U.S.* **-reling, -reled.** 9. (*tr.*) to crown with laurels. [C13 *lorer,* < OF *lorier* laurel tree, ult. < L *laurus*]

Laurentian (lɔːˈrɛnʃən) *adj.* 1. Also: **Lawrentian.** of or resembling the style of D. H. or T. E. Lawrence. 2. of, relating to, or situated near the St Lawrence River.

Laurentian Shield *n.* another name for the **Canadian Shield.** Also: **Laurentian Plateau.**

laurustinus (ˌlɔːrəˈstaɪnəs) *n.* a Mediterranean shrub with glossy evergreen leaves and white or pink fragrant flowers. [C17: < NL, < L *laurus* laurel]

lav (læv) *n. Brit. inf.* short for **lavatory.**

lava (ˈlɑːvə) *n.* 1. magma emanating from volcanoes. 2. any extrusive igneous rock formed by the solidification of lava. [C18: < It., < L *lavāre* to wash]

lavabo (ləˈveɪbəʊ) *n., pl.* **-boes** *or* **-bos.** *Chiefly R.C. Church.* 1. a. the ritual washing of the celebrant's hands after the offertory at Mass. b. (*as modifier*): *lavabo basin; lavabo towel.* 2. another name for **washbasin.** 3. a trough for washing in a convent or monastery. [C19: < L: I shall wash, the opening of Psalm 26:6]

lavage (ˈlævɪdʒ, læˈvɑːʒ) *n. Med.* the washing out of a hollow organ by flushing with water. [C19: via F, < L *lavāre* to wash]

lavatorial (ˌlævəˈtɔːrɪəl) *adj.* characterized by excessive mention of the excretory functions; vulgar or scatological: *lavatorial humour.*

lavatory (ˈlævətərɪ, -trɪ) *n., pl.* **-ries.** a. a sanitary installation for receiving and disposing of urine and faeces, consisting of a bowl fitted with a water-flushing device and connected to a drain. b. a room containing such an installation. Also called: **toilet, water closet, WC.** [C14: < LL *lavātōrium,* < L *lavāre* to wash]

lavatory paper *n. Brit.* another name for **toilet paper.**

lave (leɪv) *vb.* an archaic word for **wash.** [OE *lafian,* ? < L *lavāre* to wash]

lavender (ˈlævəndə) *n.* 1. any of various perennial shrubs or herbaceous plants of the labiate family, esp. *Lavandula vera,* cultivated for its mauve or blue flowers and as the source of a fragrant oil (**oil of lavender**). 2. the dried parts of *L. vera,* used to perfume clothes. 3. a pale or light bluish-purple colour. 4. perfume scented with lavender. [C13 *lavendre,* via F < Med. L *lavendula,* <?]

laver (ˈleɪvə) *n. Old Testament.* a large basin of water used by the priests for ritual ablutions. [C14: < OF *laveoir,* < LL *lavātōrium* washing place]

lavish (ˈlævɪʃ) *adj.* 1. prolific, abundant, or profuse. 2. generous; unstinting; liberal. 3. extravagant; prodigal; wasteful: *lavish expenditure.* ~*vb.* 4. (*tr.*) to give, expend, or apply abundantly, generously, or in profusion. [C15: adj. use of *lavas* profusion, < OF *lavasse* torrent, < L *lavāre* to wash] —ˈ**lavisher** *n.* —ˈ**lavishly** *adv.* —ˈ**lavishness** *n.*

law (lɔː) *n.* 1. a rule or set of rules, enforceable by the courts regulating the relationship between the state and its subjects, and the conduct of subjects towards one another. 2. a. a rule or body of rules made by the legislature. See **statute law.** b. a rule or body of rules made by a municipal or other authority. See **bylaw.** 3. a. the condition and control enforced by such rules. b. (*in combination*): *lawcourt.* 4. **law and order.** a. the policy of strict enforcement of the law, esp. against crime and violence. b. (*as modifier*): *law-and-order candidate.* 5. a rule of conduct: *a law of etiquette.* 6. one of a set of rules governing a particular field of activity: *the laws of tennis.* 7. **the law.** a. the legal or judicial system. b. the profession or practice of law. c. *Inf.* the police or a policeman. 8. Also called: **law of nature.** a generalization based on a recurring fact or event. 9. the science or knowledge of law; jurisprudence. 10. the principles originating and formerly applied only in courts of common law. Cf. **equity** (sense 3). 11. a general principle, formula, or rule describing a phenomenon in mathematics, science, philosophy, etc.: *the laws of thermodynamics.* 12. Also called: **Law of Moses.** (*often cap.;* preceded by *the*) the body of laws contained in the first five books of the Old Testament. 13. **go to law.** to resort to legal proceedings on some matter. 14. **lay down the law.** to speak in an authoritative or dogmatic manner. ~Related adjs.: **judicial, juridical, legal.** [OE *lagu,* < ON]

law-abiding *adj.* adhering more or less strictly to the laws: *a law-abiding citizen.*

law agent *n.* (in Scotland) a solicitor entitled to appear for a client in any Sheriff Court.

lawbreaker (ˈlɔːˌbreɪkə) *n.* a person who breaks the law. —ˈ**lawˌbreaking** *n., adj.*

law centre *n. Brit.* an independent service

financed by a local authority, which provides free legal advice and information to the general public.

lawful ('lɔːfʊl) *adj.* allowed, recognized, or sanctioned by law; legal. —'**lawfully** *adv.* —'**lawfulness** *n.*

lawgiver ('lɔːˌgɪvə) *n.* **1.** the giver of a code of laws. **2.** Also called: **lawmaker.** a maker of laws. —'**lawˌgiving** *n., adj.*

lawks (lɔːks) *interj. Brit.* an expression of surprise or dismay. [C18: var. of *Lord!*, prob. infl. in form by ALACK]

lawless ('lɔːlɪs) *adj.* **1.** without law. **2.** disobedient to the law. **3.** contrary to or heedless of the law. **4.** uncontrolled; unbridled: *lawless rage.* —'**lawlessly** *adv.* —'**lawlessness** *n.*

Law Lords *pl. n.* members of the House of Lords who sit as the highest court of appeal.

lawn[1] (lɔːn) *n.* a flat and usually level area of mown and cultivated grass. [C16: changed form of C14 *launde*, < OF *lande*, of Celtic origin] —'**lawny** *adj.*

lawn[2] (lɔːn) *n.* a fine linen or cotton fabric, used for clothing. [C15: prob. < *Laon*, town in France where made] —'**lawny** *adj.*

lawn mower *n.* a hand-operated or power-operated machine for cutting grass on lawns.

lawn tennis *n.* **1.** tennis played on a grass court. **2.** the formal name for **tennis.**

law of averages *n.* (popularly) the expectation that a possible event is bound to occur regularly with a frequency approximating to its probability.

law of supply and demand *n.* the theory that the price of an article or service is determined by the interaction of supply and demand.

law of the jungle *n.* a state of ruthless competition or self-interest.

law of thermodynamics *n.* any of three principles governing the relationships between different forms of energy. The **first law** (conservation of energy) states that energy can be transformed but not destroyed. The **second law** states that in any irreversible process entropy always increases. The **third law** states that it is impossible to reduce the temperature of a system to absolute zero in a finite number of steps.

lawrencium (lɒ'rɛnsɪəm) *n.* an element artificially produced from californium. Symbol: Lr; atomic no.: 103; half-life of most stable isotope, ^{256}Lr: 35 seconds. [C20: after Ernest O. *Lawrence* (1901–58), U.S. physicist]

Lawrentian (lɔː'rɛnʃən) *adj.* a variant spelling of **Laurentian** (sense 1).

lawsuit ('lɔːˌsuːt) *n.* a proceeding in a court of law brought by one party against another, esp. a civil action.

law term *n.* **1.** an expression or word used in law. **2.** any of various periods of time appointed for the sitting of law courts.

lawyer ('lɔːjə, 'lɔɪə) *n.* a member of the legal profession, esp. a solicitor. [C14: < LAW]

lax (læks) *adj.* **1.** lacking firmness; not strict. **2.** lacking precision or definition. **3.** not taut. **4.** *Phonetics.* (of a speech sound) pronounced with little muscular effort. [C14 (orig. used with reference to the bowels): < L *laxus* loose] —'**laxly** *adv.* —'**laxity** *or* '**laxness** *n.*

laxative ('læksətɪv) *n.* **1.** an agent stimulating evacuation of faeces. ~*adj.* **2.** stimulating evacuation of faeces. [C14 (orig.: relaxing): < Med. L *laxātīvus*, < L *laxāre* to loosen]

lay[1] (leɪ) *vb.* **laying, laid.** (*mainly tr.*) **1.** to put in a low or horizontal position; cause to lie: *to lay a cover on a bed.* **2.** to place, put, or be in a particular state or position: *he laid his finger on his lips.* **3.** (*intr.*) *Dialect or not standard.* to be in a horizontal position; lie: *he often lays in bed all the morning.* **4.** (sometimes foll. by *down*) to establish as a basis: *to lay a foundation for discussion.* **5.** to place or dispose in the proper position: *to lay a carpet.* **6.** to arrange (a table) for eating a meal. **7.** to prepare (a fire) for lighting by arranging fuel in the grate. **8.** (*also intr.*) (of birds, esp. the domestic hen) to produce (eggs). **9.** to present or put forward: *he laid his case before the magistrate.* **10.** to impute or attribute: *all the blame was laid on him.* **11.** to arrange, devise, or prepare: *to lay a trap.* **12.** to place, set, or locate: *the scene is laid in London.* **13.** to make (a bet) with (someone): *I lay you five to one on Prince.* **14.** to cause to settle: *to lay the dust.* **15.** to allay; suppress: *to lay a rumour.* **16.** to bring down forcefully: *to lay a whip on someone's back.* **17.** *Taboo sl.* to have sexual intercourse with. **18.** to press down or make smooth: *to lay the nap of cloth.* **19.** (*intr.*) *Naut.* to move or go, esp. into a specified position or direction: *to lay close to the wind.* **20. lay bare.** to reveal or explain: *he laid bare his plans.* **21. lay hold of.** to seize or grasp. **22. lay oneself open.** to make oneself vulnerable (to criticism, attack, etc.). **23. lay open.** to reveal or disclose. ~*n.* **24.** the manner or position in which something lies or is placed. **25.** *Taboo sl.* **a.** an act of sexual intercourse. **b.** a sexual partner. ~See also **layabout, lay aside,** etc. [OE *lecgan*]

▷ **Usage.** In careful English, the verb *lay* is used with an object and *lie* without one: *the soldier laid down his arms; the book was lying on the table.* All careful writers and speakers observe this distinction even in informal contexts.

lay[2] (leɪ) *vb.* the past tense of **lie**[2].

lay[3] (leɪ) *adj.* **1.** of, involving, or belonging to people who are not clergymen. **2.** nonprofessional or nonspecialist; amateur. [C14: < OF *lai*, < LL *lāicus*, ult. < Gk *laos* people]

lay[4] (leɪ) *n.* **1.** a ballad or short narrative poem, esp. one intended to be sung. **2.** a song or melody. [C13: < OF *lai*, ? of Gmc origin]

layabout ('leɪəˌbaʊt) *n.* a lazy person; loafer.

lay analyst *n.* a person without medical qualifications who practises psychoanalysis.

lay aside *vb.* (*tr., adv.*) **1.** to abandon or reject. **2.** to store or reserve for future use.

lay brother *n.* a man who has taken the vows of a religious order but is not ordained.

lay-by *n.* **1.** *Brit.* a place for drivers to stop at the side of a main road. **2.** *Naut.* an anchorage in a narrow waterway, away from the channel. **3.** a small railway siding where rolling stock may be stored or parked. **4.** *Austral. & N.Z.* a system of payment whereby a buyer pays a deposit on an article, which is reserved for him until he has paid the full price. ~*vb.* **lay by.** (*tr., adv.*) **5.** to set aside or save for future needs.

lay days *pl. n.* **1.** *Commerce.* the number of days permitted for the loading or unloading of a ship without payment of demurrage. **2.** *Naut.* the time during which a ship is kept from sailing because of loading, bad weather, etc.

lay down *vb.* (*tr., adv.*) **1.** to place on the ground, etc. **2.** to relinquish or discard: *to lay down one's life.* **3.** to formulate (a rule, principle, etc.). **4.** to build or begin to build: *the railway was laid down as far as Chester.* **5.** to record (plans) on paper. **6.** to convert (land) into pasture. **7.** to store or stock: *to lay down wine.* **8.** *Inf.* to wager or bet. **9.** *Inf.* to record (tracks) in a studio.

layer ('leɪə) *n.* **1.** a thickness of some homogeneous substance, such as a stratum or a coating on a surface. **2.** a laying hen. **3.** *Horticulture.* a shoot or branch rooted during layering. ~*vb.* **4.** to form or make a layer of (something). **5.** to take root or cause to take root by layering. [C14 *leyer, legger*, < LAY[1] + -ER[1]]

layering ('leɪərɪŋ) *n. Horticulture.* a method of propagation that induces a shoot to take root while it is still attached to the parent plant.

layette (leɪ'ɛt) *n.* a complete set of articles, including clothing, bedclothes, and other accessories, for a newborn baby. [C19: < F, < OF, < *laie*, < MDu. *laege* box]

lay figure *n.* **1.** an artist's jointed dummy, used in place of a live model, esp. for studying effects of drapery. **2.** a person considered to be subservient or unimportant. [C18: < obs. *layman*, < Du. *leeman*, lit.: joint-man]

lay in *vb.* (*tr., adv.*) to accumulate and store: *we must lay in food for the party.*

lay into *vb. (intr., prep.) Inf.* **1.** to attack forcefully. **2.** to berate severely.

layman (ˈleɪmən) *or (fem.)* **laywoman** *n., pl.* **-men** *or* **-women. 1.** a person who is not a clergyman. **2.** a person who does not have specialized or professional knowledge of a subject: *science for the layman.*

lay off *vb.* **1.** *(tr., adv.)* to suspend from work with the intention of re-employing later: *the firm had to lay off 100 men.* **2.** *(intr.) Inf.* to leave (a person, thing, or activity) alone: *lay off me, will you!* **3.** *(tr., adv.)* to mark off the boundaries of. ~*n.* **lay-off. 4.** the act of suspending employees. **5.** a period of imposed unemployment.

lay on *vb. (tr., adv.)* **1.** to provide or supply: *to lay on entertainment.* **2.** *Brit.* to install: *to lay on electricity.* **3. lay it on.** *Sl.* **a.** to exaggerate, esp. when flattering. **b.** to charge an exorbitant price. **c.** to punish or strike harshly.

lay out *vb. (tr., adv.)* **1.** to arrange or spread out. **2.** to prepare (a corpse) for burial. **3.** to plan or contrive. **4.** *Inf.* to spend (money), esp. lavishly. **5.** *Inf.* to knock unconscious. ~*n.* **layout. 6.** the arrangement or plan of something, such as a building. **7.** the arrangement of written material, photographs, or other artwork on an advertisement or page in a book, newspaper, etc. **8.** a preliminary plan indicating this. **9.** a drawing showing the relative disposition of parts in a machine, etc. **10.** the act of laying out. **11.** something laid out.

lay over *U.S.* ~*vb. (adv.)* **1.** *(tr.)* to postpone for future action. **2.** *(intr.)* to make a temporary stop in a journey. ~*n.* **layover. 3.** a break in a journey, esp. in waiting for a connection.

lay reader *n.* **1.** *Church of England.* a person licensed by a bishop to conduct religious services other than the Eucharist. **2.** *R.C. Church.* a layman chosen from among the congregation to read the epistle at Mass.

lay up *vb. (tr., adv.)* **1.** to store or reserve for future use. **2.** *(usually passive) Inf.* to incapacitate or confine through illness.

lazar (ˈlæzə) *n.* an archaic word for **leper.** [C14: via OF and Med. L, after *Lazarus,* beggar in Jesus' parable (Luke 16:19–31)]

lazaretto (ˌlæzəˈrɛtəʊ), **lazaret,** *or* **lazarette** (ˌlæzəˈrɛt) *n., pl.* **-rettos, -rets,** *or* **-rettes. 1.** Also called: **glory hole.** *Naut.* a small locker at the stern of a boat or a storeroom between decks of a ship. **2.** Also called: **lazar house, pesthouse.** (formerly) a hospital for persons with infectious diseases, esp. leprosy. [C16: It., < *lazzaro* LAZAR]

laze (leɪz) *vb.* **1.** *(intr.)* to be indolent or lazy. **2.** *(tr.;* often foll. by *away)* to spend (time) in indolence. ~*n.* **3.** the act or an instance of idling. [C16: back formation < LAZY]

lazy (ˈleɪzɪ) *adj.* **lazier, laziest. 1.** not inclined to work or exertion. **2.** conducive to or causing indolence. **3.** moving in a languid or sluggish manner: *a lazy river.* [C16: <?] —ˈ**lazily** *adv.* —ˈ**laziness** *n.*

lazybones (ˈleɪzɪˌbəʊnz) *n. Inf.* a lazy person.

lazy Susan *n.* a revolving tray, often divided into sections, for holding condiments, etc.

lb *abbrev. for:* **1.** pound (weight). [L: *libra*] **2.** *Cricket.* leg bye.

lbw *Cricket. abbrev. for* leg before wicket.

lc *abbrev. for:* **1.** left centre (of a stage, etc.). **2.** loco citato. [L: in the place cited] **3.** *Printing.* lower case.

L/C, l/c, *or* **lc** *abbrev. for* letter of credit.

LCD *abbrev. for:* **1.** liquid crystal display. **2.** Also: **lcd.** lowest common denominator.

LCJ (in Britain) *abbrev. for* Lord Chief Justice.

lcm *or* **LCM** *abbrev. for* lowest common multiple.

L/Cpl *abbrev. for* lance corporal.

LDS *abbrev. for:* **1.** Latter-day Saints. **2.** laus Deo semper. [L: praise be to God for ever] **3.** (in Britain) Licentiate in Dental Surgery.

lea (liː) *n.* **1.** *Poetic.* a meadow or field. **2.** land that has been sown with grass seed. [OE *lēah*]

LEA (in Britain) *abbrev. for* Local Education Authority.

leach (liːtʃ) *vb.* **1.** to remove or be removed from a substance by a percolating liquid. **2.** to lose or cause to lose soluble substances by the action of a percolating liquid. ~*n.* **3.** the act or process of leaching. **4.** a substance that is leached or the constituents removed by leaching. **5.** a porous vessel for leaching. [C17: var. of obs. *letch* to wet, ? < OE *leccan* to water] —ˈ**leacher** *n.*

lead[1] (liːd) *vb.* **leading, led. 1.** to show the way to (an individual or a group) by going with or ahead: *lead the party into the garden.* **2.** to guide or be guided by holding, pulling, etc.: *he led the horse by its reins.* **3.** *(tr.)* to cause to act, feel, think, or behave in a certain way; induce; influence: *he led me to believe that he would go.* **4.** (when *intr.,* foll. by *to*) (of a road, route, etc.) to serve as the means of reaching a place. **5.** *(tr.)* to go ahead so as to indicate (esp. in **lead the way**). **6.** to guide, control, or direct: *to lead an army.* **7.** *(tr.)* to direct the course of or conduct (water, a rope, or wire, etc.) along or as if along a channel. **8.** to initiate the action of (something); have the principal part in (something): *to lead a discussion.* **9.** to go at the head of or have the top position in (something): *he leads his class in geography.* **10.** *(intr.;* foll. by *with)* to have as the first or principal item: *the newspaper led with the royal birth.* **11.** *Music, Brit.* to play first violin in (an orchestra). **12.** to direct and guide (one's partner) in a dance. **13.** *(tr.)* **a.** to pass or spend: *I lead a miserable life.* **b.** to cause to pass a life of a particular kind: *to lead a person a dog's life.* **14.** *(intr.;* foll. by *to)* to tend (to) or result (in): *this will only lead to misery.* **15.** to initiate a round of cards by putting down (the first card) or to have the right to do this: *she led a diamond.* **16.** *(intr.) Boxing.* to make an offensive blow, esp. as one's habitual attacking punch. ~*n.* **17. a.** the first, foremost, or most prominent place. **b.** *(as modifier): lead singer.* **18.** example, precedence, or leadership: *the class followed the teacher's lead.* **19.** an advance or advantage held over others: *the runner had a lead of twenty yards.* **20.** anything that guides or directs; indication; clue. **21.** another name for **leash. 22.** the act or prerogative of playing the first card in a round of cards or the card so played. **23.** the principal role in a play, film, etc., or the person playing such a role. **24. a.** the principal news story in a newspaper: *the scandal was the lead in the papers.* **b.** *(as modifier): lead story.* **25.** *Music.* an important entry assigned to one part. **26.** a wire, cable, or other conductor for making an electrical connection. **27.** *Boxing.* **a.** one's habitual attacking punch. **b.** a blow made with this. **28.** a deposit of metal or ore; lode. ~See also **lead off, lead on,** etc. [OE *lǣdan;* rel. to *līthan* to travel]

lead[2] (lɛd) *n.* **1.** a heavy toxic bluish-white metallic element that is highly malleable: used in alloys, accumulators, cable sheaths, paints, and as a radiation shield. Symbol: Pb; atomic no.: 82; atomic wt.: 207.2. **2.** a lead weight suspended on a line used to take soundings of the depth of water. **3.** lead weights or shot, as used in cartridges, fishing lines, etc. **4.** a thin grooved strip of lead for holding small panes of glass or pieces of stained glass. **5.** *(pl.)* **a.** thin sheets or strips of lead used as a roof covering. **b.** a flat or low-pitched roof covered with such sheets. **6.** Also called: **leading.** *Printing.* a thin strip of type metal used for spacing between lines. **7. a.** graphite used for drawing. **b.** a thin stick of this material, esp. the core of a pencil. **8.** *(modifier)* of, consisting of, relating to, or containing lead. ~*vb. (tr.)* **9.** to fill or treat with lead. **10.** to surround, cover, or secure with lead or leads. **11.** *Printing.* to space (type) by use of leads. [OE]

lead acetate (lɛd) *n.* a white crystalline toxic solid used in dyeing cotton and in making varnishes and enamels.

leaded (ˈlɛdɪd) *adj.* (of windows) composed of small panes of glass held in place by thin grooved strips of lead: *leaded lights.*

leaden (ˈlɛdᵊn) *adj.* **1.** heavy and inert. **2.** laboured or sluggish: *leaden steps.* **3.** gloomy, spiritless, or lifeless. **4.** made partly or wholly of lead. **5.** of a dull greyish colour: *a leaden sky.* —ˈ**leadenly** *adv.* —ˈ**leadenness** *n.*

leader (ˈliːdə) *n.* **1.** a person who rules, guides, or inspires others; head. **2.** *Music.* **a.** Also called (esp. U.S. and Canad.): **concertmaster.** the principal first violinist of an orchestra, who plays solo parts, and acts as the conductor's deputy and spokesman for the orchestra. **b.** *U.S.* a conductor or director of an orchestra or chorus. **3. a.** the leading horse or dog in a team. **b.** the first man on a climbing rope. **4.** *Chiefly Brit.* the leading editorial in a newspaper. Also: **leading article. 5.** *Angling.* another word for **trace**[2]. **6.** a strip of blank film or tape used to facilitate threading a projector, developing machine, etc. **7.** (*pl.*) *Printing.* rows of dots or hyphens used to guide the reader's eye across a page, as in a table of contents. **8.** *Bot.* any of the long slender shoots that grow from the stem or branch of a tree. **9.** *Brit.* a member of the Government having primary authority in initiating legislative business (esp. in **Leader of the House of Commons** and **Leader of the House of Lords**). —ˈ**leaderless** *adj.* —ˈ**leader**ˌ**ship** *n.*

lead-free (ˈlɛdˌfriː) *adj.* See **unleaded.**

lead glass (lɛd) *n.* glass that contains lead oxide as a flux.

lead-in (ˈliːdˌɪn) *n.* **1.** an introduction to a subject. **2.** the connection between a radio transmitter, receiver, etc., and the aerial or transmission line.

leading[1] (ˈliːdɪŋ) *adj.* **1.** capable of guiding, directing, or influencing. **2.** (*prenominal*) principal or primary. **3.** in the first position.

leading[2] (ˈlɛdɪŋ) *n. Printing.* another name for **lead**[2] (sense 6).

leading aircraftman (ˈliːdɪŋ) *n. Brit. airforce.* the rank above aircraftman. —**leading aircraftwoman** *fem. n.*

leading edge (ˈliːdɪŋ) *n.* **1.** the forward edge of a propeller blade, wing, or aerofoil. Cf. **trailing edge.** ~*modifier.* **leading-edge. 2.** advanced; foremost: *leading-edge technology.*

leading light (ˈliːdɪŋ) *n.* an important or outstanding person, esp. in an organization.

leading note (ˈliːdɪŋ) *n. Music.* **1.** another word for **subtonic. 2.** (esp. in cadences) a note that tends most naturally to resolve to the note lying one semitone above it.

leading question (ˈliːdɪŋ) *n.* a question phrased in a manner that tends to suggest the desired answer, such as *What do you think of the horrible effects of pollution?*

leading rating (ˈliːdɪŋ) *n.* a rank in the Royal Navy comparable but junior to that of a corporal in the army.

leading reins *or U.S. & Canad.* **leading strings** (ˈliːdɪŋ) *pl. n.* **1.** straps or a harness and strap used to assist and control a child who is learning to walk. **2.** excessive guidance or restraint.

lead monoxide (lɛd) *n.* a poisonous insoluble oxide of lead existing in red and yellow forms: used in making glass, glazes, and cements, and as a pigment.

lead off (liːd) *vb.* (*adv.*) **1.** to initiate the action of (something); begin. ~*n.* **lead-off. 2.** an initial move or action.

lead on (liːd) *vb.* (*tr., adv.*) to lure or entice, esp. into trouble or wrongdoing.

lead pencil (lɛd) *n.* a pencil containing a thin stick of a graphite compound.

lead poisoning (lɛd) *n.* **1.** acute or chronic poisoning by lead, characterized by abdominal pain, vomiting, convulsions, and coma. **2.** *U.S. sl.* death or injury resulting from being shot with bullets.

lead screw (liːd) *n.* a threaded rod that drives the tool carriage in a lathe.

lead tetraethyl (lɛd) *n.* another name for **tetraethyl lead.**

lead time (liːd) *n.* **1.** *Manufacturing, chiefly U.S.* the time between the design of a product and its production. **2.** *Commerce.* the time from the placing of an order to the delivery of the goods.

lead up to (liːd) *vb.* (*intr., adv.* + *prep.*) **1.** to act as a preliminary or introduction to. **2.** to approach (a topic) gradually or cautiously.

leaf (liːf) *n., pl.* **leaves** (liːvz). **1.** the main organ of photosynthesis and transpiration in higher plants, usually consisting of a flat green blade attached to the stem directly or by a stalk. **2.** foliage collectively. **3. in leaf.** (of shrubs, trees, etc.) having a full complement of foliage leaves. **4.** one of the sheets of paper in a book. **5.** a hinged, sliding, or detachable part, such as an extension to a table. **6.** metal in the form of a very thin flexible sheet: *gold leaf.* **7. take a leaf out of** (*or* **from**) **someone's book.** to imitate someone, esp. in one particular course of action. **8. turn over a new leaf.** to begin a new and improved course of behaviour. ~*vb.* **9.** (when *intr.*, usually foll. by *through*) to turn (through pages, sheets, etc.) cursorily. **10.** (*intr.*) (of plants) to produce leaves. [OE] —ˈ**leafless** *adj.* —ˈ**leaf**ˌ**like** *adj.*

leafage (ˈliːfɪdʒ) *n.* a less common word for **foliage.**

leaflet (ˈliːflɪt) *n.* **1.** a printed and usually folded sheet of paper for distribution, usually free, esp. for advertising, giving information about a charity, etc. **2.** any of the subdivisions of a compound leaf such as a fern leaf. **3.** any small leaf or leaflike part. ~*vb.* **4.** to distribute leaflets (to).

leaf miner *n.* **1.** any of various insect larvae that bore into and feed on leaf tissue. **2.** the adult insect of any of these larvae.

leaf mould *n.* **1.** a nitrogen-rich material consisting of decayed leaves, etc., used as a fertilizer. **2.** any of various fungus diseases affecting the leaves of certain plants.

leaf spring *n.* **1.** one of a number of metal strips bracketed together in length to form a spring. **2.** the compound spring so formed.

leafstalk (ˈliːfˌstɔːk) *n.* the stalk attaching a leaf to a stem or branch. Technical name: **petiole.**

leafy (ˈliːfɪ) *adj.* **leafier, leafiest. 1.** covered with or having leaves. **2.** resembling a leaf or leaves. —ˈ**leafiness** *n.*

league[1] (liːg) *n.* **1.** an association or union of persons, nations, etc., formed to promote the interests of its members. **2.** an association of sporting clubs that organizes matches between member teams. **3.** a class, category, or level: *he is not in the same league.* **4. in league (with).** working or planning together with. **5.** (*modifier*) of, involving, or belonging to a league: *a league game; a league table.* ~*vb.* **leaguing, leagued. 6.** to form or be formed into a league. [C15: < OF *ligue*, < It. *liga*, ult. < L *ligāre* to bind]

league[2] (liːg) *n.* an obsolete unit of distance of varying length. It is commonly equal to 3 miles. [C14 *leuge*, < LL *leuga, leuca*, of Celtic origin]

league football *n.* **1.** Also called: **league.** *Chiefly Austral.* rugby league football. Cf. **rugby union. 2.** *Austral.* an Australian Rules competition conducted within a league. Cf. **association football.**

leaguer (ˈliːgə) *n. Chiefly U.S. & Canad.* a member of a league.

league table *n.* **1.** a list of sports clubs ranked in order according to their performance. **2.** a comparison of performance in any sphere.

leak (liːk) *n.* **1. a.** a crack, hole, etc., that allows the accidental escape or entrance of fluid, light, etc. **b.** such escaping or entering fluid, light, etc. **2. spring a leak.** to develop a leak. **3.** something resembling this in effect: *a leak in the defence system.* **4.** the loss of current from an electrical conductor because of faulty insulation, etc. **5.** a disclosure of secret information. **6.** the act or an instance of leaking. **7.** a slang word for **urination.** ~*vb.* **8.** to enter or escape or allow to enter or escape through a crack, hole, etc. **9.** (when *intr.*, often foll. by *out*) to disclose (secret information) or (of secret information) to be disclosed. **10.** (*intr.*) a slang word for **urinate.** [C15: < ON] —ˈ**leaker** *n.*

leakage (ˈliːkɪdʒ) *n.* **1.** the act or an instance of leaking. **2.** something that escapes or enters by a leak. **3.** *Physics.* an undesired flow of electric current, neutrons, etc.

leaky (ˈliːkɪ) *adj.* **leakier, leakiest.** leaking or tending to leak. —ˈ**leakiness** *n.*

leal (liːl) *adj. Arch. or Scot.* loyal; faithful. [C13: < OF *leial,* < L *lēgālis* LEGAL; rel. to LOYAL] —ˈ**leally** *adv.* —**lealty** (ˈliːəltɪ) *n.*

lean[1] (liːn) *vb.* **leaning; leant** *or* **leaned. 1.** (foll. by *against, on,* or *upon*) to rest or cause to rest against a support. **2.** to incline or cause to incline from a vertical position. **3.** (*intr.;* foll. by *to* or *towards*) to have or express a tendency or leaning. ~*n.* **4.** the condition of inclining from a vertical position. [OE *hleonian, hlinian*]

lean[2] (liːn) *adj.* **1.** (esp. of a person or animal) having no surplus flesh or bulk; not fat. **2.** not bulky or full. **3.** (of meat) having little or no fat. **4.** not rich, abundant, or satisfying. **5.** (of mixture of fuel and air) containing insufficient fuel and too much air. ~*n.* **6.** the part of meat that contains little or no fat. [OE *hlǣne,* of Gmc origin] —ˈ**leanly** *adv.* —ˈ**leanness** *n.*

lean-burn *adj.* (esp. of an internal-combustion engine) designed to use a lean mixture of fuel and air in order to reduce petrol consumption and exhaust emissions.

leaning (ˈliːnɪŋ) *n.* a tendency or inclination.

leant (lɛnt) *vb.* a past tense and past participle of **lean**[1].

lean-to *n., pl.* **-tos. 1.** a roof that has a single slope adjoining a wall or building. **2.** a shed or outbuilding with such a roof.

leap (liːp) *vb.* **leaping; leapt** *or* **leaped. 1.** (*intr.*) to jump suddenly from one place to another. **2.** (*intr.;* often foll. by *at*) to move or react quickly. **3.** (*tr.*) to jump over. **4.** to come into prominence rapidly: *the thought leapt into his mind.* **5.** (*tr.*) to cause (an animal, esp. a horse) to jump a barrier. ~*n.* **6.** the act of jumping. **7.** a spot from which a leap was or may be made. **8.** an abrupt change or increase. **9. a leap in the dark.** an action performed without knowledge of the consequences. **10. by leaps and bounds.** with unexpectedly rapid progress. [OE *hlēapan*] —ˈ**leaper** *n.*

leapfrog (ˈliːpˌfrɒg) *n.* **1.** a children's game in which each player in turn leaps over the others' bent backs. ~*vb.* **-frogging, -frogged. 2. a.** (*intr.*) to play leapfrog. **b.** (*tr.*) to leap in this way over (something). **3.** to advance or cause to advance by jumps or stages.

leapt (lɛpt, liːpt) *vb.* a past tense and past participle of **leap.**

leap year *n.* a calendar year of 366 days, February 29 (**leap day**) being the additional day, that occurs every four years (those whose number is divisible by four) except for century years whose number is not divisible by 400.

learn (lɜːn) *vb.* **learning; learnt** *or* **learned** (lɜːnd). **1.** (when *tr., may take a clause as object*) to gain knowledge of (something) or acquire skill in (some art or practice). **2.** (*tr.*) to commit to memory. **3.** (*tr.*) to gain by experience, example, etc. **4.** (*intr.;* often foll. by *of* or *about*) to become informed; know. **5.** *Not standard.* to teach. [OE *leornian*] —ˈ**learnable** *adj.* —ˈ**learner** *n.*

▷ **Usage.** Educated writers and speakers of English do not use *learn* for *teach: that will teach* (not *learn*) *him a lesson.*

learned (ˈlɜːnɪd) *adj.* **1.** having great knowledge or erudition. **2.** involving or characterized by scholarship. **3.** (*prenominal*) a title applied in referring to a member of the legal profession, esp. to a barrister: *my learned friend.* —ˈ**learnedly** *adv.* —ˈ**learnedness** *n.*

learning (ˈlɜːnɪŋ) *n.* **1.** knowledge gained by study; instruction or scholarship. **2.** the act of gaining knowledge.

learnt (lɜːnt) *vb.* a past tense and past participle of **learn.**

lease (liːs) *n.* **1.** a contract by which property is conveyed to a person for a specified period, usually for rent. **2.** the instrument by which such property is conveyed. **3.** the period of time for which it is conveyed. **4.** a prospect of renewed health, happiness, etc.: *a new lease of life.* ~*vb.* (*tr.*) **5.** to grant possession of (land, buildings, etc.) by lease. **6.** to take a lease of (property); hold under a lease. [C15: via Anglo-F < OF *lais* (n.), < *laissier* to let go, < L *laxāre* to loosen] —ˈ**leasable** *adj.* —ˈ**leaser** *n.*

leaseback (ˈliːsˌbæk) *n.* a transaction in which the buyer leases the property to the seller.

leasehold (ˈliːsˌhəʊld) *n.* **1.** land or property held under a lease. **2.** the tenure by which such property is held. **3.** (*modifier*) held under a lease. —ˈ**leaseˌholder** *n.*

leash (liːʃ) *n.* **1.** a line or rope used to walk or control a dog or other animal; lead. **2.** something resembling this in function: *he kept a tight leash on his emotions.* **3. straining at the leash.** eagerly impatient to begin something. ~*vb.* **4.** (*tr.*) to control or secure as by a leash. [C13: < OF *laisse,* < *laissier* to loose (hence, to let a dog run on a leash), ult. < L *laxus* lax]

least (liːst) *determiner.* **1. a. the.** the superlative of **little:** *you have the least talent of anyone.* **b.** (*as pronoun; functioning as sing.*): *least isn't necessarily worst.* **2. at least. a.** if nothing else: *you should at least try.* **b.** at the least. **3. at the least.** Also: **at least.** at the minimum: *at the least you should earn a hundred pounds.* **4. in the least.** (*usually used with a negative*) in the slightest degree; at all: *I don't mind in the least.* ~*adv.* **5. the least.** superlative of **little:** *they travel the least.* ~*adj.* **6.** of very little importance. [OE *lǣst,* sup. of *lǣssa* less]

least common denominator *n.* another name for **lowest common denominator.**

least common multiple *n.* another name for **lowest common multiple.**

least squares *n.* a method for determining the best value of an unknown quantity relating one or more sets of observations or measurements, esp. to find a curve that best fits a set of data.

leastways (ˈliːstˌweɪz) *or U.S. & Canad.* **leastwise** *adv. Inf.* at least; anyway; at any rate.

leather (ˈlɛðə) *n.* **1. a.** a material consisting of the skin of an animal made smooth and flexible by tanning, removing the hair, etc. **b.** (*as modifier*): *leather goods.* **2.** something, such as a garment, made of leather. ~*vb.* (*tr.*) **3.** to cover with leather. **4.** to whip as with a leather strap. [OE *lether-* (in compound words)]

leatherjacket (ˈlɛðəˌdʒækɪt) *n.* **1.** any of various tropical fishes having a leathery skin. **2.** the greyish-brown tough-skinned larva of certain craneflies, which destroy the roots of grasses, etc.

leathern (ˈlɛðən) *adj. Arch.* made of or resembling leather.

leatherneck (ˈlɛðəˌnɛk) *n. Sl.* a member of the U.S. Marine Corps. [< the custom of facing the neckband of their uniform with leather]

leathery (ˈlɛðərɪ) *adj.* having the appearance or texture of leather, esp. in toughness. —ˈ**leatheriness** *n.*

leave[1] (liːv) *vb.* **leaving, left.** (*mainly tr.*) **1.** (*also intr.*) to go or depart (from a person or place). **2.** to cause to remain behind, often by mistake, in a place: *he often leaves his keys in his coat.* **3.** to cause to be or remain in a specified state: *paying the bill left him penniless.* **4.** to renounce or abandon: *to leave a political movement.* **5.** to refrain from consuming or doing something: *the things we have left undone.* **6.** to result in; cause: *childhood problems often leave emotional scars.* **7.** to entrust or commit: *leave the shopping to her.* **8.** to pass in a specified direction: *flying out of the country, we left the cliffs on our left.* **9.** to be survived by (members of one's family): *he leaves a wife and two children.* **10.** to bequeath: *he left his investments to his children.* **11.** (*tr.*) to have as a remainder: *37 –14 leaves 23.* **12.** *Not standard.* to permit; let. **13. leave (someone) alone. a.** Also: **let alone.** See **let**[1] (sense 6). **b.** to permit to stay or be alone. [OE *lǣfan;* rel. to *belīfan* to be left as a remainder] ~See also **leave off, leave out.** —ˈ**leaver** *n.*

▷ **Usage.** In educated usage, *leave* is not used in the sense of *let* (allow): *let him go,* not *leave him go.*

leave[2] (liːv) *n.* **1.** permission to do something: *he was granted leave to speak.* **2. by** *or* **with your leave.** with your permission. **3.** permission to be absent, as from a place of work: *leave of absence.* **4.** the duration of such absence: *ten days' leave.* **5.** a farewell or departure (esp. in **take (one's) leave**). **6. on leave.** officially excused from work or duty. **7. take leave (of).** to say farewell (to). [OE *lēaf*; rel. to *alȳfan* to permit]

leave[3] (liːv) *vb.* **leaving, leaved.** (*intr.*) to produce or grow leaves.

leaved (liːvd) *adj.* **a.** having a leaf or leaves; leafed. **b.** (*in combination*): *a five-leaved stem.*

leaven ('lɛvən) *n. also* **leavening. 1.** any substance that produces fermentation in dough or batter, such as yeast, and causes it to rise. **2.** a piece of such a substance kept to ferment a new batch of dough. **3.** an agency or influence that produces a gradual change. ~*vb.* (*tr.*) **4.** to cause fermentation in (dough or batter). **5.** to pervade, causing a gradual change, esp. with some moderating or enlivening influence. [C14: via OF ult. < L *levāmen* relief, (hence, raising agent), < *levāre* to raise]

leave off *vb.* **1.** (*intr.*) to stop; cease. **2.** (*tr., adv.*) to stop wearing or using.

leave out *vb.* (*tr., adv.*) **1.** to cause to remain in the open. **2.** to omit or exclude.

leaves (liːvz) *n.* the plural of **leaf.**

leave-taking *n.* the act of departing; a farewell.

leavings ('liːvɪŋz) *pl. n.* something remaining, such as food on a plate, residue, refuse, etc.

Lebensraum ('leɪbənzˌraʊm) *n.* territory claimed by a nation or state as necessary for survival or growth. [G, lit.: living space]

lech (lɛtʃ) *Inf.* ~*vb.* **1.** (*intr.*; usually foll. by *after*) to behave lecherously (towards); lust (after). ~*n.* **2.** a lecherous act or indulgence. [C19: back formation < LECHER]

lecher ('lɛtʃə) *n.* a promiscuous or lewd man. [C12: < OF *lecheor*, < *lechier* to lick, of Gmc origin]

lecherous ('lɛtʃərəs) *adj.* characterized by or inciting lechery. —'**lecherously** *adv.*

lechery ('lɛtʃərɪ) *n., pl.* **-eries.** unrestrained and promiscuous sexuality.

lecithin ('lɛsɪθɪn) *n. Biochem.* any of a group of yellow-brown compounds that are found in many plant and animal tissues, esp. egg yolk: used in making candles, cosmetics, and inks, and as an emulsifier and stabilizer (**E322**) in foods. [C19: < Gk *lekithos* egg yolk]

lectern ('lɛktən) *n.* **1.** a reading desk in a church. **2.** any similar desk or support. [C14: < OF *lettrun*, < LL *lectrum*, ult. < *legere* to read]

lectionary ('lɛkʃənərɪ) *n., pl.* **-aries.** a book containing readings appointed to be read at divine services. [C15: < Church L *lectiōnārium*, < *lectio* a reading, < *legere* to read]

lector ('lɛktɔː) *n.* **1.** a lecturer or reader in certain universities. **2.** *R.C. Church.* **a.** a person appointed to read lessons at certain services. **b.** (in convents or monastic establishments) a member of the community appointed to read aloud during meals. [C15: < L, < *legere* to read]

lecture ('lɛktʃə) *n.* **1.** a discourse on a particular subject given or read to an audience. **2.** the text of such a discourse. **3.** a method of teaching by formal discourse. **4.** a lengthy reprimand or scolding. ~*vb.* **5.** to give or read a lecture (to an audience or class). **6.** (*tr.*) to reprimand at length. [C14: < Med. L *lectūra* reading, < *legere* to read] —'**lecturer** *n.* —'**lectureship** *n.*

led (lɛd) *vb.* the past tense and past participle of **lead**[1].

LED *Electronics. abbrev. for* light-emitting diode.

lederhosen ('leɪdəˌhəʊzən) *pl. n.* leather shorts with H-shaped braces, worn by men in Austria, Bavaria, etc. [G]

ledge (lɛdʒ) *n.* **1.** a narrow horizontal surface resembling a shelf and projecting from a wall, window, etc. **2.** a layer of rock that contains an ore; vein. **3.** a ridge of rock that lies beneath the surface of the sea. **4.** a narrow shelflike projection on a cliff or mountain. [C14 *legge*, ? < *leggen* to LAY[1]] —'**ledgy** *or* **ledged** *adj.*

ledger ('lɛdʒə) *n.* **1.** *Book-keeping.* the principal book in which the commercial transactions of a company are recorded. **2.** *Angling.* a wire trace that allows the weight to rest on the bottom and the bait to float freely. ~*vb.* **3.** (*intr.*) *Angling.* to fish using a ledger. [C15 *legger* book retained in a specific place, prob. < *leggen* to LAY[1]]

ledger line *n. Music.* a short line placed above or below the staff to accommodate notes representing pitches above or below the staff.

lee (liː) *n.* **1.** a sheltered part or side; the side away from the direction from which the wind is blowing. ~*adj.* **2.** (*prenominal*) *Naut.* on, at, or towards the side or part away from the wind: *on a lee shore.* Cf. **weather** (sense 4). [OE *hlēow* shelter]

leech[1] (liːtʃ) *n.* **1.** an annelid worm which has a sucker at each end of the body and feeds on the blood or tissues of other animals. **2.** a person who clings to or preys on another person. **3. a.** an archaic word for **physician. b.** (*in combination*): *leechcraft.* ~*vb.* (*tr.*) **4.** to use leeches to suck the blood of (a person), as a method of medical treatment. [OE *lǣce*, *lȳce*]

leech[2] (liːtʃ) *n. Naut.* the after edge of a fore-and-aft sail or either of the vertical edges of a squaresail. [C15: of Gmc origin]

leek (liːk) *n.* **1.** a vegetable with a slender white bulb, cylindrical stem, and broad flat overlapping leaves. **2.** a leek, or a representation of one, as a national emblem of Wales. [OE *lēac*]

leer (lɪə) *vb.* **1.** (*intr.*) to give an oblique, sneering, or suggestive look or grin. ~*n.* **2.** such a look. [C16: ? verbal use of obs. *leer* cheek, < OE *hlēor*] —'**leering** *adj., n.* —'**leeringly** *adv.*

leery ('lɪərɪ) *adj.* **leerier, leeriest 1.** *Now chiefly dialect.* knowing or sly. **2.** *Sl.* (foll. by *of*) suspicious or wary. [C18: ? < obs. sense (to look askance) of LEER] —'**leeriness** *n.*

lees (liːz) *pl. n.* the sediment from an alcoholic drink. [C14: pl. of obs. *lee*, < OF, prob. < Celtic]

leet (liːt) *n. Scot.* a list of candidates for an office. [C15: ? < Anglo-F *litte*, var. of LIST[1]]

leeward ('liːwəd; *Naut.* 'luːəd) *Chiefly naut.* ~*adj.* **1.** of, in, or moving to the quarter towards which the wind blows. ~*n.* **2.** the point or quarter towards which the wind blows. **3.** the side towards the lee. ~*adv.* **4.** towards the lee. ~Cf. **windward.**

leeway ('liːˌweɪ) *n.* **1.** room for free movement within limits, as in action or expenditure. **2.** sideways drift of a boat or aircraft.

left[1] (lɛft) *adj.* **1.** (*usually prenominal*) of or designating the side of something or someone that faces west when the front is turned towards the north. **2.** (*usually prenominal*) worn on a left hand, foot, etc. **3.** (*sometimes cap.*) of or relating to the political left. **4.** (*sometimes cap.*) radical or progressive. ~*adv.* **5.** on or in the direction of the left. ~*n.* **6.** a left side, direction, position, area, or part. Related adjs.: **sinister, sinistral. 7.** (*often cap.*) the supporters or advocates of varying degrees of social, political, or economic change, reform, or revolution. **8.** *Boxing.* **a.** a blow with the left hand. **b.** the left hand. [OE *left* idle, weak, var. of *lyft-* (in *lyftādl* palsy, lit.: left-disease)]

left[2] (lɛft) *vb.* the past tense and past participle of **leave**[1].

left-hand *adj.* (*prenominal*) **1.** of, relating to, located on, or moving towards the left. **2.** for use by the left hand; left-handed.

left-handed *adj.* **1.** using the left hand with greater ease than the right. **2.** performed with the left hand. **3.** designed or adapted for use by the left hand. **4.** awkward or clumsy. **5.** ironically ambiguous: *a left-handed compliment.* **6.** turning from right to left; anticlockwise. ~*adv.* **7.** with the left hand. —ˌ**left-'handedly** *adv.* —ˌ**left-'handedness** *n.* —ˌ**left-'hander** *n.*

leftist ('lɛftɪst) *adj.* **1.** of, tending towards, or relating to the political left or its principles. ~*n.*

2. a person who supports or belongs to the political left. —**ˈleftism** *n.*

left-luggage office *n. Brit.* a place at a railway station, etc., where luggage may be left for a small charge. U.S. and Canad. name: **checkroom.**

leftover (ˈlɛftˌəʊvə) *n.* **1.** (*often pl.*) an unused portion or remnant, as of material or of cooked food. ~*adj.* **2.** left as an unused portion.

leftward (ˈlɛftwəd) *adj.* **1.** on or towards the left. ~*adv.* **2.** a variant of **leftwards.**

leftwards (ˈlɛftwədz) *or* **leftward** *adv.* towards or on the left.

left wing *n.* **1.** (*often cap.*) the leftist faction of an assembly, party, group, etc.; the radical or progressive wing. **2.** *Sports.* **a.** the left-hand side of the field of play from the point of view of either team facing its opponents' goal. **b.** a player positioned in this area in certain games. ~*adj.* **left-wing. 3.** of, belonging to, or relating to the political left wing. —ˌ**left-ˈwinger** *n.*

lefty (ˈlɛftɪ) *n., pl.* **lefties.** *Inf.* **1.** a left-winger. **2.** *Chiefly U.S. & Canad.* a left-handed person.

leg (lɛg) *n.* **1.** either of the two lower limbs in humans, or any similar or analogous structure in animals that is used for locomotion or support. **2.** this part of an animal, esp. the thigh, used for food: *leg of lamb.* **3.** something similar to a leg in appearance or function, such as one of the four supporting members of a chair. **4.** a branch, limb, or part of a forked or jointed object. **5.** the part of a garment that covers the leg. **6.** a section or part of a journey or course. **7.** a single stage, lap, length, etc., in a relay race. **8.** either the opposite or adjacent side of a right-angled triangle. **9.** one of a series of games, matches, or parts of games. **10.** *Austral. & N.Z.* either one of two races on which a cumulative bet has been placed. **11.** *Cricket.* **a.** the side of the field to the left of and behind a right-handed batsman as he faces the bowler. **b.** (*as modifier*): *a leg slip; leg stump.* **12. not have a leg to stand on.** *Inf.* to have no reasonable or logical basis for an opinion or argument. **13. on his, its,** etc., **last legs.** (of a person or thing) worn out; exhausted. **14. pull (someone's) leg.** *Inf.* to tease, fool, or make fun of (someone). **15. shake a leg.** *Inf.* to hurry up: usually used in the imperative. **16. stretch one's legs.** to stand up or walk around, esp. after sitting for some time. ~*vb.* **legging, legged. 17. leg it.** *Inf.* to walk, run, or hurry. [C13: < ON *leggr,* <?]

leg. *abbrev. for:* **1.** legal. **2.** legate. **3.** legato. **4.** legislation. **5.** legislative. **6.** legislature.

legacy (ˈlɛgəsɪ) *n., pl.* **-cies. 1.** a gift by will, esp. of money or personal property. **2.** something handed down or received from an ancestor or predecessor. [C14 (meaning: office of a legate), C15 (meaning: bequest): < Med. L *lēgātia* commission; see LEGATE]

legal (ˈliːgᵊl) *adj.* **1.** established by or founded upon law; lawful. **2.** of or relating to law. **3.** recognized, enforceable, or having a remedy at law rather than in equity. **4.** relating to or characteristic of the profession of law. [C16: < L *lēgālis,* < *lēx* law] —**ˈlegally** *adv.*

legal aid *n.* financial assistance available to persons unable to meet the full cost of legal proceedings.

legalese (ˌliːgəˈliːz) *n.* the conventional language in which legal documents are written.

legalism (ˈliːgəˌlɪzəm) *n.* strict adherence to the law, esp. the letter of the law rather than its spirit. —**ˈlegalist** *n., adj.* —ˌ**legalˈistic** *adj.*

legality (lɪˈgælɪtɪ) *n., pl.* **-ties. 1.** the state or quality of being legal or lawful. **2.** adherence to legal principles.

legalize *or* **-ise** (ˈliːgəˌlaɪz) *vb.* (*tr.*) to make lawful or legal. —ˌ**legaliˈzation** *or* **-iˈsation** *n.*

legal tender *n.* currency that a creditor must by law accept in redemption of a debt.

legate (ˈlɛgɪt) *n.* **1.** a messenger, envoy, or delegate. **2.** *R.C. Church.* an emissary representing the Pope. [OE, via OF < L *lēgātus* deputy, < *lēgāre* to delegate; rel. to *lēx* law] —**ˈlegateˌship** *n.*

legatee (ˌlɛgəˈtiː) *n.* a person to whom a legacy is bequeathed.

legation (lɪˈgeɪʃən) *n.* **1.** a diplomatic mission headed by a minister. **2.** the official residence and office of a diplomatic minister. **3.** the act of sending forth a diplomatic envoy. **4.** the mission of a diplomatic envoy. **5.** the rank or office of a legate. [C15: < L *lēgātiō,* < *lēgātus* LEGATE]

legato (lɪˈgɑːtəʊ) *Music.* ~*adj., adv.* **1.** to be performed smoothly and connectedly. ~*n., pl.* **-tos. 2. a.** a style of playing with no perceptible gaps between notes. **b.** (*as modifier*): *a legato passage.* [C19: < It., lit.: bound]

leg before wicket *n. Cricket.* a manner of dismissal on the grounds that a batsman has been struck on the leg by a bowled ball that otherwise would have hit the wicket. Abbrev.: **lbw.**

leg break *n. Cricket.* a bowled ball that spins from leg to off on pitching.

legend (ˈlɛdʒənd) *n.* **1.** a popular story handed down from earlier times whose truth has not been ascertained. **2.** a group of such stories: *the Arthurian legend.* **3.** a modern story that has the characteristics of a traditional tale. **4.** a person whose fame or notoriety makes him a source of exaggerated or romanticized tales. **5.** an inscription or title, as on a coin or beneath a coat of arms. **6.** explanatory matter accompanying a table, map, chart, etc. [C14 (in the sense: a saint's life): < Med. L *legenda* passages to be read, < L *legere* to read]

legendary (ˈlɛdʒəndərɪ, -drɪ) *adj.* **1.** of or relating to legend. **2.** celebrated or described in a legend or legends. **3.** very famous or notorious.

legerdemain (ˌlɛdʒədəˈmeɪn) *n.* **1.** another name for **sleight of hand. 2.** cunning deception or trickery. [C15: < OF: light of hand]

leger line (ˈlɛdʒə) *n.* a variant spelling of **ledger line.**

legged (ˈlɛgɪd, lɛgd) *adj.* **a.** having a leg or legs. **b.** (*in combination*): *three-legged; long-legged.*

leggiero (lɛdʒˈɛərəʊ) *adj., adv. Music.* to be performed lightly and nimbly. [It.]

leggings (ˈlɛgɪŋz) *pl. n.* **1.** an extra outer covering for the lower legs. **2.** children's closefitting trousers, usually with a strap under the instep, worn for warmth in winter. **3.** a fashion garment for women consiting of closefitting trousers.

leggy (ˈlɛgɪ) *adj.* **-gier, -giest. 1.** having unusually long legs. **2.** (of a woman) having long and shapely legs. **3.** (of a plant) having an unusually long and weak stem. —**ˈlegginess** *n.*

leghorn (ˈlɛgˌhɔːn) *n.* **1.** a type of Italian wheat straw that is woven into hats. **2.** any hat made from this straw. [C19: after LEGHORN (Livorno)]

Leghorn *n.* **1.** (ˈlɛgˌhɔːn). the English name for Livorno, a port in W central Italy. **2.** (lɛˈgɔːn). a breed of domestic fowl.

legible (ˈlɛdʒəbᵊl) *adj.* (of handwriting, print, etc.) able to be read or deciphered. [C14: < LL *legibilis,* < L *legere* to read] —ˌ**legiˈbility** *n.* —**ˈlegibly** *adv.*

legion (ˈliːdʒən) *n.* **1.** a unit in the ancient Roman army of infantry with supporting cavalry of three to six thousand men. **2.** any large military force: *the French Foreign Legion.* **3.** (*usually cap.*) an association of ex-servicemen: *the British Legion.* **4.** (*often pl.*) any very large number. ~*adj.* **5.** (*usually postpositive*) very numerous. [C13: < OF, < L *legio,* < *legere* to choose]

legionary (ˈliːdʒənərɪ) *adj.* **1.** of a legion. ~*n., pl.* **-aries. 2.** a soldier belonging to a legion.

legionnaire (ˌliːdʒəˈnɛə) *n.* (*often cap.*) a member of certain military forces or associations.

Legionnaire's disease (ˌliːdʒəˈnɛəz) *n.* a serious, sometimes fatal infection, caused by bacteria (**legionella**), which has symptoms similar to those of pneumonia. [C20: after the outbreak at a meeting of the American Legion in Philadelphia in 1976]

legislate (ˈlɛdʒɪsˌleɪt) *vb.* **1.** (*intr.*) to make or pass laws. **2.** (*tr.*) to bring into effect by legislation. [C18: back formation < LEGISLATOR]

legislation (ˌlɛdʒɪsˈleɪʃən) *n.* **1.** the act or process of making laws. **2.** the laws so made.
legislative (ˈlɛdʒɪslətɪv) *adj.* **1.** of or relating to legislation. **2.** having the power or function of legislating: *a legislative assembly.* **3.** of or relating to a legislature. —ˈ**legislatively** *adv.*
legislative assembly *n.* (*often cap.*) **1.** the bicameral legislature in 28 states of the U.S. **2.** the unicameral legislature in most Canadian provinces. **3.** the lower chamber of the bicameral state legislatures in several other Commonwealth countries, such as Australia. **4.** any assembly with legislative powers.
legislative council *n.* (*often cap.*) **1.** the upper chamber of certain bicameral legislatures, such as those of the Indian and Australian states (except Queensland). **2.** the unicameral legislature of certain colonies or dependent territories. **3.** (in the U.S.) a committee of members of both chambers of a state legislature that discusses problems, constructs a legislative programme, etc.
legislator (ˈlɛdʒɪsˌleɪtə) *n.* **1.** a person concerned with the making of laws. **2.** a member of a legislature. [C17: < L *lēgis lātor,* < *lēx* law + *lātor* < *lātus,* p.p. of *ferre* to bring]
legislature (ˈlɛdʒɪsˌleɪtʃə) *n.* a body of persons vested with power to make and repeal laws.
legit (lɪˈdʒɪt) *Sl.* ~*adj.* **1.** short for **legitimate.** ~*n.* **2.** legitimate drama.
legitimate *adj.* (lɪˈdʒɪtɪmɪt). **1.** born in lawful wedlock. **2.** conforming to established standards of usage, behaviour, etc. **3.** based on correct or acceptable principles of reasoning. **4.** authorized by or in accordance with law. **5.** of, relating to, or ruling by hereditary right: *a legitimate monarch.* **6.** of or relating to serious drama as distinct from films, television, vaudeville, etc. ~*vb.* (lɪˈdʒɪtɪˌmeɪt). **7.** (*tr.*) to make, pronounce, or show to be legitimate. [C15: < Med. L *lēgitimātus* made legal, < *lēx* law] —**leˈgitimacy** *n.* —**leˈgitimately** *adv.* —**leˌgitiˈmation** *n.*
legitimatize, -tise (lɪˈdʒɪtɪməˌtaɪz) *or* **legitimize, -mise** (lɪˈdʒɪtɪˌmaɪz) *vb.* (*tr.*) to make legitimate; legalize. —**leˌgitimatiˈzation, -tiˈsation** *or* **leˌgitimiˈzation, -miˈsation** *n.*
legitimist (lɪˈdʒɪtɪmɪst) *n.* a monarchist who supports the rule of a legitimate dynasty or of its senior branch. —**leˈgitimism** *n.*
legless (ˈlɛglɪs) *adj.* **1.** without legs. **2.** *Inf.* very drunk.
Lego (ˈlɛgəʊ) *n. Trademark.* a construction toy consisting of plastic bricks that fit together with studs. [C20: < Danish *leg godt* play well]
leg-of-mutton *or* **leg-o'-mutton** *n.* (*modifier*) (of a sail, sleeve, etc.) tapering sharply.
leg-pull *n. Brit. inf.* a practical joke or mild deception.
legroom (ˈlɛgˌruːm) *n.* room to move one's legs comfortably, as in a car.
leg rope *n. Austral. & N.Z.* a rope used to secure an animal by its hind leg.
leguan (ˈlɛgʊˌɑːn) *n.* a large amphibious S African lizard. [< Du. *leguaan*]
legume (ˈlɛgjuːm, lɪˈgjuːm) *n.* **1.** the long dry fruit produced by leguminous plants; a pod. **2.** any of various table vegetables, esp. beans or peas. **3.** any leguminous plant. [C17: < F *légume,* < L *legūmen* bean, < *legere* to pick (a crop)]
leguminous (lɪˈgjuːmɪnəs) *adj.* of, relating to, or belonging to any family of flowering plants having pods (or legumes) as fruits and root nodules enabling storage of nitrogen-rich material. [C17: < L *legūmen;* see LEGUME]
legwarmer (ˈlɛgˌwɔːmə) *n.* one of a pair of garments resembling stockings without feet, often worn over jeans, tights, etc., or during exercise.
legwork (ˈlɛgˌwɜːk) *n. Inf.* work that involves travelling on foot or as if on foot.
lei (leɪ) *n.* (in Hawaii) a garland of flowers, worn around the neck. [< Hawaiian]
Leibnitzian (laɪbˈnɪtsɪən) *adj.* of the philosophy of Gottfried Leibnitz (1646–1716), German mathematician and philosopher, in which matter was conceived as existing in the form of independent units or monads, synchronized by pre-established harmony.
Leicester (ˈlɛstə) *n.* a mild dark orange cheese similar to Cheddar but looser and more moist. [after *Leicester,* a county in England]
Leics *abbrev. for* Leicestershire.
leishmaniasis (ˌliːʃməˈnaɪəsɪs) *or* **leishmaniosis** (liːʃˌmeɪnɪˈəʊsɪs, -ˌmæn-) *n.* any disease, such as kala-azar, caused by protozoa of the genus *Leishmania.* [C20: NL, after Sir W. B. *Leishman* (1865-1926), Scot. bacteriologist]
leister (ˈliːstə) *n.* **1.** a spear with three or more prongs for spearing fish, esp. salmon. ~*vb.* **2.** (*tr.*) to spear (a fish) with a leister. [C16: < Scand.]
leisure (ˈlɛʒə) *n.* **1. a.** time or opportunity for ease, relaxation, etc. **b.** (*as modifier*): *leisure activities.* **2.** ease or leisureliness. **3. at leisure. a.** having free time. **b.** not occupied or engaged. **c.** without hurrying. **4. at one's leisure.** when one has free time. [C14: < OF *leisir;* ult. < L *licēre* to be allowed] —ˈ**leisured** *adj.*
leisure centre *n.* a building designed to provide facilities for a range of leisure pursuits, such as a library, sports hall, café, and rooms for meetings.
leisurely (ˈlɛʒəlɪ) *adj.* **1.** unhurried; relaxed. ~*adv.* **2.** without haste; in a relaxed way. —ˈ**leisureliness** *n.*
leitmotiv *or* **leitmotif** (ˈlaɪtməʊˌtiːf) *n.* **1.** *Music.* a recurring short melodic phrase used, esp. in Wagnerian music dramas, to suggest a character, thing, etc. **2.** an often repeated image or theme in a literary work. [C19: < G: leading motif]
lek (lɛk) *n.* a small area in which birds of certain species, notably the black grouse, gather for sexual display and courtship. [C19: ?< dialect *lake* (vb.) < OE *lácan* to frolic, fight, or ?< Swedish *leka* to play]
lekker (ˈlɛkə) *adj. S. African sl.* pleasing, enjoyable, or likeable. [< Afrik., < Du.]
LEM (lɛm) *n. acronym for* lunar excursion module.
lemma (ˈlɛmə) *n., pl.* **-mas** *or* **-mata** (-mətə). **1.** a subsidiary proposition, assumed to be valid, that is used in the proof of another proposition. **2.** an argument or theme, esp. when used as the subject or title of a composition. **3.** *Linguistics.* a word considered as its citation form together with all the inflected forms. [C16 (meaning: proposition), C17 (meaning: title, theme): via L < Gk: premise, < *lambanein* to take (for granted)]
lemming (ˈlɛmɪŋ) *n.* **1.** any of various volelike rodents of northern and arctic regions of Europe, Asia, and North America. **2.** a member of any group following an unthinking course towards destruction. [C17: < Norwegian] —ˈ**lemmingˌlike** *adj.*
lemon (ˈlɛmən) *n.* **1.** a small Asian evergreen tree widely cultivated in warm and tropical regions for its edible fruits. Related adjs.: **citric, citrine, citrous. 2. a.** the yellow oval fruit of this tree, having juicy acidic flesh. **b.** (*as modifier*): *a lemon jelly.* **3.** Also called: **lemon yellow. a.** a greenish-yellow or pale yellow colour. **b.** (*as adj.*): *lemon wallpaper.* **4.** a distinctive tart flavour made from or in imitation of the lemon. **5.** *Sl.* a person or thing considered to be useless or defective. [C14: < Med. L *lemōn-,* < Ar. *laymūn*] —ˈ**lemony** *adj.*
lemonade (ˌlɛməˈneɪd) *n.* a drink made from lemon juice, sugar, and water or from carbonated water, citric acid, etc.
lemon balm *n.* the full name of **balm.**
lemon cheese *or* **curd** *n.* a soft spread made from lemons, sugar, eggs, and butter.
lemon grass *n.* a perennial grass with a large flower spike: grown in tropical regions as the source of an aromatic oil (**lemon grass oil**).
lemon sole *n.* a European flatfish with a variegated brown body: highly valued as a food fish.
lemon squash *n. Brit.* a drink made from a sweetened lemon concentrate and water.
lemur (ˈliːmə) *n.* **1.** any of a family of

Madagascan prosimian primates such as the ring-tailed lemur. They are typically arboreal, having foxy faces and long tails. **2.** any similar or closely related animal, such as a loris or indris. [C18: NL, adapted < L *lemurēs* ghosts; so named for its ghost-like face and nocturnal habits] —**lemuroid** (ˈlɛmjʊˌrɔɪd) *n., adj.*

lend (lɛnd) *vb.* **lending, lent. 1.** (*tr.*) to permit the use of (something) with the expectation of its return. **2.** to provide (money) temporarily, often at interest. **3.** (*intr.*) to provide loans, esp. as a profession. **4.** (*tr.*) to impart or contribute (something, esp. some abstract quality): *her presence lent beauty.* **5. lend an ear.** to listen. **6. lend oneself** *or* **itself.** to possess the right characteristics or qualities for: *the novel lends itself to serialization.* [C15 *lende* (orig. the past tense), < OE *lǣnan,* < *lǣn* loan] —**ˈlender** *n.*

▷ **Usage.** Although the use of *loan* as a verb equivalent to *lend* is widespread, it is avoided by careful speakers and writers except when referring to the formal lending of money: *the bank loaned him the money.*

lending library *n.* **1.** Also called (esp. U.S.): **circulating library.** the department of a public library providing books for use outside the building. **2.** a small commercial library.

lend-lease *n.* (during World War II) the system organized by the U.S. in 1941 by which equipment and services were provided for countries fighting Germany.

length (lɛŋkθ, lɛŋθ) *n.* **1.** the linear extent or measurement of something from end to end, usually being the longest dimension. **2.** the extent of something from beginning to end, measured in some more or less regular units or intervals: *the book was 600 pages in length.* **3.** a specified distance, esp. between two positions: *the length of a race.* **4.** a period of time, as between specified limits or moments. **5.** a piece or section of something narrow and long: *a length of tubing.* **6.** the quality, state, or fact of being long rather than short. **7.** (*usually pl.*) the amount of trouble taken in pursuing or achieving something (esp. in **to great lengths**). **8.** (*often pl.*) the extreme or limit of action (esp. in **to any length(s)**). **9.** *Prosody, phonetics.* the metrical quantity or temporal duration of a vowel or syllable. **10.** the distance from one end of a rectangular swimming bath to the other. **11. at length. a.** in depth; fully. **b.** eventually. **c.** interminably. [OE *lengthu*]

lengthen (ˈlɛŋkθən, ˈlɛŋθən) *vb.* to make or become longer. —**ˈlengthener** *n.*

lengthways (ˈlɛŋkθˌweɪz, ˈlɛŋθ-) *or* **lengthwise** *adv., adj.* in, according to, or along the direction of length.

lengthy (ˈlɛŋkθɪ, ˈlɛŋθɪ) *adj.* **lengthier, lengthiest.** of relatively great or tiresome extent or duration. —**ˈlengthily** *adv.* —**ˈlengthiness** *n.*

lenient (ˈliːnɪənt) *adj.* showing or characterized by mercy or tolerance. [C17: < L *lēnīre* to soothe, < *lēnis* soft] —**ˈleniency** *or* **ˈlenience** *n.* —**ˈleniently** *adv.*

Leninism (ˈlɛnɪˌnɪzəm) *n.* the political and economic theories of Lenin (1870-1924), Russian statesman and Marxist theorist. —**ˈLeninist** *n., adj.*

lenitive (ˈlɛnɪtɪv) *adj.* **1.** soothing or alleviating pain or distress. ~*n.* **2.** a lenitive drug. [C16: < Med. L *lēnītīvus,* < L *lēnīre* to soothe]

lenity (ˈlɛnɪtɪ) *n., pl.* **-ties.** the state or quality of being lenient. [C16: < L *lēnitās* gentleness, < *lēnis* soft]

leno (ˈliːnəʊ) *n., pl.* **-nos. 1.** (in textiles) a weave in which the warp yarns are twisted together in pairs between the weft or filling yarns. **2.** a fabric of this weave. [C19: prob. < F *linon* lawn, < *lin* flax, < L *līnum*]

lens (lɛnz) *n.* **1.** a piece of glass or other transparent material, used to converge or diverge transmitted light and form optical images. **2.** Also called: **compound lens.** a combination of such lenses for forming images or concentrating a beam of light. **3.** a device that diverges or converges a beam of electromagnetic radiation, sound, or particles. **4.** *Anat.* See **crystalline lens.** [C17: < L *lēns* lentil, referring to the similarity of a lens to the shape of a lentil]

lent (lɛnt) *vb.* the past tense and past participle of **lend.**

Lent (lɛnt) *n. Christianity.* the period of forty weekdays lasting from Ash Wednesday to Holy Saturday, observed as a time of penance and fasting commemorating Jesus' fasting in the wilderness. [OE *lencten, lengten* spring, lit.: lengthening (of hours of daylight)]

lentamente (ˌlɛntəˈmɛnteɪ) *adv. Music.* slowly. [It.]

lenten (ˈlɛntən) *adj.* **1.** (*often cap.*) of or relating to Lent. **2.** *Arch. or literary.* spare, plain, or meagre: *lenten fare.*

lenticel (ˈlɛntɪˌsɛl) *n.* any of numerous pores in the stem of a woody plant allowing exchange of gases between the plant and the exterior. [C19: < NL *lenticella,* < L *lenticula* dim. of *lēns* lentil]

lenticular (lɛnˈtɪkjʊlə) *adj.* **1.** shaped like a biconvex lens. **2.** of or concerned with a lens or lenses. **3.** shaped like a lentil seed. [C17: < L *lenticulāris* like a LENTIL]

lentil (ˈlɛntɪl) *n.* **1.** a small annual leguminous plant of the Mediterranean region and W Asia, having edible convex seeds. **2.** any of the seeds of this plant, which are cooked and eaten in soups, etc. [C13: < OF *lentille,* < L *lenticula,* dim. of *lēns* lentil]

lentivirus (ˈlɛntɪˌvaɪrəs) *n.* another name for **slow virus.** [C20: NL, < L *lentus* slow + VIRUS]

lent lily *n.* another name for the **daffodil.**

lento (ˈlɛntəʊ) *Music.* ~*adj., adv.* **1.** to be performed slowly. ~*n., pl.* **-tos. 2.** a movement or passage performed in this way. [C18: It., < L *lentus* slow]

Lent term *n.* the spring term at Cambridge University and some other educational establishments.

Leo (ˈliːəʊ) *n., Latin genitive* **Leonis** (liːˈəʊnɪs). **1.** *Astron.* a zodiacal constellation in the N hemisphere, lying between Cancer and Virgo. **2.** *Astrol.* Also called: the **Lion.** the fifth sign of the zodiac. The sun is in this sign between about July 23 and Aug. 22.

Leonid (ˈliːənɪd) *n., pl.* **Leonids** *or* **Leonides** (lɪˈɒnɪˌdiːz). any member of a meteor shower appearing to radiate from the constellation Leo. [C19: < NL *Leōnidēs,* < *leō* lion]

leonine (ˈliːəˌnaɪn) *adj.* of, characteristic of, or resembling a lion. [C14: < L *leōnīnus,* < *leō* lion]

Leonine (ˈliːəˌnaɪn) *adj.* **1.** connected with one of the popes called Leo: an epithet applied to a district of Rome fortified by Pope Leo IV (**Leonine City**). **2. Leonine verse. a.** a type of medieval hexameter or elegiac verse having internal rhyme. **b.** a type of English verse with internal rhyme.

leopard (ˈlɛpəd) *n.* **1.** Also called: **panther.** a large feline mammal of forests of Africa and Asia, usually having a tawny yellow coat with black rosette-like spots. **2.** any of several similar felines, such as the snow leopard and cheetah. **3.** *Heraldry.* a stylized leopard, painted as a lion with the face turned towards the front. [C13: < OF *lepart,* < LL, < LGk *leópardos,* < *leōn* lion + *pardos* PARD (the leopard was thought to be the result of cross-breeding)] —**ˈleopardess** *fem. n.*

leotard (ˈlɪəˌtɑːd) *n.* a tight-fitting garment covering the body from the shoulders down to the thighs and worn by acrobats, ballet dancers, etc. [C19: after Jules *Léotard,* F acrobat]

leper (ˈlɛpə) *n.* **1.** a person who has leprosy. **2.** a person who is ignored or despised. [C14: via LL < Gk *lepra,* n. use of *lepros* scaly, < *lepein* to peel]

lepido- *or before a vowel* **lepid-** *combining form.* scale or scaly: *lepidopterous.* [< Gk *lepis* scale; see LEPER]

lepidopteran (ˌlɛpɪˈdɒptərən) *n., pl.* **-terans** *or* **-tera** (-tərə). **1.** any of a large order of insects typically having two pairs of wings covered with fragile scales: comprises the butterflies and moths. ~*adj. also* **lepidopterous. 2.** of, relating to, or belonging to this order. [C19: < NL, < LEPIDO- + Gk *pteron* wing]

lepidopterist (ˌlɛpɪˈdɒptərɪst) *n.* a person who studies or collects moths and butterflies.

leprechaun (ˈlɛprəˌkɔːn) *n.* (in Irish folklore) a mischievous elf, often believed to have a treasure hoard. [C17: < Irish Gaelic *leipreachān,* < MIrish *lūchorpān,* < *lū* small + *corp* body, < L *corpus* body]

leprosy (ˈlɛprəsɪ) *n. Pathol.* a chronic infectious disease occurring mainly in tropical and subtropical regions, characterized by the formation of painful inflamed nodules beneath the skin and disfigurement and wasting of affected parts. [C16: < LEPROUS + -Y³]

leprous (ˈlɛprəs) *adj.* **1.** having leprosy. **2.** relating to or resembling leprosy. [C13: < OF, < LL *leprosus,* < *lepra* LEPER]

-lepsy *or sometimes* **-lepsia** *n. combining form.* indicating a seizure: *catalepsy.* [< NL *-lepsia,* < Gk, < *lēpsis* a seizure, < *lambanein* to seize] —**-leptic** *adj. combining form.*

lepton¹ (ˈlɛptɒn) *n., pl.* **-ta** (-tə). **1.** a Greek monetary unit worth one hundredth of a drachma. **2.** a small coin of ancient Greece. [< Gk *lepton* (*nomisma*) small (coin)]

lepton² (ˈlɛptɒn) *n. Physics.* any of a group of elementary particles and their antiparticles, such as an electron, muon, or neutrino, that participate in weak interactions. [C20: < Gk *leptos* thin, < *lepein* to peel + -ON]

lepton number *n. Physics.* a quantum number describing the behaviour of elementary particles, equal to the number of leptons present minus the number of antileptons. It is thought to be conserved in all processes.

leptospirosis (ˌlɛptəʊspaɪˈrəʊsɪs) *n.* any of several infectious diseases caused by bacteria, transmitted to man by animals and characterized by jaundice, meningitis, and kidney failure. [C20: < NL *Leptospira* (< Gk *leptos* thin + *speira* coil + -OSIS)]

lesbian (ˈlɛzbɪən) *n.* **1.** a female homosexual. ~*adj.* **2.** of or characteristic of lesbians. [C19: < the homosexuality attributed to Sappho (C6 B.C.) Gk poetess of *Lesbos*] —ˈ**lesbianism** *n.*

lese-majesty (ˈliːzˈmædʒɪstɪ) *n.* **1.** any of various offences committed against the sovereign power in a state; treason. **2.** an attack on authority or position. [C16: < F *lèse majesté,* < L *laesa mājestās* wounded majesty]

lesion (ˈliːʒən) *n.* **1.** any structural change in a bodily part resulting from injury or disease. **2.** an injury or wound. [C15: via OF < LL *laesiō* injury, < L *laedere* to hurt]

less (lɛs) *determiner.* **1. a.** the comparative of **little** (sense 1): *less sugar; less spirit than before.* **b.** (*as pronoun; functioning as sing. or pl.*): *she has less than she needs; the less you eat, the less you want.* **2.** (usually preceded by *no*) lower in rank or importance: *no less a man than the president.* **3. less of.** to a smaller extent or degree: *we see less of John these days; less of a success than I'd hoped.* ~*adv.* **4.** the comparative of a *little*: *she walks less than she should; less quickly; less beautiful.* ~*prep.* **5.** subtracting; minus: *three weeks less a day.* [OE *lǣssa* (adj.), *lǣs* (adv., n.)]

▷ **Usage.** *Less* should not be confused with *fewer. Less* refers only to quantity and not to number: *there is less water than before. Fewer* means smaller in number: *there are fewer people than before.*

-less *suffix forming adjectives.* **1.** without; lacking: *speechless.* **2.** not able to (do something) or not able to be (done, performed, etc.): *countless.* [OE *-lās,* < *lēas* lacking]

lessee (lɛˈsiː) *n.* a person to whom a lease is granted; a tenant under a lease. [C15: via Anglo-F < OF *lessé,* < *lesser* to LEASE]

lessen (ˈlɛsᵊn) *vb.* **1.** to make or become less. **2.** (*tr.*) to make little of.

lesser (ˈlɛsə) *adj.* not as great in quantity, size, or worth.

lesser celandine *n.* a Eurasian plant, related to the buttercup, having yellow flowers and heart-shaped leaves.

lesser panda *n.* See **panda** (sense 2).

lesson (ˈlɛsᵊn) *n.* **1. a.** a unit, or single period of instruction in a subject; class: *an hour-long music lesson.* **b.** the content of such a unit. **2.** material assigned for individual study. **3.** something from which useful knowledge or principles can be learned; example. **4.** the principles, knowledge, etc., gained. **5.** a reprimand or punishment intended to correct. **6.** a portion of Scripture appointed to be read at divine service. [C13: < OF *leçon,* < L *lēctiō,* < *legere* to read]

lessor (ˈlɛsɔː, lɛˈsɔː) *n.* a person who grants a lease of property.

lest (lɛst) *conj.* (*subordinating; takes a subjunctive vb.*) **1.** so as to prevent any possibility that: *keep down lest anyone see us.* **2.** (*after vbs. or phrases expressing fear, worry, anxiety, etc.*) for fear that; in case: *he was alarmed lest she should find out.* [OE *the lǣste,* earlier *thȳ lǣs the,* lit.: whereby less that]

let¹ (lɛt) *vb.* **letting, let.** (*tr.;* usually takes an infinitive without *to* or an implied infinitive) **1.** to permit; allow: *she lets him roam around.* **2.** (*imperative or dependent imperative*) **a.** used as an auxiliary to express a request, proposal, or command, or to convey a warning or threat: *let's get on; just let me catch you here again!* **b.** (in mathematical or philosophical discourse) used as an auxiliary to express an assumption or hypothesis: *let "a" equal "b".* **c.** used as an auxiliary to express resigned acceptance of the inevitable: *let the worst happen.* **3. a.** to allow the occupation of (accommodation) in return for rent. **b.** to assign (a contract for work). **4.** to allow or cause the movement of (something) in a specified direction: *to let air out of a tyre.* **5. let alone.** (*conj.*) much less; not to mention: *I can't afford wine, let alone champagne.* **6. let** *or* **leave alone** *or* **be.** refrain from annoying or interfering with: *let the poor cat alone.* **7. let go.** See **go**¹ (sense 45). **8. let loose.** to set free. ~*n.* **8.** *Brit.* the act of letting property or accommodation. ~See also **let down, let off,** etc. [OE *lǣtan* to permit]

let² (lɛt) *n.* **1.** an impediment or obstruction (esp. in **without let or hindrance**). **2.** *Tennis, squash, etc.* **a.** a minor infringement or obstruction of the ball, requiring a point to be replayed. **b.** the point so replayed. ~*vb.* **letting, letted** *or* **let. 3.** (*tr.*) *Arch.* to hinder; impede. [OE *lettan* to hinder, < *læt* late]

-let *suffix forming nouns.* **1.** small or lesser: *booklet.* **2.** an article of attire or ornament worn on a specified part of the body: *anklet.* [< OF *-elet,* < L *-āle,* < L *-ellus,* dim. suffix]

let down *vb.* (*tr., mainly adv.*) **1.** (*also prep.*) to lower. **2.** to fail to fulfil the expectations of (a person); disappoint. **3.** to undo, shorten, and resew (the hem) so as to lengthen (a dress, skirt, etc.). **4.** to untie (long hair that is bound up) and allow to fall loose. **5.** to deflate: *to let down a tyre.* ~*n.* **letdown. 6.** a disappointment.

lethal (ˈliːθəl) *adj.* **1.** able to cause or causing death. **2.** of or suggestive of death. [C16: < L *lēthālis,* < *lētum* death] —**lethality** (liːˈθælɪtɪ) *n.* —ˈ**lethally** *adv.*

lethargy (ˈlɛθədʒɪ) *n., pl.* **-gies. 1.** sluggishness, slowness, or dullness. **2.** an abnormal lack of energy. [C14: < LL *lēthargīa,* < Gk *lēthargos* drowsy, < *lēthē* forgetfulness] —**lethargic** (lɪˈθɑːdʒɪk) *adj.* —**leˈthargically** *adv.*

Lethe (ˈliːθɪ) *n.* **1.** *Greek myth.* a river in Hades that caused forgetfulness in those who drank its waters. **2.** forgetfulness. [C16: via L < Gk, < *lēthē* oblivion] —**Lethean** (lɪˈθiːən) *adj.*

let off *vb.* (*tr., mainly adv.*) **1.** (*also prep.*) to allow to disembark or leave. **2.** to explode or fire (a bomb, gun, etc.). **3.** (*also prep.*) to excuse from (work or other responsibilities): *I'll let you off for a week.* **4.** *Inf.* to allow to get away without the expected punishment, work, etc. **5.** to let (accommodation) in portions. **6.** to release (liquid, air, etc.).

let on *vb.* (*adv.;* when *tr., takes a clause as*

object) *Inf.* **1.** to allow (something, such as a secret) to be known; reveal: *he never let on that he was married.* **2.** (*tr.*) to cause or encourage to be believed; pretend.

let out *vb.* (*adv., mainly tr.*) **1.** to give vent to; emit: *to let out a howl.* **2.** to allow to go or run free; release. **3.** (*may take a clause as object*) to reveal (a secret). **4.** to make available to tenants, hirers, or contractors. **5.** to permit to flow out: *to let air out of the tyres.* **6.** to make (a garment) larger, as by unpicking (the seams) and sewing nearer the outer edge. ~*n.* **let-out. 7.** a chance to escape.

let's (lɛts) *contraction of* let us: used to express a suggestion, command, etc., by the speaker to himself and his hearers.

Lett (lɛt) *n.* another name for a **Latvian.**

letter (ˈlɛtə) *n.* **1.** any of a set of conventional symbols used in writing or printing a language, each symbol being associated with a group of phonetic values; character of the alphabet. **2.** a written or printed communication addressed to a person, company, etc., usually sent by post. **3.** (often preceded by *the*) the strict legalistic or pedantic interpretation of the meaning of an agreement, document, etc.; exact wording as distinct from actual intention (esp. in **the letter of the law**). **4. to the letter. a.** following the literal interpretation or wording exactly. **b.** attending to every detail. ~*vb.* **5.** to write or mark letters on (a sign, etc.), esp. by hand. **6.** (*tr.*) to set down or print using letters. [C13: < OF *lettre,* < L *littera* letter of the alphabet] —ˈ**letterer** *n.*

letter bomb *n.* an explosive device in an envelope, detonated when the envelope is opened.

letter box *n. Chiefly Brit.* **1. a.** a slot through which letters, etc. are delivered to a building. **b.** a private box into which letters, etc., are delivered. **2.** Also: **postbox.** a public box into which letters, etc., are put for collection.

lettered (ˈlɛtəd) *adj.* **1.** well educated in literature, the arts, etc. **2.** literate. **3.** of or characterized by learning or culture. **4.** printed or marked with letters.

letterhead (ˈlɛtəˌhɛd) *n.* a sheet of writing paper printed with one's address, name, etc.

lettering (ˈlɛtərɪŋ) *n.* **1.** the act, art, or technique of inscribing letters on to something. **2.** the letters so inscribed.

letter of credit *n.* a letter issued by a bank entitling the bearer to draw funds up to a specified maximum from that bank or its agencies.

letter of marque *or* **letters of marque** *n.* (formerly) a licence granted by a state to a private citizen to arm a ship and seize merchant vessels of another nation. Also called: **letter of marque and reprisal.**

letter-perfect *adj.* another term (esp. U.S.) for **word-perfect.**

letterpress (ˈlɛtəˌprɛs) *n.* **1. a.** a method of printing in which ink is transferred from raised surfaces to paper by pressure. **b.** matter so printed. **2.** text matter as distinct from illustrations.

letters (ˈlɛtəz) *n.* (*functioning as sing. or pl.*) **1.** literary knowledge, ability, or learning: *a man of letters.* **2.** literary culture in general. **3.** an official title, degree, etc., indicated by an abbreviation: *letters after one's name.*

letters patent *pl. n.* See **patent** (senses 1, 4).

Lettish (ˈlɛtɪʃ) *n., adj.* another word for **Latvian.**

lettuce (ˈlɛtɪs) *n.* **1.** any of various plants of the composite family cultivated in many varieties for their large edible leaves. **2.** the leaves of any of these varieties, which are eaten in salads. **3.** any of various plants that resemble true lettuce, such as lamb's lettuce. [C13: prob. < OF *laitues,* < L *lactūca,* < *lac-* milk, because of its milky juice]

let up *vb.* (*intr., adv.*) **1.** to diminish, slacken, or stop. **2.** (foll. by *on*) *Inf.* to be less harsh (towards someone). ~*n.* **let-up. 3.** *Inf.* a lessening or abatement.

leuco-, leuko- *or before a vowel* **leuc-, leuk-** *combining form.* white or lacking colour: *leucocyte; leukaemia.* [< Gk *leukos* white]

leucocyte *or esp. U.S.* **leukocyte** (ˈluːkəˌsaɪt) *n.* any of the various large unpigmented cells in the blood of vertebrates. Also called: **white blood cell, white (blood) corpuscle.** —**leucocytic** *or esp. U.S.* **leukocytic** (ˌluːkəˈsɪtɪk) *adj.*

leucoma (luːˈkəʊmə) *n. Pathol.* a white opaque scar of the cornea.

leucotomy (luːˈkɒtəmɪ) *n., pl.* **-mies.** the surgical operation of cutting some of the nerve fibres in the frontal lobes of the brain for treating intractable mental disorders.

leukaemia *or esp. U.S.* **leukemia** (luːˈkiːmɪə) *n.* an acute or chronic disease characterized by a gross proliferation of leucocytes, which crowd into the bone marrow, spleen, lymph nodes, etc., and suppress the blood-forming apparatus. [C19: < LEUCO- + Gk *haima* blood]

Lev. *Bible. abbrev. for* Leviticus.

levant (lɪˈvænt) *n.* a type of leather made from the skins of goats, sheep, or seals, having a pattern of irregular creases. [C19: shortened < *Levant morocco* (type of leather)]

Levant (lɪˈvænt) *n.* **the.** a former name for the area of the E Mediterranean now occupied by Lebanon, Syria, and Israel. [C15: < OF, < *lever* to raise (referring to the rising of the sun in the east), < L *levāre*] —**Levantine** (ˈlɛvənˌtaɪn) *adj., n.*

levanter (lɪˈvæntə) *n.* (*sometimes cap.*) **1.** an easterly wind in the W Mediterranean area. **2.** an inhabitant of the Levant.

levator (lɪˈveɪtə, -tɔː) *n. Anat.* any of various muscles that raise a part of the body. [C17: NL, < L *levāre* to raise]

levee[1] (ˈlɛvɪ) *n. U.S.* **1.** an embankment alongside a river, produced naturally by sedimentation or constructed by man to prevent flooding. **2.** an embankment that surrounds a field that is to be irrigated. **3.** a landing place on a river; quay. [C18: < F, < Med. L *levāta* < L *levāre* to raise]

levee[2] (ˈlɛvɪ, ˈlɛveɪ) *n.* **1.** a formal reception held by a sovereign just after rising from bed. **2.** (in Britain) a public court reception for men. [C17: < F, var. of *lever* a rising, < L *levāre* to raise]

level (ˈlɛvᵊl) *adj.* **1.** on a horizontal plane. **2.** having a surface of completely equal height. **3.** being of the same height as something else. **4.** (of quantities to be measured, as in recipes) even with the top of the cup, spoon, etc. **5.** equal to or even with (something or someone else). **6.** not having or showing inconsistency or irregularities. **7.** Also: **level-headed.** even-tempered; steady. **8. one's level best.** the best one can do. ~*vb.* **-elling, -elled** *or U.S.* **-eling, -eled. 9.** (*tr.;* sometimes foll. by *off*) to make (a surface) horizontal, level, or even. **10.** to make (two or more people or things) equal, as in position or status. **11.** (*tr.*) to raze to the ground. **12.** (*tr.*) to knock (a person) down as by a blow. **13.** (*tr.*) to direct (a gaze, criticism, etc.) emphatically at someone. **14.** (*intr.;* often foll. by *with*) *Inf.* to be straightforward and frank. **15.** (*intr.;* foll. by *off* or *out*) to manoeuvre an aircraft into a horizontal flight path after a dive, climb, or glide. **16.** (often foll. by *at*) to aim (a weapon) horizontally. ~*n.* **17.** a horizontal datum line or plane. **18.** a device, such as a spirit level, for determining whether a surface is horizontal. **19.** a surveying instrument used for measuring relative heights of land. **20.** position or status in a scale of values. **21.** amount or degree of progress; stage. **22.** a specified vertical position; altitude. **23.** a horizontal line or plane with respect to which measurement of elevation is based: *sea level.* **24.** a flat even surface or area of land. **25.** *Physics.* the ratio of the magnitude of a physical quantity to an arbitrary magnitude: *sound-pressure level.* **26. on the level.** *Inf.* sincere or genuine. [C14: < OF *livel,* < Vulgar L *lībellum* (unattested), < L *lībella,* dim. of *lībra* scales] —ˈ**leveller** *or U.S.* ˈ**leveler** *n.* —ˈ**levelly** *adv.* —ˈ**levelness** *n.*

level crossing *n. Brit.* a point at which a

railway and a road cross, esp. one with barriers that close the road when a train is due to pass.

level-headed *adj.* even-tempered, balanced, and reliable; steady. —ˌ**level-ˈheadedly** *adv.* —ˌ**level-ˈheadedness** *n.*

level pegging *Brit. inf.* ~*n.* **1.** equality between two contestants. ~*adj.* **2.** (of two contestants) equal.

lever (ˈliːvə) *n.* **1.** a rigid bar pivoted about a fulcrum, used to transfer a force to a load and usually to provide a mechanical advantage. **2.** any of a number of mechanical devices employing this principle. **3.** a means of exerting pressure in order to accomplish something. ~*vb.* **4.** to prise or move (an object) with a lever. [C13: < OF *leveour,* < *lever* to raise, < L *levāre* < *levis* light]

leverage (ˈliːvərɪdʒ, -vrɪdʒ) *n.* **1.** the action of a lever. **2.** the mechanical advantage gained by employing a lever. **3.** strategic advantage.

leveret (ˈlɛvərɪt, -vrɪt) *n.* a young hare, esp. one less than one year old. [C15: < Norman F *levrete,* dim. of *levre,* < L *lepus* hare]

leviable (ˈlɛvɪəbᵊl) *adj.* **1.** (of taxes, etc.) liable to be levied. **2.** (of goods, etc.) liable to bear a levy; taxable.

leviathan (lɪˈvaɪəθən) *n.* **1.** *Bible.* a monstrous beast, esp. a sea monster. **2.** any huge or powerful thing. [C14: < LL, ult. < Heb. *liwyāthān,* <?]

levigate (ˈlɛvɪˌgeɪt) *vb. Chem.* **1.** (*tr.*) to grind into a fine powder or a smooth paste. **2.** to form or cause to form a homogeneous mixture, as in the production of gels. **3.** (*tr.*) to suspend (fine particles) by grinding in a liquid, esp. as a method of separating fine from coarse particles. [C17: < L *lēvigāre,* < *lēvis* smooth] —ˌ**leviˈgation** *n.*

Levis (ˈliːvaɪz) *pl. n. Trademark.* jeans, usually blue and made of denim.

levitate (ˈlɛvɪˌteɪt) *vb.* to rise or cause to rise and float in the air, usually attributed to supernatural intervention. [C17: < L *levis* light + *-tate,* as in *gravitate*] —ˌ**leviˈtation** *n.* —ˈ**leviˌtator** *n.*

levity (ˈlɛvɪtɪ) *n., pl.* **-ties. 1.** inappropriate lack of seriousness. **2.** fickleness or instability. **3.** *Arch.* lightness in weight. [C16: < L *levitās* lightness, < *levis* light]

levy (ˈlɛvɪ) *vb.* **levying, levied.** (*tr.*) **1.** to impose and collect (a tax, tariff, fine, etc.). **2.** to conscript troops for service. **3.** to seize or attach (property) in accordance with the judgment of a court. ~*n., pl.* **levies. 4. a.** the act of imposing and collecting a tax, tariff, etc. **b.** the money so raised. **5. a.** the conscription of troops for service. **b.** a person conscripted in this way. [C15: < OF *levée* a raising, < *lever,* < L *levāre* to raise]

lewd (luːd) *adj.* characterized by or intended to excite crude sexual desire; obscene. [C14: < OE *lǣwde* ignorant] —ˈ**lewdly** *adv.* —ˈ**lewdness** *n.*

lewis (ˈluːɪs) *n.* a lifting device for heavy stone blocks consisting of a number of curved pieces of metal fitting into a dovetailed recess cut into the stone. [C18: ? < the name of the inventor]

Lewis acid *n.* a substance capable of accepting a pair of electrons from a base to form a covalent bond. Cf. **Lewis base.** [C20: after G. N. *Lewis* (1875–1946), U.S. chemist]

Lewis base *n.* a substance capable of donating a pair of electrons to an acid to form a covalent bond. Cf. **Lewis acid.** [C20: after G. N. *Lewis;* see LEWIS ACID]

Lewis gun *n.* a light air-cooled gas-operated machine gun used chiefly in World Wars I and II. [C20: after I. N. *Lewis* (1858–1931), U.S. soldier]

lewisite (ˈluːɪˌsaɪt) *n.* a colourless oily poisonous liquid having a powerful blistering action and used as a war gas. [C20: after W. L. *Lewis* (1878–1943), U.S. chemist]

lexeme (ˈlɛksiːm) *n. Linguistics.* a minimal meaningful unit that cannot be understood from the meanings of its component morphemes. [C20: < LEX(ICON) + -EME]

lexical (ˈlɛksɪkᵊl) *adj.* **1.** of or relating to items of vocabulary in a language. **2.** of or relating to a lexicon. —ˈ**lexically** *adv.*

lexicography (ˌlɛksɪˈkɒgrəfɪ) *n.* the process or profession of writing or compiling dictionaries. —ˌ**lexiˈcographer** *n.* —**lexicographic** (ˌlɛksɪkəˈgræfɪk) *or* ˌ**lexicoˈgraphical** *adj.*

lexicon (ˈlɛksɪkən) *n.* **1.** a dictionary, esp. one of an ancient language such as Greek or Hebrew. **2.** a list of terms relating to a particular subject. **3.** the vocabulary of a language or of an individual. **4.** *Linguistics.* the set of all the morphemes of a language. [C17: NL, < Gk *lexikon* n. use of *lexikos* relating to words, < Gk *lexis* word, < *legein* to speak]

lexigraphy (lɛkˈsɪgrəfɪ) *n.* a system of writing in which each word is represented by a sign. [C19: < Gk *lexis* word + -GRAPHY]

lexis (ˈlɛksɪs) *n.* the totality of vocabulary items in a language. [C20: < Gk *lexis* word]

ley (leɪ, liː) *n.* **1.** arable land temporarily under grass. **2.** Also: **ley line.** a line joining two prominent points in the landscape, thought to be the line of a prehistoric track. [C14: var. of LEA]

Leyden jar (ˈlaɪdᵊn) *n. Physics.* an early type of capacitor consisting of a glass jar with the lower part of the inside and outside coated with tinfoil. [C18: first made in Leiden (*Leyden*), city in the Netherlands]

lf *Printing. abbrev. for* light face.

LF *Radio. abbrev. for* low frequency.

LG *abbrev. for* Low German.

lh *or* **LH** *abbrev. for* left hand.

Li *the chemical symbol for* lithium.

liabilities (ˌlaɪəˈbɪlɪtɪz) *pl. n. Accounting.* business obligations not discharged and shown as balanced against assets on the balance sheet.

liability (ˌlaɪəˈbɪlɪtɪ) *n., pl.* **-ties. 1.** the state of being liable. **2.** a financial obligation. **3.** a hindrance or disadvantage.

liable (ˈlaɪəbᵊl) *adj.* (*postpositive*) **1.** legally obliged or responsible; answerable. **2.** susceptible or exposed; subject. **3.** probable or likely: *it's liable to happen soon.* [C15: ? via Anglo-F, < OF *lier* to bind, < L *ligāre*]

▷ **Usage.** Careful users of English take *liable* to mean *responsible for* and *subject to* in sentences such as *he was liable for his employees' accidents* and *he was liable to accidents.* The use of *liable* in the sense of *likely* is avoided: *he was likely* (not *liable*) *to have accidents.*

liaise (lɪˈeɪz) *vb.* (*intr.;* usually foll. by *with*) to communicate and maintain contact (with). [C20: back formation < LIAISON]

liaison (lɪˈeɪzɒn) *n.* **1.** communication and contact between groups or units. **2.** a secretive or adulterous sexual relationship. **3.** the relationship between military units necessary to ensure unity of purpose. **4.** (esp. in French) the pronunciation of a normally silent consonant at the end of a word immediately before another word commencing with a vowel, in such a way that the consonant is taken over as the initial sound of the following word, as in *ils ont* (ilzɔ̃). **5.** any thickening for soups, sauces, etc., such as egg yolks or cream. [C17: via F < OF, < *lier* to bind, < L *ligāre*]

liana (lɪˈɑːnə) *or* **liane** (lɪˈɑːn) *n.* any of various woody climbing plants of tropical forests. [C19: changed < earlier *liane* (through infl. of F *lier* to bind), < F, <?]

liar (ˈlaɪə) *n.* a person who tells lies.

Lias (ˈlaɪəs) *n.* the lowest series of rocks of the Jurassic system. [C15 (referring to a kind of limestone), C19 (geological sense): < OF *liois,* ? < *lie* dregs, so called from its appearance] —**Liassic** (laɪˈæsɪk) *adj.*

lib (lɪb) *n. Inf., sometimes derog.* short for **liberation.**

lib. *abbrev. for:* **1.** liber. [L: book] **2.** librarian. **3.** library.

Lib. *abbrev. for* Liberal.

libation (laɪˈbeɪʃən) *n.* **1. a.** the pouring-out of wine, etc., in honour of a deity. **b.** the liquid so poured out. **2.** *Usually facetious.* an alcoholic drink. [C14: < L *lībātiō,* < *lībāre* to pour an offering of drink]

libel (ˈlaɪbᵊl) *n.* **1.** *Law.* **a.** the publication of defamatory matter in permanent form, as by a written or printed statement, picture, etc. **b.** the act of publishing such matter. **2.** any defamatory or unflattering representation or statement. ~*vb.* **-belling, -belled** *or U.S.* **-beling, -beled.** (*tr.*) **3.** *Law.* to make or publish a defamatory statement or representation about (a person). **4.** to misrepresent injuriously. [C13 (in the sense: written statement), hence C14 legal sense: a plaintiff's statement, via OF < L *libellus* a little book] —**'libeller** *or* **'libelist** *n.* —**'libellous** *or* **'libelous** *adj.*

liberal ('lɪbərəl, 'lɪbrəl) *adj.* **1.** relating to or having social and political views that favour progress and reform. **2.** relating to or having policies or views advocating individual freedom. **3.** giving and generous in temperament or behaviour. **4.** tolerant of other people. **5.** abundant; lavish: *a liberal helping of cream.* **6.** not strict; free: *a liberal translation.* **7.** of or relating to an education that aims to develop general cultural interests and intellectual ability. ~*n.* **8.** a person who has liberal ideas or opinions. [C14: < L *līberālis* of freedom, < *līber* free] —**'liberally** *adv.* —**'liberalness** *n.*

Liberal ('lɪbərəl, 'lɪbrəl) *n.* **1.** a member or supporter of a Liberal Party. ~*adj.* **2.** of or relating to a Liberal Party.

liberal arts *pl. n.* the fine arts, humanities, sociology, languages, and literature. Often shortened to **arts.**

liberalism ('lɪbərəˌlɪzəm, 'lɪbrə-) *n.* liberal opinions, practices, or politics.

liberality (ˌlɪbə'rælɪtɪ) *n., pl.* **-ties. 1.** generosity; bounty. **2.** the quality or condition of being liberal.

liberalize *or* **-ise** ('lɪbərəˌlaɪz, 'lɪbrə-) *vb.* to make or become liberal. —ˌ**liberali'zation** *or* **-i'sation** *n.* —**'liberalˌizer** *or* **-ˌiser** *n.*

Liberal Party *n.* **1.** one of the major political parties in Britain. **2.** one of the major political parties in Australia, a conservative party, generally opposed to the Labor Party. **3.** any other party supporting liberal policies.

liberal studies *n.* (*functioning as sing.*) *Brit.* a supplementary arts course for those specializing in scientific, technical, or professional studies.

liberate ('lɪbəˌreɪt) *vb.* (*tr.*) **1.** to give liberty to; make free. **2.** to release (something, esp. a gas) from chemical combination. **3.** to release from occupation or subjugation by a foreign power. **4.** to free from social prejudices or injustices. **5.** *Euphemistic or facetious.* to steal. —**'liberˌator** *n.*

liberated ('lɪbəˌreɪtɪd) *adj.* **1.** given liberty; freed; released. **2.** released from occupation or subjugation by a foreign power. **3.** (esp. in feminist theory) not bound by traditional sexual and social roles.

liberation (ˌlɪbə'reɪʃən) *n.* **1.** a liberating or being liberated. **2.** the seeking of equal status or just treatment for or on behalf of any group believed to be discriminated against: *women's liberation; animal liberation.* —ˌ**liber'ationist** *n., adj.*

liberation theology *n.* the belief that Christianity involves not only faith in the Church but a commitment to change social and political conditions where it is considered exploitation and oppression exist: applied esp. to South America.

libertarian (ˌlɪbə'tɛərɪən) *n.* **1.** a believer in freedom of thought, expression, etc. **2.** a believer in the doctrine of free will. ~*adj.* **3.** of, relating to, or characteristic of a libertarian. [C18: < LIBERTY] —ˌ**liber'tarianism** *n.*

libertine ('lɪbəˌtiːn, -ˌtaɪn) *n.* **1.** a morally dissolute person. ~*adj.* **2.** morally dissolute. [C14 (in the sense: freedman, dissolute person): < L *lībertīnus* freedman, < *lībertus* freed, < *līber* free] —**'liberˌtinage** *or* **'libertinˌism** *n.*

liberty ('lɪbətɪ) *n., pl.* **-ties. 1.** the power of choosing, thinking, and acting for oneself; freedom from control or restriction. **2.** the right or privilege of access to a particular place; freedom. **3.** (*often pl.*) a social action regarded as being familiar, forward, or improper. **4.** (*often pl.*) an action that is unauthorized: *he took liberties with the translation.* **5. a.** authorized leave granted to a sailor. **b.** (*as modifier*): *liberty man; liberty boat.* **6. at liberty.** free, unoccupied, or unrestricted. **7. take liberties (with).** to be overfamiliar or overpresumptuous. [C14: < OF *liberté,* < L *lībertās,* < *līber* free]

liberty bodice *n.* a sleeveless vestlike undergarment covering the upper part of the body, formerly worn esp. by young children.

liberty hall *n.* (*sometimes caps.*) *Inf.* a place or condition of complete liberty.

libidinous (lɪ'bɪdɪnəs) *adj.* characterized by excessive sexual desire. —**li'bidinously** *adv.* —**li'bidinousness** *n.*

libido (lɪ'biːdəʊ) *n., pl.* **-dos. 1.** *Psychoanal.* psychic energy emanating from the id. **2.** sexual urge or desire. [C20 (in psychoanalysis): < L: desire] —**libidinal** (lɪ'bɪdɪn°l) *adj.* —**li'bidinally** *adv.*

libra ('laɪbrə) *n., pl.* **-brae** (-briː). an ancient Roman unit of weight corresponding to 1 pound. [C14: < L, lit.: scales]

Libra ('liːbrə) *n., Latin genitive* **Librae** ('liːbriː). **1.** *Astron.* a small faint zodiacal constellation in the S hemisphere, lying between Virgo and Scorpius. **2.** Also called: the **Scales,** the **Balance.** *Astrol.* the seventh sign of the zodiac. The sun is in this sign between about Sept. 23 and Oct. 22.

librarian (laɪ'brɛərɪən) *n.* a person in charge of or assisting in a library. —**li'brarianˌship** *n.*

library ('laɪbrərɪ) *n., pl.* **-braries. 1.** a room or set of rooms where books and other literary materials are kept. **2.** a collection of literary materials, films, tapes, gramophone records, etc., kept for borrowing or reference. **3.** the building or institution that houses such a collection: *a public library.* **4.** a set of books published as a series, often in a similar format. **5.** *Computers.* a collection of standard programs and subroutines, usually stored on disk. **6.** a collection of specific items for reference or checking against: *a library of genetic material.* [C14: < OF *librairie,* < Med. L *librāris,* n. use of L *librārius* relating to books, < *liber* book]

libration (laɪ'breɪʃən) *n.* **1.** the act of oscillating. **2.** a real or apparent oscillation of the moon enabling approximately nine per cent of the surface facing away from earth to be seen. [C17: < L, < *librāre* to balance]

librettist (lɪ'brɛtɪst) *n.* the author of a libretto.

libretto (lɪ'brɛtəʊ) *n., pl.* **-tos** *or* **-ti** (-tiː). a text written for and set to music in an opera, etc. [C18: < It., dim. of *libro* book]

Librium ('lɪbrɪəm) *n.* *Trademark.* a white crystalline compound used esp. as a tranquillizer.

Libyan ('lɪbɪən) *adj.* **1.** of or relating to Libya, a republic in N Africa, on the Mediterranean, its people, or its language. ~*n.* **2.** a native or inhabitant of Libya. **3.** the extinct Hamitic language of ancient Libya.

lice (laɪs) *n.* the plural of **louse.**

licence *or U.S.* **license** ('laɪsəns) *n.* **1.** a certificate, tag, document, etc., giving official permission to do something. **2.** formal permission or exemption. **3.** liberty of action or thought; freedom. **4.** intentional disregard of conventional rules to achieve a certain effect: *poetic licence.* **5.** excessive freedom. [C14: via OF and Med. L *licentia* permission, < L: freedom, < *licet* it is allowed]

license ('laɪsəns) *vb.* (*tr.*) **1.** to grant or give a licence for (something, such as the sale of alcohol). **2.** to give permission to or for. —**'licensable** *adj.* —**'licenser** *or* **'licensor** *n.*

licensee (ˌlaɪsən'siː) *n.* a person who holds a licence, esp. one to sell alcoholic drink.

licentiate (laɪ'sɛnʃɪɪt) *n.* **1.** a person who holds a formal attestation of competence to practise a certain profession. **2.** a higher degree awarded by certain, chiefly European, universities. **3.** a person who holds this degree. **4.** *Chiefly Presbyterian Church.* a person holding a licence to preach. [C15: < Med. L *licentiātus,* < *licentiāre* to permit] —**li'centiateˌship** *n.*

licentious (laɪ'sɛnʃəs) *adj.* **1.** sexually unrestrained or promiscuous. **2.** *Now rare.* showing disregard for convention. [C16: < L *licentiōsus* capricious, < *licentia* LICENCE] **—liˈcentiously** *adv.* **—liˈcentiousness** *n.*

lichee (ˌlaɪˈtʃiː) *n.* a variant spelling of **litchi.**

lichen (ˈlaɪkən, ˈlɪtʃən) *n.* any of various small plants which are formed by the symbiotic association of a fungus and an alga and occur as crusty patches or bushy growths on tree trunks, bare ground, etc. [C17: via L < Gk *leikhēn,* < *leikhein* to lick] **—ˈlichened** *adj.* **—ˈlichenous** *adj.*

lich gate *or* **lych gate** (lɪtʃ) *n.* a roofed gate to a churchyard, formerly used as a temporary shelter for the bier. [C15: *lich,* < OE *līc* corpse]

licit (ˈlɪsɪt) *adj.* a less common word for **lawful.** [C15: < L *licitus,* < *licēre* to be permitted] **—ˈlicitly** *adv.* **—ˈlicitness** *n.*

lick (lɪk) *vb.* **1.** (*tr.*) to pass the tongue over, esp. in order to taste or consume. **2.** to flicker or move lightly over or round (something): *the flames licked around the door.* **3.** (*tr.*) *Inf.* **a.** to defeat or vanquish. **b.** to flog or thrash. **c.** to be or do much better than. **4. lick into shape.** to put into a satisfactory condition. **5. lick one's wounds.** to retire after a defeat. *~n.* **6.** an instance of passing the tongue over something. **7.** a small amount: *a lick of paint.* **8.** short for **salt lick. 9.** *Inf.* a hit; blow. **10.** *Sl.* a short musical phrase, usually on one instrument. **11.** *Inf.* rate of movement; speed. **12. a lick and a promise.** something hastily done, esp. a hurried wash. [OE *liccian*] **—ˈlicker** *n.*

lickerish *or* **liquorish** (ˈlɪkərɪʃ) *adj. Arch.* **1.** lecherous or lustful. **2.** greedy; gluttonous. **3.** appetizing or tempting. [C16: changed < C13 *lickerous,* < OF *lechereus* lecherous; see LECHER]

lickety-split (ˈlɪkɪtɪˈsplɪt) *adv. U.S. & Canad. inf.* very quickly; speedily. [C19: < LICK + SPLIT]

licking (ˈlɪkɪŋ) *n. Inf.* **1.** a beating. **2.** a defeat.

lickspittle (ˈlɪkˌspɪtᵊl) *n.* a flattering or servile person.

licorice (ˈlɪkərɪs) *n.* the usual U.S. and Canad. spelling of **liquorice.**

lictor (ˈlɪktə) *n.* one of a group of ancient Roman officials, usually bearing fasces, who attended magistrates, etc. [C16 *lictor,* C14 *littour,* < L *ligāre* to bind]

lid (lɪd) *n.* **1.** a cover, usually removable or hinged, for a receptacle: *a saucepan lid; a desk lid.* **2.** short for **eyelid. 3. put the lid on.** *Inf.* **a.** *Brit.* to be the final blow to. **b.** to curb, prevent, or discourage. [OE *hlid*] **—ˈlidded** *adj.* **—ˈlidless** *adj.*

lido (ˈliːdəʊ) *n., pl.* **-dos.** *Brit.* a public place of recreation, including a swimming pool. [C20: after the *Lido,* island bathing beach near Venice, < L *litus* shore]

lie[1] (laɪ) *vb.* **lying, lied. 1.** (*intr.*) to speak untruthfully with intent to mislead or deceive. **2.** (*intr.*) to convey a false impression or practise deception: *the camera does not lie.* *~n.* **3.** an untrue or deceptive statement deliberately used to mislead. **4.** something that is deliberately intended to deceive. **5. give the lie to. a.** to disprove. **b.** to accuse of lying. ~Related adj.: **mendacious.** [OE *lyge* (n.), *lēogan* (vb.)]

lie[2] (laɪ) *vb.* **lying, lay, lain.** (*intr.*) **1.** (often foll. by *down*) to place oneself or be in a prostrate position, horizontal to the ground. **2.** to be situated, esp. on a horizontal surface: *the pencil is lying on the desk; India lies to the south of Russia.* **3.** to be buried: *here lies Jane Brown.* **4.** (*copula*) to be and remain (in a particular state or condition): *to lie dormant.* **5.** to stretch or extend: *the city lies before us.* **6.** (usually foll. by *on* or *upon*) to rest or weigh: *my sins lie heavily on my mind.* **7.** (usually foll. by *in*) to exist or consist inherently: *strength lies in unity.* **8.** (foll. by *with*) **a.** to be or rest (with): *the ultimate decision lies with you.* **b.** *Arch.* to have sexual intercourse (with). **9.** (of an action, claim, appeal, etc.) to subsist; be maintainable or admissible. **10.** *Arch.* to stay temporarily. *~n.* **11.** the manner, place, or style in which something is situated. **12.** the hiding place or lair of an animal. **13. lie of the land. a.** the topography of the land. **b.** the way in which a situation is developing. ~See also **lie down, lie in,** etc. [OE *licgan* akin to OHG *ligen* to lie, L *lectus* bed]

▷ **Usage.** See at **lay.**

lied (liːd; *German* liːt) *n., pl.* **lieder** (ˈliːdə; *German* ˈliːdər). *Music.* any of various musical settings for solo voice and piano of a romantic or lyrical poem. [< G: song]

lie detector *n. Inf.* a polygraph used esp. by a police interrogator to detect false or devious answers to questions, a sudden change in one or more involuntary physiological responses being considered a manifestation of guilt, fear, etc.

lie down *vb.* (*intr., adv.*) **1.** to place oneself or be in a prostrate position in order to rest. **2.** to accept without protest or opposition (esp. in **take something lying down**). *~n.* **lie-down. 3.** a rest.

lief (liːf) *adv.* **1.** *Now rare.* gladly; willingly: *I'd as lief go today as tomorrow.* *~adj.* **2.** *Arch.* **a.** ready; glad. **b.** dear; beloved. [OE *leof;* rel. to *lufu* love]

liege (liːdʒ) *adj.* **1.** (of a lord) owed feudal allegiance (esp. in **liege lord**). **2.** (of a vassal or servant) owing feudal allegiance: *a liege subject.* **3.** faithful; loyal. *~n.* **4.** a liege lord. **5.** a liegeman or true subject. [C13: < OF *lige,* < Med. L *līticus,* < *lītus, laetus* serf, of Gmc origin]

liegeman (ˈliːdʒˌmæn) *n., pl.* **-men. 1.** (formerly) a vassal. **2.** a loyal follower.

lie in *vb.* (*intr., adv.*) **1.** to remain in bed late in the morning. **2.** to be confined in childbirth. *~n.* **lie-in. 3.** a long stay in bed in the morning.

lien (ˈliːən, liːn) *n. Law.* a right to retain possession of another's property pending discharge of a debt. [C16: via OF < L *ligāmen* bond, < *ligāre* to bind]

lierne (lɪˈɜːn) *n. Archit.* a short rib that connects the intersections of the primary ribs, esp. in Gothic vaulting. [C19: < F, ? rel. to *lier* to bind]

lie to *vb.* (*intr., adv.*) *Naut.* (of a vessel) to be hove to with little or no swinging.

lieu (ljuː, luː) *n.* stead; place (esp. in **in lieu, in lieu of**). [C13: < OF, ult. < L *locus* place]

lieutenant (lɛfˈtɛnənt; *U.S.* luːˈtɛnənt) *n.* **1.** a military officer holding commissioned rank immediately junior to a captain. **2.** a naval officer holding commissioned rank immediately junior to a lieutenant commander. **3.** *U.S.* an officer in a police or fire department ranking immediately junior to a captain. **4.** a person who holds an office in subordination to or in place of a superior. [C14: < OF, lit.: place-holding] **—lieuˈtenancy** *n.*

lieutenant colonel *n.* an officer holding commissioned rank immediately junior to a colonel in certain armies, air forces, and marine corps.

lieutenant commander *n.* an officer holding commissioned rank in certain navies immediately junior to a commander.

lieutenant general *n.* an officer holding commissioned rank in certain armies, air forces, and marine corps immediately junior to a general.

lieutenant governor *n.* **1.** a deputy governor. **2.** (in the U.S.) an elected official who acts as deputy to a state governor. **3.** (in Canada) the representative of the Crown in a province: appointed by the federal government.

life (laɪf) *n., pl.* **lives** (laɪvz). **1.** the state or quality that distinguishes living beings or organisms from dead ones and from inorganic matter, characterized chiefly by metabolism, growth, and the ability to reproduce and respond to stimuli. Related adj.: **animate. 2.** the period between birth and death. **3.** a living person or being: *to save a life.* **4.** the time between birth and the present time. **5. a.** the remainder or extent of one's life. **b.** (*as modifier*): *a life sentence; life membership; life work.* **6.** *Inf.* a sentence of imprisonment for life. **7.** the amount of time that something is active or functioning: *the life of a battery.* **8.** a present condition, state, or mode of existence: *my life is* *very dull here.* **9. a.** a biography. **b.** (*as modifier*): *a life story.* **10.** a characteristic state or mode of existence: *town life.* **11.** the sum or course of human events and activities. **12.** liveliness or high spirits: *full of life.* **13.** a source of strength, animation, or vitality: *he was the life of the show.* **14.** all living things, taken as a whole: *there is no life on Mars; plant life.* **15.** (*modifier*) *Arts.* drawn or taken from a living model: *life drawing.* **16.** (in certain games) one of a number of opportunities for participation. **17. a matter of life and death.** a matter of extreme urgency. **18. as large as life.** *Inf.* real and living. **19. for the life of me (him, her,** etc.) though trying desperately. **20. not on your life.** *Inf.* certainly not. **21. the life and soul.** *Inf.* a person regarded as the main source of merriment and liveliness: *the life and soul of the party.* **22. to the life.** (of a copy or image) resembling the original exactly. **23. true to life.** faithful to reality. [OE *līf*]

life assurance *n.* a form of insurance providing for the payment of a specified sum to a named beneficiary on the death of the policyholder. Also called: **life insurance.**

life belt *n.* a buoyant ring used to keep a person afloat when in danger of drowning.

lifeblood (ˈlaɪfˌblʌd) *n.* **1.** the blood, considered as vital to life. **2.** the essential or animating force.

lifeboat (ˈlaɪfˌbəʊt) *n.* a boat used for rescuing people at sea, escaping from a sinking ship, etc.

life buoy *n.* any of various kinds of buoyant device for keeping people afloat in an emergency.

life cycle *n.* the series of changes occurring in an animal or plant between one stage and the identical stage in the next generation.

life expectancy *n.* the statistically determined average number of years of life remaining after a specified age.

lifeguard (ˈlaɪfˌgɑːd) *n.* a person at a beach or pool to guard people against the risk of drowning.

life jacket *n.* an inflatable sleeveless jacket worn to keep a person afloat when in danger of drowning.

lifeless (ˈlaɪflɪs) *adj.* **1.** without life; inanimate; dead. **2.** not sustaining living organisms. **3.** having no vitality or animation. **4.** unconscious. —**ˈlifelessly** *adv.* —**ˈlifelessness** *n.*

lifelike (ˈlaɪfˌlaɪk) *adj.* closely resembling or representing life. —**ˈlifeˌlikeness** *n.*

lifeline (ˈlaɪfˌlaɪn) *n.* **1.** a line thrown or fired aboard a vessel for hauling in a hawser for a breeches buoy. **2.** a line by which a deep-sea diver is raised or lowered. **3.** a single means of contact, communication, or support on which a person or an area, etc., relies.

lifelong (ˈlaɪfˌlɒŋ) *adj.* lasting for or as if for a lifetime.

life peer *n. Brit.* a peer whose title lapses at his death.

life preserver *n.* **1.** *Brit.* a club or bludgeon, esp. one kept for self-defence. **2.** *U.S. & Canad.* a life belt or life jacket.

lifer (ˈlaɪfə) *n. Inf.* a prisoner sentenced to imprisonment for life.

life raft *n.* a raft for emergency use at sea.

life-saver *n.* **1.** the saver of a person's life. **2.** *Austral.* an expert swimmer, esp. a member of a surf life-saving club at a surfing beach, who rescues surfers or swimmers from drowning. **3.** *Inf.* a person or thing that gives help in time of need. —**ˈlife-ˌsaving** *adj., n.*

life science *n.* any one of the branches of science concerned with the structure and behaviour of living organisms, such as biology, botany, zoology, physiology, or biochemistry.

life-size *or* **life-sized** *adj.* representing actual size.

life span *n.* the period of time during which a human being, animal, machine, etc., may be expected to live or function.

life style *n.* the particular attitudes, habits, or behaviour associated with an individual or group.

life-support *adj.* of, providing, or relating to the equipment or treatment necessary to keep a person alive.

lifetime (ˈlaɪfˌtaɪm) *n.* **1. a.** the length of time a person or animal is alive. **b.** (*as modifier*): *a lifetime supply.* **2.** the length of time that something functions, is useful, etc. **3.** Also called: **life.** *Physics.* the average time of existence of an unstable or reactive entity.

lift (lɪft) *vb.* **1.** to rise or cause to rise upwards from the ground or another support to a higher place: *to lift a sack.* **2.** to move or cause to move upwards: *to lift one's eyes.* **3.** (*tr.*) to take hold of in order to carry or remove: *to lift something down from a shelf.* **4.** (*tr.*) to raise in status, spirituality, estimation, etc.: *his position lifted him from the common crowd.* **5.** (*tr.*) to revoke or rescind: *to lift tax restrictions.* **6.** (*tr.*) to take (plants or underground crops) out of the ground for transplanting or harvesting. **7.** (*intr.*) to disappear by lifting or as if by lifting: *the fog lifted.* **8.** (*tr.*) *Inf.* to take unlawfully or dishonourably; steal. **9.** (*tr.*) *Inf.* to plagiarize. **10.** (*tr.*) *Sl.* to arrest. **11.** (*tr.*) to perform a face-lift on. ~*n.* **12.** the act or an instance of lifting. **13.** the power or force available or used for lifting. **14. a.** *Brit.* a platform, compartment, or cage raised or lowered in a vertical shaft to transport persons or goods in a building. U.S. and Canad. word: **elevator. b.** See **chair lift, ski lift. 15.** the distance or degree to which something is lifted. **16.** a ride in a car or other vehicle for part or all of a passenger's journey. **17.** a rise in the height of the ground. **18.** a rise in morale or feeling of cheerfulness usually caused by some specific thing or event. **19.** the force required to lift an object. **20.** a layer inserted in the heel of a shoe, etc., to give the wearer added height. **21.** aid; help. **22.** the component of the aerodynamic forces acting on a wing, etc., at right angles to the airflow and opposing gravity. [C13: < ON] —**ˈlifter** *n.*

liftoff (ˈlɪftˌɒf) *n.* **1.** the initial movement of a rocket from its launching pad. **2.** the instant at which this occurs. ~*vb.* **lift off. 3.** (*intr., adv.*) (of a rocket) to leave its launching pad.

lift pump *n.* a pump that raises a fluid to a higher level. Cf. **force pump.**

ligament (ˈlɪgəmənt) *n.* **1.** *Anat.* any one of the bands of tough fibrous connective tissue that restrict movement in joints, connect various bones or cartilages, support muscles, etc. **2.** any physical or abstract bond. [C14: < Med. L *ligāmentum*, < L (in the sense: bandage), < *ligāre* to bind]

ligand (ˈlɪgənd, ˈlaɪ-) *n. Chem.* an atom, molecule, radical, or ion forming a complex with a central atom. [C20: < L *ligandum*, < *ligāre* to bind]

ligate (ˈlaɪgeɪt) *vb.* (*tr.*) to tie up or constrict (something) with a ligature. [C16: < L *ligātus*, < *ligāre* to bind] —**liˈgation** *n.*

ligature (ˈlɪgətʃə, -ˌtʃʊə) *n.* **1.** the act of binding or tying up. **2.** something used to bind. **3.** a link, bond, or tie. **4.** *Surgery.* a thread or wire for tying around a vessel, duct, etc., as for constricting the flow of blood. **5.** *Printing.* a character of two or more joined letters, such as ﬁ, ﬂ, ﬃ, ﬄ. **6.** *Music.* a slur or the group of notes connected by it. ~*vb.* **7.** (*tr.*) to bind with a ligature; ligate. [C14: < LL *ligātūra*, ult. < L *ligāre* to bind]

liger (ˈlaɪgə) *n.* the hybrid offspring of a female tiger and a male lion.

ligger (ˈlɪgə) *n. Sl.* (esp. in the media) a person who habitually takes advantage of what is freely available. [C20: <?] —**ˈligging** *n.*

light[1] (laɪt) *n.* **1.** the medium of illumination that makes sight possible. **2.** Also called: **visible radiation.** electromagnetic radiation that is capable of causing a visual sensation. **3.** (*not in technical usage*) electromagnetic radiation that has a wavelength outside this range, esp. ultraviolet radiation: *ultraviolet light.* **4.** the sensation experienced when electromagnetic radiation within the visible spectrum falls on the retina of the eye. **5.** anything that illuminates, such as a lamp or candle. **6.** See **traffic light. 7.** a particular quality or type of light: *a good light for reading.* **8. a.** illumination from the sun during the day; daylight. **b.** the time this appears; daybreak; dawn. **9.** anything that allows the entrance of light, such as a window or compartment of a window. **10.** the condition of being visible or known (esp. in **bring** *or* **come to light**). **11.** an aspect or view: *he saw it in a different light.* **12.** mental understanding or spiritual insight. **13.** a person considered to be an authority or leader. **14.** brightness of countenance, esp. a sparkle in the eyes. **15. a.** the act of igniting or kindling something, such as a cigarette. **b.** something that ignites or kindles, esp. in a specified manner, such as a spark or flame. **c.** something used for igniting or kindling, such as a match. **16.** See **lighthouse. 17. in (the) light of.** in view of; taking into account; considering. **18. see the light.** to acquire insight. **19. see the light (of day). a.** to come into being. **b.** to come to public notice. **20. strike a light. a.** (*vb.*) to ignite something, esp. a match, by friction. **b.** (*interj.*) *Brit.* an exclamation of surprise. ~*adj.* **21.** full of light; well-lighted. **22.** (of a colour) reflecting or transmitting a large amount of light: *light yellow.* ~*vb.* **lighting, lighted** *or* **lit. 23.** to ignite or cause to ignite. **24.** (often foll. by *up*) to illuminate or cause to illuminate. **25.** to make or become cheerful or animated. **26.** (*tr.*) to guide or lead by light. ~See also **lights**[1], **light up.** [OE *lēoht*] —ˈ**lightish** *adj.* —ˈ**lightless** *adj.*

light[2] (laɪt) *adj.* **1.** not heavy; weighing relatively little. **2.** having relatively low density: *magnesium is a light metal.* **3.** lacking sufficient weight; not agreeing with standard or official weights. **4.** not great in degree, intensity, or number: *light rain.* **5.** without burdens, difficulties, or problems; easily borne or done: *a light heart; light work.* **6.** graceful, agile, or deft: *light fingers.* **7.** not bulky or clumsy. **8.** not serious or profound; entertaining: *light music; light verse.* **9.** without importance or consequence; insignificant: *no light matter.* **10.** frivolous or capricious. **11.** loose in morals. **12.** dizzy or unclear: *a light head.* **13.** (of bread, cake, etc.) spongy or well leavened. **14.** easily digested: *a light meal.* **15.** relatively low in alcoholic content: *a light wine.* **16.** (of a soil) having a crumbly texture. **17.** (of a vessel, lorry, etc.) **a.** designed to carry light loads. **b.** not loaded. **18.** carrying light arms or equipment: *light infantry.* **19.** (of an industry) engaged in the production of small consumer goods using light machinery. **20.** *Phonetics, prosody.* (of a syllable, vowel, etc.) unaccented or weakly stressed; short. **21. light on.** *Inf.* lacking a sufficient quantity of (something). **22. make light of.** to treat as insignificant or trifling. ~*adv.* **23.** a less common word for **lightly. 24.** with little equipment, baggage, etc.: *to travel light.* ~*vb.* **lighting, lighted** *or* **lit.** (*intr.*) **25.** (esp. of birds) to settle or land after flight. **26.** to get down from a horse, vehicle, etc. **27.** (foll. by *on* or *upon*) to come upon unexpectedly. **28.** to strike or fall on: *the choice lighted on me.* ~See also **light into, light out, lights**[2]. [OE *lēoht*] —ˈ**lightish** *adj.* —ˈ**lightly** *adv.* —ˈ**lightness** *n.*

light air *n.* very light air movement of force one (1–3 mph) on the Beaufort scale.

light breeze *n.* a very light wind of force two (4–7 mph) on the Beaufort scale.

light bulb *n.* a glass bulb containing a gas at low pressure and enclosing a thin metal filament that emits light when an electric current is passed through it. Sometimes shortened to **bulb.**

light-emitting diode *n.* a semiconductor that emits light when an electric current is applied to it: used in electronic calculators, digital watches, etc.

lighten[1] (ˈlaɪtᵊn) *vb.* **1.** to become or make light. **2.** (*intr.*) to shine; glow. **3.** (*intr.*) (of lightning) to flash. **4.** (*tr.*) *Arch.* to cause to flash.

lighten[2] (ˈlaɪtᵊn) *vb.* **1.** to make or become less heavy. **2.** to make or become less burdensome or oppressive; mitigate. **3.** to make or become more cheerful or lively.

lighter[1] (ˈlaɪtə) *n.* **1.** a small portable device for providing a naked flame to light cigarettes, etc. **2.** a person or thing that ignites something.

lighter[2] (ˈlaɪtə) *n.* a flat-bottomed barge used for transporting cargo, esp. in loading or unloading a ship. [C15: prob. < MDu.]

lighterage (ˈlaɪtərɪdʒ) *n.* **1.** the conveyance or loading and unloading of cargo by means of a lighter. **2.** the charge for this service.

light face *n.* **1.** *Printing.* a weight of type characterized by light thin lines. ~*adj. also* **light-faced. 2.** (of type) having this weight.

light-fingered *adj.* having nimble or agile fingers, esp. for thieving or picking pockets.

light flyweight *n.* **1.** an amateur boxer weighing not more than 48 kg (106 pounds). **2.** an amateur wrestler weighing not more than 48 kg (106 pounds).

light-footed *adj.* having a light or nimble tread. —ˌ**light-ˈfootedly** *adv.*

light-headed *adj.* **1.** frivolous. **2.** giddy; feeling faint or slightly delirious. —ˌ**light-ˈheadedly** *adv.* —ˌ**light-ˈheadedness** *n.*

light-hearted *adj.* cheerful or carefree in mood or disposition. —ˌ**light-ˈheartedly** *adv.* —ˌ**light-ˈheartedness** *n.*

light heavyweight *n.* **1.** Also (in Britain): **cruiserweight. a.** a professional boxer weighing 160–175 pounds (72.5–79.5 kg). **b.** an amateur boxer weighing 75–81 kg (165–179 pounds). **2. a.** a professional wrestler weighing not more than 198 pounds (90 kg). **b.** an amateur wrestler weighing not more than 90 kg (198 pounds).

lighthouse (ˈlaɪtˌhaʊs) *n.* a fixed structure in the form of a tower equipped with a light visible to mariners for warning them of obstructions, etc.

lighting (ˈlaɪtɪŋ) *n.* **1.** the act or quality of illumination or ignition. **2.** the apparatus for supplying artificial light effects to a stage, film, or television set. **3.** the distribution of light on an object or figure, as in painting, photography, etc.

lighting-up time *n.* the time when vehicles are required by law to have their lights on.

light into *vb.* (*tr., prep.*) *Inf.* to assail physically or verbally.

light middleweight *n.* an amateur boxer weighing 67–71 kg (148–157 pounds).

lightness (ˈlaɪtnɪs) *n.* the attribute of an object or colour that enables an observer to judge the extent to which the object or colour reflects or transmits incident light.

lightning (ˈlaɪtnɪŋ) *n.* **1.** a flash of light in the sky, occurring during a thunderstorm and caused by a discharge of electricity, either between clouds or between a cloud and the earth. **2.** (*modifier*) fast and sudden: *a lightning raid.* [C14: var. of *lightening*]

lightning conductor *or* **rod** *n.* a metal strip terminating in sharp points, attached to the highest part of a building, etc., to provide a safe path to earth for lightning discharges.

light opera *n.* another term for **operetta.**

light out *vb.* (*intr., adv.*) *Inf.* to depart quickly, as if being chased.

light pen *n. Computer technol.* **a.** a rodlike device which, when applied to the screen of a cathode-ray tube, can detect the time of passage of the illuminated spot across that point thus enabling a computer to determine the position on the screen being pointed at. **b.** a penlike device, used to read bar codes, that emits light and determines the intensity of that light as reflected from a small area of an adjacent surface.

lights[1] (laɪts) *pl. n.* a person's ideas, knowledge, or understanding: *he did it according to his lights.*

lights[2] (laɪts) *pl. n.* the lungs, esp. of sheep, bullocks, and pigs, used esp. for feeding pets. [C13: pl. n. use of LIGHT[2], referring to the light weight of the lungs]

lightship (ˈlaɪtˌʃɪp) *n.* a ship equipped as a lighthouse and moored where a fixed structure would prove impracticable.

light show *n.* a kaleidoscopic display of moving lights, etc., projected onto a screen, esp. during pop concerts.

lightsome (ˈlaɪtsəm) *adj. Arch. or poetic.* **1.** light-hearted or gay. **2.** airy or buoyant. **3.** not serious; frivolous.

lights out *n.* **1.** the time when those resident at an institution, such as soldiers in barracks or children at a boarding school, are expected to retire to bed. **2.** a signal indicating this.

light up *vb.* (*adv.*) **1.** to light a cigarette, pipe, etc. **2.** to illuminate or cause to illuminate. **3.** to make or become cheerful or animated.

lightweight ('laɪtˌweɪt) *adj.* **1.** of a relatively light weight. **2.** not serious; trivial. ~*n.* **3.** a person or animal of a relatively light weight. **4. a.** a professional boxer weighing 130–135 pounds (59–61 kg). **b.** an amateur boxer weighing 57–60 kg (126–132 pounds). **5. a.** a professional wrestler weighing not more than 154 pounds (70 kg). **b.** an amateur wrestler weighing not more than 68 kg (150 pounds). **6.** *Inf.* a person of little importance or influence.

light welterweight *n.* an amateur boxer weighing 60–63.5 kg (132–140 pounds).

light year *n.* a unit of distance used in astronomy, equal to the distance travelled by light in one mean solar year, i.e. 9.4607×10^{15} metres or 5.8784×10^{12} miles.

ligneous ('lɪɡnɪəs) *adj.* of or resembling wood. [C17: < L *ligneus*, < *lignum* wood]

lignin ('lɪɡnɪn) *n.* a complex polymer occurring in certain plant cell walls making the plant rigid. [C19: < L *lignum* wood + -IN]

lignite ('lɪɡnaɪt) *n.* a brown carbonaceous sedimentary rock with woody texture that consists of accumulated layers of partially decomposed vegetation: used as a fuel. Also called: **brown coal.** —**lignitic** (lɪɡ'nɪtɪk) *adj.*

lignum vitæ ('lɪɡnəm 'vaɪtɪ) *n.* **1.** either of two tropical American trees having blue or purple flowers. **2.** the heavy resinous wood of either of these trees. ~See also **guaiacum.** [NL, < LL, lit.: wood of life]

ligroin ('lɪɡrəʊɪn) *n.* a volatile fraction of petroleum: used as a solvent. [<?]

likable *or* **likeable** ('laɪkəbᵊl) *adj.* easy to like; pleasing. —'**likableness** *or* '**likeableness** *n.*

like[1] (laɪk) *adj.* **1.** (*prenominal*) similar; resembling. ~*prep.* **2.** similar to; similarly to; in the manner of: *acting like a maniac; he's so like his father.* **3.** used correlatively to express similarity: *like mother, like daughter.* **4.** such as: *there are lots of games—like draughts, for instance.* ~*adv.* **5.** a dialect word for **likely.** ~*conj.* **6.** *Not standard.* as though; as if: *you look like you've just seen a ghost.* **7.** in the same way as; in the same way that: *she doesn't dance like you do.* ~*n.* **8.** the equal or counterpart of a person or thing. **9. the like.** similar things: *dogs, foxes, and the like.* **10. the likes** (*or* **like**) **of.** people or things similar to (someone or something specified): *we don't want the likes of you around here.* [shortened < OE *gelīc*]

▷ **Usage.** The use of *like* as a conjunction (*he behaves like his father did*) is avoided in good usage, *as, as if,* or *as though* being preferred. Many careful writers and speakers do accept, however, the use of *like* as a preposition in constructions where no verb is expressed: *he looks like his father.*

like[2] (laɪk) *vb.* **1.** (*tr.*) to find (something) enjoyable or agreeable or find it enjoyable or agreeable (to do something): *he likes boxing; he likes to hear music.* **2.** (*tr.*) to be fond of. **3.** (*tr.*) to prefer or wish (to do something): *we would like you to go.* **4.** (*tr.*) to feel towards; consider; regard: *how did she like it?* **5.** (*intr.*) to feel disposed or inclined; choose; wish. ~*n.* **6.** (*usually pl.*) a favourable feeling, desire, preference, etc. (esp. in **likes and dislikes**). [OE *līcian*]

-like *suffix forming adjectives.* **1.** resembling or similar to: *lifelike.* **2.** having the characteristics of: *childlike.* [< LIKE[1] (prep.)]

likelihood ('laɪklɪˌhʊd) *or* **likeliness** *n.* **1.** the condition of being likely or probable; probability. **2.** something that is probable.

likely ('laɪklɪ) *adj.* **1.** (usually foll. by an infinitive) tending or inclined; apt: *likely to rain.* **2.** probable: *a likely result.* **3.** believable or feasible; plausible. **4.** appropriate for a purpose or activity. **5.** having good possibilities of success: *a likely candidate.* ~*adv.* **6.** probably or presumably. **7. as likely as not.** very probably. [C14: < ON *līkligr*]

like-minded *adj.* agreeing in opinions, goals, etc. —ˌ**like-'mindedly** *adv.* —ˌ**like-'mindedness** *n.*

liken ('laɪkən) *vb.* (*tr.*) to see or represent as the same or similar; compare. [C14: < LIKE[1] (adj.)]

likeness ('laɪknɪs) *n.* **1.** the condition of being alike; similarity. **2.** a painted, carved, moulded, or graphic image of a person or thing. **3.** an imitative appearance; semblance.

likewise ('laɪkˌwaɪz) *adv.* **1.** in addition; moreover; also. **2.** in like manner; similarly.

liking ('laɪkɪŋ) *n.* **1.** the feeling of a person who likes; fondness. **2.** a preference, inclination, or pleasure.

lilac ('laɪlək) *n.* **1.** any of various Eurasian shrubs or small trees of the olive family which have large sprays of purple or white fragrant flowers. **2. a.** a light or moderate purple colour. **b.** (*as adj.*): *a lilac carpet.* [C17: via F < Sp., < Ar. *līlak*, changed < Persian *nīlak* bluish, < *nīl* blue]

liliaceous (ˌlɪlɪ'eɪʃəs) *adj.* of, relating to, or belonging to a family of plants having showy flowers and a bulb or bulblike organ: includes the lily, tulip, bluebell, and onion. [C18: < LL *līliāceus*, < *līlium* lily]

Lilliputian (ˌlɪlɪ'pjuːʃɪən) *n.* **1.** a tiny person or being. ~*adj.* **2.** tiny; very small. **3.** petty or trivial. [C18: < *Lilliput*, an imaginary country of tiny inhabitants in Swift's *Gulliver's Travels* (1726)]

Lilo ('laɪˌləʊ) *n., pl.* **-los.** *Trademark.* a type of inflatable plastic or rubber mattress.

lilt (lɪlt) *n.* **1.** (in music) a jaunty rhythm. **2.** a buoyant motion. ~*vb.* (*intr.*) **3.** (of a melody) to have a lilt. **4.** to move in a buoyant manner. [C14 *lulten*, <?] —'**lilting** *adj.*

lily ('lɪlɪ) *n., pl.* **lilies.** **1.** any perennial plant of a N temperate genus, such as the tiger lily, having scaly bulbs and showy typically pendulous flowers. **2.** the bulb or flower of any of these plants. **3.** any of various similar or related plants, such as the water lily. [OE, < L *līlium*; rel. to Gk *leirion* lily] —'**lily-**ˌ**like** *adj.*

lily-livered *adj.* cowardly; timid.

lily of the valley *n., pl.* **lilies of the valley.** a small liliaceous plant of Eurasia and North America cultivated for its spikes of fragrant white bell-shaped flowers.

lily-white *adj.* **1.** of a pure white: *lily-white skin.* **2.** *Inf.* pure; irreproachable.

lima bean ('laɪmə) *n.* **1.** any of several varieties of the bean plant native to tropical America, cultivated for its flat pods containing pale green edible seeds. **2.** the seed of such a plant. [C19: after *Lima*, Peru]

limb[1] (lɪm) *n.* **1.** an arm or leg, or the analogous part on an animal, such as a wing. **2.** any of the main branches of a tree. **3.** a branching or projecting section or member; extension. **4.** a person or thing considered to be a member, part, or agent of a larger group or thing. **5.** *Chiefly Brit.* a mischievious child (esp. in **limb of Satan,** etc.). **6. out on a limb. a.** in a precarious or questionable position. **b.** *Brit.* isolated, esp. because of unpopular opinions. [OE *lim*] —'**limbless** *adj.*

limb[2] (lɪm) *n.* **1.** the edge of the apparent disc of the sun, a moon, or a planet. **2.** a graduated arc attached to instruments, such as the sextant, used for measuring angles. **3.** *Bot.* the expanded part of a leaf, petal, or sepal. [C15: < L *limbus* edge]

limbed (lɪmd) *adj.* **a.** having limbs. **b.** (*in combination*): *short-limbed; strong-limbed.*

limber[1] ('lɪmbə) *adj.* **1.** capable of being easily bent or flexed; pliant. **2.** able to move or bend freely; agile. [C16: <?] —'**limberness** *n.*

limber[2] ('lɪmbə) *n.* **1.** part of a gun carriage, consisting of an axle, pole, and two wheels. ~*vb.* **2.** (usually foll. by *up*) to attach the limber (to a gun, etc.). [C15 *lymour* shaft of a gun carriage, <?]

limber up *vb.* (*intr., adv.*) (esp. in sports) to exercise in order to be limber and agile.

limbic system (ˈlɪmbɪk) *n.* the part of the brain concerned with basic emotion, hunger, and sex. [C19 *limbic,* < F, < *limbe,* < NL *limbus,* < L: border]

limbo[1] (ˈlɪmbəʊ) *n., pl.* **-bos.** **1.** (*often cap.*) *Christianity.* the supposed abode of infants dying without baptism and the just who died before Christ. **2.** an imaginary place for lost, forgotten, or unwanted persons or things. **3.** an unknown intermediate place or condition between two extremes: *in limbo.* [C14: < Med. L *in limbo* on the border (of hell)]

limbo[2] (ˈlɪmbəʊ) *n., pl.* **-bos.** a West Indian dance in which dancers pass, while leaning backwards, under a bar. [C20: <?]

Limburger (ˈlɪmˌbɜːgə) *n.* a semihard white cheese of very strong smell and flavour. Also called: **Limburg cheese.**

lime[1] (laɪm) *n.* **1.** short for **quicklime, birdlime, slaked lime. 2.** *Agriculture.* any of certain calcium compounds, esp. calcium hydroxide, spread as a dressing on lime-deficient land. ~*vb.* (*tr.*) **3.** to spread (twigs, etc.) with birdlime. **4.** to spread a calcium compound upon (land) to improve plant growth. **5.** to catch (animals, esp. birds) as with birdlime. **6.** to whitewash (a wall, ceiling, etc.) with a mixture of lime and water (**limewash**). [OE *līm*]

lime[2] (laɪm) *n.* **1.** a small Asian citrus tree with stiff sharp spines and small round or oval greenish fruits. **2. a.** the fruit of this tree, having acid fleshy pulp rich in vitamin C. **b.** (*as modifier*): *lime juice.* ~*adj.* **3.** having the flavour of lime fruit. [C17: < F, < Ar. *līmah*]

lime[3] (laɪm) *n.* a European linden tree planted in many varieties for ornament. [C17: changed < obs. *line,* < OE *lind* LINDEN]

limeade (ˌlaɪmˈeɪd) *n.* a drink made from sweetened lime juice and plain or carbonated water.

lime green *n.* **a.** a moderate greenish-yellow colour. **b.** (*as adj.*): *a lime-green dress.*

limekiln (ˈlaɪmˌkɪln) *n.* a kiln in which calcium carbonate is calcined to produce quicklime.

limelight (ˈlaɪmˌlaɪt) *n.* **1. the.** a position of public attention or notice (esp. in **in the limelight**). **2. a.** a type of lamp, formerly used in stage lighting, in which light is produced by heating lime to white heat. **b.** Also called: **calcium light.** brilliant white light produced in this way.

limerick (ˈlɪmərɪk) *n.* a form of comic verse consisting of five anapaestic lines. [C19: allegedly < *will you come up to Limerick?,* a refrain sung between nonsense verses at a party]

limestone (ˈlaɪmˌstəʊn) *n.* a sedimentary rock consisting mainly of calcium carbonate: used as a building stone and in making cement, lime, etc.

limewater (ˈlaɪmˌwɔːtə) *n.* **1.** a clear colourless solution of calcium hydroxide in water, sometimes used in medicine as an antacid. **2.** water that contains dissolved lime or calcium salts, esp. calcium carbonate or calcium sulphate.

limey (ˈlaɪmɪ) *U.S. & Canad. sl.* ~*n.* **1.** a British person. **2.** a British sailor or ship. ~*adj.* **3.** British. [abbrev. < C19 *lime-juicer,* because British sailors drank lime juice as a protection against scurvy]

limit (ˈlɪmɪt) *n.* **1.** (*sometimes pl.*) the ultimate extent, degree, or amount of something: *the limit of endurance.* **2.** (*often pl.*) the boundary or edge of a specific area: *the city limits.* **3.** (*often pl.*) the area of premises within specific boundaries. **4.** the largest quantity or amount allowed. **5.** *Maths.* **a.** a value to which a function approaches as the independent variable approaches a specified value or infinity. **b.** a value to which a sequence a_n approaches as n approaches infinity. **c.** the limit of a sequence of partial sums of a convergent infinite series. **6.** *Maths.* one of the two specified values between which a definite integral is evaluated. **7. the limit.** *Inf.* a person or thing that is intolerably exasperating. ~*vb.* (*tr.*) **8.** to restrict or confine, as to area, extent, time, etc. [C14: < L *līmes* boundary] —ˈ**limitable** *adj.* —ˈ**limitless** *adj.* —ˈ**limitlessly** *adv.* —ˈ**limitlessness** *n.*

limitary (ˈlɪmɪtərɪ, -trɪ) *adj.* **1.** of, involving, or serving as a limit. **2.** restricted or limited.

limitation (ˌlɪmɪˈteɪʃən) *n.* **1.** something that limits a quality or achievement. **2.** the act of limiting or the condition of being limited. **3.** *Law.* a certain period of time, legally defined, within which an action, claim, etc., must be commenced.

limited (ˈlɪmɪtɪd) *adj.* **1.** having a limit; restricted; confined. **2.** without fullness or scope; narrow. **3.** (of governing powers, sovereignty, etc.) restricted or checked, by or as if by a constitution, laws, or an assembly: *limited government.* **4.** *Chiefly Brit.* (of a business enterprise) owned by shareholders whose liability for the enterprise's debts is restricted. —ˈ**limitedly** *adv.* —ˈ**limitedness** *n.*

limited liability *n. Brit.* liability restricted to the unpaid portion (if any) of the par value of the shares of a limited company.

limiter (ˈlɪmɪtə) *n.* an electronic circuit that produces an output signal whose positive or negative amplitude, or both, is limited to some predetermined value above which the peaks become flattened. Also called: **clipper.**

limn (lɪm) *vb.* (*tr.*) **1.** to represent in drawing or painting. **2.** *Arch.* to describe in words. [C15: < OF *enluminer* to illumine (a manuscript) < L *inlūmināre* to brighten, < *lūmen* light] —**limner** (ˈlɪmnə) *n.*

limnology (lɪmˈnɒlədʒɪ) *n.* the study of bodies of fresh water with reference to their plant and animal life, physical properties, geographical features, etc. [C20: < Gk *limnē* lake] —**limnological** (ˌlɪmnəˈlɒdʒɪkᵊl) *adj.* —**lim**ˈ**nologist** *n.*

limousine (ˈlɪməˌziːn, ˌlɪməˈziːn) *n.* any large and luxurious car, esp. one that has a glass division between the driver and passengers. [C20: < F, lit.: cloak (orig. one worn by shepherds in *Limousin*), hence later applied to the car]

limp[1] (lɪmp) *vb.* (*intr.*) **1.** to walk with an uneven step, esp. with a weak or injured leg. **2.** to advance in a labouring or faltering manner. ~*n.* **3.** an uneven walk or progress. [C16: prob. a back formation < obs. *limphalt* lame, < OE *lempheallt*] —ˈ**limper** *n.* —ˈ**limping** *adj., n.*

limp[2] (lɪmp) *adj.* **1.** not firm or stiff. **2.** not energetic or vital. **3.** (of the binding of a book) not stiffened with boards. [C18: prob. of Scand. origin] —ˈ**limply** *adv.* —ˈ**limpness** *n.*

limpet (ˈlɪmpɪt) *n.* **1.** any of numerous marine gastropods, such as the common limpet and keyhole limpet, that have a conical shell and are found clinging to rocks. **2.** (*modifier*) relating to or denoting certain weapons that are attached to their targets by magnetic or adhesive properties and resist removal: *limpet mines.* [OE *lempedu,* < L *lepas,* < Gk]

limpid (ˈlɪmpɪd) *adj.* **1.** clear or transparent. **2.** (esp. of writings, style, etc.) free from obscurity. **3.** calm; peaceful. [C17: < F *limpide,* < L *limpidus* clear] —**lim**ˈ**pidity** *or* ˈ**limpidness** *n.* —ˈ**limpidly** *adv.*

limp-wristed *adj.* ineffectual; effete.

limy[1] (ˈlaɪmɪ) *adj.* **limier, limiest.** of, like, or smeared with birdlime. —ˈ**liminess** *n.*

limy[2] (ˈlaɪmɪ) *adj.* **limier, limiest.** of or tasting of lime (the fruit).

linage (ˈlaɪnɪdʒ) *n.* **1.** the number of lines in a piece of written or printed matter. **2.** payment for written material calculated according to the number of lines.

linchpin (ˈlɪntʃˌpɪn) *n.* **1.** a pin placed transversely through an axle to keep a wheel in position. **2.** a person or thing regarded as an essential or coordinating element: *the linchpin of the company.* [C14 *lynspin,* < OE *lynis*]

Lincoln green (ˈlɪŋkən) *n.* **1. a.** a yellowish-green or brownish-green colour. **b.** (*as adj.*): *a Lincoln-green suit.* **2.** a cloth of this colour. [C16:

after a green fabric formerly made at *Lincoln*, in E central England]

Lincs (lɪŋks) *abbrev. for* Lincolnshire.

linctus (ˈlɪŋktəs) *n., pl.* **-tuses.** a syrupy medicinal preparation, taken to relieve coughs and sore throats. [C17 (in the sense: medicine to be licked with the tongue): < L, p.p. of *lingere* to lick]

lindane (ˈlɪndeɪn) *n.* a white poisonous crystalline powder: used as an insecticide and weedkiller. [C20: after T. van der *Linden*, Du. chemist]

linden (ˈlɪndən) *n.* any of various deciduous trees of a N temperate genus having heart-shaped leaves and small fragrant yellowish flowers: cultivated for timber and as shade trees. See also **lime**[3]. [C16: n. use of obs. adj. *linden*, < OE *linde* lime tree]

line[1] (laɪn) *n.* **1.** a narrow continuous mark, as one made by a pencil, pen, or brush across a surface. **2.** such a mark cut into or raised from a surface. **3.** a thin indented mark or wrinkle. **4.** a straight or curved continuous trace having no breadth that is produced by a moving point. **5.** *Maths.* **a.** any straight one-dimensional geometrical element whose identity is determined by two points. A **line segment** lies between any two points on a line. **b.** a set of points (x, y) that satisfies the equation $y = mx + c$, where m is the gradient and c is the intercept with the y-axis. **6.** a border or boundary: *the county line.* **7.** *Sport.* **a.** a white or coloured band indicating a boundary or division on a field, track, etc. **b.** a mark or imaginary mark at which a race begins or ends. **8.** *American football.* **a.** See **line of scrimmage. b.** the players arranged in a row on either side of the line of scrimmage at the start of each play. **9.** a specified point of change or limit: *the dividing line between sanity and madness.* **10. a.** the edge or contour of a shape. **b.** the sum or type of such contours, characteristic of a style or design: *the line of a building.* **11.** anything long, flexible, and thin, such as a wire or string: *a washing line; a fishing line.* **12.** a telephone connection: *a direct line to New York.* **13.** a conducting wire, cable, or circuit for making connections between pieces of electrical apparatus, such as a cable for electric-power transmission, telecommunications, etc. **14.** a system of travel or transportation, esp. over agreed routes: *a shipping line.* **15.** a company operating such a system. **16.** a route between two points on a railway. **17.** *Chiefly Brit.* a railway track, including the roadbed, sleepers, etc. **18.** a course or direction of movement or advance: *the line of flight of a bullet.* **19.** a course or method of action, behaviour, etc.: *take a new line with him.* **20.** a policy or prescribed course of action or way of thinking (often in **bring** *or* **come into line**). **21.** a field of study, interest, occupation, trade, or profession: *this book is in your line.* **22.** alignment; true (esp. in **in line, out of line**). **23.** one kind of product or article: *a nice line in hats.* **24.** a row of persons or things: *a line of cakes on the conveyor belt.* **25.** a chronological or ancestral series, esp. of people: *a line of prime ministers.* **26.** a row of words printed or written across a page or column. **27.** a unit of verse consisting of the number of feet appropriate to the metre being used and written or printed with the words in a single row. **28.** a short letter; note: *just a line to say thank you.* **29.** a piece of useful information or hint about something: *give me a line on his work.* **30.** one of a number of narrow horizontal bands forming a television picture. **31.** a narrow band in an electromagnetic spectrum, resulting from a transition in an atom of a gas. **32.** *Music.* **a.** any of the five horizontal marks that make up the stave. **b.** the musical part or melody notated on one such set. **c.** a discernible shape formed by sequences of notes or musical sounds: *a meandering melodic line.* **d.** (in polyphonic music) a set of staves that are held together with a bracket or brace. **33.** a defensive or fortified position, esp. one that marks the most forward position in war or a national boundary: *the front line.* **34.** a formation adopted by a body or a number of military units when drawn up abreast. **35.** the combatant forces of certain armies and navies, excluding supporting arms. **36. a.** the equator (esp. in **crossing the line**). **b.** any circle or arc on the terrestrial or celestial sphere. **37.** a U.S. and Canad. word for **queue. 38.** *Sl.* a portion of a powdered drug for snorting. **39.** *Sl.* something said for effect, esp. to solicit for money, sex, etc. **40. all along the line. a.** at every stage in a series. **b.** in every detail. **41. draw the line (at).** to object (to) or set a limit (on): *her father draws the line at her coming in after midnight.* **42. get a line on.** *Inf.* to obtain information about. **43. hold the line. a.** to keep a telephone line open. **b.** *Football.* to prevent the opponents from taking the ball forward. **c.** (of soldiers) to keep formation, as when under fire. **44. in line for.** in the running for; a candidate for: *he's in line for a directorship.* **45. in line with.** conforming to. **46. lay** *or* **put on the line. a.** to pay money. **b.** to speak frankly and directly. **c.** to risk (one's career, reputation, etc.) on something. ~*vb.* **47.** (*tr.*) to mark with a line or lines. **48.** (*tr.*) to draw or represent with a line or lines. **49.** (*tr.*) to be or put as a border to: *tulips lined the lawns.* **50.** to place in or form a row, series, or alignment. ~See also **lines, line-up.** [C13: partly < OF *ligne*, ult. < L *līnea*, n. use of *līneus* flaxen, < *līnum* flax; partly < OE *līn*, ult. also < L *līnum* flax] —**ˈlinable** *or* **ˈlineable** *adj.* —**lined** *adj.*

line[2] (laɪn) *vb.* (*tr.*) **1.** to attach an inside covering to (a garment, curtain, etc.), as for protection, to hide the seaming, or so that it should hang well. **2.** to cover or fit the inside of: *to line the walls with books.* **3.** to fill plentifully: *a purse lined with money.* [C14: ult. < L *līnum* flax, since linings were often of linen]

lineage[1] (ˈlɪnɪɪdʒ) *n.* direct descent from an ancestor, esp. a line of descendants from one ancestor. [C14: < OF *lignage*, ult. < L *līnea* LINE[1]]

lineage[2] (ˈlaɪnɪdʒ) *n.* a variant spelling of **linage.**

lineal (ˈlɪnɪəl) *adj.* **1.** being in a direct line of descent from an ancestor. **2.** of, involving, or derived from direct descent. **3.** a less common word for **linear.** [C14: via OF < LL *līneālis*, < L *līnea* LINE[1]] —**ˈlineally** *adv.*

lineament (ˈlɪnɪəmənt) *n.* (*often pl.*) **1.** a facial outline or feature. **2.** a distinctive feature. [C15: < L: line, < *līneāre* to draw a line]

linear (ˈlɪnɪə) *adj.* **1.** of, in, along, or relating to a line. **2.** of or relating to length. **3.** resembling, represented by, or consisting of a line or lines. **4.** having one dimension. **5.** designating a style in the arts, esp. painting, that obtains its effects through line rather than colour or light. **6.** *Maths.* of or relating to the first degree: *a linear equation.* **7.** narrow and having parallel edges: *a linear leaf.* **8.** *Electronics.* **a.** (of a circuit, etc.) having an output that is directly proportional to input: *linear amplifier.* **b.** having components arranged in a line. [C17: < L *līneāris* of lines] —**linearity** (ˌlɪnɪˈærɪtɪ) *n.* —**ˈlinearly** *adv.*

linear accelerator *n.* an accelerator in which charged particles are accelerated along a linear path by potential differences applied to a number of electrodes along their path.

Linear B *n.* an ancient system of writing found on clay tablets and jars of the second millennium B.C. excavated in Crete and on the Greek mainland. The script is apparently a modified form of the earlier and hitherto undeciphered **Linear A** and is generally accepted as being an early representation of Mycenaean Greek.

linear measure *n.* a unit or system of units for the measurement of length.

linear motor *n.* a form of electric motor in which the stator and the rotor are linear and parallel. It can be used to drive a train, one part of the motor being in the locomotive, the other in the track.

linear programming *n. Maths.* a technique used in economics, etc., for determining the maximum or minimum of a linear function of non-negative variables subject to constraints expressed as linear equalities or inequalities.

lineation (ˌlɪnɪˈeɪʃən) *n.* 1. the act of marking with lines. 2. an arrangement of or division into lines.

line drawing *n.* a drawing made with lines only.

lineman (ˈlaɪnmən) *n., pl.* **-men.** 1. another name for **platelayer.** 2. a person who does the chaining, taping, or marking of points for a surveyor. 3. *Austral. & N.Z.* the member of a beach life-saving team who controls the line used to help drowning swimmers and surfers. 4. *American football.* a member of a line. 5. *U.S. & Canad.* another word for **linesman** (sense 2).

line management *n.* the managers in charge of specific functions and concerned in the day-to-day operations of a company.

linen (ˈlɪnɪn) *n.* 1. **a.** a hard-wearing fabric woven from the spun fibres of flax. **b.** (*as modifier*): *a linen tablecloth.* 2. yarn or thread spun from flax fibre. 3. clothes, sheets, tablecloths, etc., made from linen cloth or from cotton. [OE *linnen*, ult. < L *līnum* flax]

line of battle *n.* a formation adopted by a military or naval force when preparing for action.

line of fire *n.* the flight path of a missile discharged or to be discharged from a firearm.

line of force *n.* a line in a field of force, such as an electric or magnetic field, for which the tangent at any point is the direction of the force at that point.

line of scrimmage *n. American football.* an imaginary line, parallel to the goal lines, on which the ball is placed at the start of each play and on either side of which the teams line up.

line-out *n. Rugby Union.* the method of restarting play when the ball goes into touch, the forwards forming two parallel lines at right angles to the touchline and jumping for the ball when it is thrown in.

line printer *n.* an electromechanical device that prints a line of characters at a time: used in printing and in computer systems.

liner[1] (ˈlaɪnə) *n.* 1. a passenger ship or aircraft, esp. one that is part of a commercial fleet. 2. See **freightliner.** 3. Also called: **eyeliner.** a cosmetic used to outline the eyes. 4. a person or thing that uses lines, esp. in drawing or copying.

liner[2] (ˈlaɪnə) *n.* 1. a material used as a lining. 2. a person who supplies or fits linings.

lines (laɪnz) *pl. n.* 1. general appearance or outline: *a car with fine lines.* 2. a plan of procedure or construction: *built on traditional lines.* 3. **a.** the spoken words of a theatrical presentation. **b.** the words of a particular role: *he forgot his lines.* 4. *Inf., chiefly Brit.* a marriage certificate: *marriage lines.* 5. a defensive position, row of trenches, or other fortification: *we broke through the enemy lines.* 6. a school punishment of writing the same sentence or phrase out a specified number of times. 7. **read between the lines.** to understand or find an implicit meaning in addition to the obvious one.

linesman (ˈlaɪnzmən) *n., pl.* **-men.** 1. an official who helps the referee or umpire in various sports, esp. by indicating when the ball has gone out of play. 2. *Chiefly Brit.* a person who installs, maintains, or repairs telephone or electric-power lines. U.S. and Canad. name: **lineman.**

line-up *n.* 1. a row or arrangement of people or things assembled for a particular purpose: *the line-up for the football match.* 2. the members of such a row or arrangement. ~*vb.* **line up.** (*adv.*) 3. to form, put into, or organize a line-up. 4. (*tr.*) to produce, organize, and assemble: *they lined up some questions.* 5. (*tr.*) to align.

ling[1] (lɪŋ) *n., pl.* **ling** *or* **lings.** 1. any of several northern coastal food fishes having an elongated body with long fins. 2. another name for **burbot** (a fish). [C13: prob. < Low G]

ling[2] (lɪŋ) *n.* another name for **heather.** [C14: < ON *lyng*]

ling. *abbrev. for* linguistics.

-ling[1] *suffix forming nouns.* 1. *Often disparaging.* a person or thing belonging to or associated with the group, activity, or quality specified: *nestling; underling.* 2. used as a diminutive: *duckling.* [OE *-ling*, of Gmc origin]

-ling[2] *suffix forming adverbs.* in a specified condition, manner, or direction: *darkling.* [OE *-ling*, adv. suffix]

lingam (ˈlɪŋgəm) *or* **linga** (ˈlɪŋgə) *n.* the Hindu phallic image of the god Siva. [C18: < Sansk.]

linger (ˈlɪŋgə) *vb.* (*mainly intr.*) 1. to delay or prolong departure. 2. to go in a slow or leisurely manner; saunter. 3. to remain just alive for some time prior to death. 4. to persist or continue, esp. in the mind. 5. to be slow to act; dither. [C13 (northern dialect) *lengeren* to dwell, < *lengen* to prolong, < OE *lengan*] —ˈ**lingerer** *n.* —ˈ**lingering** *adj.* —ˈ**lingeringly** *adv.*

lingerie (ˈlænʒərɪ) *n.* women's underwear and nightwear. [C19: < F, < *linge*, < L *līneus* linen, < *līnum* flax]

lingo (ˈlɪŋgəʊ) *n., pl.* **-goes.** *Inf.* any foreign or unfamiliar language, jargon, etc. [C17: ? < LINGUA FRANCA]

lingua franca (ˈlɪŋgwə ˈfræŋkə) *n., pl.* **lingua francas** *or* **linguae francae** (ˈlɪŋgwiː ˈfrænsiː). 1. a language used for communication among people of different mother tongues. 2. a hybrid language containing elements from several different languages used in this way. 3. any system of communication providing mutual understanding. [C17: It., lit.: Frankish tongue]

Lingua Franca *n.* a particular lingua franca spoken from the Crusades to the 18th century in the ports of the Mediterranean, based on Italian, Spanish, French, Arabic, Greek, and Turkish.

lingual (ˈlɪŋgwəl) *adj.* 1. *Anat.* of or relating to the tongue. 2. **a.** *Rare.* of or relating to language or languages. **b.** (*in combination*): *polylingual.* 3. articulated with the tongue. ~*n.* 4. a lingual consonant, such as Scots (r). —ˈ**lingually** *adv.*

linguiform (ˈlɪŋgwɪˌfɔːm) *adj.* shaped like a tongue.

linguist (ˈlɪŋgwɪst) *n.* 1. a person who is skilled in foreign languages. 2. a person who studies linguistics. [C16: < L *lingua* tongue]

linguistic (lɪŋˈgwɪstɪk) *adj.* 1. of or relating to language. 2. of or relating to linguistics. —**linˈguistically** *adv.*

linguistic atlas *n.* an atlas showing the distribution of distinctive linguistic features.

linguistics (lɪŋˈgwɪstɪks) *n.* (*functioning as sing.*) the scientific study of language.

liniment (ˈlɪnɪmənt) *n.* a medicated liquid, usually containing alcohol, camphor, and an oil, applied to the skin to relieve pain, stiffness, etc. [C15: < LL *linīmentum*, < *linere* to smear]

lining (ˈlaɪnɪŋ) *n.* 1. material used to line a garment, curtain, etc. 2. any material used as an interior covering.

link[1] (lɪŋk) *n.* 1. any of the separate rings, loops, or pieces that connect or make up a chain. 2. something that resembles such a ring, loop, or piece. 3. a connecting part or episode. 4. a connecting piece in a mechanism. 5. Also called: **radio link.** a system of transmitters and receivers that connect two locations by means of radio and television signals. 6. a unit of length equal to one hundredth of a chain. 1 link of a Gunter's chain is equal to 7.92 inches, and of an engineer's chain to 1 foot. ~*vb.* 7. (often foll. by *up*) to connect or be connected with or as if with links. 8. (*tr.*) to connect by association, etc. [C14: < ON]

link[2] (lɪŋk) *n.* (formerly) a torch used to light dark streets. [C16: ? < L *lychnus*, < Gk *lukhnos* lamp]

linkage (ˈlɪŋkɪdʒ) *n.* 1. the act of linking or the state of being linked. 2. a system of interconnected levers or rods for transmitting or regulating the motion of a mechanism. 3. *Electronics.* the product of the total number of lines of magnetic flux and the number of turns in a coil or circuit through which they pass. 4. *Genetics.* the occurrence of two genes close together on the same chromosome so that they tend to be inherited as a single unit.

linkman (ˈlɪŋkmən) *n., pl.* **-men.** a presenter of a television or radio programme, esp. a sports transmission, consisting of a number of outside broadcasts from different locations.

links (lɪŋks) *pl. n.* **1. a.** short for **golf links. b.** (*as modifier*): *a links course.* See **golf course. 2.** *Chiefly Scot.* undulating sandy ground near the shore. [OE *hlincas* pl. of *hlinc* ridge]

link-up *n.* a joining or linking together of two factions, objects, etc.

linn (lɪn) *n. Chiefly Scot.* **1.** a waterfall or a pool at the foot of it. **2.** a ravine or precipice. [C16: prob. < a confusion of two words, Scot. Gaelic *linne* pool and OE *hlynn* torrent]

Linnean *or* **Linnaean** (lɪˈniːən, -ˈneɪ-) *adj.* **1.** of or relating to Linnaeus (1707–78), Swedish botanist. **2.** relating to the system of classification of plants and animals using binomial nomenclature.

linnet (ˈlɪnɪt) *n.* a brownish Old World finch: the male has a red breast and forehead. [C16: < OF *linotte*, ult. < L *līnum* flax (because the bird feeds on flaxseeds)]

lino (ˈlaɪnəʊ) *n.* short for **linoleum.**

linocut (ˈlaɪnəʊˌkʌt) *n.* **1.** a design cut in relief on a block of linoleum. **2.** a print made from such a block.

linoleum (lɪˈnəʊlɪəm) *n.* a sheet material made of hessian, jute, etc., coated with a mixture of powdered cork, linseed oil, rosin, and pigment, used as a floor covering. Often shortened to **lino.** [C19: < L *līnum* flax + *oleum* oil]

Linotype (ˈlaɪnəʊˌtaɪp) *n.* **1.** *Trademark.* a typesetting machine, operated by a keyboard, that casts an entire line on one solid slug of metal. **2.** type produced by such a machine.

linseed (ˈlɪnˌsiːd) *n.* another name for **flaxseed.** [OE *līnsǣd*, < *līn* flax + *sǣd* seed]

linseed oil *n.* a yellow oil extracted from seeds of the flax plant. It is used in making oil paints, printer's ink, linoleum, etc.

linsey-woolsey (ˈlɪnzɪˈwʊlzɪ) *n.* **1.** a thin rough fabric of linen warp and coarse wool or cotton filling. **2.** a strange nonsensical mixture or confusion. [C15: prob. < *Lindsey*, village in Suffolk where first made + WOOL (with rhyming suffix *-sey*)]

lint (lɪnt) *n.* **1.** an absorbent cotton or linen fabric with the nap raised on one side, used to dress wounds, etc. **2.** shreds of fibre, yarn, etc. [C14: prob. < L *linteus* made of linen, < *līnum* flax] —**ˈlinty** *adj.*

lintel (ˈlɪntᵊl) *n.* a horizontal beam, as over a door or window. [C14: via OF prob. < LL *līmitāris* (unattested) of the boundary, infl. by *līminaris* of the threshold]

linter (ˈlɪntə) *n.* **1.** a machine for stripping the short fibres of ginned cotton seeds. **2.** (*pl.*) the fibres so removed.

lion (ˈlaɪən) *n.* **1.** a large gregarious predatory feline mammal of open country in parts of Africa and India, having a tawny yellow coat and, in the male, a shaggy mane. Related adj.: **leonine. 2.** a conventionalized lion, the principal beast used as an emblem in heraldry. **3.** a courageous, strong, or bellicose person. **4.** a celebrity or idol who attracts much publicity and a large following. **5. the lion's share.** the largest portion. [OE *līo*, *lēo* (ME *lioun*, < Anglo-F *liun*), both < L *leo*, Gk *leōn*] —**ˈlioness** *fem. n.*

Lion (ˈlaɪən) *n.* **the.** the constellation Leo, the fifth sign of the zodiac.

lion-hearted *adj.* very brave; courageous.

lionize *or* **-ise** (ˈlaɪəˌnaɪz) *vb.* (*tr.*) to treat as or make into a celebrity. —**ˌlioniˈzation** *or* **-iˈsation** *n.* —**ˈlionˌizer** *or* **-ˌiser** *n.*

lip (lɪp) *n.* **1.** *Anat.* **a.** either of the two fleshy folds surrounding the mouth. Related adj.: **labial. b.** (*as modifier*): *lip salve.* **2.** the corresponding part in animals, esp. mammals. **3.** any structure resembling a lip, such as the rim of a crater, the margin of a gastropod shell, etc. **4.** a nontechnical word for **labium. 5.** *Sl.* impudent talk or backchat. **6. bite one's lip. a.** to stifle one's feelings. **b.** to be annoyed or irritated. **7. keep a stiff upper lip.** to maintain one's courage or composure during a time of trouble. **8. lick** *or* **smack one's lips.** to anticipate or recall something with glee or relish. ~*vb.* **lipping, lipped. 9.** (*tr.*) to touch with the lip or lips. **10.** (*tr.*) to form or be a lip or lips for. **11.** (*tr.*) *Rare.* to murmur or whisper. **12.** (*intr.*) to use the lips in playing a wind instrument. [OE *lippa*] —**ˈlipless** *adj.* —**ˈlipˌlike** *adj.*

lipase (ˈlaɪpeɪs, ˈlɪpeɪs) *n.* any of a group of fat-digesting enzymes produced in the stomach, pancreas, and liver. [C19: < Gk *lipos* fat + -ASE]

lip gloss *n.* a cosmetic applied to the lips to give a sheen.

lipid *or* **lipide** (ˈlaɪpɪd, ˈlɪpɪd) *n. Biochem.* any of a large group of organic compounds that are esters of fatty acids or closely related substances. They are important structural materials in living organisms. Former name: **lipoid.** [C20: < F *lipide*, < Gk *lipos* fat]

lipo- *or before a vowel* **lip-** *combining form.* fat or fatty: *lipoprotein.* [< Gk *lipos* fat]

lipography (lɪˈpɒgrəfɪ) *n.* the accidental omission of words or letters in writing. [C19: < Gk *lip-*, stem of *leipein* to omit + -GRAPHY]

lipoid (ˈlɪpɔɪd, ˈlaɪ-) *adj. also* **lipoidal. 1.** resembling fat; fatty. ~*n.* **2.** a fatlike substance, such as wax. **3.** *Biochem.* a former name for **lipid.**

-lipped *adj.* having a lip or lips as specified: *tight-lipped.*

Lippizaner (ˌlɪpɪtˈsɑːnə) *n.* a breed of riding and carriage horse used by the Spanish Riding School in Vienna and usually white or grey in colour. [G, after *Lippiza*, Yugoslavia, where bred]

lip-read (ˈlɪpˌriːd) *vb.* **-reading, -read** (-ˈrɛd). to interpret (words) by lip-reading.

lip-reading *n.* a method used by the deaf to comprehend spoken words by interpreting movements of the speaker's lips. Also called: **speech-reading.** —**ˈlip-ˌreader** *n.*

lip service *n.* insincere support or respect expressed but not practised.

lipstick (ˈlɪpˌstɪk) *n.* a cosmetic for colouring the lips, usually in the form of a stick.

lip-synch *or* **lip-sync** (ˈlɪpˌsɪŋk) *vb.* to mouth (the words of a prerecorded song) on television or film.

liq. *abbrev. for:* **1.** liquid. **2.** liquor.

liquefacient (ˌlɪkwɪˈfeɪʃənt) *n.* **1.** a substance that liquefies or causes liquefaction. ~*adj.* **2.** becoming or causing to become liquid. [C19: < L *liquefacere* to make LIQUID]

liquefy (ˈlɪkwɪˌfaɪ) *vb.* **-fying, -fied.** (esp. of a gas) to become or cause to become liquid. [C15: via OF < L *liquefacere* to make liquid] —**liquefaction** (ˌlɪkwɪˈfækʃən) *n.* —**ˈliqueˌfiable** *adj.* —**ˈliqueˌfier** *n.*

liquescent (lɪˈkwɛsᵊnt) *adj.* (of a solid or gas) becoming or tending to become liquid. [C18: < L *liquescere*] —**liˈquescence** *or* **liˈquescency** *n.*

liqueur (lɪˈkjʊə; *French* likœr) *n.* **1. a.** any of several highly flavoured sweetened spirits such as kirsch or cointreau, intended to be drunk after a meal. **b.** (*as modifier*): *liqueur glass.* **2.** a small hollow chocolate sweet containing liqueur. [C18: < F; see LIQUOR]

liquid (ˈlɪkwɪd) *n.* **1.** a substance in a physical state in which it does not resist change of shape but does resist change of size. Cf. **gas** (sense 1), **solid** (sense 1). **2.** a substance that is a liquid at room temperature and atmospheric pressure. **3.** *Phonetics.* a frictionless continuant, esp. (l) or (r). ~*adj.* **4.** of, concerned with, or being a liquid or having the characteristic state of liquids: *liquid wax.* **5.** shining, transparent, or brilliant. **6.** flowing, fluent, or smooth. **7.** (of assets) in the form of money or easily convertible into money. [C14: via OF < L *liquidus*, < *liquēre* to be fluid] —**liˈquidity** *or* **ˈliquidness** *n.* —**ˈliquidly** *adv.*

liquid air *n.* air that has been liquefied by cooling: used in the production of pure oxygen, nitrogen, and as a refrigerant.

liquidambar (ˌlɪkwɪdˈæmbə) *n.* **1.** a deciduous tree of Asia and North and Central America, with star-shaped leaves, and exuding a yellow aromatic balsam. **2.** the balsam of this tree, used in medicine. [C16: NL, < L *liquidus* liquid + Med. L *ambar* AMBER]

liquidate (ˈlɪkwɪˌdeɪt) *vb.* **1.** to settle or pay off (a debt, claim, etc.). **2. a.** to terminate the operations of (a commercial firm, bankrupt estate, etc.) by assessment of liabilities and appropriation of assets for their settlement. **b.** (of a commercial firm, etc.) to terminate operations in this manner. **3.** (*tr.*) to convert (assets) into cash. **4.** (*tr.*) to eliminate or kill. —ˈ**liquiˌdator** *n.*

liquidation (ˌlɪkwɪˈdeɪʃən) *n.* **1. a.** the process of terminating the affairs of a business firm, etc., by realizing its assets to discharge its liabilities. **b.** the state of a business firm, etc., having its affairs so terminated (esp. in **to go into liquidation**). **2.** destruction; elimination.

liquid crystal display *n.* a display of numbers, esp. in an electronic calculator, using cells containing a liquid with crystalline properties (**liquid crystal**), that change their reflectivity or optical polarization when an electric field is applied to them.

liquidize *or* **-dise** (ˈlɪkwɪˌdaɪz) *vb.* **1.** to make or become liquid; liquefy. **2.** (*tr.*) to pulverize (food) in a liquidizer so as to produce a fluid.

liquidizer *or* **-diser** (ˈlɪkwɪˌdaɪzə) *n.* a kitchen appliance with blades for puréeing vegetables, blending liquids, etc. Also called: **blender.**

liquid measure *n.* a unit or system of units for measuring volumes of liquids or their containers.

liquid oxygen *n.* the clear pale blue liquid state of oxygen produced by liquefying air and allowing the nitrogen to evaporate: used in rocket fuels. Also called: **lox.**

liquid paraffin *n.* an oily liquid obtained by petroleum distillation and used as a laxative. Also called (esp. U.S. and Canad.): **mineral oil.**

liquor (ˈlɪkə) *n.* **1.** any alcoholic drink, esp. spirits, or such drinks collectively. **2.** any liquid substance, esp. that in which food has been cooked. **3.** *Pharmacol.* a solution of a pure substance in water. **4. in liquor.** drunk. [C13: via OF < L, < *liquēre* to be liquid]

liquorice *or U.S. & Canad.* **licorice** (ˈlɪkərɪs, -ərɪʃ) *n.* **1.** a perennial Mediterranean leguminous shrub. **2.** the dried root of this plant, used as a laxative and in confectionery. **3.** a sweet having a liquorice flavour. [C13: via Anglo-Norman and OF < LL *liquirītia,* < L *glycyrrhīza,* < Gk *glukurrhiza,* < *glukus* sweet + *rhiza* root]

lira (ˈlɪərə; *Italian* ˈliːra) *n., pl.* **lire** (ˈlɪərɪ; *Italian* ˈliːre) *or* **liras. 1.** the standard monetary unit of Italy. **2.** Also called: **pound.** the standard monetary unit of Turkey. [It., < L *lībra* pound]

liriodendron (ˌlɪrɪəʊˈdɛndrən) *n., pl.* **-drons** *or* **-dra** (-drə). a deciduous tulip tree of North America or a similar Chinese tree. [C18: NL, < Gk *leiron* lily + *dendron* tree]

lisle (laɪl) *n.* **a.** a strong fine cotton thread or fabric. **b.** (*as modifier*): *lisle stockings.* [C19: after *Lisle* (now Lille), town in France where this thread was orig. manufactured]

lisp (lɪsp) *n.* **1.** the articulation of *s* and *z* like or nearly like the *th* sounds in English *thin* and *then* respectively. **2.** the habit or speech defect of pronouncing *s* and *z* in this manner. **3.** the sound of a lisp in pronunciation. ~*vb.* **4.** to use a lisp in the pronunciation of (speech). **5.** to speak or pronounce imperfectly or haltingly. [OE *āwlispian,* < *wlisp* lisping (adj.), imit.] —ˈ**lisper** *n.* —ˈ**lisping** *adj., n.* —ˈ**lispingly** *adv.*

lissom *or* **lissome** (ˈlɪsəm) *adj.* **1.** supple in the limbs or body; lithe; flexible. **2.** agile; nimble. [C19: var. of *lithesome,* LITHE + -SOME[1]] —ˈ**lissomly** *or* ˈ**lissomely** *adv.* —ˈ**lissomness** *or* ˈ**lissomeness** *n.*

list[1] (lɪst) *n.* **1.** an item-by-item record of names or things, usually written or printed one under the other. **2.** *Computers.* a linearly ordered data structure. ~*vb.* **3.** (*tr.*) to make a list of. **4.** (*tr.*) to include in a list. **5.** (*tr.*) *Brit.* to declare to be a listed building. **6.** (*tr.*) *Stock Exchange.* to obtain an official quotation for (a security) so that it may be traded on the recognized market. **7.** an archaic word for **enlist.** [C17: < F, ult. rel. to LIST[2]] —ˈ**listable** *adj.* —ˈ**listing** *n.*

list[2] (lɪst) *n.* **1.** a border or edging strip, esp. of cloth. **2.** a less common word for **selvage.** ~*vb.* (*tr.*) **3.** to border with or as if with a list or lists. ~See also **lists.** [OE *līst*]

list[3] (lɪst) *vb.* **1.** (esp. of ships) to lean over or cause to lean over to one side. ~*n.* **2.** the act or an instance of leaning to one side. [C17: <?]

list[4] (lɪst) *Arch.* ~*vb.* **1.** to be pleasing to (a person). **2.** (*tr.*) to desire or choose. ~*n.* **3.** a liking or desire. [OE *lystan*]

list[5] (lɪst) *vb.* an archaic or poetic word for **listen.** [OE *hlystan*]

listed building *n.* (in Britain) a building officially recognized as having special historical or architectural interest and therefore protected from demolition or alteration.

listen (ˈlɪsᵊn) *vb.* (*intr.*) **1.** to concentrate on hearing something. **2.** to take heed; pay attention: *I warned you but you wouldn't listen.* [OE *hlysnan*] —ˈ**listener** *n.*

listen in *vb.* (*intr., adv.;* often foll. by *to*) **1.** to listen to the radio. **2.** to intercept radio communications. **3.** to listen but not contribute (to a discussion), esp. surreptitiously.

listening post *n.* **1.** *Mil.* a forward position set up to obtain early warning of enemy movement. **2.** any strategic position for obtaining information about another country or area.

lister (ˈlɪstə) *n. U.S. & Canad. agriculture.* a plough with a double mouldboard designed to throw soil to either side of a central furrow. [C19: < LIST[2]]

listless (ˈlɪstlɪs) *adj.* having or showing no interest; lacking vigour or energy. [C15: < *list* desire + -LESS] —ˈ**listlessly** *adv.* —ˈ**listlessness** *n.*

list price *n.* the selling price of merchandise as quoted in a catalogue or advertisement.

lists (lɪsts) *pl. n.* **1.** *History.* **a.** the enclosed field of combat at a tournament. **b.** the barriers enclosing the field at a tournament. **2.** any arena or scene of conflict, controversy, etc. **3. enter the lists.** to engage in a conflict, controversy, etc. [C14: pl. of LIST[2] (border)]

lit (lɪt) *vb.* **1.** a past tense and past participle of **light**[1]. **2.** a past tense and past participle of **light**[2].

lit. *abbrev. for:* **1.** literal(ly). **2.** literary. **3.** literature. **4.** litre.

litany (ˈlɪtənɪ) *n., pl.* **-nies. 1.** *Christianity.* **a.** a form of prayer consisting of a series of invocations, each followed by an unvarying response. **b. the Litany.** the general supplication in this form in the Book of Common Prayer. **2.** any tedious recital. [C13: via OF < Med. L *litanīa* < LGk *litaneia* prayer, ult. < Gk *litē* entreaty]

litchi, lichee, *or* **lychee** (ˌlaɪˈtʃiː) *n.* **1.** a Chinese tree cultivated for its round edible fruits. **2.** the fruit of this tree, which has whitish juicy pulp. [C16: < Cantonese *lai chi*]

-lite *n. combining form.* (in names of minerals) stone: *chrysolite.* [< F *-lite* or *-lithe,* < Gk *lithos* stone]

liter (ˈliːtə) *n.* the U.S. spelling of **litre.**

literacy (ˈlɪtərəsɪ) *n.* **1.** the ability to read and write. **2.** the ability to use language proficiently.

literal (ˈlɪtərəl) *adj.* **1.** in exact accordance with or limited to the primary or explicit meaning of a word or text. **2.** word for word. **3.** dull, factual, or prosaic. **4.** consisting of, concerning, or indicated by letters. **5.** true; actual. ~*n.* **6.** Also called: **literal error.** a misprint or misspelling in a text. [C14: < LL *litterālis* concerning letters, < L *littera* letter] —ˈ**literally** *adv.* —ˈ**literalness** *or* **literality** (ˌlɪtəˈrælɪtɪ) *n.*

literalism (ˈlɪtərəˌlɪzəm) *n.* **1.** the disposition to take words and statements in their literal sense. **2.** literal or realistic portrayal in art or literature. —ˈ**literalist** *n.* —ˌ**literalˈistic** *adj.*

literary (ˈlɪtərərɪ, ˈlɪtrərɪ) *adj.* **1.** of, relating to, concerned with, or characteristic of literature or scholarly writing: *a literary style.* **2.** versed in or knowledgeable about literature. **3.** (of a word) formal; not colloquial. [C17: < L *litterārius* concerning reading & writing. See LETTER] —**'literarily** *adv.* —**'literariness** *n.*

literate ('lɪtərɪt) *adj.* **1.** able to read and write. **2.** educated; learned. ~*n.* **3.** a literate person. [C15: < L *litterātus* learned. See LETTER] —**'literately** *adv.*

literati (ˌlɪtə'rɑːtiː) *pl. n.* literary or scholarly people. [C17: < L]

literature ('lɪtərɪtʃə, 'lɪtrɪ-) *n.* **1.** written material such as poetry, novels, essays, etc. **2.** the body of written work of a particular culture or people: *Scandinavian literature.* **3.** written or printed matter of a particular type or genre: *scientific literature.* **4.** the art or profession of a writer. **5.** *Inf.* printed matter on any subject. [C14: < L *litterātūra* writing; see LETTER]

lith. *abbrev. for:* **1.** lithograph. **2.** lithography.

Lith. *abbrev. for* Lithuania(n).

-lith *n. combining form.* indicating stone or rock: *megalith.* [< Gk *lithos* stone]

litharge ('lɪθɑːdʒ) *n.* another name for **lead monoxide.** [C14: via OF < L *lithargyrus,* < Gk, < *lithos* stone + *arguros* silver]

lithe (laɪð) *adj.* flexible or supple. [OE (in the sense: gentle; C15: supple)] —**'lithely** *adv.* —**'litheness** *n.*

lithia ('lɪθɪə) *n.* **1.** another name for **lithium oxide.** **2.** lithium present in mineral waters as lithium salts. [C19: NL, ult. < Gk *lithos* stone]

lithic ('lɪθɪk) *adj.* **1.** of, relating to, or composed of stone. **2.** *Pathol.* of or relating to a calculus or calculi. **3.** of or containing lithium. [C18: < Gk *lithikos* stony]

-lithic *n. and adj. combining form.* relating to the use of stone implements in a specified cultural period: *Neolithic.* [< Gk *lithikos,* < *lithos* stone]

lithium ('lɪθɪəm) *n.* a soft silvery element of the alkali metal series: the lightest known metal, used as an alloy hardener, as a reducing agent, and in batteries. Symbol: Li; atomic no.: 3; atomic wt.: 6.941. [C19: NL, < LITHO- + -IUM]

lithium oxide *n.* a white crystalline compound. It absorbs carbon dioxide and water vapour.

litho ('laɪθəʊ) *n., pl.* **-thos,** *adj., adv.* short for **lithography, lithograph, lithographic,** or **lithographically.**

litho- *or before a vowel* **lith-** *combining form.* stone: *lithograph.* [< L, < Gk, < *lithos* stone]

lithograph ('lɪθəˌgrɑːf) *n.* **1.** a print made by lithography. ~*vb.* **2.** (*tr.*) to reproduce (pictures, text, etc.) by lithography. —**lithographic** (ˌlɪθə'græfɪk) *adj.* —ˌ**litho'graphically** *adv.*

lithography (lɪ'θɒgrəfɪ) *n.* a method of printing from a metal or stone surface on which the printing areas are not raised but made ink-receptive as opposed to ink-repellent. [C18: < NL *lithographia*] —**li'thographer** *n.*

lithology (lɪ'θɒlədʒɪ) *n.* **1.** the physical characteristics of a rock, including colour, composition, and texture. **2.** the study of rocks.

lithophyte ('lɪθəˌfaɪt) *n.* **1.** a plant that grows on stony ground. **2.** an organism, such as a coral, that is partly composed of stony material.

lithosphere ('lɪθəˌsfɪə) *n.* the rigid outer layer of the earth, comprising the earth's crust and the solid upper part of the mantle.

lithotomy (lɪ'θɒtəmɪ) *n., pl.* **-mies.** the surgical removal of a calculus, esp. one in the urinary bladder. [C18: via LL < Gk]

Lithuanian (ˌlɪθjʊ'eɪnɪən) *adj.* **1.** of, relating to, or characteristic of Lithuania, an administrative division of the W Soviet Union on the Baltic Sea, its people, or their language. ~*n.* **2.** an official language of the Lithuanian SSR. **3.** a native or inhabitant of Lithuania.

litigable ('lɪtɪgəbᵊl) *adj. Law.* that may be the subject of litigation.

litigant ('lɪtɪgənt) *n.* **1.** a party to a lawsuit. ~*adj.* **2.** engaged in litigation.

litigate ('lɪtɪˌgeɪt) *vb.* **1.** to bring or contest (a claim, action, etc.) in a lawsuit. **2.** (*intr.*) to engage in legal proceedings. [C17: < L *lītigāre,* < *līt-,* stem of *līs* lawsuit + *agere* to carry on] —**'litiˌgator** *n.*

litigation (ˌlɪtɪ'geɪʃən) *n.* **1.** the act or process of bringing or contesting a lawsuit. **2.** a judicial proceeding or contest.

litigious (lɪ'tɪdʒəs) *adj.* **1.** excessively ready to go to law. **2.** of or relating to litigation. **3.** inclined to dispute or disagree. [C14: < L *lītigiōsus* quarrelsome, < *lītigium* strife] —**li'tigiously** *adv.* —**li'tigiousness** *n.*

litmus ('lɪtməs) *n.* a soluble powder obtained from certain lichens. It turns red under acid conditions and blue under basic conditions. Absorbent paper treated with it (**litmus paper**) is used as an indicator. [C16: ? < Scand.]

litotes ('laɪtəʊˌtiːz) *n., pl.* **-tes.** understatement for rhetorical effect, esp. using negation with a term in place of using an antonym of that term, as in "She was not a little upset" for "She was extremely upset". [C17: < Gk, < *litos* small]

litre *or U.S.* **liter** ('liːtə) *n.* **1.** one cubic decimetre. **2.** (formerly) the volume occupied by 1 kilogram of pure water. This is equivalent to 1.000 028 cubic decimetres or about 1.76 pints. [C19: < F, < Med. L *litra,* < Gk: a unit of weight]

LittD *or* **LitD** *abbrev. for* Doctor of Letters *or* Doctor of Literature. [L: *Litterarum Doctor*]

litter ('lɪtə) *n.* **1. a.** small refuse or waste materials carelessly dropped, esp. in public places. **b.** (*as modifier*): *litter bin.* **2.** a disordered or untidy condition or a collection of objects in this condition. **3.** a group of offspring produced at one birth by a mammal such as a sow. **4.** a layer of partly decomposed leaves, twigs, etc., on the ground in a wood or forest. **5.** straw, hay, or similar material used as bedding, protection, etc., by animals or plants. **6.** a means of conveying people, esp. sick or wounded people, consisting of a light bed or seat held between parallel sticks. **7.** see **cat litter.** ~*vb.* **8.** to make (a place) untidy by strewing (refuse). **9.** to scatter (objects, etc.) about or (of objects) to lie around or upon (anything) in an untidy fashion. **10.** (of pigs, cats, etc.) to give birth to (offspring). **11.** (*tr.*) to provide (an animal or plant) with straw or hay for bedding, protection, etc. [C13 (in the sense: bed): via Anglo-F, ult. < L *lectus* bed]

littérateur (ˌlɪtərə'tɜː; *French* literatœr) *n.* an author, esp. a professional writer. [C19: < F < L *litterātor* a grammarian]

litter lout *or U.S. & Canad.* **litterbug** ('lɪtəˌbʌg) *n. Sl.* a person who tends to drop refuse in public places.

little ('lɪtᵊl) *determiner.* **1.** (often preceded by *a*) **a.** a small quantity, extent, or duration of: *the little hope there is left; very little milk.* **b.** (*as pronoun*): *save a little for me.* **2.** not much: *little damage was done.* **3. make little of.** to regard or treat as insignificant; dismiss. **4. not a little. a.** very. **b.** a lot. **5. think little of.** to have a low opinion of. ~*adj.* **6.** of small or less than average size. **7.** young: *a little boy.* **8.** endearingly familiar; dear: *my husband's little ways.* **9.** contemptible, mean, or disagreeable: *your filthy little mind.* ~*adv.* **10.** (usually preceded by a) in a small amount; to a small extent or degree; not a lot: *to laugh a little.* **11.** (*used preceding a verb*) not at all, or hardly: *he little realized his fate.* **12.** not much or often: *we go there very little now.* **13. little by little.** by small degrees. ~See also **less, lesser, least.** [OE *lȳtel*]

Little Bear *n.* **the.** the English name for **Ursa Minor.**

Little Dipper *n.* **the.** a U.S. name for **Ursa Minor.**

little people *pl. n. Folklore.* small supernatural beings, such as elves or leprechauns.

little slam *n. Bridge, etc.* the winning of all tricks except one. Also called: **small slam.**

littoral ('lɪtərəl) *adj.* **1.** of or relating to the shore of a sea, lake, or ocean. ~*n.* **2.** a coastal or shore region. [C17: < LL *littorālis,* < *lītus* shore]

liturgical (lɪ'tɜːdʒɪkᵊl) *adj.* **1.** of or relating to public worship. **2.** of or relating to the liturgy. —**li'turgically** *adv.*

liturgy ('lɪtədʒɪ) *n., pl.* **-gies.** **1.** the forms of public services officially prescribed by a Church. **2.** (*often cap.*) Also called: **Divine Liturgy.** *Chiefly*

Eastern Churches. the Eucharistic celebration. **3.** a particular order or form of public service laid down by a Church. [C16: via Med. L, < Gk *leitourgia*, < *leitourgos* minister, < *leit-* people + *ergon* work]

Liturgy of the Hours *n. Christianity.* another name for **divine office.**

livable *or* **liveable** (ˈlɪvəbᵊl) *adj.* **1.** (of a room, house, etc.) suitable for living in. **2.** worth living; tolerable. **3.** (foll. by *with*) pleasant to live (with). —**ˈlivableness, ˈliveableness** *or* **ˌlivaˈbility, ˌliveaˈbility** *n.*

live[1] (lɪv) *vb.* (*mainly intr.*) **1.** to show the characteristics of life; be alive. **2.** to remain alive or in existence. **3.** to exist in a specified way: *to live poorly.* **4.** (usually foll. by *in* or *at*) to reside or dwell: *to live in London.* **5.** (often foll. by *on*) to continue or last: *the pain still lives in her memory.* **6.** (usually foll. by *by*) to order one's life (according to a certain philosophy, religion, etc.). **7.** (foll. by *on, upon,* or *by*) to support one's style of life; subsist: *to live by writing.* **8.** (foll. by *with*) to endure the effects (of a crime, mistake, etc.). **9.** (foll. by *through*) to experience and survive: *he lived through the war.* **10.** (*tr.*) to pass or spend (one's life, etc.). **11.** to enjoy life to the full: *he knows how to live.* **12.** (*tr.*) to put into practice in one's daily life; express: *he lives religion every day.* **13. live and let live.** to refrain from interfering in others' lives; be tolerant. ~See also **live down, live in,** etc. [OE *libban, lifian*]

live[2] (laɪv) *adj.* **1.** (*prenominal*) showing the characteristics of life. **2.** (*usually prenominal*) of, relating to, or abounding in life: *the live weight of an animal.* **3.** (*usually prenominal*) of current interest; controversial: *a live issue.* **4.** actual: *a real live cowboy.* **5.** *Inf.* full of life and energy. **6.** (of a coal, ember, etc.) glowing or burning. **7.** (esp. of a volcano) not extinct. **8.** loaded or capable of exploding: *a live bomb.* **9.** *Radio, television, etc.* transmitted or present at the time of performance, rather than being a recording: *a live show.* **10.** (of a record) **a.** recorded in concert. **b.** recorded in one studio take. **11.** connected to a source of electric power: *a live circuit.* **12.** being in a state of motion or transmitting power. **13.** acoustically reverberant. ~*adv.* **14.** during, at, or in the form of a live performance. [C16: < *on live* ALIVE]

-lived (-lɪvd) *adj.* having or having had a life as specified: *short-lived.*

lived-in *adj.* having a comfortable, natural, or homely appearance.

live down (lɪv) *vb.* (*tr., adv.*) to withstand the effects of (a crime, mistake, etc.) by waiting until others forget or forgive it.

live in (lɪv) *vb.* (*intr., adv.*) **1.** (of an employee) to dwell at one's place of employment, as in a hotel, etc. ~*adj.* **live-in. 2.** resident: *a live-in nanny; a live-in lover.*

livelihood (ˈlaɪvlɪˌhʊd) *n.* occupation or employment.

livelong (ˈlɪvˌlɒŋ) *adj. Chiefly poetic.* **1.** (of time) long or seemingly long (esp. in **all the livelong day**). **2.** whole; entire.

lively (ˈlaɪvlɪ) *adj.* **-lier, -liest. 1.** full of life or vigour. **2.** vivacious or animated, esp. when in company. **3.** busy; eventful. **4.** characterized by mental or emotional intensity; vivid. **5.** having a striking effect on the mind or senses. **6.** refreshing or invigorating: *a lively breeze.* **7.** springy or bouncy or encouraging springiness: *a lively ball.* ~*adv.* also **livelily. 8.** in a brisk or lively manner: *step lively.* —**ˈliveliness** *n.*

liven (ˈlaɪvᵊn) *vb.* (usually foll. by *up*) to make or become lively; enliven. —**ˈlivener** *n.*

live oak (laɪv) *n.* a hard-wooded evergreen oak of S North America: used for shipbuilding.

live out (lɪv) *vb.* (*intr., adv.*) (of an employee, as in a hospital or hotel) to dwell away from one's place of employment.

liver[1] (ˈlɪvə) *n.* **1.** a large highly vascular reddish-brown glandular organ in the human abdominal cavity. Its main function is the metabolic transformation of nutrients. It also secretes bile, stores glycogen, and detoxifies certain poisons. Related adj.: **hepatic. 2.** the corresponding organ in animals. **3.** the liver of certain animals used as food. **4.** a reddish-brown colour. [OE *lifer*]

liver[2] (ˈlɪvə) *n.* a person who lives in a specified way: *a fast liver.*

liveried (ˈlɪvərɪd) *adj.* (esp. of servants or footmen) wearing livery.

liverish (ˈlɪvərɪʃ) *adj.* **1.** *Inf.* having a disorder of the liver. **2.** disagreeable; peevish. —**ˈliverishness** *n.*

Liverpudlian (ˌlɪvəˈpʌdlɪən) *n.* **1.** a native or inhabitant of Liverpool, in NW England. ~*adj.* **2.** of or relating to Liverpool. [C19: < *Liverpool,* with humorous alteration of *pool* to *puddle*]

liver salts *pl. n.* a preparation of mineral salts used to treat indigestion.

liver sausage *or esp. U.S.* **liverwurst** (ˈlɪvəˌwɜːst) *n.* a sausage containing liver.

liverwort (ˈlɪvəˌwɜːt) *n.* any of a class of plants growing in wet places and resembling green seaweeds or leafy mosses. [late OE *liferwyrt*]

livery (ˈlɪvərɪ) *n., pl.* **-eries. 1.** the identifying uniform, badge, etc., of a member of a guild or one of the servants of a feudal lord. **2.** a uniform worn by some menservants. **3.** an individual or group that wears such a uniform. **4.** distinctive dress or outward appearance. **5. a.** the stabling, keeping, or hiring out of horses for money. **b.** (*as modifier*): *a livery horse.* **6. at livery.** being kept in a livery stable. [C14: via Anglo-F < OF *livrée* allocation, < *livrer* to hand over, < L *līberāre* to set free]

livery company *n. Brit.* one of the chartered companies of the City of London originating from the craft guilds.

liveryman (ˈlɪvərɪmən) *n., pl.* **-men. 1.** *Brit.* a member of a livery company. **2.** a worker in a livery stable.

livery stable *n.* a stable where horses are accommodated and from which they may be hired out.

lives (laɪvz) *n.* the plural of **life.**

livestock (ˈlaɪvˌstɒk) *n.* (*functioning as sing. or pl.*) cattle, horses, and similar animals kept for domestic use but not as pets, esp. on a farm.

live together (lɪv) *vb.* (*intr., adv.*) (esp. of an unmarried couple) to dwell in the same house or flat; cohabit.

live up (lɪv) *vb.* **1.** (*intr., adv.;* foll. by *to*) to fulfil (an expectation, obligation, principle, etc.). **2. live it up.** *Inf.* to enjoy oneself, esp. flamboyantly.

live wire (laɪv) *n.* **1.** *Inf.* an energetic or enterprising person. **2.** a wire carrying an electric current.

live with (lɪv) *vb.* (*tr., prep.*) to dwell with (a person to whom one is not married).

livid (ˈlɪvɪd) *adj.* **1.** (of the skin) discoloured, as from a bruise or contusion. **2.** of a greyish tinge or colour. **3.** *Inf.* angry or furious. [C17: via F < L *līvidus,* < *līvēre* to be black and blue] —**ˈlividly** *adv.* —**ˈlividness** *or* **liˈvidity** *n.*

living (ˈlɪvɪŋ) *adj.* **1. a.** possessing life; not dead. **b.** (*as collective n.* preceded by *the*): *the living.* **2.** having the characteristics of life (used esp. to distinguish organisms from nonliving matter). **3.** currently in use or valid: *living language.* **4.** seeming to be real: *a living image.* **5.** (of animals or plants) existing in the present age. **6.** presented by actors before a live audience: *living theatre.* **7.** (*prenominal*) (intensifier): *the living daylights.* ~*n.* **8.** the condition of being alive. **9.** the manner in which one conducts one's life: *fast living.* **10.** the means, esp. the financial means, whereby one lives. **11.** *Church of England.* another term for **benefice. 12.** (*modifier*) of, involving, or characteristic of everyday life: *living area.* **13.** (*modifier*) of or involving those now alive (esp. in **living memory**).

living death *n.* a life or lengthy experience of constant misery.

living room *n.* a room in a private house or flat used for relaxation and entertainment.

living wage *n.* a wage adequate to maintain a person and his family in reasonable comfort.

lizard (ˈlɪzəd) *n.* any of a group of reptiles typically having an elongated body, four limbs, and a long tail: includes the geckos, iguanas, chameleons, monitors, and slowworms. [C14: via OF < L *lacerta*]

LJ (in Britain) *abbrev. for* Lord Justice.

ll. *abbrev. for* lines (of written matter).

LL *abbrev. for:* **1.** Late Latin. **2.** Low Latin. **3.** Lord Lieutenant.

llama (ˈlɑːmə) *n.* **1.** a domesticated South American cud-chewing mammal of the camel family, that is used as a beast of burden and is valued for its hair, flesh, and hide. **2.** the cloth made from the wool of this animal. [C17: via Sp. < Amerind]

llano (ˈlɑːnəʊ; *Spanish* ˈʎano) *n., pl.* **-nos** (-nəʊz; *Spanish* -nɔs). an extensive grassy treeless plain, esp. in South America. [C17: Sp., < L *plānum* level ground]

LLB *abbrev. for* Bachelor of Laws. [L: *Legum Baccalaureus*]

LLD *abbrev. for* Doctor of Laws. [L: *Legum Doctor*]

LLM *abbrev. for* Master of Laws. [L: *Legum Magister*]

Lloyd's (lɔɪdz) *n.* an association of London underwriters, set up in the late 17th century. Originally concerned with marine insurance and shipping information, it now subscribes a variety of insurance policies and publishes a daily list (**Lloyd's List**) of shipping data and news. [C17: after Edward *Lloyd* (died ?1726) at whose coffee house in London the underwriters orig. carried on their business]

lm *symbol for* lumen.

lo (ləʊ) *interj.* look! see! (now often in **lo and behold**). [OE *lā*]

loach (ləʊtʃ) *n.* a carplike freshwater fish of Eurasia and Africa, having a long narrow body with barbels around the mouth. [C14: < OF *loche*, <?]

load (ləʊd) *n.* **1.** something to be borne or conveyed; weight. **2. a.** the usual amount borne or conveyed. **b.** (*in combination*): *a carload.* **3.** something that weighs down, oppresses, or burdens: *that's a load off my mind.* **4.** a single charge of a firearm. **5.** the weight that is carried by a structure. **6.** *Electrical engineering, electronics.* **a.** a device that receives or dissipates the power from an amplifier, oscillator, generator, or some other source of signals. **b.** the power delivered by a machine, generator, circuit, etc. **7.** the resistance overcome by an engine or motor when it is driving a machine, etc. **8.** an external force applied to a component or mechanism. **9. a load of.** *Inf.* a quantity of: *a load of nonsense.* **10. get a load of.** *Inf.* pay attention to. **11. have a load on.** *U.S. & Canad. sl.* to be intoxicated. ~*vb.* (*mainly tr.*) **12.** (*also intr.*) to place or receive (cargo, goods, etc.) upon (a ship, lorry, etc.). **13.** to burden or oppress. **14.** to supply in abundance: *load with gifts.* **15.** to cause to be biased: *to load a question.* **16.** (*also intr.*) to put an ammunition charge into (a firearm). **17.** *Photog.* to position (a film, cartridge, or plate) in (a camera). **18.** to weight or bias (a roulette wheel, dice, etc.). **19.** *Insurance.* to increase (a premium) to cover expenses, etc. **20.** *Computers.* to transfer (a program) to a memory. **21. load the dice. a.** to add weights to dice in order to bias them. **b.** to arrange to have a favourable or unfavourable position. [OE *lād* course; in meaning, infl. by LADE] ~See also **loads.** —ˈ**loader** *n.*

loaded (ˈləʊdɪd) *adj.* **1.** carrying a load. **2.** (of dice, a roulette wheel, etc.) weighted or otherwise biased. **3.** (of a question or statement) containing a hidden trap or implication. **4.** charged with ammunition. **5.** *Sl.* wealthy. **6.** (*postpositive*) *Sl., chiefly U.S. & Canad.* **a.** drunk. **b.** drugged.

loading (ˈləʊdɪŋ) *n.* **1.** a load or burden; weight. **2.** the addition of an inductance to electrical equipment, such as a transmission line or aerial, to improve its performance. **3.** *Austral. & N.Z.* a payment made in addition to a basic wage or salary to reward special skills, compensate for unfavourable conditions, etc.

load line *n.* a pattern of lines painted on the hull of a ship, usually near the bow, indicating the various levels that the water line should reach if the ship is properly loaded in different conditions.

loads (ləʊdz) *Inf.* ~*pl. n.* **1.** (often foll. by *of*) a lot. ~*adv.* **2.** (intensifier): *loads better.*

loadstar (ˈləʊdˌstɑː) *n.* a variant spelling of **lodestar.**

loadstone (ˈləʊdˌstəʊn) *n.* a variant spelling of **lodestone.**

loaf[1] (ləʊf) *n., pl.* **loaves** (ləʊvz). **1.** a shaped mass of baked bread. **2.** any shaped or moulded mass of food, such as sugar, cooked meat, etc. **3.** *Sl.* the head; sense: *use your loaf!* [OE *hlāf*]

loaf[2] (ləʊf) *vb.* **1.** (*intr.*) to loiter or lounge around in an idle way. **2.** (*tr.;* foll. by *away*) to spend (time) idly: *he loafed away his life.* [C19: ? back formation < LOAFER]

loafer (ˈləʊfə) *n.* **1.** a person who avoids work; idler. **2.** *Chiefly U.S. & Canad.* a moccasin-like shoe. [C19: ? < G *Landläufer* vagabond]

loam (ləʊm) *n.* **1.** rich soil consisting of a mixture of sand, clay, and decaying organic material. **2.** a paste of clay and sand used for making moulds in a foundry, plastering walls, etc. ~*vb.* **3.** (*tr.*) to cover, treat, or fill with loam. [OE *lām*] —ˈ**loamy** *adj.* —ˈ**loaminess** *n.*

loan (ləʊn) *n.* **1.** the act of lending: *the loan of a car.* **2.** property lent, esp. money lent at interest for a period of time. **3.** the adoption by speakers of one language of a form current in another language. **4.** short for **loan word. 5. on loan.** lent out; borrowed. ~*vb.* **6.** to lend (something, esp. money). [C13 *loon, lan,* < ON *lān*] —ˈ**loaner** *n.*

▷ **Usage.** See at **lend.**

loan shark *n. Inf.* a person who lends funds at illegal or exorbitant rates of interest.

loan translation *n.* the adoption by one language of a phrase or compound word whose components are literal translations of the components of a corresponding phrase or compound in a foreign language: *English "superman" from German "Übermensch".* Also called: **calque.**

loan word *n.* a word adopted, often in a modified form, from one language into another.

loath *or* **loth** (ləʊθ) *adj.* **1.** (usually foll. by *to*) reluctant or unwilling. **2. nothing loath.** willing. [OE *lāth* (in the sense: hostile)]

loathe (ləʊð) *vb.* (*tr.*) to feel strong hatred or disgust for. [OE *lāthiān,* < LOATH] —ˈ**loather** *n.*

loathing (ˈləʊðɪŋ) *n.* abhorrence; disgust.

loathly[1] (ˈləʊθlɪ) *adv.* with reluctance; unwillingly.

loathly[2] (ˈləʊðlɪ) *adj.* an archaic word for **loathsome.**

loathsome (ˈləʊðsəm) *adj.* causing loathing; abhorrent. —ˈ**loathsomely** *adv.* —ˈ**loathsomeness** *n.*

loaves (ləʊvz) *n.* the plural of **loaf**[1].

lob (lɒb) *Sport.* ~*n.* **1.** a ball struck in a high arc. **2.** *Cricket.* a ball bowled in a slow high arc. ~*vb.* **lobbing, lobbed. 3.** to hit or kick (a ball) in a high arc. **4.** *Inf.* to throw, esp. in a high arc. [C14: prob. < Low G, orig. in the sense: something dangling]

lobar (ˈləʊbə) *adj.* of, relating to, or affecting a lobe.

lobate (ˈləʊbeɪt) *adj.* **1.** having or resembling lobes. **2.** (of birds) having separate toes that are each fringed with a weblike lobe. —ˈ**lobately** *adv.* —**loˈbation** *n.*

lobby (ˈlɒbɪ) *n., pl.* **-bies. 1.** a room or corridor used as an entrance hall, vestibule, etc. **2.** *Chiefly Brit.* a hall in a legislative building used for meetings between the legislators and members of the public. **3.** Also called: **division lobby.** *Chiefly Brit.* one of two corridors in a legislative building in which members vote. **4.** a group of persons who attempt to influence legislators on behalf of a particular interest. ~*vb.* **-bying, -bied. 5.** to attempt to influence (legislators, etc.) in the formulation of policy. **6.** (*intr.*) to act in the manner of a lobbyist. **7.** (*tr.*) to apply pressure for the passage of (a bill, etc.). [C16: < Med. L *lobia* portico, < OHG *lauba* arbor, < *laub* leaf] —ˈ**lobbyer** *n.*

lobbyist (ˈlɒbɪɪst) *n.* a person employed by a particular interest to lobby. —ˈ**lobbyˌism** *n.*

lobe (ləʊb) *n.* **1.** any rounded projection forming part of a larger structure. **2.** any of the subdivisions of a bodily organ or part, delineated by shape or connective tissue. **3.** Also called: **ear lobe.** the fleshy lower part of the external ear. **4.** any of the parts, not entirely separate from each other, into which a flattened plant part, such as a leaf, is divided. [C16: < LL *lobus*, < Gk *lobos* lobe of the ear or of the liver]

lobectomy (ləʊˈbɛktəmɪ) *n., pl.* **-mies.** surgical removal of a lobe from any organ or gland in the body.

lobelia (ləʊˈbiːlɪə) *n.* any of a genus of plants having red, blue, white, or yellow five-lobed flowers with the three lower lobes forming a lip. [C18: < NL, after Matthias de *Lobel* (1538–1616), Flemish botanist]

loblolly (ˈlɒbˌlɒlɪ) *n., pl.* **-lies.** a southern U.S. pine tree with bright reddish-brown bark, green needle-like leaves, and reddish-brown cones. [C16: ? < dialect *lob* to boil + obs. dialect *lolly* thick soup]

lobola *or* **lobolo** (lɔːˈbɔːlə, ləˈbəʊ-) *n.* (in southern Africa) an African custom by which a bridegroom's family makes a payment in cattle or cash to the bride's family shortly before the marriage. [< Zulu]

lobotomy (ləʊˈbɒtəmɪ) *n., pl.* **-mies. 1.** surgical incision into a lobe of any organ. **2.** Also called: **prefrontal leucotomy.** surgical interruption of one or more nerve tracts in the frontal lobe of the brain: used in the treatment of intractable mental disorders. [C20: < LOBE + -TOMY]

lobscouse (ˈlɒbˌskaʊs) *n.* a sailor's stew of meat, vegetables, and hardtack. [C18: ? < dialect *lob* to boil + *scouse* broth]

lobster (ˈlɒbstə) *n., pl.* **-sters** *or* **-ster. 1.** any of several large marine decapod crustaceans occurring on rocky shores and having the first pair of limbs modified as large pincers. **2.** any of several similar crustaceans, esp. the spiny lobster. **3.** the flesh of any of these crustaceans, eaten as a delicacy. [OE *loppestre*, < *loppe* spider]

lobster pot *or* **trap** *n.* a round basket or trap made of open slats used to catch lobsters.

lobule (ˈlɒbjuːl) *n.* a small lobe or a subdivision of a lobe. [C17: < NL *lobulus*, < LL *lobus* LOBE] —**lobular** (ˈlɒbjʊlə) *or* **lobulate** (ˈlɒbjʊlɪt) *adj.*

lobworm (ˈlɒbˌwɜːm) *n.* **1.** another name for **lugworm. 2.** a large earthworm used as bait in fishing. [C17: < obs. *lob* lump + WORM]

local (ˈləʊkᵊl) *adj.* **1.** characteristic of or associated with a particular locality or area. **2.** of, concerned with, or relating to a particular place or point in space. **3.** *Med.* of, affecting, or confined to a limited area or part. **4.** (of a train, bus, etc.) stopping at all stations or stops. ~*n.* **5.** a train, bus, etc., that stops at all stations or stops. **6.** an inhabitant of a specified locality. **7.** *Brit. inf.* a pub close to one's home or place of work. **8.** *Med.* short for **local anaesthetic** (see **anaesthesia**). **9.** *U.S. & Canad.* an item of local interest in a newspaper. [C15: via OF < LL *locālis*, < L *locus* place] —ˈ**locally** *adv.* —ˈ**localness** *n.*

local anaesthetic *n. Med.* See **anaesthesia.**

local authority *n. Brit. & N.Z.* the governing body of a county, district, etc. U.S. equivalent: **local government.**

locale (ləʊˈkɑːl) *n.* a place or area, esp. with reference to events connected with it. [C18: < F *local* (n. use of adj.); see LOCAL]

local government *n.* **1.** government of the affairs of counties, towns, etc., by locally elected political bodies. **2.** the U.S. equivalent of **local authority.**

localism (ˈləʊkəˌlɪzəm) *n.* **1.** a pronunciation, phrase, etc., peculiar to a particular locality. **2.** another word for **provincialism.**

locality (ləʊˈkælɪtɪ) *n., pl.* **-ties. 1.** a neighbourhood or area. **2.** the site or scene of an event. **3.** the fact or condition of having a location or position in space.

localize *or* **-ise** (ˈləʊkəˌlaɪz) *vb.* **1.** to make or become local in attitude, behaviour, etc. **2.** (*tr.*) to restrict or confine (something) to a particular area or part. **3.** (*tr.*) to assign or ascribe to a particular region. —ˈ**localˌizable** *or* **-ˌisable** *adj.* —ˌ**localiˈzation** *or* **-iˈsation** *n.*

local option *n.* (esp. in Scotland, New Zealand, and the U.S.) the privilege of a municipality, county, etc., to determine by referendum whether a particular activity, esp. the sale of liquor, shall be permitted there.

locate (ləʊˈkeɪt) *vb.* **1.** (*tr.*) to discover the position, situation, or whereabouts of; find. **2.** (*tr.; often passive*) to situate or place: *located on the edge of the city.* **3.** (*intr.*) *U.S. & Canad.* to become established or settled. —**loˈcater** *n.*

▷ **Usage.** *Locate* is often used to mean "find", but many careful users of English prefer to restrict it to its more precise meaning "to find the exact position of": *she located the town on the map.*

location (ləʊˈkeɪʃən) *n.* **1.** a site or position; situation. **2.** the act or process of locating or the state of being located. **3.** a place outside a studio where filming is done: *shot on location.* **4.** (in South Africa) **a.** a Black African or Coloured township, usually located near a small town. **b.** a Black African tribal reserve in the E Cape Province. **5.** *Computers.* a position in a memory capable of holding a unit of information, such as a word, and identified by its address. [C16: < L *locatio*, < *locare* to place]

locative (ˈlɒkətɪv) *Grammar.* ~*adj.* **1.** (of a word or phrase) indicating place or direction. **2.** denoting a case of nouns, etc., that refers to the place at which the action described by the verb occurs. ~*n.* **3. a.** the locative case. **b.** a word or speech element in this case. [C19: LOCATE + -IVE, on the model of *vocative*]

loc. cit. (in textual annotation) *abbrev. for* loco citato. [L: in the place cited]

loch (lɒx, lɒk) *n.* **1.** a Scot. word for **lake**[1]. **2.** Also: **sea loch.** a long narrow bay or arm of the sea in Scotland. [C14: < Gaelic]

lochia (ˈlɒkɪə) *n.* a vaginal discharge of cellular debris, mucus, and blood following childbirth. [C17: NL < Gk *lokhia*, < *lokhos* childbirth] —ˈ**lochial** *adj.*

loci (ˈləʊsaɪ) *n.* the plural of **locus.**

lock[1] (lɒk) *n.* **1.** a device fitted to a gate, door, drawer, lid, etc., to keep it firmly closed. **2.** a similar device attached to a machine, vehicle, etc. **3. a.** a section of a canal or river that may be closed off by gates to control the water level and the raising and lowering of vessels that pass through it. **b.** (*as modifier*): *a lock gate; a lock keeper.* **4.** the jamming, fastening, or locking together of parts. **5.** *Brit.* the extent to which a vehicle's front wheels will turn: *this car has a good lock.* **6.** a mechanism that detonates the charge of a gun. **7. lock, stock, and barrel.** completely; entirely. **8.** any wrestling hold in which a wrestler seizes a part of his opponent's body. **9.** Also called: **lock forward.** *Rugby.* **a.** a player in the second row of the scrum. **b.** this position. **10.** a gas bubble in a hydraulic system or a liquid bubble in a pneumatic system that stops the fluid flow in a pipe, capillary, etc.: *an air lock.* ~*vb.* **11.** to fasten (a door, gate, etc.) or (of a door, etc.) to become fastened with a lock, bolt, etc., so as to prevent entry or exit. **12.** (*tr.*) to secure (a building) by locking all doors, windows, etc. **13.** to fix or become fixed together securely or inextricably. **14.** to become or cause to become rigid or immovable: *the front wheels of the car locked.* **15.** (when *tr., often passive*) to clasp or entangle (someone or each other) in a struggle or embrace. **16.** (*tr.*) to furnish (a canal) with locks. **17.** (*tr.*) to move (a vessel) through a system of locks. ~See also **lock out, lock up.** [OE *loc*] —ˈ**lockable** *adj.*

lock[2] (lɒk) *n.* **1.** a strand, curl, or cluster of hair. **2.** a tuft or wisp of wool, cotton, etc. **3.** (*pl.*)

Chiefly literary. hair, esp. when curly or fine. [OE *loc*]

locker (ˈlɒkə) *n.* **1. a.** a small compartment or drawer that may be locked, as one of several in a gymnasium, etc., for clothes and valuables. **b.** (*as modifier*): *a locker room.* **2.** a person or thing that locks.

locket (ˈlɒkɪt) *n.* a small ornamental case, usually on a necklace or chain, that holds a picture, keepsake, etc. [C17: < F *loquet* latch, dim. of *loc* LOCK[1]]

lockjaw (ˈlɒkˌdʒɔː) *n. Pathol.* a nontechnical name for **trismus** and (often) **tetanus.**

lock out *vb.* (*tr., adv.*) **1.** to prevent from entering by locking a door. **2.** to prevent (employees) from working during an industrial dispute, as by closing a factory. ~*n.* **lockout. 3.** the closing of a place of employment by an employer, in order to bring pressure on employees to agree to terms.

locksmith (ˈlɒkˌsmɪθ) *n.* a person who makes or repairs locks.

lock step *n.* a method of marching such that the men follow one another as closely as possible.

lock up *vb.* (*adv.*) **1.** (*tr.*) Also: **lock in, lock away.** to imprison or confine. **2.** to lock or secure the doors, windows, etc., of (a building). **3.** (*tr.*) to keep or store securely: *secrets locked up in history.* **4.** (*tr.*) to invest (funds) so that conversion into cash is difficult. ~*n.* **lockup. 5.** the action or time of locking up. **6.** a jail or block of cells. **7.** *Brit.* a small shop with no attached quarters for the owner. **8.** *Brit.* a garage or storage place separate from the main premises. ~*adj.* **lock-up. 9.** *Brit. & N.Z.* (of premises) without living quarters: *a lock-up shop.*

loco[1] (ˈləʊkəʊ) *n. Inf.* short for **locomotive.**

loco[2] (ˈləʊkəʊ) *adj.* **1.** *Sl., chiefly U.S.* insane. **2.** (of an animal) affected with loco disease. ~*n., pl.* **-cos. 3.** *U.S.* short for **locoweed.** ~*vb.* **locoed, locoing.** (*tr.*) **4.** to poison with locoweed. **5.** *U.S. sl.* to make insane. [C19: via Mexican Sp. < Sp.: crazy]

loco disease *n.* a disease of cattle, sheep, and horses characterized by paralysis and faulty vision, caused by ingestion of locoweed.

locomotion (ˌləʊkəˈməʊʃən) *n.* the act, fact, ability, or power of moving. [C17: < L *locō* from a place, ablative of *locus* place + MOTION]

locomotive (ˌləʊkəˈməʊtɪv) *n.* **1. a.** Also called: **locomotive engine.** a self-propelled engine driven by steam, electricity, or diesel power and used for drawing trains along railway tracks. **b.** (*as modifier*): *a locomotive shed; a locomotive works.* ~*adj.* **2.** of or relating to locomotion. **3.** moving or able to move, as by self-propulsion.

locomotor (ˌləʊkəˈməʊtə) *adj.* of or relating to locomotion. [C19: < L *locō* from a place + MOTOR (mover)]

locomotor ataxia *n. Pathol.* another name for **tabes dorsalis.**

locoweed (ˈləʊkəʊˌwiːd) *n.* any of several perennial leguminous plants of W North America that cause loco disease in horses, cattle, and sheep.

loculus (ˈlɒkjʊləs) *n., pl.* **loculi** (ˈlɒkjʊˌlaɪ). **1.** *Bot.* any of the chambers of an ovary or anther. **2.** *Biol.* any small cavity or chamber. [C19: NL, < L: compartment, < *locus* place] —ˈ**locular** *adj.*

locum tenens (ˈləʊkəm ˈtiːnɛnz) *n., pl.* **locum tenentes** (təˈnɛntiːz). *Chiefly Brit.* a person who stands in temporarily for another member of the same profession, esp. for a physician, chemist, or clergyman. Often shortened to **locum.** [C17: Med. L: (someone) holding the place (of another)]

locus (ˈləʊkəs) *n., pl.* **loci. 1.** (in many legal phrases) a place or area, esp. the place where something occurred. **2.** *Maths.* a set of points or lines whose location satisfies or is determined by one or more specified conditions: *the locus of points equidistant from a given point is a circle.* **3.** *Genetics.* the position of a particular gene on a chromosome. [C18: L]

locust (ˈləʊkəst) *n.* **1.** any of numerous insects, related to the grasshopper, of warm and tropical regions of the Old World, which travel in vast swarms, stripping large areas of vegetation. **2.** Also called: **locust tree.** a North American leguminous tree having prickly branches, hanging clusters of white fragrant flowers, and reddish-brown seed pods. **3.** the yellowish durable wood of this tree. **4.** any of several similar trees, such as the honey locust and carob. [C13 (the insect): < L *locusta*; applied to the tree (C17) because the pods resemble locusts]

locution (ləʊˈkjuːʃən) *n.* **1.** a word, phrase, or expression. **2.** manner or style of speech. [C15: < L *locūtiō* an utterance, < *loquī* to speak]

lode (ləʊd) *n.* **1.** a deposit of valuable ore occurring between definite limits in the surrounding rock; vein. **2.** a deposit of metallic ore filling a fissure in the surrounding rock. [OE *lād* course]

loden (ˈləʊdᵊn) *n.* **1.** a thick heavy waterproof woollen cloth with a short pile, used for coats. **2.** a dark bluish-green colour, in which the cloth is often made. [G, < OHG *lodo* thick cloth]

lodestar *or* **loadstar** (ˈləʊdˌstɑː) *n.* **1.** a star, esp. the North Star, used in navigation or astronomy as a point of reference. **2.** something that serves as a guide or model. [C14: lit.: guiding star]

lodestone *or* **loadstone** (ˈləʊdˌstəʊn) *n.* **1. a.** magnetite that is naturally magnetic. **b.** a piece of this, which can be used as a magnet. **2.** a person or thing regarded as a focus of attraction. [C16: lit.: guiding stone]

lodge (lɒdʒ) *n.* **1.** *Chiefly Brit.* a small house at the entrance to the grounds of a country mansion, usually occupied by a gatekeeper or gardener. **2.** a house or cabin used occasionally, as for some seasonal activity. **3.** (*cap. when part of a name*) a large house or hotel. **4.** a room for the use of porters in a university, college, etc. **5.** a local branch or chapter of certain societies. **6.** the building used as the meeting place of such a society. **7.** the dwelling place of certain animals, esp. beavers. **8.** a hut or tent of certain North American Indian peoples. ~*vb.* **9.** to provide or be provided with accommodation or shelter, esp. rented accommodation. **10.** (*intr.*) to live temporarily, esp. in rented accommodation. **11.** to implant, embed, or fix or be implanted, embedded, or fixed. **12.** (*tr.*) to deposit or leave for safety, storage, etc. **13.** (*tr.*) to bring (a charge or accusation) against someone. **14.** (*tr.; often foll. by in or with*) to place (authority, power, etc.) in the control (of someone). [C15: < OF *loge*, ? < OHG *louba* porch]

lodger (ˈlɒdʒə) *n.* a person who pays rent in return for accommodation in someone else's house.

lodging (ˈlɒdʒɪŋ) *n.* **1.** a temporary residence. **2.** (*sometimes pl.*) sleeping accommodation.

lodging house *n.* a private home providing accommodation and meals for lodgers.

lodgings (ˈlɒdʒɪŋz) *pl. n.* a rented room or rooms, esp. in another person's house.

lodgment *or* **lodgement** (ˈlɒdʒmənt) *n.* **1.** the act of lodging or the state of being lodged. **2.** a blockage or accumulation. **3.** a small area gained and held in enemy territory.

loess (ˈləʊɪs) *n.* a light-coloured fine-grained accumulation of clay and silt deposited by the wind. [C19: < G *Löss*, < Swiss G dialect *lösch* loose] —**loessial** (ləʊˈɛsɪəl) *adj.*

loft (lɒft) *n.* **1.** the space inside a roof. **2.** a gallery, esp. one for the choir in a church. **3.** a room over a stable used to store hay. **4.** *U.S.* an upper storey of a warehouse or factory. **5.** a raised house or coop in which pigeons are kept. **6.** *Sport.* **a.** (in golf) the angle from the vertical made by the club face to give elevation to a ball. **b.** elevation imparted to a ball. **c.** a lofting stroke or shot. ~*vb.* (*tr.*) **7.** *Sport.* to strike or kick (a ball) high in the air. **8.** to store or place in a loft. **9.** *Golf.* to slant (the face of a golf club). [OE, < ON *lopt* air, ceiling]

lofty (ˈlɒftɪ) *adj.* **loftier, loftiest. 1.** of majestic or imposing height. **2.** exalted or noble in character or nature. **3.** haughty or supercilious. **4.**

elevated, eminent, or superior. —ˈ**loftily** *adv.* —ˈ**loftiness** *n.*

log[1] (lɒg) *n.* **1. a.** a section of the trunk or a main branch of a tree, when stripped of branches. **b.** (*modifier*) constructed out of logs: *a log cabin.* **2. a.** a detailed record of a voyage of a ship or aircraft. **b.** a record of the hours flown by pilots and aircrews. **c.** a book in which these records are made; logbook. **3.** a written record of information about transmissions kept by radio stations, amateur radio operators, etc. **4.** Also called: **chip log.** a device consisting of a float with an attached line, formerly used to measure the speed of a ship. **5. like a log.** without stirring or being disturbed (in **sleep like a log**). ~*vb.* **logging, logged. 6.** (*tr.*) to fell the trees of (a forest, area, etc.) for timber. **7.** (*tr.*) to saw logs from (trees). **8.** (*intr.*) to work at the felling of timber. **9.** (*tr.*) to enter (a distance, event, etc.) in a logbook or log. **10.** (*tr.*) to travel (a specified distance or time) or move at (a specified speed). [C14: <?]

log[2] (lɒg) *n.* short for **logarithm.**

▷ **Usage.** In mathematical usage *log* is followed by a subscript number indicating the base. The absence of this number implies that the logarithm is a common logarithm.

-log *n. combining form.* a U.S. variant of **-logue.**

logan (ˈləʊgən) *n. Canad.* another name for **bogan** (a backwater).

loganberry (ˈləʊgənbərɪ, -brɪ) *n., pl.* **-ries. 1.** a trailing prickly hybrid plant of the rose family, cultivated for its edible fruit. **2.** the purplish-red acid fruit of this plant. [C19: after James H. *Logan* (1841–1928), American judge and horticulturist who first grew it (1881)]

logarithm (ˈlɒgəˌrɪðəm) *n.* the exponent indicating the power to which a fixed number, the base, must be raised to obtain a given number or variable. It is used esp. to simplify multiplication and division. Often shortened to **log.** [C17: < NL *logarithmus,* coined 1614 by John Napier (1550-1617), Scot. mathematician, < Gk *logos* ratio + *arithmos* number] —**logarithmic** (ˌlɒgəˈrɪðmɪk) *adj.*

logarithmic function *n.* **a.** the mathematical function $y = \log x$. **b.** a function that can be expressed in terms of this function.

logbook (ˈlɒgˌbʊk) *n.* **1.** a book containing the official record of trips made by a ship or aircraft. **2.** *Brit.* a former name for **registration document.**

log chip *n. Naut.* the wooden chip of a chip log. See **log** (sense 4).

loge (ləʊʒ) *n.* a small enclosure or box in a theatre or opera house. [C18: F; see LODGE]

logger (ˈlɒgə) *n.* another word for **lumberjack.**

loggerhead (ˈlɒgəˌhɛd) *n.* **1.** Also called: **loggerhead turtle.** a large-headed turtle occurring in most seas. **2.** a tool consisting of a large metal sphere attached to a long handle, used for warming liquids, melting tar, etc. **3.** *Arch. or dialect.* a blockhead; dunce. **4. at loggerheads.** engaged in dispute or confrontation. [C16: prob. < dialect *logger* wooden block + HEAD]

loggia (ˈlɒdʒə, ˈlɒdʒɪə) *n., pl.* **-gias** *or* **-gie** (-dʒɛ). a covered area on the side of a building. [C17: It., < F *loge.* See LODGE]

logging (ˈlɒgɪŋ) *n.* the work of felling, trimming, and transporting timber.

logic (ˈlɒdʒɪk) *n.* **1.** the branch of philosophy concerned with analysing the patterns of reasoning by which a conclusion is properly drawn from a set of premises, without reference to meaning or context. **2.** any formal system in which are defined axioms and rules of inference. **3.** the system and principles of reasoning used in a specific field of study. **4.** a particular method of argument or reasoning. **5.** force or effectiveness in argument or dispute. **6.** reasoned thought or argument, as distinguished from irrationality. **7.** the relationship and interdependence of a series of events, facts, etc. **8.** *Electronics, computers.* the principles underlying the units in a computer system that perform arithmetical and logical operations. See also **logic circuit.** [C14: < OF *logique* < Med. L *logica,* < Gk *logikos* concerning speech or reasoning]

logical (ˈlɒdʒɪkᵊl) *adj.* **1.** relating to, used in, or characteristic of logic: *logical connective.* **2.** using, according to, or deduced from the principles of logic: *a logical conclusion.* **3.** capable of or characterized by clear or valid reasoning. **4.** reasonable or necessary because of facts, events, etc.: *the logical candidate.* **5.** *Computers.* of, performed by, used in, or relating to the logic circuits in a computer. —ˌ**logiˈcality** *or* ˈ**logicalness** *n.* —ˈ**logically** *adv.*

logical form *n.* the structure of an argument by virtue of which it can be shown to be formally valid.

logical positivism *or* **empiricism** *n.* a philosophical theory which holds that the only meaningful statements are those that are analytic or can be tested empirically, and so rejects theology, metaphysics, etc., as meaningless.

logic circuit *n.* an electronic circuit used in computers to perform a logical operation on its two or more input signals.

logician (lɒˈdʒɪʃən) *n.* a person who specializes in or is skilled at logic.

logistics (lɒˈdʒɪstɪks) *n.* (*functioning as sing. or pl.*) **1.** the science of the movement and maintenance of military forces. **2.** the management of materials flow through an organization. **3.** the detailed planning and organization of any large complex operation. [C19: < F *logistique,* < *loger* to LODGE] —**loˈgistical** *adj.*

log jam *n. Chiefly U.S. & Canad.* **1.** blockage caused by the crowding together of a number of logs floating in a river. **2.** a deadlock; standstill.

loglog (ˈlɒglɒg) *n.* the logarithm of a logarithm (in equations, etc.).

logo (ˈləʊgəʊ, ˈlɒg-) *n., pl.* **-os.** short for **logotype** (sense 2).

logo- *combining form.* indicating word or speech: *logogram.* [< Gk *logos* word, < *legein* to speak]

logogram (ˈlɒgəˌgræm) *n.* single symbol representing an entire morpheme, word, or phrase, as for example the symbol (%) meaning *per cent.*

logorrhoea *or esp. U.S.* **logorrhea** (ˌlɒgəˈrɪə) *n.* uncontrollable or incoherent talkativeness.

logos (lɒgɒs) *n.* **1.** *Philosophy.* reason, regarded as the controlling principle of the universe. **2.** (*cap.*) the divine Word; the second person of the Trinity. [C16: Gk: word, reason]

logotype (ˈlɒgəʊˌtaɪp) *n.* **1.** *Printing.* a piece of type with several uncombined characters cast on it. **2.** Also called: **logo.** a trademark, company emblem, or similar device.

logroll (ˈlɒgˌrəʊl) *vb. Chiefly U.S.* to use logrolling in order to procure the passage of (legislation). —ˈ**logˌroller** *n.*

logrolling (ˈlɒgˌrəʊlɪŋ) *n.* **1.** *U.S.* the practice of undemocratic agreements between politicians involving mutual favours, the trading of votes, etc. **2.** another name for **birling.** See **birl.**

-logue *or U.S.* **-log** *n. combining form.* indicating speech or discourse of a particular kind: *travelogue; monologue.* [< F, < Gk *-logos*]

logwood (ˈlɒgˌwʊd) *n.* **1.** a leguminous tree of the West Indies and Central America. **2.** the heavy reddish-brown wood of this tree, yielding a dye.

-logy *n. combining form.* **1.** indicating the science or study of: *musicology.* **2.** indicating writing, discourse, or body of writings: *trilogy; phraseology; martyrology.* [< L *-logia,* < Gk, < *logos* word] —**-logical** *or* **-logic** *adj. combining form.* —**-logist** *n. combining form.*

loin (lɔɪn) *n.* **1.** *Anat.* the lower back and sides between the pelvis and the ribs. Related adj.: **lumbar. 2.** a cut of meat from this part of an animal. ~See also **loins.** [C14: < OF *loigne,* ? < Vulgar L *lumbra* (unattested), < L *lumbus* loin]

loincloth (ˈlɔɪnˌklɒθ) *n.* a piece of cloth worn round the loins. Also called: **breechcloth.**

loins (lɔɪnz) *pl. n.* **1.** the hips and the inner surface of the legs where they join the trunk of the body; crotch. **2.** *Euphemistic.* the reproductive organs.

loiter ('lɔɪtə) *vb.* (*intr.*) to stand or act aimlessly or idly. [C14: ? < MDu. *lōteren* to wobble] —**'loiterer** *n.* —**'loitering** *n., adj.*

loll (lɒl) *vb.* **1.** (*intr.*) to lie, lean, or lounge in a lazy or relaxed manner. **2.** to hang or allow to hang loosely. ~*n.* **3.** an act or instance of lolling. [C14: ? imit.] —**'loller** *n.* —**'lolling** *adj.*

Lollard ('lɒləd) *n. English history.* a follower of John Wycliffe (?1330–84), English religious reformer, during the 14th, 15th, and 16th centuries. [C14: < MDu.; mutterer, < *lollen* to mumble (prayers)] —**'Lollardism** *n.*

lollipop ('lɒlɪˌpɒp) *n.* **1.** a boiled sweet or toffee stuck on a small wooden stick. **2.** *Brit.* another word for **ice lolly.** [C18: ? < N. English dialect *lolly* the tongue + POP[1]]

lollipop man *or* **lady** *n. Brit. inf.* a person holding a circular sign on a pole who stops traffic so that children may cross the road.

lollop ('lɒləp) *vb.* (*intr.*) *Chiefly Brit.* **1.** to walk or run with a clumsy or relaxed bouncing movement. **2.** a less common word for **lounge.** [C18: prob. < LOLL + *-op* as in GALLOP, to emphasize the contrast in meaning]

lolly ('lɒlɪ) *n., pl.* **-lies. 1.** an informal word for **lollipop. 2.** *Brit.* short for **ice lolly. 3.** *Brit., Austral., & N.Z.* a slang word for **money. 4.** *Austral. & N.Z. inf.* a sweet, esp. a boiled one. **5. do the** (*or* **one's**) **lolly.** *Austral. inf.* to lose one's temper. [shortened < LOLLIPOP]

Lombard ('lɒmbəd, -bɑːd, 'lʌm-) *n.* **1.** a native or inhabitant of Lombardy, a region of N central Italy. **2.** a member of an ancient Germanic people who settled in N Italy after 568 A.D. ~*adj. also* **Lombardic. 3.** of or relating to Lombardy or the Lombards.

Lombard Street *n.* the British financial and banking world. [C16: < a street in London once occupied by Lombard bankers]

Lombardy poplar ('lɒmbədɪ, 'lʌm-) *n.* an Italian poplar tree with upwardly pointing branches giving it a columnar shape.

London pride ('lʌndən) *n.* a type of saxifrage plant having a basal rosette of leaves and pinkish-white flowers.

lone (ləʊn) *adj.* (*prenominal*) **1.** unaccompanied; solitary. **2.** single or isolated: *a lone house.* **3.** a literary word for **lonely. 4.** *Rare.* unmarried or widowed. [C14: < the mistaken division of ALONE into *a lone*] —**'loneness** *n.*

lonely ('ləʊnlɪ) *adj.* **-lier, -liest. 1.** unhappy as a result of being without companions. **2.** causing or resulting from the state of being alone. **3.** isolated, unfrequented, or desolate. **4.** without companions; solitary. —**'loneliness** *n.*

lonely hearts *adj.* (*often caps.*) of or for people who wish to meet a congenial companion or marriage partner: *a lonely hearts advertisement.*

loner ('ləʊnə) *n. Inf.* a person who avoids the company of others or prefers to be alone.

lonesome ('ləʊnsəm) *adj.* **1.** *Chiefly U.S. & Canad.* another word for **lonely.** ~*n.* **2. on** *or U.S.* **by one's lonesome.** *Inf.* on one's own. —**'lonesomely** *adv.* —**'lonesomeness** *n.*

long[1] (lɒŋ) *adj.* **1.** having relatively great extent in space or duration in time. **2. a.** (*postpositive*) of a specified number of units in extent or duration: *three hours long.* **b.** (*in combination*): *a two-foot-long line.* **3.** having or consisting of a relatively large number of items or parts: *a long list.* **4.** having greater than the average or expected range, extent, or duration: *a long match.* **5.** seeming to occupy a greater time than is really so: *she spent a long afternoon waiting.* **6. a.** (of drinks) containing a large quantity of nonalcoholic beverage. **b.** beer as opposed to spirits. **7.** (of a garment) reaching to the wearer's ankles. **8.** *Inf.* (foll. by *on*) plentifully supplied or endowed (with): *long on good ideas.* **9.** *Phonetics.* (of a speech sound, esp. a vowel) **a.** of relatively considerable duration. **b.** (in popular usage) denoting the qualities of the five English vowels in such words as *mate, mete, mite, moat, moot,* and *mute.* **10.** from end to end; lengthwise. **11.** unlikely to win, happen, succeed, etc.: *a long chance.* **12.** *Prosody.* **a.** denoting a vowel of relatively great duration. **b.** denoting a syllable containing such a vowel. **c.** carrying the emphasis. **13.** *Finance.* having or characterized by large holdings of securities or commodities in anticipation of rising prices. **14.** *Cricket.* (of a fielding position) near the boundary: *long leg.* **15. in the long run.** ultimately; after or over a period of time. ~*adv.* **16.** for a certain time or period: *how long will it last?* **17.** for or during an extensive period of time: *long into the next year.* **18.** at a distant time; quite a bit of time: *long before I met you; long ago.* **19.** *Finance.* into a position with more security or commodity holdings than are required by sale contracts and therefore dependent on rising prices for profit: *to go long.* **20. as** (*or* **so**) **long as. a.** for or during just the length of time that. **b.** inasmuch as; since. **c.** provided that; if. **21. no longer.** not any more; formerly but not now. ~*n.* **22.** a long time (esp. in **for long**). **23.** a relatively long thing, such as a signal in Morse code. **24.** *Phonetics.* a long vowel or syllable. **25.** *Finance.* a person with large holdings of a security or commodity in expectation of a rise in its price; bull. **26. before long.** soon. **27. the long and the short of it.** the essential points or facts. ~See also **longs.** [OE *lang*]

long[2] (lɒŋ) *vb.* (*intr.*; foll. by *for* or an infinitive) to have a strong desire. [OE *langian*]

long. *abbrev. for* longitude.

long- *adv.* (*in combination*) for or lasting a long time: *long-awaited; long-established; long-lasting.*

longboat ('lɒŋˌbəʊt) *n.* the largest boat carried aboard a commercial sailing vessel.

longbow ('lɒŋˌbəʊ) *n.* a large powerful hand-drawn bow, esp. as used in medieval England.

longcase clock ('lɒŋˌkeɪs) *n.* another name for **grandfather clock.**

longcloth ('lɒŋˌklɒθ) *n.* a fine plain-weave cotton cloth made in long strips.

long-dated *adj.* (of a gilt-edged security) having more than 15 years to run before redemption. Cf. **medium-dated, short-dated.**

long-day *adj.* (of certain plants) able to mature and flower only if exposed to long periods of daylight. Cf. **short-day.**

long-distance *n.* **1.** (*modifier*) covering relatively long distances: *a long-distance driver.* **2.** (*modifier*) (of telephone calls, lines, etc.) connecting points a relatively long way apart. **3.** *Chiefly U.S.* a long-distance telephone call. **4.** a long-distance telephone system or its operator. ~*adv.* **5.** by a long-distance telephone line: *he phoned long-distance.*

long-drawn-out *adj.* overprolonged or extended.

longeron ('lɒndʒərən) *n.* a main longitudinal structural member of an aircraft. [C20: < F: side support, ult. < L *longus* LONG[1]]

longevity (lɒn'dʒɛvɪtɪ) *n.* **1.** long life. **2.** relatively long duration of employment, service, etc. [C17: < LL *longaevitās,* < L *longaevus* long-lived, < *longus* LONG[1] + *aevum* age]

long face *n.* a disappointed, solemn, or miserable facial expression. —ˌ**long-'faced** *adj.*

longhand ('lɒŋˌhænd) *n.* ordinary handwriting in which letters, words, etc., are set down in full, as opposed to typing or to shorthand.

long haul *n.* **1.** a journey over a long distance, esp. one involving the transport of goods. **2.** a lengthy job.

long-headed *adj.* astute; shrewd; sagacious. —ˌ**long-'headedly** *adv.* —ˌ**long-'headedness** *n.*

longhorn ('lɒŋˌhɔːn) *n.* **1.** a long-horned breed of beef cattle, formerly common in the southwestern U.S. **2.** a British breed of beef cattle with long curved horns.

longing ('lɒŋɪŋ) *n.* **1.** a prolonged unfulfilled desire or need. ~*adj.* **2.** having or showing desire or need: *a longing look.* —**'longingly** *adv.*

longish ('lɒŋɪʃ) *adj.* rather long.

longitude ('lɒndʒɪˌtjuːd, 'lɒŋgɪ-) *n.* distance in

degrees east or west of the prime meridian at 0° measured by the angle between the plane of the prime meridian and that of the meridian through the point in question, or by the time difference. [C14: < L *longitūdō* length, < *longus* LONG[1]]

longitudinal (ˌlɒndʒɪˈtjuːdɪnᵊl, ˌlɒŋgɪ-) *adj.* **1.** of or relating to longitude or length. **2.** placed or extended lengthways. —ˌ**longiˈtudinally** *adv.*

longitudinal wave *n.* a wave that is propagated in the same direction as the displacement of the transmitting medium.

long johns *pl. n. Inf.* underpants with long legs.

long jump *n.* an athletic contest in which competitors try to cover the farthest distance possible with a running jump from a fixed board or mark. U.S. and Canad. equivalent: **broad jump.**

long-lived *adj.* having long life, existence, or currency. —ˌ**long-ˈlivedness** *n.*

long-playing *adj.* of or relating to an LP (long player).

long-range *adj.* **1.** of or extending into the future: *a long-range weather forecast.* **2.** (of vehicles, aircraft, etc.) capable of covering great distances without refuelling. **3.** (of weapons) made to be fired at a distant target.

longs (lɒŋz) *pl. n.* **1.** full-length trousers. **2.** long-dated gilt-edged securities.

longship (ˈlɒŋˌʃɪp) *n.* a narrow open vessel with oars and a square sail, used esp. by the Vikings.

longshore (ˈlɒŋˌʃɔː) *adj.* situated on, relating to, or along the shore. [C19: short form of *alongshore*]

longshore drift *n.* the process whereby beach material is gradually shifted laterally.

longshoreman (ˈlɒŋˌʃɔːmən) *n., pl.* **-men.** a U.S. and Canad. word for **docker**[1].

long shot *n.* **1.** a competitor, as in a race, considered to be unlikely to win. **2.** a bet against heavy odds. **3.** an undertaking, guess, or possibility with little chance of success. **4.** *Films, television.* a shot where the camera is or appears to be distant from the object to be photographed. **5. by a long shot.** by any means: *he still hasn't finished by a long shot.*

long-sighted *adj.* **1.** related to or suffering from hyperopia. **2.** able to see distant objects in focus. **3.** another term for **far-sighted.** —ˌ**long-ˈsightedly** *adv.* —ˌ**long-ˈsightedness** *n.*

long-standing *adj.* existing for a long time.

long-suffering *adj.* **1.** enduring pain, unhappiness, etc., without complaint. ~*n.* **2.** long and patient endurance. —ˌ**long-ˈsufferingly** *adv.*

long suit *n.* **1. a.** the longest suit in a hand of cards. **b.** a holding of four or more cards of a suit. **2.** *Inf.* an outstanding advantage, personal quality, or talent.

long-term *adj.* **1.** lasting or extending over a long time: *long-term prospects.* **2.** *Finance.* maturing after a long period: *a long-term bond.*

longtime (ˈlɒŋˌtaɪm) *adj.* of long standing.

long ton *n.* the full name for **ton**[1] (sense 1).

longueur (*French* lɔ̃gœr) *n.* a period of boredom or dullness. [lit.: length]

long vacation *n.* the long period of holiday in the summer during which universities, law courts, etc., are closed.

long wave *n.* **a.** a radio wave with a wavelength greater than 1000 metres. **b.** (*as modifier*): *a long-wave broadcast.*

longways (ˈlɒŋˌweɪz) *or U.S. & Canad.* **longwise** *adv.* another word for **lengthways.**

long weekend *n.* a weekend holiday extended by a day or days on either side.

long-winded (ˌlɒŋˈwɪndɪd) *adj.* **1.** tiresomely long. **2.** capable of energetic activity without becoming short of breath. —ˌ**long-ˈwindedly** *adv.* —ˌ**long-ˈwindedness** *n.*

lonicera (lɒˈnɪsərə) *n.* See **honeysuckle.**

loo[1] (luː) *n., pl.* **loos.** *Brit.* an informal word for **lavatory.** [C20: ? < F *lieux d'aisance* water closet]

loo[2] (luː) *n., pl.* **loos. 1.** a gambling card game. **2.** a stake used in this game. [C17: shortened < *lanterloo,* via Du. < F *lanterelu,* orig. a nonsense word from the refrain of a popular song]

loofah (ˈluːfə) *n.* the fibrous interior of the fruit of a type of gourd, which is dried and used as a bath sponge or for scrubbing. Also (esp. U.S.): **loofa, luffa.** [C19: < NL *luffa,* < Ar. *lūf*]

look (lʊk) *vb.* (*mainly intr.*) **1.** (often foll. by *at*) to direct the eyes (towards): *to look at the sea.* **2.** (often foll. by *at*) to direct one's attention (towards): *let's look at the circumstances.* **3.** (often foll. by *to*) to turn one's interests or expectations (towards): *to look to the future.* **4.** (*copula*) to give the impression of being by appearance to the eye or mind; seem: *that looks interesting.* **5.** to face in a particular direction: *the house looks north.* **6.** to expect or hope (to do something): *I look to hear from you soon.* **7.** (foll. by *for*) **a.** to search or seek: *I looked for you everywhere.* **b.** to cherish the expectation (of); hope (for): *I look for success.* **8.** (foll. by *to*) **a.** to be mindful (of): *to look to the promise one has made.* **b.** to have recourse (to): *look to your swords, men!* **9.** (foll. by *into*) to carry out an investigation. **10.** (*tr.*) to direct a look at (someone) in a specified way: *she looked her rival up and down.* **11.** (*tr.*) to accord in appearance with (something): *to look one's age.* **12. look alive, lively, sharp,** *or* **smart.** to hurry up; get busy. **13. look here.** an expression used to attract someone's attention, add emphasis to a statement, etc. ~*n.* **14.** the act or an instance of looking: *a look of despair.* **15.** a view or sight (of something): *let's have a look.* **16.** (*often pl.*) appearance to the eye or mind; aspect: *the look of innocence; I don't like the looks of this place.* **17.** style; fashion: *the new look for spring.* ~*sentence connector.* **18.** an expression demanding attention or showing annoyance, determination, etc.: *look, I've had enough of this.* ~See also **look after, look back,** etc. [OE *lōcian*] —ˈ**looker** *n.*

▷ **Usage.** See at **feel.**

look after *vb.* (*intr., prep.*) **1.** to take care of; be responsible for. **2.** to follow with the eyes.

lookalike (ˈlʊkəˌlaɪk) *n.* **a.** a person or thing that is the double of another, often well known, person or thing. **b.** (*as modifier*): *a lookalike Minister; a lookalike newspaper.*

look back *vb.* (*intr., adv.*) **1.** to cast one's mind to the past. **2.** (*usually used with a negative*) to cease to make progress: *after his first book was published, he never looked back.*

look down *vb.* (*intr., adv.;* foll. by *on* or *upon*) to express or show contempt or disdain (for).

look forward to *vb.* (*intr., adv. + prep.*) to wait or hope for, esp. with pleasure.

look-in *Inf.* ~*n.* **1.** a chance to be chosen, participate, etc. **2.** a short visit. ~*vb.* **look in. 3.** (*intr., adv.;* often foll. by *on*) to pay a short visit.

looking glass *n.* a mirror.

look on *vb.* (*intr.*) **1.** (*adv.*) to be a spectator at an event or incident. **2.** (*prep.*) Also: **look upon.** to consider or regard: *she looked on the whole affair as a joke.* —ˌ**looker-ˈon** *n.*

lookout (ˈlʊkˌaʊt) *n.* **1.** the act of keeping watch against danger, etc. **2.** a person or persons instructed or employed to keep such a watch, esp. on a ship. **3.** a strategic point from which a watch is kept. **4.** *Inf.* worry or concern: *that's his lookout.* **5.** *Chiefly Brit.* outlook, chances, or view. ~*vb.* **look out.** (*adv., mainly intr.*) **6.** to heed one's behaviour; be careful. **7.** to be on the watch: *look out for my mother at the station.* **8.** (*tr.*) to search for and find. **9.** (foll. by *on* or *over*) to face in a particular direction: *the house looks out over the moor.*

look over *vb.* **1.** (*intr., prep.*) to inspect by making a tour of (a factory, house, etc.). **2.** (*tr., adv.*) to examine (a document, letter, etc.). ~*n.* **look-over. 3.** an inspection.

look-see *n. Sl.* a brief inspection or look.

look up *vb.* (*adv.*) **1.** (*tr.*) to discover (something required to be known) by resorting to a work of reference, such as a dictionary. **2.** (*intr.*) to increase, as in quality or value: *things are looking up.* **3.** (*intr.;* foll. by *to*) to have respect (for): *I've always wanted a girlfriend I could look up to.* **4.**

(*tr.*) to visit or make contact with (a person): *I'll look you up when I'm in town.*

loom[1] (luːm) *n.* an apparatus, worked by hand or mechanically (**power loom**), for weaving yarn into a textile. [C13 (meaning any kind of tool): var. of OE *gelōma* tool]

loom[2] (luːm) *vb.* (*intr.*) **1.** to come into view indistinctly with an enlarged and often threatening aspect. **2.** (of an event) to seem ominously close. **3.** (often foll. by *over*) (of large objects) to dominate or overhang. ~*n.* **4.** a rising appearance, as of something far away. [C16: ? < East Frisian *lomen* to move slowly]

loon[1] (luːn) *n.* the U.S. and Canad. name for **diver** (the bird). [C17: of Scand. origin]

loon[2] (luːn) *n.* **1.** *Inf.* a simple-minded or stupid person. **2.** *Arch.* a person of low rank or occupation. [C15: <?]

loony *or* **looney** (ˈluːnɪ) *Sl.* ~*adj.* **loonier, looniest. 1.** lunatic; insane. **2.** foolish or ridiculous. ~*n., pl.* **loonies** *or* **looneys. 3.** a foolish or insane person. —ˈ**looniness** *n.*

loony bin *n. Sl.* a mental hospital or asylum.

loop (luːp) *n.* **1.** the round or oval shape formed by a line, string, etc., that curves around to cross itself. **2.** any round or oval-shaped thing that is closed or nearly closed. **3.** an intrauterine contraceptive device in the shape of a loop. **4.** *Electronics.* a closed electric or magnetic circuit through which a signal can circulate, as in a feedback control system. **5.** a flight manoeuvre in which an aircraft flies one complete circle in the vertical plane. **6.** Also called: **loop line.** *Chiefly Brit.* a railway branch line which leaves the main line and rejoins it after a short distance. **7.** *Maths, physics.* a closed curve on a graph: *hysteresis loop.* **8.** a continuous strip of cinematographic film. **9.** *Computers.* a series of instructions in a program, performed repeatedly until some specified condition is satisfied. ~*vb.* **10.** (*tr.*) to make a loop in or of (a line, string, etc.). **11.** (*tr.*) to fasten or encircle with a loop or something like a loop. **12.** Also: **loop the loop.** to cause (an aircraft) to perform a loop or (of an aircraft) to perform a loop. **13.** (*intr.*) to move in loops or in a path like a loop. [C14 *loupe*, <?] —ˈ**looper** *n.*

loophole (ˈluːpˌhəʊl) *n.* **1.** an ambiguity, omission, etc., as in a law, by which one can avoid a penalty or responsibility. **2.** a small gap or hole in a wall, esp. one in a fortified wall. ~*vb.* **3.** (*tr.*) to provide with loopholes.

loopy (ˈluːpɪ) *adj.* **loopier, loopiest. 1.** full of loops; curly or twisted. **2.** *Inf.* slightly mad, crazy.

loose (luːs) *adj.* **1.** free or released from confinement or restraint. **2.** not close, compact, or tight in structure or arrangement. **3.** not fitted or fitting closely: *loose clothing is cooler.* **4.** not bundled, packaged, fastened, or put in a container: *loose nails.* **5.** inexact; imprecise: *a loose translation.* **6.** (of funds, cash, etc.) not allocated or locked away; readily available: *loose change.* **7. a.** (esp. of women) promiscuous or easy. **b.** (of attitudes, ways of life, etc.) immoral or dissolute. **8. a.** lacking a sense of responsibility or propriety: *loose talk.* **b.** (*in combination*): *loosetongued.* **9. a.** (of the bowels) emptying easily, esp. excessively. **b.** (of a cough) accompanied by phlegm, mucus, etc. **10.** *Inf., chiefly U.S. & Canad.* very relaxed; easy. ~*n.* **11. the loose.** *Rugby.* the part of play when the forwards close round the ball in a ruck or loose scrum. **12. on the loose. a.** free from confinement or restraint. **b.** *Inf.* on a spree. ~*adv.* **13. a.** in a loose manner; loosely. **b.** (*in combination*): *loose-fitting.* ~*vb.* **14.** (*tr.*) to set free or release, as from confinement, restraint, or obligation. **15.** (*tr.*) to unfasten or untie. **16.** to make or become less strict, tight, firmly attached, compact, etc. **17.** (when *intr.*, often foll. by *off*) to let fly (a bullet, arrow, or other missile). [C13 (in the sense: not bound): < ON *lauss* free] —ˈ**loosely** *adv.* —ˈ**looseness** *n.*

loosebox (ˈluːsˌbɒks) *n.* an enclosed stall with a door in which an animal can be confined.

loose cover *n.* a fitted but easily removable cloth cover for a chair, sofa, etc.

loose end *n.* **1.** a detail that is left unsettled, unexplained, or incomplete. **2. at a loose end.** without purpose or occupation.

loose-jointed *adj.* **1.** supple and easy in movement. **2.** loosely built; with ill-fitting joints. —ˌ**loose-**ˈ**jointedness** *n.*

loose-leaf *adj.* (of a binder, album, etc.) capable of being opened to allow removal and addition of pages.

loosen (ˈluːsᵊn) *vb.* **1.** to make or become less tight, fixed, etc. **2.** (often foll. by *up*) to make or become less firm, compact, or rigid. **3.** (*tr.*) to untie. **4.** (*tr.*) to let loose; set free. **5.** (often foll. by *up*) to make or become less strict, severe, etc. **6.** (*tr.*) to rid or relieve (the bowels) of constipation. [C14: < LOOSE] —ˈ**loosener** *n.*

loosestrife (ˈluːsˌstraɪf) *n.* **1.** any of a genus of plants, esp. the yellow-flowered yellow loosestrife. **2. purple loosestrife.** a purple-flowered marsh plant. [C16: LOOSE + STRIFE, an erroneous translation of L *lysimachia*, as if < Gk *lusimakhos* ending strife, instead of from the name of the supposed discoverer, *Lusimakhos*]

loot (luːt) *n.* **1.** goods stolen during pillaging, as in wartime, during riots, etc. **2.** goods, money, etc., obtained illegally. **3.** *Inf.* money or wealth. ~*vb.* **4.** to pillage (a city, etc.) during war or riots. **5.** to steal (money or goods), esp. during pillaging. [C19: < Hindi *lūt*] —ˈ**looter** *n.*

lop[1] (lɒp) *vb.* **lopping, lopped.** (*tr.*; usually foll. by *off*) **1.** to sever (parts) from a tree, body, etc., esp. with swift strokes. **2.** to cut out or eliminate from as excessive. ~*n.* **3.** a part or parts lopped off, as from a tree. [C15 *loppe* branches cut off] —ˈ**lopper** *n.*

lop[2] (lɒp) *vb.* **lopping, lopped. 1.** to hang or allow to hang loosely. **2.** (*intr.*) to slouch about or move awkwardly. [C16: ? rel. to LOP[1]]

lope (ləʊp) *vb.* **1.** (*intr.*) (of a person) to move or run with a long swinging stride. **2.** (*intr.*) (of four-legged animals) to run with a regular bounding movement. **3.** to cause (a horse) to canter with a long easy stride or (of a horse) to canter in this manner. ~*n.* **4.** a long steady gait or stride. [C15: < ON *hlaupa* to LEAP]

lop-eared *adj.* (of animals) having ears that droop.

lopsided (ˌlɒpˈsaɪdɪd) *adj.* **1.** leaning to one side. **2.** greater in weight, height, or size on one side. —ˌ**lop**ˈ**sidedly** *adv.* —ˌ**lop**ˈ**sidedness** *n.*

loquacious (lɒˈkweɪʃəs) *adj.* characterized by or showing a tendency to talk a great deal. [C17: < L *loquāx* < *loquī* to speak] —**lo**ˈ**quaciously** *adv.* —**loquacity** (lɒˈkwæsɪtɪ) *or* **lo**ˈ**quaciousness** *n.*

loquat (ˈləʊkwɒt, -kwət) *n.* **1.** an ornamental evergreen tree of China and Japan, having reddish woolly branches, white flowers, and small yellow edible plumlike fruits. **2.** the fruit of this tree. [C19: < Chinese (Cantonese) *lō kwat*, lit.: rush orange]

lor (lɔː) *interj. Not standard.* an exclamation of surprise or dismay. [< LORD (interj.)]

loran (ˈlɔːrən) *n.* a radio navigation system operating over long distances. Synchronized pulses are transmitted from widely spaced radio stations to aircraft or shipping, the time of arrival of the pulses being used to determine position. [C20: *lo(ng-)ra(nge) n(avigation)*]

lord (lɔːd) *n.* **1.** a person who has power or authority over others, such as a monarch or master. **2.** a male member of the nobility, esp. in Britain. **3.** (in medieval Europe) a feudal superior, esp. the master of a manor. **4.** a husband considered as head of the household (archaic except in the facetious phrase **lord and master**). **5. my lord.** a respectful form of address used to a judge, bishop, or nobleman. ~*vb.* **6.** (*tr.*) *Now rare.* to make a lord of (a person). **7.** to act in a superior manner towards (esp. in **lord it over**). [OE *hlāford* bread keeper] —ˈ**lordless** *adj.* —ˈ**lord**ˌ**like** *adj.*

Lord (lɔːd) *n.* **1.** a title given to God or Jesus Christ. **2.** *Brit.* **a.** a title given to men of high birth, specifically to an earl, marquess, baron, or viscount. **b.** a courtesy title given to the younger sons of a duke or marquess. **c.** the ceremonial title of certain high officials or of a bishop or archbishop: *Lord Mayor; Lord Bishop of Durham.* ~*interj.* **3.** (*sometimes not cap.*) an exclamation of dismay, surprise, etc.: *Good Lord!*

Lord Chancellor *n. Brit. government.* the cabinet minister who is head of the judiciary in England and Wales, and Speaker of the House of Lords.

Lord Chief Justice *n.* the judge who is second only to the Lord Chancellor in the English legal hierarchy; president of one division of the High Court of Justice.

Lord High Chancellor *n.* another name for the **Lord Chancellor.**

Lord Lieutenant *n.* **1.** (in Britain) the representative of the Crown in a county. **2.** (formerly) the British viceroy in Ireland.

lordly (ˈlɔːdlɪ) *adj.* **-lier, -liest.** **1.** haughty; arrogant; proud. **2.** of or befitting a lord. ~*adv.* **3.** *Arch.* in the manner of a lord. —ˈ**lordliness** *n.*

Lord Mayor *n.* the mayor in the City of London and in certain other boroughs.

Lord of Misrule *n.* (formerly, in England) a person appointed master of revels at a Christmas celebration.

lordosis (lɔːˈdəʊsɪs) *n. Pathol.* forward curvature of the lumbar spine. [C18: NL < Gk, < *lordos* bent backwards] —**lordotic** (lɔːˈdɒtɪk) *adj.*

Lord President of the Council *n.* (in Britain) the cabinet minister who presides at meetings of the Privy Council.

Lord Privy Seal *n.* (in Britain) the senior cabinet minister without official duties.

Lord Provost *n.* the provost of one of the major Scottish cities.

Lords (lɔːdz) *n.* **the.** short for **House of Lords.**

Lord's (lɔːdz) *n.* a cricket ground in N London; headquarters of the MCC.

lords-and-ladies *n.* (*functioning as sing.*) another name for **cuckoopint.**

Lord's Day *n.* **the.** the Christian Sabbath; Sunday.

lordship (ˈlɔːdʃɪp) *n.* the position or authority of a lord.

Lordship (ˈlɔːdʃɪp) *n.* (preceded by *Your* or *His*) *Brit.* a title used to address or refer to a bishop, a judge of the high court, or any peer except a duke.

Lord's Prayer *n.* **the.** the prayer taught by Jesus Christ to his disciples, as in Matthew 6:9–13, Luke 11:2–4. Also called: **Our Father, Paternoster** (esp. Latin version).

Lords Spiritual *pl. n.* the Anglican archbishops and senior bishops of England and Wales who are members of the House of Lords.

Lord's Supper *n.* **the.** another term for **Holy Communion** (I Corinthians 11:20).

Lords Temporal *pl. n.* **the.** (in Britain) peers other than bishops in their capacity as members of the House of Lords.

lore (lɔː) *n.* **1.** collective knowledge or wisdom on a particular subject, esp. of a traditional nature. **2.** knowledge or learning. [OE *lār*; rel. to *leornian* to LEARN]

lorgnette (lɔːˈnjɛt) *n.* a pair of spectacles or opera glasses mounted on a handle. [C19: < F, < *lorgner* to squint, < OF *lorgne* squinting]

lorikeet (ˈlɒrɪˌkiːt, ˌlɒrɪˈkiːt) *n.* any of various small lories, such as the varied lorikeet or rainbow lorikeet. [C18: < LORY + *-keet,* as in PARAKEET]

loris (ˈlɔːrɪs) *n., pl.* **-ris.** any of several omnivorous nocturnal slow-moving prosimian primates of S and SE Asia, esp. the slow loris and slender loris, having vestigial digits and no tails. [C18: < F; <?]

lorn (lɔːn) *adj. Poetic.* forsaken or wretched. [OE *loren,* p.p. of *-lēosan* to lose]

lorry (ˈlɒrɪ) *n., pl.* **-ries.** **1.** a large motor vehicle designed to carry heavy loads, esp. one with a flat platform. U.S. and Canad. name: **truck. 2. off the back of a lorry.** *Brit. inf.* a phrase used humorously to indicate that something has been dishonestly acquired. **3.** any of various vehicles with a flat load-carrying surface, esp. one designed to run on rails. [C19: ? rel. to northern English dialect *lurry* to pull]

lory (ˈlɔːrɪ), **lowry,** *or* **lowrie** (ˈlaʊrɪ) *n., pl.* **-ries.** any of various small brightly coloured parrots of Australia and Indonesia, having a brush-tipped tongue with which to feed on nectar and pollen. [C17: via Du. < Malay *lūrī,* var. of *nūrī*]

lose (luːz) *vb.* **losing, lost.** (*mainly tr.*) **1.** to part with or come to be without, as through theft, accident, negligence, etc. **2.** to fail to keep or maintain: *to lose one's balance.* **3.** to suffer the loss or deprivation of: *to lose a parent.* **4.** to cease to have or possess. **5.** to fail to get or make use of: *to lose a chance.* **6.** (*also intr.*) to fail to gain or win (a contest, game, etc.): *to lose the match.* **7.** to fail to see, hear, perceive, or understand: *I lost the gist of his speech.* **8.** to waste: *to lose money gambling.* **9.** to wander from so as to be unable to find: *to lose one's way.* **10.** to cause the loss of: *his delay lost him the battle.* **11.** to allow to go astray or out of sight: *we lost him in the crowd.* **12.** (*usually passive*) to absorb or engross: *he was lost in contemplation.* **13.** (*usually passive*) to cause the death or destruction of: *two men were lost in the attack.* **14.** to outdistance or elude: *he soon lost his pursuers.* **15.** (*intr.*) to decrease or depreciate in value or effectiveness: *poetry always loses in translation.* **16.** (*also intr.*) (of a timepiece) to run slow (by a specified amount). **17.** (of a woman) to fail to give birth to (a viable baby), esp. as the result of a miscarriage. [OE *losian* to perish] —ˈ**losable** *adj.*

lose out *vb. Inf.* **1.** (*intr., adv.*) to be defeated or unsuccessful. **2. lose out on.** to fail to secure or make use of: *we lost out on the sale.*

loser (ˈluːzə) *n.* **1.** a person or thing that loses. **2.** *Inf.* a person or thing that seems destined to be taken advantage of, fail, etc.: *a born loser.*

losing (ˈluːzɪŋ) *adj.* unprofitable; failing: *the business was a losing concern.*

losings (ˈluːzɪŋz) *pl. n.* losses, esp. in gambling.

loss (lɒs) *n.* **1.** the act or an instance of losing. **2.** the disadvantage or deprivation resulting from losing: *a loss of reputation.* **3.** the person, thing, or amount lost: *a large loss.* **4.** (*pl.*) military personnel lost by death or capture. **5.** (*sometimes pl.*) the amount by which the costs of a business transaction or operation exceed its revenue. **6.** *Insurance.* **a.** an occurrence of something that has been insured against, thus giving rise to a claim by a policyholder. **b.** the amount of the resulting claim. **7. at a loss. a.** uncertain what to do; bewildered. **b.** rendered helpless (for lack of something): *at a loss for words.* **c.** with income less than outlay: *the firm was running at a loss.* [C14: n. prob. formed < *lost,* p.p. of *losen* to perish, < OE *lōsian* to be destroyed, < *los* destruction]

loss adjuster *n. Insurance.* a person qualified to adjust losses incurred through fire, theft, natural disaster, etc., to agree the loss and the compensation to be paid.

loss leader *n.* an article offered below cost to attract customers.

lost (lɒst) *adj.* **1.** unable to be found or recovered. **2.** unable to find one's way or ascertain one's whereabouts. **3.** confused, bewildered, or helpless: *he is lost in discussions of theory.* **4.** (sometimes foll. by *on*) not utilized, noticed, or taken advantage of (by): *rational arguments are lost on her.* **5.** no longer possessed or existing because of defeat, misfortune, or the passage of time: *a lost art.* **6.** destroyed physically: *the lost platoon.* **7.** (foll. by *to*) no longer available or open (to). **8.** (foll. by *to*) insensible or impervious (to a sense of shame, justice, etc.). **9.** (foll. by *in*) engrossed (in): *he was lost in his book.* **10.** morally fallen: *a lost woman.* **11.** damned: *a lost soul.*

Lost Generation *n.* (*sometimes not cap.*) **1.** the large number of talented young men killed in World War I. **2.** the generation of writers, esp. American authors, active after World War I.

lot (lɒt) *pron.* **1.** (*functioning as sing. or pl.; preceded by a*) a great number or quantity: *a lot to do; a lot of people.* ~*n.* **2.** a collection of objects, items, or people: *a nice lot of youngsters.* **3.** portion in life; destiny; fortune: *it falls to my lot to be poor.* **4.** any object, such as a straw or slip of paper, drawn from others at random to make a selection or choice (esp. in **draw** *or* **cast lots**). **5.** the use of lots in making a selection or choice (esp. in **by lot**). **6.** an assigned or apportioned share. **7.** an item or set of items for sale in an auction. **8.** *Chiefly U.S. & Canad.* an area of land: *a parking lot.* **9.** *Chiefly U.S. & Canad.* a film studio. **10. a bad lot.** an unpleasant or disrep|u|table person. **11. cast** *or* **throw in one's lot with.** to join with voluntarily and share the fortunes of. **12. the lot.** the entire amount or number. ~*adv.* (preceded by *a*) *Inf.* **13.** to a considerable extent, degree, or amount; very much: *to delay a lot.* **14.** a great deal of the time or often: *to sing madrigals a lot.* ~*vb.* **lotting, lotted. 15.** to draw lots for (something). **16.** (*tr.*) to divide (land, etc.) into lots. **17.** (*tr.*) another word for **allot.** ~See also **lots.** [OE *hlot*]

loth (ləʊθ) *adj.* a variant spelling of **loath.**

Lothario (ləʊˈθɑːrɪˌəʊ) *n., pl.* **-os.** (*sometimes not cap.*) a rake, libertine, or seducer. [C18: after a seducer in Nicholas Rowe's tragedy *The Fair Penitent* (1703)]

lotion (ˈləʊʃən) *n.* a liquid preparation having a soothing, cleansing, or antiseptic action, applied to the skin, eyes, etc. [C14: via OF < L *lōtiō* a washing, < *lōtus* p.p. of *lavāre* to wash]

lots (lɒts) *Inf.* ~*pl. n.* **1.** (often foll. by *of*) great numbers or quantities: *lots of people; to eat lots.* ~*adv.* **2.** a great deal. **3.** (intensifier): *the journey is lots quicker by train.*

lottery (ˈlɒtərɪ) *n., pl.* **-teries. 1.** a game of chance in which tickets are sold, which may later qualify the holder for a prize. **2.** an endeavour, the success of which is regarded as a matter of luck. [C16: < OF *loterie,* < MDu. *loterije*]

lotto (ˈlɒtəʊ) *n.* a children's game in which numbered discs are drawn at random and called out, while the players cover the corresponding numbers on cards, the winner being the first to cover all the numbers, a particular row, etc. [C18: < It., < OF *lot,* < Gmc]

lotus (ˈləʊtəs) *n.* **1.** (in Greek mythology) a fruit that induces forgetfulness and a dreamy languor in those who eat it. **2.** any of several water lilies of tropical Africa and Asia, esp. the **white lotus,** which was regarded as sacred in ancient Egypt. **3.** a related plant which is the sacred lotus of India, China, and Tibet. **4.** a representation of such a plant, common in Hindu, Buddhist, and ancient Egyptian art. **5.** any of a genus of leguminous plants of the legume family of the Old World and North America, having yellow, pink, or white pealike flowers. ~Also (rare): **lotos.** [C16: via L < Gk *lōtos,* < Semitic]

lotus-eater *n. Greek myth.* one of a people encountered by Odysseus in North Africa who lived in indolent forgetfulness, drugged by the fruit of the legendary lotus.

lotus position *n.* a seated cross-legged position used in yoga, meditation, etc.

loud (laʊd) *adj.* **1.** (of sound) relatively great in volume: *a loud shout.* **2.** making or able to make sounds of relatively great volume: *a loud voice.* **3.** clamorous, insistent, and emphatic: *loud protests.* **4.** (of colours, designs, etc.) offensive or obtrusive to look at. **5.** characterized by noisy, vulgar, and offensive behaviour. ~*adv.* **6.** in a loud manner. **7. out loud.** audibly, as distinct from silently. [OE *hlud*] —ˈ**loudish** *adj.* —ˈ**loudly** *adv.* —ˈ**loudness** *n.*

louden (ˈlaudᵊn) *vb.* to make or become louder.

loud-hailer *n.* a portable loudspeaker having a built-in amplifier and microphone. Also (U.S. and Canad.): **bullhorn.**

loudmouth (ˈlaʊdˌmaʊθ) *n. Inf.* a person who brags or talks too loudly. —**loudmouthed** (ˈlaʊdˌmaʊðd, -ˌmaʊθt) *adj.*

loudspeaker (ˌlaʊdˈspiːkə) *n.* a device for converting audio-frequency signals into sound waves. Often shortened to **speaker.**

lough (lɒx, lɒk) *n.* **1.** an Irish word for **lake**[1]. **2.** a long narrow bay or arm of the sea in Ireland. [C14: < Irish *loch* lake]

louis d'or (ˌluːɪ ˈdɔː) *n., pl.* **louis d'or** (ˌluːɪz ˈdɔː). **1.** a former French gold coin worth 20 francs. **2.** an old French coin minted in the reign of Louis XIII. ~Often shortened to **louis.** [C17: < F: golden louis, after Louis XIII]

lounge (laʊndʒ) *vb.* **1.** (*intr.;* often foll. by *about* or *around*) to sit, lie, walk, or stand in a relaxed manner. **2.** to pass (time) lazily or idly. ~*n.* **3.** a communal room in a hotel, ship, etc., used for waiting or relaxing in. **4.** *Chiefly Brit.* a living room in a private house. **5.** Also called: **lounge bar, saloon bar.** *Brit.* a more expensive bar in a pub or hotel. **6.** a sofa or couch. **7.** the act or an instance of lounging. [C16: <?]

lounger (ˈlaʊndʒə) *n.* **1.** a comfortable couch or extending chair designed for someone to relax on. **2.** a loose comfortable leisure garment. **3.** a person who lounges.

lounge suit *n.* a man's suit of matching jacket and trousers worn for the normal business day.

loupe (luːp) *n.* a magnifying glass used by jewellers, horologists, etc. [C20: < F (formerly an imperfect precious stone), < OF, <?]

lour *or* **lower** (ˈlaʊə) *vb.* (*intr.*) **1.** (esp. of the sky, weather, etc.) to be overcast, dark, and menacing. **2.** to scowl or frown. ~*n.* **3.** a menacing scowl or appearance. [C13 *louren* to scowl] —ˈ**louring** *or* ˈ**lowering** *adj.*

lourie (ˈlaʊrɪ) *n.* a type of African bird with bright plumage. [< Afrik.]

louse (laʊs) *n., pl.* **lice. 1.** a wingless bloodsucking insect, such as the head louse, body louse, and crab louse, all of which infest man. **2. biting** *or* **bird louse.** a wingless insect, such as the chicken louse: external parasites of birds and mammals, with biting mouthparts. **3.** any of various similar but unrelated insects. **4.** (*pl.* **louses**) *Sl.* an unpleasant or mean person. ~*vb.* (*tr.*) **5.** to remove lice from. **6.** (foll. by *up*) *Sl.* to ruin or spoil. [OE *lūs*]

lousewort (ˈlaʊsˌwɜːt) *n.* any of various N temperate plants having spikes of white, yellow, or mauve flowers.

lousy (ˈlaʊzɪ) *adj.* **lousier, lousiest. 1.** *Sl.* very mean or unpleasant. **2.** *Sl.* inferior or bad. **3.** infested with lice. **4.** (foll. by *with*) *Sl.* provided with an excessive amount (of): *he's lousy with money.* —ˈ**lousily** *adv.* —ˈ**lousiness** *n.*

lout (laʊt) *n.* a crude or oafish person; boor. [C16: ? < OE *lūtan* to stoop] —ˈ**loutish** *adj.*

louvre *or U.S.* **louver** (ˈluːvə) *n.* **1. a.** any of a set of horizontal parallel slats in a door or window, sloping outwards to throw off rain and admit air. **b.** Also called: **louvre boards.** the slats and frame supporting them. **2.** *Archit.* a turret that allows smoke to escape. [C14: < OF *lovier,* <?] —ˈ**louvred** *or U.S.* ˈ**louvered** *adj.*

lovable *or* **loveable** (ˈlʌvəbᵊl) *adj.* attracting or deserving affection. —ˌ**lovaˈbility,** ˌ**loveaˈbility** *or* ˈ**lovableness,** ˈ**loveableness** *n.* —ˈ**lovably** *or* ˈ**loveably** *adv.*

lovage (ˈlʌvɪdʒ) *n.* a European umbelliferous plant with greenish-white flowers and aromatic fruits, which are used for flavouring food. [C14 *loveache,* < OF *luvesche,* < LL *levisticum,* < L *ligusticum,* lit.: Ligurian (plant)]

love (lʌv) *vb.* **1.** (*tr.*) to have a great attachment to and affection for. **2.** (*tr.*) to have passionate desire, longing, and feelings for. **3.** (*tr.*) to like or desire (to do something) very much. **4.** (*tr.*) to make love to. **5.** (*intr.*) to be in love. ~*n.* **6. a.** an intense emotion of affection, warmth, fondness, and regard towards a person or thing. **b.** (*as modifier*): *love story.* **7.** a deep feeling of sexual attraction and desire. **8.** wholehearted liking for or pleasure in something. **9.** *Christianity.* God's benevolent attitude towards man. **10.** Also: **my love.** a beloved person: used esp. as an endearment. **11.** *Brit. inf.* a term of address, not necessarily for a person regarded as likable. **12.** (in tennis, squash, etc.) a score of zero. **13. fall in love.** to become in love. **14. for love.** without payment. **15. for love or money.** by any means.

16. for the love of. for the sake of. **17. in love.** in a state of strong emotional attachment and usually sexual attraction. **18. make love (to). a.** to have sexual intercourse (with). **b.** *Now arch.* to court. [OE *lufu*]

love affair *n.* a romantic or sexual relationship, esp. temporary, between two people.

love apple *n.* an archaic name for **tomato.**

lovebird (ˈlʌvˌbɜːd) *n.* any of several small African parrots often kept as cagebirds.

lovebite (ˈlʌvˌbaɪt) *n.* a temporary red mark left on a person's skin by a partner's biting or sucking it during lovemaking.

love child *n. Euphemistic.* an illegitimate child; bastard.

love-in-a-mist *n.* an erect S European plant, cultivated as a garden plant, having finely cut leaves and white or pale blue flowers.

loveless (ˈlʌvlɪs) *adj.* **1.** without love: *a loveless marriage.* **2.** receiving or giving no love. —ˈ**lovelessly** *adv.* —ˈ**lovelessness** *n.*

love-lies-bleeding *n.* any of several plants having drooping spikes of small red flowers.

lovelock (ˈlʌvˌlɒk) *n.* a long lock of hair worn on the forehead.

lovelorn (ˈlʌvˌlɔːn) *adj.* miserable because of unrequited love or unhappiness in love.

lovely (ˈlʌvlɪ) *adj.* **-lier, -liest. 1.** very attractive or beautiful. **2.** highly pleasing or enjoyable: *a lovely time.* **3.** inspiring love; lovable. ~*n., pl.* **-lies. 4.** *Sl.* a lovely woman. —ˈ**loveliness** *n.*

lovemaking (ˈlʌvˌmeɪkɪŋ) *n.* **1.** sexual play and activity between lovers, esp. including sexual intercourse. **2.** an archaic word for **courtship.**

love potion *n.* any drink supposed to arouse sexual love in the one who drinks it.

lover (ˈlʌvə) *n.* **1.** a person, now esp. a man, who has an extramarital or premarital sexual relationship with another person. **2.** (*often pl.*) either of the two people involved in a love affair. **3. a.** someone who loves a specified person or thing: *a lover of music.* **b.** (*in combination*): *a music-lover; a cat-lover.*

love seat *n.* a small upholstered sofa for two people.

lovesick (ˈlʌvˌsɪk) *adj.* pining or languishing because of love. —ˈ**loveˌsickness** *n.*

lovey-dovey (ˌlʌvɪˈdʌvɪ) *adj.* making an excessive or ostentatious display of affection.

loving (ˈlʌvɪŋ) *adj.* feeling or showing love and affection. —ˈ**lovingly** *adv.* —ˈ**lovingness** *n.*

loving cup *n.* **1.** a large vessel, usually two-handled, out of which people drink in turn at a banquet. **2.** a similar cup awarded to the winner of a competition.

low[1] (ləʊ) *adj.* **1.** having a relatively small distance from base to top; not tall or high: *a low hill; a low building.* **2. a.** situated at a relatively short distance above the ground, sea level, the horizon, or other reference position: *low cloud.* **b.** (*in combination*): *low-lying.* **3.** of less than usual height, depth, or degree: *low temperature.* **4. a.** (of numbers) small. **b.** (of measurements) expressed in small numbers. **5. a.** involving or containing a relatively small amount of something: *a low supply.* **b.** (*in combination*): *low-pressure.* **6. a.** having little value or quality. **b.** (*in combination*): *low-grade.* **7.** coarse or vulgar: *a low conversation.* **8. a.** inferior in culture or status. **b.** (*in combination*): *low-class.* **9.** in a physically or mentally depressed or weakened state. **10.** low-necked: *a low dress.* **11.** with a hushed tone; quiet or soft: *a low whisper.* **12.** of relatively small price or monetary value: *low cost.* **13.** *Music.* relating to or characterized by a relatively low pitch. **14.** (of latitudes) situated not far north or south of the equator. **15.** having little or no money. **16.** abject or servile. **17.** unfavourable: *a low opinion.* **18.** not advanced in evolution: *a low form of plant life.* **19.** deep: *a low bow.* **20.** *Phonetics.* of, relating to, or denoting a vowel whose articulation is produced by moving the back of the tongue away from the soft palate, such as for the *a* in English *father.* **21.** (of a gear) providing a relatively low forward speed for a given engine speed. **22.** (*usually cap.*) of or relating to the Low Church. ~*adv.* **23.** in a low position, level, degree, intensity, etc.: *to bring someone low.* **24.** at a low pitch; deep: *to sing low.* **25.** at a low price; cheaply: *to buy low.* **26. lay low. a.** to cause to fall by a blow. **b.** to overcome, defeat, or destroy. **27. lie low. a.** to keep or be concealed or quiet. **b.** to wait for a favourable opportunity. ~*n.* **28.** a low position, level, or degree: *an all-time low.* **29.** an area of relatively low atmospheric pressure, esp. a depression. [C12 *lāh*, < ON *lāgr*] —ˈ**lowness** *n.*

low[2] (ləʊ) *n. also* **lowing. 1.** the sound uttered by cattle; moo. ~*vb.* **2.** to make or express by a low or moo. [OE *hlōwan*]

lowan (ˈləʊən) *n.* another name for **mallee fowl.** [< Abor.]

lowborn (ˌləʊˈbɔːn) *or* **lowbred** (ˌləʊˈbrɛd) *adj. Now rare.* of ignoble or common parentage.

lowbrow (ˈləʊˌbraʊ) *Disparaging.* ~*n.* **1.** a person who has uncultivated or nonintellectual tastes. ~*adj. also* **lowbrowed. 2.** of or characteristic of such a person.

Low Church *n.* **1.** the school of thought in the Church of England stressing evangelical beliefs and practices. ~*adj.* **Low-Church. 2.** of or relating to this school.

low comedy *n.* comedy characterized by slapstick and physical action.

Low Countries *pl.n.* the lowland region of W Europe, on the North Sea: consists of Belgium, Luxembourg, and the Netherlands.

low-down *Inf.* ~*adj.* **1.** mean, underhand, or despicable. ~*n.* **lowdown. 2. the.** information.

lower[1] (ˈləʊə) *adj.* **1.** being below one or more other things: *the lower shelf.* **2.** reduced in amount or value: *a lower price.* **3.** *Maths.* (of a limit or bound) less than or equal to one or more numbers or variables. **4.** (*sometimes cap.*) *Geol.* denoting the early part of a period, formation, etc.: *Lower Silurian.* ~*vb.* **5.** (*tr.*) to cause to become low or on a lower level; bring, put, or cause to move down. **6.** (*tr.*) to reduce or bring down in estimation, dignity, value, etc.: *to lower oneself.* **7.** to reduce or be reduced: *to lower one's confidence.* **8.** (*tr.*) to make quieter: *to lower the radio.* **9.** (*tr.*) to reduce the pitch of. **10.** (*intr.*) to diminish or become less. [C12 (comp. of LOW[1]); C17 (vb.)]

lower[2] (ˈlaʊə) *vb.* a variant of **lour.**

Lower Canada *n.* (from 1791 to 1841) the official name of the S region of the present-day province of Quebec.

lower case *n.* **1.** the bottom half of a compositor's type case, in which the small letters are kept. ~*adj.* **lower-case. 2.** of or relating to small letters. ~*vb.* **lower-case. 3.** (*tr.*) to print with lower-case letters.

lower class *n.* **1.** the social stratum having the lowest position in the social hierarchy. ~*adj.* **lower-class. 2.** of or relating to the lower class. **3.** inferior or vulgar.

lower deck *n.* **1.** the deck of a ship situated immediately above the hold. **2.** *Inf.* the petty officers and seamen of a ship collectively.

lower house *n.* one of the houses of a bicameral legislature: usually the larger and more representative. Also called: **lower chamber.**

lowermost (ˈləʊəˌməʊst) *adj.* lowest.

lower regions *pl. n.* (usually preceded by *the*) hell.

lower world *n.* **1.** the earth as opposed to heaven. **2.** another name for **hell.**

lowest common denominator *n.* the smallest integer or polynomial that is exactly divisible by each denominator of a set of fractions. Abbrevs.: **lcd, LCD.** Also called: **least common denominator.**

lowest common multiple *n.* the smallest number or quantity that is exactly divisible by each member of a set of numbers or quantities. Abbrevs.: **lcm, LCM.** Also called: **least common multiple.**

low frequency *n.* a radio-frequency band or a frequency lying between 300 and 30 kilohertz.

Low German *n.* a language of N Germany, spoken esp. in rural areas: more closely related to Dutch than to standard High German. Abbrev.: **LG.** Also called: **Plattdeutsch.**

low-key *or* **low-keyed** *adj.* **1.** having a low intensity or tone. **2.** restrained or subdued.

lowland ('ləʊlənd) *n.* **1.** relatively low ground. **2.** (*often pl.*) a low generally flat region. *~adj.* **3.** of or relating to a lowland or lowlands. —'**lowlander** *n.*

Lowland ('ləʊlənd) *adj.* of or relating to the Lowlands of Scotland or the dialects of English spoken there.

Lowlands ('ləʊləndz) *pl. n.* **the.** a low, generally flat region of S central Scotland. —'**Lowlander** *n.*

Low Latin *n.* any form of Latin other than the classical, such as Medieval Latin.

low-level language *n.* a computer programming language that is closer to machine language than to human language.

lowlife ('ləʊˌlaɪf) *n., pl.* **-lifes.** *Sl.* a member or members of the criminal underworld.

low-loader *n.* a road or rail vehicle with a low platform for ease of access.

lowly ('ləʊlɪ) *adj.* **-lier, -liest. 1.** humble or low in position, rank, status, etc. **2.** full of humility; meek. **3.** simple, unpretentious, or plain. *~adv.* **4.** in a low or lowly manner. —'**lowliness** *n.*

Low Mass *n.* a Mass that has a simplified ceremonial form and is spoken rather than sung.

low-minded *adj.* having a vulgar or crude mind and character. —ˌ**low-**'**mindedly** *adv.* —ˌ**low-**'**mindedness** *n.*

low-pass filter *n. Electronics.* a filter that transmits all frequencies below a specified value, attenuating frequencies above this value.

low-pitched *adj.* **1.** pitched low in tone. **2.** (of a roof) having sides with a shallow slope.

low-pressure *adj.* **1.** having, using, or involving a pressure below normal: *a low-pressure gas.* **2.** relaxed or calm.

low profile *n.* **1.** a position or attitude characterized by a deliberate avoidance of prominence or publicity. *~adj.* **low-profile. 2.** (of a tyre) wide in relation to its height.

low-rise *adj.* **1.** of or relating to a building having only a few storeys. *~n.* **2.** such a building.

lowry *or* **lowrie** ('laʊrɪ) *n.* variant spellings of **lory.**

low-spirited *adj.* depressed or dejected. —ˌ**low-**'**spiritedly** *adv.* —ˌ**low-**'**spiritedness** *n.*

low tech *n.* **1.** short for **low technology. 2.** a style of interior design using items associated with low technology. *~adj.* **low-tech. 3.** of or using low technology. **4.** of or in the interior design style. ~Cf. **high tech.**

low technology *n.* simple unsophisticated technology that is limited to the production of basic necessities.

low-tension *adj.* subjected to, carrying, or operating at a low voltage. Abbrev.: **LT.**

low tide *n.* **1.** the tide when it is at its lowest level or the time at which it reaches this. **2.** a lowest point.

lowveld ('ləʊˌfɛlt) *n.* (in South Africa) the low grasslands of the Transvaal province. [< Afrik. *laeveld*]

low water *n.* **1.** another name for **low tide. 2.** the state of any stretch of water at its lowest level.

low-water mark *n.* **1.** the level reached at low tide. **2.** the lowest point or level; nadir.

lox[1] (lɒks) *n.* a kind of smoked salmon. [C19: < Yiddish *laks,* < MHG *lahs* salmon]

lox[2] (lɒks) *n.* short for **liquid oxygen,** esp. when used as an oxidizer for rocket fuels.

loyal ('lɔɪəl) *adj.* **1.** showing allegiance. **2.** faithful to one's country, government, etc. **3.** of or expressing loyalty. [C16: < OF *loial, leial,* < L *lēgālis* LEGAL] —'**loyally** *adv.*

loyalist ('lɔɪəlɪst) *n.* a patriotic supporter of his sovereign or government. —'**loyalism** *n.*

Loyalist ('lɔɪəlɪst) *n.* **1.** (in Northern Ireland) any of the Protestants wishing to retain Ulster's link with Britain. **2.** (in North America) an American colonist who supported Britain during the War of American Independence. **3.** (in Canada) short for **United Empire Loyalist. 4.** (during the Spanish Civil War) a supporter of the republican government.

loyalty ('lɔɪəltɪ) *n., pl.* **-ties. 1.** the state or quality of being loyal. **2.** (*often pl.*) allegiance.

lozenge ('lɒzɪndʒ) *n.* **1.** *Med.* a medicated tablet held in the mouth until it has dissolved. **2.** *Geom.* another name for **rhombus. 3.** *Heraldry.* a diamond-shaped charge. [C14: < OF *losange* of Gaulish origin] —'**lozenged** *or* '**lozengy** *adj.*

LP[1] *n.* **a.** Also called: **long player.** a long-playing gramophone record, usually 12 inches (30 cm) in diameter, designed to rotate at 33⅓ revolutions per minute. **b.** (*as modifier*): *an LP sleeve.*

LP[2] *abbrev. for:* **1.** (in Britain) Lord Provost. **2.** Also: **lp.** low pressure.

L/P *Printing. abbrev. for* letterpress.

LPG *or* **LP gas** *abbrev. for* liquefied petroleum gas.

L-plate *n. Brit.* a white rectangle with a red "L" sign fixed to the back and front of a motor vehicle to show that the driver has not passed the driving test.

Lr *the chemical symbol for* lawrencium.

LSD *n.* lysergic acid diethylamide; a crystalline compound prepared from lysergic acid, used in experimental medicine and taken illegally as a hallucinogenic drug. Informal name: **acid.**

L.S.D., £.s.d., *or* **l.s.d.** (in Britain, esp. formerly) *abbrev. for* librae, solidi, denarii. [L.: pounds, shillings, pence]

LSE *abbrev. for* London School of Economics.

LSO *abbrev. for* London Symphony Orchestra.

Lt *abbrev. for* Lieutenant.

Ltd *or* **ltd** *abbrev. for* limited (liability). U.S. equivalent: **Inc.**

Lu *the chemical symbol for* lutetium.

luau (luː'aʊ, 'luːaʊ) *n.* a feast of Hawaiian food. [< Hawaiian *lu'au*]

lubber ('lʌbə) *n.* **1.** a big, awkward, or stupid person. **2.** short for **landlubber.** [C14 *lobre,* prob. < ON] —'**lubberly** *adj., adv.* —'**lubberliness** *n.*

lubber line *n.* a mark on a ship's compass that designates the fore-and-aft axis of the vessel. Also called: **lubber's line.**

lubra ('luːbrə) *n. Austral.* an Aboriginal woman. [C19: < Abor.]

lubricant ('luːbrɪkənt) *n.* **1.** a lubricating substance, such as oil. *~adj.* **2.** serving to lubricate. [C19: < L *lūbricāns,* present participle of *lūbricāre*]

lubricate ('luːbrɪˌkeɪt) *vb.* **1.** (*tr.*) to cover or treat with an oily substance so as to lessen friction. **2.** (*tr.*) to make greasy, slippery, or smooth. **3.** (*intr.*) to act as a lubricant. [C17: < L *lūbricāre,* < *lūbricus* slippery] —ˌ**lubri**'**cation** *n.* —'**lubri**ˌ**cative** *adj.* —'**lubri**ˌ**cator** *n.*

lubricity (luː'brɪsɪtɪ) *n.* **1.** *Formal or literary.* lewdness or salaciousness. **2.** *Rare.* smoothness or slipperiness. [C15 (lewdness), C17 (slipperiness): < OF *lubricité,* < Med. L *lubricitās,* < L, < *lūbricus* slippery] —**lubricious** (luː'brɪʃəs) *or* **lubricous** ('luːbrɪkəs) *adj.*

luce (luːs) *n.* another name for the **pike** (the fish). [C14: < OF *lus,* < LL *lūcius* pike]

lucent ('luːsᵊnt) *adj.* brilliant, shining, or translucent. [C16: < L *lūcēns,* present participle of *lūcēre* to shine] —'**lucency** *n.* —'**lucently** *adv.*

lucerne (luː'sɜːn) *n. Brit.* another name for **alfalfa.**

lucid ('luːsɪd) *adj.* **1.** readily understood; clear. **2.** shining or glowing. **3.** of or relating to a period of normality between periods of insane behaviour. [C16: < L *lūcidus* full of light, < *lūx* light] —**lu**'**cidity** *or* '**lucidness** *n.* —'**lucidly** *adv.*

lucifer ('luːsɪfə) *n.* a friction match: originally a trade name.

Lucifer ('luːsɪfə) *n.* **1.** the leader of the rebellion of the angels; Satan. **2.** the planet Venus when it rises as the morning star. [OE, < L *Lūcifer* light-bearer, < *lūx* light + *ferre* to bear]

luck (lʌk) *n.* **1.** events that are beyond control and seem subject to chance; fortune. **2.** success or good fortune. **3.** something considered to bring good luck. **4. down on one's luck.** having little or no good luck to the point of suffering hardships. **5. no such luck.** *Inf.* unfortunately not. **6. try one's luck.** to attempt something that is uncertain. [C15: < MDu. *luc*]

luckless (ˈlʌklɪs) *adj.* having no luck; unlucky. —**ˈlucklessly** *adv.* —**ˈlucklessness** *n.*

lucky (ˈlʌkɪ) *adj.* **luckier, luckiest. 1.** having or bringing good fortune. **2.** happening by chance, esp. as desired. —**ˈluckily** *adv.* —**ˈluckiness** *n.*

lucky dip *n. Brit.* **1.** a box filled with sawdust containing small prizes for which children search. **2.** *Inf.* an undertaking of uncertain outcome.

lucrative (ˈluːkrətɪv) *adj.* producing a profit; profitable. [C15: < OF *lucratif;* see LUCRE] —**ˈlucratively** *adv.* —**ˈlucrativeness** *n.*

lucre (ˈluːkə) *n. Usually facetious.* money or wealth (esp. in **filthy lucre**). [C14: < L *lūcrum* gain]

lucubrate (ˈluːkjʊˌbreɪt) *vb. (intr.)* to write or study, esp. at night. [C17: < L *lūcubrāre* to work by lamplight] —**ˈlucuˌbrator** *n.*

lucubration (ˌluːkjʊˈbreɪʃən) *n.* **1.** laborious study, esp. at night. **2.** (*often pl.*) a solemn literary work.

lud (lʌd) *n. Brit.* lord (in **my lud, m'lud**): used when addressing a judge in court.

Luddite (ˈlʌdaɪt) *n. English history.* **1.** any of the textile workers opposed to mechanization, believing that its use led to unemployment, who organized machine-breaking between 1811 and 1816. **2.** any opponent of industrial change or innovation. *~adj.* **3.** of or relating to the Luddites. [C19: alleged to be after Ned *Ludd,* an 18th-century Leicestershire workman, who destroyed industrial machinery]

ludicrous (ˈluːdɪkrəs) *adj.* absurd or incongruous to the point of provoking laughter. [C17: < *lūdicrus* done in sport, < *lūdus* game] —**ˈludicrously** *adv.* —**ˈludicrousness** *n.*

ludo (ˈluːdəʊ) *n. Brit.* a simple board game in which players advance counters by throwing dice. [C19: < L: I play]

luff (lʌf) *n.* **1.** *Naut.* the leading edge of a fore-and-aft sail. *~vb.* **2.** *Naut.* to head (a sailing vessel) into the wind so that her sails flap. **3.** (*intr.*) *Naut.* (of a sail) to flap when the wind is blowing equally on both sides. **4.** to move the jib of (a crane) in order to shift a load. [C13 (in the sense: steering gear): < OF *lof,* ? < MDu. *loef* peg of a tiller]

lug[1] (lʌg) *vb.* **lugging, lugged. 1.** to carry or drag (something heavy) with great effort. **2.** (*tr.*) to introduce (an irrelevant topic) into a conversation or discussion. *~n.* **3.** the act or an instance of lugging. [C14: prob. < ON]

lug[2] (lʌg) *n.* **1.** a projecting piece by which something is connected, supported, or lifted. **2.** a box or basket for vegetables or fruit. **3.** *Inf. or Scot.* another word for **ear**[1]. **4.** *Sl.* a man, esp. a stupid or awkward one. [C15 (Scots dialect) *lugge* ear]

lug[3] (lʌg) *n. Naut.* short for **lugsail.**

luge (luːʒ) *n.* **1.** a light one-man toboggan. *~vb.* **2.** (*intr.*) to ride or race on a luge. [C20: < F]

Luger (ˈluːgə) *n. Trademark.* a German 9 mm calibre automatic pistol.

luggage (ˈlʌgɪdʒ) *n.* suitcases, trunks, etc. [C16: ? < LUG[1], infl. in form by BAGGAGE]

luggage van *n. Brit.* a railway carriage used to transport passengers' luggage, bicycles, etc.

lugger (ˈlʌgə) *n. Naut.* a small working boat rigged with a lugsail. [C18: < LUGSAIL]

lugsail (ˈlʌgsəl) *n. Naut.* a four-sided sail bent and hoisted on a yard. [C17: ? < ME (now dialect) *lugge* pole, or < *lugge* ear]

lug screw *n.* a small screw without a head.

lugubrious (lʊˈguːbrɪəs) *adj.* excessively mournful; doleful. [C17: < L *lūgubris* mournful, < *lūgēre* to grieve] —**luˈgubriously** *adv.* —**luˈgubriousness** *n.*

lugworm (ˈlʌgˌwɜːm) *n.* a worm living in burrows on sandy shores and having tufted gills: much used as bait. Sometimes shortened to **lug.**

lukewarm (ˌluːkˈwɔːm) *adj.* **1.** (esp. of water) moderately warm; tepid. **2.** having or expressing little enthusiasm or conviction. [C14 *luke* prob. < OE *hlēow* warm] —**ˌlukeˈwarmly** *adv.* —**ˌlukeˈwarmness** *n.*

lull (lʌl) *vb. (tr.)* **1.** to soothe (a person or animal) by soft sounds or motions (esp. in **lull to sleep**). **2.** to calm (someone or someone's fears, suspicions, etc.), esp. by deception. *~n.* **3.** a short period of calm or diminished activity. [C14: ? imit. of crooning sounds; rel. to MLow G *lollen* to soothe, MDu. *lollen* to talk drowsily, mumble]

lullaby (ˈlʌləˌbaɪ) *n., pl.* **-bies. 1.** a quiet song to lull a child to sleep. *~vb.* **-bying, -bied. 2.** (*tr.*) to quiet or soothe as with a lullaby. [C16: ? a blend of LULL + GOODBYE]

lumbago (lʌmˈbeɪgəʊ) *n.* pain in the lower back; backache. [C17: < LL, < L *lumbus* loin]

lumbar (ˈlʌmbə) *adj.* of, near, or relating to the part of the body between the lowest ribs and the hipbones. [C17: < NL *lumbāris,* < L *lumbus* loin]

lumbar puncture *n. Med.* insertion of a hollow needle into the lower spinal cord to withdraw cerebrospinal fluid, introduce drugs, etc.

lumber[1] (ˈlʌmbə) *n.* **1.** *Chiefly U.S. & Canad.* **a.** logs; sawn timber. **b.** (*as modifier*): *the lumber trade.* **2.** *Brit.* **a.** useless household articles that are stored away. **b.** (*as modifier*): *lumber room.* *~vb.* **3.** (*tr.*) to pile together in a disorderly manner. **4.** (*tr.*) to fill up or encumber with useless household articles. **5.** *Chiefly U.S. & Canad.* to convert (the trees) of (a forest) into marketable timber. **6.** (*tr.*) *Brit. inf.* to burden with something unpleasant, tedious, etc. [C17: ? < a n. use of LUMBER[2]] —**ˈlumberer** *n.* —**ˈlumbering** *n.*

lumber[2] (ˈlʌmbə) *vb. (intr.)* **1.** to move or proceed in an awkward heavy manner. **2.** an obsolete word for **rumble.** [C14 *lomeren*] —**ˈlumbering** *adj.*

lumberjack (ˈlʌmbəˌdʒæk) *n.* (esp. in North America) a person whose work involves felling trees, transporting the timber, etc. [C19: < LUMBER[1] + JACK[1] (man)]

lumberjacket (ˈlʌmbəˌdʒækɪt) *n.* a boldly coloured, usually checked jacket in warm cloth.

lumberyard (ˈlʌmbəˌjɑːd) *n.* the U.S. and Canad word for **timberyard.**

lumen (ˈluːmɪn) *n., pl.* **-mens** *or* **-mina** (-mɪnə). **1.** the derived SI unit of luminous flux; the flux emitted in a solid angle of 1 steradian by a point source having a uniform intensity of 1 candela. Symbol: lm **2.** *Anat.* a passage, duct, or cavity in a tubular organ. **3.** a cavity within a plant cell. [C19: NL, < L: light, aperture] —**ˈluminal** *adj.*

luminance (ˈluːmɪnəns) *n.* **1.** a state or quality of radiating or reflecting light. **2.** a measure (in candelas per square metre) of the brightness of a point on a surface that is radiating or reflecting light. Symbol: *L* [C19: < L *lūmen* light]

luminary (ˈluːmɪnərɪ) *n., pl.* **-naries. 1.** a person who enlightens or influences others. **2.** a famous person. **3.** *Literary.* something, such as the sun or moon, that gives off light. [C15: via OF, < L *lūmināre* lamp, < *lūmen* light]

luminesce (ˌluːmɪˈnɛs) *vb. (intr.)* to exhibit luminescence. [back formation < LUMINESCENT]

luminescence (ˌluːmɪˈnɛsəns) *n. Physics.* the emission of light at low temperatures by any process other than incandescence. [C19: < L *lūmen* light] —**ˌlumiˈnescent** *adj.*

luminous (ˈluːmɪnəs) *adj.* **1.** radiating or reflecting light; shining; glowing: *luminous colours.* **2.** (*not in technical use*) exhibiting luminescence: *luminous paint.* **3.** full of light; well-lit. **4.** (of a physical quantity in photometry) evaluated according to the visual sensation produced in an observer rather than by absolute energy measurements: *luminous intensity.* **5.** easily understood; lucid; clear. **6.** enlightening or wise. [C15: < L *lūminōsus* full of light, < *lūmen* light] —**luminosity** (ˌluːmɪˈnɒsɪtɪ) *n.* —**ˈluminously** *adv.* —**ˈluminousness** *n.*

luminous flux *n.* a measure of the rate of flow of luminous energy, evaluated according to its ability to produce a visual sensation. It is measured in lumens.

luminous intensity *n.* a measure of the amount of light that a point source radiates in a given direction.

lumme *or* **lummy** (ˈlʌmɪ) *interj. Brit.* an exclamation of surprise or dismay. [C19: alteration of *Lord love me*]

lummox (ˈlʌməks) *n. Inf.* a clumsy or stupid person. [C19: <?]

lump[1] (lʌmp) *n.* **1.** a small solid mass without definite shape. **2.** *Pathol.* any small swelling or tumour. **3.** a collection of things; aggregate. **4.** *Inf.* an awkward, heavy, or stupid person. **5. the lump.** *Brit.* self-employed workers in the building trade considered collectively. **6.** (*modifier*) in the form of a lump or lumps: *lump sugar.* **7. a lump in one's throat.** a tight dry feeling in one's throat, usually caused by great emotion. **8. in the lump.** collectively; en masse. ~*vb.* **9.** (*tr.;* often foll. by *together*) to collect into a mass or group. **10.** (*intr.*) to grow into lumps or become lumpy. **11.** (*tr.*) to consider as a single group, often without justification. **12.** (*tr.*) to make or cause lumps in or on. **13.** (*intr.;* often foll. by *along*) to move in a heavy manner. [C13: prob. rel. to early Du. *lompe* piece, Scand. dialect *lump* block, MHG *lumpe* rag]

lump[2] (lʌmp) *vb.* (*tr.*) *Inf.* to tolerate or put up with; endure (in **lump it**). [C16: <?]

lumpectomy (lʌmˈpɛktəmɪ) *n., pl.* **-mies.** the surgical removal of a tumour in a breast. [C20: < LUMP[1] + -ECTOMY]

lumpen (ˈlʌmpᵊn) *adj. Inf.* stupid or unthinking. [< G *Lump* vagabond, infl. by *Lumpen* rags, as in LUMPENPROLETARIAT]

lumpenproletariat (ˌlʌmpənˌprəʊlɪˈtɛərɪət) *n.* (esp. in Marxist theory) the urban social group below the proletariat, consisting of criminals, tramps, etc. [G, lit.: ragged proletariat]

lumpfish (ˈlʌmpˌfɪʃ) *n., pl.* **-fish** *or* **-fishes.** a North Atlantic fish having a globular body covered with tubercles, pelvic fins fused into a sucker, and an edible roe. Also called: **ˈlumpˌsucker.** [C16 *lump* (now obs.) lumpfish, < MDu. *lumpe*, ? rel. to LUMP[1]]

lumpish (ˈlʌmpɪʃ) *adj.* **1.** resembling a lump. **2.** stupid, clumsy, or heavy. —**ˈlumpishly** *adv.* —**ˈlumpishness** *n.*

lump sum *n.* a relatively large sum of money, paid at one time, esp. in cash.

lumpy (ˈlʌmpɪ) *adj.* **lumpier, lumpiest. 1.** full of or having lumps. **2.** (esp. of the sea) rough. **3.** (of a person) heavy or bulky. —**ˈlumpily** *adv.* —**ˈlumpiness** *n.*

Luna (ˈluːnə) *n.* the Roman goddess of the moon. [< L: moon]

lunacy (ˈluːnəsɪ) *n., pl.* **-cies. 1.** (formerly) any severe mental illness. **2.** foolishness.

luna moth *n.* a large American moth having light green wings with a yellow crescent-shaped marking on each forewing. [C19: < the markings on its wings]

lunar (ˈluːnə) *adj.* **1.** of or relating to the moon. **2.** occuring on or used on the moon: *lunar module.* **3.** relating to, caused by, or measured by the position or orbital motion of the moon. [C17: < L *lūnāris*, < *lūna* the moon]

lunar eclipse *n.* See **eclipse.**

lunar module *n.* the module used to carry astronauts on a spacecraft to the surface of the moon and back to the spacecraft.

lunar month *n.* another name for **synodic month.** See **month** (sense 6).

lunar year *n.* See **year** (sense 6).

lunate (ˈluːneɪt) *or* **lunated** *adj. Anat., bot.* shaped like a cresent. [C18: < L *lūnātus* crescent-shaped, < *lūna* moon]

lunatic (ˈluːnətɪk) *adj.* **1.** an archaic word for **insane. 2.** foolish; eccentric. ~*n.* **3.** a person who is insane. [C13 (adj.): via OF < LL *lūnāticus* crazy, moonstruck, < L *lūna* moon]

lunatic asylum *n.* another name, usually regarded as offensive, for an institution for the mentally ill.

lunatic fringe *n.* the members of a society who adopt views regarded as fanatical.

lunch (lʌntʃ) *n.* **1.** a meal eaten during the middle of the day. ~*vb.* **2.** (*intr.*) to eat lunch. **3.** (*tr.*) to provide or buy lunch for. [C16: prob. short form of LUNCHEON] —**ˈluncher** *n.*

luncheon (ˈlʌntʃən) *n.* a lunch, esp. a formal one. [C16: prob. var. of *nuncheon*, < ME *noneschench*, < *none* NOON + *schench* drink]

luncheon meat *n.* a ground mixture of meat (often pork) and cereal, usually tinned.

luncheon voucher *n.* a voucher worth a specified amount issued to employees and redeemable at a restaurant for food. Abbrev.: **LV.**

lunchroom (ˈlʌntʃˌruːm, -ˌrʊm) *n. Chiefly Canad.* a room where lunch is served or where students, employees, etc., may eat lunches they bring.

lunette (luːˈnɛt) *n.* **1.** anything that is shaped like a crescent. **2.** an oval or circular opening to admit light in a dome. **3.** a semicircular panel containing a window, mural, or sculpture. **4.** a type of fortification like a detached bastion. **5.** Also called: **lune.** *R.C. Church.* a case fitted with a bracket to hold the consecrated host. [C16: < F: crescent, < *lune* moon, < L *lūna*]

lung (lʌŋ) *n.* **1.** either one of a pair of spongy saclike respiratory organs within the thorax of higher vertebrates, which oxygenate the blood and remove its carbon dioxide. **2. at the top of one's lungs.** in one's loudest voice; yelling. [OE *lungen*]

lunge[1] (lʌndʒ) *n.* **1.** a sudden forward motion. **2.** *Fencing.* a thrust made by advancing the front foot and straightening the back leg, extending the sword arm forwards. ~*vb.* **3.** to move or cause to move with a lunge. **4.** (*intr.*) *Fencing.* to make a lunge. [C18: short form of obs. C17 *allonge*, < F *allonger* to stretch out (one's arm) < LL *ēlongāre* to lengthen] —**ˈlunger** *n.*

lunge[2] (lʌndʒ) *n.* **1.** a rope used in training or exercising a horse. ~*vb.* **2.** to exercise or train (a horse) on a lunge. [C17: < OF *longe*, shortened < *allonge*, ult. < L *longus* long]

lungfish (ˈlʌŋˌfɪʃ) *n., pl.* **-fish** *or* **-fishes.** a freshwater bony fish having an air-breathing lung, fleshy paired fins, and an elongated body.

lungwort (ˈlʌŋˌwɜːt) *n.* **1.** any of several Eurasian plants which have spotted leaves and clusters of blue or purple flowers: formerly used to treat lung diseases. **2.** See **oyster plant.**

lunula (ˈluːnjʊlə) *n., pl.* **-nulae** (-njʊˌliː). the white crescent-shaped area at the base of the human fingernail. Nontechnical name: **half-moon.** [C16: < L: small moon, < *lūna*]

Lupercalia (ˌluːpɜːˈkeɪlɪə) *n., pl.* **-lia** *or* **-lias.** an ancient Roman festival of fertility, celebrated on Feb. 15. [L, < *Lupercālis* belonging to *Lupercus*, a Roman god of the flocks] —ˌ**Luperˈcalian** *adj.*

lupin *or U.S.* **lupine** (ˈluːpɪn) *n.* a leguminous plant of North America, Europe, and Africa, with large spikes of brightly coloured flowers and flattened pods. [C14: < L *lupīnus* wolfish (see LUPINE); from the belief that the plant ravenously exhausted the soil]

lupine (ˈluːpaɪn) *adj.* of, relating to, or resembling a wolf. [C17: < L *lupīnus*, < *lupus* wolf]

lupus (ˈluːpəs) *n.* any of various ulcerative skin diseases. [C16: via Med. L < L: wolf; so called because it rapidly eats away the affected part]

lupus vulgaris (vʌlˈgɛərɪs) *n.* tuberculosis of the skin, esp. of the face. Sometimes shortened to **lupus.**

lurch[1] (lɜːtʃ) *vb.* (*intr.*) **1.** to lean or pitch suddenly to one side. **2.** to stagger. ~*n.* **3.** the act or an instance of lurching. [C19: <?]

lurch[2] (lɜːtʃ) *n.* **1. leave (someone) in the lurch.** to desert (someone) in trouble. **2.** *Cribbage.* the state of a losing player with less than 30 points at the end of a game. [C16: < F *lourche* a game similar to backgammon, < *lourche* (adj.) deceived, prob. of Gmc origin]

lurch[3] (lɜːtʃ) *vb.* (*intr.*) *Arch. or dialect.* to prowl suspiciously. [C15: ? a var. of LURK]

lurcher (ˈlɜːtʃə) *n.* **1.** a crossbred hunting dog,

esp. one trained to hunt silently. **2.** *Arch.* a person who prowls or lurks. [C16: < LURCH[3]]

lure (lʊə) *vb.* (*tr.*) **1.** (sometimes foll. by *away* or *into*) to tempt or attract by the promise of some type of reward. **2.** *Falconry.* to entice (a hawk or falcon) from the air to the falconer by a lure. ~*n.* **3.** a person or thing that lures. **4.** *Angling.* any of various types of brightly coloured artificial spinning baits. **5.** *Falconry.* a feathered decoy to which small pieces of meat can be attached. [C14: < OF *loirre* falconer's lure, < Gmc] —**'lurer** *n.*

Lurex ('lʊərɛks) *n.* **1.** *Trademark.* a thin metallic thread coated with plastic. **2.** fabric containing such thread, which makes it glitter.

lurid ('lʊərɪd) *adj.* **1.** vivid in shocking detail; sensational. **2.** horrible in savagery or violence. **3.** pallid in colour; wan. **4.** glowing with an unnatural glare. [C17: < L *lūridus* pale yellow] —**'luridly** *adv.* —**'luridness** *n.*

lurk (lɜːk) *vb.* (*intr.*) **1.** to move stealthily or be concealed, esp. for evil purposes. **2.** to be present in an unobtrusive way; be latent. ~*n.* **3.** *Austral. & N.Z. sl.* a scheme for success. [C13: prob. frequentative of LOUR] —**'lurker** *n.*

lurking ('lɜːkɪŋ) *adj.* lingering but almost unacknowledged: *a lurking suspicion.*

luscious ('lʌʃəs) *adj.* **1.** extremely pleasurable, esp. to the taste or smell. **2.** very attractive. **3.** *Arch.* cloying. [C15 *lucius, licius,* ? short for DELICIOUS] —**'lusciously** *adv.* —**'lusciousness** *n.*

lush[1] (lʌʃ) *adj.* **1.** (of vegetation) abounding in lavish growth. **2.** (esp. of fruits) succulent and fleshy. **3.** luxurious, elaborate, or opulent. [C15: prob. < OF *lasche* lazy, < L *laxus* loose] —**'lushly** *adv.* —**'lushness** *n.*

lush[2] (lʌʃ) *Sl.* ~*n. Chiefly U.S. & Canad.* **1.** a heavy drinker, esp. an alcoholic. **2.** *U.S. & Canad.* alcoholic drink. ~*vb.* **3.** *U.S. & Canad.* to drink (alcohol) to excess. [C19: <?]

lust (lʌst) *n.* **1.** a strong desire for sexual gratification. **2.** a strong desire or drive. ~*vb.* **3.** (*intr.*; often foll. by *after* or *for*) to have a lust (for). [OE] —**'lustful** *adj.* —**'lustfully** *adv.* —**'lustfulness** *n.*

lustral ('lʌstrəl) *adj.* of or relating to a ceremony of purification. [C16: < L *lūstrālis* (adj.) < LUSTRUM]

lustrate ('lʌstreɪt) *vb.* (*tr.*) to purify by means of religious rituals or ceremonies. [C17: < L *lūstrāre* to brighten] —**lus'tration** *n.*

lustre *or U.S.* **luster** ('lʌstə) *n.* **1.** reflected light; sheen; gloss. **2.** radiance or brilliance of light. **3.** great splendour of accomplishment, beauty, etc. **4.** a dress fabric of cotton and wool with a glossy surface. **5.** a vase or chandelier from which hang cut-glass drops. **6.** a drop-shaded piece of cut glass or crystal used as such a decoration. **7.** a shiny metallic surface on some pottery and porcelain. **8.** *Mineralogy.* the way in which light is reflected from the surface of a mineral. ~*vb.* **9.** to make, be, or become lustrous. [C16: < OF, < OIt. *lustro,* < L *lustrāre* to make bright] —**'lustreless** *or U.S.* **'lusterless** *adj.* —**'lustrous** *adj.*

lustreware *or U.S.* **lusterware** ('lʌstəˌwɛə) *n.* pottery with lustre decoration.

lustrum ('lʌstrəm) *or* **lustre** *n., pl.* **-trums** *or* **-tra** (-trə). a period of five years. [C16: < L: ceremony of purification, < *lustrāre* to brighten, purify]

lusty ('lʌstɪ) *adj.* **lustier, lustiest. 1.** having or characterized by robust health. **2.** strong or invigorating. —**'lustily** *adv.* —**'lustiness** *n.*

lute[1] (luːt) *n.* an ancient plucked stringed instrument with a long fretted fingerboard and a body shaped like a sliced pear. [C14: < OF *lut,* < Ar. *al 'ūd,* lit.: the wood]

lute[2] (luːt) *n.* **1.** a mixture of cement and clay used to seal the joints between pipes, etc. ~*vb.* **2.** (*tr.*) to seal (a joint or surface) with lute. [C14: via OF ult. < L *lutum* clay]

luteinizing hormone ('luːtɪɪˌnaɪzɪŋ) *n.* a hormone secreted by the anterior lobe of the pituitary gland. In female vertebrates it stimulates ovulation, and in mammals it also induces the conversion of the ruptured follicle into the corpus luteum. In male vertebrates it promotes maturation of the interstitial cells of the testes and stimulates androgen secretion. [C19: < L *lūteum* egg yolk, < *lūteus* yellow]

lutenist, lutanist, ('luːtənɪst) *or U.S. & Canad.* (*sometimes*) **lutist** ('luːtɪst) *n.* a person who plays the lute. [C17: < Med. L *lūtānista,* < *lūtāna,* apparently < OF *lut* LUTE[1]]

lutetium *or* **lutecium** (luˈtiːʃɪəm) *n.* a silvery-white metallic element of the lanthanide series. Symbol: Lu; atomic no.: 71; atomic wt.: 174.97. [C19: NL, < L *Lūtētia* ancient name of Paris, home of G. Urbain (1872–1938), F chemist, who discovered it]

Lutheran ('luːθərən) *n.* **1.** a follower of Luther (1483-1546), German leader of the Protestant Reformation, or a member of a Lutheran Church. ~*adj.* **2.** of or relating to Luther or his doctrines. **3.** of or denoting any of the Churches that follow Luther's doctrines. —**'Lutheranism** *n.*

Lutine bell ('luːtiːn, luːˈtiːn) *n.* a bell, taken from the ship *Lutine,* kept at Lloyd's in London and rung before important announcements, esp. the loss of a vessel.

lux (lʌks) *n., pl.* **lux.** the derived SI unit of illumination equal to a luminous flux of 1 lumen per square metre. [C19: < L: light]

luxate ('lʌkseɪt) *vb.* (*tr.*) *Pathol.* to put (a shoulder, knee, etc.) out of joint; dislocate. [C17: < L *luxāre* to displace, < *luxus* dislocated] —**lux'ation** *n.*

luxe (lʌks, lʊks; *French* lyks) *n.* See **de luxe.** [C16: < F < L *luxus* extravagance]

luxuriant (lʌgˈzjʊərɪənt) *adj.* **1.** rich and abundant; lush. **2.** very elaborate or ornate. **3.** extremely productive or fertile. [C16: < L *luxuriāns,* present participle of *luxuriāre* to abound to excess] —**lux'uriance** *n.* —**lux'uriantly** *adv.*

luxuriate (lʌgˈzjʊərɪˌeɪt) *vb.* (*intr.*) **1.** (foll. by *in*) to take voluptuous pleasure; revel. **2.** to flourish profusely. **3.** to live in a sumptuous way. [C17: < L *luxuriāre*] —**luxˌuri'ation** *n.*

luxurious (lʌgˈzjʊərɪəs) *adj.* **1.** characterized by luxury. **2.** enjoying or devoted to luxury. [C14: via OF < L *luxuriōsus* excessive] —**lux'uriously** *adv.* —**lux'uriousness** *n.*

luxury ('lʌkʃərɪ) *n., pl.* **-ries. 1.** indulgence in and enjoyment of rich, comfortable, and sumptuous living. **2.** (*sometimes pl.*) something considered an indulgence rather than a necessity. **3.** (*modifier*) relating to, indicating, or supplying luxury: *a luxury liner.* [C14 (in the sense: lechery): via OF < L *luxuria* excess, < *luxus* extravagance]

LV *abbrev. for* luncheon voucher.

LW *abbrev. for:* **1.** *Radio.* long wave. **2.** low water.

lx *Physics. symbol for* lux.

LXX *symbol for* Septuagint.

-ly[1] *suffix forming adjectives.* **1.** having the nature or qualities of: *godly.* **2.** occurring at certain intervals; every: *daily.* [OE *-lic*]

-ly[2] *suffix forming adverbs.* in a certain manner; to a certain degree: *quickly; recently; chiefly.* [OE *-lice,* < *-lic* -LY[1]]

lycanthropy (laɪˈkænθrəpɪ) *n.* **1.** the supposed magical transformation of a human being into a wolf. **2.** *Psychiatry.* a delusion in which a person believes that he is a wolf. [C16: < Gk *lukānthropía,* < *lukos* wolf + *anthrōpos* man] —**lycanthrope** ('laɪkənˌθrəʊp) *n.* —**lycanthropic** (ˌlaɪkənˈθrɒpɪk) *adj.*

lycée ('liːseɪ) *n., pl.* **-cées** (-seɪz). *Chiefly French.* a secondary school. [C19: F, < L: *Lyceum* a school in ancient Athens]

lyceum (laɪˈsɪəm) *n.* (now chiefly in the names of buildings) **1.** a public building for concerts, lectures, etc. **2.** *U.S.* a cultural organization responsible for presenting concerts, lectures, etc.

lychee (ˌlaɪˈtʃiː) *n.* a variant spelling of **litchi.**

lych gate (lɪtʃ) *n.* a variant spelling of **lich gate.**

lychnis ('lɪknɪs) *n.* any of a genus of plants having

red, pink, or white five-petalled flowers: includes ragged robin. [C17: NL, via L, < Gk *lukhnis* a red flower]

lycopodium (ˌlaɪkəˈpəʊdɪəm) *n.* **1.** any of a genus of club moss resembling moss but having woody tissue and spore-bearing cones. **2.** a flammable yellow powder from the spores of this plant, used in medicine and in making fireworks. [C18: NL, < Gk, < *lukos* wolf + *pous* foot]

Lycra (ˈlaɪkrə) *n. Trademark.* a type of synthetic elastic fabric and fibre used for tight-fitting garments, such as swimming costumes.

lyddite (ˈlɪdaɪt) *n.* an explosive consisting chiefly of fused picric acid. [C19: after *Lydd*, town in Kent near which the first tests were made]

lye (laɪ) *n.* **1.** any solution obtained by leaching, such as the caustic solution obtained by leaching wood ash. **2.** a concentrated solution of sodium hydroxide or potassium hydroxide. [OE *lēag*]

lying[1] (ˈlaɪɪŋ) *vb.* the present participle and gerund of **lie**[1].

lying[2] (ˈlaɪɪŋ) *vb.* the present participle and gerund of **lie**[2].

lying-in *n., pl.* **lyings-in.** confinement in childbirth

lyke-wake (ˈlaɪkˌweɪk) *n. Brit.* a watch held over a dead person, often with festivities. [C16: ? < ON]

lymph (lɪmf) *n.* the almost colourless fluid, containing chiefly white blood cells, that is collected from the tissues of the body and transported in the lymphatic system. [C17: < L *lympha* water, < earlier *limpa*, infl. in form by Gk *numphē* nymph]

lymphatic (lɪmˈfætɪk) *adj.* **1.** of, relating to, or containing lymph. **2.** of or relating to the lymphatic system. **3.** sluggish or lacking vigour. ~*n.* **4.** a lymphatic vessel. [C17 (meaning: mad): < L *lymphāticus*. Original meaning ? < a confusion between *nymph* and LYMPH]

lymphatic system *n.* an extensive network of capillary vessels that transports the interstitial fluid of the body as lymph to the venous blood circulation.

lymph gland *n.* a former name for **lymph node.**

lymph node *n.* any of numerous bean-shaped masses of tissue, situated along the course of lymphatic vessels, that help to protect against infection and are a source of lymphocytes.

lympho- *or before a vowel* **lymph-** *combining form.* indicating lymph or the lymphatic system: *lymphocyte.*

lymphocyte (ˈlɪmfəʊˌsaɪt) *n.* a type of white blood cell formed in lymphoid tissue. —**lymphocytic** (ˌlɪmfəʊˈsɪtɪk) *adj.*

lymphoid (ˈlɪmfɔɪd) *adj.* of or resembling lymph or lymphatic tissue, or relating to the lymphatic system.

lynch (lɪntʃ) *vb.* (*tr.*) (of a mob) to punish (a person) for some supposed offence by hanging without a trial. [orig. *Lynch's law;* ? after Capt. William *Lynch* (1742–1820) of Virginia, USA] —ˈ**lyncher** *n.* —ˈ**lynching** *n.*

lynchet (ˈlɪntʃɪt) *n.* a terrace or ridge formed in prehistoric or medieval times by ploughing a hillside. [OE *hlinc* ridge]

lynch law *n.* the practice of punishing a person by mob action without a proper trial.

lynx (lɪŋks) *n., pl.* **lynxes** *or* **lynx. 1.** a feline mammal of Europe and North America, with grey-brown mottled fur, tufted ears, and a short tail. **2.** the fur of this animal. **3. bay lynx.** another name for **bobcat. 4. desert lynx.** another name for **caracal.** [C14: via L < Gk *lunx*] —ˈ**lynxˌlike** *adj.*

lynx-eyed *adj.* having keen sight.

Lyon King of Arms (ˈlaɪən) *n.* the chief herald of Scotland. Also called: **Lord Lyon.** [C14: archaic spelling of LION, referring to the figure on the royal shield]

lyrate (ˈlaɪərɪt) *adj.* **1.** shaped like a lyre. **2.** (of leaves) having a large terminal lobe and smaller lateral lobes. [C18: < NL *lyrātus*, < L *lyra* LYRE]

lyre (ˈlaɪə) *n.* an ancient Greek stringed instrument consisting of a resonating tortoise shell to which a crossbar was attached by two projecting arms. It was plucked with a plectrum and used for accompanying songs. [C13: via OF < L *lyra*, < Gk *lura*]

lyrebird (ˈlaɪəˌbɜːd) *n.* either of two pheasant-like Australian birds: during courtship displays, the male spreads its tail into the shape of a lyre.

lyric (ˈlɪrɪk) *adj.* **1.** (of poetry) **a.** expressing the writer's personal feelings and thoughts. **b.** having the form and manner of a song. **2.** of or relating to such poetry. **3.** (of a singing voice) having a light quality and tone. **4.** intended for singing, esp. (in classical Greece) to the accompaniment of the lyre. ~*n.* **5.** a short poem of songlike quality. **6.** (*pl.*) the words of a popular song. ~Also (for senses 1–3): **lyrical.** [C16: < L *lyricus*, < Gk *lurikos*, < *lura* lyre] —ˈ**lyrically** *adv.* —ˈ**lyricalness** *n.*

lyrical (ˈlɪrɪkᵊl) *adj.* **1.** another word for **lyric** (senses 1–3). **2.** enthusiastic; effusive.

lyricism (ˈlɪrɪˌsɪzəm) *n.* **1.** the quality or style of lyric poetry. **2.** emotional outpouring.

lyricist (ˈlɪrɪsɪst) *n.* **1.** a person who writes the words for a song, opera, or musical play. **2.** Also called: **lyrist.** a lyric poet.

lyse (laɪs, laɪz) *vb.* to undergo or cause to undergo lysis.

lysergic acid diethylamide (lɪˈsɜːdʒɪk; daɪˌɛθɪlˈeɪmaɪd) *n.* See **LSD.**

lysin (ˈlaɪsɪn) *n.* any of a group of antibodies that cause dissolution of cells.

lysis (ˈlaɪsɪs) *n., pl.* **-ses** (-siːz). **1.** the destruction of cells by the action of a particular lysin. **2.** *Med.* the gradual reduction in the symptoms of a disease. [C19: NL, < Gk, < *luein* to release]

-lysis *n. combining form.* indicating a loosening, decomposition, or breaking down: *electrolysis; paralysis.* [< Gk, < *lusis* a loosening; see LYSIS]

Lysol (ˈlaɪsɒl) *n. Trademark.* a solution containing a mixture of cresols in water, used as an antiseptic and disinfectant.

-lyte *n. combining form.* indicating a substance that can be decomposed or broken down: *electrolyte.* [< Gk *lutos* soluble, < *luein* to loose]

-lytic *adj. combining form.* indicating a loosening or dissolving: *paralytic.* [< Gk, < *lusis;* see -LYSIS]

M

m *or* **M** (ɛm) *n., pl.* **m's, M's,** *or* **Ms. 1.** the 13th letter of the English alphabet. **2.** a speech sound represented by this letter, as in *mat.*

m *symbol for:* **1.** metre(s). **2.** mile(s). **3.** milli-. **4.** minute(s).

M *symbol for:* **1.** mach. **2.** *Currency.* mark(s). **3.** medium. **4.** mega-. **5.** million. **6.** (in Britain) motorway. ~**7.** *the Roman numeral for* 1000.

m. *abbrev. for:* **1.** *Cricket.* maiden (over). **2.** male. **3.** mare. **4.** married. **5.** masculine. **6.** meridian. **7.** month.

M. *abbrev. for:* **1.** Majesty. **2.** Master. **3.** Medieval. **4.** (in titles) Member. **5.** million. **6.** (*pl.* **MM.** *or* **MM**) Also: **M** *French.* Monsieur. [F equivalent of *Mr*]

M'- *prefix.* a variant of **Mac-.**

ma (mɑː) *n.* an informal word for **mother.**

MA *abbrev. for:* **1.** Master of Arts. **2.** Military Academy.

ma'am (mæm, mɑːm; *unstressed* məm) *n.* short for **madam:** used as a title of respect, esp. for female royalty.

mac *or* **mack** (mæk) *n. Brit. inf.* short for **mackintosh** (senses 1, 3).

Mac (mæk) *n. Chiefly U.S. & Canad.* an informal term of address to a man. [C20: abstracted < MAC-]

Mac-, Mc-, *or* **M'-** *prefix.* (in surnames of Scottish or Irish Gaelic origin) son of: *MacDonald.* [< Goidelic *mac* son of]

macabre (məˈkɑːbə, -brə) *adj.* gruesome; ghastly; grim. [C15: < OF *danse macabre* dance of death, prob. < *macabé* relating to the Maccabees, who were associated with death because of the doctrines and prayers for the dead in II Macc. (12:43–46)]

macadam (məˈkædəm) *n.* a road surface made of compressed layers of small broken stones, esp. one that is bound together with tar or asphalt. [C19: after John *McAdam* (1756–1836), Scot. engineer, the inventor]

macadamia (ˌmækəˈdeɪmɪə) *n.* **1.** an Australian tree having clusters of small white flowers and edible nutlike seeds. **2. macadamia nut.** the seed. [C19: NL, after John *Macadam* (died 1865), Australian chemist]

macadamize *or* **-ise** (məˈkædəˌmaɪz) *vb.* (*tr.*) to construct or surface (a road) with macadam. —**macˌadamiˈzation** *or* **-iˈsation** *n.* —**macˈadamˌizer** *or* **-ˌiser** *n.*

macaque (məˈkɑːk) *n.* any of various Old World monkeys of Asia and Africa. Typically the tail is short or absent and cheek pouches are present. [C17: < F, < Port. *macaco,* < W African *makaku,* < *kaku* monkey]

macaroni *or* **maccaroni** (ˌmækəˈrəʊnɪ) *n., pl.* **-nis** *or* **-nies. 1.** pasta tubes made from wheat flour. **2.** (in 18th-century Britain) a dandy who affected foreign manners and style. [C16: < It. (dialect) *maccarone,* prob. < Gk *makaria* food made from barley]

macaroon (ˌmækəˈruːn) *n.* a kind of sweet biscuit made of ground almonds, sugar, and egg whites. [C17: via F *macaron* < It. *maccarone* MACARONI]

Macassar oil (məˈkæsə) *n.* an oily preparation formerly put on the hair to make it smooth and shiny. [C19: < *Makasar,* town in Indonesia]

macaw (məˈkɔː) *n.* a large tropical American parrot having a long tail and brilliant plumage. [C17: < Port. *macau,* <?]

Macc. *abbrev. for* Maccabees (books of the Apocrypha).

McCarthyism (məˈkɑːθɪˌɪzəm) *n. Chiefly U.S.* **1.** the practice of making unsubstantiated accusations of disloyalty or Communist leanings. **2.** any use of unsupported accusations. [C20: after Joseph *McCarthy* (1908–57), U.S. senator]

McCoy (məˈkɔɪ) *n. sl.* the genuine person or thing (esp. in **the real McCoy**). [C20: ? after Kid *McCoy,* professional name of Norman Selby (1873–1940), American boxer, who was called "the real McCoy" to distinguish him from another boxer of that name]

mace[1] (meɪs) *n.* **1.** a club, usually having a spiked metal head, used esp. in the Middle Ages. **2.** a ceremonial staff carried by certain officials. **3.** See **macebearer. 4.** an early form of billiard cue. [C13: < OF, prob. < Vulgar L *mattea* (unattested); apparently rel. to L *mateola* mallet]

mace[2] (meɪs) *n.* a spice made from the dried aril round the nutmeg seed. [C14: formed as a singular < OF *macis* (wrongly assumed to be pl.), < L *macir* an oriental spice]

macebearer (ˈmeɪsˌbɛərə) *n.* a person who carries a mace in processions or ceremonies.

macedoine (ˌmæsɪˈdwɑːn) *n.* **1.** a mixture of diced vegetables. **2.** a mixture of fruit in a syrup or in jelly. **3.** any mixture; medley. [C19: < F, lit.: Macedonian, alluding to the mixture of nationalities in Macedonia]

macerate (ˈmæsəˌreɪt) *vb.* **1.** to soften or separate or be softened or separated as a result of soaking. **2.** to become or cause to become thin. [C16: < L *mācerāre* to soften] —**ˌmacerˈation** *n.* —**ˈmacerˌator** *n.*

Mach (mæk) *n.* short for **Mach number.**

mach. *abbrev. for:* **1.** machine. **2.** machinery. **3.** machinist.

machair (ˈmæxər) *n. Scot.* (in the western Highlands and islands of Scotland) a strip of sandy, grassy land just above the shore: used as grazing or arable land. [C17: < Scot. Gaelic]

machete (məˈʃɛtɪ, -ˈtʃeɪ-) *n.* a broad heavy knife used for cutting or as a weapon, esp. in parts of Central and South America. [C16 *macheto,* < Sp. *machete,* < *macho* club, ? < Vulgar L *mattea* (unattested) club]

Machiavellian (ˌmækɪəˈvɛlɪən) *adj.* **1.** of or relating to the alleged political principles of the Florentine statesman Machiavelli (1469–1527); cunning, amoral, and opportunist. ~*n.* **2.** a cunning, amoral, and opportunist person, esp. a politician. —**ˌMachiaˈvellianˌism** *n.*

machicolate (məˈtʃɪkəʊˌleɪt) *vb.* (*tr.*) to construct machicolations at the top of (a wall). [C18: < OF *machicoller,* ult. < Provençal *machacol,* < *macar* to crush + *col* neck]

machicolation (məˌtʃɪkəʊˈleɪʃən) *n.* **1.** (esp. in medieval castles) a projecting gallery or parapet having openings through which missiles could be dropped. **2.** any such opening.

machinate (ˈmækɪˌneɪt) *vb.* (*usually tr.*) to contrive, plan, or devise (schemes, plots, etc.). [C17: < L *māchinārī* to plan, < *māchina* MACHINE] —**ˈmachiˌnator** *n.*

machination (ˌmækɪˈneɪʃən) *n.* **1.** a plot or scheme. **2.** the act of devising plots or schemes.

machine (məˈʃiːn) *n.* **1.** an assembly of interconnected components arranged to transmit or modify force in order to perform useful work. **2.** a device for altering the magnitude or direction of a force, such as a lever or screw. **3.** a mechanically operated device or means of transport, such as a car or aircraft. **4.** any mechanical or electrical device that automatically performs tasks or assists in performing tasks. **5.** any intricate structure or agency. **6.** a mechanically efficient, rigid, or obedient person. **7.** an organized body of people that controls activities, policies, etc. ~*vb.* **8.** (*tr.*) to shape, cut, or remove (excess material) from (a workpiece) using a machine tool. **9.** to use a machine to carry out a process on (something). [C16: via F < L *māchina* machine, engine, < Doric Gk *makhana* pulley] —**maˈchinable** *or* **maˈchineable** *adj.* —**maˌchinaˈbility** *n.*

machine gun *n.* **1. a.** a rapid-firing automatic gun, using small-arms ammunition. **b.** (*as* *modifier): machine-gun fire.* ~*vb.* **machine-gun, -gunning, -gunned.** **2.** (*tr.*) to shoot or fire at with a machine gun. —**machine gunner** *n.*

machine language *or* **code** *n.* instructions for a computer in binary or hexadecimal code.

machine learning *n.* a branch of artificial intelligence in which a computer generates rules underlying or based on raw data that has been fed into it.

machinery (mə'ʃiːnərɪ) *n., pl.* **-eries.** **1.** machines, machine parts, or machine systems collectively. **2.** a particular machine system or set of machines. **3.** a system similar to a machine.

machine shop *n.* a workshop in which machine tools are operated.

machine tool *n.* a power-driven machine, such as a lathe, for cutting, shaping, and finishing metals, etc. —**ma'chine-ˌtooled** *adj.*

machinist (mə'ʃiːnɪst) *n.* **1.** a person who operates machines to cut or process materials. **2.** a maker or repairer of machines.

machismo (mæ'kɪzməʊ, -'tʃɪz-) *n.* strong or exaggerated masculinity. [Mexican Sp., < Sp. *macho* male, < L *masculus* MASCULINE]

Mach number *n.* (*often not cap.*) the ratio of the speed of a body in a particular medium to the speed of sound in that medium. Mach number 1 corresponds to the speed of sound. [C19: after Ernst *Mach* (1838–1916), Austrian physicist & philosopher]

macho ('mætʃəʊ) *adj.* **1.** strongly or exaggeratedly masculine. ~*n., pl.* **machos.** **2.** a strong virile man. [see MACHISMO]

mack (mæk) *n. Brit. inf.* short for **mackintosh** (senses 1, 3).

mackerel ('mækrəl) *n., pl.* **-rel** *or* **-rels.** **1.** a spiny-finned food fish occurring in northern coastal regions of the Atlantic and in the Mediterranean. It has a deeply forked tail and a greenish-blue body marked with wavy dark bands on the back. **2.** any of various related fishes. [C13: < Anglo-F, < OF *maquerel,* <?]

mackerel sky *n.* a sky patterned with cirrocumulus or small altocumulus clouds. [< similarity to pattern on mackerel's back]

mackintosh *or* **macintosh** ('mækɪnˌtɒʃ) *n.* **1.** a waterproof raincoat made of rubberized cloth. **2.** such cloth. **3.** any raincoat. [C19: after Charles *Macintosh* (1760–1843), who invented it]

McNaughten Rules *or* **McNaghten Rules** (mək'nɔːtᵊn) *pl. n.* (in English law) a set of rules established by the case of Regina *v.* McNaughten (1843) by which legal proof of criminal insanity depends on the accused being shown to be incapable of understanding what he has done.

macramé (mə'krɑːmɪ) *n.* a type of ornamental work made by knotting and weaving coarse thread. [C19: via F & It. < Turkish *makrama* towel, < Ar. *migramah* striped cloth]

macro- *or before a vowel* **macr-** *combining form.* **1.** large, long, or great in size or duration: *macroscopic.* **2.** *Pathol.* indicating abnormal enlargement or overdevelopment: *macrocephaly.* [< Gk *makros* large]

macrobiotics (ˌmækrəʊbaɪ'ɒtɪks) *n.* (*functioning as sing.*) a dietary system which advocates whole grains and vegetables grown without chemical additives. [C20: < MACRO- + Gk *biotos* life + -ICS] —ˌ**macrobi'otic** *adj.*

macrocarpa (ˌmækrəʊ'kɑːpə) *n.* a large New Zealand coniferous tree, used to form shelter belts on farms and for rough timber. [C19: < NL, < MACRO- + Gk *karpos* fruit]

macrocephaly (ˌmækrəʊ'sɛfəlɪ) *n.* the condition of having an abnormally large head or skull. —**macrocephalic** (ˌmækrəʊsɪ'fælɪk) *or* ˌ**macro'cephalous** *adj.*

macrocosm ('mækrəˌkɒzəm) *n.* a complex structure, such as the universe or society, regarded as an entirety. Cf. **microcosm.** [C16: via F & L < Gk *makros kosmos* great world] —ˌ**macro'cosmic** *adj.* —ˌ**macro'cosmically** *adv.*

macroeconomics (ˌmækrəʊˌiːkə'nɒmɪks, -ˌɛk-) *n.* (*functioning as sing.*) the branch of economics concerned with aggregates, such as national income, consumption, and investment. —ˌ**macroˌeco'nomic** *adj.*

macromolecule (ˌmækrəʊ'mɒlɪˌkjuːl) *n.* any very large molecule, such as a protein or synthetic polymer.

macron ('mækrɒn) *n.* a diacritical mark (¯) placed over a letter to represent a long vowel. [C19: < Gk *makron* something long, < *makros* long]

macroscopic (ˌmækrəʊ'skɒpɪk) *adj.* **1.** large enough to be visible to the naked eye. **2.** comprehensive; concerned with large units. [C19: see MACRO-, -SCOPIC] —ˌ**macro'scopically** *adv.*

macula ('mækjʊlə) *or* **macule** ('mækjuːl) *n., pl.* **-ulae** (-jʊˌliː) *or* **-ules.** *Anat.* **1.** a small spot or area of distinct colour, esp. the macula lutea. **2.** any small discoloured spot or blemish on the skin, such as a freckle. [C14: < L] —'**macular** *adj.* —ˌ**macu'lation** *n.*

macula lutea ('luːtɪə) *n., pl.* **maculae luteae** ('luːtɪˌiː). a small yellowish oval-shaped spot on the retina of the eye, where vision is especially sharp. [NL, lit.: yellow spot]

mad (mæd) *adj.* **madder, maddest.** **1.** mentally deranged; insane. **2.** senseless; foolish. **3.** (often foll. by *at*) *Inf.* angry; resentful. **4.** (foll. by *about, on,* or *over;* often *postpositive*) wildly enthusiastic (about) or fond (of). **5.** extremely excited or confused; frantic: *a mad rush.* **6.** wildly gay: *a mad party.* **7.** temporarily overpowered by violent reactions, emotions, etc.: *mad with grief.* **8.** (of animals) **a.** unusually ferocious: *a mad buffalo.* **b.** afflicted with rabies. **9. like mad.** *Inf.* with great energy, enthusiasm, or haste. ~*vb.* **madding, madded.** **10.** *U.S. or arch.* to make or become mad; act or cause to act as if mad. [OE *gemǣded,* p.p. of *gemǣdan* to render insane]

madam ('mædəm) *n., pl.* **madams** *or* (for sense 1) **mesdames.** **1.** a polite term of address for a woman, esp. one of relatively high social status. **2.** a woman who runs a brothel. **3.** *Brit. inf.* a precocious or pompous little girl. [C13: < OF *ma dame* my lady]

madame ('mædəm) *n., pl.* **mesdames.** a married Frenchwoman: used as a title equivalent to *Mrs,* and sometimes extended to older unmarried women to show respect. [C17: < F; see MADAM]

madcap ('mædˌkæp) *adj.* **1.** impulsive, reckless, or lively. ~*n.* **2.** an impulsive, reckless, or lively person.

madden ('mædᵊn) *vb.* to make or become mad or angry. —'**maddening** *adj.* —'**maddeningly** *adv.*

madder ('mædə) *n.* **1.** a plant having small yellow flowers and a red fleshy root. **2.** this root. **3.** a dark reddish-purple dye formerly obtained from this root. **4.** a red lake obtained from alizarin and an inorganic base; used as a pigment in inks and paints. [OE *mædere*]

madding ('mædɪŋ) *adj. Arch.* **1.** acting or behaving as if mad: *the madding crowd.* **2.** making mad; maddening. —'**maddingly** *adv.*

made (meɪd) *vb.* **1.** the past tense and past participle of **make.** ~*adj.* **2.** artificially produced. **3.** (*in combination*) produced or shaped as specified: *handmade.* **4. get** *or* **have it made.** *Inf.* to be assured of success.

Madeira (mə'dɪərə) *n.* a rich strong fortified white wine made on Madeira, a Portuguese island in the N Atlantic.

madeleine ('mædəlɪn, -ˌleɪn) *n.* a small fancy sponge cake. [C19: ? after *Madeleine* Paulmier, F pastry cook]

mademoiselle (ˌmædmwə'zɛl) *n., pl.* **mesdemoiselles.** **1.** a young unmarried French girl or woman: used as a title equivalent to *Miss.* **2.** a French teacher or governess. [C15: F, < *ma* my + *demoiselle* DAMSEL]

made-up *adj.* **1.** invented; fictional. **2.** wearing make-up. **3.** put together. **4.** (of a road) surfaced with tarmac, concrete, etc.

madhouse ('mædˌhaʊs) *n. Inf.* **1.** a mental hospital or asylum. **2.** a state of uproar or confusion.

madly ('mædlɪ) *adv.* **1.** in an insane or foolish

manner. **2.** with great speed and energy. **3.** *Inf.* extremely or excessively: *I love you madly.*

madman ('mædmən) *or* (*fem.*) **madwoman** *n., pl.* **-men** *or* **-women.** a person who is insane.

madness ('mædnɪs) *n.* **1.** insanity; lunacy. **2.** extreme anger, excitement, or foolishness. **3.** a nontechnical word for **rabies.**

Madonna (mə'dɒnə) *n.* **1.** *Chiefly R.C. Church.* a designation of the Virgin Mary. **2.** (*sometimes not cap.*) a picture or statue of the Virgin Mary. [C16: It., < *ma* my + *donna* lady]

Madonna lily *n.* a perennial widely cultivated Mediterranean lily plant with white trumpet-shaped flowers.

madras ('mædrəs, mə'dræs) *n.* a strong fine cotton or silk fabric, usually with a woven stripe. [< *Madras,* city in S India]

madrepore (ˌmædrɪ'pɔː) *n.* any coral of the genus *Madrepora,* many of which occur in tropical seas and form large coral reefs. [C18: via F < It. *madrepora* mother-stone] —ˌ**madre'poral, madreporic** (ˌmædrɪ'pɒrɪk), *or* ˌ**madre'porian** *adj.*

madrigal ('mædrɪgᵊl) *n.* **1.** *Music.* a type of 16th- or 17th-century part song for unaccompanied voices, with an amatory or pastoral text. **2.** a short love poem. [C16: < It., < Med. L *mātricāle* primitive, apparently < L *mātrīcālis,* < *matrīx* womb] —'**madrigalˌesque** *adj.* —**madrigalian** (ˌmædrɪ'gælɪən, -'geɪ-) *adj.* —'**madrigalist** *n.*

Maecenas (miː'siːnæs) *n.* a wealthy patron of the arts. [after *Maecenas* (?70–8 B.C.), Roman patron of Horace and Virgil]

maelstrom ('meɪlstrəʊm) *n.* **1.** a large powerful whirlpool. **2.** any turbulent confusion. [C17: < obs. Du. *maelstroom,* < *malen* to whirl round + *stroom* STREAM]

maenad ('miːnæd) *n.* **1.** *Classical history.* a woman participant in the orgiastic rites of Dionysus, Greek god of wine. **2.** a frenzied woman. [C16: < L *Maenas,* < Gk *mainas* madwoman] —**mae'nadic** *adj.*

maestoso (maɪ'stəʊsəʊ) *Music.* ~*adj., adv.* **1.** to be performed majestically. ~*n., pl.* **-sos. 2.** a piece or passage directed to be played in this way. [C18: It.: majestic, < L *māiestās* MAJESTY]

maestro ('maɪstrəʊ) *n., pl.* **-tri** (-trɪ) *or* **-tros. 1.** a distinguished music teacher, conductor, or musician. **2.** any master of an art: often used as a term of address. [C18: It.: master]

mae west (meɪ) *n. Sl.* an inflatable life jacket, esp. as issued to the U.S. armed forces. [C20: after *Mae West* (1892–1980), American actress, renowned for her generous bust]

Mafia ('mæfɪə) *n.* **1. the.** an international secret criminal organization founded in Sicily, and carried to the U.S. by Italian immigrants. **2.** any group considered to resemble the Mafia. [C19: < Sicilian dialect of It., lit.: hostility to the law, ? < Ar. *mahyah* bragging]

mafioso (ˌmæfɪ'əʊsəʊ) *n., pl.* **-sos** *or* **-si** (-sɪ). a person belonging to the Mafia.

mag. *abbrev. for:* **1.** magazine. **2.** magnesium. **3.** magnetic. **4.** magnetism. **5.** magnitude.

magazine (ˌmægə'ziːn) *n.* **1.** a periodic paperback publication containing articles, fiction, photographs, etc. **2. a.** a metal case holding several cartridges used in some automatic firearms. **b.** this compartment itself. **3.** a building or compartment for storing weapons, explosives, military provisions, etc. **4.** a stock of ammunition. **5.** *Photog.* another name for **cartridge** (sense 3). **6.** a rack for automatically feeding slides through a projector. [C16: via F *magasin* < It. *magazzino,* < Ar. *makhāzin,* pl. of *makhzan* storehouse, < *khazana* to store away]

magdalen ('mægdəlɪn) *or* **magdalene** ('mægdəˌliːn) *n.* **1.** *Literary.* a reformed prostitute. **2.** *Rare.* a reformatory for prostitutes. [< Mary *Magdalene* (New Testament), a woman from Magdala in Israel, often identified with the sinful woman of Luke 7:36–50]

Magdalenian (ˌmægdə'liːnɪən) *adj.* **1.** of or relating to the latest Palaeolithic culture in Europe, which ended about 10 000 years ago. ~*n* **2. the.** the Magdalenian culture. [C19: < F *magdalénien,* after *La Madeleine,* village in Dordogne, France, near which artefacts of the culture were found]

Magellanic cloud (ˌmægɪ'lænɪk) *n.* either of two small irregular galaxies situated near the S celestial pole at a distance of 160 000 light years.

magenta (mə'dʒɛntə) *n.* **1. a.** a deep purplish red. **b.** (*as adj.*): *a magenta filter.* **2.** another name for **fuchsin.** [C19: after *Magenta,* Italy, alluding to the blood shed in a battle there (1859)]

maggot ('mægət) *n.* **1.** the limbless larva of dipterous insects, esp. the housefly and blowfly. **2.** *Rare.* a fancy or whim. [C14: < earlier *mathek;* rel. to ON *mathkr* worm, OE *matha,* OHG *mado* grub]

maggoty ('mægətɪ) *adj.* **1.** of, like, or ridden with maggots. **2.** *Austral. sl.* angry.

magi ('meɪdʒaɪ) *pl. n., sing.* **magus** ('meɪgəs). **1.** See **magus. 2. the three Magi.** the wise men from the East who came to do homage to the infant Jesus (Matthew 2:1–12). [see MAGUS] —**magian** ('meɪdʒɪən) *adj.*

magic ('mædʒɪk) *n.* **1.** the art that, by use of spells, supposedly invokes supernatural powers to influence events; sorcery. **2.** the practice of this art. **3.** the practice of illusory tricks to entertain; conjuring. **4.** any mysterious or extraordinary quality or power. **5. like magic.** very quickly. ~*adj. also* **magical. 6.** of or relating to magic. **7.** possessing or considered to possess mysterious powers. **8.** unaccountably enchanting. **9.** *Inf.* wonderful; marvellous. ~*vb.* **-icking, -icked.** (*tr.*) **10.** to transform or produce by or as if by magic. **11.** (foll. by *away*) to cause to disappear as if by magic. [C14: via OF *magique,* < Gk *magikē* witchcraft, < *magos* MAGUS] —'**magically** *adv.*

magic eye *n.* a miniature cathode-ray tube in some radio receivers, on the screen of which a pattern is displayed to assist tuning. Also called: **electric eye.**

magician (mə'dʒɪʃən) *n.* **1.** another term for **conjurer. 2.** a person who practises magic. **3.** a person with extraordinary skill, influence, etc.

magic lantern *n.* an early type of slide projector.

magic mushroom *n. Inf.* any of various types of fungi that contain a hallucinogenic substance.

magic realism *or* **magical realism** *n.* a style of painting or writing that depicts images or scenes of surreal fantasy in a representational or realistic way. —**magic realist** *or* **magical realist** *n.*

magic square *n.* a square array of rows of integers arranged so that the sum of the integers is the same when taken vertically, horizontally, or diagonally.

Maginot line ('mæʒɪˌnəʊ) *n.* **1.** a line of fortifications built by France to defend its border with Germany prior to World War II; it proved ineffective. **2.** any line of defence in which blind confidence is placed. [after André *Maginot* (1877–1932), F minister of war when the fortifications were begun in 1929]

magisterial (ˌmædʒɪ'stɪərɪəl) *adj.* **1.** commanding; authoritative. **2.** domineering; dictatorial. **3.** of or relating to a teacher or person of similar status. **4.** of or relating to a magistrate. [C17: < LL *magisteriālis,* < *magister* master] —ˌ**magis'terially** *adv.*

magistracy ('mædʒɪstrəsɪ) *or* **magistrature** ('mædʒɪstrəˌtjʊə) *n., pl.* **-cies** *or* **-tures. 1.** the office or function of a magistrate. **2.** magistrates collectively. **3.** the district under the jurisdiction of a magistrate.

magistral (mə'dʒɪstrəl) *adj.* **1.** *Pharmacol.* made up according to a special prescription. **2.** of a master; masterly. [C16: < L *magistrālis,* < *magister* master] —**magistrality** (ˌmædʒɪ'strælɪtɪ) *n.*

magistrate ('mædʒɪˌstreɪt, -strɪt) *n.* **1.** a public officer concerned with the administration of law. **2.** another name for **justice of the peace.** [C17: < L *magistrātus,* < *magister* master] —'**magisˌtrateship** *n.*

magistrates' court *n.* (in England) a court held before two or more justices of the peace or a stipendiary magistrate to deal with minor crimes, certain civil actions, and preliminary hearings.

Maglemosian *or* **Maglemosean** (ˌmæglə'məʊzɪən) *n.* **1.** the first Mesolithic culture of N Europe, dating from 8000 B.C. to about 5000 B.C. ~*adj.* **2.** designating or relating to this culture. [C20: after the site at *Maglemose,* Denmark, where the culture was first classified]

magma ('mægmə) *n., pl.* **-mas** *or* **-mata** (-mətə). **1.** a paste or suspension consisting of a finely divided solid dispersed in a liquid. **2.** hot molten rock within the earth's crust which sometimes finds its way to the surface where it solidifies to form igneous rock. [C15: < L: dregs (of an ointment), < Gk: salve made by kneading, < *massein* to knead] —**magmatic** (mæg'mætɪk) *adj.*

Magna Carta *or* **Magna Charta** ('mægnə 'kɑːtə) *n. English history.* the charter granted by King John at Runnymede in 1215, recognizing the rights and privileges of the barons, church, and freemen. [Med. L: great charter]

magnanimity (ˌmægnə'nɪmɪtɪ) *n., pl.* **-ties.** generosity. [C14: via OF < L *magnanimitās,* < *magnus* great + *animus* soul]

magnanimous (mæg'nænɪməs) *adj.* generous and noble. [C16: < L *magnanimus* great-souled] —**mag'nanimously** *adv.*

magnate ('mægneɪt, -nɪt) *n.* **1.** a person of power and rank, esp. in industry. **2.** *History.* a great nobleman. [C15: back formation < earlier *magnates,* < LL: great men, < L *magnus* great] —**'magnateˌship** *n.*

magnesia (mæg'niːʃə) *n.* another name for **magnesium oxide.** [C14: via Med. L < Gk *Magnēsia,* of *Magnēs,* ancient mineral-rich region] —**mag'nesian** *or* **magnesic** (mæg'niːsɪk) *adj.*

magnesium (mæg'niːzɪəm) *n.* a light silvery-white metallic element of the alkaline earth series that burns with an intense white flame: used in light structural alloys, flashbulbs, flares, and fireworks. Symbol: Mg; atomic no.: 12; atomic wt.: 24.312. [C19: NL, < MAGNESIA]

magnesium oxide *n.* a white tasteless substance used as an antacid and laxative and in refractory materials. Formula: MgO. Also called: **magnesia.**

magnet ('mægnɪt) *n.* **1.** a body that can attract certain substances, such as iron or steel, as a result of a magnetic field; a piece of ferromagnetic substance. See also **electromagnet. 2.** a person or thing that exerts a great attraction. [C15: via L < Gk *magnēs,* shortened < *ho Magnēs lithos* the Magnesian stone. See MAGNESIA]

magnetic (mæg'nɛtɪk) *adj.* **1.** of, producing, or operated by means of magnetism. **2.** of or concerned with a magnet. **3.** of or concerned with the magnetism of the earth: *the magnetic equator.* **4.** capable of being magnetized. **5.** exerting a powerful attraction: *a magnetic personality.* —**mag'netically** *adv.*

magnetic constant *n.* a value representing the ability of free space to modify a magnetic field.

magnetic declination *n.* the angle that a compass needle makes with the direction of the geographical north pole at any given point on the earth's surface.

magnetic dip *or* **inclination** *n.* another name for **dip** (sense 24).

magnetic dipole moment *n.* a measure of the magnetic strength of a magnet or current-carrying coil, expressed as the torque produced when the magnet or coil is set with its axis perpendicular to unit magnetic field.

magnetic disk *n.* another name for **disk** (sense 2).

magnetic equator *n.* an imaginary line on the earth's surface, near the equator, at all points on which there is no magnetic dip.

magnetic field *n.* a field of force surrounding a permanent magnet or a moving charged particle, in which another permanent magnet or moving charge experiences a force.

magnetic flux *n.* a measure of the strength of a magnetic field over a given area, equal to the product of the area and the magnetic flux density through it. Symbol: ϕ

magnetic mine *n.* a mine designed to activate when a magnetic field such as that generated by the metal of a ship's hull is detected.

magnetic needle *n.* a slender magnetized rod used in certain instruments, such as the magnetic compass, for indicating the direction of a magnetic field.

magnetic north *n.* the direction in which a compass needle points, at an angle (the declination) from the direction of true (geographic) north.

magnetic pick-up *n.* a type of record-player pick-up in which the stylus moves an iron core in a coil, causing a changing magnetic field that produces the current.

magnetic pole *n.* **1.** either of two regions in a magnet where the magnetic induction is concentrated. **2.** either of two variable points on the earth's surface towards which a magnetic needle points, where the lines of force of the earth's magnetic field are vertical.

magnetic resonance *n.* the response by atoms, molecules, or nuclei subjected to a magnetic field to radio waves or other forms of energy: used in medicine for scanning.

magnetic storm *n.* a sudden severe disturbance of the earth's magnetic field, caused by emission of charged particles from the sun.

magnetic stripe *n.* (across the back of various types of bank card, credit card, etc.) a dark stripe of magnetic material consisting of several tracks onto which information may be coded and which may be read or written to electronically.

magnetic tape *n.* a long narrow plastic or metal strip coated or impregnated with iron oxide, chrome dioxide, etc., used to record sound or video signals or to store information in computers.

magnetism ('mægnɪˌtɪzəm) *n.* **1.** the property of attraction displayed by magnets. **2.** any of a class of phenomena in which a field of force is caused by a moving electric charge. **3.** the branch of physics concerned with magnetic phenomena. **4.** powerful attraction.

magnetite ('mægnɪˌtaɪt) *n.* a black magnetizable mineral that is an important source of iron.

magnetize *or* **-ise** ('mægnɪˌtaɪz) *vb.* (*tr.*) **1.** to make (a substance or object) magnetic. **2.** to attract strongly. —**ˌmagnet'izable** *or* **-'isable** *adj.* —**ˌmagneti'zation** *or* **-i'sation** *n.* —**'magnetˌizer** *or* **-ˌiser** *n.*

magneto (mæg'niːtəʊ) *n., pl.* **-tos.** a small electric generator in which the magnetic field is produced by a permanent magnet, esp. one for providing the spark in an internal-combustion engine. [C19: short for *magnetoelectric generator*]

magneto- *combining form.* indicating magnetism or magnetic properties: *magnetosphere.*

magnetoelectricity (mægˌniːtəʊɪlɛk'trɪsɪtɪ) *n.* electricity produced by the action of magnetic fields. —**magˌnetoe'lectric** *or* **magˌnetoe'lectrical** *adj.*

magnetometer (ˌmægnɪ'tɒmɪtə) *n.* any instrument for measuring the intensity or direction of a magnetic field, esp. the earth's field. —**ˌmagne'tometry** *n.*

magnetomotive (mægˌniːtəʊ'məʊtɪv) *adj.* causing a magnetic flux.

magnetosphere (mæg'niːtəʊˌsfɪə) *n.* the region surrounding the earth in which the behaviour of charged particles is dominated by the earth's magnetic field.

magnetron ('mægnɪˌtrɒn) *n.* a two-electrode electronic valve used with an applied magnetic field to generate high-power microwave oscillations, esp. for use in radar. [C20: < MAGNET + ELECTRON]

Magnificat (mæg'nɪfɪˌkæt) *n. Christianity.* the hymn of the Virgin Mary (Luke 1:46-55), used as a canticle. [< the opening phrase, *Magnificat* *anima mea Dominum* (my soul doth magnify the Lord)]

magnification (ˌmægnɪfɪˈkeɪʃən) *n.* **1.** the act of magnifying or the state of being magnified. **2.** the degree to which something is magnified. **3.** a magnified copy, photograph, drawing, etc., of something. **4.** a measure of the ability of a lens or other optical instrument to magnify.

magnificence (mægˈnɪfɪsəns) *n.* the quality of being magnificent. [C14: via F < L *magnificentia*]

magnificent (mægˈnɪfɪsᵊnt) *adj.* **1.** splendid or impressive in appearance. **2.** superb or very fine. **3.** (esp. of ideas) noble or elevated. [C16: < L *magnificentior,* irregular comp. of *magnificus* great in deeds, < *magnus* great + *facere* to do] —**magˈnificently** *adv.*

magnifico (mægˈnɪfɪkəʊ) *n., pl.* **-coes.** a magnate; grandee. [C16: It. < L *magnificus;* see MAGNIFICENT]

magnify (ˈmægnɪˌfaɪ) *vb.* **-fying, -fied. 1.** to increase, cause to increase, or be increased in apparent size, as through the action of a lens, microscope, etc. **2.** to exaggerate or become exaggerated in importance: *don't magnify your troubles.* **3.** (*tr.*) *Arch.* to glorify. [C14: via OF < L *magnificāre* to praise] —**ˈmagniˌfiable** *adj.*

magnifying glass *or* **magnifier** *n.* a convex lens used to produce an enlarged image of an object.

magniloquent (mægˈnɪləkwənt) *adj.* (of speech) lofty in style; grandiloquent. [C17: < L *magnus* great + *loquī* to speak] —**magˈniloquence** *n.* —**magˈniloquently** *adv.*

magnitude (ˈmægnɪˌtjuːd) *n.* **1.** relative importance or significance: *a problem of the first magnitude.* **2.** relative size or extent. **3.** *Maths.* a number assigned to a quantity as a basis of comparison for the measurement of similar quantities. **4.** Also called: **apparent magnitude.** *Astron.* the apparent brightness of a celestial body expressed on a numerical scale on which bright stars have a low value. **5.** Also called: **earthquake magnitude.** *Geol.* a measure of the size of an earthquake based on the quantity of energy released. [C14: < L *magnitūdō* size, < *magnus* great]

magnolia (mægˈnəʊlɪə) *n.* **1.** any tree or shrub of the genus *Magnolia* of Asia and North America: cultivated for their white, pink, purple, or yellow showy flowers. **2.** the flower of any of these plants. **3. a.** a very pale pinkish-white colour. **b.** (*as adj.*): *magnolia walls.* [C18: NL, after Pierre *Magnol* (1638–1715), F botanist]

magnox (ˈmægnɒks) *n.* an alloy consisting mostly of magnesium with small amounts of aluminium, used in fuel elements of nuclear reactors. [C20: < *mag*(*nesium*) *n*(*o*) *ox*(*idation*)]

magnox reactor *n.* a nuclear reactor using carbon dioxide as the coolant, graphite as the moderator, and uranium cased in magnox as the fuel.

magnum (ˈmægnəm) *n., pl.* **-nums.** a wine bottle holding the equivalent of two normal bottles (approximately 52 fluid ounces). [C18: < L: a big thing, < *magnus* large]

magnum opus *n.* a great work of art or literature, esp. the greatest single work of an artist. [L]

magpie (ˈmægˌpaɪ) *n.* **1.** any of various birds having a black-and-white plumage, long tail, and a chattering call. **2.** any of various similar birds of Australia. **3.** *Brit.* a person who hoards small objects. **4.** a person who chatters. **5. a.** the outmost ring but one on a target. **b.** a shot that hits this ring. [C17: < *Mag,* dim. of *Margaret,* used to signify a chatterbox + PIE[2]]

maguey (ˈmægweɪ) *n.* **1.** any of various tropical American agave plants, esp. one that yields a fibre or is used in making an alcoholic beverage. **2.** the fibre from any of these plants, used esp. for rope. [C16: Sp., of Amerind origin]

magus (ˈmeɪgəs) *n., pl.* **magi. 1.** a Zoroastrian priest. **2.** an astrologer, sorcerer, or magician of ancient times. [C14: < L, < Gk *magos,* < OPersian *magus* magician]

Magyar (ˈmægjɑː) *n.* **1.** (*pl.* **-yars**) a member of the predominant ethnic group of Hungary. **2.** the Hungarian language. ~*adj.* **3.** of or relating to the Magyars or their language. **4.** *Sewing.* of or relating to a style of sleeve cut in one piece with the bodice.

Mahabharata (ˌmɑːhəˈbɑːrətə), **Mahabharatam,** *or* **Mahabharatum** (ˌmɑːhəˈbɑːrətəm) *n.* an epic Sanskrit poem of India of which the *Bhagavad-Gita* forms a part. [Sansk., < *mahā* great + *bhārata* story]

maharajah *or* **maharaja** (ˌmɑːhəˈrɑːdʒə) *n.* any of various Indian princes, esp. any of the rulers of the former native states. [C17: Hindi, < *mahā* great + RAJAH]

maharani *or* **maharanee** (ˌmɑːhəˈrɑːniː) *n.* **1.** the wife of a maharajah. **2.** a woman holding the rank of maharajah. [C19: < Hindi, < *mahā* great + RANI]

maharishi (ˌmɑːhəˈriːʃɪ, məˈhɑːriːʃɪ) *n. Hinduism.* a Hindu teacher of religious and mystical knowledge. [< Hindi, < *mahā* great + *rishi* sage]

mahatma (məˈhɑːtmə) *n.* (*sometimes cap.*) **1.** *Hinduism.* a Brahman sage. **2.** *Theosophy.* an adept or sage. [C19: < Sansk. *mahātman,* < *mahā* great + *ātman* soul]

Mahayana (ˌmɑːhəˈjɑːnə) *n.* **a.** a liberal Buddhist school of Tibet, China, and Japan, whose adherents seek enlightenment for all sentient beings. **b.** (*as modifier*): *Mahayana Buddhism.* [< Sansk., < *mahā* great + *yāna* vehicle]

Mahdi (ˈmɑːdɪ) *n. Islam.* any of a number of Muslim messiahs expected to convert all mankind to Islam by force. [Ar. *mahdīy* one who is guided, < *madā* to guide aright] —**ˈMahdism** *n.* —**ˈMahdist** *n., adj.*

mahjong *or* **mah-jongg** (ˌmɑːˈdʒɒŋ) *n.* a game of Chinese origin, usually played by four people, using tiles bearing various designs. [< Chinese, lit.: sparrows]

mahlstick (ˈmɔːlˌstɪk) *n.* a variant spelling of **maulstick.**

mahogany (məˈhɒgənɪ) *n., pl.* **-nies. 1.** any of various tropical American trees valued for their hard reddish-brown wood. **2.** any of several trees with similar wood, such as African mahogany and Philippine mahogany. **3. a.** the wood of any of these trees. **b.** (*as modifier*): *a mahogany table.* **4. a.** a reddish-brown colour. **b.** (*as adj.*): *mahogany skin.* [C17: <?]

mahonia (məˈhəʊnɪə) *n.* any evergreen shrub of the Asian and American genus *Mahonia:* cultivated for their ornamental spiny divided leaves and clusters of small yellow flowers. [C19: NL, after Bernard *McMahon* (died 1816), American botanist]

mahout (məˈhaʊt) *n.* (in India and the East Indies) an elephant driver or keeper. [C17: Hindi *mahāut,* < Sansk. *mahāmātra* of great measure, orig. a title]

mahseer (ˈmɑːsɪə) *n.* any of various large freshwater Indian cyprinid fishes. [< Hindi]

maid (meɪd) *n.* **1.** *Arch. or literary.* a young unmarried girl; maiden. **2. a.** a female servant. **b.** (*in combination*): *a housemaid.* **3.** a spinster. [C12: form of MAIDEN]

maiden (ˈmeɪdᵊn) *n.* **1.** *Arch. or literary.* **a.** a young unmarried girl, esp. a virgin. **b.** (*as modifier*): *a maiden blush.* **2.** *Horse racing.* **a.** a horse that has never won a race. **b.** (*as modifier*): *a maiden race.* **3.** *Cricket.* See **maiden over. 4.** (*modifier*) of or relating to an older unmarried woman: *a maiden aunt.* **5.** (*modifier*) of or involving an initial experience or attempt: *a maiden voyage.* **6.** (*modifier*) (of a person or thing) untried; unused. **7.** (*modifier*) (of a place) never trodden, penetrated, or captured. [OE *mægden*] —**ˈmaidenish** *adj.* —**ˈmaidenˌlike** *adj.*

maidenhair fern *or* **maidenhair** (ˈmeɪdᵊnˌhɛə) *n.* any of various ferns of tropical and warm regions, having delicate fan-shaped fronds with small pale green leaflets. [C15: < the hairlike appearance of its fronds]

maidenhair tree *n.* another name for **ginkgo.**

maidenhead (ˈmeɪdᵊnˌhɛd) *n.* **1.** a nontechnical word for the **hymen.** **2.** virginity; maidenhood. [C13: < *maiden* + *-hed,* var. of -HOOD]

maidenhood (ˈmeɪdᵊnˌhʊd) *n.* **1.** the time during which a woman is a maiden or virgin. **2.** the condition of being a maiden or virgin.

maidenly (ˈmeɪdᵊnlɪ) *adj.* of or befitting a maiden. —ˈ**maidenliness** *n.*

maiden name *n.* a woman's surname before marriage.

maiden over *n. Cricket.* an over in which no runs are scored.

maid of honour *n.* **1.** *U.S. & Canad.* the principal unmarried attendant of a bride. **2.** *Brit.* a small tart with an almond-flavoured filling. **3.** an unmarried lady attending a queen or princess.

maidservant (ˈmeɪdˌsɜːvənt) *n.* a female servant.

maigre (ˈmeɪgə) *adj. R.C. Church.* **1.** not containing flesh, and so permissible as food on days of religious abstinence. **2.** of or designating such a day. [C17: < F: thin; see MEAGRE]

maihem (ˈmeɪhɛm) *n.* a variant spelling of **mayhem.**

mail[1] (meɪl) *n.* **1.** Also called (esp. Brit.): **post.** letters, packages, etc., that are transported and delivered by the post office. **2.** the postal system. **3.** a single collection or delivery of mail. **4.** a train, ship, or aircraft that carries mail. **5.** (*modifier*) of, involving, or used to convey mail: *a mail train.* ~*vb.* **6.** (*tr.*) *Chiefly U.S. & Canad.* to send by mail. [C13: < OF *male* bag, prob. < OHG *malha* wallet] —ˈ**mailable** *adj.*

mail[2] (meɪl) *n.* **1.** a type of flexible armour consisting of riveted metal rings or links. **2.** the hard protective shell of such animals as the turtle and lobster. ~*vb.* **3.** (*tr.*) to clothe or arm with mail. [C14: < OF *maille* mesh, < L *macula* spot]

mailbag (ˈmeɪlˌbæg) *or* **mailsack** *n.* a large bag for transporting or delivering mail.

mailbox (ˈmeɪlˌbɒks) *n.* another name (esp. U.S. and Canad.) for **letter box.**

mailing list *n.* a register of names and addresses to which advertising matter, etc., is sent by post.

maillot (mæˈjəʊ) *n.* **1.** tights worn for ballet, gymnastics, etc. **2.** a woman's swimsuit. **3.** a jersey. [< F]

mailman (ˈmeɪlˌmæn) *n., pl.* **-men.** *Chiefly U.S. & Canad.* another name for **postman.**

mail order *n.* **1.** an order for merchandise sent by post. **2. a.** a system of buying and selling merchandise through the post. **b.** (*as modifier*): *a mail-order firm.*

maim (meɪm) *vb.* (*tr.*) **1.** to mutilate, cripple, or disable a part of the body of (a person or animal). **2.** to make defective. [C14: < OF *mahaignier* to wound, prob. of Gmc origin]

mai mai (maɪ maɪ) *n. N.Z.* a duck shooter's shelter; hide. [< Maori]

main[1] (meɪn) *adj.* (*prenominal*) **1.** chief or principal. **2.** sheer or utmost (esp. in **by main force**). **3.** *Naut.* of, relating to, or denoting any gear, such as a stay or sail, belonging to the mainmast. ~*n.* **4.** a principal pipe, conduit, duct, or line in a system used to distribute water, electricity, etc. **5.** (*pl.*) **a.** the main distribution network for water, gas, or electricity. **b.** (*as modifier*): *mains voltage.* **6.** the chief or most important part or consideration. **7.** great strength or force (now esp. in **might and main**). **8.** *Literary.* the open ocean. **9.** *Arch.* short for **Spanish Main.** **10.** *Arch.* short for **mainland.** **11. in** (*or* **for**) **the main.** on the whole; for the most part. [C13: < OE *mægen* strength]

main[2] (meɪn) *n.* **1.** a throw of the dice in dice games. **2.** a cockfighting contest. **3.** a match in archery, boxing, etc. [C16: <?]

mainbrace (ˈmeɪnˌbreɪs) *n. Naut.* **1.** a brace attached to the main yard. **2. splice the mainbrace.** See **splice.**

main clause *n. Grammar.* a clause that can stand alone as a sentence.

mainframe (ˈmeɪnˌfreɪm) *Computers.* ~*adj.* **1.** denoting a high-speed general-purpose computer, usually with a large store capacity. ~*n.* **2.** such a computer. **3.** the central processing unit of a computer.

mainland (ˈmeɪnlənd) *n.* the main part of a land mass as opposed to an island or peninsula. —ˈ**mainlander** *n.*

main line *n.* **1.** *Railways.* **a.** the trunk route between two points, usually fed by branch lines. **b.** (*as modifier*): *a main-line station.* **2.** *U.S.* a main road. ~*vb.* **mainline.** **3.** (*intr.*) *Sl.* to inject a drug into a vein. ~*adj.* **mainline.** **4.** having an important position. —ˈ**mainˌliner** *n.*

mainly (ˈmeɪnlɪ) *adv.* for the most part; to the greatest extent; principally.

mainmast (ˈmeɪnˌmɑːst) *n. Naut.* the chief mast of a sailing vessel with two or more masts.

mainsail (ˈmeɪnˌseɪl; *Naut.* ˈmeɪnsᵊl) *n. Naut.* the largest and lowermost sail on the mainmast.

mainsheet (ˈmeɪnˌʃiːt) *n. Naut.* the line used to control the angle of the mainsail to the wind.

mainspring (ˈmeɪnˌsprɪŋ) *n.* **1.** the principal spring of a mechanism, esp. in a watch or clock. **2.** the chief cause or motive of something.

mainstay (ˈmeɪnˌsteɪ) *n.* **1.** *Naut.* the forestay that braces the mainmast. **2.** a chief support.

mainstream (ˈmeɪnˌstriːm) *n.* **1.** the main current (of a river, cultural trend, etc.). ~*adj.* **2.** of or relating to the style of jazz that lies between the traditional and the modern.

mainstreeting (ˈmeɪnˌstriːtɪŋ) *n. Canad.* the practice of a politician walking about the streets of a town or city to gain votes and greet supporters.

maintain (meɪnˈteɪn) *vb.* (*tr.*) **1.** to continue or retain; keep in existence. **2.** to keep in proper or good condition. **3.** to enable (a person) to support a style of living: *the money maintained us for a month.* **4.** (*takes a clause as object*) to state or assert. **5.** to defend against contradiction; uphold: *she maintained her innocence.* **6.** to defend against physical attack. [C13: < OF *maintenir,* ult. < L *manū tenēre* to hold in the hand] —**mainˈtainable** *adj.* —**mainˈtainer** *n.*

maintenance (ˈmeɪntɪnəns) *n.* **1.** the act of maintaining or the state of being maintained. **2.** a means of support; livelihood. **3.** (*modifier*) of or relating to the maintaining of buildings, machinery, etc.: *maintenance man.* **4.** *Law.* the interference in a legal action by a person having no interest in it, as by providing funds to continue the action. **5.** *Law.* a provision ordered to be made by way of periodical payments or a lump sum, as for a spouse after a divorce. [C14: < OF; see MAINTAIN]

maintop (ˈmeɪnˌtɒp) *n.* a top or platform at the head of the mainmast.

main-topmast *n. Naut.* the mast immediately above the mainmast.

maintopsail (ˌmeɪnˈtɒpseɪl; *Naut.* ˌmeɪnˈtɒpsᵊl) *n. Naut.* a topsail on the mainmast.

main yard *n. Naut.* a yard for a square mainsail.

maiolica (məˈjɒlɪkə) *n.* a variant of **majolica.**

maisonette *or* **maisonnette** (ˌmeɪzəˈnɛt) *n.* self-contained living accommodation often occupying two floors of a larger house and having its own outside entrance. [C19: < F, dim. of *maison* house]

maître d'hôtel (ˌmɛtrə dəʊˈtɛl) *n., pl.* **maîtres d'hôtel.** **1.** a head waiter or steward. **2.** the manager or owner of a hotel. [C16: < F: master of (the) hotel]

maize (meɪz) *n.* **1.** Also called: **sweet corn, Indian corn. a.** a tall annual grass cultivated for its yellow edible grains, which develop on a spike. **b.** the grain of this plant, used for food, for fodder, and as a source of oil. **2. a.** a yellow colour. **b.** (*as adj.*): *a maize gown.* [C16: < Sp. *maíz,* < Taino *mahiz*]

Maj. *abbrev. for* Major.

majestic (məˈdʒɛstɪk) *adj.* having or displaying majesty or great dignity; grand; lofty. —**maˈjestically** *adv.*

majesty (ˈmædʒɪstɪ) *n.* **1.** great dignity of bearing; loftiness; grandeur. **2.** supreme power or authority. [C13: < OF, < L *mājestās;* rel. to L *major,* comp. of *magnus* great]

Majesty (ˈmædʒɪstɪ) *n., pl.* **-ties.** (preceded by *Your, His, Her,* or *Their*) a title used to address or refer to a sovereign or the wife or widow of a sovereign.

majolica (məˈdʒɒlɪkə, məˈjɒl-) *or* **maiolica** *n.* a type of porous pottery glazed with bright metallic oxides that was originally imported into Italy via Majorca and was extensively made in Renaissance Italy. [C16: < It., < LL *Mājorica* Majorca]

major (ˈmeɪdʒə) *n.* **1.** *Mil.* an officer immediately junior to a lieutenant colonel. **2.** a person who is superior in a group or class. **3.** (often preceded by *the*) *Music.* a major key, chord, mode, or scale. **4.** *U.S., Canad., Austral., & N.Z.* **a.** the principal field of study of a student. **b.** a student who is studying a particular subject as his principal field: *a sociology major.* **5.** a person who has reached the age of legal majority. **6.** a principal or important record company, film company, etc. **7.** *Logic.* a major term or premise. ~*adj.* **8.** larger in extent, number, etc. **9.** of greater importance or priority. **10.** very serious or significant. **11.** main, chief, or principal. **12.** of, involving, or making up a majority. **13.** *Music.* **a.** (of a scale or mode) having notes separated by a whole tone, except for the third and fourth degrees, and seventh and eighth degrees, which are separated by a semitone. **b.** relating to or employing notes from the major scale: *a major key.* **c.** (*postpositive*) denoting a specified key or scale as being major: *C major.* **d.** denoting a chord or triad having a major third above the root. **e.** (in jazz) denoting a major chord with a major seventh added above the root. **14.** *Logic.* constituting the major term or major premise of a syllogism. **15.** *Chiefly U.S., Canad., Austral., & N.Z.* of or relating to a student's principal field of study at a university, etc. **16.** *Brit.* the elder: used after a schoolboy's surname if he has one or more younger brothers in the same school: *Price major.* **17.** of full legal age. ~*vb.* **18.** (*intr.;* usually foll. by *in*) *U.S., Canad., Austral., & N.Z.* to do one's principal study (in a particular subject): *to major in English literature.* **19.** (*intr.;* usually foll. by *on*) to take or deal with as the main area of interest: *the book majors on peasant dishes.* [C15 (adj.): < L, comp. of *magnus* great; C17 (n., in military sense): < F, short for SERGEANT MAJOR] —ˈ**majorship** *n.*

▷ **Usage.** The overuse of *major* in examples like *the major reason, the major differences, a major factor,* where a comparative is not really implied, is avoided by careful writers and speakers of English.

major-domo (-ˈdəʊməʊ) *n., pl.* **-mos.** **1.** the chief steward or butler of a great household. **2.** *Facetious.* a steward or butler. [C16: < Sp. *mayordomo,* < Med. L *mājor domūs* head of the household]

majorette (ˌmeɪdʒəˈrɛt) *n.* **1.** one of a group of girls who practise formation marching and baton twirling. **2.** See **drum majorette.**

major general *n. Mil.* an officer immediately junior to a lieutenant general. —ˌ**major-ˈgeneralship** *or* **major-ˈgeneralcy** *n.*

majority (məˈdʒɒrɪtɪ) *n., pl.* **-ties.** **1.** the greater number or part of something. **2.** (in an election) the number of votes or seats by which the strongest party or candidate beats the combined opposition or the runner-up. **3.** the largest party or group that votes together in a legislative or deliberative assembly. **4.** the time of reaching or state of having reached full legal age. **5.** the rank, office, or commission of major. **6.** *Euphemistic.* the dead (esp. in **join the majority, go** *or* **pass over to the majority**). **7.** (*modifier*) of, involving, or being a majority: *a majority decision.* **8. in the majority.** forming or part of the greater number of something. [C16: < Med. L *mājoritās,* < MAJOR (adj.)]

major league *n. U.S. & Canad.* a league of highest classification in baseball, football, hockey, etc.

major orders *pl. n. R.C. Church.* the three higher degrees of holy orders: bishop, priest, and deacon.

major premise *n. Logic.* the premise of a syllogism containing the predicate of its conclusion.

major term *n. Logic.* the predicate of the conclusion of a syllogism.

majuscule (ˈmædʒəˌskjuːl) *n.* **1.** a large letter, either capital or uncial, used in printing or writing. ~*adj.* **2.** relating to, printed, or written in such letters. ~Cf. **minuscule.** [C18: via F < L *mājusculus,* dim. of *mājor* bigger] —**majuscular** (məˈdʒʌskjʊlə) *adj.*

make (meɪk) *vb.* **making, made.** (*mainly tr.*) **1.** to bring into being by shaping, changing, or combining materials, ideas, etc.; form or fashion. **2.** to draw up, establish, or form: *to make one's will.* **3.** to cause to exist, bring about, or produce: *don't make a noise.* **4.** to cause, compel, or induce: *please make him go away.* **5.** to appoint or assign: *they made him chairman.* **6.** to constitute: *one swallow doesn't make a summer.* **7.** (*also intr.*) to come or cause to come into a specified state or condition: *to make merry.* **8.** (*copula*) to be or become through development: *he will make a good teacher.* **9.** to cause or ensure the success of: *your news has made my day.* **10.** to amount to: *twelve inches make a foot.* **11.** to serve as or be suitable for: *that piece of cloth will make a coat.* **12.** to prepare or put into a fit condition for use: *to make a bed.* **13.** to be the essential element in or part of: *charm makes a good salesman.* **14.** to carry out, effect, or do. **15.** (*intr.;* foll. by *to, as if to,* or *as though to*) to act with the intention or with a show of doing something: *he made as if to hit her.* **16.** to use for a specified purpose: *I will make this town my base.* **17.** to deliver or pronounce: *to make a speech.* **18.** to give information or an opinion: *what time do you make it?* **19.** to cause to seem or represent as being. **20.** to earn, acquire, or win for oneself: *to make friends.* **21.** to engage in: *to make war.* **22.** to traverse or cover (distance) by travelling: *we can make a hundred miles by nightfall.* **23.** to arrive in time for: *he didn't make the first act of the play.* **24.** *Cards.* **a.** to win a trick with (a specified card). **b.** to shuffle (the cards). **c.** *Bridge.* to fulfil (a contract) by winning the necessary number of tricks. **25.** *Cricket.* to score (runs). **26.** *Electronics.* to close (a circuit) permitting a flow of current. **27.** (*intr.*) to increase in depth: *the water in the hold was making a foot a minute.* **28.** *Inf.* to gain a place or position on or in: *to make the headlines.* **29.** *Inf., chiefly U.S.* to achieve the rank of. **30.** *Taboo sl.* to seduce. **31. make a book.** to take bets on a race or another contest. **32. make a day, night,** etc., **of it.** to cause an activity to last a day, night, etc. **33. make do.** See **do**[1] (sense 31). **34. make eyes at.** to flirt with or ogle. **35. make it. a.** *Inf.* to be successful in doing something. **b.** (foll. by *with*) *Taboo sl.* to have sexual intercourse. **36. make like.** *Sl., chiefly U.S. & Canad.* **a.** to imitate. **b.** to pretend. ~*n.* **37.** brand, type, or style. **38.** the manner or way in which something is made. **39.** disposition or character; make-up. **40.** the act or process of making. **41.** the amount or number made. **42.** *Cards.* a player's turn to shuffle. **43. on the make.** *Sl.* **a.** out for profit or conquest. **b.** in search of a sexual partner. ~See also **make away, make for,** etc. [OE *macian*] —ˈ**makable** *adj.*

make away *vb.* (*intr., adv.*) **1.** to depart in haste. **2. make away with. a.** to steal or abduct. **b.** to kill, destroy, or get rid of.

make believe *vb.* **1.** to pretend or enact a fantasy. ~*n.* **make-believe.** **2. a.** a fantasy or pretence. **b.** (*as modifier*): *a make-believe world.*

make for *vb.* (*intr., prep.*) **1.** to head towards. **2.** to prepare to attack. **3.** to help bring about.

make of *vb.* (*tr., prep.*) **1.** to interpret as the meaning of. **2.** to produce or construct from: *houses made of brick.* **3. make little, much,** etc., **of. a.** to gain little, much, etc., benefit from. **b.** to attribute little, much, etc., significance to.

make off *vb.* **1.** (*intr., adv.*) to go or run away in haste. **2. make off with.** to steal or abduct.

make out *vb.* (*adv.*) **1.** (*tr.*) to discern or perceive. **2.** (*tr.*) to understand or comprehend. **3.** (*tr.*) to write out: *he made out a cheque.* **4.** (*tr.*) to attempt to establish or prove: *he made me out to be a liar.* **5.** (*intr.*) to pretend: *he made out that he could cook.* **6.** (*intr.*) to manage or fare.

maker (ˈmeɪkə) *n.* a person who executes a legal document, esp. one who signs a promissory note.

Maker (ˈmeɪkə) *n.* **1.** a title given to God (as Creator). **2.** (**go to**) **meet one's Maker.** to die.

makeshift (ˈmeɪkˌʃɪft) *adj.* **1.** serving as a temporary or expedient means. ~*n.* **2.** something serving in this capacity.

make-up *n.* **1.** cosmetics, such as powder, lipstick, etc., applied to the face. **2. a.** the cosmetics, false hair, etc., used by an actor to adapt his appearance. **b.** the art or result of applying such cosmetics. **3.** the manner of arrangement of the parts or qualities of someone or something. **4.** the arrangement of type matter and illustrations on a page or in a book. **5.** mental or physical constitution. ~*vb.* **make up.** (*adv.*) **6.** (*tr.*) to form or constitute: *these arguments make up the case for the defence.* **7.** (*tr.*) to devise, construct, or compose, sometimes with the intent to deceive: *to make up an excuse.* **8.** (*tr.*) to supply what is lacking or deficient in; complete: *these extra people will make up our total.* **9.** (*tr.*) to put in order, arrange, or prepare: *to make up a bed.* **10.** (*intr.;* foll. by *for*) to compensate or atone (for). **11.** to settle (differences) amicably (often in **make it up**). **12.** to apply cosmetics to (the face) to enhance one's appearance or for a theatrical role. **13.** to assemble (type and illustrations) into (columns or pages). **14.** (*tr.*) to surface (a road) with tarmac, concrete, etc. **15. make up to.** *Inf.* **a.** to make friendly overtures to. **b.** to flirt with.

makeweight (ˈmeɪkˌweɪt) *n.* **1.** something put on a scale to make up a required weight. **2.** an unimportant person or thing added to make up a lack.

making (ˈmeɪkɪŋ) *n.* **1. a.** the act of a person or thing that makes or the process of being made. **b.** (*in combination*): *watchmaking.* **2. be the making of.** to cause the success of. **3. in the making.** in the process of becoming or being made. **4.** something made or the quantity of something made at one time.

makings (ˈmeɪkɪŋz) *pl. n.* **1.** potentials, qualities, or materials: *he had the makings of a leader.* **2.** Also called: **rollings.** *Sl.* the tobacco and cigarette paper used for rolling a cigarette. **3.** profits; earnings.

mako[1] (ˈmɑːkəʊ) *n., pl.* **-kos.** a blue-pointer game shark. [< Maori]

mako[2] (ˈmɑːkəʊ) *n., pl.* **-kos.** a small evergreen New Zealand tree. [< Maori]

Mal. *abbrev. for:* **1.** *Bible.* Malachi. **2.** Malay(an).

mal- *combining form.* bad or badly; wrong or wrongly; imperfect or defective: *maladjusted; malfunction.* [OF, < L *malus* bad, *male* badly]

malacca *or* **malacca cane** (məˈlækə) *n.* **1.** the stem of the rattan palm. **2.** a walking stick made from this stem. [< *Malacca,* SW Peninsular Malaysia]

malachite (ˈmæləˌkaɪt) *n.* a green mineral consisting of hydrated basic copper carbonate: a source of copper, also used for making ornaments. [C16: via OF < L *molochītēs,* < Gk *molokhitis* mallow-green stone, < *molokhē* mallow]

maladjustment (ˌmæləˈdʒʌstmənt) *n.* **1.** *Psychol.* a failure to meet the demands of society, such as coping with problems and social relationships. **2.** faulty or bad adjustment. —ˌ**maladˈjusted** *adj.*

maladminister (ˌmæləd'mɪnɪstə) *vb.* (*tr.*) to administer badly, inefficiently, or dishonestly. —ˌ**maladˌminisˈtration** *n.*

maladroit (ˌmæləˈdrɔɪt) *adj.* **1.** clumsy; not dexterous. **2.** tactless and insensitive. [C17: < F, < *mal* badly + ADROIT] —ˌ**malaˈdroitly** *adv.* —ˌ**malaˈdroitness** *n.*

malady (ˈmælədɪ) *n., pl.* **-dies. 1.** any disease or illness. **2.** any unhealthy, morbid, or desperate condition. [C13: < OF, < Vulgar L *male habitus* (unattested) in poor condition, < L *male* badly + *habitus,* < *habēre* to have]

Málaga (ˈmæləgə) *n.* a sweet fortified dessert wine from Málaga, a port in S Spain.

Malagasy (ˌmæləˈgæsɪ) *n.* **1.** (*pl.* **-gasy** *or* **-gasies**) a native or inhabitant of Madagascar. **2.** the official language of Madagascar. ~*adj.* **3.** of or relating to Madagascar, its people, or their language.

malaise (mæˈleɪz) *n.* a feeling of unease, mild sickness, or depression. [C18: < OF, < *mal* bad + *aise* EASE]

malamute *or* **malemute** (ˈmæləˌmuːt) *n.* an Alaskan Eskimo dog of the spitz type. [< the name of an Eskimo tribe]

malapropism (ˈmæləprɒpˌɪzəm) *n.* **1.** the unintentional misuse of a word by confusion with one of similar sound, esp. when creating a ridiculous effect, as in *under the affluence of alcohol.* **2.** the habit of misusing words in this manner. [C18: after Mrs *Malaprop* in Sheridan's play *The Rivals* (1775), a character who misused words, < MALAPROPOS]

malapropos (ˌmælæprəˈpəʊ) *adj.* **1.** inappropriate or misapplied. ~*adv.* **2.** in an inappropriate way or manner. ~*n.* **3.** something inopportune or inappropriate. [C17: < F *mal à propos* not to the purpose]

malaria (məˈlɛərɪə) *n.* an infectious disease characterized by recurring attacks of chills and fever, caused by the bite of an anopheles mosquito infected with any of certain protozoans. [C18: < It. *mala aria* bad air, from the belief that the disease was caused by the unwholesome air in swampy districts] —**maˈlarial, maˈlarian,** *or* **maˈlarious** *adj.*

malarkey *or* **malarky** (məˈlɑːkɪ) *n. Sl.* nonsense; rubbish. [C20: <?]

Malathion (ˌmæləˈθaɪɒn) *n. Trademark.* an insecticide consisting of an organic phosphate. [C20: < (*diethyl*) MAL(EATE) + THIO- + -ON]

Malay (məˈleɪ) *n.* **1.** a member of a people living chiefly in Malaysia and Indonesia. **2.** the language of this people. ~*adj.* **3.** of or relating to the Malays or their language.

Malayalam *or* **Malayalaam** (ˌmælɪˈɑːləm) *n.* a language of SW India.

Malayan (məˈleɪən) *adj.* **1.** of or relating to the Malay Peninsula in SE Asia. ~*n.* **2.** a native or inhabitant of the Malay Peninsula, esp. one who is a citizen of Malaysia.

Malayo-Polynesian *n.* **1.** Also called: **Austronesian.** a family of languages extending from Madagascar to the central Pacific. ~*adj.* **2.** of or relating to this family of languages.

Malaysian (məˈleɪzɪən) *adj.* **1.** of Malaysia in SE Asia. ~*n.* **2.** a native or inhabitant of Malaysia.

malcontent (ˈmælkənˌtɛnt) *adj.* **1.** disgusted or discontented. ~*n.* **2.** a person who is malcontent. [C16: < OF]

mal de mer *French.* (mal də mɛr) *n.* seasickness.

male (meɪl) *adj.* **1.** of, relating to, or designating the sex producing gametes (spermatozoa) that can fertilize female gametes (ova). **2.** of, relating to, or characteristic of a man. **3.** for or composed of men or boys: *a male choir.* **4.** (of gametes) capable of fertilizing an egg cell. **5.** (of reproductive organs) capable of producing male gametes. **6.** (of flowers) bearing stamens but lacking a functional pistil. **7.** *Electronics, engineering.* having a projecting part or parts that fit into a female counterpart: *a male plug.* ~*n.* **8.** a male person, animal, or plant. [C14: via OF < L *masculus* MASCULINE] —ˈ**maleness** *n.*

maleate (ˈmælɪˌeɪt) *n.* any salt or ester of maleic acid. [C19: < MALE(IC) ACID + -ATE[1]]

male chauvinism *n.* the belief, held or alleged to be held by certain men, that men are superior to women. —**male chauvinist** *n., adj.*

malediction (ˌmælɪˈdɪkʃən) *n.* **1.** the utterance of

a curse against someone or something. **2.** a slanderous accusation or comment. [C15: < L *maledictiō* a reviling, < *male* ill + *dīcere* to speak] —ˌ**male'dictive** *or* ˌ**male'dictory** *adj.*

malefactor ('mælɪˌfæktə) *n.* a criminal; wrongdoer. [C15: via OF < L, < *malefacere* to do evil] —'**maleˌfaction** *n.*

maleficent (mə'lɛfɪsənt) *adj.* causing evil or mischief; harmful or baleful. [C17: < L, < *maleficus* wicked, < *malum* evil] —**ma'lefic** *adj.* —**ma'leficence** *n.*

maleic acid (mə'leɪɪk) *n.* a colourless soluble crystalline substance used to synthesize other compounds, such as polyester resins. [C19: < F *maléique,* altered form of *malique;* see MALIC ACID]

male menopause *n.* a period in a man's later middle age in which he may experience an identity crisis as he feels age overtake his sexual powers.

malevolent (mə'lɛvələnt) *adj.* wishing or appearing to wish evil to others; malicious. [C16: < L *malevolens,* < *male* ill + *volens,* present participle of *velle* to wish] —**ma'levolence** *n.* —**ma'levolently** *adv.*

malfeasance (mæl'fiːzᵊns) *n. Law.* the doing of a wrongful or illegal act, esp. by a public official. Cf. **misfeasance, nonfeasance.** [C17: < OF *mal faisant,* < *mal* evil + *faisant,* < *faire* to do, < L *facere*] —**mal'feasant** *n., adj.*

malformation (ˌmælfɔː'meɪʃən) *n.* **1.** the condition of being faulty or abnormal in form or shape. **2.** *Pathol.* a deformity, esp. when congenital. —**mal'formed** *adj.*

malfunction (mæl'fʌŋkʃən) *vb.* **1.** (*intr.*) to function imperfectly or fail to function. ~*n.* **2.** failure to function or defective functioning.

malic acid ('mælɪk, 'meɪ-) *n.* a colourless crystalline compound occurring in apples and other fruits. [C18 *malic,* via F *malique* < L *mālum* apple]

malice ('mælɪs) *n.* **1.** the desire to do harm or mischief. **2.** evil intent. **3.** *Law.* the state of mind with which an act is committed and from which the intent to do wrong may be inferred. [C13: via OF < L *malitia,* < *malus* evil]

malice aforethought *n. Law.* **1.** the predetermination to do an unlawful act, esp. to kill or seriously injure. **2.** the intent with which an unlawful killing is effected, which must be proved for the crime to constitute murder.

malicious (mə'lɪʃəs) *adj.* **1.** characterized by malice. **2.** motivated by wrongful, vicious, or mischievous purposes. —**ma'liciously** *adv.* —**ma'liciousness** *n.*

malign (mə'laɪn) *adj.* **1.** evil in influence, intention, or effect. ~*vb.* **2.** (*tr.*) to slander or defame. [C14: via OF < L *malīgnus* spiteful, < *malus* evil] —**ma'ligner** *n.* —**ma'lignly** *adv.*

malignancy (mə'lɪgnənsɪ) *n., pl.* **-cies. 1.** the state or quality of being malignant. **2.** *Pathol.* a cancerous growth.

malignant (mə'lɪgnənt) *adj.* **1.** having or showing desire to harm others. **2.** tending to cause great harm; injurious. **3.** *Pathol.* (of a tumour) uncontrollable or resistant to therapy. [C16: < LL *malīgnāre* to behave spitefully, < L *malīgnus* MALIGN] —**ma'lignantly** *adv.*

malignity (mə'lɪgnɪtɪ) *n., pl.* **-ties. 1.** the condition or quality of being malign or deadly. **2.** (*often pl.*) a malign or malicious act or feeling.

malines (mə'liːn) *n.* **1.** a type of silk net used in dressmaking. **2.** another name for **Mechlin lace.** [C19: < F *Malines* (Mechelen), a Belgian city, where this lace was traditionally made]

malinger (mə'lɪŋgə) *vb.* (*intr.*) to pretend or exaggerate illness, esp. to avoid work. [C19: < F *malingre* sickly, ? < *mal* badly + OF *haingre* feeble] —**ma'lingerer** *n.*

mall (mɔːl, mæl) *n.* **1.** a shaded avenue, esp. one open to the public. **2.** a street or area lined with shops and closed to vehicles. **3.** See **pall-mall.** [C17: after *the Mall,* in St James's Park, London]

mallard ('mælɑːd) *n., pl.* **-lard** *or* **-lards.** a duck common over most of the N hemisphere, the male of which has a dark green head and reddish-brown breast: the ancestor of all domestic breeds of duck. [C14: < OF *mallart,* ? < *maslart* (unattested); see MALE, -ARD]

malleable ('mælɪəbᵊl) *adj.* **1.** (esp. of metal) able to be worked, hammered, or shaped under pressure or blows without breaking. **2.** able to be influenced; pliable or tractable. [C14: via OF < Med. L *malleābilis,* < L *malleus* hammer] —ˌ**mallea'bility** *or* (*less commonly*) '**malleableness** *n.* —'**malleably** *adv.*

mallee ('mæliː) *n.* **1.** any of several low shrubby eucalyptus trees in desert regions of Australia. **2.** (usually preceded by *the*) *Austral.* another name for the **bush** (sense 4). [C19: Abor.]

Mallee ('mæliː) *n.* a region in NW Victoria, Australia.

mallee fowl *n.* an Australian megapode.

malleolus (mə'liːələs) *n., pl.* **-li** (-ˌlaɪ). either of two rounded bony projections, one on each side of the ankle. [C17: dim. of L *malleus* hammer]

mallet ('mælɪt) *n.* **1.** a tool resembling a hammer but having a large head of wood, copper, lead, leather, etc., used for driving chisels, beating sheet metal, etc. **2.** a long stick with a head like a hammer used to strike the ball in croquet or polo. [C15: < OF *maillet* wooden hammer, dim. of *mail* MAUL (n.)]

malleus ('mælɪəs) *n., pl.* **-lei** (-lɪˌaɪ). the outermost and largest of the three small bones in the middle ear of mammals. See also **incus, stapes.** [C17: < L: hammer]

mallow ('mæləʊ) *n.* **1.** any of several malvaceous plants of Europe, having purple, pink, or white flowers. **2.** any of various related plants, such as the marsh mallow. [OE *mealuwe,* < L *malva*]

malm (mɑːm) *n.* **1.** a soft greyish limestone that crumbles easily. **2.** a chalky soil formed from this. **3.** an artificial mixture of clay and chalk used to make bricks. [OE *mealm-* (in compound words)]

malmsey ('mɑːmzɪ) *n.* a sweet Madeira wine. [C15: < Med. L *Malmasia,* corruption of Gk *Monembasia,* Gk port from which the wine was shipped]

malnutrition (ˌmælnjuː'trɪʃən) *n.* lack of adequate nutrition resulting from insufficient food, unbalanced diet, or defective assimilation.

malodorous (mæl'əʊdərəs) *adj.* having a bad smell.

malpractice (mæl'præktɪs) *n.* **1.** immoral, illegal, or unethical professional conduct or neglect of professional duty. **2.** any instance of improper professional conduct.

malt (mɔːlt) *n.* **1.** cereal grain, such as barley, that is kiln-dried after it has germinated by soaking in water. **2.** See **malt liquor, malt whisky.** ~*vb.* **3.** to make into or become malt. **4.** to make (something, esp. liquor) with malt. [OE *mealt*] —'**malty** *adj.*

malted milk *n.* **1.** a soluble powder made from dehydrated milk and malted cereals. **2.** a drink made from this powder.

Maltese (mɔːl'tiːz) *adj.* **1.** of or relating to Malta, an island in the Mediterranean, its inhabitants, or their language. ~*n.* **2.** (*pl.* **-tese**) a native or inhabitant of Malta. **3.** the official language of Malta, a form of Arabic with borrowings from Italian, etc.

Maltese cross *n.* a cross with triangular arms that taper towards the centre, sometimes having indented outer sides.

malt extract *n.* a sticky substance obtained from an infusion of malt.

Malthusian (mæl'θjuːzɪən) *adj.* **1.** of or relating to the theory of T. R. Malthus (1766–1834), English economist, stating that increases in population tend to exceed increases in the means of subsistence and that therefore sexual restraint should be exercised. ~*n.* **2.** a supporter of this theory. —**Mal'thusianism** *n.*

malting ('mɔːltɪŋ) *n.* a building in which malt is made or stored. Also called: **malt house.**

malt liquor *n.* any alcoholic drink brewed from malt.

maltose ('mɔːltəʊz) *n.* a sugar formed by the

enzymic hydrolysis of starch. [C19: < MALT + -OSE[2]]

maltreat (mælˈtriːt) *vb.* (*tr.*) to treat badly, cruelly, or inconsiderately. [C18: < F *maltraiter*] —**malˈtreater** *n.* —**malˈtreatment** *n.*

maltster (ˈmɔːltstə) *n.* a person who makes or deals in malt.

malt whisky *n.* whisky made from malted barley.

malvaceous (mælˈveɪʃəs) *adj.* of, relating to, or belonging to a family of plants that includes mallow, cotton, okra, althaea, and abutilon. [C17: < L *malvāceus*, < *malva* MALLOW]

malversation (ˌmælvɜːˈseɪʃən) *n. Rare.* professional or public misconduct. [C16: < F, < *malverser* to behave badly, < L *male versārī*]

mam (mæm) *n. Inf. or dialect.* another word for **mother.**

mama *or esp. U.S.* **mamma** (məˈmɑː) *n. Old-fashioned.* an informal word for **mother.** [C16: reduplication of childish syllable *ma*]

mamba (ˈmæmbə) *n.* any of various partly arboreal tropical African venomous snakes, esp. the **green** and **black mambas**. [< Zulu *im-amba*]

mambo (ˈmæmbəʊ) *n., pl.* **-bos. 1.** a modern Latin American dance, resembling the rumba. ~*vb.* **2.** (*intr.*) to perform this dance. [American Sp., prob. < Haitian Creole: voodoo priestess]

Mameluke *or* **Mamaluke** (ˈmæmɪˌluːk) *n.* **1.** a member of a military class, originally of Turkish slaves, ruling in Egypt from about 1250 to 1517 and remaining powerful until 1811. **2.** (in Muslim countries) a slave. [C16: via F, ult. < Ar. *mamlūk* slave, < *malaka* to possess]

mamilla *or U.S.* **mammilla** (mæˈmɪlə) *n., pl.* **-lae** (-liː). **1.** a nipple or teat. **2.** any nipple-shaped prominence. [C17: < L, dim. of *mamma* breast] —ˈ**mamillary** *or U.S.* ˈ**mammillary** *adj.*

mamma (ˈmæmə) *n., pl.* **-mae** (-miː). the milk-secreting organ of female mammals: the breast in women, the udder in cows, sheep, etc. [C17: < L: breast] —ˈ**mammary** *adj.*

mammal (ˈmæməl) *n.* any animal of the *Mammalia*, a large class of warm-blooded vertebrates having mammary glands in the female. [C19: via NL < L *mamma* breast] —**mammalian** (mæˈmeɪlɪən) *adj., n.*

mammary gland *n.* any of the milk-producing glands in mammals.

mammon (ˈmæmən) *n.* riches or wealth regarded as a source of evil and corruption. [C14: via LL < New Testament Gk *mammōnas*, < Aramaic *māmōnā* wealth] —ˈ**mammonish** *adj.* —ˈ**mammonism** *n.* —ˈ**mammonist** *or* ˈ**mammonite** *n.*

Mammon (ˈmæmən) *n. Bible.* the personification of riches and greed in the form of a false god.

mammoth (ˈmæməθ) *n.* **1.** any large extinct elephant of the Pleistocene epoch, such as the **woolly mammoth**, having a hairy coat and long curved tusks. ~*adj.* **2.** of gigantic size or importance. [C18: < Russian *mamot*, < Tartar *mamont*, ? < *mamma* earth, because of a belief that the animal made burrows]

mammy *or* **mammie** (ˈmæmɪ) *n., pl.* **-mies. 1.** a child's word for **mother. 2.** *Chiefly southern U.S.* a Black woman employed as a nurse or servant to a White family.

man (mæn) *n., pl.* **men. 1.** an adult male human being, as distinguished from a woman. **2.** (*modifier*) male; masculine: *a man child.* **3.** a human being, considered as representative of mankind. **4.** human beings collectively; mankind. **5.** Also called: **modern man. a.** a member of any of the living races of *Homo sapiens*, characterized by erect bipedal posture, a highly developed brain, and powers of articulate speech, abstract reasoning, and imagination. **b.** any extinct member of the species *Homo sapiens*, such as Cro-Magnon man. **6.** a member of any of the extinct species of the genus *Homo*, such as Java man. **7.** an adult male human being with qualities associated with the male, such as courage or virility: *be a man.* **8.** manly qualities or virtues: *the man in him was outraged.* **9. a.** a subordinate, servant, or employee. **b.** (*in combination*): *the man-days required to complete a job.* **10.** (*usually pl.*) a member of the armed forces who does not hold commissioned, warrant, or noncommissioned rank (as in **officers and men**). **11.** a member of a group, team, etc. **12.** a husband, boyfriend, etc. **13.** an expression used parenthetically to indicate an informal relationship between speaker and hearer. **14.** a movable piece in various games, such as draughts. **15.** a vassal of a feudal lord. **16.** *S. African sl.* any person. **17. as one man.** with unanimous action or response. **18. be one's own man.** to be independent or free. **19. he's your man.** he's the person needed. **20. man and boy.** from childhood. **21. sort out** *or* **separate the men from the boys.** to separate the experienced from the inexperienced. **22. to a man.** without exception. ~*interj.* **23.** *Inf.* an exclamation or expletive, often indicating surprise or pleasure. ~*vb.* **manning, manned.** (*tr.*) **24.** to provide with sufficient men for operation, defence, etc. **25.** to take one's place at or near in readiness for action. [OE *mann*]

Man. *abbrev. for:* **1.** Manila paper. **2.** Manitoba.

-man *n. combining form.* indicating a person who has a role, works in a place, or operates equipment as specified: *salesman; barman; cameraman.*

▷ **Usage.** The use of words ending in *-man* is avoided as implying a male in job advertisements, where sexual discrimination is illegal, and in many other contexts where a term that is not gender-specific is available, such as *salesperson, barperson, camera operator.*

mana (ˈmɑːnə) *n. Anthropol.* **1.** (in Polynesia, Melanesia, etc.) a concept of a life force associated with high social status and ritual power. **2.** any power achieved by ritual means; prestige; authority. [of Polynesian origin]

man about town *n.* a fashionable sophisticate, esp. one in a big city.

manacle (ˈmænək[ə]l) *n.* **1.** (*usually pl.*) a shackle, handcuff, or fetter, used to secure the hands of a prisoner, convict, etc. ~*vb.* (*tr.*) **2.** to put manacles on. **3.** to confine or constrain. [C14: via OF < L *manicula*, dim. of *manus* hand]

manage (ˈmænɪdʒ) *vb.* (*mainly tr.*) **1.** (*also intr.*) to be in charge (of); administer: *to manage a shop.* **2.** to succeed in being able (to do something); contrive. **3.** to have room, time, etc., for: *can you manage dinner tomorrow?* **4.** to exercise control or domination over. **5.** (*intr.*) to contrive to carry on despite difficulties, esp. financial ones. **6.** to wield or handle (a weapon). [C16: < It. *maneggiare* to train (esp. horses), ult. < L *manus* hand]

manageable (ˈmænɪdʒəb[ə]l) *adj.* able to be managed or controlled. —ˌ**manageaˈbility** *or* ˈ**manageableness** *n.* —ˈ**manageably** *adv.*

managed bonds *pl. n.* investment in a combination of funds, such as fixed-interest securities and property shares, in which the amount invested in each fund is dependent on the expected returns.

managed currency *n.* a currency subject to governmental control with respect to the amount in circulation and rate of exchange.

management (ˈmænɪdʒmənt) *n.* **1.** the members of the executive or administration of an organization or business. **2.** managers or employers collectively. **3.** the technique, practice, or science of managing or controlling. **4.** the skilful or resourceful use of materials, time, etc. **5.** the specific treatment of a disease, etc.

manager (ˈmænɪdʒə) *n.* **1.** a person who directs or manages an organization, industry, shop, etc. **2.** a person who controls the business affairs of an actor, entertainer, etc. **3.** a person who controls the training of a sportsman or team. **4.** a person who has a talent for managing efficiently. **5.** (in Britain) a member of either House of Parliament appointed to arrange a matter in which both Houses are concerned. —ˈ**managership** *n.*

manageress (ˌmænɪdʒəˈrɛs) *n.* a woman who is in charge of a shop, department, etc.

managerial (ˌmænɪˈdʒɪərɪəl) *adj.* of or relating to

a manager or management. —ˌmana'gerially *adv.*

managing ('mænɪdʒɪŋ) *adj.* having administrative control or authority: *a managing director.*

mañana *Spanish.* (mə'njɑːnə) *n., adv.* **a.** tomorrow. **b.** some other and later time.

man-at-arms *n., pl.* **men-at-arms.** a soldier, esp. a heavily armed mounted soldier in medieval times.

manatee (ˌmænə'tiː) *n.* a sirenian mammal occurring in tropical coastal waters of America, the West Indies, and Africa, having a prehensile upper lip and a broad flattened tail. [C16: via Sp. < Carib *Manattouï*]

manchester ('mæntʃɪstə) *n. Austral. & N.Z.* **1.** goods, such as sheets and pillowcases, which are, or were originally, made of cotton. **2. manchester department.** a section of a store which sells such goods. [< *Manchester*, city in NW England, centre of textile trade]

manchineel (ˌmæntʃɪ'niːl) *n.* a tropical American tree having fruit and milky highly caustic poisonous sap, which causes skin blisters. [C17: via F < Sp. MANZANILLA]

Manchu (mæn'tʃuː) *n.* **1.** (*pl.* **-chus** *or* **-chu**) a member of a Mongoloid people of Manchuria, a region of NE China, who conquered China in the 17th century, establishing a dynasty that lasted until 1912. **2.** the language of this people. ~*adj.* **3.** Also: **Ching.** of or relating to the dynasty of the Manchus. [< Manchu, lit.: pure]

manciple ('mænsɪp'l) *n.* a steward who buys provisions, esp. in an Inn of Court. [C13: via OF < L *mancipium* purchase, < *manceps* purchaser, < *manus* hand + *capere* to take]

Mancunian (mæŋ'kjuːnɪən) *n.* **1.** a native or inhabitant of Manchester, a city in NW England. ~*adj.* **2.** of or relating to Manchester. [< Med. L *Mancunium* Manchester]

-mancy *n. combining form.* indicating divination of a particular kind: *chiromancy.* [< OF *-mancie*, < L *-mantia*, < Gk *manteia* soothsaying] —**-mantic** *adj. combining form.*

mandala ('mændələ, mæn'dɑːlə) *n. Hindu & Buddhist art.* any of various designs symbolizing the universe, usually circular. [Sansk.: circle]

mandamus (mæn'deɪməs) *n., pl.* **-muses.** *Law.* (formerly) a writ from, now an order of, a superior court commanding an inferior tribunal, public official, etc., to carry out a public duty. [C16: L, lit.: we command, < *mandāre*]

mandarin ('mændərɪn) *n.* **1.** (in the Chinese Empire) a member of a senior grade of the bureaucracy. **2.** a high-ranking official whose powers are extensive and thought to be outside political control. **3.** a person of standing and influence, as in literary or intellectual circles, esp. one regarded as conservative or reactionary. **4. a.** a small citrus tree cultivated for its edible fruit. **b.** the fruit, resembling the tangerine. [C16: < Port. via Malay < Sansk. *mantrin* counsellor, < *mantra* counsel] —'**mandarinate** *n.*

Mandarin Chinese *or* **Mandarin** *n.* the official language of China since 1917.

Mandarin collar *n.* a high stiff round collar.

mandarin duck *n.* an Asian duck, the male of which has a distinctive brightly coloured and patterned plumage and crest.

mandate *n.* ('mændeɪt, -dɪt). **1.** an official or authoritative instruction or command. **2.** *Politics.* the support or commission given to a government and its policies or an elected representative and his policies through an electoral victory. **3.** (*often cap.*) Also called: **mandated territory.** (formerly) any of the territories under the trusteeship of the League of Nations administered by one of its member states. **4. a.** *Roman law.* a contract by which one person commissions another to act for him gratuitously. **b.** *Contract law.* a contract under which a party entrusted with goods undertakes to perform gratuitously some service in respect of such goods. **c.** *Scots Law.* a contract by which a person is engaged to act in the management of the affairs of another. ~*vb.* ('mændeɪt). (*tr.*) **5.** to assign (territory) to a nation under a mandate. **6.** to delegate authority to. [C16: < L *mandātum* something commanded, < *mandāre* to command, ? < *manus* hand + *dāre* to give] —'**mandator** *n.*

mandatory ('mændətərɪ, -trɪ) *adj.* **1.** having the nature or powers of a mandate. **2.** obligatory; compulsory. **3.** (of a state) having received a mandate over some territory. ~*n., pl.* **-ries.** *also* **mandatary. 4.** a person or state holding a mandate. —'**mandatorily** *adv.*

mandible ('mændɪb'l) *n.* **1.** the lower jawbone in vertebrates. **2.** either of a pair of mouthparts in insects and other arthropods that are usually used for biting and crushing food. **3.** *Ornithol.* either part of the bill, esp. the lower part. [C16: via OF < LL *mandibula* jaw, < *mandere* to chew] —**mandibular** (mæn'dɪbjʊlə) *adj.* —**mandibulate** (mæn'dɪbjʊlɪt, -ˌleɪt) *n., adj.*

mandolin *or* **mandoline** (ˌmændə'lɪn) *n.* a plucked stringed instrument having four pairs of strings stretched over a small light body with a fretted fingerboard: usually played with a plectrum. [C18: via F < It. *mandolino*, dim. of *mandora* lute, ult. < Gk *pandoura* musical instrument with three strings] —ˌ**mando'linist** *n.*

mandrake ('mændreɪk) *or* **mandragora** (mæn'drægərə) *n.* **1.** a Eurasian plant with purplish flowers and a forked root. It was formerly thought to have magic powers and a narcotic was prepared from its root. **2.** another name for the **May apple.** [C14: prob. via MDu. < L *mandragoras*, < Gk. The form *mandrake* was prob. adopted through folk etymology, because of the allegedly human appearance of the root and because *drake* (dragon) suggested magical powers]

mandrel *or* **mandril** ('mændrəl) *n.* **1.** a spindle on which a workpiece is supported during machining operations. **2.** a shaft or arbor on which a machining tool is mounted. [C16: ? rel. to F *mandrin* lathe]

mandrill ('mændrɪl) *n.* an Old World monkey of W Africa. It has a short tail and brown hair, and the ridged muzzle, nose, and hindquarters are red and blue. [C18: < MAN + DRILL[4]]

mane (meɪn) *n.* **1.** the long coarse hair that grows from the crest of the neck in such mammals as the lion and horse. **2.** long thick human hair. [OE *manu*] —**maned** *adj.*

manège *or* **manege** (mæ'neɪʒ) *n.* **1.** the art of training horses and riders. **2.** a riding school. [C17: via F < It. *maneggio*, < *maneggiare* to MANAGE]

manes ('mɑːneɪz) *pl. n.* (*sometimes cap.*) (in Roman legend) **1.** the spirits of the dead, often revered as minor deities. **2.** (*functioning as sing.*) the shade of a dead person. [C14: < L, prob.: the good ones, < OL *mānus* good]

maneuver (mə'nuːvə) *n., vb.* the usual U.S. spelling of **manoeuvre.**

man Friday *n.* **1.** a loyal male servant or assistant. **2.** Also: **girl Friday, person Friday.** any factotum, esp. in an office. [after the native in Daniel Defoe's novel *Robinson Crusoe* (1719)]

manful ('mænfʊl) *adj.* resolute, strong; manly. —'**manfully** *adv.* —'**manfulness** *n.*

mangabey ('mæŋgəˌbeɪ) *n.* any of several large agile arboreal Old World monkeys of central Africa, having long limbs and tail. [C18: after a region in Madagascar]

manganese ('mæŋgəˌniːz) *n.* a brittle greyish-white metallic element: used in making steel and ferromagnetic alloys. Symbol: Mn; atomic no.: 25; atomic wt.: 54.938. [C17: via F < It., prob. altered form of Med. L MAGNESIA]

mange (meɪndʒ) *n.* an infectious disorder mainly affecting domestic animals, characterized by itching and loss of hair: caused by parasitic mites. [C14: < OF *mangeue* itch, < *mangier* to eat]

mangelwurzel ('mæŋg'lˌwɜːz'l) *or* **mangoldwurzel** ('mæŋgəʊldˌwɜːz'l) *n.* a Eurasian variety of beet, cultivated as a cattle food, having a large yellowish root. [C18: < G *Mangoldwurzel*, < *Mangold* beet + *Wurzel* root]

manger ('meɪndʒə) *n.* a trough or box in a stable,

barn, etc., from which horses or cattle feed. [C14: < OF *maingeure* food trough, < *mangier* to eat, ult. < L *mandūcāre* to chew]

mangetout (ˈmɑ̃ʒˈtuː) *n.* a variety of garden pea in which the pod is also edible. Also called: **sugar pea.** [C20: < F: eat all]

mangle[1] (ˈmæŋgᵊl) *vb.* (*tr.*) **1.** to mutilate, disfigure, or destroy by cutting, crushing, or tearing. **2.** to ruin, spoil, or mar. [C14: < Norman F *mangler*, prob. < OF *mahaignier* to maim] —ˈ**mangled** *adj.* —ˈ**mangler** *n.*

mangle[2] (ˈmæŋgᵊl) *n.* **1.** Also called: **wringer.** a machine for pressing or drying textiles, clothes, etc., consisting of two heavy rollers between which the cloth is passed. ~*vb.* (*tr.*) **2.** to press or dry in a mangle. [C18: < Du. *mangel*, ult. < LL *manganum.* See MANGONEL]

mango (ˈmæŋgəʊ) *n., pl.* **-goes** *or* **-gos. 1.** a tropical Asian evergreen tree, cultivated in the tropics for its fruit. **2.** the ovoid edible fruit of this tree, having a smooth rind and sweet juicy flesh. [C16: via Port. < Malay *mangā*, < Tamil *mānkāy*, < *mān* mango tree + *kāy* fruit]

mangonel (ˈmæŋgəˌnɛl) *n. History.* a war engine for hurling stones. [C13: via OF < Med. L *manganellus*, ult. < Gk *manganon*]

mangrove (ˈmæŋgrəʊv, ˈmæn-) *n.* any of various tropical evergreen trees or shrubs, having stiltlike intertwining aerial roots and forming dense thickets along coasts. [C17 *mangrow* (changed through infl. of *grove*), < Port. *mangue*, ult. < Taino]

mangy *or* **mangey** (ˈmeɪndʒɪ) *adj.* **-gier, -giest. 1.** having or caused by mange. **2.** scruffy or shabby. —ˈ**mangily** *adv.* —ˈ**manginess** *n.*

manhandle (ˈmænˌhændᵊl, ˌmænˈhændᵊl) *vb.* (*tr.*) **1.** to handle or push (someone) about roughly. **2.** to move or do by manpower rather than by machinery.

Manhattan (mænˈhætᵊn, mən-) *n.* a mixed drink consisting of four parts whisky, one part vermouth, and a dash of bitters. [after *Manhattan*, a borough of New York City, U.S.A.]

manhole (ˈmænˌhəʊl) *n.* **1.** Also called: **inspection chamber.** a shaft with a removable cover that leads down to a sewer or drain. **2.** a hole, usually with a detachable cover, through which a man can enter a boiler, tank, etc.

manhood (ˈmænhʊd) *n.* **1.** the state or quality of being a man or being manly. **2.** men collectively. **3.** the state of being human.

man-hour *n.* a unit of work in industry, equal to the work done by one man in one hour.

manhunt (ˈmænˌhʌnt) *n.* an organized search, usually by police, for a wanted man or fugitive.

mania (ˈmeɪnɪə) *n.* **1.** a mental disorder characterized by great excitement and occasionally violent behaviour. **2.** obsessional enthusiasm or partiality. [C14: via LL < Gk: madness]

-mania *n. combining form.* indicating extreme desire or pleasure of a specified kind or an abnormal excitement aroused by something: *kleptomania; nymphomania; pyromania.* [< MANIA] —**-maniac** *n. and adj. combining form.*

maniac (ˈmeɪnɪˌæk) *n.* **1.** a wild disorderly person. **2.** a person who has a great craving or enthusiasm for something. **3.** *Psychiatry, obs.* a person afflicted with mania. [C17: < LL *maniacus* belonging to madness, < Gk]

maniacal (məˈnaɪəkᵊl) *or* **maniac** *adj.* **1.** affected with or characteristic of mania. **2.** characteristic of or befitting a maniac: *maniacal laughter.* —**maˈniacally** *adv.*

manic (ˈmænɪk) *adj.* **1.** characterizing, denoting, or affected by mania. ~*n.* **2.** a person afflicted with mania. [C19: < Gk, < MANIA]

manic-depressive *Psychiatry.* ~*adj.* **1.** denoting a mental disorder characterized by an alternation between extreme euphoria and deep depression. ~*n.* **2.** a person afflicted with this disorder.

Manichaeism *or* **Manicheism** (ˈmænɪkiːˌɪzəm) *n.* the system of religious doctrines taught by the Persian prophet Mani about the 3rd century A.D. It was based on a supposed primordial conflict between light and darkness or goodness and evil. [C14: < LL *Manichaeus*, < LGk *Manikhaios* of Mani] —ˌ**Maniˈchaean** *or* ˌ**Maniˈchean** *adj., n.* —ˈ**Manichee** *n.*

manicure (ˈmænɪˌkjʊə) *n.* **1.** care of the hands and fingernails, involving shaping the nails, removing cuticles, etc. **2.** Also called: **manicurist.** a person who gives manicures, esp. as a profession. ~*vb.* **3.** to care for (the hands and fingernails) in this way. [C19: < F, < L *manus* hand + *cūra* care]

manifest (ˈmænɪˌfɛst) *adj.* **1.** easily noticed or perceived; obvious. ~*vb.* **2.** (*tr.*) to show plainly; reveal or display. **3.** (*tr.*) to prove beyond doubt. **4.** (*intr.*) (of a disembodied spirit) to appear in visible form. ~*n.* **5.** a customs document containing particulars of a ship, its cargo, and its destination. **6. a.** a list of cargo, passengers, etc., on an aeroplane. **b.** a list of railway trucks or their cargo. [C14: < L *manifestus* plain, lit.: struck with the hand] —ˈ**maniˌfestable** *adj.* —ˈ**maniˌfestly** *adv.*

manifestation (ˌmænɪfɛˈsteɪʃən) *n.* **1.** the act of demonstrating; display. **2.** the state of being manifested. **3.** an indication or sign. **4.** a public demonstration of feeling. **5.** the materialization of a disembodied spirit. —ˌ**maniˈfestative** *adj.*

manifesto (ˌmænɪˈfɛstəʊ) *n., pl.* **-toes** *or* **-tos.** a public declaration of intent, policy, aims, etc., as issued by a political party, government, or movement. [C17: < It., < *manifestare* to MANIFEST]

manifold (ˈmænɪˌfəʊld) *adj. Formal.* **1.** of several different kinds; multiple. **2.** having many different forms, features, or elements. ~*n.* **3.** something having many varied parts, forms, or features. **4.** a chamber or pipe with a number of inlets or outlets used to collect or distribute a fluid. In an internal-combustion engine the **inlet manifold** carries the vaporized fuel from the carburettor to the inlet ports and the **exhaust manifold** carries the exhaust gases away. ~*vb.* (*tr.*) **5.** to duplicate (a page, book, etc.). **6.** to make manifold; multiply. [OE *manigfeald.* See MANY, -FOLD] —ˈ**maniˌfoldly** *adv.* —ˈ**maniˌfoldness** *n.*

manikin *or* **mannikin** (ˈmænɪkɪn) *n.* **1.** a little man; dwarf or child. **2.** an anatomical model of the body or a part of the body, esp. for use in medical or art instruction. **3.** a variant of **mannequin.** [C17: < Du. *manneken*, dim. of MAN]

Manila (məˈnɪlə) *n.* **1.** a type of cigar made in Manila, chief port of the Philippines. **2.** short for **Manila hemp** *or* **Manila paper.**

Manila hemp *or* **Manilla hemp** *n.* a fibre obtained from the abaca plant, used for rope, paper, etc.

Manila paper *or* **Manilla paper** *n.* a strong usually brown paper made from Manila hemp or similar fibres.

manilla (məˈnɪlə) *n.* an early form of currency in W Africa in the pattern of a small bracelet. [< Sp.: bracelet, dim. of *mano* hand, < L *manus*]

man in the street *n.* the typical or ordinary person.

manioc (ˈmænɪˌɒk) *or* **manioca** (ˌmænɪˈəʊkə) *n.* another name for **cassava** (sense 1). [C16: < Tupi *mandioca*]

manipulate (məˈnɪpjʊˌleɪt) *vb.* **1.** (*tr.*) to handle or use, esp. with some skill. **2.** to control or influence (something or someone) cleverly, deviously, or skilfully. **3.** to falsify (a bill, accounts, etc.) for one's own advantage. **4.** (in physiotherapy) to examine or treat manually, as in loosening a joint. [C19: back formation < *manipulation*, < L *manipulus* handful] —**manipulability** (məˌnɪpjʊləˈbɪlɪtɪ) *n.* —**maˈnipuˌlatable** *or* **maˈnipulable** *adj.* —**maˌnipuˈlation** *n.* —**maˈnipulative** *adj.* —**maˈnipuˌlator** *n.* —**maˈnipulatory** *adj.*

Manitoban (ˌmænɪˈtəʊbən) *adj.* **1.** of or denoting Manitoba, a province of W Canada. ~*n.* **2.** a native or inhabitant of Manitoba.

manitou, manitu (ˈmænɪˌtuː), *or* **manito** (ˈmænɪˌtəʊ) *n., pl.* **-tous, -tus, -tos** *or* **-tou, -tu, -to.**

(among the Algonquian Indians) a deified spirit or force. [C17: of Amerind origin]
man jack *n. Inf.* a single individual (in **every man jack, no man jack**).
mankind (ˌmænˈkaɪnd) *n.* **1.** human beings collectively; humanity. **2.** men collectively, as opposed to womankind.
manlike (ˈmænˌlaɪk) *adj.* resembling or befitting a man.
manly (ˈmænlɪ) *adj.* **-lier, -liest. 1.** possessing qualities, such as vigour or courage, generally regarded as appropriate to or typical of a man; masculine. **2.** characteristic of or befitting a man. —ˈ**manliness** *n.*
man-made *adj.* made by man; artificial.
manna (ˈmænə) *n.* **1.** *Old Testament.* the miraculous food which sustained the Israelites in the wilderness (Exodus 16:14–36). **2.** any spiritual or divine nourishment. **3.** a windfall (esp. in **manna from heaven**). **4.** a sweet substance obtained from various plants, esp. from the **manna** or **flowering ash** of S Europe, used as a mild laxative. [OE via LL < Gk, < Heb. *mān*]
manned (mænd) *adj.* **1.** supplied or equipped with men, esp. soldiers. **2.** (of spacecraft, etc.) having a human crew.
mannequin (ˈmænɪkɪn) *n.* **1.** a woman who wears the clothes displayed at a fashion show; model. **2.** a life-size dummy of the human body used to fit or display clothes. [C18: via F < Du. *manneken* MANIKIN]
manner (ˈmænə) *n.* **1.** a way of doing or being. **2.** a person's bearing and behaviour. **3.** the style or customary way of doing or accomplishing something. **4.** type or kind. **5.** mannered style, as in art; mannerism. **6. in a manner of speaking.** in a way; so to speak. **7. to the manner born.** naturally fitted to a specified role or activity. [C12: via Norman F < OF *maniere,* < Vulgar L *manuāria* (unattested) a way of handling something, noun use of L *manuārius* belonging to the hand, < *manus* hand]
mannered (ˈmænəd) *adj.* **1.** having idiosyncrasies or mannerisms; affected. **2.** (*in combination*) having manners as specified: *ill-mannered.*
mannerism (ˈmænəˌrɪzəm) *n.* **1.** a distinctive and individual gesture or trait. **2.** (*often cap.*) a principally Italian movement in art and architecture between the High Renaissance and Baroque periods (1520–1600), using distortion and exaggeration of human proportions, perspective, etc. **3.** adherence to a distinctive or affected manner, esp. in art or literature. —ˈ**mannerist** *n., adj.* —ˌ**mannerˈistic** *adj.* —ˌ**mannerˈistically** *adv.*
mannerless (ˈmænəlɪs) *adj.* having bad manners; boorish. —ˈ**mannerlessness** *n.*
mannerly (ˈmænəlɪ) *adj.* **1.** well-mannered; polite. ~*adv.* **2.** *Now rare.* with good manners; politely. —ˈ**mannerliness** *n.*
manners (ˈmænəz) *pl. n.* **1.** social conduct. **2.** a socially acceptable way of behaving.
mannikin (ˈmænɪkɪn) *n.* a variant spelling of **manikin.**
mannish (ˈmænɪʃ) *adj.* **1.** (of a woman) displaying qualities regarded as typical of a man. **2.** of or resembling a man. —ˈ**mannishly** *adv.* —ˈ**mannishness** *n.*
manoeuvre *or U.S.* **maneuver** (məˈnuːvə) *n.* **1.** a contrived, complicated, and possibly deceptive plan or action. **2.** a movement or action requiring dexterity and skill. **3. a.** a tactic or movement of a military or naval unit. **b.** (*pl.*) tactical exercises, usually on a large scale. **4.** a planned movement of an aircraft in flight. **5.** any change from the straight steady course of a ship. ~*vb.* **6.** (*tr.*) to contrive or accomplish with skill or cunning. **7.** (*intr.*) to manipulate situations, etc., in order to gain some end. **8.** (*intr.*) to perform a manoeuvre or manoeuvres. **9.** to move or deploy or be moved or deployed, as military units, etc. [C15: < F, < Med. L *manuopera* manual work, < L *manū operāre* to work with the hand] —**maˈnoeuvrable** *or U.S.* **maˈneuverable** *adj.* —**maˌnoeuvraˈbility** *or U.S.* **maˌneuveraˈbility** *n.* —**maˈnoeuvrer** *or U.S.* **maˈneuverer** *n.*
man of God *n.* **1.** a saint or prophet. **2.** a clergyman.
man-of-war *or* **man o' war** *n., pl.* **men-of-war** *or* **men o' war. 1.** a warship. **2.** See **Portuguese man-of-war.**
man-of-war bird *or* **man-o'-war bird** *n.* another name for **frigate bird.**
manometer (məˈnɒmɪtə) *n.* an instrument for comparing pressures. [C18: < F *manomètre,* < Gk *manos* sparse + *metron* measure] —**manometric** (ˌmænəʊˈmɛtrɪk) *or* ˌ**manoˈmetrical** *adj.*
manor (ˈmænə) *n.* **1.** (in medieval Europe) the manor house of a lord and the lands attached to it. **2.** a manor house. **3.** a landed estate. **4.** *Brit. sl.* a police district. [C13: < OF *manoir* dwelling, < *maneir* to dwell, < L *manēre* to remain] —**manorial** (məˈnɔːrɪəl) *adj.*
manor house *n.* (esp. formerly) the house of the lord of a manor.
manpower (ˈmænˌpaʊə) *n.* **1.** power supplied by men. **2.** a unit of power based on the rate at which a man can work; roughly 75 watts. **3.** the number of people needed or available for a job.
manqué *French.* (ˈmɒŋkeɪ) *adj.* (*postpositive*) unfulfilled; potential; would-be: *the manager is an actor manqué.* [C19: lit.: having missed]
mansard (ˈmænsɑːd, -səd) *n.* a roof having two slopes on both sides and both ends, the lower slopes being steeper than the upper. Also called: **mansard roof.** [C18: < F *mansarde,* after François *Mansart* (1598–1666), F architect]
manse (mæns) *n.* (in certain religious denominations) the house provided for a minister. [C15: < Med. L *mansus* dwelling, < p.p. of L *manēre* to stay]
manservant (ˈmænˌsɜːvənt) *n., pl.* **menservants.** a male servant, esp. a valet.
mansion (ˈmænʃən) *n.* **1.** Also called: **mansion house.** a large and imposing house. **2.** a less common word for **manor house. 3.** (*pl.*) *Brit.* a block of flats. [C14: via OF < L *mansio* a remaining, < *mansus;* see MANSE]
Mansion House *n.* **the.** the residence of the Lord Mayor of London.
man-sized *adj.* **1.** of a size appropriate for or convenient for a man. **2.** *Inf.* big; large.
manslaughter (ˈmænˌslɔːtə) *n.* **1.** *Law.* the unlawful killing of one human being by another without malice aforethought. Cf. **murder. 2.** (loosely) the killing of a human being.
manta (ˈmæntə) *n.* **1.** Also called: **manta ray, devilfish, devil ray.** any large ray (fish), having very wide winglike pectoral fins and feeding on plankton. **2.** a rough cotton cloth made in Spain and Spanish America. **3.** a piece of this used as a blanket or shawl. [Sp.: cloak, < Vulgar L; see MANTLE]
manteau (ˈmæntəʊ) *n., pl.* **-teaus** (-təʊz) *or* **-teaux** (-təʊ). a cloak or mantle. [C17: via F < L *mantellum* MANTLE]
mantel (ˈmæntᵊl) *n.* **1.** a wooden or stone frame around the opening of a fireplace, together with its decorative facing. **2.** Also called: **mantel shelf.** a shelf above this frame. [C15: < F, var. of MANTLE]
mantelet (ˈmæntᵊˌlɛt) *or* **mantlet** *n.* **1.** a woman's short mantle, worn in the mid-19th century. **2.** a portable bulletproof screen or shelter. [C14: < OF, dim. of *mantel* MANTLE]
mantelpiece (ˈmæntᵊlˌpiːs) *n.* **1.** Also called: **mantel shelf, chimneypiece.** a shelf above a fireplace often forming part of the mantel. **2.** another word for **mantel** (sense 1).
mantic (ˈmæntɪk) *adj.* **1.** of or relating to divination and prophecy. **2.** having divining or prophetic powers. [C19: < Gk *mantikos* prophetic, < *mantis* seer] —ˈ**mantically** *adv.*
-mantic *adj. combining form.* forming adjectives from nouns ending in **-mancy.**
mantilla (mænˈtɪlə) *n.* a woman's lace or silk scarf covering the shoulders and head, worn esp. in Spain. [C18: Sp., dim. of *manta* cloak]
mantis (ˈmæntɪs) *n., pl.* **-tises** *or* **-tes** (-tiːz). any carnivorous typically green insect of warm and tropical regions, having a long body and large

eyes and resting with the first pair of legs raised as if in prayer. Also called: **praying mantis.** [C17: NL, < Gk: prophet, alluding to its praying posture]

mantissa (mænˈtɪsə) *n.* the fractional part of a common logarithm representing the digits of the associated number but not its magnitude: *the mantissa of 2.4771 is .4771.* [C17: < L: something added]

mantle (ˈmæntᵊl) *n.* **1.** *Arch.* a loose wrap or cloak. **2.** anything that covers completely or envelops. **3.** a small dome-shaped or cylindrical mesh, used to increase illumination in a gas or oil lamp by becoming incandescent. **4.** *Zool.* a protective layer of epidermis in molluscs and brachiopods that secretes a substance forming the shell. **5.** *Ornithol.* the feathers of the folded wings and back, esp. when of a different colour from the remaining feathers. **6.** *Geol.* the part of the earth between the crust and the core. **7.** a less common spelling of **mantel.** ~*vb.* **8.** (*tr.*) to envelop or supply with a mantle. **9.** (*tr.*) to spread over or become spread over. **10.** (*intr.*) to blush; flush. [C13: via OF < L *mantellum,* dim. of *mantum* cloak]

mantle rock *n.* the loose rock material, including glacial drift, soils, etc., that covers the bedrock and forms the land surface.

mantra (ˈmæntrə, ˈmʌn-) *n.* **1.** *Hinduism.* any of those parts of the Vedic literature which consist of the metrical psalms of praise. **2.** *Hinduism, Buddhism.* any sacred word or syllable used as an object of concentration. [C19: < Sansk., lit.: speech, instrument of thought, < *man* to think]

mantua (ˈmæntjʊə) *n.* a woman's loose gown of the 17th and 18th centuries. [C17: changed < MANTEAU, through the infl. of *Mantua,* city in N Italy]

manual (ˈmænjʊəl) *adj.* **1.** of or relating to a hand or hands. **2.** operated or done by hand. **3.** physical, as opposed to mental or mechanical: *manual labour.* **4.** by human labour rather than automatic or computer-aided means. ~*n.* **5.** a book, esp. of instructions or information. **6.** *Music.* one of the keyboards played by hand on an organ. **7.** *Mil.* the prescribed drill with small arms. [C15: via OF < L *manuālis,* < *manus* hand] —ˈ**manually** *adv.*

manufactory (ˌmænjʊˈfæktərɪ, -trɪ) *n., pl.* **-ries.** an obsolete word for **factory.** [C17: < obs. *manufact;* see MANUFACTURE]

manufacture (ˌmænjʊˈfæktʃə) *vb.* **1.** to process or make (a product) from a raw material, esp. as a large-scale operation using machinery. **2.** (*tr.*) to invent or concoct. ~*n.* **3.** the production of goods, esp. by industrial processes. **4.** a manufactured product. **5.** the creation or production of anything. [C16: < obs. *manufact* handmade, < LL *manūfactus,* < L *manus* hand + *facere* to make] —ˌ**manuˈfacturing** *n., adj.*

manufacturer (ˌmænjʊˈfæktʃərə) *n.* a person or business concern that manufactures goods or owns a factory.

manuka (ˈmɑːnʊkə) *n.* a New Zealand tree with strong elastic wood and aromatic leaves. Also called: **tea tree.** [< Maori]

manumit (ˌmænjʊˈmɪt) *vb.* **-mitting, -mitted.** (*tr.*) to free from slavery, servitude, etc.; emancipate. [C15: < L *manūmittere* to release, < *manū* from one's hand + *ēmittere* to send away] —**manumission** (ˌmænjʊˈmɪʃən) *n.*

manure (məˈnjʊə) *n.* **1.** animal excreta, usually with straw, etc., used to fertilize land. **2.** *Chiefly Brit.* any material, esp. chemical fertilizer, used to fertilize land. ~*vb.* **3.** (*tr.*) to spread manure upon (fields or soil). [C14 (verb): < Anglo-F *mainoverer;* see MANOEUVRE] —**maˈnurer** *n.*

manus (ˈmeɪnəs) *n., pl.* **-nus.** **1.** *Anat.* the wrist and hand. **2.** the corresponding part in other vertebrates. [C19: L: hand]

manuscript (ˈmænjʊˌskrɪpt) *n.* **1.** a book or other document written by hand. **2.** the original handwritten or typed version of a book, article, etc., as submitted by an author for publication. **3.** handwriting, as opposed to printing. [C16: < Med. L *manūscriptus,* < L *manus* hand + *scribere* to write]

Manx (mæŋks) *adj.* **1.** of or relating to the Isle of Man (an island in the Irish Sea), its inhabitants, their language, or their dialect of English. ~*n.* **2.** an almost extinct language of the Isle of Man, closely related to Scottish Gaelic. **3. the Manx.** (*functioning as pl.*) the people of the Isle of Man. [C16: earlier *Maniske,* of Scand. origin, < *Mana* Isle of Man + *-iske* -ISH]

Manx cat *n.* a short-haired tailless variety of cat, believed to originate on the Isle of Man.

Manxman (ˈmæŋksmən) *or* (*fem.*) **Manxwoman** (ˈmæŋksˌwʊmən) *n., pl.* **-men** *or* **-women.** a native or inhabitant of the Isle of Man.

many (ˈmɛnɪ) *determiner.* **1.** (sometimes preceded by *a great* or *a good*) **a.** a large number of: *many times.* **b.** (*as pron.; functioning as pl.*): *many are seated already.* **2.** (foll. by *a, an,* or *another,* and a sing. noun) each of a considerable number of: *many a man.* **3.** (preceded by *as, too, that,* etc.) **a.** a great number of: *as many apples as you like.* **b.** (*as pron.; functioning as pl.*): *I have as many as you.* ~*n.* **4. the many.** the majority of mankind, esp. the common people. [OE *manig*]

many-sided *adj.* having many sides, aspects, etc. —ˌ**many-ˈsidedness** *n.*

many-valued logic *n.* any of various logics in which the truth-values that a proposition may have are not restricted to truth and falsity.

manzanilla (ˌmænzəˈnɪlə) *n.* a very dry pale sherry. [C19: < Sp.: camomile (referring to its bouquet)]

Maoism (ˈmaʊɪzəm) *n.* Marxism-Leninism as interpreted by Mao Tse-tung (1893–1976), Chinese statesman: distinguished by its theory of guerrilla warfare and its emphasis on the revolutionary potential of the peasantry. —ˈ**Maoist** *n., adj.*

Maori (ˈmaʊrɪ) *n.* **1.** (*pl.* **-ris** *or* **-ri**) a member of the people of Polynesian origin living in New Zealand and the Cook Islands since before the arrival of European settlers. **2.** the language of this people, belonging to the Malayo-Polynesian family. ~*adj.* **3.** of or relating to this people or their language. —ˈ**Maoriˌland** *n.*

map (mæp) *n.* **1.** a diagrammatic representation of the earth's surface or part of it, showing the geographical distributions, positions, etc., of features such as roads, towns, relief, rainfall, etc. **2.** a diagrammatic representation of the stars or of the surface of a celestial body. **3.** a maplike drawing of anything. **4.** *Maths.* another name for **function** (sense 5). **5.** a slang word for **face** (sense 1). **6. off the map.** no longer important; out of existence (esp. in **wipe off the map**). **7. put on the map.** to make (a town, company, etc.) well-known. ~*vb.* **mapping, mapped.** (*tr.*) **8.** to make a map of. **9.** *Maths.* to represent or transform (a function, figure, set, etc.). ~See also **map out.** [C16: < Med. L *mappa* (*mundi*) map (of the world), < L *mappa* cloth]

maple (ˈmeɪpᵊl) *n.* **1.** any tree or shrub of a N temperate genus, having winged seeds borne in pairs and lobed leaves. **2.** the hard wood of any of these trees, used for furniture and flooring. **3.** the flavour of the sap of the sugar maple. ~See also **sugar maple.** [C14: < OE *mapel-,* as in *mapeltrēow* maple tree]

maple leaf *n.* the leaf of the maple tree, the national emblem of Canada.

maple sugar *n. U.S. & Canad.* sugar made from the sap of the sugar maple.

maple syrup *n. Chiefly U.S. & Canad.* a very sweet syrup made from the sap of the sugar maple.

map out *vb.* (*tr., adv.*) to plan or design.

mapping (ˈmæpɪŋ) *n. Maths.* another name for **function** (sense 5).

map projection *n.* a means of representing or a representation of a globe or celestial sphere or part of it on a flat map.

maquette (mæˈkɛt) *n.* a sculptor's small preliminary model or sketch. [C20: < F, < It.

macchietta a little sketch, < *macchiare,* < L *macula* blemish]

maquis (mɑːˈkiː) *n., pl.* **-quis** (-ˈkiː). **1.** shrubby, mostly evergreen, vegetation found in coastal regions of the Mediterranean. **2.** (*often cap.*) **a.** the French underground movement that fought against the German occupying forces in World War II. **b.** a member of this movement. [C20: < F, < It. *macchia* thicket, < L *macula* spot]

mar (mɑː) *vb.* **marring, marred.** (*tr.*) to cause harm to; spoil or impair. [OE *merran*] —ˈ**marrer** *n.*

mar. *abbrev. for:* **1.** maritime. **2.** married.

Mar. *abbrev. for* March.

marabou (ˈmærəˌbuː) *n.* **1.** a large black-and-white African carrion-eating stork. **2.** a down feather of this bird, used to trim garments. [C19: < F, < Ar. *murābit* MARABOUT: the stork is considered a holy bird in Islam]

marabout (ˈmærəˌbuː) *n.* **1.** a Muslim holy man or hermit of North Africa. **2.** a shrine of the grave of a marabout. [C17: via F & Port. *marabuto,* < Ar. *murābit*]

maraca (məˈrækə) *n.* a percussion instrument, usually one of a pair, consisting of a gourd or plastic shell filled with dried seeds, pebbles, etc. [C20: Brazilian Port., of Amerind origin]

marae (məˈraɪ) *n. N.Z.* a traditional Maori tribal meeting place, originally one in the open air, now frequently a purpose-built building. [< Maori]

maranta (mɑːˈræntə) *n.* any of various tropical monocotyledons with ornamental leaves. [C19: after B. *Maranta* 16th-century Venetian botanist]

marasca (məˈræskə) *n.* a European cherry tree with red acid-tasting fruit. [C19: < It., var. of *amarasca,* ult. < L *amārus* bitter]

maraschino (ˌmærəˈskiːnəʊ, -ˈʃiːnəʊ) *n.* a liqueur made from marasca cherries, having a taste like bitter almonds. [C18: < It.; see MARASCA]

maraschino cherry *n.* a cherry preserved in maraschino or an imitation of this liqueur.

marasmus (məˈræzməs) *n. Pathol.* general emaciation, esp. of infants, thought to be associated with severe malnutrition or impaired utilization of nutrients. [C17: < NL, < Gk *marasmos,* < *marainein* to waste] —**maˈrasmic** *adj.*

marathon (ˈmærəθən) *n.* **1.** a race on foot of 26 miles 385 yards (42.195 kilometres). **2. a.** any long or arduous task, etc. **b.** (*as modifier*): *a marathon effort.* [referring to the feat of the messenger who ran 26 miles from Marathon to Athens to bring the news of victory in 490 B.C.]

maraud (məˈrɔːd) *vb.* to wander or raid in search of plunder. [C18: < F *marauder* to prowl, < *maraud* vagabond] —**maˈrauder** *n.* —**maˈrauding** *adj.*

marble (ˈmɑːbᵊl) *n.* **1. a.** a hard crystalline metamorphic rock resulting from the recrystallization of a limestone. **b.** (*as modifier*): *a marble bust.* **2.** a block or work of art of marble. **3.** a small round glass or stone ball used in playing marbles. ~*vb.* **4.** (*tr.*) to mottle with variegated streaks in imitation of marble. [C12: via OF < L *marmor,* < Gk *marmaros,* rel. to Gk *marmairein* to gleam] —ˈ**marbled** *adj.*

marbles (ˈmɑːbᵊlz) *n.* **1.** (*functioning as sing.*) a game in which marbles are rolled at one another, similar to bowls. **2.** (*functioning as pl.*) *Inf.* wits: *to lose one's marbles.*

marbling (ˈmɑːblɪŋ) *n.* **1.** a mottled effect or pattern resembling marble. **2.** such an effect obtained by transferring floating colours from a gum solution. **3.** the streaks of fat in lean meat.

marc (mɑːk) *n.* **1.** the remains of grapes or other fruit that have been pressed for wine-making. **2.** a brandy distilled from these. [C17: < F, < OF *marchier* to trample (grapes)]

marcasite (ˈmɑːkəˌsaɪt) *n.* **1.** a metallic pale yellow mineral consisting of iron pyrites in crystalline form used in jewellery. **2.** a cut and polished form of steel or any white metal used for making jewellery. [C15: < Med. L *marcasīta,* < Ar. *marqashītā,* ? < Persian]

marcato (mɑːˈkɑːtəʊ) *adj., adv. Music.* with each note heavily accented. [< It.: marked]

march¹ (mɑːtʃ) *vb.* **1.** (*intr.*) to walk or proceed with stately or regular steps, usually in a procession or military formation. **2.** (*tr.*) to make (a person or group) proceed. **3.** (*tr.*) to traverse or cover by marching. ~*n.* **4.** the act or an instance of marching. **5.** a regular stride. **6.** a long or exhausting walk. **7.** advance; progression (of time, etc.). **8.** a distance or route covered by marching. **9.** a piece of music, as for a march. **10. steal a march on.** to gain an advantage over, esp. by a secret enterprise or trick. [C16: < OF *marchier* to tread, prob. of Gmc origin] —ˈ**marcher** *n.*

march² (mɑːtʃ) *n.* **1.** a frontier, border, or boundary or the land lying along it, often of disputed ownership. ~*vb.* **2.** (*intr.; often foll. by upon or with*) to share a common border (with). [C13: < OF *marche,* of Gmc origin]

March (mɑːtʃ) *n.* the third month of the year, consisting of 31 days. [< OF, < L *Martius* (month) of Mars]

Marches (ˈmɑːtʃɪz) *n.* **the. 1.** the border area between England and Wales or Scotland, both characterized by continual feuding (13th–16th centuries). **2.** any of various other border regions.

March hare *n.* a hare during its breeding season in March, noted for its wild and excitable behaviour (esp. in **mad as a March hare**).

marching orders *pl. n.* **1.** military orders, esp. to infantry, giving instructions about a march, its destination, etc. **2.** *Inf.* any dismissal, esp. notice of dismissal from employment.

marchioness (ˈmɑːʃənɪs, ˌmɑːʃəˈnɛs) *n.* **1.** the wife or widow of a marquis. **2.** a woman who holds the rank of marquis. [C16: < Med. L *marchionissa,* fem. of *marchiō* MARQUIS]

marchpane (ˈmɑːtʃˌpeɪn) *n.* an archaic word for **marzipan.** [C15: < F]

Mardi Gras (ˈmɑːdɪ ˈgrɑː) *n.* the festival of Shrove Tuesday, celebrated in some cities with great revelry. [F: fat Tuesday]

mare¹ (mɛə) *n.* the adult female of a horse or zebra. [C12: < OE, of Gmc origin]

mare² (ˈmɑːreɪ, -rɪ) *n., pl.* **maria. 1.** (*cap. when part of a name*) any of a large number of huge dry plains on the surface of the moon, visible as dark markings and once thought to be seas. **2.** a similar area on the surface of Mars. [< L: sea]

mare's-nest (ˈmɛəzˌnɛst) *n.* **1.** a discovery imagined to be important but proving worthless. **2.** a disordered situation.

mare's-tail (ˈmɛəzˌteɪl) *n.* **1.** a wisp of trailing cirrus cloud, indicating strong winds at high levels. **2.** an erect pond plant with minute flowers and crowded whorls of narrow leaves.

margaric (mɑːˈgærɪk) *or* **margaritic** *adj.* of or resembling pearl. [C19: < Gk *margaron* pearl]

margarine (ˌmɑːdʒəˈriːn, ˌmɑːg-) *n.* a substitute for butter, prepared from vegetable and animal fats with added small amounts of milk, salt, vitamins, colouring matter, etc. [C19: < MARGARIC]

marge¹ (mɑːdʒ) *n. Brit. inf.* short for **margarine.**

marge² (mɑːdʒ) *n. Arch.* a margin. [C16: < F]

margin (ˈmɑːdʒɪn) *n.* **1.** an edge or rim, and the area immediately adjacent to it; border. **2.** the blank space surrounding the text on a page. **3.** a vertical line on a page delineating this space. **4.** an additional amount or one beyond the minimum necessary: *a margin of error.* **5.** *Chiefly Austral.* a payment made in addition to a basic wage, esp. for special skill or responsibility. **6.** a bound or limit. **7.** the amount by which one thing differs from another. **8.** *Commerce.* the profit on a transaction. **9.** *Econ.* the minimum return below which an enterprise becomes unprofitable. **10.** *Finance.* collateral deposited by a client with a broker as security. ~Also (archaic): **margent** (ˈmɑːdʒənt). ~*vb.* (*tr.*) **11.** to provide with a margin; border. **12.** *Finance.* to deposit a margin upon. [C14: < L *margō* border]

marginal (ˈmɑːdʒɪnᵊl) *adj.* **1.** of, in, on, or

constituting a margin. **2.** close to a limit, esp. a lower limit: *marginal legal ability.* **3.** not considered central or important; insignificant. **4.** *Econ.* relating to goods or services produced and sold at the margin of profitability: *marginal cost.* **5.** *Politics, chiefly Brit. & N.Z.* of or designating a constituency in which elections tend to be won by small margins: *a marginal seat.* **6.** designating agricultural land on the margin of cultivated zones. ~*n.* **7.** *Politics, chiefly Brit. & N.Z.* a marginal constituency. —**marginality** (ˌmɑːdʒɪˈnælɪtɪ) *n.* —ˈ**marginally** *adv.*

marginalia (ˌmɑːdʒɪˈneɪlɪə) *pl. n.* notes in the margin of a book, manuscript, or letter. [C19: NL, noun (neuter pl.) < *marginālis* marginal]

marginate (ˈmɑːdʒɪˌneɪt) *vb.* **1.** (*tr.*) to provide with a margin or margins. ~*adj.* **2.** *Biol.* having a margin of a distinct colour or form. [C18: < L *margināre*] —ˌ**marginˈation** *n.*

margrave (ˈmɑːˌgreɪv) *n.* a German nobleman ranking above a count. Margraves were originally counts appointed to govern frontier provinces, but all eventually became princes of the Holy Roman Empire. [C16: < MDu. *markgrave,* lit.: count of the MARCH[2]] —**margravate** (ˈmɑːgrəvɪt) *n.*

margravine (ˈmɑːgrəˌviːn) *n.* **1.** the wife or widow of a margrave. **2.** a woman who holds the rank of margrave. [C17: < MDu., fem. of MARGRAVE]

marguerite (ˌmɑːgəˈriːt) *n.* **1.** a cultivated garden plant whose flower heads have white or pale yellow rays around a yellow disc. **2.** any of various related plants with daisy-like flowers. [C19: < F: daisy, pearl, < L, < Gk, < *margaron*]

maria (ˈmɑːrɪə) *n.* the plural of **mare**[2].

mariachi (ˌmɑːrɪˈɑːtʃɪ) *n.* a small ensemble of street musicians in Mexico. [C20: < Mexican Sp.]

marigold (ˈmærɪˌgəʊld) *n.* **1.** any of various tropical American plants cultivated for their yellow or orange flower heads and strongly scented foliage. **2.** any of various similar or related plants, such as the marsh marigold. [C14: < *Mary* (the Virgin) + GOLD]

marijuana *or* **marihuana** (ˌmærɪˈhwɑːnə) *n.* **1.** the dried leaves and flowers of the hemp plant, used as a narcotic, esp. in cigarettes. See also **cannabis.** **2.** another name for **hemp** (the plant). [C19: < Mexican Sp.]

marimba (məˈrɪmbə) *n.* a Latin American percussion instrument consisting of a set of hardwood plates placed over tuned metal resonators, played with two soft-headed sticks in each hand. [C18: of West African origin]

marina (məˈriːnə) *n.* an elaborate docking facility for yachts and other pleasure boats. [C19: via It. & Sp. < L: MARINE]

marinade *n.* (ˌmærɪˈneɪd). **1.** a spiced liquid mixture of oil, wine, vinegar, etc., in which meat or fish is soaked before cooking. **2.** meat or fish soaked in this. ~*vb.* (ˈmærɪˌneɪd). **3.** a variant of **marinate.** [C17: < F, < Sp., < *marinar* to MARINATE]

marinate (ˈmærɪˌneɪt) *vb.* to soak in marinade. [C17: prob. < It. *marinato,* < *marinare* to pickle, ult. < L *marīnus* MARINE] —ˌ**mariˈnation** *n.*

marine (məˈriːn) *adj.* (*usually prenominal*) **1.** of, found in, or relating to the sea. **2.** of or relating to shipping, navigation, etc. **3.** of or relating to a body of seagoing troops: *marine corps.* **4.** of or relating to a government department concerned with maritime affairs. **5.** used or adapted for use at sea. ~*n.* **6.** shipping and navigation in general. **7.** (*cap. when part of a name*) a member of a marine corps or similar body. **8.** a picture of a ship, seascape, etc. **9. tell it to the marines.** *Inf.* an expression of disbelief. [C15: < OF *marin,* < L *marīnus,* < *mare* sea]

mariner (ˈmærɪnə) *n.* a formal or literary word for **seaman.** [C13: < Anglo-F, ult. < L *marīnus* MARINE]

Mariolatry (ˌmɛərɪˈɒlətrɪ) *n.* devotion to the Virgin Mary, considered as excessive. —ˌ**Mariˈolater** *n.* —ˌ**Mariˈolatrous** *adj.*

marionette (ˌmærɪəˈnɛt) *n.* a puppet or doll whose jointed limbs are moved by strings. [C17: < F, < *Marion,* dim. of *Marie* Mary + -ETTE]

Marist (ˈmɛərɪst) *n. R.C. Church.* a member of the Society of Mary, a religious congregation founded in 1824. [C19: < F *Mariste,* < *Marie* Mary (the Virgin)]

marital (ˈmærɪtᵊl) *adj.* **1.** of or relating to marriage. **2.** of or relating to a husband. [C17: < L *marītālis,* < *marītus* married (adj.), husband (n.)] —ˈ**maritally** *adv.*

maritime (ˈmærɪˌtaɪm) *adj.* **1.** of or relating to navigation, shipping, etc. **2.** of, relating to, near, or living near the sea. **3.** (of a climate) having small temperature differences between summer and winter. [C16: < L *maritimus,* < *mare* sea]

Maritime Provinces *or* **Maritimes** *pl. n.* **the.** the **Atlantic Provinces** of Canada, often excluding Newfoundland.

Maritimer (ˈmærɪˌtaɪmə) *n.* a native or inhabitant of the Maritime Provinces of Canada.

marjoram (ˈmɑːdʒərəm) *n.* **1.** Also called: **sweet marjoram.** an aromatic Mediterranean plant with sweet-scented leaves, used for seasoning food and in salads. **2.** Also called: **wild marjoram, pot marjoram, origan.** a similar and related European plant. See also **oregano.** [C14: via OF *majorane,* < Med. L *marjorana*]

mark[1] (mɑːk) *n.* **1.** a visible impression, stain, etc., on a surface, such as a spot or scratch. **2.** a sign, symbol, or other indication that distinguishes something. **3.** a cross or other symbol made instead of a signature. **4.** a written or printed sign or symbol, as for punctuation. **5.** a letter, number, or percentage used to grade academic work. **6.** a thing that indicates position or directs; marker. **7.** a desired or recognized standard: *up to the mark.* **8.** an indication of some quality, feature, or prowess. **9.** quality or importance: *a person of little mark.* **10.** a target or goal. **11.** impression or influence. **12.** *Sl.* a suitable victim, esp. for swindling. **13.** (*often cap.*) (in trade names) a model, brand, or type. **14.** *Naut.* one of the intervals distinctively marked on a sounding lead. **15.** *Rugby.* an action in which a player standing with both feet on the ground within his own 22 m line catches a forward kick, throw, or knock by an opponent and shouts "mark", which entitles him to a free kick. **16.** *Australian Rules football.* **a.** a catch of the ball from a kick of at least 10 yards, after which a free kick is taken. **b.** the spot where this occurs. **17.** (in medieval England and Germany) a piece of land held in common by the free men of a community. **18. the mark.** *Boxing.* the middle of the stomach. **19. make one's mark.** to succeed or achieve recognition. **20. on your mark** *or* **marks.** a command given to runners in a race to prepare themselves at the starting line. ~*vb.* **21.** to make or receive (a visible impression, trace, or stain) on (a surface). **22.** (*tr.*) to characterize or distinguish. **23.** (often foll. by *off* or *out*) to set boundaries or limits (on). **24.** (*tr.*) to select, designate, or doom by or as if by a mark: *to mark someone as a criminal.* **25.** (*tr.*) to put identifying or designating labels, stamps, etc., on, esp. to indicate price. **26.** (*tr.*) to pay heed or attention to: *mark my words.* **27.** to observe; notice. **28.** to grade or evaluate (scholastic work). **29.** *Brit. football, etc.* to stay close to (an opponent) to hamper his play. **30.** to keep (score) in some games. **31. mark time. a.** to move the feet alternately as in marching but without advancing. **b.** to act in a mechanical and routine way. **c.** to halt progress temporarily. ~See also **markdown, mark-up.** [OE *mearc* mark] —ˈ**marker** *n.*

mark[2] (mɑːk) *n.* **1.** See **Deutschmark, markka, Reichsmark, ostmark.** **2.** a former monetary unit and coin in England and Scotland worth two thirds of a pound sterling. **3.** a silver coin of Germany until 1924. [OE *marc* unit of weight of precious metal, ? < the marks on metal bars; apparently of Gmc origin and rel. to MARK[1]]

markdown (ˈmɑːkˌdaʊn) *n.* **1.** a price reduction. ~*vb.* **mark down. 2.** (*tr., adv.*) to reduce in price.

marked (mɑːkt) *adj.* **1.** obvious, evident, or

noticeable. 2. singled out, esp. as the target of attack: *a marked man.* 3. *Linguistics.* distinguished by a specific feature, as in phonology. For example, of the two phonemes /t/ and /d/, the /d/ is marked because it exhibits the feature of voice. —**markedly** (ˈmɑːkɪdlɪ) *adv.* —ˈ**markedness** *n.*

market (ˈmɑːkɪt) *n.* 1. a. an event or occasion, usually held at regular intervals, at which people meet to buy and sell merchandise. b. (*as modifier*): *market day.* 2. a place at which a market is held. 3. a shop that sells a particular merchandise: *an antique market.* 4. the trading or selling opportunities provided by a particular group of people: *the foreign market.* 5. demand for a particular product or commodity. 6. See **stock market.** 7. See **market price, market value.** 8. **be in the market for.** to wish to buy or acquire. 9. **on the market.** available for purchase. 10. **seller's** (*or* **buyer's**) **market.** a market characterized by excess demand (or supply) and thus favourable to sellers (or buyers). 11. **the market.** business or trade in a commodity as specified: *the sugar market.* ~*vb.* 12. (*tr.*) to offer or produce for sale. 13. (*intr.*) to buy or deal in a market. [C12: < L *mercātus,* < *mercāri* to trade, < *merx* merchandise] —ˈ**marketable** *adj.* —ˈ**marketer** *n.*

market garden *n. Chiefly Brit.* an establishment where fruit and vegetables are grown for sale. —**market gardener** *n.* —**market gardening** *n.*

marketing (ˈmɑːkɪtɪŋ) *n.* the provision of goods or services to meet consumer needs.

market maker *n. Stock Exchange.* a principal who uses his firm's money to create a market for a stock: formerly done by a jobber, the difference being that the market maker, since Big Bang, can deal direct with the public.

marketplace (ˈmɑːkɪtˌpleɪs) *n.* 1. a place where a public market is held. 2. any centre where ideas, opinions, etc., are exchanged. 3. the commercial world of buying and selling.

market price *n.* the prevailing price, as determined by supply and demand, at which goods, services, etc., may be bought or sold.

market research *n.* the study of influences upon customer behaviour and the analysis of market characteristics and trends.

market town *n. Chiefly Brit.* a town that holds a market, esp. an agricultural centre.

market value *n.* the amount obtainable on the open market for the sale of property, financial assets, or goods and services.

markhor (ˈmɑːkɔː) *or* **markhoor** (ˈmɑːkʊə) *n., pl.* **-khors, -khor** *or* **-khoors, -khoor.** a large wild Himalayan goat with large spiralled horns. [C19: < Persian, lit.: snake-eater]

marking (ˈmɑːkɪŋ) *n.* 1. a mark or series of marks. 2. the arrangement of colours on an animal, plant, etc. 3. assessment and correction of pupils' or students' written work by teachers.

markka (ˈmɑːkɑː, -kə) *n., pl.* **-kaa** (-kɑː). the standard monetary unit of Finland. [Finnish; see MARK[2]]

marksman (ˈmɑːksmən) *n., pl.* **-men.** 1. a person skilled in shooting. 2. a serviceman selected for his skill in shooting. —ˈ**marksmanship** *n.*

mark-up *n.* 1. an amount added to the cost of a commodity to provide the seller with a profit. 2. a. an increase in the price of a commodity. b. the amount of this. ~*vb.* **mark up.** (*tr., adv.*) 3. to add a percentage for profit, etc., to the cost of (a commodity). 4. to increase the price of.

marl (mɑːl) *n.* 1. a fine-grained sedimentary rock consisting of clay minerals, calcium carbonate, and silt: used as a fertilizer. ~*vb.* 2. (*tr.*) to fertilize (land) with marl. [C14: via OF, < LL *margila,* dim. of L *marga*] —ˈ**marly** *adj.*

marlin (ˈmɑːlɪn) *n., pl.* **-lin** *or* **-lins.** any of several large food and game fishes of warm and tropical seas, having a very long upper jaw. [C20: < MARLINESPIKE, < shape of the beak]

marline *or* **marlin** (ˈmɑːlɪn) *n. Naut.* a light rope, usually tarred, made of two strands laid left-handed. [C15: < Du. *marlijn,* < *marren* to tie + *lijn* line]

marlinespike *or* **marlinspike** (ˈmɑːlɪnˌspaɪk) *n. Naut.* a pointed metal tool used in separating strands of rope, etc.

marlite (ˈmɑːlaɪt) *or* **marlstone** (ˈmɑːlˌstəʊn) *n.* a type of marl that is resistant to the decomposing action of air.

marmalade (ˈmɑːməˌleɪd) *n.* a preserve made by boiling the pulp and rind of citrus fruits, esp. oranges, with sugar. [C16: via F < Port. *marmelada,* < *marmelo* quince, < L, < Gk *melimēlon,* < *meli* honey + *mēlon* apple]

marmite (ˈmɑːmaɪt) *n.* a large cooking pot. [< F: pot]

Marmite (ˈmɑːmaɪt) *n. Brit. trademark.* a yeast and vegetable extract used as a spread, flavouring, etc.

marmoreal (mɑːˈmɔːrɪəl) *adj.* of, relating to, or resembling marble. [C18: < L *marmoreus,* < *marmor* marble]

marmoset (ˈmɑːməˌzɛt) *n.* 1. any of various small South American monkeys having long hairy tails. 2. **pygmy marmoset.** a related form: the smallest monkey, inhabiting tropical forests of the Amazon. [C14: < OF *marmouset* grotesque figure, <?]

marmot (ˈmɑːmət) *n.* 1. any of various burrowing rodents of Europe, Asia, and North America. They are heavily built and have coarse fur. 2. **prairie marmot.** another name for **prairie dog.** [C17: < F *marmotte,* ? ult. < L *mūr-* (stem of *mūs*) mouse + *montis* of the mountain]

marocain (ˈmærəˌkeɪn) *n.* 1. a fabric of ribbed crepe. 2. a garment made from this fabric. [C20: < F *maroquin* Moroccan]

maroon[1] (məˈruːn) *vb.* (*tr.*) 1. to abandon ashore, esp. on an island. 2. to isolate without resources. ~*n.* 3. a descendant of a group of runaway slaves living in the remoter areas of the West Indies or Guyana. [C17 (applied to fugitive slaves): < American Sp. *cimarrón* wild, lit.: dwelling on peaks, < Sp. *cima* summit]

maroon[2] (məˈruːn) *n.* 1. a. a dark red to purplish-red colour. b. (*as adj.*): *a maroon carpet.* 2. an exploding firework, esp. one used as a warning signal. [C18: < F, lit.: chestnut]

Marq. *abbrev. for:* 1. Marquess. 2. Marquis.

marque (mɑːk) *n.* 1. a brand of product, esp. of a car. 2. See **letter of marque.** [< F, < *marquer* to MARK[1]]

marquee (mɑːˈkiː) *n.* 1. a large tent used for entertainment, exhibition, etc. 2. Also called: **marquise.** *Chiefly U.S. & Canad.* a canopy over the entrance to a theatre, hotel, etc. [C17 (orig. an officer's tent): invented sing. form of MARQUISE, erroneously taken to be pl.]

marquess (ˈmɑːkwɪs) *n.* 1. (in the British Isles) a nobleman ranking between a duke and an earl. 2. See **marquis.**

marquetry *or* **marqueterie** (ˈmɑːkɪtrɪ) *n., pl.* **-quetries** *or* **-queteries.** a pattern of inlaid veneers of wood, brass, ivory, etc., used chiefly as ornamentation in furniture. [C16: < OF, < *marqueter* to inlay, < *marque* MARK[1]]

marquis (ˈmɑːkwɪs, mɑːˈkiː) *n., pl.* **-quises** *or* **-quis.** (in various countries) a nobleman ranking above a count, corresponding to a British marquess. The title of marquis is often used in place of that of marquess. [C14: < OF *marchis,* lit.: count of the march, < *marche* MARCH[2]]

marquise (mɑːˈkiːz) *n.* 1. (in various countries) another word for **marchioness.** 2. a. a gemstone, esp. a diamond, cut in a pointed oval shape and usually faceted. b. a piece of jewellery, esp. a ring, set with such a stone or with an oval cluster of stones. 3. another name for **marquee** (sense 2). [C18: < F, fem. of MARQUIS]

marquisette (ˌmɑːkɪˈzɛt, -kwɪ-) *n.* a leno-weave fabric of cotton, silk, etc. [C20: < F, dim. of MARQUISE]

marram grass (ˈmærəm) *n.* any of several grasses that grow on sandy shores: often planted to stabilize sand dunes. [C17 *marram,* < ON *marálmr,* < *marr* sea + *hálmr* HAULM]

marri (ˈmærɪ) *n.* a species of eucalyptus of Western Australia, widely cultivated for its coloured flowers. [C19: < Abor.]

marriage (ˈmærɪdʒ) *n.* **1.** the state or relationship of being husband and wife. **2. a.** the legal union or contract made by a man and woman to live as husband and wife. **b.** (*as modifier*): *marriage certificate.* **3.** the ceremony formalizing this union; wedding. **4.** a close or intimate union, relationship, etc. [C13: < OF; see MARRY[1], -AGE]

marriageable (ˈmærɪdʒəbᵊl) *adj.* (esp. of women) suitable for marriage, usually with reference to age. —ˌ**marriageaˈbility** *n.*

marriage guidance *n.* advice given to couples who have problems in their married life.

married (ˈmærɪd) *adj.* **1.** having a husband or wife. **2.** joined in marriage. **3.** of or involving marriage or married persons. **4.** closely or intimately united. ~*n.* **5.** (*usually pl.*) a married person (esp. in **young marrieds**).

marrons glacés *French.* (marɔ̃ glase) *pl. n.* chestnuts cooked in syrup and glazed.

marrow (ˈmærəʊ) *n.* **1.** the fatty network of connective tissue that fills the cavities of bones. **2.** the vital part; essence. **3.** *Brit.* short for **vegetable marrow.** [OE *mærg*] —ˈ**marrowy** *adj.*

marrowbone (ˈmærəʊˌbəʊn) *n.* **a.** a bone containing edible marrow. **b.** (*as modifier*): *marrowbone jelly.*

marrowfat (ˈmærəʊˌfæt) *or* **marrow pea** *n.* **1.** any of several varieties of pea plant that have large seeds. **2.** the seed of such a plant.

marry[1] (ˈmærɪ) *vb.* **-rying, -ried.** **1.** to take (someone as one's husband or wife) in marriage. **2.** (*tr.*) to join or give in marriage. **3.** to unite closely or intimately. **4.** (*tr.;* sometimes foll. by *up*) to fit together or align (two things); join. **5.** (*tr.*) *Naut.* to match up (the strands of ropes) before splicing. [C13: < OF *marier,* < L *marītāre,* < *marītus* married (man), ? < *mās* male]

marry[2] (ˈmærɪ) *interj. Arch.* an exclamation of surprise, anger, etc. [C14: euphemistic for the Virgin *Mary*]

marry off *vb.* (*tr., adv.*) to find a husband or wife for (a person, esp. one's son or daughter).

Mars[1] (mɑːz) *n.* the Roman god of war.

Mars[2] (mɑːz) *n.* the fourth planet from the sun.

Marsala (mɑːˈsɑːlə) *n.* a dark sweet dessert wine from Marsala, a port in Sicily.

Marseillaise (ˌmɑːseɪˈjeɪz, -səˈleɪz) *n.* **the.** the French national anthem. [C18: < F (*chanson*) *marseillaise* song of Marseilles (first sung in Paris by the battalion of Marseilles)]

marseille (mɑːˈseɪl) *or* **marseilles** (mɑːˈseɪlz) *n.* a strong cotton fabric with a raised pattern, used for bedspreads, etc. [C18: < *Marseille quilting,* made in Marseilles]

marsh (mɑːʃ) *n.* low poorly drained land that is sometimes flooded and often lies at the edge of lakes, etc. Cf. **swamp** (sense 1). [OE *merisc*]

marshal (ˈmɑːʃəl) *n.* **1.** (in some armies and air forces) an officer of the highest rank. **2.** (in England) an officer who accompanies a judge on circuit and performs secretarial duties. **3.** (in the U.S.) **a.** a Federal court officer assigned to a judicial district whose functions are similar to those of a sheriff. **b.** (in some states) the chief police or fire officer. **4.** an officer who organizes or conducts ceremonies, parades, etc. **5.** Also called: **knight marshal.** (formerly in England) an officer of the royal family or court, esp. one in charge of protocol. ~*vb.* **-shalling, -shalled** *or U.S.* **-shaling, -shaled.** (*tr.*) **6.** to arrange in order: *to marshal the facts.* **7.** to assemble and organize (troops, vehicles, etc.) prior to onward movement. **8.** to guide or lead, esp. in a ceremonious way. **9.** to combine (coats of arms) on one shield. [C13: < OF *mareschal;* rel. to OHG *marahscalc,* < *marah* horse + *scalc* servant] —ˈ**marshalcy** *or* ˈ**marshalship** *n.*

marshalling yard *n. Railways.* a place or depot where railway wagons are shunted and made up into trains.

Marshal of the Royal Air Force *n.* a rank in the Royal Air Force comparable to that of a field marshal in the army.

marsh fever *n.* another name for **malaria.**

marsh gas *n.* a hydrocarbon gas largely composed of methane formed when organic material decays in the absence of air.

marshmallow (ˌmɑːʃˈmæləʊ) *n.* **1.** a spongy sweet containing gum arabic or gelatin, sugar, etc. **2.** a sweetened paste or confection made from the root of the marsh mallow.

marsh mallow *n.* a malvaceous plant, that grows in salt marshes and has pale pink flowers. The roots yield a mucilage formerly used to make marshmallows.

marsh marigold *n.* a yellow-flowered plant that grows in swampy places.

marshy (ˈmɑːʃɪ) *adj.* **marshier, marshiest.** of, involving, or like a marsh. —ˈ**marshiness** *n.*

marsupial (mɑːˈsjuːpɪəl, -ˈsuː-) *n.* **1.** any mammal of an order in which the young are born in an immature state and continue development in the marsupium. The order occurs mainly in Australia and South and Central America and includes the opossums and kangaroos. ~*adj.* **2.** of, relating to, or belonging to marsupials. **3.** of or relating to a marsupium. [C17: see MARSUPIUM]

marsupium (mɑːˈsjuːpɪəm, -ˈsuː-) *n., pl.* **-pia** (-pɪə). an external pouch in most female marsupials within which the newly born offspring complete their development. [C17: NL, < L: purse, < Gk, dim. of *marsipos*]

mart (mɑːt) *n.* a market or trading centre. [C15: < MDu.: MARKET]

martagon *or* **martagon lily** (ˈmɑːtəgən) *n.* a Eurasian lily plant cultivated for its mottled purplish-red flowers with reflexed petals. [C15: < F, < Turkish *martagān* a type of turban]

Martello tower (mɑːˈtɛləʊ) *n.* a small circular tower for coastal defence. [C18: after Cape *Mortella* in Corsica, where the British navy captured a tower of this type in 1794]

marten (ˈmɑːtɪn) *n., pl.* **-tens** *or* **-ten.** **1.** any of several agile arboreal mammals of Europe, Asia, and North America, having bushy tails and golden-brown to blackish fur. See also **pine marten.** **2.** the highly valued fur of these animals. ~See also **sable** (sense 1). [C15: < MDu. *martren,* < OF (*peau*) *martrine* skin of a marten, < *martre,* prob. of Gmc origin]

martial (ˈmɑːʃəl) *adj.* of, relating to, or characteristic of war, soldiers, or the military life. [C14: < L *martiālis* of MARS[1]] —ˈ**martialism** *n.* —ˈ**martialist** *n.* —ˈ**martially** *adv.*

martial art *n.* any of various philosophies of self-defence and techniques of single combat, such as judo or karate, originating in the Far East.

martial law *n.* rule of law maintained by the military in the absence of civil law.

Martian (ˈmɑːʃən) *adj.* **1.** of, occurring on, or relating to the planet Mars. ~*n.* **2.** an inhabitant of Mars, esp. in science fiction.

martin (ˈmɑːtɪn) *n.* any of various birds of the swallow family, having a square or slightly forked tail. See also **house martin.** [C15: ? < St *Martin,* bishop of Tours & patron saint of France, because the birds were believed to migrate at the time of Martinmas]

martinet (ˌmɑːtɪˈnɛt) *n.* a person who maintains strict discipline, esp. in a military force. [C17: < F, < General *Martinet,* drillmaster under Louis XIV]

martingale (ˈmɑːtɪnˌgeɪl) *n.* **1.** a strap from the reins to the girth of a horse, preventing it from carrying its head too high. **2.** any gambling system in which the stakes are raised, usually doubled, after each loss. **3.** *Naut.* a chain or cable running from a jib boom to the stern or stem. [C16: < F, <?]

martini (mɑːˈtiːnɪ) *n.* **1.** (*often cap.*) *Trademark.* an Italian vermouth. **2.** a cocktail of gin and vermouth. [C19 (sense 2): ?< the name of the inventor]

Martinmas (ˈmɑːtɪnməs) *n.* the feast of St Martin on Nov. 11; a quarter day in Scotland.

martyr (ˈmɑːtə) *n.* **1.** a person who suffers death rather than renounce his religious beliefs. **2.** a person who suffers greatly or dies for a cause, belief, etc. **3.** a person who suffers from poor health, misfortune, etc.: *a martyr to rheumatism.* ~*vb. also* **ˈmartyrize** *or* **-ise.** (*tr.*) **4.** to kill as a martyr. **5.** to make a martyr of. [OE *martir,* < Church L *martyr,* < LGk *martur-, martus* witness] —**ˈmartyrdom** *n.* —**ˌmartyriˈzation** *or* **-iˈsation** *n.*

martyrology (ˌmɑːtəˈrɒlədʒɪ) *n., pl.* **-gies. 1.** an official list of martyrs. **2.** *Christianity.* the study of the lives of the martyrs. **3.** a historical account of the lives of martyrs. —**ˌmartyrˈologist** *n.*

marvel (ˈmɑːvəl) *vb.* **-velling, -velled** *or U.S.* **-veling, -veled. 1.** (when *intr.*, often foll. by *at* or *about;* when *tr., takes a clause as object*) to be filled with surprise or wonder. ~*n.* **2.** something that causes wonder. **3.** *Arch.* astonishment. [C13: < OF *merveille,* < LL *mīrābilia,* < L *mīrābilis* < *mīrārī* to wonder at]

marvellous *or U.S.* **marvelous** (ˈmɑːvələs) *adj.* **1.** causing great wonder, surprise, etc.; extraordinary. **2.** improbable or incredible. **3.** excellent; splendid. —**ˈmarvellously** *or U.S.* **ˈmarvelously** *adv.* —**ˈmarvellousness** *or U.S.* **ˈmarvelousness** *n.*

marvel-of-Peru *n., pl.* **marvels-of-Peru.** another name for **four-o'clock** (the plant). [C16: first found in Peru]

Marxism (ˈmɑːksɪzəm) *n.* the economic and political theory and practice originated by Karl Marx (1818–83) and Friedrich Engels (1820–95), German political philosophers. It holds that actions and human institutions are economically determined, that the class struggle is the basic agency of historical change, and that capitalism will ultimately be superseded by communism. —**ˈMarxist** *n., adj.*

Marxism-Leninism *n.* the modification of Marxism by Lenin stressing that imperialism is the highest form of capitalism. —**ˈMarxist-ˈLeninist** *n., adj.*

marzipan (ˈmɑːzɪˌpæn) *n.* a paste made from ground almonds, sugar, and egg whites, used to coat fruit cakes or moulded into sweets. [C19: via G < It. *marzapane*]

-mas *n. combining form.* indicating a Christian festival: *Christmas; Michaelmas.* [< MASS]

Masai (ˈmɑːsaɪ, mɑːˈsaɪ) *n.* **1.** (*pl.* **-sais** *or* **-sai**) a member of a Nilotic people, formerly noted as warriors, living chiefly in Kenya and Tanzania. **2.** the language of this people.

masc. *abbrev. for* masculine.

mascara (mæˈskɑːrə) *n.* a cosmetic for darkening the eyelashes. [C20: < Sp.: mask]

mascon (ˈmæskɒn) *n.* any of several lunar regions of high gravity. [C20: < MAS(S) + CON(CENTRATION)]

mascot (ˈmæskət) *n.* a person, animal, or thing considered to bring good luck. [C19: < F *mascotte,* < Provençal *mascotto* charm, < *masco* witch]

masculine (ˈmæskjʊlɪn) *adj.* **1.** possessing qualities or characteristics considered typical of or appropriate to a man; manly. **2.** unwomanly. **3.** *Grammar.* denoting a gender of nouns that includes all kinds of referents as well as some male animate referents. **4.** *Prosody.* denoting an ending consisting of a single stressed syllable. **5.** *Prosody.* denoting a rhyme between pairs of single final stressed syllables. [C14: via F < L *masculīnus,* < *masculus* male, < *mās* a male] —**ˈmasculinely** *adv.* —**ˌmascuˈlinity** *n.*

maser (ˈmeɪzə) *n.* a device for amplifying microwaves, working on the same principle as a laser. [C20: *m*(*icrowave*) *a*(*mplification by*) *s*(*timulated*) *e*(*mission of*) *r*(*adiation*)]

mash (mæʃ) *n.* **1.** a soft pulpy mass or consistency. **2.** *Agriculture.* a feed of bran, meal, or malt mixed with water and fed to horses, cattle, or poultry. **3.** (esp. in brewing) a mixture of mashed malt grains and hot water, from which malt is extracted. **4.** *Brit. inf.* mashed potatoes. ~*vb.* (*tr.*) **5.** to beat or crush into a mash. **6.** to steep (malt grains) in hot water in order to extract malt. **7.** *Scot. & N English dialect.* to brew (tea). [OE *mǣsc-* (in compound words)] —**mashed** *adj.* —**ˈmasher** *n.*

mashie *or* **mashy** (ˈmæʃɪ) *n., pl.* **mashies.** *Golf.* (formerly) an iron for lofting shots, usually No. 5. [C19: ? < F *massue* club, ult. < L *mateola* mallet]

mask (mɑːsk) *n.* **1.** any covering for the whole or a part of the face worn for amusement, protection, disguise, etc. **2.** a fact, action, etc., that conceals something. **3.** another name for **masquerade. 4.** a likeness of a face or head, either sculpted or moulded, such as a death mask. **5.** an image of a face worn by an actor, esp. in classical drama, in order to symbolize a character. **6.** a variant spelling of **masque. 7.** *Surgery.* a sterile gauze covering for the nose and mouth worn to minimize the spread of germs. **8.** *Sport.* a protective covering for the face worn for fencing, ice hockey, etc. **9.** a carving in the form of a face or head, used as an ornament. **10.** a device placed over the nose and mouth to facilitate or prevent inhalation of a gas. **11.** *Photog.* a shield of paper, paint, etc., placed over an area of unexposed photographic surface to stop light falling on it. **12.** the face or head of an animal, such as a fox. **13.** *Rare.* a person wearing a mask. ~*vb.* **14.** to cover with or put on a mask. **15.** (*tr.*) to conceal; disguise: *to mask an odour.* **16.** (*tr.*) *Photog.* to shield a particular area of (an unexposed photographic surface) to prevent or reduce the action of light there. [C16: < It. *maschera,* ult. < Ar. *maskharah* clown, < *sakhira* mockery] —**masked** *adj.* —**ˈmasker** *n.*

masked ball *n.* a ball at which masks are worn.

masking tape *n.* an adhesive tape used to protect surfaces surrounding an area to be painted.

maskinonge (ˈmæskəˌnɒndʒ) *n.* another name for **muskellunge.**

masochism (ˈmæsəˌkɪzəm) *n.* **1.** *Psychiatry.* an abnormal condition in which pleasure, esp. sexual pleasure, is derived from pain or from humiliation, domination, etc., by another person. **2.** a tendency to take pleasure from one's own suffering. Cf. **sadism.** [C19: after Leopold von Sacher *Masoch* (1836–95), Austrian novelist, who described it] —**ˈmasochist** *n., adj.* —**ˌmasoˈchistic** *adj.* —**ˌmasoˈchistically** *adv.*

mason (ˈmeɪsən) *n.* **1.** a person skilled in building with stone. **2.** a person who dresses stone. ~*vb.* **3.** (*tr.*) to construct or strengthen with masonry. [C13: < OF *masson,* of Frankish origin; ? rel. to OE *macian* to make]

Mason (ˈmeɪsən) *n.* short for **Freemason.**

Mason-Dixon Line (-ˈdɪksən) *n.* in the U.S.A., the state boundary between Maryland and Pennsylvania: surveyed between 1763 and 1767 by Charles Mason and Jeremiah Dixon; popularly regarded as the dividing line between North and South.

masonic (məˈsɒnɪk) *adj.* **1.** (*often cap.*) of or relating to Freemasons or Freemasonry. **2.** of or relating to masons or masonry. —**maˈsonically** *adv.*

Masonite (ˈmeɪsəˌnaɪt) *n. Austral. trademark.* a kind of dark brown hardboard.

masonry (ˈmeɪsənrɪ) *n., pl.* **-ries. 1.** the craft of a mason. **2.** work that is built by a mason; stonework or brickwork. **3.** (*often cap.*) short for **Freemasonry.**

masque *or* **mask** (mɑːsk) *n.* **1.** a dramatic entertainment of the 16th to 17th centuries, consisting of pantomime, dancing, dialogue, and song. **2.** the words and music for this. **3.** short for **masquerade.** [C16: var. of MASK]

masquerade (ˌmæskəˈreɪd) *n.* **1.** a party or other gathering at which the guests wear masks and costumes. **2.** the disguise worn at such a function. **3.** a pretence or disguise. ~*vb.* (*intr.*) **4.** to participate in a masquerade; disguise oneself. **5.** to dissemble. [C16: < Sp. *mascarada,* < *mascara* MASK] —**ˌmasquerˈader** *n.*

mass (mæs) *n.* **1.** a large coherent body of matter

without a definite shape. **2.** a collection of the component parts of something. **3.** a large amount or number, as of people. **4.** the main part or majority. **5. in the mass.** in the main; collectively. **6.** the size of a body; bulk. **7.** *Physics.* a physical quantity expressing the amount of matter in a body. It is a measure of a body's resistance to changes in velocity (**inertial mass**) and also of the force experienced in a gravitational field (**gravitational mass**). **8.** (in painting, drawing, etc.) an area of unified colour, shade, or intensity, usually denoting a solid form or plane. ~(*modifier*) **9.** done or occurring on a large scale: *mass hysteria.* **10.** consisting of a mass or large number, esp. of people: *a mass meeting.* ~*vb.* **11.** to form (people or things) or (of people or things) to join together into a mass. ~See also **masses.** [C14: < OF *masse,* < L *massa* that which forms a lump, < Gk *maza* barley cake]

Mass (mæs, mɑːs) *n.* **1.** (in the Roman Catholic Church and certain Protestant Churches) the celebration of the Eucharist. See also **High Mass, Low Mass. 2.** a musical setting of those parts of the Eucharistic service sung by choir or congregation. [OE *mæsse,* < Church L *missa,* ult. < L *mittere* to send away; ? < the concluding dismissal in the Roman Mass, *Ite, missa est* Go, it is the dismissal]

massacre (ˈmæsəkə) *n.* **1.** the wanton or savage killing of large numbers of people, as in battle. **2.** *Inf.* an overwhelming defeat, as in a game. ~*vb.* (*tr.*) **3.** to kill indiscriminately or in large numbers. **4.** *Inf.* to defeat overwhelmingly. [C16: < OF]

massage (ˈmæsɑːʒ, -sɑːdʒ) *n.* **1.** the act of kneading, rubbing, etc., parts of the body to promote circulation, suppleness, or relaxation. ~*vb.* (*tr.*) **2.** to give a massage to. **3.** to treat (stiffness, etc.) by a massage. **4.** to manipulate (statistics, etc.) to produce a desired result; doctor. [C19: < F, < *masser* to rub]

massasauga (ˌmæsəˈsɔːgə) *n.* a North American venomous snake that has a horny rattle at the end of the tail. [C19: after the *Missisauga* River, Ontario, Canada, where it was first found]

mass defect *n. Physics.* the amount by which the mass of a particular nucleus is less than the total mass of its constituent particles.

massé *or* **massé shot** (ˈmæsɪ) *n. Billiards.* a stroke made by hitting the cue ball off centre with the cue held nearly vertically, esp. so as to make the ball move in a curve. [C19: < F, < *masser,* < *masse* sledgehammer, < OF *mace* MACE[1]]

masses (ˈmæsɪz) *pl. n.* **1.** (preceded by *the*) the body of common people. **2.** (often foll. by *of*) *Inf., chiefly Brit.* great numbers or quantities: *masses of food.*

masseur (mæˈsɜː) *or* (*fem.*) **masseuse** (mæˈsɜːz) *n.* a person who gives massages, esp. as a profession. [C19: < F *masser* to MASSAGE]

massif (ˈmæsiːf) *n.* a mass of rock or a series of connected masses forming a mountain range. [C19: < F, noun use of *massif* MASSIVE]

massive (ˈmæsɪv) *adj.* **1.** (of objects) large in mass; bulky, heavy, and usually solid. **2.** impressive or imposing. **3.** relatively intensive or large; considerable: *a massive dose.* **4.** *Geol.* **a.** (of igneous rocks) having no stratification, cleavage, etc.; homogeneous. **b.** (of sedimentary rocks) arranged in thick poorly defined strata. **5.** *Mineralogy.* without obvious crystalline structure. [C15: < F *massif,* < *masse* MASS] —ˈ**massively** *adv.* —ˈ**massiveness** *n.*

▷ **Usage.** *Massive* has in journalistic and media usage become something of a stock adjective applied to anything serious, significant, large, or important: *a massive heart attack; a massive response to the strike call.* While in some instances it is undoubtedly suitable, careful users of English should consider its applicability to the noun and avoid its use if a more appropriate adjective can be found.

mass media *pl. n.* the means of communication that reach large numbers of people, such as television, newspapers, magazines, and radio.

mass noun *n.* a noun that refers to an extended substance rather than to each of a set of objects, e.g., *water* as opposed to *lake.* In English when used indefinitely they are characteristically preceded by *some* rather than *a* or *an;* they do not have normal plural forms. Cf. **count noun.**

mass number *n.* the total number of neutrons and protons in the nucleus of a particular atom.

mass observation *n.* (*sometimes cap.*) *Chiefly Brit.* the study of the social habits of people through observation, interviews, etc.

mass-produce *vb.* (*tr.*) to manufacture (goods) to a standardized pattern on a large scale by means of extensive mechanization and division of labour. —ˌ**mass-proˈduced** *adj.* —ˌ**mass-proˈducer** *n.* —**mass production** *n.*

mass spectrometer *or* **spectroscope** *n.* an instrument in which ions, produced from a sample, are separated by electric or magnetic fields according to their ratios of charge to mass. A record is produced (**mass spectrum**) of the types of ion present and their amounts.

mast[1] (mɑːst) *n.* **1.** *Naut.* any vertical spar for supporting sails, rigging, flags, etc., above the deck of a vessel. **2.** any sturdy upright pole used as a support. **3. before the mast.** *Naut.* as an apprentice seaman. ~*vb.* **4.** (*tr.*) *Naut.* to equip with a mast or masts. [OE *mæst;* rel. to MDu. *mast* & L *mālus* pole]

mast[2] (mɑːst) *n.* the fruit of forest trees, such as beech, oak, etc., used as food for pigs. [OE *mæst;* rel. to OHG *mast* food]

mastaba *or* **mastabah** (ˈmæstəbə) *n.* a mudbrick superstructure above tombs in ancient Egypt. [< Ar.: bench]

mastectomy (mæˈstɛktəmɪ) *n., pl.* **-mies.** the surgical removal of a breast.

master (ˈmɑːstə) *n.* **1.** the man in authority, such as the head of a household, the employer of servants, or the owner of slaves or animals. **2. a.** a person with exceptional skill at a certain thing. **b.** (*as modifier*): *a master thief.* **3.** (*often cap.*) a great artist, esp. an anonymous but influential one. **4. a.** a person who has complete control of a situation, etc. **b.** an abstract thing regarded as having power or influence: *they regarded fate as the master of their lives.* **5. a.** a workman or craftsman fully qualified to practise his trade and to train others. **b.** (*as modifier*): *master carpenter.* **6. a.** an original copy, stencil, tape, etc., from which duplicates are made. **b.** (*as modifier*): *master copy.* **7.** a player of a game, esp. chess or bridge, who has won a specified number of tournament games. **8.** the principal of some colleges. **9.** a highly regarded teacher or leader. **10.** a graduate holding a master's degree. **11.** the chief executive officer aboard a merchant ship. **12.** a person presiding over a function, organization, or institution. **13.** *Chiefly Brit.* a male teacher. **14.** an officer of the Supreme Court of Judicature subordinate to a judge. **15.** the superior person or side in a contest. **16.** (*often cap.*) the heir apparent of a Scottish viscount or baron. ~(*modifier*) **17.** overall or controlling: *master plan.* **18.** designating a device or mechanism that controls others: *master switch.* **19.** main; principal: *master bedroom.* ~*vb.* (*tr.*) **20.** to become thoroughly proficient in. **21.** to overcome; defeat. **22.** to rule or control as master. [OE *magister* teacher]

Master (ˈmɑːstə) *n.* **1.** a title of address for a boy. **2.** a term of address, esp. as used by disciples addressing or referring to a religious teacher. **3.** an archaic equivalent of **Mr.**

master aircrew *n.* a warrant rank in the Royal Air Force, equal to but before a warrant officer.

master-at-arms *n., pl.* **masters-at-arms.** the senior rating in a naval unit responsible for discipline and police duties.

master builder *n.* **1.** a person skilled in the design and construction of buildings, esp. before the foundation of the profession of architecture. **2.** a self-employed builder who employs labour.

masterful (ˈmɑːstəfʊl) *adj.* **1.** having or showing mastery. **2.** fond of playing the master;

imperious. —ˈ**masterfully** *adv.* —ˈ**masterfulness** *n.*

master key *n.* a key that opens all the locks of a set. Also called: **passkey.**

masterly (ˈmɑːstəlɪ) *adj.* of the skill befitting a master. —ˈ**masterliness** *n.*

master mason *n.* 1. see **master** (sense 5a). 2. a Freemason who has reached the rank of third degree.

mastermind (ˈmɑːstəˌmaɪnd) *vb.* 1. (*tr.*) to plan and direct (a complex undertaking). ~*n.* 2. a person of great intelligence or executive talent, esp. one who directs an undertaking.

Master of Arts *n.* a degree, usually postgraduate and in a nonscientific subject, or the holder of this degree. Abbrev.: **MA.**

master of ceremonies *n.* a person who presides over a public ceremony, formal dinner, or entertainment, introducing the events, performers, etc.

Master of the Rolls *n.* (in England) a judge of the court of appeal: the senior civil judge in the country and the Keeper of the Records at the Public Record Office.

masterpiece (ˈmɑːstəˌpiːs) *or* (*less commonly*) **masterwork** (ˈmɑːstəˌwɜːk) *n.* 1. an outstanding work or performance. 2. the most outstanding piece of work of a creative artist, craftsman, etc. [C17: cf. Du. *meesterstuk*, G *Meisterstück*, a sample of work submitted to a guild by a craftsman in order to qualify for the rank of master]

masterstroke (ˈmɑːstəˌstrəʊk) *n.* an outstanding piece of strategy, skill, talent, etc.

mastery (ˈmɑːstərɪ) *n., pl.* **-teries.** 1. full command or understanding of a subject. 2. outstanding skill; expertise. 3. the power of command; control. 4. victory or superiority.

masthead (ˈmɑːstˌhɛd) *n.* 1. *Naut.* the head of a mast. 2. the name of a newspaper or periodical, its proprietors, staff, etc., printed at the top of the front page. ~*vb.* (*tr.*) 3. to send (a sailor) to the masthead as a punishment. 4. to raise (a sail) to the masthead.

mastic (ˈmæstɪk) *n.* 1. an aromatic resin obtained from the mastic tree and used as an astringent and to make varnishes and lacquers. 2. **mastic tree.** a small Mediterranean evergreen tree that yields the resin mastic. 3. any of several putty-like substances used as a filler, adhesive, or seal in wood, plaster, or masonry. 4. a liquor flavoured with mastic gum. [C14: via OF < LL *mastichum*, < L < Gk *mastikhē* resin used as chewing gum]

masticate (ˈmæstɪˌkeɪt) *vb.* 1. to chew (food). 2. to reduce (materials such as rubber) to a pulp by crushing, grinding, or kneading. [C17: < LL *masticāre*, < Gk *mastikhan* to grind the teeth] —ˌ**mastiˈcation** *n.* —ˈ**mastiˌcator** *n.*

masticatory (ˈmæstɪkətərɪ, -trɪ) *adj.* 1. of, relating to, or adapted to chewing. ~*n., pl.* **-tories.** 2. a medicinal substance chewed to increase the secretion of saliva.

mastiff (ˈmæstɪf) *n.* a breed of large powerful short-haired dog, usually fawn or brindled. [C14: < OF, ult. < L *mansuētus* tame]

mastitis (mæˈstaɪtɪs) *n.* inflammation of a breast or an udder.

masto- *or before a vowel* **mast-** *combining form.* indicating the breast, mammary glands, or something resembling a breast or nipple: *mastodon; mastoid.* [< Gk *mastos* breast]

mastodon (ˈmæstəˌdɒn) *n.* an extinct elephant-like mammal common in Pliocene times. [C19: < NL, lit.: breast-tooth, referring to the nipple-shaped projections on the teeth]

mastoid (ˈmæstɔɪd) *adj.* 1. shaped like a nipple or breast. 2. designating or relating to a nipple-like process of the temporal bone behind the ear. ~*n.* 3. the mastoid process. 4. *Inf.* mastoiditis.

mastoiditis (ˌmæstɔɪˈdaɪtɪs) *n.* inflammation of the mastoid process.

masturbate (ˈmæstəˌbeɪt) *vb.* to stimulate the genital organs of (oneself or another) to achieve sexual pleasure. [C19: < L *masturbārī*, <?; formerly thought to be derived from *manus* hand + *stuprāre* to defile] —ˌ**masturˈbation** *n.* —ˈ**masturˌbator** *n.* —**masturbatory** (ˈmæstəˌbeɪtərɪ) *adj.*

mat[1] (mæt) *n.* 1. a thick flat piece of fabric used as a floor covering, a place to wipe one's shoes, etc. 2. a smaller pad of material used to protect a surface from the heat, scratches, etc., of an object placed upon it. 3. a large piece of thick padded material put on the floor as a surface for wrestling, judo, etc. 4. any surface or mass that is densely interwoven or tangled: *a mat of weeds.* ~*vb.* **matting, matted.** 5. to tangle or weave or become tangled or woven into a dense mass. 6. (*tr.*) to cover with a mat or mats. [OE *matte*]

mat[2] (mæt) *n.* 1. a border of cardboard, cloth, etc., placed around a picture as a frame or between picture and frame. ~*adj.* 2. having a dull, lustreless, or roughened surface. ~*vb.* **matting, matted.** (*tr.*) 3. to furnish (a picture) with a mat. 4. to give (a surface) a mat finish. ~Also (for senses 2 & 4): **matt.** [C17: < F, lit.: dead]

mat[3] (mæt) *n. Printing, inf.* short for **matrix** (sense 4).

mat. *abbrev. for* matinée.

matador (ˈmætədɔː) *n.* 1. the principal bullfighter who kills the bull. 2. (in some card games) one of the highest cards. 3. a game played with dominoes in which the dots on adjacent halves must total seven. [C17: < Sp., < *matar* to kill]

matagouri (ˌmætəˈguːrɪ) *n.* a New Zealand thorny bush which forms thickets in open country. Also called: **wild Irishman.** [< Maori *tumatakuru*]

matai (ˈmɑːtaɪ) *n.* a New Zealand tree, the black pine, the wood of which is used as building timber. Also called: **black pine.** [< Maori]

match[1] (mætʃ) *n.* 1. a formal game or sports event in which people, teams, etc., compete. 2. a person or thing able to provide competition for another: *she's met her match.* 3. a person or thing that resembles, harmonizes with, or is equivalent to another in a specified respect. 4. a person or thing that is an exact copy or equal of another. 5. a. a partnership between a man and a woman, as in marriage. b. an arrangement for such a partnership. 6. a person regarded as a possible partner, as in marriage. ~*vb.* (*mainly tr.*) 7. to fit (parts) together. 8. (*also intr.*; sometimes foll. by *up*) to resemble, harmonize with, or equal (one another or something else). 9. (sometimes foll. by *with* or *against*) to compare in order to determine which is the superior. 10. (often foll. by *to* or *with*) to adapt so as to correspond with: *to match hope with reality.* 11. (often foll. by *with* or *against*) to arrange a competition between. 12. to find a match for. 13. *Electronics.* to connect (two circuits) so that their impedances are equal, to produce a maximum transfer of energy. [OE *gemæcca* spouse] —ˈ**matchable** *adj.* —ˈ**matching** *adj.*

match[2] (mætʃ) *n.* 1. a thin strip of wood or cardboard tipped with a chemical that ignites by friction on a rough surface or a surface coated with a suitable chemical (see **safety match**). 2. a length of cord or wick impregnated with a chemical so that it burns slowly. It is used to fire cannons, explosives, etc. [C14: < OF *meiche*, ? < L *myxa* wick, < Gk *muxa* lamp nozzle]

matchboard (ˈmætʃˌbɔːd) *n.* a long flimsy board tongued and grooved for lining work.

matchbox (ˈmætʃˌbɒks) *n.* a small box for holding matches.

matchless (ˈmætʃlɪs) *adj.* unequalled; incomparable; peerless. —ˈ**matchlessly** *adv.*

matchlock (ˈmætʃˌlɒk) *n.* 1. an obsolete type of gunlock igniting the powder by means of a slow match. 2. a gun having such a lock.

matchmaker (ˈmætʃˌmeɪkə) *n.* 1. a person who brings together suitable partners for marriage. 2. a person who arranges competitive matches. —ˈ**matchˌmaking** *n., adj.*

match play *n. Golf.* scoring according to the

number of holes won and lost. Cf. **stroke play.** —**match player** *n.*

match point *n.* **1.** *Tennis, squash, etc.* the final point needed to win a match. **2.** *Bridge.* the unit used for scoring in tournaments.

matchstick (ˈmætʃˌstɪk) *n.* **1.** the wooden part of a match. ~*adj.* **2.** made with or as if with matchsticks. **3.** (esp. of drawn figures) thin and straight: *matchstick men.*

matchwood (ˈmætʃˌwʊd) *n.* **1.** wood suitable for making matches. **2.** splinters or fragments.

mate[1] (meɪt) *n.* **1.** the sexual partner of an animal. **2.** a marriage partner. **3. a.** *Inf., chiefly Brit., Austral., & N.Z.* a friend, usually of the same sex: often used to any male in direct address. **b.** (*in combination*) an associate, colleague, fellow sharer, etc.: *a classmate.* **4.** one of a pair of matching items. **5.** *Naut.* **a.** short for **first mate. b.** any officer below the master on a commercial ship. **6.** (in some trades) an assistant: *a plumber's mate.* ~*vb.* **7.** to pair (a male and female animal) or (of animals) to pair for reproduction. **8.** to marry or join in marriage. **9.** (*tr.*) to join as a pair. [C14: < MLow G; rel. to OE *gemetta* table-guest, < *mete* MEAT]

mate[2] (meɪt) *n., vb. Chess.* See **checkmate.**

maté *or* **mate** (ˈmɑːteɪ) *n.* **1.** an evergreen tree cultivated in South America for its leaves, which contain caffeine. **2.** a stimulating milky beverage made from the dried leaves of this tree. ~Also called: **Paraguay tea, yerba, yerba maté.** [C18: < American Sp. (orig. referring to the vessel in which the drink was brewed), < Quechua *máti* gourd]

matelot, matlo, *or* **matlow** (ˈmætləʊ) *n. Sl., chiefly Brit.* a sailor. [C20: < F]

mater (ˈmeɪtə) *n. Brit. sl.* a word for **mother:** often used facetiously. [C16: < L]

material (məˈtɪərɪəl) *n.* **1.** the substance of which a thing is made or composed; component or constituent matter. **2.** facts, notes, etc., that a finished work may be based on or derived from. **3.** cloth or fabric. **4.** a person who has qualities suitable for a given occupation, training, etc.: *that boy is university material.* ~*adj.* **5.** of, relating to, or composed of physical substance. **6.** of, relating to, or affecting economic or physical wellbeing: *material ease.* **7.** of or concerned with physical rather than spiritual interests. **8.** of great import or consequence: *material benefit.* **9.** (often foll. by *to*) relevant. **10.** *Philosophy.* of or relating to matter as opposed to form. ~See also **materials.** [C14: via F < LL *māteriālis,* < L *māteria* MATTER] —**maˌteriˈality** *n.*

material implication *n. Logic.* a form of implication in which the proposition "if A then B" is true except when A is true and B is false.

materialism (məˈtɪərɪəˌlɪzəm) *n.* **1.** interest in and desire for money, possessions, etc., rather than spiritual or ethical values. **2.** *Philosophy.* the doctrine that matter is the only reality and that the mind, the emotions, etc., are merely functions of it. Cf. **idealism, dualism. 3.** *Ethics.* the rejection of any religious or supernatural account of things. —**maˈterialist** *n.* —**maˌterialˈistic** *adj.* —**maˌterialˈistically** *adv.*

materialize *or* **-ise** (məˈtɪərɪəˌlaɪz) *vb.* **1.** (*intr.*) to become fact; actually happen. **2.** to invest or become invested with a physical shape or form. **3.** to cause (a spirit, as of a dead person) to appear in material form or (of a spirit) to appear in such form. **4.** (*intr.*) to take shape; become tangible. —**maˌterialiˈzation** *or* **-iˈsation** *n.* —**maˈterialˌizer** *or* **-ˌiser** *n.*

▷ **Usage.** Careful writers and speakers avoid using *materialize* to mean *happen* or *occur,* esp. in formal contexts: *they talked for several hours but nothing happened* (not *materialized*). The word is often used, however, in the sense of taking shape: *after many hours of discussion, the project finally began to materialize.*

materially (məˈtɪərɪəlɪ) *adv.* **1.** to a significant extent; considerably. **2.** with respect to material objects. **3.** *Philosophy.* with respect to substance as distinct from form.

materials (məˈtɪərɪəlz) *pl. n.* the equipment necessary for a particular activity.

materia medica (məˈtɪərɪə ˈmɛdɪkə) *n.* **1.** the branch of medical science concerned with the study of drugs used in the treatment of disease. **2.** the drugs used in the treatment of disease. [C17: < Med. L: medical matter]

materiel *or* **matériel** (məˌtɪərɪˈɛl) *n.* the materials and equipment of an organization, esp. of a military force. [C19: < F: MATERIAL]

maternal (məˈtɜːnᵊl) *adj.* **1.** of, relating to, or characteristic of a mother. **2.** related through the mother's side of the family: *his maternal uncle.* [C15: < Med. L *māternālis,* < L *māternus,* < *māter* mother] —**maˈternalism** *n.* —**maˌternalˈistic** *adj.* —**maˈternally** *adv.*

maternity (məˈtɜːnɪtɪ) *n.* **1.** motherhood. **2.** the characteristics associated with motherhood; motherliness. **3.** (*modifier*) relating to pregnant women or women at the time of childbirth: *a maternity ward.*

mateship (ˈmeɪtʃɪp) *n. Austral.* friendly egalitarian comradeship.

mate's rates *pl. n. N.Z. inf.* discounted or preferential rates of payment offered to a friend or colleague: *he got the job done cheaply by a plumber friend at mate's rates.*

matey *or* **maty** (ˈmeɪtɪ) *Brit. inf.* ~*adj.* **1.** friendly or intimate. ~*n.* **2.** friend or fellow: usually used in direct address. —ˈ**mateyness** *or* ˈ**matiness** *n.*

math (mæθ) *n. U.S. & Canad. inf.* short for **mathematics.** Brit. equivalent: **maths.**

mathematical (ˌmæθəˈmætɪkᵊl) *or* **mathematic** *adj.* **1.** of, used in, or relating to mathematics. **2.** characterized by or using the precision of mathematics. **3.** using, determined by, or in accordance with the principles of mathematics. —ˌ**matheˈmatically** *adv.*

mathematical logic *n.* symbolic logic, esp. when concerned with the foundations of mathematics.

mathematician (ˌmæθəməˈtɪʃən) *n.* an expert or specialist in mathematics.

mathematics (ˌmæθəˈmætɪks) *n.* **1.** (*functioning as sing.*) a group of related sciences, including algebra, geometry, and calculus, concerned with the study of number, quantity, shape, and space and their interrelationships by using a specialized notation. **2.** (*functioning as sing. or pl.*) mathematical operations and processes involved in the solution of a problem or study of some scientific field. [C14 *mathematik* (n.), via L < Gk (adj.), < *mathēma* a science; rel. to *manthanein* to learn]

maths (mæθs) *n.* (*functioning as sing.*) *Brit. inf.* short for **mathematics.** U.S. and Canad. equivalent: **math.**

Matilda (məˈtɪldə) *n. Austral. inf.* **1.** a bushman's swag. **2. waltz Matilda.** to travel as a bushman carrying one's swag. [C20: < the Christian name]

matin, mattin (ˈmætɪn), *or* **matinal** *adj.* of or relating to matins. [C14: see MATINS]

matinée (ˈmætɪˌneɪ) *n.* a daytime, esp. afternoon, performance of a play, concert, etc. [C19: < F; see MATINS]

matinée coat *or* **jacket** *n.* a short coat for a baby.

matins *or* **mattins** (ˈmætɪnz) *n.* (*functioning as sing. or pl.*) **1. a.** *Chiefly R.C. Church.* the first of the seven canonical hours of prayer. **b.** the service of morning prayer in the Church of England. **2.** *Literary.* a morning song, esp. of birds. [C13: < OF, ult. < L *mātūtīnus* of the morning, < *Mātūta* goddess of dawn]

matlo *or* **matlow** (ˈmætləʊ) *n.* variant spellings of **matelot.**

matrass (ˈmætrəs) *n. Chem., obs.* a long-necked glass flask, used for distilling, dissolving substances, etc. [C17: < F, ? rel. to L *mētiri* to measure]

matri- *combining form.* mother or motherhood: *matriarchy.* [< L *māter* mother]

matriarch (ˈmeɪtrɪˌɑːk) *n.* **1.** a woman who dominates an organization, community, etc. **2.**

the female head of a tribe or family. **3.** a very old or venerable woman. [C17: < MATRI- + -ARCH, by false analogy with PATRIARCH] —**ˈmatriˌarchal** *or* **ˈmatriˌarchic** *adj.*

matriarchy (ˈmeɪtrɪˌɑːkɪ) *n., pl.* **-chies. 1.** a form of social organization in which a female is head of the family or society, and descent and kinship are traced through the female line. **2.** any society dominated by women.

matric (məˈtrɪk) *n. Brit.* short for **matriculation** (see **matriculate**).

matrices (ˈmeɪtrɪˌsiːz, ˈmæ-) *n.* a plural of **matrix.**

matricide (ˈmætrɪˌsaɪd, ˈmeɪ-) *n.* **1.** the act of killing one's own mother. **2.** a person who kills his mother. [C16: < L *mātrīcīdium* (the act), *mātrīcīda* (the agent). See MATRI-, -CIDE] —ˌ**matriˈcidal** *adj.*

matriculate (məˈtrɪkjʊˌleɪt) *vb.* **1.** to enrol or be enrolled in an institution, esp. a college or university. **2.** (*intr.*) to attain the academic standard required for a course at such an institution. [C16: < Med. L *mātrīculāre* to register, < *mātrīcula,* dim. of *matrix* list] —**maˌtricuˈlation** *n.*

matrilineal (ˌmætrɪˈlɪnɪəl, ˌmeɪ-) *adj.* relating to descent or kinship through the female line.

matrimony (ˈmætrɪmənɪ) *n., pl.* **-nies. 1.** the state or condition of being married. **2.** the ceremony of marriage. **3. a.** a card game in which the king and queen together are a winning combination. **b.** such a combination. [C14: via Norman F < L *mātrimōnium* wedlock, < *māter* mother] —ˌ**matriˈmonial** *adj.*

matrix (ˈmeɪtrɪks, ˈmæ-) *n., pl.* **matrices** *or* **matrixes. 1.** a substance, situation, or environment in which something has its origin, takes form, or is enclosed. **2.** the intercellular substance of bone, cartilage, connective tissue, etc. **3.** the rock in which fossils, pebbles, etc., are embedded. **4.** *Printing.* **a.** a metal mould for casting type. **b.** a papier-mâché or plastic mould impressed from the forme and used for stereotyping. **5.** a mould used in the production of gramophone records. **6.** a bed of perforated material placed beneath a workpiece in a press or stamping machine against which the punch operates. **7.** *Maths.* a rectangular array of elements set out in rows and columns, used to facilitate the solution of problems, such as transformation of coordinates. **8.** *Obs.* the womb. [C16: < L: womb, female animal used for breeding, < *māter* mother]

matron (ˈmeɪtrən) *n.* **1.** a married woman regarded as staid or dignified. **2.** a woman in charge of the domestic or medical arrangements in an institution. **3.** *U.S.* a wardress in a prison. **4.** *Brit.* the administrative head of the nursing staff in a hospital. Official name: **nursing officer.** [C14: via OF < L *mātrōna,* < *māter* mother] —ˈ**matronal** *or* ˈ**matronly** *adj.* —ˈ**matronˌhood** *or* ˈ**matronship** *n.*

matron of honour *n., pl.* **matrons of honour.** a married woman serving as chief attendant to a bride.

matt *or* **matte** (mæt) *adj., n., vb.* variant spellings of **mat**[2] (senses 2 & 4).

Matt. *Bible. abbrev. for* Matthew.

mattamore (ˈmætəˌmɔː) *n.* a subterranean storehouse or dwelling. [C17: < F, < Ar. *matmurā,* < *tamara* to store, bury]

matted (ˈmætɪd) *adj.* **1.** tangled into a thick mass. **2.** covered with or formed of matting.

matter (ˈmætə) *n.* **1.** that which makes up something, esp. a physical object; material. **2.** substance that occupies space and has mass, as distinguished from substance that is mental, spiritual, etc. **3.** substance of a specified type: *vegetable matter.* **4.** (sometimes foll. by *of* or *for*) thing; affair; concern; question: *a matter of taste.* **5.** a quantity or amount: *a matter of a few pence.* **6.** the content of written or verbal material as distinct from its style or form. **7.** (*used with a negative*) importance; consequence. **8.** *Philosophy.* **a.** (in the writings of Aristotle and the Scholastics) that which is itself formless but can receive form and become substance. **b.** that which is organized into chemical substances and living things. **9.** *Philosophy.* (in the Cartesian tradition) one of two basic modes of existence, the other being mind. **10.** *Printing.* **a.** type set up. **b.** copy to be set in type. **11.** a secretion or discharge, such as pus. **12.** *Law.* **a.** something to be proved. **b.** statements or allegations to be considered by a court. **13. for that matter.** as regards that. **14. no matter. a.** regardless of; irrespective of: *no matter what the excuse, you must not be late.* **b.** (*sentence substitute*) it is unimportant. **15. the matter.** wrong; the trouble: *there's nothing the matter.* ~*vb.* (*intr.*) **16.** to be of consequence or importance. **17.** to form and discharge pus. [C13 (n.), C16 (vb.): < L *māteria* cause, substance, esp. wood, or a substance that produces something else]

matter of course *n.* **1.** an event or result that is natural or inevitable. ~*adj.* **matter-of-course. 2.** (*usually postpositive*) occurring as a matter of course. **3.** accepting things as inevitable or natural: *a matter-of-course attitude.*

matter of fact *n.* **1.** a fact that is undeniably true. **2.** *Law.* a statement of facts the truth of which the court must determine on the basis of the evidence before it. **3. as a matter of fact.** actually; in fact. ~*adj.* **matter-of-fact. 4.** unimaginative or emotionless: *he gave a matter-of-fact account of the murder.*

matting[1] (ˈmætɪŋ) *n.* **1.** a coarsely woven fabric, usually made of a natural fibre such as straw or hemp and used as a floor covering, packing material, etc. **2.** the act or process of making mats. **3.** material for mats.

matting[2] (ˈmætɪŋ) *n.* **1.** another word for **mat**[2] (sense 1). **2.** the process of producing a mat finish.

mattins (ˈmætɪnz) *n.* a variant spelling of **matins.**

mattock (ˈmætək) *n.* a type of large pick that has one end of its blade shaped like an adze, used for loosening soil, cutting roots, etc. [OE *mattuc,* <?; rel. to L *mateola* club, mallet]

mattress (ˈmætrɪs) *n.* **1.** a large flat pad with a strong cover, filled with straw, foam rubber, etc., and often incorporating coiled springs, used as a bed or as part of a bed. **2.** a woven mat of brushwood, poles, etc., used to protect an embankment, dyke, etc., from scour. **3.** a concrete or steel raft or slab used as a foundation or footing. [C13: via OF < It. *materasso,* < Ar. *almatrah* place where something is thrown]

maturate (ˈmætjʊˌreɪt, ˈmætʃʊ-) *vb.* **1.** to mature or bring to maturity. **2.** a less common word for **suppurate.** —ˌ**matuˈration** *n.* —**maturative** (məˈtjʊərətɪv, məˈtʃʊə-) *adj.*

mature (məˈtjʊə, -ˈtʃʊə) *adj.* **1.** relatively advanced physically, mentally, etc.; grown-up. **2.** (of plans, theories, etc.) fully considered; perfected. **3.** due or payable: *a mature debenture.* **4.** *Biol.* **a.** fully developed or differentiated: *a mature cell.* **b.** fully grown; adult: *a mature animal.* **5.** (of fruit, wine, cheese, etc.) ripe or fully aged. ~*vb.* **6.** to make or become mature. **7.** (*intr.*) (of notes, bonds, etc.) to become due for payment or repayment. [C15: < L *mātūrus* early, developed] —**maˈturely** *adv.* —**maˈtureness** *n.*

maturity (məˈtjʊərɪtɪ, -ˈtʃʊə-) *n.* **1.** the state or quality of being mature; full development. **2.** *Finance.* **a.** the date upon which a bond, note, etc., becomes due for repayment. **b.** the state of a bill, note, etc., when due.

matutinal (ˌmætjʊˈtaɪnˀl) *adj.* of, occurring in, or during the morning. [C17: < LL *mātūtīnālis,* < L, < *Mātūta* goddess of the dawn]

matzo, matzoh (ˈmætsəʊ) *or* **matza, matzah** (ˈmætsə) *n., pl.* **matzos, matzohs, matzas, matzahs,** *or* **matzoth** (*Hebrew* maˈtsɔt). a large very thin biscuit of unleavened bread, traditionally eaten during Passover. [< Heb. *matsāh*]

maudlin (ˈmɔːdlɪn) *adj.* foolishly tearful or sentimental, as when drunk. [C17: < ME *Maudelen* Mary Magdalene, typically portrayed as a tearful penitent]

maugre *or* **mauger** (ˈmɔːgə) *prep. Obs.* in spite of. [C13 (meaning: ill will): < OF *maugre*, lit.: bad pleasure]

maul (mɔːl) *vb.* (*tr.*) **1.** to handle clumsily; paw. **2.** to batter or lacerate. ~*n.* **3.** a heavy two-handed hammer. **4.** *Rugby.* a loose scrum. [C13: < OF *mail*, < L *malleus* hammer] —ˈ**mauler** *n.*

maulstick *or* **mahlstick** (ˈmɔːlˌstɪk) *n.* a long stick used by artists to steady the hand holding the brush. [C17: partial translation of Du. *maalstok*, < obs. *malen* to paint + *stok* STICK]

maunder (ˈmɔːndə) *vb.* (*intr.*) to move, talk, or act aimlessly or idly. [C17: ? < obs. *maunder* to beg, < L *mendīcāre*]

maundy (ˈmɔːndɪ) *n., pl.* **maundies.** *Christianity.* the ceremonial washing of the feet of poor persons in commemoration of Jesus' washing of his disciples' feet. [C13: < OF *mandé* something commanded, < L, ult. < Christ's words: *Mandātum novum dō vōbīs* A new commandment give I unto you]

Maundy money (ˈmɔːndɪ) *n.* specially minted coins given by the British sovereign to poor people on the Thursday before Easter (**Maundy Thursday**).

mausoleum (ˌmɔːsəˈlɪəm) *n., pl.* **-leums** *or* **-lea** (-ˈlɪə). a large stately tomb. [C16: via L < Gk *mausōleion*, the tomb of *Mausolus*, king of Caria; built at Halicarnassus in the 4th cent. B.C.]

mauve (məʊv) *n.* **1. a.** any of various pale to moderate pinkish-purple or bluish-purple colours. **b.** (*as adj.*)*: a mauve flower.* **2.** a reddish-purple aniline dye. [C19: < F, < L *malva* MALLOW]

maverick (ˈmævərɪk) *n.* **1.** (in the U.S. and Canada) an unbranded animal, esp. a stray calf. **2. a.** a person of independent or unorthodox views. **b.** (*as modifier*)*: a maverick politician.* [C19: after Samuel A. *Maverick* (1803–70), Texas rancher, who did not brand his cattle]

mavis (ˈmeɪvɪs) *n.* a popular name for the **song thrush.** [C14: < OF *mauvis* thrush; <?]

maw (mɔː) *n.* **1.** the mouth, throat, crop, or stomach of an animal, esp. of a voracious animal. **2.** *Inf.* the mouth or stomach of a greedy person. [OE *maga*]

mawkish (ˈmɔːkɪʃ) *adj.* **1.** falsely sentimental, esp. in a weak or maudlin way. **2.** nauseating or insipid. [C17: < obs. *mawk* MAGGOT + -ISH] —ˈ**mawkishly** *adv.* —ˈ**mawkishness** *n.*

max. *abbrev. for* maximum.

maxi (ˈmæksɪ) *adj.* **1. a.** (of a garment) reaching the ankle. **b.** (*as n.*)*: she wore a maxi.* **c.** (*in combination*)*: a maxidress.* **2.** large or considerable. [C20: < MAXIMUM]

maxilla (mækˈsɪlə) *n., pl.* **-lae** (-liː). **1.** the upper jawbone in vertebrates. **2.** any member of one or two pairs of mouthparts in insects and other arthropods. [C17: NL, < L: jaw] —**maxˈillary** *adj.*

maxim (ˈmæksɪm) *n.* a brief expression of a general truth, principle, or rule of conduct. [C15: via F < Med. L, < *maxima*, in the phrase *maxima prōpositio* basic axiom (lit.: greatest proposition)]

maxima (ˈmæksɪmə) *n.* a plural of **maximum.**

maximal (ˈmæksɪməl) *adj.* of, relating to, or achieving a maximum; being the greatest or best possible. —ˈ**maximally** *adv.*

maximin (ˈmæksɪˌmɪn) *n.* **1.** *Maths.* the highest of a set of minimum values. **2.** (in game theory, etc.) the procedure of choosing the strategy that most benefits the least advantaged member of a group. Cf. **minimax.** [C20: < MAXI(MUM) + MIN(IMUM)]

maximize *or* **-ise** (ˈmæksɪˌmaɪz) *vb.* (*tr.*) to make as high or great as possible; increase to a maximum. —ˌ**maximiˈzation** *or* **-iˈsation** *n.* —ˈ**maxiˌmizer** *or* **-iser** *n.*

maximum (ˈmæksɪməm) *n., pl.* **-mums** *or* **-ma.** **1.** the greatest possible amount, degree, etc. **2.** the highest value of a variable quantity. ~*adj.* **3.** of, being, or showing a maximum or maximums. ~Abbrev.: **max.** [C18: < L: greatest (neuter form used as noun), < *magnus* great]

maxwell (ˈmækswəl) *n.* the cgs unit of magnetic flux equal to the flux through one square centimetre normal to a field of one gauss. It is equivalent to 10^{-8} weber. Symbol: Mx [C20: after J. C. *Maxwell* (1831–79), Scot. physicist]

may[1] (meɪ) *vb. past* **might.** (takes an infinitive without *to* or an implied infinitive) used as an auxiliary: **1.** to indicate that permission is requested by or granted to someone: *he may go.* **2.** (often foll. by *well*) to indicate possibility: *the rope may break.* **3.** to indicate ability or capacity, esp. in questions: *may I help you?* **4.** to express a strong wish: *long may she reign.* **5.** to indicate result or purpose: used only in clauses introduced by *that* or *so that: he writes so that the average reader may understand.* **6.** to express courtesy in a question: *whose child may this little girl be?* **7. be that as it may.** in spite of that: a sentence connector conceding the possible truth of a previous statement and introducing an adversative clause: *be that as it may, I still think he should come.* **8. come what may.** whatever happens. **9. that's as may be.** (foll. by a clause introduced by *but*) that may be so. [OE *mæg*, < *magan*]

▷ **Usage.** In careful written usage, *may* is used rather than *can* when reference is made to permission rather than to capability. *He may do it* is, for this reason, more appropriate than *he can do it* when the desired sense is *he is allowed to do it.* In spoken English, however, *can* is often used where the correct use of *may* results in forms that are considered to be awkward. *Can't I?* is preferred on this ground to *mayn't I?* in speech. The difference between *may* and *might* is one of emphasis: *he might be coming* usually indicates less certainty than *he may be coming.* Similarly, *might I have it?* is felt to be more hesitant than *may I have it?*

may[2] *or* **may tree** (meɪ) *n.* a Brit. name for **hawthorn.** [C16: from MAY]

May (meɪ) *n.* the fifth month of the year, consisting of 31 days. [< OF, < L *Maius* (month) of *Maia*, Roman goddess]

Maya (ˈmaɪə) *n.* **1.** (*pl.* **-ya** *or* **-yas**) Also called: **Mayan.** a member of an American Indian people of Yucatán, Belize, and N Guatemala, once having an advanced civilization. **2.** the language of this people.

May apple *n.* **1.** an American plant with edible yellowish egg-shaped fruit. **2.** the fruit.

maybe (ˈmeɪˌbiː) *adv.* **1.** perhaps. ~*sentence substitute.* **2.** possibly; neither yes nor no.

May beetle *or* **bug** *n.* another name for **cockchafer.**

Mayday (ˈmeɪˌdeɪ) *n.* the international radiotelephone distress signal. [C20: phonetic spelling of F *m'aider* help me]

May Day *n.* the first day of May, traditionally a celebration of the coming of spring: in some countries now observed as a holiday in honour of workers.

mayest (ˈmeɪɪst) *vb.* a variant of **mayst.**

mayflower (ˈmeɪˌflaʊə) *n.* **1.** any of various plants that bloom in May. **2.** *Brit.* another name for **hawthorn, cowslip,** or **marsh marigold.**

Mayflower (ˈmeɪˌflaʊə) *n.* **the.** the ship in which the Pilgrim Fathers sailed from Plymouth to America in 1620.

mayfly (ˈmeɪˌflaɪ) *n., pl.* **-flies.** any of an order of short-lived insects having large transparent wings.

mayhap (ˈmeɪˌhæp) *adv.* an archaic word for **perhaps.** [C16: shortened < *it may hap*]

mayhem *or* **maihem** (ˈmeɪhɛm) *n.* **1.** *Law.* the wilful and unlawful infliction of injury upon a person, esp. (formerly) the injuring or removing of a limb rendering him less capable of defending himself against attack. **2.** any violent destruction or confusion. [C15: < Anglo-F *mahem* injury, of Gmc origin]

Maying (ˈmeɪɪŋ) *n.* the traditional celebration of May Day.

mayn't (ˈmeɪənt, meɪnt) *contraction of* may not.

mayonnaise (ˌmeɪəˈneɪz) *n.* a thick creamy sauce made from egg yolks, oil, and vinegar or lemon juice. [C19: < F, ? < *mahonnais* of *Mahón*, a port in Minorca]

mayor (mɛə) *n.* the civic head of a municipal corporation in many countries. Scot. equivalent: **provost.** [C13: < OF *maire,* < L *maior* greater] —ˈ**mayoral** *adj.* —ˈ**mayorship** *n.*

mayoralty (ˈmɛərəltɪ) *n., pl.* **-ties.** the office or term of office of a mayor. [C14: < OF *mairalté*]

mayoress (ˈmɛərɪs) *n.* **1.** *Chiefly Brit.* the wife of a mayor. **2.** a female mayor.

maypole (ˈmeɪˌpəʊl) *n.* a tall pole around which people dance during May-Day celebrations.

May queen *n.* a girl chosen, esp. for her beauty, to preside over May-Day celebrations.

mayst (meɪst) *or* **mayest** *vb. Arch.* (used with *thou* or its relative equivalent) a singular form of the present tense of **may**[1].

mayweed (ˈmeɪˌwiːd) *n.* **1.** Also called: **dog fennel, stinking mayweed.** a widespread Eurasian weedy plant having evil-smelling leaves and daisy-like flower heads. **2. scentless mayweed.** a similar and related plant, with scentless leaves. [C16: changed < OE *mægtha* mayweed + WEED]

maze (meɪz) *n.* **1.** a complex network of paths or passages, esp. one with high hedges in a garden, designed to puzzle those walking through it. **2.** a similar system represented diagrammatically as a pattern of lines. **3.** any confusing network of streets, paths, etc. **4.** a state of confusion. ~*vb.* **5.** an archaic or dialect word for **amaze.** [C13: see AMAZE] —ˈ**mazement** *n.* —ˈ**mazy** *adj.*

mazurka *or* **mazourka** (məˈzɜːkə) *n.* **1.** a Polish national dance in triple time. **2.** a piece of music composed for this dance. [C19: < Polish: (dance) of *Mazur* (Mazovia) province in Poland]

MB *abbrev. for:* **1.** Bachelor of Medicine. **2.** *Computers.* megabyte.

MBA *abbrev. for* Master of Business Administration.

MBE *abbrev. for* Member of the Order of the British Empire (a Brit. title).

MC *abbrev. for:* **1.** Master of Ceremonies. **2.** (in the U.S.) Member of Congress. **3.** (in Britain) Military Cross.

Mc- *prefix.* a variant of **Mac-**. For entries beginning with this prefix, see under **Mac-**.

MCC (in Britain) *abbrev. for* Marylebone Cricket Club.

MCh *abbrev. for* Master of Surgery. [L *Magister Chirurgiae*]

MCP *Inf. abbrev. for* male chauvinist pig.

Md *the chemical symbol for* mendelevium.

MD *abbrev. for:* **1.** Doctor of Medicine. [< L *Medicinae Doctor*] **2.** Managing Director. **3.** mentally deficient.

MDT (in the U.S. and Canada) *abbrev. for* Mountain Daylight Time.

me (miː; *unstressed* mɪ) *pron.* (*objective*) **1.** refers to the speaker or writer: *that shocks me.* ~*n.* **2.** *Inf.* the personality of the speaker or writer or something that expresses it: *the real me.* [OE *mē* (dative)]

▷ **Usage.** Although the nominative case is traditionally required after the verb *to be,* even careful speakers say *it is me* (or *him, her,* etc.) rather than *it is I* in informal contexts. The use of *me,* etc., before an *-ing* form of the verb (*he disapproved of me coming*) is common, but careful speakers and writers use the possessive form: *he disapproved of my coming.*

ME *abbrev. for:* **1.** Marine Engineer. **2.** Mechanical Engineer. **3.** Methodist Episcopal. **4.** Middle English. **5.** Mining Engineer. **6.** (in titles) Most Excellent.

mea culpa *Latin.* (ˈmeɪɑː ˈkʊlpɑː) an acknowledgment of guilt. [lit.: my fault]

mead[1] (miːd) *n.* a wine made by fermenting a solution of honey, often with spices added. [OE *meodu*]

mead[2] (miːd) *n.* an archaic or poetic word for **meadow.** [OE *mæd*]

meadow (ˈmɛdəʊ) *n.* **1.** an area of grassland, often used for hay or for grazing of animals. **2.** a low-lying piece of grassland, often boggy and near a river. [OE *mædwe,* < *mǣd* MEAD[2]] —ˈ**meadowy** *adj.*

meadow grass *n.* a perennial grass that grows in meadows and similar places in N temperate regions.

meadow saffron *n.* another name for **autumn crocus.**

meadowsweet (ˈmɛdəʊˌswiːt) *n.* **1.** a Eurasian plant with dense heads of small fragrant cream-coloured flowers. **2.** any of several related North American plants.

meagre *or U.S.* **meager** (ˈmiːgə) *adj.* **1.** deficient in amount, quality, or extent. **2.** thin or emaciated. **3.** lacking in richness or strength. [C14: < OF *maigre,* < L *macer* lean, poor] —ˈ**meagrely** *adv.* —ˈ**meagreness** *n.*

meal[1] (miːl) *n.* **1. a.** any of the regular occasions, such as breakfast, lunch, dinner, etc., when food is served and eaten. **b.** (*in combination*): *mealtime.* **2.** the food served and eaten. **3. make a meal of.** *Inf.* to perform (a task) with unnecessarily great effort. [OE *mǣl* measure, set time, meal]

meal[2] (miːl) *n.* **1.** the edible part of a grain or pulse (excluding wheat) ground to a coarse powder. **2.** *Scot.* oatmeal. **3.** *Chiefly U.S.* maize flour. [OE *melu*]

mealie (ˈmiːlɪ) *n.* (*often pl.*) a S. African word for **maize.** [C19: < Afrik. *milie,* < Port. *milho,* < L *milium* millet]

mealie-meal *n. S. African.* meal made from finely ground maize.

meals-on-wheels *n.* (*functioning as sing.*) (in Britain) a service taking hot meals to the elderly, infirm, etc., in their own homes.

meal ticket *n. Sl.* a person, situation, etc., providing a source of livelihood or income. [< orig. U.S. sense of ticket entitling holder to a meal]

mealworm (ˈmiːlˌwɜːm) *n.* the larva of various beetles feeding on stored foods, esp. meal and flour.

mealy (ˈmiːlɪ) *adj.* **mealier, mealiest. 1.** resembling meal; powdery. **2.** containing or consisting of meal or grain. **3.** sprinkled or covered with meal or similar granules. **4.** (esp. of horses) spotted; mottled. **5.** pale in complexion. **6.** short for **mealy-mouthed.** —ˈ**mealiness** *n.*

mealy bug *n.* any of various plant-eating insects coated with a powdery waxy secretion: some species are pests of citrus fruits and greenhouse plants.

mealy-mouthed *adj.* hesitant or afraid to speak plainly; not outspoken. [C16: < MEALY (in the sense: soft, soft-spoken)]

mean[1] (miːn) *vb.* **meaning, meant.** (*mainly tr.*) **1.** (*may take a clause as object or an infinitive*) to intend to convey or express. **2.** (*may take a clause as object or an infinitive*) to intend: *she didn't mean to hurt it.* **3.** (*may take a clause as object*) to say or do in all seriousness: *the boss means what he says.* **4.** (*often passive;* often foll. by *for*) to destine or design (for a certain person or purpose): *she was meant for greater things.* **5.** (*may take a clause as object*) to denote or connote; signify; represent. **6.** (*may take a clause as object*) to produce; cause: *the weather will mean long traffic delays.* **7.** (*may take a clause as object*) to foretell; portend: *those dark clouds mean rain.* **8.** to have the importance of: *money means nothing to him.* **9.** (*intr.*) to have the intention of behaving or acting (esp. in **mean well** *or* **mean ill**). [OE *mænan*]

mean[2] (miːn) *adj.* **1.** *Chiefly Brit.* miserly, ungenerous, or petty. **2.** despicable, ignoble, or callous: *a mean action.* **3.** poor or shabby: *a mean abode.* **4.** *Inf., chiefly U.S. & Canad.* bad-tempered; vicious. **5.** *Inf.* ashamed: *he felt mean about not letting the children stay out late.* **6.** *Sl.* excellent; skilful: *he plays a mean trombone.* **7. no mean. a.** of high quality: *no mean performer.* **b.** difficult: *no mean feat.* [C12: < OE *gemǣne* common] —ˈ**meanly** *adv.* —ˈ**meanness** *n.*

mean[3] (miːn) *n.* **1.** the middle point, state, or course between limits or extremes. **2.** moderation. **3.** *Maths.* **a.** the second and third terms of a proportion, as *b* and *c* in $a/b = c/d$. **b.** another name for **average** (sense 2). **4.** *Statistics.* a statistic obtained by multiplying each possible value of a variable by its probability and then taking the sum or integral over the range of the variable. ~*adj.* **5.** intermediate or medium in size, quantity, etc. **6.** occurring halfway between extremes or limits; average. [C14: via Anglo-Norman < OF *moien,* < LL *mediānus* MEDIAN]

meander (mɪˈændə) *vb.* (*intr.*) **1.** to follow a winding course. **2.** to wander without definite aim or direction. ~*n.* **3.** (*often pl.*) a curve or bend, as in a river. **4.** (*often pl.*) a winding course or movement. **5.** an ornamental pattern, esp. as used in ancient Greek architecture. [C16: < L *maeander,* < Gk *Maiandros* the River Maeander, now the River Menderes in SW Turkey] —**meˈandering** *adj.*

mean deviation *n. Statistics.* **1.** the difference between an observed value of a variable and its mean. **2.** Also called: **mean deviation from the mean** (*or* **median**), **average deviation.** a measure of dispersion derived by computing the mean of the absolute values of the differences between observed values of a variable and the variable's mean.

meanie *or* **meany** (ˈmiːnɪ) *n.* **1.** *Inf., chiefly Brit.* a miserly or stingy person. **2.** *Chiefly U.S.* a nasty ill-tempered person.

meaning (ˈmiːnɪŋ) *n.* **1.** the sense or significance of a word, sentence, symbol, etc.; import. **2.** the purpose behind speech, action, etc. **3.** the inner, symbolic, or true interpretation, value, or message. **4.** valid content; efficacy. ~*adj.* **5.** expressive of some sense, intention, criticism, etc.: *a meaning look.* ~See also **well-meaning.**

meaningful (ˈmiːnɪŋfʊl) *adj.* **1.** having great meaning or validity. **2.** eloquent; expressive: *a meaningful silence.* —ˈ**meaningfully** *adv.* —ˈ**meaningfulness** *n.*

▷ **Usage.** *Meaningful* has become something of a vogue word and is well established in collocations such as *a meaningful experience; a meaningful relationship.* Careful writers and speakers of English, however, do not use *meaningful* in instances where other adjectives, such as real, fruitful, useful, or significant may be more exact. Examples are: *delighted to have an apparently meaningful task to perform; computers could never play any meaningful role in the lives of ordinary people.* Often, *meaningful* can be omitted without any loss of sense: *to implement meaningful reform of housing tenures.*

meaningless (ˈmiːnɪŋlɪs) *adj.* futile or empty of meaning. —ˈ**meaninglessly** *adv.* —ˈ**meaninglessness** *n.*

mean life *n. Physics.* the average time of existence of an unstable or reactive entity, such as a nucleus, elementary particle, etc.

means (miːnz) *n.* **1.** (*functioning as sing. or pl.*) the medium, method, or instrument used to obtain a result or achieve an end: *a means of communication.* **2.** (*functioning as pl.*) resources or income. **3.** (*functioning as pl.*) considerable wealth or income: *a man of means.* **4. by all means.** without hesitation or doubt; certainly. **5. by means of.** with the use or help of. **6. by no manner of means.** definitely not. **7. by no** (*or* **not by any**) **means.** on no account; in no way.

means test *n.* the checking of a person's income to determine whether he qualifies for financial or social aid from a government.

mean sun *n.* an imaginary sun moving along the celestial equator at a constant speed and completing its annual course in the same time as the sun takes to move round the ecliptic at a varying speed. It is used in the measurement of mean solar time.

meant (mɛnt) *vb.* the past tense and past participle of **mean**[1].

meantime (ˈmiːnˌtaɪm) *or* **meanwhile** (ˈmiːnˌwaɪl) *n.* **1.** the intervening time or period (esp. in **in the meantime**). ~*adv.* **2.** during the intervening time or period. **3.** at the same time, esp. in another place.

▷ **Usage.** In formal usage, *in the meantime* is preferred to *meantime,* although *meantime* is very common in informal spoken English. The most usual one-word form of the adverb in written English is *meanwhile: in the meantime* (or *meanwhile* not *meantime*), *the king had not been idle.*

mean time *or* **mean solar time** *n.* the times, at a particular place, measured in terms of the passage of the mean sun, giving 24-hour days (mean solar days) throughout a year.

meany (ˈmiːnɪ) *n., pl.* **meanies.** a variant of **meanie.**

measles (ˈmiːzəlz) *n.* (*functioning as sing.*) **1.** a highly contagious viral disease common in children, characterized by fever, profuse nasal discharge of mucus, conjunctivitis, and a rash of small red spots. See also **German measles. 2.** a disease of cattle, sheep, and pigs, caused by infestation with tapeworm larvae. [C14: < MLow G *masele* spot on the skin; infl. by ME *mesel* leper, < L *misellus,* dim. of *miser* wretched]

measly (ˈmiːzlɪ) *adj.* **-slier, -sliest. 1.** *Inf.* meagre in quality or quantity. **2.** (of meat) infested with tapeworm larvae. **3.** having or relating to measles. [C17: see MEASLES]

measurable (ˈmɛʒərəbᵊl) *adj.* able to be measured; perceptible or significant. —ˈ**measurably** *adv.*

measure (ˈmɛʒə) *n.* **1.** the extent, quantity, amount, or degree of something, as determined by measurement or calculation. **2.** a device for measuring distance, volume, etc., such as a graduated scale or container. **3.** a system of measurement: *metric measure.* **4.** a standard used in a system of measurements. **5.** a specific or standard amount of something: *a measure of grain; full measure.* **6.** a basis or standard for comparison. **7.** reasonable or permissible limit or bounds: *within measure.* **8.** degree or extent (often in **in some measure, in a measure,** etc.): *a measure of freedom.* **9.** (*often pl.*) a particular action intended to achieve an effect. **10.** a legislative bill, act, or resolution. **11.** *Music.* another word for **bar**[1] (sense 15). **12.** *Prosody.* poetic rhythm or cadence; metre. **13.** a metrical foot. **14.** *Poetic.* a melody or tune. **15.** the act of measuring; measurement. **16.** *Arch.* a dance. **17.** *Printing.* the width of a page or column of type. **18. for good measure.** as an extra precaution or beyond requirements. **19. made to measure.** (of clothes) made to fit an individual purchaser. ~*vb.* **20.** (*tr.;* often foll. by *up*) to determine the size, amount, etc., of by measurement. **21.** (*intr.*) to make a measurement. **22.** (*tr.*) to estimate or determine. **23.** (*tr.*) to function as a measurement of: *the ohm measures electrical resistance.* **24.** (*tr.*) to bring into competition or conflict with: *he measured his strength against that of his opponent.* **25.** (*intr.*) to be as specified in extent, amount, etc.: *the room measures six feet.* **26.** (*tr.*) to travel or move over as if measuring. ~See also **measure up.** [C13: < OF, < L *mēnsūra,* < *mēnsus,* p.p. of *mētīrī* to measure]

measured (ˈmɛʒəd) *adj.* **1.** determined by measurement. **2.** slow or stately. **3.** carefully considered; deliberate. —ˈ**measuredly** *adv.*

measureless (ˈmɛʒəlɪs) *adj.* limitless, vast, or infinite. —ˈ**measurelessly** *adv.*

measurement (ˈmɛʒəmənt) *n.* **1.** the act or process of measuring. **2.** an amount, extent, or size determined by measuring. **3.** a system of measures based on a particular standard.

measures (ˈmɛʒəz) *pl. n.* rock strata that are characterized by a particular type of sediment or deposit: *coal measures.*

measure up *vb.* **1.** (*adv.*) to determine the size of (something) by measurement. **2. measure up to.** to fulfil (expectations, standards, etc.).

measuring jug *n.* a graduated jug used in cooking to measure ingredients.

measuring worm *n.* the larva of a geometrid moth: it moves in a series of loops. Also called: **inchworm.**

meat (miːt) *n.* **1.** the flesh of mammals used as food. **2.** anything edible, esp. flesh with the texture of meat: *crab meat.* **3.** food, as opposed to drink. **4.** the essence or gist. **5.** an archaic word for **meal**[1]. **6. meat and drink.** a source of pleasure. [OE *mete*] —**'meatless** *adj.*

meatball ('miːtˌbɔːl) *n.* **1.** minced beef, shaped into a ball before cooking. **2.** *U.S. & Canad. sl.* a stupid or boring person.

meatus (mɪ'eɪtəs) *n., pl.* **-tuses** *or* **-tus.** *Anat.* a natural opening or channel, such as the canal leading from the outer ear to the eardrum. [C17: < L: passage, < *meāre* to pass]

meaty ('miːtɪ) *adj.* **meatier, meatiest. 1.** of, relating to, or full of meat. **2.** heavily built; fleshy or brawny. **3.** full of import or interest: *a meaty discussion.* —**'meatily** *adv.* —**'meatiness** *n.*

Mecca *or* **Mekka** ('mɛkə) *n.* **1.** a city in W Saudi Arabia: birthplace of Mohammed; the holiest city of Islam. **2.** (*sometimes not cap.*) a place that attracts many visitors.

Meccano (mɪ'kɑːnəʊ) *n. Trademark.* a construction set of miniature metal parts from which mechanical models can be made.

mech. *abbrev. for:* **1.** mechanical. **2.** mechanics. **3.** mechanism.

mechanic (mɪ'kænɪk) *n.* a person skilled in maintaining or operating machinery, motors, etc. [C14: < L *mēchanicus,* < Gk, < *mēkhanē* MACHINE]

mechanical (mɪ'kænɪk°l) *adj.* **1.** made, performed, or operated by or as if by a machine or machinery. **2.** concerned with machines or machinery. **3.** relating to or controlled or operated by physical forces. **4.** of or concerned with mechanics. **5.** (of a gesture, etc.) automatic; lacking thought, feeling, etc. **6.** *Philosophy.* accounting for phenomena by physically determining forces. —**me'chanicalism** *n.* —**me'chanically** *adv.* —**me'chanicalness** *n.*

mechanical advantage *n.* the ratio of the working force exerted by a mechanism to the applied effort.

mechanical drawing *n.* a drawing to scale of a machine, machine component, architectural plan, etc., from which dimensions can be taken.

mechanical engineering *n.* the branch of engineering concerned with the design, construction, and operation of machines.

mechanical equivalent of heat *n. Physics.* a factor for converting units of energy into heat units.

mechanician (ˌmɛkə'nɪʃən) *or* **mechanist** *n.* a person skilled in making machinery and tools; technician.

mechanics (mɪ'kænɪks) *n.* **1.** (*functioning as sing.*) the branch of science, divided into statics, dynamics, and kinematics, concerned with the equilibrium or motion of bodies in a particular frame of reference. **2.** (*functioning as sing.*) the science of designing, constructing, and operating machines. **3.** the working parts of a machine. **4.** the technical aspects of something.

mechanism ('mɛkəˌnɪzəm) *n.* **1.** a system or structure of moving parts that performs some function, esp. in a machine. **2.** something resembling a machine in the arrangement and working of its parts. **3.** any mechanical device or part of such a device. **4.** a process or technique: *the mechanism of novel writing.* **5.** *Philosophy.* the doctrine that human action can be explained in purely physical terms. **6.** *Psychoanal.* **a.** the ways in which psychological forces interact and operate. **b.** a structure having an influence on the behaviour of a person, such as a defence mechanism.

mechanistic (ˌmɛkə'nɪstɪk) *adj.* **1.** *Philosophy.* of or relating to the theory of mechanism. **2.** *Maths.* of or relating to mechanics. —**'mechanist** *n.* —ˌ**mecha'nistically** *adv.*

mechanize *or* **-ise** ('mɛkəˌnaɪz) *vb.* (*tr.*) **1.** to equip (a factory, industry, etc.) with machinery. **2.** to make mechanical, automatic, or monotonous. **3.** to equip (an army, etc.) with motorized or armoured vehicles. —ˌ**mechani'zation** *or* **-i'sation** *n.* —**'mechaˌnizer** *or* **-iser** *n.*

mechanotherapy (ˌmɛkənəʊ'θɛrəpɪ) *n.* the treatment of disorders or injuries by means of mechanical devices, esp. devices that provide exercise for bodily parts.

Mechlin lace ('mɛklɪn) *n.* bobbin lace characterized by patterns outlined by heavier thread, made at Mechlin, English name for Mechelen, a city in N Belgium. Also called: **malines.**

meconium (mɪ'kəʊnɪəm) *n.* the first faeces of a newborn infant. [C17: < NL, < L: poppy juice, < Gk, < *mēkōn* poppy]

meconopsis (ˌmiːkən'ɒpsɪs) *n.* any of various mainly Asiatic poppies. [C19: < Gk *mekon* poppy + -OPSIS]

Med (mɛd) *n. Inf.* the Mediterranean region.

med. *abbrev. for:* **1.** medical. **2.** medicine. **3.** medieval. **4.** medium.

MEd *abbrev. for* Master of Education.

médaillons (*French* medajɔ̃) *pl. n. Cookery.* small round pieces of meat, fish, vegetables, etc. Also called: **medallions.**

medal ('mɛd°l) *n.* a small flat piece of metal bearing an inscription or image, given as an award or commemoration of some outstanding event, etc. [C16: < F *médaille,* prob. < It. *medaglia,* ult. < L *metallum* METAL]

medallion (mɪ'dæljən) *n.* **1.** a large medal. **2.** an oval or circular decorative device resembling a medal, usually bearing a portrait or relief moulding, used in architecture and textile design. [C17: < F, < It., < *medaglia* MEDAL]

medallist *or U.S.* **medalist** ('mɛd°lɪst) *n.* **1.** a designer, maker, or collector of medals. **2.** *Chiefly sport.* a recipient of a medal or medals.

medal play *n. Golf.* another name for **stroke play.**

meddle ('mɛd°l) *vb.* (*intr.*) **1.** (usually foll. by *with*) to interfere officiously or annoyingly. **2.** (usually foll. by *in*) to involve oneself unwarrantedly. [C14: < OF *medler,* ult. < L *miscēre* to mix] —**'meddler** *n.* —**'meddling** *adj.*

meddlesome ('mɛd°lsəm) *adj.* intrusive or meddling. —**'meddlesomely** *adv.* —**'meddlesomeness** *n.*

Mede (miːd) *n.* a member of an Indo-European people who established an empire in SW Asia in the 7th and 6th centuries B.C. —**'Median** *n., adj.*

media ('miːdɪə) *n.* **1.** a plural of **medium. 2.** the mass media collectively.

mediaeval (ˌmɛdɪ'iːv°l) *adj.* a variant spelling of **medieval.**

media event *n.* an event that is staged for or exploited by the mass media.

medial ('miːdɪəl) *adj.* **1.** of or situated in the middle. **2.** ordinary or average in size. **3.** *Maths.* relating to an average. **4.** another word for **median** (senses 1, 2). [C16: < LL *mediālis,* < *medius* middle] —**'medially** *adv.*

median ('miːdɪən) *adj.* **1.** of, relating to, situated in, or directed towards the middle. **2.** *Statistics.* of or relating to the median. ~*n.* **3.** a middle point, plane, or part. **4.** *Geom.* **a.** a straight line joining one vertex of a triangle to the midpoint of the opposite side. **b.** a straight line joining the midpoints of the nonparallel sides of a trapezium. **5.** *Statistics.* the middle value in a frequency distribution, below and above which lie values with equal total frequencies. **6.** *Statistics.* the middle number or average of the two middle numbers in an ordered sequence of numbers. [C16: < L *mediānus,* < *medius* middle] —**'medianly** *adv.*

mediant ('miːdɪənt) *n. Music.* **a.** the third degree of a minor scale. **b.** (*as modifier*): *a mediant chord.* [C18: < It. *mediante,* < LL *mediāre* to be in the middle]

mediastinum (ˌmiːdɪə'staɪnəm) *n., pl.* **-na** (-nə). *Anat.* **1.** a membrane between two parts of an organ or cavity such as the pleural tissue between the two lungs. **2.** the part of the thoracic cavity that lies between the lungs, containing the heart, trachea, etc. [C16: < Medical L, neuter of Med. L *mediastīnus* median, < L: low grade of servant, < *medius* mean] —ˌ**medias'tinal** *adj.*

mediate *vb.* ('miːdɪˌeɪt). **1.** (*intr.;* usually foll. by *between* or *in*) to intervene (between parties or in a dispute) in order to bring about agreement. **2.**

to bring about (an agreement) between parties in a dispute. **3.** to resolve (differences) by mediation. **4.** (*intr.*) to be in an intermediate position. **5.** (*tr.*) to serve as a medium for causing (a result) or transferring (objects, information, etc.). ~*adj.* (ˈmiːdɪɪt). **6.** occurring as a result of or dependent upon mediation. [C16: < LL *mediāre* to be in the middle] —**ˈmediately** *adv.* —**ˈmediˌator** *n.*

mediation (ˌmiːdɪˈeɪʃən) *n.* the act of mediating; intercession between people, states, etc. in an attempt to reconcile disputed matters.

Medibank (ˈmɛdɪbæŋk) *n.* (in Australia), a government-run health insurance scheme.

medic[1] (ˈmɛdɪk) *n. Inf.* a doctor, medical orderly, or medical student. [C17: < MEDICAL]

medic[2] (ˈmɛdɪk) *n.* the usual U.S. spelling of **medick.**

medicable (ˈmɛdɪkəbᵊl) *adj.* potentially able to be treated or cured medically.

medical (ˈmɛdɪkᵊl) *adj.* **1.** of or relating to the science of medicine or to the treatment of patients by drugs, etc., as opposed to surgery. ~*n.* **2.** *Inf.* a medical examination. [C17: < Med. L *medicālis,* < L *medicus* physician, surgeon, < *medērī* to heal] —**ˈmedically** *adv.*

medical certificate *n.* **1.** a document stating the result of a satisfactory medical examination. **2.** a doctor's certificate giving evidence of a person's unfitness for work.

medical jurisprudence *n.* another name for **forensic medicine.**

medicament (mɪˈdɪkəmənt, ˈmɛdɪ-) *n.* a medicine or remedy. [C16: via F < L *medicāmentum,* < *medicāre* to cure]

medicate (ˈmɛdɪˌkeɪt) *vb.* (*tr.*) **1.** to cover or impregnate (a wound, etc.) with an ointment, etc. **2.** to treat (a patient) with a medicine. **3.** to add a medication to (a bandage, shampoo, etc.). [C17: < L *medicāre* to heal] —**ˈmedicative** *adj.*

medication (ˌmɛdɪˈkeɪʃən) *n.* **1.** treatment with drugs or remedies. **2.** a drug or remedy.

medicinal (mɛˈdɪsɪnᵊl) *adj.* **1.** relating to or having therapeutic properties. ~*n.* **2.** a medicinal substance. —**meˈdicinally** *adv.*

medicine (ˈmɛdɪsɪn, ˈmɛdsɪn) *n.* **1.** any drug or remedy for use in treating, preventing, or alleviating the symptoms of disease. **2.** the science of preventing, diagnosing, alleviating, or curing disease. **3.** any nonsurgical branch of medical science. **4.** the practice or profession of medicine. **5.** something regarded by primitive people as having magical or remedial properties. **6. a taste** (*or* **dose**) **of one's own medicine.** an unpleasant experience in retaliation for a similar unkind or aggressive act. **7. take one's medicine.** to accept a deserved punishment. [C13: via OF < L *medicīna* (*ars*) (art) of healing, < *medicus* doctor, < *medērī* to heal]

medicine ball *n.* a heavy ball used for physical training.

medicine man *n.* (among certain peoples, esp. North American Indians) a person believed to have supernatural powers of healing; a magician or sorcerer.

medick *or U.S.* **medic** (ˈmɛdɪk) *n.* any of various small plants having yellow or purple flowers and trifoliate leaves. [C15: < L *mēdica,* < Gk *mēdikē* (*poa*) Median (grass), a type of clover]

medico (ˈmɛdɪˌkəʊ) *n., pl.* **-cos.** *Inf.* a doctor or medical student. [C17: via It. < L *medicus*]

medieval *or* **mediaeval** (ˌmɛdɪˈiːvᵊl) *adj.* **1.** of, relating to, or in the style of the Middle Ages. **2.** *Inf.* old-fashioned; primitive. [C19: < NL *medium aevum* the middle age]

Medieval Greek *n.* the Greek language from the 7th century A.D. to shortly after the sacking of Constantinople in 1204. Also called: **Middle Greek, Byzantine Greek.**

medievalism *or* **mediaevalism** (ˌmɛdɪˈiːvəˌlɪzəm) *n.* **1.** the beliefs, life, or style of the Middle Ages or devotion to those. **2.** a belief, custom, or point of style copied or surviving from the Middle Ages.

medievalist *or* **mediaevalist** (ˌmɛdɪˈiːvəlɪst) *n.* a student or devotee of the Middle Ages.

Medieval Latin *n.* the Latin language as used throughout Europe in the Middle Ages.

mediocre (ˌmiːdɪˈəʊkə) *adj. Often derog.* average or ordinary in quality. [C16: via F < L *mediocris* moderate, lit.: halfway up the mountain, < *medius* middle + *ocris* stony mountain]

mediocrity (ˌmiːdɪˈɒkrɪtɪ, ˌmɛd-) *n., pl.* **-ties. 1.** the state or quality of being mediocre. **2.** a mediocre person or thing.

Medit. *abbrev. for* Mediterranean.

meditate (ˈmɛdɪˌteɪt) *vb.* **1.** (*intr.;* foll. by *on* or *upon*) to think about something deeply. **2.** (*intr.*) to reflect deeply on spiritual matters, esp. as a religious act. **3.** (*tr.*) to plan, consider, or think of doing (something). [C16: < L *meditārī* to reflect upon] —**ˈmeditative** *adj.* —**ˈmeditatively** *adv.* —**ˈmediˌtator** *n.*

meditation (ˌmɛdɪˈteɪʃən) *n.* **1.** the act of meditating; reflection. **2.** contemplation of spiritual matters, esp. as a religious practice.

Mediterranean (ˌmɛdɪtəˈreɪnɪən) *n.* **1.** short for the **Mediterranean Sea,** the sea between S Europe, N Africa, and SW Asia. **2.** a native or inhabitant of a Mediterranean country. ~*adj.* **3.** of, relating to, situated or dwelling near the Mediterranean Sea. **4.** denoting a postulated subdivision of the Caucasoid race, characterized by slender build and dark complexion. **5.** *Meteorol.* (of a climate) characterized by hot summers and relatively warm winters when most of the annual rainfall occurs. **6.** (*often not cap.*) *Obs.* situated in the middle of a landmass; inland. [C16: < L *mediterrāneus,* < *medius* middle + *-terrāneus,* < *terra* land]

medium (ˈmiːdɪəm) *adj.* **1.** midway between extremes; average. ~*n., pl.* **-dia** *or* **-diums. 2.** an intermediate or middle state, degree, or condition; mean: *the happy medium.* **3.** an intervening substance or agency for transmitting or producing an effect; vehicle. **4.** a means or agency for communicating or diffusing information, news, etc., to the public. **5.** a person supposedly used as a spiritual intermediary between the dead and the living. **6.** the substance in which specimens of animals and plants are preserved or displayed. **7.** *Biol.* Also called: **culture medium.** a nutritive substance in which cultures of bacteria or fungi are grown. **8.** the substance or surroundings in which an organism naturally lives or grows. **9.** *Art.* **a.** the category of a work of art, as determined by its materials and methods of production. **b.** the materials used in a work of art. **10.** any solvent in which pigments are mixed and thinned. [C16: < L: neuter sing. of *medius* middle]

▷ **Usage.** Careful writers and speakers do not use *media* as a singular noun when referring to a medium of mass communication: *television is a valuable medium* (not *media*) *for advertising.*

medium-dated *adj.* (of a gilt-edged security) having between five and fifteen years to run before redemption. Cf. **long-dated, short-dated.**

medium frequency *n.* a radio-frequency band or radio frequency lying between 3000 and 300 kilohertz. Abbrev: **MF.**

medium wave *n.* **a.** a radio wave with a wavelength between 100 and 1000 metres. **b.** (*as modifier*): *a medium-wave broadcast.*

medlar (ˈmɛdlə) *n.* **1.** a small Eurasian tree. **2.** its fruit, which resembles the crab apple and is not edible until it has begun to decay. [C14: < OF *medlier,* < L *mespilum* medlar fruit, < Gk *mespilon*]

medley (ˈmɛdlɪ) *n.* **1.** a mixture of various types or elements. **2.** a musical composition consisting of various tunes arranged as a continuous whole. **3.** Also called: **medley relay. a.** *Swimming.* a race in which a different stroke is used for each length. **b.** *Athletics.* a relay race in which each leg has a different distance. [C14: < OF *medlee,* < *medler* to mix, quarrel]

medulla (mɪˈdʌlə) *n., pl.* **-las** *or* **-lae** (-liː). **1.** *Anat.* **a.** the innermost part of an organ or structure. **b.** short for **medulla oblongata. 2.** *Bot.* another name for **pith** (sense 4). [C17: < L: marrow, prob. < *medius* middle] —**me'dullary** *or* **me'dullar** *adj.*

medulla oblongata (ˌɒblɒŋ'gɑːtə) *n., pl.* **medullа oblongatas** *or* **medullae oblongatae** (mɪ'dʌliː ˌɒblɒŋ'gɑːtiː). the lower stalklike section of the brain, continuous with the spinal cord, containing control centres for the heart and lungs. [C17: NL: oblong-shaped medulla]

medusa (mɪ'djuːzə) *n., pl.* **-sas** *or* **-sae** (-ziː). another name for **jellyfish** (sense 1). [C18: < the likeness of its tentacles to the snaky locks of *Medusa*, the Gorgon] —**me'dusoid** *adj., n.*

meed (miːd) *n. Arch.* a recompense; reward. [OE: wages]

meek (miːk) *adj.* **1.** patient, long-suffering, or submissive; humble. **2.** spineless or spiritless; compliant. [C12: rel. to ON *mjūkr* amenable] —**'meekly** *adv.* —**'meekness** *n.*

meerkat ('mɪəˌkæt) *n.* any of several South African mongooses, esp. the slender-tailed meerkat or suricate, which has a lemur-like face and four-toed feet. [C19: < Du.: sea-cat]

meerschaum ('mɪəʃəm) *n.* **1.** a white, yellowish, or pink compact earthy mineral consisting of hydrated magnesium silicate: used to make tobacco pipes and as a building stone. **2.** a tobacco pipe having a bowl made of this mineral. [C18: < G *Meerschaum* lit.: sea foam]

meet[1] (miːt) *vb.* **meeting, met. 1.** (sometimes foll. by *up* or (U.S.) *with*) to come together (with), either by design or by accident; encounter. **2.** to come into or be in conjunction or contact with (something or each other). **3.** (*tr.*) to come to or be at the place of arrival of: *to meet a train.* **4.** to make the acquaintance of or be introduced to (someone or each other). **5.** to gather in the company of (someone or each other). **6.** to come into the presence of (someone or each other) as opponents. **7.** (*tr.*) to cope with effectively; satisfy: *to meet someone's demands.* **8.** (*tr.*) to be apparent to (esp. in **meet the eye**). **9.** (*tr.*) to return or counter: *to meet a blow with another.* **10.** to agree with (someone or each other): *we met him on the price he suggested.* **11.** (*tr.;* sometimes foll. by *with*) to experience; suffer: *he met his death in a road accident.* **12.** (*intr.*) to occur together: *courage and kindliness met in him.* ~*n.* **13.** the assembly of hounds, huntsmen, etc., prior to a hunt. **14.** a meeting, esp. a sports meeting. [OE *mētan*] —**'meeter** *n.*

meet[2] (miːt) *adj. Arch.* proper, fitting, or correct. [C13: < var. of OE *gemǣte*] —**'meetly** *adv.*

meeting ('miːtɪŋ) *n.* **1.** an act of coming together; encounter. **2.** an assembly or gathering. **3.** a conjunction or union. **4.** a sporting competition, as of athletes, or of horse racing.

meeting house *n.* the place in which certain religious groups, esp. Quakers, hold their meetings for worship.

mega- *combining form.* **1.** denoting 10^6: *megawatt.* Symbol: M **2.** (in computer technology) denoting 2^{20} (1 048 576): *megabyte.* **3.** large or great: *megalith.* **4.** *Inf.* greatest: *megastar.* [< Gk *megas* huge, powerful]

megabit ('mɛgəˌbɪt) *n. Computers.* **1.** one million bits. **2.** 2^{20} bits.

megabuck ('mɛgəˌbʌk) *n. U.S. & Canad. sl.* a million dollars.

megacephaly (ˌmɛgə'sɛfəlɪ) *or* **megalocephaly** *n.* the condition of having an unusually large head or cranial capacity. —**megacephalic** (ˌmɛgəsɪ'fælɪk), **ˌmega'cephalous, ˌmegaloce'phalic,** *or* **ˌmegalo'cephalous** *adj.*

megacycle ('mɛgəˌsaɪk°l) *n.* a former unit of frequency equal to one million cycles per second; megahertz.

megadeath ('mɛgəˌdɛθ) *n.* the death of a million people, esp. in a nuclear war or attack.

megaflop ('mɛgəˌflɒp) *n. Computers.* a measure of processing speed, consisting of a million floating-point operations a second. [C20: < MEGA- + *flo(ating) p(oint)*]

megahertz ('mɛgəˌhɜːts) *n., pl.* **megahertz.** one million hertz. Former name: **megacycle.**

megalith ('mɛgəlɪθ) *n.* a stone of great size, esp. one forming part of a prehistoric monument. —**ˌmega'lithic** *adj.*

megalo- *or before a vowel* **megal-** *combining form.* indicating greatness or abnormal size: *megalopolis.* [< Gk *megas* great]

megalomania (ˌmɛgələʊ'meɪnɪə) *n.* **1.** a mental illness characterized by delusions of grandeur, power, wealth, etc. **2.** *Inf.* a lust or craving for power. —**ˌmegalo'maniac** *adj., n.* —**megalomaniacal** (ˌmɛgələʊmə'naɪək°l) *adj.*

megalopolis (ˌmɛgə'lɒpəlɪs) *n.* an urban complex, usually comprising several large towns. [C20: MEGALO- + Gk *polis* city] —**megalopolitan** (ˌmɛgələ'pɒlɪt°n) *adj., n.*

megalosaur ('mɛgələʊˌsɔː) *n.* any very large Jurassic or Cretaceous bipedal carnivorous dinosaur. [C19: < NL *megalosaurus,* < MEGALO- + Gk *sauros* lizard]

megaphone ('mɛgəˌfəʊn) *n.* a funnel-shaped instrument used to amplify the voice. See also **loud-hailer.** —**megaphonic** (ˌmɛgə'fɒnɪk) *adj.*

megapode ('mɛgəˌpəʊd) *n.* any of various ground-living gallinaceous birds of Australia, New Guinea, and adjacent islands. Their eggs incubate in mounds of sand, rotting vegetation, etc., by natural heat.

megathere ('mɛgəˌθɪə) *n.* any of various gigantic extinct American sloths, common in late Cenozoic times. [C19: < NL *megathērium,* < MEGA- + *-there,* < Gk *thērion* wild beast]

megaton ('mɛgəˌtʌn) *n.* **1.** one million tons. **2.** an explosive power, esp. of a nuclear weapon, equal to the power of one million tons of TNT.

megawatt ('mɛgəˌwɒt) *n.* one million watts.

Megger ('mɛgə) *n. Trademark.* an instrument that generates a high voltage in order to test the resistance of insulation, etc.

megilp *or* **magilp** (mə'gɪlp) *n.* an oil-painting medium of linseed oil mixed with mastic varnish or turpentine. [C18: <?]

megohm ('mɛgˌəʊm) *n.* one million ohms.

megrim ('miːgrɪm) *n. Arch.* **1.** a caprice. **2.** a migraine. **3.** (*pl.*) *Rare.* a fit of depression. **4.** (*pl.*) a disease of horses and cattle; staggers. [C14: see MIGRAINE]

meiosis (maɪ'əʊsɪs) *n., pl.* **-ses** (-ˌsiːz). **1.** a type of cell division in which a nucleus divides into four daughter nuclei, each containing half the chromosome number of the parent nucleus. **2.** *Rhetoric.* another word for **litotes.** [C16: via NL < Gk, < *meioun* to diminish, < *meiōn* less] —**meiotic** (maɪ'ɒtɪk) *adj.* —**mei'otically** *adv.*

Meistersinger ('maɪstəˌsɪŋə) *n., pl.* **-singer** *or* **-singers.** a member of one of the German guilds organized to compose and perform poetry and music, esp. in the 15th and 16th centuries. [C19: < G *Meistersinger* master singer]

melaleuca (ˌmɛlə'luːkə) *n.* any shrub or tree of the mostly Australian genus *Melaleuca,* found in sandy or swampy regions. [C19: NL < Gk *melas* black + *leukos* white, < its black trunk and white branches]

melamine ('mɛləˌmiːn) *n.* **1.** a colourless crystalline compound used in making synthetic resins. **2.** a resin produced from melamine (**melamine resin**) or a material made from this resin. [C19: < G *Melamin,* < *Melam* distillate of ammonium thiocyanate, with *-am* representing *ammonia*]

melancholia (ˌmɛlən'kəʊlɪə) *n.* a former name for **depression** (sense 3). —**ˌmelan'choliˌac** *adj., n.*

melancholy ('mɛlənkəlɪ) *n., pl.* **-cholies. 1.** a tendency to gloominess or depression. **2.** a sad thoughtful state of mind. **3.** *Arch.* **a.** a gloomy character. **b.** one of the four bodily humours; black bile. ~*adj.* **4.** characterized by, causing, or expressing sadness, dejection, etc. [C14: via OF < LL *melancholia,* < Gk, < *melas* black + *kholē* bile] —**'melanˌcholic** *adj., n.*

Melanesian (ˌmɛlə'niːʒən, -ʒɪən) *adj.* **1.** of or relating to Melanesia (a division of islands in the Pacific), its people, or their languages. ~*n.* **2.** a native or inhabitant of Melanesia: generally

Negroid with frizzy hair and small stature. **3.** a group or branch of languages spoken in Melanesia.

melange *or* **mélange** (meɪˈlɑːnʒ) *n.* a mixture; confusion. [C17: < F *mêler* to mix]

melanin (ˈmɛlənɪn) *n.* any of a group of black or dark brown pigments present in the hair, skin, and eyes of man and animals: produced in excess in certain skin diseases and in melanomas.

melanism (ˈmɛləˌnɪzəm) *n.* **1.** the condition in man and animals of having dark-coloured or black skin, feathers, etc. **2.** another name for **melanosis.** —ˌ**melaˈnistic** *adj.*

melano- *or before a vowel* **melan-** *combining form.* black or dark: *melanin; melanism; melanoma.* [< Gk *melas* black]

melanoma (ˌmɛləˈnəʊmə) *n., pl.* **-mas** *or* **-mata** (-mətə). *Pathol.* a tumour composed of darkly pigmented cells.

melanosis (ˌmɛləˈnəʊsɪs) *or* **melanism** (ˈmɛləˌnɪzəm) *n. Pathol.* a skin condition characterized by excessive deposits of melanin. —**melanotic** (ˌmɛləˈnɒtɪk) *adj.*

Melba (ˈmɛlbə) *n.* **do a Melba.** *Austral sl.* to make repeated farewell appearances. [C20: after Dame Nellie *Melba* (1861–1931), Australian operatic soprano]

Melba toast *n.* very thin crisp toast. [C20: after Dame Nellie *Melba*]

meld (mɛld) *vb.* **1.** (in some card games) to declare or lay down (cards), which then score points. ~*n.* **2.** the act of melding. **3.** a set of cards for melding. [C19: < G *melden* to announce]

melee *or* **mêlée** (ˈmɛleɪ) *n.* a noisy riotous fight or brawl. [C17: < F *mêlée,* < *mêler* to mix]

meliorate (ˈmiːlɪəˌreɪt) *vb.* a variant of **ameliorate.** —ˌ**melioˈration** *n.* —**meliorative** (ˈmiːlɪərətɪv) *adj., n.*

melisma (mɪˈlɪzmə) *n., pl.* **-mata** (-mətə) *or* **-mas.** *Music.* an expressive vocal phrase or passage consisting of several notes sung to one syllable. [C19: < Gk: melody]

melliferous (mɪˈlɪfərəs) *or* **mellific** (mɪˈlɪfɪk) *adj.* forming or producing honey. [C17: < L *mellifer,* < *mel* honey + *ferre* to bear]

mellifluous (mɪˈlɪflʊəs) *or* **mellifluent** *adj.* (of sounds or utterances) smooth or honeyed; sweet. [C15: < LL *mellifluus,* < L *mel* honey + *fluere* to flow] —**melˈlifluously** *adv.* —**melˈlifluousness** *or* **melˈlifluence** *n.*

mellow (ˈmɛləʊ) *adj.* **1.** (esp. of fruits) full-flavoured; sweet; ripe. **2.** (esp. of wines) well-matured. **3.** (esp. of colours or sounds) soft or rich. **4.** kind-hearted, esp. through maturity or old age. **5.** genial, as through the effects of alcohol. **6.** (of soil) soft and loamy. ~*vb.* **7.** to make or become mellow. [C15: ? < OE *meru* soft (as through ripeness)] —ˈ**mellowness** *n.*

melodeon *or* **melodion** (mɪˈləʊdɪən) *n. Music.* **1.** a type of small accordion. **2.** a type of keyboard instrument similar to the harmonium. [C19: < G, < *Melodie* melody]

melodic (mɪˈlɒdɪk) *adj.* **1.** of or relating to melody. **2.** of or relating to a part in a piece of music. **3.** melodious. —**meˈlodically** *adv.*

melodic minor scale *n. Music.* a minor scale modified from the natural by the sharpening of the sixth and seventh when taken in ascending order and the restoration of their original pitches when taken in descending order.

melodious (mɪˈləʊdɪəs) *adj.* **1.** having a tune that is pleasant to the ear. **2.** of or relating to melody; melodic. —**meˈlodiously** *adv.* —**meˈlodiousness** *n.*

melodist (ˈmɛlədɪst) *n.* **1.** a composer of melodies. **2.** a singer.

melodize *or* **-ise** (ˈmɛləˌdaɪz) *vb.* **1.** (*tr.*) to provide with a melody. **2.** (*tr.*) to make melodious. **3.** (*intr.*) to sing or play melodies. —ˈ**meloˌdizer** *or* **-iser** *n.*

melodrama (ˈmɛləˌdrɑːmə) *n.* **1.** a play, film, etc., characterized by extravagant action and emotion. **2.** (formerly) a romantic drama characterized by sensational incident, music, and song. **3.** overdramatic emotion or behaviour. [C19: < F *mélodrame,* < Gk *melos* song + *drame* DRAMA] —**melodramatist** (ˌmɛləˈdræmətɪst) *n.* —**melodramatic** (ˌmɛlədrəˈmætɪk) *adj.* —ˌ**melodraˈmatics** *pl. n.* —ˌ**melodraˈmatically** *adv.*

melody (ˈmɛlədɪ) *n., pl.* **-dies.** **1.** *Music.* **a.** a succession of notes forming a distinctive sequence; tune. **b.** the horizontally represented aspect of the structure of a piece of music. Cf. **harmony** (sense 4b). **2.** sounds that are pleasant because of tone or arrangement, esp. words of poetry. [C13: < OF, < LL *melōdia,* < Gk *melōidia,* < *melos* song + *aoidein* to sing]

melon (ˈmɛlən) *n.* **1.** any of several varieties of trailing plants (see **muskmelon, watermelon**), cultivated for their edible fruit. **2.** the fruit of any of these plants, which has a hard rind and juicy flesh. [C14: via OF < LL *mēlo,* form of *mēlopepō,* < Gk, < *mēlon* apple + *pepōn* gourd]

Melpomene (mɛlˈpɒmɪnɪ) *n. Greek myth.* the Muse of tragedy.

melt (mɛlt) *vb.* **melting, melted; melted** *or* **molten.** **1.** to liquefy (a solid) or (of a solid) to become liquefied, as a result of the action of heat. **2.** to become or make liquid; dissolve. **3.** (often foll. by *away*) to disappear; fade. **4.** (foll. by *down*) to melt (metal scrap) for reuse. **5.** (often foll. by *into*) to blend or cause to blend gradually. **6.** to make or become emotional or sentimental; soften. ~*n.* **7.** the act or process of melting. **8.** something melted or an amount melted. [OE *meltan* to digest] —ˈ**meltable** *adj.* —ˈ**melter** *n.* —ˈ**meltingly** *adv.*

meltdown (ˈmɛltˌdaʊn) *n.* (in a nuclear reactor) the melting of the fuel rods as a result of a defect in the cooling system, with the possible escape of radiation.

melting point *n.* the temperature at which a solid turns into a liquid.

melting pot *n.* **1.** a pot in which metals or other substances are melted, esp. in order to mix them. **2.** an area in which many races, ideas, etc., are mixed.

melton (ˈmɛltən) *n.* a heavy smooth woollen fabric with a short nap. Also called: **melton cloth.** [C19: < *Melton Mowbray,* Leicestershire, a former centre for making this]

meltwater (ˈmɛltˌwɔːtə) *n.* melted snow or ice.

mem. *abbrev. for:* **1.** member. **2.** memoir. **3.** memorandum. **4.** memorial.

member (ˈmɛmbə) *n.* **1.** a person who belongs to a club, political party, etc. **2.** any individual plant or animal in a taxonomic group. **3.** any part of an animal body, such as a limb. **4.** any part of a plant, such as a petal, root, etc. **5.** *Maths, logic.* any individual object belonging to a set or logical class. **6.** a component part of a building or construction. [C13: < L *membrum* limb, part] —ˈ**memberless** *adj.*

Member (ˈmɛmbə) *n.* (*sometimes not cap.*) **1.** short for **Member of Parliament.** **2.** short for **Member of Congress.** **3.** a member of some other legislative body.

Member of Congress *n.* a member of the U.S. Congress, esp. of the House of Representatives.

Member of Parliament *n.* a member of the House of Commons or similar legislative body, as in many Commonwealth countries.

membership (ˈmɛmbəʃɪp) *n.* **1.** the members of an organization collectively. **2.** the state of being a member.

membrane (ˈmɛmbreɪn) *n.* **1.** any thin pliable sheet of material. **2.** a pliable sheetlike usually fibrous tissue that covers, lines, or connects plant and animal organs or cells. [C16: < L *membrāna* skin covering a part of the body, < *membrum* MEMBER] —**membranous** (ˈmɛmbrənəs) *or* **membraneous** (mɛmˈbreɪnɪəs) *adj.*

memento (mɪˈmɛntəʊ) *n., pl.* **-tos** *or* **-toes.** something that reminds one of past events; a souvenir. [C15: < L, imperative of *meminisse* to remember]

memento mori (ˈmɔːriː) *n., pl.* **memento mori.**

an object, such as a skull, intended to remind people of death. [C16: L: remember you must die]

memo (ˈmɛməʊ, ˈmiːməʊ) *n., pl.* **memos.** short for **memorandum.**

memoir (ˈmɛmwɑː) *n.* **1.** a biography or historical account, esp. one based on personal knowledge. **2.** an essay, as on a specialized topic. [C16: < F, < L *memoria* MEMORY] —ˈ**memoirist** *n.*

memoirs (ˈmɛmwɑːz) *pl. n.* **1.** a collection of reminiscences about a period, series of events, etc., written from personal experience or special sources. **2.** an autobiographical record. **3.** a record, as of transactions of a society, etc.

memorabilia (ˌmɛmərəˈbɪlɪə) *pl. n., sing.* **-rabile** (-ˈræbɪlɪ). **1.** memorable events or things. **2.** objects connected with famous people or events. [C17: < L, < *memorābilis* MEMORABLE]

memorable (ˈmɛmərəbᵊl) *adj.* worth remembering or easily remembered. [C15: < L *memorābilis,* < *memorāre* to recall, < *memor* mindful] —ˌ**memoraˈbility** *n.* —ˈ**memorably** *adv.*

memorandum (ˌmɛməˈrændəm) *n., pl.* **-dums** *or* **-da** (-də). **1.** a written statement, record, or communication. **2.** a note of things to be remembered. **3.** an informal diplomatic communication. **4.** *Law.* a short written summary of the terms of a transaction. ~Often (esp. for senses 1, 2) shortened to **memo.** [C15: < L: (something) to be remembered]

memorial (mɪˈmɔːrɪəl) *adj.* **1.** serving to preserve the memory of the dead or a past event. **2.** of or involving memory. ~*n.* **3.** something serving as a remembrance. **4.** a written statement of facts submitted to a government, authority, etc., in conjunction with a petition. **5.** an informal diplomatic paper. [C14: < LL *memoriāle* a reminder, neuter of *memoriālis*] —**meˈmorially** *adv.*

memorialize *or* **-ise** (mɪˈmɔːrɪəˌlaɪz) *vb.* (*tr.*) **1.** to honour or commemorate. **2.** to present or address a memorial to.

memorize *or* **-ise** (ˈmɛməˌraɪz) *vb.* (*tr.*) to commit to memory; learn so as to remember.

memory (ˈmɛmərɪ) *n., pl.* **-ries. 1. a.** the ability of the mind to store and recall past sensations, thoughts, knowledge, etc.: *he can do it from memory.* **b.** the part of the brain that appears to have this function. **2.** the sum of everything retained by the mind. **3.** a particular recollection of an event, person, etc. **4.** the time over which recollection extends: *within his memory.* **5.** commemoration or remembrance: *in memory of our leader.* **6.** the state of being remembered, as after death. **7.** Also called: **store.** a part of a computer in which information is stored for immediate use by the central processing unit. [C14: < OF *memorie,* < L *memoria,* < *memor* mindful]

memsahib (ˈmɛmˌsɑːɪb, -hɪb) *n.* (formerly, in India) a term of respect used for a European married woman. [C19: < MA'AM + SAHIB]

men (mɛn) *n.* the plural of **man.**

menace (ˈmɛnɪs) *vb.* **1.** to threaten with violence, danger, etc. ~*n.* **2.** *Literary.* a threat. **3.** something menacing; a source of danger. **4.** *Inf.* a nuisance. [C13: ult. rel. to L *minax* threatening, < *minārī* to threaten] —ˈ**menacer** *n.* —ˈ**menacing** *adj.* —ˈ**menacingly** *adv.*

ménage (meɪˈnɑːʒ) *n.* the persons of a household. [C17: < F, < Vulgar L (unattested) *mansiōnāticum* household]

ménage à trois *French.* (menaʒ a trwɑ) *n., pl.* ***ménages à trois*** (menaʒ a trwɑ). a sexual arrangement involving a married couple and the lover of one of them. [lit.: household of three]

menagerie (mɪˈnædʒərɪ) *n.* **1.** a collection of wild animals kept for exhibition. **2.** the place where such animals are housed. [C18: < F: household management, which formerly included care of domestic animals]

mend (mɛnd) *vb.* **1.** (*tr.*) to repair (something broken or unserviceable). **2.** to improve or undergo improvement; reform (often in **mend one's ways**). **3.** (*intr.*) to heal or recover. **4.** (*intr.*) (of conditions) to improve; become better. ~*n.* **5.** the act of repairing. **6.** a mended area, esp. on a garment. **7. on the mend.** becoming better, esp. in health. [C12: < AMEND] —ˈ**mendable** *adj.* —ˈ**mender** *n.*

mendacity (mɛnˈdæsɪtɪ) *n., pl.* **-ties. 1.** the tendency to be untruthful. **2.** a falsehood. [C17: < LL *mendācitās,* < L *mendāx* untruthful] —**mendacious** (mɛnˈdeɪʃəs) *adj.* —**menˈdaciously** *adv.*

mendelevium (ˌmɛndɪˈliːvɪəm) *n.* a transuranic element artificially produced by bombardment of einsteinium. Symbol: Md; atomic no.: 101; half-life of most stable isotope, ^{258}Md: 60 days (approx.). [C20: after D. I. *Mendeleyev* (1843–1907), Russian chemist who devised the first form of the periodic table]

Mendel's laws (ˈmɛndᵊlz) *pl. n.* the principles of heredity proposed by Gregor Mendel (1822–84), Austrian monk and botanist. The **Law of Segregation** states that every somatic cell of an individual carries a pair of hereditary units for each character: the pairs separate during meiosis so that each gamete carries only one unit of each pair. The **Law of Independent Assortment** states that the separation of the units of each pair is not influenced by that of any other pair.

mendicant (ˈmɛndɪkənt) *adj.* **1.** begging. **2.** (of a member of a religious order) dependent on alms for sustenance. ~*n.* **3.** a mendicant friar. **4.** a less common word for **beggar.** [C16: < L *mendīcāre,* < *mendīcus* beggar, < *mendus* flaw] —ˈ**mendicancy** *or* **mendicity** (mɛnˈdɪsɪtɪ) *n.*

meneer (məˈnɪə) *n.* a S. African title of address equivalent to *sir* when used alone or *Mr* when placed before a name. [Afrik.]

menfolk (ˈmɛnˌfəʊk) *pl. n.* men collectively, esp. the men of a particular family.

menhaden (mɛnˈheɪdᵊn) *n., pl.* **-den.** a marine North American fish: source of fish meal, fertilizer, and oil. [C18: < Algonquian; prob. rel. to another Amerind word, *munnawhatteaúg* fertilizer]

menhir (ˈmɛnhɪə) *n.* a single standing stone, dating from prehistoric times. [C19: < Breton *men* stone + *hir* long]

menial (ˈmiːnɪəl) *adj.* **1.** consisting of or occupied with work requiring little skill, esp. domestic duties. **2.** of, involving, or befitting servants. **3.** servile. ~*n.* **4.** a domestic servant. **5.** a servile person. [C14: < Anglo-Norman *meignial,* < OF *meinie* household]

meninges (mɪˈnɪndʒiːz) *pl. n., sing.* **meninx** (ˈmiːnɪŋks). the three membranes (**dura mater, arachnoid, pia mater**) that envelop the brain and spinal cord. [C17: < Gk, pl. of *meninx* membrane] —**meningeal** (mɪˈnɪndʒɪəl) *adj.*

meningitis (ˌmɛnɪnˈdʒaɪtɪs) *n.* inflammation of the membranes that surround the brain or spinal cord, caused by infection. —**meningitic** (ˌmɛnɪnˈdʒɪtɪk) *adj.*

meningococcus (mɛˌnɪŋgəʊˈkɒkəs) *n., pl.* **-cocci** (-ˈkɒksaɪ). the bacterium that causes cerebrospinal meningitis. —**meˌningoˈcoccal** *adj.*

meniscus (mɪˈnɪskəs) *n., pl.* **-nisci** (-ˈnɪsaɪ) *or* **-niscuses. 1.** the curved upper surface of a liquid standing in a tube, produced by the surface tension. **2.** a crescent-shaped lens; a concavo-convex or convexo-concave lens. [C17: < NL, < Gk *mēniskos* crescent, dim. of *mēnē* moon] —**meˈniscoid** *adj.*

Mennonite (ˈmɛnəˌnaɪt) *n.* a member of a Protestant sect that rejects infant baptism and Church organization, and in most cases refuses military service, public office, and the taking of oaths. [C16: < G *Mennonit,* after *Menno* Simons (1496–1561), Frisian religious leader]

meno (ˈmɛnəʊ) *adv. Music.* to be played less quickly, less softly, etc. [< It., < L *minus* less]

meno- *combining form.* menstruation. [< Gk *mēn* month]

menopause (ˈmɛnəʊˌpɔːz) *n.* the period during which a woman's menstrual cycle ceases, normally at an age of 45 to 50. [C19: < F, < Gk *mēn* month + *pausis* halt] —ˌ**meno'pausal** *adj.*

menorah (mɪ'nɔːrə) *n. Judaism.* **1.** a seven-branched candelabrum used in the Temple and now an emblem of Judaism and the badge of the state of Israel. **2.** a similar lamp lit during the Chanukah festival. [< Heb.: candlestick]

menorrhagia (ˌmɛnɔː'reɪdʒɪə) *n.* excessive bleeding during menstruation.

menorrhoea (ˌmɛnə'rɪə) *n.* normal bleeding in menstruation.

menses ('mɛnsiːz) *n., pl.* **menses. 1.** another name for **menstruation. 2.** the period of time during which one menstruation occurs. **3.** the matter discharged during menstruation. [C16: < L, pl. of *mensis* month]

Menshevik ('mɛnʃɪvɪk) *or* **Menshevist** *n.* a member of the moderate wing of the Russian Social Democratic Party. Cf. **Bolshevik.** [C20: < Russian, lit.: minority, < *menshe* less, < *malo* few] —'**Menshevism** *n.*

menstruate ('mɛnstrʊˌeɪt) *vb.* (*intr.*) to undergo menstruation. [C17: < L *menstruāre,* < *mensis* month]

menstruation (ˌmɛnstrʊ'eɪʃən) *n.* the approximately monthly discharge of blood and cellular debris from the uterus by nonpregnant women from puberty to the menopause. —'**menstrual** *or* '**menstruous** *adj.*

menstruum ('mɛnstrʊəm) *n., pl.* **-struums** *or* **-strua** (-strʊə). a solvent, esp. one used in the preparation of a drug. [C17 (meaning: solvent), C14 (menstrual discharge): < Med. L, < L *mēnstruus* monthly, < *mēnsis* month; from alchemical comparison between a base metal being transmuted into gold and the supposed action of the menses]

mensurable ('mɛnsjʊrəbᵊl, -ʃə-) *adj.* a less common word for **measurable.** [C17: < LL *mēnsūrābilis,* < *mēnsūra* MEASURE] —ˌ**mensura'bility** *n.*

mensural ('mɛnʃərəl) *adj.* **1.** of or involving measure. **2.** *Music.* of or relating to music in which notes have fixed values. [C17: < LL *mēnsūrālis,* < *mēnsūra* MEASURE]

mensuration (ˌmɛnʃə'reɪʃən) *n.* **1.** the study of the measurement of geometric magnitudes such as length. **2.** the act or process of measuring. —**mensurative** ('mɛnʃərətɪv) *adj.*

-ment *suffix forming nouns, esp. from verbs.* **1.** indicating state, condition, or quality: *enjoyment.* **2.** indicating the result or product of an action: *embankment.* **3.** indicating process or action: *management.* [< F, < L *-mentum*]

mental ('mɛntᵊl) *adj.* **1.** of or involving the mind. **2.** occurring only in the mind: *mental arithmetic.* **3.** affected by mental illness: *a mental patient.* **4.** concerned with mental illness: *a mental hospital.* **5.** *Sl.* insane. [C15: < LL *mentālis,* < L *mēns* mind] —'**mentally** *adv.*

mental handicap *n.* any intellectual disability resulting from injury to the brain or from abnormal neurological development. —**mentally handicapped** *adj.*

mental healing *n.* the healing of a disorder by mental concentration or suggestion.

mentalism ('mɛntᵊˌlɪzəm) *n. Philosophy.* the doctrine that mind is the fundamental reality and that objects of knowledge exist only as aspects of the subject's consciousness. —ˌ**mental'istic** *adj.*

mentality (mɛn'tælɪtɪ) *n., pl.* **-ties. 1.** the state or quality of mental or intellectual ability. **2.** a way of thinking; mental inclination or character.

mental reservation *n.* a tacit withholding of full assent or an unexpressed qualification made when taking an oath, making a statement, etc.

menthol ('mɛnθɒl) *n.* an organic compound found in peppermint oil and used as an antiseptic, in inhalants, and as an analgesic. [C19: < G, < L *mentha* MINT[1]]

mentholated ('mɛnθəˌleɪtɪd) *adj.* containing, treated with, or impregnated with menthol.

mention ('mɛnʃən) *vb.* (*tr.*) **1.** to refer to or speak about briefly or incidentally. **2.** to acknowledge or honour. **3. not to mention (something).** to say nothing of (something too obvious to mention). ~*n.* **4.** a recognition or acknowledgment. **5.** a slight reference or allusion. **6.** the act of mentioning. [C14: via OF < L *mentiō* a calling to mind, < *mēns* mind] —'**mentionable** *adj.*

mentor ('mɛntɔː) *n.* a wise or trusted adviser or guide. [C18: < *Mentor,* adviser of Telemachus in the Odyssey]

menu ('mɛnjuː) *n.* **1.** a list of dishes served at a meal or that can be ordered in a restaurant. **2.** a list of options displayed on a visual display unit from which the operator selects an action to be carried out. [C19: < F *menu* small, detailed (list), < L *minūtus* MINUTE[2]]

menuetto (mɛnjʊ'ɛtəʊ) *n., pl.* **-tos.** *Music.* another term for **minuet.** [< It.]

meow, miaou, miaow (mɪ'aʊ, mjaʊ), *or* **miaul** (mɪ'aʊl, mjaʊl) *vb.* **1.** (*intr.*) (of a cat) to make a characteristic crying sound. ~*interj.* **2.** an imitation of this sound.

MEP (in Britain) *abbrev. for* Member of the European Parliament.

mepacrine ('mɛpəkrɪn) *n. Brit.* a drug formerly widely used to treat malaria. [C20: < ME(THYL) + PA(LUDISM + A)CR(ID)INE]

meperidine (mə'pɛrɪˌdiːn, -dɪn) *n.* the U.S. name for **pethidine.** [C20: < METHYL + PIPERIDINE]

Mephistopheles (ˌmɛfɪ'stɒfɪˌliːz) *or* **Mephisto** (mə'fɪstəʊ) *n.* a devil in medieval mythology and the one to whom Faust sold his soul in German legend. —**Mephistophelean** *or* **Mephistophelian** (ˌmɛfɪstə'fiːlɪən) *adj.*

mephitic (mɪ'fɪtɪk) *or* **mephitical** *adj.* **1.** poisonous; foul. **2.** foul-smelling; putrid. [C17: < LL *mephīticus* pestilential]

meprobamate (mə'prəʊbəˌmeɪt, ˌmɛprəʊ'bæmeɪt) *n.* a white bitter powder used as a tranquillizer. [C20: < ME(THYL) + PRO(PYL + *car)bamate* a salt or ester of an amide of carbonic acid]

-mer *suffix forming nouns. Chem.* denoting a substance of a particular class: *monomer; polymer.* [< Gk *meros* part]

mercantile ('mɜːkənˌtaɪl) *adj.* **1.** of, relating to, or characteristic of trade or traders; commercial. **2.** of or relating to mercantilism. [C17: < F, < It., < *mercante* MERCHANT]

mercantilism ('mɜːkəntɪˌlɪzəm) *n. Econ.* a theory prevalent in Europe during the 17th and 18th centuries asserting that the wealth of a nation depends on possession of precious metals and therefore that a government must maximize foreign trade surplus and foster national commercial interests, a merchant marine, the establishment of colonies, etc. —'**mercantilist** *n., adj.*

mercaptan (mɜː'kæptæn) *n.* another name (not in technical use) for **thiol.** [C19: < G, < Med. L *mercurium captans,* lit.: seizing quicksilver]

Mercator projection (mɜː'keɪtə) *n.* a map projection on which parallels and meridians form a rectangular grid, scale being exaggerated with increasing distance from the equator. Also called: **Mercator's projection.** [C17: after G. *Mercator,* Latinized name of G. *Kremer* (1512–94), Flemish cartographer]

mercenary ('mɜːsɪnərɪ, -sɪnrɪ) *adj.* **1.** influenced by greed or desire for gain. **2.** of or relating to a mercenary or mercenaries. ~*n., pl.* **-naries. 3.** a man hired to fight for a foreign army, etc. **4.** *Rare.* any person who works solely for pay. [C16: < L *mercēnārius,* < *mercēs* wages]

mercer ('mɜːsə) *n. Brit.* a dealer in textile fabrics and fine cloth. [C13: < OF *mercier* dealer, < Vulgar L, < L *merx* wares] —'**mercery** *n.*

mercerize *or* **-ise** ('mɜːsəˌraɪz) *vb.* (*tr.*) to treat (cotton yarn) with an alkali to increase its strength and reception to dye and impart a lustrous silky appearance. [C19: after John *Mercer* (1791–1866), E maker of textiles]

merchandise *n.* ('mɜːtʃənˌdaɪs, -ˌdaɪz). **1.** commercial goods; commodities. ~*vb.* ('mɜːtʃənˌdaɪz). **2.** to engage in the commercial purchase and sale of (goods or services); trade. [C13: < OF; see MERCHANT]

merchant (ˈmɜːtʃənt) *n.* **1.** a person engaged in the purchase and sale of commodities for profit; trader. **2.** *Chiefly Scot., U.S., & Canad.* a person engaged in retail trade. **3.** (esp. in historical contexts) any trader. **4.** *Derog.* a person dealing or involved in something undesirable: *a gossip merchant.* **5.** (*modifier*) **a.** of the merchant navy: *a merchant sailor.* **b.** of or concerned with trade: *a merchant ship.* ~*vb.* **6.** (*tr.*) to conduct trade in; deal in. [C13: < OF, prob. < Vulgar L, < L *mercārī* to trade, < *merx* wares]

merchantable (ˈmɜːtʃəntəbᵊl) *adj.* suitable for trading.

merchant bank *n. Brit.* a financial institution engaged primarily in accepting foreign bills and underwriting new security issues. —**merchant banker** *n.*

merchantman (ˈmɜːtʃəntmən) *n., pl.* **-men.** a merchant ship.

merchant navy *or* **marine** *n.* the ships or crew engaged in a nation's commercial shipping.

Mercian (ˈmɜːʃɪən) *adj.* **1.** of or relating to Mercia, an Anglo-Saxon kingdom in England, or its dialect. ~*n.* **2.** the dialect of Old and Middle English spoken in Mercia. **3.** a native or inhabitant of Mercia.

merciful (ˈmɜːsɪfʊl) *adj.* showing or giving mercy; compassionate. —ˈ**mercifully** *adv.* —ˈ**mercifulness** *n.*

merciless (ˈmɜːsɪlɪs) *adj.* without mercy; pitiless, cruel, or heartless. —ˈ**mercilessly** *adv.* —ˈ**mercilessness** *n.*

mercurial (mɜːˈkjʊərɪəl) *adj.* **1.** of, like, containing, or relating to mercury. **2.** volatile; lively: *a mercurial temperament.* **3.** (*sometimes cap.*) of, like, or relating to the god or the planet Mercury. ~*n.* **4.** *Med.* any salt of mercury for use as a medicine. [C14: < L *mercuriālis*] —**merˌcuriˈality** *n.* —**merˈcurially** *adv.*

mercuric (mɜːˈkjʊərɪk) *adj.* of or containing mercury in the divalent state.

mercuric chloride *n.* a white poisonous crystalline substance used as a pesticide, antiseptic, and preservative for wood. Formula: $HgCl_2$.

Mercurochrome (məˈkjʊərəˌkrəʊm) *n. Trademark.* a solution of a crystalline compound, used as tropical antibacterial agent.

mercurous (ˈmɜːkjʊrəs) *adj.* of or containing mercury in the monovalent state.

mercury (ˈmɜːkjʊrɪ) *n., pl.* **-ries. 1.** Also called: **quicksilver.** a heavy silvery-white toxic liquid metallic element: used in thermometers, barometers, mercury-vapour lamps, and dental amalgams. Symbol: Hg; atomic no.: 80; atomic wt.: 200.59. **2.** any plant of the genus *Mercurialis.* **3.** *Arch.* a messenger or courier. [C14: < L *Mercurius,* messenger of Jupiter, god of commerce; rel. to *merx* merchandise]

Mercury[1] (ˈmɜːkjʊrɪ) *n. Roman myth.* the messenger of the gods.

Mercury[2] (ˈmɜːkjʊrɪ) *n.* the second smallest planet and the nearest to the sun.

mercury-vapour lamp *n.* a lamp in which an electric discharge through mercury vapour is used to produce a greenish-blue light.

mercy (ˈmɜːsɪ) *n., pl.* **-cies. 1.** compassionate treatment of or attitude towards an offender, adversary, etc., who is in one's power or care; clemency; pity. **2.** the power to show mercy. **3.** a relieving or welcome occurrence or state of affairs. **4. at the mercy of.** in the power of. [C12: < OF, < L *mercēs* recompense, < *merx* goods]

mercy flight *n.* an aircraft flight to bring a seriously ill or injured person to hospital from an isolated community.

mercy killing *n.* another term for **euthanasia.**

mere[1] (mɪə) *adj.* being nothing more than something specified: *a mere child.* [C15: < L *merus* pure] —ˈ**merely** *adv.*

mere[2] (mɪə) *n.* **1.** *Dialect or arch.* a lake or marsh. **2.** *Obs.* the sea or an inlet of it. [OE *mere* sea, lake]

mere[3] (ˈmɛrɪ) *n.* a short flat Maori striking weapon. [< Maori]

-mere *n. combining form.* indicating a part or division. [< Gk *meros* part] —**-meric** *adj. combining form.*

meretricious (ˌmɛrɪˈtrɪʃəs) *adj.* **1.** superficially or garishly attractive. **2.** insincere. **3.** *Arch.* of, like, or relating to a prostitute. [C17: < L *merētrīcius,* < *merētrix* prostitute, < *merēre* to earn money] —ˌ**mereˈtriciously** *adv.* —ˌ**mereˈtriciousness** *n.*

merganser (mɜːˈgænsə) *n., pl.* **-sers** *or* **-ser.** any of several typically crested large marine diving ducks, having a long slender hooked bill with serrated edges. [C18: < NL, < L *mergus* waterfowl, < *mergere* to plunge + *anser* goose]

merge (mɜːdʒ) *vb.* **1.** to meet and join or cause to meet and join. **2.** to blend or cause to blend; fuse. [C17: < L *mergere* to plunge] —ˈ**mergence** *n.*

merger (ˈmɜːdʒə) *n.* **1.** *Commerce.* the combination of two or more companies. **2.** *Law.* the absorption of an estate, interest, offence, etc., into a greater one. **3.** the act of merging or the state of being merged.

meridian (məˈrɪdɪən) *n.* **1. a.** one of the imaginary lines joining the north and south poles at right angles to the equator, designated by degrees of longitude from 0° at Greenwich to 180°. **b.** the great circle running through both poles. **2.** *Astron.* the great circle on the celestial sphere passing through the north and south celestial poles and the zenith and nadir of the observer. **3.** the peak; zenith: *the meridian of his achievements.* **4.** *Obs.* noon. ~*adj.* **5.** along or relating to a meridian. **6.** of or happening at noon. **7.** relating to the peak of something. [C14: < L *merīdiānus* of midday, < *merīdiēs* midday, < *medius* MID[1] + *diēs* day]

meridional (məˈrɪdɪənᵊl) *adj.* **1.** along, relating to, or resembling a meridian. **2.** characteristic of or located in the south, esp. of Europe. ~*n.* **3.** an inhabitant of the south, esp. of France. [C14: < LL *merīdiōnālis* southern; see MERIDIAN]

meringue (məˈræŋ) *n.* **1.** stiffly beaten egg whites mixed with sugar and baked. **2.** a small cake or shell of this mixture, often filled with cream. [C18: < F, <?]

merino (məˈriːnəʊ) *n., pl.* **-nos. 1.** a breed of sheep originating in Spain. **2.** the long fine wool of this sheep. **3.** the yarn made from this wool, often mixed with cotton. ~*adj.* **4.** made from merino wool. [C18: < Sp., <?]

meristem (ˈmɛrɪˌstɛm) *n.* a plant tissue responsible for growth, whose cells divide and differentiate to form the tissues and organs of the plant. [C19: < Gk *meristos* divided, < *merizein,* < *meris* portion] —**meristematic** (ˌmɛrɪstɪˈmætɪk) *adj.*

merit (ˈmɛrɪt) *n.* **1.** worth or superior quality; excellence. **2.** (*often pl.*) a deserving or commendable quality or act. **3.** *Christianity.* spiritual credit granted or received for good works. **4.** the fact or state of deserving; desert. ~*vb.* **5.** (*tr.*) to be worthy of; deserve. [C13: via OF < L *meritum* reward, < *merēre* to deserve]

meritocracy (ˌmɛrɪˈtɒkrəsɪ) *n., pl.* **-cies. 1.** rule by persons chosen for their superior talents or intellect. **2.** the persons constituting such a group. **3.** a social system formed on such a basis. —**meritocratic** (ˌmɛrɪtəˈkrætɪk) *adj.*

meritorious (ˌmɛrɪˈtɔːrɪəs) *adj.* praiseworthy; showing merit. [C15: < L *meritōrius* earning money] —ˌ**meriˈtoriously** *adv.* —ˌ**meriˈtoriousness** *n.*

merits (ˈmɛrɪts) *pl. n.* **1.** the actual and intrinsic rights and wrongs of an issue, esp. in a law case. **2. on its (his, her,** etc.) **merits.** on the intrinsic qualities or virtues.

merle *or* **merl** (mɜːl) *n. Scot.* another name for the (European) **blackbird.** [C15: via OF < L *merula*]

merlin (ˈmɜːlɪn) *n.* a small falcon that has a dark plumage with a black-barred tail. [C14: < OF *esmerillon,* < *esmeril,* of Gmc origin]

mermaid (ˈmɜːˌmeɪd) *n.* an imaginary sea creature fabled to have a woman's head and upper body and a fish's tail. [C14: < MERE[2] + MAID]

merman (ˈmɜːˌmæn) *n., pl.* **-men.** a male counterpart of the mermaid. [C17: see MERMAID]

-merous *adj. combining form.* (in biology) having a certain number or kind of parts. [< Gk *meros* part]

Merovingian (ˌmɛrəʊˈvɪndʒɪən) *adj.* **1.** of or relating to a Frankish dynasty which ruled Gaul and W Germany from about 500 to 751 A.D. ~*n.* **2.** a member or supporter of this dynasty. [C17: < F, < Med. L *Merovingi* offspring of *Merovaeus,* L form of *Merowig,* traditional founder of the line]

merriment (ˈmɛrɪmənt) *n.* gaiety, fun, or mirth.

merry (ˈmɛrɪ) *adj.* **-rier, -riest. 1.** cheerful; jolly. **2.** very funny; hilarious. **3.** *Brit. inf.* slightly drunk. **4. make merry.** to revel; be festive. **5. play merry hell with.** *Inf.* to disturb greatly; disrupt. [OE *merige* agreeable] **—ˈmerrily** *adv.* **—ˈmerriness** *n.*

merry-andrew (-ˈændruː) *n.* a joker, clown, or buffoon. [C17: <?]

merry-go-round *n.* **1.** another name for **roundabout** (sense 1). **2.** a whirl of activity.

merrymaking (ˈmɛrɪˌmeɪkɪŋ) *n.* fun, revelry, or festivity. **—ˈmerryˌmaker** *n.*

merrythought (ˈmɛrɪˌθɔːt) *n. Brit.* a less common word for **wishbone.**

mesa (ˈmeɪsə) *n.* a flat tableland with steep edges, common in the southwestern U.S. [< Sp.: table]

mésalliance (mɛˈzælɪəns) *n.* a marriage with a person of lower social status. [C18: < F: MISALLIANCE]

mescal (mɛˈskæl) *n.* **1.** Also called: **peyote.** a spineless globe-shaped cactus of Mexico and the southwestern U.S. Its button-like tubercles (**mescal buttons**) are chewed by certain Indian tribes for their hallucinogenic effects. **2.** a colourless alcoholic spirit distilled from the fermented juice of certain agave plants. [C19: < American Sp., < Nahuatl *mexcalli* the liquor, < *metl* MAGUEY + *ixcalli* stew]

mescaline *or* **mescalin** (ˈmɛskəˌliːn, -lɪn) *n.* a hallucinogenic drug derived from mescal buttons.

mesdames (ˈmeɪˌdæm) *n.* the plural of **madame** and **madam** (sense 1).

mesdemoiselles (ˌmeɪdmwəˈzɛl) *n.* the plural of **mademoiselle.**

meseems (mɪˈsiːmz) *vb.* (*tr.; takes a clause as object*) *Arch.* it seems to me.

mesembryanthemum (mɪzˌɛmbrɪˈænθɪməm) *n.* any of a genus of plants with succulent leaves and bright flowers with rayed petals which typically open at midday. [C18: NL, < Gk *mesēmbria* noon + *anthemon* flower]

mesencephalon (ˌmɛsɛnˈsɛfəˌlɒn) *n.* the part of the brain that develops from the middle portion of the embryonic neural tube. Nontechnical name: **midbrain.**

mesentery (ˈmɛsəntərɪ, ˈmɛz-) *n., pl.* **-teries.** the double layer of peritoneum that is attached to the back wall of the abdominal cavity and supports most of the small intestine. [C16: < NL *mesenterium,* < MESO- + Gk *enteron* intestine] **—ˌmesenˈteric** *adj.* **—mesenteritis** (mɛsˌɛntəˈraɪtɪs) *n.*

mesh (mɛʃ) *n.* **1.** a network; net. **2.** an open space between the strands of a network. **3.** (*often pl.*) the strands surrounding these spaces. **4.** anything that ensnares, or holds like a net. **5.** the engagement of teeth on interacting gearwheels: *the gears are in mesh.* ~*vb.* **6.** to entangle or become entangled. **7.** (of gear teeth) to engage or cause to engage. **8.** (*intr.;* often foll. by *with*) to coordinate (with). **9.** to work or cause to work in harmony. [C16: prob. < Du. *maesche*]

mesial (ˈmiːzɪəl) *adj. Anat.* another word for **medial** (sense 1). [C19: < MESO- + -IAL]

mesmerism (ˈmɛzməˌrɪzəm) *n. Psychol.* **1.** a hypnotic state induced by the operator's imposition of his will on that of the patient. **2.** an early doctrine concerning this. [C19: after F. A. *Mesmer* (1734–1815), Austrian physician] **—mesmeric** (mɛzˈmɛrɪk) *adj.* **—ˈmesmerist** *n.*

mesmerize *or* **-ise** (ˈmɛzməˌraɪz) *vb.* (*tr.*) **1.** a former word for **hypnotize. 2.** to hold (someone) as if spellbound. **—ˌmesmeriˈzation** *or* **-iˈsation** *n.* **—ˈmesmerˌizer** *or* **-ˌiser** *n.*

mesne (miːn) *adj. Law.* **1.** intermediate or intervening: *a mesne assignment of property.* **2. mesne profits.** rents or profits accruing during the rightful owner's exclusion from his land. [C15: < legal F *meien* in the middle]

meso- *or before a vowel* **mes-** *combining form.* middle or intermediate: *mesomorph.* [< Gk *misos* middle]

mesoblast (ˈmɛsəʊˌblæst) *n.* another name for **mesoderm. —ˌmesoˈblastic** *adj.*

mesocarp (ˈmɛsəʊˌkɑːp) *n.* the middle layer of the pericarp of a fruit, such as the flesh of a peach.

mesocephalic (ˌmɛsəʊsɪˈfælɪk) *Anat.* ~*adj.* **1.** having a medium-sized head. ~*n.* **2.** an individual with such a head. **—mesocephaly** (ˌmɛsəʊˈsɛfəlɪ) *n.*

mesoderm (ˈmɛsəʊˌdɜːm) *n.* the middle germ layer of an animal embryo, giving rise to muscle, blood, bone, connective tissue, etc. **—ˌmesoˈdermal** *or* **ˌmesoˈdermic** *adj.*

Mesolithic (ˌmɛsəʊˈlɪθɪk) *n.* **1.** the period between the Palaeolithic and the Neolithic, in Europe from about 12 000 to 3000 B.C. ~*adj.* **2.** of or relating to the Mesolithic.

mesomorph (ˈmɛsəʊˌmɔːf) *n.* a type of person having a muscular body build with a relatively prominent underlying bone structure.

mesomorphic (ˌmɛsəʊˈmɔːfɪk) *adj.* **1.** *Chem.* existing in or concerned with an intermediate state of matter between a true liquid and a true solid. **2.** relating to or being a mesomorph. ~Also: **mesomorphous. —ˌmesoˈmorphism** *n.*

meson (ˈmiːzɒn) *n.* any of a group of elementary particles that has a rest mass between those of an electron and a proton, and an integral spin. [C20: < MESO- + -ON] **—meˈsonic** *or* **ˈmesic** *adj.*

mesophyte (ˈmɛsəʊˌfaɪt) *n.* any plant that grows in surroundings receiving an average supply of water.

mesosphere (ˈmɛsəʊˌsfɪə) *n.* the atmospheric layer lying between the stratosphere and the thermosphere.

Mesozoic (ˌmɛsəʊˈzəʊɪk) *adj.* **1.** of, denoting, or relating to an era of geological time that began 225 000 000 years ago and lasted about 155 000 000 years. ~*n.* **2. the.** the Mesozoic era.

mesquite *or* **mesquit** (mɛˈskiːt, ˈmɛskiːt) *n.* any of various small trees, esp. a tropical American variety, whose sugary pods (**mesquite beans**) are used as animal fodder. [C19: < Mexican Sp., < Nahautl *mizquitl*]

mess (mɛs) *n.* **1.** a state of confusion or untidiness, esp. if dirty or unpleasant. **2.** a chaotic or troublesome state of affairs; muddle. **3.** *Inf.* a dirty or untidy person or thing. **4.** *Arch.* a portion of food, esp. soft or semiliquid food. **5.** a place where service personnel eat or take recreation. **6.** a group of people, usually servicemen, who eat together. **7.** the meal so taken. ~*vb.* **8.** (*tr.;* often foll. by *up*) to muddle or dirty. **9.** (*intr.*) to make a mess. **10.** (*intr.;* often foll. by *with*) to interfere; meddle. **11.** (*intr.;* often foll. by *with* or *together*) *Mil.* to group together, esp. for eating. [C13: < OF *mes* dish of food, < LL *missus* course (at table), < L *mittere* to send forth]

mess about *or* **around** *vb.* (*adv.*) **1.** (*intr.*) to occupy oneself trivially; potter. **2.** (when *intr.,* often foll. by *with*) to interfere or meddle (with). **3.** (*intr.;* sometimes foll. by *with*) *Chiefly U.S.* to engage in adultery.

message (ˈmɛsɪdʒ) *n.* **1.** a communication, usually brief, from one person or group to another. **2.** an implicit meaning, as in a work of art. **3.** a formal communiqué. **4.** an inspired communication of a prophet or religious leader. **5.** a mission; errand. **6. get the message.** *Inf.* to understand. ~*vb.* **7.** (*tr.*) to send as a message. [C13: < OF, < Vulgar L *missāticum* (unattested) something sent, < L *missus,* p.p. of *mittere*]

messages (ˈmɛsɪdʒɪz) *pl. n. Scot. & NE English dialect.* household shopping.

message stick *n.* a stick bearing carved symbols, carried by an Australian Aborigine as identification.

messenger (ˈmɛsɪndʒə) *n.* **1.** a person who takes messages from one person or group to another. **2.** a person who runs errands. **3.** a carrier of official dispatches; courier. [C13: < OF *messagier,* < MESSAGE]

messenger RNA *n. Biochem.* a form of RNA, transcribed from a single strand of DNA, that carries genetic information required for protein synthesis from DNA to the ribosomes.

mess hall *n.* a military dining room.

Messiah (mɪˈsaɪə) *n.* **1.** *Judaism.* the awaited king of the Jews, to be sent by God to free them. **2.** Jesus Christ, when regarded in this role. **3.** an exceptional or hoped-for liberator of a country or people. [C14: < OF *Messie,* ult. < Heb. *māshīah* anointed] —**Mesˈsiahship** *n.* —**Messianic** *or* **messianic** (ˌmɛsɪˈænɪk) *adj.*

messieurs (ˈmɛsəz) *n.* the plural of **monsieur.**

mess jacket *n.* a waist-length jacket, worn by officers in the mess for formal dinners.

mess kit *n. Mil.* **1.** *Brit.* formal evening wear for officers. **2.** Also called: **mess gear.** eating utensils used esp. in the field.

messmate (ˈmɛsˌmeɪt) *n.* a person with whom one shares meals in a mess, esp. in the army.

Messrs (ˈmɛsəz) *n.* the plural of **Mr.** [C18: abbrev. < F *messieurs,* pl. of MONSIEUR]

messy (ˈmɛsɪ) *adj.* **messier, messiest.** dirty, confused, or untidy. —**ˈmessily** *adv.* —**ˈmessiness** *n.*

mestizo (mɛˈstiːzəʊ, mɪ-) *n., pl.* **-zos** *or* **-zoes.** a person of mixed parentage, esp. the offspring of a Spanish American and an American Indian. [C16: < Sp., ult. < L *miscēre* to mix] —**mestiza** (mɛˈstiːzə) *fem. n.*

mestranol (ˈmɛstrəˌnɒl, -ˌnəʊl) *n.* a synthetic oestrogen used in combination with progesterones as an oral contraceptive. [C20: < M(ETHYL) + (O)ESTR(OGEN) + (*pregn*)*an*(*e*) ($C_{21}H_{36}$) + -OL]

met (mɛt) *vb.* the past tense and past participle of **meet**[1].

met. *abbrev. for:* **1.** meteorological. **2.** meteorology. **3.** metropolitan.

meta- *or sometimes before a vowel* **met-** *prefix.* **1.** indicating change or alternation: *metabolism; metamorphosis.* **2.** (of an academic discipline) concerned with the concepts and results of that discipline: *metamathematics.* **3.** occurring or situated behind or after: *metaphysics.* **4.** (*often in italics*) denoting that an organic compound contains a benzene ring with substituents in the 1,3-positions: *meta*-cresol. **5.** denoting an isomer, polymer, or compound related to a specified compound: *metaldehyde.* **6.** denoting an oxyacid that is the least hydrated form of the anhydride or a salt of such an acid: *metaphosphoric acid.* [< Gk (prep.)]

metabolism (mɪˈtæbəˌlɪzəm) *n.* **1.** the sum total of the chemical processes that occur in living organisms, resulting in growth, production of energy, elimination of waste, etc. **2.** the sum total of the chemical processes affecting a particular substance in the body: *carbohydrate metabolism.* [C19: < Gk *metabolē* change, < *metaballein,* < META- + *ballein* to throw] —**metabolic** (ˌmɛtəˈbɒlɪk) *adj.* —ˌ**metaˈbolically** *adv.*

metabolize *or* **-ise** (mɪˈtæbəˌlaɪz) *vb.* to produce or be produced by metabolism.

metacarpus (ˌmɛtəˈkɑːpəs) *n., pl.* **-pi** (-paɪ). **1.** the skeleton of the hand between the wrist and the fingers, consisting of five long bones. **2.** the corresponding bones in other vertebrates. —ˌ**metaˈcarpal** *adj., n.*

metacentre *or U.S.* **metacenter** (ˈmɛtəˌsɛntə) *n.* the intersection of a vertical line through the centre of buoyancy of a floating body at equilibrium with a vertical line through the centre of buoyancy when the body is tilted. —ˌ**metaˈcentric** *adj.*

metage (ˈmiːtɪdʒ) *n.* **1.** the official measuring of weight or contents. **2.** a charge for this. [C16: < METE[1]]

metal (ˈmɛtᵊl) *n.* **1. a.** any of a number of chemical elements, such as iron or copper, that are often lustrous ductile solids, have basic oxides, form positive ions, and are good conductors of heat and electricity. **b.** an alloy, such as brass or steel, containing one or more of these elements. **2.** the substance of glass in a molten state or as the finished product. **3.** short for **road metal. 4.** *Heraldry.* gold or silver. **5.** the basic quality of a person or thing; stuff. **6.** (*pl.*) the rails of a railway. ~*adj.* **7.** made of metal. ~*vb.* **-alling, -alled** *or U.S.* **-aling, -aled.** (*tr.*) **8.** to fit or cover with metal. **9.** to make or mend (a road) with **road metal.** [C13: < L *metallum* mine, product of a mine, < Gk *metallon*] —**ˈmetalled** *adj.*

metal. *or* **metall.** *abbrev. for:* **1.** metallurgical. **2.** metallurgy.

metalanguage (ˈmɛtəˌlæŋgwɪdʒ) *n.* a language or system of symbols used to discuss another language or system. Cf. **object language.**

metallic (mɪˈtælɪk) *adj.* **1.** of, concerned with, or consisting of metal or a metal. **2.** suggestive of a metal: *a metallic click; metallic lustre.* **3.** *Chem.* (of a metal element) existing in the free state rather than in combination: *metallic copper.*

metallic soap *n.* any one of a number of salts or esters containing a metal, such as aluminium, calcium, magnesium, iron, and zinc. They are used as bases for ointments, fungicides, fireproofing and waterproofing agents, and dryers for paints and varnishes.

metalliferous (ˌmɛtᵊˈlɪfərəs) *adj.* containing a metallic element. [C17: < L *metallifer* yielding metal, < *metallum* metal + *ferre* to bear]

metallize, -ise, *or U.S.* **metalize** (ˈmɛtəˌlaɪz) *vb.* (*tr.*) to make metallic or to coat or treat with metal. —ˌ**metalliˈzation, -iˈsation,** *or U.S.* ˌ**metaliˈzation** *n.*

metallography (ˌmɛtəˈlɒgrəfɪ) *n.* the branch of metallurgy concerned with the composition and structure of metals and alloys. —**metallographic** (mɪˌtæləˈgræfɪk) *adj.*

metalloid (ˈmɛtəˌlɔɪd) *n.* **1.** a nonmetallic element, such as arsenic or silicon, that has some of the properties of a metal. ~*adj. also* ˌ**metalˈloidal. 2.** of or being a metalloid. **3.** resembling a metal.

metallurgy (mɛˈtælədʒɪ) *n.* the scientific study of the extraction, refining, alloying, and fabrication of metals and of their structure and properties. —**metallurgic** (ˌmɛtəˈlɜːdʒɪk) *or* ˌ**metalˈlurgical** *adj.* —**metallurgist** (mɛˈtælədʒɪst, ˈmɛtəˌlɜːdʒɪst) *n.*

metal tape *n.* a magnetic recording tape coated with pure iron: it gives enhanced recording quality.

metalwork (ˈmɛtᵊlˌwɜːk) *n.* **1.** the craft of working in metal. **2.** work in metal or articles made from metal.

metalworking (ˈmɛtᵊlˌwɜːkɪŋ) *n.* the processing of metal to change its shape, size, etc. —**ˈmetalˌworker** *n.*

metamere (ˈmɛtəˌmɪə) *n.* one of the similar body segments into which earthworms, crayfish, and similar animals are divided longitudinally. —**metameral** (mɪˈtæmərəl) *adj.*

metamerism (mɪˈtæməˌrɪzəm) *n.* **1.** Also called: **(metameric) segmentation.** the division of an animal into metameres. **2.** *Chem.* a type of isomerism in which molecular structures differ by the attachment of different groups to the same atom. —**metameric** (ˌmɛtəˈmɛrɪk) *adj.*

metamorphic (ˌmɛtəˈmɔːfɪk) *or* **metamorphous** *adj.* **1.** relating to or resulting from metamorphosis or metamorphism. **2.** (of rocks) altered considerably from the original structure and composition by pressure and heat.

metamorphism (ˌmɛtəˈmɔːfɪzəm) *n.* **1.** the process by which metamorphic rocks are formed. **2.** a variant of **metamorphosis.**

metamorphose (ˌmɛtəˈmɔːfəʊz) *vb.* to undergo or cause to undergo metamorphosis or metamorphism.

metamorphosis (ˌmɛtəˈmɔːfəsɪs) *n., pl.* **-ses** (-ˌsiːz). **1.** a complete change of physical form or substance. 2. a complete change of character, appearance, etc. 3. a person or thing that has undergone metamorphosis. 4. *Zool.* the rapid transformation of a larva into an adult that occurs in certain animals, for example the stage between chrysalis and butterfly. [C16: via L < Gk: transformation, < META- + *morphē* form]

metaphor (ˈmɛtəfə, -ˌfɔː) *n.* a figure of speech in which a word or phrase is applied to an object or action that it does not literally denote in order to imply a resemblance, for example *he is a lion in battle.* Cf. **simile.** [C16: < L, < Gk *metaphora,* < *metapherein* to transfer, < META- + *pherein* to bear] —**metaphoric** (ˌmɛtəˈfɒrɪk) *or* ˌ**metaˈphorical** *adj.* —ˌ**metaˈphorically** *adv.*

metaphrase (ˈmɛtəˌfreɪz) *n.* 1. a literal translation. ~*vb.* (*tr.*) 2. to alter or manipulate the wording of. 3. to translate literally. [C17: < Gk *metaphrazein* to translate]

metaphrast (ˈmɛtəˌfræst) *n.* a person who metaphrases, esp. one who changes the form of a text, as by rendering verse into prose. [C17: < Med. Gk *metaphrastēs* translator] —ˌ**metaˈphrastic** *or* ˌ**metaˈphrastical** *adj.* —ˌ**metaˈphrastically** *adv.*

metaphysic (ˌmɛtəˈfɪzɪk) *n.* the system of first principles and assumptions underlying an inquiry or philosophical theory.

metaphysical (ˌmɛtəˈfɪzɪkᵊl) *adj.* 1. of or relating to metaphysics. 2. (of a statement or theory) having an empirical form but in fact immune from empirical testing. 3. (popularly) abstract, abtruse, or unduly theoretical. 4. incorporeal; supernatural. —ˌ**metaˈphysically** *adv.*

Metaphysical (ˌmɛtəˈfɪzɪkᵊl) *adj.* 1. denoting or relating to certain 17th-century poets who combined intense feeling with elaborate imagery. ~*n.* 2. a poet of this group.

metaphysics (ˌmɛtəˈfɪzɪks) *n.* (*functioning as sing.*) 1. the branch of philosophy that deals with first principles, esp. of being and knowing. 2. the philosophical study of the nature of reality. 3. (popularly) abstract or subtle discussion or reasoning. [C16: < Med. L, < Gk *ta meta ta phusika* the things after the physics, from the arrangement of subjects treated in the works of Aristotle] —**metaphysician** (ˌmɛtəfɪˈzɪʃən) *or* **metaphysicist** (ˌmɛtəˈfɪzɪsɪst) *n.*

metapsychology (ˌmɛtəsaɪˈkɒlədʒɪ) *n. Psychol.* 1. the study of philosophical questions, such as the relation between mind and body, that go beyond the laws of experimental psychology. 2. any attempt to state the general laws of psychology. 3. another word for **parapsychology.** —**metapsychological** (ˌmɛtəˌsaɪkəˈlɒdʒɪkᵊl) *adj.*

metastable (ˌmɛtəˈsteɪbᵊl) *adj. Physics.* (of a body or system) having a state of apparent equilibrium although capable of changing to a more stable state. —ˌ**metastaˈbility** *n.*

metastasis (mɪˈtæstəsɪs) *n., pl.* **-ses** (-ˌsiːz). *Pathol.* the spreading of a disease organism, esp. cancer cells, from one part of the body to another. [C16: via L < Gk: transition] —**metastatic** (ˌmɛtəˈstætɪk) *adj.* —ˌ**metaˈstatically** *adv.*

metastasize *or* **-ise** (mɪˈtæstəˌsaɪz) *vb.* (*intr.*) *Pathol.* (esp. of cancer cells) to spread to a new site in the body via blood or lymph vessels.

metatarsus (ˌmɛtəˈtɑːsəs) *n., pl.* **-si** (-saɪ). 1. the skeleton of the human foot between the toes and the tarsus, consisting of five long bones. 2. the corresponding skeletal part in other vertebrates. —ˌ**metaˈtarsal** *adj., n.*

metathesis (mɪˈtæθəsɪs) *n., pl.* **-ses** (-ˌsiːz). the transposition of two sounds or letters in a word or of two words in a sentence. [C16: < LL, < Gk, < *metatithenai* to transpose] —**metathetic** (ˌmɛtəˈθɛtɪk) *or* ˌ**metaˈthetical** *adj.*

metazoan (ˌmɛtəˈzəʊən) *n.* 1. any animal having a body composed of many cells: includes all animals except sponges and protozoans. ~*adj. also* **metazoic.** 2. of or relating to the metazoans. [C19: < NL *Metazoa;* see META-, -ZOA]

mete[1] (miːt) *vb.* (*tr.*) 1. (usually foll. by *out*) *Formal.* to distribute or allot (something, often unpleasant). 2. *Poetic, dialect.* to measure. [OE *metan*]

mete[2] (miːt) *n. Rare.* a mark, limit, or boundary (esp. in **metes and bounds**). [C15: < OF, < L *mēta* goal, turning post (in race)]

metempsychosis (ˌmɛtəmsaɪˈkəʊsɪs) *n., pl.* **-ses** (-siːz). the migration of a soul from one body to another. [C16: via LL < Gk, < *metempsukhousthai,* < META- + *-em-* in + *psukhē* soul] —ˌ**metempsyˈchosist** *n.*

meteor (ˈmiːtɪə) *n.* 1. a very small meteoroid that has entered the earth's atmosphere. 2. Also called: **shooting star, falling star.** the bright streak of light appearing in the sky due to the incandescence of such a body heated by friction at its surface. [C15: < Med. L *meteōrum,* < Gk *meteōron,* < *meteōros* lofty, < *meta-* (intensifier) + *aeirein* to raise]

meteoric (ˌmiːtɪˈɒrɪk) *adj.* 1. of, formed by, or relating to meteors. 2. like a meteor in brilliance, speed, or transience. 3. *Rare.* of weather; meteorological. —ˌ**meteˈorically** *adv.*

meteorite (ˈmiːtɪəˌraɪt) *n.* a rocklike object consisting of the remains of a meteoroid that has fallen on earth. —**meteoritic** (ˌmiːtɪəˈrɪtɪk) *adj.*

meteoroid (ˈmiːtɪəˌrɔɪd) *n.* any of the small celestial bodies that are thought to orbit the sun. When they enter the earth's atmosphere, they become visible as meteors. —ˌ**meteorˈoidal** *adj.*

meteorol. *or* **meteor.** *abbrev for:* 1. meteorological. 2. meteorology.

meteorology (ˌmiːtɪəˈrɒlədʒɪ) *n.* the study of the earth's atmosphere, esp. of weather-forming processes and weather forecasting. [C17: < Gk; see METEOR, -LOGY] —**meteorological** (ˌmiːtɪərəˈlɒdʒɪkᵊl) *or* ˌ**meteoroˈlogic** *adj.* —ˌ**meteoroˈlogically** *adv.* —ˌ**meteorˈologist** *n.*

meteor shower *n.* a transient rain of meteors occurring at regular intervals and coming from a particular region in the sky.

meter[1] (ˈmiːtə) *n.* 1. any device that measures and records a quantity, such as of gas, current, voltage, etc., that has passed through it during a specified period. 2. See **parking meter.** ~*vb.* (*tr.*) 3. to measure (a rate of flow) with a meter. [C19: see METE[1]]

meter[2] (ˈmiːtə) *n.* the U.S. spelling of **metre**[1].

meter[3] (ˈmiːtə) *n.* the U.S. spelling of **metre**[2].

-meter *n. combining form.* 1. indicating an instrument for measuring: *barometer.* 2. *Prosody.* indicating a verse having a specified number of feet: *pentameter.* [< Gk *metron* measure]

Meth. *abbrev. for* Methodist.

meth- *combining form.* indicating a chemical compound derived from methane or containing methyl groups: *methacrylic acid.*

methacrylic acid (ˌmɛθəˈkrɪlɪk) *n.* a colourless crystalline water-soluble substance used in the manufacture of acrylic resins.

methadone (ˈmɛθəˌdəʊn) *or* **methadon** (ˈmɛθəˌdɒn) *n.* a narcotic analgesic drug similar to morphine but less habit-forming. [C20: < (*di*)*meth*(*yl*) + A(MINO) + *d*(*iphenyl*) + -ONE]

methane (ˈmiːθeɪn) *n.* a colourless odourless flammable gas, the main constituent of natural gas: used as a fuel.

methane series *n.* any of a series of saturated aliphatic hydrocarbons with the general formula C_nH_{2n+2}. Also called: **alkane series.**

methanoic acid (ˈmɛθəˌnəʊɪk) *n.* the modern name for **formic acid.**

methanol (ˈmɛθəˌnɒl) *n.* a colourless volatile poisonous liquid compound used as a solvent and fuel. Formula: CH_3OH. Also called: **methyl alcohol, wood alcohol.** [C20: < METHANE + -OL[1]]

methinks (mɪˈθɪŋks) *vb. past* **methought.** (*tr.; takes a clause as object*) *Arch.* it seems to me.

metho (ˈmɛθəʊ) *n. Austral. inf.* 1. another name for **methylated spirits.** 2. (*pl.* **methos**) a drinker of methylated spirits.

method (ˈmɛθəd) *n.* 1. a way of proceeding or doing something, esp. a systematic or regular one. 2. orderliness of thought, action, etc. 3. (*often pl.*) the techniques or arrangement of work for a particular field or subject. [C16: via F < L, < Gk *methodos*, lit.: a going after, < *meta-* after + *hodos* way]

Method (ˈmɛθəd) *n.* (*sometimes not cap.*) **a.** a technique of acting in which the actor bases his role on the inner motivation of the character played. **b.** (*as modifier*): *a Method actor.*

methodical (mɪˈθɒdɪkᵊl) *or* (*less commonly*) **methodic** *adj.* characterized by method or orderliness; systematic. —**meˈthodically** *adv.*

Methodism (ˈmɛθəˌdɪzəm) *n.* the system and practices of the Methodist church.

Methodist (ˈmɛθədɪst) *n.* **1.** a member of any of the Nonconformist denominations that derive from the system of faith and practice initiated by John Wesley and his followers. ~*adj.* *also* ˌ**Methodˈistic** *or* ˌ**Methodˈistical.** **2.** of or relating to Methodism or the Church embodying it (the **Methodist Church**).

methodize *or* **-ise** (ˈmɛθəˌdaɪz) *vb.* (*tr.*) to organize according to a method; systematize —ˈ**methodˌizer** *or* **-ˌiser** *n.*

methodology (ˌmɛθəˈdɒlədʒɪ) *n., pl.* **-gies.** **1.** the system of methods and principles used in a particular discipline. **2.** the branch of philosophy concerned with the science of method. —**methodological** (ˌmɛθədəˈlɒdʒɪkᵊl) *adj.* —ˌ**methodoˈlogically** *adv.* —ˌ**methodˈologist** *n.*

methought (mɪˈθɔːt) *vb. Arch.* the past tense of **methinks.**

meths (mɛθs) *n. Chiefly Brit., Austral., & N.Z.* an informal name for **methylated spirits.**

methyl (ˈmiːθaɪl, ˈmɛθɪl) *n.* **1.** (*modifier*) of, consisting of, or containing the monovalent group of atoms CH_3. **2.** a compound in which methyl groups are bound directly to a metal atom. [C19: < F *méthyle*, back formation < METHYLENE] —**methylic** (məˈθɪlɪk) *adj.*

methyl acetate *n.* a colourless volatile flammable liquid ester used as a solvent, esp. in paint removers. Formula: CH_3COOCH_3.

methyl alcohol *n.* another name for **methanol.**

methylate (ˈmɛθɪˌleɪt) *vb.* (*tr.*) to mix with methanol.

methylated spirits *n.* (*functioning as sing. or pl.*) alcohol that has been denatured by the addition of methanol and pyridine and a violet dye. Also: **methylated spirit.**

methyl chloride *n.* a colourless gas with an ether-like odour, used as a refrigerant and anaesthetic. Formula: CH_3Cl.

methylene (ˈmɛθɪˌliːn) *n.* (*modifier*) of, consisting of, or containing the divalent group of atoms $=CH_2$: *a methylene group or radical.* [C19: < F *méthylène*, < Gk *methu* wine + *hulē* wood + -ENE: orig. referring to a substance distilled from wood]

meticulous (mɪˈtɪkjʊləs) *adj.* very precise about details; painstaking. [C16 (meaning: timid): < L *meticulōsus* fearful, < *metus* fear] —**meˈticulously** *adv.* —**meˈticulousness** *n.*

métier (ˈmɛtɪeɪ) *n.* **1.** a profession or trade. **2.** a person's strong point or speciality. [C18: < F, ult. < L *ministerium* service]

Métis (mɛˈtiːs) *n., pl.* **-tis** (-ˈtiːs, -ˈtiːz). a person of mixed parentage, esp. the offspring of a French Canadian and a North American Indian. [C19: < F, < Vulgar L *mixtīcius* (unattested) of mixed race] —**Métisse** (mɛˈtiːs) *fem. n.*

metol (ˈmiːtɒl) *n.* a colourless soluble organic substance used, in the form of its sulphate, as a photographic developer. [C20: < G, arbitrary coinage]

Metonic cycle (mɪˈtɒnɪk) *n.* a cycle of 235 synodic months after which the phases of the moon recur on the same day of the month. [C17: after *Meton*, 5th-cent. B.C. Athenian astronomer]

metonymy (mɪˈtɒnɪmɪ) *n., pl.* **-mies.** the substitution of a word referring to an attribute for the thing that is meant, e.g. *the crown*, used to refer to a monarch. Cf. **synecdoche.** [C16: < LL, < Gk, < *meta-* (indicating change) + *onoma* name] —**metonymical** (ˌmɛtəˈnɪmɪkᵊl) *or* ˌ**metoˈnymic** *adj.*

metope (ˈmɛtəʊp, ˈmɛtəpɪ) *n. Archit.* a square space between triglyphs in a Doric frieze. [C16: via L < Gk, < *meta* between + *opē* one of the holes for the beam-ends]

metre[1] *or U.S.* **meter** (ˈmiːtə) *n.* **1.** a metric unit of length equal to approximately 1.094 yards. **2.** the basic SI unit of length; the length of the path travelled by light in free space during a time interval of 1/299 792 458 of a second. Symbol: m [C18: < F; see METRE[2]]

metre[2] *or U.S.* **meter** (ˈmiːtə) *n.* **1.** *Prosody.* the rhythmic arrangement of syllables in verse, usually according to the number and kind of feet in a line. **2.** *Music.* another word (esp. U.S.) for **time** (sense 22). [C14: < L *metrum*, < Gk *metron* measure]

metre-kilogram-second *n.* See **mks units.**

metric (ˈmɛtrɪk) *adj.* of or relating to the metre or metric system.

metrical (ˈmɛtrɪkᵊl) *or* **metric** *adj.* **1.** of or relating to measurement. **2.** of or in poetic metre. —ˈ**metrically** *adv.*

metricate (ˈmɛtrɪˌkeɪt) *vb.* to convert (a measuring system, instrument, etc.) from nonmetric to metric units. —ˌ**metriˈcation** *n.*

metric system *n.* any decimal system of units based on the metre. For scientific purposes SI units are used.

metric ton *n.* another name (not in technical use) for **tonne.**

metro (ˈmɛtrəʊ) *or* **métro** *French.* (metro) *n., pl.* **-ros.** an underground, or largely underground, railway system in certain cities, such as that in Paris. [C20: < F, *chemin de fer métropolitain* metropolitan railway]

Metro (ˈmɛtrəʊ) *n. Canad.* a metropolitan city administration, esp. Metropolitan Toronto.

metronome (ˈmɛtrəˌnəʊm) *n.* a device which indicates the tempo of music by producing a clicking sound from a pendulum with an adjustable period of swing. [C19: < Gk *metron* measure + *nomos* law] —**metronomic** (ˌmɛtrəˈnɒmɪk) *adj.*

metronymic (ˌmɛtrəʊˈnɪmɪk) *adj.* **1.** (of a name) derived from the name of the mother or other female ancestor. ~*n.* **2.** a metronymic name. [C19: < Gk *mētronumikos*, < *mētēr* mother + *onoma* name]

metropolis (mɪˈtrɒpəlɪs) *n., pl.* **-lises.** **1.** the main city, esp. of a country or region. **2.** a centre of activity. **3.** the chief see in an ecclesiastical province. [C16: < LL < Gk, < *mētēr* mother + *polis* city]

metropolitan (ˌmɛtrəˈpɒlɪtən) *adj.* **1.** of or characteristic of a metropolis. **2.** constituting a city and its suburbs. **3.** of, relating to, or designating an ecclesiastical metropolis. **4.** of or belonging to the home territories of a country, as opposed to overseas territories: *metropolitan France.* ~*n.* **5. a.** *Eastern Churches.* the head of an ecclesiastical province, ranking between archbishop and patriarch. **b.** *Church of England.* an archbishop. **c.** *R.C. Church.* an archbishop or bishop having authority over the dioceses in his province. —ˌ**metroˈpolitanism** *n.*

metropolitan county *n.* (in England 1974–86) any of the six conurbations with elected councils possessing powers resembling those of counties.

metropolitan district *n.* (in England since 1974) any of the districts into which the metropolitan county areas are divided.

metrorrhagia (ˌmiːtrɔːˈreɪdʒɪə, ˌmɛt-) *n.* abnormal bleeding from the uterus. [C19: NL, < Gk *mētra* womb + *-rrhagia* a breaking forth]

-metry *n. combining form.* indicating the process or science of measuring: *geometry.* [< OF *-metrie*, < L, ult. < Gk *metron* measure] —**-metric** *adj. combining form.*

mettle (ˈmɛtᵊl) *n.* **1.** courage; spirit. **2.** character. **3. on one's mettle.** roused to making one's best efforts. [C16: orig. var. of METAL]

mettled (ˈmɛtᵊld) *or* **mettlesome** (ˈmɛtᵊlsəm) *adj.* courageous, spirited, or valiant.

MeV *symbol for* million electronvolts (10^6 electronvolts).

mevrou (məˈfrəʊ) *n.* a S. African title of address

equivalent to *Mrs* when placed before a surname or *madam* when used alone. [Afrik.]

mew[1] (mjuː) *vb.* **1.** (*intr.*) (esp. of a cat) to make a characteristic high-pitched cry. ~*n.* **2.** such a sound. [C14: imit.]

mew[2] (mjuː) *n.* any seagull, esp. the common gull. [OE *mǣw*]

mew[3] (mjuː) *n.* **1.** a room or cage for hawks, esp. while moulting. ~*vb.* (*tr.*) **2.** (often foll. by *up*) to confine (hawks or falcons) in a shelter, cage, etc. **3.** to confine; conceal. [C14: < OF *mue*, < *muer* to moult, < L *mūtāre* to change]

mewl (mjuːl) *vb.* **1.** (*intr.*) (esp. of a baby) to cry weakly; whimper. ~*n.* **2.** such a cry. [C17: imit.]

mews (mjuːz) *n.* (*functioning as sing. or pl.*) *Chiefly Brit.* **1.** a yard or street lined by buildings originally used as stables but now often converted into dwellings. **2.** the buildings around a mews. [C14: pl. of MEW[3], orig. referring to royal stables built on the site of hawks' mews at Charing Cross in London]

Mex. *abbrev. for:* **1.** Mexican. **2.** Mexico.

Mexican (ˈmɛksɪkən) *adj.* **1.** of or relating to Mexico, in Central America. ~*n.* **2.** a native or inhabitant of Mexico.

MEZ *abbrev. for* Central European Time. [< G *Mitteleuropäische Zeit*]

mezcal (mɛˈskæl) *n.* a variant spelling of **mescal.**

mezcaline (ˈmɛskəˌliːn) *n.* a variant spelling of **mescaline.**

mezuzah (məˈzuzə) *n., pl.* **-zuzahs** *or* **-zuzoth** (*Hebrew* məzuˈzɔt). *Judaism.* **1.** a piece of parchment inscribed with biblical passages and fixed to the doorpost of a Jewish house. **2.** a metal case for such a parchment, sometimes worn as an ornament. [< Heb., lit.: doorpost]

mezzanine (ˈmɛzəˌniːn, ˈmɛtsəˌniːn) *n.* **1.** Also called: **mezzanine floor.** an intermediate storey, esp. a low one between the ground and first floor of a building. **2.** *Theatre, U.S. & Canad.* the first balcony. **3.** *Theatre, Brit.* a room or floor beneath the stage. [C18: < F, < It., dim. of *mezzano* middle, < L *mediānus* MEDIAN]

mezzo (ˈmɛtsəʊ) *adv. Music.* moderately; quite: *mezzo piano.* [C19: < It., lit.: half, < L *medius* middle]

mezzo-soprano *n., pl.* **-nos.** **1.** a female voice intermediate between a soprano and contralto. **2.** a singer with such a voice.

mezzotint (ˈmɛtsəʊˌtɪnt) *n.* **1.** a method of engraving a copper plate by scraping and burnishing the roughened surface. **2.** a print made from a plate so treated. ~*vb.* **3.** (*tr.*) to engrave (a copper plate) in this fashion. [C18: < It. *mezzotinto* half tint]

mf *Music. symbol for* mezzo forte. [It.: moderately loud]

MF *abbrev. for:* **1.** *Radio.* medium frequency. **2.** Middle French.

mfd *abbrev. for* manufactured.

mfg *abbrev. for* manufacturing.

MFH *Hunting. abbrev. for* Master of Foxhounds.

mfr *abbrev. for:* **1.** manufacture. **2.** manufacturer.

mg *symbol for* milligram.

Mg *the chemical symbol for* magnesium.

M. Glam *abbrev. for* Mid Glamorgan.

Mgr *abbrev. for:* **1.** manager. **2.** Monseigneur. **3.** Monsignor.

MHA (in Australia) *abbrev. for* Member of the House of Assembly.

MHG *abbrev. for* Middle High German.

mho (məʊ) *n., pl.* **mhos.** the former name for **siemens.** [C19: formed by reversing the letters of OHM (first used by Lord Kelvin)]

MHR (in the U.S. and Australia) *abbrev. for* Member of the House of Representatives.

MHz *symbol for* megahertz.

mi *or* **me** (miː) *n. Music.* (in tonic sol-fa) the third degree of any major scale; a mediant. [C16: see GAMUT]

MI *abbrev. for* Military Intelligence.

mi. *abbrev. for* mile.

MI5 *abbrev. for* Military Intelligence, section five; a former official and current popular name for the counterintelligence agency of the British Government.

MI6 *abbrev. for* Military Intelligence, section six; a former official and current popular name for the intelligence and espionage agency of the British Government.

miaou *or* **miaow** (mɪˈaʊ, mjaʊ) *vb., interj.* variant spellings of **meow.**

miasma (mɪˈæzmə) *n., pl.* **-mata** (-mətə) *or* **-mas.** **1.** an unwholesome or foreboding atmosphere. **2.** pollution in the atmosphere, esp. noxious vapours from decomposing organic matter. [C17: NL, < Gk: defilement, < *miainein* to defile] —**miˈasmal** *or* **miasmatic** (ˌmiːəzˈmætɪk) *adj.*

Mic. *Bible. abbrev. for* Micah.

mica (ˈmaɪkə) *n.* any of a group of minerals consisting of hydrous silicates of aluminium, potassium, etc., in monoclinic crystalline form, occurring in igneous and metamorphic rock. Because of their resistance to electricity and heat they are used as dielectrics, in heating elements, etc. Also called: **isinglass.** [C18: < L: crumb] —**micaceous** (maɪˈkeɪʃəs) *adj.*

mice (maɪs) *n.* the plural of **mouse.**

micelle, micell (mɪˈsɛl), *or* **micella** (mɪˈsɛlə) *n. Chem.* **a.** a charged aggregate of molecules of colloidal size in a solution. **b.** any molecular aggregate of colloidal size. [C19: < NL *micella*, dim. of L *mīca* crumb]

Mich. *abbrev. for:* **1.** Michaelmas. **2.** Michigan.

Michaelmas (ˈmɪkᵊlməs) *n.* Sept. 29, the feast of St Michael the archangel; in England, Ireland, and Wales, one of the four quarter days.

Michaelmas daisy *n. Brit.* any of various composite plants that have small autumn-blooming purple, pink, or white flowers.

Michaelmas term *n.* the autumn term at Oxford and Cambridge Universities and some other educational establishments.

Mick (mɪk) *n.* (*sometimes not cap.*) **1.** Also: **Mickey.** *Derog.* a slang name for an **Irishman** or a **Roman Catholic.** **2.** *Austral.* the tails side of a coin. [C19: < nickname for *Michael*]

mickey *or* **micky** (ˈmɪkɪ) *n. Inf.* **take the mickey out of.** to tease. [C20: <?]

Mickey Finn *n. Sl.* **a.** a drink containing a drug to make the drinker unconscious. **b.** the drug itself. ~Often shortened to **Mickey.** [C20: <?]

mickle (ˈmɪkᵊl) *or* **muckle** (ˈmʌkᵊl) *Arch. or Scot. & N English dialect.* ~*adj.* **1.** great or abundant. ~*adv.* **2.** much; greatly. ~*n.* **3.** a great amount, esp. in the proverb, *many a little makes a mickle.* **4.** *Scot.* a small amount, esp. in the proverb *mony a mickle makes a muckle.* [C13 *mikel*, < ON *mikell*, replacing OE *micel* MUCH]

micro (ˈmaɪkrəʊ) *adj.* **1.** very small. ~*n., pl.* **-cros.** **2.** short for **microcomputer, microprocessor.**

micro- *or* **micr-** *combining form.* **1.** small or minute: *microdot.* **2.** involving the use of a microscope: *microscopy.* **3.** indicating a method or instrument for dealing with small quantities: *micrometer.* **4.** (in pathology) indicating abnormal smallness or underdevelopment: *microcephaly.* **5.** denoting 10^{-6}: *microsecond.* Symbol: μ [< Gk *mikros* small]

microbe (ˈmaɪkrəʊb) *n.* any microscopic organism, esp. a disease-causing bacterium. [C19: < F, < MICRO- + Gk *bios* life] —**miˈcrobial** *or* **miˈcrobic** *adj.*

microbiology (ˌmaɪkrəʊbaɪˈɒlədʒɪ) *n.* the branch of biology involving the study of microorganisms. —**microbiological** (ˌmaɪkrəʊˌbaɪəˈlɒdʒɪkᵊl) *or* **ˌmicroˌbioˈlogic** *adj.* —**ˌmicroˌbioˈlogically** *adv.* —**ˌmicrobiˈologist** *n.*

microcephaly (ˌmaɪkrəʊˈsɛfəlɪ) *n.* the condition of having an abnormally small head or cranial capacity. —**microcephalic** (ˌmaɪkrəʊsɪˈfælɪk) *adj., n.* —**ˌmicroˈcephalous** *adj.*

microchemistry (ˌmaɪkrəʊˈkɛmɪstrɪ) *n.* chemical experimentation with minute quantities of material. —**ˌmicroˈchemical** *adj.*

microchip (ˈmaɪkrəʊˌtʃɪp) *n.* another word for **chip** (sense 7).

microcircuit (ˈmaɪkrəʊˌsɜːkɪt) *n.* a miniature electronic circuit, esp. one in which a number of permanently connected components are contained in one small chip of semiconducting material. See **integrated circuit.** —ˌ**microˈcircuitry** *n.*
microclimate (ˈmaɪkrəʊˌklaɪmɪt) *n. Ecology.* the atmospheric conditions affecting an individual or a small group of organisms, esp. when they differ from the climate of the rest of the community. —**microclimatic** (ˌmaɪkrəʊklaɪˈmætɪk) *adj.* —ˌ**microˌclimaˈtology** *n.*
microcomputer (ˌmaɪkrəʊkəmˈpjuːtə) *n.* a computer in which the central processing unit is contained in one or more silicon chips.
microcosm (ˈmaɪkrəʊˌkɒzəm) *or* **microcosmos** (ˌmaɪkrəʊˈkɒzmɒs) *n.* **1.** a miniature representation of something. **2.** man regarded as epitomizing the universe. ~Cf. **macrocosm.** [C15: via Med. L < Gk *mikros kosmos* little world] —ˌ**microˈcosmic** *or* ˌ**microˈcosmical** *adj.*
microdot (ˈmaɪkrəʊˌdɒt) *n.* **1.** a greatly reduced photographic copy (about the size of a pinhead) of a document, etc., used esp. in espionage. **2.** a tiny tablet containing LSD.
microeconomics (ˌmaɪkrəʊˌiːkəˈnɒmɪks, -ˌɛkə-) *n.* (*functioning as sing.*) the branch of economics concerned with particular commodities, firms, or individuals and the economic relationships between them. —ˌ**microˌecoˈnomic** *adj.*
microelectronics (ˌmaɪkrəʊɪlɛkˈtrɒnɪks) *n.* (*functioning as sing.*) the branch of electronics concerned with microcircuits.
microfiche (ˈmaɪkrəʊˌfiːʃ) *n.* a sheet of film, usually the size of a filing card, on which books, newspapers, documents, etc., can be recorded in miniaturized form. [C20: < F, < MICRO- + *fiche* small card]
microfilm (ˈmaɪkrəʊˌfɪlm) *n.* **1.** a strip of film on which books, documents, etc., can be recorded in miniaturized form. ~*vb.* **2.** to photograph (a page, document, etc.) on microfilm.
microgravity (ˈmaɪkrəʊˌgrævɪtɪ) *n.* another name for **weightlessness.**
microhabitat (ˌmaɪkrəʊˈhæbɪtæt) *n. Ecology.* the smallest part of the environment that supports a distinct flora and fauna, such as a fallen log in a forest.
microlight (ˈmaɪkrəʊˌlaɪt) *n.* a small private aircraft carrying no more than two people, with a wing area not less than 10 square metres: used in pleasure flying and racing.
microlith (ˈmaɪkrəʊˌlɪθ) *n. Archaeol.* a small Mesolithic flint tool which formed part of a hafted tool. —ˌ**microˈlithic** *adj.*
micrometer (maɪˈkrɒmɪtə) *n.* **1.** any of various instruments or devices for the accurate measurement of distances or angles. **2.** Also called: **micrometer gauge, micrometer calliper.** a type of gauge for the accurate measurement of small distances, thicknesses, etc. The gap between its measuring faces is adjusted by a fine screw (**micrometer screw**). —**micrometric** (ˌmaɪkrəʊˈmɛtrɪk) *or* ˌ**microˈmetrical** *adj.* —**miˈcrometry** *n.*
microminiaturization *or* **-isation** (ˌmaɪkrəʊˌmɪnɪtʃəraɪˈzeɪʃən) *n.* the production and application of very small components and the circuits and equipment in which they are used.
micron (ˈmaɪkrɒn) *n., pl.* **-crons** *or* **-cra** (-krə). a unit of length equal to 10^{-6} metre. It is being replaced by the micrometre, the equivalent SI unit. [C19: NL, < Gk *mikros* small]
Micronesian (ˌmaɪkrəʊˈniːʒən, -ʒɪən) *adj.* **1.** of or relating to Micronesia (a division of islands in the Pacific), its inhabitants, or their languages. ~*n.* **2.** a native or inhabitant of Micronesia. **3.** a group of languages spoken in Micronesia.
microorganism (ˌmaɪkrəʊˈɔːgəˌnɪzəm) *n.* any organism, such as a virus, of microscopic size.
microphone (ˈmaɪkrəˌfəʊn) *n.* a device used in sound-reproduction systems for converting sound into electrical energy. —**microphonic** (ˌmaɪkrəˈfɒnɪk) *adj.*
microprint (ˈmaɪkrəʊˌprɪnt) *n.* a greatly reduced photographic copy of print, read by a magnifying device. It is used in order to reduce the size of large books, etc.
microprocessor (ˌmaɪkrəʊˈprəʊsɛsə) *n. Computers.* a single integrated circuit performing the basic functions of the central processing unit in a small computer.
microscope (ˈmaɪkrəˌskəʊp) *n.* **1.** an optical instrument that uses a lens or combination of lenses to produce a magnified image of a small, close object. **2.** any instrument, such as the electron microscope, for producing a magnified visual image of a small object.
microscopic (ˌmaɪkrəˈskɒpɪk) *or* (*less commonly*) **microscopical** *adj.* **1.** not large enough to be seen with the naked eye but visible under a microscope. **2.** very small; minute. **3.** of, concerned with, or using a microscope. —ˌ**microˈscopically** *adv.*
microscopy (maɪˈkrɒskəpɪ) *n.* **1.** the study, design, and manufacture of microscopes. **2.** investigation by use of a microscope. —**microscopist** (maɪˈkrɒskəpɪst) *n.*
microsecond (ˈmaɪkrəʊˌsɛkənd) *n.* one millionth of a second.
microstructure (ˈmaɪkrəʊˌstrʌktʃə) *n.* structure on a microscopic scale, esp. the structure of an alloy as observed by etching, polishing, and observation under a microscope.
microsurgery (ˌmaɪkrəʊˈsɜːdʒərɪ) *n.* intricate surgery performed on cells, tissues, etc., using a specially designed operating microscope and miniature precision instruments.
microtome (ˈmaɪkrəʊˌtəʊm) *n.* an instrument used for cutting thin sections for microscopical examination. —**microtomy** (maɪˈkrɒtəmɪ) *n.*
microwave (ˈmaɪkrəʊˌweɪv) *n.* **1. a.** electromagnetic radiation in the wavelength range 0.3 to 0.001 metres: used in radar, cooking, etc. **b.** (*as modifier*): *microwave oven.* **2.** short for **microwave oven.** ~*vb.* (*tr.*) **3.** to cook in a microwave oven.
microwave detector *n. N.Z.* a device for recording the speed of a motorist.
microwave oven *n.* an oven in which food is cooked by microwaves. Often shortened to **microwave.**
microwave spectroscopy *n.* a type of spectroscopy in which information is obtained on the structure and chemical bonding of molecules and crystals by measurements of the wavelengths of microwaves emitted or absorbed by the sample. —**microwave spectroscope** *n.*
micturate (ˈmɪktjʊˌreɪt) *vb.* (*intr.*) a less common word for **urinate.** [C19: < L *micturīre* to desire to urinate, < *mingere* to urinate] —**micturition** (ˌmɪktjʊˈrɪʃən) *n.*
mid[1] (mɪd) *adj.* **1.** *Phonetics.* of, relating to, or denoting a vowel whose articulation lies approximately halfway between high and low, such as *e* in English *bet.* ~*n.* **2.** an archaic word for **middle.** [C12 *midre* (inflected form of *midd,* unattested)]
mid[2] *or* **'mid** (mɪd) *prep.* a poetic word for **amid.**
mid- *combining form.* indicating a middle part, point, time, or position: *midday; mid-April; mid-Victorian.* [OE; see MIDDLE, MID[1]]
midair (ˌmɪdˈɛə) *n.* **a.** some point above ground level, in the air. **b.** (*as modifier*): *a midair collision of aircraft.*
mid-Atlantic *adj.* characterized by a blend of British and American styles, elements, etc.: *a mid-Atlantic accent.*
midbrain (ˈmɪdˌbreɪn) *n.* the nontechnical name for **mesencephalon.**
midday (ˈmɪdˈdeɪ) *n.* **a.** the middle of the day; noon. **b.** (*as modifier*): *a midday meal.*
middelskot (ˈmɪdəlˌskɒt) *n.* (in South Africa) an intermediate payment to a farmers' cooperative for a crop or wool clip. [< Afrik. *middel* middle + *skot* payment]
midden (ˈmɪdən) *n.* **1. a.** *Arch. or dialect.* a dunghill or pile of refuse. **b.** *Dialect.* a dustbin. **2.** See **kitchen midden.** [C14: < ON]
middle (ˈmɪdəl) *adj.* **1.** equally distant from the

ends or periphery of something; central. **2.** intermediate in status, situation, etc. **3.** located between the early and late parts of a series, time sequence, etc. **4.** not extreme, esp. in size; medium. **5.** (esp. in Greek and Sanskrit grammar) denoting a voice of verbs expressing reciprocal or reflexive action. **6.** (*usually cap.*) (of a language) intermediate between the earliest and the modern forms. ~*n.* **7.** an area or point equal in distance from the ends or periphery or in time between the early and late parts. **8.** an intermediate part or section, such as the waist. **9.** *Grammar.* the middle voice. **10.** *Logic.* See **middle term.** ~*vb.* (*tr.*) **11.** to place in the middle. **12.** *Naut.* to fold in two. **13.** *Cricket.* to hit (the ball) with the middle of the bat. [OE *middel*]

middle age *n.* the period of life between youth and old age, usually (in man) considered to occur approximately between the ages of 40 and 60. —ˌ**middle-ˈaged** *adj.*

Middle Ages *n.* **the.** *European history.* **1.** (broadly) the period from the deposition of the last W Roman emperor in 476 A.D. to the Italian Renaissance (or the fall of Constantinople in 1453). **2.** (narrowly) the period from about 1000 A.D. to the 15th century. Cf. **Dark Ages.**

Middle America *n.* **1.** the territories between the U.S. and South America: Mexico, Central America, and the Antilles. **2.** the U.S. middle class, esp. those groups that are politically conservative. —**Middle American** *adj., n.*

middlebrow (ˈmɪdᵊlˌbraʊ) *Disparaging.* ~*n.* **1.** a person with conventional tastes and limited cultural appreciation. ~*adj. also* **middlebrowed. 2.** of or appealing to middlebrows.

middle C *n. Music.* the note written on the first ledger line below the treble staff or the first ledger line above the bass staff.

middle class *n.* **1.** Also called: **bourgeoisie.** a social stratum between the lower and upper classes. It consists of businessmen, professional people, etc., along with their families, and is marked by bourgeois values. ~*adj.* **middle-class. 2.** of, relating to, or characteristic of the middle class.

middle ear *n.* the sound-conducting part of the ear, containing the malleus, incus, and stapes.

Middle East *n.* **1.** (loosely) the area around the E Mediterranean, esp. Israel and the Arab countries from Turkey to North Africa and eastwards to Iran. **2.** (formerly) the area extending from the Tigris and Euphrates to Burma. —**Middle Eastern** *adj.*

Middle English *n.* the English language from about 1100 to about 1450.

middle game *n. Chess.* the central phase between the opening and the endgame.

Middle High German *n.* High German from about 1200 to about 1500.

Middle Low German *n.* Low German from about 1200 to about 1500.

middleman (ˈmɪdᵊlˌmæn) *n., pl.* **-men. 1.** a trader engaged in the distribution of goods from producer to consumer. **2.** an intermediary.

middlemost (ˈmɪdᵊlˌməʊst) *adj.* another word for **midmost.**

middle name *n.* **1.** a name between a person's first name and surname. **2.** a characteristic quality for which a person is known: *caution is my middle name.*

middle-of-the-road *adj.* **1.** not extreme, esp. in political views; moderate. **2.** of, denoting, or relating to popular music having a wide general appeal.

middle passage *n.* **the.** *History.* the journey across the Atlantic Ocean from the W coast of Africa to the West Indies: the longest part of the journey of the slave ships.

middle school *n. Brit.* a school for children aged between 8 or 9 and 12 or 13.

middle term *n. Logic.* the term that appears in both minor and major premises but not in the conclusion of a syllogism.

middle watch *n. Naut.* the watch between midnight and 4 a.m.

middleweight (ˈmɪdᵊlˌweɪt) *n.* **1. a.** a professional boxer weighing 154–160 pounds (70–72.5 kg). **b.** an amateur boxer weighing 71–75 kg (157–165 pounds). **2. a.** a professional wrestler weighing 166–176 pounds (76–80 kg). **b.** an amateur wrestler weighing 75–82 kg (162–180 pounds).

Middle West *n.* another name for the **Midwest.** —**Middle Western** *adj.* —**Middle Westerner** *n.*

middling (ˈmɪdlɪŋ) *adj.* **1.** mediocre in quality, size, etc.; neither good nor bad, esp. in health (often in **fair to middling**). ~*adv.* **2.** *Inf.* moderately: *middling well.* [C15 (N English & Scot.): < MID[1] + -LING[2]] —ˈ**middlingly** *adv.*

Middx. *abbrev. for* Middlesex.

middy (ˈmɪdɪ) *n., pl.* **-dies. 1.** *Inf.* See **midshipman** (sense 1). **2.** *Austral.* **a.** a glass of middling size, used for beer. **b.** the measure of beer it contains.

midfield (ˌmɪdˈfiːld) *n. Soccer.* **a.** the general area between the two opposing defences. **b.** (*as modifier*)*: a midfield player.*

midge (mɪdʒ) *n.* **1.** a mosquito-like dipterous insect occurring in dancing swarms, esp. near water. **2.** a small or diminutive person or animal. [OE *mycge*] —ˈ**midgy** *adj.*

midget (ˈmɪdʒɪt) *n.* **1.** a dwarf whose skeleton and features are of normal proportions. **2. a.** something small of its kind. **b.** (*as modifier*)*: a midget car.* [C19: < MIDGE + -ET]

midgut (ˈmɪdˌgʌt) *n.* **1.** the middle part of the digestive tract of vertebrates, including the small intestine. **2.** the middle part of the digestive tract of arthropods.

mid-heavyweight *n.* **a.** a professional wrestler weighing 199–209 pounds (91–95 kg). **b.** an amateur wrestler weighing 91–100 kg (199–220 pounds).

midi (ˈmɪdɪ) *adj.* (formerly) **a.** (of a skirt, coat, etc.) reaching to below the knee or midcalf. **b.** (*as n.*)*: she wore her new midi.* [C20: < MID-, on the model of MINI]

midi- *combining form.* of medium or middle size, length, etc.: *midibus; midi system.*

midinette (ˌmɪdɪˈnɛt) *n.* a Parisian seamstress or salesgirl in a clothes shop. [C20: < F, < *midi* noon + *dinette* light meal; the girls had time for only a snack at midday]

midiron (ˈmɪdˌaɪən) *n. Golf.* a club, a No. 2 iron, used for approach shots.

midi system *n.* a complete set of hi-fi sound equipment designed as a single unit that is more compact than the standard equipment.

midland (ˈmɪdlənd) *n.* **a.** the central or inland part of a country. **b.** (*as modifier*)*: a midland region.*

Midlands (ˈmɪdləndz) *n.* (*functioning as pl. or sing.*) **the.** the central counties of England: characterized by manufacturing industries. —ˈ**Midlander** *n.*

midmost (ˈmɪdˌməʊst) *adj., adv.* in the middle or midst.

midnight (ˈmɪdˌnaɪt) *n.* **1. a.** the middle of the night; 12 o'clock at night. **b.** (*as modifier*)*: the midnight hour.* **2. burn the midnight oil.** to work or study late into the night.

midnight sun *n.* the sun visible at midnight during the summer inside the Arctic and Antarctic circles.

mid-off *n. Cricket.* the fielding position on the off side closest to the bowler.

mid-on *n. Cricket.* the fielding position on the on side closest to the bowler.

midpoint (ˈmɪdˌpɔɪnt) *n.* **1.** the point on a line that is at an equal distance from either end. **2.** a point in time halfway between the beginning and end of an event.

midrib (ˈmɪdˌrɪb) *n.* the main vein of a leaf, running down the centre of the blade.

midriff (ˈmɪdrɪf) *n.* **1. a.** the middle part of the human body, esp. between waist and bust. **b.** (*as modifier*)*: midriff bulge.* **2.** *Anat.* another name for the **diaphragm** (sense 1). **3.** the part of a woman's garment covering the midriff. [OE *midhrif,* < MID[1] + *hrif* belly]

midship (ˈmɪdˌʃɪp) *Naut.* ~*adj.* **1.** in, of, or relating to the middle of a vessel. ~*n.* **2.** the middle of a vessel.

midshipman (ˈmɪdˌʃɪpmən) *n., pl.* **-men.** a probationary rank held by young naval officers under training, or an officer holding such a rank.

midships (ˈmɪdˌʃɪps) *adv., adj. Naut.* See **amidships.**

midst[1] (mɪdst) *n.* **1. in our midst.** among us. **2. in the midst of.** surrounded or enveloped by; at a point during. [C14: back formation < *amiddes* AMIDST]

midst[2] (mɪdst) *prep. Poetic.* See **amidst, amid.**

midsummer (ˈmɪdˈsʌmə) *n.* **1. a.** the middle or height of the summer. **b.** (*as modifier*): *a midsummer carnival.* **2.** another name for **summer solstice.**

Midsummer Day *or* **Midsummer's Day** *n.* June 24, the feast of St John the Baptist; in England, Ireland, and Wales, one of the four quarter days. See also **summer solstice.**

midterm (ˈmɪdˈtɜːm) *n.* **1. a.** the middle of a term in a school, university, etc. **b.** (*as modifier*): *midterm exam.* **2.** *U.S. politics.* **a.** the middle of a term of office, esp. of a presidential term, when congressional and local elections are held. **b.** (*as modifier*): *midterm elections.* **3. a.** the middle of the gestation period. **b.** (*as modifier*): *midterm pregnancy.* See **term** (sense 6).

mid-Victorian *adj.* **1.** *Brit. history.* of or relating to the middle period of the reign of Queen Victoria (1837–1901). ~*n.* **2.** a person of the mid-Victorian era.

midway (ˈmɪdˌweɪ *or, for adv., n.* ˌmɪdˈweɪ) *adj.* **1.** in or at the middle of the distance; halfway. ~*adv.* **2.** to the middle of the distance. ~*n.* **3.** *Obs.* a middle place, way, etc.

midweek (ˈmɪdˈwiːk) *n.* **a.** the middle of the week. **b.** (*as modifier*): *a midweek holiday.*

Midwest (ˈmɪdˈwɛst) *or* **Middle West** *n.* the N central part of the U.S.; the states from Ohio westwards that border on the Great Lakes, and often the upper Mississippi and Missouri valleys. —ˈ**Mid**ˈ**western** *adj.* —ˈ**Mid**ˈ**westerner** *n.*

mid-wicket *n. Cricket.* the fielding position on the on side, midway between square leg and mid-on.

midwife (ˈmɪdˌwaɪf) *n., pl.* **-wives** (-ˌwaɪvz). **1.** a nurse qualified to deliver babies and to care for women before, during, and after childbirth. **2.** a woman skilled in aiding in the delivery of babies. [C14: < OE *mid* with + *wif* woman]

midwifery (ˈmɪdˌwɪfərɪ) *n.* the training, art, or practice of a midwife; obstetrics.

midwinter (ˈmɪdˈwɪntə) *n.* **1. a.** the middle or depth of the winter. **b.** (*as modifier*): *a midwinter festival.* **2.** another name for **winter solstice.**

midyear (ˈmɪdˈjɪə) *n.* the middle of the year.

mien (miːn) *n. Literary.* a person's manner, bearing, or appearance. [C16: prob. var. of obs. *demean* appearance; rel. to F *mine* aspect]

miff (mɪf) *Inf.* ~*vb.* **1.** to take offence or to offend. ~*n.* **2.** a petulant mood. **3.** a petty quarrel. [C17: ? an imitative expression of bad temper] —ˈ**miffy** *adj.*

might[1] (maɪt) *vb.* (takes an implied infinitive or an infinitive without *to*) used as an auxiliary: **1.** making the past tense or subjunctive mood of **may**[1]: *he might have come.* **2.** (often foll. by *well*) expressing possibility: *he might well come.* In this sense *might* looks to the future and functions as a weak form of *may.* See **may**[1] (sense 2). [OE *mihte*]

▷ **Usage.** See at **may**[1].

might[2] (maɪt) *n.* **1.** power, force, or vigour, esp. of a great or supreme kind. **2.** physical strength. **3. (with) might and main.** See **main**[1] (sense 7). [OE *miht*]

mighty (ˈmaɪtɪ) *adj.* **mightier, mightiest. 1. a.** having or indicating might; powerful or strong. **b.** (*as collective n.;* preceded by *the*): *the mighty.* **2.** very large; vast. **3.** very great in extent, importance, etc. ~*adv.* **4.** *Inf., chiefly U.S. & Canad.* (intensifier): *mighty tired.* —ˈ**mightily** *adv.* —ˈ**mightiness** *n.*

▷ **Usage.** *Mighty* is used by many speakers, esp. in the south of the U.S. and in various dialects, as an intensifier equivalent to *very.* This use of *mighty* is nevertheless avoided outside informal speech by careful users of English.

mignon (ˈmɪnjɒn) *adj.* small and pretty; dainty. [C16: < F, < OF *mignot* dainty] —**mignonne** (ˈmɪnjɒn) *fem. n.*

mignonette (ˌmɪnjəˈnɛt) *n.* **1.** any of various mainly Mediterranean plants, such as **garden mignonette,** that have spikes of small greenish-white flowers. **2.** a type of fine pillow lace. **3. a.** a greyish-green colour. **b.** (*as adj.*): *mignonette ribbons.* [C18: < F, dim. of MIGNON]

migraine (ˈmiːgreɪn, ˈmaɪ-) *n.* a throbbing headache usually affecting only one side of the head and commonly accompanied by nausea and visual disturbances. [C18: (earlier form, C14 *mygrame* MEGRIM): < F, < LL *hēmicrānia* pain in half of the head, < Gk, < HEMI- + *kranion* CRANIUM] —ˈ**migrainous** *adj.*

migrant (ˈmaɪgrənt) *n.* **1.** a person or animal that moves from one region, place, or country to another. **2.** an itinerant agricultural worker. ~*adj.* **3.** moving from one region, place, or country to another; migratory.

migrate (maɪˈgreɪt) *vb.* (*intr.*) **1.** to go from one place to settle in another, esp. in a foreign country. **2.** (of birds, fishes, etc.) to journey between different habitats at specific times of the year. [C17: < L *migrāre* to change one's abode] —**mi**ˈ**grator** *n.*

migration (maɪˈgreɪʃən) *n.* **1.** the act or an instance of migrating. **2.** a group of people, birds, etc., migrating in a body. **3.** *Chem.* a movement of atoms, ions, or molecules, such as the motion of ions in solution under the influence of electric fields. —**mi**ˈ**grational** *adj.*

migratory (ˈmaɪgrətərɪ, -trɪ) *adj.* **1.** of or characterized by migration. **2.** nomadic; itinerant.

mihrab (ˈmiːræb, -rəb) *n. Islam.* the niche in a mosque showing the direction of Mecca. [< Ar.]

mikado (mɪˈkɑːdəʊ) *n., pl.* **-dos.** (*often cap.*) *Arch.* the Japanese emperor. [C18: < Japanese, < *mi-* honourable + *kado* door, palace gate]

mike[1] (maɪk) *n. Inf.* short for **microphone.**

mike[2] (maɪk) *Brit. sl.* ~*vb.* (*intr.*) **1.** to idle; wait about. ~*n.* **2.** an evasion of work: *to do a mike.* [C19: <?]

mil (mɪl) *n.* **1.** a unit of length equal to one thousandth of an inch. **2.** a unit of angular measure, used in gunnery, equal to one six-thousand-four-hundredth of a circumference. **3.** *Photog.* short for millimetre: *35-mil film.* [C18: < L *millēsimus* thousandth]

mil. *abbrev. for:* **1.** military. **2.** militia.

milady *or* **miladi** (mɪˈleɪdɪ) *n., pl.* **-dies.** (formerly) a continental title used for an English gentlewoman.

milch (mɪltʃ) *n.* **1.** (*modifier*) (esp. of cattle) yielding milk. **2. milch cow.** *Inf.* a source of easy income, esp. a person. [C13: < OE *-milce* (in compounds); rel. to OE *melcan* to milk]

mild (maɪld) *adj.* **1.** (of a taste, sensation, etc.) not powerful or strong; bland. **2.** gentle or temperate in character, climate, behaviour, etc. **3.** not extreme; moderate. **4.** feeble; unassertive. ~*n.* **5.** *Brit.* draught beer, of darker colour than bitter and flavoured with fewer hops. [OE *milde*] —ˈ**mildly** *adv.* —ˈ**mildness** *n.*

mildew (ˈmɪlˌdjuː) *n.* **1.** any of various diseases of plants that affect mainly the leaves and are caused by parasitic fungi. **2.** any fungus causing this. **3.** another name for **mould**[2]. ~*vb.* **4.** to affect or become affected with mildew. [OE *mildēaw,* < *mil-* honey + *dēaw* DEW] —ˈ**mil**ˌ**dewy** *adj.*

mild steel *n.* any of a class of strong tough steels that contain a low quantity of carbon.

mile (maɪl) *n.* **1.** Also called: **statute mile.** a unit of length used in English-speaking countries, equal to 1760 yards. 1 mile is equivalent to 1.60934 kilometres. **2.** See **nautical mile. 3.** the Roman mile, equivalent to 1620 yards. **4.** (*often pl.*) *Inf.* a great distance; great deal: *he missed by a mile.* **5.** a race extending over a mile. ~*adv.* **6. miles.** (intensifier): *that's miles better.* [OE *mīl,* < L *mīlia (passuum)* a thousand (paces)]

mileage *or* **milage** (ˈmaɪlɪdʒ) *n.* **1.** a distance expressed in miles. **2.** the total number of miles that a motor vehicle has travelled. **3.** allowance for travelling expenses, esp. as a fixed rate per mile. **4.** the number of miles a motor vehicle will travel on one gallon of fuel. **5.** *Inf.* use, benefit, or service provided by something. **6.** *Inf.* grounds, substance, or weight: *some mileage in their arguments.*

mileometer *or* **milometer** (maɪˈlɒmɪtə) *n.* a device that records the number of miles that a bicycle or motor vehicle has travelled.

milepost (ˈmaɪlˌpəʊst) *n.* **1.** *Horse racing.* a marking post on a racecourse a mile before the finishing line. **2.** *Chiefly U.S. & Canad.* a signpost that shows the distance in miles to or from a place.

miler (ˈmaɪlə) *n.* an athlete, horse, etc., that runs or specializes in races of one mile.

milestone (ˈmaɪlˌstəʊn) *n.* **1.** a stone pillar that shows the distance in miles to or from a place. **2.** a significant event in life, history, etc.

milfoil (ˈmɪlˌfɔɪl) *n.* **1.** another name for **yarrow. 2.** See **water milfoil.** [C13: < OF, < L *milifolium,* < *mille* thousand + *folium* leaf]

miliaria (ˌmɪlɪˈɛərɪə) *n.* an acute itching eruption of the skin, caused by blockage of the sweat glands. [C19: < NL, < L *miliārius* MILIARY]

miliary (ˈmɪljərɪ) *adj.* **1.** resembling or relating to millet seeds. **2.** (of a disease or skin eruption) characterized by small lesions resembling millet seeds: *miliary fever.* [C17: < L *miliārius,* < *milium* MILLET]

milieu (ˈmiːljɜː) *n., pl.* **milieus** *or French* **milieux** (miljø). surroundings, location, or setting. [C19: < F, < *mi-* MID[1] + *lieu* place]

militant (ˈmɪlɪtənt) *adj.* **1.** aggressive or vigorous, esp. in the support of a cause. **2.** warring; engaged in warfare. ~*n.* **3.** a militant person. [C15: < L *mīlitāre* to be a soldier, < *mīles* soldier] —ˈ**militancy** *n.* —ˈ**militantly** *adv.*

militarism (ˈmɪlɪtəˌrɪzəm) *n.* **1.** military spirit; pursuit of military ideals. **2.** domination by the military, esp. on a political level. **3.** a policy of maintaining a strong military organization in aggressive preparedness for war. —ˈ**militarist** *n.*

militarize *or* **-ise** (ˈmɪlɪtəˌraɪz) *vb.* (*tr.*) **1.** to convert to military use. **2.** to imbue with militarism. —ˌ**militariˈzation** *or* **-iˈsation** *n.*

military (ˈmɪlɪtərɪ, -trɪ) *adj.* **1.** of or relating to the armed forces, warlike matters, etc. **2.** of or characteristic of soldiers. ~*n., pl.* **-taries** *or* **-tary. 3.** (preceded by *the*) the armed services, esp. the army. [C16: via F < L *mīlitāris,* < *mīles* soldier] —ˈ**militarily** *adv.*

military police *n.* a corps within an army that performs police and disciplinary duties. —**military policeman** *n.*

militate (ˈmɪlɪˌteɪt) *vb.* (*intr.;* usually foll. by *against* or *for*) (of facts, etc.) to have influence or effect: *the evidence militated against his release.* [C17: < L *mīlitātus,* < *mīlitāre* to be a soldier]

▷ **Usage.** Confusion sometimes arises between *militate* and *mitigate. Militate,* which comes from the same Latin root as *military,* is an intransitive verb meaning "to have influence or effect". While it can be used in a positive sense with *for,* as in *any act that militates for peaceful cooperation,* it is typically used in a negative sense with *against* (see definition, above). *Mitigate* comes from Latin *mītis* mild and is typically used transitively. It means "to moderate; make less severe, unpleasant, etc.", and is generally restricted to formal speech or writing: *governments should endeavour to mitigate distress.*

militia (mɪˈlɪʃə) *n.* **1.** a body of citizen (as opposed to professional) soldiers. **2.** an organization containing men enlisted for service in emergency only. [C16: < L: soldiery, < *mīles* soldier] —**miˈlitiaman** *n.*

milk (mɪlk) *n.* **1. a.** a whitish fluid secreted by the mammary glands of mature female mammals and used for feeding their young until weaned. **b.** the milk of cows, goats, etc., used by man as a food or in the production of butter, cheese, etc. **2.** any similar fluid in plants, such as the juice of a coconut. **3.** a milklike pharmaceutical preparation, such as milk of magnesia. **4. cry over spilt milk.** to lament something that cannot be altered. ~*vb.* **5.** to draw milk from the udder of (an animal). **6.** (*intr.*) (of animals) to yield milk. **7.** (*tr.*) to draw off or tap in small quantities: *to milk the petty cash.* **8.** (*tr.*) to extract as much money, help, etc., as possible from: *to milk a situation of its news value.* **9.** (*tr.*) to extract venom, sap, etc., from. [OE *milc*] —ˈ**milker** *n.*

milk-and-water *adj.* (**milk and water** *when postpositive*). weak, feeble, or insipid.

milk bar *n.* **1.** a snack bar at which milk drinks and light refreshments are served. **2.** (in Australia) a shop selling, in addition to milk, basic provisions and other items.

milk chocolate *n.* chocolate that has been made with milk, having a creamy taste.

milk float *n. Brit.* a small motor vehicle used to deliver milk to houses.

milk leg *n.* inflammation and thrombosis of the femoral vein following childbirth, characterized by painful swelling of the leg.

milkmaid (ˈmɪlkˌmeɪd) *n.* a girl or woman who milks cows.

milkman (ˈmɪlkmən) *n., pl.* **-men.** a man who delivers or sells milk.

milk of magnesia *n.* a suspension of magnesium hydroxide in water, used as an antacid and laxative.

milk pudding *n. Chiefly Brit.* a pudding made by boiling or baking milk with a grain, esp. rice.

milk round *n. Brit.* **1.** a route along which a milkman regularly delivers milk. **2.** a regular series of visits, esp. as made by recruitment officers from industry to universities.

milk run *n. Aeronautics, inf.* a routine and uneventful flight. [C20: < a milkman's safe and regular routine]

milk shake *n.* a cold frothy drink made of milk, flavouring, and sometimes ice cream, whisked or beaten together.

milksop (ˈmɪlkˌsɒp) *n.* a feeble or ineffectual man or youth.

milk sugar *n.* another name for **lactose.**

milk tooth *n.* any of the first teeth to erupt; a deciduous tooth. Also called: **baby tooth.**

milkwort (ˈmɪlkˌwɜːt) *n.* any of several plants having small blue, pink, or white flowers. They were formerly believed to increase milk production in nursing women.

milky (ˈmɪlkɪ) *adj.* **milkier, milkiest. 1.** resembling milk, esp. in colour or cloudiness. **2.** of or containing milk. **3.** spiritless or spineless. —ˈ**milkily** *adv.* —ˈ**milkiness** *n.*

Milky Way *n.* **the.** the diffuse band of light stretching across the night sky that consists of millions of faint stars, nebulae, etc., and forms part of the Galaxy. [C14: translation of L *via lactea*]

mill (mɪl) *n.* **1.** a building fitted with machinery for processing materials, manufacturing goods, etc.; factory. **2.** a machine that processes materials, manufactures goods, etc., by performing a continuous or repetitive operation, such as a machine to grind flour, pulverize solids, or press fruit. **3.** a machine that tools or polishes metal. **4.** a small machine for grinding solids: *a pepper mill.* **5.** a system, institution, etc., that influences people or things in the manner of a factory: *the educational mill.* **6.** an unpleasant experience; ordeal (esp. in **go** *or* **be put through the mill**). **7.** a fist fight. ~*vb.* **8.** (*tr.*) to grind, press, or pulverize in or as if in a mill. **9.** (*tr.*) to process or produce in or with a mill. **10.** to cut or roll (metal) with or as if with a milling machine. **11.** (*tr.*) to groove or flute the edge of (a coin). **12.** (*intr.;* often foll. by *about* or *around*) to move about in a confused manner. **13.** *Arch. sl.* to fight, esp. with the fists. [OE *mylen* < LL *molīna* a mill, < L *mola* mill, < *molere* to grind] —**'millable** *adj.* —**milled** *adj.*

millboard ('mɪlˌbɔːd) *n.* strong pasteboard, used esp. in book covers. [C18: < *milled board*]

milldam ('mɪlˌdæm) *n.* a dam built in a stream to raise the water level sufficiently for it to turn a millwheel.

millefeuille *French.* (milfœj) *n. Brit.* a small iced cake made of puff pastry filled with jam and cream. [lit.: thousand leaves]

millefleurs ('miːlˌflɜː) *n.* (*functioning as sing.*) a design of stylized floral patterns, used in textiles, paperweights, etc. [F: thousand flowers]

millenarian (ˌmɪlɪ'nɛərɪən) *adj.* **1.** of or relating to a thousand or to a thousand years. **2.** of or relating to the millennium or millenarianism. ~*n.* **3.** an adherent of millenarianism.

millenarianism (ˌmɪlɪ'nɛərɪəˌnɪzəm) *n.* **1.** *Christianity.* the belief in a future millennium during which Christ will reign on earth: based on Revelation 20:1–5. **2.** any belief in a future period of ideal peace and happiness.

millenary (mɪ'lɛnərɪ) *n., pl.* **-naries.** **1.** a sum or aggregate of one thousand. **2.** another word for a **millennium.** ~*adj., n.* **3.** another word for **millenarian.** [C16: < LL *millēnārius* containing a thousand, < L *mille* thousand]

millennium (mɪ'lɛnɪəm) *n., pl.* **-niums** *or* **-nia** (-nɪə). **1. the.** *Christianity.* the period of a thousand years of Christ's awaited reign upon earth. **2.** a period or cycle of one thousand years. **3.** a time of peace and happiness, esp. in the distant future. [C17: < NL, < L *mille* thousand + *annus* year] —**mil'lennial** *adj.* —**mil'lennialist** *n.*

millepede ('mɪlɪˌpiːd) *or* **milleped** *n.* variants of **millipede.**

millepore ('mɪlɪˌpɔː) *n.* any of a genus of tropical colonial coral-like hydrozoans, having a calcareous skeleton. [C18: < NL, < L *mille* thousand + *porus* hole]

miller ('mɪlə) *n.* **1.** a person who keeps, operates, or works in a mill, esp. a corn mill. **2.** another name for **milling machine.** **3.** a person who operates a milling machine.

miller's thumb *n.* any of several small freshwater European fishes having a flattened body. [C15: < the alleged likeness of the fish's head to a thumb]

millesimal (mɪ'lɛsɪməl) *adj.* **1. a.** denoting a thousandth. **b.** (*as n.*): *a millesimal.* **2.** of, consisting of, or relating to a thousandth. [C18: < L *millēsimus*]

millet ('mɪlɪt) *n.* **1.** a cereal grass cultivated for grain and animal fodder. **2. a.** an Indian annual grass cultivated for grain and forage, having pale round shiny seeds. **b.** the seed of this plant. **3.** any of various similar or related grasses. [C14: via OF < L *milium*]

milli- *prefix.* denoting 10^{-3}: *millimetre.* Symbol: m [< F, < L *mille* thousand]

milliard ('mɪlɪˌɑːd, 'mɪljɑːd) *n. Brit.* (no longer in technical use) a thousand million. U.S. & Canad. equivalent: **billion.** [C19: < F]

millibar ('mɪlɪˌbɑː) *n.* a cgs unit of atmospheric pressure equal to 10^{-3} bar, 100 newtons per square metre or 0.7500617 millimetre of mercury.

milligram *or* **milligramme** ('mɪlɪˌgræm) *n.* one thousandth of a gram. [C19: < F]

millilitre *or U.S.* **milliliter** ('mɪlɪˌliːtə) *n.* one thousandth of a litre.

millimetre *or U.S.* **millimeter** ('mɪlɪˌmiːtə) *n.* one thousandth of a metre.

millimicron ('mɪlɪˌmaɪkrɒn) *n.* an obsolete name for a **nanometre.**

milliner ('mɪlɪnə) *n.* a person who makes or sells women's hats. [C16: orig. *Milaner,* a native of *Milan,* at that time famous for its fancy goods]

millinery ('mɪlɪnərɪ, -ɪnrɪ) *n.* **1.** hats, trimmings, etc., sold by a milliner. **2.** the business or shop of a milliner.

milling ('mɪlɪŋ) *n.* **1.** the act or process of grinding, pressing, or crushing in a mill. **2.** the grooves or fluting on the edge of a coin, etc.

milling machine *n.* a machine tool in which a horizontal arbor or vertical spindle rotates a cutting tool above a horizontal table.

million ('mɪljən) *n., pl.* **-lions** *or* **-lion.** **1.** the cardinal number that is the product of 1000 multiplied by 1000. **2.** a numeral, 1 000 000, 10^6, $\overline{M}$, etc., representing this number. **3.** (*often pl.*) *Inf.* an extremely large but unspecified number or amount: *I have millions of things to do.* ~*determiner.* **4.** (preceded by *a* or by a numeral) **a.** amounting to a million: *a million light years.* **b.** (*as pron.*): *I can see a million.* [C17: via OF < early It. *millione,* < *mille* thousand, < L]

millionaire (ˌmɪljə'nɛə) *n.* a person whose assets are worth at least a million of the standard monetary units of his country. —ˌ**million'airess** *fem. n.*

millionth ('mɪljənθ) *n.* **1. a.** one of 1 000 000 equal parts of something. **b.** (*as modifier*): *a millionth part.* **2.** one of 1 000 000 equal divisions of a scientific quantity. **3.** the fraction one divided by 1 000 000. ~*adj.* **4.** (*usually prenominal*) **a.** being the ordinal number of 1 000 000 in numbering or counting order, etc. **b.** (*as n.*): *the millionth to be manufactured.*

millipede, millepede ('mɪlɪˌpiːd), *or* **milleped** ('mɪlɪˌpɛd) *n.* any of various terrestrial herbivorous arthropods, having a cylindrical segmented body, each segment of which bears two pairs of legs. [C17: < L, < *mille* thousand + *pēs* foot]

millisecond ('mɪlɪˌsɛkənd) *n.* one thousandth of a second.

millpond ('mɪlˌpɒnd) *n.* **1.** a pool formed by damming a stream to provide water to turn a millwheel. **2.** any expanse of calm water.

millrace ('mɪlˌreɪs) *or* **millrun** *n.* **1.** the current of water that turns a millwheel. **2.** the channel for this water.

Mills bomb (mɪlz) *n.* a type of high-explosive hand grenade. [C20: after Sir William *Mills* (1856–1932), E inventor]

millstone ('mɪlˌstəʊn) *n.* **1.** one of a pair of heavy flat disc-shaped stones that are rotated one against the other to grind grain. **2.** a heavy burden, such as a responsibility or obligation.

millstream ('mɪlˌstriːm) *n.* a stream of water used to turn a millwheel.

millwheel ('mɪlˌwiːl) *n.* a wheel, esp. a waterwheel, that drives a mill.

millwork ('mɪlˌwɜːk) *n.* work done in a mill.

millwright ('mɪlˌraɪt) *n.* a person who designs, builds, or repairs grain mills or mill machinery.

milometer (maɪ'lɒmɪtə) *n.* a variant spelling of **mileometer.**

milord (mɪ'lɔːd) *n.* (formerly) a continental title used for an English gentleman. [C19: via F < E *my lord*]

milt (mɪlt) *n.* **1.** the testis of a fish. **2.** the spermatozoa and seminal fluid produced by a fish. **3.** *Rare.* the spleen, esp. of fowls and pigs. ~*vb.* **4.** to fertilize (fish roe) with milt, esp. artificially. [OE *milte* spleen; in the sense: fish sperm, prob. < MDu. *milte*] —**'milter** *n.*

mim (mɪm) *adj. Dialect.* prim, modest, or demure. [C17: ? imit. of lip-pursing]

mime (maɪm) *n.* **1.** the theatrical technique of expressing an idea or mood or portraying a character entirely by gesture and bodily movement without the use of words. **2.** Also called: **mime artist.** a performer specializing in this. **3.** a dramatic presentation using such a technique. **4.** (in the classical theatre) **a.** a comic performance with exaggerated gesture and physical action. **b.** an actor in such a performance. ~*vb.* **5.** to express (an idea, etc.) in actions or gestures without speech. **6.** (of singers or musicians) to perform as if singing a song or playing a piece of music that is actually prerecorded. [OE *mīma,* < L *mīmus* mimic actor, < Gk *mimos* imitator] —**'mimer** *n.*

Mimeograph ('mɪmɪəˌgrɑːf) *n.* **1.** *Trademark.* an office machine for printing multiple copies of text or line drawings from a stencil. **2.** a copy produced by this. ~*vb.* **3.** to print copies from (a prepared stencil) using this machine.

mimesis (mɪ'miːsɪs) *n.* **1.** *Art, literature.* the

imitative representation of nature or human behaviour. **2.** *Biol.* another name for **mimicry** (sense 2). **3.** *Rhetoric.* representation of another person's alleged words in a speech. [C16: < Gk, < *mimeisthai* to imitate]

mimetic (mɪˈmɛtɪk) *adj.* **1.** of, resembling, or relating to mimesis or imitation, as in art, etc. **2.** *Biol.* of or exhibiting mimicry. —**miˈmetically** *adv.*

mimic (ˈmɪmɪk) *vb.* **-icking, -icked.** (*tr.*) **1.** to imitate (a person, a manner, etc.), esp. for satirical effect; ape. **2.** to take on the appearance of: *certain flies mimic wasps.* **3.** to copy closely or in a servile manner. ~*n.* **4.** a person or an animal, such as a parrot, that is clever at mimicking. **5.** an animal that displays mimicry. ~*adj.* **6.** of, relating to, or using mimicry. **7.** simulated, make-believe, or mock. [C16: < L *mīmicus,* < Gk *mimikos,* < *mimos* MIME] —**ˈmimicker** *n.*

mimicry (ˈmɪmɪkrɪ) *n., pl.* **-ries.** **1.** the act or art of copying or imitating closely; mimicking. **2.** the resemblance shown by one animal species to another, which protects it from predators.

MIMinE *abbrev. for* Member of the Institute of Mining Engineers.

mimosa (mɪˈməʊsə, -zə) *n.* any of various tropical shrubs or trees having ball-like clusters of typically yellow flowers and leaves that are often sensitive to touch or light. See also **sensitive plant.** [C18: < NL, prob. < L *mīmus* MIME, because the plant's sensitivity to touch imitates the similar reaction of animals]

mimulus (ˈmɪmjʊləs) *n.* any of a genus of flowering plants of temperate regions. See **monkey flower.** [C19: Med. L, < L. *mimus* MIME, alluding to masklike flowers]

min. *abbrev. for:* **1.** mineralogy. **2.** minimum. **3.** mining. **4.** minute *or* minutes.

Min. *abbrev. for:* **1.** Minister. **2.** Ministry.

mina (ˈmaɪnə) *n.* a variant spelling of **myna.**

minaret (ˌmɪnəˈrɛt, ˈmɪnəˌrɛt) *n.* a slender tower of a mosque having one or more balconies. [C17: < F, < Turkish, < Ar. *manārat* lamp, < *nār* fire] —**ˌminaˈreted** *adj.*

minatory (ˈmɪnətərɪ, -trɪ) *or* **minatorial** *adj.* threatening or menacing. [C16: < LL *minātōrius,* < L *minārī* to threaten]

mince (mɪns) *vb.* **1.** (*tr.*) to chop, grind, or cut into very small pieces. **2.** (*tr.*) to soften or moderate: *I didn't mince my words.* **3.** (*intr.*) to walk or speak in an affected dainty manner. ~*n.* **4.** *Chiefly Brit.* minced meat. [C14: < OF *mincier,* ult. < LL *minūtia;* see MINUTIAE] —**ˈmincer** *n.*

mincemeat (ˈmɪnsˌmiːt) *n.* **1.** a mixture of dried fruit, spices, etc., used esp. for filling pies. **2.** **make mincemeat of.** *Inf.* to defeat completely.

mince pie *n.* a small round pastry tart filled with mincemeat.

mincing (ˈmɪnsɪŋ) *adj.* (of a person) affectedly elegant in gait, manner, or speech. —**ˈmincingly** *adv.*

mind (maɪnd) *n.* **1.** the part of a person responsible for thought, feelings, intention, etc. **2.** intelligence or the intellect, esp. as opposed to feelings or wishes. **3.** recollection or remembrance: *it comes to mind.* **4.** the faculty of original or creative thought; imagination: *it's all in the mind.* **5.** a person considered as an intellectual being: *great minds.* **6.** condition, state, or manner of feeling or thought: *his state of mind.* **7.** an inclination, desire, or purpose: *I have a mind to go.* **8.** attention or thoughts: *keep your mind on your work.* **9.** a sound mental state; sanity (esp. in **out of one's mind**). **10.** (in Cartesian philosophy) one of two basic modes of existence, the other being matter. **11.** **blow someone's mind.** *Sl.* **a.** (of a drug) to alter someone's mental state. **b.** to astound or surprise someone. **12.** **change one's mind.** to alter one's decision or opinion. **13.** **in** *or* **of two minds.** undecided; wavering. **14.** **give (someone) a piece of one's mind.** to criticize or censure (someone) frankly or vehemently. **15.** **make up one's mind.** to decide (something or to do something). **16.** **on one's mind.** in one's thoughts. ~*vb.* **17.** (when *tr., may take a clause as object*) to take offence at: *do you mind if I smoke?* **18.** to pay attention to (something); heed; notice: *to mind one's own business.* **19.** (*tr.; takes a clause as object*) to make certain; ensure: *mind you tell her.* **20.** (*tr.*) to take care of; have charge of: *to mind the shop.* **21.** (when *tr., may take a clause as object*) to be cautious or careful about (something): *mind how you go.* **22.** (*tr.*) to obey (someone or something); heed: *mind your father!* **23.** to be concerned (about); be troubled (about): *never mind about your hat.* **24.** **mind you.** an expression qualifying a previous statement: *Dogs are nice. Mind you, I don't like all dogs.* ~Related adj.: **mental.** ~See also **mind out.** [OE *gemynd* mind]

mind-boggling *adj. Inf.* astonishing; bewildering.

minded (ˈmaɪndɪd) *adj.* **1.** having a mind, inclination, intention, etc., as specified: *politically minded.* **2.** (*in combination*): *money-minded.*

minder (ˈmaɪndə) *n.* **1.** someone who looks after someone or something. **2.** short for **child minder.** **3.** *Sl.* an aide to someone in public life who keeps control of press and public relations. **4.** *Sl.* someone acting as a bodyguard or assistant, esp. in the criminal underworld.

mindful (ˈmaɪndfʊl) *adj.* (usually *postpositive* and foll. by *of*) keeping aware; heedful: *mindful of your duty.* —**ˈmindfully** *adv.* —**ˈmindfulness** *n.*

mindless (ˈmaɪndlɪs) *adj.* **1.** stupid or careless. **2.** requiring little or no intellectual effort. —**ˈmindlessly** *adv.* —**ˈmindlessness** *n.*

mind out *vb.* (*intr., adv.*) *Brit.* to be careful or pay attention.

mind-reader *n.* a person seemingly able to discern the thoughts of another. —**ˈmind-ˌreading** *n.*

mind's eye *n.* the visual memory or the imagination.

mine[1] (maɪn) *pron.* **1.** something or someone belonging to or associated with me: *mine is best.* **2.** **of mine.** belonging to or associated with me. ~*determiner.* **3.** (*preceding a vowel*) an archaic word for **my:** *mine eyes; mine host.* [OE *mīn*]

mine[2] (maɪn) *n.* **1.** a system of excavations made for the extraction of minerals, esp. coal, ores, or precious stones. **2.** any deposit of ore or minerals. **3.** a lucrative source or abundant supply: *a mine of information.* **4.** a device containing explosive designed to destroy ships, vehicles, or personnel, usually laid beneath the ground or in water. **5.** a tunnel dug to undermine a fortification, etc. ~*vb.* **6.** to dig into (the earth) for (minerals). **7.** to make (a hole, tunnel, etc.) by digging or boring. **8.** to place explosive mines in position below the surface of (the sea or land). **9.** to undermine (a fortification, etc.) by digging mines. **10.** another word for **undermine.** [C13: < OF, prob. of Celtic origin]

mine detector *n.* an instrument designed to detect explosive mines. —**mine detection** *n.*

mine-dump *n. S. African.* a large mound of residue esp. from gold-mining operations.

minefield (ˈmaɪnˌfiːld) *n.* **1.** an area of ground or water containing explosive mines. **2.** a subject, situation, etc., beset with hidden problems.

minelayer (ˈmaɪnˌleɪə) *n.* a warship or aircraft designed for the carrying and laying of mines.

miner (ˈmaɪnə) *n.* **1.** a person who works in a mine. **2.** any of various insects or insect larvae that bore into and feed on plant tissues. See also **leaf miner.** **3.** *Austral.* any of several honeyeaters.

mineral (ˈmɪnərəl, ˈmɪnrəl) *n.* **1.** any of a class of naturally occurring solid inorganic substances with a characteristic crystalline form and a homogeneous chemical composition. **2.** any inorganic matter. **3.** any substance obtained by mining, esp. a metal ore. **4.** (*often pl.*) *Brit.* short for **mineral water.** **5.** *Brit.* a soft drink containing carbonated water and flavourings. ~*adj.* **6.** of, relating to, containing, or resembling minerals. [C15: < Med. L *minerāle* (n.), < *minerālis* (adj.); rel. to *minera* mine, ore, <?]

mineral. *abbrev. for* mineralogy *or* mineralogical.

mineralize *or* **-ise** (ˈmɪnərəˌlaɪz) *vb.* (*tr.*) **1. a.** to impregnate (organic matter, water, etc.) with a mineral substance. **b.** to convert (such matter) into a mineral; petrify. **2.** (of gases, vapours, etc., in magma) to transform (a metal) into an ore. —ˌ**mineraliˈzation** *or* **-iˈsation** *n.* —ˈ**mineraˌlizer** *or* **-iser** *n.*

mineralogy (ˌmɪnəˈrælədʒɪ) *n.* the branch of geology concerned with the study of minerals. —**mineralogical** (ˌmɪnərəˈlɒdʒɪkᵊl) *or* ˌ**mineralˈogic** *adj.* —ˌ**minerˈalogist** *n.*

mineral oil *n. Brit.* any oil of mineral origin, esp. petroleum.

mineral water *n.* water containing dissolved mineral salts or gases, usually having medicinal properties.

mineral wool *n.* a fibrous material made by blowing steam or air through molten slag and used for packing and insulation.

miner's right *n. Austral.* a licence to prospect for and mine gold, etc.

minestrone (ˌmɪnɪˈstrəʊnɪ) *n.* a soup made from a variety of vegetables and pasta. [< It., < *minestrare* to serve]

minesweeper (ˈmaɪnˌswiːpə) *n.* a naval vessel equipped to clear mines. —ˈ**mineˌsweeping** *n.*

Ming (mɪŋ) *n.* **1.** the imperial dynasty of China from 1368 to 1644. ~*adj.* **2.** of or relating to Chinese porcelain from the Ming dynasty.

mingle (ˈmɪŋgᵊl) *vb.* **1.** to mix or cause to mix. **2.** (*intr.*; often foll. by *with*) to come into close association. [C15: < OE *mengan* to mix] —ˈ**mingler** *n.*

mingy (ˈmɪndʒɪ) *adj.* **-gier, -giest.** *Brit. inf.* miserly, stingy, or niggardly. [C20: prob. a blend of MEAN[2] + STINGY[1]]

mini (ˈmɪnɪ) *adj.* **1.** (of a woman's dress, skirt, etc.) very short; thigh-length. **2.** (*prenominal*) small; miniature. ~*n., pl.* **minis. 3.** something very small of its kind, esp. a small car or a miniskirt.

mini- *combining form.* smaller or shorter than the standard size: *minibus; miniskirt.* [C20: < MINIATURE & MINIMUM]

miniature (ˈmɪnɪtʃə) *n.* **1.** a model, copy, or representation on a very small scale. **2.** anything that is very small of its kind. **3.** a very small painting, esp. a portrait. **4.** an illuminated decoration in a manuscript. **5. in miniature.** on a small scale. ~*adj.* **6.** greatly reduced in size, etc. **7.** on a small scale; minute. [C16: < It., < Med. L, < *miniāre* to paint red (in illuminating manuscripts), < *minium* red lead] —ˈ**miniaturist** *n.*

miniaturize *or* **-ise** (ˈmɪnɪtʃəˌraɪz) *vb.* (*tr.*) to make or construct (something, esp. electronic equipment) on a very small scale; reduce in size. —ˌ**miniaturiˈzation** *or* **-iˈsation** *n.*

minibus (ˈmɪnɪˌbʌs) *n.* a small bus able to carry approximately ten passengers.

minicab (ˈmɪnɪˌkæb) *n. Brit.* a small saloon car used as a taxi.

minicomputer (ˌmɪnɪkəmˈpjuːtə) *n.* a small comparatively cheap digital computer.

minim (ˈmɪnɪm) *n.* **1.** a unit of fluid measure equal to one sixtieth of a drachm. It is approximately equal to one drop. Symbol: M, ♏ **2.** *Music.* a note having the time value of half a semibreve. **3.** a small or insignificant thing. **4.** a downward stroke in calligraphy. [C15 (*Music.*): < L *minimus* smallest]

minimal art *n.* abstract painting or sculpture in which expressiveness and illusion are minimized by the use of simple geometric shapes, flat colour, and arrangements of ordinary objects. —**minimal artist** *n.*

minimalism (ˈmɪnɪməˌlɪzəm) *n.* **1.** another name for **minimal art. 2.** a type of music based on simple elements and avoiding elaboration or embellishment. **3.** design or style in which the simplest and fewest elements are used to create the maximum effect. —ˈ**minimalist** *adj., n.*

minimax (ˈmɪnɪˌmæks) *n.* **1.** *Maths.* the lowest of a set of maximum values. **2.** (in game theory, etc.) the procedure of choosing the strategy that least benefits the most advantaged member of a group. Cf. **maximin.** [C20: < MINI(MUM) + MAX(IMUM)]

minimize *or* **-ise** (ˈmɪnɪˌmaɪz) *vb.* (*tr.*) **1.** to reduce to or estimate at the least possible degree or amount. **2.** to rank or treat at less than the true worth; belittle. —ˌ**minimiˈzation** *or* **-iˈsation** *n.* —ˈ**miniˌmizer** *or* **-iser** *n.*

minimum (ˈmɪnɪməm) *n., pl.* **-mums** *or* **-ma** (-mə). **1.** the least possible amount, degree, or quantity. **2.** the least amount recorded, allowed, or reached. **3.** (*modifier*) being the least possible, recorded, allowed, etc.: *minimum age.* ~*adj.* **4.** of or relating to a minimum or minimums. [C17: < L: smallest thing, < *minimus* least] —ˈ**minimal** *adj.* —ˈ**minimally** *adv.*

minimum lending rate *n.* the minimum rate at which a central bank, such as the Bank of England, will lend money to a customer whose credit is first class.

minimum wage *n.* the lowest wage that an employer is permitted to pay by law or union contract.

mining (ˈmaɪnɪŋ) *n.* **1.** the act, process, or industry of extracting coal, ores, etc., from the earth. **2.** *Mil.* the process of laying mines.

minion (ˈmɪnjən) *n.* **1.** a favourite or dependant, esp. a servile or fawning one. **2.** a servile agent. [C16: < F *mignon*, < OF *mignot*, of Gaulish origin]

minipill (ˈmɪnɪˌpɪl) *n.* a low-dose oral contraceptive containing progesterone only.

miniseries (ˈmɪnɪˌsɪəriːz) *n., pl.* **-series.** a television programme in several parts that is shown on consecutive days for a short period.

miniskirt (ˈmɪnɪˌskɜːt) *n.* a very short skirt, originally in the 1960s, one at least four inches above the knee. Often shortened to **mini.**

minister (ˈmɪnɪstə) *n.* **1.** (esp. in Presbyterian and some Nonconformist Churches) a clergyman. **2.** a head of a government department. **3.** any diplomatic agent accredited to a foreign government or head of state. **4.** Also called: **minister plenipotentiary.** See **envoy**[1] (sense 1). **5.** Also called: **minister resident.** a diplomat ranking after an envoy. **6.** a person who attends to the needs of others, esp. in religious matters. **7.** a person who acts as the agent or servant of a person or thing. ~*vb.* **8.** (*intr.*; often foll. by *to*) to attend to the needs (of); take care (of). **9.** (*tr.*) *Arch.* to provide; supply. [C13: via OF < L: servant; rel. to *minus* less]

ministerial (ˌmɪnɪˈstɪərɪəl) *adj.* **1.** of or relating to a minister of religion or his office. **2.** of or relating to a government minister or ministry. **3.** (*often cap.*) of or supporting the ministry against the opposition. **4.** *Law.* relating to or possessing delegated executive authority. **5.** acting as an agent or cause; instrumental. —ˌ**minisˈterially** *adv.*

minister of state *n.* **1.** (in the British Parliament) a minister, usually below cabinet rank, appointed to assist a senior minister. **2.** any government minister.

Minister of the Crown *n. Brit.* any Government minister of cabinet rank.

minister plenipotentiary *n., pl.* **ministers plenipotentiary.** another term for **envoy**[1] (sense 1).

ministrant (ˈmɪnɪstrənt) *adj.* **1.** ministering or serving as a minister. ~*n.* **2.** a person who ministers. [C17: < L *ministrans*, < *ministrāre* to wait upon]

ministration (ˌmɪnɪˈstreɪʃən) *n.* **1.** the act or an instance of serving or giving aid. **2.** the act or an instance of ministering religiously. [C14: < L *ministrātiō*, < *ministrāre* to wait upon] —**ministrative** (ˈmɪnɪstrətɪv) *adj.*

ministry (ˈmɪnɪstrɪ) *n., pl.* **-tries. 1. a.** the profession or duties of a minister of religion. **b.** the performance of these duties. **2.** ministers of religion or government ministers considered collectively. **3.** the tenure of a minister. **4. a.** a government department headed by a minister. **b.**

the buildings of such a department. [C14: < L *ministerium* service; see MINISTER]

miniver (ˈmɪnɪvə) *n.* white fur, used in ceremonial costumes. [C13: < OF *menu vair,* < *menu* small + *vair* variegated fur]

mink (mɪŋk) *n., pl.* **mink** *or* **minks.** **1.** any of several mammals of Europe, Asia, and North America, having slightly webbed feet. **2.** their highly valued fur, esp. that of the American mink. **3.** a garment made of this, esp. a woman's coat or stole. [C15: < ON]

minnesinger (ˈmɪnɪˌsɪŋə) *n.* one of the German lyric poets and musicians of the 12th to 14th centuries. [C19: < G *Minnesinger* love-singer]

minnow (ˈmɪnəʊ) *n., pl.* **-nows** *or* **-now. 1.** a small slender European freshwater cyprinid fish. **2.** a small or insignificant person. [C15: rel. to OE *myne* minnow]

Minoan (mɪˈnəʊən) *adj.* **1.** of or denoting the Bronze Age culture of Crete from about 3000 B.C. to about 1100 B.C. ~*n.* **2.** a Cretan belonging to the Minoan culture. [C19: after *Minos* in Gk myth, king of Crete, from the excavations at his supposed palace at Knossos]

minor (ˈmaɪnə) *adj.* **1.** lesser or secondary in amount, importance, etc. **2.** of or relating to the minority. **3.** below the age of legal majority. **4.** *Music.* **a.** (of a scale) having a semitone between the second and third and fifth and sixth degrees (**natural minor**). **b.** (of a key) based on the minor scale. **c.** (*postpositive*) denoting a specified key based on the minor scale: *C minor.* **d.** (of an interval) reduced by a semitone from the major. **e.** (of a chord, esp. a triad) having a minor third above the root. **f.** (esp. in jazz) of or relating to a chord built upon a minor triad and containing a minor seventh: *a minor ninth.* **5.** *Logic.* (of a term or premise) having less generality or scope than another term or proposition. **6.** *U.S. education.* of or relating to an additional secondary subject taken by a student. **7.** (*immediately postpositive*) *Brit.* the younger or junior: sometimes used after the surname of a schoolboy if he has an older brother in the same school. ~*n.* **8.** a person or thing that is lesser or secondary. **9.** a person below the age of legal majority. **10.** *U.S. & Canad. education.* a subsidiary subject. **11.** *Music.* a minor key, chord, mode, or scale. **12.** *Logic.* a minor term or premise. ~*vb.* **13.** (*intr.;* usually foll. by *in*) *U.S. education.* to take a minor. [C13: < L: less, smaller]

minor axis *n.* the shorter or shortest axis of an ellipse or ellipsoid.

minority (maɪˈnɒrɪtɪ, mɪ-) *n., pl.* **-ties. 1.** the smaller of two parts, factions, or groups. **2.** a group that is different racially, politically, etc., from a larger group of which it is a part. **3. a.** the state of being a minor. **b.** the period during which a person is below legal age. **4.** (*modifier*) relating to or being a minority: *a minority opinion.* [C16: < Med. L *minōritās,* < L MINOR]

minor league *n. U.S. & Canad.* any professional league in baseball other than a major league.

minor orders *pl. n. R.C. Church.* the four lower degrees of holy orders, namely porter, exorcist, lector, and acolyte.

minor premise *n. Logic.* the premise of a syllogism containing the subject of its conclusion.

minor term *n. Logic.* the subject of the conclusion of a syllogism.

minster (ˈmɪnstə) *n. Brit.* any of certain cathedrals and large churches, usually originally connected to a monastery. [OE *mynster,* prob. < Vulgar L *monisterium* (unattested), var. of Church L *monastērium* MONASTERY]

minstrel (ˈmɪnstrəl) *n.* **1.** a medieval musician who performed songs or recited poetry with instrumental accompaniment. **2.** a performer in a minstrel show. **3.** *Arch. or poetic.* any poet, musician, or singer. [C13: < OF *menestral,* < LL *ministeriālis* an official, < L MINISTER]

minstrel show *n.* a theatrical entertainment consisting of songs, dances, etc., performed by actors wearing black face make-up.

minstrelsy (ˈmɪnstrəlsɪ) *n., pl.* **-sies. 1.** the art of a minstrel. **2.** the poems, music, or songs of a minstrel. **3.** a troupe of minstrels.

mint[1] (mɪnt) *n.* **1.** any N temperate plant of a genus having aromatic leaves. The leaves of some species are used for seasoning and flavouring. See also **peppermint, spearmint. 2.** a sweet flavoured with mint. [OE *minte,* < L *mentha,* < Gk *minthē*] —ˈ**minty** *adj.*

mint[2] (mɪnt) *n.* **1.** a place where money is coined by governmental authority. **2.** a very large amount of money. ~*adj.* **3.** (of coins, postage stamps, etc.) in perfect condition as issued. **4. in mint condition.** in perfect condition; as if new. ~*vb.* **5.** to make (coins) by stamping metal. **6.** (*tr.*) to invent (esp. phrases or words). [OE *mynet* coin, < L *monēta* money, mint, from the temple of Juno *Monēta,* used as a mint in ancient Rome] —ˈ**minter** *n.*

mintage (ˈmɪntɪdʒ) *n.* **1.** the process of minting. **2.** the money minted. **3.** a fee paid for minting a coin. **4.** an official impression stamped on a coin.

mint julep *n. Chiefly U.S.* a long drink consisting of bourbon whiskey, crushed ice, sugar, and sprigs of mint.

minuend (ˈmɪnjʊˌɛnd) *n.* the number from which another number, the **subtrahend,** is to be subtracted. [C18: < L *minuendus* (*numerus*) (the number) to be diminished]

minuet (ˌmɪnjʊˈɛt) *n.* **1.** a stately court dance of the 17th and 18th centuries in triple time. **2.** a piece of music composed for or in the rhythm of this dance. [C17: < F *menuet* dainty, < *menu* small]

minus (ˈmaɪnəs) *prep.* **1.** reduced by the subtraction of: *four minus two* (written 4 – 2). **2.** *Inf.* deprived of; lacking: *minus the trimmings.* ~*adj.* **3. a.** indicating or involving subtraction: *a minus sign.* **b.** Also: **negative.** having a value or designating a quantity less than zero: *a minus number.* **4.** involving a disadvantage, harm, etc.: *a minus factor.* **5.** (*postpositive*) *Education.* slightly below the standard of a particular grade: *a B minus.* **6.** denoting a negative electric charge. ~*n.* **7.** short for **minus sign. 8.** a negative quantity. **9.** a disadvantage, loss, or deficit. **10.** *Inf.* something detrimental or negative. ~Mathematical symbol: – [C15: < L, neuter of MINOR]

minuscule (ˈmɪnəˌskjuːl) *n.* **1.** a lower-case letter. **2.** writing using such letters. **3.** a small cursive 7th-century style of lettering. ~*adj.* **4.** relating to, printed in, or written in small letters. Cf. **majuscule. 5.** very small. **6.** (of letters) lower-case. [C18: < F, < L (*littera*) *minuscula* very small (letter), dim. of MINOR] —**minuscular** (mɪˈnʌskjʊlə) *adj.*

minus sign *n.* the symbol –, indicating subtraction or a negative quantity.

minute[1] (ˈmɪnɪt) *n.* **1.** a period of time equal to 60 seconds; one sixtieth of an hour. **2.** Also called: **minute of arc.** a unit of angular measure equal to one sixtieth of a degree. Symbol: ′. **3.** any very short period of time; moment. **4.** a short note or memorandum. **5.** the distance that can be travelled in a minute: *it's only two minutes away.* **6. up to the minute** (**up-to-the-minute** *when prenominal*). the very latest or newest. ~*vb.* (*tr.*) **7.** to record in minutes: *to minute a meeting.* **8.** to time in terms of minutes. ~See also **minutes.** [C14: < OF, < Med. L *minūta,* n. use of L *minūtus* MINUTE[2]] —**minutely** (ˈmɪnɪtlɪ) *adv.*

minute[2] (maɪˈnjuːt) *adj.* **1.** very small; diminutive; tiny. **2.** unimportant; petty. **3.** precise or detailed. [C15: < L *minūtus,* p.p. of *minuere* to diminish] —**miˈnuteness** *n.* —**miˈnutely** *adv.*

minute gun (ˈmɪnɪt) *n.* a gun fired at one-minute intervals as a sign of distress or mourning.

minute hand (ˈmɪnɪt) *n.* the pointer on a timepiece that indicates minutes.

Minuteman (ˈmɪnɪtˌmæn) *n., pl.* **-men. 1.** (*sometimes not cap.*) (in the War of American Independence) a colonial militiaman who promised to be ready to fight at one minute's notice. **2.** a U.S. three-stage intercontinental ballistic missile.

minutes (ˈmɪnɪts) *pl. n.* an official record of the proceedings of a meeting, conference, etc.

minute steak (ˈmɪnɪt) *n.* a small piece of steak that can be cooked quickly.

minutiae (mɪˈnjuːʃɪˌiː) *pl. n., sing.* **-tia** (-ʃɪə). small, precise, or trifling details. [C18: pl. of LL *minūtia* smallness, < L *minūtus* MINUTE²]

minx (mɪŋks) *n.* a bold, flirtatious, or scheming woman. [C16: <?]

Miocene (ˈmaɪəˌsiːn) *adj.* **1.** of or denoting the fourth epoch of the Tertiary period. ~*n.* **2. the.** this epoch or rock series. [C19: Gk *meiōn* less + -CENE]

miosis *or* **myosis** (maɪˈəʊsɪs) *n., pl.* **-ses** (-siːz). **1.** excessive contraction of the pupil of the eye. **2.** a variant spelling of **meiosis** (sense 1). [C20: < Gk *muein* to shut the eyes + -OSIS] **—miotic** *or* **myotic** (maɪˈɒtɪk) *adj., n.*

miracle (ˈmɪrəkᵊl) *n.* **1.** an event contrary to the laws of nature and attributed to a supernatural cause. **2.** any amazing or wonderful event. **3.** a marvellous example of something: *a miracle of engineering.* **4.** short for **miracle play. 5.** (*modifier*) being or seeming a miracle: *a miracle cure.* [C12: < L *mīrāculum,* < *mīrāri* to wonder at]

miracle play *n.* a medieval play based on a biblical story or the life of a saint. Cf. **mystery play.**

miraculous (mɪˈrækjʊləs) *adj.* **1.** of, like, or caused by a miracle; marvellous. **2.** surprising. **3.** having the power to work miracles. **—miˈraculously** *adv.* **—miˈraculousness** *n.*

mirage (mɪˈrɑːʒ) *n.* **1.** an image of a distant object or sheet of water, often inverted or distorted, caused by atmospheric refraction by hot air. **2.** something illusory. [C19: < F, < (*se*) *mirer* to be reflected]

mire (ˈmaɪə) *n.* **1.** a boggy or marshy area. **2.** mud, muck, or dirt. ~*vb.* **3.** to sink or cause to sink in a mire. **4.** (*tr.*) to make dirty or muddy. **5.** (*tr.*) to involve, esp. in difficulties. [C14: < ON *mýrr*]

mirepoix (mɪəˈpwɑː) *n.* a mixture of sautéed root vegetables used as a base for braising meat or for various sauces. [F, prob. after Duke of *Mirepoix,* 18th-cent. F general]

mirk (mɜːk) *n.* a variant spelling of **murk. —ˈmirky** *adj.* **—ˈmirkily** *adv.* **—ˈmirkiness** *n.*

mirror (ˈmɪrə) *n.* **1.** a surface, such as polished metal or glass coated with a metal film, that reflects an image of an object placed in front of it. **2.** such a reflecting surface mounted in a frame. **3.** any reflecting surface. **4.** a thing that reflects or depicts something else. ~*vb.* **5.** (*tr.*) to reflect, represent, or depict faithfully: *he mirrors his teacher's ideals.* [C13: < OF < *mirer* to look at, < L *mīrārī* to wonder at]

mirror carp *n.* a variety of carp with a smooth shiny body surface.

mirror image *n.* **1.** an image as observed in a mirror. **2.** an object that corresponds to another but has left and right reversed as if seen in a mirror.

mirror writing *n.* backward writing that forms a mirror image of normal writing.

mirth (mɜːθ) *n.* laughter, gaiety, or merriment. [OE *myrgth*] **—ˈmirthful** *adj.* **—ˈmirthfulness** *n.* **—ˈmirthless** *adj.* **—ˈmirthlessness** *n.*

MIRV (mɜːv) *n. acronym for* multiple independently targeted re-entry vehicle: a missile that has several warheads, each one being directed to a different enemy target.

mis- *prefix.* **1.** wrong or bad; wrongly or badly: *misunderstanding; misfortune; mistreat; mislead.* **2.** lack of; not: *mistrust.* [OE *mis*(*se*)-]

misadventure (ˌmɪsədˈvɛntʃə) *n.* **1.** an unlucky event; misfortune. **2.** *Law.* accidental death not due to crime or negligence.

misalliance (ˌmɪsəˈlaɪəns) *n.* an unsuitable alliance or marriage. **—ˌmisalˈly** *vb.*

misanthrope (ˈmɪzənˌθrəʊp) *or* **misanthropist** (mɪˈzænθrəpɪst) *n.* a person who dislikes or distrusts other people or mankind in general. [C17: < Gk *mīsanthrōpos,* < *misos* hatred + *anthrōpos* man] **—misanthropic** (ˌmɪzənˈθrɒpɪk) *or* **ˌmisanˈthropical** *adj.* **—misanthropy** (mɪˈzænθrəpɪ) *n.*

misapply (ˌmɪsəˈplaɪ) *vb.* **-plying, -plied.** (*tr.*) **1.** to apply wrongly or badly. **2.** another word for **misappropriate. —misapplication** (ˌmɪsæplɪˈkeɪʃən) *n.*

misapprehend (ˌmɪsæprɪˈhɛnd) *vb.* (*tr.*) to misunderstand. **—misapprehension** (ˌmɪsæprɪˈhɛnʃən) *n.* **—ˌmisappreˈhensive** *adj.* **—ˌmisappreˈhensiveness** *n.*

misappropriate (ˌmɪsəˈprəʊprɪˌeɪt) *vb.* (*tr.*) to appropriate for a wrong or dishonest use; embezzle or steal. **—ˌmisapˌpropriˈation** *n.*

misbecome (ˌmɪsbɪˈkʌm) *vb.* **-coming, -came.** (*tr.*) to be unbecoming to or unsuitable for.

misbegotten (ˌmɪsbɪˈgɒtᵊn) *adj.* **1.** unlawfully obtained. **2.** badly conceived, planned, or designed. **3.** *Literary and dialect.* illegitimate; bastard.

misbehave (ˌmɪsbɪˈheɪv) *vb.* to behave (oneself) badly. **—ˌmisbeˈhaver** *n.* **—misbehaviour** *or U.S.* **misbehavior** (ˌmɪsbɪˈheɪvjə) *n.*

misbelief (ˌmɪsbɪˈliːf) *n.* a false or unorthodox belief. **—ˌmisbeˈliever** *n.*

misc. *abbrev. for:* **1.** miscellaneous. **2.** miscellany.

miscalculate (ˌmɪsˈkælkjʊˌleɪt) *vb.* (*tr.*) to calculate wrongly. **—ˌmiscalcuˈlation** *n.*

miscall (ˌmɪsˈkɔːl) *vb.* (*tr.*) **1.** to call by the wrong name. **2.** *Dialect.* to abuse or malign. **—ˌmisˈcaller** *n.*

miscarriage (mɪsˈkærɪdʒ) *n.* **1.** (*also* ˈmɪskær-). spontaneous expulsion of a fetus from the womb, esp. prior to the 20th week of pregnancy. **2.** an act of mismanagement or failure: *a miscarriage of justice.* **3.** *Brit.* the failure of freight to reach its destination.

miscarry (mɪsˈkærɪ) *vb.* **-rying, -ried.** (*intr.*) **1.** to expel a fetus prematurely from the womb; abort. **2.** to fail. **3.** *Brit.* (of freight, mail, etc.) to fail to reach a destination.

miscast (ˌmɪsˈkɑːst) *vb.* **-casting, -cast.** (*tr.*) **1.** to cast badly. **2.** (*often passive*) **a.** to cast (a role) in (a play, film, etc.) inappropriately: *Falstaff was miscast.* **b.** to assign an inappropriate role to: *he was miscast as Othello.*

miscegenation (ˌmɪsɪdʒɪˈneɪʃən) *n.* interbreeding of races, esp. where differences of pigmentation are involved. [C19: < L *miscēre* to mingle + *genus* race]

miscellanea (ˌmɪsəˈleɪnɪə) *pl. n.* a collection of miscellaneous items, esp. literary works. [C16: < L: neuter pl. of *miscellāneus* MISCELLANEOUS]

miscellaneous (ˌmɪsəˈleɪnɪəs) *adj.* **1.** composed of or containing a variety of things; mixed. **2.** having varied capabilities, sides, etc. [C17: < L *miscellāneus,* < *miscellus* mixed, < *miscēre* to mix] **—ˌmiscelˈlaneously** *adv.* **—ˌmiscelˈlaneousness** *n.* **—miscellanist** (mɪˈsɛlənɪst) *n.*

miscellany (mɪˈsɛlənɪ; *U.S.* ˈmɪsəˌleɪnɪ) *n., pl.* **-nies.** (*sometimes pl.*) a miscellaneous collection of items, esp. essays, poems, etc. [C16: < F *miscellanées* (pl.) MISCELLANEA]

mischance (mɪsˈtʃɑːns) *n.* **1.** bad luck. **2.** a stroke of bad luck.

mischief (ˈmɪstʃɪf) *n.* **1.** wayward but not malicious behaviour, usually of children, that causes trouble, irritation, etc. **2.** a playful inclination to behave in this way or to tease or disturb. **3.** a person who causes mischief. **4.** injury or harm caused by a person or thing. **5.** a source of trouble, difficulty, etc. [C13: < OF

ˌmisaˈdapt *vb.*
ˌmisadˈdress *vb.*
ˌmisadˌminisˈtration *n.*
ˌmisaˈlign *vb.*
ˌmisaˈlignment *n.*
ˌmisarˈrange *vb.*
ˌmisarˈrangement *n.*

meschief, < *meschever* to meet with calamity; < *mes-* MIS- + *chever,* < *chef* end]

mischievous (ˈmɪstʃɪvəs) *adj.* **1.** inclined to acts of mischief. **2.** teasing; slightly malicious. **3.** causing or intended to cause harm. —**ˈmischievously** *adv.* —**ˈmischievousness** *n.*

miscible (ˈmɪsɪbᵊl) *adj.* capable of mixing: *miscible with water.* [C16: < Med. L *miscibilis,* < L *miscēre* to mix] —ˌ**misciˈbility** *n.*

misconceive (ˌmɪskənˈsiːv) *vb.* to have the wrong idea; fail to understand. —ˌ**misconˈceiver** *n.*

misconception (ˌmɪskənˈsɛpʃən) *n.* a false or mistaken view, opinion, or attitude.

misconduct *n.* (mɪsˈkɒndʌkt). **1.** behaviour, such as adultery or professional negligence, that is regarded as immoral or unethical. ~*vb.* (ˌmɪskənˈdʌkt). (*tr.*) **2.** to conduct (oneself) in such a way. **3.** to manage (something) badly.

misconstrue (ˌmɪskənˈstruː) *vb.* **-struing, -strued.** (*tr.*) to interpret mistakenly. —ˌ**misconˈstruction** *n.*

miscreant (ˈmɪskrɪənt) *n.* **1.** a wrongdoer or villain. **2.** *Arch.* an unbeliever or heretic. ~*adj.* **3.** evil or villainous. **4.** *Arch.* unbelieving or heretical. [C14: < OF *mescreant* unbelieving, < *mes-* MIS- + *creant,* ult. < L *credere* to believe]

miscue (ˌmɪsˈkjuː) *n.* **1.** *Billiards, etc.* a faulty stroke in which the cue tip slips off the cue ball or misses it. **2.** *Inf.* a blunder or mistake. ~*vb.* **-cuing, -cued.** (*intr.*) **3.** *Billiards.* to make a miscue. **4.** *Theatre.* to fail to answer one's cue.

misdate (mɪsˈdeɪt) *vb.* (*tr.*) to date (a letter, event, etc.) wrongly.

misdeal (ˌmɪsˈdiːl) *vb.* **-dealing, -dealt.** **1.** (*intr.*) to deal out cards incorrectly. ~*n.* **2.** a faulty deal. —ˌ**misˈdealer** *n.*

misdeed (ˌmɪsˈdiːd) *n.* an evil or illegal action.

misdemean (ˌmɪsdɪˈmiːn) *vb.* a rare word for **misbehave.**

misdemeanour *or U.S.* **misdemeanor** (ˌmɪsdɪˈmiːnə) *n.* **1.** *Criminal law.* (formerly) an offence generally less heinous than a felony. **2.** any minor offence or transgression.

misdirect (ˌmɪsdɪˈrɛkt) *vb.* (*tr.*) **1.** to give (a person) wrong directions or instructions. **2.** to address (a letter, parcel, etc.) wrongly. —ˌ**misdiˈrection** *n.*

misdoubt (mɪsˈdaʊt) *vb.* an archaic word for **doubt** or **suspect.**

mise en scène *French.* (miz ɑ̃ sɛn) *n.* **1. a.** the arrangement of properties, scenery, etc., in a play. **b.** the objects so arranged; stage setting. **2.** the environment of an event.

miser (ˈmaɪzə) *n.* **1.** a person who hoards money or possessions, often living miserably. **2.** a selfish person. [C16: < L: wretched]

miserable (ˈmɪzərəbᵊl) *adj.* **1.** unhappy or depressed; wretched. **2.** causing misery, discomfort, etc.: *a miserable life.* **3.** contemptible: *a miserable villain.* **4.** sordid or squalid: *miserable living conditions.* **5.** mean; stingy. [C16: < OF, < L *miserābilis,* < *miserārī* to pity, < *miser* wretched] —**ˈmiserableness** *n.* —**ˈmiserably** *adv.*

misère (mɪˈzɛə) *n.* **1.** a call in solo whist, etc. declaring a hand that will win no tricks. **2.** a hand that will win no tricks. [C19: < F: misery]

Miserere (ˌmɪzəˈrɛərɪ, -ˈrɪərɪ) *n.* the 51st psalm, the Latin version of which begins "Miserere mei, Deus" ("Have mercy on me, O God").

misericord *or* **misericorde** (mɪˈzɛrɪˌkɔːd) *n.* **1.** a ledge projecting from the underside of the hinged seat of a choir stall in a church, on which the occupant can support himself while standing. **2.** *Christianity.* **a.** a relaxation of certain monastic rules for infirm or aged monks or nuns. **b.** a monastery or room where this can be enjoyed. **3.** a medieval dagger used to give the death stroke to a wounded foe. [C14: < OF, < L *misericordia* compassion, < *miserēre* to pity + *cor* heart]

miserly (ˈmaɪzəlɪ) *adj.* of or resembling a miser; avaricious. —**ˈmiserliness** *n.*

misery (ˈmɪzərɪ) *n., pl.* **-eries.** **1.** intense unhappiness, suffering, etc. **2.** a cause of such unhappiness, etc. **3.** squalid or poverty-stricken conditions. **4.** *Brit. inf.* a person who is habitually depressed: *he is such a misery.* [C14: via Anglo-Norman < L *miseria,* < *miser* wretched]

misfeasance (mɪsˈfiːzəns) *n. Law.* the improper performance of an act that is lawful in itself. Cf. **malfeasance, nonfeasance.** [C16: < OF *mesfaisance,* < *mesfaire* to perform misdeeds]

misfile (ˌmɪsˈfaɪl) *vb.* to file (papers, records, etc.) wrongly.

misfire (ˌmɪsˈfaɪə) *vb.* (*intr.*) **1.** (of a firearm or its projectile) to fail to fire or explode as expected. **2.** (of a motor engine or vehicle, etc.) to fail to fire at the appropriate time. **3.** to fail to operate or occur as intended. ~*n.* **4.** the act or an instance of misfiring.

misfit *n.* (ˈmɪsˌfɪt). **1.** a person not suited to a particular social environment. **2.** something that does not fit or fits badly. ~*vb.* (ˌmɪsˈfɪt), **-fitting, -fitted.** (*intr.*) **3.** to fail to fit or be fitted.

misfortune (mɪsˈfɔːtʃən) *n.* **1.** evil fortune; bad luck. **2.** an unfortunate or disastrous event.

misgive (mɪsˈgɪv) *vb.* **-giving, -gave, -given.** to make or be apprehensive or suspicious.

misgiving (mɪsˈgɪvɪŋ) *n.* (*often pl.*) a feeling of uncertainty, apprehension, or doubt.

misguide (ˌmɪsˈgaɪd) *vb.* (*tr.*) to guide or direct wrongly or badly.

misguided (ˌmɪsˈgaɪdɪd) *adj.* foolish or unreasonable, esp. in action or behaviour. —ˌ**misˈguidedly** *adv.*

mishandle (ˌmɪsˈhændᵊl) *vb.* (*tr.*) to handle or treat badly or inefficiently.

mishap (ˈmɪshæp) *n.* **1.** an unfortunate accident. **2.** bad luck.

mishit *Sport.* ~*n.* (ˈmɪsˌhɪt). **1.** a faulty shot or stroke. ~*vb.* (ˌmɪsˈhɪt), **-hitting, -hit.** **2.** to hit (a ball) with a faulty stroke.

mishmash (ˈmɪʃˌmæʃ) *n.* a confused collection or mixture. [C15: reduplication of MASH]

Mishna (ˈmɪʃnə) *n., pl.* **Mishnayoth** (mɪʃˈnɑːjəʊt). *Judaism.* a compilation of precepts collected in the late second century A.D. It forms the earlier part of the Talmud. [C17: < Heb., < *shānāh* to repeat] —**Mishnaic** (mɪʃˈneɪɪk) *or* **ˈMishnic** *adj.*

misinform (ˌmɪsɪnˈfɔːm) *vb.* (*tr.*) to give incorrect information to. —**misinformation** (ˌmɪsɪnfəˈmeɪʃən) *n.*

misinterpret (ˌmɪsɪnˈtɜːprɪt) *vb.* (*tr.*) to interpret badly, misleadingly, or incorrectly. —ˌ**misinˌterpreˈtation** *n.* —ˌ**misinˈterpreter** *n.*

misjudge (ˌmɪsˈdʒʌdʒ) *vb.* to judge (a person or persons) wrongly or unfairly. —ˌ**misˈjudger** *n.* —ˌ**misˈjudgment** *or* ˌ**misˈjudgement** *n.*

mislay (mɪsˈleɪ) *vb.* **-laying, -laid.** (*tr.*) **1.** to lose (something) temporarily, esp. by forgetting where it is. **2.** to lay (something) badly.

mislead (mɪsˈliːd) *vb.* **-leading, -led.** (*tr.*) **1.** to give false or confusing information to. **2.** to lead or guide in the wrong direction. —**misˈleader** *n.* —**misˈleading** *adj.*

mismatch (ˌmɪsˈmætʃ) *vb.* **1.** to match badly, esp. in marriage. ~*n.* **2.** a bad match.

misnomer (ˌmɪsˈnəʊmə) *n.* **1.** an incorrect or unsuitable name for a person or thing. **2.** the act of referring to a person by the wrong name. [C15:

ˌ**misconˈjecture** *vb.*
misˈcopy *vb.*
ˌ**misˈcount** *vb., n.*
ˌ**misdiagˈnosis** *n.*
misˈeduˌcate *vb.*
ˌ**miseduˈcation** *n.*
ˌ**misemˈploy** *vb.*
misˈestiˌmate *vb., n.*
ˌ**misestiˈmation** *n.*
misˈgauge *vb.*
ˌ**misˈgovern** *vb.*
ˌ**misˈgovernment** *n.*
ˌ**misˈhear** *vb.*
ˌ**misiˌdentifiˈcation** *n.*
ˌ**misiˈdentiˌfy** *vb.*
ˌ**misˈmanage** *vb.*
ˌ**misˈmanagement** *n.*
misˈmarriage *n.*
misˈmeasure *vb.*
misˈname *vb.*

via Anglo-Norman < OF *mesnommer* to misname, < L *nōmināre* to call by name]

miso- *or before a vowel* **mis-** *combining form.* indicating hatred: *misogyny.* [< Gk *misos* hatred]

misogamy (mɪˈsɒgəmɪ, maɪ-) *n.* hatred of marriage. —**miˈsogamist** *n.*

misogyny (mɪˈsɒdʒɪnɪ, maɪ-) *n.* hatred of women. [C17: < Gk, < MISO- + *gunē* woman] —**miˈsogynist** *n.* —**miˈsogynous** *adj.*

misplace (ˌmɪsˈpleɪs) *vb.* (*tr.*) **1.** to put (something) in the wrong place, esp. to lose (something) temporarily by forgetting where it was placed. **2.** (*often passive*) to bestow (trust, affection, etc.) unadvisedly. —ˌ**misˈplacement** *n.*

misplaced modifier *n. Grammar.* a participle intended to modify a noun but having the wrong grammatical relationship to it, for example *having left* in the sentence *Having left Europe for good, Peter's future seemed bleak.*

misplay (ˌmɪsˈpleɪ) *vb.* **1.** (*tr.*) to play badly or wrongly in games or sports. ~*n.* **2.** a wrong or unskilful play.

misprint *n.* (ˈmɪsˌprɪnt). **1.** an error in printing, made through damaged type, careless reading, etc. ~*vb.* (ˌmɪsˈprɪnt). **2.** (*tr.*) to print (a letter) incorrectly.

misprision[1] (mɪsˈprɪʒən) *n.* **a.** a failure to inform the authorities of the commission of an act of treason. **b.** the deliberate concealment of the commission of a felony. [C15: via Anglo-F < OF *mesprision* error, < *mesprendre* to mistake, < *mes-* MIS- + *prendre* to take]

misprision[2] (mɪsˈprɪʒən) *n. Arch.* **1.** contempt. **2.** failure to appreciate the value of something. [C16: < MISPRIZE]

misprize *or* **-ise** (mɪsˈpraɪz) *vb.* to fail to appreciate the value of; disparage. [C15: < OF *mesprisier,* < *mes-* MIS- + *prisier* to PRIZE[2]]

mispronounce (ˌmɪsprəˈnaʊns) *vb.* to pronounce (a word) wrongly. —**mispronunciation** (ˌmɪsprəˌnʌnsɪˈeɪʃən) *n.*

misquote (ˌmɪsˈkwəʊt) *vb.* to quote (a text, speech, etc.) inaccurately. —ˌ**misquoˈtation** *n.*

misread (ˌmɪsˈriːd) *vb.* **-reading, -read** (-ˈrɛd). (*tr.*) **1.** to read incorrectly. **2.** to misinterpret.

misrepresent (ˌmɪsrɛprɪˈzɛnt) *vb.* (*tr.*) to represent wrongly or inaccurately. —ˌ**misrepresenˈtation** *n.* —ˌ**misrepreˈsentative** *adj.*

misrule (ˌmɪsˈruːl) *vb.* **1.** (*tr.*) to govern inefficiently or without justice. ~*n.* **2.** inefficient or unjust government. **3.** disorder.

miss[1] (mɪs) *vb.* **1.** to fail to reach, hit, meet, find, or attain (some aim, target, etc.). **2.** (*tr.*) to fail to attend or be present for: *to miss an appointment.* **3.** (*tr.*) to fail to see, hear, understand, or perceive. **4.** (*tr.*) to lose, overlook, or fail to take advantage of: *to miss an opportunity.* **5.** (*tr.*) to leave out; omit: *to miss an entry in a list.* **6.** (*tr.*) to discover or regret the loss or absence of: *she missed him.* **7.** (*tr.*) to escape or avoid (something, esp. a danger), usually narrowly: *he missed death by inches.* ~*n.* **8.** a failure to reach, hit, etc. **9. give (something) a miss.** *Inf.* to avoid (something): *give the pudding a miss.* ~See also **miss out.** [OE *missan* (meaning: to fail to hit)]

miss[2] (mɪs) *n. Inf.* **1.** an unmarried woman or girl. **2.** (in the fashion trade) a size in young women's clothes. [C17: < MISTRESS]

Miss (mɪs) *n.* a title of an unmarried woman or girl, usually used before the surname or sometimes alone in direct address. [C17: shortened < MISTRESS]

▷ **Usage.** When reference is made to two or more unmarried women with the same surname, *the Misses Smith* is more formal than *the Miss Smiths.* See also **Ms.**

missal (ˈmɪsᵊl) *n. R.C. Church.* a book containing the prayers, rites, etc., of the Masses for a complete year. [C14: < Church L *missale* (n.), < *missālis* concerning the MASS]

misshape *vb.* (ˌmɪsˈʃeɪp). **-shaping, -shaped** *or* **-shapen.** **1.** (*tr.*) to shape badly; deform. ~*n.* (ˈmɪsˌʃeɪp). **2.** something that is badly shaped.

misshapen (ˌmɪsˈʃeɪpᵊn) *adj.* badly shaped; deformed. —ˌ**misˈshapenness** *n.*

missile (ˈmɪsaɪl) *n.* **1.** any object or weapon that is thrown at a target or shot from an engine, gun, etc. **2.** a rocket-propelled weapon that flies either in a fixed trajectory (**ballistic missile**) or in a trajectory controlled during flight (**guided missile**). [C17: < L *missilis,* < *mittere* to send]

missilery *or* **missilry** (ˈmɪsaɪlrɪ) *n.* **1.** missiles collectively. **2.** the design, operation, or study of missiles.

missing (ˈmɪsɪŋ) *adj.* **1.** not present; absent or lost. **2.** not able to be traced and not known to be dead: *nine men were missing after the attack.* **3. go missing.** to become lost or disappear.

missing link *n.* **1.** (*sometimes cap.;* usually preceded by *the*) a hypothetical extinct animal, formerly thought to be intermediate between the anthropoid apes and man. **2.** any missing section or part in a series.

mission (ˈmɪʃən) *n.* **1.** a specific task or duty assigned to a person or group of people. **2.** a person's vocation (often in **mission in life**). **3.** a group of persons representing or working for a particular country, business, etc., in a foreign country. **4.** a special embassy sent to a foreign country for a specific purpose. **5. a.** a group of people sent by a religious body, esp. a Christian church, to a foreign country to do religious and social work. **b.** the campaign undertaken by such a group. **6. a.** a building in which missionary work is performed. **b.** the area assigned to a particular missionary. **7.** the dispatch of aircraft or spacecraft to achieve a particular task. **8.** a charitable centre that offers shelter or aid to the destitute or underprivileged. **9.** (*modifier*) of or relating to an ecclesiastical mission: *a mission station.* ~*vb.* **10.** (*tr.*) to direct a mission to or establish a mission in (a given region). [C16: < L *missiō,* < *mittere* to send]

missionary (ˈmɪʃənərɪ) *n., pl.* **-aries. a.** Also called: **missioner.** a member of a religious mission. **b.** (*as modifier*): *missionary work.*

missionary position *n. Inf.* a position for sexual intercourse in which the man lies on top of the woman and they are face to face. [C20: < the belief that missionaries advocated this as the proper position to primitive peoples among whom it was unknown]

missis *or* **missus** (ˈmɪsɪz, -ɪs) *n.* **1.** (usually preceded by *the*) *Inf.* one's wife or the wife of the person addressed or referred to. **2.** an informal term of address for a woman. [C19: spoken version of MISTRESS]

Mississippian (ˌmɪsɪˈsɪpɪən) *adj.* **1.** of or relating to the state of Mississippi, U.S.A. or the Mississippi river. **2.** (in North America) of or denoting the lower of two subdivisions of the Carboniferous period (see also **Pennsylvanian** (sense 2)). ~*n.* **3.** an inhabitant or native of the state of Mississippi. **4. the.** the Mississippian period or rock system.

missive (ˈmɪsɪv) *n.* **1.** a formal or official letter. **2.** a formal word for **letter.** [C15: < Med. L *missivus,* < *mittere* to send]

miss out *vb.* (*adv.*) **1.** (*tr.*) to leave out; overlook. **2.** (*intr.;* often foll. by *on*) to fail to experience: *you missed out on the celebrations.*

misspell (ˌmɪsˈspɛl) *vb.* **-spelling, -spelt** *or* **-spelled.** to spell (a word or words) wrongly.

misspelling (ˌmɪsˈspɛlɪŋ) *n.* a wrong spelling.

misspend (ˌmɪsˈspɛnd) *vb.* **-spending, -spent.** to spend thoughtlessly or wastefully.

ˌ**misperˈception** *n.*
misˈphrase *vb.*
ˌ**misproˈportion** *n.*
misˈpunctuˌate *vb.*
ˌ**mispunctuˈation** *n.*
ˌ**misreˈmember** *vb.*
ˌ**misreˈport** *vb.*
misˈrhymed *adj.*
ˌ**misˈstate** *vb.*
ˌ**misˈstatement** *n.*

misstep (ˌmɪsˈstɛp) *n.* 1. a false step. 2. an error.
missy (ˈmɪsɪ) *n., pl.* **missies.** *Inf.* an affectionate or disparaging form of address to a young girl.
mist (mɪst) *n.* 1. a thin fog resulting from condensation in the air near the earth's surface. 2. *Meteorol.* such an atmospheric condition with a horizontal visibility of 1–2 kilometres. 3. a fine spray of liquid, such as that produced by an aerosol container. 4. condensed water vapour on a surface. 5. something that causes haziness or lack of clarity, such as a film of tears. ~*vb.* 6. to cover or be covered with or as if with mist. [OE]
mistake (mɪˈsteɪk) *n.* 1. an error or blunder in action, opinion, or judgment. 2. a misconception or misunderstanding. ~*vb.* **-taking, -took, -taken.** 3. (*tr.*) to misunderstand; misinterpret: *she mistook his meaning.* 4. (*tr.;* foll. by *for*) to take (for), interpret (as), or confuse (with): *she mistook his direct manner for honesty.* 5. (*tr.*) to choose badly or incorrectly: *he mistook his path.* 6. (*intr.*) to make a mistake. [C13 (meaning: to do wrong, err): < ON *mistaka* to take erroneously] —**misˈtakable** *adj.*
mistaken (mɪˈsteɪkən) *adj.* 1. (*usually predicative*) wrong in opinion, judgment, etc. 2. arising from error in opinion, judgment, etc.: *a mistaken viewpoint.* —**misˈtakenly** *adv.* —**misˈtakenness** *n.*
mister (ˈmɪstə) (*sometimes cap.*) ~*n.* 1. an informal form of address for a man. 2. *Naval.* a. the official form of address for subordinate or senior warrant officers. b. the official form of address for all officers in a merchant ship, other than the captain. 3. *Brit.* the form of address for a surgeon. 4. the form of address for officials holding certain positions: *mister chairman.* ~*vb.* 5. (*tr.*) *Inf.* to call (someone) mister. [C16: var. of MASTER]
Mister (ˈmɪstə) *n.* the full form of **Mr.**
misterioso (mɪˌstɛrɪˈəʊsəʊ) *adv. Music.* in a mysterious manner; mysteriously. [It.]
mistigris (ˈmɪstɪgriː) *n.* 1. the joker or a blank card used as a wild card in a variety of draw poker. 2. the game. [C19: < F: jack of clubs, game in which this card was wild]
mistime (ˌmɪsˈtaɪm) *vb.* (*tr.*) to time (an action, utterance, etc.) wrongly.
mistle thrush *or* **missel thrush** (ˈmɪsᵊl) *n.* a large European thrush with a brown back and spotted breast, noted for feeding on mistletoe berries. [C18: < OE *mistel* MISTLETOE]
mistletoe (ˈmɪsᵊlˌtəʊ) *n.* 1. a Eurasian evergreen shrub with waxy white berries: grows as a partial parasite on various trees: used as a Christmas decoration. 2. any of several similar and related American plants. [OE *misteltān,* < *mistel* mistletoe + *tān* twig; rel. to ON *mistilteinn*]
mistook (mɪˈstʊk) *vb.* the past tense of **mistake.**
mistral (ˈmɪstrəl, mɪˈstrɑːl) *n.* a strong cold dry wind that blows through the Rhône valley and S France to the Mediterranean coast, mainly in the winter. [C17: via F < Provençal, < L *magistrālis* MAGISTRAL]
mistreat (ˌmɪsˈtriːt) *vb.* (*tr.*) to treat badly. —ˌ**misˈtreatment** *n.*
mistress (ˈmɪstrɪs) *n.* 1. a woman who has a continuing extramarital sexual relationship with a man. 2. a woman in a position of authority, ownership, or control. 3. a woman having control over something specified: *mistress of her own destiny.* 4. *Chiefly Brit.* short for **schoolmistress.** 5. an archaic or dialect word for **sweetheart.** [C14: < OF; see MASTER, -ESS]
Mistress (ˈmɪstrɪs) *n.* an archaic or dialect title equivalent to **Mrs.**
Mistress of the Robes *n.* (in Britain) a lady of high rank in charge of the Queen's wardrobe.
mistrial (mɪsˈtraɪəl) *n.* 1. a trial made void because of some error. 2. *U.S.* an inconclusive trial, as when a jury cannot agree on a verdict.
mistrust (ˌmɪsˈtrʌst) *vb.* 1. to have doubts or suspicions about (someone or something). ~*n.* 2. distrust. —ˌ**misˈtrustful** *adj.* —ˌ**misˈtrustfully** *adv.* —ˌ**misˈtrustfulness** *n.*
misty (ˈmɪstɪ) *adj.* **-tier, -tiest.** 1. consisting of or resembling mist. 2. obscured as by mist. 3. indistinct; blurred. —ˈ**mistily** *adv.* —ˈ**mistiness** *n.*
misunderstand (ˌmɪsʌndəˈstænd) *vb.* **-standing, -stood.** to fail to understand properly.
misunderstanding (ˌmɪsʌndəˈstændɪŋ) *n.* 1. a failure to understand properly. 2. a disagreement.
misunderstood (ˌmɪsʌndəˈstʊd) *adj.* not properly or sympathetically understood: *a misunderstood adolescent.*
misuse *n.* (ˌmɪsˈjuːs), *also* **misusage.** 1. erroneous, improper, or unorthodox use: *misuse of words.* 2. cruel or inhumane treatment. ~*vb.* (ˌmɪsˈjuːz). (*tr.*) 3. to use wrongly. 4. to treat badly or harshly. —ˌ**misˈuser** *n.*
mite[1] (maɪt) *n.* any of numerous small terrestrial or aquatic free-living or parasitic arachnids. [OE *mīte*]
mite[2] (maɪt) *n.* 1. a very small particle, creature, or object. 2. a very small contribution or sum of money. See also **widow's mite.** 3. a former Flemish coin of small value. 4. **a mite.** *Inf.* somewhat: *he's a mite foolish.* [C14: < MLow G, MDu. *mīte*]
Mithraism (ˈmɪθreɪˌɪzəm) *or* **Mithraicism** (mɪθˈreɪɪˌsɪzəm) *n.* the ancient religion of Mithras, the Persian god of light. —**Mithraic** (mɪθˈreɪɪk) *adj.* —ˈ**Mithraist** *n., adj.*
mithridatism (ˈmɪθrɪdeɪˌtɪzəm) *n.* immunity to large doses of poison by prior ingestion of gradually increased doses. [C19: < LL *mithradatium,* after Mithradates VI (?132-63 B.C.), King of Pontus, alluding to his legendary immunity to poison] —**mithridatic** (ˌmɪθrɪˈdætɪk, -ˈdeɪ-) *adj.*
mitigate (ˈmɪtɪˌgeɪt) *vb.* to make or become less severe or harsh; moderate. [C15: < L *mītigāre,* < *mītis* mild + *agere* to make] —**mitigable** (ˈmɪtɪgəbᵊl) *adj.* —ˌ**mitiˈgation** *n.* —ˈ**mitiˌgative** *or* ˈ**mitiˌgatory** *adj.* —ˈ**mitiˌgator** *n.*
▷ **Usage.** See at **militate.**
mitochondrion (ˌmaɪtəʊˈkɒndrɪən) *n., pl.* **-dria** (-drɪə). a small spherical or rodlike body, in the cytoplasm of most cells: contains enzymes responsible for energy production. [C19: NL, < Gk *mitos* thread + *khondrion* small grain]
mitosis (maɪˈtəʊsɪs, mɪ-) *n.* a method of cell division, in which the nucleus divides into daughter nuclei, each containing the same number of chromosomes as the parent nucleus. [C19: < NL, < Gk *mitos* thread] —**mitotic** (maɪˈtɒtɪk, mɪ-) *adj.*
mitral (ˈmaɪtrəl) *adj.* 1. of or like a mitre. 2. *Anat.* of or relating to the mitral valve.
mitral valve *n.* the valve between the left atrium and the left ventricle of the heart.
mitre *or U.S.* **miter** (ˈmaɪtə) *n.* 1. *Christianity.* the liturgical headdress of a bishop or abbot, consisting of a tall pointed cleft cap with two bands hanging down at the back. 2. Also called: **mitre joint.** a corner joint formed by cutting bevels of equal angles at the ends of each piece of material. 3. a bevelled surface of a mitre joint. ~*vb.* (*tr.*) 4. to make a mitre joint between (two pieces of material). 5. to confer a mitre upon: *a mitred abbot.* [C14: < OF, < L *mitra,* < Gk: turban]
mitre box *n.* an open-ended box with sides slotted to guide a saw in cutting mitre joints.
mitt (mɪt) *n.* 1. any of various glovelike hand coverings, such as one that does not cover the fingers. 2. short for **mitten** (sense 1). 3. *Baseball.* a large round thickly padded leather mitten worn by the catcher. 4. (*often pl.*) a slang word for **hand.** 5. *Sl.* a boxing glove. [C18: < MITTEN]
mitten (ˈmɪtᵊn) *n.* 1. a glove having one section

misˈtitle *vb.* **misˈtype** *vb.*

for the thumb and a single section for the other fingers. Sometimes shortened to **mitt.** **2.** *Sl.* a boxing glove. [C14: < OF *mitaine*, <?]

mittimus (ˈmɪtɪməs) *n., pl.* **-muses.** *Law.* a warrant of commitment to prison or a command to a jailer to hold someone in prison. [C15: < L: we send, the first word of such a command]

mix (mɪks) *vb.* **1.** (*tr.*) to combine or blend (ingredients, liquids, objects, etc.) together into one mass. **2.** (*intr.*) to become or have the capacity to become combined, joined, etc.: *some chemicals do not mix.* **3.** (*tr.*) to form (something) by combining constituents: *to mix cement.* **4.** (*tr.; often foll. by in or into*) to add as an additional element (to a mass or compound): *to mix flour into a batter.* **5.** (*tr.*) to do at the same time: *to mix study and pleasure.* **6.** (*tr.*) to consume (different alcoholic drinks) in close succession. **7.** to come or cause to come into association socially: *Pauline mixed well.* **8.** (*intr.; often foll. by with*) to go together; complement. **9.** (*tr.*) to crossbreed (differing strains of plants or breeds of livestock), esp. more or less at random. **10.** *Music.* to balance and adjust (individual performers' parts) to make an overall sound by electronic means. **11. mix it.** *Inf.* to cause mischief or trouble, often for a person named: *she tried to mix it for John.* ~*n.* **12.** the act or an instance of mixing. **13.** the result of mixing; mixture. **14.** a mixture of ingredients, esp. one commercially prepared for making a cake, bread, etc. **15.** *Inf.* a state of confusion. **16.** *Music.* the sound produced by mixing. ~See also **mix-up.** [C15: back formation < *mixt* mixed, via OF < L *mixtus*, < *miscēre* to mix] —ˈ**mixable** *adj.*

mixed (mɪkst) *adj.* **1.** formed or blended together by mixing. **2.** composed of different elements, races, sexes, etc.: *a mixed school.* **3.** consisting of conflicting elements, thoughts, attitudes, etc.: *mixed feelings.* **4.** *Maths.* (of a number) consisting of the sum of an integer and a fraction or a decimal fraction, as 5½ or 17.43. —**mixedness** (ˈmɪksɪdnɪs) *n.*

mixed bag *n. Inf.* something composed of diverse elements, characteristics, people, etc.

mixed blessing *n.* an event, situation, etc., having both advantages and disadvantages.

mixed doubles *pl. n. Tennis.* a doubles game with a man and a woman as partners on each side.

mixed farming *n.* combined arable and livestock farming (on **mixed farms**).

mixed marriage *n.* a marriage between persons of different races or religions.

mixed metaphor *n.* a combination of incongruous metaphors, as *when the Nazi jackboots sing their swan song.*

mixed-up *adj.* in a state of mental confusion.

mixer (ˈmɪksə) *n.* **1.** a person or thing that mixes. **2.** *Inf.* **a.** a person considered in relation to his ability to mix socially. **b.** a person who creates trouble for others. **3.** a kitchen appliance, usually electrical, used for mixing foods, etc. **4.** a drink such as ginger ale, fruit juice, etc., used in preparing cocktails. **5.** *Electronics.* a device in which two or more input signals are combined to give a single output signal.

mixer tap *n.* a tap in which hot and cold water supplies have a joint outlet but are controlled separately.

mixture (ˈmɪkstʃə) *n.* **1.** the act of mixing or state of being mixed. **2.** something mixed; a result of mixing. **3.** *Chem.* a substance consisting of two or more substances mixed together without any chemical bonding between them. **4.** *Pharmacol.* a liquid medicine in which an insoluble compound is suspended in the liquid. **5.** *Music.* an organ stop that controls several ranks of pipes. **6.** the mixture of petrol vapour and air in an internal-combustion engine. [C16: < L *mixtūra*, < *mixtus*, p.p. of *miscere* to mix]

mix-up *n.* **1.** a confused condition or situation. **2.** *Inf.* a fight. ~*vb.* **mix up.** (*tr., adv.*) **3.** to make into a mixture. **4.** to confuse or confound: *Tom mixes John up with Bill.* **5.** (*often passive*) to put (someone) into a state of confusion: *I'm all mixed up.* **6.** (*foll. by in or with; usually passive*) to involve (in an activity or group, esp. one that is illegal): *mixed up in the drugs racket.*

mizzen *or* **mizen** (ˈmɪzᵊn) *Naut.* ~*n.* **1.** a sail set on a mizzenmast. **2.** short for **mizzenmast.** ~*adj.* **3.** of or relating to a mizzenmast: *a mizzen staysail.* [C15: < F *misaine*, < It. *mezzana*, *mezzano* middle]

mizzenmast *or* **mizenmast** (ˈmɪzᵊnˌmɑːst; *Naut.* ˈmɪzᵊnməst) *n. Naut.* (on a vessel with three or more masts) the third mast from the bow.

mizzle[1] (ˈmɪzᵊl) *vb., n.* a dialect word for **drizzle.** [C15: ? < Low G *miseln* to drizzle] —ˈ**mizzly** *adj.*

mizzle[2] (ˈmɪzᵊl) *vb.* (*intr.*) *Brit. sl.* to decamp. [C18: <?]

mk *Currency. symbol for:* **1.** mark. **2.** markka.

mks units *pl. n.* a metric system of units based on the metre, kilogram, and second as the units of length, mass, and time; it forms the basis of the SI units.

mkt *abbrev. for* market.

ml *symbol for:* **1.** mile. **2.** millilitre.

ML *abbrev. for* Medieval Latin.

MLA *abbrev. for:* **1.** Member of the Legislative Assembly. **2.** Modern Language Association (of America).

MLC (in Australia and India) *abbrev. for* Member of the Legislative Council.

MLitt *abbrev. for* Master of Letters. [L *Magister Litterarum*]

Mlle *or* **Mlle.** *pl.* **Mlles** *or* **Mlles.** the French equivalent of **Miss.** [< F *Mademoiselle*]

MLR *abbrev. for* minimum lending rate.

mm *symbol for* millimetre.

MM **1.** the French equivalent of **Messrs.** [< F *Messieurs*] **2.** *abbrev. for* Military Medal.

Mme *pl.* **Mmes** the French equivalent of **Mrs.** [< F *Madame, Mesdames*]

MMus *abbrev. for* Master of Music.

Mn *the chemical symbol for* manganese.

MNA (in Canada) *abbrev. for* Member of the National Assembly (of Quebec).

mnemonic (nɪˈmɒnɪk) *adj.* **1.** aiding or meant to aid one's memory. **2.** of or relating to memory or mnemonics. ~*n.* **3.** something, such as a verse, to assist memory. [C18: < Gk *mnēmonikos*, < *mnēmōn* mindful, < *mnasthai* to remember] —**mneˈmonically** *adv.*

mnemonics (nɪˈmɒnɪks) *n.* (*usually functioning as sing.*) **1.** the art or practice of improving or of aiding the memory. **2.** a system of rules to aid the memory.

mo (məʊ) *n. Inf.* **1.** *Chiefly Brit.* short for **moment** (sense 1) (esp. in **half a mo**). **2.** *Austral.* short for **moustache** (sense 1).

Mo *the chemical symbol for* molybdenum.

MO *abbrev. for* Medical Officer.

m.o. *or* **MO** *abbrev. for:* **1.** mail order. **2.** money order.

-mo *suffix forming nouns.* (in bookbinding) indicating book size by specifying the number of leaves formed by folding one sheet of paper: *16mo* or *sixteenmo.* [abstracted < DUODECIMO]

moa (ˈməʊə) *n.* any of various recently extinct large flightless birds of New Zealand (see **ratite**). [C19: < Maori]

moa hunter *n. N.Z.* an anthropologists' term for an early Maori.

moan (məʊn) *n.* **1.** a low prolonged mournful sound expressive of suffering or pleading. **2.** any similar mournful sound, esp. that made by the wind. **3.** *Inf.* a grumble or complaint. ~*vb.* **4.** to utter (words, etc.) in a low mournful manner. **5.** (*intr.*) to make a sound like a moan. **6.** (*usually intr.*) *Inf.* to grumble or complain. [C13: rel. to OE *mǣnan* to grieve over] —ˈ**moaner** *n.* —ˈ**moanful** *adj.* —ˈ**moaning** *n., adj.*

moat (məʊt) *n.* **1.** a wide water-filled ditch surrounding a fortified place, such as a castle. ~*vb.* **2.** (*tr.*) to surround with or as if with a moat. [C14: < OF *motte* mound]

mob (mɒb) *n.* **1. a.** a riotous or disorderly crowd of people; rabble. **b.** (*as modifier*): *mob law.* **2.** *Often derog.* a group or class of people, animals, or things. **3.** *Often derog.* the masses. **4.** *Sl.* a gang of criminals. **5.** *Austral. & N.Z.* a large number of anything. **6.** *Austral. & N.Z.* a flock or herd of animals. **7. mobs of.** *Austral. & N.Z. inf.* lots of. ~*vb.* **mobbing, mobbed.** (*tr.*) **8.** to attack in a group resembling a mob. **9.** to surround, esp. in order to acclaim. **10.** to crowd into (a building, etc.). [C17: shortened < L *mōbile vulgus* the fickle populace]

mobcap (ˈmɒbˌkæp) *n.* a woman's large cotton cap with a pouched crown, worn esp. during the 18th century. [C18: < obs. *mob* woman, esp. loose-living, + CAP]

mobile (ˈməʊbaɪl) *adj.* **1.** having freedom of movement; movable. **2.** changing quickly in expression: *a mobile face.* **3.** *Sociol.* (of individuals or social groups) moving within and between classes, occupations, and localities. **4.** (of military forces) able to move freely and quickly. **5.** (*postpositive*) *Inf.* having transport available: *are you mobile?* ~*n.* **6. a.** a sculpture suspended in midair with delicately balanced parts that are set in motion by air currents. **b.** (*as modifier*): *mobile sculpture.* [C15: via OF < L *mōbilis*, < *movēre* to move] —**mobility** (məʊˈbɪlɪtɪ) *n.*

-mobile (məʊˌbiːl) *suffix forming nouns.* indicating a vehicle designed for a particular person or purpose: *Popemobile.*

mobile home *n.* living quarters mounted on wheels and capable of being towed by a motor vehicle.

mobilize *or* **-lise** (ˈməʊbɪˌlaɪz) *vb.* **1.** to prepare for war or another emergency by organizing (national resources, the armed services, etc.). **2.** (*tr.*) to organize for a purpose. **3.** (*tr.*) to put into motion or use. —ˈ**mobiˌlizable** *or* ˈ**-ˌlisable** *adj.* —ˌ**mobiliˈzation** *or* **-liˈsation** *n.*

Möbius strip (ˈmɜːbɪəs) *n. Maths.* a one-sided continuous surface, formed by twisting a long narrow rectangular strip of material through 180° and joining the ends. [C19: after August *Möbius* (1790–1868), G mathematician]

mobocracy (mɒˈbɒkrəsɪ) *n., pl.* **-cies. 1.** rule or domination by a mob. **2.** the mob that rules.

mobster (ˈmɒbstə) *n.* a U.S. slang word for **gangster.**

moccasin (ˈmɒkəsɪn) *n.* **1.** a shoe of soft leather, esp. deerskin, worn by North American Indians. **2.** any soft shoe resembling this. **3.** short for **water moccasin.** [C17: of Amerind origin]

moccasin flower *n.* any of several North American orchids with a pink solitary flower. See also **lady's-slipper, cypripedium.**

mocha (ˈmɒkə) *n.* **1.** a dark brown coffee originally imported from the port of Mocha in Arabia. **2.** a flavouring made from coffee and chocolate. **3.** a soft glove leather, made from goatskin or sheepskin. **4. a.** a dark brown colour. **b.** (*as adj.*): *mocha shoes.*

mock (mɒk) *vb.* **1.** (when *intr.*, often foll. by *at*) to behave with scorn or contempt (towards); show ridicule (for). **2.** (*tr.*) to imitate, esp. in fun; mimic. **3.** (*tr.*) to deceive, disappoint, or delude. **4.** (*tr.*) to defy or frustrate. ~*n.* **5.** the act of mocking. **6.** a person or thing mocked. **7.** a counterfeit; imitation. **8.** (*often pl.*) *Inf.* (in England and Wales) school examinations taken as practice before public exams. ~*adj.* (*prenominal*) **9.** sham or counterfeit. **10.** serving as an imitation or substitute, esp. for practice purposes: *a mock battle.* ~See also **mock-up.** [C15: < OF *mocquer*] —ˈ**mocker** *n.* —ˈ**mocking** *n., adj.* —ˈ**mockingly** *adv.*

mockers (ˈmɒkəz) *pl. n. Inf.* **put the mockers on.** to ruin the chances of success of. [C20: ? < MOCK]

mockery (ˈmɒkərɪ) *n., pl.* **-eries. 1.** ridicule, contempt, or derision. **2.** a derisive action or comment. **3.** an imitation or pretence, esp. a derisive one. **4.** a person or thing that is mocked. **5.** a person, thing, or action that is inadequate.

mock-heroic *adj.* **1.** (of a literary work, esp. a poem) imitating the style of heroic poetry in order to satirize an unheroic subject. ~*n.* **2.** burlesque imitation of the heroic style.

mockingbird (ˈmɒkɪŋˌbɜːd) *n.* any of various American songbirds, noted for their ability to mimic the song of other birds.

mock orange *n.* **1.** Also called: **syringa, philadelphus.** a shrub with white fragrant flowers resembling those of the orange. **2.** an Australian shrub with white flowers and dark shiny leaves.

mock turtle soup *n.* an imitation turtle soup made from a calf's head.

mock-up *n.* **1.** a working full-scale model of a machine, apparatus, etc., for testing, research, etc. **2.** a layout of printed matter. ~*vb.* **mock up. 3.** (*tr., adv.*) to build or make a mock-up of.

mod[1] (mɒd) *n. Brit.* **a.** a member of a group of teenagers, originally in the mid-1960s, noted for their clothes-consciousness. **b.** a member of a revived group of this type in the late 1970s and early 1980s. [C20: < MODERNIST]

mod[2] (mɒd) *n.* an annual Highland Gaelic meeting with musical and literary competitions. [C19: < Gaelic *mōd* assembly, < ON]

MOD (in Britain) *abbrev. for* Ministry of Defence.

mod. *abbrev. for:* **1.** moderate. **2.** moderato. **3.** modern.

modal (ˈməʊdᵊl) *adj.* **1.** of or relating to mode or manner. **2.** *Grammar.* (of a verb form or auxiliary verb) expressing a distinction of mood, such as that between possibility and actuality. **3.** qualifying, or expressing a qualification of, the truth of some statement. **4.** *Metaphysics.* of or relating to the form of a thing as opposed to its attributes, substance, etc. **5.** *Music.* of or relating to a mode. **6.** of or relating to a statistical mode. —**moˈdality** *n.* —ˈ**modally** *adv.*

modal logic *n.* **1.** the logical study of such philosophical concepts as necessity, possibility, contingency, etc. **2.** the logical study of concepts whose formal properties resemble certain moral, epistemological, and psychological concepts.

mod cons *pl. n. Inf.* modern conveniences; the usual installations of a modern house, such as hot water, heating, etc.

mode (məʊd) *n.* **1.** a manner or way of doing, acting, or existing. **2.** the current fashion or style. **3.** *Music.* **a.** any of the various scales of notes within one octave, esp. any of the twelve natural diatonic scales taken in ascending order used in plainsong, folk song, and art music until 1600. **b.** (in the music of classical Greece) any of the descending diatonic scales from which the liturgical modes evolved. **c.** either of the two main scale systems in music since 1600: *major mode; minor mode.* **4.** *Logic, linguistics.* another name for **mood**[2]. **5.** *Philosophy.* a complex combination of ideas which is not simply the sum of its component ideas. **6.** the predominating value in a set of values as determined from statistical data or by observation. [C14: < L *modus* manner]

model (ˈmɒdᵊl) *n.* **1. a.** a representation, usually on a smaller scale, of a device, structure, etc. **b.** (*as modifier*): *a model train.* **2. a.** a standard to be imitated. **b.** (*as modifier*): *a model wife.* **3.** a representative form, style, or pattern. **4.** a person who poses for a sculptor, painter, or photographer. **5.** a person who wears clothes to display them to prospective buyers; mannequin. **6.** a preparatory sculpture in clay, wax, etc., from which the finished work is copied. **7.** a design or style of a particular product. ~*vb.* **-elling, -elled** *or U.S.* **-eling, -eled. 8.** to make a model of (something or someone). **9.** to form in clay, wax, etc.; mould. **10.** to display (clothing and accessories) as a mannequin. **11.** to plan or create according to a model or models. [C16: < OF *modelle*, < It., < L *modulus*, dim. of *modus* MODE] —ˈ**modeller** *or U.S.* ˈ**modeler** *n.*

modem (ˈməʊdɛm) *n. Computers.* a device for connecting two computers by a telephone line, consisting of a modulator that converts computer signals into audio signals and a corresponding demodulator. [C20: < *mo(dulator) dem(odulator)*]

moderate *adj.* (ˈmɒdərɪt). **1.** not extreme or

excessive. **2.** not violent; mild or temperate. **3.** of average quality or extent: *moderate success.* ~*n.* (ˈmɒdərɪt). **4.** a person who holds moderate views, esp. in politics. ~*vb.* (ˈmɒdəˌreɪt). **5.** to become or cause to become less extreme or violent. **6.** (when *intr.*, often foll. by *over*) to preside over a meeting, discussion, etc. **7.** *Physics.* to slow down (neutrons), esp. by using a moderator. [C14: < L *moderātus,* < *moderārī* to restrain]

moderate breeze *n.* a wind of force 4 on the Beaufort scale, reaching speeds of 13 to 18 mph.

moderation (ˌmɒdəˈreɪʃən) *n.* **1.** the state or an instance of being moderate. **2.** the act of moderating. **3. in moderation.** within moderate or reasonable limits.

moderato (ˌmɒdəˈrɑːtəʊ) *adv. Music.* **1.** at a moderate tempo. **2.** a direction indicating that the tempo specified is to be used with restraint: *allegro moderato.* [It.]

moderator (ˈmɒdəˌreɪtə) *n.* **1.** a person or thing that moderates. **2.** *Presbyterian Church.* a minister appointed to preside over a Church court, synod, or general assembly. **3.** a presiding officer at a public or legislative assembly. **4.** a material, such as heavy water, used for slowing down neutrons in nuclear reactors. **5.** an examiner at Oxford or Cambridge Universities in first public examinations. **6.** (in Britain and New Zealand) one who is responsible for consistency of standards in the grading of some public examinations. —ˈ**moderˌatorship** *n.*

modern (ˈmɒdən) *adj.* **1.** of, involving, or befitting the present or a recent time; contemporary. **2.** of, relating to, or characteristic of contemporary styles or schools of art, literature, music, etc., esp. those of an experimental kind. **3.** belonging or relating to the period in history from the end of the Middle Ages to the present. ~*n.* **4.** a contemporary person. [C16: < OF, < LL *modernus,* < *modō* (adv.) just recently, < *modus* MODE] —**moˈdernity** *or* ˈ**modernness** *n.*

Modern English *n.* the English language since about 1450.

Modern Hebrew *n.* the official language of Israel; a revived form of ancient Hebrew.

modernism (ˈmɒdəˌnɪzəm) *n.* **1.** modern tendencies, thoughts, etc., or the support of these. **2.** something typical of contemporary life or thought. **3.** (*cap.*) *R.C. Church.* the movement at the end of the 19th and beginning of the 20th centuries that sought to adapt doctrine to modern thought. —ˈ**modernist** *n., adj.* —ˌ**modernˈistic** *adj.* —ˌ**modernˈistically** *adv.*

modernize *or* **-ise** (ˈmɒdəˌnaɪz) *vb.* **1.** (*tr.*) to make modern in appearance or style. **2.** (*intr.*) to adopt modern ways, ideas, etc. —ˌ**moderniˈzation** *or* **-iˈsation** *n.* —ˈ**modernˌizer** *or* **-ˌiser** *n.*

modest (ˈmɒdɪst) *adj.* **1.** having or expressing a humble opinion of oneself or one's accomplishments or abilities. **2.** reserved or shy. **3.** not ostentatious or pretentious. **4.** not extreme or excessive. **5.** decorous or decent. [C16: via OF < L *modestus* moderate, < *modus* MODE] —ˈ**modestly** *adv.*

modesty (ˈmɒdɪstɪ) *n., pl.* **-ties.** the quality or condition of being modest.

modicum (ˈmɒdɪkəm) *n.* a small amount or portion. [C15: < L: a little way, < *modicus* moderate]

modification (ˌmɒdɪfɪˈkeɪʃən) *n.* **1.** the act of modifying or the condition of being modified. **2.** something modified. **3.** a small change or adjustment. **4.** *Grammar.* the relation between a modifier and the word or phrase that it modifies. —ˈ**modifiˌcatory** *or* ˈ**modifiˌcative** *adj.*

modifier (ˈmɒdɪˌfaɪə) *n.* **1.** Also called: **qualifier.** *Grammar.* a word or phrase that qualifies the sense of another word; for example, the noun *alarm* is a modifier of *clock* in *alarm clock* and the phrase *every day* is an adverbial modifier of *walks* in *he walks every day.* **2.** a person or thing that modifies.

▷ **Usage.** Nouns are frequently used in English to modify other nouns: *police officer; chicken farm.* They should be used with restraint, however, esp. when the appropriate adjective can be used: *lunar research* (not *moon research*); *educational system* (not *education system*).

modify (ˈmɒdɪˌfaɪ) *vb.* **-fying, -fied.** (*mainly tr.*) **1.** to change the structure, character, intent, etc., of. **2.** to make less extreme or uncompromising. **3.** *Grammar.* (of a word or phrase) to bear the relation of modifier to (another word or phrase). **4.** *Linguistics.* to change (a vowel) by umlaut. **5.** (*intr.*) to be or become modified. [C14: < OF *modifier,* < L *modificāre* to limit, < *modus* measure + *facere* to make] —ˈ**modiˌfiable** *adj.*

modish (ˈməʊdɪʃ) *adj.* in the current fashion or style. —ˈ**modishly** *adv.* —ˈ**modishness** *n.*

modiste (məʊˈdiːst) *n.* a fashionable dressmaker or milliner. [C19: < F, < *mode* fashion]

modular (ˈmɒdjʊlə) *adj.* of, consisting of, or resembling a module or modulus.

modulate (ˈmɒdjʊˌleɪt) *vb.* **1.** (*tr.*) to change the tone, pitch, or volume of. **2.** (*tr.*) to adjust or regulate the degree of. **3.** *Music.* **a.** to change or cause to change from one key to another. **b.** (often foll. by *to*) to make or become in tune (with a pitch, key, etc.). **4.** *Physics, electronics.* to superimpose the amplitude, frequency, phase, etc., of a wave or signal onto another wave or signal or onto an electron beam. [C16: < L *modulātus* in due measure, melodious, < *modulārī,* < *modus* measure] —ˌ**moduˈlation** *n.* —ˈ**moduˌlator** *n.*

module (ˈmɒdjuːl) *n.* **1.** a standard unit of measure, esp. one used to coordinate the dimensions of buildings and components. **2.** a standard self-contained unit or item, such as an assembly of electronic components, or a standardized piece of furniture, that can be used in combination with other units. **3.** *Astronautics.* any of several self-contained separable units making up a spacecraft or launch vehicle, each of which has one or more specified tasks. **4.** *Education.* a short course of study that together with other such courses counts towards a qualification. [C16: < L *modulus,* dim. of *modus* MODE]

modulus (ˈmɒdjʊləs) *n., pl.* **-li** (-ˌlaɪ). **1.** *Physics.* a coefficient expressing a specified property of a specified substance. See **modulus of elasticity.** **2.** *Maths.* another name for the **absolute value** of a complex number. **3.** *Maths.* the number by which a logarithm to one base is multiplied to give the corresponding logarithm to another base. **4.** *Maths.* an integer that can be divided exactly into the difference between two other integers: *7 is a modulus of 25 and 11.* [C16: < L, dim. of *modus* measure]

modulus of elasticity *n.* the ratio of the stress applied to a body or substance to the resulting strain within the elastic limit. Also called: **elastic modulus.**

modus operandi (ˈməʊdəs ˌɒpəˈrændiː, -ˈrændaɪ) *n., pl.* **modi operandi** (ˈməʊdiː ˌɒpəˈrændiː, ˈməʊdaɪ ˌɒpəˈrændaɪ). procedure; method of operating. [C17: > L]

modus vivendi (ˈməʊdəs vɪˈvɛndiː, -ˈvɛndaɪ) *n., pl.* **modi vivendi** (ˈməʊdiː vɪˈvɛndiː, ˈməʊdaɪ vɪˈvɛndaɪ). a working arrangement between conflicting interests; practical compromise. [C19: > L: way of living]

mog (mɒg) *or* **moggy** *n., pl.* **mogs** *or* **moggies.** *Brit.* a slang name for **cat.** [C20: dialect, orig. a pet name for a cow]

Mogadon (ˈmɒgəˌdɒn) *n. Trademark.* a minor tranquillizer used to treat insomnia.

mogul (ˈməʊgʌl, məʊˈgʌl) *n.* an important or powerful person. [C18: < MOGUL]

Mogul (ˈməʊgʌl, məʊˈgʌl) *n.* **1.** a member of the Muslim dynasty of Indian emperors established in 1526. **2.** a Muslim Indian, Mongol, or Mongolian. ~*adj.* **3.** of or relating to the Moguls or their empire. [C16: < Persian *mughul* Mongolian]

MOH (in Britain) *abbrev. for* Medical Officer of Health.

mohair (ˈməʊˌhɛə) *n.* **1.** Also called: **angora.** the long soft silky hair of the Angora goat. **2. a.** a fabric made from the yarn of this hair and cotton or wool. **b.** (*as modifier*): *a mohair suit.* [C16: (infl. by *hair*), ult. < Ar. *mukhayyar,* lit.: choice]

Moham. *abbrev. for* Mohammedan.

Mohammedan (məʊˈhæmɪdᵊn) *n., adj.* another word (not in Muslim use) for **Muslim.**

Mohammedanism (məʊˈhæmɪdᵊˌnɪzəm) *n.* another word (not in Muslim use) for **Islam.**

Mohawk (ˈməʊhɔːk) *n.* **1.** (*pl.* **-hawks** *or* **-hawk**) a member of a North American Indian people formerly living along the Mohawk River. **2.** the Iroquoian language of this people.

mohican (məʊˈhiːkən) *n.* a punk hairstyle in which the head is shaved at the sides and the remaining strip of hair is worn stiffly erect and sometimes brightly coloured.

moidore (ˈmɔɪdɔː) *n.* a former Portuguese gold coin. [C18: < Port. *moeda de ouro* money of gold]

moiety (ˈmɔɪɪtɪ) *n., pl.* **-ties.** **1.** a half. **2.** one of two parts or divisions of something. [C15: < OF *moitié,* < L *mediētās* middle, < *medius*]

moil (mɔɪl) *Arch. or dialect.* ~*vb.* **1.** to moisten or soil or become moist, soiled, etc. **2.** (*intr.*) to toil or drudge (esp. in **toil and moil**). ~*n.* **3.** toil; drudgery. **4.** confusion; turmoil. [C14 (to moisten; later: to work hard in unpleasantly wet conditions) < OF *moillier,* ult. < L *mollis* soft]

moire (mwɑː) *n.* a fabric, usually silk, having a watered effect. [C17: < F, earlier *mouaire,* < MOHAIR]

moiré (ˈmwɑːreɪ) *adj.* **1.** having a watered or wavelike pattern. ~*n.* **2.** such a pattern, impressed on fabrics by means of engraved rollers. **3.** any fabric having such a pattern; moire. **4.** Also: **moiré pattern.** a pattern seen when two geometrical patterns, such as grids, are visually superimposed. [C17: < F, < *moire* MOHAIR]

moist (mɔɪst) *adj.* **1.** slightly damp or wet. **2.** saturated with or suggestive of moisture. [C14: < OF, ult. rel. to L *mūcidus* musty] —ˈ**moistly** *adv.* —ˈ**moistness** *n.*

moisten (ˈmɔɪsᵊn) *vb.* to make or become moist.

moisture (ˈmɔɪstʃə) *n.* water or other liquid diffused as vapour or condensed on or in objects.

moisturize *or* **-ise** (ˈmɔɪstʃəˌraɪz) *vb.* (*tr.*) to add moisture to (the air, the skin, etc.). —ˈ**moisturˌizer** *or* **-ˌiser** *n.*

moke (məʊk) *n. Brit. sl.* a donkey. [C19: < ?]

mol *Chem. symbol for* mole³.

mol. *abbrev. for:* **1.** molecular. **2.** molecule.

molal (ˈməʊləl) *adj. Chem.* of or consisting of a solution containing one mole of solute per thousand grams of solution. [C20: < MOLE³ + -AL¹]

molar¹ (ˈməʊlə) *n.* **1.** any of the 12 grinding teeth in man. **2.** a corresponding tooth in other mammals. ~*adj.* **3.** of or relating to any of these teeth. **4.** used for or capable of grinding. [C16: < L *molāris,* < *mola* millstone]

molar² (ˈməʊlə) *adj.* **1.** (of a physical quantity) per unit amount of substance: *molar volume.* **2.** (not recommended in technical usage) (of a solution) containing one mole of solute per litre of solution. [C19: < L *mōlēs* a mass]

molasses (məˈlæsɪz) *n.* (*functioning as sing.*) **1.** the thick brown uncrystallized bitter syrup obtained from sugar during refining. **2.** the U.S. and Canad. name for **treacle** (sense 1). [C16: < Port. *melaço,* < LL *mellāceum* must, < L *mel* honey]

mold (məʊld) *n., vb.* the U.S. spelling of **mould.**

moldboard (ˈməʊldˌbɔːd) *n.* the U.S. spelling of **mouldboard.**

molder (ˈməʊldə) *vb.* the U.S. spelling of **moulder.**

molding (ˈməʊldɪŋ) *n.* the U.S. spelling of **moulding.**

moldy (ˈməʊldɪ) *adj.* the U.S. spelling of **mouldy.**

mole¹ (məʊl) *n. Pathol.* a nontechnical name for **naevus.** [OE *māl*]

mole² (məʊl) *n.* **1.** any small burrowing mammal of a family of Europe, Asia, and North and Central America. They have velvety, typically dark fur and forearms specialized for digging. **2.** *Inf.* a spy who has infiltrated an organization and become a trusted member of it. [C14: < MDu. *mol,* of Gmc origin]

mole³ (məʊl) *n.* the basic SI unit of amount of substance; the amount that contains as many elementary entities as there are atoms in 0.012 kilogram of carbon-12. The entity may be an atom, a molecule, an ion, a radical, etc. Symbol: mol [C20: < G *Mol,* short for *Molekül* MOLECULE]

mole⁴ (məʊl) *n.* **1.** a breakwater. **2.** a harbour protected by a breakwater. [C16: < F *môle,* < L *mōlēs* mass]

Molech (ˈməʊlɛk) *n. Bible.* a variant spelling of **Moloch.**

molecular (məʊˈlɛkjʊlə, mə-) *adj.* of or relating to molecules. —**moˈlecularly** *adv.*

molecular biology *n.* the study of the structure and function of biological molecules, esp. nucleic acids and proteins.

molecular formula *n.* a chemical formula indicating the numbers and types of atoms in a molecule: *H_2SO_4 is the molecular formula of sulphuric acid.*

molecular weight *n.* the sum of all the atomic weights (relative atomic masses) of the atoms in a molecule; the ratio of the average mass per molecule of a specified isotopic composition of a substance to 1/12 the mass of an atom of carbon-12. Abbrev.: **mol. wt.**

molecule (ˈmɒlɪˌkjuːl) *n.* **1.** the simplest unit of a chemical compound that can exist, consisting of two or more atoms held together by chemical bonds. **2.** a very small particle. [C18: via F < NL *mōlēcula,* dim. of L *mōlēs* mass]

molehill (ˈməʊlˌhɪl) *n.* **1.** the small mound of earth thrown up by a burrowing mole. **2. make a mountain out of a molehill.** to exaggerate an unimportant matter out of all proportion.

moleskin (ˈməʊlˌskɪn) *n.* **1.** the dark grey dense velvety pelt of a mole, used as a fur. **2.** a hard-wearing cotton fabric of twill weave. **3.** (*modifier*): *a moleskin waistcoat.*

molest (məˈlɛst) *vb.* (*tr.*) **1.** to disturb or annoy by malevolent interference. **2.** to accost or attack, esp. with the intention of assaulting sexually. [C14: < L *molestāre* to annoy, < *molestus* troublesome, < *mōlēs* mass] —**molestation** (ˌməʊlɛˈsteɪʃən) *n.* —**moˈlester** *n.*

moll (mɒl) *n. Sl.* **1.** the female accomplice of a gangster. **2.** a prostitute. [C17: < *Moll,* familiar form of *Mary*]

mollify (ˈmɒlɪˌfaɪ) *vb.* **-fying, -fied.** (*tr.*) **1.** to pacify; soothe. **2.** to lessen the harshness or severity of. [C15: < OF *mollifier,* via LL, < L *mollis* soft + *facere* to make] —ˈ**molliˌfiable** *adj.* —ˌ**mollifiˈcation** *n.* —ˈ**molliˌfier** *n.*

mollusc *or U.S.* **mollusk** (ˈmɒləsk) *n.* any of various invertebrates having a soft unsegmented body and often a shell, secreted by a fold of skin (the mantle). The group includes the gastropods (snails, slugs, etc.), bivalves (clams, mussels, etc.), and cephalopods (squid, octopuses, etc.). [C18: via NL < L *molluscus,* < *mollis* soft] —**molluscan** *or U.S.* **molluskan** (mɒˈlʌskən) *adj., n.*

molly (ˈmɒlɪ) *n., pl.* **-lies.** any of various brightly coloured tropical or subtropical American freshwater fishes. [C19: < NL *Mollienisia,* < Comte F. N. *Mollien* (1758–1850), F statesman]

mollycoddle (ˈmɒlɪˌkɒdᵊl) *vb.* **1.** (*tr.*) to treat with indulgent care; pamper. ~*n.* **2.** a pampered person. [C19: < obs. sl. *molly* an effeminate boy, < *Molly* girl's name + CODDLE]

Moloch (ˈməʊlɒk) *or* **Molech** (ˈməʊlɛk) *n. Old Testament.* a Semitic deity to whom parents sacrificed their children.

Molotov cocktail (ˈmɒləˌtɒf) *n.* an elementary incendiary weapon, usually a bottle of petrol with a short delay fuse or wick; petrol bomb. [C20: after V. M. *Molotov,* Soviet statesman (1890–1986)]

molt (məʊlt) *vb., n.* the usual U.S. spelling of **moult.** —ˈ**molter** *n.*

molten (ˈməʊltən) *adj.* **1.** liquefied; melted. **2.** made by having been melted: *molten casts.* ~*vb.* **3.** the past participle of **melt.**

molto (ˈmɒltəʊ) *adv. Music.* very: *allegro molto; molto adagio.* [< It., < L *multum* (adv.) much]

mol. wt. *abbrev. for* molecular weight.
moly (ˈməʊlɪ) *n., pl.* **-lies.** **1.** *Greek myth.* a magic herb given by Hermes to Odysseus to nullify the spells of Circe. **2.** a variety of wild garlic of S Europe having yellow flowers. [C16: < L *mōly,* < Gk *mōlu*]
molybdenite (mɒˈlɪbdɪˌnaɪt) *n.* a soft grey mineral consisting of molybdenum sulphide in hexagonal crystalline form with rhenium as an impurity. Formula: MoS_2.
molybdenum (mɒˈlɪbdɪnəm) *n.* a very hard silvery-white metallic element occurring principally in molybdenite: used in alloys, esp. to harden and strengthen steels. Symbol: Mo; atomic no.: 42; atomic wt.: 95.94. [C19: < NL, < L *molybdaena* galena, < Gk, < *molubdos* lead]
mom (mɒm) *n. Chiefly U.S. & Canad.* an informal word for **mother.**
moment (ˈməʊmənt) *n.* **1.** a short indefinite period of time. **2.** a specific instant or point in time: *at that moment the phone rang.* **3. the moment.** the present point of time: *at the moment it's fine.* **4.** import, significance, or value: *a man of moment.* **5.** *Physics.* **a.** a tendency to produce motion, esp. rotation about a point or axis. **b.** the product of a physical quantity, such as force or mass, and its distance from a fixed reference point. See also **moment of inertia.** [C14: < OF, < L *mōmentum,* < *movēre* to move]
momentarily (ˈməʊməntərəlɪ, -trɪlɪ) *adv.* **1.** for an instant; temporarily. **2.** from moment to moment; every instant. ~*adv.* **3.** *U.S. & Canad.* very soon. Also (for senses 1, 2): **momently.**
momentary (ˈməʊməntərɪ, -trɪ) *adj.* **1.** lasting for only a moment; temporary. **2.** *Rare.* occurring or present at each moment. —ˈ**momentariness** *n.*
moment of inertia *n.* the tendency of a body to resist angular acceleration, expressed as the sum of the products of the mass of each particle in the body and the square of its perpendicular distance from the axis of rotation.
moment of truth *n.* **1.** a moment when a person or thing is put to the test. **2.** the point in a bullfight when the matador is about to kill the bull.
momentous (məʊˈmɛntəs) *adj.* of great significance. —**moˈmentously** *adv.* —**moˈmentousness** *n.*
momentum (məʊˈmɛntəm) *n., pl.* **-ta** (-tə) *or* **-tums.** **1.** *Physics.* the product of a body's mass and its velocity. **2.** the impetus of a body resulting from its motion. **3.** driving power or strength. [C17: < L: movement; see MOMENT]
momma (ˈmɒmə) *n. Chiefly U.S.* **1.** an informal or childish word for **mother.** **2.** *Inf.* a buxom and voluptuous woman.
mon. *abbrev. for* monetary.
Mon. *abbrev. for* Monday.
mon- *combining form.* a variant of **mono-** before a vowel.
monad (ˈmɒnæd, ˈməʊ-) *n.* **1.** (*pl.* **-ads** *or* **-ades** (-əˌdiːz)). *Philosophy.* any fundamental singular metaphysical entity, esp. if autonomous. **2.** a single-celled organism. **3.** an atom, ion, or radical with a valency of one. ~Also (for senses 1, 2): **monas.** [C17: < LL *monas,* < Gk: unit, < *monos* alone] —**monadic** (mɒˈnædɪk) *adj.*
monadelphous (ˌmɒnəˈdɛlfəs) *adj.* **1.** (of stamens) having united filaments forming a tube around the style. **2.** (of flowers) having monadelphous stamens. [C19: < MONO- + Gk *adelphos* brother]
monadnock (məˈnædnɒk) *n.* a residual hill of hard rock in an otherwise eroded area. [C19: after Mount *Monadnock,* New Hampshire, U.S.]
monandrous (mɒˈnændrəs) *adj.* **1.** having only one male sexual partner over a period of time. **2.** (of plants) having flowers with only one stamen. **3.** (of flowers) having only one stamen. [C19: < MONO- + -ANDROUS] —**moˈnandry** *n.*
monarch (ˈmɒnək) *n.* **1.** a sovereign head of state, esp. a king, queen, or emperor, who rules usually by hereditary right. **2.** a supremely powerful or pre-eminent person or thing. **3.** Also called: **milkweed.** a large migratory orange-and-black butterfly that feeds on the milkweed plant. [C15: < LL *monarcha,* < Gk; see MONO-, -ARCH] —**monarchal** (mɒˈnɑːkᵊl) *or* **moˈnarchial** *adj.* —**moˈnarchical** *or* **moˈnarchic** *adj.* —ˈ**monarchism** *n.* —ˈ**monarchist** *n., adj.* —ˌ**monarˈchistic** *adj.*
monarchy (ˈmɒnəkɪ) *n., pl.* **-chies.** **1.** a form of government in which supreme authority is vested in a single and usually hereditary figure, such as a king. **2.** a country reigned over by a monarch.
monarda (mɒˈnɑːdə) *n.* any of various mintlike North American plants. [C19: < NL, after N. *Monardés* (1493–1588), Sp. botanist]
monastery (ˈmɒnəstərɪ) *n., pl.* **-teries.** the residence of a religious community, esp. of monks, living in seclusion from secular society and bound by religious vows. [C15: < Church L *monastērium,* ult. < Gk *monazein* to live alone, < *monos* alone] —**monasterial** (ˌmɒnəˈstɪərɪəl) *adj.*
monastic (məˈnæstɪk) *adj.* **1.** of or relating to monasteries or monks, nuns, etc. **2.** resembling this sort of life. ~*n.* **3.** a person committed to this way of life, esp. a monk.
monasticism (məˈnæstɪˌsɪzəm) *n.* the monastic system, movement, or way of life.
monatomic (ˌmɒnəˈtɒmɪk) *or* **monoatomic** (ˌmɒnəʊəˈtɒmɪk) *adj. Chem.* **1.** (of an element) having or consisting of single atoms. **2.** (of a compound or molecule) having only one atom or group that can be replaced in a chemical reaction.
monaural (mɒˈnɔːrəl) *adj.* **1.** relating to, having, or hearing with only one ear. **2.** another word for **monophonic.** —**monˈaurally** *adv.*
monazite (ˈmɒnəˌzaɪt) *n.* a yellow to reddish-brown mineral consisting of a phosphate of thorium, cerium, and lanthanum in monoclinic crystalline form. [C19: < G, < Gk *monazein* to live alone, so called because of its rarity]
Monday (ˈmʌndɪ) *n.* the second day of the week; first day of the working week. [OE *mōnandæg* moon's day, translation of LL *lūnae diēs*]
monecious (mɒˈniːʃəs) *adj.* a variant spelling of **monoecious.**
Monel metal *or* **Monell metal** (mɒˈnɛl) *n. Trademark.* any of various silvery corrosion-resistant alloys. [C20: after A. *Monell* (died 1921), president of the International Nickel Co., New York, which introduced the alloys]
monetarism (ˈmʌnɪtəˌrɪzəm) *n.* **1.** the theory that inflation is caused by an excess quantity of money in an economy. **2.** an economic policy based on this theory and on a belief in the efficiency of free market forces. —ˈ**monetarist** *n., adj.*
monetary (ˈmʌnɪtərɪ, -trɪ) *adj.* of or relating to money or currency. [C19: < LL *monētārius,* < L *monēta* MONEY] —ˈ**monetarily** *adv.*
monetize *or* **-ise** (ˈmʌnɪˌtaɪz) *vb.* (*tr.*) **1.** to establish as legal tender. **2.** to give a legal value to (a coin). —ˌ**monetiˈzation** *or* **-iˈsation** *n.*
money (ˈmʌnɪ) *n.* **1.** a medium of exchange that functions as legal tender. **2.** the official currency, in the form of banknotes, coins, etc., issued by a government or other authority. **3.** a particular denomination or form of currency: *silver money.* **4.** (*Law or arch. pl.* **moneys** *or* **monies**) a pecuniary sum or income. **5.** an unspecified amount of paper currency or coins: *money to lend.* **6. for one's money.** in one's opinion. **7. in the money.** *Inf.* well-off; rich. **8. one's money's worth.** full value for the money one has paid for something. **9. put money on.** to place a bet on. ~Related adj.: **pecuniary.** [C13: < OF *moneie,* < L *monēta;* see MINT[2]]
moneybags (ˈmʌnɪˌbægz) *n.* (*functioning as sing.*) *Inf.* a very rich person.
moneychanger (ˈmʌnɪˌtʃeɪndʒə) *n.* **1.** a person engaged in the business of exchanging currencies or money. **2.** *Chiefly U.S.* a machine for dispensing coins.
moneyed *or* **monied** (ˈmʌnɪd) *adj.* **1.** having a great deal of money; rich. **2.** arising from or characterized by money.

money-grubbing *adj. Inf.* seeking greedily to obtain money. —ˈ**money-ˌgrubber** *n.*

moneylender (ˈmʌnɪˌlɛndə) *n.* a person who lends money at interest as a living. —ˈ**money-ˌlending** *adj., n.*

moneymaker (ˈmʌnɪˌmeɪkə) *n.* **1.** a person who is intent on accumulating money. **2.** a person or thing that is or might be profitable. —ˈ**money-ˌmaking** *adj., n.*

money of account *n.* another name (esp. U.S. and Canad.) for **unit of account.**

money-spinner *n. Inf.* an enterprise, idea, person, or thing that is a source of wealth.

monger (ˈmʌŋgə) *n.* **1.** (*in combination except in archaic use*) a trader or dealer: *ironmonger.* **2.** (*in combination*) a promoter of something: *warmonger.* [OE *mangere,* ult. < L *mangō* dealer] —ˈ**mongering** *n., adj.*

mongol (ˈmɒŋgᵊl) *n.* (not in technical use) a person affected by Down's syndrome.

Mongol (ˈmɒŋgɒl, -gᵊl) *n.* another word for **Mongolian.**

mongolian (mɒŋˈgəʊlɪən) *adj.* (not in technical use) of, relating to, or affected by Down's syndrome.

Mongolian (mɒŋˈgəʊlɪən) *adj.* **1.** of or relating to Mongolia, a region in Central Asia, its people, or their language. ~*n.* **2.** a native or inhabitant of Mongolia. **3.** the language of Mongolia.

Mongolic (mɒŋˈgɒlɪk) *n.* **1.** a branch or subfamily of the Altaic family of languages, including Mongolian and Kalmuck. **2.** another word for **Mongoloid.**

mongolism (ˈmɒŋgəˌlɪzəm) *n. Pathol.* a former name (not in technical use) for **Down's syndrome.** [C20: the condition produces facial features similar to those of the Mongoloid peoples]

mongoloid (ˈmɒŋgəˌlɔɪd) *adj.* (not in technical use) **1.** relating to or characterized by Down's syndrome. ~*n.* **2.** a person affected by Down's syndrome.

Mongoloid (ˈmɒŋgəˌlɔɪd) *adj.* **1.** of or relating to a major racial group of mankind, characterized by yellowish complexion, straight black hair, slanting eyes, short nose, and scanty facial hair, including most of the peoples of Asia, the Eskimos, and the North American Indians. ~*n.* **2.** a member of this group.

mongoose (ˈmɒŋˌguːs) *n., pl.* **-gooses.** any of various small predatory mammals occurring in Africa and from S Europe to SE Asia, typically having a long tail and brindled coat. [C17: < Marathi (a language of India) *mangūs*]

mongrel (ˈmʌŋgrəl) *n.* **1.** a plant or animal, esp. a dog, of mixed or unknown breeding. **2.** *Derog.* a person of mixed race. ~*adj.* **3.** of mixed origin, breeding, character, etc. [C15: < obs. *mong* mixture] —ˈ**mongrelism** *n.* —ˈ**mongreˌlize** *or* **-ise** *vb.* —ˌ**mongreliˈzation** *or* **-iˈsation** *n.* —ˈ**mongrelly** *adj.*

'mongst (mʌŋst) *prep. Poetic.* short for **amongst.**

monied (ˈmʌnɪd) *adj.* a less common spelling of **moneyed.**

monies (ˈmʌnɪz) *n. Law, arch.* a plural of **money.**

moniker *or* **monicker** (ˈmɒnɪkə) *n. Sl.* a person's name or nickname. [C19: < Shelta *munnik,* altered < Irish Gaelic *ainm* name]

monism (ˈmɒnɪzəm) *n.* **1.** *Philosophy.* the doctrine that reality consists of only one basic substance or element, such as mind or matter. Cf. **dualism, pluralism.** **2.** the attempt to explain anything in terms of one principle only. —ˈ**monist** *n., adj.* —**moˈnistic** *adj.*

monition (məʊˈnɪʃən) *n.* **1.** a warning or caution; admonition. **2.** *Christianity.* a formal notice from a bishop or ecclesiastical court requiring a person to refrain from committing a specific offence. [C14: via OF < L *monitiō,* < *monēre* to warn]

monitor (ˈmɒnɪtə) *n.* **1.** a person or piece of equipment that warns, checks, controls, or keeps a continuous record of something. **2.** *Education.* **a.** a senior pupil with various supervisory duties, etc. **b.** a pupil assisting a teacher in classroom organization, etc. **3.** a television set used in a studio for viewing or checking a programme being transmitted. **4. a.** a loudspeaker used in a recording studio to determine quality or balance. **b.** a loudspeaker used on stage to enable musicians to hear themselves. **5.** any of various large predatory lizards inhabiting warm regions of Africa, Asia, and Australia. **6.** (formerly) a small heavily armoured warship used for coastal assault. ~*vb.* **7.** to act as a monitor of. **8.** (*tr.*) to observe or record (the activity or performance of) (an engine or other device). **9.** (*tr.*) to check (the technical quality of) (a radio or television broadcast). [C16: < L, < *monēre* to advise] —**monitorial** (ˌmɒnɪˈtɔːrɪəl) *adj.* —ˈ**monitorship** *n.* —ˈ**monitress** *fem. n.*

monitory (ˈmɒnɪtərɪ, -trɪ) *adj. also* **monitorial.** **1.** warning or admonishing. ~*n., pl.* **-ries.** **2.** *Rare.* a letter containing a monition.

monk (mʌŋk) *n.* a male member of a religious community bound by vows of poverty, chastity, and obedience. Related adj.: **monastic.** [OE *munuc,* < LL *monachus,* < LGk: solitary (man), < Gk *monos* alone] —ˈ**monkish** *adj.*

monkey (ˈmʌŋkɪ) *n.* **1.** any of numerous long-tailed primates excluding lemurs, tarsiers, etc.: see **Old World monkey, New World monkey.** **2.** any primate except man. **3.** a naughty or mischievous person, esp. a child. **4.** the head of a pile-driver (**monkey engine**) or of some similar mechanical device. **5.** *U.S. & Canad. sl.* an addict's dependence on a drug (esp. in **have a monkey on one's back**). **6.** *Sl.* a butt of derision; someone made to look a fool (esp. in **make a monkey of**). **7.** *Sl.* (esp. in bookmaking) £500. **8.** *U.S. & Canad. sl.* $500. ~*vb.* **9.** (*intr.;* usually foll. by *around, with,* etc.) to meddle, fool, or tinker. **10.** (*tr.*) *Rare.* to imitate; ape. [C16: ? < Low G; cf. MLow G *Moneke,* name of the ape's son in the tale of Reynard the Fox]

monkey business *n. Inf.* mischievous, suspect, or dishonest behaviour or acts.

monkey flower *n.* any of various plants of the genus *Mimulus,* cultivated for their yellow or red flowers.

monkey jacket *n.* a short close-fitting jacket, esp. a waist-length jacket similar to a mess jacket.

monkey nut *n. Brit.* another name for a **peanut.**

monkey puzzle *n.* a South American coniferous tree having branches shaped like a candelabrum and stiff sharp leaves. Also called: **Chile pine.**

monkey's wedding *n. S. African inf.* a combination of rain and sunshine. [<?]

monkey tricks *or U.S.* **monkey shines** *pl. n. Inf.* mischievous behaviour or acts.

monkey wrench *n.* a wrench with adjustable jaws.

monkfish (ˈmʌŋkˌfɪʃ) *n., pl.* **-fish** *or* **-fishes.** **1.** any of various angler fishes. **2.** another name for **angelfish** (sense 3).

monk's cloth *n.* a heavy cotton fabric of basket weave, used mainly for bedspreads.

monkshood (ˈmʌŋkshʊd) *n.* any of several poisonous N temperate plants that have hooded blue-purple flowers.

mono (ˈmɒnəʊ) *adj.* **1.** short for **monophonic.** ~*n.* **2.** monophonic sound.

mono- *or before a vowel* **mon-** *combining form.* **1.** one; single: *monorail.* **2.** indicating that a chemical compound contains a single specified atom or group: *monoxide.* [< Gk *monos*]

monoacid (ˌmɒnəʊˈæsɪd), **monacid, monoacidic** (ˌmɒnəʊəˈsɪdɪk), *or* **monacidic** *adj. Chem.* (of a base) capable of reacting with only one molecule of a monobasic acid; having only one hydroxide ion per molecule.

monobasic (ˌmɒnəʊˈbeɪsɪk) *adj. Chem.* (of an acid, such as hydrogen chloride) having only one replaceable hydrogen atom per molecule.

monocarpic (ˌmɒnəʊˈkɑːpɪk) *or* **monocarpous** *adj.* (of some flowering plants) producing fruit only once before dying.

monochromatic (ˌmɒnəʊkrəʊˈmætɪk) *or* **monochroic** (ˌmɒnəʊˈkrəʊɪk) *adj.* (of light or other electromagnetic radiation) having only one wavelength.

monochrome (ˈmɒnəˌkrəʊm) *n.* **1.** a black-and-white photograph or transparency. **2.** *Photog.* black-and-white. **3. a.** a painting, drawing, etc., done in a range of tones of a single colour. **b.** the technique or art of this. **4.** (*modifier*) executed in or resembling monochrome: *a monochrome print.* ~Also called (for senses 3, 4): **monotint.** [C17: via Med. L < Gk *monokhrōmos* of one colour] —ˌ**mono**ˈ**chromic** *adj.* —ˈ**mono**ˌ**chromist** *n.*

monocle (ˈmɒnəkᵊl) *n.* a lens for correcting defective vision of one eye, held in position by the facial muscles. [C19: < F, < LL, < MONO- + *oculus* eye] —ˈ**monocled** *adj.*

monocline (ˈmɒnəʊˌklaɪn) *n.* a fold in stratified rocks in which the strata are inclined in the same direction from the horizontal. [C19: < MONO- + Gk *klīnein* to lean] —ˌ**mono**ˈ**clinal** *adj., n.*

monoclinic (ˌmɒnəʊˈklɪnɪk) *adj. Crystallog.* relating to or belonging to the crystal system characterized by three unequal axes, one pair of which are not at right angles to each other. [C19: < MONO- + Gk *klīnein* to lean]

monoclinous (ˌmɒnəʊˈklaɪnəs, ˈmɒnəʊˌklaɪnəs) *adj.* (of flowering plants) having the male and female reproductive organs on the same flower. Cf. **diclinous.** [C19: < MONO- + Gk *klīne* bed] —ˈ**mono**ˌ**clinism** *n.*

monoclonal antibody (ˌmɒnəʊˈkləʊnᵊl) *n.* an antibody, produced by a single clone of cells grown in culture, that is both pure and specific and capable of proliferating indefinitely: used in diagnosis, therapy, and biotechnology.

monocotyledon (ˌmɒnəʊˌkɒtɪˈliːdᵊn) *n.* any of various flowering plants having a single embryonic seed leaf, leaves with parallel veins, and flowers with parts in threes: includes grasses, lilies, palms, and orchids. Cf. **dicotyledon.** —ˌ**mono**ˌ**coty**ˈ**ledonous** *adj.*

monocracy (mɒˈnɒkrəsɪ) *n., pl.* **-cies.** government by one person. —**monocrat** (ˈmɒnəˌkræt) *n.* —ˌ**mono**ˈ**cratic** *adj.*

monocular (mɒˈnɒkjʊlə) *adj.* having or intended for the use of only one eye. [C17: < LL *monoculus* one-eyed] —**mo**ˈ**nocularly** *adv.*

monoculture (ˈmɒnəʊˌkʌltʃə) *n.* the continuous growing of one type of crop.

monocycle (ˈmɒnəˌsaɪkᵊl) *n.* another name for **unicycle.**

monocyte (ˈmɒnəʊˌsaɪt) *n.* the largest type of white blood cell that acts as part of the immune system by engulfing particles, such as invading microorganisms.

monody (ˈmɒnədɪ) *n., pl.* **-dies. 1.** (in Greek tragedy) an ode sung by a single actor. **2.** any poem of lament for someone's death. **3.** *Music.* a style of composition consisting of a single vocal part, usually with accompaniment. [C17: via LL < Gk *monōidia*, < MONO- + *aeidein* to sing] —**monodic** (mɒˈnɒdɪk) *adj.* —ˈ**monodist** *n.*

monoecious (mɒˈniːʃəs) *adj.* **1.** (of some flowering plants) having the male and female reproductive organs in separate flowers on the same plant. **2.** (of some animals and lower plants) hermaphrodite. [C18: < NL *monoecia*, < MONO- + Gk *oikos* house]

monofilament (ˌmɒnəˈfɪləmənt) *or* **monofil** (ˈmɒnəfɪl) *n.* synthetic thread or yarn composed of a single strand rather than twisted fibres.

monogamy (mɒˈnɒgəmɪ) *n.* **1.** the state or practice of having only one husband or wife over a period of time. **2.** *Zool.* the practice of having only one mate. [C17: via F < LL *monogamia*, < Gk; see MONO- + -GAMY] —**mo**ˈ**nogamist** *n.* —**mo**ˈ**nogamous** *adj.*

monogenesis (ˌmɒnəʊˈdʒɛnɪsɪs) *or* **monogeny** (mɒˈnɒdʒɪnɪ) *n.* **1.** the hypothetical descent of all organisms from a single cell. **2.** asexual reproduction in animals. **3.** the direct development of an ovum into an organism resembling the adult. **4.** the hypothetical descent of all human beings from a single pair of ancestors.

monogram (ˈmɒnəˌgræm) *n.* a design of one or more letters, esp. initials, on clothing, stationery, etc. [C17: < LL *monogramma*, < Gk; see MONO-, -GRAM] —**monogrammatic** (ˌmɒnəgrəˈmætɪk) *adj.*

monograph (ˈmɒnəˌgrɑːf) *n.* **1.** a paper, book, or other work concerned with a single subject or aspect of a subject. ~*vb.* (*tr.*) **2.** to write a monograph on. —**monographer** (mɒˈnɒgrəfə) *or* **mo**ˈ**nographist** *n.* —ˌ**mono**ˈ**graphic** *adj.*

monogyny (mɒˈnɒdʒɪnɪ) *n.* the custom of having only one female sexual partner over a period of time. —**mo**ˈ**nogynous** *adj.*

monohull (ˈmɒnəʊˌhʌl) *n.* a sailing vessel with a single hull.

monokini (ˈmɒnəʊˌkiːnɪ) *n.* a woman's one-piece bathing garment usually equivalent to the bottom half of a bikini. [C20: < MONO- + BIKINI (as if *bikini* were from BI-)]

monolayer (ˈmɒnəʊˌleɪə) *n.* a single layer of atoms or molecules adsorbed on a surface. Also called: **molecular film.**

monolingual (ˌmɒnəʊˈlɪŋgwəl) *adj.* knowing or expressed in only one language.

monolith (ˈmɒnəlɪθ) *n.* **1.** a large block of stone or anything that resembles one in appearance, intractability, etc. **2.** a statue, obelisk, column, etc., cut from one block of stone. **3.** a large hollow foundation piece sunk as a caisson and filled with concrete. [C19: via F < Gk *monolithos* made from a single stone] —ˌ**mono**ˈ**lithic** *adj.*

monologue (ˈmɒnəˌlɒg) *n.* **1.** a long speech made by one actor in a play, film, etc., esp. when alone. **2.** a dramatic piece for a single performer. **3.** any long speech by one person, esp. when interfering with conversation. [C17: via F < Gk *monologos* speaking alone] —**monologic** (ˌmɒnəˈlɒdʒɪk) *or* ˌ**mono**ˈ**logical** *adj.* —**monologist** (ˈmɒnəˌlɒgɪst) *n.* —**monologize** *or* **-ise** (mɒˈnɒlədʒaɪz) *vb.*

monomania (ˌmɒnəʊˈmeɪnɪə) *n.* an excessive mental preoccupation with one thing, idea, etc. —ˌ**mono**ˈ**mani**ˌ**ac** *n., adj.* —**monomaniacal** (ˌmɒnəʊməˈnaɪəkᵊl) *adj.*

monomark (ˈmɒnəmɑːk) *n. Brit.* a series of letters or figures to identify goods, personal articles, etc.

monomer (ˈmɒnəmə) *n. Chem.* a compound whose molecules can join together to form a polymer. —**monomeric** (ˌmɒnəˈmɛrɪk) *adj.*

monometallism (ˌmɒnəʊˈmɛtᵊˌlɪzəm) *n.* **1.** the use of one metal, esp. gold or silver, as the sole standard of value and currency. **2.** the economic policies supporting a monometallic standard. —**monometallic** (ˌmɒnəʊmɪˈtælɪk) *adj.* —ˌ**mono**ˈ**metallist** *n.*

monomial (mɒˈnəʊmɪəl) *n.* **1.** *Maths.* an expression consisting of a single term, such as *5ax*. ~*adj.* **2.** consisting of a single algebraic term. [C18: MONO- + (BIN)OMIAL]

monomorphic (ˌmɒnəʊˈmɔːfɪk) *or* **monomorphous** *adj.* **1.** (of an individual organism) showing little or no change in structure during the entire life history. **2.** (of a species) existing or having parts that exist in only one form. **3.** (of a chemical compound) having only one crystalline form.

mononucleosis (ˌmɒnəʊˌnjuːklɪˈəʊsɪs) *n.* **1.** *Pathol.* the presence of a large number of monocytes in the blood. **2.** See **infectious mononucleosis.**

monophonic (ˌmɒnəʊˈfɒnɪk) *adj.* **1.** Also: **monaural.** (of a system of broadcasting, recording, or reproducing sound) using only one channel between source and loudspeaker. Sometimes shortened to **mono.** Cf. **stereophonic. 2.** *Music.* of or relating to a style of musical composition consisting of a single melodic line.

monophthong (ˈmɒnəfˌθɒŋ) *n.* a simple or pure vowel. [C17: < Gk *monophthongos*, < MONO- + *thongos* sound]

Monophysite (mɒˈnɒfɪˌsaɪt) *n. Christianity.* a person who holds that there is only one nature in the person of Christ, which is primarily divine with human attributes. [C17: via Church L < LGk, < MONO- + *phusis* nature] —**Monophysitic** (ˌmɒnəʊfɪˈsɪtɪk) *adj.*

monoplane (ˈmɒnəʊˌpleɪn) *n.* an aeroplane with only one pair of wings. Cf. **biplane.**

monopolize *or* **-lise** (məˈnɒpəˌlaɪz) *vb.* (*tr.*) **1.** to have, control, or make use of fully, excluding others. **2.** to obtain, maintain, or exploit a monopoly of (a market, commodity, etc.). **—mo,nopoli'zation** *or* **-li'sation** *n.* **—mo'nopo,lizer** *or* **-,liser** *n.*

monopoly (mə'nɒpəlɪ) *n., pl.* **-lies.** **1.** exclusive control of the market supply of a product or service. **2. a.** an enterprise exercising this control. **b.** the product or service so controlled. **3.** *Law.* the exclusive right granted to a person, company, etc., by the state to purchase, manufacture, use, or sell some commodity or to trade in a specified area. **4.** exclusive control, possession, or use of something. [C16: < LL, < Gk *monopōlion,* < MONO- + *pōlein* to sell] **—mo'nopolist** *n.* **—mo,nopo'listic** *adj.*

Monopoly (mə'nɒpəlɪ) *n. Trademark.* a board game for two to six players who throw dice to advance their tokens, the object being to acquire the property on which their tokens land.

monorail ('mɒnəʊ,reɪl) *n.* a single-rail railway, often elevated and with suspended cars.

monosaccharide (,mɒnəʊ'sækə,raɪd) *n.* a simple sugar, such as glucose or fructose, that does not hydrolyse to yield other sugars.

monosodium glutamate (,mɒnəʊ'səʊdɪəm 'gluːtə,meɪt) *n.* a white crystalline substance that has little flavour itself but enhances protein flavours: used as a food additive.

monosyllabic (,mɒnəsɪ'læbɪk) *adj.* **1.** (of a word) containing only one syllable. **2.** characterized by monosyllables; curt. **—,monosyl'labically** *adv.*

monosyllable ('mɒnə,sɪləbᵊl) *n.* a word of one syllable, esp. one used as a sentence.

monotheism ('mɒnəʊθɪ,ɪzəm) *n.* the belief or doctrine that there is only one God. **—'mono,theist** *n., adj.* **—,monothe'istic** *adj.* **—,monothe'istically** *adv.*

monotint ('mɒnə,tɪnt) *n.* another word for **monochrome** (senses 3, 4).

monotone ('mɒnə,təʊn) *n.* **1.** a single unvaried pitch level in speech, sound, etc. **2.** utterance, etc., without change of pitch. **3.** lack of variety in style, expression, etc. *~adj.* **4.** unvarying.

monotonous (mə'nɒtənəs) *adj.* **1.** tedious, esp. because of repetition. **2.** in unvarying tone. **—mo'notonously** *adv.* **—mo'notonousness** *n.*

monotony (mə'nɒtənɪ) *n., pl.* **-nies.** **1.** wearisome routine; dullness. **2.** lack of variety in pitch or cadence.

monotreme ('mɒnəʊ,triːm) *n.* any mammal of a primitive order of Australia and New Guinea, having a single opening (cloaca) for the passage of eggs or sperm, faeces, and urine. The group contains only the echidnas and the platypus. [C19: via NL < MONO- + Gk *trēma* hole] **—monotrematous** (,mɒnəʊ'triːmətəs) *adj.*

monotype ('mɒnə,taɪp) *n.* **1.** a single print made from a metal or glass plate on which a picture has been painted. **2.** *Biol.* a monotypic genus or species.

Monotype ('mɒnə,taɪp) *n.* **1.** *Trademark.* any of various typesetting systems, esp. originally one in which each character was cast individually from hot metal. **2.** type produced by such a system.

monotypic (,mɒnəʊ'tɪpɪk) *adj.* **1.** (of a genus or species) consisting of only one type of animal or plant. **2.** of or relating to a monotype.

monovalent (,mɒnəʊ'veɪlənt) *adj. Chem.* **a.** having a valency of one. **b.** having only one valency. ~Also: **univalent.** **—,mono'valence** *or* **,mono'valency** *n.*

monoxide (mɒ'nɒksaɪd) *n.* an oxide that contains one oxygen atom per molecule.

Monseigneur *French.* (mɔ̃sɛɲœr) *n., pl.* ***Messeigneurs*** (mesɛɲœr). a title given to French bishops, prelates, and princes. [lit.: my lord]

monsieur (məs'jɜː) *n., pl.* **messieurs.** a French title of address equivalent to *sir* when used alone or *Mr* before a name. [lit.: my lord]

Monsignor (mɒn'siːnjə) *n., pl.* **Monsignors** *or* **Monsignori** (*Italian* monsiŋ'ɲoːri). *R.C. Church.* an ecclesiastical title attached to certain offices. [C17: < It., < F MONSEIGNEUR]

monsoon (mɒn'suːn) *n.* **1.** a seasonal wind of S Asia from the southwest in summer and from the northeast in winter. **2.** the rainy season when the SW monsoon blows, from about April to October. **3.** any wind that changes direction with the seasons. [C16: < obs. Du. *monssoen,* < Port., < Ar. *mawsim* season] **—mon'soonal** *adj.*

mons pubis ('mɒnz 'pjuːbɪs) *n., pl.* **montes pubis** ('mɒntiːz). the fatty flesh in human males over the junction of the pubic bones. Compare **mons veneris.** [C17: NL: hill of the pubes]

monster ('mɒnstə) *n.* **1.** an imaginary beast, usually made up of various animal or human parts. **2.** a person, animal, or plant with a marked deformity. **3.** a cruel, wicked, or inhuman person. **4. a.** a very large person, animal, or thing. **b.** (*as modifier*): *a monster cake.* [C13: < OF *monstre,* < L *monstrum* portent, < *monēre* to warn]

monstera (mɒn'stɪərə) *n.* any of various tropical evergreen climbing plants. [<?]

monstrance ('mɒnstrəns) *n. R.C. Church.* a receptacle in which the consecrated Host is exposed for adoration. [C16: < Med. L *mōnstrantia,* < L *mōnstrāre* to show]

monstrosity (mɒn'strɒsɪtɪ) *n., pl.* **-ties.** **1.** an outrageous or ugly person or thing; monster. **2.** the state or quality of being monstrous.

monstrous ('mɒnstrəs) *adj.* **1.** abnormal, hideous, or unnatural in size, character, etc. **2.** (of plants and animals) abnormal in structure. **3.** outrageous, atrocious, or shocking. **4.** huge. **5.** of, relating to, or resembling a monster. **—'monstrously** *adv.* **—'monstrousness** *n.*

mons veneris ('mɒnz 'vɛnərɪs) *n., pl.* **montes veneris** ('mɒntiːz). the fatty flesh in human females over the junction of the pubic bones. Compare **mons pubis.** [C17: NL: hill of Venus]

montage (mɒn'tɑːʒ) *n.* **1.** the art or process of composing pictures of miscellaneous elements, such as other pictures or photographs. **2.** such a composition. **3.** a method of film editing by juxtaposition or partial superimposition of several shots to form a single image. **4.** a film sequence of this kind. [C20: < F, < *monter* to MOUNT¹]

montane ('mɒnteɪn) *adj.* of or inhabiting mountainous regions. [C19: < L *montānus,* < *mons* MOUNTAIN]

montbretia (mɒn'briːʃə) *n.* any plant of an African genus related to the iris with ornamental orange or yellow flowers. [C19: NL, after A. F. E. Coquebert de *Montbret* (1780–1801), F botanist]

monte ('mɒntɪ) *n.* a gambling card game of Spanish origin. [C19: < Sp.: mountain, hence pile of cards]

Montessori method (,mɒntɪ'sɔːrɪ) *n.* a method of nursery education in which children are allowed to develop at their own pace through practical play. [C20: after Maria *Montessori* (1870–1952), Italian educationalist]

month (mʌnθ) *n.* **1.** one of the twelve divisions (**calendar months**) of the calendar year. **2.** a period of time extending from one date to a corresponding date in the next calendar month. **3.** a period of four weeks or of 30 days. **4.** the period of time (**solar month**) taken by the moon to return to the same longitude after one complete revolution around the earth; 27.321 58 days (approximately 27 days, 7 hours, 43 minutes, 4.5 seconds). **5.** the period of time (**sidereal month**) taken by the moon to make one complete revolution around the earth, measured between two successive conjunctions with a particular star; 27.321 66 days (approximately 27 days, 7 hours, 43 minutes, 11 seconds). **6.** Also called: **lunation.** the period of time (**lunar** or **synodic month**) taken by the moon to make one complete revolution around the earth, measured between two successive new moons; 29.530 59 days (approximately 29 days, 12 hours, 44 minutes, 3 seconds). [OE *mōnath*]

monthly ('mʌnθlɪ) *adj.* **1.** occurring, done, appearing, payable, etc., once every month. **2.** lasting or valid for a month. *~adv.* **3.** once a month. *~n., pl.* **-lies.** **4.** a book, periodical, magazine, etc., published once a month. **5.** *Inf.* a menstrual period.

monument (ˈmɒnjʊmənt) *n.* **1.** an obelisk, statue, building, etc., erected in commemoration of a person or event. **2.** a notable building or site, esp. one preserved as public property. **3.** a tomb or tombstone. **4.** a literary or artistic work regarded as commemorative of its creator or a particular period. **5.** *U.S.* a boundary marker. **6.** an exceptional example: *his lecture was a monument of tedium.* [C13: < L *monumentum,* < *monēre* to remind]

monumental (ˌmɒnjʊˈmɛntᵊl) *adj.* **1.** like a monument, esp. in large size, endurance, or importance. **2.** of, relating to, or being a monument. **3.** *Inf.* (intensifier): *monumental stupidity.* —ˌ**monuˈmentally** *adv.*

moo (muː) *vb.* **1.** (*intr.*) (of a cow, bull, etc.) to make a characteristic deep long sound; low. ~*interj.* **2.** an instance or imitation of this sound.

mooch (muːtʃ) *vb. Sl.* **1.** (*intr.; often with around*) to loiter or walk aimlessly. **2.** (*intr.*) to lurk; skulk. **3.** (*tr.*) to cadge. **4.** (*tr.*) *Chiefly U.S. & Canad.* to steal. [C17: ? < OF *muchier* to skulk] —ˈ**moocher** *n.*

mood[1] (muːd) *n.* **1.** a temporary state of mind or temper: *a cheerful mood.* **2.** a sullen or gloomy state of mind, esp. when temporary: *she's in a mood.* **3.** a prevailing atmosphere or feeling. **4. in the mood.** in a favourable state of mind. [OE *mōd* mind, feeling]

mood[2] (muːd) *n.* **1.** *Grammar.* a category of the verb or verbal inflections that expresses semantic and grammatical differences, including such forms as the indicative, subjunctive, and imperative. **2.** *Logic.* one of the possible arrangements of the syllogism, classified by whether the component propositions are universal or particular and affirmative or negative. ~Also called: **mode.** [C16: < MOOD[1], infl. in meaning by MODE]

moody (ˈmuːdɪ) *adj.* **moodier, moodiest. 1.** sullen, sulky, or gloomy. **2.** temperamental or changeable. —ˈ**moodily** *adv.* —ˈ**moodiness** *n.*

Moog (muːg, məʊg) *n. Music, trademark.* a type of synthesizer. [C20: after Robert *Moog* (born 1934), U.S. engineer]

mooi (mɔɪ) *adj. S. African sl.* pleasing; nice. [< Afrik.]

moolvie *or* **moolvi** (ˈmuːlviː) *n.* (esp. in India) a Muslim doctor of the law, teacher, or learned man: also used as a title of respect. [C17: < Urdu, < Ar. *mawlawīy;* cf. MULLAH]

Moomba (ˈmuːmbə) *n.* an annual carnival that takes place in Melbourne, Australia, in March. [< Abor. *moom* buttocks, anus; *moomba* orig. thought to be Abor. word meaning "Let's get together and have fun"]

moon (muːn) *n.* **1.** the natural satellite of the earth. **2.** the face of the moon as it is seen during its revolution around the earth, esp. at one of its phases: *new moon; full moon.* **3.** any natural satellite of a planet. **4.** moonlight. **5.** something resembling a moon. **6.** a month, esp. a lunar one. **7. over the moon.** *Inf.* extremely happy; ecstatic. ~*vb.* **8.** (when *tr.*, often foll. by *away;* when *intr.*, often foll. by *around*) to be idle in a listless way, as if in love, or to idle (time) away. **9.** (*intr.*) *Sl.* to expose one's buttocks to passers-by. [OE *mōna*] —ˈ**moonless** *adj.*

moonbeam (ˈmuːnˌbiːm) *n.* a ray of moonlight.

mooncalf (ˈmuːnˌkɑːf) *n., pl.* **-calves** (-ˌkɑːvz). **1.** a born fool; dolt. **2.** a person who idles time away.

moon-faced *adj.* having a round face.

moonlight (ˈmuːnˌlaɪt) *n.* **1.** light from the sun received on earth after reflection by the moon. **2.** (*modifier*) illuminated by the moon: *a moonlight walk.* ~*vb.* **-lighting, -lighted. 3.** (*intr.*) *Inf.* to work at a secondary job, esp. at night and illegally. —ˈ**moonˌlighter** *n.*

moonlight flit *n. Brit. inf.* a hurried departure at night, esp. from rented accommodation to avoid payments of rent owed.

moonlit (ˈmuːnlɪt) *adj.* illuminated by the moon.

moonquake (ˈmuːnˌkweɪk) *n.* a light tremor of the moon, detected on the moon's surface.

moonscape (ˈmuːnˌskeɪp) *n.* the general surface of the moon or a representation of it.

moonshine (ˈmuːnˌʃaɪn) *n.* **1.** another word for **moonlight** (sense 1). **2.** *U.S. & Canad.* illegally distilled or smuggled whisky. **3.** foolish talk or thought.

moonshot (ˈmuːnˌʃɒt) *n.* the launching of a spacecraft, rocket, etc., to the moon.

moonstone (ˈmuːnˌstəʊn) *n.* a gem variety of orthoclase or albite that is white and translucent.

moonstruck (ˈmuːnˌstrʌk) *or* **moonstricken** (ˈmuːnˌstrɪkən) *adj.* deranged or mad.

moony (ˈmuːnɪ) *adj.* **moonier, mooniest. 1.** *Inf.* dreamy or listless. **2.** of or like the moon.

moor[1] (mʊə, mɔː) *n.* a tract of unenclosed ground, usually covered with heather, coarse grass, bracken, and moss. [OE *mōr*]

moor[2] (mʊə, mɔː) *vb.* to secure (a ship, boat, etc.) with cables, ropes, or anchors, or (of a ship, boat, etc.) to be secured in this way. [C15: of Gmc origin; rel. to OE *mǣrelsrāp* rope for mooring] —**moorage** (ˈmʊərɪdʒ) *n.*

Moor (mʊə, mɔː) *n.* a member of a Muslim people of North Africa, of mixed Arab and Berber descent. [C14: via OF < L *Maurus,* < Gk *Mauros,* ? < Berber] —ˈ**Moorish** *adj.*

moorcock (ˈmʊəˌkɒk, ˈmɔː-) *n.* the male of the red grouse.

moorhen (ˈmʊəˌhɛn, ˈmɔː-) *n.* **1.** a bird of the rail family, inhabiting ponds, lakes, etc., having a black plumage, red bill, and a red shield above the bill. **2.** the female of the red grouse.

mooring (ˈmʊərɪŋ, ˈmɔː-) *n.* **1.** a place for anchoring a vessel. **2.** a permanent anchor with a floating buoy, to which vessels can moor.

moorings (ˈmʊərɪŋz, ˈmɔː-) *pl. n.* **1.** *Naut.* the ropes, anchors, etc., used in mooring a vessel. **2.** (*sometimes sing.*) something that provides security or stability.

Moorish idol *n.* a tropical marine spiny-finned fish that is common around coral reefs. It has a deeply compressed body with yellow and black stripes.

moorland (ˈmʊələnd) *n. Brit.* an area of moor.

moose (muːs) *n., pl.* **moose.** a large North American deer having large flattened palmate antlers: also occurs in Europe and Asia where it is called an elk. [C17: of Amerind origin]

moot (muːt) *adj.* **1.** subject or open to debate: *a moot point.* ~*vb.* **2.** (*tr.*) to suggest or bring up for debate. **3.** (*intr.*) to plead or argue hypothetical cases, as an academic exercise or as training for law students. ~*n.* **4.** a discussion or debate of a hypothetical case or point, held as an academic activity. **5.** (in Anglo-Saxon England) an assembly dealing with local legal and administrative affairs. [OE *gemōt*]

moot court *n.* a mock court trying hypothetical legal cases.

mop (mɒp) *n.* **1.** an implement with a wooden handle and a head made of twists of cotton or a piece of synthetic sponge, used for polishing or washing floors, or washing dishes. **2.** something resembling this, such as a tangle of hair. ~*vb.* **mopping, mopped.** (*tr.*) **3.** (often foll. by *up*) to clean or soak up as with a mop. ~See also **mop up.** [C15 *mappe,* ult. < L *mappa* napkin]

mope (məʊp) *vb.* (*intr.*) **1.** to be gloomy or apathetic. **2.** to move or act in an aimless way. ~*n.* **3.** a gloomy person. [C16: ? < obs. *mope* fool & rel. to *mop* grimace] —ˈ**moper** *n.* —ˈ**mopy** *adj.*

moped (ˈməʊpɛd) *n. Brit.* a light motorcycle not over 50cc. [C20: < MOTOR + PEDAL[1]]

mopes (məʊps) *pl. n.* **the.** low spirits.

mopoke (ˈməʊˌpəʊk) *n.* **1.** a small spotted owl of Australia and New Zealand. **2.** (in Australia) a frogmouth (bird) with reddish-brown or grey plumage. **3.** *Austral. & N.Z. sl.* a slow or lugubrious person. ~Also called: **morepork.** [C19: imit. of the bird's cry]

moppet (ˈmɒpɪt) *n.* a less common word for **poppet** (sense 1). [C17: < obs. *mop* rag doll; <?]

mop up *vb.* (*tr., adv.*) **1.** to clean with a mop. **2.** *Inf.* to complete (a task, etc.). **3.** *Mil.* to clear (remaining enemy forces) after a battle, as by killing, taking prisoner, etc.

moquette (mɒˈkɛt) *n.* a thick velvety fabric used for carpets, upholstery, etc. [C18: < F; <?]

MOR *abbrev. for* middle-of-the-road: used esp. in radio programming.

Mor. *abbrev. for* Morocco.

mora *or* **morra** (ˈmɔːrə) *n.* a guessing game played with the fingers, esp. in Italy and China. [C18: < It. *mora*]

moraine (mɒˈreɪn) *n.* a mass of debris, carried by glaciers and forming ridges and mounds when deposited. [C18: < F, < Savoy dialect *morena*, <?] —**moˈrainal** *or* **moˈrainic** *adj.*

moral (ˈmɒrəl) *adj.* **1.** concerned with or relating to human behaviour, esp. the distinction between good and bad or right and wrong behaviour: *moral sense.* **2.** adhering to conventionally accepted standards of conduct. **3.** based on a sense of right and wrong according to conscience: *moral courage; moral law.* **4.** having psychological rather than tangible effects: *moral support.* **5.** having the effects but not the appearance of (victory or defeat): *a moral victory.* **6.** having a strong probability: *a moral certainty.* ~*n.* **7.** the lesson to be obtained from a fable or event. **8.** a concise truth; maxim. **9.** (*pl.*) principles of behaviour in accordance with standards of right and wrong. **10.** *Austral. sl.* a certainty: *a moral to win.* [C14: < L *mōrālis* relating to morals or customs, < *mōs* custom] —**ˈmorally** *adv.*

morale (mɒˈrɑːl) *n.* the degree of mental or moral confidence of a person or group. [C18: morals, < F, n. use of MORAL (adj.)]

moralist (ˈmɒrəlɪst) *n.* **1.** a person who seeks to regulate the morals of others. **2.** a person who lives in accordance with moral principles. —ˌ**moralˈistic** *adj.* —ˌ**moralˈistically** *adv.*

morality (məˈrælɪtɪ) *n., pl.* **-ties.** **1.** the quality of being moral. **2.** conformity, or degree of conformity, to conventional standards of moral conduct. **3.** a system of moral principles. **4.** an instruction or lesson in morals. **5.** short for **morality play.**

morality play *n.* a type of drama between the 14th and 16th centuries concerned with the conflict between personified virtues and vices.

moralize *or* **-lise** (ˈmɒrəˌlaɪz) *vb.* **1.** (*intr.*) to make moral pronouncements. **2.** (*tr.*) to interpret or explain in a moral sense. **3.** (*tr.*) to improve the morals of. —ˌ**moraliˈzation** *or* **-liˈsation** *n.* —ˈ**moraˌlizer** *or* **-ˌliser** *n.*

moral majority *n.* a presumed majority of people believed to be in favour of a stricter code of public morals. [C20: after *Moral Majority*, a right-wing U.S. religious organization, based on SILENT MAJORITY]

moral philosophy *n.* the branch of philosophy dealing with ethics.

Moral Rearmament *n.* a worldwide movement for moral and spiritual renewal founded by Frank Buchman in 1938. Also called: **Buchmanism.** Former name: **Oxford Group.**

moral theology *n.* the branch of theology dealing with ethics.

morass (məˈræs) *n.* **1.** a tract of swampy low-lying land. **2.** a disordered or muddled situation or circumstance, esp. one that impedes progress. [C17: < Du. *moeras*, ult. < OF *marais* MARSH]

moratorium (ˌmɒrəˈtɔːrɪəm) *n., pl.* **-ria** (-rɪə) *or* **-riums.** **1.** a legally authorized postponement of the fulfilment of an obligation. **2.** an agreed suspension of activity. [C19: NL, < LL *morātōrius* dilatory, < *mora* delay]

Moravian (məˈreɪvɪən, mɒ-) *adj.* **1.** of or relating to Moravia, its people, or their dialect of Czech. **2.** of or relating to the Moravian Church. ~*n.* **3.** the Moravian dialect. **4.** a native or inhabitant of Moravia. **5.** a member of the Moravian Church. —**Moˈravianism** *n.*

moray (mɒˈreɪ) *n., pl.* **-rays.** a voracious marine coastal eel marked with brilliant colours. [C17: < Port. *moréia*, < L *mūrēna*, < Gk *muraina*]

morbid (ˈmɔːbɪd) *adj.* **1.** having an unusual interest in death or unpleasant events. **2.** gruesome. **3.** relating to or characterized by disease. [C17: < L *morbidus* sickly, < *morbus* illness] —**morˈbidity** *n.* —ˈ**morbidly** *adv.* —ˈ**morbidness** *n.*

morbid anatomy *n.* the branch of medical science concerned with the study of the structure of diseased organs and tissues.

morbific (mɔːˈbɪfɪk) *adj.* causing disease.

mordant (ˈmɔːdᵊnt) *adj.* **1.** sarcastic or caustic. **2.** having the properties of a mordant. **3.** pungent. ~*n.* **4.** a substance used before the application of a dye, possessing the ability to fix colours. **5.** an acid or other corrosive fluid used to etch lines on a printing plate. [C15: < OF: biting, < *mordre* to bite, < L *mordēre*] —ˈ**mordancy** *n.* —ˈ**mordantly** *adv.*

mordent (ˈmɔːdᵊnt) *n. Music.* a melodic ornament consisting of the rapid alternation of a note with a note one degree lower than it. [C19: < G, < It. *mordente*, < *mordere* to bite]

more (mɔː) *determiner.* **1. a.** the comparative of **much** or **many:** *more joy than you know; more sausages.* **b.** (*as pron.; functioning as sing. or pl.*): *he has more than she has; even more are dying.* **2. a.** additional; further: *no more bananas.* **b.** (*as pron.; functioning as sing. or pl.*): *I can't take any more; more than expected.* **3. more of.** to a greater extent or degree: *we see more of Sue; more of a nuisance.* ~*adv.* **4.** used to form the comparative of some adjectives and adverbs: *a more believable story; more quickly.* **5.** the comparative of **much:** *people listen to the radio more now.* **6. more or less. a.** as an estimate; approximately. **b.** to an unspecified extent or degree: *the party was ruined, more or less.* [OE *māra*]

▷ **Usage.** See at **most.**

moreish *or* **morish** (ˈmɔːrɪʃ) *adj. Inf.* (of food) causing a desire for more.

morel (mɒˈrɛl) *n.* an edible fungus in which the mushroom has a pitted cap. [C17: < F *morille*, prob. of Gmc origin]

morello (məˈrɛləʊ) *n., pl.* **-los.** a variety of small very dark sour cherry. [C17: ? < Med. L *amārellum*, dim. of L *amārus* bitter, but also infl. by It. *morello* blackish]

morendo (mɒrˈɛndəʊ) *adv. Music.* gradually dying away. [It.: dying]

moreover (mɔːˈrəʊvə) *sentence connector.* in addition to what has already been said.

morepork (ˈmɔːˌpɔːk) *n.* another name, esp. in New Zealand, for **mopoke.**

mores (ˈmɔːreɪz) *pl. n.* the customs and conventions embodying the fundamental values of a group or society. [C20: < L, pl. of *mōs* custom]

morganatic (ˌmɔːgəˈnætɪk) *adj.* of or designating a marriage between a person of high rank and a person of low rank, by which the latter is not elevated to the higher rank and any issue have no rights to the succession of the higher party's titles, property, etc. [C18: < Med. L *mātrimōnium ad morganāticum* marriage based on the morning-gift (a token present after consummation representing the husband's only liability); *morganātica*, ult. < OHG *morgan* morning] —ˌ**morgaˈnatically** *adv.*

morgen (ˈmɔːgən) *n.* **1.** a South African unit of area, equal to about two acres or 0.8 hectare. **2.** a unit of area, formerly used in Prussia and Scandinavia, equal to about two thirds of an acre. [C17: < Du.: morning, a morning's ploughing]

morgue (mɔːg) *n.* **1.** another word for **mortuary.** **2.** *Inf.* a room or file containing clippings, etc., used for reference in a newspaper. [C19: < F *le Morgue*, a Paris mortuary]

moribund (ˈmɒrɪˌbʌnd) *adj.* **1.** near death. **2.** without force or vitality. [C18: < L, < *morī* to die] —ˌ**moriˈbundity** *n.* —ˈ**moriˌbundly** *adv.*

Morisco (məˈrɪskəʊ) *or* **Moresco** (məˈrɛskəʊ) *n., pl.* **-cos** *or* **-coes.** **1.** a Spanish Moor. **2.** a morris dance. ~*adj.* **3.** another word for **Moorish;** see **Moor.** [C16: < Sp., < *Moro* MOOR]

morish (ˈmɔːrɪʃ) *adj.* a variant spelling of **moreish.**

Mormon (ˈmɔːmən) *n.* **1.** a member of the

Church of Jesus Christ of Latter-day Saints, founded in 1830 in New York by Joseph Smith. **2.** a prophet whose supposed revelations were recorded by Joseph Smith in the Book of Mormon. ~*adj.* **3.** of or relating to the Mormons, their Church, or their beliefs. —ˈ**Mormonism** *n.*

morn (mɔːn) *n.* a poetic word for **morning.** [OE *morgen*]

mornay (ˈmɔːneɪ) *adj.* (*often immediately postpositive*) denoting a cheese sauce: *eggs mornay.* [? after Philippe de *Morney* (1549-1623), F Huguenot leader]

morning (ˈmɔːnɪŋ) *n.* **1.** the first part of the day, ending at noon. **2.** sunrise; daybreak; dawn. **3.** the beginning or early period. **4. the morning after.** *Inf.* the aftereffects of excess, esp. a hangover. **5.** (*modifier*) of, used in, or occurring in the morning: *morning coffee.* [C13 *morwening,* < MORN, on the model of EVENING]

morning-after pill *n.* an oral contraceptive that is effective if taken some hours after intercourse.

morning dress *n.* formal day dress for men, comprising a cutaway frock coat (**morning coat**), usually with grey trousers and top hat.

morning-glory *n., pl.* **-ries.** any of various mainly tropical plants of the convolvulus family, with trumpet-shaped blue, pink, or white flowers, which close in late afternoon.

mornings (ˈmɔːnɪŋz) *adv. Inf.* in the morning, esp. regularly, or during every morning.

morning sickness *n.* nausea occurring shortly after rising: a symptom of pregnancy.

morning star *n.* a planet, usually Venus, seen just before sunrise. Also called: **daystar.**

Moro (ˈmɔːrəʊ) *n.* **1.** (*pl.* **-ros** *or* **-ro**) a member of a group of predominantly Muslim peoples of the S Philippines. **2.** the language of these peoples. [C19: via Sp. < L *Maurus* MOOR]

Moroccan (məˈrɒkən) *adj.* **1.** of or denoting Morocco, a kingdom in NW Africa, or its inhabitants, their customs, etc. ~*n.* **2.** a native or inhabitant of Morocco.

morocco (məˈrɒkəʊ) *n.* a fine soft leather made from goatskins, used for bookbinding, shoes, etc. [C17: after *Morocco,* where it was orig. made]

moron (ˈmɔːrɒn) *n.* **1.** a foolish or stupid person. **2.** a person having an intelligence quotient of between 50 and 70. [C20: < Gk *mōros* foolish] —**moronic** (məˈrɒnɪk) *adj.* —**moˈronically** *adv.* —ˈ**moronism** *or* **moˈronity** *n.*

morose (məˈrəʊs) *adj.* ill-tempered or gloomy. [C16: < L *mōrōsus* peevish, < *mōs* custom, will] —**moˈrosely** *adv.* —**moˈroseness** *n.*

-morph *n. combining form.* indicating shape, form, or structure of a specified kind: *ectomorph.* [< Gk *-morphos,* < *morphē* shape] —**-morphic** *or* **-morphous** *adj. combining form.* —**-morphy** *n. combining form.*

morpheme (ˈmɔːfiːm) *n. Linguistics.* a speech element having a meaning or grammatical function that cannot be subdivided into further such elements. [C20: < F, < Gk *morphē* form, on the model of PHONEME] —**morˈphemic** *adj.* —**morˈphemically** *adv.*

morphine (ˈmɔːfiːn) *or* **morphia** (ˈmɔːfɪə) *n.* an alkaloid extracted from opium: used in medicine as an anaesthetic and sedative. [C19: < F, < *Morpheus,* in Gk myth, the god of sleep & dreams]

morphogenesis (ˌmɔːfəʊˈdʒɛnɪsɪs) *n.* **1.** the development of form in an organism during its growth. **2.** the evolutionary development of form in an organism or part of an organism. —**morphogenetic** (ˌmɔːfəʊdʒɪˈnɛtɪk) *adj.*

morphology (mɔːˈfɒlədʒɪ) *n.* **1.** the branch of biology concerned with the form and structure of organisms. **2.** the form and structure of words in a language. **3.** the form and structure of anything. —**morphologic** (ˌmɔːfəˈlɒdʒɪk) *or* ˌ**morphoˈlogical** *adj.* —ˌ**morphoˈlogically** *adv.* —**morˈphologist** *n.*

Morris chair (ˈmɒrɪs) *n.* an armchair with an adjustable back. [C19: after William *Morris* (1834-96), E writer, painter, & craftsman]

morris dance *n.* any of various old English folk dances usually performed by men (**morris men**) adorned with bells and often representing characters from folk tales. Often shortened to **morris.** [C15 *moreys daunce* Moorish dance] —**morris dancing** *n.*

morro (ˈmɒrəʊ) *n., pl.* **-ros** (-rəʊz). a rounded hill or promontory. [< Sp.]

morrow (ˈmɒrəʊ) *n.* (usually preceded by *the*) *Arch. or poetic.* **1.** the next day. **2.** the period following a specified event. **3.** the morning. [C13 *morwe,* < OE *morgen* morning]

Morse code (mɔːs) *n.* a telegraph code used internationally for transmitting messages. Letters, numbers, etc., are represented by groups of shorter dots and longer dashes, or by groups of the corresponding sounds. [C19: after Samuel *Morse* (1791-1872), U.S. inventor]

morsel (ˈmɔːsᵊl) *n.* **1.** a small slice or mouthful of food. **2.** a small piece; bit. [C13: < OF, < *mors* a bite, < L *morsus,* < *mordēre* to bite]

mortal (ˈmɔːtᵊl) *adj.* **1.** (of living beings, esp. human beings) subject to death. **2.** of or involving life or the world. **3.** ending in or causing death; fatal: *a mortal blow.* **4.** deadly or unrelenting: *a mortal enemy.* **5.** of or like the fear of death: *mortal terror.* **6.** great or very intense: *mortal pain.* **7.** conceivable or possible: *there was no mortal reason to go.* **8.** *Sl.* long and tedious: *for three mortal hours.* ~*n.* **9.** a mortal being. **10.** *Inf.* a person: *a mean mortal.* [C14: < L *mortālis,* < *mors* death] —ˈ**mortally** *adv.*

mortality (mɔːˈtælɪtɪ) *n., pl.* **-ties. 1.** the condition of being mortal. **2.** great loss of life, as in war or disaster. **3.** the number of deaths in a given period. **4.** mankind; humanity.

mortal sin *n. Christianity.* a sin regarded as involving total loss of grace.

mortar (ˈmɔːtə) *n.* **1.** a mixture of cement or lime or both with sand and water, used as a bond between bricks or stones or as a covering on a wall. **2.** a cannon having a short barrel and relatively wide bore that fires low-velocity shells in high trajectories. **3.** a vessel, usually bowl-shaped, in which substances are pulverized with a pestle. ~*vb.* (*tr.*) **4.** to join (bricks or stones) or cover (a wall) with mortar. **5.** to fire on with mortars. [C13: < L *mortārium* basin in which mortar is mixed; in some senses, via OF *mortier* substance mixed inside such a vessel]

mortarboard (ˈmɔːtəˌbɔːd) *n.* **1.** a black tasselled academic cap with a flat square top. **2.** a small square board with a handle on the underside for carrying mortar.

mortgage (ˈmɔːgɪdʒ) *n.* **1.** a conditional conveyance of property, esp. real property, as security for the repayment of a loan. **2.** the deed effecting such a transaction. **3.** the loan itself. ~*vb.* (*tr.*) **4.** to convey (property) by mortgage. **5.** *Inf.* to pledge. [C14: < OF, lit.: dead pledge] —ˈ**mortgageable** *adj.*

mortgagee (ˌmɔːgɪˈdʒiː) *n. Law.* the party to a mortgage who makes the loan.

mortgagor (ˌmɔːgɪˈdʒɔː) *or* **mortgager** *n. Property law.* a person who borrows money by mortgaging his property to the lender as security.

mortician (mɔːˈtɪʃən) *n. Chiefly U.S.* another word for **undertaker.** [C19: < MORTUARY + *-ician,* as in *physician*]

mortification (ˌmɔːtɪfɪˈkeɪʃən) *n.* **1.** a feeling of humiliation. **2.** something causing this. **3.** *Christianity.* the practice of mortifying the senses. **4.** another word for **gangrene.**

mortify (ˈmɔːtɪˌfaɪ) *vb.* **-fying, -fied. 1.** (*tr.*) to humiliate or cause to feel shame. **2.** (*tr.*) *Christianity.* to subdue and bring under control by self-denial, disciplinary exercises, etc. **3.** (*intr.*) to undergo tissue death or become gangrenous. [C14: via OF < Church L *mortificāre* to put to death, < L *mors* death + *facere* to do] —ˈ**mortiˌfier** *n.* —ˈ**mortiˌfying** *adj.*

mortise *or* **mortice** (ˈmɔːtɪs) *n.* **1.** a slot or recess cut into a piece of wood, stone, etc., to receive a matching projection (tenon) of another piece, or a mortise lock. ~*vb.* (*tr.*) **2.** to cut a slot or recess in (a piece of wood, stone, etc.). **3.** to join (two pieces of wood, stone, etc.) by means of a mortise and tenon. [C14: < OF *mortoise,* ? < Ar. *murtazza* fastened in position]

mortise lock *n.* a lock set into a mortise in a door so that the mechanism of the lock is enclosed by the door.

mortmain (ˈmɔːtˌmeɪn) *n. Law.* the state or condition of lands, buildings, etc., held inalienably, as by an ecclesiastical or other corporation. [C15: < OF *mortemain,* < Med. L *mortua manus* dead hand, inalienable ownership]

mortuary (ˈmɔːtʃʊərɪ) *n., pl.* **-aries.** **1.** Also called: **morgue.** a building where dead bodies are kept before cremation or burial. ~*adj.* **2.** of or relating to death or burial. [C14 (as n., a funeral gift to a parish priest): via Med. L *mortuārium* (n.) < L *mortuārius* of the dead]

morwong (ˈmɔːˌwɒŋ) *n.* a food fish of Australasian coastal waters. [< Abor.]

mosaic (məˈzeɪɪk) *n.* **1.** a design or decoration made up of small pieces of coloured glass, stone, etc. **2.** the process of making a mosaic. **3. a.** a mottled yellowing that occurs in the leaves of plants affected with any of various virus diseases. **b.** Also called: **mosaic disease.** any of the diseases, such as **tobacco mosaic,** that produce this discoloration. **4.** a light-sensitive surface on a television camera tube, consisting of a large number of granules of photoemissive material. [C16: via F & It. < Med. L, < LGk: mosaic work, < Gk: of the Muses, < *mousa* MUSE] —**mosaicist** (məˈzeɪɪsɪst) *n.*

Mosaic (məʊˈzeɪɪk) *adj.* of or relating to Moses or the laws and traditions ascribed to him.

Mosaic law *n. Bible.* the laws ascribed to Moses and contained in the Pentateuch.

moschatel (ˌmɒskəˈtɛl) *n.* a small N temperate plant with greenish-white musk-scented flowers. Also called: **townhall clock, five-faced bishop.** [C18: via F < It. *moscatella,* dim. of *moscato* MUSK]

mosey (ˈməʊzɪ) *vb.* (*intr.*) *Inf.* (often foll. by *along* or *on*) to amble. [C19: <?]

Moslem (ˈmɒzləm) *n., pl.* **-lems** *or* **-lem,** *adj.* a variant spelling of **Muslim.**

mosque (mɒsk) *n.* a Muslim place of worship. [C14: earlier *mosquee,* < OF via It. *moschea,* ult. < Ar. *masjid* temple]

mosquito (məˈskiːtəʊ) *n., pl.* **-toes** *or* **-tos.** any dipterous insect of the family Culicidae: the females have a long proboscis adapted for piercing the skin of man and animals to suck their blood. See also **aedes, anopheles, culex.** [C16: < Sp., dim. of *mosca* fly, < L *musca*]

mosquito net *or* **netting** *n.* a fine curtain or net to keep mosquitoes out.

moss (mɒs) *n.* **1.** any of a class of plants, typically growing in dense mats on trees, rocks, moist ground, etc. **2.** a clump or growth of any of these plants. **3.** any of various similar but unrelated plants, such as Spanish moss and reindeer moss. **4.** *Scot. & N English.* a peat bog or marsh. [OE *mos* swamp] —ˈ**moss**ˌ**like** *adj.* —ˈ**mossy** *adj.* —ˈ**mossiness** *n.*

moss agate *n.* a variety of chalcedony with dark greenish mossy markings.

mossie (ˈmɒsɪ) *n.* another name for the **cape sparrow.** [<?]

mosso (ˈmɒsəʊ) *adv. Music.* to be performed with rapidity. [It., p.p. of *muovere* to MOVE]

moss rose *n.* a variety of rose that has a mossy stem and calyx and fragrant pink flowers.

moss stitch *n.* a knitting stitch made up of alternate plain and purl stitches.

mosstrooper (ˈmɒsˌtruːpə) *n.* a raider in the Borders of England and Scotland in the mid-17th century. [C17 *moss,* in dialect sense: bog]

most (məʊst) *determiner.* **1. a.** a great majority of; nearly all: *most people like eggs.* **b.** (*as pron.; functioning as sing. or pl.*): *most of them don't know; most of it is finished.* **2. the most. a.** the superlative of **many** and **much:** *you have the most money; the most apples.* **b.** (*as pron.*): *the most he can afford is two pounds.* **3. at (the) most.** at the maximum: *that girl is four at the most.* **4. make the most of.** to use to the best advantage: *she makes the most of her accent.* ~*adv.* **5. the most.** used to form the superlative of some adjectives and adverbs: *the most beautiful daughter of all.* **6.** the superlative of **much:** *people welcome a drink most after work.* **7.** (intensifier): *a most absurd story.* [OE *mǣst* or *mǣst,* whence ME *moste, mēst*]

▷ **Usage.** The meanings of *most* and *mostly* should not be confused. In *she was most affected by the news, most* is equivalent to *very* and is generally acceptable. In *she was mostly affected by the news,* the implication is that there was something else, in addition to the news, which affected her, although less so. *More* and *most* should also be distinguished when used in comparisons. *More* applies to cases involving two persons, objects, etc., *most* to cases involving three or more: *John is the more intelligent of the two; he is the most intelligent of the students.*

-most *suffix. forming the superlative degree of some adjectives and adverbs: hindmost; uppermost.* [OE *-mǣst, -mest,* orig. a sup. suffix, later mistakenly taken as < *mǣst* (adv.) most]

mostly (ˈməʊstlɪ) *adv.* **1.** almost entirely; chiefly. **2.** on many or most occasions; usually.

Most Reverend *n.* (in Britain) a courtesy title applied to Anglican and Roman Catholic archbishops.

mot (məʊ) *n.* short for **bon mot.** [C16: via F < Vulgar L *mottum* (unattested) utterance, < L *muttum,* < *muttīre* to mutter]

MOT (in Britain and New Zealand) *abbrev. for:* **1.** Ministry of Transport (*Brit.,* now Transport Industries). **2.** *Brit.* the MOT test or test certificate.

mote (məʊt) *n.* a tiny speck. [OE *mot*]

motel (məʊˈtɛl) *n.* a roadside hotel for motorists. [C20: < *motor* + *hotel*]

motet (məʊˈtɛt) *n.* a polyphonic choral composition used as an anthem in the Roman Catholic service. [C14: < OF, dim. of *mot* word; see MOT]

moth (mɒθ) *n.* any of numerous insects that typically have stout bodies with antennae of various shapes (but not clubbed), including large brightly coloured species, such as hawk moths, and small inconspicuous types, such as the clothes moths. Cf. **butterfly** (sense 1). [OE *moththe*]

mothball (ˈmɒθˌbɔːl) *n.* **1.** a small ball of camphor or naphthalene used to repel clothes moths in stored clothing, etc. **2. put in mothballs.** to postpone work on (a project, activity, etc.). ~*vb.* (*tr.*) **3.** to prepare (a ship) for a long period of storage by sealing with plastic. **4.** to take (a factory, etc.) out of operation but maintain it for future use. **5.** to postpone work on (a project, activity, etc.).

moth-eaten *adj.* **1.** decayed, decrepit, or outdated. **2.** eaten away by or as if by moths.

mother[1] (ˈmʌðə) *n.* **1. a.** a female who has given birth to offspring. **b.** (*as modifier*): *a mother bird.* **2.** (*often cap., esp. as a term of address*) a person's own mother. **3.** a female substituting in the function of a mother. **4.** (*often cap.*) *Chiefly arch.* a term of address for an old woman. **5. a.** motherly qualities, such as maternal affection: *it appealed to the mother in her.* **b.** (*as modifier*): *mother love.* **c.** (*in combination*): *mothercraft.* **6. a.** a female or thing that creates, nurtures, protects, etc., something. **b.** (*as modifier*): *mother church; mother earth.* **7.** a title given to certain members of female religious orders. **8.** (*modifier*) native or innate: *mother wit.* ~*vb.* (*tr.*) **9.** to give birth to or produce. **10.** to nurture, protect, etc. as a mother. [OE *mōdor*] —ˈ**motherless** *adj.*

mother[2] (ˈmʌðə) *n.* a stringy slime containing various bacteria that forms on the surface of liquids undergoing fermentation. Also called: **mother of vinegar.** [C16: ? < MOTHER[1], but cf. Sp. *madre* scum, Du. *modder* dregs, MLow G *modder* decaying object, *mudde* sludge]

Mother Carey's chicken (ˈkɛərɪz) *n.* another name for **storm petrel.** [<?]

mother country *n.* **1.** the original country of colonists or settlers. **2.** a person's native country.

Mother Goose *n.* the imaginary author of a

collection of nursery rhymes. [C18: translated < F *Contes de ma mère l'Oye* (1697), a collection of tales by Charles Perrault]

motherhood ('mʌðə,hʊd) *n.* **1.** the state of being a mother. **2.** the qualities characteristic of a mother.

Mothering Sunday ('mʌðərɪŋ) *n. Brit.* the fourth Sunday in Lent, when mothers traditionally receive presents from their children. Also called: **Mother's Day.**

mother-in-law *n., pl.* **mothers-in-law.** the mother of one's wife or husband.

motherland ('mʌðə,lænd) *n.* a person's native country.

mother lode *n. Mining.* the principal lode in a system.

motherly ('mʌðəlɪ) *adj.* of or resembling a mother, esp. in warmth or protectiveness. —'**motherliness** *n.*

mother-of-pearl *n.* a hard iridescent substance that forms the inner layer of the shells of certain molluscs, such as the oyster. It is used to make buttons, etc. Also called: **nacre.**

Mother's Day *n.* **1.** *U.S. & Canad.* the second Sunday in May, observed as a day in honour of mothers. **2.** See **Mothering Sunday.**

mother ship *n.* a ship providing facilities and supplies for a number of small vessels.

mother superior *n., pl.* **mother superiors** *or* **mothers superior.** the head of a community of nuns.

mother tongue *n.* **1.** the language first learned by a child. **2.** a language from which another has evolved.

mother wit *n.* native practical intelligence; common sense.

mothproof ('mɒθ,pruːf) *adj.* **1.** (esp. of clothes) chemically treated so as to repel clothes moths. ~*vb.* **2.** (*tr.*) to make (clothes, etc.) mothproof.

mothy ('mɒθɪ) *adj.* **mothier, mothiest. 1.** moth-eaten. **2.** containing moths; full of moths.

motif (məʊ'tiːf) *n.* **1.** a distinctive idea, esp. a theme elaborated on in a piece of music, literature, etc. **2.** Also called: **motive.** a recurring shape in a design. **3.** a single decoration, such as a symbol or name on a jumper, sweatshirt, etc. [C19: < F; see MOTIVE]

motile ('məʊtaɪl) *adj.* capable of moving spontaneously and independently. [C19: < L *mōtus* moved, < *movēre* to move] —**motility** (məʊ'tɪlɪtɪ) *n.*

motion ('məʊʃən) *n.* **1.** the process of continual change in the physical position of an object; movement. **2.** a movement or action, esp. of part of the human body; a gesture. **3. a.** the capacity for movement. **b.** a manner of movement, esp. walking; gait. **4.** a mental impulse. **5.** a formal proposal to be discussed and voted on in a debate, meeting, etc. **6.** *Law.* an application made to a judge or court for an order or ruling necessary to the conduct of legal proceedings. **7.** *Brit.* **a.** the evacuation of the bowels. **b.** excrement. **8. a.** part of a moving mechanism. **b.** the action of such a part. **9. go through the motions. a.** to act or perform the task (of doing something) mechanically or without sincerity. **b.** to mimic the action (of something) by gesture. **10. in motion.** operational or functioning (often in **set in motion, set the wheels in motion**). ~*vb.* **11.** (when *tr., may take a clause as object or an infinitive*) to signal or direct (a person) by a movement or gesture. [C15: < L *mōtiō* a moving, < *movēre* to move] —'**motionless** *adj.*

motion picture *n.* a U.S. and Canad. term for **film** (sense 1).

motivate ('məʊtɪ,veɪt) *vb.* (*tr.*) to give incentive to. —,**moti'vation** *n.*

motivational research (,məʊtɪ'veɪʃən'l) *n.* the application of psychology to the study of consumer behaviour, esp. the planning of advertising and sales campaigns. Also called: **motivation research.**

motive ('məʊtɪv) *n.* **1.** the reason for a certain course of action, whether conscious or unconscious. **2.** a variant of **motif** (sense 2). ~*adj.* **3.** of or causing motion: *a motive force.* **4.** of or acting as a motive; motivating. ~*vb.* (*tr.*) **5.** to motivate. [C14: < OF *motif*, < LL *mōtīvus* (adj.) moving, < L *mōtus*, p.p. of *movēre* to move] —'**motiveless** *adj.*

motive power *n.* **1.** any source of energy used to produce motion. **2.** the means of supplying power to an engine, vehicle, etc.

mot juste *French.* (mo ʒyst) *n., pl.* ***mots justes*** (mo ʒyst). the appropriate word or expression.

motley ('mɒtlɪ) *adj.* **1.** made up of elements of varying type, quality, etc. **2.** multicoloured. ~*n.* **3.** a motley collection. **4.** the particoloured attire of a jester. [C14: ? < *mot* speck]

moto ('məʊtəʊ) *n. Music.* movement. [It.]

motocross ('məʊtə,krɒs) *n.* **1.** a motorcycle race across rough ground. **2.** another name for **rallycross.** [C20: < MOTO(R) + CROSS(-COUNTRY)]

motor ('məʊtə) *n.* **1. a.** the engine, esp. an internal-combustion engine, of a vehicle. **b.** (*as modifier*): *a motor scooter.* **2.** Also called: **electric motor.** a machine that converts electrical energy into mechanical energy. **3.** any device that converts another form of energy into mechanical energy to produce motion. **4. a.** *Chiefly Brit.* a car. **b.** (*as modifier*): *motor spares.* ~*adj.* **5.** producing or causing motion. **6.** *Physiol.* **a.** of or relating to nerves or neurons that carry impulses that cause muscles to contract. **b.** of or relating to movement or to muscles that induce movement. ~*vb.* **7.** (*intr.*) to travel by car. **8.** (*tr.*) *Brit.* to transport by car. **9.** (*intr.*) *Inf.* to move fast; make good progress. [C16: < L *mōtor* a mover, < *movēre* to move]

motorbicycle ('məʊtə,baɪsɪk'l) *n.* **1.** a motorcycle. **2.** a moped.

motorbike ('məʊtə,baɪk) *n.* a less formal name for **motorcycle.**

motorboat ('məʊtə,bəʊt) *n.* any boat powered by a motor.

motorbus ('məʊtə,bʌs) *n.* a bus driven by an internal-combustion engine.

motorcade ('məʊtə,keɪd) *n.* a parade of cars. [C20: < MOTOR + CAVALCADE]

motorcar ('məʊtə,kɑː) *n.* **1.** a more formal word for **car. 2.** a self-propelled electric railway car.

motorcycle ('məʊtə,saɪk'l) *n.* **1.** Also called: **motorbike.** a two-wheeled vehicle that is driven by a petrol engine. ~*vb.* (*intr.*) **2.** to ride on a motorcycle. —'**motor,cyclist** *n.*

motorist ('məʊtərɪst) *n.* a driver of a car.

motorize *or* **-ise** ('məʊtə,raɪz) *vb.* (*tr.*) **1.** to equip with a motor. **2.** to provide (military units) with motor vehicles. —,**motori'zation** *or* **-i'sation** *n.*

motorman ('məʊtəmən) *n., pl.* **-men. 1.** the driver of an electric train. **2.** the operator of a motor.

motormouth ('məʊtə,maʊθ) *n. Sl.* a garrulous person.

motor scooter *n.* a light motorcycle with small wheels and an enclosed engine. Often shortened to **scooter.**

motor vehicle *n.* a road vehicle driven esp. by an internal-combustion engine.

motorway ('məʊtə,weɪ) *n. Brit.* a main road for fast-moving traffic, having separate carriageways for vehicles travelling in opposite directions.

Motown ('məʊ,taʊn) *n.* music combining rhythm and blues and pop, or gospel rhythms and modern ballad harmony. [C20: < *Mo(tor) Town,* nickname for Detroit, Michigan, where it originated]

motte (mɒt) *n. History.* a mound on which a castle was erected. [C14: see MOAT]

MOT test *n.* (in Britain) a compulsory annual test of the roadworthiness of motor vehicles over a certain age.

mottle ('mɒt'l) *vb.* **1.** (*tr.*) to colour with streaks or blotches of different shades. ~*n.* **2.** a mottled appearance, as of the surface of marble. [C17: back formation < MOTLEY]

motto ('mɒtəʊ) *n., pl.* **-toes** *or* **-tos. 1.** a short saying expressing the guiding maxim or ideal of a family, organization, etc., esp. when part of a coat of arms. **2.** a verse or maxim contained in a paper cracker. **3.** a quotation prefacing a book or chapter of a book. [C16: via It. < L *muttum* utterance]

moue *French.* (mu) *n.* a pouting look.

moufflon (ˈmuːflɒn) *n.* a wild short-fleeced mountain sheep of Corsica and Sardinia. [C18: via F < Romance *mufrone,* < LL *mufrō*]

mouillé (ˈmwiːeɪ) *adj. Phonetics.* palatalized, as in the sounds represented by Spanish *ll* or *ñ,* (pronounced as (ʎ) and (ɲ)), or French *ll* (representing a (j) sound). [C19: < F, p.p. of *mouiller* to moisten, < L *mollis* soft]

moujik (ˈmuːʒɪk) *n.* a variant spelling of **muzhik.**

mould[1] *or U.S.* **mold** (məʊld) *n.* **1.** a shaped cavity used to give a definite form to fluid or plastic material. **2.** a frame on which something may be constructed. **3.** something shaped in or made on a mould. **4.** shape, form, design, or pattern. **5.** specific nature, character, or type. ~*vb.* (*tr.*) **6.** to make in a mould. **7.** to shape or form, as by using a mould. **8.** to influence or direct: *to mould opinion.* **9.** to cling to: *the skirt moulds her figure.* **10.** *Metallurgy.* to make (a material) into a mould used in casting. [C13 (n.): < OF *modle,* < L *modulus* a small measure] —ˈ**mouldable** *or U.S.* ˈ**moldable** *adj.* —ˈ**moulder** *or U.S.* ˈ**molder** *n.*

mould[2] *or U.S.* **mold** (məʊld) *n.* **1.** a coating or discoloration caused by various fungi that develop in a damp atmosphere on the surface of food, fabrics, etc. **2.** any of the fungi that cause this growth. ~*vb.* **3.** to become or cause to become covered with this growth. ~Also called: **mildew.** [C15: dialect (N English) *mowlde* mouldy, < p.p. of *moulen* to become mouldy, prob. < ON]

mould[3] *or U.S.* **mold** (məʊld) *n.* loose soil, esp. when rich in organic matter. [OE *molde*]

mouldboard *or U.S.* **moldboard** (ˈməʊldˌbɔːd) *n.* the curved blade of a plough, which turns over the furrow.

moulder *or U.S.* **molder** (ˈməʊldə) *vb.* (often foll. by *away*) to crumble or cause to crumble, as through decay. [C16: verbal use of MOULD[3]]

moulding *or U.S.* **molding** (ˈməʊldɪŋ) *n.* **1.** *Archit.* **a.** a shaped outline, esp. one used on cornices, etc. **b.** a shaped strip made of wood, stone, etc. **2.** something moulded.

mouldy *or U.S.* **moldy** (ˈməʊldɪ) *adj.* **-dier, -diest.** **1.** covered with mould. **2.** stale or musty, esp. from age or lack of use. **3.** *Sl.* boring; dull. —ˈ**mouldiness** *or U.S.* ˈ**moldiness** *n.*

moult *or U.S.* **molt** (məʊlt) *vb.* **1.** (of birds, mammals, arthropods, etc.) to shed (feathers, hair, or cuticle). ~*n.* **2.** the periodic process of moulting. [C14 *mouten,* < OE *mūtian,* as in *bimūtian* to exchange for, < L *mūtāre* to change] —ˈ**moulter** *or U.S.* ˈ**molter** *n.*

mound (maʊnd) *n.* **1.** a raised mass of earth, debris, etc. **2.** any heap or pile. **3.** a small natural hill. **4.** an artificial ridge of earth, stone, etc., as used for defence. ~*vb.* **5.** (often foll. by *up*) to gather into a mound; heap. **6.** (*tr.*) to cover or surround with a mound: *to mound a grave.* [C16: earthwork, ? < OE *mund* hand, hence defence]

Mound Builder *n.* a member of a group of prehistoric inhabitants of the Mississippi region of the U.S., who built altar mounds, tumuli, etc.

mound-builder *n.* another name for **megapode.**

mount[1] (maʊnt) *vb.* **1.** to go up (a hill, stairs, etc.); climb. **2.** to get up on (a horse, a platform, etc.). **3.** (*intr.;* often foll. by *up*) to increase; accumulate: *excitement mounted.* **4.** (*tr.*) to fix onto a backing, setting, or support: *to mount a photograph; to mount a slide.* **5.** (*tr.*) to provide with a horse for riding, or to place on a horse. **6.** (of male animals) to climb onto (a female animal) for copulation. **7.** (*tr.*) to prepare (a play, etc.) for production. **8.** (*tr.*) to plan and organise (a campaign, etc.). **9.** (*tr.*) to prepare (a skeleton, etc.) for exhibition as a specimen. **10.** (*tr.*) to place or carry (weapons) in such a position that they can be fired. **11. mount guard.** See **guard.** ~*n.* **12.** a backing, setting, or support onto which something is fixed. **13.** the act or manner of mounting. **14.** a horse for riding. **15.** a slide used in microscopy. [C16: < OF *munter,* < Vulgar L *montāre* (unattested) < L *mons* MOUNT[2]] —ˈ**mountable** *adj.* —ˈ**mounter** *n.*

mount[2] (maʊnt) *n.* a mountain or hill: used in literature and (when cap.) in proper names: *Mount Everest.* [OE *munt,* < L *mons* mountain, but infl. in ME by OF *mont*]

mountain (ˈmaʊntɪn) *n.* **1. a.** a natural upward projection of the earth's surface, higher and steeper than a hill. **b.** (*as modifier*): *mountain scenery.* **c.** (*in combination*): *a mountaintop.* **2.** a huge heap or mass: *a mountain of papers.* **3.** anything of great quantity or size. **4.** a surplus of a commodity, esp. in the European Economic Community: *a butter mountain.* [C13: < OF *montaigne,* ult. < L *montānus,* < *mons* mountain]

mountain ash *n.* **1.** any of various trees, such as the European mountain ash or rowan, having clusters of small white flowers and bright red berries. **2.** any of several Australian eucalyptus trees, such as *Eucalyptus regnans.*

mountain avens *n.* See **avens** (sense 2).

mountain cat *n.* any of various wild feline mammals, such as the bobcat, lynx, or puma.

mountaineer (ˌmaʊntɪˈnɪə) *n.* **1.** a person who climbs mountains. **2.** a person living in a mountainous area. ~*vb.* **3.** (*intr.*) to climb mountains. —ˌ**mountainˈeering** *n.*

mountain goat *n.* any wild goat inhabiting mountainous regions.

mountain laurel *n.* any of various ericaceous shrubs or trees of E North America having leathery poisonous leaves and clusters of pink or white flowers. Also called: **calico bush.**

mountain lion *n.* another name for **puma.**

mountainous (ˈmaʊntɪnəs) *adj.* **1.** of or relating to mountains: *a mountainous region.* **2.** like a mountain, esp. in size or impressiveness.

mountain sickness *n.* nausea, headache, and shortness of breath caused by climbing to high altitudes. Also called: **altitude sickness.**

mountebank (ˈmaʊntɪˌbæŋk) *n.* **1.** (formerly) a person who sold quack medicines in public places. **2.** a charlatan; fake. ~*vb.* **3.** (*intr.*) to play the mountebank. [C16: < It. *montambanco* a climber on a bench, < *montare* to MOUNT[1] + *banco* BENCH] —ˌ**mounteˈbankery** *n.*

mounted (ˈmaʊntɪd) *adj.* **1.** riding horses: *mounted police.* **2.** provided with a support, backing, etc.

Mountie *or* **Mounty** (ˈmaʊntɪ) *n., pl.* **Mounties.** *Inf.* a member of the Royal Canadian Mounted Police. [< MOUNTED]

mounting (ˈmaʊntɪŋ) *n.* another word for **mount**[1] (sense 12).

mounting-block *n.* a block of stone formerly used to aid a person when mounting a horse.

mourn (mɔːn) *vb.* **1.** to feel or express sadness for the death or loss of (someone or something). **2.** (*intr.*) to observe the customs of mourning, as by wearing black. [OE *murnan*] —ˈ**mourner** *n.*

mournful (ˈmɔːnfʊl) *adj.* **1.** evoking grief; sorrowful. **2.** gloomy; sad. —ˈ**mournfully** *adv.* —ˈ**mournfulness** *n.*

mourning (ˈmɔːnɪŋ) *n.* **1.** the act or feelings of one who mourns; grief. **2.** the conventional symbols of grief, such as the wearing of black. **3.** the period of time during which a death is officially mourned. ~*adj.* **4.** of or relating to mourning. —ˈ**mourningly** *adv.*

mourning band *n.* a piece of black material, esp. an armband, worn to indicate mourning.

mourning dove *n.* a brown North American dove with a plaintive song.

mouse *n.* (maʊs), *pl.* **mice** (maɪs). **1.** any of numerous small long-tailed rodents that are similar to but smaller than rats. See also **fieldmouse, harvest mouse, house mouse.** **2.** any of various related rodents, such as the jumping mouse. **3.** a quiet, timid, or cowardly person. **4.** *Computers.* a hand-held device used to control cursor movements and computing functions without keying. **5.** *Sl.* a black eye. ~*vb.* (maʊz).

6. to stalk and catch (mice, etc.). **7.** (*intr.*) to go about stealthily. [OE *mūs*] —ˈ**mouse**ˌ**like** *adj.*

mouser (ˈmaʊzə, ˈmaʊsə) *n.* a cat or other animal that is used to catch mice.

mousetrap (ˈmaʊsˌtræp) *n.* **1.** any trap for catching mice, esp. one with a spring-loaded metal bar that is released by the taking of the bait. **2.** *Brit. inf.* cheese of indifferent quality.

moussaka *or* **mousaka** (mʊˈsɑːkə) *n.* a dish originating in the Balkan States, consisting of meat, aubergines, and tomatoes, topped with cheese sauce. [C20: < Mod. Gk]

mousse (muːs) *n.* **1.** a light creamy dessert made with eggs, cream, fruit, etc., set with gelatin. **2.** a similar dish made from fish or meat. **3.** short for **styling mousse.** [C19: < F: froth]

mousseline (*French* muslin) *n.* **1.** a fine fabric made of rayon or silk. **2.** a type of fine glass. [C17: F: MUSLIN]

moustache *or U.S.* **mustache** (məˈstɑːʃ) *n.* **1.** the unshaved growth of hair on the upper lip. **2.** a similar growth of hair or bristles (in animals). **3.** a mark like a moustache. [C16: via F < It. *mostaccio,* ult. < Doric Gk *mustax* upper lip] —**mous**ˈ**tached** *or U.S.* **mus**ˈ**tached** *adj.*

moustache cup *n.* a cup with a partial cover to protect a drinker's moustache.

Mousterian (muːˈstɪərɪən) *n.* **1.** a culture characterized by flint flake tools and associated with Neanderthal man, dating from before 70 000–32 000 B.C. ~*adj.* **2.** of or relating to this culture. [C20: < F *moustérien,* < archaeological finds of the same period in the cave of *Le Moustier,* Dordogne, France]

mousy *or* **mousey** (ˈmaʊsɪ) *adj.* **mousier, mousiest. 1.** resembling a mouse, esp. in hair colour. **2.** shy or ineffectual. **3.** infested with mice. —ˈ**mousily** *adv.* —ˈ**mousiness** *n.*

mouth *n.* (maʊθ), *pl.* **mouths** (maʊðz). **1.** the opening through which many animals take in food and issue vocal sounds. **2.** the system of organs surrounding this opening, including the lips, tongue, teeth, etc. **3.** the visible part of the lips on the face. **4.** a person regarded as a consumer of food: *four mouths to feed.* **5.** a particular manner of speaking: *a foul mouth.* **6.** *Inf.* boastful, rude, or excessive talk: *he is all mouth.* **7.** the point where a river issues into a sea or lake. **8.** the opening of a container, such as a jar. **9.** the opening of a cave, tunnel, volcano, etc. **10.** that part of the inner lip of a horse on which the bit acts. **11.** a pout; grimace. **12. down in** *or* **at the mouth.** in low spirits. ~*vb.* (maʊð). **13.** to speak or say (something) insincerely, esp. in public. **14.** (*tr.*) to form (words) with movements of the lips but without speaking. **15.** (*tr.*) to take (something) into the mouth or to move (something) around inside the mouth. **16.** (*intr.;* usually foll. by *at*) to make a grimace. [OE *mūth*] —**mouther** (ˈmaʊðə) *n.*

mouthful (ˈmaʊθˌfʊl) *n., pl.* **-fuls. 1.** as much as is held in the mouth at one time. **2.** a small quantity, as of food. **3.** a long word or phrase that is difficult to say. **4.** *Brit. inf.* an abusive response.

mouth organ *n.* another name for **harmonica.**

mouthpart (ˈmaʊθˌpɑːt) *n.* any of the paired appendages in arthropods that surround the mouth and are specialized for feeding.

mouthpiece (ˈmaʊθˌpiːs) *n.* **1.** the part of a wind instrument into which the player blows. **2.** the part of a telephone receiver into which a person speaks. **3.** the part of a container forming its mouth. **4.** a person who acts as a spokesman, as for an organization. **5.** a publication expressing the official views of an organization.

mouthwash (ˈmaʊθˌwɒʃ) *n.* a medicated solution for gargling and cleansing the mouth.

mouthy (ˈmaʊðɪ) *adj.* **mouthier, mouthiest.** bombastic; excessively talkative.

mouton (ˈmuːtɒn) *n.* sheepskin processed to resemble the fur of another animal, esp. beaver or seal. [< F: sheep]

movable *or* **moveable** (ˈmuːvəbᵊl) *adj.* **1.** able to be moved; not fixed. **2.** (esp. of Easter) varying in date from year to year. **3.** (usually spelt **moveable**) *Law.* denoting or relating to personal property as opposed to realty. ~*n.* **4.** (*often pl.*) a movable article, esp. a piece of furniture. —ˌ**mova**ˈ**bility** *or* ˈ**movableness** *n.* —ˈ**movably** *adv.*

move (muːv) *vb.* **1.** to go or take from one place to another; change in position. **2.** (*usually intr.*) to change (one's dwelling, place of business, etc.). **3.** to be or cause to be in motion; stir. **4.** (*intr.*) (of machines, etc.) to work or operate. **5.** (*tr.*) to cause (to do something); prompt. **6.** (*intr.*) to begin to act: *move soon or we'll lose the order.* **7.** (*intr.*) to associate oneself with a specified social circle: *to move in exalted spheres.* **8.** (*intr.*) to make progress. **9.** (*tr.*) to arouse affection, pity, or compassion in; touch. **10.** (in board games) to change the position of (a piece) or (of a piece) to change position. **11.** (*intr.*) (of merchandise) to be disposed of by being bought. **12.** (when *tr., often takes a clause as object;* when *intr.,* often foll. by *for*) to suggest (a proposal) formally, as in debating or parliamentary procedure. **13.** (*intr.;* usually foll. by *on* or *along*) to go away or to another place; leave. **14.** to cause (the bowels) to evacuate or (of the bowels) to be evacuated. ~*n.* **15.** the act of moving; movement. **16.** one of a sequence of actions, usually part of a plan; manoeuvre. **17.** the act of moving one's residence, place of business, etc. **18.** (in board games) **a.** a player's turn to move his piece. **b.** a manoeuvre of a piece. **19. get a move on.** *Inf.* **a.** to get started. **b.** to hurry up. **20. on the move. a.** travelling from place to place. **b.** advancing; succeeding. **c.** very active; busy. [C13: < Anglo-F *mover,* < L *movēre*]

move in *vb.* (*mainly adv.*) **1.** (*also prep.*) Also (when *prep.*): **move into.** to occupy or take possession of (a new residence, place of business, etc.). **2.** (*intr.;* often foll. by *on*) *Inf.* to creep close (to), as in preparing to capture. **3.** (*intr.;* often foll. by *on*) *Inf.* to try to gain power or influence (over).

movement (ˈmuːvmənt) *n.* **1. a.** the act, process, or result of moving. **b.** an instance of moving. **2.** the manner of moving. **3. a.** a group of people with a common ideology. **b.** the organized action of such a group. **4.** a trend or tendency. **5.** the driving and regulating mechanism of a watch or clock. **6.** (*often pl.*) a person's location and activities during a specific time. **7. a.** the evacuation of the bowels. **b.** the matter evacuated. **8.** *Music.* a principal self-contained section of a symphony, sonata, etc. **9.** tempo or pace, as in music or literature. **10.** *Fine arts.* the appearance of motion in painting, sculpture, etc. **11.** *Prosody.* the rhythmical structure of verse. **12.** a positional change by one or a number of military units. **13.** a change in the market price of a security or commodity.

mover (ˈmuːvə) *n.* **1.** *Inf.* a person, business, idea, etc., that is advancing or progressing. **2.** a person or thing that moves. **3.** a person who moves a proposal, as in a debate. **4.** *U.S. & Canad.* a removal firm or a person who works for one.

movie (ˈmuːvɪ) *n.* **a.** an informal word for **film** (sense 1). **b.** (*as modifier*): *movie ticket.*

moving (ˈmuːvɪŋ) *adj.* **1.** arousing or touching the emotions. **2.** changing or capable of changing position. **3.** causing motion. —ˈ**movingly** *adv.*

moving staircase *or* **stairway** *n.* less common terms for **escalator** (sense 1).

mow (məʊ) *vb.* **mowing, mowed, mowed** *or* **mown. 1.** to cut down (grass, crops, etc.), with a hand implement or machine. **2.** (*tr.*) to cut the growing vegetation of (a field, lawn, etc.). [OE *māwan*] —ˈ**mower** *n.*

mow down *vb.* (*tr., adv.*) to kill in large numbers, esp. by gunfire.

mown (məʊn) *vb.* the past participle of **mow.**

mozzarella (ˌmɒtsəˈrɛlə) *n.* a moist white Italian curd cheese made originally from buffalo milk. [< It., dim. of *mozza* a type of cheese, < *mozzare* to cut off]

mp **1.** *abbrev. for* melting point. **2.** *Music. symbol for* mezzo piano. [It.: moderately soft]

MP *abbrev. for:* **1.** (in Britain, Canada, etc.) Member of Parliament. **2.** (in Britain) Metropolitan Police. **3.** Military Police. **4.** Mounted Police.

mpg *abbrev. for* miles per gallon.

mph *abbrev. for* miles per hour.

MPhil *or* **MPh** *abbrev. for* Master of Philosophy.

MPP (in Canada) *abbrev. for* Member of Provincial Parliament.

Mr (ˈmɪstə) *n., pl.* **Messrs.** a title used before a man's name or before some office that he holds: *Mr Jones; Mr President.* [C17: abbrev. of MISTER]

MR *abbrev. for:* **1.** (in Britain) Master of the Rolls. **2.** motivation(al) research.

MRC (in Britain) *abbrev. for* Medical Research Council.

m-RNA *abbrev. for* messenger RNA.

Mrs (ˈmɪsɪz) *n., pl.* **Mrs** *or* **Mesdames.** a title used before the name or names of a married woman. [C17: orig. abbrev. of MISTRESS]

Ms (mɪz, məs) *n.* a title substituted for **Mrs** or **Miss** to avoid making a distinction between married and unmarried women.

▷ **Usage.** *Ms* as a form of address, while not universally liked, has gained wide acceptance in recent years particularly in written English. It fulfils the need for a title corresponding to *Mr* in contexts where it is thought desirable to avoid differentiating between married and unmarried women or where such distinction is irrelevant. It may also be used as a form of address on letters if it is not known whether the recipient is *Miss* or *Mrs.*

MS *abbrev. for:* **1.** Master of Surgery. **2.** (on gravestones, etc.) memoriae sacrum. [L: sacred to the memory of] **3.** multiple sclerosis.

MS. *or* **ms.** *pl.* **MSS.** *or* **mss.** *abbrev. for* manuscript.

MSc *abbrev. for* Master of Science.

MSC (in Britain) *abbrev. for* Manpower Services Commission.

MSG *abbrev. for* monosodium glutamate.

Msgr *abbrev. for* Monsignor.

MST *abbrev. for* Mountain Standard Time.

Mt *or* **mt** *abbrev. for:* **1.** mount: *Mt Everest.* **2.** Also: **mtn.** mountain.

MTech *abbrev. for* Master of Technology.

mtg *abbrev. for:* **1.** meeting. **2.** Also: **mtge.** mortgage.

mu (mjuː) *n.* the 12th letter in the Greek alphabet (Μ, μ).

much (mʌtʃ) *determiner.* **1. a.** (*usually used with a negative*) a great quantity or degree of: *there isn't much honey left.* **b.** (*as pron.*): *much has been learned from this.* **2. a bit much.** *Inf.* rather excessive. **3. make much of. a.** (*used with a negative*) to make sense of: *he couldn't make much of her babble.* **b.** to give importance to: *she made much of this fact.* **c.** to pay flattering attention to: *the reporters made much of the film star.* **4. not much of.** not to any appreciable degree or extent: *he's not much of an actor really.* **5. not up to much.** *Inf.* of a low standard: *this beer is not up to much.* ~*adv.* **6.** considerably: *they're much better now.* **7.** practically; nearly (esp. in **much the same**). **8.** (*usually used with a negative*) often; a great deal: *it doesn't happen much in this country.* **9. (as) much as.** even though; although: *much as I'd like to, I can't come.* ~See also **more, most.** [OE *mycel*]

muchness (ˈmʌtʃnɪs) *n.* **1.** *Arch. or inf.* magnitude. **2. much of a muchness.** *Brit.* very similar.

mucilage (ˈmjuːsɪlɪdʒ) *n.* **1.** a sticky preparation, such as gum or glue, used as an adhesive. **2.** a complex glutinous carbohydrate secreted by certain plants. [C14: via OF < LL *mūcilāgo* mouldy juice, < L, < *mucēre* to be mouldy] —**mucilaginous** (ˌmjuːsɪˈlædʒɪnəs) *adj.*

muck (mʌk) *n.* **1.** farmyard dung or decaying vegetable matter. **2.** an organic soil rich in humus and used as a fertilizer. **3.** dirt or filth. **4.** *Sl., chiefly Brit.* rubbish. **5. make a muck of.** *Sl., chiefly Brit.* to ruin or spoil. ~*vb.* (*tr.*) **6.** to spread manure upon (fields, etc.). **7.** to soil or pollute. **8.** (usually foll. by *up*) *Brit. sl.* to ruin or spoil. **9.** (often foll. by *out*) to clear muck from. [C13: prob. < ON] —ˈ**mucky** *adj.*

muck about *vb. Brit. sl.* **1.** (*intr.*) to waste time; misbehave. **2.** (when *intr.,* foll. by *with*) to interfere (with), annoy, or waste the time (of).

mucker (ˈmʌkə) *n. Brit. sl.* **a.** a friend; mate. **b.** a coarse person. —ˈ**muckerish** *adj.*

muck in *vb.* (*intr., adv.*) *Brit. sl.* to share duties, work, etc. (with other people).

muckrake (ˈmʌkˌreɪk) *vb.* (*intr.*) to seek out and expose scandal, esp. concerning public figures. —ˈ**muckˌraker** *n.* —ˈ**muckˌraking** *n.*

musksweat (ˈmʌkˌswɛt) *n. Brit. inf.* profuse sweat or a state of profuse sweating.

mucous (ˈmjuːkəs) *adj.* of, resembling, or secreting mucus. [C17: < L *mūcōsus* slimy, < MUCUS] —**mucosity** (mjuːˈkɒsɪtɪ) *n.*

mucous membrane *n.* a mucus-secreting membrane that lines body cavities or passages that are open to the external environment.

mucus (ˈmjuːkəs) *n.* the slimy protective secretion of the mucous membranes. [C17: < L: nasal secretions; cf. *mungere* to blow the nose]

mud (mʌd) *n.* **1.** a fine-grained soft wet deposit that occurs on the ground after rain, at the bottom of ponds, etc. **2.** *Inf.* slander or defamation. **3. clear as mud.** *Inf.* not at all clear. **4. here's mud in your eye.** *Inf.* a humorous drinking toast. **5. (someone's) name is mud.** *Inf.* (someone) is disgraced. **6. throw** (*or* **sling**) **mud at.** *Inf.* slander; vilify. ~*vb.* **mudding, mudded.** **7.** (*tr.*) to soil or cover with mud. [C14: prob. < MLow G *mudde*]

mud bath *n.* **1.** a medicinal bath in heated mud. **2.** a dirty or muddy occasion, state, etc.

mudbrick (ˈmʌdˌbrɪk) *n.* a brick made with mud.

muddle (ˈmʌdᵊl) *vb.* (*tr.*) **1.** (often foll. by *up*) to mix up (objects, items, etc.). **2.** to confuse. **3.** *U.S.* to mix or stir (alcoholic drinks, etc.). ~*n.* **4.** a state of physical or mental confusion. [C16: ? < MDu. *moddelen* to make muddy] —ˈ**muddled** *adj.* —ˈ**muddler** *n.* —ˈ**muddling** *adj.,n.*

muddleheaded (ˌmʌdᵊlˈhɛdɪd) *adj.* mentally confused or vague. —ˌ**muddleˈheadedness** *n.*

muddle through *vb.* (*intr., adv.*) *Chiefly Brit.* to succeed in spite of lack of organization.

muddy (ˈmʌdɪ) *adj.* **-dier, -diest.** **1.** covered or filled with mud. **2.** not clear or bright: *muddy colours.* **3.** cloudy: *a muddy liquid.* **4.** (esp. of thoughts) confused or vague. ~*vb.* **-dying, -died.** **5.** to become or cause to become muddy. —ˈ**muddily** *adv.* —ˈ**muddiness** *n.*

mudfish (ˈmʌdˌfɪʃ) *n., pl.* **-fish** *or* **-fishes.** any of various fishes, such as the bowfin, that live at the muddy bottoms of rivers, lakes, etc.

mud flat *n.* a tract of low muddy land that is covered at high tide and exposed at low tide.

mudguard (ˈmʌdˌgɑːd) *n.* a curved part of a motorcycle, bicycle, etc., attached above the wheels to reduce the amount of water or mud thrown up by them. U.S. and Canad. name: **fender.**

mud hen *n.* any of various birds that frequent marshes, esp. the coots, rails, etc.

mudlark (ˈmʌdˌlɑːk) *n.* **1.** (formerly) a person who made a living by picking up odds and ends in the mud of tidal rivers. **2.** *Sl., now rare.* a street urchin. **3.** *Austral. sl.* a racehorse that runs well on a wet or muddy course.

mud map *n. Austral.* **1.** a rough map drawn on the ground with a stick. **2.** any rough sketch map.

mudpack (ˈmʌdˌpæk) *n.* a cosmetic astringent paste containing fuller's earth.

mud puppy *n.* an aquatic North American salamander having persistent larval features.

mudskipper (ˈmʌdˌskɪpə) *n.* any of various gobies that occur in tropical coastal regions of Africa and Asia and can move on land by means of their strong pectoral fins.

mudslinging (ˈmʌdˌslɪŋɪŋ) *n.* casting malicious slurs on an opponent, esp. in politics. —ˈ**mudˌslinger** *n.*

mudstone (ˈmʌdˌstəʊn) *n.* a dark grey clay rock similar to shale.

mud turtle *n.* any of various small turtles that inhabit muddy rivers in North and Central America.

muesli (ˈmjuːzlɪ) *n.* a mixture of rolled oats, nuts, fruit, etc., eaten with milk. [Swiss G, < G *Mus* mush, purée + *-li*, dim. suffix]

muezzin (muːˈɛzɪn) *n.* *Islam.* the official of a mosque who calls the faithful to prayer from the minaret. [C16: < Ar. *mu'adhdhin*]

muff[1] (mʌf) *n.* an open-ended cylinder of fur or cloth into which the hands are placed for warmth. [C16: prob. < Du. *mof*, ult. < F *mouffle* MUFFLE[1]]

muff[2] (mʌf) *vb.* **1.** to perform (an action) awkwardly. **2.** (*tr.*) to bungle (a shot, catch, etc.). ~*n.* **3.** any unskilful play, esp. a dropped catch. **4.** any bungled action. **5.** a bungler. [C19: <?]

muffin (ˈmʌfɪn) *n.* **1.** *Brit.* a thick round baked yeast roll, usually toasted and served with butter. **2.** *U.S. & Canad.* a small cup-shaped sweet bread roll, usually eaten hot with butter. [C18: ? < Low G *muffen* cakes]

muffin man *n.* *Brit.* (formerly) an itinerant seller of muffins.

muffle[1] (ˈmʌfᵊl) *vb.* (*tr.*) **1.** (often foll. by *up*) to wrap up (the head) in a scarf, cloak, etc., esp. for warmth. **2.** to deaden (a sound or noise), esp. by wrapping. **3.** to prevent (the expression of something) by (someone). ~*n.* **4.** something that muffles. **5.** a kiln with an inner chamber for firing porcelain, enamel, etc. [C15: prob. < OF; cf. OF *moufle* mitten, *emmouflé* wrapped up]

muffle[2] (ˈmʌfᵊl) *n.* the fleshy hairless part of the upper lip and nose in ruminants and some rodents. [C17: < F *mufle*, <?]

muffler (ˈmʌflə) *n.* **1.** a thick scarf, collar, etc. **2.** the U.S. and Canad. name for **silencer** (sense 1).

mufti (ˈmʌftɪ) *n.* civilian dress, esp. as worn by a person who normally wears a military uniform. [C19: ? < MUFTI]

Mufti (ˈmʌftɪ) *n., pl.* **-tis.** a Muslim legal expert and adviser on the law of the Koran. [C16: < Ar. *muftī*, < *aftā* to give a (legal) decision]

mug[1] (mʌg) *n.* **1.** a drinking vessel with a handle, usually cylindrical and made of earthenware. **2.** Also called: **mugful.** the quantity held by a mug or its contents. [C16: prob. of Scand. origin]

mug[2] (mʌg) *n.* **1.** *Sl.* a person's face or mouth. **2.** *Sl.* a gullible person, esp. one who is swindled easily. **3. a mug's game.** a worthless activity. ~*vb.* **mugging, mugged. 4.** (*tr.*) *Inf.* to attack or rob (someone) violently. [C18: ? < MUG[1], since drinking vessels were sometimes modelled into the likeness of a face] —ˈ**mugger** *n.*

muggins (ˈmʌgɪnz) *n.* (*functioning as sing.*) **1.** *Brit. sl.* **a.** a simpleton. **b.** a title used humorously to refer to oneself. **2.** a card game. [C19: prob. < the surname *Muggins*]

muggy (ˈmʌgɪ) *adj.* **-gier, -giest.** (of weather, air, etc.) unpleasantly warm and humid. [C18: dialect *mug* drizzle, prob. of Scand. origin] —ˈ**mugginess** *n.*

mug shot *n.* *Inf.* a photograph of a person's face, esp. one resembling a police-file picture.

mug up *vb.* (*adv.*) *Brit. sl.* to study (a subject) hard, esp. for an exam. [C19: < ?]

Muhammadan *or* **Muhammedan** (mʊˈhæmədᵊn) *n., adj.* another word (not in Muslim use) for **Muslim.**

mujaheddin *or* **mujahedeen** (ˌmuːdʒəhəˈdiːn) *pl. n.* (preceded by *the; sometimes cap.*) (in Afghanistan and Iran) fundamentalist Muslim guerrillas. [C20: < Ar. *mujāhidīn* fighters, ult. < JIHAD]

mukluk (ˈmʌklʌk) *n.* a soft boot, usually of sealskin, worn by Eskimos. [< Eskimo *muklok* large seal]

mulatto (mjuːˈlætəʊ) *n., pl.* **-tos** *or* **-toes. 1.** a person having one Negro and one White parent. ~*adj.* **2.** of a light brown colour; tawny. [C16: < Sp. *mulato* young mule, var. of *mulo* MULE[1]]

mulberry (ˈmʌlbərɪ, -brɪ) *n., pl.* **-ries. 1.** a tree having edible blackberry-like fruit, such as the white mulberry, the leaves of which are used to feed silkworms. **2.** the fruit of any of these trees. **3.** any of several similar or related trees. **4. a.** a dark purple colour. **b.** (*as adj.*): *a mulberry dress.* [C14: < L *mōrum*, < Gk *moron;* rel. to OE *mōrberie*]

mulch (mʌltʃ) *n.* **1.** half-rotten vegetable matter, peat, etc., used to prevent soil erosion or enrich the soil. ~*vb.* **2.** (*tr.*) to cover (the surface of land) with mulch. [C17: < obs. *mulch* soft; rel. to OE *mylisc* mellow]

mulct (mʌlkt) *vb.* (*tr.*) **1.** to cheat or defraud. **2.** to fine (a person). ~*n.* **3.** a fine or penalty. [C15: via F < L *multa* a fine]

mule[1] (mjuːl) *n.* **1.** the sterile offspring of a male donkey and a female horse, used as a beast of burden. **2.** any hybrid animal: *a mule canary.* **3.** Also called: **spinning mule.** a machine that spins cotton into yarn and winds the yarn on spindles. **4.** *Inf.* an obstinate or stubborn person. [C13: < OF *mul*, < L *mūlus* ass, mule]

mule[2] (mjuːl) *n.* a backless shoe or slipper. [C16: < OF < L *mulleus* a magistrate's shoe]

muleta (mjuːˈlɛtə) *n.* the small cape attached to a stick used by the matador during a bullfight. [Sp.: small mule, crutch, < *mula* MULE[1]]

muleteer (ˌmjuːlɪˈtɪə) *n.* a person who drives mules.

mulga (ˈmʌlgə) *n.* *Austral.* **1.** any of various Australian acacia shrubs. **2.** scrub comprised of a dense growth of acacia. **3.** *Inf.* the outback; bush. [< Abor.]

muliebrity (ˌmjuːlɪˈɛbrɪtɪ) *n.* **1.** the condition of being a woman. **2.** femininity. [C16: via LL < L *muliēbris* womanly, < *mulier* woman]

mulish (ˈmjuːlɪʃ) *adj.* stubborn; obstinate. —ˈ**mulishly** *adv.* —ˈ**mulishness** *n.*

mull[1] (mʌl) *vb.* (*tr.*) (often foll. by *over*) to study or ponder. [C19: prob. < MUDDLE]

mull[2] (mʌl) *vb.* (*tr.*) to heat (wine, ale, etc.) with sugar and spices. [C17: <?] —**mulled** *adj.*

mull[3] (mʌl) *n.* a light muslin fabric of soft texture. [C18: earlier *mulmull*, < Hindi *malmal*]

mull[4] (mʌl) *n.* *Scot.* a promontory. [C14: rel. to Gaelic *maol*, Icelandic *múli*]

mullah *or* **mulla** (ˈmʌlə, ˈmʊlə) *n.* (formerly) a Muslim scholar, teacher, or religious leader: also used as a title of respect. [C17: < Turkish *molla*, Persian & Hindi *mulla*, < Ar. *mawlā* master]

mullein (ˈmʌlɪn) *n.* any of various Mediterranean herbaceous plants such as the common mullein or Aaron's rod, typically having tall spikes of yellow flowers and broad hairy leaves. [C15: < OF *moleine*, prob. < OF *mol* soft, < L *mollis*]

muller (ˈmʌlə) *n.* a flat heavy implement of stone or iron used to grind material against a slab of stone, etc. [C15: prob. < *mullen* to grind to powder]

mullet (ˈmʌlɪt) *n.* any of various teleost food fishes such as the grey mullet or red mullet. [C15: via OF < L *mullus*, < Gk *mullos*]

mulligatawny (ˌmʌlɪgəˈtɔːnɪ) *n.* a curry-flavoured soup of Anglo-Indian origin, made with meat stock. [C18: < Tamil *milakutanni*, < *milaku* pepper + *tanni* water]

mullion (ˈmʌlɪən) *n.* **1.** a vertical member between the casements or panes of a window. ~*vb.* **2.** (*tr.*) to furnish (a window, screen, etc.) with mullions. [C16: var. of ME *munial*, < OF *moinel*, <?]

mullock (ˈmʌlək) *n.* *Austral.* **1.** waste material from a mine. **2. poke mullock at.** *Inf.* to ridicule. [C14: rel. to OE *myl* dust, ON *mylja* to crush]

mulloway (ˈmʌləˌweɪ) *n.* a large Australian marine food fish. [C19: <?]

multangular (mʌlˈtæŋgjʊlə) *or* **multiangular** *adj.* having many angles.

multi- *combining form.* **1.** many or much: *multimillion.* **2.** more than one: *multistorey.* [< L *multus* much, many]

ˌ**multiˈaxial** *adj.*
ˌ**multiˈcellular** *adj.*
ˈ**multiˌcoloured** *adj.*
ˌ**multiˈcultural** *adj.*
ˌ**multidiˈmensional** *adj.*
ˌ**multidiˈrectional** *adj.*
ˌ**multiˈfaceted** *adj.*

multifarious (ˌmʌltɪˈfɛərɪəs) *adj.* having many parts of great variety. [C16: < LL *multifārius* manifold, < L *multifāriam* on many sides] —ˌ**multiˈfariously** *adv.* —ˌ**multiˈfariousness** *n.*

multiflora rose (ˌmʌltɪˈflɔːrə) *n.* an Asian climbing shrubby rose having clusters of small fragrant flowers.

multiform (ˈmʌltɪˌfɔːm) *adj.* having many forms. —ˌ**multiˈformity** *n.*

multigym (ˈmʌltɪˌdʒɪm) *n.* an exercise apparatus incorporating a variety of weights, used for toning the muscles.

multilateral (ˌmʌltɪˈlætərəl, -ˈlætrəl) *adj.* **1.** of or involving more than two nations or parties: *a multilateral pact.* **2.** having many sides. —ˌ**multiˈlaterally** *adv.*

multilingual (ˌmʌltɪˈlɪŋgwəl) *adj.* **1.** able to speak more than two languages. **2.** written or expressed in more than two languages.

multimedia (ˌmʌltɪˈmiːdɪə) *pl. n.* the combined use of media such as television, slides, etc.

multimillionaire (ˌmʌltɪˌmɪljəˈnɛə) *n.* a person with a fortune of several million pounds, dollars, etc.

multinational (ˌmʌltɪˈnæʃənˀl) *adj.* **1.** (of a large business company) operating in several countries. ~*n.* **2.** such a company.

multiparous (mʌlˈtɪpərəs) *adj.* (of certain species of mammal) producing many offspring at one birth. [C17: < NL *multiparus*]

multipartite (ˌmʌltɪˈpɑːtaɪt) *adj.* **1.** divided into many parts or sections. **2.** *Government.* a less common word for **multilateral.**

multiple (ˈmʌltɪpˀl) *adj.* **1.** having or involving more than one part, individual, etc. **2.** *Electronics, U.S. & Canad.* (of a circuit) having a number of conductors in parallel. ~*n.* **3.** the product of a given number or polynomial and any other one: *6 is a multiple of 2.* **4.** short for **multiple store.** [C17: via F < LL *multiplus*, < L MULTIPLEX] —ˈ**multiply** *adv.*

multiple-choice *adj.* having a number of possible given answers out of which the correct one must be chosen.

multiple personality *n. Psychiatry.* a mental disorder in which an individual's personality appears to have become separated into two or more distinct personalities. Nontechnical name: **split personality.**

multiple sclerosis *n.* a chronic progressive disease of the central nervous system, resulting in speech and visual disorders, tremor, muscular incoordination, partial paralysis, etc.

multiple store *n.* one of several retail enterprises under the same ownership and management. Also called: **multiple shop.**

multiplex (ˈmʌltɪˌplɛks) *n.* **1.** *Telecomm.* **a.** the use of a common communications channel for sending two or more messages or signals. **b.** (*as modifier*): *a multiplex transmitter.* ~*adj.* **2.** a less common word for **multiple.** ~*vb.* **3.** to send (messages or signals) or (of messages and signals) to be sent by multiplex. [C16: < L: having many folds, < MULTI- + *plicāre* to fold]

multiplicand (ˌmʌltɪplɪˈkænd) *n.* a number to be multiplied by another number, the **multiplier.** [C16: < L *multiplicandus*, gerund of *multiplicāre* to MULTIPLY]

multiplication (ˌmʌltɪplɪˈkeɪʃən) *n.* **1.** a mathematical operation, the inverse of division, in which the product of two or more numbers or quantities is calculated. Usually written $a \times b$, $a.b$, ab. **2.** the act of multiplying or state of being multiplied. **3.** the act or process in animals, plants, or people, of reproducing or breeding.

multiplication sign *n.* the symbol ×, placed between numbers to be multiplied.

multiplication table *n.* one of a group of tables giving the results of multiplying two numbers together.

multiplicity (ˌmʌltɪˈplɪsɪtɪ) *n., pl.* **-ties. 1.** a large number or great variety. **2.** the state of being multiple.

multiplier (ˈmʌltɪˌplaɪə) *n.* **1.** a person or thing that multiplies. **2.** the number by which another number, the **multiplicand,** is multiplied. **3.** *Physics.* any instrument, such as a photomultiplier, for increasing an effect. **4.** *Econ.* the ratio of the total change in income (resulting from successive rounds of spending) to an initial autonomous change in expenditure.

multiply (ˈmʌltɪˌplaɪ) *vb.* **-plying, -plied. 1.** to increase or cause to increase in number, quantity, or degree. **2.** (*tr.*) to combine (two numbers or quantities) by multiplication. **3.** (*intr.*) to increase in number by reproduction. [C13: < OF *multiplier*, < L *multiplicāre* to multiply, < *multus* much, many + *plicāre* to fold] —ˈ**multiˌpliable** *or* **multiplicable** (ˈmʌltɪpˈɪkəbˀl) *adj.*

multistage (ˈmʌltɪˌsteɪdʒ) *adj.* **1.** (of a rocket or missile) having several stages, each of which can be jettisoned after it has burnt out. **2.** (of a turbine, compressor, or supercharger) having more than one rotor. **3.** (of any process or device) having more than one stage.

multistorey (ˌmʌltɪˈstɔːrɪ) *adj.* **1.** (of a building) having many storeys. ~*n.* **2.** a multi-storey car park.

multitrack (ˈmʌltɪˌtræk) *adj.* (in sound recording) using tape containing two or more tracks, usually four to twenty-four.

multitude (ˈmʌltɪˌtjuːd) *n.* **1.** a large gathering of people. **2. the.** the common people. **3.** a large number. **4.** the state or quality of being numerous. [C14: via OF < L *multitūdō*]

multitudinous (ˌmʌltɪˈtjuːdɪnəs) *adj.* **1.** very numerous. **2.** *Rare.* great in extent, variety, etc. **3.** *Poetic.* crowded. —ˌ**multiˈtudinously** *adv.* —ˌ**multiˈtudinousness** *n.*

multi-user *adj.* (of a computer) capable of being used by several people at once.

multivalent (ˌmʌltɪˈveɪlənt) *adj.* another word for **polyvalent.** —ˌ**multiˈvalency** *n.*

mum[1] (mʌm) *n.* **1.** *Chiefly Brit.* an informal word for **mother. 2.** *Austral. & N.Z.* an informal word for **wife** (sense 1). [C19: a child's word]

mum[2] (mʌm) *adj.* **1.** keeping information, etc., to oneself; silent. ~*n.* **2. mum's the word.** (*interj.*) silence or secrecy is to be observed. [C14: suggestive of closed lips]

mum[3] (mʌm) *vb.* **mumming, mummed.** (*intr.*) to act in a mummer's play. [C16: verbal use of MUM[2]]

mumble (ˈmʌmbˀl) *vb.* **1.** to utter indistinctly, as with the mouth partly closed. **2.** *Rare.* to chew (food) ineffectually. ~*n.* **3.** an indistinct or low utterance or sound. [C14 *momelen*, < MUM[2]] —ˈ**mumbler** *n.* —ˈ**mumbling** *adj.* —ˈ**mumblingly** *adv.*

mumbo jumbo (ˈmʌmbəʊ) *n., pl.* **mumbo jumbos. 1.** foolish religious reverence, ritual, or incantation. **2.** meaningless or unnecessarily complicated language. **3.** an object of superstitious awe or reverence. [C18: prob. < W African *mama dyumbo*, name of a tribal god]

mu meson (mjuː) *n.* a former name for **muon.**

mummer (ˈmʌmə) *n.* **1.** one of a group of masked performers in a folk play or mime. **2.** *Humorous or derog.* an actor. [C15: < OF *momeur*, < *momer* to mime]

mummery (ˈmʌmərɪ) *n., pl.* **-meries. 1.** a performance by mummers. **2.** hypocritical or ostentatious ceremony.

mummify (ˈmʌmɪˌfaɪ) *vb.* **-fying, -fied. 1.** (*tr.*) to preserve (a body) as a mummy. **2.** (*intr.*) to dry up; shrivel. —ˌ**mummifiˈcation** *n.*

mummy[1] (ˈmʌmɪ) *n., pl.* **-mies. 1.** an embalmed or preserved body, esp. as prepared for burial in ancient Egypt. **2.** a mass of pulp. **3.** a dark brown pigment. [C14: < OF *momie*, < Med. L, < Ar.: asphalt, < Persian *mūm* wax]

mummy[2] (ˈmʌmɪ) *n., pl.* **-mies.** *Chiefly Brit.* a child's word for **mother.** [C19: var. of MUM[1]]

ˌ**multiˈfoliate** *adj.*
ˈ**multiˌhull** *n.*
ˌ**multiˈpolar** *adj.*
ˌ**multiˈpurpose** *adj.*
ˌ**multiˈracial** *adj.*

mumps (mʌmps) *n.* (*functioning as sing. or pl.*) **1.** an acute contagious viral disease of the parotid salivary glands, characterized by swelling of the affected parts, fever, and pain beneath the ear. **2.** sulks. [C16: < *mump* to grimace] —**ˈmumpish** *adj.*

mumsy (ˈmʌmzɪ) *adj.* **-sier, -siest.** homely or drab. —**ˈmumsiness** *n.*

mun. *abbrev. for* municipal.

munch (mʌntʃ) *vb.* to chew (food) steadily, esp. with a crunching noise. [C14 *monche,* imit.]

mundane (mʌnˈdeɪn, ˈmʌndeɪn) *adj.* **1.** everyday, ordinary, or banal. **2.** relating to the world or worldly matters. [C15: < F *mondain,* via LL, < L *mundus* world] —**munˈdanely** *adv.* —**munˈdaneness** *n.*

mung bean (mʌŋ) *n.* **1.** an E Asian bean plant grown for forage and as the source of bean sprouts for cookery. **2.** the seed of this plant.

municipal (mjuːˈnɪsɪpᵊl) *adj.* of or relating to a town, city, or borough or its local government. [C16: < L *mūnicipium* a free town, < *mūniceps* citizen, < *mūnia* responsibilities + *capere* to take] —**muˈnicipally** *adv.*

municipality (mjuːˌnɪsɪˈpælɪtɪ) *n., pl.* **-ties. 1.** a city, town, or district enjoying local self-government. **2.** the governing body of such a unit.

municipalize *or* **-ise** (mjuːˈnɪsɪpəˌlaɪz) *vb.* (*tr.*) **1.** to bring under municipal ownership or control. **2.** to make a municipality of. —**muˌnicipaliˈzation** *or* **-iˈsation** *n.*

munificent (mjuːˈnɪfɪsənt) *adj.* **1.** (of a person) generous; bountiful. **2.** (of a gift) liberal. [C16: back formation < L *mūnificentia* liberality, < *mūnificus,* < *mūnus* gift + *facere* to make] —**muˈnificence** *n.* —**muˈnificently** *adv.*

muniments (ˈmjuːnɪmənts) *pl. n. Law.* the title deeds and other documentary evidence relating to the title to land. [C15: via OF < L *munire* to defend]

munition (mjuːˈnɪʃən) *vb.* (*tr.*) to supply with munitions. [C16: via F < L *mūnītiō* fortification, < *mūnīre* to fortify]

munitions (mjuːˈnɪʃənz) *pl. n.* (*sometimes sing.*) military equipment and stores, esp. ammunition.

Munro (mʌnˈrəʊ) *n., pl.* **-ros.** *Mountaineering.* any Scottish peak over 3000 feet high. [C20: after H. T. *Munro,* who listed these in 1891]

muntjac *or* **muntjak** (ˈmʌntˌdʒæk) *n.* any small Asian deer typically having a chestnut-brown coat and small antlers. [C18: prob. < Javanese *mindjangan* deer]

muon (ˈmjuːɒn) *n.* a positive or negative elementary particle with a mass 207 times that of an electron. It was originally called the **mu meson.** [C20: short for MU MESON]

mural (ˈmjʊərəl) *n.* **1.** a large painting on a wall. ~*adj.* **2.** of or relating to a wall. [C15: < L *mūrālis,* < *mūrus* wall] —**ˈmuralist** *n.*

murder (ˈmɜːdə) *n.* **1.** the unlawful premeditated killing of one human being by another. Cf. **manslaughter. 2.** *Inf.* something dangerous, difficult, or unpleasant: *driving around London is murder.* **3. cry blue murder.** *Inf.* to make an outcry. **4. get away with murder.** *Inf.* to escape censure; do as one pleases. ~*vb.* (*mainly tr.*) **5.** (*also intr.*) to kill (someone) unlawfully with premeditation or during the commission of a crime. **6.** to kill brutally. **7.** *Inf.* to destroy; ruin. **8.** *Inf.* to defeat completely; beat decisively: *the home team murdered their opponents.* [OE *morthor*] —**ˈmurderer** *n.* —**ˈmurderess** *fem. n.*

murderous (ˈmɜːdərəs) *adj.* **1.** intending, capable of, or guilty of murder. **2.** *Inf.* very dangerous or difficult: *a murderous road.* —**ˈmurderously** *adv.* —**ˈmurderousness** *n.*

murex (ˈmjʊərɛks) *n., pl.* **murices** (ˈmjʊərɪˌsiːz). any of a genus of spiny-shelled marine gastropods: formerly used as a source of the dye Tyrian purple. [C16: < L *mūrex* purple fish]

muriatic acid (ˌmjʊərɪˈætɪk) *n.* a former name for **hydrochloric acid.** [C17: < L *muriāticus* pickled, < *muria* brine]

murk *or* **mirk** (mɜːk) *n.* **1.** gloomy darkness. ~*adj.* **2.** an archaic variant of **murky.** [C13: prob. < ON *myrkr* darkness]

murky *or* **mirky** (ˈmɜːkɪ) *adj.* **murkier, murkiest** *or* **mirkier, mirkiest. 1.** gloomy or dark. **2.** cloudy or impenetrable as with smoke or fog. —**ˈmurkily** *or* **ˈmirkily** *adv.* —**ˈmurkiness** *or* **ˈmirkiness** *n.*

murmur (ˈmɜːmə) *n.* **1.** a continuous low indistinct sound, as of distant voices. **2.** an indistinct utterance: *a murmur of satisfaction.* **3.** a complaint; grumble: *he made no murmur at my suggestion.* **4.** *Med.* any abnormal soft blowing sound heard usually over the chest (**heart murmur**). ~*vb.* **5.** to utter (something) in a murmur. **6.** (*intr.*) to complain. [C14: as n., < L *murmur;* vb. via OF *murmurer* < L *murmurāre* to rumble] —**ˈmurmurer** *n.* —**ˈmurmuring** *n., adj.* —**ˈmurmuringly** *adv.* —**ˈmurmurous** *adj.*

murphy (ˈmɜːfɪ) *n., pl.* **-phies.** a dialect or informal word for **potato.** [C19: < the common Irish surname *Murphy*]

murrain (ˈmʌrɪn) *n.* **1.** any plaguelike disease in cattle. **2.** *Arch.* a plague. [C14: < OF *morine,* < *morir* to die, < L *morī*]

Murray cod (ˈmʌrɪ) *n.* a large greenish Australian freshwater food fish. [after *Murray* River in SE Australia]

murther (ˈmɜːðə) *n., vb.* an archaic word for **murder.** —**ˈmurtherer** *n.*

mus. *abbrev. for:* **1.** museum. **2.** music. **3.** musical.

MusB *or* **MusBac** *abbrev. for* Bachelor of Music.

muscadine (ˈmʌskədɪn, -ˌdaɪn) *n.* **1.** a woody climbing plant of the southeastern U.S. **2.** the musk-scented purple grape produced by this plant: used to make wine. [C16: < MUSCATEL]

muscae volitantes (ˈmʌsiː vɒlɪˈtæntiːz) *pl. n. Pathol.* moving black specks or threads seen before the eyes, caused by opaque fragments floating in the vitreous humour or a defect in the lens. [C18: NL: flying flies]

muscat (ˈmʌskət, -kæt) *n.* **1.** any of various grapevines that produce sweet white grapes used for making wine or raisins. **2.** another name for **muscatel** (sense 1). [C16: via OF < Provençal, < *musc* MUSK]

muscatel (ˌmʌskəˈtɛl) *or* **muscadel** *n.* **1.** Also called: **muscat.** a rich sweet wine made from muscat grapes. **2.** the grape or raisin from a muscat vine. [C14: < OF *muscadel,* < OProvençal, < *moscadel,* < *muscat* musky]

muscle (ˈmʌsᵊl) *n.* **1.** a tissue composed of bundles of elongated cells capable of contraction and relaxation to produce movement in an organ or part. **2.** an organ composed of muscle tissue. **3.** strength or force. ~*vb.* **4.** (*intr.;* often foll. by *in, on,* etc.) *Inf.* to force one's way (in). [C16: < Medical L *musculus* little mouse, < the imagined resemblance of some muscles to mice] —**ˈmuscly** *adj.*

muscle-bound *adj.* **1.** having overdeveloped and inelastic muscles. **2.** lacking flexibility.

muscleman (ˈmʌsᵊlˌmæn) *n., pl.* **-men. 1.** a man with highly developed muscles. **2.** a henchman employed by a gangster to intimidate or use violence upon victims.

Muscovite (ˈmʌskəˌvaɪt) *n.* **1.** a native or inhabitant of Moscow. ~*adj.* **2.** an archaic word for **Russian.**

Muscovy duck (ˈmʌskəvɪ) *or* **musk duck** *n.* a large crested widely domesticated South American duck, having a greenish-black plumage with white markings and a large red caruncle on the bill. [C17: orig. *musk duck,* a name later mistakenly associated with *Muscovy,* an arch. name for Russia]

muscular (ˈmʌskjʊlə) *adj.* **1.** having well-developed muscles; brawny. **2.** of, relating to, or consisting of muscle. [C17: < NL *muscularis,* < *musculus* MUSCLE] —**muscularity** (ˌmʌskjʊˈlærɪtɪ) *n.* —**ˈmuscularly** *adv.*

muscular dystrophy *n.* a genetic disease characterized by progressive deterioration and wasting of muscle fibres.

musculature (ˈmʌskjʊlətʃə) *n.* **1.** the arrangement of muscles in an organ or part. **2.** the total muscular system of an organism.

MusD *or* **MusDoc** *abbrev. for* Doctor of Music.

muse[1] (mju:z) *vb.* **1.** (when *intr.*, often foll. by *on* or *about*) to reflect (about) or ponder (on), usually in silence. **2.** (*intr.*) to gaze thoughtfully. ~*n.* **3.** a state of abstraction. [C14: < OF *muser*, ? < *mus* snout, < Med. L *mūsus*]

muse[2] (mju:z) *n.* (often preceded by *the*) a goddess that inspires a creative artist, esp. a poet. [C14: < OF, < L *Mūsa*, < Gk *Mousa* a Muse]

Muse (mju:z) *n. Greek myth.* any of nine sister goddesses, each of whom was regarded as the protectress of a different art or science.

musette (mju:ˈzɛt) *n.* **1.** a type of bagpipe popular in France during the 17th and 18th centuries. **2.** a dance, originally accompanied by a musette. [C14: < OF, dim. of *muse* bagpipe]

museum (mju:ˈzɪəm) *n.* a building where objects of historical, artistic, or scientific interest are exhibited and preserved. [C17: via L < Gk *Mouseion* home of the Muses, < *Mousa* MUSE]

museum piece *n.* **1.** an object of sufficient age or interest to be kept in a museum. **2.** *Inf.* a person or thing regarded as antiquated.

mush[1] (mʌʃ) *n.* **1.** a soft pulpy mass or consistency. **2.** *U.S.* a thick porridge made from corn meal. **3.** *Inf.* cloying sentimentality. [C17: < obs. *moose* porridge; prob. rel. to MASH]

mush[2] (mʌʃ) *Canad.* ~*interj.* **1.** an order to dogs in a sled team to start up or go faster. ~*vb.* **2.** to travel by or drive a dogsled. ~*n.* **3.** a journey with a dogsled. [C19: ? < imperative of F *marcher* to advance]

mushroom (ˈmʌʃru:m, -rʊm) *n.* **1. a.** the fleshy spore-producing body of any of various fungi, typically consisting of a cap at the end of a stem. Some species, such as the field mushroom, are edible. Cf. **toadstool. b.** (*as modifier*): *mushroom soup.* **2. a.** something resembling a mushroom in shape or rapid growth. **b.** (*as modifier*): *mushroom expansion.* ~*vb.* (*intr.*) **3.** to grow rapidly: *demand mushroomed overnight.* **4.** to assume a mushroom-like shape. [C15: < OF *mousseron*, < LL *mussiriō*, <?]

mushroom cloud *n.* the large mushroom-shaped cloud produced by a nuclear explosion.

mushy (ˈmʌʃɪ) *adj.* **mushier, mushiest. 1.** soft and pulpy. **2.** *Inf.* excessively sentimental or emotional. —ˈ**mushily** *adv.* —ˈ**mushiness** *n.*

music (ˈmju:zɪk) *n.* **1.** an art form consisting of sequences of sounds in time, esp. tones of definite pitch organized melodically, harmonically and rhythmically. **2.** the sounds so produced, esp. by singing or musical instruments. **3.** written or printed music, such as a score or set of parts. **4.** any sequence of sounds perceived as pleasing or harmonious. **5. face the music.** *Inf.* to confront the consequences of one's actions. [C13: via OF < L *mūsica*, < Gk *mousikē* (*tekhnē*) (art) belonging to the Muses, < *Mousa* MUSE]

musical (ˈmju:zɪkᵊl) *adj.* **1.** of, relating to, or used in music. **2.** harmonious; melodious: *musical laughter.* **3.** talented in or fond of music. **4.** involving or set to music. ~*n.* **5.** Also called: **musical comedy.** a light romantic play or film having dialogue interspersed with songs and dances. —ˌ**musiˈcality** *n.* —ˈ**musically** *adv.*

musical box *or* **music box** *n.* a mechanical instrument that plays tunes by means of pins on a revolving cylinder striking the tuned teeth of a comblike metal plate, contained in a box.

musical chairs *n.* (*functioning as sing.*) **1.** a party game in which players walk around chairs while music is played, there being one more player than chairs. Whenever the music stops, the player who fails to find a chair is eliminated. **2.** any situation involving several people in a series of interrelated changes.

musicassette (ˈmju:zɪkəˌsɛt) *n.* an audio cassette of prerecorded music.

music centre *n.* a single hi-fi unit containing a turntable, amplifier, radio and cassette player.

music drama *n.* **1.** an opera in which the musical and dramatic elements are of equal importance and strongly interfused. **2.** the genre of such operas. [C19: < G *Musikdrama*, coined by Wagner to describe his later operas]

music hall *n. Chiefly Brit.* **1.** a variety entertainment consisting of songs, comic turns, etc. U.S. and Canad. name: **vaudeville. 2.** a theatre at which such entertainments are staged.

musician (mju:ˈzɪʃən) *n.* a person who plays or composes music, esp. as a profession. —**muˈsicianly** *adj.* —**muˈsicianship** *n.*

musicology (ˌmju:zɪˈkɒlədʒɪ) *n.* the scholarly study of music. —**musicological** (ˌmju:zɪkəˈlɒdʒɪkᵊl) *adj.* —ˌ**musiˈcologist** *n.*

music paper *n.* paper ruled or printed with a stave for writing music.

musique concrète *French.* (myzik kɔ̃krɛt) *n.* another term for **concrete music.**

musk (mʌsk) *n.* **1.** a strong-smelling glandular secretion of the male musk deer, used in perfumery. **2.** a similar substance produced by certain other animals, such as the civet and otter, or manufactured synthetically. **3.** a North American plant which has yellow flowers and was formerly cultivated for its musky scent. **4.** the smell of musk or a similar heady smell. **5.** (*modifier*) containing or resembling musk: *musk oil.* [C14: < LL *muscus*, < Gk, < Persian, prob. < Sansk. *mushká* scrotum (from the appearance of the musk deer's musk bag), dim. of *mūsh* MOUSE]

musk deer *n.* a small central Asian mountain deer. The male secretes musk.

musk duck *n.* **1.** another name for **Muscovy duck. 2.** a duck inhabiting swamps, lakes, and streams in Australia. The male emits a musky odour.

muskeg (ˈmʌsˌkɛg) *n. Chiefly Canad.* **1.** undrained boggy land. **2.** a bog or swamp of this nature. [C19: of Amerind origin: grassy swamp]

muskellunge (ˈmʌskəˌlʌndʒ) *or* **maskinonge** (ˈmæskɪˌnɒndʒ) *n., pl.* **-lunges, -nonges** *or* **-lunge, -nonge.** a large North American freshwater game fish, related to the pike. Often shortened (informally) to **musky** or **muskie.** [C18 *maskinunga*, of Amerind origin]

musket (ˈmʌskɪt) *n.* a long-barrelled muzzle-loading shoulder gun used between the 16th and 18th centuries by infantry soldiers. [C16: < F *mousquet*, < It. *moschetto* arrow, earlier: sparrow hawk, < *moscha* a fly, < L *musca*]

musketeer (ˌmʌskɪˈtɪə) *n.* (formerly) a soldier armed with a musket.

musketry (ˈmʌskɪtrɪ) *n.* **1.** muskets or musketeers collectively. **2.** the technique of using small arms.

muskmelon (ˈmʌskˌmɛlən) *n.* **1.** any of several varieties of the melon, such as the cantaloupe and honeydew. **2.** the fruit of any of these melons, having ribbed or warty rind and sweet yellow, white, orange, or green flesh with a musky aroma.

musk ox *n.* a large bovid mammal, which has a dark shaggy coat, short legs, and widely spaced downward-curving horns, and emits a musky smell: now confined to the tundras of Canada and Greenland.

muskrat (ˈmʌskˌræt) *n., pl.* **-rats** *or* **-rat. 1.** a North American beaver-like amphibious rodent, closely related to but larger than the voles. **2.** the brown fur of this animal. ~Also called: **musquash.**

musk rose *n.* a Mediterranean rose, cultivated for its white musk-scented flowers.

musky (ˈmʌskɪ) *adj.* **muskier, muskiest.** resembling the smell of musk; having a heady or pungent sweet aroma. —ˈ**muskiness** *n.*

Muslim (ˈmʊzlɪm, ˈmʌz-) *or* **Moslem** *n., pl.* **-lims** *or* **-lim. 1.** a follower of the religion of Islam. ~*adj.* **2.** of or relating to Islam, its doctrines, culture, etc. ~Also (but not in Muslim use): **Mohammedan, Muhammadan.** [C17: < Ar., lit.: one who surrenders] —ˈ**Muslimism** *or* ˈ**Moslemism** *n.*

muslin (ˈmʌzlɪn) *n.* a fine plain-weave cotton fabric. [C17: < F *mousseline*, < It., < Ar. *mawṣilīy* of Mosul (Iraq), where it was first produced]

musquash (ˈmʌskwɒʃ) *n.* another name for **muskrat,** esp. the fur. [C17: of Amerind origin]

muss (mʌs) *U.S. & Canad. inf.* ~*vb.* **1.** (*tr.;* often foll. by *up*) to make untidy; rumple. ~*n.* **2.** a state of disorder; muddle. [C19: prob. a blend of MESS + FUSS] —ˈ**mussy** *adj.*

mussel (ˈmʌsəl) *n.* **1.** any of various marine bivalves, esp. the edible mussel, having a dark slightly elongated shell and living attached to rocks, etc. **2.** any of various freshwater bivalves, attached to rocks, sand, etc., having a flattened oval shell (a source of mother-of-pearl). [OE *muscle,* < Vulgar L *muscula* (unattested), < L *musculus,* dim. of *mūs* mouse]

Mussulman (ˈmʌsəlmən) *n. pl.* **-mans.** an archaic word for **Muslim.** [C16: < Persian *Musulmān* (pl.) < Ar. *Muslimūn,* pl. of MUSLIM]

must[1] (mʌst; *unstressed* məst, məs) *vb.* (takes an infinitive without *to* or an implied infinitive) used as an auxiliary: **1.** to express obligation or compulsion: *you must pay your dues.* In this sense, *must* does not form a negative. If used with a negative infinitive it indicates obligatory prohibition. **2.** to indicate necessity: *I must go to the bank tomorrow.* **3.** to indicate the probable correctness of a statement: *he must be there by now.* **4.** to indicate inevitability: *all good things must come to an end.* **5.** to express resolution: **a.** on the part of the speaker: *I must finish this.* **b.** on the part of another or others: *let him get drunk if he must.* **6.** (used emphatically) to express conviction or certainty on the part of the speaker: *you must be joking.* **7.** (foll. by *away*) used with an implied verb of motion to express compelling haste: *I must away.* ~*n.* **8.** an essential or necessary thing: *strong shoes are a must for hill walking.* [OE *mōste,* p.t. of *mōtan* to be allowed, be obliged to]

must[2] (mʌst) *n.* the pressed juice of grapes or other fruit ready for fermentation. [OE, < L *mustum* new wine, < *mustus* newborn]

must[3] (mʌst) *n.* mustiness or mould. [C17: back formation < MUSTY]

mustache (məˈstɑːʃ) *n.* the U.S. spelling of **moustache.** —**musˈtached** *adj.*

mustachio (məˈstɑːʃɪˌəʊ) *n., pl.* **-chios.** (*often pl.*) *Often humorous.* a moustache, esp. when bushy or elaborately shaped. [C16: < Sp. *mostacho* & It. *mostaccio*] —**musˈtachioed** *adj.*

mustang (ˈmʌstæŋ) *n.* a small breed of horse, often wild or half wild, found in the southwestern U.S. [C19: < Mexican Sp. *mestengo,* < *mesta* a group of stray animals]

mustard (ˈmʌstəd) *n.* **1.** any of several Eurasian plants, esp. black mustard and white mustard, having yellow flowers and slender pods: cultivated for their pungent seeds. **2.** a paste made from the powdered seeds of any of these plants and used as a condiment. **3. a.** a brownish-yellow colour. **b.** (*as adj.*): *a mustard carpet.* **4.** *Sl., chiefly U.S.* zest or enthusiasm. [C13: < OF *moustarde,* < L *mustum* MUST[2], since the original was made by adding must]

mustard and cress *n.* seedlings of white mustard and garden cress, used in salads, etc.

mustard gas *n.* an oily liquid vesicant compound used in chemical warfare. Its vapour causes blindness and burns.

mustard plaster *n. Med.* a mixture of powdered black mustard seeds applied to the skin for its counterirritant effects.

musteline (ˈmʌstɪˌlaɪn, -lɪn) *adj.* of or belonging to a family of typically predatory mammals, including weasels, ferrets, badgers, skunks, and otters. [C17: < L *mustēlīnus,* < *mustēla* weasel]

muster (ˈmʌstə) *vb.* **1.** to call together (numbers of men) for duty, inspection, etc., or (of men) to assemble in this way. **2. muster in** *or* **out.** *U.S.* to enlist into or discharge from military service. **3.** (*tr.;* sometimes foll. by *up*) to summon or gather: *to muster one's arguments; to muster up courage.* **4.** (*tr.*) *Austral. & N.Z.* to round up (stock). ~*n.* **5.** an assembly of military personnel for duty, etc. **6.** a collection, assembly, or gathering. **7.** *Austral. & N.Z.* the act of rounding up stock. **8. pass muster.** to be acceptable. [C14: < OF *moustrer,* < L *monstrāre* to show, < *monstrum* portent]

musth *or* **must** (mʌst) *n.* (often preceded by *in*) a state of frenzied sexual excitement in the males of certain large mammals, esp. elephants. [C19: < Urdu *mast,* < Persian: drunk]

musty (ˈmʌstɪ) *adj.* **-tier, -tiest. 1.** smelling or tasting old, stale, or mouldy. **2.** old-fashioned, dull, or hackneyed: *musty ideas.* [C16: ? var. of obs. *moisty*] —ˈ**mustily** *adv.* —ˈ**mustiness** *n.*

mutable (ˈmjuːtəbəl) *adj.* able to or tending to change. [C14: < L *mūtābilis* fickle, < *mūtāre* to change] —ˌ**mutaˈbility** *or* (*less commonly*) ˈ**mutableness** *n.* —ˈ**mutably** *adv.*

mutagen (ˈmjuːtədʒən) *n.* a substance that can induce genetic mutation. [C20: < MUTATION + -GEN] —**mutagenic** (ˌmjuːtəˈdʒɛnɪk) *adj.*

mutant (ˈmjuːtənt) *n.* **1.** Also called: **mutation.** an animal, organism, or gene that has undergone mutation. ~*adj.* **2.** of, undergoing, or resulting from mutation. [C20: < L *mutāre* to change]

mutate (mjuːˈteɪt) *vb.* to undergo or cause to undergo mutation. [C19: < L *mūtātus,* p.p. of *mūtāre* to change]

mutation (mjuːˈteɪʃən) *n.* **1.** the act or process of mutating; change; alteration. **2.** a change or alteration. **3.** a change in the chromosomes or genes of a cell which may affect the structure and development of the resultant offspring. **4.** another word for **mutant** (sense 1). **5.** a physical characteristic of an individual resulting from this type of chromosomal change. **6.** *Phonetics.* **a.** (in Germanic languages) another name for **umlaut. b.** (in Celtic languages) a phonetic change in certain initial consonants caused by a preceding word. —**muˈtational** *adj.* —**muˈtationally** *adv.*

mutatis mutandis *Latin.* (muːˈtɑːtɪs muːˈtændɪs) the necessary changes having been made.

mutch (mʌtʃ) *n.* a close-fitting linen cap formerly worn by women and children in Scotland. [C15: < MDu. *mutse* cap, < Med. L *almucia* AMICE]

mute (mjuːt) *adj.* **1.** not giving out sound or speech; silent. **2.** unable to speak; dumb. **3.** unspoken or unexpressed. **4.** *Law.* (of a person arraigned on indictment) refusing to answer a charge. **5.** *Phonetics.* another word for **plosive. 6.** (of a letter in a word) silent. ~*n.* **7.** a person who is unable to speak. **8.** *Law.* a person who refuses to plead. **9.** any of various devices used to soften the tone of stringed or brass instruments. **10.** *Phonetics.* a plosive consonant. **11.** a silent letter. **12.** an actor in a dumb show. **13.** a hired mourner. ~*vb.* (*tr.*) **14.** to reduce the volume of (a musical instrument) by means of a mute, soft pedal, etc. **15.** to subdue the strength of (a colour, tone, lighting, etc.). [C14 *muwet* < OF *mu,* < L *mūtus* silent] —ˈ**mutely** *adv.* —ˈ**muteness** *n.*

mute swan *n.* a Eurasian swan with a pure white plumage and an orange-red bill.

muti (ˈmuːtɪ) *n. S. African.* medicine, esp. herbal. [< Zulu *umuthi* tree, shrub]

mutilate (ˈmjuːtɪˌleɪt) *vb.* (*tr.*) **1.** to deprive of a limb, essential part, etc.; maim. **2.** to expurgate, damage, etc. (a text, book, etc.). [C16: < L *mutilāre* to cut off; rel. to *mutilus* maimed] —ˌ**mutiˈlation** *n.* —ˈ**mutiˌlative** *adj.* —ˈ**mutiˌlator** *n.*

mutineer (ˌmjuːtɪˈnɪə) *n.* a person who mutinies.

mutinous (ˈmjuːtɪnəs) *adj.* **1.** openly rebellious. **2.** characteristic or indicative of mutiny. —ˈ**mutinously** *adv.* —ˈ**mutinousness** *n.*

mutiny (ˈmjuːtɪnɪ) *n., pl.* **-nies. 1.** open rebellion against constituted authority, esp. by seamen or soldiers against their officers. ~*vb.* **-nying, -nied. 2.** (*intr.*) to engage in mutiny. [C16: < obs. *mutine,* < OF *mutin* rebellious, < *meute* mutiny, ult. < L *movēre* to move]

mutism (ˈmjuːˌtɪzəm) *n.* **1.** the state of being mute. **2.** *Psychiatry.* **a.** a refusal to speak. **b.** the lack of development of speech.

mutt (mʌt) *n. Sl.* **1.** an inept, ignorant, or stupid person. **2.** a mongrel dog; cur. [C20: < MUTTONHEAD]

mutter (ˈmʌtə) *vb.* **1.** to utter (something) in a low and indistinct tone. **2.** (*intr.*) to grumble or complain. **3.** (*intr.*) to make a low continuous murmuring sound. ~*n.* **4.** a muttered sound or complaint. [C14 *moteren*] —**'muttering** *n., adj.*

mutton ('mʌtᵊn) *n.* **1.** the flesh of sheep, esp. of mature sheep, used as food. **2. mutton dressed (up) as lamb.** an older person, thing, or idea dressed up to look young or new. [C13 *moton* sheep, < OF, < Med. L *multō*, of Celtic origin] —**'muttony** *adj.*

mutton bird *n.* any of several shearwaters, having a dark plumage with greyish underparts. In New Zealand, applied to one collected for food, esp. by Maoris. [C19: < the taste of its flesh]

mutton chop *n.* a piece of mutton from the loin.

muttonchops ('mʌtᵊn,tʃɒps) *pl. n.* side whiskers trimmed in the shape of chops.

muttonhead ('mʌtᵊn,hɛd) *n. Sl.* a stupid or ignorant person; fool. —**'mutton,headed** *adj.*

mutual ('mjuːtʃʊəl) *adj.* **1.** experienced or expressed by each of two or more people about the other; reciprocal: *mutual distrust.* **2.** *Inf.* common to or shared by both: *a mutual friend.* **3.** denoting an insurance company, etc., in which the policyholders share the profits and expenses and there are no shareholders. [C15: < OF *mutuel*, < L *mūtuus* reciprocal (orig.: borrowed); rel. to *mūtāre* to change] —**mutuality** (,mjuːtʃʊ'ælɪtɪ) *n.* —**'mutually** *adv.*

▷ **Usage.** *Mutual* was originally used when only two people, or groups of people, were concerned, but is nowadays often extended to cover more than two and to mean "common" rather than "reciprocal": *several of the group felt that this course would be in their mutual interest.* It is used especially in instances where "common" might be ambiguous: *he sent an emissary who was a mutual friend to ask me to reconsider my decision.*

mutual induction *n.* the production of an electromotive force in a circuit by a current change in a second circuit magnetically linked to the first.

mutual insurance *n.* a system of insurance by which all policyholders become company members under contract to pay premiums into a common fund out of which claims are paid. See also **mutual** (sense 3).

mutuel ('mjuːtʃʊəl) *n.* short for **pari-mutuel.**

muu-muu ('muː,muː) *n.* a loose brightly coloured dress worn by women in Hawaii. [< Hawaiian]

Muzak ('mjuːzæk) *n. Trademark.* recorded light music played in shops, restaurants, factories, etc.

muzhik *or* **moujik** ('muːʒɪk) *n.* a Russian peasant, esp. under the tsars. [C16: < Russian: peasant]

muzzle ('mʌzᵊl) *n.* **1.** the projecting part of the face, usually the jaws and nose, of animals such as the dog and horse. **2.** a guard or strap fitted over an animal's nose and jaws to prevent it biting or eating. **3.** the front end of a gun barrel. ~*vb.* (*tr.*) **4.** to prevent from being heard or noticed. **5.** to put a muzzle on (an animal). [C15 *mosel*, < OF *musel*, dim. of *muse* snout, < Med. L *mūsus*, <?] —**'muzzler** *n.*

muzzle-loader *n.* a firearm receiving its ammunition through the muzzle. —**'muzzle-,loading** *adj.*

muzzle velocity *n.* the velocity of a projectile as it leaves a firearm's muzzle.

muzzy ('mʌzɪ) *adj.* **-zier, -ziest. 1.** blurred or hazy. **2.** confused or befuddled. [C18: <?] —**'muzzily** *adv.* —**'muzziness** *n.*

MVO (in Britain) *abbrev. for* Member of the Royal Victorian Order.

MW **1.** *symbol for* megawatt. **2.** *Radio. abbrev. for* medium wave.

Mx *Physics. symbol for* maxwell.

my (maɪ) *determiner.* **1.** of, belonging to, or associated with the speaker or writer (me): *my own ideas.* **2.** used in various forms of address: *my lord.* ~*interj.* **3.** an exclamation of surprise, awe, etc.: *my, how you've grown!* [C12 *mī*, var. of OE *mīn* when preceding a word beginning with a consonant]

myalgia (maɪ'ældʒɪə) *n.* pain in a muscle or a group of muscles. [C19: < MYO- + -ALGIA]

myalism ('maɪə,lɪzəm) *n.* a kind of witchcraft practised esp. in the West Indies. [C19: < *myal*, prob. West African]

myall ('maɪəl) *n.* **1.** any of several Australian acacias having hard scented wood. **2.** an Australian Aborigine living independently of society. [C19: Abor. name]

mycelium (maɪ'siːlɪəm) *n., pl.* **-lia** (-lɪə). the vegetative body of fungi: a mass of branching filaments (hyphae). [C19 (lit.: nail of fungus): < MYCO- + Gk *hēlos* nail] —**my'celial** *adj.*

Mycenaean (,maɪsɪ'niːən) *adj.* **1.** of or relating to ancient Mycenae, a city in S Greece, or its inhabitants. **2.** of or relating to the Aegean civilization of Mycenae (1400 to 1100 B.C.).

-mycete *n. combining form.* indicating a member of a class of fungi: *myxomycete.* [< NL *-mycetes*, < Gk *mukētes*, pl. of *mukēs* fungus]

myco- *or before a vowel* **myc-** *combining form.* indicating fungus: *mycology.* [< Gk *mukēs* fungus]

mycology (maɪ'kɒlədʒɪ) *n.* the branch of botany concerned with the study of fungi. —**mycological** (,maɪkə'lɒdʒɪkᵊl) *or* **,myco'logic** *adj.* —**my'cologist** *n.*

mycosis (maɪ'kəʊsɪs) *n.* any infection or disease caused by fungus. —**mycotic** (maɪ'kɒtɪk) *adj.*

mycotoxin (,maɪkə'tɒksɪn) *n.* any of various toxic substances produced by fungi, some of which may affect food. —**,mycotox'ology** *n.*

myelin ('maɪəlɪn) *or* **myeline** ('maɪə,liːn) *n.* a white tissue forming an insulating sheath (**myelin sheath**) around certain nerve fibres. Damage to the myelin sheath causes neurological disease, as in multiple sclerosis.

myelitis (,maɪə'laɪtɪs) *n.* inflammation of the spinal cord or of the bone marrow.

myeloma (,maɪə'ləʊmə) *n., pl.* **-mas** *or* **-mata** (-mətə). a usually malignant tumour of the bone marrow.

myna, mynah, *or* **mina** ('maɪnə) *n.* any of various tropical Asian starlings, some of which can mimic human speech. [C18: < Hindi *mainā*, < Sansk. *madana*]

Mynheer (mə'nɪə) *n.* a Dutch title of address equivalent to *Sir* when used alone or to *Mr* before a name. [C17: < Du. *mijnheer* my lord]

myo- *or before a vowel* **my-** *combining form.* muscle: *myocardium.* [< Gk *mus* MUSCLE]

myocardium (,maɪəʊ'kɑːdɪəm) *n., pl.* **-dia** (-dɪə). the muscular tissue of the heart. [C19: *myo-* + *cardium*, < Gk *kardia* heart] —**,myo'cardial** *adj.*

myology (maɪ'ɒlədʒɪ) *n.* the branch of medical science concerned with muscles.

myope ('maɪəʊp) *n.* any person afflicted with myopia. [C18: via F < Gk *muōps*; see MYOPIA]

myopia (maɪ'əʊpɪə) *n.* inability to see distant objects clearly because the images are focused in front of the retina; short-sightedness. [C18: via NL < Gk *muōps* short-sighted, < *mūein* to close (the eyes), + *ōps* eye] —**myopic** (maɪ'ɒpɪk) *adj.* —**my'opically** *adv.*

myosin ('maɪəsɪn) *n.* the chief protein of muscle. [C19: < MYO- + -OSE² + -IN]

myosotis (,maɪə'səʊtɪs) *n.* any plant of the genus *Myosotis.* See **forget-me-not.** [C18: NL < Gk *muosōtis* mouse-ear (referring to its furry leaves), < *mus* mouse + *ous* ear]

myriad ('mɪrɪəd) *adj.* **1.** innumerable. ~*n.* (*also used in pl.*) **2.** a large indefinite number. **3.** *Arch.* ten thousand. [C16: via LL < Gk *murias* ten thousand]

myriapod ('mɪrɪə,pɒd) *n.* **1.** any of a group of terrestrial arthropods having a long segmented body and many walking limbs, such as the centipedes and millipedes. ~*adj.* **2.** of, relating to, or belonging to this group. [C19: < NL *Myriapoda.* See MYRIAD, -POD]

Myrmidon ('mɜːmɪ,dɒn, -dᵊn) *n.* **1.** *Greek myth.* one of a race of people who were led against Troy by Achilles. **2.** (*often not cap.*) a follower or henchman.

myrobalan (maɪ'rɒbələn, mɪ-) *n.* **1.** the dried plumlike fruit of various tropical trees used in dyeing, tanning, ink, and medicine. **2.** a dye extracted from this fruit. [C16: via L < Gk *murobalanos*, < *muron* ointment + *balanos* acorn]

myrrh (mɜː) *n.* **1.** any of several trees and shrubs of Africa and S Asia that exude an aromatic resin. **2.** the resin obtained from such a plant, used in perfume, incense, and medicine. [OE *myrre*, via L < Gk *murrha*, ult. < Akkadian *murrū*]

myrtle (ˈmɜːt^{ə}l) *n.* an evergreen shrub or tree, esp. a S European shrub with pink or white flowers and aromatic blue-black berries. [C16: < Med. L *myrtilla*, < L *myrtus*, < Gk *murtos*]

myself (maɪˈsɛlf) *pron.* **1. a.** the reflexive form of *I* or *me*. **b.** (intensifier): *I myself know of no answer.* **2.** (*preceded by a copula*) my usual self: *I'm not myself today.* **3.** *Not standard.* used instead of *I* or *me* in compound noun phrases: *John and myself are voting together.*

▷ **Usage.** The use of *myself* for *I* or *me* is often the result of an attempt to be elegant or correct. However, careful users of English only employ *myself* when it follows *I* or *me* in the same clause: *I cut myself,* but *he gave it to me* (not *myself*). The same is true of the other reflexives. This rule does permit constructions such as *he wrote it himself* (unassisted) and *he himself wrote it* (without an intermediary), but these are only to be used to reinforce a previous reference to the same individual.

mysterious (mɪˈstɪərɪəs) *adj.* **1.** characterized by or indicative of mystery. **2.** puzzling, curious. —**mysˈteriously** *adv.* —**mysˈteriousness** *n.*

mystery[1] (ˈmɪstərɪ, -trɪ) *n., pl.* **-teries. 1.** an unexplained or inexplicable event, phenomenon, etc. **2.** a person or thing that arouses curiosity or suspense because of an unknown, obscure, or enigmatic quality. **3.** the state or quality of being obscure, inexplicable, or enigmatic. **4.** a story, film, etc., which arouses suspense and curiosity because of facts concealed. **5.** *Christianity.* any truth that is divinely revealed but otherwise unknowable. **6.** *Christianity.* a sacramental rite, such as the Eucharist, or (*when pl.*) the consecrated elements of the Eucharist. **7.** (*often pl.*) any rites of certain ancient Mediterranean religions. **8.** short for **mystery play.** [C14: via L < Gk *mustērion* secret rites]

mystery[2] (ˈmɪstərɪ) *n., pl.* **-teries.** *Arch.* **1.** a trade, occupation, or craft. **2.** a guild of craftsmen. [C14: < Med. L *mistērium*, < L *ministerium* occupation, < *minister* official]

mystery play *n.* (in the Middle Ages) a type of drama based on the life of Christ. Cf. **miracle play.**

mystery tour *n.* an excursion to an unspecified destination.

mystic (ˈmɪstɪk) *n.* **1.** a person who achieves mystical experience or an apprehension of divine mysteries ~*adj.* **2.** another word for **mystical.** [C14: via L < Gk *mustikos*, < *mustēs* mystery initiate; rel. to *muein* to initiate into sacred rites]

mystical (ˈmɪstɪk^{ə}l) *adj.* **1.** relating to or characteristic of mysticism. **2.** *Christianity.* having a divine or sacred significance that surpasses human apprehension. **3.** having occult or metaphysical significance. —ˈ**mystically** *adv.*

mysticism (ˈmɪstɪˌsɪzəm) *n.* **1.** belief in or experience of a reality surpassing normal human understanding or experience. **2.** a system of contemplative prayer and spirituality aimed at achieving direct intuitive experience of the divine. **3.** obscure or confused belief or thought.

mystify (ˈmɪstɪˌfaɪ) *vb.* **-fying, -fied.** (*tr.*) **1.** to confuse, bewilder, or puzzle. **2.** to make obscure. [C19: < F *mystifier*, < *mystère* MYSTERY[1] or *mystique* MYSTIC] —ˌ**mystifiˈcation** *n.* —ˈ**mystiˌfying** *adj.*

mystique (mɪˈstiːk) *n.* an aura of mystery, power, and awe that surrounds a person or thing. [C20: < F (adj.): MYSTIC]

myth (mɪθ) *n.* **1. a.** a story about superhuman beings of an earlier age, usually of how natural phenomena, social customs, etc., came into existence. **b.** another word for **mythology** (senses 1, 3). **2.** a person or thing whose existence is fictional or unproven. [C19: via LL < Gk *muthos* fable]

myth. *abbrev. for:* **1.** mythological. **2.** mythology.

mythical (ˈmɪθɪk^{ə}l) *or* **mythic** *adj.* **1.** of or relating to myth. **2.** imaginary or fictitious. —ˈ**mythically** *adv.*

mythicize *or* **-cise** (ˈmɪθɪˌsaɪz) *vb.* (*tr.*) to make into or treat as a myth. —ˈ**mythicist** *n.*

mytho- *combining form.* myth: *mythopoeia.*

mythologize *or* **-gise** (mɪˈθɒləˌdʒaɪz) *vb.* **1.** to tell, study, or explain (myths). **2.** (*intr.*) to create or make up myths. **3.** (*tr.*) to convert into a myth. —**myˈtholoˌgizer** *or* **-ˌgiser** *n.*

mythology (mɪˈθɒlədʒɪ) *n., pl.* **-gies. 1.** a body of myths, esp. one associated with a particular culture, person, etc. **2.** a body of stories about a person, institution, etc. **3.** myths collectively. **4.** the study of myths. —**mythological** (ˌmɪθəˈlɒdʒɪk^{ə}l) *adj.* —**myˈthologist** *n.*

mythomania (ˌmɪθəʊˈmeɪnɪə) *n. Psychiatry.* the tendency to lie or exaggerate, occurring in some mental disorders. —ˌ**mythoˈmaniˌac** *n., adj.*

mythopoeia (ˌmɪθəʊˈpiːə) *n.* the composition or making of myths. [C19: < Gk, ult. < *muthos* myth + *poiein* to make] —ˌ**mythoˈpoeic** *adj.*

mythos (ˈmaɪθɒs, ˈmɪθɒs) *n., pl.* **-thoi** (-θɔɪ). **1.** the complex of beliefs, values, attitudes, etc., characteristic of a specific group or society. **2.** another word for **myth** or **mythology.**

myxo (ˈmɪksəʊ) *n. Austral. sl.* myxomatosis.

myxo- *or before a vowel* **myx-** *combining form.* mucus or slime: *myxomatosis.* [< Gk *muxa*]

myxoedema *or U.S.* **myxedema** (ˌmɪksɪˈdiːmə) *n.* a disease resulting from underactivity of the thyroid gland characterized by puffy eyes, face, and hands and mental sluggishness. See also **cretinism.**

myxoma (mɪkˈsəʊmə) *n., pl.* **-mas** *or* **-mata** (-mətə). a tumour composed of mucous connective tissue, usually situated in subcutaneous tissue. —**myxomatous** (mɪkˈsɒmətəs) *adj.*

myxomatosis (ˌmɪksəməˈtəʊsɪs) *n.* an infectious and usually fatal viral disease of rabbits characterized by swelling of the mucous membranes and formation of skin tumours.

myxomycete (ˌmɪksəʊmaɪˈsiːt) *n.* any of a group of organisms having a naked mass of protoplasm and characteristics of both plants and animals: usually classified as fungi.

myxovirus (ˈmɪksəʊˌvaɪrəs) *n.* any of a group of viruses that cause influenza, mumps, etc.

N

n *or* **N** (ɛn) *n., pl.* **n's, N's,** *or* **Ns.** **1.** the 14th letter of the English alphabet. **2.** a speech sound represented by this letter.

n[1] *symbol for:* **1.** neutron. **2.** *Optics.* index of refraction. **3.** nano-.

n[2] (ɛn) *determiner.* an indefinite number (of): *there are n objects in a box.*

N *symbol for:* **1.** Also: **kt.** *Chess.* knight. **2.** newton(s). **3.** *Chem.* nitrogen. **4.** North. **5.** noun. **6.** (*in combination*) nuclear: *N-power; N-plant.*

n. *abbrev. for:* **1.** neuter. **2.** new. **3.** nominative. **4.** noon. **5.** note. **6.** noun. **7.** number.

N. *abbrev. for:* **1.** National(ist). **2.** Navy. **3.** New. **4.** Norse.

Na *the chemical symbol for* sodium. [L *natrium*]

NA *abbrev. for* North America.

NAAFI *or* **Naafi** (ˈnæfɪ) *n.* **1.** *acronym for* Navy, Army, and Air Force Institutes: an organization providing canteens, shops, etc., for British military personnel at home or overseas. **2.** a canteen, shop, etc., run by this organization.

naartjie (ˈnɑːtʃɪ) *n. S. African.* a tangerine. [< Afrik., < Tamil]

nab (næb) *vb.* **nabbing, nabbed.** (*tr.*) *Inf.* **1.** to arrest (a criminal, etc.). **2.** to seize suddenly; snatch. [C17: ? of Scand. origin]

nabob (ˈneɪbɒb) *n.* **1.** *Inf.* a rich or important man. **2.** (formerly) a European who made a fortune in India. **3.** another name for a **nawab.** [C17: < Port. *nababo,* < Hindi *nawwāb;* see NAWAB]

NAC *abbrev. for* National Advisory Council.

nacelle (nəˈsɛl) *n.* a streamlined enclosure on an aircraft, not part of the fuselage, to accommodate an engine, passengers, crew, etc. [C20: < F: small boat, < LL *nāvicella,* a dim. of L *nāvis* ship]

Nachtmusik (ˈnæxtmuːˌziːk) *n.* a piece of music of a serenade-like character. [G: lit., night music]

NACODS (ˈneɪkɒdz) *n.* (in Britain) *acronym for* National Association of Colliery Overmen, Deputies, and Shotfirers.

nacre (ˈneɪkə) *n.* the technical name for **mother-of-pearl.** [C16: via F < OIt. *naccara,* < Ar. *naqqārah* shell, drum] —ˈ**nacred** *adj.*

nacreous (ˈneɪkrɪəs) *adj.* relating to, consisting of, or having the lustre of mother-of-pearl.

NACRO *or* **Nacro** (ˈnækrəʊ) *n.* (in Britain) *acronym for* National Association for the Care and Resettlement of Offenders.

nadir (ˈneɪdɪə, ˈnæ-) *n.* **1.** the point on the celestial sphere directly below an observer and diametrically opposite the zenith. **2.** the lowest point; depths. [C14: < OF, < Ar. *nazīr as-samt,* lit.: opposite the zenith]

nae (neɪ) *or* **na** (nɑː) a Scot. word for **no**[2] or **not.**

naevus *or U.S.* **nevus** (ˈniːvəs) *n., pl.* **-vi** (-vaɪ). any pigmented blemish on the skin; birthmark or mole. [C19: < L; rel. to (*g*)*natus* born, produced by nature] —ˈ**naevoid** *or U.S.* ˈ**nevoid** *adj.*

naff (næf) *adj. Brit. sl.* inferior or useless. [C19: ? < back slang on *fan,* short for FANNY]

naff off *sentence substitute. Brit sl.* a forceful expression of dismissal or contempt.

nag[1] (næg) *vb.* **nagging, nagged.** **1.** to scold or annoy constantly. **2.** (when *intr.,* often foll. by *at*) to be a constant source of discomfort or worry (to). ~*n.* **3.** a person, esp. a woman, who nags. [C19: of Scand. origin] —ˈ**nagger** *n.*

nag[2] (næg) *n.* **1.** *Often derog.* a horse. **2.** a small riding horse. [C14: of Gmc origin]

nagana (nəˈgɑːnə) *n.* a disease of hoofed animals of central and southern Africa, transmitted by tsetse flies. [< Zulu *u-nakane*]

Nah. *Bible. abbrev. for* Nahum.

Nahuatl (ˈnɑːwɑːtᵊl, nɑːˈwɑːtᵊl) *n.* **1.** (*pl.* **-tl** *or* **-tls**) a member of one of a group of Central American and Mexican Indian peoples including the Aztecs. **2.** the language of these peoples.

naiad (ˈnaɪæd) *n., pl.* **-ads** *or* **-ades** (-əˌdiːz). **1.** *Greek myth.* a nymph dwelling in a lake, river, or spring. **2.** the aquatic larva of the dragonfly, mayfly, and related insects. **3.** Also called: **water nymph.** a submerged aquatic plant, having narrow leaves and small flowers. [C17: via L < Gk *nāias* water nymph; rel. to *náein* to flow]

naïf (nɑːˈiːf) *adj., n.* a less common word for **naive.**

nail (neɪl) *n.* **1.** a fastening device, usually made of metal, having a point at one end and a head at the other. **2.** anything resembling such a device in function or shape. **3.** the horny plate covering part of the dorsal surface of the fingers or toes. Related adj.: **ungual.** **4.** the claw of a mammal, bird, or reptile. **5.** a unit of length, formerly used for measuring cloth, equal to two and a quarter inches. **6. hit the nail on the head.** to do or say something correct or telling. **7. on the nail.** (of payments) at once. ~*vb.* (*tr.*) **8.** to attach with or as if with nails. **9.** *Inf.* to arrest, catch, or seize. **10.** *Inf.* to hit or bring down, as with a shot. **11.** *Inf.* to expose or detect (a lie or liar). **12.** to fix (one's eyes, attention, etc.) on. **13.** to stud with nails. [OE *nægl*] —ˈ**nailer** *n.*

nail-biting *n.* **1.** the act or habit of biting one's fingernails. **2. a.** anxiety or tension. **b.** (*as modifier*): *nail-biting suspense.*

nailbrush (ˈneɪlˌbrʌʃ) *n.* a small stiff-bristled brush for cleaning the fingernails.

nailfile (ˈneɪlˌfaɪl) *n.* a small file of metal or of board coated with emery, used to trim the nails.

nail polish *or* **varnish** *or esp. U.S.* **enamel** *n.* a quick-drying cosmetic lacquer applied to colour the nails or make them shiny or esp. both.

nail set *n.* a punch for driving the head of a nail below or flush with the surrounding surface.

nainsook (ˈneɪnsʊk, ˈnæn-) *n.* a light soft plain-weave cotton fabric. [C19: < Hindi, < *nain* eye + *sukh* delight]

naira (ˈnaɪrə) *n.* the standard monetary unit of Nigeria. [C20: altered < *Nigeria*]

naive, naïve (nɑːˈiːv, naɪˈiːv), *or* **naïf** *adj.* **1.** having or expressing innocence and credulity; ingenuous. **2.** lacking developed powers of reasoning or criticism: *a naive argument.* [C17: < F fem. of *naïf,* < OF: native, spontaneous, < L *nātīvus* NATIVE] —**naˈively, naˈïvely,** *or* **naˈïfly** *adv.* —**naˈiveness, naˈïveness,** *or* **naˈïfness** *n.*

naivety (naɪˈiːvtɪ), **naiveté,** *or* **naïveté** (ˌnɑːiːvˈteɪ) *n., pl.* **-ties** *or* **-tés.** **1.** the state or quality of being naive. **2.** a naive act or statement.

naked (ˈneɪkɪd) *adj.* **1.** having the body unclothed; undressed. **2.** having no covering; exposed: *a naked flame.* **3.** with no qualification or concealment: *the naked facts.* **4.** unaided by any optical instrument (esp. in **the naked eye**). **5.** with no protection or shield. **6.** (usually foll. by *of*) destitute: *naked of weapons.* **7.** (of animals) lacking hair, feathers, scales, etc. **8.** *Law.* **a.** unsupported by authority: *a naked contract.* **b.** lacking some essential condition to render valid; incomplete. [OE *nacod*] —ˈ**nakedly** *adv.* —ˈ**nakedness** *n.*

naked ladies *n.* (*functioning as sing.*) another name for **autumn crocus.**

naked lady *n.* a pink orchid found in Australia and New Zealand.

naked singularity *n. Astron.* a hypothetical location at which there would be a discontinuity in the space-time continuum as a result of the gravitational collapse of a spherical mass. See also **black hole.**

NALGO (ˈnælgəʊ) *n.* (in Britain) *acronym for* National and Local Government Officers' Association.

namby-pamby (ˌnæmbɪˈpæmbɪ) *adj.* **1.** sentimental or prim in a weak insipid way. **2.** clinging, feeble, or spineless. ~*n., pl.* **-bies.** **3.** a person who is namby-pamby. [C18: a nickname of

Ambrose Phillips (died 1749), whose pastoral verse was ridiculed for being insipid]

name (neɪm) *n.* **1.** a word or term by which a person or thing is commonly and distinctively known. **2.** mere outward appearance as opposed to fact: *he was ruler in name only.* **3.** a word or phrase descriptive of character, usually abusive: *to call a person names.* **4.** reputation, esp., if unspecified, good reputation: *he's made quite a name for himself.* **5. a.** a famous person or thing: *a name in the advertising world.* **b.** *Chiefly U.S. & Canad.* (*as modifier*): *a name product.* **6. in the name of. a.** for the sake of. **b.** by the authority of. **7. name of the game. a.** anything that is significant or important. **b.** normal conditions, circumstances, etc.: *in gambling, losing money's the name of the game.* **8. to one's name.** belonging to one: *I haven't a penny to my name.* ~*vb.* (*tr.*) **9.** to give a name to. **10.** to refer to by name; cite: *he named three French poets.* **11.** to fix or specify: *they have named a date for the meeting.* **12.** to appoint or nominate: *he was named Journalist of the Year.* **13. name names.** to cite people, esp. in order to blame or accuse them. **14. name the day.** to choose the day for one's wedding. [OE *nama,* rel. to L *nomen,* Gk *noma*] —ˈ**namable** *or* ˈ**nameable** *adj.*

name-calling *n.* verbal abuse, esp. as a crude form of argument.

name day *n.* **1.** *R.C. Church.* the feast day of a saint whose name one bears. **2.** another name for **ticket day.**

name-dropping *n. Inf.* the practice of referring frequently to famous people, esp. as though they were intimate friends, in order to impress others. —ˈ**name-**ˌ**dropper** *n.*

nameless (ˈneɪmlɪs) *adj.* **1.** without a name. **2.** indescribable: *a nameless horror seized him.* **3.** too unpleasant or disturbing to be mentioned: *nameless atrocities.* —ˈ**namelessness** *n.*

namely (ˈneɪmlɪ) *adv.* that is to say.

nameplate (ˈneɪmˌpleɪt) *n.* a small panel on or next to the door of a room or building, bearing the occupant's name and profession.

namesake (ˈneɪmˌseɪk) *n.* a person or thing named after another, or with the same name as another. [C17: prob. describing people connected *for the name's sake*]

nametape (ˈneɪmˌteɪp) *n.* a tape attached to clothing, etc., bearing the owner's name.

nana[1] (ˈnænə) *n.* a child's word for **grandmother.**

nana[2] (ˈnɑːnə) *n. Austral. sl.* **1.** the head. **2. do one's nana.** to become very angry. **3. off one's nana.** mad; insane. [C19: prob. < BANANA]

nan bread *or* **naan** (nɑːn) *n.* (in Indian cookery) a slightly leavened bread in a large flat leaf shape. [< Hindi]

nancy (ˈnænsɪ) *n., pl.* **-cies.** an effeminate or homosexual boy or man. Also called: **nance, nancy boy.** [C20: < the girl's name *Nancy*]

NAND circuit *or* **gate** (nænd) *n. Electronics.* a computer logic circuit having two or more input wires and one output wire that has an output signal if one or more of the input signals are at a low voltage. Cf. **OR circuit.** [C20: < *not* + AND; see NOT CIRCUIT, AND CIRCUIT]

nankeen (næŋˈkiːn) *or* **nankin** (ˈnænkɪn) *n.* **1.** a hard-wearing buff-coloured cotton fabric. **2. a.** a pale greyish-yellow colour. **b.** (*as adj.*): *a nankeen carpet.* [C18: after *Nanking,* China, where it originated]

nanny (ˈnænɪ) *n., pl.* **-nies. 1.** a nurse or nursemaid for children. **2.** a child's word for **grandmother.** [C19: child's name for a nurse]

nannygai (ˈnænɪˌgaɪ) *n., pl.* **-gais.** an edible red Australian sea fish. [< Abor.]

nanny goat *n.* a female goat.

nano- *combining form.* denoting 10^{-9}: *nanosecond.* Symbol: n [< L *nānus* dwarf, < Gk *nanos*]

nanometre (ˈnænəʊˌmiːtə) *n.* one thousand-millionth of a metre. Symbol: nm

nanosecond (ˈnænəʊˌsɛkənd) *n.* one thousand-millionth of a second. Symbol: ns

Nansen bottle (ˈnænsən) *n.* an instrument used by oceanographers for obtaining samples of sea water from a desired depth. [C19: after F. *Nansen* (1861-1930), Norwegian arctic explorer & statesman]

nap[1] (næp) *vb.* **napping, napped.** (*intr.*) **1.** to sleep for a short while; doze. **2.** to be inattentive or off guard (esp. in **catch someone napping**). ~*n.* **3.** a short light sleep; doze. [OE *hnappian*]

nap[2] (næp) *n.* **1. a.** the raised fibres of velvet or similar cloth. **b.** the direction in which these fibres lie. **2.** any similar downy coating. **3.** *Austral. inf.* blankets; bedding. ~*vb.* **napping, napped. 4.** (*tr.*) to raise the nap of (velvet, etc.) by brushing. [C15: prob. < MDu. *noppe*]

nap[3] (næp) *n.* **1.** Also called: **napoleon.** a card game similar to whist, usually played for stakes. **2.** a call in this game, undertaking to win all five tricks. **3.** *Horse racing.* a tipster's choice for a certain winner. **4. nap hand.** a position in which there is a very good chance of success if a risk is taken. ~*vb.* **napping, napped.** (*tr.*) **5.** *Horse racing.* to name (a horse) as likely to win a race. [C19: < NAPOLEON, the card game]

napalm (ˈneɪpɑːm, ˈnæ-) *n.* **1.** a thick and highly incendiary liquid, usually consisting of petrol gelled with aluminium soaps, used in firebombs, flame-throwers, etc. ~*vb.* **2.** (*tr.*) to attack with napalm. [C20: < NA(PHTHENE) + *palm*(*itate*) salt of PALMITIC ACID]

nape (neɪp) *n.* the back of the neck. [C13: <?]

napery (ˈneɪpərɪ) *n. Rare.* household linen, esp. table linen. [C14: < OF *naperie,* < *nape* tablecloth, < L *mappa*]

naphtha (ˈnæfθə, ˈnæp-) *n.* a distillation product from coal tar or petroleum: used as a solvent and in petrol. [C16: via L < Gk, < Iranian]

naphthalene (ˈnæfθəˌliːn, ˈnæp-) *n.* a white crystalline hydrocarbon with a characteristic penetrating odour, used in mothballs and in dyes, explosives, etc. Formula: $C_{10}H_8$. [C19: < NAPHTHA + ALCOHOL + -ENE] —**naphthalic** (næfˈθælɪk, næp-) *adj.*

naphthene (ˈnæfθiːn, ˈnæp-) *n.* any of various cyclic methylene hydrocarbons found in petroleum. [C20: < NAPHTHA + -ENE]

naphthol (ˈnæfθɒl, ˈnæp-) *n.* a white crystalline solid having two isomeric forms, used in dyes and as an antioxidant. Formula: $C_{10}H_7OH$. [C19: < NAPHTHA + -OL[1]]

Napierian logarithm (nəˈpɪərɪən, neɪ-) *n.* another name for **natural logarithm.**

Napier's bones (ˈneɪpɪəz) *pl. n.* a set of graduated rods formerly used for multiplication and division. [C17: based on a method invented by John *Napier* (1550-1617), Scot. mathematician]

napkin (ˈnæpkɪn) *n.* **1.** Also called: **table napkin.** a usually square piece of cloth or paper used while eating to protect the clothes, wipe the mouth, etc.; serviette. **2.** *Rare.* a small piece of cloth. **3.** a more formal name for **nappy**[1]. **4.** a less common term for **sanitary towel.** [C15: < OF, < *nape* tablecloth, < L *mappa* cloth]

napoleon (nəˈpəʊlɪən) *n.* **1.** a former French gold coin worth 20 francs. **2.** *Cards.* the full name for **nap**[3] (sense 1). [C19: < F *napoléon,* after *Napoleon* I, Emperor of the French (1804-15)]

Napoleonic (nəˌpəʊlɪˈɒnɪk) *adj.* relating to or characteristic of Napoleon I or his era.

nappe (næp) *n.* **1.** a large sheet or mass of rock, originally a recumbent fold, that has been thrust from its original position by earth movements. **2.** the sheet of water that flows over a dam or weir. **3.** *Geom.* either of the two parts into which a cone is divided by the vertex. [C20: < F: tablecloth]

nappy[1] (ˈnæpɪ) *n., pl.* **-pies.** *Brit.* a piece of soft towelling or other absorbent material wrapped around a baby in order to absorb its excrement. Also called: **napkin.** U.S. and Canad. name: **diaper.** [C20: changed from NAPKIN]

nappy[2] (ˈnæpɪ) *adj.* **-pier, -piest. 1.** having a nap; downy; fuzzy. **2.** (of beer) **a.** having a head; frothy. **b.** strong or heady.

narcissism (ˈnɑːsɪˌsɪzəm) *or* **narcism** (ˈnɑːsɪzəm) *n.* **1.** an exceptional interest in or admiration for oneself, esp. one's physical appearance. **2.** sexual satisfaction derived from contemplation of one's own physical endowments. [C19: after *Narcissus*, a beautiful youth in Gk myth., who fell in love with his reflection in a pool] —**ˈnarcissist** *n.* —ˌ**narcisˈsistic** *adj.*

narcissus (nɑːˈsɪsəs) *n., pl.* **-cissuses** *or* **-cissi** (-ˈsɪsaɪ). a plant of a Eurasian genus whose yellow, orange, or white flowers have a crown surrounded by spreading segments. [C16: via L < Gk *nárkissos*, ? < *narkē* numbness, because of narcotic properties attributed to the plant]

narco- *or sometimes before a vowel* **narc-** *combining form.* **1.** indicating numbness or torpor: *narcolepsy.* **2.** connected with or derived from illicit drug production: *narcoeconomies.* [< Gk *narkē* numbness]

narcoanalysis (ˌnɑːkəʊəˈnælɪsɪs) *n.* psychoanalysis of a patient in a trance induced by a narcotic drug.

narcolepsy (ˈnɑːkəˌlɛpsɪ) *n. Pathol.* a rare condition characterized by sudden episodes of deep sleep. —ˌ**narcoˈleptic** *adj.*

narcosis (nɑːˈkəʊsɪs) *n.* unconsciousness induced by narcotics or general anaesthetics.

narcosynthesis (ˌnɑːkəʊˈsɪnθɪsɪs) *n.* a method of treating severe personality disorders by working with the patient while he is under the influence of a barbiturate drug.

narcotic (nɑːˈkɒtɪk) *n.* **1.** any of a group of drugs, such as opium and morphine, that produce numbness and stupor. **2.** anything that relieves pain or induces sleep, mental numbness, etc. ~*adj.* **3.** of or relating to narcotics or narcotics addicts. **4.** of or relating to narcosis. [C14: via Med. L < Gk *narkōtikós*, < *narkoūn* to numb, < *narkē* numbness] —**narˈcotically** *adv.*

narcotism (ˈnɑːkəˌtɪzəm) *n.* stupor or addiction induced by narcotic drugs.

narcotize *or* **-tise** (ˈnɑːkəˌtaɪz) *vb.* (*tr.*) to place under the influence of a narcotic drug. —ˌ**narcotiˈzation** *or* **-tiˈsation** *n.*

nard (nɑːd) *n.* **1.** another name for **spikenard. 2.** any of several plants whose aromatic roots were formerly used in medicine. [C14: via L < Gk *nárdos*, ? ult. < Sansk. *nalada* Indian spikenard]

nardoo (ˈnɑːduː) *n.* (in Australia) **1.** any of certain cloverlike ferns that grow in swampy areas. **2.** the spores of such a plant, used as food. [C19: < Abor.]

nares (ˈnɛəriːz) *pl. n., sing.* **naris** (ˈnɛərɪs). *Anat.* the nostrils. [C17: < L; rel. to OE *nasu*, L *nāsus* nose] —**ˈnarial** *adj.*

narghile, nargile, *or* **nargileh** (ˈnɑːgɪlɪ, -ˌleɪ) *n.* another name for **hookah.** [C19: < F *narguilé*, < Persian *nārgīleh* a pipe having a bowl made of coconut shell, < *nārgīl* coconut]

nark (nɑːk) *Sl.* ~*n.* **1.** *Brit., Austral., & N.Z.* an informer or spy: *copper's nark.* **2.** *Brit.* someone who complains in an irritating or whining manner. ~*vb.* **3.** *Brit., Austral., & N.Z.* to annoy, upset, or irritate. **4.** (*intr.*) *Brit., Austral., & N.Z.* to inform or spy, esp. for the police. **5.** (*intr.*) *Brit.* to complain irritatingly. [C19: prob. < Romany *nāk* nose]

narky (ˈnɑːkɪ) *adj.* **narkier, narkiest.** *Sl.* irritable, complaining, or sarcastic.

Narraganset (ˌnærəˈgænsɪt) *n.* **1.** (*pl.* **-set** *or* **-sets**) a member of a North American Indian people formerly living in Rhode Island. **2.** the language of this people, belonging to the Algonquian family.

narrate (nəˈreɪt) *vb.* **1.** to tell (a story); relate. **2.** to speak in accompaniment of (a film, etc.). [C17: < L *narrāre* to recount, < *gnārus* knowing] —**narˈratable** *adj.* —**narˈrator** *n.*

narration (nəˈreɪʃən) *n.* **1.** the act or process of narrating. **2.** a narrated account or story.

narrative (ˈnærətɪv) *n.* **1.** an account or story, as of events, experiences, etc. **2.** the part of a literary work, etc., that relates events. **3.** the process or technique of narrating. ~*adj.* **4.** telling a story: *a narrative poem.* **5.** of or relating to narration: *narrative art.*

narrow (ˈnærəʊ) *adj.* **1.** small in breadth, esp. in comparison to length. **2.** limited in range or extent. **3.** limited in outlook. **4.** limited in means or resources. **5.** barely adequate or successful (esp. in **a narrow escape**). **6.** painstakingly thorough: *a narrow scrutiny.* **7.** *Finance.* denoting an assessment of liquidity as including notes and coin in circulation with the public, banks' till money, and banks' balances: *narrow money.* Cf. **broad** (sense 12). **8.** *Phonetics.* another word for **tense**[1] (sense 4). ~*vb.* **9.** to make or become narrow; limit; restrict. ~*n.* **10.** a narrow place, esp. a pass or strait. ~See also **narrows.** [OE *nearu*] —**ˈnarrowly** *adv.* —**ˈnarrowness** *n.*

narrow boat *n.* a long bargelike boat with a beam of 2.1 metres (7 feet), used on canals.

narrow gauge *n.* **1.** a railway track with a smaller distance between the lines than the standard gauge of 56½ inches. ~*adj.* **narrow-gauge. 2.** of or denoting a railway with a narrow gauge.

narrow-minded *adj.* having a biased or illiberal viewpoint; bigoted, intolerant, or prejudiced. —ˌ**narrow-ˈmindedness** *n.*

narrows (ˈnærəʊz) *pl. n.* a narrow part of a strait, river, current, etc.

narthex (ˈnɑːθɛks) *n.* **1.** a portico at the west end of a church, esp. one at right angles to the nave. **2.** a rectangular entrance hall between the porch and nave of a church. [C17: via L < Med. Gk: enclosed porch (earlier: box), < Gk *narthēx* giant fennel, the stems of which were used to make boxes]

narwhal, narwal (ˈnɑːwəl), *or* **narwhale** (ˈnɑː-ˌweɪl) *n.* an arctic toothed whale having a black-spotted whitish skin and, in the male, a long spiral tusk. [C17: of Scand. origin; cf. Danish, Norwegian *narhval*, < ON *nāhvalr*, < *nār* corpse + *hvalr* whale]

nary (ˈnɛərɪ) *adv. Dialect or inf.* not; never: *nary a man was left.* [C19: var. of *ne'er a* never a]

NASA (ˈnæsə) *n.* (in the U.S.) *acronym for* National Aeronautics and Space Administration.

nasal (ˈneɪzᵊl) *adj.* **1.** of the nose. **2.** *Phonetics.* pronounced with the soft palate lowered allowing air to escape via the nasal cavity. ~*n.* **3.** a nasal speech sound, such as English *m, n,* or *ng.* [C17: < F < LL *nāsālis*, < L *nāsus* nose] —**nasality** (neɪˈzælɪtɪ) *n.* —**ˈnasally** *adv.*

nasalize *or* **-lise** (ˈneɪzᵊˌlaɪz) *vb.* (*tr.*) to pronounce nasally. —ˌ**nasaliˈzation** *or* **-liˈsation** *n.*

nascent (ˈnæsᵊnt, ˈneɪ-) *adj.* starting to grow or develop; being born. [C17: < L *nascēns*, present participle of *nāscī* to be born] —**ˈnascency** *n.*

naso- *combining form.* nose: *nasopharynx.* [< L *nāsus* nose]

nastic movement (ˈnæstɪk) *n.* a response of plant parts that is independent of the direction of the external stimulus, such as the opening of buds caused by an alteration in light intensity. [C19 *nastic*, < Gk *nastos* close-packed, < *nassein* to press down]

nasturtium (nəˈstɜːʃəm) *n.* a plant having round leaves and yellow, red, or orange trumpet-shaped spurred flowers. [C17: < L: kind of cress, < *nāsus* nose + *tortus* twisted; because the pungent smell causes one to wrinkle one's nose]

nasty (ˈnɑːstɪ) *adj.* **-tier, -tiest. 1.** unpleasant or repugnant. **2.** dangerous or painful: *a nasty wound.* **3.** spiteful or ill-natured. **4.** obscene or indecent. ~*n., pl.* **-ties. 5.** an offensive or unpleasant person or thing: *a video nasty.* [C14: <?; prob. rel. to Swedish dialect *nasket* & Du. *nestig* dirty] —**ˈnastily** *adv.* —**ˈnastiness** *n.*

NAS/UWT (in Britain) *abbrev. for* National Association of Schoolmasters/Union of Women Teachers.

nat. *abbrev. for:* **1.** national. **2.** native. **3.** natural.

natal (ˈneɪtᵊl) *adj.* of or relating to birth. [C14: < L *nātālis* of one's birth, < *nātus*, < *nascī* to be born]

natant (ˈneɪtᵊnt) *adj.* floating or swimming. [C18: < L *natāns*, present participle of *natāre* to swim]

natation (nəˈteɪʃən) *n.* a literary word for **swimming.** [C16: < L *natātiō* a swimming, < *natāre* to swim]

natatory (nəˈteɪtərɪ) *or* **natatorial** (ˌnætəˈtɔːrɪəl) *adj.* of or relating to swimming. [C18: < LL *natātōrius*, < L *natāre* to swim]

natch (nætʃ) *sentence substitute. Inf.* short for **naturally.**

nates (ˈneɪtiːz) *pl. n., sing.* **-tis** (-tɪs). a technical word for the **buttocks.** [C17: < L]

NATFHE (in Britain) *abbrev. for* National Association of Teachers in Further and Higher Education.

natheless (ˈneɪθlɪs) *or* **nathless** (ˈnæθlɪs) *Arch. sentence connector.* nonetheless. [OE *nāthylǣs*, < *nā* never + *thӯ* for that + *lǣs* less]

nation (ˈneɪʃən) *n.* **1.** an aggregation of people or peoples of one or more cultures, races, etc., organized into a single state: *the Australian nation.* **2.** a community of persons not constituting a state but bound by common descent, language, history, etc.: *the French-Canadian nation.* [C13: via OF < L *nātiō* birth, tribe, < *nascī* to be born] —ˈ**nation**ˌ**hood** *n.*

national (ˈnæʃənᵊl) *adj.* **1.** of or relating to a nation as a whole. **2.** characteristic of a particular nation: *the national dress of Poland.* ~*n.* **3.** a citizen or subject. **4.** a national newspaper. —ˈ**nationally** *adv.*

national anthem *n.* a patriotic song adopted by a nation for use on public occasions.

national assistance *n.* the former name for **supplementary benefit.**

national bank *n.* **1.** (in the U.S.) a commercial bank incorporated under a Federal charter and legally required to be a member of the Federal Reserve System. **2.** a bank operated by a government.

National Country Party *n.* an Australian political party drawing its main support from rural areas. Often shortened to: **National Party.**

national debt *n.* the total outstanding borrowings of a nation's central government.

National Economic Development Council *n.* an advisory body on economic policy in Britain, composed of representatives of government, management, and trade unions. Abbrevs.: **NEDC,** (inf.) **Neddy.**

National Enterprise Board *n.* a public corporation established in 1975 to help the economy of the UK, develop its industrial efficiency, and support its productive employment. Abbrev.: **NEB.**

National Football *n.* (in Australia) another name for **Australian Rules.**

national grid *n. Brit.* **1.** a network of high-voltage electric power lines linking major electric power stations. **2.** the metric coordinate system used in ordnance survey maps.

National Guard *n.* **1.** (*sometimes not cap.*) the armed force that was established in France in 1789 and existed intermittently until 1871. **2.** (in the U.S.) a state military force that can be called into federal service by the president.

National Health Service *n.* (in Britain) the system of national medical services since 1948, financed mainly by taxation. Abbrev.: **NHS.**

national income *n. Econ.* the total of all incomes accruing over a specified period to residents of a country.

national insurance *n.* (in Britain) state insurance based on weekly contributions from employees and employers and providing payments to the unemployed, the sick, the retired, etc., as well as medical services.

nationalism (ˈnæʃənəˌlɪzəm) *n.* **1.** a sentiment based on common cultural characteristics that binds a population and often produces a policy of national independence. **2.** loyalty to one's country; patriotism. **3.** exaggerated or fanatical devotion to a national community. —ˈ**nationalist** *n., adj.* —ˌ**national**ˈ**istic** *adj.*

Nationalist Party *n.* (in South Africa) the largest political party in Parliament: composed mainly of centre to right-wing Afrikaners.

nationality (ˌnæʃəˈnælɪtɪ) *n., pl.* **-ties.** **1.** the fact of being a citizen of a particular nation. **2.** a body of people sharing common descent, history, language, etc.; a nation. **3.** a national group: *30 different nationalities are found in this city.* **4.** national character. **5.** the fact of being a nation; national status.

nationalize *or* **-lise** (ˈnæʃənəˌlaɪz) *vb.* (*tr.*) **1.** to put (an industry, resources, etc.) under state control. **2.** to make national in character or status. **3.** a less common word for **naturalize.** —ˌ**nationali**ˈ**zation** *or* **-li**ˈ**sation** *n.*

national park *n.* an area of countryside designated by a national government as being of notable scenic, environmental, or historical importance.

National Party *n.* **1.** (in New Zealand) the more conservative of the two main political parties. **2.** (in Australia) another name for **National Country Party.**

National Savings Bank *n.* (in Britain) a government savings bank, run through the Post Office.

national service *n. Chiefly Brit.* compulsory military service.

National Socialism *n. German history.* the doctrines and practices of the Nazis, involving the supremacy of Hitler as Führer, anti-Semitism, state control of the economy, and national expansion. —**National Socialist** *n., adj.*

national superannuation *n. N.Z.* a government pension given on the attainment of a specified age; old age pension.

National Trust *n.* (in Britain) an organization concerned with the preservation of historic buildings and areas of the countryside of great beauty.

nationwide (ˈneɪʃənˌwaɪd) *adj.* covering or available to the whole of a nation; national.

native (ˈneɪtɪv) *adj.* **1.** relating or belonging to a person by virtue of conditions existing at birth: *a native language.* **2.** natural or innate: *native wit.* **3.** born in a specified place: *a native Indian.* **4.** (when *postpositive,* foll. by *to*) originating in: *kangaroos are native to Australia.* **5.** relating to the indigenous inhabitants of a country: *the native art of the New Guinea Highlands.* **6.** (of metals) found naturally in the elemental form; not chemically combined as in an ore. **7.** unadulterated by civilization, artifice, or adornment; natural. **8.** *Arch.* related by birth or race. **9.** **go native.** (of a settler) to adopt the lifestyle of the local population, esp. when it appears less civilized. ~*n.* **10.** (usually foll. by *of*) a person born in a particular place: *a native of Geneva.* **11.** (usually foll. by *of*) a species of animal or plant originating in a particular place. **12.** a member of an indigenous people of a country, esp. a non-White people, as opposed to colonial immigrants. [C14: < L *nātīvus* innate, natural, < *nascī* to be born] —ˈ**natively** *adv.* —ˈ**nativeness** *n.*

native bear *n.* an Australian name for **koala.**

native-born *adj.* born in the country or area indicated.

native companion *n.* (in Australia) another name for **brolga.**

native dog *n. Austral.* a dingo.

nativity (nəˈtɪvɪtɪ) *n., pl.* **-ties.** birth or origin. [C14: < LL *nātīvitas* birth; see NATIVE]

Nativity (nəˈtɪvɪtɪ) *n.* **1.** the birth of Christ. **2.** the feast of Christmas as a commemoration of this. **3.** **a.** an artistic representation of the circumstances of the birth of Christ. **b.** (*as modifier*): *a Nativity play.*

NATO *or* **Nato** (ˈneɪtəʊ) *n. acronym for* North Atlantic Treaty Organization: an international organization established (1949) for purposes of collective security.

natron (ˈneɪtrən) *n.* a whitish or yellow mineral that consists of hydrated sodium carbonate and occurs in saline deposits and salt lakes. [C17: via F & Sp. < Ar. *natrūn*, < Gk *nitron* NITRE]

NATSOPA (nætˈsəʊpə) *n.* (in Britain) *acronym for* National Society of Operative Printers, Graphical and Media Personnel.

natter (ˈnætə) *Chiefly Brit. inf.* ~*vb.* **1.** (*intr.*) to talk idly and at length; chatter. ~*n.* **2.** prolonged idle chatter. [C19: < *gnatter* to grumble, imit.]

natterjack (ˈnætəˌdʒæk) *n.* a European toad having a greyish-brown body marked with reddish warty processes. [C18: <?]

natty (ˈnætɪ) *adj.* **-tier, -tiest.** *Inf.* smart; spruce; dapper. [C18: < obs. *netty,* < *net* NEAT[1]] —ˈ**nattily** *adv.* —ˈ**nattiness** *n.*

natural (ˈnætʃrəl) *adj.* **1.** of, existing in, or produced by nature: *natural science; natural cliffs.* **2.** in accordance with human nature. **3.** as is normal or to be expected: *the natural course of events.* **4.** not acquired; innate: *a natural gift for sport.* **5.** being so through innate qualities: *a natural leader.* **6.** not supernatural or strange: *natural phenomena.* **7.** genuine or spontaneous. **8.** lifelike: *she looked more natural without make-up.* **9.** not affected by man; wild: *in the natural state this animal is not ferocious.* **10.** being or made from organic material; not synthetic: *a natural fibre like cotton.* **11.** born out of wedlock. **12.** not adopted but rather related by blood: *her natural parents.* **13.** *Music.* **a.** not sharp or flat. **b.** (*postpositive*) denoting a note that is neither sharp nor flat. **c.** (of a key or scale) containing no sharps or flats. **14.** based on the principles and findings of human reason rather than on revelation: *natural religion.* ~*n.* **15.** *Inf.* a person or thing regarded as certain to qualify for success, selection, etc.: *the horse was a natural for first place.* **16.** *Music.* **a.** Also called (U.S.): **cancel.** an accidental cancelling a previous sharp or flat. Usual symbol: ♮ **b.** a note affected by this accidental. **17.** *Obs.* an imbecile; idiot. —ˈ**naturalness** *n.*

natural childbirth *n.* a method of childbirth characterized by the absence of anaesthetics, in which the expectant mother is given special breathing and relaxing exercises.

natural gas *n.* a gaseous mixture, consisting mainly of methane, trapped below ground; used extensively as a fuel.

natural history *n.* **1.** the study of animals and plants in the wild state. **2.** the sum of these phenomena in a given place or at a given time. —**natural historian** *n.*

naturalism (ˈnætʃrəˌlɪzəm) *n.* **1.** a movement, esp. in art and literature, advocating detailed realistic and factual description. **2.** the belief that all religious truth is based not on revelation but rather on the study of natural causes and processes. **3.** *Philosophy.* a scientific account of the world in terms of causes and natural forces. **4.** action or thought caused by natural instincts.

naturalist (ˈnætʃrəlɪst) *n.* **1.** a person who is versed in or interested in botany or zoology. **2.** a person who advocates or practises naturalism.

naturalistic (ˌnætʃrəˈlɪstɪk) *adj.* **1.** of or reproducing nature in effect or characteristics. **2.** of or characteristic of naturalism. **3.** of naturalists. —ˌ**naturalˈistically** *adv.*

naturalize *or* **-lise** (ˈnætʃrəˌlaɪz) *vb.* **1.** (*tr.*) to give citizenship to (a person of foreign birth). **2.** to be or cause to be adopted in another place, as a word, custom, etc. **3.** (*tr.*) to introduce (a plant or animal from another region) and cause it to adapt to local conditions. **4.** (*intr.*) (of a plant or animal) to adapt successfully to a foreign environment. **5.** (*tr.*) to make natural or more lifelike. —ˌ**naturaliˈzation** *or* **-liˈsation** *n.*

natural language *n.* a language that has evolved naturally as a means of communication among people, as opposed to an invented language or a code.

natural logarithm *n.* a logarithm to the base e. Usually written $\log_e$ or ln. Also called: **Napierian logarithm.**

naturally (ˈnætʃrəlɪ) *adv.* **1.** in a natural way. **2.** instinctively. ~*adv., sentence substitute.* **3.** of course; surely.

natural number *n.* any of the positive integers 1, 2, 3, 4,...

natural philosophy *n.* physical science, esp. physics. —**natural philosopher** *n.*

natural resources *pl. n.* naturally occurring materials such as coal, fertile land, etc.

natural science *n.* the sciences that are involved in the study of the physical world and its phenomena, including biology, physics, chemistry, and geology.

natural selection *n.* a process resulting in the survival of those individuals from a population of animals or plants that are best adapted to the prevailing environmental conditions.

natural theology *n.* the attempt to derive theological truth, and esp. the existence of God, from empirical facts by reasoned argument. Cf. **revealed religion.**

natural wastage *n.* the loss of employees, etc., through not replacing those who retire or resign rather than dismissal or redundancy.

nature (ˈneɪtʃə) *n.* **1.** fundamental qualities; identity or essential character. **2.** (*often cap.*) the whole system of the existence, forces, and events of all physical life that are not controlled by man. **3.** plant and animal life, as distinct from man. **4.** a wild primitive state untouched by man. **5.** natural unspoilt countryside. **6.** disposition or temperament. **7.** desires or instincts governing behaviour. **8.** the normal biological needs of the body. **9.** sort; character. **10. against nature.** unnatural or immoral. **11. by nature.** essentially or innately. **12. call of nature.** *Inf.* the need to urinate or defecate. **13. from nature.** using natural models in drawing, painting, etc. **14. in** (*or* **of**) **the nature of.** essentially the same as; by way of. [C13: via OF < L *nātūra,* < *nātus,* p.p. of *nascī* to be born]

nature reserve *n.* an area of land that is protected and managed in order to preserve its flora and fauna.

nature strip *n. Austral. inf.* a grass strip running along in front of a house or beside a road or between carriageways.

nature study *n.* the study of the natural world, esp. animals and plants, by direct observation at an elementary level.

nature trail *n.* a path through countryside designed and usually signposted to draw attention to natural features of interest.

naturism (ˈneɪtʃəˌrɪzəm) *n.* another name for **nudism.** —ˈ**naturist** *n., adj.*

naught (nɔːt) *n.* **1.** *Arch. or literary.* nothing; ruin or failure. **2.** a variant spelling (esp. U.S.) of **nought. 3. set at naught.** to disregard or scorn; disdain. ~*adv.* **4.** *Arch. or literary.* not at all: *it matters naught.* ~*adj.* **5.** *Obs.* worthless, ruined, or wicked. [OE *nāwiht,* < *nā* NO[1] + *wiht* thing, person]

naughty (ˈnɔːtɪ) *adj.* **-tier, -tiest. 1.** (esp. of children) mischievous or disobedient. **2.** mildly indecent; titillating. [C14: (orig.: needy, poor): < NAUGHT] —ˈ**naughtily** *adv.* —ˈ**naughtiness** *n.*

nauplius (ˈnɔːplɪəs) *n., pl.* **-plii** (-plɪˌaɪ). the larva of many crustaceans, having a rounded unsegmented body with three pairs of limbs. [C19: < L: type of shellfish, < Gk *Nauplios,* one of the sons of the Greek god Poseidon]

nausea (ˈnɔːzɪə, -sɪə) *n.* **1.** the sensation that precedes vomiting. **2.** a feeling of revulsion. [C16: via L < Gk: seasickness, < *naus* ship]

nauseate (ˈnɔːzɪˌeɪt, -sɪ-) *vb.* **1.** (*tr.*) to arouse feelings of disgust or revulsion in. **2.** to feel or cause to feel sick. —ˈ**nauseˌating** *adj.*

nauseous (ˈnɔːzɪəs, -sɪəs) *adj.* **1.** causing nausea. **2.** distasteful; repulsive. —ˈ**nauseously** *adv.* —ˈ**nauseousness** *n.*

nautch *or* **nauch** (nɔːtʃ) *n.* an intricate traditional Indian dance performed by professional dancing girls. [C18: < Hindi *nāc,* < Sansk., < *nrtyati* he acts or dances]

nautical (ˈnɔːtɪkəl) *adj.* of or involving ships, navigation, or seamen. [C16: < L *nauticus,* < Gk *nautikos,* < *naus* ship] —ˈ**nautically** *adv.*

nautical mile *n.* a unit of length, used esp. in navigation, equal to 1852 metres (6076.103 feet). Also called: **international nautical mile, air mile.**

nautilus (ˈnɔːtɪləs) *n., pl.* **-luses** *or* **-li** (-ˌlaɪ). **1.** any of a genus of cephalopod molluscs, esp. the pearly nautilus. **2.** short for **paper nautilus.** [C17: via L < Gk *nautilos* sailor, < *naus* ship]

Navaho *or* **Navajo** (ˈnævəˌhəʊ) *n.* **1.** (*pl.* **-ho, -hos, -hoes** *or* **-jo, -jos, -joes**) a member of a North

American Indian people of Arizona, New Mexico, and Utah. **2.** the language of this people.

naval (ˈneɪvᵊl) *adj.* **1.** of, characteristic of, or having a navy. **2.** of or relating to ships; nautical. [C16: < L *nāvālis*, < *nāvis* ship]

naval architecture *n.* the designing of ships. —**naval architect** *n.*

navarin (ˈnævərɪn) *n.* a stew of mutton or lamb with root vegetables. [< F]

nave[1] (neɪv) *n.* the central space in a church, extending from the narthex to the chancel and often flanked by aisles. [C17: via Med. L < L *nāvis* ship, from the similarity of shape]

nave[2] (neɪv) *n.* the central block or hub of a wheel. [OE *nafu, nafa*]

navel (ˈneɪvᵊl) *n.* **1.** the scar in the centre of the abdomen, usually forming a slight depression, where the umbilical cord was attached. Technical name: **umbilicus.** Related adj.: **umbilical. 2.** a central part or point. [OE *nafela*]

navel orange *n.* a sweet orange that has at its apex a navel-like depression enclosing an underdeveloped secondary fruit.

navelwort (ˈneɪvᵊlˌwɜːt) *n.* another name for **pennywort** (sense 1).

navicular (nəˈvɪkjʊlə) *Anat.* ~*adj.* **1.** shaped like a boat. ~*n.* **2.** a small boat-shaped bone of the wrist or foot. [C16: < LL *nāviculāris*, < L *nāvicula*, dim. of *nāvis* ship]

navigable (ˈnævɪgəbᵊl) *adj.* **1.** wide, deep, or safe enough to be sailed through: *a navigable channel.* **2.** capable of being steered: *a navigable raft.* —ˌ**navigaˈbility** *n.* —ˈ**navigably** *adv.*

navigate (ˈnævɪˌgeɪt) *vb.* **1.** to direct or plot the path or position of (a ship, an aircraft, etc.). **2.** (*tr.*) to travel over, through, or on in a boat, aircraft, etc. **3.** *Inf.* to direct (oneself) carefully or safely: *he navigated his way to the bar.* **4.** (*intr.*) (of a passenger in a motor vehicle) to give directions to the driver; point out the route. [C16: < L *nāvigāre* to sail, < *nāvis* ship + *agere* to drive]

navigation (ˌnævɪˈgeɪʃən) *n.* **1.** the skill or process of plotting a route and directing a ship, aircraft, etc., along it. **2.** the act or practice of navigating: *dredging made navigation of the river possible.* —ˌ**naviˈgational** *adj.*

navigator (ˈnævɪˌgeɪtə) *n.* **1.** a person who performs navigation. **2.** (esp. formerly) a person who explores by ship. **3.** an instrument for assisting a pilot to navigate an aircraft.

navvy (ˈnævɪ) *n., pl.* **-vies.** *Brit. inf.* a labourer on a building site, etc. [C19: < *navigator* builder of a *navigation* (in the sense canal)]

navy (ˈneɪvɪ) *n., pl.* **-vies. 1.** the warships and auxiliary vessels of a nation or ruler. **2.** (*often cap.*) the branch of a country's armed services comprising such ships, their crews, and all their supporting services. **3.** short for **navy blue. 4.** *Arch. or literary.* a fleet of ships. [C14: via OF < Vulgar L *nāvia* (unattested) ship, < L *nāvis* ship]

navy blue *n.* **a.** a dark greyish-blue colour. **b.** (*as adj.*): *a navy-blue suit.* [C19: < the colour of the British naval uniform]

Navy List *n.* (in Britain) an official list of all commissioned officers of the Royal Navy.

navy yard *n.* a naval shipyard, esp. in the U.S.

nawab (nəˈwɑːb) *n.* (formerly) a Muslim ruling prince or powerful landowner in India. [C18: < Hindi *nawwāb*, < Ar. *nuwwāb*, pl. of *na'ib* viceroy]

nay (neɪ) *sentence substitute.* **1.** a word for **no**[1]: archaic or dialectal except in voting by voice. ~*n.* **2.** a person who votes in the negative. ~*adv.* **3.** (*sentence modifier*) *Arch.* an emphatic form of **no**[1]. [C12: < ON *nei*, < *ne* not + *ei* ever]

Nazarene (ˌnæzəˈriːn) *n.* **1.** an early name for a **Christian** (Acts 24:5) or (when preceded by *the*) for **Jesus Christ. 2.** a member of one of several groups of Jewish-Christians found principally in Syria. ~*adj.* **3.** of Nazareth in N Israel, or the Nazarenes.

Nazarite (ˈnæzəˌraɪt) *or* **Nazirite** *n.* a religious ascetic of ancient Israel. [C16: < L *Nazaraeus*, < Heb. *nāzar* to consecrate + -ITE[1]]

Nazi (ˈnɑːtsɪ) *n., pl.* **-zis. 1.** a member of the fascist National Socialist German Workers' Party, which seized political control in Germany in 1933 under Adolf Hitler. ~*adj.* **2.** characteristic of or relating to the Nazis. [C20: < G, phonetic spelling of the first two syllables of *Nationalsozialist* National Socialist] —**Nazism** (ˈnɑːtˌsɪzəm) *or* **Naziism** (ˈnɑːtsɪˌɪzəm) *n.*

Nb *the chemical symbol for* niobium.

NB *abbrev. for* New Brunswick.

NB, N.B., nb, *or* **n.b.** *abbrev. for* nota bene. [L: note well]

NCB (in Britain) *abbrev. for* National Coal Board: now **British Coal.**

NCO *abbrev. for* noncommissioned officer.

NCP (in Australia) *abbrev. for* National Country Party.

NCU (in Britain) *abbrev. for* National Communications Union.

nd *abbrev. for* no date.

Nd *the chemical symbol for* neodymium.

NDP (in Canada) *abbrev. for* New Democratic Party.

NDT (in Canada) *abbrev. for* Newfoundland Daylight Time.

Ne *the chemical symbol for* neon.

NE[1] *symbol for* northeast(ern).

NE[2] *or* **N.E.** *abbrev. for* New England.

ne- *combining form.* a variant of **neo-,** esp. before a vowel: *Nearctic.*

Neanderthal man (nɪˈændəˌtɑːl) *n.* a type of primitive man occurring throughout much of Europe in late Palaeolithic times. [C19: < the anthropological findings (1857) in the Neandertal, a valley near Düsseldorf, Germany]

neap (niːp) *adj.* **1.** of, relating to, or constituting a neap tide. ~*n.* **2.** short for **neap tide.** [OE, as in *nēpflōd* neap tide, <?]

Neapolitan (ˌnɪəˈpɒlɪtᵊn) *n.* **1.** a native or inhabitant of Naples. ~*adj.* **2.** of or relating to Naples. [C15: < L *Neāpolītānus*, ult. < Gk *Neapolis* new town]

Neapolitan ice cream *n.* ice cream with several layers of different colours and flavours.

neap tide *n.* either of the tides that occur at the first or last quarter of the moon when the tide-generating forces of the sun and moon oppose each other and produce the smallest rise and fall in tidal level. Cf. **spring tide** (sense 1).

near (nɪə) *prep.* **1.** at or to a place or time not far away from; close to. ~*adv.* **2.** at or to a place or time not far away; close by. **3.** short for **nearly**: *I was damn near killed.* ~*adj.* **4.** (*postpositive*) at or in a place not far away. **5.** (*prenominal*) only just successful or only just failing: *a near escape.* **6.** (*postpositive*) *Inf.* miserly, mean. **7.** (*prenominal*) closely connected or intimate: *a near relation.* ~*vb.* **8.** to come or draw close (to). ~*n.* **9.** Also called: **nearside. a.** the left side of a horse, vehicle, etc. **b.** (*as modifier*): *the near foreleg.* [OE *nēar* (adv.), comp. of *nēah* close] —ˈ**nearness** *n.*

nearby *adj.* (ˈnɪəˌbaɪ), *adv.* (ˌnɪəˈbaɪ). not far away; close at hand.

Nearctic (nɪˈɑːktɪk) *adj.* of a zoogeographical region consisting of North America, north of the tropic of Cancer, and Greenland.

Near East *n.* **1.** another term for the **Middle East. 2.** (formerly) the Balkan States and the area of the Ottoman Empire.

near gale *n. Meteorol.* a wind of force seven on the Beaufort scale or from 32-38 mph.

nearly (ˈnɪəlɪ) *adv.* **1.** almost. **2. not nearly.** nowhere near: *not nearly enough.* **3.** closely: *the person most nearly concerned.*

near miss *n.* **1.** a bomb, shell, etc., that does not exactly hit the target. **2.** any attempt or shot that just fails to be successful. **3.** an incident in which two aircraft, etc., narrowly avoid collision.

nearside (ˈnɪəˌsaɪd) *n.* **1.** (usually preceded by *the*) *Chiefly Brit.* **a.** the side of a vehicle, etc., nearer the kerb. **b.** (*as modifier*): *the nearside door.* **2. a.** the left side of an animal, etc. **b.** (*as modifier*): *the nearside flank.*

near-sighted (ˌnɪəˈsaɪtɪd) *adj.* relating to or suffering from myopia. —ˌ**near-ˈsightedly** *adv.*

near thing *n. Inf.* an event or action whose outcome is nearly a failure, success, disaster, etc.

neat[1] (niːt) *adj.* **1.** clean, tidy, and orderly. **2.** liking or insisting on order and cleanliness. **3.** smoothly or competently done; efficient: *a neat job.* **4.** pat or slick: *his excuse was suspiciously neat.* **5.** (of alcoholic drinks, etc.) undiluted. **6.** (of language) concise and well-phrased. **7.** *Sl., chiefly U.S. & Canad.* pleasing; admirable; excellent. [C16: < OF *net,* < L *nitidus* clean, < *nitēre* to shine] —**ˈneatly** *adv.* —**ˈneatness** *n.*

neat[2] (niːt) *n., pl.* **neat.** *Arch. or dialect.* a domestic bovine animal. [OE *neat*]

neaten (ˈniːtᵊn) *vb.* (*tr.*) to make neat; tidy.

neath *or* **ˈneath** (niːθ) *prep. Arch.* short for **beneath.**

neat's-foot oil *n.* a yellow oil obtained by boiling the feet and shinbones of cattle.

neb (nɛb) *n. Arch. or dialect.* **1.** the peak of a cap. **2.** the beak of a bird or the nose or snout of an animal. **3.** the projecting end of anything. [OE *nebb*]

NEB *abbrev. for:* **1.** New English Bible. **2.** National Enterprise Board.

nebula (ˈnɛbjʊlə) *n., pl.* **-lae** (-ˌliː) *or* **-las. 1.** *Astron.* a diffuse cloud of particles and gases visible either as a hazy patch of light or an irregular dark region. **2.** *Pathol.* opacity of the cornea. [C17: < L: mist, cloud] —**ˈnebular** *adj.*

nebular hypothesis *n.* the theory that the solar system evolved from nebular matter.

nebulosity (ˌnɛbjʊˈlɒsɪtɪ) *n., pl.* **-ties. 1.** the state of being nebulous. **2.** *Astron.* a nebula.

nebulous (ˈnɛbjʊləs) *adj.* **1.** lacking definite form, shape, or content; vague or amorphous. **2.** of a nebula. **3.** *Rare.* misty or hazy. —**ˈnebulousness** *n.*

NEC *abbrev. for* National Executive Committee.

necessaries (ˈnɛsɪsərɪz) *pl. n.* (*sometimes sing.*) what is needed; essential items: *the necessaries of life.*

necessarily (ˈnɛsɪsərɪlɪ, ˌnɛsɪˈsɛrɪlɪ) *adv.* **1.** as an inevitable or natural consequence. **2.** as a certainty: *he won't necessarily come.*

necessary (ˈnɛsɪsərɪ) *adj.* **1.** needed to achieve a certain desired result; required. **2.** inevitable: *the necessary consequences of your action.* **3.** *Logic.* **a.** (of a statement, formula, etc.) true under all interpretations. **b.** (of a proposition) determined to be true by its meaning, so that its denial would be self-contradictory. Cf. **sufficient** (sense 2). **4.** *Rare.* compelled, as by necessity or law; not free. ~*n.* **5.** *Inf.* (preceded by *the*) the money required for a particular purpose. **6. do the necessary.** *Inf.* to do something that is necessary in a particular situation. ~See also **necessaries.** [C14: < L *necessārius* indispensable, < *necesse* unavoidable]

necessitarianism (nɪˌsɛsɪˈtɛərɪəˌnɪzəm) *n. Philosophy.* the belief that human actions and choices are causally determined and cannot be willed. —**neˌcessiˈtarian** *n., adj.*

necessitate (nɪˈsɛsɪˌteɪt) *vb.* (*tr.*) **1.** to cause as an unavoidable result. **2.** (*usually passive*) to compel or require (someone to do something).

necessitous (nɪˈsɛsɪtəs) *adj.* very needy; destitute; poverty-stricken.

necessity (nɪˈsɛsɪtɪ) *n., pl.* **-ties. 1.** (*sometimes pl.*) something needed; prerequisite: *necessities of life.* **2.** a condition or set of circumstances that inevitably requires a certain result: *it is a matter of necessity to wear formal clothes when meeting the Queen.* **3.** the state or quality of being obligatory or unavoidable. **4.** urgent requirement, as in an emergency. **5.** poverty or want. **6.** *Rare.* compulsion through laws of nature; fate. **7.** *Logic.* the property of being necessary. **8. of necessity.** inevitably.

neck (nɛk) *n.* **1.** the part of an organism connecting the head with the body. **2.** the part of a garment around the neck. **3.** something resembling a neck in shape or position: *the neck of a bottle.* **4.** *Anat.* a constricted portion of an organ or part. **5.** a narrow strip of land; peninsula or isthmus. **6.** a strait or channel. **7.** the part of a violin, cello, etc., that extends from the body to the tuning pegs and supports the fingerboard. **8.** a solid block of lava from an extinct volcano, exposed after erosion of the surrounding rock. **9.** the length of a horse's head and neck taken as an approximate distance by which one horse beats another in a race: *to win by a neck.* **10.** *Archit.* the narrow band at the top of the shaft of a column. **11.** *Inf.* impudence or cheek. **12. get it in the neck.** *Inf.* to be reprimanded or punished severely. **13. neck and neck.** absolutely level in a race or competition. **14. neck of the woods.** *Inf.* a particular area: *what brings you to this neck of the woods?* **15. neck or nothing.** at any cost. **16. save one's** *or* **someone's neck.** *Inf.* to escape from or help someone else to escape from a difficult or dangerous situation. **17. stick one's neck out.** *Inf.* to risk criticism, ridicule, etc., by speaking one's mind. ~*vb.* **18.** (*intr.*) *Inf.* to kiss or fondle someone or one another passionately. [OE *hnecca*]

neckband (ˈnɛkˌbænd) *n.* a band around the neck of a garment as finishing, decoration, or a base for a collar.

neckcloth (ˈnɛkˌklɒθ) *n.* a large ornamental usually white cravat worn formerly by men.

neckerchief (ˈnɛkətʃɪf, -ˌtʃiːf) *n.* a piece of ornamental cloth, often square, worn round the neck. [C14: < NECK + KERCHIEF]

necking (ˈnɛkɪŋ) *n. Inf.* the activity of kissing and embracing lovingly.

necklace (ˈnɛklɪs) *n.* **1.** a chain, band, or cord, often bearing beads, pearls, jewels, etc., worn around the neck as an ornament, esp. by women. **2.** (in South Africa) **a.** a tyre soaked in petrol, placed round a person's neck, and set on fire in order to burn the person to death. **b.** (*as modifier*): *necklace victims.* ~*vb.* (*tr.*) **3.** (in South Africa) to kill a person by means of a necklace.

neckline (ˈnɛkˌlaɪn) *n.* the shape or position of the upper edge of a dress, blouse, etc.

necktie (ˈnɛkˌtaɪ) *n.* the U.S. name for **tie** (sense 10).

neckwear (ˈnɛkˌwɛə) *n.* articles of clothing, such as ties, scarves, etc., worn round the neck.

necro- *or before a vowel* **necr-** *combining form.* indicating death, a dead body, or dead tissue: *necrosis.* [< Gk *nekros* corpse]

necrobiosis (ˌnɛkrəʊbaɪˈəʊsɪs) *n. Physiol.* the normal degeneration and death of cells.

necrolatry (nɛˈkrɒlətrɪ) *n.* the worship of the dead.

necrology (nɛˈkrɒlədʒɪ) *n., pl.* **-gies. 1.** a list of people recently dead. **2.** a less common word for **obituary.** —**necrological** (ˌnɛkrəˈlɒdʒɪkᵊl) *adj.*

necromancy (ˈnɛkrəʊˌmænsɪ) *n.* **1.** the art of supposedly conjuring up the dead, esp. in order to obtain from them knowledge of the future. **2.** black magic; sorcery. [C13: (sense 1) ult. < Gk *nekromanteia,* < *nekros* corpse; (sense 2) < Med. L *nigromantia,* < L *niger* black, which replaced *necro-* through folk etymology] —**ˈnecroˌmancer** *n.* —**ˌnecroˈmantic** *adj.*

necrophilia (ˌnɛkrəʊˈfɪlɪə) *n.* sexual attraction for or sexual intercourse with dead bodies. Also called: **necromania, necrophilism.** —**necrophile** (ˈnɛkrəʊˌfaɪl) *n.* —**ˌnecroˈphilic** *adj.*

necropolis (nɛˈkrɒpəlɪs) *n., pl.* **-lises** *or* **-leis** (-ˌleɪs). a burial site or cemetery. [C19: < Gk, < *nekros* dead + *polis* city]

necropsy (ˈnɛkrɒpsɪ) *or* **necroscopy** (nɛˈkrɒskəpɪ) *n., pl.* **-sies** *or* **-pies.** another name for **autopsy.** [C19: < Gk *nekros* dead body + *opsis* sight]

necrosis (nɛˈkrəʊsɪs) *n.* **1.** the death of one or more cells in the body, usually within a localized area, as from an interruption of the blood supply. **2.** death of plant tissue due to disease, frost, etc. [C17: NL, < Gk *nekrōsis,* < *nekroun* to kill, < *nekros* corpse] —**necrotic** (nɛˈkrɒtɪk) *adj.*

nectar (ˈnɛktə) *n.* **1.** a sugary fluid produced in the nectaries of flowers and collected by bees. **2.** *Classical myth.* the drink of the gods. Cf. **ambrosia** (sense 1). **3.** any delicious drink. [C16: via L < Gk *néktar*] —**ˈnectarous** *adj.*

nectarine (ˈnɛktərɪn) *n.* **1.** a variety of peach tree. **2.** the fruit of this tree, which has a smooth skin. [C17: apparently < NECTAR]

nectary (ˈnɛktərɪ) *n., pl.* **-ries.** any of various structures secreting nectar that occur in the flowers, leaves, stipules, etc., of a plant. [C18: < NL *nectarium,* < NECTAR]

ned (nɛd) *n. Sl.* a hooligan. [<?]

NEDC *abbrev. for* National Economic Development Council. Also (inf.): **Neddy** (ˈnɛdɪ).

neddy (ˈnɛdɪ) *n., pl.* **-dies.** a child's word for a **donkey.** [C18: < *Ned,* pet form of *Edward*]

née *or* **nee** (neɪ) *adj.* indicating the maiden name of a married woman: *Mrs Bloggs née Blandish.* [C19: < F: p.p. (fem.) of *naître* to be born, < L *nasci*]

need (niːd) *vb.* **1.** (*tr.*) to be in want of: *to need money.* **2.** (*tr.*) to be obliged: *to need to do more work.* **3.** (takes an infinitive without *to*) used as an auxiliary to express necessity or obligation and does not add *-s* when used with *he, she, it,* and singular nouns: *need he go?* **4.** (*intr.*) *Arch.* to be essential to: *there needs no reason for this.* ~*n.* **5.** the fact or an instance of feeling the lack of something: *he has need of a new coat.* **6.** a requirement: *the need for vengeance.* **7.** necessity or obligation: *no need to be frightened.* **8.** distress: *a friend in need.* **9.** poverty or destitution. ~See also **needs.** [OE *nēad, nied*]

needful (ˈniːdfʊl) *adj.* **1.** necessary; required. **2.** *Arch.* poverty-stricken. ~*n.* **3. the needful.** *Inf.* what is necessary, esp. money. —ˈ**needfulness** *n.*

needle (ˈniːdᵊl) *n.* **1.** a pointed slender piece of metal with a hole in it through which thread is passed for sewing. **2.** a somewhat larger rod with a point at one end, used in knitting. **3.** a similar instrument with a hook at one end for crocheting. **4. a.** another name for **stylus** (sense 3). **b.** a small thin pointed device used to transmit the vibrations from a gramophone record to the pick-up. **5.** *Med.* the long hollow pointed part of a hypodermic syringe, which is inserted into the body. **6.** *Surgery.* a pointed instrument, often curved, for suturing, puncturing, or ligating. **7.** a long narrow stiff leaf in which water loss is greatly reduced: *pine needles.* **8.** any slender sharp spine. **9.** a pointer on the scale of a measuring instrument. **10.** short for **magnetic needle. 11.** a sharp pointed instrument used in engraving. **12.** anything long and pointed, such as an obelisk. **13.** *Inf.* **a.** anger or intense rivalry, esp. in a sporting encounter. **b.** (*as modifier*): *a needle match.* **14. have** *or* **get the needle.** *Brit. inf.* to feel dislike, nervousness, or annoyance: *she got the needle after he had refused her invitation.* ~*vb.* (*tr.*) **15.** *Inf.* to goad or provoke, as by constant criticism. **16.** to sew, embroider, or prick (fabric) with a needle. [OE *nǣdl*]

needlecord (ˈniːdᵊlˌkɔːd) *n.* a corduroy fabric with narrow ribs.

needlepoint (ˈniːdᵊlˌpɔɪnt) *n.* **1.** embroidery done on canvas with various stitches so as to resemble tapestry. **2.** another name for **point lace.**

needless (ˈniːdlɪs) *adj.* not required; unnecessary. —ˈ**needlessly** *adv.* —ˈ**needlessness** *n.*

needle time *n.* the limited time allocated by a radio channel to the broadcasting of music from records.

needlewoman (ˈniːdᵊlˌwʊmən) *n., pl.* **-women.** a woman who does needlework; seamstress.

needlework (ˈniːdᵊlˌwɜːk) *n.* sewing and embroidery.

needs (niːdz) *adv.* **1.** (preceded or foll. by *must*) of necessity: *we must needs go.* ~*pl. n.* **2.** what is required; necessities: *his needs are modest.*

needy (ˈniːdɪ) *adj.* **needier, neediest. a.** in need of practical or emotional support; distressed. **b.** (*as collective n.;* preceded by *the*): *the needy.*

ne'er (nɛə) *adv.* a poetic contraction of **never.**

ne'er-do-well *n.* **1.** an improvident, irresponsible, or lazy person. ~*adj.* **2.** useless; worthless: *your ne'er-do-well schemes.*

nefarious (nɪˈfɛərɪəs) *adj.* evil; wicked; sinful. [C17: < L *nefārius,* < *nefās* unlawful deed, < *nē* not + *fās* divine law] —**neˈfariously** *adv.* —**neˈfariousness** *n.*

neg. *abbrev. for* negative(ly).

negate (nɪˈgeɪt) *vb.* (*tr.*) **1.** to nullify; invalidate. **2.** to contradict. [C17: < L *negāre,* < *neg-,* var. of *nec* not + *aio* I say] —**neˈgator** *or* **neˈgater** *n.*

negation (nɪˈgeɪʃən) *n.* **1.** the opposite or absence of something. **2.** a negative thing or condition. **3.** the act of negating. **4.** *Logic.* a proposition that is the denial of another proposition and is true only if the original proposition is false.

negative (ˈnɛgətɪv) *adj.* **1.** expressing a refusal or denial: *a negative answer.* **2.** lacking positive qualities, such as enthusiasm or optimism. **3.** showing opposition or resistance. **4.** measured in a direction opposite to that regarded as positive. **5.** *Biol.* indicating movement or growth away from a stimulus: *negative geotropism.* **6.** *Med.* indicating absence of the disease or condition for which a test was made. **7.** another word for **minus** (senses 3b, 4). **8.** *Physics.* **a.** (of an electric charge) having the same polarity as the charge of an electron. **b.** (of a body, system, ion, etc.) having a negative electric charge; having an excess of electrons. **9.** short for **electronegative. 10.** of or relating to a photographic negative. **11.** *Logic.* (of a categorial proposition) denying the satisfaction by the subject of the predicate, as in *some men are irrational; no pigs have wings.* ~*n.* **12.** a statement or act of denial or refusal. **13.** a negative thing. **14.** *Photog.* a piece of photographic film or a plate, previously exposed and developed, showing an image that, in black-and-white photography, has a reversal of tones. **15.** *Physics.* a negative object, such as a terminal or a plate in a voltaic cell. **16.** a sentence or other linguistic element with a negative meaning, as the English word *not.* **17.** a quantity less than zero. **18.** *Logic.* a negative proposition. **19. in the negative.** indicating denial or refusal. ~*vb.* (*tr.*) **20.** to deny; negate. **21.** to show to be false; disprove. **22.** to refuse consent to or approval of: *the proposal was negatived.* —ˈ**negatively** *adv.* —ˈ**negativeness** *or* ˌ**negaˈtivity** *n.*

negative feedback *n.* See **feedback.**

negative resistance *n.* a characteristic of certain electronic components in which an increase in the applied voltage increases the resistance, producing a proportional decrease in current.

negative sign *n.* the symbol (-) used to indicate a negative quantity or a subtraction.

negativism (ˈnɛgətɪvˌɪzəm) *n.* **1.** a tendency to be unconstructively critical. **2.** any sceptical or derisive system of thought. —ˈ**negativist** *n., adj.*

neglect (nɪˈglɛkt) *vb.* (*tr.*) **1.** to fail to give due care, attention, or time to: *to neglect a child.* **2.** to fail (to do something) through carelessness: *he neglected to tell her.* **3.** to disregard. ~*n.* **4.** lack of due care or attention; negligence: *the child starved through neglect.* **5.** the act or an instance of neglecting or the state of being neglected. [C16: < L *neglegere,* < *nec* not + *legere* to select]

neglectful (nɪˈglɛktfʊl) *adj.* (when *postpositive,* foll. by *of*) careless; heedless.

negligee, negligée, *or* **negligé** (ˈnɛglɪˌʒeɪ) *n.* **1.** a woman's light dressing gown, esp. one that is lace-trimmed. **2.** any informal attire. [C18: < F *négligée,* p.p. (fem.) of *négliger* to NEGLECT]

negligence (ˈnɛglɪdʒəns) *n.* **1.** the state of being negligent. **2.** a negligent act. **3.** *Law.* a civil wrong whereby the defendant is in breach of a legal duty of care, resulting in injury to the plaintiff.

negligent (ˈnɛglɪdʒənt) *adj.* **1.** lacking attention, care, or concern; neglectful. **2.** careless or nonchalant. —ˈ**negligently** *adv.*

negligible (ˈnɛglɪdʒəbᵊl) *adj.* so small, unimportant, etc., as to be not worth considering. —ˈ**negligibly** *adv.*

negotiable (nɪˈgəʊʃəbᵊl) *adj.* **1.** able to be negotiated. **2.** (of a bill of exchange, promissory note, etc.) legally transferable in title from one party to another. —**neˌgotiaˈbility** *n.*

negotiate (nɪˈgəʊʃɪˌeɪt) *vb.* **1.** to talk (with

others) to achieve (an agreement, etc.). **2.** (*tr.*) to succeed in passing round or over. **3.** (*tr.*) *Finance.* **a.** to transfer (a negotiable commercial paper) to another in return for value received. **b.** to sell (financial assets). **c.** to arrange for (a loan). [C16: < L *negōtiārī* to do business, < *negōtium* business, < *nec* not + *ōtium* leisure] —**neˌgotiˈation** *n.* —**neˈgotiˌator** *n.*

Negress (ˈniːgrɪs) *n.* a female Negro.

Negrillo (nɪˈgrɪləʊ) *n., pl.* **-los** *or* **-loes.** a member of a dwarfish Negro race of central and southern Africa. [C19: < Sp., dim. of *negro* black]

Negrito (nɪˈgriːtəʊ) *n., pl.* **-tos** *or* **-toes.** a member of any of various dwarfish Negroid peoples of SE Asia and Melanesia. [C19: < Sp., dim. of *negro* black]

negritude (ˈniːgrɪˌtjuːd, ˈnɛg-) *n.* **1.** the fact of being a Negro. **2.** awareness and cultivation of the Negro heritage, values, and culture. [C20: < F, < *nègre* NEGRO]

Negro (ˈniːgrəʊ) *n., pl.* **-groes.** **1.** a member of any of the dark-skinned indigenous peoples of Africa and their descendants elsewhere. ~*adj.* **2.** relating to or characteristic of Negroes. [C16: < Sp. or Port.: black, < L *niger*] —**ˈNegroˌism** *n.*

Negroid (ˈniːgrɔɪd) *adj.* **1.** denoting, relating to, or belonging to one of the major racial groups of mankind, characterized by brown-black skin, crisp or woolly hair, a broad flat nose, and full lips. ~*n.* **2.** a member of this racial group.

negus (ˈniːgəs) *n., pl.* **-guses.** a hot drink of port and lemon juice, usually spiced and sweetened. [C18: after Col. Francis *Negus* (died 1732), its E inventor]

Negus (ˈniːgəs) *n., pl.* **-guses.** a title of the emperor of Ethiopia. [< Amharic: king]

Neh. *Bible. abbrev. for* Nehemiah.

neigh (neɪ) *n.* **1.** the high-pitched cry of a horse. ~*vb.* **2.** to make a neigh or utter with a sound like a neigh. [OE *hnǣgan*]

neighbour *or U.S.* **neighbor** (ˈneɪbə) *n.* **1.** a person who lives near or next to another. **2. a.** a person or thing near or next to another. **b.** (*as modifier*): *neighbour states.* ~*vb.* **3.** (when *intr.*, often foll. by *on*) to be or live close to. [OE *nēahbūr*, < *nēah* NIGH + *būr, gebūr* dweller; see BOOR] —**ˈneighbouring** *or U.S.* **ˈneighboring** *adj.*

neighbourhood *or U.S.* **neighborhood** (ˈneɪbəˌhʊd) *n.* **1.** the immediate environment; surroundings. **2.** a district where people live. **3.** the people in a particular area. **4.** *Maths.* the set of all points whose distance from a given point is less than a specified value. **5.** (*modifier*) living or situated in and serving the needs of a local area: *a neighbourhood community worker.* **6. in the neighbourhood of.** approximately.

neighbourhood watch *n.* a scheme under which members of a community agree together to take responsibility for keeping an eye on each other's property, as a way of preventing crime.

neighbourly *or U.S.* **neighborly** (ˈneɪbəlɪ) *adj.* kind, friendly, or sociable, as befits a neighbour. —**ˈneighbourliness** *or U.S.* **ˈneighborliness** *n.*

neither (ˈnaɪðə, ˈniːðə) *determiner.* **1. a.** not one nor the other (of two). **b.** (*as pronoun*): *neither can win.* ~*conj.* **2.** (*coordinating*) **a.** (used preceding alternatives joined by *nor*) not: *neither John nor Mary nor Joe went.* **b.** another word for **nor** (sense 2). ~*adv.* (*sentence modifier*) **3.** *Not standard.* another word for **either** (sense 4). [C13 (lit.: *ne either* not either): changed < OE *nāwther*, < *nāhwæther*, < *nā* not + *hwæther* which of two]

▷ **Usage.** A verb following a compound subject that uses *neither...(nor)* should be in the singular if both subjects are in the singular: *neither Jack nor John has done the work.* Where the subjects are different in number, the verb usually agrees with the subject nearest to it: *neither they nor Jack was able to come.* It may be considered preferable to rephrase the sentence in order to avoid this construction.

nekton (ˈnɛktɒn) *n.* the population of free-swimming animals that inhabits the middle depths of a sea or lake. [C19: via G < Gk *nēkton* a swimming thing, < *nēkhein* to swim]

nelly (ˈnɛlɪ) *n.* **not on your nelly.** (*sentence substitute*). *Brit. sl.* certainly not.

nelson (ˈnɛlsən) *n.* any wrestling hold in which a wrestler places his arm or arms under his opponent's arm or arms from behind and exerts pressure with his palms on the back of his opponent's neck. [C19: < a proper name]

nematic (nɪˈmætɪk) *adj. Chem.* (of a substance) existing in or having a mesomorphic state in which a linear orientation of the molecules causes anisotropic properties. [C20: NEMAT(O)- (referring to the threadlike chains of molecules in liquid) + -IC]

nemato- *or before a vowel* **nemat-** *combining form.* indicating a threadlike form: *nematocyst.* [< Gk *nēma* thread]

nematocyst (ˈnɛmətəˌsɪst, nɪˈmætə-) *n.* a structure in coelenterates, such as jellyfish, consisting of a capsule containing a hollow coiled thread that can sting or paralyse.

nematode (ˈnɛməˌtəʊd) *n.* any of a class of unsegmented worms having a tough outer cuticle, including the hookworm and filaria. Also called: **nematode worm, roundworm.**

Nembutal (ˈnɛmbjʊˌtɑːl) *n.* a trademark for **pentobarbitone sodium.**

nemertean (nɪˈmɜːtɪən) *or* **nemertine** (ˈnɛməˌtaɪn) *n.* **1.** any of a class of soft flattened ribbon-like marine worms having an eversible threadlike proboscis. ~*adj.* **2.** of or belonging to the *Nemertea.* [C19: via NL < Gk *Nēmertēs* a NEREID]

nemesia (nɪˈmiːʒə) *n.* any plant of a southern African genus cultivated for their brightly coloured flowers. [C19: NL, < Gk *nemesion*, name of a plant resembling this]

Nemesis (ˈnɛmɪsɪs) *n., pl.* **-ses** (-ˌsiːz). **1.** *Greek myth.* the goddess of retribution and vengeance. **2.** (*sometimes not cap.*) any agency of retribution and vengeance. [C16: via L < Gk: righteous wrath, < *némein* to distribute what is due]

nemophila (nɛˈmɒfɪlə) *n.* an annual trailing plant with blue flowers. [< Gk *nemos* grove + *philos* loving]

neo- *or sometimes before a vowel* **ne-** *combining form.* **1.** (*sometimes cap.*) new, recent, or a modern form: *neoclassicism.* **2.** (*usually cap.*) the most recent subdivision of a geological period: *Neogene.* [< Gk *neos* new]

neoclassicism (ˌniːəʊˈklæsɪˌsɪzəm) *n.* **1.** a late 18th- and early 19th-century style in architecture and art, based on classical models. **2.** *Music.* a movement of the 1920s that sought to avoid the emotionalism of late romantic music. —**neoclassical** (ˌniːəʊˈklæsɪkᵊl) *or* **ˌneoˈclassic** *adj.*

neocolonialism (ˌniːəʊkəˈləʊnɪəˌlɪzəm) *n.* political control by an outside power of a country that is in theory independent, esp. through the domination of its economy. —**ˌneocoˈlonialist** *n., adj.*

Neo-Darwinism (ˌniːəʊˈdɑːwɪnˌɪzəm) *n.* a modern theory of evolution that relates Darwinism to the occurrence of inheritable variation by genetic mutation.

neodymium (ˌniːəʊˈdɪmɪəm) *n.* a toxic silvery-white metallic element of the lanthanide series. Symbol: Nd; atomic no.: 60; atomic wt.: 144.24. [C19: NL; see NEO- + DIDYMIUM]

Neolithic (ˌniːəˈlɪθɪk) *n.* **1.** the cultural period that was characterized by primitive farming and the use of polished stone and flint tools and weapons. ~*adj.* **2.** relating to this period.

neologism (nɪˈɒləˌdʒɪzəm) *or* **neology** *n., pl.* **-gisms** *or* **-gies.** **1.** a newly coined word, or a phrase or familiar word used in a new sense. **2.** the practice of using or introducing neologisms. [C18: via F < NEO- + *-logism*, < Gk *logos* word] —**neˈologist** *n.*

neologize *or* **-gise** (nɪˈɒləˌdʒaɪz) *vb.* (*intr.*) to invent or use neologisms.

neomycin (ˌniːəʊˈmaɪsɪn) *n.* an antibiotic obtained from the bacterium *Streptomyces fradiae*, administered in the treatment of skin and eye infections. [C20: < NEO- + Gk *mukēs* fungus + -IN]

neon (ˈniːɒn) *n.* 1. a colourless odourless rare gaseous element occurring in trace amounts in the atmosphere: used in illuminated signs and lights. Symbol: Ne; atomic no.: 10; atomic wt.: 20.179. 2. (*modifier*) of or illuminated by neon: *neon sign.* [C19: via NL < Gk *neon* new]

neonatal (ˌniːəʊˈneɪtᵊl) *adj.* occurring in or relating to the first few weeks of life in human babies. —ˈ**neoˌnate** *n.*

neon lamp *n.* a glass bulb or tube containing neon at low pressure that gives a pink or red glow when a voltage is applied.

neophyte (ˈniːəʊˌfaɪt) *n.* 1. a person newly converted to a religious faith. 2. a novice in a religious order. 3. a beginner. [C16: via Church L < New Testament Gk *neophutos* recently planted, < *néos* new + *phuton* a plant]

neoplasm (ˈniːəʊˌplæzəm) *n. Pathol.* any abnormal new growth of tissue; tumour.

Neo-Platonism (ˌniːəʊˈpleɪtəˌnɪzəm) *n.* a philosophical system which was developed in the 3rd century A.D. as a synthesis of Platonic, Pythagorean, and Aristotelian elements. —ˌ**Neo-**ˈ**Platonist** *n.*

neoprene (ˈniːəʊˌpriːn) *n.* a synthetic rubber obtained by the polymerization of chloroprene, a colourless liquid derivative of butadiene, resistant to oil and ageing and used in waterproof products. [C20: < NEO- + PR(OPYL) + -ENE]

neoteny (nɪˈɒtənɪ) *n.* the persistence of larval features in the adult form of an animal. [C19: < NL *neotenia,* < Gk NEO- + *teinein* to stretch]

neoteric (ˌniːəʊˈtɛrɪk) *Rare.* ~*adj.* 1. belonging to a new fashion or trend; modern. ~*n.* 2. a new writer or philosopher. [C16: via LL < Gk *neōterikos* young, fresh, < *neoteros* younger, more recent, < *neos* new, recent]

Nepali (nɪˈpɔːlɪ) *or* **Nepalese** (ˌnɛpəˈliːz) *n.* 1. the official language of Nepal, also spoken in parts of India. 2. (*pl.* **-pali, -palis,** *or* **-palese**) a native or inhabitant of Nepal. ~*adj.* 3. of or relating to Nepal, its inhabitants, or their language.

nepenthe (nɪˈpɛnθɪ) *or* **nepenthes** (nɪˈpɛnθiːz) *n.* a drug that ancient writers referred to as a means of forgetting grief or trouble. [C16: via L < Gk *nēpenthes* sedative made from a herb, < *nē-* not + *penthos* grief]

nepeta (ˈnɛpɛtə, nəˈpɛtə) *n.* any of a genus of plants found in N temperate regions. It includes catmint. [< L]

nephew (ˈnɛvjuː, ˈnɛf-) *n.* a son of one's sister or brother. [C13: < OF *neveu,* < L *nepōs*]

nephology (nɪˈfɒlədʒɪ) *n.* the study of clouds. [C19: < Gk *nephos* cloud + -LOGY]

nephridium (nɪˈfrɪdɪəm) *n., pl.* **-ia** (-ɪə). a simple excretory organ of many invertebrates, consisting of a tube through which waste products pass to the exterior. [C19: NL: little kidney]

nephrite (ˈnɛfraɪt) *n.* a tough fibrous mineral: a variety of jade. [C18: via G < Gk *nephros* kidney; it was thought to be beneficial in kidney disorders]

nephritic (nɪˈfrɪtɪk) *adj.* 1. of or relating to the kidneys. 2. relating to or affected with nephritis.

nephritis (nɪˈfraɪtɪs) *n.* inflammation of a kidney.

nephro- *or before a vowel* **nephr-** *combining form.* kidney or kidneys: *nephritis.* [< Gk *nephros*]

ne plus ultra *Latin.* (ˈneɪ ˈplʊs ˈʊltrɑː) *n.* the extreme or perfect point or state. [lit.: not more beyond (that is, go no further), allegedly a warning to sailors inscribed on the Pillars of Hercules at Gibraltar]

nepotism (ˈnɛpəˌtɪzəm) *n.* favouritism shown to relatives or close friends by those with power. [C17: < It. *nepotismo,* < *nepote* NEPHEW, from the former papal practice of granting favours to nephews or other relatives] —ˈ**nepotist** *n.*

Neptune[1] (ˈnɛptjuːn) *n.* the Roman god of the sea. Greek counterpart: **Poseidon.**

Neptune[2] (ˈnɛptjuːn) *n.* the eighth planet from the sun, having two satellites, Triton and Nereid.

neptunium (nɛpˈtjuːnɪəm) *n.* a silvery metallic element synthesized in the production of plutonium and occurring in trace amounts in uranium ores. Symbol: Np; atomic no.: 93; half-life of most stable isotope, ^{237}Np: 2.14 × 10^6 years. [C20: < NEPTUNE[2], the planet beyond Uranus, because neptunium is the element beyond uranium in the periodic table]

NERC *abbrev. for* Natural Environment Research Council.

Nereid (ˈnɪərɪɪd) *n., pl.* **Nereides** (nəˈriːədiːz). *Greek myth.* any of 50 sea nymphs who were the daughters of the sea god Nereus. [C17: via L < Gk]

nerine (nɪːˈraɪniː) *n.* any of a genus of bulbous plants native to South Africa and grown elsewhere as greenhouse plants for their pink, red, or orange flowers: includes the Guernsey lily. [after the water nymph *Nerine* in Roman myth]

neroli oil *or* **neroli** (ˈnɪərəlɪ) *n.* a brown oil distilled from the flowers of various orange trees: used in perfumery. [C17: after Anne Marie de la Tremoïlle of *Neroli,* French-born It. princess believed to have discovered it]

nervate (ˈnɜːveɪt) *adj.* (of leaves) having veins.

nervation (nɜːˈveɪʃən) *or* **nervature** (ˈnɜːvətʃə) *n.* a less common word for **venation.**

nerve (nɜːv) *n.* 1. any of the cordlike bundles of fibres that conduct impulses between the brain or spinal cord and another part of the body. 2. bravery or steadfastness. 3. **lose one's nerve.** to become timid, esp. failing to perform some audacious act. 4. *Inf.* effrontery; impudence. 5. muscle or sinew (often in **strain every nerve**). 6. a vein in a leaf or an insect's wing. ~*vb.* (*tr.*) 7. to give courage to (oneself); steel (oneself). 8. to provide with nerve or nerves. ~See also **nerves.** [C16: < L *nervus;* rel. to Gk *neuron*]

nerve cell *n.* another name for **neuron.**

nerve centre *n.* 1. a group of nerve cells associated with a specific function. 2. a principal source of control over any complex activity.

nerve fibre *n.* a threadlike extension of a nerve cell; axon.

nerve gas *n.* any of various poisonous gases that have a paralysing effect on the central nervous system that can be fatal.

nerve impulse *n.* the electrical wave transmitted along a nerve fibre, usually following stimulation of the nerve-cell body.

nerveless (ˈnɜːvlɪs) *adj.* 1. calm and collected. 2. listless or feeble. —ˈ**nervelessly** *adv.*

nerve-racking *or* **nerve-wracking** *adj.* very distressing, exhausting, or harrowing.

nerves (nɜːvz) *pl. n. Inf.* 1. the imagined source of emotional control: *my nerves won't stand it.* 2. anxiety, tension, or imbalance: *she's all nerves.* 3. **get on one's nerves.** to irritate or upset one.

nervine (ˈnɜːviːn) *adj.* 1. having a soothing effect upon the nerves. ~*n.* 2. a nervine agent. [C17: < NL *nervīnus,* < L *nervus* NERVE]

nervous (ˈnɜːvəs) *adj.* 1. very excitable or sensitive; highly strung. 2. (often foll. by *of*) apprehensive or worried. 3. of or containing nerves: *nervous tissue.* 4. affecting the nerves or nervous tissue: *a nervous disease.* 5. *Arch.* vigorous or forceful. —ˈ**nervously** *adv.* —ˈ**nervousness** *n.*

nervous breakdown *n.* any mental illness not primarily of organic origin, in which the patient ceases to function properly, often accompanied by severely impaired concentration, anxiety, insomnia, and lack of self-esteem.

nervous system *n.* the sensory and control apparatus of animals, consisting of a network of nerve cells (see **neuron**).

nervure (ˈnɜːvjʊə) *n.* 1. *Entomol.* any of the chitinous rods that form the framework of an insect's wing; vein. 2. *Bot.* any of the veins of a leaf. [C19: < F; see NERVE, -URE]

nervy (ˈnɜːvɪ) *adj.* **nervier, nerviest.** 1. *Brit. inf.* tense or apprehensive. 2. having or needing bravery or endurance. 3. *U.S. & Canad. inf.* brash or cheeky. 4. *Arch.* muscular; sinewy.

nescience (ˈnɛsɪəns) *n.* a formal or literary word for **ignorance.** [C17: < LL *nescientia,* < L *nescīre* to be ignorant of, < *ne* not + *scīre* to know] —ˈ**nescient** *adj.*

ness (nɛs) *n. Arch.* a promontory or headland. [OE *næs* headland]

-ness *suffix forming nouns chiefly from adjectives and participles.* indicating state, condition, or quality: *greatness; selfishness.* [OE *-nes,* of Gmc origin]

nest (nɛst) *n.* **1.** a place or structure in which birds, fishes, etc., lay eggs or give birth to young. **2.** a number of animals of the same species occupying a common habitat: *an ants' nest.* **3.** a place fostering something undesirable: *a nest of thievery.* **4.** a cosy or secluded place. **5.** a set of things, usually of graduated sizes, designed to fit together: *a nest of tables.* ~*vb.* **6.** (*intr.*) to make or inhabit a nest. **7.** (*intr.*) to hunt for birds' nests. **8.** (*tr.*) to place in a nest. **9.** *Computers.* to position data within other data at different ranks or levels so that the different levels of data can be used or accessed recursively. [OE]

nest egg *n.* **1.** a fund of money kept in reserve; savings. **2.** a natural or artificial egg left in a nest to induce hens to lay their eggs in it.

nestle (ˈnɛsᵊl) *vb.* **1.** (*intr.; often foll. by up or down*) to snuggle, settle, or cuddle closely. **2.** (*intr.*) to be in a sheltered position; lie snugly. **3.** (*tr.*) to shelter or place snugly or partly concealed, as in a nest. [OE *nestlian*]

nestling (ˈnɛstlɪŋ, ˈnɛslɪŋ) *n.* **a.** a young bird not yet fledged. **b.** (*as modifier*): *a nestling thrush.* [C14: < NEST + -LING[1]]

net[1] (nɛt) *n.* **1.** an openwork fabric of string, wire, etc.; mesh. **2.** a device made of net, used to protect or enclose things or to trap animals. **3.** a thin light mesh fabric used for curtains, etc. **4.** a plan, strategy, etc., intended to trap or ensnare: *the murderer slipped through the police net.* **5.** *Tennis, badminton, etc.* **a.** a strip of net that divides the playing area into two equal parts. **b.** a shot that hits the net. **6.** the goal in soccer, hockey, etc. **7.** (*often pl.*) *Cricket.* **a.** a pitch surrounded by netting, used for practice. **b.** a practice session in a net. **8.** another word for **network** (sense 2). ~*vb.* **netting, netted.** **9.** (*tr.*) to ensnare. **10.** (*tr.*) to shelter or surround with a net. **11.** (*intr.*) *Tennis, badminton, etc.* to hit a shot into the net. **12.** to make a net out of (rope, string, etc.). [OE *net;* rel. to Gothic *nati,* Du. *net*]

net[2] *or* **nett** (nɛt) *adj.* **1.** remaining after all deductions, as for taxes, expenses, losses, etc.: *net profit.* Cf. **gross** (sense 2). **2.** (of weight) after deducting tare. **3.** final; conclusive (esp. in **net result**). ~*n.* **4.** net income, profits, weight, etc. ~*vb.* **netting, netted.** **5.** (*tr.*) to yield or earn as clear profit. [C14: clean, neat, < F *net* NEAT[1]]

netball (ˈnɛtˌbɔːl) *n.* a game for two teams of seven players (usually women) played on a hard court. Points are scored by shooting the ball through a net hanging from a ring at the top of a pole.

net domestic product *n. Econ.* the gross domestic product minus an allowance for the depreciation of capital goods.

nether (ˈnɛðə) *adj.* below, beneath, or underground: *nether regions.* [OE *niothera, nithera,* lit.: further down, < *nither* down]

nethermost (ˈnɛðəˌməʊst) *adj.* **the.** farthest down; lowest.

nether world *n.* **1.** the underworld. **2.** hell. ~Also called: **nether regions.**

net national product *n.* gross national product minus an allowance for the depreciation of capital goods.

net profit *n.* gross profit minus all operating costs not included in the calculation of gross profit, esp. wages, overheads, and depreciation.

net statutory income *n.* (in Britain) the total taxable income of a person for the tax assessment year, after the deduction of personal allowances.

netsuke (ˈnɛtsʊkɪ) *n.* (in Japan) a carved toggle, esp. of wood or ivory, originally used to tether a medicine box, purse, etc., worn dangling from the waist. [C19: < Japanese]

nett (nɛt) *adj., n., vb.* a variant spelling of **net**[2].

netting (ˈnɛtɪŋ) *n.* any netted fabric or structure.

nettle (ˈnɛtᵊl) *n.* **1.** a plant having serrated leaves with stinging hairs and greenish flowers. **2.** any of various other plants with stinging hairs or spines. **3.** any of various plants that resemble nettles, such as the dead-nettle. **4. grasp the nettle.** to attempt something with boldness and courage. ~*vb.* (*tr.*) **5.** to bother; irritate. **6.** to sting as a nettle does. [OE *netele*]

nettle rash *n.* a nontechnical name for **urticaria.**

network (ˈnɛtˌwɜːk) *n.* **1.** an interconnected group or system: *a network of shops.* **2.** a system of intersecting lines, roads, veins, etc. **3.** another name for **net**[1] (sense 1) or **netting.** **4.** *Radio & TV.* a group of broadcasting stations that all transmit the same programme simultaneously. **5.** *Electronics, computers.* a system of interconnected components or circuits. ~*vb.* **6.** *Radio & TV.* to broadcast over a network. **7.** (of computers, terminals, etc.) to connect or be connected. **8.** (*intr.*) to form business contacts through informal social meetings.

neume *or* **neum** (njuːm) *n. Music.* one of a series of notational symbols used before the 14th century. [C15: < Med. L *neuma* group of notes sung on one breath, < Gk *pneuma* breath]

neural (ˈnjʊərəl) *adj.* of or relating to a nerve or the nervous system. —ˈ**neurally** *adv.*

neuralgia (njʊˈrældʒə) *n.* severe spasmodic pain along the course of one or more nerves. —**neuˈralgic** *adj.*

neurasthenia (ˌnjʊərəsˈθiːnɪə) *n.* (no longer in technical use) a neurosis characterized by extreme lassitude and inability to cope with any but the most trivial tasks.

neuritis (njʊˈraɪtɪs) *n.* inflammation of a nerve or nerves, often accompanied by pain and loss of function in the affected part. —**neuritic** (njʊˈrɪtɪk) *adj.*

neuro- *or before a vowel* **neur-** *combining form.* indicating a nerve or the nervous system: *neurology.* [< Gk *neuron* nerve; rel. to L *nervus*]

neuroglia (njʊˈrɒglɪə) *n.* the delicate web of connective tissue that surrounds and supports nerve cells. [C19: < NEURO- + LGk *glia* glue]

neurolemma (ˌnjʊərəʊˈlɛmə) *n.* the thin membrane that forms a sheath around nerve fibres. [C19: NL, < NEURO- + Gk *eilēma* covering]

neurology (njʊˈrɒlədʒɪ) *n.* the study of the anatomy, physiology, and diseases of the nervous system. —**neurological** (ˌnʊərəˈlɒdʒɪkᵊl) *adj.*

neuromuscular (ˌnjʊərəʊˈmʌskjʊlə) *adj.* of, relating to, or affecting nerves and muscles.

neuron (ˈnjʊərɒn) *or* **neurone** (ˈnjʊərəʊn) *n.* a cell specialized to conduct nerve impulses: consists of a cell body, axon, and dendrites. Also called: **nerve cell.** —**neuronic** (njʊˈrɒnɪk) *adj.*

neuropathology (ˌnjʊərəʊpəˈθɒlədʒɪ) *n.* the study of diseases of the nervous system.

neuropathy (njʊˈrɒpəθɪ) *n.* any disease of the nervous system. —**neuropathic** (ˌnjʊərəʊˈpæθɪk) *adj.* —ˌ**neuroˈpathically** *adv.*

neurophysiology (ˌnjʊərəʊˌfɪzɪˈɒlədʒɪ) *n.* the study of the functions of the nervous system. —**neurophysiological** (ˌnjʊərəʊˌfɪzɪəˈlɒdʒɪkᵊl) *adj.*

neuropterous (njʊˈrɒptərəs) *or* **neuropteran** *adj.* of or belonging to an order of insects having two pairs of large much-veined wings and biting mouthparts. [C18: < NL *Neuroptera,* < NEURO- + Gk *pteron* wing]

neurosis (njʊˈrəʊsɪs) *n., pl.* **-ses** (-siːz). a relatively mild mental disorder, characterized by hysteria, anxiety, depression, or obsessive behaviour.

neurosurgery (ˌnjʊərəʊˈsɜːdʒərɪ) *n.* the branch of surgery concerned with the nervous system. —ˌ**neuroˈsurgical** *adj.*

neurotic (njʊˈrɒtɪk) *adj.* **1.** of or afflicted by neurosis. ~*n.* **2.** a person who is afflicted with a neurosis or who tends to be emotionally unstable. —**neuˈrotically** *adv.* —**neuˈrotiˌcism** *n.*

neurotomy (njʊˈrɒtəmɪ) *n., pl.* **-mies.** the surgical cutting of a nerve.

neurotransmitter (ˌnjʊərəʊtrænzˈmɪtə) *n.* a chemical by which a nerve cell communicates with another nerve cell or with a muscle.

neurovascular (ˌnuərəʊˈvæskjʊlə) *adj.* of or affecting both the nerves and the blood vessels.

neuter (ˈnjuːtə) *adj.* **1.** *Grammar.* **a.** denoting or belonging to a gender of nouns which do not specify the sex of their referents. **b.** (*as n.*): *German "Mädchen" (meaning "girl") is a neuter.* **2.** (of animals and plants) having nonfunctional, underdeveloped, or absent reproductive organs. **3.** giving no indication of sex. *~n.* **4.** a sexually underdeveloped female insect, such as a worker bee. **5.** a castrated animal. *~vb.* **6.** (*tr.*) to castrate (an animal). [C14: < L, < *ne* not + *uter* either (of two)]

neutral (ˈnjuːtrəl) *adj.* **1.** not siding with any party to a war or dispute. **2.** of or belonging to a neutral party, country, etc. **3.** of no distinctive quality or type. **4.** (of a colour) **a.** having no hue; achromatic. **b.** dull, but harmonizing with most other colours. **5.** a less common term for **neuter** (sense 2). **6.** *Chem.* neither acidic nor alkaline. **7.** *Physics.* having zero charge or potential. **8.** *Phonetics.* (of a vowel) articulated with the tongue relaxed in mid-central position: *"about" begins with a neutral vowel.* *~n.* **9.** a neutral person, nation, etc. **10.** a citizen of a neutral state. **11.** the position of the controls of a gearbox that leaves the transmission disengaged. [C16: < L *neutrālis*; see NEUTER] —ˈ**neutrally** *adv.*

neutralism (ˈnjuːtrəˌlɪzəm) *n.* (in international affairs) the policy of noninvolvement or nonalignment with power blocs. —ˈ**neutralist** *n.*

neutrality (njuːˈtrælɪtɪ) *n.* **1.** the state of being neutral. **2.** the condition of being chemically or electrically neutral.

neutralize *or* **-ise** (ˈnjuːtrəˌlaɪz) *vb.* (*mainly tr.*) **1.** (*also intr.*) to render or become neutral by counteracting, mixing, etc. **2.** (*also intr.*) to make or become electrically or chemically neutral. **3.** to exclude (a country) from warfare or alliances by international agreement: *the great powers neutralized Belgium in the 19th century.* —ˌ**neutraliˈzation** *or* **-iˈsation** *n.* —ˈ**neutralˌizer** *or* **-ˌiser** *n.*

neutretto (njuːˈtrɛtəʊ) *n., pl.* **-tos.** *Physics.* **1.** the neutrino associated with the muon. **2.** (formerly) any of various hypothetical neutral particles. [C20: < NEUTR(INO) + diminutive suffix *-etto*]

neutrino (njuːˈtriːnəʊ) *n., pl.* **-nos.** *Physics.* a stable elementary particle with zero rest mass and spin ½ that travels at the speed of light. [C20: < It., dim. of *neutrone* NEUTRON]

neutron (ˈnjuːtrɒn) *n.* *Physics.* a neutral elementary particle with approximately the same mass as a proton. In the nucleus of an atom it is stable but when free it decays. [C20: < NEUTRAL, on the model of ELECTRON]

neutron bomb *n.* a type of nuclear weapon designed to cause little blast or long-lived radioactive contamination. The neutrons destroy all life in the target area. Technical name: **enhanced radiation weapon.**

neutron number *n.* the number of neutrons in the nucleus of an atom. Symbol: *N*

neutron star *n.* a star, composed solely of neutrons, that has collapsed under its own gravity.

névé (ˈnɛveɪ) *n.* a mass of porous ice, formed from snow, that has not yet become frozen into glacier ice. [C19: < Swiss F *névé* glacier, < LL *nivātus* snow-cooled, < *nix* snow]

never (ˈnɛvə) *adv., sentence substitute.* **1.** at no time; not ever. **2.** certainly not; by no means; in no case. *~sentence substitute.* **3.** Also: **well I never!** surely not! [OE *nǣfre*, < *ne* not + *æfre* EVER]

▷ **Usage.** In good usage, *never* is not used with simple past tenses to mean *not* (*I was asleep at midnight, so I did not see* (not *never saw*) *her go*).

nevermore (ˌnɛvəˈmɔː) *adv.* *Literary.* never again.

never-never *Inf.* *~n.* **1.** *Brit.* the hire-purchase system of buying. **2.** *Austral.* remote desert country. *~adj.* **3.** imaginary; idyllic (esp. in **never-never land**).

nevertheless (ˌnɛvəðəˈlɛs) *sentence connector.* in spite of that; however; yet.

new (njuː) *adj.* **1. a.** recently made or brought into being. **b.** (*as collective n.; preceded by the*): *the new.* **2.** of a kind never before existing; novel: *a new concept in marketing.* **3.** recently discovered: *a new comet.* **4.** markedly different from what was before: *the new liberalism.* **5.** (often foll. by *to* or *at*) recently introduced (to); inexperienced (in) or unaccustomed (to): *new to this neighbourhood.* **6.** (*cap. in names or titles*) more or most recent of things with the same name: *the New Testament.* **7.** (*prenominal*) fresh; additional: *send some new troops.* **8.** (often foll. by *to*) unknown: *this is new to me.* **9.** (of a cycle) beginning or occurring again: *a new year.* **10.** (*prenominal*) (of crops) harvested early. **11.** changed, esp. for the better: *she returned a new woman.* **12.** up-to-date; fashionable. *~adv.* (*usually in combination*) **13.** recently, freshly: *new-laid eggs.* **14.** anew; again. *~*See also **news.** [OE *nīowe*] —ˈ**newness** *n.*

New Australian *n.* an Australian name for a recent immigrant, esp. one from Europe.

newborn (ˈnjuːˌbɔːn) *adj.* **1.** recently or just born. **2.** (of hope, faith, etc.) reborn.

New Canadian *n.* *Canad.* a recent immigrant to Canada.

new chum *n.* **1.** *Austral. & N.Z. inf.* a recent British immigrant. **2.** *Austral.* a novice in any activity.

newcomer (ˈnjuːˌkʌmə) *n.* a person who has recently arrived or started to participate in something.

newel (ˈnjuːəl) *n.* **1.** the central pillar of a winding staircase, esp. one that is made of stone. **2.** Also called: **newel post.** the post at the top or bottom of a flight of stairs that supports the handrail. [C14: < OF *nouel* knob, < Med. L *nōdellus*, dim. of *nōdus* NODE]

newfangled (ˈnjuːˈfæŋgᵊld) *adj.* newly come into existence or fashion, esp. excessively modern. [C14 *newefangel* liking new things, < *new* + *-fangel*, < OE *fōn* to take]

newish (ˈnjuːɪʃ) *adj.* fairly new.

New Jerusalem *n.* *Christianity.* heaven.

New Latin *n.* the form of Latin used since the Renaissance, esp. for scientific nomenclature.

New Look *n.* **the.** a fashion in women's clothes introduced in 1947, characterized by long full skirts.

newly (ˈnjuːlɪ) *adv.* **1.** recently. **2.** again; anew: *newly raised hopes.* **3.** in a new manner; differently: *a newly arranged hairdo.*

newlywed (ˈnjuːlɪˌwɛd) *n.* (*often pl.*) a recently married person.

new maths *n.* (*functioning as sing.*) *Brit.* an approach to mathematics in which the basic principles of set theory are introduced at an elementary level.

new moon *n.* the moon when it appears as a narrow waxing crescent.

news (njuːz) *n.* (*functioning as sing.*) **1.** important or interesting recent happenings. **2.** information about such events, as in the mass media. **3. the news.** a presentation, such as a radio broadcast, of information of this type. **4.** interesting or important information not previously known. **5.** a person, fashion, etc., widely reported in the mass media: *she is news in the film world.* [C15: < ME *newes*, pl. of *newe* new (adj.), a model of OF *noveles* or Med. L *nova* new things] —ˈ**newsless** *adj.*

news agency *n.* an organization that collects news reports for newspapers, etc. Also called: **press agency.**

newsagent (ˈnjuːzˌeɪdʒənt) *or U.S.* **newsdealer** *n.* a shopkeeper who sells newspapers, stationery, etc.

newscast (ˈnjuːzˌkɑːst) *n.* a radio or television broadcast of the news. [C20: < NEWS + (BROAD)CAST] —ˈ**newsˌcaster** *n.*

news conference *n.* another term for **press conference.**

newsflash (ˈnjuːzˌflæʃ) *n.* a brief item of

important news, often interrupting a radio or television programme.

newsletter (ˈnjuːzˌlɛtə) *n.* **1.** Also called: **news-sheet.** a printed periodical bulletin circulated to members of a group. **2.** *History.* a written or printed account of the news.

newsmonger (ˈnjuːzˌmʌŋgə) *n. Old-fashioned.* a gossip.

newspaper (ˈnjuːzˌpeɪpə) *n.* a weekly or daily publication consisting of folded sheets and containing articles on the news, features, reviews, and advertisements. Often shortened to **paper.**

newspaperman (ˈnjuːzˌpeɪpəˌmæn) *n., pl.* **-men. 1.** a person who works for a newspaper as a reporter or editor. **2.** the owner or proprietor of a newspaper. **3.** a person who sells newspapers in the street.

newspeak (ˈnjuːˌspiːk) *n.* the language of bureaucrats and politicians, regarded as deliberately ambiguous and misleading. [C20: < *1984,* a novel by George Orwell]

newsprint (ˈnjuːzˌprɪnt) *n.* an inexpensive wood-pulp paper used for newspapers.

newsreader (ˈnjuːzˌriːdə) *n.* a news announcer on radio or television.

newsreel (ˈnjuːzˌriːl) *n.* a short film with a commentary presenting current events.

newsroom (ˈnjuːzˌruːm, -ˌrʊm) *n.* a room in a newspaper office, television station, etc., where news is received and prepared for publication or broadcasting.

newsstand (ˈnjuːzˌstænd) *n.* a portable stand or stall from which newspapers are sold.

New Style *n.* the present method of reckoning dates using the Gregorian calendar.

news vendor *n.* a person who sells newspapers.

newsworthy (ˈnjuːzˌwɜːðɪ) *adj.* sufficiently interesting to be reported in a news bulletin, etc.

newsy (ˈnjuːzɪ) *adj.* **newsier, newsiest.** full of news, esp. gossipy or personal news.

newt (njuːt) *n.* any of various small semiaquatic amphibians having a long slender body and tail and short feeble legs. [C15: < *a newt,* a mistaken division of *an ewt; ewt,* < OE *eveta* EFT]

New Testament *n.* a collection of writings composed soon after Christ's death and added to the Jewish writings of the Old Testament to make up the Christian Bible.

newton (ˈnjuːtᵊn) *n.* the derived SI unit of force that imparts an acceleration of 1 metre per second per second to a mass of 1 kilogram. Symbol: N [C20: after Sir Isaac *Newton* (1643-1727), E scientist]

Newtonian telescope (njuːˈtəʊnɪən) *n.* a type of astronomical reflecting telescope in which light is reflected from a large concave mirror onto a plane mirror, and through a hole in the side of the body of the telescope to form an image.

Newton's law of gravitation *n.* the principle that two particles attract each other with forces directly proportional to the product of their masses divided by the square of the distance between them.

Newton's laws of motion *pl. n.* three laws of mechanics describing the motion of a body. **The first law** states that a body remains at rest or in uniform motion unless acted upon by a force. **The second law** states that a body's rate of change of momentum is proportional to the force causing it. **The third law** states that when a force acts on a body an equal and opposite force acts simultaneously on another body.

new town *n.* (in Britain) a town planned as a complete unit and built with government sponsorship, esp. to accommodate overspill population.

new wave *n.* a movement in art, politics, etc., that consciously breaks with traditional ideas, esp. **the New Wave,** a movement in the French cinema of the 1960s, characterized by a fluid use of the camera.

New World *n.* **the.** the Americas; the western hemisphere.

New World monkey *n.* any of a family of monkeys of Central and South America, many of which are arboreal and have a prehensile tail.

New Year *n.* the first day or days of the year in various calendars, usually a holiday.

New Year's Day *n.* January 1, celebrated as a holiday in many countries. Often shortened to (U.S. and Canad. inf.) **New Year's.**

New Year's Eve *n.* the evening of Dec. 31. See also **Hogmanay.**

New Zealander (ˈziːləndə) *n.* **1.** a native or inhabitant of New Zealand. **2.** in earlier usage, a Maori.

next (nɛkst) *adj.* **1.** immediately following: *the next patient to be examined.* **2.** immediately adjoining: *the next room.* **3.** closest to in degree: *the next-best thing.* **4. the next (Sunday) but one.** the (Sunday) after the next. ~*adv.* **5.** at a time immediately to follow: *the patient to be examined next.* **6. next to. a.** adjacent to: *the house next to ours.* **b.** following in degree: *next to your mother, who do you love most?* **c.** almost: *next to impossible.* ~*prep.* **7.** *Arch.* next to. [OE *nēhst,* sup. of *nēah* NIGH]

next door *adj.* (**next-door** *when prenominal*), *adv.* at or to the adjacent house, flat, etc.

next of kin *n.* a person's closest relative.

nexus (ˈnɛksəs) *n., pl.* **nexus. 1.** a means of connection; link; bond. **2.** a connected group or series. [C17: < L, < *nectere* to bind]

Nez Percé (ˈnɛz ˈpɜːs) *n.* **1.** (*pl.* **Nez Percés** (ˈpɜːsɪz) *or* **Nez Percé**) a member of a North American Indian people of the Pacific coast. **2.** the language of this people.

NF (in Britain) *abbrev. for* National Front.

Nfld. *or* **NF.** *abbrev. for* Newfoundland.

NFU (in Britain) *abbrev. for* National Farmers' Union.

NG *abbrev. for:* **1.** (in the U.S.) National Guard. **2.** New Guinea. **3.** Also: **ng.** no good.

NGA (in Britain) *abbrev. for* National Graphical Association.

ngaio (ˈnaɪəʊ) *n., pl.* **ngaios.** a small evergreen New Zealand tree. [< Maori]

ngati (ˈnɑːtiː) *n., pl.* **ngati.** *N.Z.* a tribe or clan. [< Maori]

NHI (in Britain) *abbrev. for* National Health Insurance.

NHS (in Britain) *abbrev. for* National Health Service.

Ni *the chemical symbol for* nickel.

NI *abbrev. for:* **1.** (in Britain) National Insurance. **2.** Northern Ireland. **3.** (in New Zealand) North Island.

niacin (ˈnaɪəsɪn) *n.* another name for **nicotinic acid.** [C20: < NI(COTINIC) AC(ID) + -IN]

nib (nɪb) *n.* **1.** the writing point of a pen, esp. an insertable tapered metal part. **2.** a point, tip, or beak. **3.** (*pl.*) crushed cocoa beans. ~*vb.* **nibbing, nibbed.** (*tr.*) **4.** to provide with a nib. **5.** to sharpen the nib of. [C16 (in the sense: beak): <?]

nibble (ˈnɪbᵊl) *vb.* (when *intr.,* often foll. by *at*) **1.** (esp. of animals) to take small repeated bites (of). **2.** to take dainty or tentative bites: *to nibble at a cake.* **3.** to bite (at) gently. ~*n.* **4.** a small mouthful. **5.** an instance of nibbling. [C15: rel. to Low G *nibbelen*] —ˈ**nibbler** *n.*

niblick (ˈnɪblɪk) *n. Golf.* (formerly) a club giving a great deal of lift. [C19: <?]

nibs (nɪbz) *n.* **his nibs.** *Sl.* a mock title used of someone in authority. [C19: <?]

nice (naɪs) *adj.* **1.** pleasant: *a nice day.* **2.** kind or friendly: *a nice gesture of help.* **3.** good or satisfactory: *they made a nice job of it.* **4.** subtle or discriminating: *a nice point in the argument.* **5.** precise; skilful: *a nice fit.* **6.** *Now rare.* fastidious; respectable: *he was not too nice about his methods.* **7.** *Obs.* **a.** foolish or ignorant. **b.** delicate. **c.** shy; modest. **d.** wanton. [C13 (orig.: foolish): < OF *nice* simple, silly, < L *nescius,* < *nescīre* to be ignorant] —ˈ**nicely** *adv.* —ˈ**niceness** *n.* —ˈ**nicish** *adj.*

nice-looking *adj. Inf.* attractive in appearance; pretty or handsome.

nicety (ˈnaɪsɪtɪ) *n., pl.* **-ties. 1.** a subtle point: *a* *nicety of etiquette.* **2.** (*usually pl.*) a refinement or delicacy: *the niceties of first-class travel.* **3.** subtlety, delicacy, or precision. **4. to a nicety.** with precision.

niche (nɪtʃ, niːʃ) *n.* **1.** a recess in a wall, esp. one that contains a statue, etc. **2.** a position particularly suitable for the person occupying it: *he found his niche in politics.* **3.** *Ecology.* the status of a plant or animal within its community, which determines its activities, relationships with other organisms, etc. ~*vb.* **4.** (*tr.*) to place (a statue) in a niche; ensconce (oneself). [C17: < F, < OF *nichier* to nest, < Vulgar L *nīdicāre* (unattested), < L *nīdus* NEST]

Nichrome (ˈnaɪˌkrəʊm) *n. Trademark.* any of various alloys containing nickel, iron, and chromium, used in electrical heating elements, furnaces, etc.

nick (nɪk) *n.* **1.** a small notch or indentation. **2.** *Brit. sl.* a prison or police station. **3. in good nick.** *Inf.* in good condition. **4. in the nick of time.** just in time. ~*vb.* **5.** (*tr.*) to chip or cut. **6.** *Sl., chiefly Brit.* **a.** to steal. **b.** to arrest. **7.** (*intr.; often foll. by off*) *Inf.* to depart rapidly. **8. nick (someone) for.** *U.S. & Canad. sl.* to defraud (someone) to the extent of. **9.** to divide and reset (the tail muscles of a horse) to give the tail a high carriage. **10.** (*tr.*) to guess, catch, etc., exactly. [C15: ? changed < C14 *nocke* NOCK]

nickel (ˈnɪkᵊl) *n.* **1.** a malleable silvery-white metallic element that is corrosion-resistant: used in alloys, in electroplating, and as a catalyst in organic synthesis. Symbol: Ni; atomic no.: 28; atomic wt.: 58.71. **2.** a U.S. or Canadian coin worth five cents. ~*vb.* **-elling, -elled** *or U.S.* **-eling, -eled. 3.** (*tr.*) to plate with nickel. [C18: < G *Kupfernickel* niccolite, lit.: copper demon; it was mistakenly thought to contain copper]

nickelodeon (ˌnɪkəˈləʊdɪən) *n. U.S.* **1.** an early form of jukebox. **2.** (formerly) a Pianola, esp. one operated by inserting a five-cent piece. [C20: < NICKEL + (MEL)ODEON]

nickel plate *n.* a thin layer of nickel deposited on a surface, usually by electrolysis.

nickel silver *n.* any of various white alloys containing copper, zinc, and nickel: used in making tableware, etc. Also called: **German silver.**

nicker[1] (ˈnɪkə) *vb.* (*intr.*) **1.** (of a horse) to neigh softly. **2.** to snigger. [C18: ? < NEIGH]

nicker[2] (ˈnɪkə) *n., pl.* **-er.** *Brit. sl.* a pound sterling. [C20: <?]

nick-nack (ˈnɪkˌnæk) *n.* a variant spelling of **knick-knack.**

nickname (ˈnɪkˌneɪm) *n.* **1.** a familiar, pet, or derisory name given to a person, animal, or place. **2.** a shortened or familiar form of a person's name: *Joe is a nickname for Joseph.* ~*vb.* **3.** (*tr.*) to call by a nickname. [C15 *a nekename*, mistaken division of *an ekename* an additional name]

Nicol prism (ˈnɪkᵊl) *n.* a device composed of two prisms of Iceland spar or calcite cut at specified angles and cemented together. It is used for producing plane-polarized light. [C19: after William *Nicol* (?1768–1851), Scot. physicist, its inventor]

nicotiana (nɪˌkəʊʃɪˈɑːnə) *n.* a plant of an American and Australian genus, having white, yellow, or purple fragrant flowers. Also called: **tobacco plant.** [C16: see NICOTINE]

nicotinamide (ˌnɪkəˈtɪnəˌmaɪd) *n.* the amide of nicotinic acid: a component of the vitamin B complex. Formula: $C_6H_6ON_2$.

nicotine (ˈnɪkəˌtiːn) *n.* a colourless oily acrid toxic liquid that turns yellowish-brown in air and light: the principal alkaloid in tobacco. [C19: < F, < NL *herba nicotiana* Nicot's plant, after J. *Nicot* (1530-1600), F diplomat who introduced tobacco into France] —ˈ**nicoˌtined** *adj.* —**nicotinic** (ˌnɪkəˈtɪnɪk) *adj.*

nicotinic acid *n.* a vitamin of the B complex that occurs in milk, liver, yeast, etc. Lack of it in the diet leads to the disease pellagra.

nicotinism (ˈnɪkətiːˌnɪzəm) *n. Pathol.* a toxic condition of the body caused by nicotine.

nictitate (ˈnɪktɪˌteɪt) *or* **nictate** (ˈnɪkteɪt) *vb.* a technical word for **blink.** [C19: < Med. L *nictitāre* to wink repeatedly, < L *nictāre* to blink] —ˌ**nictiˈtation** *or* **nicˈtation** *n.*

nictitating membrane *n.* (in reptiles, birds, and some mammals) a thin fold of skin beneath the eyelid that can be drawn across the eye.

nidicolous (nɪˈdɪkələs) *adj.* (of young birds) remaining in the nest some time after hatching. [C19: < L *nīdus* nest + *colere* to inhabit]

nidifugous (nɪˈdɪfjʊgəs) *adj.* (of young birds) leaving the nest very soon after hatching. [C19: < L *nīdus* nest + *fugere* to flee]

nidify (ˈnɪdɪˌfaɪ) *or* **nidificate** (ˈnɪdɪfɪˌkeɪt) *vb.* **-fying, -fied.** (*intr.*) (of birds) to make or build a nest. [C17: < L *nīdificāre*, < *nīdus* a nest + *facere* to make] —ˌ**nidifiˈcation** *n.*

niece (niːs) *n.* a daughter of one's sister or brother. [C13: < OF: niece, granddaughter, ult. < L *neptis* granddaughter]

niello (nɪˈɛləʊ) *n., pl.* **-li** (-lɪ) *or* **-los. 1.** a black compound of sulphur and silver, lead, or copper used to incise a design on a metal surface. **2.** this process. **3.** an object decorated with niello. [C19: < It. < L *nigellus* blackish, < *niger* black]

niff (nɪf) *Brit. sl.* ~*n.* **1.** a bad smell. ~*vb.* (*intr.*) **2.** to stink. [C20: ? < SNIFF] —ˈ**niffy** *adj.*

nifty (ˈnɪftɪ) *adj.* **-tier, -tiest.** *Inf.* **1.** pleasing, apt, or stylish. **2.** quick; agile. [C19: <?] —ˈ**niftily** *adv.* —ˈ**niftiness** *n.*

nigella (naɪˈdʒɛlə) *n.* another name for **love-in-a-mist.**

Nigerian (naɪˈdʒɪərɪən) *n.* **1.** a native or inhabitant of Nigeria, a country in West Africa. ~*adj.* **2.** of Nigeria, its people, culture, etc.

niggard (ˈnɪgəd) *n.* **1.** a stingy person. ~*adj.* **2.** *Arch.* miserly. [C14: ? < ON]

niggardly (ˈnɪgədlɪ) *adj.* **1.** stingy. **2.** meagre: *a niggardly salary.* ~*adv.* **3.** stingily; grudgingly. —ˈ**niggardliness** *n.*

nigger (ˈnɪgə) *Derog.* ~*n.* **1.** another name for a Negro. **2.** a member of any dark-skinned race. **3. nigger in the woodpile.** a hidden snag. [C18: < C16 dialect *neeger*, < F *nègre*, < Sp. NEGRO]

niggle (ˈnɪgᵊl) *vb.* **1.** (*intr.*) to find fault continually. **2.** (*intr.*) to be preoccupied with details; fuss. **3.** (*tr.*) to irritate; worry. ~*n.* **4.** a trivial objection or complaint. **5.** a slight feeling as of misgiving, uncertainty, etc. [C16: < Scand.] —ˈ**niggler** *n.* —ˈ**niggly** *adj.*

niggling (ˈnɪglɪŋ) *adj.* **1.** petty. **2.** fussy. **3.** irritating. **4.** requiring painstaking work. **5.** persistently troubling.

nigh (naɪ) *adj., adv., prep.* an archaic, poetic, or dialect word for **near.** [OE *nēah, nēh*]

night (naɪt) *n.* **1.** the period of darkness that occurs each 24 hours, as distinct from day. **2.** (*modifier*) of, occurring, working, etc., at night: *a night nurse.* **3.** this period considered as a unit: *four nights later they left.* **4.** the period between sunset and retiring to bed; evening. **5.** the time between bedtime and morning. **6.** the weather at night: *a clear night.* **7.** the activity or experience of a person during a night. **8.** (*sometimes cap.*) any evening designated for a special observance or function. **9.** nightfall or dusk. **10.** a state or period of gloom, ignorance, etc. **11. make a night of it.** to celebrate for most of the night. ~Related adj.: **nocturnal.** ~See also **nights.** [OE *niht*]

night blindness *n. Pathol.* a nontechnical term for **nyctalopia.** —ˈ**night-ˌblind** *adj.*

nightcap (ˈnaɪtˌkæp) *n.* **1.** a bedtime drink. **2.** a soft cap formerly worn in bed.

nightclothes (ˈnaɪtˌkləʊðz) *pl. n.* clothes worn in bed.

nightclub (ˈnaɪtˌklʌb) *n.* a place of entertainment open until late at night, usually offering food, drink, a floor show, dancing, etc.

nightdress (ˈnaɪtˌdrɛs) *n. Brit.* a loose dress worn in bed by women. Also called: **nightgown, nightie.**

nightfall (ˈnaɪtˌfɔːl) *n.* the approach of darkness; dusk.

night fighter *n.* an interceptor aircraft used for operations at night.

nightgown (ˈnaɪtˌgaʊn) *n.* **1.** another name for **nightdress. 2.** a man's nightshirt.

nighthawk (ˈnaɪtˌhɔːk) *n.* **1.** any of various nocturnal American birds. **2.** *Inf.* another name for **night owl.**

nightie *or* **nighty** (ˈnaɪtɪ) *n., pl.* **nighties.** *Inf.* short for **nightdress.**

nightingale (ˈnaɪtɪŋˌgeɪl) *n.* a brownish European songbird with a broad reddish-brown tail: well known for its musical song, usually heard at night. [OE *nihtegale,* < NIGHT + *galan* to sing]

nightjar (ˈnaɪtˌdʒɑː) *n.* any of a family of nocturnal birds which have large eyes and feed on insects. [C17: NIGHT + JAR[2], so called from its discordant cry]

night latch *n.* a door lock operated by means of a knob on the inside and a key on the outside.

nightlife (ˈnaɪtˌlaɪf) *n.* social life or entertainment taking place at night.

night-light *n.* a dim light burning at night, esp. for children.

nightlong (ˈnaɪtˌlɒŋ) *adj., adv.* throughout the night.

nightly (ˈnaɪtlɪ) *adj.* **1.** happening or relating to each night. **2.** happening at night. ~*adv.* **3.** at night or each night.

nightmare (ˈnaɪtˌmɛə) *n.* **1.** a terrifying or deeply distressing dream. **2. a.** an event or condition resembling a terrifying dream. **b.** (*as modifier*): *a nightmare drive.* **3.** a thing that is feared. **4.** (formerly) an evil spirit supposed to suffocate sleeping people. [C13 (meaning: incubus; C16: bad dream): < NIGHT + OE *mare, mære* evil spirit, < Gmc] —**ˈnightˌmarish** *adj.*

night owl *or* **nighthawk** *n. Inf.* a person who is or prefers to be up and about late at night.

nights (naɪts) *adv. Inf.* at night, esp. regularly: *he works nights.*

night safe *n.* a safe built into the outside wall of a bank, in which customers can deposit money at times when the bank is closed.

night school *n.* an educational institution that holds classes in the evening.

nightshade (ˈnaɪtˌʃeɪd) *n.* any of various solanaceous plants, such as deadly nightshade and black nightshade. [OE *nihtscada,* apparently NIGHT + SHADE, referring to the poisonous or soporific qualities of these plants]

night shift *n.* **1.** a group of workers who work a shift during the night. **2.** the period worked.

nightshirt (ˈnaɪtˌʃɜːt) *n.* a loose knee-length or longer shirtlike garment worn in bed by men.

nightspot (ˈnaɪtˌspɒt) *n.* an informal word for **nightclub.**

night-time *n.* the time from sunset to sunrise; night as distinct from day.

night watch *n.* **1.** a watch or guard kept at night, esp. for security. **2.** the period of time the watch is kept. **3.** a night watchman.

night watchman *n.* **1.** Also called: **night watch.** a person who keeps guard at night on a factory, public building, etc. **2.** *Cricket.* a batsman sent in to bat to play out time when a wicket has fallen near the end of a day's play.

nightwear (ˈnaɪtˌwɛə) *n.* apparel worn in bed or before retiring to bed; pyjamas, etc.

nigrescent (naɪˈgrɛsᵊnt) *adj.* blackish; dark. [C18: < L *nigrescere* to grow black, < *niger* black] —**niˈgrescence** *n.*

nihilism (ˈnaɪɪˌlɪzəm) *n.* **1.** a complete denial of all established authority and institutions. **2.** *Philosophy.* an extreme form of scepticism that systematically rejects all values, belief in existence, etc. **3.** a revolutionary doctrine of destruction for its own sake. **4.** the practice of terrorism. [C19: < L *nihil* nothing] —**ˈnihilist** *n., adj.* —**ˌnihilˈistic** *adj.* —**nihility** (naɪˈhɪlɪtɪ) *n.*

nihil obstat (ˈnaɪhɪl ˈɒbstæt) the phrase used by a Roman Catholic censor to declare publication inoffensive to faith or morals. [L, lit.: nothing hinders]

-nik *suffix forming nouns.* denoting a person associated with a specified state or quality: *beatnik.* [C20: < Russian *-nik,* as in SPUTNIK, and infl. by Yiddish *-nik* (agent suffix)]

nil (nɪl) *n.* nothing: used esp. in the scoring of certain games. [C19: < L]

Nile green (naɪl) *n.* **a.** a pale bluish-green colour. **b.** (*as adj.*): *a Nile-green dress.*

nilgai (ˈnɪlgaɪ) *or* **nilghau** (ˈnɪlgɔː) *n., pl.* **-gai, -gais** *or* **-ghau, -ghaus.** a large Indian antelope, the male of which has small horns. [C19: < Hindi *nīlgāw,* < Sansk. *nīla* blue + *go* bull]

Nilotic (naɪˈlɒtɪk) *adj.* **1.** of the Nile. **2.** of or belonging to a Negroid pastoral people inhabiting the S Sudan, parts of Kenya and Uganda, and neighbouring countries. **3.** relating to the group of languages spoken by the Nilotic peoples. [C17: via L < Gk *Neilotikós,* < *Neilos* the River Nile]

nimble (ˈnɪmbᵊl) *adj.* **1.** agile, quick, and neat in movement. **2.** alert; acute. [OE *nǣmel* quick to grasp, & *numol* quick at seizing, both < *niman* to take] —**ˈnimbleness** *n.* —**ˈnimbly** *adv.*

nimbostratus (ˌnɪmbəʊˈstreɪtəs, -ˈstrɑːtəs) *n., pl.* **-ti** (-taɪ). a dark rain-bearing stratus cloud.

nimbus (ˈnɪmbəs) *n., pl.* **-bi** (-baɪ) *or* **-buses. 1. a.** a dark grey rain-bearing cloud. **b.** (*in combination*): *cumulonimbus clouds.* **2. a.** an emanation of light surrounding a saint or deity. **b.** a representation of this emanation. **3.** a surrounding aura. [C17: < L: cloud]

Nimrod (ˈnɪmrɒd) *n.* **1.** a hunter famous for his prowess (Genesis 10:8–9). **2.** a person dedicated to or skilled in hunting.

nincompoop (ˈnɪnkəmˌpuːp, ˈnɪŋ-) *n.* a stupid person; fool; idiot. [C17: <?]

nine (naɪn) *n.* **1.** the cardinal number that is the sum of one and eight. **2.** a numeral, 9, IX, etc., representing this number. **3.** something representing, represented by, or consisting of nine units, such as a playing card with nine symbols on it. **4.** Also: **nine o'clock.** nine hours after noon or midnight: *the play starts at nine.* **5. dressed (up) to the nines.** *Inf.* elaborately dressed. **6. 999** (in Britain) the telephone number of the emergency services. **7. nine to five.** normal office hours: *a nine-to-five job.* ~*determiner.* **8. a.** amounting to nine: *nine days.* **b.** (*as pronoun*): *nine are ready.* [OE *nigon*]

nine-days wonder *n.* something that arouses great interest but only for a short period.

ninefold (ˈnaɪnˌfəʊld) *adj.* **1.** equal to or having nine times as many or as much. **2.** composed of nine parts. ~*adv.* **3.** by nine times as much.

ninepins (ˈnaɪnˌpɪnz) *n.* **1.** (*functioning as sing.*) another name for **skittles. 2.** (*sing.*) one of the pins used in this game.

nineteen (ˈnaɪnˈtiːn) *n.* **1.** the cardinal number that is the sum of ten and nine. **2.** a numeral, 19, XIX, etc., representing this number. **3.** something represented by, representing, or consisting of 19 units. **4. talk nineteen to the dozen.** to talk incessantly. ~*determiner.* **5. a.** amounting to nineteen: *nineteen pictures.* **b.** (*as pronoun*): *only nineteen voted.* [OE *nigontīne*]

nineteenth (ˌnaɪnˈtiːnθ) *adj.* **1.** (*usually prenominal*) **a.** coming after the eighteenth in numbering, position, etc.; being the ordinal number of *nineteen.* Often written: 19th. **b.** (*as n.*): *the nineteenth was rainy.* ~*n.* **2. a.** one of 19 equal parts of something. **b.** (*as modifier*): *a nineteenth part.* **3.** the fraction equal to one divided by 19 (1/19).

nineteenth hole *n. Golf, sl.* the bar in a golf clubhouse. [C20: < its being the next objective after a standard 18-hole round]

ninetieth (ˈnaɪntɪɪθ) *adj.* **1.** (*usually prenominal*) **a.** being the ordinal number of *ninety* in numbering, position, etc. Often written: 90th. **b.** (*as n.*): *ninetieth in succession.* ~*n.* **2. a.** one of 90 equal parts of something. **b.** (*as modifier*): *a ninetieth part.* **3.** the fraction one divided by 90 (1/90).

ninety (ˈnaɪntɪ) *n., pl.* **-ties. 1.** the cardinal number that is the product of ten and nine. **2.** a numeral, 90, XC, etc., representing this number. **3.** something represented by, representing, or consisting of 90 units. ~*determiner.* **4. a.**

amounting to ninety: *ninety times.* **b.** (*as pronoun*): *at least ninety are missing.* [OE *nigontig*]

ninny (ˈnɪnɪ) *n., pl.* **-nies.** a dull-witted person. [C16: ? < *an innocent* simpleton]

ninth (naɪnθ) *adj.* **1.** (*usually prenominal*) **a.** coming after the eighth in order, position, etc.; being the ordinal number of *nine.* Often written: 9th. **b.** (*as n.*): *ninth in line.* ~*n.* **2. a.** one of nine equal parts. **b.** (*as modifier*): *a ninth part.* **3.** the fraction one divided by nine (1/9). **4.** *Music.* an interval of one octave plus a second. ~*adv.* **5.** Also: **ninthly.** after the eighth person, position, event, etc. [OE *nigotha*]

niobium (naɪˈəʊbɪəm) *n.* a ductile white superconductive metallic element that occurs principally in the black mineral columbite and tantalite. Symbol: Nb; atomic no.: 41; atomic wt.: 92.906. Former name: **columbium.** [C19: < NL, < *Niobe* (daughter of Tantalus); because it occurred in TANTALITE]

nip[1] (nɪp) *vb.* **nipping, nipped.** (*mainly tr.*) **1.** to compress, as between a finger and the thumb; pinch. **2.** (often foll. by *off*) to remove by clipping, biting, etc. **3.** (when *intr.*, often foll. by *at*) to give a small sharp bite (to): *the dog nipped at his heels.* **4.** (esp. of the cold) to affect with a stinging sensation. **5.** to harm through cold: *the frost nipped the young plants.* **6.** to check or destroy the growth of (esp. in **nip in the bud**). **7.** (*intr.*; foll. by *along, up, out,* etc.) *Brit. inf.* to hurry; dart. **8.** *Sl., chiefly U.S. & Canad.* to snatch. ~*n.* **9.** a pinch, snip, etc. **10.** severe frost or cold: *the first nip of winter.* **11. put the nips in.** *Austral. & N.Z. sl.* to exert pressure on someone, esp. in order to extort money. **12.** *Arch.* a taunting remark. **13. nip and tuck.** *U.S. & Canad.* neck and neck. [C14: < ON]

nip[2] (nɪp) *n.* **1.** a small drink of spirits; dram. ~*vb.* **nipping, nipped. 2.** to drink spirits, esp. habitually in small amounts. [C18: < *nipperkin* a vessel holding a half-pint or less, <?]

nipper (ˈnɪpə) *n.* **1.** a person or thing that nips. **2.** the large pincer-like claw of a lobster, crab, etc. **3.** *Inf., chiefly Brit.* a small child.

nippers (ˈnɪpəz) *pl. n.* an instrument or tool, such as a pair of pliers, for snipping or squeezing.

nipple (ˈnɪpᵊl) *n.* **1.** the small conical projection in the centre of each breast, which in women contains the outlet of the milk ducts. **2.** something resembling a nipple in shape or function. **3.** Also called: **grease nipple.** a small drilled bush, usually screwed into a bearing, through which grease is introduced. [C16: < earlier *neble, nible,* ? < NEB, NIB]

nipplewort (ˈnɪpᵊlˌwɜːt) *n.* an annual Eurasian plant with pointed oval leaves and small yellow flower heads.

nippy (ˈnɪpɪ) *adj.* **-pier, -piest. 1.** (of weather) frosty or chilly. **2.** *Brit. inf.* **a.** quick; nimble; active. **b.** (of a motor vehicle) small and relatively powerful. **3.** (of dogs) inclined to bite. —**ˈnippily** *adv.*

NIREX (ˈnaɪrɛks) *n. acronym for* Nuclear Industry Radioactive Waste Executive.

nirvana (nɪəˈvɑːnə, nɜː-) *n. Buddhism, Hinduism.* final release from the cycle of reincarnation attained by extinction of all desires and individual existence, culminating (in Buddhism) in absolute blessedness, or (in Hinduism) in absorption into Brahman. [C19: < Sansk.: extinction, < *nir-* out + *vāti* it blows]

nisi (ˈnaɪsaɪ) *adj.* (*postpositive*) *Law.* (of a court order) coming into effect on a specified date unless cause is shown why it should not: *a decree nisi.* [C19: <: unless, if not]

Nissen hut (ˈnɪsᵊn) *n.* a military shelter of semicircular cross section, made of corrugated steel sheet. [C20: after Lt Col. Peter *Nissen* (1871–1930), British mining engineer, its inventor]

nit[1] (nɪt) *n.* **1.** the egg of a louse, esp. adhering to human hair. **2.** the larva of a louse. [OE *hnitu*]

nit[2] (nɪt) *n.* a unit of luminance equal to 1 candela per square metre. [C20: < L *nitor* brightness]

nit[3] (nɪt) *n. Inf., chiefly Brit.* short for **nitwit.**

nit[4] (nɪt) *n.* a unit of information equal to 1.44 bits. Also called: **nepit.** [C20: < *N(apierian dig)it*]

nit[5] (nɪt) *n.* **keep nit.** *Austral. inf.* to keep watch, esp. during illegal activity. [C19: < *nix!* a shout of warning] —**ˈnit-ˌkeeper** *n.*

nit-picking *Inf.* ~*n.* **1.** a concern with insignificant details, esp. with the intention of finding fault. ~*adj.* **2.** showing such a concern; fussy. [C20: < NIT[1] + PICK[1]] —**ˈnit-ˌpicker** *n.*

nitrate (ˈnaɪtreɪt) *n.* **1.** any salt or ester of nitric acid. **2.** a fertilizer containing nitrate salts. ~*vb.* **3.** (*tr.*) to treat with nitric acid or a nitrate. **4.** to convert or be converted into a nitrate. —**niˈtration** *n.*

nitre *or U.S.* **niter** (ˈnaɪtə) *n.* another name for **potassium nitrate** or **sodium nitrate.** [C14: via OF < L *nitrum,* prob. < Gk *nitron*]

nitric (ˈnaɪtrɪk) *adj.* of or containing nitrogen.

nitric acid *n.* a colourless corrosive liquid important in the manufacture of fertilizers, explosives, and many other chemicals. Formula: HNO_3. Former name: **aqua fortis.**

nitride (ˈnaɪtraɪd) *n.* a compound of nitrogen with a more electropositive element.

nitrification (ˌnaɪtrɪfɪˈkeɪʃən) *n.* **1.** the oxidation of the ammonium compounds in dead organic material into nitrites and nitrates by soil nitrobacteria, making nitrogen available to plants. **2.** the addition of a nitro group to an organic compound.

nitrify (ˈnaɪtrɪˌfaɪ) *vb.* **-fying, -fied.** (*tr.*) **1.** to treat or cause to react with nitrogen. **2.** to treat (soil) with nitrates. **3.** (of nitrobacteria) to convert (ammonium compounds) into nitrates by oxidation. —**ˈnitriˌfiable** *adj.*

nitrite (ˈnaɪtraɪt) *n.* any salt or ester of nitrous acid.

nitro- *or before a vowel* **nitr-** *combining form.* **1.** indicating that a chemical compound contains a nitro group, $-NO_2$: *nitrobenzene.* **2.** indicating that a chemical compound is a nitrate ester: *nitrocellulose.* [< Gk *nitron* NATRON]

nitrobacteria (ˌnaɪtrəʊbækˈtɪərɪə) *pl. n., sing.* **-terium** (-ˈtɪərɪəm). soil bacteria that are involved in nitrification.

nitrobenzene (ˌnaɪtrəʊˈbɛnziːn) *n.* a yellow oily liquid compound, used as a solvent and in the manufacture of aniline. Formula: $C_6H_5NO_2$.

nitrocellulose (ˌnaɪtrəʊˈsɛljʊˌləʊs) *n.* another name (not in chemical usage) for **cellulose nitrate.**

nitrogen (ˈnaɪtrədʒən) *n.* a colourless odourless relatively unreactive gaseous element that forms 78 per cent of the air and is an essential constituent of proteins and nucleic acids. Symbol: N; atomic no.: 7; atomic wt.: 14.0067.

nitrogen cycle *n.* the natural circulation of nitrogen by living organisms. Nitrates in the soil, derived from dead organic matter by bacterial action, are absorbed and synthesized into complex organic compounds by plants and reduced to nitrates again when the plants and the animals feeding on them die and decay.

nitrogen dioxide *n.* a red-brown poisonous gas that is an intermediate in the manufacture of nitric acid, a nitrating agent, and an oxidizer for rocket fuels. Formula: NO_2.

nitrogen fixation *n.* **1.** the conversion of atmospheric nitrogen into nitrogen compounds by soil bacteria in the root nodules of legumes, and by certain algae. **2.** a process in which atmospheric nitrogen is converted into a nitrogen compound, used esp. for fertilizer.

nitrogenize *or* **-ise** (naɪˈtrɒdʒɪˌnaɪz) *vb.* to combine or treat with nitrogen or a nitrogen compound. —**niˌtrogeniˈzation** *or* **-iˈsation** *n.*

nitrogen mustard *n.* any of a class of organic compounds resembling mustard gas in their molecular structure: important in the treatment of cancer.

nitrogenous (naɪˈtrɒdʒɪnəs) *adj.* containing nitrogen or a nitrogen compound.

nitroglycerin (ˌnaɪtrəʊˈglɪsərɪn) *or* **nitroglycerine** (ˌnaɪtrəʊˈglɪsəˌriːn) *n.* a pale yellow viscous explosive liquid made from glycerol and nitric and sulphuric acids. Formula: $CH_2NO_3CHNO_3CH_2NO_3$. Also called: **trinitroglycerin.**

nitromethane (ˌnaɪtrəʊˈmiːθeɪn) *n.* an oily colourless liquid obtained from methane and used as a solvent and rocket fuel.

nitrous (ˈnaɪtrəs) *adj.* of, derived from, or containing nitrogen, esp. in a low valency state. [C17: < L *nitrōsus* full of natron]

nitrous acid *n.* a weak monobasic acid known only in solution and in the form of nitrite salts. Formula: HNO_2.

nitrous oxide *n.* a colourless gas with a sweet smell: used as an anaesthetic in dentistry. Formula: N_2O. Also called: **laughing gas.**

nitty (ˈnɪtɪ) *adj.* **-tier, -tiest.** infested with nits.

nitty-gritty (ˈnɪtɪˈgrɪtɪ) *n.* **the.** *Inf.* the basic facts of a matter, situation, etc.; the core. [C20: ? rhyming compound < GRIT]

nitwit (ˈnɪtˌwɪt) *n. Inf.* a foolish or dull person. [C20: ? < NIT[1] + WIT[1]]

nix[1] (nɪks) *Inf.* ~*sentence substitute.* **1.** another word for **no**[1]. ~*n.* **2.** a refusal. **3.** nothing. [C18: < G, inf. form of *nichts* nothing]

nix[2] (nɪks) *or* (*fem.*) **nixie** (ˈnɪksɪ) *n. Germanic myth.* a water sprite, usually unfriendly to humans. [C19: < G *Nixe*, < OHG *nihhus*]

NMR *abbrev. for* nuclear magnetic resonance.

NNE *symbol for* north-northeast.

NNW *symbol for* north-northwest.

no[1] (nəʊ) *sentence substitute.* **1.** used to express denial, disagreement, refusal, etc. ~*n., pl.* **noes** *or* **nos. 2.** an answer or vote of *no.* **3. not take no for an answer.** to continue in a course of action, etc., despite refusals. **4.** (*often pl.*) a person who votes in the negative. **5. the noes have it.** there is a majority of votes in the negative. [OE *nā*, < *ne* not, no + *ā* ever]

no[2] (nəʊ) *determiner.* **1.** not any, not a, or not one: *there's no money left; no card in the file.* **2.** not at all: *she's no youngster.* **3.** (foll. by comparative adjectives and adverbs) not: *no less than forty; no taller than a child.* [OE *nā*, < *nān* NONE]

No[1] *or* **Noh** (nəʊ) *n., pl.* **No** *or* **Noh.** the stylized classic drama of Japan, developed in the 15th century or earlier, using music, dancing, and themes from religious stories or myths. [< Japanese *nō* talent, < Chinese *neng*]

No[2] *the chemical symbol for* nobelium.

No. *abbrev. for:* **1.** north(ern). **2.** Also: **no.** (*pl.* **Nos.** *or* **nos.**) number. [< F *numéro*]

n.o. *Cricket. abbrev. for* not out.

no-account *U.S. dialect.* ~*adj.* **1.** worthless; good-for-nothing. ~*n.* **2.** a worthless person.

nob[1] (nɒb) *n. Cribbage.* **1.** the jack of the suit turned up. **2. one for his nob.** the call made with this jack, scoring one point. [C19: <?]

nob[2] (nɒb) *n. Sl., chiefly Brit.* a person of wealth or social distinction. [C19: <?]

no-ball *n.* **1.** *Cricket.* an illegal ball, as for overstepping the crease, for which the batting side scores a run unless the batsman hits the ball, in which case he can only be out by being run out. **2.** *Rounders.* an illegal ball, esp. one bowled too high or too low. ~*interj.* **3.** *Cricket, rounders.* a call by the umpire indicating a no-ball.

nobble (ˈnɒbᵊl) *vb.* (*tr.*) *Brit. sl.* **1.** to disable (a racehorse), esp. with drugs. **2.** to win over or outwit (a person) by underhand means. **3.** to suborn (a person, esp. a juror) by threats, bribery, etc. **4.** to steal. **5.** to grab. **6.** to kidnap. [C19: < *nobbler*, from a false division of *an hobbler* (one who hobbles horses) as *a nobbler*]

nobelium (nəʊˈbiːlɪəm) *n.* a transuranic element produced artificially from curium. Symbol: No; atomic no.: 102; half-life of most stable isotope, ^{255}No: 180 seconds (approx.). [C20: NL, after *Nobel* Institute, Stockholm, where it was discovered]

Nobel prize (nəʊˈbɛl) *n.* a prize for outstanding contributions to chemistry, physics, physiology and medicine, literature, economics, and peace that may be awarded annually; established 1901. [C20: after Alfred *Nobel* (1833-96), Swedish chemist and philanthropist]

nobility (nəʊˈbɪlɪtɪ) *n., pl.* **-ties. 1.** a privileged class whose titles are conferred by descent or royal decree. **2.** the quality of being good; dignity: *nobility of mind.* **3.** (in the British Isles) the class of people holding the title of dukes, marquesses, earls, viscounts, or barons and their feminine equivalents; peerage.

nobilmente (ˌnəʊbɪlˈmɛnteɪ) *adj, adv. Music.* to be performed in a noble manner. [It.]

noble (ˈnəʊbᵊl) *adj.* **1.** of or relating to a hereditary class with special status, often derived from a feudal period. **2.** of or characterized by high moral qualities; magnanimous: *a noble deed.* **3.** having dignity or eminence; illustrious. **4.** imposing; magnificent: *a noble avenue of trees.* **5.** superior; excellent: *a noble strain of horses.* **6.** *Chem.* **a.** (of certain elements) chemically unreactive. **b.** (of certain metals, esp. copper, silver, and gold) resisting oxidation. ~*n.* **7.** a person belonging to a privileged class whose status is usually indicated by a title. **8.** (in the British Isles) a person holding the title of duke, marquess, earl, viscount, or baron, or a feminine equivalent. **9.** a former British gold coin having the value of one third of a pound. [C13: via OF < L *nōbilis*, orig., capable of being known, hence well-known, < *noscere* to know] —ˈ**nobleness** *n.* —ˈ**nobly** *adv.*

nobleman (ˈnəʊbᵊlmən) *or* (*fem.*) **noblewoman** *n., pl.* **-men** *or* **-women.** a person of noble rank, title, or status; peer; aristocrat.

noble savage *n.* (in romanticism) an idealized view of primitive man.

noblesse oblige (nəʊˈblɛs əʊˈbliːʒ) *n. Often ironic.* the supposed obligation of nobility to be honourable and generous. [F, lit.: nobility obliges]

nobody (ˈnəʊbədɪ) *pron.* **1.** no person; no-one. ~*n., pl.* **-bodies. 2.** an insignificant person.

▷ **Usage.** See at **everyone.**

nock (nɒk) *n.* **1.** a notch on an arrow that fits on the bowstring. **2.** either of the grooves at each end of a bow that hold the bowstring. ~*vb.* (*tr.*) **3.** to fit (an arrow) on a bowstring. [C14: rel. to Swedish *nock* tip]

no-claim bonus *n.* a reduction on an insurance premium, esp. one covering a motor vehicle, if no claims have been made within a specified period. Also called: **no-claims bonus.**

noctambulism (nɒkˈtæmbjʊˌlɪzəm) *or* **noctambulation** *n.* another word for **somnambulism.** [C19: < L *nox* night + *ambulāre* to walk]

noctilucent (ˌnɒktɪˈluːsᵊnt) *adj.* shining at night, as certain high-altitude clouds, believed to consist of meteor dust that reflects sunlight. [< L, < *nox* night + *lūcēre* to shine]

noctuid (ˈnɒktjʊɪd) *n.* any of a large family of nocturnal moths that includes the underwings. [C19: via NL < L *noctua* night owl, < *nox* night]

noctule (ˈnɒktjuːl) *n.* any of several large Old World insectivorous bats. [C18: prob. < LL *noctula* small owl, < L *noctua* night owl]

nocturnal (nɒkˈtɜːnᵊl) *adj.* **1.** of, used during, occurring in, or relating to the night. **2.** (of animals) active at night. **3.** (of plants) having flowers that open at night and close by day. [C15: < LL *nocturnālis*, < L *nox* night] —ˌ**nocturˈnality** *n.* —**nocˈturnally** *adv.*

nocturne (ˈnɒktɜːn) *n.* **1.** a short, lyrical piece of music, esp. one for the piano. **2.** a painting of a night scene.

nod (nɒd) *vb.* **nodding, nodded. 1.** to lower and raise (the head) briefly, as to indicate agreement, etc. **2.** (*tr.*) to express by nodding: *she nodded approval.* **3.** (*intr.*) (of flowers, trees, etc.) to sway or bend forwards and back. **4.** (*intr.*) to let the head fall forwards through drowsiness; be almost asleep. **5.** (*intr.*) to be momentarily careless: *even Homer sometimes nods.* ~*n.* **6.** a quick down-and-up movement of the head, as in assent, command, etc. **7. nodding acquaintance.** a slight, casual, or superficial knowledge (of a subject or person). **8. on the nod.** *Inf.* agreed, as in committee, without formal procedure. **9.** See **land of Nod.** ~See also **nod off.** [C14 *nodde*, <?] —ˈ**nodding** *adj., n.*

noddle[1] (ˈnɒdᵊl) *n. Inf., chiefly Brit.* the head or brains: *use your noddle!* [C15: <?]

noddle[2] (ˈnɒdᵊl) *vb. Inf., chiefly Brit.* to nod (the head), as through drowsiness. [C18: < NOD]

noddy (ˈnɒdɪ) *n., pl.* **-dies. 1.** any of several tropical terns, typically having a dark plumage. **2.** a fool or dunce. [C16: ? n. use of obs. *noddy* foolish, drowsy, ? < NOD (vb.); the bird is so called because it allows itself to be caught by hand]

node (nəʊd) *n.* **1.** a knot, swelling, or knob. **2.** the point on a plant stem from which the leaves or lateral branches grow. **3.** *Physics.* a point at which the amplitude of one of the two kinds of displacement in a standing wave has zero or minimum value. **4.** Also called: **crunode.** *Maths.* a point at which two branches of a curve intersect. **5.** *Maths., linguistics.* one of the objects of which a graph or a tree consists. **6.** *Astron.* either of the two points at which the orbit of a body intersects the plane of the ecliptic. **7.** *Anat.* any natural bulge or swelling, such as those along the course of a lymphatic vessel (**lymph node**). [C16: < L *nōdus* knot] —ˈ**nodal** *adj.*

nod off *vb.* (*intr., adv.*) *Inf.* to fall asleep.

nodule (ˈnɒdjuːl) *n.* **1.** a small knot, lump, or node. **2.** any of the knoblike outgrowths on the roots of clover and other legumes that contain bacteria involved in nitrogen fixation. **3.** a small rounded lump of rock or mineral substance, esp. in a matrix of different rock material. [C17: < L *nōdulus,* < *nōdus* knot] —ˈ**nodular,** ˈ**nodulose,** *or* ˈ**nodulous** *adj.*

Noel *or* **Noël** (nəʊˈɛl) *n.* (in carols, etc.) another word for **Christmas.** [C19: < F, < L *nātālis* a birthday]

noetic (nəʊˈɛtɪk) *adj.* of or relating to the mind. [C17: < Gk *noētikos,* < *noein* to think]

nog *or* **nogg** (nɒg) *n.* **1.** Also called: **flip.** a drink, esp. an alcoholic one, containing beaten egg. **2.** *East Anglian dialect.* strong local beer. [C17 (orig.: a strong beer): <?]

noggin (ˈnɒgɪn) *n.* **1.** a small quantity of spirits. **2.** a small mug. **3.** *Inf.* the head. [C17: <?]

no-go area *n.* a district in a town that is barricaded off, usually by a paramilitary organization, which the police, army, etc., can only enter by force.

Noh (nəʊ) *n.* a variant spelling of **No**[1].

noir (nwɑː) *adj.* (of a film) showing characteristics of a *film noir,* in plot or style. [C20: < French, lit.: black]

noise (nɔɪz) *n.* **1.** a sound, esp. one that is loud or disturbing. **2.** loud shouting; clamour; din. **3.** any undesired electrical disturbance in a circuit, etc. **4.** (*pl.*) conventional comments or sounds conveying a reaction: *sympathetic noises.* **5. make a noise.** to talk a great deal or complain (about). ~*vb.* **6.** (*tr.;* usually foll. by *abroad* or *about*) to spread (news, gossip, etc.). [C13: < OF, < L: NAUSEA]

noiseless (ˈnɔɪzlɪs) *adj.* making little or no sound. —ˈ**noiselessly** *adv.* —ˈ**noiselessness** *n.*

noisette (nwɑːˈzɛt) *adj.* **1.** flavoured with hazelnuts. **2.** nutbrown, as butter browned over heat. ~*n.* **3.** a small round or oval piece of meat. **4.** a hazelnut chocolate. [< F: hazelnut]

noisome (ˈnɔɪsəm) *adj.* **1.** (esp. of smells) offensive. **2.** harmful or noxious. [C14: < obs. *noy,* var. of ANNOY + -SOME[1]] —ˈ**noisomeness** *n.*

noisy (ˈnɔɪzɪ) *adj.* **noisier, noisiest. 1.** making a loud or constant noise. **2.** full of or characterized by noise. —ˈ**noisily** *adv.* —ˈ**noisiness** *n.*

nolens volens *Latin.* (ˈnəʊlɛnz ˈvəʊlɛnz) *adv.* whether willing or unwilling.

nolle prosequi (ˈnɒlɪ ˈprɒsɪˌkwaɪ) *n. Law.* an entry made on the court record when the plaintiff or prosecutor undertakes not to continue the action or prosecution. [L: do not pursue]

nomad (ˈnəʊmæd) *n.* **1.** a member of a people or tribe who move from place to place to find pasture and food. **2.** a wanderer. [C16: via F < L *nomas* wandering shepherd, < Gk] —**noˈmadic** *adj.* —ˈ**nomadism** *n.*

no-man's-land *n.* **1.** land between boundaries, esp. an unoccupied zone between opposing forces. **2.** an unowned or unclaimed piece of land. **3.** an ambiguous area of activity.

nom de guerre (ˈnɒm də ˈgɛə) *n., pl.* **noms de guerre** (ˈnɒm də ˈgɛə). an assumed name. [F, lit.: war name]

nom de plume (ˈnɒm də ˈpluːm) *n., pl.* **noms de plume** (ˈnɒm də ˈpluːm). another term for **pen name.** [F]

nomenclature (nəʊˈmɛnklətʃə; *U.S.* ˈnəʊmənˌkleɪtʃər) *n.* the terminology used in a particular science, art, activity, etc. [C17: < L *nōmenclātūra* list of names]

nominal (ˈnɒmɪnᵊl) *adj.* **1.** in name only; theoretical: *the nominal leader.* **2.** minimal in comparison with real worth; token: *a nominal fee.* **3.** of, constituting, or giving a name. **4.** *Grammar.* of or relating to a noun or noun phrase. ~*n.* **5.** *Grammar.* a noun, noun phrase, or syntactically similar structure. [C15: < L *nōminālis,* < *nōmen* name] —ˈ**nominally** *adv.*

nominalism (ˈnɒmɪnᵊˌlɪzəm) *n.* the philosophical theory that a general word, such as *dog,* is merely a name and does not denote a real object, the general idea "dog". —ˈ**nominalist** *n.*

nominal value *n.* another name for **par value.**

nominate (ˈnɒmɪˌneɪt) *vb.* (*mainly tr.*) **1.** to propose as a candidate, esp. for an elective office. **2.** to appoint to an office or position. **3.** (*intr.*) *Austral.* to stand as a candidate in an election. [C16: < L *nōmināre* to call by name, < *nōmen* name] —ˌ**nomiˈnation** *n.* —ˈ**nomiˌnator** *n.*

nominative (ˈnɒmɪnətɪv) *adj.* **1.** *Grammar.* denoting a case of nouns and pronouns in inflected languages that is used esp. to identify the subject of a finite verb. **2.** appointed rather than elected to a position, office, etc. ~*n.* **3.** *Grammar.* **a.** the nominative case. **b.** a word or speech element in the nominative case. [C14: < L *nōminātīvus* belonging to naming, < *nōmen* name] —**nominatival** (ˌnɒmɪnəˈtaɪvᵊl) *adj.*

nominee (ˌnɒmɪˈniː) *n.* a person who is nominated to an office or as a candidate. [C17: < NOMINATE + -EE]

nomogram (ˈnɒməˌgræm, ˈnəʊmə-) *or* **nomograph** *n.* an arrangement of two linear or logarithmic scales such that an intersecting straight line enables intermediate values or values on a third scale to be read off. [C20: < Gk *nomos* law + -GRAM]

-nomy *n. combining form.* indicating a science or the laws governing a certain field of knowledge: *agronomy; economy.* [< Gk *-nomia* law] —**-nomic** *adj. combining form.*

non- *prefix.* **1.** indicating negation: *nonexistent.* **2.** indicating refusal or failure: *noncooperation.* **3.** indicating exclusion from a specified class: *nonfiction.* **4.** indicating lack or absence: *nonobjective; nonevent.* [< L *nōn* not]

nonage (ˈnəʊnɪdʒ) *n.* **1.** *Law.* the state of being under any of various ages at which a person may legally enter into certain transactions, such as marrying, etc. **2.** any period of immaturity.

nonagenarian (ˌnəʊnədʒɪˈnɛərɪən) *n.* **1.** a person who is from 90 to 99 years old. ~*adj.* **2.** of, relating to, or denoting a nonagenarian. [C19: < L *nōnāgēnārius,* < *nōnāginta* ninety]

nonaggression (ˌnɒnəˈgrɛʃən) *n.* **a.** restraint of aggression, esp. between states. **b.** (*as modifier*): *a nonaggression pact.*

nonagon (ˈnɒnəˌgɒn) *n.* a polygon having nine sides. —**nonagonal** (nɒnˈægənᵊl) *adj.*

nonaligned (ˌnɒnəˈlaɪnd) *adj.* (of states, etc.) not

ˌ**nonacaˈdemic** *adj.*
ˌ**nonacˈceptance** *n.*
ˌ**nonadˈdictive** *adj.*
ˌ**nonalcoˈholic** *adj.*
ˌ**nonapˈpearance** *n.*
ˌ**nonatˈtendance** *n.*
ˌ**nonatˈtributable** *adj.*
nonˈbasic *adj.*
ˌ**nonbelˈligerent** *adj.*
ˌ**nonbioˈlogical** *adj.*
nonˈbreakable *adj.*
nonˈcarboˌnated *adj.*
non-ˈCatholic *adj., n.*

part of a major alliance or power bloc. —ˌ**nonaˈlignment** *n.*

nonce (nɒns) *n.* the present time or occasion (now only in **for the nonce**). [C12: < *for the nonce,* a mistaken division of *for then anes,* < *then* dative singular of *the* + *anes* ONCE]

nonce word *n.* a word coined for a single occasion.

nonchalant (ˈnɒnʃələnt) *adj.* casually unconcerned or indifferent; uninvolved. [C18: < F, < *nonchaloir* to lack warmth, < NON- + *chaloir* < L *calēre* to be warm] —ˈ**nonchalance** *n.*

non-com (ˈnɒnˌkɒm) *n.* short for **noncommissioned officer.**

noncombatant (nɒnˈkɒmbətənt) *n.* **1.** a civilian in time of war. **2.** a member of the armed forces whose duties do not include fighting, such as a chaplain or surgeon.

noncommissioned officer (ˌnɒnkəˈmɪʃənd) *n.* (in the armed forces) a person, such as a sergeant or corporal, who is appointed from the ranks as a subordinate officer.

noncommittal (ˌnɒnkəˈmɪtᵊl) *adj.* not involving or revealing commitment to any particular opinion or course of action.

non compos mentis *Latin.* (ˈnɒn ˈkɒmpəs ˈmɛntɪs) *adj.* mentally incapable of managing one's own affairs; of unsound mind. [L: not in control of one's mind]

nonconformist (ˌnɒnkənˈfɔːmɪst) *n.* **1.** a person who does not conform to generally accepted patterns of behaviour or thought. ~*adj.* **2.** of or characterized by behaviour that does not conform to accepted patterns. —ˌ**nonconˈformity** *or* ˌ**nonconˈformism** *n.*

Nonconformist (ˌnɒnkənˈfɔːmɪst) *n.* **1.** a member of a Protestant denomination that dissents from an Established Church, esp. the Church of England. ~*adj.* **2.** of, relating to, or denoting Nonconformists. —ˌ**Nonconˈformity** *or* ˌ**Nonconˈformism** *n.*

noncontributory (ˌnɒnkənˈtrɪbjʊtərɪ) *adj.* **1.** denoting an insurance or pension scheme for employees, the premiums of which are paid entirely by the employer. **2.** (of a state benefit) not dependent on national insurance contributions.

nondescript (ˈnɒndɪˌskrɪpt) *adj.* **1.** having no outstanding features. ~*n.* **2.** a nondescript person or thing. [C17: < NON- + L *dēscriptus,* p.p. of *dēscribere* to copy]

none[1] (nʌn) *pron.* (*functioning as sing. or pl.*) **1.** not any of a particular class: *none of my letters has arrived.* **2.** no-one; nobody: *there were none to tell the tale.* **3.** not any (of): *none of it looks edible.* **4. none other.** no other person: *none other than the Queen herself.* **5. none the.** (*foll. by a comparative adj.*) in no degree: *she was none the worse for her ordeal.* **6. none too.** not very: *he was none too pleased.* [OE *nān,* lit.: not one]

▷ **Usage.** See at **everyone.**

none[2] (nəʊn) *n.* another word for **nones.**

nonentity (nɒnˈɛntɪtɪ) *n., pl.* **-ties. 1.** an insignificant person or thing. **2.** a nonexistent thing. **3.** the state of not existing; nonexistence.

nones (nəʊnz) *n.* (*functioning as sing. or pl.*) **1.** (in the Roman calendar) the ninth day before the ides of each month: the seventh day of March, May, July, and October, and the fifth of each other month. **2.** *Chiefly R.C. Church.* the fifth of the seven canonical hours of the divine office, originally fixed at the ninth hour of the day, about 3 p.m. [OE *nōn,* < L *nōna hora* ninth hour, < *nōnus* ninth]

nonesuch *or* **nonsuch** (ˈnʌnˌsʌtʃ) *n. Arch.* a matchless person or thing; nonpareil.

nonet (nəʊˈnɛt) *n.* **1.** a piece of music for nine instruments or nine voices. **2.** a group of nine singers or instrumentalists.

nonetheless (ˌnʌnðəˈlɛs) *sentence connector.* despite that; however; nevertheless.

non-Euclidean geometry *n.* the branch of modern geometry in which certain axioms of Euclidean geometry are denied.

nonevent (ˌnɒnɪˈvɛnt) *n.* a disappointing or insignificant occurrence, esp. one predicted to be important.

nonexecutive director (ˌnɒnɪgˈzɛkjʊtɪv) *n.* a director of a commercial company who is not a full-time employee of the company.

nonfeasance (nɒnˈfiːzᵊns) *n. Law.* a failure to act when under an obligation to do so. Cf. **malfeasance, misfeasance.** [C16: < NON- + *feasance* (obs.) doing, < F *faisance,* < *faire* to do, L *facere*]

nonferrous (nɒnˈfɛrəs) *adj.* **1.** denoting any metal other than iron. **2.** not containing iron.

nonflammable (nɒnˈflæməbᵊl) *adj.* incapable of burning or not easily set on fire.

nong (nɒŋ) *n. Austral. sl.* a stupid or incompetent person. [C19: ? < obs. E dialect *nigmenog* silly fellow, <?]

nonillion (nəʊˈnɪljən) *n.* **1.** (in Britain, France, and Germany) the number represented as one followed by 54 zeros (10^{54}). **2.** (in the U.S. and Canada) the number represented as one followed by 30 zeros (10^{30}). Brit. word: **quintillion.** [C17: < F, < L *nōnus* ninth, on the model of MILLION]

---

nonˈcerebral *adj.*
non-ˈChristian *adj., n.*
nonˈclassic *or* **nonˈclassical** *adj.*
nonˈclassiˌfied *adj.*
nonˈclerical *adj.*
nonˈclinical *adj.*
ˌ**noncolˈlegiate** *adj.*
ˌ**noncomˈbining** *adj.*
ˌ**noncomˈmercial** *adj.*
ˌ**noncomˈmissioned** *adj.*
ˌ**noncomˈmunicant** *n.*
ˌ**noncomˈmunicative** *adj.*
nonˈcommunist *n., adj.*
ˌ**noncomˈpetitive** *adj.*
ˌ**noncomˈpliance** *n.*
ˌ**nonconˈciliatory** *adj.*
ˌ**nonconˈclusive** *adj.*
ˌ**nonconˈductive** *adj.*
ˌ**nonconˈductor** *n.*
ˌ**nonconfiˈdential** *adj.*
ˌ**nonconˈflicting** *adj.*
ˌ**nonconˈsecutive** *adj.*
ˌ**nonconˈsenting** *adj.*
ˌ**nonconˈstructive** *adj.*
ˌ**nonconˈtagious** *adj.*
ˌ**nonconˈtributing** *adj.*
ˌ**noncontroˈversial** *adj.*
ˌ**nonconˈventional** *adj.*
ˌ**nonconˈvertible** *adj.*
ˌ**noncoˌoperˈation** *n.*
ˌ**noncorˈroborative** *adj.*
ˌ**noncorˈroding** *adj.*
ˌ**noncreˈative** *adj.*
nonˈcriminal *adj.*
nonˈcritical *adj.*
nonˈcultiˌvated *adj.*
ˌ**nondeˈciduous** *adj.*
ˌ**nondeˈlivery** *n.*
ˌ**nondemoˈcratic** *adj.*
ˌ**nondeˈmonstrable** *adj.*
ˌ**nondeˌnomiˈnational** *adj.*
ˌ**nondepartˈmental** *adj.*
ˌ**nondeˈpendence** *n.*
ˌ**nondeˈtachable** *adj.*
nonˈdetoˌnating *adj.*
nonˈdisciˌplinary *adj.*
ˌ**nondisˈcrimiˌnating** *adj.*
ˌ**nondiˈvisible** *adj.*
ˌ**nondocˈtrinal** *adj.*
ˌ**nondogˈmatic** *adj.*
nonˈdrinker *n.*
nonˈdrip *adj.*
nonˈdriver *n.*
nonˈearning *adj.*
ˌ**nonecoˈnomic** *adj.*
ˌ**nonefˈfective** *adj.*
ˌ**noneˈlastic** *adj.*
ˌ**noneˈquivalent** *adj.*
ˌ**nonesˈsential** *adj., n.*
nonˈethical *adj.*
ˌ**nonexˈchangeable** *adj.*
ˌ**nonexˈistence** *n.*
ˌ**nonexˈistent** *adj.*
ˌ**nonexˈplosive** *adj.*
nonˈfactual *adj.*
nonˈfatal *adj.*
nonˈfattening *adj.*
nonˈfinite *adj.*
nonˈflexible *adj.*
nonˈfluid *adj.*
nonˈfreezing *adj.*
ˌ**nonfulˈfilment** *n.*
nonˈfunctional *adj.*
nonˈfusible *adj.*
nonˈgaseous *adj.*
ˌ**nongovernˈmental** *adj.*
ˌ**nonharˈmonic** *adj.*
nonˈhuman *adj.*
ˌ**noninˈfectious** *adj.*
ˌ**noninˈflammable** *adj.*
ˌ**noninˈflected** *adj.*
ˌ**noninˈheritable** *adj.*
ˌ**nonintelˈlectual** *adj.*
ˌ**noninterˈsecting** *adj.*

nonintervention (ˌnɒnɪntəˈvɛnʃən) *n.* refusal to intervene, esp. the abstention by a state from intervening in the affairs of other states or in its own internal disputes.

nonjuror (nɒnˈdʒʊərə) *n.* a person who refuses to take an oath, as of allegiance.

Nonjuror (nɒnˈdʒʊərə) *n.* any of a group of clergy in England and Scotland who declined to take the oath of allegiance to William and Mary in 1689.

nonmetal (nɒnˈmɛtᵊl) *n.* any of a number of chemical elements that have acidic oxides and are poor conductors of heat and electricity. —ˌ**nonmeˈtallic** *adj.*

nonmoral (nɒnˈmɒrəl) *adj.* not involving morality or ethics; neither moral nor immoral.

nonobjective (ˌnɒnəbˈdʒɛktɪv) *adj.* of or designating an art movement in which things are depicted in an abstract or purely formalized way.

no-nonsense (ˌnəʊˈnɒnsəns) *adj.* sensible, practical, and straightforward: *a severe no-nonsense look.*

nonpareil (ˈnɒnpərəl, ˌnɒnpəˈreɪl) *n.* a person or thing that is unsurpassed; peerless example. [C15: < F, < NON- + *pareil* similar]

nonplus (nɒnˈplʌs) *vb.* **-plussing, -plussed** *or U.S.* **-plusing, -plused.** **1.** (*tr.*) to put at a loss; confound. ~*n., pl.* **-pluses. 2.** a state of utter perplexity prohibiting action or speech. [C16: < L *nōn plūs* no further]

non-profit-making *adj.* not yielding a profit, esp. because organized or established for some other reason: *a non-profit-making organization.*

nonproliferation (ˌnɒnprəˌlɪfərˈeɪʃən) *n.* **a.** limitation of the production or spread of something, esp. nuclear or chemical weapons. **b.** (*as modifier*): *a nonproliferation treaty.*

non-pros (ˌnɒnˈprɒs) *n.* **1.** short for **non prosequitur.** ~*vb.* **-prossing, -prossed. 2.** (*tr.*) to enter a judgment of non prosequitur against (a plaintiff).

non prosequitur (ˈnɒn prəʊˈsɛkwɪtə) *n. Law.* (formerly) a judgment in favour of a defendant when the plaintiff failed to take the necessary steps in an action within the time allowed. [L, lit.: he does not prosecute]

nonrepresentational (ˌnɒnrɛprɪzɛnˈteɪʃənᵊl) *adj. Art.* another word for **abstract.**

nonresistant (ˌnɒnrɪˈzɪstənt) *adj.* **1.** incapable of resisting something, such as a disease; susceptible. **2.** *History.* (esp. in 17th-century England) practising passive obedience to royal authority even when its commands were unjust.

nonrestrictive (ˌnɒnrɪˈstrɪktɪv) *adj.* **1.** not limiting. **2.** *Grammar.* denoting a relative clause that is not restrictive. Cf. **restrictive** (sense 2).

nonsense (ˈnɒnsəns) *n.* **1.** something that has or makes no sense; unintelligible language; drivel. **2.** conduct or action that is absurd. **3.** foolish behaviour: *she'll stand no nonsense.* **4.** things of little or no value; trash. ~*interj.* **5.** an exclamation of disagreement. —**nonsensical** (nɒnˈsɛnsɪkᵊl) *adj.* —**nonˈsensically** *adv.* —**nonˈsensicalness** *or* **nonˌsensiˈcality** *n.*

nonsense verse *n.* verse in which the sense is nonexistent or absurd.

non sequitur (ˈnɒn ˈsɛkwɪtə) *n.* **1.** a statement having little or no relevance to what preceded it. **2.** *Logic.* a conclusion that does not follow from the premises. [L, lit.: it does not follow]

nonsmoker (nɒnˈsməʊkə) *n.* **1.** a person who does not smoke. **2.** a train compartment in which smoking is forbidden. —**nonˈsmoking** *adj.*

nonstandard (nɒnˈstændəd) *adj.* **1.** denoting or characterized by idiom, vocabulary, etc., that is not regarded as correct and acceptable by educated native speakers of a language; not standard. **2.** deviating from a given standard.

nonstarter (nɒnˈstɑːtə) *n.* **1.** a horse that fails to run in a race for which it has been entered. **2.** a person or thing that has little chance of success.

nonstick (ˈnɒnˈstɪk) *adj.* (of saucepans, etc.) coated with a substance that prevents food sticking to them.

nonstop (ˈnɒnˈstɒp) *adj., adv.* without making a stop: *a nonstop flight.*

nonsuch (ˈnʌnˌsʌtʃ) *n.* a variant spelling of **nonesuch.**

nonsuit (nɒnˈsuːt) *Law.* ~*n.* **1.** an order of a judge dismissing a suit when the plaintiff fails to show he has a good cause of action or fails to produce any evidence. ~*vb.* **2.** (*tr.*) to order the dismissal of the suit of (a person).

non troppo (ˈnɒn ˈtrɒpəʊ) *adv. Music.* (preceded by a direction, esp. a tempo marking) not to be observed too strictly (esp. in **allegro ma non troppo, adagio ma non troppo**). [It.]

non-U (nɒnˈjuː) *adj. Brit. inf.* (esp. of language) not characteristic of or used by the upper class.

nonunion (nɒnˈjuːnjən) *adj.* **1.** not belonging or related to a trade union: *nonunion workers.* **2.** not

---

ˌ**noninˈtoxiˌcating** *adj.*
nonˈiron *adj.*
nonˈirritant *adj., n.*
nonˈlethal *adj.*
nonˈlinear *adj.*
nonˈliterary *adj.*
nonˈlogical *adj.*
nonˈluminous *adj.*
ˌ**nonmagˈnetic** *adj.*
ˌ**nonmaˈlignant** *adj.*
nonˈmaritime *adj.*
nonˈmember *n.*
nonˈmembership *n.*
nonˈmetric *adj.*
nonˈmigratory *adj.*
nonˈmilitant *adj.*
ˌ**nonminisˈterial** *adj.*
nonˈnavigable *adj.*
ˌ**non-neˈgotiable** *adj.*
non-ˈnuclear *adj.*
ˌ**nonobˈservance** *n.*
ˌ**nonocˈcurrence** *n.*
ˌ**nonoperˈational** *adj.*
nonˈoperative *adj.*
ˌ**nonorˈganic** *adj.*
nonˈparalˌlel *adj.*
ˌ**nonpaˈrental** *adj.*
ˌ**nonparliaˈmentary** *adj.*
ˌ**nonpaˈrochial** *adj.*
ˌ**nonparˈticiˌpating** *adj.*
ˌ**nonpartiˈsan** *or* ˌ**nonpartiˈzan** *adj.*
nonˈparty *adj.*
nonˈpaying *adj.*
nonˈpayment *n.*
nonˈpermanent *adj.*
nonˈpermeable *adj.*
nonˈphysical *adj.*
nonˈplaying *adj.*
nonˈpoisonous *adj.*
nonˈporous *adj.*
nonˈpractising *adj.*
nonˈpredatory *adj.*
ˌ**nonpreˈscriptive** *adj.*
ˌ**nonproˈfessional** *adj.*
nonˈracial *adj.*
nonˈradical *adj.*
ˌ**nonradioˈactive** *adj.*
nonˈreader *n.*
ˌ**nonrecogˈnition** *n.*
ˌ**nonreˈcoverable** *adj.*
nonˈregistered *adj.*
ˌ**nonreˈligious** *adj.*
ˌ**nonreˈnewable** *adj.*
ˌ**nonrepreˈsentative** *adj.*
nonˈresident *n., adj.*
ˌ**nonresiˈdential** *adj.*
ˌ**nonreˈstricted** *adj.*
ˌ**nonreˈturnable** *adj.*
nonˈrigid *adj.*
nonˈscheduled *adj.*
ˌ**nonscienˈtific** *adj.*
nonˈseasonal *adj.*
ˌ**nonsecˈtarian** *adj.*
nonˈsecular *adj.*
nonˈsegreˌgated *adj.*
ˌ**nonseˈlective** *adj.*
nonˈsexist *adj.*
nonˈsexual *adj.*
nonˈskilled *adj.*
nonˈslip *adj.*
nonˈsocial *adj.*
nonˈsoluble *adj.*
nonˈspeaking *adj.*
nonˈspecialist *n.*
nonˈspiritual *adj.*
nonˈstaining *adj.*
ˌ**nonstaˈtistical** *adj.*
nonˈstructural *adj.*
ˌ**nonsubˈscriber** *n.*
nonˈsurgical *adj.*
nonˈswimmer *n.*
nonˈtaxable *adj.*
nonˈteaching *adj.*
nonˈtechnical *adj.*
ˌ**nonterriˈtorial** *adj.*
nonˈtoxic *adj.*
ˌ**nontransˈferable** *adj.*
nonˈtropical *adj.*
nonˈvenomous *adj.*
nonˈverbal *adj.*
nonˈvintage *adj.*
nonˈviolent *adj.*
nonˈvocal *adj.*

favouring or employing union labour: *a nonunion shop*. **3.** not produced by union labour.

nonvoter (nɒnˈvəʊtə) *n.* **1.** a person who does not vote. **2.** a person not eligible to vote.

nonvoting (nɒnˈvəʊtɪŋ) *adj.* **1.** of or relating to a nonvoter. **2.** *Finance.* (of shares, etc.) not entitling the holder to vote at company meetings.

noodle¹ (ˈnuːdᵊl) *n.* (*often pl.*) a ribbon-like strip of pasta. [C18: < G *Nudel* <?]

noodle² (ˈnuːdᵊl) *n.* **1.** *U.S. & Canad. sl.* the head. **2.** a simpleton. [C18: ? a blend of NODDLE¹ & NOODLE¹]

nook (nʊk) *n.* **1.** a corner or narrow recess. **2.** a secluded or sheltered place. [C13: <?]

noon (nuːn) *n.* **1.** the middle of the day; 12 o'clock. **2.** *Poetic.* the most important part; culmination. [OE *nōn*, < L *nōna* (*hōra*) ninth hour (orig. 3 p.m., the ninth hour from sunrise)]

noonday (ˈnuːnˌdeɪ) *n.* the middle of the day; noon.

no-one *or* **no one** *pron.* no person; nobody.

▷ **Usage.** See at **everyone.**

noontime (ˈnuːnˌtaɪm) *or* **noontide** *n.* the middle of the day; noon.

noose (nuːs) *n.* **1.** a loop in the end of a rope, such as a lasso or hangman's halter, usually tied with a slipknot. **2.** something that restrains or traps. **3. put one's head in a noose.** to bring about one's own downfall. ~*vb.* (*tr.*) **4.** to secure as in a noose. **5.** to make a noose of or in. [C15: ? < Provençal *nous*, < L *nōdus* NODE]

no-par *adj.* (of securities) without a par value.

nor (nɔː; *unstressed* nə) *conj.* (*coordinating*) **1.** (used to join alternatives, the first of which is preceded by *neither*) and not: *neither measles nor mumps.* **2.** (foll. by a verb) (and) not...either: *they weren't talented—nor were they particularly funny.* **3.** *Poetic.* neither: *nor wind nor rain.* [C13: contraction of OE *nōther*, < *nāhwæther* NEITHER]

Nor. *abbrev. for:* **1.** Norman. **2.** north. **3.** Norway. **4.** Norwegian.

noradrenaline (ˌnɔːrəˈdrɛnəlɪn, -liːn) *or* **noradrenalin** *n.* a hormone secreted by the adrenal medulla, increasing blood pressure and heart rate. U.S. name: **norepinephrine.**

NOR circuit *or* **gate** (nɔː) *n. Computers.* a logic circuit having two or more input wires and one output wire that has a high-voltage output signal only if all input signals are at a low voltage. Cf. **AND circuit.** [C20: < NOR; the action performed is similar to the operation of the conjunction *nor* in logic]

nordic (ˈnɔːdɪk) *adj. Skiing.* of competitions in cross-country racing and ski-jumping. Cf. **alpine** (sense 4).

Nordic (ˈnɔːdɪk) *adj.* of or belonging to a subdivision of the Caucasoid race typified by the tall blond blue-eyed long-headed inhabitants of Scandinavia. [C19: < F *nordique*, < *nord* NORTH]

norepinephrine (ˌnɔːrɛpɪˈnɛfrɪn, -riːn) *n.* the U.S. name for **noradrenaline.**

Norfolk jacket (ˈnɔːfək) *n.* a man's single-breasted belted jacket with one or two chest pockets and a box pleat down the back. [C19: worn in *Norfolk* for duck shooting]

noria (ˈnɔːrɪə) *n.* a water wheel with buckets attached to its rim for raising water from a stream into irrigation canals, etc. [C18: via Sp. < Ar. *nā'ūra*, < *na'ara* to creak]

nork (nɔːk) *n.* (*usually pl.*) *Austral. taboo sl.* a female breast. [C20: <?]

norm (nɔːm) *n.* **1.** an average level of achievement or performance, as of a group. **2.** a standard of achievement or behaviour that is required, desired, or designated as normal. [C19: < L *norma* carpenter's square]

normal (ˈnɔːmᵊl) *adj.* **1.** usual; regular; common; typical: *the normal level.* **2.** constituting a standard: *if we take this as normal.* **3.** *Psychol.* **a.** being within certain limits of intelligence, ability, etc. **b.** conforming to the conventions of one's group. **4.** (of laboratory animals) maintained in a natural state for purposes of comparison with animals treated with drugs, etc. **5.** *Chem.* (of a solution) containing a number of grams equal to the equivalent weight of the solute in each litre of solvent. **6.** *Geom.* another word for **perpendicular** (sense 1). ~*n.* **7.** the usual, average, or typical state, degree, form, etc. **8.** anything that is normal. **9.** *Geom.* a perpendicular line or plane. [C16: < L *normālis* conforming to the carpenter's square, < *norma* NORM] —**normality** (nɔːˈmælɪtɪ) *or esp. U.S.* ˈ**normalcy** *n.*

normal curve *n. Statistics.* a symmetrical bell-shaped curve representing the probability density function of a normal distribution.

normal distribution *n. Statistics.* a continuous distribution of a random variable with its mean, median, and mode equal.

normalize *or* **-ise** (ˈnɔːməˌlaɪz) *vb.* (*tr.*) **1.** to bring or make into the normal state. **2.** to bring into conformity with a standard. **3.** to heat (steel) above a critical temperature and allow it to cool in air to relieve internal stresses; anneal. —ˌ**normaliˈzation** *or* **-iˈsation** *n.*

normally (ˈnɔːməlɪ) *adv.* **1.** as a rule; usually; ordinarily. **2.** in a normal manner.

Norman (ˈnɔːmən) *n.* **1.** (in the Middle Ages) a member of the people of Normandy in N France, descended from the 10th-century Scandinavian conquerors of the country and the native French. **2.** a native or inhabitant of Normandy. **3.** another name for **Norman French.** ~*adj.* **4.** of or characteristic of the Normans or their dialect of French. **5.** of or characteristic of Normandy. **6.** denoting or having the style of Romanesque architecture used in Britain from the Norman Conquest until the 12th century, characterized by the rounded arch, massive masonry walls, etc.

Norman Conquest *n.* the invasion and settlement of England by the Normans, following the Battle of Hastings (1066).

Norman French *n.* the medieval Norman and English dialect of Old French.

normative (ˈnɔːmətɪv) *adj.* **1.** implying, creating, or prescribing a norm or standard, as in language: *normative grammar.* **2.** expressing value judgments as contrasted with stating facts.

Norn¹ (nɔːn) *n. Norse myth.* any of the three virgin goddesses of fate. [C18: ON]

Norn² (nɔːn) *n.* the medieval Norse language of the Orkneys, Shetlands, and parts of N Scotland. [C17: < ON *norrœ́na* Norwegian, < *northr* north]

Norse (nɔːs) *adj.* **1.** of ancient and medieval Scandinavia or its inhabitants. **2.** of or characteristic of Norway. ~*n.* **3. a.** the N group of Germanic languages, spoken in Scandinavia. **b.** any one of these languages, esp. in their ancient or medieval forms. **4. the Norse.** (*functioning as pl.*) **a.** the Norwegians. **b.** the Vikings.

Norseman (ˈnɔːsmən) *n., pl.* **-men.** another name for a **Viking.**

north (nɔːθ) *n.* **1.** one of the four cardinal points of the compass, at 0° or 360°, that is 90° from east and west and 180° from south. **2.** the direction along a meridian towards the North Pole. **3.** the direction in which a compass needle points; magnetic north. **4. the north.** (*often cap.*) any area lying in or towards the north. **5.** (*usually cap.*) *Cards.* the player or position at the table corresponding to north on the compass. ~*adj.* **6.** in, towards, or facing the north. **7.** (esp. of the wind) from the north. ~*adv.* **8.** in, to, or towards the north. [OE]

North (nɔːθ) *n.* **the. 1.** the northern area of England, generally regarded as reaching the southern boundaries of Yorkshire, Derbyshire, and Cheshire. **2.** (in the U.S.) the states north of the Mason-Dixon Line that were known as the Free States during the Civil War. **3.** the northern part of North America, esp. Alaska, the Yukon and the Northwest Territories. **4.** the countries of the world that are economically and technically advanced. ~*adj.* **5.** of or denoting the northern part of a specified country, area, etc.

Northants (nɔːˈθænts) *abbrev. for* Northamptonshire.

northbound (ˈnɔːθˌbaʊnd) *adj.* going or leading towards the north.

north by east *n.* one point on the compass east of north.

north by west *n.* one point on the compass west of north.

North Country *n.* (usually preceded by *the*) another name for **North** (sense 1).

Northd *abbrev. for* Northumberland.

northeast (ˌnɔːθˈiːst; *Naut.* ˌnɔːrˈiːst) *n.* **1.** the point of the compass or direction midway between north and east. **2.** (*often cap.;* usually preceded by *the*) any area lying in or towards this direction. ~*adj. also* **northeastern.** **3.** (*sometimes cap.*) of or denoting the northeastern part of a specified country, area, etc.: *northeast Lincolnshire.* **4.** in, towards, or facing the northeast. **5.** (esp. of the wind) from the northeast. ~*adv.* **6.** in, to, or towards the northeast. —ˌ**northˈeasternmost** *adj.*

Northeast (ˌnɔːθˈiːst) *n.* (usually preceded by *the*) the northeastern part of England, esp. Northumberland and Durham.

northeast by east *n.* one point on the compass east of northeast.

northeast by north *n.* one point on the compass north of northeast.

northeaster (ˌnɔːθˈiːstə; *Naut.* ˌnɔːrˈiːstə) *n.* a strong wind or storm from the northeast.

northeasterly (ˌnɔːθˈiːstəlɪ; *Naut.* ˌnɔːrˈiːstəlɪ) *adj., adv.* **1.** in, towards, or (esp. of a wind) from the northeast. ~*n., pl.* **-lies.** **2.** a wind or storm from the northeast.

northeastward (ˌnɔːθˈiːstwəd; *Naut.* ˌnɔːrˈiːstwəd) *adj.* **1.** towards or (esp. of a wind) from the northeast. ~*n.* **2.** a direction towards or area in the northeast. —ˌ**northˈeastwardly** *adj., adv.*

norther (ˈnɔːðə) *n. Chiefly southern U.S.* a wind or storm from the north.

northerly (ˈnɔːðəlɪ) *adj.* **1.** of or situated in the north. ~*adv., adj.* **2.** towards the north. **3.** from the north: *a northerly wind.* ~*n., pl.* **-lies.** **4.** a wind from the north. —ˈ**northerliness** *n.*

northern (ˈnɔːðən) *adj.* **1.** in or towards the north. **2.** (esp. of winds) proceeding from the north. **3.** (*sometimes cap.*) of or characteristic of the north or North.

Northerner (ˈnɔːðənə) *n.* (*sometimes not cap.*) a native or inhabitant of the north of any specified region, esp. England, the U.S., or the far north of Canada.

northern hemisphere *n.* (*often caps.*) that half of the globe lying north of the equator.

northern lights *pl. n.* another name for **aurora borealis.**

northernmost (ˈnɔːðənˌməʊst) *adj.* situated or occurring farthest north.

northing (ˈnɔːθɪŋ, -ðɪŋ) *n.* **1.** *Navigation.* movement or distance covered in a northerly direction, esp. as expressed in the resulting difference in latitude. **2.** *Astron.* a north or positive declination.

Northland (ˈnɔːθlənd) *n.* **1.** the peninsula containing Norway and Sweden. **2.** (in Canada) the far north. —ˈ**Northlander** *n.*

Northman (ˈnɔːθmən) *n., pl.* **-men.** another name for a **Viking.**

north-northeast *n.* **1.** the point on the compass or the direction midway between north and northeast. ~*adj., adv.* **2.** in, from, or towards this direction.

north-northwest *n.* **1.** the point on the compass or the direction midway between northwest and north. ~*adj., adv.* **2.** in, from, or towards this direction.

North Pole *n.* **1.** the northernmost point on the earth's axis, at a latitude of 90°N, characterized by very low temperatures. **2.** Also called: **north celestial pole.** *Astron.* the point of intersection of the earth's extended axis and the northern half of the celestial sphere. **3.** (*usually not cap.*) the pole of a freely suspended magnet, which is attracted to the earth's magnetic North Pole.

North-Sea gas *n.* (in Britain) natural gas obtained from deposits below the North Sea.

North Star *n.* **the.** another name for **Polaris.**

northward (ˈnɔːθwəd; *Naut.* ˈnɔːðəd) *adj.* **1.** moving, facing, or situated towards the north. ~*n.* **2.** the northward part, direction, etc. ~*adv. also* **northwards.** **3.** towards the north.

northwest (ˌnɔːθˈwɛst; *Naut.* ˌnɔːˈwɛst) *n.* **1.** the point of the compass or direction midway between north and west. **2.** (*often cap.;* usually preceded by *the*) any area lying in or towards this direction. ~*adj. also* **northwestern.** **3.** (*sometimes cap.*) of or denoting the northwestern part of a specified country, area, etc.: *northwest Greenland.* ~*adj., adv.* **4.** in, to, or towards the northwest. —ˌ**northˈwesternmost** *adj.*

Northwest (ˌnɔːθˈwɛst) *n.* (usually preceded by *the*) the northwestern part of England, esp. Lancashire and the Lake District.

northwest by north *n.* one point on the compass north of northwest.

northwest by west *n.* one point on the compass south of northwest.

northwester (ˌnɔːθˈwɛstə; *Naut.* ˌnɔːˈwɛstə) *n.* a strong wind or storm from the northwest.

northwesterly (ˌnɔːθˈwɛstəlɪ; *Naut.* ˌnɔːˈwɛstəlɪ) *adj., adv.* **1.** in, towards, or (esp. of a wind) from the northwest. ~*n., pl.* **-lies.** **2.** a wind or storm from the northwest.

Northwest Territories *pl. n.* the part of Canada north of the provinces and east of the Yukon Territory.

northwestward (ˌnɔːθˈwɛstwəd; *Naut.* ˌnɔːˈwɛstwəd) *adj.* **1.** towards or (esp. of a wind) from the northwest. ~*n.* **2.** a direction towards or area in the northwest. —ˌ**northˈwestwardly** *adj., adv.*

Norw. *abbrev. for:* **1.** Norway. **2.** Norwegian.

Norway lobster (ˈnɔːˌweɪ) *n.* a European lobster fished for food.

Norway rat *n.* another name for **brown rat.**

Norway spruce *n.* a European spruce tree having drooping branches and dark green needle-like leaves.

Norwegian (nɔːˈwiːdʒən) *adj.* **1.** of or characteristic of Norway, its language, or its people. ~*n.* **2.** any of the various North Germanic languages of Norway. **3.** a native or inhabitant of Norway.

Nos. *or* **nos.** *abbrev. for* numbers.

nose (nəʊz) *n.* **1.** the organ of smell and entrance to the respiratory tract, consisting of a prominent structure divided into two hair-lined air passages. Related adj.: **nasal.** **2.** the sense of smell itself: in animals, the ability to follow trails by scent (esp. in **a good nose**). **3.** the scent, aroma, bouquet of something, esp. wine. **4.** instinctive skill in discovering things (sometimes in **follow one's nose**): *he had a nose for good news stories.* **5.** any part resembling a nose in form or function, such as a nozzle or spout. **6.** the forward part of a vehicle, aircraft, etc. **7.** narrow margin of victory (in **(win) by a nose**). **8. cut off one's nose to spite one's face.** to carry out a vengeful action that hurts oneself more than another. **9. get up (someone's) nose.** *Inf.* to annoy or irritate (someone). **10. keep one's nose clean.** to stay out of trouble. **11. lead by the nose.** to make (someone) do unquestioningly all one wishes; dominate. **12. look down one's nose at.** *Inf.* to be disdainful of. **13. on the nose.** *Sl.* **a.** (in horse-race betting) to win only: *I bet twenty pounds on the nose on that horse.* **b.** *Chiefly U.S. & Canad.* precisely; exactly. **c.** *Austral.* bad or bad-smelling. **14. pay through the nose.** *Inf.* to pay an exorbitant price. **15. put someone's nose out of joint.** *Inf.* to thwart or offend someone. **16. rub someone's nose in it.** *Inf.* to remind someone unkindly of a failing or error. **17. turn up one's nose (at).** *Inf.* to behave disdainfully (towards). **18. with one's nose in the air.** haughtily. ~*vb.* **19.** (*tr.*) (esp. of horses, dogs, etc.) to rub, touch, or sniff with the nose; nuzzle. **20.** to smell or sniff. **21.** (*intr.;* usually foll. by *after* or *for*) to search (for) by or as if by scent. **22.** to move or cause to move forwards slowly and carefully: *we nosed the car into the garage.* **23.** (*intr.;* foll. by *into, around, about,* etc.) to pry or snoop (into) or meddle (in). [OE *nosu*] —ˈ**noseless** *adj.* —ˈ**noseˌlike** *adj.*

nosebag (ˈnəʊzˌbæg) *n.* a bag, fastened around the head of a horse and covering the nose, in which feed is placed.

noseband (ˈnəʊzˌbænd) *n.* the detachable part of a horse's bridle that goes around the nose.

nosebleed (ˈnəʊzˌbliːd) *n.* bleeding from the nose as the result of injury, etc.

nose cone *n.* the conical forward section of a missile, spacecraft, etc., designed to withstand high temperatures, esp. during re-entry into the earth's atmosphere.

nose dive *n.* **1.** a sudden plunge with the nose or front pointing downwards, esp. of an aircraft. **2.** *Inf.* a sudden drop or sharp decline: *prices took a nose dive.* ~*vb.* **nose-dive.** (*intr.*) **3.** to perform a nose dive.

nose flute *n.* (esp. in the South Sea Islands) a type of flute blown through the nose.

nosegay (ˈnəʊzˌgeɪ) *n.* a small bunch of flowers; posy. [C15: < NOSE + *gay* (arch.) toy]

nosepiece (ˈnəʊzˌpiːs) *n.* **1.** a piece of armour to protect the nose. **2.** the connecting part of a pair of spectacles that rests on the nose; bridge. **3.** the part of a microscope to which one or more objective lenses are attached. **4.** a less common word for **noseband.**

nose rag *n. Sl.* a handkerchief.

nose ring *n.* a ring fixed through the nose, as for leading a bull.

nose wheel *n.* a wheel fitted to the forward end of a vehicle, esp. the landing wheel under the nose of an aircraft.

nosey (ˈnəʊzɪ) *adj.* a variant spelling of **nosy.**

nosh (nɒʃ) *Sl.* ~*n.* **1.** food or a meal. ~*vb.* **2.** to eat. [C20: < Yiddish; cf. G *naschen* to nibble]

nosh-up *n. Brit. sl.* a large and satisfying meal.

no-side *n. Rugby.* the end of a match, signalled by the referee's whistle.

nosology (nɒˈsɒlədʒɪ) *n.* the branch of medicine concerned with the classification of diseases. [C18: < Gk *nosos* disease] —**nosological** (ˌnɒsəˈlɒdʒɪkᵊl) *adj.*

nostalgia (nɒˈstældʒə, -dʒɪə) *n.* **1.** a yearning for past circumstances, events, etc. **2.** the evocation of this emotion, as in a book, film, etc. **3.** homesickness. [C18: NL, < Gk *nostos* a return home + -ALGIA] —**nosˈtalgic** *adj.* —**nosˈtalgically** *adv.*

nostoc (ˈnɒstɒk) *n.* a blue-green gelatinous alga occurring in moist places. [C17: NL, coined by Paracelsus (1493–1541) Swiss physician]

nostril (ˈnɒstrɪl) *n.* either of the two external openings of the nose. [OE *nosthyrl,* < *nosu* NOSE + *thyrel* hole]

nostrum (ˈnɒstrəm) *n.* **1.** a patent or quack medicine. **2.** a favourite remedy. [C17: < L: our own (make), < *noster* our]

nosy *or* **nosey** (ˈnəʊzɪ) *adj.* **nosier, nosiest.** *Inf.* prying or inquisitive. —ˈ**nosily** *adv.* —ˈ**nosiness** *n.*

nosy parker *n. Inf., chiefly Brit.* a prying person. [C20: arbitrary use of surname *Parker*]

not (nɒt) *adv.* **1. a.** used to negate the sentence, phrase, or word that it modifies: *I will not stand for it.* **b.** (*in combination*)*: they cannot go.* **2. not that.** (*conj.*) Also (arch.): **not but what.** which is not to say or suppose that: *I expect to lose the game—not that I mind.* ~*sentence substitute.* **3.** used to indicate denial or refusal: *certainly not.* [C14 *not,* var. of *nought* nothing, < OE *nāwiht,* < *nā* no + *wiht* creature, thing]

nota bene *Latin.* (ˈnəʊtə ˈbiːnɪ) note well; take note. Abbrevs.: **NB, N.B., nb, n.b.**

notability (ˌnəʊtəˈbɪlɪtɪ) *n., pl.* **-ties. 1.** the quality of being notable. **2.** a distinguished person.

notable (ˈnəʊtəbᵊl) *adj.* **1.** worthy of being noted or remembered; remarkable; distinguished. ~*n.* **2.** a notable person. [C14: via OF < L *notābilis,* < *notāre* to NOTE] —ˈ**notably** *adv.*

notarize *or* **-rise** (ˈnəʊtəˌraɪz) *vb.* (*tr.*) *U.S.* to attest to (a document, etc.), as a notary.

notary (ˈnəʊtərɪ) *n., pl.* **-ries. 1.** a notary public. **2.** (formerly) a clerk licensed to prepare legal documents. **3.** *Arch.* a clerk or secretary. [C14: < L *notārius* clerk, < *nota* a mark, note] —**notarial** (nəʊˈtɛərɪəl) *adj.* —ˈ**notaryship** *n.*

notary public *n., pl.* **notaries public.** a public official, usually a solicitor, who is legally authorized to administer oaths, attest and certify certain documents, etc.

notation (nəʊˈteɪʃən) *n.* **1.** any series of signs or symbols used to represent quantities or elements in a specialized system, such as music or mathematics. **2.** the act or process of notating. **3.** a note or record. [C16: < L *notātiō,* < *notāre* to NOTE] —**noˈtational** *adj.*

notch (nɒtʃ) *n.* **1.** a V-shaped cut or indentation; nick. **2.** a nick made in a tally stick. **3.** *U.S. & Canad.* a narrow gorge. **4.** *Inf.* a step or level (esp. in **a notch above**). ~*vb.* (*tr.*). **5.** to cut or make a notch in. **6.** to record with or as if with a notch. **7.** (usually foll. by *up*) *Inf.* to score or achieve: *the team notched up its fourth win.* [C16: < incorrect division of *an otch* (as *a notch*), < OF *oche* notch, < L *obsecāre,* < *secāre* to cut]

NOT circuit *or* **gate** (nɒt) *n. Computers.* a logic circuit that has a high-voltage output signal if the input signal is low, and vice versa: used extensively in computers. Also called: **inverter, negator.** [C20: the action performed on electrical signals is similar to the operation of *not* in logical constructions]

note (nəʊt) *n.* **1.** a brief record in writing, esp. a jotting for future reference. **2.** a brief informal letter. **3.** a formal written communication, esp. from one government to another. **4.** a short written statement giving any kind of information. **5.** a critical comment, explanatory statement, or reference in a book. **6.** short for **banknote. 7.** a characteristic atmosphere: *a note of sarcasm.* **8.** a distinctive vocal sound, as of a species of bird or animal. **9.** any of a series of graphic signs representing the pitch and duration of a musical sound. **10.** Also called (esp. U.S. and Canad.): **tone.** *Chiefly Brit.* a musical sound of definite fundamental frequency or pitch. **11.** *Chiefly Brit.* a key on a piano, organ, etc. **12.** a sound used as a signal or warning: *the note to retreat was sounded.* **13.** short for **promissory note. 14.** *Arch. or poetic.* a melody. **15. of note. a.** distinguished or famous. **b.** important: *nothing of note.* **16. strike the right** (*or* **a false**) **note.** to behave appropriately (or inappropriately). **17. take note.** (often foll. by *of*) to pay attention (to). ~*vb.* (*tr.; may take a clause as object*) **18.** to notice; perceive. **19.** to pay close attention to: *they noted every movement.* **20.** to make a written note of: *she noted the date in her diary.* **21.** to remark upon: *I note that you do not wear shoes.* **22.** to write down (music, a melody, etc.) in notes. **23.** a less common word for **annotate.** [C13: via OF < L *nota* sign] —ˈ**noteless** *adj.*

notebook (ˈnəʊtˌbʊk) *n.* a book for recording notes or memoranda.

notecase (ˈnəʊtˌkeɪs) *n.* a less common word for **wallet** (sense 1).

noted (ˈnəʊtɪd) *adj.* **1.** celebrated; famous. **2.** of special significance; noticeable. —ˈ**notedly** *adv.*

notelet (ˈnəʊtlɪt) *n.* a folded card with a printed design on the front, for writing a short letter.

notepaper (ˈnəʊtˌpeɪpə) *n.* paper for writing letters; writing paper.

noteworthy (ˈnəʊtˌwɜːðɪ) *adj.* worthy of notice; notable. —ˈ**noteˌworthiness** *n.*

nothing (ˈnʌθɪŋ) *pron.* **1.** (*indefinite*) no thing; not anything: *I can give you nothing.* **2.** no part or share: *to have nothing to do with this crime.* **3.** a matter of no importance: *it doesn't matter, it's nothing.* **4.** indicating the absence of anything perceptible; nothingness. **5.** indicating the absence of meaning, value, worth, etc.: *to amount to nothing.* **6.** zero quantity; nought. **7. be nothing to. a.** not to concern or be significant to (someone). **b.** to be not nearly as good, etc., as. **8. have** *or* **be nothing to do with.** to have no connection with. **9. nothing but.** no more than; only. **10. nothing doing.** *Inf.* an expression of dismissal, refusal, etc. **11. nothing if not.** at the very least; certainly. **12. nothing less than** *or*

nothing short of. downright; truly. **13. there's nothing to it.** it is very simple, easy, etc. **14. think nothing of. a.** to regard as easy or natural. **b.** to have no compunction about. **c.** to have a very low opinion of. ~*adv.* **15.** in no way; not at all: *he looked nothing like his brother.* ~*n.* **16.** *Inf.* a person or thing of no importance or significance. **17. sweet nothings.** words of endearment or affection. [OE *nāthing, nān thing,* < *nān* NONE[1] + THING]

▷ **Usage.** *Nothing* always takes a singular verb in careful usage, although a plural verb is often heard in informal speech in sentences such as *nothing but books were on the shelf.*

nothingness (ˈnʌθɪŋnɪs) *n.* **1.** the state of being nothing; nonexistence. **2.** absence of consciousness or life. **3.** complete insignificance. **4.** something that is worthless.

notice (ˈnəʊtɪs) *n.* **1.** observation; attention: *to escape notice.* **2. take notice.** to pay attention. **3. take no notice of.** to ignore or disregard. **4.** a warning; announcement. **5.** a displayed placard or announcement giving information. **6.** advance notification of intention to end an arrangement, contract, etc., as of employment (esp. in **give notice**). **7. at short notice.** with notification only a little in advance. **8.** *Chiefly Brit.* dismissal from employment. **9.** favourable, interested, or polite attention: *she was beneath his notice.* **10.** a theatrical or literary review: *the play received very good notices.* ~*vb.* **11.** to become aware (of); perceive; note. **12.** (*tr.*) to point out or remark upon. **13.** (*tr.*) to pay polite or interested attention to. **14.** (*tr.*) to acknowledge (an acquaintance, etc.). [C15: via OF < L *notitia* fame, < *nōtus* known]

noticeable (ˈnəʊtɪsəbˀl) *adj.* easily seen or detected; perceptible. —ˈ**noticeably** *adv.*

notice board *n. Brit.* a board on which notices, advertisements, bulletins, etc., are displayed. U.S. and Canad. name: **bulletin board.**

notifiable (ˈnəʊtɪˌfaɪəbˀl) *adj.* denoting certain infectious diseases, outbreaks of which must be reported to the public health authorities.

notification (ˌnəʊtɪfɪˈkeɪʃən) *n.* **1.** the act of notifying. **2.** a formal announcement. **3.** something that notifies; a notice.

notify (ˈnəʊtɪˌfaɪ) *vb.* **-fying, -fied.** (*tr.*) **1.** to tell. **2.** *Chiefly Brit.* to make known; announce. [C14: < OF *notifier,* < L *notificāre,* < *nōtus* known + *facere* to make] —ˈ**notiˌfier** *n.*

notion (ˈnəʊʃən) *n.* **1.** a vague idea; impression. **2.** an idea, concept, or opinion. **3.** an inclination or whim. ~See also **notions.** [C16: < L *nōtiō* a becoming acquainted (with), examination (of), < *noscere* to know]

notional (ˈnəʊʃənˀl) *adj.* **1.** expressing or consisting of ideas. **2.** not evident in reality; hypothetical or imaginary: *a notional tax credit.* **3.** characteristic of a notion, esp. in being speculative or abstract. **4.** *Grammar.* **a.** (of a word) having lexical meaning. **b.** another word for **semantic.** —ˈ**notionally** *adv.*

notions (ˈnəʊʃənz) *pl. n. Chiefly U.S. & Canad.* pins, cotton, ribbon, etc., used for sewing; haberdashery.

notochord (ˈnəʊtəˌkɔːd) *n.* a fibrous longitudinal rod in all embryo and some adult chordate animals, immediately above the gut, that supports the body. [C19: < Gk *nōton* the back + CHORD[1]]

notorious (nəʊˈtɔːrɪəs) *adj.* **1.** well-known for some bad or unfavourable quality, deed, etc.; infamous. **2.** *Rare.* generally known or widely acknowledged. [C16: < Med. L *notōrius* well-known, < *nōtus* known] —**notoriety** (ˌnəʊtəˈraɪɪtɪ) *n.* —**no**ˈ**toriously** *adv.*

notornis (nəʊˈtɔːnɪs) *n.* a rare flightless rail of New Zealand. [C19: NL, < Gk *notos* south + *ornis* bird]

not proven (ˈprəʊvˀn) *adj.* (*postpositive*) a third verdict available to Scottish courts, returned when there is insufficient evidence against the accused to convict.

no-trump *Cards.* ~*n. also* **no-trumps. 1.** a bid or contract to play without trumps. ~*adj. also* **no-trumper. 2.** (of a hand) suitable for playing without trumps.

Notts (nɒts) *abbrev. for* Nottinghamshire.

notwithstanding (ˌnɒtwɪθˈstændɪŋ) *prep.* **1.** (*often immediately postpositive*) in spite of; despite. ~*conj.* **2.** (*subordinating*) although. ~*sentence connector.* **3.** nevertheless.

nougat (ˈnuːgɑː) *n.* a hard chewy pink or white sweet containing chopped nuts, cherries, etc. [C19: via F < Provençal *nogat,* < *noga* nut, < L *nux* nut]

nought (nɔːt) *n. also* **naught, ought, aught. 1.** another name for **zero:** used esp. in numbering. ~*n., adj., adv.* **2.** a variant spelling of **naught.** [OE *nōwiht,* < *ne* not, no + *ōwiht* something]

noughts and crosses *n.* (*functioning as sing.*) a game in which two players, one using a nought, "O", the other a cross, "X", alternately mark squares formed by two pairs of crossed lines, the winner being the first to get three of his symbols in a row. U.S. and Canad. term: **tick-tack-toe,** (U.S.) **crisscross.**

noun (naʊn) *n.* **a.** a word or group of words that refers to a person, place, or thing. **b.** (*as modifier*): *a noun phrase.* Abbrev.: **N, n.** [C14: via Anglo-F < L *nōmen* NAME] —ˈ**nounal** *adj.* Related adj.: **nominal.**

nourish (ˈnʌrɪʃ) *vb.* (*tr.*) **1.** to provide with the materials necessary for life and growth. **2.** to encourage (an idea, etc.); foster: *to nourish resentment.* [C14: < OF *norir,* < L *nūtrīre* to feed] —ˈ**nourisher** *n.* —ˈ**nourishing** *adj.*

nourishment (ˈnʌrɪʃmənt) *n.* **1.** the act or state of nourishing. **2.** a substance that nourishes; food.

nous (naʊs) *n.* **1.** *Metaphysics.* mind or reason, esp. regarded as the principle governing all things. **2.** *Brit. sl.* common sense. [C17: < Gk: mind]

nouveau riche (ˌnuːvəʊ ˈriːʃ) *n., pl.* **nouveaux riches** (ˌnuːvəʊ ˈriːʃ). (often preceded by *the*) a person who has acquired wealth recently and is regarded as vulgarly ostentatious or lacking in social graces. [C19: < F lit.: new rich]

nouvelle cuisine (ˈnuːvɛl kwiːˈziːn) *n.* a style of preparing food, often raw or only lightly cooked, with unusual combinations of flavours. [C20: F, lit.: new cookery]

Nov. *abbrev. for* November.

nova (ˈnəʊvə) *n., pl.* **-vae** (-viː) *or* **-vas.** a faint variable star that undergoes an explosion and fast increase of luminosity, decreasing to its original luminosity in months or years. [C19: NL *nova* (*stella*) new (star), < L *novus* new]

novel[1] (ˈnɒvˀl) *n.* **1.** an extended fictional work in prose dealing with character, action, thought, etc., esp. in the form of a story. **2. the novel.** the literary genre represented by novels. [C15: < OF *novelle,* < L *novella* (*narrātiō*) new (story); see NOVEL[2]]

novel[2] (ˈnɒvˀl) *adj.* of a kind not seen before; fresh; new; original: *a novel suggestion.* [C15: < L *novellus,* dim. of *novus* new]

novelette (ˌnɒvəˈlɛt) *n.* **1.** an extended prose narrative or short novel. **2.** a novel that is regarded as slight, trivial, or sentimental. **3.** a short piece of lyrical music, esp. for piano.

novelettish (ˌnɒvəˈlɛtɪʃ) *adj.* characteristic of a novelette; trite or sentimental.

novelist (ˈnɒvəlɪst) *n.* a writer of novels.

novelistic (ˌnɒvəˈlɪstɪk) *adj.* of or characteristic of novels, esp. in style or method of treatment.

novella (nəʊˈvɛlə) *n., pl.* **-las** *or* **-le** (-leɪ). **1.** a short narrative tale, esp. one having a satirical point, such as those in Boccaccio's *Decameron.* **2.** a short novel. [C20: < It.; see NOVEL[1]]

novelty (ˈnɒvˀltɪ) *n., pl.* **-ties. 1. a.** the quality of being new and interesting. **b.** (*as modifier*): *novelty value.* **2.** a new or unusual experience. **3.** (*often pl.*) a small usually cheap new ornament or trinket. [C14: < OF *novelté;* see NOVEL[2]]

November (nəʊˈvɛmbə) *n.* the eleventh month of the year, consisting of 30 days. [C13: via OF < L: ninth month, < *novem* nine]

novena (nəʊˈviːnə) *n., pl.* **-nae** (-niː). *R.C. Church.* a devotion consisting of prayers or services on nine consecutive days. [C19: < Med. L, < L *novem* nine]

novice (ˈnɒvɪs) *n.* **1.** a person who is new to or inexperienced in a certain task, situation, etc.; beginner; tyro. **2.** a probationer in a religious order. **3.** a racehorse that has not won a specified number of races. [C14: via OF < L *novicius,* < *novus* new]

novitiate *or* **noviciate** (nəʊˈvɪʃɪɪt, -ˌeɪt) *n.* **1.** the state of being a novice, esp. in a religious order, or the period for which this lasts. **2.** the part of a religious house where the novices live. [C17: < F *noviciat,* < L *novīcius* NOVICE]

Novocaine (ˈnəʊvəˌkeɪn) *n.* a trademark for **procaine hydrochloride.** See **procaine.**

now (naʊ) *adv.* **1.** at or for the present time. **2.** immediately. **3.** in these times; nowadays. **4.** given the present circumstances: *now we'll have to stay to the end.* **5.** (preceded by *just*) very recently: *he left just now.* **6.** (often preceded by *just*) very soon: *he is leaving just now.* **7.** **(every) now and again** *or* **then.** occasionally; on and off. **8. now now!** an exclamation used to rebuke or pacify someone. ~*conj.* **9.** (*subordinating;* often foll. by *that*) seeing that: *now you're in charge, things will be better.* ~*sentence connector.* **10. a.** used as a hesitation word: *now, I can't really say.* **b.** used for emphasis: *now listen to this.* **c.** used at the end of a command: *run along, now.* ~*n.* **11.** the present time: *now is the time to go.* ~*adj.* **12.** *Inf.* of the moment; fashionable: *the now look.* [OE *nū*]

nowadays (ˈnaʊəˌdeɪz) *adv.* in these times. [C14: < NOW + *adays* < OE *a* on + *daeges* genitive of DAY]

noway (ˈnəʊˌweɪ) *adv.* **1.** not at all. ~*sentence substitute.* **no way. 2.** used to make an emphatic refusal, denial, etc.

Nowel *or* **Nowell** (nəʊˈɛl) *n.* an archaic spelling of **Noel.**

nowhere (ˈnəʊwɛə) *adv.* **1.** in, at, or to no place; not anywhere. **2. get nowhere (fast).** *Inf.* to fail completely to make any progress. **3. nowhere near.** far from; not nearly. ~*n.* **4.** a nonexistent or insignificant place. **5. middle of nowhere.** a completely isolated place.

nowise (ˈnəʊˌwaɪz) *adv.* in no manner; not at all.

nowt (naʊt) *n. N English.* a dialect word for **nothing.** [< NAUGHT]

noxious (ˈnɒkʃəs) *adj.* poisonous or harmful. [C17: < L *noxius* harmful, < *noxa* injury] —ˈ**noxiously** *adv.* —ˈ**noxiousness** *n.*

nozzle (ˈnɒzᵊl) *n.* a projecting pipe or spout from which fluid is discharged. [C17 *nosle, nosel,* dim. of NOSE]

Np *the chemical symbol for* neptunium.

NP *or* **np.** *abbrev. for* Notary Public.

NPA *abbrev. for* Newspaper Publishers' Association.

NPL *abbrev. for* National Physical Laboratory.

NS *abbrev. for:* **1.** New Style (method of reckoning dates). **2.** Nova Scotia. **3.** Nuclear Ship.

NSB (in Britain) *abbrev. for* National Savings Bank.

NSC (in Britain) *abbrev. for* National Safety Council.

NSPCC (in Britain) *abbrev. for* National Society for the Prevention of Cruelty to Children.

NST (in Canada) *abbrev. for* Newfoundland Standard Time.

NSW *abbrev. for* New South Wales.

NT *abbrev. for:* **1.** (in Britain) National Trust. **2.** New Testament. **3.** Northern Territory. **4.** no-trump.

-n't *contraction of* not: used as an enclitic after *be* and *have* when they function as main verbs and after auxiliary verbs or verbs operating syntactically as auxiliaries: *can't; don't; isn't.*

nth (ɛnθ) *adj.* **1.** *Maths.* of or representing an unspecified ordinal number, usually the greatest in a series: *the nth power.* **2.** *Inf.* being the last or most extreme of a long series: *for the nth time.* **3. to the nth degree.** *Inf.* to the utmost extreme.

NTP *abbrev. for* normal temperature and pressure. Also: **STP.**

nt. wt. *or* **nt wt** *abbrev. for* net weight.

n-type *adj.* **1.** (of a semiconductor) having more conduction electrons than mobile holes. **2.** associated with or resulting from the movement of electrons in a semiconductor.

nu (njuː) *n.* the 13th letter in the Greek alphabet (N, ν), a consonant. [< Gk, of Semitic origin]

nuance (njuːˈɑːns, ˈnjuːɑːns) *n.* a subtle difference in colour, meaning, tone, etc. [C18: < F, < *nuer* to show light and shade, ult. < L *nūbēs* a cloud]

nub (nʌb) *n.* **1.** a small lump or protuberance. **2.** a small piece or chunk. **3.** the point or gist: *the nub of a story.* [C16: var. of *knub,* < MLow G *knubbe* KNOB] —ˈ**nubbly** *or* ˈ**nubby** *adj.*

nubble (ˈnʌbᵊl) *n.* a small lump. [C19: dim. of NUB]

nubile (ˈnjuːbaɪl) *adj.* (of a girl) **1.** ready or suitable for marriage by virtue of age or maturity. **2.** sexually attractive. [C17: < L *nūbilis,* < *nūbere* to marry] —**nubility** (njuːˈbɪlɪtɪ) *n.*

nucha (ˈnjuːkə) *n., pl.* **-chae** (-kiː). *Zool., anat.* the back or nape of the neck. [C14: < Med. L, < Ar.: spinal marrow] —ˈ**nuchal** *adj.*

nuclear (ˈnjuːklɪə) *adj.* **1.** of or involving the nucleus of an atom: *nuclear fission.* **2.** *Biol.* of, relating to, or contained within the nucleus of a cell: *a nuclear membrane.* **3.** of, forming, or resembling any other kind of nucleus. **4.** of or operated by energy from fission or fusion of atomic nuclei: *a nuclear weapon.* **5.** involving or possessing nuclear weapons: *nuclear war.*

nuclear bomb *n.* a bomb whose force is due to uncontrolled nuclear fusion or nuclear fission.

nuclear energy *n.* energy released during a nuclear reaction as a result of fission or fusion. Also called: **atomic energy.**

nuclear family *n. Sociol., anthropol.* a primary social unit consisting of parents and their offspring.

nuclear fission *n.* the splitting of an atomic nucleus into approximately equal parts, either spontaneously or as a result of the impact of a particle usually with an associated release of energy. Sometimes shortened to **fission.**

nuclear fuel *n.* a fuel that provides nuclear energy, used in nuclear submarines, etc.

nuclear fusion *n.* a reaction in which two nuclei combine to form a nucleus with the release of energy. Sometimes shortened to **fusion.**

nuclear magnetic resonance *n.* a technique for determining the magnetic moments of nuclei by subjecting a substance to high-frequency radiation and a large magnetic field. It is used for determining structure, esp. in body scanning.

nuclear physics *n.* (*functioning as sing.*) the branch of physics concerned with the structure and behaviour of the nucleus and the particles of which it consists.

nuclear power *n.* power, esp. electrical or motive, produced by a nuclear reactor. Also called: **atomic power.**

nuclear reaction *n.* a process in which the structure and energy content of an atomic nucleus is changed by interaction with another nucleus or particle.

nuclear reactor *n.* a device in which a nuclear reaction is maintained and controlled for the production of nuclear energy. Sometimes shortened to **reactor.**

nuclear winter *n.* a period of low temperatures and little light that has been suggested would occur after a nuclear war.

nuclease (ˈnjuːklɪˌeɪz) *n.* any of a group of enzymes that hydrolyse nucleic acids to simple nucleotides.

nucleate *adj.* (ˈnjuːklɪɪt, -ˌeɪt). **1.** having a nucleus. ~*vb.* (ˈnjuːklɪˌeɪt). (*intr.*) **2.** to form a nucleus.

nuclei (ˈnjuːklɪˌaɪ) *n.* a plural of **nucleus.**

nucleic acid (njuːˈkliːɪk, -ˈkleɪ-) *n. Biochem.* any of a group of complex compounds with a high molecular weight that are vital constituents of all living cells. See also **RNA, DNA.**

nucleo- *or before a vowel* **nucle-** *combining*

form. **1.** nucleus or nuclear. **2.** nucleic acid. [< Latin *nucleus* kernel, < *nux* nut]

nucleolus (ˌnjuːklɪˈəʊləs) *n., pl.* **-li** (-laɪ). a small rounded body within a resting cell nucleus that contains RNA and proteins and is involved in protein synthesis. Also called: **nucleole.** [C19: < L, dim. of NUCLEUS] —ˌ**nucleˈolar** *adj.*

nucleon (ˈnjuːklɪˌɒn) *n.* a proton or neutron, esp. one present in an atomic nucleus.

nucleonics (ˌnjuːklɪˈɒnɪks) *n.* (*functioning as sing.*) the branch of physics concerned with the applications of nuclear energy. —ˌ**nucleˈonic** *adj.* —ˌ**nucleˈonically** *adv.*

nucleoside (ˈnjuːklɪəˌsaɪd) *n. Biochem.* a compound containing a purine or pyrimidine base linked to a sugar (usually ribose or deoxyribose).

nucleotide (ˈnjuːklɪəˌtaɪd) *n. Biochem.* a compound consisting of a nucleoside linked to phosphoric acid.

nucleus (ˈnjuːklɪəs) *n., pl.* **-clei** *or* **-cleuses. 1.** a central or fundamental thing around which others are grouped; core. **2.** a centre of growth or development; basis: *the nucleus of an idea.* **3.** *Biol.* the spherical or ovoid compartment of a cell that contains the chromosomes and associated molecules that control the characteristics and growth of the cell. **4.** *Astron.* the central portion in the head of a comet, consisting of small solid particles of ice and frozen gases. **5.** *Physics.* the positively charged dense region at the centre of an atom, composed of protons and neutrons, about which electrons orbit. **6.** *Chem.* a fundamental group of atoms in a molecule serving as the base structure for related compounds. [C18: < L: kernel, < *nux* nut]

nuclide (ˈnjuːklaɪd) *n.* a species of atom characterized by its atomic number and its mass number. [C20: < NUCLEO- + *-ide,* < Gk *eidos* shape]

nude (njuːd) *adj.* **1.** completely undressed. **2.** having no covering; bare; exposed. **3.** *Law.* **a.** lacking some essential legal requirement. **b.** (of a contract, etc.) made without consideration and void unless under seal. ~*n.* **4.** the state of being naked (esp. in **in the nude**). **5.** a naked figure, esp. in painting, sculpture, etc. [C16: < L *nūdus*] —ˈ**nudely** *adv.*

nudge (nʌdʒ) *vb.* (*tr.*) **1.** to push (someone) gently, esp. with the elbow, to get attention; jog. **2.** to push slowly or lightly: *as I drove out, I just nudged the gatepost.* ~*n.* **3.** a gentle poke or push. [C17: ? < Scand.] —ˈ**nudger** *n.*

nudibranch (ˈnjuːdɪˌbræŋk) *n.* a marine gastropod of an order characterized by a shell-less, often beautifully coloured, body bearing external gills. Also called: **sea slug.** [C19: < L *nudus* naked + *branche,* < L *branchia* gills]

nudism (ˈnjuːdɪzəm) *n.* the practice of nudity, esp. for reasons of health, etc. —ˈ**nudist** *n., adj.*

nudity (ˈnjuːdɪtɪ) *n., pl.* **-ties.** the state or fact of being nude; nakedness.

nugatory (ˈnjuːgətərɪ, -trɪ) *adj.* **1.** of little value; trifling. **2.** not valid: *a nugatory law.* [C17: < L *nūgātōrius,* < *nūgārī* to jest, < *nūgae* trifles]

nugget (ˈnʌgɪt) *n.* **1.** a small piece or lump, esp. of gold in its natural state. **2.** something small but valuable or excellent. [C19: <?]

nuggety (ˈnʌgɪtɪ) *adj.* **1.** of or resembling a nugget. **2.** *Austral. & N.Z. inf.* (of a person) thickset; stocky.

nuisance (ˈnjuːsəns) *n.* **1.** a person or thing that causes annoyance or bother. **2.** *Law.* something unauthorized that is obnoxious or injurious to the community at large or to an individual, esp. in relation to his ownership of property. **3. nuisance value.** the usefulness of a person's or thing's capacity to cause difficulties or irritation. [C15: via OF < *nuire* to injure, < L *nocēre*]

NUJ (in Britain) *abbrev. for* National Union of Journalists.

nuke (njuːk) *Sl., chiefly U.S.* ~*vb.* (*tr.*) **1.** to attack or destroy with nuclear weapons. ~*n.* **2.** a nuclear bomb.

null (nʌl) *adj.* **1.** without legal force; invalid; (esp. in **null and void**). **2.** without value or consequence; useless. **3.** lacking distinction; characterless. **4.** nonexistent; amounting to nothing. **5.** *Maths.* **a.** quantitatively zero. **b.** relating to zero. **c.** (of a set) having no members. **6.** *Physics.* involving measurement in which conditions are adjusted so that an instrument has a zero reading, as with a Wheatstone bridge. [C16: < L *nullus* none, < *ne* not + *ullus* any]

nullah (ˈnʌlɑː) *n.* (in India) a stream or drain. [C18: < Hindi *nālā*]

nulla-nulla (ˌnʌləˈnʌlə) *n. Austral.* a wooden club used as a weapon by Aborigines. Also called: **nulla.** [< Abor.]

null hypothesis *n. Statistics.* the residual hypothesis if the alternative hypothesis tested against it fails to achieve a predetermined significance level.

nullify (ˈnʌlɪˌfaɪ) *vb.* **-fying, -fied.** (*tr.*) **1.** to render legally void or of no effect. **2.** to render ineffective or useless; cancel out. [C16: < LL *nullificāre* to despise, < L *nullus* of no account + *facere* to make] —ˌ**nullifiˈcation** *n.*

nullity (ˈnʌlɪtɪ) *n., pl.* **-ties. 1.** the state of being null. **2.** a null or legally invalid act or instrument. **3.** something null, ineffective, characterless, etc. [C16: < Med. L *nullitās,* < L *nullus* no, not any]

NUM (in Britain) *abbrev. for* National Union of Mineworkers.

num. *abbrev. for:* **1.** number. **2.** numeral.

Num. *Bible. abbrev. for* Numbers.

numb (nʌm) *adj.* **1.** deprived of feeling through cold, shock, etc. **2.** unable to move; paralysed. ~*vb.* **3.** (*tr.*) to make numb; deaden, shock, or paralyse. [C15 *nomen,* lit.: taken (with paralysis), < OE *niman* to take] —ˈ**numbly** *adv.* —ˈ**numbness** *n.*

numbat (ˈnʌmˌbæt) *n.* a small Australian marsupial having a long snout and tongue and strong claws for hunting and feeding on termites. [C20: < Abor.]

number (ˈnʌmbə) *n.* **1.** a concept of quantity that is or can be derived from a single unit, the sum of a collection of units, or zero. Every number occupies a unique position in a sequence, enabling it to be used in counting. See also **cardinal number, ordinal number. 2.** the symbol used to represent a number; numeral. **3.** a numeral or string of numerals used to identify a person or thing: *a telephone number.* **4.** the person or thing so identified or designated: *she was number seven in the race.* **5.** sum or quantity: *a large number of people.* **6.** one of a series, as of a magazine; issue. **7. a.** a self-contained piece of pop or jazz music. **b.** a self-contained part of an opera or other musical score. **8.** a group of people, esp. an exclusive group: *he was not one of our number.* **9.** *Sl.* a person, esp. a sexually attractive girl: *who's that nice little number?* **10.** *Inf.* an admired article: *that little number is by Dior.* **11.** a grammatical category for the variation in form of nouns, pronouns, and any words agreeing with them, depending on how many persons or things are referred to. **12. any number of.** several or many. **13. by numbers.** *Mil.* (of a drill procedure, etc.) performed step by step, each move being made on the call of a number. **14. get** *or* **have someone's number.** *Inf.* to discover a person's true character or intentions. **15. one's number is up.** *Brit. inf.* one is finished; one is ruined or about to die. **16. without** *or* **beyond number.** innumerable. ~*vb.* (*mainly tr.*) **17.** to assign a number to. **18.** to add up to; total. **19.** (*also intr.*) to list (items) one by one; enumerate. **20.** (*also intr.*) to put or be put into a group, category, etc.: *they were numbered among the worst hit.* **21.** to limit the number of: *his days were numbered.* [C13: < OF *nombre,* < L *numerus*]

number crunching *n. Computers.* the large-scale processing of numerical data.

numberless (ˈnʌmbəlɪs) *adj.* **1.** too many to be counted; countless. **2.** not containing numbers.

number one *n.* **1.** the first in a series or sequence. **2.** an informal phrase for **oneself, myself,** etc.: *to look after number one.* **3.** *Inf.* the most important person; chief: *he's number one in* *the organization.* **4.** *Inf.* the best-selling pop record in any one week. ~*adj.* **5.** first in importance, urgency, quality, etc.: *number one priority.*

numberplate (ˈnʌmbəˌpleɪt) *n.* a plate mounted on the front and back of a motor vehicle bearing the registration number. Usual U.S. term: **license plate,** (Canad.) **licence plate.**

Number Ten *n.* 10 Downing Street, the British prime minister's official London residence.

number theory *n.* the study of integers, their properties, and the relationship between integers.

numbfish (ˈnʌmˌfɪʃ) *n., pl.* **-fish** *or* **-fishes.** any of several electric rays. [C18: so called because it numbs its victims]

numbles (ˈnʌmbᵊlz) *pl. n. Arch.* the heart, lungs, liver, etc., of a deer or other animal. [C14: < OF *nombles,* pl. of *nomble* thigh muscle of a deer, changed < L *lumbulus,* dim. of *lumbus* loin]

numbskull (ˈnʌmˌskʌl) *n.* a variant spelling of **numskull.**

numen (ˈnjuːmɛn) *n., pl.* **-mina** (-mɪnə). **1.** (esp. in ancient Roman religion) a deity or spirit presiding over a thing or place. **2.** a guiding principle, force, or spirit. [C17: < L: a nod (indicating a command), divine power]

numerable (ˈnjuːmərəbᵊl) *adj.* able to be numbered or counted. —ˈ**numerably** *adv.*

numeral (ˈnjuːmərəl) *n.* **1.** a symbol or group of symbols used to express a number: for example, *6* (*Arabic*), *VI* (*Roman*), *110* (*binary*). ~*adj.* **2.** of, consisting of, or denoting a number. [C16: < LL *numerālis* belonging to number, < L *numerus*]

numerate *adj.* (ˈnjuːmərɪt). **1.** able to use numbers, esp. in arithmetical operations. ~*vb.* (ˈnjuːməˌreɪt). (*tr.*) **2.** to read (a numerical expression). **3.** a less common word for **enumerate.** [C18 (vb.): < L *numerus* number + -ATE[1], by analogy with *literate*] —**numeracy** (ˈnjuːmərəsɪ) *n.*

numeration (ˌnjuːməˈreɪʃən) *n.* **1.** the act or process of writing, reading, or naming numbers. **2.** a system of numbering. —ˈ**numerative** *adj.*

numerator (ˈnjuːməˌreɪtə) *n.* **1.** *Maths.* the dividend of a fraction: the numerator of 7/8 is 7. Cf. **denominator. 2.** a person or thing that numbers; enumerator.

numerical (njuːˈmɛrɪkᵊl) *or* **numeric** *adj.* **1.** of, relating to, or denoting a number or numbers. **2.** measured or expressed in numbers: *numerical value.* —**nuˈmerically** *adv.*

numerology (ˌnjuːməˈrɒlədʒɪ) *n.* the study of numbers, such as the figures in a birth date, and of their supposed influence on human affairs. —**numerological** (ˌnjuːmərəˈlɒdʒɪkᵊl) *adj.*

numerous (ˈnjuːmərəs) *adj.* **1.** being many. **2.** consisting of many parts: *a numerous collection.* —ˈ**numerously** *adv.* —ˈ**numerousness** *n.*

numinous (ˈnjuːmɪnəs) *adj.* **1.** denoting, being, or relating to a numen; divine. **2.** arousing spiritual or religious emotions. **3.** mysterious or awe-inspiring. [C17: < L *numin-,* NUMEN + -OUS]

numismatics (ˌnjuːmɪzˈmætɪks) *n.* (*functioning as sing.*) the study or collection of coins, medals, etc. Also called: ˌ**numismaˈtology.** [C18: < F *numismatique,* < L *nomisma,* < Gk: piece of currency, < *nomizein* to have in use, < *nōmos* use] —ˌ**numisˈmatic** *adj.* —ˌ**numisˈmatically** *adv.*

nummulite (ˈnʌmjʊˌlaɪt) *n.* any of a family of large fossil protozoans common in Tertiary times. [C19: < NL, < L *nummulus,* < *nummus* coin]

numskull *or* **numbskull** (ˈnʌmˌskʌl) *n.* a stupid person; dolt; blockhead.

nun (nʌn) *n.* a female member of a religious order. [OE *nunne,* < Church L *nonna,* < LL: form of address used for an elderly woman] —ˈ**nunhood** *n.* —ˈ**nunlike** *adj.*

nun buoy *n. Naut.* a red buoy, conical at the top, marking the right side of a channel leading into a harbour. [C18: < obs. *nun* child's spinning top + BUOY]

Nunc Dimittis (ˈnʌŋk dɪˈmɪtɪs, ˈnʊŋk) *n.* **1.** the Latin name for the Canticle of Simeon (Luke 2:29–32). **2.** a musical setting of this. [from the opening words (Vulgate): now let depart]

nunciature (ˈnʌnsɪətʃə) *n.* the office or term of office of a nuncio. [C17: < It. *nunziatura;* see NUNCIO]

nuncio (ˈnʌnʃɪˌəʊ, -sɪ-) *n., pl.* **-cios.** *R.C. Church.* a diplomatic representative of the Holy See. [C16: via It. < L *nuntius* messenger]

nunnery (ˈnʌnərɪ) *n., pl.* **-neries.** the convent or religious house of a community of nuns.

NUPE (ˈnjuːpɪ) *n.* (in Britain) *acronym for* National Union of Public Employees.

nuptial (ˈnʌpʃəl, -tʃəl) *adj.* **1.** relating to marriage; conjugal: *nuptial vows.* **2.** *Zool.* of or relating to mating: *the nuptial flight of a queen bee.* [C15: < L *nuptiālis,* < *nuptiae* marriage, < *nubere* to marry] —ˈ**nuptially** *adv.*

nuptials (ˈnʌpʃəlz, -tʃəlz) *pl. n.* (*sometimes sing.*) a marriage ceremony; wedding.

NUR (in Britain) *abbrev. for* National Union of Railwaymen.

nurd (nɜːd) *n. Sl.* a stupid and feeble person. —ˈ**nurdish** *adj.*

nurse (nɜːs) *n.* **1.** a person, often a woman, who is trained to tend the sick and infirm, assist doctors, etc. **2.** short for **nursemaid. 3.** a woman employed to breast-feed another woman's child; wet nurse. **4.** a worker in a colony of social insects that takes care of the larvae. ~*vb.* (*mainly tr.*) **5.** (*also intr.*) to tend (the sick). **6.** (*also intr.*) to feed (a baby) at the breast. **7.** to try to cure (an ailment). **8.** to clasp fondly: *she nursed the child in her arms.* **9.** to look after (a child) as one's employment. **10.** to harbour; preserve: *to nurse a grudge.* **11.** to give special attention to, esp. in order to promote goodwill: *to nurse a difficult constituency.* **12.** *Billiards.* to keep (the balls) together for a series of cannons. [C16: < earlier *norice,* OF *nourice,* < LL *nūtrīcia,* < L *nūtrīcius* nourishing, < *nūtrīre* to nourish] —ˈ**nursing** *n., adj.*

nursemaid (ˈnɜːsˌmeɪd) *or* **nurserymaid** *n.* a woman employed to look after someone else's children. Often shortened to **nurse.**

nursery (ˈnɜːsrɪ) *n., pl.* **-ries. 1.** a room in a house set apart for children. **2.** a place where plants, young trees, etc., are grown commercially. **3.** an establishment providing daycare for babies and young children; crèche. **4.** anywhere serving to foster or nourish new ideas, etc. **5.** Also called: **nursery cannon.** *Billiards.* **a.** a series of cannons with the three balls adjacent to a cushion, esp. near a corner pocket. **b.** a cannon in such a series.

nurseryman (ˈnɜːsrɪmən) *n., pl.* **-men.** a person who owns or works in a nursery in which plants are grown.

nursery rhyme *n.* a short traditional verse or song for children, such as *Little Jack Horner.*

nursery school *n.* a school for young children, usually from three to five years old.

nursery slopes *pl. n.* gentle slopes used by beginners in skiing.

nursery stakes *pl. n.* a race for two-year-old horses.

nurse shark *n.* any of various sharks having an external groove on each side of the head between the mouth and nostril. [C15 *nusse fisshe* (later infl. in spelling by NURSE), ? < a division of obs. *an huss* shark, dogfish (<?) as *a nuss*]

nursing home *n.* a private hospital or residence for aged or infirm persons.

nursing officer *n.* (in Britain) the official name for **matron** (sense 4).

nursling *or* **nurseling** (ˈnɜːslɪŋ) *n.* a child or young animal that is being suckled, nursed, or fostered.

nurture (ˈnɜːtʃə) *n.* **1.** the act or process of promoting the development, etc., of a child. **2.** something that nourishes. ~*vb.* (*tr.*) **3.** to feed or support. **4.** to educate or train. [C14: < OF *norriture,* < L *nūtrīre* to nourish] —ˈ**nurtural** *adj.* —ˈ**nurturer** *n.*

NUS (in Britain) *abbrev. for:* **1.** National Union of Seamen. **2.** National Union of Students.

nut (nʌt) *n.* **1.** a dry one-seeded indehiscent fruit that usually possesses a woody wall. **2.** (*not in technical use*) any similar fruit, such as the walnut, having a hard shell and an edible kernel. **3.** the edible kernel of such a fruit. **4.** *Sl.* an eccentric or mad person. **5.** *Sl.* the head. **6.** **do one's nut.** *Brit. sl.* to be extremely angry. **7.** **off one's nut.** *Sl.* mad or foolish. **8.** a person or thing that presents difficulties (esp. in **a tough nut to crack**). **9.** the female component of a screwed assembly, having an internal spiral thread, esp. a small metallic block, usually hexagonal or square, that fits onto a bolt. **10.** Also called (U.S. and Canad.): **frog.** *Music.* **a.** the ridge at the upper end of the fingerboard of a violin, cello, etc., over which the strings pass to the tuning pegs. **b.** the end of a violin bow that is held by the player. **11.** a small usually gingery biscuit. **12.** *Brit.* a small piece of coal. ~*vb.* **nutting, nutted. 13.** (*intr.*) to gather nuts. ~See also **nuts.** [OE *hnutu*]

NUT (in Britain) *abbrev. for* National Union of Teachers.

nutant (ˈnjuːtᵊnt) *adj. Bot.* having the apex hanging down. [C18: < L *nūtāre* to nod]

nutation (njuːˈteɪʃən) *n.* **1.** *Astron.* a periodic variation in the precession of the earth's axis causing the earth's poles to oscillate about their mean position. **2.** the spiral growth of a shoot or similar plant organ, caused by variation in the growth rate in different parts. **3.** the act of nodding. [C17: < L *nūtātiō*, < *nūtāre* to nod]

nutbrown (ˈnʌtˈbraʊn) *adj.* reddish-brown.

nutcase (ˈnʌtˌkeɪs) *n. Sl.* an insane or very foolish person.

nutcracker (ˈnʌtˌkrækə) *n.* **1.** (*often pl.*) a device for cracking the shells of nuts. **2.** either an Old World bird or a North American bird (**Clark's nutcracker**) having speckled plumage and feeding on nuts, seeds, etc.

nutgall (ˈnʌtˌgɔːl) *n.* a nut-shaped gall caused by gall wasps on the oak and other trees.

nuthatch (ˈnʌtˌhætʃ) *n.* a songbird having strong feet and bill, and feeding on insects, seeds, and nuts. [C14 *notehache*, < *note* nut + *hache* hatchet, from its habit of splitting nuts]

nuthouse (ˈnʌtˌhaʊs) *n. Sl.* a mental hospital.

nutmeg (ˈnʌtˌmɛg) *n.* **1.** an East Indian evergreen tree cultivated in the tropics for its hard aromatic seed. See also **mace**[2]. **2.** the seed of this tree, used as a spice. [C13: < OF *nois muguede*, < OProvençal *noz muscada* musk-scented nut, < L *nux* NUT + *muscus* MUSK]

nutria (ˈnjuːtrɪə) *n.* another name for **coypu,** esp. the fur. [C19: < Sp., var. of *lutria*, ult. < L *lūtra* otter]

nutrient (ˈnjuːtrɪənt) *n.* **1.** any of the mineral substances that are absorbed by the roots of plants. **2.** any substance that nourishes an animal. ~*adj.* **3.** providing or contributing to nourishment. [C17: < L *nūtrīre* to nourish]

nutriment (ˈnjuːtrɪmənt) *n.* any material providing nourishment. [C16: < L *nūtrīmentum*, < *nūtrīre* to nourish] —**nutrimental** (ˌnjuːtrɪˈmɛntᵊl) *adj.*

nutrition (njuːˈtrɪʃən) *n.* **1.** a process in animals and plants involving the intake and assimilation of nutrient materials. **2.** the act or process of nourishing. **3.** the study of nutrition, esp. in humans. [C16: < LL *nūtrītiō*, < *nūtrīre* to nourish] —**nuˈtritional** *adj.* —**nuˈtritionist** *n.*

nutritious (njuːˈtrɪʃəs) *adj.* nourishing. [C17: < L *nūtrīcius*, < *nūtrix* NURSE] —**nuˈtritiously** *adv.* —**nuˈtritiousness** *n.*

nutritive (ˈnjuːtrɪtɪv) *adj.* **1.** providing nourishment. **2.** of, concerning, or promoting nutrition. ~*n.* **3.** a nutritious food.

nuts (nʌts) *adj.* **1.** a slang word for **insane. 2.** (foll. by *about* or *on*) *Sl.* extremely fond (of) or enthusiastic (about). ~*interj.* **3.** *Sl.* an expression of contempt, refusal, or defiance.

nuts and bolts *pl. n. Inf.* the essential or practical details.

nutshell (ˈnʌtˌʃɛl) *n.* **1.** the shell around the kernel of a nut. **2.** **in a nutshell.** in essence; briefly.

nutter (ˈnʌtə) *n. Brit. sl.* a mad or eccentric person.

nutty (ˈnʌtɪ) *adj.* **-tier, -tiest. 1.** containing nuts. **2.** resembling nuts. **3.** a slang word for **insane. 4.** (foll. by *over* or *about*) *Inf.* extremely enthusiastic (about). —ˈ**nuttiness** *n.*

nux vomica (ˈnʌks ˈvɒmɪkə) *n.* **1.** an Indian tree with orange-red berries containing poisonous seeds. **2.** any of the seeds of this tree, which contain strychnine and other poisonous alkaloids. **3.** a medicine manufactured from the seeds of this tree, formerly used as a heart stimulant. [C16: < Med. L: vomiting nut]

nuzzle (ˈnʌzᵊl) *vb.* **1.** to push or rub gently with the nose or snout. **2.** (*intr.*) to nestle; lie close. **3.** (*tr.*) to dig out with the snout. [C15 *nosele*, < NOSE (n.)]

NW *symbol for* northwest(ern).

NWMP (in Canada) *abbrev. for* North West Mounted Police.

NWT *abbrev. for* Northwest Territories (of Canada).

NY *or* **N.Y.** *abbrev. for* New York (city or state).

nyala (ˈnjɑːlə) *n., pl.* **-la** *or* **-las. 1.** a spiral-horned southern African antelope with a fringe of white hairs along the length of the back and neck. **2.** **mountain nyala.** a similar Ethiopian animal lacking the white crest. [< Zulu]

NYC *abbrev. for* New York City.

nyctalopia (ˌnɪktəˈləʊpɪə) *n.* inability to see normally in dim light. Nontechnical name: **night blindness.** [C17: via LL < Gk *nuktálōps*, < *nux* night + *alaos* blind + *ōps* eye]

nyctitropism (nɪkˈtɪtrəˌpɪzəm) *n.* a tendency of some plant parts to assume positions at night that are different from their daytime positions. [C19: *nyct-*, < Gk *nukt-*, *nux* night + -TROPISM]

nye (naɪ) *n.* a flock of pheasants. Also called: **nide, eye.** [C15: < OF *ni*, < L *nīdus* nest]

nylon (ˈnaɪlɒn) *n.* **1.** a class of synthetic polyamide materials of which monofilaments are used for bristles, etc., and fibres can be spun into yarn. **2.** yarn or cloth made of nylon, used for clothing, stockings, etc. [C20: orig. a trademark]

nylons (ˈnaɪlɒnz) *pl. n.* stockings made of nylon.

nymph (nɪmf) *n.* **1.** *Myth.* a spirit of nature envisaged as a beautiful maiden. **2.** *Chiefly poetic.* a beautiful young woman. **3.** the larva of insects such as the dragonfly. It resembles the adult, apart from having underdeveloped wings, and develops without a pupal stage. [C14: via OF < L, < Gk *numphē*] —ˈ**nymphal** *or* **nymphean** (ˈnɪmfɪən) *adj.* —ˈ**nymphlike** *adj.*

nympha (ˈnɪmfə) *n., pl.* **-phae** (-fiː). *Anat.* either one of the labia minora. [C17: < L: bride]

nymphet (ˈnɪmfɪt) *n.* a young girl who is sexually precocious and desirable. [C17 (meaning: a young nymph): dim. of NYMPH]

nympho (ˈnɪmfəʊ) *n., pl.* **-phos.** *Inf.* short for **nymphomaniac.**

nympholepsy (ˈnɪmfəˌlɛpsɪ) *n., pl.* **-sies.** a state of violent emotion, esp. when associated with a desire for something that one cannot have. [C18: < Gk *numpholēptos* caught by nymphs, < *numphē* nymph + *lambanein* to seize] —ˈ**nymphoˌlept** *n.* —ˌ**nymphoˈleptic** *adj.*

nymphomania (ˌnɪmfəˈmeɪnɪə) *n.* a neurotic compulsion in women to have sexual intercourse with many men without being able to have lasting relationships with them. [C18: NL, < Gk *numphē* nymph + -MANIA] —ˌ**nymphoˈmaniac** *n., adj.*

nystagmus (nɪˈstægməs) *n.* involuntary movement of the eye comprising a smooth drift followed by a flick back. [C19: NL, < Gk *nustagmos*] —**nysˈtagmic** *adj.*

N.Z., NZ, *or* **N. Zeal.** *abbrev. for* New Zealand.

NZBC (formerly) *abbrev. for* New Zealand Broadcasting Commission.

NZEF (in New Zealand) *abbrev. for* New Zealand Expeditionary Force, the New Zealand army that served 1914-18. **2NZEF** is used to refer to the Second New Zealand Expeditionary Force, in World War II.

o *or* **O** (əʊ) *n., pl.* **o's, O's,** *or* **Os. 1.** the 15th letter and fourth vowel of the English alphabet. **2.** any of several speech sounds represented by this letter, as in *code, pot, cow,* or *form.* **3.** another name for **nought.**

O[1] *symbol for:* **1.** *Chem.* oxygen. **2.** a human blood type of the ABO group. **3.** Old.

O[2] (əʊ) *interj.* **1.** a variant of **oh. 2.** an exclamation introducing an invocation, entreaty, wish, etc.: *O God! O for the wings of a dove!*

o. *abbrev. for:* **1.** octavo. **2.** old. **3.** only. **4.** order. **5.** *Pharmacol.* pint. [< L *octarius*]

O. *abbrev. for:* **1.** Ocean. **2.** octavo. **3.** old.

o' (ə) *prep. Inf. or arch.* shortened form of **of:** *a cup o' tea.*

O'- *prefix.* (in surnames of Irish Gaelic origin) descendant of: *O'Corrigan.* [< Irish Gaelic *ó, ua* descendant]

-o *suffix forming nouns.* indicating a diminutive or slang abbreviation: *wino.*

oaf (əʊf) *n.* a stupid or loutish person. [C17: var. of OE *ælf* ELF] —**ˈoafish** *adj.* —**ˈoafishness** *n.*

oak (əʊk) *n.* **1.** any deciduous or evergreen tree or shrub having acorns as fruits and lobed leaves. **2. a.** the wood of any of these trees, used esp. as building timber and for making furniture. **b.** (*as modifier*): *an oak table.* **3.** any of various trees that resemble the oak, such as the poison oak. **4.** anything made of oak, esp. a heavy outer door to a set of rooms in an Oxford college. **5.** the leaves of an oak tree, worn as a garland. [OE *āc*]

oak apple *or* **gall** *n.* any of various brownish round galls on oak trees, containing the larvae of certain wasps.

oaken (ˈəʊkən) *adj.* made of the wood of the oak.

Oaks (əʊks) *n.* (*functioning as sing.*) **the.** a horse race for fillies held annually at Epsom since 1779: one of the classics of English flat racing. [named after an estate near Epsom]

oakum (ˈəʊkəm) *n.* loose fibre obtained by unravelling old rope, used esp. for caulking seams in wooden ships. [OE *ācuma,* var. of *ācumba,* lit.: off-combings, < *ā-* off + *-cumba,* < *cemban* to COMB]

O & M *abbrev. for* organization and method (in studies of working methods).

OAP (in Britain) *abbrev. for* old age pension *or* pensioner.

oar (ɔː) *n.* **1.** a long shaft of wood for propelling a boat by rowing, having a broad blade that is dipped into and pulled against the water. **2.** short for **oarsman. 3. put one's oar in.** to interfere or interrupt. ~*vb.* **4.** to row or propel with or as if with oars. [OE *ār,* of Gmc origin] —**ˈoarless** *adj.* —**ˈoarˌlike** *adj.*

oarfish (ˈɔːˌfɪʃ) *n., pl.* **-fish** *or* **-fishes.** a very long ribbonfish with long slender ventral fins. [C19: referring to the flattened oarlike body]

oarlock (ˈɔːˌlɒk) *n.* the usual U.S. and Canad. word for **rowlock.**

oarsman (ˈɔːzmən) *n., pl.* **-men.** a man who rows, esp. one who rows in a racing boat. —**ˈoarsmanship** *n.*

OAS *abbrev. for:* **1.** *Organisation de l'Armée Secrète;* an organization which opposed Algerian independence by acts of terrorism. **2.** Organization of American States.

oasis (əʊˈeɪsɪs) *n., pl.* **-ses** (-siːz). **1.** a fertile patch in a desert occurring where the water table approaches or reaches the ground surface. **2.** a place of peace, safety, or happiness. [C17: via L < Gk, prob. < Egyptian]

oast (əʊst) *n. Chiefly Brit.* **1.** a kiln for drying hops. **2.** Also called: **oast house.** a building containing such kilns, usually having a conical or pyramidal roof. [OE *āst*]

oat (əʊt) *n.* **1.** an erect annual grass grown in temperate regions for its edible seed. **2.** (*usually pl.*) the seeds or fruits of this grass. **3.** any of various other grasses such as the wild oat. **4.** *Poetic.* a flute made from an oat straw. **5. feel one's oats.** *U.S. & Canad. inf.* **a.** to feel exuberant. **b.** to feel self-important. **6. sow one's (wild) oats.** to indulge in adventure or promiscuity during youth. [OE *āte,* <?]

oatcake (ˈəʊtˌkeɪk) *n.* a crisp brittle unleavened biscuit made of oatmeal.

oaten (ˈəʊtᵊn) *adj.* made of oats or oat straw.

oath (əʊθ) *n., pl.* **oaths** (əʊðz). **1.** a solemn pronouncement to affirm the truth of a statement or to pledge a person to some course of action. **2.** the form of such a pronouncement. **3.** an irreverent or blasphemous expression, esp. one involving the name of a deity; curse. **4. my oath.** *Austral. sl.* certainly; yes indeed. **5. on, upon,** *or* **under oath. a.** under the obligation of an oath. **b.** *Law.* having sworn to tell the truth, usually with one's hand on the Bible. **6. take an oath.** to declare formally with a pledge, esp. before giving evidence. [OE *āth*]

oatmeal (ˈəʊtˌmiːl) *n.* **1.** meal ground from oats, used for making porridge, oatcakes, etc. **2. a.** a greyish-yellow colour. **b.** (*as adj.*): *an oatmeal coat.*

OAU *abbrev. for* Organization of African Unity.

OB *Brit. abbrev. for:* **1.** Old Boy. **2.** outside broadcast.

ob. *abbrev. for:* **1.** (on tombstones, etc.) obiit. [L: he (or she) died] **2.** obiter. [L: incidentally; in passing] **3.** oboe.

ob- *prefix.* inverse or inversely: *obovate.* [< OF, < L *ob.* In compound words < L, *ob-* (and *oc-, of-, op-*) indicates: to, towards (*object*); against (*oppose*); away from (*obsolete*); before (*obstetric*); and is used as an intensifier (*oblong*)]

Obad. *Bible. abbrev. for* Obadiah.

obbligato *or* **obligato** (ˌɒblɪˈgɑːtəʊ) *Music.* ~*adj., n.* **1.** not to be omitted in performance ~*n., pl.* **-tos** *or* **-ti** (-tiː). **2.** an essential part in a score: *with oboe obbligato.* [C18: < It., < *obbligare* to OBLIGE]

obconic (ɒbˈkɒnɪk) *adj. Bot.* (of a fruit) shaped like a cone and attached at the pointed end.

obcordate (ɒbˈkɔːdeɪt) *adj. Bot.* heart-shaped and attached at the pointed end: *obcordate leaves.*

obdurate (ˈɒbdjʊrɪt) *adj.* **1.** not easily moved by feelings or supplication; hardhearted. **2.** impervious to persuasion. [C15: < L *obdūrāre* to make hard, < *ob-* (intensive) + *dūrus* hard] —**ˈobduracy** *or* **ˈobdurateness** *n.* —**ˈobdurately** *adv.*

OBE *abbrev. for* Officer of the Order of the British Empire (a Brit. title).

obeah (ˈəʊbɪə) *n.* **1.** a kind of witchcraft practised by the Negroes of the West Indies. **2.** a charm used in this. [of W African origin]

obedience (əˈbiːdɪəns) *n.* **1.** the condition or quality of being obedient. **2.** the act or an instance of obeying; dutiful or submissive behaviour. **3.** the authority vested in a Church or similar body. **4.** the collective group of persons submitting to this authority.

obedient (əˈbiːdɪənt) *adj.* obeying or willing to obey. [C13: < OF, < L *oboediens,* present participle of *oboedīre* to OBEY] —**oˈbediently** *adv.*

obeisance (əʊˈbeɪsəns) *n.* **1.** an attitude of deference or homage. **2.** a gesture expressing obeisance. [C14: < OF *obéissant,* present participle of *obéir* to OBEY] —**oˈbeisant** *adj.*

obelisk (ˈɒbɪlɪsk) *n.* **1.** a stone pillar having a square or rectangular cross section and sides that taper towards a pyramidal top. **2.** *Printing.* another name for **dagger** (sense 2). [C16: via L < Gk *obeliskos* a little spit, < *obelos* spit] —ˌ**obeˈliscal** *adj.* —ˌ**obeˈliskoid** *adj.*

obelus (ˈɒbɪləs) *n., pl.* **-li** (-ˌlaɪ). **1.** a mark (— or ÷) used in editions of ancient documents to indicate spurious words or passages. **2.** another name for **dagger** (sense 2). [C14: via LL < Gk *obelos* spit]

obese (əʊˈbiːs) *adj.* excessively fat or fleshy; corpulent. [C17: < L *obēsus*, < *ob-* (intensive) + *edere* to eat] —**oˈbesity** *or* **oˈbeseness** *n.*

obey (əˈbeɪ) *vb.* **1.** to carry out (instructions or orders); comply with (demands). **2.** to behave or act in accordance with (one's feelings, whims, etc.). [C13: < OF *obéir*, < L *oboedīre*, < *ob-* towards + *audīre* to hear] —**oˈbeyer** *n.*

obfuscate (ˈɒbfʌsˌkeɪt) *vb.* (*tr.*) **1.** to obscure or darken. **2.** to perplex or bewilder. [C16: < L *ob-* (intensive) + *fuscāre* to blacken, < *fuscus* dark] —ˌ**obfusˈcation** *n.* —ˈ**obfusˌcatory** *adj.*

obi (ˈəʊbɪ) *n., pl.* **obis** *or* **obi.** a broad sash tied in a large flat bow at the back, worn as part of the Japanese national costume. [C19: < Japanese]

obit (ˈɒbɪt, ˈəʊbɪt) *n. Inf.* **1.** short for **obituary. 2.** a memorial service.

obiter dictum (ˈɒbɪtə ˈdɪktəm, ˈəʊ-) *n., pl.* **obiter dicta** (ˈdɪktə). **1.** *Law.* an observation by a judge on some point of law not directly in issue in the case before him. **2.** any comment or remark made in passing. [L: something said in passing]

obituary (əˈbɪtjʊərɪ) *n., pl.* **-aries.** a published announcement of a death, often accompanied by a short biography of the dead person. [C18: < Med. L *obituārius*, < L *obīre* to fall] —**oˈbituarist** *n.*

obj. *abbrev. for:* **1.** objection. **2.** *Grammar.* object(ive).

object[1] (ˈɒbdʒɪkt) *n.* **1.** a tangible and visible thing. **2.** a person or thing seen as a focus for feelings, thought, etc. **3.** an aim or objective. **4.** *Inf.* a ridiculous or pitiable person, spectacle, etc. **5.** *Philosophy.* that towards which cognition is directed as contrasted with the thinking subject. **6.** *Grammar.* a noun, pronoun, or noun phrase whose referent is the recipient of the action of a verb. See also **direct object, indirect object. 7.** *Grammar.* a noun, pronoun, or noun phrase that is governed by a preposition. **8. no object.** not a hindrance or obstacle: *money is no object.* [C14: < LL *objectus* something thrown before (the mind), < L *obicere*; see OBJECT[2]]

object[2] (əbˈdʒɛkt) *vb.* **1.** (*tr.; takes a clause as object*) to state as an objection. **2.** (*intr.;* often foll. by *to*) to raise or state an objection (to); present an argument (against). [C15: < L *obicere*, < *ob-* against + *jacere* to throw] —**obˈjector** *n.*

object glass *n. Optics.* another name for **objective** (sense 10).

objectify (əbˈdʒɛktɪˌfaɪ) *vb.* **-fying, -fied.** (*tr.*) to represent concretely; present as an object. —**obˌjectifiˈcation** *n.*

objection (əbˈdʒɛkʃən) *n.* **1.** an expression or feeling of opposition or dislike. **2.** a cause for such an expression or feeling. **3.** the act of objecting.

objectionable (əbˈdʒɛkʃənəbᵊl) *adj.* unpleasant, offensive, or repugnant. —**obˌjectionaˈbility** *or* **obˈjectionableness** *n.* —**obˈjectionably** *adv.*

objective (əbˈdʒɛktɪv) *adj.* **1.** existing independently of perception or an individual's conceptions. **2.** undistorted by emotion or personal bias. **3.** of or relating to actual and external phenomena as opposed to thoughts, feelings, etc. **4.** *Med.* (of disease symptoms) perceptible to persons other than the individual affected. **5.** *Grammar.* denoting a case of nouns and pronouns, esp. in languages having only two cases, that is used to identify the direct object of a finite verb or preposition. See also **accusative. 6.** of or relating to a goal or aim. ~*n.* **7.** the object of one's endeavours; goal; aim. **8.** an actual phenomenon; reality. **9.** *Grammar.* the objective case. **10.** Also called: **object glass.** *Optics.* the lens or combination of lenses nearest to the object in an optical instrument. ~Abbrev.: **obj.** Cf. **subjective.** —**objectival** (ˌɒbdʒɛkˈtaɪvəl) *adj.* —**obˈjectively** *adv.* —ˌ**objecˈtivity** *or* (*less commonly*) **obˈjectiveness** *n.*

objectivism (əbˈdʒɛktɪˌvɪzəm) *n.* **1.** the tendency to stress what is objective. **2.** the philosophical doctrine that reality is objective, and that sense data correspond with it. —**obˈjectivist** *n., adj.* —**obˌjectivˈistic** *adj.*

object language *n.* a language described by another language. Cf. **metalanguage.**

object lesson *n.* a convincing demonstration of some principle or ideal.

object program *n.* a computer program transcribed from the equivalent source program into machine language by the compiler or assembler.

objet d'art *French.* (ɔbʒɛ dar) *n., pl.* ***objets d'art*** (ɔbʒɛ dar). a small object considered to be of artistic worth. [F: object of art]

objurgate (ˈɒbdʒəˌgeɪt) *vb.* (*tr.*) to scold or reprimand. [C17: < L *objurgāre*, < *ob-* against + *jurgāre* to scold] —ˌ**objurˈgation** *n.* —ˈ**objurˌgator** *n.* —**objurgatory** (ɒbˈdʒɜːgətərɪ, -trɪ) *adj.*

obl. *abbrev. for:* **1.** oblique. **2.** oblong.

oblate[1] (ˈɒbleɪt) *adj.* having an equatorial diameter of greater length than the polar diameter: *the earth is an oblate sphere.* Cf. **prolate.** [C18: < NL *oblātus* lengthened, < L *ob-* towards + *lātus*, p.p. of *ferre* to bring]

oblate[2] (ˈɒbleɪt) *n.* a person dedicated to a monastic or religious life. [C19: < F *oblat*, < Med. L *oblātus*, < L *offerre* to OFFER]

oblation (ɒˈbleɪʃən) *n.* **1.** *Christianity.* the offering of the Eucharist to God. **2.** any offering made for religious or charitable purposes. [C15: < Church L *oblātiō*; see OBLATE[2]] —**oblatory** (ˈɒblətərɪ, -trɪ) *or* **obˈlational** *adj.*

obligate (ˈɒblɪˌgeɪt) *vb.* **1.** to compel, constrain, or oblige morally or legally. **2.** (in the U.S.) to bind (property, funds, etc.) as security. ~*adj.* **3.** compelled, bound, or restricted. **4.** *Biol.* able to exist under only one set of environmental conditions. [C16: < L *obligāre* to OBLIGE] —ˈ**obligable** *adj.* —**obˈligative** *adj.* —ˈ**obliˌgator** *n.*

obligation (ˌɒblɪˈgeɪʃən) *n.* **1.** a moral or legal requirement; duty. **2.** the act of obligating or the state of being obligated. **3.** *Law.* **a.** a written contract containing a penalty. **b.** an instrument acknowledging indebtedness to secure the repayment of money borrowed. **4.** a person or thing to which one is bound morally or legally. **5.** a service or favour for which one is indebted.

obligato (ˌɒblɪˈgɑːtəʊ) *adj., n. Music.* a variant spelling of **obbligato.**

obligatory (ɒˈblɪgətərɪ, -trɪ) *adj.* **1.** required to be done, obtained, possessed, etc. **2.** of the nature of or constituting an obligation. —**obˈligatorily** *adv.*

oblige (əˈblaɪdʒ) *vb.* **1.** (*tr.; often passive*) to bind or constrain (someone to do something) by legal, moral, or physical means. **2.** (*tr.; usually passive*) to make indebted or grateful (to someone) by doing a favour. **3.** to do a service or favour to (someone): *she obliged the guests with a song.* [C13: < OF *obliger*, < L *obligāre*, < *ob-* towards + *ligāre* to bind] —**oˈbliger** *n.*

obligee (ˌɒblɪˈdʒiː) *n.* a person in whose favour an obligation, contract, or bond is created; creditor.

obliging (əˈblaɪdʒɪŋ) *adj.* ready to do favours; agreeable; kindly. —**oˈbligingly** *adv.* —**oˈbligingness** *n.*

obligor (ˌɒblɪˈgɔː) *n.* a person who binds himself by contract to perform some obligation; debtor.

oblique (əˈbliːk) *adj.* **1.** at an angle; slanting; sloping. **2.** *Geom.* **a.** (of lines, planes, etc.) neither perpendicular nor parallel to one another or to another line, plane, etc. **b.** not related to or containing a right angle. **3.** indirect or evasive. **4.** *Grammar.* denoting any case of nouns, pronouns, etc., other than the nominative and vocative. **5.** *Biol.* having asymmetrical sides or planes: *an oblique leaf.* ~*n.* **6.** something oblique, esp. a line. **7.** another name for **solidus** (sense 1). ~*vb.* (*intr.*) **8.** to take or have an oblique direction. **9.** (of a military formation) to move forward at an angle. [C15: < OF, < L *oblīquus*, <?] —**oˈbliquely** *adv.* —**oˈbliqueness** *n.* —**obliquity** (əˈblɪkwɪtɪ) *n.*

oblique angle *n.* an angle that is not a right angle or any multiple of a right angle.

obliterate (əˈblɪtəˌreɪt) *vb.* (*tr.*) to destroy every trace of; wipe out completely. [C16: < L *oblitterāre* to erase, < *ob-* out + *littera* letter] —**oˌbliteˈration** *n.* —**oˈbliterative** *adj.* —**oˈbliterˌator** *n.*

oblivion (əˈblɪvɪən) *n.* **1.** the condition of being forgotten or disregarded. **2.** *Law.* amnesty; pardon. [C14: via OF < L *oblīviō* forgetfulness, < *oblīviscī* to forget]

oblivious (əˈblɪvɪəs) *adj.* (usually foll. by *of*) unaware or forgetful. —**obˈliviously** *adv.* —**obˈliviousness** *n.*

oblong (ˈɒbˌlɒŋ) *adj.* **1.** having an elongated, esp. rectangular, shape. ~*n.* **2.** a figure or object having this shape. [C15: < L *oblongus*, < *ob-* (intensive) + *longus* LONG[1]]

obloquy (ˈɒbləkwɪ) *n., pl.* **-quies.** **1.** defamatory or censorious statements, esp. when directed against one person. **2.** disgrace brought about by public abuse. [C15: < L *obloquium* contradiction, < *ob-* against + *loquī* to speak]

obnoxious (əbˈnɒkʃəs) *adj.* **1.** extremely unpleasant. **2.** *Obs.* exposed to harm, injury, etc. [C16: < L *obnoxius*, < *ob-* to + *noxa* injury, < *nocēre* to harm] —**obˈnoxiously** *adv.* —**obˈnoxiousness** *n.*

oboe (ˈəʊbəʊ) *n.* **1.** a woodwind instrument consisting of a conical tube fitted with a mouthpiece having a double reed. It has a penetrating nasal tone. **2.** a person who plays this instrument in an orchestra. ~Arch. form: **hautboy.** [C18: via It. *oboe*, phonetic approximation to F *haut bois*, lit.: high wood (referring to its pitch)] —**ˈoboist** *n.*

oboe d'amore (dɑːˈmɔːreɪ) *n.* a type of oboe pitched a minor third lower than the oboe itself: used chiefly in baroque music.

obs. *abbrev. for:* **1.** observation. **2.** obsolete.

obscene (əbˈsiːn) *adj.* **1.** offensive or outrageous to accepted standards of decency or modesty. **2.** *Law.* (of publications, etc.) having a tendency to deprave or corrupt. **3.** disgusting; repellent. [C16: < L *obscēnus* inauspicious] —**obˈscenely** *adv.*

obscenity (əbˈsɛnɪtɪ) *n., pl.* **-ties.** **1.** the state or quality of being obscene. **2.** an obscene act, statement, work, etc.

obscurant (əbˈskjʊərənt) *n.* an opposer of reform and enlightenment. —**obscurantism** (ˌɒbskjʊəˈrænˌtɪzəm) *n.* —ˌ**obscuˈrantist** *n., adj.*

obscure (əbˈskjʊə) *adj.* **1.** unclear. **2.** indistinct, vague, or indefinite. **3.** inconspicuous or unimportant. **4.** hidden, secret, or remote. **5.** (of a vowel) reduced to a neutral vowel (ə). **6.** gloomy, dark, clouded, or dim. ~*vb.* (*tr.*) **7.** to make unclear, vague, or hidden. **8.** to cover or cloud over. **9.** *Phonetics.* to pronounce (a vowel) so that it becomes a neutral sound represented by (ə). [C14: via OF < L *obscūrus* dark] —**obscuration** (ˌɒbskjʊˈreɪʃən) *n.* —**obˈscurely** *adv.* —**obˈscureness** *n.*

obscurity (əbˈskjʊərɪtɪ) *n., pl.* **-ties.** **1.** the state or quality of being obscure. **2.** an obscure person or thing.

obsequies (ˈɒbsɪkwɪz) *pl. n., sing.* **-quy.** funeral rites. [C14: via Anglo-Norman < Med. L *obsequiae* (infl. by L *exsequiae*), < *obsequium* compliance]

obsequious (əbˈsiːkwɪəs) *adj.* **1.** obedient or attentive in an ingratiating or servile manner. **2.** *Now rare.* submissive or compliant. [C15: < L *obsequiōsus* compliant, < *obsequi* to follow] —**obˈsequiously** *adv.* —**obˈsequiousness** *n.*

observance (əbˈzɜːvəns) *n.* **1.** recognition of or compliance with a law, custom, practice, etc. **2.** a ritual, ceremony, or practice, esp. of a religion. **3.** observation or attention. **4.** the degree of strictness of a religious order in following its rule. **5.** *Arch.* respectful or deferential attention.

observant (əbˈzɜːvənt) *adj.* **1.** paying close attention to detail; watchful or heedful. **2.** adhering strictly to rituals, ceremonies, laws, etc. —**obˈservantly** *adv.*

observation (ˌɒbzəˈveɪʃən) *n.* **1.** the act of observing or the state of being observed. **2.** a comment or remark. **3.** detailed examination of phenomena prior to analysis, diagnosis, or interpretation: *the patient was under observation.* **4.** the facts learned from observing. **5.** *Navigation.* **a.** a sight taken with an instrument to determine the position of an observer relative to that of a given heavenly body. **b.** the data so taken. —ˌ**obserˈvational** *adj.* —ˌ**obserˈvationally** *adv.*

observatory (əbˈzɜːvətərɪ, -trɪ) *n., pl.* **-ries.** **1.** an institution or building specially designed and equipped for observing meteorological and astronomical phenomena. **2.** any building or structure providing an extensive view of its surroundings.

observe (əbˈzɜːv) *vb.* **1.** (*tr.; may take a clause as object*) to see; perceive; notice: *we have observed that you steal.* **2.** (when *tr., may take a clause as object*) to watch (something) carefully; pay attention to (something). **3.** to make observations of (something), esp. scientific ones. **4.** (when *intr.*, usually foll. by *on* or *upon;* when *tr., may take a clause as object*) to make a comment or remark: *the speaker observed that times had changed.* **5.** (*tr.*) to abide by, keep, or follow (a custom, tradition, etc.). [C14: via OF < L *observāre*, < *ob-* to + *servāre* to watch] —**obˈservable** *adj.* —**obˈserver** *n.*

obsess (əbˈsɛs) *vb.* (*tr.;* when passive, foll. by *with* or *by*) to preoccupy completely; haunt. [C16: < L *obsessus* besieged, p.p. of *obsidēre*, < *ob-* in front of + *sedēre* to sit] —**obˈsessive** *adj.* —**obˈsessively** *adv.* —**obˈsessiveness** *n.*

obsession (əbˈsɛʃən) *n.* **1.** *Psychiatry.* a persistent idea or impulse, often associated with anxiety and mental illness. **2.** a persistent preoccupation, idea, or feeling. **3.** the act of obsessing or the state of being obsessed. —**obˈsessional** *adj.* —**obˈsessionally** *adv.*

obsidian (ɒbˈsɪdɪən) *n.* a dark glassy volcanic rock formed by very rapid solidification of lava. [C17: < L *obsidiānus*, erroneous transcription of *obsiānus* (*lapis*) (stone of) *Obsius*, (in Pliny) the discoverer of a stone resembling obsidian]

obsolesce (ˌɒbsəˈlɛs) *vb.* (*intr.*) to become obsolete.

obsolescent (ˌɒbsəˈlɛsᵊnt) *adj.* becoming obsolete or out of date. [C18: < L *obsolescere;* see OBSOLETE] —ˌ**obsoˈlescence** *n.*

obsolete (ˈɒbsəˌliːt, ˌɒbsəˈliːt) *adj.* **1.** out of use or practice; not current. **2.** out of date; unfashionable or outmoded. **3.** *Biol.* (of parts, organs, etc.) vestigial; rudimentary. [C16: < L *obsolētus* worn out, p.p. of *obsolēre* (unattested), < *ob-* opposite to + *solēre* to be used] —**ˈobsoˌletely** *adv.* —**ˈobsoˌleteness** *n.*

obstacle (ˈɒbstəkᵊl) *n.* **1.** a person or thing that opposes or hinders something. **2.** *Brit.* a fence or hedge used in showjumping. [C14: via OF < L *obstāculum*, < *obstāre*, < *ob-* against + *stāre* to stand]

obstacle race *n.* a race in which competitors have to negotiate various obstacles.

obstetric (ɒbˈstɛtrɪk) *or* **obstetrical** *adj.* of or relating to childbirth or obstetrics. [C18: via NL < L *obstetrīcius*, < *obstetrix* a midwife, lit.: woman who stands opposite, < *obstāre* to stand in front of; see OBSTACLE] —**obˈstetrically** *adv.*

obstetrician (ˌɒbstɛˈtrɪʃən) *n.* a physician who specializes in obstetrics.

obstetrics (ɒbˈstɛtrɪks) *n.* (*functioning as sing.*) the branch of medicine concerned with childbirth and the treatment of women before and after childbirth.

obstinacy (ˈɒbstɪnəsɪ) *n., pl.* **-cies.** **1.** the state or quality of being obstinate. **2.** an obstinate act, attitude, etc.

obstinate (ˈɒbstɪnɪt) *adj.* **1.** adhering fixedly to a particular opinion, attitude, course of action, etc. **2.** self-willed or headstrong. **3.** difficult to subdue or alleviate; persistent: *an obstinate fever.* [C14: < L *obstinātus*, p.p. of *obstināre* to persist in, < *ob-* (intensive) + *stin-*, var. of *stare* to stand] —**ˈobstinately** *adv.*

obstreperous (əbˈstrɛpərəs) *adj.* noisy or rough, esp. in resisting restraint or control. [C16: < L, <

obstrepere, < *ob-* against + *strepere* to roar] **—ob'streperously** *adv.* **—ob'streperousness** *n.*

obstruct (əb'strʌkt) *vb.* (*tr.*) **1.** to block (a road, passageway, etc.) with an obstacle. **2.** to make (progress or activity) difficult. **3.** to impede or block a clear view of. [C17: < L: built against, p.p. of *obstruere,* < *ob-* against + *struere* to build] **—ob'structive** *adj., n.* **—ob'structively** *adv.* **—ob'structiveness** *n.* **—ob'structor** *n.*

obstruction (əb'strʌkʃən) *n.* **1.** a person or thing that obstructs. **2.** the act or an instance of obstructing. **3.** delay of business, esp. in a legislature by means of procedural devices. **4.** *Sport.* the act of unfairly impeding an opposing player. **—ob'structional** *adj.*

obstructionist (əb'strʌkʃənɪst) *n.* a person who deliberately obstructs business, etc., esp. in a legislature. **—ob'structionism** *n.*

obtain (əb'teɪn) *vb.* **1.** (*tr.*) to gain possession of; acquire; get. **2.** (*intr.*) to be customary, valid, or accepted: *a new law obtains in this case.* [C15: via OF < L *obtinēre* to take hold of] **—ob'tainable** *adj.* **—ob,taina'bility** *n.* **—ob'tainer** *n.* **—ob'tainment** *n.*

obtrude (əb'truːd) *vb.* **1.** to push (oneself, one's opinions, etc.) on others in an unwelcome way. **2.** (*tr.*) to push out or forward. [C16: < L *obtrūdere,* < *ob-* against + *trūdere* to push forward] **—ob'truder** *n.* **—obtrusion** (əb'truːʒən) *n.*

obtrusive (əb'truːsɪv) *adj.* **1.** obtruding or tending to obtrude. **2.** sticking out; protruding; noticeable. **—ob'trusively** *adv.* **—ob'trusiveness** *n.*

obtuse (əb'tjuːs) *adj.* **1.** mentally slow or emotionally insensitive. **2.** *Maths.* (of an angle) lying between 90° and 180°. **3.** not sharp or pointed. **4.** indistinctly felt, heard, etc.; dull: *obtuse pain.* **5.** (of a leaf or similar flat part) having a rounded or blunt tip. [C16: < L *obtūsus* dulled, p.p. of *obtundere* to beat down] **—ob'tusely** *adv.* **—ob'tuseness** *n.*

obverse ('ɒbvɜːs) *adj.* **1.** facing or turned towards the observer. **2.** forming or serving as a counterpart. **3.** (of leaves) narrower at the base than at the top. ~*n.* **4.** a counterpart or complement. **5.** *Logic.* a proposition derived from another by replacing the original predicate by its negation and changing the proposition from affirmative to negative or vice versa, as *no sum is correct* from *every sum is incorrent.* **6.** the side of a coin that bears the main design or device. [C17: < L *obversus* turned towards, p.p. of *obvertere*] **—ob'versely** *adv.*

obvert (ɒb'vɜːt) *vb.* (*tr.*) **1.** *Logic.* to deduce the obverse of (a proposition). **2.** *Rare.* to turn so as to show the main or other side. [C17: < L *obvertere* to turn towards] **—ob'version** *n.*

obviate ('ɒbvɪ,eɪt) *vb.* (*tr.*) to do away with. [C16: < LL *obviātus* prevented, p.p. of *obviāre;* see OBVIOUS] **—,obvi'ation** *n.*

obvious ('ɒbvɪəs) *adj.* **1.** easy to see or understand; evident. **2.** exhibiting motives, feelings, intentions, etc., clearly or without subtlety. **3.** naive or unsubtle: *the play was rather obvious.* [C16: < L *obvius,* < *obviam* in the way] **—'obviously** *adv.* **—'obviousness** *n.*

Oc. *abbrev. for* Ocean.

OC *abbrev. for* Officer Commanding.

o/c *abbrev. for* overcharge.

ocarina (,ɒkə'riːnə) *n.* an egg-shaped wind instrument with a protruding mouthpiece and six to eight finger holes, producing an almost pure tone. [C19: < It.: little goose, < *oca* goose, ult. < L *avis* bird]

Occam's *or* **Ockham's razor** ('ɒkəmz) *n.* a maxim, attributed to William of Occam, English nominalist philosopher (died ? 1349), stating that in explaining something assumptions must not be needlessly multiplied.

occas. *abbrev. for* occasional(ly).

occasion (ə'keɪʒən) *n.* **1.** (sometimes foll. by *of*) the time of a particular happening or event. **2.** (sometimes foll. by *for*) a reason or cause (to do or be something); grounds: *there was no occasion to complain.* **3.** an opportunity (to do something); chance. **4.** a special event, time, or celebration: *the party was quite an occasion.* **5. on occasion.** every so often. **6. rise to the occasion.** to have the courage, wit, etc., to meet the special demands of a situation. **7. take occasion.** to avail oneself of an opportunity (to do something). ~*vb.* **8.** (*tr.*) to bring about, esp. incidentally or by chance. [C14: < L *occāsiō* a falling down, < *occidere*]

occasional (ə'keɪʒənᵊl) *adj.* **1.** taking place from time to time; not frequent or regular. **2.** of, for, or happening on special occasions. **3.** serving as an occasion (for something). **—oc'casionally** *adv.*

occasional table *n.* a small table with no regular use.

occident ('ɒksɪdənt) *n.* a literary or formal word for **west.** Cf. **orient.** [C14: via OF < L *occidere* to fall (with reference to the setting sun)] **—,occi'dental** *adj.*

Occident ('ɒksɪdənt) *n.* (usually preceded by *the*) **1.** the countries of Europe and America. **2.** the western hemisphere. **—,Occi'dental** *adj.*

occipital (ɒk'sɪpɪtᵊl) *adj.* **1.** of or relating to the back of the head or skull. ~*n.* **2.** short for **occipital bone.** [See OCCIPUT]

occipital bone *n.* the bone that forms the back part of the skull and part of its base.

occipital lobe *n.* the posterior portion of each cerebral hemisphere, concerned with the interpretation of visual sensory impulses.

occiput ('ɒksɪ,pʌt) *n., pl.* **occiputs** *or* **occipita** (ɒk'sɪpɪtə). the back part of the head or skull. [C14: < L, < *ob-* at the back of + *caput* head]

occlude (ə'kluːd) *vb.* **1.** (*tr.*) to block or stop up (a passage or opening); obstruct. **2.** (*tr.*) to prevent the passage of. **3.** (*tr.*) *Chem.* (of a solid) to incorporate (a substance) by absorption or adsorption. **4.** *Meteorol.* to form or cause to form an occluded front. **5.** *Dentistry.* to produce or cause to produce occlusion, as in chewing. [C16: < L *occlūdere,* < *ob-* (intensive) + *claudere* to close] **—oc'cludent** *adj.*

occluded front *n. Meteorol.* the line or plane occurring where the cold front of a depression has overtaken the warm front, raising the warm sector from ground level. Also called: **occlusion.**

occlusion (ə'kluːʒən) *n.* **1.** the act of occluding or the state of being occluded. **2.** *Meteorol.* another term for **occluded front.** **3.** *Dentistry.* the normal position of the teeth when the jaws are closed. **—oc'clusive** *adj.*

occult *adj.* (ɒ'kʌlt, 'ɒkʌlt). **1. a.** of or characteristic of mystical or supernatural phenomena or influences. **b.** (*as n.*): *the occult.* **2.** beyond ordinary human understanding. **3.** secret or esoteric. ~*vb.* (ɒ'kʌlt). **4.** *Astron.* (of a celestial body) to hide (another celestial body) from view by occultation or (of a celestial body) to become hidden by occultation. **5.** to hide or become hidden or shut off from view. **6.** (*intr.*) (of lights, esp. in lighthouses) to shut off at regular intervals. [C16: < L *occultus,* p.p. of *occulere,* < *ob-* over, up + *-culere,* rel. to *celāre* to conceal] **—'occul,tism** *n.* **—'occultist** *n.* **—oc'cultness** *n.*

occultation (,ɒkʌl'teɪʃən) *n.* the temporary disappearance of one celestial body as it moves out of sight behind another body.

occupancy ('ɒkjʊpənsɪ) *n., pl.* **-cies.** **1.** the act of occupying; possession of a property. **2.** *Law.* the possession and use of property by or without agreement and without any claim to ownership. **3.** *Law.* the act of taking possession of unowned property, esp. land, with the intent of thus acquiring ownership. **4.** the condition or fact of being an occupant, esp. a tenant. **5.** the period of time during which one is an occupant, esp. of property.

occupant ('ɒkjʊpənt) *n.* **1.** a person, thing, etc., holding a position or place. **2.** *Law.* a person who has possession of something, esp. an estate, house, etc.; tenant. **3.** *Law.* a person who acquires by occupancy the title to something previously without an owner.

occupation (,ɒkjʊ'peɪʃən) *n.* **1.** a person's regular work or profession; job. **2.** any activity on which time is spent by a person. **3.** the act of occupying or the state of being occupied. **4.** the control of a country by a foreign military power. **5.** the period of time that a nation, place, or position is occupied. **6.** (*modifier*) for the use of the occupier of a particular property: *occupation road.* —ˌ**occuˈpational** *adj.*

occupational psychology *n.* the scientific study of mental or emotional problems associated with the working environment.

occupational therapy *n. Med.* creative activity, such as a craft or hobby to help a patient recover from a physical or mental illness.

occupier (ˈɒkjʊˌpaɪə) *n.* **1.** *Brit.* a person who is in possession or occupation of a house or land. **2.** a person or thing that occupies.

occupy (ˈɒkjʊˌpaɪ) *vb.* **-pying, -pied.** (*tr.*) **1.** to live or be established in (a house, flat, office, etc.). **2.** (*often passive*) to keep (a person) busy or engrossed. **3.** (*often passive*) to take up (time or space). **4.** to take and hold possession of, esp. as a demonstration: *students occupied the college buildings.* **5.** to fill or hold (a position or rank). [C14: < OF *occuper,* < L *occupāre* to seize hold of]

occur (əˈkɜː) *vb.* **-curring, -curred.** (*intr.*) **1.** to happen; take place; come about. **2.** to be found or be present; exist. **3.** (foll. by *to*) to be realized or thought of (by); suggest itself (to). [C16: < L *occurrere* to run up to]

▷ **Usage.** In careful English, *occur* and *happen* are not used of prearranged events: *the wedding took place* (not *occurred* or *happened*) *in the afternoon.*

occurrence (əˈkʌrəns) *n.* **1.** something that occurs; a happening; event. **2.** the act or an instance of occurring: *a crime of frequent occurrence.* —**ocˈcurrent** *adj.*

ocean (ˈəʊʃən) *n.* **1.** a very large stretch of sea, esp. one of the five oceans of the world, the Atlantic, Pacific, Indian, Arctic, and Antarctic. **2.** the body of salt water covering approximately 70 per cent of the earth's surface. **3.** a huge quantity or expanse: *an ocean of replies.* **4.** *Literary.* the sea. [C13: via OF < L *ōceanus,* < *Oceanus,* Gk god of the stream believed to flow round the earth]

oceanarium (ˌəʊʃəˈnɛərɪəm) *n., pl.* **-iums** *or* **-ia** (-ɪə). a large saltwater aquarium for marine life.

ocean-going *adj.* (of a ship, boat, etc.) suited for travel on the open ocean.

oceanic (ˌəʊʃɪˈænɪk) *adj.* **1.** of or relating to the ocean. **2.** living in the depths of the ocean: *oceanic fauna.* **3.** huge or overwhelming.

Oceanid (əʊˈsɪənɪd) *n., pl.* **Oceanids** *or* **Oceanides** (ˌəʊsɪˈænɪˌdiːz). *Greek myth.* an ocean nymph.

oceanography (ˌəʊʃəˈnɒgrəfɪ, ˌəʊʃɪə-) *n.* the branch of science dealing with the physical, chemical, geological, and biological features of the oceans. —ˌ**oceanˈographer** *n.* —**oceanographic** (ˌəʊʃənəˈgræfɪk, ˌəʊʃɪə-) *or* ˌ**oceanoˈgraphical** *adj.*

oceanology (ˌəʊʃəˈnɒlədʒɪ, ˌəʊʃɪə-) *n.* the study of the sea, esp. of its economic geography.

ocellus (ɒˈsɛləs) *n., pl.* **-li** (-laɪ). **1.** the simple eye of insects and some other invertebrates, consisting basically of light-sensitive cells. **2.** any eyelike marking in animals, such as the eyespot on the tail feather of a peacock. [C19: via NL < L: small eye, < *oculus* eye] —**oˈcellar** *adj.* —**ocellate** (ˈɒsɪˌleɪt) *or* ˈ**ocelˌlated** *adj.* —ˌ**ocelˈlation** *n.*

ocelot (ˈɒsɪˌlɒt, ˈəʊ-) *n.* a feline mammal inhabiting Central and South America and having a dark-spotted buff-brown coat. [C18: via F < Nahuatl *ocelotl* jaguar]

och (ɒx) *interj. Scot. & Irish.* an expression of surprise, contempt, disagreement, etc.

oche (ˈɒkɪ) *n. Darts.* the mark or ridge on the floor behind which a player must stand to throw. [<?]

ochlocracy (ɒkˈlɒkrəsɪ) *n., pl.* **-cies.** rule by the mob; mobocracy. [C16: via F, < Gk *okhlokratia,* < *okhlos* mob + *kratos* power] —**ochlocrat** (ˈɒkləˌkræt) *n.* —ˌ**ochloˈcratic** *adj.*

ochone (ɒˈxəʊn) *interj. Scot. & Irish.* an expression of sorrow or regret. [< Gaelic *ochóin*]

ochre *or U.S.* **ocher** (ˈəʊkə) *n.* **1.** any of various natural earths containing ferric oxide, silica, and alumina: used as yellow or red pigments. **2. a.** a moderate yellow-orange to orange colour. **b.** (*as adj.*): *an ochre dress.* ~*vb.* **ochreing, ochred** *or U.S.* **ochering** *or* **ochring, ochered** *or* **ochred. 3.** (*tr.*) to colour with ochre. [C15: < OF *ocre,* < L *ōchra,* < Gk *ōkhros* pale yellow] —**ochreous** (ˈəʊkrɪəs, ˈəʊkərəs), **ochrous** (ˈəʊkrəs), **ochry** (ˈəʊkərɪ, ˈəʊkrɪ) *or U.S.* ˈ**ocherous,** ˈ**ochery** *adj.*

-ock *suffix forming nouns.* indicating smallness: *hillock.* [OE *-oc, -uc*]

ocker (ˈɒkə) *Austral. sl.* ~*n.* **1.** (*often cap.*) an uncultivated or boorish Australian. ~*adj.* **2.** typical of such a person. [C20: after an Australian TV character]

Ockham's razor (ˈɒkəmz) *n.* a variant spelling of **Occam's razor.**

o'clock (əˈklɒk) *adv.* **1.** used after a number from one to twelve to indicate the hour of the day or night. **2.** used after a number to indicate direction or position relative to the observer, twelve o'clock being directly ahead and other positions being obtained by comparisons with a clock face. [C18: abbrev. for *of the clock*]

OCR *abbrev. for* optical character reader *or* recognition.

oct. *abbrev. for* octavo.

Oct. *abbrev. for* October.

oct- *combining form.* a variant of **octo-** before a vowel.

octa- *combining form.* a variant of **octo-.**

octad (ˈɒktæd) *n.* **1.** a group or series of eight. **2.** *Chem.* an element with a valency of eight. [C19: < Gk *oktás,* < *oktō* eight] —**ocˈtadic** *adj.*

octagon (ˈɒktəˌgən) *n.* a polygon having eight sides. [C17: via L < Gk *oktagōnos* having eight angles] —**octagonal** (ɒkˈtægənᵊl) *adj.*

octahedron (ˌɒktəˈhiːdrən) *n., pl.* **-drons** *or* **-dra** (-drə). a solid figure having eight plane faces.

octal notation *or* **octal** (ˈɒktəl) *n. Computers.* a number system having a base 8, one octal digit being equivalent to a group of three bits.

octane (ˈɒkteɪn) *n.* a liquid hydrocarbon found in petroleum. Formula: C_8H_{18}.

octane number *or* **rating** *n.* a measure of the antiknock quality of a petrol expressed as a percentage.

octant (ˈɒktənt) *n.* **1.** *Maths.* **a.** any of the eight parts into which the three planes containing the Cartesian coordinate axes divide space. **b.** an eighth part of a circle. **2.** *Astron.* the position of a celestial body when it is at an angular distance of 45° from another body. **3.** an instrument used for measuring angles, similar to a sextant but having a graduated arc of 45°. [C17: < L *octans* half quadrant, < *octo* eight]

octavalent (ˌɒktəˈveɪlənt) *adj. Chem.* having a valency of eight.

octave (ˈɒktɪv) *n.* **1. a.** the interval between two musical notes one of which has twice the pitch of the other and lies eight notes away from it counting inclusively along the diatonic scale. **b.** one of these two notes, esp. the one of higher pitch. **c.** (*as modifier*): *an octave leap.* **2.** *Prosody.* a rhythmic group of eight lines of verse. **3.** (ˈɒkteɪv). **a.** a feast day and the seven days following. **b.** the final day of this period. **4.** the eighth of eight basic positions in fencing. **5.** any set or series of eight. ~*adj.* **6.** consisting of eight parts. [C14: (orig.: eighth day) via OF < Med. L *octāva diēs* eighth day (after a festival), < L *octo* eight]

octavo (ɒkˈteɪvəʊ) *n., pl.* **-vos. 1.** a book size resulting from folding a sheet of paper of a specified size to form eight leaves: *demi-octavo.* Often written: **8vo, 8°. 2.** a book of this size. [C16: < NL *in octavo* in an eighth (of a sheet)]

octennial (ɒkˈtɛnɪəl) *adj.* **1.** occurring every eight years. **2.** lasting for eight years. [C17: < L *octennium,* < *octo* eight + *annus* year] —**ocˈtennially** *adv.*

octet (ɒkˈtɛt) *n.* **1.** any group of eight, esp. singers or musicians. **2.** a piece of music composed for such a group. **3.** *Prosody.* another word for **octave** (sense 2). **4.** *Chem.* a stable group of eight electrons. ~Also (for senses 1, 2, 3): **octette.** [C19: < L *octo* eight, on the model of DUET]

octillion (ɒkˈtɪljən) *n.* **1.** (in Britain and Germany) the number represented as one followed by 48 zeros (10^{48}). **2.** (in the U.S., Canada, and France) the number represented as one followed by 27 zeros (10^{27}). [C17: < F, on the model of MILLION] —**ocˈtillionth** *adj., n.*

octo-, octa-, *or before a vowel* **oct-** *combining form.* eight: *octosyllabic; octagon.* [< L *octo,* Gk *oktō*]

October (ɒkˈtəʊbə) *n.* the tenth month of the year, consisting of 31 days. [OE, < L, < *octo* eight, since it was the eighth month in Roman reckoning]

Octobrist (ɒkˈtəʊbrɪst) *n.* a member of a Russian political party favouring the constitutional reforms granted in a manifesto issued by Nicholas II in Oct. 1905.

octocentenary (ˌɒktəʊsɛnˈtiːnərɪ) *n., pl.* **-naries.** an 800th anniversary.

octogenarian (ˌɒktəʊdʒɪˈnɛərɪən) *n.* **1.** a person who is from 80 to 89 years old. ~*adj.* **2.** of or relating to an octogenarian. [C19: < L *octōgēnārius* containing eighty, < *octōgēnī* eighty each]

octopus (ˈɒktəpəs) *n., pl.* **-puses. 1.** a cephalopod mollusc having a soft oval body with eight long suckered tentacles and occurring at the sea bottom. **2.** a powerful influential organization, etc., with far-reaching effects, esp. harmful ones. [C18: via NL < Gk *oktōpous* having eight feet]

octoroon *or* **octaroon** (ˌɒktəˈruːn) *n.* a person having one quadroon and one White parent and therefore having one-eighth Negro blood. Cf. **quadroon.** [C19: OCTO- + *-roon* as in QUADROON]

octosyllable (ˈɒktəˌsɪləbᵊl) *n.* **1.** a line of verse composed of eight syllables. **2.** a word of eight syllables. —**octosyllabic** (ˌɒktəʊsɪˈlæbɪk) *adj.*

octroi (ˈɒktrwɑː) *n.* **1.** a duty on goods brought into certain towns. **2.** the place where it is collected. **3.** the officers responsible for its collection. [C17: < F *octroyer* to concede, < Med. L *auctorizāre* to AUTHORIZE]

octuple (ˈɒktjʊpᵊl) *n.* **1.** a quantity or number eight times as great as another. ~*adj.* **2.** eight times as much or as many. **3.** consisting of eight parts. ~*vb.* **4.** (*tr.*) to multiply by eight. [C17: < L *octuplus,* < *octo* eight + *-plus* as in *duplus* double]

ocular (ˈɒkjʊlə) *adj.* **1.** of or relating to the eye. ~*n.* **2.** another name for **eyepiece.** [C16: < L *oculāris* < *oculus* eye] —**ˈocularly** *adv.*

ocularist (ˈɒkjʊlərɪst) *n.* a person who makes artificial eyes.

oculist (ˈɒkjʊlɪst) *n. Med.* a former term for **ophthalmologist.** [C17: via F < L *oculus* eye]

od (ɒd, əʊd), **odyl,** *or* **odyle** (ˈɒdɪl) *n. Arch.* a hypothetical force formerly thought to be responsible for many natural phenomena, such as magnetism, light, and hypnotism. [C19: coined by Baron Karl von Reichenbach (1788–1869), G scientist] —**ˈodic** *adj.*

OD[1] (ˌəʊˈdiː) *Inf.* ~*n.* **1.** an overdose of a drug. ~*vb.* (*intr.*) **OD'ing, OD'd. 2.** to take an overdose of a drug. [C20: < *o*(*ver*)*d*(*ose*)]

OD[2] *abbrev. for:* **1.** Officer of the Day. **2.** Also: **o.d.** *Mil.* olive drab. **3.** Also: **O/D** *Banking.* **a.** on demand. **b.** overdrawn. **4.** ordnance datum. **5.** outside diameter.

odalisque *or* **odalisk** (ˈəʊdəlɪsk) *n.* a female slave or concubine. [C17: via F, changed < Turkish *ōdalik,* < *ōdah* room + *-lik,* n. suffix]

odd (ɒd) *adj.* **1.** unusual or peculiar in appearance, character, etc. **2.** occasional, incidental, or random: *odd jobs.* **3.** leftover or additional: *odd bits of wool.* **4. a.** not divisible by two. **b.** represented or indicated by a number that is not divisible by two: *graphs are on odd pages.* Cf. **even**[1] (sense 7). **5.** being part of a matched pair or set when the other or others are missing: *an odd sock.* **6.** (*in combination*) used to designate an indefinite quantity more than the quantity specified in round numbers: *fifty-odd pounds.* **7.** out of the way. **8. odd man out.** a person or thing excluded from others forming a group, unit, etc. ~*n.* **9.** *Golf.* **a.** one stroke more than the score of one's opponent. **b.** a handicap of one stroke. **10.** a thing or person that is odd in sequence or number. ~See also **odds.** [< ON *oddi* triangle, point] —**ˈoddly** *adv.* —**ˈoddness** *n.*

oddball (ˈɒdˌbɔːl) *Inf.* ~*n.* **1.** Also: **odd bod, odd fish.** a strange or eccentric person or thing. ~*adj.* **2.** strange or peculiar.

Oddfellow (ˈɒdˌfɛləʊ) *n.* a member of a secret benevolent and fraternal association founded in England in the 18th century.

oddity (ˈɒdɪtɪ) *n., pl.* **-ties. 1.** an odd person or thing. **2.** an odd quality or characteristic. **3.** the condition of being odd.

odd-jobman *or* **odd-jobber** *n.* a person who does casual work, esp. domestic repairs.

oddment (ˈɒdmənt) *n.* **1.** (*often pl.*) an odd piece or thing; leftover. **2.** *Printing.* **a.** pages that do not make a complete signature. **b.** any individual part of a book excluding the main text.

odd pricing *n.* pricing goods in such a way as to imply that a bargain is being offered, as £5.99 instead of £6.

odds (ɒdz) *pl. n.* **1.** (foll. by *on* or *against*) the probability, expressed as a ratio, that a certain event will take place: *the odds against the outsider are a hundred to one.* **2.** the amount, expressed as a ratio, by which the wager of one better is greater than that of another: *he was offering odds of five to one.* **3.** the likelihood that a certain state of affairs will be so: *the odds are that he is drunk.* **4.** an equalizing allowance, esp. one given to a weaker side in a contest. **5.** the advantage that one contender is judged to have over another. **6.** *Brit.* a significant difference (esp. in **it makes no odds**). **7. at odds.** on bad terms. **8. give** *or* **lay odds.** to offer a bet with favourable odds. **9. over the odds. a.** more than is expected, necessary, etc. **b.** unfair or excessive. **10. take odds.** to accept a bet with favourable odds. **11. what's the odds?** *Brit. inf.* what difference does it make?

odds and ends *pl. n.* miscellaneous items or articles.

odds-on *adj.* **1.** (of a horse, etc.) rated at even money or less to win. **2.** regarded as more or most likely to win, succeed, happen, etc.

ode (əʊd) *n.* **1.** a lyric poem, typically addressed to a particular subject, with lines of varying lengths and complex rhythms. **2.** (formerly) a poem meant to be sung. [C16: via F < LL *ōda,* < Gk *ōidē,* < *aeidein* to sing]

-ode[1] *n. combining form.* denoting resemblance: *nematode.* [< Gk *-ōdēs,* < *eidos* shape]

-ode[2] *n. combining form.* denoting a path or way: *electrode.* [< Gk *-odos,* < *hodos* a way]

odeum (ˈəʊdɪəm) *n., pl.* **odea** (ˈəʊdɪə). (esp. in ancient Greece and Rome) a building for musical performances. Also called: **odeon.** [C17: < L, < Gk *ōideion,* < *ōidē* ODE]

odious (ˈəʊdɪəs) *adj.* offensive; repugnant. [C17: < L; see ODIUM] —**ˈodiousness** *n.*

odium (ˈəʊdɪəm) *n.* **1.** the dislike accorded to a hated person or thing. **2.** hatred; repugnance. [C17: < L; rel. to *ōdī* I hate, Gk *odussasthai* to be angry]

odometer (ɒˈdɒmɪtə, əʊ-) *n.* the usual U.S. and Canad. name for **mileometer.** [C18 *hodometer,* < Gk *hodos* way + -METER] —**oˈdometry** *n.*

-odont *adj. and n. combining form.* -toothed: *acrodont.* [< Gk *odōn* tooth]

odonto- *or before a vowel* **odont-** *combining form.* indicating a tooth or teeth: *odontology.* [< Gk *odōn* tooth]

odontoglossum (ɒˌdɒntəˈglɒsəm) *n.* a tropical American epiphytic orchid having clusters of brightly coloured flowers.

odontology (ˌɒdɒnˈtɒlədʒɪ) *n.* the branch of science concerned with the anatomy, development, and diseases of teeth. —**odontological** (ɒˌdɒntəˈlɒdʒɪkᵊl) *adj.* —**ˌodonˈtologist** *n.*

odoriferous (ˌəʊdəˈrɪfərəs) *adj.* having or emitting an odour, esp. a fragrant one. —ˌ**odor'iferously** *adv.* —ˌ**odor'iferousness** *n.*

odorous ('əʊdərəs) *adj.* having or emitting a characteristic smell or odour. —'**odorously** *adv.* —'**odorousness** *n.*

odour *or U.S.* **odor** ('əʊdə) *n.* **1.** the property of a substance that gives it a characteristic scent or smell. **2.** a pervasive quality about something: *an odour of dishonesty.* **3.** repute or regard (in **in good odour, in bad odour**). **4.** *Arch.* a sweet-smelling fragrance. [C13: < OF *odur,* < L *odor*] —'**odourless** *or U.S.* '**odorless** *adj.*

Odyssey ('ɒdɪsɪ) *n.* **1.** a Greek epic poem, attributed to Homer, describing the ten-year homeward wanderings of Odysseus after the fall of Troy. **2.** (*often not cap.*) any long eventful journey. —**Odyssean** (ˌɒdɪ'siːən) *adj.*

Oe *symbol for* oersted.

OE *abbrev. for* Old English (language).

OECD *abbrev. for* Organization for Economic Cooperation and Development.

OED *abbrev. for* Oxford English Dictionary.

oedema *or* **edema** (ɪ'diːmə) *n., pl.* **-mata** (-mətə). **1.** *Pathol.* an excessive accumulation of serous fluid in the intercellular spaces of tissue. **2.** *Bot.* an abnormal swelling in a plant caused by parenchyma or an accumulation of water in the tissues. [C16: via NL < Gk *oidēma,* < *oidein* to swell] —**oedematous, edematous** (ɪ'dɛmətəs) *or* **oe'demaˌtose, e'demaˌtose** *adj.*

Oedipus complex ('iːdɪpəs) *n. Psychoanal.* the usually unconscious desire of a child, esp. a male child, to possess sexually the parent of the opposite sex while excluding the parent of the same sex. —'**oedipal** *or* ˌ**oedi'pean** *adj.*

OEEC *abbrev. for* Organization for European Economic Cooperation. It was superseded by the OECD in 1961.

oenology *or* **enology** (iː'nɒlədʒɪ) *n.* the study of wine. [C19: < Gk *oinos* wine + -LOGY] —**oenological** *or* **enological** (ˌiːnə'lɒdʒɪk°l) *adj.* —**oe'nologist** *or* **e'nologist** *n.*

oenothera (iː'nɒθərə) *n.* any of various hardy biennial or herbaceous perennial plants having yellow flowers. Also called: **evening primrose.** [< Gk *oinothēras,* ? < *onothēras* a plant whose roots smell of wine]

o'er (ɔː, əʊə) *prep., adv.* a poetic contraction of **over.**

oersted ('ɜːstɛd) *n.* the cgs unit of magnetic field strength; the field strength that would cause a unit magnetic pole to experience a force of 1 dyne in free space. It is equivalent to 79.58 amperes per metre. Symbol: Oe [C20: after H. C. *Oersted* (1777–1851), Danish physicist who discovered electromagnetism]

oesophagus *or U.S.* **esophagus** (iː'sɒfəgəs) *n., pl.* **-gi** (-ˌgaɪ). the part of the alimentary canal between the pharynx and the stomach; gullet. [C16: via NL < Gk *oisophagos,* < *oisein,* future infinitive of *pherein* to carry + *-phagos,* < *phagein* to eat] —**oesophageal** *or U.S.* **esophageal** (iːˌsɒfə'dʒiːəl) *adj.*

oestradiol (ˌiːstrə'daɪɒl, ˌɛstrə-) *or U.S.* **estradiol** *n.* the most potent oestrogenic hormone secreted by the mammalian ovary: synthesized and used to treat oestrogen deficiency and cancer of the breast. [C20: < NL, < OESTRIN + DI-[1] + -OL[1]]

oestrin ('iːstrɪn) *n.* an obsolete term for **oestrogen.** [C20: < OESTR(US) + -IN]

oestrogen ('iːstrədʒən, 'ɛstrə-) *or U.S.* **estrogen** *n.* any of several hormones that induce oestrus, stimulate changes in the female reproductive organs, and promote development of female secondary sexual characteristics. [C20: < OESTRUS + -GEN] —**oestrogenic** (ˌiːstrə'dʒɛnɪk, ˌɛstrə-) *or U.S.* **estrogenic** (ˌɛstrə'dʒɛnɪk, ˌiːstrə-) *adj.* —ˌ**oestro'genically** *or U.S.* ˌ**estro'genically** *adv.*

oestrous cycle ('iːstrəs) *n.* a hormonally controlled cycle of activity of the reproductive organs in many female mammals.

oestrus ('iːstrəs, 'ɛstrəs) *or U.S.* **estrus** *n.* a regularly occurring period of sexual receptivity in most female mammals, except humans, during which ovulation occurs and copulation can take place; heat. [C17: < L *oestrus* gadfly, hence frenzy, < Gk *oistros*] —'**oestrous** *or U.S.* '**estrous** *adj.*

oeuvre *French.* (œvrə) *n.* **1.** a work of art, literature, music, etc. **2.** the total output of a writer, painter, etc. [ult. < L *opera,* pl. of *opus* work]

of (ɒv; *unstressed* əv) *prep.* **1.** used with a verbal noun or gerund to link it with a following noun that is either the subject or the object of the verb embedded in the gerund: *the breathing of a fine swimmer* (subject); *the breathing of clean air* (object). **2.** used to indicate possession, origin, or association: *the house of my sister; to die of hunger.* **3.** used after words or phrases expressing quantities: *a pint of milk.* **4.** constituted by, containing, or characterized by: *a family of idiots; a rod of iron; a man of some depth.* **5.** used to indicate separation, as in time or space: *within a mile of the town; within ten minutes of the beginning of the concert.* **6.** used to mark apposition: *the city of Naples; a speech on the subject of archaeology.* **7.** about; concerning: *speak to me of love.* **8.** used in passive constructions to indicate the agent: *he was beloved of all.* **9.** *Inf.* used to indicate a day or part of a period of time when some activity habitually occurs: *I go to the pub of an evening.* **10.** *U.S.* before the hour of: *a quarter of nine.* [OE (as prep. & adv.); rel. to L *ab*]

▷ **Usage.** See at **off.**

OF *abbrev. for* Old French (language).

off (ɒf) *prep.* **1.** used to indicate actions in which contact is absent, as between an object and a surface: *to lift a cup off the table.* **2.** used to indicate the removal of something that is appended to or in association with something else: *to take the tax off potatoes.* **3.** out of alignment with: *we are off course.* **4.** situated near to or leading away from: *just off the High Street.* **5.** not inclined towards: *I've gone off you.* ~*adv.* **6.** (*particle*) so as to deactivate or disengage: *turn off the radio.* **7.** (*particle*) **a.** so as to get rid of: *sleep off a hangover.* **b.** so as to be removed from, esp. as a reduction: *he took ten per cent off.* **8.** spent away from work or other duties: *take the afternoon off.* **9. a.** on a trip, journey, or race: *I saw her off at the station.* **b.** (*particle*) so as to be completely absent, used up, or exhausted: *this stuff kills off all vermin.* **10.** out from the shore or land: *the ship stood off.* **11. a.** out of contact; at a distance: *the ship was 10 miles off.* **b.** out of the present location: *the girl ran off.* **12.** away in the future: *August is less than a week off.* **13.** (*particle*) so as to be no longer taking place: *the match has been rained off.* **14.** (*particle*) removed from contact with something, as clothing from the body: *the girl took all her clothes off.* **15. off and on.** intermittently; from time to time: *he comes here off and on.* **16. off with.** (*interj.*) a command or an exhortation to remove or cut off (something specified): *off with his head; off with that coat.* ~*adj.* **17.** not on; no longer operative: *the off position on the dial.* **18.** (*postpositive*) not taking place; cancelled or postponed: *the meeting is off.* **19.** in a specified condition regarding money, provisions, etc.: *well off; how are you off for bread?* **20.** unsatisfactory or disappointing: *his performance was rather off; an off year for good tennis.* **21.** (*postpositive*) in a condition as specified: *I'd be better off without this job.* **22.** (*postpositive*) no longer on the menu: *haddock is off.* **23.** (*postpositive*) (of food or drink) having gone bad, sour, etc.: *this milk is off.* ~*n.* **24.** *Cricket.* **a.** the part of the field on that side of the pitch to which the batsman presents his bat when taking strike. **b.** (*in combination*) a fielding position in this part of the field: *mid-off.* **c.** (*as modifier*): *the off stump.* [orig. var. of OF; fully distinguished from it in the 17th cent.]

▷ **Usage.** In educated usage, *off* is not followed by *from* or *of*: *he stepped off* (not *off of*) *the platform.* Careful writers also avoid using the word in the place of *from*: *they bought apples from* (rather than *off*) *the man.*

off. *abbrev. for:* **1.** offer. **2.** office. **3.** officer. **4.** official.

offal ('ɒfᵊl) *n.* **1.** the edible internal parts of an animal, such as the heart, liver, and tongue. **2.** dead or decomposing organic matter. **3.** refuse; rubbish. [C14: < OFF + FALL, referring to parts fallen or cut off]

offbeat ('ɒfˌbiːt) *n.* **1.** *Music.* any of the normally unaccented beats in a bar, such as the second and fourth beats in a bar of four-four time. ~*adj.* **2. a.** unusual, unconventional, or eccentric. **b.** (*as n.*): *he liked the offbeat in fashion.*

off-Broadway *adj.* **1.** designating the kind of experimental, low-budget, or noncommercial productions associated with theatre outside the Broadway area in New York. **2.** (of theatres) not located in Broadway.

off colour *adj.* (**off-colour** *when prenominal*). **1.** *Chiefly Brit.* slightly ill; unwell. **2.** indecent or indelicate; risqué.

offcut ('ɒfˌkʌt) *n.* a piece of paper, wood, fabric, etc., remaining after the main pieces have been cut; remnant.

offence *or U.S.* **offense** (əˈfɛns) *n.* **1.** a violation or breach of a law, rule, etc. **2.** any public wrong or crime. **3.** annoyance, displeasure, or resentment. **4. give offence (to).** to cause annoyance or displeasure (to). **5. take offence.** to feel injured, humiliated, or offended. **6.** a source of annoyance, displeasure, or anger. **7.** attack; assault. **8.** *Arch.* injury or harm.

offend (əˈfɛnd) *vb.* **1.** to hurt the feelings, sense of dignity, etc., of (a person, etc.). **2.** (*tr.*) to be disagreeable to; disgust: *the smell offended him.* **3.** (*intr. except in archaic uses*) to break (a law). [C14: via OF *offendre* to strike against, < L *offendere*] **—ofˈfender** *n.* **—ofˈfending** *adj.*

offensive (əˈfɛnsɪv) *adj.* **1.** unpleasant or disgusting, as to the senses. **2.** causing anger or annoyance; insulting. **3.** for the purpose of attack rather than defence. ~*n.* **4.** (usually preceded by *the*) an attitude or position of aggression. **5.** an assault, attack, or military initiative, esp. a strategic one. **—ofˈfensively** *adv.* **—ofˈfensiveness** *n.*

offer ('ɒfə) *vb.* **1.** to present (something, someone, oneself, etc.) for acceptance or rejection. **2.** (*tr.*) to present as part of a requirement: *she offered English as a second subject.* **3.** (*tr.*) to provide or make accessible: *this stream offers the best fishing.* **4.** (*intr.*) to present itself: *if an opportunity should offer.* **5.** (*tr.*) to show or express willingness or the intention (to do something). **6.** (*tr.*) to put forward (a proposal, opinion, etc.) for consideration. **7.** (*tr.*) to present for sale. **8.** (*tr.*) to propose as payment; bid or tender. **9.** (when *tr.*, often foll. by *up*) to present (a prayer, sacrifice, etc.) as or during an act of worship. **10.** (*tr.*) to show readiness for: *to offer battle.* **11.** (*intr.*) *Arch.* to make a proposal of marriage. ~*n.* **12.** something, such as a proposal or bid, that is offered. **13.** the act of offering or the condition of being offered. **14.** a proposal of marriage. **15. on offer.** for sale at a reduced price. [OE, < L *offerre* to present, < *ob-* to + *ferre* to bring]

offering ('ɒfərɪŋ) *n.* **1.** something that is offered. **2.** a contribution to the funds of a religious organization. **3.** a sacrifice, as of an animal, to a deity.

offertory ('ɒfətərɪ) *n., pl.* **-tories.** *Christianity.* **1.** the oblation of the bread and wine at the Eucharist. **2.** the offerings of the worshippers at this service. **3.** the prayers said or sung while the worshippers' offerings are being brought to the altar during the **offertory procession.** [C14: < Church L *offertōrium* place appointed for offerings, < L *offerre* to OFFER]

offhand (ˌɒfˈhænd) *adj. also* **offhanded,** *adv.* **1.** without care, thought, attention, or consideration; sometimes, brusque or ungracious: *an offhand manner.* **2.** without preparation or warning; impromptu. **—ˌoffˈhandedly** *adv.* **—ˌoffˈhandedness** *n.*

office ('ɒfɪs) *n.* **1. a.** a room or rooms in which business, professional duties, clerical work, etc., are carried out. **b.** (*as modifier*): *office furniture; an office boy.* **2.** (*often pl.*) the building or buildings in which the work of an organization, such as a business, is carried out. **3.** a commercial or professional business: *the architect's office approved the plans.* **4.** the group of persons working in an office: *it was a happy office until she came.* **5.** (*cap. when part of a name*) (in Britain) a department of the national government: *the Home Office.* **6.** (*cap. when part of a name*) (in the U.S.) **a.** a governmental agency, esp. of the Federal government. **b.** a subdivision of such an agency: *Office of Science and Technology.* **7. a.** a position of trust, responsibility, or duty, esp. in a government or organization: *to seek office.* **b.** (*in combination*): *an office-holder.* **8.** duty or function: *the office of an administrator.* **9.** (*often pl.*) a minor task or service: *domestic offices.* **10.** (*often pl.*) an action performed for another, usually a beneficial action: *through his good offices.* **11.** a place where tickets, information, etc., can be obtained: *a ticket office.* **12.** *Christianity.* **a.** (*often pl.*) a ceremony or service, prescribed by ecclesiastical authorities, esp. one for the dead. **b.** *R.C. Church.* the official daily service. **c.** short for **divine office. 13.** (*pl.*) the parts of a house or estate where work is done, goods are stored, etc. **14.** (*usually pl.*) *Brit., euphemistic.* a lavatory (esp. in **usual offices**). **15. in** (*or* **out of**) **office.** (of a government) in (*or* out of) power. **16. the office.** a hint or signal. [C13: via OF < L *officium* service, duty, < *opus* work, service + *facere* to do]

office block *n.* a large building designed to provide office accommodation.

office boy *n.* a boy employed in an office for running errands and other minor jobs.

officer ('ɒfɪsə) *n.* **1.** a person in the armed services who holds a position of responsibility, authority, and duty. **2.** See **police officer. 3.** a person authorized to serve as master or mate of a vessel. **4.** a person appointed or elected to a position of responsibility or authority in a government, society, etc. **5.** a government official: *a customs officer.* **6.** (in the Order of the British Empire) a member of the grade below commander. ~*vb.* (*tr.*) **7.** to furnish with officers. **8.** to act as an officer over (some section, group, organization, etc.).

officer of the day *n.* a military officer whose duty is to take charge of the security of the unit or camp for a day. Also called: **orderly officer.**

official (əˈfɪʃəl) *adj.* **1.** of or relating to an office, its administration, or its duration. **2.** sanctioned by, recognized by, or derived from authority: *an official statement.* **3.** having a formal ceremonial character: *an official dinner.* ~*n.* **4.** a person who holds a position in an organization, government department, etc., esp. a subordinate position. **—ofˈficially** *adv.*

officialdom (əˈfɪʃəldəm) *n.* **1.** the outlook or behaviour of officials, esp. those rigidly adhering to regulations; bureaucracy. **2.** officials or bureaucrats collectively.

officialese (əˌfɪʃəˈliːz) *n.* language characteristic of official documents, esp. when verbose or pedantic.

Official Receiver *n.* an officer appointed by the Department of Trade and Industry to receive the income and manage the estate of a bankrupt. See also **receiver** (sense 2).

officiant (əˈfɪʃɪənt) *n.* a person who presides and officiates at a religious ceremony.

officiate (əˈfɪʃɪˌeɪt) *vb.* (*intr.*) **1.** to hold the position, responsibility, or function of an official. **2.** to conduct a religious or other ceremony. [C17: < Med. L *officiāre,* < L *officium;* see OFFICE] **—ofˌficiˈation** *n.* **—ofˈficiˌator** *n.*

officious (əˈfɪʃəs) *adj.* **1.** unnecessarily or obtrusively ready to offer advice or services. **2.** *Diplomacy.* informal or unofficial. [C16: < L *officiōsus* kindly, < *officium* service; see OFFICE] **—ofˈficiously** *adv.* **—ofˈficiousness** *n.*

offing ('ɒfɪŋ) *n.* **1.** the part of the sea that can be seen from the shore. **2. in the offing.** likely to occur soon.

offish (ˈɒfɪʃ) *adj. Inf.* aloof or distant in manner. —ˈ**offishly** *adv.* —ˈ**offishness** *n.*

off key *adj.* (**off-key** *when prenominal*), *adv.* **1.** *Music.* **a.** not in the correct key. **b.** out of tune. **2.** out of keeping; discordant.

off-licence *n. Brit.* **1.** a shop or a counter in a pub or hotel where alcoholic drinks are sold for consumption elsewhere. U.S. equivalents: **package store, liquor store.** **2.** a licence permitting such sales.

off limits *adj.* (**off-limits** *when prenominal*). **1.** *U.S., chiefly mil.* not to be entered; out of bounds. ~*adv.* **2.** in or into an area forbidden by regulations.

off line *adj.* (**off-line** *when prenominal*). **1.** of or concerned with a part of a computer system not connected to the central processing unit but controlled by a computer storage device. Cf. **on line.** **2.** disconnected from a computer; switched off.

off-load *vb.* (*tr.*) to get rid of (something unpleasant), as by delegation to another.

off-peak *adj.* of or relating to services as used outside periods of intensive use.

off-putting *adj. Brit. inf.* arousing reluctance or aversion.

off-sales *pl. n. Brit.* sales of alcoholic drink for consumption off the premises by a pub or an off-licence attached to a pub.

off season *adj.* (**off-season** *when prenominal*). **1.** denoting or occurring during a period of little activity in a trade or business. ~*n.* **2.** such a period. ~*adv.* **3.** in an off-season period.

offset *n.* (ˈɒfˌsɛt). **1.** something that counterbalances or compensates for something else. **2. a.** a printing method in which the impression is made onto an intermediate surface, such as a rubber blanket, which transfers it to the paper. **b.** (*modifier*) relating to, involving, or printed by offset: *offset letterpress.* **3.** another name for **setoff.** **4.** *Bot.* a short runner in certain plants that produces roots and shoots at the tip. **5.** a ridge projecting from a range of hills or mountains. **6.** a narrow horizontal or sloping surface formed where a wall is reduced in thickness towards the top. **7.** *Surveying.* a measurement of distance to a point at right angles to a survey line. ~*vb.* (ˌɒfˈsɛt), **-setting, -set.** **8.** (*tr.*) to counterbalance or compensate for. **9.** (*tr.*) to print (text, etc.) using the offset process. **10.** (*tr.*) to construct an offset in (a wall). **11.** (*intr.*) to project or develop as an offset.

offshoot (ˈɒfˌʃuːt) *n.* **1.** a shoot or branch growing from the main stem of a plant. **2.** something that develops or derives from a principal source or origin.

offshore (ˌɒfˈʃɔː) *adj., adv.* **1.** from, away from, or at some distance from the shore. ~*adj.* **2.** sited or conducted at sea: *offshore industries.* **3.** based or operating abroad: *offshore funds.*

offside *adj., adv.* (ˌɒfˈsaɪd). **1.** *Sport.* (in football, etc.) in a position illegally ahead of the ball when it is played. Cf. **onside.** ~*n.* (ˈɒfˌsaɪd). **2.** (usually preceded by *the*) *Chiefly Brit.* **a.** the side of a vehicle, etc., nearest the centre of the road. **b.** (*as modifier*): *the offside passenger door.*

off-sider *n. Austral. & N.Z.* a partner or assistant.

offspring (ˈɒfˌsprɪŋ) *n.* **1.** the immediate descendant or descendants of a person, animal, etc.; progeny. **2.** a product, outcome, or result.

offstage (ˈɒfˈsteɪdʒ) *adj., adv.* out of the view of the audience; off the stage.

off-the-peg *adj.* (of clothing) ready to wear; not produced especially for the person buying.

off-the-wall *adj.* (**off the wall** *when postpositive*). *Sl.* new or unexpected in an unconventional or eccentric way. [C20: ? < the use of the phrase in handball and squash to describe a shot that is unexpected]

off-white *n.* **1.** a colour consisting of white with a tinge of grey or yellow. ~*adj.* **2.** of such a colour: *an off-white coat.*

oft (ɒft) *adv.* short for **often** (archaic or poetic except in combinations such as **oft-repeated** and **oft-recurring**). [OE *oft;* rel. to OHG *ofto*]

OFT (in Britain) *abbrev. for* Office of Fair Trading.

Oftel (ˈɒfˌtɛl) *n.* (in Britain) *acronym for* Office of Telecommunications: a Government body that monitors British Telecom.

often (ˈɒfᵊn) *adv.* **1.** frequently or repeatedly; much of the time. Arch. equivalents: ˈ**often-ˌtimes,** ˈ**oftˌtimes.** **2. as often as not.** quite frequently. **3. every so often.** at intervals. **4. more often than not.** in more than half the instances. ~*adj.* **5.** *Arch.* repeated; frequent. [C14: var. of OFT before vowels and *h*]

ogee (ˈəʊdʒiː) *n. Archit.* **1.** Also called: **talon.** a moulding having a cross section in the form of a letter S. **2.** short for **ogee arch.** [C15: prob. var. of OGIVE]

ogee arch *n. Archit.* a pointed arch having an S-shaped curve on both sides. Sometimes shortened to **ogee.**

Ogen melon (ˈəʊgɛn) *n.* a variety of small melon with sweet pale orange flesh. [C20: after a kibbutz in Israel where it was first developed]

ogham *or* **ogam** (ˈɒgəm) *n.* an ancient alphabetical writing system used by the Celts in Britain, consisting of straight lines drawn or carved perpendicular to or at an angle to another long straight line. [C17: < OIrish *ogom,* < ?, but associated with the name *Ogma,* legendary inventor of this alphabet]

ogive (ˈəʊdʒaɪv, əʊˈdʒaɪv) *n.* **1.** a diagonal rib or groin of a Gothic vault. **2.** another name for **lancet arch.** [C17: < OF, <?] —**oˈgival** *adj.*

ogle (ˈəʊgᵊl) *vb.* **1.** to look at (someone, esp. a woman) amorously. **2.** (*tr.*) to stare or gape at. ~*n.* **3.** a flirtatious or lewd look. [C17: prob. < Low G *oegeln,* < *oegen* to look at] —ˈ**ogler** *n.*

O grade *n.* (in Scotland) **1. a.** the basic level of the Scottish Certificate of Education. **b.** (*as modifier*): *O-grade history.* **2.** a pass in a subject at O grade: *she has ten O grades.*

ogre (ˈəʊgə) *n.* **1.** (in folklore) a giant, usually given to eating human flesh. **2.** any monstrous or cruel person. [C18: < F, ? < L *Orcus,* god of the infernal regions] —ˈ**ogreish** *adj.* —ˈ**ogress** *fem. n.*

oh (əʊ) *interj.* an exclamation expressive of surprise, pain, pleasure, etc.

OHG *abbrev. for* Old High German.

ohm (əʊm) *n.* the derived SI unit of electric resistance; the resistance between two points on a conductor when a constant potential difference of 1 volt between them produces a current of 1 ampere. Symbol: Ω [C19: after Georg Simon *Ohm* (1787-1854), G physicist] —ˈ**ohmage** *n.*

ohmmeter (ˈəʊmˌmiːtə) *n.* an instrument for measuring electrical resistance.

OHMS (in Britain and the Commonwealth) *abbrev. for* On Her (*or* His) Majesty's Service.

Ohm's law (əʊmz) *n.* the principle that the electric current passing through a conductor is directly proportional to the potential difference across it, provided that the temperature remains constant. The constant of proportionality is the resistance of the conductor.

oho (əʊˈhəʊ) *interj.* an exclamation expressing surprise, exultation, or derision.

-oid *suffix forming adjectives and associated nouns.* indicating likeness, resemblance, or similarity: *anthropoid.* [< Gk *-oeidēs* resembling, < *eidos* form]

-oidea *suffix forming plural proper nouns.* forming the names of zoological classes or superfamilies: *Canoidea.* [< NL, < L *-oīdēs* -OID]

oil (ɔɪl) *n.* **1.** any of a number of viscous liquids with a smooth sticky feel. They are usually flammable, insoluble in water, soluble in organic solvents, and are obtained from plants and animals, from mineral deposits, and by synthesis. See also **essential oil.** **2. a.** another name for **petroleum.** **b.** (*as modifier*): *an oil engine; an oil rig.* **3. a.** any of a number of substances usually derived from petroleum and used for lubrication.

b. (*in combination*): *an oilcan.* c. (*as modifier*): *an oil pump.* 4. Also called: **fuel oil.** a fraction of petroleum used as a fuel in domestic heating, marine engines, etc. 5. *Brit.* a. paraffin, esp. when used as a domestic fuel. b. (*as modifier*): *an oil lamp.* 6. any substance of a consistency resembling that of oil: *oil of vitriol.* 7. the solvent, usually linseed oil, with which pigments are mixed to make artists' paints. 8. a. (*often pl.*) oil colour or paint. b. (*as modifier*): *an oil painting.* 9. an oil painting. 10. *Austral. & N.Z. sl.* facts or news. 11. **strike oil.** a. to discover petroleum while drilling for it. b. *Inf.* to become very rich or successful. ~*vb.* (*tr.*) 12. to lubricate, smear, polish, etc., with oil or an oily substance. 13. **oil one's tongue.** *Inf.* to speak flatteringly or glibly. 14. **oil someone's palm.** *Inf.* to bribe someone. 15. **oil the wheels.** to make things run smoothly. [C12: < OF *oile*, < L *oleum* (olive) oil, < *olea* olive tree, < Gk *elaia* OLIVE] —'**oiler** *n.* —'**oil-**ˌ**like** *adj.*

oil cake *n.* stock feed consisting of compressed cubes made from the residue of the crushed seeds of oil-bearing crops such as linseed.

oilcan ('ɔɪlˌkæn) *n.* a container with a long nozzle for applying lubricating oil to machinery.

oilcloth ('ɔɪlˌklɒθ) *n.* 1. waterproof material made by treating one side of a cotton fabric with a drying oil or a synthetic resin. 2. another name for **linoleum.**

oil drum *n.* a metal drum used to contain or transport oil.

oilfield ('ɔɪlˌfiːld) *n.* an area containing reserves of petroleum, esp. one that is already being exploited.

oilfired ('ɔɪlˌfaɪəd) *adj.* (of central heating, etc.) using oil as fuel.

oilman ('ɔɪlmən) *n., pl.* **-men.** 1. a person who owns or operates oil wells. 2. a person who sells oil.

oil minister *n.* a government official in charge of or representing the interests of an oil-producing country.

oil of vitriol *n.* another name for **sulphuric acid.**

oil paint *n.* paint made of pigment ground in oil, usually linseed oil.

oil painting *n.* 1. a picture painted with oil paints. 2. the art or process of painting with oil paints. 3. **he's** *or* **she's no oil painting.** *Inf.* he *or* she is not regarded as good-looking.

oil palm *n.* a tropical African palm tree, the fruits of which yield palm oil.

oil rig *n.* See **rig** (sense 6).

oilskin ('ɔɪlˌskɪn) *n.* 1. a. a cotton fabric treated with oil and pigment to make it waterproof. b. (*as modifier*): *an oilskin hat.* 2. (*often pl.*) a protective outer garment of this fabric.

oil slick *n.* a mass of floating oil covering an area of water.

oilstone ('ɔɪlˌstəʊn) *n.* a stone with a fine grain lubricated with oil and used for sharpening cutting tools. See also **whetstone.**

oil well *n.* a boring into the earth or sea bed for the extraction of petroleum.

oily ('ɔɪlɪ) *adj.* **oilier, oiliest.** 1. soaked in or smeared with oil or grease. 2. consisting of, containing, or resembling oil. 3. flatteringly servile or obsequious. —'**oilily** *adv.* —'**oiliness** *n.*

oink (ɔɪŋk) *interj.* an imitation or representation of the grunt of a pig or the cry of a goose.

ointment ('ɔɪntmənt) *n.* 1. a fatty or oily medicated preparation applied to the skin to heal or protect. 2. a similar substance used as a cosmetic. [C14: < OF *oignement*, < L *unguentum* UNGUENT]

Oireachtas ('ɛrəkθəs) *n.* the parliament of the Republic of Ireland. [Irish Gaelic: assembly, < OIrish *airech* nobleman]

Ojibwa (əʊ'dʒɪbwə) *n.* 1. (*pl.* **-was** *or* **-wa**) a member of a North American Indian people living west of Lake Superior. 2. the language of this people.

O.K. (ˌəʊ'keɪ) *Inf.* ~*sentence substitute.* 1. an expression of approval or agreement. ~*adj.* (*usually postpositive*), *adv.* 2. in good or satisfactory condition. ~*vb.* **O.K.ing** (ˌəʊ'keɪɪŋ), **O.K.ed** (ˌəʊ'keɪd). 3. (*tr.*) to approve or endorse. ~*n., pl.* **O.K.s.** 4. approval or agreement. ~Also: **okay.** [C19: ? < *o(ll) k(orrect)*, jocular alteration of *all correct*]

okapi (əʊ'kɑːpɪ) *n., pl.* **-pis** *or* **-pi.** a ruminant mammal of the forests of central Africa, having a reddish-brown coat with horizontal white stripes on the legs, and small horns. [C20: < a Central African word]

okay (ˌəʊ'keɪ) *sentence substitute, adj., adv., vb., n.* a variant spelling of **O.K.**

okra ('əʊkrə) *n.* 1. an annual plant of the Old World tropics, with yellow-and-red flowers and edible oblong sticky green pods. 2. the pod of this plant, eaten in soups, stews, etc. See also **gumbo** (sense 1). [C18: of West African origin]

-ol[1] *suffix forming nouns.* denoting a chemical compound containing a hydroxyl group, esp. alcohols and phenols: *ethanol; quinol.* [< ALCOHOL]

-ol[2] *n. combining form.* (not used systematically) a variant of **-ole**[1].

old (əʊld) *adj.* 1. having lived or existed for a relatively long time: *an old man; an old tradition; an old house.* 2. a. of or relating to advanced years or a long life: *old age.* b. (*as collective n.; preceded by the*): *the old.* c. **old and young.** people of all ages. 3. decrepit or senile. 4. worn with age or use: *old clothes; an old car.* 5. a. (*postpositive*) having lived or existed for a specified period: *a child who is six years old.* b. (*in combination*): *a six-year-old child.* c. (*as n. in combination*): *a six-year-old.* 6. (*cap. when part of a name or title*) earlier or earliest of two or more things with the same name: *the old edition; the Old Testament.* 7. (*cap. when part of a name*) designating the form of a language in which the earliest known records are written: *Old English.* 8. (*prenominal*) familiar through long acquaintance or repetition: *an old friend; an old excuse.* 9. practised; hardened: *old in cunning.* 10. (*prenominal; often preceded by good*) cherished; dear: used as a term of affection or familiarity: *good old George.* 11. *Inf.* (with any of several nouns) used as a familiar form of address to a person: *old thing; old bean; old stick.* 12. skilled through long experience (esp. in **an old hand**). 13. out of date; unfashionable. 14. remote or distant in origin or time of origin: *an old culture.* 15. (*prenominal*) former; previous: *my old house was small.* 16. a. (*prenominal*) established for a relatively long time: *an old member.* b. (*in combination*): *old-established.* 17. sensible, wise, or mature: *old beyond one's years.* 18. (intensifier) (esp. in **a high old time, any old thing, any old how,** etc.). 19. **good old days.** an earlier period of time regarded as better than the present. 20. **little old.** *Inf.* indicating affection, esp. humorous affection. 21. **the old one** (*or* **gentleman**). *Inf.* a jocular name for **Satan.** ~*n.* 22. an earlier or past time: *in days of old.* [OE *eald*] —'**oldish** *adj.* —'**oldness** *n.*

old age pension *n.* a former name for **retirement pension.** —**old age pensioner** *n.*

Old Bailey ('beɪlɪ) *n.* the Central Criminal Court of England.

Old Bill (bɪl) *n.* (*functioning as pl., preceded by the*) *Brit. sl.* policemen collectively. [C20: ? < the World War I cartoon of a soldier with a drooping moustache]

old boy *n.* 1. (*sometimes caps.*) *Brit.* a male ex-pupil of a school. 2. *Inf., chiefly Brit.* a. a familiar name used to refer to a man. b. an old man.

old boy network *n. Brit. inf.* the appointment to power of former pupils of the same small group of public schools or universities.

Old Contemptibles *pl. n.* the British expeditionary force to France in 1914. [< the Kaiser's alleged reference to them as a "contemptible little army"]

old country *n.* the country of origin of an immigrant or an immigrant's ancestors.

Old Dart *n.* **the.** *Austral. sl.* Britain, esp. England. [C19: <?]

olden (ˈəʊldᵊn) *adj.* an archaic or poetic word for **old** (often in **in olden days** and **in olden times**).

Old English *n.* **1.** Also called: **Anglo-Saxon.** the English language from the time of the earliest Saxon settlements in the fifth century A.D. to about 1100. Abbrev.: **OE. 2.** *Printing.* a Gothic typeface commonly used in England up to the 18th century.

Old English sheepdog *n.* a breed of large bobtailed sheepdog with a profuse shaggy coat.

older (ˈəʊldə) *adj.* **1.** the comparative of **old. 2.** Also (of people): **elder.** of greater age.

old-fashioned *adj.* **1.** belonging to, characteristic of, or favoured by former times; outdated: *old-fashioned ideas.* **2.** favouring or adopting the dress, manners, fashions, etc., of a former time. **3.** *Scot. & N English dialect.* old for one's age: *an old-fashioned child.* ~*n.* **4.** a cocktail containing spirit, bitters, fruit, etc.

Old French *n.* the French language in its earliest forms, from about the 9th century up to about 1400. Abbrev.: **OF.**

old girl *n.* **1.** (*sometimes caps.*) *Brit.* a female ex-pupil of a school. **2.** *Inf., chiefly Brit.* **a.** a familiar name used to refer to a woman. **b.** an old woman.

Old Glory *n.* a nickname for the flag of the United States of America.

old gold *n.* **a.** a dark yellow colour, sometimes with a brownish tinge. **b.** (*as adj.*)*: an old-gold carpet.*

old guard *n.* **1.** a group that works for a long-established or old-fashioned cause or principle. **2.** the conservative element in a political party or other group. [C19: after Napoleon's imperial guard]

old hat *adj.* (*postpositive*) old-fashioned or trite.

Old High German *n.* a group of West Germanic dialects that eventually developed into modern German; High German up to about 1200. Abbrev.: **OHG.**

oldie (ˈəʊldɪ) *n. Inf.* an old joke, song, film, person, etc.

Old Irish *n.* the Celtic language of Ireland up to about 900 A.D.

old lady *n.* an informal term for **mother** or **wife.**

Old Latin *n.* the Latin language before the classical period, up to about 100 B.C.

Old Low German *n.* the Saxon and Low Franconian dialects of German up to about 1200; the old form of modern Low German and Dutch. Abbrev.: **OLG.**

old maid *n.* **1.** a woman regarded as unlikely ever to marry; spinster. **2.** *Inf.* a prim, fastidious, or excessively cautious person. **3.** a card game in which players try to avoid holding the unpaired card at the end of the game. —ˌ**old-ˈmaidish** *adj.*

old man *n.* **1.** an informal term for **father** or **husband. 2.** (*sometimes caps.*) *Inf.* a man in command, such as an employer, foreman, or captain of a ship. **3.** *Sometimes facetious.* an affectionate term used in addressing a man. **4.** Also called: **southernwood.** an aromatic shrubby wormwood of S Europe, having drooping yellow flowers. **5.** *Christianity.* the unregenerate aspect of human nature.

old man's beard *n.* any of various plants having long trailing parts, esp. traveller's joy and Spanish moss.

old master *n.* **1.** one of the great European painters of the period 1500 to 1800. **2.** a painting by one of these.

old moon *n.* a phase of the moon lying between last quarter and new moon, when it appears as a waning crescent.

Old Nick (nɪk) *n. Inf.* a jocular name for **Satan.**

Old Norse *n.* the language or group of dialects of medieval Scandinavia and Iceland from about 700 to about 1350. Abbrev.: **ON.**

Old Pretender *n.* James Francis Edward Stuart, 1688-1766, son of James II and pretender to the British throne.

Old Prussian *n.* the former language of the non-German Prussians, belonging to the Baltic branch of the Indo-European family: extinct by 1700.

old rose *n.* **a.** a greyish-pink colour. **b.** (*as adj.*)*: old-rose gloves.*

Old Saxon *n.* the Saxon dialect of Low German up to about 1200, from which modern Low German is derived. Abbrev.: **OS.**

old school *n.* **1.** *Chiefly Brit.* one's former school. **2.** a group of people favouring traditional ideas or conservative practices.

old school tie *n.* **1.** *Brit.* a distinctive tie that indicates which school the wearer attended. **2.** the attitudes, loyalties, values, etc., associated with British public schools.

Old South *n.* the American South before the Civil War.

oldster (ˈəʊldstə) *n. Inf.* an older person.

old style *n. Printing.* a type style reviving the characteristics of **old face,** a type style that originated in the 18th century and was characterized by having little contrast between thick and thin strokes.

Old Style *n.* the former method of reckoning dates using the Julian calendar. Cf. **New Style.**

Old Testament *n.* the collection of books comprising the sacred Scriptures of the Hebrews; the first part of the Christian Bible.

old-time *adj.* (*prenominal*) of or relating to a former time; old-fashioned: *old-time dancing.*

old-timer *n.* **1.** a person who has been in a certain place, occupation, etc., for a long time. **2.** *U.S.* an old man.

old wives' tale *n.* a belief, usually superstitious or erroneous, passed on by word of mouth as a piece of traditional wisdom.

old woman *n.* **1.** an informal term for **mother** or **wife. 2.** a timid, fussy, or cautious person. —ˌ**old-ˈwomanish** *adj.*

Old World *n.* that part of the world that was known before the discovery of the Americas; the eastern hemisphere.

old-world *adj.* of or characteristic of former times, esp., in Europe, quaint or traditional.

Old World monkey *n.* any monkey such as a macaque, baboon, or mandrill, which has nostrils that are close together and a nonprehensile tail.

-ole[1] *or* **-ol** *n. combining form.* **1.** denoting an organic unsaturated compound containing a 5-membered ring: *thiazole.* **2.** denoting an aromatic organic ether: *anisole.* [< L *oleum* oil, < Gk *elaion,* < *elaia* olive]

-ole[2] *suffix of nouns.* indicating something small: *arteriole.* [< L *-olus,* dim. suffix]

oleaceous (ˌəʊlɪˈeɪʃəs) *adj.* of, relating to, or belonging to a family of trees and shrubs which includes the ash, jasmine, privet, lilac, and olive. [C19: via NL < L *olea* OLIVE; see also OIL]

oleaginous (ˌəʊlɪˈædʒɪnəs) *adj.* **1.** resembling or having the properties of oil. **2.** containing or producing oil. [C17: < L *oleāginus,* < *olea* OLIVE; see also OIL]

oleander (ˌəʊlɪˈændə) *n.* a poisonous evergreen Mediterranean shrub or tree with fragrant white, pink, or purple flowers. Also called: **rosebay.** [C16: < Med. L, var. of *arodandrum,* ? < L RHODODENDRON]

oleate (ˈəʊlɪˌeɪt) *n.* any salt or ester of oleic acid.

oleic acid (əʊˈliːɪk) *n.* a colourless oily liquid unsaturated acid occurring, as the glyceride, in almost all natural fats; used in making soaps, ointments, cosmetics, and lubricating oils. [C19 *oleic,* < L *oleum* oil + -IC]

olein (ˈəʊlɪɪn) *n.* another name for **triolein.** [C19: < F *oléine,* < L *oleum* oil + -IN]

oleo- *combining form.* oil: *oleomargarine.* [< L *oleum* OIL]

oleomargarine (ˌəʊlɪəʊˌmɑːdʒəˈriːn) *or* **oleomargarin** (ˌəʊlɪəʊˈmɑːdʒərɪn) *n.* another name (esp. U.S.) for **margarine.**

oleoresin (ˌəʊlɪəʊˈrɛzɪn) *n.* **1.** a semisolid mixture of a resin and essential oil, obtained from certain plants. **2.** *Pharmacol.* a liquid preparation of resins and oils, obtained by extraction from plants. —ˌ**oleoˈresinous** *adj.*

oleum (ˈəʊlɪəm) *n., pl.* **olea** (ˈəʊlɪə) *or* **oleums.**

another name for **fuming sulphuric acid.** [< L: oil, referring to its oily consistency]

O level *n. Brit.* **1. a.** the basic level of the General Certificate of Education. **b.** (*as modifier*): *O-level maths.* **2.** a pass in a particular subject at O level: *he has eight O levels.*

olfaction (ɒlˈfækʃən) *n.* **1.** the sense of smell. **2.** the act or function of smelling.

olfactory (ɒlˈfæktərɪ, -trɪ) *adj.* **1.** of or relating to the sense of smell. ~*n., pl.* **-ries. 2.** (*usually pl.*) an organ or nerve concerned with the sense of smell. [C17: < L *olfactus,* p.p. of *olfacere,* < *olere* to smell + *facere* to make]

OLG *abbrev. for* Old Low German.

oligarch (ˈɒlɪˌgɑːk) *n.* a member of an oligarchy.

oligarchy (ˈɒlɪˌgɑːkɪ) *n., pl.* **-chies. 1.** government by a small group of people. **2.** a state or organization so governed. **3.** a small body of individuals ruling such a state. **4.** *Chiefly U.S.* a small clique of private citizens who exert a strong influence on government. [C16: via Med. L < Gk *oligarkhia,* < *oligos* few + -ARCHY] —ˌ**oliˈgarchic** *or* ˌ**oliˈgarchical** *adj.*

oligo- *or before a vowel* **olig-** *combining form.* indicating a few or little: *oligopoly.* [< Gk *oligos* little, few]

Oligocene (ˈɒlɪgəʊˌsiːn, ɒˈlɪg-) *adj.* **1.** of, denoting, or formed in the third epoch of the Tertiary period. ~*n.* **2. the.** the Oligocene epoch or rock series. [C19: OLIGO- + -CENE]

oligochaete (ˈɒlɪgəʊˌkiːt) *n.* **1.** any freshwater or terrestrial annelid worm having bristles borne singly along the length of the body: includes the earthworms. ~*adj.* **2.** of or relating to this type of worm. [C19: < NL < OLIGO- + Gk *khaitē* long hair]

oligopoly (ˌɒlɪˈgɒpəlɪ) *n., pl.* **-lies.** *Econ.* a market situation in which control over the supply of a commodity is held by a small number of producers. [C20: < OLIGO- + Gk *pōlein* to sell] —ˌ**oliˌgopoˈlistic** *adj.*

oligotrophic (ˌɒlɪgəʊˈtrɒfɪk) *adj.* (of lakes and similar habitats) poor in nutrients and plant life and rich in oxygen. [C20: < OLIGO- + Gk *trophein* to nourish + -IC] —**oligotrophy** (ˌɒlɪˈgɒtrəfɪ) *n.*

olio (ˈəʊlɪˌəʊ) *n., pl.* **olios. 1.** a dish of many different ingredients. **2.** a miscellany or potpourri. [C17: < Sp. *olla* stew, < L: jar]

olivaceous (ˌɒlɪˈveɪʃəs) *adj.* of an olive colour.

olive (ˈɒlɪv) *n.* **1.** an evergreen oleaceous tree of the Mediterranean region having white fragrant flowers and edible fruits that are black when ripe. **2.** the fruit of this plant, eaten as a relish and used as a source of olive oil. **3.** the wood of the olive tree, used for ornamental work. **4. a.** a yellow-green colour like that of an unripe olive. **b.** (*as adj.*): *an olive coat.* ~*adj.* **5.** of, relating to, or made of the olive tree, its wood, or its fruit. [C13: via OF < L *oliva,* rel. to Gk *elaia* olive tree]

olive branch *n.* **1.** a branch of an olive tree used to symbolize peace. **2.** any offering of peace or conciliation.

olive crown *n.* (esp. in ancient Greece and Rome) a garland of olive leaves awarded as a token of victory.

olive drab *n. U.S.* **1. a.** a dull but fairly strong greyish-olive colour. **b.** (*as adj.*): *an olive-drab jacket.* **2.** cloth or clothes in this colour, esp. the uniform of the U.S. Army.

olive green *n.* **a.** a colour that is greener, stronger, and brighter than olive; deep yellowish-green. **b.** (*as adj.*): *an olive-green coat.*

olive oil *n.* a pale yellow oil pressed from ripe olive fruits and used in cooking, medicines, etc.

olivine (ˈɒlɪˌviːn, ˌɒlɪˈviːn) *n.* any of a group of hard glassy olive-green minerals consisting of magnesium iron silicate in crystalline form. [C18: < G, after its colour]

olla (ˈɒlə) *n.* **1.** a cooking pot. **2.** short for **olla podrida.** [Sp., < L *olla,* var. of *aulla* pot]

olla podrida (ˈɒlə pɒˈdriːdə) *n.* **1.** a Spanish dish, consisting of a stew with beans, sausages, etc. **2.** an assortment; miscellany. [Sp., lit.: rotten pot]

ology (ˈɒlədʒɪ) *n., pl.* **-gies.** *Inf.* a science or other branch of knowledge. [C19: abstracted < words such as *theology, biology,* etc.; see -LOGY]

-ology *n. combining form.* See **-logy.**

oloroso (ˌɒləˈrəʊsəʊ) *n., pl.* **-sos.** a full-bodied golden-coloured sweet sherry. [< Sp.: fragrant]

Olympiad (əˈlɪmpɪˌæd) *n.* **1.** a staging of the modern Olympic Games. **2.** the four-year period between consecutive celebrations of the Olympic Games; a unit of ancient Greek chronology dating back to 776 B.C. **3.** an international contest in chess, bridge, etc.

Olympian (əˈlɪmpɪən) *adj.* **1.** of or relating to Mount Olympus or to the classical Greek gods. **2.** majestic or godlike in manner or bearing. **3.** of or relating to ancient Olympia, a plain in Greece, or its inhabitants. ~*n.* **4.** a god of Mount Olympus. **5.** an inhabitant of ancient Olympia. **6.** *Chiefly U.S.* a competitor in the Olympic Games.

Olympic (əˈlɪmpɪk) *adj.* **1.** of or relating to the Olympic Games. **2.** of or relating to ancient Olympia.

Olympic Games *n.* (*functioning as sing. or pl.*) **1.** the greatest Panhellenic festival, held every fourth year in honour of Zeus at ancient Olympia, consisting of games and festivities. **2.** Also called: **the Olympics.** the modern revival of these games, consisting of international athletic and sporting contests held every four years in a selected country.

OM *abbrev. for* Order of Merit (a Brit. title).

-oma *n. combining form.* indicating a tumour: *carcinoma.* [< Gk *-ōma*]

omasum (əʊˈmeɪsəm) *n., pl.* **-sa** (-sə). another name for **psalterium.** [C18: < L: bullock's tripe]

ombre *or U.S.* **omber** (ˈɒmbə) *n.* an 18th-century card game. [C17: < Sp. *hombre* man, referring to the player who attempts to win the stakes]

ombudsman (ˈɒmbʊdzmən) *n., pl.* **-men.** an official who investigates citizens' complaints against the government or its servants. Also called (Brit.): **Parliamentary Commissioner.** [C20: < Swedish: commissioner]

-ome *n. combining form.* denoting a mass or part of a specified kind: *rhizome.* [var. of -OMA]

omega (ˈəʊmɪgə) *n.* **1.** the 24th and last letter of the Greek alphabet (Ω, ω). **2.** the ending or last of a series. [C16: < Gk *ō mega* big o]

omega minus *n.* an unstable negatively charged elementary particle, classified as a baryon, that has a mass 3276 times that of the electron.

omelette *or esp. U.S.* **omelet** (ˈɒmlɪt) *n.* a savoury or sweet dish of beaten eggs cooked in fat. [C17: < F *omelette,* changed < *alumette,* < *alumelle* sword blade, changed by mistaken division < *la lemelle,* < L (see LAMELLA); apparently from the flat shape of the omelette]

omen (ˈəʊmən) *n.* **1.** a phenomenon or occurrence regarded as a sign of future happiness or disaster. **2.** prophetic significance. ~*vb.* **3.** (*tr.*) to portend. [C16: < L]

omentum (əʊˈmɛntəm) *n., pl.* **-ta** (-tə). *Anat.* a double fold of peritoneum connecting the stomach with other abdominal organs. [C16: < L: membrane, esp. a caul, <?]

omertà *Italian.* (omerˈta) *n.* a conspiracy of silence.

omicron (əʊˈmaɪkrɒn, ˈɒmɪkrɒn) *n.* the 15th letter in the Greek alphabet (Ο, ο). [< Gk *ō mikron* small o]

ominous (ˈɒmɪnəs) *adj.* **1.** foreboding evil. **2.** serving as or having significance as an omen. [C16: < L *ōminōsus,* < OMEN] —ˈ**ominously** *adv.* —ˈ**ominousness** *n.*

omission (əʊˈmɪʃən) *n.* **1.** something that has been omitted or neglected. **2.** the act of omitting or the state of having been omitted. [C14: < L *omissiō,* < *omittere* to OMIT] —**oˈmissive** *adj.*

omit (əʊˈmɪt) *vb.* **omitting, omitted.** (*tr.*) **1.** to neglect to do or include. **2.** to fail (to do something). [C15: < L *omittere,* < *ob-* away + *mittere* to send] —**omissible** (əʊˈmɪsɪbᵊl) *adj.* —**oˈmitter** *n.*

omni- *combining form.* all or everywhere: *omnipresent.* [< L *omnis* all]

omnibus (ˈɒmnɪˌbʌs, -bəs) *n., pl.* **-buses. 1.** a

formal word for **bus** (sense 1). **2.** Also called: **omnibus volume.** a collection of works by one author or several works on a similar topic, reprinted in one volume. *~adj.* **3.** (*prenominal*) of, dealing with, or providing for many different things or cases. [C19: < L, lit.: for all, dative pl. of *omnis* all]

omnicompetent (ˌɒmnɪˈkɒmpɪtənt) *adj.* able to judge or deal with all matters. —ˌ**omniˈcompetence** *n.*

omnidirectional (ˌɒmnɪdɪˈrɛkʃənˀl, -daɪ-) *adj.* (of an antenna) capable of transmitting and receiving radio signals equally in any direction of the horizontal plane.

omnifarious (ˌɒmnɪˈfɛərɪəs) *adj.* of many or all varieties or forms. [C17: < LL *omnifārius,* < L *omnis* all + *-farius* doing] —ˌ**omniˈfariously** *adv.* —ˌ**omniˈfariousness** *n.*

omnific (ɒmˈnɪfɪk) *or* **omnificent** (ɒmˈnɪfɪsənt) *adj. Rare.* creating all things. [C17: via Med. L < L *omni-* + *-ficus,* < *facere* to do] —**omˈnificence** *n.*

omnipotent (ɒmˈnɪpətənt) *adj.* **1.** having very great or unlimited power. *~n.* **2. the Omnipotent.** an epithet for God. [C14: via OF < L *omnipotens* all-powerful, < OMNI- + *potens,* < *posse* to be able] —**omˈnipotence** *n.* —**omˈnipotently** *adv.*

omnipresent (ˌɒmnɪˈprɛzˀnt) *adj.* (esp. of a deity) present in all places at the same time. —ˌ**omniˈpresence** *n.*

omniscient (ɒmˈnɪsɪənt) *adj.* **1.** having infinite knowledge or understanding. **2.** having very great or seemingly unlimited knowledge. [C17: < Med. L *omnisciens,* < L OMNI- + *scīre* to know] —**omˈniscience** *n.* —**omˈnisciently** *adv.*

omnium-gatherum (ˈɒmnɪəmˈgæðərəm) *n. Often facetious.* a miscellaneous collection. [C16: < L *omnium* of all, + Latinized form of E *gather*]

omnivorous (ɒmˈnɪvərəs) *adj.* **1.** eating any type of food indiscriminately. **2.** taking in or assimilating everything, esp. with the mind. [C17: < L *omnivorus* all-devouring, < OMNI- + *vorāre* to eat greedily] —ˈ**omniˌvore** *n.* —**omˈnivorously** *adv.* —**omˈnivorousness** *n.*

omphalos (ˈɒmfəˌlɒs) *n.* **1.** (in the ancient world) a sacred conical object, esp. a stone. The famous omphalos at Delphi was assumed to mark the centre of the earth. **2.** the central point. **3.** *Literary.* another word for **navel.** [Gk: navel]

on (ɒn) *prep.* **1.** in contact or connection with the surface of; at the upper surface of: *an apple on the ground; a mark on the tablecloth.* **2.** attached to: *a puppet on a string.* **3.** carried with: *I've no money on me.* **4.** in the immediate vicinity of; close to or along the side of: *a house on the sea.* **5.** within the time limits of (a day or date): *he arrived on Thursday.* **6.** being performed upon or relayed through the medium of: *what's on the television?* **7.** at the occasion of: *on his retirement.* **8.** used to indicate support, subsistence, contingency, etc.: *he lives on bread.* **9. a.** regularly taking (a drug): *she's on the pill.* **b.** addicted to: *he's on heroin.* **10.** by means of (something considered as a mode of transport) (esp. in **on foot, on horseback,** etc.). **11.** in the process or course of: *on a journey; on strike.* **12.** concerned with or relating to: *a programme on archaeology.* **13.** used to indicate the basis or grounds, as of a statement or action: *I have it on good authority.* **14.** against: used to indicate opposition: *they marched on the city at dawn.* **15.** used to indicate a meeting or encounter: *he crept up on her.* **16.** (used with an adj. preceded by *the*) indicating the manner or way in which an action is carried out: *on the sly; on the cheap.* *~adv.* (*often used as a particle*) **17.** in the position or state required for the commencement or sustained continuation, as of a mechanical operation: *the radio's been on all night.* **18. a.** attached to, surrounding, or placed in contact with something: *the girl had nothing on.* **b.** taking place: *what's on tonight?* **19.** in a manner indicating continuity, persistence, etc.: *don't keep on about it; the play went on all afternoon.* **20.** in a direction towards something, esp. forwards: *we drove on towards London; march on!* **21. on and off.** intermittently; from time to time. **22. on and on.** without ceasing; continually. *~adj.* **23.** functioning; operating: *the on position on a radio.* **24.** (*postpositive*) *Inf.* **a.** staked or wagered as a bet: *ten pounds on that horse.* **b.** performing, as on stage, etc.: *I'm on in five minutes.* **c.** definitely taking place: *the match is on for Friday.* **d.** charged to: *the drinks are on me.* **e.** tolerable or practicable, acceptable, etc.: *your plan just isn't on.* **25.** *Cricket.* (of a bowler) bowling. **26. on at.** *Inf.* nagging: *she was always on at her husband.* *~n.* **27.** *Cricket.* **a.** (*modifier*) relating to or denoting the leg side of a cricket field or pitch: *an on drive.* **b.** (*in combination*) used to designate certain fielding positions on the leg side: *mid-on.* [OE *an, on*]

ON *abbrev. for* Old Norse.

-on *suffix forming nouns.* **1.** indicating a chemical substance: *interferon.* **2.** (in physics) indicating an elementary particle or quantum: *electron; photon.* **3.** (in chemistry) indicating an inert gas: *neon; radon.* [< ION]

onager (ˈɒnədʒə) *n., pl.* **-gri** (-ˌgraɪ) *or* **-gers. 1.** a Persian variety of the wild ass. **2.** an ancient war engine for hurling stones, etc. [C14: < LL: military engine for stone throwing, < L: wild ass, < Gk *onagros,* < *onos* ass + *agros* field]

onanism (ˈəʊnəˌnɪzəm) *n.* **1.** the withdrawal of the penis from the vagina before ejaculation. **2.** masturbation. [C18: after *Onan,* son of Judah; see Genesis 38:9] —ˈ**onanist** *n., adj.* —ˌ**onanˈistic** *adj.*

ONC (in Britain) *abbrev. for* Ordinary National Certificate.

once (wʌns) *adv.* **1.** one time; on one occasion or in one case. **2.** at some past time: *I could speak French once.* **3.** by one step or degree (of relationship): *a cousin once removed.* **4.** (*in conditional clauses, negatives, etc.*) ever; at all: *if you once forget it.* **5.** multiplied by one. **6. once and away. a.** conclusively. **b.** occasionally. **7. once and for all.** conclusively; for the last time. **8. once in a while.** occasionally; now and then. **9. once or twice** *or* **once and again.** a few times. **10. once upon a time.** used to begin fairy tales and children's stories. *~conj.* **11.** (*subordinating*) as soon as; if ever: *once you begin, you'll enjoy it.* *~n.* **12.** one occasion or case: *you may do it, this once.* **13. all at once. a.** suddenly. **b.** simultaneously. **14. at once. a.** immediately. **b.** simultaneously. **15. for once.** this time, if (or but) at no other time. [C12 *ones, anes,* adverbial genitive of *on, an* ONE]

once-over *n. Inf.* **1.** a quick examination or appraisal. **2.** a quick but comprehensive piece of work. **3.** a violent beating or thrashing. ~Esp. in **give (a person** or **thing) the** (or **a**) **once-over.**

oncer (ˈwʌnsə) *n.* **1.** *Brit. sl.* a one-pound note. **2.** *Austral. sl.* a person elected to Parliament who can only expect to serve one term. **3.** *Austral. & N.Z.* something which happens only once. [C20: < ONCE]

oncogene (ˈɒŋkəʊˌdʒiːn) *n.* any of several genes, present in all cells, that when abnormally activated can cause cancer. [C20: < Gk *onkos* mass, tumour + GENE] —**oncogenic** (ˌɒŋkəʊˈdʒɛnɪk) *adj.*

oncoming (ˈɒnˌkʌmɪŋ) *adj.* **1.** coming nearer in space or time; approaching. *~n.* **2.** the approach or onset: *the oncoming of winter.*

oncost (ˈɒnˌkɒst) *n. Brit.* **1.** another word for **overhead** (sense 5). **2.** (*sometimes pl.*) another word for **overheads.**

OND (in Britain) *abbrev. for* Ordinary National Diploma.

on dit *French* (ɔ̃ di) *n., pl.* ***on dits*** (ɔ̃ di). a rumour; piece of gossip. [lit.: it is said, they say]

one (wʌn) *determiner.* **1. a.** single; lone; not two or more. **b.** (*as pron.*): *one is enough for now; one at a time.* **c.** (*in combination*): *one-eyed.* **2. a.** distinct from all others; only; unique: *one girl in a million.* **b.** (*as pron.*): *one of a kind.* **3. a.** a specified (person, item, etc.) as distinct from another or others of its kind: *raise one hand and then the other.* **b.** (*as pron.*): *which one is correct?* **4.** a certain, indefinite, or unspecified (time); some: *one day you'll be sorry.* **5.** *Inf.* an emphatic word for **a**[1] or **an**[1]: *it was one hell of a fight.* **6.** a certain (person): *one Miss Jones was named.* **7. (all) in one.** combined; united. **8. all one. a.** all the same. **b.** of no consequence: *it's all one to me.* **9. at one.** (often foll. by *with*) in a state of agreement or harmony. **10. be made one.** to become married. **11. many a one.** many people. **12. neither one thing nor the other.** indefinite, undecided, or mixed. **13. never a one.** none. **14. one and all.** everyone, without exception. **15. one by one.** one at a time; individually. **16. one or two.** a few. **17. one way and another.** on balance. **18. one with another.** on average. ~*pron.* **19.** an indefinite person regarded as typical of every person: *one can't say any more than that.* **20.** any indefinite person: used as the subject of a sentence to form an alternative grammatical construction to that of the passive voice: *one can catch fine trout in this stream.* **21.** *Arch.* an unspecified person: *one came to him.* ~*n.* **22.** the smallest natural number and the first cardinal number; unity. **23.** a numeral (1, I, i, etc.) representing this number. **24.** *Inf.* a joke or story (esp. in **the one about**). **25.** something representing, represented by, or consisting of one unit. **26.** Also: **one o'clock.** one hour after noon or midnight. **27.** a blow or setback (esp. in **one in the eye for**). **28. the Evil one.** Satan. **29. the Holy One** *or* **the One above.** God. ~Related prefixes: **mono-, uni-.** [OE *ān*]

▷ **Usage.** Where the pronoun *one* is repeated, as in *one might think one would be unwise to say that, he* is sometimes substituted: *one might think he would be unwise to say that.* Careful writers avoid *one* followed by *he,* however, because of possible ambiguity: *he* in this case could refer either to the same person as *one* or to some other person.

-one *suffix forming nouns.* indicating that a chemical compound is a ketone: *acetone.* [arbitrarily < Gk *-ōnē,* fem. patronymic suffix, but ? infl. by *-one* in OZONE]

one another *pron.* the reflexive form of plural pronouns when the action, attribution, etc., is reciprocal: *they kissed one another; knowing one another.* Also: **each other.**

one-armed bandit *n. Inf.* a fruit machine operated by pulling down a lever at one side.

one-horse *adj.* **1.** drawn by or using one horse. **2.** (*prenominal*) *Inf.* small or obscure: *a one-horse town.*

one-liner *n. Inf.* a short joke or witty remark.

one-man *adj.* consisting of or done by or for one man: *a one-man band; a one-man show.*

oneness (ˈwʌnnɪs) *n.* **1.** the state or quality of being one; singleness. **2.** the state of being united; agreement. **3.** uniqueness. **4.** sameness.

one-night stand *n.* **1.** a performance given only once at any one place. **2.** *Inf.* a sexual encounter lasting only one evening or night.

one-off *n. Brit.* **a.** something that is carried out or made only once. **b.** (*as modifier*): *a one-off job.*

one-on-one *adj.* the U.S. term for **one-to-one** (sense 2).

one-parent family *n.* a household consisting of at least one dependent child and the mother or father, the other parent being dead or permanently absent. Also called: **single-parent family.**

one-piece *adj.* (of a garment, esp. a bathing costume) made in one piece.

onerous (ˈɒnərəs, ˈəʊ-) *adj.* **1.** laborious or oppressive. **2.** *Law.* (of a contract, etc.) having or involving burdens or obligations. [C14: < L *onerōsus* burdensome, < *onus* load] —ˈ**onerously** *adv.* —ˈ**onerousness** *n.*

oneself (wʌnˈsɛlf) *pron.* **1. a.** the reflexive form of *one.* **b.** (intensifier): *one doesn't do that oneself.* **2.** (*preceded by a copula*) one's normal or usual self: *one doesn't feel oneself after such an experience.*

one-sided *adj.* **1.** considering or favouring only one side of a matter, problem, etc. **2.** having all the advantage on one side. **3.** larger or more developed on one side. **4.** having, existing on, or occurring on one side only. —ˌ**one-**ˈ**sidedly** *adv.* —ˌ**one-**ˈ**sidedness** *n.*

one-step *n.* an early 20th-century ballroom dance with long quick steps, the precursor of the foxtrot.

One Thousand Guineas *n.* See **Thousand Guineas.**

one-time *adj.* (*prenominal*) at some time in the past; former.

one-to-one *adj.* **1.** (of two or more things) corresponding exactly. **2.** denoting a relationship or encounter in which someone is involved with only one other person: *one-to-one tuition.* **3.** *Maths.* involving the pairing of each member of one set with only one member of another set, without remainder.

one-track *adj.* **1.** *Inf.* obsessed with one idea, subject, etc. **2.** having or consisting of a single track.

one-up *adj. Inf.* having an advantage or lead over someone or something. —ˌ**one-**ˈ**upmanship** *n.*

one-way *adj.* **1.** moving or allowing travel in one direction only: *one-way traffic.* **2.** entailing no reciprocal obligation, action, etc.: *a one-way agreement.*

ongoing (ˈɒnˌgəʊɪŋ) *adj.* **1.** actually in progress: *ongoing projects.* **2.** continually moving forward; developing. **3.** remaining in existence; continuing.

onion (ˈʌnjən) *n.* **1.** an alliaceous plant having greenish-white flowers: cultivated for its rounded edible bulb. **2.** the bulb of this plant, consisting of concentric layers of white succulent leaf bases with a pungent odour and taste. **3. know one's onions.** *Brit. sl.* to be fully acquainted with a subject. [C14: via Anglo-Norman < OF *oignon,* < L *unio* onion] —ˈ**oniony** *adj.*

onionskin (ˈʌnjənˌskɪn) *n.* a glazed translucent paper.

on line *adj.* (**on-line** *when prenominal*). of or concerned with a peripheral device that is directly connected to and controlled by the central processing unit of a computer. Cf. **off line.**

onlooker (ˈɒnˌlʊkə) *n.* a person who observes without taking part. —ˈ**on**ˌ**looking** *adj.*

only (ˈəʊnlɪ) *adj.* (*prenominal*) **1. the.** being single or very few in number: *the only men left in town were too old to bear arms.* **2.** (of a child) having no siblings. **3.** unique by virtue of being superior to anything else; peerless. **4. one and only. a.** (*adj.*) incomparable; unique. **b.** (*as n.*) the object of all one's love: *you are my one and only.* ~*adv.* **5.** without anyone or anything else being included; alone: *you have one choice only; only a genius can do that.* **6.** merely or just: *it's only Henry.* **7.** no more or no greater than: *we met only an hour ago.* **8.** used in conditional clauses introduced by *if* to emphasize the impossibility of the condition ever being fulfilled: *if I had only known, this would never have happened.* **9.** not earlier than; not...until: *I only found out yesterday.* **10. if only** *or* **if...only.** an expression used to introduce a wish, esp. one felt to be unrealizable. **11. only if.** never...except when. **12. only too. a.** (intensifier): *he was only too pleased to help.* **b.** most regrettably (esp. in **only too true**). ~*sentence connector.* **13.** but; however: used to introduce an exception or condition: *play outside: only don't go into the street.* [OE *ānlīc,* < *ān* ONE + *-līc* -LY[1]]

▷ **Usage.** In informal English, *only* is often used as a sentence connector: *it would have been possible, only he was not present at the time.* This use is avoided in careful usage, esp. in formal contexts: *it would have been possible had he been present.* In formal speech and writing, *only* is placed directly before the word or words that it modifies: *she could interview only three applicants in the morning.* In all but the most formal contexts, however, it is generally regarded as acceptable to put *only* before the verb: *she could only interview three applicants in the morning.*

o.n.o. *abbrev. for* or near(est) offer.

onomastics (ˌɒnəˈmæstɪks) *n.* (*functioning as sing.*) the study of proper names, esp. of their origins. [< Gk *onomastikos,* < *onomazein* to name, < *onoma* NAME]

onomatopoeia (ˌɒnəˌmætəˈpiːə) *n.* **1.** the formation of words whose sound is imitative of the sound of the noise or action designated, such as *hiss.* **2.** the use of such words for poetic or rhetorical effect. [C16: via LL < Gk *onoma* name + *poiein* to make] —ˌ**onoˌmatoˈpoeic** *or* **onomatopoetic** (ˌɒnəˌmætəpəʊˈɛtɪk) *adj.* —ˌ**onoˌmatoˈpoeically** *or* ˌ**onoˌmatopoˈetically** *adv.*

onrush (ˈɒnˌrʌʃ) *n.* a forceful forward rush or flow.

onset (ˈɒnˌsɛt) *n.* **1.** an attack; assault. **2.** a start; beginning.

onshore (ˈɒnˈʃɔː) *adj., adv.* **1.** towards the land: *an onshore gale.* **2.** on land; not at sea.

onside (ˌɒnˈsaɪd) *adj., adv. Football, etc.* (of a player) in a legal position, as when behind the ball or with a required number of opponents between oneself and the opposing team's goal line. Cf. **offside.**

onslaught (ˈɒnˌslɔːt) *n.* a violent attack. [C17: < MDu. *aenslag,* < *aan* ON + *slag* a blow]

Ont. *abbrev. for* Ontario.

Ontarian (ɒnˈtɛərɪən) *or* **Ontarioan** (ɒnˈtɛərɪˌəʊən) *adj.* **1.** of or denoting Ontario, a province of central Canada. ~*n.* **2.** a native or inhabitant of Ontario.

onto *or* **on to** (ˈɒntu; *unstressed* ˈɒntə) *prep.* **1.** to a position that is on: *step onto the train.* **2.** having become aware of (something illicit or secret): *the police are onto us.* **3.** into contact with: *get onto the factory.*

▷ **Usage.** *Onto* is generally accepted as a word in its own right. *On to* is still used, however, where *on* is considered to be part of the verb: *he moved on to the next platform* as contrasted with *he jumped onto the next platform.*

onto- *combining form.* existence or being: *ontogeny; ontology.* [< LGk, < *ōn* (stem *ont-*) being, present participle of *einai* to be]

ontogeny (ɒnˈtɒdʒənɪ) *or* **ontogenesis** (ˌɒntəˈdʒɛnɪsɪs) *n.* the entire sequence of events involved in the development of an individual organism. Cf. **phylogeny.** —**ontogenic** (ˌɒntəˈdʒɛnɪk) *or* **ontogenetic** (ˌɒntədʒɪˈnɛtɪk) *adj.* —ˌ**ontoˈgenically** *or* ˌ**ontogeˈnetically** *adv.*

ontology (ɒnˈtɒlədʒɪ) *n.* **1.** *Philosophy.* the branch of metaphysics that deals with the nature of being. **2.** *Logic.* the set of entities presupposed by a theory. —ˌ**ontoˈlogical** *adj.* —ˌ**ontoˈlogically** *adv.*

onus (ˈəʊnəs) *n., pl.* **onuses.** a responsibility, task, or burden. [C17: L: burden]

onward (ˈɒnwəd) *adj.* **1.** directed or moving forwards, onwards, etc. ~*adv.* **2.** a variant of **onwards.**

onwards (ˈɒnwədz) *or* **onward** *adv.* at or towards a point or position ahead, in advance, etc.

onychophoran (ˌɒnɪˈkɒfərən) *n.* a wormlike invertebrate having a segmented body and short unjointed limbs, and breathing by means of tracheae. [< NL *Onychophora,* < Gk *onukh-* claw + -PHORE]

-onym *n. combining form.* indicating a name or word: *pseudonym.* [< Gk *-onumon,* < var. of *onoma* name]

onyx (ˈɒnɪks) *n.* **1.** a variety of chalcedony with alternating black-and-white parallel bands, used as a gemstone. **2.** a variety of calcite used as an ornamental stone; onyx marble. [C13: < L, < Gk: fingernail (so called from its veined appearance)]

oo- *or* **oö-** *combining form.* egg or ovum: *oosperm.* [< Gk *ōion* EGG[1]]

oocyte (ˈəʊəˌsaɪt) *n.* an immature female germ cell that gives rise to an ovum after two meiotic divisions.

oodles (ˈuːdᵊlz) *pl. n. Inf.* great quantities: *oodles of money.* [C20: <?]

oogamy (əʊˈɒgəmɪ) *n.* sexual reproduction involving a small motile male gamete and a large much less motile female gamete. —**oˈogamous** *adj.*

Ookpik (ˈuːkpɪk) *n. Canad. trademark.* a sealskin doll resembling an owl, first made in 1963 by an Inuit and used abroad as a symbol of Canadian handicrafts. [< Eskimo *ukpik* a snowy owl]

oolite (ˈəʊəˌlaɪt) *n.* any sedimentary rock, esp. limestone, consisting of tiny spherical concentric grains within a fine matrix. [C18: < F, < NL *oolitēs,* lit.: egg stone; prob. a translation of G *Rogenstein* roe stone] —**oolitic** (ˌəʊəˈlɪtɪk) *adj.*

oology (əʊˈɒlədʒɪ) *n.* the branch of ornithology concerned with the study of birds' eggs. —**oological** (ˌəʊəˈlɒdʒɪkᵊl) *adj.* —**oˈologist** *n.*

oolong (ˈuːˌlɒŋ) *n.* a kind of dark tea, grown in China, that is partly fermented before being dried. [C19: < Chinese *wu lung,* < *wu* black + *lung* dragon]

oomiak *or* **oomiac** (ˈuːmɪˌæk) *n.* a variant of **umiak.**

oompah (ˈuːmˌpɑː) *n.* a representation of the sound made by a deep brass instrument, esp. in military band music.

oomph (ʊmf) *n. Inf.* **1.** enthusiasm, vigour, or energy. **2.** sex appeal. [C20: < ?]

oops (ʊps, uːps) *interj.* an exclamation of surprise or of apology as when someone drops something or makes a mistake.

ooze[1] (uːz) *vb.* **1.** (*intr.*) to flow or leak out slowly, as through pores or small holes. **2.** to exude or emit (moisture, etc.). **3.** (*tr.*) to overflow with: *to ooze charm.* **4.** (*intr.;* often foll. by *away*) to disappear or escape gradually. ~*n.* **5.** a slow flowing or leaking. **6.** an infusion of vegetable matter, such as oak bark, used in tanning. [OE *wōs* juice]

ooze[2] (uːz) *n.* **1.** a soft thin mud found at the bottom of lakes and rivers. **2.** a fine-grained marine deposit consisting of the hard parts of planktonic organisms. **3.** muddy ground, esp. of bogs. [OE *wāse* mud]

oozy[1] (ˈuːzɪ) *adj.* **oozier, ooziest.** moist or dripping.

oozy[2] (ˈuːzɪ) *adj.* **oozier, ooziest.** of, resembling, or containing mud; slimy. —ˈ**oozily** *adv.* —ˈ**ooziness** *n.*

OP *abbrev. for* Ordo Praedicatorum (the Dominicans). [L: Order of Preachers]

op. *abbrev. for:* **1.** opera. **2.** operation. **3.** operator. **4.** optical. **5.** opposite. **6.** opus.

o.p. *or* **O.P.** *abbrev. for* out of print.

opacity (əʊˈpæsɪtɪ) *n., pl.* **-ties. 1.** the state or quality of being opaque. **2.** the degree to which something is opaque. **3.** an opaque object or substance. **4.** obscurity of meaning; unintelligibility.

opah (ˈəʊpə) *n.* a large soft-finned deep-sea teleost fish having a deep, brilliantly coloured body. Also called: **moonfish, kingfish.** [C18: of West African origin]

opal (ˈəʊpᵊl) *n.* an amorphous form of hydrated silicon dioxide that can be of almost any colour. It is used as a gemstone. [C16: < L *opalus,* < Gk *opallios,* < Sansk. *upala* precious stone] —ˈ**opal-ˌlike** *adj.*

opalescent (ˌəʊpəˈlɛsᵊnt) *adj.* having or emitting an iridescence like that of an opal. —ˌ**opaˈlesce** *vb.* (*intr.*) —ˌ**opalˈescence** *n.*

opaline (ˈəʊpəˌlaɪn) *adj.* **1.** opalescent. ~*n.* **2.** an opaque or semiopaque whitish glass.

opaque (əʊˈpeɪk) *adj.* **1.** not transmitting light; not transparent or translucent. **2.** not reflecting light; lacking lustre or shine; dull. **3.** hard to understand; unintelligible. **4.** unintelligent; dense. ~*n.* **5.** *Photog.* an opaque pigment used to block out areas on a negative. ~*vb.* **opaquing, opaqued.** (*tr.*) **6.** to make opaque. **7.** *Photog.* to block out areas on (a negative), using an opaque. [C15: < L *opācus* shady] —**oˈpaquely** *adv.* —**oˈpaqueness** *n.*

op. cit. (in textual annotations) *abbrev. for* opere citato. [L: in the work cited]

ope (əʊp) *vb., adj.* an archaic or poetic word for **open.**

OPEC (ˈəʊpɛk) *n. acronym for* Organization of Petroleum-Exporting Countries.

open (ˈəʊpᵊn) *adj.* **1.** not closed or barred. **2.** affording free passage, access, view, etc.; not blocked or obstructed. **3.** not sealed, fastened, or wrapped. **4.** having the interior part accessible: *an open drawer.* **5.** extended, expanded, or unfolded: *an open flower.* **6.** ready for business. **7.** able to be obtained; available: *the position is no longer open.* **8.** unobstructed by buildings, trees, etc.: *open countryside.* **9.** free to all to join, enter, use, visit, etc.: *an open competition.* **10.** unengaged or unoccupied: *the doctor has an hour open for you to call.* **11.** (of a season or period) not restricted for purposes of hunting game or quarry of various kinds. **12.** not decided or finalized: *an open question.* **13.** ready to entertain new ideas; not biased or prejudiced. **14.** unreserved or candid. **15.** liberal or generous: *an open hand.* **16.** extended or eager to receive (esp. in **with open arms**). **17.** exposed to view; blatant: *open disregard of the law.* **18.** liable or susceptible: *you will leave yourself open to attack.* **19.** (of climate or seasons) free from frost; mild. **20.** free from navigational hazards, such as ice, sunken ships, etc. **21.** having large or numerous spacing or apertures: *open ranks.* **22.** full of small openings or gaps; porous: *an open texture.* **23.** *Music.* **a.** (of a string) not stopped with the finger. **b.** (of a pipe, such as an organ pipe) not closed at either end. **c.** (of a note) played on such a string or pipe. **24.** *Commerce.* in operation; active: *an open account.* **25.** (of a cheque) not crossed. **26.** (of a return ticket) not specifying a date for travel. **27.** *Sport.* (of a goal, court, etc.) unguarded or relatively unprotected. **28.** (of a wound) exposed to the air. **29.** (esp. of the large intestine) free from obstruction. **30.** undefended and of no military significance: *an open city.* **31.** *Phonetics.* **a.** denoting a vowel pronounced with the lips relatively wide apart. **b.** denoting a syllable that does not end in a consonant, as in *pa.* **32.** *Maths.* (of a set) containing points whose neighbourhood consists of other points of the same set. ~*vb.* **33.** to move from a closed or fastened position: *to open a window.* **34.** (when *intr.*, foll. by *on* or *onto*) to render, be, or become accessible or unobstructed: *to open a road; to open a parcel.* **35.** (*intr.*) to come into or appear in view: *the lake opened before us.* **36.** to extend or unfold or cause to extend or unfold: *to open a newspaper.* **37.** to disclose or uncover or be disclosed or uncovered: *to open one's heart.* **38.** to cause (the mind) to become receptive or (of the mind) to become receptive. **39.** to operate or cause to operate: *to open a shop.* **40.** (when *intr.*, sometimes foll. by *out*) to make or become less compact or dense in structure: *to open ranks.* **41.** to set or be set in action; start: *to open the batting.* **42.** (*tr.*) to arrange for (a bank account, etc.), usually by making an initial deposit. **43.** to turn to a specified point in (a book, etc.): *open at page one.* **44.** *Law.* to make the opening statement in (a case before a court of law). **45.** (*intr.*) *Cards.* to bet, bid, or lead first on a hand. ~*n.* **46.** (often after *the*) any wide or unobstructed space or expanse, esp. of land or water. **47.** See **open air.** **48.** *Sport.* a competition which all may enter. **49. bring** (*or* **come**) **into the open.** to make (*or* become) evident or public. ~See also **open up.** [OE] —ˈ**openable** *adj.* —ˈ**opener** *n.* —ˈ**openly** *adv.* —ˈ**openness** *n.*

open air *n.* **a.** the place or space where the air is unenclosed; the outdoors. **b.** (*as modifier*): *an open-air concert.*

open-and-shut *adj.* easily decided or solved; obvious: *an open-and-shut case.*

opencast mining (ˈəʊpᵊnˌkɑːst) *n. Brit.* mining by excavating from the surface. Also called (esp. U.S.): **strip mining,** (Austral. and N.Z.) **open cut mining.** [C18: < OPEN + arch. *cast* ditch, cutting]

open chain *n.* a chain of atoms in a molecule that is not joined at its ends into the form of a ring.

open circuit *n.* an incomplete electrical circuit in which no current flows.

open day *n.* an occasion on which an institution, such as a school, is open for inspection by the public.

open door *n.* **1.** a policy or practice by which a nation grants opportunities for trade to all other nations equally. **2.** free and unrestricted admission. ~*adj.* **open-door.** **3.** open to all; accessible.

open-ended *adj.* without definite limits, as of duration or amount: *an open-ended contract.*

open-eyed *adj.* **1.** with the eyes wide open, as in amazement. **2.** watchful; alert.

open-faced *adj.* **1.** having an ingenuous expression. **2.** (of a watch) having no lid or cover other than the glass.

open-handed *adj.* generous. —ˌ**open-ˈhandedly** *adv.* —ˌ**open-ˈhandedness** *n.*

open-hearted *adj.* **1.** kindly and warm. **2.** disclosing intentions and thoughts clearly; candid. —ˌ**open-ˈheartedness** *n.*

open-hearth furnace *n.* (esp. formerly) a steel-making reverbatory furnace in which pig iron and scrap are contained in a shallow hearth and heated by producer gas.

open-heart surgery *n.* surgical repair of the heart during which the blood circulation is often maintained mechanically.

open house *n.* **1.** a U.S. and Canad. name for **at-home.** **2. keep open house.** to be always ready to receive guests.

opening (ˈəʊpənɪŋ) *n.* **1.** the act of making or becoming open. **2.** a vacant or unobstructed space, esp. one that will serve as a passageway; gap. **3.** *Chiefly U.S.* a tract in a forest in which trees are scattered or absent. **4.** the first part or stage of something. **5. a.** the first performance of something, esp. a theatrical production. **b.** (*as modifier*): *the opening night.* **6.** a specific or formal sequence of moves at the start of any of certain games, esp. chess or draughts. **7.** an opportunity or chance. **8.** *Law.* the preliminary statement made by counsel to the court or jury.

opening batsman *n. Cricket.* one of the two batsmen beginning an innings.

opening time *n. Brit.* the time at which pubs can legally start selling alcoholic drinks.

open letter *n.* a letter, esp. one of protest, addressed to a person but also made public, as through the press.

open market *n.* a market in which prices are determined by supply and demand, there are no barriers to entry, and trading is not restricted to a specific area.

open-minded *adj.* having a mind receptive to new ideas, arguments, etc.; unprejudiced. —ˌ**open-ˈmindedness** *n.*

open-mouthed *adj.* **1.** having an open mouth, esp. in surprise. **2.** greedy or ravenous. **3.** clamorous or vociferous.

open-plan *adj.* having no or few dividing walls between areas: *an open-plan office floor.*

open prison *n.* a penal establishment in which the prisoners are trusted to serve their sentences and so do not need to be locked up.

open punctuation *n.* punctuation which has relatively few semicolons, commas, etc. Cf. **close punctuation.**

open-reel *adj.* another term for **reel-to-reel.**

open secret *n.* something that is supposed to be secret but is widely known.

open sesame *n.* a very successful means of achieving a result. [< the magical words used in the *Arabian Nights' Entertainment* to open the robbers' den]

open shop *n.* an establishment in which persons are employed irrespective of their membership of a trade union.

open slather *n.* See **slather.**

Open University *n.* **the.** (in Britain) a university founded in 1969 for mature students studying by television and radio lectures, correspondence courses, local counselling, and summer schools.

open up *vb.* (*adv.*) **1.** (*intr.*) to start firing a gun or guns. **2.** (*intr.*) to speak freely or without restraint. **3.** (*intr.*) *Inf.* (of a motor vehicle) to accelerate. **4.** (*tr.*) to render accessible: *the motorway opened up the remoter areas.* **5.** (*intr.*) to make or become more exciting or lively: *the game opened up after half-time.*

open verdict *n.* a finding by a coroner's jury of death without stating the cause.

openwork (ˈəʊpᵊnˌwɜːk) *n.* ornamental work, as of metal or embroidery, having a pattern of openings or holes.

opera[1] (ˈɒpərə, ˈɒprə) *n.* **1.** an extended dramatic work in which music constitutes a dominating feature. **2.** the branch of music or drama represented by such works. **3.** the score, libretto, etc., of an opera. **4.** a theatre where opera is performed. [C17: via It. < L: work, a work, pl. of *opus* work]

opera[2] (ˈɒpərə) *n.* a plural of **opus.**

operable (ˈɒpərəbᵊl, ˈɒprə-) *adj.* **1.** capable of being treated by a surgical operation. **2.** capable of being operated. **3.** capable of being put into practice. —ˌ**operaˈbility** *n.* —ˈ**operably** *adv.*

opéra bouffe (ˈɒpərə ˈbuːf) *n., pl.* **opéras bouffes** (ˈɒpərə ˈbuːf). a type of light or satirical opera common in France during the 19th century. [F: comic opera]

opera buffa (ˈbuːfə) *n., pl.* **opera buffas.** comic opera, esp. that originating in Italy during the 18th century. [It.: comic opera]

opéra comique (kɒˈmiːk) *n., pl.* **opéras comiques.** (ˈɒpərə kɒˈmiːk). a type of opera current in France during the 19th century and characterized by spoken dialogue. [F: comic opera: it originated in satirical parodies of grand opera]

opera glasses *pl. n.* small low-powered binoculars used by audiences in theatres, etc.

opera hat *n.* a collapsible top hat operated by a spring.

opera house *n.* a theatre designed for opera.

operand (ˈɒpəˌrænd) *n.* a quantity or function upon which a mathematical operation is performed. [C19: < L *operandum* (something) to be worked upon, < *operārī* to work]

operant (ˈɒpərənt) *adj.* **1.** producing effects; operating. ~*n.* **2.** a person or thing that operates.

opera seria (ˈsɪərɪə) *n., pl.* **opera serias.** a type of opera current in 18th-century Italy based on a serious plot, esp. a mythological tale. [It.: serious opera]

operate (ˈɒpəˌreɪt) *vb.* **1.** to function or cause to function. **2.** (*tr.*) to control the functioning of. **3.** to manage, direct, run, or pursue (a business, system, etc.). **4.** (*intr.*) to perform a surgical operation (upon a person or animal). **5.** (*intr.*) to produce a desired effect. **6.** (*tr.; usually foll. by on*) to treat or process in a particular or specific way. **7.** (*intr.*) to conduct military or naval operations. **8.** (*intr.*) to deal in securities on a stock exchange. [C17: < L *operārī* to work]

operatic (ˌɒpəˈrætɪk) *adj.* **1.** of or relating to opera. **2.** histrionic or exaggerated. —ˌ**operˈatically** *adv.*

operating cycle *n.* the time taken by a firm to convert its raw materials into finished goods and thereafter sell them and collect payment.

operating theatre *n.* a room in which surgical operations are performed.

operation (ˌɒpəˈreɪʃən) *n.* **1.** the act, process, or manner of operating. **2.** the state of being in effect, in action, or operative (esp. in **in** *or* **into operation**). **3.** a process, method, or series of acts, esp. of a practical or mechanical nature. **4.** *Surgery.* any manipulation of the body or one of its organs or parts to repair damage, arrest the progress of a disease, remove foreign matter, etc. **5. a.** a military or naval action, such as a campaign, manoeuvre, etc. **b.** (*cap. and prenominal when part of a name*): *Operation Crossbow.* **6.** *Maths.* any procedure, such as addition, in which one or more numbers or quantities are operated upon according to specific rules. **7.** a commercial or financial transaction.

operational (ˌɒpəˈreɪʃənᵊl) *adj.* **1.** of or relating to an operation. **2.** in working order and ready for use. **3.** *Mil.* capable of, needed in, or actually involved in operations. —ˌ**operˈationally** *adv.*

operationalism (ˌɒpəˈreɪʃənəˌlɪzəm) *or* **operationism** (ˌɒpəˈreɪʃəˌnɪzəm) *n. Philosophy.* the theory that scientific terms are derived by the experimental operations which determine their applicability. —ˌ**operˌationalˈistic** *adj.*

operations research *n.* the analysis of problems in business and industry involving quantitative techniques. Also called: **operational research.**

operative (ˈɒpərətɪv) *adj.* **1.** in force, effect, or operation. **2.** exerting force or influence. **3.** producing a desired effect; significant: *the operative word.* **4.** of or relating to a surgical procedure. ~*n.* **5.** a worker, esp. one with a special skill. **6.** *U.S.* a private detective. —ˈ**operatively** *adv.* —ˈ**operativeness** *or* ˌ**operaˈtivity** *n.*

operator (ˈɒpəˌreɪtə) *n.* **1.** a person who operates a machine, instrument, etc., esp. a telephone switchboard. **2.** a person who owns or operates an industrial or commercial establishment. **3.** a speculator, esp. one who operates on currency or stock markets. **4.** *Inf.* a person who manipulates affairs and other people. **5.** *Maths.* any symbol, term, letter, etc., used to indicate or express a specific operation or process, such as ∫ (the integral operator).

operculum (əʊˈpɜːkjʊləm) *n., pl.* **-la** (-lə) *or* **-lums.** **1.** *Zool.* **a.** the hard bony flap covering the gill slits in fishes. **b.** the bony plate in certain gastropods covering the opening of the shell when the body is withdrawn. **2.** *Biol. & Bot.* any other covering or lid in various organisms. [C18: via NL < L: lid, < *operīre* to cover] —**oˈpercular** *or* **operculate** (əʊˈpɜːkjʊlɪt, -ˌleɪt) *adj.*

operetta (ˌɒpəˈrɛtə) *n.* a type of comic or light-hearted opera. [C18: < It.: a small OPERA[1]] —ˌ**operˈettist** *n.*

ophicleide (ˈɒfɪˌklaɪd) *n. Music.* an obsolete keyed wind instrument of bass pitch. [C19: < F *ophicléide,* < Gk *ophis* snake + *kleis* key]

ophidian (əʊˈfɪdɪən) *adj.* **1.** snakelike. **2.** of, relating to, or belonging to the suborder of reptiles that comprises the snakes. ~*n.* **3.** any reptile of this suborder; a snake. [C19: < NL *Ophidia,* name of suborder, < Gk *ophidion,* < *ophis* snake]

ophthalmia (ɒfˈθælmɪə) *n.* inflammation of the eye, often including the conjunctiva. [C16: via LL < Gk, < *ophthalmos* eye; see OPTIC]

ophthalmic (ɒfˈθælmɪk) *adj.* of or relating to the eye.

ophthalmic optician *n.* See **optician.**

ophthalmo- *or before a vowel* **ophthalm-** *combining form.* indicating the eye or the eyeball. [< Gk *ophthalmos* EYE]

ophthalmology (ˌɒfθælˈmɒlədʒɪ) *n.* the branch of medicine concerned with the eye and its diseases. —**ophthalmological** (ɒfˌθælməˈlɒdʒɪkᵊl) *adj.* —ˌ**ophthalˈmologist** *n.*

ophthalmoscope (ɒfˈθælməˌskəʊp) *n.* an instrument for examining the interior of the eye. —**ophthalmoscopic** (ɒfˌθælməˈskɒpɪk) *adj.*

-opia *n. combining form.* indicating a visual defect or condition: *myopia.* [< Gk, < *ōps* eye] —**-opic** *adj. combining form.*

opiate *n.* (ˈəʊpɪɪt). **1.** any of various narcotic drugs containing opium. **2.** any other narcotic or sedative drug. **3.** something that soothes, deadens, or induces sleep. ~*adj.* (ˈəʊpɪɪt). **4.** containing or consisting of opium. **5.** inducing relaxation; soporific. ~*vb.* (ˈəʊpɪˌeɪt). (*tr.*) *Rare.* **6.** to treat with an opiate. **7.** to dull or deaden. [C16: < Med. L *opiātus,* < L *opium* OPIUM]

opine (əʊˈpaɪn) *vb.* (when *tr., usually takes a clause as object*) to hold or express an opinion: *he opined that it was a mistake.* [C16: < L *opīnārī*]

opinion (əˈpɪnjən) *n.* **1.** judgment or belief not founded on certainty or proof. **2.** the prevailing or popular feeling or view: *public opinion.* **3.** evaluation, impression, or estimation of the value or worth of a person or thing. **4.** an evaluation or judgment given by an expert: *a medical opinion.* **5.** the advice given by counsel on a case submitted to him for his view on the legal points involved. **6. a matter of opinion.** a point open to question. **7. be of the opinion (that).** to believe (that). [C13: via OF < L *opīniō* belief, < *opīnārī* to think]

opinionated (əˈpɪnjəˌneɪtɪd) *adj.* holding obstinately and unreasonably to one's own opinions; dogmatic. —**oˈpinionˌatedly** *adv.* —**oˈpinionˌatedness** *n.*

opinionative (əˈpɪnjənətɪv) *adj. Rare.* **1.** of or relating to opinion. **2.** another word for **opinionated.** —**oˈpinionatively** *adv.* —**oˈpinionativeness** *n.*

opinion poll *n.* another term for a **poll** (sense 3).

opium (ˈəʊpɪəm) *n.* **1.** an addictive narcotic drug extracted from the seed capsules of the opium poppy: used in medicine as an analgesic and hypnotic. **2.** something having a tranquillizing or stupefying effect. [C14: < L: poppy juice, < Gk *opion,* dim. of *opos,* juice of a plant]

opium poppy *n.* a poppy of SW Asia, with greyish-green leaves and typically white or reddish flowers: widely cultivated as a source of opium.

opossum (əˈpɒsəm) *n., pl.* **-sums** *or* **-sum.** **1.** a thick-furred marsupial, esp. the **common opossum** of North and South America, having an elongated snout and a hairless prehensile tail. **2.** *Austral. & N.Z.* any of various similar animals, esp. a phalanger. ~Often shortened to **possum.** [C17: < Algonquian *aposoum*]

opp. *abbrev. for:* **1.** opposed. **2.** opposite.

opponent (əˈpəʊnənt) *n.* **1.** a person who opposes another in a contest, battle, etc. **2.** *Anat.* an opponent muscle. ~*adj.* **3.** opposite, as in position. **4.** *Anat.* (of a muscle) bringing two parts into opposition. **5.** opposing; contrary. [C16: < L *oppōnere* to oppose] —**opˈponency** *n.*

opportune (ˈɒpəˌtjuːn) *adj.* **1.** occurring at a time that is suitable or advantageous. **2.** fit or suitable for a particular purpose or occurrence. [C15: via OF < L *opportūnus,* < *ob-* to + *portus* harbour (orig.: coming to the harbour, obtaining timely protection)] —**ˈopporˌtunely** *adv.* —**ˈopporˌtuneness** *n.*

opportunist (ˌɒpəˈtjuːnɪst) *n.* **1.** a person who adapts his actions, responses, etc., to take advantage of opportunities, circumstances, etc. ~*adj.* **2.** taking advantage of opportunities and circumstances in this way. —**ˌopporˈtunism** *n.*

opportunistic (ˌɒpətjʊˈnɪstɪk) *adj.* **1.** of or characterized by opportunism. **2.** *Med.* (of an infection) caused by any microorganism that is harmless to a healthy person but debilitates a person whose immune system has been weakened.

opportunity (ˌɒpəˈtjuːnɪtɪ) *n., pl.* **-ties.** **1.** a favourable, appropriate, or advantageous combination of circumstances. **2.** a chance or prospect.

opportunity shop *n. Austral. & N.Z.* a shop selling used goods for charitable funds.

opposable (əˈpəʊzəbᵊl) *adj.* **1.** capable of being opposed. **2.** Also: **apposable.** (of the thumb of primates, esp. man) capable of being moved into a position facing the other digits so as to be able to touch the ends of each. **3.** capable of being placed opposite something else. —**opˌposaˈbility** *n.* —**opˈposably** *adv.*

oppose (əˈpəʊz) *vb.* **1.** (*tr.*) to fight against, counter, or resist strongly. **2.** (*tr.*) to be hostile or antagonistic to; be against. **3.** (*tr.*) to place or set in opposition; contrast or counterbalance. **4.** (*tr.*) to place opposite or facing. **5.** (*intr.*) to be or act in opposition. [C14: via OF < L *oppōnere,* < *ob-* against + *pōnere* to place] —**opˈposer** *n.* —**opˈposing** *adj.* —**oppositive** (əˈpɒzɪtɪv) *adj.*

opposite (ˈɒpəzɪt, -sɪt) *adj.* **1.** situated or being on the other side or at each side of something between. **2.** facing or going in contrary directions: *opposite ways.* **3.** diametrically different in character, tendency, belief, etc. **4.** *Bot.* **a.** (of leaves) arranged in pairs on either side of the stem. **b.** (of parts of a flower) arranged opposite the middle of another part. **5.** *Maths.* (of a side in a triangle) facing a specified angle. Abbrev.: **opp.** ~*n.* **6.** a person or thing that is opposite; antithesis. ~*prep.* **7.** Also: **opposite to.** facing; corresponding to (something on the other side of a division). **8.** as a co-star with: *she played opposite Olivier.* ~*adv.* **9.** on opposite sides: *she lives opposite.* —**ˈoppositely** *adv.* —**ˈoppositeness** *n.*

opposite number *n.* a person holding an equivalent and corresponding position on another side or situation.

opposition (ˌɒpəˈzɪʃən) *n.* **1.** the act of opposing or the state of being opposed. **2.** hostility, unfriendliness, or antagonism. **3.** a person or group antagonistic or opposite in aims to another. **4. a.** (usually preceded by *the*) a political party or group opposed to the ruling party or government. **b.** (*cap. as part of a name, esp. in Britain and Commonwealth countries): Her Majesty's Loyal Opposition.* **c. in opposition.** (of a political party) opposing the government. **5.** a position facing or opposite another. **6.** something that acts as an obstacle to some course or progress. **7.** *Astron.* the position of an outer planet or the moon when it is in line with the earth as seen from the sun and is approximately at its nearest to the earth. **8.** *Astrol.* an exact aspect of 180° between two planets, etc., an orb of 8° being allowed. **9.** *Logic.* the relation between propositions having the same subject and predicate but differing in quality, quantity, or both, as with *all men are wicked; no men are wicked; some men are not wicked.* —**ˌoppoˈsitional** *adj.* —**ˌoppoˈsitionist** *n.* —**ˌoppoˈsitionless** *adj.*

oppress (əˈprɛs) *vb.* (*tr.*) **1.** to subjugate by cruelty, force, etc. **2.** to afflict or torment. **3.** to lie heavy on (the mind, etc.). [C14: via OF < Med. L *oppressāre,* < L *opprimere,* < *ob-* against + *premere* to press] —**opˈpressing** *adj.* —**opˈpression** *n.* —**opˈpressor** *n.*

oppressive (əˈprɛsɪv) *adj.* **1.** cruel, harsh, or tyrannical. **2.** heavy, constricting, or depressing. —**opˈpressively** *adv.* —**opˈpressiveness** *n.*

opprobrious (əˈprəʊbrɪəs) *adj.* **1.** expressing scorn, disgrace, or contempt. **2.** shameful or infamous. —**opˈprobriously** *adv.* —**opˈprobriousness** *n.*

opprobrium (əˈprəʊbrɪəm) *n.* **1.** the state of being abused or scornfully criticized. **2.** reproach or censure. **3.** a cause of disgrace or ignominy. [C17: < L *ob-* against + *probrum* a shameful act]

oppugn (əˈpjuːn) *vb.* (*tr.*) to call into question; dispute. [C15: < L *oppugnāre,* < *ob-* against + *pugnāre* to fight, < *pugnus* clenched fist] —**opˈpugner** *n.*

opsin (ˈɒpsɪn) *n.* the protein that together with retinene makes up the purple visual pigment rhodopsin. [C20: back formation < RHODOPSIN]

-opsis *n. combining form.* indicating a specified appearance or resemblance: *meconopsis.* [< Gk *opsis* sight]

opsit-bank (ˈɒpsɪt-) *n. S. African.* a bench for two people, formerly used for courting couples. [< Afrik., < Du.]

opsonin (ˈɒpsənɪn) *n.* a constituent of blood serum that renders bacteria more susceptible to ingestion by phagocytes. [C20: < Gk *opsōnion* victuals] —**opsonic** (ɒpˈsɒnɪk) *adj.*

opt (ɒpt) *vb.* (when *intr.,* foll. by *for*) to show preference (for) or choose (to do something). See also **opt in, opt out.** [C19: < F *opter,* < L *optāre* to choose]

opt. *abbrev. for:* **1.** *Grammar.* optative. **2.** optical. **3.** optician. **4.** optimum. **5.** optional.

optative (ˈɒptətɪv) *adj.* **1.** indicating or expressing choice or wish. **2.** *Grammar.* denoting a mood of verbs in Greek and Sanskrit expressing a wish. ~*n.* **3.** *Grammar.* **a.** the optative mood. **b.** a verb in this mood. [C16: via F *optatif,* < LL *optātīvus,* < L *optāre* to desire]

optic (ˈɒptɪk) *adj.* **1.** of or relating to the eye or vision. **2.** a less common word for **optical.** ~*n.* **3.** an informal word for **eye**[1]. **4.** *Brit., trademark.* a device attached to an inverted bottle for dispensing measured quantities of liquid. [C16: < Med. L *opticus*, < Gk *optikos*, < *optos* visible; rel. to *ōps* eye]

optical (ˈɒptɪkᵊl) *adj.* **1.** of, relating to, producing, or involving light. **2.** of or relating to the eye or to the sense of sight; optic. **3.** (esp. of a lens) aiding vision or correcting a visual disorder. —**ˈoptically** *adv.*

optical activity *n.* the ability of substances that are optical isomers to rotate the plane of polarization of a transmitted beam of plane-polarized light.

optical character reader *n.* a computer peripheral device enabling letters, numbers, or other characters usually printed on paper to be optically scanned and input to a storage device, such as magnetic tape. The device uses the process of **optical character recognition.** Abbrev. (for both *reader* and *recognition*): **OCR.**

optical crown *n.* an optical glass of low dispersion and relatively low refractive index.

optical disc *n.* a small computer disc that can store a very large amount of visual data in digital form: used esp. for long-term storage, as of archive material.

optical fibre *n.* a communications cable consisting of a thin glass fibre in a protective sheath. Light transmitted along the fibre may be modulated with vision, sound, or data signals. See also **fibre optics.**

optical flint *n.* an optical glass of high dispersion and high refractive index containing lead oxide, used in the manufacture of lenses, artificial gems, and cut glass.

optical glass *n.* any of several types of clear homogeneous glass of known refractive index used in the construction of lenses, etc.

optical isomerism *n.* isomerism of chemical compounds in which the two isomers differ only in that their molecules are mirror images of each other. —**optical isomer** *n.*

optician (ɒpˈtɪʃən) *n.* a general name used to refer to: **a.** an **ophthalmic optician.** one qualified to examine the eyes and prescribe and supply spectacles and contact lenses. **b.** a **dispensing optician.** one who supplies and fits spectacle frames and lenses, but is not qualified to prescribe lenses.

optics (ˈɒptɪks) *n.* (*functioning as sing.*) the branch of science concerned with vision and the generation, nature, propagation, and behaviour of electromagnetic light.

optimal (ˈɒptɪməl) *adj.* another word for **optimum** (sense 2).

optimism (ˈɒptɪˌmɪzəm) *n.* **1.** the tendency to expect the best in all things. **2.** hopefulness; confidence. **3.** the doctrine of the ultimate triumph of good over evil. **4.** the philosophical doctrine that this is the best of all possible worlds. ~Cf. **pessimism.** [C18: < F *optimisme*, < L *optimus* best, sup. of *bonus* good] —**ˈoptimist** *n.* —ˌ**optiˈmistic** *adj.* —ˌ**optiˈmistically** *adv.*

optimize *or* **-mise** (ˈɒptɪˌmaɪz) *vb.* **1.** (*tr.*) to take the full advantage of. **2.** (*tr.*) to plan or carry out (an economic activity) with maximum efficiency. **3.** (*intr.*) to be optimistic. **4.** (*tr.*) to write or modify (a computer program) to achieve maximum efficiency. —ˌ**optimiˈzation** *or* **-miˈsation** *n.*

optimum (ˈɒptɪməm) *n., pl.* **-ma** (-mə) *or* **-mums. 1.** a condition, degree, amount, or compromise that produces the best possible result. ~*adj.* **2.** most favourable or advantageous; best: *optimum conditions.* [C19: < L: the best (thing), < *optimus* best; see OPTIMISM]

opt in *vb.* (*intr., adv.*) to choose to be involved in or part of a scheme, etc.

option (ˈɒpʃən) *n.* **1.** the act or an instance of choosing or deciding. **2.** the power or liberty to choose. **3.** an exclusive opportunity, usually for a limited period, to buy something at a future date: *a six-month option on the Canadian rights to this book.* **4.** *Stock Exchange.* the right, purchased from a dealer, to buy or sell shares at a fixed price at some time in the future. **5.** See **local option. 6.** something chosen; choice. **7. keep** (*or* **leave**) **one's options open.** not to commit oneself. **8. soft option.** an easy alternative. [C17: < L *optiō* free choice, < *optāre* to choose]

optional (ˈɒpʃənᵊl) *adj.* possible but not compulsory; left to personal choice. —**ˈoptionally** *adv.*

optometrist (ɒpˈtɒmɪtrɪst) *n.* a person who is qualified to examine the eyes and prescribe and supply spectacles and contact lenses. Also called (esp. Brit.): **ophthalmic optician.**

optometry (ɒpˈtɒmɪtrɪ) *n.* the science or practice of testing visual acuity and prescribing corrective lenses. —**optometric** (ˌɒptəˈmɛtrɪk) *adj.*

opt out *vb.* (*intr., adv.*; often foll. by *of*) to choose not to be involved (in) or part (of).

opulent (ˈɒpjʊlənt) *adj.* **1.** having or indicating wealth. **2.** abundant or plentiful. [C17: < L *opulens*, < *opēs* (pl.) wealth] —**ˈopulence** *or* (*less commonly*) **ˈopulency** *n.* —**ˈopulently** *adv.*

opuntia (ɒˈpʌnʃɪə) *n.* a cactus, esp. the prickly pear, having fleshy branched stems and green, red, or yellow flowers. [C17: NL, < L *Opuntia* (*herba*) the Opuntian (plant), < *Opus*, ancient town of Locris, Greece]

opus (ˈəʊpəs) *n., pl.* **opuses** *or* **opera. 1.** an artistic composition, esp. a musical work. **2.** (*often cap.*) (usually followed by a number) a musical composition by a particular composer, generally catalogued in order of publication: *Beethoven's opus 61.* Abbrev.: **op.** [C18: < L: a work]

or[1] (ɔː; *unstressed* ə) *conj.* (*coordinating*) **1.** used to join alternatives. **2.** used to join rephrasings of the same thing: *twelve, or a dozen.* **3.** used to join two alternatives when the first is preceded by *either* or *whether*: *either yes or no.* **4. one or two, four or five,** etc. a few. **5.** a poetic word for **either** or **whether,** as the first element in correlatives, with *or* also preceding the second alternative. [C13: contraction of *other*, changed (through infl. of EITHER) < OE *oththe*]

▷ **Usage.** See at **either** and **neither.**

or[2] (ɔː) *adj.* (*usually postpositive*) *Heraldry.* of the metal gold. [C16: via F < L *aurum* gold]

OR *abbrev. for:* **1.** operational research. **2.** *Mil.* other ranks.

-or[1] *suffix forming nouns from verbs.* a person or thing that does what is expressed by the verb: *actor; conductor; generator; sailor.* [via OF *-eur*, *-eor*, < L *-or* or *-ātor*]

-or[2] *suffix forming nouns.* **1.** indicating state, condition, or activity: *terror; error.* **2.** the U.S. spelling of **-our.**

ora (ˈɔːrə) *n.* the plural of **os**[2].

orache *or esp. U.S.* **orach** (ˈɒrɪtʃ) *n.* any of several herbaceous plants or small shrubs of the goosefoot family, esp. **garden orache,** which is cultivated as a vegetable. They have typically greyish-green lobed leaves and inconspicuous flowers. [C15: < OF *arache*, < L *atriplex*, < Gk *atraphaxus*, <?]

oracle (ˈɒrəkᵊl) *n.* **1.** a prophecy revealed through the medium of a priest or priestess at the shrine of a god. **2.** a shrine at which an oracular god is consulted. **3.** an agency through which a prophecy is transmitted. **4.** any person or thing believed to indicate future action with infallible authority. [C14: via OF < L *ōrāculum*, < *ōrāre* to request]

Oracle (ˈɒrəkᵊl) *n. Trademark. acronym for* Optional Reception of Announcements by Coded Line Electronics: the teletext service of Independent Television.

oracular (ɒˈrækjʊlə) *adj.* **1.** of or relating to an oracle. **2.** wise and prophetic. **3.** mysterious or ambiguous. —**oˈracularly** *adv.*

oracy (ˈɔːrəsɪ) *n.* the capacity to express oneself in and understand speech. [C20: < L *or-*, *os* mouth, by analogy with *literacy*]

oral (ˈɔːrəl, ˈɒrəl) *adj.* **1.** spoken or verbal. **2.** relating to, affecting, or for use in the mouth: *an oral thermometer.* **3.** denoting a drug to be taken by mouth: *an oral contraceptive.* **4.** of, relating to, or using spoken words. **5.** *Psychoanal.* relating to a stage of psychosexual development during which the child's interest is concentrated on the mouth. ~*n.* **6.** an examination in which the questions and answers are spoken rather than written. [C17: < LL *orālis,* < L *ōs* face] —ˈ**orally** *adv.*

oral history *n.* the memories of living people about events or social conditions in their earlier lives taped and preserved as historical evidence.

oral society *n.* a society that has not developed literacy.

orange (ˈɒrɪndʒ) *n.* **1.** any of several citrus trees, esp. **sweet orange** and the Seville orange, cultivated in warm regions for their round edible fruit. **2. a.** the fruit of any of these trees, having a yellowish-red bitter rind and segmented juicy flesh. **b.** (*as modifier*): *orange peel.* **3.** the hard wood of any of these trees. **4.** any of a group of colours, such as that of the skin of an orange, that lie between red and yellow in the visible spectrum. **5.** a dye or pigment producing these colours. **6.** orange cloth or clothing: *dressed in orange.* **7.** any of several trees or herbaceous plants that resemble the orange, such as mock orange. ~*adj.* **8.** of the colour orange. [C14: via OF *auranja,* < Ar. *nāranj,* < Persian, < Sansk. *nāranga*]

Orange (ˈɒrɪndʒ) *adj.* of or relating to the Orangemen.

orangeade (ˌɒrɪndʒˈeɪd) *n.* an effervescent or still orange-flavoured drink.

orange blossom *n.* the flowers of the orange tree, traditionally worn by brides.

Orangeman (ˈɒrɪndʒmən) *n., pl.* **-men.** a member of a society founded as a secret order in Ireland (1795) to uphold Protestantism. [C18: after William, prince of *Orange,* later William III]

Orangeman's Day *n.* the 12th of July, celebrated by Protestants in Northern Ireland and elsewhere, to commemorate the anniversary of the Battle of the Boyne (1690).

orange pekoe *n.* a superior grade of black tea growing in India and Sri Lanka.

orangery (ˈɒrɪndʒərɪ, -dʒrɪ) *n., pl.* **-eries.** a building, such as a greenhouse, in which orange trees are grown.

orange stick *n.* a small stick used to clean the fingernails and cuticles.

orangewood (ˈɒrɪndʒˌwʊd) *n.* **a.** the hard fine-grained yellowish wood of the orange tree. **b.** (*as modifier*): *an orangewood table.*

orang-utan (ɔːˌræŋuːˈtæn, ˌɔːræŋˈuːtæn) *or* **orang-outang** (ɔːˌræŋuːˈtæŋ, ˌɔːræŋˈuːtæŋ) *n.* a large anthropoid ape of the forests of Sumatra and Borneo, with shaggy reddish-brown hair and strong arms. Sometimes shortened to **orang.** [C17: < Malay *orang hutan,* < *ōrang* man + *hūtan* forest]

orate (ɔːˈreɪt) *vb.* (*intr.*) **1.** to make or give an oration. **2.** to speak pompously and lengthily.

oration (ɔːˈreɪʃən) *n.* **1.** a formal public declaration or speech. **2.** any rhetorical, lengthy, or pompous speech. [C14: < L *ōrātiō* speech, harangue, < *ōrāre* to plead, pray]

orator (ˈɒrətə) *n.* **1.** a public speaker, esp. one versed in rhetoric. **2.** a person given to lengthy or pompous speeches. **3.** *Obs.* the plaintiff in a cause of action in chancery.

oratorio (ˌɒrəˈtɔːrɪəʊ) *n., pl.* **-rios.** a dramatic but unstaged musical composition for soloists, chorus, and orchestra, based on a religious theme. [C18: < It., lit.: ORATORY[2], referring to the Church of the Oratory at Rome where musical services were held]

oratory[1] (ˈɒrətərɪ, -trɪ) *n.* **1.** the art of public speaking. **2.** rhetorical skill or style. [C16: < L (*ars*) *ōrātōria* (the art of) public speaking] —ˌ**oraˈtorical** *adj.* —ˌ**oraˈtorically** *adv.*

oratory[2] (ˈɒrətərɪ, -trɪ) *n., pl.* **-ries.** a small room or secluded place, set apart for private prayer. [C14: < Anglo-Norman, < Church L *ōrātōrium* place of prayer, < *ōrāre* to plead, pray]

orb (ɔːb) *n.* **1.** (in regalia) an ornamental sphere surmounted by a cross. **2.** a sphere; globe. **3.** *Poetic.* another word for **eye**[1]. **4.** *Obs. or poetic.* **a.** a celestial body, esp. the earth or sun. **b.** the orbit of a celestial body. ~*vb.* **5.** to make or become circular or spherical. **6.** (*tr.*) an archaic word for **encircle.** [C16: < L *orbis* circle, disc]

orbicular (ɔːˈbɪkjʊlə), **orbiculate,** *or* **orbiculated** *adj.* **1.** circular or spherical. **2.** (of a leaf or similar flat part) circular or nearly circular. —**orbicularity** (ɔːˌbɪkjʊˈlærɪtɪ) *n.* —**orˈbicularly** *adv.*

orbit (ˈɔːbɪt) *n.* **1.** *Astron.* the curved path followed by a planet, satellite, etc., in its motion around another celestial body. **2.** a range or field of action or influence; sphere. **3.** the bony cavity containing the eyeball; eye socket. **4.** *Zool.* **a.** the skin surrounding the eye of a bird. **b.** the hollow in which lies the eye or eyestalk of an insect. **5.** *Physics.* the path of an electron around the nucleus of an atom. **6. go into orbit.** *Inf.* to reach an extreme and often uncontrolled state: *when he realized the price he nearly went into orbit.* ~*vb.* **7.** to move around (a body) in a curved path. **8.** (*tr.*) to send (a satellite, spacecraft, etc.) into orbit. **9.** (*intr.*) to move in or as if in an orbit. [C16: < L *orbita* course, < *orbis* circle] —ˈ**orbital** *adj.* —ˈ**orbitally** *adv.*

orbital velocity *n.* the velocity required by a spacecraft to enter and maintain a given orbit.

orc (ɔːk) *n.* **1.** any of various whales, such as the killer and grampus. **2.** a mythical monster. [C16: via L *orca,* ? < Gk *orux* whale]

Orcadian (ɔːˈkeɪdɪən) *n.* **1.** a native or inhabitant of the Orkneys. ~*adj.* **2.** of or relating to the Orkneys. [< L *Orcades* the Orkney Islands]

orchard (ˈɔːtʃəd) *n.* **1.** an area of land devoted to the cultivation of fruit trees. **2.** a collection of fruit trees especially cultivated. [OE *orceard, ortigeard,* < *ort-,* < L *hortus* garden + *geard* YARD[2]]

orchestra (ˈɔːkɪstrə) *n.* **1.** a large group of musicians, esp. one whose members play a variety of different instruments. **2.** a group of musicians, each playing the same type of instrument. **3.** Also called: **orchestra pit.** the space reserved for musicians in a theatre, immediately in front of or under the stage. **4.** *Chiefly U.S. & Canad.* the stalls in a theatre. **5.** (in ancient Greek theatre) the semicircular space in front of the stage. [C17: via L < Gk: the space in the theatre for the chorus, < *orkheisthai* to dance] —**orchestral** (ɔːˈkɛstrəl) *adj.* —**orˈchestrally** *adv.*

orchestrate (ˈɔːkɪˌstreɪt) *vb.* (*tr.*) **1.** to score or arrange (a piece of music) for orchestra. **2.** to arrange, organize, or build up for special or maximum effect. —ˌ**orchesˈtration** *n.* —ˈ**orchesˌtrator** *n.*

orchid (ˈɔːkɪd) *n.* a terrestrial or epiphytic plant having flowers of unusual shapes and beautiful colours, usually with one petal larger than the other two. The flowers are specialized for pollination by certain insects. [C19: < NL *Orchideae;* see ORCHIS]

orchil (ˈɔːkɪl, -tʃɪl) *or* **archil** *n.* **1.** a purplish dye obtained by treating various lichens with aqueous ammonia. **2.** the lichens yielding this dye. [C15: < OF *orcheil,* <?]

orchis (ˈɔːkɪs) *n.* **1.** a N temperate terrestrial orchid having fleshy tubers and spikes of typically pink flowers. **2.** any of various temperate or tropical orchids such as the fringed orchis. [C16: via L < Gk *orkhis* testicle; so called from the shape of its roots]

OR circuit *or* **gate** (ɔː) *n. Computers.* a logic circuit having two or more input wires and one output wire that gives a high-voltage output signal if one or more input signals are at a high voltage: used extensively as a basic circuit in computers. [C20: < its similarity to the function of *or* in logical constructions]

ord. *abbrev. for:* **1.** order. **2.** ordinal. **3.** ordinance. **4.** ordinary.

ordain (ɔːˈdeɪn) *vb.* (*tr.*) **1.** to consecrate (someone) as a priest; confer holy orders upon. **2.** (*may take a clause as object*) to decree, appoint, or predestine irrevocably. **3.** (*may take a clause as object*) to order, establish, or enact with authority. [C13: < Anglo-Norman *ordeiner*, < LL *ordināre*, < L *ordo* ORDER] —**or'dainer** *n.* —**or'dainment** *n.*

ordeal (ɔː'diːl) *n.* **1.** a severe or trying experience. **2.** *History.* a method of trial in which the innocence of an accused person was determined by subjecting him to physical danger, esp. by fire or water. [OE *ordāl, ordēl* verdict]

order ('ɔːdə) *n.* **1.** a state in which all components or elements are arranged logically, comprehensibly, or naturally. **2.** an arrangement or disposition of things in succession; sequence: *alphabetical order.* **3.** an established or customary method or state, esp. of society. **4.** a peaceful or harmonious condition of society: *order reigned in the streets.* **5.** (*often pl.*) a class, rank, or hierarchy: *the lower orders.* **6.** *Biol.* any of the taxonomic groups into which a class is divided and which contains one or more families. **7.** an instruction that must be obeyed; command. **8. a.** a commission or instruction to produce or supply something in return for payment. **b.** the commodity produced or supplied. **c.** (*as modifier*): *order form.* **9.** a procedure followed by an assembly, meeting, etc. **10.** (*cap. when part of a name*) a body of people united in a particular aim or purpose. **11.** (*usually cap.*) Also called: **religious order.** a group of persons who bind themselves by vows in order to devote themselves to the pursuit of religious aims. **12.** (*often pl.*) another name for **holy orders, major orders,** or **minor orders. 13.** *History.* a society of knights constituted as a fraternity, such as the Knights Templars. **14. a.** a group of people holding a specific honour for service or merit, conferred on them by a sovereign or state. **b.** the insignia of such a group. **15. a.** any of the five major classical styles of architecture classified by the style of columns and entablatures used. **b.** any style of architecture. **16.** *Christianity.* **a.** the sacrament by which bishops, priests, etc., have their offices conferred upon them. **b.** any of the degrees into which the ministry is divided. **c.** the office of an ordained Christian minister. **17.** *Maths.* **a.** the number of times a function must be differentiated to obtain a given derivative. **b.** the order of the highest derivative in a differential equation. **c.** the number of rows or columns in a determinant or square matrix. **d.** the number of members of a finite group. **18.** *Mil.* (often preceded by *the*) the dress, equipment, or formation directed for a particular purpose or undertaking: *battle order.* **19. a tall order.** something difficult, demanding, or exacting. **20. in order. a.** in sequence. **b.** properly arranged. **c.** appropriate or fitting. **21. in order that.** (*conj.*) with the purpose that; so that. **22. in order to.** (*prep.;* foll. by an infinitive) so that it is possible to: *to eat in order to live.* **23. keep order.** to maintain or enforce order. **24. of** *or* **in the order of.** having an approximately specified size or quantity. **25. on order.** having been ordered but not having been delivered. **26. out of order. a.** not in sequence. **b.** not working. **c.** not following the rules or customary procedure. **27. to order. a.** according to a buyer's specifications. **b.** on request or demand. ~*vb.* **28.** (*tr.*) to give a command to (a person or animal to do or be something). **29.** to request (something) to be supplied or made, esp. in return for payment. **30.** (*tr.*) to instruct or command to move, go, etc. (to a specified place): *they ordered her into the house.* **31.** (*tr.; may take a clause as object*) to authorize; prescribe: *the doctor ordered a strict diet.* **32.** (*tr.*) to arrange, regulate, or dispose (articles, etc.) in their proper places. **33.** (*tr.*) (of fate) to will; ordain. ~*interj.* **34.** an exclamation demanding that orderly behaviour be restored. [C13: < OF *ordre,* < L *ordō*] —**'orderer** *n.*

order in council *n.* (in Britain) a decree of the Cabinet, usually made under the authority of a statute: in theory a decree of the sovereign and Privy Council.

orderly ('ɔːdəlɪ) *adj.* **1.** in order, properly arranged, or tidy. **2.** obeying or appreciating method, system, and arrangement. **3.** *Mil.* of or relating to orders: *an orderly book.* ~*n., pl.* **-lies. 4.** *Med.* a male hospital attendant. **5.** *Mil.* a junior rank detailed to carry orders or perform minor tasks for a more senior officer. —**'orderliness** *n.*

orderly room *n. Mil.* a room in the barracks of a battalion or company used for general administrative purposes.

Order of Merit *n. Brit.* an order conferred on civilians and servicemen for eminence in any field.

order of the day *n.* **1.** the general directive of a commander in chief or the specific instructions of a commanding officer. **2.** *Inf.* the prescribed or only thing offered or available. **3.** (in Parliament) any item of public business ordered to be considered on a specific day. **4.** an agenda or programme.

Order of the Garter *n.* See **Garter.**

order paper *n.* a list indicating the order in which business is to be conducted, esp. in Parliament.

ordinal ('ɔːdɪnᵊl) *adj.* **1.** denoting a certain position in a sequence of numbers. **2.** of, relating to, or characteristic of an order in biological classification. ~*n.* **3.** short for **ordinal number. 4.** a book containing the forms of services for the ordination of ministers. **5.** *R.C. Church.* a service book.

ordinal number *n.* a number denoting relative position in a sequence, such as *first, second, third.* Sometimes shortened to **ordinal.**

ordinance ('ɔːdɪnəns) *n.* an authoritative regulation, decree, law, or practice. [C14: < OF *ordenance,* < L *ordināre* to set in order]

ordinarily ('ɔːdᵊnrɪlɪ) *adv.* in ordinary, normal, or usual practice; usually; normally.

ordinary ('ɔːdᵊnrɪ) *adj.* **1.** of common or established type or occurrence. **2.** familiar, everyday, or unexceptional. **3.** uninteresting or commonplace. **4.** having regular or ex officio jurisdiction: *an ordinary judge.* **5.** *Maths.* (of a differential equation) containing two variables only and derivatives of one of the variables with respect to the other. ~*n., pl.* **-naries. 6.** a common or average situation, amount, or degree (esp. in **out of the ordinary**). **7.** a normal or commonplace person or thing. **8.** *Civil law.* a judge who exercises jurisdiction in his own right. **9.** (*usually cap.*) an ecclesiastic, esp. a bishop, holding an office to which certain jurisdictional powers are attached. **10.** *R.C. Church.* **a.** the parts of the Mass that do not vary from day to day. **b.** a prescribed form of divine service, esp. the Mass. **11.** the U.S. name for **penny-farthing. 12.** *Heraldry.* any of several conventional figures, such as the bend, and the cross, commonly charged upon shields. **13.** *History.* a clergyman who visited condemned prisoners. **14.** *Brit. obs.* **a.** a meal provided regularly at a fixed price. **b.** the inn, etc., providing such meals. **15. in ordinary.** *Brit.* (used esp. in titles) in regular service or attendance: *physician in ordinary to the sovereign.* [C16 (adj.) & C13 (some n. senses): ult. < L *ordinārius* orderly, < *ordō* order]

Ordinary level *n.* a formal name for **O level.**

ordinary rating *n.* a rank in the Royal Navy comparable to that of a private in the army.

ordinary seaman *n.* a seaman of the lowest rank, being insufficiently experienced to be an able-bodied seaman.

ordinary shares *pl. n. Brit.* shares representing part of the capital issued by a company and entitling their holders to a variable dividend according to the profitability of the company and to a claim on net assets. U.S. equivalent: **common stock.** Cf. **preference shares.**

ordinate ('ɔːdɪnɪt) *n.* the vertical or *y*-coordinate of a point in a two-dimensional system of Cartesian coordinates. Cf. **abscissa.** [C16: < NL (*linea*) *ordināte* (*applicāta*) (line applied) in an orderly manner < *ordināre* to arrange in order]

ordination (ˌɔːdɪ'neɪʃən) *n.* **1. a.** the act of conferring holy orders. **b.** the reception of holy orders. **2.** the condition of being ordained or regulated. **3.** an arrangement or order.

ordnance (ˈɔːdnəns) *n.* **1.** cannon or artillery. **2.** military supplies; munitions. **3. the.** a department of an army or government dealing with military supplies. [C14: var. of ORDINANCE]

ordnance datum *n.* mean sea level calculated from observation taken at Newlyn, Cornwall, and used as the official basis for height calculation on British maps. Abbrev.: **OD.**

Ordnance Survey *n.* the official map-making body of the British or Irish government.

Ordovician (ˌɔːdəʊˈvɪʃɪən) *adj.* **1.** of, denoting, or formed in the second period of the Palaeozoic era, between the Cambrian and Silurian periods. ~*n.* **2. the.** the Ordovician period or rock system. [C19: < L *Ordovices*, ancient Celtic tribe in N Wales]

ordure (ˈɔːdjʊə) *n.* excrement; dung. [C14: via OF, < *ord* dirty, < L *horridus* shaggy]

ore (ɔː) *n.* any naturally occurring mineral or aggregate of minerals from which economically important constituents, esp. metals, can be extracted. [OE *ār, ōra*]

öre (ˈørə) *n., pl.* **öre.** a Scandinavian monetary unit worth one hundredth of a Swedish krona and (**øre**) one hundredth of a Danish and Norwegian krone.

oread (ˈɔːrɪˌæd) *n. Greek myth.* a mountain nymph. [C16: via L < Gk *Oreias*, < *oros* mountain]

oregano (ˌɒrɪˈgɑːnəʊ) *n.* **1.** a Mediterranean variety of wild marjoram (*Origanum vulgare*), with pungent leaves. **2.** the dried powdered leaves of this plant, used to season food. [C18: American Sp., < Sp., < L *orīganum*, < Gk *origanon* an aromatic herb, ? marjoram]

orfe (ɔːf) *n.* a small slender European cyprinoid fish, occurring in two colour varieties, namely the **silver orfe** and the **golden orfe,** popular aquarium fishes. [C17: < G; rel. to L *orphus*, Gk *orphos* the sea perch]

organ (ˈɔːgən) *n.* **1. a.** Also called: **pipe organ.** a large complex musical keyboard instrument in which sound is produced by means of a number of pipes arranged in sets or stops, supplied with air from a bellows. **b.** (*as modifier*): *organ stop; organ loft.* **2.** any instrument, such as a harmonium, in which sound is produced in this way. **3.** a fully differentiated structural and functional unit, such as a kidney or a root, in an animal or plant. **4.** an agency or medium of communication, esp. a periodical issued by a specialist group or party. **5.** an instrument with which something is done or accomplished. **6.** a euphemistic word for **penis.** [C13: < OF *organe*, < L *organum* implement, < Gk *organon* tool]

organdie *or esp. U.S.* **organdy** (ˈɔːgəndɪ) *n., pl.* **-dies.** a fine and slightly stiff cotton fabric used for dresses, etc. [C19: < F *organdi*, <?]

organelle (ˌɔːgəˈnɛl) *n.* a structural and functional unit in a cell or unicellular organism. [C20: < NL *organella*, < L *organum*; see ORGAN]

organ-grinder *n.* a street musician playing a hand organ for money.

organic (ɔːˈgænɪk) *adj.* **1.** of, relating to, or derived from living plants and animals. **2.** of or relating to animal or plant constituents or products having a carbon basis. **3.** of or relating to one or more organs of an animal or plant. **4.** of, relating to, or belonging to the class of chemical compounds that are formed from carbon: *an organic compound.* **5.** constitutional in the structure of something; fundamental; integral. **6.** of or characterized by the coordination of integral parts; organized. **7.** of or relating to the essential constitutional laws regulating the government of a state: *organic law.* **8.** of, relating to, or grown with the use of fertilizers or pesticides deriving from animal or vegetable matter. ~*n.* **9.** any substance, such as a fertilizer or pesticide, that is derived from animal or vegetable matter. —**orˈganically** *adv.*

organic chemistry *n.* the branch of chemistry concerned with the compounds of carbon.

organism (ˈɔːgəˌnɪzəm) *n.* **1.** any living animal or plant, including any bacterium or virus. **2.** anything resembling a living creature in structure, behaviour, etc. —ˌ**organˈismal** *or* ˌ**organˈismic** *adj.* —ˌ**organˈismally** *adv.*

organist (ˈɔːgənɪst) *n.* a person who plays the organ.

organization *or* **-isation** (ˌɔːgənaɪˈzeɪʃən) *n.* **1.** the act of organizing or the state of being organized. **2.** an organized structure or whole. **3.** a business or administrative concern united and constructed for a particular end. **4.** a body of administrative officials, as of a government department, etc. **5.** order, tidiness, or system; method. —ˌ**organiˈzational** *or* **-iˈsational** *adj.*

organize *or* **-ise** (ˈɔːgəˌnaɪz) *vb.* **1.** to form (parts or elements of something) into a structured whole; coordinate. **2.** (*tr.*) to arrange methodically or in order. **3.** (*tr.*) to provide with an organic structure. **4.** (*tr.*) to enlist (the workers) (of a factory, etc.) in a trade union. **5.** (*intr.*) to join or form an organization or trade union. **6.** (*tr.*) *Inf.* to put (oneself) in an alert and responsible frame of mind. [C15: < Med. L *organizare*, < L *organum* ORGAN] —ˈ**organˌizer** *or* **-ˌiser** *n.*

organometallic (ɔːˌgænəʊmɪˈtælɪk) *adj.* of, concerned with, or being an organic compound with one or more metal atoms in its molecules.

organon (ˈɔːgəˌnɒn) *or* **organum** *n., pl.* **-na** (-nə), **-nons** *or* **-na, -nums. 1.** *Epistemology.* a system of logical or scientific rules, esp. that of Aristotle. **2.** *Arch.* a sense organ, regarded as an instrument for acquiring knowledge. [C16: < Gk: implement; see ORGAN]

organotin (ɔːgænəʊˈtɪn) *adj.* of, concerned with, or being an organic compound with one or more tin atoms in its molecules: used as a pesticide, hitherto considered to decompose safely, now found to be toxic in the food chain.

organza (ɔːˈgænzə) *n.* a thin stiff fabric of silk, cotton, nylon, rayon, etc. [C20: <?]

orgasm (ˈɔːgæzəm) *n.* **1.** the most intense point during sexual excitement. **2.** *Rare.* intense or violent excitement. [C17: < NL *orgasmus*, < Gk *orgasmos*, < *organ* to mature, swell] —**orˈgasmic** *or* **orˈgastic** *adj.*

orgeat (ˈɔːʒɑː) *n.* a drink made from barley or almonds, and orangeflower water. [C18: via F, < *orge* barley, < L *hordeum*]

orgy (ˈɔːdʒɪ) *n., pl.* **-gies. 1.** a wild gathering marked by promiscuous sexual activity, excessive drinking, etc. **2.** an act of immoderate or frenzied indulgence. **3.** (*often pl.*) secret religious rites of Dionysus, Bacchus, etc., marked by drinking, dancing, and songs. [C16: < F *orgies*, < L *orgia*, < Gk: nocturnal festival] —ˌ**orgiˈastic** *adj.*

oribi (ˈɒrɪbɪ) *n., pl.* **-bi** *or* **-bis.** a small African antelope of the grasslands and bush south of the Sahara, with fawn-coloured coat and, in the male, ridged spikelike horns. [C18: < Afrik., prob. < Hottentot *arab*]

oriel (ˈɔːrɪəl) *n.* a bay window, esp. one that is supported by one or more brackets or corbels. Also called: **oriel window.** [C14: < OF *oriol* gallery, ? < Med. L *auleolum* niche]

orient *n.* (ˈɔːrɪənt). **1.** *Poetic.* another word for **east.** Cf. **occident. 2.** *Arch.* the eastern sky or the dawn. **3. a.** the iridescent lustre of a pearl. **b.** (*as modifier*): *orient pearls.* **4.** a pearl of high quality. ~*adj.* (ˈɔːrɪənt). **5.** *Now chiefly poetic.* oriental. **6.** *Arch.* (of the sun, stars, etc.) rising. ~*vb.* (ˈɔːrɪˌɛnt). **7.** to adjust or align (oneself or something else) according to surroundings or circumstances. **8.** (*tr.*) to position or set (a map, etc.) with reference to the compass or other specific directions. **9.** (*tr.*) to build (a church) with the chancel end facing in an easterly direction. [C18: via F < L *oriēns* rising (sun), < *orīrī* to rise]

▷ **Usage.** See at **orientate.**

Orient (ˈɔːrɪənt) *n.* (usually preceded by *the*) **1.** the countries east of the Mediterranean. **2.** the eastern hemisphere.

oriental (ˌɔːrɪˈɛntᵊl) *adj.* another word for **eastern.**

Oriental (ˌɔːrɪˈɛntᵊl) *adj.* **1.** (*sometimes not cap.*) of or relating to the Orient. **2.** of or denoting a region consisting of southeastern Asia from India to Borneo, Java, and the Philippines. ~*n.* **3.** (*sometimes not cap.*) an inhabitant, esp. a native, of the Orient.

Orientalism (ˌɔːrɪˈɛntəˌlɪzəm) *n.* **1.** knowledge of or devotion to the Orient. **2.** an Oriental quality, style, or trait. —ˌ**Oriˈentalist** *n.* —ˌ**Oriˌentalˈistic** *adj.*

orientate (ˈɔːrɪɛnˌteɪt) *vb.* another word for **orient** (senses 7, 8, 9).

▷ **Usage.** Careful users avoid *orientate* as an unnecessary back formation from *orientation*, since *orient* has the same range of meanings. Nevertheless, there can be little doubt that either form is acceptable. The excessive use of *orientate* and *orientation* in such phrases as *orientation course* (preparatory course), *profits-orientated systems* (those designed to produce high profits), and *student-orientated lectures* (lectures written with students in mind) is frowned on in careful usage as jargon.

orientation (ˌɔːrɪɛnˈteɪʃən) *n.* **1.** the act or process of orienting or the state of being oriented. **2.** positioning with relation to the compass or other specific directions. **3.** the adjustment or alignment of oneself or one's ideas to surroundings or circumstances. **4.** Also called: **orientation course.** *Chiefly U.S. & Canad.* **a.** a course, lecture, etc., introducing a new situation or environment. **b.** (*as modifier*): *an orientation talk.* **5.** *Psychol.* the knowledge of one's own temporal, social, and practical circumstances. **6.** the siting of a church on an east-west axis. —ˌ**orienˈtational** *adj.*

-oriented *suffix forming adjectives.* geared or directed towards: *sports-oriented.*

orienteer (ˌɔːrɪənˈtɪə) *vb.* (*intr.*) **1.** to take part in orienteering. ~*n.* **2.** a person who takes part in orienteering.

orienteering (ˌɔːrɪɛnˈtɪərɪŋ) *n.* a sport in which contestants race on foot over a course consisting of checkpoints found with the aid of a map and a compass. [C20: < Swedish *orientering*]

orifice (ˈɒrɪfɪs) *n. Chiefly technical.* an opening or mouth into a cavity; vent; aperture. [C16: via F < LL *ōrificium*, < L *ōs* mouth + *facere* to make]

oriflamme (ˈɒrɪˌflæm) *n.* a scarlet flag adopted as the national banner of France in the Middle Ages. [C15: via OF, < L *aurum* gold + *flamma* flame]

orig. *abbrev. for:* **1.** origin. **2.** original(ly).

origami (ˌɒrɪˈgɑːmɪ) *n.* the art or process, originally Japanese, of paper folding. [< Japanese, < *ori* a fold + *kami* paper]

origan (ˈɒrɪgən) *n.* another name for **marjoram** (sense 2). [C16: < L *orīganum*, < Gk *origanon* an aromatic herb]

origanum (ˌɒrɪˈgɑːnəm) *n.* See **oregano.**

origin (ˈɒrɪdʒɪn) *n.* **1.** a primary source; derivation. **2.** the beginning of something; first part. **3.** (*often pl.*) ancestry or parentage; birth; extraction. **4.** *Anat.* **a.** the end of a muscle, opposite its point of insertion. **b.** the beginning of a nerve or blood vessel or the site where it first starts to branch out. **5.** *Maths.* **a.** the point of intersection of coordinate axes or planes. **b.** the point whose coordinates are all zero. [C16: < F *origine*, < L *orīgō* beginning, < *orīrī* to spring from]

original (əˈrɪdʒɪnᵊl) *adj.* **1.** of or relating to an origin or beginning. **2.** fresh and unusual; novel. **3.** able to think of or carry out new ideas or concepts. **4.** being that from which a copy, translation, etc., is made. ~*n.* **5.** the first and genuine form of something, from which others are derived. **6.** a person or thing used as a model in art or literature. **7.** a person whose way of thinking is unusual or creative. **8.** the first form or occurrence of something. —**oˈriginally** *adv.*

originality (əˌrɪdʒɪˈnælɪtɪ) *n., pl.* **-ties. 1.** the quality or condition of being original. **2.** the ability to create or innovate.

original sin *n.* a state of sin held to be innate in mankind as the descendants of Adam.

originate (əˈrɪdʒɪˌneɪt) *vb.* **1.** to come or bring into being. **2.** (*intr.*) *U.S. & Canad.* (of a bus, train, etc.) to begin its journey at a specified point. —**oˌrigiˈnation** *n.* —**oˈrigiˌnator** *n.*

oriole (ˈɔːrɪˌəʊl) *n.* **1.** a tropical Old World songbird, such as the **golden oriole**, having a long pointed bill and a mostly yellow-and-black plumage. **2.** an American songbird, esp. the Baltimore oriole, with a typical male plumage of black with either orange or yellow. [C18: < Med. L *oryolus*, < L *aureolus*, dim. of *aureus*, < *aurum* gold]

Orion (əˈraɪən) *n.* a constellation containing two first-magnitude stars (Betelgeuse and Rigel) and a distant low-density emission nebula (the **Orion Nebula**).

orison (ˈɒrɪzᵊn) *n. Literary.* another word for **prayer**[1]. [C12: < OF *oreison*, < LL *ōrātiō*, < L: speech, < *ōrāre* to speak]

Oriya (ɒˈriːə) *n.* **1.** (*pl.* **-ya**) a member of a people of India living chiefly in Orissa. **2.** the state language of Orissa, belonging to the Indo-European family.

Orlon (ˈɔːlɒn) *n. Trademark.* a crease-resistant acrylic fibre or fabric used for clothing, etc.

orlop *or* **orlop deck** (ˈɔːlɒp) *n. Naut.* (in a vessel with four or more decks) the lowest deck. [C15: < Du. *overloopen* to spill]

ormer (ˈɔːmə) *n.* **1.** Also called: **sea-ear.** an edible marine gastropod mollusc that has an ear-shaped shell perforated with holes and occurs near the Channel Islands. **2.** any other abalone. [C17: < F, apparently < L *auris* ear + *mare* sea]

ormolu (ˈɔːməˌluː) *n.* **1. a.** a gold-coloured alloy of copper, tin, or zinc used to decorate furniture, etc. **b.** (*as modifier*): *an ormolu clock.* **2.** gold prepared for gilding. [C18: < F *or moulu* ground gold]

ornament *n.* (ˈɔːnəmənt). **1.** anything that enhances the appearance of a person or thing. **2.** decorations collectively: *she was totally without ornament.* **3.** a small decorative object. **4.** something regarded as a source of pride or beauty. **5.** *Music.* any of several decorations, such as the trill, etc. ~*vb.* (ˈɔːnəˌmɛnt). (*tr.*) **6.** to decorate with or as if with ornaments. **7.** to serve as an ornament to. [C14: < L *ornāmentum*, < *ornāre* to adorn] —ˌ**ornamenˈtation** *n.*

ornamental (ˌɔːnəˈmɛntᵊl) *adj.* **1.** of value as an ornament; decorative. **2.** (of a plant) used to decorate houses, gardens, etc. ~*n.* **3.** a plant cultivated for show or decoration. —ˌ**ornaˈmentally** *adv.*

ornate (ɔːˈneɪt) *adj.* **1.** heavily or elaborately decorated. **2.** (of style in writing, etc.) overembellished; flowery. [C15: < L *ornāre* to decorate] —**orˈnately** *adv.* —**orˈnateness** *n.*

ornery (ˈɔːnərɪ) *adj. U.S. & Canad. dialect or inf.* **1.** stubborn or vile-tempered. **2.** low; treacherous: *an ornery trick.* **3.** ordinary. [C19: alteration of ORDINARY] —ˈ**orneriness** *n.*

ornitho- *or before a vowel* **ornith-** *combining form.* bird or birds. [< Gk *ornis*, *ornith-* bird]

ornithology (ˌɔːnɪˈθɒlədʒɪ) *n.* the study of birds. —**ornithological** (ˌɔːnɪθəˈlɒdʒɪkᵊl) *adj.* —ˌ**ornithoˈlogically** *adv.* —ˌ**orniˈthologist** *n.*

ornithorhynchus (ˌɔːnɪθəʊˈrɪŋkəs) *n.* the technical name for **duck-billed platypus.** [C19: NL, < ORNITHO- + Gk *rhunkhos* bill]

oro-[1] *combining form.* mountain: *orogeny.* [< Gk *oros*]

oro-[2] *combining form.* oral; mouth: *oromaxillary.* [< L, < *ōs*]

orogeny (ɒˈrɒdʒɪnɪ) *or* **orogenesis** (ˌɒrəʊˈdʒɛnɪsɪs) *n.* the formation of mountain ranges. —**orogenic** (ˌɒrəʊˈdʒɛnɪk) *or* **orogenetic** (ˌɒrəʊdʒɪˈnɛtɪk) *adj.*

orotund (ˈɒrəʊˌtʌnd) *adj.* **1.** (of the voice) resonant; booming. **2.** (of speech or writing) bombastic; pompous. [C18: < L *ore rotundo* with rounded mouth]

orphan (ˈɔːfən) *n.* **1. a.** a child, one or both of whose parents are dead. **b.** (*as modifier*): *an orphan child.* ~*vb.* **2.** (*tr.*) to deprive of one or both parents. [C15: < LL *orphanus*, < Gk *orphanos*]

orphanage (ˈɔːfənɪdʒ) *n.* **1.** an institution for

orphans and abandoned children. **2.** the state of being an orphan.

Orphean (ˈɔːfɪən) *adj.* **1.** of or relating to Orpheus, a poet and lyre-player in Greek mythology. **2.** melodious or enchanting.

Orphic (ˈɔːfɪk) *adj.* **1.** of or relating to Orpheus or Orphism, a mystery religion of ancient Greece. **2.** (*sometimes not cap.*) mystical or occult. —ˈ**Orphically** *adv.*

orpine (ˈɔːpaɪn) *or* **orpin** (ˈɔːpɪn) *n.* a succulent perennial N temperate plant with toothed leaves and heads of small purplish-white flowers. [C14: < OF, apparently < *orpiment*, a yellow mineral (? referring to the yellow flowers of a related species)]

orrery (ˈɒrərɪ) *n., pl.* **-ries.** a mechanical model of the solar system in which the planets can be moved at the correct relative velocities around the sun. [C18: orig. made for Charles Boyle, Earl of *Orrery*]

orris *or* **orrice** (ˈɒrɪs) *n.* **1.** any of various irises that have fragrant rhizomes. **2.** Also: **orrisroot.** the rhizome of such a plant, prepared and used as perfume. [C16: var. of IRIS]

orthicon (ˈɔːθɪˌkɒn) *n.* a television camera tube in which an optical image produces a corresponding electrical charge pattern on a mosaic surface that is scanned from behind by an electron beam. The resulting discharge of the mosaic provides the output signal current. See also **image orthicon.** [C20: < ORTHO- + ICON(OSCOPE)]

ortho- *or before a vowel* **orth-** *combining form.* **1.** straight or upright: *orthorhombic.* **2.** perpendicular or at right angles: *orthogonal.* **3.** correct or right: *orthodontics.* **4.** (*often in italics*) denoting an organic compound containing a benzene ring with substituents attached to adjacent carbon atoms (the 1,2- positions). **5.** denoting an oxyacid regarded as the highest hydrated form of the anhydride or a salt of such an acid: *orthophosphoric acid.* **6.** denoting a diatomic substance in which the spins of the two atoms are parallel: *orthohydrogen.* [< Gk *orthos* straight, upright]

orthochromatic (ˌɔːθəʊkrəʊˈmætɪk) *adj. Photog.* of or relating to an emulsion giving a rendering of relative light intensities of different colours that corresponds approximately to the colour sensitivity of the eye, esp. one that is insensitive to red light. Sometimes shortened to **ortho.** —**orthochromatism** (ˌɔːθəʊˈkrəʊməˌtɪzəm) *n.*

orthoclase (ˈɔːθəʊˌkleɪs, -ˌkleɪz) *n.* a white or coloured feldspar mineral consisting of an aluminium silicate of potassium in monoclinic crystalline form.

orthodontics (ˌɔːθəʊˈdɒntɪks) *or* **orthodontia** (ˌɔːθəʊˈdɒntɪə) *n.* (*functioning as sing.*) the branch of dentistry concerned with preventing or correcting irregularities of the teeth. —ˌ**orthoˈdontic** *adj.* —ˌ**orthoˈdontist** *n.*

orthodox (ˈɔːθəˌdɒks) *adj.* **1.** conforming with established standards, as in religion, behaviour, or attitudes. **2.** conforming to the Christian faith as established by the early Church. [C16: via Church L < Gk *orthodoxos*, < *orthos* correct + *doxa* belief] —ˈ**orthoˌdoxy** *n.*

Orthodox (ˈɔːθəˌdɒks) *adj.* **1.** of or relating to the Orthodox Church of the East. **2.** (*sometimes not cap.*) of or relating to Orthodox Judaism.

Orthodox Church *n.* **1.** the collective body of those Eastern Churches that were separated from the western Church in the 11th century and are in communion with the Greek patriarch of Constantinople. **2.** any of these Churches.

Orthodox Judaism *n.* a form of Judaism characterized by traditional interpretation and strict observance of the Mosaic Law.

orthoepy (ˈɔːθəʊˌɛpɪ) *n.* the study of correct or standard pronunciation. [C17: < Gk *orthoepeia*, < ORTHO- straight + *epos* word] —**orthoepic** (ˌɔːθəʊˈɛpɪk) *adj.* —ˌ**orthoˈepically** *adv.*

orthogenesis (ˌɔːθəʊˈdʒɛnɪsɪs) *n.* **1.** *Biol.* **a.** evolution of a group of organisms in a particular direction, which is generally predetermined. **b.** the theory that proposes such a development. **2.** the theory that there is a series of stages through which all cultures pass in the same order. —**orthogenetic** (ˌɔːθəʊdʒɪˈnɛtɪk) *adj.* —ˌ**orthogeˈnetically** *adv.*

orthogonal (ɔːˈθɒgənᵊl) *adj.* relating to, consisting of, or involving right angles; perpendicular. —**orˈthogonally** *adv.*

orthographic (ˌɔːθəˈgræfɪk) *or* **orthographical** *adj.* of or relating to spelling. —ˌ**orthoˈgraphically** *adv.*

orthography (ɔːˈθɒgrəfɪ) *n., pl.* **-phies. 1.** a writing system. **2. a.** spelling considered to be correct. **b.** the principles underlying spelling. **3.** the study of spelling. —**orˈthographer** *or* **orˈthographist** *n.*

orthopaedics *or U.S.* **orthopedics** (ˌɔːθəʊˈpiːdɪks) *n.* (*functioning as sing.*) **1.** the branch of surgery concerned with disorders of the spine and joints and the repair of deformities of these parts. **2. dental orthopaedics.** another name for **orthodontics.** —ˌ**orthoˈpaedic** *or U.S.* ˌ**orthoˈpedic** *adj.* —ˌ**orthoˈpaedist** *or U.S.* ˌ**orthoˈpedist** *n.*

orthopteran (ɔːˈθɒptərən) *n.* **1.** Also: **orthopteron** (*pl.* **-tera** (-tərə)) any orthopterous insect. ~*adj.* **2.** another word for **orthopterous.**

orthopterous (ɔːˈθɒptərəs) *adj.* of, relating to, or belonging to a large order of insects, including crickets, locusts, and grasshoppers, having leathery forewings and membranous hind wings.

orthoptic (ɔːˈθɒptɪk) *adj.* relating to normal binocular vision.

orthoptics (ɔːˈθɒptɪks) *n.* (*functioning as sing.*) the science or practice of correcting defective vision, as by exercises to strengthen weak eye muscles. —**orˈthoptist** *n.*

orthorhombic (ˌɔːθəʊˈrɒmbɪk) *adj. Crystallog.* relating to the crystal system characterized by three mutually perpendicular unequal axes.

ortolan (ˈɔːtələn) *n.* **1.** a brownish Old World bunting regarded as a delicacy. **2.** any of various other small birds eaten as delicacies, esp. the bobolink. [C17: via F < L *hortulānus*, < *hortulus*, dim. of *hortus* garden]

-ory[1] *suffix forming nouns.* **1.** indicating a place for: *observatory.* **2.** something having a specified use: *directory.* [via OF *-orie*, < L *-ōrium*, *-ōria*]

-ory[2] *suffix forming adjectives.* of or relating to; characterized by; having the effect of: *contributory.* [via OF *-orie*, < L *-ōrius*]

oryx (ˈɒrɪks) *n., pl.* **-yxes** *or* **-yx.** any large African antelope of the genus *Oryx*, typically having long straight nearly upright horns. [C14: via L < Gk *orux* stonemason's axe, used also of the pointed horns of an antelope]

os[1] (ɒs) *n., pl.* **ossa** (ˈɒsə). *Anat.* the technical name for **bone.** [C16: < L: bone]

os[2] (ɒs) *n., pl.* **ora.** *Anat., zool.* a mouth or mouthlike part or opening. [C18: < L]

Os *the chemical symbol for* osmium.

OS *abbrev. for:* **1.** Old Saxon (language). **2.** Old Style. **3.** Ordinary Seaman. **4.** (in Britain) Ordnance Survey. **5.** outsize.

Osage orange (əʊˈseɪdʒ) *n.* **1.** a North American thorny tree, grown for hedges and ornament. **2.** the warty orange-like fruit of this plant. [< *Osage* Amerind tribe]

Oscar (ˈɒskə) *n.* any of several small gold statuettes awarded annually in the United States for outstanding achievements in films. Official name: **Academy Award.** [C20: said to have been named after a remark made by an official that it reminded him of his uncle Oscar]

oscillate (ˈɒsɪˌleɪt) *vb.* **1.** (*intr.*) to move or swing from side to side regularly. **2.** (*intr.*) to waver between opinions, courses of action, etc. **3.** *Physics.* to undergo or produce or cause to undergo or produce oscillation. [C18: < L *oscillāre* to swing]

oscillating universe theory *n.* the theory that the universe is oscillating between periods of expansion and contraction.

oscillation (ˌɒsɪˈleɪʃən) *n.* **1.** *Statistics, physics.* **a.** regular fluctuation in value, position, or state about a mean value, such as the variation in an alternating current. **b.** a single cycle of such a fluctuation. **2.** the act or process of oscillating. **—oscillatory** ('ɒsɪlətərɪ, -trɪ) *adj.*

oscillator ('ɒsɪˌleɪtə) *n.* **1.** a circuit or instrument for producing an alternating current or voltage of a required frequency. **2.** any instrument for producing oscillations. **3.** a person or thing that oscillates.

oscillogram (ɒ'sɪləˌɡræm) *n.* the recording obtained from an oscillograph or the trace on an oscilloscope screen.

oscillograph (ɒ'sɪləˌɡrɑːf) *n.* a device for producing a graphical record of the variation of an oscillating quantity, such as an electric current. **—oscillographic** (ɒˌsɪlə'ɡræfɪk) *adj.* **—oscillography** (ˌɒsɪ'lɒɡrəfɪ) *n.*

oscilloscope (ɒ'sɪləˌskəʊp) *n.* an instrument for producing a representation of a rapidly changing quantity on the screen of a cathode-ray tube.

oscine ('ɒsaɪn, 'ɒsɪn) *adj.* of, relating to, or belonging to the suborder of passerine birds that includes most of the songbirds. [C17: via NL < L *oscen* singing bird]

oscitancy ('ɒsɪtənsɪ) *or* **oscitance** *n., pl.* **-tancies** *or* **-tances.** **1.** the state of being drowsy, lazy, or inattentive. **2.** the act of yawning. ~Also called: **oscitation.** [C17: < L *oscitāre* to yawn] **—'oscitant** *adj.*

oscular ('ɒskjʊlə) *adj.* **1.** *Zool.* of or relating to a mouthlike aperture, esp. of a sponge. **2.** of or relating to the mouth or to kissing.

osculate ('ɒskjʊˌleɪt) *vb.* **1.** *Usually humorous.* to kiss. **2.** (*intr.*) (of an organism) to be intermediate between two taxonomic groups. **3.** *Geom.* to touch in osculation. [C17: < L *ōsculārī* to kiss]

osculation (ˌɒskjʊ'leɪʃən) *n.* **1.** *Maths.* a point at which two branches of a curve have a common tangent, each branch extending in both directions of the tangent. **2.** *Rare.* the act of kissing. **—osculatory** ('ɒskjʊlətərɪ, -trɪ) *adj.*

-ose[1] *suffix forming adjectives.* possessing; resembling: *grandiose.* [< L *-ōsus*; see -OUS]

-ose[2] *suffix forming nouns.* **1.** indicating a carbohydrate, esp. a sugar: *lactose.* **2.** indicating a decomposition product of protein: *albumose.* [< GLUCOSE]

osier ('əʊzɪə) *n.* **1.** any of various willow trees, whose flexible branches or twigs are used for making baskets, etc. **2.** a twig or branch from such a tree. **3.** any of several North American dogwoods, esp. the red osier. [C14: < OF, prob. < Med. L *ausēria*, ? of Gaulish origin]

-osis *suffix forming nouns.* **1.** indicating a process or state: *metamorphosis.* **2.** indicating a diseased condition: *tuberculosis.* **3.** indicating the formation or development of something: *fibrosis.* [< Gk, suffix used to form nouns from verbs with infinitives in *-oein* or *-oun*]

Osmanli (ɒz'mænlɪ) *adj.* **1.** of or relating to the Ottoman Empire. ~*n.* **2.** (formerly) a subject of the Ottoman Empire. [C19: < Turkish, < *Osman* I (1259–1326), Turkish Sultan]

osmiridium (ˌɒzmɪ'rɪdɪəm) *n.* a very hard corrosion-resistant white or grey natural alloy of osmium and iridium: used in pen nibs, etc. [C19: < OSM(IUM) + IRIDIUM]

osmium ('ɒzmɪəm) *n.* a very hard brittle bluish-white metal, the heaviest known element, occurring with platinum and alloyed with iridium in osmiridium. Symbol: Os; atomic no.: 76; atomic wt.: 190.2. [C19: < Gk *osmē* smell, from its penetrating odour]

osmose ('ɒzməʊs, -məʊz, 'ɒs-) *vb.* to undergo or cause to undergo osmosis. [C19 (n.): abstracted < the earlier terms *endosmose* and *exosmose;* rel. to Gk *ōsmos* push]

osmosis (ɒz'məʊsɪs, ɒs-) *n.* **1.** the tendency of the solvent of a less concentrated solution of dissolved molecules to pass through a semipermeable membrane into a more concentrated solution until both solutions are of the same concentration. **2.** diffusion through any membrane or porous barrier, as in dialysis. [C19: Latinized form < OSMOSE, < Gk *ōsmos* push] **—osmotic** (ɒz'mɒtɪk, ɒs-) *adj.* **—os'motically** *adv.*

osmotic pressure *n.* the pressure necessary to prevent osmosis into a given solution when the solution is separated from the pure solvent by a semipermeable membrane.

osmunda (ɒz'mʌndə) *or* **osmund** ('ɒzmənd) *n.* any of a genus of ferns having large spreading fronds. [C13: < OF *osmonde*, <?]

osprey ('ɒsprɪ, -preɪ) *n.* **1.** a large broad-winged fish-eating diurnal bird of prey, with a dark back and whitish head and underparts. Often called (U.S. and Canad.): **fish hawk.** **2.** any of the feathers of various other birds, used esp. as trimming for hats. [C15: < OF *ospres*, apparently < L *ossifraga*, lit.: bone-breaker, < *os* bone + *frangere* to break]

ossein ('ɒsɪɪn) *n.* a protein that forms the organic matrix of bone. [C19: < L *osseus* bony, < *os* bone]

osseous ('ɒsɪəs) *adj.* consisting of or containing bone, bony. [C17: < L *osseus*, < *os* bone] **—'osseously** *adv.*

ossify ('ɒsɪˌfaɪ) *vb.* **-fying, -fied.** **1.** to convert or be converted into bone. **2.** (*intr.*) (of habits, attitudes, etc.) to become inflexible. [C18: < F *ossifier*, < L *os* bone + *facere* to make] **—ˌossifi'cation** *n.* **—'ossiˌfier** *n.*

ossuary ('ɒsjʊərɪ) *n., pl.* **-aries.** any container for the burial of human bones, such as an urn or vault. [C17: < LL *ossuārium*, < L *os* bone]

osteal ('ɒstɪəl) *adj.* **1.** of or relating to bone or to the skeleton. **2.** composed of bone; osseous. [C19: < Gk *osteon* bone]

osteitis (ˌɒstɪ'aɪtɪs) *n.* inflammation of a bone. **—osteitic** (ˌɒstɪ'ɪtɪk) *adj.*

ostensible (ɒ'stɛnsɪbᵊl) *adj.* **1.** apparent; seeming. **2.** pretended. [C18: via F < Med. L *ostensibilis*, < L *ostendere* to show, < *ob-* before + *tendere* to extend] **—osˌtensi'bility** *n.* **—os'tensibly** *adv.*

ostensive (ɒ'stɛnsɪv) *adj.* **1.** obviously or manifestly demonstrative. **2.** (of a definition) giving examples of objects to which a word or phrase is properly applied. **3.** a less common word for **ostensible.** [C17: < LL *ostentīvus*, < L *ostendere* to show; see OSTENSIBLE] **—os'tensively** *adv.*

ostentation (ˌɒstɛn'teɪʃən) *n.* pretentious, showy, or vulgar display. **—ˌosten'tatious** *adj.* **—ˌosten'tatiously** *adv.* **—ˌosten'tatiousness** *n.*

osteo- *or before a vowel* **oste-** *combining form.* indicating bone or bones. [< Gk *osteon*]

osteoarthritis (ˌɒstɪəʊɑː'θraɪtɪs) *n.* chronic inflammation of the joints, esp. those that bear weight, with pain and stiffness. **—osteoarthritic** (ˌɒstɪəʊɑː'θrɪtɪk) *adj., n.*

osteology (ˌɒstɪ'ɒlədʒɪ) *n.* the study of the structure and function of bones. **—osteological** (ˌɒstɪə'lɒdʒɪkᵊl) *adj.* **—ˌosteo'logically** *adv.* **—ˌoste'ologist** *n.*

osteoma (ˌɒstɪ'əʊmə) *n., pl.* **-mata** (-mətə) *or* **-mas.** a benign tumour composed of bone or bonelike tissue.

osteomalacia (ˌɒstɪəʊmə'leɪʃɪə) *n.* a disease characterized by softening of the bones, resulting from a deficiency of vitamin D and of calcium and phosphorus. [C19: < NL, < OSTEO- + Gk *malakia* softness] **—ˌosteoma'lacial** *or* **osteomalacic** (ˌɒstɪəʊmə'læsɪk) *adj.*

osteomyelitis (ˌɒstɪəʊˌmaɪɪ'laɪtɪs) *n.* inflammation of bone marrow, caused by infection.

osteopathy (ˌɒstɪ'ɒpəθɪ) *n.* a system of healing based on the manipulation of bones or other parts of the body. **—'osteoˌpath** *n.* **—osteopathic** (ˌɒstɪə'pæθɪk) *adj.* **—ˌosteo'pathically** *adv.*

osteoplasty ('ɒstɪəˌplæstɪ) *n., pl.* **-ties.** the branch of surgery concerned with bone repair or bone grafting.

osteoporosis (ˌɒstɪəʊpɔː'rəʊsɪs) *n.* porosity and brittleness of the bones caused by lack of calcium in the bone matrix. [C19: < OSTEO- + PORE[2] + -OSIS] **—osteoporotic** (ˌɒstɪəʊpɔː'rɒtɪk) *adj.*

ostinato (ˌɒstɪ'nɑːtəʊ) *n., pl.* **-tos.** **a.** a continuously reiterated musical phrase. **b.** (*as* *modifier*): *an ostinato passage.* [It.: < L *obstinātus* OBSTINATE]

ostler *or* **hostler** (ˈɒslə) *n. Arch.* a stableman, esp. one at an inn. [C15: var. of *hostler*, < HOSTEL]

ostmark (ˈɒstmɑːk) *n.* the standard monetary unit of East Germany, divided into 100 pfennigs. [lit.: east mark]

ostracize *or* **-ise** (ˈɒstrəˌsaɪz) *vb.* (*tr.*) **1.** to exclude or banish (a person) from a particular group, society, etc. **2.** (in ancient Greece) to punish by temporary exile. [C17: < Gk *ostrakizein* to select someone for banishment by voting on potsherds, < *ostrakon* potsherd] —ˈ**ostracism** *n.* —ˈ**ostraˌcizable** *or* **-isable** *adj.* —ˈ**ostraˌcizer** *or* **-iser** *n.*

ostrich (ˈɒstrɪtʃ) *n., pl.* **-triches** *or* **-trich.** **1.** a fast-running flightless African bird that is the largest living bird with stout two-toed feet and dark feathers, except on the naked head, neck, and legs. **2. American ostrich.** another name for **rhea. 3.** a person who refuses to recognize the truth, reality, etc. [C13: < OF *ostrice*, < L *avis* bird + LL *struthio* ostrich, < Gk *strouthion*]

OT *abbrev. for:* **1.** occupational therapy. **2.** Old Testament. **3.** overtime.

otalgia (əʊˈtældʒɪə, -dʒə) *n.* the technical name for **earache.**

OTC (in Britain) *abbrev. for:* **1.** Officers' Training Corps. **2.** *Stock Exchange.* over the counter: denoting dealings between brokers in areas for which no official market prices are quoted.

OTE *abbrev. for* on target earnings: referring to the salary a salesman should be able to achieve.

other (ˈʌðə) *determiner.* **1. a.** (when used before a singular noun, usually preceded by *the*) the remaining (one or ones in a group of which one or some have been specified): *I'll read the other sections of the paper later.* **b. the other.** (*as pron.; functioning as sing.*): *one walks while the other rides.* **2.** (a) different (one or ones from that or those already specified or understood): *no other man but you.* **3.** additional; further: *there are no other possibilities.* **4.** (preceded by *every*) alternate; two: *it buzzes every other minute.* **5. other than. a.** apart from; besides: *a lady other than his wife.* **b.** different from: *he couldn't be other than what he is.* Archaic form: **other from. 6. no other.** *Arch.* nothing else: *I can do no other.* **7. or other.** (preceded by a phrase or word with *some*) used to add vagueness to the preceding pronoun, noun, or noun phrase: *he's somewhere or other.* **8. other things being equal.** conditions being the same or unchanged. **9. the other day, night,** etc. a few days, nights, etc., ago. **10. the other thing.** an unexpressed alternative. ~*pron.* **11.** another: *show me one other.* **12.** (*pl.*) additional or further ones. **13.** (*pl.*) other people or things. **14. the others.** the remaining ones (of a group). ~*adv.* **15.** (usually used with a negative and foll. by *than*) otherwise; differently: *they couldn't behave other than they do.* [OE *ōther*] —ˈ**otherness** *n.*

other-directed *adj.* guided by values derived from external influences.

other ranks *pl. n.* (*rarely sing.*) *Chiefly Brit.* (in the armed forces) all those who do not hold a commissioned rank.

otherwise (ˈʌðəˌwaɪz) *sentence connector.* **1.** or else; if not, then: *go home — otherwise your mother will worry.* ~*adv.* **2.** differently: *I wouldn't have thought otherwise.* **3.** in other respects: *an otherwise hopeless situation.* ~*adj.* **4.** (*predicative*) of an unexpected nature; different: *the facts are otherwise.* ~*pron.* **5.** something different in outcome: *success or otherwise.* [C14: < OE *on ōthre wisan* in other manner]

other world *n.* the spirit world or afterlife.

otherworldly (ˌʌðəˈwɜːldlɪ) *adj.* **1.** of or relating to the spiritual or imaginative world. **2.** impractical or unworldly. —ˌ**otherˈworldliness** *n.*

otic (ˈəʊtɪk, ˈɒtɪk) *adj.* of or relating to the ear. [C17: < Gk *ōtikos*, < *ous* ear]

-otic *suffix forming adjectives.* **1.** relating to or affected by: *sclerotic.* **2.** causing: *narcotic.* [< Gk *-ōtikos*]

otiose (ˈəʊtɪˌəʊs, -ˌəʊz) *adj.* **1.** serving no useful purpose: *otiose language.* **2.** *Rare.* indolent; lazy. [C18: < L *ōtiōsus* leisured, < *ōtium* leisure] —**otiosity** (ˌəʊtɪˈɒsɪtɪ) *or* ˈ**otiˌoseness** *n.*

otitis (əʊˈtaɪtɪs) *n.* inflammation of the ear.

oto- *or before a vowel* **ot-** *combining form.* indicating the ear. [< Gk *ous, ōt-* ear]

otolaryngology (ˌəʊtəʊˌlærɪŋˈgɒlədʒɪ) *n.* another name for **otorhinolaryngology. —otolaryngological** (ˌəʊtəʊləˌrɪŋgəˈlɒdʒɪkᵊl) *adj.* —ˌ**otoˌlarynˈgologist** *n.*

otolith (ˈəʊtəʊˌlɪθ) *n.* any of the granules of calcium carbonate in the inner ear of vertebrates. Movement of otoliths, caused by a change in the animal's position, stimulates sensory hair cells, which convey information to the brain. —ˌ**otoˈlithic** *adj.*

otology (əʊˈtɒlədʒɪ) *n.* the branch of medicine concerned with the ear. —**otological** (ˌəʊtəˈlɒdʒɪkᵊl) *adj.* —**oˈtologist** *n.*

otorhinolaryngology (ˌəʊtəʊˌraɪnəʊˌlærɪŋˈgɒlədʒɪ) *n.* the branch of medicine concerned with the ear, nose, and throat. Sometimes called **otolaryngology.**

otoscope (ˈəʊtəʊˌskəʊp) *n.* a medical instrument for examining the external ear. —**otoscopic** (ˌəʊtəʊˈskɒpɪk) *adj.*

OTT *Sl. abbrev. for* over the top.

ottava rima (əʊˈtɑːvə ˈriːmə) *n. Prosody.* a stanza form consisting of eight iambic pentameter lines, rhyming a b a b a b c c. [It.: eighth rhyme]

otter (ˈɒtə) *n., pl.* **-ters** *or* **-ter. 1.** a freshwater carnivorous mammal, esp. the **Eurasian otter**, typically having smooth fur, a streamlined body, and webbed feet. **2.** the fur of this animal. **3.** a type of fishing tackle consisting of a weighted board to which hooked and baited lines are attached. [OE *otor*]

otter hound *n.* a large rough-coated dog of a breed formerly used for otter hunting.

ottoman (ˈɒtəmən) *n., pl.* **-mans. 1. a.** a low padded seat, usually armless, sometimes in the form of a chest. **b.** a cushioned footstool. **2.** a corded fabric. [C17: < F *ottomane*, fem. of OTTOMAN]

Ottoman (ˈɒtəmən) *or* **Othman** (ˈɒθmən) *adj.* **1.** *History.* of or relating to the Ottomans or the Ottoman Empire. **2.** denoting or relating to the Turkish language. ~*n., pl.* **-mans. 3.** a member of a Turkish people in the late 13th century. [C17: < F, via Med. L, < Ar. *Othmāni* Turkish, < Turkish *Othman* or *Osman* I (1259–1326), Turkish Sultan]

Ottoman Empire *n.* the former Turkish empire in Europe, Asia, and Africa, which lasted from the late 13th century until the end of World War I.

ou (əʊ) *n. S. African. sl.* a man. [< Afrik., ? < Du.]

OU *abbrev. for:* **1.** the Open University. **2.** Oxford University.

ouananiche (ˌwɑːnəˈniːʃ) *n.* a landlocked variety of the Atlantic salmon found in lakes in SE Canada. [< Canad. F, of Amerind origin, < *wananish*, dim. of *wanans* salmon]

oubaas (ˈəʊˌbɑːs) *n. S. African.* a man in authority. [< Afrik., < Du. *oud* old + *baas* boss]

oubliette (ˌuːblɪˈɛt) *n.* a dungeon, the only entrance to which is through the top. [C19: < F, < *oublier* to forget]

ouch (aʊtʃ) *interj.* an exclamation of sharp sudden pain.

ought[1] (ɔːt) *vb.* (foll. by *to; takes an infinitive or implied infinitive*) used as an auxiliary: **1.** to indicate duty or obligation: *you ought to pay.* **2.** to express prudent expediency: *you ought to see him.* **3.** (usually with reference to future time) to express probability or expectation: *you ought to finish this by Friday.* **4.** to express a desire or wish on the part of the speaker: *you ought to come next week.* [OE *āhte*, p.t. of *āgan* to OWE]

▷ **Usage.** In careful English, *ought* is not used with *did* or *had. I ought not to do it,* not *I didn't ought to do it; I ought not to have done it,* not *I hadn't ought to have done it.*

ought[2] (ɔːt) *pron., adv.* a variant spelling of **aught.**

ought[3] (ɔːt) *n.* a less common word for **nought** (zero). [C19: mistaken division of *a nought* as *an ought;* see NOUGHT]

Ouija (ˈwiːdʒə) *n. Trademark.* a board on which are marked the letters of the alphabet. Answers to questions are spelt out by a pointer and are supposedly formed by spirits. [C19: < F *oui* yes + G *ja* yes]

ouma (ˈəʊmɑː) *n.* (in South Africa) **1.** grandmother, esp. in titular use with her surname. **2.** *Sl.* any elderly woman. [< Afrik., < Du. *oma* grandmother]

ounce[1] (aʊns) *n.* **1.** a unit of weight equal to one sixteenth of a pound (avoirdupois). Abbrev.: **oz. 2.** a unit of weight equal to one twelfth of a Troy or Apothecaries' pound; 1 ounce is equal to 480 grains. **3.** short for **fluid ounce. 4.** a small portion or amount. [C14: < OF *unce,* < L *uncia* a twelfth]

ounce[2] (aʊns) *n.* another name for **snow leopard.** [C18: < OF *once,* by mistaken division of *lonce* as if *l'once,* < L LYNX]

oupa (ˈəʊpɑː) *n. S. African.* **1.** grandfather, esp. in titular use with surname. **2.** *Sl.* any elderly man. [Afrik.]

our (ˈaʊə) *determiner.* **1.** of, belonging to, or associated in some way with us: *our best vodka; our parents are good to us.* **2.** belonging to or associated with all people or people in general: *our nearest planet is Venus.* **3.** a formal word for *my* used by editors or other writers, and monarchs. [OE *ūre* (genitive pl.), < US]

-our *suffix forming nouns.* indicating state, condition, or activity: *behaviour; labour.* [in OF *-eur,* < L *-or,* n. suffix]

Our Father *n.* another name for the **Lord's Prayer,** taken from its opening words.

ours (ˈaʊəz) *pron.* **1.** something or someone belonging to or associated with us: *ours have blue tags.* **2. of ours.** belonging to or associated with us.

ourself (aʊəˈsɛlf) *pron. Arch.* a variant of **myself,** formerly used by monarchs or editors.

ourselves (aʊəˈsɛlvz) *pron.* **1. a.** the reflexive form of *we* or *us.* **b.** (intensifier): *we ourselves will finish it.* **2.** (*preceded by a copula*) our usual selves: *we are ourselves when we're together.* **3.** *Not standard.* used instead of *we* or *us* in compound noun phrases: *other people and ourselves.*

▷ **Usage.** See at **myself.**

-ous *suffix forming adjectives.* **1.** having or full of: *dangerous; spacious.* **2.** (in chemistry) indicating that an element is chemically combined in the lower of two possible valency states: *ferrous.* Cf. **-ic** (sense 2). [< OF, < L *-ōsus* or *-us,* Gk *-os,* adj. suffixes]

ousel (ˈuːzᵊl) *n.* a variant spelling of **ouzel.**

oust (aʊst) *vb.* (*tr.*) **1.** to force out of a position or place; supplant or expel. **2.** *Property law.* to deprive (a person) of the possession of land, etc. [C16: < Anglo-Norman *ouster,* < L *obstāre* to withstand]

ouster (ˈaʊstə) *n. Property law.* the act of dispossessing of freehold property; eviction.

out (aʊt) *adv.* (*when predicative, can in some senses be regarded as adj.*) **1.** (*often used as a particle*) at or to a point beyond the limits of some location; outside: *get out at once.* **2.** (*particle*) used to indicate exhaustion or extinction: *the sugar's run out; put the light out.* **3.** not in a particular place, esp., not at home. **4.** public; revealed: *the secret is out.* **5.** on sale or on view to the public: *the book is being brought out next May.* **6.** (of the sun, stars, etc.) visible. **7.** in flower: *the roses are out now.* **8.** not in fashion, favour, or current usage. **9.** not or not any longer worth considering: *that plan is out.* **10.** not allowed: *smoking on duty is out.* **11.** (of a fire or light) no longer burning or providing illumination. **12.** not working: *the radio's out.* **13.** Also: **out on strike.** on strike. **14.** (of a jury) withdrawn to consider a verdict in private. **15.** (*particle*) out of consciousness: *she passed out.* **16.** (*particle*) used to indicate a burst of activity as indicated by the verb: *fever broke out.* **17.** (*particle*) used to indicate obliteration of an object: *the graffiti was painted out.* **18.** (*particle*) used to indicate an approximate drawing or description: *chalk out.* **19.** at or to the fullest length or extent: *spread out.* **20.** loudly; clearly: *calling out.* **21.** desirous of or intent on (something or doing something): *I'm out for as much money as I can get.* **22.** (*particle*) used to indicate a goal or object achieved at the end of the action specified by the verb: *he worked it out.* **23.** (*preceded by a superlative*) existing: *the friendliest dog out.* **24.** an expression in signalling, radio, etc., to indicate the end of a transmission. **25.** used up; exhausted: *our supplies are completely out.* **26.** worn into holes: *out at the elbows.* **27.** inaccurate, deficient, or discrepant: *out by six pence.* **28.** not in office or authority. **29.** completed or concluded, as of time: *before the year is out.* **30.** *Obs.* (of a young woman) in or into society: *Lucinda had a large party when she came out.* **31.** *Sport.* denoting the state in which a player is caused to discontinue active participation, esp. in some specified role. **32. out of. a.** at or to a point outside: *out of his reach.* **b.** away from; not in: *stepping out of line; out of focus.* **c.** because of; motivated by: *out of jealousy.* **d.** from (a material or source): *made out of plastic.* **e.** not or no longer having any of (a substance, material, etc.): *we're out of sugar.* **f.** no longer in a specified state or condition: *out of work; out of practice.* **g.** (of a horse) born of. ~*adj.* **33.** directed or indicating direction outwards: *the out tray.* **34.** (of an island) remote from the mainland. ~*prep.* **35.** *Nonstandard or U.S.* out of; out through: *he ran out the door.* ~*interj.* **36. a.** an exclamation of dismissal, reproach, etc. **b.** (in wireless telegraphy) an expression used to signal that the speaker is signing off. **37. out with it.** a command to make something known immediately, without missing any details. ~*n.* **38.** *Chiefly U.S.* a method of escape from a place, difficult situation, etc. **39.** *Baseball.* an instance of causing a batter to be out by fielding. ~*vb.* **40.** (*tr.*) to put or throw out. **41.** (*intr.*) to be made known or effective despite efforts to the contrary (esp. in **the truth will out**). [OE *ūt*]

out- *prefix.* **1.** excelling or surpassing in a particular action: *outlast; outlive.* **2.** indicating an external location or situation away from the centre: *outpost; outpatient.* **3.** indicating emergence, an issuing forth, etc.: *outcrop; outgrowth.* **4.** indicating the result of an action: *outcome.*

outage (ˈaʊtɪdʒ) *n.* **1.** a quantity of goods missing or lost after storage or shipment. **2.** a period of power failure, machine stoppage, etc.

out and away *adv.* by far.

out-and-out *adj.* (*prenominal*) thoroughgoing; complete.

outback (ˈaʊtˌbæk) *n.* **a.** the remote bush country of Australia. **b.** (*as modifier*): *outback life.*

outbalance (ˌaʊtˈbæləns) *vb.* another word for **outweigh.**

outboard (ˈaʊtˌbɔːd) *adj.* **1.** (of a boat's engine) portable, with its own propeller, and designed to be attached externally to the stern. **2.** in a position away from, or further away from, the centre line of a vessel or aircraft, esp. outside the hull or fuselage. ~*adv.* **3.** away from the centre line of a vessel or aircraft, esp. outside the hull or fuselage. ~*n.* **4.** an outboard motor.

outbound (ˈaʊtˌbaʊnd) *adj.* going out; outward bound.

outbrave (ˌaʊtˈbreɪv) *vb.* (*tr.*) **1.** to surpass in bravery. **2.** to confront defiantly.

ˌ**out**ˈ**act** *vb.*
ˌ**out**ˈ**bargain** *vb.*
ˌ**out**ˈ**bid** *vb.*
ˌ**out**ˈ**box** *vb.*

outbreak (ˈaʊtˌbreɪk) *n.* a sudden, violent, or spontaneous occurrence, esp. of disease or strife.
outbuilding (ˈaʊtˌbɪldɪŋ) *n.* a building separate from a main building; outhouse.
outburst (ˈaʊtˌbɜːst) *n.* **1.** a sudden and violent expression of emotion. **2.** an explosion or eruption.
outcast (ˈaʊtˌkɑːst) *n.* **1.** a person who is rejected or excluded from a social group. **2.** a vagabond or wanderer. **3.** anything thrown out or rejected. *~adj.* **4.** rejected, abandoned, or discarded; cast out.
outcaste (ˈaʊtˌkɑːst) *n.* **1.** a person who has been expelled from a caste. **2.** a person having no caste. *~vb.* **3.** (*tr.*) to cause (someone) to lose his caste.
outclass (ˌaʊtˈklɑːs) *vb.* (*tr.*) **1.** to surpass in class, quality, etc. **2.** to defeat easily.
outcome (ˈaʊtˌkʌm) *n.* something that follows from an action or situation; result; consequence.
outcrop *n.* (ˈaʊtˌkrɒp). **1.** part of a rock formation or mineral vein that appears at the surface of the earth. **2.** an emergence; appearance. *~vb.* (ˌaʊtˈkrɒp), **-cropping, -cropped. 3.** (*intr.*) (of rock strata, mineral veins, etc.) to protrude through the surface of the earth.
outcry *n.* (ˈaʊtˌkraɪ), *pl.* **-cries. 1.** a widespread or vehement protest. **2.** clamour; uproar. *~vb.* (ˌaʊtˈkraɪ), **-crying, -cried. 3.** (*tr.*) to cry louder or make more noise than (someone or something).
outdated (ˌaʊtˈdeɪtɪd) *adj.* old-fashioned or obsolete.
outdo (ˌaʊtˈduː) *vb.* **-doing, -did, -done.** (*tr.*) to surpass or exceed in performance.
outdoor (ˈaʊtˈdɔː) *adj.* (*prenominal*) taking place, existing, or intended for use in the open air: *outdoor games; outdoor clothes.* Also: **out-of-door.**
outdoors (ˌaʊtˈdɔːz) *adv.* **1.** Also: **out-of-doors.** in the open air; outside. *~n.* **2.** the world outside or far away from human habitation.
outer (ˈaʊtə) *adj.* (*prenominal*) **1.** being or located on the outside; external. **2.** further from the middle or central part. *~n.* **3.** *Archery.* **a.** the white outermost ring on a target. **b.** a shot that hits this ring. **4.** *Austral. & N.Z.* the unsheltered part of the spectator area at a sports ground. **5. on the outer.** *Austral. & N.Z.* excluded or neglected.
outer bar *n.* (in England) a collective name for junior barristers who plead from outside the bar of the court.
outermost (ˈaʊtəˌməʊst) *adj.* furthest from the centre or middle; outmost.
outer space *n.* any region of space beyond the atmosphere of the earth.
outfall (ˈaʊtˌfɔːl) *n.* the end of a river, sewer, drain, etc., from which it discharges.
outfield (ˈaʊtˌfiːld) *n.* **1.** *Cricket.* the area of the field relatively far from the pitch; the deep. Cf. **infield** (sense 1). **2.** *Baseball.* **a.** the area of the playing field beyond the lines connecting first, second, and third bases. **b.** the positions of the left fielder, centre fielder, and right fielder taken collectively. **3.** *Agriculture.* farmland most distant from the farmstead. —**ˈoutˌfielder** *n.*
outfit (ˈaʊtˌfɪt) *n.* **1.** a set of articles or equipment for a particular task, etc. **2.** a set of clothes, esp. a carefully selected one. **3.** *Inf.* any group or association regarded as a cohesive unit, such as a military company, etc. *~vb.* **-fitting, -fitted. 4.** to furnish or be furnished with an outfit, equipment, etc. —**ˈoutˌfitter** *n.*
outflank (ˌaʊtˈflæŋk) *vb.* (*tr.*) **1.** to go around the flank of (an opposing army, etc.). **2.** to get the better of.
outflow (ˈaʊtˌfləʊ) *n.* **1.** anything that flows out, such as liquid, money, etc. **2.** the amount that flows out. **3.** the act or process of flowing out.
outfox (ˌaʊtˈfɒks) *vb.* (*tr.*) to surpass in guile or cunning.
outgeneral (ˌaʊtˈdʒɛnərəl) *vb.* **-alling, -alled** *or U.S.* **-aling, -aled.** (*tr.*) to surpass in generalship.
outgo *vb.* (ˌaʊtˈgəʊ), **-going, -went, -gone. 1.** (*tr.*) to exceed or outstrip. *~n.* (ˈaʊtˌgəʊ). **2.** cost; outgoings; outlay. **3.** something that goes out; outflow.
outgoing (ˈaʊtˌgəʊɪŋ) *adj.* **1.** departing; leaving. **2.** retiring from office. **3.** friendly and sociable. *~n.* **4.** the act of going out.
outgoings (ˈaʊtˌgəʊɪŋz) *pl.n.* expenditure.
outgrow (ˌaʊtˈgrəʊ) *vb.* **-growing, -grew, -grown.** (*tr.*) **1.** to grow too large for (clothes, shoes, etc.). **2.** to lose (a habit, idea, reputation, etc.) in the course of development or time. **3.** to grow larger or faster than.
outgrowth (ˈaʊtˌgrəʊθ) *n.* **1.** a thing growing out of a main body. **2.** a development, result, or consequence. **3.** the act of growing out.
outgun (ˌaʊtˈgʌn) *vb.* **-gunning, -gunned.** (*tr.*) **1.** to surpass in fire power. **2.** to surpass in shooting. **3.** *Inf.* to surpass or excel.
outhouse (ˈaʊtˌhaʊs) *n.* a building near to, but separate from, a main building; outbuilding.
outing (ˈaʊtɪŋ) *n.* a short outward and return journey; trip; excursion.
outjockey (ˌaʊtˈdʒɒkɪ) *vb.* (*tr.*) to outwit by deception.
outlandish (aʊtˈlændɪʃ) *adj.* **1.** grotesquely unconventional in appearance, habits, etc. **2.** *Arch.* foreign. —**outˈlandishly** *adv.* —**outˈlandishness** *n.*
outlaw (ˈaʊtˌlɔː) *n.* **1.** (formerly) a person excluded from the law and deprived of its protection. **2.** any fugitive from the law, esp. a habitual transgressor. *~vb.* (*tr.*) **3.** to put (a person) outside the law and deprive of its protection. **4.** to ban. —**ˈoutˌlawry** *n.*
outlay *n.* (ˈaʊtˌleɪ). **1.** an expenditure of money, effort, etc. *~vb.* (ˌaʊtˈleɪ), **-laying, -laid. 2.** (*tr.*) to spend (money, etc.).
outlet (ˈaʊtlɛt, -lɪt) *n.* **1.** an opening or vent permitting escape or release. **2. a.** a market for a product or service. **b.** a commercial establishment retailing the goods of a particular producer or wholesaler. **3.** a channel that drains a body of water. **4.** a point in a wiring system from which current can be taken to supply electrical devices.
outlier (ˈaʊtˌlaɪə) *n.* **1.** an outcrop of rocks that is entirely surrounded by older rocks. **2.** a person, thing, or part situated away from a main or related body. **3.** a person who lives away from his place of work, duty, etc.
outline (ˈaʊtˌlaɪn) *n.* **1.** a preliminary or schematic plan, draft, etc. **2.** (*usually pl.*) the important features of a theory, work, etc. **3.** the line by which an object or figure is or appears to be bounded. **4. a.** a drawing or manner of drawing consisting only of external lines. **b.** (*as modifier*): *an outline map.* *~vb.* (*tr.*) **5.** to draw or display the outline of. **6.** to give the main features or general idea of.
outlive (ˌaʊtˈlɪv) *vb.* (*tr.*) **1.** to live longer than (someone). **2.** to live beyond (a date or period): *he outlived the century.* **3.** to live through (an experience).
outlook (ˈaʊtˌlʊk) *n.* **1.** a mental attitude or point of view. **2.** the probable or expected condition or outcome of something: *the weather outlook.* **3.** the view from a place. **4.** view or prospect. **5.** the act or state of looking out.
outlying (ˈaʊtˌlaɪɪŋ) *adj.* distant or remote from the main body or centre, as of a town or region.
outmanoeuvre *or U.S.* **outmaneuver** (ˌaʊtməˈnuːvə) *vb.* (*tr.*) to secure a strategic advantage over by skilful manoeuvre.
outmoded (ˌaʊtˈməʊdɪd) *adj.* no longer fashion-

ˌ**outˈdance** *vb.*
ˌ**outˈdare** *vb.*
ˌ**outˈdistance** *vb.*
ˌ**outˈdrink** *vb.*
ˌ**outˈface** *vb.*
ˌ**outˈfight** *vb.*
ˌ**outˈfly** *vb.*
ˌ**outˈguess** *vb.*
ˌ**outˈhit** *vb.*
ˌ**outˈjump** *vb.*
ˌ**outˈlast** *vb.*
ˌ**outˈmatch** *vb.*

able or widely accepted. —ˌ**outˈmodedly** *adv.* —ˌ**outˈmodedness** *n.*

outmost (ˈaʊtˌməʊst) *adj.* another word for **outermost.**

out of bounds *adj.* (*postpositive*), *adv.* **1.** (often foll. by *to*) not to be entered (by); barred (to). **2.** outside specified or prescribed limits.

out of date *adj.* (**out-of-date** *when prenominal*), *adv.* no longer valid, current, or fashionable; outmoded.

out-of-door *adj.* (*prenominal*) another term for **outdoor.**

out-of-doors *adv., adj.* (*postpositive*) in the open air; outside. Also: **outdoors.**

out of pocket *adj.* (**out-of-pocket** *when prenominal*). **1.** (*postpositive*) having lost money, as in a commercial enterprise. **2.** without money to spend. **3.** (*prenominal*) (of expenses) unbudgeted and paid for in cash.

out of the way *adj.* (**out-of-the-way** *when prenominal*). **1.** distant from more populous areas. **2.** uncommon or unusual.

outpatient (ˈaʊtˌpeɪʃənt) *n.* a nonresident hospital patient. Cf. **inpatient.**

outpoint (ˌaʊtˈpɔɪnt) *vb.* (*tr.*) to score more points than.

outport (ˈaʊtˌpɔːt) *n.* **1.** *Chiefly Brit.* a subsidiary port built in deeper water than the original port. **2.** *Canad.* a small fishing village of Newfoundland.

outpost (ˈaʊtˌpəʊst) *n.* **1.** *Mil.* **a.** a position stationed at a distance from the area occupied by a major formation. **b.** the troops assigned to such a position. **2.** an outlying settlement or position.

outpour *n.* (ˈaʊtˌpɔː). **1.** the act of flowing or pouring out. **2.** something that pours out. ~*vb.* (ˌaʊtˈpɔː). **3.** to pour or cause to pour out freely or rapidly.

outpouring (ˈaʊtˌpɔːrɪŋ) *n.* **1.** a passionate or exaggerated outburst; effusion. **2.** another word for **outpour** (senses 1, 2).

output (ˈaʊtˌpʊt) *n.* **1.** the act of production or manufacture. **2.** the amount produced, as in a given period: *a weekly output.* **3.** the material produced, manufactured, etc. **4.** *Electronics.* **a.** the power, voltage, or current delivered by a circuit or component. **b.** the point at which the signal is delivered. **5.** the power, energy, or work produced by an engine or a system. **6.** *Computers.* **a.** the information produced by a computer. **b.** the operations and devices involved in producing this information. **7.** (*modifier*) of or relating to electronic or computer output: *output signal.* ~*vb.* **8.** (*tr.*) *Computers.* to cause (data) to be emitted as output.

outrage (ˈaʊtˌreɪdʒ) *n.* **1.** a wantonly vicious or cruel act. **2.** a gross violation of decency, morality, honour, etc. **3.** profound indignation, anger, or hurt, caused by such an act. ~*vb.* (*tr.*) **4.** to cause profound indignation, anger, or resentment in. **5.** to offend grossly. **6.** to commit an act of wanton viciousness, cruelty, or indecency on. **7.** a euphemistic word for **rape**[1]. [C13 (meaning: excess): via F < *outré* beyond, < L *ultrā*]

outrageous (aʊtˈreɪdʒəs) *adj.* **1.** being or having the nature of an outrage. **2.** grossly offensive to decency, authority, etc. **3.** violent or unrestrained in behaviour or temperament. **4.** extravagant or immoderate. —**outˈrageously** *adv.* —**outˈrageousness** *n.*

outrank (ˌaʊtˈræŋk) *vb.* (*tr.*) **1.** to be of higher rank than. **2.** to take priority over.

outré (ˈuːtreɪ) *adj.* deviating from what is usual or proper. [C18: < F, p.p. of *outrer* to pass beyond]

outride (ˌaʊtˈraɪd) *vb.* **-riding, -rode, -ridden.** (*tr.*) **1.** to outdo by riding faster, farther, or better than. **2.** (of a vessel) to ride out (a storm).

outrider (ˈaʊtˌraɪdə) *n.* **1.** a person who goes in advance to investigate, discover a way, etc.; scout. **2.** a person who rides in front of or beside a carriage, esp. as an attendant or guard. **3.** *U.S.* a mounted herdsman.

outrigger (ˈaʊtˌrɪgə) *n.* **1.** a framework for supporting a pontoon outside and parallel to the hull of a boat to provide stability. **2.** a boat equipped with such a framework, esp. one of the canoes of the South Pacific. **3.** any projecting framework attached to a boat, aircraft, building, etc., to act as a support. **4.** *Rowing.* another name for **rigger** (sense 2). [C18: < OUT- + RIG + -ER[1]]

outright *adj.* (ˈaʊtˌraɪt). (*prenominal*) **1.** without qualifications or limitations: *outright ownership.* **2.** complete; total. **3.** straightforward; direct. ~*adv.* (ˌaʊtˈraɪt). **4.** without restrictions. **5.** without reservation or concealment: *ask outright.* **6.** instantly: *he was killed outright.*

outrush (ˌaʊtˈrʌʃ) *n.* a flowing or rushing out.

outset (ˈaʊtˌsɛt) *n.* a start; beginning (esp. in **from** (*or* **at**) **the outset**).

outside *prep.* (ˌaʊtˈsaɪd). **1.** (sometimes foll. by *of*) on or to the exterior of: *outside the house.* **2.** beyond the limits of. **3.** apart from; other than: *no-one knows outside you.* ~*adj.* (ˈaʊtˌsaɪd). **4.** (*prenominal*) situated on the exterior: *an outside lavatory.* **5.** remote; unlikely. **6.** not a member of. **7.** the greatest possible or probable (prices, odds, etc.). ~*adv.* (ˌaʊtˈsaɪd). **8.** outside a specified thing or place; out of doors. **9.** *Sl.* not in prison. ~*n.* (ˈaʊtˈsaɪd). **10.** the external side or surface. **11.** the external appearance or aspect. **12.** (of a pavement, etc.) the side nearest the road or away from a wall. **13.** *Sport.* an outside player, as in football. **14.** (*pl.*) the outer sheets of a ream of paper. **15.** *Canad.* (in the north) the settled parts of Canada. **16. at the outside.** *Inf.* at the most or at the greatest extent: *two days at the outside.*

▷ **Usage.** In careful usage, *outside* and *inside* are preferred to *outside of* and *inside of*: *she waits outside* (not *outside of*) *the school.*

outside broadcast *n. Radio, television.* a broadcast not made from a studio.

outsider (ˌaʊtˈsaɪdə) *n.* **1.** a person or thing excluded from or not a member of a set, group, etc. **2.** a contestant, esp. a horse, thought unlikely to win in a race. **3.** *Canad.* a person who does not live in the Arctic regions.

outsize (ˈaʊtˌsaɪz) *adj.* **1.** Also: **outsized.** very large or larger than normal. ~*n.* **2.** something outsize, such as a garment or person. **3.** (*modifier*) relating to or dealing in outsize clothes: *an outsize shop.*

outskirts (ˈaʊtˌskɜːts) *pl. n.* (*sometimes sing.*) outlying or bordering areas, districts, etc., as of a city.

outsmart (ˌaʊtˈsmɑːt) *vb.* (*tr.*) *Inf.* to get the better of; outwit.

outspan *S. African.* ~*n.* (ˈaʊtˌspæn). **1.** an area on a farm kept available for travellers to rest and refresh animals, etc. **2.** the act of unharnessing or unyoking. ~*vb.* (ˌaʊtˈspæn), **-spanning, -spanned.** **3.** to unharness or unyoke (animals). [C19: partial translation of Afrik. *uitspan*, < *uit* out + *spannen* to stretch]

outspoken (ˌaʊtˈspəʊkən) *adj.* **1.** candid or bold in speech. **2.** said or expressed with candour or boldness.

outspread *vb.* (ˌaʊtˈsprɛd), **-spreading, -spread.** **1.** to spread out. ~*adj.* (ˈaʊtˈsprɛd). **2.** spread or stretched out. **3.** scattered or diffused widely. ~*n.* (ˈaʊtˌsprɛd). **4.** a spreading out.

outstanding (ˌaʊtˈstændɪŋ) *adj.* **1.** superior; excellent. **2.** prominent, remarkable, or striking. **3.** unsettled, unpaid, or unresolved. **4.** (of shares, bonds, etc.) issued and sold. **5.** projecting or jutting upwards or outwards. —ˌ**outˈstandingly** *adv.*

ˌ**outˈnumber** *vb.*
ˌ**outˈpace** *vb.*
ˌ**outperˈform** *vb.*
ˌ**outˈplay** *vb.*
ˌ**outˈrace** *vb.*
ˌ**outˈrange** *vb.*
ˌ**outˈreach** *vb.*
ˌ**outˈrival** *vb.*
ˌ**outˈrun** *vb.*
ˌ**outˈsell** *vb.*
ˌ**outˈshine** *vb.*
ˌ**outˈshoot** *vb.*
ˌ**outˈsing** *vb.*
ˌ**outˈsit** *vb.*
ˌ**outˈstare** *vb.*

outstation (ˈaʊtˌsteɪʃən) *n.* a station or post at a distance from the base station or in a remote region.
outstay (ˌaʊtˈsteɪ) *vb.* (*tr.*) **1.** to stay longer than. **2.** to stay beyond (a limit). **3. outstay one's welcome.** See **overstay** (sense 2).
outstretch (ˌaʊtˈstrɛtʃ) *vb.* (*tr.*) **1.** to extend or expand; stretch out. **2.** to stretch or extend beyond.
outstrip (ˌaʊtˈstrɪp) *vb.* **-stripping, -stripped.** (*tr.*) **1.** to surpass in a sphere of activity, competition, etc. **2.** to be or grow greater than. **3.** to go faster than and leave behind.
outtake (ˈaʊtˌteɪk) *n.* an unreleased take from a recording session, film, or television programme.
out tray *n.* (in an office, etc.) a tray for outgoing correspondence, documents, etc.
outturn (ˈaʊtˌtɜːn) *n.* another word for **output** (sense 2).
outvote (ˌaʊtˈvəʊt) *vb.* (*tr.*) to defeat by a majority of votes.
outward (ˈaʊtwəd) *adj.* **1.** of or relating to what is apparent or superficial. **2.** of or relating to the outside of the body. **3.** belonging or relating to the external, as opposed to the mental, spiritual, or inherent. **4.** of, relating to, or directed towards the outside or exterior. **5. the outward man. a.** *Theol.* the body as opposed to the soul. **b.** *Facetious.* clothing. ~*adv.* **6.** (of a ship) away from port. **7.** a variant of **outwards.** ~*n.* **8.** the outward part; exterior. —**ˈoutwardness** *n.*
Outward Bound movement *n.* (in Britain) a scheme to provide adventure training for young people.
outwardly (ˈaʊtwədlɪ) *adv.* **1.** in outward appearance. **2.** with reference to the outside or outer surface; externally.
outwards (ˈaʊtwədz) *or* **outward** *adv.* towards the outside; out.
outwear (ˌaʊtˈwɛə) *vb.* **-wearing, -wore, -worn.** (*tr.*) **1.** to use up or destroy by wearing. **2.** to last or wear longer than. **3.** to outlive, outgrow, or develop beyond. **4.** to deplete or exhaust in strength, determination, etc.
outweigh (ˌaʊtˈweɪ) *vb.* (*tr.*) **1.** to prevail over; overcome. **2.** to be more important or significant than. **3.** to be heavier than.
outwit (ˌaʊtˈwɪt) *vb.* **-witting, -witted.** (*tr.*) to get the better of by cunning or ingenuity.
outwith (ˌaʊtˈwɪθ) *prep. Scot.* outside; beyond.
outwork *n.* (ˈaʊtˌwɜːk). **1.** (*often pl.*) defences which lie outside main defensive works. **2.** work done away from the factory, etc., by which it has been commissioned. ~*vb.* (ˌaʊtˈwɜːk), **-working, -worked** *or* **-wrought.** (*tr.*) **3.** to work better, harder, etc., than. **4.** to work out to completion. —**ˈoutˌworker** *n.*
ouzel *or* **ousel** (ˈuːzᵊl) *n.* **1.** short for **water ouzel.** See **dipper** (sense 2). **2.** an archaic name for the (European) **blackbird.** [OE *ōsle*]
ouzo (ˈuːzəʊ) *n., pl.* **ouzos.** a strong aniseed-flavoured spirit from Greece. [Mod. Gk *ouzon,* <?]
ova (ˈəʊvə) *n.* the plural of **ovum.**
oval (ˈəʊvᵊl) *adj.* **1.** having the shape of an ellipse or ellipsoid. ~*n.* **2.** anything that is oval in shape, such as a sports ground. **3.** *Austral.* **a.** an Australian Rules ground. **b.** any sports field. [C16: < Med. L *ōvālis,* < L *ōvum* egg] —**ˈovally** *adv.* —**ˈovalness** *or* **ovality** (əʊˈvælɪtɪ) *n.*
ovariectomy (əʊˌvɛərɪˈɛktəmɪ) *n., pl.* **-mies.** *Surgery.* surgical removal of an ovary or ovarian tumour.
ovary (ˈəʊvərɪ) *n., pl.* **-ries.** **1.** either of the two female reproductive organs, which produce ova and secrete oestrogen hormones. **2.** the corresponding organ in vertebrate and invertebrate animals. **3.** *Bot.* the hollow basal region of a carpel containing one or more ovules. [C17: < NL *ōvārium,* < L *ōvum* egg] —**ovarian** (əʊˈvɛərɪən) *adj.*
ovate (ˈəʊveɪt) *adj.* **1.** shaped like an egg. **2.** (esp. of a leaf) shaped like the longitudinal section of an egg, with the broader end at the base. [C18: < L *ōvātus* egg-shaped] —**ˈovately** *adv.*
ovation (əʊˈveɪʃən) *n.* **1.** an enthusiastic reception, esp. one of prolonged applause. **2.** a victory procession less glorious than a triumph awarded to a Roman general. [C16: < L *ovātiō* rejoicing, < *ovāre* to exult] —**oˈvational** *adj.*
oven (ˈʌvᵊn) *n.* **1.** an enclosed heated compartment or receptacle for baking or roasting food. **2.** a similar device, usually lined with a refractory material, used for drying substances, firing ceramics, heat-treating, etc. [OE *ofen*] —**ˈovenˌlike** *adj.*
ovenbird (ˈʌvᵊnˌbɜːd) *n.* **1.** any of numerous small brownish South American passerine birds that build oven-shaped clay nests. **2.** a common North American warbler that has an olive-brown striped plumage with an orange crown and builds a cup-shaped nest on the ground.
oven-ready *adj.* (of various foods) bought already prepared so that they are ready to be cooked in the oven.
ovenware (ˈʌvᵊnˌwɛə) *n.* heat-resistant dishes in which food can be both cooked and served.
over (ˈəʊvə) *prep.* **1.** directly above; on the top of; via the top or upper surface of: *over one's head.* **2.** on or to the other side of: *over the river.* **3.** during; through or throughout (a period of time). **4.** in or throughout all parts of: *to travel over England.* **5.** throughout the whole extent of: *over the racecourse.* **6.** above; in preference to. **7.** by the agency of (an instrument of telecommunication): *over the radio.* **8.** more than: *over a century ago.* **9.** on the subject of; about: *an argument over nothing.* **10.** while occupied in: *discussing business over golf.* **11.** having recovered from the effects of. **12. over and above.** added to; in addition to. ~*adv.* **13.** in a state, condition, situation, or position that is placed or put over something: *to climb over.* **14.** (*particle*) so as to cause to fall: *knocking over a policeman.* **15.** at or to a point across intervening space, water, etc. **16.** throughout a whole area: *the world over.* **17.** (*particle*) from beginning to end, usually cursorily: *to read a document over.* **18.** throughout a period of time: *stay over for this week.* **19.** (esp. in signalling and radio) it is now your turn to speak, act, etc. **20.** more than is expected or usual: *not over well.* **21. over again.** once more. **22. over against. a.** opposite to. **b.** contrasting with. **23. over and over.** (often foll. by *again*) repeatedly. ~*adj.* **24.** (*postpositive*) finished; no longer in progress. ~*adv., adj.* **25.** remaining; surplus (often in **left over**). ~*n.* **26.** *Cricket.* **a.** a series of six balls bowled by a bowler from the same end of the pitch. **b.** the play during this. [OE *ofer*]
over- *prefix.* **1.** excessive or excessively; beyond an agreed or desirable limit: *overcharge; overdue.* **2.** indicating superior rank: *overseer.* **3.** indicating location or movement above: *overhang.* **4.** indicating movement downwards: *overthrow.*
overage (ˌəʊvərˈeɪdʒ) *adj.* beyond a specified age.
overall *adj.* (ˈəʊvərˌɔːl). (*prenominal*) **1.** from one end to the other. **2.** including or covering everything: *the overall cost.* ~*adv.* (ˌəʊvərˈɔːl). **3.** in general; on the whole. ~*n.* (ˈəʊvərˌɔːl). **4.** *Brit.* a protective work garment usually worn over ordinary clothes. **5.** (*pl.*) hard-wearing work trousers with a bib and shoulder straps or jacket attached.

ˌoutˈstep *vb.*
ˌoutˈtalk *vb.*
ˌoutˈthink *vb.*
ˌoutˈvalue *vb.*
ˌoutˈwalk *vb.*
ˌoveraˈbundance *n.*
ˌoveracˈcentuˌate *vb.*
ˌoverˈact *vb.*
ˌoverˈactive *adj.*
ˌoverafˈfect *vb.*
ˌoveragˈgressive *adj.*
ˌoveramˈbitious *adj.*
ˌoverˈanaˌlyse *vb.*
ˌoverˌaniˈmation *n.*
ˌoverˈanxious *adj.*
ˌoverapˈpreciative *adj.*
ˌoverˌappreˈhensive *adj.*

overarch (ˌəʊvərˈɑːtʃ) *vb.* (*tr.*) to form an arch over.

overarm (ˈəʊvərˌɑːm) *adj.* **1.** *Sport, esp. cricket.* bowled, thrown, or performed with the arm raised above the shoulder. ~*adv.* **2.** with the arm raised above the shoulder.

overawe (ˌəʊvərˈɔː) *vb.* (*tr.*) to subdue, restrain, or overcome by affecting with a feeling of awe.

overbalance *vb.* (ˌəʊvəˈbæləns). **1.** to lose or cause to lose balance. **2.** (*tr.*) another word for **outweigh.** ~*n.* (ˈəʊvəˌbæləns). **3.** excess of weight, value, etc.

overbear (ˌəʊvəˈbɛə) *vb.* **-bearing, -bore, -borne.** **1.** (*tr.*) to dominate or overcome. **2.** (*tr.*) to press or bear down with weight or physical force. **3.** to produce (fruit, etc.) excessively.

overbearing (ˌəʊvəˈbɛərɪŋ) *adj.* **1.** domineering or dictatorial in manner or action. **2.** of particular or overriding importance or significance. —ˌ**overˈbearingly** *adv.*

overblown (ˌəʊvəˈbləʊn) *adj.* **1.** overdone or excessive. **2.** bombastic; turgid: *overblown prose.* **3.** (of flowers) past the stage of full bloom.

overboard (ˈəʊvəˌbɔːd) *adv.* **1.** from on board a vessel into the water. **2. go overboard.** *Inf.* **a.** to be extremely enthusiastic. **b.** to go to extremes. **3. throw overboard.** to reject or abandon.

overbuild (ˌəʊvəˈbɪld) *vb.* **-building, -built.** (*tr.*) **1.** to build over or on top of. **2.** to erect too many buildings in (an area). **3.** to build too large or elaborately.

overburden *vb.* (ˌəʊvəˈbɜːdᵊn). **1.** (*tr.*) to load with excessive weight, work, etc. ~*n.* (ˈəʊvəˌbɜːdᵊn). **2.** an excessive burden or load. **3.** *Geol.* the sedimentary rock material that covers coal seams, mineral veins, etc. —ˌ**overˈburdensome** *adj.*

overcast *adj.* (ˈəʊvəˌkɑːst). **1.** covered over or obscured, esp. by clouds. **2.** *Meteorol.* (of the sky) cloud-covered. **3.** gloomy or melancholy. **4.** sewn over by overcasting. ~*vb.* (ˌəʊvəˈkɑːst). **5.** to sew (an edge, as of a hem) with long stitches passing successively over the edge. ~*n.* (ˈəʊvəˌkɑːst). **6.** *Meteorol.* the state of the sky when it is cloud-covered.

overcharge *vb.* (ˌəʊvəˈtʃɑːdʒ). **1.** to charge too much. **2.** (*tr.*) to fill or load beyond capacity. **3.** *Literary.* another word for **exaggerate.** ~*n.* (ˈəʊvəˌtʃɑːdʒ). **4.** an excessive price or charge. **5.** an excessive load.

overcloud (ˌəʊvəˈklaʊd) *vb.* **1.** to make or become covered with clouds. **2.** to make or become dark or dim.

overcoat (ˈəʊvəˌkəʊt) *n.* a warm heavy coat worn over the outer clothes in cold weather.

overcome (ˌəʊvəˈkʌm) *vb.* **-coming, -came, -come.** **1.** (*tr.*) to get the better of in a conflict. **2.** (*tr.; often passive*) to render incapable or powerless by laughter, sorrow, exhaustion, etc. **3.** (*tr.*) to surmount obstacles, objections, etc. **4.** (*intr.*) to be victorious.

overcrop (ˌəʊvəˈkrɒp) *vb.* **-cropping, -cropped.** (*tr.*) to exhaust (land) by excessive cultivation.

overdo (ˌəʊvəˈduː) *vb.* **-doing, -did, -done.** (*tr.*) **1.** to take or carry too far; do to excess. **2.** to exaggerate, overelaborate, or overplay. **3.** to cook or bake too long. **4. overdo it** *or* **things.** to overtax one's strength, capacity, etc.

overdose *n.* (ˈəʊvəˌdəʊs). **1.** (esp. of drugs) an excessive dose. ~*vb.* (ˌəʊvəˈdəʊs). **2.** to take an excessive dose or give an excessive dose to. —ˌ**overˈdosage** *n.*

overdraft (ˈəʊvəˌdrɑːft) *n.* **1.** a withdrawal of money in excess of the credit balance on a bank account. **2.** the amount of money withdrawn thus.

overdraw (ˌəʊvəˈdrɔː) *vb.* **-drawing, -drew, -drawn.** **1.** to draw on (a bank account) in excess of the credit balance. **2.** (*tr.*) to exaggerate in describing or telling.

overdress *vb.* (ˌəʊvəˈdrɛs). **1.** to dress (oneself or another) too elaborately or finely. ~*n.* (ˈəʊvəˌdrɛs). **2.** a dress that may be worn over a jumper, blouse, etc.

overdrive *n.* (ˈəʊvəˌdraɪv). **1.** a very high gear in a motor vehicle used at high speeds to reduce wear. ~*vb.* (ˌəʊvəˈdraɪv), **-driving, -drove, -driven.** **2.** (*tr.*) to drive too hard or too far; overwork or overuse.

overdub (in multitrack recording) ~*vb.* (ˌəʊvəˈdʌb), **-dubbing, -dubbed.** **1.** to add (new sound) on a spare track or tracks. ~*n.* (ˈəʊvəˌdʌb). **2.** the blending of various layers of sound in one recording by this method.

overdue (ˌəʊvəˈdjuː) *adj.* past the time specified, required, or preferred for arrival, occurrence, payment, etc.

overestimate *vb.* (ˌəʊvərˈɛstɪˌmeɪt). **1.** (*tr.*) to estimate too highly. ~*n.* (ˌəʊvərˈɛstɪmɪt). **2.** an estimate that is too high. —ˌ**overˌestiˈmation** *n.*

overexpose (ˌəʊvərɪksˈpəʊz) *vb.* (*tr.*) **1.** to expose too much or for too long. **2.** *Photog.* to expose (a film, etc.) for too long or with too bright a light.

overflow *vb.* (ˌəʊvəˈfləʊ), **-flowing, -flowed, -flown.** **1.** to flow or run over (a limit, brim, etc.). **2.** to fill or be filled beyond capacity so as to spill or run over. **3.** (*intr.;* usually foll. by *with*) to be filled with happiness, tears, etc. **4.** (*tr.*) to spread or cover over; flood or inundate. ~*n.* (ˈəʊvəˌfləʊ). **5.** overflowing matter, esp. liquid. **6.** any outlet that enables surplus liquid to be discharged or drained off. **7.** the amount by which a limit, capacity, etc., is exceeded.

overfold (ˈəʊvəˌfəʊld) *n. Geol.* a fold in the form of an anticline in which one limb is more steeply inclined than the other.

ˌ**overasˈsert** *vb.*
ˌ**overasˈsertive** *adj.*
ˌ**overasˈsessment** *n.*
ˌ**overatˈtentive** *adj.*
ˌ**overˈbid** *vb.*
ˈ**overˌbid** *n.*
ˌ**overˈbold** *adj.*
ˌ**overˈbook** *vb.*
ˌ**overˈbusy** *adj.*
ˌ**overˈbuy** *vb.*
ˌ**overcaˈpacity** *n.*
ˌ**overˈcareful** *adj.*
ˌ**overˈcautious** *adj.*
ˌ**overˈcivil** *adj.*
ˌ**overˈcommon** *adj.*
ˌ**overˈcompenˌsate** *vb.*
ˌ**overcomˈpetitive** *adj.*
ˌ**overcomˈplacency** *n.*
ˌ**overˈcomplex** *adj.*
ˌ**overˈcompliˌcate** *vb.*
ˌ**overconˈcern** *n.*
ˌ**overˈconfident** *adj.*
ˌ**overˌconsciˈentious** *adj.*
ˌ**overconˈservative** *adj.*
ˌ**overconˈsiderate** *adj.*
ˌ**overconˈsumption** *n.*
ˌ**overˈcook** *vb.*
ˌ**overˈcostly** *adj.*
ˌ**overˈcritical** *adj.*
ˌ**overˈcrowd** *vb.*
ˌ**overˈcurious** *adj.*
ˌ**overˈdecoˌrate** *vb.*
ˌ**overˈdelicate** *adj.*
ˌ**overdeˈpendence** *n.*
ˌ**overdeˈpendent** *adj.*
ˌ**overˈdetailed** *adj.*
ˌ**overdeˈvelop** *vb.*
ˌ**overˈdiligent** *adj.*
ˌ**overdiˈlute** *vb.*
ˌ**overˈdistant** *adj.*
ˌ**overdiˈversiˌfy** *vb.*
ˌ**overˈdramaˌtize** *or* **-ise** *vb.*
ˌ**overˈdrink** *vb.*
ˌ**overˈeager** *adj.*
ˌ**overˈeat** *vb.*
ˌ**overˈeduˌcate** *vb.*
ˌ**overefˈfusive** *adj.*
ˌ**overeˈlaborate** *adj., vb.*
ˌ**overemˈbellish** *vb.*
ˌ**overeˈmotional** *adj.*
ˌ**overˈemphasis** *n.*
ˌ**overˈemphaˌsize** *or* **-ise** *vb.*
ˌ**overenˈthusiasm** *n.*
ˌ**overenˌthusiˈastic** *adj.*
ˌ**overexˈcitable** *adj.*
ˌ**overˈexerˌcise** *vb.*
ˌ**overexˈert** *vb.*
ˌ**overexˈpand** *vb.*
ˌ**overexˈpansion** *n.*
ˌ**overexˈpenditure** *n.*
ˌ**overexˈplicit** *adj.*
ˌ**overexˈpressive** *adj.*
ˌ**overexˈtend** *vb.*
ˌ**overfaˈmiliar** *adj.*
ˌ**overˈfanciful** *adj.*
ˌ**overˈfar** *adj., adv.*
ˌ**overfasˈtidious** *adj.*
ˌ**overˈfeed** *vb.*
ˌ**overˈfill** *vb.*
ˌ**overˈfish** *vb.*
ˌ**overˈfly** *vb.*
ˌ**overˈfond** *adj.*
ˌ**overˈfull** *adj.*
ˈ**overˌgarment** *n.*
ˌ**overˌgeneraliˈzation** *or* **-iˈsation** *n.*

overgrow (ˌəʊvəˈgrəʊ) *vb.* **-growing, -grew, -grown.** **1.** (*tr.*) to grow over or across (an area, path, etc.). **2.** (*tr.*) to choke or supplant by a stronger growth. **3.** (*tr.*) to grow too large for. **4.** (*intr.*) to grow beyond normal size. —**ˈoverˌgrowth** *n.*

overhand (ˈəʊvəˌhænd) *adj.* **1.** thrown or performed with the hand raised above the shoulder. **2.** sewn with thread passing over two edges in one direction. ~*adv.* **3.** with the hand above the shoulder; overarm. **4.** with shallow stitches passing over two edges. ~*vb.* **5.** to sew (two edges) overhand.

overhang *vb.* (ˌəʊvəˈhæŋ), **-hanging, -hung.** **1.** to project or extend beyond (a surface, building, etc.). **2.** (*tr.*) to hang or be suspended over. **3.** (*tr.*) to menace, threaten, or dominate. ~*n.* (ˈəʊvəˌhæŋ). **4.** a formation, object, etc., that extends beyond or hangs over something, such as an outcrop of rock overhanging a mountain face. **5.** the amount or extent of projection.

overhaul *vb.* (ˌəʊvəˈhɔːl). (*tr.*) **1.** to examine carefully for faults, necessary repairs, etc. **2.** to make repairs or adjustments to (a car, machine, etc.). **3.** to overtake. ~*n.* (ˈəʊvəˌhɔːl). **4.** a thorough examination and repair.

overhead *adj.* (ˈəʊvəˌhɛd). **1.** situated or operating above head height or some other reference level. **2.** (*prenominal*) inclusive: *the overhead price included meals.* ~*adv.* (ˌəʊvəˈhɛd). **3.** over or above head height, esp. in the sky. ~*n.* (ˈəʊvəˌhɛd). **4. a.** a stroke in racket games played from above head height. **b.** (*as modifier*): *an overhead smash.* **5.** (*modifier*) of, concerned with, or resulting from overheads: *overhead costs.*

overhead camshaft *n.* a type of camshaft situated above the cylinder head in an internal-combustion engine.

overhead projector *n.* a projector that throws an enlarged image of a transparency onto a surface above and behind the person using it.

overheads (ˈəʊvəˌhɛdz) *pl. n.* business expenses, such as rent, that are not directly attributable to any department or product and can therefore be assigned only arbitrarily.

overhead-valve engine *n.* a type of internal-combustion engine in which the inlet and exhaust valves are in the cylinder head above the pistons. U.S. name: **valve-in-head engine.**

overhear (ˌəʊvəˈhɪə) *vb.* **-hearing, -heard.** (*tr.*) to hear (a person, remark, etc.) without the knowledge of the speaker.

overheat (ˌəʊvəˈhiːt) *vb.* **1.** to make or become excessively hot. **2.** (*tr.; often passive*) to make very agitated, irritated, etc. **3.** (*tr.*) to stimulate excessively: *overheat the economy.* ~*n.* **4.** the condition of being overheated.

overjoy (ˌəʊvəˈdʒɔɪ) *vb.* (*tr.*) to give great delight to. —ˌ**overˈjoyed** *adj.*

overkill (ˈəʊvəˌkɪl) *n.* **1.** the capability to deploy more weapons, esp. nuclear weapons, than is necessary to ensure military advantage. **2.** any capacity or treatment that is greater than that required or appropriate.

overland (ˈəʊvəˌlænd) *adj.* (*prenominal*), *adv.* **1.** over or across land. ~*vb.* **2.** *Austral.* to drive (cattle or sheep) overland. —**ˈoverˌlander** *n.*

overlap *vb.* (ˌəʊvəˈlæp), **-lapping, -lapped.** **1.** (of two things) to extend or lie partly over (each other). **2.** to cover and extend beyond (something). **3.** (*intr.*) to coincide partly in time, subject, etc. ~*n.* (ˈəʊvəˌlæp). **4.** a part that overlaps or is overlapped. **5.** the amount, length, etc., overlapping. **6.** *Geol.* the horizontal extension of the lower beds in a series of rock strata beyond the upper beds.

overlay *vb.* (ˌəʊvəˈleɪ), **-laying, -laid.** (*tr.*) **1.** to lay or place over or upon (something else). **2.** (often foll. by *with*) to cover, overspread, or conceal (with). **3.** (foll. by *with*) to cover (a surface) with an applied decoration: *ebony overlaid with silver.* **4.** to achieve the correct printing pressure all over (a forme or plate) by adding to the appropriate areas of the packing. ~*n.* (ˈəʊvəˌleɪ). **5.** something that is laid over something else; covering. **6.** an applied decoration or layer, as of gold leaf. **7.** a transparent sheet giving extra details to a map or diagram over which it is designed to be placed. **8.** *Printing.* material, such as paper, used to overlay a forme or plate.

overleaf (ˌəʊvəˈliːf) *adv.* on the other side of the page.

overlie (ˌəʊvəˈlaɪ) *vb.* **-lying, -lay, -lain.** (*tr.*) **1.** to lie or rest upon. Cf. **overlay. 2.** to kill (a baby or newborn animal) by lying upon it.

overlong (ˌəʊvəˈlɒŋ) *adj., adv.* too or excessively long.

overlook *vb.* (ˌəʊvəˈlʊk). (*tr.*) **1.** to fail to notice or take into account. **2.** to disregard deliberately or indulgently. **3.** to afford a view of from above: *the house overlooks the bay.* **4.** to rise above. **5.** to look at carefully. **6.** to cast the evil eye upon (someone). ~*n.* (ˈəʊvəˌlʊk). *U.S.* **7.** a high place affording a view. **8.** an act of overlooking.

overlord (ˈəʊvəˌlɔːd) *n.* a supreme lord or master. —**ˈoverˌlordship** *n.*

overly (ˈəʊvəlɪ) *adv.* too; excessively.

overman *vb.* (ˌəʊvəˈmæn), **-manning, -manned.** **1.** (*tr.*) to supply with an excessive number of men. ~*n.* (ˈəʊvəˌmæn), *pl.* **-men.** **2.** a man who oversees others. **3.** a superman.

overmaster (ˌəʊvəˈmɑːstə) *vb.* (*tr.*) to overpower.

overmatch *Chiefly U.S.* ~*vb.* (ˌəʊvəˈmætʃ). (*tr.*) **1.** to be more than a match for. **2.** to match with a superior opponent. ~*n.* (ˈəʊvəˌmætʃ). **3.** a person superior in ability. **4.** a match in which one contestant is superior.

overmuch (ˌəʊvəˈmʌtʃ) *adv., adj.* **1.** too much; very much. ~*n.* **2.** an excessive amount.

overnice (ˌəʊvəˈnaɪs) *adj.* too fastidious, precise, etc.

overnight *adv.* (ˌəʊvəˈnaɪt). **1.** for the duration of the night. **2.** in or as if in the course of one night; suddenly: *the situation changed overnight.* ~*adj.* (ˈəʊvəˌnaɪt). (*usually prenominal*) **3.** done in, occurring in, or lasting the night: *an overnight stop.* **4.** staying for one night. **5.** for use during a single night. **6.** occurring in or as if in the course of one night; sudden: *an overnight victory.*

overpass *n.* (ˈəʊvəˌpɑːs). **1.** another name for **flyover** (sense 1). ~*vb.* (ˌəʊvəˈpɑːs), **-passing, -passed, -past.** (*tr.*) *Now rare.* **2.** to pass over, through, or across. **3.** to exceed. **4.** to ignore.

overplay (ˌəʊvəˈpleɪ) *vb.* **1.** (*tr.*) to exaggerate the importance of. **2.** to act or behave in an exaggerated manner. **3. overplay one's hand.** to overestimate the worth or strength of one's position.

ˌ**overˈgenerous** *adj.*
ˌ**overˈhastily** *adv.*
ˌ**overˈhasty** *adj.*
ˌ**overˌidealˈistic** *adj.*
ˌ**overiˈdealˌize** *or* **-ˌise** *vb.*
ˌ**overimˈaginative** *adj.*
ˌ**overimˈpress** *vb.*
ˌ**overinˈcline** *vb.*
ˌ**overinˈdulge** *vb.*
ˌ**overinˈdulgence** *n.*
ˌ**overinˈflate** *vb.*
ˌ**overˈinfluence** *vb.*
ˌ**overinˈsistent** *adj.*
ˌ**overinˈsure** *vb.*
ˌ**overinˈtense** *adj.*
ˌ**overˈinterest** *n.*
ˌ**overinˈvest** *vb.*
ˌ**overˈissue** *vb., n.*
ˌ**overˈladen** *adj.*
ˌ**overˈlarge** *adj.*
ˌ**overˈlavish** *adj.*
ˌ**overˈleap** *vb.*
ˌ**overˈload** *vb.*
ˈ**overˌload** *n.*
ˌ**overˈmany** *adj.*
ˌ**overˈmeasure** *n.*
ˌ**overˈmodest** *adj.*
ˌ**overˈmodiˌfy** *vb.*
ˌ**overˌoptiˈmistic** *adj.*
ˌ**overparˈticular** *adj.*
ˌ**overˈpay** *vb.*
ˌ**overˌpessiˈmistic** *adj.*
ˌ**overˈpopuˌlate** *vb.*
ˌ**overˌpopuˈlation** *n.*

overpower (ˌəʊvəˈpaʊə) *vb.* (*tr.*) **1.** to conquer or subdue by superior force. **2.** to have such a strong effect on as to make helpless or ineffective. **3.** to supply with more power than necessary. —ˌ**overˈpowering** *adj.*

overprint *vb.* (ˌəʊvəˈprɪnt). **1.** (*tr.*) to print (additional matter or another colour) on a sheet of paper. ~*n.* (ˈəʊvəˌprɪnt). **2.** additional matter or another colour printed onto a previously printed sheet. **3.** additional matter applied to a finished postage stamp by printing, stamping, etc.

overrate (ˌəʊvəˈreɪt) *vb.* (*tr.*) to assess too highly.

overreach (ˌəʊvəˈriːtʃ) *vb.* **1.** (*tr.*) to defeat or thwart (oneself) by attempting to do or gain too much. **2.** (*tr.*) to aim for but miss by going too far. **3.** to get the better of (a person) by trickery. **4.** (*tr.*) to reach beyond or over. **5.** (*intr.*) to reach or go too far. **6.** (*intr.*) (of a horse) to strike the back of a forefoot with the edge of the opposite hind foot.

overreact (ˌəʊvərɪˈækt) *vb.* (*intr.*) to react excessively to something. —ˌ**overreˈaction** *n.*

override *vb.* (ˌəʊvəˈraɪd), **-riding, -rode, -ridden.** (*tr.*) **1.** to set aside or disregard with superior authority or power. **2.** to supersede or annul. **3.** to dominate or vanquish by or as if by trampling down. **4.** to take manual control of (a system that is usually under automatic control). **5.** to extend or pass over, esp. to overlap. **6.** to ride (a horse, etc.) too hard. **7.** to ride over. ~*n.* (ˈəʊvəˌraɪd). **8.** a device that can override an automatic control.

overrider (ˈəʊvəˌraɪdə) *n.* either of two attachments fitted to the bumper of a motor vehicle to prevent it interlocking with that of another vehicle.

overriding (ˌəʊvəˈraɪdɪŋ) *adj.* taking precedence.

overrule (ˌəʊvəˈruːl) *vb.* (*tr.*) **1.** to disallow the arguments of (a person) by the use of authority. **2.** to rule or decide against (an argument, decision, etc.). **3.** to prevail over, dominate, or influence. **4.** to exercise rule over.

overrun *vb.* (ˌəʊvəˈrʌn), **-running, -ran, -run.** **1.** (*tr.*) to swarm or spread over rapidly. **2.** to run over (something); overflow. **3.** to extend or run beyond a limit. **4.** (*intr.*) (of an engine) to run with a closed throttle at a speed dictated by that of the vehicle it drives. **5.** (*tr.*) to print (a book, journal, etc.) in a greater quantity than ordered. **6.** (*tr.*) *Printing.* to transfer (set type) from one column, line, or page, to another. **7.** (*tr.*) *Arch.* to run faster than. ~*n.* (ˈəʊvəˌrʌn). **8.** the act or an instance of overrunning. **9.** the amount or extent of overrunning. **10.** the number of copies of a publication in excess of the quantity ordered.

overseas *adv.* (ˌəʊvəˈsiːz). **1.** beyond the sea; abroad. ~*adj.* (ˈəʊvəˈsiːz). **2.** of, to, in, from, or situated in countries beyond the sea. **3.** Also: **oversea.** of or relating to passage over the sea. ~*n.* (ˌəʊvəˈsiːz). **4.** (*functioning as sing.*) *Inf.* a foreign country or foreign countries collectively.

oversee (ˌəʊvəˈsiː) *vb.* **-seeing, -saw, -seen.** (*tr.*) **1.** to watch over and direct; supervise. **2.** to watch secretly or accidentally. **3.** *Arch.* to scrutinize; inspect.

overseer (ˈəʊvəˌsiːə) *n.* **1.** a person who oversees others, esp. workmen. **2.** *Brit. history.* a minor official of a parish attached to the poorhouse.

oversell (ˌəʊvəˈsɛl) *vb.* **-selling, -sold.** **1.** (*tr.*) to sell more of (a commodity, etc.) than can be supplied. **2.** to use excessively aggressive methods in selling (commodities). **3.** (*tr.*) to exaggerate the merits of.

overset (ˌəʊvəˈsɛt) *vb.* **-setting, -set.** (*tr.*) **1.** to disturb or upset. **2.** *Printing.* to set (type or copy) in excess of the space available.

oversew (ˈəʊvəˌsəʊ, ˌəʊvəˈsəʊ) *vb.* **-sewing, -sewed, -sewn.** to sew (two edges) with close stitches that pass over them both.

oversexed (ˌəʊvəˈsɛkst) *adj.* having an excessive preoccupation with sexual activity.

overshadow (ˌəʊvəˈʃædəʊ) *vb.* (*tr.*) **1.** to render insignificant or less important in comparison. **2.** to cast a shadow or gloom over.

overshoe (ˈəʊvəˌʃuː) *n.* a protective shoe worn over an ordinary shoe.

overshoot *vb.* (ˌəʊvəˈʃuːt), **-shooting, -shot.** **1.** to shoot or go beyond (a mark or target). **2.** (of an aircraft) to fly or taxi too far along a runway. **3.** (*tr.*) to pass swiftly over or down over, as water over a wheel. ~*n.* (ˈəʊvəˌʃuːt). **4.** an act or instance of overshooting. **5.** the extent of such overshooting.

overshot (ˈəʊvəˌʃɒt) *adj.* **1.** having or designating an upper jaw that projects beyond the lower jaw. **2.** (of a water wheel) driven by a flow of water that passes over the wheel.

oversight (ˈəʊvəˌsaɪt) *n.* **1.** an omission or mistake, esp. one made through failure to notice something. **2.** supervision.

oversize *adj.* (ˌəʊvəˈsaɪz). **1.** Also: **oversized.** larger than the usual size. ~*n.* (ˈəʊvəˌsaɪz). **2.** a size larger than the usual or proper size. **3.** something that is oversize.

overskirt (ˈəʊvəˌskɜːt) *n.* an outer skirt, esp. one that reveals a decorative underskirt.

overspend *vb.* (ˌəʊvəˈspɛnd), **-spending, -spent.** **1.** to spend in excess of (one's desires or what one can afford or is allocated). **2.** (*tr.; usually passive*) to wear out; exhaust. ~*n.* (ˈəʊvəˌspɛnd). **3.** the amount by which someone or something is overspent.

overspill *n.* (ˈəʊvəˌspɪl). **1. a.** something that spills over or is in excess. **b.** (*as modifier*): *overspill population.* ~*vb.* (ˌəʊvəˈspɪl), **-spilling, -spilt** *or* **-spilled.** **2.** (*intr.*) to overflow.

overstate (ˌəʊvəˈsteɪt) *vb.* (*tr.*) to state too strongly; exaggerate or overemphasize. —ˌ**overˈstatement** *n.*

overstay (ˌəʊvəˈsteɪ) *vb.* (*tr.*) **1.** to stay beyond the time, limit, or duration of. **2. overstay** *or* **outstay one's welcome.** to stay (at a party, etc.), longer than pleases the host or hostess.

overstep (ˌəʊvəˈstɛp) *vb.* **-stepping, -stepped.** (*tr.*) to go beyond (a certain or proper limit).

overstrung (ˌəʊvəˈstrʌŋ) *adj.* **1.** too highly strung; tense. **2.** (of a piano) having two sets of strings crossing each other at an oblique angle.

overstuff (ˌəʊvəˈstʌf) *vb.* (*tr.*) **1.** to force too much into. **2.** to cover (furniture, etc.) entirely with upholstery.

oversubscribe (ˌəʊvəsəbˈskraɪb) *vb.* (*tr.; often passive*) to subscribe or apply for in excess of available supply.

overt (ˈəʊvɜːt, əʊˈvɜːt) *adj.* **1.** open to view; observable. **2.** *Law.* open; deliberate. [C14: via OF, < *ovrir* to open, < L *aperīre*] —ˈ**overtly** *adv.*

overtake (ˌəʊvəˈteɪk) *vb.* **-taking, -took, -taken.** **1.** *Chiefly Brit.* to move past (another vehicle or person) travelling in the same direction. **2.** (*tr.*) to pass or do better than, after catching up with. **3.** (*tr.*) to come upon suddenly or unexpectedly:

ˌ**overpreˈcise** *adj.*
ˌ**overˈprice** *vb.*
ˌ**overproˈduce** *vb.*
ˌ**overproˈduction** *n.*
ˌ**overproˈtective** *adj.*
ˌ**overˈproud** *adj.*
ˌ**overˈpubliˌcize** *or* **-ise** *vb.*
ˌ**overreˈliance** *n.*
ˌ**overˈrighteous** *adj.*
ˌ**overˈripe** *adj.*
ˌ**overroˈmantiˌcize** *or* **-ise** *vb.*
ˌ**overˈsceptical** *adj.*
ˌ**overˈscrupulous** *adj.*
ˌ**overˈsensitive** *adj.*
ˌ**overˈsimpliˌfy** *vb.*
ˌ**overˈsleep** *vb.*
ˈ**overˌsleeve** *n.*
ˌ**oversoˈlicitous** *adj.*
ˌ**overˈsparing** *adj.*
ˌ**overˈspecialˌize** *or* **-ˌise** *vb.*
ˌ**overˈspread** *vb.*
ˌ**overˈstaff** *vb.*
ˌ**overˈsteer** *vb.*
ˌ**overˈstimuˌlate** *vb.*
ˌ**overˈstock** *vb.*
ˌ**overˈstrain** *vb.*
ˌ**overˈstretch** *vb.*
ˌ**overˈstrict** *adj.*
ˌ**overˈsubtle** *adj.*
ˌ**oversupˈply** *vb., n.*
ˌ**oversusˈceptible** *adj.*
ˌ**oversusˈpicious** *adj.*

night overtook him. **4.** (*tr.*) to catch up with; draw level with.

overtax (ˌəʊvəˈtæks) *vb.* (*tr.*) **1.** to tax too heavily. **2.** to impose too great a strain on.

overthrow *vb.* (ˌəʊvəˈθrəʊ), **-throwing, -threw, -thrown.** **1.** (*tr.*) to effect the downfall or destruction of (a ruler, institution, etc.), esp. by force. **2.** (*tr.*) to throw or turn over. **3.** to throw (something, esp. a ball) too far. ~*n.* (ˈəʊvəˌθrəʊ). **4.** downfall; destruction. **5.** *Cricket.* **a.** a ball thrown back too far by a fielder. **b.** a run scored because of this.

overthrust (ˈəʊvəˌθrʌst) *n. Geol.* a reverse fault in which the rocks on the upper surface of a fault plane have moved over the rocks on the lower surface.

overtime *n.* (ˈəʊvəˌtaɪm). **1. a.** work at a regular job done in addition to regular working hours. **b.** (*as modifier*): *overtime pay.* **2.** the rate of pay established for such work. **3.** time in excess of a set period. **4.** *Sport, U.S. & Canad.* extra time. ~*adv.* (ˈəʊvəˌtaɪm). **5.** beyond the regular or stipulated time. ~*vb.* (ˌəʊvəˈtaɪm). **6.** (*tr.*) to exceed the required time for (a photographic exposure, etc.).

overtone (ˈəʊvəˌtəʊn) *n.* **1.** (*often pl.*) additional meaning or nuance: *overtones of despair.* **2.** *Music, acoustics.* any of the tones, with the exception of the fundamental, that constitute a musical sound and contribute to its quality.

overture (ˈəʊvəˌtjʊə) *n.* **1.** *Music.* **a.** a piece of orchestral music that is played at the beginning of an opera or oratorio, often containing the main musical themes of the work. **b.** a one-movement orchestral piece, usually having a descriptive or evocative title. **2.** (*often pl.*) a proposal, act, or gesture initiating a relationship, negotiation, etc. **3.** something that introduces what follows. ~*vb.* (*tr.*) **4.** to make or present an overture to. **5.** to introduce with an overture. [C14: via OF < LL *apertūra* opening, < L *aperīre* to open]

overturn *vb.* (ˌəʊvəˈtɜːn). **1.** to turn or cause to turn from an upright or normal position. **2.** (*tr.*) to overthrow or destroy. **3.** (*tr.*) to invalidate; reverse. ~*n.* (ˈəʊvəˌtɜːn). **4.** the act of overturning or the state of being overturned.

overview (ˈəʊvəˌvjuː) *n.* a general survey.

overweening (ˌəʊvəˈwiːnɪŋ) *adj.* **1.** (of a person) excessively arrogant or presumptuous. **2.** (of opinions, appetites, etc.) excessive; immoderate. [C14: < OVER + *weening* < OE *wēnan* WEEN] —ˌ**overˈweeningness** *n.*

overweight *adj.* (ˌəʊvəˈweɪt). **1.** weighing more than is usual, allowed, or healthy. ~*n.* (ˈəʊvəˌweɪt). **2.** extra or excess weight. ~*vb.* (ˌəʊvəˈweɪt). (*tr.*) **3.** to give too much emphasis or consideration to. **4.** to add too much weight to. **5.** to weigh down.

overwhelm (ˌəʊvəˈwɛlm) *vb.* (*tr.*) **1.** to overpower the thoughts, emotions, or senses of. **2.** to overcome with irresistible force. **3.** to cover over or bury completely. **4.** to weigh or rest upon overpoweringly. —ˌ**overˈwhelming** *adj.*

overwind (ˌəʊvəˈwaɪnd) *vb.* **-winding, -wound.** (*tr.*) to wind (a watch, etc.) beyond the proper limit.

overwork *vb.* (ˌəʊvəˈwɜːk). (*mainly tr.*) **1.** (*also intr.*) to work too hard or too long. **2.** to use too much: *to overwork an excuse.* **3.** to decorate the surface of. ~*n.* (ˈəʊvəˌwɜːk). **4.** excessive or excessively tiring work.

overwrite (ˌəʊvəˈraɪt) *vb.* **-writing, -wrote, -written.** **1.** to write (something) in an excessively ornate style. **2.** to write too much about (someone or something). **3.** to write on top of (other writing). **4.** to record on a storage medium, such as a magnetic disk, thus destroying what was originally recorded there.

overwrought (ˌəʊvəˈrɔːt) *adj.* **1.** full of nervous tension; agitated. **2.** too elaborate; fussy: *an overwrought style.* **3.** (*often postpositive* and foll. by *with*) with the surface decorated or adorned.

ovi- *or* **ovo-** *combining form.* egg or ovum: *oviform; ovoviviparous.* [< L *ōvum*]

oviduct (ˈɒvɪˌdʌkt, ˈəʊ-) *n.* the tube through which ova are conveyed from an ovary. Also called (in mammals): **Fallopian tube.** —**oviducal** (ˌɒvɪˈdjuːkᵊl, ˌəʊ-) *or* ˌ**oviˈductal** *adj.*

oviform (ˈəʊvɪˌfɔːm) *adj. Biol.* shaped like an egg.

ovine (ˈəʊvaɪn) *adj.* of, relating to, or resembling a sheep. [C19: < LL *ovīnus*, < L *ovis* sheep]

oviparous (əʊˈvɪpərəs) *adj.* (of fishes, reptiles, birds, etc.) producing eggs that hatch outside the body of the mother. Cf. **ovoviviparous, viviparous** (sense 1). —**oviparity** (ˌəʊvɪˈpærɪtɪ) *n.* —**oˈviparously** *adv.*

ovipositor (ˌəʊvɪˈpɒzɪtə) *n.* **1.** the egg-laying organ of most female insects, consisting of a pair of specialized appendages at the end of the abdomen. **2.** a similar organ in certain female fishes, formed by an extension of the edges of the genital opening. [C19:< OVI- + L *positor*, < *ponere* to place] —ˌ**oviˈposit** *vb.* (*intr.*)

ovoid (ˈəʊvɔɪd) *adj.* **1.** egg-shaped. ~*n.* **2.** something that is ovoid.

ovoviviparous (ˌəʊvəʊvaɪˈvɪpərəs) *adj.* (of certain reptiles, fishes, etc.) producing eggs that hatch within the body of the mother. Cf. **oviparous, viviparous** (sense 1). —**ovoviviparity** (ˌəʊvəʊˌvaɪvɪˈpærɪtɪ) *n.*

ovulate (ˈɒvjʊˌleɪt) *vb.* (*intr.*) to produce or discharge eggs from an ovary. [C19: < OVULE] —ˌ**ovuˈlation** *n.*

ovule (ˈɒvjuːl) *n.* **1.** a small body in seed-bearing plants that contains the egg cell and develops into the seed after fertilization. **2.** *Zool.* an immature ovum. [C19: via F < Med. L *ōvulum* a little egg, < L *ōvum* egg] —ˈ**ovular** *adj.*

ovum (ˈəʊvəm) *n., pl.* **ova.** an unfertilized female gamete; egg cell. [< L: egg]

ow (aʊ) *interj.* an exclamation of pain.

owe (əʊ) *vb.* (*mainly tr.*) **1.** to be under an obligation to pay (someone) to the amount of. **2.** (*intr.*) to be in debt: *he still owes for his house.* **3.** (often foll. by *to*) to have as a result (of). **4.** to feel the need or obligation to do, give, etc. **5.** to hold or maintain in the mind or heart (esp. in **owe a grudge**). [OE *āgan* to have (C12: to have to)]

Owen gun (ˈəʊɪn) *n.* a type of simple, recoil-operated sub-machine-gun first used by Australian forces in World War II.

owing (ˈəʊɪŋ) *adj.* **1.** (*postpositive*) owed; due. **2.** **owing to.** because of or on account of.

▷ **Usage.** See at **due.**

owl (aʊl) *n.* **1.** a nocturnal bird of prey having large front-facing eyes, a small hooked bill, soft feathers, and a short neck. **2.** any of various breeds of owl-like fancy domestic pigeon. **3.** a person who looks or behaves like an owl, esp. in having a solemn manner. [OE *ūle*] —ˈ**owlish** *adj.* —ˈ**owl-ˌlike** *adj.*

owlet (ˈaʊlɪt) *n.* a young or nestling owl.

own (əʊn) *determiner.* (*preceded by a possessive*) **1. a.** (intensifier): *John's own idea.* **b.** (*as pron.*): *I'll use my own.* **2.** on behalf of oneself or in relation to oneself: *he is his own worst enemy.* **3.** **come into one's own. a.** to fulfil one's potential. **b.** to receive what is due to one. **4. hold one's own.** to maintain one's situation or position, esp. in spite of opposition or difficulty. **5. on one's own. a.** without help. **b.** by oneself; alone. ~*vb.* **6.** (*tr.*) to have as one's possession. **7.** (when *intr.*, often foll. by *up, to,* or *up to*) to confess or admit; acknowledge. **8.** (*tr.; takes a clause as object*) *Now rare.* to concede: *I own that you are right.* [OE *āgen*, orig. p.p. of *āgan* to have. See OWE] —ˈ**owner** *n.* —ˈ**ownership** *n.*

ˌ**overˈtechnical** *adj.*
ˌ**overˈtire** *vb.*
ˌ**overˈtop** *vb.*
ˌ**overˈtrade** *vb.*
ˌ**overˈtrain** *vb.*
ˌ**overˈtrump** *vb.*
ˌ**overˈuse** *vb., n.*
ˌ**overˈvalue** *vb.*
ˌ**overˈwater** *vb.*
ˌ**overˈweigh** *vb.*
ˌ**overˈwilling** *adj.*
ˌ**overˈzealous** *adj.*

own brand *n.* a product which displays the name of the retailer rather than the producer.

owner-occupier *n.* someone who has bought or is buying the house in which he lives.

own goal *n.* **1.** *Soccer.* a goal scored by a player accidentally kicking the ball into his own team's net. **2.** *Inf.* any action that results in disadvantage to the person who took it or to his associates.

ox (ɒks) *n., pl.* **oxen. 1.** an adult castrated male of any domesticated species of cattle used for draught work and meat. **2.** any bovine mammal, esp. any of the domestic cattle. [OE *oxa*]

oxalic acid (ɒk'sælɪk) *n.* a colourless poisonous crystalline acid found in many plants: used as a bleach and a cleansing agent for metals. Formula: $(COOH)_2$. [C18: < F *oxalique,* < L *oxalis* garden sorrel; see OXALIS]

oxalis ('ɒksəlɪs, ɒk'sælɪs) *n.* a plant having clover-like leaves which contain oxalic acid and white, pink, red, or yellow flowers. See also **wood sorrel.** [C18: via L < Gk: sorrel, sour wine, < *oxus* acid, sharp]

oxblood ('ɒks,blʌd) *or* **oxblood red** *adj.* of a dark reddish-brown colour.

oxbow ('ɒks,bəʊ) *n.* **1.** a U-shaped piece of wood fitted under and around the neck of a harnessed ox and attached to the yoke. **2.** Also called: **oxbow lake.** a small curved lake lying on the flood plain of a river and constituting the remnant of a former meander.

Oxbridge ('ɒks,brɪdʒ) *n.* **a.** the British universities of Oxford and Cambridge, esp. considered as ancient and prestigious academic institutions, bastions of privilege and superiority, etc. **b.** (*as modifier*): *Oxbridge arrogance.*

oxen ('ɒksən) *n.* the plural of **ox.**

oxeye ('ɒks,aɪ) *n.* **1.** a Eurasian composite plant having daisy-like flower heads with yellow rays and dark centres. **2.** any of various North American plants having daisy-like flowers. **3. oxeye daisy.** a type of hardy perennial chrysanthemum.

ox-eyed *adj.* having large round eyes, like those of an ox.

Oxfam ('ɒks,fæm) *n. acronym for* Oxford Committee for Famine Relief.

Oxford ('ɒksfəd) *n.* (*sometimes not cap.*) **1.** a type of stout laced shoe with a low heel. **2.** a lightweight fabric of plain or twill weave used for men's shirts, etc. [<*Oxford,* city in S England]

Oxford bags *pl. n.* trousers with very wide baggy legs.

Oxford blue *n.* **1. a.** a dark blue colour. **b.** (*as adj.*): *an Oxford-blue scarf.* **2.** a person who has been awarded a blue from Oxford University.

Oxford Movement *n.* a movement within the Church of England that began at Oxford in 1833. It affirmed the continuity of the Church with early Christianity and strove to restore the High-Church ideals of the 17th century. Also called: **Tractarianism.**

oxidant ('ɒksɪdənt) *n.* a substance that acts or is used as an oxidizing agent. Also called (esp. in rocketry): **oxidizer.**

oxidation (,ɒksɪ'deɪʃən) *n.* **a.** the act or process of oxidizing. **b.** (*as modifier*): *an oxidation state.* —**'oxi,date** *vb.* —**,oxi'dational** *adj.* —**'oxi,dative** *adj.*

oxidation-reduction *n.* **a.** a reversible chemical process usually involving the transfer of electrons, in which one reaction is an oxidation and the reverse reaction is a reduction. **b.** (*as modifier*): *an oxidation-reduction reaction.* ~Also: **redox.**

oxide ('ɒksaɪd) *n.* **1.** any compound of oxygen with another element. **2.** any organic compound in which an oxygen atom is bound to two alkyl groups; an ether. [C18: < F, < *ox(ygène)* + *(ac)ide*]

oxidize *or* **-ise** ('ɒksɪ,daɪz) *vb.* **1.** to undergo or cause to undergo a chemical reaction with oxygen, as in formation of an oxide. **2.** to form or cause to form a layer of metal oxide, as in rusting. **3.** to lose or cause to lose hydrogen atoms. **4.** to undergo or cause to undergo a decrease in the number of electrons. —**,oxidi'zation** *or* **-i'sation** *n.*

oxidizing agent *n. Chem.* a substance that oxidizes another substance, being itself reduced in the process.

oxlip ('ɒks,lɪp) *n.* **1.** a Eurasian woodland plant, with small drooping pale yellow flowers. **2.** a similar and related plant that is a natural hybrid between the cowslip and primrose. [OE *oxanslyppe,* lit.: ox's slippery dropping; see SLIP[3]]

Oxon *abbrev. for* Oxfordshire. [< L *Oxonia*]

Oxon. *abbrev. for* (in degree titles, etc.) of Oxford. [< L *Oxoniensis*]

Oxonian (ɒk'səʊnɪən) *adj.* **1.** of or relating to Oxford or Oxford University. ~*n.* **2.** a member of Oxford University. **3.** an inhabitant or native of Oxford.

oxpecker ('ɒks,pɛkə) *n.* either of two African starlings, having flattened bills with which they obtain food from the hides of cattle. Also called: **tick-bird.**

oxtail ('ɒks,teɪl) *n.* the skinned tail of an ox, used esp. in soups and stews.

oxter ('əʊkstə) *n. Scot., Irish, & N English dialect.* the armpit. [C16: < OE *oxta*]

oxtongue ('ɒks,tʌŋ) *n.* **1.** any of various Eurasian composite plants having oblong bristly leaves and clusters of dandelion-like flowers. **2.** any of various other plants having bristly tongue-shaped leaves. **3.** the tongue of an ox, braised or boiled as food.

oxy-[1] *combining form.* denoting something sharp; acute: *oxytone.* [< Gk, < *oxus*]

oxy-[2] *combining form.* containing or using oxygen: *oxyacetylene.*

oxyacetylene (,ɒksɪə'sɛtɪ,liːn) *n.* **a.** a mixture of oxygen and acetylene; used in a blowpipe for cutting or welding metals at high temperatures. **b.** (*as modifier*): *an oxyacetylene burner.*

oxyacid (,ɒksɪ'æsɪd) *n.* any acid that contains oxygen. Also called: **oxygen acid.**

oxygen ('ɒksɪdʒən) *n.* **a.** a colourless odourless highly reactive gaseous element: the most abundant element in the earth's crust. Symbol: O; atomic no.: 8; atomic wt.: 15.9994. **b.** (*as modifier*): *an oxygen mask.* —**oxygenic** (,ɒksɪ'dʒɛnɪk) *or* **oxygenous** (ɒk'sɪdʒɪnəs) *adj.*

oxygenate ('ɒksɪdʒɪ,neɪt) *or* **oxygenize** *or* **-ise** *vb.* to enrich or be enriched with oxygen: *to oxygenate blood.* —**,oxygen'ation** *n.* —**'oxyge-n,izer** *or* **-iser** *n.*

oxygen tent *n. Med.* a transparent enclosure covering a bedridden patient, into which oxygen is released to help maintain respiration.

oxyhaemoglobin (,ɒksɪ,hiːməʊ'gləʊbɪn) *n. Biochem.* the bright red product formed when oxygen from the lungs combines with haemoglobin in the blood.

oxyhydrogen (,ɒksɪ'haɪdrɪdʒən) *n.* **a.** a mixture of hydrogen and oxygen used to provide an intense flame for welding. **b.** (*as modifier*): *an oxyhydrogen blowpipe.*

oxymoron (,ɒksɪ'mɔːrɒn) *n., pl.* **-mora** (-'mɔːrə). *Rhetoric.* an epigrammatic effect, by which contradictory terms are used in conjunction: *beautiful tyrant.* [C17: via NL < Gk *oxumōron,* < *oxus* sharp + *mōros* stupid]

oyer and terminer ('ɔɪə; 'tɜːmɪnə) *n.* **1.** *English law.* (formerly) a commission issued to judges to try cases on assize. **2.** the court in which such a hearing was held. [C15: < Anglo-Norman, < *oyer* to hear + *terminer* to judge]

oyez *or* **oyes** ('əʊ'jɛs, -'jɛz) *sentence substitute.* **1.** a cry, usually uttered three times, by a public crier or court official for silence and attention before making a proclamation. ~*n.* **2.** such a cry. [C15: via Anglo-Norman < OF *oiez!* hear!]

oyster ('ɔɪstə) *n.* **1. a.** an edible marine bivalve mollusc having a rough irregularly shaped shell and occurring on the sea bed, mostly in coastal waters. **b.** (*as modifier*): *oyster farm; oyster knife.* **2.** any of various similar and related molluscs, such as the pearl oyster and the saddle oyster. **3.** the oyster-shaped piece of dark meat in the hollow of the pelvic bone of a fowl. **4.**

something from which advantage, delight, profit, etc., may be derived: *the world is his oyster.* **5.** *Inf.* a very uncommunicative person. ~*vb.* **6.** (*intr.*) to dredge for, gather, or raise oysters. [C14 *oistre,* < OF *uistre,* < L *ostrea,* < Gk *ostreon;* rel. to Gk *osteon* bone, *ostrakon* shell]

oyster bed *n.* a place, esp. on the sea bed, where oysters breed and grow naturally or are cultivated for food or pearls. Also called: **oyster bank, oyster park.**

oystercatcher (ˈɔɪstəˌkætʃə) *n.* a shore bird having a black or black-and-white plumage and a long stout laterally compressed red bill.

oyster crab *n.* any of several small soft-bodied crabs that live as commensals in the mantles of oysters.

oyster plant *n.* **1.** another name for **salsify** (sense 1). **2.** Also called: **sea lungwort.** a prostrate coastal plant with clusters of blue flowers.

oz *or* **oz.** *abbrev. for* ounce. [< It. *onza*]

Oz (ɒz) *n. Austral. sl.* Australia.

Ozalid (ˈɒzəlɪd) *n.* **1.** *Trademark.* a method of duplicating type matter, illustrations, etc., when printed on translucent paper. **2.** a reproduction produced by this method.

ozocerite *or* **ozokerite** (əʊˈzəʊkəˌraɪt) *n.* a brown or greyish wax that occurs associated with petroleum and is used for making candles and waxed paper. [C19: < G *Ozokerit,* < Gk *ozein* odour + *kēros* beeswax]

ozone (ˈəʊzəʊn, əʊˈzəʊn) *n.* **1.** a colourless gas with a chlorine-like odour, formed by an electric discharge in oxygen: a strong oxidizing agent, used in bleaching, sterilizing water, purifying air, etc. Formula: O_3. **2.** *Inf.* clean bracing air, as found at the seaside. [C19: < G *Ozon,* < Gk: smell] —**ozonic** (əʊˈzɒnɪk) *or* **ˈozonous** *adj.*

ozonize *or* **-ise** (ˈəʊzəʊˌnaɪz) *vb.* (*tr.*) **1.** to convert (oxygen) into ozone. **2.** to treat (a substance) with ozone. —ˌ**ozoniˈzation** *or* **-iˈsation** *n.* —ˈ**ozonˌizer** *or* **-ˌiser** *n.*

ozonosphere (əʊˈzəʊnəˌsfɪə, -ˈzɒnə-) *or* **ozone layer** *n.* a region of ozone concentration in the stratosphere that absorbs high-energy solar ultraviolet rays.

P

p *or* **P** (piː) *n., pl.* **p's, P's,** or **Ps.** **1.** the 16th letter of the English alphabet. **2.** a speech sound represented by this letter. **3. mind one's p's and q's.** to be careful to behave correctly and use polite or suitable language.

p *symbol for:* **1.** (in Britain) penny *or* pence. **2.** *Music.* piano: an instruction to play quietly. **3.** *Physics.* pico-. **4.** *Physics.* **a.** momentum. **b.** proton. **c.** pressure.

P *symbol for:* **1.** *Chem.* phosphorus. **2.** *Physics.* **a.** parity. **b.** poise. **c.** power. **d.** pressure. **3.** (on road signs) parking. **4.** *Chess.* pawn. **5.** *Currency.* **a.** peseta. **b.** peso. **6.** (of a medicine or drug) available only from a chemist's shop, but not requiring a prescription to obtain it.

p. *abbrev. for:* **1.** (*pl.* **pp.**) page. **2.** part. **3.** participle. **4.** past. **5.** per. **6.** pint. **7.** pipe. **8.** population. **9.** post. [L: after] **10.** pro. [L: in favour of; for]

pa (pɑː) *n.* an informal word for **father.**

Pa *the chemical symbol for* protactinium.

PA *abbrev. for:* **1.** personal assistant. **2.** *Mil.* Post Adjutant. **3.** power of attorney. **4.** press agent. **5.** Press Association. **6.** private account. **7.** public-address system. **8.** publicity agent. **9.** Publishers Association. **10.** purchasing agent.

p.a. *abbrev. for* per annum. [L: yearly]

pabulum (ˈpæbjʊləm) *n. Rare.* **1.** food. **2.** food for thought. [C17: < L, < *pascere* to feed]

PABX (in Britain) *abbrev. for* private automatic branch exchange. See also **PBX.**

paca (ˈpɑːkə, ˈpækə) *n.* a large burrowing rodent of Central and South America, having white-spotted brown fur. [C17: < Sp., < Amerind]

pace[1] (peɪs) *n.* **1. a.** a single step in walking. **b.** the distance covered by a step. **2.** a measure of length equal to the average length of a stride, approximately 3 feet. **3.** speed of movement, esp. of walking or running. **4.** rate or style of proceeding at some activity: *to live at a fast pace.* **5.** manner or action of stepping, walking, etc.; gait. **6.** any of the manners in which a horse or other quadruped walks or runs. **7.** a manner of moving, sometimes developed in the horse, in which the two legs on the same side are moved at the same time. **8. keep pace with.** to proceed at the same speed as. **9. put (someone) through his paces.** to test the ability of (someone). **10. set the pace.** to determine the rate at which a group runs or walks or proceeds at some other activity. ~*vb.* **11.** (*tr.*) to set or determine the pace for, as in a race. **12.** (often foll. by *about, up and down,* etc.) to walk with regular slow or fast paces, as in boredom, agitation, etc.: *to pace the room.* **13.** (*tr.;* often foll. by *out*) to measure by paces: *to pace out the distance.* **14.** (*intr.*) to walk with slow regular strides. **15.** (*intr.*) (of a horse) to move at the pace (the specially developed gait). [C13: via OF < L *passūs* step, < *pandere* to extend (the legs as in walking)]

pace[2] (ˈpeɪsɪ; *Latin* ˈpɑːkɛ) *prep.* with due deference to: used to acknowledge politely someone who disagrees. [C19: < L, < *pāx* peace]

pacemaker (ˈpeɪsˌmeɪkə) *n.* **1.** a person, horse, vehicle, etc., used in a race or speed trial to set the pace. **2.** a person, organization, etc., regarded as being the leader in a particular activity. **3.** Also called: **cardiac pacemaker.** a small area of specialized tissue within the wall of the heart whose spontaneous electrical activity initiates and controls the heartbeat. **4.** Also called: **artificial pacemaker.** an electronic device to assume the functions of the natural cardiac pacemaker.

pacer (ˈpeɪsə) *n.* **1.** a horse trained to move at a special gait. **2.** another word for **pacemaker** (sense 1).

pacesetter (ˈpeɪsˌsɛtə) *n.* another word for **pacemaker** (senses 1, 2).

paceway (ˈpeɪsˌweɪ) *n. Austral.* a racecourse for trotting and pacing.

pachisi (pəˈtʃiːzɪ) *n.* an Indian game somewhat resembling backgammon, played on a cruciform board using six cowries as dice. [C18: < Hindi, < *pacīs* twenty-five (the highest throw)]

pachyderm (ˈpækɪˌdɜːm) *n.* any very large thick-skinned mammal, such as an elephant, rhinoceros, or hippopotamus. [C19: < F *pachyderme,* < Gk *pakhudermos,* < *pakhus* thick + *derma* skin] —ˌ**pachyˈdermatous** *adj.*

pacific (pəˈsɪfɪk) *adj.* **1.** tending or conducive to peace; conciliatory. **2.** not aggressive. **3.** free from conflict; peaceful. [C16: < OF, < L *pācificus,* < *pāx* peace + *facere* to make] —**paˈcifically** *adv.*

Pacific (pəˈsɪfɪk) *n.* **1. the.** short for **Pacific Ocean.** ~*adj.* **2.** of or relating to the Pacific Ocean or its islands.

Pacific Ocean *n.* the world's largest and deepest ocean, lying between Asia and Australia and North and South America.

pacifier (ˈpæsɪˌfaɪə) *n.* **1.** a person or thing that pacifies. **2.** *U.S. & Canad.* a baby's dummy or teething ring.

pacifism (ˈpæsɪˌfɪzəm) *n.* **1.** the belief that violence of any kind is unjustifiable and that one should not participate in war, etc. **2.** the belief that international disputes can be settled by arbitration rather than war. —ˈ**pacifist** *n., adj.*

pacify (ˈpæsɪˌfaɪ) *vb.* **-fying, -fied.** (*tr.*) **1.** to calm the anger or agitation of; mollify. **2.** to restore to peace or order. [C15: < OF *pacifier;* see PACIFIC] —ˈ**paciˌfiable** *adj.* —**pacification** (ˌpæsɪfɪˈkeɪʃən) *n.*

pack[1] (pæk) *n.* **1. a.** a bundle or load, esp. one carried on the back. **b.** (*as modifier*): *a pack animal.* **2.** a collected amount of anything. **3.** a complete set of similar things, esp. a set of 52 playing cards. **4.** a group of animals of the same kind, esp. hunting animals: *a pack of hounds.* **5.** any group or band that associates together, esp. for criminal purposes. **6.** any group or set regarded dismissively: *a pack of fools; a pack of lies.* **7.** *Rugby.* the forwards of a team. **8.** the basic organizational unit of Cub Scouts and Brownie Guides. **9.** a small package, carton, or container, used to retail commodities, esp. foodstuffs, cigarettes, etc. **10.** short for **pack ice. 11.** the quantity of something, such as food, packaged for preservation. **12.** *Med.* a sheet or blanket, either damp or dry, for wrapping about the body, esp. for its soothing effect. **13.** another name for **rucksack** *or* **backpack. 14.** Also called: **face pack.** a cream treatment that cleanses and tones the skin. **15.** a parachute folded and ready for use. **16. go to the pack.** *Austral. & N.Z. inf.* to fall into a worse state or condition. **17.** *Computers.* another name for **deck** (sense 5). ~*vb.* **18.** to place or arrange (articles) in (a container), such as clothes in a suitcase. **19.** (*tr.*) to roll up into a bundle. **20.** (when *passive,* often foll. by *out*) to press tightly together; cram: *the audience packed into the foyer; the hall was packed out.* **21.** to form (snow, ice, etc.) into a hard compact mass or (of snow, etc.) to become compacted. **22.** (*tr.*) to press in or cover tightly. **23.** (*tr.*) to load (a horse, donkey, etc.) with a burden. **24.** (often foll. by *off* or *away*) to send away or go away, esp. hastily. **25.** (*tr.*) to seal (a joint) by inserting a layer of compressible material between the faces. **26.** (*tr.*) *Med.* to treat with a pack. **27.** (*tr.*) *Sl.* to be capable of inflicting (a blow, etc.): *he packs a mean punch.* **28.** (*tr.*) *U.S. inf.* to carry or wear habitually: *he packs a gun.* **29.** (*tr.;* often foll. by *in, into, to,* etc.) *U.S., Canad., & N.Z.* to carry (goods, etc.), esp. on the back. **30. send packing.** *Inf.* to dismiss peremptorily. ~See also **pack in, pack up.** [C13: <?] —ˈ**packable** *adj.*

pack[2] (pæk) *vb.* (*tr.*) to fill (a legislative body, committee, etc.) with one's own supporters: *to pack a jury.* [C16: ? changed < PACT]

package (ˈpækɪdʒ) *n.* **1.** any wrapped or boxed object or group of objects. **2. a.** a proposition, offer, or thing for sale in which separate items are offered together as a unit. **b.** (*as modifier*): *a package holiday; a package deal.* **3.** the act or process of packing or packaging. **4.** *Computers.* a set of programs designed for a specific type of problem. **5.** the usual U.S. and Canad. word for **packet** (sense 1). ~*vb.* (*tr.*) **6.** to wrap in or put into a package. **7.** to design and produce a package for (retail goods). **8.** to group (separate items) together as a single unit. —ˈ**packager** *n.*

packaging (ˈpækɪdʒɪŋ) *n.* **1.** the box or wrapping in which a product is offered for sale. **2.** the presentation of a person, product, etc., to the public in a way designed to build up a favourable image.

pack drill *n.* a military punishment of marching about carrying a full pack of equipment.

packer (ˈpækə) *n.* **1.** a person or company whose business is to pack goods, esp. food: *a meat packer.* **2.** a person or machine that packs.

packet (ˈpækɪt) *n.* **1.** a small or medium-sized container of cardboard, paper, etc., often together with its contents: *a packet of biscuits.* Usual U.S. and Canad. word: **package. 2.** a small package; parcel. **3.** Also called: **packet boat.** a boat that transports mail, passengers, goods, etc., on a fixed short route. **4.** *Sl.* a large sum of money: *to cost a packet.* ~*vb.* **5.** (*tr.*) to wrap up in a packet or as a packet. [C16: < OF *pacquet,* < *pacquer* to pack, < ODu. *pak* a pack]

packhorse (ˈpækˌhɔːs) *n.* a horse used to transport goods, equipment, etc.

pack ice *n.* a large area of floating ice, consisting of pieces that have become massed together.

pack in *vb.* (*tr., adv.*) *Brit. & N.Z. inf.* to stop doing (something) (esp. in **pack it in**).

packing (ˈpækɪŋ) *n.* **1. a.** material used to cushion packed goods. **b.** (*as modifier*): *a packing needle.* **2.** the packaging of foodstuffs. **3.** any substance or material used to make joints watertight or gastight.

pack rat *n.* a rat of W North America, having a long tail that is furry in some species.

packsaddle (ˈpækˌsædᵊl) *n.* a saddle hung with packs, equipment, etc., used on a pack animal.

packthread (ˈpækˌθrɛd) *n.* a strong twine for sewing or tying up packages.

pack up *vb.* (*adv.*) **1.** to put (things) away in a proper or suitable place. **2.** *Inf.* to give up (an attempt) or stop doing (something). **3.** (*intr.*) (of an engine, etc.) to fail to operate; break down.

pact (pækt) *n.* an agreement or compact between two or more parties, nations, etc. [C15: < OF *pacte,* < L *pactum,* < *pacīscī* to agree]

pad[1] (pæd) *n.* **1.** a thick piece of soft material used to make something comfortable, give it shape, or protect it. **2.** Also called: **stamp pad, ink pad.** a block of firm absorbent material soaked with ink for transferring to a rubber stamp. **3.** Also called: **notepad, writing pad.** a number of sheets of paper fastened together along one edge. **4.** a flat piece of stiff material used to back a piece of blotting paper. **5. a.** the fleshy cushion-like underpart of the foot of a cat, dog, etc. **b.** any of the parts constituting such a structure. **6.** any of various level surfaces or flat-topped structures, such as a launch pad. **7.** the large flat floating leaf of the water lily. **8.** *Sl.* a person's residence. ~*vb.* **padding, padded.** (*tr.*) **9.** to line, stuff, or fill out with soft material, esp. in order to protect or shape. **10.** (often foll. by *out*) to inflate with irrelevant or false information: *to pad out a story.* [C16: <?]

pad[2] (pæd) *vb.* **padding, padded. 1.** (*intr.;* often foll. by *along, up,* etc.) to walk with a soft or muffled tread. **2.** (when *intr.,* often foll. by *around*) to travel (a route, etc.) on foot, esp. at a slow pace; tramp: *to pad around the country.* ~*n.* **3.** a dull soft sound, esp. of footsteps. [C16: ? < MDu. *paden,* < *pad* PATH]

padded cell *n.* a room, esp. one in a mental hospital, with padded surfaces in which violent inmates are placed.

padding (ˈpædɪŋ) *n.* **1.** any soft material used to pad clothes, etc. **2.** superfluous material put into a speech or written work to pad it out; waffle. **3.** inflated or false entries in a financial account, esp. an expense account.

paddle[1] (ˈpædᵊl) *n.* **1.** a short light oar with a flat blade at one or both ends, used without a rowlock. **2.** Also called: **float.** a blade of a water wheel or paddle wheel. **3.** a period of paddling: *to go for a paddle upstream.* **4. a.** a paddle wheel used to propel a boat. **b.** (*as modifier*): *a paddle steamer.* **5.** any of various instruments shaped like a paddle and used for beating, mixing, etc. **6.** a table-tennis bat. **7.** the flattened limb of a seal, turtle, etc., specialized for swimming. ~*vb.* **8.** to propel (a canoe, etc.) with a paddle. **9. paddle one's own canoe. a.** to be self-sufficient. **b.** to mind one's own business. **10.** (*tr.*) to stir or mix with or as if with a paddle. **11.** to row (a boat) steadily, but not at full pressure. **12.** (*intr.*) to swim with short rapid strokes, like a dog. **13.** (*tr.*) *U.S. & Canad. inf.* to spank. [C15: <?] —ˈ**paddler** *n.*

paddle[2] (ˈpædᵊl) *vb.* (*mainly intr.*) **1.** to walk or play barefoot in shallow water, mud, etc. **2.** to dabble the fingers, hands, or feet in water. **3.** to walk unsteadily, like a baby. **4.** (*tr.*) *Arch.* to fondle with the fingers. ~*n.* **5.** the act of paddling in water. [C16: <?] —ˈ**paddler** *n.*

paddle wheel *n.* a large wheel fitted with paddles, turned by an engine to propel a vessel.

paddock (ˈpædək) *n.* **1.** a small enclosed field, usually near a house or stable. **2.** (in horse racing) the enclosure in which horses are paraded and mounted before a race. **3.** *Austral. & N.Z.* any area of fenced land. [C17: var. of dialect *parrock,* < OE *pearruc* enclosure, of Gmc origin. See PARK]

paddy[1] (ˈpædɪ) *n., pl.* **-dies. 1.** Also called: **paddy field.** a field planted with rice. **2.** rice as a growing crop or when harvested but not yet milled. [< Malay *pādī*]

paddy[2] (ˈpædɪ) *n., pl.* **-dies.** *Brit. inf.* a fit of temper. [C19: < *Paddy* inf. name for an Irishman]

pademelon *or* **paddymelon** (ˈpædɪˌmɛlən) *n.* a small wallaby of coastal scrubby regions of Australia. [C19: of Abor. origin]

padlock (ˈpædˌlɒk) *n.* **1.** a detachable lock having a hinged or sliding shackle, which can be used to secure a door, lid, etc., by passing the shackle through rings or staples. ~*vb.* **2.** (*tr.*) to fasten as with a padlock. [C15 *pad,* <?]

padre (ˈpɑːdrɪ) *n. Inf.* (*sometimes cap.*) **1.** father: used to address or refer to a priest. **2.** a chaplain to the armed forces. [via Sp. or It. < L *pater* father]

padsaw (ˈpædˌsɔː) *n.* a small narrow saw used for cutting curves. [C19: < PAD[1] (in the sense: a handle that can be fitted to various tools) + SAW[1]]

paean *or U.S.* (*sometimes*) **pean** (ˈpiːən) *n.* **1.** a hymn sung in ancient Greece in thanksgiving to a deity. **2.** any song of praise. **3.** enthusiastic praise: *the film received a paean from the critics.* [C16: via L < Gk *paiān* hymn to Apollo, from his title *Paiān,* the physician of the gods]

paediatrician *or U.S.* **pediatrician** (ˌpiːdɪəˈtrɪʃən) *n.* a medical practitioner who specializes in paediatrics.

paediatrics *or U.S.* **pediatrics** (ˌpiːdɪˈætrɪks) *n.* (*functioning as sing.*) the branch of medical science concerned with children and their diseases. —ˌ**paediˈatric** *or U.S.* ˌ**pediˈatric** *adj.*

paedo-, *before a vowel* **paed-,** *or esp. U.S.* **pedo-, ped-** *combining form.* indicating a child or children: *paedophilia.* [< Gk *pais, paid-* child]

paedomorphosis (ˌpiːdəˈmɔːfəsɪs) *n.* the resemblance of adult animals to the young of their ancestors.

paedophilia *or esp. U.S.* **pedophilia** (ˌpiːdəʊˈfɪlɪə) *n.* the condition of being sexually attracted to children. —**paedophile** *or esp. U.S.* **pedophile** (ˈpiːdəʊˌfaɪl) *or* ˌ**paedoˈphiliˌac** *or esp. U.S.* ˌ**pedoˈphiliˌac** *n., adj.*

paella (paɪˈɛlə) *n., pl.* **-las** (-ləz). **1.** a Spanish dish made from rice, shellfish, chicken, and vegetables. **2.** the pan in which a paella is cooked. [< Catalan, < OF *paelle*, < L *patella* small pan]

paeony (ˈpiːənɪ) *n., pl.* **-nies.** a variant spelling of **peony.**

pagan (ˈpeɪgən) *n.* **1.** a member of a group professing any religion other than Christianity, Judaism, or Islam. **2.** a person without any religion; heathen. ~*adj.* **3.** of or relating to pagans. **4.** heathen; irreligious. [C14: < Church L *pāgānus* civilian (hence, not a soldier of Christ), < L: villager, < *pāgus* village] —ˈ**pagandom** *n.* —ˈ**paganish** *adj.* —ˈ**paganism** *n.*

paganize *or* **-ise** (ˈpeɪgəˌnaɪz) *vb.* to become pagan or convert to paganism.

page[1] (peɪdʒ) *n.* **1.** one side of one of the leaves of a book, newspaper, etc., or the written or printed matter it bears. **2.** such a leaf considered as a unit. **3.** an episode, phase, or period: *a glorious page in the revolution.* ~*vb.* **4.** another word for **paginate.** [C15: via OF < L *pāgina*]

page[2] (peɪdʒ) *n.* **1.** a boy employed to run errands, carry messages, etc., for the guests in a hotel, club, etc. **2.** a youth in attendance at official functions or ceremonies, esp. weddings. **3.** *Medieval history.* **a.** a boy in training for knighthood in personal attendance on a knight. **b.** a youth in the personal service of a person of rank. ~*vb.* (*tr.*) **4.** to call out the name of (a person), esp. by a loudspeaker system, so as to give him a message. **5.** to call (a person) by an electronic device, such as a bleep. **6.** to act as a page to or attend as a page. [C13: via OF < It. *paggio*, prob. < Gk *paidion* boy, < *pais* child]

pageant (ˈpædʒənt) *n.* **1.** an elaborate colourful display portraying scenes from history, etc. **2.** any magnificent or showy display, procession, etc. [C14: < Med. L *pāgina* scene of a play, < L: PAGE[1]]

pageantry (ˈpædʒəntrɪ) *n., pl.* **-ries. 1.** spectacular display or ceremony. **2.** *Arch.* pageants collectively.

pageboy (ˈpeɪdʒˌbɔɪ) *n.* **1.** a smooth medium-length hairstyle with the ends of the hair curled under. **2.** a less common word for **page**[2]**.**

pager (ˈpeɪdʒə) *n.* an electronic device used to call a person.

page-three *modifier. Brit.* denoting a scantily dressed attractive girl, as photographed on page three of some tabloid newspapers.

paginate (ˈpædʒɪˌneɪt) *vb.* (*tr.*) to number the pages of (a book, manuscript, etc.) in sequence. Cf. **foliate.** —ˌ**pagiˈnation** *n.*

pagoda (pəˈgəʊdə) *n.* an Indian or Far Eastern temple, esp. a tower, usually pyramidal and having many storeys. [C17: < Port. *pagode*, ult. < Sansk. *bhagavatī* divine]

pagoda tree *n.* a Chinese leguminous tree with ornamental white flowers.

paid (peɪd) *vb.* **1.** the past tense and past participle of **pay**[1]. **2. put paid to.** *Chiefly Brit. & N.Z.* to end or destroy: *breaking his leg put paid to his hopes of running in the Olympics.*

pail (peɪl) *n.* **1.** a bucket, esp. one made of wood or metal. **2.** Also called: **pailful.** the quantity that fills a pail. [OE *pægel*]

paillasse (ˈpælɪˌæs, ˌpælɪˈæs) *n.* a variant spelling (esp. U.S.) of **palliasse.**

pain (peɪn) *n.* **1.** the sensation of acute physical hurt or discomfort caused by injury, illness, etc. **2.** emotional suffering or mental distress. **3. on pain of.** subject to the penalty of. **4.** Also called: **pain in the neck.** *Inf.* a person or thing that is a nuisance. ~*vb.* (*tr.*) **5.** to cause (a person) hurt, grief, anxiety, etc. **6.** *Inf.* to annoy; irritate. ~See also **pains.** [C13: < OF *peine*, < L *poena* punishment, grief, < Gk *poinē* penalty] —ˈ**painless** *adj.*

pained (peɪnd) *adj.* having or expressing pain or distress, esp. mental or emotional distress.

painful (ˈpeɪnfʊl) *adj.* **1.** causing pain; distressing: *a painful duty.* **2.** affected with pain. **3.** tedious or difficult. **4.** *Inf.* extremely bad. —ˈ**painfully** *adv.* —ˈ**painfulness** *n.*

painkiller (ˈpeɪnˌkɪlə) *n.* **1.** an analgesic drug or agent. **2.** anything that relieves pain.

pains (peɪnz) *pl. n.* **1.** care or trouble (esp. in **take pains, be at pains to**). **2.** painful sensations experienced during contractions in childbirth; labour pains.

painstaking (ˈpeɪnzˌteɪkɪŋ) *adj.* extremely careful, esp. as to fine detail. —ˈ**painsˌtakingly** *adv.* —ˈ**painsˌtakingness** *n.*

paint (peɪnt) *n.* **1.** a substance used for decorating or protecting a surface, esp. a mixture consisting of a solid pigment suspended in a liquid that dries to form a hard coating. **2.** a dry film of paint on a surface. **3.** *Inf.* face make-up, such as rouge. **4.** short for **greasepaint.** ~*vb.* **5.** to make (a picture) of (a figure, landscape, etc.) with paint applied to a surface such as canvas. **6.** to coat (a surface, etc.) with paint, as in decorating. **7.** (*tr.*) to apply (liquid, etc.) onto (a surface): *she painted the cut with antiseptic.* **8.** (*tr.*) to apply make-up onto (the face, lips, etc.). **9.** (*tr.*) to describe vividly in words. **10. paint the town red.** *Inf.* to celebrate uninhibitedly. [C13: < OF *peint* painted, < *peindre* to paint, < L *pingere* to paint] —ˈ**painty** *adj.*

paintbox (ˈpeɪntˌbɒks) *n.* a box containing a tray of dry watercolour paints.

paintbrush (ˈpeɪntˌbrʌʃ) *n.* a brush used to apply paint.

painted lady *n.* a migratory butterfly with pale brownish-red mottled wings.

painter[1] (ˈpeɪntə) *n.* **1.** a person who paints surfaces as a trade. **2.** an artist who paints pictures. —ˈ**painterly** *adj.*

painter[2] (ˈpeɪntə) *n.* a line attached to the bow of a boat for tying it up. [C15: prob. < OF *penteur* strong rope]

painting (ˈpeɪntɪŋ) *n.* **1.** the art of applying paints to canvas, etc. **2.** a picture made in this way. **3.** the act of applying paint to a surface.

pair (pɛə) *n., pl.* **pairs** *or* (*functioning as sing. or pl.*) **pair. 1.** two identical or similar things matched for use together: *a pair of socks.* **2.** two persons, animals, things, etc., used or grouped together: *a pair of horses; a pair of scoundrels.* **3.** an object considered to be two identical or similar things joined together: *a pair of trousers.* **4.** two people joined in love or marriage. **5.** a male and a female animal of the same species kept for breeding purposes. **6.** *Parliament.* **a.** two opposed members who both agree not to vote on a specified motion. **b.** the agreement so made. **7.** two playing cards of the same rank or denomination. **8.** one member of a matching pair: *I can't find the pair to this glove.* ~*vb.* **9.** (often foll. by *off*) to arrange or fall into groups of twos. **10.** to group or be grouped in matching pairs. **11.** to join or be joined in marriage; mate or couple. **12.** (when *tr.*, *usually passive*) *Parliament.* to form or cause to form a pair. [C13: < OF *paire*, < L *paria* equal (things), < *pār* equal]

▷ **Usage.** Like other collective nouns, *pair* takes a singular or a plural verb according to whether it is seen as a unit or as a collection of two things: *the pair of cuff links was gratefully received; that pair* (the two of them) *are on very good terms.*

paisley (ˈpeɪzlɪ) *n.* **1.** a pattern of small curving shapes with intricate detailing. **2.** a soft fine wool fabric traditionally printed with this pattern. **3.** a shawl made of this fabric, popular in the late 19th century. **4.** (*modifier*) of or decorated with this pattern: *a paisley scarf.* [C19: after *Paisley*, town in Scotland]

pajamas (pəˈdʒɑːməz) *pl. n.* the U.S. spelling of **pyjamas.**

pakeha (ˈpɑːkɪˌhɑː) *n. N.Z.* a European, as distinct from a Maori: *Maori and pakeha.* [< Maori]

Paki (ˈpækɪ) *Brit. sl. derog.* ~*n., pl.* **Pakis. 1.** a Pakistani or person of Pakistani descent. ~*adj.* **2.** Pakistani or of Pakistani descent.

Pakistani (ˌpɑːkɪˈstɑːnɪ) *adj.* **1.** of or relating to

Pakistan, a country in the Indian subcontinent. ~*n., pl.* **-nis.** **2.** a native or inhabitant of Pakistan.

pakora (pəˈkɔːrə) *n.* an Indian dish consisting of pieces of vegetable, chicken, etc., dipped in spiced batter and deep-fried. [C20: < Hindi]

pal (pæl) *Inf.* ~*n.* **1.** a close friend; comrade. ~*vb.* **palling, palled.** **2.** (*intr.;* usually foll. by *with*) to associate as friends. [C17: < E Gypsy: brother, ult. < Sansk. *bhrātar* BROTHER]

PAL (pæl) *n. acronym for* phase alternation line: a colour-television broadcasting system used generally in Europe.

palace (ˈpælɪs) *n.* (*cap. when part of a name*) **1.** the official residence of a reigning monarch. **2.** the official residence of various high-ranking people, as of an archbishop. **3.** a large and richly furnished building resembling a royal palace. [C13: < OF *palais,* < L *Palātium* Palatine, the site of the palace of the emperors in Rome]

paladin (ˈpælədɪn) *n.* **1.** one of the legendary twelve peers of Charlemagne's court. **2.** a knightly champion. [C16: via F < It. *paladino,* < L *palātīnus* imperial official]

palaeo-, *before a vowel* **palae-** *or esp. U.S.* **paleo-, pale-** *combining form.* old, ancient, or prehistoric: *palaeography.* [< Gk *palaios* old]

palaeobotany *or U.S.* **paleobotany** (ˌpælɪəʊˈbɒtənɪ) *n.* the study of fossil plants. —ˌ**palaeoˈbotanist** *or U.S.* ˌ**paleoˈbotanist** *n.*

Palaeocene *or U.S.* **Paleocene** (ˈpælɪəʊˌsiːn) *adj.* **1.** of, denoting, or formed in the first epoch of the Tertiary period. ~*n.* **2. the.** the Palaeocene epoch or rock series. [C19: < F, < *paléo* PALAEO- + Gk *kainos* new]

palaeoclimatology *or U.S.* **paleoclimatology** (ˌpælɪəʊˌklaɪməˈtɒlədʒɪ) *n.* the study of climates of the geological past.

palaeography *or U.S.* **paleography** (ˌpælɪˈɒgrəfɪ) *n.* **1.** the study of the handwritings of the past, and often the manuscripts, etc., so that they may be dated, read, etc. **2.** a handwriting of the past. —ˌ**palaeˈographer** *or U.S.* ˌ**paleˈographer** *n.* —**palaeographic** (ˌpælɪəʊˈgræfɪk), ˌ**palaeoˈgraphical** *or U.S.* ˌ**paleoˈgraphic,** ˌ**paleoˈgraphical** *adj.*

Palaeolithic *or U.S.* **Paleolithic** (ˌpælɪəʊˈlɪθɪk) *n.* **1.** the period of the emergence of primitive man and the manufacture of unpolished chipped stone tools, about 2.5 million to 3 million years ago. ~*adj.* **2.** (*sometimes not cap.*) of or relating to this period.

palaeomagnetism *or U.S.* **paleomagnetism** (ˌpælɪəʊˈmægnɪtɪzəm) *n.* the study of the fossil magnetism in rocks, used to determine the past configuration of the earth's constituents.

palaeontology *or U.S.* **paleontology** (ˌpælɪɒnˈtɒlədʒɪ) *n.* the study of fossils to determine the structure and evolution of extinct animals and plants and the age and conditions of deposition of the rock strata in which they are found. [C19: < PALAEO- + ONTO- + -LOGY] —**palaeontological** *or U.S.* **paleontological** (ˌpælɪˌɒntəˈlɒdʒɪkᵊl) *adj.* —ˌ**palaeonˈtologist** *or U.S.* ˌ**paleonˈtologist** *n.*

Palaeozoic *or U.S.* **Paleozoic** (ˌpælɪəʊˈzəʊɪk) *adj.* **1.** of, denoting, or relating to an era of geological time that began with the Cambrian period and lasted until the end of the Permian period. ~*n.* **2. the.** the Palaeozoic era.

palanquin *or* **palankeen** (ˌpælənˈkiːn) *n.* a covered litter, formerly used in the Orient, carried on the shoulders of four men. [C16: < Port. *palanquim,* < Prakrit *pallanka,* < Sansk. *paryanka* couch]

palatable (ˈpælətəbᵊl) *adj.* **1.** pleasant to taste. **2.** acceptable or satisfactory. —ˌ**palataˈbility** *or* ˈ**palatableness** *n.* —ˈ**palatably** *adv.*

palatal (ˈpælətᵊl) *adj.* **1.** Also: **palatine.** of or relating to the palate. **2.** *Phonetics.* of, relating to, or denoting a speech sound articulated with the blade of the tongue touching the hard palate. ~*n.* **3.** Also called: **palatine.** the bony plate that forms the palate. **4.** *Phonetics.* a palatal speech sound, such as (j). —ˈ**palatally** *adv.*

palatalize *or* **-lise** (ˈpælətəˌlaɪz) *vb.* (*tr.*) to pronounce (a speech sound) with the blade of the tongue touching the palate. —ˌ**palataliˈzation** *or* **-liˈsation** *n.*

palate (ˈpælɪt) *n.* **1.** the roof of the mouth, separating the oral and nasal cavities. See **hard palate, soft palate.** **2.** the sense of taste: *she had no palate for the wine.* **3.** relish or enjoyment. [C14: < L *palātum,* ? of Etruscan origin]

palatial (pəˈleɪʃəl) *adj.* of, resembling, or suitable for a palace; sumptuous. —**paˈlatially** *adv.*

palatinate (pəˈlætɪnɪt) *n.* a territory ruled by a palatine prince or noble or count palatine.

palatine[1] (ˈpæləˌtaɪn) *adj.* **1.** (of an individual) possessing royal prerogatives in a territory. **2.** of or relating to a count palatine, county palatine, palatinate, or palatine. **3.** of or relating to a palace. ~*n.* **4.** *Feudal history.* the lord of a palatinate. **5.** any of various important officials at the late Roman, Merovingian, or Carolingian courts. [C15: via F < L *palātīnus* belonging to the palace, < *palātium;* see PALACE]

palatine[2] (ˈpæləˌtaɪn) *adj.* **1.** of the palate. ~*n.* **2.** either of two bones forming the hard palate. [C17: < F *palatin,* < L *palātum* palate]

palaver (pəˈlɑːvə) *n.* **1.** tedious or time-consuming business, esp. when of a formal nature: *all the palaver of filling in forms.* **2.** confused talk and activity; hubbub. **3.** (often used humorously) a conference. **4.** *Now rare.* talk intended to flatter or persuade. ~*vb.* **5.** (*intr.*) (often used humorously) to have a conference. **6.** (*intr.*) to talk confusedly. **7.** (*tr.*) to flatter or cajole. [C18: < Port. *palavra* talk, < L *parabola* PARABLE]

pale[1] (peɪl) *adj.* **1.** lacking brightness or colour: *pale morning light.* **2.** (of a colour) whitish. **3.** dim or wan: *the pale stars.* **4.** feeble: *a pale effort.* ~*vb.* **5.** to make or become pale or paler; blanch. **6.** (*intr.;* often foll. by *before*) to lose superiority (in comparison to): *her beauty paled before that of her hostess.* [C13: < OF *palle,* < L *pallidus,* < *pallēre* to look wan] —ˈ**palely** *adv.* —ˈ**paleness** *n.* —ˈ**palish** *adj.*

pale[2] (peɪl) *n.* **1.** a wooden post or strip used as an upright member in a fence. **2.** an enclosing barrier, esp. a fence made of pales. **3.** an area enclosed by a pale. **4.** *Heraldry.* a vertical stripe, usually in the centre of a shield. **5. beyond the pale.** outside the limits of social convention. [C14: < OF *pal,* < L *pālus* stake]

paleface (ˈpeɪlˌfeɪs) *n.* a derogatory term for a White person, said to have been used by North American Indians.

paleo- *or before a vowel* **pale-** *combining form.* variants (esp. U.S.) of **palaeo-.**

Palestine Liberation Organization (ˈpælɪˌstaɪn) *n.* an organization founded in 1964 with the aim of creating a state for Palestinian Arabs and removing the state of Israel.

Palestinian (ˌpælɪˈstɪnɪən) *adj.* **1.** of or relating to Palestine, a former country in the Middle East. ~*n.* **2.** a native or inhabitant of this area. **3.** a descendant of an inhabitant of this area, displaced when Israel became a state.

palette (ˈpælɪt) *n.* **1.** Also: **pallet.** a flat piece of wood, plastic, etc., used by artists as a surface on which to mix their paints. **2.** the range of colours characteristic of a particular artist, painting, or school of painting: *a restricted palette.* [C17: < F, dim. of *pale* shovel, < L *pala* spade]

palette *or* **pallet knife** *n.* a spatula with a thin flexible blade used in painting and cookery.

palfrey (ˈpɔːlfrɪ) *n. Arch.* a light saddle horse, esp. ridden by women. [C12: < OF *palefrei,* < Med. L, < LL *paraverēdus,* < Gk *para* beside + L *verēdus* light fleet horse, of Celtic origin]

Pali (ˈpɑːlɪ) *n.* an ancient language of India derived from Sanskrit; the language of the Buddhist scriptures. [C19: < Sansk. *pāli-bhāsa,* < *pāli* canon + *bhāsa* language, of Dravidian origin]

palimony (ˈpælɪmənɪ) *n. U.S.* alimony awarded to a nonmarried partner after the break-up of a long-term relationship. [C20: < PAL + ALIMONY]

palimpsest (ˈpælɪmpˌsɛst) *n.* **1.** a manuscript on which two or more texts have been written, each one being erased to make room for the next. ~*adj.* **2.** (of a text) written on a palimpsest. **3.**

(of a document, etc.) used as a palimpsest. [C17: < L *palimpsestus,* < Gk *palimpsēstos,* < *palin* again + *psēstos* rubbed smooth]

palindrome (ˈpælɪnˌdrəʊm) *n.* a word or phrase the letters of which, when taken in reverse order, read the same: *able was I ere I saw Elba.* [C17: < Gk *palindromos* running back again] —**palindromic** (ˌpælɪnˈdrɒmɪk) *adj.*

paling (ˈpeɪlɪŋ) *n.* **1.** a fence made of pales. **2.** pales collectively. **3.** a single pale. **4.** the act of erecting pales.

palisade (ˌpælɪˈseɪd) *n.* **1.** a strong fence made of stakes driven into the ground, esp. for defence. **2.** one of the stakes used in such a fence. ~*vb.* **3.** (*tr.*) to enclose with a palisade. [C17: via F < OProvençal *palissada,* ult. < L *pālus* stake]

pall[1] (pɔːl) *n.* **1.** a cloth covering, usually black, spread over a coffin or tomb. **2.** a coffin, esp. during the funeral ceremony. **3.** a dark heavy covering; shroud: *the clouds formed a pall over the sky.* **4.** a depressing or oppressive atmosphere: *her bereavement cast a pall on the party.* **5.** *Heraldry.* a Y-shaped bearing. **6.** *Christianity.* a small square linen cloth with which the chalice is covered at the Eucharist. ~*vb.* **7.** (*tr.*) to cover or depress with a pall. [OE *pæll,* < L *pallium* cloak]

pall[2] (pɔːl) *vb.* **1.** (*intr.;* often foll. by *on*) to become boring, insipid, or tiresome (to): *history classes palled on me.* **2.** to cloy or satiate, or become cloyed or satiated. [C14: var. of APPAL]

Palladian (pəˈleɪdɪən) *adj.* denoting, relating to, or having the style of architecture created by Andrea Palladio. [C18: after Andrea *Palladio* (1508–80), It. architect] —**Palˈladianˌism** *n.*

palladium[1] (pəˈleɪdɪəm) *n.* a ductile malleable silvery-white element of the platinum metal group: used as a catalyst and, alloyed with gold, in jewellery, etc. Symbol: Pd; atomic no.: 46; atomic wt.: 106.4. [C19: after the asteroid *Pallas,* at the time (1803) a recent discovery]

palladium[2] (pəˈleɪdɪəm) *n.* something believed to ensure protection; safeguard. [C17: after the *Palladium,* a statue of Pallas Athena, Gk goddess of wisdom]

pallbearer (ˈpɔːlˌbɛərə) *n.* a person who carries or escorts the coffin at a funeral.

pallet[1] (ˈpælɪt) *n.* a straw-filled mattress or bed. [C14: < Anglo-Norman *paillet,* < OF *paille* straw, < L *palea* straw]

pallet[2] (ˈpælɪt) *n.* **1.** an instrument with a handle and a flat, sometimes flexible, blade used by potters for shaping. **2.** a portable platform for storing and moving goods. **3.** *Horology.* the locking lever that engages and disengages to give impulses to the balance. **4.** a variant spelling of **palette** (sense 1). **5.** *Music.* a flap valve that opens to admit air to the wind chest of an organ. [C16: < OF *palette* a little shovel, < L *pala* spade]

palliasse *or esp. U.S.* **paillasse** (ˈpælɪˌæs, ˌpælɪˈæs) *n.* a straw-filled mattress; pallet. [C18: < F *paillasse,* < It. *pagliaccio,* ult. < L *palea* PALLET[1]]

palliate (ˈpælɪˌeɪt) *vb.* (*tr.*) **1.** to lessen the severity of (pain, disease, etc.) without curing; alleviate. **2.** to cause (an offence, etc.) to seem less serious; extenuate. [C16: < LL *palliāre* to cover up, < L *pallium* a cloak] —ˌ**palliˈation** *n.*

palliative (ˈpælɪətɪv) *adj.* **1.** relieving without curing. ~*n.* **2.** something that palliates, such as a sedative drug. —ˈ**palliatively** *adv.*

pallid (ˈpælɪd) *adj.* lacking colour, brightness, or vigour: *a pallid complexion; a pallid performance.* [C17: < L *pallidus,* < *pallēre* to be PALE[1]] —ˈ**pallidly** *adv.* —ˈ**pallidness** *or* **palˈlidity** *n.*

pall-mall (ˈpælˈmæl) *n. Obs.* **1.** a game in which a ball is driven by a mallet along an alley and through an iron ring. **2.** the alley itself. [C17: < obs. F, < It. *pallamaglio,* < *palla* ball + *maglio* mallet]

pallor (ˈpælə) *n.* a pale condition, esp. when unnatural: *fear gave his face a deathly pallor.* [C17: < L: whiteness (of the skin), < *pallēre* to be PALE[1]]

pally (ˈpælɪ) *adj.* **-lier, -liest.** *Inf.* on friendly terms.

palm[1] (pɑːm) *n.* **1.** the inner part of the hand from the wrist to the base of the fingers. **2.** a linear measure based on the breadth or length of a hand, equal to three to four inches (7.5 to 10 centimetres) or seven to ten inches (17.5 to 25 centimetres) respectively. **3.** the part of a glove that covers the palm. **4. a.** one side of the blade of an oar. **b.** the face of the fluke of an anchor. **5.** a flattened part of the antlers of certain deer. **6. in the palm of one's hand.** at one's mercy or command. ~*vb.* (*tr.*) **7.** to conceal in or about the hand, as in sleight-of-hand tricks, etc. ~See also **palm off.** [C14 *paume,* via OF < L *palma*] —**palmar** (ˈpælmə) *adj.*

palm[2] (pɑːm) *n.* **1.** any treelike plant of a tropical and subtropical family having a straight unbranched trunk crowned with large pinnate or palmate leaves. **2.** a leaf or branch of any of these trees, a symbol of victory, success, etc. **3.** merit or victory. [OE, < L *palma,* from the likeness of its spreading fronds to a hand; see PALM[1]] —**palmaceous** (pælˈmeɪʃəs) *adj.*

palmate (ˈpælmeɪt, -mɪt) *or* **palmated** *adj.* **1.** shaped like an open hand: *palmate antlers.* **2.** *Bot.* having five lobes that spread out from a common point: *palmate leaves.* **3.** (of most water birds) having three toes connected by a web.

palmer (ˈpɑːmə) *n.* (in medieval Europe) **1.** a pilgrim bearing a palm branch as a sign of his visit to the Holy Land. **2.** any pilgrim. [C13: < OF *palmier,* < Med. L, < L *palma* PALM[2]]

palmetto (pælˈmɛtəʊ) *n., pl.* **-tos** *or* **-toes.** any of several small chiefly tropical palms with fan-shaped leaves. [C16: < Sp. *palmito* a little PALM[2]]

palmistry (ˈpɑːmɪstrɪ) *n.* the process or art of telling fortunes, etc., by the configuration of lines and bumps on a person's hand. Also called: **chiromancy.** [C15 *pawmestry,* < *paume* PALM[1]; the second element is unexplained] —ˈ**palmist** *n.*

palmitic acid (pælˈmɪtɪk) *n.* a white crystalline solid that is a saturated fatty acid: used in the manufacture of soap and candles. [C19: < F]

palm off *vb.* (*tr., adv.;* often foll. by *on*) **1.** to offer, sell, or spend fraudulently: *to palm off a counterfeit coin.* **2.** to divert in order to be rid of: *I palmed the unwelcome visitor off on John.*

palm oil *n.* an oil obtained from the fruit of certain palms, used as an edible fat and in soap, etc.

Palm Sunday *n.* the Sunday before Easter commemorating Christ's triumphal entry into Jerusalem.

palmy (ˈpɑːmɪ) *adj.* **palmier, palmiest. 1.** prosperous, flourishing, or luxurious: *a palmy life.* **2.** covered with, relating to, or resembling palms.

palmyra (pælˈmaɪrə) *n.* a tall tropical Asian palm with large fan-shaped leaves used for thatching and weaving. [C17: < Port. *palmeira* palm tree; ? infl. by *Palmyra,* city in Syria]

palomino (ˌpæləˈmiːnəʊ) *n., pl.* **-nos.** a golden horse with a white mane and tail. [American Sp., < Sp.: dovelike, < L, < *palumbēs* ring dove]

palp (pælp) *or* **palpus** (ˈpælpəs) *n., pl.* **palps** *or* **palpi** (ˈpælpaɪ). either of a pair of sensory appendages that arise from the mouthparts of crustaceans and insects. [C19: < F, < L *palpus* a touching]

palpable (ˈpælpəbᵊl) *adj.* **1.** (*usually prenominal*) easily perceived by the senses or the mind; obvious: *a palpable lie.* **2.** capable of being touched; tangible. [C14: < LL *palpābilis* that may be touched, < L *palpāre* to touch] —ˌ**palpaˈbility** *n.* —ˈ**palpably** *adv.*

palpate (ˈpælpeɪt) *vb.* (*tr.*) *Med.* to examine (an area of the body) by the sense of touch. [C19: < L *palpāre* to stroke] —**palˈpation** *n.*

palpebral (ˈpælpɪbrəl) *adj.* of or relating to the eyelid. [C19: < LL, < L *palpebra* eyelid]

palpitate (ˈpælpɪˌteɪt) *vb.* (*intr.*) **1.** (of the heart) to beat rapidly. **2.** to flutter or tremble. [C17: < L *palpitāre* to throb, < *palpāre* to stroke] —ˈ**palpitant** *adj.* —ˌ**palpiˈtation** *n.*

palsy (ˈpɔːlzɪ) *Pathol.* ~*n., pl.* **-sies. 1.** paralysis, esp. of a specified type: *cerebral palsy.* ~*vb.*

-sying, -sied. (*tr.*) 2. to paralyse. [C13 *palesi,* < OF *paralisie,* < L PARALYSIS] —'**palsied** *adj.*

palter ('pɔːltə) *vb.* (*intr.*) 1. to act or talk insincerely. 2. to haggle. [C16: <?]

paltry ('pɔːltrɪ) *adj.* **-trier, -triest.** 1. insignificant; meagre. 2. worthless or petty. [C16: < Low Gmc *palter, paltrig* ragged] —'**paltrily** *adv.* —'**paltriness** *n.*

paludal (pə'ljuːdᵊl) *adj. Rare.* 1. of or relating to marshes. 2. malarial. [C19: < L *palus* marsh]

paludism ('pæljʊˌdɪzəm) *n.* a less common word for **malaria.** [C19: < L *palus* marsh]

palynology (ˌpælɪ'nɒlədʒɪ) *n.* the study of living and fossil pollen grains and plant spores. [C20: < Gk *palunein* to scatter + -LOGY] —**palynological** (ˌpælɪnə'lɒdʒɪkᵊl) *adj.* —ˌ**paly'nologist** *n.*

pampas ('pæmpəz) *n.* (*functioning as sing. or more often pl.*) **a.** the extensive grassy plains of temperate South America, esp. in Argentina. **b.** (*as modifier*): *pampas dwellers.* [C18: < American Sp. *pampa* (sing.), < Amerind *bamba* plain] —**pampean** ('pæmpɪən, pæm'piːən) *adj.*

pampas grass ('pæmpəs, -pəz) *n.* any of various large South American grasses, widely cultivated for their large feathery silver-coloured flower branches.

pamper ('pæmpə) *vb.* (*tr.*) 1. to treat with affectionate and usually excessive indulgence; coddle; spoil. 2. *Arch.* to feed to excess. [C14: of Gmc origin] —'**pamperer** *n.*

pamphlet ('pæmflɪt) *n.* 1. a brief publication generally having a paper cover; booklet. 2. a brief treatise, often on a subject of current interest, in pamphlet form. [C14 *pamflet,* < Med. L *Pamphilus* title of a 12th-century amatory poem < Gk *Pamphilos* proper name]

pamphleteer (ˌpæmflɪ'tɪə) *n.* 1. a person who writes or issues pamphlets. ~*vb.* 2. (*intr.*) to write or issue pamphlets.

pan[1] (pæn) *n.* 1. **a.** a wide metal vessel used in cooking. **b.** (*in combination*): *saucepan.* 2. Also called: **panful.** the amount such a vessel will hold. 3. any of various similar vessels used in industry, etc. 4. a dish used esp. by gold prospectors for separating gold from gravel by washing and agitating. 5. either of the two dishlike receptacles on a balance. 6. Also called: **lavatory pan.** *Brit.* the bowl of a lavatory. 7. **a.** a natural or artificial depression in the ground where salt can be obtained by the evaporation of brine. **b.** a natural depression containing water or mud. 8. See **hardpan, brainpan.** 9. a small cavity containing priming powder in the locks of old guns. 10. a hard substratum of soil. ~*vb.* **panning, panned.** 11. (when *tr.,* often foll. by *off* or *out*) to wash (gravel) in a pan to separate particles of (valuable minerals) from it. 12. (*intr.;* often foll. by *out*) (of gravel, etc.) to yield valuable minerals by this process. 13. (*tr.*) *Inf.* to criticize harshly: *the critics panned his new play.* ~See also **pan out.** [OE *panne*]

pan[2] (pæn) *vb.* **panning, panned.** 1. to move (a film camera) or (of a film camera) to be moved so as to follow a moving object or obtain a panoramic effect. ~*n.* 2. the act of panning. [C20: shortened < PANORAMIC]

pan- *combining form.* 1. all or every: *panchromatic.* 2. including or relating to all parts or members: *Pan-American; pantheistic.* [< Gk *pan,* neuter of *pas* all]

panacea (ˌpænə'sɪə) *n.* a remedy for all diseases or ills. [C16: via L < Gk *panakeia,* < *pan* all + *akēs* remedy] —ˌ**pana'cean** *adj.*

panache (pə'næʃ, -'nɑːʃ) *n.* 1. a dashing manner; swagger: *he rides with panache.* 2. a plume on a helmet. [C16: via F < OIt. *pennacchio,* < LL *pinnāculum* feather, < L *pinna* feather]

panada (pə'nɑːdə) *n.* a mixture of flour, water, etc., or of breadcrumbs soaked in milk, used as a thickening. [C16: < Sp., < *pan* bread, < L *pānis*]

Panama hat (ˌpænə'mɑː) *n.* (*sometimes not cap.*) a hat made of the plaited leaves of a palmlike plant of Central and South America. Often shortened to **panama** or **Panama.**

Pan-American *adj.* of, relating to, or concerning North, South, and Central America collectively or the advocacy of political or economic unity among American countries. —'**Pan-A'merican**ˌ**ism** *n.*

panatella (ˌpænə'tɛlə) *n.* a long slender cigar. [American Sp. *panetela* long slim biscuit, < It. *panatella* small loaf, < *pane* bread, < L *pānis*]

pancake ('pænˌkeɪk) *n.* 1. a thin flat cake made from batter and fried on both sides. 2. a stick or flat cake of compressed make-up. 3. Also called: **pancake landing.** an aircraft landing made by levelling out a few feet from the ground and then dropping onto it. ~*vb.* 4. to cause (an aircraft) to make a pancake landing or (of an aircraft) to make a pancake landing.

Pancake Day *n.* another name for **Shrove Tuesday.** See **Shrovetide.**

panchromatic (ˌpænkrəʊ'mætɪk) *adj. Photog.* (of an emulsion or film) made sensitive to all colours. —**panchromatism** (pæn'krəʊməˌtɪzəm) *n.*

pancreas ('pæŋkrɪəs) *n.* a large elongated glandular organ, situated behind the stomach, that secretes insulin and pancreatic juice. [C16: via NL < Gk *pankreas,* < *pan-* + *kreas* flesh] —**pancreatic** (ˌpæŋkrɪ'ætɪk) *adj.*

pancreatic juice *n.* the clear alkaline secretion of the pancreas that is released into the duodenum and contains digestive enzymes.

pancreatin ('pæŋkrɪətɪn) *n.* the powdered extract of the pancreas of certain animals, used in medicine as an aid to the digestion.

panda ('pændə) *n.* 1. Also called: **giant panda.** a large black-and-white herbivorous bearlike mammal, related to the raccoons and inhabiting the bamboo forests of China. 2. **lesser** *or* **red panda.** a closely related smaller animal resembling a raccoon, of the mountain forests of S Asia, having a reddish-brown coat and ringed tail. [C19: via F < a native Nepalese word]

panda car *n. Brit.* a police patrol car.

pandanus (pæn'deɪnəs) *n., pl.* **-nuses.** any of various Old World tropical palmlike plants having leaves and roots yielding a fibre used for making mats, etc. [C19: via NL < Malay *pandan*]

pandect ('pændɛkt) *n.* 1. a treatise covering all aspects of a particular subject. 2. (*often pl.*) the complete body of laws of a country; legal code, esp. the digest of Roman civil law made in the 6th century by order of Justinian. [C16: via LL < Gk *pandektēs* containing everything, < PAN- + *dektēs* receiver]

pandemic (pæn'dɛmɪk) *adj.* 1. (of a disease) affecting persons over a wide geographical area; extensively epidemic. ~*n.* 2. a pandemic disease. [C17: < LL *pandēmus,* < Gk *pandēmos* general, < PAN- + *demos* the people]

pandemonium (ˌpændɪ'məʊnɪəm) *n.* 1. wild confusion; uproar. 2. a place of uproar and chaos. [C17: coined by Milton for the capital of hell in *Paradise Lost,* < PAN- + Gk *daimōn* DEMON]

pander ('pændə) *vb.* 1. (*intr.;* foll. by *to*) to give gratification (to weaknesses or desires). 2. (*arch.* when *tr.*) to act as a go-between in a sexual intrigue (for). ~*n. also* **panderer.** 3. a person who caters for vulgar desires. 4. a person who procures a sexual partner for another; pimp. [C16 (n.): < *Pandare* Pandarus, in legend, the procurer of Cressida for Troilus]

pandit ('pʌndɪt; *spelling pron.* 'pændɪt) *n. Hinduism.* a variant of **pundit** (sense 3).

P & L *abbrev. for* profit and loss.

P & O *abbrev. for* Peninsular and Oriental (Steamship Company).

p & p *Brit. abbrev. for* postage and packing.

pane (peɪn) *n.* 1. a sheet of glass in a window or door. 2. a panel of a window, door, wall, etc. 3. a flat section or face, as of a cut diamond. [C13: < OF *pan* portion, < L *pannus* rag]

panegyric (ˌpænɪ'dʒɪrɪk) *n.* a formal public commendation; eulogy. [C17: via F & L < Gk, < *panēguris* public gathering] —ˌ**pane'gyrical** *adj.* —ˌ**pane'gyrically** *adv.* —ˌ**pane'gyrist** *n.* —**panegyrize** *or* **-rise** ('pænɪdʒɪˌraɪz) *vb.*

panel ('pænᵊl) *n.* 1. a flat section of a wall, door, etc. 2. any distinct section of something formed from a sheet of material, esp. of a car body. **3.** a piece of material inserted in a skirt, etc. **4. a.** a group of persons selected to act as a team in a quiz, to discuss a topic before an audience, etc. **b.** (*as modifier*): *a panel game.* **5.** *Law.* **a.** a list of persons summoned for jury service. **b.** the persons on a jury. **6.** *Scots Law.* a person accused of a crime. **7. a.** a thin board used as a surface or backing for an oil painting. **b.** a painting done on such a surface. **8.** any picture with a length much greater than its breadth. **9.** See **instrument panel. 10.** *Brit.* (formerly) **a.** a list of patients insured under the National Health Insurance Scheme. **b.** a list of medical practitioners available for consultation by these patients. ~*vb.* **-elling, -elled** *or U.S.* **-eling, -eled.** (*tr.*) **11.** to furnish or decorate with panels. **12.** *Law.* **a.** to empanel (a jury). **b.** (in Scotland) to bring (a person) to trial; indict. [C13: < OF: portion, < *pan* piece of cloth, < L *pannus*]

panel beater *n.* a person who beats out the bodywork of motor vehicles, etc.

panelling *or U.S.* **paneling** ('pænᵊlɪŋ) *n.* **1.** panels collectively, as on a wall or ceiling. **2.** material used for making panels.

panellist *or U.S.* **panelist** ('pænᵊlɪst) *n.* a member of a panel, esp. on radio or television.

panel pin *n.* a slender nail with a narrow head.

panel saw *n.* a saw with a long narrow blade for cutting thin wood.

panel van *n. Austral. & N.Z.* a small van.

pang (pæŋ) *n.* a sudden brief sharp feeling, as of loneliness, physical pain, or hunger. [C16: var. of earlier *prange*, of Gmc origin]

panga ('pæŋgə) *n.* a broad heavy knife of E Africa. [< a native E African word]

pangolin (pæŋ'gəʊlɪn) *n.* a mammal of tropical Africa, S Asia, and Indonesia, having a scaly body and a long snout for feeding on ants and termites. Also called: **scaly anteater.** [C18: < Malay *peng-gōling*, < *gōling* to roll over; < its ability to roll into a ball]

panhandle[1] ('pæn,hændᵊl) *n.* (*sometimes cap.*) (in the U.S.) a narrow strip of land that projects from one state into another.

panhandle[2] ('pæn,hændᵊl) *vb. U.S. inf.* to beg from (passers-by). [C19: prob. a back formation < *panhandler* a person who begs with a pan] —'**pan,handler** *n.*

Panhellenic (,pænhɛ'lɛnɪk) *adj.* of or relating to all the Greeks or all Greece.

panic ('pænɪk) *n.* **1.** a sudden overwhelming feeling of terror or anxiety, esp. one affecting a whole group of people. **2.** (*modifier*) of or resulting from such terror: *panic measures.* **3.** (*modifier*) for use in an emergency: *panic stations; panic button.* ~*vb.* **-icking, -icked. 4.** to feel or cause to feel panic. [C17: < F *panique*, < NL, < Gk *panikos* emanating from *Pan*, Gk god of the fields, considered as the source of irrational fear] —'**panicky** *adj.*

panic button *n.* a button or switch that operates a safety device, for use in an emergency.

panic grass *n.* any of various grasses, such as millet, grown in warm and tropical regions for fodder and grain. [C15 *panic*, < L *pānicum*, prob. a back formation < *pānicula* PANICLE]

panicle ('pænɪkᵊl) *n.* a compound raceme, as in the oat. [C16: < L *pānicula* tuft, dim. of *panus* thread, ult. < Gk *penos* web] —'**panicled** *adj.* —**paniculate** (pə'nɪkjʊ,leɪt, -lɪt) *adj.*

panic-stricken *or* **panic-struck** *adj.* affected by panic.

panjandrum (pæn'dʒændrəm) *n.* a pompous self-important official or person of rank. [C18: after a character in a nonsense work (1755) by S. Foote, E playwright]

pan loaf *n. Scot.* a loaf of bread with a light crust all the way round. Often shortened to **pan.**

pannage ('pænɪdʒ) *n. Arch.* **1.** the right to pasture pigs in a forest. **2.** payment for this. **3.** acorns, beech mast, etc., on which pigs feed. [C13: < OF *pasnage*, ult. < L *pastion-*, *pastiō* feeding, < *pascere* to feed]

pannier ('pænɪə) *n.* **1.** a large basket, esp. one of a pair slung over a beast of burden. **2.** one of a pair of bags slung either side of the back wheel of a motorcycle, etc. **3.** (esp. in the 18th century) **a.** a hooped framework to distend a woman's skirt. **b.** one of two puffed-out loops of material worn drawn back onto the hips. [C13: < OF *panier*, < L *pānārium* basket for bread, < *pānis* bread]

pannikin ('pænɪkɪn) *n. Chiefly Brit.* a small metal cup or pan. [C19: < PAN[1] + -KIN]

pannikin boss *n. Austral. sl.* a minor overseer.

panoply ('pænəplɪ) *n., pl.* **-plies. 1.** a complete or magnificent array. **2.** the entire equipment of a warrior. [C17: via F < Gk, < PAN- + *hopla* armour] —'**panoplied** *adj.*

panoptic (pæn'ɒptɪk) *adj.* taking in all parts, aspects, etc., in a single view; all-embracing. [C19: < Gk *panoptēs* seeing everything]

panorama (,pænə'rɑːmə) *n.* **1.** an extensive unbroken view in all directions. **2.** a wide or comprehensive survey of a subject. **3.** a large extended picture of a scene, unrolled before spectators a part at a time so as to appear continuous. **4.** another name for **cyclorama.** [C18: < PAN- + Gk *horāma* view] —**panoramic** (,pænə'ræmɪk) *adj.* —,**pano'ramically** *adv.*

pan out *vb.* (*intr., adv.*) *Inf.* to work out; result.

panpipes ('pæn,paɪps) *pl. n.* (*often sing.; often cap.*) a number of reeds or whistles of graduated lengths bound together to form a musical wind instrument. Also called: **pipes of Pan, syrinx.**

pansy ('pænzɪ) *n., pl.* **-sies. 1.** a garden plant having flowers with rounded velvety petals, white, yellow, or purple in colour. See also **wild pansy. 2.** *Sl.* an effeminate or homosexual man or boy. [C15: < OF *pensée* thought, < *penser* to think, < L *pensāre*]

pant (pænt) *vb.* **1.** to breathe with noisy deep gasps, as when out of breath from exertion. **2.** to say (something) while breathing thus. **3.** (*intr.; often foll. by for*) to have a frantic desire (for). **4.** (*intr.*) to throb rapidly. ~*n.* **5.** the act or an instance of panting. **6.** a short deep gasping noise. [C15: < OF *pantaisier*, < Gk *phantasioun* to have visions, < *phantasia* FANTASY]

pantalets *or* **pantalettes** (,pæntə'lɛts) *pl. n.* **1.** long drawers extending below the skirts: worn during the 19th century. **2.** ruffles for the ends of such drawers. [C19: dim. of PANTALOONS]

pantaloon (,pæntə'luːn) *n.* **1.** (in pantomime) an absurd old man, the butt of the clown's tricks. **2.** (*usually cap.*) (in commedia dell'arte) a lecherous old merchant dressed in pantaloons. [C16: < F *Pantalon*, < It. *Pantalone*, prob. < *San Pantaleone*, a fourth-century Venetian saint]

pantaloons (,pæntə'luːnz) *pl. n.* **1.** *History.* **a.** men's tight-fitting trousers fastened below the calf or under the shoe. **b.** children's trousers resembling these. **2.** *Inf.* any trousers, esp. baggy ones.

pantechnicon (pæn'tɛknɪkən) *n. Brit.* **1.** a large van, esp. one used for furniture removals. **2.** a warehouse where furniture is stored. [C19: < PAN- + Gk *tekhnikon* relating to the arts, < *tekhnē* art; orig. a London bazaar, later used as a furniture warehouse]

pantheism ('pænθɪ,ɪzəm) *n.* **1.** the doctrine that regards God as identical with the material universe or the forces of nature. **2.** readiness to worship all gods. —'**pantheist** *n.* —,**panthe'istic** *or* ,**panthe'istical** *adj.* —,**panthe'istically** *adv.*

pantheon ('pænθɪən) *n.* **1.** (esp. in ancient Greece or Rome) a temple to all the gods. **2.** all the gods of a religion. **3.** a building commemorating a nation's dead heroes. [C14: via L < Gk *Pantheion*, < PAN- + *-theios* divine, < *theos* god]

panther ('pænθə) *n., pl.* **-thers** *or* **-ther. 1.** another name for **leopard** (sense 1), esp. the black variety (**black panther**). **2.** *U.S. & Canad.* any of various related animals, esp. the puma. [C14: < OF *pantère*, < L *panthēra*, < Gk *panthēr*]

panties ('pæntɪz) *pl. n.* a pair of women's or children's underpants.

pantihose ('pæntɪ,həʊz) *pl. n.* See **panty hose.**

pantile ('pæn,taɪl) *n.* a roofing tile, with an S-shaped cross section, so that the downward curve of one tile overlaps the upward curve of the next.

pantisocracy (ˌpæntɪˈsɒkrəsɪ) *n., pl.* **-cies.** a community, social group, etc., in which all have rule and everyone is equal. [C18: (coined by Robert Southey, E poet) < Gk, < PANTO- + *isos* equal + -CRACY]

panto (ˈpæntəʊ) *n., pl.* **-tos.** *Brit. inf.* short for **pantomime** (sense 1).

panto- *or before a vowel* **pant-** *combining form.* all: *pantisocracy; pantograph; pantomime.* [< Gk *pant-, pas*]

pantograph (ˈpæntəˌgrɑːf) *n.* **1.** an instrument consisting of pivoted levers for copying drawings, maps, etc., to any scale. **2.** a sliding type of current collector, esp. a diamond-shaped frame mounted on a train roof in contact with an overhead wire. **3.** a device used to suspend a studio lamp so that its height can be adjusted. —**pantographic** (ˌpæntəˈgræfɪk) *adj.*

pantomime (ˈpæntəˌmaɪm) *n.* **1.** (in Britain) a kind of play performed at Christmas time characterized by farce, music, lavish sets, stock roles, and topical jokes. **2.** a theatrical entertainment in which words are replaced by gestures and bodily actions. **3.** action without words as a means of expression. **4.** *Inf., chiefly Brit.* a confused or farcical situation. ~*vb.* **5.** another word for **mime.** [C17: via L < Gk *pantomīmos*] —**pantomimic** (ˌpæntəˈmɪmɪk) *adj.* —**pantomimist** (ˈpæntəˌmaɪmɪst) *n.*

pantothenic acid (ˌpæntəˈθenɪk) *n.* an oily acid that is a vitamin of the B complex: occurs widely in animal and vegetable foods. [C20: < Gk *pantothen* from every side]

pantry (ˈpæntrɪ) *n., pl.* **-tries.** a small room in which provisions, cooking utensils, etc., are kept; larder. [C13: via Anglo-Norman < OF *paneterie* store for bread, ult. < L *pānis* bread]

pants (pænts) *pl. n.* **1.** *Brit.* an undergarment covering the body from the waist to the thighs or knees. **2.** the usual U.S. and Canad. name for **trousers. 3. bore, scare,** etc., **the pants off.** *Inf.* to bore, scare, etc., extremely. [C19: shortened < *pantaloons*]

panty girdle (ˈpæntɪ) *n.* a foundation garment with a crotch, often of lighter material than a girdle.

panty hose *pl. n.* the U.S. name for **tights** (sense 1). Also (Canad. and N.Z.) **pantyhose,** (Austral.) **pantihose.**

panzer (ˈpænzə; *German* ˈpantsər) *n.* **1.** (*modifier*) of or relating to the fast mechanized armoured units employed by the German army in World War II: *a panzer attack.* **2.** a vehicle belonging to a panzer unit, esp. a tank. **3.** (*pl.*) armoured troops. [C20: < G, < MHG, < OF *panciere* coat of mail, < L *pantex* PAUNCH]

pap[1] (pæp) *n.* **1.** any soft or semiliquid food, esp. for babies or invalids; mash. **2.** worthless or oversimplified ideas, etc.; drivel. **3.** *S. African.* maize porridge. [C15: < MLow G *pappe,* via Med. L < L *pappāre* to eat]

pap[2] (pæp) *n.* **1.** *Arch. or Scot. & N English dialect.* a nipple or teat. **2.** something resembling a breast, such as one of a pair of rounded hilltops. [C12: < ON, imit. of a sucking sound]

papa (pəˈpɑː) *n. Old-fashioned.* an informal word for **father.** [C17: < F, a children's word for father]

papacy (ˈpeɪpəsɪ) *n., pl.* **-cies. 1.** the office or term of office of a pope. **2.** the system of government in the Roman Catholic Church that has the pope as its head. [C14: < Med. L *pāpātia,* < *pāpa* POPE]

papain (pəˈpeɪɪn, -ˈpaɪɪn) *n.* an enzyme occurring in the unripe fruit of the papaya tree: used as a meat tenderizer and in medicine as an aid to protein digestion. [C19: < PAPAYA]

papal (ˈpeɪpᵊl) *adj.* of or relating to the pope or the papacy. —ˈ**papally** *adv.*

paparazzo (ˌpæpəˈrætsəʊ) *n., pl.* **-razzi** (-ˈrætsiː). a freelance photographer who specializes in candid-camera shots of famous people. [C20: < It.]

papaver (pæˈpɑːvə) *n.* any of a genus of hardy annual or perennial plants with showy flowers; poppy. [L: poppy]

papaveraceous (pəˌpeɪvəˈreɪʃəs) *adj.* of or relating to a family of plants having large showy flowers and a cylindrical seed capsule with pores beneath the lid: includes the poppies and greater celandine. [C19: < NL, < L *papāver* poppy]

papaverine (pəˈpeɪvəˌriːn, -rɪn) *n.* a white crystalline alkaloid found in opium and used to treat coronary spasms and certain types of colic. [C19: < L *papāver* poppy]

papaw (pəˈpɔː) *or* **pawpaw** *n.* **1.** Also called: **custard apple. a.** a bush or small tree of Central North America, having small fleshy edible fruit. **b.** the fruit of this tree. **2.** another name for **papaya.** [C16: < Sp. PAPAYA]

papaya (pəˈpaɪə) *n.* **1.** a West Indian evergreen tree with a crown of large dissected leaves and large green hanging fruit. **2.** the fruit of this tree, having a yellow sweet edible pulp and small black seeds. ~Also called: **papaw, pawpaw.** [C15 *papaye,* < Sp. *papaya,* of Amerind origin]

paper (ˈpeɪpə) *n.* **1.** a substance made from cellulose fibres derived from rags, wood, etc., and formed into flat thin sheets suitable for writing on, decorating walls, wrapping, etc. **2.** a single piece of such material, esp. if written or printed on. **3.** (*usually pl.*) documents for establishing the identity of the bearer. **4.** (*pl.*) Also called: **ship's papers.** official documents relating to a ship. **5.** (*pl.*) collected diaries, letters, etc. **6.** See **newspaper, wallpaper. 7.** *Government.* See **white paper, green paper. 8.** a lecture or treatise on a specific subject. **9.** a short essay. **10. a.** a set of examination questions. **b.** the student's answers. **11.** *Commerce.* See **commercial paper. 12.** *Theatre sl.* a free ticket. **13. on paper.** in theory, as opposed to fact. ~*adj.* **14.** made of paper: *paper cups do not last long.* **15.** thin like paper: *paper walls.* **16.** (*prenominal*) existing only as recorded on paper but not yet in practice: *paper expenditure.* **17.** taking place in writing: *paper battles.* ~*vb.* **18.** to cover (walls) with wallpaper. **19.** (*tr.*) to cover or furnish with paper. **20.** (*tr.*) *Theatre sl.* to fill (a performance, etc.) by giving away free tickets (esp. in **paper the house**). ~See also **paper over.** [C14: < L PAPYRUS] —ˈ**paperer** *n.* —ˈ**papery** *adj.*

paperback (ˈpeɪpəˌbæk) *n.* **1.** a book or edition with covers made of flexible card. ~*adj.* **2.** of or denoting a paperback or publication of paperbacks. ~*vb.* **3.** (*tr.*) to publish a paperback edition of a book.

paperbark (ˈpeɪpəˌbɑːk) *n.* any of several Australian trees of swampy regions, having papery bark that can be peeled off in thin layers.

paperboy (ˈpeɪpəˌbɔɪ) *n.* a boy employed to deliver newspapers, etc. —ˈ**paperˌgirl** *fem. n.*

paper chase *n.* a cross-country run in which a runner lays a trail of paper for others to follow.

paperclip (ˈpeɪpəˌklɪp) *n.* a clip for holding sheets of paper together, esp. one of bent wire.

paper-cutter *n.* a machine for cutting paper, usually a blade mounted over a table.

paperhanger (ˈpeɪpəˌhæŋə) *n.* a person who hangs wallpaper as an occupation.

paperknife (ˈpeɪpəˌnaɪf) *n., pl.* **-knives.** a knife with a comparatively blunt blade for opening sealed envelopes, etc.

paper money *n.* paper currency issued by the government or the central bank as legal tender and which circulates as a substitute for specie.

paper mulberry *n.* a small E Asian tree, the inner bark of which was formerly used for making paper in Japan. See also **tapa.**

paper nautilus *n.* a cephalopod mollusc of warm and tropical seas, having a papery external spiral shell. Also called: **argonaut.**

paper over *vb.* (*tr., adv.*) to conceal (something controversial or unpleasant).

paper tape *n.* a strip of paper used in computers, telex machines, etc., for recording information in the form of punched holes.

paper tiger *n.* a nation, institution, etc., that

appears powerful but is in fact weak or insignificant. [C20: translation of a Chinese phrase first applied to the U.S.]

paperweight (ˈpeɪpəˌweɪt) *n.* a small heavy object to prevent loose papers from scattering.

paperwork (ˈpeɪpəˌwɜːk) *n.* clerical work, such as the writing of reports or letters.

Paphian (ˈpeɪfɪən) *adj.* **1.** of or relating to Aphrodite, who was worshipped at Paphos, a village in SW Cyprus. **2.** *Literary.* of sexual love.

papier-mâché (ˌpæpjeɪˈmæʃeɪ) *n.* **1.** a hard strong substance made of paper pulp or layers of paper mixed with paste, size, etc., and moulded when moist. *~adj.* **2.** made of papier-mâché. [C18: < F, lit.: chewed paper]

papilionaceous (pəˌpɪlɪəˈneɪʃəs) *adj.* of, relating to, or belonging to a family of leguminous plants having irregular flowers: includes peas, beans, clover, alfalfa, gorse, and broom. [C17: < NL, < L *pāpiliō* butterfly]

papilla (pəˈpɪlə) *n., pl.* **-lae** (-liː). **1.** the small projection of tissue at the base of a hair, tooth, or feather. **2.** any similar protuberance. [C18: < L: nipple] **—paˈpillary** *or* **ˈpapillate** *adj.*

papilloma (ˌpæpɪˈləʊmə) *n., pl.* **-mata** (-mətə) *or* **-mas.** *Pathol.* a benign tumour forming a rounded mass. [C19: < PAPILLA + -OMA]

papillon (ˈpæpɪˌlɒn) *n.* a breed of toy dog with large ears. [F: butterfly, < L *pāpiliō*]

papillote (ˈpæpɪˌləʊt) *n.* **1.** a paper frill around cutlets, etc. **2. en papillote** (ɑ̃ papijɔt). (of food) cooked in oiled greaseproof paper or foil. [C18: < F PAPILLON]

papist (ˈpeɪpɪst) *n., adj.* (*often cap.*) *Usually disparaging.* another term for **Roman Catholic.** [C16: < F *papiste*, < Church L *pāpa* POPE] **—paˈpistical** *or* **paˈpistic** *adj.* **—ˈpapistry** *n.*

papoose (pəˈpuːs) *n.* an American Indian baby. [C17: < Algonquian *papoos*]

pappus (ˈpæpəs) *n., pl.* **pappi** (ˈpæpaɪ). a ring of fine feathery hairs surrounding the fruit in composite plants, such as the thistle. [C18: via NL < Gk *pappos* old man, old man's beard, hence: pappus, down] **—ˈpappose** *or* **ˈpappous** *adj.*

paprika (ˈpæprɪkə, pæˈpriː-) *n.* **1.** a mild powdered seasoning made from a sweet variety of red pepper. **2.** the fruit or plant from which this seasoning is obtained. [C19: via Hungarian < Serbian, < *papar* PEPPER]

Pap test *or* **smear** (pæp) *n. Med.* an examination of stained cells in a smear taken of bodily secretions, esp. from the uterus, for detection of cancer. [C20: after George *Papanicolaou* (1883–1962), U.S. anatomist, who devised it]

papule (ˈpæpjuːl) *or* **papula** (ˈpæpjʊlə) *n., pl.* **-ules** *or* **-ulae** (-jʊˌliː). *Pathol.* a small solid usually round elevation of the skin. [C19: < L *papula* pustule] **—ˈpapular** *adj.*

papyrology (ˌpæpɪˈrɒlədʒɪ) *n.* the study of ancient papyri. **—ˌpapyˈrologist** *n.*

papyrus (pəˈpaɪrəs) *n., pl.* **-ri** (-raɪ) *or* **-ruses.** **1.** a tall aquatic plant of S Europe and N and central Africa. **2.** a kind of paper made from the stem pith of this plant, used by the ancient Egyptians, Greeks, and Romans. **3.** an ancient document written on this paper. [C14: via L < Gk *papūros* reed used in making paper]

par (pɑː) *n.* **1.** an accepted standard, such as an average (esp. in **up to par**). **2.** a state of equality (esp. in **on a par with**). **3.** *Finance.* the established value of the unit of one national currency in terms of the unit of another. **4.** *Commerce.* **a.** See **par value. b.** equality between the current market value of a share, bond, etc., and its face value, indicated by **at par; above** (*or* **below**) **par** indicates that the market value is above (or below) face value. **5.** *Golf.* a standard score for a hole or course that a good player should make: *par for the course was 72.* *~adj.* **6.** average or normal. **7.** (*usually prenominal*) of or relating to par: *par value.* [C17: < L *pār* equal]

par. *abbrev. for:* **1.** paragraph. **2.** parallel. **3.** parenthesis. **4.** parish.

para (ˈpærə) *n. Inf.* **1. a.** a soldier in an airborne unit. **b.** an airborne unit. **2.** a paragraph.

para-[1] *or before a vowel* **par-** *prefix.* **1.** beside; near: *parameter.* **2.** beyond: *parapsychology.* **3.** resembling: *paratyphoid fever.* **4.** defective; abnormal: *paranoia.* **5.** (*usually in italics*) denoting that an organic compound contains a benzene ring with substituents attached to atoms that are directly opposite (the 1,4- positions): *para*-cresol. **6.** denoting an isomer, polymer, or compound related to a specified compound: *paraldehyde.* **7.** denoting the form of a diatomic substance in which the spins of the two constituent atoms are antiparallel: *parahydrogen.* [< Gk *para* (prep.) alongside, beyond]

para-[2] *combining form.* indicating an object that acts as a protection against something: *parachute; parasol.* [via F < It. *para-*, < *parare* to defend, ult. < L *parāre* to prepare]

para-aminobenzoic acid (əˌmaɪnəʊbɛnˈzəʊɪk, -ˌmiː-) *n. Biochem.* an acid present in yeast and liver: used in the manufacture of dyes and pharmaceuticals.

parabasis (pəˈræbəsɪs) *n., pl.* **-ses** (-ˌsiːz). (in classical Greek comedy) an address by the chorus. [C19: < Gk, < *parabanein* to step forward]

parabiosis (ˌpærəbaɪˈəʊsɪs) *n.* **1.** the natural union of two individuals, such as Siamese twins. **2.** a similar union induced for experimental or therapeutic purposes. [C20: < PARA-[1] + Gk *biōsis* manner of life, < *bios* life] **—parabiotic** (ˌpærəbaɪˈɒtɪk) *adj.*

parable (ˈpærəbᵊl) *n.* **1.** a short story that uses familiar events to illustrate a religious or ethical situation. **2.** any of the stories of this kind told by Jesus Christ. [C14: < OF *parabole*, < L *parabola* comparison, < Gk *parabolē* analogy, < *paraballein* to throw alongside]

parabola (pəˈræbələ) *n.* a conic section formed by the intersection of a cone by a plane parallel to its side. [C16: via NL < Gk *parabolē* a setting alongside; see PARABLE]

parabolic[1] (ˌpærəˈbɒlɪk) *adj.* **1.** of, relating to, or shaped like a parabola. **2.** shaped like a paraboloid: *a parabolic mirror.*

parabolic[2] (ˌpærəˈbɒlɪk) *or* **parabolical** *adj.* of or like a parable. **—ˌparaˈbolically** *adv.*

parabolic aerial *n.* a formal name for **dish aerial.**

paraboloid (pəˈræbəˌlɔɪd) *n.* a geometric surface whose sections parallel to two coordinate planes are parabolic and whose sections parallel to the third plane are either elliptical or hyperbolic. **—paˌraboˈloidal** *adj.*

paracetamol (ˌpærəˈsiːtəˌmɒl, -ˈsɛtə-) *n.* a mild analgesic drug. [C20: < *para-acetamidophenol*]

parachronism (pəˈrækrəˌnɪzəm) *n.* an error in dating, esp. by giving too late a date. [C17: < PARA-[1] + *-chronism*, as in ANACHRONISM]

parachute (ˈpærəˌʃuːt) *n.* **1.** a device used to retard the fall of a person or package from an aircraft, consisting of a large fabric canopy connected to a harness. *~vb.* **2.** (of troops, supplies, etc.) to land or cause to land by parachute from an aircraft. [C18: < F, < PARA-[2] + *chute* fall] **—ˈparaˌchutist** *n.*

Paraclete (ˈpærəˌkliːt) *n. Christianity.* the Holy Ghost as comforter or advocate. [C15: via OF < Church L *Paraclētus*, < LGk *Paraklētos* advocate, < Gk *parakalein* to summon help]

parade (pəˈreɪd) *n.* **1.** an ordered, esp. ceremonial, march or procession, as of troops being reviewed. **2.** Also called: **parade ground.** a place where military formations regularly assemble. **3.** a visible show or display: *to make a parade of one's grief.* **4.** a public promenade or street of shops. **5.** a successive display of things or people. **6. on parade. a.** on display. **b.** showing oneself off. *~vb.* **7.** (when *intr.*, often foll. by *through* or *along*) to walk or march, esp. in a procession. **8.** (*tr.*) to exhibit or flaunt: *he was parading his medals.* **9.** (*tr.*) to cause to assemble in formation, as for a military parade. **10.** (*intr.*) to walk about in a public place. [C17: < F: a making ready, a boasting display] **—paˈrader** *n.*

paradigm (ˈpærəˌdaɪm) *n.* **1.** the set of all the

inflected forms of a word. **2.** a pattern or model. **3.** (in the philosophy of science) a general conception of the nature of scientific endeavour within which a given enquiry is undertaken. [C15: via F & L < Gk *paradeigma* pattern, < *paradeiknunai* to compare] —**paradigmatic** (ˌpærədɪɡˈmætɪk) *adj.*

paradise (ˈpærəˌdaɪs) *n.* **1.** heaven as the ultimate abode or state of the righteous. **2.** *Islam.* the sensual garden of delights that the Koran promises the faithful after death. **3.** Also called: **limbo.** (according to some theologians) the intermediate abode or state of the just prior to the Resurrection of Jesus. **4.** the Garden of Eden. **5.** any place or condition that fulfils all one's desires or aspirations. **6.** a park in which foreign animals are kept. [OE, < Church L *paradīsus,* < Gk *paradeisos* garden, of Persian origin] —**paradisiacal** (ˌpærədɪˈsaɪəkᵊl), **paradisiac** (ˌpærəˈdɪsɪˌæk), *or* **paradisaical** (ˌpærədɪˈseɪɪkᵊl) *adj.*

paradise duck *n.* a New Zealand duck with bright plumage.

paradox (ˈpærəˌdɒks) *n.* **1.** a seemingly absurd or self-contradictory statement that is or may be true: *religious truths are often expressed in paradox.* **2.** a self-contradictory proposition, such as *I always tell lies.* **3.** a person or thing exhibiting apparently contradictory characteristics. **4.** an opinion that conflicts with common belief. [C16: < LL *paradoxum,* < Gk *paradoxos* opposed to existing notions] —ˌ**paraˈdoxical** *adj.* —ˌ**paraˈdoxically** *adv.*

paradoxical sleep *n. Physiol.* sleep that appears to be deep but that is characterized by rapid eye movements, heavier breathing, and increased electrical activity of the brain.

paraffin (ˈpærəfɪn) *n.* **1.** Also called: **paraffin oil,** (esp. U.S. and Canad.) **kerosene.** a liquid mixture consisting mainly of alkane hydrocarbons, used as an aircraft fuel, in domestic heaters, and as a solvent. **2.** another name for **alkane. 3.** See **paraffin wax. 4.** See **liquid paraffin.** ~*vb.* (*tr.*) **5.** to treat with paraffin. [C19: < G, < L *parum* too little + *affinis* adjacent; so called from its chemical inertia]

paraffin wax *n.* a white insoluble odourless waxlike solid consisting mainly of alkane hydrocarbons, used in candles, waterproof paper, and as a sealing agent. Also called: **paraffin.**

paragliding (ˈpærəˌɡlaɪdɪŋ) *n.* the sport of cross-country gliding using a specially designed parachute shaped like flexible wings. The parachutist glides from an aeroplane to a predetermined landing area.

paragon (ˈpærəɡən) *n.* a model of excellence; pattern: *a paragon of virtue.* [C16: via F < OIt. *paragone* comparison, < Med. Gk *parakonē,* < PARA-¹ + *akonē* whetstone]

paragraph (ˈpærəˌɡrɑːf) *n.* **1.** (in a piece of writing) one of a series of subsections each usually devoted to one idea and each marked by the beginning of a new line, indention, etc. **2.** *Printing.* the character ¶, used to indicate the beginning of a new paragraph. **3.** a short article, etc., in a newspaper. ~*vb.* (*tr.*) **4.** to form into paragraphs. **5.** to express or report in a paragraph. [C16: < Med. L *paragraphus,* < Gk *paragraphos* line drawing attention to part of a text, < *paragraphein* to write beside] —**paragraphic** (ˌpærəˈɡræfɪk) *adj.*

paragraphia (ˌpærəˈɡrɑːfɪə) *n. Psychiatry.* the habitual writing of a different word or letter from the one intended, often the result of a mental disorder. [C20: < NL; see PARA-¹, -GRAPH]

Paraguayan (ˈpærəˌɡwaɪən) *adj.* **1.** of or relating to Paraguay, a republic in South America. ~*n.* **2.** a native or inhabitant of Paraguay.

Paraguay tea (ˈpærəˌɡwaɪ) *n.* another name for **maté.**

parahydrogen (ˌpærəˈhaɪdrədʒən) *n. Chem.* the form of molecular hydrogen in which the nuclei of the two atoms in each molecule spin in opposite directions.

parakeet *or* **parrakeet** (ˈpærəˌkiːt) *n.* any of numerous small long-tailed parrots. [C16: < Sp. *periquito* & OF *paroquet* parrot, <?]

paraldehyde (pəˈrældɪˌhaɪd) *n.* a colourless liquid substance that is a cyclic trimer of acetaldehyde: used as a hypnotic.

paralipsis (ˌpaerəˈlɪpsɪs) *or* **paraleipsis** (ˌpærəˈlaɪpsɪs) *n., pl.* **-ses** (-siːz). a rhetorical device in which an idea is emphasized by the pretence that it is too obvious to discuss, as in *there are many practical drawbacks, not to mention the cost.* [C16: via LL < Gk: neglect, < *paraleipein* to leave aside]

parallax (ˈpærəˌlæks) *n.* **1.** an apparent change in the position of an object resulting from a change in position of the observer. **2.** *Astron.* the angle subtended at a celestial body, esp. a star, by the radius of the earth's orbit. [C17: via F < NL *parallaxis,* < Gk: change, < *parallassein* to change] —**parallactic** (ˌpærəˈlæktɪk) *adj.*

parallel (ˈpærəˌlɛl) *adj.* (when *postpositive,* usually foll. by *to*) **1.** separated by an equal distance at every point; never touching or intersecting: *parallel walls.* **2.** corresponding; similar: *parallel situations.* **3.** *Music.* Also: **consecutive.** (of two or more parts or melodies) moving in similar motion but keeping the same interval apart throughout: *parallel fifths.* **4.** *Grammar.* denoting syntactic constructions in which the constituents of one construction correspond to those of the other. **5.** *Computers.* operating on several items of information, instructions, etc., simultaneously. ~*n.* **6.** *Maths.* one of a set of parallel lines, planes, etc. **7.** an exact likeness. **8.** a comparison. **9.** Also called: **parallel of latitude.** any of the imaginary lines around the earth parallel to the equator, designated by degrees of latitude. **10. a.** a configuration of two or more electrical components connected between two points in a circuit so that the same voltage is applied to each (esp. in **in parallel**). Cf. **series** (sense 6). **b.** (*as modifier*): *a parallel circuit.* **11.** *Printing.* the character (‖) used as a reference mark. ~*vb.* **-leling, -leled.** (*tr.*) **12.** to make parallel. **13.** to supply a parallel to. **14.** to be a parallel to or correspond with: *your experience parallels mine.* [C16: via F & L < Gk *parallēlos* alongside one another]

parallel bars *pl. n. Gymnastics.* a pair of wooden bars on uprights used for various exercises.

parallelepiped (ˌpærəˌlɛlɪˈpaɪpɛd) *or* **parallelepipedon** (ˌpærəˌlɛlɪˈpaɪpɪdən) *n.* a geometric solid whose six faces are parallelograms. [C16: < Gk, < *parallēlos* PARALLEL + *epipedon* plane surface, < EPI- + *pedon* ground]

parallelism (ˈpærəˌlɛlɪzəm) *n.* **1.** the state of being parallel. **2.** *Grammar.* the repetition of a syntactic construction in successive sentences for rhetorical effect. **3** *Philosophy.* the doctrine that mental and physical processes are regularly correlated but are not casually connected, so that, for example, pain always accompanies, but is not caused by, a pinprick.

parallelogram (ˌpærəˈlɛləˌɡræm) *n.* a quadrilateral whose opposite sides are parallel and equal in length. [C16: via F < LL, < Gk *parallēlogrammon,* < *parallēlos* PARALLEL + *grammē* line]

parallelogram rule *n. Maths, physics.* a rule for finding the resultant of two vectors by constructing a parallelogram with two adjacent sides representing the magnitudes and directions of the vectors, the diagonal through the point of intersection of the vectors representing their resultant.

paralogism (pəˈræləˌdʒɪzəm) *n.* **1.** *Logic, obs.* an argument that is unintentionally invalid. Cf. **sophism. 2.** any invalid argument or conclusion. [C16: via LL < Gk *paralogismos,* < *paralogizesthai* to argue fallaciously, < PARA-¹ + *-logizesthai,* ult. < *logos* word] —**paˈralogist** *n.*

paralyse *or U.S.* **-lyze** (ˈpærəˌlaɪz) *vb.* (*tr.*) **1.** *Pathol.* to affect with paralysis. **2.** *Med.* to render (a part of the body) insensitive to pain, touch, etc. **3.** to make immobile; transfix. [C19: < F *paralyser,* < *paralysie* PARALYSIS] —ˌ**paralyˈsation** *or U.S.* **-lyˈzation** *n.* —ˈ**paraˌlyser** *or U.S.* **-ˌlyzer** *n.*

paralysis (pəˈrælɪsɪs) *n., pl.* **-ses** (-ˌsiːz). **1.** *Pathol.* **a.** impairment or loss of voluntary muscle function or of sensation (**sensory paralysis**) in a part or area of the body. **b.** a disease characterized by such impairment or loss; palsy. **2.** cessation or impairment of activity: *paralysis of industry by strikes.* [C16: via L < Gk *paralusis;* see PARA-[1], -LYSIS]

paralytic (ˌpærəˈlɪtɪk) *adj.* **1.** of, relating to, or of the nature of paralysis. **2.** afflicted with or subject to paralysis. **3.** *Brit. inf.* very drunk. ~*n.* **4.** a person afflicted with paralysis.

paramagnetism (ˌpærəˈmægnɪˌtɪzəm) *n. Physics.* a weakly magnetic condition of substances with a relative permeability just greater than unity: used in some low temperature techniques. —**paramagnetic** (ˌpærəmægˈnɛtɪk) *adj.*

paramatta *or* **parramatta** (ˌpærəˈmætə) *n.* a lightweight twill-weave dress fabric of wool with silk or cotton, now used esp. for rubber-proofed garments. [C19: after *Parramatta,* New South Wales, Australia, where orig. produced]

paramecium (ˌpærəˈmiːsɪəm) *n., pl.* **-cia** (-sɪə). any of a genus of freshwater protozoa having an oval body covered with cilia and a ventral groove for feeding. [C18: NL, < Gk *paramēkēs* elongated, < PARA-[1] + *mēkos* length]

paramedic (ˌpærəˈmɛdɪk) *or* **paramedical** *n.* **1.** a person, such as a laboratory technician, who supplements the work of the medical profession. ~*adj.* **2.** of or designating such a person.

parameter (pəˈræmɪtə) *n.* **1.** an arbitrary constant that determines the specific form of a mathematical expression, such as *a* and *b* in $y = ax^2 + b$. **2.** a characteristic constant of a statistical population, such as its variance or mean. **3.** *Inf.* any constant or limiting factor: *a designer must work within the parameters of budget and practicality.* [C17: < NL; see PARA-[1], -METER] —**parametric** (ˌpærəˈmɛtrɪk) *adj.*

parametric amplifier *n.* a type of high-frequency amplifier in which energy is transferred to the input signal through a circuit with a varying reactance.

paramilitary (ˌpærəˈmɪlɪtərɪ, -trɪ) *adj.* **1.** denoting or relating to a group of personnel with military structure functioning either as a civil force or in support of military forces. **2.** denoting or relating to a force with military structure conducting armed operations against a ruling power.

paramount (ˈpærəˌmaʊnt) *adj.* of the greatest importance or significance. [C16: via Anglo-Norman < OF *paramont,* < *par* by + *-amont* above, < L *ad montem* to the mountain] —ˈ**paraˌmountcy** *n.* —ˈ**paraˌmountly** *adv.*

paramour (ˈpærəˌmʊə) *n.* **1.** *Now usually derog.* a lover, esp. adulterous. **2.** an archaic word for **beloved.** [C13: < OF, lit.: through love]

parang (ˈpɑːræŋ) *n.* a Malay short stout straight-edged knife used in Borneo. [C19: < Malay]

paranoia (ˌpærəˈnɔɪə) *n.* **1.** a mental disorder characterized by any of several types of delusions, as of grandeur or persecution. **2.** *Inf.* intense fear or suspicion, esp. when unfounded. [C19: via NL < Gk: frenzy, < *paranoos* distraught, < PARA-[1] + *noos* mind] —ˈ**paraˌnoid, paranoiac** (ˌpærəˈnɔɪɪk) *or* **paranoic** (ˌpærəˈnəʊɪk) *adj., n.*

paranormal (ˌpærəˈnɔːməl) *adj.* **1.** beyond normal explanation. ~*n.* **2. the.** paranormal happenings generally.

parapet (ˈpærəpɪt, -ˌpɛt) *n.* **1.** a low wall or railing along the edge of a balcony, roof, etc. **2.** *Mil.* a rampart, mound of sandbags, etc., in front of a trench giving protection from fire. [C16: < It. *parapetto,* lit.: chest-high wall, < L *pectus* breast]

paraph (ˈpærəf) *n.* a flourish after a signature, originally to prevent forgery. [C14: via F < Med. L *paraphus,* var. of *paragraphus* PARAGRAPH]

paraphernalia (ˌpærəfəˈneɪlɪə) *pl. n.* (*sometimes functioning as sing.*) **1.** miscellaneous articles or equipment. **2.** *Law.* (formerly) articles of personal property given to a married woman by her husband and regarded in law as her possessions. [C17: via Med. L < L *parapherna* personal property of a married woman, apart from her dowry, < Gk, < PARA-[1] + *phernē* dowry, < *pherein* to carry]

paraphrase (ˈpærəˌfreɪz) *n.* **1.** an expression of a statement or text in other words. ~*vb.* **2.** to put into other words; restate. [C16: via F < L *paraphrasis,* < Gk, < *paraphrazein* to recount] —**paraphrastic** (ˌpærəˈfræstɪk) *adj.*

paraplegia (ˌpærəˈpliːdʒə) *n. Pathol.* paralysis of the lower half of the body, usually as the result of disease or injury of the spine. [C17: via NL < Gk: a blow on one side, < PARA-[1] + *plēssein* to strike] —ˌ**paraˈplegic** *adj., n.*

parapraxis (ˌpærəˈpræksɪs) *n., pl.* **-praxes** (-ˈpræksiːz) *Psychoanal.* a minor error in action, such as a slip of the tongue. [C20: < PARA-[1] + Gk *praxis* a deed]

parapsychology (ˌpærəsaɪˈkɒlədʒɪ) *n.* the study of mental phenomena, such as telepathy, which are beyond the scope of normal physical explanation. —ˌ**parapsyˈchologist** *n.*

Paraquat (ˈpærəˌkwɒt) *n. Trademark.* a yellow extremely poisonous weedkiller.

parascending (ˈpærəˌsɛndɪŋ) *n.* a sport in which a parachutist, starting from ground level, is towed by a vehicle until he is airborne and then descends in the normal way.

paraselene (ˌpærəsɪˈliːnɪ) *n., pl.* **-nae** (-niː). a bright image of the moon on a lunar halo. Also called: **mock moon.** [C17: NL, < PARA-[1] + Gk *selēnē* moon]

parasite (ˈpærəˌsaɪt) *n.* **1.** an animal or plant that lives in or on another (the host) from which it obtains nourishment. **2.** a person who habitually lives at the expense of others; sponger. [C16: via L < Gk *parasitos* one who lives at another's expense, < PARA-[1] + *sitos* grain] —**parasitic** (ˌpærəˈsɪtɪk) *or* ˌ**paraˈsitical** *adj.* —ˌ**paraˈsitically** *adv.* —ˈ**parasiˌtism** *n.*

parasitize *or* **-tise** (ˈpærəsɪˌtaɪz) *vb.* (*tr.*) **1.** to infest with parasites. **2.** to live on (another organism) as a parasite. —ˌ**parasitiˈzation** *or* **-tiˈsation** *n.*

parasitology (ˌpærəsaɪˈtɒlədʒɪ) *n.* the branch of biology that is concerned with the study of parasites. —ˌ**parasitˈologist** *n.*

parasol (ˈpærəˌsɒl) *n.* an umbrella used for protection against the sun; sunshade. [C17: via F < It. *parasole,* < PARA-[2] + *sole* sun, < L *sōl*]

parasympathetic (ˌpærəˌsɪmpəˈθɛtɪk) *adj. Anat., Physiol.* of or relating to the division of the autonomic nervous system that acts by slowing the heartbeat, constricting the bronchi of the lungs, stimulating the smooth muscles of the digestive tract, etc. Cf. **sympathetic** (sense 4).

parasynthesis (ˌpærəˈsɪnθɪsɪs) *n.* formation of words by compounding a phrase and adding an affix, as *light-headed, light* + *head* with the affix *-ed.* —**parasynthetic** (ˌpærəsɪnˈθɛtɪk) *adj.*

parataxis (ˌpærəˈtæksɪs) *n.* the juxtaposition of clauses without the use of a conjunction, as *None of my friends stayed—they all left early.* [C19: NL < Gk, < *paratassein,* lit.: to arrange side by side] —**paratactic** (ˌpærəˈtæktɪk) *adj.*

parathion (ˌpærəˈθaɪɒn) *n.* a toxic oil used as an insecticide. [< PARA-[1] + Gk *theion* sulphur]

parathyroid gland (ˌpærəˈθaɪrɔɪd) *n.* any one of the small egg-shaped endocrine glands situated near or embedded within the thyroid gland.

paratroops (ˈpærəˌtruːps) *pl. n.* troops trained and equipped to be dropped by parachute into a battle area. Also called: **paratroopers.**

paratyphoid fever (ˌpærəˈtaɪfɔɪd) *n.* a disease resembling but less severe than typhoid fever, caused by bacteria of the genus *Salmonella.*

paravane (ˈpærəˌveɪn) *n.* a torpedo-shaped device towed from the bow of a vessel so that the cables will cut the anchors of any moored mines. [C20: < PARA-[2] + VANE]

par avion *French.* (par avjɔ̃) *adv.* by aeroplane: used in labelling mail sent by air.

parazoan (ˌpærəˈzəʊən) *n., pl.* **-zoa** (-ˈzəʊə). any

multicellular invertebrate of a division of the animal kingdom, the sponges. [C19: < *parazoa*, on the model of *protozoa* & *metazoa*, < PARA-[1] + Gk *zōon* animal]

parboil (ˈpɑːˌbɔɪl) *vb.* (*tr.*) **1.** to boil until partially cooked. **2.** to subject to uncomfortable heat. [C15: < OF *parboillir*, < LL *perbullīre* to boil thoroughly (see PER-, BOIL[1]); modern meaning due to confusion of *par-* with *part*]

parbuckle (ˈpɑːˌbʌkᵊl) *n.* **1.** a rope sling for lifting or lowering a heavy cylindrical object, such as a cask. ~*vb.* **2.** (*tr.*) to raise or lower (an object) with such a sling. [C17 *parbunkel*: <?]

parcel (ˈpɑːsᵊl) *n.* **1.** something wrapped up; package. **2.** a group of people or things having some common characteristic. **3.** a quantity of some commodity offered for sale; lot. **4.** a distinct portion of land. ~*vb.* **-celling, -celled** *or U.S.* **-celing, -celed.** (*tr.*) **5.** (often foll. by *up*) to make a parcel of; wrap up. **6.** (often foll. by *out*) to divide (up) into portions. [C14: < OF *parcelle*, < L *particula* PARTICLE]

parch (pɑːtʃ) *vb.* **1.** to deprive or be deprived of water; dry up: *the sun parches the fields.* **2.** (*tr.; usually passive*) to make very thirsty. **3.** (*tr.*) to roast (corn, etc.) lightly. [C14: <?]

Parcheesi (pɑːˈtʃiːzɪ) *n. Trademark.* a board game derived from the ancient game of pachisi.

parchment (ˈpɑːtʃmənt) *n.* **1.** the skin of certain animals, such as sheep, treated to form a durable material, as for manuscripts. **2.** a manuscript, etc., made of this material. **3.** a type of stiff yellowish paper resembling parchment. [C13: < OF *parchemin*, via L < Gk *pergamēnē*, < *Pergamēnos* of Pergamum (where parchment was made); OF *parchemin* was infl. by *parche* leather, < L *Parthica* (*pellis*) Parthian (leather)]

pard (pɑːd) *n. Arch.* a leopard or panther. [C13: via OF < L *pardus*, < Gk *pardos*]

pardon (ˈpɑːdᵊn) *vb.* (*tr.*) **1.** to excuse or forgive (a person) for (an offence, mistake, etc.): *to pardon someone; to pardon a fault.* ~*n.* **2.** forgiveness. **3. a.** release from punishment for an offence. **b.** the warrant granting such release. **4.** a Roman Catholic indulgence. ~*sentence substitute.* **5.** Also: **pardon me; I beg your pardon. a.** sorry; excuse me. **b.** what did you say? [C13: < OF, < Med. L *perdōnum*, < *perdōnāre* to forgive freely, < L *per* (intensive) + *dōnāre* to grant] —ˈ**pardonable** *adj.* —ˈ**pardonably** *adv.*

pardoner (ˈpɑːdᵊnə) *n.* (before the Reformation) a person licensed to sell ecclesiastical indulgences.

pare (pɛə) *vb.* (*tr.*) **1.** to peel (the outer layer) from (something). **2.** to cut the edges from (the nails). **3.** to decrease bit by bit. [C13: < OF *parer* to adorn, < L *parāre* to make ready] —ˈ**parer** *n.*

paregoric (ˌpærəˈgɒrɪk) *n.* a medicine consisting of opium, benzoic acid, and camphor, formerly widely used to relieve diarrhoea and coughing. [C17 (meaning: relieving pain): via LL < Gk *parēgoros* relating to soothing speech, < PARA-[1] (beside) + *agora* assembly]

pareira (pəˈrɛərə) *n.* the root of a South American climbing plant, used as a diuretic, tonic, and as a source of curare. [C18: < Port. *pareira brava*, lit.: wild vine]

parenchyma (pəˈrɛŋkɪmə) *n.* **1.** a soft plant tissue consisting of simple thin-walled cells: constitutes the greater part of fruits, stems, roots, etc. **2.** animal tissue that constitutes the essential part of an organ as distinct from the blood vessels, connective tissue, etc. [C17: via NL < Gk *parenkhuma* something poured in beside, < PARA-[1] + *enkhuma* infusion] —**parenchymatous** (ˌpærɛŋˈkɪmətəs) *adj.*

parent (ˈpɛərənt) *n.* **1.** a father or mother. **2.** a person acting as a father or mother; guardian. **3.** *Rare.* an ancestor. **4.** a source or cause. **5.** an organism or organization that has produced one or more organisms similar to itself. **6.** *Physics, chem.* a precursor, such as a nucleus or compound, of a derived entity. [C15: via OF < L *parens* parent, < *parere* to bring forth] —**paˈrental** *adj.* —ˈ**parenthood** *n.*

parentage (ˈpɛərəntɪdʒ) *n.* **1.** ancestry. **2.** derivation from a particular origin. **3.** a less common word for **parenthood.**

parent company *n.* a company that owns a number of subsidiary companies.

parenteral (pæˈrɛntərəl) *adj. Med.* **1.** (esp. of the route by which a drug is administered) by means other than through the digestive tract, esp. by injection. **2.** designating a drug to be injected. [C20: < PARA-[1] + ENTERO- + -AL[1]]

parenthesis (pəˈrɛnθɪsɪs) *n., pl.* **-ses** (-ˌsiːz). **1.** a phrase, often explanatory or qualifying, inserted into a passage with which it is not grammatically connected, and marked off by brackets, dashes, etc. **2.** Also called: **bracket.** either of a pair of characters, (), used to enclose such a phrase or as a sign of aggregation in mathematical or logical expressions. **3.** an interlude; interval. **4. in parenthesis.** inserted as a parenthesis. [C16: via LL < Gk: something placed in besides, < *parentithenai*, < PARA-[1] + EN-[2] + *tithenai* to put] —**parenthetic** (ˌpærənˈθɛtɪk) *or* ˌ**parenˈthetical** *adj.* —ˌ**parenˈthetically** *adv.*

parenthesize *or* **-sise** (pəˈrɛnθɪˌsaɪz) *vb.* (*tr.*) **1.** to place in parentheses. **2.** to insert as a parenthesis. **3.** to intersperse (a speech, writing, etc.) with parentheses.

parenting (ˈpɛərəntɪŋ) *n.* all the skills and experience of bringing up children.

parent teacher association *n.* a social group of the parents of children at a school and their teachers formed in order to foster better understanding between them and to organize fund-raising activities on behalf of the school.

parergon (pəˈrɛəgɒn) *n., pl.* **-ga** (-gə). work that is not one's main employment. [C17: < L, < Gk, < PARA-[1] + *ergon* work]

paresis (pəˈriːsɪs, ˈpærɪsɪs) *n., pl.* **-ses** (-ˌsiːz). *Pathol.* incomplete or slight paralysis of motor functions. [C17: via NL < Gk: a relaxation, < *parienai* to let go] —**paretic** (pəˈrɛtɪk) *adj.*

par excellence *French.* (par ɛksɛlɑ̃s; *English* pɑːr ˈɛksələns) *adv.* to a degree of excellence; beyond comparison. [F, lit.: by (way of) excellence]

parfait (pɑːˈfeɪ) *n.* a rich frozen dessert made from eggs and cream, fruit, etc. [< F: PERFECT]

parget (ˈpɑːdʒɪt) *n.* **1.** Also called: **pargeting. a.** plaster, mortar, etc., used to line chimney flues or cover walls. **b.** plasterwork that has incised ornamental patterns. ~*vb.* (*tr.*) **2.** to cover or decorate with parget. [C14: < OF *pargeter* to throw over, < *par* PER- + *geter* to throw]

parhelic circle *n. Meteorol.* a luminous band at the same altitude as the sun, parallel to the horizon, caused by reflection of the sun's rays by ice crystals in the atmosphere.

parhelion (pɑːˈhiːlɪən) *n., pl.* **-lia** (-lɪə). one of several bright spots on the parhelic circle or solar halo, caused by the diffraction of light by ice crystals in the atmosphere. Also called: **mock sun.** [C17: via L < Gk *parēlion*, < PARA-[1] (beside) + *hēlios* sun] —**parˈhelic** *or* **parheliacal** (ˌpɑːhɪˈlaɪəkᵊl) *adj.*

pariah (pəˈraɪə, ˈpærɪə) *n.* **1.** a social outcast. **2.** (formerly) a member of a low caste in South India. [C17: < Tamil *paraiyan* drummer, < *parai* drum: members were drummers at festivals]

pariah dog *n.* another term for **pye-dog.**

parietal (pəˈraɪɪtᵊl) *adj.* **1.** *Anat., biol.* of or forming the walls of a bodily cavity: *the parietal bones of the skull.* **2.** of or relating to the side of the skull. **3.** (of plant ovaries) having ovules attached to the walls. **4.** *U.S.* living or having authority within a college. ~*n.* **5.** a parietal bone. [C16: < LL *parietālis*, < L *pariēs* wall]

parietal lobe *n.* the portion of each cerebral hemisphere concerned with the perception of sensations of touch, temperature, and taste and with muscular movements.

pari-mutuel (ˌpærɪˈmjuːtʃʊəl) *n., pl.* **pari-mutuels** *or* **paris-mutuels** (ˌpærɪˈmjuːtʃʊəlz). a system of betting in which those who have bet on the winners of a race share in the total amount wagered less a percentage for the management. [C19: < F, lit.: mutual wager]

paring (ˈpɛərɪŋ) *n.* (*often pl.*) something pared or cut off.

pari passu *Latin.* (ˌpærɪ ˈpæsuː, ˈpɑːrɪ) *adv. Usually legal.* with equal speed or progress.

Paris Commune (ˈpærɪs) *n. French history.* the council established in Paris in the spring of 1871 in opposition to the National Assembly and esp. to the peace negotiated with Prussia following the Franco-Prussian War.

Paris green *n.* an emerald-green poisonous substance used as a pigment and insecticide.

parish (ˈpærɪʃ) *n.* **1.** a subdivision of a diocese, having its own church and a clergyman. **2.** the churchgoers of such a subdivision. **3.** (in England and, formerly, Wales) the smallest unit of local government. **4.** (in Louisiana) a county. **5.** (in Quebec and New Brunswick, Canada) a subdivision of a county. **6.** the people living in a parish. **7. on the parish.** *History.* receiving parochial relief. [C13: < OF *paroisse,* < Church L, < LGk, < *paroikos* Christian, sojourner, < Gk: neighbour, < PARA-[1] (beside) + *oikos* house]

parish clerk *n.* a person designated to assist in various church duties.

parish council *n.* (in England and, formerly, Wales) the administrative body of a parish. See **parish** (sense 3).

parishioner (pəˈrɪʃənə) *n.* a member of a particular parish.

parish pump *adj.* of only local interest; parochial.

parish register *n.* a book in which the births, baptisms, marriages, and deaths in a parish are recorded.

parity (ˈpærɪtɪ) *n., pl.* **-ties. 1.** equality of rank, pay, etc. **2.** close or exact analogy or equivalence. **3.** *Finance.* the amount of a foreign currency equivalent to a specific sum of domestic currency. **4.** equality between prices of commodities or securities in two separate markets. **5.** *Physics.* **a.** a property of a physical system characterized by the behaviour of the sign of its wave function when reflected in space. The wave function either remains unchanged (**even parity**) or changes in sign (**odd parity**). **b.** a quantum number describing this property, equal to +1 for even parity systems and -1 for odd parity systems. Symbol: *P* **6.** *Maths.* a relationship between two integers. If both are odd or both even they have the same parity; if one is odd and one even they have different parity. [C16: < LL *pāritās;* see PAR]

parity check *n.* a check made of computer data to ensure that the total number of bits of value 1 (or 0) in each unit of information remains odd or even after transfer between a peripheral device and the memory or vice versa.

park (pɑːk) *n.* **1.** a large area of land preserved in a natural state for recreational use by the public. **2.** a piece of open land in a town with public amenities. **3.** a large area of land forming a private estate. **4.** an area designed to accommodate a number of related enterprises: *a business park.* **5.** *U.S. & Canad.* a playing field or sports stadium. **6. the park.** *Brit. inf.* a soccer pitch. **7.** a gear selector position on the automatic transmission of a motor vehicle that acts as a parking brake. **8.** the area in which the equipment and supplies of a military formation are assembled. ~*vb.* **9.** to stop and leave (a vehicle) temporarily. **10.** to manoeuvre (a motor vehicle) into a space for it to be left: *try to park without hitting the kerb.* **11.** (*tr.*) *Inf.* to leave or put somewhere: *park yourself in front of the fire.* **12.** (*intr.*) *Mil.* to arrange equipment in a park. **13.** (*tr.*) to enclose in or as a park. [C13: < OF *parc,* < Med. L *parricus* enclosure, < Gmc]

parka (ˈpɑːkə) *n.* a warm weatherproof coat with a hood, originally worn by Eskimos. [C19: < Aleutian: skin]

parkin (ˈpɑːkɪn) *n. Brit.* moist spicy ginger cake usually containing oatmeal. [C19: <?]

parking lot *n.* the U.S. and Canad. term for **car park.**

parking meter *n.* a timing device, usually coin-operated, that indicates how long a vehicle may be left parked.

parking orbit *n.* an orbit around the earth or moon in which a spacecraft can be placed temporarily in order to prepare for the next step in its programme.

parking ticket *n.* a summons served for a parking offence.

Parkinson's disease (ˈpɑːkɪnsənz) *n.* a progressive chronic disorder of the central nervous system characterized by impaired muscular coordination and tremor. Also called: **parkinsonism.** [C19: after James *Parkinson* (1755–1824), E surgeon, who first described it]

Parkinson's law *n.* the notion, expressed facetiously as a law of economics, that work expands to fill the time available for its completion. [C20: after C. N. *Parkinson* (born 1909), E economist, who formulated it]

park keeper *n.* (in Britain) an official who patrols and supervises a public park.

parkland (ˈpɑːkˌlænd) *n.* grassland with scattered trees.

parky (ˈpɑːkɪ) *adj.* **parkier, parkiest.** (*usually postpositive*) *Brit. inf.* (of the weather) chilly; cold. [C19: ? < PERKY]

Parl. *abbrev. for:* **1.** Parliament. **2.** Also: **parl.** parliamentary.

parlance (ˈpɑːləns) *n.* a particular manner of speaking, esp. when specialized; idiom: *political parlance.* [C16: < OF, < *parler* to talk, via Med. L < LL *parabola* speech]

parlando (pɑːˈlændəʊ) *adj., adv. Music.* to be performed as though speaking. [It.: speaking]

parley (ˈpɑːlɪ) *n.* **1.** a discussion, esp. between enemies under a truce to decide terms of surrender, etc. ~*vb.* **2.** (*intr.*) to discuss, esp. with an enemy. [C16: < F, < *parler* to talk, < Med. L *parabolāre,* < LL *parabola* speech]

parliament (ˈpɑːləmənt) *n.* **1.** an assembly of the representatives of a political nation or people, often the supreme legislative authority. **2.** any legislative or deliberative assembly, conference, etc. [C13: < Anglo-L *parliamentum,* < OF *parlement,* < *parler* to speak; see PARLEY]

Parliament (ˈpɑːləmənt) *n.* **1.** the highest legislative authority in Britain, consisting of the House of Commons, which exercises effective power, the House of Lords, and the sovereign. **2.** a similar legislature in another country or state. **3.** any of the assemblies of such a body created by a general election and royal summons and dissolved before the next election.

parliamentarian (ˌpɑːləmɛnˈtɛərɪən) *n.* **1.** an expert in parliamentary procedures. ~*adj.* **2.** of or relating to a parliament.

parliamentary (ˌpɑːləˈmɛntərɪ) *adj.* (*sometimes cap.*) **1.** of or proceeding from a parliament or Parliament: *a parliamentary decree.* **2.** conforming to the procedures of a parliament or Parliament: *parliamentary conduct.* **3.** having a parliament or Parliament.

Parliamentary Commissioner *n.* (in Britain) the official name for **ombudsman.**

parliamentary private secretary *n.* (in Britain) a backbencher in Parliament who assists a minister. Abbrev.: **PPS.**

parliamentary secretary *n.* a member of Parliament appointed to assist a minister of the Crown with his departmental responsibilities.

parlour *or U.S.* **parlor** (ˈpɑːlə) *n.* **1.** *Old-fashioned.* a living room, esp. one kept tidy for the reception of visitors. **2.** a small room for guests away from the public rooms in an inn, club, etc. **3.** *Chiefly U.S., Canad., & N.Z.* a room or shop equipped as a place of business: *a billiard parlor.* **4.** a building equipped for milking cows in. [C13: < Anglo-Norman *parlur,* < OF *parleur* room in convent for receiving guests, < *parler* to speak; see PARLEY]

parlous (ˈpɑːləs) *Arch. or humorous.* ~*adj.* **1.** dangerous or difficult. **2.** cunning. ~*adv.* **3.** extremely. [C14 *perlous,* var. of PERILOUS] —ˈ**parlously** *adv.*

Parmesan cheese (ˌpɑːmɪˈzæn, ˈpɑːmɪzən) *n.* a hard dry cheese used grated, esp. on pasta dishes and soups. [C16: < F, < It. *parmegiano* of Parma, Italy]

Parnassus (pɑːˈnæsəs) *n.* **1. Mount.** a mountain in central Greece: in ancient times sacred to Apollo and the Muses. **2. a.** the world of poetry. **b.** a centre of poetic or other creative activity.

parochial (pəˈrəʊkɪəl) *adj.* **1.** narrow in outlook or scope; provincial. **2.** of or relating to a parish. [C14: via OF < Church L *parochiālis*; see PARISH] —**paˈrochialˌism** *n.* —**paˈrochially** *adv.*

parody (ˈpærədɪ) *n., pl.* **-dies. 1.** a musical, literary, or other composition that mimics the style of another composer, author, etc., in a humorous or satirical way. **2.** something so badly done as to seem an intentional mockery; travesty. ~*vb.* **-dying, -died. 3.** (*tr.*) to make a parody of. [C16: via L < Gk *paroidiā* satirical poem, < PARA-[1] + *ōidē* song] —**parodic** (pəˈrɒdɪk) *or* **paˈrodical** *adj.* —**ˈparodist** *n.*

parol (ˈpærəl, pəˈrəʊl) *Law.* ~*n.* **1.** an oral statement; word of mouth (now only in **by parol**). ~*adj.* **2. a.** (of a contract, lease, etc.) made orally or in writing but not under seal. **b.** expressed or given by word of mouth: *parol evidence.* [C15: < OF *parole* speech; see PAROLE]

parole (pəˈrəʊl) *n.* **1. a.** the freeing of a prisoner before his sentence has expired, on the condition that he is of good behaviour. **b.** the duration of such conditional release. **2.** a promise given by a prisoner, as to be of good behaviour if granted liberty or partial liberty. **3.** *Linguistics.* language as manifested in the individual speech acts of particular speakers. **4. on parole.** conditionally released from detention. ~*vb.* (*tr.*) **5.** to place (a person) on parole. [C17: < OF, < *parole d'honneur* word of honour; *parole* < LL *parabola* speech] —**parolee** (pəˌrəʊˈliː) *n.*

paronomasia (ˌpærənəʊˈmeɪzɪə) *n. Rhetoric.* a play on words, esp. a pun. [C16: via L < Gk, < *paronomazein* to make a change in naming, < PARA-[1] (besides) + *onomazein* to name, < *onoma* a name]

parotid (pəˈrɒtɪd) *adj.* **1.** relating to or situated near the parotid gland. ~*n.* **2.** See **parotid gland.** [C17: via F, via L < Gk *parōtis*, < PARA-[1] (near) + *-ōtis*, < *ous* ear]

parotid gland *n.* a large salivary gland, in man situated in front of and below each ear.

parotitis (ˌpærəˈtaɪtɪs) *n.* inflammation of the parotid gland. See also **mumps.**

-parous *adj. combining form.* giving birth to: *oviparous.* [< L *-parus*, < *parere* to bring forth]

paroxysm (ˈpærəkˌsɪzəm) *n.* **1.** an uncontrollable outburst: *a paroxysm of giggling.* **2.** *Pathol.* **a.** a sudden attack or recurrence of a disease. **b.** any fit or convulsion. [C17: via F < Med. L *paroxysmus* annoyance, < Gk, < *paroxunein* to goad, < PARA-[1] (intensifier) + *oxunein* to sharpen, < *oxus* sharp] —ˌ**paroxˈysmal** *adj.*

parquet (ˈpɑːkeɪ, -kɪ) *n.* **1.** a floor covering of pieces of hardwood fitted in a decorative pattern; parquetry. **2.** Also called: **parquet floor.** a floor so covered. **3.** *U.S.* the stalls of a theatre. ~*vb.* (*tr.*) **4.** to cover a floor with parquet. [C19: < OF: small enclosure, < *parc* enclosure; see PARK]

parquetry (ˈpɑːkɪtrɪ) *n.* a geometric pattern of inlaid pieces of wood, esp. as used to cover a floor.

parr (pɑː) *n., pl.* **parrs** *or* **parr.** a salmon up to two years of age. [C18: <?]

parrakeet (ˈpærəˌkiːt) *n.* a variant spelling of **parakeet.**

parramatta (ˌpærəˈmætə) *n.* a variant spelling of **paramatta.**

parricide (ˈpærɪˌsaɪd) *n.* **1.** the act of killing either of one's parents. **2.** a person who kills his or her parent. [C16: < L *parricīdium* murder of a parent or relative, & < *parricīda* one who murders a relative, < *parri-* (rel. to Gk *pēos* kinsman) + -CIDE] —ˌ**parriˈcidal** *adj.*

parrot (ˈpærət) *n.* **1.** any of several related tropical and subtropical birds having a short hooked bill, bright plumage, and an ability to mimic sounds. **2.** a person who repeats or imitates the words or actions of another. ~*vb.* **3.** (*tr.*) to repeat or imitate without understanding. [C16: prob. < F *paroquet*, <?]

parrot-fashion *adv. Inf.* without regard for meaning; by rote: *she learned it parrot-fashion.*

parrot fever *or* **disease** *n.* another name for **psittacosis.**

parrotfish (ˈpærətˌfɪʃ) *n., pl.* **-fish** *or* **-fishes.** a brightly coloured tropical marine percoid fish having parrot-like jaws.

parry (ˈpærɪ) *vb.* **-rying, -ried. 1.** to ward off (an attack, etc.) by blocking or deflecting, as in fencing. **2.** (*tr.*) to evade (questions, etc.), esp. adroitly. ~*n., pl.* **-ries. 3.** an act of parrying. **4.** a skilful evasion, as of a question. [C17: < F *parer* to ward off, < L *parāre* to prepare]

parse (pɑːz) *vb. Grammar.* to assign constituent structure to (a sentence or the words in a sentence). [C16: < L *pars* (*ōrātionis*) part (of speech)]

parsec (ˈpɑːˌsɛk) *n.* a unit of astronomical distance equivalent to 3.0857×10^{16} metres or 3.262 light years. [C20: < PARALLAX + SECOND[2]]

Parsee *or* **Parsi** (ˌpɑːˈsiː, ˈpɑːˌsiː) *n.* an adherent of a Zoroastrian religion, the practitioners of which were driven out of Persia by the Muslims in the eighth century A.D. It is now found chiefly in western India. [C17: < Persian *Pārsī* a Persian, < OPersian *Pārsa* Persia] —ˈ**Parseeˌism** *or* ˈ**Parsiˌism** *n.*

parser (ˈpaːzə) *n. Computers.* a program that interprets ordinary language typed into a computer by recognizing key words or analysing sentence structure and then translating it into the appropriate machine language.

parsimony (ˈpɑːsɪmənɪ) *n.* extreme care in spending; niggardliness. [C15: < L *parcimōnia*, < *parcere* to spare] —**parsimonious** (ˌpɑːsɪˈməʊnɪəs) *adj.* —ˌ**parsiˈmoniously** *adv.*

parsley (ˈpɑːslɪ) *n.* **1.** a S European umbelliferous plant, widely cultivated for its curled aromatic leaves, which are used in cooking. **2.** any of various similar and related plants, such as fool's-parsley and cow parsley. [C14 *persely*, < OE *petersilie* + OF *persil*, *peresil*, both ult. < L *petroselīnum* rock parsley, < Gk, < *petra* rock + *selinon* parsley]

parsnip (ˈpɑːsnɪp) *n.* **1.** an umbelliferous plant cultivated for its long whitish root. **2.** the root of this plant, eaten as a vegetable. [C14: < OF *pasnaie*, < L *pastināca*, < *pastināre* to dig, < *pastinum* two-pronged tool for digging]

parson (ˈpɑːsᵊn) *n.* **1.** a parish priest in the Church of England. **2.** any clergyman. [C13: < Med. L *persōna* parish priest, < L: personage; see PERSON]

parsonage (ˈpɑːsᵊnɪdʒ) *n.* the residence of a parson, as provided by the parish.

parson bird *n.* another name for **tui.**

parson's nose *n.* the fatty extreme end portion of the tail of a fowl when cooked.

part (pɑːt) *n.* **1.** a piece or portion of a whole. **2.** an integral constituent of something: *dancing is part of what we teach.* **3.** an amount less than the whole; bit: *they only recovered part of the money.* **4.** one of several equal divisions: *mix two parts flour to one part water.* **5.** an actor's role in a play. **6.** a person's proper role or duty: *everyone must do his part.* **7.** (*often pl.*) region; area: *you're well known in these parts.* **8.** *Anat.* any portion of a larger structure. **9.** a component that can be replaced in a machine, etc. **10.** the U.S. and Canad. word for **parting** (sense 1). **11.** *Music.* one of a number of separate melodic lines which is assigned to one or more instrumentalists or singers. **12. for one's part.** as far as one is concerned. **13. for the most part.** generally. **14. in part.** to some degree; partly. **15. of many parts.** having many different abilities. **16. on the part of.** on behalf of. **17. part and parcel.** an essential ingredient. **18. play a part. a.** to pretend to be what one is not. **b.** to have something to do with; be instrumental. **19. take in good part.** to respond to (teasing, etc.) with good humour. **20. take part in.** to participate in. **21. take someone's**

part. to support one person in an argument, etc. ~*vb.* **22.** to divide or separate from one another; take or come apart: *to part the curtains; the seams parted when I washed the dress.* **23.** to go away or cause to go away from one another: *the couple parted amicably.* **24.** (*intr.*; foll. by *from*) to leave; say goodbye to. **25.** (*intr.*; foll. by *with*) to relinquish, esp. reluctantly: *I couldn't part with my teddy bear.* **26.** (*tr.*; foll. by *from*) to cause to relinquish, esp. reluctantly: *he's not easily parted from his cash.* **27.** (*intr.*) to split; separate: *the path parts here.* **28.** (*tr.*) to arrange (the hair) in such a way that a line of scalp is left showing. **29.** (*intr.*) *Euphemistic.* to die. **30.** (*intr.*) *Arch.* to depart. ~*adv.* **31.** to some extent; partly. ~See also **parts.** [C13: via OF < L *partīre* to divide, < *pars* a part]

part. *abbrev. for:* **1.** participle. **2.** particular.

partake (pɑːˈteɪk) *vb.* **-taking, -took, -taken.** (*mainly intr.*) **1.** (foll. by *in*) to have a share; participate. **2.** (foll. by *of*) to take or receive a portion, esp. of food or drink. **3.** (foll. by *of*) to suggest or have some of the quality (of): *music partaking of sadness.* [C16: back formation < *partaker*, earlier *part taker*, based on L *particeps* participant] —**parˈtaker** *n.*

parterre (pɑːˈtɛə) *n.* **1.** a formally patterned flower garden. **2.** the pit of a theatre. [C17: < F, < *par* along + *terre* ground]

parthenogenesis (ˌpɑːθɪnəʊˈdʒɛnɪsɪs) *n.* a type of reproduction, occurring in some insects and flowers, in which the unfertilized ovum develops directly into a new individual. [C19: < Gk *parthenos* virgin + *genesis* birth] —**parthenogenetic** (ˌpɑːθɪˌnəʊdʒɪˈnɛtɪk) *adj.*

Parthian shot (ˈpɑːθɪən) *n.* a hostile remark or gesture delivered while departing. [< the custom of archers from Parthia, an ancient Asian empire, who shot their arrows backwards while retreating]

partial (ˈpɑːʃəl) *adj.* **1.** relating to only a part; not general or complete: *a partial eclipse.* **2.** biased: *a partial judge.* **3.** (*postpositive*; foll. by *to*) having a particular liking (for). **4.** *Maths.* designating or relating to an operation in which only one of a set of independent variables is considered at a time. ~*n.* **5.** Also called: **partial tone.** *Music, acoustics.* any of the component tones of a single musical sound. **6.** *Maths.* a partial derivative. [C15: < OF *parcial*, < LL *partiālis* incomplete, < L *pars* part] —ˈ**partially** *adv.* —ˈ**partialness** *n.*

▷ **Usage.** In strict usage, a difference is sometimes made between the meanings of *partially* "not fully or completely", and *partly* "concerning only a part" or "in part". The distinction can be helpful in a sentence such as *the book, which was written partly in English and partly in French, was only partially completed when he died.* In practice, however, the two words are used interchangeably.

partial derivative *n.* the derivative of a function of two or more variables with respect to one of the variables, the other or others being considered constant. Written $\partial f/\partial x$.

partiality (ˌpɑːʃɪˈælɪtɪ) *n., pl.* **-ties. 1.** favourable bias. **2.** (usually foll. by *for*) liking or fondness. **3.** the state of being partial.

partible (ˈpɑːtəbᵊl) *adj.* (esp. of property or an inheritance) divisible; separable. [C16: < LL *partibilis*, < *part-*, *pars* part]

participate (pɑːˈtɪsɪˌpeɪt) *vb.* (*intr.*; often foll. by *in*) to take part, be or become actively involved, or share (in). [C16: < L *participāre*, < *pars* part + *capere* to take] —**parˈticipant** *adj., n.* —**parˌticiˈpation** *n.* —**parˈticiˌpator** *n.* —**parˈticipatory** *adj.*

participle (ˈpɑːtɪsɪpᵊl) *n.* a nonfinite form of verbs, in English and other languages, used adjectivally and in the formation of certain compound tenses. See also **present participle, past participle.** [C14: via OF < L *participium*, < *particeps*, < *pars* part + *capere* to take] —**participial** (ˌpɑːtɪˈsɪpɪəl) *adj.* —ˌ**partiˈcipially** *adv.*

particle (ˈpɑːtɪkᵊl) *n.* **1.** an extremely small piece of matter; speck. **2.** a very tiny amount; iota: *it doesn't make a particle of difference.* **3.** a function word, esp. (in certain languages) a word belonging to an uninflected class having grammatical function: *"up" is sometimes regarded as an adverbial particle.* **4.** a common affix, such as *re-, un-,* or *-ness.* **5.** *Physics.* a body with finite mass that can be treated as having negligible size, and internal structure. **6.** See **elementary particle.** [C14: < L *particula* a small part, < *pars* part]

particle accelerator *n.* a machine for accelerating charged elementary particles to very high energies, used in nuclear physics.

parti-coloured (ˈpɑːtɪˌkʌləd) *adj.* having different colours in different parts; variegated. [C16 *parti*, < (obs.) *party* of more than one colour, < OF: striped, < L *partīre* to divide]

particular (pəˈtɪkjʊlə) *adj.* **1.** (*prenominal*) of or belonging to a single or specific person, thing, category, etc.; specific; special: *the particular demands of the job.* **2.** (*prenominal*) exceptional or marked: *a matter of particular importance.* **3.** (*prenominal*) relating to or providing specific details or circumstances: *a particular account.* **4.** exacting or difficult to please, esp. in details; fussy. **5.** (of the solution of a differential equation) obtained by giving specific values to the arbitrary constants in a general equation. **6.** *Logic.* (of a proposition) affirming or denying something about only some members of a class of objects, as in *some men are not wicked.* Cf. **universal** (sense 9). ~*n.* **7.** a separate distinct item that helps to form a generalization: opposed to *general.* **8.** (*often pl.*) an item of information; detail: *complete in every particular.* **9. in particular.** especially or exactly. [C14: < OF *particuler*, < LL *particulāris* concerning a part, < L *particula* PARTICLE] —**parˈticularly** *adv.*

particularism (pəˈtɪkjʊləˌrɪzəm) *n.* **1.** exclusive attachment to the interests of one group, class, sect, etc. **2.** the principle of permitting each state in a federation the right to further its own interests. **3.** *Christian theol.* the doctrine that divine grace is restricted to the elect. —**parˈticularist** *n., adj.*

particularity (pəˌtɪkjʊˈlærɪtɪ) *n., pl.* **-ties. 1.** (*often pl.*) a specific circumstance: *the particularities of the affair.* **2.** great attentiveness to detail; fastidiousness. **3.** the quality of being precise: *a description of great particularity.* **4.** the state or quality of being particular as opposed to general; individuality.

particularize *or* **-ise** (pəˈtɪkjʊləˌraɪz) *vb.* **1.** to treat in detail; give details (about). **2.** (*intr.*) to go into detail. —**parˌticulariˈzation** *or* **-iˈsation** *n.*

particulate (pɑːˈtɪkjʊlɪt, -ˌleɪt) *n.* **1.** a substance consisting of separate particles. ~*adj.* **2.** of or made up of separate particles.

parting (ˈpɑːtɪŋ) *n.* **1.** *Brit.* the line of scalp showing when sections of hair are combed in opposite directions. U.S. and Canad. equivalent: **part. 2.** the act of separating or the state of being separated. **3. a.** a departure or leave-taking, esp. one causing a final separation. **b.** (*as modifier*): *a parting embrace.* **4.** a place or line of separation or division. **5.** a euphemism for **death.** ~*adj.* (*prenominal*) **6.** *Literary.* departing: *the parting day.* **7.** serving to divide or separate.

partisan *or* **partizan** (ˌpɑːtɪˈzæn, ˈpɑːtɪˌzæn) *n.* **1.** an adherent or devotee of a cause, party, etc. **2.** a member of an armed resistance group within occupied territory. ~*adj.* **3.** of, relating to, or characteristic of a partisan. **4.** excessively devoted to one party, faction, etc.; one-sided. [C16: via F < OIt. *partigiano*, < *parte* faction, < L *pars* part] —ˌ**partiˈsanship** *or* ˌ**partiˈzanship** *n.*

partita (pɑːˈtiːtə) *n., pl.* **-te** (-teɪ) *or* **-tas** *Music.* a type of suite. [It.: divided (piece), < L *partīre* to divide]

partite (ˈpɑːtaɪt) *adj.* **1.** (*in combination*) composed of or divided into a specified number of parts: *bipartite.* **2.** (esp. of plant leaves) divided almost to the base to form two or more parts. [C16: < L *partīre* to divide]

partition (pɑːˈtɪʃən) *n.* **1.** a division into parts;

separation. 2. something that separates, such as a large screen dividing a room in two. 3. a part or share. 4. *Property law.* a division of property, esp. realty, among joint owners. ~*vb.* (*tr.*) 5. (often foll. by *off*) to separate or apportion into sections: *to partition a room off with a large screen.* 6. *Property law.* to divide (property, esp. realty) among joint owners. [C15: via OF < L *partītiō*, < *partīre* to divide] —**par'titioner** *or* **par'titionist** *n.*

partitive ('pɑːtɪtɪv) *adj.* 1. *Grammar.* indicating that a noun involved in a construction refers only to a part of what it otherwise refers to. The phrase *some of the butter* is a partitive construction. 2. serving to separate or divide into parts. ~*n.* 3. *Grammar.* a partitive linguistic element or feature. [C16: < Med. L *partītīvus* serving to divide, < L *partīre* to divide] —'**partitively** *adv.*

partly ('pɑːtlɪ) *adv.* not completely.

▷ **Usage.** See at **partial.**

partner ('pɑːtnə) *n.* 1. an ally or companion: *a partner in crime.* 2. a member of a partnership. 3. one of a pair of dancers or players on the same side in a game: *my bridge partner.* 4. either member of a couple in a relationship. ~*vb.* 5. to be or cause to be a partner (of). [C14: var. (infl. by PART) of *parcener* one who shares equally with another, < OF *parçonier*, ult. < L *partīre* to divide]

partnership ('pɑːtnəʃɪp) *n.* 1. a. a contractual relationship between two or more persons carrying on a joint business venture. b. the deed creating such a relationship. c. the persons associated in such a relationship. 2. the state or condition of being a partner.

part of speech *n.* a class of words sharing important syntactic or semantic features; a group of words in a language that may occur in similar positions or fulfil similar functions in a sentence. The chief parts of speech in English are noun, pronoun, adjective, determiner, adverb, verb, preposition, conjunction, and interjection.

parton ('pɑːˌtɒn) *n. Physics.* a hypothetical elementary particle postulated as a constituent of neutrons and protons. [< PART + -ON]

partook (pɑː'tʊk) *vb.* the past tense of **partake.**

partridge ('pɑːtrɪdʒ) *n., pl.* **-tridges** *or* **-tridge.** any of various small Old World game birds of the pheasant family, esp. the common or European partridge. [C13: < OF *perdriz*, < L *perdix*, < Gk]

parts (pɑːts) *pl. n.* 1. personal abilities or talents: *a man of many parts.* 2. short for **private parts.**

part song *n.* 1. a song composed in harmonized parts. 2. (*in more technical usage*) a piece of homophonic choral music in which the topmost part carries the melody.

part-time *adj.* 1. for less than the entire time appropriate to an activity: *a part-time job.* ~*adv.* **part time.** 2. on a part-time basis: *he works part time.* ~Cf. **full-time.** —ˌ**part-'timer** *n.*

parturient (pɑː'tjʊərɪənt) *adj.* 1. of or relating to childbirth. 2. giving birth. 3. producing a new idea, etc. [C16: via L *parturīre*, < *parere* to bring forth] —**par'turiency** *n.*

parturition (ˌpɑːtjʊ'rɪʃən) *n.* the act or process of giving birth. [C17: < LL *parturītiō*, < *parturīre* to be in labour]

part work *n. Brit.* a series of magazines issued weekly or monthly, which are designed to be bound together to form a complete book.

party ('pɑːtɪ) *n., pl.* **-ties.** 1. a. a social gathering for pleasure, often held as a celebration. b. (*as modifier*): *party spirit.* c. (*in combination*): *partygoer.* 2. a group of people associated in some activity: *a rescue party.* 3. a. (*often cap.*) a group of people organized together to further a common political aim, etc. b. (*as modifier*): *party politics.* 4. a person, esp. one entering into a contract. 5. the person or persons taking part in legal proceedings: *a party to the action.* 6. *Inf., humorous.* a person. ~*vb.* **-ties, -tying, -tied.** (*intr.*) 7. *Inf.* to celebrate; revel. ~*adj.* 7. *Heraldry.* (of a shield) divided vertically into two colours, metals, or furs. [C13: < OF *partie* part, < L *partīre* to divide; see PART]

party line *n.* 1. a telephone line serving two or more subscribers. 2. the policies or dogma of a political party, etc.

party wall *n. Property law.* a wall separating two properties or pieces of land and over which each of the adjoining owners has certain rights.

par value *n.* the value imprinted on the face of a share certificate or bond and used to assess dividend, capital ownership, or interest.

parvenu *or* (*fem.*) **parvenue** ('pɑːvəˌnjuː) *n.* 1. a person who, having risen socially or economically, is considered to be an upstart. ~*adj.* 2. of or characteristic of a parvenu. [C19: < F, < *parvenir* to attain, < L *pervenīre*, < *per* through + *venīre* to come]

parvovirus ('pɑːvəʊˌvaɪrəs) *n.* any of a group of viruses characterized by their very small size, each of which is specific to a particular species, as for example canine parvovirus. [C20: NL, < L *parvus* little + VIRUS]

pas (pɑː) *n., pl.* **pas.** a dance step or movement, esp. in ballet. [C18: < F, lit.: step]

pascal ('pæskᵊl) *n.* the derived SI unit of pressure; the pressure exerted on an area of 1 square metre by a force of 1 newton; equivalent to 10 dynes per square centimetre or 1.45×10^{-4} pound per square inch. Symbol: Pa [C20: after B. *Pascal* (1623–62), F mathematician & scientist]

PASCAL ('pæsˌkæl) *n.* a high-level computer-programming language developed as a teaching language.

Pascal's triangle *n.* a triangular figure consisting of rows of numbers, each number being obtained by adding together the two numbers on either side of it in the row above. [C17: after B. *Pascal*; see PASCAL]

paschal ('pæskᵊl) *adj.* 1. of or relating to **Passover** (sense 1). 2. of or relating to **Easter.** [C15: < OF *pascal*, via Church L < Heb. *pesakh* Passover]

Paschal Lamb *n.* 1. (*sometimes not caps.*) *Old Testament.* the lamb killed and eaten on the first day of the Passover. 2. Christ regarded as this sacrifice.

pas de basque (ˌpɑː də 'bɑː) *n., pl.* **pas de basque.** a dance step performed usually on the spot and used esp. in reels and jigs. [< F, lit.: Basque step]

pas de deux (*French* pɑddø) *n., pl.* **pas de deux.** *Ballet.* a sequence for two dancers. [F: step for two]

pash (pæʃ) *n. Sl.* infatuation. [C20: < PASSION]

pasha *or* **pacha** ('pɑːʃə, 'pæʃə) *n.* (formerly) a high official of the Ottoman Empire or the modern Egyptian kingdom: placed after a name when used as a title. [C17: < Turkish *paşa*]

pashm ('pæʃəm) *n.* the underfur of various Tibetan animals, esp. goats, used for Cashmere shawls. [< Persian, lit.: wool]

Pashto, Pushto ('pʌʃtəʊ), *or* **Pushtu** *n.* 1. a language of Afghanistan and NW Pakistan. 2. (*pl.* **-to** *or* **-tos, -tu** *or* **-tus**) a speaker of the Pashto language; a Pathan. ~*adj.* 3. denoting or relating to this language or a speaker of it.

paso doble ('pæsəʊ 'dəʊbleɪ) *n., pl.* **paso dobles** *or* **pasos dobles.** 1. a modern ballroom dance in fast duple time. 2. a piece of music composed for or in the rhythm of this dance. [Sp.: double step]

pas op ('pɑːs ˌɒp) *interj. S. African.* beware. [Afrik.]

pasqueflower ('pɑːskˌflaʊə) *n.* 1. a small purple-flowered plant of N and Central Europe and W Asia. 2. any of several related North American plants. [C16: < F *passefleur*, < *passer* to excel + *fleur* flower; changed to *pasqueflower* Easter flower, because it blooms at Easter]

pasquinade (ˌpæskwɪ'neɪd) *n.* an abusive lampoon or satire, esp. one posted in a public place. [C17: < It. *Pasquino* name given to an ancient Roman statue disinterred in 1501, which was annually posted with satirical verses]

pass (pɑːs) *vb.* 1. to go onwards or move by or past (a person, thing, etc.). 2. to run, extend, or lead through, over, or across (a place): *the route passes through the city.* **3.** to go through or cause to go through (an obstacle or barrier): *to pass a needle through cloth.* **4.** to move or cause to move onwards or over: *he passed his hand over her face.* **5.** (*tr.*) to go beyond or exceed: *this victory passes all expectation.* **6.** to gain or cause to gain an adequate mark or grade in (an examination, course, etc.). **7.** (often foll. by *away* or *by*) to elapse or allow to elapse: *we passed the time talking.* **8.** (*intr.*) to take place or happen: *what passed at the meeting?* **9.** to speak or exchange or be spoken or exchanged: *angry words passed between them.* **10.** to spread or cause to spread: *we passed the news round the class.* **11.** to transfer or exchange or be transferred or exchanged: *the bomb passed from hand to hand.* **12.** (*intr.*) to undergo change or transition: *to pass from joy to despair.* **13.** (when *tr.*, often foll. by *down*) to transfer or be transferred by inheritance: *the house passed to the younger son.* **14.** to agree to or be agreed to by a legislative body, etc.: *the assembly passed 10 resolutions.* **15.** (*tr.*) (of a legislative measure) to undergo (a procedural stage) and be agreed: *the bill passed the committee stage.* **16.** (when *tr.*, often foll. by *on* or *upon*) to pronounce (judgment, findings, etc.): *the court passed sentence.* **17.** to go or allow to go without comment or censure: *the insult passed unnoticed.* **18.** (*intr.*) to opt not to exercise a right, as by not answering a question or not making a bid or a play in card games. **19.** to discharge (urine, etc.) from the body. **20.** (*intr.*) to come to an end or disappear: *his anger soon passed.* **21.** (*intr.*; usually foll. by *for* or *as*) to be likely to be mistaken for (someone or something else): *you could easily pass for your sister.* **22.** (*intr.*; foll. by *away, on,* or *over*) *Euphemistic.* to die. **23.** *Sport.* to hit, kick, or throw (the ball, etc.) to another player. **24. bring to pass.** *Arch.* to cause to happen. **25. come to pass.** *Arch.* to happen. ~*n.* **26.** the act of passing. **27.** a route through a range of mountains where there is a gap between peaks. **28.** a permit, licence, or authorization to do something without restriction. **29. a.** a document allowing entry to and exit from a military installation. **b.** a document authorizing leave of absence. **30.** *Brit.* **a.** the passing of a college or university examination to a satisfactory standard but not as high as honours. **b.** (*as modifier*): *a pass degree.* **31.** a dive, sweep, or bombing or landing run by an aircraft. **32.** a motion of the hand or of a wand as part of a conjuring trick. **33.** *Inf.* an attempt to invite sexual intimacy. **34.** a state of affairs, esp. a bad one (esp. in **a pretty pass**). **35.** *Sport.* the transfer of a ball, etc., from one player to another. **36.** *Fencing.* a thrust or lunge. **37.** *Bridge, etc.* the act of passing (making no bid). ~*sentence substitute.* **38.** *Bridge, etc.* a call indicating that a player has no bid to make. ~See also **pass off, pass out,** etc. [C13: < OF *passer* to pass, surpass, < L *passūs* step]

pass. *abbrev. for:* **1.** passive. **2.** passenger. **3.** passage.

passable (ˈpɑːsəbᵊl) *adj.* **1.** adequate, fair, or acceptable. **2.** (of an obstacle) capable of being crossed. **3.** (of currency) valid for circulation. **4.** (of a proposed law) able to be enacted. —ˈ**passableness** *n.* —ˈ**passably** *adv.*

passacaglia (ˌpæsəˈkɑːljə) *n.* **1.** an old Spanish dance in slow triple time. **2.** a slow instrumental piece characterized by a series of variations on a particular theme played over a repeated bass part. [C17: earlier *passacalle,* < Sp. *pasacalle* street dance, < *paso* step + *calle* street]

passage (ˈpæsɪdʒ) *n.* **1.** a channel, opening, etc., through or by which a person may pass. **2.** *Music.* a section or division of a piece, movement, etc. **3.** a way, as in a hall or lobby. **4.** a section of a written work, speech, etc. **5.** a journey, esp. by ship. **6.** the act or process of passing from one place, condition, etc., to another: *passage of a gas through a liquid.* **7.** the permission, right, or freedom to pass: *to be denied passage through a country.* **8.** the enactment of a law by a legislative body. **9.** *Rare.* an exchange, as of blows, words, etc. [C13: < OF < *passer* to PASS]

passageway (ˈpæsɪdʒˌweɪ) *n.* a way, esp. one in or between buildings; passage.

pass band *n.* the band of frequencies that is transmitted with maximum efficiency through a circuit, filter, etc.

passbook (ˈpɑːsˌbʊk) *n.* **1.** a book for keeping a record of withdrawals from and payments into a building society. **2.** another name for **bankbook. 3.** *S. African.* an official document to identify the bearer, his race, residence, and employment.

passé (ˈpɑːseɪ, ˈpæseɪ) *adj.* **1.** out-of-date: *passé ideas.* **2.** past the prime; faded: *a passé society beauty.* [C18: < F, p.p. of *passer* to PASS]

passenger (ˈpæsɪndʒə) *n.* **1. a.** a person travelling in a car, train, boat, etc., not driven by him. **b.** (*as modifier*): *a passenger seat.* **2.** *Chiefly Brit.* a member of a group or team who is not participating fully in the work. [C14: < OF *passager* passing, < PASSAGE]

passenger pigeon *n.* a gregarious North American pigeon, now extinct.

passe-partout (ˌpæspɑːˈtuː) *n.* **1.** a mounting for a picture in which strips of gummed paper bind together the glass, picture, and backing. **2.** the gummed paper used for this. **3.** a mat on which a photograph, etc., is mounted. **4.** something that secures entry everywhere, esp. a master key. [C17: < F, lit.: pass everywhere]

passepied (pɑːsˈpjeɪ) *n., pl.* **-pieds** (-ˈpjeɪ). **1.** a lively minuet in triple time, popular in the 17th century. **2.** a piece of music composed for or in the rhythm of this dance. [C17: < F: pass foot]

passer-by *n., pl.* **passers-by.** a person that is passing or going by, esp. on foot.

passerine (ˈpæsəˌraɪn, -ˌriːn) *adj.* **1.** of, relating to, or belonging to an order of birds characterized by the perching habit: includes the larks, finches, starlings, etc. ~*n.* **2.** any bird belonging to this order. [C18: < L *passer* sparrow]

passim *Latin.* (ˈpæsɪm) *adv.* here and there; throughout: used to indicate that what is referred to occurs frequently in the work cited.

passing (ˈpɑːsɪŋ) *adj.* **1.** transitory or momentary: *a passing fancy.* **2.** cursory or casual in action or manner: *a passing reference.* ~*adv., adj.* **3.** *Arch.* to an extreme degree: *the events were passing strange.* ~*n.* **4.** a place where or means by which one may pass, cross, ford, etc. **5.** a euphemistic word for **death. 6. in passing.** by the way; incidentally.

passing bell *n.* a bell rung to announce a death or a funeral. Also called: **death knell.**

passing note *or U.S.* **passing tone** *n.* a nonharmonic note through which a melody passes from one harmonic note to the next.

passion (ˈpæʃən) *n.* **1.** ardent love or affection. **2.** intense sexual love. **3.** a strong affection or enthusiasm for an object, concept, etc.: *a passion for poetry.* **4.** any strongly felt emotion, such as love, hate, envy, etc. **5.** an outburst of anger: *he flew into a passion.* **6.** the object of an intense desire, ardent affection, or enthusiasm. **7.** an outburst expressing intense emotion: *he burst into a passion of sobs.* **8.** the sufferings and death of a Christian martyr. [C12: via F < Church L *passiō* suffering, < L *patī* to suffer] —ˈ**passional** *adj.* —ˈ**passionless** *adj.*

Passion (ˈpæʃən) *n.* **1.** the sufferings of Christ from the Last Supper to his death on the cross. **2.** any of the four Gospel accounts of this. **3.** a musical setting of this: *the St Matthew Passion.*

passionate (ˈpæʃənɪt) *adj.* **1.** manifesting or exhibiting intense sexual feeling or desire. **2.** capable of, revealing, or characterized by intense emotion. **3.** easily roused to anger; quick-tempered. —ˈ**passionately** *adv.*

passionflower (ˈpæʃənˌflaʊə) *n.* any plant of a tropical American genus cultivated for their red, yellow, greenish, or purple showy flowers: some species have edible fruit. [C17: < alleged resemblance between parts of the flower and the instruments of the Crucifixion]

passion fruit *n.* the edible fruit of any of various passionflowers, esp. granadilla.

Passion play *n.* a play depicting the Passion of Christ.

passive (ˈpæsɪv) *adj.* **1.** not active or not participating perceptibly in an activity, organization, etc. **2.** unresisting and receptive to external forces; submissive. **3.** affected or acted upon by an external object or force. **4.** *Grammar.* denoting a voice of verbs in sentences in which the grammatical subject is the recipient of the action described by the verb, as *was broken* in the sentence *The glass was broken by a boy.* **5.** *Chem.* (of a substance, esp. a metal) apparently chemically unreactive. **6.** *Electronics, telecomm.* **a.** capable only of attenuating a signal: *a passive network.* **b.** not capable of amplifying a signal or controlling a function: *a passive communications satellite.* **7.** *Finance.* (of a bond, share, debt, etc.) yielding no interest. ~*n.* **8.** *Grammar.* **a.** the passive voice. **b.** a passive verb. [C14: < L *passīvus* susceptible of suffering, < *patī* to undergo] —ˈ**passively** *adv.* —**pasˈsivity** *or* ˈ**passiveness** *n.*

passive resistance *n.* resistance to a government, law, etc., without violence, as by fasting, demonstrating, or refusing to cooperate.

passive smoking *n.* the inhalation of smoke from other people's cigarettes by a nonsmoker.

passkey (ˈpɑːsˌkiː) *n.* **1.** any of various keys, esp. a latchkey. **2.** another term for **master key** or **skeleton key.**

pass law *n.* (in South Africa) a law restricting the movement of Black Africans.

pass off *vb.* (*adv.*) **1.** to be or cause to be accepted in a false character: *he passed the fake diamonds off as real.* **2.** (*intr.*) to come to a gradual end; disappear: *eventually the pain passed off.* **3.** (*intr.*) to take place: *the meeting passed off without disturbance.* **4.** (*tr.*) to set aside or disregard: *I managed to pass off his insult.*

pass out *vb.* (*adv.*) **1.** (*intr.*) *Inf.* to become unconscious; faint. **2.** (*intr.*) *Brit.* (esp. of an officer cadet) to qualify for a military commission, etc. **3.** (*tr.*) to distribute.

pass over *vb.* **1.** (*tr., adv.*) to take no notice of; disregard: *they passed me over in the last round of promotions.* **2.** (*intr., prep.*) to disregard (something bad or embarrassing).

Passover (ˈpɑːsˌəʊvə) *n.* **1.** an eight-day Jewish festival celebrated in commemoration of the passing over or sparing of the Israelites in Egypt (Exodus 12). **2.** another term for the **Paschal Lamb.** [C16: < *pass over,* translation of Heb. *pesah,* < *pāsah* to pass over]

passport (ˈpɑːspɔːt) *n.* **1.** an official document issued by a government, identifying an individual, granting him permission to travel abroad, and requesting the protection of other governments for him. **2.** a quality, asset, etc., that gains a person admission or acceptance. [C15: < F *passeport,* < *passer* to PASS + PORT[1]]

pass up *vb.* (*tr., adv.*) *Inf.* to let go by; ignore: *I won't pass up this opportunity.*

password (ˈpɑːsˌwɜːd) *n.* **1.** a secret word, phrase, etc., that ensures admission by proving identity, membership, etc. **2.** an action, quality, etc., that gains admission or acceptance.

past (pɑːst) *adj.* **1.** completed, finished, and no longer in existence: *past happiness.* **2.** denoting or belonging to the time that has elapsed at the present moment: *the past history of the world.* **3.** denoting a specific unit of time that immediately precedes the present one: *the past month.* **4.** (*prenominal*) denoting a person who has held an office or position; former: *a past president.* **5.** *Grammar.* denoting any of various tenses of verbs that are used in describing actions, events, or states that have been begun or completed at the time of utterance. ~*n.* **6. the past.** the period of time that has elapsed: *forget the past.* **7.** the history, experience, or background of a nation, person, etc. **8.** an earlier period of someone's life, esp. one regarded as disreputable. **9.** *Grammar.* **a.** a past tense. **b.** a verb in a past tense. ~*adv.* **10.** at a time before the present; ago: *three years past.* **11.** on or onwards: *I greeted him but he just walked past.* ~*prep.* **12.** beyond in time: *it's past midnight.* **13.** beyond in place or position: *the library is past the church.* **14.** moving beyond: *he walked past me.* **15.** beyond or above the reach, limit, or scope of: *his foolishness is past comprehension.* **16. past it.** *Inf.* unable to perform the tasks one could do when one was younger. **17. not put it past someone.** to consider someone capable of (the action specified). [C14: < *passed,* p.p. of PASS]

pasta (ˈpæstə) *n.* any of several variously shaped edible preparations made from a flour and water dough, such as spaghetti. [It., < LL: PASTE]

paste (peɪst) *n.* **1.** a mixture of a soft or malleable consistency, such as toothpaste. **2.** an adhesive made from water and flour or starch, used for joining pieces of paper, etc. **3.** a preparation of food, such as meat, that has been pounded to a creamy mass, for spreading on bread, etc. **4.** any of various sweet doughy confections: *almond paste.* **5.** dough, esp. for making pastry. **6. a.** a hard shiny glass used for making imitation gems. **b.** an imitation gem made of this glass. **7.** the combined ingredients of porcelain. See also **hard paste, soft paste.** ~*vb.* (*tr.*) **8.** (often foll. by *on* or *onto*) to attach as by using paste: *he pasted posters onto the wall.* **9.** (usually foll. by *with*) to cover (a surface) with paper, etc.: *he pasted the wall with posters.* **10.** *Sl.* to thrash or beat; defeat. [C14: via OF < LL *pasta* dough, < Gk *pastē* barley porridge, < *passein* to sprinkle]

pasteboard (ˈpeɪstˌbɔːd) *n.* **1.** a stiff board formed from layers of paper or pulp pasted together. ~*adj.* **2.** flimsy or fake.

pastel (ˈpæstᵊl, pæˈstɛl) *n.* **1. a.** a substance made of ground pigment bound with gum. **b.** a crayon of this. **c.** a drawing done in such crayons. **2.** the medium or technique of pastel drawing. **3.** a pale delicate colour. ~*adj.* **4.** (of a colour) pale; delicate: *pastel blue.* [C17: via F < It. *pastello,* < LL *pastellus* woad, dim. of *pasta* PASTE] —ˈ**pastelist** *or* ˈ**pastellist** *n.*

pastern (ˈpæstən) *n.* the part of a horse's foot between the fetlock and the hoof. [C14: < OF *pasturon,* < *pasture* a hobble, < L *pāstōrius* of a shepherd, < PASTOR]

paste-up *n. Printing.* a sheet of paper or board on which are pasted artwork, proofs, etc., for photographing prior to making a plate.

pasteurism (ˈpæstəˌrɪzəm, -stjə-, ˈpɑː-) *n. Med.* a method of securing immunity from rabies or of treating patients with other viral infections by the serial injection of progressively more virulent suspensions of the causative virus. Also called: **Pasteur treatment.** [C19: after Louis *Pasteur* (1822–95), F chemist & bacteriologist]

pasteurization *or* **-isation** (ˌpæstəraɪˈzeɪʃən, -stjə-, ˌpɑː-) *n.* the process of heating beverages, such as milk, beer, wine, or cider, or solid foods, such as cheese or crab meat, to destroy harmful microorganisms.

pasteurize *or* **-ise** (ˈpæstəˌraɪz, -stjə-, ˈpɑː-) *vb.* (*tr.*) to subject (milk, beer, etc.) to pasteurization. —ˈ**pasteuˌrizer** *or* **-iser** *n.*

pastiche (pæˈstiːʃ) *or* **pasticcio** (pæˈstɪtʃəʊ) *n., pl.* **-tiches** *or* **-ticcios.** **1.** a work of art that mixes styles, materials, etc. **2.** a work of art in the style of another artist. [C19: F *pastiche,* It. *pasticcio,* lit.: piecrust (hence, something blended) < LL *pasta* PASTE]

pastille *or* **pastil** (ˈpæstɪl) *n.* **1.** a small flavoured or medicated lozenge. **2.** an aromatic substance burnt to fumigate the air. [C17: via F < L *pastillus* small loaf, < *pānis* bread]

pastime (ˈpɑːsˌtaɪm) *n.* an activity or entertainment which makes time pass pleasantly.

past master *n.* **1.** a person with talent for, or experience in, a particular activity. **2.** a person who has held the office of master in a guild, etc.

pastor (ˈpɑːstə) *n.* **1.** a clergyman or priest in charge of a congregation. **2.** a person who exercises spiritual guidance over a number of people. **3.** a S Asian starling having a black head and wings and a pale pink body. [C14: < L: shepherd, < *pascere* to feed] —ˈ**pastorship** *n.*

pastoral (ˈpɑːstərəl) *adj.* **1.** of, characterized by, or depicting rural life, scenery, etc. **2.** (of a literary work) dealing with an idealized form of rural existence. **3.** (of land) used for pasture. **4.** of or relating to a clergyman or priest in charge of a congregation or his duties as such. **5.** of or relating to shepherds, their work, etc. ~*n.* **6.** a literary work or picture portraying rural life, esp. in an idealizing way. **7.** *Music.* a variant spelling of **pastorale.** **8. a.** a letter from a clergyman to the people under his charge. **b.** the letter of a bishop to the clergy or people of his diocese. **c.** Also called: **pastoral staff.** the crosier carried by a bishop. [C15: < L, < PASTOR] —ˈ**pastoralism** *n.* —ˈ**pastorally** *adv.*

pastorale (ˌpæstəˈrɑːl) *n., pl.* **-rales.** *Music.* **1.** a composition evocative of rural life, sometimes with a droning accompaniment. **2.** a musical play based on a rustic story. [C18: It., < L: PASTORAL]

pastoralist (ˈpɑːstərəlɪst) *n. Austral.* a grazier raising sheep, cattle, etc., on a large scale.

pastorate (ˈpɑːstərɪt) *n.* **1.** the office or term of office of a pastor. **2.** a body of pastors.

pastourelle (ˌpɑːstuːˈrɛl) *n. Music.* **1.** a pastoral piece of music. **2.** one of the figures in a quadrille. [C19: < F: little shepherdess]

past participle *n.* a participial form of verbs used to modify a noun that is logically the object of a verb, also used in certain compound tenses and passive forms of the verb.

past perfect *Grammar.* ~*adj.* **1.** denoting a tense of verbs used in relating past events where the action had already occurred at the time of the action of a main verb that is itself in a past tense. In English this is a compound tense formed with *had* plus the past participle. ~*n.* **2. a.** the past perfect tense. **b.** a verb in this tense.

pastrami (pəˈstrɑːmɪ) *n.* highly seasoned smoked beef. [< Yiddish, < Romanian *pastramă*, < *păstra* to preserve]

pastry (ˈpeɪstrɪ) *n., pl.* **-tries.** **1.** a dough of flour, water, and fat. **2.** baked foods, such as tarts, made with this dough. **3.** an individual cake or pastry pie. [C16: < PASTE]

pasturage (ˈpɑːstʃərɪdʒ) *n.* **1.** the business of grazing cattle. **2.** another word for **pasture.**

pasture (ˈpɑːstʃə) *n.* **1.** land covered with grass or herbage and grazed by or suitable for grazing by livestock. **2.** the grass or herbage growing on it. ~*vb.* **3.** (*tr.*) to cause (livestock) to graze or (of livestock) to graze (a pasture). [C13: via OF < LL *pāstūra*, < *pascere* to feed]

pasty[1] (ˈpeɪstɪ) *adj.* **pastier, pastiest.** **1.** of or like the colour, texture, etc., of paste. **2.** (esp. of the complexion) pale or unhealthy-looking. —ˈ**pastily** *adv.* —ˈ**pastiness** *n.*

pasty[2] (ˈpæstɪ) *n., pl.* **pasties.** a round of pastry folded over a filling of meat, vegetables, etc. [C13: < OF *pastée*, < LL *pasta* dough]

PA system *n.* See **public-address system.**

pat[1] (pæt) *vb.* **patting, patted.** **1.** to hit (something) lightly with the palm of the hand or some other flat surface: *to pat a ball.* **2.** to slap (a person or animal) gently, esp. on the back, as an expression of affection, congratulation, etc. **3.** (*tr.*) to shape, smooth, etc., with a flat instrument or the palm. **4.** (*intr.*) to walk or run with light footsteps. **5. pat (someone) on the back.** *Inf.* to congratulate. ~*n.* **6.** a light blow with something flat. **7.** a gentle slap. **8.** a small mass of something: *a pat of butter.* **9.** the sound of patting. **10. pat on the back.** *Inf.* a gesture or word indicating approval. [C14: ? imit.]

pat[2] (pæt) *adv.* **1.** Also: **off pat.** exactly or fluently memorized: *he recited it pat.* **2.** opportunely or aptly. **3. stand pat. a.** *Chiefly U.S. & Canad.* to refuse to abandon a belief, decision, etc. **b.** (in poker, etc.) to play without adding new cards to the hand dealt. ~*adj.* **4.** exactly right; apt: *a pat reply.* **5.** too exactly fitting; glib: *a pat answer to a difficult problem.* **6.** exactly right: *a pat hand in poker.* [C17: ? adv. use ("with a light stroke") of PAT[1]]

pat[3] (pæt) *n.* **on one's pat.** *Austral. inf.* alone. [C20: rhyming slang, < *Pat* Malone]

pat. *abbrev. for* patent(ed).

patagium (pəˈteɪdʒɪəm) *n., pl.* **-gia** (-dʒɪə). **1.** a web of skin in bats and gliding mammals that functions as a wing. **2.** a membranous fold of skin connecting a bird's wing to the shoulder. [C19: NL, < L, < Gk *patageion* gold border on a tunic]

patch (pætʃ) *n.* **1.** a piece of material used to mend a garment, etc., or to make patchwork, a sewn-on pocket, etc. **2. a.** a small plot of land. **b.** its produce: *a patch of cabbages.* **3.** *Med.* **a.** a protective covering for an injured eye. **b.** any protective dressing. **4.** an imitation beauty spot made of black silk, etc., worn esp. in the 18th century. **5.** an identifying piece of fabric worn on the shoulder of a uniform. **6.** a small contrasting section: *a patch of cloud in the blue sky.* **7.** a scrap; remnant. **8. not a patch on.** not nearly as good as. **9. strike** *or* **hit a bad patch.** to have a difficult time. ~*vb.* (*tr.*) **10.** to mend or supply (a garment, etc.) with a patch or patches. **11.** to put together or produce with patches. **12.** (of material) to serve as a patch to. **13.** (often foll. by *up*) to mend hurriedly or in a makeshift way. **14.** (often foll. by *up*) to make (up) or settle (a quarrel, etc.). **15.** to connect (electric circuits) together temporarily by means of a patch board. [C16 *pacche*, ? < F *pieche* PIECE] —ˈ**patcher** *n.*

patch board *or* **panel** *n.* a device with a large number of sockets into which electrical plugs can be inserted to form many different temporary circuits: used in telephone exchanges, computer systems, etc. Also called: **plugboard.**

patchouli *or* **patchouly** (ˈpætʃʊlɪ, pəˈtʃuːlɪ) *n., pl.* **-lis** *or* **-lies.** **1.** any of several Asiatic trees, the leaves of which yield a heavy fragrant oil. **2.** the perfume made from this oil. [C19: < Tamil *paccilai*, < *paccu* green + *ilai* leaf]

patch pocket *n.* a pocket on the outside of a garment.

patch test *n. Med.* a test to detect an allergic reaction by applying small amounts of a suspected substance to the skin.

patchwork (ˈpætʃˌwɜːk) *n.* **1.** needlework done by sewing pieces of different materials together. **2.** something made up of various parts.

patchy (ˈpætʃɪ) *adj.* **patchier, patchiest.** **1.** irregular in quality, occurrence, intensity, etc.: *a patchy essay.* **2.** having or forming patches. —ˈ**patchily** *adv.* —ˈ**patchiness** *n.*

pate (peɪt) *n.* the head, esp. with reference to baldness or (in facetious use) intelligence. [C14: <?]

pâté (ˈpæteɪ) *n.* **1.** a spread of finely minced liver, poultry, etc., served usually as an hors d'oeuvre. **2.** a savoury pie. [C18: < F: PASTE]

pâté de foie gras (pɑte də fwa grɑ) *n., pl.* **pâtés de foie gras** (pɑte). a smooth rich paste made from the liver of a specially fattened goose. [F: pâté of fat liver]

patella (pəˈtɛlə) *n., pl.* **-lae** (-liː). *Anat.* a small flat triangular bone in front of and protecting the knee joint. Nontechnical name: **kneecap.** [C17: < L, < *patina* shallow pan] —**paˈtellar** *adj.*

paten (ˈpætᵊn) *n.* a plate, usually made of silver or gold, esp. for the bread in the Eucharist. [C13: < OF *patene*, < Med. L, < L *patina* pan]

patency (ˈpeɪtᵊnsɪ) *n.* the condition of being obvious.

patent (ˈpeɪtᵊnt, ˈpætᵊnt) *n.* **1. a.** a government grant to an inventor assuring him the sole right to make, use, and sell his invention for a limited period. **b.** a document conveying such a grant. **2.** an invention, privilege, etc., protected by a patent. **3. a.** an official document granting a right. **b.** any right granted by such a document. ~*adj.* **4.** open or available for inspection (esp. in **letters patent, patent writ**). **5.** (ˈpeɪtᵊnt). obvious: *their scorn was patent to everyone.* **6.** concerning protection, appointment, etc., of or by a patent or patents. **7.** proprietary. **8.** (esp. of a bodily passage or duct) being open or unobstructed. ~*vb.* (*tr.*) **9.** to obtain a patent for. **10.** to grant by a patent. [C14: via OF < L *patēre* to lie open;

n. use, short for *letters patent*, < Med. L *litterae patentes* letters lying open (to public inspection)] —**'patentable** *adj.* —**,paten'tee** *n.* —**,paten'tor** *n.*

▷ **Usage.** The pronunciation "'pæt³nt" is heard in *letters patent* and *Patent Office* and is the usual U.S. pronunciation for all senses. In Britain "'pæt³nt" is sometimes heard for senses 1, 2, and 3, but "peɪt³nt" is commoner and is regularly used in collocations like *patent leather*.

patent leather ('peɪt³nt) *n.* leather processed with lacquer to give a hard glossy surface.

patently ('peɪt³ntlɪ) *adv.* obviously.

patent medicine ('peɪt³nt) *n.* a medicine with a patent, available without a prescription.

Patent Office ('pæt³nt) *n.* a government department that issues patents.

Patent Rolls ('pæt³nt) *pl. n.* (in Britain) the register of patents issued.

pater ('peɪtə) *n. Brit. sl.* another word for **father:** now chiefly used facetiously. [< L]

paterfamilias (,peɪtəfə'mɪlɪ,æs) *n., pl.* **patresfamilias** (,pɑːtreɪzfə'mɪlɪ,æs). the male head of a household. [L: father of the family]

paternal (pə'tɜːn³l) *adj.* **1.** relating to or characteristic of a father; fatherly. **2.** (*prenominal*) related through the father: *his paternal grandfather.* **3.** inherited or derived from the male parent. [C17: < LL *paternālis*, < L *pater* father] —**pa'ternally** *adv.*

paternalism (pə'tɜːnə,lɪzəm) *n.* the attitude or policy of a government or other authority that manages the affairs of a country, company, etc., in the manner of a father, esp. in usurping individual responsibility. —**pa'ternalist** *n., adj.* —**pa,ternal'istic** *adj.* —**pa,ternal'istically** *adv.*

paternity (pə'tɜːnɪtɪ) *n.* **1. a.** the fact or state of being a father. **b.** (*as modifier*): *a paternity suit was filed against the man.* **2.** descent or derivation from a father. **3.** authorship or origin. [C15: < LL *paternitās*, < L *pater* father]

paternoster (,pætə'nɒstə) *n.* **1.** *R.C. Church.* the beads at the ends of each decade of the rosary at which the Paternoster is recited. **2.** a type of fishing tackle in which short lines and hooks are attached at intervals to the main line. **3.** a type of lift in which platforms are attached to continuous chains: passengers enter while it is moving. [L, lit.: our father (from the opening of the Lord's Prayer)]

Paternoster (,pætə'nɒstə) *n.* (*sometimes not cap.*) *R.C. Church.* **1.** the Lord's Prayer, esp. in Latin. **2.** the recital of this as an act of devotion.

Paterson's curse ('pætəs³nz) *n.* an Australian name for **viper's bugloss.**

path (pɑːθ) *n., pl.* **paths** (pɑːðz). **1.** a road or way, esp. a narrow trodden track. **2.** a surfaced walk, as through a garden. **3.** the course or direction in which something moves: *the path of a whirlwind.* **4.** a course of conduct: *the path of virtue.* [OE *pæth*] —**'pathless** *adj.*

path. *abbrev. for:* **1.** pathological. **2.** pathology.

-path *n. combining form.* **1.** denoting a person suffering from a specified disease or disorder: *neuropath.* **2.** denoting a practitioner of a particular method of treatment: *osteopath.* [back formation < -PATHY]

Pathan (pə'tɑːn) *n.* a member of the Pashto-speaking people of Afghanistan, NW Pakistan, and elsewhere. [C17: < Hindi]

pathetic (pə'θɛtɪk) *adj.* **1.** evoking or expressing pity, sympathy, etc. **2.** distressingly inadequate: *the old man sat huddled before a pathetic fire.* **3.** *Brit. sl.* ludicrously or contemptibly uninteresting or worthless. **4.** *Obs.* of or affecting the feelings. [C16: < F *pathétique*, via LL < Gk *pathetikos* sensitive, < *pathos* suffering] —**pa'thetically** *adv.*

pathetic fallacy *n.* (in literature) the presentation of inanimate objects in nature as possessing human feelings.

pathfinder ('pɑːθ,faɪndə) *n.* **1.** a person who makes or finds a way, esp. through unexplored areas or fields of knowledge. **2.** an aircraft or parachutist that indicates a target area by dropping flares, etc. **3.** a radar device used for navigation or homing onto a target.

patho- *or before a vowel* **path-** *combining form.* disease: *pathology.* [< Gk *pathos* suffering]

pathogen ('pæθə,dʒɛn) *n.* any agent that can cause disease. —**,patho'genic** *adj.*

pathogenesis (,pæθə'dʒɛnɪsɪs) *or* **pathogeny** (pə'θɒdʒɪnɪ) *n.* the development of a disease. —**pathogenetic** (,pæθədʒɪ'nɛtɪk) *adj.*

pathological (,pæθə'lɒdʒɪk³l) *or* (*less commonly*) **pathologic** *adj.* **1.** of or relating to pathology. **2.** relating to, involving, or caused by disease. **3.** *Inf.* compulsively motivated: *a pathological liar.* —**,patho'logically** *adv.*

pathology (pə'θɒlədʒɪ) *n., pl.* **-gies. 1.** the branch of medicine concerned with the cause, origin, and nature of disease, including the changes occurring as a result of disease. **2.** the manifestations of disease, esp. changes occurring in tissues or organs. —**pa'thologist** *n.*

pathos ('peɪθɒs) *n.* **1.** the quality or power, esp. in literature or speech, of arousing feelings of pity, sorrow, etc. **2.** a feeling of sympathy or pity. [C17: < Gk: suffering]

pathway ('pɑːθ,weɪ) *n.* **1.** a path. **2.** *Biochem.* a chain of reactions associated with a particular metabolic process.

-pathy *n. combining form.* **1.** indicating feeling or perception: *telepathy.* **2.** indicating disease: *psychopathy.* **3.** indicating a method of treating disease: *osteopathy.* [< Gk *patheia* suffering; see PATHOS] —**-pathic** *adj. combining form.*

patience ('peɪʃəns) *n.* **1.** tolerant and even-tempered perseverance. **2.** the capacity for calmly enduring pain, trying situations, etc. **3.** *Brit.* any of various card games for one player only. U.S. word: **solitaire.** [C13: via OF < L *patientia* endurance, < *patī* to suffer]

patient ('peɪʃənt) *adj.* **1.** enduring trying circumstances with even temper. **2.** tolerant; understanding. **3.** capable of accepting delay with equanimity. **4.** persevering or diligent: *a patient worker.* ~*n.* **5.** a person who is receiving medical care. [C14: see PATIENCE] —**'patiently** *adv.*

patina[1] ('pætɪnə) *n., pl.* **-nas. 1.** a film formed on the surface of a metal, esp. the green oxidation of bronze or copper. **2.** any fine layer on a surface: *a patina of frost.* **3.** the sheen on a surface caused by long handling. [C18: < It.: coating, < L: PATINA[2]]

patina[2] ('pætɪnə) *n., pl.* **-nae** (-,niː). a broad shallow dish used in ancient Rome. [< L, < Gk *patanē* platter]

patio ('pætɪ,əʊ) *n., pl.* **-tios. 1.** an open inner courtyard, esp. one in a Spanish or Spanish-American house. **2.** an area adjoining a house, esp. one that is paved. [C19: < Sp.: courtyard]

patisserie (pə'tiːsərɪ) *n.* **1.** a shop where fancy pastries are sold. **2.** such pastries. [C18: F, < *pâtissier* pastry cook, ult. < LL *pasta* PASTE]

Patna rice ('pætnə) *n.* a variety of long-grain rice, used for savoury dishes. [after *Patna*, city in NE India]

patois ('pætwɑː) *n., pl.* **patois** ('pætwɑːz). **1.** a regional dialect of a language, usually considered substandard. **2.** the jargon of a particular group. [C17: < OF: rustic speech, ? < *patoier* to handle awkwardly, < *patte* paw]

pat. pend. *abbrev. for* patent pending.

patri- *combining form.* father: *patricide; patriarch.* [< L *pater*, Gk *patēr* father]

patrial ('peɪtrɪəl) *n.* (in Britain, formerly) a person having by statute the right of abode in the United Kingdom. [C20: < L *patria* native land]

patriarch ('peɪtrɪ,ɑːk) *n.* **1.** the male head of a tribe or family. **2.** a very old or venerable man. **3.** *Bible.* **a.** any of a number of persons regarded as the fathers of the human race. **b.** any of the three ancestors of the Hebrew people: Abraham, Isaac, or Jacob. **c.** any of Jacob's twelve sons, regarded as the ancestors of the twelve tribes of Israel. **4.** *Early Christian Church.* the bishop of one of several principal sees, esp. those of Rome, Antioch, and Alexandria. **5.** *Eastern Orthodox*

Church. the bishops of the four ancient principal sees of Constantinople, Antioch, Alexandria, and Jerusalem, and also of Russia, Rumania, and Serbia. **6.** *R.C. Church.* **a.** a title given to the pope. **b.** a title given to a number of bishops, esp. of the Uniat Churches, indicating their rank as immediately below that of the pope. **7.** the oldest or most venerable member of a group, community, etc. **8.** a person regarded as the founder of a community, tradition, etc. [C12: via OF < Church L *patriarcha*] —ˌ**patriˈarchal** *adj.*

patriarchate (ˈpeɪtrɪˌɑːkɪt) *n.* the office, jurisdiction, province, or residence of a patriarch.

patriarchy (ˈpeɪtrɪˌɑːkɪ) *n., pl.* **-chies. 1.** a form of social organization in which a male is the head of the family and descent, kinship, and title are traced through the male line. **2.** any society governed by such a system.

patrician (pəˈtrɪʃən) *n.* **1.** a member of the hereditary aristocracy of ancient Rome. **2.** (in medieval Europe) a member of the upper class in numerous Italian republics and German free cities. **3.** an aristocrat. **4.** a person of refined conduct, tastes, etc. ~*adj.* **5.** (esp. in ancient Rome) of, relating to, or composed of patricians. **6.** aristocratic. [C15: < OF *patricien,* < L *patricius* noble, < *pater* father]

patricide (ˈpætrɪˌsaɪd) *n.* **1.** the act of killing one's father. **2.** a person who kills his father. —ˌ**patriˈcidal** *adj.*

patrilineal (ˌpætrɪˈlɪnɪəl) *adj.* tracing descent, kinship, or title through the male line.

patrimony (ˈpætrɪmənɪ) *n., pl.* **-nies. 1.** an inheritance from one's father or other ancestor. **2.** the endowment of a church. [C14 *patrimoyne,* < OF, < L *patrimonium* paternal inheritance] —**patrimonial** (ˌpætrɪˈməʊnɪəl) *adj.*

patriot (ˈpeɪtrɪət, ˈpæt-) *n.* a person who vigorously supports his country and its way of life. [C16: via F < LL *patriōta,* < Gk *patriōtēs,* < *patris* native land; rel. to Gk *patēr* father; cf. L *pater* father, *patria* fatherland] —**patriotic** (ˌpætrɪˈɒtɪk) *adj.* —ˌ**patriˈotically** *adv.*

patriotism (ˈpætrɪəˌtɪzəm) *n.* devotion to one's own country and concern for its defence.

patristic (pəˈtrɪstɪk) *or* **patristical** *adj.* of or relating to the Fathers of the Church, their writings, or the study of these. —**paˈtristics** *n.* (*functioning as sing.*)

patrol (pəˈtrəʊl) *n.* **1.** the action of going round a town, etc., at regular intervals for purposes of security or observation. **2.** a person or group that carries out such an action. **3.** a military detachment with the mission of security or combat with enemy forces. **4.** a division of a troop of Scouts or Guides. ~*vb.* **-trolling, -trolled. 5.** to engage in a patrol of (a place). [C17: < F *patrouiller,* < *patouiller* to flounder in mud, < *patte* paw] —**paˈtroller** *n.*

patrol car *n.* a police car used for patrolling streets and motorways.

patrology (pəˈtrɒlədʒɪ) *n.* **1.** the study of the writings of the Fathers of the Church. **2.** a collection of such writings. [C17: < Gk *patr-, patēr* father + -LOGY] —**paˈtrologist** *n.*

patrol wagon *n.* the usual U.S., Austral., and N.Z. term for **Black Maria.**

patron[1] (ˈpeɪtrən) *n.* **1.** a person who sponsors or aids artists, charities, etc.; protector or benefactor. **2.** a customer of a shop, hotel, etc., esp. a regular one. **3.** See **patron saint.** [C14: via OF < L *patrōnus* protector, < *pater* father] —ˈ**patroness** *fem. n.*

patron[2] (patrɔ̃) *n.* the owner of a restaurant, hotel. etc., esp. of a French one. [F]

patronage (ˈpætrənɪdʒ) *n.* **1. a.** the support given or custom brought by a patron. **b.** the position of a patron. **2.** (in politics) **a.** the practice of making appointments to office, granting contracts, etc. **b.** the favours, etc., so distributed. **3. a.** a condescending manner. **b.** any kindness done in a condescending way.

patronize *or* **-ise** (ˈpætrəˌnaɪz) *vb.* **1.** to behave or treat in a condescending way. **2.** (*tr.*) to act as a patron by sponsoring or bringing trade to. —ˈ**patronˌizer** *or* -ˌ**iser** *n.* —ˈ**patronˌizing** *or* -ˌ**ising** *adj.* —ˈ**patronˌizingly** *or* -ˌ**isingly** *adv.*

patron saint *n.* a saint regarded as the particular guardian of a country, person, etc.

patronymic (ˌpætrəˈnɪmɪk) *adj.* **1.** (of a name) derived from the name of its bearer's father or ancestor. ~*n.* **2.** a patronymic name. [C17: via LL < Gk *patronumikos,* < *pater* father + *onoma* NAME]

patroon (pəˈtruːn) *n. U.S.* a Dutch land holder in New Netherland and New York with manorial rights in the colonial era. [C18: < Du.: PATRON[1]]

patsy (ˈpætsɪ) *n., pl.* **-sies.** *Sl., chiefly U.S. & Canad.* a person who is easily cheated, victimized, etc. [C20: <?]

patten (ˈpætᵊn) *n.* a wooden clog or sandal on a raised wooden platform or metal ring. [C14: < OF *patin,* prob. < *patte* paw]

patter[1] (ˈpætə) *vb.* **1.** (*intr.*) to walk or move with quick soft steps. **2.** to strike with or make a quick succession of light tapping sounds. ~*n.* **3.** a quick succession of light tapping sounds, as of feet: *the patter of mice.* [C17: < PAT[1]]

patter[2] (ˈpætə) *n.* **1.** the glib rapid speech of comedians, etc. **2.** quick idle talk; chatter. **3.** the jargon of a particular group, etc.; lingo. ~*vb.* **4.** (*intr.*) to speak glibly and rapidly. **5.** to repeat (prayers, etc.) in a mechanical or perfunctory manner. [C14: < L *pater* in *Pater Noster* Our Father]

pattern (ˈpætᵊn) *n.* **1.** an arrangement of repeated or corresponding parts, decorative motifs, etc. **2.** a decorative design: *a paisley pattern.* **3.** a style: *various patterns of cutlery.* **4.** a plan or diagram used as a guide in making something: *a paper pattern for a dress.* **5.** a standard way of moving, acting, etc.: *traffic patterns.* **6.** a model worthy of imitation: *a pattern of kindness.* **7.** a representative sample. **8.** a wooden or metal shape or model used in a foundry to make a mould. ~*vb.* (*tr.*) **9.** (often foll. by *after* or *on*) to model. **10.** to arrange as or decorate with a pattern. [C14 *patron,* < Med. L *patrōnus* example, < L: PATRON[1]]

patty (ˈpætɪ) *n., pl.* **-ties. 1.** a small cake of minced food. **2.** a small pie. [C18: < F PÂTÉ]

patu (ˈpɑːtuː) *n., pl.* **patus.** *N.Z.* a short Maori club, now ceremonial only. [< Maori]

patulous (ˈpætjʊləs) *adj. Bot.* spreading widely or expanded: *patulous branches.* [C17: < L *patulus* open, < *patēre* to lie open]

paua (ˈpɑːʊɑ) *n.* an edible abalone of New Zealand, having an iridescent shell used for jewellery, etc. [< Maori]

paucity (ˈpɔːsɪtɪ) *n.* **1.** insufficiency; dearth. **2.** smallness of number; fewness. [C15: < L *paucitās* scarcity, < *paucus* few]

Pauli exclusion principle (ˈpɔːlɪ) *n. Physics.* the principle that two identical fermions cannot occupy the same quantum state in a body such as an atom. [C20: after Wolfgang *Pauli* (1900–58), U.S. physicist]

Pauline (ˈpɔːlaɪn) *adj.* relating to Saint Paul or his doctrines.

Paul Jones (pɔːl dʒəʊnz) *n.* an old-time dance in which partners are exchanged. [C19: after John Paul *Jones* (1747–92), U.S. naval commander in the War of Independence]

paulownia (pɔːˈləʊnɪə) *n.* a tree of a Japanese genus, esp. one having large heart-shaped leaves and clusters of purplish or white flowers. [C19: NL, after Anna *Paulovna,* daughter of Paul I of Russia]

paunch (pɔːntʃ) *n.* **1.** the belly or abdomen, esp. when protruding. **2.** another name for **rumen.** ~*vb.* (*tr.*) **3.** to stab in the stomach; disembowel. [C14: < Anglo-Norman *paunche,* < OF *pance,* < L *panticēs* (pl.) bowels] —ˈ**paunchy** *adj.* —ˈ**paunchiness** *n.*

pauper (ˈpɔːpə) *n.* **1.** a person who is extremely poor. **2.** (formerly) a person supported by public charity. [C16: < L: poor] —ˈ**pauperˌism** *n.*

pauperize *or* **-ise** (ˈpɔːpəˌraɪz) *vb.* (*tr.*) to make a pauper of; impoverish.

pause (pɔːz) *vb.* (*intr.*) **1.** to cease an action

temporarily. **2.** to hesitate; delay: *she replied without pausing.* ~*n.* **3.** a temporary stop or rest, esp. in speech or action; short break. **4.** *Prosody.* another word for **caesura.** **5.** Also called: **fermata.** *Music.* a continuation of a note or rest beyond its normal length. Usual symbol: 𝄐 **6. give pause to.** to cause to hesitate. [C15: < L *pausa* pause, < Gk *pausis,* < *pauein* to halt]

pav (pæv) *n. Austral. & N.Z. inf.* short for **pavlova.**

pavane *or* **pavan** (pəˈvɑːn, ˈpævᵊn) *n.* **1.** a slow and stately dance of the 16th and 17th centuries. **2.** a piece of music composed for or in the rhythm of this dance. [C16 *pavan,* via F < Sp. *pavana,* < OIt. *padovana* Paduan (dance), < *Padova* Padua]

pave (peɪv) *vb.* (*tr.*) **1.** to cover (a road, etc.) with a firm surface suitable for travel, as with paving stones or concrete. **2.** to serve as the material for a pavement or other hard layer: *bricks paved the causeway.* **3.** (often foll. by *with*) to cover with a hard layer (of): *shelves paved with marble.* **4.** to prepare or make easier (esp. in **pave the way**). [C14: < OF *paver,* < L *pavīre* to ram down] —ˈ**paver** *n.*

pavement (ˈpeɪvmənt) *n.* **1.** a hard-surfaced path for pedestrians alongside and a little higher than a road. U.S. and Canad. word: **sidewalk.** **2.** the material used in paving. [C13: < L *pavīmentum* hard floor, < *pavīre* to beat hard]

pavilion (pəˈvɪljən) *n.* **1.** *Brit.* a building at a sports ground, esp. a cricket pitch, in which players change, etc. **2.** a summerhouse or other decorative shelter. **3.** a building or temporary structure, esp. one that is open and ornamental, for housing exhibitions, etc. **4.** a large ornate tent, esp. one with a peaked top, as used by medieval armies. **5.** one of a set of buildings that together form a hospital or other large institution. ~*vb.* (*tr.*) *Literary.* **6.** to place as in a pavilion: *pavilioned in splendour.* **7.** to provide with a pavilion or pavilions. [C13: < OF *pavillon* canopied structure, < L *pāpiliō* butterfly, tent]

paving (ˈpeɪvɪŋ) *n.* **1.** a paved surface; pavement. **2.** material used for a pavement.

pavlova (pævˈləʊvə) *n.* a meringue cake topped with whipped cream and fruit. [C20: after Anna *Pavlova* (1885–1931), Russian ballerina]

Pavlovian (pævˈləʊvɪən) *adj.* **1.** of or relating to the work of Ivan Pavlov (1849–1936), Soviet physiologist, on conditioned reflexes. **2.** (of a reaction or response) automatic; involuntary.

paw (pɔː) *n.* **1.** any of the feet of a four-legged mammal, bearing claws or nails. **2.** *Inf.* a hand, esp. one that is large, clumsy, etc. ~*vb.* **3.** to scrape or contaminate with the paws or feet. **4.** (*tr.*) *Inf.* to touch or caress in a clumsy, rough, or overfamiliar manner. [C13: via OF < Gmc]

pawky (ˈpɔːkɪ) *adj.* **pawkier, pawkiest.** *Dialect or Scot.* having a dry wit. [C17: < Scot. *pawk* trick, <?] —ˈ**pawkily** *adv.* —ˈ**pawkiness** *n.*

pawl (pɔːl) *n.* a pivoted lever shaped to engage with a ratchet wheel to prevent motion in a particular direction. [C17: ? < Du. *pal* pawl]

pawn[1] (pɔːn) *vb.* (*tr.*) **1.** to deposit (an article) as security for the repayment of a loan, esp. from a pawnbroker. **2.** to stake: *to pawn one's honour.* ~*n.* **3.** an article deposited as security. **4.** the condition of being so deposited (esp. in **in pawn**). **5.** a person or thing that is held as a security. **6.** the act of pawning. [C15: < OF *pan* security, < L *pannus* cloth, apparently because clothing was often left as a surety] —ˈ**pawnage** *n.*

pawn[2] (pɔːn) *n.* **1.** a chess man of the lowest theoretical value. **2.** a person, group, etc., manipulated by another. [C14: < Anglo-Norman *poun,* < OF, < Med. L *pedō* infantryman, < L *pēs* foot]

pawnbroker (ˈpɔːnˌbrəʊkə) *n.* a dealer licensed to lend money at a specified rate of interest on the security of movable personal property, which can be sold if the loan is not repaid within a specified period. —ˈ**pawnˌbroking** *n.*

pawnshop (ˈpɔːnˌʃɒp) *n.* the premises of a pawnbroker.

pawn ticket *n.* a receipt for goods pawned.

pawpaw (ˈpɔːˌpɔː) *n.* another name for **papaw** or **papaya.**

pax (pæks) *n.* **1.** *Chiefly R.C. Church.* **a.** the kiss of peace. **b.** a small metal or ivory plate, formerly used to convey the kiss of peace from the celebrant at Mass to those attending it. ~*interj.* **2.** *Brit. school sl.* a call signalling an end to hostilities or claiming immunity from the rules of a game. [L: peace]

PAX (in Britain) *abbrev. for* private automatic exchange.

pay[1] (peɪ) *vb.* **paying, paid.** **1.** to discharge (a debt, obligation, etc.) by giving or doing something: *he paid his creditors.* **2.** (when *intr.,* often foll. by *for*) to give (money, etc.) to (a person) in return for goods or services: *they pay their workers well; they pay by the hour.* **3.** to give or afford (a person, etc.) a profit or benefit: *it pays one to be honest.* **4.** (*tr.*) to give or bestow (a compliment, regards, attention, etc.). **5.** (*tr.*) to make (a visit or call). **6.** (*intr.;* often foll. by *for*) to give compensation or make amends. **7.** (*tr.*) to yield a return of: *the shares pay 15 per cent.* **8.** *Austral. inf.* to acknowledge or accept (something) as true, just, etc. **9. pay one's way. a.** to contribute one's share of expenses. **b.** to remain solvent without outside help. ~*n.* **10. a.** money given in return for work or services; a salary or wage. **b.** (*as modifier*): *a pay slip; a pay claim.* **11.** paid employment (esp. in **in the pay of**). **12.** (*modifier*) requiring the insertion of money before or during use: *a pay phone.* **13.** (*modifier*) rich enough in minerals to be profitably worked: *pay gravel.* ~See also **pay back, pay for,** etc. [C12: < OF *payer,* < L *pācāre* to appease (a creditor), < *pāx* peace] —ˈ**payer** *n.*

pay[2] (peɪ) *vb.* **paying, payed.** (*tr.*) *Naut.* to caulk (the seams of a wooden vessel) with pitch or tar. [C17: < OF *peier,* < L *picāre,* < *pix* pitch]

payable (ˈpeɪəbᵊl) *adj.* **1.** (often foll. by *on*) to be paid: *payable on the third of each month.* **2.** that is capable of being paid. **3.** capable of being profitable. **4.** (of a debt, etc.) imposing an obligation on the debtor to pay, esp. at once.

pay back *vb.* (*tr., adv.*) **1.** to retaliate against: *to pay someone back for an insult.* **2.** to give or do (something equivalent) in return for a favour, insult, etc. **3.** to repay (a loan, etc.).

pay bed *n.* an informal name for **private pay bed.**

payday (ˈpeɪˌdeɪ) *n.* the day on which wages or salaries are paid.

pay dirt *n. Chiefly U.S.* **1.** soil, gravel, ore, etc. that contains sufficient minerals to make it worthwhile mining. **2.** *Inf.* **hit** (*or* **strike**) **pay dirt.** to become wealthy, successful, etc.

PAYE (in Britain and New Zealand) *abbrev. for* pay as you earn; a system by which income tax levied on wage and salary earners is paid by employers directly to the government.

payee (peɪˈiː) *n.* the person to whom a cheque, money order, etc., is made out.

pay for *vb.* (*prep.*) **1.** to make payment for. **2.** (*intr.*) to suffer or be punished, as for a mistake, wrong decision, etc.

paying guest *n.* a euphemism for **lodger.**

payload (ˈpeɪˌləʊd) *n.* **1.** that part of a cargo earning revenue. **2. a.** the passengers, cargo, or bombs carried by an aircraft. **b.** the equipment carried by a rocket, satellite, or spacecraft. **3.** the explosive power of a warhead, bomb, etc., carried by a missile or aircraft.

paymaster (ˈpeɪˌmɑːstə) *n.* an official of a government, business, etc., responsible for the payment of wages and salaries.

payment (ˈpeɪmənt) *n.* **1.** the act of paying. **2.** a sum of money paid. **3.** something given in return; punishment or reward.

paynim (ˈpeɪnɪm) *n. Arch.* **1.** a heathen or pagan. **2.** a Muslim. [C13: < OF *paienime,* < LL *pāgānismus* paganism, < *pāgānus* PAGAN]

pay off *vb.* **1.** (*tr., adv.*) to pay all that is due in wages, etc., and discharge from employment. **2.** (*tr., adv.*) to pay the complete amount of (a debt, bill, etc.). **3.** (*intr., adv.*) to turn out to be profitable, effective, etc.: *the gamble paid off.* **4.** (*tr., adv.* or *intr., prep.*) to take revenge on (a person) or for (a wrong done): *to pay someone off for an insult.* **5.** (*tr., adv.*) *Inf.* to give a bribe to. ~*n.* **payoff.** **6.** the final settlement, esp. in retribution. **7.** *Inf.* the climax, consequence, or outcome of events, a story, etc. **8.** the final payment of a debt, salary, etc. **9.** the time of such a payment. **10.** *Inf.* a bribe.

payola (peɪˈəʊlə) *n. Inf.* **1.** a bribe given to secure special treatment, esp. to a disc jockey to promote a commercial product. **2.** the practice of paying or receiving such bribes. [C20: < PAY[1] + *-ola,* as in PIANOLA]

pay out *vb.* (*adv.*) **1.** to distribute (money, etc.); disburse. **2.** (*tr.*) to release (a rope) gradually, hand over hand.

payroll (ˈpeɪˌrəʊl) *n.* **1.** a list of employees, specifying the salary or wage of each. **2.** the total of these amounts or the actual money equivalent.

payt *abbrev. for* payment.

pay up *vb.* (*adv.*) to pay (money) promptly, in full, or on demand.

Pb *the chemical symbol for* lead. [< NL *plumbum*]

PB *Athletics. abbrev. for* personal best.

PBX (in Britain) *abbrev. for* private branch exchange; a telephone system that handles the internal and external calls of a building, firm, etc.

pc *abbrev. for:* **1.** per cent. **2.** personal computer. **3.** postcard. **4.** (in prescriptions) post cibum. [Latin: after meals]

PC *abbrev. for:* **1.** Parish Council(lor). **2.** (in Britain) Police Constable. **3.** (in Britain) Privy Council(lor). **4.** (in Canada) Progressive Conservative.

pc. *abbrev. for:* **1.** (*pl.* **pcs.**) piece. **2.** price.

PCB *abbrev. for* polychlorinated biphenyl; any of a group of compounds in which chlorine atoms replace the hydrogen atoms in biphenyl: used in electrical insulators and in the manufacture of plastics; a toxic pollutant.

PCP *n. Trademark.* phencyclidine; a depressant drug used illegally as a hallucinogen.

pd *abbrev. for:* **1.** paid. **2.** Also: **PD.** per diem. **3.** potential difference.

Pd *the chemical symbol for* palladium.

PDSA (in Britain) *abbrev. for* People's Dispensary for Sick Animals.

PDT (in the U.S. and Canada) *abbrev. for* Pacific Daylight Time.

PE *abbrev. for:* **1.** physical education. **2.** potential energy. **3.** Presiding Elder. **4.** Also: **p.e.** printer's error. **5.** *Statistics.* probable error. **6.** Protestant Episcopal.

pea (piː) *n.* **1.** an annual climbing plant with small white flowers and long green pods containing edible green seeds: cultivated in temperate regions. **2.** the seed of this plant, eaten as a vegetable. **3.** any of several other leguminous plants, such as the sweet pea. [C17: < PEASE (incorrectly assumed to be a pl.)]

peace (piːs) *n.* **1. a.** the state existing during the absence of war. **b.** (*as modifier*): *peace negotiations.* **2.** (*often cap.*) a treaty marking the end of a war. **3.** a state of harmony between people or groups. **4.** law and order within a state: *a breach of the peace.* **5.** absence of mental anxiety (often in **peace of mind**). **6.** a state of stillness, silence, or serenity. **7. at peace. a.** in a state of harmony or friendship. **b.** in a state of serenity. **c.** dead: *the old lady is at peace now.* **8. hold** *or* **keep one's peace.** to keep silent. **9. keep the peace.** to maintain law and order. ~*vb.* **10.** (*intr.*) *Obs. except as an imperative.* to be or become silent or still. ~*modifier.* **11.** denoting a person or thing symbolizing support for international peace: *peace women.* [C12: < OF *pais,* < L *pāx*]

peaceable (ˈpiːsəbᵊl) *adj.* **1.** inclined towards peace. **2.** tranquil; calm. —ˈ**peaceableness** *n.* —ˈ**peaceably** *adv.*

Peace Corps *n.* an agency of the U.S. government that sends volunteers to developing countries to work on educational projects, etc.

peaceful (ˈpiːsfʊl) *adj.* **1.** not in a state of war or disagreement. **2.** calm; tranquil. **3.** of, relating to, or in accord with a time of peace. **4.** inclined towards peace. —ˈ**peacefully** *adv.* —ˈ**peacefulness** *n.*

peacekeeping (ˈpiːsˌkiːpɪŋ) *n.* **a.** the maintenance of peace, esp. the prevention of further fighting between hostile forces. **b.** (*as modifier*): *a UN peacekeeping force.*

peacemaker (ˈpiːsˌmeɪkə) *n.* a person who establishes peace, esp. between others. —ˈ**peaceˌmaking** *n.*

peace offering *n.* **1.** something given to an adversary in the hope of procuring or maintaining peace. **2.** *Judaism.* a sacrificial meal shared between the offerer and Jehovah.

peace pipe *n.* a long decorated pipe smoked by North American Indians, esp. as a token of peace. Also called: **calumet.**

peace sign *n.* a gesture made with the palm of the hand outwards and the index and middle fingers raised in a V.

peacetime (ˈpiːsˌtaɪm) *n.* **a.** a period without war; time of peace. **b.** (*as modifier*): *a peacetime agreement.*

peach[1] (piːtʃ) *n.* **1.** a small tree with pink flowers and rounded edible fruit: cultivated in temperate regions. **2.** the soft juicy fruit of this tree, which has a downy reddish-yellow skin, yellowish-orange sweet flesh, and a single stone. **3. a.** a pinkish-yellow to orange colour. **b.** (*as adj.*): *a peach dress.* **4.** *Inf.* a person or thing that is especially pleasing. [C14 *peche,* < OF, < Med. L *persica,* < L *Persicum mālum* Persian apple]

peach[2] (piːtʃ) *vb.* (*intr.*) *Sl.* to inform against an accomplice. [C15: var. of earlier *apeche,* < F, < LL *impedicāre* to entangle; see IMPEACH]

peach brandy *n.* (esp. in S. Africa) a coarse brandy made from fermented peaches.

peach melba *n.* a dessert made of halved peaches, vanilla ice cream, and raspberries.

peachy (ˈpiːtʃɪ) *adj.* **peachier, peachiest.** **1.** of or like a peach, esp. in colour or texture. **2.** *Inf.* excellent; fine. —ˈ**peachiness** *n.*

peacock (ˈpiːˌkɒk) *n., pl.* **-cocks** *or* **-cock.** **1.** a male peafowl, having a crested head and a very large fanlike tail marked with blue and green eyelike spots. **2.** another name for **peafowl.** **3.** a vain strutting person. ~*vb.* **4.** to display (oneself) proudly. [C14 *pecok, pe-* < OE *pāwa* (< L *pāvō* peacock) + COCK[1]] —ˈ**peaˌcockish** *adj.* —ˈ**peaˌhen** *fem. n.*

peacock blue *n.* **a.** a greenish-blue colour. **b.** (*as adj.*): *a peacock-blue car.*

peafowl (ˈpiːˌfaʊl) *n., pl.* **-fowls** *or* **-fowl.** either of two large pheasants of India and Ceylon and of SE Asia. The males (see **peacock** (sense 1)) have a characteristic bright plumage.

pea green *n.* **a.** a yellowish-green colour. **b.** (*as adj.*): *a pea-green teapot.*

pea jacket *or* **peacoat** (ˈpiːˌkəʊt) *n.* a sailor's short heavy woollen overcoat. [C18: < Du. *pijjekker,* < *pij* coat of coarse cloth + *jekker* jacket]

peak[1] (piːk) *n.* **1.** a pointed end, edge, or projection: *the peak of a roof.* **2.** the pointed summit of a mountain. **3.** a mountain with a pointed summit. **4.** the point of greatest development, strength, etc.: *the peak of his career.* **5. a.** a sharp increase followed by a sharp decrease: *a voltage peak.* **b.** the maximum value of this quantity. **c.** (*as modifier*): *peak voltage.* **6.** Also called: **visor.** a projecting piece on the front of some caps. **7.** *Naut.* **a.** the extreme forward (**forepeak**) or aft (**afterpeak**) part of the hull. **b.** (of a fore-and-aft quadrilateral sail) the after uppermost corner. **c.** the after end of a gaff. ~*vb.* **8.** to form or reach or cause to form or reach a peak. **9.** (*tr.*) *Naut.* to set (a gaff) or tilt (oars) vertically. ~*adj.* **10.** of or relating to a period of greatest use or demand: *peak viewing hours.* [C16: ? < PIKE[2], infl. by BEAK[1]]

peak[2] (piːk) *vb.* (*intr.*) to become wan, emaciated, or sickly. [C16: <?] —ˈ**peaky** *or* ˈ**peakish** *adj.*

peaked (piːkt) *adj.* having a peak; pointed.

peak load *n.* the maximum load on an electrical power-supply system.

peal (piːl) *n.* **1.** a loud prolonged usually reverberating sound, as of bells, thunder, or laughter. **2.** *Bell-ringing.* a series of changes rung in accordance with specific rules. **3.** (*not in technical usage*) the set of bells in a belfry. ~*vb.* **4.** (*intr.*) to sound with a peal or peals. **5.** (*tr.*) to give forth loudly and sonorously. **6.** (*tr.*) to ring (bells) in peals. [C14 *pele,* var. of *apele* APPEAL]

peanut (ˈpiːˌnʌt) *n.* **a.** a leguminous plant widely cultivated for its edible seeds. **b.** the edible nutlike seed of this plant, used for food and as a source of oil. Also called: **groundnut, monkey nut.** ~See also **peanuts.**

peanut butter *n.* a brownish oily paste made from peanuts.

peanuts (ˈpiːˌnʌts) *n. Sl.* a trifling amount of money.

pear (pɛə) *n.* **1.** a widely cultivated tree, having white flowers and edible fruits. **2.** the sweet gritty-textured juicy fruit of this tree, which has a globular base and tapers towards the apex. **3.** the wood of this tree, used for making furniture. [OE *pere,* ult. < L *pirum*]

pearl[1] (pɜːl) *n.* **1.** a hard smooth lustrous typically rounded structure occurring on the inner surface of the shell of a clam or oyster around an invading particle such as a sand grain; much valued as a gem. **2.** any artificial gem resembling this. **3.** See **mother-of-pearl. 4.** a person or thing that is like a pearl, esp. in beauty or value. **5.** a pale greyish-white colour, often with a bluish tinge. ~*adj.* **6.** of, made of, or set with pearl or mother-of-pearl. **7.** having the shape or colour of a pearl. ~*vb.* **8.** (*tr.*) to set with or as if with pearls. **9.** to shape into or assume a pearl-like form or colour. **10.** (*intr.*) to dive or search for pearls. [C14: < OF, < Vulgar L *pernula* (unattested), < L *perna* sea mussel]

pearl[2] (pɜːl) *n., vb.* a variant spelling of **purl**[1] (senses 2, 3, 5).

pearl ash *n.* the granular crystalline form of potassium carbonate.

pearl barley *n.* barley ground into small round grains, used esp. in soups and stews.

pearly (ˈpɜːlɪ) *adj.* **pearlier, pearliest. 1.** resembling a pearl, esp. in lustre. **2.** decorated with pearls or mother-of-pearl. ~*n., pl.* **pearlies.** *Brit.* **3.** a London costermonger or his wife who wear on ceremonial occasions a traditional dress of dark clothes covered with pearl buttons. **4.** (*pl.*) the clothes or the buttons themselves. —ˈ**pearliness** *n.*

Pearly Gates *pl. n. Inf.* the entrance to heaven.

pearly king *or* (*fem.*) **pearly queen** *n.* the London costermonger whose ceremonial clothes display the most lavish collection of pearl buttons.

pearly nautilus *n.* any of several cephalopod molluscs of warm and tropical seas, having a partitioned pale pearly external shell with brown stripes. Also called: **chambered nautilus.**

pearmain (ˈpɛəˌmeɪn) *n.* any of several varieties of apple having a red skin. [C15: < OF *permain* a type of pear, ? < L *Parmēnsis* of Parma]

peart (pɪət) *adj. Dialect.* lively; spirited; brisk. [C15: var. of PERT] —ˈ**peartly** *adv.*

peasant (ˈpɛzᵊnt) *n.* **1.** a member of a class of low social status that depends on either cottage industry or agricultural labour as a means of subsistence. **2.** *Inf.* a person who lives in the country; rustic. **3.** *Inf.* an uncouth or uncultured person. [C15: < Anglo-F, < OF *païsant,* < *païs* country, < L *pāgus* rural area]

peasantry (ˈpɛzᵊntrɪ) *n.* peasants as a class.

pease (piːz) *n., pl.* **pease.** *Arch. or dialect.* another word for **pea.** [OE *peose,* via LL < L *pisa* peas, pl. of *pisum,* < Gk *pison*]

peasecod *or* **peascod** (ˈpiːzˌkɒd) *n. Arch.* the pod of a pea plant. [C14: < PEASE + COD[2]]

pease pudding *n.* (esp. in Britain) a dish of split peas that have been soaked and boiled.

peashooter (ˈpiːˌʃuːtə) *n.* a tube through which dried peas are blown, used as a toy weapon.

peasouper (ˌpiːˈsuːpə) *n.* **1.** *Inf., chiefly Brit.* dense dirty yellowish fog. **2.** *Canad.* a disparaging name for a **French Canadian.**

peat (piːt) *n.* **a.** a compact brownish deposit of partially decomposed vegetable matter saturated with water: found in uplands and bogs and used as a fuel (when dried) and as a fertilizer. **b.** (*as modifier*): *peat bog.* [C14: < Anglo-L *peta,* ? < Celtic] —ˈ**peaty** *adj.*

peat moss *n.* any of various mosses, esp. sphagnum, that grow in wet places and decay to form peat. See also **sphagnum.**

pebble (ˈpɛbᵊl) *n.* **1.** a small smooth rounded stone, esp. one worn by the action of water. **2. a.** a transparent colourless variety of rock crystal, used for making certain lenses. **b.** such a lens. **3.** (*modifier*) *Inf.* (of a lens or of spectacles) thick, with a high degree of magnification or distortion. **4. a.** a grainy irregular surface, esp. on leather. **b.** leather having such a surface. ~*vb.* (*tr.*) **5.** to cover with pebbles. **6.** to impart a grainy surface to (leather). [OE *papolstān,* < *papol-* (? imit.) + *stān* stone] —ˈ**pebbly** *adj.*

pebble dash *n. Brit.* a finish for external walls consisting of small stones embedded in plaster.

pecan (pɪˈkæn, ˈpiːkən) *n.* **1.** a hickory tree of the southern U.S. having deeply furrowed bark and edible nuts. **2.** the smooth oval nut of this tree, which has a sweet oily kernel. [C18: < Algonquian *paccan*]

peccable (ˈpɛkəbᵊl) *adj.* liable to sin. [C17: via F < Med. L *peccābilis,* < L *peccāre* to sin]

peccadillo (ˌpɛkəˈdɪləʊ) *n., pl.* **-los** *or* **-loes.** a petty sin or fault. [C16: < Sp., < *pecado* sin, < L *peccātum,* < *peccāre* to transgress]

peccant (ˈpɛkənt) *adj. Rare.* **1.** guilty of an offence; corrupt. **2.** violating or disregarding a rule; faulty. **3.** producing disease; morbid. [C17: < L *peccans,* < *peccāre* to sin] —ˈ**peccancy** *n.*

peccary (ˈpɛkərɪ) *n., pl.* **-ries** *or* **-ry.** either of two piglike mammals of forests of southern North America, Central and South America. [C17: < Carib]

peck[1] (pɛk) *n.* **1.** a unit of dry measure equal to 8 quarts or one quarter of a bushel. **2.** a container used for measuring this quantity. **3.** a large quantity or number. [C13: < Anglo-Norman, <?]

peck[2] (pɛk) *vb.* **1.** (when *intr.,* sometimes foll. by *at*) to strike with the beak or with a pointed instrument. **2.** (*tr.;* sometimes foll. by *out*) to dig (a hole, etc.) by pecking. **3.** (*tr.*) (of birds) to pick up (corn, worms, etc.) by pecking. **4.** (*intr.;* often foll. by *at*) to nibble or pick (at one's food). **5.** *Inf.* to kiss (a person) quickly and lightly. **6.** (*intr.;* foll. by *at*) to nag. ~*n.* **7.** a quick light blow, esp. from a bird's beak. **8.** a mark made by such a blow. **9.** *Inf.* a quick light kiss. [C14: <?]

pecker (ˈpɛkə) *n. Brit. sl.* spirits (esp. in **keep one's pecker up**).

pecking order *n.* **1.** Also called: **peck order.** a natural hierarchy in a group of gregarious birds, such as domestic fowl. **2.** any hierarchical order, as among people in a particular group.

peckish (ˈpɛkɪʃ) *adj. Inf., chiefly Brit.* feeling slightly hungry. [C18: < PECK[2]]

pecten (ˈpɛktɪn) *n., pl.* **-tens** *or* **-tines** (-tɪˌniːz). **1.** a comblike structure in the eye of birds and reptiles, consisting of a network of blood vessels projecting inwards from the retina. **2.** any other comblike part or organ. [C18: < L: a comb, < *pectere* to comb]

pectin (ˈpɛktɪn) *n. Biochem.* any of the acidic polysaccharides that occur in ripe fruit and vegetables: used in the manufacture of jams because of their ability to solidify to a gel. [C19: < Gk *pēktos* congealed, < *pegnuein* to set] —ˈ**pectic** *or* ˈ**pectinous** *adj.*

pectoral (ˈpɛktərəl) *adj.* **1.** of or relating to the chest, breast, or thorax: *pectoral fins.* **2.** worn on the breast or chest: *a pectoral medallion.* ~*n.* **3.** a pectoral organ or part, esp. a muscle or fin. **4.** a medicine for disorders of the chest or lungs. **5.** anything worn on the chest or breast for decoration or protection. [C15: < L *pectorālis,* < *pectus* breast] —ˈ**pectorally** *adv.*

pectoral fin *n.* either of a pair of fins, situated

just behind the head in fishes, that help to control the direction of movement during locomotion.

pectoral muscle *n.* either of two large chest muscles (**pectoralis major** and **pectoralis minor**), that assist in movements of the shoulder and upper arm.

peculate (ˈpɛkjʊˌleɪt) *vb.* to appropriate or embezzle (public money, etc.). [C18: < L *pecūlārī,* < *pecūlium* private property (orig., cattle); see PECULIAR] —ˌ**pecuˈlation** *n.* —ˈ**pecuˌlator** *n.*

peculiar (pɪˈkjuːlɪə) *adj.* **1.** strange or unusual; odd: *a peculiar idea.* **2.** distinct from others; special. **3.** (*postpositive;* foll. by *to*) belonging characteristically or exclusively (to): *peculiar to North America.* [C15: < L *pecūliāris* concerning private property, < *pecūlium,* lit.: property in cattle, < *pecus* cattle] —**peˈculiarly** *adv.*

peculiarity (pɪˌkjuːlɪˈærɪtɪ) *n., pl.* **-ties. 1.** a strange or unusual habit or characteristic. **2.** a distinguishing trait, etc., that is characteristic of a particular person; idiosyncrasy. **3.** the state or quality of being peculiar.

pecuniary (pɪˈkjuːnɪərɪ) *adj.* **1.** of or relating to money. **2.** *Law.* (of an offence) involving a monetary penalty. [C16: < L *pecūniāris,* < *pecūnia* money] —**peˈcuniarily** *adv.*

pecuniary advantage *n. Law.* financial advantage that is dishonestly obtained by deception and that constitutes a criminal offence.

-ped *or* **-pede** *n. combining form.* foot or feet: *quadruped; centipede.* [< L *pēs, ped-* foot]

pedagogue *or U.S.* (*sometimes*) **pedagog** (ˈpɛdəˌgɒg) *n.* **1.** a teacher or educator. **2.** a pedantic or dogmatic teacher. [C14: < L *paedagōgus,* < Gk *paidagōgos* slave who looked after his master's son, < *pais* boy + *agōgos* leader] —ˌ**pedaˈgogic** *or* ˌ**pedaˈgogical** *adj.* —ˌ**pedaˈgogically** *adv.*

pedagogy (ˈpɛdəˌgɒgɪ, -ˌgɒdʒɪ, -ˌgəʊdʒɪ) *n.* the principles, practice, or profession of teaching.

pedal[1] (ˈpɛdᵊl) *n.* **1. a.** any foot-operated lever, esp. one of the two levers that drive the chainwheel of a bicycle, the foot brake, clutch control, or accelerator of a car, one of the levers on an organ controlling deep bass notes, or one of the levers on a piano used to mute or sustain tone. **b.** (*as modifier*): *a pedal cycle.* ~*vb.* **-alling, -alled** *or U.S.* **-aling, -aled. 2.** to propel (a bicycle, etc.) by operating the pedals. **3.** (*intr.*) to operate the pedals of an organ, piano, etc. **4.** to work (pedals of any kind). [C17: < L *pedālis;* see PEDAL[2]]

pedal[2] (ˈpiːdᵊl) *adj.* of or relating to the foot or feet. [C17: < L *pedālis,* < *pēs* foot]

pedal point (ˈpɛdᵊl) *n. Music.* a sustained bass note, over which the other parts move bringing changing harmonies. Often shortened to **pedal.**

pedant (ˈpɛdᵊnt) *n.* **1.** a person who relies too much on academic learning or who is concerned chiefly with insignificant detail. **2.** *Arch.* a schoolmaster or teacher. [C16: via OF < It. *pedante* teacher] —**pedantic** (pɪˈdæntɪk) *adj.* —**peˈdantically** *adv.*

pedantry (ˈpɛdᵊntrɪ) *n., pl.* **-ries.** the habit or an instance of being a pedant, esp. in the display of useless knowledge or minute observance of petty rules or details.

pedate (ˈpɛdeɪt) *adj.* **1.** (of a plant leaf) deeply divided into several lobes. **2.** *Zool.* having or resembling a foot: *a pedate appendage.* [C18: < L *pedātus* equipped with feet, < *pēs* foot]

peddle (ˈpɛdᵊl) *vb.* **1.** to go from place to place selling (goods, esp. small articles). **2.** (*tr.*) to sell (illegal drugs, esp. narcotics). **3.** (*tr.*) to advocate (ideas, etc.) persistently: *to peddle a new philosophy.* [C16: back formation < PEDLAR]

peddler (ˈpɛdlə) *n.* **1.** a person who sells illegal drugs, esp. narcotics. **2.** the usual U.S. spelling of **pedlar.**

pederasty *or* **paederasty** (ˈpɛdəˌræstɪ) *n.* homosexual relations between men and boys. [C17: < NL *paederastia,* < Gk, < *pais* boy + *erastēs* lover, < *eran* to love] —ˈ**pederˌast** *or* ˈ**paederˌast** *n.* —ˌ**pederˈastic** *or* ˌ**paederˈastic** *adj.*

pedestal (ˈpɛdɪstᵊl) *n.* **1.** a base that supports a column, statue, etc. **2.** a position of eminence or supposed superiority (esp. in **place, put,** *or* **set on a pedestal**). [C16: < F *piédestal,* < OIt. *piedestallo,* < *pie* foot + *di* of + *stallo* a stall]

pedestrian (pɪˈdɛstrɪən) *n.* **1. a.** a person travelling on foot; walker. **b.** (*as modifier*): *a pedestrian precinct.* ~*adj.* **2.** dull; commonplace: *a pedestrian style of writing.* [C18: < L *pedester,* < *pēs* foot]

pedestrian crossing *n. Brit.* a path across a road marked as a crossing for pedestrians.

pedestrianize *or* **-ise** (pɪˈdɛstrɪəˌnaɪz) *vb.* (*tr.*) to convert (a street, etc.) into an area for the use of pedestrians only. —**peˌdestrianiˈzation** *or* **-iˈsation** *n.*

pedi- *combining form.* indicating the foot: *pedicure.* [< L *pēs, ped-* foot]

pedicab (ˈpɛdɪˌkæb) *n.* a pedal-operated tricycle, available for hire in some Asian countries, with an attached seat for one or two passengers.

pedicel (ˈpɛdɪˌsɛl) *n.* **1.** the stalk bearing a single flower of an inflorescence. **2.** Also called: **peduncle.** *Biol.* any short stalk bearing an organ or organism. ~Also called: **pedicle.** [C17: < NL *pedicellus,* < L *pedīculus,* < *pēs* foot]

pediculosis (pɪˌdɪkjʊˈləʊsɪs) *n. Pathol.* the state of being infested with lice. [C19: via NL < L *pedīculus* louse] —**pediculous** (pɪˈdɪkjʊləs) *adj.*

pedicure (ˈpɛdɪˌkjʊə) *n.* treatment of the feet, either by a medical expert or a cosmetician. [C19: via F < L *pēs* foot + *curāre* to care for]

pedigree (ˈpɛdɪˌgriː) *n.* **1. a.** the line of descent of a purebred animal. **b.** (*as modifier*): *a pedigree bull.* **2.** a document recording this. **3.** a genealogical table, esp. one indicating pure ancestry. [C15: < OF *pie de grue* crane's foot, alluding to the spreading lines used in a genealogical chart] —ˈ**pediˌgreed** *adj.*

pediment (ˈpɛdɪmənt) *n.* a low-pitched gable, esp. one that is triangular as used in classical architecture. [C16: < obs. *periment,* ? workman's corruption of PYRAMID] —ˌ**pediˈmental** *adj.*

pedipalp (ˈpɛdɪˌpælp) *n.* either member of the second pair of head appendages of arachnids: specialized for feeding, locomotion, etc. [C19: < NL *pedipalpi,* < L *pēs* foot + *palpus* palp]

pedlar *or esp. U.S.* **peddler** (ˈpɛdlə) *n.* a person who peddles; hawker. [C14: changed < *peder,* < *ped, pedde* basket, <?]

pedo- *or before a vowel* **ped-** a variant (esp. U.S.) of **paedo-.**

pedology (pɪˈdɒlədʒɪ) *n.* the study of soils. [C20: < Gk *pedon* ground, earth + -OLOGY]

pedometer (pɪˈdɒmɪtə) *n.* a device that records the number of steps taken in walking and hence the distance travelled.

peduncle (pɪˈdʌŋkᵊl) *n.* **1.** the stalk of a plant bearing an inflorescence or solitary flower. **2.** *Anat., pathol.* any stalklike structure. **3.** *Biol.* another name for **pedicel** (sense 2). [C18: < NL *pedunculus,* < L *pedīculus* little foot] —**peduncular** (pɪˈdʌŋkjʊlə) *or* **pedunculate** (pɪˈdʌŋkjʊlɪt, -ˌleɪt) *adj.*

pee (piː) *Inf.* ~*vb.* **peeing, peed. 1.** (*intr.*) to urinate. ~*n.* **2.** urine. **3.** the act of urinating. [C18: euphemistic for PISS, based on the initial letter]

peek (piːk) *vb.* **1.** (*intr.*) to glance quickly or furtively. ~*n.* **2.** such a glance. [C14 *pike,* rel. to M Du *kiken* to peek]

peekaboo (ˈpiːkəˌbuː) *n.* **1.** a game for young children, in which one person hides his face and suddenly reveals it and cries "peekaboo". ~*adj.* **2.** (of a garment) made of fabric that is sheer or patterned with small holes. [C16: < PEEK + BOO]

peel[1] (piːl) *vb.* **1.** (*tr.*) to remove (the skin, rind, etc.) of (a fruit, egg, etc.). **2.** (*intr.*) (of paint, etc.) to be removed from a surface, esp. by weathering. **3.** (*intr.*) (of a surface) to lose its outer covering of paint, etc., esp. by weathering. **4.** (*intr.*) (of a person or part of the body) to shed skin in flakes or (of skin) to be shed in flakes, esp. as a result of sunburn. ~*n.* **5.** the skin or rind of a fruit, etc. ~See also **peel off.** [OE *pilian* to strip off the outer layer, < L *pilāre* to make bald, < *pilus* a hair] —ˈ**peeler** *n.*

peel[2] (piːl) *n.* a long-handled shovel used by bakers for moving bread in an oven. [C14 *pele,* < OF, < L *pāla* spade, < *pangere* to drive in]

peel[3] (piːl) *n. Brit.* a fortified tower of the 16th century on the borders of Scotland. [C14 (fence made of stakes): < OF *piel* stake, < L *pālus*]

peeler (ˈpiːlə) *n. Irish & obs. Brit. sl.* another word for **policeman.** [C19: < the founder of the police force, Sir Robert *Peel* (1788–1850), Brit. statesman & prime minister]

peeling (ˈpiːlɪŋ) *n.* a strip of skin, rind, bark, etc., that has been peeled off: *a potato peeling.*

peel off *vb.* (*adv.*) **1.** to remove or be removed by peeling. **2.** (*intr.*) *Sl.* to undress. **3.** (*intr.*) (of an aircraft) to turn away as by banking, and leave a formation.

peen (piːn) *n.* **1.** the end of a hammer head opposite the striking face, often rounded or wedge-shaped. ~*vb.* **2.** (*tr.*) to strike with the peen of a hammer or a stream of metal shot. [C17: var. of *pane,* ? < F *panne,* ult. < L *pinna* point]

peep[1] (piːp) *vb.* (*intr.*) **1.** to look furtively or secretly, as through a small aperture or from a hidden place. **2.** to appear partially or briefly: *the sun peeped through the clouds.* ~*n.* **3.** a quick or furtive look. **4.** the first appearance: *the peep of dawn.* [C15: var. of PEEK]

peep[2] (piːp) *vb.* (*intr.*) **1.** (esp. of young birds) to utter shrill small noises. **2.** to speak in a weak voice. ~*n.* **3.** a peeping sound. [C15: imit.]

peeper (ˈpiːpə) *n.* **1.** a person who peeps. **2.** (*often pl.*) a slang word for **eye**[1] (sense 1).

peephole (ˈpiːpˌhəʊl) *n.* a small aperture, as in a door for observing callers before opening.

Peeping Tom *n.* a man who furtively observes women undressing; voyeur. [C19: after the tailor who, according to legend, peeped at Lady Godiva when she rode naked through Coventry]

peepshow (ˈpiːpˌʃəʊ) *n.* a box with a peephole through which a series of pictures can be seen.

peepul (ˈpiːpᵊl) *or* **pipal** *n.* an Indian tree resembling the banyan: regarded as sacred by Buddhists. Also called: **bo tree.** [C18: < Hindi *pīpal,* < Sansk. *pippala*]

peer[1] (pɪə) *n.* **1.** a member of a nobility; nobleman. **2.** a person who holds any of the five grades of the British nobility: duke, marquess, earl, viscount, and baron. See also **life peer. 3.** a person who is an equal in social standing, rank, age, etc.: *to be tried by one's peers.* [C14 (in sense 3): < OF *per,* < L *pār* equal]

peer[2] (pɪə) *vb.* (*intr.*) **1.** to look intently with or as if with difficulty: *to peer into the distance.* **2.** to appear partially or dimly: *the sun peered through the fog.* [C16: < Flemish *pieren* to look with narrowed eyes]

peerage (ˈpɪərɪdʒ) *n.* **1.** the whole body of peers; aristocracy. **2.** the position, rank, or title of a peer. **3.** (esp. in the British Isles) a book listing the peers and giving their genealogy.

peeress (ˈpɪərɪs) *n.* **1.** the wife or widow of a peer. **2.** a woman holding the rank of a peer in her own right.

peer group *n.* a social group composed of individuals of approximately the same age.

peerless (ˈpɪəlɪs) *adj.* having no equals; matchless.

peeve (piːv) *Inf.* ~*vb.* **1.** (*tr.*) to irritate; vex; annoy. ~*n.* **2.** something that irritates; vexation. [C20: back formation < PEEVISH] —**peeved** *adj.*

peevish (ˈpiːvɪʃ) *adj.* fretful or irritable. [C14: <?] —ˈ**peevishly** *adv.* —ˈ**peevishness** *n.*

peewee (ˈpiːwiː) *n.* a small black-and-white Australian bird with long thin legs. [imit.]

peewit *or* **pewit** (ˈpiːwɪt) *n.* another name for **lapwing.** [C16: imit. of its call]

peg (pɛg) *n.* **1.** a small cylindrical pin or dowel used to join two parts together. **2.** a pin pushed or driven into a surface: used to mark scores, define limits, support coats, etc. **3.** any of several pins on a violin, etc., which can be turned so as to tune strings wound around them. **4.** Also called: **clothes peg.** *Brit.* a split or hinged pin for fastening wet clothes to a line to dry. U.S. and Canad. equivalent: **clothespin. 5.** *Brit.* a small drink of wine or spirits. **6.** an opportunity or pretext for doing something: *a peg on which to hang a theory.* **7.** *Inf.* a level of self-esteem, importance, etc. (esp. in **bring** *or* **take down a peg**). **8.** *Inf.* See **peg leg. 9. off the peg.** *Chiefly Brit.* (of clothes) ready-to-wear, as opposed to tailor-made. ~*vb.* **pegging, pegged. 10.** (*tr.*) to knock or insert a peg into. **11.** (*tr.*) to secure with pegs: *to peg a tent.* **12.** (*tr.*) to mark (a score) with pegs, as in some card games. **13.** (*tr.*) *Inf.* to throw (stones, etc.) at a target. **14.** (*intr.;* foll. by *away, along,* etc.) *Chiefly Brit.* to work steadily: *he pegged away at his job for years.* **15.** (*tr.*) to stabilize (the price of a commodity, an exchange rate, etc.). [C15: < Low Gmc *pegge*]

pegboard (ˈpɛgˌbɔːd) *n.* **1.** a board having a pattern of holes into which small pegs can be fitted, used for playing certain games or keeping a score. **2.** another name for **solitaire** (sense 1). **3.** hardboard perforated by a pattern of holes in which articles may be hung, as for display.

peg leg *n. Inf.* **1.** an artificial leg, esp. one made of wood. **2.** a person with an artificial leg.

pegmatite (ˈpɛgməˌtaɪt) *n.* any of a class of coarse-grained intrusive igneous rocks consisting chiefly of quartz and feldspar. [C19: < Gk *pegma* something joined together]

peg out *vb.* (*adv.*) **1.** (*intr.*) *Inf.* to collapse or die. **2.** (*intr.*) *Cribbage.* to score the point that wins the game. **3.** (*tr.*) to mark or secure with pegs: *to peg out one's claims to a piece of land.*

peg top *n.* a child's spinning top, usually made of wood with a metal centre pin.

peg-top *adj.* (of skirts, trousers, etc.) wide at the hips then tapering off towards the ankle.

PEI *abbrev. for* Prince Edward Island.

peignoir (ˈpeɪnwɑː) *n.* a woman's dressing gown. [C19: < F, < *peigner* to comb, since the garment was worn while the hair was combed]

pejoration (ˌpiːdʒəˈreɪʃən) *n.* **1.** semantic change whereby a word acquires unfavourable connotations. **2.** the process of worsening.

pejorative (pɪˈdʒɒrətɪv, ˈpiːdʒər-) *adj.* **1.** (of words, expressions, etc.) having an unpleasant or disparaging connotation. ~*n.* **2.** a pejorative word, etc. [C19: < F *péjoratif,* < LL *pējōrātus,* p.p. of *pējōrāre* to make worse, < L *pēior* worse] —**peˈjoratively** *adv.*

pekan (ˈpɛkən) *n.* another name for **fisher** (the animal). [C18: < Canad. F *pékan,* < Amerind]

peke (piːk) *n. Inf.* a Pekingese dog.

Pekingese (ˌpiːkɪŋˈiːz) *or* **Pekinese** (ˌpiːkəˈniːz) *n.* **1.** (*pl.* **-ese**) a small breed of pet dog with a profuse straight coat, curled plumed tail, and short wrinkled muzzle. **2.** the dialect of Mandarin Chinese spoken in Peking. **3.** (*pl.* **-ese**) a native or inhabitant of Peking, in NE China. ~*adj.* **4.** of Peking or its inhabitants.

Peking man (piːˈkɪŋ) *n.* an early type of man, of the Lower Palaeolithic age, remains of which were found in a cave near Peking.

pekoe (ˈpiːkəʊ) *n.* a high-quality tea made from the downy tips of the young buds of the tea plant. [C18: < Chinese *peh ho,* < *peh* white + *ho* down]

pelage (ˈpɛlɪdʒ) *n.* the coat of a mammal, consisting of hair, wool, fur, etc. [C19: via F < OF *pel* animal's coat, < L *pilus* hair]

Pelagianism (pɛˈleɪdʒɪəˌnɪzəm) *n. Christianity.* a heretical doctrine, first formulated by Pelagius, a 5th-century British monk, that rejected the concept of original sin. —**Peˈlagian** *n., adj.*

pelagic (pɛˈlædʒɪk) *adj.* **1.** of or relating to the open sea: *pelagic whaling.* **2.** (of marine life) occurring in the upper waters of open sea. [C17: < L *pelagicus,* < *pelagus,* < Gk *pelagos* sea]

pelargonium (ˌpɛləˈgəʊnɪəm) *n.* any plant of a chiefly southern African genus having circular or lobed leaves and red, pink, or white aromatic flowers: includes many cultivated geraniums. [C19: via NL < Gk *pelargos* stork, on the model of GERANIUM; from the likeness of the seed vessels to a stork's bill]

pelf (pɛlf) *n. Contemptuous.* money or wealth; lucre. [C14: < OF *pelfre* booty]

pelham (ˈpɛləm) *n.* a horse's bit for a double bridle, less severe than a curb but more severe than a snaffle. [prob. < the name *Pelham*]

pelican (ˈpɛlɪkən) *n.* any aquatic bird of a tropical and warm water family. They have a long straight flattened bill, with a distensible pouch for engulfing fish. [OE *pellican,* < LL *pelicānus,* < Gk *pelekān*]

pelican crossing *n.* a type of road crossing with a pedestrian-operated traffic-light system. [C20: < *pe(destrian) li(ght) con(trolled) crossing,* with *-con* adapted to *-can* of *pelican*]

pelisse (pɛˈliːs) *n.* **1.** a fur-trimmed cloak. **2.** a loose coat, usually fur-trimmed, worn esp. by women in the early 19th century. [C18: via OF < Med. L *pellicia* cloak, < L *pellis* skin]

pellagra (pəˈleɪgrə, -ˈlæ-) *n. Pathol.* a disease caused by a dietary deficiency of nicotinic acid, characterized by scaling of the skin, inflammation of the mouth, diarrhoea, mental impairment, etc. [C19: via It. < *pelle* skin + *-agra,* < Gk *agra* paroxysm] —**pelˈlagrous** *adj.*

pellet (ˈpɛlɪt) *n.* **1.** a small round ball, esp. of compressed matter. **2. a.** an imitation bullet used in toy guns. **b.** a piece of small shot. **3.** a stone ball formerly used in a catapult. **4.** *Ornithol.* a mass of undigested food that is regurgitated by birds of prey. **5.** a small pill. ~*vb.* (*tr.*) **6.** to strike with pellets. **7.** to make or form into pellets. [C14: < OF *pelote,* < Vulgar L *pilota* (unattested), < L *pila* ball]

pellitory (ˈpɛlɪtərɪ, -trɪ) *n., pl.* **-ries. 1.** any of various plants of a S and W European genus, esp. wall pellitory, that grow in crevices and have long narrow leaves and small pink flowers. **2. pellitory of Spain.** a small Mediterranean plant, the root of which contains an oil formerly used to relieve toothache. [C16 *peletre,* < OF *piretre,* < L, < Gk *purethron,* < *pur* fire, from the hot pungent taste of the root]

pell-mell (ˈpɛlˈmɛl) *adv.* **1.** in a confused headlong rush: *the hounds ran pell-mell into the yard.* **2.** in a disorderly manner: *the things were piled pell-mell in the room.* ~*adj.* **3.** disordered; tumultuous: *a pell-mell rush for the exit.* ~*n.* **4.** disorder; confusion. [C16: < OF *pesle-mesle,* jingle based on *mesler* to MEDDLE]

pellucid (pɛˈluːsɪd) *adj.* **1.** transparent or translucent. **2.** extremely clear in style and meaning. [C17: < L *pellūcidus,* var. of *perlūcidus,* < *perlūcēre* to shine through] —ˌ**pelluˈcidity** *or* **pelˈlucidness** *n.* —**pelˈlucidly** *adv.*

pelmet (ˈpɛlmɪt) *n.* an ornamental drapery or board fixed above a window to conceal the curtain rail. [C19: prob. < F *palmette* palm-leaf decoration on cornice moulding]

pelota (pəˈlɒtə) *n.* any of various games played in Spain, Spanish America, SW France, etc., by two players who use a basket strapped to their wrists or a wooden racket to propel a ball against a specially marked wall. [C19: < Sp.: ball, < OF *pelote;* see PELLET]

pelt[1] (pɛlt) *vb.* **1.** (*tr.*) to throw (missiles, etc.) at (a person, etc.). **2.** (*tr.*) to hurl (insults, etc.) at (a person, etc.). **3.** (*intr.;* foll. by *along,* etc.) to hurry. **4.** (*intr.*) to rain heavily. ~*n.* **5.** a blow. **6.** speed (esp. in **at full pelt**). [C15:<?]

pelt[2] (pɛlt) *n.* **1.** the skin of a fur-bearing animal, esp. when it has been removed from the carcass. **2.** the hide of an animal, stripped of hair. [C15: ? back formation < PELTRY]

peltate (ˈpɛlteɪt) *adj.* (of leaves) having the stalk attached to the centre of the lower surface. [C18: < L *peltātus* equipped with a *pelta* small shield]

peltry (ˈpɛltrɪ) *n., pl.* **-ries.** the pelts of animals collectively. [C15: < OF *peleterie* collection of pelts, < L *pilus* hair]

pelvic fin *n.* either of a pair of fins attached to the pelvic girdle of fishes that help to control the direction of movement during locomotion.

pelvic inflammatory disease *n.* inflammation of a woman's womb, Fallopian tubes, or ovaries as a result of infection with one of a group of bacteria.

pelvis (ˈpɛlvɪs) *n., pl.* **-vises** *or* **-ves** (-viːz). **1.** the large funnel-shaped structure at the lower end of the trunk of most vertebrates. **2.** Also called: **pelvic girdle.** the bones that form this structure. **3.** any anatomical cavity or structure shaped like a funnel or cup. [C17: < L: basin] —ˈ**pelvic** *adj.*

pemmican *or* **pemican** (ˈpɛmɪkən) *n.* a small pressed cake of shredded dried meat, pounded into paste, used originally by American Indians and now chiefly for emergency rations. [C19: < Amerind *pimikân,* < *pimii* grease]

pemphigus (ˈpɛmfɪgəs, pɛmˈfaɪ-) *n. Pathol.* any of a group of blistering skin diseases. [C18: via NL < Gk *pemphix* bubble]

pen[1] (pɛn) *n.* **1.** an implement for writing or drawing using ink, formerly consisting of a sharpened and split quill, and now of a metal nib attached to a holder. See also **ballpoint, fountain pen. 2.** the writing end of such an implement; nib. **3.** style of writing. **4. the pen.** writing as an occupation. ~*vb.* **penning, penned. 5.** (*tr.*) to write or compose. [OE *pinne,* < LL *penna* (quill) pen, < L: feather]

pen[2] (pɛn) *n.* **1.** an enclosure in which domestic animals are kept. **2.** any place of confinement. **3.** a dock for servicing submarines, esp. having a bombproof roof. ~*vb.* **penning, penned** *or* **pent. 4.** (*tr.*) to enclose in a pen. [OE *penn*]

pen[3] (pɛn) *n. U.S. & Canad. inf.* short for **penitentiary** (sense 1).

pen[4] (pɛn) *n.* a female swan. [C16: <?]

PEN (pɛn) *n. acronym for* International Association of Poets, Playwrights, Editors, Essayists, and Novelists.

Pen. *abbrev. for* Peninsula.

penal (ˈpiːnᵊl) *adj.* **1.** of, relating to, constituting, or prescribing punishment. **2.** used or designated as a place of punishment: *a penal institution.* [C15: < LL *poenālis* concerning punishment, < L *poena* penalty] —ˈ**penally** *adv.*

penal code *n.* the codified body of the laws that relate to crime and its punishment.

penalize *or* **-ise** (ˈpiːnəˌlaɪz) *vb.* (*tr.*) **1.** to impose a penalty on (someone), as for breaking a law or rule. **2.** to inflict a disadvantage on. **3.** *Sport.* to award a free stroke, point, or penalty against (a player or team). **4.** to declare (an act) legally punishable. —ˌ**penaliˈzation** *or* **-iˈsation** *n.*

penalty (ˈpɛnᵊltɪ) *n., pl.* **-ties. 1.** a legal or official punishment, such as a term of imprisonment. **2.** some other form of punishment, such as a fine or forfeit for not fulfilling a contract. **3.** loss, suffering, or other unfortunate result of one's own action, error, etc. **4.** *Sport, games, etc.* a handicap awarded against a player or team for illegal play, such as a free shot at goal by the opposing team. [C16: < Med. L *poenālitās* penalty; see PENAL]

penalty area *n.* another name for **penalty box** (sense 1).

penalty box *n.* **1.** *Soccer.* a rectangular area in front of the goal, within which a penalty is awarded for a foul by the defending team. **2.** *Ice hockey.* a bench for players serving time penalties.

penalty rates *pl. n. Austral. & N.Z.* rates of pay for employees working outside normal hours.

penance (ˈpɛnəns) *n.* **1.** voluntary self-punishment to atone for a sin, crime, etc. **2.** a feeling of regret for one's wrongdoings. **3.** *Christianity.* a punishment usually consisting of prayer, fasting, etc., imposed by church authority as a condition of absolution. **4.** *R.C. Church.* a sacrament in which repentant sinners are absolved on condition of confession of their sins to a priest and of performing a penance. ~*vb.* **5.** (*tr.*) (of ecclesiastical authorities) to impose a penance upon (a sinner). [C13: via OF < L *paenitentia* repentance]

penates (pəˈnɑːtiːz) *pl. n.* See **lares and penates.**

pence (pɛns) *n.* a plural of **penny.**

▷ **Usage.** Since the decimalization of British currency and the introduction of the abbreviation

p, as in *10p, 85p,* etc., the abbreviation has tended to replace *pence* in speech, as in *4p* (ˌfɔːˈpiː), etc.

penchant (ˈpɒŋʃɒn) *n.* strong inclination or liking; bent or taste. [C17: < F, < *pencher* to incline, < L *pendēre* to be suspended]

pencil (ˈpɛnsᵊl) *n.* **1.** a thin cylindrical instrument used for writing, drawing, etc., consisting of a rod of graphite or other marking substance usually encased in wood and sharpened. **2.** something similar in shape or function: *a styptic pencil.* **3.** a narrow set of lines or rays, such as light rays, diverging from or converging to a point. **4.** *Rare.* an artist's individual style. **5.** a type of artist's brush. ~*vb.* **-cilling, -cilled** *or U.S.* **-ciling, -ciled.** (*tr.*) **6.** to draw, colour, or write with a pencil. **7.** to mark with a pencil. [C14: < OF *pincel,* < L *pēnicillus* painter's brush, < *pēniculus* a little tail] —ˈ**penciller** *or U.S.* ˈ**penciler** *n.*

pend (pɛnd) *vb.* (*intr.*) to await judgment or settlement. [C15: < L *pendēre* to hang]

pendant (ˈpɛndənt) *n.* **1. a.** an ornament that hangs from a piece of jewellery. **b.** a necklace with such an ornament. **2.** a hanging light, esp. a chandelier. **3.** a carved ornament that is suspended from a ceiling or roof. ~*adj.* **4.** a variant spelling of **pendent.** [C14: < OF, < *pendre* to hang, < L *pendēre* to hang down]

pendent (ˈpɛndənt) *adj.* **1.** dangling. **2.** jutting. **3.** (of a grammatical construction) incomplete. **4.** a less common word for **pending.** ~*n.* **5.** a variant spelling of **pendant.** [C15: < OF *pendant,* < *pendre* to hang; see PENDANT] —ˈ**pendency** *n.*

pendentive (pɛnˈdɛntɪv) *n.* any of four triangular sections of vaulting with concave sides, positioned at a corner of a rectangular space to support a dome. [C18: < F *pendentif,* < L *pendens* hanging, < *pendere* to hang]

pending (ˈpɛndɪŋ) *prep.* **1.** while waiting for. ~*adj.* (*postpositive*) **2.** not yet decided, confirmed, or finished. **3.** imminent: *these developments have been pending for some time.*

pendragon (pɛnˈdrægən) *n.* a supreme war chief or leader of the ancient Britons. [Welsh, lit.: head dragon]

pendulous (ˈpɛndjʊləs) *adj.* hanging downwards, esp. so as to swing from side to side. [C17: < L *pendulus,* < *pendēre* to hang down] —ˈ**pendulously** *adv.* —ˈ**pendulousness** *n.*

pendulum (ˈpɛndjʊləm) *n.* **1.** a body mounted so that it can swing freely under the influence of gravity. **2.** such a device used to regulate a clock mechanism. **3.** something that changes fairly regularly: *the pendulum of public opinion.* [C17: < L *pendulus* PENDULOUS]

peneplain *or* **peneplane** (ˈpiːnɪˌpleɪn) *n.* a relatively flat land surface produced by erosion. [C19: < L *paene* almost + PLAIN[1]]

penetrant (ˈpɛnɪtrənt) *adj.* **1.** sharp; penetrating. ~*n.* **2.** *Chem.* a substance that lowers the surface tension of a liquid and thus causes it to penetrate or be absorbed more easily. **3.** a person or thing that penetrates.

penetrate (ˈpɛnɪˌtreɪt) *vb.* **1.** to find or force a way into or through (something); pierce; enter. **2.** to diffuse through (a substance, etc.); permeate. **3.** (*tr.*) to see through: *their eyes could not penetrate the fog.* **4.** (*tr.*) (of a man) to insert the penis into the vagina of (a woman). **5.** (*tr.*) to grasp the meaning of (a principle, etc.). **6.** (*intr.*) to be understood: *his face lit up as the new idea penetrated.* [C16: < L *penetrāre*] —ˈ**penetrable** *adj.* —ˌ**penetraˈbility** *n.* —ˈ**peneˌtrator** *n.*

penetrating (ˈpɛnɪˌtreɪtɪŋ) *adj.* tending to or able to penetrate: *a penetrating mind; a penetrating voice.* —ˈ**peneˌtratingly** *adv.*

penetration (ˌpɛnɪˈtreɪʃən) *n.* **1.** the act or an instance of penetrating. **2.** the ability or power to penetrate. **3.** keen insight or perception. **4.** *Mil.* an offensive manoeuvre that breaks through an enemy's defensive position.

pen friend *n.* a person with whom one exchanges letters, often a person in another country whom one has not met. Also called: **pen pal.**

penguin (ˈpɛŋgwɪn) *n.* a flightless marine bird of cool southern, esp. Antarctic, regions: they have wings modified as flippers, webbed feet, and feathers lacking barbs. [C16: ? < Welsh *pen gwyn,* < *pen* head + *gwyn* white]

penicillin (ˌpɛnɪˈsɪlɪn) *n.* any of a group of antibiotics with powerful action against bacteria: obtained from the fungus *Penicillium.* [C20: < PENICILLIUM]

penicillium (ˌpɛnɪˈsɪlɪəm) *n., pl.* **-cilliums** *or* **-cillia** (-ˈsɪlɪə). any saprophytic fungus of the genus *Penicillium,* which commonly grow as a green or blue mould on stale food. [C19: NL, < L *pēnicillus* tuft of hairs; < the appearance of the sporangia of this fungus]

penillion *or* **pennillion** (pɪˈnɪlɪən) *pl. n., sing.* **penill** (pɪˈnɪl). the Welsh art or practice of singing poetry in counterpoint to a traditional melody played on the harp. [< Welsh: verses]

peninsula (pɪˈnɪnsjʊlə) *n.* a narrow strip of land projecting into a sea or lake from the mainland. [C16: < L, lit.: almost an island, < *paene* almost + *insula* island] —**penˈinsular** *adj.*

penis (ˈpiːnɪs) *n., pl.* **-nises** *or* **-nes** (-niːz). the male organ of copulation in higher vertebrates, also used for urine excretion in many mammals. [C17: < L: penis] —**penile** (ˈpiːnaɪl) *adj.*

penitent (ˈpɛnɪtənt) *adj.* **1.** feeling regret for one's sins; repentant. ~*n.* **2.** a person who is penitent. **3.** *Christianity.* **a.** a person who repents his sins and seeks forgiveness for them. **b.** *R.C. Church.* a person who confesses his sins and submits to a penance. [C14: < Church L *paenitēns* regretting, < *paenitēre* to repent, <?] —ˈ**penitence** *n.* —ˈ**penitently** *adv.*

penitential (ˌpɛnɪˈtɛnʃəl) *adj.* **1.** of, showing, or constituting penance. ~*n.* **2.** *Chiefly R.C. Church.* a book or compilation of instructions for confessors. **3.** a less common word for **penitent** (senses 2, 3). —ˌ**peniˈtentially** *adv.*

penitentiary (ˌpɛnɪˈtɛnʃərɪ) *n., pl.* **-ries. 1.** (in the U.S. and Canada) a state or federal prison. **2.** *R.C. Church.* **a.** a cardinal who presides over a tribunal that decides all matters affecting the sacrament of penance. **b.** this tribunal itself. ~*adj.* **3.** another word for **penitential** (sense 1). **4.** *U.S. & Canad.* (of an offence) punishable by imprisonment in a penitentiary. [C15 (meaning also: an officer dealing with penances): < Med. L *poenitēntiārius,* < L *paenitēns* PENITENT]

penknife (ˈpɛnˌnaɪf) *n., pl.* **-knives.** a small knife with one or more blades that fold into the handle; pocketknife.

penman (ˈpɛnmən) *n., pl.* **-men. 1.** a person skilled in handwriting. **2.** a person who writes by hand in a specified way: *a bad penman.* **3.** an author. **4.** *Rare.* a scribe.

penmanship (ˈpɛnmənʃɪp) *n.* style or technique of writing by hand.

penna (ˈpɛnə) *n., pl.* **-nae** (-niː). *Ornithol.* any large feather that has a vane and forms part of the main plumage of a bird. [L: feather]

pen name *n.* an author's pseudonym. Also called: **nom de plume.**

pennant (ˈpɛnənt) *n.* **1.** a type of pennon, esp. one flown from vessels as identification or for signalling. **2.** *Chiefly U.S., Canad., & Austral.* **a.** a flag serving as an emblem of championship in certain sports. **b.** (*as modifier*): *pennant cricket.* [C17: prob. a blend of PENDANT & PENNON]

pennate (ˈpɛneɪt) *adj. Biol.* **1.** having feathers, wings, or winglike structures. **2.** another word for **pinnate.** [C19: < L *pennātus,* < *penna* wing]

penni (ˈpɛnɪ) *n., pl.* **-nia** (-nɪə) *or* **-nis.** a Finnish monetary unit worth one hundredth of a markka. [Finnish, < Low G *pennig* PENNY]

penniless (ˈpɛnɪlɪs) *adj.* very poor; almost totally without money. —ˈ**pennilessly** *adv.* —ˈ**pennilessness** *n.*

pennon (ˈpɛnən) *n.* **1.** a long flag, often tapering and divided at the end, originally a knight's personal flag. **2.** a small tapering or triangular flag borne on a ship or boat. **3.** a poetic word for **wing.** [C14: via OF ult. < L *penna* feather]

Pennsylvania Dutch (ˌpɛnsɪlˈveɪnɪə) *n.* **1.** a dialect of German spoken in E Pennsylvania. **2.**

(preceded by *the; functioning as pl.*) a group of German-speaking people in E Pennsylvania, descended from 18th-century settlers from SW Germany and Switzerland.

Pennsylvanian (ˌpɛnsɪlˈveɪnɪən) *adj.* **1.** of the state of Pennsylvania, in the U.S. **2.** (in North America) of, denoting, or formed in the upper of two divisions of the Carboniferous period. ~*n.* **3.** an inhabitant or native of the state of Pennsylvania. **4.** (preceded by *the*) the Pennsylvanian period or rock system.

penny (ˈpɛnɪ) *n., pl.* **pennies** *or* **pence** (pɛns). **1.** Also called: **new penny.** *Brit.* a bronze coin having a value equal to one hundredth of a pound. Abbrev.: **p. 2.** *Brit.* (before 1971) a bronze or copper coin having a value equal to one twelfth of a shilling. Abbrev.: **d. 3.** (*pl.* **pennies**). *U.S. & Canad.* a cent. **4.** a coin of similar value, as used in several other countries. **5.** (*used with a negative*) *Inf., chiefly Brit.* the least amount of money: *I don't have a penny.* **6. a pretty penny.** *Inf.* a considerable sum of money. **7. spend a penny.** *Brit. inf.* to urinate. **8. the penny dropped.** *Inf., chiefly Brit.* the explanation of something was finally realized. [OE *penig, pening*]

penny arcade *n. Chiefly U.S.* a public place with various coin-operated machines for entertainment.

Penny Black *n.* the first adhesive postage stamp, issued in Britain in 1840.

penny-dreadful *n., pl.* **-fuls.** *Brit. inf.* a cheap, often lurid book or magazine.

penny-farthing *n. Brit.* an early type of bicycle with a large front wheel and a small rear wheel, the pedals being on the front wheel.

penny-pinching *adj.* **1.** excessively careful with money; miserly. ~*n.* **2.** miserliness. —**ˈpenny-ˌpincher** *n.*

pennyroyal (ˌpɛnɪˈrɔɪəl) *n.* **1.** a Eurasian plant with hairy leaves and small mauve flowers, yielding an aromatic oil used in medicine. **2.** a similar and related plant of E North America. [C16: var. of Anglo-Norman *puliol real,* < OF *pouliol* (< L *pūleium* pennyroyal) + *real* ROYAL]

pennyweight (ˈpɛnɪˌweɪt) *n.* a unit of weight equal to 24 grains or one twentieth of an ounce (Troy).

penny whistle *n.* a type of flageolet with six finger holes, esp. a cheap metal one. Also called: **tin whistle.**

penny-wise *adj.* **1.** greatly concerned with saving small sums of money. **2. penny-wise and pound-foolish.** careful about trifles but wasteful in large ventures.

pennywort (ˈpɛnɪˌwɜːt) *n.* **1.** a Eurasian rock plant with whitish-green tubular flowers and rounded leaves. **2.** a marsh plant of Europe and North Africa, having circular leaves and greenish-pink flowers. **3.** any of various other plants with rounded penny-like leaves.

pennyworth (ˈpɛnɪˌwɜːθ) *n.* **1.** the amount that can be bought for a penny. **2.** a small amount: *he hasn't got a pennyworth of sense.*

penology (piːˈnɒlədʒɪ) *n.* **1.** the branch of the social sciences concerned with the punishment of crime. **2.** the science of prison management. [C19: < Gk *poinē* punishment] —**penological** (ˌpiːnəˈlɒdʒɪkəl) *adj.* —**peˈnologist** *n.*

pen pal *n.* another name for **pen friend.**

penpusher (ˈpɛnˌpʊʃə) *n.* a person who writes a lot, esp. a clerk involved with boring paperwork. —**ˈpenˌpushing** *adj., n.*

pension[1] (ˈpɛnʃən) *n.* **1.** a regular payment made by the state to people over a certain age to enable them to subsist without having to work. **2.** a regular payment made by an employer to former employees after they retire. **3.** any regular payment made by way of patronage, or in recognition of merit, service, etc.: *a pension paid to a disabled soldier.* ~*vb.* **4.** (*tr.*) to grant a pension to. [C14: via OF < L *pēnsiō* a payment, < *pendere* to pay] —**ˈpensionable** *adj.* —**ˈpensionary** *adj.* —**ˈpensioner** *n.*

pension[2] *French.* (pɑ̃sjɔ̃) *n.* (in France and some other countries) a relatively cheap boarding house. [C17: < F; extended meaning of *pension* grant; see PENSION[1]]

pension off *vb.* (*tr., adv.*) **1.** to cause to retire from a job and pay a pension to. **2.** to discard, because of age: *to pension off submarines.*

pensive (ˈpɛnsɪv) *adj.* **1.** deeply or seriously thoughtful, often with a tinge of sadness. **2.** expressing or suggesting pensiveness. [C14: < OF *pensif,* < *penser* to think, < L *pensāre* to consider] —**ˈpensively** *adv.* —**ˈpensiveness** *n.*

penstemon (pɛnˈstiːmən) *n.* a variant (esp. U.S.) of **pentstemon.**

penstock (ˈpɛnˌstɒk) *n.* **1.** a conduit that supplies water to a hydroelectric power plant. **2.** a channel bringing water from the head gates to a water wheel. **3.** a sluice for controlling water flow. [C17: < PEN[2] + STOCK]

pent (pɛnt) *vb.* a past tense and past participle of **pen**[2].

penta- *combining form.* five: *pentagon; pentameter.* [< Gk *pente*]

pentacle (ˈpɛntəkəl) *n.* **1.** another name for **pentagram.** [C16: < It. *pentacolo* something having five corners]

pentad (ˈpɛntæd) *n.* **1.** a group or series of five. **2.** the number or sum of five. **3.** a period of five years. **4.** *Chem.* a pentavalent element, atom, or radical. [C17: < Gk *pentas* group of five]

pentadactyl (ˌpɛntəˈdæktɪl) *adj.* (of the limbs of amphibians, reptiles, birds, and mammals) having a hand or foot bearing five digits.

pentagon (ˈpɛntəˌgɒn) *n.* a polygon having five sides. —**pentagonal** (pɛnˈtægənəl) *adj.*

Pentagon (ˈpɛntəˌgɒn) *n.* **1.** the five-sided building in Arlington, Virginia, that houses the headquarters of the U.S. Department of Defense. **2.** the military leadership of the U.S.

pentagram (ˈpɛntəˌgræm) *n.* **1.** a star-shaped figure with five points. **2.** such a figure used by the Pythagoreans, Black magicians, etc. ~Also called: **pentacle, pentangle.**

pentahedron (ˌpɛntəˈhiːdrən) *n., pl.* **-drons** *or* **-dra** (-drə). a solid figure having five plane faces. —ˌ**pentaˈhedral** *adj.*

pentamerous (pɛnˈtæmərəs) *adj.* consisting of five parts, esp. (of flowers) having the petals, sepals, and other parts arranged in groups of five.

pentameter (pɛnˈtæmɪtə) *n.* **1.** a verse line consisting of five metrical feet. **2.** (in classical prosody) a verse line consisting of two dactyls, one stressed syllable, two dactyls, and a final stressed syllable. ~*adj.* **3.** designating a verse line consisting of five metrical feet.

pentane (ˈpɛnteɪn) *n.* an alkane hydrocarbon having three isomers, esp. the isomer with a straight chain of carbon atoms (*n*-pentane) which is a colourless flammable liquid used as a solvent.

pentangle (ˈpɛnˌtæŋgəl) *n.* another name for **pentagram.**

pentanoic acid (ˌpɛntəˈnəʊɪk) *n.* a colourless liquid carboxylic acid with an unpleasant odour, used in making perfumes, flavourings, and pharmaceuticals.

Pentateuch (ˈpɛntəˌtjuːk) *n.* the first five books of the Old Testament. [C16: < Church L *pentateuchus,* < Gk PENTA- + *teukhos* tool (in LGk: scroll)] —ˌ**Pentaˈteuchal** *adj.*

pentathlon (pɛnˈtæθlən) *n.* an athletic contest consisting of five different events. [C18: < Gk *pentathlon,* < PENTA- + *athlon* contest]

pentatomic (ˌpɛntəˈtɒmɪk) *adj. Chem.* having five atoms in the molecule.

pentatonic scale (ˌpɛntəˈtɒnɪk) *n. Music.* any of several scales consisting of five notes.

pentavalent (ˌpɛntəˈveɪlənt) *adj. Chem.* having a valency of five. Also: **quinquevalent.**

Pentecost (ˈpɛntɪˌkɒst) *n.* **1.** a Christian festival occurring on Whit Sunday commemorating the descent of the Holy Ghost on the apostles. **2.** *Judaism.* the harvest festival, celebrated on the fiftieth day after the second day of Passover. [OE, < Church L, < Gk *pentēkostē* fiftieth (day after the Resurrection)]

Pentecostal (ˌpɛntɪˈkɒstəl) *adj.* **1.** (*usually prenominal*) of or relating to any of various

Christian groups that emphasize the charismatic aspects of Christianity and adopt a fundamental attitude to the Bible. **2.** of or relating to Pentecost or the influence of the Holy Spirit. ~*n.* **3.** a member of a Pentecostal Church. —ˌ**Penteˈcostalist** *n., adj.*

penthouse (ˈpɛntˌhaus) *n.* **1.** a flat or maisonette built onto the top floor or roof of a block of flats. **2.** a construction on the roof of a building, esp. one used to house machinery, etc. **3.** a shed built against a building, esp. one that has a sloping roof. [C14 *pentis* (later *penthouse*), < OF *apentis*, < LL *appendicium* appendage, < L *appendere* to hang from; see APPEND]

pentobarbitone sodium (ˌpɛntəˈbɑːbɪˌtəʊn) *n.* a barbiturate drug used in medicine as a sedative and hypnotic.

pentode (ˈpɛntəʊd) *n.* **1.** an electronic valve having five electrodes: a cathode, anode, and three grids. **2.** (*modifier*) (of a transistor) having three terminals at the base or gate. [C20: < PENTA- + Gk *hodos* way]

Pentothal sodium (ˈpɛntəˌθæl) *n.* a trademark for **thiopentone sodium.**

pentstemon (pɛntˈstiːmən) *or esp. U.S.* **penstemon** *n.* any plant of a North American genus having white, pink, red, blue, or purple flowers with five stamens, one of which is sterile. [C18: NL, < PENTA- + Gk *stēmōn* thread (here: stamen)]

pent-up *adj.* not released; repressed: *pent-up emotions.*

pentyl acetate (ˈpɛntaɪl, -tɪl) *n.* a colourless combustible liquid used as a solvent for paints, in the extraction of penicillin, in photographic film, and as a flavouring. Also called: **amyl acetate.**

penult (ˈpɛnʌlt, pɪˈnʌlt) *n.* the last syllable but one in a word. [C16: L *paenultima syllaba*, < *paene ultima* almost the last]

penultimate (pɪˈnʌltɪmɪt) *adj.* **1.** next to the last. ~*n.* **2.** anything next to last, esp. a penult.

penumbra (pɪˈnʌmbrə) *n., pl.* **-brae** (-briː) *or* **-bras. 1.** a fringe region of half shadow resulting from the partial obstruction of light by an opaque object. **2.** *Astron.* the lighter and outer region of a sunspot. **3.** *Painting.* the area in which light and shade blend. [C17: via NL < L *paene* almost + *umbra* shadow] —**peˈnumbral** *adj.*

penurious (pɪˈnjʊərɪəs) *adj.* **1.** niggardly with money. **2.** lacking money or means. **3.** scanty. —**peˈnuriously** *adv.* —**peˈnuriousness** *n.*

penury (ˈpɛnjʊrɪ) *n.* **1.** extreme poverty. **2.** extreme scarcity. [C15: < L *pēnūria* dearth, <?]

peon[1] (ˈpiːən, ˈpiːɒn) *n.* **1.** a Spanish-American farm labourer or unskilled worker. **2.** (formerly, in Spanish America) a debtor compelled to work off his debts. **3.** any very poor person. [C19: < Sp. *peón* peasant, < Med. L *pedō* man who goes on foot, < L *pēs* foot] —ˈ**peonage** *n.*

peon[2] (pjuːn, ˈpiːən, ˈpiːɒn) *n.* (in India, Sri Lanka, etc., esp. formerly) **1.** a messenger or attendant, esp. in an office. **2.** a native policeman. **3.** a foot soldier. [C17: < Port. *peão* orderly; see PEON[1]]

peony *or* **paeony** (ˈpiːənɪ) *n., pl.* **-nies. 1.** any of a genus of shrubs and plants of Eurasia and North America, having large pink, red, white, or yellow flowers. **2.** the flower of any of these plants. [OE *peonie*, < L *paeōnia*, < Gk *paiōnia*; rel. to *paiōnios* healing, < *paiōn* physician]

people (ˈpiːpᵊl) *n.* (*usually functioning as pl.*) **1.** persons collectively or in general. **2.** a group of persons considered together: *blind people.* **3.** (*pl.* **peoples**) the persons living in a country and sharing the same nationality: *the French people.* **4.** one's family: *he took her home to meet his people.* **5.** persons loyal to someone powerful: *the king's people accompanied him in exile.* **6. the people. a.** the mass of persons without special distinction, privileges, etc. **b.** the body of persons in a country, etc., esp. those entitled to vote. ~*vb.* **7.** (*tr.*) to provide with or as if with people or inhabitants. [C13: < OF *pople*, < L *populus*]

▷ **Usage.** See at **person.**

people's democracy *n.* (in Communist ideology) a country or government in transition from bourgeois democracy to socialism.

people's front *n.* a less common term for **popular front.**

pep (pɛp) *n.* **1.** high spirits, energy, or vitality. ~*vb.* **pepping, pepped. 2.** (*tr.*; usually foll. by *up*) to liven by imbuing with new vigour. [C20: short for PEPPER]

PEP *abbrev. for* political and economic planning.

peperomia (ˌpɛpəˈrəʊmɪə) *n.* any of a genus of tropical plants cultivated for their ornamental foliage. [C19: NL < Gk *peperi* pepper + *omoros* similar]

peplum (ˈpɛpləm) *n., pl.* **-lums** *or* **-la** (-lə). a flared ruffle attached to the waist of a jacket, bodice, etc. [C17: < L: full upper garment, < Gk *peplos* shawl]

pepo (ˈpiːpəʊ) *n., pl.* **-pos.** the fruit of any of various plants, such as the melon, cucumber, and pumpkin, having a firm rind, fleshy watery pulp, and numerous seeds. [C19: < L: pumpkin, < Gk *pepōn* edible gourd, < *peptein* to ripen]

pepper (ˈpɛpə) *n.* **1.** a woody climbing plant, *Piper nigrum*, of the East Indies, having small black berry-like fruits. **2.** the dried fruit of this plant, which is ground to produce a sharp hot condiment. See also **black pepper, white pepper. 3.** any of various other plants of the genus *Piper.* **4.** Also called: **capsicum.** any of various tropical plants, the fruits of which are used as a vegetable and a condiment. See also **sweet pepper, red pepper, cayenne pepper. 5.** the fruit of any of these capsicums, which has a mild or pungent taste. **6.** the condiment made from the fruits of any of these plants. ~*vb.* (*tr.*) **7.** to season with pepper. **8.** to sprinkle liberally; dot: *his prose was peppered with alliteration.* **9.** to pelt with small missiles. [OE *piper*, < L, < Gk *peperi*]

pepper-and-salt *adj.* **1.** (of cloth, etc.) marked with a fine mixture of black and white. **2.** (of hair) streaked with grey.

peppercorn (ˈpɛpəˌkɔːn) *n.* **1.** the small dried berry of the pepper plant. **2.** something trifling.

peppercorn rent *n.* a rent that is very low or nominal.

pepper mill *n.* a small hand mill used to grind peppercorns.

peppermint (ˈpɛpəˌmɪnt) *n.* **1.** a temperate mint plant with purple or white flowers and downy leaves, which yield a pungent oil. **2.** the oil from this plant, which is used as a flavouring. **3.** a sweet flavoured with peppermint.

pepper pot *n.* **1.** a small container with perforations in the top for sprinkling pepper. **2.** a West Indian stew of meat, etc., highly seasoned with an extract of bitter cassava.

pepper tree *n.* any of several evergreen trees of a chiefly South American genus having yellowish-white flowers and bright red ornamental fruits.

peppery (ˈpɛpərɪ) *adj.* **1.** flavoured with or tasting of pepper. **2.** quick-tempered; irritable. **3.** full of bite and sharpness: *a peppery speech.* —ˈ**pepperiness** *n.*

pep pill *n. Inf.* a tablet containing a stimulant drug.

peppy (ˈpɛpɪ) *adj.* **-pier, -piest.** *Inf.* full of vitality; bouncy or energetic. —ˈ**peppily** *adv.* —ˈ**peppiness** *n.*

pepsin (ˈpɛpsɪn) *n.* an enzyme produced in the stomach, which, when activated by acid, splits proteins into peptones. [C19: via G < Gk *pepsis*, < *peptein* to digest]

pep talk *n. Inf.* an enthusiastic talk designed to increase confidence, production, cooperation, etc.

peptic (ˈpɛptɪk) *adj.* **1.** of, relating to, or promoting digestion. **2.** of, relating to, or caused by pepsin or the action of the digestive juices. [C17: < Gk *peptikos* capable of digesting, < *peptein* to digest]

peptic ulcer *n. Pathol.* an ulcer of the mucous membrane lining those parts of the alimentary tract exposed to digestive juices, including the oesophagus, the stomach, and the duodenum.

peptide (ˈpɛptaɪd) *n.* any of a group of compounds consisting of two or more amino acids linked by chemical bonding between their respective carboxyl and amino groups.

peptide bond *n. Biochem.* a chemical amide linkage, =CHCONHCH=, formed by the condensation of the amino group of one amino acid with the carboxyl group of another.

peptone (ˈpɛptəʊn) *n. Biochem.* any of a group of compounds that form an intermediary group in the digestion of proteins to amino acids. [C19: < G *Pepton,* < Gk *pepton* something digested, < *peptein* to digest] —**peptonic** (pɛpˈtɒnɪk) *adj.*

per (pɜː; *unstressed* pə) *determiner.* **1.** for every: *three pence per pound.* ~*prep.* **2.** (esp. in some Latin phrases) by; through. **3. as per.** according to: *as per specifications.* **4. as per usual.** *Inf.* as usual. [C15: < L: by, for each]

per. *abbrev. for:* **1.** period. **2.** person.

per- *prefix.* **1.** indicating that a chemical compound contains a high proportion of a specified element: *peroxide.* **2.** indicating that a chemical element is in a higher than usual state of oxidation: *permanganate.* [< L *per* through. In compound words borrowed from L, *per-* indicates: through (*pervade*); throughout (*permanent*); away (*perfidy*); and is used as an intensifier (*permutation*)]

peracid (pɜːrˈæsɪd) *n.* an acid, such as perchloric acid, in which the element forming the acid radical exhibits its highest valency.

peradventure (pərədˈvɛntʃə, ˌpɜːr-) *Arch.* ~*adv.* **1.** by chance; perhaps. ~*n.* **2.** chance or doubt. [C13: < OF *par aventure* by chance]

perambulate (pəˈræmbjʊˌleɪt) *vb.* **1.** to walk about (a place). **2.** (*tr.*) to walk round in order to inspect. [C16: < L *perambulāre* to traverse, < *per-* through + *ambulāre* to walk] —**perˌambuˈlation** *n.* —**perambulatory** (pəˈræmbjʊlətərɪ, -trɪ) *adj.*

perambulator (pəˈræmbjʊˌleɪtə) *n.* a formal word for **pram**[1].

per annum (pər ˈænəm) *adv.* every year or by the year. [L]

percale (pəˈkeɪl, -ˈkɑːl) *n.* a close-textured woven cotton fabric, used esp. for sheets. [C17: via F < Persian *pargālah* piece of cloth]

per capita (pə ˈkæpɪtə) *adj., adv.* of or for each person. [L, lit.: according to heads]

perceive (pəˈsiːv) *vb.* **1.** to become aware of (something) through the senses; recognize or observe. **2.** (*tr.; may take a clause as object*) to come to comprehend; grasp. [C13: < OF *perçoivre,* < L *percipere* to seize entirely] —**perˈceivable** *adj.* —**perˈceivably** *adv.*

per cent (pə ˈsɛnt) *adv.* **1.** Also: **per centum.** in or for every hundred. ~*n. also* **percent. 2.** a percentage or proportion. **3.** (*often pl.*) securities yielding a rate of interest as specified: *he bought three percents.* [C16: < Med. L *per centum* out of every hundred]

percentage (pəˈsɛntɪdʒ) *n.* **1.** proportion or rate per hundred parts. **2.** *Commerce.* the interest, tax, commission, or allowance on a hundred items. **3.** any proportion in relation to the whole. **4.** *Inf.* profit or advantage.

percentile (pəˈsɛntaɪl) *n.* one of 99 actual or notional values of a variable dividing its distribution into 100 groups with equal frequencies. Also called: **centile.**

percept (ˈpɜːsɛpt) *n.* **1.** a concept that depends on recognition by the senses, such as sight, of some external object or phenomenon. **2.** an object or phenomenon that is perceived. [C19: < L *perceptum,* < *percipere* to PERCEIVE]

perceptible (pəˈsɛptəbᵊl) *adj.* able to be perceived; noticeable or recognizable. —**perˌceptiˈbility** *n.* —**perˈceptibly** *adv.*

perception (pəˈsɛpʃən) *n.* **1.** the act or the effect of perceiving. **2.** insight or intuition gained by perceiving. **3.** the ability or capacity to perceive. **4.** way of perceiving; view. **5.** the process by which an organism detects and interprets information from the external world by means of the sensory receptors. [C15: < L *perceptiō* comprehension; see PERCEIVE] —**perˈceptional** *adj.* —**perceptual** (pəˈsɛptjʊəl) *adj.*

perceptive (pəˈsɛptɪv) *adj.* **1.** quick at perceiving; observant. **2.** perceptual. **3.** able to perceive. —**perˈceptively** *adv.* —**ˌpercepˈtivity** *or* **perˈceptiveness** *n.*

perch[1] (pɜːtʃ) *n.* **1.** a pole, branch, or other resting place above ground on which a bird roosts. **2.** a similar resting place for a person or thing. **3.** another name for **rod** (sense 7). ~*vb.* **4.** (usually foll. by *on*) to alight, rest, or cause to rest on or as if on a perch: *the bird perched on the branch; the cap was perched on his head.* [C13 *perche* stake, < OF, < L *pertica* long staff]

perch[2] (pɜːtʃ) *n., pl.* **perch** *or* **perches. 1.** any of a family of freshwater spiny-finned teleost fishes of Europe and North America: valued as food and game fishes. **2.** any of various similar or related fishes. [C13: < OF *perche,* < L *perca,* < Gk *perkē*]

perchance (pəˈtʃɑːns) *adv. Arch. or poetic.* **1.** perhaps; possibly. **2.** by chance; accidentally. [C14: < Anglo-F *par chance*]

Percheron (ˈpɜːʃəˌrɒn) *n.* a compact heavy breed of carthorse. [C19: < F, < *le Perche,* region of NW France, where the breed originated]

perchloric acid (pəˈklɔːrɪk) *n.* a colourless syrupy oxyacid of chlorine containing a greater proportion of oxygen than chloric acid. It is a powerful oxidizing agent. Formula: $HClO_4$.

percipient (pəˈsɪpɪənt) *adj.* **1.** able to perceive. **2.** perceptive. ~*n.* **3.** a person who perceives. [C17: < L *percipiens* observing, < *percipere* to grasp] —**perˈcipience** *n.* —**perˈcipiently** *adv.*

percolate *vb.* (ˈpɜːkəˌleɪt). **1.** to cause (a liquid) to pass through a fine mesh, porous substance, etc., or (of a liquid) to pass through a fine mesh, etc.; trickle: *rain percolated through the roof.* **2.** to permeate; penetrate gradually: *water percolated the road.* **3.** to make (coffee) or (of coffee) to be made in a percolator. ~*n.* (ˈpɜːkəlɪt, -ˌleɪt). **4.** a product of percolation. [C17: < L *percolāre,* < PER- + *cōlāre* to strain, < *cōlum* a strainer; see COLANDER] —**percolable** (ˈpɜːkələbᵊl) *adj.* —**ˌpercoˈlation** *n.*

percolator (ˈpɜːkəˌleɪtə) *n.* a kind of coffeepot in which boiling water is forced up through a tube and filters down through the coffee grounds into a container.

per contra (ˈpɜː ˈkɒntrə) *adv.* on the contrary. [< L]

percuss (pəˈkʌs) *vb.* (*tr.*) **1.** to strike sharply, rapidly, or suddenly. **2.** *Med.* to tap on (a body surface) with the fingertips or a special hammer to aid diagnosis. [C16: < L *percutere,* < *per-* through + *quatere* to shake] —**perˈcussor** *n.*

percussion (pəˈkʌʃən) *n.* **1.** the act, an instance, or an effect of percussing. **2.** *Music.* the family of instruments in which sound arises from the striking of materials with sticks or hammers. **3.** *Music.* instruments of this family constituting a section of an orchestra, etc. **4.** *Med.* the act of percussing a body surface. **5.** the act of exploding a percussion cap. [C16: < L *percussiō,* < *percutere* to hit; see PERCUSS] —**perˈcussive** *adj.* —**perˈcussively** *adv.* —**perˈcussiveness** *n.*

percussion cap *n.* a detonator consisting of a paper or thin metal cap containing material that explodes when struck.

percussion instrument *n.* any of various musical instruments that produce a sound when their resonating surfaces are struck directly, as with a stick or mallet, or by leverage action.

percussionist (pəˈkʌʃənɪst) *n. Music.* a person who plays any of several percussion instruments.

percutaneous (ˌpɜːkjʊˈteɪnɪəs) *adj. Med.* effected through the skin, as in the absorption of an ointment.

per diem (ˈpɜː ˈdaɪɛm, ˈdiːɛm) *adv.* **1.** every day or by the day. ~*n.* **2.** an allowance for daily expenses. [< L]

perdition (pəˈdɪʃən) *n.* **1.** *Christianity.* **a.** final and irrevocable spiritual ruin. **b.** this state as one that the wicked are said to be destined to endure forever. **2.** another word for **hell. 3.** *Arch.* utter ruin or destruction. [C14: < LL *perditiō* ruin, < L *perdere* to lose, < PER- (away) + *dāre* to give]

perdurable (pəˈdjʊərəbᵊl) *adj. Rare.* extremely

durable. [C13: < LL *perdūrābilis,* < L *per-* (intensive) + *dūrābilis* long-lasting, < *dūrus* hard]

père *French.* (pɛr; *English* pɛə) *n.* an addition to a French surname to specify the father rather than the son of the same name: *Dumas père.*

Père David's deer *n.* a large grey deer, surviving only in captivity. [C20: after Father A. *David* (died 1900), F missionary]

peregrinate (ˈpɛrɪgrɪˌneɪt) *vb.* **1.** (*intr.*) to travel or wander about from place to place; voyage. **2.** (*tr.*) to travel through (a place). [C16: < L, < *peregrīnārī* to travel; see PEREGRINE] —ˌ**peregriˈnation** *n.* —ˈ**peregriˌnator** *n.*

peregrine (ˈpɛrɪgrɪn) *adj. Arch.* **1.** coming from abroad. **2.** travelling. [C14: < L *peregrīnus* foreign, < *pereger* being abroad, < *per* through + *ager* land (that is, beyond one's own land)]

peregrine falcon *n.* a falcon occurring in most parts of the world, having a dark plumage on the back and wings and lighter underparts.

peremptory (pəˈrɛmptərɪ) *adj.* **1.** urgent or commanding: *a peremptory ring on the bell.* **2.** not able to be remitted or debated; decisive. **3.** dogmatic. **4.** *Law.* **a.** admitting of no denial or contradiction; precluding debate. **b.** obligatory rather than permissive. [C16: < Anglo-Norman *peremptorie,* < L *peremptōrius* decisive, < *perimere* to take away completely] —**perˈemptorily** *adv.* —**perˈemptoriness** *n.*

perennial (pəˈrɛnɪəl) *adj.* **1.** lasting throughout the year or through many years. **2.** everlasting; perpetual. ~*n.* **3.** a woody or herbaceous plant that continues its growth for at least three years. [C17: < L *perennis* continual, < *per* through + *annus* year] —**perˈennially** *adv.*

perestroika (ˌpɛrəˈstrɔɪkə) *n.* the policy of restructuring the Soviet economy, etc., under Gorbachov. [C20: Russian, lit.: reconstruction]

perfect *adj.* (ˈpɜːfɪkt). **1.** having all essential elements. **2.** unblemished; faultless: *a perfect gemstone.* **3.** correct or precise: *perfect timing.* **4.** utter or absolute: *a perfect stranger.* **5.** excellent in all respects: *a perfect day.* **6.** *Maths.* exactly divisible into equal integral or polynomial roots: *36 is a perfect square.* **7.** *Bot.* **a.** (of flowers) having functional stamens and pistils. **b.** (of plants) having all parts present. **8.** *Grammar.* denoting a tense of verbs used in describing an action that has been completed. In English this is formed with *have* or *has* plus the past participle. **9.** *Music.* **a.** of or relating to the intervals of the unison, fourth, fifth, and octave. **b.** (of a cadence) ending on the tonic chord, giving a feeling of conclusion. Also: **final.** ~*n.* (ˈpɜːfɪkt). **10.** *Grammar.* **a.** the perfect tense. **b.** a verb in this tense. ~*vb.* (pəˈfɛkt). (*tr.*) **11.** to make perfect; improve to one's satisfaction: *he is in Paris to perfect his French.* **12.** to make fully accomplished. [C13: < L *perfectus,* < *perficere* to perform, < *per-* through + *facere* to do]

▷ **Usage.** See at **unique.**

perfect gas *n.* another name for **ideal gas.**

perfectible (pəˈfɛktəbᵊl) *adj.* capable of becoming or being made perfect. —**perˌfectiˈbility** *n.*

perfection (pəˈfɛkʃən) *n.* **1.** the act of perfecting or the state or quality of being perfect. **2.** the highest degree of a quality, etc. **3.** an embodiment of perfection. [C13: < L *perfectiō* a completing, < *perficere* to finish]

perfectionism (pəˈfɛkʃəˌnɪzəm) *n.* **1.** *Philosophy.* the doctrine that man can attain perfection in this life. **2.** the demand for the highest standard of excellence. —**perˈfectionist** *n., adj.*

perfective (pəˈfɛktɪv) *adj.* **1.** tending to perfect. **2.** *Grammar.* denoting an aspect of verbs used to express that the action or event described by the verb is or was completed: *I lived in London for ten years* is perfective; *I have lived in London for ten years* is imperfective, since the implication is that I still live in London.

perfectly (ˈpɜːfɪktlɪ) *adv.* **1.** completely, utterly, or absolutely. **2.** in a perfect way.

perfect number *n.* an integer, such as 28, that is equal to the sum of all its possible factors, excluding itself.

perfect participle *n.* another name for **past participle.**

perfect pitch *n.* another name (not in technical usage) for **absolute pitch** (sense 1).

perfervid (pɜːˈfɜːvɪd) *adj. Literary.* extremely ardent or zealous. [C19: < NL *perfervidus*]

perfidious (pəˈfɪdɪəs) *adj.* guilty, treacherous, or faithless; deceitful. [C18: < L, < *perfidus* faithless] —**perˈfidiously** *adv.* —**perˈfidiousness** *n.* —ˈ**perfidy** *n.*

perfoliate (pəˈfəʊlɪɪt, -ˌeɪt) *adj.* (of a leaf) having a base that completely encloses the stem, so that the stem appears to pass through it. [C17: < NL *perfoliātus,* < L *per-* through + *folium* leaf] —**perˌfoliˈation** *n.*

perforate *vb.* (ˈpɜːfəˌreɪt). **1.** to make a hole or holes in (something). **2.** (*tr.*) to punch rows of holes between (stamps, etc.) for ease of separation. ~*adj.* (ˈpɜːfərɪt). **3.** *Biol.* pierced by small holes: *perforate shells.* **4.** *Philately.* another word for **perforated.** [C16: < L *perforāre,* < *per-* through + *forāre* to pierce] —**perforable** (ˈpɜːfərəbᵊl) *adj.* —ˈ**perfoˌrator** *n.*

perforated (ˈpɜːfəˌreɪtɪd) *adj.* **1.** pierced with holes. **2.** (esp. of stamps) having perforations.

perforation (ˌpɜːfəˈreɪʃən) *n.* **1.** the act of perforating or the state of being perforated. **2.** a hole or holes made in something. **3. a.** a method of making individual stamps, etc. easily separable by punching holes along their margins. **b.** the holes punched in this way. Abbrev.: **perf.**

perforce (pəˈfɔːs) *adv.* by necessity; unavoidably. [C14: < OF *par force*]

perform (pəˈfɔːm) *vb.* **1.** to carry out (an action). **2.** (*tr.*) to fulfil: *to perform someone's request.* **3.** to present or enact (a play, concert, etc.): *the group performed Hamlet.* [C14: < Anglo-Norman *perfourmer* (infl. by *forme* FORM), < OF *parfournir,* < *par-* PER- + *fournir* to provide] —**perˈformable** *adj.* —**perˈformer** *n.*

performance (pəˈfɔːməns) *n.* **1.** the act, process, or art of performing. **2.** an artistic or dramatic production: *last night's performance was terrible.* **3.** manner or quality of functioning: *a machine's performance.* **4.** *Inf.* mode of conduct or behaviour, esp. when distasteful: *what did you mean by that performance at the restaurant?* **5.** *Inf.* any tiresome procedure: *the performance of preparing to go out in the snow.*

performance art *n.* a theatrical presentation that incorporates various art forms, such as dance, sculpture, etc.

performative (pəˈfɔːmətɪv) *adj. Linguistics, philosophy.* **1. a.** denoting an utterance that itself constitutes the act described by the verb. For example, the sentence *I confess that I was there* is itself a confession. **b.** (*as n.*)*: that sentence is a performative.* **2. a.** denoting a verb that may be used as the main verb in such an utterance. **b.** (*as n.*)*: "promise" is a performative.*

perfume *n.* (ˈpɜːfjuːm). **1.** a mixture of alcohol and fragrant essential oils extracted from flowers, etc., or made synthetically. **2.** a scent or odour, esp. a fragrant one. ~*vb.* (pəˈfjuːm). **3.** (*tr.*) to impart a perfume to. [C16: < F *parfum,* prob. < OProvençal *perfum,* < *perfumar* to make scented, < *per* through (< L) + *fumar* to smoke, < L *fumāre* to smoke]

perfumer (pəˈfjuːmə) *n.* a person who makes or sells perfume.

perfumery (pəˈfjuːmərɪ) *n., pl.* **-eries. 1.** a place where perfumes are sold. **2.** a factory where perfumes are made. **3.** the process of making perfumes. **4.** perfumes in general.

perfunctory (pəˈfʌŋktərɪ) *adj.* **1.** done superficially, only as a matter of routine. **2.** dull or indifferent. [C16: < LL *perfunctōrius* negligent, < *perfunctus* dispatched, < *perfungī* to fulfil] —**perˈfunctorily** *adv.* —**perˈfunctoriness** *n.*

perfuse (pəˈfjuːz) *vb.* (*tr.*) to suffuse or permeate (a liquid, colour, etc.) through or over (something). [C16: < L *perfūsus* wetted, < *perfundere* to pour over]

pergola (ˈpɜːgələ) *n.* a horizontal trellis or framework, supported on posts, that carries climbing plants. [C17: via It. < L *pergula* projection from a roof, < *pergere* to go forward]

perhaps (pəˈhæps; *informal* præps) *adv.* **1. a.** possibly; maybe. **b.** (*as sentence modifier*): *he'll arrive tomorrow, perhaps.* ~*sentence substitute.* **2.** it may happen, be so, etc.; maybe. [C16 *perhappes*, < *per* by + *happes* chance]

peri (ˈpɪərɪ) *n., pl.* **-ris. 1.** (in Persian folklore) one of a race of beautiful supernatural beings. **2.** any beautiful fairy-like creature. [C18: < Persian: fairy, < Avestan *pairikā* witch]

peri- *prefix.* **1.** enclosing, encircling, or around: *pericardium; pericarp.* **2.** near or adjacent: *perihelion.* [< Gk *peri* around]

perianth (ˈpɛrɪˌænθ) *n.* the outer part of a flower, consisting of the calyx and corolla. [C18: < F *périanthe*, < NL, < PERI- + Gk *anthos* flower]

periapt (ˈpɛrɪˌæpt) *n. Rare.* a charm or amulet. [C16: via F < Gk *periapton*, < PERI- + *haptos* clasped, < *haptein* to fasten]

pericarditis (ˌpɛrɪkɑːˈdaɪtɪs) *n.* inflammation of the pericardium.

pericardium (ˌpɛrɪˈkɑːdɪəm) *n., pl.* **-dia** (-dɪə). the membranous sac enclosing the heart. [C16: via NL < Gk *perikardion*, < PERI- + *kardia* heart] —ˌ**periˈcardial** *or* ˌ**periˈcardiˌac** *adj.*

pericarp (ˈpɛrɪˌkɑːp) *n.* the part of a fruit enclosing the seeds that develops from the wall of the ovary. [C18: via F < NL *pericarpium*] —ˌ**periˈcarpial** *adj.*

perichondrium (ˌpɛrɪˈkɒndrɪəm) *n., pl.* **-dria** (-drɪə). the fibrous membrane that covers the cartilage. [C18: NL, < PERI- + Gk *chondros* cartilage]

periclase (ˈpɛrɪˌkleɪs) *n.* a mineral consisting of magnesium oxide. [C19: < NL *periclasia*, < Gk *peri* very + *klasis* a breaking, referring to its perfect cleavage]

pericline (ˈpɛrɪˌklaɪn) *n.* **1.** a white translucent variety of albite in the form of elongated crystals. **2.** Also called: **dome.** a dome-shaped formation of stratified rock with its slopes following the direction of folding. [C19: < Gk *periklinēs* sloping on all sides] —ˌ**periˈclinal** *adj.*

pericranium (ˌpɛrɪˈkreɪnɪəm) *n., pl.* **-nia** (-nɪə). the fibrous membrane covering the external surface of the skull. [C16: NL, < Gk *perikranion*]

peridot (ˈpɛrɪˌdɒt) *n.* a pale green transparent variety of the olivine chrysolite, used as a gemstone. [C14: < OF *peritot*, <?]

perigee (ˈpɛrɪˌdʒiː) *n.* the point in its orbit around the earth when the moon or a satellite is nearest the earth. [C16: via F < Gk *perigeion*, < PERI- + *gea* earth] —ˌ**periˈgean** *adj.*

periglacial (ˌpɛrɪˈgleɪʃəl) *adj.* relating to a region bordering a glacier: *periglacial climate.*

perihelion (ˌpɛrɪˈhiːlɪən) *n., pl.* **-lia** (-lɪə). the point in its orbit when a planet or comet is nearest the sun. [C17: < NL *perihēlium*, < PERI- + Gk *hēlios* sun]

peril (ˈpɛrɪl) *n.* exposure to risk or harm; danger or jeopardy. [C13: via OF < L *perīculum*]

perilous (ˈpɛrɪləs) *adj.* very hazardous or dangerous: *a perilous journey.* —ˈ**perilously** *adv.* —ˈ**perilousness** *n.*

perilune (ˈpɛrɪˌluːn) *n.* the point in a lunar orbit when a spacecraft is nearest the moon. [C20: < PERI- + *-lune*, < L *lūna* moon]

perimeter (pəˈrɪmɪtə) *n.* **1.** *Maths.* **a.** the curve or line enclosing a plane area. **b.** the length of this curve or line. **2. a.** any boundary around something. **b.** (*as modifier*): *a perimeter fence.* **3.** a medical instrument for measuring the field of vision. [C16: < F *périmètre*, < L *perimetros*] —**perimetric** (ˌpɛrɪˈmɛtrɪk) *adj.*

perinatal (ˌpɛrɪˈneɪtᵊl) *adj.* of or occurring in the period from about three months before to one month after birth.

perineum (ˌpɛrɪˈniːəm) *n., pl.* **-nea** (-ˈniːə). **1.** the region of the body between the anus and the genital organs. **2.** the surface of the human trunk between the thighs. [C17: < NL, < Gk *perinaion*, < PERI- + *inein* to empty] —ˌ**periˈneal** *adj.*

period (ˈpɪərɪəd) *n.* **1.** a portion of time of indefinable length: *he spent a period away from home.* **2. a.** a portion of time specified in some way: *Picasso's blue period.* **b.** (*as modifier*): *period costume.* **3.** a nontechnical name for an occurence of menstruation. **4.** *Geol.* a unit of geological time during which a system of rocks is formed: *the Jurassic period.* **5.** a division of time, esp. of the academic day. **6.** *Physics, maths.* the time taken to complete one cycle of a regularly recurring phenomenon; the reciprocal of frequency. Symbol: *T* **7.** *Astron.* **a.** the time required by a body to make one complete rotation on its axis. **b.** the time interval between two successive maxima or minima of light variation of a variable star. **8.** *Chem.* one of the horizontal rows of elements in the periodic table. Each period starts with an alkali metal and ends with a rare gas. **9.** another term (esp. U.S. and Canad.) for **full stop. 10.** a complete sentence, esp. one with several clauses. **11.** a completion or end. [C14 *peryod*, < L *periodus*, < Gk *periodos* circuit, < PERI- + *hodos* way]

periodic (ˌpɪərɪˈɒdɪk) *adj.* **1.** happening or recurring at intervals; intermittent. **2.** of, relating to, or resembling a period. **3.** having or occurring in repeated periods or cycles. —ˌ**periˈodically** *adv.* —**periodicity** (ˌpɪərɪəˈdɪsɪtɪ) *n.*

periodical (ˌpɪərɪˈɒdɪkᵊl) *n.* **1.** a publication issued at regular intervals, usually monthly or weekly. ~*adj.* **2.** of or relating to such publications. **3.** published at regular intervals. **4.** periodic or occasional.

periodic function *n. Maths.* a function whose value is repeated at constant intervals.

periodic law *n.* the principle that the chemical properties of the elements are periodic functions of their atomic weights or, more accurately, of their atomic numbers.

periodic sentence *n. Rhetoric.* a sentence in which the completion of the main clause is left to the end, thus creating an effect of suspense.

periodic table *n.* a table of the elements, arranged in order of increasing atomic number, based on the periodic law.

periodontics (ˌpɛrɪəˈdɒntɪks) *n.* (*functioning as sing.*) the branch of dentistry concerned with diseases affecting the tissues and structures that surround teeth. [C19: < PERI- + *-odontics*, < Gk *odōn* tooth] —ˌ**perioˈdontical** *adj.*

periosteum (ˌpɛrɪˈɒstɪəm) *n., pl.* **-tea** (-tɪə). a thick fibrous two-layered membrane covering the surface of bones. [C16: NL, < Gk *periosteon*, < PERI- + *osteon* bone] —ˌ**periˈosteal** *adj.*

peripatetic (ˌpɛrɪpəˈtɛtɪk) *adj.* **1.** itinerant. **2.** *Brit.* employed in two or more educational establishments and travelling from one to another: *a peripatetic football coach.* ~*n.* **3.** a peripatetic person. [C16: < L *peripatēticus*, < Gk, < *peripatein* to pace to and fro] —ˌ**peripaˈtetically** *adv.*

Peripatetic (ˌpɛrɪpəˈtɛtɪk) *adj.* **1.** of or relating to the teachings of Aristotle, who used to teach philosophy while walking about the Lyceum in ancient Athens. ~*n.* **2.** a student of Aristotelianism.

peripeteia (ˌpɛrɪpɪˈtaɪə, -ˈtɪə) *n.* (esp. in drama) an abrupt turn of events or reversal of circumstances. [C16: < Gk, < PERI- + *piptein* to fall (to change suddenly, lit.: to fall around)]

peripheral (pəˈrɪfərəl) *adj.* **1.** not relating to the most important part of something; incidental. **2.** of or relating to a periphery. **3.** *Anat.* of, relating to, or situated near the surface of the body: *a peripheral nerve.* —**peˈripherally** *adv.*

peripheral device *or* **unit** *n. Computers.* any device, such as a card punch, line printer, etc., concerned with input/output, storage, etc. Often shortened to **peripheral.**

periphery (pəˈrɪfərɪ) *n., pl.* **-eries. 1.** the outermost boundary of an area. **2.** the outside surface of something. [C16: < LL *peripheria*, < Gk, < PERI- + *pherein* to bear]

periphrasis (pəˈrɪfrəsɪs) *n., pl.* **-rases** (-rəˌsiːz). **1.** a roundabout way of expressing something; circumlocution. **2.** an expression of this kind. [C16: via L < Gk, < PERI- + *phrazein* to declare]

periphrastic (ˌpɛrɪˈfræstɪk) *adj.* **1.** employing or involving periphrasis. **2.** expressed in two or more words rather than by an inflected form of one: used esp. of a tense of a verb where the alternative word is an auxiliary verb, as in *He does go.* —ˌ**periˈphrastically** *adv.*

perisarc (ˈpɛrɪˌsɑːk) *n.* the outer chitinous layer secreted by colonial hydrozoan coelenterates. [C19: < PERI- + -*sarc*, < Gk *sarx* flesh]

periscope (ˈpɛrɪˌskəʊp) *n.* any of a number of optical instruments that enable the user to view objects that are not in the direct line of vision, such as one in a submarine for looking above the surface of the water. They have a system of mirrors or prisms to reflect the light. [C19: < Gk *periskopein* to look around] —**periscopic** (ˌpɛrɪˈskɒpɪk) *adj.*

perish (ˈpɛrɪʃ) *vb.* **1.** (*intr.*) to be destroyed or die, esp. in an untimely way. **2.** (*tr.* sometimes foll. by *with* or *from*) to cause to suffer: *we were perished with cold.* **3.** to rot or cause to rot: *leather perishes if exposed to bad weather.* ~*n.* **4. do a perish.** *Austral. inf.* to die or come near to dying of thirst or starvation. [C13: < OF *périr*, < L *perīre* to pass away entirely]

perishable (ˈpɛrɪʃəbᵊl) *adj.* **1.** liable to rot. ~*n.* **2.** (*often pl.*) a perishable article, esp. food. —ˌ**perishaˈbility** *or* ˈ**perishableness** *n.*

perishing (ˈpɛrɪʃɪŋ) *adj.* **1.** *Inf.* (of weather, etc.) extremely cold. **2.** *Sl.* (intensifier qualifying something undesirable): *it's a perishing nuisance!* —ˈ**perishingly** *adv.*

perisperm (ˈpɛrɪˌspɜːm) *n.* the nutritive tissue surrounding the embryo in certain seeds.

perissodactyl (pəˌrɪsəʊˈdæktɪl) *n.* **1.** any of an order of placental mammals having hooves with an odd number of toes: includes horses, tapirs, and rhinoceroses. ~*adj.* **2.** of, relating to, or belonging to this order. [C19: < NL *perissodactylus*, < Gk *perissos* uneven + *daktulos* digit]

peristalsis (ˌpɛrɪˈstælsɪs) *n.*, *pl.* **-ses** (-siːz). *Physiol.* the succession of waves of involuntary muscular contraction of various bodily tubes, esp. of the alimentary tract, where it effects transport of food and waste products. [C19: < NL, < PERI- + Gk *stalsis* compression, < *stellein* to press together] —ˌ**periˈstaltic** *adj.*

peristome (ˈpɛrɪˌstəʊm) *n.* **1.** a fringe of pointed teeth surrounding the opening of a moss capsule. **2.** any of various parts surrounding the mouth of invertebrates such as echinoderms, earthworms, and protozoans. [C18: < NL *peristoma*, < PERI- + Gk *stoma* mouth]

peristyle (ˈpɛrɪˌstaɪl) *n.* **1.** a colonnade round a court or building. **2.** an area surrounded by a colonnade. [C17: via F < L *peristȳlum*, < Gk *peristulon*, < PERI- + *stulos* column]

peritoneum (ˌpɛrɪtəˈniːəm) *n.*, *pl.* **-nea** (-ˈniːə) *or* **-neums.** a serous sac that lines the walls of the abdominal cavity and covers the viscera. [C16: via LL < Gk *peritonaion*, < *peritonos* stretched around] —ˌ**peritoˈneal** *adj.*

peritonitis (ˌpɛrɪtəˈnaɪtɪs) *n.* inflammation of the peritoneum.

periwig (ˈpɛrɪˌwɪg) *n.* a wig, such as a peruke. [C16 *perwyke*, changed < F *perruque* wig, PERUKE]

periwinkle[1] (ˈpɛrɪˌwɪŋkᵊl) *n.* any of various edible marine gastropods having a spirally coiled shell. Often shortened to **winkle.** [C16: <?]

periwinkle[2] (ˈpɛrɪˌwɪŋkᵊl) *n.* any of several Eurasian evergreen plants having trailing stems and blue flowers. [C14 *pervenke*, < OE *perwince*, < LL *pervinca*]

perjure (ˈpɜːdʒə) *vb.* (*tr.*) *Criminal law.* to render (oneself) guilty of perjury. [C15: < OF *parjurer*, < L *perjūrāre*, < PER- + *jūrāre* to make an oath, < *jūs* law] —ˈ**perjurer** *n.*

perjured (ˈpɜːdʒəd) *adj.* *Criminal law.* **1. a.** having sworn falsely. **b.** having committed perjury. **2.** involving or characterized by perjury: *perjured evidence.*

perjury (ˈpɜːdʒərɪ) *n.*, *pl.* **-juries.** *Criminal law.* the offence committed by a witness in judicial proceedings who, having been lawfully sworn, wilfully gives false evidence. [C14: < Anglo-F *parjurie*, < L *perjūrium* a false oath; see PERJURE] —**perjurious** (pɜːˈdʒʊərɪəs) *adj.*

perk[1] (pɜːk) *adj.* **1.** pert; brisk; lively. ~*vb.* **2.** See **perk up.** [C16: see PERK UP]

perk[2] (pɜːk) *vb. Inf.* short for **percolate** (sense 3).

perk[3] (pɜːk) *n. Brit. inf.* short for **perquisite.**

perk up *vb.* (*adv.*) **1.** to make or become more cheerful, hopeful, or lively. **2.** to rise or cause to rise briskly: *the dog's ears perked up.* **3.** (*tr.*) to make smarter in appearance: *she perked up her outfit with a bright scarf.* [C14 *perk*, ? < Norman F *perquer*; see PERCH[1]]

perky (ˈpɜːkɪ) *adj.* **perkier, perkiest. 1.** jaunty; lively. **2.** confident; spirited. —ˈ**perkily** *adv.* —ˈ**perkiness** *n.*

perlite (ˈpɜːlaɪt) *n.* a variety of obsidian consisting of masses of globules. [C19: < F, < *perle* PEARL[1]]

perm[1] (pɜːm) *n.* **1.** a hairstyle produced by treatment with heat, chemicals, etc., which gives long-lasting waves or curls. Also called (esp. formerly): **permanent wave.** ~*vb.* (*tr.*) **2.** to give a perm to (hair).

perm[2] (pɜːm) *n. Inf.* short for **permutate, permutation** (sense 4).

permafrost (ˈpɜːməˌfrɒst) *n.* ground that is permanently frozen. [C20: < PERMA(NENT) + FROST]

permalloy (pɜːmˈælɔɪ) *n.* any of various alloys containing iron and nickel and sometimes smaller amounts of chromium and molybdenum.

permanence (ˈpɜːmənəns) *n.* the state or quality of being permanent.

permanency (ˈpɜːmənənsɪ) *n.*, *pl.* **-cies. 1.** a person or thing that is permanent. **2.** another word for **permanence.**

permanent (ˈpɜːmənənt) *adj.* **1.** existing or intended to exist for an indefinite period: *a permanent structure.* **2.** not expected to change; not temporary: *a permanent condition.* [C15: < L *permanens* continuing, < *permanēre* to stay to the end] —ˈ**permanently** *adv.*

permanent magnet *n.* a magnet, often of steel, that retains its magnetization after the magnetic field producing it has been removed.

permanent press *n.* a chemical treatment for clothing that makes the fabric crease-resistant and sometimes provides a garment with a permanent crease or pleats.

permanent wave *n.* another name (esp. formerly) for **perm**[1] (sense 1).

permanent way *n. Chiefly Brit.* the track of a railway, including the sleepers, rails, etc.

permanganate (pəˈmæŋgəˌneɪt, -nɪt) *n.* a salt of permanganic acid.

permanganic acid (ˌpɜːmænˈgænɪk) *n.* a monobasic acid known only in solution and in the form of permanganate salts. Formula: $HMnO_4$.

permeability (ˌpɜːmɪəˈbɪlɪtɪ) *n.* **1.** the state or quality of being permeable. **2.** a measure of the ability of a medium to modify a magnetic field, expressed as the ratio of the magnetic flux density in the medium to the field strength; measured in henries per metre. Symbol: μ

permeable (ˈpɜːmɪəbᵊl) *adj.* capable of being permeated, esp. by liquids. [C15: < LL *permeābilis*, < L *permeāre* to pervade; see PERMEATE] —ˈ**permeably** *adv.*

permeance (ˈpɜːmɪəns) *n.* **1.** the act of permeating. **2.** the reciprocal of the reluctance of a magnetic circuit. —ˈ**permeant** *adj., n.*

permeate (ˈpɜːmɪˌeɪt) *vb.* **1.** to penetrate or pervade (a substance, area, etc.): *a lovely smell permeated the room.* **2.** to pass through or cause to pass through by osmosis or diffusion: *to permeate a membrane.* [C17: < L *permeāre*, < *per-* through + *meāre* to pass] —ˌ**permeˈation** *n.* —ˈ**permeative** *adj.*

Permian (ˈpɜːmɪən) *adj.* **1.** of, denoting, or formed in the last period of the Palaeozoic era, between the Carboniferous and Triassic periods. ~*n.* **2. the.** the Permian period or rock system. [C19: after *Perm*, Russian port]

permissible (pəˈmɪsəbᵊl) *adj.* permitted; allowable. —**perˌmissiˈbility** *n.* —**perˈmissibly** *adv.*

permission (pəˈmɪʃən) *n.* authorization to do something.

permissive (pəˈmɪsɪv) *adj.* **1.** tolerant; lenient: *permissive parents.* **2.** indulgent in matters of sex: *a permissive society.* **3.** granting permission. —**perˈmissively** *adv.* —**perˈmissiveness** *n.*

permit *vb.* (pəˈmɪt), **-mitting, -mitted.** **1.** (*tr.*) to grant permission to do something: *you are permitted to smoke.* **2.** (*tr.*) to consent to or tolerate: *she will not permit him to come.* **3.** (when *intr.*, often foll. by *of;* when *tr.*, often foll. by an infinitive) to allow the possibility (of): *the passage permits of two interpretations; his work permits him to relax nowadays.* ~*n.* (ˈpɜːmɪt). **4.** an official document granting authorization; licence. **5.** permission. [C15: < L *permittere,* < *per-* through + *mittere* to send] —**perˈmitter** *n.*

permittivity (ˌpɜːmɪˈtɪvɪtɪ) *n., pl.* **-ties.** a measure of the ability of a substance to transmit an electric field.

permutate (ˈpɜːmjʊˌteɪt) *vb.* to alter the sequence or arrangement (of): *endlessly permutating three basic designs.*

permutation (ˌpɜːmjʊˈteɪʃən) *n.* **1.** *Maths.* **a.** an ordered arrangement of the numbers, terms, etc., of a set into specified groups: *the permutations of a, b, and c, taken two at a time, are ab, ba, ac, ca, bc, cb.* **b.** a group formed in this way. **2.** a combination of items, etc., made by reordering. **3.** an alteration; transformation. **4.** a fixed combination for selections of results on football pools. Usually shortened to **perm.** [C14: < L *permūtātiō,* < *permūtāre* to change thoroughly] —ˌ**permuˈtational** *adj.*

permute (pəˈmjuːt) *vb.* (*tr.*) **1.** to change the sequence of. **2.** *Maths.* to subject to permutation. [C14: < L *permūtāre,* < PER- + *mūtāre* to change]

pernicious (pəˈnɪʃəs) *adj.* **1.** wicked or malicious: *pernicious lies.* **2.** causing grave harm; deadly. [C16: < L *perniciōsus,* < *perniciēs* ruin, < PER- (intensive) + *nex* death] —**perˈniciously** *adv.* —**perˈniciousness** *n.*

pernicious anaemia *n.* a form of anaemia characterized by lesions of the spinal cord, weakness, sore tongue, diarrhoea, etc.: associated with inadequate absorption of vitamin B_{12}.

pernickety (pəˈnɪkɪtɪ) *adj. Inf.* **1.** excessively precise; fussy. **2.** (of a task) requiring close attention. [C19: orig. Scot. <?]

peroneal (ˌpɛrəˈniːəl) *adj. Anat.* of or relating to the fibula. [C19: < NL *peronē,* < Gk: fibula]

perorate (ˈpɛrəˌreɪt) *vb.* (*intr.*) **1.** to speak at length, esp. in a formal manner. **2.** to conclude a speech or sum up.

peroration (ˌpɛrəˈreɪʃən) *n.* the conclusion of a speech or discourse, in which points made previously are summed up. [C15: < L *perōrātiō,* < PER- (thoroughly) + *orāre* to speak]

perovskite (pɛˈrɒvskaɪt) *n.* a yellow, brown, or greyish-black mineral. [C19: after *Perovski,* Russian mineralogist]

peroxide (pəˈrɒksaɪd) *n.* **1.** short for **hydrogen peroxide,** esp. when used for bleaching hair. **2.** any of a class of metallic oxides, such as sodium peroxide, Na_2O_2. **3.** (*not in technical usage*) any of certain dioxides, such as manganese peroxide, MnO_2, that resemble peroxides in their formula. **4.** any of a class of organic compounds whose molecules contain two oxygen atoms bound together. **5.** (*modifier*) of, relating to, bleached with, or resembling peroxide: *a peroxide blonde.* ~*vb.* **6.** (*tr.*) to bleach (the hair) with peroxide.

perpendicular (ˌpɜːpənˈdɪkjʊlə) *adj.* **1.** at right angles. **2.** denoting, relating to, or having the style of Gothic architecture used in England during the 14th and 15th centuries, characterized by tracery having vertical lines. **3.** upright; vertical. ~*n.* **4.** *Geom.* a line or plane perpendicular to another. **5.** any instrument used for indicating the vertical line through a given point. [C14: < L *perpendiculāris,* < *perpendiculum* a plumb line, < *per-* through + *pendēre* to hang] —**perpendicularity** (ˌpɜːpənˌdɪkjʊˈlærɪtɪ) *n.* —ˌ**perpenˈdicularly** *adv.*

perpetrate (ˈpɜːpɪˌtreɪt) *vb.* (*tr.*) to perform or be responsible for (a deception, crime, etc.). [C16: < L *perpetrāre,* < *per-* (thoroughly) + *patrāre* to perform] —ˌ**perpeˈtration** *n.* —ˈ**perpeˌtrator** *n.*

perpetual (pəˈpɛtjʊəl) *adj.* **1.** (*usually prenominal*) eternal; permanent. **2.** (*usually prenominal*) seemingly ceaseless because often repeated: *your perpetual complaints.* [C14: via OF < L *perpetuālis* universal, < *perpes* continuous, < *per-* (thoroughly) + *petere* to go towards] —**perˈpetually** *adv.*

perpetual motion *n.* motion of a hypothetical mechanism that continues indefinitely without any external source of energy. It is impossible in practice because of friction.

perpetuate (pəˈpɛtjʊˌeɪt) *vb.* (*tr.*) to cause to continue: *to perpetuate misconceptions.* [C16: < L *perpetuāre* to continue without interruption, < *perpetuus* PERPETUAL] —**perˌpetuˈation** *n.*

perpetuity (ˌpɜːpɪˈtjuːɪtɪ) *n., pl.* **-ties.** **1.** eternity. **2.** the state of being perpetual. **3.** *Property law.* a limitation preventing the absolute disposal of an estate for longer than the period allowed by law. **4.** an annuity that is payable indefinitely. **5. in perpetuity.** for ever. [C15: < OF *perpetuite,* < L *perpetuitās* continuity; see PERPETUAL]

perplex (pəˈplɛks) *vb.* (*tr.*) **1.** to puzzle; bewilder; confuse. **2.** to complicate: *to perplex an issue.* [C15: < obs. *perplex* (adj.) intricate, < L *perplexus* entangled, < *per-* (thoroughly) + *plectere* to entwine] —**perplexedly** (pəˈplɛksɪdlɪ, -ˈplɛkstlɪ) *adv.* —**perˈplexingly** *adv.*

perplexity (pəˈplɛksɪtɪ) *n., pl.* **-ties.** **1.** the state of being perplexed. **2.** the state of being intricate or complicated. **3.** something that perplexes.

per pro (ˈpɜː ˈprəʊ) *prep.* by delegation to: through the agency of: used when signing documents on behalf of someone else. [L: abbrev. of *per prōcūrātiōnem*]

▷ **Usage.** In formal correspondence, when Brenda Smith is signing on behalf of Peter Jones, she should write *Peter Jones per pro* (or *pp*) *Brenda Smith,* not the other way about.

perquisite (ˈpɜːkwɪzɪt) *n.* **1.** an incidental benefit gained from a certain type of employment, such as the use of a company car. **2.** a customary benefit received in addition to a regular income. **3.** a customary tip. **4.** something expected or regarded as an exclusive right. ~Often shortened (informal) to **perk.** [C15: < Med. L *perquīsītum,* < L *perquīrere* to seek earnestly for something]

Perrier water *or* **Perrier** (ˈpɛrɪeɪ) *n. Trademark.* a sparkling mineral water from the south of France. [C20: after a spring, *Source Perrier,* at Vergèze, France]

perron (ˈpɛrən) *n.* an external flight of steps, esp. one at the front entrance of a building. [C14: < OF, < *pierre* stone, < L *petra*]

perry (ˈpɛrɪ) *n., pl.* **-ries.** wine made of pears, similar in taste to cider. [C14 *pereye,* < OF *peré,* ult. < L *pirum* pear]

pers. *abbrev. for:* **1.** person. **2.** personal.

Pers. *abbrev. for* Persia(n).

perse (pɜːs) *n.* **a.** a dark greyish-blue colour. **b.** (*as adj.*): *perse cloth.* [C14: < OF, < Med. L *persus,* ? changed < L *Persicus* Persian]

per se (ˈpɜː ˈseɪ) *adv.* by or in itself; intrinsically. [L]

persecute (ˈpɜːsɪˌkjuːt) *vb.* (*tr.*) **1.** to oppress, harass, or maltreat, esp. because of race, religion, etc. **2.** to bother persistently. [C15: < OF, < *persecuteur,* < LL *persecūtor* pursuer, < *persequī* to take vengeance upon] —ˌ**perseˈcution** *n.* —ˈ**perseˌcutive** *adj.* —ˈ**perseˌcutor** *n.*

persecution complex *n. Psychol.* an acute irrational fear that other people are plotting one's downfall.

perseverance (ˌpɜːsɪˈvɪərəns) *n.* **1.** continued steady belief or efforts; persistence. **2.** *Christian theol.* continuance in a state of grace.

perseveration (pɜːˌsɛvəˈreɪʃən) *n. Psychol.* the tendency for an impression, idea, or feeling to dissipate only slowly and to recur during subsequent experiences.

persevere (ˌpɜːsɪˈvɪə) *vb.* (*intr.*; often foll. by *in*) to show perseverance. [C14: < OF *perseverer*, < L, < *perseverus* very strict; see SEVERE]

Persian (ˈpɜːʃən) *adj.* **1.** of or relating to ancient Persia or modern Iran, their inhabitants, or their languages. ~*n.* **2.** a native, citizen, or inhabitant of modern Iran; an Iranian. **3.** the language of Iran or Persia in any of its ancient or modern forms.

Persian carpet *or* **rug** *n.* a carpet or rug made in Persia or the Near East by knotting silk or wool yarn by hand onto a woven backing in rich colours and flowing or geometric designs.

Persian cat *n.* a long-haired variety of domestic cat.

Persian lamb *n.* **1.** a black loosely curled fur from the karakul lamb. **2.** a karakul lamb.

persiennes (ˌpɜːsɪˈɛnz) *pl. n.* outside window shutters having louvres. [C19: < F, < *persien* Persian]

persiflage (ˈpɜːsɪˌflɑːʒ) *n.* light frivolous conversation, style, or treatment; friendly teasing. [C18: via F < *persifler* to tease, < *per-* (intensive) + *siffler* to whistle, < L *sībilāre* to whistle]

persimmon (pɜːˈsɪmən) *n.* **1.** any of several tropical trees, typically having hard wood and large orange-red fruit. **2.** the sweet fruit of any of these trees, which is edible when completely ripe. [C17: < Amerind]

persist (pəˈsɪst) *vb.* (*intr.*) **1.** (often foll. by *in*) to continue steadfastly or obstinately despite opposition. **2.** to continue without interruption: *the rain persisted throughout the night.* [C16: < L *persistere*, < *per-* (intensive) + *sistere* to stand steadfast] —**perˈsister** *n.*

persistence (pəˈsɪstəns) *or* **persistency** *n.* **1.** the quality of persisting; tenacity. **2.** the act of persisting; continued effort or existence.

persistent (pəˈsɪstənt) *adj.* **1.** showing persistence. **2.** incessantly repeated; unrelenting: *your persistent questioning.* **3.** (of plant parts) remaining attached to the plant after the normal time of withering. **4.** *Zool.* (of parts normally present only in young stages) present in the adult. **5.** (of a chemical, esp. when used as a insecticide) slow to break down. —**perˈsistently** *adv.*

person (ˈpɜːsᵊn) *n., pl.* **persons.** **1.** an individual human being. **2.** the body of a human being: *guns hidden on his person.* **3.** a grammatical category into which pronouns and forms of verbs are subdivided depending on whether they refer to the speaker, the person addressed, or some other individual, thing, etc. **4.** a human being or a corporation recognized in law as having certain rights and obligations. **5. in person.** actually present: *the author will be there in person.* [C13: < OF *persone*, < L *persōna* mask, ? < Etruscan *phersu* mask]

▷ **Usage.** *People* is the word usually used to refer to more than one individual: *there were a hundred people at the reception. Persons* is rarely used, except in official English: *several persons were interviewed.*

-person *n. combining form.* sometimes used instead of *-man* and *-woman* or *-lady: chairperson.*

▷ **Usage.** See at **-man.**

persona (pɜːˈsəʊnə) *n., pl.* **-nae** (-niː). **1.** (*often pl.*) a character in a play, novel, etc. **2.** (in Jungian psychology) the mechanism that conceals a person's true thoughts and feelings, esp. in adaptation to the outside world. [L: mask]

personable (ˈpɜːsənəbᵊl) *adj.* pleasant in appearance and personality. —ˈ**personableness** *n.* —ˈ**personably** *adv.*

personage (ˈpɜːsənɪdʒ) *n.* **1.** an important or distinguished person. **2.** another word for **person** (sense 1). **3.** *Rare.* a figure in literature, history, etc.

persona grata *Latin.* (pɜːˈsəʊnə ˈgrɑːtə) *n., pl.* ***personae gratae*** (pɜːˈsəʊniː ˈgrɑːtiː). an acceptable person, esp. a diplomat.

personal (ˈpɜːsənᵊl) *adj.* **1.** of or relating to the private aspects of a person's life: *personal letters.* **2.** (*prenominal*) of or relating to a person's body, its care, or its appearance: *personal hygiene.* **3.** (*prenominal*) belonging to or intended for a particular person and no-one else: *for your personal use.* **4.** (*prenominal*) undertaken by an individual: *a personal appearance by a celebrity.* **5.** referring to or involving a person's individual personality, intimate affairs, etc., esp. in an offensive way: *personal remarks; don't be so personal.* **6.** having the attributes of an individual conscious being: *a personal God.* **7.** of, relating to, or denoting grammatical person. **8.** *Law.* of or relating to movable property, as money, etc.

▷ **Usage.** *Personal* is sometimes used unnecessarily for emphasis: *my personal opinion is that he will not.* In formal contexts it is preferable to restrict it to instances where a distinction is made between private and official views, policies, etc.: *the prime minister gave me her personal opinion, which was not that of the cabinet.*

personal column *n.* a newspaper column containing personal messages and advertisements.

personal computer *n.* a small inexpensive computer used in word processing, computer games, etc.

personality (ˌpɜːsəˈnælɪtɪ) *n., pl.* **-ties.** **1.** *Psychol.* the sum total of all the behavioural and mental characteristics by means of which an individual is recognized as being unique. **2.** the distinctive character of a person that makes him socially attractive: *a salesman needs a lot of personality.* **3.** a well-known person in a certain field, such as entertainment. **4.** a remarkable person. **5.** (*often pl.*) a personal remark.

personalize *or* **-ise** (ˈpɜːsənəˌlaɪz) *vb.* (*tr.*) **1.** to endow with personal or individual qualities. **2.** to mark (stationery, clothing, etc.) with a person's initials, name, etc. **3.** to take (a remark, etc.) personally. **4.** another word for **personify.** —ˌ**personaliˈzation** *or* **-iˈsation** *n.*

personally (ˈpɜːsənəlɪ) *adv.* **1.** without the help or intervention of others: *I'll attend to it personally.* **2.** (*sentence modifier*) in one's own opinion or as regards oneself: *personally, I hate onions.* **3.** as if referring to oneself: *to take the insults personally.* **4.** as a person: *we like him personally, but professionally he's incompetent.*

personal pronoun *n.* a pronoun having a definite person or thing as an antecedent and functioning grammatically in the same way as the noun that it replaces. The personal pronouns include *I, you, he, she, it, we,* and *they.*

personal property *n. Law.* movable property, such as furniture or money. Also called: **personalty.** Cf. **real property.**

personal stereo *n.* a small audio cassette player worn attached to a belt and used with lightweight headphones.

persona non grata *Latin.* (pɜːˈsəʊnə nɒn ˈgrɑːtə) *n., pl.* ***personae non gratae*** (pɜːˈsəʊniː nɒn ˈgrɑːtiː). **1.** an unacceptable or unwelcome person. **2.** a diplomat who is not acceptable to the government to whom he is accredited.

personate (ˈpɜːsəˌneɪt) *vb.* (*tr.*) **1.** to act the part of (a character in a play); portray. **2.** *Criminal law.* to assume the identity of (another person) with intent to deceive. —ˌ**personˈation** *n.* —ˈ**personative** *adj.* —ˈ**personˌator** *n.*

personification (pɜːˌsɒnɪfɪˈkeɪʃən) *n.* **1.** the attribution of human characteristics to things, abstract ideas, etc. **2.** the representation of an abstract quality or idea in the form of a person, creature, etc., as in art and literature. **3.** a person or thing that personifies. **4.** a person or thing regarded as an embodiment of a quality: *he is the personification of optimism.*

personify (pɜːˈsɒnɪˌfaɪ) *vb.* **-fying, -fied.** (*tr.*) **1.** to attribute human characteristics to (a thing or abstraction). **2.** to represent (an abstract quality) in human or animal form. **3.** (of a person or thing) to represent (an abstract quality), as in art. **4.** to be the embodiment of. —**perˈsoniˌfier** *n.*

personnel (ˌpɜːsəˈnɛl) *n.* **1.** the people employed in an organization or for a service. **2. a.** the department that interviews, appoints, or keeps records of employees. **b.** (*as modifier*): *a personnel officer.* [C19: < F, ult. < LL *persōnālis* personal (adj.); see PERSON]

perspective (pəˈspɛktɪv) *n.* **1.** a way of regarding situations, facts, etc., and judging their relative importance. **2.** the proper or accurate point of view or the ability to see it; objectivity: *try to get some perspective on your troubles.* **3.** a view over some distance in space or time; prospect. **4.** the theory or art of suggesting three dimensions on a two-dimensional surface, in order to recreate the appearance and spatial relationships that objects or a scene in recession present to the eye. **5.** the appearance of objects, buildings, etc., relative to each other, as determined by their distance from the viewer, or the effects of this distance on their appearance. [C14: < Med. L *perspectīva ars* the science of optics, < L *perspicere* to inspect carefully] —**perˈspectively** *adv.*

Perspex (ˈpɜːspɛks) *n. Trademark.* any of various clear acrylic resins.

perspicacious (ˌpɜːspɪˈkeɪʃəs) *adj.* acutely perceptive or discerning. [C17: < L *perspicax,* < *perspicere* to look at closely] —ˌ**perspiˈcaciously** *adv.* —**perspicacity** (ˌpɜːspɪˈkæsɪtɪ) *or* ˌ**perspiˈcaciousness** *n.*

perspicuous (pəˈspɪkjʊəs) *adj.* (of speech or writing) easily understood; lucid. [C15: < L *perspicuus* transparent, < *perspicere* to explore thoroughly] —**perˈspicuously** *adv.* —**perˈspicuousness** *or* **perspicuity** (ˌpɜːspɪˈkjuːɪtɪ) *n.*

perspiration (ˌpɜːspəˈreɪʃən) *n.* **1.** the salty fluid secreted by the sweat glands of the skin. **2.** the act of secreting this fluid. —**perspiratory** (pəˈspaɪərətərɪ) *adj.*

perspire (pəˈspaɪə) *vb.* to secrete or exude (perspiration) through the pores of the skin. [C17: < L *perspīrāre* to blow, < *per-* (through) + *spīrare* to breathe] —**perˈspiringly** *adv.*

persuade (pəˈsweɪd) *vb.* (*tr.; may take a clause as object or an infinitive*) **1.** to induce, urge, or prevail upon successfully: *he finally persuaded them to buy it.* **2.** to cause to believe; convince: *even with the evidence, the police were not persuaded.* [C16: < L *persuādēre,* < *per-* (intensive) + *suādēre* to urge, advise] —**perˈsuadable** *or* **perˈsuasible** *adj.* —**perˌsuadaˈbility** *or* **perˌsuasiˈbility** *n.* —**perˈsuader** *n.*

persuasion (pəˈsweɪʒən) *n.* **1.** the act of persuading or of trying to persuade. **2.** the power to persuade. **3.** a strong belief. **4.** an established creed or belief, esp. a religious one. **5.** a sect, party, or faction. [C14: < L *persuāsiō*]

persuasive (pəˈsweɪsɪv) *adj.* having the power or tending to persuade: *a persuasive salesman.* —**perˈsuasively** *adv.* —**perˈsuasiveness** *n.*

pert (pɜːt) *adj.* **1.** saucy, impudent, or forward. **2.** jaunty: *a pert little hat.* **3.** *Obs.* clever or brisk. [C13: var. of earlier *apert,* < L *apertus* open, < *aperīre* to open] —ˈ**pertly** *adv.* —ˈ**pertness** *n.*

pert. *abbrev. for* pertaining.

pertain (pəˈteɪn) *vb.* (*intr.;* often foll. by *to*) **1.** to have reference or relevance. **2.** to be appropriate. **3.** to belong (to) or be a part (of). [C14: < L *pertinēre,* < *per-* (intensive) + *tenēre* to hold]

pertinacious (ˌpɜːtɪˈneɪʃəs) *adj.* **1.** doggedly resolute in purpose or belief; unyielding. **2.** stubbornly persistent. [C17: < L *pertināx,* < *per-* (intensive) + *tenāx* clinging, < *tenēre* to hold] —ˌ**pertiˈnaciously** *adv.* —**pertinacity** (ˌpɜːtɪˈnæsɪtɪ) *or* ˌ**pertiˈnaciousness** *n.*

pertinent (ˈpɜːtɪnənt) *adj.* relating to the matter at hand; relevant. [C14: < L *pertinēns,* < *pertinēre* to PERTAIN] —ˈ**pertinence** *or* ˈ**pertinency** *n.* —ˈ**pertinently** *adv.*

perturb (pəˈtɜːb) *vb.* (*tr.; often passive*) **1.** to disturb the composure of; trouble. **2.** to throw into disorder. **3.** *Physics, astron.* to cause (a planet, electron, etc.) to undergo a perturbation. [C14: < OF *pertourber,* < L *perturbāre* to confuse, < *per-* (intensive) + *turbāre* to agitate] —**perˈturbable** *adj.* —**perˈturbing** *adj.*

perturbation (ˌpɜːtəˈbeɪʃən) *n.* **1.** the act of perturbing or the state of being perturbed. **2.** a cause of disturbance. **3.** *Physics.* a secondary influence on a system that modifies simple behaviour, such as the effect of the other electrons on one electron in an atom. **4.** *Astron.* a small continuous deviation in the orbit of a planet or comet, due to the attraction of neighbouring planets.

pertussis (pəˈtʌsɪs) *n.* the technical name for **whooping cough.** [C18: NL, < L *per-* (intensive) + *tussis* cough] —**perˈtussal** *adj.*

Peru Current (pəˈruː) *n.* a cold ocean current flowing northwards off the Pacific coast of South America. Also called: **Humboldt Current.**

peruke (pəˈruːk) *n.* a wig for men in the 17th and 18th centuries. Also called: **periwig.** [C16: < F *perruque,* < It. *perrucca* wig, <?]

peruse (pəˈruːz) *vb.* (*tr.*) **1.** to read or examine with care; study. **2.** to browse or read in a leisurely way. [C15 (meaning: to use up): < PER- (intensive) + USE] —**peˈrusal** *n.* —**peˈruser** *n.*

perv (pɜːv) *Sl.* ~*n.* **1.** a pervert. **2.** *Austral.* a lascivious look. ~*vb. also* **perve.** (*intr.*) **3.** *Austral.* to behave like a voyeur.

pervade (pɜːˈveɪd) *vb.* (*tr.*) to spread through or throughout, esp. subtly or gradually; permeate. [C17: < L *pervādere,* < *per-* through + *vādere* to go] —**pervasion** (pɜːˈveɪʒən) *n.* —**pervasive** (pɜːˈveɪsɪv) *adj.* —**perˈvasively** *adv.* —**perˈvasiveness** *n.*

perverse (pəˈvɜːs) *adj.* **1.** deliberately deviating from what is regarded as normal, good, or proper. **2.** persistently holding to what is wrong. **3.** wayward or contrary; obstinate. [C14: < OF *pervers,* < L *perversus* turned the wrong way] —**perˈversely** *adv.* —**perˈverseness** *or* **perˈversity** *n.*

perversion (pəˈvɜːʃən) *n.* **1.** any abnormal means of obtaining sexual satisfaction. **2.** the act of perverting or the state of being perverted. **3.** a perverted form or usage.

pervert *vb.* (pəˈvɜːt). (*tr.*) **1.** to use wrongly or badly. **2.** to interpret wrongly or badly; distort. **3.** to lead into deviant or perverted beliefs or behaviour; corrupt. **4.** to debase. ~*n.* (ˈpɜːvɜːt). **5.** a person who practises sexual perversion. [C14: < OF *pervertir,* < L *pervertere* to turn the wrong way] —**perˈverted** *adj.* —**perˈverter** *n.* —**perˈvertible** *adj.* —**perˈversive** *adj.*

pervious (ˈpɜːvɪəs) *adj.* **1.** able to be penetrated; permeable. **2.** receptive to new ideas, etc.; open-minded. [C17: < L *pervius,* < *per-* (through) + *via* a way] —ˈ**perviously** *adv.* —ˈ**perviousness** *n.*

pes (peɪz, piːz) *n., pl.* **pedes** (ˈpɛdiːz). the technical name for the human **foot.** [C19: NL: foot]

peseta (pəˈseɪtə; *Spanish* peˈseta) *n.* the standard monetary unit of Spain, divided into 100 céntimos. [C19: < Sp., dim. of PESO]

pesky (ˈpɛskɪ) *adj.* **peskier, peskiest.** *U.S. & Canad. inf.* troublesome. [C19: prob. changed < *pesty;* see PEST] —ˈ**peskily** *adv.* —ˈ**peskiness** *n.*

peso (ˈpeɪsəʊ; *Spanish* ˈpeso) *n., pl.* **-sos** (-səʊz; *Spanish* -sos). the standard monetary unit of Argentina, Bolivia, Colombia, Cuba, the Dominican Republic, Mexico, the Philippines, and Uruguay. [C16: < Sp.: weight, < L *pēnsum* something weighed out, < *pendere* to weigh]

pessary (ˈpɛsərɪ) *n., pl.* **-ries.** *Med.* **1.** a device for inserting into the vagina, either as a support for the uterus or (**diaphragm pessary**) as a contraceptive. **2.** a vaginal suppository. [C14: < LL *pessārium,* < L *pessum,* < Gk *pessos* plug]

pessimism (ˈpɛsɪˌmɪzəm) *n.* **1.** the tendency to expect the worst in all things. **2.** the doctrine of the ultimate triumph of evil over good. **3.** the doctrine that this world is corrupt and that man's sojourn in it is a preparation for some other existence. [C18: < L *pessimus* worst, sup. of *malus* bad] —ˈ**pessimist** *n.* —ˌ**pessiˈmistic** *adj.* —ˌ**pessiˈmistically** *adv.*

pest (pɛst) *n.* **1.** a person or thing that annoys, esp. by imposing itself when it is not wanted; nuisance. **2.** any organism that damages crops, or injures or irritates livestock or man. **3.** *Rare.* an epidemic disease. [C16: < L *pestis* plague, <?]

pester (ˈpɛstə) *vb.* (*tr.*) to annoy or nag continually. [C16: < OF *empestrer* to hobble (a horse), < Vulgar L *impāstōriāre* (unattested) to use a hobble, ult. < L *pastor* herdsman]

pesticide (ˈpɛstɪˌsaɪd) *n.* a chemical used for killing pests, esp. insects. —ˌ**pestiˈcidal** *adj.*

pestiferous (pɛˈstɪfərəs) *adj.* **1.** *Inf.* troublesome; irritating. **2.** breeding, carrying, or spreading infectious disease. **3.** corrupting; pernicious. [C16: < L *pestifer*, < *pestis* contagion + *ferre* to bring]

pestilence (ˈpɛstɪləns) *n.* **1. a.** any epidemic of a deadly infectious disease, such as the plague. **b.** such a disease. **2.** an evil influence.

pestilent (ˈpɛstɪlənt) *adj.* **1.** annoying; irritating. **2.** highly destructive morally or physically; pernicious. **3.** likely to cause epidemic or infectious disease. [C15: < L *pestilens* unwholesome, < *pestis* plague] —ˈ**pestilently** *adv.* —**pestilential** (ˌpɛstɪˈlɛnʃəl) *adj.* —ˌ**pestiˈlentially** *adv.*

pestle (ˈpɛsᵊl) *n.* **1.** a club-shaped instrument for mixing or grinding substances in a mortar. **2.** a tool for pounding or stamping. ~*vb.* **3.** to pound (a substance or object) with or as if with a pestle. [C14: < OF *pestel*, < L *pistillum*]

pet[1] (pɛt) *n.* **1.** a tame animal kept for companionship, amusement, etc. **2.** a person who is fondly indulged; favourite: *teacher's pet.* ~*adj.* **3.** kept as a pet: *a pet dog.* **4.** of or for pet animals: *pet food.* **5.** particularly cherished: *a pet hatred.* **6.** familiar or affectionate: *a pet name.* ~*vb.* **petting, petted. 7.** (*tr.*) to treat (a person, animal, etc.) as a pet; pamper. **8.** (*tr.*) to pat or fondle (an animal, child, etc.). **9.** (*intr.*) *Inf.* (of two people) to caress each other in an erotic manner. [C16: <?] —ˈ**petter** *n.*

pet[2] (pɛt) *n.* a fit of sulkiness, esp. at what is felt to be a slight; pique. [C16: <?]

Pet. *Bible. abbrev. for* Peter.

peta- *prefix.* denoting 10^{15}: *petametres.* Symbol: P [C20: so named because it is the SI prefix after TERA-; on the model of PENTA-, the prefix after TETRA-]

petal (ˈpɛtᵊl) *n.* any of the separate parts of the corolla of a flower: often brightly coloured. [C18: < NL *petalum*, < Gk *petalon* leaf] —ˈ**petaline** *adj.* —ˈ**petalled** *adj.* —ˈ**petal-**ˌ**like** *adj.*

-petal *adj. combining form.* seeking: *centripetal.* [< NL *-petus*, < L *petere* to seek]

petard (pɪˈtɑːd) *n.* **1.** (formerly) a device containing explosives used to breach a wall, doors, etc. **2. hoist with one's own petard.** being the victim of one's own schemes, etc. [C16: < F: firework, < *péter* to break wind, < L *pēdere*]

petaurist (pətˈɒrɪst) *n.* another name for **flying phalanger.** [C19: < L, < Gk *petauristēs* performer on the springboard]

petcock (ˈpɛtˌkɒk) *n.* a small valve for checking the water content of a steam boiler or draining waste from the cylinder of a steam engine. [C19: < PET[1] or ? F *pet*, < *péter* to break wind + COCK[1]]

petechia (pɪˈtiːkɪə) *n., pl.* **-chiae** (-kɪˌiː). a minute discoloured spot on the surface of the skin. [C18: via NL < It. *petecchia* freckle, <?] —**peˈtechial** *adj.*

peter[1] (ˈpiːtə) *vb.* (*intr.*; foll. by *out* or *away*) to fall (off) in volume, intensity, etc., and finally cease. [C19: <?]

peter[2] (ˈpiːtə) *n. Sl.* **1.** a safe, till, or cashbox. **2.** a prison cell. [C17 (meaning a case): < the name *Peter*]

peterman (ˈpiːtəmən) *n., pl.* **-men.** *Sl.* a burglar skilled in safe-breaking. [C19: < PETER[2]]

Peter Pan *n.* a youthful, boyish, or immature man. [C20: after the main character in *Peter Pan* (1904), a play by J. M. Barrie]

Peter Principle *n.* **the.** the theory, usually taken facetiously, that all members in a hierarchy rise to their own level of incompetence. [C20: < the book *The Peter Principle* (1969) by Dr Lawrence J. *Peter* and Raymond Hull]

petersham (ˈpiːtəʃəm) *n.* **1.** a thick corded ribbon used to stiffen belts, etc. **2.** a heavy woollen fabric used for coats, etc. **3.** a kind of overcoat made of such fabric. [C19: after Viscount *Petersham* (died 1851), E army officer]

Peter's pence *or* **Peter pence** *n.* **1.** an annual tax, originally of one penny, formerly levied for the maintenance of the Papal See. **2.** a voluntary contribution made by Roman Catholics for the same purpose. [C13: referring to St *Peter*, considered as the first pope]

pethidine (ˈpɛθɪˌdiːn) *n.* a white crystalline water-soluble drug used as an analgesic. [C20: ? a blend of PIPERIDINE + ETHYL]

petiole (ˈpɛtɪˌəʊl) *n.* **1.** the stalk by which a leaf is attached to the plant. **2.** *Zool.* a slender stalk or stem, as between the thorax and abdomen of ants. [C18: via F < L *petiolus* little foot, < *pēs* foot] —**petiolate** (ˈpɛtɪəˌleɪt) *adj.*

petit (ˈpɛtɪ) *adj.* (*prenominal*) *Chiefly law.* of lesser importance; small. [C14: < OF: little, <?]

petit bourgeois (ˈbʊəʒwɑː) *n., pl.* **petits bourgeois** (ˈbʊəʒwɑːz). **1.** Also called: **petite bourgeoisie, petty bourgeoisie.** the section of the middle class with the lowest social status, as shopkeepers, lower clerical staff, etc. **2.** a member of this stratum. ~*adj.* **3.** of, relating to, or characteristic of the petit bourgeois, esp. indicating a sense of self-righteousness and conformity to established standards of behaviour.

petite (pəˈtiːt) *adj.* (of a woman) small, delicate, and dainty. [C18: < F, fem. of *petit* small]

petit four (fɔː) *n., pl.* **petits fours** (fɔːz). any of various very small fancy cakes and biscuits. [F, lit.: little oven]

petition (pɪˈtɪʃən) *n.* **1.** a written document signed by a large number of people demanding some form of action from a government or other authority. **2.** any formal request to a higher authority; entreaty. **3.** *Law.* a formal application in writing made to a court asking for some specific judicial action: *a petition for divorce.* **4.** the action of petitioning. ~*vb.* **5.** (*tr.*) to address or present a petition to (a person in authority, government, etc.): *to petition Parliament.* **6.** (*intr.*; foll. by *for*) to seek by petition: *to petition for a change in the law.* [C14: < L *petītiō*, < *petere* to seek] —**peˈtitionary** *adj.*

petitioner (pɪˈtɪʃənə) *n.* **1.** a person who presents a petition. **2.** *Chiefly Brit.* the plaintiff in a divorce suit.

petitio principii (pɪˈtɪʃɪˌəʊ prɪnˈkɪpɪˌaɪ) *n. Logic.* a form of fallacious reasoning in which the conclusion has been assumed in the premises; begging the question. [C16: L, translation of Gk *to en arkhei aiteisthai* an assumption at the beginning]

petit jury *n.* a jury of 12 persons empanelled to determine the facts of a case and decide the issue pursuant to the direction of the court on points of law. Also called: **petty jury.** —**petit juror** *n.*

petit larceny *n.* (formerly, in England) the stealing of property valued at 12 pence or under. Abolished 1827. Also called: **petty larceny.**

petit mal (mæl) *n.* a mild form of epilepsy characterized by periods of impairment or loss of consciousness for up to 30 seconds. Cf. **grand mal.** [C19: F: little illness]

petit point (ˈpɛtɪ ˈpɔɪnt; *French* pəti pwɛ̃) *n.* **1.** a small diagonal needlepoint stitch used for fine detail. **2.** work done with such stitches. [F: small point]

Petrarchan sonnet (pɛˈtrɑːkən) *n.* a sonnet form of the Italian poet Petrarch (1304–74), having an octave rhyming a b b a a b b a and a sestet rhyming either c d e c d e or c d c d c d.

petrel (ˈpɛtrəl) *n.* any of a family of oceanic birds having a hooked bill and tubular nostrils: includes albatrosses, storm petrels, and shearwaters. [C17: var. of earlier *pitteral*, associated by folk etymology with St *Peter*, because the bird appears to walk on water]

Petri dish (ˈpiːtrɪ) *n.* a shallow dish, often with a cover, used in laboratories, esp. for producing cultures of microorganisms. [C19: after J. R. *Petri* (1852–1921), G bacteriologist]

petrifaction (ˌpɛtrɪˈfækʃən) *or* **petrification** (ˌpɛtrɪfɪˈkeɪʃən) *n.* **1.** the act or process of forming petrified organic material. 2. the state of being petrified.

petrify (ˈpɛtrɪˌfaɪ) *vb.* **-fying, -fied.** 1. (*tr.; often passive*) to convert (organic material) into a fossilized form by impregnation with dissolved minerals so that the original appearance is preserved. 2. to make or become dull, unresponsive, etc.; deaden. 3. (*tr.; often passive*) to stun or daze with horror, fear, etc. [C16: < F *pétrifier*, ult. < Gk *petra* stone] —**ˈpetriˌfier** *n.*

petro- *or before a vowel* **petr-** *combining form.* 1. indicating stone or rock: *petrology.* 2. indicating petroleum, its products, etc.: *petrochemical.* [< Gk *petra* rock or *petros* stone]

petrochemical (ˌpɛtrəʊˈkɛmɪkəl) *n.* 1. any substance, such as acetone or ethanol, obtained from petroleum. ~*adj.* 2. of, concerned with, or obtained from petrochemicals or related to petrochemistry. —ˌ**petroˈchemistry** *n.*

petrodollar (ˈpɛtrəʊˌdɒlə) *n.* money earned by a country by the exporting of petroleum.

petroglyph (ˈpɛtrəˌglɪf) *n.* a drawing or carving on rock, esp. a prehistoric one. [C19: via F < Gk *petra* stone + *gluphē* carving]

petrography (pɛˈtrɒgrəfɪ) *n.* the branch of petrology concerned with the description and classification of rocks. —**peˈtrographer** *n.* —**petrographic** (ˌpɛtrəˈgræfɪk) *or* ˌ**petroˈgraphical** *adj.*

petrol (ˈpɛtrəl) *n.* any one of various volatile flammable liquid mixtures of hydrocarbons, obtained from petroleum and used as a solvent and a fuel for internal-combustion engines. U.S. and Canad. name: **gasoline.** [C16: via F < Med. L PETROLEUM]

petrolatum (ˌpɛtrəˈleɪtəm) *n.* a translucent gelatinous substance obtained from petroleum; used as a lubricant and in medicine as an ointment base. Also called: **petroleum jelly.**

petrol bomb *n.* 1. a device filled with petrol that bursts into flames on impact. ~*vb.* **petrol-bomb.** (*tr.*) 2. to attack with petrol bombs.

petroleum (pəˈtrəʊlɪəm) *n.* a dark-coloured thick flammable crude oil occurring in sedimentary rocks, consisting mainly of hydrocarbons. Fractional distillation separates the crude oil into petrol, paraffin, diesel oil, lubricating oil, etc. Fuel oil, paraffin wax, asphalt, and carbon black are extracted from the residue. [C16: < Med. L, < L *petra* stone + *oleum* oil]

petroleum jelly *n.* another name for **petrolatum.**

petrology (pɛˈtrɒlədʒɪ) *n., pl.* **-gies.** the study of the composition, origin, structure, and formation of rocks. —**petrological** (ˌpɛtrəˈlɒdʒɪkəl) *adj.* —**peˈtrologist** *n.*

petrol station *n. Brit.* another term for **filling station.**

petrous (ˈpɛtrəs, ˈpiː-) *adj. Anat.* denoting the dense part of the temporal bone that surrounds the inner ear. [C16: < L *petrōsus* full of rocks] —**petrosal** (pɛˈtrəʊsəl) *adj.*

petticoat (ˈpɛtɪˌkəʊt) *n.* 1. a woman's underskirt. 2. *Inf.* a. a humorous or mildly disparaging name for a woman. b. (*as modifier*): *petticoat politics.* [C15: see PETTY, COAT]

pettifogger (ˈpɛtɪˌfɒgə) *n.* 1. a lawyer who conducts unimportant cases, esp. one who resorts to trickery. 2. any person who quibbles. [C16: < PETTY + *fogger*, <?, perhaps < *Fugger*, a family (C15–16) of G financiers] —**ˈpettiˌfoggery** *n.* —**ˈpettiˌfog** *vb.* **-fogging, -fogged.** (*intr.*) —**ˈpettiˌfogging** *adj.*

pettish (ˈpɛtɪʃ) *adj.* peevish; petulant. [C16: < PET[2]] —**ˈpettishly** *adv.* —**ˈpettishness** *n.*

petty (ˈpɛtɪ) *adj.* **-tier, -tiest.** 1. trivial; trifling: *petty details.* 2. narrow-minded, mean: *petty spite.* 3. minor or subordinate in rank: *petty officialdom.* 4. *Law.* a variant of **petit.** [C14: < OF PETIT] —**ˈpettily** *adv.* —**ˈpettiness** *n.*

petty cash *n.* a small cash fund for minor incidental expenses.

petty jury *n.* a variant of **petit jury.**

petty larceny *n.* a variant of **petit larceny.**

petty officer *n.* a noncommissioned officer in a naval service comparable in rank to a sergeant in an army or marine corps.

petty sessions *n.* (*functioning as sing. or pl.*) another term for **magistrates' court.**

petulant (ˈpɛtjʊlənt) *adj.* irritable, impatient, or sullen in a peevish or capricious way. [C16: via OF < L *petulāns* bold, < *petulāre* (unattested) to attack playfully, < *petere* to assail] —**ˈpetulance** *or* **ˈpetulancy** *n.* —**ˈpetulantly** *adv.*

petunia (pɪˈtjuːnɪə) *n.* any plant of a tropical American genus cultivated for their colourful funnel-shaped flowers. [C19: via NL < obs. F *petun* variety of tobacco, < Tupi *petyn*]

petuntse (pɪˈtʌntsɪ, -ˈtʊn-) *n.* a fusible mineral used in hard-paste porcelain. [C18: < Chinese, < *pe* white + *tun* heap + *tzu* offspring]

pew (pjuː) *n.* 1. (in a church) **a.** one of several long benchlike seats with backs, used by the congregation. **b.** an enclosed compartment reserved for the use of a family or other small group. 2. *Brit. inf.* a seat (esp. in **take a pew).** [C14 *pywe,* < OF, < L *podium* a balcony, < Gk *podion* supporting structure, < *pous* foot]

pewit *or* **peewit** (ˈpiːwɪt) *n.* other names for **lapwing.** [C13: imit. of the bird's cry]

pewter (ˈpjuːtə) *n.* 1. **a.** any of various alloys containing tin, lead, and sometimes copper and antimony. **b.** (*as modifier*): *pewter ware; a pewter tankard.* 2. plate or kitchen utensils made from pewter. [C14: < OF *peaultre,* <?] —**ˈpewterer** *n.*

peyote (peɪˈəʊtɪ, pɪ-) *n.* another name for **mescal** (the plant). [Mexican Sp., < Nahuatl *peyotl*]

pF *abbrev. for* picofarad.

pf. *abbrev for:* 1. perfect. 2. Also: **pfg.** pfennig. 3. preferred.

pfennig (ˈfɛnɪg; *German* ˈpfɛnɪç) *n., pl.* **-nigs** *or* **-nige** (*German* -nɪgə). a German monetary unit worth one hundredth of a mark. [G: PENNY]

PG *symbol for* a film certified for viewing by anyone, but which contains scenes that may be unsuitable for children, for whom parental guidance is necessary. [C20: < abbrev. of *parental guidance*]

pg. *abbrev. for* page.

Pg. *abbrev. for:* 1. Portugal. 2. Portuguese.

pH *n.* potential of hydrogen; a measure of the acidity or alkalinity of a solution. Pure water has a pH of 7, acid solutions have a pH less than 7, and alkaline solutions a pH greater than 7.

phacelia (fæˈsiːlɪə) *n.* any of a genus of N American plants having clusters of blue flowers. [NL < Gk *phakelos* a cluster]

phaeton (ˈfeɪtən) *n.* a light four-wheeled horse-drawn carriage with or without a top. [C18: < F, < L, < Gk *Phaethon* son of Helios (the sun god), who borrowed his father's chariot]

-phage *n. combining form.* indicating something that eats or consumes something specified: *bacteriophage.* [< Gk *-phagos;* see PHAGO-] —**-phagous** *adj. combining form.*

phago- *or before a vowel* **phag-** *combining form.* eating, consuming, or destroying: *phagocyte.* [< Gk *phagein* to consume]

phagocyte (ˈfægəˌsaɪt) *n.* a cell or protozoan that engulfs particles, such as microorganisms. —**phagocytic** (ˌfægəˈsɪtɪk) *adj.*

phagocytosis (ˌfægəsaɪˈtəʊsɪs) *n.* the process by which a cell, such as a white blood cell, ingests microorganisms, other cells, etc.

-phagy *or* **-phagia** *n. combining form.* indicating an eating or devouring: *anthropophagy.* [< Gk *-phagia;* see PHAGO-]

phalange (ˈfælændʒ) *n., pl.* **phalanges** (fæˈlændʒiːz). *Anat.* another name for **phalanx** (sense 4). [C16: via F, ult. < Gk PHALANX]

phalangeal (fəˈlændʒɪəl) *adj. Anat.* of or relating to a phalanx or phalanges.

phalanger (fəˈlændʒə) *n.* any of various Australasian arboreal marsupials having dense fur and a long tail. Also called (Austral.): **possum.** See also **flying phalanger.** [C18: via NL < Gk *phalaggion* spider's web, referring to its webbed hind toes]

phalanx (ˈfælæŋks) *n., pl.* **phalanxes** *or* **phalan-**

ges (fæˈlændʒiːz). **1.** an ancient Greek and Macedonian battle formation of hoplites presenting long spears from behind a wall of overlapping shields. **2.** any closely ranked unit or mass of people: *the police formed a phalanx to protect the embassy.* **3.** a number of people united for a common purpose. **4.** *Anat.* any of the bones of the fingers or toes. **5.** *Bot.* a bundle of stamens. [C16: via L < Gk: infantry formation in close ranks, bone of finger or toe]

phalarope (ˈfæləˌrəʊp) *n.* any of a family of aquatic shore birds of northern oceans and lakes, having a long slender bill and lobed toes. [C18: via F < NL *Phalaropus,* < Gk *phalaris* coot + *pous* foot]

phallic (ˈfælɪk) *adj.* **1.** of, relating to, or resembling a phallus: *a phallic symbol.* **2.** *Psychoanal.* relating to a stage of psychosexual development during which a male child's interest is concentrated on the genital organs. **3.** of or relating to phallicism.

phallicism (ˈfælɪˌsɪzəm) *or* **phallism** *n.* the worship or veneration of the phallus.

phallus (ˈfæləs) *n., pl.* **-li** (-laɪ) *or* **-luses. 1.** another word for **penis. 2.** an image of the male sexual organ, esp. as a symbol of reproductive power. [C17: via LL < Gk *phallos*]

-phane *n. combining form.* indicating something resembling a specified substance: *cellophane.* [< Gk *phainein* to shine, appear]

phanerogam (ˈfænərəʊˌgæm) *n.* any plant of a former major division which included all seed-bearing plants; a former name for **spermatophyte.** [C19: < NL *phanerogamus,* < Gk *phaneros* visible + *gamos* marriage] —ˌ**phaneroˈgamic** *or* **phanerogamous** (ˌfænəˈrɒgəməs) *adj.*

phantasm (ˈfæntæzəm) *n.* **1.** a phantom. **2.** an illusory perception of an object, person, etc. [C13: < OF *fantasme,* < L *phantasma,* < Gk] —**phanˈtasmal** *or* **phanˈtasmic** *adj.*

phantasmagoria (ˌfæntæzməˈgɔːrɪə) *or* **phantasmagory** (fænˈtæzməgərɪ) *n.* **1.** *Psychol.* a shifting medley of real or imagined figures, as in a dream. **2.** *Films.* a sequence of pictures made to vary in size rapidly. **3.** a shifting scene composed of different elements. [C19: prob. < F, < PHANTASM + *-agorie,* ? < Gk *ageirein* to gather together] —**phantasmagoric** (ˌfæntæzməˈgɒrɪk) *or* ˌ**phantasmaˈgorical** *adj.*

phantasy (ˈfæntəsɪ) *n., pl.* **-sies.** an archaic spelling of **fantasy.**

phantom (ˈfæntəm) *n.* **1. a.** an apparition or spectre. **b.** (*as modifier*): *a phantom army marching through the sky.* **2.** the visible representation of something abstract, esp. as in a dream or hallucination: *phantoms of evil haunted his sleep.* **3.** something apparently unpleasant or horrific that has no material form. [C13: < OF *fantosme,* < L *phantasma*]

phantom limb *n.* the illusion that a limb still exists following its amputation, sometimes with the sensation of pain (**phantom limb pain**).

-phany *n. combining form.* indicating a manifestation: *theophany.* [< Gk *-phania,* < *phainein* to show] —**-phanous** *adj. combining form.*

phar., Phar., pharm., *or* **Pharm.** *abbrev. for:* **1.** pharmaceutical. **2.** pharmacist. **3.** pharmacopoeia. **4.** pharmacy.

Pharaoh (ˈfɛərəʊ) *n.* the title of the ancient Egyptian kings. [OE *Pharaon,* via L, Gk, & Heb., ult. < Egyptian *pr-'o* great house] —**Pharaonic** (fɛəˈrɒnɪk) *adj.*

Pharisaic (ˌfærɪˈseɪɪk) *or* **Pharisaical** *adj.* **1.** *Judaism.* of, relating to, or characteristic of the Pharisees or Pharisaism. **2.** (*often not cap.*) righteously hypocritical. —ˌ**Phariˈsaically** *adv.*

Pharisaism (ˈfærɪseɪˌɪzəm) *n.* **1.** *Judaism.* the tenets and customs of the Pharisees. **2.** (*often not cap.*) observance of the external forms of religion without genuine belief; hypocrisy.

Pharisee (ˈfærɪˌsiː) *n.* **1.** a member of an ancient Jewish sect teaching strict observance of Jewish traditions. **2.** (*often not cap.*) a self-righteous or hypocritical person. [OE *Farīsēus,* ult. < Aramaic *perīshāiyā,* pl. of *perīsh* separated]

pharmaceutical (ˌfɑːməˈsjuːtɪkᵊl) *or* (*less commonly*) **pharmaceutic** *adj.* of or relating to drugs or pharmacy. [C17: < LL *pharmaceuticus,* < Gk *pharmakeus* purveyor of drugs; see PHARMACY] —ˌ**pharmaˈceutically** *adv.*

pharmaceutics (ˌfɑːməˈsjuːtɪks) *n.* **1.** (*functioning as sing.*) another term for **pharmacy** (sense 1). **2.** pharmaceutical remedies.

pharmacist (ˈfɑːməsɪst) *n.* a person qualified to prepare and dispense drugs.

pharmaco- *combining form.* indicating drugs: *pharmacology.* [< Gk *pharmakon* drug]

pharmacognosy (ˌfɑːməˈkɒgnəsɪ) *n.* the study of crude drugs of plant and animal origin. [C19: < PHARMACO- + *gnosy,* < Gk *gnosis* knowledge] —ˌ**pharmaˈcognosist** *n.*

pharmacology (ˌfɑːməˈkɒlədʒɪ) *n.* the science or study of drugs, including their characteristics, action, and uses. —**pharmacological** (ˌfɑːməkəˈlɒdʒɪkᵊl) *adj.* —ˌ**pharmacoˈlogically** *adv.* —ˌ**pharmaˈcologist** *n.*

pharmacopoeia *or U.S.* (*sometimes*) **pharmacopeia** (ˌfɑːməkəˈpiːə) *n.* an authoritative book containing a list of medicinal drugs with their uses, preparation, dosages, formulas, etc. [C17: via NL < Gk *pharmakopoiia* art of preparing drugs, < PHARMACO- + *-poiia,* < *poiein* to make] —ˌ**pharmacoˈpoeial** *adj.*

pharmacy (ˈfɑːməsɪ) *n., pl.* **-cies. 1.** Also: **pharmaceutics.** the practice or art of preparing and dispensing drugs. **2.** a dispensary. [C14: < Med. L *pharmacia,* < Gk *pharmakeia* making of drugs, < *pharmakon* drug]

pharos (ˈfɛərɒs) *n.* any marine lighthouse or beacon. [C16: after a large Hellenistic lighthouse on an island off Alexandria in Egypt]

pharyngeal (ˌfærɪnˈdʒiːəl) *or* **pharyngal** (fəˈrɪŋgᵊl) *adj.* **1.** of, relating to, or situated in or near the pharynx. **2.** *Phonetics.* pronounced with an articulation in or constriction of the pharynx. [C19: < NL *pharyngeus;* see PHARYNX]

pharyngitis (ˌfærɪnˈdʒaɪtɪs) *n.* inflammation of the pharynx.

pharynx (ˈfærɪŋks) *n., pl.* **pharynges** (fæˈrɪndʒiːz) *or* **pharynxes.** the part of the alimentary canal between the mouth and the oesophagus. [C17: via NL < Gk *pharunx* throat]

phase (feɪz) *n.* **1.** any distinct or characteristic period or stage in a sequence of events: *there were two phases to the resolution.* **2.** *Astron.* one of the recurring shapes of the portion of the moon or an inferior planet illuminated by the sun. **3.** *Physics.* the fraction of a cycle of a periodic quantity that has been completed at a specific reference time, expressed as an angle. **4.** *Physics.* a particular stage in a periodic process or phenomenon. **5. in phase.** (of two waveforms) reaching corresponding phases at the same time. **6. out of phase.** (of two waveforms) not in phase. **7.** *Chem.* a distinct state of matter characterized by homogeneous composition and properties and the possession of a clearly defined boundary. **8.** *Zool.* a variation in the normal form of an animal, esp. a colour variation, brought about by seasonal or geographical change. ~*vb.* (*tr.*) **9.** (*often passive*) to execute, arrange, or introduce gradually or in stages: *the withdrawal was phased over several months.* **10.** (sometimes foll. by *with*) to cause (a part, process, etc.) to function or coincide with (another part, etc.): *he tried to phase the intake and output of the machine; he phased the intake with the output.* **11.** *Chiefly U.S.* to arrange (processes, goods, etc.) to be supplied or executed when required. [C19: < NL *phases,* pl. of *phasis,* < Gk: aspect] —ˈ**phasic** *adj.*

phase in *vb.* (*tr., adv.*) to introduce in a gradual or cautious manner: *the legislation was phased in over two years.*

phase modulation *n.* a type of modulation in which the phase of a radio carrier wave is varied by an amount proportional to the instantaneous amplitude of the modulating signal.

phase out *vb.* (*tr., adv.*) **1.** to discontinue or

withdraw gradually. ~*n.* **phase-out.** **2.** *Chiefly U.S.* the action or an instance of phasing out: *a phase-out of conventional forces.*

phase rule *n.* the principle that in any system in equilibrium the number of degrees of freedom is equal to the number of components less the number of phases plus two.

-phasia *n. combining form.* indicating speech disorder of a specified kind: *aphasia.* [< Gk, < *phanai* to speak] **—-phasic** *adj. and n. combining form.*

phatic (ˈfætɪk) *adj.* (of speech) used to establish social contact and to express sociability rather than specific meaning. [C20: < Gk *phat(os)* spoken + -IC]

PhD *abbrev. for* Doctor of Philosophy. Also: **DPhil.**

pheasant (ˈfɛzᵊnt) *n.* **1.** any of various long-tailed gallinaceous birds, having a brightly-coloured plumage in the male: native to Asia but introduced elsewhere. **2.** any of various other related birds, including the quails and partridges. **3.** *U.S. & Canad.* any of several other gallinaceous birds, esp. the ruffed grouse. [C13: < OF *fesan,* < L *phāsiānus,* < Gk *phasianos ornis* Phasian bird, after the River *Phasis,* in Colchis, an ancient country on the Black Sea]

phellem (ˈfɛləm) *n. Bot.* the technical name for **cork** (sense 4). [C20: < Gk *phellos* cork + PHLOEM]

phenacetin (fɪˈnæsɪtɪn) *n.* a white crystalline solid used in medicine to relieve pain and fever. Also called: **acetophenetidin.** [C19: < PHENO- + ACETYL + -IN]

pheno- *or before a vowel* **phen-** *combining form.* **1.** showing or manifesting: *phenotype.* **2.** indicating that a molecule contains benzene rings: *phenobarbitone.* [< Gk *phaino-* shining, < *phainein* to show; its use in a chemical sense is exemplified in *phenol,* so called because orig. prepared from illuminating gas]

phenobarbitone (ˌfiːnəʊˈbɑːbɪˌtəʊn) *or* **phenobarbital** (ˌfiːnəʊˈbɑːbɪtᵊl) *n.* a white crystalline derivative of barbituric acid used as a sedative for treating insomnia and epilepsy.

phenocryst (ˈfiːnəˌkrɪst, ˈfɛn-) *n.* any of several large crystals in igneous rocks such as porphyry. [C19: < PHENO- (shining) + CRYSTAL]

phenol (ˈfiːnɒl) *n.* **1.** Also called: **carbolic acid.** a white crystalline derivative of benzene, used as an antiseptic and disinfectant and in the manufacture of resins, explosives, and pharmaceuticals. Formula: C_6H_5OH. **2.** *Chem.* any of a class of organic compounds whose molecules contain one or more hydroxyl groups bound directly to a carbon atom in an aromatic ring. **—pheˈnolic** *adj.*

phenolic resin *n.* any one of a class of resins derived from phenol, used in paints, adhesives, and as thermosetting plastics.

phenology (fɪˈnɒlədʒɪ) *n.* the study of recurring phenomena, such as animal migration, esp. as influenced by climatic conditions. [C19: < PHENO(MENON) + -LOGY] **—phenological** (ˌfiːnəˈlɒdʒɪkᵊl) *adj.* **—pheˈnologist** *n.*

phenolphthalein (ˌfiːnɒlˈθeɪliːn, -lɪɪn, -ˈθæl-) *n.* a colourless crystalline compound used in medicine as a laxative and in chemistry as an indicator. [< PHENO- + *phthal-,* short form of NAPHTHALENE + -IN]

phenomena (fɪˈnɒmɪnə) *n.* a plural of **phenomenon.**

phenomenal (fɪˈnɒmɪnᵊl) *adj.* **1.** of or relating to a phenomenon. **2.** extraordinary; outstanding; remarkable: *a phenomenal achievement.* **3.** *Philosophy.* known or perceived by the senses rather than the mind. **—pheˈnomenally** *adv.*

phenomenalism (fɪˈnɒmɪnəˌlɪzəm) *n. Philosophy.* the doctrine that statements about physical objects and the external world can be analysed in terms of possible or actual experiences, and that entities, such as physical objects, are only mental constructions out of phenomenal appearances. **—pheˈnomenalist** *n., adj.*

phenomenology (fɪˌnɒmɪˈnɒlədʒɪ) *n. Philosophy.* **1.** the movement that concentrates on the detailed description of conscious experience. **2.** the science of phenomena as opposed to the science of being. **—phenomenological** (fɪˌnɒmɪnəˈlɒdʒɪkᵊl) *adj.*

phenomenon (fɪˈnɒmɪnən) *n., pl.* **-ena** (-ɪnə) *or* **-enons.** **1.** anything that can be perceived as an occurrence or fact by the senses. **2.** any remarkable occurrence or person. **3.** *Philosophy.* **a.** the object of perception, experience, etc. **b.** (in the writings of Kant (1724–1804), German philosopher) a thing as it appears, as distinguished from its real nature as a thing-in-itself. [C16: via LL < Gk *phainomenon,* < *phainesthai* to appear, < *phainein* to show]

▷ **Usage.** Although *phenomena* is often treated as if it were singular, correct usage is to employ *phenomenon* with a singular construction and *phenomena* with a plural: *that is an interesting phenomenon* (not *phenomena*)*; several new phenomena were recorded in his notes.*

phenotype (ˈfiːnəʊˌtaɪp) *n.* the physical constitution of an organism as determined by the interaction of its genetic constitution and the environment. **—phenotypic** (ˌfiːnəʊˈtɪpɪk) *or* **ˌphenoˈtypical** *adj.* **—ˌphenoˈtypically** *adv.*

phenyl (ˈfiːnaɪl, ˈfɛnɪl) *n.* (*modifier*) of, containing, or consisting of the monovalent group C_6H_5, derived from benzene: *a phenyl group.*

phenylalanine (ˌfiːnaɪlˈæləˌniːn) *n.* an essential amino acid; a component of proteins.

phenylketonuria (ˌfiːnaɪlˌkiːtəˈnjʊərɪə) *n.* a congenital metabolic disorder characterized by the abnormal accumulation of phenylalanine in the body fluids, resulting in mental deficiency. [C20: NL; see PHENYL, KETONE, -URIA]

pheromone (ˈfɛrəˌməʊn) *n.* a chemical substance, secreted externally by certain animals, such as insects, affecting the behaviour of other animals of the same species. [C20 *phero-,* < Gk *pherein* to bear + (HOR)MONE]

phew (fjuː) *interj.* an exclamation of relief, surprise, disbelief, weariness, etc.

phi (faɪ) *n., pl.* **phis.** the 21st letter in the Greek alphabet, Φ, ϕ.

phial (ˈfaɪəl) *n.* a small bottle for liquids, etc.; vial. [C14: < OF *fiole,* < L *phiola* saucer, < Gk *phialē* wide shallow vessel]

Phi Beta Kappa (ˈfaɪ ˈbeɪtə ˈkæpə, ˈbiːtə) *n.* (in the U.S.) **1.** a national honorary society, founded in 1776, membership of which is based on high academic ability. **2.** a member of this society. [< the initials of the Gk motto *philosophia biou kubernētēs* philosophy the guide of life]

phil. *abbrev. for:* **1.** philharmonic. **2.** philosophy.

Phil. *abbrev. for:* **1.** Philadelphia. **2.** *Bible.* Philippians. **3.** Philippines.

philadelphus (ˌfɪləˈdɛlfəs) *n.* any of a N temperate genus of shrubs cultivated for their strongly scented showy flowers. See also **mock orange** (sense 1). [C19: NL, < Gk *philadelphon* mock orange, lit.: loving one's brother]

philander (fɪˈlændə) *vb.* (*intr.;* often foll. by *with*) (of a man) to flirt with women. [C17: < Gk *philandros* fond of men, used as a name for a lover in literary works] **—phiˈlanderer** *n.*

philanthropic (ˌfɪlənˈθrɒpɪk) *or* **philanthropical** *adj.* showing concern for humanity, esp. by performing charitable actions, donating money, etc. **—ˌphilanˈthropically** *adv.*

philanthropy (fɪˈlænθrəpɪ) *n., pl.* **-pies.** **1.** the practice of performing charitable or benevolent actions. **2.** love of mankind in general. [C17: < LL *philanthrōpia,* < Gk: love of mankind, < *philos* loving + *anthrōpos* man] **—phiˈlanthropist** *or* **philanthrope** (ˈfɪlənˌθrəʊp) *n.*

philately (fɪˈlætəlɪ) *n.* the collection and study of postage stamps. [C19: < F *philatélie,* < PHILO- + Gk *ateleia* exemption from charges (here referring to stamps)] **—philatelic** (ˌfɪləˈtɛlɪk) *adj.* **—ˌphilaˈtelically** *adv.* **—phiˈlatelist** *n.*

-phile *or* **-phil** *n. combining form.* indicating a person or thing having a fondness for something specified: *bibliophile.* [< Gk *philos* loving]

Philem. *Bible. abbrev. for* Philemon.

philharmonic (ˌfɪlhɑːˈmɒnɪk, ˌfɪlə-) *adj.* **1.** fond of music. **2.** (*cap. when part of a name*) denoting an orchestra, choir, society, etc., devoted to music. *~n.* **3.** (*cap. when part of a name*) a specific philharmonic choir, orchestra, or society. [C18: < F *philharmonique,* < It. *filarmonico* music-loving]

philhellene (fɪlˈhɛliːn) *n.* **1.** a lover of Greece and Greek culture. **2.** *European history.* a supporter of the cause of Greek national independence. —**philhellenic** (ˌfɪlhɛˈliːnɪk) *adj.*

-philia *n. combining form.* **1.** indicating a tendency towards: *haemophilia.* **2.** indicating an abnormal liking for: *necrophilia.* [< Gk *philos* loving] —**-philiac** *n. combining form.* —**-philous** *or* **-philic** *adj. combining form.*

philibeg (ˈfɪlɪˌbɛg) *n.* a variant spelling of **filibeg.**

philippic (fɪˈlɪpɪk) *n.* a bitter or impassioned speech of denunciation; invective. [C16: after the orations of Demosthenes, 4th-century orator, against Philip of Macedon (382–336 B.C.)]

Philippine (ˈfɪlɪˌpiːn) *n., adj.* another word for **Filipino.**

Philistine (ˈfɪlɪˌstaɪn) *n.* **1.** a person who is hostile towards culture, the arts, etc.; a smug boorish person. **2.** a member of the non-Semitic people who inhabited ancient Philistia, a country on the coast of SW Palestine. *~adj.* **3.** (*sometimes not cap.*) boorishly uncultured. **4.** of or relating to the ancient Philistines. —**Philistinism** (ˈfɪlɪstɪˌnɪzəm) *n.*

phillumenist (fɪˈljuːmənɪst, -ˈluː-) *n.* a person who collects matchbox labels. [C20: < PHILO- + L *lumen* light + -IST]

philo- *or before a vowel* **phil-** *combining form.* indicating a love of: *philology; philanthropic.* [< Gk *philos* loving]

philodendron (ˌfɪləˈdɛndrən) *n., pl.* **-drons** *or* **-dra** (-drə). an evergreen climbing plant of a tropical American genus: cultivated as a house plant. [C19: NL < Gk: lover of trees]

philogyny (fɪˈlɒdʒɪnɪ) *n. Rare.* fondness for women. [C17: < Gk *philogunia,* < PHILO- + *gunē* woman] —**phiˈlogynist** *n.*

philology (fɪˈlɒlədʒɪ) *n.* (no longer in scholarly use) **1.** comparative and historical linguistics. **2.** the scientific analysis of written records and literary texts. **3.** the study of literature. [C17: < L *philologia,* < Gk: love of language] —**philological** (ˌfɪləˈlɒdʒɪkᵊl) *adj.* —ˌ**philoˈlogically** *adv.* —**phiˈlologist** *or* (*less commonly*) **phiˈlologer** *n.*

philomel (ˈfɪləˌmɛl) *or* **philomela** (ˌfɪləʊˈmiːlə) *n.* poetic names for a **nightingale.** [C14 *philomene,* via Med. L < L *philomēla,* < Gk]

philoprogenitive (ˌfɪləʊprəʊˈdʒɛnɪtɪv) *adj. Rare.* **1.** fond of children. **2.** producing many offspring.

philos. *abbrev. for:* **1.** philosopher. **2.** philosophical.

philosopher (fɪˈlɒsəfə) *n.* **1.** a student, teacher, or devotee of philosophy. **2.** a person of philosophical temperament, esp. one who is patient, wise, and stoical. **3.** (formerly) an alchemist or devotee of occult science.

philosopher's stone *n.* a stone or substance thought by alchemists to be capable of transmuting base metals into gold.

philosophical (ˌfɪləˈsɒfɪkᵊl) *or* **philosophic** *adj.* **1.** of or relating to philosophy or philosophers. **2.** reasonable, wise, or learned. **3.** calm and stoical, esp. in the face of difficulties or disappointments. —ˌ**philoˈsophically** *adv.*

philosophical analysis *n.* a philosophical method in which language and experience are analysed in an attempt to provide new insights into various philosophical problems.

philosophize *or* **-phise** (fɪˈlɒsəˌfaɪz) *vb.* **1.** (*intr.*) to make philosophical pronouncements and speculations. **2.** (*tr.*) to explain philosophically. —**phiˈlosoˌphizer** *or* **-ˌphiser** *n.*

philosophy (fɪˈlɒsəfɪ) *n., pl.* **-phies.** **1.** the academic discipline concerned with making explicit the nature and significance of ordinary and scientific beliefs and investigating the intelligibility of concepts by means of rational argument concerning their presuppositions, implications, and interrelationships. **2.** the particular doctrines relating to these issues of a specific individual or school: *the philosophy of Descartes.* **3.** the basic principles of a discipline: *the philosophy of law.* **4.** any system of belief, values, or tenets. **5.** a personal outlook or viewpoint. **6.** serenity of temper. [C13: < OF *filosofie,* < L *philosophia,* < Gk, < *philosophos* lover of wisdom]

-philous *or* **-philic** *adj. combining form.* indicating love of or fondness for: *heliophilous.* [< L *-philus,* < Gk *-philos*]

philtre *or U.S.* **philter** (ˈfɪltə) *n.* a drink supposed to arouse desire. [C16: < L *philtrum,* < Gk *philtron* love potion, < *philos* loving]

phimosis (faɪˈməʊsɪs) *n.* abnormal tightness of the foreskin, preventing its being retracted. [C17: via NL < Gk: a muzzling]

phiz (fɪz) *n. Sl., chiefly Brit.* the face or a facial expression. Also called: **phizog** (fɪˈzɒg). [C17: colloquial shortening of PHYSIOGNOMY]

phlebitis (flɪˈbaɪtɪs) *n.* inflammation of a vein. [C19: via NL < Gk] —**phlebitic** (flɪˈbɪtɪk) *adj.*

phlebo- *or before a vowel* **phleb-** *combining form.* indicating a vein: *phlebotomy.* [< Gk *phleps, phleb-* vein]

phlebotomy (flɪˈbɒtəmɪ) *n., pl.* **-mies.** surgical incision into a vein. [C14: < OF *flebothomie,* < LL *phlebotomia,* < Gk]

phlegm (flɛm) *n.* **1.** the viscid mucus secreted by the walls of the respiratory tract. **2.** *Arch.* one of the four bodily humours. **3.** apathy; stolidity. **4.** imperturbability; coolness. [C14: < OF *fleume,* < LL *phlegma,* < Gk: inflammation, < *phlegein* to burn] —ˈ**phlegmy** *adj.*

phlegmatic (flɛgˈmætɪk) *or* **phlegmatical** *adj.* **1.** having a stolid or unemotional disposition. **2.** not easily excited. —**phlegˈmatically** *adv.*

phloem (ˈfləʊɛm) *n.* tissue in higher plants that conducts synthesized food substances to all parts of the plant. [C19: via G < Gk *phloos* bark]

phlogiston (flɒˈdʒɪstɒn, -tən) *n. Chem.* a hypothetical substance formerly thought to be present in all combustible materials. [C18: via NL < Gk, < *phlogizein* to set alight]

phlox (flɒks) *n., pl.* **phlox** *or* **phloxes.** any of a chiefly North American genus of plants cultivated for their clusters of white, red, or purple flowers. [C18: via L < Gk: a plant of glowing colour, lit.: flame]

phlyctena (flɪkˈtiːnə) *n., pl.* **-nae** (-niː). *Pathol.* a small blister, vesicle, or pustule. [C17: via NL < Gk *phluktaina,* < *phluzein* to swell]

-phobe *n. combining form.* indicating one that fears or hates: *xenophobe.* [< Gk *-phobos* fearing] —**-phobic** *adj. combining form.*

phobia (ˈfəʊbɪə) *n. Psychiatry.* an abnormal intense and irrational fear of a given situation, organism, or object. [C19: < Gk *phobos* fear] —ˈ**phobic** *adj., n.*

-phobia *n. combining form.* indicating an extreme abnormal fear of or aversion to: *acrophobia; claustrophobia.* [via L < Gk, < *phobos* fear] —**-phobic** *adj. combining form.*

phocomelia (ˌfəʊkəʊˈmiːlɪə) *n.* a congenital deformity characterized esp. by short stubby hands or feet attached close to the body. [C19: via NL < Gk *phōkē* a seal + *melos* a limb]

phoebe (ˈfiːbɪ) *n.* any of several greyish-brown North American flycatchers. [C19: imit.]

Phoenician (fəˈnɪʃɪən, -ˈniːʃən) *n.* **1.** a member of an ancient Semitic people of NW Syria. **2.** the extinct language of this people. *~adj.* **3.** of Phoenicia, an ancient E Mediterranean maritime country, the Phoenicians, or their language.

phoenix *or U.S.* **phenix** (ˈfiːnɪks) *n.* **1.** a legendary Arabian bird said to set fire to itself and rise anew from the ashes every 500 years. **2.** a person or thing of surpassing beauty or quality. [OE *fenix,* via L < Gk *phoinix*]

phon (fɒn) *n.* a unit of loudness that measures the intensity of a sound by the number of decibels it is above a reference tone. [C20: via G < Gk *phōnē* sound]

phonate (fəʊˈneɪt) *vb.* (*intr.*) to articulate speech sounds, esp. voiced speech sounds. [C19: < Gk *phōnē* voice] —**phoˈnation** *n.*

phone[1] (fəʊn) *n., vb.* short for **telephone.**

phone[2] (fəʊn) *n. Phonetics.* a single speech sound. [C19: < Gk *phōnē* sound, voice]

-phone *combining form.* **1.** (*forming nouns*) indicating a device giving off sound: *telephone.* **2.** (*forming nouns and adjectives*) (a person) speaking a particular language: *Francophone.* [< Gk *phōnē* voice, sound] —**-phonic** *adj. combining form.*

phonecard (ˈfəʊnˌkɑːd) *n.* **1.** a public telephone that is operated by a special card instead of coins. **2.** the card used.

phone-in *n.* **a.** a radio or television programme in which listeners' or viewers' questions, comments, etc., are telephoned to the studio and broadcast live as part of a discussion. **b.** (*as modifier*): *a phone-in programme.*

phoneme (ˈfəʊniːm) *n. Linguistics.* one of the set of speech sounds in any given language that serve to distinguish one word from another. [C20: via F < Gk *phōnēma* sound, speech] —**phonemic** (fəˈniːmɪk) *adj.*

phonemics (fəˈniːmɪks) *n.* (*functioning as sing.*) that aspect of linguistics concerned with the classification and analysis of the phonemes of a language. —**phoˈnemicist** *n.*

phonetic (fəˈnɛtɪk) *adj.* **1.** of or relating to phonetics. **2.** denoting any perceptible distinction between one speech sound and another. **3.** conforming to pronunciation: *phonetic spelling.* [C19: < NL *phōnēticus,* < Gk, < *phōnein* to make sounds, speak] —**phoˈnetically** *adv.*

phonetics (fəˈnɛtɪks) *n.* (*functioning as sing.*) the science concerned with the study of speech processes, including the production, perception, and analysis of speech sounds. —**phonetician** (ˌfəʊnɪˈtɪʃən) *or* **phonetist** (ˈfəʊnɪtɪst) *n.*

phoney *or esp. U.S.* **phony** (ˈfəʊnɪ) *Inf.* ~*adj.* **-nier, -niest. 1.** not genuine; fake. **2.** (of a person) insincere or pretentious. ~*n., pl.* **-neys** *or esp. U.S.* **-nies. 3.** an insincere or pretentious person. **4.** something that is not genuine; a fake. [C20: <?] —**ˈphoneyness** *or esp. U.S.* **ˈphoniness** *n.*

phonics (ˈfɒnɪks) *n.* (*functioning as sing.*) **1.** an obsolete name for **acoustics** (sense 1). **2.** a method of teaching people to read by training them to associate letters with their phonetic values. —**ˈphonic** *adj.* —**ˈphonically** *adv.*

phono- *or before a vowel* **phon-** *combining form.* indicating a sound or voice: *phonograph; phonology.* [< Gk *phōnē* sound, voice]

phonogram (ˈfəʊnəˌgræm) *n.* any written symbol standing for a sound, syllable, morpheme, or word. —ˌ**phonoˈgramic** *or* ˌ**phonoˈgrammic** *adj.*

phonograph (ˈfəʊnəˌgrɑːf) *n.* **1.** an early form of gramophone capable of recording and reproducing sound on wax cylinders. **2.** another U.S. and Canad. word for **gramophone** or **record player.**

phonography (fəʊˈnɒgrəfɪ) *n.* **1.** a writing system that represents sounds by individual symbols. **2.** the employment of such a writing system. —**phonographic** (ˌfəʊnəˈgræfɪk) *adj.*

phonology (fəˈnɒlədʒɪ) *n., pl.* **-gies. 1.** the study of the sound system of a language or of languages in general. **2.** such a sound system. —**phonological** (ˌfəʊnəˈlɒdʒɪkəl, ˌfɒn-) *adj.* —ˌ**phonoˈlogically** *adv.* —**phoˈnologist** *n.*

phonon (ˈfəʊnɒn) *n. Physics.* a quantum of vibrational energy in the acoustic vibrations of a crystal lattice. [C20: < PHONO- + -ON]

-phony *n. combining form.* indicating a specified type of sound: *cacophony; euphony.* [< Gk *-phōnia,* < *phōnē* sound] —**-phonic** *adj. combining form.*

phooey (ˈfuːɪ) *interj. Inf.* an exclamation of scorn, contempt, etc. [C20: prob. var. of PHEW]

-phore *n. combining form.* indicating one that bears or produces: *semaphore.* [< NL *-phorus,* < Gk *-phoros* bearing, < *pherein* to bear] —**-phorous** *adj. combining form.*

-phoresis *n. combining form.* indicating a transmission: *electrophoresis.* [< Gk *phorēsis* being carried, < *pherein* to bear]

phormium (ˈfɔːmɪəm) *n.* any of a genus of plants of the lily family with tough leathery evergreen leaves. Also called: **New Zealand flax, flax lily.** [C19: NL < Gk *phormos* basket]

phosgene (ˈfɒzdʒiːn) *n.* a colourless poisonous gas: used in chemical warfare and in the manufacture of pesticides, dyes, and polyurethane resins. [C19: < Gk *phos* light + *-gene,* var. of -GEN]

phosphate (ˈfɒsfeɪt) *n.* **1.** any salt or ester of any phosphoric acid. **2.** (*often pl.*) any of several chemical fertilizers containing phosphorous compounds. [C18: < F *phosphat;* see PHOSPHORUS, -ATE[1]] —**phosphatic** (fɒsˈfætɪk) *adj.*

phosphatide (ˈfɒsfəˌtaɪd) *n.* another name for **phospholipid.**

phosphene (ˈfɒsfiːn) *n.* the sensation of light caused by pressure on the eyelid of a closed eye. [C19: < Gk *phos* light + *phainein* to show]

phosphide (ˈfɒsfaɪd) *n.* any compound of phosphorus with another element, esp. a more electropositive element.

phosphine (ˈfɒsfiːn) *n.* a colourless inflammable gas that is slightly soluble in water and has a strong fishy odour: used as a pesticide.

phosphite (ˈfɒsfaɪt) *n.* any salt or ester of phosphorous acid.

phospho- *or before a vowel* **phosph-** *combining form.* containing phosphorus: *phosphoric.* [< F, < *phosphore* PHOSPHORUS]

phospholipid (ˌfɒsfəˈlɪpɪd) *n.* any of a group of fatty compounds: important constituents of all membranes. Also called: **phosphatide.**

phosphor (ˈfɒsfə) *n.* a substance capable of emitting light when irradiated with particles of electromagnetic radiation. [C17: < F, ult. < Gk *phōsphoros* PHOSPHORUS]

phosphorate (ˈfɒsfəˌreɪt) *vb.* to treat or combine with phosphorus.

phosphor bronze *n.* any of various hard corrosion-resistant alloys containing phosphorus: used in gears, bearings, cylinder casings, etc.

phosphoresce (ˌfɒsfəˈrɛs) *vb.* (*intr.*) to exhibit phosphorescence.

phosphorescence (ˌfɒsfəˈrɛsəns) *n.* **1.** *Physics.* a fluorescence that persists after the bombarding radiation producing it has stopped. **2.** the light emitted in phosphorescence. **3.** the emission of light in which insufficient heat is evolved to cause fluorescence. Cf. **fluorescence.** —ˌ**phosphoˈrescent** *adj.*

phosphoric (fɒsˈfɒrɪk) *adj.* of or containing phosphorus in the pentavalent state.

phosphoric acid *n.* **1.** Also called: **orthophosphoric acid.** a colourless solid tribasic acid used in the manufacture of fertilizers and soap. **2.** any oxyacid of phosphorus produced by reaction between phosphorus pentoxide and water.

phosphorous (ˈfɒsfərəs) *adj.* of or containing phosphorus in the trivalent state.

phosphorous acid *n.* **1.** Also called: **orthophosphorous acid.** a white or yellowish hygroscopic crystalline dibasic acid. **2.** any oxyacid of phosphorus containing less oxygen than the corresponding phosphoric acid.

phosphorus (ˈfɒsfərəs) *n.* **1.** an allotropic nonmetallic element occurring in phosphates and living matter. Ordinary phosphorus is a toxic flammable phosphorescent white solid; the red form is less reactive and nontoxic: used in matches, pesticides, and alloys. The radioisotope **phosphorus-32** (**radiophosphorus**), with a half-life of 14.3 days, is used in radiotherapy and as a tracer. Symbol: P; atomic no.: 15; atomic wt.: 30.974. **2.** a less common name for a **phosphor.** [C17: via L < Gk *phōsphoros* light-bringing, < *phōs* light + *pherein* to bring]

Phosphorus (ˈfɒsfərəs) *n.* a morning star, esp. Venus.

phossy jaw (ˈfɒsɪ) *n.* a gangrenous condition of the lower jawbone caused by prolonged exposure to phosphorus fumes. [C19: *phossy,* colloquial shortening of PHOSPHORUS]

phot (fɒt, fəʊt) *n.* a unit of illumination equal to one lumen per square centimetre. 1 phot is equal to 10 000 lux. [C20: < Gk *phōs* light]

phot. *abbrev. for:* **1.** photograph. **2.** photographic. **3.** photography.

photic (ˈfəʊtɪk) *adj.* **1.** of or concerned with light. **2.** designating the zone of the sea where photosynthesis takes place.

photo (ˈfəʊtəʊ) *n., pl.* **-tos.** short for **photograph.**

photo- *combining form.* **1.** of, relating to, or produced by light: *photosynthesis.* **2.** indicating a photographic process: *photolithography.* [< Gk *phōs, phōt-* light]

photo call *n.* a time arranged for photographers, esp. press photographers, to take pictures of a celebrity.

photocell (ˈfəʊtəʊˌsɛl) *n.* a device in which the photoelectric or photovoltaic effect or photoconductivity is used to produce a current or voltage when exposed to light or other electromagnetic radiation. They are used in exposure meters, burglar alarms, etc. Also called: **photoelectric cell, electric eye.**

photochemistry (ˌfəʊtəʊˈkɛmɪstrɪ) *n.* the branch of chemistry concerned with the chemical effects of light and other electromagnetic radiations. —**photochemical** (ˌfəʊtəʊˈkɛmɪkᵊl) *adj.*

photocomposition (ˌfəʊtəʊˌkɒmpəˈzɪʃən) *n.* another name (esp. U.S. and Canad.) for **filmsetting.**

photoconductivity (ˌfəʊtəʊˌkɒndʌkˈtɪvɪtɪ) *n.* the change in the electrical conductivity of certain substances, such as selenium, as a result of the absorption of electromagnetic radiation. —**photoconductive** (ˌfəʊtəʊkənˈdʌktɪv) *adj.* —ˌ**photoconˈductor** *n.*

photocopier (ˈfəʊtəʊˌkɒpɪə) *n.* an instrument using light-sensitive photographic materials to reproduce written, printed, or graphic work.

photocopy (ˈfəʊtəʊˌkɒpɪ) *n., pl.* **-copies. 1.** a photographic reproduction of written, printed, or graphic work. ~*vb.* **-copying, -copied. 2.** to reproduce (written, printed, or graphic work) on photographic material.

photoelectric (ˌfəʊtəʊɪˈlɛktrɪk) *adj.* of or concerned with electric or electronic effects caused by light or other electromagnetic radiation. —**photoelectricity** (ˌfəʊtəʊɪlɛkˈtrɪsɪtɪ) *n.*

photoelectric cell *n.* another name for **photocell.**

photoelectric effect *n.* **1.** the ejection of electrons from a solid by an incident beam of sufficiently energetic electromagnetic radiation. **2.** any phenomenon involving electricity and electromagnetic radiation, such as photoemission.

photoelectron (ˌfəʊtəʊɪˈlɛktrɒn) *n.* an electron ejected from an atom, molecule, or solid by an incident photon.

photoemission (ˌfəʊtəʊɪˈmɪʃən) *n.* the emission of electrons due to the impact of electromagnetic radiation.

photoengraving (ˌfəʊtəʊɪnˈgreɪvɪŋ) *n.* **1.** a photomechanical process for producing letterpress printing plates. **2.** a plate made by this process. **3.** a print made from such a plate. —ˌ**photoenˈgrave** *vb. (tr.)*

photo finish *n.* **1.** a finish of a race in which contestants are so close that a photograph is needed to decide the result. **2.** any race or competition in which the winners are separated by a very small margin.

Photofit (ˈfəʊtəʊˌfɪt) *n. Trademark.* **a.** a method of combining photographs of facial features, hair, etc., into a composite picture of a face: used by the police to trace suspects, criminals, etc. **b.** (*as modifier*): *a Photofit picture.*

photoflash (ˈfəʊtəʊˌflæʃ) *n.* another name for **flashbulb.**

photoflood (ˈfəʊtəʊˌflʌd) *n.* a highly incandescent tungsten lamp used for indoor photography, television, etc.

photog. *abbrev. for:* **1.** photograph. **2.** photographer. **3.** photographic. **4.** photography.

photogenic (ˌfəʊtəˈdʒɛnɪk) *adj.* **1.** (esp. of a person) having a general facial appearance that looks attractive in photographs. **2.** *Biol.* producing or emitting light. —ˌ**photoˈgenically** *adv.*

photogram (ˈfəʊtəˌgræm) *n.* **1.** a picture, usually abstract, produced on a photographic material without the use of a camera. **2.** *Obs.* a photograph.

photogrammetry (ˌfəʊtəʊˈgræmɪtrɪ) *n.* the process of making measurements from photographs, used esp. in the construction of maps from aerial photographs.

photograph (ˈfəʊtəˌgrɑːf) *n.* **1.** an image of an object, person, scene, etc., in the form of a print or slide recorded by a camera. Often shortened to **photo.** ~*vb.* **2.** to take a photograph of (an object, person, scene, etc.).

photographic (ˌfəʊtəˈgræfɪk) *adj.* **1.** of or relating to photography. **2.** like a photograph in accuracy or detail. **3.** (of a person's memory) able to retain facts, appearances, etc., in precise detail. —ˌ**photoˈgraphically** *adv.*

photography (fəˈtɒgrəfɪ) *n.* **1.** the process of recording images on sensitized material by the action of light, x-rays, etc. **2.** the art, practice, or occupation of taking photographs. —**phoˈtographer** *n.*

photogravure (ˌfəʊtəʊgrəˈvjʊə) *n.* **1.** any of various methods in which an intaglio plate for printing is produced by the use of photography. **2.** matter printed from such a plate. [C19: < PHOTO- + F *gravure* engraving]

photojournalism (ˌfəʊtəʊˈdʒɜːnᵊˌlɪzəm) *n.* journalism in which photographs are the predominant feature. —ˌ**photoˈjournalist** *n.*

photokinesis (ˌfəʊtəʊkɪˈniːsɪs, -kaɪ-) *n. Biol.* the movement of an organism in response to the stimulus of light.

photolithography (ˌfəʊtəʊlɪˈθɒgrəfɪ) *n.* **1.** a lithographic printing process using photographically made plates. Often shortened to **photolitho. 2.** *Electronics.* a process used in the manufacture of semiconductor devices and printed circuits in which a particular pattern is transferred from a photograph onto a substrate. —ˌ**photoliˈthographer** *n.*

photoluminescence (ˌfəʊtəʊˌluːmɪˈnɛsəns) *n.* luminescence resulting from the absorption of light or infrared or ultraviolet radiation.

photolysis (fəʊˈtɒlɪsɪs) *n.* chemical decomposition caused by light or other electromagnetic radiation. —**photolytic** (ˌfəʊtəʊˈlɪtɪk) *adj.*

photomechanical (ˌfəʊtəʊmɪˈkænɪkᵊl) *adj.* of or relating to any of various methods by which printing plates are made using photography. —ˌ**photomeˈchanically** *adv.*

photometer (fəʊˈtɒmɪtə) *n.* an instrument used in photometry, usually one that compares the illumination produced by a particular light source with that produced by a standard source.

photometry (fəʊˈtɒmɪtrɪ) *n.* **1.** the measurement of the intensity of light. **2.** the branch of physics concerned with such measurements. —**phoˈtometrist** *n.*

photomicrograph (ˌfəʊtəʊˈmaɪkrəˌgrɑːf) *n.* a photograph of a microscope image. —**photomicrography** (ˌfəʊtəʊmaɪˈkrɒgrəfɪ) *n.*

photomontage (ˌfəʊtəʊmɒnˈtɑːʒ) *n.* **1.** the technique of producing a composite picture by combining several photographs. **2.** the composite picture so produced.

photomultiplier (ˌfəʊtəʊˈmʌltɪˌplaɪə) *n.* a device sensitive to electromagnetic radiation which produces a detectable pulse of current.

photon (ˈfəʊtɒn) *n.* a quantum of electromagnetic radiation with energy equal to the product of the frequency of the radiation and the Planck constant.

photo-offset *n. Printing.* an offset process in which the plates are produced photomechanically.

photoperiodism (ˌfəʊtəʊˈpɪərɪəˌdɪzəm) *n.* the response of plants and animals by behaviour, growth, etc., to the period of daylight in every 24 hours (**photoperiod**). —ˌ**photoˌperiˈodic** *adj.*

photophobia (ˌfəʊtəʊˈfəʊbɪə) *n.* **1.** *Pathol.* abnormal sensitivity of the eyes to light. **2.**

Psychiatry. abnormal fear of sunlight or well-lit places. —ˌ**photo'phobic** *adj.*

photopolymer (ˌfəʊtəʊ'pɒlɪmə) *n.* a polymeric material that is sensitive to light: used in printing plates, microfilms, etc.

photoreceptor (ˌfəʊtəʊrɪ'sɛptə) *n. Zool., physiol.* a light-sensitive cell or organ that conveys impulses through the sensory neuron connected to it.

photosensitive (ˌfəʊtəʊ'sɛnsɪtɪv) *adj.* sensitive to electromagnetic radiation, esp. light. —ˌ**photoˌsensi'tivity** *n.* —ˌ**photo'sensitize** *or* **-tise** *vb.* (*tr.*)

photoset ('fəʊtəʊˌsɛt) *vb.* **-setting, -set.** another word for **filmset.** —'**photoˌsetter** *n.*

photosphere ('fəʊtəʊˌsfɪə) *n.* the visible surface of the sun. —**photospheric** (ˌfəʊtəʊ'sfɛrɪk) *adj.*

Photostat ('fəʊtəʊˌstæt) *n.* **1.** *Trademark.* a machine or process used to make photographic copies of written, printed, or graphic matter. **2.** any copy made by such a machine. ~*vb.* **statting** *or* **stating, statted** *or* **stated.** **3.** to make a Photostat copy (of). —ˌ**photo'static** *adj.*

photosynthesis (ˌfəʊtəʊ'sɪnθɪsɪs) *n.* (in plants) the synthesis of organic compounds from carbon dioxide and water using light energy absorbed by chlorophyll. —ˌ**photo'synthesize** *or* **-sise** *vb.* —**photosynthetic** (ˌfəʊtəʊsɪn'θɛtɪk) *adj.* —ˌ**photosyn'thetically** *adv.*

phototaxis (ˌfəʊtəʊ'tæksɪs) *n.* the movement of an entire organism in response to light.

phototropism (ˌfəʊtəʊ'trəʊpɪzəm) *n.* the growth response of plant parts to the stimulus of light, producing a bending towards the light source. —ˌ**photo'tropic** *adj.*

photovoltaic effect (ˌfəʊtəʊvɒl'teɪɪk) *n.* the effect when electromagnetic radiation falls on a thin film of one solid deposited on the surface of a dissimilar solid producing a difference in potential between the two materials.

phrasal verb *n.* a phrase that consists of a verb plus an adverbial or prepositional particle, esp. one the meaning of which cannot be deduced from the constituents: *"take in" meaning "deceive" is a phrasal verb.*

phrase (freɪz) *n.* **1.** a group of words forming a syntactic constituent of a sentence. Cf. **clause** (sense 1). **2.** an idiomatic or original expression. **3.** manner or style of speech or expression. **4.** *Music.* a small group of notes forming a coherent unit of melody. ~*vb.* (*tr.*) **5.** *Music.* to divide (a melodic line, part, etc.) into musical phrases, esp. in performance. **6.** to express orally or in a phrase. [C16: < L *phrasis,* < Gk: speech, < *phrazein* to tell] —'**phrasal** *adj.*

phrase book *n.* a book containing frequently used expressions and their equivalents in a foreign language.

phrase marker *n. Linguistics.* a representation, esp. a tree diagram, of the constituent structure of a sentence.

phraseogram ('freɪzɪəˌgræm) *n.* a symbol representing a phrase, as in shorthand.

phraseology (ˌfreɪzɪ'ɒlədʒɪ) *n., pl.* **-gies.** **1.** the manner in which words or phrases are used. **2.** a set of phrases used by a particular group of people. —**phraseological** (ˌfreɪzɪə'lɒdʒɪkᵊl) *adj.*

phrasing ('freɪzɪŋ) *n.* **1.** the way in which something is expressed, esp. in writing; wording. **2.** *Music.* the division of a melodic line, part, etc., into musical phrases.

phrenetic (frɪ'nɛtɪk) *adj.* an obsolete spelling of **frenetic.** —**phre'netically** *adv.*

phrenic ('frɛnɪk) *adj.* **1. a.** of or relating to the diaphragm. **b.** (*as n.*): *the phrenic.* **2.** *Obs.* of or relating to the mind. [C18: < NL *phrenicus,* < Gk *phrēn* mind, diaphragm]

phrenology (frɪ'nɒlədʒɪ) *n.* (formerly) the branch of science concerned with determination of the strength of the faculties by the shape and size of the skull overlying the parts of the brain thought to be responsible for them. —**phrenological** (ˌfrɛnə'lɒdʒɪkᵊl) *adj.* —**phre'nologist** *n.*

phrensy ('frɛnzɪ) *n., pl.* **-sies** an obsolete spelling of **frenzy.**

Phrygian ('frɪdʒɪən) *adj.* **1.** of or relating to ancient Phrygia, a country of W central Asia Minor, its inhabitants, or their extinct language. **2.** *Music.* of or relating to an authentic mode represented by the natural diatonic scale from E to E. ~*n.* **3.** a native or inhabitant of ancient Phrygia. **4.** an ancient language of Phrygia.

Phrygian cap *n.* a conical cap of soft material worn during ancient times, that became a symbol of liberty during the French Revolution.

phthisis ('θaɪsɪs, 'fθaɪ-, 'taɪ-) *n.* any disease that causes wasting of the body, esp. pulmonary tuberculosis. [C16: via L < Gk, < *phthinein* to waste away]

phut (fʌt) *Inf.* ~*n.* **1.** a representation of a muffled explosive sound. ~*adv.* **2. go phut.** to break down or collapse. [C19: imit.]

phycomycete (ˌfaɪkəʊ'maɪsiːt) *n.* any of a class of filamentous fungi: includes certain mildews and moulds. [< Gk *phukos* seaweed + -MYCETE]

phyla ('faɪlə) *n.* the plural of **phylum.**

phylactery (fɪ'læktərɪ) *n., pl.* **-teries.** **1.** *Judaism.* either of the pair of blackened square cases containing parchments inscribed with biblical passages, bound by leather thongs to the head and left arm, and worn by Jewish men during weekday morning prayers. **2.** a reminder. **3.** *Arch.* an amulet or charm. [C14: < LL *phylactērium,* < Gk *phulaktērion* outpost, < *phulax* a guard]

phyletic (faɪ'lɛtɪk) *adj.* of or relating to the evolutionary development of organisms. [C19: < Gk *phuletikos* tribal]

-phyll *or* **-phyl** *n. combining form.* leaf: *chlorophyll.* [< Gk *phullon*]

phyllo- *or before a vowel* **phyll-** *combining form.* leaf: *phyllopod.* [< Gk *phullon* leaf]

phyllode ('fɪləʊd) *n.* a flattened leafstalk that resembles and functions as a leaf. [C19: < NL *phyllodium,* < Gk *phullōdēs* leaflike]

phylloquinone (ˌfɪləʊkwɪ'nəʊn) *n.* a viscous fat-soluble liquid occurring in plants: essential for the production of prothrombin, required in blood clotting. Also called: **vitamin K_1.**

phyllotaxis (ˌfɪlə'tæksɪs) *or* **phyllotaxy** *n., pl.* **-taxes** (-'tæksiːz) *or* **-taxies.** **1.** the arrangement of the leaves on a stem. **2.** the study of this arrangement. —ˌ**phyllo'tactic** *adj.*

-phyllous *adj. combining form.* having leaves of a specified number or type: *monophyllous.* [< Gk *-phullos* of a leaf]

phylloxera (ˌfɪlɒk'sɪərə, fɪ'lɒksərə) *n., pl.* **-rae** (-riː) *or* **-ras.** any of a genus of homopterous insects, such as vine phylloxera, typically feeding on plant juices. [C19: NL, < PHYLLO- + *xēros* dry]

phylo- *or before a vowel* **phyl-** *combining form.* tribe; race; phylum: *phylogeny.* [< Gk *phulon* race]

phylogeny (faɪ'lɒdʒɪnɪ) *or* **phylogenesis** (ˌfaɪləʊ'dʒɛnɪsɪs) *n., pl.* **-nies** *or* **-geneses** (-'dʒɛnɪˌsiːz). *Biol.* the sequence of events involved in the evolution of a species, genus, etc. Cf. **ontogeny.** [C19: < PHYLO- + -GENY] —**phylogenic** (ˌfaɪləʊ'dʒɛnɪk) *or* **phylogenetic** (ˌfaɪləʊdʒɪ'nɛtɪk) *adj.*

phylum ('faɪləm) *n., pl.* **-la.** **1.** a major taxonomic division of the animals and plants that contain one or more classes. **2.** a group of related language families or linguistic stocks. [C19: NL, < Gk *phulon* race]

phys. *abbrev. for:* **1.** physical. **2.** physician. **3.** physics. **4.** physiological. **5.** physiology.

physalis (faɪ'seɪlɪs) *n.* any of a genus of plants producing inflated orange seed vessels. See **Chinese lantern.** [NL < Gk *physallis* bladder]

physic ('fɪzɪk) *n.* **1.** *Rare.* a medicine, esp. a cathartic. **2.** *Arch.* the art or skill of healing. ~*vb.* **-icking, -icked.** (*tr.*) **3.** *Arch.* to treat (a patient) with medicine. [C13: < OF *fisique,* via L, < Gk *phusikē,* < *phusis* nature]

physical ('fɪzɪkᵊl) *adj.* **1.** of or relating to the body, as distinguished from the mind or spirit. **2.** of, relating to, or resembling material things or nature: *the physical universe.* **3.** of or concerned with matter and energy. **4.** of or relating to physics. —'**physically** *adv.*

physical anthropology *n.* the branch of anthropology dealing with the genetic aspect of human development and its physical variations.

physical chemistry *n.* the branch of chemistry concerned with the way in which the physical properties of substances depend on their chemical structure, properties, and reactions.

physical education *n.* training and practice in sports, gymnastics, etc. Abbrev.: **PE.**

physical geography *n.* the branch of geography that deals with the natural features of the earth's surface.

physical jerks *pl. n. Brit. inf.* See **jerk**[1] (sense 6).

physical science *n.* any of the sciences concerned with nonliving matter, such as physics, chemistry, astronomy, and geology.

physical therapy *n.* another term for **physiotherapy.**

physician (fɪˈzɪʃən) *n.* **1.** a person legally qualified to practise medicine, esp. other than surgery; doctor of medicine. **2.** *Arch.* any person who treats diseases; healer. [C13: < OF *fisicien,* < *fisique* PHYSIC]

physicist (ˈfɪzɪsɪst) *n.* a person versed in or studying physics.

physics (ˈfɪzɪks) *n.* (*functioning as sing.*) **1.** the branch of science concerned with the properties of matter and energy and the relationships between them. It is based on mathematics and traditionally includes mechanics, optics, electricity and magnetism, acoustics, and heat. Modern physics, based on quantum theory, includes atomic, nuclear, particle, and solid-state studies. **2.** physical properties of behaviour: *the physics of the electron.* **3.** *Arch.* natural science. [C16: < L *physica,* translation of Gk *ta phusika* natural things, < *phusis* nature]

physio- *or before a vowel* **phys-** *combining form.* **1.** of or relating to nature or natural functions: *physiology.* **2.** physical: *physiotherapy.* [< Gk *phusio,* ult. < *phuein* to make grow]

physiocrat (ˈfɪzɪəʊˌkræt) *n.* a believer in the 18th-century French economic theory that the inherent natural order governing society was based on land and its natural products as the only true form of wealth. [C18: < F *physiocrate;* see PHYSIO-, -CRAT] —**physiocracy** (ˌfɪzɪˈɒkrəsɪ) *n.*

physiognomy (ˌfɪzɪˈɒnəmɪ) *n.* **1.** a person's features considered as an indication of personality. **2.** the art or practice of judging character from facial features. **3.** the outward appearance of something. [C14: < OF *phisonomie,* via Med. L, < LGk *phusiognōmia,* < *phusis* nature + *gnōmōn* judge] —**physiognomic** (ˌfɪzɪəˈnɒmɪk) *or* **ˌphysiogˈnomical** *adj.* —**ˌphysiogˈnomically** *adv.* —**ˌphysiˈognomist** *n.*

physiography (ˌfɪzɪˈɒgrəfɪ) *n.* another name for **geomorphology** or **physical geography.** —**ˌphysiˈographer** *n.* —**physiographic** (ˌfɪzɪəˈgræfɪk) *or* **ˌphysioˈgraphical** *adj.*

physiol. *abbrev. for:* **1.** physiological. **2.** physiology.

physiology (ˌfɪzɪˈɒlədʒɪ) *n.* **1.** the branch of science concerned with the functioning of organisms. **2.** the processes and functions of all or part of an organism. [C16: < L *physiologia,* < Gk] —**ˌphysiˈologist** *n.* —**physiological** (ˌfɪzɪəˈlɒdʒɪkəl) *adj.* —**ˌphysioˈlogically** *adv.*

physiotherapy (ˌfɪzɪəʊˈθɛrəpɪ) *n.* the treatment of disease, injury, etc., by physical means, such as massage or exercises, rather than by drugs. —**ˌphysioˈtherapist** *n.*

physique (fɪˈziːk) *n.* the general appearance of the body with regard to size, shape, muscular development, etc. [C19: via F < *physique* (adj.) natural, < L *physicus* physical]

-phyte *n. combining form.* indicating a plant of a specified type or habitat: *lithophyte.* [< Gk *phuton* plant] —**-phytic** *adj. combining form.*

phyto- *or before a vowel* **phyt-** *combining form.* indicating a plant or vegetation: *phytogenesis.* [< Gk *phuton* plant, < *phuein* to make grow]

phytogenesis (ˌfaɪtəʊˈdʒɛnɪsɪs) *or* **phytogeny** (faɪˈtɒdʒənɪ) *n.* the branch of botany concerned with the origin and evolution of plants.

phyton (ˈfaɪtɒn) *n.* a unit of plant structure, usually considered as the smallest part of the plant that is capable of growth when detached from the parent plant. [C20: < Gk; see -PHYTE]

phytopathology (ˌfaɪtəʊpəˈθɒlədʒɪ) *n.* the branch of botany concerned with diseases of plants.

phytoplankton (ˌfaɪtəˈplæŋktən) *n.* the plant constituent of plankton, mainly unicellular algae.

phytotoxin (ˌfaɪtəˈtɒksɪn) *n.* a toxin, such as strychnine, that is produced by a plant.

pi[1] (paɪ) *n., pl.* **pis. 1.** the 16th letter in the Greek alphabet (Π, π). **2.** *Maths.* a transcendental number, fundamental to mathematics, that is the ratio of the circumference of a circle to its diameter. Approximate value: 3.141 592... ; symbol: π [C18 (mathematical use): representing the first letter of Gk *periphereia* PERIPHERY]

pi[2] *or* **pie** (paɪ) *n., pl.* **pies. 1.** a jumbled pile of printer's type. **2.** a jumbled mixture. ~*vb.* **piing, pied** *or* **pieing, pied.** (*tr.*) **3.** to spill and mix (set type) indiscriminately. **4.** to mix up. [C17: <?]

pi[3] (paɪ) *adj. Brit. sl.* See **pious** (senses 2, 3).

piacevole (piːætʃˈeɪvəʊleɪ) *adv. Music.* in an agreeable, pleasant manner. [It.]

piacular (paɪˈækjʊlə) *adj.* **1.** making expiation. **2.** requiring expiation. [C17: < L *piāculum* propitiatory sacrifice, < *piāre* to appease]

piaffe (pɪˈæf) *n. Dressage.* a slow trot done on the spot. [C18: < F, < *piaffer* to strut]

pia mater (ˈpaɪə ˈmeɪtə) *n.* the innermost of the three membranes (see **meninges**) that cover the brain and spinal cord. [C16: < Med. L, lit.: pious mother]

pianism (ˈpiːəˌnɪzəm) *n.* technique, skill, or artistry in playing the piano. —**ˌpiaˈnistic** *adj.*

pianissimo (pɪəˈnɪsɪˌməʊ) *adj., adv. Music.* to be performed very quietly. Symbol: *pp* [C18: < It., sup. of *piano* soft]

pianist (ˈpɪənɪst) *n.* a person who plays the piano.

piano[1] (pɪˈænəʊ) *n., pl.* **-anos.** a musical stringed instrument played by depressing keys that cause hammers to strike the strings and produce audible vibrations. [C19: short for PIANOFORTE]

piano[2] (ˈpjɑːnəʊ) *adj., adv. Music.* to be performed softly. [C17: < It., < L *plānus* flat]

piano accordion (pɪˈænəʊ) *n.* an accordion in which the right hand plays a piano-like keyboard. See **accordion.** —**piano accordionist** *n.*

pianoforte (pɪˌænəʊˈfɔːtɪ) *n.* the full name for **piano**[1]. [C18: < It., orig. (*gravecembalo col*) *piano e forte* (harpsichord with) soft & loud; see PIANO[2], FORTE[2]]

Pianola (pɪəˈnəʊlə) *n. Trademark.* a type of mechanical piano in which the keys are depressed by air pressure, this air flow being regulated by perforations in a paper roll.

piano roll (pɪˈænəʊ) *n.* a perforated roll of paper for a Pianola.

piastre *or* **piaster** (pɪˈæstə) *n.* **1.** the standard monetary unit of the former republic of South Vietnam. **2. a.** a fractional monetary unit of Egypt, Lebanon, Sudan, and Syria worth one hundredth of a pound. **b.** Also called: **kurus.** a Turkish monetary unit worth one hundredth of a lira. **c.** a Libyan monetary unit worth one hundredth of a dinar. [C17: < F *piastre,* < It. *piastra d'argento* silver plate]

piazza (pɪˈætsə; *Italian* ˈpjattsa) *n.* **1.** a large open square in an Italian town. **2.** *Chiefly Brit.* a covered passageway or gallery. [C16: < It.: marketplace, < L *platēa* courtyard, < Gk *plateia;* see PLACE]

pibroch (ˈpiːbrɒk; *Gaelic* ˈpiːbrɒx) *n.* a form of music for Scottish bagpipes, consisting of a theme and variations. [C18: < Gaelic *piobaireachd,* < *piobair* piper]

pic (pɪk) *n., pl.* **pics** *or* **pix.** *Inf.* a photograph or illustration. [C20: shortened < PICTURE]

pica[1] (ˈpaɪkə) *n.* **1.** another word for **em. 2.** (formerly) a size of printer's type equal to 12 point. **3.** a typewriter type size having 10 characters to the inch. [C15: < Anglo-L *pīca* list of ecclesiastical regulations, apparently < L *pīca* magpie, with reference to its habit of collecting things; the connection between the orig. sense & the typography meanings is obscure]

pica[2] (ˈpaɪkə) *n. Pathol.* an abnormal craving to ingest substances such as clay, dirt, or hair. [C16: < Medical L, < L: magpie, an allusion to its omnivorous feeding habits]

picador (ˈpɪkəˌdɔː) *n. Bullfighting.* a horseman who pricks the bull with a lance to weaken it. [C18: < Sp., lit.: pricker, < *picar* to prick]

picaresque (ˌpɪkəˈrɛsk) *adj.* of or relating to a type of fiction in which the hero, a rogue, goes through a series of episodic adventures. [C19: via F < Sp. *picaresco,* < *pícaro* a rogue]

picaroon (ˌpɪkəˈruːn) *n. Arch.* an adventurer or rogue. [C17: < Sp. *picarón,* < *pícaro*]

picayune (ˌpɪkəˈjuːn) *adj. also* **picayunish.** *U.S. & Canad. inf.* **1.** of small value or importance. **2.** mean; petty. ~*n.* **3.** any coin of little value, esp. a five-cent piece. **4.** an unimportant person or thing. [C19: < F *picaillon* coin from Piedmont, < Provençal *picaioun,* <?]

piccalilli (ˈpɪkəˌlɪlɪ) *n.* a pickle of mixed vegetables in a mustard sauce. [C18 *piccalillo,* ? based on PICKLE]

piccanin (ˈpɪkəˌnɪn) *n. S. African inf.* a Black African child. [var. of PICCANINNY]

piccaninny *or esp. U.S.* **pickaninny** (ˌpɪkəˈnɪnɪ) *n., pl.* **-nies.** a small Negro or Aboriginal child. [C17: ? < Port. *pequenino* tiny one, < *pequeno* small]

piccolo (ˈpɪkəˌləʊ) *n., pl.* **-los.** a woodwind instrument an octave higher than the flute. [C19: < It.: small]

pick[1] (pɪk) *vb.* **1.** to choose (something) deliberately or carefully, as from a number; select. **2.** to pluck or gather (fruit, berries, or crops) from (a tree, bush, field, etc.). **3.** (*tr.*) to remove loose particles from (the teeth, the nose, etc.). **4.** (esp. of birds) to nibble or gather (corn, etc.). **5.** (*tr.*) to pierce, dig, or break up (a hard surface) with a pick. **6.** (*tr.*) to form (a hole, etc.) in this way. **7.** (when *intr.,* foll. by *at*) to nibble (at) fussily or without appetite. **8.** to separate (strands, fibres, etc.), as in weaving. **9.** (*tr.*) to provoke (an argument, fight, etc.) deliberately. **10.** (*tr.*) to steal (money or valuables) from (a person's pocket). **11.** (*tr.*) to open (a lock) with an instrument other than a key. **12.** to pluck the strings of (a guitar, banjo, etc.). **13.** (*tr.*) to make (one's way) carefully on foot: *they picked their way through the rubble.* **14. pick and choose.** to select fastidiously, fussily, etc. **15. pick someone's brains.** to obtain information or ideas from someone. ~*n.* **16.** freedom or right of selection (esp. in **take one's pick**). **17.** a person, thing, etc., that is chosen first or preferred: *the pick of the bunch.* **18.** the act of picking. **19.** the amount of a crop picked at one period or from one area. ~See also **pick at, pick off,** etc. [C15: < earlier *piken* to pick, infl. by F *piquer* to pierce] —ˈ**picker** *n.*

pick[2] (pɪk) *n.* **1.** a tool with a handle carrying a long steel head curved and tapering to a point at one or both ends, used for loosening soil, breaking rocks, etc. **2.** any of various tools used for picking, such as an ice pick or toothpick. **3.** a plectrum. [C14: ? a var. of PIKE[2]]

pickaback (ˈpɪkəˌbæk) *n., adv.* another word for **piggyback.**

pick at *vb.* (*intr., prep.*) to make criticisms of in a niggling or petty manner.

pickaxe *or U.S.* **pickax** (ˈpɪkˌæks) *n.* **1.** a large pick or mattock. ~*vb.* **2.** to use a pickaxe on (earth, rocks, etc.). [C15: < earlier *pikois* (but infl. also by AXE), < OF, < *pic* PICK[2]]

pickerel (ˈpɪkərəl, ˈpɪkrəl) *n., pl.* **-el** *or* **-els.** **1.** a small pike. **2.** any of several North American freshwater game fishes of the pike family. [C14: dim. of PIKE[1]]

picket (ˈpɪkɪt) *n.* **1.** a pointed stake that is driven into the ground to support a fence, etc. **2.** an individual or group standing outside an establishment to make a protest, to dissuade or prevent employees or clients from entering, etc. **3.** a small detachment of troops positioned to give early warning of attack. ~*vb.* **4.** to post or serve as pickets at (a factory, embassy, etc.). **5.** to guard (a main body or place) by using or acting as a picket. **6.** (*tr.*) to fasten (a horse or other animal) to a picket. **7.** (*tr.*) to fence (an area, etc.) with pickets. [C18: < F *piquet,* < OF *piquer* to prick; see PIKE[2]] —ˈ**picketer** *n.*

picket fence *n.* a fence consisting of pickets driven into the ground.

picket line *n.* a line of people acting as pickets.

pickings (ˈpɪkɪŋz) *pl. n.* (*sometimes sing.*) money, profits, etc., acquired easily; spoils.

pickle (ˈpɪkᵊl) *n.* **1.** (*often pl.*) vegetables, such as onions, etc., preserved in vinegar, brine, etc. **2.** any food preserved in this way. **3.** a liquid or marinade, such as spiced vinegar, for preserving vegetables, meat, fish, etc. **4.** *Chiefly U.S. & Canad.* a cucumber that has been preserved and flavoured in a pickling solution, as brine or vinegar. **5.** *Inf.* an awkward or difficult situation: *to be in a pickle.* **6.** *Brit. inf.* a mischievous child. ~*vb.* (*tr.*) **7.** to preserve in a pickling liquid. **8.** to immerse (a metallic object) in a liquid, such as an acid, to remove surface scale. [C14: ? < MDu. *pekel*] —ˈ**pickler** *n.*

pickled (ˈpɪkᵊld) *adj.* **1.** preserved in a pickling liquid. **2.** *Inf.* intoxicated; drunk.

picklock (ˈpɪkˌlɒk) *n.* **1.** a person who picks locks. **2.** an instrument for picking locks.

pick-me-up *n. Inf.* a tonic or restorative, esp. a special drink taken as a stimulant.

pick off *vb.* (*tr., adv.*) to aim at and shoot one by one.

pick on *vb.* (*intr., prep.*) to select for something unpleasant, esp. in order to bully or blame.

pick out *vb.* (*tr., adv.*) **1.** to select for use or special consideration, etc., as from a group. **2.** to distinguish (an object from its surroundings), as in painting: *she picked out the woodwork in white.* **3.** to recognize (a person or thing): *we picked out his face among the crowd.* **4.** to distinguish (sense or meaning) as from a mass of detail or complication. **5.** to play (a tune) tentatively, as by ear.

pickpocket (ˈpɪkˌpɒkɪt) *n.* a person who steals from the pockets of others in public places.

pick-up *n.* **1.** the light balanced arm of a record player that carries the wires from the cartridge to the preamplifier. **2.** an electromagnetic transducer that converts vibrations into electric signals. **3.** another name for **cartridge** (sense 2). **4.** a small truck with an open body used for light deliveries. **5.** *Inf., chiefly U.S.* an ability to accelerate rapidly: *this car has good pick-up.* **6.** *Inf.* a casual acquaintance, usually one made with sexual intentions. **7.** *Inf.* **a.** a stop to collect passengers, goods, etc. **b.** the people or things collected. **8.** *Inf.* an improvement. **9.** *Sl.* a pick-me-up. ~*vb.* **pick up.** (*adv.*) **10.** (*tr.*) to gather up in the hand or hands. **11.** (*reflexive*) to raise (oneself) after a fall or setback. **12.** (*tr.*) to obtain casually, incidentally, etc. **13.** (*intr.*) to improve in health, condition, activity, etc.: *the market began to pick up.* **14.** (*tr.*) to learn gradually or as one goes along. **15.** to resume; return to. **16.** (*tr.*) to accept the responsibility for paying (a bill). **17.** (*tr.*) to collect or give a lift to (passengers, goods, etc.). **18.** (*tr.*) *Inf.* to become acquainted with, esp. with a view to having sexual relations. **19.** (*tr.*) *Inf.* to arrest. **20.** to increase (speed). **21.** (*tr.*) to receive (electrical signals, a radio signal, sounds, etc.).

Pickwickian (pɪkˈwɪkɪən) *adj.* **1.** of, relating to, or resembling Mr Pickwick in Charles Dickens' *The Pickwick Papers,* esp. in being naive or benevolent. **2.** (of the use or meaning of a word, etc.) odd or unusual.

picky (ˈpɪkɪ) *adj.* **pickier, pickiest.** *Inf.* fussy; finicky. —ˈ**pickily** *adv.* —ˈ**pickiness** *n.*

picnic (ˈpɪknɪk) *n.* **1.** a trip or excursion on which people bring food to be eaten in the open air. **2. a.** any informal meal eaten outside. **b.** (*as modifier*): *a picnic lunch.* **3.** *Inf.* an easy or agreeable task. ~*vb.* **-nicking, -nicked.** **4.** (*intr.*)

to eat or take part in a picnic. [C18: < F *piquenique*, <?] —ˈ**picnicker** *n.*

picnic races *pl. n. Austral.* horse races for amateur riders held in rural areas.

pico- *prefix.* denoting 10^{-12}: *picofarad.* Symbol: p [< Sp. *pico* small quantity, odd number, peak]

picot (ˈpiːkəʊ) *n.* any of a pattern of small loops, as on lace. [C19: < F: small point, < *pic* point]

picotee (ˌpɪkəˈtiː) *n.* a type of carnation having pale petals edged with a darker colour. [C18: < F *picoté* marked with points, < *picot* PICOT]

picric acid (ˈpɪkrɪk) *n.* a toxic sparingly soluble crystalline yellow acid; 2,4,6-trinitrophenol: used as a dye, antiseptic, and explosive. [C19: < Gk *pikros* bitter + -IC]

Pict (pɪkt) *n.* a member of any of the peoples who lived in N Britain in the first to the fourth centuries A.D. [OE *Peohtas;* later forms < LL *Pictī* painted men, < *pingere* to paint] —ˈ**Pictish** *adj.*

pictograph (ˈpɪktəˌgrɑːf) *n.* **1.** a picture or symbol standing for a word or group of words, as in written Chinese. **2.** a chart on which symbols are used to represent values. ~Also called: **pictogram.** [C19: < L *pictus,* < *pingere* to paint] —**pictographic** (ˌpɪktəˈgræfɪk) *adj.* —**pictography** (pɪkˈtɒgrəfɪ) *n.*

pictorial (pɪkˈtɔːrɪəl) *adj.* **1.** relating to, consisting of, or expressed by pictures. **2.** (of language, style, etc.) suggesting a picture; vivid; graphic. ~*n.* **3.** a magazine, newspaper, etc., containing many pictures. [C17: < LL *pictōrius,* < L *pictor* painter, < *pingere* to paint] —**picˈtorially** *adv.*

picture (ˈpɪktʃə) *n.* **1. a.** a visual representation of something, such as a person or scene, produced on a surface, as in a photograph, painting, etc. **b.** (*as modifier*): *picture gallery; picture postcard.* **2.** a mental image: *a clear picture of events.* **3.** a verbal description, esp. one that is vivid. **4.** a situation considered as an observable scene: *the political picture.* **5.** a person or thing resembling another: *he was the picture of his father.* **6.** a person, scene, etc., typifying a particular state: *the picture of despair.* **7.** the image on a television screen. **8.** a motion picture; film. **9. the pictures.** *Chiefly Brit.* a cinema or film show. **10.** another name for **tableau vivant. 11. in the picture.** informed about a situation. ~*vb.* (*tr.*) **12.** to visualize or imagine. **13.** to describe or depict, esp. vividly. **14.** (*often passive*) to put in a picture or make a picture of: *they were pictured sitting on the rocks.* [C15: < L *pictūra* painting, < *pingere* to paint]

picture card *n.* another name for **court card.**

picture hat *n.* a hat with a very wide brim.

picture moulding *n.* **1.** the edge around a framed picture. **2.** Also called: **picture rail.** the moulding or rail near the top of a wall from which pictures are hung.

picture palace *or* **house** *n. Brit., old-fashioned.* another name for **cinema.**

picturesque (ˌpɪktʃəˈrɛsk) *adj.* **1.** visually pleasing, esp. in being striking or quaint: *a picturesque view.* **2.** (of language) graphic; vivid. [C18: < F *pittoresque* (but also infl. by PICTURE), < It., < *pittore* painter, < L *pictor*] —ˌ**picturˈesquely** *adv.* —ˌ**picturˈesqueness** *n.*

picture tube *n.* another name for **television tube.**

picture window *n.* a large window having a single pane of glass, usually facing a view.

picture writing *n.* **1.** any writing system that uses pictographs. **2.** a system of artistic expression and communication using pictures.

piddle (ˈpɪdᵊl) *vb.* **1.** (*intr.*) *Inf.* to urinate. **2.** (when *tr.,* often foll. by *away*) to spend (one's time) aimlessly; fritter. [C16: <?] —ˈ**piddler** *n.*

piddling (ˈpɪdlɪŋ) *adj. Inf.* petty; trifling; trivial.

piddock (ˈpɪdək) *n.* a marine bivalve boring into rock, clay, or wood by means of sawlike shell valves. [C19: <?]

pidgin (ˈpɪdʒɪn) *n.* a language made up of elements of two or more other languages and used for contacts, esp. trading contacts, between the speakers of other languages. [C19: ? < Chinese pronunciation of E *business*]

pidgin English *n.* a pidgin in which one of the languages involved is English.

pie[1] (paɪ) *n.* **1.** a baked sweet or savoury filling in a pastry-lined dish, often covered with a pastry crust. **2. pie in the sky.** illusory hope or promise of some future good. [C14: <?]

pie[2] (paɪ) *n.* an archaic or dialect name for **magpie.** [C13: via OF < L *pīca* magpie]

pie[3] (paɪ) *n., vb. Printing.* a variant spelling of **pi**[2].

piebald (ˈpaɪˌbɔːld) *adj.* **1.** marked in two colours, esp. black and white. ~*n.* **2.** a black-and-white horse. [C16: PIE[2] + BALD; see also PIED]

pie cart *n. N.Z.* a mobile van selling warmed-up food and drinks.

piece (piːs) *n.* **1.** an amount or portion forming a separate mass or structure; bit: *a piece of wood.* **2.** a small part, item, or amount forming part of a whole, esp. when broken off or separated: *a piece of bread.* **3.** a length by which a commodity is sold, esp. cloth, wallpaper, etc. **4.** an instance or occurrence: *a piece of luck.* **5.** an example or specimen of a style or type: *a beautiful piece of Dresden.* **6.** *Inf.* an opinion or point of view: *to state one's piece.* **7.** a literary, musical, or artistic composition. **8.** a coin: *a fifty-pence piece.* **9.** a small object used in playing certain games: *chess pieces.* **10.** a firearm or cannon. **11.** any chessman other than a pawn. **12.** *Brit. dialect.* a packed lunch taken to work. **13.** *N.Z.* fragments of fleece wool. **14. go to pieces. a.** (of a person) to lose control of oneself; have a breakdown. **b.** (of a building, organization, etc.) to disintegrate. **15. nasty piece of work.** *Brit. inf.* a cruel or mean person. **16. of a piece.** of the same kind; alike. ~*vb.* (*tr.*) **17.** (often foll. by *together*) to fit or assemble piece by piece. **18.** (often foll. by *up*) to patch or make up (a garment, etc.) by adding pieces. [C13 *pece,* < OF, of Gaulish origin]

pièce de résistance *French.* (pjɛs də rezistɑ̃s) *n.* **1.** the principal or most outstanding item in a series. **2.** the main dish of a meal.

piece goods *pl. n.* goods, esp. fabrics, made in standard widths and lengths.

piecemeal (ˈpiːsˌmiːl) *adv.* **1.** by degrees; bit by bit; gradually. **2.** in or into pieces. ~*adj.* **3.** fragmentary or unsystematic: *a piecemeal approach.* [C13 *pecemele,* < PIECE + *-mele,* < OE *mælum* quantity taken at one time]

piece of eight *n., pl.* **pieces of eight.** a former Spanish coin worth eight reals; peso.

piecework (ˈpiːsˌwɜːk) *n.* work paid for according to the quantity produced.

pie chart *n.* a circular graph divided into sectors proportional to the magnitudes of the quantities represented.

piecrust table (ˈpaɪˌkrʌst) *n.* a round table, edged with moulding suggestive of a pie crust.

pied (paɪd) *adj.* having markings of two or more colours. [C14: < PIE[2]; an allusion to the magpie's colouring]

pied-à-terre (ˌpjeɪtɑːˈtɛə) *n., pl.* **pieds-à-terre** (ˈpjeɪtɑːˈteə). a flat or other lodging for occasional use. [< F, lit.: foot on (the) ground]

piedmont (ˈpiːdmɒnt) *adj.* (*prenominal*) (of glaciers, plains, etc.) formed or situated at the foot of a mountain. [via F < It. *piémonte,* < *pié,* var. of *piede* foot + *mont* mountain]

pied wagtail *n.* a British songbird with a black throat and back, long black tail, and white underparts and face.

pie-eyed *adj. Sl.* drunk.

pier (pɪə) *n.* **1.** a structure with a deck that is built out over water, and used as a landing place, promenade, etc. **2.** a pillar that bears heavy loads. **3.** the part of a wall between two adjacent openings. **4.** another name for **buttress** (sense 1). [C12 *per,* < Anglo-L *pera* pier supporting a bridge]

pierce (pɪəs) *vb.* (*mainly tr.*) **1.** to form or cut (a hole) in (something) as with a sharp instrument. **2.** to thrust into sharply or violently: *the thorn pierced his heel.* **3.** to force (a way, route, etc.) through (something). **4.** (of light, etc.) to shine through or penetrate (darkness). **5.** (*also intr.*) to discover or realize (something) suddenly or (of an idea, etc.) to become suddenly apparent. **6.** (of sounds or cries) to sound sharply through (the silence, etc.). **7.** to move or affect deeply or sharply: *the cold pierced their bones.* **8.** (*intr.*) to penetrate: *piercing cold.* [C13 *percen,* < OF *percer,* ult. < L *pertundere,* < *per* through + *tundere* to strike] —**ˈpiercing** *adj.* —**ˈpiercingly** *adv.*

pier glass *n.* a tall narrow mirror, designed to hang on the wall between windows.

pieris (ˈpaɪrɪs) *n.* an evergreen shrub with white flowers like lily of the valley in spring. [< L, < Gk *Pīeria* the haunt of the Muses]

Pierrot (ˈpɪərəʊ; *French* pjɛro) *n.* **1.** a male character from French pantomime with a whitened face, white costume, and pointed hat. **2.** (*usually not cap.*) a clown so made up.

pier table *n.* a side table designed to stand against a wall between windows.

pietà (pɪɛˈtɑː) *n.* a sculpture, painting, or drawing of the dead Christ, supported by the Virgin Mary. [It.: pity, < L *pietās* PIETY]

pietism (ˈpaɪɪˌtɪzəm) *n.* exaggerated or affected piety. —**ˈpietist** *n.* —**ˌpieˈtistic** *or* **ˌpieˈtistical** *adj.*

piet-my-vrou (ˈpɪtˌmeɪˈfrəʊ) *n. S. African.* a red-breasted cuckoo. [imit.]

piety (ˈpaɪɪtɪ) *n., pl.* **-ties. 1.** dutiful devotion to God and observance of religious principles. **2.** the quality of being pious. **3.** a pious action, saying, etc. **4.** *Now rare.* devotion and obedience to parents or superiors. [C13 *piete,* < OF, < L *pietās* piety, dutifulness, < *pius* pious]

piezoelectric effect (paɪˌiːzəʊɪˈlɛktrɪk) *or* **piezoelectricity** (paɪˌiːzəʊɪlɛkˈtrɪsɪtɪ) *n. Physics.* **a.** the production of electricity or electric polarity by applying a mechanical stress to certain crystals. **b.** the converse effect in which stress is produced in a crystal as a result of an applied potential difference. [C19: < Gk *piezein* to press] —**piˌezoeˈlectrically** *adv.*

piffle (ˈpɪfᵊl) *Inf.* ~*n.* **1.** nonsense. ~*vb.* **2.** (*intr.*) to talk or behave feebly. [C19: <?]

piffling (ˈpɪflɪŋ) *adj. Inf.* worthless; trivial.

pig (pɪg) *n.* **1.** any artiodactyl mammal of an African and Eurasian family, esp. the domestic pig, typically having a long head with a movable snout and a thick bristle-covered skin. Related adj.: **porcine. 2.** *Inf.* a dirty, greedy, or bad-mannered person. **3.** the meat of swine; pork. **4.** *Derog.* a slang word for **policeman. 5. a.** a mass of metal cast into a simple shape. **b.** the mould used. **6.** *Brit. inf.* something that is difficult or unpleasant. **7. a pig in a poke.** something bought or received without prior sight or knowledge. **8. make a pig of oneself.** *Inf.* to overindulge oneself. ~*vb.* **pigging, pigged. 9.** (*intr.*) (of a sow) to give birth. **10.** (*intr.*) Also: **pig it.** *Inf.* to live in squalor. **11.** (*tr.*) *Inf.* to devour (food) greedily. [C13 *pigge,* <?]

pigeon[1] (ˈpɪdʒɪn) *n.* **1.** any of numerous related birds having a heavy body, small head, short legs, and long pointed wings. **2.** *Sl.* a victim or dupe. [C14: < OF *pijon* young dove, < LL *pīpiō* young bird, < *pīpīre* to chirp]

pigeon[2] (ˈpɪdʒɪn) *Brit. inf.* concern or responsibility (often in **it's his, her,** etc., **pigeon**). [C19: altered < PIDGIN]

pigeon breast *n.* a deformity of the chest characterized by an abnormal protrusion of the breastbone, caused by rickets.

pigeonhole (ˈpɪdʒɪnˌhəʊl) *n.* **1.** a small compartment for papers, letters, etc., as in a bureau. **2.** a hole or recess in a dovecote for pigeons to nest in. ~*vb.* (*tr.*) **3.** to put aside or defer. **4.** to classify or categorize.

pigeon-toed *adj.* having the toes turned inwards.

pigface (ˈpɪgˌfeɪs) *n. Austral.* a creeping succulent plant having bright-coloured flowers and red fruits and often grown for ornament.

piggery (ˈpɪgərɪ) *n., pl.* **-geries. 1.** a place where pigs are kept. **2.** great greediness.

piggish (ˈpɪgɪʃ) *adj.* **1.** like a pig, esp. in appetite or manners. **2.** *Inf., chiefly Brit.* obstinate or mean. —**ˈpiggishly** *adv.* —**ˈpiggishness** *n.*

piggy (ˈpɪgɪ) *n., pl.* **-gies. 1.** a child's word for a **pig. 2.** a child's word for a **toe.** ~*adj.* **-gier, -giest. 3.** another word for **piggish.**

piggyback (ˈpɪgɪˌbæk) *or* **pickaback** *n.* **1.** a ride on the back and shoulders of another person. **2.** a system whereby a vehicle, aircraft, etc., is transported for part of its journey on another vehicle. ~*adv.* **3.** on the back and shoulders of another person. **4.** on or as an addition. ~*adj.* **5.** of or for a piggyback: *a piggyback ride; piggyback lorry trains.* **6.** of or relating to a type of heart transplant in which the transplanted heart functions in conjunction with the patient's own heart.

piggy bank *n.* a child's coin bank shaped like a pig with a slot for coins.

pig-headed *adj.* stupidly stubborn. —**ˌpigˈheadedly** *adv.* —**ˌpigˈheadedness** *n.*

pig iron *n.* crude iron produced in a blast furnace and poured into moulds.

Pig Islander *n. N.Z. inf.* a New Zealander.

piglet (ˈpɪglɪt) *n.* a young pig.

pigmeat (ˈpɪgˌmiːt) *n.* a less common name for pork, ham, or bacon.

pigment (ˈpɪgmənt) *n.* **1.** a substance occurring in plant or animal tissue and producing a characteristic colour. **2.** any substance used to impart colour. **3.** a powder that is mixed with a liquid to give a paint, ink, etc. [C14: < L *pigmentum,* < *pingere* to paint] —**ˈpigmentary** *adj.*

pigmentation (ˌpɪgmənˈteɪʃən) *n.* **1.** coloration in plants, animals, or man caused by the presence of pigments. **2.** the deposition of pigment in animals, plants, or man.

Pigmy (ˈpɪgmɪ) *n., pl.* **-mies.** a variant spelling of **Pygmy.**

pignut (ˈpɪgˌnʌt) *n.* **1.** Also called: **hognut. a.** the bitter nut of any of several North American hickory trees. **b.** any of the trees bearing such a nut. **2.** another name for **earthnut.**

pig-root *vb.* (*intr.*) *Austral. & N.Z. sl.* (of a horse) to buck slightly.

pigskin (ˈpɪgˌskɪn) *n.* **1.** the skin of the domestic pig. **2.** leather made of this skin. **3.** *U.S. & Canad. inf.* a football. ~*adj.* **4.** made of pigskin.

pigsticking (ˈpɪgˌstɪkɪŋ) *n.* the sport of hunting wild boar. —**ˈpigˌsticker** *n.*

pigsty (ˈpɪgˌstaɪ) *or U.S. & Canad.* **pigpen** *n., pl.* **-sties. 1.** a pen for pigs; sty. **2.** *Brit.* an untidy place.

pigswill (ˈpɪgˌswɪl) *n.* waste food or other edible matter fed to pigs. Also called: **pig's wash.**

pigtail (ˈpɪgˌteɪl) *n.* **1.** a plait of hair or one of two plaits on either side of the face. **2.** a twisted roll of tobacco.

pika (ˈpaɪkə) *n.* a burrowing mammal of mountainous regions of North America and Asia, having short rounded ears, a rounded body, and rudimentary tail. [C19: < E Siberian *piika*]

pikau (ˈpiːkaʊ) *n. N.Z.* a pack, knapsack, or rucksack. [Maori]

pike[1] (paɪk) *n., pl.* **pike** *or* **pikes. 1.** any of several large predatory freshwater teleost fishes having a broad flat snout, strong teeth, and an elongated body covered with small scales. **2.** any of various similar fishes. [C14: short for *pikefish,* < OE *pīc* point, with reference to the shape of its jaw]

pike[2] (paɪk) *n.* **1.** a medieval weapon consisting of a metal spearhead joined to a long pole. **2.** a point or spike. ~*vb.* **3.** (*tr.*) to pierce using a pike. [OE *pīc* point, <?] —**ˈpikeman** *n.*

pike[3] (paɪk) *n.* short for **turnpike** (senses 1, 2).

pike[4] (paɪk) *n. Northern English dialect.* a pointed or conical hill. [OE *pīc*]

pike[5] (paɪk) *or* **piked** (paɪkt) *adj.* (of the body position of a diver) bent at the hips but with the legs straight.

pike[6] (paɪk) *vb.* (*intr.*; foll. by *out*) *Austral. sl.* to shirk. [< PIKER]

pikeperch (ˈpaɪkˌpɜːtʃ) *n., pl.* **-perch** *or* **-perches.** any of various pikelike freshwater teleost fishes of the perch family of Europe.

piker (ˈpaɪkə) *n. U.S., Austral., & N.Z. sl.* **1.** a lazy person; shirker. **2.** a mean person. [C19: < *Pike* county, Missouri, U.S.A.]

pikestaff (ˈpaɪkˌstɑːf) *n.* the wooden handle of a pike.

pilaster (pɪˈlæstə) *n.* a shallow rectangular column attached to the face of a wall. [C16: < F *pilastre,* < L *pīla* pillar] —**piˈlastered** *adj.*

pilau (pɪˈlaʊ), **pilaf, pilaff** (ˈpɪlæf), *or* **pilaw** (pɪˈlɔː) *n.* a dish originating from the East, consisting of rice flavoured with spices and cooked in stock, to which meat, poultry, or fish may be added. [C17: < Turkish *pilâw,* < Persian]

pilchard (ˈpɪltʃəd) *n.* a European food fish of the herring family, with a rounded body covered with large scales. [C16 *pylcher,* <?]

pile[1] (paɪl) *n.* **1.** a collection of objects laid on top of one another; heap; mound. **2.** *Inf.* a large amount of money (esp. in **make a pile**). **3.** (*often pl.*) *Inf.* a large amount: *a pile of work.* **4.** a less common word for **pyre. 5.** a large building or group of buildings. **6.** *Physics.* a structure of uranium and a moderator used for producing atomic energy; nuclear reactor. ~*vb.* **7.** (often foll. by *up*) to collect or be collected into or as if into a pile: *snow piled up in the drive.* **8.** (*intr.;* foll. by *in, into, off, out,* etc.) to move in a group, esp. in a hurried or disorganized manner: *to pile off the bus.* **9. pile it on.** *Inf.* to exaggerate. ~See also **pile up.** [C15: via OF < L *pīla* stone pier]

pile[2] (paɪl) *n.* **1.** a long column of timber, concrete, or steel, driven into the ground as a foundation for a structure. ~*vb.* (*tr.*) **2.** to drive (piles) into the ground. **3.** to support (a structure) with piles. [OE *pīl,* < L *pīlum*]

pile[3] (paɪl) *n.* **1.** the yarns in a fabric that stand up or out from the weave, as in carpeting, velvet, etc. **2.** soft fine hair, fur, wool, etc. [C15: < Anglo-Norman *pyle,* < L *pilus* hair]

pileate (ˈpaɪlɪɪt, -ˌeɪt, ˈpɪl-) *or* **pileated** (ˈpaɪlɪˌeɪtɪd, ˈpɪl-) *adj.* **1.** (of birds) having a crest. **2.** *Bot.* having a pileus. [C18: < L *pīleātus* wearing a felt cap, < PILEUS]

pile-driver *n.* a machine that drives piles into the ground.

pileous (ˈpaɪlɪəs, ˈpɪl-) *adj. Biol.* **1.** hairy. **2.** of or relating to hair. [C19: ult. < L *pilus* a hair]

piles (paɪlz) *pl. n.* a nontechnical name for **haemorrhoids.** [C15: < L *pilae* balls (referring to the external piles)]

pileum (ˈpaɪlɪəm, ˈpɪl-) *n., pl.* **-lea** (-lɪə). the top of a bird's head from the base of the bill to the occiput. [C19: NL, < L PILEUS]

pile up *vb.* (*adv.*) **1.** to gather or be gathered in a pile. **2.** *Inf.* to crash or cause to crash. ~*n.* **pile-up. 3.** *Inf.* a multiple collision of vehicles.

pileus (ˈpaɪlɪəs) *n., pl.* **-lei** (-lɪˌaɪ). the upper cap-shaped part of a mushroom. [C18: (botanical use): NL, < L: felt cap]

pilewort (ˈpaɪlˌwɜːt) *n.* any of several plants, such as lesser celandine, thought to be effective in treating piles.

pilfer (ˈpɪlfə) *vb.* to steal (minor items), esp. in small quantities. [C14 *pylfre* (n.) < OF *pelfre* booty] —**ˈpilferage** *n.* —**ˈpilferer** *n.*

pilgrim (ˈpɪlgrɪm) *n.* **1.** a person who undertakes a journey to a sacred place. **2.** any wayfarer. [C12: < Provençal *pelegrin,* < L *peregrīnus* foreign, < *per* through + *ager* land]

pilgrimage (ˈpɪlgrɪmɪdʒ) *n.* **1.** a journey to a shrine or other sacred place. **2.** a journey or long search made for exalted or sentimental reasons. ~*vb.* **3.** (*intr.*) to make a pilgrimage.

Pilgrim Fathers *or* **Pilgrims** *pl. n.* **the.** the English Puritans who sailed on the Mayflower to New England, where they founded Plymouth Colony in SE Massachusetts (1620).

piliferous (paɪˈlɪfərəs) *adj.* (esp. of plants) bearing or ending in a hair or hairs. [C19: < L *pilus* hair + -FEROUS] —**ˈpiliˌform** *adj.*

piling (ˈpaɪlɪŋ) *n.* **1.** the act of driving piles. **2.** a number of piles. **3.** a structure formed of piles.

pill[1] (pɪl) *n.* **1.** a small spherical or ovoid mass of a medicinal substance, intended to be swallowed whole. **2. the pill.** (*sometimes cap.*) *Inf.* an oral contraceptive. **3.** something unpleasant that must be endured (esp. in **bitter pill to swallow**). **4.** *Sl.* a ball or disc. **5.** *Sl.* an unpleasant or boring person. ~*vb.* **6.** (*tr.*) to give pills to. [C15: < MFlemish *pille,* < L *pilula* a little ball, < *pila* ball]

pill[2] (pɪl) *vb.* **1.** *Arch. or dialect.* to peel or skin (something). **2.** *Arch.* to pillage or plunder (a place, etc.). [OE *pilian,* < L *pilāre* to strip]

pillage (ˈpɪlɪdʒ) *vb.* **1.** to rob (a town, village, etc.) of (booty or spoils). ~*n.* **2.** the act of pillaging. **3.** something obtained by pillaging; booty. [C14: via OF < *piller* to despoil, prob. < *peille* rag, < L *pīleus* felt cap] —**ˈpillager** *n.*

pillar (ˈpɪlə) *n.* **1.** an upright structure of stone, brick, metal, etc. that supports a superstructure. **2.** something resembling this in shape or function: *a pillar of smoke.* **3.** a prominent supporter: *a pillar of the Church.* **4. from pillar to post.** from one place to another. [C13: < OF *pilier,* < L *pīla*]

pillar box *n.* (in Britain) a red pillar-shaped public letter box situated on a pavement.

pillbox (ˈpɪlˌbɒks) *n.* **1.** a box for pills. **2.** a small enclosed fortified emplacement, made of reinforced concrete. **3.** a small round hat.

pillion (ˈpɪljən) *n.* **1.** a seat or place behind the rider of a motorcycle, scooter, horse, etc. ~*adv.* **2.** on a pillion: *to ride pillion.* [C16: < Gaelic; cf. Scot. *pillean,* Irish *pillīn* couch]

pilliwinks (ˈpɪlɪˌwɪŋks) *pl. n.* a medieval instrument of torture for the fingers. [C14: <?]

pillory (ˈpɪlərɪ) *n., pl.* **-ries. 1.** a wooden framework into which offenders were formerly locked by the neck and wrists and exposed to public abuse and ridicule. **2.** exposure to public scorn or abuse. ~*vb.* **-rying, -ried.** (*tr.*) **3.** to expose to public scorn or ridicule. **4.** to punish by putting in a pillory. [C13: < Anglo-L *pillorium,* < OF *pilori,* <?]

pillow (ˈpɪləʊ) *n.* **1.** a cloth case stuffed with feathers, foam rubber, etc., used to support the head, esp. during sleep. **2.** Also called: **cushion.** a padded cushion or board on which pillow lace is made. **3.** anything like a pillow in shape or function. ~*vb.* (*tr.*) **4.** to rest (one's head) on or as if on a pillow. **5.** to serve as a pillow for. [OE *pylwe,* < L *pulvīnus* cushion]

pillowcase (ˈpɪləʊˌkeɪs) *or* **pillowslip** (ˈpɪləʊˌslɪp) *n.* a removable washable cover of cotton, linen, nylon, etc., for a pillow.

pillow fight *n.* a mock fight in which participants thump each other with pillows.

pillow lace *n.* lace made by winding thread around bobbins on a padded cushion or board. Cf. **point lace.**

pilose (ˈpaɪləʊz) *adj. Biol.* covered with fine soft hairs: *pilose leaves.* [C18: < L *pilōsus,* < *pilus* hair] —**pilosity** (paɪˈlɒsɪtɪ) *n.*

pilot (ˈpaɪlət) *n.* **1.** a person who is qualified to operate an aircraft or spacecraft in flight. **2. a.** a person who is qualified to steer or guide a ship into or out of a port, river mouth, etc. **b.** (*as modifier*): *a pilot ship.* **3.** a person who steers a ship. **4.** a person who acts as a leader or guide. **5.** *Machinery.* a guide used to assist in joining two mating parts together. **6.** an experimental programme on radio or television. **7.** (*modifier*) serving as a test or trial: *a pilot project.* **8.** (*modifier*) serving as a guide: *a pilot beacon.* ~*vb.* (*tr.*) **9.** to act as pilot of. **10.** to control the course of. **11.** to guide or lead (a project, people, etc.). [C16: < F *pilote,* < Med. L *pilotus,* ult. < Gk *pēdon* oar]

pilotage (ˈpaɪlətɪdʒ) *n.* **1.** the act of piloting an aircraft or ship. **2.** a pilot's fee.

pilot balloon *n.* a meteorological balloon used to observe air currents.

pilot fish *n.* a small fish of tropical and subtropical seas, marked with dark vertical bands: often accompanies sharks.

pilot house *n. Naut.* an enclosed structure on the bridge of a vessel from which it can be navigated; a wheelhouse.

pilot lamp *n.* a small light in an electric circuit or device that lights when the current is on.

pilot light *n.* **1.** a small auxiliary flame that

ignites the main burner of a gas appliance. **2.** a small electric light used as an indicator.

pilot officer *n.* the most junior commissioned rank in the British Royal Air Force and in certain other air forces.

pilot study *n.* a small-scale experiment undertaken to decide whether and how to launch a full-scale project.

Pilsner (ˈpɪlznə) *or* **Pilsener** *n.* a type of pale beer with a strong flavour of hops. [after *Pilsen,* W Czechoslovakia, where it was orig. brewed]

pilule (ˈpɪljuːl) *n.* a small pill. [C16: via F < L *pilula* little ball, < *pila* ball] —ˈ**pilular** *adj.*

pimento (pɪˈmɛntəʊ) *n., pl.* **-tos.** another name for **allspice** or **pimiento.** [C17: < Sp. *pimiento* pepper plant, < Med. L *pigmenta* spiced drink, < L *pigmentum* PIGMENT]

pi meson *n.* another name for **pion.**

pimiento (pɪˈmjɛntəʊ, -ˈmɛn-) *n., pl.* **-tos.** a Spanish pepper with a red fruit used as a vegetable. Also called: **pimento.** [var. of PIMENTO]

pimp[1] (pɪmp) *n.* **1.** a man who solicits for a prostitute or brothel. **2.** a man who procures sexual gratification for another; procurer; pander. ~*vb.* **3.** (*intr.*) to act as a pimp. [C17: <?]

pimp[2] (pɪmp) *Sl., chiefly Austral. & N.Z.* ~*n.* **1.** a spy or informer. ~*vb.* **2.** (*intr.;* often foll. by *on*) to inform (on). [<?]

pimpernel (ˈpɪmpəˌnɛl, -nᵊl) *n.* any of several plants, such as the scarlet pimpernel, typically having small star-shaped flowers. [C15: < OF *pimpernelle,* ult. < L *piper* PEPPER]

pimple (ˈpɪmpᵊl) *n.* a small round usually inflamed swelling of the skin. [C14: rel. to OE *pipilian* to break out in spots] —ˈ**pimpled** *adj.* —ˈ**pimply** *adj.* —ˈ**pimpliness** *n.*

pin (pɪn) *n.* **1.** a short stiff straight piece of wire pointed at one end and either rounded or having a flattened head at the other: used mainly for fastening pieces of cloth, paper, etc. **2.** short for **cotter pin, hairpin, panel pin, rolling pin,** or **safety pin.** **3.** an ornamental brooch, esp. a narrow one. **4.** a badge worn fastened to the clothing by a pin. **5.** something of little or no importance (esp. in **not care** *or* **give a pin (for)**). **6.** a peg or dowel. **7.** anything resembling a pin in shape, function, etc. **8.** (in various bowling games) a usually club-shaped wooden object set up in groups as a target. **9.** Also called: **safety pin.** a clip on a hand grenade that prevents its detonation until removed or released. **10.** *Naut.* **a.** See **belaying pin.** **b.** the sliding closure for a shackle. **11.** *Music.* a metal tuning peg on a piano. **12.** *Surgery.* a metal rod, esp. of stainless steel, for holding together adjacent ends of fractured bones during healing. **13.** *Chess.* a position in which a piece is pinned against a more valuable piece or the king. **14.** *Golf.* the flagpole marking the hole on a green. **15.** (*usually pl.*) *Inf.* a leg. ~*vb.* **pinning, pinned.** (*tr.*) **16.** to attach, hold, or fasten with or as if with a pin or pins. **17.** to transfix with a pin, spear, etc. **18.** (foll. by *on*) *Inf.* to place (the blame for something): *he pinned the charge on his accomplice.* **19.** *Chess.* to cause (an enemy piece) to be effectively immobilized since moving it would reveal a check or expose a more valuable piece to capture. ~See also **pin down.** [OE *pinn*]

pinaceous (paɪˈneɪʃəs) *adj.* of, relating to, or belonging to a family of conifers with needle-like leaves: includes pine, spruce, fir, larch, and cedar. [C19: via NL < L *pīnus* a pine]

pinafore (ˈpɪnəˌfɔː) *n.* **1.** *Chiefly Brit.* an apron, esp. one with a bib. **2.** Also called: **pinafore dress.** a dress with a sleeveless bodice or bib top, worn over a jumper or blouse. [C18: < PIN + AFORE]

pinaster (paɪˈnæstə) *n.* a Mediterranean pine tree with paired needles and prickly cones. Also called: **maritime** (*or* **cluster**) **pinaster.** [C16: < L: wild pine, < *pīnus* pine]

pinball (ˈpɪnˌbɔːl) *n.* **a.** a game in which the player shoots a small ball through several hazards on a table, electrically operated machine, etc. **b.** (*as modifier*): *a pinball machine.*

pince-nez (ˈpænsˌneɪ, ˈpɪns-; *French* pɛ̃sne) *n., pl.* **pince-nez.** eyeglasses that are held in place only by means of a clip over the bridge of the nose. [C19: F, lit.: pinch-nose]

pincers (ˈpɪnsəz) *pl. n.* **1.** Also called: **pair of pincers.** a gripping tool consisting of two hinged arms with handles at one end and, at the other, curved bevelled jaws that close on the workpiece. **2.** the pair or pairs of jointed grasping appendages in lobsters and certain other arthropods. [C14: < OF *pinceour,* < OF *pincier* to pinch]

pinch (pɪntʃ) *vb.* **1.** to press (something, esp. flesh) tightly between two surfaces, esp. between a finger and thumb. **2.** to confine, squeeze, or painfully press (toes, fingers, etc.) because of lack of space: *these shoes pinch.* **3.** (*tr.*) to cause stinging pain to: *the cold pinched his face.* **4.** (*tr.*) to make thin or drawn-looking, as from grief, lack of food, etc. **5.** (usually foll. by *on*) to provide (oneself or another person) with meagre allowances, amounts, etc. **6. pinch pennies.** to live frugally because of meanness or to economize. **7.** (usually foll. by *off, out,* or *back*) to remove the tips of (buds, shoots, etc.) to correct or encourage growth. **8.** (*tr.*) *Inf.* to steal or take without asking. **9.** (*tr.*) *Inf.* to arrest. ~*n.* **10.** a squeeze or sustained nip. **11.** the quantity of a substance, such as salt, that can be taken between a thumb and finger. **12.** a very small quantity. **13.** (usually preceded by *the*) sharp, painful, or extreme stress, need, etc.: *feeling the pinch of poverty.* **14.** *Sl.* a robbery. **15.** *Sl.* a police raid or arrest. **16. at a pinch.** if absolutely necessary. [C16: prob. < OF *pinchier* (unattested)]

pinchbeck (ˈpɪntʃˌbɛk) *n.* **1.** an alloy of copper and zinc, used as imitation gold. **2.** a spurious or cheap imitation. ~*adj.* **3.** made of pinchbeck. **4.** sham or cheap. [C18 (the alloy), C19 (something spurious): after C. *Pinchbeck* (?1670–1732), E watchmaker who invented it]

pinchpenny (ˈpɪntʃˌpɛnɪ) *adj.* **1.** niggardly; miserly. ~*n., pl.* **-nies.** **2.** a miserly person.

pincushion (ˈpɪnˌkʊʃən) *n.* a small well-padded cushion in which pins are stuck ready for use.

pin down *vb.* (*tr., adv.*) **1.** to force (someone) to make a decision or carry out a promise. **2.** to define clearly: *he had a vague suspicion that he couldn't quite pin down.* **3.** to confine to a place.

pine[1] (paɪn) *n.* **1.** any of a genus of evergreen resinous coniferous trees of the N hemisphere, with long needle-shaped leaves **(pine needles)** and brown cones. **2.** the wood of any of these trees. [OE *pīn,* < L *pīnus* pine]

pine[2] (paɪn) *vb.* **1.** (*intr.;* often foll. by *for* or an infinitive) to feel great longing or desire; yearn. **2.** (*intr.;* often foll. by *away*) to become ill or thin through worry, longing, etc. [OE *pīnian* to torture, < *pīn* pain, < Med. L *pēna,* < L *poena* PAIN]

pineal eye (ˈpɪnɪəl) *n.* an outgrowth of the pineal gland that forms an eyelike structure on the top of the head in certain cold-blooded vertebrates. [C19: < F, < L *pīnea* pine cone]

pineal gland *or* **body** *n.* a pea-sized organ situated at the base of the brain that secretes a hormone, melatonin, into the bloodstream. Technical names: **epiphysis, epiphysis cerebri.**

pineapple (ˈpaɪnˌæpᵊl) *n.* **1.** a tropical American plant cultivated for its large fleshy edible fruit. **2.** the fruit of this plant, consisting of an inflorescence clustered around a fleshy axis and surmounted by a tuft of leaves. **3.** *Mil. sl.* a hand grenade. [C14 *pinappel* pine cone; C17: applied to the fruit because of its appearance]

pine cone *n.* the seed-producing structure of a pine tree. See **cone** (sense 3a).

pine marten *n.* a marten of N European and Asian coniferous woods, having dark brown fur with a creamy-yellow patch on the throat.

pinene (ˈpaɪniːn) *n.* either of two isomeric terpenes, found in many essential oils and constituting the main part of oil of turpentine. [C20: < PINE[1] + -ENE]

pine tar *n.* a brown or black semisolid or viscous substance, produced by the destructive distillation of pine wood, used in roofing compositions, paints, medicines, etc.

pinfeather (ˈpɪnˌfɛðə) *n. Ornithol.* a feather emerging from the skin and still enclosed in its horny sheath.

pinfold (ˈpɪnˌfəʊld) *n.* **1.** a pound for stray cattle. ~*vb.* **2.** (*tr.*) to gather or confine in or as if in a pinfold. [OE *pundfald*]

ping (pɪŋ) *n.* **1.** a short high-pitched resonant sound, as of a bullet striking metal or a sonar echo. ~*vb.* **2.** (*intr.*) to make such a noise. [C19: imit.]

pinger (ˈpɪŋə) *n.* a device that makes a pinging sound, esp. one that can be preset to ring at a particular time.

Ping-Pong (ˈpɪŋˌpɒŋ) *n. Trademark.* another name for **table tennis.** Also: **ping pong.**

pinhead (ˈpɪnˌhɛd) *n.* **1.** the head of a pin. **2.** something very small. **3.** *Inf.* a stupid person. —ˈ**pinˌheaded** *adj.* —ˈ**pinˌheadedness** *n.*

pinhole (ˈpɪnˌhəʊl) *n.* a small hole made with or as if with a pin.

pinion[1] (ˈpɪnjən) *n.* **1.** *Chiefly poetic.* a bird's wing. **2.** the part of a bird's wing including the flight feathers. ~*vb.* (*tr.*) **3.** to hold or bind (the arms) of (a person) so as to restrain or immobilize him. **4.** to confine or shackle. **5.** to make (a bird) incapable of flight by removing the flight feathers. [C15: < OF *pignon* wing, < L *pinna* wing]

pinion[2] (ˈpɪnjən) *n.* a cogwheel that engages with a larger wheel or rack. [C17: < F *pignon* cogwheel, < OF *peigne* comb, < L *pecten*]

pink[1] (pɪŋk) *n.* **1.** a pale reddish colour. **2.** pink cloth or clothing: *dressed in pink.* **3.** any of various Old World plants, such as the garden pink, cultivated for their fragrant flowers. See also **carnation** (sense 1). **4.** the flower of any of these plants. **5.** the highest or best degree, condition, etc. (esp. in **in the pink**). **6. a.** a huntsman's scarlet coat. **b.** a huntsman who wears a scarlet coat. ~*adj.* **7.** of the colour pink. **8.** *Brit. inf.* left-wing. **9.** (of a huntsman's coat) scarlet or red. ~*vb.* **10.** (*intr.*) another word for **knock** (sense 7). [C16 (the flower), C18 (the colour): ? short for PINKEYE] —ˈ**pinkish** *or* ˈ**pinky** *adj.* —ˈ**pinkness** *n.*

pink[2] (pɪŋk) *vb.* (*tr.*) **1.** to prick lightly with a sword, etc. **2.** to decorate (leather, etc.) with a perforated or punched pattern. **3.** to cut with pinking shears. [C14: ? of Low G origin]

pink[3] (pɪŋk) *n.* a sailing vessel with a narrow overhanging transom. [C15: < MDu. *pinke,* <?]

pinkeye (ˈpɪŋkˌaɪ) *n.* **1.** Also called: **acute conjunctivitis.** an acute contagious inflammation of the conjunctiva of the eye, characterized by redness, discharge, etc. **2.** Also called: **infectious keratitis.** a similar condition affecting the cornea of horses and cattle. [C16: partial translation of obs. Du. *pinck oogen* small eyes]

pinkie *or* **pinky** (ˈpɪŋkɪ) *n., pl.* **-ies.** *Scot., U.S., & Canad.* the little finger. [C19: < Du. *pinkje*]

pinking shears *pl. n.* scissors with a serrated edge on one or both blades, producing a wavy edge to material cut, thus preventing fraying.

pink salmon *n.* **1.** any salmon having pale pink flesh. **2.** the flesh of such a fish.

pin money *n.* **1.** an allowance by a husband to his wife for personal expenditure. **2.** money saved or earned for incidental expenses.

pinna (ˈpɪnə) *n., pl.* **-nae** (-niː) *or* **-nas.** **1.** any leaflet of a pinnate compound leaf. **2.** *Zool.* a feather, wing, fin, etc. **3.** another name for **auricle** (sense 2). [C18: via NL < L: wing]

pinnace (ˈpɪnɪs) *n.* any of various kinds of ship's tender. [C16: < F *pinace,* ? < OSp. *pinaza,* lit.: something made of pine, ult. < L *pīnus* pine]

pinnacle (ˈpɪnəkᵊl) *n.* **1.** the highest point, esp. of fame, success, etc. **2.** a towering peak, as of a mountain. **3.** a slender upright structure in the form of a spire on the top of a buttress, gable, or tower. ~*vb.* (*tr.*) **4.** to set as on a pinnacle. **5.** to furnish with a pinnacle or pinnacles. **6.** to crown with a pinnacle. [C14: via OF < LL *pinnăculum* a peak, < L *pinna* wing]

pinnate (ˈpɪneɪt, ˈpɪnɪt) *adj.* **1.** like a feather in appearance. **2.** (of compound leaves) having the leaflets growing opposite each other in pairs on either side of the stem. [C18: < L *pinnātus,* < *pinna* feather] —ˈ**pinnately** *adv.* —**pin**ˈ**nation** *n.*

pinniped (ˈpɪnɪˌpɛd) *adj.* **1.** of, relating to, or belonging to an order of aquatic placental mammals having a streamlined body and limbs specialized as flippers: includes seals, sea lions, and the walrus. ~*n.* **2.** any pinniped animal. [C19: < NL *pinnipēs,* < L *pinna* fin + *pēs* foot]

pinnule (ˈpɪnjuːl) *n.* **1.** any of the lobes of a leaflet of a pinnate compound leaf, which is itself pinnately divided. **2.** *Zool.* any feather-like part, such as any of the arms of a sea lily. [C16: < L *pinnula,* dim. of *pinna* feather] —ˈ**pinnular** *adj.*

pinny (ˈpɪnɪ) *n., pl.* **-nies.** a child's or informal name for **pinafore** (sense 1).

pinochle *or* **pinocle** (ˈpiːnʌkᵊl) *n.* **1.** a card game for two to four players similar to bezique. **2.** the combination of queen of spades and jack of diamonds in this game. [C19: <?]

pinpoint (ˈpɪnˌpɔɪnt) *vb.* (*tr.*) **1.** to locate or identify exactly: *to pinpoint a problem; to pinpoint a place on a map.* ~*n.* **2.** an insignificant or trifling thing. **3.** the point of a pin. **4.** (*modifier*) exact: *a pinpoint aim.*

pinprick (ˈpɪnˌprɪk) *n.* **1.** a slight puncture made by or as if by a pin. **2.** a small irritation. ~*vb.* **3.** (*tr.*) to puncture with or as if with a pin.

pins and needles *n.* (*functioning as sing.*) *Inf.* **1.** a tingling sensation in the fingers, toes, legs, etc., caused by the return of normal blood circulation after its temporary impairment. **2. on pins and needles.** in a state of anxious suspense.

pinstripe (ˈpɪnˌstraɪp) *n.* (in textiles) a very narrow stripe in fabric or the fabric itself.

pint (paɪnt) *n.* **1.** a unit of liquid measure of capacity equal to one eighth of a gallon. 1 Brit. pint is equal to 0.568 litre, 1 U.S. pint to 0.473 litre. **2.** a unit of dry measure of capacity equal to one half of a quart. 1 U.S. dry pint is equal to one sixty-fourth of a U.S. bushel or 0.5506 litre. **3.** a measure having such a capacity. **4.** *Brit. inf.* **a.** a pint of beer. **b.** a drink of beer: *he's gone out for a pint.* [C14: < OF *pinte,* <?; ? < Med. L *pincta* marks used in measuring liquids, ult. < L *pingere* to paint]

pinta (ˈpaɪntə) *n. Inf.* a pint of milk. [C20: phonetic rendering of *pint of*]

pintail (ˈpɪnˌteɪl) *n., pl.* **-tails** *or* **-tail.** a greyish-brown duck with a pointed tail.

pintle (ˈpɪntᵊl) *n.* **1.** a pin or bolt forming the pivot of a hinge. **2.** the link bolt, hook, or pin on a vehicle's towing bracket. **3.** the needle or plunger of the injection valve of an oil engine. [OE *pintel* penis]

pinto (ˈpɪntəʊ) *U.S. & Canad.* ~*adj.* **1.** marked with patches of white; piebald. ~*n., pl.* **-tos.** **2.** a pinto horse. [C19: < American Sp. (orig.: painted, spotted), ult. < L *pingere* to paint]

pint-size *or* **pint-sized** *adj. Inf.* very small.

pin tuck *n.* a narrow, ornamental fold, esp. used on shirt fronts and dress bodices.

pin-up *n.* **1.** *Inf.* **a.** a picture of a sexually attractive person, esp. when partially or totally undressed. **b.** (*as modifier*): *a pin-up magazine.* **2.** *Sl.* a person who has appeared in such a picture. **3.** a photograph of a famous personality.

pinus radiata (ˈpaɪnəs ˌreɪdɪˈɑːtə) *n.* a pine tree grown in New Zealand and Australia to produce building timber.

pinwheel (ˈpɪnˌwiːl) *n.* another name for a **Catherine wheel** (sense 1).

pinworm (ˈpɪnˌwɜːm) *n.* a parasitic nematode worm, infecting the colon, rectum, and anus of humans. Also called: **threadworm.**

piny (ˈpaɪnɪ) *adj.* **pinier, piniest.** of, resembling, or covered with pine trees.

Pinyin (ˈpɪnˈjɪn) *n.* a system of spelling used to transliterate Chinese characters into the Roman alphabet.

pion (ˈpaɪɒn) *or* **pi meson** *n. Physics.* a meson having a positive or negative charge and a rest mass 273 times that of the electron, or no charge and a rest mass 264 times that of the electron.

pioneer (ˌpaɪəˈnɪə) *n.* **1. a.** a colonist, explorer, or settler of a new land, region, etc. **b.** (*as modifier*): *a pioneer wagon.* **2.** an innovator or developer of something new. **3.** *Mil.* a member of an infantry group that digs entrenchments, makes roads, etc. ~*vb.* **4.** to be a pioneer (in or of). **5.** (*tr.*) to initiate, prepare, or open up: *to pioneer a medical programme.* [C16: < OF *paonier* infantryman, < *paon* PAWN[2]]

pious (ˈpaɪəs) *adj.* **1.** having or expressing reverence for a god or gods; religious; devout. **2.** marked by reverence. **3.** marked by false reverence; sanctimonious. **4.** sacred; not secular. [C17: < L *pius*] —ˈ**piously** *adv.* —ˈ**piousness** *n.*

pip[1] (pɪp) *n.* **1.** the seed of a fleshy fruit, such as an apple or pear. **2.** any of the segments marking the surface of a pineapple. [C18: short for PIPPIN]

pip[2] (pɪp) *n.* **1.** a short high-pitched sound, a sequence of which can act as a time signal, esp. on radio. **2.** a radar blip. **3. a.** a device, such as a spade, diamond, heart, or club on a playing card. **b.** any of the spots on dice or dominoes. **4.** *Inf.* the emblem worn on the shoulder by junior officers in the British Army, indicating their rank. ~*vb.* **pipping, pipped. 5.** (of a young bird) **a.** (*intr.*) to chirp; peep. **b.** to pierce (the shell of its egg) while hatching. **6.** (*intr.*) to make a short high-pitched sound. [C16 (in the sense: spot); C17 (vb.); C20 (in the sense: short high-pitched sound): ? imit.]

pip[3] (pɪp) *n.* **1.** a contagious disease of poultry characterized by the secretion of thick mucus in the mouth and throat. **2.** *Facetious sl.* a minor human ailment. **3.** *Brit. sl.* a bad temper or depression (esp. in **give (someone) the pip**). ~*vb.* **pipping, pipped. 4.** *Brit. sl.* to cause to be annoyed or depressed. [C15: < MDu. *pippe*, ult. < L *pituita* phlegm]

pip[4] (pɪp) *vb.* **pipping, pipped.** (*tr.*) *Brit. sl.* **1.** to wound, esp. with a gun. **2.** to defeat (a person), esp. when his success seems certain (often in **pip at the post**). **3.** to blackball or ostracize. [C19 (orig. in the sense: to blackball): prob. < PIP[2]]

pipal (ˈpiːpᵊl) *n.* a variant of **peepul.**

pipe[1] (paɪp) *n.* **1.** a long tube of metal, plastic, etc., used to convey water, oil, gas, etc. **2.** a long tube or case. **3.** an object made in various shapes and sizes, consisting of a small bowl with an attached tubular stem, in which tobacco or other substances are smoked. **4.** Also called: **pipeful.** the amount of tobacco that fills the bowl of a pipe. **5. put that in your pipe and smoke it.** *Inf.* accept that fact if you can. **6.** *Zool., bot.* any of various hollow organs, such as the respiratory passage of certain animals. **7. a.** any musical instrument whose sound production results from the vibration of an air column in a simple tube. **b.** any of the tubular devices on an organ. **8. the pipes.** See **bagpipes. 9.** a shrill voice or sound, as of a bird. **10. a.** a boatswain's pipe. **b.** the sound it makes. **11.** (*pl.*) *Inf.* the respiratory tract or vocal cords. **12.** *Metallurgy.* a conical hole in the head of an ingot. **13.** a cylindrical vein of rich ore. **14.** Also called: **volcanic pipe.** a vertical cylindrical passage in a volcano through which molten lava is forced during eruption. ~*vb.* **15.** to play (music) on a pipe. **16.** (*tr.*) to summon or lead by a pipe: *to pipe the dancers.* **17.** to utter (something) shrilly. **18. a.** to signal orders to (the crew) by a boatswain's pipe. **b.** (*tr.*) to signal the arrival or departure of: *to pipe the admiral aboard.* **19.** (*tr.*) to convey (water, gas, etc.) by a pipe or pipes. **20.** (*tr.*) to provide with pipes. **21.** (*tr.*) to trim (an article, esp. of clothing) with piping. **22.** to force cream or icing, etc., through a shaped nozzle to decorate food. ~See also **pipe down, pipe up.** [OE *pīpe* (n.), *pīpian* (vb.), ult. < L *pīpāre* to chirp]

pipe[2] (paɪp) *n.* **1.** a large cask for wine, oil, etc. **2.** a measure of capacity for wine equal to four barrels or 105 Brit. gallons. **3.** a cask holding this quantity with its contents. [C14: via OF (in the sense: tube), ult. < L *pīpāre* to chirp]

pipeclay (ˈpaɪpˌkleɪ) *n.* **1.** a fine white pure clay, used in the manufacture of tobacco pipes and pottery and for whitening leather and similar materials. ~*vb.* **2.** (*tr.*) to whiten with pipeclay.

pipe cleaner *n.* a short length of thin wires twisted so as to hold tiny tufts of yarn: used to clean the stem of a tobacco pipe.

piped music *n.* light popular music prerecorded and played through amplifiers in a shop, restaurant, factory, etc., as background music.

pipe down *vb.* (*intr., adv.*) *Inf.* to stop talking, making noise, etc.

pipe dream *n.* a fanciful or impossible plan or hope. [alluding to dreams produced by smoking an opium pipe]

pipefish (ˈpaɪpˌfɪʃ) *n., pl.* **-fish** *or* **-fishes.** any of various teleost fishes having a long tubelike snout and an elongated body covered with bony plates. Also called: **needlefish.**

pipefitting (ˈpaɪpˌfɪtɪŋ) *n.* **a.** the act or process of bending and joining pipes. **b.** the branch of plumbing involving this. —ˈ**pipeˌfitter** *n.*

pipeline (ˈpaɪpˌlaɪn) *n.* **1.** a long pipe used to transport oil, natural gas, etc. **2.** a medium of communication, esp. a private one. **3. in the pipeline.** in the process of being completed, delivered, or produced. ~*vb.* (*tr.*) **4.** to convey by pipeline. **5.** to supply with a pipeline.

pipe major *n.* the noncommissioned officer responsible for the training of a pipe band.

pipe organ *n.* another name for **organ** (the musical instrument).

piper (ˈpaɪpə) *n.* **1.** a person who plays a pipe or bagpipes. **2. pay the piper and call the tune.** to bear the cost of an undertaking and control it.

piperidine (pɪˈpɛrɪˌdiːn) *n.* a liquid compound with a peppery ammoniacal odour: used in making rubbers and curing epoxy resins.

piperine (ˈpɪpəˌraɪn) *n.* an alkaloid that is the active ingredient of pepper, used as a flavouring and as an insecticide. [C19: < L *piper* PEPPER]

piperonal (ˈpɪpərəʊˌnæl) *n.* a white fragrant aldehyde used in flavourings, perfumery, and suntan lotions.

pipette (pɪˈpɛt) *n.* a slender glass tube for transferring or measuring out known volumes of liquid. [C19: via F: little pipe]

pipe up *vb.* (*intr., adv.*) **1.** to commence singing or playing a musical instrument: *the band piped up.* **2.** to speak up, esp. in a shrill voice.

pipi (ˈpɪpiː) *n., pl.* **pipi** *or* **pipis. 1.** an edible shellfish of New Zealand. **2.** an Australian mollusc of sandy beaches, widely used as bait. [< Maori]

piping (ˈpaɪpɪŋ) *n.* **1.** pipes collectively, as in the plumbing of a house. **2.** a cord of icing, whipped cream, etc., often used to decorate desserts and cakes. **3.** a thin strip of covered cord or material, used to edge hems, etc. **4.** the sound of a pipe or bagpipes. **5.** the art or technique of playing a pipe or bagpipes. **6.** a shrill voice or sound, esp. a whistling sound. ~*adj.* **7.** making a shrill sound. **8. piping hot.** extremely hot.

pipistrelle (ˌpɪpɪˈstrɛl) *n.* any of a genus of numerous small brownish insectivorous bats, occurring in most parts of the world. [C18: via F < It. *pipistrello*, < L *vespertīliō* a bat, < *vesper* evening, because of its nocturnal habits]

pipit (ˈpɪpɪt) *n.* any of various songbirds, esp. the **meadow pipit,** having brownish speckled plumage and a long tail. [C18: prob. imit.]

pipkin (ˈpɪpkɪn) *n.* a small earthenware vessel. [C16: ? dim. of PIPE[2]; see -KIN]

pippin (ˈpɪpɪn) *n.* any of several varieties of eating apple. [C13: < OF *pepin*, <?]

pipsissewa (pɪpˈsɪsəwə) *n.* any of several ericaceous plants of an Asian and American genus, having jagged evergreen leaves and white or pinkish flowers. Also called: **wintergreen.** [C19: < Algonquian *pipisisikweu*, lit.: it breaks it into pieces, so called because believed to be efficacious in treating bladder stones]

pipsqueak (ˈpɪpˌskwiːk) *n. Inf.* a person or thing that is insignificant or contemptible.

piquant (ˈpiːkənt, -kɑːnt) *adj.* **1.** having an agreeably pungent or tart taste. **2.** lively or stimulating to the mind. [C16: < F (lit.: prickling),

< *piquer* to prick, goad] —ˈ**piquancy** *n.* —ˈ**piquantly** *adv.*

pique (piːk) *n.* **1.** a feeling of resentment or irritation, as from having one's pride wounded. ~*vb.* **piquing, piqued.** (*tr.*) **2.** to cause to feel resentment or irritation. **3.** to excite or arouse. **4.** (foll. by *on* or *upon*) to pride or congratulate (oneself). [C16: < F, < *piquer* to prick]

piqué (ˈpiːkeɪ) *n.* a close-textured fabric of cotton, silk, or spun rayon woven with lengthwise ribs. [C19: < F *piqué* pricked, < *piquer* to prick]

piquet (pɪˈkɛt, -ˈkeɪ) *n.* a card game for two people played with a reduced pack. [C17: < F, <?]

piracy (ˈpaɪrəsɪ) *n., pl.* **-cies. 1.** *Brit.* robbery on the seas. **2.** a felony, such as robbery or hijacking, committed aboard a ship or aircraft. **3.** the unauthorized use or appropriation of patented or copyrighted material, ideas, etc. [C16: < Anglo-L *pirātia*, < LGk *peirāteia;* see PIRATE]

piranha *or* **piraña** (pɪˈrɑːnjə) *n.* any of various small freshwater voracious fishes of tropical America, having strong jaws and sharp teeth. [C19: via Port. < Tupi: fish with teeth, < *pirá* fish + *sainha* tooth]

pirate (ˈpaɪrɪt) *n.* **1.** a person who commits piracy. **2. a.** a vessel used by pirates. **b.** (*as modifier*): *a pirate ship.* **3.** a person who illicitly uses or appropriates someone else's literary, artistic, or other work. **4. a.** a person or group of people who broadcast illegally. **b.** (*as modifier*): *a pirate radio station.* ~*vb.* **5.** (*tr.*) to use, appropriate, or reproduce (artistic work, ideas, etc.) illicitly. [C15: < L *pīrāta*, < Gk *peirātēs* one who attacks, < *peira* an attack] —**piratic** (paɪˈrætɪk) *or* **piˈratical** *adj.* —**piˈratically** *adv.*

pirogue (pɪˈrəʊg) *or* **piragua** (pɪˈrɑːgwə, -ˈræg-) *n.* any of various kinds of dugout canoes. [C17: via F < Sp., of Amerind origin]

pirouette (ˌpɪrʊˈɛt) *n.* **1.** a body spin, esp. in dancing, on the toes or the ball of the foot. ~*vb.* **2.** (*intr.*) to perform a pirouette. [C18: < F, < OF *pirouet* spinning top]

piscatorial (ˌpɪskəˈtɔːrɪəl) *or* **piscatory** (ˈpɪskətərɪ, -trɪ) *adj.* **1.** of or relating to fish, fishing, or fishermen. **2.** devoted to fishing. [C19: < L *piscātōrius*, < *piscātor* fisherman] —ˌ**piscaˈtorially** *adv.*

Pisces (ˈpaɪsiːz, ˈpɪ-) *n., Latin genitive* **Piscium** (ˈpaɪsɪəm). **1.** *Astron.* a faint extensive zodiacal constellation lying between Aquarius and Aries on the ecliptic. **2.** *Astrol.* Also called: the **Fishes.** the twelfth sign of the zodiac. The sun is in this sign between about Feb. 19 and March 20. **3. a.** a taxonomic group that comprises all fishes. See **fish** (sense 1). **b.** a taxonomic group that comprises the bony fishes only. See **teleost.** [C14: L: the fish (pl.)]

pisci- *combining form.* fish: *pisciculture.* [< L *piscis*]

pisciculture (ˈpɪsɪˌkʌltʃə) *n.* the rearing and breeding of fish under controlled conditions. —ˌ**pisciˈcultural** *adj.* —ˌ**pisciˈculturist** *n., adj.*

piscina (pɪˈsiːnə) *n., pl.* **-nae** (-niː) *or* **-nas.** *R.C. Church.* a stone basin, with a drain, in a church or sacristy where water used at Mass is poured away. [C16: < L: fish pond, < *piscis* a fish]

piscine (ˈpɪsaɪn) *adj.* of, relating to, or resembling a fish.

piscivorous (pɪˈsɪvərəs) *adj.* feeding on fish.

pish (pʃ, pɪʃ) *interj.* **1.** an exclamation of impatience or contempt. ~*vb.* **2.** to make this exclamation at (someone or something).

pisiform (ˈpɪsɪˌfɔːm) *adj.* **1.** *Zool., bot.* resembling a pea. ~*n.* **2.** a small pealike bone on the ulnar side of the carpus. [C18: via NL < L *pīsum* pea + *forma* shape]

pismire (ˈpɪsˌmaɪə) *n.* an archaic or dialect word for an **ant.** [C14 (lit.: urinating ant, from the odour of formic acid): < PISS + obs. *mire* ant, < ON]

piss (pɪs) *Taboo sl.* ~*vb.* **1.** (*intr.*) to urinate. **2.** (*tr.*) to discharge as or in one's urine: *to piss blood.* ~*n.* **3.** an act of urinating. **4.** urine. [C13: < OF *pisser*, prob. imit.]

pissed (pɪst) *adj. Brit. taboo sl.* drunk.

piss off *vb.* (*adv.*) *Taboo sl.* **1.** (*tr.; often passive*) to annoy, irritate, or disappoint. **2.** (*intr.*) *Chiefly Brit.* to go away; depart: often used to dismiss a person.

pistachio (pɪˈstɑːʃɪˌəʊ) *n., pl.* **-chios. 1.** a tree of the Mediterranean region and W Asia, with small hard-shelled nuts. **2.** Also called: **pistachio nut.** the nut of this tree, having an edible green kernel. **3.** the sweet flavour of the pistachio nut, used in ice creams, etc. ~*adj.* **4.** of a yellowish-green colour. [C16: via It. & L < Gk *pistakion* pistachio nut, < *pistakē* pistachio tree, < Persian *pistah*]

piste (piːst) *n.* a slope or course for skiing. [C18: via OF < OIt. *pista*, < *pistare* to tread down]

pistil (ˈpɪstɪl) *n.* the female reproductive part of a flower, consisting of one or more separate or fused carpels. [C18: < L *pistillum* pestle]

pistillate (ˈpɪstɪlɪt, -ˌleɪt) *adj.* (of plants) **1.** having pistils but no anthers. **2.** having or producing pistils.

pistol (ˈpɪstᵊl) *n.* **1.** a short-barrelled handgun. **2. hold a pistol to a person's head.** to threaten a person in order to force him to do what one wants. ~*vb.* **-tolling, -tolled** *or U.S.* **-toling, -toled. 3.** (*tr.*) to shoot with a pistol. [C16: < F *pistole*, < G, < Czech *pišťala* pistol, pipe]

pistole (pɪsˈtəʊl) *n.* any of various gold coins of varying value, formerly used in Europe. [C16: < OF, shortened < *pistolet*, lit.: little PISTOL]

pistol grip *n.* **a.** a handle shaped like the butt of a pistol. **b.** (*as modifier*): *a pistol-grip camera.*

pistol-whip *vb.* **-whipping, -whipped.** (*tr.*) *U.S.* to beat or strike with a pistol barrel.

piston (ˈpɪstən) *n.* a disc or cylindrical part that slides to and fro in a hollow cylinder. In an internal-combustion engine it is attached by a pivoted connecting rod to a crankshaft or flywheel, thus converting reciprocating motion into rotation. [C18: via F < OIt. *pistone*, < *pistare* to grind, < L *pinsere* to beat]

piston ring *n.* a split ring that fits into a groove on the rim of a piston to provide a spring-loaded seal against the cylinder wall.

piston rod *n.* **1.** the rod that connects the piston of a reciprocating steam engine to the crosshead. **2.** a less common name for a **connecting rod.**

pit[1] (pɪt) *n.* **1.** a large, usually deep opening in the ground. **2. a.** a mine or excavation, esp. for coal. **b.** the shaft in a mine. **c.** (*as modifier*): *pit pony; pit prop.* **3.** a concealed danger or difficulty. **4. the pit.** hell. **5.** Also called: **orchestra pit.** the area that is occupied by the orchestra in a theatre, located in front of the stage. **6.** an enclosure for fighting animals or birds. **7.** *Anat.* **a.** a small natural depression on the surface of a body, organ, or part. **b.** the floor of any natural bodily cavity: *the pit of the stomach.* **8.** *Pathol.* a small indented scar at the site of a former pustule; pockmark. **9.** a working area at the side of a motor-racing track for servicing or refuelling vehicles. **10.** *U.S.* a section on the floor of a commodity exchange devoted to a special line of trading. **11.** the ground floor of the auditorium of a theatre. **12.** another word for **pitfall** (sense 2). ~*vb.* **pitting, pitted. 13.** (*tr.;* often foll. by *against*) to match in opposition, esp. as antagonists. **14.** to mark or become marked with pits. **15.** (*tr.*) to place or bury in a pit. [OE *pytt*, < L *puteus*]

pit[2] (pɪt) *Chiefly U.S. & Canad.* ~*n.* **1.** the stone of a cherry, etc. ~*vb.* **pitting, pitted.** (*tr.*) **2.** to extract the stone from (a fruit). [C19: < Du.: kernel]

pitapat (ˈpɪtəˌpæt) *adv.* **1.** with quick light taps. ~*vb.* **-patting, -patted. 2.** (*intr.*) to make quick light taps. ~*n.* **3.** such taps. [C16: imit.]

pitch[1] (pɪtʃ) *vb.* **1.** to hurl or throw (something); cast; fling. **2.** (*usually tr.*) to set up (a camp, tent, etc.). **3.** (*tr.*) to set the level, character, or slope of. **4.** (*intr.*) to slope downwards. **5.** (*intr.*) to fall forwards or downwards. **6.** (*intr.*) (of a vessel) to dip and raise its bow and stern alternately. **7.** (*tr.; foll. by up*) *Cricket.* to bowl (a ball) so that it bounces near the batsman. **8.** (*intr.*) (of a missile, aircraft, etc.) to deviate from a stable flight attitude by movement of the longitudinal axis about the lateral axis. **9.** (*tr.*) (in golf, etc.) to hit (a ball) steeply into the air. **10.** (*tr.*) *Music.* **a.** to sing or play accurately (a note, interval, etc.). **b.** (*usually passive*) (of a wind instrument) to specify or indicate its basic key or harmonic series by its size, manufacture, etc. **11.** *Baseball.* **a.** (*tr.*) to throw (a baseball) to a batter. **b.** (*intr.*) to act as a pitcher in a baseball game. *~n.* **12.** the degree of elevation or depression. **13. a.** the angle of descent of a downward slope. **b.** such a slope. **14.** the extreme height or depth. **15.** *Mountaineering.* a section of a route between two belay points. **16.** the degree of slope of a roof. **17.** the distance between corresponding points on adjacent members of a body of regular form, esp. the distance between teeth on a gearwheel or between threads on a screw thread. **18.** the pitching motion of a ship, missile, etc. **19.** *Music.* **a.** the auditory property of a note that is conditioned by its frequency relative to other notes: *high pitch; low pitch.* **b.** an absolute frequency assigned to a specific note, fixing the relative frequencies of all other notes. **20.** *Cricket.* the rectangular area between the stumps, 22 yards long and 10 feet wide; the wicket. **21.** the act or manner of pitching a ball, as in cricket, etc. **22.** *Chiefly Brit.* a vendor's station, esp. on a pavement. **23.** *Sl.* a persuasive sales talk, esp. one routinely repeated. **24.** *Chiefly Brit.* (in many sports) the field of play. **25.** *Golf.* Also called: **pitch shot.** an approach shot in which the ball is struck in a high arc. **26. queer someone's pitch.** *Brit. inf.* to upset someone's plans. ~See also **pitch in, pitch into.** [C13 *picchen*]

pitch² (pɪtʃ) *n.* **1.** any of various heavy dark viscid substances obtained as a residue from the distillation of tars. **2.** any of various similar substances, such as asphalt, occurring as natural deposits. **3.** crude turpentine obtained as sap from pine trees. *~vb.* **4.** (*tr.*) to apply pitch to (something). [OE *pic,* < L *pix*]

pitch-black *adj.* **1.** extremely dark; unlit: *the room was pitch-black.* **2.** of a deep black colour.

pitchblende (ˈpɪtʃˌblɛnd) *n.* a blackish mineral that occurs in veins, frequently associated with silver: the principal source of uranium and radium. [C18: partial translation of G *Pechblende,* < *Pech* PITCH² (from its black colour) + BLENDE]

pitch-dark *adj.* extremely or completely dark.

pitched battle *n.* **1.** a battle ensuing from the deliberate choice of time and place. **2.** any fierce encounter, esp. one with large numbers.

pitcher¹ (ˈpɪtʃə) *n.* a large jug, usually rounded with a narrow neck and often of earthenware, used mainly for holding water. [C13: < OF *pichier,* < Med. L *picārium,* var. of *bicārium* BEAKER]

pitcher² (ˈpɪtʃə) *n. Baseball.* the player on the fielding team who throws the ball to the batter.

pitcher plant *n.* any of various insectivorous plants, having leaves modified to form pitcher-like organs that attract and trap insects, which are then digested.

pitchfork (ˈpɪtʃˌfɔːk) *n.* **1.** a long-handled fork with two or three long curved tines for tossing hay. *~vb.* (*tr.*) **2.** to use a pitchfork on (something). **3.** to thrust (someone) unwillingly into a position.

pitch in *vb.* (*intr., adv.*) **1.** to cooperate or contribute. **2.** to begin energetically.

pitch into *vb.* (*intr., prep.*) *Inf.* **1.** to assail physically or verbally. **2.** to get on with doing (something).

pitch pine *n.* **1.** any of various coniferous trees of North America: valued as a source of turpentine and pitch. **2.** the wood of any of these trees.

pitch pipe *n.* a small pipe that sounds a note or notes of standard frequency. It is used for establishing the correct starting note for unaccompanied singing.

pitchy (ˈpɪtʃɪ) *adj.* **pitchier, pitchiest. 1.** full of or covered with pitch. **2.** resembling pitch. —**ˈpitchiness** *n.*

piteous (ˈpɪtɪəs) *adj.* exciting or deserving pity. —**ˈpiteously** *adv.* —**ˈpiteousness** *n.*

pitfall (ˈpɪtˌfɔːl) *n.* **1.** an unsuspected difficulty or danger. **2.** a trap in the form of a concealed pit, designed to catch men or wild animals. [OE *pytt* PIT¹ + *fealle* trap]

pith (pɪθ) *n.* **1.** the soft fibrous tissue lining the inside of the rind in fruits such as the orange. **2.** the essential or important part, point, etc. **3.** weight; substance. **4.** *Bot.* the central core of unspecialized cells surrounded by conducting tissue in stems. **5.** the soft central part of a bone, feather, etc. *~vb.* (*tr.*) **6.** to kill (animals) by severing the spinal cord. **7.** to remove the pith from (a plant). [OE *pitha*]

pithead (ˈpɪtˌhɛd) *n.* the top of a mine shaft and the buildings, hoisting gear, etc., around it.

pithecanthropus (ˌpɪθɪkænˈθrəʊpəs) *n., pl.* **-pi** (-ˌpaɪ). any primitive apelike man of the former genus *Pithecanthropus,* now included in the genus *Homo.* See **Java man.** [C19: NL, < Gk *pithēkos* ape + *anthrōpos* man]

pith helmet *n.* a lightweight hat made of the pith of the sola, an E Indian swamp plant, that protects the wearer from the sun. Also called: **topee, topi.**

pithos (ˈpɪθɒs, ˈpaɪ-) *n., pl.* **-thoi** (-θɔɪ). a large ceramic container for oil or grain. [< Gk]

pithy (ˈpɪθɪ) *adj.* **pithier, pithiest. 1.** terse and full of meaning or substance. **2.** of, resembling, or full of pith. —**ˈpithily** *adv.* —**ˈpithiness** *n.*

pitiable (ˈpɪtɪəbᵊl) *adj.* exciting or deserving pity or contempt. —**ˈpitiableness** *n.* —**ˈpitiably** *adv.*

pitiful (ˈpɪtɪfʊl) *adj.* **1.** arousing or deserving pity. **2.** arousing or deserving contempt. **3.** *Arch.* full of pity or compassion. —**ˈpitifully** *adv.* —**ˈpitifulness** *n.*

pitiless (ˈpɪtɪlɪs) *adj.* having or showing little or no pity or mercy. —**ˈpitilessly** *adv.* —**ˈpitilessness** *n.*

pitman (ˈpɪtmən) *n., pl.* **-men.** *Chiefly Scot. & N English.* a person who works in a pit, esp. a coal miner.

piton (ˈpiːtɒn) *n. Mountaineering.* a metal spike that may be driven into a crevice and used to secure a rope, etc. [C20: < F: ringbolt]

pits (pɪts) *pl. n.* **the.** *Sl.* the worst possible person, place, or thing. [C20: < ? *armpits*]

pitta bread *or* **pitta** (ˈpɪtə) *n.* a flat rounded slightly leavened bread, originally from the Middle East. [< Mod. Gk: a cake]

pittance (ˈpɪtᵊns) *n.* a small amount or portion, esp. a meagre allowance of money. [C16: < OF *pietance* ration, ult. < L *pietās* duty]

pitter-patter (ˈpɪtəˌpætə) *n.* **1.** the sound of light rapid taps or pats, as of raindrops. *~vb.* **2.** (*intr.*) to make such a sound. *~adv.* **3.** with such a sound.

pituitary (pɪˈtjuːɪtərɪ) *n., pl.* **-taries. 1.** See **pituitary gland.** *~adj.* **2.** of or relating to the pituitary gland. [C17: < LL *pītuītārius* slimy, < *pītuīta* phlegm]

pituitary gland *or* **body** *n.* the master endocrine gland, attached by a stalk to the base of the brain. Its two lobes secrete hormones affecting skeletal growth, development of the sex glands, and the functioning of the other endocrine glands.

pit viper *n.* any venomous snake of a New World family, having a heat-sensitive organ in a pit on each side of the head: includes the rattlesnakes.

pity (ˈpɪtɪ) *n., pl.* **pities. 1.** sympathy or sorrow felt for the sufferings of another. **2. have** (*or* **take**) **pity on.** to have sympathy or show mercy for. **3.** something that causes regret. **4.** an unfortunate chance: *what a pity you can't come.* *~vb.* **pitying, pitied.** (*tr.*) **5.** to feel pity for. [C13: < OF *pité,* < L *pietās* duty] —**ˈpitying** *adj.* —**ˈpityingly** *adv.*

pityriasis (ˌpɪtəˈraɪəsɪs) *n.* any of a group of skin diseases characterized by the shedding of dry flakes of skin. [C17: via NL < Gk *pituriasis* scurfiness, < *pituron* bran]

più (pju:) *adv.* (*in combination*) *Music.* more (quickly, etc.): *più allegro.* [It., < L *plus* more]
piupiu (ˈpi:u:ˌpi:u:) *n.* a skirt made from leaves of the New Zealand flax, worn by Maoris on ceremonial occasions. [< Maori]
pivot (ˈpɪvət) *n.* **1.** a short shaft or pin supporting something that turns; fulcrum. **2.** the end of a shaft or arbor that terminates in a bearing. **3.** a person or thing upon which progress, success, etc., depends. **4.** the person or position from which a military formation takes its reference when altering position, etc. ~*vb.* **5.** (*tr.*) to mount on or provide with a pivot or pivots. **6.** (*intr.*) to turn on or as if on a pivot. [C17: < OF]
pivotal (ˈpɪvətᵊl) *adj.* **1.** of, involving, or acting as a pivot. **2.** of crucial importance.
pix[1] (pɪks) *n.* a plural of **pic.**
pix[2] (pɪks) *n.* a less common spelling of **pyx.**
pixel (ˈpɪksɛl) *n.* any of a number of very small picture elements that make up a picture, as on a visual display unit. [C20: < *pix* pictures + *el(ement)*]
pixie *or* **pixy** (ˈpɪksɪ) *n., pl.* **pixies.** (in folklore) a fairy or elf. [C17: <?]
pixilated *or* **pixillated** (ˈpɪksɪˌleɪtɪd) *adj. Chiefly U.S.* **1.** eccentric or whimsical. **2.** *Sl.* drunk. [C20: < PIXIE + *-lated,* as in *stimulated, titillated,* etc.]
pizza (ˈpi:tsə) *n.* a dish of Italian origin consisting of a baked disc of dough covered with cheese and tomatoes, etc. [C20: < It., ? < Vulgar L *picea* (unattested), ? rel. to Med. Gk *pitta* cake]
pizzazz *or* **pizazz** (pəˈzæz) *n. Inf.* an attractive combination of energy and style; sparkle. Also: **bezazz.**
pizzeria (ˌpi:tsəˈri:ə) *n.* a place where pizzas are made, sold, or eaten.
pizzicato (ˌpɪtsɪˈkɑ:təʊ) *Music.* ~*adj., adv.* **1.** (in music for the violin family) to be plucked with the finger. ~*n.* **2.** this style or technique of playing. [C19: < It.: pinched, < *pizzicare* to twist]
pizzle (ˈpɪzᵊl) *n. Arch. or dialect.* the penis of an animal, esp. a bull. [C16: of Gmc origin]
pk *pl.* **pks** *abbrev. for:* **1.** pack. **2.** park. **3.** peak.
pkg. *pl.* **pkgs.** *abbrev. for* package.
pl *abbrev. for:* **1.** place. **2.** plate. **3.** plural.
Pl. (in street names) *abbrev. for* Place.
PLA *abbrev. for* Port of London Authority.
plaas (plɑ:s) *n. S. African.* a farm. [< Afrik., < Du.]
placable (ˈplækəbᵊl) *adj.* easily placated or appeased. [C15: via OF < L *plācābilis,* < *plācāre* to appease] —ˌ**placaˈbility** *n.*
placard (ˈplækɑ:d) *n.* **1.** a notice for public display; poster. **2.** a small plaque or card. ~*vb.* (*tr.*) **3.** to post placards on or in. **4.** to advertise by placards. **5.** to display as a placard. [C15: < OF *plaquart,* < *plaquier* to plate, lay flat; see PLAQUE]
placate (pləˈkeɪt) *vb.* (*tr.*) to pacify or appease. [C17: < L *plācāre*] —**plaˈcation** *n.* —**plaˈcatory** *adj.*
place (pleɪs) *n.* **1.** a particular point or part of space or of a surface, esp. that occupied by a person or thing. **2.** a geographical point, such as a town, city, etc. **3.** a position or rank in a sequence or order. **4.** an open square lined with houses in a city or town. **5.** space or room. **6.** a house or living quarters. **7.** a country house with grounds. **8.** any building or area set aside for a specific purpose. **9.** a passage in a book, play, film, etc.: *to lose one's place.* **10.** proper, right, or customary surroundings (esp. in **out of place, in place**). **11.** right, prerogative, or duty: *it is your place to give a speech.* **12.** appointment, position, or job: *a place at college.* **13.** position, condition, or state: *if I were in your place.* **14. a.** a space or seat, as at a dining table. **b.** (*as modifier*): *place mat.* **15.** *Maths.* the relative position of a digit in a number. **16.** any of the best times in a race. **17.** *Horse racing.* **a.** *Brit.* the first, second, or third position at the finish. **b.** *U.S. & Canad.* the first or usually the second position at the finish. **c.** (*as modifier*): *a place bet.* **18. all over the place.** in disorder or disarray. **19. give place (to).** to make room (for) or be superseded (by). **20. go places.** *Inf.* **a.** to travel. **b.** to become successful. **21. in place of. a.** instead of; in lieu of: *go in place of my sister.* **b.** in exchange for: *he gave her it in place of her ring.* **22. know one's place.** to be aware of one's inferior position. **23. put someone in his** (*or* **her**) **place.** to humble someone who is arrogant, conceited, forward, etc. **24. take one's place.** to take up one's usual or specified position. **25. take place.** to happen or occur. **26. take the place of.** to be a substitute for. ~*vb.* (*mainly tr.*) **27.** to put or set in a particular or appropriate place. **28.** to find or indicate the place of. **29.** to identify or classify by linking with an appropriate context: *to place a face.* **30.** to regard or view as being: *to place prosperity above sincerity.* **31.** to make (an order, bet, etc.). **32.** to find a home or job for (someone). **33.** to appoint to an office or position. **34.** (often foll. by *with*) to put under the care (of). **35.** to direct or aim carefully. **36.** (*passive*) *Brit.* to cause (a racehorse, greyhound, athlete, etc.) to arrive in first, second, third, or sometimes fourth place. **37.** (*intr.*) *U.S. & Canad.* (of a racehorse, greyhound, etc.) to finish among the first three in a contest, esp. in second position. **38.** to invest (funds). **39.** (*tr.*) to insert (an advertisement) in a newspaper, journal, etc. [C13: via OF < L *platēa* courtyard, < Gk *plateia,* < *platus* broad]
placebo (pləˈsi:bəʊ) *n., pl.* **-bos** *or* **-boes. 1.** *Med.* an inactive substance administered to a patient usually to compare its effects with those of a real drug but sometimes for the psychological benefit to the patient through his believing he is receiving treatment. **2.** something said or done to please or humour another. **3.** *R.C. Church.* a traditional name for the vespers of the office for the dead. [C13 (in the ecclesiastical sense): < L *Placebo Domino* I shall please the Lord; C19 (in the medical sense)]
placebo effect *n. Med.* a positive therapeutic effect claimed by a patient after receiving a placebo believed by him to be an active drug.
place card *n.* a card placed on a dinner table before a seat, indicating who is to sit there.
place kick *Football, etc.* ~*n.* **1.** a kick in which the ball is placed in position before it is kicked. ~*vb.* **place-kick. 2.** to kick (a ball) in this way.
placement (ˈpleɪsmənt) *n.* **1.** the act of placing or the state of being placed. **2.** arrangement or position. **3.** the process of finding employment.
placenta (pləˈsɛntə) *n., pl.* **-tas** *or* **-tae** (-ti:). **1.** the vascular organ formed in the uterus of most mammals during pregnancy, consisting of both maternal and embryonic tissues and providing oxygen and nutrients for the fetus. **2.** *Bot.* the part of the ovary of flowering plants to which the ovules are attached. [C17: via L < Gk *plakoeis* flat cake, < *plax* flat] —**plaˈcental** *adj.*
placer (ˈplæsə) *n.* **a.** surface sediment containing particles of gold or some other valuable mineral. **b.** (*in combination*): *placer-mining.* [C19: < American Sp.: deposit, < Sp. *plaza* PLACE]
place setting *n.* the cutlery, crockery, and glassware laid for one person at a dining table.
placet (ˈpleɪsɛt) *n.* a vote or expression of assent by saying *placet.* [C16: < L, lit.: it pleases]
placid (ˈplæsɪd) *adj.* having a calm appearance or nature. [C17: < L *placidus* peaceful] —**placidity** (pləˈsɪdɪtɪ) *or* ˈ**placidness** *n.* —ˈ**placidly** *adv.*
placket (ˈplækɪt) *n. Dressmaking.* **1.** a piece of cloth sewn in under a closure with buttons, zips, etc. **2.** the closure itself. [C16: ? < MDu. *plackaet* breastplate, < Med. L *placca* metal plate]
placoid (ˈplækɔɪd) *adj.* **1.** platelike or flattened. **2.** (of the scales of sharks) toothlike; composed of dentine with an enamel tip and basal pulp cavity. [C19: < Gk *plac-, plax* flat]
plafond (pləˈfɒn; *French* plafɔ̃) *n.* a ceiling, esp. one having ornamentation. [C17: < F, < *plat* flat + *fond* bottom, < L *fundus*]
plagal (ˈpleɪgᵊl) *adj.* **1.** (of a cadence) progressing from the subdominant to the tonic chord, as in the *Amen* of a hymn. **2.** (of a mode) commencing upon the dominant of an authentic mode, but

sharing the same final as the authentic mode. ~Cf. **authentic** (sense 4). [C16: < Med. L *plagālis*, < *plaga*, ? < Gk *plagos* side]

plage (plɑːʒ) *n.* another name for **flocculus** (sense 1). [F, lit.: beach]

plagiarism (ˈpleɪdʒəˌrɪzəm) *n.* **1.** the act of plagiarizing. **2.** something plagiarized. [C17: < L *plagiārus* plunderer, < *plagium* kidnapping] —ˈ**plagiarist** *n.* —ˌ**plagiaˈristic** *adj.*

plagiarize *or* **-ise** (ˈpleɪdʒəˌraɪz) *vb.* to appropriate (ideas, passages, etc.) from (another work or author). —ˈ**plagiaˌrizer** *or* **-iser** *n.*

plagioclase (ˈpleɪdʒɪəʊˌkleɪz) *n.* a series of feldspar minerals consisting of a mixture of sodium and calcium aluminium silicates in triclinic crystalline form. [C19: < Gk, < *plagos* side + -CLASE] —**plagioclastic** (ˌpleɪdʒɪəʊˈklæstɪk) *adj.*

plague (pleɪg) *n.* **1.** any widespread and usually highly contagious disease with a high fatality rate. **2.** an infectious disease of rodents, esp. rats, transmitted to man by the bite of the rat flea. **3.** See **bubonic plague**. **4.** something that afflicts or harasses. **5.** *Inf.* an annoyance or nuisance. **6.** a pestilence, affliction, or calamity on a large scale, esp. when regarded as sent by God. ~*vb.* **plaguing, plagued.** (*tr.*) **7.** to afflict or harass. **8.** to bring down a plague upon. **9.** *Inf.* to annoy. [C14: < LL *plāga* pestilence, < L: a blow]

plaguy *or* **plaguey** (ˈpleɪgɪ) *Arch., inf.* ~*adj.* **1.** disagreeable or vexing. ~*adv.* **2.** disagreeably or annoyingly. —ˈ**plaguily** *adv.*

plaice (pleɪs) *n., pl.* **plaice** *or* **plaices.** **1.** a European flatfish having an oval brown body marked with red or orange spots and valued as a food fish. **2.** *U.S. & Canad.* any of various other related fishes. [C13: < OF *plaïz*, < LL *platessa* flatfish, < Gk *platus* flat]

plaid (plæd, pleɪd) *n.* **1.** a long piece of cloth of a tartan pattern, worn over the shoulder as part of Highland costume. **2. a.** a crisscross weave or cloth. **b.** (*as modifier*): *a plaid scarf.* [C16: < Scot. Gaelic *plaide*, <?]

Plaid Cymru (ˌplaɪd ˈkʌmrɪ) *n.* the Welsh nationalist party. [Welsh]

plain[1] (pleɪn) *adj.* **1.** flat or smooth; level. **2.** not complicated; clear: *the plain truth.* **3.** not difficult; simple or easy: *a plain task.* **4.** honest or straightforward. **5.** lowly, esp. in social rank or education. **6.** without adornment or show: *a plain coat.* **7.** (of fabric) without pattern or of simple untwilled weave. **8.** not attractive. **9.** not mixed; simple: *plain vodka.* **10.** *Knitting.* of or done in plain. ~*n.* **11.** a level or almost level tract of country. **12.** a simple stitch in knitting made by passing the wool round the front of the needle. ~*adv.* **13.** (intensifier): *just plain tired.* [C13: < OF: simple, < L *plānus* level, clear] —ˈ**plainly** *adv.* —ˈ**plainness** *n.*

plain[2] (pleɪn) *vb.* a dialect or poetic word for **complain.** [C14 *pleignen*, < OF *plaindre* to lament, < L *plangere* to beat]

plainchant (ˈpleɪnˌtʃɑːnt) *n.* another name for **plainsong.** [C18: < F, for Med. L *cantus plānus*]

plain chocolate *n.* chocolate with a slightly bitter flavour and dark colour.

plain clothes *pl. n.* **a.** ordinary clothes, as distinguished from uniform, as worn by a police detective on duty. **b.** (*as modifier*): *a plain-clothes policeman.*

plain flour *n.* flour to which no raising agent has been added.

plain sailing *n.* **1.** *Inf.* smooth or easy progress. **2.** *Naut.* sailing in a body of water that is unobstructed; clear sailing.

plainsman (ˈpleɪnzmən) *n., pl.* **-men.** a person who lives in a plains region, esp. in the Great Plains of North America.

plainsong (ˈpleɪnˌsɒŋ) *n.* the style of unison unaccompanied vocal music used in the medieval Church, esp. in Gregorian chant. [C16: translation of Med. L *cantus plānus*]

plain-spoken *adj.* candid; frank; blunt.

plaint (pleɪnt) *n.* **1.** *Arch.* a complaint or lamentation. **2.** *Law.* a statement in writing of grounds of complaint made to a court of law. [C13: < OF *plainte*, < L *planctus* lamentation, < *plangere* to beat]

plaintiff (ˈpleɪntɪf) *n.* a person who brings a civil action in a court of law. [C14: < legal F *plaintif*, < OF *plaintif* (adj.) complaining, < *plainte* PLAINT]

plaintive (ˈpleɪntɪv) *adj.* expressing melancholy; mournful. [C14: < OF *plaintif* grieving, < PLAINT] —ˈ**plaintively** *adv.* —ˈ**plaintiveness** *n.*

plait (plæt) *n.* **1.** a length of hair, etc., that has been plaited. **2.** a rare spelling of **pleat.** ~*vb.* **3.** (*tr.*) to intertwine (strands or strips) in a pattern. [C15 *pleyt*, < OF *pleit*, < L *plicāre* to fold]

plan (plæn) *n.* **1.** a detailed scheme, method, etc., for attaining an objective. **2.** (*sometimes pl.*) a proposed, usually tentative idea for doing something. **3.** a drawing to scale of a horizontal section through a building taken at a given level. **4.** an outline, sketch, etc. ~*vb.* **planning, planned.** **5.** to form a plan (for) or make plans (for). **6.** (*tr.*) to make a plan of (a building). **7.** (*tr.; takes a clause as object or an infinitive*) to have in mind as a purpose; intend. [C18: via F < L *plānus* flat]

planar (ˈpleɪnə) *adj.* **1.** of or relating to a plane. **2.** lying in one plane; flat. [C19: < LL *plānāris* on level ground, < L *plānus* flat]

planarian (pləˈnɛərɪən) *n.* any of various free-living mostly aquatic flatworms, having a three-branched intestine. [C19: < NL *Plānāria* type genus, < LL *plānārius* flat; see PLANE[1]]

planar process *n.* a method of producing diffused junctions in semiconductor devices. A pattern of holes is etched into an oxide layer formed on a silicon substrate, into which impurities are diffused through the holes.

planchet (ˈplɑːntʃɪt) *n.* a piece of metal ready to be stamped as a coin, medal, etc.; flan. [C17: < F: little board, < *planche* PLANK]

planchette (plɑːnˈʃɛt) *n.* a heart-shaped board on wheels with a pencil attached that writes messages under supposed spirit guidance. [C19: < F: little board, < *planche* PLANK]

Planck constant (plæŋk) *or* **Planck's constant** *n.* a fundamental constant equal to the energy of any quantum of radiation divided by its frequency. [C19: after Max *Planck* (1858–1947), G physicist]

plane[1] (pleɪn) *n.* **1.** *Maths.* a flat surface in which a straight line joining any two of its points lies entirely on that surface. **2.** a level surface. **3.** a level of existence, attainment, etc. **4. a.** short for **aeroplane. b.** a wing or supporting surface of an aircraft. ~*adj.* **5.** level or flat. **6.** *Maths.* lying entirely in one plane. ~*vb.* (*intr.*) **7.** to glide. **8.** (of a boat) to rise partly and skim over the water when moving at a certain speed. [C17: < L *plānum* level surface]

plane[2] (pleɪn) *n.* **1.** a tool with a steel blade set obliquely in a wooden or iron body, for smoothing timber surfaces, cutting grooves, etc. **2.** a flat tool, usually metal, for smoothing the surface of clay or plaster in a mould. ~*vb.* (*tr.*) **3.** to smooth or cut (timber, etc.) using a plane. **4.** (often foll. by *off*) to remove using a plane. [C14: via OF < LL *plāna* plane, < *plānāre* to level]

plane[3] (pleɪn) *n.* See **plane tree.**

plane geometry *n.* the study of the properties of plane curves, figures, etc.

plane polarization *n.* a type of polarization in which waves of light or other radiation are restricted to vibration in a single plane.

planet (ˈplænɪt) *n.* **1.** Also called: **major planet.** any of the nine celestial bodies, Mercury, Venus, earth, Mars, Jupiter, Saturn, Uranus, Neptune, or Pluto, that revolve around the sun in elliptical orbits. **2.** any celestial body revolving around a star. **3.** *Astrol.* any of the planets of the solar system, excluding the earth but including the sun and moon, each thought to rule one or sometimes two signs of the zodiac. [C12: via OF < LL *planēta*, < Gk *planētēs* wanderer, < *planaein* to wander]

plane table *n.* a surveying instrument consisting of a drawing board mounted on adjustable legs.

planetarium (ˌplænɪˈtɛərɪəm) *n., pl.* **-iums** *or* **-ia** (-ɪə). **1.** an instrument for simulating the apparent motions of the sun, moon, and planets by projecting images of these bodies onto a domed ceiling. **2.** a building in which such an instrument is housed. **3.** a model of the solar system.

planetary (ˈplænɪtərɪ, -trɪ) *adj.* **1.** of a planet. **2.** mundane; terrestrial. **3.** wandering or erratic. **4.** *Astrol.* under the influence of one of the planets. **5.** (of a gear) having an axis that rotates around that of another gear.

planetesimal hypothesis (ˌplænɪˈtɛsɪməl) *n.* the discredited theory that the close passage of a star to the sun caused many small bodies (**planetesimals**) to be drawn from the sun, eventually coalescing to form the planets. [C20: *planetesimal,* < PLANET + INFINITESIMAL]

planetoid (ˈplænɪˌtɔɪd) *n.* another name for **asteroid** (sense 1). —ˌ**planeˈtoidal** *adj.*

plane tree *or* **plane** *n.* a tree with ball-shaped heads of fruit and leaves with pointed lobes. [C14 *plane,* < OF, < L *platanus,* < Gk, < *platos* wide, referring to the leaves]

plangent (ˈplændʒənt) *adj.* **1.** having a loud deep sound. **2.** resonant and mournful. [C19: < L *plangere* to beat (esp. the breast, in grief)]

planimeter (plæˈnɪmɪtə) *n.* a mechanical instrument for measuring the area of an irregular plane figure by moving a point attached to an arm. —**plaˈnimetry** *n.*

planish (ˈplænɪʃ) *vb.* (*tr.*) to give a final finish to (metal, etc.) by hammering or rolling. [C16: < OF *planir* to smooth out, < L *plānus* flat]

planisphere (ˈplænɪˌsfɪə) *n.* a projection or representation of all or part of a sphere on a plane surface. [C14: < Med. L *plānisphaerium,* < L *plānus* flat + Gk *sphaira* globe]

plank (plæŋk) *n.* **1.** a stout length of sawn timber. **2.** something that supports or sustains. **3.** one of the policies in a political party's programme. **4.** **walk the plank.** to be forced by pirates, etc., to walk to one's death off the end of a plank jutting out from the side of a ship. ~*vb.* **5.** (*tr.*) to cover or provide with planks. [C13: < OF *planke,* < LL *planca* board, < *plancus* flat-footed]

planking (ˈplæŋkɪŋ) *n.* a number of planks.

plankton (ˈplæŋktən) *n.* the organisms inhabiting the surface layer of a sea or lake, consisting of small drifting plants and animals. [C19: via G < Gk *planktos* wandering, < *plazesthai* to roam]

planning permission *n.* (in Britain) formal permission granted by a local authority for the development or changed use of land or buildings.

plano- *or sometimes before a vowel* **plan-** *combining form.* indicating flatness or planeness: *plano-concave.* [< L *plānus* flat]

plano-concave (ˌpleɪnəʊˈkɒnkeɪv) *adj.* (of a lens) having one side concave and the other plane.

plano-convex (ˌpleɪnəʊˈkɒnvɛks) *adj.* (of a lens) having one side convex and the other plane.

plant[1] (plɑːnt) *n.* **1.** any living organism that typically synthesizes its food from inorganic substances, lacks specialized sense organs, and has no powers of locomotion. **2.** such an organism that is smaller than a shrub or tree; a herb. **3.** a cutting, seedling, or similar structure, esp. when ready for transplantation. **4.** *Inf.* a thing positioned secretly for discovery by another, esp. in order to incriminate an innocent person. ~*vb.* (*tr.*) **5.** (often foll. by *out*) to set (seeds, crops, etc.) into (ground) to grow. **6.** to place firmly in position. **7.** to establish; found. **8.** (foll. by *with*) to stock or furnish. **9.** to implant in the mind. **10.** *Sl.* to deliver (a blow). **11.** *Inf.* to position or hide, esp. in order to deceive or observe. **12.** *Inf.* to hide or secrete, esp. for some illegal purpose or in order to incriminate someone. [OE, < *planta* a shoot] —ˈ**plantable** *adj.*

plant[2] (plɑːnt) *n.* **1.** the land, buildings, and equipment used in carrying on an industry or business. **2.** a factory or workshop. **3.** mobile mechanical equipment for construction, road-making, etc. [C20: special use of PLANT[1]]

plantain[1] (ˈplæntɪn) *n.* any of various N temperate plants, esp. the great plantain, which has a rosette of broad leaves and a slender spike of small greenish flowers. See also **ribwort.** [C14 *plauntein,* < OF, < L *plantāgō,* < *planta* sole of the foot]

plantain[2] (ˈplæntɪn) *n.* a large tropical plant with a green-skinned banana-like fruit which is eaten as a staple food in many tropical regions. [C16: Sp. *platano* plantain, PLANE TREE]

plantain lily *n.* any of several Asian plants of the genus *Hosta,* having broad ribbed leaves.

plantar (ˈplæntə) *adj.* of or on the sole of the foot. [C18: < L *plantāris,* < *planta* sole of the foot]

plantation (plænˈteɪʃən) *n.* **1.** an estate, esp. in tropical countries, where cash crops such as rubber, oil palm, etc., are grown on a large scale. **2.** a group of cultivated trees or plants. **3.** (formerly) a colony or group of settlers.

planter (ˈplɑːntə) *n.* **1.** the owner or manager of a plantation. **2.** a machine designed for rapid and efficient planting of seeds. **3.** a colonizer or settler. **4.** a decorative pot for house plants.

plantigrade (ˈplæntɪˌgreɪd) *adj.* **1.** walking with the entire sole of the foot touching the ground, as man and bears. ~*n.* **2.** a plantigrade animal. [C19: via F < NL *plantigradus,* < L *planta* sole of the foot + *gradus* a step]

plant louse *n.* another name for an **aphid.**

plaque (plæk, plɑːk) *n.* **1.** an ornamental or commemorative inscribed tablet. **2.** a small flat brooch or badge. **3.** *Pathol.* any small abnormal patch on or within the body. **4.** short for **dental plaque.** [C19: < F, < *plaquier* to plate, < MDu. *placken* to beat into a thin plate]

plash (plæʃ) *vb., n.* a less common word for **splash.** [OE *plæsc,* prob. imit.] —ˈ**plashy** *adj.*

-plasia *or* **-plasy** *n. combining form.* indicating growth, development, or change. [< NL, < Gk *plasis* a moulding, < *plassein* to mould] —**-plastic** *adj. combining form.*

plasm (ˈplæzəm) *n.* **1.** protoplasm of a specified type: *germ plasm.* **2.** a variant of **plasma.**

-plasm *n. combining form.* (in biology) indicating the material forming cells: *protoplasm.* [< Gk *plasma* something moulded; see PLASMA] —**-plasmic** *adj. combining form.*

plasma (ˈplæzmə) *or* **plasm** *n.* **1.** the clear yellowish fluid portion of blood or lymph in which the corpuscles and cells are suspended. **2.** Also called: **blood plasma.** a sterilized preparation of such fluid, taken from the blood, for use in transfusions. **3.** a former name for **protoplasm** or **cytoplasm.** **4.** *Physics.* a hot ionized gas containing positive ions and electrons. **5.** a green variety of chalcedony. [C18: < LL: something moulded, < Gk, < *plassein* to mould] —**plasmatic** (plæzˈmætɪk) *or* ˈ**plasmic** *adj.*

plasma torch *n.* an electrical device for converting a gas into a plasma, used for melting metal, etc.

plasmid (ˈplæzmɪd) *n.* a small circle of bacterial DNA that is independent of the main bacterial chromosome. Plasmids often contain genes for drug resistances and can be transmitted between bacteria of the same and different species: used in genetic engineering. [C20: < PLASM + -ID[1]]

plasmodium (plæzˈməʊdɪəm) *n., pl.* **-dia** (-dɪə). **1.** an amoeboid mass of protoplasm, containing many nuclei: a stage in the life cycle of certain organisms. **2.** a parasitic protozoan which causes malaria. [C19: NL; see PLASMA, -ODE[1]] —**plasˈmodial** *adj.*

plasmolysis (plæzˈmɒlɪsɪs) *n.* the shrinkage of protoplasm away from cell walls that occurs as a result of excessive water loss, esp. in plant cells.

-plast *n. combining form.* indicating a living cell or particle of living matter: *protoplast.* [< Gk *plastos* formed, < *plassein* to form]

plaster (ˈplɑːstə) *n.* **1.** a mixture of lime, sand, and water that is applied to a wall or ceiling as a soft paste that hardens when dry. **2.** *Brit.* an adhesive strip of material for dressing a cut, wound, etc. **3.** short for **mustard plaster** or **plaster of Paris.** ~*vb.* **4.** to coat (a wall, ceiling, etc.) with plaster. **5.** (*tr.*) to apply like plaster: *she* *plastered make-up on her face.* **6.** (*tr.*) to cause to lie flat or to adhere. **7.** (*tr.*) to apply a plaster cast to. **8.** (*tr.*) *Sl.* to strike or defeat with great force. [OE, < Med. L *plastrum* medicinal salve, building plaster, via L < Gk *emplastron* curative dressing] —ˈ**plasterer** *n.*

plasterboard (ˈplɑːstəˌbɔːd) *n.* a thin rigid board, in the form of a layer of plaster compressed between two layers of fibreboard, used to form or cover walls, etc.

plastered (ˈplɑːstəd) *adj. Sl.* intoxicated; drunk.

plaster of Paris *n.* **1.** a white powder that sets to a hard solid when mixed with water, used for making sculptures and casts, as an additive for lime plasters, and for making casts for setting broken limbs. **2.** the hard plaster produced when this powder is mixed with water. [C15: < Med. L *plastrum parisiense,* orig. made from the gypsum of *Paris*]

plastic (ˈplæstɪk) *n.* **1.** any one of a large number of synthetic materials that have a polymeric structure and can be moulded when soft and then set. Plastics are used in the manufacture of many articles and in coatings, artificial fibres, etc. ~*adj.* **2.** made of plastic. **3.** easily influenced; impressionable. **4.** capable of being moulded or formed. **5. a.** of moulding or modelling: *the plastic arts.* **b.** produced or apparently produced by moulding: *the plastic draperies of Giotto's figures.* **6.** having the power to form or influence: *the plastic forces of the imagination.* **7.** *Biol.* able to change, develop, or grow: *plastic tissues.* **8.** *Sl.* superficially attractive yet unoriginal or artificial: *plastic food.* [C17: < L *plasticus* relating to moulding, < Gk *plastikos,* < *plassein* to form] —ˈ**plastically** *adv.* —**plasticity** (plæˈstɪsɪtɪ) *n.*

-plastic *adj. combining form.* growing or forming. [< Gk *plastikos;* see PLASTIC]

plastic bomb *n.* a bomb consisting of plastic explosive fitted around a detonator.

plastic bullet *n.* a bullet consisting of a cylinder of plastic about four inches long, generally causing less severe injuries than an ordinary bullet, and used esp. for riot control. Also called: **baton round.**

plastic explosive *n.* an adhesive jelly-like explosive substance.

Plasticine (ˈplæstɪˌsiːn) *n. Trademark.* a soft coloured material used, esp. by children, for modelling.

plasticize *or* **-cise** (ˈplæstɪˌsaɪz) *vb.* to make or become plastic, as by the addition of a plasticizer. —ˌ**plasticiˈzation** *or* **-ciˈsation** *n.*

plasticizer *or* **-ciser** (ˈplæstɪˌsaɪzə) *n.* any of a number of substances added to materials. Their uses include softening and improving the flexibility of plastics and preventing dried paint coatings from becoming too brittle.

plastic surgery *n.* the branch of surgery concerned with therapeutic or cosmetic repair or re-formation of missing, injured, or malformed tissues or parts. —**plastic surgeon** *n.*

plastid (ˈplæstɪd) *n.* any of various small particles in the cells of plants and some animals which contain starch, oil, protein, etc. [C19: via G < Gk *plastēs* sculptor, < *plassein* to form]

plastron (ˈplæstrən) *n.* the bony plate forming the ventral part of the shell of a tortoise or turtle. [C16: via F < It. *piastrone,* < *piastra* breastplate, < L *emplastrum* PLASTER] —ˈ**plastral** *adj.*

-plasty *n. combining form.* indicating plastic surgery: *rhinoplasty.* [< Gk *-plastia;* see -PLAST]

plat[1] (plæt) *n.* a small area of ground; plot. [C16 (also in ME place names): orig. a var. of PLOT[2]]

plat[2] (plæt) *vb.* **platting, platted,** *n.* a dialect variant spelling of **plait.** [C16]

platan (ˈplæt°n) *n.* another name for **plane tree.** [C14: see PLANE TREE]

plate (pleɪt) *n.* **1. a.** a shallow usually circular dish made of porcelain, earthenware, glass, etc., on which food is served. **b.** (*as modifier*): *a plate rack.* **2. a.** Also called: **plateful.** the contents of a plate. **b.** *Austral. & N.Z.* a plate of cakes, sandwiches, etc., brought by a guest to a party: *everyone was asked to bring a plate.* **3.** an entire course of a meal: *a cold plate.* **4.** any shallow receptacle, esp. for receiving a collection in church. **5.** flat metal of uniform thickness obtained by rolling, usually having a thickness greater than about three millimetres. **6.** a thin coating of metal usually on another metal, as produced by electrodeposition. **7.** metal or metalware that has been coated in this way: *Sheffield plate.* **8.** dishes, cutlery, etc., made of gold or silver. **9.** a sheet of metal, plastic, rubber, etc., having a printing surface produced by a process such as stereotyping. **10.** a print taken from such a sheet or from a woodcut. **11.** a thin flat sheet of a substance, such as metal or glass. **12.** a small piece of metal, plastic, etc., designed to bear an inscription and to be fixed to another surface. **13.** armour made of overlapping or articulated pieces of thin metal. **14.** *Photog.* a sheet of glass, or sometimes metal, coated with photographic emulsion on which an image can be formed by exposure to light. **15.** a device for straightening teeth. **16.** an informal word for **denture** (sense 1). **17.** *Anat.* any flat platelike structure. **18. a.** a cup awarded to the winner of a sporting contest, esp. a horse race. **b.** a race or contest for such a prize. **19.** any of the rigid layers of the earth's lithosphere. **20.** *Electronics, chiefly U.S.* the anode in an electronic valve. **21.** a horizontal timber joist that supports rafters. **22.** a light horseshoe for flat racing. **23.** *R.C. Church.* Also called: **Communion plate.** a flat plate held under the chin of a communicant in order to catch any fragments of the consecrated Host. **24. on a plate.** acquired without trouble: *he was handed the job on a plate.* **25. on one's plate.** waiting to be done or dealt with. ~*vb.* (*tr.*) **26.** to coat (a surface, usually metal) with a thin layer of other metal by electrolysis, etc. **27.** to cover with metal plates, as for protection. **28.** *Printing.* to make a stereotype or electrotype from (type or another plate). **29.** to form (metal) into plate, esp. by rolling. [C13: < OF: thin metal sheet, something flat, < Vulgar L *plattus* (unattested)]

plateau (ˈplætəʊ) *n., pl.* **-eaus** *or* **-eaux** (-əʊz). **1.** a wide mainly level area of elevated land. **2.** a relatively long period of stability; levelling off: *the rising prices reached a plateau.* [C18: < F, < OF *platel* something flat, < *plat* flat]

plated (ˈpleɪtɪd) *adj.* **a.** coated with a layer of metal. **b.** (*in combination*): *gold-plated.*

plate glass *n.* glass formed into a thin sheet by rolling, used for windows, etc.

platelayer (ˈpleɪtˌleɪə) *n. Brit.* a workman who lays and maintains railway track. U.S. equivalent: **trackman.**

platelet (ˈpleɪtlɪt) *n.* a minute particle occurring in the blood of vertebrates and involved in the clotting of the blood. [C19: a small PLATE]

platen (ˈplæt°n) *n.* **1.** a flat plate in a printing press that presses the paper against the type. **2.** the roller on a typewriter, against which the keys strike. [C15: < OF *platine,* < *plat* flat]

plater (ˈpleɪtə) *n.* **1.** a person or thing that plates. **2.** *Horse racing.* a mediocre horse entered chiefly for minor races.

plate tectonics *n.* (*functioning as sing.*) *Geol.* the study of the earth's crust with reference to the theory that the lithosphere is divided into rigid blocks (plates) that float on semimolten rock and are thus able to interact with each other at their boundaries.

platform (ˈplætfɔːm) *n.* **1.** a raised floor or other horizontal surface. **2.** a raised area at a railway station, from which passengers have access to the trains. **3.** See **drilling platform.** **4.** the declared principles, aims, etc., of a political party, etc. **5. a.** the thick raised sole of some shoes. **b.** (*as modifier*): *platform shoes.* **6.** a vehicle or level place on which weapons are mounted and fired. [C16: < F *plateforme,* < *plat* flat + *forme* layout]

platform ticket *n.* a ticket for admission to railway platforms but not for travel.

plating (ˈpleɪtɪŋ) *n.* **1.** a coating or layer of material, esp. metal. **2.** a layer or covering of metal plates.

platiniridium (ˌplætɪnɪˈrɪdɪəm) *n.* any alloy of platinum and iridium.

platinize *or* **-nise** (ˈplætɪˌnaɪz) *vb.* (*tr.*) to coat with platinum. —ˌ**platiniˈzation** *or* **-niˈsation** *n.*

platinum (ˈplætɪnəm) *n.* a ductile malleable silvery-white metallic element, very resistant to heat and chemicals: used in jewellery, laboratory apparatus, electrical contacts, dentistry, electroplating, and as a catalyst. Symbol: Pt; atomic no.: 78; atomic wt.: 195.09. [C19: NL, < Sp. *platina* silvery element, < *plata* silver, < Provençal: silver plate + the suffix *-um*]

platinum black *n. Chem.* a black powder consisting of very finely divided platinum metal.

platinum-blond *or* (*fem.*) **platinum-blonde** *adj.* **1.** (of hair) of a pale silver-blond colour. **2. a.** having hair of this colour. **b.** (*as n.*): *she was a platinum blonde.*

platinum metal *n.* any of the group of precious metallic elements consisting of ruthenium, rhodium, palladium, osmium, iridium, and platinum.

platitude (ˈplætɪˌtjuːd) *n.* **1.** a trite, dull, or obvious remark. **2.** staleness or insipidity of thought or language; triteness. [C19: < F, lit.: flatness, < *plat* flat] —ˌ**platiˈtudinous** *adj.*

platitudinize *or* **-ise** (ˌplætɪˈtjuːdɪˌnaɪz) *vb.* (*intr.*) to speak or write in platitudes.

Platonic (pləˈtɒnɪk) *adj.* **1.** of or relating to Plato or his teachings. **2.** (*often not cap.*) free from physical desire: *Platonic love.* —**Plaˈtonically** *adv.*

Platonic solid *n.* any of the five possible regular polyhedrons: cube, tetrahedron, octahedron, icosahedron, and dodecahedron.

Platonism (ˈpleɪtəˌnɪzəm) *n.* the teachings of Plato (?427–?347 B.C.), Greek philosopher, and his followers; esp. the philosophical theory that the meanings of general words are real entities (forms) and that particular objects have properties in common by virtue of their relationship with these forms. —ˈ**Platonist** *n.*

platoon (pləˈtuːn) *n.* **1.** *Mil.* a subunit of a company, usually comprising three sections of ten to twelve men. **2.** a group of people sharing a common activity, etc. [C17: < F *peloton* little ball, group of men, < *pelote* ball; see PELLET]

Plattdeutsch (*German* ˈplatdɔytʃ) *n.* another name for **Low German.** [lit.: flat German]

platteland (ˈplatəˌlant) *n.* **the.** (in South Africa) the area outside the cities and chief towns. [C20: < Afrik., < Du *plat* flat + *land* country]

platter (ˈplætə) *n.* a large shallow usually oval dish or plate. [C14: < Anglo-Norman *plater*, < *plat* dish, < OF *plat* flat; see PLATE]

platy- *combining form.* indicating something flat, as **platyhelminth,** the flatworm. [< Gk *platus* flat]

platypus (ˈplætɪpəs) *n., pl.* **-puses.** See **duck-billed platypus.** [C18: NL, < PLATY- + *-pus*, < Gk *pous* foot]

platyrrhine (ˈplætɪˌraɪn) *or* **platyrrhinian** (ˌplætɪˈrɪnɪən) *adj.* **1.** (esp. of New World monkeys) having widely separated nostrils opening to the side of the face. **2.** (of a human) having an unusually short wide nose. [C19: < NL *platyrrhinus*, < PLATY- + *-rrhinus*, < Gk *rhis* nose]

plaudit (ˈplɔːdɪt) *n.* (*usually pl.*) **1.** an expression of enthusiastic approval. **2.** a round of applause. [C17: < earlier *plaudite*, < L: applaud!, < *plaudere* to APPLAUD]

plausible (ˈplɔːzɪbᵊl) *adj.* **1.** apparently reasonable, valid, truthful, etc.: *a plausible excuse.* **2.** apparently trustworthy or believable: *a plausible speaker.* [C16: < L *plausibilis* worthy of applause, < *plaudere* to APPLAUD] —ˌ**plausiˈbility** *or* ˈ**plausibleness** *n.* —ˈ**plausibly** *adv.*

play (pleɪ) *vb.* **1.** to occupy oneself in (a sport or diversion). **2.** (*tr.*) to contend against (an opponent) in a sport or game: *Ed played Tony at chess and lost.* **3.** to fulfil or cause to fulfil (a particular role) in a team game: *he plays in the defence.* **4.** (*intr.;* often foll. by *about* or *around*) to behave carelessly, esp. in a way that is unconsciously cruel or hurtful: *to play about with a young girl's affections.* **5.** (when *intr.*, often foll. by *at*) to perform or act the part (of) in or as in a dramatic production. **6.** to perform (a dramatic production). **7. a.** to have the ability to perform on (a musical instrument): *David plays the harp.* **b.** to perform as specified: *he plays out of tune.* **8.** (*tr.*) **a.** to reproduce (a piece of music, note, etc.) on an instrument. **b.** to perform works by: *to play Brahms.* **9.** to discharge or cause to discharge: *he played the water from the hose onto the garden.* **10.** to cause (a radio, etc.) to emit sound. **11.** to move freely, quickly, or irregularly: *lights played on the scenery.* **12.** (*tr.*) *Stock Exchange.* to speculate or operate aggressively for gain in (a market). **13.** (*tr.*) *Angling.* to attempt to tire (a hooked fish) by alternately letting out and reeling in line. **14.** to put (a card, counter, piece, etc.) into play. **15.** to gamble. **16. play fair** (*or* **false**). (often foll. by *with*) to prove oneself fair (*or* unfair) in one's dealings. **17. play for time.** to delay the outcome of some activity so as to gain time to one's own advantage. **18. play into the hands of.** to act directly to the advantage of (an opponent). ~*n.* **19.** a dramatic composition written for performance by actors on a stage, etc.; drama. **20.** the performance of a dramatic composition. **21. a.** games, exercise, or other activity undertaken for pleasure, esp. by children. **b.** (*in combination*): *playroom.* **22.** conduct: *fair play.* **23.** the playing of a game or the period during which a game is in progress: *rain stopped play.* **24.** *U.S.* a manoeuvre in a game: *a brilliant play.* **25.** the situation of a ball, etc., that is within the defined area and being played according to the rules (in **in play, out of play**). **26.** gambling. **27.** activity or operation: *the play of the imagination.* **28.** freedom of movement: *too much play in the rope.* **29.** light, free, or rapidly shifting motion: *the play of light on the water.* **30.** fun, jest, or joking: *I only did it in play.* **31. call into play.** to bring into operation. **32. make a play for.** *Inf.* to make an obvious attempt to gain. ~See also **play along, playback,** etc. [OE *plega* (n.), *plegan* (vb.)] —ˈ**playable** *adj.*

play-act *vb.* **1.** (*intr.*) to pretend or make believe. **2.** (*intr.*) to behave in an overdramatic or affected manner. **3.** to act in or as in (a play). —ˈ**play-ˌacting** *n.* —ˈ**play-ˌactor** *n.*

play along *vb.* (*adv.*) **1.** (*intr.;* usually foll. by *with*) to cooperate (with), esp. as a temporary measure. **2.** (*tr.*) to manipulate as if in a game, esp. for one's own advantage: *he played the widow along until she gave him her money.*

playback (ˈpleɪˌbæk) *n.* **1.** the act or process of reproducing a recording, esp. on magnetic tape. **2.** the part of a tape recorder serving to reproduce or used for reproducing recorded material. ~*vb.* **play back.** (*adv.*) **3.** to reproduce (recorded material) on (a magnetic tape) by means of a tape recorder.

playbill (ˈpleɪˌbɪl) *n.* **1.** a poster or bill advertising a play. **2.** the programme of a play.

playboy (ˈpleɪˌbɔɪ) *n.* a man, esp. one of private means, who devotes himself to the pleasures of nightclubs, female company, etc.

play down *vb.* (*tr., adv.*) to make little or light of; minimize the importance of.

player (ˈpleɪə) *n.* **1.** a person who participates in or is skilled at some game or sport. **2.** a person who plays a game or sport professionally. **3.** a person who plays a musical instrument. **4.** an actor.

player piano *n.* a mechanical piano; Pianola.

playful (ˈpleɪfʊl) *adj.* **1.** full of high spirits and fun: *a playful kitten.* **2.** good-natured and humorous: *a playful remark.* —ˈ**playfully** *adv.*

playgoer (ˈpleɪˌgəʊə) *n.* a person who goes to theatre performances, esp. frequently.

playground (ˈpleɪˌgraʊnd) *n.* **1.** an outdoor area for children's play, esp. one having swings, slides, etc., or adjoining a school. **2.** a place popular as a sports or holiday resort.

playgroup (ˈpleɪˌgruːp) *n.* a regular meeting of small children for supervised creative play.

playhouse (ˈpleɪˌhaʊs) *n.* **1.** a theatre. **2.** *U.S.* a small house for children to play in.

playing card *n.* one of a pack of 52 rectangular pieces of stiff card, used for playing a wide variety of games, each card having one or more symbols of the same kind on the face, but an identical design on the reverse.

playing field *n. Chiefly Brit.* a field or open space used for sport.

playlet (ˈpleɪlɪt) *n.* a short play.

playlist (ˈpleɪˌlɪst) *n.* a list of records chosen for playing, as on a radio station.

playmate (ˈpleɪˌmeɪt) *or* **playfellow** *n.* a friend or partner in play or recreation.

play off *vb.* (*adv.*) **1.** (*tr.;* usually foll. by *against*) to manipulate as if in playing a game: *to play one person off against another.* **2.** (*intr.*) to take part in a play-off. ~*n.* **play-off. 3.** *Sport.* an extra contest to decide the winner when competitors are tied. **4.** *Chiefly U.S. & Canad.* a contest or series of games to determine a championship.

play on *vb.* (*intr.*) **1.** (*adv.*) to continue to play. **2.** (*prep.*) Also: **play upon.** to exploit or impose upon (the feelings or weakness of another).

play on words *n.* another term for **pun[1]**.

playpen (ˈpleɪˌpɛn) *n.* a small enclosure, usually portable, in which a young child can be left to play in safety.

playschool (ˈpleɪˌskuːl) *n.* an informal nursery group for preschool children.

plaything (ˈpleɪˌθɪŋ) *n.* **1.** a toy. **2.** a person regarded or treated as a toy.

playtime (ˈpleɪˌtaɪm) *n.* a time for play or recreation, esp. the school break.

play up *vb.* (*adv.*) **1.** (*tr.*) to highlight: *to play up one's best features.* **2.** *Brit. inf.* to behave irritatingly (towards). **3.** (*intr.*) *Brit. inf.* (of a machine, etc.) to function erratically: *the car is playing up again.* **4.** to hurt; give (one) trouble: *my back's playing up again.* **5. play up to. a.** to support (another actor) in a performance. **b.** to try to gain favour with by flattery.

playwright (ˈpleɪˌraɪt) *n.* a person who writes plays.

plaza (ˈplɑːzə) *n.* **1.** an open space or square, esp. in Spain. **2.** *Chiefly U.S. & Canad.* a modern complex of shops, buildings, and parking areas. [C17: < Sp., < L *platēa* courtyard; see PLACE]

PLC *or* **plc** *abbrev. for* Public Limited Company.

plea (pliː) *n.* **1.** an earnest entreaty or request. **2. a.** *Law.* something alleged by or on behalf of a party to legal proceedings in support of his claim or defence. **b.** *Criminal law.* the answer made by an accused to the charge: *a plea of guilty.* **c.** (in Scotland and formerly in England) a suit or action at law. [C13: < Anglo-Norman *plai,* < OF *plaid* lawsuit, < Med. L *placitum* court order (lit.: what is pleasing), < L *placēre* to please]

plead (pliːd) *vb.* **pleading, pleaded, plead** (plɛd), *or esp. Scot. & U.S.* **pled. 1.** (when *intr.,* often foll. by *with*) to appeal earnestly or humbly (to). **2.** (*tr.; may take a clause as object*) to give as an excuse: *to plead ignorance.* **3.** *Law.* to declare oneself to be (guilty or not guilty) in answer to the charge. **4.** *Law.* to advocate (a case) in a court of law. **5.** (*intr.*) *Law.* **a.** to file pleadings. **b.** to address a court as an advocate. [C13: < OF *plaidier,* < Med. L *placitāre* to have a lawsuit, < L *placēre* to please] —ˈ**pleadable** *adj.* —ˈ**pleader** *n.*

pleadings (ˈpliːdɪŋz) *pl. n. Law.* the formal written statements presented alternately by the plaintiff and defendant in a lawsuit.

pleasance (ˈplɛzəns) *n.* **1.** a secluded part of a garden laid out with trees, walks, etc. **2.** *Arch.* enjoyment or pleasure. [C14 *plesaunce,* < OF *plaisance,* ult. < *plaisir* to PLEASE]

pleasant (ˈplɛzᵊnt) *adj.* **1.** giving or affording pleasure; enjoyable. **2.** having pleasing or agreeable manners, appearance, habits, etc. **3.** *Obs.* merry and lively. [C14: < OF *plaisant,* < *plaisir* to PLEASE] —ˈ**pleasantly** *adv.*

pleasantry (ˈplɛzᵊntrɪ) *n., pl.* **-ries. 1.** (*often pl.*) an agreeable or amusing remark, etc., often one made in order to be polite: *they exchanged pleasantries.* **2.** an agreeably humorous manner or style. [C17: < F *plaisanterie,* < *plaisant* PLEASANT]

please (pliːz) *vb.* **1.** to give satisfaction, pleasure, or contentment to (a person). **2.** to be the will of or have the will (to): *if it pleases you; the court pleases.* **3. if you please.** if you will or wish, sometimes used in ironic exclamation. **4. pleased with.** happy because of. **5. please oneself.** to do as one likes. ~*adv.* **6.** (*sentence modifier*) used in making polite requests, pleading, etc. **7. yes please.** a polite formula for accepting an offer, invitation, etc. [C14 *plese,* < OF *plaisir,* < L *placēre*] —**pleased** *adj.* —**pleasedly** (ˈpliːzɪdlɪ) *adv.*

pleasing (ˈpliːzɪŋ) *adj.* giving pleasure; likable or gratifying. —ˈ**pleasingly** *adv.*

pleasurable (ˈplɛʒərəbᵊl) *adj.* enjoyable, agreeable, or gratifying. —ˈ**pleasurably** *adv.*

pleasure (ˈplɛʒə) *n.* **1.** an agreeable or enjoyable sensation or emotion: *the pleasure of hearing good music.* **2.** something that gives enjoyment: *his garden was his only pleasure.* **3. a.** amusement, recreation, or enjoyment. **b.** (*as modifier*): *a pleasure ground.* **4.** *Euphemistic.* sexual gratification: *he took his pleasure of her.* **5.** a person's preference. ~*vb.* **6.** (when *intr.,* often foll. by *in*) *Arch.* to give pleasure to or take pleasure (in). [C14 *plesir,* < OF]

pleat (pliːt) *n.* **1.** any of various types of fold formed by doubling back fabric, etc., and pressing, stitching, or steaming into place. ~*vb.* **2.** (*tr.*) to arrange (material, part of a garment, etc.) in pleats. [C16: var. of PLAIT]

pleb (plɛb) *n.* **1.** short for **plebeian. 2.** *Brit. inf., often derog.* a common vulgar person.

plebeian (pləˈbiːən) *adj.* **1.** of or characteristic of the common people, esp. those of ancient Rome. **2.** lacking refinement; philistine or vulgar: *plebeian tastes.* ~*n.* **3.** one of the common people, esp. one of the Roman plebs. **4.** a person who is coarse, vulgar, etc. [C16: < L *plēbēius* of the people, < *plēbs* the common people of ancient Rome] —**pleˈbeianˌism** *n.*

plebiscite (ˈplɛbɪˌsaɪt, -sɪt) *n.* **1.** a direct vote by the electorate of a state, region, etc., on some question, usually of national importance. **2.** any expression of public opinion on some matter. ~See also **referendum.** [C16: < OF *plēbiscite,* < L *plēbiscītum* decree of the people, < *plēbs* the populace + *scīscere* to decree, < *scīre* to know] —**plebiscitary** (pləˈbɪsɪtərɪ, -trɪ) *adj.*

plectrum (ˈplɛktrəm) *or* **plectron** (ˈplɛktrən) *n., pl.* **-tra** (-trə), **-trums** *or* **-tra, -trons.** any implement for plucking a string, such as a small piece of plastic, wood, etc., used to strum a guitar. [C17: < L, < Gk *plektron,* < *plessein* to strike]

pled (plɛd) *vb. U.S. or* (*esp. in legal usage*) *Scot.* a past tense and past participle of **plead.**

pledge (plɛdʒ) *n.* **1.** a formal or solemn promise or agreement. **2. a.** collateral for the payment of a debt or the performance of an obligation. **b.** the condition of being collateral (esp. in **in pledge**). **3.** a token: *the gift is a pledge of their sincerity.* **4.** an assurance of support or goodwill, conveyed by drinking a toast: *we drank a pledge to their success.* **5.** a person who binds himself, as by becoming bail or surety for another. **6. take** *or* **sign the pledge.** to make a vow to abstain from alcoholic drink. ~*vb.* **7.** to promise formally or solemnly. **8.** (*tr.*) to bind by or as if by a pledge: *they were pledged to secrecy.* **9.** to give or offer (one's word, freedom, property, etc.) as a guarantee, as for the repayment of a loan. **10.** to drink a toast to (a person, cause, etc.). [C14: < OF *plege,* < LL *plebium* security, < *plebīre* to pledge, of Gmc origin] —ˈ**pledgable** *adj.* —ˈ**pledger** *or* ˈ**pledgor** *n.*

pledgee (plɛdʒˈiː) *n.* **1.** a person to whom a pledge is given. **2.** a person to whom property is delivered as a pledge.

pledget (ˈplɛdʒɪt) *n.* a small flattened pad of wool, cotton, etc., esp. for use as a pressure bandage to be applied to wounds. [C16: <?]

-plegia *n. combining form.* indicating a

specified type of paralysis: *paraplegia*. [< Gk, < *plēgē* stroke, < *plēssein* to strike] **—-plegic** *adj. and n. combining form.*

pleiad (ˈplaɪəd) *n.* a brilliant or talented group, esp. one with seven members. [C16: orig. F *Pléiade*, name given by Ronsard to himself and six other poets, ult. after the *Pleiades*, the seven daughters of the Gk god Atlas]

Pleiocene (ˈplaɪəʊˌsiːn) *adj., n.* a variant spelling of **Pliocene.**

Pleistocene (ˈplaɪstəˌsiːn) *adj.* **1.** of, denoting, or formed in the first epoch of the Quaternary period. It was characterized by extensive glaciations of the N hemisphere and the evolutionary development of man. *~n.* **2. the.** the Pleistocene epoch or rock series. [C19: < Gk *pleistos* most + *kainos* recent]

plenary (ˈpliːnərɪ, ˈplɛn-) *adj.* **1.** full, unqualified, or complete: *plenary powers; plenary indulgence.* **2.** (of assemblies, councils, etc.) attended by all the members. [C15: < LL *plēnārius*, < L *plēnus* full] **—ˈplenarily** *adv.*

plenipotentiary (ˌplɛnɪpəˈtɛnʃərɪ) *adj.* **1.** (esp. of a diplomatic envoy) invested with or possessing full authority. **2.** conferring full authority. **3.** (of power or authority) full; absolute. *~n., pl.* **-aries.** **4.** a person invested with full authority to transact business, esp. a diplomat authorized to represent a country. See also **envoy**[1] (sense 1). [C17: < Med. L *plēnipotentiārius*, < L *plēnus* full + *potentia* POWER]

plenitude (ˈplɛnɪˌtjuːd) *n.* **1.** abundance. **2.** the condition of being full or complete. [C15: via OF < L *plēnitūdō*, < *plēnus* full]

plenteous (ˈplɛntɪəs) *adj.* **1.** ample; abundant: *a plenteous supply of food.* **2.** producing or yielding abundantly: *a plenteous grape harvest.* [C13 *plenteus*, < OF, < *plentif*, < *plenté* PLENTY] **—ˈplenteously** *adv.* **—ˈplenteousness** *n.*

plentiful (ˈplɛntɪfʊl) *adj.* **1.** ample; abundant. **2.** having or yielding an abundance: *a plentiful year.* **—ˈplentifully** *adv.* **—ˈplentifulness** *n.*

plenty (ˈplɛntɪ) *n., pl.* **-ties.** **1.** (often foll. by *of*) a great number, amount, or quantity; lots: *plenty of time; there are plenty of cars on display here.* **2.** ample supplies or resources: *the age of plenty.* **3. in plenty.** existing in abundance: *food in plenty.* *~determiner.* **4. a.** very many; ample: *plenty of people believe in ghosts.* **b.** (as *pron.*): *that's plenty, thanks.* *~adv.* **5.** *Inf.* fully or abundantly: *the coat was plenty big enough.* [C13: < OF *plenté*, < LL *plēnitās* fullness, < L *plēnus* full]

plenum (ˈpliːnəm) *n., pl.* **-nums** *or* **-na** (-nə). **1.** an enclosure containing gas at a higher pressure than the surrounding environment. **2.** a fully attended meeting. **3.** (esp. in the philosophy of the Stoics) space regarded as filled with matter. [C17: < L: space filled with matter, < *plēnus* full]

pleochroism (plɪˈɒkrəʊˌɪzəm) *n.* a property of certain crystals of absorbing light waves selectively and therefore of showing different colours when looked at from different directions. [C19: < Gk *pleiōn* more, < *polus* many + *-chroism* < *khrōs* skin colour] **—pleochroic** (ˌpliːəˈkrəʊɪk) *adj.*

pleomorphism (ˌpliːəˈmɔːfɪzəm) *or* **pleomorphy** (ˈpliːəˌmɔːfɪ) *n.* **1.** the occurrence of more than one different form in the life cycle of a plant or animal. **2.** another word for **polymorphism** (sense 2). **—ˌpleoˈmorphic** *adj.*

pleonasm (ˈpliːəˌnæzəm) *n. Rhetoric.* **1.** the use of more words than necessary or an instance of this, such as *a tiny little child.* **2.** a word or phrase that is superfluous. [C16: < L *pleonasmus*, < Gk *pleonasmos* excess, < *pleonazein* to be redundant] **—ˌpleoˈnastic** *adj.*

plesiosaur (ˈpliːsɪəˌsɔː) *n.* any of various marine reptiles of Jurassic and Cretaceous times, having a long neck, short tail, and paddle-like limbs. [C19: < NL *plēsiosaurus*, < Gk *plēsios* near + *sauros* a lizard]

plethora (ˈplɛθərə) *n.* **1.** superfluity or excess; overabundance. **2.** *Pathol., obs.* a condition caused by dilation of superficial blood vessels, characterized esp. by a reddish face. [C16: via Med. L < Gk *plēthōrē* fullness, < *plēthein* to grow full] **—plethoric** (plɛˈθɒrɪk) *adj.*

pleura (ˈplʊərə) *n., pl.* **pleurae** (ˈplʊəriː). the thin transparent membrane enveloping the lungs and lining the walls of the thoracic cavity. [C17: via Med. L < Gk: side, rib] **—ˈpleural** *adj.*

pleurisy (ˈplʊərɪsɪ) *n.* inflammation of the pleura, characterized by pain that is aggravated by deep breathing or coughing. [C14: < OF *pleurisie*, < LL, < Gk *pleuritis*, < *pleura* side] **—pleuritic** (plʊˈrɪtɪk) *adj., n.*

pleuro- *or before a vowel* **pleur-** *combining form.* **1.** of or relating to the side. **2.** indicating the pleura. [< Gk *pleura* side]

pleuropneumonia (ˌplʊərəʊnjuːˈməʊnɪə) *n.* the combined disorder of pleurisy and pneumonia.

Plexiglas (ˈplɛksɪˌglɑːs) *n. U.S. trademark.* a transparent plastic, polymethyl methacrylate, used for combs, plastic sheeting, etc.

plexor (ˈplɛksə) *or* **plessor** *n. Med.* a small hammer with a rubber head for use in percussion of the chest and testing reflexes. [C19: < Gk *plēxis* a stroke, < *plēssein* to strike]

plexus (ˈplɛksəs) *n., pl.* **-uses** *or* **-us.** **1.** any complex network of nerves, blood vessels, or lymphatic vessels. **2.** an intricate network or arrangement. [C17: NL, < L *plectere* to braid]

pliable (ˈplaɪəbᵊl) *adj.* easily moulded, bent, influenced, or altered. **—ˌpliaˈbility** *or* **ˈpliableness** *n.* **—ˈpliably** *adv.*

pliant (ˈplaɪənt) *adj.* **1.** easily bent; supple: *a pliant young tree.* **2.** adaptable; yielding readily to influence; compliant. [C14: < OF, < *plier* to fold; see PLY[2]] **—ˈpliancy** *n.* **—ˈpliantly** *adv.*

plicate (ˈplaɪkeɪt) *or* **plicated** *adj.* having or arranged in parallel folds or ridges; pleated: *a plicate leaf; plicate rock strata.* [C18: < L *plicātus* folded, < *plicāre* to fold] **—pliˈcation** *n.*

plié (ˈpliːeɪ) *n.* a classic ballet practice posture with back erect and knees bent. [F: bent]

plier (ˈplaɪə) *n.* a person who plies a trade.

pliers (ˈplaɪəz) *pl. n.* a gripping tool consisting of two hinged arms usually with serrated jaws. [C16: < PLY[1]]

plight[1] (plaɪt) *n.* a condition of extreme hardship, danger, etc. [C14 *plit*, < OF *pleit* fold; prob. infl. by OE *pliht* PLIGHT[2]]

plight[2] (plaɪt) *vb. (tr.)* **1.** to promise formally or pledge (allegiance, support, etc.). **2. plight one's troth.** to make a promise, esp. of marriage. *~n.* **3.** *Arch. or dialect.* a solemn promise, esp. of engagement; pledge. [OE *pliht* peril] **—ˈplighter** *n.*

plimsoll *or* **plimsole** (ˈplɪmsəl) *n. Brit.* a light rubber-soled canvas shoe worn for various sports. Also called: **gym shoe.** [C20: < the resemblance of the sole to a Plimsoll line]

Plimsoll line (ˈplɪmsəl) *n.* another name for **load line.** [C19: after Samuel *Plimsoll* (1824–98), English MP, who advocated its adoption]

plinth (plɪnθ) *n.* **1.** the rectangular slab or block that forms the lowest part of the base of a column, pedestal, or pier. **2.** Also called: **plinth course.** the lowest part of the wall of a building, esp. one that is formed of a course of stone or brick. **3.** a flat block on either side of a door-frame, where the architrave meets the skirting. [C17: < L *plinthus*, < Gk *plinthos* brick]

Pliocene *or* **Pleiocene** (ˈplaɪəʊˌsiːn) *adj.* **1.** of, denoting, or formed in the last epoch of the Tertiary period, during which many modern mammals appeared. *~n.* **2. the.** the Pliocene epoch or rock series. [C19: < Gk *pleiōn* more, < *polus* many + *-cene* < *kainos* recent]

plissé (ˈpliːseɪ, ˈplɪs-) *n.* **1.** fabric with a wrinkled finish, achieved by treatment involving caustic soda: *cotton plissé.* **2.** such a finish on a fabric. [F: pleated]

PLO *abbrev. for* Palestine Liberation Organization.

plod (plɒd) *vb.* **plodding, plodded.** **1.** to make (one's way) or walk along (a path, etc.) with heavy usually slow steps. **2.** (*intr.*) to work slowly and perseveringly. *~n.* **3.** the act of plodding.

[C16: imit.] —ˈ**plodder** *n.* —ˈ**plodding** *adj.* —ˈ**ploddingly** *adv.*

-ploid *adj. and n. combining form.* indicating a specific multiple of a single set of chromosomes: *diploid.* [< Gk *-pl(oos)* -fold + -OID] —**-ploidy** *n. combining form.*

plonk[1] (plɒŋk) *vb.* **1.** (often foll. by *down*) to drop or be dropped heavily: *he plonked the money on the table.* ~*n.* **2.** the act or sound of plonking. [var. of PLUNK]

plonk[2] (plɒŋk) *n. Inf.* alcoholic drink, usually wine, esp. of inferior quality. [C20: ? < F *blanc* white, as in *vin blanc* white wine]

plop (plɒp) *n.* **1.** the characteristic sound made by an object dropping into water without a splash. ~*vb.* **plopping, plopped. 2.** to fall or cause to fall with the sound of a plop: *the stone plopped into the water.* ~*interj.* **3.** an exclamation imitative of this sound: *to go plop.* [C19: imit.]

plosion (ˈpləʊʒən) *n. Phonetics.* the sound of an abrupt break or closure, esp. the audible release of a stop. Also called: **explosion.**

plosive (ˈpləʊsɪv) *Phonetics.* ~*adj.* **1.** accompanied by plosion. ~*n.* **2.** a plosive consonant; stop. [C20: < F, < *explosif* EXPLOSIVE]

plot[1] (plɒt) *n.* **1.** a secret plan to achieve some purpose, esp. one that is illegal or underhand. **2.** the story or plan of a play, novel, etc. **3.** *Mil.* a graphic representation of an individual or tactical setting that pinpoints an artillery target. **4.** *Chiefly U.S.* a diagram or plan. ~*vb.* **plotting, plotted. 5.** to plan secretly (something illegal, revolutionary, etc.); conspire. **6.** (*tr.*) to mark (a course, as of a ship or aircraft) on a map. **7.** (*tr.*) to make a plan or map of. **8. a.** to locate and mark (points) on a graph by means of coordinates. **b.** to draw (a curve) through these points. **9.** (*tr.*) to construct the plot of (a literary work, etc.). [C16: < PLOT[2], infl. by obs. *complot* conspiracy, < OF, <?] —ˈ**plotter** *n.*

plot[2] (plɒt) *n.* a small piece of land: *a vegetable plot.* [OE]

plough *or esp. U.S.* **plow** (plaʊ) *n.* **1.** an agricultural implement with sharp blades for cutting or turning over the earth. **2.** any of various similar implements, such as a device for clearing snow. **3.** ploughed land. **4. put one's hand to the plough.** to begin or undertake a task. ~*vb.* **5.** to till (the soil, etc.) with a plough. **6.** to make (furrows or grooves) in (something) with or as if with a plough. **7.** (when *intr.*, usually foll. by *through*) to move (through something) in the manner of a plough. **8.** (*intr.*; foll. by *through*) to work at slowly or perseveringly. **9.** (*intr.*; foll. by *into* or *through*) (of a vehicle) to run uncontrollably into something in its path. **10.** (*intr.*) *Brit. sl.* to fail an examination. [OE *plōg* plough land] —ˈ**plougher** *or esp. U.S.* ˈ**plower** *n.*

Plough (plaʊ) *n.* **the.** the group of the seven brightest stars in the constellation Ursa Major. Also called: **Charles's Wain.** Usual U.S. name: the **Big Dipper.**

plough back *vb.* (*tr., adv.*) to reinvest (the profits of a business) in the same business.

ploughman *or esp. U.S.* **plowman** (ˈplaʊmən) *n., pl.* **-men.** a man who ploughs, esp. using horses.

ploughman's lunch *n.* a snack lunch, served esp. in a pub, consisting of bread and cheese with pickle.

ploughshare *or esp. U.S.* **plowshare** (ˈplaʊˌʃɛə) *n.* the horizontal pointed cutting blade of a mouldboard plough.

plover (ˈplʌvə) *n.* **1.** any of a family of shore birds, typically having a round head, straight bill, and large pointed wings. **2. green plover.** another name for **lapwing.** [C14: < OF *plovier* rainbird, < L *pluvia* rain]

plow (plaʊ) *n., vb.* the usual U.S. spelling of **plough.**

ploy (plɔɪ) *n.* **1.** a manoeuvre or tactic in a game, conversation, etc. **2.** any business, job, hobby, etc., with which one is occupied: *angling is his latest ploy.* **3.** *Chiefly Brit.* a frolic, escapade, or practical joke. [C18: orig. Scot. & N English, obs. n. sense of EMPLOY meaning an occupation]

PLP (in Britain) *abbrev. for* Parliamentary Labour Party.

PLR *abbrev. for* Public Lending Right.

pluck (plʌk) *vb.* **1.** (*tr.*) to pull off (feathers, fruit, etc.) from (a fowl, tree, etc.). **2.** (when *intr.*, foll. by *at*) to pull or tug. **3.** (*tr.*; foll. by *off, away,* etc.) *Arch.* to pull (something) forcibly or violently (from something or someone). **4.** (*tr.*) to sound (the strings) of (a musical instrument) with the fingers, a plectrum, etc. **5.** (*tr.*) *Sl.* to fleece or swindle. ~*n.* **6.** courage, usually in the face of difficulties or hardship. **7.** a sudden pull or tug. **8.** the heart, liver, and lungs, esp. of an animal used for food. [OE *pluccian, plyccan*] —ˈ**plucker** *n.*

pluck up *vb.* (*tr., adv.*) **1.** to pull out; uproot. **2.** to muster (courage, one's spirits, etc.).

plucky (ˈplʌkɪ) *adj.* **pluckier, pluckiest.** having or showing courage in the face of difficulties, danger, etc. —ˈ**pluckily** *adv.* —ˈ**pluckiness** *n.*

plug (plʌg) *n.* **1.** a piece of wood, cork, or other material, used to stop up holes or waste pipes or as a wedge for taking a screw or nail. **2.** a device having one or more pins to which an electric cable is attached: used to make an electrical connection when inserted into a socket. **3.** Also called: **volcanic plug.** a mass of solidified magma filling the neck of an extinct volcano. **4.** See **sparking plug. 5. a.** a cake of pressed or twisted tobacco, esp. for chewing. **b.** a small piece of such a cake. **6.** *Inf.* a favourable mention of a product, show, etc., as on television. ~*vb.* **plugging, plugged. 7.** (*tr.*) to stop up or secure (a hole, gap, etc.) with or as if with a plug. **8.** (*tr.*) to insert or use (something) as a plug: *to plug a finger into one's ear.* **9.** (*tr.*) *Inf.* to make favourable and often-repeated mentions of (a song, product, show, etc.), as on television. **10.** (*tr.*) *Sl.* to shoot: *he plugged six rabbits.* **11.** (*tr.*) *Sl.* to punch. **12.** (*intr.*; foll. by *along, away,* etc.) *Inf.* to work steadily or persistently. [C17: < MDu. *plugge*] —ˈ**plugger** *n.*

plughole (ˈplʌgˌhəʊl) *n.* a hole in a sink, etc., through which waste water drains and which can be closed with a plug.

plug in *vb.* (*tr., adv.*) to connect (an electrical appliance, etc.) with a power source by means of an electrical plug.

plug-ugly *adj.* **1.** *Inf.* extremely ugly. ~*n., pl.* **-uglies. 2.** *U.S. sl.* a city tough; ruffian. [C19: <?]

plum (plʌm) *n.* **1.** a small rosaceous tree with an edible oval fruit that is purple, yellow, or green and contains an oval stone. **2.** the fruit of this tree. **3.** a raisin, as used in a cake or pudding. **4. a.** a dark reddish-purple colour. **b.** (*as adj.*): *a plum carpet.* **5.** *Inf.* **a.** something of a superior or desirable kind, such as a financial bonus. **b.** (*as modifier*): *a plum job.* [OE *plūme*]

plumage (ˈpluːmɪdʒ) *n.* the layer of feathers covering the body of a bird. [C15: < OF, < *plume* feather, < L *plūma* down]

plumate (ˈpluːmeɪt, -mɪt) *or* **plumose** *adj. Zool., bot.* **1.** of or possessing feathers or plumes. **2.** covered with small hairs: *a plumate seed.* [C19: < L *plūmātus* covered with feathers; see PLUME]

plumb (plʌm) *n.* **1.** a weight, usually of lead, suspended at the end of a line and used to determine water depth or verticality. **2.** the perpendicular position of a freely suspended plumb line (esp. in **out of plumb, off plumb**). ~*adv. also* **plum. 3.** vertical or perpendicular. **4.** *Inf., chiefly U.S.* (intensifier): *plumb stupid.* **5.** *Inf.* exactly; precisely. ~*vb.* **6.** (*tr.*; often foll. by *up*) to test the alignment of or adjust to the vertical with a plumb line. **7.** (*tr.*) to experience (the worst extremes of): *to plumb the depths of despair.* **8.** (*tr.*) to understand or master (something obscure): *to plumb a mystery.* **9.** to connect or join (a device such as a tap) to a water pipe or drainage system. [C13: < OF *plomb* (unattested) lead line, < *plon* lead, < L *plumbum*] —ˈ**plumbable** *adj.*

plumbago (plʌmˈbeɪgəʊ) *n., pl.* **-gos. 1.** a plant of warm regions, having clusters of blue, white, or red flowers. **2.** another name for **graphite.** [C17:

< L: lead ore, translation of Gk *polubdaina*, < *polubdos* lead]

plumber (ˈplʌmə) *n.* a person who installs and repairs pipes, fixtures, etc., for water, drainage, and gas. [C14: < OF *plommier* worker in lead, < LL *plumbārius*, < L *plumbum* lead]

plumbing (ˈplʌmɪŋ) *n.* **1.** the trade or work of a plumber. **2.** the pipes, fixtures, etc., used in a water, drainage, or gas installation. **3.** the act or procedure of using a plumb.

plumbism (ˈplʌmˌbɪzəm) *n.* chronic lead poisoning. [C19: < L *plumbum* lead]

plumb line *n.* a string with a metal weight, or **plumb bob,** at one end that, when suspended, points directly towards the earth's centre of gravity and so is used to determine verticality, depth, etc.

plumb rule *n.* a plumb line attached to a narrow board, used by builders, surveyors, etc.

plume (pluːm) *n.* **1.** a feather, esp. one that is large or ornamental. **2.** a feather or cluster of feathers worn esp. formerly as a badge or ornament in a headband, hat, etc. **3.** *Biol.* any feathery part. **4.** something that resembles a plume: *a plume of smoke.* **5.** a token or decoration of honour; prize. ~*vb.* (*tr.*) **6.** to adorn with feathers or plumes. **7.** (of a bird) to clean or preen (itself or its feathers). **8.** (foll. by *on* or *upon*) to pride or congratulate (oneself). [C14: < OF, < L *plūma* downy feather]

plummet (ˈplʌmɪt) *vb.* **1.** (*intr.*) to drop down; plunge. ~*n.* **2.** the weight on a plumb line; plumb bob. **3.** a lead plumb used by anglers. [C14: < OF *plommet* ball of lead, < *plomb* lead, < L *plumbum*]

plummy (ˈplʌmɪ) *adj.* **-mier, -miest. 1.** of, full of, or resembling plums. **2.** *Brit. inf.* (of speech) deep, refined, and somewhat drawling. **3.** *Brit. inf.* choice; desirable.

plumose (ˈpluːməʊs, -məʊz) *adj.* another word for **plumate.** [C17: < L *plūmōsus* feathery]

plump[1] (plʌmp) *adj.* **1.** well filled out or rounded; chubby: *a plump turkey.* **2.** bulging; full: *a plump wallet.* ~*vb.* **3.** (often foll. by *up* or *out*) to make or become plump: *to plump up a pillow.* [C15 (meaning: dull, rude), C16 (in current senses): ? < MDu. *plomp* blunt] —ˈ**plumply** *adv.* —ˈ**plumpness** *n.*

plump[2] (plʌmp) *vb.* **1.** (often foll. by *down, into,* etc.) to drop or fall suddenly and heavily. **2.** (*intr.;* foll. by *for*) to give support (to) or make a choice (of) one out of a group or number. ~*n.* **3.** a heavy abrupt fall or the sound of this. ~*adv.* **4.** suddenly or heavily. **5.** straight down; directly: *the helicopter landed plump in the middle of the field.* ~*adj., adv.* **6.** in a blunt, direct, or decisive manner. [C14: prob. imit.]

plum pudding *n. Brit.* a boiled or steamed pudding made with flour, suet, sugar, and dried fruit.

plumule (ˈpluːmjuːl) *n.* **1.** the embryonic shoot of seed-bearing plants. **2.** a down feather of young birds. [C18: < LL *plūmula* a little feather]

plumy (ˈpluːmɪ) *adj.* **plumier, plumiest. 1.** plumelike; feathery. **2.** consisting of, covered with, or adorned with feathers.

plunder (ˈplʌndə) *vb.* **1.** to steal (valuables, goods, sacred items, etc.) from (a town, church, etc.) by force, esp. in time of war; loot. **2.** (*tr.*) to rob or steal (choice or desirable things) from (a place): *to plunder an orchard.* ~*n.* **3.** anything taken by plundering; booty. **4.** the act of plundering; pillage. [C17: prob. < Du. *plunderen* (orig.: to plunder household goods)] —ˈ**plunderer** *n.*

plunge (plʌndʒ) *vb.* **1.** (usually foll. by *into*) to thrust or throw (something, oneself, etc.): *they plunged into the sea.* **2.** to throw or be thrown into a certain condition: *the room was plunged into darkness.* **3.** (usually foll. by *into*) to involve or become involved deeply (in). **4.** (*intr.*) to move or dash violently or with great speed or impetuosity. **5.** (*intr.*) to descend very suddenly or steeply: *the ship plunged in heavy seas; a plunging neckline.* **6.** (*intr.*) *Inf.* to speculate or gamble recklessly, for high stakes, etc. ~*n.* **7.** a leap or dive. **8.** *Inf.* a swim; dip. **9.** a pitching or tossing motion. **10. take the plunge.** *Inf.* to resolve to do something dangerous or irrevocable. [C14: < OF *plongier,* < Vulgar L *plumbicāre* (unattested) to sound with a plummet, < L *plumbum* lead]

plunger (ˈplʌndʒə) *n.* **1.** a rubber suction cup used to clear blocked drains, etc. **2.** a device or part of a machine that has a plunging or thrusting motion; piston. **3.** *Inf.* a reckless gambler.

plunk (plʌŋk) *vb.* **1.** to pluck (the strings) of (a banjo, etc.) or (of such an instrument) to give forth a sound when plucked. **2.** (often foll. by *down*) to drop or be dropped, esp. heavily or suddenly. ~*n.* **3.** the act or sound of plunking. [C20: imit.]

pluperfect (pluːˈpɜːfɪkt) *adj., n. Grammar.* another term for **past perfect.** [C16: < L *plūs quam perfectum* more than perfect]

plural (ˈplʊərəl) *adj.* **1.** containing, involving, or composed of more than one. **2.** denoting a word indicating that more than one referent is being referred to or described. ~*n.* **3.** *Grammar.* **a.** the plural number. **b.** a plural form. [C14: < OF *plurel,* < LL *plūrālis* concerning many, < L *plūs* more] —ˈ**plurally** *adv.*

pluralism (ˈplʊərəˌlɪzəm) *n.* **1.** the holding by a single person of more than one ecclesiastical benefice or office; plurality. **2.** *Sociol.* a theory of society as several autonomous but interdependent groups. **3.** the existence in a society of groups having distinctive ethnic origin, cultural forms, religions, etc. **4.** *Philosophy.* **a.** the metaphysical doctrine that reality consists of more than two basic types of substance. Cf. **monism, dualism. b.** the metaphysical doctrine that reality consists of independent entities rather than one unchanging whole. —ˈ**pluralist** *n., adj.* —ˌ**pluralˈistic** *adj.*

plurality (plʊəˈrælɪtɪ) *n., pl.* **-ties. 1.** the state of being plural. **2.** *Maths.* a number greater than one. **3.** the U.S. term for **relative majority. 4.** a large number. **5.** the greater number; majority. **6.** another word for **pluralism** (sense 1).

pluralize *or* **-ise** (ˈplʊərəˌlaɪz) *vb.* **1.** (*intr.*) to hold more than one ecclesiastical benefice or office at the same time. **2.** to make or become plural.

pluri- *combining form.* denoting several. [< L *plur-, plus* more, *plures* several]

plus (plʌs) *prep.* **1.** increased by the addition of: *four plus two.* **2.** with or with the addition of: *a good job, plus a new car.* ~*adj.* **3.** (*prenominal*) indicating or involving addition: *a plus sign.* **4.** another word for **positive** (senses 7, 8). **5.** on the positive part of a scale or coordinate axis: *a value of +x.* **6.** indicating the positive side of an electrical circuit. **7.** involving advantage: *a plus factor.* **8.** (*postpositive*) *Inf.* having a value above that which is stated: *she had charm plus.* **9.** (*postpositive*) slightly above a specified standard: *he received a B+ grade for his essay.* ~*n.* **10.** short for **plus sign. 11.** a positive quantity. **12.** *Inf.* something positive or to the good. **13.** a gain, surplus, or advantage. ~Mathematical symbol: + [C17: < L: more]

▷ **Usage.** *Plus, together with,* and *along with* do not create compound subjects in the way that *and* does: the number of the verb depends on that of the subject to which *plus, together with,* or *along with* is added: *this task, plus all the others, was* (not *were*) *undertaken by the government.*

plus fours *pl. n.* men's baggy knickerbockers reaching below the knee, now only worn for golf, etc. [C20: because made with four inches of material to hang over at the knee]

plush (plʌʃ) *n.* **1.** a fabric with a cut pile that is longer and softer than velvet. ~*adj.* **2.** Also: **plushy.** *Inf.* lavishly appointed; rich; costly. [C16: < F *pluche,* < OF *peluchier* to pluck, ult. < L *pilus* a hair] —ˈ**plushly** *adv.*

plus sign *n.* the symbol +, indicating addition or positive quantity.

Pluto[1] (ˈpluːtəʊ) *n. Gk myth.* the god of the underworld; Hades.

Pluto[2] (ˈpluːtəʊ) *n.* the smallest planet and the farthest known from the sun. [L, < Gk *Ploutōn,* lit.: the rich one]

plutocracy (pluːˈtɒkrəsɪ) *n., pl.* **-cies.** **1.** the rule of society by the wealthy. **2.** a state or government characterized by the rule of the wealthy. **3.** a class that exercises power by virtue of its wealth. [C17: < Gk *ploutokratia,* < *ploutos* wealth + *-kratia* rule] **—plutocratic** (ˌpluːtəˈkrætɪk) *adj.* **—ˌplutoˈcratically** *adv.*

plutocrat (ˈpluːtəˌkræt) *n.* a member of a plutocracy.

pluton (ˈpluːtɒn) *n.* any mass of igneous rock that has solidified below the surface of the earth. [C20: back formation < PLUTONIC]

plutonic (pluːˈtɒnɪk) *adj.* (of igneous rocks) derived from magma that has cooled and solidified below the surface of the earth. [C20: after PLUTO[1]]

plutonium (pluːˈtəʊnɪəm) *n.* a highly toxic metallic transuranic element. It occurs in trace amounts in uranium ores and is produced in a nuclear reactor by neutron bombardment of uranium-238. The most stable isotope, **plutonium-239,** readily undergoes fission and is used as a reactor fuel. Symbol: Pu; atomic no.: 94; half-life of ^{239}Pu: 24 360 years. [C20: after PLUTO[2] because Pluto lies beyond Neptune and plutonium was discovered soon after NEPTUNIUM]

pluvial (ˈpluːvɪəl) *adj.* **1.** of, characterized by, or due to the action of rain; rainy. ~*n.* **2.** *Geol.* a period of persistent heavy rainfall. [C17: < L *pluviālis* rainy, < *pluvia* rain]

pluviometer (ˌpluːvɪˈɒmɪtə) *n.* another name for **rain gauge.** **—pluviometric** (ˌpluːvɪəˈmɛtrɪk) *adj.* **—ˌpluvioˈmetrically** *adv.*

ply[1] (plaɪ) *vb.* **plying, plied.** (*mainly tr.*) **1.** to carry on, pursue, or work at (a job, trade, etc.). **2.** to manipulate or wield (a tool, etc.). **3.** to sell (goods, wares, etc.), esp. at a regular place. **4.** (usually foll. by *with*) to provide (with) or subject (to) repeatedly or persistently: *he plied us with drink; he plied the speaker with questions.* **5.** (*intr.*) to work steadily or diligently. **6.** (*also intr.*) (esp. of a ship, etc.) to travel regularly along (a route) or in (an area): *to ply the trade routes.* [C14 *plye,* short for *aplye* to APPLY]

ply[2] (plaɪ) *n., pl.* **plies.** **1. a.** a layer, fold, or thickness, as of yarn. **b.** (*in combination*): *four-ply.* **2.** a thin sheet of wood glued to other similar sheets to form plywood. **3.** one of the strands twisted together to make rope, yarn, etc. [C15: < OF *pli* fold, < *plier* to fold, < L *plicāre*]

Plymouth Brethren (ˈplɪməθ) *pl. n.* a religious sect founded about 1827, strongly Puritanical in outlook and having no organized ministry.

plywood (ˈplaɪˌwʊd) *n.* a structural board consisting of thin layers of wood glued together under pressure, with the grain of one layer at right angles to the grain of the adjoining layer.

pm *abbrev. for* premium.

Pm *the chemical symbol for* promethium.

PM *abbrev. for:* **1.** Past Master (of a fraternity). **2.** Paymaster. **3.** Postmaster. **4.** Prime Minister. **5.** *Mil.* Provost Marshal.

p.m., P.M., pm, *or* **PM** *abbrev. for:* **1.** (indicating the time from midday to midnight) post meridiem. [L: after noon] **2.** post-mortem (examination).

PMG *abbrev. for:* **1.** Paymaster General. **2.** Postmaster General.

PMS *abbrev. for* premenstrual syndrome.

PMT *abbrev. for* premenstrual tension.

PNdB *abbrev. for* perceived noise decibel.

pneumatic (njʊˈmætɪk) *adj.* **1.** of or concerned with air, gases, or wind. **2.** (of a machine or device) operated by compressed air or by a vacuum. **3.** containing compressed air: *a pneumatic tyre.* **4.** (of the bones of birds) containing air spaces which reduce their weight as an adaptation to flying. ~*n.* **5.** a pneumatic tyre. [C17: < LL *pneumaticus* of air or wind, < Gk, < *pneuma* breath, wind] **—pneuˈmatically** *adv.*

pneumatics (njʊˈmætɪks) *n.* (*functioning as sing.*) the branch of physics concerned with the mechanical properties of gases, esp. air.

pneumatology (ˌnjuːməˈtɒlədʒɪ) *n.* **1.** the branch of theology concerned with the Holy Ghost and other spiritual beings. **2.** an obsolete name for **psychology** (the science).

pneumatophore (njuːˈmætəʊˌfɔː) *n.* **1.** a specialized root of certain swamp plants, such as the mangrove, that branches upwards and undergoes gaseous exchange with the atmosphere. **2.** a polyp such as the Portuguese man-of-war, that is specialized as a float.

pneumococcus (ˌnjuːməʊˈkɒkəs) *n., pl.* **-cocci** (-ˈkɒksaɪ). a bacterium that causes pneumonia.

pneumoconiosis (ˌnjuːməʊˌkəʊnɪˈəʊsɪs) *or* **pneumonoconiosis** (ˌnjuːmənəʊˌkəʊnɪˈəʊsɪs) *n.* any disease of the lungs or bronchi caused by the inhalation of metallic or mineral particles. [C19: shortened < *pneumonoconiosis,* < Gk *pneumōn* lung + *-coniosis,* < *konis* dust]

pneumoencephalogram (ˌnjuːməʊɛnˈsɛfələˌgræm) *n.* See **encephalogram.**

pneumogastric (ˌnjuːməʊˈgæstrɪk) *adj. Anat.* **1.** of or relating to the lungs and stomach. **2.** a former term for **vagus.**

pneumonectomy (ˌnjuːməʊˈnɛktəmɪ) *or* **pneumectomy** *n., pl.* **-mies.** the surgical removal of a lung or part of a lung. [C20: < Gk *pneumōn* lung + -ECTOMY]

pneumonia (njuːˈməʊnɪə) *n.* inflammation of one or both lungs, in which the air sacs (alveoli) become filled with liquid. [C17: NL < Gk < *pneumōn* lung] **—pneumonic** (njuːˈmɒnɪk) *adj.*

pneumothorax (ˌnjuːməʊˈθɔːræks) *n.* the abnormal presence of air between the lung and the wall of the chest (pleural cavity), resulting in collapse of the lung.

p-n junction *n. Electronics.* a boundary between a p-type and n-type semiconductor that functions as a rectifier and is used in diodes and junction transistors.

po (pəʊ) *n., pl.* **pos.** *Brit.* an informal word for **chamber pot.** [C19: < POT[1]]

Po *the chemical symbol for* polonium.

PO *abbrev. for:* **1.** Personnel Officer. **2.** petty officer. **3.** Pilot Officer. **4.** Also: **p.o.** postal order. **5.** Post Office.

poach[1] (pəʊtʃ) *vb.* **1.** to catch (game, fish, etc.) illegally by trespassing on private property. **2.** to encroach on or usurp (another person's rights, duties, etc.) or steal (an idea, employee, etc.). **3.** *Tennis, badminton, etc.* to take or play (shots that should belong to one's partner). **4.** to break up (land) into wet muddy patches, as by riding over it. [C17: < OF *pocher,* of Gmc origin] **—ˈpoacher** *n.*

poach[2] (pəʊtʃ) *vb.* to simmer (eggs, fish, etc.) very gently in water, milk, stock, etc. [C15: < OF *pochier* to enclose in a bag (as the yolks are enclosed by the whites)] **—ˈpoacher** *n.*

pochard (ˈpəʊtʃəd) *n., pl.* **-chards** *or* **-chard.** any of various diving ducks, esp. a European variety, the male of which has a grey-and-black body and a reddish head. [C16: <?]

pock (pɒk) *n.* **1.** any pustule resulting from an eruptive disease, esp. from smallpox. **2.** another word for **pockmark** (sense 1). [OE *pocc*] **—ˈpocky** *adj.*

pocket (ˈpɒkɪt) *n.* **1.** a small bag or pouch in a garment for carrying small articles, money, etc. **2.** any bag or pouch or anything resembling this. **3.** *S. African.* a bag or sack of vegetables or fruit. **4.** a cavity in the earth, etc., such as one containing ore. **5.** a small enclosed or isolated area: *a pocket of resistance.* **6.** any of the six holes with pouches or nets let into the corners and sides of a billiard table. **7. in one's pocket.** under one's control. **8. in** *or* **out of pocket.** having made a profit or loss. **9. line one's pockets.** to make money, esp. by dishonesty when in a position of trust. **10.** (*modifier*) small: *a pocket edition.* ~*vb.* (*tr.*) **11.** to put into one's pocket. **12.** to take surreptitiously or unlawfully; steal. **13.** (*usually passive*) to confine in or as if in a pocket. **14.** to conceal or keep back: *he pocketed his pride and* *asked for help.* **15.** *Billiards, etc.* to drive (a ball) into a pocket. [C15: < Anglo-Norman *poket* a little bag, < *poque* bag, < MDu. *poke* bag] —ˈ**pocketless** *adj.*

pocket battleship *n.* a small heavily armed battle cruiser specially built to conform with treaty limitations on tonnage and armament.

pocket billiards *n.* (*functioning as sing.*) *Billiards.* **1.** another name for **pool**[2] (sense 5). **2.** any game played on a table in which the object is to pocket the balls, esp. snooker and pool.

pocketbook (ˈpɒkɪtˌbʊk) *n. Chiefly U.S.* a small bag or case for money, papers, etc.

pocket borough *n.* (before the Reform Act of 1832) an English borough constituency controlled by one person or family who owned the land.

pocketful (ˈpɒkɪtfʊl) *n., pl.* **-fuls.** as much as a pocket will hold.

pocketknife (ˈpɒkɪtˌnaɪf) *n., pl.* **-knives.** a small knife with one or more blades that fold into the handle; penknife.

pocket money *n.* **1.** *Brit.* a small weekly sum of money given to children by parents as an allowance. **2.** money for day-to-day spending, incidental expenses, etc.

pockmark (ˈpɒkˌmɑːk) *n.* **1.** Also called: **pock.** a pitted scar left on the skin after the healing of a smallpox or similar pustule. **2.** any pitting of a surface that resembles or suggests such scars. ~*vb.* **3.** (*tr.*) to scar or pit with pockmarks.

poco (ˈpəʊkəʊ; *Italian* ˈpɔːko) *or* **un poco** *adj., adv.* (*in combination*) *Music.* a little; to a small degree. [< It.: little, < L *paucus* few]

poco a poco *adv.* (*in combination*) *Music.* little by little: *poco a poco rall.* [It.]

pod (pɒd) *n.* **1. a.** the fruit of any leguminous plant, consisting of a long two-valved case that contains seeds. **b.** the seedcase as distinct from the seeds. **2.** any similar fruit. **3.** a streamlined structure attached to an aircraft and used to house a jet engine, fuel tank, armament, etc. ~*vb.* **podding, podded. 4.** (*tr.*) to remove the pod from. [C17: ? back formation < earlier *podware* bagged vegetables]

-pod *or* **-pode** *n. combining form.* indicating a certain type or number of feet: *arthropod; tripod.* [< Gk *-podos* footed, < *pous* foot]

podagra (pəˈdægrə) *n.* gout of the foot or big toe. [C15: via L < Gk, < *pous* foot + *agra* a trap]

poddy (ˈpɒdɪ) *n., pl.* **-dies.** *Austral.* a handfed calf or lamb. [? < *poddy* (adj.) fat]

podgy (ˈpɒdʒɪ) *adj.* **podgier, podgiest. 1.** short and fat; chubby. **2.** (of the face, arms, etc.) unpleasantly chubby and pasty-looking. [C19: < *podge* a short plump person] —ˈ**podgily** *adv.* —ˈ**podginess** *n.*

podium (ˈpəʊdɪəm) *n., pl.* **-diums** *or* **-dia** (-dɪə). **1.** a small raised platform used by lecturers, conductors, etc. **2.** a plinth that supports a colonnade or wall. **3.** a low wall surrounding the arena of an ancient amphitheatre. **4.** *Zool.* any footlike organ, such as the tube foot of a starfish. [C18: < L: platform, < Gk *podion* little foot, < *pous* foot]

-podium *n. combining form.* a part resembling a foot: *pseudopodium.* [< NL: footlike; see PODIUM]

podophyllin (ˌpɒdəʊˈfɪlɪn) *n.* a bitter yellow resin obtained from the dried underground stems of the May apple and mandrake: used as a cathartic. [C19: < NL *Podophyllum,* genus of herbs, < *podo-,* < Gk *pous* foot + *phullon* leaf]

-podous *adj. combining form.* having feet of a certain kind or number: *cephalopodous.*

podzol (ˈpɒdzɒl) *or* **podsol** (ˈpɒdsɒl) *n.* a type of soil characteristic of coniferous forest regions having a greyish-white colour in its upper layers from which certain minerals have leached. [C20: < Russian: ash ground]

poem (ˈpəʊɪm) *n.* **1.** a composition in verse, usually characterized by words chosen for their sound and suggestive power as well as for their sense, and using such techniques as metre, rhyme, and alliteration. **2.** a literary composition that is not in verse but exhibits the intensity of imagination and language common to it: *a prose poem.* **3.** anything resembling a poem in beauty, effect, etc. [C16: < L *poēma,* < Gk, var. of *poiēma* something created, < *poiein* to make]

poesy (ˈpəʊɪzɪ) *n., pl.* **-sies. 1.** an archaic word for **poetry. 2.** *Poetic.* the art of writing poetry. [C14: via OF < L *poēsis,* < Gk, < *poiēsis* poetic art, < *poiein* to make]

poet (ˈpəʊɪt) *or* (*sometimes when fem.*) **poetess** *n.* **1.** a person who writes poetry. **2.** a person with great imagination and creativity. [C13: < L *poēta,* < Gk *poiētēs* maker, poet]

poetaster (ˌpəʊɪˈtæstə, -ˈteɪ-) *n.* a writer of inferior verse. [C16: < Med. L; see POET, -ASTER]

poetic (pəʊˈɛtɪk) *or* **poetical** *adj.* **1.** of poetry. **2.** characteristic of poetry, as in being elevated, sublime, etc. **3.** characteristic of a poet. **4.** recounted in verse. —**poˈetically** *adv.*

poeticize (pəʊˈɛtɪˌsaɪz), **poetize** (ˈpəʊɪˌtaɪz) *or* **poeticise, poetise** *vb.* **1.** (*tr.*) to put into poetry or make poetic. **2.** (*intr.*) to speak or write poetically.

poetic justice *n.* fitting retribution.

poetic licence *n.* justifiable departure from conventional rules of form, fact, etc., as in poetry.

poetics (pəʊˈɛtɪks) *n.* (*usually functioning as sing.*) **1.** the principles and forms of poetry or the study of these. **2.** a treatise on poetry.

poet laureate *n., pl.* **poets laureate.** *Brit.* the poet appointed as court poet of Britain who is given a lifetime post in the Royal Household.

poetry (ˈpəʊɪtrɪ) *n.* **1.** literature in metrical form; verse. **2.** the art or craft of writing verse. **3.** poetic qualities, spirit, or feeling in anything. **4.** anything resembling poetry in rhythm, beauty, etc. [C14: < Med. L *poētria,* < L *poēta* POET]

po-faced *adj.* wearing a disapproving stern expression. [C20: changed < *poor-faced*]

pogo stick (ˈpəʊgəʊ) *n.* a stout pole with a handle at the top, steps for the feet and a spring at the bottom, so that the user can spring up, down, and along on it. [C20: <?]

pogrom (ˈpɒgrəm) *n.* an organized persecution or extermination of an ethnic group, esp. of Jews. [C20: via Yiddish < Russian: destruction, < *po-* like + *grom* thunder]

pohutukawa (pəˌhuːtuːˈkɑːwə) *n.* a New Zealand tree which grows on the coast and produces red flowers in the summer. Also called: **Christmas tree.**

poi (pɔɪ) *n. N.Z.* a ball of woven New Zealand flax swung rhythmically by Maori women while performing poi dances.

poi dance *n. N.Z.* a women's formation dance that involves singing and manipulating a poi.

-poiesis *n. combining form.* indicating the act of making or producing something specified. [< Gk, < *poiēsis* a making; see POESY] —**-poietic** *adj. combining form.*

poignant (ˈpɔɪnjənt, -nənt) *adj.* **1.** sharply distressing or painful to the feelings. **2.** to the point; cutting or piercing: *poignant wit.* **3.** keen or pertinent in mental appeal: *a poignant subject.* **4.** pungent in smell. [C14: < OF, < L *pungens* pricking, < *pungere* to sting] —ˈ**poignancy** *or* ˈ**poignance** *n.* —ˈ**poignantly** *adv.*

poikilothermic (ˌpɔɪkɪləʊˈθɜːmɪk) *or* **poikilothermal** (ˌpɔɪkɪləʊˈθɜːməl) *adj.* (of all animals except birds and mammals) having a body temperature that varies with the temperature of the surroundings. [C19: < Gk *poikilos* various + THERMAL] —ˌ**poikiloˈthermy** *n.*

poinciana (ˌpɔɪnsɪˈɑːnə) *n.* a tree of a tropical genus having large orange or red flowers. [C17: NL, after M. de *Poinci,* 17th-cent. governor of the French Antilles]

poind (pɔɪnd) *vb.* (*tr.*) *Scots Law.* **1.** to take (property of a debtor, etc.) in execution of distress; distrain. **2.** to impound (stray cattle, etc.). [C15: < Scot., var. of OE *pyndan* to impound]

poinsettia (pɔɪnˈsɛtɪə) *n.* a shrub of Mexico and Central America, widely cultivated for its showy scarlet bracts, which resemble petals. [C19: NL, after J. P. *Poinsett* (1799–1851), U.S. Minister to Mexico]

point (pɔɪnt) *n.* **1.** a dot or tiny mark. **2.** a location, spot, or position. **3.** any dot used in writing or printing, such as a decimal point or a full stop. **4.** the sharp tapered end of a pin, knife, etc. **5.** *Maths.* **a.** a geometric element having no dimensions whose position is located by means of its coordinates. **b.** a location: *point of inflection.* **6.** a small promontory. **7.** a specific condition or degree. **8.** a moment: *at that point he left the room.* **9.** a reason, aim, etc.: *the point of this exercise is to train new teachers.* **10.** an essential element in an argument: *I take your point.* **11.** a suggestion or tip. **12.** a detail or item. **13.** a characteristic, physical attribute, etc.: *he has his good points.* **14.** a distinctive characteristic or quality of an animal, esp. one used as a standard in judging livestock. **15.** (*often pl.*) any of the extremities, such as the tail, ears, or feet, of a domestic animal. **16.** (*often pl.*) *Ballet.* the tip of the toes. **17.** a single unit for measuring or counting, as in the scoring of a game. **18.** *Printing.* a unit of measurement equal to one twelfth of a pica. There are approximately 72 points to the inch. **19.** *Finance.* a unit of value used to quote security and commodity prices and their fluctuations. **20.** *Navigation.* **a.** one of the 32 marks on the compass indicating direction. **b.** the angle of 11°15′ between two adjacent marks. **21.** *Cricket.* a fielding position at right angles to the batsman on the off side and relatively near the pitch. **22.** either of the two electrical contacts that make or break the current flow in the distributor of an internal-combustion engine. **23.** *Brit.* (*often pl.*) a junction of railway tracks in which a pair of rails can be moved so that a train can be directed onto either of two lines. U.S. and Canad. equivalent: **switch.** **24.** (*often pl.*) a piece of ribbon, cord, etc., with metal tags at the end: used during the 16th and 17th centuries to fasten clothing. **25.** *Brit.* short for **power point.** **26.** the position of the body of a pointer or setter when it discovers game. **27.** *Boxing.* a mark awarded for a scoring blow, knockdown, etc. **28.** any diacritic used in a writing system, esp. in a phonetic transcription, to indicate modifications of vowels or consonants. **29.** *Jewellery.* a unit of weight equal to 0.01 carat. **30.** the act of pointing. **31. at** (*or* **on**) **the point of.** at the moment immediately before: *on the point of leaving the room.* **32. beside the point.** irrelevant. **33. case in point.** a specific or relevant instance. **34. make a point of. a.** to make (something) one's regular habit. **b.** to do (something) because one thinks it important. **35. not to put too fine a point on it.** to speak plainly and bluntly. **36. score points off.** to gain an advantage at someone else's expense. **37. to the point.** relevant. **38. up to a point.** not completely. ~*vb.* **39.** (usually foll. by *at* or *to*) to indicate the location or direction of by or as by extending (a finger or other pointed object) towards it: *he pointed to the front door; don't point that gun at me.* **40.** (*intr.;* usually foll. by *at* or *to*) to indicate or identify a specific person or thing among several: *all evidence pointed to Donald as the murderer.* **41.** (*tr.*) to direct or face in a specific direction: *point me in the right direction.* **42.** (*tr.*) to sharpen or taper. **43.** (*intr.*) (of gun dogs) to indicate the place where game is lying by standing rigidly with the muzzle turned in its direction. **44.** (*tr.*) to finish or repair the joints of (brickwork, masonry, etc.) with mortar or cement. **45.** (*tr.*) *Music.* to mark (a psalm text) with vertical lines to indicate the points at which the music changes during chanting. **46.** (*tr.*) *Phonetics.* to provide (a letter or letters) with diacritics. **47.** (*tr.*) to provide (a Hebrew or similar text) with vowel points. ~See also **point off, point out, point up.** [C13: < OF: spot, < L *punctum* a point, < *pungere* to pierce]

point-blank *adj.* **1. a.** aimed or fired at a target so close that it is unnecessary to make allowance for the drop in the course of the projectile. **b.** permitting such aim or fire without loss of accuracy: *at point-blank range.* **2.** aimed or fired at nearly zero range. **3.** plain or blunt: *a point-blank question.* ~*adv.* **4.** directly or straight. **5.** plainly or bluntly. [C16: < POINT + BLANK (in the sense: centre spot of an archery target)]

point duty *n.* the stationing of a policeman or traffic warden at a road junction to control and direct traffic.

pointe (pɔɪnt) *n. Ballet.* the tip of the toe (esp. in **on pointes**). [< F: point]

pointed (ˈpɔɪntɪd) *adj.* **1.** having a point. **2.** cutting or incisive: *a pointed wit.* **3.** obviously directed at a particular person or aspect: *pointed criticism.* **4.** emphasized or made conspicuous: *pointed ignorance.* **5.** (of an arch or style of architecture) Gothic. **6.** *Music.* (of a psalm text) marked to show changes in chanting. **7.** (of Hebrew text) with vowel points marked. —ˈ**pointedly** *adv.*

pointer (ˈpɔɪntə) *n.* **1.** a person or thing that points. **2.** an indicator on a measuring instrument. **3.** a long rod or cane used by a lecturer to point to parts of a map, blackboard, etc. **4.** one of a breed of large smooth-coated gun dogs, usually white with black, liver, or lemon markings. **5.** a helpful piece of information.

pointillism (ˈpwæntɪˌlɪzəm) *n.* the technique of painting elaborated from impressionism, in which dots of unmixed colour are juxtaposed on a white ground so that from a distance they fuse in the viewer's eye into appropriate intermediate tones. [C19: < F, < *pointiller* to mark with tiny dots, < *pointille* little point, < It., < *punto* POINT] —ˈ**pointillist** *n., adj.*

pointing (ˈpɔɪntɪŋ) *n.* the act or process of repairing or finishing joints in brickwork, masonry, etc., with mortar.

point lace *n.* lace made by a needle with buttonhole stitch on a paper pattern. Also called: **needlepoint.** Cf. **pillow lace.**

pointless (ˈpɔɪntlɪs) *adj.* **1.** without a point. **2.** without meaning, relevance, or force. **3.** *Sport.* without a point scored. —ˈ**pointlessly** *adv.*

point off *vb.* (*tr., adv.*) to mark off from the right-hand side (a number of decimal places) in a whole number to create a mixed decimal: *point off three decimal places in 12345 and you get 12.345.*

point of honour *n., pl.* **points of honour.** a circumstance, event, etc., that involves the defence of one's principles, social honour, etc.

point of no return *n.* **1.** a point at which an irreversible commitment must be made to an action, progression, etc. **2.** a point in a journey at which, if one continues, supplies will be insufficient for a return to the starting place.

point of order *n., pl.* **points of order.** a question raised in a meeting as to whether the rules governing procedures are being breached.

point of sale *n.* (in retail distribution) **a.** the place and time when a sale is made. **b.** (*as modifier*): *a point-of-sale display.*

point of view *n., pl.* **points of view.** **1.** a position from which someone or something is observed. **2.** a mental viewpoint or attitude.

point out *vb.* (*tr., adv.*) to indicate or specify.

pointsman (ˈpɔɪntsˌmæn, -mən) *n., pl.* **-men.** **1.** a person who operates railway points. **2.** a policeman or traffic warden on point duty.

point source *n. Optics.* a source of light or other radiation that can be considered to have negligible dimensions.

point-to-point *n. Brit.* a steeplechase organized by a recognized hunt or other body, usually restricted to amateurs riding horses that have been regularly used in hunting.

point up *vb.* (*tr., adv.*) to emphasize, esp. by identifying: *he pointed up the difficulties.*

poise[1] (pɔɪz) *n.* **1.** composure or dignity of manner. **2.** physical balance. **3.** equilibrium; stability. **4.** the position of hovering. ~*vb.* **5.** to be or cause to be balanced or suspended. **6.** (*tr.*) to hold, as in readiness: *to poise a lance.* [C16: < OF *pois* weight, < L *pēnsum,* < *pendere* to weigh]

poise[2] (pwɑːz, pɔɪz) *n.* the cgs unit of viscosity; the viscosity of a fluid in which a tangential force of 1 dyne per square centimetre maintains a difference in velocity of 1 centimetre per second between two parallel planes 1 centimetre apart. Symbol: P [C20: after Jean Louis Marie *Poiseuille* (1799–1869), F physician]

poised (pɔɪzd) *adj.* **1.** self-possessed; dignified. **2.** balanced and prepared for action.

poison (ˈpɔɪzᵊn) *n.* **1.** any substance that can impair function or otherwise injure the body. **2.** something that destroys, corrupts, etc. **3.** a substance that retards a chemical reaction or the activity of a catalyst. **4.** a substance that absorbs neutrons in a nuclear reactor and thus slows down the reaction. ~*vb.* (*tr.*) **5.** to give poison to (a person or animal), esp. with intent to kill. **6.** to add poison to. **7.** to taint or infect with or as if with poison. **8.** (foll. by *against*) to turn (a person's mind) against: *he poisoned her mind against me.* **9.** to retard or stop (a chemical or nuclear reaction) by the action of a poison. [C13: < OF *puison* potion, < L *pōtiō* a drink, esp. a poisonous one, < *pōtāre* to drink] —ˈ**poisoner** *n.*

poison ivy *n.* any of several North American shrubs or climbing plants that cause an itching rash on contact.

poisonous (ˈpɔɪzənəs) *adj.* **1.** having the effects or qualities of a poison. **2.** capable of killing or inflicting injury. **3.** corruptive or malicious. —ˈ**poisonously** *adv.* —ˈ**poisonousness** *n.*

poison-pen letter *n.* a letter written in malice, usually anonymously, and intended to abuse, frighten, or insult the recipient.

poison sumach *n.* a swamp shrub of the southeastern U.S. that causes an itching rash on contact with the skin.

Poisson distribution (ˈpwɑːsᵊn) *n. Statistics.* a distribution that represents the number of events occurring randomly in a fixed time at an average rate λ. [C19: after S. D. *Poisson* (1781–1840), F mathematician]

poke[1] (pəʊk) *vb.* **1.** (*tr.*) to jab or prod, as with the elbow, a stick, etc. **2.** (*tr.*) to make (a hole) by or as by poking. **3.** (when *intr.*, often foll. by *at*) to thrust (at). **4.** (*tr.*) *Inf.* to hit with the fist; punch. **5.** (usually foll. by *in, through,* etc.) to protrude or cause to protrude: *don't poke your arm out of the window.* **6.** (*tr.*) to stir (a fire, etc.) by poking. **7.** (*intr.*) to meddle or intrude. **8.** (*intr.;* often foll. by *about* or *around*) to search or pry. **9. poke one's nose into.** to interfere with or meddle in. ~*n.* **10.** a jab or prod. **11.** *Inf.* a blow with one's fist; punch. [C14: < Low G & MDu. *poken* to prod]

poke[2] (pəʊk) *n.* **1.** *Dialect.* a pocket or bag. **2. a pig in a poke.** See **pig.** [C13: < OF *poque,* of Gmc origin]

poke[3] (pəʊk) *n.* **1.** Also called: **poke bonnet.** a bonnet with a brim that projects at the front, popular in the 18th and 19th centuries. **2.** the brim itself. [C18: < POKE[1] (in the sense: to project)]

poker[1] (ˈpəʊkə) *n.* a metal rod, usually with a handle, for stirring a fire.

poker[2] (ˈpəʊkə) *n.* a card game of bluff and skill in which bets are made on the hands dealt, the highest-ranking hand winning the pool. [C19: prob. < F *poque* similar card game]

poker face *n. Inf.* a face without expression, as that of a poker player attempting to conceal the value of his cards. —ˈ**poker-ˌfaced** *adj.*

poker machine *n. Austral. & N.Z.* a fruit machine.

pokerwork (ˈpəʊkəˌwɜːk) *n.* the art of producing pictures or designs on wood by charring it with a heated tool.

pokeweed (ˈpəʊkˌwiːd), **pokeberry,** *or* **pokeroot** *n.* a tall North American plant that has a poisonous purple root used medicinally. [C18 *poke,* < Algonquian *puccoon* plant used in dyeing, < *pak* blood]

pokie (ˈpəʊkɪ) *n. Austral. inf.* short for **poker machine.**

poky *or* **pokey** (ˈpəʊkɪ) *adj.* **pokier, pokiest. 1.** (esp. of rooms) small and cramped. **2.** *Inf., chiefly U.S.* without speed or energy; slow. [C19: < POKE[1] (in sl. sense: to confine)] —ˈ**pokily** *adv.* —ˈ**pokiness** *n.*

pol. *abbrev. for:* **1.** political. **2.** politics.

Pol. *abbrev. for:* **1.** Poland. **2.** Polish.

polar (ˈpəʊlə) *adj.* **1.** at, near, or relating to either of the earth's poles or the area inside the Arctic or Antarctic Circles: *polar regions.* **2.** having or relating to a pole or poles. **3.** pivotal or guiding in the manner of the Pole Star. **4.** directly opposite, as in tendency or character. **5.** *Chem.* (of a molecule) having an uneven distribution of electrons and thus a permanent dipole moment: *water has polar molecules.*

polar bear *n.* a white carnivorous bear of coastal regions of the North Pole.

polar circle *n.* a term for either the **Arctic Circle** or **Antarctic Circle.**

polar coordinates *pl. n.* a pair of coordinates for locating a point in a plane by means of the length of a radius vector, *r,* which pivots about the origin to establish the angle, θ, that the position of the point makes with a fixed line. Usually written (*r,* θ).

polar distance *n.* the angular distance of a star, planet, etc., from the celestial pole; the complement of the declination.

polar front *n. Meteorol.* a front dividing cold polar air from warmer temperate or tropical air.

Polari (pəˈlɑːrɪ) *n.* an English slang derived from the Lingua Franca of Mediterranean ports; brought to England by sailors from the 16th century onwards. [C19: < It. *parlare* to speak]

polarimeter (ˌpəʊləˈrɪmɪtə) *n.* an instrument for measuring the polarization of light. —**polarimetric** (ˌpəʊlərɪˈmɛtrɪk) *adj.*

Polaris (pəˈlɑːrɪs) *n.* **1.** Also called: the **Pole Star,** the **North Star.** the brightest star in the constellation Ursa Minor, situated slightly less than 1° from the north celestial pole. **2.** a type of U.S. two-stage intermediate-range ballistic missile, usually fired by a submerged submarine. [< Med. L *stella polāris* polar star]

polariscope (pəʊˈlærɪˌskəʊp) *n.* an instrument for detecting polarized light or for observing objects under polarized light, esp. for detecting strain in transparent materials.

polarity (pəʊˈlærɪtɪ) *n., pl.* **-ties. 1.** the condition of having poles. **2.** the condition of a body or system in which it has opposing physical properties, esp. magnetic poles or electric charge. **3.** the particular state of a part that has polarity: *an electrode with positive polarity.* **4.** the state of having or expressing two directly opposite tendencies, opinions, etc.

polarization *or* **-isation** (ˌpəʊləraɪˈzeɪʃən) *n.* **1.** the condition of having or giving polarity. **2.** *Physics.* the phenomenon in which waves of light or other radiation are restricted to certain directions of vibration.

polarize *or* **-ise** (ˈpəʊləˌraɪz) *vb.* **1.** to acquire or cause to acquire polarity or polarization. **2.** (*tr.*) to cause (people) to adopt extreme opposing positions: *to polarize opinion.* —ˈ**polarˌizer** *or* **-ˌiser** *n.*

polar lights *pl. n.* the aurora borealis in the N hemisphere or the aurora australis in the S hemisphere.

polarography (ˌpəʊləˈrɒgrəfɪ) *n.* a technique for analysing and studying ions in solution by using an electrolytic cell with a very small cathode and obtaining a graph (**polarogram**) of the current against the potential to determine the concentration and nature of the ions.

Polaroid (ˈpəʊləˌrɔɪd) *n. Trademark.* **1.** a type of plastic sheet that can polarize a transmitted beam of normal light because it is composed of long parallel molecules. It only transmits plane-polarized light if these molecules are parallel to the plane of polarization. **2. Polaroid Land Camera.** any of several types of camera yielding a finished print by means of a special developing and processing technique that occurs inside the camera and takes only a few seconds.

polder (ˈpəʊldə, ˈpɒl-) *n.* a stretch of land

reclaimed from the sea or a lake, esp. in the Netherlands. [C17: < MDu. *polre*]

pole[1] (pəʊl) *n.* **1.** a long slender usually round piece of wood, metal, or other material. **2.** the piece of timber on each side of which a pair of carriage horses are hitched. **3.** another name for **rod** (sense 7). **4. up the pole.** *Brit., Austral., & N.Z. inf.* **a.** slightly mad. **b.** mistaken; on the wrong track. ~*vb.* **5.** (*tr.*) to strike or push with a pole. **6.** (*tr.*) **a.** to set out (an area of land or garden) with poles. **b.** to support (a crop, such as hops) on poles. **7.** to punt (a boat). [OE *pāl*, < L *pālus* a stake]

pole[2] (pəʊl) *n.* **1.** either of the two antipodal points where the earth's axis of rotation meets the earth's surface. See also **North Pole, South Pole. 2.** *Physics.* **a.** either of the two regions at the extremities of a magnet to which the lines of force converge. **b.** either of two points at which there are opposite electric charges, as at the terminals of a battery. **3.** *Biol.* either end of the axis of a cell, spore, ovum, or similar body. **4.** either of two mutually exclusive or opposite actions, opinions, etc. **5. poles apart** (*or* **asunder**). having widely divergent opinions, tastes, etc. [C14: < L *polus* end of an axis, < Gk *polos* pivot]

Pole (pəʊl) *n.* a native, inhabitant, or citizen of Poland or a speaker of Polish.

poleaxe *or U.S.* **poleax** (ˈpəʊlˌæks) *n.* **1.** another term for a battle-axe or a butcher's axe. ~*vb.* **2.** (*tr.*) to hit or fell with or as if with a poleaxe. [C14 *pollax* battle-axe, < POLL + AXE]

polecat (ˈpəʊlˌkæt) *n., pl.* **-cats** *or* **-cat. 1.** a dark brown musteline mammal of Europe, Asia, and N Africa, that is closely related to but larger than the weasel and gives off an unpleasant smell. **2.** *U.S.* a nontechnical name for **skunk** (sense 1). [C14 *polcat*, ? < OF *pol* cock, < L *pullus*, + CAT; from its preying on poultry]

polemic (pəˈlɛmɪk) *adj. also* **polemical. 1.** of or involving dispute or controversy. ~*n.* **2.** an argument or controversy, esp. over a doctrine, belief, etc. **3.** a person engaged in such controversy. [C17: < Med. L *polemicus*, < Gk *polemikos* relating to war, < *polemos* war] —**poˈlemically** *adv.* —**polemicist** (pəˈlɛmɪsɪst) *n.*

polemics (pəˈlɛmɪks) *n.* (*functioning as sing.*) the art or practice of dispute or argument, as in attacking or defending a doctrine or belief.

pole star *n.* a guiding principle, rule, etc.

Pole Star *n.* **the.** the star closest to the N celestial pole at any particular time. At present this is Polaris, but it will eventually be replaced owing to precession of the earth's axis.

pole vault *n.* **1. the.** a field event in which competitors attempt to clear a high bar with the aid of an extremely flexible long pole. ~*vb.* **pole-vault. 2.** (*intr.*) to perform a pole vault or compete in the pole vault. —**ˈpole-ˌvaulter** *n.*

poley (ˈpəʊlɪ) *adj. Austral.* (of cattle) hornless or polled.

police (pəˈliːs) *n.* **1.** (*often preceded by the*) the organized civil force of a state, concerned with maintenance of law and order. **2.** (*functioning as pl.*) the members of such a force collectively. **3.** any organized body with a similar function: *security police.* ~*vb.* (*tr.*) **4.** to regulate, control, or keep in order by means of a police or similar force. **5.** to observe or record the activity or enforcement of: *a committee was set up to police the new agreement on picketing.* [C16: via F < L *polītīa* administration; see POLITY]

police dog *n.* a dog, often an Alsatian, trained to help the police, as in tracking.

policeman (pəˈliːsmən) *or* (*fem.*) **policewoman** *n., pl.* **-men** *or* **-women.** a member of a police force, esp. one holding the rank of constable.

police officer *n.* a member of a police force, esp. a constable; policeman.

police state *n.* a state or country in which a repressive government maintains control through the police.

police station *n.* the office or headquarters of the police force of a district.

policing (pəˈliːsɪŋ) *n.* the policies, techniques, and practice of a police force in keeping order, preventing crime, etc.

policy[1] (ˈpɒlɪsɪ) *n., pl.* **-cies. 1.** a plan of action adopted or pursued by an individual, government, party, business, etc. **2.** wisdom, shrewdness, or sagacity. **3.** (*often pl.*) *Scot.* the improved grounds surrounding a country house. [C14: < OF *policie*, < L *polītīa* administration, POLITY]

policy[2] (ˈpɒlɪsɪ) *n., pl.* **-cies.** a document containing a contract of insurance. [C16: < OF *police* certificate, < OIt. < L *apodixis* proof, < Gk *apodeixis*] —**ˈpolicyˌholder** *n.*

polio (ˈpəʊlɪəʊ) *n.* short for **poliomyelitis.**

poliomyelitis (ˌpəʊlɪəʊˌmaɪəˈlaɪtɪs) *n.* an acute infectious viral disease, esp. affecting children. In its paralytic form the brain and spinal cord are involved, causing paralysis and wasting of muscle. Also called: **infantile paralysis.** [C19: NL, < Gk *polios* grey + *muelos* marrow]

polish (ˈpɒlɪʃ) *vb.* **1.** to make or become smooth and shiny by rubbing, esp. with wax or an abrasive. **2.** (*tr.*) to make perfect or complete. **3.** to make or become elegant or refined. ~*n.* **4.** a finish or gloss. **5.** the act of polishing. **6.** a substance used to produce a shiny, often protective surface. **7.** elegance or refinement, esp. in style, manner, etc. [C13 *polis*, < OF *polir*, < L *polīre* to polish] —**ˈpolisher** *n.*

Polish (ˈpəʊlɪʃ) *adj.* **1.** of, relating to, or characteristic of Poland, its people, or their language. ~*n.* **2.** the official language of Poland.

polished (ˈpɒlɪʃt) *adj.* **1.** accomplished: *a polished actor.* **2.** impeccably or professionally done: *a polished performance.* **3.** (of rice) having had the outer husk removed by milling.

polish off *vb.* (*tr., adv.*) *Inf.* **1.** to finish or process completely. **2.** to dispose of or kill.

polish up *vb.* (*adv.*) **1.** to make or become smooth and shiny by polishing. **2.** (when *intr.*, foll. by *on*) to study or practise until adept (at); improve: *he's polishing up on his German.*

Politburo (ˈpɒlɪtˌbjʊərəʊ) *n.* **1.** the executive and policy-making committee of a Communist Party. **2.** the supreme policy-making authority in most Communist countries. [C20: < Russian: contraction of *Politicheskoe Buro* political bureau]

polite (pəˈlaɪt) *adj.* **1.** showing a great regard for others, as in manners, speech, etc.; courteous. **2.** cultivated or refined: *polite society.* **3.** elegant or polished: *polite letters.* [C15: < L *polītus* polished] —**poˈlitely** *adv.* —**poˈliteness** *n.*

politesse (ˌpɒlɪˈtɛs) *n.* formal or genteel politeness. [C18: via F < It. *politezza*, ult. < L *polīre* to polish]

politic (ˈpɒlɪtɪk) *adj.* **1.** artful or shrewd; ingenious. **2.** crafty or unscrupulous; cunning. **3.** wise or prudent, esp. in statesmanship: *a politic choice.* **4.** an archaic word for **political.** ~ See also **body politic.** [C15: < OF *politique*, < L *polīticus* concerning civil administration, < Gk, < *politēs* citizen, < *polis* city] —**ˈpoliticly** *adv.*

political (pəˈlɪtɪkᵊl) *adj.* **1.** of or relating to the state, government, public administration, etc. **2. a.** of or relating to government policy-making as distinguished from administration or law. **b.** of or relating to the civil aspects of government as distinguished from the military. **3.** of, dealing with, or relating to politics: *a political person.* **4.** of or relating to the parties and the partisan aspects of politics. **5.** organized with respect to government: *a political unit.* —**poˈlitically** *adv.*

political economy *n.* the former name for **economics** (sense 1).

political prisoner *n.* a person imprisoned for holding or expressing particular political beliefs.

political science *n.* the study of the state, government, and politics: one of the social sciences. —**political scientist** *n.*

politician (ˌpɒlɪˈtɪʃən) *n.* **1.** a person actively engaged in politics, esp. a full-time professional member of a deliberative assembly. **2.** a person who is experienced or skilled in government or administration; statesman. **3.** *Disparaging, chief-*

ly U.S. a person who engages in politics out of a wish for personal gain.
politicize *or* **-ise** (pəˈlɪtɪˌsaɪz) *vb.* **1.** (*tr.*) to render political in tone, interest, or awareness. **2.** (*intr.*) to participate in political discussion or activity. —**poˌliticiˈzation** *or* **-iˈsation** *n.*
politicking (ˈpɒlɪtɪkɪŋ) *n.* political activity, esp. seeking votes.
politico (pəˈlɪtɪˌkəʊ) *n., pl.* **-cos.** *Chiefly U.S.* an informal word for a **politician** (senses 1, 3). [C17: < It. or Sp.]
politics (ˈpɒlɪtɪks) *n.* **1.** (*functioning as sing.*) the art and science of directing and administrating states and other political units; government. **2.** (*functioning as sing.*) the complex or aggregate of relationships of people in society, esp. those relationships involving authority or power. **3.** (*functioning as pl.*) political activities or affairs: *party politics.* **4.** (*functioning as sing.*) the business or profession of politics. **5.** (*functioning as sing. or pl.*) any activity concerned with the acquisition of power, etc.: *company politics are frequently vicious.* **6.** manoeuvres or factors leading up to or influencing (something): *the politics of the decision.* **7.** (*functioning as pl.*) opinions, sympathies, etc., with respect to politics: *his conservative politics.*
polity (ˈpɒlɪtɪ) *n., pl.* **-ties.** **1.** a form of government or organization of a society, etc.; constitution. **2.** a politically organized society, etc. **3.** the management of public affairs. **4.** political organization. [C16: < L *polītīa,* < Gk *politeia* citizenship, civil administration, < *politēs* citizen, < *polis* city]
polka (ˈpɒlkə) *n.* **1.** a 19th-century Bohemian dance with three steps and a hop, in fast duple time. **2.** a piece of music composed for or in the rhythm of this dance. ~*vb.* **-kaing, -kaed.** **3.** (*intr.*) to dance a polka. [C19: via F < Czech *pulka* half-step]
polka dot *n.* one of a pattern of small circular regularly spaced spots on a fabric.
poll (pəʊl) *n.* **1.** the casting, recording, or counting of votes in an election; a voting. **2.** the result of such a voting: *a heavy poll.* **3.** Also called: **opinion poll. a.** a canvassing of a representative sample of people on some question in order to determine the general opinion. **b.** the results of such a canvassing. **4.** any counting or enumeration, esp. for taxation or voting purposes. **5.** the back part of the head of an animal. ~*vb.* (*mainly tr.*) **6.** to receive (a vote or quantity of votes): *he polled 10 000 votes.* **7.** to receive, take, or record the votes of: *he polled the whole town.* **8.** to canvass (a person, group, area, etc.) as part of a survey of opinion. **9.** (*sometimes intr.*) to cast (a vote) in an election. **10.** to clip or shear. **11.** to remove or cut short the horns of (cattle). [C13 (in the sense: a human head) & C17 (in the sense: votes): < MLow G *polle* hair of the head, head, top of a tree]
pollack *or* **pollock** (ˈpɒlək) *n., pl.* **-lacks, -lack** *or* **-locks, -lock.** a gadoid food fish that has a projecting lower jaw and occurs in northern seas. [C17: < earlier Scot. *podlok,* <?]
pollan (ˈpɒlən) *n.* any of several varieties of whitefish that occur in lakes in Northern Ireland. [C18: prob. < Irish *poll* lake]
pollard (ˈpɒləd) *n.* **1.** an animal, such as a sheep or deer, that has either shed its horns or antlers or has had them removed. **2.** a tree that has had its branches cut back to encourage a more bushy growth. ~*vb.* **3.** (*tr.*) to convert into a pollard; poll. [C16: hornless animal; see POLL]
pollen (ˈpɒlən) *n.* a substance produced by the anthers of seed-bearing plants, consisting of numerous fine grains containing the male gametes. [C16: < L: powder] —**pollinic** (pəˈlɪnɪk) *adj.*
pollen analysis *n.* another name for **palynology.**
pollen count *n.* a measure of the pollen present in the air over a 24-hour period, often published to enable sufferers from hay fever to predict the severity of their attacks.
pollex (ˈpɒlɛks) *n., pl.* **-lices** (-lɪˌsiːz). the first digit of the forelimb of amphibians, reptiles, birds, and mammals, such as the thumb of man. [C19: < L: thumb, big toe] —**pollical** (ˈpɒlɪkᵊl) *adj.*
pollinate (ˈpɒlɪˌneɪt) *vb.* (*tr.*) to transfer pollen from the anthers to the stigma of (a flower). —ˌ**polliˈnation** *n.* —ˈ**polliˌnator** *n.*
polling booth *n.* a semienclosed space in which a voter stands to mark a ballot paper during an election.
polling station *n.* a building, such as a school, designated as the place to which voters go during an election in order to cast their votes.
polliwog *or* **pollywog** (ˈpɒlɪˌwɒg) *n. Dialect, U.S., & Canad.* a tadpole. [C15 *polwygle*]
pollster (ˈpəʊlstə) *n.* a person who conducts opinion polls.
poll tax *n.* a tax levied per head of adult population.
pollutant (pəˈluːtᵊnt) *n.* a substance that pollutes, esp. a chemical produced as a waste product of an industrial process.
pollute (pəˈluːt) *vb.* (*tr.*) **1.** to contaminate, as with poisonous or harmful substances. **2.** to make morally corrupt. **3.** to desecrate. [C14 *polute,* < L *polluere* to defile] —**polˈluter** *n.* —**polˈlution** *n.*
Pollyanna (ˌpɒlɪˈænə) *n.* a person who is optimistic. [C20: after the chief character in *Pollyanna* (1913), a novel by Eleanor Porter (1868–1920), U.S. writer]
polo (ˈpəʊləʊ) *n.* **1.** a game similar to hockey played on horseback using long-handled mallets (**polo sticks**) and a wooden ball. **2.** short for **water polo.** **3.** Also called: **polo neck. a.** a collar on a garment, worn rolled over to fit closely round the neck. **b.** a garment, esp. a sweater, with such a collar. [C19: < Balti (dialect of Kashmir): ball, < Tibetan *pulu*]
polonaise (ˌpɒləˈneɪz) *n.* **1.** a ceremonial marchlike dance in three-four time from Poland. **2.** a piece of music composed for or in the rhythm of this dance. **3.** a woman's costume with a tight bodice and an overskirt drawn back to show a decorative underskirt. [C18: < F *danse polonaise* Polish dance]
polonium (pəˈləʊnɪəm) *n.* a very rare radioactive element that occurs in trace amounts in uranium ores. Symbol: Po; atomic no.: 84; half-life of most stable isotope, ^{209}Po: 103 years. [C19: NL, < Med. L *Polōnia* Poland; in honour of the nationality of its discoverer, Marie Curie]
polony (pəˈləʊnɪ) *n., pl.* **-nies.** *Brit.* another name for **Bologna sausage.**
poltergeist (ˈpɒltəˌgaɪst) *n.* a spirit believed to manifest its presence by noises and acts of mischief, such as throwing furniture about. [C19: < G, < *poltern* to be noisy + *Geist* GHOST]
poltroon (pɒlˈtruːn) *n.* an abject or contemptible coward. [C16: < OF *poultron,* < OIt. *poltrone* lazy good-for-nothing, apparently < *poltrīre* to lie indolently in bed]
poly (ˈpɒlɪ) *n., pl.* **polys.** *Inf.* short for **polytechnic.**
poly- *combining form.* **1.** more than one; many or much: *polyhedron.* **2.** having an excessive or abnormal number or amount: *polyphagia.* [< Gk *polus* much, many]
polyamide (ˌpɒlɪˈæmaɪd, -mɪd) *n.* any of a class of synthetic polymeric materials, including nylon.
polyandry (ˈpɒlɪˌændrɪ) *n.* **1.** the practice or condition of being married to more than one husband at the same time. **2.** the practice in animals of a female mating with more than one male during one breeding season. **3.** the condition in flowers of having a large indefinite number of stamens. [C18: < Gk *poluandria,* < POLY- + *-andria* < *anēr* man] —ˌ**polyˈandrous** *adj.*
polyanthus (ˌpɒlɪˈænθəs) *n., pl.* **-thuses.** any of several hybrid garden primroses with brightly coloured flowers. [C18: NL, < Gk: having many flowers]
polyatomic (ˌpɒlɪəˈtɒmɪk) *adj.* (of a molecule) containing more than two atoms.
poly bag (ˈpɒlɪ) *n. Brit. inf.* a polythene bag, esp.

one used to store or protect food or household articles.

polybasic (ˌpɒlɪˈbeɪsɪk) *adj.* (of an acid) having two or more replaceable hydrogen atoms per molecule.

polycarpic (ˌpɒlɪˈkɑːpɪk) *or* **polycarpous** *adj.* (of a plant) able to produce flowers and fruit several times in succession. —**ˈpolyˌcarpy** *n.*

polycentrism (ˌpɒlɪˈsɛntrɪzəm) *n.* the fact or advocacy of the existence of more than one predominant ideological or political centre in a political system, alliance, etc., in the Communist world.

polychaete (ˈpɒlɪˌkiːt) *n.* **1.** a marine annelid worm having a distinct head and paired fleshy appendages (parapodia) that bear bristles and are used in swimming. ~*adj. also* **polychaetous. 2.** of or denoting such a creature. [C19: < NL, < Gk *polukhaitēs* having much hair]

polychromatic (ˌpɒlɪkrəʊˈmætɪk), **polychromic** (ˌpɒlɪˈkrəʊmɪk), *or* **polychromous** *adj.* **1.** having various or changing colours. **2.** (of light or other radiation) containing radiation with more than one wavelength. —**polychromatism** (ˌpɒlɪˈkrəʊməˌtɪzəm) *n.*

polyclinic (ˌpɒlɪˈklɪnɪk) *n.* a hospital or clinic able to treat a wide variety of diseases.

polycotyledon (ˌpɒlɪˌkɒtɪˈliːdᵊn) *n.* any of various plants, esp. gymnosperms, that have or appear to have more than two cotyledons. —**ˌpolyˌcotyˈledonous** *adj.*

polycyclic (ˌpɒlɪˈsaɪklɪk) *adj.* **1.** (of a molecule or compound) having molecules that contain two or more closed rings of atoms. **2.** *Biol.* having two or more rings or whorls: *polycyclic shells.* ~*n.* **3.** a polycyclic compound.

polydactyl (ˌpɒlɪˈdæktɪl) *adj. also* **polydactylous. 1.** (of man and other vertebrates) having more than the normal number of digits. ~*n.* **2.** a human or other vertebrate having more than the normal number of digits.

polyester (ˌpɒlɪˈɛstə) *n.* any of a large class of synthetic materials that are polymers containing recurring -COO- groups: used as plastics, textile fibres, and adhesives.

polyethylene (ˌpɒlɪˈɛθɪˌliːn) *n.* another name for **polythene.**

polygamy (pəˈlɪgəmɪ) *n.* **1.** the practice of having more than one wife or husband at the same time. **2.** the condition of having male, female, and hermaphrodite flowers on the same plant or on separate plants of the same species. **3.** the practice in male animals of having more than one mate during one breeding season. [C16: via F < Gk *polugamia*] —**poˈlygamist** *n.* —**poˈlygamous** *adj.* —**poˈlygamously** *adv.*

polygene (ˈpɒlɪˌdʒiːn) *n.* any of a group of genes that each produce a small quantitative effect on a particular characteristic, such as height.

polygenesis (ˌpɒlɪˈdʒɛnɪsɪs) *n.* **1.** *Biol.* evolution of organisms from different ancestral groups. **2.** the hypothetical descent of different races from different ultimate ancestors. —**polygenetic** (ˌpɒlɪdʒɪˈnɛtɪk) *adj.*

polyglot (ˈpɒlɪˌglɒt) *adj.* **1.** having a command of many languages. **2.** written in or containing many languages. ~*n.* **3.** a person with a command of many languages. **4.** a book, esp. a Bible, containing several versions of the same text written in various languages. **5.** a mixture of languages. [C17: < Gk *poluglōttos,* lit.: many-tongued]

polygon (ˈpɒlɪˌgɒn) *n.* a closed plane figure bounded by three or more straight sides that meet in pairs in the same number of vertices and do not intersect other than at these vertices. Specific polygons are named according to the number of sides, such as triangle, pentagon, etc. [C16: via L < Gk *polugōnon* figure with many angles] —**polygonal** (pəˈlɪgənᵊl) *adj.* —**poˈlygonally** *adv.*

polygonum (pəˈlɪgənəm) *n.* a plant having stems with knotlike joints and spikes of small white, green, or pink flowers. [C18: NL, < Gk *polugonon* knotgrass, < *polu-* POLY- + *-gonon,* < *gonu* knee]

polygraph (ˈpɒlɪˌgrɑːf) *n.* **1.** an instrument for the simultaneous recording of several involuntary physiological activities, including pulse rate and perspiration, used esp. as a lie detector. **2.** a device for producing copies of written matter. [C18: < Gk *polugraphos* writing copiously]

polygyny (pəˈlɪdʒɪnɪ) *n.* **1.** the practice or condition of being married to more than one wife at the same time. **2.** the practice in animals of a male mating with more than one female during one breeding season. **3.** the condition in flowers of having many styles. [C18: < POLY- + *-gyny,* < Gk *gunē* a woman] —**poˈlygynous** *adj.*

polyhedron (ˌpɒlɪˈhiːdrən) *n., pl.* **-drons** *or* **-dra** (-drə). a solid figure consisting of four or more plane faces (all polygons), pairs of which meet along an edge, three or more edges meeting at a vertex. Specific polyhedrons are named according to the number of faces, such as tetrahedron, icosahedron, etc. [C16: < Gk *poluedron,* < POLY- + *hedron* side] —**ˌpolyˈhedral** *adj.*

Polyhymnia (ˌpɒlɪˈhɪmnɪə) *n. Greek myth.* the Muse of singing, mime, and sacred dance. [L, < Gk *Polumnia* full of songs]

polymath (ˈpɒlɪˌmæθ) *n.* a person of great and varied learning. [C17: < Gk *polumathēs* having much knowledge] —**polymathy** (pəˈlɪməθɪ) *n.*

polymer (ˈpɒlɪmə) *n.* a naturally occurring or synthetic compound, such as starch or Perspex, that has large molecules made up of many relatively simple repeated units. —**polymerism** (pəˈlɪməˌrɪzəm, ˈpɒlɪmə-) *n.*

polymeric (ˌpɒlɪˈmɛrɪk) *adj.* of, concerned with, or being a polymer: *a polymeric compound.* [C19: < Gk *polumerēs* having many parts]

polymerization *or* **-isation** (pəˌlɪməraɪˈzeɪʃən, ˌpɒlɪməraɪ-) *n.* the act or process of forming a polymer or copolymer.

polymerize *or* **-ise** (ˈpɒlɪməˌraɪz, pəˈlɪmə-) *vb.* to react or cause to react to form a polymer.

polymerous (pəˈlɪmərəs) *adj. Biol.* having or being composed of many parts.

polymorph (ˈpɒlɪˌmɔːf) *n.* a species of animal or plant, or a crystalline form of a chemical compound, that exhibits polymorphism. [C19: < Gk *polumorphos* having many forms]

polymorphism (ˌpɒlɪˈmɔːfɪzəm) *n.* **1.** the occurrence of more than one form of individual in a single species within an interbreeding population. **2.** the existence or formation of different types of crystal of the same chemical compound.

polymorphous (ˌpɒlɪˈmɔːfəs) *or* **polymorphic** *adj.* **1.** having, taking, or passing through many different forms or stages. **2.** exhibiting or undergoing polymorphism.

Polynesian (ˌpɒlɪˈniːʒən, -ʒɪən) *adj.* **1.** of or relating to Polynesia, a group of Pacific islands, or to its people, or any of their languages. ~*n.* **2.** a member of the people that inhabit Polynesia, generally of Caucasoid features with light skin and wavy hair. **3.** a branch of the Malayo-Polynesian family of languages, including Maori and Hawaiian.

polyneuritis (ˌpɒlɪnjʊˈraɪtɪs) *n.* inflammation of many nerves at the same time.

polynomial (ˌpɒlɪˈnəʊmɪəl) *adj.* **1.** of, consisting of, or referring to two or more names or terms. ~*n.* **2. a.** a mathematical expression consisting of a sum of terms each of which is the product of a constant and one or more variables raised to a positive or zero integral power. **b.** Also called: **multinomial.** any mathematical expression consisting of the sum of a number of terms. **3.** *Biol.* a taxonomic name consisting of more than two terms, such as *Parus major minor* in which *minor* designates the subspecies.

polynucleotide (ˌpɒlɪˈnjuːklɪəˌtaɪd) *n. Biochem.* a molecular chain of nucleotides chemically bonded by a series of ester linkages between the phosphoryl group of one nucleotide and the hydroxyl group of the sugar in the adjacent nucleotide.

polynya (ˈpɒlənˌjɑː) *n.* a stretch of open water surrounded by ice, esp. near the mouths of large rivers, in arctic seas. [C19: < Russian, < *poly* open]

polyp (ˈpɒlɪp) *n.* **1.** *Zool.* one of the two forms of individual that occur in coelenterates. It usually has a hollow cylindrical body with a ring of tentacles around the mouth. **2.** Also called: **polypus.** *Pathol.* a small growth arising from the surface of a mucous membrane. [C16 *polip,* < F *polype* nasal polyp, < L *pōlypus,* < Gk *polupous* having many feet] —ˈ**polypous** *or* ˈ**polypoid** *adj.*

polypeptide (ˌpɒlɪˈpɛptaɪd) *n.* any of a group of natural or synthetic polymers made up of amino acids chemically linked together; includes the proteins.

polypetalous (ˌpɒlɪˈpɛtələs) *adj.* (of flowers) having many distinct or separate petals.

polyphagia (ˌpɒlɪˈfeɪdʒə) *n.* **1.** an abnormal desire to consume excessive amounts of food. **2.** the habit of certain animals, esp. certain insects, of feeding on many different types of food. [C17: NL, < Gk, < *poluphagos* eating much] —**polyphagous** (pəˈlɪfəgəs) *adj.*

polyphase (ˈpɒlɪˌfeɪz) *adj.* **1.** (of an electrical system, circuit, or device) having or using alternating voltages of the same frequency, the phases of which are cyclically displaced by fractions of a period. **2.** having more than one phase.

polyphone (ˈpɒlɪˌfəʊn) *n.* a letter or character having more than one phonetic value, such as *c* in English.

polyphonic (ˌpɒlɪˈfɒnɪk) *adj.* **1.** *Music.* composed of relatively independent parts; contrapuntal. **2.** many-voiced. **3.** *Phonetics.* denoting a polyphone. —ˌ**polyˈphonically** *adv.*

polyphony (pəˈlɪfənɪ) *n., pl.* **-nies. 1.** polyphonic style of composition or a piece of music utilizing it. **2.** the use of polyphones in a writing system. [C19: < Gk *poluphōnia* diversity of tones] —**poˈlyphonous** *adj.* —**poˈlyphonously** *adv.*

polyploid (ˈpɒlɪˌplɔɪd) *adj.* (of cells, organisms, etc.) having more than twice the basic (haploid) number of chromosomes. —ˌ**polyˈploidal** *adj.* —ˈ**polyˌploidy** *n.*

polypod (ˈpɒlɪˌpɒd) *adj.* **1.** (esp. of insect larvae) having many legs or similar appendages. ~*n.* **2.** an animal of this type.

polypody (ˈpɒlɪˌpəʊdɪ) *n., pl.* **-dies.** any of various ferns having deeply divided leaves and round naked sporangia. [C15: < L *polypodium,* < Gk, < POLY- + *pous* foot]

polypropylene (ˌpɒlɪˈprəʊpɪˌliːn) *n.* any of various tough flexible synthetic thermoplastic materials made by polymerizing propylene.

polypus (ˈpɒlɪpəs) *n., pl.* **-pi** (-paɪ). *Pathol.* another word for **polyp** (sense 2). [C16: via L < Gk: POLYP]

polysaccharide (ˌpɒlɪˈsækəˌraɪd, -rɪd) *or* **polysaccharose** (ˌpɒlɪˈsækəˌrəʊz, -ˌrəʊs) *n.* any one of a class of carbohydrates whose molecules contain linked monosaccharide units: includes starch, inulin, and cellulose.

polysemy (ˌpɒlɪˈsiːmɪ, pəˈlɪsəmɪ) *n.* the existence of several meanings in a single word. [C20: < NL *polysēmia,* < Gk *polusēmos* having many meanings] —ˌ**polyˈsemous** *adj.*

polysomic (ˌpɒlɪˈsəʊmɪk) *adj.* of, relating to, or designating a basically diploid chromosome complement, in which some but not all the chromosomes are represented more than twice.

polystyrene (ˌpɒlɪˈstaɪriːn) *n.* a synthetic thermoplastic material obtained by polymerizing styrene; used as a white rigid foam (**expanded polystyrene**) for insulating and packing and as a glasslike material in light fittings.

polysyllable (ˈpɒlɪˌsɪləbˀl) *n.* a word consisting of more than two syllables. —**polysyllabic** (ˌpɒlɪsɪˈlæbɪk) *adj.* —ˌ**polysylˈlabically** *adv.*

polysyndeton (ˌpɒlɪˈsɪndɪtən) *n. Rhetoric.* the use of several conjunctions in close succession, esp. where some might be omitted, as in *he ran and jumped and laughed for joy.* [C16: POLY- + *-syndeton,* < Gk *sundetos* bound together]

polytechnic (ˌpɒlɪˈtɛknɪk) *n.* **1.** *Brit.* a college offering advanced courses in many fields at and below degree standard. ~*adj.* **2.** of or relating to technical instruction and training. [C19: via F < Gk *polutekhnos* skilled in many arts]

polytetrafluoroethylene (ˌpɒlɪˌtɛtrəˌflʊərəʊˈɛθɪˌliːn) *n.* a white thermoplastic material with a waxy texture, made by polymerizing tetrafluoroethylene. It is used for making gaskets, hoses, insulators, bearings, and for coating metal surfaces. Abbrev.: **PTFE.** Also called (trademark): **Teflon.**

polytheism (ˈpɒlɪθiːˌɪzəm, ˌpɒlɪˈθiːɪzəm) *n.* the worship of or belief in more than one god. —ˌ**polytheˈistic** *adj.* —ˌ**polytheˈistically** *adv.*

polythene (ˈpɒlɪˌθiːn) *n.* any one of various light thermoplastic materials made from ethylene with properties depending on the molecular weight of the polymer. Also called: **polyethylene.**

polytonality (ˌpɒlɪtəʊˈnælɪtɪ) *or* **polytonalism** *n. Music.* the simultaneous use of more than two different keys or tonalities. —ˌ**polyˈtonal** *adj.* —ˌ**polyˈtonally** *adv.*

polyunsaturated (ˌpɒlɪʌnˈsætʃəˌreɪtɪd) *adj.* of or relating to a class of animal and vegetable fats, the molecules of which consist of long carbon chains with many double bonds. Polyunsaturated compounds do not contain cholesterol.

polyurethane (ˌpɒlɪˈjʊərəˌθeɪn) *n.* a class of synthetic materials commonly used as a foam for insulation and packing.

polyvalent (ˌpɒlɪˈveɪlənt, pəˈlɪvələnt) *adj.* **1.** *Chem.* having more than one valency. **2.** (of a vaccine) effective against several strains of the same disease-producing microorganism, antigen, or toxin. —ˌ**polyˈvalency** *n.*

polyvinyl (ˌpɒlɪˈvaɪnɪl, -ˈvaɪnˀl) *n.* (*modifier*) designating a plastic or resin formed by polymerization of a vinyl derivative.

polyvinyl acetate *n.* a colourless odourless tasteless resin used in emulsion paints and adhesives and for sealing porous surfaces.

polyvinyl chloride *n.* the full name of **PVC.**

polyvinyl resin *n.* any of a class of thermoplastic resins made by polymerizing a vinyl compound. The commonest type is PVC.

polyzoan (ˌpɒlɪˈzəʊən) *n., adj.* another word for **bryozoan.** [C19: < NL, *Polyzoa* class name, < POLY- + *-zoan,* < Gk *zoion* an animal]

pom (pɒm) *n. Austral. & N.Z. sl.* short for **pommy.**

POM *abbrev. for* prescription only medicine (*or* medication).

pomace (ˈpʌmɪs) *n.* **1.** the pulpy residue of apples or similar fruit after crushing and pressing, as in cider-making. **2.** any pulpy substance left after crushing, mashing, etc. [C16: < Med. L *pōmācium* cider, < L *pōmum* apple]

pomaceous (pɒˈmeɪʃəs) *adj.* of, relating to, or bearing pomes, such as the apple and quince trees. [C18: < NL *pōmāceus,* < L *pōmum* apple]

pomade (pəˈmɑːd) *n.* **1.** a perfumed oil or ointment put on the hair, as to make it smooth and shiny. ~*vb.* **2.** (*tr.*) to put pomade on. ~Also: **pomatum.** [C16: < F *pommade,* < It. *pomato* (orig. made partly from apples), < L *pōmum* apple]

pomander (pəʊˈmændə) *n.* **1.** a mixture of aromatic substances in a sachet or an orange, formerly carried as scent or as a protection against disease. **2.** a container for such a mixture. [C15: < OF *pome d'ambre,* < Med. L *pōmum ambrae* apple of amber]

pome (pəʊm) *n.* the fleshy fruit of the apple and related plants, consisting of an enlarged receptacle enclosing the ovary and seeds. [C15: < OF, < LL *pōma,* pl. of L *pōmum* apple]

pomegranate (ˈpɒmɪˌgrænɪt, ˈpɒmˌgrænɪt) *n.* **1.** an Asian shrub or small tree cultivated in semitropical regions for its edible fruit. **2.** the many-chambered globular fruit of this tree, which has tough reddish rind, juicy red pulp, and many seeds. [C14: < OF *pome grenate,* < L *pōmum* apple + *grenate,* < *grānātus* full of seeds]

pomelo (ˈpɒmɪˌləʊ) *n., pl.* **-los. 1.** Also called: **shaddock.** the edible yellow fruit, resembling a grapefruit, of a tropical tree widely grown in oriental regions. **2.** *U.S.* another name for **grapefruit.** [C19: < Du. *pompelmoes*]

Pomeranian (ˌpɒməˈreɪnɪən) *adj.* **1.** of or relating to Pomerania, a region of N central

Europe. ~*n.* **2.** a breed of toy dog of the spitz type with a long thick straight coat.

pomfret (ˈpʌmfrɪt, ˈpɒm-) *or* **pomfret-cake** *n.* a small black rounded confection of liquorice. Also called: **Pontefract cake.** [C19: < *Pomfret,* earlier form of *Pontefract,* Yorks., where orig. made]

pomiculture (ˈpɒmɪˌkʌltʃə) *n.* the cultivation of fruit. [C19: < L *pōmum* fruit + CULTURE]

pommel (ˈpʌməl, ˈpɒm-) *n.* **1.** the raised part on the front of a saddle. **2.** a knob at the top of a sword or similar weapon. ~*vb.* **-melling, -melled** *or U.S.* **-meling, -meled.** **3.** a less common word for **pummel.** [C14: < OF *pomel* knob, < Vulgar L *pōmellum* (unattested) little apple, < L *pōmum* apple]

pommy (ˈpɒmɪ) *n., pl.* **-mies.** (*sometimes cap.*) *Sl.* a mildly offensive word used by Australians and New Zealanders for a British person. Sometimes shortened to **pom.** [C20: <?, ? a blend of IMMIGRANT & POMEGRANATE (alluding to the red cheeks of British immigrants)]

pomology (pɒˈmɒlədʒɪ) *n.* the branch of horticulture concerned with the study and cultivation of fruit. [C19: < NL *pōmologia,* < L *pōmum* fruit] —**pomological** (ˌpɒməˈlɒdʒɪkᵊl) *adj.*

pomp (pɒmp) *n.* **1.** stately or magnificent display; ceremonial splendour. **2.** vain display, esp. of dignity or importance. **3.** *Obs.* a procession or pageant. [C14: < OF *pompe,* < L *pompa* procession, < Gk *pompē*]

pompadour (ˈpɒmpəˌdʊə) *n.* an early 18th-century hairstyle for women, having the front hair arranged over a pad to give it greater height and bulk. [C18: after the Marquise de *Pompadour,* mistress of Louis XV of France, who originated it]

pompano (ˈpɒmpəˌnəʊ) *n., pl.* **-no** *or* **-nos.** **1.** any of several food fishes of American coastal regions of the Atlantic. **2.** a spiny-finned food fish of North American coastal regions of the Pacific. [C19: < Sp. *pámpano,* <?]

pom-pom (ˈpɒmpɒm) *n.* an automatic rapid-firing small-calibre cannon, esp. a type of anti-aircraft cannon used in World War II. Also called: **pompom.** [C19: imit.]

pompon (ˈpɒmpɒn) *or* **pompom** *n.* **1.** a ball of tufted silk, wool, feathers, etc., worn on a hat for decoration. **2. a.** the small globelike flower head of certain varieties of dahlia and chrysanthemum. **b.** (*as modifier*): *pompon dahlia.* [C18: < F, < OF *pompe* knot of ribbons, <?]

pomposo (pɒmˈpəʊsəʊ) *adv. Music.* in a pompous manner. [It.]

pompous (ˈpɒmpəs) *adj.* **1.** exaggeratedly or ostentatiously dignified or self-important. **2.** ostentatiously lofty in style: *a pompous speech.* **3.** *Rare.* characterized by ceremonial pomp or splendour. —**pomposity** (pɒmˈpɒsɪtɪ) *or* ˈ**pompousness** *n.* —ˈ**pompously** *adv.*

'pon (pɒn) *Poetic or arch. contraction of* upon.

ponce (pɒns) *Derog. sl., chiefly Brit.* ~*n.* **1.** a man given to ostentatious or effeminate display. **2.** another word for **pimp**[1]. ~*vb.* **3.** (*intr.; often foll. by around* or *about*) to act like a ponce. [C19: < Polari, < Sp. *pu(n)to* male prostitute or F *pront* prostitute]

poncho (ˈpɒntʃəʊ) *n., pl.* **-chos.** a cloak of a kind originally worn in South America, made of a rectangular or circular piece of cloth with a hole in the middle for the head. [C18: < American Sp., of Amerind origin, < *pantho* woollen material]

pond (pɒnd) *n.* a pool of still water, often artificially created. [C13 *ponde* enclosure]

ponder (ˈpɒndə) *vb.* (when *intr.,* sometimes foll. by *on* or *over*) to give thorough or deep consideration (to); meditate (upon). [C14: < OF *ponderer,* < L *ponderāre* to weigh, consider, < *pondus* weight] —ˈ**ponderable** *adj.*

ponderous (ˈpɒndərəs) *adj.* **1.** heavy; huge. **2.** (esp. of movement) lacking ease or lightness; lumbering or graceless. **3.** dull or laborious: *a ponderous oration.* [C14: < L *ponderōsus* of great weight, < *pondus* weight] —ˈ**ponderously** *adv.* —ˈ**ponderousness** *or* **ponderosity** (ˌpɒndəˈrɒsɪtɪ) *n.*

pond lily *n.* another name for **water lily.**

pondok (ˈpɒndɒk) *or* **pondokie** *n. Derog.* (in southern Africa) a crudely made house built of tin sheet, reeds, etc. [C20: < Malay *pondók* leaf house]

pond scum *n.* a greenish layer floating on the surface of stagnant waters, consisting of algae.

pondweed (ˈpɒndˌwiːd) *n.* **1.** any of various water plants of the genus *Potamogeton,* which grow in ponds and slow streams. **2.** Also called: **waterweed.** *Brit.* any of various water plants, such as mare's-tail, that have thin or much-divided leaves.

pone[1] (pəʊn, ˈpəʊnɪ) *n. Cards.* the player to the right of the dealer, or the nondealer in two-handed games. [C19: < L: put!, that is, play, < *ponere* to put]

pone[2] (pəʊn) *n. Southern U.S.* bread made of maize. Also called: **pone bread, corn pone.** [C17: of Amerind origin]

pong (pɒŋ) *Brit. inf.* ~*n.* **1.** a disagreeable or offensive smell; stink. ~*vb.* **2.** (*intr.*) to stink. [C20: ? < Romany *pan* to stink] —ˈ**pongy** *adj.*

ponga (ˈpɒŋə) *n.* a tall New Zealand tree fern with large leathery leaves.

pongee (pɒnˈdʒiː, ˈpɒndʒiː) *n.* **1.** a thin plain-weave silk fabric from China or India, left in its natural colour. **2.** a cotton or rayon fabric similar to this. [C18: < Mandarin Chinese (Peking) *pen-chī* woven at home, < *pen* own + *chi* loom]

pongid (ˈpɒŋgɪd, ˈpɒndʒɪd) *n.* **1.** any primate of the family Pongidae, which includes the gibbons and the great apes. ~*adj.* **2.** of this family. [< NL *Pongo* type genus, < Congolese *mpongo* ape]

pongo (ˈpɒŋgəʊ) *n., pl.* **-gos.** an anthropoid ape, esp. an orang-utan or (formerly) a gorilla. [C17: < Congolese *mpongo*]

poniard (ˈpɒnjəd) *n.* **1.** a small dagger with a slender blade. ~*vb.* **2.** (*tr.*) to stab with a poniard. [C16: < OF *poignard,* < *poing* fist, < L *pugnus*]

pons Varolii (pɒnz vəˈrəʊlɪˌaɪ) *n., pl.* **pontes Varolii** (ˈpɒntiːz). a broad white band of connecting nerve fibres that bridges the hemispheres of the cerebellum in mammals. Sometimes shortened to **pons.** [C16: NL, lit.: bridge of Varoli, after Costanzo *Varoli* (?1543–75), It. anatomist]

pontifex (ˈpɒntɪˌfɛks) *n., pl.* **pontifices** (pɒnˈtɪfɪˌsiːz). (in ancient Rome) any of the senior members of the Pontifical College, presided over by the **Pontifex Maximus.** [C16: < L, ? < Etruscan but infl. by folk etymology as if meaning lit.: bridge-maker]

pontiff (ˈpɒntɪf) *n.* a former title of the pagan high priest at Rome, later used of popes and occasionally of other bishops, and now confined to the pope. [C17: < F *pontife,* < L PONTIFEX]

pontifical (pɒnˈtɪfɪkᵊl) *adj.* **1.** of, relating to, or characteristic of a pontiff. **2.** having an excessively authoritative manner; pompous. ~*n.* **3.** *R.C. Church, Church of England.* a book containing the prayers and ritual instructions for ceremonies restricted to a bishop. —**ponˈtifically** *adv.*

pontificals (pɒnˈtɪfɪkᵊlz) *pl. n. Chiefly R.C. Church.* the insignia and special vestments worn by a bishop, esp. when celebrating High Mass.

pontificate *vb.* (pɒnˈtɪfɪˌkeɪt). (*intr.*) **1.** to speak or behave in a pompous or dogmatic manner. **2.** to serve or officiate at a Pontifical Mass. ~*n.* (pɒnˈtɪfɪkɪt). **3.** the office or term of office of a pope.

pontoon[1] (pɒnˈtuːn) *n.* **a.** a watertight float or vessel used where buoyancy is required in water, as in supporting a bridge, in salvage work, or where a temporary or mobile structure is required in military operations. **b.** (*as modifier*): *a pontoon bridge.* [C17: < F *ponton,* < L *pontō* punt, < *pōns* bridge]

pontoon[2] (pɒnˈtuːn) *n.* a gambling game in which players try to obtain card combinations better than the banker's but never worth more than 21 points. Also called: **twenty-one** (esp. U.S.), **vingt-**

et-un. [C20: prob. an alteration of F *vingt-et-un,* lit.: twenty-one]

pony (ˈpəʊnɪ) *n., pl.* **-nies.** **1.** any of various breeds of small horse, usually under 14.2 hands. **2.** a small drinking glass, esp. for liqueurs. **3.** anything small of its kind. **4.** *Brit. sl.* a sum of £25, esp. in bookmaking. **5.** Also called: **trot.** *U.S. sl.* a translation used by students, often illicitly; crib. [C17: < Scot. *powney,* ? < obs. F *poulenet* a little colt, < L *pullus* young animal, foal]

ponytail (ˈpəʊnɪˌteɪl) *n.* a hairstyle for girls and women in which the hair is gathered together tightly by a band at the back of the head into a loose-hanging fall.

pony trekking *n.* the act of riding ponies cross-country, esp. as a pastime.

pooch (puːtʃ) *n. Chiefly U.S. & Canad.* a slang word for **dog.** [<?]

poodle (ˈpuːdᵊl) *n.* **1.** a breed of dog with curly hair, which is generally clipped from ribs to tail. **2.** a servile person; lackey. [C19: < G *Pudel,* short for *Pudelhund,* < *pudeln* to splash + *Hund* dog; formerly trained as water dogs]

poof (pʊf, puːf), **poove** (puːv), *or* **poofter** (ˈpuːftə) *n. Brit. derog. sl.* a male homosexual. [C20: < F *pouffe* puff]

pooh (puː) *interj.* an exclamation of disdain, contempt, or disgust.

Pooh-Bah (ˈpuːˈbɑː) *n.* a pompous self-important official holding several offices at once and fulfilling none of them. [C19: after the character, the Lord-High-Everything-Else, in *The Mikado* (1885), by Gilbert & Sullivan]

pooh-pooh (ˈpuːˈpuː) *vb.* (*tr.*) to express disdain or scorn for; dismiss or belittle.

pool[1] (puːl) *n.* **1.** a small body of still water, usually fresh; small pond. **2.** a small isolated collection of spilt liquid, puddle: *a pool of blood.* **3.** a deep part of a stream or river where the water runs very slowly. **4.** an underground accumulation of oil or gas. **5.** See **swimming pool.** [OE *pōl*]

pool[2] (puːl) *n.* **1.** any communal combination of resources, funds, etc.: *a typing pool.* **2.** the combined stakes of the betters in many gambling games; kitty. **3.** *Commerce.* a group of producers who agree to establish and maintain output levels and high prices, each member of the group being allocated a maximum quota. **4.** *Finance, chiefly U.S.* a joint fund organized by security-holders for speculative or manipulative purposes on financial markets. **5.** any of various billiard games in which the object is to pot all the balls with the cue ball, esp. that played with 15 coloured and numbered balls, popular in the U.S.; pocket billiards. ~*vb.* (*tr.*) **6.** to combine (investments, money, interests, etc.) into a common fund, as for a joint enterprise. **7.** *Commerce.* to organize a pool of (enterprises). [C17: < F *poule,* lit.: hen used to signify stakes in a card game, < Med. L *pulla* hen, < L *pullus* young animal]

pools (puːlz) *pl. n.* **the.** *Brit.* an organized nationwide principally postal gambling pool betting on the result of football matches. Also called: **football pools.**

poop[1] (puːp) *Naut.* ~*n.* **1.** a raised structure at the stern of a vessel, esp. a sailing ship. **2.** Also called: **poop deck.** a raised deck at the stern of a ship. ~*vb.* **3.** (*tr.*) (of a wave or sea) to break over the stern of (a vessel). **4.** (*intr.*) (of a vessel) to ship a wave or sea over the stern, esp. repeatedly. [C15: < OF *pupe,* < L *puppis*]

poop[2] (puːp) *vb. U.S. & Canad. sl.* **1.** (*tr.; usually passive*) to cause to become exhausted; tire: *he was pooped after the race.* **2.** (*intr.;* usually foll. by *out*) to give up or fail: *he pooped out of the race.* [C14 *poupen* to blow, ? imit.]

poor (pʊə, pɔː) *adj.* **1.** lacking financial or other means of subsistence; needy. **2.** characterized by or indicating poverty: *the country had a poor economy.* **3.** scanty or inadequate: *a poor salary.* **4.** (when *postpositive,* usually foll. by *in*) badly supplied (with resources, etc.): *a region poor in wild flowers.* **5.** inferior. **6.** contemptible or despicable. **7.** disappointing or disagreeable: *a poor play.* **8.** (*prenominal*) deserving of pity; unlucky: *poor John is ill again.* [C13: < OF *povre,* < L *pauper*] —ˈ**poorness** *n.*

poor box *n.* a box, esp. one in a church, used for the collection of alms or money for the poor.

poorhouse (ˈpʊəˌhaʊs, ˈpɔː-) *n.* another name for **workhouse** (sense 1).

poor law *n. English history.* a law providing for the relief or support of the poor from parish funds.

poorly (ˈpʊəlɪ, ˈpɔː-) *adv.* **1.** badly. ~*adj.* **2.** (*usually postpositive*) *Inf.* in poor health; rather ill.

poort (pʊət) *n.* (in South Africa) a steep narrow mountain pass, usually following a river or stream. [C19: < Afrik., < Du.: gateway]

poor White *n. Often offens.* **a.** a poverty-stricken and underprivileged White person, esp. in the southern U.S. and South Africa. **b.** (*as modifier*): *poor White trash.*

pop[1] (pɒp) *vb.* **popping, popped.** **1.** to make or cause to make a light sharp explosive sound. **2.** to burst open with such a sound. **3.** (*intr.;* often foll. by *in, out,* etc.) *Inf.* to come (to) or go (from) rapidly or suddenly. **4.** (*intr.*) (esp. of the eyes) to protrude: *her eyes popped with amazement.* **5.** to shoot at (a target) with a firearm. **6.** (*tr.*) to place with a sudden movement: *she popped some tablets into her mouth.* **7.** (*tr.*) *Inf.* to pawn: *he popped his watch yesterday.* **8.** (*tr.*) *Sl.* to take (a drug) in pill form or as an injection. **9. pop the question.** *Inf.* to propose marriage. ~*n.* **10.** a light sharp explosive sound; crack. **11.** *Inf.* a flavoured nonalcoholic carbonated beverage. ~*adv.* **12.** with a popping sound. ~See also **pop off.** [C14: imit.]

pop[2] (pɒp) *n.* **1. a.** music of general appeal, esp. among young people, that originated as a distinctive genre in the 1950s. It is generally characterized by a heavy rhythmic element and the use of electrical amplification. **b.** (*as modifier*): *a pop group.* **2.** *Inf.* a piece of popular or light classical music. ~*adj.* **3.** *Inf.* short for **popular.**

pop[3] (pɒp) *n.* **1.** an informal word for **father.** **2.** *Inf.* a name used in addressing an old man.

POP *abbrev. for* Post Office Preferred (size of envelopes, etc.).

pop. *abbrev. for:* **1.** popular(ly). **2.** population.

pop art *n.* a movement in modern art that imitates the methods, styles, and themes of popular culture and mass media, such as comic strips, advertising, and science fiction.

popcorn (ˈpɒpˌkɔːn) *n.* **1.** a variety of maize having hard pointed kernels that puff up and burst when heated. **2.** the puffed edible kernels of this plant.

pope (pəʊp) *n.* **1.** (*often cap.*) the bishop of Rome as head of the Roman Catholic Church. **2.** *Eastern Orthodox Churches.* a title sometimes given to a parish priest or to the Greek Orthodox patriarch of Alexandria. [OE *papa,* < Church L: bishop, esp. of Rome, < LGk *papas* father-in-God, < Gk *pappas* father] —ˈ**popedom** *n.*

popery (ˈpəʊpərɪ) *n.* a derogatory name for **Roman Catholicism.**

popeyed (ˈpɒpˌaɪd) *adj.* **1.** having bulging prominent eyes. **2.** staring in astonishment.

popgun (ˈpɒpˌgʌn) *n.* a toy gun that fires a pellet or cork by means of compressed air.

popinjay (ˈpɒpɪnˌdʒeɪ) *n.* **1.** a conceited, foppish, or excessively talkative person. **2.** an archaic word for **parrot.** **3.** the figure of a parrot used as a target. [C13 *papeniai,* < OF *papegay* a parrot, < Sp., < Ar. *babaghā*]

popish (ˈpəʊpɪʃ) *adj. Derog.* belonging to or characteristic of Roman Catholicism.

poplar (ˈpɒplə) *n.* **1.** a tree of N temperate regions, having triangular leaves, flowers borne in catkins, and light soft wood. **2.** *U.S.* the tulip tree. [C14: < OF *poplier,* < L *pōpulus*]

poplin (ˈpɒplɪn) *n.* a strong fabric, usually of cotton, in plain weave with fine ribbing. [C18: < F *papeline,* ? < *Poperinge,* a centre of textile manufacture in Flanders]

popliteal (pɒpˈlɪtɪəl, ˌpɒplɪˈtiːəl) *adj.* of, relating to, or near the part of the leg behind the knee.

[C18: < NL *popliteus* the muscle behind the knee joint, < L *poples* the ham of the knee]

pop off *vb.* (*intr., adv.*) *Inf.* **1.** to depart suddenly or unexpectedly. **2.** to die, esp. suddenly.

poppadom *or* **poppadum** (ˈpɒpədəm) *n.* a thin round crisp Indian bread, fried or roasted and served with curry, etc. [< Hindi]

popper (ˈpɒpə) *n.* **1.** a person or thing that pops. **2.** *Brit.* an informal name for **press stud. 3.** *Chiefly U.S. & Canad.* a container for cooking popcorn in. **4.** *Sl.* an amyl nitrite capsule, crushed and inhaled by drug users.

poppet (ˈpɒpɪt) *n.* **1.** a term of affection for a small child or sweetheart. **2.** Also called: **poppet valve.** a mushroom-shaped valve that is lifted from its seating by applying an axial force to its stem. **3.** *Naut.* a temporary supporting brace for a vessel hauled on land. [C14: early var. of PUPPET]

popping crease *n. Cricket.* a line four feet in front of and parallel with the bowling crease, at or behind which the batsman stands. [C18: < POP[1] (in the obs. sense: to hit) + CREASE]

popple (ˈpɒpᵊl) *vb.* (*intr.*) **1.** (of boiling water or a choppy sea) to heave or toss; bubble. **2.** (often foll. by *along*) (of a stream or river) to move with an irregular tumbling motion. [C14: imit.]

poppy (ˈpɒpɪ) *n., pl.* **-pies. 1.** any of numerous papaveraceous plants having red, orange, or white flowers and a milky sap. **2.** any of several similar or related plants, such as the California poppy and Welsh poppy. **3.** any of the drugs, such as opium, that are obtained from these plants. **4. a.** a strong red to reddish-orange colour. **b.** (*as adj.*): *a poppy dress.* **5.** an artificial red poppy flower worn to mark Remembrance Sunday. [OE *popæg*, ult. < L *papāver*]

poppycock (ˈpɒpɪˌkɒk) *n. Inf.* nonsense. [C19: < Du. dialect *pappekak*, lit.: soft excrement]

Poppy Day *n.* an informal name for **Remembrance Sunday.**

poppyhead (ˈpɒpɪˌhɛd) *n.* **1.** the hard dry seed-containing capsule of a poppy. **2.** a carved ornament, esp. one used on the top of the end of a pew or bench in Gothic church architecture.

poppy seed *n.* the small grey seeds of one type of poppy flower, used esp. on loaves.

pop socks *pl. n.* knee-length nylon stockings.

popsy (ˈpɒpsɪ) *n., pl.* **-sies.** *Old-fashioned Brit. sl.* an attractive young woman. [C19: dim. < *pop*, shortened < POPPET; orig. a nursery term]

populace (ˈpɒpjʊləs) *n.* (*sometimes functioning as pl.*) **1.** local inhabitants. **2.** the common people; masses. [C16: via F < It. *popolaccio* the common herd, < *popolo* people, < L *populus*]

popular (ˈpɒpjʊlə) *adj.* **1.** widely favoured or admired. **2.** favoured by an individual or limited group: *I'm not very popular with her.* **3.** prevailing among the general public; common: *popular discontent.* **4.** appealing to or comprehensible to the layman: *a popular lecture on physics.* ~*n.* **5.** (*usually pl.*) a cheap newspaper with a mass circulation. [C15: < L *populāris* of the people, democratic] —**popularity** (ˌpɒpjʊˈlærɪtɪ) *n.* —ˈ**popularly** *adv.*

popular front *n.* (*often cap.*) any of the left-wing groups or parties that were organized from 1935 onwards to oppose the spread of fascism.

popularize *or* **-ise** (ˈpɒpjʊləˌraɪz) *vb.* (*tr.*) **1.** to make popular. **2.** to make or cause to become easily understandable or acceptable. —ˌ**populariˈzation** *or* **-iˈsation** *n.* —ˈ**popularˌizer** *or* **-ˌiser** *n.*

populate (ˈpɒpjʊˌleɪt) *vb.* (*tr.*) **1.** (*often passive*) to live in; inhabit. **2.** to provide a population for; colonize or people. [C16: < Med. L *populāre*, < L *populus* people]

population (ˌpɒpjʊˈleɪʃən) *n.* **1.** (*sometimes functioning as pl.*) all the persons inhabiting a specified place. **2.** the number of such inhabitants. **3.** (*sometimes functioning as pl.*) all the people of a particular class in a specific area: *the Chinese population of San Francisco.* **4.** the act or process of providing a place with inhabitants; colonization. **5.** *Ecology.* a group of individuals of the same species inhabiting a given area. **6.** *Astron.* either of two main groups of stars classified according to age and location. **7.** *Statistics.* the entire aggregate of individuals or items from which samples are drawn.

population explosion *n.* a rapid increase in the size of a population caused by such factors as a sudden decline in infant mortality or an increase in life expectancy.

Populist (ˈpɒpjʊlɪst) *n.* **1.** *U.S. history.* a member of the People's Party, formed largely by agrarian interests to contest the 1892 presidential election. **2.** (*often not cap.*) a politician or other person who claims to support the interests of the ordinary people. ~*adj.* **3.** of or relating to the People's Party or any individual or movement with similar aims. —ˈ**Populism** *n.*

populous (ˈpɒpjʊləs) *adj.* containing many inhabitants. [C15: < LL *populōsus*] —ˈ**populously** *adv.* —ˈ**populousness** *n.*

porangi (ˈpɔːræŋɪ) *adj. N.Z. inf.* crazy; mad. [< Maori]

porbeagle (ˈpɔːˌbiːgᵊl) *n.* any of several voracious sharks of northern seas. Also called: **mackerel shark.** [C18: < Cornish *porgh-bugel*, <?]

porcelain (ˈpɔːslɪn) *n.* **1.** a more or less translucent ceramic material, the principal ingredients being kaolin and petuntse (hard paste) or other clays, bone ash, etc. **2.** an object made of this or such objects collectively. **3.** (*modifier*) of, relating to, or made from this material: *a porcelain cup.* [C16: < F *porcelaine*, < It. *porcellana* cowrie shell, lit.: relating to a sow, < *porcella* little sow, < *porca* sow, < L; see PORK] —**porcellaneous** (ˌpɔːsəˈleɪnɪəs) *adj.*

porch (pɔːtʃ) *n.* **1.** a low structure projecting from the doorway of a house and forming a covered entrance. **2.** *U.S. & Canad.* a veranda. [C13: < F *porche*, < L *porticus* portico]

porcine (ˈpɔːsaɪn) *adj.* of or characteristic of pigs. [C17: < L *porcīnus*, < *porcus* a pig]

porcupine (ˈpɔːkjʊˌpaɪn) *n.* any of various large rodents that have a body covering of protective spines or quills. [C14 *porc despyne* pig with spines, < OF *porc espin;* see PORK, SPINE] —ˈ**porcuˌpinish** *adj.* —ˈ**porcuˌpiny** *adj.*

porcupine fish *n.* any of various fishes of temperate and tropical seas having a body that is covered with sharp spines and can be inflated into a globe. Also called: **globefish.**

porcupine grass *n. Austral.* another name for **spinifex** (sense 2).

pore[1] (pɔː) *vb.* (*intr.*) **1.** (foll. by *over*) to make a close intent examination or study (of): *he pored over the documents for several hours.* **2.** (foll. by *over, on,* or *upon*) to think deeply (about). **3.** (foll. by *over, on,* or *upon*) *Rare.* to gaze fixedly (upon). [C13 *pouren*]

pore[2] (pɔː) *n.* **1.** any small opening in the skin or outer surface of an animal. **2.** any other small hole, such as a space in a rock, etc. [C14: < LL *porus*, < Gk *poros* passage, pore]

porgy (ˈpɔːgɪ) *n., pl.* **-gy** *or* **-gies.** any of various perchlike fishes, many of which occur in American Atlantic waters. [C18: < Sp. *pargo*, < L *phager*, < Gk *phagros* sea bream]

poriferan (pɔːˈrɪfərən) *n.* any invertebrate of the phylum *Porifera*, which comprises the sponges. [C19: < NL *porifer* bearing pores]

pork (pɔːk) *n.* the flesh of pigs used as food. [C13: < OF *porc*, < L *porcus* pig]

porker (ˈpɔːkə) *n.* a pig, esp. a young one, fattened to provide meat.

pork pie *n.* a pie filled with minced seasoned pork.

porkpie hat (ˈpɔːkˌpaɪ) *n.* a hat with a round flat crown and a brim that can be turned up or down.

porky (ˈpɔːkɪ) *adj.* **porkier, porkiest. 1.** characteristic of pork. **2.** *Inf.* fat; obese.

porn (pɔːn) *or* **porno** (ˈpɔːnəʊ) *n., adj. Inf.* short for **pornography** or **pornographic.**

pornography (pɔːˈnɒgrəfɪ) *n.* **1.** writings, pictures, films, etc., designed to stimulate sexual excitement. **2.** the production of such material. ~Sometimes (informal) shortened to **porn** or **porno.** [C19: < Gk *pornographos* writing of harlots] —**por'nographer** *n.* —**pornographic** (ˌpɔːnəˈgræfɪk) *adj.* —ˌ**porno'graphically** *adv.*

poromeric (ˌpɔːrəˈmɛrɪk) *adj.* **1.** (of a plastic) permeable to water vapour. ~*n.* **2.** a substance having this characteristic, esp. one used in place of leather in making shoe uppers. [C20: < PORO(SITY) + (POLY)MER + -IC]

porous (ˈpɔːrəs) *adj.* **1.** able to absorb water, air, or other fluids. **2.** *Biol. & geol.* having pores. [C14: < Med. L *porōsus,* < LL *porus* PORE[2]] —ˈ**porously** *adv.* —**porosity** (pɔːˈrɒsɪtɪ) *or* ˈ**porousness** *n.*

porphyria (pɔːˈfɪrɪə) *n.* a hereditary disease of body metabolism, producing abdominal pain, mental confusion, etc. [C19: < NL, < *porphyrin* a purple substance excreted by patients suffering from this condition, < Gk *porphura* purple]

porphyry (ˈpɔːfɪrɪ) *n., pl.* **-ries. 1.** a reddish-purple rock consisting of large crystals of feldspar in a finer groundmass of feldspar, hornblende, etc. **2.** any igneous rock with large crystals embedded in a finer groundmass of minerals. [C14 *porfurie,* < LL, < Gk *porphuritēs* (*lithos*) purple (stone), < *porphuros* purple] —ˌ**porphyˈritic** *adj.*

porpoise (ˈpɔːpəs) *n., pl.* **-poise** *or* **-poises.** any of various small cetacean mammals having a blunt snout and many teeth. [C14: < F *pourpois,* < Med. L *porcopiscus,* < L *porcus* pig + *piscis* fish]

porridge (ˈpɒrɪdʒ) *n.* **1.** a dish made from oatmeal or another cereal, cooked in water or milk to a thick consistency. **2.** *Sl.* a term of imprisonment. [C16: var. (infl. by ME *porray* pottage) of POTTAGE]

porringer (ˈpɒrɪndʒə) *n.* a small dish, often with a handle, for soup, porridge, etc. [C16: changed < ME *potinger, poteger,* < OF, < *potage* soup; see POTTAGE]

port[1] (pɔːt) *n.* **1.** a town or place alongside navigable water with facilities for the loading and unloading of ships. **2.** See **port of entry.** [OE, < L *portus*]

port[2] (pɔːt) *n.* **1.** Also called (formerly): **larboard.** the left side of an aircraft or vessel when facing the nose or bow. Cf. **starboard** (sense 1). ~*vb.* **2.** to turn or be turned towards the port. [C17: <?]

port[3] (pɔːt) *n.* a sweet fortified dessert wine. [C17: after *Oporto,* Portugal, from where it came orig.]

port[4] (pɔːt) *n.* **1.** *Naut.* **a.** an opening in the side of a ship, fitted with a watertight door, for access to the holds. **b.** See **porthole** (sense 1). **2.** a small opening in a wall, armoured vehicle, etc., for firing through. **3.** an aperture by which fluid enters or leaves the cylinder head of an engine, compressor, etc. **4.** *Electronics.* a logical circuit for the input and ouput of data. **5.** *Chiefly Scot.* a gate in a town or fortress. [OE, < L *porta* gate]

port[5] (pɔːt) *vb.* (*tr.*) *Mil.* to carry (a rifle, etc.) in a position diagonally across the body with the muzzle near the left shoulder. [C14: < OF, < *porter* to carry, < L *portāre*]

port[6] (pɔːt) *n. Austral.* a travelling bag, such as a suitcase. [C20: shortened < PORTMANTEAU]

Port. *abbrev. for:* **1.** Portugal. **2.** Portuguese.

portable (ˈpɔːtəbᵊl) *adj.* **1.** able to be carried or moved easily, esp. by hand. ~*n.* **2.** an article designed to be readily carried by hand, such as a television, typewriter, etc. [C14: < LL *portābilis,* < L *portāre* to carry] —ˌ**portaˈbility** *n.* —ˈ**portably** *adv.*

portage (ˈpɔːtɪdʒ) *n.* **1.** the act of carrying; transport. **2.** the cost of carrying or transporting. **3.** the transporting of boats, supplies, etc., overland between navigable waterways. **4.** the route used for such transport. ~*vb.* **5.** to transport (boats, supplies, etc.) thus. [C15: < F, < OF *porter* to carry]

Portakabin (ˈpɔːtəˌkæbɪn) *n. Trademark.* a portable building quickly set up for use as a temporary office, etc.

portal (ˈpɔːtᵊl) *n.* an entrance, gateway, or doorway, esp. one that is large and impressive. [C14: via OF < Med. L *portāle,* < L *porta* gate]

portal vein *n.* any vein connecting two capillary networks, esp. in the liver.

portamento (ˌpɔːtəˈmɛntəʊ) *n., pl.* **-ti** (-tɪ). *Music.* a smooth slide from one note to another in which intervening notes are not separately discernible. [C18: < It.: a carrying, < L *portāre* to carry]

portative (ˈpɔːtətɪv) *adj.* **1.** a less common word for **portable. 2.** concerned with the act of carrying. [C14: < F, < L *portāre* to carry]

portcullis (pɔːtˈkʌlɪs) *n.* an iron or wooden grating suspended vertically in grooves in the gateway of a castle or town and able to be lowered so as to bar the entrance. [C14 *port colice,* < OF *porte coleïce* sliding gate, < *porte* door + *coleïce,* < *couler* to slide, < LL *cōlāre* to filter]

Porte (pɔːt) *n.* short for Sublime Porte; the court or government of the Ottoman Empire. [C17: shortened < F *Sublime Porte* High Gate, rendering the Turkish title *Babi Ali,* the imperial gate, regarded as the seat of government]

porte-cochere (ˌpɔːtkɒˈʃɛə) *n.* **1.** a large covered entrance for vehicles leading into a courtyard. **2.** a large roof projecting over a drive to shelter travellers entering or leaving vehicles. [C17: < F: carriage entrance]

portend (pɔːˈtɛnd) *vb.* (*tr.*) to give warning of; foreshadow. [C15: < L *portendere* to indicate]

portent (ˈpɔːtɛnt) *n.* **1.** a sign of a future event; omen. **2.** momentous or ominous significance: *a cry of dire portent.* **3.** a marvel. [C16: < L *portentum* sign, < *portendere* to portend]

portentous (pɔːˈtɛntəs) *adj.* **1.** of momentous or ominous significance. **2.** miraculous, amazing, or awe-inspiring. **3.** self-important or pompous.

porter[1] (ˈpɔːtə) *n.* **1.** a man employed to carry luggage, parcels, supplies, etc., at a railway station or hotel. **2.** *U.S. & Canad.* a railway employee who waits on passengers, esp. in a sleeper. [C14: < OF *portour,* < LL *portātōr,* < L *portāre* to carry] —ˈ**porterage** *n.*

porter[2] (ˈpɔːtə) *n.* **1.** *Chiefly Brit.* a person in charge of a gate or door; doorman or gatekeeper. **2.** a person employed as a caretaker and doorkeeper who also answers inquiries. **3.** a person in charge of the maintenance of a building, esp. a block of flats. [C13: < OF *portier,* < LL *portārius,* < L *porta* door]

porter[3] (ˈpɔːtə) *n. Brit.* a dark sweet ale brewed from black malt. [C18: < *porter's ale,* apparently because it was a favourite beverage of porters]

porterhouse (ˈpɔːtəˌhaʊs) *n.* **1.** Also called: **porterhouse steak.** a thick choice steak of beef cut from the middle ribs or sirloin. **2.** (formerly) a place in which porter, beer, etc., and sometimes chops and steaks, were served. [C19 (sense 1): said to be after a porterhouse in New York]

portfire (ˈpɔːtˌfaɪə) *n.* a slow-burning fuse used for firing rockets and fireworks and, in mining, for igniting explosives. [C17: < F *porte-feu,* < *porter* to carry + *feu* fire]

portfolio (pɔːtˈfəʊlɪəʊ) *n., pl.* **-os. 1.** a flat case, esp. of leather, used for carrying maps, drawings, etc. **2.** the contents of such a case, such as drawings or photographs, that demonstrate recent work. **3.** such a case used for carrying ministerial or state papers. **4.** the responsibilities or role of the head of a government department: *the portfolio for foreign affairs.* **5. Minister without portfolio.** a cabinet minister who is not responsible for any government department. **6.** the complete investments held by an individual investor or a financial organization. [C18: < It. *portafoglio,* < *portāre* to carry + *foglio* leaf, < L *folium*]

portfolio management *n.* the service provided by an investment adviser who manages a financial portfolio on behalf of the investor.

porthole (ˈpɔːtˌhəʊl) *n.* **1.** a small aperture in the side of a vessel to admit light and air, fitted with a watertight cover. Sometimes shortened to **port. 2.** an opening in a wall or parapet through which a gun can be fired.

portico (ˈpɔːtɪkəʊ) *n., pl.* **-coes** *or* **-cos. 1.** a covered entrance to a building; porch. **2.** a covered walkway in the form of a roof supported by columns or pillars, esp. one built on to the exterior of a building. [C17: via It. < L *porticus*]

portière (ˌpɔːtɪˈɛə; *French* pɔrtjɛr) *n.* a curtain hung in a doorway. [C19: via F < Med. L *portāria*, < L *porta* door] —ˌ**portiˈèred** *adj.*

portion (ˈpɔːʃən) *n.* **1.** a part of a whole. **2.** a part allotted or belonging to a person or group. **3.** an amount of food served to one person; helping. **4.** *Law.* **a.** a share of property, esp. one coming to a child from the estate of his parents. **b.** a dowry. **5.** a person's lot or destiny. ~*vb.* (*tr.*) **6.** to divide up; share out. **7.** to give a share to (a person). [C13: via OF < L *portiō*] —ˈ**portionless** *adj.*

Portland cement (ˈpɔːtlənd) *n.* a cement that hardens under water and is made by heating clay and crushed chalk or limestone. [C19: after the *Isle of Portland*, a peninsula in Dorset, because its colour resembles that of the stone quarried there]

portly (ˈpɔːtlɪ) *adj.* **-lier, -liest. 1.** stout or corpulent. **2.** *Arch.* stately; impressive. [C16: < PORT[5] (in the sense: deportment)] —ˈ**portliness** *n.*

portmanteau (pɔːtˈmæntəʊ) *n., pl.* **-teaus** *or* **-teaux** (-təʊz). **1.** (formerly) a large travelling case made of stiff leather, esp. one hinged at the back so as to open out into two compartments. **2.** (*modifier*) embodying several uses or qualities: *the heroine is a portmanteau figure of all the virtues.* [C16: < F: cloak carrier]

portmanteau word *n.* another name for **blend** (sense 7). [C19: < the idea that two meanings are packed into one word]

port of call *n.* **1.** a port where a ship stops. **2.** any place visited on a traveller's itinerary.

port of entry *n. Law.* an airport, harbour, etc., where customs officials are stationed to supervise the entry into and exit from a country of persons and merchandise.

portrait (ˈpɔːtrɪt, -treɪt) *n.* **1.** a painting or other likeness of an individual, esp. of the face. **2.** a verbal description, esp. of a person's character. [C16: < F, < *portraire* to PORTRAY] —ˈ**portraitist** *n.*

portraiture (ˈpɔːtrɪtʃə) *n.* **1.** the practice or art of making portraits. **2. a.** a portrait. **b.** portraits collectively. **3.** a verbal description.

portray (pɔːˈtreɪ) *vb.* (*tr.*) **1.** to make a portrait of. **2.** to depict in words. **3.** to play the part of (a character) in a play or film. [C14: < OF *portraire* to depict, < L *prōtrahere* to drag forth] —**porˈtrayal** *n.* —**porˈtrayer** *n.*

Port-Salut (ˈpɔːsəˈluː) *n.* a mild semihard whole-milk cheese of a round flat shape. [C19: named after the Trappist monastery at *Port du Salut* in NW France where it was first made]

Portuguese (ˌpɔːtjʊˈgiːz) *n.* **1.** the official language of Portugal and Brazil; it belongs to the Romance group of the Indo-European family. **2.** (*pl.* **-guese**) a native, citizen, or inhabitant of Portugal. ~*adj.* **3.** of Portugal, its inhabitants, or their language.

Portuguese man-of-war *n.* any of several large hydrozoans having an aerial float and long stinging tentacles. Sometimes shortened to **man-of-war.**

portulaca (ˌpɔːtjʊˈlækə, -ˈleɪkə) *n.* any of a genus of plants of tropical and subtropical America, having yellow, pink, or purple showy flowers. [C16: < L: PURSLANE]

POSB (in New Zealand and formerly in Britain) *abbrev. for* Post Office Savings Bank.

pose[1] (pəʊz) *vb.* **1.** to assume or cause to assume a physical attitude, as for a photograph or painting. **2.** (*intr.;* often foll. by *as*) to present oneself (as something one is not). **3.** (*intr.*) to affect an attitude in order to impress others. **4.** (*tr.*) to put forward or ask: *to pose a question.* **5.** (*intr.*) *Sl.* to adopt a particular style of appearance and stand or strut around, esp. in bars, discotheques, etc., in order to attract attention. ~*n.* **6.** a physical attitude, esp. one deliberately adopted for an artist or photographer. **7.** a mode of behaviour that is adopted for effect. [C14: < OF *poser* to set in place, < LL *pausāre* to cease, put down (infl. by L *pōnere* to place)]

pose[2] (pəʊz) *vb.* (*tr.*) *Rare.* to puzzle or baffle. [C16: < obs. *appose*, < L *appōnere* to put to]

poser[1] (ˈpəʊzə) *n.* **1.** a person who poses. **2.** *Inf.* a person who likes to be seen in trendsetting clothes in fashionable bars, discos, etc.

poser[2] (ˈpəʊzə) *n.* a baffling or insoluble question.

poseur (pəʊˈzɜː) *n.* a person who strikes an attitude or assumes a pose in order to impress others. [C19: < F, < *poser* to POSE[1]]

posh (pɒʃ) *adj. Inf., chiefly Brit.* **1.** smart, elegant, or fashionable. **2.** upper-class or genteel. [C19: often said to be an acronym of *port out, starboard home*, the most desirable location for a cabin in British ships sailing to & from the East, being the shaded side; but more likely < obs. sl. *posh* (n.) a dandy]

posit (ˈpɒzɪt) *vb.* (*tr.*) **1.** to assume or put forward as fact or the factual basis for an argument; postulate. **2.** to put in position. [C17: < L *pōnere* to place]

position (pəˈzɪʃən) *n.* **1.** place, situation, or location: *he took up a position to the rear.* **2.** the appropriate or customary location: *the telescope is in position for use.* **3.** the manner in which a person or thing is placed; arrangement. **4.** *Mil.* an area or point occupied for tactical reasons. **5.** point of view; stand: *what's your position on this issue?* **6.** social status, esp. high social standing. **7.** a post of employment; job. **8.** the act of positing a fact or viewpoint. **9.** something posited, such as an idea. **10.** *Sport.* the part of a field or playing area where a player is placed or where he generally operates. **11.** *Music.* the vertical spacing or layout of the written notes in a chord. **12.** (in classical prosody) the situation in which a short vowel may be regarded as long, that is, when it occurs before two or more consonants. **13.** *Finance.* the market commitment of an investor in securities or a trader in commodities: *a short position.* **14. in a position.** (foll. by an infinitive) able (to). ~*vb.* (*tr.*) **15.** to put in the proper or appropriate place; locate. **16.** *Sport.* to place (oneself or another player) in a particular part of the field or playing area. [C15: < LL *positiō* a positioning, affirmation, < *pōnere* to place] —**poˈsitional** *adj.*

positional notation *n.* the method of denoting numbers by the use of a finite number of digits, each digit having its value multiplied by its place value, as in $936 = (9 \times 100) + (3 \times 10) + 6$.

positive (ˈpɒzɪtɪv) *adj.* **1.** expressing certainty or affirmation: *a positive answer.* **2.** possessing actual or specific qualities; real: *a positive benefit.* **3.** tending to emphasize what is good or laudable; constructive: *he takes a very positive attitude when correcting pupils' mistakes.* **4.** tending towards progress or improvement. **5.** *Philosophy.* constructive rather than sceptical. **6.** (*prenominal*) *Inf.* (intensifier): *a positive delight.* **7.** *Maths.* having a value greater than zero: *a positive number.* **8.** *Maths.* **a.** measured in a direction opposite to that regarded as negative. **b.** having the same magnitude as but opposite sense to an equivalent negative quantity. **9.** *Grammar.* denoting the usual form of an adjective as opposed to its comparative or superlative form. **10.** *Physics.* **a.** (of an electric charge) having an opposite polarity to the charge of an electron and the same polarity as the charge of a proton. **b.** (of a body, system, ion, etc.) having a positive electric charge. **11.** short for **electropositive. 12.** *Med.* (of the results of an examination or test) indicating the presence of a suspected disorder or organism. ~*n.* **13.** something that is positive. **14.** *Maths.* a quantity greater than zero. **15.** *Photog.* a print or slide showing a photographic image whose colours or tones correspond to those of the original subject. **16.** *Grammar.* the positive degree of an adjective or adverb. **17.** a positive object, such as a terminal or plate in a voltaic cell. [C13: < LL *positīvus*, < *pōnere* to place] —ˈ**positiveness** *n.*

positive discrimination *n.* the provision of special opportunities for a disadvantaged group.

positive feedback *n.* See **feedback** (sense 1).

positively (ˈpɒzɪtɪvlɪ) *adv.* **1.** in a positive manner. **2.** (intensifier): *he disliked her; in fact, he positively hated her.*

positive vetting *n.* the checking of a person's background, to assess his suitability for a position that may involve national security.

positivism ('pɒzɪtɪˌvɪzəm) *n.* **1.** a form of empiricism, esp. as established by Auguste Comte, that rejects metaphysics and theology and holds that experimental investigation and observation are the only sources of substantial knowledge. See also **logical positivism.** **2.** the quality of being definite, certain, etc. —**'positivist** *n., adj.*

positron ('pɒzɪˌtrɒn) *n. Physics.* the antiparticle of the electron, having the same mass but an equal and opposite charge. [C20: < *posi*(*tive* + *elec*)*tron*]

positronium (ˌpɒzɪ'trəʊnɪəm) *n. Physics.* a short-lived entity consisting of a positron and an electron bound together.

posology (pə'sɒlədʒɪ) *n.* the branch of medicine concerned with the determination of appropriate doses of drugs or agents. [C19: < F *posologie,* < Gk *posos* how much]

poss. *abbrev. for:* **1.** possession. **2.** possessive. **3.** possible. **4.** possibly.

posse ('pɒsɪ) *n.* **1.** *U.S.* short for **posse comitatus,** the able-bodied men of a district forming a group upon whom the sheriff may call for assistance in maintaining law and order. **2.** (in W Canada), a troop of trained horses and riders who perform at stampedes. **3.** *Law.* possibility (esp. in **in posse**). [C16: < Med. L (n.): power, < L (vb.): to be able]

posse comitatus (ˌkɒmɪ'tɑːtəs) *n.* the formal legal term for **posse** (sense 1). [Med. L: strength (manpower) of the county]

possess (pə'zɛs) *vb.* (*tr.*) **1.** to have as one's property; own. **2.** to have as a quality, characteristic, etc.: *to possess good eyesight.* **3.** to have knowledge of: *to possess a little French.* **4.** to gain control over or dominate: *whatever possessed you to act so foolishly?* **5.** (foll. by *of*) to cause to be the owner or possessor: *I am possessed of the necessary information.* **6.** to have sexual intercourse with. **7.** *Now rare.* to maintain (oneself or one's feelings) in a certain state or condition: *possess yourself in patience until I tell you the news.* [C15: < OF *possesser,* < L *possidēre*] —**pos'sessor** *n.* —**pos'sessory** *adj.*

possessed (pə'zɛst) *adj.* **1.** (foll. by *of*) owning or having. **2.** (*usually postpositive*) under the influence of a powerful force, such as a spirit or strong emotion. **3.** a less common term for **self-possessed.**

possession (pə'zɛʃən) *n.* **1.** the act of possessing or state of being possessed: *in possession of the crown.* **2.** anything that is owned or possessed. **3.** (*pl.*) wealth or property. **4.** the state of being controlled by or as if by evil spirits. **5.** the occupancy of land, property, etc., whether or not accompanied by ownership: *to take possession of a house.* **6.** a territory subject to a foreign state: *colonial possessions.* **7.** *Sport.* control of the ball, puck, etc., as exercised by a player or team: *he got possession in his own half.*

possessive (pə'zɛsɪv) *adj.* **1.** of or relating to possession. **2.** having or showing an excessive desire to possess or dominate: *a possessive husband.* **3.** *Grammar.* **a.** another word for **genitive. b.** denoting an inflected form of a noun or pronoun used to convey the idea of possession, association, etc., as *my* or *Harry's.* ~*n.* **4.** *Grammar.* **a.** the possessive case. **b.** a word or speech element in the possessive case. —**pos'sessively** *adv.* —**pos'sessiveness** *n.*

posset ('pɒsɪt) *n.* a drink of hot milk curdled with ale, beer, etc., flavoured with spices, formerly used as a remedy for colds. [C15 *poshoote,* <?]

possibility (ˌpɒsɪ'bɪlɪtɪ) *n., pl.* **-ties. 1.** the state or condition of being possible. **2.** anything that is possible. **3.** a competitor, candidate, etc., who has a moderately good chance of winning, being chosen, etc. **4.** (*often pl.*) a future prospect or potential: *my new house has great possibilities.*

possible ('pɒsɪbᵊl) *adj.* **1.** capable of existing, taking place, or proving true without contravention of any natural law. **2.** capable of being achieved: *it is not possible to finish in three weeks.* **3.** having potential: *the idea is a possible money-spinner.* **4.** feasible but less than probable: *it is possible that man will live on Mars.* **5.** *Logic.* (of a statement, formula, etc.) capable of being true under some interpretation or in some circumstances. ~*n.* **6.** another word for **possibility** (sense 3). [C14: < L *possibilis* that may be, < *posse* to be able]

possibly ('pɒsɪblɪ) *sentence substitute, adv.* **1. a.** perhaps or maybe. **b.** (*as sentence modifier*): *possibly he'll come.* ~*adv.* **2.** by any chance; at all: *he can't possibly come.*

possum ('pɒsəm) *n.* **1.** an informal name for **opossum. 2.** an Australian and New Zealand name for **phalanger. 3. play possum.** to pretend to be dead, ignorant, asleep, etc., in order to deceive an opponent. **4. stir the possum** *Austral. sl.* to cause trouble.

post[1] (pəʊst) *n.* **1.** a length of wood, metal, etc., fixed upright to serve as a support, marker, point of attachment, etc. **2.** *Horse racing.* **a.** either of two upright poles marking the beginning (**starting post**) and end (**winning post**) of a racecourse. **b.** the finish of a horse race. ~*vb.* (*tr.*) **3.** (sometimes foll. by *up*) to fasten or put up (a notice) in a public place. **4.** to announce by or as if by means of a poster: *to post banns.* **5.** to publish (a name) on a list. **6.** to denounce publicly; brand. [OE, < L *postis*]

post[2] (pəʊst) *n.* **1.** a position to which a person is appointed or elected; appointment; job. **2.** a position to which a person, such as a sentry, is assigned for duty. **3.** a permanent military establishment. **4.** *Brit.* either of two military bugle calls (**first post** and **last post**) giving notice of the time to retire for the night. **5.** See **trading post.** ~*vb.* **6.** (*tr.*) to assign to or station at a particular place or position. **7.** *Chiefly Brit.* to transfer to a different unit or ship on taking up a new appointment, etc. [C16: < F *poste,* < It. *posto,* ult. < L *pōnere* to place]

post[3] (pəʊst) *n.* **1.** *Chiefly Brit.* letters, packages, etc., that are transported and delivered by the Post Office; mail. **2.** *Chiefly Brit.* a single collection or delivery of mail. **3.** *Brit.* an official system of mail delivery. **4.** (formerly) any of a series of stations furnishing relays of men and horses to deliver mail over a fixed route. **5.** a rider who carried mail between such stations. **6.** *Brit.* a postbox or post office: *take this to the post.* **7.** any of various book sizes, esp. 5¼ by 8¼ inches (**post octavo**). **8. by return of post.** *Brit.* by the next mail in the opposite direction. ~*vb.* **9.** (*tr.*) *Chiefly Brit.* to send by post. U.S. and Canad. word: **mail. 10.** (*tr.*) *Book-keeping.* **a.** to enter (an item) in a ledger. **b.** (often foll. by *up*) to compile or enter all paper items in (a ledger). **11.** (*tr.*) to inform of the latest news. **12.** (*intr.*) (formerly) to travel with relays of post horses. **13.** *Arch.* to travel or dispatch with speed; hasten. ~*adv.* **14.** with speed; rapidly. **15.** (formerly) by means of post horses. [C16: via F < It. *poste,* < L *posita* something placed, < *pōnere* to put]

post- *prefix.* **1.** after in time or sequence; following; subsequent: *postgraduate.* **2.** behind; posterior to: *postorbital.* [< L, < *post* after, behind]

postage ('pəʊstɪdʒ) *n.* the charge for delivering a piece of mail.

postage meter *n. Chiefly U.S. & Canad.* a postal franking machine. Also called: **postal meter.**

postage stamp *n.* **1.** a printed paper label with a gummed back for attaching to mail as an official indication that the required postage has been paid. **2.** a mark printed on an envelope, etc., serving the same function.

postal ('pəʊstᵊl) *adj.* of or relating to a Post Office or to the mail-delivery service. —**'postally** *adv.*

postal note *n. Austral. & N.Z.* the usual name for **postal order.**

postal order *n.* a written order for the payment of a sum of money, to a named payee, obtainable and payable at a post office.

postbag ('pəʊstˌbæg) *n.* **1.** *Chiefly Brit.* another name for **mailbag.** **2.** the mail received by a magazine, radio programme, public figure, etc.

postbox (ˈpəʊstˌbɒks) *n.* another name for **letter box** (sense 2).

postcard (ˈpəʊstˌkɑːd) *n.* a card, often bearing a photograph, picture, etc., on one side (**picture postcard**), for sending a message by post without an envelope. Also called (U.S.): **postal card.**

post chaise *n.* a closed four-wheeled horse-drawn coach used as a rapid means for transporting mail and passengers in the 18th and 19th centuries. [C18: < POST³ + CHAISE]

postcode (ˈpəʊstˌkəʊd) *n.* a code of letters and digits used as part of a postal address to aid the sorting of mail. Also called: **postal code.** U.S. name: **zip code.**

postdate (pəʊstˈdeɪt) *vb.* (*tr.*) **1.** to write a future date on (a document, etc.), as on a cheque to prevent it being paid until then. **2.** to assign a date to (an event, period, etc.) that is later than its previously assigned date of occurrence. **3.** to be or occur at a later date than.

postdoctoral (pəʊstˈdɒktərəl) *adj.* of, relating to, or designating studies, research, or professional work above the level of a doctorate.

poster (ˈpəʊstə) *n.* **1.** a placard or bill posted in a public place as an advertisement. **2.** a person who posts bills.

poste restante (ˈpəʊst rɪˈstænt) *n.* **1.** an address on mail indicating that it should be kept at a specified post office until collected by the addressee. **2.** the mail-delivery service or post-office department that handles mail having this address. ~U.S. and Canad. equivalent: **general delivery.** [F, lit.: mail remaining]

posterior (pɒˈstɪərɪə) *adj.* **1.** situated at the back of or behind something. **2.** coming after or following another in a series. **3.** coming after in time. ~*n.* **4.** the buttocks; rump. [C16: < L: latter, < *posterus* coming next, < *post* after] —**posˈteriorly** *adv.*

posterity (pɒˈsterɪtɪ) *n.* **1.** future or succeeding generations. **2.** all of one's descendants. [C14: < F *postérité*, < L *posteritās*, < *posterus* coming after, < *post* after]

postern (ˈpɒstən) *n.* a back door or gate, esp. one that is for private use. [C13: < OF *posterne*, < LL *posterula* (*jānua*) a back (entrance), < *posterus* coming behind]

poster paint *or* **colour** *n.* a gum-based opaque watercolour paint used for writing posters, etc.

post-free *adv., adj.* **1.** *Brit.* with the postage prepaid; post-paid. **2.** free of postal charge.

postglacial (pəʊstˈgleɪsɪəl, -ʃəl) *adj.* formed or occurring after a glacial period.

postgraduate (pəʊstˈgrædjʊɪt) *n.* a student who has obtained a degree from a university, etc., and is pursuing studies for a more advanced qualification. Also (U.S. and Canad.): **graduate.**

posthaste (ˈpəʊstˈheɪst) *adv.* **1.** with great haste. ~*n.* **2.** *Arch.* great haste.

post horn *n.* a simple valveless natural horn consisting of a long tube of brass or copper.

post horse *n.* (formerly) a horse kept at an inn or post house for use by postriders or for hire to travellers.

post house *n.* (formerly) a house or inn where horses were kept for postriders or for hire to travellers.

posthumous (ˈpɒstjʊməs) *adj.* **1.** happening or continuing after one's death. **2.** (of a book, etc.) published after the author's death. **3.** (of a child) born after the father's death. [C17: < L *postumus* the last, but modified as though < L *post* after + *humus* earth, that is, after the burial] —**ˈposthumously** *adv.*

posthypnotic suggestion (ˌpəʊsthɪpˈnɒtɪk) *n.* a suggestion made to the subject while he is in a hypnotic trance, to be acted upon at some time after emerging from the trance.

postiche (pɒˈstiːʃ) *adj.* **1.** (of architectural ornament) inappropriately applied; sham. **2.** false or artificial; spurious. ~*n.* **3.** another term for **hairpiece** (sense 2). **4.** anything that is false; sham or pretence. [C19: < F, < It. *apposticcio* (n.), < LL *appositīcius* (adj.); see APPOSITE]

postilion *or* **postillion** (pɒˈstɪljən) *n.* a person who rides the near horse of the leaders in order to guide a team of horses drawing a coach. [C16: < F *postillon*, < It. *postiglione*, < *posta* POST³]

postimpressionism (ˌpəʊstɪmˈprɛʃəˌnɪzəm) *n.* a movement in painting in France at the end of the 19th century which rejected the naturalism and momentary effects of impressionism but adapted its use of pure colour to paint subjects with greater subjective emotion. —ˌ**postimˈpressionist** *n., adj.*

posting (ˈpəʊstɪŋ) *n.* an appointment to a position or post.

postliminy (pəʊstˈlɪmɪnɪ) *or* **postliminium** (ˌpəʊstlɪˈmɪnɪəm) *n., pl.* **-nies** *or* **-ia** (-ɪə). *International law.* the right by which persons and property seized in war are restored to their former status on recovery. [C17: < L *post* behind + *limen, liminis* threshold]

postlude (ˈpəʊstluːd) *n. Music.* a final or concluding piece or movement. [C19: < POST- + *-lude*, < L *lūdus* game; cf. PRELUDE]

postman (ˈpəʊstmən) *or* (*fem.*) **postwoman** *n., pl.* **-men** *or* **-women.** a person who carries and delivers mail as a profession.

postman's knock *n.* a children's party game in which a kiss is exchanged for a pretend letter.

postmark (ˈpəʊstˌmɑːk) *n.* **1.** any mark stamped on mail by postal officials, usually showing the date and place of posting. ~*vb.* **2.** (*tr.*) to put such a mark on (mail).

postmaster (ˈpəʊstˌmɑːstə) *or* (*fem.*) **postmistress** *n.* an official in charge of a local post office.

postmaster general *n., pl.* **postmasters general.** the executive head of the postal service in certain countries.

postmeridian (ˌpəʊstməˈrɪdɪən) *adj.* after noon; in the afternoon or evening. [C17: < L *postmerīdiānus* in the afternoon]

post meridiem (ˈpəʊst məˈrɪdɪəm) the full form of **p.m.** [C17: L: after noon]

post mill *n.* a windmill built around a central post on which the whole mill can be turned so that the sails catch the wind.

postmillennialism (ˌpəʊstmɪˈlɛnɪəˌlɪzəm) *n. Christian theol.* the doctrine or belief that the Second Coming of Christ will be preceded by the millennium. —ˌ**postmilˈlennialist** *n.*

postmodernism (pəʊstˈmɒdəˌnɪzəm) *n.* (in the arts, architecture, etc.) a rejection of all the hitherto accepted certainties that underpinned modern style and content. —**postˈmodernist** *n., adj.*

postmortem (pəʊstˈmɔːtəm) *adj.* **1.** (*prenominal*) occurring after death. ~*n.* **2.** analysis or study of a recent event: *a postmortem on a game of chess.* **3.** See **postmortem examination.** [C18: < L, lit.: after death]

postmortem examination *n.* dissection and examination of a dead body to determine the cause of death. Also called: **autopsy, necropsy.**

post-obit (pəʊstˈəʊbɪt, -ˈɒbɪt) *Chiefly law.* ~*n.* **1.** a bond given by a borrower, payable after the death of a specified person, esp. one given to a moneylender by an expectant heir promising to repay when his interest falls into possession. ~*adj.* **2.** taking effect after death. [C18: < L *post obitum* after death]

post office *n.* a building or room where postage

---

postˈclassical *adj.*
postˈcoital *adj.*
ˌ**postconsoˈnantal** *adj.*
ˌ**postconvaˈlescent** *adj.*
ˌ**post-Darˈwinian** *adj.*
ˌ**postdeˌvelopˈmental** *adj.*
ˌ**postdiagˈnostic** *adj.*
ˌ**postdiˈgestive** *adj.*
ˌ**posteˈlection** *adj.*
post-ˈMarxian *adj.*
ˌ**postmenoˈpausal** *adj.*
postˈnatal *adj.*
postˈnuptial *adj.*

stamps are sold and other postal business is conducted.

Post Office *n.* a government department or authority in many countries responsible for postal services and often telecommunications.

post office box *n.* a private numbered place in a post office, in which letters received are kept until called for.

postoperative (pəʊstˈɒpərətɪv) *adj.* of or occurring in the period following a surgical operation.

post-paid *adv., adj.* with the postage prepaid.

postpone (pəʊstˈpəʊn, pəˈspəʊn) *vb.* (*tr.*) **1.** to put off or delay until a future time. **2.** to put behind in order of importance; defer. [C16: < L *postpōnere* to put after] —**postˈponement** *n.*

postpositive (pəʊstˈpɒzɪtɪv) *adj.* **1.** (of an adjective or other modifier) placed after the word modified, either immediately after, as in *two men abreast,* or as part of a complement, as in *those men are bad.* ~*n.* **2.** a postpositive modifier.

postprandial (pəʊstˈprændɪəl) *adj. usually humorous.* after a meal.

postrider (ˈpəʊstˌraɪdə) *n.* (formerly) a person who delivered post on horseback.

postscript (ˈpəʊsˌskrɪpt, ˈpəʊst-) *n.* **1.** a message added at the end of a letter, after the signature. **2.** any supplement, as to a document or book. [C16: < LL *postscribere* to write after]

postulant (ˈpɒstjʊlənt) *n.* a person who makes a request or application, esp. a candidate for admission to a religious order. [C18: < L *postulāns* asking, < *postulāre* to ask]

postulate *vb.* (ˈpɒstjʊˌleɪt). (*tr.; may take a clause as object*) **1.** to assume to be true or existent; take for granted. **2.** to ask, demand, or claim. **3.** to nominate (a person) to a post or office subject to approval by a higher authority. ~*n.* (ˈpɒstjʊlɪt). **4.** something taken as self-evident or assumed as the basis of an argument. **5.** a prerequisite. **6.** a fundamental principle, **7.** *Logic, maths.* an unproved statement that should be taken for granted: used as an initial premise in a process of reasoning. [C16: < L *postulāre* to ask for] —ˌ**postuˈlation** *n.*

postulator (ˈpɒstjʊˌleɪtə) *n. R.C. Church.* a person who presents a plea for the beatification or canonization of some deceased person.

posture (ˈpɒstʃə) *n.* **1.** a position or attitude of the limbs or body. **2.** a characteristic manner of bearing the body: *good posture.* **3.** the disposition of the parts of a visible object. **4.** a mental attitude. **5.** a state or condition. **6.** a false or affected attitude; pose. ~*vb.* **7.** to assume or cause to assume a bodily attitude. **8.** (*intr.*) to assume an affected posture; pose. [C17: via F < It. *postura,* < L *positūra,* < *pōnere* to place] —ˈ**postural** *adj.* —ˈ**posturer** *n.*

postviral syndrome (ˌpəʊstˈvaɪrəl) *n.* a condition that sometimes occurs after a viral infection in which the sufferer may experience extreme muscular fatigue or various other symptoms over a long period. Abbrev.: **PVS.**

posy (ˈpəʊzɪ) *n., pl.* **-sies. 1.** a small bunch of flowers. **2.** *Arch.* a brief motto or inscription, esp. one on a trinket or a ring. [C16: var. of POESY]

pot[1] (pɒt) *n.* **1.** a container, usually round and deep and often having a handle and lid, used for cooking and other domestic purposes. **2.** the amount that a pot will hold; potful. **3.** a large mug or tankard. **4.** *Austral.* any of various measures used for serving beer. **5.** the money or stakes in the pool in gambling games. **6.** a wicker trap for catching fish, esp. crustaceans: *a lobster pot.* **7.** *Billiards, etc.* a shot by which a ball is pocketed. **8.** a chamber pot, esp. a small one designed for a baby or toddler. **9.** (*often pl.*) *Inf.* a large amount (esp. of money). **10.** *Inf.* a prize or trophy. **11.** *Chiefly Brit.* short for **chimneypot. 12.** short for **flowerpot, teapot. 13.** See **potbelly. 14. go to pot.** to go to ruin. ~*vb.* **potting, potted.** (*mainly tr.*) **15.** to put or preserve (meat, etc.) in a pot. **16.** to plant (a cutting, seedling, etc.) in soil in a flowerpot. **17.** to cause (a baby or toddler) to use or sit on a pot. **18.** to shoot (game) for food rather than for sport. **19.** (*also intr.*) to shoot casually or without careful aim. **20.** (*also intr.*) to shape clay as a potter. **21.** *Billiards, etc.* to pocket (a ball). **22.** *Inf.* to capture or win. [LOE *pott,* < Med. L *pottus* (unattested), ? < L *pōtus* a drink]

pot[2] (pɒt) *n. Sl.* cannabis used as a drug in any form. [C20: ? shortened < Mexican Indian *potiguaya*]

potable (ˈpəʊtəbᵊl) *adj.* drinkable. [C16: < LL *pōtābilis* drinkable, < L *pōtāre* to drink] —ˌ**potaˈbility** *n.*

potae (ˈpɒtaɪ) *n. N.Z.* a hat. [Maori]

potage *French.* (pɔtaʒ; *English* pəʊˈtɑːʒ) *n.* any thick soup. [C16: < OF; see POTTAGE]

potamic (pəˈtæmɪk) *adj.* of or relating to rivers. [C19: < Gk *potamos* river]

potash (ˈpɒtˌæʃ) *n.* **1.** another name for **potassium carbonate** or **potassium hydroxide. 2.** potassium chemically combined in certain compounds: *chloride of potash.* [C17 *pot ashes,* translation of obs. Du. *potaschen;* because orig. obtained by evaporating the lye of wood ashes in pots]

potassium (pəˈtæsɪəm) *n.* a light silvery element of the alkali metal group that is highly reactive and rapidly oxidizes in air. Symbol: K; atomic no.: 19; atomic wt.: 39.102. [C19: NL *potassa* potash] —**poˈtassic** *adj.*

potassium-argon dating *n.* a technique for determining the age of minerals based on the occurrence in natural potassium of a small fixed amount of radioisotope ^{40}K that decays to the stable argon isotope ^{40}Ar with a half-life of 1.28×10^9 years. Measurement of the ratio of these isotopes thus gives the age of the mineral.

potassium bromide *n.* a white crystalline soluble substance with a bitter saline taste used in making photographic papers and plates and in medicine as a sedative. Formula: KBr.

potassium carbonate *n.* a white odourless substance used in making glass and soft soap and as an alkaline cleansing agent. Formula: K_2CO_3.

potassium chlorate *n.* a white crystalline soluble substance used in explosives and as a disinfectant and bleaching agent. Formula: $KClO_3$.

potassium cyanide *n.* a white poisonous granular soluble solid substance used in photography. Formula: KCN.

potassium hydrogen tartrate *n.* a white soluble crystalline salt used in baking powders, soldering fluxes, and laxatives. Formula: $KHC_4H_4O_6$. Also called: **cream of tartar.**

potassium hydroxide *n.* a white deliquescent alkaline solid used in the manufacture of soap, liquid shampoos, and detergents. Formula: KOH.

potassium nitrate *n.* a colourless or white crystalline compound used in gunpowders, pyrotechnics, fertilizers, and as a preservative for foods (**E 252**). Formula: KNO_3. Also called: **saltpetre, nitre.**

potassium permanganate *n.* a dark purple poisonous odourless soluble crystalline solid, used as a bleach, disinfectant, and antiseptic. Formula: $KMnO_4$.

potation (pəʊˈteɪʃən) *n.* **1.** the act of drinking. **2.** a drink or draught, esp. of alcoholic drink. [C15: < L *pōtātiō,* < *pōtāre* to drink]

potato (pəˈteɪtəʊ) *n., pl.* **-toes. 1. a.** a plant of South America widely cultivated for its edible tubers. **b.** the starchy oval tuber of this plant, which has a brown or red skin and is cooked and eaten as a vegetable. **2.** any of various similar plants, esp. the sweet potato. [C16: < Sp. *patata* white potato, < Taino *batata* sweet potato]

potato beetle *n.* another name for the **Colorado beetle.**

potato chip *n.* (*usually pl.*) **1.** another name for

ˌ**postpiˈtuitary** *adj.*
ˌ**post-Reforˈmation** *adj.*
ˌ**post-Soˈcratic** *adj.*
ˌ**post-Vicˈtorian** *adj.*
ˈ**postˈwar** *adj.*

chip (sense 4). **2.** the U.S. and Canad. term for **crisp** (sense 10).

potato crisp *n.* (*usually pl.*) another name for **crisp** (sense 10).

potbelly (ˈpɒtˌbɛlɪ) *n., pl.* **-lies. 1.** a protruding or distended belly. **2.** a person having such a belly. —ˈ**potˌbellied** *adj.*

potboiler (ˈpɒtˌbɔɪlə) *n. Inf.* an artistic work of little merit produced quickly to make money.

pot-bound *adj.* (of a pot plant) having grown to fill all the available root space and therefore lacking room for continued growth.

potboy (ˈpɒtˌbɔɪ) *or* **potman** (ˈpɒtmən) *n., pl.* **-boys** *or* **-men.** *Chiefly Brit.* (esp. formerly) a man employed at a public house to serve beer, etc.

potch (pɒtʃ) *n. Chiefly Austral., sl.* inferior quality opal. [C20: <?]

poteen (ˈpɒtiːn) *or* **poitín** (pɒˈtʃiːn) *n.* (in Ireland) illicit spirit, often distilled from potatoes. [C19: < Irish *poitín* little pot, < *pota* pot]

potent[1] (ˈpəʊtᵊnt) *adj.* **1.** possessing great strength; powerful. **2.** (of arguments, etc.) persuasive or forceful. **3.** influential or authoritative. **4.** tending to produce violent physical or chemical effects: *a potent poison.* **5.** (of a male) capable of having sexual intercourse. [C15: < L *potēns* able, < *posse* to be able] —ˈ**potency** *or* ˈ**potence** *n.* —ˈ**potently** *adv.*

potent[2] (ˈpəʊtᵊnt) *adj. Heraldry.* (of a cross) having flat bars across the ends of the arms. [C17: < obs. *potent* a crutch, < L *potentia* power]

potentate (ˈpəʊtᵊnˌteɪt) *n.* a ruler or monarch. [C14: < LL *potentātus,* < L: rule, < *potens* powerful, < *posse* to be able]

potential (pəˈtɛnʃəl) *adj.* **1. a.** possible but not yet actual. **b.** (*prenominal*) capable of being or becoming; latent. **2.** *Grammar.* (of a verb) expressing possibility, as English *may* and *might.* ~*n.* **3.** latent but unrealized ability: *Jones has great potential as a sales manager.* **4.** *Grammar.* a potential verb or verb form. **5.** short for **electric potential.** [C14: < OF *potencial,* < LL *potentiālis,* < L *potentia* power] —**poˈtentially** *adv.*

potential difference *n.* the difference in electric potential between two points in an electric field; the work that has to be done in transferring unit positive charge from one point to the other, measured in volts. Abbrev.: **pd.**

potential energy *n.* the energy of a body or system as a result of its position in an electric, magnetic, or gravitational field. Abbrev.: **PE.**

potentiality (pəˌtɛnʃɪˈælɪtɪ) *n., pl.* **-ties. 1.** latent or inherent capacity for growth, fulfilment, etc. **2.** a person or thing that possesses this.

potentiate (pəˈtɛnʃɪˌeɪt) *vb.* (*tr.*) **1.** to cause to be potent. **2.** *Med.* to increase (the individual action or effectiveness) of two drugs by administering them in combination.

potentilla (ˌpəʊtᵊnˈtɪlə) *n.* any rosaceous plant or shrub of the N temperate genus *Potentilla,* having five-petalled flowers. [C16: NL, < Med. L: garden valerian, < L *potēns* powerful]

potentiometer (pəˌtɛnʃɪˈɒmɪtə) *n.* **1.** an instrument for determining a potential difference of electromotive force. **2.** a device used in electronic circuits, esp. as a volume control. Sometimes shortened to **pot.** —**poˌtentiˈometry** *n.*

potful (ˈpɒtfʊl) *n.* the amount held by a pot.

pother (ˈpɒðə) *n.* **1.** a commotion, fuss, or disturbance. **2.** a choking cloud of smoke, dust, etc. ~*vb.* **3.** to make or be troubled or upset. [C16: <?]

potherb (ˈpɒtˌhɜːb) *n.* any plant having leaves, flowers, stems, etc., that are used in cooking.

pothole (ˈpɒtˌhəʊl) *n.* **1.** *Geog.* **a.** a deep hole in limestone areas resulting from action by running water. **b.** a circular hole in the bed of a river produced by abrasion. **2.** a deep hole produced in a road surface by wear or weathering.

potholing (ˈpɒtˌhəʊlɪŋ) *n. Brit.* a sport in which participants explore underground caves. —ˈ**potˌholer** *n.*

pothook (ˈpɒtˌhʊk) *n.* **1.** a curved or S-shaped hook used for suspending a pot over a fire. **2.** a long hook used for lifting hot pots, lids, etc. **3.** an S-shaped mark, often made by children when learning to write.

pothouse (ˈpɒtˌhaʊs) *n. Brit.* (formerly) a small tavern or pub.

pothunter (ˈpɒtˌhʌntə) *n.* **1.** a person who hunts for profit without regard to the rules of sport. **2.** *Inf.* a person who enters competitions for the sole purpose of winning prizes.

potion (ˈpəʊʃən) *n.* a drink, esp. of medicine, poison, or some supposedly magic beverage. [C13: via OF < L *pōtiō* a drink, esp. a poisonous one, < *pōtāre* to drink]

potlatch (ˈpɒtˌlætʃ) *n. Anthropol.* a competitive ceremonial activity among certain North American Indians, involving a lavish distribution of gifts to emphasize the wealth and status of the chief or clan. [C19: of Amerind origin, < *patshatl* a present]

potluck (ˈpɒtˈlʌk) *n. Inf.* **1.** whatever food happens to be available without special preparation. **2.** whatever is available (esp. in **take potluck**).

pot marigold *n.* a Central European and Mediterranean plant grown for its rayed orange-and-yellow showy flowers.

potoroo (ˌpɒtəˈruː) *n.* another name for **kangaroo rat.** [< Abor.]

potpourri (ˌpəʊˈpʊərɪ) *n., pl.* **-ris. 1.** a collection of mixed flower petals dried and preserved in a pot to scent the air. **2.** a collection of unrelated items; miscellany. **3.** a medley of popular tunes. [C18: < F, lit.: rotten pot, translation of Sp. *olla podrida* miscellany]

pot roast *n.* meat cooked slowly in a covered pot with very little water.

potsherd (ˈpɒtˌʃɜːd) *or* **potshard** (ˈpɒtˌʃɑːd) *n.* a broken fragment of pottery. [C14: < POT[1] + *schoord* piece of broken crockery; see SHARD]

pot shot *n.* **1.** a chance shot taken casually, hastily, or without careful aim. **2.** a shot fired to kill game in disregard of the rules of sport. **3.** a shot fired at quarry within easy range.

pot still *n.* a type of still in which heat is applied directly to the pot in which the wash is contained: used in distilling whisky.

pottage (ˈpɒtɪdʒ) *n.* a thick soup. [C13: < OF *potage* contents of a pot, < *pot* POT[1]]

potted (ˈpɒtɪd) *adj.* **1.** placed or grown in a pot. **2.** cooked or preserved in a pot: *potted shrimps.* **3.** *Inf.* abridged: *a potted version of a novel.*

potter[1] (ˈpɒtə) *n.* a person who makes pottery.

potter[2] (ˈpɒtə) *or esp. U.S. & Canad.* **putter** *vb.* **1.** (*intr.;* often foll. by *about* or *around*) to busy oneself in a desultory though agreeable manner. **2.** (*intr.;* often foll. by *along* or *about*) to move with little energy or direction: *to potter about town.* **3.** (*tr.;* usually foll. by *away*) to waste (time): *to potter the day away.* [C16 (in the sense: to poke repeatedly): < OE *potian* to thrust] —ˈ**potterer** *or esp. U.S.* ˈ**putterer** *n.*

Potteries (ˈpɒtərɪz) *pl. n.* **the.** (*sometimes functioning as sing.*) a region of W central England, in Staffordshire, in which the china industries are concentrated.

potter's field *n.* **1.** *New Testament.* the land bought by the Sanhedrin with the money paid for the betrayal of Jesus, to be used as a burial place for strangers (Acts 1:19; Matthew 27:7). **2.** *U.S.* a cemetery where the poor or unidentified are buried at the public's expense.

potter's wheel *n.* a device with a horizontal rotating disc, on which clay is moulded by hand.

pottery (ˈpɒtərɪ) *n., pl.* **-teries. 1.** articles made from earthenware and baked in a kiln. **2.** a place where such articles are made. **3.** the craft or business of making such articles. [C15: < OF *poterie,* < *potier* potter, < *pot* POT[1]]

potting shed *n.* a building in which plants are set in flowerpots and in which empty pots, potting compost, etc., are stored.

pottle (ˈpɒtᵊl) *n. Arch.* a liquid measure equal to half a gallon. [C14 *potel,* < OF: a small pot]

potto (ˈpɒtəʊ) *n., pl.* **-tos.** a short-tailed prosimian primate having vertebral spines protruding through the skin in the neck region. Also called: **kinkajou.** [C18: of W African origin]

Pott's disease (pɒts) *n.* a disease of the spine, characterized by weakening and gradual disintegration of the vertebrae. [C18: after Percivall *Pott* (1714–88), E surgeon]

Pott's fracture *n.* a fracture of the lower part of the fibula, usually with the dislocation of the ankle. [C18: see POTT'S DISEASE]

potty[1] (ˈpɒtɪ) *adj.* **-tier, -tiest.** *Brit. inf.* **1.** foolish or slightly crazy. **2.** trivial or insignificant. **3.** (foll. by *about*) very keen (on). [C19: ? < POT[1]] —ˈ**pottiness** *n.*

potty[2] (ˈpɒtɪ) *n., pl.* **-ties.** a child's word for **chamber pot.**

pouch (paʊtʃ) *n.* **1.** a small flexible baglike container: *a tobacco pouch.* **2.** a saclike structure in any of various animals, such as the cheek fold in rodents. **3.** *Anat.* any sac, pocket, or pouchlike cavity. **4.** a Scot. word for **pocket.** ~*vb.* **5.** (*tr.*) to place in or as if in a pouch. **6.** to arrange or become arranged in a pouchlike form. **7.** (*tr.*) (of certain birds and fishes) to swallow. [C14: < OF *pouche,* < OF *poche* bag] —ˈ**pouchy** *adj.*

pouf *or* **pouffe** (puːf) *n.* **1.** a large solid cushion used as a seat. **2. a.** a woman's hairstyle, fashionable esp. in the 18th century, in which the hair is piled up in rolled puffs. **b.** a pad set in the hair to make such puffs. **3.** (*also* pʊf). *Brit. derog. sl.* less common spellings of **poof.** [C19: < F]

poulard *or* **poularde** (ˈpuːlɑːd) *n.* a hen that has been spayed for fattening. Cf. **capon.** [C18: < OF *pollarde,* < *polle* hen]

poult (pəʊlt) *n.* the young of a gallinaceous bird, esp. of domestic fowl. [C15: var. of *poulet* PULLET]

poulterer (ˈpəʊltərə) *n. Brit.* another word for a **poultryman.** [C17: < obs. *poulter,* < OF *pouletier,* < *poulet* PULLET]

poultice (ˈpəʊltɪs) *n. Med.* a local moist and often heated application for the skin used to improve the circulation, treat inflamed areas, etc. [C16: < earlier *pultes,* < L *puls* a thick porridge]

poultry (ˈpəʊltrɪ) *n.* domestic fowls collectively. [C14: < OF *pouletrie,* < *pouletier* poultry dealer]

poultryman (ˈpəʊltrɪmən) *or* **poulterer** *n., pl.* **-trymen** *or* **-terers. 1.** Also called: **chicken farmer.** a person who rears domestic fowls for their eggs or meat. **2.** a dealer in poultry.

pounce[1] (paʊns) *vb.* **1.** (*intr.;* often foll. by *on* or *upon*) to spring or swoop, as in capturing prey. ~*n.* **2.** the act of pouncing; a spring or swoop. **3.** the claw of a bird of prey. [C17: apparently < ME *punson* pointed tool] —ˈ**pouncer** *n.*

pounce[2] (paʊns) *n.* **1.** a very fine resinous powder, esp. of cuttlefish bone, formerly used to dry ink. **2.** a fine powder, esp. of charcoal, that is tapped through perforations in paper in order to transfer the design to another surface. ~*vb.* (*tr.*) **3.** to dust (paper) with pounce. **4.** to transfer (a design) by means of pounce. [C18: < OF *ponce,* < L *pūmex* pumice]

pouncet box (ˈpaʊnsɪt) *n.* a box with a perforated top used for perfume. [C16 *pouncet,* ? alteration of *pounced* perforated]

pound[1] (paʊnd) *vb.* **1.** (when *intr.,* often foll. by *on* or *at*) to strike heavily and often. **2.** (*tr.*) to beat to a pulp; pulverize. **3.** (*tr.;* foll. by *out*) to produce, as by typing heavily. **4.** to walk or move with heavy steps or thuds. **5.** (*intr.*) to throb heavily. ~*n.* **6.** the act of pounding. [OE *pūnian*] —ˈ**pounder** *n.*

pound[2] (paʊnd) *n.* **1.** an avoirdupois unit of weight that is divided into 16 ounces and is equal to 0.453 592 kilograms. Abbrev.: **lb. 2.** a troy unit of weight divided into 12 ounces equal to 0.373 242 kilograms. **3. a.** the standard monetary unit of the United Kingdom, divided into 100 pence. Official name: **pound sterling. b.** (*as modifier*)*: a pound note.* **4.** the standard monetary unit of various other countries, including Cyprus, Egypt, Ireland, Israel, and Malta. **5.** Also called: **pound Scots.** a former Scottish monetary unit originally worth an English pound but later declining in value to 1 shilling 8 pence. [OE *pund,* < L *pondō*]

pound[3] (paʊnd) *n.* **1.** an enclosure for keeping officially removed vehicles or distrained goods or animals, esp. stray dogs. **2.** a place where people are confined. **3.** a trap for animals. ~*vb.* **4.** (*tr.*) to confine in or as if in a pound; impound, imprison, or restrain. [C14: < LOE *pund-,* as in *pundfeald* PINFOLD]

poundage (ˈpaʊndɪdʒ) *n.* **1.** a charge of so much per pound of weight. **2.** a charge of so much per pound sterling. **3.** a weight expressed in pounds.

poundal (ˈpaʊndᵊl) *n.* the fps unit of force; the force that imparts an acceleration of 1 foot per second per second to a mass of 1 pound. Abbrev.: **pdl.** [C19: < POUND[2] + QUINTAL]

-pounder (ˈpaʊndə) *n.* (*in combination*) **1.** something weighing a specified number of pounds: *a 200-pounder.* **2.** something worth a specified number of pounds: *a ten-pounder.* **3.** a gun that discharges a shell weighing a specified number of pounds: *a two-pounder.*

pound sterling *n.* See **pound**[2] (sense 3).

pour (pɔː) *vb.* **1.** to flow or cause to flow in a stream. **2.** (*tr.*) to emit in a profuse way. **3.** (*intr.;* often foll. by *down*) Also: **pour with rain.** to rain heavily. **4.** (*intr.*) to move together in large numbers; swarm. **5.** (*intr.*) to serve tea, coffee, etc.: *shall I pour?* **6. it never rains but it pours.** events, esp. unfortunate ones, come in rapid succession. **7. pour oil on troubled waters.** to calm a quarrel, etc. ~*n.* **8.** a pouring, downpour, etc. [C13: <?] —ˈ**pourer** *n.*

pourboire *French.* (purbwar) *n.* a tip; gratuity. [lit.: for drinking]

poussin (*French* pusɛ̃) *n.* a young chicken reared for eating. [< F]

pout[1] (paʊt) *vb.* **1.** to thrust out (the lips), as when sullen or (of the lips) to be thrust out. **2.** (*intr.*) to swell out; protrude. **3.** (*tr.*) to utter with a pout. ~*n.* **4.** Also: **the pouts.** a fit of sullenness. **5.** the act or state of pouting. [C14: <?] —ˈ**poutingly** *adv.*

pout[2] (paʊt) *n., pl.* **pout** *or* **pouts. 1.** short for **eelpout. 2.** Also called: **horned pout.** a N American catfish with barbels round the mouth. **3.** any of various gadoid food fishes. [OE *-pūte,* as in *ǣlepūte* eelpout]

pouter (ˈpaʊtə) *n.* **1.** a person or thing that pouts. **2.** a breed of domestic pigeon with a large crop capable of being greatly puffed out.

poverty (ˈpɒvətɪ) *n.* **1.** the condition of being without adequate food, money, etc. **2.** scarcity: *a poverty of wit.* **3.** a lack of elements conducive to fertility in soil. [C12: < OF *poverté,* < L *paupertās* restricted means, < *pauper* poor]

poverty-stricken *adj.* suffering from extreme poverty.

poverty trap *n.* the situation of being unable to raise one's living standard because one is dependent on state benefits which are reduced if one gains any extra income.

pow (paʊ) *interj.* an exclamation imitative of a collision, explosion, etc.

POW *abbrev. for* prisoner of war.

powan (ˈpaʊən) *n.* a freshwater whitefish occurring in some Scottish lakes. [C17: Scot. var. of POLLAN]

powder (ˈpaʊdə) *n.* **1.** a substance in the form of tiny loose particles. **2.** any of various preparations in this form, such as gunpowder, face powder, or soap powder. ~*vb.* **3.** to turn into powder; pulverize. **4.** (*tr.*) to cover or sprinkle with or as if with powder. [C13: < OF *poldre,* < L *pulvis* dust] —ˈ**powderer** *n.* —ˈ**powdery** *adj.*

powder blue *n.* a dusty pale blue colour.

powder burn *n.* a superficial burn of the skin caused by a momentary intense explosion.

powder flask *n.* a small flask or case formerly used to carry gunpowder.

powder horn *n.* a powder flask consisting of the hollow horn of an animal.

powder keg *n.* **1.** a small barrel to hold gunpowder. **2.** a potential source of violence, disaster, etc.

powder metallurgy *n.* the science and technology of producing solid metal components from metal powder by compaction and sintering.

powder monkey *n.* (formerly) a boy who carried powder from the magazine to the guns on warships.

powder puff *n.* a soft pad of fluffy material used for applying cosmetic powder to the skin.

powder room *n.* a ladies' cloakroom.

powdery mildew *n.* a plant disease characterized by a white powdery growth on stems and leaves, caused by parasitic fungi.

power ('paʊə) *n.* **1.** ability to do something. **2.** (*often pl.*) a specific ability, capacity, or faculty. **3.** political, financial, social, etc., force or influence. **4.** control or dominion or a position of control, dominion, or authority. **5.** a state or other political entity with political, industrial, or military strength. **6.** a person or group that exercises control, influence, or authority: *he's a power in the state.* **7.** a prerogative, privilege, or liberty. **8.** legal authority to act for another. **9. a.** a military force. **b.** military potential. **10.** *Maths.* **a.** the value of a number or quantity raised to some exponent. **b.** another name for **exponent** (sense 4). **11.** *Physics, engineering.* a measure of the rate of doing work expressed as the work done per unit time. It is measured in watts, horsepower, etc. **12. a.** the rate at which electrical energy is fed into or taken from a device or system. It is measured in watts. **b.** (*as modifier*): *a power amplifier.* **13.** the ability to perform work. **14. a.** mechanical energy as opposed to manual labour. **b.** (*as modifier*): *a power tool.* **15.** a particular form of energy: *nuclear power.* **16. a.** a measure of the ability of a lens or optical system to magnify an object. **b.** another word for **magnification. 17.** *Inf.* a large amount: *a power of good.* **18. in one's power.** (*often foll. by an infinitive*) able or allowed (to). **19. in (someone's) power.** under the control of (someone). **20. the powers that be.** established authority. ~*vb.* **21.** (*tr.*) to give or provide power to. **22.** (*tr.*) to fit (a machine) with a motor or engine. **23.** *Inf.* to move or cause to move by the exercise of physical power. [C13: < Anglo-Norman *poer,* < Vulgar L *potēre* (unattested), < L *posse* to be able]

powerboat ('paʊəˌbəʊt) *n.* a boat, esp. a fast one, propelled by an inboard or outboard motor.

powerboating ('paʊəˌbəʊtɪŋ) *n.* the sport of driving powerboats in racing competitions.

power cut *n.* a temporary interruption or reduction in the supply of electrical power.

power dive *n.* **1.** a steep dive by an aircraft with its engines at high power. ~*vb.* **power-dive. 2.** to cause (an aircraft) to perform a power dive or (of an aircraft) to perform a power dive.

powerful ('paʊəfʊl) *adj.* **1.** having great power. **2.** extremely effective or efficient: *a powerful drug.* ~*adv.* **3.** *Dialect.* very: *he ran powerful fast.* —'**powerfully** *adv.* —'**powerfulness** *n.*

powerhouse ('paʊəˌhaʊs) *n.* **1.** an electrical generating station or plant. **2.** *Inf.* a forceful or powerful person or thing.

powerless ('paʊəlɪs) *adj.* without power or authority. —'**powerlessly** *adv.* —'**powerlessness** *n.*

power of attorney *n.* **1.** legal authority to act for another person in certain specified matters. **2.** the document conferring such authority.

power pack *n.* a device for converting the current from a supply into direct or alternating current at the voltage required by a particular electrical or electronic device.

power plant *n.* **1.** the complex, including machinery, associated equipment, and the structure housing it, that is used in the generation of power, esp. electrical power. **2.** the equipment supplying power to a particular machine.

power point *n.* an electrical socket mounted on or recessed into a wall.

power station *n.* an electrical generating station.

power steering *n.* a form of steering used on vehicles, where the torque applied to the steering wheel is augmented by engine power. Also called: **power-assisted steering.**

power structure *n.* the structure or distribution of power and authority in a community.

powwow ('paʊˌwaʊ) *n.* **1.** a talk, conference, or meeting. **2.** a magical ceremony of certain North American Indians. **3.** (among certain North American Indians) a medicine man. **4.** a meeting of North American Indians. ~*vb.* **5.** (*intr.*) to hold a powwow. [C17: of Amerind origin]

pox (pɒks) *n.* **1.** any disease characterized by the formation of pustules on the skin that often leave pockmarks when healed. **2.** (usually preceded by *the*) an informal name for **syphilis. 3. a pox on (someone *or* something).** (*interj.*) *Arch.* an expression of intense disgust or aversion. [C15: changed < *pocks,* pl. of POCK]

pozzuolana (ˌpɒtswəˈlɑːnə) *or* **pozzolana** (ˌpɒtsəˈlɑːnə) *n.* **1.** a type of porous volcanic ash used in making hydraulic cements. **2.** any of various artificial substitutes for this ash used in cements. [C18: < It.: of *Pozzuoli,* port in SW Italy]

pp *abbrev. for:* **1.** past particple. **2.** per procurationem. See **per pro.** ~**3.** *Music. symbol for* pianissimo.

pp *or* **PP** *abbrev. for:* **1.** parcel post. **2.** post-paid. **3.** (in prescriptions) post prandium. [Latin: after a meal] **4.** prepaid.

PP *abbrev. for:* **1.** Parish Priest. **2.** past President.

pp. *abbrev. for* pages.

ppd *abbrev. for:* **1.** post-paid. **2.** prepaid.

PPE *abbrev. for* philosophy, politics, and economics: a university course.

ppm *Chem. abbrev. for* parts per million.

ppr *or* **p.pr.** *abbrev. for* present participle.

PPS *abbrev. for:* **1.** parliamentary private secretary. **2.** Also: **pps** post postscriptum. [L: after postscript; additional postscript]

PQ *abbrev. for:* **1.** (in Canada) Parti Québecois. **2.** Province of Quebec.

pr *abbrev. for:* **1.** (*pl.* **prs**) pair. **2.** paper. **3.** power.

Pr *the chemical symbol for* praseodymium.

PR *abbrev. for:* **1.** proportional representation. **2.** public relations. **3.** Puerto Rico.

pr. *abbrev. for:* **1.** price. **2.** pronoun.

practicable ('præktɪkəbᵊl) *adj.* **1.** capable of being done; feasible. **2.** usable. [C17: < F *praticable,* < *pratiquer* to practise; see PRACTICAL] —ˌ**practicaˈbility** *or* '**practicableness** *n.* —'**practicably** *adv.*

▷ **Usage.** See at **practical.**

practical ('præktɪkᵊl) *adj.* **1.** of, involving, or concerned with experience or actual use; not theoretical. **2.** of or concerned with ordinary affairs, work, etc. **3.** adapted or adaptable for use. **4.** of, involving, or trained by practice. **5.** being such for all general purposes; virtual. ~*n.* **6.** an examination or lesson in a practical subject. [C17: < earlier *practic,* < F *pratique,* via LL < Gk *praktikos,* < *prassein* to experience] —ˌ**practiˈcality** *or* '**practicalness** *n.*

▷ **Usage.** In careful usage, a distinction is made between *practical* and *practicable. Practical* refers to a person, idea, project, etc., as being more concerned with or relevant to practice than theory: *he is a very practical person; the idea had no practical application. Practicable* refers to a project or idea as being capable of being done or put into effect: *the plan was expensive, yet practicable.*

practical joke *n.* a prank or trick usually intended to make the victim appear foolish. —**practical joker** *n.*

practically ('præktɪkəlɪ, -klɪ) *adv.* **1.** virtually; almost: *it rained practically every day.* **2.** in actuality rather than in theory: *what can we do practically to help?*

practice ('præktɪs) *n.* **1.** a usual or customary action: *it was his practice to rise at six.* **2.** repetition of an activity in order to achieve mastery and fluency. **3.** the condition of having mastery of a skill or activity through repetition (esp. in **in practice, out of practice**). **4.** the exercise of a profession: *he set up practice as a lawyer.* **5.** the act of doing something: *he put his plans into practice.* **6.** the established method of conducting proceedings in a court of law. ~*vb.* **7.** the U.S. spelling of **practise.** [C16: < Med. L *practicāre* to practise, < Gk *praktikē* practical work, < *prattein* to do]

practise *or U.S.* **practice** (ˈpræktɪs) *vb.* **1.** to do or cause to do repeatedly in order to gain skill. **2.** (*tr.*) to do (something) habitually or frequently: *they practise ritual murder.* **3.** to observe or pursue (something): *to practise Christianity.* **4.** to work at (a profession, etc.): *he practises medicine.* **5.** (foll. by *on* or *upon*) to take advantage of (someone, someone's credulity, etc.). [C15: see PRACTICE]

practised *or U.S.* **practiced** (ˈpræktɪst) *adj.* **1.** expert; skilled; proficient. **2.** acquired or perfected by practice.

practitioner (prækˈtɪʃənə) *n.* **1.** a person who practises a profession or art. **2.** *Christian Science.* a person authorized to practise spiritual healing. [C16: < *practician,* < OF, < *pratiquer* to PRACTISE]

prae- *prefix.* an archaic variant of **pre-**.

praedial *or* **predial** (ˈpriːdɪəl) *adj.* **1.** of or relating to land, farming, etc. **2.** attached to or occupying land. [C16: < Med. L *praediālis,* < L *praedium* farm, estate]

praesidium (prɪˈsɪdɪəm) *n.* a variant of **presidium.**

praetor *or esp. U.S.* **pretor** (ˈpriːtə, -tɔː) *n.* (in ancient Rome) any of several senior magistrates ranking just below the consuls. [C15: < L: one who leads the way, prob. < *praeīre,* < *prae* before + *īre* to go] —**praeˈtorian** *or* **preˈtorian** *adj., n.* —ˈ**praetorship** *or* ˈ**pretorship** *n.*

pragmatic (prægˈmætɪk) *adj.* **1.** advocating behaviour that is dictated more by practical consequences than by theory. **2.** *Philosophy.* of pragmatism. **3.** involving everyday or practical business. **4.** of or concerned with the affairs of a state or community. **5.** *Rare.* meddlesome; officious. Also (for senses 3, 5): **pragmatical.** [C17: < LL *prāgmaticus,* < Gk *prāgmatikos* < *pragma* act, < *prattein* to do] —**pragˌmatiˈcality** *n.* —**pragˈmatically** *adv.*

pragmatic sanction *n.* an edict, decree, or ordinance issued with the force of fundamental law by a sovereign.

pragmatism (ˈprægməˌtɪzəm) *n.* **1.** action or policy dictated by consideration of the practical consequences rather than by theory. **2.** *Philosophy.* the doctrine that the content of a concept consists only in its practical applicability. —ˈ**pragmatist** *n., adj.*

prairie (ˈprɛərɪ) *n.* (*often pl.*) a treeless grassy plain of the central U.S. and S Canada. [C18: < F, < OF *praierie,* < L *prātum* meadow]

prairie chicken, fowl, grouse, *or* **hen** *n.* either of two mottled brown-and-white grouse of North America.

prairie dog *n.* any of several rodents that live in large complex burrows in the prairies of North America. Also called: **prairie marmot.**

prairie oyster *n.* a drink consisting of raw unbeaten egg, vinegar or Worcester sauce, salt, and pepper: a supposed cure for a hangover.

prairie schooner *n. Chiefly U.S.* a horse-drawn covered wagon used in the 19th century to cross the prairies of North America.

prairie wolf *n.* another name for **coyote.**

praise (preɪz) *n.* **1.** the act of expressing commendation, admiration, etc. **2.** the rendering of homage and gratitude to a deity. **3. sing someone's praises.** to commend someone highly. ~*vb.* (*tr.*) **4.** to express commendation, admiration, etc., for. **5.** to proclaim the glorious attributes of (a deity) with homage and thanksgiving. [C13: < OF *preisier,* < LL *pretiāre* to esteem highly, < L *pretium* prize]

praiseworthy (ˈpreɪzˌwɜːðɪ) *adj.* deserving of praise; commendable. —ˈ**praiseˌworthily** *adv.* —ˈ**praiseˌworthiness** *n.*

Prakrit (ˈprɑːkrɪt) *n.* any of the vernacular Indic languages as distinguished from Sanskrit: spoken from about 300 B.C. to the Middle Ages. [C18: < Sansk. *prākrta* original] —**Praˈkritic** *adj.*

praline (ˈprɑːliːn) *n.* **1.** a confection of nuts with caramelized sugar. **2.** Also called: **sugared almond.** a sweet consisting of an almond encased in sugar. [C18: < F, after César de Choiseul, comte de Plessis-*Praslin* (1598–1675), F field marshal whose chef first concocted it]

pralltriller (ˈprɑːlˌtrɪlə) *n.* an ornament used in 18th-century music consisting of an inverted mordent with an added initial upper note. [G: bouncing trill]

pram¹ (præm) *n. Brit.* a cotlike four-wheeled carriage for a baby. U.S. term: **baby carriage.** [C19: shortened & altered < PERAMBULATOR]

pram² (prɑːm) *n. Naut.* a light tender with a flat bottom and a bow formed from the ends of the side and bottom planks meeting in a small raised transom. [C16: < MDu. *prame*]

prance (prɑːns) *vb.* **1.** (*intr.*) to swagger or strut. **2.** (*intr.*) to caper, gambol, or dance about. **3.** (*intr.*) (of a horse) to move with high lively springing steps. **4.** (*tr.*) to cause to prance. ~*n.* **5.** the act or an instance of prancing. [C14 *prauncen,* <?] —ˈ**prancer** *n.* —ˈ**prancing** *adj.*

prandial (ˈprændɪəl) *adj. Facetious.* of or relating to a meal. [C19: < L *prandium* meal, luncheon]

prang (præŋ) *Chiefly Brit. sl.* ~*n.* **1.** an accident or crash in an aircraft, car, etc. **2.** an aircraft bombing raid. ~*vb.* **3.** to crash or damage (an aircraft, car, etc.). **4.** to damage (a town, etc.) by bombing. [C20: ? imit.]

prank¹ (præŋk) *n.* a mischievous trick or joke. [C16: <?] —ˈ**prankish** *adj.* —ˈ**prankster** *n.*

prank² (præŋk) *vb.* **1.** (*tr.*) to dress or decorate showily or gaudily. **2.** (*intr.*) to make an ostentatious display. [C16: < MDu. *pronken*]

prase (preɪz) *n.* a light green translucent variety of chalcedony. [C14: < F, < L *prasius* a leek-green stone, < Gk *prasios,* < *prason* a leek]

praseodymium (ˌpreɪzɪəʊˈdɪmɪəm) *n.* a malleable ductile silvery-white element of the lanthanide series of metals. Symbol: Pr; atomic no.: 59; atomic wt.: 140.91. [C20: NL, < Gk *prasios* of a leek-green colour + DIDYMIUM]

prate (preɪt) *vb.* **1.** (*intr.*) to talk idly and at length; chatter. **2.** (*tr.*) to utter in an idle or empty way. ~*n.* **3.** idle or trivial talk; chatter. [C15: of Gmc origin] —ˈ**prater** *n.* —ˈ**prating** *adj.*

pratfall (ˈprætˌfɔːl) *n. U.S. & Canad. sl.* a fall upon one's buttocks. [C20: < C16 *prat* buttocks (<?) + FALL]

pratincole (ˈprætɪŋˌkəʊl, ˈpreɪ-) *n.* any of various swallow-like shore birds of the Old World, having long pointed wings, short legs, and a short bill. [C18: < NL *pratincola* field-dwelling, < L *prātum* meadow + *incola* inhabitant]

prattle (ˈprætᵊl) *vb.* **1.** (*intr.*) to talk in a foolish or childish way; babble. **2.** (*tr.*) to utter in a foolish or childish way. ~*n.* **3.** foolish or childish talk. [C16: < MLow G *pratelen* to chatter] —ˈ**prattler** *n.* —ˈ**prattling** *adj.*

prau (praʊ) *n.* a variant of **proa.**

prawn (prɔːn) *n.* **1.** any of various small edible marine decapod crustaceans having a slender flattened body with a long tail and two pairs of pincers. **2. come the raw prawn with.** *Austral. inf.* to attempt to deceive. [C15: <?]

praxis (ˈpræksɪs) *n., pl.* **praxes** (ˈpræksiːz) *or* **praxises. 1.** the practice of a field of study, as opposed to the theory. **2.** a practical exercise. **3.** accepted practice or custom. [C16: via Med. L < Gk: deed, action, < *prassein* to do]

pray (preɪ) *vb.* **1.** (when *intr.,* often foll. by *for;* when *tr., usually takes a clause as object*) to utter prayers (to God or other object of worship). **2.** (when *tr., usually takes a clause as object or an infinitive*) to beg or implore: *she prayed to be allowed to go.* ~*sentence substitute.* **3.** *Arch.* I beg you; please: *pray, leave us alone.* [C13: < OF *preier,* < L *precārī* to implore, < *prex* an entreaty]

prayer¹ (prɛə) *n.* **1.** a personal communication or

petition addressed to a deity, esp. in the form of supplication, adoration, praise, contrition, or thanksgiving. **2.** a similar personal communication that does not involve adoration, addressed to beings closely associated with a deity, such as saints. **3.** the practice of praying: *prayer is our solution to human problems.* **4.** (*often pl.*) a form of devotion spent mainly or wholly praying: *morning prayers.* **5.** (*cap. when part of a recognized name*) a form of words used in praying: *the Lord's Prayer.* **6.** an object or benefit prayed for. **7.** an earnest request or entreaty. [C13 *preiere,* < OF, < Med. L, < L *precārius* obtained by begging, < *prex* prayer] —ˈ**prayerful** *adj.*

prayer[2] (ˈpreɪə) *n.* a person who prays.

prayer book (prɛə) *n.* a book containing the prayers used at church services or recommended for private devotions.

prayer rug (prɛə) *n.* the small carpet on which a Muslim kneels and prostrates himself while saying his prayers. Also called: **prayer mat.**

prayer wheel (prɛə) *n. Buddhism.* (esp. in Tibet) a wheel or cylinder inscribed with or containing prayers, each revolution of which is counted as an uttered prayer, so that such prayers can be repeated by turning it.

praying mantis *or* **mantid** *n.* another name for **mantis.**

PRB *abbrev. for* Pre-Raphaelite Brotherhood.

pre- *prefix.* before in time, position, etc.: *predate; pre-eminent.* [< L *prae* before]

preach (priːtʃ) *vb.* **1.** to make known (religious truth) or give religious or moral instruction or exhortation in (sermons). **2.** to advocate (a virtue, action, etc.), esp. in a moralizing way. [C13: < OF *prechier,* < Church L *praedicāre,* < L: to proclaim in public; see PREDICATE]

preacher (ˈpriːtʃə) *n.* a person who preaches, esp. a Protestant clergyman.

preachify (ˈpriːtʃɪˌfaɪ) *vb.* **-fying, -fied.** (*intr.*) *Inf.* to preach or moralize in a tedious manner. —ˌ**preachifiˈcation** *n.*

preachment (ˈpriːtʃmənt) *n.* **1.** the act of preaching. **2.** a tedious or pompous sermon.

preachy (ˈpriːtʃɪ) *adj.* **preachier, preachiest.** *Inf.* inclined to or marked by preaching.

preamble (priːˈæmbᵊl) *n.* **1.** a preliminary or introductory statement, esp. attached to a statute setting forth its purpose. **2.** a preliminary event, fact, etc. [C14: < OF *préambule,* < LL *praeambulum,* < L *prae-* before + *ambulāre* to walk]

preamplifier (priːˈæmplɪˌfaɪə) *n.* an electronic amplifier used to improve the signal-to-noise ratio of an electronic device. It boosts a low-level signal to an intermediate level before it is transmitted to the main amplifier.

prebend (ˈprɛbənd) *n.* **1.** the stipend assigned by a cathedral or collegiate church to a canon or member of the chapter. **2.** the land, tithe, or other source of such a stipend. **3.** a less common word for **prebendary. 4.** *Church of England.* the office of a prebendary. [C15: < OF *prébende,* < Med. L *praebenda* stipend, < L *praebēre* to offer, < *prae* forth + *habēre* to have] —**prebendal** (prɪˈbɛndᵊl) *adj.*

prebendary (ˈprɛbəndərɪ, -drɪ) *n., pl.* **-daries. 1.** a canon or member of the chapter of a cathedral or collegiate church who holds a prebend. **2.** *Church of England.* an honorary canon with the title of prebendary.

Precambrian *or* **Pre-Cambrian** (priːˈkæmbrɪən) *adj.* **1.** of, denoting, or formed in the earliest geological era, which lasted for about 4 000 000 000 years before the Cambrian period. ~*n.* **2. the.** the Precambrian era.

precancel (priːˈkænsᵊl) *vb.* **-celling, -celled** *or U.S.* **-celing, -celed.** (*tr.*) to cancel (postage stamps) before placing them on mail.

precarious (prɪˈkɛərɪəs) *adj.* **1.** liable to failure or catastrophe; insecure; perilous. **2.** *Arch.* dependent on another's will. [C17: < L *precārius* obtained by begging, < *prex* PRAYER[1]] —**preˈcariously** *adv.* —**preˈcariousness** *n.*

precast (ˈpriːˌkɑːst) *adj.* (esp. of concrete when employed as a structural element in building) cast in a particular form before being used.

precaution (prɪˈkɔːʃən) *n.* **1.** an action taken to avoid a dangerous or undesirable event. **2.** caution practised beforehand; circumspection. [C17: < F, < LL *praecautiō,* < L, < *prae* before + *cavēre* to beware] —**preˈcautionary** *adj.*

precede (prɪˈsiːd) *vb.* **1.** to go or be before (someone or something) in time, place, rank, etc. **2.** (*tr.*) to preface or introduce. [C14: via OF < L *praecēdere* to go before]

precedence (ˈprɛsɪdəns) *or* **precedency** *n.* **1.** the act of preceding or the condition of being precedent. **2.** the ceremonial order or priority to be observed on formal occasions: *the officers are seated according to precedence.* **3.** a right to preferential treatment: *I take precedence over you.*

precedent *n.* (ˈprɛsɪdənt). **1.** *Law.* a judicial decision that serves as an authority for deciding a later case. **2.** an example or instance used to justify later similar occurrences. ~*adj.* (prɪˈsiːdᵊnt, ˈprɛsɪdənt). **3.** preceding.

precedented (ˈprɛsɪˌdɛntɪd) *adj.* (of a decision, etc.) supported by having a precedent.

precedential (ˌprɛsɪˈdɛnʃəl) *adj.* **1.** of or serving as a precedent. **2.** having precedence.

preceding (prɪˈsiːdɪŋ) *adj.* (*prenominal*) going or coming before; former.

precentor (prɪˈsɛntə) *n.* **1.** a cleric who directs the choral services in a cathedral. **2.** a person who leads a congregation or choir in the sung parts of church services. [C17: < LL *praecentor,* < *prae* before + *canere* to sing] —**precentorial** (ˌpriːsɛnˈtɔːrɪəl) *adj.* —**preˈcentorˌship** *n.*

precept (ˈpriːsɛpt) *n.* **1.** a rule or principle for action. **2.** a guide or rule for morals; maxim. **3.** a direction, esp. for a technical operation. **4.** *Law.* **a.** a writ or warrant. **b.** (in England) an order to collect money under a rate. [C14: < L *praeceptum* injunction, < *praecipere* to admonish, < *prae* before + *capere* to take] —**preˈceptive** *adj.*

preceptor (prɪˈsɛptə) *n. Rare.* a tutor or instructor. —**preceptorial** (ˌpriːsɛpˈtɔːrɪəl) *or* **preˈceptoral** *adj.* —**preˈceptress** *fem. n.*

precession (prɪˈsɛʃən) *n.* **1.** the act of preceding. **2.** See **precession of the equinoxes. 3.** the motion of a spinning body, such as a top, gyroscope, or planet, in which it wobbles so that the axis of rotation sweeps out a cone. [C16: < LL *praecessiō,* < L *praecēdere* to precede] —**preˈcessional** *adj.* —**preˈcessionally** *adv.*

precession of the equinoxes *n.* the slightly earlier occurrence of the equinoxes each year due to the slow continuous westward shift of the equinoctial points along the ecliptic.

precinct (ˈpriːsɪŋkt) *n.* **1. a.** an enclosed area or

ˌ**preabˈsorb** *vb.*
ˌ**preacˈcept** *vb.*
ˌ**preacˈcustom** *vb.*
ˌ**preacˈquaint** *vb.*
ˌ**preaˈdapt** *vb.*
ˌ**preadˈdress** *vb.*
ˌ**preadˈjust** *vb.*
ˌ**preadoˈlescent** *n., adj.*
preˈadverˌtise *vb.*
ˌ**prealˈlot** *vb.*
ˌ**preanˈnounce** *vb.*
ˌ**preapˈpearance** *n.*
ˌ**preappliˈcation** *n.*
ˌ**preapˈpoint** *vb.*
preˈarm *vb.*
ˌ**prearˈrange** *vb.*
ˌ**prearˈranged** *adj.*
ˌ**prearˈrangement** *n.*
ˌ**preascerˈtain** *vb.*
ˌ**preasˈsemble** *vb.*
ˌ**preasˈsign** *vb.*
ˌ**preasˈsumption** *n.*
ˌ**preasˈsurance** *n.*
preˈboil *vb.*
ˌ**pre-Byzˈanˌtine** *adj.*
preˈcancerous *adj.*
pre-ˈCeltic *adj.*
preˈcensor *vb.*
ˌ**pre-Chauˈcerian** *adj.*
preˈcheck *vb.*
preˈchill *vb.*
pre-ˈChristian *adj.*

building marked by a fixed boundary such as a wall. **b.** such a boundary. **2.** an area in a town, often closed to traffic, that is designed or reserved for a particular activity: *a shopping precinct.* **3.** *U.S.* **a.** a district of a city for administrative or police purposes. **b.** a polling district. [C15: < Med. L *praecinctum* (something) surrounded, < L *praecingere* to gird around]

precincts (ˈpriːsɪŋkts) *pl. n.* the surrounding region or area.

preciosity (ˌprɛʃɪˈɒsɪtɪ) *n., pl.* **-ties.** fastidiousness or affectation.

precious (ˈprɛʃəs) *adj.* **1.** beloved; dear; cherished. **2.** very costly or valuable. **3.** very fastidious or affected, as in speech, manners, etc. **4.** *Inf.* worthless: *you and your precious ideas!* ~*adv.* **5.** *Inf.* (intensifier): *there's precious little left.* [C13: < OF *precios,* < L *pretiōsus* valuable, < *pretium* price] —**ˈpreciously** *adv.* —**ˈpreciousness** *n.*

precious metal *n.* gold, silver, or platinum.

precious stone *n.* any of certain rare minerals, such as diamond, ruby, or opal, that are highly valued as gemstones.

precipice (ˈprɛsɪpɪs) *n.* **1.** the steep sheer face of a cliff or crag. **2.** the cliff or crag itself. [C16: < L *praecipitium* steep place, < *praeceps* headlong] —**ˈprecipiced** *adj.*

precipitant (prɪˈsɪpɪtənt) *adj.* **1.** hasty or impulsive; rash. **2.** rushing or falling rapidly or without heed. **3.** abrupt or sudden. ~*n.* **4.** *Chem.* a substance that causes a precipitate to form. —**preˈcipitance** *or* **preˈcipitancy** *n.*

precipitate *vb.* (prɪˈsɪpɪˌteɪt). **1.** (*tr.*) to cause to happen too soon; bring on. **2.** to throw or fall from or as from a height. **3.** to cause (moisture) to condense and fall as snow, rain, etc., or (of moisture, rain, etc.) to condense and fall thus. **4.** *Chem.* to undergo or cause to undergo a process in which a dissolved substance separates from solution as a fine suspension of solid particles. ~*adj.* (prɪˈsɪpɪtɪt). **5.** rushing ahead. **6.** done rashly or with undue haste. **7.** sudden and brief. ~*n.* (prɪˈsɪpɪtɪt). **8.** *Chem.* a precipitated solid. [C16: < L *praecipitāre* to throw down headlong, < *praeceps* steep, < *prae* before + *caput* head] —**preˈcipitable** *adj.* —**preˌcipitaˈbility** *n.* —**preˈcipitately** *adv.* —**preˈcipiˌtator** *n.*

precipitation (prɪˌsɪpɪˈteɪʃən) *n.* **1.** *Meteorol.* **a.** rain, snow, sleet, dew, etc., formed by condensation of water vapour in the atmosphere. **b.** the deposition of these on the earth's surface. **2.** the formation of a chemical precipitate. **3.** the act of precipitating or the state of being precipitated. **4.** rash or undue haste.

precipitous (prɪˈsɪpɪtəs) *adj.* **1.** resembling a precipice. **2.** very steep. **3.** hasty or precipitate. —**preˈcipitously** *adv.* —**preˈcipitousness** *n.*

precis *or* **précis** (ˈpreɪsiː) *n., pl.* **precis** *or* **précis** (ˈpreɪsiːz). **1.** a summary of a text; abstract. ~*vb.* **2.** (*tr.*) to make a precis of. [C18: < F: PRECISE]

precise (prɪˈsaɪs) *adj.* **1.** strictly correct in amount or value: *a precise sum.* **2.** particular: *this precise location.* **3.** using or operating with total accuracy: *precise instruments.* **4.** strict in observance of rules, standards, etc.: *a precise mind.* [C16: < F *précis,* < L *praecīdere* to curtail, < *prae* before + *caedere* to cut] —**preˈcisely** *adv.* —**preˈciseness** *n.*

precision (prɪˈsɪʒən) *n.* **1.** the quality of being precise; accuracy. **2.** (*modifier*) characterized by a high degree of exactness: *precision grinding.* [C17: < L *praecīsiō* a cutting off; see PRECISE] —**preˈcisionism** *n.* —**preˈcisionist** *n.*

preclude (prɪˈkluːd) *vb.* (*tr.*) **1.** to exclude or debar. **2.** to make impossible, esp. beforehand. [C17: < L *praeclūdere* to shut up, < *prae* before + *claudere* to close] —**preclusion** (prɪˈkluːʒən) *n.* —**preclusive** (prɪˈkluːsɪv) *adj.*

precocial (prɪˈkəʊʃəl) *adj.* **1.** denoting birds whose young, after hatching, are covered with down and capable of leaving the nest within a few days. ~*n.* **2.** a precocial bird. ~Cf. **altricial.**

precocious (prɪˈkəʊʃəs) *adj.* **1.** ahead in development, such as the mental development of a child. **2.** *Bot.* flowering or ripening early. [C17: < L *praecox,* < *prae* early + *coquere* to ripen] —**preˈcociously** *adv.* —**preˈcociousness** *or* **precocity** (prɪˈkɒsɪtɪ) *n.*

precognition (ˌpriːkɒgˈnɪʃən) *n. Psychol.* the alleged ability to foresee future events. [C17: < LL *praecognitiō* foreknowledge, < *praecognoscere* to foresee] —**precognitive** (priːˈkɒgnɪtɪv) *adj.*

preconceive (ˌpriːkənˈsiːv) *vb.* (*tr.*) to form an idea of beforehand. —**preconception** (ˌpriːkənˈsɛpʃən) *n.*

precondition (ˌpriːkənˈdɪʃən) *n.* **1.** a necessary or required condition; prerequisite. ~*vb.* **2.** (*tr.*) *Psychol.* to present successively two stimuli to (an organism) without reinforcement so that they become associated; if a response is then conditioned to the second stimulus on its own, the same response will be evoked by the first stimulus.

preconize *or* **-ise** (ˈpriːkəˌnaɪz) *vb.* (*tr.*) **1.** to announce or commend publicly. **2.** to summon publicly. **3.** (of the pope) to approve the appointment of (a nominee) to one of the higher dignities in the Roman Catholic Church. [C15: < Med. L *praecōnīzāre* to make an announcement, < L *praecō* herald] —**ˌpreconiˈzation** *or* **-iˈsation** *n.*

precursor (prɪˈkɜːsə) *n.* **1.** a person or thing that precedes and announces someone or something to come. **2.** a predecessor. **3.** a substance that gives rise to another more important substance. [C16: < L *praecursor* one who runs in front, < *praecurrere,* < *prae* in front + *currere* to run]

precursory (prɪˈkɜːsərɪ) *or* **precursive** *adj.* **1.** serving as a precursor. **2.** preliminary.

pred. *abbrev. for* predicate.

predacious *or* **predaceous** (prɪˈdeɪʃəs) *adj.* (of animals) habitually hunting and killing other animals for food. [C18: < L *praeda* plunder] —**preˈdaciousness, preˈdaceousness,** *or* **predacity** (prɪˈdæsɪtɪ) *n.*

predate (priːˈdeɪt) *vb.* (*tr.*) **1.** to affix a date to (a document, paper, etc.) that is earlier than the actual date. **2.** to assign a date to (an event, period, etc.) that is earlier than the actual or previously assigned date of occurrence. **3.** to be or occur at an earlier date than; precede in time.

predation (prɪˈdeɪʃən) *n.* a relationship between two species of animal in a community, in which one hunts, kills, and eats the other.

predator (ˈprɛdətə) *n.* **1.** any carnivorous animal. **2.** a predatory person or thing.

predatory (ˈprɛdətərɪ) *adj.* **1.** *Zool.* another word for **predacious. 2.** of or characterized by plundering, robbing, etc. [C16: < L *praedātōrius* rapacious, < *praedārī* to pillage, < *praeda* booty] —**ˈpredatorily** *adv.* —**ˈpredatoriness** *n.*

predecease (ˌpriːdɪˈsiːs) *vb.* to die before (some other person).

predecessor (ˈpriːdɪˌsɛsə) *n.* **1.** a person who precedes another, as in an office. **2.** something that precedes something else. **3.** an ancestor. [C14: via OF < LL *praedēcessor,* < *prae* before + *dēcēdere* to go away]

predella (prɪˈdɛlə) *n., pl.* **-le** (-liː). **1.** a painting or a series of small paintings in a long strip forming the lower edge of an altarpiece or the face of an altar step. **2.** a platform in a church upon which the altar stands. [C19: < It.: step, prob. < OHG *bret* board]

---

preˈclassical *adj.*
preˈcollege *adj.*
ˌpreconˈcession *n.*
ˌpreconˈdemn *vb.*
ˌpreconˈstruct *vb.*
ˌpreconsulˈtation *n.*
ˌpreconˈtrive *vb.*
ˌpreconˈviction *n.*
preˈcook *vb.*
ˌpre-Darˈwinian *adj.*
preˈdesigˌnate *vb.*

predestinarian (ˌpriːdɛstɪˈnɛərɪən) *n.* **1.** a person who believes in divine predestination. *~adj.* **2.** of or relating to predestination or those who believe in it.

predestinate *vb.* (priːˈdɛstɪˌneɪt). **1.** another word for **predestine.** *~adj.* (priːˈdɛstɪnɪt, -ˌneɪt). **2.** predestined.

predestination (priːˌdɛstɪˈneɪʃən) *n.* **1.** *Christian theol.* **a.** the act of God foreordaining every event from eternity. **b.** the doctrine or belief, esp. associated with Calvin, that the final salvation of some of mankind is foreordained from eternity by God. **2.** the act of predestining or the state of being predestined.

predestine (priːˈdɛstɪn) *or* **predestinate** *vb.* (*tr.*) **1.** to determine beforehand. **2.** *Christian theol.* (of God) to decree from eternity (any event, esp. the final salvation of individuals). [C14: < L *praedestināre* to resolve beforehand]

predetermine (ˌpriːdɪˈtɜːmɪn) *vb.* (*tr.*) **1.** to determine beforehand. **2.** to influence or bias. —**ˌpredeˈterminable** *adj.* —**ˌpredeˈterminate** *adj.* —**ˌpredeˌtermiˈnation** *n.*

predicable (ˈprɛdɪkəbᵊl) *adj.* **1.** capable of being predicated or asserted. *~n.* **2.** a quality that can be predicated. **3.** *Logic, obs.* any of the five Aristotelian classes of predicates, namely genus, species, difference, property, and relation. [C16: < L *praedicābilis,* < *praedicāre* to assert publicly; see PREDICATE] —**ˌpredicaˈbility** *n.*

predicament **1.** (prɪˈdɪkəmənt). *n.* a perplexing, embarrassing, or difficult situation. **2.** (ˈprɛdɪkəmənt). *Logic.* a logical category. [C14: < LL *praedicāmentum* what is predicated, < *praedicāre* to announce; see PREDICATE]

predicant (ˈprɛdɪkənt) *adj.* **1.** of or relating to preaching. *~n.* **2.** a member of a religious order founded for preaching, esp. a Dominican. [C17: < L *praedicāns* preaching, < *praedicāre* to say publicly; see PREDICATE]

predicate *vb.* (ˈprɛdɪˌkeɪt). (*mainly tr.*) **1.** (*also intr.; when tr., may take a clause as object*) to declare or affirm. **2.** to imply or connote. **3.** (foll. by *on* or *upon*) *Chiefly U.S.* to base (a proposition, argument, etc.). **4.** *Logic.* to assert (a property or condition) of the subject of a proposition. *~n.* (ˈprɛdɪkɪt). **5.** *Grammar.* the part of a sentence in which something is asserted or denied of the subject of a sentence. **6.** *Logic.* a term, property, or condition that is affirmed or denied concerning the subject of a proposition. *~adj.* (ˈprɛdɪkɪt). **7.** of or relating to something that has been predicated. [C16: < L *praedicāre* to assert publicly, < *prae* in front + *dīcere* to say] —**ˌprediˈcation** *n.*

predicate calculus *n.* the system of symbolic logic concerned not only with relations between propositions as wholes but also with the representation by symbols of individuals and predicates in propositions. See also **propositional calculus.**

predicative (prɪˈdɪkətɪv) *adj. Grammar.* relating to or occurring within the predicate of a sentence: *a predicative adjective.* Cf. **attributive.** —**preˈdicatively** *adv.*

predict (prɪˈdɪkt) *vb.* (*tr.; may take a clause as object*) to state or make a declaration about in advance; foretell. [C17: < L *praedīcere* to mention beforehand] —**preˈdictable** *adj.* —**preˌdictaˈbility** *n.* —**preˈdictably** *adv.* —**preˈdictor** *n.*

prediction (prɪˈdɪkʃən) *n.* **1.** the act of predicting. **2.** something predicted; a forecast.

predigest (ˌpriːdaɪˈdʒɛst, -dɪ-) *vb.* (*tr.*) to treat (food) artificially to aid subsequent digestion in the body. —**ˌprediˈgestion** *n.*

predikant (ˌprɛdɪˈkænt) *n.* a minister in the Dutch Reformed Church, esp. in South Africa. [< Du., < OF *predicant,* < LL, < *praedicāre* to PREACH]

predilection (ˌpriːdɪˈlɛkʃən) *n.* a predisposition, preference, or bias. [C18: < F *prédilection,* < Med. L *praedīligere* to prefer, < L *prae* before + *dīligere* to love]

predispose (ˌpriːdɪˈspəʊz) *vb.* (*tr.*) (often foll. by *to* or *towards*) to incline or make (someone) susceptible to something beforehand. —**ˌpredisˈposal** *n.* —**ˌpredispoˈsition** *n.*

predominant (prɪˈdɒmɪnənt) *adj.* **1.** superior in power, influence, etc., over others. **2.** prevailing. —**preˈdominance** *n.* —**preˈdominantly** *adv.*

predominate *vb.* (prɪˈdɒmɪˌneɪt). (*intr.*) **1.** (often foll. by *over*) to have power, influence, or control. **2.** to prevail or preponderate. *~adj.* (prɪˈdɒmɪnɪt). **3.** another word for **predominant.** [C16: < Med. L *praedomināri,* < L *prae* before + *dominārī* to bear rule] —**preˈdominately** *adv.* —**preˌdomiˈnation** *n.*

pre-eminent (prɪˈɛmɪnənt) *adj.* extremely eminent or distinguished; outstanding. —**preˈeminence** *n.* —**pre-ˈeminently** *adv.*

pre-empt (prɪˈɛmpt) *vb.* **1.** (*tr.*) to acquire in advance of or to the exclusion of others; appropriate. **2.** (*tr.*) *Chiefly U.S.* to occupy (public land) in order to acquire a prior right to purchase. **3.** (*intr.*) *Bridge.* to make a high opening bid, often on a weak hand, to shut out opposition bidding. —**pre-ˈemptor** *n.*

pre-emption (prɪˈɛmpʃən) *n.* **1.** *Law.* the purchase of or right to purchase property in preference to others. **2.** *International law.* the right of a government to intercept and seize property of the subjects of another state while in transit, esp. in time of war. [C16: < Med. L *praeemptiō,* < *praeemere* to buy beforehand]

pre-emptive (prɪˈɛmptɪv) *adj.* **1.** of, involving, or capable of pre-emption. **2.** *Bridge.* (of a high bid) made to shut out opposition bidding. **3.** *Mil.* designed to reduce or destroy an enemy's attacking strength before it can use it: *a pre-emptive strike.*

preen (priːn) *vb.* **1.** (of birds) to maintain (feathers) in a healthy condition by arrangement, cleaning, and other contact with the bill. **2.** to dress or array (oneself) carefully; primp. **3.** (usually foll. by *on*) to pride or congratulate (oneself). [C14 *preinen,* prob. < *prunen,* infl. by *prenen* to prick; suggestive of the pricking movement of the bird's beak] —**ˈpreener** *n.*

pref. *abbrev. for:* **1.** preface. **2.** prefatory. **3.** preference. **4.** preferred. **5.** prefix.

prefab (ˈpriːˌfæb) *n.* a building that is prefabricated, esp. a small house.

prefabricate (priːˈfæbrɪˌkeɪt) *vb.* (*tr.*) to manufacture sections of (a building) so that they can be easily transported to and rapidly assembled on a building site. —**preˌfabriˈcation** *n.*

preface (ˈprɛfɪs) *n.* **1.** a statement written as an introduction to a literary or other work, typically explaining its scope, intention, method, etc.; foreword. **2.** anything introductory. *~vb.* (*tr.*) **3.** to furnish with a preface. **4.** to serve as a preface to. [C14: < Med. L *praefātia,* < L *praefātiō* a saying beforehand, < *praefārī* to utter in advance] —**ˈprefacer** *n.*

prefatory (ˈprɛfətərɪ, -trɪ) *or* **prefatorial** (ˌprɛfəˈtɔːrɪəl) *adj.* of or serving as a preface; introductory. [C17: < L *praefārī* to say in advance]

prefect (ˈpriːfɛkt) *n.* **1.** (in France, Italy, etc.) the chief administrative officer in a department. **2.** (in France, etc.) the head of a police force. **3.** *Brit.* a schoolchild appointed to a position of limited power over his fellows. **4.** (in ancient

---

ˌpredisˈsolve *vb.*
ˌpredisˈtinguish *vb.*
ˌprediˈvide *vb.*
preˈdoom *vb.*
ˌpredyˈnastic *adj.*
ˌpre-eˈlect *vb.*
ˌpre-eˈlection *n.*
ˌpre-enˈgage *vb.*
ˌpre-enˈgagement *n.*
ˌpre-enˈlistment *n.*
ˌpre-esˈtablish *vb.*
pre-ˈestiˌmate *vb.*
ˌpre-exˈamine *vb.*
ˌpre-exˈist *vb.*
ˌpre-exˈistence *n.*
ˌpre-exˈpose *vb.*

Rome) any of several magistrates or military commanders. **5.** *R.C. Church.* one of two senior masters in a Jesuit school or college. [C14: < L *praefectus* one put in charge, < *praeficere* to place in authority over, < *prae* before + *facere* to do] —**prefectorial** (ˌpriːfɛkˈtɔːrɪəl) *adj.*

prefecture (ˈpriːfɛkˌtjʊə) *n.* **1.** the office, position, or area of authority of a prefect. **2.** the official residence of a prefect in France, etc.

prefer (prɪˈfɜː) *vb.* **-ferring, -ferred. 1.** (when *tr., may take a clause as object or an infinitive*) to like better or value more highly: *I prefer to stand.* **2.** *Law.* (esp. of the police) to put (charges) before a court, magistrate, etc., for consideration and judgment. **3.** (*tr.; often passive*) to advance in rank over another or others; promote. [C14: < L *praeferre* to carry in front, prefer]

preferable (ˈprɛfərəbᵊl) *adj.* preferred or more desirable. —**ˈpreferably** *adv.*

preference (ˈprɛfərəns, ˈprɛfrəns) *n.* **1.** the act of preferring. **2.** something or someone preferred. **3.** *International trade.* the granting of favour or precedence to particular foreign countries, as by levying differential tariffs.

preference shares *pl. n. Brit.* fixed-interest shares issued by a company and giving their holders a prior right over ordinary shareholders to payment of dividend and to repayment of capital if the company is liquidated. U.S. name: **preferred stock.** Cf. **ordinary shares.**

preferential (ˌprɛfəˈrɛnʃəl) *adj.* **1.** showing or resulting from preference. **2.** giving, receiving, or originating from preference in international trade. —**ˌpreferˈentially** *adv.*

preferment (prɪˈfɜːmənt) *n.* **1.** the act of promoting to a higher position, office, etc. **2.** the state of being preferred for promotion or social advancement. **3.** the act of preferring.

prefigure (priːˈfɪgə) *vb.* (*tr.*) **1.** to represent or suggest in advance. **2.** to imagine beforehand. —**ˌprefiguˈration** *n.* —**preˈfigurement** *n.*

prefix *n.* (ˈpriːfɪks). **1.** *Grammar.* an affix that precedes the stem to which it is attached, as for example *un-* in *unhappy.* Cf. **suffix** (sense 1). **2.** something coming or placed before. ~*vb.* (priːˈfɪks, ˈpriːfɪks). (*tr.*) **3.** to put or place before. **4.** *Grammar.* to add (a morpheme) as a prefix to the beginning of a word. —**prefixion** (priːˈfɪkʃən) *n.*

prefrontal (priːˈfrʌntᵊl) *adj.* in or relating to the foremost part of the frontal lobe of the brain.

preglacial (priːˈgleɪsɪəl, -ʃəl) *adj.* formed or occurring before a glacial period, esp. before the Pleistocene epoch.

pregnable (ˈprɛgnəbᵊl) *adj.* capable of being assailed or captured. [C15 *prenable,* < OF *prendre* to take, < L *prehendere* to catch]

pregnant (ˈprɛgnənt) *adj.* **1.** carrying a fetus or fetuses within the womb. **2.** full of meaning or significance. **3.** inventive or imaginative. **4.** prolific or fruitful. [C16: < L *praegnāns* with child, < *prae* before + (*g*)*nascī* to be born] —**ˈpregnancy** *n.* —**ˈpregnantly** *adv.*

prehensile (prɪˈhɛnsaɪl) *adj.* adapted for grasping, esp. by wrapping around a support: *a prehensile tail.* [C18: < F *préhensile,* < L *prehendere* to grasp] —**prehensility** (ˌpriːhɛnˈsɪlɪtɪ) *n.*

prehension (prɪˈhɛnʃən) *n.* **1.** the act of grasping. **2.** apprehension by the mind.

prehistoric (ˌpriːhɪˈstɒrɪk) *or* **prehistorical** *adj.* of or relating to man's development before the appearance of the written word. —**ˌprehisˈtorically** *adv.* —**preˈhistory** *n.*

pre-ignition (ˌpriːɪgˈnɪʃən) *n.* ignition of all or part of the explosive charge in an internal-combustion engine before the exact instant necessary for correct operation.

prejudge (priːˈdʒʌdʒ) *vb.* (*tr.*) to judge beforehand, esp. without sufficient evidence.

prejudice (ˈprɛdʒʊdɪs) *n.* **1.** an opinion formed beforehand, esp. an unfavourable one based on inadequate facts. **2.** the act or condition of holding such opinions. **3.** intolerance of or dislike for people of a specific race, religion, etc. **4.** disadvantage or injury resulting from prejudice. **5. in** (*or* **to**) **the prejudice of.** to the detriment of. **6. without prejudice.** *Law.* without dismissing or detracting from an existing right or claim. ~*vb.* (*tr.*) **7.** to cause to be prejudiced. **8.** to disadvantage or injure by prejudice. [C13: < OF *préjudice,* < L *praejūdicium,* < *prae* before + *jūdicium* sentence, < *jūdex* a judge]

prejudicial (ˌprɛdʒʊˈdɪʃəl) *adj.* causing prejudice; damaging. —**ˌprejuˈdicially** *adv.*

prelacy (ˈprɛləsɪ) *n., pl.* **-cies. 1.** Also called: **prelature. a.** the office or status of a prelate. **b.** prelates collectively. **2.** *Often derog.* government of the Church by prelates.

prelapsarian (ˌpriːlæpˈsɛərɪən) *adj.* of or relating to the human state before the Fall: *prelapsarian innocence.*

prelate (ˈprɛlɪt) *n.* a Church dignitary of high rank, such as a cardinal, bishop, or abbot. [C13: < OF *prélat,* < Church L *praelātus,* < L *praeferre* to hold in special esteem] —**prelatic** (prɪˈlætɪk) *or* **preˈlatical** *adj.*

preliminaries (prɪˈlɪmɪnərɪz) *pl. n.* the full word for **prelims.**

preliminary (prɪˈlɪmɪnərɪ) *adj.* **1.** (*usually prenominal*) occurring before or in preparation; introductory. ~*n., pl.* **-naries. 2.** a preliminary event or occurrence. **3.** an eliminating contest held before the main competition. [C17: < NL *praelīmināris,* < L *prae* before + *līmen* threshold] —**preˈliminarily** *adv.*

prelims (ˈpriːlɪmz, prəˈlɪmz) *pl. n.* **1.** Also called: **front matter.** the pages of a book, such as the title page and contents, before the main text. **2.** the first public examinations taken for the bachelor's degree in some universities. **3.** (in Scotland) the school examinations taken before public examinations. [C19: a contraction of PRELIMINARIES]

prelude (ˈprɛljuːd) *n.* **1. a.** a piece of music that precedes a fugue, or forms the first movement of a suite, or an introduction to an act in an opera, etc. **b.** (esp. for piano) a self-contained piece of music. **2.** an introduction or preceding event, occurrence, etc. ~*vb.* **3.** to serve as a prelude to (something). **4.** (*tr.*) to introduce by a prelude. [C16: < Med. L *praelūdium,* < *prae* before + L *lūdere* to play] —**preludial** (prɪˈljuːdɪəl) *adj.*

premarital (priːˈmærɪtᵊl) *adj.* (esp. of sexual relations) occurring before marriage.

premature (ˌprɛməˈtjʊə, ˈprɛməˌtjʊə) *adj.* **1.** occurring or existing before the normal or expected time. **2.** impulsive or hasty: *a premature judgment.* **3.** (of an infant) born before the end of the full period of gestation. [C16: < L *praemātūrus* very early < *prae* in advance + *mātūrus* ripe] —**ˌpremaˈturely** *adv.*

premedical (priːˈmɛdɪkᵊl) *adj.* **1.** of or relating to a course of study prerequisite for entering medical school. **2.** of or relating to a person engaged in such a course of study.

premedication (ˌpriːmɛdɪˈkeɪʃən) *n. Surgery.* any drugs administered to sedate and otherwise prepare a patient for general anaesthesia.

premeditate (prɪˈmɛdɪˌteɪt) *vb.* to plan or consider (something, such as a violent crime) beforehand. —**preˈmediˌtator** *n.*

premeditation (prɪˌmɛdɪˈteɪʃən) *n.* **1.** *Law.* prior resolve to do some act or to commit a crime. **2.** the act of premeditating.

premenstrual tension *or* **syndrome** *n.* symp-

ˈpreˈflight *adj.*
preˈform *vb.*
ˌpreforˈmation *n.*
preˈfranked *adj.*
preˈfreeze *vb.*
ˌpre-Gerˈmanic *adj.*
pre-ˈGreek *adj.*
preˈharden *vb.*
preˈheat *vb.*
ˌpre-Hoˈmeric *adj.*
preˈindiˌcate *vb.*
ˌpreinˈdustrial *adj.*
ˌpreinˈform *vb.*
ˌpreinˈstruct *vb.*
pre-ˈMarxian *adj.*
preˈmenstrual *adj.*

toms, esp. nervous tension, that may be experienced because of hormonal changes in the days before a menstrual period starts.

premier (ˈprɛmjə) *n.* **1.** another name for **prime minister. 2.** any of the heads of government of the Canadian provinces and the Australian states. **3.** *Austral.* a team that wins a premiership. ~*adj.* (*prenominal*) **4.** first in importance, rank, etc. **5.** first in occurrence; earliest. [C15: < OF: first, < L *prīmārius* principal, < *prīmus* first]

premiere (ˈprɛmɪˌɛə, ˈprɛmɪə) *n.* **1.** the first public performance of a film, play, opera, etc. **2.** the leading lady in a theatre company. ~*vb.* **3.** (*tr.*) to give a premier of: *the show will be premiered on Broadway.* [C19: < F, fem. of *premier* first]

premiership (ˈprɛmjəʃɪp) *n.* **1.** the office of premier. **2.** *Austral.* **a.** a championship competition held among a number of sporting clubs. **b.** a victory in such a championship.

premillennialism (ˌpriːmɪˈlɛnɪəˌlɪzəm) *n.* the doctrine or belief that the millennium will be preceded by the Second Coming of Christ. —ˌ**premilˈlennialist** *n.* —ˌ**premilleˈnarian** *n., adj.*

premise *n. also* **premiss.** (ˈprɛmɪs). **1.** *Logic.* a statement that is assumed to be true for the purpose of an argument from which a conclusion is drawn. ~*vb.* (prɪˈmɪz, ˈprɛmɪs). **2.** (when *tr., may take a clause as object*) to state or assume (a proposition) as a premise in an argument, etc. [C14: < OF *prémisse,* < Med. L *praemissa* sent on before, < L *praemittere* to dispatch in advance]

premises (ˈprɛmɪsɪz) *pl. n.* **1.** a piece of land together with its buildings, esp. considered as a place of business. **2.** *Law.* (in a deed, etc.) the matters referred to previously; the aforesaid.

premium (ˈpriːmɪəm) *n.* **1.** an amount paid in addition to a standard rate, price, wage, etc.; bonus. **2.** the amount paid or payable, usually in regular instalments, for an insurance policy. **3.** the amount above nominal or par value at which something sells. **4.** an offer of something free or at a reduced price as an inducement to buy a commodity or service. **5.** a prize given to the winner of a competition. **6.** *U.S.* an amount sometimes charged for a loan of money in addition to the interest. **7.** great value or regard: *to put a premium on someone's services.* **8. at a premium. a.** in great demand, usually because of scarcity. **b.** above par. [C17: < L *praemium* prize]

Premium Savings Bonds *pl. n.* (in Britain) bonds issued by the Treasury since 1956 for purchase by the public. No interest is paid but there is a monthly draw for cash prizes of various sums. Also called: **premium bonds.**

premolar (priːˈməʊlə) *adj.* **1.** situated before a molar tooth. ~*n.* **2.** any one of eight bicuspid teeth in the human adult, two on each side of both jaws between the first molar and the canine.

premonition (ˌprɛməˈnɪʃən) *n.* **1.** an intuition of a future, usually unwelcome, occurrence; foreboding. **2.** an early warning of a future event. [C16: < LL *praemonitiō,* < L *praemonēre* to admonish beforehand, < *prae* before + *monēre* to warn] —**premonitory** (prɪˈmɒnɪtərɪ, -trɪ) *adj.*

Premonstratensian (ˌpriːmɒnstrəˈtɛnsɪən) *adj.* **1.** of or denoting an order of regular canons founded in 1119 at Prémontré, in France. ~*n.* **2.** a member of this order.

prenatal (priːˈneɪtᵊl) *adj.* **1.** occurring or present before birth; during pregnancy. ~*n.* **2.** *Inf.* a prenatal examination. ~Also: **antenatal.**

prenominal (priːˈnɒmɪnᵊl) *adj.* placed before a noun, esp. (of an adjective or sense of an adjective) used only before a noun.

prentice (ˈprɛntɪs) *n.* an archaic word for **apprentice.**

preoccupation (priːˌɒkjʊˈpeɪʃən) *n.* **1.** the state of being preoccupied, esp. mentally. **2.** something that preoccupies the mind.

preoccupied (priːˈɒkjʊˌpaɪd) *adj.* **1.** engrossed or absorbed in something, esp. one's own thoughts. **2.** already occupied or used.

preoccupy (priːˈɒkjʊˌpaɪ) *vb.* **-pying, -pied.** (*tr.*) **1.** to engross the thoughts or mind of. **2.** to occupy before or in advance of another. [C16: < L *praeoccupāre* to capture in advance]

preordain (ˌpriːɔːˈdeɪn) *vb.* (*tr.*) to ordain, decree, or appoint beforehand.

prep (prɛp) *n. Inf.* short for **preparation** (sense 5) or (chiefly U.S.) **preparatory school.**

prep. *abbrev. for:* **1.** preparation. **2.** preparatory. **3.** preposition.

preparation (ˌprɛpəˈreɪʃən) *n.* **1.** the act or process of preparing. **2.** the state of being prepared; readiness. **3.** (*often pl.*) a measure done in order to prepare for something; provision: *to make preparations for something.* **4.** something that is prepared, esp. a medicine. **5.** (esp. in a boarding school) **a.** homework. **b.** the period reserved for this. Usually shortened to **prep. 6.** *Music.* **a.** the anticipation of a dissonance so that the note producing it in one chord is first heard in the preceding chord as a consonance. **b.** a note so employed.

preparative (prɪˈpærətɪv) *adj.* **1.** preparatory. ~*n.* **2.** something that prepares. —**preˈparatively** *adv.*

preparatory (prɪˈpærətərɪ, -trɪ) *adj.* **1.** serving to prepare. **2.** introductory. **3.** occupied in preparation. **4. preparatory to.** before: *a drink preparatory to eating.* —**preˈparatorily** *adv.*

preparatory school *n.* **1.** (in Britain) a private school, usually single-sex and for children between the ages of 6 and 13, generally preparing pupils for public school. **2.** (in the U.S.) a private secondary school preparing pupils for college. ~Often shortened to **prep school.**

prepare (prɪˈpɛə) *vb.* **1.** to make ready or suitable in advance for some use, event, etc.: *to prepare a meal; to prepare to go.* **2.** to put together using parts or ingredients; construct. **3.** (*tr.*) to equip or outfit, as for an expedition. **4.** (*tr.*) *Music.* to soften the impact of (a dissonant note) by the use of preparation. **5. be prepared.** (*foll. by an infinitive*) to be willing and able: *I'm not prepared to reveal these figures.* [C15: < L *praeparāre,* < *prae* before + *parāre* to make ready] —**preˈparer** *n.*

preparedness (prɪˈpɛərɪdnɪs) *n.* the state of being prepared, esp. militarily ready for war.

prepay (priːˈpeɪ) *vb.* **-paying, -paid.** (*tr.*) to pay for in advance. —**preˈpayable** *adj.*

prepense (prɪˈpɛns) *adj.* (*postpositive*) (usually in legal contexts) premeditated (esp. in **malice prepense**). [C18: < Anglo-Norman *purpensé,* < OF *purpenser* to consider in advance, < L *pēnsāre* to consider]

preponderant (prɪˈpɒndərənt) *adj.* greater in weight, force, influence, etc. —**preˈponderance** *n.* —**preˈponderantly** *adv.*

preponderate (prɪˈpɒndəˌreɪt) *vb.* (*intr.*) **1.** (often foll. by *over*) to be more powerful, important, numerous, etc. (than). **2.** to be of greater weight than something else. [C17: < LL *praeponderāre* to be of greater weight, < *pondus* weight] —**preˌponderˈation** *n.*

preposition (ˌprɛpəˈzɪʃən) *n.* a word or group of words used before a noun or pronoun to relate it grammatically or semantically to some other constituent of a sentence. [C14: < L *praepositiō* a putting before, < *pōnere* to place] —ˌ**prepoˈsitional** *adj.* —ˌ**prepoˈsitionally** *adv.*

▷ **Usage.** The practice of ending a sentence with a preposition (*they are the people I hate talking to*) has been much condemned, but careful users avoid it only where it would be stylistically clumsy.

---

preˈmix *vb.*
preˈnuptial *adj.*
preˈpack *vb.*
preˈpackage *vb.*
preˈpacked *adj.*
preˈpalatal *adj.*
preˈplan *vb.*

prepossess (ˌpriːpəˈzɛs) *vb.* (*tr.*) **1.** to preoccupy or engross mentally. **2.** to influence in advance, esp. to make a favourable impression on beforehand. —ˌ**preposˈsession** *n.*

prepossessing (ˌpriːpəˈzɛsɪŋ) *adj.* creating a favourable impression; attractive.

preposterous (prɪˈpɒstərəs) *adj.* contrary to nature, reason, or sense; absurd; ridiculous. [C16: < L *praeposterus* reversed, < *prae* in front + *posterus* following] —**preˈposterously** *adv.* —**preˈposterousness** *n.*

prepotency (prɪˈpəutᵊnsɪ) *n.* **1.** the quality of possessing greater power or influence. **2.** *Genetics.* the ability of one parent to transmit more characteristics to its offspring than the other parent. **3.** *Bot.* the ability of pollen from one source to bring about fertilization more readily than that from other sources. —**preˈpotent** *adj.*

preppy (ˈprɛpɪ) *Inf.* ~*adj.* **1.** of or denoting a style of neat, understated, and often expensive clothes; young but classic. ~*n., pl.* **-pies. 2.** a person exhibiting such style. [C20: orig. U.S., < *preppy* a person who attends a PREPARATORY SCHOOL]

prep school *n. Inf.* See **preparatory school.**

prepuce (ˈpriːpjuːs) *n.* **1.** the retractable fold of skin covering the tip of the penis. Nontechnical name: **foreskin. 2.** a similar fold of skin covering the tip of the clitoris. [C14: < L *praepūtium*]

prequel (ˈpriːkwəl) *n.* a film that is made about an earlier stage of a story or character's life because the later part of it has already made a successful film. [C20: < PRE- + (*se*)*quel*]

Pre-Raphaelite (ˌpriːˈræfəlaɪt) *n.* **1.** a member of the **Pre-Raphaelite Brotherhood,** an association of painters and writers founded in 1848 to revive the fidelity to nature and the vivid realistic colour considered typical of Italian painting before Raphael. ~*adj.* **2.** of, in the manner of, or relating to Pre-Raphaelite painting and painters. —ˌ**Pre-ˈRaphaelitˌism** *n.*

prerequisite (priːˈrɛkwɪzɪt) *adj.* **1.** required as a prior condition. ~*n.* **2.** something required as a prior condition.

prerogative (prɪˈrɒgətɪv) *n.* **1.** an exclusive privilege or right exercised by a person or group of people holding a particular office or hereditary rank. **2.** any privilege or right. **3.** a power, privilege, or immunity restricted to a sovereign or sovereign government. ~*adj.* **4.** having or able to exercise a prerogative. [C14: < L *praerogātīva* privilege, earlier: group with the right to vote first, < *prae* before + *rogāre* to ask]

pres. *abbrev. for:* **1.** present (time). **2.** presidential.

Pres. *abbrev. for* President.

presage *n.* (ˈprɛsɪdʒ). **1.** an intimation or warning of something about to happen; portent; omen. **2.** a sense of what is about to happen; foreboding. ~*vb.* (ˈprɛsɪdʒ, prɪˈseɪdʒ). (*tr.*) **3.** to have a presentiment of. **4.** to give a forewarning of; portend. [C14: < L *praesāgium,* < *praesāgīre* to perceive beforehand] —**preˈsageful** *adj.* —**preˈsager** *n.*

presale (ˈpriːˌseɪl) *n.* the practice of arranging the sale of a product before it is available. —**preˈsell** *vb.* (*tr.*)

presbyopia (ˌprɛzbɪˈəupɪə) *n.* a progressively diminishing ability of the eye to focus, noticeable from middle to old age, caused by loss of elasticity of the crystalline lens. [C18: NL, < Gk *presbus* old man + *ōps* eye] —**presbyopic** (ˌprɛzbɪˈɒpɪk) *adj.*

presbyter (ˈprɛzbɪtə) *n.* **1. a.** an elder of a congregation in the early Christian Church. **b.** (in some Churches having episcopal politics) an official who is subordinate to a bishop and has administrative and sacerdotal functions. **2.** (in some hierarchical Churches) another name for **priest. 3.** (in the Presbyterian Church) an elder. [C16: < LL, < Gk *presbuteros* an older man, < *presbus* old man] —ˌ**presbyˈterial** *adj.*

presbyterian (ˌprɛzbɪˈtɪərɪən) *adj.* **1.** of or designating Church government by presbyters or lay elders. ~*n.* **2.** an upholder of this type of Church government. —ˌ**presbyˈterianism** *n.*

Presbyterian (ˌprɛzbɪˈtɪərɪən) *adj.* **1.** of or relating to any of various Protestant Churches governed by presbyters or lay elders and adhering to various modified forms of Calvinism. ~*n.* **2.** a member of a Presbyterian Church. —ˌ**Presbyˈterianism** *n.*

presbytery (ˈprɛzbɪtərɪ) *n., pl.* **-teries. 1.** *Presbyterian Church.* **a.** a local Church court. **b.** the congregations within the jurisdiction of any such court. **2.** the part of a church east of the choir, in which the main altar is situated; a sanctuary. **3.** presbyters or elders collectively. **4.** *R.C. Church.* the residence of a parish priest. [C15: < OF *presbiterie,* < Church L, < Gk *presbyterion;* see PRESBYTER]

prescience (ˈprɛsɪəns) *n.* knowledge of events before they take place; foreknowledge. [C14: < L *praescīre* to foreknow] —ˈ**prescient** *adj.*

prescribe (prɪˈskraɪb) *vb.* **1.** (*tr.*) to lay down as a rule or directive. **2.** *Med.* to recommend or order the use of (a drug or other remedy). [C16: < L *praescrībere* to write previously] —**preˈscriber** *n.*

prescript (ˈpriːskrɪpt) *n.* something laid down or prescribed. [C16: < L *praescriptum* something written down beforehand, < *praescrībere* to PRESCRIBE]

prescription (prɪˈskrɪpʃən) *n.* **1. a.** written instructions from a physician to a pharmacist stating the form, dosage, strength, etc., of a drug to be issued to a specific patient. **b.** the drug or remedy prescribed. **2.** written instructions for an optician on the proper grinding of lenses for spectacles. **3.** the act of prescribing. **4.** something that is prescribed. **5.** a long-established custom or a claim based on one. **6.** *Law.* **a.** the uninterrupted possession of property over a stated time, after which a right or title is acquired (**positive prescription**). **b.** the barring of adverse claims to property, etc., after a specified time has elapsed, allowing the possessor to acquire title (**negative prescription**). [C14: < legal L *praescriptiō* an order; see PRESCRIBE]

prescriptive (prɪˈskrɪptɪv) *adj.* **1.** making or giving directions, rules, or injunctions. **2.** sanctioned by long-standing custom. **3.** based upon legal prescription: *a prescriptive title.* —**preˈscriptively** *adv.* —**preˈscriptiveness** *n.*

presence (ˈprɛzəns) *n.* **1.** the state or fact of being present. **2.** immediate proximity. **3.** personal appearance or bearing, esp. of a dignified nature. **4.** an imposing or dignified personality. **5.** an invisible spirit felt to be nearby. **6.** *Electronics.* a recording control that boosts mid-range frequencies. **7.** *Obs.* assembly or company. [C14: via OF < L *praesentia* a being before, < *praeesse* to be before]

presence chamber *n.* the room in which a great person, such as a monarch, receives guests, assemblies, etc.

presence of mind *n.* the ability to remain calm and act constructively during times of crisis.

present[1] (ˈprɛzᵊnt) *adj.* **1.** (*prenominal*) in existence at the time at which something is spoken or written. **2.** (*postpositive*) being in a specified place, thing, etc.: *the murderer is present in this room.* **3.** (*prenominal*) now being dealt with or under discussion: *the present author.* **4.** *Grammar.* denoting a tense of verbs used when the action or event described is occurring at the time of utterance or when the speaker does not

---

preˈprandial *adj.*
ˌ**prepubliˈcation** *adj.*
ˌ**prereˈcord** *vb.*
ˌ**pre-Reforˈmation** *adj.*
preˈregister *vb.*
ˌ**preregisˈtration** *n.*
ˌ**pre-Reˈnaissance** *adj.*
pre-ˈRoman *adj.*
ˌ**pre-Roˈmantic** *adj.*
ˈ**preˈschool** *adj.*
ˌ**preseˈlect** *vb.*

wish to make any explicit temporal reference. **5.** *Arch.* instant: *present help is at hand.* ~*n.* **6.** *Grammar.* **a.** the present tense. **b.** a verb in this tense. **7. at present.** now. **8. for the present.** for the time being; temporarily. **9. the present.** the time being; now. ~See also **presents.** [C13: < L *praesens,* < *praeesse* to be in front of]

present[2] *vb.* (prɪˈzɛnt). (*mainly tr.*) **1.** to introduce (a person) to another, esp. to someone of higher rank. **2.** to introduce to the public: *to present a play.* **3.** to introduce and compere (a radio or television show). **4.** to show; exhibit: *he presented a brave face to the world.* **5.** to bring or suggest to the mind: *to present a problem.* **6.** to put forward; submit: *she presented a proposal for a new book.* **7.** to award: *to present a prize; to present a university with a foundation scholarship.* **8.** to offer formally: *to present one's compliments.* **9.** to hand over for action or settlement: *to present a bill.* **10.** to depict in a particular manner: *the actor presented Hamlet as a very young man.* **11.** to salute someone with (one's weapon) (usually in **present arms**). **12.** to aim (a weapon). **13.** to nominate (a clergyman) to a bishop for institution to a benefice in his diocese. **14.** to lay (a charge, etc.) before a court, magistrate, etc., for consideration or trial. **15.** to bring a formal charge or accusation against (a person); indict. **16.** (*intr.*) *Med.* to seek treatment for a particular problem: *she presented with postnatal depression.* **17.** (*intr.*) *Inf.* to produce a specified impression: *she presents well in public.* **18. present oneself.** to appear, esp. at a specific time and place. ~*n.* (ˈprɛzᵊnt). **19.** a gift. [C13: < OF *presenter,* < L *praesentāre* to exhibit, < *praesens* PRESENT[1]]

presentable (prɪˈzɛntəbᵊl) *adj.* **1.** fit to be presented or introduced to other people. **2.** fit to be displayed or offered. —**preˈsentableness** *or* **preˌsentaˈbility** *n.* —**preˈsentably** *adv.*

presentation (ˌprɛzənˈteɪʃən) *n.* **1.** the act of presenting or state of being presented. **2.** the manner of presenting; delivery or overall impression. **3.** a verbal report, often with illustrative material: *a presentation on the company results.* **4. a.** an offering, as of a gift. **b.** (*as modifier*): *a presentation copy of a book.* **5.** a performance or representation, as of a play. **6.** the formal introduction of a person, as at court; debut. **7.** the act or right of nominating a clergyman to a benefice. —ˌ**presenˈtational** *adj.*

presentationism (ˌprɛzənˈteɪʃəˌnɪzəm) *n. Philosophy.* the theory that objects are identical with our perceptions of them. Cf. **representationalism.** —ˌ**presenˈtationist** *n., adj.*

presentative (prɪˈzɛntətɪv) *adj.* **1.** *Philosophy.* able to be known or perceived immediately. **2.** conferring the right of ecclesiastical presentation.

present-day *n.* (*modifier*) of the modern day; current: *I don't like present-day fashions.*

presenter (prɪˈzɜntə) *n.* **1.** a person who presents something or someone. **2.** *Radio, television.* a person who introduces a show, links items, etc.

presentient (prɪˈsɛnʃənt) *adj.* characterized by or experiencing a presentiment. [C19: < L *praesentiens,* < *praesentire,* < *prae-* PRE- + *sentire* to feel]

presentiment (prɪˈzɛntɪmənt) *n.* a sense of something about to happen; premonition. [C18: < obs. F, < *pressentir* to sense beforehand]

presently (ˈprɛzəntlɪ) *adv.* **1.** in a short while; soon. **2.** *Chiefly Scot., U.S., & Canad.* at the moment. **3.** an archaic word for **immediately.**

presentment (prɪˈzɛntmənt) *n.* **1.** the act of presenting or state of being presented; presentation. **2.** something presented, such as a picture, play, etc. **3.** *Law.* a statement on oath by a jury of something within their own knowledge or observation. **4.** *Commerce.* the presenting of a bill of exchange, promissory note, etc.

present participle (ˈprɛzᵊnt) *n.* a participial form of verbs used adjectivally when the action it describes is contemporaneous with that of the main verb of a sentence and also used in the formation of certain compound tenses. In English this form ends in *-ing.*

present perfect (ˈprɛzᵊnt) *adj., n. Grammar.* another term for **perfect** (senses 8, 10).

presents (ˈprɛzənts) *pl. n. Law.* used in a deed or document to refer to itself: *know all men by these presents.*

preservative (prɪˈzɜːvətɪv) *n.* **1.** something that preserves, esp. a chemical added to foods. ~*adj.* **2.** tending or intended to preserve.

preserve (prɪˈzɜːv) *vb.* (*mainly tr.*) **1.** to keep safe from danger or harm; protect. **2.** to protect from decay or dissolution; maintain: *to preserve old buildings.* **3.** to maintain possession of; keep up: *to preserve a façade of indifference.* **4.** to prevent from decomposition or chemical change. **5.** to prepare (food), as by salting, so that it will resist decomposition. **6.** to make preserves of (fruit, etc.). **7.** to rear and protect (game) in restricted places for hunting or fishing. **8.** (*intr.*) to maintain protection for game in preserves. ~*n.* **9.** something that preserves or is preserved. **10.** a special domain: *archaeology is the preserve of specialists.* **11.** (*usually pl.*) fruit, etc., prepared by cooking with sugar. **12.** areas where game is reared for private hunting or fishing. [C14: via OF, < LL *praeservāre,* lit.: to keep safe in advance, < L *prae* before + *servāre* to keep safe] —**preˈservable** *adj.* —**preservation** (ˌprɛzəˈveɪʃən) *n.* —**preˈserver** *n.*

preshrunk (priːˈʃrʌŋk) *adj.* (of fabrics) having undergone shrinking during manufacture so that further shrinkage will not occur.

preside (prɪˈzaɪd) *vb.* (*intr.*) **1.** to sit in or hold a position of authority, as over a meeting. **2.** to exercise authority; control. [C17: via F < L *praesidēre* to superintend, < *prae* before + *sedēre* to sit]

presidency (ˈprɛzɪdənsɪ) *n., pl.* **-cies. 1.** the office, dignity, or term of a president. **2.** (*often cap.*) the office of president of a republic, esp. of the President of the U.S.

president (ˈprɛzɪdənt) *n.* **1.** (*often cap.*) the head of state of a republic, esp. of the U.S. **2.** (in the U.S.) the chief executive officer of a company, corporation, etc. **3.** a person who presides over an assembly, meeting, etc. **4.** the chief executive officer of certain establishments of higher education. [C14: via OF < LL *praesidens* ruler; see PRESIDE] —**presidential** (ˌprɛzɪˈdɛnʃəl) *adj.* —ˌ**presiˈdentially** *adv.* —ˈ**presidentship** *n.*

presidium *or* **praesidium** (prɪˈsɪdɪəm) *n.* **1.** (*often cap.*) (in Communist countries) a permanent committee of a larger body, such as a legislature, that acts for it when it is in recess. **2.** a collective presidency. [C20: < Russian *prezidium,* < L *praesidium,* < *praesidēre* to superintend; see PRESIDE]

press[1] (prɛs) *vb.* **1.** to apply or exert weight, force, or steady pressure (on): *he pressed the button on the camera.* **2.** (*tr.*) to squeeze or compress so as to alter in shape. **3.** to apply heat or pressure to (clothing) so as to smooth out creases. **4.** to make (objects) from soft material by pressing with a mould, etc., esp. to make gramophone records from plastic. **5.** (*tr.*) to clasp; embrace. **6.** (*tr.*) to extract or force out (juice) by pressure (from). **7.** (*tr.*) to force or compel. **8.** to importune (a person) insistently: *they pressed for an answer.* **9.** to harass or cause harassment. **10.** (*tr.*) to plead or put forward strongly: *to press a claim.* **11.** (*intr.*) to be urgent. **12.** (*tr.; usually passive*) to have little of: *we're hard pressed for time.* **13.** (when *intr.*, often foll. by *on* or *forward*) to hasten or advance or cause to hasten or advance in a forceful manner. **14.** (*intr.*) to crowd; push. **15.** (*tr.*) *Arch.* to trouble or

---

preˈset *vb.*
preˈshape *vb.*
preˈshrink *vb.*
preˈsoak *vb.*
ˌ**pre-SoˈCratic** *adj.*

oppress. ~*n.* **16.** any machine that exerts pressure to form, shape, or cut materials or to extract liquids, compress solids, or hold components together while an adhesive joint is formed. **17.** See **printing press. 18.** the art or process of printing. **19. to (the) press.** to be printed: *when is this book going to press?* **20. a. the press.** news media collectively, esp. newspapers. **b.** (*as modifier*): *press relations.* **21.** the opinions and reviews in the newspapers, etc.: *the play received a poor press.* **22.** the act of pressing or state of being pressed. **23.** the act of crowding or pushing together. **24.** a closely packed throng; crowd. **25.** a cupboard, esp. a large one used for storing clothes or linen. **26.** a wood or metal clamp to prevent tennis rackets, etc., from warping when not in use. [C14 *pressen,* < OF *presser,* < L, < *premere* to press]

press[2] (prɛs) *vb.* (*tr.*) **1.** to recruit (men) by forcible measures for military service. **2.** to use for a purpose other than intended (esp. in **press into service**). ~*n.* **3.** recruitment into military service by forcible measures, as by a press gang. [C16: back formation < *prest* to recruit soldiers; also infl. by PRESS[1]]

press agent *n.* a person employed to obtain favourable publicity, such as notices in newspapers, for an organization, actor, etc.

press box *n.* an area reserved for reporters, as in a sports stadium.

press conference *n.* an interview for press reporters given by a politician, film star, etc.

press gallery *n.* an area for newspaper reporters, esp. in a legislative assembly.

press gang *n.* **1.** (formerly) a detachment of men used to press civilians for service in the navy or army. ~*vb.* **press-gang.** (*tr.*) **2.** to force (a person) to join the navy or army by a press gang. **3.** to induce (a person) to perform a duty by forceful persuasion.

pressing (ˈprɛsɪŋ) *adj.* **1.** demanding immediate attention. **2.** persistent or importunate. ~*n.* **3.** a large specified number of gramophone records produced at one time from a master record. —**ˈpressingly** *adv.*

pressman (ˈprɛsmən, -ˌmæn) *n., pl.* **-men. 1.** a journalist. **2.** a person who operates a printing press.

press of sail *n. Naut.* the most sail a vessel can carry under given conditions. Also called: **press of canvas.**

press release *n.* an official announcement or account of a news item circulated to the press.

pressroom (ˈprɛsˌruːm, -ˌrʊm) *n.* the room in a printing establishment that houses the printing presses.

press stud *n.* a fastening device consisting of one part with a projecting knob that snaps into a hole on another like part, used esp. on clothing. Canad. equivalent: **dome fastener.**

press-up *n.* an exercise in which the body is alternately raised from and lowered to the floor by the arms only, the trunk being kept straight. Also called (U.S. and Canad.): **push-up.**

pressure (ˈprɛʃə) *n.* **1.** the state of pressing or being pressed. **2.** the exertion of force by one body on the surface of another. **3.** a moral force that compels: *to bring pressure to bear.* **4.** urgent claims or demands: *to work under pressure.* **5.** a burdensome condition that is hard to bear: *the pressure of grief.* **6.** the force applied to a unit area of a surface, usually measured in pascals, millibars, torrs, or atmospheres. **7.** short for **atmospheric pressure** or **blood pressure.** ~*vb.* (*tr.*) **8.** to constrain or compel, as by moral force. **9.** another word for **pressurize.** [C14: < LL *pressūra* a pressing, < L *premere* to press]

pressure cooker *n.* a strong hermetically sealed pot in which food may be cooked quickly under pressure at a temperature above the normal boiling point of water. —**ˈpressure-ˌcook** *vb.*

pressure group *n.* a group of people who seek to exert pressure on legislators, public opinion, etc., in order to promote their own ideas or welfare.

pressure point *n.* any of several points on the body above an artery that, when firmly pressed, will control bleeding from the artery at a point farther away from the heart.

pressure suit *n.* an inflatable suit worn by a person flying at high altitudes or in space, to provide protection from low pressure.

pressurize *or* **-ise** (ˈprɛʃəˌraɪz) *vb.* (*tr.*) **1.** to increase the pressure in (an enclosure, such as an aircraft cabin) in order to maintain approximately atmospheric pressure when the external pressure is low. **2.** to increase pressure on (a fluid). **3.** to make insistent demands of (someone); coerce. —**ˌpressuriˈzation** *or* **-iˈsation** *n.*

pressurized-water reactor *n.* a type of nuclear reactor that uses water under pressure as both coolant and moderator.

presswork (ˈprɛsˌwɜːk) *n.* the operation of, or matter printed by, a printing press.

Prestel (ˈprɛstɛl) *n. Trademark.* (in Britain) the Post Office public viewdata service.

Prester John (ˈprɛstə) *n.* a legendary Christian priest and king, believed in the Middle Ages to have ruled in the Far East, but identified in the 14th century with the king of Ethiopia. [C14 *Prestre Johan,* < Med. L *presbyter Iohannes* Priest John]

prestidigitation (ˌprɛstɪˌdɪdʒɪˈteɪʃən) *n.* another name for **sleight of hand.** [C19: < F: quick-fingeredness, < L *praestigiae* tricks, prob. infl. by F *preste* nimble, & L *digitus* finger] —**ˌprestiˈdigiˌtator** *n.*

prestige (prɛˈstiːʒ) *n.* **1.** high status or reputation achieved through success, influence, wealth, etc.; renown. **2. a.** the power to impress; glamour. **b.** (*modifier*): *a prestige car.* [C17: via F < L *praestigiae* tricks] —**prestigious** (prɛˈstɪdʒəs) *adj.*

prestissimo (prɛˈstɪsɪˌməʊ) *Music.* ~*adj., adv.* **1.** to be played as fast as possible. ~*n., pl.* **-mos. 2.** a piece to be played in this way. [C18: < It.: very quickly, < *presto* fast]

presto (ˈprɛstəʊ) *adj., adv.* **1.** *Music.* to be played very fast. ~*adv.* **2.** immediately (esp. in **hey presto**). ~*n., pl.* **-tos. 3.** *Music.* a passage directed to be played very quickly. [C16: < It.: fast, < LL *praestus* (adj.) ready to hand, L *praestō* (adv.) present]

prestressed concrete (ˌpriːˈstrɛst) *n.* concrete that contains steel wires that are stretched to counteract the stresses that will occur under load.

presumably (prɪˈzjuːməblɪ) *adv.* (*sentence modifier*) one supposes that: *presumably he won't see you, if you're leaving tomorrow.*

presume (prɪˈzjuːm) *vb.* **1.** (when *tr., often takes a clause as object*) to take (something) for granted; assume. **2.** (when *tr., often foll. by an infinitive*) to dare (to do something): *do you presume to copy my work?* **3.** (*intr.;* foll. by *on* or *upon*) to rely or depend: *don't presume on his agreement.* **4.** (*intr.;* foll. by *on* or *upon*) to take advantage (of): *don't presume upon his good nature too far.* **5.** (*tr.*) *Law.* to take as proved until contrary evidence is produced. [C14: via OF < L *praesūmere* to take in advance, < *prae* before + *sūmere* to ASSUME] —**presumedly** (prɪˈzjuːmɪdlɪ) *adv.* —**preˈsuming** *adj.*

presumption (prɪˈzʌmpʃən) *n.* **1.** the act of presuming. **2.** bold or insolent behaviour. **3.** a belief or assumption based on reasonable evidence. **4.** a basis on which to presume. **5.** *Law.* an inference of the truth of a fact from other facts proved. [C13: via OF < L *praesumptiō* anticipation, < *praesūmere* to take beforehand; see PRESUME]

presumptive (prɪˈzʌmptɪv) *adj.* **1.** based on presumption or probability. **2.** affording reasonable ground for belief. —**preˈsumptively** *adv.*

presumptuous (prɪˈzʌmptjʊəs) *adj.* characterized by presumption or tending to presume; bold; forward. —**preˈsumptuously** *adv.* —**preˈsumptuousness** *n.*

presuppose (ˌpriːsəˈpəʊz) *vb.* (*tr.*) **1.** to take for granted. **2.** to require as a necessary prior condition. —**presupposition** (ˌpriːsʌpəˈzɪʃən) *n.*

pretence *or U.S.* **pretense** (prɪˈtɛns) *n.* **1.** the act of pretending. **2.** a false display; affectation. **3.** a claim, esp. a false one, to a right, title, or distinction. **4.** make-believe. **5.** a pretext.

pretend (prɪˈtɛnd) *vb.* **1.** (when *tr., usually takes a clause as object or an infinitive*) to claim or allege (something untrue). **2.** (*tr.; may take a clause as object or an infinitive*) to make believe, as in a play: *you pretend to be Ophelia.* **3.** (*intr.;* foll. by *to*) to present a claim, esp. a dubious one: *to pretend to the throne.* **4.** (*intr.;* foll. by *to*) *Obs.* to aspire as a candidate or suitor (for). ~*adj.* **5.** make-believe; imaginary. [C14: < L *praetendere* to stretch forth, feign]

pretender (prɪˈtɛndə) *n.* **1.** a person who pretends or makes false allegations. **2.** a person who mounts a claim, as to a throne or title.

pretension (prɪˈtɛnʃən) *n.* **1.** (*often pl.*) a false claim, esp. to merit, worth, or importance. **2.** a specious or unfounded allegation; pretext. **3.** the quality of being pretentious.

pretentious (prɪˈtɛnʃəs) *adj.* **1.** making claim to distinction or importance, esp. undeservedly. **2.** ostentatious. —**preˈtentiously** *adv.* —**preˈtentiousness** *n.*

preterite *or esp. U.S.* **preterit** (ˈprɛtərɪt) *Grammar.* ~*n.* **1.** a tense of verbs used to relate past action, formed in English by inflection of the verb, as *jumped, swam.* **2.** a verb in this tense. ~*adj.* **3.** denoting this tense. [C14: < LL *praeteritum* (*tempus*) past (time), < L *praeterīre* to go by, < *preter-* beyond + *īre* to go]

pretermit (ˌpriːtəˈmɪt) *vb.* **-mitting, -mitted.** (*tr.*) *Rare.* **1.** to disregard. **2.** to fail to do; neglect; omit. [C16: < L *praetermittere* to let pass, < *preter-* beyond + *mittere* to send]

preternatural (ˌpriːtəˈnætʃrəl) *adj.* **1.** beyond what is ordinarily found in nature; abnormal. **2.** another word for **supernatural.** [C16: < Med. L *praeternātūrālis,* < L *praeter natūram* beyond the scope of nature] —ˌ**preterˈnaturally** *adv.*

pretext (ˈpriːtɛkst) *n.* **1.** a fictitious reason given in order to conceal the real one. **2.** a pretence. [C16: < L *praetextum* disguise, < *praetexere* to weave in front, disguise]

pretor (ˈpriːtə, -tɔː) *n.* a variant (esp. U.S.) spelling of **praetor.**

prettify (ˈprɪtɪˌfaɪ) *vb.* **-fying, -fied.** (*tr.*) to make pretty, esp. in a trivial fashion; embellish. —ˌ**prettifiˈcation** *n.* —ˈ**prettiˌfier** *n.*

pretty (ˈprɪtɪ) *adj.* **-tier, -tiest.** **1.** pleasing or appealing in a delicate or graceful way. **2.** dainty, neat, or charming. **3.** *Inf., often ironical.* excellent, grand, or fine: *here's a pretty mess!* **4.** commendable; good of its kind: *he replied with a pretty wit.* **5.** *Inf.* effeminate; foppish. **6.** *Arch. or Scot.* vigorous or brave. **7. sitting pretty.** *Inf.* in a favourable or satisfactory state. ~*n., pl.* **-ties. 8.** a pretty person or thing. ~*adv. Inf.* **9.** fairly; somewhat. **10.** very. ~*vb.* **-tying, -tied. 11.** (*tr.;* often foll. by *up*) to make pretty; adorn. [OE *prættig* clever] —ˈ**prettily** *adv.* —ˈ**prettiness** *n.*

▷ **Usage.** The use of *pretty* as an adverb meaning *fairly* or *quite* is accepted informal usage but is avoided in formal contexts by careful writers of English: *the profit was fairly* (not *pretty*) *large that year.*

pretty-pretty *adj. Inf.* excessively or ostentatiously pretty.

pretzel (ˈprɛtsəl) *n.* a brittle savoury biscuit, in the form of a knot or stick, eaten esp. in Germany and the U.S. [C19: < G, < OHG *brezitella*]

prevail (prɪˈveɪl) *vb.* (*intr.*) **1.** (often foll. by *over* or *against*) to prove superior; gain mastery: *skill will prevail.* **2.** to be the most important feature; be prevalent. **3.** to exist widely; be in force. **4.** (often foll. by *on* or *upon*) to succeed in persuading or inducing. [C14: < L *praevalēre* to be superior in strength] —**preˈvailer** *n.*

prevailing (prɪˈveɪlɪŋ) *adj.* **1.** generally accepted; widespread: *the prevailing opinion.* **2.** most frequent; predominant: *the prevailing wind is from the north.* —**preˈvailingly** *adv.*

prevalent (ˈprɛvələnt) *adj.* **1.** widespread or current. **2.** superior in force or power; predominant. —ˈ**prevalence** *n.* —ˈ**prevalently** *adv.*

prevaricate (prɪˈværɪˌkeɪt) *vb.* (*intr.*) to speak or act falsely or evasively with intent to deceive. [C16: < L *praevāricārī* to walk crookedly, < *prae* beyond + *vāricare* to straddle the legs] —**preˌvariˈcation** *n.* —**preˈvariˌcator** *n.*

prevent (prɪˈvɛnt) *vb.* **1.** (*tr.*) to keep from happening, esp. by taking precautionary action. **2.** (*tr.;* often foll. by *from*) to keep (someone from doing something). **3.** (*intr.*) to interpose or act as a hindrance. **4.** (*tr.*) *Arch.* to anticipate or precede. [C15: < L *praevenīre,* < *prae* before + *venīre* to come] —**preˈventable** *or* **preˈventible** *adj.* —**preˈventably** *or* **preˈventibly** *adv.*

▷ **Usage.** *Prevent* in the sense of definition 2, above, is in strict usage followed either by *from* or by the possessive case: *there is nothing to prevent Mary from going* or *there is nothing to prevent Mary's going.* The use of prevent in a construction such as *there is nothing to prevent Mary going* is regarded by careful writers and speakers of English as less acceptable and should be restricted to informal contexts.

prevention (prɪˈvɛnʃən) *n.* **1.** the act of preventing. **2.** a hindrance or impediment.

preventive (prɪˈvɛntɪv) *adj.* **1.** tending or intended to prevent or hinder. **2.** *Med.* tending to prevent disease; prophylactic. **3.** (in Britain) of, relating to, or belonging to the customs and excise service or the coastguard. ~*n.* **4.** something that serves to prevent or hinder. **5.** *Med.* any drug or agent that tends to prevent disease. Also (for senses 1, 2, 4, 5): **preventative.** —**preˈventively** *or* **preˈventatively** *adv.*

preview (ˈpriːvjuː) *n.* **1.** an advance view or sight. **2.** an advance showing before public presentation of a film, art exhibition, etc., usually before an invited audience. ~*vb.* **3.** (*tr.*) to view in advance.

previous (ˈpriːvɪəs) *adj.* **1.** (*prenominal*) existing or coming before something else. **2.** (*postpositive*) *Inf.* taking place or done too soon; premature. **3. previous to.** before. [C17: < L *praevius* leading the way, < *prae* before + *via* way] —ˈ**previously** *adv.* —ˈ**previousness** *n.*

previous question *n.* **1.** (in the House of Commons) a motion to drop the present topic under debate, put in order to prevent a vote. **2.** (in the House of Lords and U.S. legislative bodies) a motion to vote on a bill without delay.

previse (prɪˈvaɪz) *vb.* (*tr.*) *Rare.* **1.** to predict or foresee. **2.** to notify in advance. [C16: < L *praevidēre* to foresee] —**prevision** (prɪˈvɪʒən) *n.*

prey (preɪ) *n.* **1.** an animal hunted or captured by another for food. **2.** a person or thing that becomes the victim of a hostile person, influence, etc. **3. bird** *or* **beast of prey.** a bird or animal that preys on others for food. **4.** an archaic word for **booty.** ~*vb.* (*intr.;* often foll. by *on* or *upon*) **5.** to hunt food by killing other animals. **6.** to make a victim (of others), as by profiting at their expense. **7.** to exert a depressing or obsessive effect (on the mind, spirits, etc.). [C13: < OF *preie,* < L *praeda* booty] —ˈ**preyer** *n.*

priapic (praɪˈæpɪk, -ˈeɪ-) *or* **priapean** (ˌpraɪəˈpiːən) *adj.* **1.** (*sometimes cap.*) of or relating to Priapus, in classical antiquity the god of male procreative power and of gardens and vineyards. **2.** a less common word for **phallic.**

priapism (ˈpraɪəˌpɪzəm) *n. Pathol.* prolonged painful erection of the penis, caused by

---

preˈsurgical *adj.*
preˈtest *vb.*
ˈ**preˈwar** *adj.*
preˈwarm *vb.*

neurological disorders, etc. [C17: < LL *priăpismus*, ult. < Gk *Priapus*; see PRIAPIC]

price (praɪs) *n.* **1.** the sum in money or goods for which anything is or may be bought or sold. **2.** the cost at which anything is obtained. **3.** the cost of bribing a person. **4.** a sum of money offered as a reward for a capture or killing. **5.** value or worth, esp. high worth. **6.** *Gambling.* another word for **odds.** **7. at any price.** whatever the price or cost. **8. at a price.** at a high price. **9. what price (something)?** what are the chances of (something) happening now? ~*vb.* (*tr.*) **10.** to fix the price of. **11.** to discover the price of. **12. price out of the market.** to charge so highly for as to prevent the sale, hire, etc., of. [C13 *pris*, < OF, < L *pretium*] —ˈ**pricer** *n.*

price control *n.* the establishment and maintenance of maximum price levels for basic goods and services by a government.

price-fixing *n.* **1.** the setting of prices by agreement among producers and distributors. **2.** another name for **price control** or **resale price maintenance.**

priceless (ˈpraɪslɪs) *adj.* **1.** of inestimable worth; invaluable. **2.** *Inf.* extremely amusing or ridiculous. —ˈ**pricelessly** *adv.* —ˈ**pricelessness** *n.*

price ring *n.* a group of traders formed to maintain the prices of their goods.

pricey *or* **pricy** (ˈpraɪsɪ) *adj.* **pricier, priciest.** an informal word for **expensive.**

prick (prɪk) *vb.* (*mainly tr.*) **1. a.** to make (a small hole) in (something) by piercing lightly with a sharp point. **b.** to wound in this manner. **2.** (*intr.*) to cause or have a piercing or stinging sensation. **3.** to cause to feel a sharp emotional pain: *knowledge of such poverty pricked his conscience.* **4.** to puncture. **5.** to outline by dots or punctures. **6.** (*also intr.*; usually foll. by *up*) to rise or raise erect: *the dog pricked his ears up.* **7.** (usually foll. by *out* or *off*) to transplant (seedlings) into a larger container. **8.** *Arch.* to urge on, esp. to spur a horse on. **9. prick up one's ears.** to start to listen attentively; become interested. ~*n.* **10.** the act of pricking or the sensation of being pricked. **11.** a mark made by a sharp point; puncture. **12.** a sharp emotional pain: *a prick of conscience.* **13.** a taboo slang word for **penis.** **14.** *Sl., derog.* an obnoxious or despicable person. **15.** an instrument or weapon with a sharp point. **16.** the track of an animal, esp. a hare. **17. kick against the pricks.** to hurt oneself by struggling against something in vain. [OE *prica* point, puncture] —ˈ**pricker** *n.*

pricket (ˈprɪkɪt) *n.* **1.** a male deer in the second year of life having unbranched antlers. **2.** a sharp metal spike on which to stick a candle. [C14 *priket*, < *prik* PRICK]

prickle (ˈprɪkᵊl) *n.* **1.** *Bot.* a pointed process arising from the outer layer of a stem, leaf, etc., and containing no woody tissue. Cf. **thorn.** **2.** a pricking or stinging sensation. ~*vb.* **3.** to feel or cause to feel a stinging sensation. **4.** (*tr.*) to prick, as with a thorn. [OE *pricel*]

prickly (ˈprɪklɪ) *adj.* **-lier, -liest.** **1.** having or covered with prickles. **2.** stinging. **3.** irritable. **4.** full of difficulties: *a prickly problem.* —ˈ**prickliness** *n.*

prickly heat *n.* a nontechnical name for **miliaria.**

prickly pear *n.* **1.** any of various tropical cactuses having flattened or cylindrical spiny joints and oval fruit that is edible in some species. **2.** the fruit of any of these plants.

pride (praɪd) *n.* **1.** a feeling of honour and self-respect; a sense of personal worth. **2.** excessive self-esteem; conceit. **3.** a source of pride. **4.** satisfaction or pleasure in one's own or another's success, achievements, etc. (esp. in **take (a) pride in**). **5.** the better or superior part of something. **6.** the most flourishing time. **7.** a group (of lions). **8.** courage; spirit. **9.** *Arch.* pomp or splendour. **10. pride of place.** the most important position. ~*vb.* **11.** (*tr.*; foll. by *on* or *upon*) to take pride in (oneself) for. [OE *prȳda*] —ˈ**prideful** *adj.* —ˈ**pridefully** *adv.*

prie-dieu (priːˈdjɜː) *n.* a piece of furniture consisting of a low surface for kneeling upon and a narrow front surmounted by a rest, for use when praying. [C18: < F, < *prier* to pray + *Dieu* God]

prier *or* **pryer** (ˈpraɪə) *n.* a person who pries.

priest (priːst) *n.* **1.** a person ordained to act as a mediator between God and man in administering the sacraments, preaching, etc. **2.** (in episcopal Churches) a minister in the second grade of the hierarchy of holy orders, ranking below a bishop but above a deacon. **3.** a minister of any religion. **4.** an official who offers sacrifice on behalf of the people and performs other religious ceremonies. ~*vb.* **5.** (*tr.*) to make a priest; ordain. [OE *prēost*, apparently < PRESBYTER] —ˈ**priestess** *fem. n.* —ˈ**priest,hood** *n.* —ˈ**priest,like** *adj.* —ˈ**priestly** *adj.*

priestcraft (ˈpriːst,krɑːft) *n.* **1.** the art and skills involved in the work of a priest. **2.** *Derog.* the influence of priests upon politics.

priest-hole *or* **priest's hole** *n.* a secret chamber in certain houses in England, built as a hiding place for Roman Catholic priests when they were proscribed in the 16th and 17th centuries.

prig[1] (prɪg) *n.* a person who is smugly self-righteous and narrow-minded. [C18: <?] —ˈ**priggery** *or* ˈ**priggishness** *n.* —ˈ**priggish** *adj.* —ˈ**priggishly** *adv.*

prig[2] (prɪg) *Brit. sl.* ~*vb.* **prigging, prigged.** **1.** another word for **steal.** ~*n.* **2.** another word for **thief.** [C16: <?]

prim (prɪm) *adj.* **primmer, primmest.** **1.** affectedly proper, precise, or formal. ~*vb.* **primming, primmed.** **2.** (*tr.*) to make prim. **3.** to purse (the mouth) primly or (of the mouth) to be so pursed. [C18: <?] —ˈ**primly** *adv.* —ˈ**primness** *n.*

prima ballerina (ˈpriːmə) *n.* a leading female ballet dancer. [< It., lit.: first ballerina]

primacy (ˈpraɪməsɪ) *n., pl.* **-cies.** **1.** the state of being first in rank, grade, etc. **2.** *Christianity.* the office, rank, or jurisdiction of a primate, senior bishop, or pope.

prima donna (ˈpriːmə ˈdɒnə) *n., pl.* **prima donnas.** **1.** a leading female operatic star. **2.** *Inf.* a temperamental person. [C19: < It.: first lady]

prima facie (ˈpraɪmə ˈfeɪʃɪ) *adv.* at first sight; as it seems at first. [C15: < L, < *prīmus* first + *faciēs* FACE]

prima-facie evidence *n. Law.* evidence that is sufficient to establish a fact or to raise a presumption of the truth unless controverted.

primal (ˈpraɪməl) *adj.* **1.** first or original. **2.** chief or most important. [C17: < Med. L *prīmālis*, < L *prīmus* first]

primaquine (ˈpraɪmə,kwiːn) *n.* a synthetic drug used in the treatment of malaria. [C20: < *prima-*, < L *prīmus* first + QUIN(OLIN)E]

primarily (ˈpraɪmərəlɪ) *adv.* **1.** principally; chiefly; mainly. **2.** at first; originally.

primary (ˈpraɪmərɪ) *adj.* **1.** first in importance, degree, rank, etc. **2.** first in position or time, as in a series. **3.** fundamental; basic. **4.** being the first stage; elementary. **5.** (*prenominal*) of or relating to the education of children up to the age of 11. **6.** (of the flight feathers of a bird's wing) growing from the manus. **7. a.** being the part of an electric circuit, such as a transformer, in which a changing current induces a current in a neighbouring circuit: *a primary coil.* **b.** (of a current) flowing in such a circuit. **8. a.** (of a product) consisting of a natural raw material; unmanufactured. **b.** (of production or industry) involving the extraction or winning of such products. **9.** (of Latin, Greek, or Sanskrit tenses) referring to present or future time. **10.** *Geol., obs.* relating to the Palaeozoic or earlier eras. ~*n., pl.* **-ries.** **11.** a person or thing that is first in rank, occurrence, etc. **12.** (in the U.S.) a preliminary election in which the voters of a state or region choose a party's convention delegates, nominees for office, etc. Full name: **primary election.** **13.**

short for **primary colour** or **primary school.** **14.** any of the flight feathers growing from the manus of a bird's wing. **15.** a primary coil, winding, inductance, or current in an electric circuit. **16.** *Astron.* a celestial body around which one or more specified secondary bodies orbit: *the sun is the primary of the earth.* [C15: < L *prīmārius* principal, < *prīmus* first]

primary accent *or* **stress** *n. Linguistics.* the strongest accent in a word or breath group, as that on the first syllable of *agriculture.*

primary cell *n.* an electric cell that generates an electromotive force by the direct and usually irreversible conversion of chemical energy into electrical energy. Also called: **voltaic cell.**

primary colour *n.* **1.** any of three colours (usually red, green, and blue) that can be mixed to match any other colour, including white light but excluding black. **2.** any one of the colours cyan, magenta, or yellow. An equal mixture of the three produces a black pigment. **3.** any one of the colours red, yellow, green, or blue. All other colours look like a mixture of two or more of these colours.

primary school *n.* **1.** (in England and Wales) a school for children below the age of 11. It is usually divided into an infant and a junior section. **2.** (in Scotland) a school for children below the age of 12. **3.** (in the U.S. and Canad.) a school equivalent to the first three or four grades of elementary school.

primate[1] (ˈpraɪmeɪt) *n.* **1.** any placental mammal of the order *Primates,* typically having flexible hands, good eyesight, and, in the higher apes, a highly developed brain: includes lemurs, apes, and man. ~*adj.* **2.** of, relating to, or belonging to the order *Primates.* [C18: < NL *primates,* pl. of *prīmās* principal, < *prīmus* first] —**primatial** (praɪˈmeɪʃəl) *adj.*

primate[2] (ˈpraɪmeɪt) *n.* **1.** another name for an **archbishop.** **2. Primate of all England.** the Archbishop of Canterbury. **3. Primate of England.** the Archbishop of York. [C13: < OF, < L *prīmās* principal, < *prīmus* first]

prime (praɪm) *adj.* **1.** (*prenominal*) first in quality or value; first-rate. **2.** (*prenominal*) fundamental; original. **3.** (*prenominal*) first in importance; chief. **4.** *Maths.* **a.** having no factors except itself or one: $x^2 + x + 3$ *is a prime polynomial.* **b.** (foll. by *to*) having no common factors (with): *20 is prime to 21.* **5.** *Finance.* having the best credit rating: *prime investments.* ~*n.* **6.** the time when a thing is at its best. **7.** a period of power, vigour, etc. (esp. in **the prime of life**). **8.** *Maths.* short for **prime number.** **9.** *Chiefly R.C. Church.* the second of the seven canonical hours of the divine office, originally fixed for the first hour of the day, at sunrise. **10.** the first of eight basic positions from which a parry or attack can be made in fencing. ~*vb.* **11.** to prepare (something). **12.** (*tr.*) to apply a primer, such as paint or size, to (a surface). **13.** (*tr.*) to fill (a pump) with its working fluid before starting, in order to expel air from it before starting. **14. prime the pump. a.** see **pump priming. b.** to make an initial input in order to set a process going. **15.** (*tr.*) to increase the quantity of fuel in the float chamber of (a carburettor) in order to facilitate the starting of an engine. **16.** (*tr.*) to insert a primer into (a gun, mine, etc.) preparatory to detonation or firing. **17.** (*tr.*) to provide with facts beforehand; brief. [(adj.) C14: < L *prīmus* first; (n.) C13: < L *prīma* (*hora*) the first (hour); (vb.) C16: <?] —ˈ**primeness** *n.*

prime cost *n.* the portion of the cost of a commodity that varies directly with the amount of it produced, principally comprising materials and labour. Also called: **variable cost.**

prime meridian *n.* the 0° meridian from which the other meridians are calculated, usually taken to pass through Greenwich.

prime minister *n.* **1.** the head of a parliamentary government. **2.** the chief minister of a sovereign or a state.

prime mover *n.* **1.** the original force behind an idea, enterprise, etc. **2. a.** the source of power, such as fuel, wind, electricity, etc., for a machine. **b.** the means of extracting power from such a source, such as a steam engine.

prime number *n.* an integer that cannot be factorized into other integers but is only divisible by itself or 1, such as 2, 3, 7, and 11.

primer[1] (ˈpraɪmə) *n.* an introductory text, such as a school textbook. [C14: via Anglo-Norman, < Med. L *primārius* (*liber*) a first (book), < L *prīmārius* PRIMARY]

primer[2] (ˈpraɪmə) *n.* **1.** a person or thing that primes. **2.** a device, such as a tube containing explosive, for detonating the main charge in a gun, mine, etc. **3.** a substance, such as paint, applied to a surface as a base, sealer, etc. [C15: see PRIME (vb.)]

prime rate *n.* the lowest commercial interest rate charged by a bank at a particular time.

primers (ˈprɪməz) *n.* (*functioning as sing.*) *N.Z. inf.* the youngest classes in a primary school: *in the primers.*

prime time *n.* the peak viewing time on television, for which advertising rates are the highest.

primeval *or* **primaeval** (praɪˈmiːvᵊl) *adj.* of or belonging to the first ages of the world. [C17: < L *prīmaevus* youthful, < *prīmus* first + *aevum* age] —**priˈmevally** *or* **priˈmaevally** *adv.*

priming (ˈpraɪmɪŋ) *n.* **1.** something used to prime. **2.** a substance used to ignite an explosive charge.

primitive (ˈprɪmɪtɪv) *adj.* **1.** of or belonging to the beginning; original. **2.** characteristic of an early state, esp. in being crude or uncivilized: *a primitive dwelling.* **3.** *Anthropol.* denoting a preliterate and nonindustrial social system. **4.** *Biol.* of, relating to, or resembling an early stage in development: *primitive amphibians.* **5.** showing the characteristics of primitive painters; untrained, childlike, or naive. **6.** *Geol.* of or denoting rocks formed in or before the Palaeozoic era. **7.** denoting a word from which another word is derived, as for example *hope,* from which *hopeless* is derived. **8.** *Protestant theol.* of or associated with a group that breaks away from a sect, denomination, or Church in order to return to what is regarded as the original simplicity of the Gospels. ~*n.* **9.** a primitive person or thing. **10. a.** an artist whose work does not conform to traditional standards of Western painting, such as a painter from an African civilization. **b.** a painter of the pre-Renaissance era in European painting. **c.** a painter of any era whose work appears childlike or untrained. **11.** a work by such an artist. **12.** a word from which another word is derived. **13.** *Maths.* a curve or other form from which another is derived. [C14: < L *prīmitīvus* earliest of its kind < *prīmus* first] —ˈ**primitively** *adv.* —ˈ**primitiveness** *n.*

primitivism (ˈprɪmɪtɪˌvɪzəm) *n.* **1.** the condition of being primitive. **2.** the belief that the value of primitive cultures is superior to that of the modern world. —ˈ**primitivist** *n., adj.*

primo (ˈpriːməʊ) *n., pl.* **-mos** *or* **-mi** (-miː). *Music.* **1.** the upper or right-hand part of a piano duet. **2. tempo primo.** at the same speed as at the beginning of the piece. [It.: first, < L *prīmus*]

primogenitor (ˌpraɪməʊˈdʒɛnɪtə) *n.* **1.** a forefather; ancestor. **2.** an earliest parent or ancestor, as of a race. [C17: alteration of PROGENITOR after PRIMOGENITURE]

primogeniture (ˌpraɪməʊˈdʒɛnɪtʃə) *n.* **1.** the state of being a first-born. **2.** *Law.* the right of an eldest son to succeed to the estate of his ancestor to the exclusion of all others. [C17: < Med. L *prīmōgenitūra* birth of a first child, < L *prīmō* at first + LL *genitūra* a birth] —**primogenitary** (ˌpraɪməʊˈdʒɛnɪtərɪ, -trɪ) *adj.*

primordial (praɪˈmɔːdɪəl) *adj.* **1.** existing at or from the beginning; primeval. **2.** constituting an origin; fundamental. **3.** *Biol.* relating to an early stage of development. [C14: < LL *prīmōrdiālis* original, < L *prīmus* first + *ōrdīrī* to begin] —**priˌmordiˈality** *n.* —**priˈmordially** *adv.*

primp (prɪmp) *vb.* to dress (oneself), esp. in fine clothes; prink. [C19: prob. < PRIM]

primrose (ˈprɪmˌrəʊz) *n.* **1.** any of various temperate plants of the genus *Primula,* esp. a European variety which has pale yellow flowers. **2.** short for **evening primrose. 3.** Also called: **primrose yellow.** a light yellow, sometimes with a greenish tinge. ~*adj.* **4.** of or abounding in primroses. **5.** of the colour primrose. [C15: < OF *primerose,* < Med. L *prīma rosa* first rose]

primrose path *n.* (often preceded by *the*) a pleasurable way of life.

primula (ˈprɪmjʊlə) *n.* any plant of the N temperate genus *Primula,* having white, yellow, pink, or purple funnel-shaped flowers with five spreading petals: includes the primrose, oxlip, cowslip, and polyanthus. [C18: NL, < Med. L *prīmula* (*vēris*) little first one (of the spring)]

primum mobile *Latin.* (ˈpraɪmʊm ˈməʊbɪlɪ) *n.* **1.** a prime mover. **2.** *Astron.* the outermost empty sphere in the Ptolemaic system that was thought to revolve around the earth from east to west in 24 hours carrying with it the inner spheres of the planets, sun, moon, and fixed stars. [C15: < Med. L: first moving (thing)]

Primus (ˈpraɪməs) *n. Trademark.* a portable paraffin cooking stove, used esp. by campers. Also called: **Primus stove.**

prince (prɪns) *n.* **1.** (in Britain) a son of the sovereign or of one of the sovereign's sons. **2.** a nonreigning male member of a sovereign family. **3.** the monarch of a small territory that was at some time subordinate to an emperor or king. **4.** any monarch. **5.** a nobleman in various countries, such as Italy and Germany. **6.** an outstanding member of a specified group: *a merchant prince.* [C13: via OF < L *princeps* first man, ruler] —ˈ**princedom** *n.* —ˈ**prince**ˌ**like** *adj.*

prince consort *n.* the husband of a female sovereign, who is himself a prince.

princeling (ˈprɪnslɪŋ) *n.* **1.** a young prince. **2.** Also called: **princelet.** the ruler of an insignificant territory.

princely (ˈprɪnslɪ) *adj.* **-lier, -liest. 1.** generous or lavish. **2.** of or characteristic of a prince. ~*adv.* **3.** in a princely manner. —ˈ**princeliness** *n.*

Prince of Darkness *n.* another name for **Satan.**

Prince of Peace *n. Bible.* the future Messiah (Isaiah 9:6): held by Christians to be Christ.

Prince of Wales (weɪlz) *n.* the eldest son and heir apparent of the British sovereign.

prince regent *n.* a prince who acts as regent during the minority, disability, or absence of the legal sovereign.

prince's-feather *n.* **1.** a garden plant with spikes of bristly brownish-red flowers. **2.** a tall tropical plant with hanging spikes of pink flowers.

princess (prɪnˈsɛs) *n.* **1.** (in Britain) a daughter of the sovereign or of one of the sovereign's sons. **2.** a nonreigning female member of a sovereign family. **3.** the wife and consort of a prince. **4.** *Arch.* a female sovereign. **5.** Also: **princess dress.** a style of dress having a fitted bodice and A-line skirt without a seam at the waistline.

princess royal *n.* the eldest daughter of a British or (formerly) a Prussian sovereign.

principal (ˈprɪnsɪpᵊl) *adj.* (*prenominal*) **1.** first in importance, rank, value, etc. **2.** denoting capital or property as opposed to interest, etc. ~*n.* **3.** a person who is first in importance or directs some event, organization, etc. **4.** *Law.* **a.** a person who engages another to act as his agent. **b.** an active participant in a crime. **c.** the person primarily liable to fulfil an obligation. **5.** the head of a school or other educational institution. **6.** (in Britain) a civil servant of an executive grade who is in charge of a section. **7.** *Finance.* **a.** capital or property, as contrasted with income. **b.** the original amount of a debt on which interest is calculated. **8.** a main roof truss or rafter. **9.** *Music.* either of two types of open diapason organ stops. [C13: via OF < L *principālis* chief, < *princeps* chief man] —ˈ**principally** *adv.* —ˈ**principalship** *n.*

principal boy *n.* the leading male role in a pantomime, played by a woman.

principality (ˌprɪnsɪˈpælɪtɪ) *n., pl.* **-ties. 1.** a territory ruled by a prince or from which a prince draws his title. **2.** the authority of a prince.

principal parts *pl. n. Grammar.* the main inflected forms of a verb, from which all other inflections may be deduced.

principate (ˈprɪnsɪˌpeɪt) *n.* **1.** a state ruled by a prince. **2.** a form of rule in the early Roman Empire in which some republican forms survived.

principle (ˈprɪnsɪpᵊl) *n.* **1.** a standard or rule of personal conduct: *he'd stoop to anything—he has no principles.* **2.** a set of such moral rules: *a man of principle.* **3.** a fundamental or general truth. **4.** the essence of something. **5.** a source; origin. **6.** a law concerning a natural phenomenon or the behaviour of a system: *the principle of the conservation of mass.* **7.** *Chem.* a constituent of a substance that gives the substance its characteristics. **8. in principle.** in theory. **9. on principle.** because of or in demonstration of a principle. [C14: < L *principium* beginning, basic tenet]

principled (ˈprɪnsɪpᵊld) *adj.* **a.** having high moral principles. **b.** (*in combination*): *high-principled.*

prink (prɪŋk) *vb.* **1.** to dress (oneself, etc.) finely; deck out. **2.** (*intr.*) to preen oneself. [C16: prob. changed < PRANK[2] (to adorn)]

print (prɪnt) *vb.* **1.** to reproduce (text, pictures, etc.), esp. in large numbers, by applying ink to paper or other material. **2.** to produce or reproduce (a manuscript, data, etc.) in print, as for publication. **3.** to write (letters, etc.) in the style of printed matter. **4.** to mark or indent (a surface) by pressing (something) onto it. **5.** to produce a photographic print from (a negative). **6.** (*tr.*) to fix in the mind or memory. **7.** (*tr.*) to make (a mark) by applying pressure. ~*n.* **8.** printed matter such as newsprint. **9.** a printed publication such as a book. **10. in print. a.** in printed or published form. **b.** (of a book, etc.) offered for sale by the publisher. **11. out of print.** no longer available from a publisher. **12.** a design or picture printed from an engraved plate, wood block, or other medium. **13.** printed text, esp. with regard to the typeface: *small print.* **14.** a positive photographic image produced from a negative image on film. **15. a.** a fabric with a printed design. **b.** (*as modifier*): *a print dress.* **16. a.** a mark made by pressing something onto a surface. **b.** a stamp, die, etc., that makes such an impression. **17.** See **fingerprint.** ~See also **print out.** [C13 *priente,* < OF: something printed, < *preindre* to make an impression, < L *premere* to press] —ˈ**printable** *adj.*

printed circuit *n.* an electronic circuit in which certain components and the connections between them are formed by etching a metallic coating or by electrodeposition on one or both sides of a thin insulating board.

printer (ˈprɪntə) *n.* **1.** a person or business engaged in printing. **2.** a machine or device that prints. **3.** *Computers.* an output device for printing results on paper.

printer's devil *n.* an apprentice or errand boy in a printing establishment.

printing (ˈprɪntɪŋ) *n.* **1.** the business or art of producing printed matter. **2.** printed text. **3.** Also called: **impression.** all the copies of a book, etc., printed at one time. **4.** a form of writing in which letters resemble printed letters.

printing press *n.* any of various machines used for printing.

printmaker (ˈprɪntˌmeɪkə) *n.* a person who makes print or prints, esp. a craftsman or artist.

print out *vb.* (*tr., adv.*) **1.** (of a computer output device) to produce (printed information). ~*n.* **print-out. 2.** such printed information.

print shop *n.* a place in which printing is carried out.

prior[1] (ˈpraɪə) *adj.* **1.** (*prenominal*) previous. **2. prior to.** before; until. [C18: < L: previous]

prior[2] (ˈpraɪə) *n.* **1.** the superior of a community in certain religious orders. **2.** the deputy head of a monastery or abbey, immediately below the abbot. [C11: < LL: head, < L (adj.): previous, < OL *pri* before] —ˈ**priorate** *n.* —ˈ**prioress** *fem. n.*

priority (praɪˈɒrɪtɪ) *n., pl.* **-ties.** **1.** the condition of being prior; antecedence; precedence. **2.** the right of precedence over others. **3.** something given specified attention: *my first priority.*

priory (ˈpraɪərɪ) *n., pl.* **-ories.** a religious house governed by a prior, sometimes being subordinate to an abbey. [C13: < Med. L *priōria*]

prise *or* **prize** (praɪz) *vb.* (*tr.*) **1.** to force open by levering. **2.** to extract or obtain with difficulty: *they had to prise the news out of him.* [C17: < OF *prise* a taking, < *prendre* to take, < L *prehendere;* see PRIZE¹]

prism (ˈprɪzəm) *n.* **1.** a transparent polygonal solid, often having triangular ends and rectangular sides, for dispersing light into a spectrum or for reflecting light: used in binoculars, periscopes, etc. **2.** *Maths.* a polyhedron having parallel bases and sides that are parallelograms. [C16: < Med. L *prisma,* < Gk: something shaped by sawing, < *prizein* to saw]

prismatic (prɪzˈmætɪk) *adj.* **1.** of or produced by a prism. **2.** exhibiting bright spectral colours: *prismatic light.* **3.** *Crystallog.* another word for **orthorhombic.** —**prisˈmatically** *adv.*

prison (ˈprɪzᵊn) *n.* **1.** a public building used to house convicted criminals and accused persons awaiting trial. **2.** any place of confinement. [C12: < OF *prisun,* < L *prēnsiō* a capturing, < *prehendere* to lay hold of]

prisoner (ˈprɪzənə) *n.* **1.** a person kept in custody as a punishment for a crime, while awaiting trial, or for some other reason. **2.** a person confined by any of various restraints: *we are all prisoners of time.* **3. take (someone) prisoner.** to capture and hold (someone) as a prisoner.

prisoner of war *n.* a person, esp. a serviceman, captured by an enemy in time of war. Abbrev.: **POW.**

prisoner's base *n.* a children's game involving two teams, members of which chase and capture each other.

prissy (ˈprɪsɪ) *adj.* **-sier, -siest.** fussy and prim, esp. in a prudish way. [C20: prob. < PRIM + SISSY] —ˈ**prissily** *adv.* —ˈ**prissiness** *n.*

pristine (ˈprɪstaɪn, -tiːn) *adj.* **1.** of or involving the earliest period, state, etc.; original. **2.** pure; uncorrupted. [C15: < L *pristinus* primitive]

prithee (ˈprɪðɪ) *interj. Arch.* pray thee; please. [C16: shortened < *I pray thee*]

privacy (ˈpraɪvəsɪ, ˈprɪvəsɪ) *n.* **1.** the condition of being private. **2.** secrecy.

private (ˈpraɪvɪt) *adj.* **1.** not widely or publicly known: *they had private reasons for the decision.* **2.** confidential; secret: *a private conversation.* **3.** not for general or public use: *a private bathroom.* **4.** of or provided by a private individual or organization rather than by the state. **5.** (*prenominal*) individual; special: *my own private recipe.* **6.** (*prenominal*) having no public office, rank, etc.: *a private man.* **7.** (*prenominal*) denoting a soldier of the lowest military rank. **8.** (of a place) retired; not overlooked. ~*n.* **9.** a soldier of the lowest rank in many armies and marine corps. **10. in private.** in secret. [C14: < L *prīvātus* belonging to one individual, withdrawn from public life, < *prīvāre* to deprive] —ˈ**privately** *adv.*

private bill *n.* a bill presented to Parliament or Congress on behalf of a private individual, corporation, etc.

private company *n.* a limited company that does not issue shares for public subscription and whose owners do not enjoy an unrestricted right to transfer their shareholdings. Cf. **public company.**

private detective *n.* an individual privately employed to investigate a crime or make other inquiries. Also called: **private investigator.**

private enterprise *n.* economic activity undertaken by private individuals or organizations under private ownership.

privateer (ˌpraɪvəˈtɪə) *n.* **1.** an armed privately owned vessel commissioned for war service by a government. **2.** Also called: **privateersman.** a member of the crew of a privateer. ~*vb.* **3.** (*intr.*) to serve as a privateer.

private eye *n. Inf.* a private detective.

private hotel *n.* **1.** a hotel in which the proprietor has the right to refuse to accept a person as a guest. **2.** *Austral. & N.Z.* a hotel not having a licence to sell alcoholic liquor.

private income *n.* an income from sources other than employment, such as investment. Also called: **private means.**

private life *n.* the social life or personal relationships of an individual, esp. of a celebrity.

private member *n.* a member of a legislative assembly not having an appointment in the government.

private member's bill *n.* a parliamentary bill sponsored by a Member of Parliament who is not a government minister.

private parts *or* **privates** *pl. n.* euphemistic terms for **genitals.**

private patient *n. Brit.* a patient receiving medical treatment not paid for by the National Health Service.

private pay bed *n.* (in Britain) a hospital bed reserved for private patients who are charged by the health service for use of hospital facilities.

private practice *n. Brit.* medical practice that is not part of the National Health Service.

private school *n.* a school under the financial and managerial control of a private body, accepting mostly fee-paying pupils.

private secretary *n.* **1.** a secretary entrusted with the personal and confidential matters of a business executive. **2.** a civil servant who acts as aide to a minister or senior government official.

private sector *n.* the part of a country's economy that consists of privately owned enterprises.

privation (praɪˈveɪʃən) *n.* **1.** loss or lack of the necessities of life, such as food and shelter. **2.** hardship resulting from this. **3.** the state of being deprived. [C14: < L *prīvātiō* deprivation]

privative (ˈprɪvətɪv) *adj.* **1.** causing privation. **2.** expressing lack or negation, as for example the English suffix *-less* and prefix *un-.* [C16: < L *prīvātīvus* indicating loss] —ˈ**privatively** *adv.*

privatize *or* **-ise** (ˈpraɪvɪˌtaɪz) *vb.* (*tr.*) to take into, or return to, private ownership, a company or concern that has previously been owned by the state. —ˌ**privatiˈzation** *or* **-iˈsation** *n.*

privet (ˈprɪvɪt) *n.* **a.** any of a genus of shrubs, esp. one having oval dark green leaves, white flowers, and purplish-black berries. **b.** (*as modifier*): *a privet hedge.* [C16: <?]

privilege (ˈprɪvɪlɪdʒ) *n.* **1.** a benefit, immunity, etc., granted under certain conditions. **2.** the advantages and immunities enjoyed by a small usually powerful group or class, esp. to the disadvantage of others: *one of the obstacles to social harmony is privilege.* **3.** *U.S. Stock Exchange.* a speculative contract permitting its purchaser to make optional purchases or sales of securities at a specified time over a limited period. ~*vb.* (*tr.*) **4.** to bestow a privilege or privileges upon. **5.** (foll. by *from*) to free or exempt. [C12: < OF *privilège,* < L *prīvilēgium* law relevant to rights of an individual, < *prīvus* an individual + *lēx* law]

privileged (ˈprɪvɪlɪdʒd) *adj.* **1.** enjoying or granted as a privilege or privileges. **2.** *Law.* **a.** not actionable as a libel or slander. **b.** (of a communication, document, etc.) that a witness cannot be compelled to divulge.

privity (ˈprɪvɪtɪ) *n., pl.* **-ties.** **1.** a legally recognized relationship existing between two parties, such as that between the parties to a contract: *privity of contract.* **2.** secret knowledge that is shared. [C13: < OF *privité*]

privy (ˈprɪvɪ) *adj.* **privier, priviest.** **1.** (*postpositive;* foll. by *to*) participating in the knowledge of something secret. **2.** *Arch.* secret, hidden, etc. ~*n., pl.* **privies.** **3.** a lavatory, esp. an outside one. **4.** *Law.* a person in privity with another. See **privity.** [C13: < OF *privé* something private, < L *prīvātus* PRIVATE] —ˈ**privily** *adv.*

privy council *n.* **1.** the council of state of a monarch, esp. formerly. **2.** *Arch.* a secret council.

Privy Council *n.* **1.** the private council of the British sovereign, consisting of all current and former ministers of the Crown and other distinguished subjects, all of whom are appointed for life. **2.** (in Canada), a ceremonial body of advisers of the governor general, the chief of them being the Federal cabinet ministers. —**Privy Councillor** *n.*

privy purse *n.* (*often cap.*) **1.** an allowance voted by Parliament for the private expenses of the monarch. **2.** an official of the royal household responsible for dealing with the monarch's private expenses. Full name: **Keeper of the Privy Purse.**

privy seal *n.* (*often cap.*) (in Britain) a seal affixed to certain documents issued by royal authority: of less importance than the great seal.

prize[1] (praɪz) *n.* **1. a.** a reward or honour for having won a contest, competition, etc. **b.** (*as modifier*): *prize jockey; prize essay.* **2.** something given to the winner of any game of chance, lottery, etc. **3.** something striven for. **4.** any valuable property captured in time of war, esp. a vessel. [C14: < OF *prise* a capture, < L *prehendere* to seize; infl. by ME *prise* reward]

prize[2] (praɪz) *vb.* (*tr.*) to esteem greatly; value highly. [C15 *prise*, < OF *preisier* to PRAISE]

prize court *n. Law.* a court having jurisdiction to determine how property captured at sea in wartime is to be distributed.

prizefight (ˈpraɪzˌfaɪt) *n.* a boxing match for a prize or purse. —ˈ**prizeˌfighter** *n.* —ˈ**prizeˌfighting** *n.*

prize ring *n.* **1.** the enclosed area or ring used by prizefighters. **2. the prize ring.** the sport of prizefighting.

pro[1] (prəʊ) *adv.* **1.** in favour of a motion, issue, course of action, etc. ~*prep.* **2.** in favour of. ~*n., pl.* **pros. 3.** (*usually pl.*) an argument or vote in favour of a proposal or motion. See also **pros and cons.** [< L *prō* (prep.) in favour of]

pro[2] (prəʊ) *n., pl.* **pros,** *adj. Inf.* **1.** short for **professional. 2.** a prostitute. [C19]

PRO *abbrev. for:* **1.** Public Records Office. **2.** public relations officer.

pro-[1] *prefix.* **1.** in favour of; supporting: *pro-Chinese.* **2.** acting as a substitute for: *proconsul; pronoun.* [< L *prō* (adv. & prep.). In compound words borrowed < L, *prō-* indicates: forward, out (*project*); away from (*prodigal*); onward (*proceed*); in front of (*provide, protect*); on behalf of (*procure*); substitute for (*pronominal*); and sometimes intensive force (*promiscuous*)]

pro-[2] *prefix.* before in time or position; anterior; forward: *prognathous.* [< Gk *pro* (prep.) before (in time, position, etc.)]

proa (ˈprəʊə) *or* **prau** *n.* any of several kinds of canoe-like boats used in the South Pacific, esp. one equipped with an outrigger and sails. [C16: < Malay *parāhū* a boat]

pro-am (ˈprəʊˈæm) *adj.* (of a golf tournament, etc.) involving both professional and amateur players.

probability (ˌprɒbəˈbɪlɪtɪ) *n., pl.* **-ties. 1.** the condition of being probable. **2.** an event or other thing that is probable. **3.** *Statistics.* a measure of the degree of confidence one may have in the occurrence of an event, measured on a scale from zero (impossibility) to one (certainty).

probable (ˈprɒbəbˀl) *adj.* **1.** likely to be or to happen but not necessarily so. **2.** most likely: *the probable cause of the accident.* ~*n.* **3.** a person who is probably to be chosen for a team, event, etc. [C14: via OF < L *probābilis* that may be proved, < *probāre* to prove]

probably (ˈprɒbəblɪ) *adv.* **1.** (*sentence modifier*) in all likelihood or probability: *I'll probably see you tomorrow.* ~*sentence substitute.* **2.** I believe such a thing may be the case.

probang (ˈprəʊbæŋ) *n. Surgery.* a long flexible rod, often with a small sponge at one end, for inserting into the oesophagus, as to apply medication. [C17: var., apparently by association with PROBE, of *provang*, coined by W. Rumsey (1584–1660), Welsh judge, its inventor; <?]

probate (ˈprəʊbɪt, -beɪt) *n.* **1.** the process of officially proving the validity of a will. **2.** the official certificate stating a will to be genuine and conferring on the executors power to administer the estate. **3.** (*modifier*) relating to probate: *a probate court.* ~*vb.* **4.** (*tr.*) *Chiefly U.S.* to establish officially the validity of (a will). [C15: < L *probāre* to inspect]

probation (prəˈbeɪʃən) *n.* **1.** a system of dealing with offenders by placing them under the supervision of a probation officer. **2. on probation. a.** under the supervision of a probation officer. **b.** undergoing a test period. **3.** a trial period, as for a teacher. —**proˈbational** *or* **proˈbationary** *adj.*

probationer (prəˈbeɪʃənə) *n.* a person on probation.

probation officer *n.* an officer of a court who supervises offenders placed on probation and assists and befriends them.

probe (prəʊb) *vb.* **1.** (*tr.*) to search into closely. **2.** to examine (something) with or as if with a probe. ~*n.* **3.** something that probes or tests. **4.** *Surgery.* a slender instrument for exploring a wound, sinus, etc. **5.** a thorough inquiry, such as one by a newspaper into corrupt practices. **6.** *Electronics.* a lead connecting to or containing a monitoring circuit used for testing. **7.** anything which provides or acts as a coupling, esp. a flexible tube extended from an aircraft to link it with another so that it can refuel. **8.** See **space probe.** [C16: < Med. L *proba* investigation, < L *probāre* to test] —ˈ**probeable** *adj.* —ˈ**prober** *n.*

probity (ˈprəʊbɪtɪ) *n.* confirmed integrity. [C16: < L *probitās* honesty, < *probus* virtuous]

problem (ˈprɒbləm) *n.* **1. a.** any thing, matter, person, etc., that is difficult to deal with. **b.** (*as modifier*): *a problem child.* **2.** a puzzle, question, etc., set for solution. **3.** *Maths.* a statement requiring a solution usually by means of several operations or constructions. **4.** (*modifier*) designating a literary work that deals with difficult moral questions: *a problem play.* [C14: < LL *problēma*, < Gk: something put forward]

problematic (ˌprɒbləˈmætɪk) *or* **problematical** *adj.* **1.** having the nature of a problem; uncertain; questionable. **2.** *Logic, obs.* (of a proposition) asserting that a property may or may not hold. —ˌ**problemˈatically** *adv.*

pro bono publico *Latin.* (ˈprəʊ ˈbəʊnəʊ ˈpʊblɪkəʊ) for the public good.

proboscidean *or* **proboscidian** (ˌprəʊbɒˈsɪdɪən) *adj.* **1.** of or belonging to an order of massive herbivorous placental mammals having tusks and a long trunk: contains the elephants. ~*n.* **2.** any proboscidean animal.

proboscis (prəʊˈbɒsɪs) *n., pl.* **-cises** *or* **-cides** (-sɪˌdiːz). **1.** a long flexible prehensile trunk or snout, as of an elephant. **2.** the elongated mouthpart of certain insects. **3.** any similar organ. **4.** *Inf., facetious.* a person's nose. [C17: via L < Gk *proboskis* trunk of an elephant, < *boskein* to feed]

procaine (ˈprəʊkeɪn, prəʊˈkeɪn) *n.* a colourless or white crystalline water-soluble substance used, as the hydrochloride, as a local anaesthetic. [C20: < PRO-[1] + (CO)CAINE]

procathedral (ˌprəʊkəˈθiːdrəl) *n.* a church serving as a cathedral.

procedure (prəˈsiːdʒə) *n.* **1.** a way of acting or progressing, esp. an established method. **2.** the established form of conducting the business of a

---

ˌ**proaˈmendment** *adj.*
ˌ**pro-Aˈmerican** *adj., n.*
ˌ**proannexˈation** *adj.*
ˌ**proapˈproval** *adj.*
ˌ**proarbiˈtration** *adj.*
ˌ**proautoˈmation** *adj.*
proˈbiblical *adj.*
pro-ˈBolshevik *adj., n.*
pro-ˈBritish *adj.*
proˈbusiness *adj.*
proˈcapitalist *adj.*
pro-ˈCatholic *adj., n.*

legislature, the enforcement of a legal right, etc. **3.** *Computers.* another name for **subroutine.** —**pro'cedural** *adj.* —**pro'cedurally** *adv.*

proceed (prə'siːd) *vb.* (*intr.*) **1.** (often foll. by *to*) to advance or carry on, esp. after stopping. **2.** (often foll. by *with*) to continue: *he proceeded with his reading.* **3.** (often foll. by *against*) to institute or carry on a legal action. **4.** to originate; arise: *evil proceeds from the heart.* [C14: < L *prōcēdere* to advance] —**pro'ceeder** *n.*

proceeding (prə'siːdɪŋ) *n.* **1.** an act or course of action. **2. a.** a legal action. **b.** any step taken in a legal action. **3.** (*pl.*) the minutes of the meetings of a society, etc. **4.** (*pl.*) legal action; litigation. **5.** (*pl.*) the events of an occasion.

proceeds ('prəʊsiːdz) *pl. n.* **1.** the profit or return derived from a commercial transaction, investment, etc. **2.** the result, esp. the total sum, accruing from some undertaking.

process[1] ('prəʊsɛs) *n.* **1.** a series of actions which produce a change or development: *the process of digestion.* **2.** a method of doing or producing something. **3.** progress or course of time. **4. in the process of.** during or in the course of. **5. a.** a summons commanding a person to appear in court. **b.** the whole proceedings in an action at law. **6.** a natural outgrowth or projection of a part or organism. **7.** (*modifier*) relating to the general preparation of a printing forme or plate by the use, at some stage, of photography. ~*vb.* (*tr.*) **8.** to subject to a routine procedure; handle. **9.** to treat or prepare by a special method, esp. to treat (food) in order to preserve it: *to process cheese.* **10. a.** to institute legal proceedings against. **b.** to serve a process on. **11.** *Photog.* **a.** to develop, rinse, fix, wash, and dry (exposed film, etc.). **b.** to produce final prints or slides from (undeveloped film). **12.** *Computers.* to perform operations on (data) according to programmed instructions in order to obtain the required information. [C14: < OF *procès,* < L *prōcessus* an advancing, < *prōcēdere* to proceed]

process[2] (prə'sɛs) *vb.* (*intr.*) to proceed in a procession. [C19: back formation < PROCESSION]

process industry *n.* a manufacturing industry, such as oil refining, which converts bulk raw materials into a workable form.

procession (prə'sɛʃən) *n.* **1.** the act of proceeding in a regular formation. **2.** a group of people or things moving forwards in an orderly, regular, or ceremonial manner. **3.** *Christianity.* the emanation of the Holy Spirit. ~*vb.* **4.** (*intr.*) *Rare.* to go in procession. [C12: via OF < L *prōcessiō* a marching forwards]

processional (prə'sɛʃənəl) *adj.* **1.** of or suitable for a procession. ~*n.* **2.** *Christianity.* **a.** a book containing the prayers, hymns, etc., prescribed for processions. **b.** a hymn, etc., used in a procession.

processor ('prəʊsɛsə) *n.* **1.** *Computers.* another name for **central processing unit. 2.** a person or thing that carries out a process.

process-server *n.* a sheriff's officer who serves legal documents such as writs for appearance in court.

procès-verbal *French.* (prɔsɛvɛrbal) *n., pl.* **-baux** (-bo). a written record of an official proceeding; minutes. [C17: < F: see PROCESS[1], VERBAL]

prochronism ('prəʊkrəˌnɪzəm) *n.* an error in dating that places an event earlier than it actually occurred. [C17: < PRO-[2] + Gk *khronos* time + -ISM, by analogy with ANACHRONISM]

proclaim (prə'kleɪm) *vb.* (*tr.*) **1.** (*may take a clause as object*) to announce publicly. **2.** (*may take a clause as object*) to indicate plainly. **3.** to praise or extol. [C14: < L *prōclāmāre* to shout aloud] —**proclamation** (ˌprɒklə'meɪʃən) *n.* —**pro'claimer** *n.* —**proclamatory** (prə'klæmətərɪ, -trɪ) *adj.*

proclitic (prəʊ'klɪtɪk) *adj.* **1. a.** denoting a monosyllabic word or form having no stress and pronounced as a prefix of the following word, as in English *'t* for *it* in *'twas.* **b.** (in classical Greek) denoting a word that throws its accent onto the following word. ~*n.* **2.** a proclitic word or form. [C19: < NL *proclīticus,* < Gk *proklinein* to lean forwards; on the model of ENCLITIC]

proclivity (prə'klɪvɪtɪ) *n., pl.* **-ties.** a tendency or inclination. [C16: < L *prōclīvitās,* < *prōclīvis* steep, < *clīvus* a slope]

proconsul (prəʊ'kɒnsᵊl) *n.* **1.** a governor of a colony or other dependency. **2.** (in ancient Rome) the governor of a senatorial province. —**proconsular** (prəʊ'kɒnsjʊlə) *adj.* —**pro'consulate** *or* **pro'consulship** *n.*

procrastinate (prəʊ'kræstɪˌneɪt, prə-) *vb.* (*usually intr.*) to put off (an action) until later; delay. [C16: < L *prōcrāstināre* to postpone until tomorrow, < PRO-[1] + *crās* tomorrow] —**proˌcrasti'nation** *n.* —**pro'crastiˌnator** *n.*

procreate ('prəʊkrɪˌeɪt) *vb.* **1.** to beget or engender (offspring). **2.** (*tr.*) to bring into being. [C16: < L *prōcreāre,* < PRO-[1] + *creāre* to create] —**'procreant** *or* **'procreˌative** *adj.* —**ˌprocre'ation** *n.* —**'procreˌator** *n.*

Procrustean (prəʊ'krʌstɪən) *adj.* designed to produce conformity by ruthless methods. [C19: < *Procrustes,* Gk robber who fitted travellers into his bed by stretching or lopping off their limbs]

proctology (prɒk'tɒlədʒɪ) *n.* the branch of medical science concerned with the rectum. [< Gk *prōktos* rectum + -OLOGY]

proctor ('prɒktə) *n.* **1.** a member of the staff of certain universities having duties including the enforcement of discipline. **2.** (formerly) an agent, esp. one engaged to conduct another's case in a court. **3.** *Church of England.* one of the elected representatives of the clergy in Convocation. [C14: syncopated var. of PROCURATOR] —**proctorial** (prɒk'tɔːrɪəl) *adj.*

procumbent (prəʊ'kʌmbənt) *adj.* **1.** (of stems) trailing loosely along the ground. **2.** leaning forwards or lying on the face. [C17: < L *prōcumbere* to fall forwards]

procurator ('prɒkjʊˌreɪtə) *n.* **1.** (in ancient Rome) a civil official of the emperor's administration, often employed as the governor of a minor province. **2.** *Rare.* a person engaged by another to manage his affairs. [C13: < L: a manager, < *prōcūrāre* to attend to] —**procuracy** ('prɒkjʊrəsɪ) *or* **'procuˌratorship** *n.* —**procuratorial** (ˌprɒkjʊrə'tɔːrɪəl) *adj.*

procurator fiscal *n.* (in Scotland) a legal officer who performs the functions of public prosecutor and coroner.

procure (prə'kjʊə) *vb.* **1.** (*tr.*) to obtain or acquire; secure. **2.** to obtain (women or girls) to act as prostitutes. [C13: < L *prōcūrāre* to look after] —**pro'curable** *adj.* —**pro'curement, pro'cural,** *or* **procuration** (ˌprɒkjʊ'reɪʃən) *n.*

procurer (prə'kjʊərə) *n.* a person who procures, esp. one who procures women as prostitutes.

prod (prɒd) *vb.* **prodding, prodded. 1.** to poke or jab with or as if with a pointed object. **2.** (*tr.*) to rouse to action. ~*n.* **3.** the act or an instance of prodding. **4.** a sharp object. **5.** a stimulus or reminder. [C16: <?] —**'prodder** *n.*

prod. *abbrev. for:* **1.** produce. **2.** produced. **3.** product.

prodigal ('prɒdɪgᵊl) *adj.* **1.** recklessly wasteful or extravagant, as in disposing of goods or money. **2.** lavish: *prodigal of compliments.* ~*n.* **3.** a person who spends lavishly or squanders money. [C16: < Med. L *prōdigālis* wasteful, < L, < *prōdigere* to squander, < *agere* to drive] —**ˌprodi'gality** *n.* —**'prodigally** *adv.*

prodigious (prə'dɪdʒəs) *adj.* **1.** vast in size, extent, power, etc. **2.** wonderful or amazing. [C16: < L *prōdigiōsus* marvellous, < *prōdigium;*

ˌprocentrali'zation *or* **-i'sation** *adj.*
pro'church *adj.*
pro'clerical *adj.*
pro-'Communist *adj., n.*
ˌprocon'scription *adj.*
ˌproconser'vation *adj.*
ˌpro-Dar'winian *adj., n.*
ˌprodemo'cratic *adj.*

see PRODIGY] **—pro'digiously** *adv.* **—pro'digiousness** *n.*

prodigy ('prɒdɪdʒɪ) *n., pl.* **-gies.** 1. a person, esp. a child, of unusual or marvellous talents. 2. anything that is a cause of wonder. 3. something monstrous or abnormal. [C16: < L *prōdigium* an unnatural happening]

produce *vb.* (prə'djuːs). 1. to bring (something) into existence; yield. 2. (*tr.*) to make: *she produced a delicious dinner.* 3. (*tr.*) to give birth to. 4. (*tr.*) to present to view: *to produce evidence.* 5. (*tr.*) to bring before the public: *he produced a film last year.* 6. (*tr.*) to act as producer of. 7. (*tr.*) *Geom.* to extend (a line). ~*n.* ('prɒdjuːs). 8. anything produced; a product. 9. agricultural products collectively: *farm produce.* [C15: < L *prōdūcere* to bring forward] **—pro'ducible** *adj.* **—pro,duci'bility** *n.*

producer (prə'djuːsə) *n.* 1. a person or thing that produces. 2. *Brit.* a person responsible for the artistic direction of a play. 3. *U.S. & Canad.* a person who organizes the stage production of a play, including the finance, management, etc. 4. the person who takes overall administrative responsibility for a film or television programme. Cf. **director** (sense 4). 5. *Econ.* a person or business enterprise that generates goods or services for sale. Cf. **consumer** (sense 1). 6. *Chem.* an apparatus or plant for making producer gas.

producer gas *n.* a mixture of carbon monoxide and nitrogen produced by passing air over hot coke, used mainly as a fuel.

product ('prɒdʌkt) *n.* 1. something produced by effort, or some mechanical or industrial process. 2. the result of some natural process. 3. a result or consequence. 4. *Maths.* the result of the multiplication of two or more numbers, quantities, etc. [C15: < L *prōductum* (something) produced, < *prōdūcere* to bring forth]

production (prə'dʌkʃən) *n.* 1. the act of producing. 2. anything that is produced; a product. 3. the amount produced or the rate at which it is produced. 4. *Econ.* the creation or manufacture of goods and services with exchange value. 5. any work created as a result of literary or artistic effort. 6. the presentation of a play, opera, etc. 7. *Brit.* the artistic direction of a play. 8. (*modifier*) manufactured by mass production: *a production model of a car.* **—pro'ductional** *adj.*

production line *n.* a factory system in which parts or components of the end product are transported by a conveyor through a number of different sites at each of which a manual or machine operation is performed on them.

productive (prə'dʌktɪv) *adj.* 1. producing or having the power to produce; fertile. 2. yielding favourable results. 3. *Econ.* **a.** producing goods and services that have exchange value: *productive assets.* **b.** relating to such production: *the productive processes of an industry.* 4. (*postpositive;* foll. by *of*) resulting in: *productive of good results.* **—pro'ductively** *adv.* **—productivity** (,prɒdʌk'tɪvɪtɪ) *or* **pro'ductiveness** *n.*

proem ('prəʊɛm) *n.* an introduction or preface, such as to a work of literature. [C14: < L *prooemium* introduction, < Gk *prooimion,* < PRO-[2] + *hoimē* song] **—proemial** (prəʊ'iːmɪəl) *adj.*

Prof. *abbrev. for* Professor.

profane (prə'feɪn) *adj.* 1. having or indicating contempt, irreverence, or disrespect for a divinity or something sacred. 2. not designed for religious purposes; secular. 3. not initiated into the inner mysteries or sacred rites. 4. coarse or blasphemous: *profane language.* ~*vb.* (*tr.*) 5. to treat (something sacred) with irreverence. 6. to put to an unworthy use. [C15: < L *profānus* outside the temple] **—profanation** (,prɒfə'neɪʃən) *n.* **—pro'fanely** *adv.* **—pro'faneness** *n.* **—pro'faner** *n.*

profanity (prə'fænɪtɪ) *n., pl.* **-ties.** 1. the state or quality of being profane. 2. vulgar or irreverent action, speech, etc.

profess (prə'fɛs) *vb.* 1. (*tr.*) to affirm or acknowledge: *to profess ignorance; to profess a belief in God.* 2. (*tr.*) to claim (something), often insincerely or falsely: *to profess to be a skilled driver.* 3. to receive or be received into a religious order, as by taking vows. [C14: < L *prōfitērī* to confess openly]

professed (prə'fɛst) *adj.* (*prenominal*) 1. avowed or acknowledged. 2. alleged or pretended. 3. professing to be qualified as: *a professed philosopher.* 4. having taken vows of a religious order. **—professedly** (prə'fɛsɪdlɪ) *adv.*

profession (prə'fɛʃən) *n.* 1. an occupation requiring special training in the liberal arts or sciences, esp. one of the three learned professions, law, theology, or medicine. 2. the body of people in such an occupation. 3. an avowal; declaration. 4. Also called: **profession of faith.** a declaration of faith in a religion, esp. as made on entering the Church or an order belonging to it. [C13: < Med. L *professiō* the taking of vows upon entering a religious order, < L: public acknowledgment; see PROFESS]

professional (prə'fɛʃənᵊl) *adj.* 1. of, suitable for, or engaged in as a profession. 2. engaging in an activity as a means of livelihood. 3. **a.** extremely competent in a job, etc. **b.** (of a piece of work or anything performed) produced with competence or skill. 4. undertaken or performed by people who are paid. ~*n.* 5. a person who belongs to one of the professions. 6. a person who engages for his livelihood in some activity also pursued by amateurs. 7. a person who engages in an activity with great competence. 8. an expert player of a game who gives instruction, esp. to members of a club by whom he is hired. **—pro'fessiona,lism** *n.* **—pro'fessionally** *adv.*

professional foul *n. Football.* a deliberate foul committed as a last-ditch tactic to prevent an opponent from scoring.

professor (prə'fɛsə) *n.* 1. the principal teacher in a field of learning at a university or college; a holder of a university chair. 2. *Chiefly U.S. & Canad.* any teacher in a university or college. 3. a person who professes his opinions, beliefs, etc. [C14: < Med. L: one who has made his profession in a religious order, < L: a public teacher; see PROFESS] **—professorial** (,prɒfɪ'sɔːrɪəl) *adj.* **—,profes'sorially** *adv.* **—,profes'soriate** *or* **pro'fessorship** *n.*

proffer ('prɒfə) *vb.* 1. (*tr.*) to offer for acceptance. ~*n.* 2. the act of proffering. [C13: < OF *proffrir,* < PRO-[1] + *offrir* to offer]

proficient (prə'fɪʃənt) *adj.* 1. having great facility (in an art, occupation, etc.); skilled. ~*n.* 2. an expert. [C16: < L *prōficere* to make progress] **—pro'ficiency** *n.* **—pro'ficiently** *adv.*

profile ('prəʊfaɪl) *n.* 1. a side view or outline of an object, esp. of a human head. 2. a short biographical sketch. 3. a graph, table, etc., representing the extent to which a person, field, or object exhibits various tested characteristics: *a population profile.* 4. a vertical section of soil or rock showing the different layers. 5. the outline of the shape of a river valley either from source to mouth (**long profile**) or at right angles to the flow of the river (**cross profile**). ~*vb.* 6. (*tr.*) to draw, write, or make a profile of. [C17: < It. *profilo,* < *profilare* to sketch lightly, < L *filum* thread] **—'profiler** *or* **profilist** ('prəʊfɪlɪst) *n.*

profit ('prɒfɪt) *n.* 1. (*often pl.*) excess of revenues over outlays and expenses in a business enterprise. 2. the monetary gain derived from a transaction. 3. income derived from property or an investment, as contrasted with capital gains. 4. *Econ.* the income accruing to a successful entrepreneur and held to be the motivating factor of a capitalist economy. 5. a gain, benefit, or

---

,prodis'armament *adj.*
,prodisso'lution *adj.*
,proen'forcement *adj.*
,pro-Euro'pean *adj., n.*
,pro'fascist *adj., n.*
pro'feminist *adj., n.*

advantage. ~*vb.* **6.** to gain or cause to gain profit. [C14: < L *prōfectus* advance, < *prōficere* to make progress] —'**profitless** *adj.*

profitable ('prɒfɪtəbᵊl) *adj.* affording gain or profit. —ˌ**profita'bility** *n.* —'**profitably** *adv.*

profit and loss *n. Book-keeping.* an account compiled at the end of a financial year showing that year's revenue and expense items and indicating gross and net profit or loss.

profit centre *n.* a section of a commercial organization which is allocated financial targets in its own right.

profiteer (ˌprɒfɪ'tɪə) *n.* **1.** a person who makes excessive profits, esp. by charging exorbitant prices for goods in short supply. ~*vb.* **2.** (*intr.*) to make excessive profits.

profiterole ('prɒfɪtəˌrəʊl, prə'fɪtəˌrəʊl) *n.* a small case of choux pastry with a sweet or savoury filling. [C16: < F, lit.: a small profit]

profit-sharing *n.* a system in which a portion of the net profit of a business is distributed to its employees, usually in proportion to their wages or their length of service.

profligate ('prɒflɪgɪt) *adj.* **1.** shamelessly immoral or debauched. **2.** wildly extravagant or wasteful. ~*n.* **3.** a profligate person. [C16: < L *prōflīgātus* corrupt, < *prōflīgāre* to overthrow, < PRO-[1] + *flīgere* to beat] —**profligacy** ('prɒflɪgəsɪ) *n.* —'**profligately** *adv.*

pro forma ('prəʊ 'fɔːmə) *adj.* **1.** prescribing a set form or procedure. ~*adv.* **2.** performed in a set manner. [L: for form's sake]

profound (prə'faʊnd) *adj.* **1.** penetrating deeply into subjects or ideas: *a profound mind.* **2.** showing or requiring great knowledge or understanding: *a profound treatise.* **3.** situated at or extending to a great depth. **4.** stemming from the depths of one's nature: *profound regret.* **5.** intense or absolute: *profound silence.* **6.** thoroughgoing; extensive: *profound changes.* ~*n.* **7.** *Arch. or literary.* a great depth; abyss. [C14: < OF *profund,* < L *profundus* deep, < *fundus* bottom] —**pro'foundly** *adv.* —**profundity** (prə'fʌndɪtɪ) *n.*

profuse (prə'fjuːs) *adj.* **1.** plentiful or abundant: *profuse compliments.* **2.** (often foll. by *in*) free or generous in the giving (of): *profuse in thanks.* [C15: < L *profundere* to pour lavishly] —**pro'fusely** *adv.* —**pro'fuseness** *or* **pro'fusion** *n.*

progenitive (prəʊ'dʒɛnɪtɪv) *adj.* capable of bearing offspring. —**pro'genitiveness** *n.*

progenitor (prəʊ'dʒɛnɪtə) *n.* **1.** a direct ancestor. **2.** an originator or founder. [C14: < L: ancestor, < *gignere* to beget]

progeny ('prɒdʒɪnɪ) *n., pl.* **-nies. 1.** the immediate descendant or descendants of a person, animal, etc. **2.** a result or outcome. [C13: < L *prōgeniēs* lineage; see PROGENITOR]

progesterone (prəʊ'dʒɛstəˌrəʊn) *n.* a steroid hormone, secreted mainly by the corpus luteum in the ovary, that prepares and maintains the uterus for pregnancy. [C20: < PRO-[1] + GE(STATION) + STER(OL) + -ONE]

prognathous (prɒg'neɪθəs) *or* **prognathic** (prɒg'næθɪk) *adj.* having a projecting lower jaw. [C19: < PRO-[2] + Gk *gnathos* jaw]

prognosis (prɒg'nəʊsɪs) *n., pl.* **-noses** (-'nəʊsiːz). **1.** *Med.* a prediction of the course or outcome of a disease. **2.** any prediction. [C17: via L < Gk: knowledge beforehand]

prognostic (prɒg'nɒstɪk) *adj.* **1.** of or serving as a prognosis. **2.** predicting. ~*n.* **3.** *Med.* any symptom or sign used in making a prognosis. **4.** a sign of some future occurrence. [C15: < OF *pronostique,* < L *prognōsticum,* < Gk, < *progignōskein* to know in advance]

prognosticate (prɒg'nɒstɪˌkeɪt) *vb.* **1.** to foretell (future events); prophesy. **2.** (*tr.*) to foreshadow or portend. [C16: < Med. L *prognōsticāre* to predict] —**progˌnosti'cation** *n.* —**prog'nosticative** *adj.* —**prog'nostiˌcator** *n.*

program *or* (*sometimes*) **programme** ('prəʊgræm) *n.* **1.** a sequence of coded instructions fed into a computer, enabling it to perform specified logical and arithmetical operations on data. ~*vb.* **-gramming, -grammed. 2.** (*tr.*) to feed a program into (a computer). **3.** (*tr.*) to arrange (data) in a suitable form so that it can be processed by a computer. **4.** (*intr.*) to write a program. —'**programmer** *n.*

programmable *or* **programable** (prəʊ'græməbəl) *adj.* capable of being programmed for automatic operation or computer processing.

programme *or U.S.* **program** ('prəʊgræm) *n.* **1.** a written or printed list of the events, performers, etc., in a public performance. **2.** a performance presented at a scheduled time, esp. on radio or television. **3.** a specially arranged selection of things to be done: *what's the programme for this afternoon?* **4.** a plan, schedule, or procedure. **5.** a syllabus or curriculum. ~*vb.* **-gramming, -grammed** *or U.S.* **-graming, -gramed. 6.** to design or schedule (something) as a programme. ~*n., vb.* **7.** *Computers.* a variant spelling of **program.** [C17: < LL *programma,* < Gk: written public notice, < PRO-[2] + *graphein* to write] —ˌ**program'matic** *adj.*

programmed learning *n.* a teaching method in which the material to be learnt is broken down into easily understandable parts on which the pupil is able to test himself.

programme music *n.* music that is intended to depict or evoke a scene or idea.

programming language *n.* a language system by which instructions to a computer are coded, using a set of characters that is mutually comprehensible to user and computer.

progress *n.* ('prəʊgrɛs). **1.** movement forwards, esp. towards a place or objective. **2.** satisfactory development or advance. **3.** advance towards completion or perfection. **4.** (*modifier*) of or relating to progress: *a progress report.* **5.** (formerly) a stately royal journey. **6. in progress.** taking place. ~*vb.* (prə'grɛs). **7.** (*intr.*) to move forwards or onwards. **8.** (*intr.*) to move towards completion or perfection. **9.** (*tr.*) to be responsible for the satisfactory progress of (a project, etc.) to completion. [C15: < L *prōgressus,* < *prōgredī* to advance, < *gradī* to step]

progression (prə'grɛʃən) *n.* **1.** the act of progressing; advancement. **2.** the act or an instance of moving from one thing in a sequence to the next. **3.** *Maths.* a sequence of numbers in which each term differs from the succeeding term by a constant relation. See also **arithmetic progression, geometric progression, harmonic progression. 4.** *Music.* movement from one note or chord to the next. —**pro'gressional** *adj.*

progressive (prə'grɛsɪv) *adj.* **1.** of or relating to progress. **2.** progressing by steps or degrees. **3.** (*often cap.*) favouring or promoting political or social reform: *a progressive policy.* **4.** denoting an educational system that allows flexibility in learning procedures, based on activities determined by the needs and capacities of the individual child. **5.** (esp. of a disease) advancing in severity, complexity, or extent. **6.** (of a dance, card game, etc.) involving a regular change of partners. **7.** denoting an aspect of verbs in some languages, including English, used to express continuous activity: *a progressive aspect of the verb "to walk" is "is walking".* ~*n.* **8.** a person who advocates progress, as in education, politics, etc. **9. a.** the progressive aspect of a verb. **b.** a verb in this aspect. —**pro'gressively** *adv.* —**pro'gressiveness** *n.* —**pro'gressivism** *n.* —**pro'gressivist** *n.*

prohibit (prə'hɪbɪt) *vb.* (*tr.*) **1.** to forbid by law or other authority. **2.** to hinder or prevent. [C15: < L *prohibēre* to prevent, < PRO-[1] + *habēre* to hold] —**pro'hibiter** *or* **pro'hibitor** *n.*

prohibition (ˌprəʊɪ'bɪʃən) *n.* **1.** the act of prohibiting or state of being prohibited. **2.** an

pro'foreign *adj.*

pro-'Freudian *adj., n.*

order or decree that prohibits. **3.** (*sometimes cap.*) (esp. in the U.S.) a policy of legally forbidding the manufacture, sale, or consumption of alcoholic beverages. **4.** *Law.* an order of a superior court forbidding an inferior court to determine a matter outside its jurisdiction. —ˌ**prohiˈbitionary** *adj.* —ˌ**prohiˈbitionist** *n.*

Prohibition (ˌprəʊɪˈbɪʃən) *n.* the period (1920–33) when the manufacture, sale, and transportation of intoxicating liquors was banned in the U.S. —ˌ**Prohiˈbitionist** *n.*

prohibitive (prəˈhɪbɪtɪv) *or* (*less commonly*) **prohibitory** (prəˈhɪbɪtərɪ, -trɪ) *adj.* **1.** prohibiting or tending to prohibit. **2.** (esp. of prices) tending or designed to discourage sale or purchase. —**proˈhibitively** *adv.* —**proˈhibitiveness** *n.*

project *n.* (ˈprɒdʒɛkt). **1.** a proposal, scheme, or design. **2. a.** a task requiring considerable or concerted effort, such as one by students. **b.** the subject of such a task. ~*vb.* (prəˈdʒɛkt). **3.** (*tr.*) to propose or plan. **4.** (*tr.*) to throw forwards. **5.** to jut or cause to jut out. **6.** (*tr.*) to make a prediction based on known data and observations. **7.** (*tr.*) to transport in the imagination: *to project oneself into the future.* **8.** (*tr.*) to cause (an image) to appear on a surface. **9.** to cause (one's voice) to be heard clearly at a distance. **10.** *Psychol.* **a.** (*intr.*) (esp. of a child) to believe that others share one's subjective mental life. **b.** to impute to others (one's hidden desires). **11.** (*tr.*) *Geom.* to draw a projection of. **12.** (*intr.*) to communicate effectively, esp. to a large gathering. [C14: < L *prōicere* to throw down]

projectile (prəˈdʒɛktaɪl) *n.* **1.** an object thrown forwards. **2.** any self-propelling missile, esp. a rocket. **3.** any object that can be fired from a gun, such as a shell. ~*adj.* **4.** designed to be hurled forwards. **5.** projecting forwards. **6.** *Zool.* another word for **protrusile.** [C17: < NL *prōjectilis* jutting forwards]

projection (prəˈdʒɛkʃən) *n.* **1.** the act of projecting or the state of being projected. **2.** a part that juts out. **3.** See **map projection. 4.** the representation of a line, figure, or solid on a given plane as it would be seen from a particular direction or in accordance with an accepted set of rules. **5.** a scheme or plan. **6.** a prediction based on known evidence and observations. **7. a.** the process of showing film on a screen. **b.** the images shown. **8.** *Psychol.* **a.** the belief that others share one's subjective mental life. **b.** the process of projecting one's own hidden desires and impulses. —**proˈjectional** *adj.* —**proˈjective** *adj.*

projectionist (prəˈdʒɛkʃənɪst) *n.* a person responsible for the operation of film projection machines.

projective geometry *n.* the branch of geometry concerned with the properties of solids that are invariant under projection and section.

projector (prəˈdʒɛktə) *n.* **1.** an optical instrument that projects an enlarged image of individual slides. Full name: **slide projector. 2.** an optical instrument in which a film is wound past a lens so that the frames can be viewed as a continuously moving sequence. Full name: **film** *or* **cine projector. 3.** a device for projecting a light beam. **4.** a person who devises projects.

prokaryote *or* **procaryote** (prəʊˈkærɪɒt) *n.* an organism having cells in which the genetic material is in a single filament of DNA, not enclosed in a nucleus. Cf. **eukaryote.** [< PRO-² + KARYO- + *-ote* as in *zygote*]

prolapse (ˈprəʊlæps, prəʊˈlæps) *Pathol.* ~*n.* **1.** Also: **prolapsus** (prəʊˈlæpsəs). the sinking or falling down of an organ or part. ~*vb.* (*intr.*) **2.** (of an organ, etc.) to sink from its normal position. [C17: < L *prōlābi* to slide along]

prolate (ˈprəʊleɪt) *adj.* having a polar diameter of greater length than the equatorial diameter. Cf. **oblate**¹. [C17: < L *prōferre* to enlarge] —ˈ**prolately** *adv.*

prole (prəʊl) *n., adj. Derog. sl., chiefly Brit.* short for **proletarian.**

prolegomenon (ˌprəʊlɛˈgɒmɪnən) *n., pl.* **-na** (-nə). (*often pl.*) a preliminary discussion, esp. a formal critical introduction to a lengthy text. [C17: < Gk, < *prolegein,* < PRO-² + *legein* to say] —ˌ**proleˈgomenal** *adj.*

prolepsis (prəʊˈlɛpsɪs) *n., pl.* **-ses** (-siːz). **1.** a rhetorical device by which objections are anticipated and answered in advance. **2.** use of a word after a verb in anticipation of its becoming applicable through the action of the verb, as *flat* in *hammer it flat.* [C16: via LL < Gk: anticipation, < *prolambanein* to anticipate, < PRO-² + *lambanein* to take] —**proˈleptic** *adj.*

proletarian (ˌprəʊlɪˈtɛərɪən) *adj.* **1.** of or belonging to the proletariat. ~*n.* **2.** a member of the proletariat. [C17: < L *prōlētārius* one whose only contribution to the state was his offspring, < *prōlēs* offspring] —ˌ**proleˈtarianism** *n.*

proletariat (ˌprəʊlɪˈtɛərɪət) *n.* **1.** all wage-earners collectively. **2.** the lower or working class. **3.** (in Marxist theory) the class of wage-earners, esp. industrial workers, in a capitalist society, whose only possession of significant material value is their labour. **4.** (in ancient Rome) the lowest class of citizens, who had no property. [C19: via F < L *prōlētārius* PROLETARIAN]

proliferate (prəˈlɪfəˌreɪt) *vb.* **1.** to grow or reproduce (new parts, cells, etc.) rapidly. **2.** to grow or increase rapidly. [C19: < Med. L *prōlifer* having offspring, < L *prōlēs* offspring + *ferre* to bear] —**proˌliferˈation** *n.* —**proˈliferative** *adj.*

prolific (prəˈlɪfɪk) *adj.* **1.** producing fruit, offspring, etc., in abundance. **2.** producing constant or successful results. **3.** (often foll. by *in* or *of*) rich or fruitful. [C17: < Med. L *prōlificus,* < L *prōlēs* offspring] —**proˈlifically** *adv.* —**proˈlificness** *or* **proˈlificacy** *n.*

prolix (ˈprəʊlɪks, prəʊˈlɪks) *adj.* **1.** (of a speech, book, etc.) so long as to be boring. **2.** long-winded. [C15: < L *prōlixus* stretched out widely, < *līquī* to flow] —**proˈlixity** *n.* —**proˈlixly** *adv.*

prolocutor (prəʊˈlɒkjʊtə) *n.* a chairman, esp. of the lower house of clergy in a convocation of the Anglican Church. [C15: < L: advocate, < *loqui* to speak] —**proˈlocutorship** *n.*

prologue *or U.S.* (*often*) **prolog** (ˈprəʊlɒg) *n.* **1.** the prefatory lines introducing a play or speech. **2.** a preliminary act or event. **3.** (in early opera) **a.** an introductory scene in which a narrator summarizes the main action of the work. **b.** a brief independent play preceding the opera, esp. one in honour of a patron. ~*vb.* **-loguing, -logued** *or U.S.* **-loging, -loged. 4.** (*tr.*) to introduce with a prologue. [C13: < L *prologus,* < Gk, < PRO-² + *logos* discourse]

prolong (prəˈlɒŋ) *vb.* (*tr.*) to lengthen; extend. [C15: < LL *prōlongāre* to extend, < L PRO-¹ + *longus* long] —**prolongation** (ˌprəʊlɒŋˈgeɪʃən) *n.*

prolusion (prəˈluːʒən) *n.* **1.** a preliminary written exercise. **2.** an introductory essay. [C17: < L *prōlūsiō,* < *prōlūdere* to practise beforehand, < PRO-¹ + *lūdere* to play] —**prolusory** (prəˈluːzərɪ) *adj.*

prom (prɒm) *n.* **1.** *Brit.* short for **promenade** (sense 1) or **promenade concert. 2.** *U.S. & Canad. inf.* a formal dance held at a high school or college.

PROM (prɒm) *n. Computers. acronym for* Programmable Read Only Memory.

promenade (ˌprɒməˈnɑːd) *n.* **1.** *Chiefly Brit.* a public walk, esp. at a seaside resort. **2.** a leisurely walk, esp. one in a public place for pleasure or display. **3.** a marchlike step in dancing. **4.** a marching sequence in a square or country dance. ~*vb.* **5.** to take a promenade in or through (a place). **6.** (*intr.*) *Dancing.* to perform a

---

ˌ**proimmiˈgration** *adj.*
proˈindustry *adj.*
ˌ**prointeˈgration** *adj.*
ˌ**prointerˈvention** *adj.*
ˌ**proinˈvestment** *adj.*
proˈlabour *adj.*

promenade. **7.** (*tr.*) to display or exhibit (someone or oneself) on or as if on a promenade. [C16: < F, < *promener* to lead out for a walk, < LL *prōmināre* to drive (cattle) along, < *mināre* to drive, prob. < *minārī* to threaten] —ˌ**prome'nader** *n.*

promenade concert *n.* a concert at which some of the audience stand rather than sit.

promenade deck *n.* an upper covered deck of a passenger ship for the use of the passengers.

promethazine (prəʊ'mɛθəˌziːn) *n.* an antihistamine drug used to treat allergies and to prevent vomiting. [C20: < PRO(PYL) + (DI-[1]) + METH(YL + AMINE) + AZINE]

Promethean (prə'miːθɪən) *adj.* **1.** of or relating to Prometheus, in Greek myth the Titan who stole fire from Olympus to give to mankind. He was punished by being chained to a rock and having an eagle tear out his liver. **2.** creative, original, or life-enhancing.

promethium (prə'miːθɪəm) *n.* a radioactive element of the lanthanide series artificially produced by the fission of uranium. Symbol: Pm; atomic no.: 61; half-life of most stable isotope, ^{145}Pm: 17.7 years. [C20: NL < *Prometheus;* see PROMETHEAN]

prominence ('prɒmɪnəns) *n.* **1.** the state of being prominent. **2.** something that is prominent, such as a protuberance. **3.** relative importance. **4.** *Astron.* an eruption of incandescent gas from the sun's surface, visible during a total eclipse.

prominent ('prɒmɪnənt) *adj.* **1.** jutting or projecting outwards. **2.** standing out from its surroundings; noticeable. **3.** widely known; eminent. [C16: < L *prōminēre* to jut out, < PRO-[1] + *ēminēre* to project] —'**prominently** *adv.*

promiscuous (prə'mɪskjʊəs) *adj.* **1.** indulging in casual and indiscriminate sexual relationships. **2.** consisting of a number of dissimilar parts or elements mingled indiscriminately. **3.** indiscriminate in selection. **4.** casual or heedless. [C17: < L *prōmiscuus* indiscriminate, < PRO-[1] + *miscēre* to mix] —**pro'miscuously** *adv.* —**promiscuity** (ˌprɒmɪ'skjuːɪtɪ) *or* **pro'miscuousness** *n.*

promise ('prɒmɪs) *vb.* **1.** (often foll. by *to;* when *tr., may take a clause as object or an infinitive*) to give an assurance of (something to someone): *I promise that I will come.* **2.** (*tr.*) to undertake to give (something to someone): *he promised me a car for my birthday.* **3.** (when *tr., takes an infinitive*) to cause people to expect that one is likely (to be or do something): *she promises to be a fine soprano.* **4.** (*tr.; usually passive*) *Obs.* to betroth: *I'm promised to Bill.* **5.** (*tr.*) to assure (someone) of the authenticity or inevitability of something: *there'll be trouble, I promise you.* ~*n.* **6.** an assurance given by one person to another agreeing or guaranteeing to do or not to do something. **7.** indication of forthcoming excellence: *a writer showing considerable promise.* **8.** the thing of which an assurance is given. [C14: < L *prōmissum* a promise, < *prōmittere* to send forth] —ˌ**promi'see** *n.* —'**promiser** *or* (*Law*) '**promisor** *n.*

Promised Land *n.* **1.** *Old Testament.* the land of Canaan, promised by God to Abraham and his descendants as their heritage (Genesis 12:7). **2.** *Christianity.* heaven. **3.** any longed-for place where one expects to find greater happiness.

promising ('prɒmɪsɪŋ) *adj.* showing promise of future success. —'**promisingly** *adv.*

promissory ('prɒmɪsərɪ) *adj.* **1.** containing, relating to, or having the nature of a promise. **2.** *Insurance.* stipulating how the provisions of an insurance contract will be fulfilled.

promissory note *n. Commerce.* a document containing a signed promise to pay a stated sum of money to a specified person at a designated date or on demand. Also called: **note, note of hand.**

promo ('prəʊməʊ) *n., pl.* **-mos.** *Inf.* something used to promote a product, esp. a videotape film used to promote a pop record. [C20: shortened < *promotion*]

promontory ('prɒməntərɪ, -trɪ) *n., pl.* **-ries. 1.** a high point of land, esp. of rocky coast, that juts out into the sea. **2.** *Anat.* any of various projecting structures. [C16: < L *prōmunturium* headland]

promote (prə'məʊt) *vb.* (*tr.*) **1.** to encourage the progress or existence of. **2.** to raise to a higher rank, status, etc. **3.** to advance (a pupil or student) to a higher course, class, etc. **4.** to work for: *to promote reform.* **5.** to encourage the sale of (a product) by advertising or securing financial support. [C14: < L *prōmovēre* to push onwards] —**pro'motion** *n.* —**pro'motional** *adj.*

promoter (prə'məʊtə) *n.* **1.** a person or thing that promotes. **2.** a person who helps to organize, develop, or finance an undertaking. **3.** a person who organizes and finances a sporting event, esp. a boxing match.

prompt (prɒmpt) *adj.* **1.** performed or executed without delay. **2.** quick or ready to act or respond. ~*adv.* **3.** *Inf.* punctually. ~*vb.* **4.** (*tr.*) to urge (someone to do something). **5.** to remind (an actor, singer, etc.) of lines forgotten during a performance. **6.** (*tr.*) to refresh the memory of. **7.** (*tr.*) to give rise to by suggestion: *his affairs will prompt discussion.* ~*n.* **8.** *Commerce.* **a.** the time limit allowed for payment of the debt incurred by purchasing on credit. **b.** Also called: **prompt note.** a memorandum sent to a purchaser to remind him of the time limit and the sum due. **9.** anything that serves to remind. [C15: < L *promptus* evident, < *prōmere* to produce, < *emere* to buy] —'**promptly** *adv.* —'**promptness** *n.*

prompter ('prɒmptə) *n.* **1.** a person offstage who reminds the actors of forgotten lines or cues. **2.** a person, thing, etc., that prompts.

promptitude ('prɒmptɪˌtjuːd) *n.* the quality of being prompt; punctuality.

prompt side *n. Theatre.* the side of the stage where the prompter is, usually to the actor's left in Britain and to his right in the United States.

promulgate ('prɒməlˌgeɪt) *vb.* (*tr.*) **1.** to put into effect (a law, decree, etc.), esp. by formal proclamation. **2.** to announce officially. **3.** to make widespread. [C16: < L *prōmulgāre* to bring to public knowledge] —ˌ**promul'gation** *n.* —'**promulˌgator** *n.*

pron. *abbrev. for:* **1.** pronominal. **2.** pronoun. **3.** pronounced. **4.** pronunciation.

pronate (prəʊ'neɪt) *vb.* (*tr.*) to turn (the forearm or hand) so that the palmar surface is directed downwards. [C19: < LL *prōnāre* to bow] —**pro'nation** *n.* —**pro'nator** *n.*

prone (prəʊn) *adj.* **1.** lying flat or face downwards; prostrate. **2.** sloping or tending downwards. **3.** having an inclination to do something. [C14: < L *prōnus* bent forward, < PRO-[1]] —'**pronely** *adv.* —'**proneness** *n.*

-prone *adj. combining form.* liable or disposed to suffer: *accident-prone.*

prong (prɒŋ) *n.* **1.** a sharply pointed end of an instrument, such as on a fork. **2.** any pointed projecting part. ~*vb.* **3.** (*tr.*) to prick or spear with or as if with a prong. [C15] —**pronged** *adj.*

pronghorn ('prɒŋˌhɔːn) *n.* a ruminant mammal inhabiting rocky deserts of North America and having small branched horns. Also called: **American antelope.**

pronominal (prəʊ'nɒmɪn^{ə}l) *adj.* relating to or playing the part of a pronoun. [C17: < LL *prōnōminālis,* < *prōnōmen* a PRONOUN] —**pro'nominally** *adv.*

pronoun ('prəʊˌnaʊn) *n.* one of a class of words that serves to replace a noun or noun phrase that has already been or is about to be mentioned in the sentence or context. Abbrev.: **pron.** [C16: < L *prōnōmen,* < PRO-[1] + *nōmen* noun]

pronounce (prə'naʊns) *vb.* **1.** to utter or

---

pro'military *adj.*
ˌ**promi'nority** *adj.*
pro'modern *adj.*
pro'monarchist *adj., n.*
pro'nationalist *adj., n.*

articulate (a sound or sounds). **2.** (*tr.*) to utter (words) in the correct way. **3.** (*tr.; may take a clause as object*) to proclaim officially: *I now pronounce you man and wife.* **4.** (when *tr., may take a clause as object*) to declare as one's judgment: *to pronounce the death sentence upon someone.* [C14: < L *prōnuntiāre* to announce] —**pro'nounceable** *adj.* —**pro'nouncer** *n.*

pronounced (prə'naʊnst) *adj.* **1.** strongly marked or indicated. **2.** (of a sound) articulated with vibration of the vocal cords; voiced. —**pronouncedly** (prə'naʊnsɪdlɪ) *adv.*

pronouncement (prə'naʊnsmənt) *n.* **1.** an official or authoritative announcement. **2.** the act of declaring or uttering formally.

pronto ('prɒntəʊ) *adv. Inf.* at once. [C20: < Sp.: quick, < L *promptus* PROMPT]

pronunciation (prəˌnʌnsɪ'eɪʃən) *n.* **1.** the act, instance, or manner of pronouncing sounds. **2.** the supposedly correct manner of pronouncing sounds in a given language. **3.** a phonetic transcription of a word.

proof (pru:f) *n.* **1.** any evidence that establishes or helps to establish the truth, validity, quality, etc., of something. **2.** *Law.* the whole body of evidence upon which the verdict of a court is based. **3.** *Maths, logic.* a sequence of steps or statements that establishes the truth of a proposition. **4.** the act of testing the truth of something (esp. in **put to the proof**). **5.** *Scots Law.* trial before a judge without a jury. **6.** *Printing.* a trial impression made from composed type for the correction of errors. **7.** (in engraving, etc.) a print made by an artist or under his supervision for his own satisfaction before he hands the plate over to a professional printer. **8.** *Photog.* a trial print from a negative. **9. a.** the alcoholic strength of proof spirit. **b.** the strength of a liquor as measured on a scale in which the strength of proof spirit is 100 degrees. ~*adj.* **10.** (*usually postpositive;* foll. by *against*) impervious (to): *the roof is proof against rain.* **11.** having the alcoholic strength of proof spirit. **12.** of proved impenetrability: *proof armour.* ~*vb.* **13.** (*tr.*) to take a proof from (type matter, a plate, etc.). **14.** to proofread (text) or inspect (a print, etc.), as for approval. **15.** to render (something) proof, esp. to waterproof. [C13: < OF *preuve* a test, < LL *proba,* < L *probāre* to test]

-proof *adj., vb. combining form.* (to make) impervious to; secure against (damage by): *waterproof.* [< PROOF (adj.)]

proofread ('pru:fˌri:d) *vb.* **-reading, -read** (-ˌrɛd). to read (copy or printer's proofs) and mark errors to be corrected. —'**proofˌreader** *n.*

proof spirit *n.* (in Britain) a mixture of alcohol and water or an alcoholic beverage that contains 49.28 per cent of alcohol by weight, 57.1 per cent by volume at 51°F: used until 1980 as a standard of alcoholic liquids.

prop[1] (prɒp) *vb.* **propping, propped.** (*tr.;* often foll. by *up*) **1.** to support with a rigid object, such as a stick. **2.** (usually also foll. by *against*) to place or lean. **3.** to sustain or support. ~*n.* **4.** something that gives rigid support, such as a stick. **5.** short for **clothes prop. 6.** a person or thing giving support, as of a moral nature. **7.** *Rugby.* either of the forwards at either end of the front row of a scrum. [C15]

prop[2] (prɒp) *n.* short for **property** (sense 8).

prop[3] (prɒp) *n.* an informal word for **propeller.**

prop. *abbrev. for:* **1.** proper(ly). **2.** property. **3.** proposition. **4.** proprietor.

propaedeutic (ˌprəʊpɪ'dju:tɪk) *n.* **1.** (*often pl.*) preparatory instruction basic to further study of an art or science. ~*adj. also* **propaedeutical. 2.** of, relating to, or providing such instruction. [C19: < Gk *propaideuein* to teach in advance, < PRO-[2] + *paideuein* to rear]

propaganda (ˌprɒpə'gændə) *n.* **1.** the organized dissemination of information, allegations, etc., to assist or damage the cause of a government, movement, etc. **2.** such information, allegations, etc. [C18: < It., use of *propāgandā* in the NL title *Sacra Congregatio de Propaganda Fide* Sacred Congregation for Propagating the Faith] —ˌ**propa'gandism** *n.* —ˌ**propa'gandist** *n., adj.*

Propaganda (ˌprɒpə'gændə) *n. R.C. Church.* a congregation responsible for directing the work of the foreign missions.

propagandize *or* **-ise** (ˌprɒpə'gændaɪz) *vb.* **1.** (*tr.*) to spread by, or subject to, propaganda. **2.** (*intr.*) to spread or organize propaganda.

propagate ('prɒpəˌgeɪt) *vb.* **1.** *Biol.* to reproduce or cause to reproduce; breed. **2.** (*tr.*) *Horticulture.* to produce (plants) by layering, grafting, cuttings, etc. **3.** (*tr.*) to promulgate. **4.** *Physics.* to transmit, esp. in the form of a wave: *to propagate sound.* **5.** (*tr.*) to transmit (characteristics) from one generation to the next. [C16: < L *propāgāre* to increase (plants) by cuttings, < *propāgēs* a cutting, < *pangere* to fasten] —ˌ**propa'gation** *n.* —ˌ**propa'gational** *adj.* —'**propagative** *adj.* —'**propaˌgator** *n.*

propane ('prəʊpeɪn) *n.* a flammable gaseous alkane found in petroleum and used as a fuel. Formula: $CH_3CH_2CH_3$. [C19: < PROPIONIC (ACID) + -ANE]

pro patria *Latin.* ('prəʊ 'pætrɪˌɑ:) for one's country.

propel (prə'pɛl) *vb.* **-pelling, -pelled.** (*tr.*) to impel, drive, or cause to move forwards. [C15: < L *prōpellere*] —**pro'pellant** *or* **pro'pellent** *n.*

propeller (prə'pɛlə) *n.* **1.** a device having blades radiating from a central hub that is rotated to produce thrust to propel a ship, aircraft, etc. **2.** a person or thing that propels.

propelling pencil *n.* a pencil consisting of a metal or plastic case containing a replaceable lead. As the point is worn away the lead can be extended, usually by turning part of the case.

propene ('prəʊpi:n) *n.* a colourless gaseous alkene obtained by cracking petroleum. Formula: $CH_3CH{:}CH_2$. Also called: **propylene.**

propensity (prə'pɛnsɪtɪ) *n., pl.* **-ties. 1.** a natural tendency. **2.** *Obs.* partiality. [C16: < L *prōpensus* inclined to, < *prōpendēre* to hang forwards]

proper ('prɒpə) *adj.* **1.** (*usually prenominal*) appropriate or usual: *in its proper place.* **2.** suited to a particular purpose: *use the proper knife to cut the bread.* **3.** correct in behaviour. **4.** vigorously or excessively moral. **5.** up to a required or regular standard. **6.** (*immediately postpositive*) (of an object, quality, etc.) referred to so as to exclude anything not directly connected with it: *his claim is connected with the deed proper.* **7.** (*postpositive;* foll. by *to*) belonging to or characteristic of a person or thing. **8.** (*prenominal*) *Brit. inf.* (intensifier): *I felt a proper fool.* **9.** (*usually postpositive*) (of heraldic colours) considered correct for the natural colour of the object depicted: *three martlets proper.* **10.** *Arch.* pleasant or good. **11. good and proper.** *Inf.* thoroughly. ~*n.* **12.** the parts of the Mass that vary according to the particular day or feast on which the Mass is celebrated. [C13: via OF < L *prōprius* special] —'**properly** *adv.* —'**properness** *n.*

proper fraction *n.* a fraction in which the numerator has a lower absolute value than the denominator, as $\frac{1}{2}$ or $x/(3 + x^2)$.

proper motion *n.* the very small continuous change in the direction of motion of a star relative to the sun.

proper noun *or* **name** *n.* the name of a person, place, or object, as for example *Iceland, Patrick,* or *Uranus.* Cf. **common noun.**

propertied ('prɒpətɪd) *adj.* owning land or property.

property ('prɒpətɪ) *n., pl.* **-ties. 1.** something of value, either tangible, such as land, or intangible, such as copyrights. **2.** *Law.* the right to possess, use, and dispose of anything. **3.** possessions collectively. **4. a.** land or real estate. **b.** (*as modifier*): *property rights.* **5.** *Chiefly Austral.* a ranch or station. **6.** a quality or characteristic attribute, such as the density or strength of a material. **7.** *Logic, obs.* Also called: **proprium** ('prəʊpɪəm). an attribute that is not essential to a species but is common and peculiar to it. **8.** any movable object used on the set of a stage play or film. Usually shortened to **prop**. [C13: < OF *propriété*, < L *proprietās* something personal, < *proprius* one's own]

property centre *n.* a service for buying and selling property, including conveyancing, provided by a group of local solicitors. In full: **solicitors' property centre.**

property man *n.* a member of the stage crew in charge of the stage properties. Usually shortened to **propman.**

prophecy (ˈprɒfɪsɪ) *n., pl.* **-cies. 1. a.** a message of divine truth revealing God's will. **b.** the act of uttering such a message. **2.** a prediction or guess. **3.** the charismatic endowment of a prophet. [C13: ult. < Gk *prophētēs* PROPHET]

prophesy (ˈprɒfɪˌsaɪ) *vb.* **-sying, -sied. 1.** to foretell (something) by or as if by divine inspiration. **2.** (*intr.*) *Arch.* to give instructions in religious subjects. [C14 *prophecien*, < PROPHECY] **—ˈprophe͵siable** *adj.* **—ˈprophe͵sier** *n.*

prophet (ˈprɒfɪt) *n.* **1.** a person who supposedly speaks by divine inspiration, esp. one through whom a divinity expresses his will. **2.** a person who predicts the future: *a prophet of doom.* **3.** a spokesman for a movement, doctrine, etc. [C13: < OF *prophète*, < L, < Gk *prophētēs* one who declares the divine will, < PRO-² + *phanai* to speak] **—ˈprophetess** *fem. n.*

Prophet (ˈprɒfɪt) *n.* **the. 1.** the principal designation of Mohammed as the founder of Islam. **2.** a name for Joseph Smith as the founder of the Mormon Church.

prophetic (prəˈfɛtɪk) *adj.* **1.** of or relating to a prophet or prophecy. **2.** of the nature of a prophecy; predictive. **—proˈphetically** *adv.*

prophylactic (ˌprɒfɪˈlæktɪk) *adj.* **1.** protecting from or preventing disease. **2.** protective or preventive. *~n.* **3.** a prophylactic drug or device. **4.** *Chiefly U.S.* another name for **condom.** [C16: via F < Gk *prophulaktikos*, < *prophulassein* to guard by taking advance measures, < PRO-² + *phulax* a guard]

prophylaxis (ˌprɒfɪˈlæksɪs) *n.* the prevention of disease or control of its possible spread.

propinquity (prəˈpɪŋkwɪtɪ) *n.* **1.** nearness in place or time. **2.** nearness in relationship. [C14: < L *propinquitās*, < *propinquus* near, < *prope* nearby]

propionic acid (ˌprəʊpɪˈɒnɪk) *n.* a colourless liquid carboxylic acid used in inhibiting the growth of moulds in bread. [C19: < Gk *pro-* first + *pionic*, < *piōn* fat, because it is first in order of the fatty acids]

propitiate (prəˈpɪʃɪˌeɪt) *vb.* (*tr.*) to appease or make well disposed; conciliate. [C17: < L *propitiāre*, < *propitius* gracious] **—proˈpitiable** *adj.* **—pro͵pitiˈation** *n.* **—proˈpitiative** *adj.* **—proˈpiti͵ator** *n.* **—proˈpitiatory** *adj.*

propitious (prəˈpɪʃəs) *adj.* **1.** favourable or auspicious. **2.** gracious or favourably inclined. [C15: < L *propitius* well disposed, < *prope* close to] **—proˈpitiously** *adv.* **—proˈpitiousness** *n.*

propjet (ˈprɒpˌdʒɛt) *n.* another name for **turboprop.**

propolis (ˈprɒpəlɪs) *n.* a greenish-brown resinous aromatic substance collected by bees from the buds of trees for use in the construction of hives. Also called: **bee glue, hive dross.** [C17: via L < Gk: suburb, bee glue, < *pro-* before + *polis* city]

proponent (prəˈpəʊnənt) *n.* a person who argues in favour of something or puts forward a proposal, etc. [C16: < L *prōpōnere* to PROPOSE]

proportion (prəˈpɔːʃən) *n.* **1.** relative magnitude or extent; ratio. **2.** correct or desirable relationship between parts; symmetry. **3.** a part considered with respect to the whole. **4.** (*pl.*) dimensions or size: *a building of vast proportions.* **5.** a share or quota. **6.** a relationship that maintains a constant ratio between two variable quantities: *prices increase in proportion to manufacturing costs.* **7.** *Maths.* a relationship between four numbers or quantities in which the ratio of the first pair equals the ratio of the second pair. *~vb.* (*tr.*) **8.** to adjust in relative amount, size, etc. **9.** to cause to be harmonious in relationship of parts. [C14: < L *prōportiō*, < *prō portione*, lit.: for (its, one's) PORTION] **—proˈportionable** *adj.* **—proˈportionably** *adv.* **—proˈportionment** *n.*

proportional (prəˈpɔːʃənᵊl) *adj.* **1.** of, involving, or being in proportion. *~n.* **2.** *Maths.* an unknown term in a proportion: *in* $a/b = c/x$, *x is the fourth proportional.* **—pro͵portionˈality** *n.* **—proˈportionally** *adv.*

proportional representation *n.* representation of parties in an elective body in proportion to the votes they win. Abbrev.: **PR.**

proportionate *adj.* (prəˈpɔːʃənɪt). **1.** being in proper proportion. *~vb.* (prəˈpɔːʃəˌneɪt). **2.** (*tr.*) to make proportionate. **—proˈportionately** *adv.*

proposal (prəˈpəʊzᵊl) *n.* **1.** the act of proposing. **2.** something proposed, as a plan. **3.** an offer, esp. of marriage.

propose (prəˈpəʊz) *vb.* **1.** (when *tr., may take a clause as object*) to put forward (a plan, etc.) for consideration. **2.** (*tr.*) to nominate, as for a position. **3.** (*tr.*) to intend (to do something): *I propose to leave town now.* **4.** (*tr.*) to announce the drinking of (a toast). **5.** (*intr.;* often foll. by *to*) to make an offer of marriage. [C14: < OF *proposer*, < L *prōpōnere* to display, < PRO-¹ + *pōnere* to place] **—proˈposable** *adj.* **—proˈposer** *n.*

proposition (ˌprɒpəˈzɪʃən) *n.* **1.** a proposal for consideration. **2.** *Logic.* the content of a sentence that affirms or denies something and is capable of being true or false. **3.** *Maths.* a statement or theorem, usually containing its proof. **4.** *Inf.* a person or matter to be dealt with: *he's a difficult proposition.* **5.** *Inf.* an invitation to engage in sexual intercourse. *~vb.* **6.** (*tr.*) to propose a plan, deal, etc., to, esp. to engage in sexual intercourse. [C14 *proposicioun*, < L *prōpositiō* a setting forth; see PROPOSE] **—͵propoˈsitional** *adj.*

propositional calculus *n.* the system of symbolic logic concerned only with the relations between propositions as wholes, taking no account of their internal structure. Cf. **predicate calculus.**

propound (prəˈpaʊnd) *vb.* (*tr.*) **1.** to put forward for consideration. **2.** *English law.* to produce (a will or similar instrument) to the proper court or authority for its validity to be established. [C16 *propone*, < L *prōpōnere* to set forth, < PRO-¹ + *pōnere* to place] **—proˈpounder** *n.*

propranolol (prəʊˈprænəˌlɒl) *n.* a drug used in the treatment of heart disease.

proprietary (prəˈpraɪɪtərɪ, -trɪ) *adj.* **1.** of or belonging to property or proprietors. **2.** privately owned and controlled. **3.** *Med.* denoting a drug manufactured and distributed under a trade name. *~n., pl.* **-taries. 4.** *Med.* a proprietary drug. **5.** a proprietor or proprietors collectively. **6. a.** right to property. **b.** property owned. **7.** (in Colonial America) an owner of a **proprietary colony,** a colony which was granted by the Crown to a particular person or group. [C15: < LL *proprietārius* an owner, < *proprius* one's own] **—proˈprietarily** *adv.*

proprietary name *n.* a name which is restricted in use by virtue of being a trade name.

proprietor (prəˈpraɪətə) *n.* **1.** an owner of a business. **2.** a person enjoying exclusive right of ownership to some property. **—proprietorial** (prə͵praɪəˈtɔːrɪəl) *adj.* **—proˈprietress** *or* **proˈprietrix** *fem. n.*

propriety (prəˈpraɪətɪ) *n., pl.* **-ties. 1.** the quality or state of being appropriate or fitting. **2.** conformity to the prevailing standard of behaviour, speech, etc. **3. the proprieties.** the standards of behaviour considered correct by polite society. [C15: < OF *propriété*, < L *proprietās* a peculiarity, < *proprius* one's own]

proprioceptor (ˌprəʊprɪəˈsɛptə) *n. Physiol.* any receptor, as in the inner ear, muscles, etc., that supplies information about the state of the body. [C20: < *proprio-*, < L *proprius* one's own + RECEPTOR] **—͵proprioˈceptive** *adj.*

---

pro-ˈProtestant *adj., n.*

proptosis (prɒpˈtəʊsɪs) *n., pl.* **-ses** (-siːz). *Pathol.* the forward displacement of an organ or part, such as the eyeball. [C17: via LL < Gk, < *propiptein* to fall forwards]
propulsion (prəˈpʌlʃən) *n.* **1.** the act of propelling or the state of being propelled. **2.** a propelling force. [C15: < L *prōpellere* to propel] —**propulsive** (prəˈpʌlsɪv) *or* **proˈpulsory** *adj.*
propyl (ˈprəʊpɪl) *n.* (*modifier*) of or containing the monovalent group of atoms C_3H_7-. [C19: < PROP(IONIC ACID) + -YL]
propylaeum (ˌprɒpɪˈliːəm) *or* **propylon** (ˈprɒpɪˌlɒn) *n., pl.* **-laea** (-ˈliːə) *or* **-lons, -la** (-lə). a portico, esp. one that forms the entrance to a temple. [C18: via L < Gk *propulaion* before the gate, < PRO-[2] + *pulē* gate]
propylene (ˈprəʊpɪˌliːn) *n.* another name for **propene.** [C19]
propylene glycol *n.* a colourless viscous compound used as an antifreeze and brake fluid.
pro rata (ˈprəʊ ˈrɑːtə) in proportion. [Med. L]
prorate (prəʊˈreɪt, ˈprəʊreɪt) *vb. Chiefly U.S. & Canad.* to divide, assess, or distribute proportionately. [C19: < PRO RATA] —**proˈratable** *adj.* —**proˈration** *n.*
prorogue (prəˈrəʊg) *vb.* to discontinue the meetings of (a legislative body) without dissolving it. [C15: < L *prorogāre,* lit.: to ask publicly] —**prorogation** (ˌprəʊrəˈgeɪʃən) *n.*
prosaic (prəʊˈzeɪɪk) *adj.* **1.** lacking imagination. **2.** having the characteristics of prose. [C16: < LL *prōsaicus,* < L *prōsa* PROSE] —**proˈsaically** *adv.*
pros and cons *pl. n.* the various arguments in favour of and against a motion, course of action, etc. [C16: < L *prō* for + *con,* < *contrā* against]
proscenium (prəˈsiːnɪəm) *n., pl.* **-nia** (-nɪə) *or* **-niums. 1.** the arch or opening separating the stage from the auditorium together with the area immediately in front of the arch. **2.** (in ancient theatres) the stage itself. [C17: via L < Gk *proskēnion,* < *pro-* before + *skēnē* scene]
prosciutto (prəʊˈʃuːtəʊ; *Italian* proˈʃutto) *n.* cured ham from Italy: usually served as an hors d'oeuvre. [It., lit.: dried beforehand]
proscribe (prəʊˈskraɪb) *vb.* (*tr.*) **1.** to condemn or prohibit. **2.** to outlaw; banish; exile. [C16: < L *prōscrībere* to put up a public notice, < *prō-* in public + *scrībere* to write] —**proˈscriber** *n.* —**proscription** (prəʊˈskrɪpʃən) *n.*
prose (prəʊz) *n.* **1.** spoken or written language distinguished from poetry by its lack of a marked metrical structure. **2.** a passage set for translation into a foreign language. **3.** commonplace or dull discourse, expression, etc. **4.** (*modifier*) written in prose. **5.** (*modifier*) matter-of-fact. ~*vb.* **6.** to write (something) in prose. **7.** (*intr.*) to speak or write in a tedious style. [C14: via OF < L *prōsa ōrātiō* straightforward speech, < *prorsus* prosaic, < *prōvertere* to turn forwards] —ˈ**proseˌlike** *adj.*
prosecute (ˈprɒsɪˌkjuːt) *vb.* **1.** (*tr.*) to bring a criminal action against (a person). **2.** (*intr.*) **a.** to seek redress by legal proceedings. **b.** to institute or conduct a prosecution. **3.** (*tr.*) to practise (a profession or trade). **4.** (*tr.*) to continue to do (a task, etc.). [C15: < L *prōsequī* to follow] —ˈ**proseˌcutable** *adj.* —ˈ**proseˌcutor** *n.*
prosecution (ˌprɒsɪˈkjuːʃən) *n.* **1.** the act of prosecuting or the state of being prosecuted. **2. a.** the institution and conduct of legal proceedings against a person. **b.** the proceedings brought in the name of the Crown to put an accused on trial. **3.** the lawyers acting for the Crown to put the case against a person. **4.** the following up or carrying on of something begun.
proselyte (ˈprɒsɪˌlaɪt) *n.* **1.** a person newly converted to a religious faith, esp. a Gentile converted to Judaism. ~*vb.* **2.** a less common word for **proselytize.** [C14: < Church L *prosēlytus,* < Gk *prosēlutos* recent arrival, convert, < *proserchesthai* to draw near] —**proselytism** (ˈprɒsɪlɪˌtɪzəm) *n.* —**proselytic** (ˌprɒsɪˈlɪtɪk) *adj.*
proselytize *or* **-ise** (ˈprɒsɪlɪˌtaɪz) *vb.* to convert (someone) from one religious faith to another. —ˈ**proselytˌizer** *or* -ˌ**iser** *n.*
prosencephalon (ˌprɒsɛnˈsɛfəlɒn) *n., pl.* **-la** (-lə). the part of the brain that develops from the anterior portion of the neural tube. Nontechnical name: **forebrain.** [C19: < NL, < Gk *prosō* forward + *enkephalos* brain]
prosenchyma (prɒsˈɛŋkɪmə) *n.* a plant tissue consisting of long narrow cells with pointed ends: occurs in conducting tissue. [C19: < NL, < Gk *pros-* towards + *enkhuma* infusion]
prosimian (prəʊˈsɪmɪən) *n.* **1.** any of a primitive suborder of primates, including lemurs, lorises, and tarsiers. ~*adj.* **2.** of or belonging to this suborder. [C19: via NL < L *sīmia* ape]
prosit *German.* (ˈproːzɪt) *sentence substitute.* good health! cheers! [G, < L, lit.: may it prove beneficial]
prosody (ˈprɒsədɪ) *n.* **1.** the study of poetic metre and of the art of versification. **2.** a system of versification. **3.** the patterns of stress and intonation in a language. [C15: < L *prosōdia* accent of a syllable, < Gk *prosōidia* song set to music, < *pros* towards + *ōidē,* < *aoidē* song; see ODE] —**prosodic** (prəˈsɒdɪk) *adj.* —ˈ**prosodist** *n.*
prosopopoeia *or* **prosopopeia** (ˌprɒsəpəˈpiːə) *n.* **1.** *Rhetoric.* another word for **personification. 2.** a figure of speech that represents an imaginary, absent, or dead person speaking or acting. [C16: via L < Gk *prosōpopoiia* dramatization, < *prosōpon* face + *poiein* to make]
prospect *n.* (ˈprɒspɛkt). **1.** (*sometimes pl.*) a probability of future success. **2.** a view or scene. **3.** a mental outlook. **4.** expectation, or what one expects. **5.** a prospective buyer, project, etc. **6.** a survey or observation. **7.** *Mining.* **a.** a known or likely deposit of ore. **b.** the location of a deposit of ore. **c.** the yield of mineral obtained from a sample of ore. ~*vb.* (prəˈspɛkt). **8.** (when *intr.,* often foll. by *for*) to explore (a region) for gold or other valuable minerals. **9.** (*tr.*) to work (a mine) to discover its profitability. **10.** (*intr.;* often foll. by *for*) to search (for). [C15: < L *prōspectus* distant view, < *prōspicere* to look into the distance]
prospective (prəˈspɛktɪv) *adj.* **1.** looking towards the future. **2.** (*prenominal*) expected or likely. —**proˈspectively** *adv.*
prospector (prəˈspɛktə) *n.* a person who searches for gold, petroleum, etc.
prospectus (prəˈspɛktəs) *n., pl.* **-tuses. 1.** a formal statement giving details of a forthcoming event, such as the issue of shares. **2.** a brochure giving details of courses, as at a school.
prosper (ˈprɒspə) *vb.* (*usually intr.*) to thrive, succeed, etc., or cause to thrive, etc., in a healthy way. [C15: < L *prosperāre* to succeed, < *prosperus* fortunate, < PRO-[1] + *spēs* hope]
prosperity (prɒˈspɛrɪtɪ) *n.* the condition of prospering; success or wealth.
prosperous (ˈprɒspərəs) *adj.* **1.** flourishing; prospering. **2.** wealthy. —ˈ**prosperously** *adv.*
prostaglandin (ˌprɒstəˈglændɪn) *n.* any of a group of hormone-like compounds found in all mammalian tissues, which stimulate the muscles and affect the nervous system. [C20: < *prosta(te) gland* + -IN; orig. believed to be secreted by the prostate gland]
prostate (ˈprɒsteɪt) *n.* **1.** Also called: **prostate gland.** a gland in male mammals that surrounds the neck of the bladder and secretes a liquid constituent of the semen. ~*adj.* **2.** Also: **prostatic** (prɒˈstætɪk). of the prostate gland. [C17: via Med. L < Gk *prostatēs* something standing in front (of the bladder), < *pro-* in front + *histanai* to cause to stand]
prosthesis (ˈprɒsθɪsɪs) *n., pl.* **-ses** (-ˌsiːz). **1.** *Surgery.* **a.** the replacement of a missing bodily

---

ˌ**proreˈform** *adj.*
ˌ**prorestoˈration** *adj.*
ˌ**proreˈvision** *adj.*
ˌ**prorevoˈlutionary** *adj.*
ˌ**proˈslavery** *adj.*
pro-ˈSoviet *adj.*

part with an artificial substitute. **b.** an artificial part such as a limb, eye, or tooth. **2.** *Linguistics.* another word for **prothesis.** [C16: via LL < Gk: an addition, < *prostithenai* to add, < *pros-* towards + *tithenai* to place] —**prosthetic** (prɒsˈθɛtɪk) *adj.* —**prosˈthetically** *adv.*

prosthetics (prɒsˈθɛtɪks) *n.* (*functioning as sing.*) the branch of surgery concerned with prosthesis.

prostitute (ˈprɒstɪˌtjuːt) *n.* **1.** a woman who engages in sexual intercourse for money. **2.** a man who engages in such activity, esp. in homosexual practices. **3.** a person who offers his talent for unworthy purposes. ~*vb.* (*tr.*) **4.** to offer (oneself or another) in sexual intercourse for money. **5.** to offer for unworthy purposes. [C16: < L *prōstituere* to expose to prostitution, < *prō-* in public + *statuere* to cause to stand] —ˌ**prostiˈtution** *n.* —ˈ**prostiˌtutor** *n.*

prostrate *adj.* (ˈprɒstreɪt). **1.** lying face downwards, as in submission. **2.** exhausted physically or emotionally. **3.** helpless or defenceless. **4.** (of a plant) growing closely along the ground. ~*vb.* (prɒˈstreɪt). (*tr.*) **5.** to cast (oneself) down, as in submission. **6.** to lay or throw down flat. **7.** to make helpless. **8.** to make exhausted. [C14: < L *prōsternere* to throw to the ground, < *prō-* before + *sternere* to lay low] —**prosˈtration** *n.*

prostyle (ˈprəʊstaɪl) *adj.* **1.** (of a building) having a row of columns in front, esp. as in the portico of a Greek temple. ~*n.* **2.** a prostyle building, portico, etc. [C17: < L *prostȳlos,* < Gk: with pillars in front, < PRO-[2] + *stulos* pillar]

prosy (ˈprəʊzɪ) *adj.* **prosier, prosiest.** **1.** of the nature of or similar to prose. **2.** dull, tedious, or long-winded. —ˈ**prosily** *adv.* —ˈ**prosiness** *n.*

Prot. *abbrev. for:* **1.** Protectorate. **2.** Protestant.

protactinium (ˌprəʊtækˈtɪnɪəm) *n.* a toxic radioactive element that occurs in uranium ores and is produced by neutron irradiation of thorium. Symbol: Pa; atomic no.: 91; half-life of most stable isotope, ^{231}Pa: 32 500 years.

protagonist (prəʊˈtægənɪst) *n.* **1.** the principal character in a play, story, etc. **2.** a supporter, esp. when important or respected, of a cause, party, etc. [C17: < Gk *prōtagōnistēs,* < *prōtos* first + *agōnistēs* actor] —**proˈtagonism** *n.*

▷ **Usage.** The use of *protagonist* as in definition 2 is regarded as unacceptable by some people on the grounds that the word derives from the Greek *prōtos* first, higher ranking, not from Latin *pro* in favour of. While the second sense has undoubtedly developed as a result of confusion over the etymology it is now well established in English; careful writers and speakers may, however, prefer to avoid this use and employ an alternative word such as *proponent, champion,* or *advocate.* In either of its uses, the word has the sense of *chief* and so does not need to be qualified by this or any similar adjective: *a protagonist of the movement* not *a leading protagonist of the movement.*

protasis (ˈprɒtəsɪs) *n., pl.* **-ses** (-siːz). **1.** *Logic, grammar.* the antecedent of a conditional statement, such as *it rains* in *if it rains the game will be cancelled.* **2.** (in classical drama) the introductory part of a play. [C17: via L < Gk: a proposal, < *pro-* before + *teinein* to extend]

protea (ˈprəʊtɪə) *n.* a shrub of tropical and southern Africa, having flowers with coloured bracts arranged in showy heads. [C20: < NL, < *Proteus,* a sea god who could change shape, referring to the many forms of the plant]

protean (prəʊˈtiːən, ˈprəʊtɪən) *adj.* readily taking on various shapes or forms; variable. [C16: < *Proteus;* see PROTEA]

protease (ˈprəʊtɪˌeɪs) *n.* any enzyme involved in proteolysis. [C20: < PROTEIN + -ASE]

protect (prəˈtɛkt) *vb.* (*tr.*) **1.** to defend from trouble, harm, etc. **2.** *Econ.* to assist (domestic industries) by the imposition of protective tariffs on imports. **3.** *Commerce.* to provide funds in advance to guarantee payment of (a note, etc.). [C16: < L *prōtegere* to cover before]

protection (prəˈtɛkʃən) *n.* **1.** the act of protecting or the condition of being protected. **2.** something that protects. **3. a.** the imposition of duties on imports, for the protection of domestic industries against overseas competition, etc. **b.** Also called: **protectionism.** the system or theory of such restrictions. **4.** *Inf.* **a.** Also called: **protection money.** money demanded by gangsters for freedom from molestation. **b.** freedom from molestation purchased in this way. —**proˈtectionˌism** *n.* —**proˈtectionist** *n., adj.*

protective (prəˈtɛktɪv) *adj.* **1.** giving or capable of giving protection. **2.** *Econ.* of or intended for protection of domestic industries. ~*n.* **3.** something that protects. **4.** a condom. —**proˈtectively** *adv.* —**proˈtectiveness** *n.*

protective coloration *n.* the coloration of an animal that enables it to blend with its surroundings and therefore escape the attention of predators.

protector (prəˈtɛktə) *n.* **1.** a person or thing that protects. **2.** *History.* a person who exercised royal authority during the minority, absence, or incapacity of the monarch. —**proˈtectress** *fem. n.*

Protector (prəˈtɛktə) *n.* short for **Lord Protector,** the title borne by Oliver Cromwell (1653–58) and by Richard Cromwell (1658–59) as heads of state during the period known as the Protectorate.

protectorate (prəˈtɛktərɪt) *n.* **1. a.** a territory largely controlled by but not annexed to a stronger state. **b.** the relation of a protecting state to its protected territory. **2.** the office or period of office of a protector.

protégé *or* (*fem.*) **protégée** (ˈprəʊtɪˌʒeɪ) *n.* a person who is protected and aided by the patronage of another. [C18: < F *protéger* to PROTECT]

protein (ˈprəʊtiːn) *n.* any of a large group of nitrogenous compounds of high molecular weight that are essential constituents of all living organisms. [C19: via G < Gk *prōteios* primary, < *protos* first + -IN] —ˌ**proteinˈaceous, proˈteinic,** *or* **proˈteinous** *adj.*

pro tempore *Latin.* (ˈprəʊ ˈtɛmpərɪ) *adv., adj.* for the time being. Often shortened to **pro tem** (prəʊ ˈtɛm).

proteolysis (ˌprəʊtɪˈɒlɪsɪs) *n.* the hydrolysis of proteins into simpler compounds by the action of enzymes. [C19: < NL, < *proteo-* (< PROTEIN) + -LYSIS] —**proteolytic** (ˌprəʊtɪəˈlɪtɪk) *adj.*

protest *n.* (ˈprəʊtɛst). **1. a.** public, often organized, manifestation of dissent. **b.** (*as modifier*): *a protest march.* **2.** a formal or solemn objection. **3.** a formal notarial statement drawn up on behalf of a creditor and declaring that the debtor has dishonoured a bill of exchange, etc. **4.** the act of protesting. ~*vb.* (prəˈtɛst). **5.** (when *intr.,* foll. by *against, at, about,* etc.; when *tr., may take a clause as object*) to make a strong objection (to something, esp. a supposed injustice or offence). **6.** (when *tr., may take a clause as object*) to disagree; object: *"I'm O.K." she protested.* **7.** (when *tr., may take a clause as object*) to assert in a formal or solemn manner. **8.** (*tr.*) *Chiefly U.S.* to object forcefully to: *leaflets protesting Dr King's murder.* [C14: < L *prōtestārī* to make a formal declaration, < *prō-* before + *testārī* to assert] —**proˈtestant** *adj., n.* —**proˈtester** *or* **proˈtestor** *n.* —**proˈtestingly** *adv.*

Protestant (ˈprɒtɪstənt) *n.* **a.** an adherent of Protestantism. **b.** (*as modifier*): *the Protestant Church.*

Protestantism (ˈprɒtɪstənˌtɪzəm) *n.* the religion of any of the Churches of Western Christendom that are separated from the Roman Catholic Church and adhere substantially to principles established during the Reformation.

---

proˈsyndicalism *n.*

protestation (ˌprəʊtɛsˈteɪʃən) *n.* **1.** the act of protesting. **2.** a strong declaration.

prothalamion (ˌprəʊθəˈleɪmɪən) *or* **prothalamium** *n., pl.* **-mia** (-mɪə). a song or poem in celebration of a marriage. [C16: < Gk *pro-* before + *thalamos* marriage]

prothallus (prəʊˈθæləs) *or* **prothallium** (prəʊˈθælɪəm) *n., pl.* **-li** (-laɪ) *or* **-lia** (-lɪə). *Bot.* the small flat green disc of tissue that bears the reproductive organs of pteridophytes. [C19: < NL, < *pro-* before + Gk *thallus* a young shoot]

prothesis (ˈprɒθɪsɪs) *n., pl.* **-ses** (-siːz). **1.** a development of a language by which a syllable is prefixed to a word to facilitate pronunciation: *Latin "scala" gives Spanish "escala" by prothesis.* **2.** *Eastern Orthodox Church.* the solemn preparation of the Eucharistic elements before consecration. [C16: via LL < Gk: a setting out in public, < *pro-* forth + *thesis* a placing] **—prothetic** (prəˈθɛtɪk) *adj.* **—proˈthetically** *adv.*

prothrombin (prəʊˈθrɒmbɪn) *n. Biochemistry.* a zymogen found in blood that gives rise to thrombin on activation.

protist (ˈprəʊtɪst) *n.* any organism belonging to a large group, including bacteria, protozoans, and fungi, regarded as distinct from plants and animals. [C19: < NL *Protista* most primitive organisms, < Gk *prōtistos* the very first, < *prōtos* first]

protium (ˈprəʊtɪəm) *n.* the most common isotope of hydrogen, having a mass number of 1. [C20: NL, < PROTO- + -IUM]

proto- *or sometimes before a vowel* **prot-** *combining form.* **1.** first: *protomartyr.* **2.** primitive or original: *prototype.* **3.** first in a series of chemical compounds: *protoxide.* [< Gk *prōtos* first, < *pro* before]

protocol (ˈprəʊtəˌkɒl) *n.* **1.** the formal etiquette and procedure for state and diplomatic ceremonies. **2.** a record of an agreement, esp. in international negotiations, etc. **3. a.** an amendment to a treaty or convention. **b.** an annexe appended to a treaty to deal with subsidiary matters. **4.** *Chiefly U.S.* a record of data or observations on a particular experiment or proceeding. [C16: < Med. L *prōtocollum,* < LGk *prōtokollon* sheet glued to the front of a manuscript, < PROTO- + *kolla* glue]

protohuman (ˌprəʊtəʊˈhjuːmən) *n.* **1.** any of various prehistoric primates that resembled modern man. *~adj.* **2.** of these primates.

Proto-Indo-European *n.* the prehistoric unrecorded language that was the ancestor of all Indo-European languages.

protomartyr (ˌprəʊtəʊˈmɑːtə) *n.* **1.** St Stephen as the first Christian martyr. **2.** the first martyr to lay down his life in any cause.

proton (ˈprəʊtɒn) *n.* a stable, positively charged elementary particle, found in atomic nuclei in numbers equal to the atomic number of the element. [C20: < Gk *prōtos* first]

protoplasm (ˈprəʊtəˌplæzəm) *n. Biol.* the living contents of a cell: a complex translucent colourless colloidal substance. [C19: < NL, < PROTO- + Gk *plasma* form] **—ˌprotoˈplasmic, ˌprotoˈplasmal,** *or* **ˌprotoplasˈmatic** *adj.*

prototype (ˈprəʊtəˌtaɪp) *n.* **1.** one of the first units manufactured of a product, which is tested so that the design can be changed if necessary before the product is manufactured commercially. **2.** a person or thing that serves as an example of a type. **3.** *Biol.* the ancestral or primitive form of a species. **—ˌprotoˈtypal, prototypic** (ˌprəʊtəˈtɪpɪk), *or* **ˌprotoˈtypical** *adj.*

protozoan (ˌprəʊtəˈzəʊən) *n., pl.* **-zoa** (-ˈzəʊə). **1.** Also **protozoon.** any minute invertebrate of a phylum including amoebas and foraminifers. *~adj. also* **protozoic. 2.** of or belonging to this group. [C19: via NL < Gk PROTO- + *zoion* animal]

protract (prəˈtrækt) *vb. (tr.)* **1.** to lengthen or extend (a speech, etc.). **2.** (of a muscle) to draw, thrust, or extend (a part, etc.) forwards. **3.** to plot using a protractor and scale. [C16: < L *prōtrahere* to prolong, < PRO-[1] + *trahere* to drag] **—proˈtracted** *adj.* **—protractedly** *adv.* **—proˈtraction** *n.*

protractile (prəˈtræktaɪl) *adj.* able to be extended: *protractile muscle.*

protractor (prəˈtræktə) *n.* **1.** an instrument for measuring or drawing angles on paper, usually a flat semicircular transparent plastic sheet graduated in degrees. **2.** *Anat.* a former term for **extensor.**

protrude (prəˈtruːd) *vb.* **1.** to thrust forwards or outwards. **2.** to project or cause to project. [C17: < L, < PRO-[2] + *trudere* to thrust] **—proˈtrusion** *n.* **—proˈtrusive** *adj.*

protrusile (prəˈtruːsaɪl) *adj. Zool.* capable of being thrust forwards: *protrusile jaws.*

protuberant (prəˈtjuːbərənt) *adj.* swelling out; bulging. [C17: < LL *prōtūberāre* to swell, < PRO-[1] + *tūber* swelling] **—proˈtuberance** *or* **proˈtuberancy** *n.* **—proˈtuberantly** *adv.*

proud (praʊd) *adj.* **1.** (foll. by *of,* an infinitive, or a clause) pleased or satisfied, as with oneself, one's possessions, achievements, etc. **2.** feeling honoured or gratified by some distinction. **3.** having an inordinately high opinion of oneself; haughty. **4.** characterized by or proceeding from a sense of pride: *a proud moment.* **5.** having a proper sense of self-respect. **6.** stately or distinguished. **7.** bold or fearless. **8.** (of a surface, edge, etc.) projecting or protruding. **9.** (of animals) restive or excited, often sexually. *~adv.* **10. do (someone) proud. a.** to entertain (someone) on a grand scale: *they did us proud at the hotel.* **b.** to honour (someone): *his honesty did him proud.* [LOE *prūd,* < OF *prud, prod* brave, < LL *prōde* useful, < L *prōdesse* to be of value] **—ˈproudly** *adv.* **—ˈproudness** *n.*

proud flesh *n.* a mass of tissue formed around a healing wound.

Prov. *abbrev. for:* **1.** Provençal. **2.** *Bible.* Proverbs. **3.** Province. **4.** Provost.

prove (pruːv) *vb.* **proving, proved; proved** *or* **proven.** (*mainly tr.*) **1.** (*may take a clause as object or an infinitive*) to demonstrate the truth or validity of, esp. by using an established sequence of procedures. **2.** to establish the quality of, esp. by experiment. **3.** *Law.* to establish the genuineness of (a will). **4.** to show (oneself) able or courageous. **5.** (*copula*) to be found (to be): *this has proved useless.* **6.** (*intr.*) (of dough) to rise in a warm place before baking. [C12: < OF *prover,* < L *probāre* to test, < *probus* honest] **—ˈprovable** *adj.* **—ˈprovably** *adv.* **—ˌprovaˈbility** *n.*

proven (ˈpruːvᵊn, ˈprəʊ-) *vb.* **1.** a past participle of **prove. 2.** See **not proven.** *~adj.* **3.** tried; tested: *a proven method.*

provenance (ˈprɒvɪnəns) *n.* a place of origin, as of a work of art. [C19: < F, < *provenir,* < L *prōvenīre* to originate, < *venīre* to come]

Provençal (ˌprɒvɒnˈsɑːl; *French* prɔvɑ̃sal) *adj.* **1.** denoting or characteristic of Provence, a former province of SE France, its inhabitants, their dialect of French, or their Romance language. *~n.* **2.** a language of Provence, closely related to French and Italian, belonging to the Romance group of the Indo-European family. **3.** a native or inhabitant of Provence.

provender (ˈprɒvɪndə) *n.* **1.** fodder for livestock. **2.** food in general. [C14: < OF *provendre,* < LL *praebenda* grant, < L *praebēre* to proffer]

proverb (ˈprɒvɜːb) *n.* **1.** a short memorable saying embodying some commonplace fact. **2.** a person or thing exemplary of a characteristic: *Antarctica is a proverb for extreme cold.* **3.** *Bible.* a wise saying providing guidance. [C14: via OF < L *prōverbium,* < *verbum* word]

proverbial (prəˈvɜːbɪəl) *adj.* **1.** (*prenominal*) commonly or traditionally referred to as an example of some peculiarity, characteristic, etc.

---

proˈunion *adj.* **ˌprouniˈversity** *adj.*

2. of, embodied in, or resembling a proverb. —**pro'verbially** *adv.*

provide (prə'vaɪd) *vb.* (*mainly tr.*) **1.** to furnish or supply. **2.** to afford; yield: *this meeting provides an opportunity to talk.* **3.** (*intr.;* often foll. by *for* or *against*) to take careful precautions: *he provided against financial ruin by wise investment.* **4.** (*intr.;* foll. by *for*) to supply means of support (to): *he provides for his family.* **5.** (of a person, law, etc.) to state as a condition; stipulate. **6.** to confer and induct into ecclesiastical offices. [C15: < L *prōvidēre* to provide for, < *prō-* beforehand + *vidēre* to see] —**pro'vider** *n.*

providence ('prɒvɪdəns) *n.* **1. a.** *Christianity.* God's foreseeing protection and care of his creatures. **b.** such protection and care as manifest by some other force. **2.** a supposed manifestation of such care and guidance. **3.** the foresight or care exercised by a person in the management of his affairs.

Providence ('prɒvɪdəns) *n. Christianity.* God, esp. as showing foreseeing care of his creatures.

provident ('prɒvɪdənt) *adj.* **1.** providing for future needs. **2.** exercising foresight in the management of one's affairs. **3.** characterized by foresight. [C15: < L *prōvidens* foreseeing, < *prōvidēre* to PROVIDE] —'**providently** *adv.*

providential (ˌprɒvɪ'dɛnʃəl) *adj.* characteristic of or presumed to proceed from or as if from divine providence. —ˌ**provi'dentially** *adv.*

provident society *n.* a mutual insurance society catering esp. for those on a low income, providing sickness, death, and pension benefits.

providing (prə'vaɪdɪŋ) *or* **provided** *conj.* (*subordinating;* sometimes foll. by *that*) on the condition or understanding (that): *I'll play, providing you pay me.*

province ('prɒvɪns) *n.* **1.** a territory governed as a unit of a country or empire. **2.** (*pl.;* usually preceded by *the*) those parts of a country lying outside the capital and other large cities and regarded as outside the mainstream of sophisticated culture. **3.** an area of learning, activity, etc. **4.** the extent of a person's activities or office. **5.** an ecclesiastical territory, having an archbishop or metropolitan at its head. **6.** an administrative and territorial subdivision of a religious order. **7.** *History.* a region of the Roman Empire outside Italy ruled by a governor from Rome. [C14: < OF, < L *prōvincia* conquered territory]

provincewide ('prɒvɪnsˌwaɪd) *Canad.* ~*adj.* **1.** covering or available to the whole of a province: *a provincewide referendum.* ~*adv.* **2.** throughout a province: *an advertising campaign to go provincewide.*

provincial (prə'vɪnʃəl) *adj.* **1.** of or connected with a province. **2.** characteristic of or connected with the provinces. **3.** having attitudes and opinions supposedly common to people living in the provinces; unsophisticated; limited. **4.** *N.Z.* denoting a football team representing a province, one of the historical administrative areas of New Zealand. ~*n.* **5.** a person lacking the sophistications of city life; rustic or narrow-minded individual. **6.** a person coming from or resident in a province or the provinces. **7.** the head of an ecclesiastical province. **8.** the head of a territorial subdivision of a religious order. —**provinciality** (prəˌvɪnʃɪ'ælɪtɪ) *n.* —**pro'vincially** *adv.*

provincialism (prə'vɪnʃəˌlɪzəm) *n.* **1.** narrowness of mind; lack of sophistication. **2.** a word or attitude characteristic of a provincial. **3.** attention to the affairs of one's local area rather than the whole nation. **4.** the state or quality of being provincial.

provision (prə'vɪʒən) *n.* **1.** the act of supplying food, etc. **2.** something that is supplied. **3.** preparations (esp. in **make provision for**). **4.** (*pl.*) food and other necessities, as for an expedition. **5.** a condition or stipulation incorporated in a document; proviso. **6.** the conferring of and induction into ecclesiastical offices. ~*vb.* **7.** (*tr.*) to supply with provisions. [C14: < L *prōvīsiō* a providing; see PROVIDE] —**pro'visioner** *n.*

provisional (prə'vɪʒənᵊl) *adj.* subject to later alteration; temporary or conditional: *a provisional decision.* —**pro'visionally** *adv.*

Provisional (prə'vɪʒənᵊl) *adj.* **1.** designating one of the two factions of the IRA and Sinn Féin that have existed since a split in late 1969. The Provisional movement advocates terrorism to achieve Irish unity. ~*n.* **2.** Also called: **Provo.** a member of the Provisional IRA or Sinn Féin.

proviso (prə'vaɪzəʊ) *n., pl.* **-sos** *or* **-soes. 1.** a clause in a document or contract that embodies a condition or stipulation. **2.** a condition or stipulation. [C15: < Med. L *prōvīsō quod* it being provided that, < L *prōvīsus* provided]

provisory (prə'vaɪzərɪ) *adj.* **1.** containing a proviso; conditional. **2.** provisional. **3.** making provision. —**pro'visorily** *adv.*

Provo ('prəʊvəʊ) *n., pl.* **-vos.** another name for a **Provisional.**

provocation (ˌprɒvə'keɪʃən) *n.* **1.** the act of provoking or inciting. **2.** something that causes indignation, anger, etc.

provocative (prə'vɒkətɪv) *adj.* serving or intended to provoke or incite, esp. to anger or sexual desire: *a provocative look; a provocative remark.* —**pro'vocatively** *adv.*

provoke (prə'vəʊk) *vb.* (*tr.*) **1.** to anger or infuriate. **2.** to incite or stimulate. **3.** to promote (anger, indignation, etc.) in a person. **4.** to cause; bring about: *the accident provoked an inquiry.* [C15: < L *prōvocāre* to call forth] —**pro'voking** *adj.* —**pro'vokingly** *adv.*

provost ('prɒvəst) *n.* **1.** the head of certain university colleges or schools. **2.** (formerly) the principal magistrate of a Scottish burgh; now only a courtesy title. **3.** *Church of England.* the senior dignitary of one of the more recent cathedral foundations. **4.** *R.C. Church.* **a.** the head of a cathedral chapter. **b.** (formerly) the member of a monastic community second in authority under the abbot. **5.** (in medieval times) an overseer, steward, or bailiff. [OE *profost,* < Med. L *prōpositus* placed at the head (of), < L *praepōnere* to place first]

provost marshal (prə'vəʊ) *n.* the officer in charge of military police in a camp or city.

prow (praʊ) *n.* the bow of a vessel. [C16: < OF *proue,* < L *prora,* < Gk *prōra*]

prowess ('praʊɪs) *n.* **1.** outstanding or superior skill or ability. **2.** bravery or fearlessness, esp. in battle. [C13: < OF *proesce,* < *prou* good]

prowl (praʊl) *vb.* **1.** (when *intr.,* often foll. by *around* or *about*) to move stealthily around (a place) as if in search of prey or plunder. ~*n.* **2.** the act of prowling. **3. on the prowl. a.** moving around stealthily. **b.** pursuing members of the opposite sex. [C14 *prollen,* <?] —'**prowler** *n.*

prox. *abbrev. for* proximo (next month).

proximal ('prɒksɪməl) *adj. Anat.* situated close to the centre, median line, or point of attachment or origin. —'**proximally** *adv.*

proximate ('prɒksɪmɪt) *adj.* **1.** next or nearest in space or time. **2.** very near; close. **3.** immediately preceding or following in a series. **4.** a less common word for **approximate.** [C16: < LL *proximāre* to draw near, < L *proximus* next, < *prope* near] —'**proximately** *adv.*

proximity (prɒk'sɪmɪtɪ) *n.* **1.** nearness in space or time. **2.** nearness or closeness in a series. [C15: < L *proximitās* closeness; see PROXIMATE]

proximo ('prɒksɪməʊ) *adv. Now rare except when abbreviated in formal correspondence.* in or during the next or coming month: *a letter of the seventh proximo.* Abbrev.: **prox.** Cf. **instant, ultimo.** [C19: < L: in or on the next]

proxy ('prɒksɪ) *n., pl.* **proxies. 1.** a person authorized to act on behalf of someone else; agent: *to vote by proxy.* **2.** the authority, esp. in the form of a document, given to a person to act on behalf

'**pro'war** *adj.*

of someone else. [C15 *prokesye,* < *procuracy,* < L *prōcūrātiō* procuration; see PROCURE]

prude (pruːd) *n.* a person who affects or shows an excessively modest, prim, or proper attitude, esp. regarding sex. [C18: < F, < *prudefemme,* < OF *prode femme* respectable woman; see PROUD] —ˈ**prudery** *n.* —ˈ**prudish** *adj.* —ˈ**prudishly** *adv.*

prudence (ˈpruːdəns) *n.* **1.** caution in practical affairs; discretion. **2.** care taken in the management of one's resources. **3.** consideration for one's own interests. **4.** the quality of being prudent.

prudent (ˈpruːdᵊnt) *adj.* **1.** discreet or cautious in managing one's activities; circumspect. **2.** practical and careful in providing for the future. **3.** exercising good judgment. [C14: < L *prūdēns* far-sighted, < *prōvidens* acting with foresight; see PROVIDENT] —ˈ**prudently** *adv.*

prudential (pruːˈdɛnʃəl) *adj.* **1.** characterized by or resulting from prudence. **2.** exercising sound judgment. —**pruˈdentially** *adv.*

pruinose (ˈpruːɪˌnəʊs, -ˌnəʊz) *adj. Bot.* coated with a powdery or waxy bloom. [C19: < L *pruīnōsus* frost-covered, < *pruīna* hoarfrost]

prune[1] (pruːn) *n.* **1.** a purplish-black partially dried fruit of any of several varieties of plum tree. **2.** *Sl., chiefly Brit.* a dull or foolish person. **3.** **prunes and prisms.** denoting an affected and mincing way of speaking. [C14: < OF *prune,* < L *prūnum* plum, < Gk *prounon*]

prune[2] (pruːn) *vb.* **1.** to remove (dead or superfluous twigs, branches, etc.) from (a tree, shrub, etc.), esp. by cutting off. **2.** to remove (anything undesirable or superfluous) from (a book, etc.). [C15: < OF *proignier* to clip, prob. < *provigner* to prune vines, ult. < L *propāgo* a cutting] —ˈ**prunable** *adj.* —ˈ**pruner** *n.*

prunella (pruːˈnɛlə) *n.* a strong fabric, esp. a twill-weave worsted, formerly used for academic gowns and the uppers of some shoes. [C17: ? < *prunelle,* a green French liqueur, with reference to the colour of the cloth]

pruning hook *n.* a tool with a curved steel blade terminating in a hook, used for pruning.

prurient (ˈprʊərɪənt) *adj.* **1.** unusually or morbidly interested in sexual thoughts or practices. **2.** exciting lustfulness. [C17: < L *prūrīre* to lust after, itch] —ˈ**prurience** *n.* —ˈ**pruriently** *adv.*

prurigo (prʊəˈraɪgəʊ) *n.* a chronic inflammatory disease of the skin characterized by intense itching. [C19: < L: an itch] —**pruriginous** (prʊəˈrɪdʒɪnəs) *adj.*

pruritus (prʊəˈraɪtəs) *n. Pathol.* any intense sensation of itching. [C17: < L: an itching; see PRURIENT] —**pruritic** (prʊəˈrɪtɪk) *adj.*

Prussian (ˈprʌʃən) *adj.* **1.** of Prussia, a former state in N Germany, or its people, esp. of the Junkers and their formal military tradition. ~*n.* **2.** a native or inhabitant of Prussia. **3.** **Old Prussian.** the extinct Baltic language of the non-German inhabitants of Prussia.

Prussian blue *n.* **1.** a dark blue insoluble crystalline compound of iron, ferric ferrocyanide, used as a pigment in paints. **2. a.** the blue or deep greenish-blue colour of this. **b.** (*as adj.*): *a Prussian-blue carpet.*

prussic acid (ˈprʌsɪk) *n.* the extremely poisonous aqueous solution of hydrogen cyanide. [C18: < F *acide prussique* Prussian acid, because obtained from Prussian blue]

pry[1] (praɪ) *vb.* **prying, pried.** **1.** (*intr.;* often foll. by *into*) to make an impertinent or uninvited inquiry (about a private matter, topic, etc.). ~*n., pl.* **pries.** **2.** the act of prying. **3.** a person who pries. [C14: <?]

pry[2] (praɪ) *vb.* **prying, pried.** the U.S. and Canad. word for **prise.** [C14: <?]

pryer (ˈpraɪə) *n.* a variant spelling of **prier.**

Przewalski's horse (ˌpɜːʒəˈvælskɪz) *n.* a rare wild horse of W Mongolia, having an erect mane and no forelock. [C19: after the Russian explorer Nikolai *Przewalski* (1839–88), who discovered it]

PS *abbrev. for:* **1.** Passenger Steamer. **2.** Police Sergeant. **3.** Also: **ps.** postscript. **4.** private secretary. **5.** prompt side.

Ps. *or* **Psa.** *Bible. abbrev. for* Psalm(s).

psalm (sɑːm) *n.* **1.** (*often cap.*) any of the sacred songs that constitute a book (Psalms) of the Old Testament. **2.** a musical setting of one of these. **3.** any sacred song. [OE, < LL *psalmus,* < Gk *psalmos* song accompanied on the harp, < *psallein* to play (the harp)] —**psalmic** (ˈsɑːmɪk, ˈsæl-) *adj.*

psalmist (ˈsɑːmɪst) *n.* the composer of a psalm or psalms, esp. (when *cap.* and preceded by *the*) David, traditionally regarded as the author of the Book of Psalms.

psalmody (ˈsɑːmədɪ, ˈsæl-) *n., pl.* **-dies.** **1.** the act of singing psalms or hymns. **2.** the art of setting psalms to music. [C14: via LL < Gk *psalmōdia* singing accompanied by a harp, < *psalmos* (see PSALM) + *ōidē* ODE] —ˈ**psalmodist** *n.* —**psalmodic** (sælˈmɒdɪk) *adj.*

Psalter (ˈsɔːltə) *n.* **1.** another name for the Book of Psalms, esp. in the version in the Book of Common Prayer. **2.** a translation, musical, or metrical version of the Psalms. **3.** a book containing a version of Psalms. [OE *psaltere,* < LL *psaltērium,* < Gk *psaltērion* stringed instrument, < *psallein* to play a stringed instrument]

psalterium (sɔːlˈtɪərɪəm) *n., pl.* **-teria** (-ˈtɪərɪə). the third compartment of the stomach of ruminants. Also called: **omasum.** [C19: < L *psaltērium* PSALTER; from the similarity of its folds to the pages of a book]

psaltery (ˈsɔːltərɪ) *n., pl.* **-teries.** *Music.* an ancient stringed instrument similar to the lyre, but having a trapezoidal sounding board over which the strings are stretched.

p's and q's *pl. n.* behaviour; manners (esp. in **mind one's p's and q's**). [altered < *p(lea)se and (than)k yous*]

PSBR (in Britain) *abbrev. for* public sector borrowing requirement; the money required by the public sector of the economy for expenditure on items that are not financed from income.

psephology (sɛˈfɒlədʒɪ) *n.* the statistical and sociological study of elections. [C20: < Gk *psephos* pebble, vote + -LOGY, from the ancient Greeks' custom of voting with pebbles] —**psephological** (ˌsɛfəˈlɒdʒɪkᵊl) *adj.* —ˌ**psephoˈlogically** *adv.* —**pseˈphologist** *n.*

pseud (sjuːd) *n.* **1.** *Inf.* a false or pretentious person. ~*adj.* **2.** another word for **pseudo.**

Pseudepigrapha (ˌsjuːdɪˈpɪgrəfə) *pl. n.* various Jewish writings from the first century B.C. to the first century A.D. that claim to have been divinely revealed but which have been excluded from the Greek canon of the Old Testament. [C17: < Gk *pseudepigraphos* falsely entitled, < PSEUDO- + *epigraphein* to inscribe] —**Pseudepigraphic** (ˌsjuːdɛpɪˈgræfɪk) *or* ˌ**Pseudepiˈgraphical** *adj.*

pseudo (ˈsjuːdəʊ) *adj. Inf.* not genuine.

pseudo- *or sometimes before a vowel* **pseud-** *combining form.* **1.** false, pretending, or unauthentic: *pseudo-intellectual.* **2.** having a close resemblance to: *pseudopodium.* [< Gk *pseudēs* false, < *pseudein* to lie]

pseudocarp (ˈsjuːdəʊˌkɑːp) *n.* a fruit, such as the apple, that includes parts other than the ripened ovary. —ˌ**pseudoˈcarpous** *adj.*

pseudomorph (ˈsjuːdəʊˌmɔːf) *n.* a mineral that

ˌ**pseudoanˈtique** *adj.*
ˌ**pseudoarˈchaic** *adj.*
ˌ**pseudoˌaristoˈcratic** *adj.*
ˌ**pseudoarˈtistic** *adj.*
ˌ**pseudo-Boˈhemian** *adj.*
ˌ**pseudoˈclassic** *or* ˌ**pseudoˈclassical** *adj.*
ˌ**pseudoˈclassiˌcism** *n.*
ˌ**pseudoˈcultiˌvated** *adj.*
ˌ**pseudoˌdemoˈcratic** *adj.*
ˌ**pseudo-Eˌlizaˈbethan** *adj.*
ˌ**pseudo-ˈGeorgian** *adj.*
ˌ**pseudo-ˈGothic** *adj.*
ˌ**pseudo-ˈGrecian** *adj.*
ˌ**pseudohisˈtorical** *adj.*
ˌ**pseudoˈliterary** *adj.*
ˌ**pseudoˌmediˈeval** *adj.*
ˌ**pseudoˈmodern** *adj.*

has an uncharacteristic crystalline form as a result of assuming the shape of another mineral that it has replaced. —ˌ**pseudo'morphic** *or* ˌ**pseudo'morphous** *adj.* —ˌ**pseudo'morphism** *n.*

pseudonym ('sjuːdəˌnɪm) *n.* a fictitious name adopted esp. by an author. [C19: via F < Gk *pseudōnumon*] —ˌ**pseudo'nymity** *n.* —**pseudonymous** (sjuː'dɒnɪməs) *adj.*

pseudopodium (ˌsjuːdəʊ'pəʊdɪəm) *n., pl.* **-dia** (-dɪə). a temporary projection from the cell of a protozoan, etc., used for feeding and locomotion.

psf *abbrev. for* pounds per square foot.

pshaw (pʃɔː) *interj. Becoming rare.* an exclamation of disgust, impatience, disbelief, etc.

psi[1] (psaɪ) *n.* **1.** the 23rd letter of the Greek alphabet (Ψ, ψ), a composite consonant, transliterated as *ps.* **2.** paranormal or psychic phenomena collectively.

psi[2] *abbrev. for* pounds per square inch.

psilocybin (ˌsɪlə'saɪbɪn, ˌsaɪlə-) *n.* a crystalline phosphate ester that is the active principle of the hallucinogenic fungus *Psilocybe mexicana.* Formula: $C_{12}H_{17}N_2O_4P$. [C20: < NL *Psilocybe* (< Gk *psilos* bare + *kubē* head) + -IN]

psi particle *n.* a type of elementary particle thought to be formed from charmed quarks. See **charm** (sense 7).

psittacine ('sɪtəˌsaɪn, -sɪn) *adj.* of, relating to, or resembling a parrot. [C19: < LL *psittacīnus,* < L *psittacus* a parrot]

psittacosis (ˌsɪtə'kəʊsɪs) *n.* a viral disease of parrots and other birds that can be transmitted to man, in whom it produces pneumonia. Also called: **parrot fever.** [C19: < NL, < L *psittacus* a parrot, < Gk *psittakos;* see -OSIS]

psoas ('səʊəs) *n.* either of two muscles of the loins that aid in flexing and rotating the thigh. [C17: < NL, < Gk *psoai* (pl.)]

psoriasis (sə'raɪəsɪs) *n.* a skin disease characterized by the formation of reddish spots and patches covered with silvery scales. [C17: via NL < Gk: itching disease, < *psōra* itch] —**psoriatic** (ˌsɔːrɪ'ætɪk) *adj.*

psst (pst) *interj.* an exclamation of beckoning, esp. one made surreptitiously.

PST (in the U.S. and Canada) *abbrev. for* Pacific Standard Time.

PSV *abbrev. for* public service vehicle.

psych *or* **psyche** (saɪk) *vb.* (*tr.*) *Inf.* to psychoanalyse. See also **psych out, psych up.** [C20: shortened < PSYCHOANALYSE]

psyche ('saɪkɪ) *n.* the human mind or soul. [C17: < L, < Gk *psukhē* breath, soul]

psychedelic (ˌsaɪkɪ'dɛlɪk) *adj.* **1.** relating to or denoting new or altered perceptions or sensory experiences, as through the use of hallucinogenic drugs. **2.** denoting any of the drugs, esp. LSD, that produce these effects. **3.** *Inf.* (of painting, etc.) having the vivid colours and complex patterns popularly associated with the visual effects of psychedelic states. [C20: < PSYCHE + Gk *delos* visible] —ˌ**psyche'delically** *adv.*

psychiatry (saɪ'kaɪətrɪ) *n.* the branch of medicine concerned with the diagnosis and treatment of mental disorders. —**psychiatric** (ˌsaɪkɪ'ætrɪk) *or* ˌ**psychi'atrical** *adj.* —ˌ**psychi'atrically** *adv.* —**psy'chiatrist** *n.*

psychic ('saɪkɪk) *adj.* **1. a.** outside the possibilities defined by natural laws, as mental telepathy. **b.** (of a person) sensitive to forces not recognized by natural laws. **2.** mental as opposed to physical. ~*n.* **3.** a person who is sensitive to parapsychological forces or influences. —'**psychical** *adj.* —'**psychically** *adv.*

psycho ('saɪkəʊ) *n., pl.* **-chos,** *adj.* an informal word for **psychopath** or **psychopathic.**

psycho- *or sometimes before a vowel* **psych-** *combining form.* indicating the mind or psychological or mental processes: *psychology; psychosomatic.* [< Gk *psukhē* spirit, breath]

psychoactive (ˌsaɪkəʊ'æktɪv) *adj.* (of drugs such as LSD and barbiturates) capable of affecting mental activity. Also: **psychotropic.**

psychoanalyse *or esp. U.S.* **-lyze** (ˌsaɪkəʊ'ænəˌlaɪz) *vb.* (*tr.*) to examine or treat (a person) by psychoanalysis.

psychoanalysis (ˌsaɪkəʊə'nælɪsɪs) *n.* a method of studying the mind and treating mental and emotional disorders based on revealing and investigating the role of the unconscious mind. —**psychoanalyst** (ˌsaɪkəʊ'ænəlɪst) *n.* —**psychoanalytic** (ˌsaɪkəʊˌænə'lɪtɪk) *or* ˌ**psychoˌana'lytical** *adj.* —ˌ**psychoˌana'lytically** *adv.*

psychobiology (ˌsaɪkəʊbaɪ'ɒlədʒɪ) *n. Psychol.* the attempt to understand the psychology of organisms in terms of their biological functions and structures. —**psychobiological** (ˌsaɪkəʊˌbaɪə'lɒdʒɪk°l) *adj.* —ˌ**psychobi'ologist** *n.*

psychochemical (ˌsaɪkəʊ'kɛmɪk°l) *n.* **1.** any of various chemical compounds whose primary effect is the alteration of the normal state of consciousness. ~*adj.* **2.** of such compounds.

psychodrama ('saɪkəʊˌdrɑːmə) *n. Psychiatry.* a form of group therapy in which individuals act out situations from their past.

psychodynamics (ˌsaɪkəʊdaɪ'næmɪks) *n.* (*functioning as sing.*) *Psychol.* the study of interacting motives and emotions. —ˌ**psychody'namic** *adj.*

psychogenic (ˌsaɪkəʊ'dʒɛnɪk) *adj. Psychol.* (esp. of disorders or symptoms) of mental, rather than organic, origin. —ˌ**psycho'genically** *adv.*

psychokinesis (ˌsaɪkəʊkɪ'niːsɪs, -kaɪ-) *n.* (in parapsychology) alteration of the state of an object supposedly by mental influence alone. [C20: < PSYCHO- + Gk *kinēsis* motion]

psycholinguistics (ˌsaɪkəʊlɪŋ'gwɪstɪks) *n.* (*functioning as sing.*) the psychology of language, including language acquisition by children, language disorders, etc. —ˌ**psycho'linguist** *n.*

psychological (ˌsaɪkə'lɒdʒɪk°l) *adj.* **1.** of or relating to psychology. **2.** of or relating to the mind or mental activity. **3.** having no real or objective basis; arising in the mind: *his backaches are all psychological.* **4.** affecting the mind. —ˌ**psycho'logically** *adv.*

psychological moment *n.* the most appropriate time for producing a desired effect.

psychological warfare *n.* the military application of psychology, esp. to attempts to influence morale in time of war.

psychologize *or U.S.* **-gise** (saɪ'kɒləˌdʒaɪz) *vb.* (*intr.*) **1.** to make interpretations of mental processes. **2.** to carry out investigation in psychology.

psychology (saɪ'kɒlədʒɪ) *n., pl.* **-gies.** **1.** the scientific study of all forms of human and animal behaviour. **2.** *Inf.* the mental make-up of an individual that causes him to think or act in the way he does. —**psy'chologist** *n.*

psychometrics (ˌsaɪkəʊ'mɛtrɪks) *n.* (*functioning as sing.*) **1.** the branch of psychology concerned with the design and use of psychological tests. **2.** the application of statistical techniques to psychological testing.

psychometry (saɪ'kɒmɪtrɪ) *n. Psychol.* **1.** measurement and testing of mental states and processes. **2.** (in parapsychology) the supposed ability to deduce facts about events by touching objects related to them. —**psychometric** (ˌsaɪkəʊ'mɛtrɪk) *or* ˌ**psycho'metrical** *adj.* —ˌ**psycho' metrically** *adv.*

psychomotor (ˌsaɪkəʊ'məʊtə) *adj.* of, relating to, or characterizing movements of the body associated with mental activity.

psychoneurosis (ˌsaɪkəʊnjʊ'rəʊsɪs) *n., pl.* **-roses** (-'rəʊsiːz). another word for **neurosis.**

psychopath ('saɪkəʊˌpæθ) *n.* a person afflicted with a personality disorder characterized by a tendency to commit antisocial and sometimes

---

ˌ**pseudo'mythical** *adj.*
ˌ**pseudoˌori'ental** *adj.*
ˌ**pseudoˌphilo'sophical** *adj.*
ˌ**pseudopro'fessional** *adj.*
ˌ**pseudoˌpsycho'logical** *adj.*
ˌ**pseudo'scholarly** *adj.*
ˌ**pseudo'science** *n.*
ˌ**pseudoˌscien'tific** *adj.*
ˌ**pseudo-Vic'torian** *adj.*

violent acts and a failure to feel guilt for such acts. —ˌpsycho'pathic *adj.* —ˌpsycho'pathically *adv.*

psychopathology (ˌsaɪkəʊpə'θɒlədʒɪ) *n.* the scientific study of mental disorders. —**psychopathological** (ˌsaɪkəʊˌpæθə'lɒdʒɪkᵊl) *adj.*

psychopathy (saɪ'kɒpəθɪ) *n.* any mental disorder or disease.

psychopharmacology (ˌsaɪkəʊˌfɑːmə'kɒlədʒɪ) *n.* the study of drugs that affect the mind.

psychophysics (ˌsaɪkəʊ'fɪzɪks) *n.* (*functioning as sing.*) the branch of psychology concerned with the relationship between physical stimuli and their effects on the organism. —ˌ**psycho'physical** *adj.*

psychophysiology (ˌsaɪkəʊˌfɪzɪ'ɒlədʒɪ) *n.* the branch of psychology concerned with the physiological basis of mental processes. —**psychophysiological** (ˌsaɪkəʊˌfɪzɪə'lɒdʒɪkᵊl) *adj.*

psychosexual (ˌsaɪkəʊ'sɛksjʊəl) *adj.* of or relating to the mental aspects of sex, such as sexual fantasies. —ˌ**psycho'sexually** *adv.*

psychosis (saɪ'kəʊsɪs) *n., pl.* **-choses** (-'kəʊsiːz). any form of severe mental disorder in which the individual's contact with reality becomes highly distorted. [C19: NL, < PSYCHO- + -OSIS]

psychosocial (ˌsaɪkəʊ'səʊʃəl) *adj.* of or relating to processes or factors that are both social and psychological in origin.

psychosomatic (ˌsaɪkəʊsə'mætɪk) *adj.* of disorders, such as stomach ulcers, thought to be caused or aggravated by psychological factors such as stress.

psychosurgery (ˌsaɪkəʊ'sɜːdʒərɪ) *n.* any surgical procedure on the brain, such as a frontal lobotomy, to relieve serious mental disorders. —**psychosurgical** (ˌsaɪkəʊ'sɜːdʒɪkᵊl) *adj.*

psychotherapy (ˌsaɪkəʊ'θɛrəpɪ) *n.* the treatment of nervous disorders by psychological methods. —ˌ**psychoˌthera'peutic** *adj.* —ˌ**psychoˌthera'peutically** *adv.* —ˌ**psycho'therapist** *n.*

psychotic (saɪ'kɒtɪk) *Psychiatry.* ~*adj.* **1.** of or characterized by psychosis. ~*n.* **2.** a person suffering from psychosis. —**psy'chotically** *adv.*

psychotomimetic (saɪˌkɒtəʊmɪ'mɛtɪk) *adj.* (of drugs such as LSD and mescaline) capable of inducing psychotic symptoms.

psych out *vb.* (*mainly tr., adv.*) *Inf.* **1.** to guess correctly the intentions of (another). **2.** to analyse (a problem, etc.) psychologically. **3.** to intimidate or frighten.

psychrometer (saɪ'krɒmɪtə) *n.* a type of hygrometer consisting of two thermometers, one of which has a dry bulb and the other a bulb that is kept moist and ventilated.

psych up *vb.* (*tr., adv.*) *Inf.* to get (oneself or another) into a state of psychological readiness for an action, performance, etc.

pt *abbrev. for:* **1.** part. **2.** patient. **3.** payment. **4.** point. **5.** port. **6.** pro tempore.

Pt *abbrev. for:* (in place names): **1.** Point. **2.** Port. ~**3.** *the chemical symbol for* platinum.

PT *abbrev. for:* **1.** physical therapy. **2.** physical training. **3.** postal telegraph.

pt. *abbrev. for:* **1.** pint. **2.** preterite.

PTA *abbrev. for:* **1.** Parent-Teacher Association. **2.** (in Britain) Passenger Transport Authority.

ptarmigan ('tɑːmɪgən) *n., pl.* **-gans** *or* **-gan.** any of several arctic and subarctic grouse, esp. one which has a white winter plumage. [C16: changed (? infl. by Gk *pteron* wing) < Scot. Gaelic *tarmachan,* <?]

Pte *Mil. abbrev. for* private.

pteridology (ˌtɛrɪ'dɒlədʒɪ) *n.* the branch of botany concerned with the study of ferns. [C19: < *pterido-,* < Gk *pteris* fern + -LOGY] —**pteridological** (ˌtɛrɪdəʊ'lɒdʒɪkᵊl) *adj.*

pteridophyte ('tɛrɪdəʊˌfaɪt) *n.* a plant, such as a fern, reproducing by spores and having vascular tissue, roots, stems, and leaves. [C19: < *pterido-,* < Gk *pteris* fern + -PHYTE]

ptero- *combining form.* a wing, or a part resembling a wing: *pterodactyl.* [< Gk *pteron*]

pterodactyl (ˌtɛrə'dæktɪl) *n.* an extinct flying reptile having membranous wings supported on an elongated fourth digit.

pteropod ('tɛrəˌpɒd) *n.* a small marine gastropod mollusc in which the foot is expanded into two winglike lobes for swimming. Also called: **sea butterfly.**

pterosaur ('tɛrəˌsɔː) *n.* any of an order of extinct flying reptiles of Jurassic and Cretaceous times: included the pterodactyls.

-pterous *or* **-pteran** *adj. combining form.* indicating a specified number or type of wings: *dipterous.* [< Gk *-pteros,* < *pteron* wing]

pterygoid process ('tɛrɪˌgɔɪd) *n. Anat.* either of two long bony plates extending downwards from each side of the sphenoid bone within the skull. [C18 *pterygoid,* < Gk *pterugoeidēs,* < *pterux* wing; see -OID]

PTO *or* **pto** *abbrev. for* please turn over.

Ptolemaic (ˌtɒlɪ'meɪɪk) *adj.* **1.** of or relating to Ptolemy, the 2nd-century A.D. Greek astronomer, or to his conception of the universe. **2.** of or relating to the Macedonian dynasty that ruled Egypt from the death of Alexander the Great (323 B.C.) to the death of Cleopatra (30 B.C.).

Ptolemaic system *n.* the theory of planetary motion developed by Ptolemy from the hypotheses of earlier philosophers, stating that the earth lay at the centre of the universe with the sun, the moon, and the known planets revolving around it in complicated orbits. Beyond the largest of these orbits lay a sphere of fixed stars.

ptomaine *or* **ptomain** ('təʊmeɪn) *n.* any of a group of amines formed by decaying organic matter. [C19: < It. *ptomaina,* < Gk *ptoma* corpse, < *piptein* to fall]

ptomaine poisoning *n.* a popular term for **food poisoning.** Ptomaines were once erroneously thought to be a cause of food poisoning.

ptosis ('təʊsɪs) *n., pl.* **ptoses** ('təʊsiːz). prolapse or drooping of a part, esp. the eyelid. [C18: < Gk: a falling] —**ptotic** ('tɒtɪk) *adj.*

pty *Austral., N.Z., & S. African. abbrev. for* proprietary.

ptyalin ('taɪəlɪn) *n. Biochemistry.* an amylase secreted in the saliva of man and other animals. [C19: < Gk *ptualon* saliva, < *ptuein* to spit]

p-type *adj.* **1.** (of a semiconductor) having a density of mobile holes in excess of that of conduction electrons. **2.** associated with or resulting from the movement of holes in a semiconductor: *p-type conductivity.*

Pu *the chemical symbol for* plutonium.

pub (pʌb) *n.* **1.** *Chiefly Brit.* a building with a bar and one or more public rooms licensed for the sale and consumption of alcoholic drink, often also providing light meals. Formal name: **public house.** **2.** *Austral. & N.Z.* a hotel. ~*vb.* **pubbing, pubbed.** **3.** (*intr.*) *Inf.* to visit a pub or pubs (esp. in **go pubbing**).

pub. *abbrev. for:* **1.** public. **2.** publication. **3.** published. **4.** publisher. **5.** publishing.

pub-crawl *Inf., chiefly Brit.* ~*n.* **1.** a drinking tour of a number of pubs or bars. ~*vb.* **2.** (*intr.*) to make such a tour.

puberty ('pjuːbətɪ) *n.* the period at the beginning of adolescence when the sex glands become functional. Also called: **pubescence.** [C14: < L *pūbertās* maturity, < *pūber* adult] —'**pubertal** *adj.*

pubes ('pjuːbiːz) *n., pl.* **pubes.** **1.** the region above the external genital organs, covered with hair from the time of puberty. **2.** pubic hair. **3.** the pubic bones. **4.** the plural of **pubis.** [< L]

pubescent (pjuː'bɛsᵊnt) *adj.* **1.** arriving or arrived at puberty. **2.** (of certain plants and animals or their parts) covered with a layer of fine short hairs or down. [C17: < L *pūbēscere* to reach manhood, < *pūber* adult] —**pu'bescence** *n.*

pubic ('pjuːbɪk) *adj.* of or relating to the pubes or pubis: *pubic hair.*

pubis ('pjuːbɪs) *n., pl.* **-bes.** one of the three sections of the hipbone that forms part of the pelvis. [C16: shortened < NL *os pūbis* bone of the PUBES]

public ('pʌblɪk) *adj.* **1.** of or concerning the people as a whole. **2.** open to all: *public gardens.*

3. performed or made openly: *public proclamation.* **4.** (*prenominal*) well-known: *a public figure.* **5.** (*usually prenominal*) maintained at the expense of, serving, or for the use of a community: *a public library.* **6.** open, acknowledged, or notorious: *a public scandal.* **7. go public.** (of a private company) to issue shares for subscription by the public. ~*n.* **8.** the community or people in general. **9.** a section of the community grouped because of a common interest, activity, etc.: *the racing public.* [C15: < L *pūblicus,* changed < *pōplicus* of the people, < *populus* people] —ˈ**publicly** *adv.*

public-address system *n.* a system of microphones, amplifiers, and loudspeakers for increasing the sound level, used in auditoriums, public gatherings, etc. Sometimes shortened to **PA system.**

publican (ˈpʌblɪkən) *n.* **1.** (in Britain) a person who keeps a public house. **2.** (in ancient Rome) a public contractor, esp. one who farmed the taxes of a province. [C12: < OF *publicain,* < L *pūblicānus* tax gatherer, < *pūblicum* state revenues]

publication (ˌpʌblɪˈkeɪʃən) *n.* **1.** the act or process of publishing a printed work. **2.** any printed work offered for sale or distribution. **3.** the act or an instance of making information public. [C14: via OF < L *pūblicātiō* confiscation of property, < *pūblicāre* to seize for public use]

public bar *n. Brit.* a bar in a public house usually serving drinks at a cheaper price than in the lounge bar.

public company *n.* a limited company whose shares may be purchased by the public and traded freely on the open market and whose share capital is not less than a statutory minimum. Cf. **private company.**

public convenience *n.* a public lavatory.

public corporation *n.* (in Britain) an organization established to run a nationalized industry or state-owned enterprise. The chairman and board members are appointed by a government minister, and the government has overall control.

public domain *n.* **1.** the status of a published work upon which the copyright has expired or which has not been subject to copyright. **2. in the public domain.** generally known or accessible.

public enemy *n.* a notorious person, such as a criminal, who is regarded as a menace to the public.

public house *n.* **1.** *Brit.* the formal name for a **pub.** **2.** *U.S. & Canad.* an inn, tavern, or small hotel.

publicist (ˈpʌblɪsɪst) *n.* **1.** a person who publicizes something, esp. a press or publicity agent. **2.** a journalist. **3.** *Rare.* a person learned in public or international law.

publicity (pʌˈblɪsɪtɪ) *n.* **1. a.** the technique or process of attracting public attention to people, products, etc., as by the use of the mass media. **b.** (*as modifier*): *a publicity agent.* **2.** public interest aroused by such a technique or process. **3.** information used to draw public attention to people, products, etc. **4.** the state of being public. [C18: via F < Med. L *pūblicitās;* see PUBLIC]

publicize *or* **-ise** (ˈpʌblɪˌsaɪz) *vb.* (*tr.*) to bring to public notice; advertise.

public lending right *n.* the right of authors to receive payment when their books are borrowed from public libraries.

public nuisance *n.* **1.** *Law.* an illegal act causing harm to members of a community rather than to any individual. **2.** *Inf.* a person generally considered objectionable.

public opinion *n.* the attitude of the public, esp. as a factor in determining action, policy, etc.

public prosecutor *n. Law.* an official in charge of prosecuting important cases.

Public Record Office *n.* an institution in which official records are stored and kept available for inspection by the public.

public relations *n.* (*functioning as sing. or pl.*) **1. a.** the practice of creating, promoting, or maintaining goodwill and a favourable image among the public towards an institution, public body, etc. **b.** the professional staff employed for this purpose. Abbrev.: **PR.** **c.** the techniques employed. **d.** (*as modifier*): *the public-relations industry.* **2.** the relationship between an organization and the public.

public school *n.* **1.** (in England and Wales) a private independent fee-paying secondary school. **2.** in certain Canadian provinces, a public elementary school as distinguished from a separate school. **3.** any school that is part of a free local educational system.

public sector *n.* the part of an economy which consists of state-owned institutions, including nationalized industries and services provided by local authorities.

public servant *n.* **1.** an elected or appointed holder of a public office. **2.** the Austral. and N.Z. equivalent of **civil servant.**

public service *n.* the Austral. and N.Z. equivalent of the **civil service.**

public-spirited *adj.* having or showing active interest in the good of the community.

public utility *n.* an enterprise concerned with the provision to the public of essentials, such as electricity or water. Also called (in the U.S.): **public-service corporation.**

public works *pl. n.* engineering projects and other constructions, financed and undertaken by a government for the community.

publish (ˈpʌblɪʃ) *vb.* **1.** to produce and issue (printed matter) for distribution and sale. **2.** (*intr.*) to have one's written work issued for publication. **3.** (*tr.*) to announce formally or in public. **4.** (*tr.*) to communicate (defamatory matter) to someone other than the person defamed: *to publish a libel.* [C14: < OF *puplier,* < L *pūblicāre* to make PUBLIC] —ˈ**publishable** *adj.*

publisher (ˈpʌblɪʃə) *n.* **1.** a company or person engaged in publishing periodicals, books, music, etc. **2.** *U.S. & Canad.* the proprietor of a newspaper.

puce (pjuːs) *n., adj.* (of) a colour varying from deep red to dark purplish brown. [C18: shortened < F *couleur puce* flea colour, < L *pūlex* flea]

puck[1] (pʌk) *n.* a small disc of hard rubber used in ice hockey. [C19: <?]

puck[2] (pʌk) *n.* a mischievous or evil spirit. [OE *pūca,* <?] —ˈ**puckish** *adj.*

pucka (ˈpʌkə) *adj.* a less common spelling of **pukka.**

pucker (ˈpʌkə) *vb.* **1.** to gather (a soft surface such as the skin) into wrinkles, or (of such a surface) to be so gathered. ~*n.* **2.** a wrinkle, crease, or irregular fold. [C16: ? rel. to POKE[2], from the baglike wrinkles]

pudding (ˈpʊdɪŋ) *n.* **1.** a sweetened usually cooked dessert made in many forms and of various ingredients. **2.** a savoury dish, usually consisting partially of pastry or batter: *steak-and-kidney pudding.* **3.** the dessert course in a meal. **4.** a sausage-like mass of meat, oatmeal, etc., stuffed into a prepared skin or bag and boiled. [C13 *poding*] —ˈ**puddingy** *adj.*

pudding stone *n.* a conglomerate rock in which there is a difference in colour and composition between the pebbles and the matrix.

puddle (ˈpʌdᵊl) *n.* **1.** a small pool of water, esp. of rain. **2.** a small pool of any liquid. **3.** a worked mixture of wet clay and sand that is impervious to water and is used to line a pond or canal. ~*vb.* (*tr.*) **4.** to make (clay, etc.) into puddle. **5.** to subject (iron) to puddling. [C14 *podel,* dim. of OE *pudd* ditch, <?] —ˈ**puddler** *n.* —ˈ**puddly** *adj.*

puddling (ˈpʌdlɪŋ) *n.* a process for converting pig iron into wrought iron by heating it with ferric oxide in a furnace and stirring it to oxidize the carbon.

pudency (ˈpjuːdᵊnsɪ) *n.* modesty or prudishness. [C17: < LL *pudentia,* < L *pudēre* to feel shame]

pudendum (pjuːˈdɛndəm) *n., pl.* **-da** (-də). (*often pl.*) the human external genital organs collectively, esp. of a female. [C17: < LL, < L *pudenda* the shameful (parts), < *pudēre* to be ashamed] —**puˈdendal** *or* **pudic** (ˈpjuːdɪk) *adj.*

pudgy (ˈpʌdʒɪ) *adj.* **pudgier, pudgiest.** a variant spelling (esp. U.S.) of **podgy.** [C19: <?] —ˈ**pudgily** *adv.* —ˈ**pudginess** *n.*

pueblo (ˈpwɛbləʊ; *Spanish* ˈpweβlo) *n., pl.* **-los** (-ləʊz; *Spanish* -los). **1.** a communal village, built by certain Indians of the southwestern U.S. and parts of Latin America, consisting of one or more flat-roofed houses. **2.** (in Spanish America) a village or town. [C19: < Sp.: people, < L *populus*]

Pueblo (ˈpwɛbləʊ) *n., pl.* **-lo** *or* **-los.** a member of any of the North American Indian peoples who live in pueblos.

puerile (ˈpjʊəraɪl) *adj.* **1.** exhibiting silliness; immature; trivial. **2.** of or characteristic of a child. [C17: < L *puerīlis* childish, < *puer* a boy] —ˈ**puerilely** *adv.* —**puerility** (pjʊəˈrɪlɪtɪ) *n.*

puerperal (pjuːˈɜːpərəl) *adj.* of or occurring during the period following childbirth. [C18: < NL *puerperālis*, < L *puerperium* childbirth, ult. < *puer* boy + *parere* to bear]

puerperal fever *n.* a serious, formerly widespread, form of blood poisoning caused by infection contracted during childbirth.

puerperal psychosis *n.* a mental disorder sometimes occurring in women after childbirth, characterized by deep depression.

puff (pʌf) *n.* **1.** a short quick gust or emission, as of wind, smoke, etc. **2.** the amount of wind, smoke, etc., released in a puff. **3.** the sound made by a puff. **4.** an instance of inhaling and expelling the breath as in smoking. **5.** a light aerated pastry usually filled with cream, jam, etc. **6.** a powder puff. **7.** exaggerated praise, as of a book, product, etc., esp. through an advertisement. **8.** a piece of clothing fabric gathered up so as to bulge in the centre while being held together at the edges. **9.** a cylindrical roll of hair pinned in place in a coiffure. **10.** *U.S.* a quilted bed cover. **11.** one's breath (esp. in **out of puff**). **12.** *Derog. sl.* a male homosexual. ~*vb.* **13.** to blow or breathe or cause to blow or breathe in short quick draughts. **14.** (*tr.; often foll. by out; usually passive*) to cause to be out of breath. **15.** to take draws at (a cigarette, etc.). **16.** (*intr.*) to move with or by the emission of puffs: *the steam train puffed up the incline.* **17.** (often foll. by *up, out,* etc.) to swell, as with air, pride, etc. **18.** (*tr.*) to praise with exaggerated empty words, often in advertising. **19.** (*tr.*) to apply (powder, dust, etc.) to (something). [OE *pyffan*] —ˈ**puffy** *adj.*

puff adder *n.* **1.** a large venomous African viper that inflates its body when alarmed. **2.** another name for **hognose snake.**

puffball (ˈpʌfˌbɔːl) *n.* **1.** any of various fungi having a round fruiting body that discharges a cloud of brown spores when mature. **2.** short for **puffball skirt.**

puffball skirt *n.* a skirt or a dress with a skirt that puffs out wide and is nipped into a narrow hem.

puffer (ˈpʌfə) *n.* **1.** a person or thing that puffs. **2.** Also called: **globefish.** a marine fish with an elongated spiny body that can be inflated to form a globe.

puffin (ˈpʌfɪn) *n.* any of various northern diving birds, having a black-and-white plumage and a brightly coloured vertically flattened bill. [C14: ? of Cornish origin]

puff pastry *or U.S.* **puff paste** *n.* a dough used for making a rich flaky pastry.

puff-puff *n. Brit.* a children's name for a steam locomotive or railway train.

pug[1] (pʌg) *n.* a small compact breed of dog with a smooth coat, lightly curled tail, and a short wrinkled nose. [C16: <?] —ˈ**puggish** *adj.*

pug[2] (pʌg) *vb.* **pugging, pugged.** (*tr.*) **1.** to mix (clay) with water to form a malleable mass or paste, often in a **pug mill.** **2.** to fill or stop with clay or a similar substance. [C19: <?]

pug[3] (pʌg) *n.* a slang name for **boxer** (sense 1). [C20: shortened < PUGILIST]

pugging (ˈpʌgɪŋ) *n.* material such as clay, sawdust, etc., inserted between wooden flooring and ceiling to deaden sound. Also called: **pug.**

puggree, pugree (ˈpʌgrɪ) *or* **puggaree, pugaree** (ˈpʌgərɪ) *n.* **1.** the usual Indian word for **turban.** **2.** a scarf, usually pleated, around the crown of some hats, esp. sun helmets. [C17: < Hindi *pagrī*, < Sansk. *parikara*]

pugilism (ˈpjuːdʒɪˌlɪzəm) *n.* the art, practice, or profession of fighting with the fists; boxing. [C18: < L *pugil* a boxer] —ˈ**pugilist** *n.* —ˌ**pugiˈlistic** *adj.* —ˌ**pugiˈlistically** *adv.*

pugnacious (pʌgˈneɪʃəs) *adj.* readily disposed to fight; belligerent. [C17: < L *pugnāx*] —**pugˈnaciously** *adv.* —**pugnacity** (pʌgˈnæsɪtɪ) *n.*

pug nose *n.* a short stubby upturned nose. [C18: < PUG[1]] —ˈ**pug-ˌnosed** *adj.*

puisne (ˈpjuːnɪ) *adj.* (esp. of a subordinate judge) of lower rank. [C16: < Anglo-F, < OF *puisné* born later, < L *posteā* afterwards + *nascī* to be born]

puissance (ˈpjuːɪsᵊns, ˈpwiːsɑːns) *n.* **1.** a competition in showjumping that tests a horse's ability to jump large obstacles. **2.** *Arch. or poetic.* power. [C15: < OF; see PUISSANT]

puissant (ˈpjuːɪsᵊnt) *adj. Arch. or poetic.* powerful. [C15: < OF, ult. < L *potēns* mighty, < *posse* to have power] —ˈ**puissantly** *adv.*

puke (pjuːk) *Sl.* ~*vb.* **1.** to vomit. ~*n.* **2.** the act of vomiting. **3.** the matter vomited. [C16: prob. imit.]

pukeko (ˈpʊkəkəʊ) *n., pl.* **-kos.** a New Zealand wading bird with bright plumage. [< Maori]

pukka *or* **pucka** (ˈpʌkə) *adj. Anglo-Indian.* properly or perfectly done, constructed, etc.; good; genuine. [C17: < Hindi *pakkā* firm, < Sansk. *pakva*]

pulchritude (ˈpʌlkrɪˌtjuːd) *n. Formal or literary.* physical beauty. [C15: < L *pulchritūdō*, < *pulcher* beautiful] —ˌ**pulchriˈtudinous** *adj.*

pule (pjuːl) *vb.* (*intr.*) to cry plaintively; whimper. [C16: ? imit.] —ˈ**puler** *n.*

Pulitzer prize (ˈpʊlɪtzə) *n.* one of a group of prizes awarded yearly since 1917 for excellence in American journalism, literature, and music. [after Joseph *Pulitzer* (1847-1911), Hungarian-born U.S. newspaper publisher]

pull (pʊl) *vb.* (*mainly tr.*) **1.** (*also intr.*) to exert force on (an object) so as to draw it towards the source of the force. **2.** to remove; extract: *to pull a tooth.* **3.** to strip of feathers, hair, etc.; pluck. **4.** to draw the entrails from (a fowl). **5.** to rend or tear. **6.** to strain (a muscle or tendon). **7.** (usually foll. by *off*) *Inf.* to bring about: *to pull off a million-pound deal.* **8.** (often foll. by *on*) *Inf.* to draw out (a weapon) for use: *he pulled a knife on his attacker.* **9.** *Inf.* to attract: *the pop group pulled a crowd.* **10.** (*intr.;* usually foll. by *on* or *at*) to drink or inhale deeply: *to pull at one's pipe.* **11.** to make (a grimace): *to pull a face.* **12.** (*also intr.;* foll. by *away, out, over,* etc.) to move (a vehicle) or (of a vehicle) to be moved in a specified manner. **13.** (*intr.*) to possess or exercise the power to move: *this car doesn't pull well on hills.* **14.** *Printing.* to take (a proof) from type. **15.** *Golf, baseball, etc.* to hit (a ball) so that it veers away from the direction in which the player intended to hit it. **16.** *Cricket.* to hit (a ball pitched straight or on the off side) to the leg side. **17.** (*also intr.*) to row (a boat) or take a stroke of (an oar) in rowing. **18.** (of a rider) to restrain (a horse), esp. to prevent it from winning a race. **19. pull a fast one.** *Sl.* to play a sly trick. **20. pull apart** *or* **to pieces.** to criticize harshly. **21. pull (one's) punches. a.** *Inf.* to restrain the force of one's criticisms or actions. **b.** *Boxing.* to restrain the force of one's blows. ~*n.* **22.** an act or an instance of pulling or being pulled. **23.** the force or effort used in pulling: *the pull of the moon affects the tides.* **24.** the act or an instance of taking in drink or smoke. **25.** *Printing.* a proof taken from type: *the first pull was smudged.* **26.** something used for pulling, such as a handle. **27.** *Inf.* special advantage or influence: *his uncle is chairman of the company, so he has quite a lot of pull.* **28.** *Inf.* the power to attract attention or support. **29.** a period of rowing. **30.** a single stroke of an oar in rowing. **31.** the act of pulling the ball in golf, cricket, etc. **32.** the act of reining in a horse. ~See also **pull down, pull in,** etc. [OE *pullian*] —**ˈpuller** *n.*

pull down *vb.* (*tr., adv.*) to destroy or demolish: *the old houses were pulled down.*

pullet (ˈpʊlɪt) *n.* a young hen of the domestic fowl, less than one year old. [C14: < OF *poulet* chicken, < L *pullus* a young animal or bird]

pulley (ˈpʊlɪ) *n.* **1.** a wheel with a grooved rim in which a rope can run in order to change the direction of a force applied to the rope, etc. **2.** a number of such wheels pivoted in parallel in a block, used to raise heavy loads. **3.** a wheel with a flat, convex, or grooved rim mounted on a shaft and driven by or driving a belt passing around it. [C14 *poley,* < OF *polie,* < Vulgar L *polidium* (unattested), apparently < LGk *polidion* (unattested) a little pole, < Gk *polos* axis]

pull in *vb.* (*adv.*) **1.** (*intr.;* often foll. by *to*) to reach a destination: *the train pulled in at the station.* **2.** (*intr.*) Also: **pull over.** (of a motor vehicle) **a.** to draw in to the side of the road. **b.** to stop (at a café, lay-by, etc.). **3.** (*tr.*) to attract: *his appearance will pull in the crowds.* **4.** (*tr.*) *Brit. sl.* to arrest. **5.** (*tr.*) to earn or gain (money). ~*n.* **pull-in. 6.** *Brit.* a roadside café, esp. for lorry drivers.

Pullman (ˈpʊlmən) *n., pl.* **-mans.** a luxurious railway coach. Also called: **Pullman car.** [C19: after G. M. *Pullman* (1831–97), its U.S. inventor]

pull off *vb.* (*tr.*) **1.** to remove (clothing) forcefully. **2.** (*adv.*) to succeed in performing (a difficult feat).

pull out *vb.* (*adv.*) **1.** (*tr.*) to extract. **2.** (*intr.*) to depart: *the train pulled out of the station.* **3.** *Mil.* to withdraw or be withdrawn: *the troops were pulled out of the ruined city.* **4.** (*intr.*) (of a motor vehicle) **a.** to draw away from the side of the road. **b.** to draw out from behind another vehicle to overtake. **5.** (*intr.*) to abandon a position or situation. **6.** (foll. by *of*) to level out (from a dive). ~*n.* **pull-out. 7.** an extra leaf of a book that folds out. **8.** a removable section of a magazine, etc.

pullover (ˈpʊlˌəʊvə) *n.* a garment, esp. a sweater, that is pulled on over the head.

pull through *vb.* to survive or recover or cause to survive or recover, esp. after a serious illness or crisis. Also: **pull round.**

pull together *vb.* **1.** (*intr., adv.*) to cooperate, or work harmoniously. **2. pull oneself together.** *Inf.* to regain one's self-control or composure.

pullulate (ˈpʌljʊˌleɪt) *vb.* (*intr.*) **1.** (of animals, etc.) to breed abundantly. **2.** (of plants) to sprout, bud, or germinate. [C17: < L *pullulāre* to sprout, < *pullulus* a baby animal, < *pullus* young animal] —**ˌpulluˈlation** *n.*

pull up *vb.* (*adv.*) **1.** (*tr.*) to remove by the roots. **2.** (often foll. by *with* or *on*) to move level (with) or ahead (of), esp. in a race. **3.** to stop: *the car pulled up suddenly.* **4.** (*tr.*) to rebuke.

pulmonary (ˈpʌlmənərɪ, ˈpʊl-) *adj.* **1.** of or affecting the lungs. **2.** having lungs or lunglike organs. [C18: < L *pulmōnārius,* < *pulmō* a lung]

pulmonary artery *n.* either of the two arteries that convey oxygen-depleted blood from the heart to the lungs.

pulmonary vein *n.* any one of the four veins that convey oxygen-rich blood from the lungs to the heart.

pulp (pʌlp) *n.* **1.** soft or fleshy plant tissue, such as the succulent part of a fleshy fruit. **2.** a moist mixture of cellulose fibres, as obtained from wood, from which paper is made. **3. a.** a magazine or book containing trite or sensational material, and usually printed on cheap rough paper. **b.** (*as modifier*): *a pulp novel.* **4.** *Dentistry.* the soft innermost part of a tooth, containing nerves and blood vessels. **5.** any soft soggy mass. **6.** *Mining.* pulverized ore. ~*vb.* **7.** to reduce (a material) to pulp or (of a material) to be reduced to pulp. **8.** (*tr.*) to remove the pulp from (fruit, etc.). [C16: < L *pulpa*] —**ˈpulpy** *adj.*

pulpit (ˈpʊlpɪt) *n.* **1.** a raised platform, usually surrounded by a barrier, set up in churches as the appointed place for preaching, etc. **2.** a medium for expressing an opinion, such as a newspaper column. **3.** (usually preceded by *the*) **a.** the preaching of the Christian message. **b.** the clergy or their influence. [C14: < L *pulpitum* a platform]

pulpwood (ˈpʌlpˌwʊd) *n.* pine, spruce, or any other soft wood used to make paper.

pulque (ˈpʊlkɪ) *n.* a light alcoholic drink from Mexico made from the juice of various agave plants. [C17: < Mexican Sp., apparently < Nahuatl, < *puliuhqui* decomposed, since it will only keep for a day]

pulsar (ˈpʌlˌsɑː) *n.* any of a number of very small stars first discovered in 1967, which rotate fast, emitting regular pulses of polarized radiation. [C20: < PULS(ATING ST)AR, on the model of QUASAR]

pulsate (pʌlˈseɪt) *vb.* (*intr.*) **1.** to expand and contract with a rhythmical beat; throb. **2.** *Physics.* to vary in intensity, magnitude, etc. **3.** to quiver or vibrate. [C18: < L *pulsāre* to push] —**pulsative** (ˈpʌlsətɪv) *adj.* —**pulˈsation** *n.* —**pulˈsator** *n.* —**pulsatory** (ˈpʌlsətərɪ, -trɪ) *adj.*

pulsatilla (ˌpʌlsəˈtɪlə) *n.* any of a genus of plants related to the anemone, with feathery or hairy foliage. [C16: < Med. L, < *pulsāta* beaten (by the wind)]

pulsating star *n.* a type of variable star, the variation in brightness resulting from expansion and subsequent contraction of the star.

pulse[1] (pʌls) *n.* **1.** *Physiol.* **a.** the rhythmical contraction and expansion of an artery at each beat of the heart. **b.** a single such pulsation. **2.** *Physics, electronics.* **a.** a transient sharp change in some quantity normally constant in a system. **b.** one of a series of such transient disturbances, usually recurring at regular intervals. **3. a.** a recurrent rhythmical series of beats, vibrations, etc. **b.** any single beat, wave, etc., in such a series. **4.** an inaudible electronic "ping" to operate a slide projector. **5.** bustle, vitality, or excitement: *the pulse of a city.* **6. keep one's finger on the pulse.** to be well informed about current events, opinions, etc. ~*vb.* **7.** (*intr.*) to beat, throb, or vibrate. **8.** (*tr.*) to provide an electronic pulse to operate (a slide projector). [C14 *pous,* < L *pulsus* a beating, < *pellere* to beat] —**ˈpulseless** *adj.*

pulse[2] (pʌls) *n.* **1.** the edible seeds of any of several leguminous plants, such as peas, beans, and lentils. **2.** the plant producing any of these. [C13 *pols,* < OF, < L *puls* pottage of pulse]

pulsejet (ˈpʌlsˌdʒɛt) *n.* a type of ramjet engine in which air is admitted through movable vanes that are closed by the pressure resulting from each intermittent explosion of the fuel in the combustion chamber, thus causing a pulsating thrust. Also called: **pulsejet engine, pulsojet.**

pulse modulation *n. Electronics.* a type of modulation in which a train of pulses is used as the carrier wave, one or more of its parameters, such as amplitude, being modulated or modified in order to carry information.

pulsimeter (pʌlˈsɪmɪtə) *n. Med.* an instrument for measuring the rate of the pulse.

pulverize *or* **-ise** (ˈpʌlvəˌraɪz) *vb.* **1.** to reduce (a substance) to fine particles, as by grinding, or (of a substance) to be so reduced. **2.** (*tr.*) to destroy completely. [C16: < LL *pulverizare,* < L *pulvis* dust] —**ˈpulverˌizable** *or* **-ˌisable** *adj.* —**ˌpulveriˈzation** *or* **-iˈsation** *n.* —**ˈpulverˌizer** *or* **-ˌiser** *n.*

pulverulent (pʌlˈvɛrʊlənt) *adj.* consisting of, covered with, or crumbling to dust or fine particles. [C17: < L *pulverulentus,* < *pulvis* dust]

puma (ˈpjuːmə) *n.* a large American feline mammal that resembles a lion, having a plain greyish-brown coat and long tail. Also called: **cougar, mountain lion.** [C18: via Sp. < Quechua]

pumice (ˈpʌmɪs) *n.* **1.** Also called: **pumice stone.** a light porous volcanic rock used for scouring and, in powdered form, as an abrasive and for polishing. ~*vb.* **2.** (*tr.*) to rub or polish with pumice. [C15 *pomys,* < OF *pomis,* < L *pūmex*] —**pumiceous** (pjuːˈmɪʃəs) *adj.*

pummel (ˈpʌməl) *vb.* **-melling, -melled** *or U.S.* **-meling, -meled.** (*tr.*) to strike repeatedly with or as if with the fists. Also (less commonly): **pommel.** [C16: see POMMEL]

pump[1] (pʌmp) *n.* **1.** any device for compressing, driving, raising, or reducing the pressure of a fluid, esp. by means of a piston or set of rotating impellers. ~*vb.* **2.** (when *tr.*, usually foll. by *from, out,* etc.) to raise or drive (air, liquid, etc., esp. into or from something) with a pump. **3.** (*tr.;* usually foll. by *in* or *into*) to supply in large amounts: *to pump capital into a project.* **4.** (*tr.*) to deliver (bullets, etc.) repeatedly. **5.** to operate (something, esp. a handle) in the manner of a pump or (of something) to work in this way: *to pump the pedals of a bicycle.* **6.** (*tr.*) to obtain (information) from (a person) by persistent questioning. **7.** (*intr.;* usually foll. by *from* or *out of*) (of liquids) to flow freely in large spurts: *oil pumped from the fissure.* **8. pump iron.** *Sl.* to exercise with weights; do body-building exercises. [C15: < MDu. *pumpe* pipe, prob. < Sp. *bomba,* imit.]

pump[2] (pʌmp) *n.* **1.** a low-cut low-heeled shoe without fastenings, worn esp. for dancing. **2.** a type of shoe with a rubber sole, used in games such as tennis; plimsoll. [C16: <?]

pumpernickel (ˈpʌmpəˌnɪkᵊl) *n.* a slightly sour black bread, originating in Germany, made of coarse rye flour. [C18: < G, <?]

pumpkin (ˈpʌmpkɪn) *n.* **1.** any of several creeping plants of the genus *Cucurbita.* **2.** the large round fruit of any of these plants, which has a thick orange rind, pulpy flesh, and numerous seeds. [C17: < earlier *pumpion,* < OF, < L *pepo,* < Gk, < *peptein* to ripen]

pump priming *n.* **1.** the process of introducing fluid into a pump to improve starting and to expel air from it. **2.** government expenditure designed to stimulate economic activity in stagnant or depressed areas. **3.** another term for **deficit financing.**

pun[1] (pʌn) *n.* **1.** the use of words to exploit ambiguities and innuendoes for humorous effect; a play on words. An example is: *"Ben Battle was a soldier bold, And used to war's alarms: But a cannonball took off his legs, So he laid down his arms."* (Thomas Hood). ~*vb.* **punning, punned. 2.** (*intr.*) to make puns. [C17: ? < It. *puntiglio* wordplay; see PUNCTILIO]

pun[2] (pʌn) *vb.* **punning, punned.** (*tr.*) *Brit.* to pack (earth, rubble, etc.) by pounding. [C16: var. of POUND[1]]

puna *Spanish.* (ˈpuna) *n.* **1.** a high cold dry plateau. **2.** another name for **mountain sickness.** [C17: < American Sp., of Amerind origin]

punch[1] (pʌntʃ) *vb.* **1.** to strike at, esp. with a clenched fist. **2.** (*tr.*) *Western U.S.* to herd or drive (cattle), esp. for a living. **3.** (*tr.*) to poke with a stick, etc. ~*n.* **4.** a blow with the fist. **5.** *Inf.* point or vigour: *his arguments lacked punch.* [C15: ? var. of *pounce,* < OF *poinçonner* to stamp] —ˈ**puncher** *n.*

punch[2] (pʌntʃ) *n.* **1.** a tool or machine for piercing holes in a material. **2.** a tool or machine used for stamping a design on something or shaping it by impact. **3.** the solid die of a punching machine. **4.** *Computers.* a device for making holes in a card or paper tape. ~*vb.* **5.** (*tr.*) to pierce, cut, stamp, shape, or drive with a punch. [C14: shortened < *puncheon,* < OF *ponçon;* see PUNCHEON[2]]

punch[3] (pʌntʃ) *n.* any mixed drink containing fruit juice and, usually, alcoholic liquor, generally hot and spiced. [C17: ? < Hindi *pānch,* < Sansk. *pañca* five; it orig. had five ingredients]

Punch (pʌntʃ) *n.* the main character in the traditional children's puppet show **Punch and Judy.**

punchball (ˈpʌntʃˌbɔːl) *n.* **1.** Also called (U.S. and Canad.): **punching bag.** a stuffed or inflated ball or bag, either suspended or supported by a flexible rod, that is punched for exercise, esp. boxing training. **2.** *U.S.* a game resembling baseball.

punchbowl (ˈpʌntʃˌbəʊl) *n.* **1.** a large bowl for serving punch, often having small drinking glasses hooked around the rim. **2.** *Brit.* a bowl-shaped depression in the land.

punch-drunk *adj.* **1.** demonstrating or characteristic of the behaviour of a person who has suffered repeated blows to the head, esp. a professional boxer. **2.** dazed; stupefied.

punched card *or esp. U.S.* **punch card** *n.* a card on which data can be coded in the form of punched holes. In computing, there are usually 80 columns and 12 rows, each column containing a pattern of holes representing one character.

punched tape *or U.S.* (*sometimes*) **perforated tape** *n.* other terms for **paper tape.**

puncheon[1] (ˈpʌntʃən) *n.* a large cask of variable capacity, usually between 70 and 120 gallons. [C15 *poncion,* < OF *ponchon,* <?]

puncheon[2] (ˈpʌntʃən) *n.* **1.** a short wooden post used as a vertical strut. **2.** a less common name for **punch**[2] (sense 1). [C14 *ponson,* < OF *ponçon,* < L *punctiō* a puncture, < *pungere* to prick]

Punchinello (ˌpʌntʃɪˈnɛləʊ) *n., pl.* **-los** *or* **-loes. 1.** a clown from Italian puppet shows, the prototype of Punch. **2.** (*sometimes not cap.*) any grotesque or absurd character. [C17: < earlier *Polichinello,* < It. *Polecenella,* < *pulcino* chicken, ult. < L *pullus* young animal]

punch line *n.* the culminating part of a joke, funny story, etc., that gives it its point.

punch-up *n. Brit. inf.* a fight or brawl.

punchy (ˈpʌntʃɪ) *adj.* **punchier, punchiest. 1.** an informal word for **punch-drunk. 2.** *Inf.* incisive or forceful. —ˈ**punchily** *adv.* —ˈ**punchiness** *n.*

punctate (ˈpʌŋkteɪt) *adj.* having or marked with minute spots or depressions. [C18: < NL *punctātus,* < L *punctum* a point] —**puncˈtation** *n.*

punctilio (pʌŋkˈtɪlɪˌəʊ) *n., pl.* **-tilios. 1.** strict attention to minute points of etiquette. **2.** a petty formality or fine point of etiquette. [C16: < It. *puntiglio* small point, < L *punctum* point]

punctilious (pʌŋkˈtɪlɪəs) *adj.* **1.** paying scrupulous attention to correctness in etiquette. **2.** attentive to detail. —**puncˈtiliously** *adv.* —**puncˈtiliousness** *n.*

punctual (ˈpʌŋktjʊəl) *adj.* **1.** arriving or taking place at an arranged time. **2.** (of a person) having the characteristic of always keeping to arranged times. **3.** *Obs.* precise; exact. **4.** *Maths.* consisting of or confined to a point. [C14: < Med. L *punctuālis* concerning detail, < L *punctum* point] —ˌ**punctuˈality** *n.* —ˈ**punctually** *adv.*

punctuate (ˈpʌŋktjʊˌeɪt) *vb.* (*mainly tr.*) **1.** (*also intr.*) to insert punctuation marks into (a written text). **2.** to interrupt or insert at frequent intervals: *a meeting punctuated by heckling.* **3.** to give emphasis to. [C17: < Med. L *punctuāre* to prick, < L, < *pungere* to puncture]

punctuation (ˌpʌŋktjʊˈeɪʃən) *n.* **1.** the use of symbols not belonging to the alphabet of a writing system to indicate aspects of the intonation and meaning not otherwise conveyed in the written language. **2.** the symbols used for this purpose.

punctuation mark *n.* any of the signs used in punctuation, such as a comma.

puncture (ˈpʌŋktʃə) *n.* **1.** a small hole made by a sharp object. **2.** a perforation and loss of pressure in a pneumatic tyre. **3.** the act of puncturing or perforating. ~*vb.* **4.** (*tr.*) to pierce a hole in (something) with a sharp object. **5.** to cause (something pressurized, esp. a tyre) to lose pressure by piercing, or (of a tyre, etc.) to collapse in this way. **6.** (*tr.*) to depreciate (a person's self-esteem, pomposity, etc.). [C14: < L *punctūra,* < *pungere* to prick]

pundit (ˈpʌndɪt) *n.* **1.** a self-appointed expert. **2.** (formerly) a learned person. **3.** Also: **pandit.** a Brahman learned in Sanskrit and, esp. in Hindu religion, philosophy or law. [C17: < Hindi *paṇḍit,* < Sansk. *paṇḍita* learned man]

punga (ˈpʌŋə) *n.* a variant spelling of **ponga.**

pungent (ˈpʌndʒənt) *adj.* **1.** having an acrid smell or sharp bitter flavour. **2.** (of wit, satire, etc.) biting; caustic. **3.** *Biol.* ending in a sharp point. [C16: < L *pungens* piercing, < *pungere* to prick] —ˈ**pungency** *n.* —ˈ**pungently** *adv.*

Punic (ˈpjuːnɪk) *adj.* **1.** of or relating to ancient

Carthage or the Carthaginians. **2.** treacherous; faithless. ~*n.* **3.** the language of the Carthaginians; a late form of Phoenician. [C15: < L *Pūnicus,* var. of *Poenicus* Carthaginian, < Gk *Phoinix*]

punish (ˈpʌnɪʃ) *vb.* **1.** to force (someone) to undergo a penalty for some crime or misdemeanour. **2.** (*tr.*) to inflict punishment for (some crime, etc.). **3.** (*tr.*) to treat harshly, esp. as by overexertion: *to punish a horse.* **4.** (*tr.*) *Inf.* to consume in large quantities: *to punish the bottle.* [C14 *punisse,* < OF *punir,* < L *pūnīre* to punish, < *poena* penalty] —**ˈpunishable** *adj.* —**ˈpunisher** *n.* —**ˈpunishing** *adj.*

punishment (ˈpʌnɪʃmənt) *n.* **1.** a penalty for a crime or offence. **2.** the act of punishing or state of being punished. **3.** *Inf.* rough treatment.

punitive (ˈpjuːnɪtɪv) *adj.* relating to, involving, or with the intention of inflicting punishment: *a punitive expedition.* [C17: < Med. L *pūnītīvus* concerning punishment, < L *pūnīre* to punish] —**ˈpunitively** *adv.*

Punjabi (pʌnˈdʒɑːbɪ) *n.* **1.** (*pl.* **-bis**) a member of the chief people of the Punjab, in NW India. **2.** the language of the Punjab, belonging to the Indic branch of the Indo-European family. ~*adj.* **3.** of the Punjab, its people, or their language.

punk[1] (pʌŋk) *n.* **1.** an inferior or worthless person or thing. **2. a.** a youth movement of the late 1970s, characterized by anti-Establishment slogans and the wearing of worthless articles such as safety pins for decoration. **b.** (*as modifier*): *a punk record.* **3.** worthless articles collectively. **4.** short for **punk rock. 5.** *Obs.* a young male homosexual; catamite. **6.** *Obs.* a prostitute. ~*adj.* **7.** rotten or worthless. [C16: <?]

punk[2] (pʌŋk) *n.* dried decayed wood or other substance that smoulders when ignited: used as tinder. [C18: <?]

punka *or* **punkah** (ˈpʌŋkə) *n.* **1.** a fan made of a palm leaf or leaves. **2.** a large fan made of palm leaves, etc., worked mechanically to cool a room. [C17: < Hindi *pankhā,* < Sansk. *paksaka* fan, < *paksa* wing]

punk rock *n.* rock music in a style of the late 1970s, characterized by offensive or aggressive lyrics and performance. —**punk rocker** *n.*

punnet (ˈpʌnɪt) *n. Chiefly Brit.* a small basket for fruit. [C19: ? dim. of dialect *pun* POUND[2]]

punster (ˈpʌnstə) *n.* a person who is fond of making puns, esp. one who makes a tedious habit of this.

punt[1] (pʌnt) *n.* **1.** an open flat-bottomed boat with square ends, propelled by a pole. ~*vb.* **2.** to propel (a boat, esp. a punt) by pushing with a pole on the bottom of a river, etc. [OE *punt* shallow boat, < L *pontō* punt]

punt[2] (pʌnt) *n.* **1.** a kick in certain sports, such as rugby, in which the ball is released and kicked before it hits the ground. ~*vb.* **2.** to kick (a ball, etc.) using a punt. [C19: ? var. of dialect *bunt* to push]

punt[3] (pʌnt) *Chiefly Brit.* ~*vb.* **1.** (*intr.*) to gamble; bet. ~*n.* **2.** a gamble or bet, esp. against the bank, as in roulette, or on horses. **3.** Also called: **punter.** a person who bets. **4. take a punt at.** *Austral. & N.Z. inf.* to make an attempt at. [C18: < F *ponter* to punt, < *ponte* bet laid against the banker, < Sp. *punto* point, < L *punctum*]

punter[1] (ˈpʌntə) *n.* a person who punts a boat.

punter[2] (ˈpʌntə) *n.* a person who kicks a ball.

punter[3] (ˈpʌntə) *n.* **1.** one who gambles or bets. **2.** *Inf.* any person, esp. when a customer. **3.** *Sl.* a prostitute's client.

puny (ˈpjuːnɪ) *adj.* **-nier, -niest. 1.** small and weakly. **2.** paltry; insignificant. [C16: < OF *puisne* PUISNE] —**ˈpuniness** *n.*

pup (pʌp) *n.* **1. a.** a young dog; puppy. **b.** the young of various other animals, such as the seal. **2. in pup.** (of a bitch) pregnant. **3.** *Inf., chiefly Brit.* a conceited young man (esp. in **young pup**). **4. sell (someone) a pup.** to swindle (someone) by selling him something worthless. ~*vb.* **pupping, pupped. 5.** (of dogs, seals, etc.) to give birth to (young). [C18: back formation < PUPPY]

pupa (ˈpjuːpə) *n., pl.* **-pae** (-piː) *or* **-pas.** an insect at the immobile nonfeeding stage of development between larva and adult, when many internal changes occur. [C19: via NL, < L: a doll] —**ˈpupal** *adj.*

pupate (pjuːˈpeɪt) *vb.* (*intr.*) (of an insect larva) to develop into a pupa. —**puˈpation** *n.*

pupil[1] (ˈpjuːpᵊl) *n.* **1.** a student who is taught by a teacher. **2.** *Civil & Scots Law.* a boy under 14 or a girl under 12 who is in the care of a guardian. [C14: < L *pupillus* an orphan, < *pūpus* a child] —**ˈpupillage** *or U.S.* **ˈpupilage** *n.* —**ˈpupillary** *or* **ˈpupilary** *adj.*

pupil[2] (ˈpjuːpᵊl) *n.* the dark circular aperture at the centre of the iris of the eye, through which light enters. [C16: < L *pūpilla,* dim. of *pūpa* doll; from the tiny reflections in the eye] —**ˈpupillary** *or* **ˈpupilary** *adj.*

pupiparous (pjuːˈpɪpərəs) *adj.* (of certain dipterous flies) producing young that have already reached the pupa stage at the time of hatching. [C19: < NL *pupiparus,* < PUPA + *parere* to bring forth]

puppet (ˈpʌpɪt) *n.* **1. a.** a small doll or figure moved by strings attached to its limbs or by the hand inserted in its cloth body. **b.** (*as modifier*): *a puppet theatre.* **2. a.** a person, state, etc., that appears independent but is controlled by another. **b.** (*as modifier*): *a puppet government.* [C16 *popet,* ? < OF *poupette* little doll, ult. < L *pūpa* doll]

puppeteer (ˌpʌpɪˈtɪə) *n.* a person who manipulates puppets.

puppetry (ˈpʌpɪtrɪ) *n.* **1.** the art of making and manipulating puppets and presenting puppet shows. **2.** unconvincing or specious presentation.

puppy (ˈpʌpɪ) *n., pl.* **-pies. 1.** a young dog; pup. **2.** *Inf., contemptuous.* a brash or conceited young man; pup. [C15 *popi,* < OF *popée* doll] —**ˈpuppyhood** *n.* —**ˈpuppyish** *adj.*

puppy fat *n.* fatty tissue that develops in childhood or adolesence and usually disappears with maturity.

puppy love *n.* another term for **calf love.**

Purana (pʊˈrɑːnə) *n.* any of a class of Sanskrit writings not included in the Vedas, characteristically recounting the birth and deeds of Hindu gods and the creation of the universe. [C17: < Sansk.: ancient, < *purā* formerly]

Purbeck marble *or* **stone** (ˈpɜːbɛk) *n.* a fossil-rich limestone that takes a high polish. [C15: after *Purbeck,* Dorset, where quarried]

purblind (ˈpɜːˌblaɪnd) *adj.* **1.** partly or nearly blind. **2.** lacking in insight or understanding; obtuse. [C13: see PURE, BLIND]

purchase (ˈpɜːtʃɪs) *vb.* (*tr.*) **1.** to obtain (goods, etc.) by payment. **2.** to obtain by effort, sacrifice, etc.: *to purchase one's freedom.* **3.** to draw or lift (a load) with mechanical apparatus. ~*n.* **4.** something that is purchased. **5.** the act of buying. **6.** acquisition of an estate by any lawful means other than inheritance. **7.** the mechanical advantage achieved by a lever. **8.** a firm foothold, grasp, etc., as for climbing something. [C13: < OF *porchacier* to strive to obtain; see CHASE[1]] —**ˈpurchasable** *adj.* —**ˈpurchaser** *n.*

purchase tax *n.* (in Britain, formerly) a tax levied on nonessential consumer goods and added to selling prices by retailers.

purdah (ˈpɜːdə) *n.* **1.** the custom in some Muslim and Hindu communities of keeping women in seclusion, with clothing that conceals them completely when they go out. **2.** a screen in a Hindu house used to keep the women out of view. [C19: < Hindi *parda* veil, < Persian *pardah*]

pure (pjʊə) *adj.* **1.** not mixed with any extraneous or dissimilar materials, elements, etc. **2.** free from tainting or polluting matter: *pure water.* **3.** free from moral taint or defilement: *pure love.* **4.** (*prenominal*) (intensifier): *a pure coincidence.* **5.** (of a subject, etc.) studied in its theoretical aspects rather than for its practical applications: *pure mathematics.* **6.** (of a vowel) pronounced with more or less unvarying quality without any glide. **7.** (of a consonant) not accompanied by another consonant. **8.** of unmixed descent. **9.** *Genetics, biol.* breeding true; homozygous. [C13: < OF *pur,* < L *pūrus* unstained] —ˈ**purely** *adv.* —ˈ**pureness** *n.*

purebred *adj.* (ˈpjʊəˈbrɛd). **1.** denoting a pure strain obtained through many generations of controlled breeding. ~*n.* (ˈpjʊəˌbrɛd). **2.** a purebred animal.

purée (ˈpjʊəreɪ) *n.* **1.** a smooth thick pulp of sieved fruit, vegetables, meat, or fish. ~*vb.* **-réeing, -réed.** **2.** (*tr.*) to make (cooked foods) into a purée. [C19: < F *purer* to PURIFY]

purfle (ˈpɜːfᵊl) *n. also* **purfling. 1.** a ruffled or curved ornamental band, as on clothing, furniture, etc. ~*vb.* **2.** (*tr.*) to decorate with such a band. [C14: < OF *purfiler* to decorate with a border, < *fil* thread, < L *filum*]

purgation (pɜːˈgeɪʃən) *n.* the act of purging or state of being purged; purification.

purgative (ˈpɜːgətɪv) *Med.* ~*n.* **1.** a drug or agent for purging the bowels. ~*adj.* **2.** causing evacuation of the bowels. —ˈ**purgatively** *adv.*

purgatory (ˈpɜːgətərɪ, -trɪ) *n.* **1.** *Chiefly R.C. Church.* a state or place in which the souls of those who have died in a state of grace are believed to undergo a limited amount of suffering to expiate their venial sins. **2.** a place or condition of suffering or torment, esp. one that is temporary. [C13: < OF *purgatoire,* < Med. L *pūrgātōrium,* lit.: place of cleansing, < L *pūrgāre* to purge] —ˌ**purgaˈtorial** *adj.*

purge (pɜːdʒ) *vb.* **1.** (*tr.*) to rid (something) of (impure elements). **2.** (*tr.*) to rid (a state, political party, etc.) of (dissident people). **3.** (*tr.*) **a.** to empty (the bowels) by evacuation of faeces. **b.** to cause (a person) to evacuate his bowels. **4. a.** to clear (a person) of a charge. **b.** to free (oneself) of guilt, as by atonement. **5.** (*intr.*) to be purified. ~*n.* **6.** the act or process of purging. **7.** the elimination of opponents or dissidents from a state, political party, etc. **8.** a purgative drug or agent. [C14: < OF *purger,* < L *pūrgāre* to purify]

purificator (ˈpjʊərɪfɪˌkeɪtə) *n. Christianity.* a small white linen cloth used to wipe the chalice and paten at the Eucharist.

purify (ˈpjʊərɪˌfaɪ) *vb.* **-fying, -fied. 1.** to free (something) of contaminating or debasing matter. **2.** (*tr.*) to free (a person, etc.) from sin or guilt. **3.** (*tr.*) to make clean, as in a ritual. [C14: < OF *purifier,* < LL *pūrificāre* to cleanse, < *pūrus* pure + *facere* to make] —ˌ**purifiˈcation** *n.* —**purificatory** (ˈpjʊərɪfɪˌkeɪtərɪ, -trɪ) *adj.* —ˈ**puriˌfier** *n.*

Purim (ˈpʊərɪm; *Hebrew* puːˈriːm) *n.* a Jewish holiday in February or March to commemorate the deliverance of the Jews from the massacre planned by Haman (Esther 9). [Heb. *pūrīm,* pl. of *pūr* lot; from the casting of lots by Haman]

purine (ˈpjʊəriːn) *or* **purin** (ˈpjʊərɪn) *n.* **1.** a colourless crystalline solid that can be prepared from uric acid. Formula: $C_5H_4N_4$. **2.** any of a number of nitrogenous bases that are derivatives of purine. [C19: < G *Purin*]

puriri (puːˈriːriː) *n.* a New Zealand tree with hard timber and red berries. [< Maori]

purism (ˈpjʊəˌrɪzəm) *n.* insistence on traditional canons of correctness of form or purity of style or content. —ˈ**purist** *adj., n.* —**puˈristic** *adj.*

puritan (ˈpjʊərɪtᵊn) *n.* **1.** a person who adheres to strict moral or religious principles, esp. one opposed to luxury and sensual enjoyment. ~*adj.* **2.** characteristic of a puritan. [C16: < LL *pūritās* purity] —ˈ**puritanˌism** *n.*

Puritan (ˈpjʊərɪtᵊn) (in the late 16th and 17th centuries) ~*n.* **1.** any of the extreme English Protestants who wished to purify the Church of England of most of its ceremony and other aspects that they deemed to be Catholic. ~*adj.* **2.** of or relating to the Puritans. —ˈ**Puritanˌism** *n.*

puritanical (ˌpjʊərɪˈtænɪkᵊl) *adj.* **1.** *Usually disparaging.* strict in moral or religious outlook, esp. in shunning sensual pleasures. **2.** (*sometimes cap.*) of or relating to a puritan or the Puritans. —ˌ**puriˈtanically** *adv.*

purity (ˈpjʊərɪtɪ) *n.* the state or quality of being pure.

purl[1] (pɜːl) *n.* **1.** a knitting stitch made by doing a plain stitch backwards. **2.** a decorative border, as of lace. **3.** gold or silver wire thread. ~*vb.* **4.** to knit in purl stitch. **5.** to edge (something) with a purl. ~Also (for senses 2, 3, 5): **pearl.** [C16: < dialect *pirl* to twist into a cord]

purl[2] (pɜːl) *vb.* **1.** (*intr.*) (of a stream, etc.) to flow with a gentle swirling or rippling movement and a murmuring sound. ~*n.* **2.** a swirling movement of water; eddy. **3.** a murmuring sound, as of a shallow stream. [C16: rel. to Norwegian *purla* to bubble]

purler (ˈpɜːlə) *n. Inf.* a headlong or spectacular fall (esp. in **come a purler**).

purlieu (ˈpɜːljuː) *n.* **1.** *English history.* land on the edge of a forest once included within the bounds of the royal forest but later separated although still subject to some of the forest laws. **2.** (*usually pl.*) a neighbouring area; outskirts. **3.** (*often pl.*) a place one frequents; haunt. [C15 *purlewe,* < Anglo-F *puralé* a going through (infl. also by OF *lieu* place), < OF *puraler,* < *pur* through + *aler* to go]

purlin *or* **purline** (ˈpɜːlɪn) *n.* a horizontal beam that provides intermediate support for the common rafters of a roof construction. [C15: <?]

purloin (pɜːˈlɔɪn) *vb.* to steal. [C15: < OF *porloigner* to put at a distance, < *por-* for + *loin* distant, < L *longus* long] —**purˈloiner** *n.*

purple (ˈpɜːpᵊl) *n.* **1.** a colour between red and blue. **2.** a dye or pigment producing such a colour. **3.** cloth of this colour, often used to symbolize royalty or nobility. **4.** (usually preceded by *the*) high rank; nobility. **5. a.** the official robe of a cardinal. **b.** the rank of a cardinal as signified by this. ~*adj.* **6.** of the colour purple. **7.** (of writing) excessively elaborate or full of imagery: *purple prose.* [OE, < L *purpura* purple dye, < Gk *porphura* the purple fish (murex)] —ˈ**purpleness** *n.* —ˈ**purplish** *or* ˈ**purply** *adj.*

purple heart *n.* **1.** any of several tropical American trees. **2.** *Inf., chiefly Brit.* a heart-shaped purple tablet consisting mainly of amphetamine.

Purple Heart *n.* a decoration awarded to members of the U.S. Armed Forces for a wound received in action.

purple patch *n.* **1.** Also called: **purple passage.** a section in a piece of writing characterized by fanciful or ornate language. **2.** *Austral. sl.* a period of good fortune.

purport *vb.* (pɜːˈpɔːt). (*tr.*) **1.** to claim to be (true, official, etc.) by manner or appearance, esp. falsely. **2.** (esp. of speech or writing) to signify or imply. ~*n.* (ˈpɜːpɔːt). **3.** meaning; significance. **4.** object; intention. [C15: < Anglo-F: contents, < OF *porporter* to convey, < L *portāre*]

purpose (ˈpɜːpəs) *n.* **1.** the reason for which anything is done, created, or exists. **2.** a fixed design or idea that is the object of an action or other effort. **3.** determination: *a man of purpose.* **4.** practical advantage or use: *to work to good purpose.* **5.** that which is relevant (esp. in **to** *or* **from the purpose**). **6.** *Arch.* purport. **7. on purpose.** intentionally. ~*vb.* **8.** (*tr.*) to intend or determine to do (something). [C13: < OF *porpos,* < *porposer* to plan, < L *prōpōnere* to PROPOSE] —ˈ**purposeless** *adj.*

purpose-built *adj.* made to serve a specific purpose.

purposeful (ˈpɜːpəsfʊl) *adj.* **1.** having a definite purpose in view. **2.** determined. —ˈ**purposefully** *adv.* —ˈ**purposefulness** *n.*

purposely (ˈpɜːpəslɪ) *adv.* on purpose.

purposive (ˈpɜːpəsɪv) *adj.* **1.** having or indicating conscious intention. **2.** serving a purpose; useful. —ˈ**purposively** *adv.* —ˈ**purposiveness** *n.*

purpura (ˈpɜːpjʊrə) *n. Pathol.* any of several blood diseases marked by purplish spots caused by subcutaneous bleeding. [C18: via L < Gk *porphura* a shellfish yielding purple dye]

purr (pɜː) *vb.* **1.** (*intr.*) (esp. of cats) to make a low vibrant sound, usually considered as expressing pleasure, etc. **2.** (*tr.*) to express (pleasure, etc.) by this sound or by a sound suggestive of purring. ~*n.* **3.** a purring sound. [C17: imit.]

purse (pɜːs) *n.* **1.** a small bag or pouch for carrying money, esp. coins. **2.** *U.S. & Canad.* a woman's handbag. **3.** anything resembling a small bag or pouch in form or function. **4.** wealth; funds; resources. **5.** a sum of money that is offered, esp. as a prize. ~*vb.* **6.** (*tr.*) to contract (the mouth, lips, etc.) into a small rounded shape. [OE *purs,* prob. < LL *bursa* bag, ult. < Gk: leather]

purser (ˈpɜːsə) *n.* an officer aboard a ship or aircraft who keeps the accounts and attends to the welfare of the passengers.

purse seine *n.* a large net that encloses fish and is then closed at the bottom by means of a line resembling the string formerly used to draw shut the neck of a money pouch.

purse strings *pl. n.* control of expenditure (esp. in **hold** *or* **control the purse strings**).

purslane (ˈpɜːslɪn) *n.* a plant with fleshy leaves used (esp. formerly) in salads and as a potherb. [C14 *purcelane,* < OF *porcelaine,* < LL, < L *porcillāca,* var. of *portulāca*]

pursuance (pəˈsjuːəns) *n.* the carrying out or pursuing of an action, plan, etc.

pursuant (pəˈsjuːənt) *adj.* **1.** (*usually postpositive;* often foll. by *to*) *Chiefly law.* in agreement or conformity. **2.** *Arch.* pursuing. [C17: rel. to ME *poursuivant* following after, < OF; see PURSUE] —**purˈsuantly** *adv.*

pursue (pəˈsjuː) *vb.* **-suing, -sued.** (*mainly tr.*) **1.** (*also intr.*) to follow (a fugitive, etc.) in order to capture or overtake. **2.** to follow closely or accompany: *ill health pursued her.* **3.** to seek or strive to attain (some desire, etc.). **4.** to follow the precepts of (a plan, policy, etc.). **5.** to apply oneself to (studies, interests, etc.). **6.** to follow persistently or seek to become acquainted with. **7.** to continue to discuss or argue (a point, subject, etc.). [C13: < Anglo-Norman *pursiwer,* < OF *poursivre,* < L *prōsequī* to follow after] —**purˈsuer** *n.*

pursuit (pəˈsjuːt) *n.* **1. a.** the act of pursuing. **b.** (*as modifier*): *a pursuit plane.* **2.** an occupation or pastime. **3.** (in cycling) a race in which the riders set off at intervals along the track and attempt to overtake each other. [C14: < OF *poursieute,* < *poursivre* to PURSUE]

pursuivant (ˈpɜːsɪvənt) *n.* **1.** the lowest rank of heraldic officer. **2.** *History.* a state or royal messenger. **3.** *History.* a follower or attendant. [C14: < OF, < *poursivre* to PURSUE]

purulent (ˈpjʊərʊlənt) *adj.* of, relating to, or containing pus. [C16: < L *pūrulentus,* < *pūs*] —ˈ**purulence** *n.* —ˈ**purulently** *adv.*

purvey (pəˈveɪ) *vb.* (*tr.*) **1.** to sell or provide (commodities, esp. foodstuffs) on a large scale. **2.** to publish (lies, scandal, etc.). [C13: < OF *porveeir,* < L *prōvidēre* to PROVIDE] —**purˈveyor** *n.*

purveyance (pəˈveɪəns) *n.* **1.** *History.* the collection or requisition of provisions for a sovereign. **2.** *Rare.* the act of purveying.

purview (ˈpɜːvjuː) *n.* **1.** scope of operation. **2.** breadth or range of outlook. **3.** *Law.* the body of a statute, containing the enacting clauses. [C15: < Anglo-Norman *purveu,* < *porveeir* to furnish; see PURVEY]

pus (pʌs) *n.* the yellow or greenish fluid product of inflammation. [C16: < L *pūs*]

push (pʊʃ) *vb.* **1.** (when *tr.,* often foll. by *off, away,* etc.) to apply steady force to in order to move. **2.** to thrust (one's way) through something, such as a crowd. **3.** (*tr.*) to encourage or urge (a person) to some action, decision, etc. **4.** (when *intr.,* often foll. by *for*) to be an advocate or promoter (of): *to push for acceptance of one's theories.* **5.** (*tr.*) to use one's influence to help (a person): *to push one's own candidate.* **6.** to bear upon (oneself or another person) in order to achieve better results, etc. **7.** (*tr.*) to rely too much on: *to push one's luck.* **8.** *Cricket, etc.* to hit (a ball) with a stiff pushing stroke. **9.** (*tr.*) *Inf.* to sell (narcotic drugs) illegally. **10.** (*intr.;* foll. by *out, into,* etc.) to extend: *the cliffs pushed out to the sea.* ~*n.* **11.** the act of pushing; thrust. **12.** a part or device that is pressed to operate some mechanism. **13.** *Inf.* drive, energy, etc. **14.** *Inf.* a special effort or attempt to advance, as of an army: *to make a push.* **15.** *Austral. sl.* a group, gang, or clique. **16.** *Cricket, etc.* a stiff pushing stroke. **17. at a push.** *Inf.* with difficulty; only just. **18. the push.** *Inf., chiefly Brit.* dismissal, esp. from employment. ~See also **push off, push in,** etc. [C13: < OF *pousser,* < L *pulsāre,* < *pellere* to drive]

push-bike *n. Brit.* an informal name for **bicycle.**

push button *n.* **1.** an electrical switch operated by pressing a button, which closes or opens a circuit. ~*modifier.* **push button. 2. a.** operated by a push button: *a push-button radio.* **b.** initiated as simply as by pressing a button: *push-button warfare.*

pushcart (ˈpʊʃˌkɑːt) *n.* another name (esp. U.S. and Canad.) for **barrow**[1] (sense 3).

pushchair (ˈpʊʃˌtʃɛə) *n. Brit.* a chair-shaped carriage for a small child. U.S. and Canad. word: **stroller.** Austral. words: **pusher, stroller.**

pushed (pʊʃt) *adj.* (often foll. by *for*) *Inf.* short (of) or in need (of time, money, etc.).

pusher (ˈpʊʃə) *n.* **1.** *Inf.* a person who sells illegal drugs, esp. narcotics such as heroin. **2.** *Inf.* an aggressively ambitious person. **3.** a person or thing that pushes. **4.** *Austral.* the usual name for **pushchair.**

push in *vb.* (*intr., adv.*) to force one's way into a group of people, queue, etc.

pushing (ˈpʊʃɪŋ) *adj.* **1.** enterprising or aggressively ambitious. **2.** impertinently self-assertive. ~*adv.* **3.** almost or nearly (a certain age, speed, etc.): *pushing fifty.* —ˈ**pushingly** *adv.*

push off *vb.* (*adv.*) **1.** Also: **push out.** to move into open water, as by being cast off from a mooring. **2.** (*intr.*) *Inf.* to go away; leave.

pushover (ˈpʊʃˌəʊvə) *n. Inf.* **1.** something that is easily achieved. **2.** a person, team, etc., that is easily taken advantage of or defeated.

push-pull *n.* (*modifier*) using two similar electronic devices made to operate out of phase with each other to produce a signal that replicates the input waveform: *a push-pull amplifier.*

push-start *vb.* (*tr.*) **1.** to start (a motor vehicle) by pushing it while it is in gear, thus turning the engine. ~*n.* **2.** this process.

push through *vb.* (*tr.*) to compel to accept: *the bill was pushed through Parliament.*

Pushto (ˈpʌʃtəʊ) *or* **Pushtu** (ˈpʌʃtuː) *n., adj.* variant spellings of **Pashto.**

push-up *n.* the U.S. and Canad. term for **press-up.**

pushy (ˈpʊʃɪ) *adj.* **pushier, pushiest.** *Inf.* **1.** offensively assertive. **2.** aggressively or ruthlessly ambitious. —ˈ**pushily** *adv.* —ˈ**pushiness** *n.*

pusillanimous (ˌpjuːsɪˈlænɪməs) *adj.* characterized by a lack of courage or determination. [C16: < LL *pusillanimis* < L *pusillus* weak + *animus* courage] —**pusillanimity** (ˌpjuːsɪləˈnɪmɪtɪ) *n.* —ˌ**pusilˈlanimously** *adv.*

puss (pʊs) *n.* **1.** an informal name for a **cat. 2.** *Sl.* a girl or woman. **3.** an informal name for a **hare.** [C16: rel. to MLow G *pūs*]

pussy[1] (ˈpʊsɪ) *n., pl.* **pussies. 1.** Also called: **puss, pussycat.** an informal name for a **cat. 2.** a furry catkin. **3.** *Taboo sl.* the female pudenda. [C18: < PUSS]

pussy[2] (ˈpʌsɪ) *adj.* **-sier, -siest.** containing or full of pus.

pussyfoot (ˈpʊsɪˌfʊt) *vb.* (*intr.*) *Inf.* **1.** to move about stealthily or warily like a cat. **2.** to avoid committing oneself.

pussy willow (ˈpʊsɪ) *n.* a willow tree with silvery silky catkins.

pustulant (ˈpʌstjʊlənt) *adj.* **1.** causing the formation of pustules. ~*n.* **2.** an agent causing such formation.

pustulate *vb.* (ˈpʌstjʊˌleɪt). **1.** to form or cause to form into pustules. ~*adj.* (ˈpʌstjʊlɪt). **2.** covered with pustules. —ˌ**pustuˈlation** *n.*

pustule (ˈpʌstjuːl) *n.* **1.** a small inflamed elevated area of skin containing pus. **2.** any spot resembling a pimple. [C14: < L *pustula* a blister, var. of *pūsula*] —**pustular** (ˈpʌstjʊlə) *adj.*

put (pʊt) *vb.* **putting, put.** (*mainly tr.*) **1.** to cause to be (in a position or place): *to put a book on the table.* **2.** to cause to be (in a state, relation, etc.): *to put one's things in order.* **3.** (foll. by *to*) to cause (a person) to experience or suffer: *to put to death.* **4.** to set or commit (to an action, task, or duty), esp. by force: *he put him to work.* **5.** to render or translate: *to put into English.* **6.** to set (words) in a musical form (esp. in **put to music**). **7.** (foll. by *at*) to estimate: *he put the distance at fifty miles.* **8.** (foll. by *to*) to utilize: *he put his knowledge to use.* **9.** (foll. by *to*) to couple (a female animal) with a male for breeding: *the farmer put his heifer to the bull.* **10.** to express: *to put it bluntly.* **11.** to make (an end or limit): *he put an end to the proceedings.* **12.** to present for consideration; propose: *he put the question to the committee.* **13.** to invest (money) in or expend (time, energy, etc.) on: *he put five thousand pounds into the project.* **14.** to impart: *to put zest into a party.* **15.** to throw or cast. **16. not know where to put oneself.** to feel embarrassed. **17. stay put.** to remain in one place; remain stationary. ~*n.* **18.** a throw, esp. in putting the shot. **19.** Also called: **put option.** *Stock Exchange.* an option to sell a stated number of securities at a specified price during a limited period. ~See also **put about, put across,** etc. [C12 *puten* to push]

put about *vb.* (*adv.*) **1.** *Naut.* to change course. **2.** (*tr.*) to make widely known: *he put about the news of the air disaster.* **3.** (*tr.; usually passive*) to disconcert or disturb.

put across *vb.* (*tr.*) **1.** (*adv.*) to communicate in a comprehensible way: *he couldn't put things across very well.* **2. put one across.** *Inf.* to get (someone) to believe a claim, excuse, etc., by deception: *they put one across their teacher.*

put aside *vb.* (*tr., adv.*) **1.** to move (an object, etc.) to one side, esp. in rejection. **2.** to save: *to put money aside for a rainy day.* **3.** to disregard: *let us put aside our differences.*

putative (ˈpjuːtətɪv) *adj.* (*prenominal*) **1.** commonly regarded as being: *the putative father.* **2.** considered to exist or have existed; inferred. [C15: < LL *putātīvus* supposed, < L *putāre* to consider] —ˈ**putatively** *adv.*

put away *vb.* (*tr., adv.*) **1.** to return (something) to the proper place. **2.** to save: *to put away money for the future.* **3.** to lock up in a prison, mental institution, etc.: *they put him away for twenty years.* **4.** to eat or drink, esp. in large amounts.

put back *vb.* (*tr., adv.*) **1.** to return to its former place. **2.** to move to a later time: *the wedding was put back a fortnight.* **3.** to impede the progress of: *the strike put back production.*

put by *vb.* (*tr., adv.*) to set aside for the future; save.

put down *vb.* (*tr., adv.*) **1.** to make a written record of. **2.** to repress: *to put down a rebellion.* **3.** to consider: *they put him down for an ignoramus.* **4.** to attribute: *I put the mistake down to inexperience.* **5.** to put (an animal) to death, because of old age or illness. **6.** to table on the agenda: *the MPs put down a motion on the increase in crime.* **7.** *Sl.* to reject or humiliate. ~*n.* **put-down. 8.** a cruelly crushing remark.

put forth *vb.* (*tr., adv.*) *Formal.* **1.** to propose. **2.** (of a plant) to produce or bear (leaves, etc.).

put forward *vb.* (*tr., adv.*) **1.** to propose; suggest. **2.** to offer the name of; nominate.

put in *vb.* (*adv.*) **1.** (*intr.*) *Naut.* to bring a vessel into port. **2.** (often foll. by *for*) to apply (for a job, etc.). **3.** (*tr.*) to submit: *he put in his claims form.* **4.** to intervene with (a remark) during a conversation. **5.** (*tr.*) to devote (time, effort, etc.): *he put in three hours overtime last night.* **6.** (*tr.*) to establish or appoint: *he put in a manager.* **7.** (*tr.*) *Cricket.* to cause to bat: *England won the toss and put the visitors in to bat.*

put off *vb.* (*tr.*) **1.** (*adv.*) to postpone: *they have put off the dance until tomorrow.* **2.** (*adv.*) to evade (a person) by postponement or delay: *they tried to put him off, but he came anyway.* **3.** (*adv.*) to cause aversion: *he was put off by her appearance.* **4.** (*prep.*) to cause to lose interest in: *the accident put him off driving.*

put on *vb.* (*tr., mainly adv.*) **1.** to clothe oneself in. **2.** (*usually passive*) to adopt (an attitude or feeling) insincerely: *his misery was just put on.* **3.** to present (a play, show, etc.). **4.** to add: *she put on weight.* **5.** to cause (an electrical device) to function. **6.** (*also prep.*) to wager (money) on a horse race, game, etc. **7.** (*also prep.*) to impose: *to put a tax on cars.* **8.** *Cricket.* to cause (a bowler) to bowl.

put out *vb.* (*tr., adv.*) **1.** (*often passive*) **a.** to annoy; anger. **b.** to disturb; confuse. **2.** to extinguish (a fire, light, etc.). **3.** to poke forward: *to put out one's tongue.* **4.** to be a source of inconvenience to: *I hope I'm not putting you out.* **5.** to publish; broadcast: *the authorities put out a leaflet.* **6.** to render unconscious. **7.** to dislocate: *he put out his shoulder in the accident.* **8.** to give out (work to be done) at different premises. **9.** to lend (money) at interest. **10.** *Cricket, etc.* to dismiss (a player or team).

put over *vb.* (*tr., adv.*) **1.** *Inf.* to communicate (facts, information, etc.). **2.** *Chiefly U.S.* to postpone. **3. put (a fast) one over on.** *Inf.* to get (someone) to believe a claim, excuse, etc., by deception: *he put one over on his boss.*

put-put (ˈpʌtˌpʌt) *Inf.* ~*n.* **1.** a light chugging or popping sound, as made by a petrol engine. ~*vb.* **-putting, -putted. 2.** (*intr.*) to make such a sound.

putrefy (ˈpjuːtrɪˌfaɪ) *vb.* **-fying, -fied.** (of organic matter) to decompose or rot with an offensive smell. [C15: < OF *putrefier* + L *putrefacere*, < *puter* rotten + *facere* to make] —**putrefaction** (ˌpjuːtrɪˈfækʃən) *n.* —ˌ**putreˈfactive** *or* **putrefacient** (ˌpjuːtrɪˈfeɪʃənt) *adj.*

putrescent (pjuːˈtrɛsᵊnt) *adj.* **1.** becoming putrid; rotting. **2.** characterized by or undergoing putrefaction. [C18: < L *putrescere* to become rotten] —**puˈtrescence** *n.*

putrid (ˈpjuːtrɪd) *adj.* **1.** (of organic matter) in a state of decomposition: *putrid meat.* **2.** morally corrupt. **3.** sickening; foul: *a putrid smell.* **4.** *Inf.* deficient in quality or value: *a putrid film.* [C16: < L *putridus*, < *putrēre* to be rotten] —**puˈtridity** *or* ˈ**putridness** *n.* —ˈ**putridly** *adv.*

Putsch (pʊtʃ) *n.* a violent and sudden uprising; political revolt. [C20: < G: < Swiss G: a push, imit.]

putt (pʌt) *Golf.* ~*n.* **1.** a stroke on the green with a putter to roll the ball into or near the hole. ~*vb.* **2.** to strike (the ball) in this way. [C16: of Scot. origin]

puttee *or* **putty** (ˈpʌtɪ) *n., pl.* **-tees** *or* **-ties.** (*often pl.*) a strip of cloth worn wound around the leg from the ankle to the knee, esp. as part of a uniform in World War I. [C19: < Hindi *paṭṭī*, < Sansk. *paṭṭikā*, < *paṭṭa* cloth]

putter[1] (ˈpʌtə) *n. Golf.* **1.** a club with a short shaft for putting, usually having a solid metal head. **2.** a golfer who putts: *he is a good putter.*

putter[2] (ˈpʌtə) *vb.* the usual U.S. and Canad. word for **potter**[1]. —ˈ**putterer** *n.*

putter[3] (ˈpʊtə) *n.* **1.** a person who puts: *the putter of a question.* **2.** a person who puts the shot.

put through *vb.* (*tr., mainly adv.*) **1.** to carry out to a conclusion: *he put through his plan.* **2.** (*also prep.*) to organize the processing of: *she put through his application to join the organization.* **3.** to connect by telephone. **4.** to make (a telephone call).

putting green (ˈpʌtɪŋ) *n.* **1.** (on a golf course) the area of closely mown grass at the end of a fairway where the hole is. **2.** an area of smooth grass with several holes for putting games.

putto (ˈpʊtəʊ) *n., pl.* **-ti** (-tiː). a representation of a small boy, a cherub or cupid, esp. in baroque painting or sculpture. [< It., < L *putus* boy]

putty (ˈpʌtɪ) *n., pl.* **-ties. 1.** a stiff paste made of whiting and linseed oil that is used to fix glass into frames and to fill cracks in woodwork, etc. **2.** any substance with a similar function or appearance.

3. a mixture of lime and water with sand or plaster of Paris used on plaster as a finishing coat. 4. (*as modifier*): *a putty knife.* 5. a person who is easily influenced: *he's putty in her hands.* 6. a. a colour varying from greyish yellow to greyish brown. b. (*as adj.*): *putty wool.* ~*vb.* **-tying, -tied.** 7. (*tr.*) to fix, fill, or coat with putty. [C17: < F *potée* a potful]

put up *vb.* (*adv., mainly tr.*) 1. to build; erect: *to put up a statue.* 2. to accommodate or be accommodated at: *can you put me up for tonight?* 3. to increase (prices). 4. to submit (a plan, case, etc.). 5. to offer: *to put a house up for sale.* 6. to give: *to put up a good fight.* 7. to provide (money) for: *they put up five thousand for the new project.* 8. to preserve or can (jam, etc.). 9. to pile up (long hair) on the head in any of several styles. 10. (*also intr.*) to nominate or be nominated as a candidate: *he put up for president.* 11. *Arch.* to return (a weapon) to its holder: *put up your sword!* 12. **put up to. a.** to inform or instruct (a person) about (tasks, duties, etc.). **b.** to incite to. 13. **put up with.** *Inf.* to endure; tolerate. ~*adj.* **put-up.** 14. dishonestly or craftily prearranged (esp. in **put-up job**).

put upon *vb.* (*intr., prep.; usually passive*) 1. to presume on (a person's generosity, good nature, etc.): *he's always being put upon.* 2. to impose hardship on: *he was sorely put upon.*

puzzle ('pʌzᵊl) *vb.* 1. to perplex or be perplexed. 2. (*intr.;* foll. by *over*) to ponder about the cause of: *he puzzled over her absence.* 3. (*tr.;* usually foll. by *out*) to solve by mental effort: *he puzzled out the meaning.* ~*n.* 4. a person or thing that puzzles. 5. a problem that cannot be easily solved. 6. the state of being puzzled. 7. a toy, game, or question presenting a problem that requires skill or ingenuity for its solution. [C16: <?] —**'puzzlement** *n.* —**'puzzler** *n.* —**'puzzling** *adj.* —**'puzzlingly** *adv.*

PVC *abbrev. for* polyvinyl chloride; a synthetic thermoplastic material made by polymerizing vinyl chloride. The flexible forms are used in insulation, shoes, etc. Rigid PVC is used for moulded articles.

PVS *abbrev. for* postviral syndrome.

Pvt. *Mil. abbrev. for* private.

PW *abbrev. for* policewoman.

PWR *abbrev. for* pressurized-water reactor.

pyaemia *or* **pyemia** (paɪ'iːmɪə) *n.* blood poisoning characterized by pus-forming microorganisms in the blood. [C19: < NL, < Gk *puon* pus + *haima* blood] —**py'aemic** *or* **py'emic** *adj.*

pye-dog, pie-dog, *or* **pi-dog** ('paɪˌdɒg) *n.* an ownerless half-wild Asian dog. [C19: Anglo-Indian, < Hindi *pāhī* outsider]

pyelitis (ˌpaɪə'laɪtɪs) *n.* inflammation of the pelvis of the kidney. [C19: NL, < Gk *puelos* trough] —**pyelitic** (ˌpaɪə'lɪtɪk) *adj.*

pygmy *or* **pigmy** ('pɪgmɪ) *n., pl.* **-mies.** 1. an abnormally undersized person. 2. something that is a very small example of its type. 3. a person of little importance or significance. 4. (*modifier*) very small. [C14 *pigmeis* the Pygmies, < L *Pygmaeus* a Pygmy, < Gk *pugmaios* undersized, < *pugmē* fist] —**pygmaean** *or* **pygmean** (pɪg'miːən) *adj.*

Pygmy *or* **Pigmy** ('pɪgmɪ) *n., pl.* **-mies.** a member of one of the dwarf peoples of Equatorial Africa, noted for their hunting and forest culture.

Pyjama cricket *n. Austral. inf.* one-day cricket, esp. when played at night in coloured uniforms.

pyjamas *or U.S.* **pajamas** (pə'dʒɑːməz) *pl. n.* 1. loose-fitting nightclothes comprising a jacket or top and trousers. 2. full loose-fitting ankle-length trousers worn by either sex in various Eastern countries. [C19: < Hindi, < Persian *pai* leg + *jāma* garment]

pyknic ('pɪknɪk) *adj.* characterized by a broad squat fleshy physique with a large chest and abdomen. [C20: < Gk *puknos* thick]

pylon ('paɪlən) *n.* 1. a large vertical steel tower-like structure supporting high-tension electrical cables. 2. a post or tower for guiding pilots or marking a turning point in a race. 3. a streamlined aircraft structure for attaching an engine pod, etc., to the main body of the aircraft. 4. a monumental gateway, such as one at the entrance to an ancient Egyptian temple. [C19: < Gk *pulōn* a gateway]

pylorus (paɪ'lɔːrəs) *n., pl.* **-ri** (-raɪ). the small circular opening at the base of the stomach through which partially digested food passes to the duodenum. [C17: via LL < Gk *pulōrus* gatekeeper, < *pulē* gate + *ouros* guardian]

pyo- *or before a vowel* **py-** *combining form.* denoting pus: *pyosis.* [< Gk *puon*]

pyorrhoea *or esp. U.S.* **pyorrhea** (ˌpaɪə'rɪə) *n. Pathol.* 1. any condition characterized by a discharge of pus. 2. See **pyorrhoea alveolaris.**

pyorrhoea alveolaris (ˌælvɪə'lɑːrɪs) *n. Dentistry.* inflammation of the gums characterized by the discharge of pus and loosening of the teeth.

pyracantha (ˌpaɪrə'kænθə) *n.* any of a genus of shrubs with yellow, orange, or scarlet berries, widely cultivated for ornament. [C17: < Gk *purakantha,* < PYRO- + *akantha* thorn]

pyramid ('pɪrəmɪd) *n.* 1. a huge masonry construction that has a square base and, as in the case of the ancient Egyptian royal tombs, four sloping triangular sides. 2. an object or structure resembling such a construction. 3. *Maths.* a solid having a polygonal base and triangular sides that meet in a common vertex. 4. *Crystallography.* a crystal form in which three planes intersect all three axes of the crystal. 5. *Finance.* a group of enterprises containing a series of holding companies structured so that the top holding company controls the entire group with a relatively small proportion of the total capital invested. 6. (*pl.*) a game similar to billiards. ~*vb.* 7. to build up or be arranged in the form of a pyramid. 8. *Finance.* to form (companies) into a pyramid. [C16 (earlier *pyramis*): < L *pyramis,* < Gk *puramis,* prob. < Egyptian] —**pyramidal** (pɪ'ræmɪdᵊl), ˌ**pyra'midical,** *or* ˌ**pyra'midic** *adj.* —**py'ramidally** *or* ˌ**pyra'midically** *adv.*

pyramid selling *n.* a practice adopted by some manufacturers of advertising for distributors and selling them batches of goods. The first distributors then advertise for more distributors who are sold subdivisions of the original batches at an increased price. This process continues until the final distributors are left with a stock that is unsaleable except at a loss.

pyre ('paɪə) *n.* a pile of wood or other combustible material, esp. one for cremating a corpse. [C17: < L *pyra,* < Gk *pura* hearth, < *pur* fire]

pyrethrin (paɪ'riːθrɪn) *n.* either of two oily compounds found in pyrethrum and used as insecticides. [C19: < PYRETHRUM + -IN]

pyrethrum (paɪ'riːθrəm) *n.* 1. any of several cultivated Eurasian chrysanthemums with white, pink, red, or purple flowers. 2. any insecticide prepared from the dried flowers of any of these plants. [C16: via L < Gk *purethron* feverfew, prob. < *puretos* fever; see PYRETIC]

pyretic (paɪ'rɛtɪk) *adj. Pathology.* of, relating to, or characterized by fever. [C18: < NL *pyreticus,* < Gk *puretos* fever, < *pur* fire]

Pyrex ('paɪrɛks) *n. Trademark.* **a.** any of a variety of glasses that have low coefficients of expansion, making them suitable for heat-resistant glassware used in cookery and chemical apparatus. **b.** (*as modifier*): *a Pyrex dish.*

pyrexia (paɪ'rɛksɪə) *n.* a technical name for **fever.** [C18: < NL, < Gk *purexis,* < *puressein* to be feverish, < *pur* fire] —**py'rexial** *or* **py'rexic** *adj.*

pyridine ('pɪrɪˌdiːn) *n.* a colourless hygroscopic liquid with a characteristic odour: used as a solvent and in preparing other organic chemicals. Formula: C_5H_5N. [C19: < PYRO- + -ID[2] + -INE[2]]

pyridoxine (ˌpɪrɪ'dɒksiːn) *n. Biochemistry.* a derivative of pyridine that is a precursor of the compounds pyridoxal and pyridoxamine. Also called: **vitamin B_6.**

pyrimidine (paɪ'rɪmɪˌdiːn) *n.* 1. a liquid or crystalline organic compound with a penetrating odour. Formula: $C_4H_4N_2$. 2. any of a number of similar compounds having a basic structure that is derived from pyrimidine, and which are constituents of nucleic acids. [C20: var. of PYRIDINE]

pyrite (ˈpaɪraɪt) *n.* a yellow mineral consisting of iron sulphide in cubic crystalline form. It occurs in igneous and metamorphic rocks and in veins, associated with various metals, and is used mainly in the manufacture of sulphuric acid and paper. Formula: FeS_2. Also called: **iron pyrites, pyrites.** [C16: < L *pyrites* flint, < Gk *puritēs* (*lithos*) fire(stone), < *pur* fire] —**pyritic** (paɪˈrɪtɪk) *or* **pyˈritous** *adj.*

pyrites (paɪˈraɪtiːz; *in combination* ˈpaɪraɪts) *n., pl.* **-tes.** 1. another name for **pyrite.** 2. any of a number of other disulphides of metals, esp. of copper and tin.

pyro- *or before a vowel* **pyr-** *combining form.* 1. denoting fire or heat: *pyromania; pyrometer.* 2. *Chem.* denoting a new substance obtained by heating another: *pyroboric acid is obtained by heating boric acid.* 3. *Mineralogy.* **a.** having a property that changes upon the application of heat. **b.** having a flame-coloured appearance: *pyroxylin.* [< Gk *pur* fire]

pyroelectricity (ˌpaɪrəʊɪlɛkˈtrɪsɪtɪ) *n.* the development of opposite charges at the ends of the axis of certain crystals as a result of a change in temperature.

pyrogallol (ˌpaɪrəʊˈgælɒl) *n.* a crystalline soluble phenol with weakly acidic properties: used as a photographic developer and for absorbing oxygen in gas analysis. Formula: $C_6H_3(OH)_3$. [C20: < PYRO- + GALL(IC ACID) + -OL[1]]

pyrogenic (ˌpaɪrəʊˈdʒɛnɪk) *or* **pyrogenous** (paɪˈrɒdʒɪnəs) *adj.* 1. produced by or producing heat. 2. *Pathology.* causing or resulting from fever. 3. *Geol.* less common words for **igneous.**

pyrography (paɪˈrɒgrəfɪ) *n.* another name for **pokerwork.**

pyroligneous (ˌpaɪrəʊˈlɪgnɪəs) *or* **pyrolignic** *adj.* (of a substance) produced by the action of heat on wood, esp. by destructive distillation.

pyrolysis (paɪˈrɒlɪsɪs) *n.* 1. the application of heat to chemical compounds in order to cause decomposition. 2. such chemical decomposition. —**pyrolytic** (ˌpaɪrəʊˈlɪtɪk) *adj.*

pyromania (ˌpaɪrəʊˈmeɪnɪə) *n. Psychiatry.* the uncontrollable impulse and practice of setting things on fire. —ˌ**pyroˈmaniˌac** *n.*

pyrometer (paɪˈrɒmɪtə) *n.* an instrument for measuring high temperatures, esp. by measuring the brightness or total quantity of the radiation produced. —**pyrometric** (ˌpaɪrəʊˈmɛtrɪk) *or* ˌ**pyroˈmetrical** *adj.* —ˌ**pyroˈmetrically** *adv.* —**pyˈrometry** *n.*

pyrope (ˈpaɪrəʊp) *n.* a deep yellowish-red garnet that consists of magnesium aluminium silicate and is used as a gemstone. [C14 (used loosely of a red gem; modern sense C19): < OF *pirope,* < L *pyrōpus* bronze, < Gk *purōpus* fiery-eyed]

pyrophoric (ˌpaɪrəʊˈfɒrɪk) *adj.* 1. (of a chemical) igniting spontaneously on contact with air. 2. (of an alloy) producing sparks when struck or scraped: *lighter flints are made of pyrophoric alloy.* [C19: < NL *pyrophorus,* < Gk *purophoros* fire-bearing, < *pur* fire + *pherein* to bear]

pyrosis (paɪˈrəʊsɪs) *n. Pathology.* a technical name for **heartburn.** [C18: < NL, < Gk: a burning, < *puroun* to burn, < *pur* fire]

pyrostat (ˈpaɪrəʊˌstæt) *n.* 1. a device that activates an alarm or extinguisher in the event of a fire. 2. a thermostat for use at high temperatures. —ˌ**pyroˈstatic** *adj.*

pyrotechnics (ˌpaɪrəʊˈtɛknɪks) *n.* 1. (*functioning as sing.*) the art of making fireworks. 2. (*functioning as sing. or pl.*) a firework display. 3. (*functioning as sing. or pl.*) brilliance of display, as in the performance of music. —ˌ**pyroˈtechnic** *or* ˌ**pyroˈtechnical** *adj.*

pyroxene (paɪˈrɒksiːn) *n.* any of a large group of minerals consisting of the silicates of magnesium, iron, and calcium. They occur in basic igneous rocks. [C19: PYRO- + *-xene* < Gk *xenos* foreign, because mistakenly thought to have originated elsewhere when found in igneous rocks]

pyroxylin (paɪˈrɒksɪlɪn) *n.* a yellow substance obtained by nitrating cellulose with a mixture of nitric and sulphuric acids; guncotton: used to make collodion, plastics, lacquers, and adhesives.

pyrrhic (ˈpɪrɪk) *Prosody.* ~*n.* 1. a metrical foot of two short or unstressed syllables. ~*adj.* 2. of or composed in pyrrhics. [C16: via L, < Gk *purrhikhē,* said to be after its inventor *Purrhikhos*]

Pyrrhic victory *n.* a victory in which the victor's losses are as great as those of the defeated. Also called: **Cadmean victory.** [after *Pyrrhus,* who defeated the Romans at Asculum in 279 B.C. but suffered heavy losses]

Pyrrhonism (ˈpɪrəˌnɪzəm) *n.* the doctrine of Pyrrho (?365-?275 B.C.), Greek sceptic philosopher, that certain knowledge is impossible to obtain.

pyruvic acid (paɪˈruːvɪk) *n.* a liquid formed during the metabolism of proteins and carbohydrates, helping to release energy to the body. [C19: < PYRO- + L *ūva* grape]

Pythagoras' theorem (paɪˈθægərəs) *n.* the theorem that in a right-angled triangle the square of the length of the hypotenuse equals the sum of the squares of the other two sides. [after *Pythagoras* (?580-?500 B.C.), Gk philosopher & mathematician]

Pythagorean (paɪˌθægəˈriːən) *adj.* 1. of or relating to Pythagoras. ~*n.* 2. a follower of Pythagoras.

Pythian (ˈpɪθɪən) *adj. also* **Pythic.** 1. of or relating to Delphi or its oracle. ~*n.* 2. the priestess of Apollo at the oracle of Delphi. [C16: via L *Pȳthius* < Gk *Puthios* of Delphi]

python (ˈpaɪθən) *n.* any of a family of large nonvenomous snakes of Africa, S Asia, and Australia. They reach a length of more than 20 feet and kill their prey by constriction. [C16: NL, after *Python,* a dragon killed by Apollo] —**pythonic** (paɪˈθɒnɪk) *adj.*

pythoness (ˈpaɪθənɛs) *n.* a woman, such as Apollo's priestess at Delphi, believed to be possessed by an oracular spirit. [C14 *phitonesse,* ult. < Gk *Puthōn* Python; see PYTHON]

pyuria (paɪˈjʊərɪə) *n. Pathol.* any condition characterized by the presence of pus in the urine. [C19: < NL, < Gk *puon* pus + *ouron* urine]

pyx (pɪks) *n.* 1. Also called: **pyx chest.** the chest in which coins from the British mint are placed to be tested for weight, etc. 2. *Christianity.* any receptacle in which the Eucharistic Host is kept. [C14: < L *pyxis* small box, < Gk, < *puxos* box tree]

pyxidium (pɪkˈsɪdɪəm) *or* **pyxis** (ˈpɪksɪs) *n., pl.* **-ia** (-ɪə) *or* **pyxides** (ˈpɪksɪˌdiːz). the dry fruit of such plants as the plantain: a capsule whose upper part falls off when mature so that the seeds are released. [C19: via NL < Gk *puxidion* a little box, < *puxis* box]

pyxis (ˈpɪksɪs) *n., pl.* **pyxides** (ˈpɪksɪˌdiːz). 1. a small box used by the ancient Greeks and Romans to hold medicines, etc. 2. another name for **pyxidium.** [C14: via L < Gk: box]

Q

q *or* **Q** (kjuː) *n., pl.* **q's, Q's,** *or* **Qs.** **1.** the 17th letter of the English alphabet. **2.** a speech sound represented by this letter.

q *symbol for* quintal.

Q *symbol for:* **1.** *Physics.* heat. **2.** *Chess.* queen. **3.** question.

q. *abbrev. for:* **1.** quart. **2.** quarter. **3.** quarterly. **4.** query. **5.** question. **6.** quire.

Q. *abbrev. for:* **1.** quartermaster. **2.** (*pl.* **Qq., qq.**) Also: **q.** quarto. **3.** Quebec. **4.** Queen. **5.** question. **6.** *Electronics.* Q factor.

QANTAS (ˈkwɒntəs) *n.* the national airline of Australia. [C20: < *Q(ueensland) a(nd) N(orthern) T(erritory) A(erial) S(ervices Ltd)*]

QARANC *abbrev. for* Queen Alexandra's Royal Army Nursing Corps.

QB *abbrev. for* Queen's Bench.

QC *abbrev. for* Queen's Counsel.

QED *abbrev. for* quod erat demonstrandum. [L: which was to be shown or proved]

Q factor *n.* **1.** a measure of the relationship between stored energy and rate of energy dissipation in certain electrical components, devices, etc. **2.** Also called: **Q value.** the heat released in a nuclear reaction. ~Symbol: Q [C20: short for *quality factor*]

Q fever *n.* an acute disease characterized by fever and pneumonia, transmitted to man by a rickettsia. [C20: < *q(uery) fever* (the cause being orig. unknown)]

Qld *abbrev. for* Queensland.

QM *abbrev. for* Quartermaster.

QMG *abbrev. for* Quartermaster General.

qr. *pl.* **qrs.** *abbrev. for:* **1.** quarter. **2.** quarterly. **3.** quire.

Q-ship *n.* a merchant ship with concealed guns, used to decoy enemy ships. [C20: < *Q* short for QUERY]

QSM (in New Zealand) *abbrev. for* Queen's Service Medal.

QSO *abbrev. for:* **1.** quasi-stellar object. **2.** (in New Zealand) Queen's Service Order.

qt *pl.* **qt** *or* **qts** *abbrev. for* quart.

q.t. *Inf.* **1.** *abbrev. for* quiet. **2. on the q.t.** secretly.

qua (kweɪ, kwɑː) *prep.* in the capacity of; by virtue of being. [C17: < L, ablative sing. (fem.) of *qui* who]

quack[1] (kwæk) *vb.* (*intr.*) **1.** (of a duck) to utter a harsh guttural sound. **2.** to make a noise like a duck. ~*n.* **3.** the sound made by a duck. [C17: imit.]

quack[2] (kwæk) *n.* **1. a.** an unqualified person who claims medical knowledge or other skills. **b.** (*as modifier*): *a quack doctor.* **2.** *Brit., Austral., & N.Z. inf.* a doctor; physician or surgeon. ~*vb.* **3.** (*intr.*) to act in the manner of a quack. [C17: short for QUACKSALVER] —ˈ**quackish** *adj.*

quackery (ˈkwækərɪ) *n., pl.* **-eries.** the activities or methods of a quack.

quack grass *n.* another name for **couch grass.**

quacksalver (ˈkwækˌsælvə) *n.* an archaic word for **quack**[2]. [C16: < Du., < *quack,* apparently: to hawk + *salf* SALVE]

quad[1] (kwɒd) *n.* short for **quadrangle.**

quad[2] (kwɒd) *n. Printing.* a block of type metal used for spacing. [C19: shortened < QUADRAT]

quad[3] (kwɒd) *n.* short for **quadruplet.**

quad[4] (kwɒd) *adj., n. Inf.* short for **quadraphonic** *or* **quadraphonics.**

Quadragesima (ˌkwɒdrəˈdʒɛsɪmə) *n.* the first Sunday in Lent. Also called: **Quadragesima Sunday.** [C16: < Med. L *quadrāgēsima dies* the fortieth day]

Quadragesimal (ˌkwɒdrəˈdʒɛsɪməl) *adj.* of, relating to, or characteristic of Lent.

quadrangle (ˈkwɒdˌræŋgᵊl) *n.* **1.** *Geom.* a plane figure consisting of four points connected by four lines. **2.** a rectangular courtyard, esp. one having buildings on all four sides. **3.** the building surrounding such a courtyard. [C15: < LL *quadrangulum* figure having four corners] —**quadrangular** (kwɒˈdræŋgjʊlə) *adj.*

quadrant (ˈkwɒdrənt) *n.* **1.** *Geom.* **a.** a quarter of the circumference of a circle. **b.** the area enclosed by two perpendicular radii of a circle. **c.** any of the four sections into which a plane is divided by two coordinate axes. **2.** a piece of a mechanism in the form of a quarter circle. **3.** an instrument formerly used in astronomy and navigation for measuring the altitudes of stars. [C14: < L *quadrāns* a quarter] —**quadrantal** (kwɒˈdræntᵊl) *adj.*

quadraphonics *or* **quadrophonics** (ˌkwɒdrəˈfɒnɪks) *n.* (*functioning as sing.*) a system of sound recording and reproduction that uses four independent loudspeakers to give directional sources of sound. —ˌ**quadraˈphonic** *or* ˌ**quadroˈphonic** *adj.*

quadrat (ˈkwɒdrət) *n.* **1.** *Ecology.* an area of vegetation selected at random for study. **2.** *Printing.* an archaic name for **quad**[2]. [C14 (meaning "a square"): var. of QUADRATE]

quadrate *n.* (ˈkwɒdrɪt, -reɪt). **1.** a cube, square, or a square or cubelike object. **2.** one of a pair of bones of the upper jaw of fishes, amphibians, reptiles, and birds. ~*adj.* (ˈkwɒdrɪt, -reɪt). **3.** of or relating to this bone. **4.** square or rectangular. ~*vb.* (kwɒˈdreɪt). **5.** (*tr.*) to make square or rectangular. **6.** (often foll. by *with*) to conform or cause to conform. [C14: < L *quadrāre* to make square]

quadratic (kwɒˈdrætɪk) *Maths.* ~*n.* **1.** Also called: **quadratic equation.** an equation containing one or more terms in which the variable is raised to the power of two, but no terms in which it is raised to a higher power. ~*adj.* **2.** of or relating to the second power.

quadrature (ˈkwɒdrətʃə) *n.* **1.** *Maths.* the process of determining a square having an area equal to that of a given figure or surface. **2.** the process of making square or dividing into squares. **3.** *Astron.* a configuration in which two celestial bodies form an angle of 90° with a third body. **4.** *Electronics.* the relationship between two waves that are 90° out of phase.

quadrella (kwɒˈdrɛlə) *n. Austral.* a form of betting in which the punter must select the winner of four specified races.

quadrennial (kwɒˈdrɛnɪəl) *adj.* **1.** occurring every four years. **2.** lasting four years. ~*n.* **3.** a period of four years. —**quadˈrennially** *adv.*

quadrennium (kwɒˈdrɛnɪəm) *n., pl.* **-niums** *or* **-nia** (-nɪə). a period of four years. [C17: < L *quadriennium,* < QUADRI- + *annus* year]

quadri- *or before a vowel* **quadr-** *combining form.* four: *quadrilateral.* [< L; cf. *quattuor* four]

quadric (ˈkwɒdrɪk) *Maths.* ~*adj.* **1.** having or characterized by an equation of the second degree. **2.** of the second degree. ~*n.* **3.** a quadric curve, surface, or function.

quadriceps (ˈkwɒdrɪˌsɛps) *n., pl.* **-cepses** (-ˌsɛpsɪz) *or* **-ceps.** *Anat.* a large four-part muscle of the front of the thigh, which extends the leg. [C19: NL, < QUADRI- + *-ceps* as in BICEPS]

quadrifid (ˈkwɒdrɪfɪd) *adj. Bot.* divided into four lobes or other parts: *quadrifid leaves.*

quadrilateral (ˌkwɒdrɪˈlætərəl) *adj.* **1.** having or formed by four sides. ~*n.* **2.** Also called: **tetragon.** a polygon having four sides.

quadrille[1] (kwɒˈdrɪl) *n.* **1.** a square dance for four couples. **2.** a piece of music for such a dance. [C18: via F < Sp. *cuadrilla,* dim. of *cuadro* square, < L *quadra*]

quadrille[2] (kwɒˈdrɪl, kwə-) *n.* an old card game for four players. [C18: < F, < Sp. *cuartillo,* < *cuarto* fourth, < L *quartus,* infl. by QUADRILLE[1]]

quadrillion (kwɒˈdrɪljən) *n.* **1.** (in Britain,

France, and Germany) the number represented as one followed by 24 zeros (10^{24}). U.S. and Canad. word: **septillion.** **2.** (in the U.S. and Canada) the number represented as one followed by 15 zeros (10^{15}). *~determiner.* **3.** amounting to this number: *a quadrillion atoms.* [C17: < F *quadrillon,* < QUADRI- + *-illion,* on the model of *million*] —**quad'rillionth** *adj.*

quadrinomial (ˌkwɒdrɪˈnəʊmɪəl) *n.* an algebraic expression containing four terms.

quadriplegia (ˌkwɒdrɪˈpliːdʒɪə) *n.* paralysis of all four limbs. Also called: **tetraplegia.** [C20: < QUADRI- + Gk *plēssein* to strike] —**quadriplegic** (ˌkwɒdrɪˈpliːdʒɪk) *adj.*

quadrivalent (ˌkwɒdrɪˈveɪlənt) *adj. Chem.* another word for **tetravalent.** —ˌ**quadri'valency** *or* ˌ**quadri'valence** *n.*

quadrivium (kwɒˈdrɪvɪəm) *n., pl.* **-ia** (ɪə). (in medieval learning) a course consisting of arithmetic, geometry, astronomy, and music. [< Med. L, < L: crossroads, < QUADRI- + *via* way]

quadroon (kwɒˈdruːn) *n.* a person who is one-quarter Negro. [C18: < Sp. *cuarterón,* < *cuarto* quarter, < L *quartus*]

quadrumanous (kwɒˈdruːmənəs) *adj.* (of monkeys and apes) having all four feet specialized for use as hands. [C18: < NL *quadrumanus,* < QUADRI- + L *manus* hand]

quadruped (ˈkwɒdrʊˌpɛd) *n.* **1.** an animal, esp. a mammal, that has all four limbs specialized for walking. *~adj.* **2.** having four feet. [C17: < L *quadrupēs,* < *quadru-* (see QUADRI-) + *pēs* foot] —**quadrupedal** (kwɒˈdruːpɪdᵊl) *adj.*

quadruple (ˈkwɒdrʊpᵊl, kwɒˈdruːpᵊl) *vb.* **1.** to multiply by four or increase fourfold. *~adj.* **2.** four times as much or as many; fourfold. **3.** consisting of four parts. **4.** *Music.* having four beats in each bar. *~n.* **5.** a quantity or number four times as great as another. [C16: via OF < L *quadruplus,* < *quadru-* (see QUADRI-) + *-plus* -fold] —ˈ**quadruply** *adv.*

quadruplet (ˈkwɒdrʊplɪt, kwɒˈdruːplɪt) *n.* **1.** one of four offspring born at one birth. **2.** a group of four similar things. **3.** *Music.* a group of four notes to be played in a time value of three.

quadruplicate *adj.* (kwɒˈdruːplɪkɪt). **1.** fourfold or quadruple. *~vb.* (kwɒˈdruːplɪˌkeɪt). **2.** to multiply or be multiplied by four. *~n.* (kwɒˈdruːplɪkɪt). **3.** a group or set of four things. [C17: < L *quadruplicāre* to increase fourfold]

quaestor (ˈkwiːstə) *or U.S. (sometimes)* **questor** (ˈkwɛstə) *n.* any of several magistrates of ancient Rome, usually a financial administrator. [C14: < L, < *quaerere* to inquire] —**quaestorial** (kwɛˈstɔːrɪəl) *adj.*

quaff (kwɒf) *vb.* to drink heartily or in one draught. [C16: ? imit.; cf. MLow G *quassen* to eat or drink excessively] —ˈ**quaffer** *n.*

quag (kwæg) *n.* a quagmire. [C16: ? rel. to QUAKE]

quagga (ˈkwægə) *n., pl.* **-gas** *or* **-ga.** a recently extinct member of the horse family of southern Africa: it had zebra-like stripes on the head and shoulders. [C18: < obs. Afrik., < Hottentot *quăgga*]

quaggy (ˈkwægɪ) *adj.* **-gier, -giest. 1.** resembling a quagmire; boggy. **2.** soft or flabby.

quagmire (ˈkwægˌmaɪə) *n.* **1.** a soft wet area of land that gives way under the feet; bog. **2.** an awkward, complex, or embarrassing situation. [C16: < QUAG + MIRE]

quahog (ˈkwɑːˌhɒg) *n.* an edible clam native to the Atlantic coast of North America, having a large heavy rounded shell. [C18: < Amerind, short for *poquauhock,* < *pohkeni* dark + *hogki* shell]

quaich *or* **quaigh** (kweɪx) *n. Scot.* a small shallow drinking cup, usually with two handles. [< Gaelic *cuach* cup]

Quai d'Orsay (*French* ke dɔrsɛ) *n.* the quay along the south bank of the Seine, Paris, where the French foreign office is situated.

quail[1] (kweɪl) *n., pl.* **quails** *or* **quail.** any of various small Old World game birds having rounded bodies and small tails. [C14: < OF *quaille,* < Med. L *quaccula,* prob. imit.]

quail[2] (kweɪl) *vb.* (*intr.*) to shrink back with fear; cower. [C15: ? < OF *quailler,* < L *coāgulāre* to curdle]

quaint (kweɪnt) *adj.* **1.** attractively unusual, esp. in an old-fashioned style. **2.** odd or inappropriate. [C13 (in the sense: clever): < OF *cointe,* < L *cognitus* known, < *cognoscere* to ascertain] —ˈ**quaintly** *adv.* —ˈ**quaintness** *n.*

quair (kwɛə) *n. Scot.* a book. [var. of QUIRE[1]]

quake (kweɪk) *vb.* (*intr.*) **1.** to shake or tremble with or as with fear. **2.** to convulse or quiver, as from instability. *~n.* **3.** a quaking. **4.** *Inf.* an earthquake. [OE *cwacian*]

Quaker (ˈkweɪkə) *n.* **1.** a member of the Society of Friends, a Christian sect founded by George Fox about 1650. Quakers reject sacraments, ritual, and formal ministry, and have promoted many causes for social reform. *~adj.* **2.** of the Society of Friends or its beliefs or practices. [C17: orig. a derog. nickname] —ˈ**Quakeress** *fem. n.* —ˈ**Quakerish** *adj.* —ˈ**Quakerism** *n.*

quaking (ˈkweɪkɪŋ) *adj.* unstable or unsafe to walk on, as a bog or quicksand.

quaking grass *n.* any of various grasses having delicate branches that shake in the wind.

quaky (ˈkweɪkɪ) *adj.* **quakier, quakiest.** inclined to quake; shaky. —ˈ**quakiness** *n.*

qualification (ˌkwɒlɪfɪˈkeɪʃən) *n.* **1.** an ability, quality, or attribute, esp. one that fits a person to perform a particular job or task. **2.** a condition that modifies or limits; restriction. **3.** a qualifying or being qualified.

qualified (ˈkwɒlɪˌfaɪd) *adj.* **1.** having the abilities, qualities, attributes, etc., necessary to perform a particular job or task. **2.** limited, modified, or restricted; not absolute.

qualify (ˈkwɒlɪˌfaɪ) *vb.* **-fying, -fied. 1.** to provide or be provided with the abilities or attributes necessary for a task, office, duty, etc.: *his degree qualifies him for the job.* **2.** (*tr.*) to make less strong, harsh, or violent; moderate or restrict. **3.** (*tr.*) to modify or change the strength or flavour of. **4.** (*tr.*) *Grammar.* another word for **modify. 5.** (*tr.*) to attribute a quality to; characterize. **6.** (*intr.*) to progress to the final stages of a competition, as by winning preliminary contests. [C16: < OF *qualifier,* < Med. L *quālificāre* to characterize, < L *quālis* of what kind + *facere* to make] —ˈ**qualiˌfiable** *adj.* —ˈ**qualiˌfier** *n.*

qualitative (ˈkwɒlɪtətɪv) *adj.* involving or relating to distinctions based on quality or qualities. —ˈ**qualitatively** *adv.*

qualitative analysis *n.* See **analysis** (sense 4).

quality (ˈkwɒlɪtɪ) *n., pl.* **-ties. 1.** a distinguishing characteristic or attribute. **2.** the basic character or nature of something. **3.** a feature of personality. **4.** degree or standard of excellence, esp. a high standard. **5.** (formerly) high social status or the distinction associated with it. **6.** musical tone colour; timbre. **7.** *Logic.* the characteristic of a proposition that makes it affirmative or negative. **8.** *Phonetics.* the distinctive character of a vowel, determined by the configuration of the mouth, tongue, etc. **9.** (*modifier*) having or showing excellence or superiority: *a quality product.* [C13: < OF *qualité,* < L *quālitās* state, < *quālis* of what sort]

quality control *n.* control of the relative quality of a manufactured product, usually by statistical sampling techniques.

qualm (kwɑːm) *n.* **1.** a sudden feeling of sickness or nausea. **2.** a pang of doubt, esp. concerning moral conduct; scruple. **3.** a sudden sensation of misgiving. [OE *cwealm* death or plague] —ˈ**qualmish** *adj.*

quandary (ˈkwɒndrɪ) *n., pl.* **-ries.** a difficult situation; predicament; dilemma. [C16: <?; ? rel. to L *quandō* when]

quandong, quandang (ˈkwɒnˌdɒŋ), *or* **quantong** (ˈkwɒnˌtɒŋ) *n.* **1.** Also called: **native peach. a.** a small Australian tree. **b.** the edible fruit or nut of this tree. **2. silver quandong. a.** an Australian tree. **b.** its timber. [< Abor.]

quango (ˈkwæŋgəʊ) *n., pl.* **-gos.** *acronym for* quasi-autonomous nongovernmental organization.

quant (kwɒnt) *n.* **1.** a long pole for propelling a boat, esp. a punt. ~*vb.* **2.** to propel (a boat) with a quant. [C15: prob. < L *contus* pole, < Gk *kontos*]

quanta (ˈkwɒntə) *n.* the plural of **quantum.**

quantic (ˈkwɒntɪk) *n.* a homogeneous function of two or more variables in a rational and integral form. [C19: < L *quantus* how great]

quantifier (ˈkwɒntɪˌfaɪə) *n.* **1.** *Logic.* a symbol indicating the quantity of a term: *the existential quantifier corresponds to the words "there is something, such that".* **2.** *Grammar.* a word or phrase, such as *some, all,* or *no,* expressing quantity.

quantify (ˈkwɒntɪˌfaɪ) *vb.* **-fying, -fied.** (*tr.*) **1.** to discover or express the quantity of. **2.** *Logic.* to specify the quantity of (a term) by using a quantifier, such as *all, some,* or *no.* [C19: < Med. L *quantificāre,* < L *quantus* how much + *facere* to make] —ˈ**quantifiable** *adj.* —ˌ**quantifiˈcation** *n.*

quantitative (ˈkwɒntɪtətɪv) *or* **quantitive** *adj.* **1.** involving or relating to considerations of amount or size. **2.** capable of being measured. **3.** *Prosody.* of a metrical system that is based on the length of syllables. —ˈ**quantitatively** *or* ˈ**quantitively** *adv.*

quantitative analysis *n.* See **analysis** (sense 4).

quantity (ˈkwɒntɪtɪ) *n., pl.* **-ties. 1. a.** a specified or definite amount, number, etc. **b.** (*as modifier*): *a quantity estimate.* **2.** the aspect of anything that can be measured, weighed, counted, etc. **3. unknown quantity.** a person or thing whose action, effort, etc., is unknown or unpredictable. **4.** a large amount. **5.** *Maths.* an entity having a magnitude that may be denoted by a numerical expression. **6.** *Physics.* a specified magnitude or amount. **7.** *Logic.* the characteristic of a proposition that makes it universal or particular. **8.** *Prosody.* the relative duration of a syllable or the vowel in it. [C14: < OF *quantité,* < L *quantitās* amount, < *quantus* how much]

quantity surveyor *n.* a person who estimates the cost of the materials and labour necessary for a construction job.

quantize *or* **-ise** (ˈkwɒntaɪz) *vb.* (*tr.*) **1.** *Physics.* to restrict (a physical quantity) to one of a set of fixed values. **2.** *Maths.* to limit to values that are multiples of a basic unit. —ˌ**quantiˈzation** *or* **-iˈsation** *n.*

quantum (ˈkwɒntəm) *n., pl.* **-ta. 1.** *Physics.* **a.** the smallest quantity of some physical property that a system can possess according to the quantum theory. **b.** a particle with such a unit of energy. **2.** amount or quantity, esp. a specific amount. ~*adj.* **3.** of or designating a major breakthrough or sudden advance: *a quantum leap forward.* [C17: < L *quantus* (adj.) how much]

quantum mechanics *n.* (*functioning as sing.*) the branch of mechanics, based on the quantum theory, used for interpreting the behaviour of elementary particles and atoms, which do not obey Newtonian mechanics.

quantum number *n. Physics.* one of a set of integers or half-integers characterizing the energy states of a particle or system of particles.

quantum theory *n.* a theory concerning the behaviour of physical systems based on the idea that they can only possess certain properties, such as energy and angular momentum, in discrete amounts (quanta).

quaquaversal (ˌkwɑːkwəˈvɜːsəl) *adj. Geol.* directed outwards in all directions from a common centre. [C18: < L *quāquā* in every direction + *versus* towards]

quarantine (ˈkwɒrənˌtiːn) *n.* **1.** a period of isolation or detention, esp. of persons or animals arriving from abroad, to prevent the spread of disease. **2.** the place where such detention is enforced. **3.** any period or state of enforced isolation. ~*vb.* **4.** (*tr.*) to isolate in or as if in quarantine. [C17: < It. *quarantina* period of forty days, < *quaranta* forty, < L *quadrāgintā*]

quarantine flag *n. Naut.* the yellow signal flag for the letter Q, flown alone from a vessel to indicate that there is no disease aboard or, with a second signal flag, to indicate that there is disease aboard. Also called: **yellow jack.**

quark[1] (kwɑːk) *n. Physics.* any of at least five hypothetical elementary particles postulated to be fundamental units of all baryons and mesons. [C20: coined by James Joyce in the novel *Finnegans Wake* (1939), & given special application in physics]

quark[2] (kwɑːk) *n.* a type of low-fat soft cheese. [< G]

quarrel[1] (ˈkwɒrəl) *n.* **1.** an angry disagreement; argument. **2.** a cause of dispute; grievance. ~*vb.* **-relling, -relled** *or U.S.* **-reling, -reled.** (*intr.; often foll. by with*) **3.** to engage in a disagreement or dispute; argue. **4.** to find fault; complain. [C14: < OF *querele,* < L *querēlla* complaint, < *querī* to complain] —ˈ**quarreller** *or U.S.* ˈ**quarreler** *n.*

quarrel[2] (ˈkwɒrəl) *n.* **1.** an arrow having a four-edged head, fired from a crossbow. **2.** a small square or diamond-shaped pane of glass. [C13: < OF *quarrel* pane, < Med. L *quadrellus,* dim. of L *quadrus* square]

quarrelsome (ˈkwɒrəlsəm) *adj.* inclined to quarrel or disagree; belligerent.

quarrian *or* **quarrion** (ˈkwɒrɪən) *n.* a cockatiel of inland Australia that feeds on seeds and grasses. [C20: prob. < Abor.]

quarry[1] (ˈkwɒrɪ) *n., pl.* **-ries. 1.** an open surface excavation for the extraction of building stone, slate, marble, etc. **2.** a copious source, esp. of information. ~*vb.* **-rying, -ried. 3.** to extract (stone, slate, etc.) from or as if from a quarry. **4.** (*tr.*) to excavate a quarry in. **5.** to obtain (something) diligently and laboriously. [C15: < OF *quarriere,* < *quarre* (unattested) square-shaped stone, < L *quadrāre* to make square]

quarry[2] (ˈkwɒrɪ) *n., pl.* **-ries. 1.** an animal, etc., that is hunted, esp. by other animals; prey. **2.** anything pursued. [C14 *quirre* entrails offered to the hounds, < OF *cuirée* what is placed on the hide, < *cuir* hide, < L *corium* leather; prob. also infl. by OF *coree* entrails, < L *cor* heart]

quarryman (ˈkwɒrɪmən) *n., pl.* **-men.** a man who works in or manages a quarry.

quarry tile *n.* an unglazed floor tile.

quart (kwɔːt) *n.* **1.** a unit of liquid measure equal to a quarter of a gallon or two pints. 1 U.S. quart (0.946 litre) is equal to 0.8326 U.K. quart. 1 U.K. quart (1.136 litres) is equal to 1.2009 U.S. quarts. **2.** a unit of dry measure equal to 2 pints or one eighth of a peck. [C14: < OF *quarte,* < L *quartus* fourth]

quartan (ˈkwɔːtᵊn) *adj.* (of a fever) occurring every third day. [C13: < L *febris quartāna* fever occurring every fourth day, reckoned inclusively]

quarte (kɑːt) *n.* the fourth of eight basic positions from which a parry or attack can be made in fencing. [C18: F < OF *quarte,* < L *quartus* fourth]

quarter (ˈkwɔːtə) *n.* **1.** one of four equal parts of an object, quantity, etc. **2.** the fraction equal to one divided by four (¼). **3.** *U.S., Canad., etc.* a 25-cent piece. **4.** a unit of weight equal to a quarter of a hundredweight. 1 U.S. quarter is equal to 25 pounds; 1 Brit. quarter is equal to 28 pounds. **5.** short for **quarter-hour. 6.** a fourth part of a year; three months. **7.** *Astron.* **a.** one fourth of the moon's period of revolution around the earth. **b.** either of two phases of the moon when half of the lighted surface is visible. **8.** *Inf.* a unit of weight equal to a quarter of a pound or 4 ounces. **9.** *Brit.* a unit of capacity for grain, etc., usually equal to 8 U.K. bushels. **10.** *Sport.* one of the four periods into which certain games are divided. **11.** *Naut.* the part of a vessel's side towards the stern. **12.** a region or district of a town or city: *the Spanish quarter.* **13.** a region, direction, or point of the compass. **14.** (*sometimes pl.*) an unspecified person or group of people: *to get word from the highest quarter.* **15.** mercy or pity, as shown to a defeated opponent (esp. in **ask for** *or* **give quarter**). **16.** any of the four limbs, including the adjacent parts, of a quadruped or bird. **17.** *Heraldry.* one of four quadrants into which a shield may be divided. ~*vb.* **18.** (*tr.*) to divide into four equal parts. **19.** (*tr.*) to divide into any number of parts. **20.** (*tr.*) (esp. formerly) to dismember (a human body). **21.** to billet or be billeted in lodgings, esp. (of military personnel) in civilian lodgings. **22.** (*intr.*) (of hounds) to range over an area of ground in search of game or the scent of quarry. **23.** (*intr.*) *Naut.* (of the wind) to blow onto a vessel's quarter. **24.** (*tr.*) *Heraldry.* **a.** to divide (a shield) into four separate bearings. **b.** to place (one set of arms) in diagonally opposite quarters to another. ~*adj.* **25.** being or consisting of one of four equal parts. ~See also **quarters.** [C13: < OF *quartier,* < L *quartārius* a fourth part, < *quartus* fourth]

quarterback (ˈkwɔːtəˌbæk) *n.* a player in American football who directs attacking play.

quarter-bound *adj.* (of a book) having a binding consisting of two types of material, the better type being used on the spine.

quarter day *n.* any of four days in the year when certain payments become due. In England, Wales, and Ireland these are Lady Day, Midsummer Day, Michaelmas, and Christmas. In Scotland they are Candlemas, Whit Sunday, Lammas, and Martinmas.

quarterdeck (ˈkwɔːtəˌdɛk) *n. Naut.* the after part of the weather deck of a ship, traditionally the deck for official or ceremonial use.

quartered (ˈkwɔːtəd) *adj.* **1.** *Heraldry.* (of a shield) divided into four sections, each having contrasting arms or having two sets of arms, each repeated in diagonally opposite corners. **2.** (of a log) sawn into four equal parts along two diameters at right angles to each other.

quarterfinal (ˌkwɔːtəˈfaɪnᵊl) *n.* the round before the semifinal in a competition.

quarter-hour *n.* **1.** a period of 15 minutes. **2.** either of the points on a timepiece that mark 15 minutes before or after the hour.

quartering (ˈkwɔːtərɪŋ) *n.* **1.** *Mil.* the allocation of accommodation to service personnel. **2.** *Heraldry.* **a.** the marshalling of several coats of arms on one shield, usually representing intermarriages. **b.** any coat of arms marshalled in this way.

quarterlight (ˈkwɔːtəˌlaɪt) *n. Brit.* a small pivoted window in the door of a car for ventilation.

quarterly (ˈkwɔːtəlɪ) *adj.* **1.** occurring, done, paid, etc., at intervals of three months. **2.** of, relating to, or consisting of a quarter. ~*n., pl.* **-lies. 3.** a periodical issued every three months. ~*adv.* **4.** once every three months.

quartermaster (ˈkwɔːtəˌmɑːstə) *n.* **1.** an officer responsible for accommodation, food, and equipment in a military unit. **2.** a rating in the navy, usually a petty officer, with particular responsibility for navigational duties.

quarter-miler *n.* an athlete who specializes in running the quarter mile.

quartern (ˈkwɔːtən) *n.* **1.** a fourth part of certain weights or measures. **2.** Also called: **quartern loaf.** *Brit.* **a.** a type of loaf 4 inches square. **b.** any loaf weighing 1600 g. [C13: < OF *quarteron,* < *quart* a quarter]

quarter note *n.* the usual U.S. and Canad. name for **crotchet** (sense 1).

quarter plate *n.* a photographic plate measuring 8.3 × 10.8 cm.

quarters (ˈkwɔːtəz) *pl. n.* **1.** accommodation, esp. as provided for military personnel. **2.** the stations assigned to crew members of a warship: *general quarters.*

quarter sessions *n.* (*functioning as sing. or pl.*) (formerly) any of various courts held four times a year before justices of the peace or a recorder.

quarterstaff (ˈkwɔːtəˌstɑːf) *n., pl.* **-staves** (-ˌsteɪvz). a stout iron-tipped wooden staff about 6ft. long, formerly used as a weapon. [C16: < ?]

quarter tone *n. Music.* a quarter of a whole tone.

quartet *or* **quartette** (kwɔːˈtɛt) *n.* **1.** a group of four singers or instrumentalists or a piece of music composed for such a group. **2.** any group of four. [C18: < It. *quartetto,* dim. of *quarto* fourth]

quartic (ˈkwɔːtɪk) *adj., n.* another word for **biquadratic.** [C19: < L *quartus* fourth]

quartile (ˈkwɔːtaɪl) *n.* **1.** *Statistics.* one of three values of a variable dividing its distribution into four groups with equal frequencies. ~*adj.* **2.** *Statistics.* of a quartile. **3.** *Astrol.* denoting an aspect of two heavenly bodies when their longitudes differ by 90°. [C16: < Med. L *quartīlis,* < L *quartus* fourth]

quarto (ˈkwɔːtəʊ) *n., pl.* **-tos.** a book size resulting from folding a sheet of paper into four leaves or eight pages. [C16: < NL *in quartō* in quarter]

quartz (kwɔːts) *n.* a hard glossy mineral consisting of silicon dioxide in crystalline form. It occurs as colourless rock crystal and as several impure coloured varieties including agate, chalcedony, flint, and amethyst. Formula: SiO_2. [C18: < G *Quarz,* of Slavic origin]

quartz clock *or* **watch** *n.* a clock or watch that is operated by a vibrating quartz crystal.

quartz crystal *n.* a thin plate or rod cut from a piece of piezoelectric quartz and ground so that it vibrates at a particular frequency.

quartz glass *n.* a colourless glass composed of almost pure silica, resistant to very high temperatures.

quartz-iodine lamp *or* **quartz lamp** *n.* an electric light bulb consisting of a quartz envelope enclosing an inert gas containing iodine vapour and a tungsten filament: used for car headlights, cine projectors, etc.

quartzite (ˈkwɔːtsaɪt) *n.* **1.** a sandstone composed of quartz. **2.** a very hard rock consisting of intergrown quartz crystals.

quasar (ˈkweɪzɑː, -sɑː) *n.* any of a class of quasi-stellar objects that are powerful sources of radio waves and other forms of energy. Many have large red shifts which imply distances of several thousand million light years. [C20: *quas(i-stell)ar (radio source)*]

quash (kwɒʃ) *vb.* (*tr.*) **1.** to subdue forcefully and completely. **2.** to annul or make void (a law, etc.). **3.** to reject (an indictment, etc.) as invalid. [C14: < OF *quasser,* < L *quassāre* to shake]

quasi- *combining form.* **1.** almost but not really; seemingly: *a quasi-religious cult.* **2.** resembling but not actually being; so-called: *a quasi-scholar.* [< L, lit.: as if]

quasi-stellar object (ˈkwɑːzɪ, ˈkweɪsaɪ) *n.* a member of any of several classes of astronomical bodies, including **quasars** and **quasi-stellar galaxies,** both of which have exceptionally large red shifts. Abbrev.: **QSO.**

quassia (ˈkwɒʃə) *n.* **1.** any of a genus of tropical American trees having bitter bark and wood. **2.** the wood of this tree or a bitter compound extracted from it, formerly used as a tonic and vermifuge, now used in insecticides. [C18: < NL, after Graman *Quassi,* a slave who discovered (1730) the medicinal value of the root]

quatercentenary (ˌkwætəsɛnˈtiːnərɪ) *n., pl.* **-naries.** a 400th anniversary. [C19: < L *quater* four times + CENTENARY] —**quatercentennial** (ˌkwætəsɛnˈtɛnɪəl) *adj., n.*

quaternary (kwəˈtɜːnərɪ) *adj.* **1.** consisting of fours or by fours. **2.** fourth in a series. **3.** *Chem.* containing or being an atom bound to four other atoms or groups. ~*n., pl.* **-naries. 4.** the number four or a set of four. [C15: < L *quaternārius* each containing four, < *quaternī* by fours, < *quattuor* four]

Quaternary (kwəˈtɜːnərɪ) *adj.* **1.** of or denoting the most recent period of geological time, which succeeded the Tertiary period one million years ago. ~*n.* **2. the.** the Quaternary period or rock system.

quaternion (kwəˈtɜːnɪən) *n.* **1.** *Maths.* a generalized complex number consisting of four components, $x = x_0 + x_1i + x_2j + x_3k$, where x, $x_0 \ldots x_3$ are real numbers and $i^2 = j^2 = k^2 = -1$, $ij = -ji = k$, etc. **2.** a set of four. [C14: < LL, < L *quaternī* four at a time]

quatrain (ˈkwɒtreɪn) *n.* a stanza or poem of four lines. [C16: < F, < L *quatre* four, < L *quattuor*]

quatrefoil (ˈkætrəˌfɔɪl) *n.* **1.** a leaf composed of four leaflets. **2.** *Archit.* a carved ornament having four foils arranged about a common centre. [C15: < OF, < *quatre* four + *-foil* leaflet]

quattrocento (ˌkwætrəʊˈtʃɛntəʊ) *n.* the 15th century, esp. in reference to Renaissance Italian art and literature. [It., lit.: four hundred (short for fourteen hundred)]

quaver (ˈkweɪvə) *vb.* **1.** to say or sing (something) with a trembling voice. **2.** (*intr.*) (esp. of the voice) to quiver or tremble. **3.** (*intr.*) *Rare.* to sing or play trills. ~*n.* **4.** *Music.* a note having the time value of an eighth of a semibreve. Usual U.S. and Canad. name: **eighth note. 5.** a tremulous sound or note. [C15 (in the sense: to vibrate): < *quaven* to tremble, of Gmc origin] —ˈ**quavering** *adj.* —ˈ**quaveringly** *adv.*

quay (kiː) *n.* a wharf, typically one built parallel to the shoreline. [C14 *keye,* < OF *kai,* of Celtic origin]

quayage (ˈkiːɪdʒ) *n.* **1.** a system of quays. **2.** a charge for the use of a quay.

quayside (ˈkiːˌsaɪd) *n.* the edge of a quay along the water.

Que. *abbrev. for* Quebec.

quean (kwiːn) *n.* **1.** *Arch.* **a.** a boisterous impudent woman. **b.** a prostitute. **2.** *Scot.* an unmarried girl. [OE *cwene*]

queasy (ˈkwiːzɪ) *adj.* **-sier, -siest. 1.** having the feeling that one is about to vomit; nauseous. **2.** feeling or causing uneasiness. [C15: <?] —ˈ**queasily** *adv.* —ˈ**queasiness** *n.*

Quebecker *or* **Quebecer** (kwɪˈbɛkə, kəˈbɛkə) *n.* a native or inhabitant of Quebec.

Québecois (*French* kebɛkwa) *n., pl.* **-cois** (-kwa). a native or inhabitant of the province of Quebec, esp. a French-speaking one.

quebracho (keɪˈbrɑːtʃəʊ) *n., pl.* **-chos** (-tʃəʊz). **1.** either of two South American trees having a tannin-rich hard wood used in tanning and dyeing. **2.** a South American tree, whose bark yields alkaloids used in medicine and tanning. **3.** the wood or bark of any of these trees. [C19: < American Sp., < *quiebracha,* < *quebrar* to break (< L *crepāre* to rattle) + *hacha* axe (< F)]

Quechua (ˈkɛtʃwə) *n.* **1.** (*pl.* **-uas** *or* **-ua**) a member of any of a group of South American Indian peoples of the Andes, including the Incas. **2.** the language or family of languages spoken by these peoples. —ˈ**Quechuan** *adj., n.*

queen (kwiːn) *n.* **1.** a female sovereign who is the official ruler or head of state. **2.** the wife of a king. **3.** a woman or a thing personified as a woman considered the best or most important of her kind: *the queen of ocean liners.* **4.** *Sl.* an effeminate male homosexual. **5.** the only fertile female in a colony of bees, ants, etc. **6.** an adult female cat. **7.** a playing card bearing the picture of a queen. **8.** the most powerful chess piece, able to move in a straight line in any direction or diagonally. ~*vb.* **9.** *Chess.* to promote (a pawn) to a queen when it reaches the eighth rank. **10.** (*tr.*) to crown as queen. **11.** (*intr.*) to reign as queen. **12. queen it.** (often foll. by *over*) *Inf.* to behave in an overbearing manner. [OE *cwēn*]

Queen-Anne *n.* **1.** a style of furniture popular in England about 1700–20 and in America about 1720–70, characterized by the use of curves, walnut veneer, and the cabriole leg. ~*adj.* **2.** in or of this style. **3.** of a style of architecture popular in early 18th-century England, characterized by red-brick construction with classical ornamentation.

Queen Anne's lace *n.* another name for the **wild carrot.**

queen bee *n.* **1.** the fertile female bee in a hive. **2.** *Inf.* a woman in a position of dominance over her associates.

queen consort *n.* the wife of a reigning king.

queen dowager *n.* the widow of a king.

queenly (ˈkwiːnlɪ) *adj.* **-lier, -liest. 1.** resembling or appropriate to a queen. ~*adv.* **2.** in a manner appropriate to a queen.

queen mother *n.* the widow of a former king who is also the mother of the reigning sovereign.

queen olive *n.* a variety of olive having large fleshy fruit suitable for pickling.

queen post *n.* one of a pair of vertical posts that connect the tie beam of a truss to the principal rafters. Cf. **king post.**

Queen's Award for Industry *n.* (in Britain) an award given to firms that have outstanding export records or have made technological advances.

Queen's Bench *n.* (in England when the sovereign is female) one of the divisions of the High Court of Justice.

Queensberry rules (ˈkwiːnzbərɪ) *pl. n.* **1.** the code of rules followed in modern boxing. **2.** *Inf.* gentlemanly conduct, esp. in a dispute. [C19: after the ninth Marquess of *Queensberry,* who originated the rules in 1869]

Queen's Counsel *n.* **1.** (in England when the sovereign is female) a barrister appointed Counsel to the Crown on the recommendation of the Lord Chancellor. **2.** (in Canada) an honorary title which may be bestowed by the government on lawyers with long experience.

Queen's English *n.* (when the British sovereign is female) standard Southern British English.

queen's evidence *n. English law.* (when the sovereign is female) evidence given for the Crown against his former associates in crime by an accomplice (esp. in **turn queen's evidence).** U.S. equivalent: **state's evidence.**

Queen's Guide *n.* (in Britain and the Commonwealth when the sovereign is female) a Guide who has passed the highest tests of proficiency.

queen's highway *n.* **1.** (in Britain when the sovereign is female) any public road or right of way. **2.** (in Canada) a main road maintained by the provincial government.

Queensland nut (ˈkwiːnzˌlænd) *n.* another name for **macadamia.**

Queen's Scout *n.* (in Britain and the Commonwealth when the sovereign is female) a Scout who has passed the highest tests of proficiency. U.S. equivalent: **Eagle Scout.**

queer (kwɪə) *adj.* **1.** differing from the normal or usual; odd or strange. **2.** dubious; shady. **3.** faint, giddy, or queasy. **4.** *Inf., derog.* homosexual. **5.** *Inf.* eccentric or slightly mad. **6.** *Sl.* worthless or counterfeit. ~*n.* **7.** *Inf., derog.* a homosexual. ~*vb.* (*tr.*) *Inf.* **8.** to spoil or thwart (esp. in **queer someone's pitch). 9.** to put in a difficult position. [C16: ? < G *quer* oblique, ult. < OHG *twërh*] —ˈ**queerly** *adv.* —ˈ**queerness** *n.*

queer fish *n. Brit. inf.* an odd person.

queer street *n.* (*sometimes cap.*) *Inf.* a difficult situation, such as debt or bankruptcy (in **in queer street).**

quell (kwɛl) *vb.* (*tr.*) **1.** to suppress (rebellion, etc.); subdue. **2.** to overcome or allay. [OE *cwellan* to kill] —ˈ**queller** *n.*

quench (kwɛntʃ) *vb.* (*tr.*) **1.** to satisfy (one's thirst, desires, etc.); slake. **2.** to put out (a fire, etc.); extinguish. **3.** to put down; suppress; subdue. **4.** to cool (hot metal) by plunging it into cold water. [OE *ācwencan* to extinguish] —ˈ**quenchable** *adj.* —ˈ**quencher** *n.*

quenelle (kəˈnɛl) *n.* a ball of finely sieved meat or fish. [C19: < F, < G *Knödel* dumpling, < OHG *knodo* knot]

querist (ˈkwɪərɪst) *n.* a person who makes inquiries or queries; questioner.

quern (kwɜːn) *n.* a stone hand mill for grinding corn. [OE *cweorn*]

querulous (ˈkwɛrʊləs, ˈkwɛrjʊ-) *adj.* **1.** inclined to make whining or peevish complaints. **2.** characterized by or proceeding from a complaining fretful attitude or disposition. [C15: < L *querulus,* < *querī* to complain] —ˈ**querulously** *adv.* —ˈ**querulousness** *n.*

query (ˈkwɪərɪ) *n., pl.* **-ries. 1.** a question, esp. one expressing doubt. **2.** a question mark. ~*vb.* **-rying, -ried.** (*tr.*) **3.** to express uncertainty, doubt, or an objection concerning (something). **4.** to express as a query. **5.** *U.S.* to put a question to (a person); ask. [C17: < earlier *quere*, < L *quaere* ask!, < *quaerere* to seek]

quest (kwɛst) *n.* **1.** a looking for or seeking; search. **2.** (in medieval romance) an expedition by a knight or knights to accomplish some task, such as finding the Holy Grail. **3.** the object of a search; a goal or target. ~*vb.* (*mainly intr.*) **4.** (foll. by *for* or *after*) to go in search (of). **5.** (of dogs, etc.) to search for game. **6.** (*also tr.*) *Arch.* to seek or pursue. [C14: < OF *queste*, < L *quaesita* sought, < *quaerere* to seek] —ˈ**quester** *n.* —ˈ**questing** *adj.* —ˈ**questingly** *adv.*

question (ˈkwɛstʃən) *n.* **1.** a form of words addressed to a person in order to elicit information or evoke a response; interrogative sentence. **2.** a point at issue: *it's only a question of time until she dies.* **3.** a difficulty or uncertainty. **4. a.** an act of asking. **b.** an investigation into some problem. **5.** a motion presented for debate. **6. put the question.** to require members of a deliberative assembly to vote on a motion presented. **7.** *Law.* a matter submitted to a court or other tribunal. **8. beyond (all) question.** beyond (any) dispute or doubt. **9. call in** *or* **into question. a.** to make (something) the subject of disagreement. **b.** to cast doubt upon the validity, truth, etc., of (something). **10. in question.** under discussion: *this is the man in question.* **11. out of the question.** beyond consideration; unthinkable or impossible. **12. put to the question.** (formerly) to interrogate by torture. ~*vb.* (*mainly tr.*) **13.** to put a question or questions to (a person); interrogate. **14.** to make (something) the subject of dispute. **15.** to express uncertainty about the validity, truth, etc., of (something); doubt. [C13: via OF < L *quaestiō*, < *quaerere* to seek] —ˈ**questioner** *n.*

questionable (ˈkwɛstʃənəbᵊl) *adj.* **1.** (esp. of a person's morality or honesty) admitting of some doubt; dubious. **2.** of disputable value or authority. —ˈ**questionableness** *n.* —ˈ**questionably** *adv.*

questioning (ˈkwɛstʃənɪŋ) *adj.* **1.** proceeding from or characterized by a feeling of doubt or uncertainty. **2.** intellectually stimulated. —ˈ**questioningly** *adv.*

questionless (ˈkwɛstʃənlɪs) *adj.* **1.** blindly adhering; unquestioning. **2.** a less common word for **unquestionable.** —ˈ**questionlessly** *adv.*

question mark *n.* **1.** the punctuation mark ?, used at the end of questions and in other contexts where doubt or ignorance is implied. **2.** this mark used for any other purpose, as to draw attention to a possible mistake.

question master *n. Brit.* the chairman of a radio or television quiz or panel game.

questionnaire (ˌkwɛstʃəˈnɛə, ˌkɛs-) *n.* a set of questions on a form, submitted to a number of people in order to collect statistical information.

question time *n.* (in parliamentary bodies of the British type) the time set aside each day for questions to government ministers.

quetzal (ˈkɛtsəl) *n., pl.* **-zals** *or* **-zales** (-ˈsɑːlɛs). **1.** a crested bird of Central and N South America, which has a brilliant green, red, and white plumage and, in the male, long tail feathers. **2.** the standard monetary unit of Guatemala. [via American Sp. < Nahuatl *quetzalli* brightly coloured tail feather]

queue (kjuː) *Chiefly Brit.* ~*n.* **1.** a line of people, vehicles, etc., waiting for something. **2.** a pigtail. ~*vb.* **queuing, queued. 3.** (*intr.*, often foll. by *up*) to form or remain in a line while waiting. Usual U.S. word: **line.** [C16 (in the sense: tail); C18 (in the sense: pigtail): via F < L *cauda* tail]

queue-jump *vb.* (*intr.*) **1.** to take a place in a queue ahead of those already queuing; push in. **2.** to obtain some advantage out of turn or unfairly. —ˈ**queue-**ˌ**jumper** *n.*

quibble (ˈkwɪbᵊl) *vb.* (*intr.*) **1.** to make trivial objections. **2.** *Arch.* to play on words; pun. ~*n.* **3.** a trivial objection or equivocation, esp. one used to avoid an issue. **4.** *Arch.* a pun. [C17: prob. < obs. *quib*, ? < L *quibus* (< *quī* who, which), as used in legal documents, with reference to their obscure phraseology] —ˈ**quibbler** *n.* —ˈ**quibbling** *adj.*

quiche (kiːʃ) *n.* an open savoury tart with an egg custard filling to which bacon, onion, cheese, etc., are added. [F, < G *Kuchen* cake]

quick (kwɪk) *adj.* **1.** performed or occurring during a comparatively short time: *a quick move.* **2.** lasting a short time; brief. **3.** accomplishing something in a time that is shorter than normal: *a quick worker.* **4.** characterized by rapidity of movement; fast. **5.** immediate or prompt. **6.** (*postpositive*) eager or ready to perform (an action): *quick to criticize.* **7.** responsive to stimulation; alert; lively. **8.** eager or enthusiastic for learning. **9.** easily excited or aroused. **10.** nimble in one's movements or actions; deft: *quick fingers.* **11.** *Arch.* **a.** alive; living. **b.** (*as n.*) living people (esp. in **the quick and the dead**). **12. quick with child.** *Arch.* pregnant. ~*n.* **13.** any area of sensitive flesh, esp. that under a toenail or fingernail. **14.** the most important part (of a thing). **15. cut (someone) to the quick.** to hurt (someone's) feelings deeply. ~*adv. Inf.* **16.** in a rapid manner; swiftly. **17.** *Inf.* soon: *I hope he comes quick.* ~*sentence substitute.* **18.** a command to perform an action immediately. [OE *cwicu* living] —ˈ**quickly** *adv.* —ˈ**quickness** *n.*

quick-change artist *n.* an actor or entertainer who undertakes several rapid changes of costume during his performance.

quicken (ˈkwɪkən) *vb.* **1.** to make or become faster; accelerate. **2.** to impart to or receive vigour, enthusiasm, etc.: *science quickens man's imagination.* **3.** to make or become alive; revive. **4. a.** (of an unborn fetus) to begin to show signs of life. **b.** (of a pregnant woman) to reach the stage of pregnancy at which movements of the fetus can be felt.

quick-freeze *vb.* **-freezing, -froze, -frozen.** (*tr.*) to preserve (food) by subjecting it to rapid refrigeration at temperatures of 0°C or lower.

quickie (ˈkwɪkɪ) *n. Inf.* **1.** Also called (esp. Brit.): **quick one.** a speedily consumed alcoholic drink. **2.** anything made or done rapidly.

quicklime (ˈkwɪkˌlaɪm) *n.* another name for **calcium oxide.**

quick march *n.* **1.** a march at quick time or the order to proceed at such a pace. ~*sentence substitute.* **2.** a command to commence such a march.

quicksand (ˈkwɪkˌsænd) *n.* a deep mass of loose wet sand that sucks anything on top of it inextricably into it.

quickset (ˈkwɪkˌsɛt) *Chiefly Brit.* ~*n.* **1. a.** a plant or cutting, esp. of hawthorn, set so as to form a hedge. **b.** such plants or cuttings collectively. **2.** a hedge composed of such plants. ~*adj.* **3.** composed of such plants.

quicksilver (ˈkwɪkˌsɪlvə) *n.* **1.** another name for **mercury** (sense 1). ~*adj.* **2.** rapid or unpredictable in movement or change.

quickstep (ˈkwɪkˌstɛp) *n.* **1.** a modern ballroom dance in rapid quadruple time. **2.** a piece of music composed for or in the rhythm of this dance. ~*vb.* **-stepping, -stepped. 3.** (*intr.*) to perform this dance.

quick-tempered *adj.* readily roused to anger; irascible.

quickthorn (ˈkwɪkˌθɔːn) *n.* hawthorn, esp. when planted as a hedge. [C17: prob. < *quick* in the sense "fast-growing": cf. QUICKSET]

quick time *n. Mil.* the normal marching rate of 120 paces to the minute.

quick-witted *adj.* having a keenly alert mind, esp. as used to avert danger, make an effective reply, etc. —ˌ**quick-**ˈ**wittedly** *adv.* —ˌ**quick-**ˈ**wittedness** *n.*

quid[1] (kwɪd) *n.* a piece of tobacco, suitable for chewing. [OE *cwidu* chewing resin]

quid[2] (kwɪd) *n., pl.* **quid.** *Brit. sl.* **1.** a pound (sterling). **2. (be) quids in.** (to be) in a very favourable or advantageous position. [C17: <?]

quiddity (ˈkwɪdɪtɪ) *n., pl.* **-ties. 1.** the essential nature of something. **2.** a petty or trifling distinction; quibble. [C16: < Med. L *quidditās*, < L *quid* what]

quidnunc (ˈkwɪdˌnʌŋk) *n.* a person eager to learn news and scandal; gossipmonger. [C18: < L, lit.: what now]

quid pro quo (ˈkwɪd prəʊ ˈkwəʊ) *n., pl.* **quid pro quos.** **1.** a reciprocal exchange. **2.** something given in compensation, esp. an advantage or object given in exchange for another. [C16: < L: something for something]

quiescent (kwɪˈɛsᵊnt) *adj.* quiet, inactive, or dormant. [C17: < L *quiescere* to rest] —**quiˈescence** *or* **quiˈescency** *n.* —**quiˈescently** *adv.*

quiet (ˈkwaɪət) *adj.* **1.** characterized by an absence of noise. **2.** calm or tranquil: *the sea is quiet tonight.* **3.** free from activities, distractions, etc.; untroubled: *a quiet life.* **4.** short of work, orders, etc.; not busy: *business is quiet today.* **5.** private; not public; secret: *a quiet word with someone.* **6.** free from anger, impatience, or other extreme emotion. **7.** free from pretentiousness; modest or reserved: *quiet humour.* **8.** *Astron.* (of the sun) exhibiting a very low number of sunspots, solar flares, etc.; inactive. ~*n.* **9.** the state of being silent, peaceful, or untroubled. **10.** **on the quiet.** without other people knowing. ~*vb.* **11.** a less common word for **quieten.** [C14: < L *quiētus*, p.p. of *quiēscere* to rest, < *quiēs* repose] —ˈ**quietness** *n.*

quieten (ˈkwaɪətᵊn) *vb. Chiefly Brit.* **1.** (often foll. by *down*) to make or become calm, silent, etc. **2.** (*tr.*) to allay (fear, doubts, etc.).

quietism (ˈkwaɪəˌtɪzəm) *n.* **1.** a form of religious mysticism originating in Spain in the late 17th century, requiring complete passivity to God's will. **2.** passivity and calmness of mind towards external events. —ˈ**quietist** *n., adj.*

quietly (ˈkwaɪətlɪ) *adv.* **1.** in a quiet manner. **2.** **just quietly.** *Austral.* confidentially.

quietude (ˈkwaɪəˌtjuːd) *n.* the state or condition of being quiet, peaceful, calm, or tranquil.

quietus (kwaɪˈiːtəs, -ˈeɪtəs) *n., pl.* **-tuses.** **1.** anything that serves to quash, eliminate, or kill. **2.** a release from life; death. **3.** the discharge or settlement of debts, duties, etc. [C16: < L *quiētus est*, lit.: he is at rest]

quiff (kwɪf) *n. Brit.* a tuft of hair brushed up above the forehead. [C19: <?]

quill (kwɪl) *n.* **1. a.** any of the large stiff feathers of the wing or tail of a bird. **b.** the long hollow part of a feather; calamus. **2.** Also called: **quill pen.** a feather made into a pen for writing. **3.** any of the stiff hollow spines of a porcupine or hedgehog. **4.** a device, formerly made from a crow quill, for plucking a harpsichord string. **5.** a small roll of bark, esp. one of dried cinnamon. **6.** a bobbin or spindle. **7.** a fluted fold, as in a ruff. ~*vb.* (*tr.*) **8.** to wind (thread, etc.) onto a spool or bobbin. **9.** to make or press fluted folds in (a ruff, etc.). [C15 (in the sense: hollow reed or pipe): <?; cf. MLow G *quiele* quill]

quilt (kwɪlt) *n.* **1.** a cover for a bed, consisting of a soft filling sewn between two layers of material, usually with crisscross seams. **2.** short for **continental quilt.** **3.** a bedspread. **4.** anything resembling a quilt. ~*vb.* (*tr.*) **5.** to stitch together (two pieces of fabric) with (a thick padding or lining) between them. **6.** to create (a garment, etc.) in this way. **7.** to pad with material. [C13: < OF *coilte* mattress, < L *culcita* stuffed item of bedding] —ˈ**quilted** *adj.* —ˈ**quilter** *n.*

quilting (ˈkwɪltɪŋ) *n.* **1.** material for quilts. **2.** the act of making a quilt. **3.** quilted work.

quin (kwɪn) *n. Brit.* short for **quintuplet** (sense 1). U.S. and Canad. word: **quint.**

quinary (ˈkwaɪnərɪ) *adj.* **1.** of or by fives. **2.** fifth in a series. **3.** (of a number system) having a base of five. [C17: < L *quīnārius* containing five, < *quīnī* five each]

quince (kwɪns) *n.* **1.** a small widely cultivated Asian tree with edible pear-shaped fruits. **2.** the fruit of this tree, much used in preserves. [C14 *qwince* pl. of *quyn*, < OF *coin*, < L *cotōneum*, < Gk *kudōnion* quince]

quincentenary (ˌkwɪnsɛnˈtiːnərɪ) *n., pl.* **-naries.** a 500th anniversary. [C19: irregularly < L *quinque* five + CENTENARY] —**quincentennial** (ˌkwɪnsɛnˈtɛnɪəl) *adj., n.*

quincunx (ˈkwɪnkʌŋks) *n.* a group of five objects arranged in the shape of a rectangle with one at each of the four corners and the fifth in the centre. [C17: < L: five twelfths, < *quinque* five + *uncia* twelfth; in ancient Rome, this was a coin worth five twelfths of an AS[2] and marked with five spots] —**quincuncial** (kwɪnˈkʌnʃəl) *adj.*

quinella (kwɪˈnɛlə) *n. Austral.* a form of betting in which the punter must select the first and second place-winners, in any order. [< American Sp. *quiniela*]

quinidine (ˈkwɪnɪˌdiːn) *n.* a crystalline alkaloid drug used to treat heart arrhythmias.

quinine (kwɪˈniːn; *U.S.* ˈkwaɪnaɪn) *n.* a bitter crystalline alkaloid extracted from cinchona bark, the salts of which are used as a tonic, analgesic, etc., and in malaria therapy. [C19: < Sp. *quina* cinchona bark, < Quechua *kina* bark]

quinol (ˈkwɪnɒl) *n.* another name for **hydroquinone.**

quinoline (ˈkwɪnəˌliːn, -lɪn) *n.* an oily colourless insoluble compound synthesized by heating aniline, nitrobenzene, glycerol, and sulphuric acid: used as a food preservative and in the manufacture of dyes and antiseptics.

quinquagenarian (ˌkwɪŋkwədʒɪˈnɛərɪən) *n.* **1.** a person between 50 and 59 years old. ~*adj.* **2.** being between 50 and 59 years old. **3.** of a quinquagenarian. [C16: < L *quinquāgēnārius* containing fifty, < *quinquāgēnī* fifty each]

Quinquagesima (ˌkwɪŋkwəˈdʒɛsɪmə) *n.* the Sunday preceding Lent. Also called: **Quinquagesima Sunday.** [C14: via Med. L < L *quinquāgēsima diēs* fiftieth day]

quinquecentenary (ˌkwɪŋkwɪsɛnˈtiːnərɪ) *n., pl.* **-naries.** another name for **quincentenary.**

quinquennial (kwɪnˈkwɛnɪəl) *adj.* **1.** occurring once every five years or over a period of five years. ~*n.* **2.** a fifth anniversary. —**quinˈquennially** *adv.*

quinquennium (kwɪnˈkwɛnɪəm) *n., pl.* **-nia** (-nɪə). a period or cycle of five years. [C17: < L *quinque* five + *annus* year]

quinquereme (ˌkwɪŋkwɪˈriːm) *n.* an ancient Roman galley with five banks of oars. [C16: < L *quinquerēmis*, < *quinque-* five + *rēmus* oar]

quinquevalent (ˌkwɪŋkwɪˈveɪlənt) *adj. Chem.* another word for **pentavalent.** —ˌ**quinqueˈvalency** *or* ˌ**quinqueˈvalence** *n.*

quinsy (ˈkwɪnzɪ) *n.* inflammation of the tonsils and surrounding tissues with the formation of abscesses. [C14: via OF & Med. L < Gk *kunankhē*, < *kuōn* dog + *ankhein* to strangle]

quint[1] *n.* **1.** (kwɪnt). an organ stop sounding a note a fifth higher. **2.** (kɪnt). *Piquet.* a sequence of five cards in the same suit. [C17: < F *quinte*, < L *quintus* fifth]

quint[2] (kwɪnt) *n.* the U.S. and Canad. word for **quin.**

quintain (ˈkwɪntɪn) *n.* (esp. in medieval Europe) a post or target set up for tilting exercises for mounted knights or foot soldiers. [C14: < OF *quintaine*, < L: street in a Roman camp between the fifth & sixth maniples (the maniple was a unit of 120-200 soldiers in ancient Rome), < *quintus* fifth]

quintal (ˈkwɪntᵊl) *n.* **1.** a unit of weight equal to (esp. in Britain) 112 pounds or (esp. in U.S.) 100 pounds. **2.** a unit of weight equal to 100 kilograms. [C15: via OF < Ar. *qintār*, possibly < L *centēnārius* consisting of a hundred]

quintan (ˈkwɪntən) *adj.* (of a fever) occurring every fourth day. [C17: < L *febris quintāna* fever occurring every fifth day, reckoned inclusively]

quinte (kænt) *n.* the fifth of eight basic positions from which a parry or attack can be made in fencing. [C18: F < L *quintus* fifth]

quintessence (kwɪnˈtɛsəns) *n.* **1.** the most typical representation of a quality, state, etc. **2.** an extract of a substance containing its principle in its most concentrated form. **3.** (in ancient philosophy) ether, the fifth essence or element, which was thought to be the constituent matter of the heavenly bodies and latent in all things. [C15: via F < Med. L *quinta essentia* the fifth essence, translation of Gk] —**quintessential** (ˌkwɪntɪˈsɛnʃəl) *adj.* —ˌ**quintesˈsentially** *adv.*

quintet *or* **quintette** (kwɪnˈtɛt) *n.* **1.** a group of five singers or instrumentalists or a piece of music composed for such a group. **2.** any group of five. [C19: < It. *quintetto,* < *quinto* fifth]

quintillion (kwɪnˈtɪljən) *n., pl.* **-lions** *or* **-lion. 1.** (in Britain, France, and Germany) the number represented as one followed by 30 zeros (10^{30}). U.S. and Canad. word: **nonillion. 2.** (in the U.S. and Canada) the number represented as one followed by 18 zeros (10^{18}). Brit. word: **trillion.** [C17: < L *quintus* fifth + *-illion,* as in MILLION] —**quinˈtillionth** *adj.*

quintuple (ˈkwɪntjʊpᵊl, kwɪnˈtjuːpᵊl) *vb.* **1.** to multiply by five. ~*adj.* **2.** five times as much or as many; fivefold. **3.** consisting of five parts. ~*n.* **4.** a quantity or number five times as great as another. [C16: < F, < L *quintus,* on the model of QUADRUPLE]

quintuplet (ˈkwɪntjʊplɪt, kwɪnˈtjuːplɪt) *n.* **1.** one of five offspring born at one birth. **2.** a group of five similar things. **3.** *Music.* a group of five notes to be played in a time value of three or four.

quintuplicate *adj.* (kwɪnˈtjuːplɪkɪt). **1.** fivefold or quintuple. ~*vb.* (kwɪnˈtjuːplɪˌkeɪt). **2.** to multiply or be multiplied by five. ~*n.* (kwɪnˈtjuːplɪkɪt). **3.** a group or set of five things.

quip (kwɪp) *n.* **1.** a sarcastic remark. **2.** a witty saying. **3.** *Arch.* another word for **quibble.** ~*vb.* **quipping, quipped. 4.** (*intr.*) to make a quip. [C16: < earlier *quippy,* prob. < L *quippe* indeed, to be sure] —ˈ**quipster** *n.*

quire[1] (ˈkwaɪə) *n.* **1.** a set of 24 or 25 sheets of paper. **2.** four sheets of paper folded to form 16 pages. **3.** a set of all the sheets in a book. [C15 *quayer,* < OF *quaier,* < L *quaternī* four at a time, < *quater* four times]

quire[2] (ˈkwaɪə) *n.* an obsolete spelling of **choir.**

quirk (kwɜːk) *n.* **1.** a peculiarity of character; mannerism or foible. **2.** an unexpected twist or turn: *a quirk of fate.* **3.** a continuous groove in an architectural moulding. **4.** a flourish, as in handwriting. [C16: <?] —ˈ**quirky** *adj.* —ˈ**quirkiness** *n.*

quirt (kwɜːt) *U.S.* ~*n.* **1.** a whip with a leather thong at one end. ~*vb.* (*tr.*) **2.** to strike with a quirt. [C19: < Sp. *cuerda* CORD]

quisling (ˈkwɪzlɪŋ) *n.* a traitor who aids an occupying enemy force; collaborator. [C20: after Major Vidkun *Quisling* (1887–1945), Norwegian collaborator with the Nazis]

quit (kwɪt) *vb.* **quitting, quitted,** *or* (*chiefly U.S.*) **quit. 1.** (*tr.*) to depart from; leave. **2.** to resign; give up (a job). **3.** (*intr.*) (of a tenant) to give up occupancy of premises and leave them. **4.** to desist or cease from (something or doing something). **5.** (*tr.*) to pay off (a debt). **6.** (*tr.*) *Arch.* to conduct or acquit (oneself); comport (oneself). ~*adj.* **7.** (*usually predicative;* foll. by *of*) free (from); released (from). [C13: < OF *quitter,* < L *quiētus* QUIET]

▷ **Usage.** Some users of English have felt that *quit* in the sense of *leave* is informal, but this use is quite standard at all levels of language. Careful users do not use *quit* to mean *cease* (*he never quit moaning*) because this is felt to be an Americanism.

quitch grass (kwɪtʃ) *n.* another name for **couch grass.** Sometimes shortened to **quitch.** [OE *cwice;* ? rel. to *cwicu* living, QUICK (with the implication that the grass cannot be killed)]

quitclaim (ˈkwɪtˌkleɪm) *Law.* ~*n.* **1.** a renunciation of a claim or right. ~*vb.* **2.** (*tr.*) to renounce (a claim). [C14: < Anglo-F *quiteclame,* < *quite* QUIT + *clamer* to declare (< L *clamāre* to shout)]

quite (kwaɪt) *adv.* **1.** completely or absolutely: *you're quite right.* **2.** (*not used with a negative*) somewhat: *she's quite pretty.* **3.** in actuality; truly. **4. quite a** *or* **an.** (*not used with a negative*) of an exceptional, considerable, or noticeable kind: *quite a girl.* **5. quite something.** a remarkable or noteworthy thing or person. ~*sentence substitute.* **6.** Also: **quite so.** an expression used to indicate agreement. [C14: adverbial use of *quite* (adj.) QUIT]

▷ **Usage.** See at **very.**

quitrent (ˈkwɪtˌrɛnt) *n.* (formerly) a rent payable by a freeholder or copyholder to his lord in lieu of services.

quits (kwɪts) *adj.* (*postpositive*) *Inf.* **1.** on an equal footing; even. **2. call it quits.** to agree to end a dispute, contest, etc., agreeing that honours are even.

quittance (ˈkwɪtᵊns) *n.* **1.** release from debt or other obligation. **2.** a receipt or other document certifying this. [C13: < OF, < *quitter* to release from obligation; see QUIT]

quitter (ˈkwɪtə) *n.* a person who gives up easily.

quiver[1] (ˈkwɪvə) *vb.* **1.** (*intr.*) to shake with a tremulous movement; tremble. ~*n.* **2.** the state, process, or noise of shaking or trembling. [C15: < obs. *cwiver* quick, nimble] —ˈ**quivering** *adj.* —ˈ**quivery** *adj.*

quiver[2] (ˈkwɪvə) *n.* a case for arrows. [C13: < OF *cuivre*]

qui vive (ˌkiː ˈviːv) *n.* **on the qui vive.** on the alert; attentive. [C18: < F, lit.: long live who?, sentry's challenge (equivalent to "Whose side are you on?")]

quixotic (kwɪkˈsɒtɪk) *adj.* preoccupied with an unrealistically optimistic or chivalrous approach to life; impractically idealistic. [C18: after DON QUIXOTE] —**quixˈotically** *adv.*

quiz (kwɪz) *n., pl.* **quizzes. 1. a.** an entertainment in which the knowledge of the players is tested by a series of questions. **b.** (*as modifier*): *a quiz programme.* **2.** any set of quick questions designed to test knowledge. **3.** an investigation by close questioning. **4.** *Obs.* a practical joke. **5.** *Obs.* a puzzling individual. **6.** *Obs.* a person who habitually looks quizzically at others. ~*vb.* **quizzing, quizzed.** (*tr.*) **7.** to investigate by close questioning; interrogate. **8.** *U.S. & Canad. inf.* to test the knowledge of (a student or class). **9.** (*tr.*) *Obs.* to look quizzically at, esp. through a small monocle. [C18: <?] —ˈ**quizzer** *n.*

quizzical (ˈkwɪzɪkᵊl) *adj.* questioning and mocking or supercilious. —ˈ**quizzically** *adv.*

quod (kwɒd) *n. Chiefly Brit.* a slang word for **jail.** [C18: <?]

quod erat demonstrandum *Latin.* (ˈkwɒd ˈɛræt ˌdɛmənˈstrændum) (at the conclusion of a proof, esp. of a theorem in Euclidean geometry) which was to be proved. Abbrev.: **QED.**

quodlibet (ˈkwɒdlɪˌbɛt) *n.* **1.** a light piece of music. **2.** a subtle argument, esp. one prepared as an exercise on a theological topic. [C14: < L, < *quod* what + *libet* pleases, that is, whatever you like]

quoin (kwɔɪn, kɔɪn) *n.* **1.** an external corner of a wall. **2.** a stone forming the external corner of a wall. **3.** another name for **keystone** (sense 1). **4.** *Printing.* a wedge or an expanding device used to lock type up in a chase. **5.** a wedge used for any of various other purposes. [C16: var. of *coin* (in former sense of corner)]

quoit (kɔɪt) *n.* a ring of iron, plastic, etc., used in the game of quoits. [C15: <?]

quoits (kɔɪts) *pl. n.* (*usually functioning as sing.*) a game in which quoits are tossed at a stake in the ground in attempts to encircle it.

quokka (ˈkwɒkə) *n.* a small wallaby of Western Australia, now rare. [of Abor. origin]

quondam (ˈkwɒndæm) *adj.* (*prenominal*) of an earlier time; former. [C16: < L]

quorate (ˈkwɔːˌreɪt) *adj. Brit.* consisting of or being a quorum: *the meeting was quorate.*

quorum (ˈkwɔːrəm) *n.* a minimum number of members in an assembly, etc., required to be present before any business can be transacted. [C15: < L, lit.: of whom, occurring in L commissions in the formula *quorum vos...duos* (etc.) *volumus* of whom we wish that you be...two (etc.)]

quota (ˈkwəʊtə) *n.* **1.** the proportional share or part that is due from, due to, or allocated to a person or group. **2.** a prescribed number or quantity, as of items to be imported or students admitted to a college, etc. [C17: < L *quota pars* how big a share?, < *quotus* of what number]

quotable (ˈkwəʊtəbᵊl) *adj.* apt or suitable for quotation. —ˌ**quotaˈbility** *n.*

quotation (kwəʊˈteɪʃən) *n.* **1.** a phrase or passage from a book, etc., remembered and spoken, esp. to support a point. **2.** the act or habit of quoting. **3.** *Commerce.* a statement of the current market price of a security or commodity. **4.** an estimate of costs submitted by a contractor to a prospective client. **5.** *Printing.* a quadrat used to fill up spaces.

quotation mark *n.* either of the punctuation marks used to begin or end a quotation, respectively " and " or ' and '. Also called: **inverted comma.**

quote (kwəʊt) *vb.* **1.** to recite a quotation. **2.** (*tr.*) to put quotation marks round (a phrase, etc.). **3.** *Stock Exchange.* to state (a current market price) of (a security or commodity). ~*n.* **4.** an informal word for **quotation. 5.** (*often pl.*) an informal word for **quotation mark.** ~*interj.* **6.** an expression used to indicate that the words that follow it form a quotation. [C14: < Med. L *quotāre* to assign reference numbers to passages, < L *quot* how many]

quoted company *n.* a company whose shares are quoted on the stock exchange.

quote-unquote *interj.* an expression used before or part before and part after a quotation to identify it as such, and sometimes to dissociate the writer or speaker from it.

quoth (kwəʊθ) *vb. Arch.* (used with all pronouns except *thou* and *you,* and with nouns) said. [OE *cwæth,* third person sing. of *cwethan* to say]

quotha (ˈkwəʊθə) *interj. Arch.* an expression of mild sarcasm, used in picking up a word or phrase used by someone else. [C16: < *quoth a* quoth he]

quotidian (kwəʊˈtɪdɪən) *adj.* **1.** (esp. of fever) recurring daily. **2.** commonplace. ~*n.* **3.** a fever characterized by attacks that recur daily. [C14: < L *quotīdiānus,* var. of *cottīdiānus* daily]

quotient (ˈkwəʊʃənt) *n.* **1. a.** the result of the division of one number or quantity by another. **b.** the integral part of the result of division. **2.** a ratio of two numbers or quantities to be divided. [C15: < L *quotiens* how often]

quo vadis (ˈkwəʊ ˈvɑːdɪs) whither goest thou? [L < the Vulgate version of John 16:5]

quo warranto (ˈkwəʊ wɒˈræntəʊ) *n. Law.* a proceeding initiated to determine or (formerly) a writ demanding by what authority a person claims an office, franchise, or privilege. [< Med. L: by what warrant]

Qur'an (kʊˈrɑːn, -ˈræn) *n.* a variant spelling of **Koran.**

q.v. (denoting a cross-reference) *abbrev. for* quod vide. [NL: which (word, item, etc.) see]

qwerty *or* **QWERTY keyboard** (ˈkwɜːtɪ) *n.* the standard English language typewriter keyboard layout with the characters q, w, e, r, t, and y at the top left of the keyboard.

R

r *or* **R** (ɑː) *n., pl.* **r's, R's,** *or* **Rs. 1.** the 18th letter of the English alphabet. **2.** a speech sound represented by this letter. **3.** See **three Rs, the.**

R *symbol for:* **1.** *Chem.* gas constant. **2.** *Chem.* radical. **3.** *Currency.* **a.** rand. **b.** rupee. **4.** Réaumur (scale). **5.** *Physics, electronics.* resistance. **6.** roentgen *or* röntgen. **7.** *Chess.* rook. **8.** Royal.

r. *abbrev. for:* **1.** rare. **2.** recto. **3.** Also: r rod (unit of length). **4.** ruled. **5.** *Cricket.* run(s).

R. *abbrev. for:* **1.** rabbi. **2.** rector. **3.** Regiment. **4.** Regina. [L: Queen] **5.** Republican. **6.** Rex. [L: King] **7.** River. **8.** Royal.

R. *or* **r.** *abbrev. for:* **1.** radius. **2.** railway. **3.** registered (trademark). **4.** right. **5.** river. **6.** road. **7.** rouble.

Ra *the chemical symbol for* radium.

RA *abbrev. for:* **1.** rear admiral. **2.** *Astron.* right ascension. **3.** (in Britain) Royal Academician *or* Academy. **4.** (in Britain) Royal Artillery.

RAAF *abbrev. for* Royal Australian Air Force.

rabbet (ˈræbɪt) *or* **rebate** *n.* **1.** a recess, groove, or step, usually of rectangular section, cut into a piece of timber to receive a mating piece. ~*vb.* (*tr.*) **2.** to cut a rabbet in (timber). **3.** to join (pieces of timber) using a rabbet. [C15: < OF *rabattre* to beat down]

rabbi (ˈræbaɪ) *n., pl.* **-bis. 1.** the spiritual leader of a Jewish congregation; the chief religious minister of a synagogue. **2.** a scholar learned in Jewish Law, esp. one authorized to teach it. [Heb., < *rabh* master + *-ī* my]

rabbinate (ˈræbɪnɪt) *n.* **1.** the position, function, or tenure of office of a rabbi. **2.** rabbis collectively.

rabbinic (rəˈbɪnɪk) *or* **rabbinical** (rəˈbɪnɪkᵊl) *adj.* of or relating to the rabbis, their teachings, writings, views, language, etc. —**rabˈbinically** *adv.*

Rabbinic (rəˈbɪnɪk) *n.* the form of the Hebrew language used by the rabbis of the Middle Ages.

rabbit (ˈræbɪt) *n., pl.* **-bits** *or* **-bit. 1.** any of various common gregarious burrowing mammals of Europe and North Africa. They are closely related and similar to hares but are smaller and have shorter ears. **2.** the fur of such an animal. **3.** *Brit. inf.* a poor performer at a game or sport. ~*vb.* (*intr.*) **4.** to hunt or shoot rabbits. **5.** (often foll. by *on* or *away*) *Brit. inf.* to talk inconsequentially; chatter. [C14: ? < Walloon *robett,* dim. of Flemish *robbe* rabbit, <?]

rabbit fever *n. Pathol.* another name for **tularaemia.**

rabbit punch *n.* a short sharp blow to the back of the neck that can cause loss of consciousness or even death. Austral. name: **rabbit killer.**

rabble (ˈræbᵊl) *n.* **1.** a disorderly crowd; mob. **2. the rabble.** *Contemptuous.* the common people. [C14 (in the sense: a pack of animals): <?]

rabble-rouser *n.* a person who manipulates the passions of the mob; demagogue. —ˈ**rabble-ˌrousing** *adj., n.*

Rabelaisian (ˌræbəˈleɪzɪən, -ʒən) *adj.* **1.** of, relating to, or resembling the work of François Rabelais (?1494–1553), French writer, esp. by broad, often bawdy humour and sharp satire. ~*n.* **2.** a student or admirer of Rabelais. —ˌ**Rabeˈlaisianism** *n.*

rabid (ˈræbɪd, ˈreɪ-) *adj.* **1.** relating to or having rabies. **2.** zealous; fanatical; violent; raging. [C17: < L *rabidus* frenzied, < *rabere* to be mad] —**rabidity** (rəˈbɪdɪtɪ) *or* ˈ**rabidness** *n.* —ˈ**rabidly** *adv.*

rabies (ˈreɪbiːz) *n. Pathol.* an acute infectious viral disease of the nervous system transmitted by the saliva of infected animals, esp. dogs. [C17: < L: madness, < *rabere* to rave] —**rabic** (ˈræbɪk) *or* **rabietic** (ˌreɪbɪˈɛtɪk) *adj.*

RAC *abbrev. for:* **1.** Royal Armoured Corps. **2.** Royal Automobile Club.

raccoon *or* **racoon** (rəˈkuːn) *n., pl.* **-coons** *or* **-coon. 1.** an omnivorous mammal, esp. the **North American raccoon,** inhabiting forests of North and Central America. Raccoons have a pointed muzzle, long tail, and greyish-black fur with black bands around the tail and across the face. **2.** the fur of the raccoon. [C17: < Algonquian *ărăhkun,* < *ărăhkuněm* he scratches with his hands]

race[1] (reɪs) *n.* **1.** a contest of speed, as in running, etc. **2.** any competition or rivalry. **3.** rapid or constant onward movement: *the race of time.* **4.** a rapid current of water, esp. one through a narrow channel that has a tidal range greater at one end than the other. **5.** a channel of a stream, esp. one for conducting water to or from a water wheel for energy: *a mill race.* **6. a.** a channel or groove that contains ball bearings or roller bearings. **b.** the inner or outer cylindrical ring in a ball bearing or roller bearing. **7.** *Austral. & N.Z.* a narrow passage or enclosure in a sheep yard through which sheep pass individually, as to a sheep dip. **8.** *Austral.* a wire tunnel through which footballers pass from the changing room onto a football field. **9.** *Arch.* the span or course of life. ~*vb.* **10.** to engage in a contest of speed with (another). **11.** to engage in a race, esp. as a profession: *to race pigeons.* **12.** to move or go as fast as possible. **13.** to run (an engine, propeller, etc.) or (of an engine, propeller, etc.) to run at high speed, esp. after reduction of the load or resistance. ~See also **races.** [C13: < ON *rās* running]

race[2] (reɪs) *n.* **1.** a group of people of common ancestry, distinguished from others by physical characteristics, such as hair type, colour of skin, stature, etc. **2. the human race.** human beings collectively. **3.** a group of animals or plants having common characteristics that distinguish them from other members of the same species, usually forming a geographically isolated group; subspecies. **4.** a group of people sharing the same interests, characteristics, etc.: *the race of authors.* [C16: < F, < It. *razza,* <?]

racecard (ˈreɪsˌkɑːd) *n.* a card at a race meeting with the races and runners, etc., printed on it.

racecourse (ˈreɪsˌkɔːs) *n.* a long broad track, over which horses are raced. Also called (esp. U.S. and Canad.): **racetrack.**

racehorse (ˈreɪsˌhɔːs) *n.* a horse specially bred for racing.

raceme (rəˈsiːm) *n.* an inflorescence in which the flowers are borne along the main stem. [C18: < L *racēmus* bunch of grapes] —ˈ**raceˌmose** *adj.*

race meeting *n.* a prearranged fixture for racing horses (or greyhounds) over a set course.

racemic (rəˈsiːmɪk, -ˈsɛm-) *adj. Chem.* of, concerned with, or being a mixture of dextrorotatory and laevorotatory isomers in such proportions that the mixture has no optical activity. [C19: < RACEME + -IC] —**racemism** (ˈræsɪˌmɪzəm) *n.*

racer (ˈreɪsə) *n.* **1.** a person, animal, or machine that races. **2.** a turntable used to traverse a heavy gun. **3.** any of several slender nonvenomous North American snakes, such as the **striped racer.**

race relations *n.* **1.** (*functioning as pl.*) the relations between members of two or more human races, esp. within a single community. **2.** (*functioning as sing.*) the branch of sociology concerned with such relations.

race riot *n.* a riot among members of different races in the same community.

races (ˈreɪsɪz) *pl. n.* **the races.** a series of contests of speed between horses (or greyhounds) over a set course.

racetrack (ˈreɪsˌtræk) *n.* **1.** a circuit or course,

esp. an oval one, used for motor racing, etc. **2.** the usual U.S. and Canad. word for **racecourse.**

raceway (ˈreɪsˌweɪ) *n.* **1.** another word for **race**[1] (senses 5, 6). **2.** *Chiefly U.S.* a racetrack.

rachis *or* **rhachis** (ˈreɪkɪs) *n., pl.* **rachises, rhachises** *or* **rachides, rhachides** (ˈrækɪˌdiːz, ˈreɪ-). **1.** *Bot.* the main axis or stem of an inflorescence or compound leaf. **2.** *Ornithol.* the shaft of a feather, esp. the part that carries the barbs. **3.** another name for **spinal column.** [C17: via NL < Gk *rhakhis* ridge] **—rachial, rhachial** (ˈreɪkɪəl) *or* **rachidial, rhachidial** (rəˈkɪdɪəl) *adj.*

rachitis (rəˈkaɪtɪs) *n. Pathol.* another name for **rickets. —rachitic** (rəˈkɪtɪk) *adj.*

Rachmanism (ˈrækməˌnɪzəm) *n.* extortion or exploitation by a landlord of tenants of slum property. [C20: after Perec *Rachman* (1920–62), British property-owner]

racial (ˈreɪʃəl) *adj.* **1.** denoting or relating to the division of the human species into races on grounds of physical characteristics. **2.** characteristic of any such group. **—ˈracially** *adv.*

racialism (ˈreɪʃəˌlɪzəm) *or* **racism** *n.* **1.** the belief that races have distinctive cultural characteristics determined by hereditary factors and that this endows some races with an intrinsic superiority. **2.** abusive or aggressive behaviour towards members of another race on the basis of such a belief. **—ˈracialist** *or* **ˈracist** *n., adj.*

rack[1] (ræk) *n.* **1.** a framework for holding, carrying, or displaying a specific load or object. **2.** a toothed bar designed to engage a pinion to form a mechanism that will adjust the position of something. **3.** (preceded by *the*) an instrument of torture that stretched the body of the victim. **4.** a cause or state of mental or bodily stress, suffering, etc. (esp. in **on the rack**). **5.** *U.S. & Canad.* (in pool, snooker, etc.) **a.** the triangular frame used to arrange the balls for the opening shot. **b.** the balls so grouped. Brit. equivalent: **frame.** ~*vb.* (*tr.*) **6.** to torture on the rack. **7.** to cause great suffering to: *guilt racked his conscience.* **8.** to strain or shake (something) violently: *the storm racked the town.* **9.** to place or arrange in or on a rack. **10.** to move (parts of machinery or a mechanism) using a toothed rack. **11.** to raise (rents) exorbitantly. **12. rack one's brains.** to strain in mental effort. [C14 *rekke,* prob. < MDu. *rec* framework] **—ˈracker** *n.*

rack[2] (ræk) *n.* destruction; wreck (obs. except in **go to rack and ruin**). [C16: var. of WRACK[1]]

rack[3] (ræk) *n.* another word for **single-foot.** [C16: ? based on ROCK[2]]

rack[4] (ræk) *n.* **1.** a group of broken clouds moving in the wind. ~*vb.* **2.** (*intr.*) (of clouds) to be blown along by the wind. [OE *wrǣc* what is driven]

rack[5] (ræk) *vb.* (*tr.*) to clear (wine, beer, etc.) as by siphoning it off from the dregs. [C15: < OProvençal *arraca,* < *raca* dregs of grapes after pressing]

rack-and-pinion *n.* **1.** a device for converting rotary into linear motion and vice versa, in which a gearwheel (the pinion) engages with a flat toothed bar (the rack). ~*adj.* **2.** (of a type of steering gear in motor vehicles) having a track rod with a rack along part of its length that engages with a pinion attached to the steering column.

racket[1] (ˈrækɪt) *n.* **1.** a noisy disturbance or loud commotion; clamour; din. **2.** an illegal enterprise carried on for profit, such as extortion, fraud, etc. **3.** *Sl.* a business or occupation: *what's your racket?* **4.** *Music.* a medieval woodwind instrument of deep bass pitch. ~*vb.* **5.** (*intr.;* often foll. by *about*) *Now rare.* to go about gaily or noisily, in search of pleasure, etc. [C16: prob. imit.] **—ˈrackety** *adj.*

racket[2] *or* **racquet** (ˈrækɪt) *n.* **1.** a bat consisting of an open network of strings stretched in an oval frame with a handle, used to strike a tennis ball, etc. **2.** a snowshoe shaped like a tennis racket. ~*vb.* **3.** (*tr.*) to strike (a ball, etc.) with a racket. ~See also **rackets.** [C16: < F *raquette,* < Ar. *rāhat* palm of the hand]

racketeer (ˌrækɪˈtɪə) *n.* **1.** a person engaged in illegal enterprises for profit. ~*vb.* **2.** (*intr.*) to operate an illegal enterprise. **—ˌracketˈeering** *n.*

racket press *n.* a device consisting of a frame closed by a spring mechanism, for keeping taut the strings of a tennis racket, squash racket, etc.

rackets (ˈrækɪts) *n.* (*functioning as sing.*) **a.** a game similar to squash played in a four-walled court by two or four players using rackets and a small hard ball. **b.** (*as modifier*): *a rackets court.*

rack railway *n.* a steep mountain railway having a middle rail fitted with a rack that engages a pinion on the locomotive to provide traction. Also called: **cog railway.**

rack-rent *n.* **1.** a high rent that annually equals the value of the property upon which it is charged. **2.** any extortionate rent. ~*vb.* **3.** to charge an extortionate rent for. **—ˈrack-ˌrenter** *n.*

racon (ˈreɪkɒn) *n.* another name for **radar beacon.** [C20: < RA(DAR) + (BEA)CON]

raconteur (ˌrækɒnˈtɜː) *n.* a person skilled in telling stories. [C19: F, < *raconter* to tell]

racoon (rəˈkuːn) *n., pl.* **-coons** *or* **-coon.** a variant spelling of **raccoon.**

racquet (ˈrækɪt) *n.* a variant spelling of **racket**[2].

racy (ˈreɪsɪ) *adj.* **racier, raciest. 1.** (of a person's manner, literary style, etc.) having a distinctively lively and spirited quality. **2.** having a characteristic or distinctive flavour: *a racy wine.* **3.** suggestive; slightly indecent; risqué. **—ˈracily** *adv.* **—ˈraciness** *n.*

rad[1] (ræd) *n.* a unit of absorbed ionizing radiation dose equivalent to an energy absorption per unit mass of 0.01 joule per kilogram of irradiated material. [C20: < RADIATION]

rad[2] *symbol for* radian.

rad. *abbrev. for:* **1.** radical. **2.** radius.

RADA (ˈrɑːdə) *n.* (in Britain) *acronym for* Royal Academy of Dramatic Art.

radar (ˈreɪdɑː) *n.* **1.** a method for detecting the position and velocity of a distant object. A narrow beam of extremely high-frequency radio pulses is transmitted and reflected by the object back to the transmitter. The direction of the reflected beam and the time between transmission and reception of a pulse determine the position of the object. **2.** the equipment used in such detection. [C20: *ra*(*dio*) *d*(*etecting*) *a*(*nd*) *r*(*anging*)]

radar beacon *n.* a device for transmitting a coded radar signal in response to a signal from an aircraft or ship. The coded signal is then used by the navigator to determine his position. Also called: **racon.**

radarscope (ˈreɪdɑːˌskəʊp) *n.* a cathode-ray oscilloscope on which radar signals can be viewed.

radar trap *n.* a device using radar to detect motorists who exceed the speed limit.

raddle (ˈrædᵊl) *vb.* **1.** (*tr.*) *Chiefly Brit.* to paint (the face) with rouge. ~*n., vb.* **2.** another word for **ruddle.** [C16: var. of RUDDLE]

raddled (ˈrædᵊld) *adj.* (esp. of a person) unkempt or run-down in appearance.

radial (ˈreɪdɪəl) *adj.* **1.** (of lines, etc.) emanating from a common central point; arranged like the radii of a circle. **2.** of, like, or relating to a radius or ray. **3.** short for **radial-ply. 4.** *Anat.* of or relating to the radius or forearm. **5.** *Astron.* (of velocity) in a direction along the line of sight of a celestial object and measured by means of the red shift (or blue shift) of the spectral lines of the object. ~*n.* **6.** a radial part or section. [C16: < Med. L *radiālis,* < RADIUS] **—ˈradially** *adv.*

radial engine *n.* an internal-combustion engine having a number of cylinders arranged about a central crankcase.

radial-ply *adj.* (of a motor tyre) having the fabric cords in the outer casing running radially to enable the sidewalls to be flexible.

radial symmetry *n.* a type of structure of an organism in which a vertical cut through the axis in any of two or more planes produces two halves that are mirror images of each other. Cf. **bilateral symmetry.**

radian (ˈreɪdɪən) *n.* an SI unit of plane angle; the

angle between two radii of a circle that cut off on the circumference an arc equal in length to the radius. 1 radian is equivalent to 57.296 degrees. Symbol: rad. [C19: < RADIUS]

radiance (ˈreɪdɪəns) *or* **radiancy** *n., pl.* **-ances** *or* **-ancies. 1.** the quality or state of being radiant. **2.** a measure of the amount of electromagnetic radiation leaving or arriving at a point on a surface.

radiant (ˈreɪdɪənt) *adj.* **1.** sending out rays of light; bright; shining. **2.** characterized by health, happiness, etc.: *a radiant smile.* **3.** emitted or propagated by or as radiation; radiated: *radiant heat.* **4.** sending out heat by radiation: *a radiant heater.* **5.** *Physics.* (of a physical quantity in photometry) evaluated by absolute energy measurements: *radiant flux.* ~*n.* **6.** a point or object that emits radiation, esp. the part of a heater that gives out heat. **7.** *Astron.* the point in the sky from which a meteor shower appears to emanate. [C15: < L *radiāre* to shine, < *radius* ray of light] —ˈ**radiancy** *n.* —ˈ**radiantly** *adv.*

radiant energy *n.* energy that is emitted or propagated in the form of particles or electromagnetic radiation.

radiant heat *n.* heat transferred in the form of electromagnetic radiation rather than by conduction or convection; infrared radiation.

radiata pine (ˌreɪdɪˈɑːtə) *n.* a pine tree grown in Australia and New Zealand to produce building timber. Often shortened to **radiata.** [< NL]

radiate *vb.* (ˈreɪdɪˌeɪt). **1.** Also: **eradiate.** to emit (heat, light, or other forms of radiation) or (of heat, light, etc.) to be emitted as radiation. **2.** (*intr.*) (of lines, beams, etc.) to spread out from a centre or be arranged in a radial pattern. **3.** (*tr.*) (of a person) to show (happiness, etc.) to a great degree. ~*adj.* (ˈreɪdɪɪt, -ˌeɪt). **4.** having rays; radiating. **5.** (of a capitulum) consisting of ray flowers. **6.** (of animals) showing radial symmetry. [C17: < L *radiāre* to emit rays] —ˈ**radiative** *adj.*

radiation (ˌreɪdɪˈeɪʃən) *n.* **1.** *Physics.* **a.** the emission or transfer of radiant energy as particles, electromagnetic waves, sound, etc. **b.** the particles, etc., emitted, esp. the particles and gamma rays emitted in nuclear decay. **2.** Also called: **radiation therapy.** *Med.* treatment using a radioactive substance. **3.** the act, state, or process of radiating or being radiated. —ˌ**radiˈational** *adj.*

radiation sickness *n. Pathol.* illness caused by overexposure of the body to ionizing radiations from radioactive material or x-rays.

radiator (ˈreɪdɪˌeɪtə) *n.* **1.** a device for heating a room, building, etc., consisting of a series of pipes through which hot water or steam passes. **2.** a device for cooling an internal-combustion engine, consisting of thin-walled tubes through which water passes. **3.** *Electronics.* the part of an aerial or transmission line that radiates electromagnetic waves.

radical (ˈrædɪkᵊl) *adj.* **1.** of, relating to, or characteristic of the basic or inherent constitution of a person or thing; fundamental: *a radical fault.* **2.** concerned with or tending to concentrate on fundamental aspects of a matter; searching or thoroughgoing: *radical thought.* **3.** favouring or tending to produce extreme or fundamental changes in political, economic, or social conditions, institutions, etc.: *a radical party.* **4.** of or arising from the root or the base of the stem of a plant: *radical leaves.* **5.** *Maths.* of, relating to, or containing roots of numbers or quantities. **6.** *Linguistics.* of or relating to the root of a word. ~*n.* **7.** a person who favours extreme or fundamental change in existing institutions or in political, social, or economic conditions. **8.** *Maths.* a root of a number or quantity, such as $\sqrt[3]{5}$, $\sqrt{x}$. **9.** *Chem.* **a.** short for **free radical. b.** another name for **group** (sense 9). **10.** *Linguistics.* another word for **root**[1] (sense 8). [C14: < LL *rādīcālis* having roots, < L *rādix* a root] —ˈ**radicalness** *n.*

radicalism (ˈrædɪkəˌlɪzəm) *n.* **1.** the principles, desires, or practices of political radicals. **2.** a radical movement, esp. in politics. —ˌ**radicalˈistic** *adj.* —ˌ**radicalˈistically** *adv.*

radically (ˈrædɪkəlɪ) *adv.* thoroughly; completely; fundamentally: *to alter radically.*

radical sign *n.* the symbol $\sqrt{}$ placed before a number or quantity to indicate the extraction of a root, esp. a square root. The value of a higher root is indicated by a raised digit in front of the symbol, as in $\sqrt[3]{}$.

radicand (ˈrædɪˌkænd, ˌrædɪˈkænd) *n.* a number or quantity from which a root is to be extracted, usually preceded by a radical sign: 3 *is the radicand of* $\sqrt{3}$. [C20: < L *rādīcandum*, lit.: that which is to be rooted, < *rādīcāre*, < *rādīx* root]

radicchio (ræˈdiːkɪəʊ) *n., pl.* **-chios.** an Italian variety of chicory, having purple leaves streaked with white that are eaten raw in salads.

radices (ˈreɪdɪˌsiːz) *n.* a plural of **radix.**

radicle (ˈrædɪkᵊl) *n.* **1.** *Bot.* **a.** the part of the embryo of seed-bearing plants that develops into the main root. **b.** a very small root or rootlike part. **2.** *Anat.* any bodily structure resembling a rootlet, esp. one of the smallest branches of a vein or nerve. **3.** *Chem.* a variant spelling of **radical** (sense 9). [C18: < L *rādīcula*, < *rādīx* root]

radii (ˈreɪdɪˌaɪ) *n.* a plural of **radius.**

radio (ˈreɪdɪəʊ) *n., pl.* **-dios. 1.** the use of electromagnetic waves, lying in the radio-frequency range, for broadcasting, two-way communications, etc. **2.** an electronic device designed to receive, demodulate, and amplify radio signals from sound broadcasting stations, etc. **3.** the broadcasting, content, etc., of radio programmes: *he thinks radio is poor these days.* **4.** the occupation or profession concerned with any aspect of the broadcasting of radio programmes. **5.** short for **radiotelegraph, radiotelegraphy,** or **radiotelephone. 6.** (*modifier*) **a.** of, relating to, or sent by radio signals: *a radio station.* **b.** of, concerned with, using, or operated by radio frequencies: *radio spectrum.* **c.** relating to or produced for radio: *radio drama.* ~*vb.* **-dioing, -dioed. 7.** to transmit (a message, etc.) to (a person, etc.) by means of radio waves. ~Also called (esp. Brit.): **wireless.** [C20: short for *radiotelegraphy*]

radio- *combining form.* **1.** denoting radio, broadcasting, or radio frequency: *radiogram.* **2.** indicating radioactivity or radiation: *radiocarbon; radiochemistry.* [< F, < L *radius* ray]

radioactive (ˌreɪdɪəʊˈæktɪv) *adj.* exhibiting, using, or concerned with radioactivity. —ˌ**radioˈactively** *adv.*

radioactive decay *n.* disintegration of a nucleus that occurs spontaneously or as a result of electron capture. Also called: **disintegration.**

radioactive series *n. Physics.* a series of nuclides each of which undergoes radioactive decay into the next member of the series, ending with a stable element, usually lead.

radioactivity (ˌreɪdɪəʊækˈtɪvɪtɪ) *n.* the spontaneous emission of radiation from atomic nuclei. The radiation can consist of alpha, beta, or gamma radiation.

radio astronomy *n.* a branch of astronomy in which the radio telescope is used to detect and analyse radio signals received on earth from radio sources in space.

radio beacon *n.* a fixed radio transmitting station that broadcasts a characteristic signal by means of which a vessel or aircraft can determine its bearing or position.

radiobiology (ˌreɪdɪəʊbaɪˈɒlədʒɪ) *n.* the branch of biology concerned with the effects of radiation on living organisms and the study of biological processes using radioactive substances as tracers. —**radiobiological** (ˌreɪdɪəʊˌbaɪəˈlɒdʒɪkᵊl) *adj.* —ˌ**radioˌbioˈlogically** *adv.* —ˌ**radiobiˈologist** *n.*

radiocarbon (ˌreɪdɪəʊˈkɑːbᵊn) *n.* a radioactive isotope of carbon, esp. carbon-14. See **carbon** (sense 1).

radiocarbon dating *n.* See **carbon dating.**

radiochemistry (ˌreɪdɪəʊˈkɛmɪstrɪ) *n.* the chemistry of radioactive elements and their compounds. —ˌ**radio'chemical** *adj.* —ˌ**radio'chemist** *n.*

radio compass *n.* any navigational device that gives a bearing by determining the direction of incoming radio waves transmitted from a particular radio station or beacon. See also **goniometer** (sense 2).

radio control *n.* remote control by means of radio signals from a transmitter. —'**radio-con'trolled** *adj.*

radioelement (ˌreɪdɪəʊ'ɛlɪmənt) *n.* an element that is naturally radioactive.

radio frequency *n.* **1. a.** any frequency that lies in the range 10 kilohertz to 300 000 megahertz and can be used for broadcasting. Abbrevs.: **rf, RF. b.** (*as modifier*): *a radio-frequency amplifier.* **2.** the frequency transmitted by a particular radio station.

radiogram ('reɪdɪəʊˌgræm) *n.* **1.** *Brit.* a unit comprising a radio and record player. **2.** a message transmitted by radiotelegraphy. **3.** another name for **radiograph.**

radiograph ('reɪdɪəʊˌgrɑːf) *n.* an image produced on a specially sensitized photographic film or plate by radiation, usually by x-rays or gamma rays.

radiography (ˌreɪdɪ'ɒgrəfɪ) *n.* the production of radiographs of opaque objects for use in medicine, surgery, industry, etc. —ˌ**radi'ographer** *n.* —**radiographic** (ˌreɪdɪəʊ'græfɪk) *adj.* —ˌ**radio'graphically** *adv.*

radio-immuno-assay ('reɪdɪəʊˌɪmjʊnəʊ'æseɪ) *n.* a sensitive immunological assay, making use of radioactive labelling, of such things as hormone levels in the blood.

radioisotope (ˌreɪdɪəʊ'aɪsətəʊp) *n.* a radioactive isotope. —**radioisotopic** (ˌreɪdɪəʊˌaɪsə'tɒpɪk) *adj.*

radiolarian (ˌreɪdɪəʊ'lɛərɪən) *n.* any of various marine protozoans typically having a siliceous shell and stiff radiating pseudopodia. [C19: < NL *Radiolaria,* < LL *radiolus* little sunbeam, < L *radius* ray]

radiology (ˌreɪdɪ'ɒlədʒɪ) *n.* the use of x-rays and radioactive substances in the diagnosis and treatment of disease. —ˌ**radi'ologist** *n.*

radiometer (ˌreɪdɪ'ɒmɪtə) *n.* any instrument for the detection or measurement of radiant energy. —**radiometric** (ˌreɪdɪəʊ'mɛtrɪk) *adj.* —ˌ**radi'ometry** *n.*

radiopaging ('reɪdɪəʊˌpeɪdʒɪŋ) *n.* a system whereby a person carrying a small radio receiver (**pager**) is alerted when it emits a sound or other signal in response to a call from a distant location.

radiopaque (ˌreɪdɪəʊ'peɪk) *or* **radio-opaque** *adj.* not permitting x-rays or other radiation to pass through. —**radiopacity** (ˌreɪdɪəʊ'pæsɪtɪ) *or* ˌ**radio-o'pacity** *n.*

radioscopy (ˌreɪdɪ'ɒskəpɪ) *n.* another word for **fluoroscopy.** —**radioscopic** (ˌreɪdɪəʊ'skɒpɪk) *adj.* —ˌ**radio'scopically** *adv.*

radiosonde ('reɪdɪəʊˌsɒnd) *n.* an airborne instrument to send meteorological information back to earth by radio. [C20: RADIO- + F *sonde* sounding line]

radio source *n.* a celestial object, such as a supernova remnant or quasar, that is a source of radio waves.

radio spectrum *n.* the range of electromagnetic frequencies used in radio transmission, between 10 kilohertz and 300 000 megahertz.

radio star *n.* a former name for **radio source.**

radiotelegraphy (ˌreɪdɪəʊtɪ'lɛgrəfɪ) *n.* a type of telegraphy in which messages (usually in Morse code) are transmitted by radio waves. —ˌ**radio'teleˌgraph** *vb., n.* —**radiotelegraphic** (ˌreɪdɪəʊˌtɛlɪ'græfɪk) *adj.*

radiotelephone (ˌreɪdɪəʊ'tɛlɪˌfəʊn) *n.* **1.** a device for communications by means of radio waves rather than by transmitting along wires or cables. ~*vb.* **2.** to telephone (a person) by radiotelephone. —**radiotelephonic** (ˌreɪdɪəʊˌtɛlɪ'fɒnɪk) *adj.* —**radiotelephony** (ˌreɪdɪəʊtɪ'lɛfənɪ) *n.*

radio telescope *n.* an instrument used in radio astronomy to pick up and analyse radio waves from space and also to transmit radio waves.

radioteletype (ˌreɪdɪəʊ'tɛlɪˌtaɪp) *n.* **1.** a teleprinter that transmits or receives information by means of radio waves. **2.** a network of such devices widely used for communicating news, messages, etc. Abbrevs.: **RTT, RTTY.**

radiotherapy (ˌreɪdɪəʊ'θɛrəpɪ) *n.* the treatment of disease by means of alpha or beta particles emitted from an implanted or ingested radioisotope, or by means of a beam of high-energy radiation. —**radiotherapeutic** (ˌreɪdɪəʊˌθɛrə'pjuːtɪk) *adj.* —ˌ**radio'therapist** *n.*

radio wave *n.* an electromagnetic wave of radio frequency.

radish ('rædɪʃ) *n.* **1.** any of a genus of plants of Europe and Asia, with petals arranged like a cross, cultivated for their edible roots. **2.** the root of this plant, which has a pungent taste and is eaten raw in salads. [OE *rǣdic,* < L *rādīx* root]

radium ('reɪdɪəm) *n.* **a.** a highly radioactive luminescent white element of the alkaline earth group of metals. It occurs in pitchblende and other uranium ores. Symbol: Ra; atomic no.: 88; half-life of most stable isotope, ^{226}Ra: 1620 years. **b.** (*as modifier*): *radium needle.* [C20: < L *radius* ray]

radium therapy *n.* treatment of disease, esp. cancer, by exposing affected tissues to radiation from radium.

radius ('reɪdɪəs) *n., pl.* **-dii** *or* **-diuses. 1.** a straight line joining the centre of a circle or sphere to any point on the circumference or surface. **2.** the length of this line, usually denoted by the symbol *r.* **3.** *Anat.* the outer, slightly shorter of the two bones of the human forearm, extending from the elbow to the wrist. **4.** a corresponding bone in other vertebrates. **5.** any of the veins of an insect's wing. **6.** a group of ray flowers, occurring in such plants as the daisy. **7. a.** any radial or radiating part, such as a spoke. **b.** (*as modifier*): *a radius arm.* **8.** a circular area of a size indicated by the length of its radius: *the police stopped every lorry within a radius of four miles.* **9.** the operational limit of a ship, aircraft, etc. [C16: < L: rod, ray, spoke]

radix ('reɪdɪks) *n., pl.* **-dices** *or* **-dixes. 1.** *Maths.* any number that is the base of a number system or of a system of logarithms: *10 is the radix of the decimal system.* **2.** *Biol.* the root or point of origin of a part or organ. **3.** *Linguistics.* a less common word for **root**[1] (sense 8). [C16: < L *rādīx* root]

radix point *n.* a point, such as the decimal point in the decimal system, separating the integral part of a number from the fractional part.

radome ('reɪdəʊm) *n.* a protective housing for a radar antenna made from a material that is transparent to radio waves. [C20: RA(DAR) + DOME]

radon ('reɪdɒn) *n.* a colourless radioactive element of the rare gas group, the most stable isotope of which, radon-222, is a decay product of radium. Symbol: Rn; atomic no.: 86; half-life of ^{222}Rn: 3.82 days. [C20: < RADIUM + -ON]

radula ('rædjʊlə) *n., pl.* **-lae** (-ˌliː). a horny tooth-bearing strip on the tongue of molluscs that is used for rasping food. [C19: < LL: a scraping iron, < L *rādere* to scrape] —'**radular** *adj.*

RAF (*Not standard* ræf) *abbrev. for* Royal Air Force.

Rafferty ('ræfətɪ) *or* **Rafferty's rules** *pl. n.* *Austral. & N.Z. sl.* no rules at all. [C20: <?]

raffia *or* **raphia** ('ræfɪə) *n.* **1.** a palm tree, native to Madagascar, that has large plumelike leaves, the stalks of which yield a useful fibre. **2.** the fibre obtained from this plant, used for weaving, etc. **3.** any of several related palms or the fibre obtained from them. [C19: < Malagasy]

raffish ('ræfɪʃ) *adj.* **1.** careless or unconventional in dress, manners, etc.; rakish. **2.** tawdry; flashy; vulgar. [C19: < *raff* rubbish, rabble] —'**raffishly** *adv.* —'**raffishness** *n.*

raffle ('ræf'l) *n.* **1. a.** a lottery in which the prizes are goods rather than money. **b.** (*as modifier*): *a* *raffle ticket.* ~*vb.* **2.** (*tr.;* often foll. by *off*) to dispose of (goods) in a raffle. [C14 (a dice game): < OF, <?] —ˈ**raffler** *n.*

rafflesia (ræˈfliːzɪə) *n.* any of various tropical Asian parasitic leafless plants, the flowers of which grow up to 45 cm (18 inches) across, smell of putrid meat, and are pollinated by carrion flies. [C19: NL, after Sir Stamford *Raffles,* (1781–1826), E colonial administrator, who discovered it]

raft (rɑːft) *n.* **1.** a buoyant platform of logs, planks, etc., used as a vessel or moored platform. **2.** a thick slab of reinforced concrete laid over soft ground to provide a foundation for a building. ~*vb.* **3.** to convey on or travel by raft, or make a raft from. [C15: < ON *raptr* RAFTER]

rafter (ˈrɑːftə) *n.* any one of a set of parallel sloping beams that form the framework of a roof. [OE *ræfter*]

RAFVR *abbrev. for* Royal Air Force Volunteer Reserve.

rag[1] (ræg) *n.* **1. a.** a small piece of cloth, such as one torn from a discarded garment, or such pieces of cloth collectively. **b.** (*as modifier*)*: a rag doll.* **2.** a fragmentary piece of any material; scrap; shred. **3.** *Inf.* a newspaper, esp. one considered as worthless, sensational, etc. **4.** *Inf.* an item of clothing. **5.** *Inf.* a handkerchief. **6.** *Brit. sl., esp. naval.* a flag or ensign. [C14: prob. back formation < RAGGED < OE *raggig*]

rag[2] (ræg) *vb.* **ragging, ragged.** (*tr.*) **1.** to draw attention facetiously and persistently to the shortcomings of (a person). **2.** *Brit.* to play rough practical jokes on. ~*n.* **3.** *Brit.* a boisterous practical joke. **4.** (in British universities, etc.) **a.** a period in which various events are organized to raise money for charity. **b.** (*as modifier*)*: rag day.* [C18: <?]

rag[3] (ræg) *Jazz.* ~*n.* **1.** a piece of ragtime music. ~*vb.* **ragging, ragged. 2.** (*tr.*) to compose or perform in ragtime. [C20: < RAGTIME]

raga (ˈrɑːgə) *n.* (in Indian music) **1.** any of several conventional patterns of melody and rhythm that form the basis for freely interpreted compositions. **2.** a composition based on one of these patterns. [C18: < Sansk. *rāga* tone, colour]

ragamuffin (ˈrægəˌmʌfɪn) *n.* a ragged unkempt person, esp. a child. [C14 *Ragamoffyn,* a demon in the poem *Piers Plowman* (1393); prob. based on RAG[1]]

rag-and-bone man *n. Brit.* a man who buys and sells discarded clothing, etc. U.S. equivalent: **junkman.**

ragbag (ˈrægˌbæg) *n.* **1.** a bag for storing odd rags. **2.** a confused assortment; jumble.

ragbolt (ˈrægˌbəʊlt) *n.* a bolt that has angled projections on it to prevent it working loose.

rage (reɪdʒ) *n.* **1.** intense anger; fury. **2.** violent movement or action, esp. of the sea, wind, etc. **3.** great intensity of hunger or other feelings. **4.** a fashion or craze (esp. in **all the rage**). **5.** *Austral. & N.Z. inf.* a dance or party. ~*vb.* (*intr.*) **6.** to feel or exhibit intense anger. **7.** (esp. of storms, fires, etc.) to move or surge with great violence. **8.** (esp. of a disease) to spread rapidly and uncontrollably. [C13: via OF < L *rabiēs* madness]

ragged (ˈrægɪd) *adj.* **1.** (of clothes) worn to rags; tattered. **2.** (of a person) dressed in tattered clothes. **3.** having a neglected or unkempt appearance: *ragged weeds.* **4.** having a rough or uneven surface or edge; jagged. **5.** uneven or irregular: *a ragged beat; a ragged shout.* [C13: prob. < *ragge* RAG[1]] —ˈ**raggedly** *adv.* —ˈ**raggedness** *n.*

ragged robin *n.* a plant related to the carnation family and native to Europe and Asia, that has pink or white flowers with ragged petals. See also **catchfly.**

raggedy (ˈrægɪdɪ) *adj. Inf., chiefly U.S. & Canad.* somewhat ragged; tattered: *a raggedy doll.*

ragi, raggee, *or* **raggy** (ˈrægɪ) *n.* a cereal grass, cultivated in Africa and Asia for its edible grain. [C18: < Hindi]

raglan (ˈræglən) *n.* **1.** a coat, jumper, etc., with sleeves that continue to the collar instead of having armhole seams. ~*adj.* **2.** cut in this design: *a raglan sleeve.* [C19: after Lord *Raglan* (1788–1855), Brit. field marshal]

ragout (ræˈguː) *n.* **1.** a richly seasoned stew of meat and vegetables. ~*vb.* **-gouting** (-ˈguːɪŋ), **-gouted** (-ˈguːd). **2.** (*tr.*) to make into a ragout. [C17: < F, < *ragoûter* to stimulate the appetite again, < *ra-* RE- + *goûter* < L *gustāre* to taste]

ragtag (ˈrægˌtæg) *n. Derog.* the common people; rabble (esp. in **ragtag and bobtail**). [C19]

ragtime (ˈrægˌtaɪm) *n.* a style of jazz piano music, developed by Scott Joplin around 1900, having a two-four rhythm base and a syncopated melody. [C20: prob. < RAGGED + TIME]

rag trade *n. Inf.* the clothing business.

ragweed (ˈrægˌwiːd) *n.* a North American plant of the composite family such as the **common ragweed.** Its green tassel-like flowers produce large amounts of pollen, which causes hay fever. Also called: **ambrosia.**

ragworm (ˈrægˌwɜːm) *n.* any polychaete worm living chiefly in burrows in sand and having a flattened body with a row of fleshy lateral appendages along each side. U.S. name: **clamworm.**

ragwort (ˈrægˌwɜːt) *n.* any of several European plants of the composite family that have yellow daisy-like flowers. See also **groundsel.**

rah (rɑː) *interj. Inf., chiefly U.S.* short for **hurrah.**

raid (reɪd) *n.* **1.** a sudden surprise attack. **2.** an attempt by speculators to force down commodity prices by rapid selling. ~*vb.* **3.** to make a raid against (a person, thing, etc.). [C15: Scot. dialect, < OE *rād* military expedition] —ˈ**raider** *n.*

rail[1] (reɪl) *n.* **1.** a horizontal bar of wood, etc., supported by vertical posts, functioning as a fence, barrier, etc. **2.** a horizontal bar fixed to a wall on which to hang things: *a picture rail.* **3.** a horizontal framing member in a door. Cf. **stile**[2]. **4.** short for **railing. 5.** one of a pair of parallel bars laid on a track, roadway, etc., that serve as a guide and running surface for the wheels of a train, tramcar, etc. **6. a.** short for **railway. b.** (*as modifier*)*: rail transport.* **7.** *Naut.* a trim for finishing the top of a bulwark. **8. off the rails. a.** into or in a state of disorder. **b.** eccentric or mad. ~*vb.* (*tr.*) **9.** to provide with a rail or railings. **10.** (usually foll. by *in* or *off*) to fence (an area) with rails. [C13: < OF *raille* rod, < L *rēgula* ruler]

rail[2] (reɪl) *vb.* (*intr.;* foll. by *at* or *against*) to complain bitterly or vehemently. [C15: < OF *railler* to mock, < OProvençal *ralhar* to chatter, < LL *ragere* to yell] —ˈ**railer** *n.*

rail[3] (reɪl) *n.* any of various small cranelike wading marsh birds with short wings and neck, long legs, and dark plumage. [C15: < OF *raale,* ? < L *rādere* to scrape]

railcar (ˈreɪlˌkɑː) *n.* a passenger-carrying railway vehicle consisting of a single coach with its own power unit.

railcard (ˈreɪlˌkɑːd) *n. Brit.* an identity card issued to people, such as senior citizens or students, entitled to cheap rail fares.

railhead (ˈreɪlˌhɛd) *n.* **1.** a terminal of a railway. **2.** the farthest point reached by completed track on an unfinished railway.

railing (ˈreɪlɪŋ) *n.* **1.** (*often pl.*) a fence, balustrade, or barrier that consists of rails supported by posts. **2.** rails collectively or material for making rails.

raillery (ˈreɪlərɪ) *n., pl.* **-leries. 1.** light-hearted satire or ridicule; banter. **2.** a bantering remark. [C17: < F, < *railler* to tease; see RAIL[2]]

railroad (ˈreɪlˌrəʊd) *n.* **1.** the usual U.S. word for **railway.** ~*vb.* **2.** (*tr.*) *Inf.* to force (a person) into (an action) with haste or by unfair means.

railway (ˈreɪlˌweɪ) *or U.S.* **railroad** *n.* **1.** a permanent track composed of a line of parallel metal rails fixed to sleepers, for transport of passengers and goods in trains. **2.** any track for the wheels of a vehicle to run on: *a cable railway.* **3.** the entire equipment, rolling stock, buildings, property, and system of tracks used in such a transport system. **4.** the organization responsible for operating a railway network. **5.** (*modifier*) of, relating to, or used on a railway: *a railway engine.*

raiment (ˈreɪmənt) *n. Arch. or poetic.* attire; clothing. [C15: < *arrayment,* < OF *areement;* see ARRAY]

rain (reɪn) *n.* **1. a.** precipitation from clouds in the form of drops of water, formed by the condensation of water vapour in the atmosphere. **b.** a fall of rain; shower. **c.** (*in combination*): *a raindrop.* **2.** a large quantity of anything falling rapidly or in quick succession: *a rain of abuse.* **3. (come) rain or (come) shine.** regardless of the weather or circumstances. **4. right as rain.** *Brit. inf.* perfectly all right. ~*vb.* **5.** (*intr.;* with *it* as subject) to be the case that rain is falling. **6.** (often with *it* as subject) to fall or cause to fall like rain. **7.** (*tr.*) to bestow in large measure: *to rain abuse on someone.* **8. rained off.** cancelled or postponed on account of rain. U.S. and Canad. term: **rained out.** ~See also **rains.** [OE *regn*] —ˈ**rainless** *adj.*

rainbow (ˈreɪnˌbəʊ) *n.* **1. a.** a bow-shaped display in the sky of the colours of the spectrum, caused by the refraction and reflection of the sun's rays through rain. **b.** (*as modifier*): *a rainbow pattern.* **2.** an illusory hope: *to chase rainbows.* **3.** (*modifier*) of or relating to a political grouping together by several minorities, esp. of different races: *the rainbow coalition.*

rainbow trout *n.* a freshwater trout of North American origin, marked with many black spots and two longitudinal red stripes.

rain check *n. U.S. & Canad.* **1.** a ticket stub for a baseball game that allows readmission on a future date if the event is cancelled because of rain. **2.** the deferral of acceptance of an offer. **3. take a rain check.** *Inf.* to accept or request the postponement of an offer.

raincoat (ˈreɪnˌkəʊt) *n.* a coat made of a waterproof material.

rainfall (ˈreɪnˌfɔːl) *n.* **1.** precipitation in the form of raindrops. **2.** *Meteorol.* the amount of precipitation in a specified place and time.

rainforest (ˈreɪnˌfɒrɪst) *n.* dense forest found in tropical areas of heavy rainfall.

rain gauge *n.* an instrument for measuring rainfall or snowfall, consisting of a cylinder covered by a funnel-like lid.

rainproof (ˈreɪnˌpruːf) *adj.* **1.** Also: ˈ**rainˌtight.** (of garments, materials, etc.) impermeable to rainwater. ~*vb.* **2.** (*tr.*) to make rainproof.

rains (reɪnz) *pl. n.* **the rains.** the season of heavy rainfall, esp. in the tropics.

rain shadow *n.* the relatively dry area on the leeward side of high ground in the path of rain-bearing winds.

rainstorm (ˈreɪnˌstɔːm) *n.* a storm with heavy rain.

rainwater (ˈreɪnˌwɔːtə) *n.* pure water from rain (as distinguished from spring water, tap water, etc., which may contain minerals and impurities).

rainy (ˈreɪnɪ) *adj.* **rainier, rainiest. 1.** characterized by a large rainfall: *a rainy climate.* **2.** wet or showery; bearing rain. —ˈ**rainily** *adv.* —ˈ**raininess** *n.*

rainy day *n.* a future time of need, esp. financial.

raise (reɪz) *vb.* (*mainly tr.*) **1.** to move or elevate to a higher position or level; lift. **2.** to set or place in an upright position. **3.** to construct, build, or erect: *to raise a barn.* **4.** to increase in amount, size, value, etc.: *to raise prices.* **5.** to increase in degree, strength, intensity, etc.: *to raise one's voice.* **6.** to advance in rank or status; promote. **7.** to arouse or awaken from sleep or death. **8.** to stir up or incite; activate: *to raise a mutiny.* **9. raise Cain** (*or* **the devil, hell, the roof,** etc.). **a.** to create a disturbance, esp. by making a great noise. **b.** to protest vehemently. **10.** to give rise to; cause or provoke: *to raise a smile.* **11.** to put forward for consideration: *to raise a question.* **12.** to cause to assemble or gather together: *to raise an army.* **13.** to grow or cause to grow: *to raise a crop.* **14.** to bring up; rear: *to raise a family.* **15.** to cause to be heard or known; utter or express: *to raise a shout.* **16.** to bring to an end; remove: *to raise a siege.* **17.** to cause (bread, etc.) to rise, as by the addition of yeast. **18.** *Poker.* to bet more than (the previous player). **19.** *Bridge.* to bid (one's partner's suit) at a higher level. **20.** *Naut.* to cause (something) to seem to rise above the horizon by approaching: *we raised land after 20 days.* **21.** to establish radio communications with: *we raised Moscow last night.* **22.** to obtain (money, funds, etc.). **23.** to bring (a surface, a design, etc.) into relief; cause to project. **24.** to cause (a blister, etc.) to form on the skin. **25.** *Maths.* to multiply (a number) by itself a specified number of times: *8 is 2 raised to the power 3.* **26. raise one's glass (to).** to drink a toast (to). **27. raise one's hat.** *Old-fashioned.* to take one's hat briefly off one's head as a greeting or mark of respect. ~*n.* **28.** the act or an instance of raising. **29.** *Chiefly U.S. & Canad.* an increase, esp. in salary, wages, etc.; rise. [C12: < ON *reisa*] —ˈ**raisable** *or* ˈ**raiseable** *adj.*

raised beach *n.* a wave-cut platform raised above the shoreline by a relative fall in the water level.

raisin (ˈreɪzᵊn) *n.* a dried grape. [C13: < OF: grape, ult. < L *racēmus* cluster of grapes] —ˈ**raisiny** *adj.*

raison d'être *French.* (rɛzɔ̃ dɛtrə) *n., pl.* ***raisons d'être*** (rɛzɔ̃ dɛtrə). reason or justification for existence.

raj (rɑːdʒ) *n.* **1.** (in India) government; rule. **2.** (cap. and preceded by *the*) the British government in India before 1947. [C19: < Hindi, < Sansk., < *rājati* he rules]

rajah *or* **raja** (ˈrɑːdʒə) *n.* **1.** (in India, formerly) a ruler: sometimes used as a title preceding a name. **2.** a Malayan or Javanese prince or chieftain. [C16: < Hindi, < Sansk. *rājan* king]

Rajput *or* **Rajpoot** (ˈrɑːdʒpʊt) *n. Hinduism.* one of a Hindu military caste claiming descent from the Kshatriya, the original warrior caste. [C16: < Hindi, < Sansk. *rājan* king]

rake[1] (reɪk) *n.* **1.** a hand implement consisting of a row of teeth set in a headpiece attached to a long shaft and used for gathering hay, straw, etc., or for smoothing loose earth. **2.** any of several mechanical farm implements equipped with rows of teeth or rotating wheels mounted with tines and used to gather hay, straw, etc. **3.** any of various implements similar in shape or function. **4.** the act of raking. ~*vb.* **5.** to scrape, gather, or remove (leaves, refuse, etc.) with a rake. **6.** to level or prepare (a surface) with a rake. **7.** (*tr.;* sometimes foll. by *out*) to clear (ashes, etc.) from (a fire). **8.** (*tr.;* foll. by *up* or *together*) to gather (items or people) with difficulty, as from a scattered area or limited supply. **9.** (*tr.;* often foll. by *through, over,* etc.) to search or examine carefully. **10.** (when *intr.,* foll. by *against, along,* etc.) to scrape or graze: *the ship raked the side of the quay.* **11.** (*tr.*) to direct (gunfire) along the length of (a target): *machine-guns raked the column.* **12.** (*tr.*) to sweep (one's eyes) along the length of (something); scan. ~See also **rake in, rake-off,** etc. [OE *raca*] —ˈ**raker** *n.*

rake[2] (reɪk) *n.* a dissolute man, esp. one in fashionable society; roué. [C17: short for *rakehell* a dissolute man]

rake[3] (reɪk) *vb.* (*mainly intr.*) **1.** to incline from the vertical by a perceptible degree, esp. (of a ship's mast) towards the stern. **2.** (*tr.*) to construct with a backward slope. ~*n.* **3.** the degree to which an object, such as a ship's mast, inclines from the perpendicular, esp. towards the stern. **4.** *Theatre.* the slope of a stage from the back towards the footlights. **5.** the angle between the working face of a cutting tool and a plane perpendicular to the surface of the workpiece. [C17: <?; ? rel. to G *ragen* to project, Swedish *raka*]

rake in *vb.* (*tr., adv.*) *Inf.* to acquire (money) in large amounts.

rake-off *Sl.* ~*n.* **1.** a share of profits, esp. one that is illegal or given as a bribe. ~*vb.* **rake off. 2.** (*tr., adv.*) to take or receive (such a share of profits).

rake up *vb.* (*tr., adv.*) to revive, discover, or

bring to light (something forgotten): *to rake up an old quarrel.*

raki *or* **rakee** (rɑːˈkiː, ˈrækɪ) *n.* a strong spirit distilled in Turkey from grain, usually flavoured with aniseed or other aromatics. [C17: < Turkish *rāqī*]

rakish[1] (ˈreɪkɪʃ) *adj.* dissolute; profligate. [C18: < RAKE[2]] —ˈ**rakishly** *adv.* —ˈ**rakishness** *n.*

rakish[2] (ˈreɪkɪʃ) *adj.* **1.** dashing; jaunty: *a hat set at a rakish angle.* **2.** *Naut.* (of a ship or boat) having lines suggestive of speed. [C19: prob. < RAKE[3]]

rale *or* **râle** (rɑːl) *n. Med.* an abnormal crackling sound heard on auscultation of the chest, usually caused by the accumulation of fluid in the lungs. [C19: < F, < *râler* to breathe with a rattling sound]

rallentando (ˌrælenˈtændəʊ) *adj., adv. Music.* becoming slower. Also: **ritardando.** [C19: It., < *rallentare* to slow down]

rally[1] (ˈrælɪ) *vb.* **-lying, -lied.** **1.** to bring (a group, unit, etc.) into order, as after dispersal, or (of such a group) to reform and come to order. **2.** (when *intr.*, foll. by *to*) to organize (supporters, etc.) for a common cause or (of such people) to come together for a purpose. **3.** to summon up (one's strength, spirits, etc.) or (of a person's health, strength, or spirits) to revive or recover. **4.** (*intr.*) *Stock Exchange.* to increase sharply after a decline. **5.** (*intr.*) *Tennis, squash, etc.* to engage in a rally. ~*n., pl.* **-lies.** **6.** a large gathering of people for a common purpose. **7.** a marked recovery of strength or spirits, as during illness. **8.** a return to order after dispersal or rout, as of troops, etc. **9.** *Stock Exchange.* a sharp increase in price or trading activity after a decline. **10.** *Tennis, squash, etc.* an exchange of several shots before one player wins the point. **11.** a type of motoring competition over public roads. [C16: < OF *rallier*, < RE- + *alier* to write] —ˈ**rallier** *n.*

rally[2] (ˈrælɪ) *vb.* **-lying, -lied.** to mock or ridicule (someone) in a good-natured way; chaff; tease. [C17: < OF *railler* to tease; see RAIL[2]]

rallycross (ˈrælɪˌkrɒs) *n.* a form of motor sport in which cars race over a one-mile circuit of rough grass with some hard-surfaced sections.

rally round *vb.* (*intr.*) to come to the aid of (someone); offer moral or practical support.

ram (ræm) *n.* **1.** an uncastrated adult male sheep. **2.** a piston or moving plate, esp. one driven hydraulically or pneumatically. **3.** the falling weight of a pile driver. **4.** short for **battering ram.** **5.** a pointed projection in the stem of an ancient warship for puncturing the hull of enemy ships. **6.** a warship equipped with a ram. ~*vb.* **ramming, rammed.** **7.** (*tr.*; usually foll. by *into*) to force or drive, as by heavy blows: *to ram a post into the ground.* **8.** (of a moving object) to crash with force (against another object) or (of two moving objects) to collide in this way. **9.** (*tr.*; often foll. by *in* or *down*) to stuff or cram (something into a hole, etc.). **10.** (*tr.*; foll. by *onto, against*, etc.) to thrust violently: *he rammed the books onto the desk.* **11.** (*tr.*) to present (an idea, argument, etc.) forcefully or aggressively (esp. in **ram (something) down someone's throat**). **12.** (*tr.*) to drive (a charge) into a firearm. [OE *ramm*] —ˈ**rammer** *n.*

Ram (ræm) *n.* **the.** the constellation Aries, the first sign of the zodiac.

RAM[1] (ræm) *n. Computers. acronym for* random access memory: a temporary storage space which loses its contents when the computer is switched off.

RAM[2] *abbrev. for* Royal Academy of Music.

Ramadan *or* **Rhamadhan** (ˌræməˈdɑːn) *n.* **1.** a period of 30 days in the ninth month of the Muslim year, during which strict fasting is observed from sunrise to sunset. **2.** the fast itself. [C16: < Ar., lit.: the hot month, < *ramad* dryness]

Raman effect (ˈrɑːmən) *n.* the change in wavelength of light that is scattered by electrons within a material. The effect is used in **Raman spectroscopy** for studying the properties of molecules. [C20: after Sir Chandasekhara *Raman* (1888–1970), Indian physicist]

ramble (ˈræmbᵊl) *vb.* (*intr.*) **1.** to stroll about freely, as for relaxation, with no particular direction. **2.** (of paths, streams, etc.) to follow a winding course; meander. **3.** to grow or develop in a random fashion. **4.** (of speech, writing, etc.) to lack organization. ~*n.* **5.** a leisurely stroll, esp. in the countryside. [C17: prob. rel. to MDu. *rammelen* to ROAM (of animals)]

rambler (ˈræmblə) *n.* **1.** a weak-stemmed plant that straggles over other vegetation. **2.** a person who rambles, esp. one who takes country walks. **3.** a person who lacks organization in his speech or writing.

rambling (ˈræmblɪŋ) *adj.* **1.** straggling or sprawling haphazardly: *a rambling old house.* **2.** (of speech or writing) diffuse and disconnected. **3.** (of a plant, esp. a rose) climbing and straggling. **4.** nomadic; wandering.

Ramboesque (ˌræmbəʊˈɛsk) *adj.* looking or behaving like or characteristic of Rambo, a fictional film character noted for his mindless brutality and aggression. [C20: after *Rambo, First Blood II,* released in Britain 1985] —ˈ**Ramboˌism** *n.*

rambunctious (ræmˈbʌŋkʃəs) *adj. Inf.* boisterous; unruly. [C19: prob. < Icelandic *ram* (intensifying prefix) + *-bunctious*, < BUMPTIOUS] —**ramˈbunctiousness** *n.*

rambutan (ræmˈbuːtᵊn) *n.* **1.** a tree related to the soapberry, native to SE Asia, that has bright red edible fruit covered with hairs. **2.** the fruit of this tree. [C18: < Malay, < *rambut* hair]

RAMC *abbrev. for* Royal Army Medical Corps.

ramekin *or* **ramequin** (ˈræmɪkɪn) *n.* **1.** a savoury dish made from a cheese mixture baked in a fireproof container. **2.** the container itself. [C18: F *ramequin*, of Gmc origin]

ramification (ˌræmɪfɪˈkeɪʃən) *n.* **1.** the act or process of ramifying or branching out. **2.** an offshoot or subdivision. **3.** a structure of branching parts.

ramify (ˈræmɪˌfaɪ) *vb.* **-fying, -fied.** **1.** to divide into branches or branchlike parts. **2.** (*intr.*) to develop complicating consequences. [C16: < F *ramifier*, < L *rāmus* branch + *facere* to make]

ramjet *or* **ramjet engine** (ˈræmˌdʒɛt) *n.* **a.** a type of jet engine in which fuel is burned in a duct using air compressed by the forward speed of the aircraft. **b.** an aircraft powered by such an engine.

ramose (ˈreɪməʊs, ræˈməʊs) *or* **ramous** (ˈreɪməs) *adj.* having branches. [C17: < L *rāmōsus*, < *rāmus* branch] —ˈ**ramosely** *or* ˈ**ramously** *adv.* —**ramosity** (ræˈmɒsɪtɪ) *n.*

ramp (ræmp) *n.* **1.** a sloping floor, path, etc., that joins two surfaces at different levels. **2.** a movable stairway by which passengers enter and leave an aircraft. **3.** the act of ramping. **4.** *Brit. sl.* a swindle, esp. one involving exorbitant prices. ~*vb.* (*intr.*) **5.** (often foll. by *about* or *around*) (esp. of animals) to rush around in a wild excited manner. **6.** to act in a violent or threatening manner (esp. in **ramp and rage**). [C18 (n.): < C13 *rampe*, < OF *ramper* to crawl or rear, prob. of Gmc origin]

rampage *vb.* (ræmˈpeɪdʒ). **1.** (*intr.*) to rush about in a violent or agitated fashion. ~*n.* (ˈræmpeɪdʒ, ræmˈpeɪdʒ). **2.** angry or destructive behaviour. **3. on the rampage.** behaving violently or destructively. [C18: < Scot., <?; ? based on RAMP] —**ramˈpageous** *adj.* —**ramˈpageously** *adv.* —**ramˈpager** *n.*

rampant (ˈræmpənt) *adj.* **1.** unrestrained or violent in behaviour, etc. **2.** growing or developing unchecked. **3.** (*postpositive*) *Heraldry.* (of a beast) standing on the hind legs, the right foreleg raised above the left. **4.** (of an arch) having one abutment higher than the other. [C14: < OF *ramper* to crawl, rear; see RAMP] —ˈ**rampancy** *n.* —ˈ**rampantly** *adv.*

rampart (ˈræmpɑːt) *n.* **1.** the surrounding embankment of a fort, often including any walls, parapets, etc., that are built on the bank. **2.** any defence or bulwark. ~*vb.* **3.** (*tr.*) to provide with a rampart; fortify. [C16: < OF, < RE- + *emparer* to take possession of, < OProvençal *antparar*, < L *ante* before + *parāre* to prepare]

rampike (ˈræmˌpaɪk) *n. Canad.* a tall tree that has been burned or is bare of branches.

rampion (ˈræmpɪən) *n.* a plant, native to Europe and Asia, that has clusters of bell-shaped bluish flowers and an edible white tuberous root used in salads. [C16: prob. < OF *raiponce*, < OIt. *raponzo*, < *rapa* turnip, < L *rāpum*]

ramrod (ˈræmˌrɒd) *n.* **1.** a rod for cleaning the barrel of a rifle, etc. **2.** a rod for ramming in the charge of a muzzle-loading firearm.

ramshackle (ˈræmˌʃækᵊl) *adj.* (esp. of buildings) rickety, shaky, or derelict. [C17 *ramshackled*, < obs. *ransackle* to RANSACK]

ramsons (ˈræmzənz, -sənz) *pl. n.* (*usually functioning as sing.*) **1.** a broad-leaved garlic native to Europe and Asia. **2.** the bulbous root of this plant, eaten as a relish. [OE *hramesa*]

ran (ræn) *vb.* the past tense of **run.**

RAN *abbrev. for* Royal Australian Navy.

ranch (rɑːntʃ) *n.* **1.** a large tract of land, esp. one in North America, together with the necessary personnel, buildings, and equipment, for rearing livestock, esp. cattle. **2. a.** any large farm for the rearing of a particular kind of livestock or crop: *a mink ranch.* **b.** the buildings, land, etc., connected with it. ~*vb.* **3.** (*intr.*) to run a ranch. **4.** (*tr.*) to raise (animals) on or as if on a ranch. [C19: < Mexican Sp. *rancho* small farm] —ˈ**rancher** *n.*

rancherie (ˈrɑːntʃərɪ) *n.* (in British Columbia, Canada) a settlement of North American Indians, esp. on a reserve. [< Sp. *rancheria*]

rancid (ˈrænsɪd) *adj.* **1.** (of food) having an unpleasant stale taste or smell as the result of decomposition. **2.** (of a taste or smell) rank or sour; stale. [C17: < L *rancidus*, < *rancēre* to stink] —ˈ**rancidness** *or* **rancidity** (rænˈsɪdɪtɪ) *n.*

rancour *or U.S.* **rancor** (ˈræŋkə) *n.* malicious resentfulness or hostility; spite. [C14: < OF, < LL *rancor* rankness] —ˈ**rancorous** *adj.* —ˈ**rancorously** *adv.*

rand[1] (rænd, rɒnt) *n.* the standard monetary unit of the Republic of South Africa, divided into 100 cents. [C20: < Afrik., < *Witwatersrand*, S Transvaal, referring to the gold-mining there; rel. to RAND[2]]

rand[2] (rænd) *n.* **1.** *Shoemaking.* a leather strip put in the heel of a shoe before the lifts are put on. **2.** *Dialect.* **a.** a strip or margin; border. **b.** a strip of cloth; selvage. [OE; rel. to OHG *rant* border, rim of a shield, ON *rönd* shield, rim]

Rand (rænd) *n.* **the.** short for Witwatersrand, an area in South Africa rich in mineral deposits, esp. gold.

R & B *abbrev. for* rhythm and blues.

R & D *abbrev. for* research and development.

random (ˈrændəm) *adj.* **1.** lacking any definite plan or prearranged order; haphazard: *a random selection.* **2.** *Statistics.* **a.** having a value which cannot be determined but only described in terms of probability: *a random variable.* **b.** chosen without regard to any characteristics of the individual members of the population so that each has an equal chance of being selected: *random sampling.* ~*n.* **3. at random.** not following any prearranged order. [C14: < OF *randon*, < *randir* to gallop, of Gmc origin] —ˈ**randomly** *adv.* —ˈ**randomness** *n.*

random access *n.* another name for **direct access.**

randomize *or* **-ise** (ˈrændəˌmaɪz) *vb.* (*tr.*) to set up (a selection process, sample, etc.) in a deliberately random way in order to enhance the statistical validity of any results obtained. —ˌ**randomiˈzation** *or* **-iˈsation** *n.* —ˈ**randomˌizer** *or* **-ˌiser** *n.*

R and R *U.S. mil. abbrev. for* rest and recreation.

randy (ˈrændɪ) *adj.* **randier, randiest. 1.** *Inf., chiefly Brit.* sexually eager or lustful. **2.** *Chiefly Scot.* lacking any sense of propriety; reckless. ~*n., pl.* **randies. 3.** *Chiefly Scot.* a rude or reckless person. [C17: prob. < obs. *rand* to RANT] —ˈ**randily** *adv.* —ˈ**randiness** *n.*

ranee (ˈrɑːnɪ) *n.* a variant spelling of **rani.**

rang (ræŋ) *vb.* the past tense of **ring**[2].

▷ **Usage.** See at **ring**[2].

rangatira (ˌrʌŋgəˈtɪərə) *n. N.Z.* a Maori chief of either sex. [< Maori]

range (reɪndʒ) *n.* **1.** the limits within which a person or thing can function effectively: *the range of vision.* **2.** the limits within which any fluctuation takes place: *a range of values.* **3.** the total products of a manufacturer, designer, or stockist: *the new spring range.* **4. a.** the maximum effective distance of a projectile fired from a weapon. **b.** the distance between a target and a weapon. **5.** an area set aside for shooting practice or rocket testing. **6.** the total distance which a ship, aircraft, or land vehicle is capable of covering without taking on fresh fuel. *the range of this car is about 160 miles.* **7.** *Maths.* (of a function or variable) the set of values that a function or variable can take. **8.** *U.S. & Canad.* **a.** an extensive tract of open land on which livestock can graze. **b.** (*as modifier*): *range cattle.* **9.** the geographical region in which a species of plant or animal normally grows or lives. **10.** a rank, row, or series of items. **11.** a series or chain of mountains. **12.** a large stove with burners and one or more ovens, usually heated by solid fuel. **13.** the act or process of ranging. ~*vb.* **14.** to establish or be situated in a line, row, or series. **15.** (*tr.; often reflexive,* foll. by *with*) to put into a specific category; classify: *she ranges herself with the angels.* **16.** (foll. by *on*) to aim or point (a telescope, gun, etc.) or (of a gun, telescope, etc.) to be pointed or aimed. **17.** to establish the distance of (a target) from (a weapon). **18.** (*intr.*) (of a gun or missile) to have a specified range. **19.** (when *intr.*, foll. by *over*) to wander about (in) an area; roam (over). **20.** (*intr.;* foll. by *over*) (of an animal or plant) to live or grow in its normal habitat. **21.** (*tr.*) to put (cattle) to graze on a range. **22.** (*intr.*) to fluctuate within specific limits. **23.** (*intr.*) to extend or run in a specific direction. **24.** (*intr.*) *Naut.* (of a vessel) to swing back and forth while at anchor. **25.** (*tr.*) to make (lines of printers' type) level or even at the margin. [C13: < OF: row, < *ranger* to position, < *renc* line]

rangefinder (ˈreɪndʒˌfaɪndə) *n.* an instrument for determining the distance of an object from the observer, esp. in order to sight a gun or focus a camera.

ranger (ˈreɪndʒə) *n.* **1.** *Brit.* (*sometimes cap.*) an official in charge of a forest, park, nature reserve, etc. **2.** *Orig. U.S.* a person employed to patrol a State or national park. Brit. equivalent: **warden. 3.** *U.S.* one of a body of armed troops employed to police a State or district: *a Texas ranger.* **4.** (in the U.S.) a commando specially trained in making raids. **5.** a person who wanders about; a rover.

Ranger *or* **Ranger Guide** (ˈreɪndʒə) *n. Brit.* a member of the senior branch of the Guides.

rangiora (ˌræŋgɪˈɔːrə) *n.* a broad-leaved shrub of New Zealand. [< Maori]

rangy (ˈreɪndʒɪ) *adj.* **rangier, rangiest. 1.** having long slender limbs. **2.** adapted to wandering or roaming. **3.** allowing considerable freedom of movement; spacious. —ˈ**rangily** *adv.* —ˈ**ranginess** *n.*

rani *or* **ranee** (ˈrɑːnɪ) *n.* a queen or princess; the wife of a rajah. [C17: < Hindi: queen, < Sansk. *rājñī*]

rank[1] (ræŋk) *n.* **1.** a position, esp. an official one, within a social organization: *the rank of captain.* **2.** high social or other standing; status. **3.** a line or row of people or things. **4.** the position of an item in any ordering or sequence. **5.** *Brit.* a place where taxis wait to be hired. **6.** a line of soldiers drawn up abreast of each other. **7.** any of the eight horizontal rows of squares on a chessboard. **8. close ranks.** to maintain discipline or solidarity. **9. pull rank.** to get one's own way by virtue of one's superior position or rank. **10. rank and file.**

a. the ordinary soldiers, excluding the officers. **b.** the great mass or majority of any group, as opposed to the leadership. **c.** (*modifier*): *rank-and-file support.* ~*vb.* **11.** (*tr.*) to arrange (people or things) in rows or lines; range. **12.** to accord or be accorded a specific position in an organization or group. **13.** (*tr.*) to array a set of objects as a sequence: *to rank students by their test scores.* **14.** (*intr.*) to be important; rate: *money ranks low in her order of priorities.* **15.** *Chiefly U.S.* to take precedence or surpass in rank. [C16: < OF *ranc* row, rank, of Gmc origin]

rank[2] (ræŋk) *adj.* **1.** showing vigorous and profuse growth: *rank weeds.* **2.** highly offensive or disagreeable, esp. in smell or taste. **3.** (*prenominal*) complete or absolute; utter: *a rank outsider.* **4.** coarse or vulgar; gross: *his language was rank.* [OE *ranc* straight, noble] —ˈ**rankly** *adv.* —ˈ**rankness** *n.*

ranker (ˈræŋkə) *n.* **1.** a soldier in the ranks. **2.** a commissioned officer who entered service as a noncommissioned recruit.

ranking (ˈræŋkɪŋ) *adj.* **1.** *Chiefly U.S. & Canad.* prominent; high ranking. **2.** *Caribbean sl.* possessed of style; exciting. ~*n.* **3.** a position on a scale; rating: *a ranking in a tennis tournament.*

rankle (ˈræŋkᵊl) *vb.* (*intr.*) to cause severe and continuous irritation, anger, or bitterness; fester. [C14 *ranclen,* < OF *draoncle* ulcer, < L *dracunculus* dim. of *dracō* serpent]

ransack (ˈrænsæk) *vb.* (*tr.*) **1.** to search through every part of (a house, box, etc.); examine thoroughly. **2.** to plunder; pillage. [C13: < ON *rann* house + *saka* to search] —ˈ**ransacker** *n.*

ransom (ˈrænsəm) *n.* **1.** the release of captured prisoners, property, etc., on payment of a stipulated price. **2.** the price demanded or stipulated for such a release. **3. hold to ransom. a.** to keep (prisoners, etc.) in confinement until payment for their release is received. **b.** to attempt to force (a person) to comply with one's demands. **4. a king's ransom.** a very large amount of money or valuables. ~*vb.* (*tr.*) **5.** to pay a stipulated price and so obtain the release of (prisoners, property, etc.). **6.** to set free (prisoners, property, etc.) upon receiving the payment demanded. **7.** to redeem; rescue: *Christ ransomed men from sin.* [C14: < OF *ransoun,* < L *redemptiō* a buying back] —ˈ**ransomer** *n.*

rant (rænt) *vb.* **1.** to utter (something) in loud, violent, or bombastic tones. ~*n.* **2.** loud, declamatory, or extravagant speech; bombast. [C16: < Du. *ranten* to rave] —ˈ**ranter** *n.* —ˈ**ranting** *adj., n.* —ˈ**rantingly** *adv.*

ranunculaceous (rəˌnʌŋkjʊˈleɪʃəs) *adj.* of, relating to, or belonging to a N temperate family of flowering plants typically having flowers with five petals and numerous anthers and styles. The family includes the buttercup, clematis, and columbine.

ranunculus (rəˈnʌŋkjʊləs) *n., pl.* **-luses** *or* **-li** (-ˌlaɪ). any of a genus of ranunculaceous plants having finely divided leaves and typically yellow five-petalled flowers. The genus includes buttercup, crowfoot, and spearwort. [C16: < L: tadpole, < *rāna* frog]

RAOC *abbrev. for* Royal Army Ordnance Corps.

rap[1] (ræp) *vb.* **rapping, rapped. 1.** to strike (a fist, stick, etc.) against (something) with a sharp quick blow; knock. **2.** (*intr.*) to make a sharp loud sound, esp. by knocking. **3.** (*tr.*) to rebuke or criticize sharply. **4.** (*tr.; foll. by out*) to put (forth) in sharp rapid speech; utter in an abrupt fashion: *to rap out orders.* **5.** (*intr.*) *Sl.* to talk, esp. volubly. **6.** (*intr.*) to perform a rhythmic monologue with musical backing. **7. rap over the knuckles.** to reprimand. ~*n.* **8.** a sharp quick blow or the sound produced by such a blow. **9.** a sharp rebuke or criticism. **10.** *Sl.* voluble talk; chatter. **11. a.** a fast, rhythmic monologue over a musical backing. **b.** (*as modifier*): *rap music.* **12. beat the rap.** *U.S. & Canad. sl.* to escape punishment or be acquitted of a crime. **13. take the rap.** *Sl.* to suffer the punishment for a crime, whether guilty or not. [C14: prob. < ON; cf. Swedish *rappa* to beat]

rap[2] (ræp) *n.* (*used with a negative*) the least amount (esp. in **not care a rap**). [C18: prob. < *ropaire* counterfeit coin formerly current in Ireland]

rap[3] (ræp) *vb., n. Austral. inf.* a variant spelling of **wrap** (senses 7, 12).

rapacious (rəˈpeɪʃəs) *adj.* **1.** practising pillage or rapine. **2.** greedy or grasping. **3.** (of animals, esp. birds) subsisting by catching living prey. [C17: < L *rapāx,* < *rapere* to seize] —**raˈpaciously** *adv.* —**rapacity** (rəˈpæsɪtɪ) *or* **raˈpaciousness** *n.*

rape[1] (reɪp) *n.* **1.** the offence of forcing a person, esp. a woman, to submit to sexual intercourse against that person's will. **2.** the act of despoiling a country in warfare. **3.** any violation or abuse: *the rape of justice.* **4.** *Arch.* abduction: *the rape of the Sabine women.* ~*vb.* (*mainly tr.*) **5.** to commit rape upon (a person). **6.** *Arch.* to carry off by force; abduct. [C14: < L *rapere* to seize] —ˈ**rapist** *n.*

rape[2] (reɪp) *n.* a Eurasian plant that is cultivated for its seeds, **rapeseed,** which yield a useful oil, **rape oil,** and as a fodder plant. Also called: **colza, cole.** [C14: < L *rāpum* turnip]

rape[3] (reɪp) *n.* (*often pl.*) the skins and stalks of grapes left after wine-making: used in making vinegar. [C17: < F *râpe,* of Gmc origin]

raphia (ˈræfɪə) *n.* a variant spelling of **raffia.**

raphide (ˈreɪfaɪd) *or* **raphis** (ˈreɪfɪs) *n., pl.* **raphides** (ˈræfɪˌdiːz). needle-shaped crystals, usually of calcium oxalate, that occur in many plant cells. [C18: < F, < Gk *rhaphis* needle]

rapid (ˈræpɪd) *adj.* **1.** (of an action) performed or occurring during a short interval of time; quick. **2.** acting or moving quickly; fast: *a rapid worker.* ~See also **rapids.** [C17: < L *rapidus* tearing away, < *rapere* to seize] —ˈ**rapidly** *adv.* —**rapidity** (rəˈpɪdɪtɪ) *or* ˈ**rapidness** *n.*

rapid eye movement *n.* movement of the eyeballs during paradoxical sleep, while the sleeper is dreaming. Abbrev.: **REM.**

rapid fire *n.* **1.** a fast rate of gunfire. ~*adj.* **rapid-fire. 2.** firing shots rapidly. **3.** done, delivered, or occurring in rapid succession.

rapids (ˈræpɪdz) *pl. n.* part of a river where the water is very fast and turbulent.

rapier (ˈreɪpɪə) *n.* **1.** a long narrow two-edged sword with a guarded hilt, used as a thrusting weapon, popular in the 16th and 17th centuries. **2.** a smaller single-edged 18th-century sword, used principally in France. [C16: < OF *espee rapiere,* lit.: rasping sword]

rapine (ˈræpaɪn) *n.* the seizure of property by force; pillage. [C15: < L *rapīna* plundering, < *rapere* to snatch]

rappee (ræˈpiː) *n.* a moist English snuff. [C18: < F *tabac râpé,* lit.: scraped tobacco]

rappel (ræˈpɛl) *vb.* **-pelling, -pelled,** *n.* **1.** another word for **abseil.** ~*n.* **2.** (formerly) a drumbeat to call soldiers to arms. [C19: < F, < *rappeler* to call back, < L *appellāre* to summon]

rapport (ræˈpɔː) *n.* (often foll. by *with*) a sympathetic relationship or understanding. See also **en rapport.** [C15: < F, < *rapporter* to bring back, < RE- + *aporter,* < L *apportāre,* < *ad* to + *portāre* to carry]

rapprochement *French.* (raprɔʃmɑ̃) *n.* a resumption of friendly relations, esp. between two countries. [C19: lit.: bringing closer]

rapscallion (ræpˈskæljən) *n.* a disreputable person; rascal or rogue. [C17: < earlier *rascallion;* see RASCAL]

rapt[1] (ræpt) *adj.* **1.** totally absorbed; engrossed; spellbound, esp. through or as if through emotion: *rapt with wonder.* **2.** characterized by or proceeding from rapture: *a rapt smile.* [C14: < L *raptus* carried away, < *rapere* to seize] —ˈ**raptly** *adv.*

rapt[2] (ræpt) *adj. Austral. inf.* a variant spelling of **wrapped** (sense 3).

raptor (ˈræptə) *n.* another name for **bird of prey.** [C17: < L: plunderer, < *rapere* to take by force]

raptorial (ræpˈtɔːrɪəl) *adj. Zool.* **1.** (of the feet of birds) adapted for seizing prey. **2.** of or relating to birds of prey. [C19: < L *raptor* robber, < *rapere* to snatch]

rapture (ˈræptʃə) *n.* **1.** the state of mind resulting from feelings of high emotion; joyous ecstasy. **2.** (*often pl.*) an expression of ecstatic joy. **3.** *Arch.* the act of transporting a person from one sphere of existence to another. ~*vb.* **4.** (*tr.*) *Arch. or literary.* to enrapture. [C17: < Med. L *raptūra*, < L *raptus* RAPT[1]] —ˈ**rapturous** *adj.*

rara avis (ˈrɛərə ˈeɪvɪs) *n., pl.* **rarae aves** (ˈrɛəriː ˈeɪviːz). an unusual, uncommon, or exceptional person or thing. [L: rare bird]

rare[1] (rɛə) *adj.* **1.** not widely known; not frequently used or experienced; uncommon or unusual: *a rare word.* **2.** not widely distributed; not generally occurring: *a rare herb.* **3.** (of a gas, esp. the atmosphere at high altitudes) having a low density; thin; rarefied. **4.** uncommonly great; extreme: *kind to a rare degree.* **5.** exhibiting uncommon excellence: *rare skill.* [C14: < L *rārus* sparse] —ˈ**rareness** *n.*

rare[2] (rɛə) *adj.* (of meat, esp. beef) undercooked. [OE *hrēr*; rel. to *hreaw* RAW]

rarebit (ˈrɛəbɪt) *n.* another term for **Welsh rabbit.** [C18: by folk etymology < (WELSH) RABBIT; see RARE[2], BIT[1]]

rare earth *n.* **1.** any oxide of a lanthanide. **2.** Also called: **rare-earth element.** any element of the lanthanide series.

raree show (ˈrɛəriː) *n.* **1.** a street show or carnival. **2.** another name for **peepshow.** [C17: *raree* < RARE[1]]

rarefaction (ˌrɛərɪˈfækʃən) *or* **rarefication** (ˌrɛərɪfɪˈkeɪʃən) *n.* the act or process of making less dense or the state of being less dense. —ˌ**rareˈfactive** *adj.*

rarefied (ˈrɛərɪˌfaɪd) *adj.* **1.** exalted in nature or character; lofty: *a rarefied spiritual existence.* **2.** current within only a small group. **3.** thin: *air rarefied at altitude.*

rarefy (ˈrɛərɪˌfaɪ) *vb.* **-fying, -fied.** to make or become rarer or less dense; thin out. [C14: < OF *rarefier*, < L *rārēfacere*, < *rārus* RARE[1] + *facere* to make] —ˈ**rareˌfiable** *adj.* —ˈ**rareˌfier** *n.*

rare gas *n.* another name for **inert gas.**

rarely (ˈrɛəlɪ) *adv.* **1.** hardly ever; seldom. **2.** to an unusual degree; exceptionally. **3.** *Dialect.* uncommonly well; excellently: *he did rarely at market yesterday.*

raring (ˈrɛərɪŋ) *adj.* ready; willing; enthusiastic (esp. in **raring to go**). [C20: < *rare*, var. of REAR[2]]

rarity (ˈrɛərɪtɪ) *n., pl.* **-ties. 1.** a rare person or thing, esp. something valued because it is uncommon. **2.** the state of being rare.

rasbora (ræzˈbɔːrə) *n.* any of the small cyprinid fishes of tropical Asia and East Africa. Many species are brightly coloured and are popular aquarium fishes. [< NL, < an East Indian language]

rascal (ˈrɑːskᵊl) *n.* **1.** a disreputable person; villain. **2.** a mischievous or impish rogue. **3.** an affectionate or mildly reproving term, esp. for a child: *you little rascal.* **4.** *Obs.* a person of lowly birth. ~*adj.* **5.** (*prenominal*) *Obs.* **a.** belonging to the rabble. **b.** dishonest; knavish. [C14: < OF *rascaille* rabble, ? < OF *rasque* mud]

rascality (rɑːˈskælɪtɪ) *n., pl.* **-ties.** mischievous or disreputable character or action.

rascally (ˈrɑːskəlɪ) *adj.* **1.** dishonest or mean; base. ~*adv.* **2.** in a dishonest or mean fashion.

rase (reɪz) *vb.* a variant spelling of **raze.**

rash[1] (ræʃ) *adj.* **1.** acting without due thought; impetuous. **2.** resulting from excessive haste or impetuosity: *a rash word.* [C14: < OHG *rasc* hurried, clever] —ˈ**rashly** *adv.* —ˈ**rashness** *n.*

rash[2] (ræʃ) *n.* **1.** *Pathol.* any skin eruption. **2.** a series of unpleasant and unexpected occurrences: *a rash of forest fires.* [C18: < OF *rasche*, < *raschier* to scratch, < L *rādere* to scrape]

rasher (ˈræʃə) *n.* a thin slice of bacon or ham. [C16: <?]

rasp (rɑːsp) *n.* **1.** a harsh grating noise. **2.** a coarse file with rows of raised teeth. ~*vb.* **3.** (*tr.*) to scrape or rub (something) roughly, esp. with a rasp; abrade. **4.** to utter with or make a harsh grating noise. **5.** to irritate (one's nerves); grate (upon). [C16: < OF *raspe*, of Gmc origin; cf. OHG *raspōn* to scrape] —ˈ**rasper** *n.* —ˈ**rasping** *adj.* —ˈ**raspish** *adj.*

raspberry (ˈrɑːzbərɪ, -brɪ) *n., pl.* **-ries. 1.** a prickly rosaceous shrub of North America and Europe that has pinkish-white flowers and typically red berry-like fruits (drupelets). See also **bramble. 2. a.** the fruit of any such plant. **b.** (*as modifier*): *raspberry jelly.* **3. a.** a dark purplish-red colour. **b.** (*as adj.*): *a raspberry dress.* **4.** a spluttering noise made with the tongue and lips to express contempt (esp. in **blow a raspberry**). [C17: < earlier *raspis* raspberry, <? + BERRY]

Rastafarian (ˌræstəˈfɛərɪən) *n.* **1.** a member of a Jamaican cult that regards Ras Tafari, the former emperor of Ethiopia, Haile Selassie, as God. ~*adj.* **2.** of, characteristic of, or relating to the Rastafarians. ~Often shortened to **Rasta.**

raster (ˈræstə) *n.* a pattern of horizontal scanning lines traced by an electron beam, esp. on a television screen. [C20: via G < L: rake, < *rādere* to scrape]

rat (ræt) *n.* **1.** any of numerous long-tailed Old World rodents, that are similar to but larger than mice and are now distributed all over the world. **2.** *Inf.* a person who deserts his friends or associates, esp. in time of trouble. **3.** *Inf.* a worker who works during a strike; blackleg; scab. **4.** *Inf.* a despicable person. **5. have** *or* **be rats.** *Austral. sl.* to be mad or eccentric. **6. smell a rat.** to detect something suspicious. ~*vb.* **ratting, ratted. 7.** (*intr.*; usually foll. by *on*) **a.** to divulge secret information (about); betray the trust (of). **b.** to default (on); abandon. **8.** to hunt and kill rats. [OE *rætt*]

rata (ˈrɑːtə) *n.* a New Zealand tree with red flowers. [< Maori]

ratable *or* **rateable** (ˈreɪtəbᵊl) *adj.* **1.** able to be rated or evaluated. **2.** *Brit.* (of property) liable to payment of rates. —ˌ**rataˈbility** *or* ˌ**rateaˈbility** *n.* —ˈ**ratably** *or* ˈ**rateably** *adv.*

ratable value *or* **rateable value** *n. Brit.* a fixed value assigned to a property by a local authority, on the basis of which variable annual rates are charged.

ratafia (ˌrætəˈfɪə) *or* **ratafee** (ˌrætəˈfiː) *n.* **1.** any liqueur made from fruit or from brandy with added fruit. **2.** a flavouring essence made from almonds. **3.** *Chiefly Brit.* Also called: **ratafia biscuit.** a small macaroon flavoured with almonds. [C17: < West Indian Creole F]

ratan (ræˈtæn) *n.* a variant spelling of **rattan.**

ratatat-tat (ˈrætəˌtætˈtæt) *or* **ratatat** (ˈrætəˈtæt) *n.* the sound of knocking on a door.

ratatouille (ˌrætəˈtwiː) *n.* a vegetable casserole made of tomatoes, aubergines, peppers, etc., fried in oil and stewed slowly. [C19: < F, < *touiller* to stir, < L, < *tudes* hammer]

ratbag (ˈrætˌbæg) *n. Sl.* an eccentric, stupid, or unreliable person.

rat-catcher *n.* a person whose job is to destroy or drive away vermin, esp. rats.

ratchet (ˈrætʃɪt) *n.* **1.** a device in which a toothed rack or wheel is engaged by a pawl to permit motion in one direction only. **2.** the toothed rack or wheel forming part of such a device. [C17: < F *rochet*, < OF *rocquet* blunt head of a lance, of Gmc origin]

rate[1] (reɪt) *n.* **1.** a quantity or amount considered in relation to or measured against another quantity or amount: *a rate of 70 miles an hour.* **2.** a price or charge with reference to a standard or scale: *rate of interest.* **3.** a charge made per unit for a commodity, service, etc. **4.** See **rates. 5.** the relative speed of progress or change of something variable; pace: *the rate of production has doubled.* **6. a.** relative quality; class or grade. **b.** (*in combination*): *first-rate ideas.* **7. at any rate.** in any case; at all events; anyway. ~*vb.* (*mainly tr.*) **8.** (*also intr.*) to assign or receive a position on a scale of relative values; rank: *he is rated fifth in the world.* **9.** to estimate the value of; evaluate: *we rate your services highly.* **10.** to be worthy of; deserve: *this hotel does not rate four stars.* **11.** to consider; regard: *I rate him among my friends.* **12.** *Brit.* to assess the value of (property) for the purpose of local taxation. [C15: < OF, < Med. L *rata*, < L *prō ratā parte* according to a fixed proportion, < *ratus* fixed, < *rērī* to think, decide]

▷ **Usage.** The use of the verb *rate* alone with the sense of thinking highly of something is avoided in careful usage: *the clients do not think highly of* (not *do not rate*) *the new system.*

rate² (reɪt) *vb.* (*tr.*) to scold or criticize severely; rebuke harshly. [C14: ? rel. to Swedish *rata* to chide]

rateable (ˈreɪtəbᵊl) *adj.* a variant spelling of **ratable.**

rate-cap (ˈreɪtˌkæp) *vb.* (*tr.*) **-capping, -capped.** (in Britain) to impose on (a local authority) an upper limit on the rate it may levy. —**ˈrate-ˌcapping** *n.*

ratel (ˈreɪtᵊl) *n.* a carnivorous mammal related to the badger family, inhabiting wooded regions of Africa and S Asia. It has a massive body, strong claws, and a thick coat that is paler on the back. It feeds on honey and small animals. [C18: < Afrik.]

rate of exchange *n.* See **exchange rate.**

ratepayer (ˈreɪtˌpeɪə) *n. Brit.* a person who pays local rates, esp. a householder.

rates (reɪts) *pl. n. Brit.* a tax on property levied by a local authority.

rather (ˈrɑːðə) *adv.* (*in senses 1-4, not used with a negative*) **1.** relatively or fairly; somewhat: *it's rather dull.* **2.** to a significant or noticeable extent; quite: *she's rather pretty.* **3.** to a limited extent or degree: *I rather thought that was the case.* **4.** with better or more just cause: *this text is rather to be deleted than rewritten.* **5.** more readily or willingly; sooner: *I would rather not see you tomorrow.* ~*sentence connector.* **6.** on the contrary: *it's not cold. Rather, it's very hot.* ~*sentence substitute.* (ˈrɑːˈðɜː). **7.** an expression of strong affirmation: *Is it worth seeing? Rather!* [OE *hrathor* comp. of *hræth* READY, quick]

▷ **Usage.** Both *would* and *had* are used with *rather* in sentences such as *I would rather* (or *had rather*) *go to the film than to the play. Had rather* is less common and now widely regarded as slightly old-fashioned.

ratify (ˈrætɪˌfaɪ) *vb.* **-fying, -fied.** (*tr.*) to give formal approval or consent to. [C14: via OF < L *ratus* fixed (see RATE¹) + *facere* to make] —**ˈratiˌfiable** *adj.* —**ˌratifiˈcation** *n.* —**ˈratiˌfier** *n.*

rating¹ (ˈreɪtɪŋ) *n.* **1.** a classification according to order or grade; ranking. **2.** an ordinary seaman. **3.** *Sailing.* a handicap assigned to a racing boat based on its dimensions, draught, etc. **4.** the estimated financial or credit standing of a business enterprise or individual. **5.** *Radio, television, etc.* a figure based on statistical sampling indicating what proportion of the total audience tune in to a specific programme.

rating² (ˈreɪtɪŋ) *n.* a sharp scolding or rebuke.

ratio (ˈreɪʃɪəʊ) *n., pl.* **-tios. 1.** a measure of the relative size of two classes expressible as a proportion: *the ratio of boys to girls is 2 to 1.* **2.** *Maths.* a quotient of two numbers or quantities. See also **proportion** (sense 6). [C17: < L: a reckoning, < *rērī* to think]

ratiocinate (ˌrætɪˈɒsɪˌneɪt) *vb.* (*intr.*) to think or argue logically and methodically; reason. [C17: < L *ratiōcinārī* to calculate, < *ratiō* REASON] —**ˌratiˌociˈnation** *n.* —**ˌratiˈociˌnative** *adj.* —**ˌratiˈociˌnator** *n.*

ration (ˈræʃən) *n.* **1. a.** a fixed allowance of food, provisions, etc., esp. a statutory one for civilians in time of scarcity or soldiers in time of war. **b.** (*as modifier*): *a ration book.* **2.** a sufficient or adequate amount: *you've had your ration of television for today.* ~*vb.* (*tr.*) **3.** (often foll. by *out*) to distribute (provisions), esp. to an army. **4.** to restrict the distribution or consumption of (a commodity) by (people): *the government has rationed sugar.* ~See also **rations.** [C18: via F < L *ratiō* REASON]

rational (ˈræʃənᵊl) *adj.* **1.** using reason or logic in thinking out a problem. **2.** in accordance with the principles of logic or reason; reasonable. **3.** of sound mind; sane: *the patient seemed quite rational.* **4.** endowed with the capacity to reason: *man is a rational being.* **5.** *Maths.* **a.** expressible as a ratio of two integers: *a rational number.* **b.** (of an expression, equation, etc.) containing no variable either in irreducible radical form or raised to a fractional power. ~*n.* **6.** a rational number. [C14: < L *ratiōnālis*, < *ratiō* REASON] —**ˌratioˈnality** *n.* —**ˈrationally** *adv.* —**ˈrationalness** *n.*

rationale (ˌræʃəˈnɑːl) *n.* a reasoned exposition, esp. one defining the fundamental reasons for an action, etc. [C17: < NL, < L *ratiōnālis*]

rationalism (ˈræʃənəˌlɪzəm) *n.* **1.** reliance on reason rather than intuition to justify one's beliefs or actions. **2.** *Philosophy.* the doctrine that knowledge is acquired by reason without regard to experience. **3.** the belief that knowledge and truth are ascertained by rational thought and not by divine or supernatural revelation. —**ˈrationalist** *n.* —**ˌrationalˈistic** *adj.* —**ˌrationalˈistically** *adv.*

rationalize *or* **-ise** (ˈræʃənəˌlaɪz) *vb.* **1.** to justify (one's actions) with plausible reasons, esp. after the event. **2.** to apply logic or reason to (something). **3.** (*tr.*) to eliminate unnecessary equipment, etc., from (a factory, etc.), in order to make it more efficient. **4.** (*tr.*) *Maths.* to eliminate radicals without changing the value of (an expression) or the roots of (an equation). —**ˌrationaliˈzation** *or* **-iˈsation** *n.* —**ˈrationalˌizer** *or* **-ˌiser** *n.*

rational number *n.* any real number of the form *a*/*b*, where *a* and *b* are integers and *b* is not zero, as 7 or 7/3.

rations (ˈræʃənz) *pl. n.* (*sometimes sing.*) a fixed daily allowance of food, esp. to military personnel or when supplies are limited.

ratite (ˈrætaɪt) *adj.* **1.** (of flightless birds) having a breastbone that lacks a keel for the attachment of flight muscles. **2.** of or denoting the flightless birds, that have a flat breastbone, feathers lacking vanes, and reduced wings. ~*n.* **3.** a bird, such as an ostrich that belongs to this group; a flightless bird. [C19: < L *ratis* raft]

rat kangaroo *n.* any of several ratlike kangaroos that occur in Australia and Tasmania.

ratline *or* **ratlin** (ˈrætlɪn) *n. Naut.* any of a series of light lines tied across the shrouds of a sailing vessel for climbing aloft. [C15: <?]

ratoon *or* **rattoon** (ræˈtuːn) *n.* **1.** a new shoot that grows from near the root of crop plants, esp. the sugar cane, after the old growth has been cut back. ~*vb.* **2.** to propagate by such a growth. [C18: < Sp. *retoño*, < RE- + *otoñar* to sprout in autumn, < *otoño* AUTUMN]

rat race *n.* a continual routine of hectic competitive activity: *working in the City is a real rat race.*

ratsbane (ˈrætsˌbeɪn) *n.* rat poison, esp. arsenic oxide.

rat-tail *n.* **1. a.** a horse's tail that has no hairs. **b.** a horse having such a tail. **2.** a style of spoon in which the line of the handle is prolonged in a tapering moulding along the back of the bowl.

rattan *or* **ratan** (ræˈtæn) *n.* **1.** a climbing palm having tough stems used for wickerwork and canes. **2.** the stems of such a plant collectively. **3.** a stick made from one of these stems. [C17: < Malay *rōtan*]

ratter (ˈrætə) *n.* **1.** a dog or cat that catches and kills rats. **2.** another word for **rat** (sense 3).

rattle (ˈrætᵊl) *vb.* **1.** to make a rapid succession of short sharp sounds, as of loose pellets colliding when shaken in a container. **2.** to shake with such a sound. **3.** to send, move, drive, etc., with such a sound: *the car rattled along the country road.* **4.** (*intr.*; foll. by *on*) to chatter idly: *he rattled on about his work.* **5.** (*tr.*; foll. by *off, out,* etc.) to recite perfunctorily or rapidly. **6.** (*tr.*) *Inf.* to disconcert; make frightened or anxious. ~*n.* **7.** a rapid succession of short sharp sounds. **8.** a baby's toy filled with small pellets that rattle when shaken. **9.** a series of loosely connected horny segments on the tail of a rattlesnake, vibrated to produce a rattling sound. **10.** any of various European scrophulariaceous plants having a capsule in which the seeds rattle, such as the **red rattle** and the **yellow rattle**. **11.** idle chatter. **12.** *Med.* another name for **rale**. [C14: < MDu. *ratelen*, imit.] —**ˈrattly** *adj.*

rattlebrain (ˈrætᵊlˌbreɪn), **rattlehead**, *or* **rattlepate** *n. Sl.* a light-minded person, full of idle talk.

rattler (ˈrætlə) *n.* **1.** a person or thing that rattles. **2.** *Inf.* a rattlesnake.

rattlesnake (ˈrætᵊlˌsneɪk) *n.* any of the venomous New World snakes such as the **black** or **timber rattlesnake** belonging to the family of pit vipers. They have a series of loose horny segments on the tail that are vibrated to produce a buzzing or whirring sound.

rattletrap (ˈrætᵊlˌtræp) *n. Inf.* a broken-down old vehicle, esp. an old car.

rattling (ˈrætlɪŋ) *adv. Inf.* (intensifier qualifying something good, fine, etc.): *a rattling good lunch.*

ratty (ˈrætɪ) *adj.* **-tier, -tiest. 1.** *Brit. & N.Z. inf.* irritable; annoyed. **2.** *Inf.* (of the hair) straggly, unkempt, or greasy. **3.** *U.S. & Canad. sl.* shabby; dilapidated. **4.** *Austral. sl.* mad, eccentric, or odd. **5.** of, like, or full of rats. —**ˈrattily** *adv.* —**ˈrattiness** *n.*

raucous (ˈrɔːkəs) *adj.* (of voices, cries, etc.) harshly or hoarsely loud. [C18: < L *raucus* hoarse] —**ˈraucously** *adv.* —**ˈraucousness** *n.*

raunchy (ˈrɔːntʃɪ) *adj.* **-chier, -chiest.** *Sl.* **1. a.** lecherous or smutty. **b.** openly sexual; earthy. **2.** *Chiefly U.S.* slovenly; dirty. [C20: <?] —**ˈraunchily** *adv.* —**ˈraunchiness** *n.*

raupo (ˈraʊpəʊ) *n., pl.* **-pos.** a marsh reed common in New Zealand. [< Maori]

rauwolfia (rɔːˈwʊlfɪə, raʊ-) *n.* **1.** a tropical flowering tree or shrub of SE Asia with latex in its stem. **2.** the powdered root of this plant: a source of various drugs, esp. reserpine. [C19: NL, after Leonhard *Rauwolf* (died 1596), G botanist]

ravage (ˈrævɪdʒ) *vb.* **1.** to cause extensive damage to. ~*n.* **2.** (*often pl.*) destructive action: *the ravages of time.* [C17: < F, < OF *ravir* to snatch away, RAVISH] —**ˈravager** *n.*

rave (reɪv) *vb.* **1.** to utter (something) in a wild or incoherent manner, as when delirious. **2.** (*intr.*) to speak in an angry uncontrolled manner. **3.** (*intr.*) (of the sea, wind, etc.) to rage or roar. **4.** (*intr.*; foll. by *over* or *about*) *Inf.* to write or speak (about) with great enthusiasm. **5.** (*intr.*) *Brit. sl.* to enjoy oneself wildly or uninhibitedly. ~*n.* **6.** *Inf.* **a.** enthusiastic or extravagant praise. **b.** (*as modifier*): *a rave review.* **7.** Also called: **rave-up.** *Brit. sl.* a party. [C14 *raven*, apparently < OF *resver* to wander]

ravel (ˈrævᵊl) *vb.* **-elling, -elled** *or U.S.* **-eling, -eled. 1.** to tangle (threads, fibres, etc.) or (of threads, etc.) to become entangled. **2.** (often foll. by *out*) to tease or draw out (the fibres of a fabric) or (of a fabric) to fray out in loose ends; unravel. **3.** (*tr.*; usually foll. by *out*) to disentangle or resolve: *to ravel out a complicated story.* ~*n.* **4.** a tangle or complication. [C16: < MDu. *ravelen*] —**ˈraveller** *n.* —**ˈravelly** *adj.*

raven[1] (ˈreɪvᵊn) *n.* **1.** a large passerine bird of the crow family, having a large straight bill, long wedge-shaped tail, and black plumage. **2. a.** a shiny black colour. **b.** (*as adj.*): *raven hair.* [OE *hræfn*]

raven[2] (ˈrævᵊn) *vb.* **1.** to seize or seek (plunder, prey, etc.). **2.** to eat (something) voraciously or greedily. [C15: < OF *raviner* to attack impetuously; see RAVENOUS]

ravening (ˈrævənɪŋ) *adj.* (of animals) voracious; predatory. —**ˈraveningly** *adv.*

ravenous (ˈrævənəs) *adj.* **1.** famished; starving. **2.** rapacious; voracious. [C16: < OF *ravineux*, < L *rapīna* plunder, < *rapere* to seize] —**ˈravenously** *adv.* —**ˈravenousness** *n.*

raver (ˈreɪvə) *n. Brit. sl.* a person who leads a wild or uninhibited social life.

ravine (rəˈviːn) *n.* a deep narrow steep-sided valley. [C15: < OF: torrent, < L *rapīna* robbery, infl. by L *rapidus* RAPID, both < *rapere* to snatch]

raving (ˈreɪvɪŋ) *adj.* **1. a.** delirious; frenzied. **b.** (*as adv.*): *raving mad.* **2.** *Inf.* (intensifier): *a raving beauty.* ~*n.* **3.** (*usually pl.*) frenzied or wildly extravagant talk or utterances. —**ˈravingly** *adv.*

ravioli (ˌrævɪˈəʊlɪ) *n.* small squares of pasta containing a savoury mixture of meat, cheese, etc. [C19: It. dialect, lit.: little turnips, < It. *rava* turnip, < L *rāpa*]

ravish (ˈrævɪʃ) *vb.* (*tr.*) **1.** (*often passive*) to enrapture. **2.** to rape. **3.** *Arch.* to carry off by force. [C13: < OF *ravir*, < L *rapere* to seize] —**ˈravisher** *n.* —**ˈravishment** *n.*

ravishing (ˈrævɪʃɪŋ) *adj.* delightful; lovely; entrancing. —**ˈravishingly** *adv.*

raw (rɔː) *adj.* **1.** (of food) not cooked. **2.** (*prenominal*) in an unfinished, natural, or unrefined state; not treated by manufacturing or other processes: *raw materials.* **3.** (of the skin, a wound, etc.) having the surface exposed or abraded, esp. painfully. **4.** (of an edge of material) unhemmed; liable to fray. **5.** ignorant, inexperienced, or immature: *a raw recruit.* **6.** (*prenominal*) not selected or modified: *raw statistics.* **7.** frank or realistic: *a raw picture of a marriage.* **8.** (of spirits) undiluted. **9.** *Chiefly U.S.* coarse, vulgar, or obscene. **10.** (of the weather) harshly cold and damp. **11.** *Inf.* unfair; unjust (esp. in **a raw deal**). ~*n.* **12. in the raw. a.** *Inf.* without clothes; naked. **b.** in a natural or unmodified state. **13. the raw.** *Brit. inf.* a sensitive point: *his criticism touched me on the raw.* [OE *hreaw*] —**ˈrawish** *adj.* —**ˈrawly** *adv.* —**ˈrawness** *n.*

rawboned (ˈrɔːˈbəʊnd) *adj.* having a lean bony physique.

rawhide (ˈrɔːˌhaɪd) *n.* **1.** untanned hide. **2.** a whip or rope made of strips cut from such a hide.

rawinsonde (ˈreɪwɪnˌsɒnd) *n.* a hydrogen balloon carrying meteorological instruments and a radar target, enabling the velocity of winds in the atmosphere to be measured. [C20: blend of *radar* + *wind* + *radiosonde*]

raw material *n.* **1.** material on which a particular manufacturing process is carried out. **2.** a person or thing regarded as suitable for some particular purpose: *raw material for the army.*

raw silk *n.* **1.** untreated silk fibres reeled from the cocoon. **2.** fabric woven from such fibres.

ray[1] (reɪ) *n.* **1.** a narrow beam of light; gleam. **2.** a slight indication: *a ray of solace.* **3.** *Maths.* a straight line extending from a point. **4.** a thin beam of electromagnetic radiation or particles. **5.** any of the bony or cartilaginous spines of the fin of a fish that form the support for the soft part of the fin. **6.** any of the arms or branches of a starfish. ~*vb.* **7.** (of an object) to emit (light) in rays or (of light) to issue in the form of rays. **8.** (*intr.*) (of lines, etc.) to extend in rays or on radiating paths. **9.** (*tr.*) to adorn (an ornament, etc.) with rays or radiating lines. [C14: < OF *rai*, < L *radius* spoke]

ray[2] (reɪ) *n.* any of various marine selachian fishes typically having a flattened body, greatly enlarged winglike pectoral fins, gills on the undersurface of the fins, and a long whiplike tail. [C14: < OF *raie*, < L *raia*]

ray[3] (reɪ) *n. Music.* (in tonic sol-fa) the second degree of any major scale; supertonic. [C14: see GAMUT]

ray flower *or* **floret** *n.* any of the small strap-shaped flowers in the flower head of certain composite plants, such as the daisy.

ray gun *n.* (in science fiction) a gun that emits rays to paralyse, stun, or destroy.

rayless (ˈreɪlɪs) *adj.* **1.** dark; gloomy. **2.** lacking rays: *a rayless flower.*

raylet (ˈreɪlɪt) *n.* a small ray.

rayon (ˈreɪɒn) *n.* **1.** any of a number of textile fibres made from wood pulp or other forms of cellulose. **2.** any fabric made from such a fibre.

3. (*as modifier*): *a rayon shirt.* [C20: < F, < OF *rai* RAY[1]]

raze *or* **rase** (reɪz) *vb.* (*tr.*) **1.** to demolish (buildings, etc.) completely (esp. in **raze to the ground**). **2.** to delete; erase. **3.** *Arch.* to graze. [C16: < OF *raser*, < L *rādere* to scrape] —ˈ**razer** *or* ˈ**raser** *n.*

razoo (rɑːˈzuː) *n., pl.* **-zoos.** *Austral. & N.Z. inf.* an imaginary coin: *not a brass razoo; they took every last razoo.* [C20: <?]

razor (ˈreɪzə) *n.* **1.** a sharp implement used esp. for shaving the face. **2. on a razor's edge** *or* **razor-edge.** in an acute dilemma. ~*vb.* **3.** (*tr.*) to cut or shave with a razor. [C13: < OF *raseor*, < *raser* to shave; see RAZE]

razorback (ˈreɪzəˌbæk) *n.* **1.** Also called: **finback.** another name for the **common rorqual** (see **rorqual**). **2.** a wild pig of the U.S., having a narrow body, long legs, and a ridged back.

razorbill (ˈreɪzəˌbɪl) *or* **razor-billed auk** *n.* a common auk of the North Atlantic, having a thick laterally compressed bill with white markings.

razor-shell *n.* any of various sand-burrowing bivalve molluscs which have a long tubular shell. U.S. name: **razor clam.**

razor wire *n.* strong wire with pieces of sharp metal set across it at close intervals.

razz (ræz) *U.S. & Canad. sl.* ~*vb.* **1.** (*tr.*) to make fun of; deride. ~*n.* **2.** short for **raspberry** (sense 4).

razzle-dazzle (ˈræzəlˈdæzəl) *or* **razzmatazz** (ˈræzməˈtæz) *n. Sl.* **1.** noisy or showy fuss or activity. **2.** a spree or frolic. [C19: rhyming compound < DAZZLE]

Rb *the chemical symbol for* rubidium.

RC *abbrev. for:* **1.** Red Cross. **2.** Roman Catholic.

RCA *abbrev. for:* **1.** Radio Corporation of America. **2.** Royal College of Art.

RCAF *abbrev. for* Royal Canadian Air Force.

RC CH *abbrev. for* Roman Catholic Church.

RCM *abbrev. for* Royal College of Music.

RCMP *abbrev. for* Royal Canadian Mounted Police.

RCN *abbrev. for:* **1.** Royal Canadian Navy. **2.** Royal College of Nursing.

RCP *abbrev. for* Royal College of Physicians.

RCS *abbrev. for:* **1.** Royal College of Science. **2.** Royal College of Surgeons. **3.** Royal Corps of Signals.

rd *abbrev. for:* **1.** road. **2.** rod (unit of length). **3.** round. **4.** *Physics.* rutherford.

Rd *abbrev. for* Road.

RDC (in Britain, formerly) *abbrev. for* Rural District Council.

re[1] (reɪ, riː) *n. Music.* a variant of **ray**[1].

re[2] (riː) *prep.* with reference to. [C18: < L *rē*, ablative case of *rēs* thing]

▷ **Usage.** *Re*, in contexts such as *re your letter, your remarks have been noted* or *he spoke to me re your complaint*, is common in business. In general English *with reference to* is preferable in the former case and *about* or *concerning* in the latter. The use of *re* is often restricted to the letter heading.

Re *the chemical symbol for* rhenium.

RE *abbrev. for:* **1.** Religious Education. **2.** Royal Engineers.

re- *prefix.* **1.** indicating return to a previous condition, withdrawal, etc.: *rebuild; renew.* **2.** indicating repetition of an action: *remarry.* [L]

▷ **Usage.** Verbs with *re-* indicate repetition or restoration. It is unnecessary to add an adverb such as *back* or *again: This must not occur again* (not *recur again*).

reach (riːtʃ) *vb.* **1.** (*tr.*) to arrive at or get to (a place, person, etc.) in the course of movement or action: *to reach the office.* **2.** to extend as far as (a point or place): *to reach the ceiling; can you reach?* **3.** (*tr.*) to come to (a certain condition or situation): *to reach the point of starvation.* **4.** (*intr.*) to extend in influence or operation: *the Roman conquest reached throughout England.* **5.** (*tr.*) *Inf.* to pass or give (something to a person) with the outstretched hand. **6.** (*intr.;* foll. by *out, for,* or *after*) to make a movement (towards), as if to grasp or touch. **7.** (*tr.*) to make contact or communication with (someone): *we tried to reach him all day.* **8.** (*tr.*) to strike, esp. in fencing or boxing. **9.** (*tr.*) to amount to (a certain sum): *to reach five million.* **10.** (*intr.*) *Naut.* to sail on a tack with the wind on or near abeam. ~*n.* **11.** the act of reaching. **12.** the extent or distance of reaching: *within reach.* **13.** the range of influence, power, etc. **14.** an open stretch of water, esp. on a river. **15.** *Naut.* the direction or distance sailed by a vessel on one tack. [OE *rǣcan*] —ˈ**reachable** *adj.* —ˈ**reacher** *n.*

reach-me-down *n.* **1. a.** (*often pl.*) a cheaply ready-made or second-hand garment. **b.** (*as modifier*): *reach-me-down finery.* **2.** (*modifier*) not original; derivative: *reach-me-down ideas.*

react (rɪˈækt) *vb.* **1.** (*intr.;* foll. by *to, upon,* etc.) (of a person or thing) to act in response to another person, a stimulus, etc. **2.** (*intr.;* foll. by *against*) to act in an opposing or contrary manner. **3.** (*intr.*) *Physics.* to exert an equal force in the opposite direction to an acting force. **4.** *Chem.* to undergo or cause to undergo a chemical reaction. [C17: < LL *reagere*, < RE- + L *agere* to do] —**reˈactive** *adj.*

re-act (riːˈækt) *vb.* (*tr.*) to act or perform again.

reactance (rɪˈæktəns) *n.* the opposition to the flow of alternating current by the capacitance or inductance of an electrical circuit.

reactant (rɪˈæktənt) *n.* a substance that participates in a chemical reaction.

reaction (rɪˈækʃən) *n.* **1.** a response to some foregoing action or stimulus. **2.** the reciprocal action of two things acting together. **3.** opposition to change, esp. political change, or a desire to return to a former system. **4.** a response indicating a person's feelings or emotional attitude. **5.** *Med.* **a.** any effect produced by the action of a drug. **b.** any effect produced by a substance (allergen) to which a person is allergic. **6.** *Chem.* a process that involves changes in the structure and energy content of atoms, molecules, or ions. **7.** the equal and opposite force that acts on a body whenever it exerts a force on another body. —**reˈactional** *adj.*

reactionary (rɪˈækʃənərɪ, -ʃənrɪ) *or* **reactionist** *adj.* **1.** of, relating to, or characterized by reaction, esp. against radical political or social change. ~*n., pl.* **-aries** *or* **-ists.** **2.** a person opposed to radical change. —**reˈactionism** *n.*

reaction engine *or* **motor** *n.* an engine, such as a jet engine, that ejects gas at high velocity and develops its thrust from the ensuing reaction.

reaction turbine *n.* a turbine in which the working fluid is accelerated by expansion in both the static nozzles and the rotor blades.

reactivate (rɪˈæktɪˌveɪt) *vb.* (*tr.*) to make (something) active again. —**reˌactiˈvation** *n.*

reactor (rɪˈæktə) *n.* **1.** *Chem.* a substance, such as a reagent, that undergoes a reaction. **2.** short for **nuclear reactor.** **3.** a vessel in which a chemical reaction takes place. **4.** a coil of low resistance and high inductance that introduces reactance into a circuit. **5.** *Med.* a person sensitive to a particular drug or agent.

read[1] (riːd) *vb.* **reading, read** (rɛd). **1.** to comprehend the meaning of (something written or printed) by looking at and interpreting the written or printed characters. **2.** (when *tr.*, often foll. by *out*) to look at, interpret, and speak aloud (something written or printed). **3.** (*tr.*) to interpret the significance or meaning of through

---

ˌ**reabˈsorb** *vb.*
ˌ**reacˈcept** *vb.*
ˌ**reacˈceptance** *n.*
ˌ**reacˈclaim** *vb.*
ˌ**reacˈcredit** *vb.*
ˌ**reacˈcustom** *vb.*
ˌ**reaˈcidiˌfy** *vb.*
ˌ**reacˈquaint** *vb.*
ˌ**reacˈquaintance** *n.*
ˌ**reacˈquire** *vb.*
ˌ**reacquiˈsition** *n.*

scrutiny and recognition: *to read a map.* **4.** (*tr.*) to interpret or understand the meaning of (signs, characters, etc.) other than by visual means: *to read Braille.* **5.** (*tr.*) to have sufficient knowledge of (a language) to understand the written or printed word. **6.** (*tr.*) to discover or make out the true nature or mood of: *to read someone's mind.* **7.** to interpret or understand (something read) in a specified way: *I read this speech as satire.* **8.** (*tr.*) to adopt as a reading in a particular passage: *for "boon" read "bone".* **9.** (*intr.*) to have or contain a certain form or wording: *the sentence reads as follows.* **10.** to undertake a course of study in (a subject): *to read history.* **11.** to gain knowledge by reading: *he read about the war.* **12.** (*tr.*) to register, indicate, or show: *the meter reads 100.* **13.** (*tr.*) to put into a specified condition by reading: *to read a child to sleep.* **14.** (*tr.*) to hear and understand, esp. when using a two-way radio: *we are reading you loud and clear.* **15.** *Computers.* to obtain (data) from a storage device, such as magnetic tape. **16. read a lesson** (*or* **lecture**). *Inf.* to censure or reprimand. ~*n.* **17.** matter suitable for reading: *this book is a very good read.* **18.** the act or a spell of reading. ~See also **read into, read out,** etc. [OE *rǣdan* to advise, explain]

read[2] (rɛd) *vb.* **1.** the past tense and past participle of **read**[1]. ~*adj.* **2.** having knowledge gained from books (esp. in **widely read** and **well-read**). **3. take (something) as read.** to take (something) for granted as a fact; understand or presume.

readable (ˈriːdəbᵊl) *adj.* **1.** (of handwriting, etc.) able to be read or deciphered; legible. **2.** (of style of writing) interesting, easy, or pleasant to read. —ˌ**readaˈbility** *or* ˈ**readableness** *n.* —ˈ**readably** *adv.*

reader (ˈriːdə) *n.* **1.** a person who reads. **2.** *Chiefly Brit.* a member of staff below a professor but above a senior lecturer at a university. **3. a.** a book that is part of a planned series for those learning to read. **b.** a standard textbook, esp. for foreign-language learning. **4.** a person who reads aloud in public. **5.** a person who reads and assesses the merit of manuscripts submitted to a publisher. **6.** a proofreader. **7.** short for **lay reader.**

readership (ˈriːdəʃɪp) *n.* all the readers collectively of a particular publication or author: *a readership of five million.*

reading (ˈriːdɪŋ) *n.* **1. a.** the act of a person who reads. **b.** (*as modifier*): *a reading room.* **2. a.** ability to read. **b.** (*as modifier*): *a child of reading age.* **3.** any matter that can be read; written or printed text. **4.** a public recital or rendering of a literary work. **5.** the form of a particular word or passage in a given text, esp. where more than one version exists. **6.** an interpretation, as of a piece of music, a situation, or something said or written. **7.** knowledge gained from books: *a person of little reading.* **8.** a measurement indicated by a gauge, dial, scientific instrument, etc. **9.** *Parliamentary procedure.* **a.** the formal recital of the body or title of a bill in a legislative assembly in order to begin one of the stages of its passage. **b.** one of the three stages in the passage of a bill through a legislative assembly. See **first reading, second reading, third reading.** **10.** the formal recital of something written, esp. a will.

read into (riːd) *vb.* (*tr., prep.*) to discern in or infer from a statement (meanings not intended by the speaker or writer).

read out (riːd) *vb.* (*adv.*) **1.** (*tr.*) to read (something) aloud. **2.** (*tr.*) *U.S.* to expel (someone) from a political party or other society. **3.** to retrieve information from a computer memory or storage device. ~*n.* **read-out.** **4. a.** the act of retrieving information from a computer memory or storage device. **b.** the information retrieved.

read up (riːd) *vb.* (*adv.;* when *intr.,* often foll. by *on*) to acquire information about (a subject) by reading intensively.

read-write head (ˈriːdˈraɪt) *n. Computers.* an electromagnet that can both read and write information on a magnetic tape or disk.

ready (ˈrɛdɪ) *adj.* **readier, readiest.** **1.** in a state of completion or preparedness, as for use or action. **2.** willing or eager: *ready helpers.* **3.** prompt or rapid: *a ready response.* **4.** (*prenominal*) quick in perceiving; intelligent: *a ready mind.* **5.** (*postpositive*) (foll. by *to*) on the point (of) or liable (to): *ready to collapse.* **6.** (*postpositive*) conveniently near (esp. in **ready to hand**). **7. make** *or* **get ready.** to prepare (oneself or something) for use or action. ~*n.* **8.** *Inf.* (*often preceded by* the) short for **ready money.** **9. at** *or* **to the ready. a.** (of a rifle) in the position adopted prior to aiming and firing. **b.** poised for use or action: *with pen at the ready.* ~*vb.* **readying, readied.** (*tr.*) **10.** to put in a state of readiness; prepare. [OE (*ge*)*rǣde*] —ˈ**readily** *adv.* —ˈ**readiness** *n.*

ready-made *adj.* **1.** made for purchase and immediate use by any customer. **2.** extremely convenient or ideally suited: *a ready-made solution.* **3.** unoriginal or conventional: *ready-made phrases.* ~*n.* **4.** a ready-made article, esp. a garment.

ready-mix *n.* **1.** (*modifier*) consisting of ingredients blended in advance, esp. of food that is ready to cook or eat after addition of milk or water: *a ready-mix cake.* **2.** concrete that is mixed before or during delivery to a building site.

ready money *n.* funds for immediate use; cash. Also: **the ready, the readies.**

ready reckoner *n.* a table of numbers used to facilitate simple calculations, esp. one for working out interest, etc.

ready-to-wear *adj.* (**ready to wear** *when postpositive*). **1.** (of clothes) not tailored for the wearer; of a standard size. ~*n.* **2.** an article or suit of such clothes.

reafforest (ˌriːəˈfɒrɪst) *or* **reforest** *vb.* (*tr.*) to replant (an area that was formerly forested). —ˌ**reafˌforestˈation** *or* ˌ**reforestˈation** *n.*

reagent (riːˈeɪdʒənt) *n.* a substance for use in a chemical reaction, esp. for use in chemical synthesis and analysis.

real[1] (rɪəl) *adj.* **1.** existing or occurring in the physical world; not imaginary, fictitious, or theoretical; actual. **2.** (*prenominal*) true; actual; not false: *the real reason.* **3.** (*prenominal*) deserving the name; rightly so called: *a real friend.* **4.** not artificial or simulated; genuine: *real fur.* **5.** *Philosophy.* existent or relating to actual existence (as opposed to nonexistent, potential, contingent, or apparent). **6.** (*prenominal*) *Econ.* (of prices, incomes, etc.) considered in terms of purchasing power rather than nominal currency value. **7.** (*prenominal*) denoting or relating to immovable property such as land and tenements: *real estate.* **8.** *Maths.* involving or containing real numbers alone; having no imaginary part. **9.** *Inf.* (intensifier): *a real genius.* **10. the real thing.** the genuine article, not a substitute. ~*n.* **11. for real.** *Sl.* not as a test or trial; in earnest. **12. the real.** that which exists in fact; reality. [C15: < OF *réel,* < LL *reālis,* < L *rēs* thing] —ˈ**realness** *n.*

real[2] (reɪˈɑːl) *n., pl.* **reals** *or* **reales** (*Spanish* reˈales). a former small Spanish or Spanish-American silver coin. [C17: < Sp., lit.: royal, < L *rēgālis;* see REGAL]

real ale *n.* any beer which is allowed to ferment in the barrel and which is pumped up from the keg without using carbon dioxide.

ˌ**reaˈdapt** *vb.*
ˌ**readˈdress** *vb.*
ˌ**readˈjourn** *vb.*
ˌ**readˈjournment** *n.*
ˌ**reaˈdjust** *vb.*
ˌ**readˈmission** *n.*
ˌ**readˈmit** *vb.*
ˌ**reaˈdopt** *vb.*
ˌ**reafˈfirm** *vb.*
ˌ**reaffirˈmation** *n.*

real estate *n.* another term, chiefly U.S. and Canad., for **real property.**

realgar (rɪˈælgə) *n.* a rare orange-red soft mineral consisting of arsenic sulphide in monoclinic crystalline form. [C14: via Med. L < Ar. *rahj al-ghar* powder of the mine]

realism (ˈrɪəˌlɪzəm) *n.* **1.** awareness or acceptance of the physical universe, events, etc., as they are, as opposed to the abstract or ideal. **2.** a style of painting and sculpture that seeks to represent the familiar or typical in real life. **3.** any similar style in other arts, esp. literature. **4.** *Philosophy.* the thesis that general terms refer to entities that have a real existence separate from the individuals which fall under them. **5.** *Philosophy.* the theory that physical objects continue to exist whether they are perceived or not. —**ˈrealist** *n.*

realistic (ˌrɪəˈlɪstɪk) *adj.* **1.** showing awareness and acceptance of reality. **2.** practical or pragmatic rather than ideal or moral. **3.** (of a book, etc.) depicting what is real and actual. **4.** of or relating to philosophical realism. —ˌ**realˈistically** *adv.*

reality (rɪˈælɪtɪ) *n., pl.* **-ties. 1.** the state of things as they are or appear to be, rather than as one might wish them to be. **2.** something that is real. **3.** the state of being real. **4.** *Philosophy.* **a.** that which exists, independent of human awareness. **b.** the totality of facts. **5. in reality.** actually; in fact.

realize *or* **-ise** (ˈrɪəˌlaɪz) *vb.* **1.** (when *tr., may take a clause as object*) to become conscious or aware of (something). **2.** (*tr., often passive*) to bring (a plan, ambition, etc.) to fruition. **3.** (*tr.*) to give (a drama or film) the appearance of reality. **4.** (*tr.*) (of goods, property, etc.) to sell for or make (a certain sum): *this table realized £800.* **5.** (*tr.*) to convert (property or goods) into cash. **6.** (*tr.*) (of a musicologist or performer) to reconstruct (a composition) from an incomplete set of parts. —**ˈrealˌizable** *or* **-ˌisable** *adj.* —**ˈrealˌizably** *or* **-ˌisably** *adv.* —ˌ**realiˈzation** *or* **-iˈsation** *n.* —**ˈrealˌizer** *or* **-ˌiser** *n.*

real life *n.* actual human life, as lived by real people, esp. contrasted with the lives of fictional characters: *miracles don't happen in real life.*

really (ˈrɪəlɪ) *adv.* **1.** in reality; in actuality; assuredly: *it's really quite harmless.* **2.** truly; genuinely: *really beautiful.* ~*interj.* **3.** an exclamation of dismay, disapproval, doubt, surprise, etc. **4. not really?** an exclamation of surprise or polite doubt.

▷ **Usage.** See at **very.**

realm (rɛlm) *n.* **1.** a royal domain; kingdom: *peer of the realm.* **2.** a field of interest, study, etc.: *the realm of the occult.* [C13: < OF *reialme,* < L *regimen* rule, infl. by OF *reial,* < L *rēgālis* REGAL]

real number *n.* any rational or irrational number. See **number.**

real presence *n.* the doctrine that the body of Christ is actually present in the Eucharist.

real property *n. Property law.* immoveable property, esp. freehold land. Cf. **personal property.**

real tennis *n.* an ancient form of tennis played in a four-walled indoor court.

real-time *adj.* denoting or relating to a data-processing system in which a computer is on-line to a source of data and processes the data as it is generated.

realtor (ˈrɪəltə, -ˌtɔː) *n.* a U.S. word for an **estate agent,** esp. an accredited one. [C20: < REALTY + -OR[1]]

realty (ˈrɪəltɪ) *n.* another term for **real property.**

ream[1] (riːm) *n.* **1.** a number of sheets of paper, formerly 480 sheets (**short ream**), now 500 sheets (**long ream**) or 516 sheets (**printer's ream** or **perfect ream**). One ream is equal to 20 quires. **2.** (*often pl.*) *Inf.* a large quantity, esp. of written matter: *he wrote reams.* [C14: < OF, < Sp., < Ar. *rizmah* bale]

ream[2] (riːm) *vb.* (*tr.*) **1.** to enlarge (a hole) by use of a reamer. **2.** *U.S.* to extract (juice) from (a citrus fruit) using a reamer. [C19: ? < C14 *remen* to open up, < OE *rȳman* to widen]

reamer (ˈriːmə) *n.* **1.** a steel tool with a cylindrical or tapered shank around which longitudinal teeth are ground, used for smoothing the bores of holes accurately to size. **2.** *U.S.* a utensil with a conical projection used for extracting juice from citrus fruits.

reap (riːp) *vb.* **1.** to cut or harvest (a crop) from (a field). **2.** (*tr.*) to gain or get (something) as a reward for or result of some action or enterprise. [OE *riopan*] —**ˈreapable** *adj.*

reaper (ˈriːpə) *n.* **1.** a person who reaps or a machine for reaping. **2. the grim reaper.** death.

rear[1] (rɪə) *n.* **1.** the back or hind part. **2.** the area or position that lies at the back: *a garden at the rear of the house.* **3.** the section of a military force farthest from the front. **4.** an informal word for **buttocks** (see **buttock**). **5. bring up the rear.** to be at the back in a procession, race, etc. **6. in the rear.** at the back. **7.** (*modifier*) of or in the rear: *the rear side.* [C17: prob. < REARWARD or REARGUARD]

rear[2] (rɪə) *vb.* **1.** (*tr.*) to care for and educate (children) until maturity; raise. **2.** (*tr.*) to breed (animals) or grow (plants). **3.** (*tr.*) to place or lift (a ladder, etc.) upright. **4.** (*tr.*) to erect (a monument, building, etc.). **5.** (*intr.; often foll. by up*) (esp. of horses) to lift the front legs in the air and stand nearly upright. **6.** (*intr.; often foll. by up or over*) (esp. of tall buildings) to rise high; tower. **7.** (*intr.*) to start with anger, resentment, etc. [OE *rǣran*] —**ˈrearer** *n.*

rear admiral *n.* an officer holding flag rank in any of certain navies junior to a vice admiral.

rearguard (ˈrɪəˌgɑːd) *n.* **1.** a detachment detailed to protect the rear of a military formation, esp. in retreat. **2.** an entrenched or conservative element, as in a political party. **3.** (*modifier*) of, relating to, or characteristic of a rearguard: *a rearguard action.* [C15: < OF *rereguarde,* < *rer,* < L *retro* back + *guarde* GUARD]

rear light *or* **lamp** *n.* a red light, usually one of a pair, attached to the rear of a motor vehicle. U.S. and Canad. names: **taillight, tail lamp.**

rearm (riːˈɑːm) *vb.* **1.** to arm again. **2.** (*tr.*) to equip (an army, etc.) with better weapons. —**reˈarmament** *n.*

rearmost (ˈrɪəˌməʊst) *adj.* nearest the rear; coming last.

rear-view mirror *n.* a mirror on a motor vehicle enabling the driver to see traffic behind him.

rearward (ˈrɪəwəd) *adj., adv.* **1.** Also (for adv. only): **rearwards.** towards or in the rear. ~*n.* **2.** a position in the rear, esp. the rear division of a military formation. [C14 (*as n.:* the part of an army behind the main body of troops): < Anglo-F *rerewarde,* var. of *reregarde;* see REARGUARD]

reason (ˈriːzᵊn) *n.* **1.** the faculty of rational argument, deduction, judgment, etc. **2.** sound mind; sanity. **3.** a cause or motive, as for a belief, action, etc. **4.** an argument in favour or a justification for something. **5.** *Philosophy.* the intellect regarded as a source of knowledge, as contrasted with experience. **6.** *Logic.* a premise

---

ˌ**reaˈlign** *vb.*
ˌ**reaˈlignment** *n.*
reˈalloˌcate *vb.*
ˌ**realloˈcation** *n.*
ˌ**realˈlot** *vb.*
reˈalter *vb.*
ˌ**realterˈation** *n.*
reˈanaˌlyse *vb.*
ˌ**reaˈnalysis** *n.*
reˈaniˌmate *vb.*
ˌ**reaniˈmation** *n.*
ˌ**reapˈpear** *vb.*
ˌ**reapˈpearance** *n.*
ˌ**reappliˈcation** *n.*
ˌ**reapˈply** *vb.*
ˌ**reapˈpoint** *vb.*
ˌ**reapˈpointment** *n.*
ˌ**reapˈportion** *vb.*
ˌ**reapˈpraisal** *n.*
ˌ**reapˈpraise** *vb.*
reˈargue *vb.*
ˌ**rearˈrange** *vb.*
ˌ**rearˈrangement** *n.*
ˌ**rearˈrest** *vb., n.*

of an argument in favour of the given conclusion. **7. by reason of.** because of. **8. in** *or* **within reason.** within moderate or justifiable bounds. **9. it stands to reason.** it is logical or obvious. **10. listen to reason.** to be persuaded peaceably. **11. reasons of State.** political justifications for an immoral act. ~*vb.* **12.** (when *tr., takes a clause as object*) to think logically or draw (logical conclusions) from facts or premises. **13.** (*intr.;* usually foll. by *with*) to seek to persuade by reasoning. **14.** (*tr.;* often foll. by *out*) to work out or resolve (a problem) by reasoning. [C13: < OF *reisun,* < L *ratiō* reckoning, < *rērī* to think] —**'reasoner** *n.*

▷ **Usage.** Careful users of English avoid the expression *the reason is because...* since *the reason is...* and *because* mean the same thing. *Because* should be replaced by *that: the reason is that...*

reasonable ('riːzənəbᵊl) *adj.* **1.** showing reason or sound judgment. **2.** having the ability to reason. **3.** having modest or moderate expectations. **4.** moderate in price. **5.** fair; average: *reasonable weather.* —**'reasonably** *adv.* —**'reasonableness** *n.*

reasoned ('riːzᵊnd) *adj.* well thought-out or well presented: *a reasoned explanation.*

reasoning ('riːzənɪŋ) *n.* **1.** the act or process of drawing conclusions from facts, evidence, etc. **2.** the arguments, proofs, etc., so adduced.

reassure (ˌriːə'ʃʊə) *vb.* (*tr.*) **1.** to relieve (someone) of anxieties; restore confidence to. **2.** to insure again. —**ˌreas'surance** *n.* —**ˌreas'surer** *n.* —**ˌreas'suringly** *adv.*

Réaumur ('reɪəˌmjʊə) *adj.* indicating measurement on the Réaumur scale.

Réaumur scale *n.* a scale of temperature in which the freezing point of water is taken as 0° and the boiling point as 80°. [C18: after René de *Réaumur* (1683–1757), F physicist, who introduced it]

reave (riːv) *vb.* **reaving, reaved** *or* **reft.** *Arch.* **1.** to carry off (property, prisoners, etc.) by force. **2.** (*tr.;* foll. by *of*) to deprive; strip. See **reive.** [OE *reāfian*]

rebate[1] *n.* ('riːbeɪt). **1.** a refund of a fraction of the amount payable; discount. ~*vb.* (rɪ'beɪt). (*tr.*) **2.** to deduct (a part) of a payment from (the total). **3.** *Arch.* to reduce. [C15: < OF *rabattre* to beat down, hence reduce, < RE- + *abatre* to put down] —**re'batable** *or* **re'bateable** *adj.* —**'rebater** *n.*

rebate[2] ('riːbeɪt, 'ræbɪt) *n., vb.* another word for **rabbet.**

rebec *or* **rebeck** ('riːbɛk) *n.* a medieval stringed instrument resembling the violin but having a lute-shaped body. [C16: < OF *rebebe,* < Ar. *rebāb;* ? infl. by OF *bec* beak]

rebel *vb.* (rɪ'bɛl), **-belling, -belled.** (*intr.;* often foll. by *against*) **1.** to resist or rise up against a government or authority, esp. by force of arms. **2.** to dissent from an accepted moral code or convention of behaviour, etc. **3.** to show repugnance (towards). ~*n.* ('rɛbᵊl). **4. a.** a person who rebels. **b.** (*as modifier*): *a rebel soldier.* **5.** a person who dissents from some accepted moral code or convention of behaviour, etc. [C13: < OF *rebelle,* < L *rebellis* insurgent, < RE- + *bellum* war]

rebellion (rɪ'bɛljən) *n.* **1.** organized opposition to a government or other authority. **2.** dissent from an accepted moral code or convention of behaviour, etc. [C14: via OF < L *rebelliō* revolt (of those conquered); see REBEL]

rebellious (rɪ'bɛljəs) *adj.* **1.** showing a tendency towards rebellion. **2.** (of a problem, etc.) difficult to overcome; refractory. —**re'belliously** *adv.* —**re'belliousness** *n.*

rebirth (riː'bɜːθ) *n.* **1.** a revival or renaissance: *the rebirth of learning.* **2.** a second or new birth.

rebore *n.* ('riːˌbɔː). **1.** the process of boring out the cylinders of a worn reciprocating engine and fitting oversize pistons. ~*vb.* (riː'bɔː). **2.** (*tr.*) to carry out this process.

rebound *vb.* (rɪ'baʊnd). (*intr.*) **1.** to spring back, as from a sudden impact. **2.** to misfire, esp. so as to hurt the perpetrator. ~*n.* ('riːbaʊnd). **3.** the act or an instance of rebounding. **4. on the rebound. a.** in the act of springing back. **b.** *Inf.* in a state of recovering from rejection, etc.: *he married her on the rebound from an unhappy love affair.* [C14: < OF *rebondir,* < RE- + *bondir* to BOUND[2]]

rebounder (rɪ'baʊndə) *n.* a type of small trampoline used for aerobic exercising.

rebozo (rɪ'bəʊzəʊ) *n., pl.* **-zos.** a long wool or linen scarf covering the shoulders and head, worn by Latin American women. [C19: < Sp., < *rebozar* to muffle]

rebuff (rɪ'bʌf) *vb.* (*tr.*) **1.** to snub, reject, or refuse (help, sympathy, etc.). **2.** to beat back (an attack); repel. ~*n.* **3.** a blunt refusal or rejection; snub. [C16: < OF *rebuffer,* < It., < *ribuffo* a reprimand, < *ri-* RE- + *buffo* puff, gust, apparently imit.]

rebuke (rɪ'bjuːk) *vb.* **1.** (*tr.*) to scold or reprimand (someone). ~*n.* **2.** a reprimand or scolding. [C14: < OF *rebuker,* < RE- + *buchier* to hack down, < *busche* log, of Gmc origin] —**re'bukable** *adj.* —**re'buker** *n.* —**re'bukingly** *adv.*

rebus ('riːbəs) *n., pl.* **-buses. 1.** a puzzle consisting of pictures, symbols, etc., representing syllables and words; the word *hear* might be represented by H and a picture of an ear. **2.** a heraldic device that is a pictorial representation of the name of the bearer. [C17: < F *rébus,* < L *rēbus* by things < RES]

rebut (rɪ'bʌt) *vb.* **-butting, -butted.** (*tr.*) to refute or disprove, esp. by offering a contrary contention or argument. [C13: < OF *reboter,* < RE- + *boter* to thrust, BUTT[3]] —**re'buttable** *adj.* —**re'buttal** *n.*

rebutter (rɪ'bʌtə) *n.* **1.** *Law.* a defendant's pleading in reply to a plaintiff's surrejoinder. **2.** a person who rebuts.

rec. *abbrev. for:* **1.** receipt. **2.** recipe. **3.** record.

recalcitrant (rɪ'kælsɪtrənt) *adj.* **1.** not susceptible to control; refractory. ~*n.* **2.** a recalcitrant person. [C19: via F < L, < RE- + *calcitrāre* to kick, < *calx* heel] —**re'calcitrance** *n.*

recalescence (ˌriːkə'lɛsəns) *n.* a sudden spontaneous increase in the temperature of cooling iron. [C19: < L *recalēscere* to grow warm again, < RE- + *calēscere,* < *calēre* to be hot] —**ˌrecal'esce** *vb.* (*intr.*) —**ˌreca'lescent** *adj.*

recall (rɪ'kɔːl) *vb.* (*tr.*) **1.** (*may take a clause as object*) to bring back to mind; recollect; remember. **2.** to order to return. **3.** to revoke or take back. **4.** to cause (one's thoughts, attention, etc.) to return from a reverie or digression. ~*n.* **5.** the act of recalling or state of being recalled. **6.** revocation or cancellation. **7.** the ability to remember things; recollection. **8.** *Mil.* (formerly) a signal to call back troops, etc. **9.** *U.S.* the process by which elected officials may be deprived of office by popular vote. —**re'callable** *adj.*

recant (rɪ'kænt) *vb.* to repudiate or withdraw (a former belief or statement), esp. formally in public. [C16: < L *recantāre,* < RE- + *cantāre* to

---

ˌreas'semble *vb.*
ˌreas'sembly *n.*
ˌreas'sert *vb.*
ˌreas'sertion *n.*
ˌreas'sess *vb.*
ˌreas'sessment *n.*
ˌreas'sign *vb.*
ˌreas'sume *vb.*
ˌreas'sumption *n.*
ˌreat'tain *vb.*
ˌreat'tempt *vb., n.*
ˌrea'waken *vb.*
re'baptism *n.*
ˌrebap'tize *or* **-'tise** *vb.*
re'bid *vb.*
re'bind *vb.*
re'born *adj.*
re'broadcast *vb.*
re'build *vb.*
re'burial *n.*
re'bury *vb.*
re'calcuˌlate *vb.*

sing] —**recantation** (ˌriːkænˈteɪʃən) *n.* —**reˈcanter** *n.*

recap *vb.* (ˈriːˌkæp, riːˈkæp), **-capping, -capped,** *n.* (ˈriːˌkæp). *Inf.* short for **recapitulate** or **recapitulation.** —**reˈcappable** *adj.*

recapitulate (ˌriːkəˈpɪtjʊˌleɪt) *vb.* **1.** to restate the main points of (an argument, speech, etc.). **2.** (*tr.*) (of an animal) to repeat (stages of its evolutionary development) during the embryonic stages of its life. [C16: < LL *recapitulāre*, lit.: to put back under headings; see CAPITULATE] —ˌ**recaˈpitulative** *or* ˌ**recaˈpitulatory** *adj.*

recapitulation (ˌriːkəˌpɪtjʊˈleɪʃən) *n.* **1.** the act of recapitulating, esp. summing up, as at the end of a speech. **2.** Also called: **palingenesis.** *Biol.* the apparent repetition in the embryonic development of an animal of the changes that occurred during its evolutionary history. **3.** *Music.* the repeating of earlier themes, esp. in the final section of a movement in sonata form.

recapture (riːˈkæptʃə) *vb.* (*tr.*) **1.** to capture or take again. **2.** to recover, renew, or repeat (a lost or former ability, sensation, etc.). ~*n.* **3.** the act of recapturing or fact of being recaptured.

recce (ˈrɛkɪ) *n., vb.,* **-ceing, -ced** *or* **-ceed.** a slang word for **reconnaissance** or **reconnoitre.**

recd *or* **rec'd** *abbrev. for* received.

recede (rɪˈsiːd) *vb.* (*intr.*) **1.** to withdraw from a point or limit; go back: *the tide receded.* **2.** to become more distant: *hopes of rescue receded.* **3.** to slope backwards: *apes have receding foreheads.* **4. a.** (of a man's hair) to cease to grow at the temples and above the forehead. **b.** (of a man) to start to go bald in this way. **5.** to decline in value. **6.** (usually foll. by *from*) to draw back or retreat, as from a promise. [C15: < L *recēdere* to go back, < RE- + *cēdere* to yield]

re-cede (riːˈsiːd) *vb.* (*tr.*) to restore to a former owner.

receipt (rɪˈsiːt) *n.* **1.** a written acknowledgment by a receiver of money, goods, etc., that payment or delivery has been made. **2.** the act of receiving or fact of being received. **3.** (*usually pl.*) an amount or article received. **4.** *Obs.* another word for **recipe.** ~*vb.* **5.** (*tr.*) to acknowledge payment of (a bill), as by marking it. [C14: < OF *receite*, < Med. L *recepta*, < L *recipere* to RECEIVE]

receivable (rɪˈsiːvəbᵊl) *adj.* **1.** suitable for or capable of being received, esp. as payment or legal tender. **2.** (of a bill, etc.) awaiting payment: *accounts receivable.* ~*n.* **3.** (*usually pl.*) the part of the assets of a business represented by accounts due for payment.

receive (rɪˈsiːv) *vb.* (*mainly tr.*) **1.** to take (something offered) into one's hand or possession. **2.** to have (an honour, blessing, etc.) bestowed. **3.** to accept delivery or transmission of (a letter, etc.). **4.** to be informed of (news). **5.** to hear and consent to or acknowledge (a confession, etc.). **6.** (of a container) to take or hold (a substance, commodity, or certain amount). **7.** to support or sustain (the weight of something); bear. **8.** to apprehend or perceive (ideas, etc.). **9.** to experience, undergo, or meet with: *to receive a crack on the skull.* **10.** (*also intr.*) to be at home to (visitors). **11.** to greet or welcome (guests), esp. in formal style. **12.** to admit (a person) to a place, society, condition, etc.: *he was received into the priesthood.* **13.** to accept or acknowledge (a precept or principle) as true or valid. **14.** to convert (incoming radio signals) into sounds, pictures, etc., by means of a receiver. **15.** (*also intr.*) *Tennis, etc.* to play at the other end from the server. **16.** (*also intr.*) to partake of (the Christian Eucharist). **17.** (*intr.*) *Chiefly Brit.* to buy and sell stolen goods. [C13: < OF *receivre*, < L *recipere*, < RE- + *capere* to take]

received (rɪˈsiːvd) *adj.* generally accepted or believed: *received wisdom.*

Received Pronunciation *n.* the accent of standard Southern British English. Abbrev.: **RP.**

receiver (rɪˈsiːvə) *n.* **1.** a person who receives something; recipient. **2.** a person appointed by a court to manage property pending the outcome of litigation, during the infancy of the owner, or after the owner has been declared bankrupt or insane. **3.** *Chiefly Brit.* a person who receives stolen goods knowing that they have been stolen. **4.** the equipment in a telephone, radio, or television that receives incoming electrical signals or modulated radio waves and converts them into the original audio or video signals. **5.** the detachable part of a telephone that is held to the ear. **6.** *Chem.* a vessel in which the distillate is collected during distillation. **7.** *U.S. sport.* a player whose function is to receive the ball.

receivership (rɪˈsiːvəʃɪp) *n. Law.* **1.** the office or function of a receiver. **2.** the condition of being administered by a receiver.

receiving order *n. Brit.* a court order appointing a receiver to manage the property of a debtor or bankrupt.

recension (rɪˈsɛnʃən) *n.* **1.** a critical revision of a literary work. **2.** a text revised in this way. [C17: < L *recēnsiō*, < *recēnsēre*, < RE- + *cēnsēre* to assess]

recent (ˈriːsᵊnt) *adj.* having appeared, happened, or been made not long ago; modern, fresh, or new. [C16: < L *recens* fresh; rel. to Gk *kainos* new] —ˈ**recently** *adv.* —ˈ**recentness** *or* ˈ**recency** *n.*

Recent (ˈriːsᵊnt) *adj., n. Geol.* another word for **Holocene.**

receptacle (rɪˈsɛptəkᵊl) *n.* **1.** an object that holds something; container. **2.** *Bot.* **a.** the enlarged or modified tip of the flower stalk that bears the parts of the flower. **b.** the part of lower plants that bears the reproductive organs or spores. [C15: < L *receptāculum* store-place, < *receptāre*, < *recipere* to RECEIVE]

reception (rɪˈsɛpʃən) *n.* **1.** the act of receiving or state of being received. **2.** the manner in which something, such as a guest or a new idea, is received: *a cold reception.* **3.** a formal party for guests, such as after a wedding. **4.** an area in an office, hotel, etc., where visitors or guests are received and appointments or reservations dealt with. **5.** short for **reception room.** **6.** the quality or fidelity of a received radio broadcast: *the reception was poor.* [C14: < L *receptiō*, < *recipere* to RECEIVE]

reception centre *n.* temporary accommodation provided in an emergency for homeless people.

receptionist (rɪˈsɛpʃənɪst) *n.* a person employed in an office, surgery, etc., to receive clients or guests, arrange appointments, etc.

reception room *n.* **1.** a room in a private house suitable for entertaining guests. **2.** a room in a hotel suitable for receptions, etc.

receptive (rɪˈsɛptɪv) *adj.* **1.** able to apprehend quickly. **2.** tending to receive new ideas or suggestions favourably. **3.** able to hold or receive. —**reˈceptively** *adv.* —**receptivity** (ˌriːsɛpˈtɪvɪtɪ) *or* **reˈceptiveness** *n.*

receptor (rɪˈsɛptə) *n.* **1.** *Physiol.* a sensory nerve ending that changes specific stimuli into nerve impulses. **2.** any of various devices that receive information, signals, etc.

recess *n.* (rɪˈsɛs, ˈriːsɛs). **1.** a space, such as a niche or alcove, set back or indented. **2.** (*often pl.*) a secluded or secret place: *recesses of the mind.* **3.** a cessation of business, such as the closure of Parliament during a vacation. **4.** *Anat.* a small cavity or depression in a bodily organ. **5.** *U.S. & Canad.* a break between classes at a school. ~*vb.* (rɪˈsɛs). **6.** (*tr.*) to place or set (something) in a recess. **7.** (*tr.*) to build a recess in (a wall, etc.). [C16: < L *recessus* a retreat, < *recēdere* to RECEDE]

recession[1] (rɪˈsɛʃən) *n.* **1.** a temporary depression in economic activity or prosperity. **2.** the

---

reˌcapitaliˈzation *or* **-iˈsation** *n.*
reˈcapitalˌize *or* **-ˌise** *vb.*
reˈcast *vb.*

withdrawal of the clergy and choir in procession after a church service. **3.** the act of receding. **4.** a part of a building, wall, etc., that recedes. [C17: < L *recessio;* see RECESS]

recession[2] (riːˈsɛʃən) *n.* the act of restoring possession to a former owner. [C19: < RE- + CESSION]

recessional (rɪˈsɛʃənᵊl) *adj.* **1.** of or relating to recession. ~*n.* **2.** a hymn sung as the clergy and choir withdraw after a church service.

recessive (rɪˈsɛsɪv) *adj.* **1.** tending to recede or go back. **2.** *Genetics.* **a.** (of a gene) capable of producing its characteristic phenotype in the organism only when its allele is identical. **b.** (of a character) controlled by such a gene. Cf. **dominant** (sense 4). **3.** *Linguistics.* (of stress) tending to be placed on or near the initial syllable of a polysyllabic word. ~*n.* **4.** *Genetics.* a recessive gene or character. —**reˈcessively** *adv.* —**reˈcessiveness** *n.*

recharge (ˌriːˈtʃɑːdʒ) *vb.* (*tr.*) **1.** to cause (an accumulator, capacitor, etc.) to take up and store electricity again. **2.** to revive or renew (one's energies) (esp. in **recharge one's batteries**). —**reˈchargeable** *adj.*

recherché (rəˈʃɛəʃeɪ) *adj.* **1.** known only to connoisseurs; choice or rare. **2.** studiedly refined or elegant. [C18: < F: p.p. of *rechercher* to make a thorough search for]

recidivism (rɪˈsɪdɪˌvɪzəm) *n.* habitual relapse into crime. [C19: < L *recidīvus* falling back, < RE- + *cadere* to fall] —**reˈcidivist** *n., adj.* —**reˌcidiˈvistic** *or* **reˈcidivous** *adj.*

recipe (ˈrɛsɪpɪ) *n.* **1.** a list of ingredients and directions for making something, esp. when preparing food. **2.** *Med.* (formerly) a medical prescription. **3.** a method for achieving some desired objective: *a recipe for success.* [C14: < L, lit.: take (it)! < *recipere* to take]

recipient (rɪˈsɪpɪənt) *n.* **1.** a person who or thing that receives. ~*adj.* **2.** receptive. [C16: via F < L, < *recipere* to RECEIVE] —**reˈcipience** *or* **reˈcipiency** *n.*

reciprocal (rɪˈsɪprəkᵊl) *adj.* **1.** of, relating to, or designating something given by each of two people, countries, etc., to the other; mutual: *reciprocal trade.* **2.** given or done in return: *a reciprocal favour.* **3.** (of a pronoun) indicating that action is given and received by each subject; for example, *each other* in *they started to shout at each other.* **4.** *Maths.* of or relating to a number or quantity divided into one. ~*n.* **5.** something that is reciprocal. **6.** Also called: **inverse.** *Maths.* a number or quantity that when multiplied by a given number or quantity gives a product of one: *the reciprocal of 2 is 0.5.* [C16: < L *reciprocus* alternating] —**reˌciproˈcality** *n.* —**reˈciprocally** *adv.*

reciprocate (rɪˈsɪprəˌkeɪt) *vb.* **1.** to give or feel in return. **2.** to move or cause to move backwards and forwards. **3.** (*intr.*) to be correspondent or equivalent. [C17: < L *reciprocāre,* < *reciprocus* RECIPROCAL] —**reˌciproˈcation** *n.* —**reˈciprocative** *or* **reˈciproˌcatory** *adj.* —**reˈciproˌcator** *n.*

reciprocating engine *n.* an engine in which one or more pistons move backwards and forwards inside a cylinder or cylinders.

reciprocity (ˌrɛsɪˈprɒsɪtɪ) *n.* **1.** reciprocal action or relation. **2.** a mutual exchange of commercial or other privileges. [C18: via F < L *reciprocus* RECIPROCAL]

recision (rɪˈsɪʒən) *n.* the act of cancelling or rescinding; annulment: *the recision of a treaty.* [C17: < L *recīsiō,* < *recīdere* to cut back]

recital (rɪˈsaɪtᵊl) *n.* **1.** a musical performance by a soloist. **2.** the act of reciting or repeating something learned or prepared. **3.** an account, narration, or description. **4.** (*often pl.*) *Law.* the preliminary statement in a deed showing the reason for its existence and explaining the operative part. —**reˈcitalist** *n.*

recitation (ˌrɛsɪˈteɪʃən) *n.* **1.** the act of reciting from memory, esp. a formal reading of verse before an audience. **2.** something recited.

recitative[1] (ˌrɛsɪtəˈtiːv) *n.* a passage in a musical composition, esp. the narrative parts in an oratorio, reflecting the natural rhythms of speech. [C17: < It. *recitativo;* see RECITE]

recitative[2] (rɪˈsaɪtətɪv) *adj.* of or relating to recital.

recite (rɪˈsaɪt) *vb.* **1.** to repeat (a poem, etc.) aloud from memory before an audience. **2.** (*tr.*) to give a detailed account of. **3.** (*tr.*) to enumerate (examples, etc.). [C15: < L *recitāre* to cite again, < RE- + *citāre* to summon] —**reˈcitable** *adj.* —**reˈciter** *n.*

reck (rɛk) *vb. Arch.* (*used mainly with a negative*) **1.** to mind or care about (something): *to reck nought.* **2.** (*usually impersonal*) to concern or interest (someone). [OE *reccan*]

reckless (ˈrɛklɪs) *adj.* having or showing no regard for danger or consequences; heedless; rash: *a reckless driver.* [OE *recceleās;* see RECK, -LESS] —ˈ**recklessly** *adv.* —ˈ**recklessness** *n.*

reckon (ˈrɛkən) *vb.* **1.** to calculate or ascertain by calculating; compute. **2.** (*tr.*) to include; count as part of a set or class. **3.** (*usually passive*) to consider or regard: *he is reckoned clever.* **4.** (when *tr., takes a clause as object*) to think or suppose; be of the opinion: *I reckon you don't know.* **5.** (*intr.;* foll. by *with*) to settle accounts (with). **6.** (*intr.;* foll. by *with* or *without*) to take into account or fail to take into account: *they reckoned without John.* **7.** (*intr.;* foll. by *on* or *upon*) to rely or depend: *I reckon on your support.* **8.** (*tr.*) *Inf.* to have a high opinion of. **9. to be reckoned with.** of considerable importance or influence. [OE (*ge*)*recenian* recount]

▷ **Usage.** Some senses of *reckon* are considered informal. The usage *I reckon on your support* is avoided in formal contexts, while in the sentence *It will snow tonight, I reckon,* the words *believe, suppose, think,* or *imagine* are preferred.

reckoner (ˈrɛkənə) *n.* any of various devices or tables used to facilitate reckoning, esp. a ready reckoner.

reckoning (ˈrɛkənɪŋ) *n.* **1.** the act of counting or calculating. **2.** settlement of an account or bill. **3.** a bill or account. **4.** retribution for one's actions (esp. in **day of reckoning**). **5.** *Navigation.* short for **dead reckoning.**

reclaim (rɪˈkleɪm) *vb.* (*tr.*) **1.** to regain possession of. **2.** to convert (desert, marsh, etc.) into land suitable for growing crops. **3.** to recover (useful substances) from waste products. **4.** to convert (someone) from sin, folly, vice, etc. ~*n.* **5.** the act of reclaiming or state of being reclaimed. [C13: < OF *réclamer,* < L *reclāmāre* to cry out, < RE- + *clāmāre* to shout] —**reˈclaimable** *adj.* —**reˈclaimant** *or* **reˈclaimer** *n.*

reclamation (ˌrɛkləˈmeɪʃən) *n.* **1.** the conversion of desert, marsh, etc., into land suitable for cultivation. **2.** the recovery of useful substances from waste products. **3.** the act of reclaiming or state of being reclaimed.

réclame *French.* (reklam) *n.* **1.** public acclaim or attention; publicity. **2.** the capacity for attracting publicity.

reclinate (ˈrɛklɪˌneɪt) *adj. Bot.* naturally curved or bent backwards so that the upper part rests on the ground. [C18: < L *reclīnātus* bent back]

recline (rɪˈklaɪn) *vb.* to rest in a leaning position. [C15: < OF *recliner,* < L *reclīnāre,* < RE- + *clīnāre* to LEAN[1]] —**reˈclinable** *adj.* —**reclination** (ˌrɛklɪˈneɪʃən) *n.*

recliner (rɪˈklaɪnə) *n.* a person or thing that reclines, esp. a type of armchair having a back that can be adjusted to slope at various angles.

---

reˈchallenge *vb.*
reˈcheck *vb., n.*
reˈchristen *vb.*
reˈcircuˌlate *vb.*
ˌreclassifiˈcation *n.*
reˈclassiˌfy *vb.*
reˈclothe *vb.*

recluse (rɪˈkluːs) *n.* **1.** a person who lives in seclusion, esp. to devote himself to prayer and religious meditation; a hermit. *~adj.* **2.** solitary; retiring. [C13: < OF *reclus,* < LL *reclūdere* to shut away, < L RE- + *claudere* to close] —**reclusion** (rɪˈkluːʒən) *n.* —**reˈclusive** *adj.*

recognition (ˌrɛkəgˈnɪʃən) *n.* **1.** the act of recognizing or fact of being recognized. **2.** acceptance or acknowledgment of a claim, duty, etc. **3.** a token of thanks. **4.** formal acknowledgment of a government or of the independence of a country. [C15: < L *recognitiō,* < *recognoscere,* < RE- + *cognoscere* to know] —**recognitive** (rɪˈkɒgnɪtɪv) *or* **reˈcognitory** *adj.*

recognizance *or* **recognisance** (rɪˈkɒgnɪzəns) *n. Law.* **a.** a bond entered into before a court or magistrate by which a person binds himself to do a specified act, as to appear in court on a stated day, keep the peace, or pay a debt. **b.** a monetary sum pledged to the performance of such an act. [C14: < OF *reconoissance,* < *reconoistre* to RECOGNIZE] —**reˈcognizant** *or* **reˈcognisant** *adj.*

recognize *or* **-ise** (ˈrɛkəgˌnaɪz) *vb.* (*tr.*) **1.** to perceive (a person or thing) to be the same as or belong to the same class as something previously seen or known; know again. **2.** to accept or be aware of (a fact, problem, etc.): *to recognize necessity.* **3.** to give formal acknowledgment of the status or legality of (a government, a representative, etc.). **4.** *Chiefly U.S. & Canad.* to grant (a person) the right to speak in a deliberative body. **5.** to give a token of thanks for (a service rendered, etc.). **6.** to make formal acknowledgment of (a claim, etc.). **7.** to show approval or appreciation of (something good). **8.** to acknowledge or greet (a person). [C15: < L *recognoscere,* < RE- + *cognoscere* to know] —ˈ**recogˌnizable** *or* **-isable** *adj.* —ˌ**recogˌnizaˈbility** *or* **-isaˈbility** *n.* —ˈ**recogˌnizably** *or* **-isably** *adv.* —ˈ**recogˌnizer** *or* **-iser** *n.*

recoil *vb.* (rɪˈkɔɪl). (*intr.*) **1.** to jerk back, as from an impact or violent thrust. **2.** (often foll. by *from*) to draw back in fear, horror, or disgust. **3.** (foll. by *on* or *upon*) to go wrong, esp. so as to hurt the perpetrator. **4.** (of an atom, etc.) to change momentum as a result of the emission of a particle. *~n.* (rɪˈkɔɪl, ˈriːkɔɪl). **5. a.** the backward movement of a gun when fired. **b.** the distance moved. **6.** the motion acquired by an atom, etc., as a result of its emission of a particle. **7.** the act of recoiling. [C13: < OF *reculer,* < RE- + *cul* rump, < L *cūlus*] —**reˈcoiler** *n.*

recollect (ˌrɛkəˈlɛkt) *vb.* (when *tr., often takes a clause as object*) to recall from memory; remember. [C16: < L *recolligere,* < RE- + *colligere* to COLLECT] —ˌ**recolˈlection** *n.* —ˌ**recolˈlective** *adj.* —ˌ**recolˈlectively** *adv.*

recombinant DNA (riːˈkɒmbɪnənt) *n.* DNA molecules that are extracted from different sources and chemically joined together.

recombination (ˌriːkɒmbɪˈneɪʃən) *n. Genetics.* any of several processes by which genetic material of different origins becomes combined.

recommend (ˌrɛkəˈmɛnd) *vb.* (*tr.*) **1.** (*may take a clause as object or an infinitive*) to advise as the best course or choice; counsel. **2.** to praise or commend: *to recommend a new book.* **3.** to make attractive or advisable: *the trip has little to recommend it.* **4.** *Arch.* to entrust (a person or thing) to someone else's care; commend. [C14: via Med. L < L RE- + *commendāre* to COMMEND] —ˌ**recomˈmendable** *adj.* —ˌ**recomˈmendatory** *adj.* —ˌ**recomˈmender** *n.*

recommendation (ˌrɛkəmɛnˈdeɪʃən) *n.* **1.** the act of recommending. **2.** something that recommends, esp. a letter. **3.** something that is recommended, such as a course of action.

recommit (ˌriːkəˈmɪt) *vb.* **-mitting, -mitted.** (*tr.*) **1.** to send (a bill) back to a committee for further consideration. **2.** to commit again. —ˌ**recomˈmitment** *or* ˌ**recomˈmittal** *n.*

recompense (ˈrɛkəmˌpɛns) *vb.* (*tr.*) **1.** to pay or reward for service, work, etc. **2.** to compensate for loss, injury, etc. *~n.* **3.** compensation for loss, injury, etc. **4.** reward, remuneration, or repayment. [C15: < OF *recompenser,* < L RE- + *compensāre* to balance in weighing] —ˈ**recomˌpensable** *adj.* —ˈ**recomˌpenser** *n.*

reconcile (ˈrɛkənˌsaɪl) *vb.* (*tr.*) **1.** (*often passive;* usually foll. by *to*) to make (oneself or another) no longer opposed; cause to acquiesce in something unpleasant: *she reconciled herself to poverty.* **2.** to become friendly with (someone) after estrangement or to re-establish friendly relations between (two or more people). **3.** to settle (a quarrel). **4.** to make (two apparently conflicting things) compatible or consistent with each other. **5.** to reconsecrate (a desecrated church, etc.). [C14: < L *reconciliāre,* < RE- + *conciliāre* to make friendly, CONCILIATE] —ˈ**reconˌcilement** *n.* —ˈ**reconˌciler** *n.* —**reconciliation** (ˌrɛkənˌsɪlɪˈeɪʃən) *n.* —**reconciliatory** (ˌrɛkənˈsɪlɪətərɪ, -trɪ) *adj.*

recondite (rɪˈkɒndaɪt, ˈrɛkənˌdaɪt) *adj.* **1.** requiring special knowledge; abstruse. **2.** dealing with abstruse or profound subjects. [C17: < L *reconditus* hidden away, < RE- + *condere* to conceal] —**reˈconditely** *adv.* —**reˈconditeness** *n.*

recondition (ˌriːkənˈdɪʃən) *vb.* (*tr.*) to restore to good condition or working order: *to recondition an engine.* —ˌ**reconˈditioned** *adj.*

reconnaissance (rɪˈkɒnɪsəns) *n.* **1.** the act of reconnoitring. **2.** the process of obtaining information about the position, etc., of an enemy. **3.** a preliminary inspection of an area of land. [C18: < F, < OF *reconoistre* to explore, RECOGNIZE]

reconnoitre *or U.S.* **reconnoiter** (ˌrɛkəˈnɔɪtə) *vb.* **1.** to survey or inspect (an enemy's position, region of land, etc.). *~n.* **2.** the act or process of reconnoitring; a reconnaissance. [C18: < obs. F *reconnoître* to inspect, explore; see RECOGNIZE] —ˌ**reconˈnoitrer** *or U.S.* ˌ**reconˈnoiterer** *n.*

reconsider (ˌriːkənˈsɪdə) *vb.* to consider (something) again, with a view to changing one's policy or course of action. —ˌ**reconˌsiderˈation** *n.*

reconstitute (riːˈkɒnstɪˌtjuːt) *vb.* (*tr.*) **1.** to restore (food, etc.) to its former or natural state, as by the addition of water to a concentrate. **2.** to reconstruct; form again. —**reconstituent** (ˌriːkənˈstɪtjʊənt) *adj., n.* —ˌ**reconstiˈtution** *n.*

reconstruct (ˌriːkənˈstrʌkt) *vb.* (*tr.*) **1.** to construct or form again; rebuild. **2.** to form a picture of (a crime, past event, etc.) by piecing together evidence. —ˌ**reconˈstructible** *adj.* —ˌ**reconˈstruction** *n.* —ˌ**reconˈstructive** *or* ˌ**reconˈstructional** *adj.* —ˌ**reconˈstructor** *n.*

reconvert (ˌriːkənˈvɜːt) *vb.* (*tr.*) **1.** to change (something) back to a previous state or form. **2.** to bring (someone) back to his former religion. —**reconversion** (ˌriːkənˈvɜːʃən) *n.*

record *n.* (ˈrɛkɔːd). **1.** an account in permanent form, esp. in writing, preserving knowledge or information. **2.** a written account of some transaction that serves as legal evidence of the transaction. **3.** a written official report of the proceedings of a court of justice or legislative body. **4.** anything serving as evidence or as a memorial: *the First World War is a record of human folly.* **5.** (*often pl.*) information or data on

---

ˌ**recodifiˈcation** *n.*
reˈcodify *vb.*
ˌ**recoloniˈzation** *or* **-niˈsation** *n.*
reˈcoloˌnize *or* **-ˌnise** *vb.*
reˈcolour *vb.*
ˌ**recomˈbine** *vb.*
ˌ**recomˈmence** *vb.*
ˌ**recomˈmencement** *n.*
ˌ**recomˈpose** *vb.*
ˌ**reconˈfirm** *vb.*
ˌ**reconfirˈmation** *n.*
ˌ**reconˈnect** *vb.*
ˌ**reconˈnection** *n.*
reˈconquer *vb.*
reˈconquest *n.*
reˈconseˌcrate *vb.*
ˌ**reconseˈcration** *n.*
ˌ**reconˈsign** *vb.*
ˌ**reconˈsignment** *n.*
ˌ**reconˈsoliˌdate** *vb.*
ˌ**reconˌsoliˈdation** *n.*
ˌ**reconˈvene** *vb.*
ˌ**reconˈvey** *vb.*
ˌ**reconˈvict** *vb.*

a specific subject collected methodically over a long period: *weather records.* **6. a.** the best or most outstanding amount, rate, height, etc., ever attained, as in some field of sport: *a world record.* **b.** (*as modifier*): *a record time.* **7.** the sum of one's recognized achievements, career, or performance. **8.** a list of crimes of which an accused person has previously been convicted. **9. have a record.** to be a known criminal. **10.** Also called: **gramophone record, disc.** a thin disc of a plastic material upon which sound has been recorded. **11.** the markings made by a recording instrument such as a seismograph. **12.** *Computers.* a group of data or piece of information preserved as a unit in machine-readable form. **13. for the record.** for the sake of strict factual accuracy. **14. go on record.** to state one's views publicly. **15. off the record.** confidential or confidentially. **16. on record. a.** stated in a public document. **b.** publicly known. **17. set** *or* **put the record straight.** to correct an error. ~*vb.* (rɪˈkɔːd). (*mainly tr.*) **18.** to set down in some permanent form so as to preserve the true facts of: *to record the minutes of a meeting.* **19.** to contain or serve to relate (facts, information, etc.). **20.** to indicate, show, or register: *his face recorded his disappointment.* **21.** to remain as or afford evidence of: *these ruins record the life of the Romans in Britain.* **22.** (*also intr.*) to make a recording of (music, speech, etc.) for reproduction, esp. on a record player or tape recorder, or for later broadcasting. **23.** (*also intr.*) (of an instrument) to register or indicate (information) on a scale: *the barometer recorded a low pressure.* [C13: < OF *recorder,* < L *recordārī* to remember, < RE- + *cor* heart] —**reˈcordable** *adj.*

recorded delivery *n.* a Post Office service by which an official record of posting and delivery is obtained for a letter or package.

recorder (rɪˈkɔːdə) *n.* **1.** a person who records, such as an official or historian. **2.** something that records, esp. an apparatus that provides a permanent record of experiments, etc. **3.** short for **tape recorder. 4.** *Music.* a wind instrument of the flute family, blown through a fipple in the mouth end, having a reedlike quality of tone. **5.** (in England) a barrister or solicitor of at least ten years' standing appointed to sit as a part-time judge in the crown court. —**reˈcordership** *n.*

recording (rɪˈkɔːdɪŋ) *n.* **1. a.** the act or process of making a record, esp. of sound on a gramophone record or magnetic tape. **b.** (*as modifier*): *recording studio.* **2.** the record or tape so produced. **3.** something that has been recorded, esp. a radio or television programme.

Recording Angel *n.* an angel who supposedly keeps a record of every person's good and bad acts.

record player *n.* a device for reproducing the sounds stored on a record. A stylus vibrates in accordance with the undulations of the walls of the groove in the record as it rotates.

recount (rɪˈkaʊnt) *vb.* (*tr.*) to tell the story or details of; narrate. [C15: < OF *reconter,* < RE- + *conter* to tell; see COUNT[1]] —**reˈcountal** *n.*

re-count *vb.* (riːˈkaʊnt). **1.** to count (votes, etc.) again. ~*n.* (ˈriːˌkaʊnt). **2.** a second or further count, esp. of votes in an election.

recoup (rɪˈkuːp) *vb.* **1.** to regain or make good (a financial or other loss). **2.** (*tr.*) to reimburse or compensate (someone), as for a loss. **3.** *Law.* to keep back (something due), having rightful claim to do so. ~*n.* **4.** *Rare.* the act of recouping; recoupment. [C15: < OF *recouper* to cut back, < RE- + *couper,* < *coper* to behead] —**reˈcoupable** *adj.* —**reˈcoupment** *n.*

recourse (rɪˈkɔːs) *n.* **1.** the act of resorting to a person, course of action, etc., in difficulty (esp. in **have recourse to**). **2.** a person, organization, or course of action that is turned to for help, etc. **3.** the right to demand payment, esp. from the drawer or endorser of a bill of exchange or other negotiable instrument when the person accepting it fails to pay. **4. without recourse.** a qualified endorsement on such a negotiable instrument, by which the endorser protects himself from liability to subsequent holders. [C14: < OF *recours,* < LL *recursus* a running back, < RE- + L *currere* to run]

recover (rɪˈkʌvə) *vb.* **1.** (*tr.*) to find again or obtain the return of (something lost). **2.** to regain (loss of money, time, etc.). **3.** (of a person) to regain (health, spirits, composure, etc.). **4.** to regain (a former and better condition): *industry recovered after the war.* **5.** *Law.* **a.** (*tr.*) to gain (something) by the judgment of a court of law: *to recover damages.* **b.** (*intr.*) to succeed in a lawsuit. **6.** (*tr.*) to obtain (useful substances) from waste. **7.** (*intr.*) (in fencing, rowing, etc.) to make a recovery. [C14: < OF *recoverer,* < L *recuperāre* RECUPERATE] —**reˈcoverable** *adj.* —**reˌcoveraˈbility** *n.* —**reˈcoverer** *n.*

re-cover (riːˈkʌvə) *vb.* (*tr.*) **1.** to cover again. **2.** to provide (furniture, etc.) with a new cover.

recovery (rɪˈkʌvərɪ) *n., pl.* **-eries. 1.** the act or process of recovering, esp. from sickness, a shock, or a setback. **2.** restoration to a former or better condition. **3.** the regaining of something lost. **4.** the extraction of useful substances from waste. **5.** the retrieval of a space capsule after a spaceflight. **6.** *Law.* the obtaining of a right, etc., by the judgment of a court. **7.** *Fencing.* a return to the position of guard after making an attack. **8.** *Swimming, rowing, etc.* the action of bringing the arm, an oar, etc., forward for another stroke. **9.** *Golf.* a stroke played from the rough or a bunker to the fairway or green.

recreant (ˈrɛkrɪənt) *Arch.* ~*adj.* **1.** cowardly; faint-hearted. **2.** disloyal. ~*n.* **3.** a disloyal or cowardly person. [C14: < OF, < *recroire* to surrender, < RE- + L *crēdere* to believe] —**ˈrecreance** *or* **ˈrecreancy** *n.* —**ˈrecreantly** *adv.*

recreate (ˈrɛkrɪˌeɪt) *vb. Rare.* to amuse (oneself or someone else). [C15: < L *recreāre* to invigorate, renew, < RE- + *creāre* to CREATE] —**ˈrecreative** *adj.* —**ˈrecreatively** *adv.* —**ˈrecreˌator** *n.*

re-create (ˌriːkrɪˈeɪt) *vb.* to create anew; reproduce. —**ˌre-creˈation** *n.* —**ˌre-creˈator** *n.*

recreation (ˌrɛkrɪˈeɪʃən) *n.* **1.** refreshment of health or spirits by relaxation and enjoyment. **2.** an activity that promotes this. **3. a.** an interval of free time between school lessons. **b.** (*as modifier*): *recreation period.* —**ˌrecreˈational** *adj.*

recriminate (rɪˈkrɪmɪˌneɪt) *vb.* (*intr.*) to return an accusation against someone or engage in mutual accusations. [C17: via Med. L, < L *crīmināri* to accuse, < *crīmen* accusation] —**reˌcrimiˈnation** *n.* —**reˈcriminative** *or* **reˈcriminatory** *adj.* —**reˈcrimiˌnator** *n.*

recrudesce (ˌriːkruːˈdɛs) *vb.* (*intr.*) (of a disease, trouble, etc.) to break out or appear again after a period of dormancy. [C19: < L *recrūdēscere,* < RE- + *crūdēscere* to grow worse, < *crūdus* bloody, raw] —**ˌrecruˈdescence** *n.*

recruit (rɪˈkruːt) *vb.* **1. a.** to enlist (men) for military service. **b.** to raise or strengthen (an army, etc.) by enlistment. **2.** (*tr.*) to enrol or obtain (members, support, etc.). **3.** to furnish or be furnished with a fresh supply; renew. **4.** *Arch.* to recover (health, spirits, etc.). ~*n.* **5.** a newly joined member of a military service. **6.** any new member or supporter. [C17: < F *recrute* lit.: new growth, < *recroître,* < L, < RE- + *crēscere* to grow] —**reˈcruitable** *adj.* —**reˈcruiter** *n.* —**reˈcruitment** *n.*

recta (ˈrɛktə) *n.* a plural of **rectum.**

rectal (ˈrɛktəl) *adj.* of or relating to the rectum. —**ˈrectally** *adv.*

rectangle (ˈrɛkˌtæŋgᵊl) *n.* a parallelogram having four right angles. [C16: < Med. L

---

reˈcross *vb.* **reˈcrystalˌlize** *or* **-ˌlise** *vb.*

rectangulum, < L *rectus* straight + *angulus* angle]

rectangular (rɛkˈtæŋgjʊlə) *adj.* **1.** shaped like a rectangle. **2.** having or relating to right angles. **3.** mutually perpendicular: *rectangular coordinates.* **4.** having a base or section shaped like a rectangle. —**rec,tanguˈlarity** *n.* —**recˈtangularly** *adv.*

rectangular coordinates *pl. n.* the Cartesian coordinates in a system of mutually perpendicular axes.

rectangular hyperbola *n.* a hyperbola with perpendicular asymptotes.

recti (ˈrɛktaɪ) *n.* the plural of **rectus.**

recti- *or before a vowel* **rect-** *combining form.* straight or right: *rectangle.* [< L *rectus*]

rectifier (ˈrɛktɪˌfaɪə) *n.* **1.** an electronic device that converts an alternating current to a direct current. **2.** *Chem.* an apparatus for condensing a hot vapour to a liquid in distillation; condenser. **3.** a thing or person that rectifies.

rectify (ˈrɛktɪˌfaɪ) *vb.* **-fying, -fied.** (*tr.*) **1.** to put right; correct; remedy. **2.** to separate (a substance) from a mixture or refine (a substance) by fractional distillation. **3.** to convert (alternating current) into direct current. **4.** *Maths.* to determine the length of (a curve). [C14: via OF < Med. L *rectificāre*, < L *rectus* straight + *facere* to make] —**ˈrectiˌfiable** *adj.* —**ˌrectifiˈcation** *n.*

rectilinear (ˌrɛktɪˈlɪnɪə) *or* **rectilineal** *adj.* **1.** in, moving in, or characterized by a straight line. **2.** consisting of, bounded by, or formed by a straight line. —**ˌrectiˈlinearly** *or* **ˌrectiˈlineally** *adv.*

rectitude (ˈrɛktɪˌtjuːd) *n.* **1.** moral or religious correctness. **2.** correctness of judgment. [C15: < LL *rectitūdō*, < L *rectus* right, < *regere* to rule]

recto (ˈrɛktəʊ) *n., pl.* **-tos.** **1.** the front of a sheet of printed paper. **2.** the right-hand pages of a book. Cf. **verso** (sense 1b). [C19: < L *rectō foliō* on the right-hand page]

rectocele (ˈrɛktəʊˌsiːl) *n. Pathol.* a protrusion or herniation of the rectum into the vagina.

rector (ˈrɛktə) *n.* **1.** *Church of England.* a clergyman in charge of a parish in which, as its incumbent, he would formerly have been entitled to the whole of the tithes. **2.** *R.C. Church.* a cleric in charge of a college, religious house, or congregation. **3.** *Protestant Episcopal Church.* a clergyman in charge of a parish. **4.** *Chiefly Brit.* the head of certain schools, colleges, or universities. **5.** (in Scotland) a high-ranking official in a university. **6.** (in South Africa) a principal of an Afrikaans university. [C14: < L: director, ruler, < *regere* to rule] —**ˈrectorate** *n.* —**rectorial** (rɛkˈtɔːrɪəl) *adj.* —**ˈrectorship** *n.*

rectory (ˈrɛktərɪ) *n., pl.* **-ries.** **1.** the official house of a rector. **2.** *Church of England.* the office and benefice of a rector.

rectrix (ˈrɛktrɪks) *n., pl.* **rectrices** (ˈrɛktrɪˌsiːz, rɛkˈtraɪsiːz). any of the large stiff feathers of a bird's tail, used in controlling the direction of flight. [C17: < LL, fem. of L *rector* RECTOR]

rectum (ˈrɛktəm) *n., pl.* **-tums** *or* **-ta.** the lower part of the alimentary canal, between the sigmoid flexure of the colon and the anus. [C16: < NL *rectum intestinum* the straight intestine]

rectus (ˈrɛktəs) *n., pl.* **-ti.** *Anat.* a straight muscle. [C18: < NL *rectus musculus*]

recumbent (rɪˈkʌmbənt) *adj.* **1.** lying down; reclining. **2.** (of an organ) leaning or resting against another organ. [C17: < L *recumbere* to lie back, < RE- + *cumbere* to lie] —**reˈcumbence** *or* **reˈcumbency** *n.* —**reˈcumbently** *adv.*

recuperate (rɪˈkuːpəˌreɪt, -ˈkjuː-) *vb.* **1.** (*intr.*) to recover from illness or exhaustion. **2.** to recover (financial losses, etc.). [C16: < L *recuperāre* to recover, < RE- + *capere* to gain] —**reˌcuperˈation** *n.* —**reˈcuperative** *adj.*

recur (rɪˈkɜː) *vb.* **-curring, -curred.** (*intr.*) **1.** to happen again. **2.** (of a thought, etc.) to come back to the mind. **3.** (of a problem, etc.) to come up again. **4.** *Maths.* (of a digit or group of digits) to be repeated an infinite number of times at the end of a decimal fraction. [C15: < L *recurrere*, < RE- + *currere* to run] —**reˈcurring** *adj.*

recurrent (rɪˈkʌrənt) *adj.* **1.** tending to happen again or repeatedly. **2.** *Anat.* (of certain nerves, etc.) turning back, so as to run in the opposite direction. —**reˈcurrence** *n.* —**reˈcurrently** *adv.*

recurrent fever *n.* another name for **relapsing fever.**

recurring decimal *n.* a rational number that contains a pattern of digits repeated indefinitely after the decimal point.

recursion (rɪˈkɜːʃən) *n.* **1.** the act or process of returning or running back. **2.** *Maths, logic.* the application of a function to its own values to generate an infinite sequence of values. [C17: < L *recursio*, < *recurrere* RECUR] —**reˈcursive** *adj.*

recurve (rɪˈkɜːv) *vb.* to curve or bend (something) back or down or (of something) to be so curved or bent. [C16: < L *recurvāre*, < RE- + *curvāre* to CURVE]

recusant (ˈrɛkjʊzənt) *n.* **1.** (in 16th to 18th century England) a Roman Catholic who did not attend the services of the Church of England. **2.** any person who refuses to submit to authority. ~*adj.* **3.** (formerly, of Catholics) refusing to attend services of the Church of England. **4.** refusing to submit to authority. [C16: < L *recūsāns* refusing, < *recūsāre*, < RE- + *causārī* to dispute, < *causa* a CAUSE] —**ˈrecusance** *or* **ˈrecusancy** *n.*

recycle (riːˈsaɪkᵊl) *vb.* (*tr.*) **1.** to pass (a substance) through a system again for further treatment or use. **2.** to reclaim for further use: *to recycle water.* ~*n.* **3.** the repetition of a fixed sequence of events.

red[1] (rɛd) *n.* **1.** any of a group of colours, such as that of a ripe tomato or fresh blood. **2.** a pigment or dye of or producing these colours. **3.** red cloth or clothing: *dressed in red.* **4.** a red ball in snooker, etc. **5.** (in roulette) one of two colours on which players may place even bets. **6.** short for **red wine.** **7. in the red.** *Inf.* in debt. **8. see red.** *Inf.* to become very angry. ~*adj.* **redder, reddest.** **9.** of the colour red. **10.** reddish in colour or having parts or marks that are reddish: *red deer.* **11.** having the face temporarily suffused with blood, being a sign of anger, shame, etc. **12.** (of the complexion) rosy; florid. **13.** (of the eyes) bloodshot. **14.** (of the hands) stained with blood. **15.** bloody or violent: *red revolution.* ~*vb.* **redding, redded.** **16.** another word for **redden.** [OE *rēad*] —**ˈreddish** *adj.* —**ˈredness** *n.*

red[2] (rɛd) *vb.* **redding, red** *or* **redded.** (*tr.*) a variant spelling of **redd.**

Red (rɛd) *Inf.* ~*adj.* **1.** Communist, Socialist, or Soviet. **2.** radical, leftist, or revolutionary. ~*n.* **3.** a member or supporter of a Communist or Socialist Party or a national of the Soviet Union. **4.** a radical, leftist, or revolutionary. [C19: < the colour chosen to symbolize revolutionary socialism]

redact (rɪˈdækt) *vb.* (*tr.*) to put (a literary work, etc.) into appropriate form for publication; edit. [C15: < L *redigere* to bring back, < *red-* RE- + *agere* to drive] —**reˈdaction** *n.* —**reˈdactional** *adj.* —**reˈdactor** *n.*

red admiral *n.* a butterfly of temperate Europe and Asia, having black wings with red and white markings. See also **white admiral.**

red algae *pl. n.* the numerous algae which contain a red pigment in addition to chlorophyll. The group includes carrageen and dulse.

redback (ˈrɛdˌbæk) *n. Austral.* a small, venomous spider, the female of which has a red stripe on its back. Also called: **redback spider.**

red bark *n.* a kind of cinchona containing a high proportion of alkaloids.

red biddy *n. Inf.* cheap red wine fortified with methylated spirits.

red blood cell *n.* another name for **erythrocyte.**

red-blooded *adj. Inf.* vigorous; virile. —**ˌredˈbloodedness** *n.*

redbreast (ˈrɛdˌbrɛst) *n.* any of various birds having a red breast, esp. the Old World robin.

redbrick (ˈrɛdˌbrɪk) *n.* (*modifier*) denoting,

relating to, or characteristic of a provincial British university of relatively recent foundation.

redcap ('rɛd,kæp) *n.* **1.** *Brit. inf.* a military policeman. **2.** *U.S. & Canad.* a porter at an airport or station.

red card *n. Soccer.* a piece of red pasteboard displayed by a referee to indicate that a player has been sent off.

red carpet *n.* **1.** a strip of red carpeting laid for important dignitaries to walk on. **2. a.** deferential treatment accorded to a person of importance. **b.** (*as modifier*): *a red-carpet reception.*

red cedar *n.* **1.** any of several North American coniferous trees, esp. a juniper that has fragrant reddish wood. **2.** the wood of any of these trees. **3.** any of several Australian timber trees.

red cent *n.* (*used with a negative*) *Inf., chiefly U.S.* a cent considered as a trivial amount of money (esp. in **not have a red cent,** etc.).

redcoat ('rɛd,kəʊt) *n.* **1.** (formerly) a British soldier. **2.** *Canad. inf.* another name for **Mountie.**

red coral *n.* any of several corals, the skeletons of which are pinkish red in colour and used to make ornaments, etc.

red corpuscle *n.* another name for **erythrocyte.**

Red Crescent *n.* the emblem of the Red Cross Society in a Muslim country.

Red Cross *n.* **1.** an international humanitarian organization (**Red Cross Society**) formally established by the Geneva Convention of 1864. **2.** the emblem of this organization, consisting of a red cross on a white background.

redcurrant (,rɛd'kʌrənt) *n.* **1.** a N temperate shrub having greenish flowers and small edible rounded red berries. **2. a.** the fruit of this shrub. **b.** (*as modifier*): *redcurrant jelly.*

redd *or* **red** (rɛd) *Scot. & N English dialect.* ~*vb.* **redding, redd** *or* **redded. 1.** (*tr.; often foll. by up*) to bring order to; tidy (up). ~*n.* **2.** the act or an instance of redding. [C15: *redden* to clear, ? a variant of RID] —'**redder** *n.*

red deer *n.* a large deer formerly widely distributed in the woodlands of Europe and Asia. The coat is reddish brown in summer and the short tail is surrounded by a patch of light-coloured hair.

redden ('rɛdᵊn) *vb.* **1.** to make or become red. **2.** (*intr.*) to flush with embarrassment, anger, etc.

reddle ('rɛdᵊl) *n., vb.* a variant spelling of **ruddle.**

red duster *n. Brit.* an informal name for the **Red Ensign.**

red dwarf *n.* one of a class of stars of relatively small mass and low luminosity.

rede (ri:d) *Arch.* ~*n.* **1.** advice or counsel. **2.** an explanation. ~*vb.* (*tr.*) **3.** to advise; counsel. **4.** to explain. [OE *rǣdan* to rule]

red earth *n.* a clayey zonal soil of tropical savanna lands, formed by extensive chemical weathering and coloured by iron compounds.

redeem (rɪ'di:m) *vb.* (*tr.*) **1.** to recover possession or ownership of by payment of a price or service; regain. **2.** to convert (bonds, shares, etc.) into cash. **3.** to pay off (a loan, etc.). **4.** to recover (something pledged, mortgaged, or pawned). **5.** to convert (paper money) into bullion or specie. **6.** to fulfil (a promise, pledge, etc.). **7.** to exchange (coupons, etc.) for goods. **8.** to reinstate in someone's estimation or good opinion: *he redeemed himself by his altruistic action.* **9.** to make amends for. **10.** to recover from captivity, esp. by a money payment. **11.** *Christianity.* (of Christ as Saviour) to free (humanity) from sin by death on the Cross. [C15: < OF *redimer,* < L *redimere,* < *red-* RE- + *emere* to buy] —**re'deemable** *or* **re'demptible** *adj.* —**re'deemer** *n.*

Redeemer (rɪ'di:mə) *n.* **the.** Jesus Christ as having brought redemption to mankind.

redeeming (rɪ'di:mɪŋ) *adj.* serving to compensate for faults or deficiencies.

redemption (rɪ'dɛmpʃən) *n.* **1.** the act or process of redeeming. **2.** the state of being redeemed. **3.** *Christianity.* **a.** deliverance from sin through the incarnation, sufferings, and death of Christ. **b.** atonement for guilt. [C14: via OF < L *redemptiō* a buying back; see REDEEM] —**re'demptional, re'demptive,** *or* **re'demptory** *adj.* —**re'demptively** *adv.*

Red Ensign *n.* the ensign of the British Merchant Navy, having the Union Jack on a red background at the upper corner of the vertical edge alongside the hoist. It was also the national flag of Canada until 1965.

redeploy (,ri:dɪ'plɔɪ) *vb.* to assign new positions or tasks to (labour, troops, etc.). —,**rede'ployment** *n.*

redevelopment area (,ri:dɪ'vɛləpmənt) *n.* an urban area in which all or most of the buildings are demolished and rebuilt.

redeye ('rɛd,aɪ) *n.* **1.** *U.S. sl.* inferior whisky. **2.** another name for **rudd.**

red-faced *adj.* **1.** flushed with embarrassment or anger. **2.** having a florid complexion. —**red-facedly** (,rɛd'feɪsɪdlɪ, -'feɪstlɪ) *adv.*

redfin ('rɛd,fɪn) *n.* any of various small cyprinid fishes with reddish fins.

redfish ('rɛd,fɪʃ) *n., pl.* **-fish** *or* **-fishes. 1.** a male salmon that has recently spawned. Cf. **blackfish** (sense 2). **2.** *Canad.* another name for **kokanee.**

red flag *n.* **1.** a symbol of socialism, communism, or revolution. **2.** a warning of danger or a signal to stop.

red fox *n.* the common European fox which has a reddish-brown coat.

red giant *n.* a giant star that emits red light.

red grouse *n.* a reddish-brown grouse of upland moors of Great Britain.

Red Guard *n.* a member of a Communist Chinese youth movement.

red-handed *adj.* (*postpositive*) in the act of committing a crime or doing something wrong or shameful (esp. in **catch red-handed**). [C19 (earlier, C15 *red hand*)] —,**red-'handedly** *adv.* —,**red-'handedness** *n.*

red hat *n.* the broad-brimmed crimson hat given to cardinals as the symbol of their rank.

redhead ('rɛd,hɛd) *n.* a person with red hair. —'**red,headed** *adj.*

red heat *n.* **1.** the temperature at which a substance is red-hot. **2.** the state or condition of being red-hot.

red herring *n.* **1.** anything that diverts attention from a topic or line of inquiry. **2.** a herring cured by salting and smoking.

red-hot *adj.* **1.** (esp. of metal) heated to the temperature at which it glows red. **2.** extremely hot. **3.** keen, excited, or eager. **4.** furious; violent: *red-hot anger.* **5.** very recent or topical: *red-hot information.* **6.** *Austral. sl.* extreme, unreasonable, or unfair.

red-hot poker *n.* a liliaceous plant: widely cultivated for its showy spikes of red or yellow flowers.

Red Indian *n., adj.* another name, now considered offensive, for **American Indian.** [see REDSKIN]

redingote ('rɛdɪŋ,gəʊt) *n.* **1.** a man's full-skirted outer coat of the 18th and 19th centuries. **2.** a woman's coat of the 18th century, with an open-fronted skirt, revealing a decorative underskirt. **3.** a woman's coat with a close-fitting top and a full skirt. [C19: < F, < E *riding coat*]

redintegrate (rɛ'dɪntɪ,greɪt) *vb.* (*tr.*) to make whole or complete again; restore to a perfect state; renew. [C15: < L *redintegrāre* to renew, < *red-* RE- + *integer* complete] —**re,dinte'gration** *n.* —**red'integrative** *adj.*

---

re'deco,rate *vb.*
re'dedi,cate *vb.*
re,dedi'cation *n.*
,rede'fine *vb.*
,rede'scribe *vb.*
,rede'sign *vb.*
,rede'termine *vb.*
,rede'velop *vb.*
,rede'veloper *n.*
,rede'velopment *n.*
,redi'rect *vb.*
,redi'rection *vb.*
,redis'cover *vb.*
,redis'covery *n.*

redistribution (ˌriːdɪstrɪˈbjuːʃən) *n.* **1.** the act or an instance of distributing again. **2.** a revision of the number of seats in the Canadian House of Commons allocated to each province, made every ten years on the basis of a new census.

redivivus (ˌrɛdɪˈvaɪvəs) *adj. Rare.* returned to life; revived. [C17: < LL, < L *red-* RE- + *vīvus* alive]

red lead (lɛd) *n.* a bright-red poisonous insoluble oxide of lead.

red-letter day *n.* a memorably important or happy occasion. [C18: < the red letters used in ecclesiastical calendars to indicate saints' days and feasts]

red light *n.* **1.** a signal to stop, esp. a red traffic signal. **2.** a danger signal. **3. a.** a red lamp indicating that a house is a brothel. **b.** (*as modifier*): *a red-light district.*

redline (ˈrɛdˌlaɪn) *vb.* (*tr.*) (esp. of a bank or group of banks) to refuse to consider giving a loan to (a person or country) because of the presumed risks involved.

red meat *n.* any meat that is dark in colour, esp. beef and lamb. Cf. **white meat.**

red mullet *n.* a food fish of European waters with a pair of long barbels beneath the chin and a reddish coloration. U.S. name: **goatfish.**

redneck (ˈrɛdˌnɛk) *n. Disparaging.* **1.** (in the southwestern U.S.) a poor uneducated White farm worker. **2.** a person or institution that is extremely reactionary. ~*adj.* **3.** reactionary and bigoted: *redneck laws.*

redo (riːˈduː) *vb.* **-doing, -did, -done.** (*tr.*) **1.** to do over again. **2.** *Inf.* to redecorate, esp. thoroughly: *we redid the house last summer.*

red ochre *n.* any of various natural red earths containing ferric oxide: used as pigments.

redolent (ˈrɛdəʊlənt) *adj.* **1.** having a pleasant smell; fragrant. **2.** (*postpositive;* foll. by *of* or *with*) having the odour or smell (of): *a room redolent of flowers.* **3.** (*postpositive;* foll. by *of* or *with*) reminiscent or suggestive (of): *a picture redolent of the 18th century.* [C14: < L *redolens* smelling (of), < *redolēre* to give off an odour, < *red-* RE- + *olēre* to smell] —ˈ**redolence** *or* ˈ**redolency** *n.* —ˈ**redolently** *adv.*

redouble (rɪˈdʌbᵊl) *vb.* **1.** to make or become much greater in intensity, number, etc.: *to redouble one's efforts.* **2.** to send back (sounds) or (of sounds) to be sent back. **3.** *Bridge.* to double (an opponent's double). ~*n.* **4.** the act of redoubling.

redoubt (rɪˈdaʊt) *n.* **1.** an outwork or fieldwork defending a hilltop, pass, etc. **2.** a temporary defence work built inside a fortification as a last defensive position. [C17: via F < obs. It. *ridotta,* < Med. L *reductus* shelter, < L *redūcere,* < RE- + *dūcere* to lead]

redoubtable (rɪˈdaʊtəbᵊl) *adj.* **1.** to be feared; formidable. **2.** worthy of respect. [C14: < OF, < *redouter* to dread, < RE- + *douter* to be afraid, DOUBT] —**reˈdoubtableness** *n.* —**reˈdoubtably** *adv.*

redound (rɪˈdaʊnd) *vb.* **1.** (*intr.;* foll. by *to*) to have an advantageous or disadvantageous effect (on): *brave deeds redound to your credit.* **2.** (*intr.;* foll. by *on* or *upon*) to recoil or rebound. **3.** (*tr.*) *Arch.* to reflect; bring: *his actions redound dishonour upon him.* [C14: < OF *redonder,* < L *redundāre* to stream over, < *red-* RE- + *undāre* to rise in waves]

redox (ˈriːdɒks) *n.* (*modifier*) another term for **oxidation-reduction.** [C20: < RED(UCTION) + OX(IDATION)]

red pepper *n.* **1.** any of several varieties of the pepper plant cultivated for their hot pungent red podlike fruits. **2.** the fruit of any of these plants. **3.** the ripe red fruit of the sweet pepper. **4.** another name for **cayenne pepper.**

Red Planet *n.* **the.** an informal name for **Mars**[2].

redpoll (ˈrɛdˌpɒl) *n.* either of two widely distributed types of finches, having a greyish-brown plumage with a red crown and pink breast.

red rag *n.* a provocation; something that infuriates. [so called because red objects supposedly infuriate bulls]

redress (rɪˈdrɛs) *vb.* (*tr.*) **1.** to put right (a wrong), esp. by compensation; make reparation for. **2.** to correct or adjust (esp. in **redress the balance**). **3.** to make compensation to (a person) for a wrong. ~*n.* **4.** the act or an instance of setting right a wrong; remedy or cure. **5.** compensation, amends, or reparation for a wrcng, injury, etc. [C14: < OF *redrecier* to set up again, < RE- + *drecier* to straighten; see DRESS] —**reˈdressable** *or* **reˈdressible** *adj.* —**reˈdresser** *or* **reˈdressor** *n.*

re-dress (riːˈdrɛs) *vb.* (*tr.*) to dress (something) again.

Red River cart *n. Canad. history.* a strongly-built, two-wheeled, ox- or horse-drawn cart used in W Canada.

red rose *n. English history.* the emblem of the House of Lancaster.

red salmon *n.* any salmon having reddish flesh, esp. the sockeye salmon.

redshank (ˈrɛdˌʃæŋk) *n.* any of various large common European sandpipers, esp. the **spotted redshank,** having red legs.

red shift *n.* a shift in the spectral lines of a stellar spectrum towards the red end of the visible region relative to the wavelength of these lines in the terrestrial spectrum.

redskin (ˈrɛdˌskɪn) *n.* an informal name, now considered offensive, for an **American Indian.** [so called because one now extinct tribe painted themselves with red ochre]

red snapper *n.* any of various marine percoid food fishes of the snapper family, having a reddish coloration, common in American coastal regions of the Atlantic.

red spider *n.* short for **red spider mite** (see **spider mite**).

Red Spot *n.* a reddish oval spot, about 48 000 kilometres long, seen to drift around the S hemisphere of Jupiter.

red squirrel *n.* a reddish-brown squirrel, inhabiting woodlands of Europe and parts of Asia.

redstart (ˈrɛdˌstɑːt) *n.* **1.** a European songbird of the thrush family: the male has a black throat, orange-brown tail and breast, and grey back. **2.** a North American warbler. [OE *rēad* red + *steort* tail]

red tape *n.* obstructive official routine or procedure; time-consuming bureaucracy. [C18: from the red tape used to bind official government documents]

reduce (rɪˈdjuːs) *vb.* (*mainly tr.*) **1.** (*also intr.*) to make or become smaller in size, number, etc. **2.** to bring into a certain state, condition, etc.: *to reduce a forest to ashes; he was reduced to tears.* **3.** (*also intr.*) to make or become slimmer; lose or cause to lose excess weight. **4.** to impoverish (esp. in **in reduced circumstances**). **5.** to bring into a state of submission to one's authority; subjugate: *the whole country was reduced after three months.* **6.** to bring down the price of (a commodity). **7.** to lower the rank or status of; demote: *reduced to the ranks.* **8.** to set out systematically as an aid to understanding; simplify: *his theories have been reduced in a treatise.* **9.** *Maths.* to modify or simplify the form of (an expression or equation), esp. by substitution of one term by another. **10.** to thin out (paint) by adding oil, turpentine, etc. **11.** (*also intr.*) *Chem.* **a.** to undergo or cause to undergo a chemical reaction with hydrogen. **b.** to lose or cause to lose oxygen atoms. **c.** to undergo or cause to undergo an increase in the number of electrons. **12.** *Photog.* to lessen the density of (a negative or

---

ˌ**redisˈtribute** *vb.*
ˌ**rediˈvide** *vb.*
ˌ**rediˈvision** *n.*
ˈ**reˌdraft** *n.*
reˈdraft *vb.*
reˈdraw *vb.*
reˈdrill *vb.*

print). **13.** *Surgery.* to manipulate or reposition (a broken or displaced bone, organ, or part) back to its normal site. [C14: < L *redūcere* to bring back, < RE- + *dūcere* to lead] **—reˈducible** *adj.* **—reˌduciˈbility** *n.* **—reˈducibly** *adv.*

reducer (rɪˈdjuːsə) *n.* **1.** *Photog.* a chemical solution used to lessen the density of a negative or print by oxidizing some of the blackened silver to soluble silver compounds. **2.** a pipe fitting connecting two pipes of different diameters. **3.** a person or thing that reduces.

reducing agent *n. Chem.* a substance that reduces another substance in a chemical reaction, being itself oxidized in the process.

reducing glass *n.* a lens or curved mirror that produces an image smaller than the object observed.

reductase (rɪˈdʌkteɪz) *n.* any enzyme that catalyses a biochemical reduction reaction. [C20: < REDUCTION + -ASE]

reductio ad absurdum (rɪˈdʌktɪəʊ æd æbˈsɜːdəm) *n.* **1.** a method of disproving a proposition by showing that its inevitable consequences would be absurd. **2.** a method of indirectly proving a proposition by assuming its negation to be true and showing that this leads to an absurdity. **3.** application of a principle or proposed principle to an instance in which it is absurd. [L, lit.: reduction to the absurd]

reduction (rɪˈdʌkʃən) *n.* **1.** the act or process or an instance of reducing. **2.** the state or condition of being reduced. **3.** the amount by which something is reduced. **4.** a form of an original resulting from a reducing process, such as a copy on a smaller scale. **5.** *Maths.* **a.** the process of converting a fraction into its decimal form. **b.** the process of dividing out the common factors in the numerator and denominator of a fraction. **—reˈductive** *adj.*

reduction formula *n. Maths.* a formula expressing the values of a trigonometric function of any angle greater than 90° in terms of a function of an acute angle.

reductionism (rɪˈdʌkʃəˌnɪzəm) *n.* **1.** the analysis of complex things, data, etc., into less complex constituents. **2.** *Often disparaging.* any theory or method that holds that a complex idea, system, etc., can be completely understood in terms of its simpler parts or components. **—reˈductionist** *n., adj.* **—reˌductionˈistic** *adj.*

redundancy (rɪˈdʌndənsɪ) *n., pl.* **-cies. 1. a.** the state or condition of being redundant or superfluous, esp. superfluous in one's job. **b.** (*as modifier*): *a redundancy payment.* **2.** excessive proliferation or profusion, esp. of superfluity.

redundant (rɪˈdʌndənt) *adj.* **1.** surplus to requirements; unnecessary or superfluous. **2.** verbose or tautological. **3.** deprived of one's job because it is no longer necessary. [C17: < L *redundans* overflowing, < *redundāre* to stream over; see REDOUND] **—reˈdundantly** *adv.*

red underwing *n.* a large noctuid moth having hind wings coloured red and black.

reduplicate *vb.* (rɪˈdjuːplɪˌkeɪt). **1.** to make or become double; repeat. **2.** to repeat (a sound or syllable) in a word or (of a sound or syllable) to be repeated. ~*adj.* (rɪˈdjuːplɪkɪt). **3.** doubled or repeated. **4.** (of petals or sepals) having the margins curving outwards. **—reˌdupliˈcation** *n.* **—reˈduplicative** *adj.*

red-water *n.* a disease of cattle which destroys the red blood cells, characterized by the passage of red or blackish urine.

red wine *n.* wine made from black grapes and coloured by their skins.

redwing (ˈrɛdˌwɪŋ) *n.* a small European thrush having a speckled breast, reddish flanks, and brown back.

redwood (ˈrɛdˌwʊd) *n.* a giant coniferous tree of coastal regions of California, having reddish fibrous bark and durable timber.

reebok (ˈriːbʌk, -bɒk) *n., pl.* **-boks** *or* **-bok.** a variant spelling of **rhebok.**

re-echo (riːˈɛkəʊ) *vb.* **-oing, -oed. 1.** to echo (a sound that is already an echo); resound. **2.** (*tr.*) to repeat like an echo.

reed (riːd) *n.* **1.** any of various widely distributed tall grasses that grow in swamps and shallow water and have jointed hollow stalks. **2.** the stalk, or stalks collectively, of any of these plants, esp. as used for thatching. **3.** *Music.* **a.** a thin piece of cane or metal inserted into the tubes of certain wind instruments, which sets in vibration the air column inside the tube. **b.** a wind instrument or organ pipe that sounds by means of a reed. **4.** one of the several vertical parallel wires on a loom that may be moved upwards to separate the warp threads. **5.** a small semicircular architectural moulding. **6.** an archaic word for **arrow. 7. broken reed.** a weak, unreliable, or ineffectual person. ~*vb.* (*tr.*) **8.** to fashion into or supply with reeds or reeding. **9.** to thatch using reeds. [OE *hreod*]

reedbuck (ˈriːdˌbʌk) *n., pl.* **-bucks** *or* **-buck.** an antelope of Africa south of the Sahara, having a buff-coloured coat and inward-curving horns.

reed bunting *n.* a common European bunting that has a brown streaked plumage with, in the male, a black head.

reed grass *n.* a tall perennial grass of rivers and ponds of Europe, Asia, and Canada.

reeding (ˈriːdɪŋ) *n.* **1.** a set of small semicircular architectural mouldings. **2.** the milling on the edges of a coin.

reedling (ˈriːdlɪŋ) *n.* a titlike Eurasian songbird, common in reed beds, which belongs to the family of Old World flycatchers and has a tawny back and tail and, in the male, a grey-and-black head. Also called: **bearded tit.**

reed mace *n.* a tall reedlike marsh plant, with straplike leaves and flowers in long brown spikes. Also called: (popularly) **bulrush, cat's-tail.**

reed organ *n.* **1.** a wind instrument, such as the harmonium, accordion, or harmonica, in which the sound is produced by reeds, each reed producing one note only. **2.** a type of pipe organ in which all the pipes are fitted with reeds.

reed pipe *n.* **1.** a wind instrument, such as a clarinet, whose sound is produced by a vibrating reed. **2.** an organ pipe sounded by a vibrating reed.

reed stop *n.* an organ stop controlling a rank of reed pipes.

reed warbler *n.* any of various common Old World warblers that inhabit marshy regions and have a brown plumage.

reedy (ˈriːdɪ) *adj.* **reedier, reediest. 1.** (of a place) abounding in reeds. **2.** of or like a reed. **3.** having a tone like a reed instrument; shrill or piping. **—ˈreedily** *adv.* **—ˈreediness** *n.*

reef[1] (riːf) *n.* **1.** a ridge of rock, sand, coral, etc., the top of which lies close to the surface of the sea. **2.** a vein of ore, esp. one of gold-bearing quartz. **3.** (*cap.*) **the. a.** the Great Barrier Reef in Australia. **b.** the Witwatersrand in South Africa, a gold-bearing ridge. [C16: < MDu. *ref,* < ON *rif* RIB[1], REEF[2]]

reef[2] (riːf) *Naut.* ~*n.* **1.** the part gathered in when sail area is reduced, as in a high wind. ~*vb.* **2.** to reduce the area of (sail) by taking in a reef. **3.** (*tr.*) to shorten or bring inboard (a spar). [C14: < MDu. *rif;* rel. to ON *rif* reef, RIB[1]]

reefer (ˈriːfə) *n.* **1.** *Naut.* a person who reefs, such as a midshipman. **2.** another name for **reefing jacket. 3.** *Sl.* a hand-rolled cigarette containing cannabis. [C19: < REEF[2]; applied to the cigarette < its resemblance to the rolled reef of a sail]

reefing jacket *n.* a man's short double-breasted jacket of sturdy wool.

reef knot *n.* a knot consisting of two overhand knots turned opposite ways. Also called: **square knot.**

---

re-ˈedit *vb.* **re-ˈeduˌcate** *vb.* **re-ˌeduˈcation** *n.*

reef point *n. Naut.* one of several short lengths of line stitched through a sail for tying a reef.

reek (riːk) *vb.* **1.** (*intr.*) to give off or emit a strong unpleasant odour; smell or stink. **2.** (*intr.*; often foll. by *of*) to be permeated (by): *the letter reeks of subservience.* **3.** (*tr.*) to treat with smoke; fumigate. **4.** (*tr.*) *Chiefly dialect.* to give off or emit (smoke, fumes, etc.). ~*n.* **5.** a strong offensive smell; stink. **6.** *Chiefly dialect.* smoke or steam; vapour. [OE *rēocan*] —**'reeky** *adj.*

reel[1] (riːl, rɪəl) *n.* **1.** any of various cylindrical objects or frames that turn on an axis and onto which film, tape, wire, etc., may be wound. U.S. equivalent: **spool. 2.** *Angling.* a device for winding, casting, etc., consisting of a revolving spool with a handle, attached to a fishing rod. ~*vb.* (*tr.*) **3.** to wind (cotton, thread, etc.) onto a reel. **4.** (foll. by *in, out,* etc.) to wind or draw with a reel: *to reel in a fish.* [OE *hrēol*] —**'reelable** *adj.* —**'reeler** *n.*

reel[2] (riːl, rɪəl) *vb.* (*mainly intr.*) **1.** to sway, esp. under the shock of a blow or through dizziness or drunkenness. **2.** to whirl about or have the feeling of whirling about: *his brain reeled.* ~*n.* **3.** a staggering or swaying motion or sensation. [C14 *relen,* prob. < REEL[1]]

reel[3] (riːl, rɪəl) *n.* **1.** any of various lively Scottish dances for a fixed number of couples who combine in square and circular formations. **2.** a piece of music composed for or in the rhythm of this dance. [C18: < REEL[2]]

reel-fed *adj. Printing.* involving or printing on a web of paper: *a reel-fed press.*

reelman ('riːlmən, 'rɪəl-) *n., pl.* **-men.** *Austral. & N.Z.* the member of a beach life-saving team who controls the reel on which the line is wound.

reel off *vb.* (*tr., adv.*) to recite or write fluently and without apparent effort.

reel-to-reel *adj.* **1.** (of magnetic tape) wound from one reel to another in use. **2.** (of a tape recorder) using magnetic tape wound from one reel to another, as opposed to cassettes.

re-entrant (riː'ɛntrənt) *adj.* **1.** (of an angle) pointing inwards. ~*n.* **2.** an angle or part that points inwards.

re-entry (riː'ɛntrɪ) *n., pl.* **-tries. 1.** the act of retaking possession of land, etc. **2.** the return of a spacecraft into the earth's atmosphere.

reeve[1] (riːv) *n.* **1.** *English history.* the local representative of the king in a shire until the early 11th century. **2.** (in medieval England) a manorial steward who supervised the daily affairs of the manor. **3.** *Canad. government.* (in some provinces) a president of a local council, esp. in a rural area. **4.** (formerly) a minor local official in England and the U.S. [OE *gerēva*]

reeve[2] (riːv) *vb.* **reeving, reeved** *or* **rove.** (*tr.*) *Naut.* **1.** to pass (a rope or cable) through an eye or other narrow opening. **2.** to fasten by passing through or around something. [C17: ? < Du. *rēven* REEF[2]]

reeve[3] (riːv) *n.* the female of the ruff (the bird). [C17: <?]

re-export *vb.* (ˌriːɪk'spɔːt, ˌriː'ɛkspɔːt). **1.** to export (imported goods, esp. after processing). ~*n.* (riː'ɛkspɔːt). **2.** the act of re-exporting. **3.** a re-exported commodity. —ˌ**re-expor'tation** *n.* —ˌ**re-ex'porter** *n.*

ref (rɛf) *n. Inf.* short for **referee.**

ref. *abbrev. for:* **1.** referee. **2.** reference. **3.** reformed.

refection (rɪ'fɛkʃən) *n.* refreshment with food and drink. [C14: < L *refectiō* a restoring, < *reficere,* < RE- + *facere* to make]

refectory (rɪ'fɛktərɪ, -trɪ) *n., pl.* **-ries.** a dining hall in a religious or academic institution. [C15: < LL *refectōrium,* < L *refectus* refreshed]

refectory table *n.* a long narrow dining table supported by two trestles.

refer (rɪ'fɜː) *vb.* **-ferring, -ferred.** (often foll. by *to*). **1.** (*intr.*) to make mention (of). **2.** (*tr.*) to direct the attention of (someone) for information, facts, etc.: *the reader is referred to Chomsky, 1965.* **3.** (*intr.*) to seek information (from): *he referred to his notes.* **4.** (*intr.*) to be relevant (to); pertain or relate (to). **5.** (*tr.*) to assign or attribute: *Cromwell referred his victories to God.* **6.** (*tr.*) to hand over for consideration, reconsideration, or decision: *to refer a complaint to another department.* **7.** (*tr.*) to hand back to the originator as unacceptable or unusable. **8.** (*tr.*) *Brit.* to fail (a student) in an examination. **9. refer to drawer.** a request by a bank that the payee consult the drawer concerning a cheque payable by that bank. **10.** (*tr.*) to direct (a patient, client, etc.) to another doctor, agency, etc. [C14: < L *referre,* < RE- + *ferre* to BEAR[1]] —**referable** ('rɛfərəbəl) *or* **referrable** (rɪ'fɜːrəbəl) *adj.* —**re'ferral** *n.* —**re'ferrer** *n.*

▷ **Usage.** The common practice of adding *back* to *refer* is tautologous, since this meaning is already contained in the *re-* of *refer: this refers to* (not *back to*) *what has already been said.* However, when *refer* is used in the sense of passing a document or question for further consideration to the person from whom it was received, it may be appropriate to say *he referred the matter back.*

referee (ˌrɛfə'riː) *n.* **1.** a person to whom reference is made, esp. for an opinion, information, or a decision. **2.** the umpire or judge in any of various sports, esp. football and boxing. **3.** a person who is willing to testify to the character or capabilities of someone. **4.** *Law.* a person appointed by a court to report on a matter. ~*vb.* **-eeing, -eed. 5.** to act as a referee (in); preside (over).

reference ('rɛfərəns, 'rɛfrəns) *n.* **1.** the act or an instance of referring. **2.** something referred, esp. proceedings submitted to a referee in law. **3.** a direction of the attention to a passage elsewhere or to another book, etc. **4.** a book or passage referred to. **5.** a mention or allusion: *this book contains several references to the Civil War.* **6.** the relation between a word or phrase and the object or idea to which it refers. **7. a.** a source of information or facts. **b.** (*as modifier*): *a reference book; a reference library.* **8.** a written testimonial regarding one's character or capabilities. **9.** a person referred to for such a testimonial. **10. a.** (foll. by *to*) relation or delimitation, esp. to or by membership of a specific group: *without reference to sex or age.* **b.** (*as modifier*): *a reference group.* **11. terms of reference.** the specific limits of responsibility that determine the activities of an investigating body, etc. ~*vb.* (*tr.*) **12.** to furnish or compile a list of references for (a publication, etc.). **13.** to make a reference to; refer to. ~*prep.* **14.** *Business jargon.* with reference to: *reference your letter of the 9th inst.* Abbrev.: **re.** —**referential** (ˌrɛfə'rɛnʃəl) *adj.*

referendum (ˌrɛfə'rɛndəm) *n., pl.* **-dums** *or* **-da** (-də). **1.** submission of an issue of public importance to the direct vote of the electorate. **2.** a vote on such a measure. ~See also **plebiscite.** [C19: < L: something to be carried back, < *referre* to REFER]

referent ('rɛfərənt) *n.* the object or idea to which a word or phrase refers. [C19: < L *referens* < *referre* to REFER]

ˌ**re-e'lect** *vb.*
ˌ**re-e'lection** *n.*
re-'eligible *adj.*
ˌ**re-e'merge** *vb.*
ˌ**re-e'mergence** *n.*
ˌ**re-e'mergent** *adj.*
re-'emphaˌsize *or* **-ˌsise** *vb.*
ˌ**re-em'ploy** *vb.*
ˌ**re-em'ployment** *n.*
ˌ**re-en'act** *vb.*
ˌ**re-en'actment** *n.*
ˌ**re-en'force** *vb.*
ˌ**re-en'forcement** *n.*
re-'enter *vb.*
ˌ**re-e'quip** *vb.*
ˌ**re-e'rect** *vb.*
ˌ**re-es'tablish** *vb.*
ˌ**re-e'valuˌate** *vb.*
ˌ**re-eˌvalu'ation** *n.*
ˌ**re-ex'amine** *vb.*
ˌ**re-ex'hibit** *vb.*
ˌ**re-ex'perience** *vb.*
re'face *vb.*

referred pain *n. Psychol.* pain felt at some place other than its actual place of origin.

refill *vb.* (riːˈfɪl). **1.** to fill (something) again. ~*n.* (ˈriːfɪl). **2.** a replacement for a consumable substance in a permanent container. **3.** a second or subsequent filling. —**reˈfillable** *adj.*

refine (rɪˈfaɪn) *vb.* **1.** to make or become free from impurities or foreign matter; purify. **2.** (*tr.*) to separate (a mixture) into pure constituents, as in an oil refinery. **3.** to make or become elegant or polished. **4.** (*intr.*; often foll. by *on* or *upon*) to enlarge or improve (upon) by making subtle or fine distinctions. **5.** (*tr.*) to make (language) more subtle or polished. [C16: < RE- + FINE[1]] —**reˈfinable** *adj.* —**reˈfiner** *n.*

refined (rɪˈfaɪnd) *adj.* **1.** not coarse or vulgar; genteel, elegant, or polite. **2.** subtle; discriminating. **3.** freed from impurities; purified.

refinement (rɪˈfaɪnmənt) *n.* **1.** the act of refining or the state of being refined. **2.** a fine or delicate point or distinction; a subtlety. **3.** fineness or precision of thought, expression, manners, etc. **4.** an improvement to a piece of equipment, etc.

refinery (rɪˈfaɪnərɪ) *n., pl.* **-eries.** a factory for the purification of some crude material, such as sugar, oil, etc.

refit *vb.* (riːˈfɪt), **-fitting, -fitted. 1.** to make or be made ready for use again by repairing, re-equipping, or resupplying. ~*n.* (ˈriːˌfɪt). **2.** a repair or re-equipping, as of a ship, for further use. —**reˈfitment** *n.*

refl. *abbrev. for:* **1.** reflection. **2.** reflective. **3.** reflex(ive).

reflate (riːˈfleɪt) *vb.* to inflate or be inflated again. [C20: back formation < REFLATION]

reflation (riːˈfleɪʃən) *n.* **1.** an increase in economic activity. **2.** an increase in the supply of money and credit designed to cause such economic activity. ~Cf. **inflation** (sense 2). [C20: < RE- + *-flation*, as in INFLATION]

reflect (rɪˈflɛkt) *vb.* **1.** to undergo or cause to undergo a process in which light, other electromagnetic radiation, sound, particles, etc., are thrown back after impinging on a surface. **2.** (of a mirror, etc.) to form an image of (something) by reflection. **3.** (*tr.*) to show or express: *his tactics reflect his desire for power.* **4.** (*tr.*) to bring as a consequence: *their success reflected great credit on them.* **5.** (*intr.*; foll. by *on* or *upon*) to cause to be regarded in a specified way: *her behaviour reflects well on her.* **6.** (*intr.*; often foll. by *on* or *upon*) to cast dishonour or honour, credit or discredit, etc. (on). **7.** (*intr.*; usually foll. by *on*) to think, meditate, or ponder. [C15: < L *reflectere*, < RE- + *flectere* to bend] —**reˈflectingly** *adv.*

reflectance (rɪˈflɛktəns) *or* **reflection factor** *n.* a measure of the ability of a surface to reflect light or other electromagnetic radiation, equal to the ratio of the reflected flux to the incident flux.

reflecting telescope *n.* a type of telescope in which the initial image is formed by a concave mirror. Also called: **reflector.** Cf. **refracting telescope.**

reflection *or* **reflexion** (rɪˈflɛkʃən) *n.* **1.** the act of reflecting or the state of being reflected. **2.** something reflected or the image so produced, as by a mirror. **3.** careful or long consideration or thought. **4.** attribution of discredit or blame. **5.** *Maths.* a transformation in which the direction of one axis is reversed or changes the polarity of one of the variables. **6.** *Anat.* the bending back of a structure or part upon itself. —**reˈflectional** *or* **reˈflexional** *adj.*

reflection density *n. Physics.* a measure of the extent to which a surface reflects light or other electromagnetic radiation. Symbol: *D*

reflective (rɪˈflɛktɪv) *adj.* **1.** characterized by quiet thought or contemplation. **2.** capable of reflecting: *a reflective surface.* **3.** produced by reflection. —**reˈflectively** *adv.*

reflectivity (ˌriːflɛkˈtɪvɪtɪ) *n.* **1.** *Physics.* a measure of the ability of a surface to reflect radiation, equal to the reflectance of a layer of material sufficiently thick for the reflectance not to depend on the thickness. **2.** Also: **reflectiveness.** the quality or capability of being reflective.

reflector (rɪˈflɛktə) *n.* **1.** a person or thing that reflects. **2.** a surface or object that reflects light, sound, heat, etc. **3.** another name for **reflecting telescope.**

reflet (rəˈfleɪ) *n.* an iridescent glow or lustre, as on ceramic ware. [C19: < F: a reflection, < It. *riflesso*, < L *reflexus*, < *reflectere* to reflect]

reflex *n.* (ˈriːflɛks). **1. a.** an immediate involuntary response, such as coughing, evoked by a given stimulus. **b.** (*as modifier*): *a reflex action.* See also **reflex arc. 2. a.** a mechanical response to a particular situation, involving no conscious decision. **b.** (*as modifier*): *a reflex response.* **3.** a reflection; an image produced by or as if by reflection. ~*adj.* (ˈriːflɛks). **4.** *Maths.* (of an angle) between 180° and 360°. **5.** (*prenominal*) turned, reflected, or bent backwards. ~*vb.* (rɪˈflɛks). **6.** (*tr.*) to bend, turn, or reflect backwards. [C16: < L *reflexus* bent back, < *reflectere* to reflect] —**reˈflexible** *adj.* —**reˌflexiˈbility** *n.*

reflex arc *n. Physiol.* the neural pathway over which impulses travel to produce a reflex action.

reflex camera *n.* a camera in which the image is composed and focused on a large ground-glass viewfinder screen.

reflexion (rɪˈflɛkʃən) *n. Brit.* a less common spelling of **reflection.** —**reˈflexional** *adj.*

reflexive (rɪˈflɛksɪv) *adj.* **1.** denoting a class of pronouns that refer back to the subject of a sentence or clause. Thus, in *that man thinks a great deal of himself,* the pronoun *himself* is reflexive. **2.** denoting a verb used transitively with the reflexive pronoun as its direct object, as in *to dress oneself.* **3.** *Physiol.* of or relating to a reflex. ~*n.* **4.** a reflexive pronoun or verb. —**reˈflexively** *adv.* —**reˈflexiveness** *or* **reflexivity** (ˌriːflɛkˈsɪvɪtɪ) *n.*

reflexology (ˌriːflɛkˈsɒlədʒɪ) *n.* a form of therapy in alternative medicine in which the soles of the feet are massaged: designed to stimulate the blood supply and nerves and thus relieve tension. —ˌ**reflexˈologist** *n.*

reflux (ˈriːflʌks) *vb.* **1.** *Chem.* to boil or be boiled in a vessel attached to a condenser, so that the vapour condenses and flows back into the vessel. ~*n.* **2.** *Chem.* **a.** an act of refluxing. **b.** (*as modifier*): *a reflux condenser.* **3.** the act or an instance of flowing back; ebb. [C15: < Med. L *refluxus*, < L *refluere* to flow back]

reform (rɪˈfɔːm) *vb.* **1.** (*tr.*) to improve (an existing institution, law, etc.) by alteration or correction of abuses. **2.** to give up or cause to give up a reprehensible habit or immoral way of life. ~*n.* **3.** an improvement or change for the better, esp. as a result of correction of legal or political abuses or malpractices. **4.** a principle, campaign, or measure aimed at achieving such change. **5.** improvement of morals or behaviour. [C14: via OF < L *reformāre* to form again] —**reˈformable** *adj.* —**reˈformative** *adj.* —**reˈformer** *n.*

re-form (riːˈfɔːm) *vb.* to form anew. —ˌ**reforˈmation** *n.*

reformation (ˌrɛfəˈmeɪʃən) *n.* **1.** the act or an instance of reforming or the state of being reformed. **2.** (*usually cap.*) a religious and political movement of 16th-century Europe that began as an attempt to reform the Roman Catholic Church and resulted in the establishment of the Protestant Churches. —ˌ**reforˈmational** *adj.*

---

reˈfilm *vb.*
refiˈnance *vb.*
reˈfinish *vb.*
reˈfloat *vb.*
reˈfocus *vb.*
reˈfold *vb.*
reˈforge *vb.*

reformatory (rɪˈfɔːmətərɪ, -trɪ) *n., pl.* **-ries.** **1.** Also called: **reform school.** (formerly) a place of instruction where young offenders were sent for corrective training. ~*adj.* **2.** having the purpose or function of reforming.

Reformed (rɪˈfɔːmd) *adj.* **1.** of or designating a Protestant Church, esp. the Calvinist. **2.** of or designating Reform Judaism.

reformism (rɪˈfɔːmɪzəm) *n.* a doctrine advocating reform, esp. political or religious reform rather than abolition. —**reˈformist** *n., adj.*

Reform Judaism *n.* a movement in Judaism which does not require strict observance of the law, but adapts Judaism to the contemporary world.

refract (rɪˈfrækt) *vb.* **1.** to cause to undergo refraction. **2.** (*tr.*) to measure the amount of refraction of (the eye, a lens, etc.). [C17: < L *refractus* broken up, < *refringere,* < RE- + *frangere* to break] —**reˈfractable** *adj.* —**reˈfractive** *adj.*

refracting telescope *n.* a type of telescope in which the image is formed by a set of lenses. Also called: **refractor.** Cf. **reflecting telescope.**

refraction (rɪˈfrækʃən) *n.* **1.** *Physics.* the change in direction of a propagating wave, such as light or sound, in passing from one medium to another in which it has a different velocity. **2.** the amount by which a wave is refracted. **3.** the ability of the eye to refract light. —**reˈfractional** *adj.*

refractive index *n. Physics.* a measure of the extent to which a medium refracts light; the ratio of the speed of light in free space to that in the medium.

refractometer (ˌriːfrækˈtɒmɪtə) *n.* any instrument for measuring the refractive index. —**refractometric** (rɪˌfræktəˈmɛtrɪk) *adj.* —ˌ**refracˈtometry** *n.*

refractor (rɪˈfræktə) *n.* **1.** an object or material that refracts. **2.** another name for **refracting telescope.**

refractory (rɪˈfræktərɪ) *adj.* **1.** unmanageable or obstinate. **2.** *Med.* not responding to treatment. **3.** *Physiol.* (of a nerve or muscle) incapable of responding to stimulation. **4.** (of a material) able to withstand high temperatures without fusion or decomposition. ~*n., pl.* **-ries.** **5.** a material, such as fire clay, that is able to withstand high temperatures. —**reˈfractorily** *adv.* —**reˈfractoriness** *n.*

refrain[1] (rɪˈfreɪn) *vb.* (*intr.;* usually foll. by *from*) to abstain (from action); forbear. [C14: < L *refrēnāre* to check with a bridle, < RE- + *frēnum* a bridle] —**reˈfrainer** *n.* —**reˈfrainment** *n.*

refrain[2] (rɪˈfreɪn) *n.* **1.** a regularly recurring melody, such as the chorus of a song. **2.** a much repeated saying or idea. [C14: via OF, ult. < L *refringere* to break into pieces]

refrangible (rɪˈfrændʒɪbəl) *adj.* capable of being refracted. [C17: < L *refringere* to break up, < RE- + *frangere* to break] —**reˌfrangiˈbility** *or* **reˈfrangibleness** *n.*

refresh (rɪˈfrɛʃ) *vb.* **1.** (*usually tr. or reflexive*) to make or become fresh or vigorous, as through rest, drink, or food; revive or reinvigorate. **2.** (*tr.*) to enliven (something worn or faded), as by adding new decorations. **3.** to pour cold water over previously blanched and drained food. **4.** (*tr.*) to stimulate (the memory, etc.). **5.** (*tr.*) to replenish, as with new equipment or stores. [C14: < OF *refreschir;* see RE-, FRESH] —**reˈfresher** *n.* —**reˈfreshing** *adj.*

refresher course *n.* a short educational course for people to review their subject and developments in it.

refreshment (rɪˈfrɛʃmənt) *n.* **1.** the act of refreshing or the state of being refreshed. **2.** (*pl.*) snacks and drinks served as a light meal.

refrigerant (rɪˈfrɪdʒərənt) *n.* **1.** a fluid capable of changes of phase at low temperatures: used as the working fluid of a refrigerator. **2.** a cooling substance, such as ice or solid carbon dioxide. **3.** *Med.* an agent that provides a sensation of coolness or reduces fever. ~*adj.* **4.** causing cooling or freezing.

refrigerate (rɪˈfrɪdʒəˌreɪt) *vb.* to make or become frozen or cold, esp. for preservative purposes; chill or freeze. [C16: < L *refrīgerāre* to make cold, < RE- + *frīgus* cold] —**reˌfrigerˈation** *n.* —**reˈfrigerative** *adj.* —**reˈfrigeratory** *adj., n.*

refrigerator (rɪˈfrɪdʒəˌreɪtə) *n.* a chamber in which food, drink, etc., are kept cool. Informal name: **fridge.**

refringent (rɪˈfrɪndʒənt) *adj. Physics.* of, concerned with, or causing refraction; refractive. [C18: < L *refringere;* see REFRACT] —**reˈfringency** *or* **reˈfringence** *n.*

reft (rɛft) *vb.* a past tense and past participle of **reave.**

refuel (riːˈfjuːəl) *vb.* **-elling, -elled** *or U.S.* **-eling, -eled.** to supply or be supplied with fresh fuel.

refuge (ˈrɛfjuːdʒ) *n.* **1.** shelter or protection, as from the weather or danger. **2.** any place, person, action, or thing that offers protection, help, or relief. [C14: via OF < L *refugium,* < *refugere,* < RE- + *fugere* to escape]

refugee (ˌrɛfjʊˈdʒiː) *n.* **a.** a person who has fled from some danger or problem, esp. political persecution. **b.** (*as modifier*): *a refugee camp.* —ˌ**refuˈgeeism** *n.*

refugium (rɪˈfjuːdʒɪəm) *n., pl.* **-gia** (-dʒɪə). a geographical region that has remained unaltered by a climatic change affecting surrounding regions and that therefore forms a haven for relict fauna and flora. [C20: L: REFUGE]

refulgent (rɪˈfʌldʒənt) *adj. Literary.* shining, brilliant, or radiant. [C16: < L *refulgēre,* < RE- + *fulgēre* to shine] —**reˈfulgence** *or* **reˈfulgency** *n.* —**reˈfulgently** *adv.*

refund *vb.* (rɪˈfʌnd). (*tr.*) **1.** to give back (money, etc.), as when an article purchased is unsatisfactory. **2.** to reimburse (a person). ~*n.* (ˈriːˌfʌnd). **3.** return of money to a purchaser or the amount so returned. [C14: < L *refundere,* < RE- + *fundere* to pour] —**reˈfundable** *adj.* —**reˈfunder** *n.*

re-fund (riːˈfʌnd) *vb.* (*tr.*) *Finance.* to discharge (an old or matured debt) by new borrowing, as by a new bond issue. [C20: < RE- + FUND]

refurbish (riːˈfɜːbɪʃ) *vb.* (*tr.*) to renovate, re-equip, or restore. —**reˈfurbishment** *n.*

refusal (rɪˈfjuːzəl) *n.* **1.** the act or an instance of refusing. **2.** the opportunity to reject or accept; option.

refuse[1] (rɪˈfjuːz) *vb.* **1.** (*tr.*) to decline to accept (something offered): *to refuse promotion.* **2.** to decline to give or grant (something) to (a person, etc.). **3.** (when *tr., takes an infinitive*) to express determination not (to do something); decline: *he refuses to talk about it.* **4.** (of a horse) to be unwilling to take (a jump). [C14: < OF *refuser,* < L *refundere* to pour back] —**reˈfusable** *adj.* —**reˈfuser** *n.*

refuse[2] (ˈrɛfjuːs) *n.* **a.** anything thrown away; waste; rubbish. **b.** (*as modifier*): *a refuse collection.* [C15: < OF *refuser* to REFUSE[1]]

refusenik *or* **refusnik** (rɪˈfjuːznɪk) *n.* a Jew in the Soviet Union who has been refused permission to emigrate. [C20: < REFUSE[1] + -NIK]

refute (rɪˈfjuːt) *vb.* (*tr.*) to prove (a statement, theory, charge, etc.) of (a person) to be false or incorrect; disprove. [C16: < L *refūtāre* to rebut] —**refutable** (ˈrɛfjʊtəbəl, rɪˈfjuː-) *adj.* —ˈ**refutably** *adv.* —ˌ**refuˈtation** *n.* —**reˈfuter** *n.*

▷ **Usage.** *Refute* is often used incorrectly as a synonym of *deny.* In careful usage, however, to *deny* something is to state that it is untrue; to *refute* something is to assemble evidence in order to prove it untrue: *all he could do was deny the allegations since he was unable to refute them.*

reg. *abbrev. for:* **1.** regiment. **2.** register(ed). **3.** registrar. **4.** regular(ly). **5.** regulation.

---

reˈformuˌlate *vb.*
ˌ**reformuˈlation** *n.*
reˈfreeze *vb.*
reˈfurnish *vb.*

regain (rɪˈgeɪn) *vb.* (*tr.*) **1.** to take or get back; recover. **2.** to reach again. —**reˈgainer** *n.*

regal (ˈriːgᵊl) *adj.* of, relating to, or befitting a king or queen; royal. [C14: < L *rēgālis*, < *rēx* king] —**reˈgality** *n.* —**ˈregally** *adv.*

regale (rɪˈgeɪl) *vb.* (*tr.*; usually foll. by *with*) **1.** to give delight or amusement to: *he regaled them with stories.* **2.** to provide with choice or abundant food or drink. ~*n.* **3.** *Arch.* **a.** a feast. **b.** a delicacy of food or drink. [C17: < F *régaler*, < *gale* pleasure] —**reˈgalement** *n.*

regalia (rɪˈgeɪlɪə) *n.* (*pl.*, *sometimes functioning as sing.*) **1.** the ceremonial emblems or robes of royalty, high office, an order, etc. **2.** any splendid or special clothes; finery. [C16: < Med. L: royal privileges, < L *rēgālis* REGAL]

regard (rɪˈgɑːd) *vb.* **1.** to look closely or attentively at (something or someone); observe steadily. **2.** (*tr.*) to hold (a person or thing) in respect, admiration, or affection: *we regard your work very highly.* **3.** (*tr.*) to look upon or consider in a specified way: *she regarded her brother as her responsibility.* **4.** (*tr.*) to relate to; concern; have a bearing on. **5.** to take notice of or pay attention to (something); heed: *he has never regarded the conventions.* **6. as regards.** (*prep.*) in respect of; concerning. ~*n.* **7.** a gaze; look. **8.** attention; heed: *he spends without regard to his bank balance.* **9.** esteem, affection, or respect. **10.** reference, relation, or connection (esp. in **with regard to** *or* **in regard to**). **11.** (*pl.*) good wishes or greetings (esp. in **with kind regards,** used at the close of a letter). **12. in this regard.** on this point. [C14: < OF *regarder* to look at, care about, < RE- + *garder* to GUARD]

regardant (rɪˈgɑːdᵊnt) *adj.* (*usually postpositive*) *Heraldry.* (of a beast) shown looking backwards over its shoulder. [C15: < OF; see REGARD]

regardful (rɪˈgɑːdfʊl) *adj.* **1.** (often foll. by *of*) showing regard (for); heedful (of). **2.** showing regard, respect, or consideration. —**reˈgardfully** *adv.*

regarding (rɪˈgɑːdɪŋ) *prep.* in respect of; on the subject of.

regardless (rɪˈgɑːdlɪs) *adj.* **1.** (usually foll. by *of*) taking no regard or heed; heedless. ~*adv.* **2.** in spite of everything; disregarding drawbacks. —**reˈgardlessly** *adv.* —**reˈgardlessness** *n.*

regatta (rɪˈgætə) *n.* an organized series of races of yachts, rowing boats, etc. [C17: < obs. It. *rigatta* contest, <?]

regd *abbrev. for* registered.

regelation (ˌriːdʒɪˈleɪʃən) *n.* the rejoining together of two pieces of ice as a result of melting under pressure at the interface between them and subsequent refreezing. —**ˈregeˌlate** *vb.*

regency (ˈriːdʒənsɪ) *n.*, *pl.* **-cies.** **1.** government by a regent. **2.** the office of a regent. **3.** a territory under the jurisdiction of a regent. [C15: < Med. L *regentia*, < L *regere* to rule]

Regency (ˈriːdʒənsɪ) *n.* (preceded by *the*) **1.** (in Britain) the period (1811–20) of the regency of the Prince of Wales (later George IV). **2.** (in France) the period (1715-23) of the regency of Philip, Duke of Orleans. ~*adj.* **3.** characteristic of or relating to the Regency periods or to the styles of architecture, art, etc., produced in them.

regenerate *vb.* (rɪˈdʒɛnəˌreɪt). **1.** to undergo or cause to undergo moral, spiritual, or physical renewal or invigoration. **2.** to form or be formed again; come or bring into existence once again. **3.** to replace (lost or damaged tissues or organs) by new growth, or to cause (such tissues) to be replaced. **4.** (*tr.*) *Electronics.* to use positive feedback to improve the demodulation and amplification of a signal. ~*adj.* (rɪˈdʒɛnərɪt). **5.** morally, spiritually, or physically renewed or reborn. —**reˈgeneracy** *n.* —**reˌgenerˈation** *n.* —**reˈgenerative** *adj.* —**reˈgeneratively** *adv.* —**reˈgenerˌator** *n.*

regent (ˈriːdʒənt) *n.* **1.** the ruler or administrator of a country during the minority, absence, or incapacity of its monarch. **2.** *U.S. & Canad.* a member of the governing board of certain schools and colleges. ~*adj.* **3.** (*usually postpositive*) acting or functioning as a regent: *a queen regent.* [C14: < L *regēns*, < *regere* to rule] —**ˈregental** *adj.* —**ˈregentship** *n.*

regent-bird *n. Austral.* a bowerbird, the male of which has showy yellow and velvety-black plumage. [after the Prince *Regent*]

reggae (ˈrɛgeɪ) *n.* a type of West Indian popular music having four beats to the bar, the upbeat being strongly accented. [C20: of West Indian origin]

regicide (ˈrɛdʒɪˌsaɪd) *n.* **1.** the killing of a king. **2.** a person who kills a king. [C16: < L *rēx* king + -CIDE] —ˌ**regiˈcidal** *adj.*

regime *or* **régime** (reɪˈʒiːm) *n.* **1.** a system of government or a particular administration: *a fascist regime.* **2.** a social system or order. **3.** *Med.* another word for **regimen** (sense 1). [C18: < F, < L *regimen* guidance, < *regere* to rule]

regimen (ˈrɛdʒɪˌmɛn) *n.* **1.** Also called: **regime.** *Med.* a systematic course of therapy, often including a recommended diet. **2.** administration or rule. [C14: < L: guidance]

regiment *n.* (ˈrɛdʒɪmənt). **1.** a military formation varying in size from a battalion to a number of battalions. **2.** a large number in regular or organized groups. ~*vb.* (ˈrɛdʒɪˌmɛnt). (*tr.*) **3.** to force discipline or order on, esp. in a domineering manner. **4.** to organize into a regiment. **5.** to form into organized groups. [C14: via OF < LL *regimentum* government, < L *regere* to rule] —ˌ**regiˈmental** *adj.* —ˌ**regiˈmentally** *adv.* —ˌ**regimenˈtation** *n.*

regimentals (ˌrɛdʒɪˈmɛntᵊlz) *pl. n.* **1.** the uniform and insignia of a regiment. **2.** military dress.

Regina (rɪˈdʒaɪnə) *n.* queen: now used chiefly in documents, inscriptions, etc. Cf. **Rex.**

region (ˈriːdʒən) *n.* **1.** any large, indefinite, and continuous part of a surface or space. **2.** an area considered as a unit for geographical, functional, social, or cultural reasons. **3.** an administrative division of a country, or a Canadian province. **4.** a realm or sphere of activity or interest. **5.** range, area, or scope: *in what region is the price likely to be?* **6.** a division or part of the body: *the lumbar region.* [C14: < L *regiō*, < *regere* to govern]

regional (ˈriːdʒənᵊl) *adj.* of, characteristic of, or limited to a region. —**ˈregionally** *adv.*

regionalism (ˈriːdʒənəˌlɪzəm) *n.* **1.** division of a country into administrative regions having partial autonomy. **2.** loyalty to one's home region; regional patriotism. —**ˈregionalist** *n.*, *adj.*

régisseur *French.* (reʒisœr) *n.* an official in a dance company with varying duties, usually including directing productions. [F, < *régir* to manage]

register (ˈrɛdʒɪstə) *n.* **1.** an official or formal list recording names, events, or transactions. **2.** the book in which such a list is written. **3.** an entry in such a list. **4.** a recording device that accumulates data, totals sums of money, etc.: *a cash register.* **5.** a movable plate that controls the flow of air into a furnace, chimney, room, etc. **6.** *Music.* **a.** the timbre characteristic of a certain manner of voice production. **b.** any of the stops on an organ as classified in respect of its tonal quality: *the flute register.* **7.** *Printing.* the exact correspondence of lines of type, etc., on the two sides of a printed sheet of paper. **8.** a form of a language associated with a particular social situation or subject matter. **9.** the act or an instance of registering. ~*vb.* **10.** (*tr.*) to enter or cause someone to enter (an event, person's name, ownership, etc.) on a register. **11.** to show or be shown on a scale or other measuring instrument: *the current didn't register on the meter.* **12.** to show or be shown in a person's face, bearing, etc.:

---

reˈgalvaˌnize *or* **-ˌnise** *vb.*
reˈgather *vb.*
reˈgermiˌnate *vb.*
ˌ**regermiˈnation** *n.*
reˈgild *vb.*

his face registered surprise. **13.** (*intr.*) *Inf.* to have an effect; make an impression: *the news of her uncle's death just did not register.* **14.** to send (a letter, package, etc.) by registered post. **15.** (*tr.*) *Printing.* to adjust (a printing press, forme, etc.) to ensure that the printed matter is in register. [C14: < Med. L *registrum,* < L *regerere* to transcribe, < RE- + *gerere* to bear] —ˈ**registrable** *adj.*

register office *n. Brit.* a government office where civil marriages are performed and births, marriages, and deaths are recorded. Often called: **registry office.**

registered post *n.* **1.** a Post Office service by which compensation is paid for loss or damage to mail for which a registration fee has been paid. **2.** mail sent by this service.

Registered Trademark *n.* See **trademark** (sense 1).

register ton *n.* the full name for **ton**[1] (sense 6).

registrar (ˌrɛdʒɪˈstrɑː, ˈrɛdʒɪˌstrɑː) *n.* **1.** a person who keeps official records. **2.** an administrative official responsible for student records, enrolment procedure, etc., in a school, college, or university. **3.** *Brit. & N.Z.* a hospital doctor senior to a houseman but junior to a consultant. **4.** *Austral.* the chief medical administrator of a large hospital. **5.** *Chiefly U.S.* a person employed by a company to maintain a register of its security issues. —ˈ**regisˌtrarship** *n.*

registration (ˌrɛdʒɪˈstreɪʃən) *n.* **1. a.** the act of registering or state of being registered. **b.** (*as modifier*): *a registration number.* **2.** an entry in a register. **3.** a group of people, such as students, who register at a particular time. **4.** *Austral.* **a.** a tax payable by the owner of a motor vehicle. **b.** the period paid for.

registration document *n. Brit.* a document giving identification details of a motor vehicle, including its manufacturer, date of registration, and owner's name.

registration number *n.* a sequence of letters and numbers assigned to a motor vehicle when it is registered, usually indicating the year and place of registration, displayed on numberplates at the front and rear of the vehicle.

registration plate *n. Austral. & N.Z.* the numberplate of a vehicle.

registry (ˈrɛdʒɪstrɪ) *n., pl.* **-tries. 1.** a place where registers are kept. **2.** the registration of a ship's country of origin: *a ship of Liberian registry.* **3.** another word for **registration.**

registry office *n. Brit.* another term for **register office.**

Regius professor (ˈriːdʒɪəs) *n. Brit.* a person appointed by the Crown to a university chair founded by a royal patron. [C17: *regius,* < L: royal, < *rex* king]

reglet (ˈrɛglɪt) *n.* **1.** a flat narrow architectural moulding. **2.** *Printing.* a strip of oiled wood used for spacing between lines. [C16: < OF, lit.: a little rule, < *régle* rule, < L *rēgula*]

regmaker (ˈrɛxˌmɑːkə) *n. S. African.* a drink to relieve the symptoms of a hangover. [< Afrik., right maker]

regnal (ˈrɛgnəl) *adj.* **1.** of a sovereign or reign. **2.** designating a year of a sovereign's reign calculated from the date of accession. [C17: < Med. L *rēgnālis,* < L *rēgnum* sovereignty; see REIGN]

regnant (ˈrɛgnənt) *adj.* **1.** (*postpositive*) reigning. **2.** prevalent; current. [C17: < L *regnāre* to REIGN] —ˈ**regnancy** *n.*

regorge (rɪˈgɔːdʒ) *vb.* **1.** (*tr.*) to vomit up; disgorge. **2.** (*intr.*) (esp. of water) to flow or run back. [C17: < F *regorger;* see GORGE]

regress *vb.* (rɪˈgrɛs). **1.** (*intr.*) to return or revert, as to a former place, condition, or mode of behaviour. **2.** (*tr.*) *Statistics.* to measure the extent to which (a dependent variable) is associated with one or more independent variables. ~*n.* (ˈriːgrɛs). **3.** movement in a backward direction; retrogression. [C14: < L *regressus,* < *regredī* to go back, < RE- + *gradī* to go] —**reˈgressive** *adj.* —**reˈgressor** *n.*

regression (rɪˈgrɛʃən) *n.* **1.** *Psychol.* the adoption by an adult of behaviour more appropriate to a child. **2.** *Statistics.* **a.** the measure of the association between one variable (the dependent variable) and other variables (the independent variables). **b.** (*as modifier*): *regression curve.* **3.** the act of regressing.

regret (rɪˈgrɛt) *vb.* **-gretting, -gretted.** (*tr.*) **1.** (*may take a clause as object or an infinitive*) to feel sorry, repentant, or upset about. **2.** to bemoan or grieve the death or loss of. ~*n.* **3.** a sense of repentance, guilt, or sorrow. **4.** a sense of loss or grief. **5.** (*pl.*) a polite expression of sadness, esp. in a formal refusal of an invitation. [C14: < OF *regreter,* < ON] —**reˈgretful** *adj.* —**reˈgretfully** *adv.* —**reˈgretfulness** *n.* —**reˈgrettable** *adj.* —**reˈgrettably** *adv.*

regroup (riːˈgruːp) *vb.* **1.** to reorganize (military forces), esp. after an attack or a defeat. **2.** (*tr.*) to rearrange into a new grouping.

Regt *abbrev. for:* **1.** Regent. **2.** Regiment.

regulable (ˈrɛgjʊləbᵊl) *adj.* able to be regulated.

regular (ˈrɛgjʊlə) *adj.* **1.** normal, customary, or usual. **2.** according to a uniform principle, arrangement, or order. **3.** occurring at fixed or prearranged intervals: *a regular call on a customer.* **4.** following a set rule or normal practice; methodical or orderly. **5.** symmetrical in appearance or form; even: *regular features.* **6.** (*prenominal*) organized, elected, conducted, etc., in a proper or officially prescribed manner. **7.** (*prenominal*) officially qualified or recognized: *he's not a regular doctor.* **8.** (*prenominal*) (intensifier): *a regular fool.* **9.** *U.S. & Canad. inf.* likable, dependable, or nice: *a regular guy.* **10.** denoting or relating to the personnel or units of the permanent military services: *a regular soldier.* **11.** (of flowers) having any of their parts, esp. petals, alike in size, etc.; symmetrical. **12.** *Grammar.* following the usual pattern of formation in a language. **13.** *Maths.* **a.** (of a polygon) equilateral and equiangular. **b.** (of a polyhedron) having identical regular polygons as faces. **c.** (of a prism) having regular polygons as bases. **d.** (of a pyramid) having a regular polygon as a base and the altitude passing through the centre of the base. **14.** *Bot.* (of a flower) having radial symmetry. **15.** (*postpositive*) subject to the rule of an established religious order or community: *canons regular.* ~*n.* **16.** a professional long-term serviceman in a military unit. **17.** *Inf.* a person who does something regularly, such as attending a theatre. **18.** a member of a religious order or congregation, as contrasted with a secular. [C14: < OF *reguler,* < L *rēgulāris* of a bar of wood or metal, < *rēgula* ruler, model] —ˌ**reguˈlarity** *n.* —ˈ**regularˌize** *or* **-ˌise** *vb.* —ˈ**regularly** *adv.*

regulate (ˈrɛgjʊˌleɪt) *vb.* (*tr.*) **1.** to adjust (the amount of heat, sound, etc.) as required; control. **2.** to adjust (an instrument or appliance) so that it operates correctly. **3.** to bring into conformity with a rule, principle, or usage. [C17: < LL *rēgulāre* to control, < L *rēgula* ruler] —ˈ**regulative** *or* ˈ**regulatory** *adj.* —ˈ**regulatively** *adv.*

regulation (ˌrɛgjʊˈleɪʃən) *n.* **1.** the act or process of regulating. **2.** a rule, principle, or condition that governs procedure or behaviour. **3.** (*modifier*) as required by official rules: *regulation uniform.* **4.** (*modifier*) normal; usual; conforming to accepted standards: *a regulation haircut.*

regulator (ˈrɛgjʊˌleɪtə) *n.* **1.** a person or thing that regulates. **2.** the mechanism by which the speed of a timepiece is regulated. **3.** any of various mechanisms or devices, such as a governor valve, for controlling fluid flow, pressure, temperature, etc.

---

reˈglaze *vb.*
reˈgrade *vb.*
reˈgrow *vb.*
reˈgrowth *n.*

regulo (ˈrɛgjʊləʊ) *n.* any of a number of temperatures to which a gas oven may be set: *cook at regulo 4.* [C20: < *Regulo*, trademark for a type of thermostatic control on gas ovens]

regulus (ˈrɛgjʊləs) *n., pl.* **-luses** *or* **-li** (-ˌlaɪ). impure metal forming beneath the slag during the smelting of ores. [C16: < L: a petty king, < *rēx* king; formerly used for *antimony*, because it combines readily with gold, the king of metals] —ˈ**reguline** *adj.*

regurgitate (rɪˈgɜːdʒɪˌteɪt) *vb.* **1.** to vomit forth (partially digested food). **2.** (of some birds and animals) to bring back to the mouth (undigested or partly digested food to feed the young). **3.** (*intr.*) to be cast up or out, esp. from the mouth. [C17: < Med. L *regurgitāre*, < RE- + *gurgitāre* to flood, < L *gurges* whirlpool] —**reˈgurgitant** *n., adj.* —**reˌgurgiˈtation** *n.*

rehabilitate (ˌriːəˈbɪlɪˌteɪt) *vb.* (*tr.*) **1.** to help (a physically or mentally disabled person or an ex-prisoner) to readapt to society or a new job, as by vocational guidance, retraining, or therapy. **2.** to restore to a former position or rank. **3.** to restore the good reputation of. [C16: < Med. L *rehabilitāre* to restore, < RE- + L *habilitās* skill] —ˌ**rehaˌbiliˈtation** *n.* —ˌ**rehaˈbilitative** *adj.*

Rehabilitation Department *n. N.Z.* a government department set up after World War II to assist ex-servicemen. Often shortened to **rehab.**

rehash (riːˈhæʃ) *vb.* **1.** (*tr.*) to rework, reuse, or make over (old or already used material). ~*n.* **2.** something consisting of old, reworked, or reused material. [C19: < RE- + HASH[1] (to chop into pieces)]

rehearsal (rɪˈhɜːsᵊl) *n.* **1.** a session of practising a play, concert, etc., in preparation for public performance. **2. in rehearsal.** being prepared for public performance.

rehearse (rɪˈhɜːs) *vb.* **1.** to practise (a play, concert, etc.), in preparation for public performance. **2.** (*tr.*) to run through; recount; recite: *he rehearsed the grievances of the committee.* **3.** (*tr.*) to train or drill (a person) for public performance. [C16: < Anglo-Norman *rehearser*, < OF *rehercier* to harrow a second time, < RE- + *herce* harrow] —**reˈhearser** *n.*

reheat *vb.* (riːˈhiːt). **1.** to heat or be heated again: *to reheat yesterday's soup.* **2.** (*tr.*) to add fuel to (the exhaust gases of an aircraft jet engine) to produce additional heat and thrust. ~*n.* (ˈriːhiːt), *also* **reheating. 3.** a process in which additional fuel is ignited in the exhaust gases of a jet engine to produce additional thrust. —**reˈheater** *n.*

rehoboam (ˌriːəˈbəʊəm) *n.* a wine bottle holding the equivalent of six normal bottles. [after *Rehoboam*, a son of King Solomon, < Heb., lit.: the nation is enlarged]

Reich (raɪk) *n.* **1.** the Holy Roman Empire (962–1806) (**First Reich**). **2.** the Hohenzollern empire in Germany from 1871 to 1918 (**Second Reich**). **3.** the Nazi dictatorship in Germany from 1933–45 (**Third Reich**). [G: kingdom]

Reichsmark (ˈraɪksˌmɑːk) *n., pl.* **-marks** *or* **-mark.** the standard monetary unit of Germany between 1924 and 1948.

Reichstag (ˈraɪksˌtɑːg) *n.* **1.** the legislative assembly of Germany (1867–1933). **2.** the building in Berlin in which this assembly met.

reify (ˈriːɪˌfaɪ) *vb.* **-fying, -fied.** (*tr.*) to consider or make (an abstract idea or concept) real or concrete. [C19: < L *rēs* thing] —ˌ**reifiˈcation** *n.* —ˌ**reifiˈcatory** *adj.* —ˈ**reiˌfier** *n.*

reign (reɪn) *n.* **1.** the period during which a monarch is the official ruler of a country. **2.** a period during which a person or thing is dominant or powerful: *the reign of violence.* ~*vb.* (*intr.*) **3.** to exercise the power and authority of a sovereign. **4.** to be accorded the rank and title of a sovereign without having ruling authority. **5.** to predominate; prevail: *darkness reigns.* **6.** (*usually present participle*) to be the most recent winner of a contest, etc.: *the reigning champion.* [C13: < OF *reigne*, < L *rēgnum* kingdom, < *rēx* king]

reimburse (ˌriːɪmˈbɜːs) *vb.* (*tr.*) to repay or compensate (someone) for (money already spent, losses, damages, etc.). [C17: < RE- + *imburse*, < Med. L *imbursāre* to put in a moneybag, < *bursa* PURSE] —ˌ**reimˈbursable** *adj.* —ˌ**reimˈbursement** *n.* —ˌ**reimˈburser** *n.*

reimport *vb.* (ˌriːɪmˈpɔːt, riːˈɪmpɔːt). **1.** (*tr.*) to import (goods manufactured from exported raw materials). ~*n.* (riːˈɪmpɔːt). **2.** the act of reimporting. **3.** a reimported commodity. —ˌ**reimporˈtation** *n.*

rein (reɪn) *n.* **1.** (*often pl.*) one of a pair of long straps, usually connected together and made of leather, used to control a horse. **2.** a similar device used to control a very young child. **3.** any form or means of control: *to take up the reins of government.* **4.** the direction in which a rider turns (in **on a left rein**). **5.** something that restrains, controls, or guides. **6. give (a) free rein.** to allow considerable freedom; remove restraints. **7. keep a tight rein on.** to control carefully; limit: *we have to keep a tight rein on expenditure.* ~*vb.* **8.** (*tr.*) to check, restrain, hold back, or halt with or as if with reins. **9.** to control or guide (a horse) with a rein or reins: *they reined left.* ~See also **rein in.** [C13: < OF *resne*, < L *retinēre* to hold back, < RE- + *tenēre* to hold]

reincarnate *vb.* (riːˈɪnkɑːneɪt). (*tr.; often passive*) **1.** to cause to undergo reincarnation; be born again. ~*adj.* (ˌriːɪnˈkɑːnɪt). **2.** born again in a new body.

reincarnation (ˌriːɪnkɑːˈneɪʃən) *n.* **1.** the belief that on the death of the body the soul transmigrates to or is born again in another body. **2.** the incarnation or embodiment of a soul in a new body after it has left the old one at physical death. **3.** embodiment again in a new form, as of a principle or idea. —ˌ**reincarˈnationist** *n., adj.*

reindeer (ˈreɪnˌdɪə) *n., pl.* **-deer** *or* **-deers.** a large deer, having large branched antlers in the male and female and inhabiting the arctic regions. It also occurs in North America, where it is known as a caribou. [C14: < ON *hreindȳri*, < *hreinn* reindeer + *dyr* animal]

reindeer moss *n.* any of various lichens which occur in arctic and subarctic regions, providing food for reindeer.

reinforce (ˌriːɪnˈfɔːs) *vb.* (*tr.*) **1.** to give added strength or support to. **2.** to give added emphasis to; stress or increase: *his rudeness reinforced my determination.* **3.** to give added support to (a military force) by providing more men, supplies, etc. [C17: < F *renforcer*] —ˌ**reinˈforcement** *n.*

reinforced concrete *n.* concrete with steel bars, mesh, etc., embedded in it to enable it to withstand tensile and shear stresses.

rein in *vb.* (*adv.*) to stop (a horse) by pulling on the reins.

reins (reɪnz) *pl. n. Arch.* the kidneys or loins. [C14: < OF, < L *rēnēs* the kidneys]

reinstate (ˌriːɪnˈsteɪt) *vb.* (*tr.*) to restore to a former rank or condition. —ˌ**reinˈstatement** *n.* —ˌ**reinˈstator** *n.*

---

reˈhang *vb.*
reˈharness *vb.*
reˈhear *vb.*
reˈheel *vb.*
reˈhire *vb.*
reˈhouse *vb.*
ˌ**reimˈpose** *vb.*
ˌ**reimˈprison** *vb.*
ˌ**reinˈcorpoˌrate** *vb.*
ˌ**reinˌcorpoˈration** *n.*
ˌ**reinˈcur** *vb.*
ˌ**reinˈduce** *vb.*
ˌ**reinˈduction** *n.*
ˌ**reinˈfect** *vb.*
ˌ**reinˈfection** *n.*
ˌ**reinˈfuse** *vb.*
ˌ**reinˈfusion** *n.*
ˌ**reinˈocuˌlate** *vb.*
ˌ**reinˌocuˈlation** *n.*
ˌ**reinˈsert** *vb.*
ˌ**reinˈsertion** *n.*
ˌ**reinˈspect** *vb.*
ˌ**reinˈspection** *n.*
ˌ**reinˈstruct** *vb.*
ˌ**reinˈstruction** *n.*
ˌ**reinˈsure** *vb.*

reinsurer (ˌriːɪnˈʃʊərə) *n.* an insurance company which will accept business from other insurance companies, thus enabling the risks to be spread. —ˌ**reinˈsurance** *n.*

reiterate (riːˈɪtəˌreɪt) *vb.* (*tr.; may take a clause as object*) to say or do again or repeatedly. [C16: < L *reiterāre,* < RE- + *iterāre* to do again, < *iterum* again] —**reˌiterˈation** *n.* —**reˈiterative** *adj.* —**reˈiteratively** *adv.*

reive (riːv) *vb.* (*intr.*) *Scot. & N English dialect.* to go on a plundering raid. [var. of REAVE] —ˈ**reiver** *n.*

reject *vb.* (rɪˈdʒɛkt). (*tr.*) **1.** to refuse to accept, use, believe, etc. **2.** to throw out as useless or worthless; discard. **3.** to rebuff (a person). **4.** (of an organism) to fail to accept (a foreign tissue graft or organ transplant). ~*n.* (ˈriːdʒɛkt). **5.** something rejected as imperfect, unsatisfactory, or useless. [C15: < L *rēicere* to throw back, < RE- + *jacere* to hurl] —**reˈjecter** *or* **reˈjector** *n.* —**reˈjection** *n.* —**reˈjective** *adj.*

rejig (riːˈdʒɪg) *vb.* **-jigging, -jigged.** (*tr.*) **1.** to re-equip (a factory or plant). **2.** *Inf.* to rearrange, manipulate, etc., sometimes in an unscrupulous way. ~*n.* **3.** the act or process of rejigging. —**reˈjigger** *n.*

rejoice (rɪˈdʒɔɪs) *vb.* (when *tr., takes a clause as object or an infinitive;* when *intr.,* often foll. by *in*) to feel or express great joy or happiness. [C14: < OF *resjoir,* < RE- + *joir* to be glad, < L *gaudēre* to rejoice] —**reˈjoicer** *n.*

rejoin[1] (riːˈdʒɔɪn) *vb.* **1.** to come again into company with (someone or something). **2.** (*tr.*) to put or join together again; reunite.

rejoin[2] (rɪˈdʒɔɪn) *vb.* (*tr.*) **1.** to answer or reply. **2.** *Law.* to answer (a plaintiff's reply). [C15: < OF *rejoign-,* stem of *rejoindre;* see RE-, JOIN]

rejoinder (rɪˈdʒɔɪndə) *n.* **1.** a reply or response to a question or remark. **2.** *Law.* (in pleading) the answer made by a defendant to the plaintiff's reply. [C15: < OF *rejoindre* to REJOIN[2]]

rejuvenate (rɪˈdʒuːvɪˌneɪt) *vb.* (*tr.*) **1.** to give new youth, restored vitality, or youthful appearance to. **2.** (*usually passive*) *Geog.* to cause (a river) to begin eroding more vigorously to a new lower base level. [C19: < RE- + L *juvenis* young] —**reˌjuveˈnation** *n.* —**reˈjuveˌnator** *n.*

rejuvenesce (rɪˌdʒuːvəˈnɛs) *vb.* **1.** to make or become youthful or restored to vitality. **2.** *Biol.* to convert (cells) or (of cells) to be converted into a more active form. —**reˌjuveˈnescence** *n.* —**reˌjuveˈnescent** *adj.*

rel. *abbrev. for:* **1.** relating. **2.** relative(ly). **3.** released. **4.** religion. **5.** religious.

relapse (rɪˈlæps) *vb.* (*intr.*) **1.** to lapse back into a former state or condition, esp. one involving bad habits. **2.** to become ill again after apparent recovery. ~*n.* **3.** the act or an instance of relapsing. **4.** the return of ill health after an apparent or partial recovery. [C16: < L *relabī,* < RE- + *labī* to slip, slide] —**reˈlapser** *n.*

relapsing fever *n.* any of various infectious diseases characterized by recurring fever, caused by the bite of body lice or ticks. Also called: **recurrent fever.**

relate (rɪˈleɪt) *vb.* **1.** (*tr.*) to tell or narrate (a story, etc.). **2.** (often foll. by *to*) to establish association (between two or more things) or (of something) to have relation or reference (to something else). **3.** (*intr.;* often foll. by *to*) to form a sympathetic or significant relationship (with other people, things, etc.). [C16: < L *relātus* brought back, < *referre,* < RE- + *ferre* to bear] —**reˈlatable** *adj.* —**reˈlater** *n.*

▷ **Usage.** *Relate* is frequently applied to personal relationships, as in sense 3, but this usage is vague and is avoided by careful speakers and writers.

related (rɪˈleɪtɪd) *adj.* **1.** connected; associated. **2.** connected by kinship or marriage. —**reˈlatedness** *n.*

relation (rɪˈleɪʃən) *n.* **1.** the state or condition of being related or the manner in which things are related. **2.** connection by blood or marriage; kinship. **3.** a person who is connected by blood or marriage; relative. **4.** reference or regard (esp. in **in** *or* **with relation to**). **5.** the position, association, connection, or status of one person or thing with regard to another. **6.** the act of relating or narrating. **7.** an account or narrative. **8.** *Law.* the statement of grounds of complaint made by a relator. **9.** *Logic, maths.* **a.** an association between ordered pairs of objects, numbers, etc., such as ... is greater than .... **b.** the set of ordered pairs whose members have such an association. ~See also **relations.** [C14: < L *relātiō* a narration, a relation (between philosophical concepts)]

relational (rɪˈleɪʃənᵊl) *adj.* **1.** *Grammar.* indicating or expressing syntactic relation, as for example the case endings in Latin. **2.** having relation or being related.

relations (rɪˈleɪʃənz) *pl. n.* **1.** social, political, or personal connections or dealings between or among individuals, groups, nations, etc. **2.** family or relatives. **3.** *Euphemistic.* sexual intercourse.

relationship (rɪˈleɪʃənʃɪp) *n.* **1.** the state of being connected or related. **2.** association by blood or marriage; kinship. **3.** the mutual dealings, connections, or feelings that exist between two countries, people, etc. **4.** an emotional or sexual affair or liaison.

relative (ˈrɛlətɪv) *adj.* **1.** having meaning or significance only in relation to something else; not absolute. **2.** (*prenominal*) (of a scientific quantity) being measured or stated relative to some other substance or measurement: *relative density.* **3.** (*prenominal*) comparative or respective: *the relative qualities of speed and accuracy.* **4.** (*postpositive;* foll. by *to*) in proportion (to); corresponding (to): *earnings relative to production.* **5.** having reference (to); pertinent (to). **6.** *Grammar.* denoting or belonging to a class of words that function as subordinating conjunctions in introducing relative clauses such as *who, which,* and *that.* Cf. **demonstrative. 7.** *Grammar.* denoting or relating to a clause (**relative clause**) that modifies a noun or pronoun occurring earlier in the sentence. **8.** (of a musical key or scale) having the same key signature as another key or scale. ~*n.* **9.** a person who is related by blood or marriage; relation. **10.** a relative pronoun, clause, or grammatical construction. [C16: < LL *relātīvus* referring] —ˈ**relatively** *adv.* —ˈ**relativeness** *n.*

relative aperture *n. Photog.* the ratio of the equivalent focal length of a lens to the effective aperture of the lens.

relative atomic mass *n.* another name for **atomic weight.**

relative density *n.* the ratio of the density of a substance to the density of a standard substance under specified conditions. For liquids and solids the standard is usually water at 4°C. For gases the standard is air or hydrogen at the same temperature and pressure as the substance. See also **specific gravity, vapour density.**

relative frequency *n. Statistics.* the ratio of the actual number of favourable events to the total possible number of events.

relative humidity *n.* the mass of water vapour present in the air expressed as a percentage of the mass present in an equal volume of saturated air at the same temperature.

relative majority *n. Brit.* the excess of votes or

---

reˈinteˌgrate *vb.*
ˌ**reinteˈgration** *n.*
ˌ**reinˈterpret** *vb.*
ˌ**reinˌterpreˈtation** *n.*
ˌ**reinˈterroˌgate** *vb.*
ˌ**reinˌterroˈgation** *n.*
ˌ**reintroˈduce** *vb.*
ˌ**reintroˈduction** *n.*
ˌ**reinˈvade** *vb.*
ˌ**reinˈvasion** *n.*
ˌ**reinˈvestiˌgate** *vb.*
ˌ**reinˌvestiˈgation** *n.*
reˈjudge *vb.*
reˈkey *vb.*
reˈkindle *vb.*
reˈlabel *vb.*

seats won by the winner of an election over the runner-up when no candidate or party has more than 50 per cent. Cf. **absolute majority.**

relative molecular mass *n.* another name for **molecular weight.**

relative permeability *n.* the ratio of the permeability of a medium to that of free space.

relative permittivity *n.* the ratio of the permittivity of a substance to that of free space.

relativism (ˈrɛlətɪˌvɪzəm) *n.* any theory holding that truth or moral or aesthetic value, etc., is not universal or absolute but may differ between individuals or cultures. —**ˈrelativist** *n., adj.* —**ˌrelativˈistic** *adj.*

relativity (ˌrɛləˈtɪvɪtɪ) *n.* **1.** either of two theories developed by Albert Einstein, the **special theory of relativity,** which requires that the laws of physics shall be the same as seen by any two different observers in uniform relative motion, and the **general theory of relativity,** which considers observers with relative acceleration and leads to a theory of gravitation. **2.** the state or quality of being relative.

relator (rɪˈleɪtə) *n.* **1.** a person who relates a story; narrator. **2.** *English law.* a person who gives information upon which the attorney general brings an action.

relatum (rɪˈleɪtəm) *n., pl.* **-ta** (-tə). *Logic.* one of the objects between which a relation is said to hold.

relax (rɪˈlæks) *vb.* **1.** to make (muscles, a grip, etc.) less tense or rigid or (of muscles, a grip, etc.) to become looser or less rigid. **2.** (*intr.*) to take rest, as from work or effort. **3.** to lessen the force of (effort, concentration) or (of effort) to become diminished. **4.** to make (rules or discipline) less rigid or strict or (of rules, etc.) to diminish in severity. **5.** (*intr.*) (of a person) to become less formal; unbend. [C15: < L *relaxāre* to loosen, < RE- + *laxāre,* < *laxus* loose] —**reˈlaxed** *adj.* —**relaxedly** (rɪˈlæksɪdlɪ) *adv.* —**reˈlaxer** *n.*

relaxant (rɪˈlæksᵊnt) *n.* **1.** *Med.* a drug or agent that relaxes, esp. one that relaxes tense muscles. ~*adj.* **2.** of or tending to produce relaxation.

relaxation (ˌriːlækˈseɪʃən) *n.* **1.** rest or refreshment, as after work or effort; recreation. **2.** a form of rest or recreation: *his relaxation is cricket.* **3.** a partial lessening of a punishment, duty, etc. **4.** the act of relaxing or state of being relaxed. **5.** *Physics.* the return of a system to equilibrium after a displacement from this state.

relaxin (rɪˈlæksɪn) *n.* **1.** a mammalian polypeptide hormone secreted during pregnancy, which relaxes the pelvic ligaments. **2.** a preparation of this hormone, used to facilitate childbirth. [C20: < RELAX + -IN]

relay *n.* (ˈriːleɪ). **1.** a person or team of people relieving others, as on a shift. **2.** a fresh team of horses, etc., posted along a route to relieve others. **3.** the act of relaying or process of being relayed. **4.** short for **relay race. 5.** an automatic device that controls a valve, switch, etc., by means of an electric motor, solenoid, or pneumatic mechanism. **6.** *Electronics.* an electrical device in which a small change in current or voltage controls the switching on or off of circuits. **7.** *Radio.* **a.** a combination of a receiver and transmitter designed to receive radio signals and retransmit them. **b.** (*as modifier*)*: a relay station.* ~*vb.* (rɪˈleɪ). (*tr.*) **8.** to carry or spread (news or information) by relays. **9.** to supply or replace with relays. **10.** to retransmit (a signal) by means of a relay. **11.** *Brit.* to broadcast (a performance) by sending out signals through a transmitting station. [C15 *relaien,* < OF *relaier* to leave behind, < RE- + *laier* to leave, ult. < L *laxāre* to loosen]

relay race *n.* a race between two or more teams of contestants in which each contestant covers a specified portion of the distance.

release (rɪˈliːs) *vb.* (*tr.*) **1.** to free (a person or animal) from captivity or imprisonment. **2.** to free (someone) from obligation or duty. **3.** to free (something) from (one's grip); let fall. **4.** to issue (a record, film, or book) for sale or circulation. **5.** to make (news or information) known or allow (news, etc.) to be made known. **6.** *Law.* to relinquish (a right, claim, or title) in favour of someone else. ~*n.* **7.** the act of freeing or state of being freed. **8.** the act of issuing for sale or publication. **9.** something issued for sale or public showing, esp. a film or a record: *a new release from Bob Dylan.* **10.** a news item, etc., made available for publication, broadcasting, etc. **11.** *Law.* the surrender of a claim, right, title, etc., in favour of someone else. **12.** a control mechanism for starting or stopping an engine. [C13: < OF *relesser,* < L *relaxāre* to slacken] —**reˈleaser** *n.*

relegate (ˈrɛlɪˌgeɪt) *vb.* (*tr.*) **1.** to move to a position of less authority, importance, etc.; demote. **2.** (*usually passive*) *Chiefly Brit.* to demote (a football team, etc.) to a lower division. **3.** to assign or refer (a matter) to another. **4.** (foll. by *to*) to banish or exile. **5.** to assign (something) to a particular group or category. [C16: < L *relēgāre,* < RE- + *lēgāre* to send] —**ˈreleˌgatable** *adj.* —**ˌreleˈgation** *n.*

relent (rɪˈlɛnt) *vb.* (*intr.*) **1.** to change one's mind about some decision, esp. a harsh one; become more mild or amenable. **2.** (of the pace or intensity of something) to slacken. **3.** (of the weather) to become more mild. [C14: < RE- + L *lentāre* to bend, < *lentus* flexible]

relentless (rɪˈlɛntlɪs) *adj.* **1.** (of an enemy, etc.) implacable; inflexible; inexorable. **2.** (of pace or intensity) sustained; unremitting. —**reˈlentlessly** *adv.* —**reˈlentlessness** *n.*

relevant (ˈrɛlɪvənt) *adj.* having direct bearing on the matter in hand; pertinent. [C16: < Med. L *relevans,* < L *relevāre,* < RE- + *levāre* to raise, RELIEVE] —**ˈrelevance** *or* **ˈrelevancy** *n.* —**ˈrelevantly** *adv.*

reliable (rɪˈlaɪəbᵊl) *adj.* able to be trusted; dependable. —**reˌliaˈbility** *or* **reˈliableness** *n.* —**reˈliably** *adv.*

reliance (rɪˈlaɪəns) *n.* **1.** dependence, confidence, or trust. **2.** something or someone upon which one relies. —**reˈliant** *adj.* —**reˈliantly** *adv.*

relic (ˈrɛlɪk) *n.* **1.** something that has survived from the past, such as an object or custom. **2.** something treasured for its past associations; keepsake. **3.** (*usually pl.*) a remaining part or fragment. **4.** *R.C. Church, Eastern Church.* part of the body of a saint or his belongings, venerated as holy. **5.** *Inf.* an old or old-fashioned person or thing. **6.** (*pl.*) *Arch.* the remains of a dead person; corpse. [C13: < OF *relique,* < L *reliquiae* remains, < *relinquere* to leave behind]

relict (ˈrɛlɪkt) *n.* **1.** *Ecology.* **a.** a group of animals or plants that exists as a remnant of a formerly widely distributed group. **b.** (*as modifier*)*: a relict fauna.* **2.** *Geol.* a mountain, lake, glacier, etc., that is a remnant of a pre-existing formation after a destructive process has occurred. **3.** an archaic word for **widow. 4.** an archaic word for **relic.** [C16: < L *relictus* left behind, < *relinquere* to RELINQUISH]

relief (rɪˈliːf) *n.* **1.** a feeling of cheerfulness or optimism that follows the removal of anxiety, pain, or distress. **2.** deliverance from or alleviation of anxiety, pain, etc. **3. a.** help or assistance, as to the poor or needy. **b.** (*as modifier*)*: relief work.* **4.** a diversion from monotony. **5.** a person who replaces another at some task or duty. **6.** a bus, plane, etc., that carries additional passengers when a scheduled service is full. **7.** a road (**relief road**) carrying traffic round an urban area; bypass. **8. a.** the act of freeing a beleaguered town, fortress, etc.: *the relief of Mafikeng.* **b.** (*as modifier*)*: a relief column.* **9.** Also called: **relievo, rilievo.** *Sculpture, archit.* **a.** the projection of forms or figures from a flat ground, so that they are partly or wholly free of it. **b.** a piece of work of this kind. **10.** a

reˈlearn *vb.*　　reˈlet *vb.*

printing process that employs raised surfaces from which ink is transferred to the paper. **11.** any vivid effect resulting from contrast: *comic relief.* **12.** variation in altitude in an area; difference between highest and lowest level. **13.** *Law.* redress of a grievance or hardship: *to seek relief through the courts.* **14. on relief.** *U.S. & Canad.* (of people) in receipt of government aid because of personal need. [C14: < OF, < *relever;* see RELIEVE]

relief map *n.* a map that shows the configuration and height of the land surface, usually by means of contours.

relieve (rɪˈliːv) *vb.* (*tr.*) **1.** to bring alleviation of (pain, distress, etc.) to (someone). **2.** to bring aid or assistance to (someone in need, etc.). **3.** to take over the duties or watch of (someone). **4.** to bring aid or a relieving force to (a besieged town, etc.). **5.** to free (someone) from an obligation. **6.** to make (something) less unpleasant, arduous, or monotonous. **7.** to bring into relief or prominence, as by contrast. **8.** (foll. by *of*) *Inf.* to take from: *the thief relieved him of his watch.* **9. relieve oneself.** to urinate or defecate. [C14: < OF *relever,* < L *relevāre* to lift up, relieve, < RE- + *levāre* to lighten] —**reˈlievable** *adj.* —**reˈliever** *n.*

relieved (rɪˈliːvd) *adj.* (*postpositive;* often foll. by *at, about,* etc.) experiencing relief, esp. from worry or anxiety.

religieuse *French.* (rəliʒjøz) *n.* a nun. [C18: fem. of RELIGIEUX]

religieux *French.* (rəliʒjø) *n., pl.* **-gieux** (-ʒjø). a member of a monastic order or clerical body. [C17: < L *religiōsus* religious]

religion (rɪˈlɪdʒən) *n.* **1.** belief in, worship of, or obedience to a supernatural power or powers considered to be divine or to have control of human destiny. **2.** any formal or institutionalized expression of such belief: *the Christian religion.* **3.** the attitude and feeling of one who believes in a transcendent controlling power or powers. **4.** *Chiefly R.C. Church.* the way of life entered upon by monks and nuns: *to enter religion.* **5.** something of overwhelming importance to a person: *football is his religion.* [C12: via OF < L *religiō* fear of the supernatural, piety, prob. < *religāre,* < RE- + *ligāre* to bind]

religionism (rɪˈlɪdʒəˌnɪzəm) *n.* extreme religious fervour. —**reˈligionist** *n., adj.*

religiose (rɪˈlɪdʒɪˌəʊs) *adj.* affectedly or extremely pious; sanctimoniously religious. —**reˈligiˌosely** *adv.* —**religiosity** (rɪˌlɪdʒɪˈɒsɪtɪ) *n.*

religious (rɪˈlɪdʒəs) *adj.* **1.** of, relating to, or concerned with religion. **2. a.** pious; devout; godly. **b.** (*as collective n.;* preceded by *the*): *the religious.* **3.** appropriate to or in accordance with the principles of a religion. **4.** scrupulous, exact, or conscientious. **5.** *Christianity.* of or relating to a way of life dedicated to religion and defined by a monastic rule. ~*n.* **6.** *Christianity.* a monk or nun. —**reˈligiously** *adv.* —**reˈligiousness** *n.*

relinquish (rɪˈlɪŋkwɪʃ) *vb.* (*tr.*) **1.** to give up (a task, struggle, etc.); abandon. **2.** to surrender or renounce (a claim, right, etc.). **3.** to release; let go. [C15: < F *relinquir,* < L *relinquere,* < RE- + *linquere* to leave] —**reˈlinquisher** *n.* —**reˈlinquishment** *n.*

reliquary (ˈrɛlɪkwərɪ) *n., pl.* **-quaries.** a receptacle or repository for relics, esp. relics of saints. [C17: < OF *reliquaire,* < *relique* RELIC]

relique (rəˈliːk, ˈrɛlɪk) *n.* an archaic spelling of **relic.**

reliquiae (rɪˈlɪkwɪˌiː) *pl. n.* fossil remains of animals or plants. [C19: < L: remains]

relish (ˈrɛlɪʃ) *vb.* (*tr.*) **1.** to savour or enjoy (an experience) to the full. **2.** to anticipate eagerly; look forward to. **3.** to enjoy the taste or flavour of (food, etc.); savour. ~*n.* **4.** liking or enjoyment, as of something eaten or experienced (esp. in **with relish**). **5.** pleasurable anticipation: *he didn't have much relish for the idea.* **6.** an appetizing or spicy food added to a main dish to enhance its flavour. **7.** an appetizing taste or flavour. **8.** a zestful trace or touch: *there was a certain relish in all his writing.* [C16: < earlier *reles* aftertaste, < OF, < *relaisser* to leave behind; see RELEASE] —ˈ**relishable** *adj.*

relive (riːˈlɪv) *vb.* (*tr.*) to experience (a sensation, event, etc.) again, esp. in the imagination. —**reˈlivable** *adj.*

relocate (ˌriːləʊˈkeɪt) *vb.* to move or be moved to a new place, esp. (of an employee, a business, etc.) to a new area or place of employment. —ˌ**reloˈcation** *n.*

reluctance (rɪˈlʌktəns) *or* **reluctancy** *n.* **1.** lack of eagerness or willingness; disinclination. **2.** *Physics.* a measure of the resistance of a closed magnetic circuit to a magnetic flux. [C16: < L *reluctārī* to resist, < RE- + *luctārī* to struggle]

reluctant (rɪˈlʌktənt) *adj.* not eager; unwilling; disinclined. [C17: < L *reluctārī* to resist] —**reˈluctantly** *adv.*

reluctivity (ˌrɛlʌkˈtɪvɪtɪ) *n., pl.* **-ties.** *Physics.* a specific or relative reluctance of a magnetic material. [C19: < obs. *reluct* to struggle + *-ivity*]

rely (rɪˈlaɪ) *vb.* **-lying, -lied.** (*intr.;* foll. by *on* or *upon*) **1.** to be dependent (on): *he relies on his charm.* **2.** to have trust or confidence (in): *you can rely on us.* [C14: < OF *relier* to fasten together, < L *religāre,* < RE- + *ligāre* to tie]

REM *abbrev. for* rapid eye movement.

remain (rɪˈmeɪn) *vb.* (*mainly intr.*) **1.** to stay behind or in the same place: *to remain at home.* **2.** (*copula*) to continue to be: *to remain cheerful.* **3.** to be left, as after use, the passage of time, etc. **4.** to be left to be done, said, etc.: *it remains to be pointed out.* [C14: < OF *remanoir,* < L *remanēre,* < RE- + *manēre* to stay]

remainder (rɪˈmeɪndə) *n.* **1.** a part or portion that is left, as after use, subtraction, expenditure, the passage of time, etc.: *the remainder of the milk.* **2.** *Maths.* **a.** the amount left over when one quantity cannot be exactly divided by another: *for 10 ÷ 3, the remainder is 1.* **b.** another name for **difference** (sense 7). **3.** *Property law.* a future interest in property; an interest in a particular estate that will pass to one at some future date, as on the death of the current possessor. **4.** a number of copies of a book left unsold when demand ceases, which are sold at a reduced price. ~*vb.* **5.** (*tr.*) to sell (copies of a book) as a remainder.

remains (rɪˈmeɪnz) *pl. n.* **1.** any pieces, fragments, etc., that are left unused or still extant, as after use, consumption, the passage of time: *archaeological remains.* **2.** the body of a dead person; corpse. **3.** Also called: **literary remains.** the unpublished writings of an author at the time of his death.

remake *n.* (ˈriːˌmeɪk). **1.** something that is made again, esp. a new version of an old film. **2.** the act of making again. ~*vb.* (riːˈmeɪk), **-making, -made. 3.** (*tr.*) to make again or anew.

remand (rɪˈmɑːnd) *vb.* (*tr.*) **1.** *Law.* (of a court or magistrate) to send (a prisoner or accused person) back into custody. **2.** to send back. ~*n.* **3.** the sending of a prisoner or accused person back into custody to await trial. **4.** the act of remanding or state of being remanded. **5. on remand.** in custody or on bail awaiting trial. [C15: < Med. L *remandāre* to send back word, < L RE- + *mandāre* to command]

remand centre *n.* (in England) an institution to which accused persons are sent for detention while awaiting appearance before a court.

remanence (ˈrɛmənəns) *n. Physics.* the ability of a material to retain magnetization after the removal of the magnetizing field. [C17: < L *remanēre* to stay behind]

remark (rɪˈmɑːk) *vb.* **1.** (when *intr.,* often foll. by *on* or *upon;* when *tr., may take a clause as object*) to pass a casual comment (about); reflect in informal speech or writing. **2.** (*tr.; may take a*

reˈlight *vb.* **reˈload** *vb.*

clause as object) to perceive; observe; notice. ~*n.* **3.** a brief casually expressed thought or opinion. **4.** notice, comment, or observation: *the event passed without remark.* **5.** a variant of **remarque.** [C17: < OF *remarquer* to observe, < RE- + *marquer* to note, MARK[1]] —**re'marker** *n.*

remarkable (rɪ'mɑːkəbᵊl) *adj.* **1.** worthy of note or attention: *a remarkable achievement.* **2.** unusual, striking, or extraordinary: *a remarkable sight.* —**re'markableness** *n.* —**re'markably** *adv.*

remarque (rɪ'mɑːk) *n.* a mark in the margin of an engraved plate to indicate the stage of production. [C19: < F; see REMARK]

remaster (riː'mɑːstə) *vb.* (*tr.*) to make a new master audio recording, now usually digital, from (an earlier original recording), in order to produce compact discs or stereo records with improved sound reproduction.

REME ('riːmɪ) *n. acronym for* Royal Electrical and Mechanical Engineers.

remedial (rɪ'miːdɪəl) *adj.* **1.** affording a remedy; curative. **2.** denoting or relating to special teaching for backward and slow learners: *remedial education.* —**re'medially** *adv.*

remedy ('rɛmɪdɪ) *n., pl.* **-dies. 1.** (usually foll. by *for* or *against*) any drug or agent that cures a disease or controls its symptoms. **2.** (usually foll. by *for* or *against*) anything that serves to cure defects, improve conditions, etc.: *a remedy for industrial disputes.* **3.** the legally permitted variation from the standard weight or quality of coins. ~*vb.* (*tr.*) **4.** to relieve or cure (a disease, etc.) by a remedy. **5.** to put to rights (a fault, error, etc.); correct. [C13: < Anglo-Norman *remedie,* < L *remedium* a cure, < *remedērī,* < RE- + *medērī* to heal] —**remediable** (rɪ'miːdɪəbᵊl) *adj.* —**re'mediably** *adv.* —**'remediless** *adj.*

remember (rɪ'mɛmbə) *vb.* **1.** to become aware of (something forgotten) again; bring back to one's consciousness. **2.** to retain (an idea, intention, etc.) in one's conscious mind: *remember to do one's shopping.* **3.** (*tr.*) to give money, etc., to (someone), as in a will or in tipping. **4.** (*tr.;* foll. by *to*) to mention (a person's name) to another person, as by way of greeting: *remember me to your mother.* **5.** (*tr.*) to mention (a person) favourably, as in prayer. **6.** (*tr.*) to commemorate (a person, event, etc.): *to remember the dead of the wars.* **7. remember oneself.** to recover one's good manners after a lapse. [C14: < OF *remembrer,* < LL *rememorārī* to recall to mind, < L RE- + *memor* mindful] —**re'memberer** *n.*

remembrance (rɪ'mɛmbrəns) *n.* **1.** the act of remembering or state of being remembered. **2.** something that is remembered; reminiscence. **3.** a memento or keepsake. **4.** the extent in time of one's power of recollection. **5.** the act of honouring some past event, person, etc.

Remembrance Day *n.* **1.** (in Britain) another name for **Remembrance Sunday. 2.** (in Canada) a statutory holiday observed on November 11 in memory of the dead of both World Wars.

remembrancer (rɪ'mɛmbrənsə) *n.* **1.** *Arch.* a reminder, memento, or keepsake. **2.** (*usually cap.*) (in Britain) any of several officials of the Exchequer, esp. one (**Queen's** *or* **King's Remembrancer**) whose duties include collecting debts due to the Crown. **3.** (*usually cap.*) an official (**City Remembrancer**) appointed by the Corporation of the City of London to represent its interests to Parliament.

Remembrance Sunday *n.* (in Britain) the Sunday closest to November 11, on which the dead of both World Wars are commemorated. Also called: **Remembrance Day.**

remex ('riːmɛks) *n., pl.* **remiges** ('rɛmɪˌdʒiːz). any of the large flight feathers of a bird's wing. [C18: < L: rower, < *rēmus* oar] —**remigial** (rɪ'mɪdʒɪəl) *adj.*

remind (rɪ'maɪnd) *vb.* (*tr.;* usually foll. by *of; may take a clause as object or an infinitive*) to cause (a person) to remember (something or to do something); put (a person) in mind (of something): *remind me to phone home; flowers remind me of holidays.* —**re'minder** *n.*

remindful (rɪ'maɪndfʊl) *adj.* **1.** serving to remind. **2.** (*postpositive*) mindful.

reminisce (ˌrɛmɪ'nɪs) *vb.* (*intr.*) to talk or write about old times, past experiences, etc.

reminiscence (ˌrɛmɪ'nɪsəns) *n.* **1.** the act of recalling or narrating past experiences. **2.** (*often pl.*) some past experience, event, etc., that is recalled. **3.** an event, phenomenon, or experience that reminds one of something else. **4.** *Philosophy.* the doctrine that the mind has seen the universal forms of all things in a previous disembodied existence.

reminiscent (ˌrɛmɪ'nɪsᵊnt) *adj.* **1.** (*postpositive;* foll. by *of*) stimulating memories (of) or comparisons (with). **2.** characterized by reminiscence. **3.** (of a person) given to reminiscing. [C18: < L *reminiscī* to call to mind, < RE- + *mēns* mind] —**ˌremi'niscently** *adv.*

remise (rɪ'maɪz) *vb.* **1.** (*tr.*) *Law.* to give up or relinquish (a right, claim, etc.). **2.** (*intr.*) *Fencing.* to make a remise. ~*n.* **3.** *Fencing.* a second thrust made on the same lunge after the first has missed. **4.** *Obs.* a coach house. [C17: < F *remettre* to put back, < L *remittere,* < RE- + *mittere* to send]

remiss (rɪ'mɪs) *adj.* (*postpositive*) **1.** lacking in care or attention to duty; negligent. **2.** lacking in energy. [C15: < L *remissus,* < *remittere,* < RE- + *mittere* to send] —**re'missly** *adv.* —**re'missness** *n.*

remissible (rɪ'mɪsɪbᵊl) *adj.* able to be remitted. [C16: < L *remissibilis;* see REMIT] —**reˌmissi'bility** *n.*

remission (rɪ'mɪʃən) *or* (*less commonly*) **remittal** (rɪ'mɪtᵊl) *n.* **1.** the act of remitting or state of being remitted. **2.** a reduction of the term of a sentence of imprisonment, as for good conduct. **3.** forgiveness for sin. **4.** discharge or release from penalty, obligation, etc. **5.** lessening of intensity; abatement, as in the symptoms of a disease. **6.** *Rare.* the act of sending a remittance. —**re'missive** *adj.* —**re'missively** *adv.*

remit *vb.* (rɪ'mɪt), **-mitting, -mitted.** (*mainly tr.*) **1.** (*also intr.*) to send (payment, etc.), as for goods or service, esp. by post. **2.** *Law.* (esp. of an appeal court) to send back (a case) to an inferior court for further consideration. **3.** to cancel or refrain from exacting (a penalty or punishment). **4.** (*also intr.*) to relax (pace, intensity, etc.) or (of pace) to slacken or abate. **5.** to postpone; defer. **6.** *Arch.* to pardon or forgive (crime, sins, etc.). ~*n.* ('riːmɪt, rɪ'mɪt). **7.** area of authority (of a committee, etc.). **8.** *Law.* the transfer of a case from one court or jurisdiction to another. **9.** the act of remitting. [C14: < L *remittere,* < RE- + *mittere* to send] —**re'mittable** *adj.* —**re'mitter** *n.*

remittance (rɪ'mɪtəns) *n.* **1.** payment for goods or services received or as an allowance, esp. when sent by post. **2.** the act of remitting.

remittance man *n.* a man living abroad on money sent from home, esp. in the days of the British Empire.

remittent (rɪ'mɪtᵊnt) *adj.* (of the symptoms of a disease) characterized by periods of diminished severity. —**re'mittence** *n.* —**re'mittently** *adv.*

remix *vb.* (riː'mɪks). **1.** to change the balance and separation of (a recording). ~*n.* ('riːmɪks). **2.** a remixed version of a recording.

remnant ('rɛmnənt) *n.* **1.** (*often pl.*) a part left over after use, processing, etc. **2.** a surviving trace or vestige: *a remnant of imperialism.* **3.** a piece of material from the end of a roll. ~*adj.* **4.** remaining; left over. [C14: < OF *remenant* remaining, < *remanoir* to REMAIN]

---

re'marriage *n.*
re'marry *vb.*
'reˌmatch *n.*
re'measure *vb.*
re'measurement *n.*
ˌremilitari'zation *or* **-ri'sation** *n.*
re'militaˌrize *or* **-ˌrise** *vb.*
re'model *vb.*
ˌremodifi'cation *n.*

remonetize *or* **-ise** (riːˈmʌnɪˌtaɪz) *vb.* (*tr.*) to reinstate as legal tender: *to remonetize silver.* —**reˌmonetiˈzation** *or* **-iˈsation** *n.*

remonstrance (rɪˈmɒnstrəns) *n.* **1.** the act of remonstrating. **2.** a protest or reproof, esp. a petition protesting against something.

remonstrant (rɪˈmɒnstrənt) *n.* **1.** a person who remonstrates, esp. one who signs a remonstrance. ~*adj.* **2.** *Rare.* remonstrating.

remonstrate (ˈrɛmənˌstreɪt) *vb.* (*intr.*) (usually foll. by *with, against,* etc.) to argue in protest or objection: *to remonstrate with the government.* [C16: < Med. L *remonstrāre* to point out (errors, etc.), < L RE- + *monstrāre* to show] —ˌ**remonˈstration** *n.* —**remonstrative** (rɪˈmɒnstrətɪv) *adj.* —ˈ**remonˌstrator** *n.*

remontant (rɪˈmɒntənt) *adj.* **1.** (esp. of roses) flowering more than once in a single season. ~*n.* **2.** a rose having such a growth. [C19: < F: coming up again, < *remonter*]

remora (ˈrɛmərə) *n.* a marine spiny-finned fish which has a flattened elongated body and attaches itself to larger fish, rocks, etc., by a sucking disc on the top of the head. [C16: < L, < RE- + *mora* delay; from its alleged habit of delaying ships]

remorse (rɪˈmɔːs) *n.* **1.** a sense of deep regret and guilt for some misdeed. **2.** compunction; pity; compassion. [C14: < Med. L *remorsus* a gnawing, < L *remordēre,* < RE- + *mordēre* to bite] —**reˈmorseful** *adj.* —**reˈmorsefully** *adv.* —**reˈmorsefulness** *n.* —**reˈmorseless** *adj.*

remote (rɪˈməʊt) *adj.* **1.** located far away; distant. **2.** far from society or civilization; out-of-the-way. **3.** distant in time. **4.** distantly related or connected: *a remote cousin.* **5.** slight or faint (esp. in **not the remotest idea**). **6.** (of a person's manner) aloof or abstracted. [C15: < L *remōtus* far removed, < *removēre,* < RE- + *movēre* to move] —**reˈmotely** *adv.* —**reˈmoteness** *n.*

remote control *n.* control of a system or activity from a distance, usually by radio, ultrasonic, or electrical signals. —**reˈmote-conˈtrolled** *adj.*

rémoulade (ˌrɛməˈleɪd) *n.* a mayonnaise sauce flavoured with herbs, mustard, and capers, served with salads, cold meat, etc. [C19: < F, < dialect *ramolas* horseradish, < L *armoracea*]

remould *vb.* (ˌriːˈməʊld). (*tr.*) **1.** to mould again. **2.** to bond a new tread onto the casing of (a worn pneumatic tyre). ~*n.* (ˈriːˌməʊld). **3.** a tyre made by this process.

remount *vb.* (riːˈmaʊnt). **1.** to get on (a horse, bicycle, etc.) again. **2.** (*tr.*) to mount (a picture, jewel, exhibit, etc.) again. ~*n.* (ˈriːˌmaʊnt). **3.** a fresh horse.

removal (rɪˈmuːvᵊl) *n.* **1.** the act of removing or state of being removed. **2. a.** a change of residence. **b.** (*as modifier*): *a removal company.* **3.** dismissal from office.

removalist (rɪˈmuːvəlɪst) *n. Austral.* a person or company that transports household effects to a new home.

remove (rɪˈmuːv) *vb.* (*mainly tr.*) **1.** to take away and place elsewhere. **2.** to dismiss (someone) from office. **3.** to do away with; abolish; get rid of. **4.** *Euphemistic.* to assassinate; kill. **5.** (*intr.*) *Formal.* to change the location of one's home or place of business. ~*n.* **6.** the act of removing, esp. (formal) a removal of one's residence or place of work. **7.** the degree of difference: *only one remove from madness.* **8.** *Brit.* (in certain schools) a class or form. [C14: < OF *removoir,* < L *removēre;* see MOVE] —**reˈmovable** *adj.* —**reˌmovaˈbility** *n.* —**reˈmover** *n.*

removed (rɪˈmuːvd) *adj.* **1.** separated by distance or abstract distinction. **2.** (*postpositive*) separated by a degree of descent or kinship: *the child of a person's first cousin is his first cousin once removed.*

remunerate (rɪˈmjuːnəˌreɪt) *vb.* (*tr.*) to reward or pay for work, service, etc. [C16: < L *remūnerārī* to reward, < RE- + *mūnerāre* to give, < *mūnus* a gift] —**reˌmunerˈation** *n.* —**reˈmunerable** *adj.* —**reˈmunerative** *adj.* —**reˈmuneratively** *adv.* —**reˈmunerˌator** *n.*

renaissance (rəˈneɪsəns; *U.S. also* ˈrɛnəˌsɒns) *or* **renascence** *n.* a revival or rebirth, esp. of culture and learning. [C19: < F, < L RE- + *nascī* to be born]

Renaissance (rəˈneɪsəns; *U.S. also* ˈrɛnəˌsɒns) *n.* **1. the.** the great revival of art, literature, and learning in Europe in the 14th, 15th, and 16th centuries. **2.** the spirit, culture, art, science, and thought of this period. ~*adj.* **3.** of, characteristic of, or relating to the Renaissance, its culture, etc.

renal (ˈriːnᵊl) *adj.* of, relating to, resembling, or situated near the kidney. [C17: < F, < LL *rēnālis,* < L *rēnēs* kidneys, <?]

renal pelvis *n.* a small funnel-shaped cavity of the kidney into which urine is discharged before passing into the ureter.

renascent (rɪˈnæsᵊnt, -ˈneɪ-) *adj.* becoming active or vigorous again; reviving: *renascent nationalism.* [C18: < L *renascī* to be born again]

rencounter (rɛnˈkaʊntə) *Arch.* ~*n. also* **rencontre** (rɛnˈkɒntə). **1.** an unexpected meeting. **2.** a hostile clash, as of two armies, adversaries, etc.; skirmish. ~*vb.* **3.** to meet (someone) unexpectedly. [C16: < F *rencontre,* < *rencontrer;* as ENCOUNTER]

rend (rɛnd) *vb.* **rending, rent. 1.** to tear with violent force or to be torn in this way; rip. **2.** (*tr.*) to tear or pull (one's clothes, etc.), esp. as a manifestation of rage or grief. **3.** (*tr.*) (of a noise or cry) to disturb (the silence) with a shrill or piercing tone. [OE *rendan*] —ˈ**rendible** *adj.*

render (ˈrɛndə) *vb.* (*tr.*) **1.** to present or submit (accounts, etc.) for payment, etc. **2.** to give or provide (aid, charity, a service, etc.). **3.** to show (obedience), as expected. **4.** to give or exchange, as by way of return or requital: *to render blow for blow.* **5.** to cause to become: *grief had rendered him simple-minded.* **6.** to deliver (a verdict or opinion) formally. **7.** to portray or depict (something), as in painting, music, or acting. **8.** to translate (something). **9.** (sometimes foll. by *up*) to yield or give: *the tomb rendered up its secret.* **10.** (often foll. by *back*) to return (something); give back. **11.** to cover the surface of (brickwork, etc.) with a coat of plaster. **12.** (often foll. by *down*) to extract (fat) from (meat) by melting. ~*n.* **13.** a first thin coat of plaster applied to a surface. **14.** one who or that which rends. [C14: < OF *rendre,* < L *reddere* to give back (infl. by L *prendere* to grasp), < RE- + *dare* to give] —ˈ**renderable** *adj.* —ˈ**renderer** *n.* —ˈ**rendering** *n.*

rendezvous (ˈrɒndɪˌvuː) *n., pl.* **-vous** (-ˌvuːz). **1.** a meeting or appointment to meet at a specified time and place. **2.** a place where people meet. ~*vb.* (*intr.*) **3.** to meet at a specified time or place. [C16: < F, < *rendez-vous!* present yourselves! < *se rendre* to present oneself; see RENDER]

rendition (rɛnˈdɪʃən) *n.* **1.** a performance of a musical composition, dramatic role, etc. **2.** a translation. **3.** the act of rendering. [C17: < obs. F, < LL *redditiō;* see RENDER]

renegade (ˈrɛnɪˌgeɪd) *n.* **1. a.** a person who deserts his cause or faith for another; traitor. **b.** (*as modifier*): *a renegade priest.* **2.** any outlaw or rebel. [C16: < Sp. *renegado,* ult. < L RE- + *negāre* to deny]

renege *or* **renegue** (rɪˈniːg, -ˈneɪg) *vb.* **1.** (*intr.;* often foll. by *on*) to go back (on one's promise, etc.). ~*vb., n.* **2.** *Cards.* other words for **revoke.** [C16 (in the sense: to deny, renounce): < Med. L *renegāre* to renounce] —**reˈneger** *or* **reˈneguer** *n.*

renew (rɪˈnjuː) *vb.* (*mainly tr.*) **1.** to take up again. **2.** (*also intr.*) to begin (an activity) again; recommence. **3.** to restate or reaffirm (a promise, etc.). **4.** (*also intr.*) to make (a lease,

---

reˈmodiˌfy *vb.*
reˈname *vb.*
ˌ**reneˈgotiable** *adj.*
ˌ**reneˈgotiˌate** *vb.*
ˌ**renegotiˈation** *n.*

etc.) valid for a further period. **5.** to regain or recover (vigour, strength, activity, etc.). **6.** to restore to a new or fresh condition. **7.** to replace (an old or worn-out part or piece). **8.** to replenish (a supply, etc.). —**reˈnewable** *adj.* —**reˈnewal** *n.* —**reˈnewer** *n.*

reni- *combining form.* kidney or kidneys: *reniform.* [< L *rēnēs*]

reniform (ˈrɛnɪˌfɔːm) *adj.* having the shape or profile of a kidney: *a reniform leaf.*

renin (ˈriːnɪn) *n.* a proteolytic enzyme secreted by the kidneys, which plays an important part in the maintenance of blood pressure. [C20: < RENI- + -IN]

rennet (ˈrɛnɪt) *n.* **1.** the membrane lining the fourth stomach of a young calf. **2.** a substance prepared esp. from the stomachs of calves and used for curdling milk in making cheese. [C15: rel. to OE *gerinnan* to curdle, RUN]

rennin (ˈrɛnɪn) *n.* an enzyme that occurs in gastric juice and is an active constituent of rennet. It coagulates milk. [C20: < RENNET + -IN]

renounce (rɪˈnaʊns) *vb.* **1.** (*tr.*) to give up formally (a claim or right): *to renounce a title.* **2.** (*tr.*) to repudiate: *to renounce Christianity.* **3.** (*tr.*) to give up (some habit, etc.) voluntarily: *to renounce one's old ways.* **4.** (*intr.*) *Cards.* to fail to follow suit because one has no more cards of the suit led. ~*n.* **5.** *Cards.* a failure to follow suit. [C14: < OF *renoncer,* < L *renuntiāre,* < RE- + *nuntiāre* to announce, < *nuntius* messenger] —**reˈnouncement** *n.* —**reˈnouncer** *n.*

renovate (ˈrɛnəˌveɪt) *vb.* (*tr.*) **1.** to restore (something) to good condition. **2.** to revive or refresh (one's spirits, health, etc.). [C16: < L *renovāre,* < RE- + *novāre* to make new] —ˌ**renoˈvation** *n.* —ˈ**renoˌvative** *adj.* —ˈ**renoˌvator** *n.*

renown (rɪˈnaʊn) *n.* widespread reputation, esp. of a good kind; fame. [C14: < Anglo-Norman *renoun,* < OF *renom,* < *renomer* to celebrate, < RE- + *nomer* to name, < L *nōmināre*] —**reˈnowned** *adj.*

rent[1] (rɛnt) *n.* **1.** a payment made periodically by a tenant to a landlord or owner for the occupation or use of land, buildings, etc. **2.** *Econ.* the return derived from the cultivation of land in excess of production costs. **3. for rent.** *Chiefly U.S. & Canad.* available for use and occupation subject to the payment of rent. ~*vb.* **4.** (*tr.*) to grant (a person) the right to use one's property in return for periodic payments. **5.** (*tr.*) to occupy or use (property) in return for periodic payments. **6.** (*intr.;* often foll. by *at*) to be let or rented (for a specified rental). [C12: < OF *rente* revenue, < Vulgar L *rendere* (unattested) to yield; see RENDER] —ˈ**rentable** *adj.* —ˈ**renter** *n.*

rent[2] (rɛnt) *n.* **1.** a slit or opening made by tearing or rending. **2.** a breach or division. ~*vb.* **3.** the past tense and past participle of **rend.**

rental (ˈrɛntᵊl) *n.* **1. a.** the amount paid by a tenant as rent. **b.** an income derived from rents received. **2.** property available for renting. ~*adj.* **3.** of or relating to rent.

rent boy *n.* a young male prostitute.

rent-free *adj., adv.* without payment of rent.

rentier *French.* (rɑ̃tje) *n.* a person whose income consists primarily of fixed unearned amounts, such as rent or interest. [< *rente;* see RENT[1]]

rent-roll *n.* **1.** a register of lands and buildings owned by a person, company, etc., showing the rent due from each tenant. **2.** the total income arising from rented property.

renunciation (rɪˌnʌnsɪˈeɪʃən) *n.* **1.** the act or an instance of renouncing. **2.** a formal declaration renouncing something. [C14: < L *renunciātiō* a declaration, < *renuntiāre* to report] —**reˈnunciative** *or* **reˈnunciatory** *adj.*

rep[1] *or* **repp** (rɛp) *n.* a silk, wool, rayon, or cotton fabric with a transversely corded surface. [C19: < F *reps,* ? < E *ribs*] —**repped** *adj.*

rep[2] (rɛp) *n.* *Theatre.* short for **repertory company.**

rep[3] (rɛp) *n.* **1.** short for **representative** (sense 2). **2.** *N.Z. inf.* a rugby player selected to represent his district.

rep[4] (rɛp) *n.* *U.S. inf.* short for **reputation.**

rep. *abbrev. for:* **1.** report. **2.** reporter. **3.** reprint.

Rep. *abbrev. for:* **1.** *U.S.* Representative. **2.** Republic. **3.** *U.S.* Republican.

repair[1] (rɪˈpɛə) *vb.* (*tr.*) **1.** to restore (something damaged or broken) to good condition or working order. **2.** to heal (a breach or division) in (something): *to repair a broken marriage.* **3.** to make amends for (a mistake, injury, etc.). ~*n.* **4.** the act, task, or process of repairing. **5.** a part that has been repaired. **6.** state or condition: *in good repair.* [C14: < OF *reparer,* < L *reparāre,* < RE- + *parāre* to make ready] —**reˈpairable** *adj.* —**reˈpairer** *n.*

repair[2] (rɪˈpɛə) *vb.* (*intr.*) **1.** (usually foll. by *to*) to go (to a place). **2.** (usually foll. by *to*) to have recourse (to) for help, etc.: *to repair to one's lawyer.* ~*n.* **3.** a haunt or resort. [C14: < OF *repairier,* < LL *repatriāre* to return to one's native land, < L RE- + *patria* fatherland]

repairman (rɪˈpɛəˌmæn) *n., pl.* **-men.** a man whose job it is to repair machines, etc.

repand (rɪˈpænd) *adj. Bot.* having a wavy margin: *a repand leaf.* [C18: < L *repandus* bent backwards, < RE- + *pandus* curved] —**reˈpandly** *adv.*

reparable (ˈrɛpərəbᵊl, ˈrɛprə-) *adj.* able to be repaired, recovered, or remedied. [C16: < L *reparābilis,* < *reparāre* to REPAIR[1]] —ˈ**reparably** *adv.*

reparation (ˌrɛpəˈreɪʃən) *n.* **1.** the act or process of making amends. **2.** (*usually pl.*) compensation exacted as an indemnity from a defeated nation by the victors. **3.** the act or process of repairing or state of having been repaired. [C14 *reparacioun,* ult. < L *reparāre* to REPAIR[1]] —**reparative** (rɪˈpærətɪv) *or* **reˈparatory** *adj.*

repartee (ˌrɛpɑːˈtiː) *n.* **1.** a sharp, witty, or aphoristic remark made as a reply. **2.** skill in making sharp witty replies. [C17: < F *repartie,* < *repartir* to retort, < RE- + *partir* to go away]

repast (rɪˈpɑːst) *n.* a meal or the food provided at a meal: *a light repast.* [C14: < OF, < *repaistre* to feed, < LL *repāscere,* < L RE- + *pāscere* to feed, pasture (of animals)]

repatriate *vb.* (riːˈpætrɪˌeɪt). **1.** (*tr.*) to send back (a person) to the country of his birth or citizenship. ~*n.* (riːˈpætrɪɪt). **2.** a person who has been repatriated. [C17: < LL *repatriāre,* < RE- + *patria* fatherland] —**reˌpatriˈation** *n.*

repay (rɪˈpeɪ) *vb.* **-paying, -paid. 1.** to pay back (money, etc.) to (a person); refund or reimburse. **2.** to make a return for (something): *to repay kindness.* —**reˈpayable** *adj.* —**reˈpayment** *n.*

repeal (rɪˈpiːl) *vb.* (*tr.*) **1.** to annul or rescind officially: revoke: *these laws were repealed.* ~*n.* **2.** an instance or the process of repealing; annulment. [C14: < OF *repeler,* < RE- + *apeler* to call, APPEAL] —**reˈpealable** *adj.* —**reˈpealer** *n.*

repeat (rɪˈpiːt) *vb.* **1.** (when *tr., may take a clause as object*) to do or experience (something) again once or several times, esp. to say or write (something) again. **2.** (*intr.*) to occur more than once: *the last figure repeats.* **3.** (*tr.; may take a clause as object*) to reproduce (the words, sounds,

---

reˈnomiˌnate *vb.*
ˌ**renomiˈnation** *n.*
ˌ**renotifiˈcation** *n.*
reˈnotiˌfy *vb.*
reˈnumber *vb.*
ˌ**reoccuˈpation** *n.*
reˈoccuˌpy *vb.*
ˌ**reocˈcurrence** *n.*
reˈopen *vb.*
reˈorder *vb., n.*
ˌ**reorganiˈzation** *or* **-iˈsation** *n.*
reˈorganˌize *or* **-ˌise** *vb.*
reˈorganˌizer *or* **-ˌiser** *n.*
reˈoriˌent *vb.*
ˌ**reorienˈtation** *n.*
reˈpack *vb.*
reˈpackage *vb.*
reˈpaint *vb.*
reˈpaper *vb.*

etc.) uttered by someone else; echo. **4.** (*tr.*) to utter (a poem, etc.) from memory; recite. **5.** (*intr.*) (of food) to be tasted again after ingestion as the result of belching. **6.** (*tr.; may take a clause as object*) to tell to another person (the secrets imparted to one by someone else). **7.** (*intr.*) (of a clock) to strike the hour or quarter-hour just past. **8.** (*intr.*) *U.S.* to vote (illegally) more than once in a single election. **9. repeat oneself.** to say or do the same thing more than once, esp. so as to be tedious. ~*n.* **10. a.** the act or an instance of repeating. **b.** (*as modifier*): *a repeat performance.* **11.** a word, action, etc., that is repeated. **12.** an order made out for goods, etc., that duplicates a previous order. **13.** *Radio, television.* a broadcast of a programme which has been broadcast before. **14.** *Music.* a passage that is an exact restatement of the passage preceding it. [C14: < OF *repeter,* < L *repetere,* < RE- + *petere* to seek] **—re'peatable** *adj.*

repeated (rɪ'piːtɪd) *adj.* done, made, or said again and again; continual. **—re'peatedly** *adv.*

repeater (rɪ'piːtə) *n.* **1.** a person or thing that repeats. **2.** Also called: **repeating firearm.** a firearm capable of discharging several shots without reloading. **3.** a timepiece which strikes the hour or quarter-hour just past, when a spring is pressed. **4.** *Electrical engineering.* a device that amplifies or augments incoming electrical signals and retransmits them.

repeating decimal *n.* another name for **recurring decimal.**

repechage (ˌrɛpɪ'ʃɑːʒ) *n.* a heat of a competition, esp. in rowing or fencing, in which eliminated contestants have another chance to qualify for the next round or the final. [C19: < F *repêchage,* lit.: fishing out again, < RE- + *pêcher* to fish + -AGE]

repel (rɪ'pɛl) *vb.* **-pelling, -pelled.** (*mainly tr.*) **1.** to force or drive back (something or somebody). **2.** (*also intr.*) to produce a feeling of aversion or distaste in (someone or something); be disgusting (to). **3.** to be effective in keeping away, controlling, or resisting: *a spray that repels flies.* **4.** to have no affinity for; fail to mix with or absorb: *water and oil repel each other.* **5.** to disdain to accept (something); turn away from or spurn: *she repelled his advances.* [C15: < L *repellere,* < RE- + *pellere* to push] **—re'peller** *n.* **—re'pellingly** *adv.*

▷ **Usage.** See at **repulse.**

repellent (rɪ'pɛlənt) *adj.* **1.** distasteful or repulsive. **2.** driving or forcing away or back; repelling. ~*n. also* **repellant. 3.** something, esp. a chemical substance, that repels: *insect repellent.* **4.** a substance with which fabrics are treated to increase their resistance to water. **—re'pellence** *or* **re'pellency** *n.* **—re'pellently** *adv.*

repent[1] (rɪ'pɛnt) *vb.* to feel remorse (for); be contrite (about); show penitence (for). [C13: < OF *repentir,* < RE- + *pentir,* < L *paenitēre* to repent] **—re'penter** *n.*

repent[2] ('riːpᵊnt) *adj. Bot.* lying or creeping along the ground: *repent stems.* [C17: < L *rēpere* to creep]

repentance (rɪ'pɛntəns) *n.* **1.** remorse or contrition for one's past actions. **2.** an act or the process of being repentant; penitence. **—re'pentant** *adj.*

repercussion (ˌriːpə'kʌʃən) *n.* **1.** (*often pl.*) a result or consequence of an action or event: *the repercussions of the war are still felt.* **2.** a recoil after impact; a rebound. **3.** a reflection, esp. of sound; echo or reverberation. [C16: < L *repercussiō,* < *repercutere* to strike back] **—ˌreper'cussive** *adj.*

repertoire ('rɛpəˌtwɑː) *n.* **1.** all the works collectively that a company, actor, etc., is competent to perform. **2.** the entire stock of things available in a field or of a kind. **3. in repertoire.** denoting the performance of two or more plays, etc., by the same company in the same venue on different evenings over a period of time: *"Tosca" returns to Leeds next month in repertoire with "Wozzeck".* [C19: < F, < LL *repertōrium* inventory; see REPERTORY]

repertory ('rɛpətərɪ, -trɪ) *n., pl.* **-ries. 1.** the entire stock of things available in a field or of a kind; repertoire. **2.** a building or place where a stock of things is kept; repository. **3.** short for **repertory company.** [C16: < LL *repertōrium* storehouse, < L *reperīre* to obtain, < RE- + *parere* to bring forth] **—repertorial** (ˌrɛpə'tɔːrɪəl) *adj.*

repertory company *n.* a theatrical company that performs plays from a repertoire. U.S. name: **stock company.**

repetend ('rɛpɪˌtɛnd) *n.* **1.** *Maths.* the digit in a recurring decimal that repeats itself. **2.** anything repeated. [C18: < L *repetendum* what is to be repeated, < *repetere* to REPEAT]

répétiteur *French.* (repetitœr) *n.* a member of an opera company who coaches the singers.

repetition (ˌrɛpɪ'tɪʃən) *n.* **1.** the act or an instance of repeating; reiteration. **2.** a thing, word, action, etc., that is repeated. **3.** a replica or copy. **—repetitive** (rɪ'pɛtɪtɪv) *adj.*

repetitious (ˌrɛpɪ'tɪʃəs) *adj.* characterized by unnecessary repetition. **—ˌrepe'titiously** *adv.* **—ˌrepe'titiousness** *n.*

repine (rɪ'paɪn) *vb.* (*intr.*) to be fretful or low-spirited through discontent. [C16: < RE- + PINE[2]]

replace (rɪ'pleɪs) *vb.* (*tr.*) **1.** to take the place of; supersede. **2.** to substitute a person or thing for (another); put in place of: *to replace an old pair of shoes.* **3.** to restore to its rightful place. **—re'placeable** *adj.* **—re'placer** *n.*

replacement (rɪ'pleɪsmənt) *n.* **1.** the act or process of replacing. **2.** a person or thing that replaces another.

replay *n.* ('riːˌpleɪ). **1.** Also called: **action replay.** a showing again of a sequence of action in slow motion immediately after it happens. **2.** a second match between a pair or group of contestants. ~*vb.* (riː'pleɪ). **3.** to play again (a record, sporting contest, etc.).

replenish (rɪ'plɛnɪʃ) *vb.* (*tr.*) **1.** to make full or complete again by supplying what has been used up. **2.** to put fresh fuel on (a fire). [C14: < OF *replenir,* < RE- + *plenir,* < L *plēnus* full] **—re'plenisher** *n.* **—re'plenishment** *n.*

replete (rɪ'pliːt) *adj.* (*usually postpositive*) **1.** (often foll. by *with*) copiously supplied (with); abounding (in). **2.** having one's appetite completely or excessively satisfied; gorged; satiated. [C14: < L *replētus,* < *replēre,* < RE- + *plēre* to fill] **—re'pletely** *adv.* **—re'pleteness** *n.* **—re'pletion** *n.*

replevin (rɪ'plɛvɪn) *Law.* ~*n.* **1.** the recovery of goods unlawfully taken, made subject to establishing the validity of the recovery in a legal action and returning the goods if the decision is adverse. **2.** (formerly) a writ of replevin. ~*vb.* **3.** another word for **replevy.** [C15: < Anglo-F, < OF *replevir* to give security for, < RE- + *plevir* to PLEDGE]

replevy (rɪ'plɛvɪ) *Law.* ~*vb.* **-plevying, -plevied.** (*tr.*) **1.** to recover possession of (goods) by replevin. ~*n., pl.* **-plevies. 2.** another word for **replevin.** [C15: < OF *replevir; see* REPLEVIN] **—re'pleviable** *or* **re'plevisable** *adj.*

replica ('rɛplɪkə) *n.* an exact copy or reproduction, esp. on a smaller scale. [C19: < It., lit.: a reply, < *replicare,* < L: to bend back, repeat]

replicate *vb.* ('rɛplɪˌkeɪt). (*mainly tr.*) **1.** (*also intr.*) to make or be a copy (of); reproduce. **2.** to fold (something) over on itself; bend back. ~*adj.* ('rɛplɪkɪt). **3.** folded back on itself: *a replicate leaf.* [C19: < L *replicātus* bent back; see REPLICA] **—ˌrepli'cation** *n.* **—'replicative** *adj.*

reply (rɪ'plaɪ) *vb.* **-plying, -plied.** (*mainly intr.*) **1.** to make answer (to) in words or writing or by an action; respond. **2.** (*tr.; takes a clause as*

---

re'people *vb.*
re'phrase *vb.*
re'plan *vb.*
re'plant *vb.*

object) to say (something) in answer: *he replied that he didn't want to come.* **3.** *Law.* to answer a defendant's plea. **4.** to return (a sound); echo. ~*n., pl.* **-plies. 5.** an answer; response. **6.** the answer made by a plaintiff or petitioner to a defendant's case. [C14: < OF *replier* to fold again, reply, < L *replicāre,* < RE- + *plicāre* to fold] **—re'plier** *n.*

repoint (ˌriːˈpɔɪnt) *vb.* (*tr.*) to repair the joints of (brickwork, masonry, etc.) with mortar or cement.

report (rɪˈpɔːt) *n.* **1.** an account prepared after investigation and published or broadcast. **2.** a statement made widely known; rumour: *according to report, he is not dead.* **3.** an account of the deliberations of a committee, body, etc.: *a report of parliamentary proceedings.* **4.** *Brit.* a statement on the progress of each schoolchild. **5.** a written account of a case decided at law. **6.** comment on a person's character or actions; reputation: *he is of good report here.* **7.** a sharp loud noise, esp. one made by a gun. ~*vb.* (when *tr., may take a clause as object;* when *intr.,* often foll. by *on*) **8.** to give an account (of); describe. **9.** to give an account of the results of an investigation (into): *to report on housing conditions.* **10.** (of a committee, legislative body, etc.) to make a formal report on (a bill). **11.** (*tr.*) to complain about (a person), esp. to a superior. **12.** to present (oneself) or be present at an appointed place or for a specific purpose: *report to the manager's office.* **13.** (*intr.*) to say or show that one is (in a certain state): *to report fit.* **14.** (*intr.;* foll. by *to*) to be responsible (to) and under the authority (of). **15.** (*intr.*) to act as a reporter. **16.** *Law.* to take down in writing details of (the proceedings of a court of law, etc.) as a record or for publication. [C14: < OF, < *reporter,* < L *reportāre,* < RE- + *portāre* to carry] **—re'portable** *adj.* **—re'portedly** *adv.*

reportage (rɪˈpɔːtɪdʒ, ˌrɛpɔːˈtɑːʒ) *n.* **1.** the act or process of reporting news or other events of general interest. **2.** a journalist's style of reporting.

reported speech *n.* another term for **indirect speech.**

reporter (rɪˈpɔːtə) *n.* **1.** a person who reports, esp. one employed to gather news for a newspaper or broadcasting organization. **2.** a person authorized to report the proceedings of a legislature.

report stage *n.* the stage preceding the third reading in the passage of a bill through Parliament.

repose[1] (rɪˈpəʊz) *n.* **1.** a state of quiet restfulness; peace or tranquillity. **2.** dignified calmness of manner; composure. ~*vb.* **3.** to lie or lay down at rest. **4.** (*intr.*) to lie when dead, as in the grave. **5.** (*intr.;* foll. by *on, in,* etc.) *Formal.* to be based (on): *your plan reposes on a fallacy.* [C15: < OF *reposer,* < LL *repausāre,* < RE- + *pausāre* to stop] **—re'posal** *n.* **—re'poser** *n.* **—re'poseful** *adj.* **—re'posefully** *adv.*

repose[2] (rɪˈpəʊz) *vb.* (*tr.*) **1.** to put (trust) in a person or thing. **2.** to place or put (an object) somewhere. [C15: < L *repōnere* to store up, < RE- + *pōnere* to put] **—re'posal** *n.*

repository (rɪˈpɒzɪtərɪ, -trɪ) *n., pl.* **-ries. 1.** a place or container in which things can be stored for safety. **2.** a place where things are kept for exhibition; museum. **3.** a place of burial; sepulchre. **4.** a person to whom a secret is entrusted; confidant. [C15: < L *repositōrium,* < *repōnere* to place]

repossess (ˌriːpəˈzɛs) *vb.* (*tr.*) to take back possession of (property), esp. for nonpayment of money due under a hire-purchase agreement. **—repossession** (ˌriːpəˈzɛʃən) *n.* **—ˌrepos'sessor** *n.*

repoussé (rəˈpuːseɪ) *adj.* **1.** raised in relief, as a design on a thin piece of metal hammered through from the underside. ~*n.* **2.** a design or surface made in this way. [C19: < F, < *repousser,* < RE- + *pousser* to PUSH]

repp (rɛp) *n.* a variant spelling of **rep**[1].

reprehend (ˌrɛprɪˈhɛnd) *vb.* (*tr.*) to find fault with; criticize. [C14: < L *reprehendere* to hold fast, rebuke, < RE- + *prendere* to grasp] **—ˌrepre'hender** *n.* **—ˌrepre'hension** *n.*

reprehensible (ˌrɛprɪˈhɛnsɪbᵊl) *adj.* open to criticism or rebuke; blameworthy. [C14: < LL *reprehensibilis,* < L *reprehendere;* see REPREHEND] **—ˌrepreˌhensi'bility** *n.* **—ˌrepre'hensibly** *adv.*

represent (ˌrɛprɪˈzɛnt) *vb.* (*tr.*) **1.** to stand as an equivalent of; correspond to. **2.** to act as a substitute or proxy (for). **3.** to act as or be the authorized delegate or agent for (a person, country, etc.): *an MP represents his constituency.* **4.** to serve or use as a means of expressing: *letters represent the sounds of speech.* **5.** to exhibit the characteristics of; exemplify; typify: *romanticism in music is represented by Beethoven.* **6.** to present an image of through the medium of a picture or sculpture; portray. **7.** to bring clearly before the mind. **8.** to set forth in words; state or explain. **9.** to describe as having a specified character or quality: *he represented her as a saint.* **10.** to act out the part of on stage; portray. [C14: < L *repraesentāre* to exhibit, < RE- + *praesentāre* to PRESENT[2]] **—ˌrepre'sentable** *adj.* **—ˌrepreˌsenta'bility** *n.*

re-present (ˌriːprɪˈzɛnt) *vb.* (*tr.*) to present again. **—re-presentation** (ˌriːˌprɛzənˈteɪʃən) *n.*

representation (ˌrɛprɪzɛnˈteɪʃən) *n.* **1.** the act or an instance of representing or the state of being represented. **2.** anything that represents, such as a verbal or pictorial portrait. **3.** anything that is represented, such as an image brought clearly to mind. **4.** the principle by which delegates act for a constituency. **5.** a body of representatives. **6.** an instance of acting for another in a particular capacity, such as executor. **7.** a dramatic production or performance. **8.** (*often pl.*) a statement of facts, true or alleged, esp. one set forth by way of remonstrance or expostulation.

representational (ˌrɛprɪzɛnˈteɪʃənᵊl) *adj.* **1.** *Art.* depicting objects, scenes, etc., directly as seen; naturalistic. **2.** of or relating to representation.

representationalism (ˌrɛprɪzɛnˈteɪʃənəˌlɪzəm) *or* **representationism** *n.* **1.** *Philosophy.* the doctrine that in perceptions of objects what is before the mind is not the object but a representation of it. Cf. **presentationism. 2.** *Art.* the practice of depicting objects, scenes, etc., directly as seen. **—ˌrepresenˌtational'istic** *adj.* **—ˌrepresen'tationist** *n., adj.*

representative (ˌrɛprɪˈzɛntətɪv) *n.* **1.** a person or thing that represents another. **2.** a person who represents and tries to sell the products or services of a firm. **3.** a typical example. **4.** a person representing a constituency in a deliberative, legislative, or executive body, esp. (*cap.*) a member of the **House of Representatives** (the lower house of Congress). ~*adj.* **5.** serving to represent; symbolic. **6. a.** exemplifying a class or kind; typical. **b.** containing or including examples of all the interests, types, etc., in a group. **7.** acting as deputy or proxy for another. **8.** representing a constituency or the whole people in the process of government: *a representative council.* **9.** of or relating to the political representation of the people: *representative government.* **10.** of or relating to a mental picture or representation. **—ˌrepre'sentatively** *adv.* **—ˌrepre'sentativeness** *n.*

repress (rɪˈprɛs) *vb.* (*tr.*) **1.** to keep (feelings, etc.) under control; suppress or restrain. **2.** to put into a state of subjugation: *to repress a people.* **3.** *Psychol.* to banish (unpleasant thoughts) from one's conscious mind. [C14: < L *reprimere* to press back, < RE- + *premere* to PRESS[1]] **—re'pressed** *adj.* **—re'presser** *or* **re'pressor** *n.*

---

re'popuˌlate *vb.* **ˌrepo'sition** *vb., n.* **re'pot** *vb.*

—**re'pressible** *adj.* —**re'pression** *n.* —**re'pressive** *adj.*

re-press (riː'prɛs) *vb.* (*tr.*) to press again, esp. to reproduce more gramophone records by a second pressing.

reprieve (rɪ'priːv) *vb.* (*tr.*) **1.** to postpone or remit the punishment of (a person, esp. one condemned to death). **2.** to give temporary relief to (a person or thing), esp. from otherwise irrevocable harm. ~*n.* **3.** a postponement or remission of punishment. **4.** a warrant granting a postponement. **5.** a temporary relief from pain or harm; respite. [C16: < OF *repris* (something) taken back, < *reprendre,* < L *reprehendere;* ? also infl. by obs. E *repreve* to reprove] —**re'prievable** *adj.* —**re'priever** *n.*

reprimand ('rɛprɪˌmɑːnd) *n.* **1.** a reproof or formal admonition; rebuke. ~*vb.* **2.** (*tr.*) to admonish or rebuke, esp. formally. [C17: < F *réprimande,* < L *reprimenda* (things) to be repressed; see REPRESS] —ˌ**repri'manding** *adj.*

reprint *n.* ('riːˌprɪnt). **1.** a reproduction in print of any matter already published. **2.** a reissue of a printed work using the same type, plates, etc., as the original. ~*vb.* (riː'prɪnt). **3.** (*tr.*) to print again. —**re'printer** *n.*

reprisal (rɪ'praɪzᵊl) *n.* **1.** the act or an instance of retaliation in any form. **2.** (*often pl.*) retaliatory action against an enemy in wartime. **3.** (formerly) the forcible seizure of the property or subjects of one nation by another. [C15: < OF *reprisaille,* < OIt., < *riprendere* to recapture, < L *reprehendere;* see REPREHEND]

reprise (rɪ'priːz) *Music.* ~*n.* **1.** the repeating of an earlier theme. ~*vb.* **2.** to repeat (an earlier theme). [C14: < OF, < *reprendre* to take back, < L *reprehendere;* see REPREHEND]

repro ('riːprəʊ) *n., pl.* **-pros. 1.** short for **reproduction** (sense 2): *repro furniture.* **2.** short for **reproduction proof.**

reproach (rɪ'prəʊtʃ) *vb.* (*tr.*) **1.** to impute blame to (a person) for an action or fault; rebuke. ~*n.* **2.** the act of reproaching. **3.** rebuke or censure; reproof. **4.** disgrace or shame: *to bring reproach upon one's family.* **5. above** *or* **beyond reproach.** perfect; beyond criticism. [C15: < OF *reprochier,* < L RE- + *prope* near] —**re'proachable** *adj.* —**re'proacher** *n.* —**re'proachingly** *adv.*

reproachful (rɪ'prəʊtʃfʊl) *adj.* full of or expressing reproach. —**re'proachfully** *adv.* —**re'proachfulness** *n.*

reprobate ('rɛprəʊˌbeɪt) *adj.* **1.** morally unprincipled; depraved. **2.** *Christianity.* condemned to eternal punishment in hell. ~*n.* **3.** an unprincipled, depraved, or damned person. **4.** a disreputable or roguish person. ~*vb.* (*tr.*) **5.** to disapprove of; condemn. **6.** (of God) to condemn to eternal punishment in hell. [C16: < LL *reprobātus* held in disfavour, < L RE- + *probāre* to test, APPROVE] —**reprobacy** ('rɛprəbəsɪ) *n.* —'**reproˌbater** *n.* —ˌ**repro'bation** *n.*

reprocess (riː'prəʊsɛs) *vb.* (*tr.*) to treat again (something already made and used) in order to make it reusable in some form. —**re'processing** *n., adj.*

reproduce (ˌriːprə'djuːs) *vb.* (*mainly tr.*) **1.** to make a copy, representation, or imitation of; duplicate. **2.** (*also intr.*) *Biol.* to undergo or cause to undergo a process of reproduction. **3.** to produce again; bring back into existence again; re-create. **4.** (*intr.*) to come out (well, badly, etc.) when copied. —ˌ**repro'ducer** *n.* —ˌ**repro'ducible** *adj.* —ˌ**repro'ducibly** *adv.* —ˌ**reproˌduci'bility** *n.*

reproduction (ˌriːprə'dʌkʃən) *n.* **1.** *Biol.* any of various processes, either sexual or asexual, by which an animal or plant produces one or more individuals similar to itself. **2. a.** an imitation or facsimile of a work of art. **b.** (*as modifier*): *a reproduction portrait.* **3.** the quality of sound from an audio system. **4.** the act or process of reproducing.

reproduction proof *n. Printing.* a proof of very good quality used for photographic reproduction to make a printing plate.

reproductive (ˌriːprə'dʌktɪv) *adj.* of, relating to, characteristic of, or taking part in reproduction. —ˌ**repro'ductively** *adv.* —ˌ**repro'ductiveness** *n.*

reprography (rɪ'prɒgrəfɪ) *n.* the art or process of copying, reprinting, or reproducing printed material. —**reprographic** (ˌrɛprə'græfɪk) *adj.* —ˌ**repro'graphically** *adv.*

reproof (rɪ'pruːf) *n.* an act or expression of rebuke or censure. Also: **reproval** (rɪ'pruːvᵊl). [C14 *reproffe,* < OF *reprove,* < LL *reprobāre* to disapprove of; see REPROBATE]

re-proof (riː'pruːf) *vb.* (*tr.*) **1.** to treat (a coat, jacket, etc.) so as to renew its texture, waterproof qualities, etc. **2.** to provide a new proof of (a book, galley, etc.).

reprove (rɪ'pruːv) *vb.* (*tr.*) to rebuke or scold. [C14: < OF *reprover,* < LL *reprobāre,* < L RE- + *probāre* to examine] —**re'provable** *adj.* —**re'prover** *n.* —**re'provingly** *adv.*

reptant ('rɛptənt) *adj. Biol.* creeping, crawling, or lying along the ground. [C17: < L *reptāre* to creep]

reptile ('rɛptaɪl) *n.* **1.** any of the cold-blooded vertebrates characterized by lungs, an outer covering of horny scales or plates, and young produced in eggs, such as the tortoises, turtles, snakes, lizards, and crocodiles. **2.** a grovelling insignificant person: *you miserable little reptile!* ~*adj.* **3.** creeping, crawling, or squirming. [C14: < LL *reptilis* creeping, < L *rēpere* to crawl] —**reptilian** (rɛp'tɪlɪən) *n., adj.*

republic (rɪ'pʌblɪk) *n.* **1.** a form of government in which the people or their elected representatives possess the supreme power. **2.** a political or national unit possessing such a form of government. **3.** a constitutional form in which the head of state is an elected or nominated president. [C17: < F *république,* < L *rēspublica,* lit.: the public thing, < *rēs* thing + *publica* PUBLIC]

republican (rɪ'pʌblɪkən) *adj.* **1.** of, resembling, or relating to a republic. **2.** supporting or advocating a republic. ~*n.* **3.** a supporter or advocate of a republic.

Republican (rɪ'pʌblɪkən) *adj.* **1.** of, belonging to, or relating to a Republican Party. **2.** of, belonging to, or relating to the Irish Republican Army. ~*n.* **3.** a member or supporter of a Republican Party. **4.** a member or supporter of the Irish Republican Army.

republicanism (rɪ'pʌblɪkəˌnɪzəm) *n.* **1.** the principles or theory of republican government. **2.** support for a republic. **3.** (*often cap.*) support for a Republican Party.

Republican Party *n.* **1.** one of the two major political parties in the U.S.: established around 1854. **2.** any of a number of political parties in other countries, usually so named to indicate their opposition to monarchy.

repudiate (rɪ'pjuːdɪˌeɪt) *vb.* (*tr.*) **1.** to reject the authority or validity of; refuse to accept or ratify. **2.** to refuse to acknowledge or pay (a debt). **3.** to cast off or disown (a son, lover, etc.). [C16: < L *repudiāre* to put away, < *repudium* separation, divorce, < RE- + *pudēre* to be ashamed] —**re'pudiable** *adj.* —**reˌpudi'ation** *n.* —**re'pudiative** *adj.* —**re'pudiˌator** *n.*

repugnant (rɪ'pʌgnənt) *adj.* **1.** repellent to the senses; causing aversion. **2.** distasteful; offensive; disgusting. **3.** contradictory; inconsistent or incompatible. [C14: < L *repugnāns* resisting, < *repugnāre,* < RE- + *pugnāre* to fight] —**re'pugnance** *n.* —**re'pugnantly** *adv.*

repulse (rɪ'pʌls) *vb.* (*tr.*) **1.** to drive back or ward off (an attacking force); repel; rebuff. **2.** to reject with coldness or discourtesy: *she repulsed his advances.* ~*n.* **3.** the act or an instance of

---

re'price *vb.*
ˌ**repro'grammable** *or*
ˌ**repro'gramable** *adj.*
ˌ**republi'cation** *n.*
re'publish *vb.*

driving back or warding off; rebuff. **4.** a cold discourteous rejection or refusal. [C16: < L *repellere* to drive back] —**re'pulser** *n.*

▷ **Usage.** The verbs *repulse* and *repel* share the meaning of physically driving back or away, but they can be carefully distinguished in other senses. Although the related adjective *repulsive* has the meaning of causing feelings of disgust, *repulse* does not mean to drive away by arousing disgust. Instead, *repel* is normally used in this sense, and *repulse* is used when the required meaning is to reject coldly or drive away with discourtesy.

repulsion (rɪˈpʌlʃən) *n.* **1.** a feeling of disgust or aversion. **2.** *Physics.* a force separating two objects, such as the force between two like electric charges.

repulsive (rɪˈpʌlsɪv) *adj.* **1.** causing or occasioning repugnance; loathsome; disgusting or distasteful. **2.** tending to repel, esp. by coldness and discourtesy. **3.** *Physics.* concerned with, producing, or being a repulsion. —**re'pulsively** *adv.* —**re'pulsiveness** *n.*

reputable (ˈrɛpjʊtəbᵊl) *adj.* **1.** having a good reputation; honoured, trustworthy, or respectable. **2.** (of words) acceptable as good usage; standard. —**'reputably** *adv.*

reputation (ˌrɛpjʊˈteɪʃən) *n.* **1.** the estimation in which a person or thing is generally held; opinion. **2.** a high opinion generally held about a person or thing; esteem. **3.** notoriety or fame, esp. for some specified characteristic. [C14: < L *reputātiō*, < *reputāre* to calculate; see REPUTE]

repute (rɪˈpjuːt) *vb.* **1.** (*tr.; usually passive*) to consider (a person or thing) to be as specified: *he is reputed to be rich.* ~*n.* **2.** public estimation; reputation: *a writer of little repute.* [C15: < OF *reputer*, < L *reputāre*, < RE- + *putāre* to think]

reputed (rɪˈpjuːtɪd) *adj.* (*prenominal*) generally reckoned or considered; supposed: *the reputed writer of two epic poems.* —**re'putedly** *adv.*

request (rɪˈkwɛst) *vb.* (*tr.*) **1.** to express a desire for, esp. politely; ask for or demand: *to request a bottle of wine.* ~*n.* **2.** the act or an instance of requesting, esp. in the form of a written statement, etc.; petition or solicitation. **3. by request.** in accordance with someone's desire. **4. in request.** in demand; popular: *he is in request all over the world.* **5. on request.** on the occasion of a demand or request: *application forms are available on request.* [C14: < OF *requeste*, < Vulgar L *requaerere*; see REQUIRE, QUEST] —**re'quester** *n.*

request stop *n.* a point on a route at which a bus, etc., will stop only if signalled to do so. U.S. equivalent: **flag stop.**

Requiem (ˈrɛkwɪəm) *n.* **1.** *R.C. Church.* a Mass celebrated for the dead. **2.** a musical setting of this Mass. **3.** any piece of music composed or performed as a memorial to a dead person. [C14: < L *requiēs* rest, from the introit, *Requiem aeternam dona eis* Rest eternal grant unto them]

requiem shark *n.* any of a family of sharks occurring mostly in tropical seas and characterized by a nictitating membrane.

requiescat (ˌrɛkwɪˈɛskæt) *n.* a prayer for the repose of the souls of the dead. [L, < *requiescat in pace* may he rest in peace]

require (rɪˈkwaɪə) *vb.* (*mainly tr.; may take a clause as object or an infinitive*) **1.** to have need of; depend upon; want. **2.** to impose as a necessity; make necessary: *this work requires precision.* **3.** (*also intr.*) to make formal request (for); insist upon. **4.** to call upon or oblige (a person) authoritatively; order or command: *to require someone to account for his actions.* [C14: < OF *requerre*, via Vulgar L < L *requīrere* to seek to know; also infl. by *quaerere* to seek] —**re'quirer** *n.*

requirement (rɪˈkwaɪəmənt) *n.* **1.** something demanded or imposed as an obligation. **2.** a thing desired or needed. **3.** the act or an instance of requiring.

requisite (ˈrɛkwɪzɪt) *adj.* **1.** absolutely essential; indispensable. ~*n.* **2.** something indispensable; necessity. [C15: < L *requīsītus* sought after, < *requīrere* to seek for] —**'requisitely** *adv.*

requisition (ˌrɛkwɪˈzɪʃən) *n.* **1.** a request or demand, esp. an authoritative or formal one. **2.** an official form on which such a demand is made. **3.** the act of taking something over, esp. temporarily for military or public use. ~*vb.* (*tr.*) **4.** to demand and take for use, esp. by military or public authority. **5.** (*may take an infinitive*) to require (someone) formally to do (something): *to requisition a soldier to drive an officer's car.* —ˌ**requi'sitionary** *adj.* —ˌ**requi'sitionist** *n.*

requite (rɪˈkwaɪt) *vb.* (*tr.*) to make return to (a person for a kindness or injury); repay with a similar action. [C16: RE- + obs. *quite* to discharge, repay; see QUIT] —**re'quitable** *adj.* —**re'quital** *n.* —**re'quitement** *n.* —**re'quiter** *n.*

reredos (ˈrɪədɒs) *n.* **1.** a screen or wall decoration at the back of an altar. **2.** another word for **fireback.** [C14: < OF *areredos*, < *arere* behind + *dos* back, < L *dorsum*]

rerun *vb.* (riːˈrʌn), **-running, -ran.** (*tr.*) **1.** to broadcast or put on (a film, etc.) again. **2.** to run (a race, etc.) again. ~*n.* (ˈriːˌrʌn). **3.** a film, etc., that is broadcast again; repeat. **4.** a race that is run again.

res (reɪs) *n., pl.* **res.** *Latin.* a thing, matter, or object.

res. *abbrev. for:* **1.** research. **2.** reserve. **3.** residence. **4.** resides. **5.** resigned. **6.** resolution.

resale price maintenance (ˈriːseɪl) *n.* the practice by which a manufacturer establishes a fixed or minimum price for the resale of a brand product by retailers or other distributors. U.S. equivalent: **fair trade.** Abbrev.: **rpm.**

rescind (rɪˈsɪnd) *vb.* (*tr.*) to annul or repeal. [C17: < L *rēscindere* to cut off, < *re-* (intensive) + *scindere* to cut] —**re'scindable** *adj.* —**re'scinder** *n.* —**re'scindment** *n.*

rescission (rɪˈsɪʒən) *n.* the act of rescinding.

rescript (ˈriːˌskrɪpt) *n.* **1.** (in ancient Rome) a reply by the emperor to a question on a point of law. **2.** any official announcement or edict; a decree. **3.** something rewritten. [C16: < L *rēscriptum* reply, < *rēscribere* to write back]

rescue (ˈrɛskjuː) *vb.* **-cuing, -cued.** (*tr.*) **1.** to bring (someone or something) out of danger, etc.; deliver or save. **2.** to free (a person) from legal custody by force. **3.** *Law.* to seize (goods) by force. ~*n.* **4. a.** the act or an instance of rescuing. **b.** (*as modifier*): *a rescue party.* **5.** the forcible removal of a person from legal custody. **6.** *Law.* the forcible seizure of goods or property. [C14 *rescowen*, < OF *rescourre*, < RE- + *escourre* to pull away, < L *excutere* to shake off, < *quatere* to shake] —**'rescuer** *n.*

research (rɪˈsɜːtʃ) *n.* **1.** systematic investigation to establish facts or collect information on a subject. ~*vb.* **2.** to carry out investigations into (a subject, etc.). [C16: < OF *recercher* to seek, search again, < RE- + *cercher* to SEARCH] —**re'searchable** *adj.* —**re'searcher** *n.*

research and development *n.* a commercial company's application of scientific research to develop new products. Abbrev.: **R & D.**

reseat (riːˈsiːt) *vb.* (*tr.*) **1.** to show (a person) to a new seat. **2.** to put a new seat on (a chair, etc.). **3.** to provide new seats for (a theatre, etc.). **4.** to re-form the seating of (a valve).

resect (rɪˈsɛkt) *vb.* (*tr.*) *Surgery.* to cut out part of (a bone, organ, or other structure or part). [C17: < L *resecāre*, < RE- + *secāre* to cut]

resection (rɪˈsɛkʃən) *n.* **1.** *Surgery.* excision of

---

re'purchase *vb., n.*
re'puriˌfy *vb.*
re'read *vb.*
ˌ**rere'cording** *n.*
re'roof *vb.*
re'route *vb.*
re'salable *or* **re'saleable** *adj.*
re'schedule *vb.*
re'seal *vb.*
re'sealable *adj.*

part of a bone, organ, or other part. **2.** *Surveying.* a method of fixing the position of a point by making angular observations to three fixed points. —**re'sectional** *adj.*

resemblance (rɪ'zɛmbləns) *n.* **1.** the state or quality of resembling; likeness or similarity. **2.** the degree or extent to which a likeness exists. **3.** semblance; likeness. —**re'semblant** *adj.*

resemble (rɪ'zɛmbᵊl) *vb.* (*tr.*) to possess some similarity to; be like. [C14: < OF *resembler,* < RE- + *sembler* to look like, < L *similis* like] —**re'sembler** *n.*

resent (rɪ'zɛnt) *vb.* (*tr.*) to feel bitter, indignant, or aggrieved at. [C17: < F *ressentir,* < RE- + *sentir* to feel, < L *sentīre* to perceive; see SENSE] —**re'sentful** *adj.* —**re'sentment** *n.*

reserpine ('rɛsəpɪn) *n.* an insoluble alkaloid, extracted from the roots of a rauwolfia, used medicinally to lower blood pressure and as a sedative and tranquillizer. [C20: < G *Reserpin,* prob. < the NL name of the plant]

reservation (ˌrɛzə'veɪʃən) *n.* **1.** the act or an instance of reserving. **2.** something reserved, esp. accommodation or a seat. **3.** (*often pl.*) a stated or unstated qualification of opinion that prevents one's wholehearted acceptance of a proposal, etc. **4.** an area of land set aside, esp. (in the U.S. and Canada) for American Indian peoples. **5.** *Brit.* the strip of land between the two carriageways of a dual carriageway. **6.** the act or process of keeping back, esp. for oneself; withholding. **7.** *Law.* a right or interest retained by the grantor in property dealings.

reserve (rɪ'zɜːv) *vb.* (*tr.*) **1.** to keep back or set aside, esp. for future use or contingency; withhold. **2.** to keep for oneself; retain: *I reserve the right to question these men later.* **3.** to obtain or secure by advance arrangement: *I have reserved two tickets for tonight's show.* **4.** to delay delivery of (a judgment). ~*n.* **5. a.** something kept back or set aside, esp. for future use or contingency. **b.** (*as modifier*): *a reserve stock.* **6.** the state or condition of being reserved: *I have plenty in reserve.* **7.** a tract of land set aside for a special purpose: *a nature reserve.* **8.** *Austral. & N.Z.* a public park. **9.** *Canad.* an Indian reservation. **10.** *Sport.* a substitute. **11.** (*often pl.*) **a.** a part of an army not committed to immediate action in a military engagement. **b.** that part of a nation's armed services not in active service. **12.** coolness or formality of manner; restraint, silence, or reticence. **13.** (*often pl.*) *Finance.* liquid assets or a portion of capital not invested or a portion of profits not distributed by a bank or business enterprise and held to meet future liabilities or contingencies. **14. without reserve.** without reservations; fully. [C14: < OF *reserver,* < L *reservāre,* < RE- + *servāre* to keep] —**re'servable** *adj.* —**re'server** *n.*

re-serve (riː'sɜːv) *vb.* (*tr.*) to serve again.

reserve bank *n.* one of the twelve banks forming part of the U.S. Federal Reserve System.

reserve currency *n.* foreign currency that is acceptable as a medium of international payments and is held in reserve by many countries.

reserved (rɪ'zɜːvd) *adj.* **1.** set aside for use by a particular person. **2.** cool or formal in manner; restrained or reticent. **3.** destined; fated: *a man reserved for greatness.* —**reservedly** (rɪ'zɜːvɪdlɪ) *adv.* —**re'servedness** *n.*

reserved list *n. Brit.* a list of retired naval, army, or air-force officers available for recall to active service in an emergency.

reserved occupation *n. Brit.* an occupation from which one will not be called up for military service in time of war.

reserve-grade *adj. Austral.* denoting a sporting team of the second rank in a club.

reserve price *n. Brit.* the minimum price acceptable to the owner of property being auctioned or sold. Also called (esp. Scot. and U.S.): **upset price.**

reservist (rɪ'zɜːvɪst) *n.* one who serves in the reserve formations of a nation's armed forces.

reservoir ('rɛzəˌvwɑː) *n.* **1.** a natural or artificial lake or large tank used for collecting and storing water for community use. **2.** *Biol.* a cavity in an organism containing fluid. **3.** a place where a great stock of anything is accumulated. **4.** a large supply of something: *a reservoir of talent.* [C17: < F *réservoir,* < *réserver* to RESERVE]

reservoir rock *n.* porous and permeable rock containing producible oil or gas in its pore spaces.

reset[1] *vb.* (riː'sɛt), **-setting, -set.** (*tr.*) **1.** to set again (a broken bone, matter in type, a gemstone, etc.). **2.** to restore (a gauge, etc.) to zero. ~*n.* ('riːˌsɛt). **3.** the act or an instance of setting again. **4.** a thing that is set again. —**re'setter** *n.*

reset[2] *Scot.* ~*vb.* (riː'sɛt), **-setting, -set. 1.** to receive or handle (goods) knowing they have been stolen. ~*n.* ('riːsɛt). **2.** the receiving of stolen goods. [C14: < OF *receter,* < L *receptāre,* < *recipere* to receive] —**re'setter** *n.*

res gestae ('dʒɛstiː) *pl. n.* **1.** things done or accomplished; achievements. **2.** *Law.* incidental facts and circumstances that are admissible in evidence because they explain the matter at issue. [L]

reside (rɪ'zaɪd) *vb.* (*intr.*) *Formal.* **1.** to live permanently (in a place); have one's home (in): *he resides in London.* **2.** (of things, qualities, etc.) to be inherently present (in); be vested (in): *political power resides in military strength.* [C15: < L *residēre* to sit back, < RE- + *sedēre* to sit] —**re'sider** *n.*

residence ('rɛzɪdəns) *n.* **1.** the place in which one resides; abode or home. **2.** a large imposing house; mansion. **3.** the fact of residing in a place or a period of residing. **4. in residence. a.** actually resident: *the Queen is in residence.* **b.** designating a creative artist resident and active for a set period at a college, gallery, etc.: *writer in residence.*

residency ('rɛzɪdənsɪ) *n., pl.* **-cies. 1.** a variant of **residence. 2.** *U.S. & Canad.* the period, following internship, during which a physician undergoes specialized training. **3.** (in India, formerly) the official house of the governor general at the court of a native prince.

resident ('rɛzɪdənt) *n.* **1.** a person who resides in a place. **2.** (esp. formerly) a representative of the British government in a British protectorate. **3.** (in India, formerly) a representative of the British governor general at the court of a native prince. **4.** a bird or animal that does not migrate. **5.** *Brit. & N.Z.* a junior doctor who lives in the hospital where he works. **6.** *U.S. & Canad.* a physician who lives in the hospital while undergoing specialist training after completing his internship. ~*adj.* **7.** living in a place; residing. **8.** living or staying at a place in order to discharge a duty, etc. **9.** (of qualities, etc.) existing or inherent (in). **10.** (of birds and animals) not in the habit of migrating. —'**residentship** *n.*

residential (ˌrɛzɪ'dɛnʃəl) *adj.* **1.** suitable for or allocated for residence: *a residential area.* **2.** relating to residence. —ˌ**resi'dentially** *adv.*

residentiary (ˌrɛzɪ'dɛnʃərɪ) *adj.* **1.** residing in a place, esp. officially. **2.** obliged to reside in an official residence: *a residentiary benefice.* ~*n., pl.* **-tiaries. 3.** a clergyman obliged to reside in the place of his official appointment.

residual (rɪ'zɪdjʊəl) *adj.* **1.** of, relating to, or designating a residue or remainder; remaining; leftover. **2.** *U.S.* of or relating to the payment of residuals. ~*n.* **3.** something left over as a residue; remainder. **4.** *Statistics.* **a.** the difference between the mean of a set of observations and one particular observation. **b.** the difference between the numerical value of one particular observation and the theoretical result. **5.** (*often*

---

re'settle *vb.*
re'settlement *n.*
re'ship *vb.*
re'shuffle *vb., n.*

pl.) payment made to an actor, musician, etc., for subsequent use of film in which the person appears. —**re'sidually** *adv.*

residuary (rɪ'zɪdjʊərɪ) *adj.* **1.** of, relating to, or constituting a residue; residual. **2.** *Law.* entitled to the residue of an estate after payment of debts and distribution of specific gifts.

residue ('rɛzɪˌdjuː) *n.* **1.** matter remaining after something has been removed. **2.** *Law.* what is left of an estate after the discharge of debts and distribution of specific gifts. [C14: < OF *residu,* < L *residuus* remaining over, < *residēre* to stay behind]

residuum (rɪ'zɪdjʊəm) *n., pl.* **-ua** (-jʊə). a more formal word for **residue.**

resign (rɪ'zaɪn) *vb.* **1.** (when *intr.,* often foll. by *from*) to give up tenure of (a job, office, etc.). **2.** (*tr.*) to reconcile (oneself) to; yield: *to resign oneself to death.* **3.** (*tr.*) to give up (a right, claim, etc.); relinquish. [C14: < OF *resigner,* < L *resignāre* to unseal, destroy, < RE- + *signāre* to seal] —**re'signer** *n.*

re-sign (riː'saɪn) *vb.* to sign again.

resignation (ˌrɛzɪg'neɪʃən) *n.* **1.** the act of resigning. **2.** a formal document stating one's intention to resign. **3.** a submissive unresisting attitude; passive acquiescence.

resigned (rɪ'zaɪnd) *adj.* characteristic of or proceeding from an attitude of resignation; acquiescent or submissive. —**resignedly** (rɪ'zaɪnɪdlɪ) *adv.* —**re'signedness** *n.*

resile (rɪ'zaɪl) *vb.* (*intr.*) to spring or shrink back; recoil or resume original shape. [C16: < OF *resilir,* < L *resilīre* to jump back, < RE- + *salīre* to jump] —**re'silement** *n.*

resilient (rɪ'zɪlɪənt) *adj.* **1.** (of an object) capable of regaining its original shape or position after bending, stretching, or other deformation; elastic. **2.** (of a person) recovering easily and quickly from illness, hardship, etc. —**re'silience** *or* **re'siliency** *n.* —**re'siliently** *adv.*

resin ('rɛzɪn) *n.* **1.** Also called: **rosin.** any of a group of solid or semisolid amorphous compounds that are obtained directly from certain plants as exudations. **2.** any of a large number of synthetic, usually organic, materials that have a polymeric structure, esp. such a substance in a raw state before it is moulded or treated with plasticizer, etc. ~*vb.* **3.** (*tr.*) to treat or coat with resin. [C14: < OF *resine,* < L *rēsīna,* < Gk *rhētinē* resin from a pine] —'**resinous** *adj.* —'**resinously** *adv.* —'**resinousness** *n.*

resinate ('rɛzɪˌneɪt) *vb.* (*tr.*) to impregnate with resin.

resipiscence (ˌrɛsɪ'pɪsəns) *n. Literary.* acknowledgment that one has been mistaken. [C16: < LL *resipiscentia,* < *resipiscere* to recover one's senses, < L *sapere* to know] —ˌ**resi'piscent** *adj.*

resist (rɪ'zɪst) *vb.* **1.** to stand firm (against); not yield (to); fight (against). **2.** (*tr.*) to withstand the deleterious action of; be proof against: *to resist corrosion.* **3.** (*tr.*) to oppose; refuse to accept or comply with: *to resist arrest.* **4.** (*tr.*) to refrain from, esp. in spite of temptation (esp. in **cannot resist (something)**). ~*n.* **5.** a substance used to protect something, esp. a coating that prevents corrosion. [C14: < L *resistere,* < RE- + *sistere* to stand firm] —**re'sister** *n.* —**re'sistible** *adj.* —**reˌsisti'bility** *n.* —**re'sistibly** *adv.* —**re'sistless** *adj.*

resistance (rɪ'zɪstəns) *n.* **1.** the act or an instance of resisting. **2.** the capacity to withstand something, esp. the body's natural capacity to withstand disease. **3. a.** the opposition to a flow of electric current through a circuit component, medium, or substance. It is measured in ohms. Symbol: R **b.** (*as modifier*): *a resistance thermometer.* **4.** any force that tends to retard or oppose motion: *air resistance; wind resistance.* **5.** *Physics.* the magnitude of the real part of the acoustic or mechanical impedance. **6. line of least resistance.** the easiest, but not necessarily the best or most honourable, course of action. **7.** See **passive resistance.** —**re'sistant** *adj., n.*

Resistance (rɪ'zɪstəns) *n.* **the.** an illegal organization fighting for national liberty in a country under enemy occupation.

resistance thermometer *n.* an accurate type of thermometer in which temperature is calculated from the resistance of a coil of wire or of a semiconductor placed at the point at which the temperature is to be measured.

resistivity (ˌriːzɪs'tɪvɪtɪ) *n.* **1.** the electrical property of a material that determines the resistance of a piece of given dimensions. It is measured in ohms. Former name: **specific resistance. 2.** the power or capacity to resist; resistance.

resistor (rɪ'zɪstə) *n.* an electrical component designed to introduce a known value of resistance into a circuit.

resit (riː'sɪt) *vb.* **-sitting, -sat.** (*tr.*) **1.** to sit (an examination) again. ~*n.* **2.** an examination which one must sit again.

res judicata (ˌdʒuːdɪ'kɑːtə) *or* **res adjudicata** *n. Law.* a matter already adjudicated upon that cannot be raised again. [L]

resoluble (rɪ'zɒljʊbᵊl, 'rɛzəl-) *or* **resolvable** *adj.* able to be resolved or analysed. [C17: < LL *resolubilis,* < L *resolvere;* see RESOLVE] —**reˌsolu'bility, reˌsolva'bility** *or* **re'solubleness, re'solvableness** *n.*

re-soluble (riː'sɒljʊbᵊl) *adj.* capable of being dissolved again. —**re-'solubleness** *or* **re-ˌsolu'bility** *n.* —**re-'solubly** *adv.*

resolute ('rɛzəˌluːt) *adj.* **1.** firm in purpose or belief; steadfast. **2.** characterized by resolution; determined: *a resolute answer.* [C16: < L *resolutus,* < *resolvere* to RESOLVE] —'**resoˌlutely** *adv.* —'**resoˌluteness** *n.*

resolution (ˌrɛzə'luːʃən) *n.* **1.** the act or an instance of resolving. **2.** firmness or determination. **3.** something resolved or determined; decision. **4.** a formal expression of opinion by a meeting. **5.** a judicial decision on some matter; verdict; judgment. **6.** the act of separating something into its constituent parts or elements. **7.** *Med.* subsidence of the symptoms of a disease, esp. the disappearance of inflammation without pus. **8.** *Music.* the process in harmony whereby a dissonant note or chord is followed by a consonant one. **9.** the ability of a television or film image to reproduce fine detail. **10.** *Physics.* another word for **resolving power.** —ˌ**reso'lutioner** *or* ˌ**reso'lutionist** *n.*

resolve (rɪ'zɒlv) *vb.* (*mainly tr.*) **1.** (*takes a clause as object or an infinitive*) to decide or determine firmly. **2.** to express (an opinion) formally, esp. by a vote. **3.** (*also intr.;* usually foll. by *into*) to separate or cause to separate (into) (constituent parts). **4.** (*usually reflexive*) to change; alter: *the ghost resolved itself into a tree.* **5.** to make up the mind of; cause to decide: *the tempest resolved him to stay at home.* **6.** to find the answer or solution to. **7.** to explain away or dispel: *to resolve a doubt.* **8.** to bring to an end; conclude: *to resolve an argument.* **9.** *Med.* to cause (an inflammation) to subside, esp. without the formation of pus. **10.** *Music.* (*also intr.*) to follow (a dissonant note or chord) by one producing a consonance. **11.** *Physics.* to distinguish between (separate parts) of (an image) as in a microscope, telescope, or other optical instrument. ~*n.* **12.** something determined or decided; resolution: *he had made a resolve to work all day.* **13.** firmness of purpose; determination: *nothing can break his resolve.* [C14: < L *resolvere* to unfasten, reveal, < RE- + *solvere* to loosen] —**re'solvable** *adj.* —**reˌsolva'bility** *n.* —**re'solver** *n.*

resolved (rɪ'zɒlvd) *adj.* fixed in purpose or intention; determined. —**resolvedly** (rɪ'zɒlvɪdlɪ) *adv.* —**re'solvedness** *n.*

resolvent (rɪ'zɒlvənt) *adj.* **1.** serving to dissolve

re'site *vb.*

or separate something into its elements; resolving. ~*n.* 2. a drug or agent able to reduce swelling or inflammation.

resolving power *n.* 1. Also called: **resolution.** *Physics.* the ability of a microscope or telescope to produce separate images of closely placed objects. 2. *Photog.* the ability of an emulsion to show up fine detail in an image.

resonance (ˈrɛzənəns) *n.* 1. the condition or quality of being resonant. 2. sound produced by a body vibrating in sympathy with a neighbouring source of sound. 3. the condition of a body or system when it is subjected to a periodic disturbance of the same frequency as the natural frequency of the body or system. 4. amplification of speech sounds by sympathetic vibration in the bone structure of the head and chest, resounding in the cavities of the nose, mouth, and pharynx. 5. *Electronics.* the condition of an electrical circuit when the frequency is such that the capacitive and inductive reactances are equal in magnitude. 6. *Med.* the sound heard when tapping a hollow bodily structure, esp. the chest or abdomen. 7. *Chem.* the phenomenon in which the electronic structure of a molecule can be represented by two or more hypothetical structures involving single, double, and triple chemical bonds. 8. *Physics.* the condition of a system in which there is a sharp maximum probability for the absorption of electromagnetic radiation or capture of particles. [C16: < L *resonāre* to RESOUND]

resonant (ˈrɛzənənt) *adj.* 1. resounding or re-echoing. 2. producing resonance: *resonant walls.* 3. full of, or intensified by, resonance: *a resonant voice.* —ˈ**resonantly** *adv.*

resonate (ˈrɛzəˌneɪt) *vb.* 1. to resound or cause to resound; reverberate. 2. *Chem., electronics.* to exhibit or cause to exhibit resonance. [C19: < L *resonāre*] —ˌ**resoˈnation** *n.*

resonator (ˈrɛzəˌneɪtə) *n.* any body or system that displays resonance, esp. a tuned electrical circuit or a conducting cavity in which microwaves are generated by a resonant current.

resorb (rɪˈsɔːb) *vb.* (*tr.*) to absorb again. [C17: < L *resorbēre,* < RE- + *sorbēre* to suck in] —**reˈsorbent** *adj.* —**reˈsorption** *n.* —**reˈsorptive** *adj.*

resorcinol (rɪˈzɔːsɪˌnɒl) *n.* a colourless crystalline phenol, used in making dyes, drugs, resins, and adhesives. Formula: $C_6H_4(OH)_2$. [C19: NL, < RESIN + *orcinol,* a crystalline solid] —**reˈsorcinal** *adj.*

resort (rɪˈzɔːt) *vb.* (*intr.*) 1. (usually foll. by *to*) to have recourse (to) for help, use, etc.: *to resort to violence.* 2. to go, esp. often or habitually: *to resort to the beach.* ~*n.* 3. a place to which many people go for recreation, etc.: *a holiday resort.* 4. the use of something as a means, help, or recourse. 5. **last resort.** the last possible course of action open to one. [C14: < OF *resortir,* < RE- + *sortir* to emerge] —**reˈsorter** *n.*

re-sort (riːˈsɔːt) *vb.* (*tr.*) to sort again.

resound (rɪˈzaʊnd) *vb.* (*intr.*) 1. to ring or echo with sound; reverberate. 2. to make a prolonged echoing noise: *the trumpet resounded.* 3. (of sounds) to echo or ring. 4. to be widely famous: *his fame resounded throughout India.* [C14: < OF *resoner,* < L *resonāre* to sound again]

re-sound (riːˈsaʊnd) *vb.* to sound or cause to sound again.

resounding (rɪˈzaʊndɪŋ) *adj.* 1. clear and emphatic: *a resounding vote of confidence.* 2. resonant; reverberating. —**reˈsoundingly** *adv.*

resource (rɪˈzɔːs, -ˈsɔːs) *n.* 1. capability, ingenuity, and initiative; quick-wittedness: *a man of resource.* 2. (*often pl.*) a source of economic wealth, esp. of a country or business enterprise. 3. a supply or source of aid or support; something resorted to in time of need. 4. a means of doing something; expedient. [C17: < OF *ressourse* relief, < *resourdre,* < L *resurgere,* < RE- + *surgere* to rise] —**reˈsourceless** *adj.*

resourceful (rɪˈzɔːsfʊl, -ˈsɔːs-) *adj.* ingenious, capable, and full of initiative. —**reˈsourcefully** *adv.* —**reˈsourcefulness** *n.*

respect (rɪˈspɛkt) *n.* 1. an attitude of deference, admiration, or esteem; regard. 2. the state of being honoured or esteemed. 3. a detail, point, or characteristic: *they differ in some respects.* 4. reference or relation (esp. in **in respect of, with respect to**). 5. polite or kind regard; consideration: *respect for people's feelings.* 6. (*often pl.*) an expression of esteem or regard (esp. in **pay one's respects**). ~*vb.* (*tr.*) 7. to have an attitude of esteem towards: *to respect one's elders.* 8. to pay proper attention to; not violate: *to respect Swiss neutrality.* 9. *Arch.* to concern or refer to. [C14: < L *rēspicere* to look back, pay attention to, < RE- + *specere* to look] —**reˈspecter** *n.*

respectable (rɪˈspɛktəbᵊl) *adj.* 1. having or deserving the respect of other people; estimable; worthy. 2. having good social standing or reputation. 3. having socially or conventionally acceptable morals, etc.: *a respectable woman.* 4. relatively or fairly good; considerable: *a respectable salary.* 5. fit to be seen by other people; presentable. —**reˌspectaˈbility** *n.* —**reˈspectably** *adv.*

respectful (rɪˈspɛktfʊl) *adj.* full of, showing, or giving respect. —**reˈspectfully** *adv.* —**reˈspectfulness** *n.*

respecting (rɪˈspɛktɪŋ) *prep.* concerning; regarding.

respective (rɪˈspɛktɪv) *adj.* belonging or relating separately to each of several people or things; several: *we took our respective ways home.* —**reˈspectiveness** *n.*

respectively (rɪˈspɛktɪvlɪ) *adv.* (in listing a number of items or attributes that refer to another list) separately in the order given: *he gave Janet and John a cake and a chocolate respectively.*

respirable (ˈrɛspɪrəbᵊl) *adj.* 1. able to be breathed. 2. suitable or fit for breathing. —ˌ**respiraˈbility** *n.*

respiration (ˌrɛspɪˈreɪʃən) *n.* 1. the process in living organisms of taking in oxygen from the surroundings and giving out carbon dioxide. 2. the chemical breakdown of complex organic substances that takes place in the cells and tissues of animals and plants, during which energy is released and carbon dioxide produced. —**respiratory** (ˈrɛspɪrətərɪ, -trɪ) *or* ˌ**respiˈrational** *adj.*

respirator (ˈrɛspɪˌreɪtə) *n.* 1. an apparatus for providing long-term artificial respiration. 2. a device worn over the mouth and nose to prevent inhalation of noxious fumes or to warm cold air before it is breathed.

respiratory quotient *n. Biol.* the ratio of the volume of carbon dioxide expired to the volume of oxygen consumed by an organism, tissue, or cell in a given time.

respire (rɪˈspaɪə) *vb.* 1. to inhale and exhale (air); breathe. 2. (*intr.*) to undergo the process of respiration. [C14: < L *rēspīrāre* to exhale, < RE- + *spīrāre* to breathe]

respite (ˈrɛspɪt, -paɪt) *n.* 1. a pause from exertion; interval of rest. 2. a temporary delay. 3. a temporary stay of execution; reprieve. ~*vb.* 4. (*tr.*) to grant a respite to; reprieve. [C13: < OF *respit,* < L *respectus* a looking back; see RESPECT]

resplendent (rɪˈsplɛndənt) *adj.* having a brilliant or splendid appearance. [C15: < *rēsplendēre,* < RE- + *splendēre* to shine] —**reˈsplendence** *or* **reˈsplendency** *n.* —**reˈsplendently** *adv.*

respond (rɪˈspɒnd) *vb.* 1. to state or utter (something) in reply. 2. (*intr.*) to act in reply; react: *to respond by issuing an invitation.* 3. (*intr.;* foll. by *to*) to react favourably: *this patient will respond to treatment.* 4. an archaic word for **correspond.** ~*n.* 5. *Archit.* a pilaster or an engaged column that supports an arch or a lintel. 6. *Christianity.* a choral anthem chanted in response to a lesson read. [C14: < OF *respondre,* < L *rēspondēre* to return like for like, < RE- + *spondēre* to pledge] —**reˈspondence** *or* **reˈspondency** *n.* —**reˈsponder** *n.*

respondent (rɪˈspɒndənt) *n.* 1. *Law.* a person

against whom a petition is brought. ~*adj.* **2.** a less common word for **responsive.**

response (rɪˈspɒns) *n.* **1.** the act of responding; reply or reaction. **2.** *Bridge.* a bid replying to a partner's bid or double. **3.** (*usually pl.*) *Christianity.* a short sentence or phrase recited or sung in reply to the officiant at a church service. **4.** *Electronics.* the ratio of the output to the input level of an electrical device. **5.** a glandular, muscular, or electrical reaction that arises from stimulation of the nervous system. [C14: < L *rēsponsum* answer, < *rēspondēre* to RESPOND] —**reˈsponseless** *adj.*

responser *or* **responsor** (rɪˈspɒnsə) *n.* a radio or radar receiver used to receive and display signals from a transponder.

responsibility (rɪˌspɒnsɪˈbɪlɪtɪ) *n., pl.* **-ties. 1.** the state or position of being responsible. **2.** a person or thing for which one is responsible.

responsible (rɪˈspɒnsɪbᵊl) *adj.* **1.** (*postpositive; usually foll. by for*) having control or authority (over). **2.** (*postpositive; foll. by to*) being accountable for one's actions and decisions (to): *responsible to one's commanding officer.* **3.** (of a position, duty, etc.) involving decision and accountability. **4.** (often foll. by *for*) being the agent or cause (of some action): *responsible for a mistake.* **5.** able to take rational decisions without supervision; accountable for one's own actions. **6.** able to meet financial obligations; of sound credit. [C16: < L *rēsponsus,* < *rēspondēre* to RESPOND] —**reˈsponsibleness** *n.* —**reˈsponsibly** *adv.*

responsive (rɪˈspɒnsɪv) *adj.* **1.** reacting or replying quickly or favourably, as to a suggestion, initiative, etc. **2.** (of an organism) reacting to a stimulus. —**reˈsponsively** *adv.* —**reˈsponsiveness** *n.*

responsory (rɪˈspɒnsərɪ) *n., pl.* **-ries.** an anthem or chant recited or sung after a lesson in a church service. [C15: < LL *rēsponsōrium,* < L *rēspondēre* to answer]

rest[1] (rɛst) *n.* **1. a.** relaxation from exertion or labour. **b.** (*as modifier*)*: a rest period.* **2.** repose; sleep. **3.** any relief or refreshment, as from worry. **4.** calm; tranquillity. **5.** death regarded as repose: *eternal rest.* **6.** cessation from motion. **7. at rest. a.** not moving. **b.** calm. **c.** dead. **d.** asleep. **8.** a pause or interval. **9.** a mark in a musical score indicating a pause of specific duration. **10.** *Prosody.* a pause at the end of a line; caesura. **11.** a shelter or lodging: *a seaman's rest.* **12.** a thing or place on which to put something for support or to steady it. **13.** *Billiards, snooker.* any of various special poles sometimes used as supports for the cue. **14. come to rest.** to slow down and stop. **15. lay to rest.** to bury (a dead person). **16. set (someone's mind) at rest.** to reassure (someone) or settle (someone's mind). ~*vb.* **17.** to take or give rest, as by sleeping, lying down, etc. **18.** to place or position (oneself, etc.) for rest or relaxation. **19.** (*tr.*) to place or position for support or steadying: *to rest one's elbows on the table.* **20.** (*intr.*) to be at ease; be calm. **21.** to cease or cause to cease from motion or exertion. **22.** (*intr.*) to remain without further attention or action: *let the matter rest.* **23.** to direct (one's eyes) or (of one's eyes) to be directed: *her eyes rested on the child.* **24.** to depend or cause to depend; base; rely: *the whole argument rests on one crucial fact.* **25.** (*intr.;* foll. by *with, on, upon,* etc.) to be a responsibility (of): *it rests with us to apportion blame.* **26.** *Law.* to finish the introduction of evidence in (a case). **27.** to put pastry in a cool place to allow the gluten to contract. **28. rest on one's oars.** to stop doing anything for a time. [OE *ræst, reste,* of Gmc origin] —**ˈrester** *n.*

rest[2] (rɛst) *n.* (usually preceded by *the*) **1.** something left or remaining; remainder. **2.** the others: *the rest of the world.* ~*vb.* **3.** (*copula*) to continue to be (as specified); remain: *rest assured.* [C15: < OF *rester* to remain, < L *rēstāre,* < RE- + *stāre* to stand]

rest area *n. Austral. & N.Z.* a motorists' stopping place, usually off a highway, equipped with tables, seats, etc.

restaurant (ˈrɛstəˌrɒŋ, ˈrɛstrɒŋ) *n.* a commercial establishment where meals are prepared and served to customers. [C19: < F, < *restaurer* to RESTORE]

restaurant car *n. Brit.* a railway coach in which meals are served. Also called: **dining car.**

restaurateur (ˌrɛstərəˈtɜː) *n.* a person who owns or runs a restaurant. [C18: via F < LL *restaurātor,* < L *restaurāre* to RESTORE]

rest-cure *n.* **1.** a rest taken as part of a course of medical treatment, so as to relieve stress, anxiety, etc. **2.** an easy time or assignment: usually used with a negative: *it's no rest-cure, I assure you.*

restful (ˈrɛstfʊl) *adj.* **1.** giving or conducive to rest. **2.** being at rest; tranquil; calm. —**ˈrestfully** *adv.* —**ˈrestfulness** *n.*

restharrow (ˈrɛstˌhærəʊ) *n.* any of a genus of Eurasian papilionaceous plants with tough woody stems and roots. [C16: < *rest,* var. of ARREST (to hinder, stop) + HARROW]

resting (ˈrɛstɪŋ) *adj.* **1.** not moving or working; at rest. **2.** *Euphemistic.* (of an actor) out of work. **3.** (esp. of plant spores) undergoing a period of dormancy before germination.

restitution (ˌrɛstɪˈtjuːʃən) *n.* **1.** the act of giving back something that has been lost or stolen. **2.** *Law.* compensating for loss or injury by reverting as far as possible to the original position. **3.** the return of an object or system to its original state, esp. after elastic deformation. [C13: < L *rēstitūtiō,* < *rēstituere* to rebuild, < RE- + *statuere* to set up] —**ˈrestiˌtutive** *or* **ˌrestiˈtutory** *adj.*

restive (ˈrɛstɪv) *adj.* **1.** restless, nervous, or uneasy. **2.** impatient of control or authority. [C16: < OF *restif* balky, < *rester* to remain] —**ˈrestively** *adv.* —**ˈrestiveness** *n.*

restless (ˈrɛstlɪs) *adj.* **1.** unable to stay still or quiet. **2.** ceaselessly active or moving: *the restless wind.* **3.** worried; anxious; uneasy. **4.** not restful; without repose: *a restless night.* —**ˈrestlessly** *adv.* —**ˈrestlessness** *n.*

rest mass *n.* the mass of an object that is at rest relative to an observer. It is the mass used in Newtonian mechanics.

restoration (ˌrɛstəˈreɪʃən) *n.* **1.** the act of restoring to a former or original condition, place, etc. **2.** the giving back of something lost, stolen, etc. **3.** something restored, replaced, or reconstructed. **4.** a model or representation of an extinct animal, etc. **5.** (*usually cap.*) *Brit. history.* the re-establishment of the monarchy in 1660 or the reign of Charles II (1660–85).

restorative (rɪˈstɒrətɪv) *adj.* **1.** tending to revive or renew health, spirits, etc. ~*n.* **2.** anything that restores or revives, esp. a drug.

restore (rɪˈstɔː) *vb.* (*tr.*) **1.** to return (something) to its original or former condition. **2.** to bring back to health, good spirits, etc. **3.** to return (something lost, stolen, etc.) to its owner. **4.** to reintroduce or re-enforce: *to restore discipline.* **5.** to reconstruct (an extinct animal, etc.). [C13: < OF, < L *rēstaurāre* to rebuild, < RE- + *-staurāre,* as in *instaurāre* to renew] —**reˈstorable** *adj.* —**reˈstorer** *n.*

restrain (rɪˈstreɪn) *vb.* (*tr.*) **1.** to hold (someone) back from some action, esp. by force. **2.** to deprive (someone) of liberty, as by imprisonment. **3.** to limit or restrict. [C14 *restreyne,* < OF *restreindre,* < L *rēstringere,* < RE- + *stringere* to draw, bind] —**reˈstrainable** *adj.* —**restrainedly** (rɪˈstreɪnɪdlɪ) *adv.* —**reˈstrainer** *n.*

restraint (rɪˈstreɪnt) *n.* **1.** the ability to control or moderate one's impulses, passions, etc. **2.** the act

reˈspray *vb.*
ˈreˌspray *n.*
reˈstart *vb., n.*
reˈstate *vb.*
reˈstock *vb.*

of restraining or the state of being restrained. **3.** something that restrains; restriction. [C15: < OF *restreinte,* < *restreindre* to RESTRAIN]

restraint of trade *n.* action interfering with the freedom to compete in business.

restrict (rɪˈstrɪkt) *vb.* (often foll. by *to*) to confine or keep within certain, often specified, limits or selected bounds. [C16: < L *rēstrictus* bound up, < *rēstringere;* see RESTRAIN]

restricted (rɪˈstrɪktɪd) *adj.* **1.** limited or confined. **2.** not accessible to the general public or (*esp. U.S.*) out of bounds to military personnel. **3.** *Brit.* denoting a zone in which a speed limit or waiting restrictions for vehicles apply. **—reˈstrictedly** *adv.* **—reˈstrictedness** *n.*

restriction (rɪˈstrɪkʃən) *n.* **1.** something that restricts; a restrictive measure, law, etc. **2.** the act of restricting or the state of being restricted. **—reˈstrictionist** *n., adj.*

restrictive (rɪˈstrɪktɪv) *adj.* **1.** restricting or tending to restrict. **2.** *Grammar.* denoting a relative clause or phrase that restricts the number of possible referents of its antecedent. The relative clause in *Americans who live in New York* is restrictive; the relative clause in *Americans, who are generally extrovert,* is nonrestrictive. **—reˈstrictively** *adv.* **—reˈstrictiveness** *n.*

restrictive practice *n. Brit.* **1.** a trading agreement against the public interest. **2.** a practice of a union or other group tending to limit the freedom of other workers or employers.

rest room *n. U.S. & Canad.* a room in a public building with toilets, washbasins, and, sometimes, couches.

result (rɪˈzʌlt) *n.* **1.** something that ensues from an action, policy, etc.; outcome; consequence. **2.** a number, quantity, or value obtained by solving a mathematical problem. **3.** *U.S.* a decision of a legislative body. **4.** (*often pl.*) the final score or outcome of a sporting contest. **5.** *Sport.* a win. ~*vb.* (*intr.*) **6.** (often foll. by *from*) to be the outcome or consequence (of). **7.** (foll. by *in*) to issue or terminate (in a specified way, etc.); end: *to result in tragedy.* [C15: < L *resultāre* to rebound, spring from, < RE- + *saltāre* to leap]

resultant (rɪˈzʌltənt) *adj.* **1.** that results; resulting. ~*n.* **2.** *Maths, physics.* a single vector that is the vector sum of two or more other vectors.

resume (rɪˈzjuːm) *vb.* **1.** to begin again or go on with (something interrupted). **2.** (*tr.*) to occupy again, take back, or recover: *to resume one's seat; resume the presidency.* **3.** *Arch.* to summarize; make a résumé of. [C15: < L *resūmere,* < RE- + *sūmere* to take up] **—reˈsumable** *adj.* **—reˈsumer** *n.*

résumé (ˈrɛzjʊˌmeɪ) *n.* **1.** a short descriptive summary, as of events, etc. **2.** *U.S.* another name for **curriculum vitae.** [C19: < F, < *résumer* to RESUME]

resumption (rɪˈzʌmpʃən) *n.* the act of resuming or beginning again. [C15: via OF < LL *resumptiō,* < L *resūmere* to RESUME] **—reˈsumptive** *adj.* **—reˈsumptively** *adv.*

resupinate (rɪˈsjuːpɪnɪt) *adj. Bot.* (of plant parts) reversed or inverted in position, so as to appear to be upside down. [C18: < L *resupīnātus* bent back, < *resupīnāre,* < RE- + *supīnāre* to place on the back] **—reˌsupiˈnation** *n.*

resurge (rɪˈsɜːdʒ) *vb.* (*intr.*) *Rare.* to rise again as if from the dead. [C16: < L *resurgere* to rise again, reappear, < RE- + *surgere* to lift, arise]

resurgent (rɪˈsɜːdʒənt) *adj.* rising again, as to new life, vigour, etc.: *resurgent nationalism.* **—reˈsurgence** *n.*

resurrect (ˌrɛzəˈrɛkt) *vb.* **1.** to rise or raise from the dead; bring or be brought back to life. **2.** (*tr.*) to bring back into use or activity; revive. **3.** (*tr.*) *Facetious.* (formerly) to exhume and steal (a body) from its grave.

resurrection (ˌrɛzəˈrɛkʃən) *n.* **1.** a supposed act or instance of a dead person coming back to life. **2.** belief in the possibility of this as part of a religious or mystical system. **3.** the condition of those who have risen from the dead: *we shall all live in the resurrection.* **4.** (*usually cap.*) *Christian theol.* the rising again of Christ from the tomb three days after his death. **5.** (*usually cap.*) the rising again from the dead of all men at the Last Judgment. [C13: via OF < LL *resurrectiō,* < L *resurgere* to rise again] **—ˌresurˈrectional** *or* **ˌresurˈrectionary** *adj.*

resurrectionism (ˌrɛzəˈrɛkʃəˌnɪzəm) *n.* belief that men will rise again from the dead, esp. according to Christian doctrine.

resurrectionist (ˌrɛzəˈrɛkʃənɪst) *n.* **1.** *Facetious.* (formerly) a body snatcher. **2.** a person who believes in the Resurrection.

resurrection plant *n.* any of several unrelated desert plants that form a tight ball when dry and unfold and bloom when moistened.

resuscitate (rɪˈsʌsɪˌteɪt) *vb.* (*tr.*) to restore to consciousness; revive. [C16: < L *resuscitāre,* < RE- + *suscitāre* to raise, < *sub-* up from below + *citāre* to rouse, < *citus* quick] **—reˌsusciˈtation** *n.* **—reˈsuscitative** *adj.* **—reˈsusciˌtator** *n.*

ret (rɛt) *vb.* **retting, retted.** (*tr.*) to moisten or soak (flax, hemp, etc.) in order to separate the fibres from the woody tissue by beating. [C15: of Gmc origin]

ret. *abbrev. for:* **1.** retain. **2.** retired. **3.** return(ed).

retable (rɪˈteɪbᵊl) *n.* an ornamental screenlike structure above and behind an altar. [C19: < F, < Sp. *retablo,* < L *retrō* behind + *tabula* board]

retail (ˈriːteɪl) *n.* **1.** the sale of goods individually or in small quantities to consumers. Cf. **wholesale.** ~*adj.* **2.** of, relating to, or engaged in such selling: *retail prices.* ~*adv.* **3.** in small amounts or at a retail price. ~*vb.* **4.** to sell or be sold in small quantities to consumers. **5.** (rɪˈteɪl). (*tr.*) to relate (gossip, scandal, etc.) in detail. [C14: < OF *retaillier,* < RE- + *taillier* to cut; see TAILOR] **—ˈretailer** *n.*

retail price index *n.* a measure of the changes in the average level of retail prices of selected goods, usually on a monthly basis. Abbrev.: **RPI.**

retain (rɪˈteɪn) *vb.* (*tr.*) **1.** to keep in one's possession. **2.** to be able to hold or contain: *soil that retains water.* **3.** (of a person) to be able to remember (information, etc.) without difficulty. **4.** to hold in position. **5.** to keep for one's future use, as by paying a retainer or nominal charge. **6.** *Law.* to engage the services of (a barrister) by payment of a preliminary fee. [C14: < OF *retenir,* < L *retinēre* to hold back, < RE- + *tenēre* to hold] **—reˈtainable** *adj.* **—reˈtainment** *n.*

retained object *n. Grammar.* a direct or indirect object of a passive verb. The phrase *the drawings* in *she was given the drawings* is a retained object.

retainer (rɪˈteɪnə) *n.* **1.** *History.* a supporter or dependant of a person of rank. **2.** a servant, esp. one who has been with a family for a long time. **3.** a clip, frame, or similar device that prevents a part of a machine, etc., from moving. **4.** a fee paid in advance to secure first option on the services of a barrister, jockey, etc. **5.** a reduced rent paid for a flat, etc., to reserve it for future use.

retaining wall *n.* a wall constructed to hold back earth, loose rock, etc. Also called: **revetment.**

retake *vb.* (riːˈteɪk), **-taking, -took, -taken.** (*tr.*) **1.** to take back or capture again: *to retake a fortress.* **2.** *Films.* to shoot (a scene) again. **3.** to tape (a recording) again. ~*n.* (ˈriːˌteɪk). **4.** *Films.* a rephotographed scene. **5.** a retaped recording. **—reˈtaker** *n.*

retaliate (rɪˈtælɪˌeɪt) *vb.* (*intr.*) **1.** to take retributory action, esp. by returning some injury or wrong in kind. **2.** to cast (accusations) back upon a person. [C17: < LL *retāliāre,* < L RE- + *tālis* of such kind] —**re,tali'ation** *n.* —**re'taliative** *or* **re'taliatory** *adj.*

retard (rɪ'tɑːd) *vb.* (*tr.*) to delay or slow down (the progress or speed) of (something). [C15: < OF *retarder,* < L *retardāre,* < RE- + *tardāre* to make slow, < *tardus* sluggish]

retardant (rɪ'tɑːdᵊnt) *n.* **1.** a substance that reduces the rate of a chemical reaction. ~*adj.* **2.** having a slowing effect.

retardation (ˌriːtɑː'deɪʃən) *or* **retardment** (rɪ'tɑːdmənt) *n.* **1.** the act of retarding or the state of being retarded. **2.** something that retards. —**re'tardative** *or* **re'tardatory** *adj.*

retarded (rɪ'tɑːdɪd) *adj.* underdeveloped, usually mentally and esp. having an IQ of 70 to 85.

retarder (rɪ'tɑːdə) *n.* **1.** a person or thing that retards. **2.** a substance added to slow down the rate of a chemical change, such as one added to cement to delay its setting.

retch (rɛtʃ, riːtʃ) *vb.* **1.** (*intr.*) to undergo an involuntary spasm of ineffectual vomiting. ~*n.* **2.** an involuntary spasm of ineffectual vomiting. [OE *hrǣcan;* rel. to ON *hrǣkja* to spit]

retd *abbrev. for:* **1.** retired. **2.** retained. **3.** returned.

rete ('riːtɪ) *n., pl.* **retia** ('riːʃɪə, -tɪə). *Anat.* any network of nerves or blood vessels; plexus. [C14 (referring to a metal network used with an astrolabe): < L *rēte* net] —**retial** ('riːʃɪəl) *adj.*

retention (rɪ'tɛnʃən) *n.* **1.** the act of retaining or state of being retained. **2.** the capacity to hold or retain liquid, etc. **3.** the capacity to remember. **4.** *Pathol.* the abnormal holding within the body of urine, faeces, etc. [C14: < L *retentiō,* < *retinēre* to RETAIN]

retentive (rɪ'tɛntɪv) *adj.* having the capacity to retain or remember. —**re'tentively** *adv.* —**re'tentiveness** *n.*

retiarius (ˌriːtɪ'ɛərɪəs, ˌriːʃɪ-) *n., pl.* **-arii** (-'ɛərɪˌaɪ). (in ancient Rome) a gladiator armed with a net and trident. [L, < *rēte* net]

reticent ('rɛtɪsənt) *adj.* not communicative; not saying all that one knows; taciturn; reserved. [C19: < L *reticēre* to keep silent, < RE- + *tacēre* to be silent] —'**reticence** *n.* —'**reticently** *adv.*

reticle ('rɛtɪkᵊl) *or* (*less commonly*) **reticule** *n.* a network of fine lines, wires, etc., placed in the focal plane of an optical instrument. [C17: < L *rēticulum* a little net, < *rēte* net]

reticulate *adj.* (rɪ'tɪkjʊlɪt), *also* **reticular. 1.** in the form of a network or having a network of parts: *a reticulate leaf.* ~*vb.* (rɪ'tɪkjʊˌleɪt). **2.** to form or be formed into a net. [C17: < LL *rēticulātus* made like a net] —**re'ticulately** *adv.* —**re,ticu'lation** *n.*

reticule ('rɛtɪˌkjuːl) *n.* **1.** (formerly) a woman's small bag or purse, usually with a drawstring and made of net, beading, brocade, etc. **2.** a less common variant of **reticle.** [C18: < F *réticule,* < L *rēticulum* RETICLE]

reticulum (rɪ'tɪkjʊləm) *n., pl.* **-la** (-lə). **1.** any fine network, esp. one in the body composed of cells, fibres, etc. **2.** the second compartment of the stomach of ruminants. [C17: < L: little net, < *rēte* net]

retiform ('riːtɪˌfɔːm, 'rɛt-) *adj. Rare.* netlike; reticulate. [C17: < L *rēte* net + *forma* shape]

retina ('rɛtɪnə) *n., pl.* **-nas** *or* **-nae** (-ˌniː). the light-sensitive membrane forming the inner lining of the posterior wall of the eyeball. [C14: < Med. L, ? < L *rēte* net] —'**retinal** *adj.*

retinene ('rɛtɪˌniːn) *n.* a yellow pigment, the aldehyde of vitamin A, that is involved in the formation of rhodopsin. [C20: < RETINA + -ENE]

retinitis (ˌrɛtɪ'naɪtɪs) *n.* inflammation of the retina. [C20: < NL, < RETINA + -ITIS]

retinoscopy (ˌrɛtɪ'nɒskəpɪ) *n. Ophthalmol.* a procedure for detecting errors of refraction in the eye by means of an instrument (**retinoscope**) that reflects a beam of light from a mirror into the eye. —**retinoscopic** (ˌrɛtɪnə'skɒpɪk) *adj.* —ˌ**retino'scopically** *adv.* —ˌ**reti'noscopist** *n.*

retinue ('rɛtɪˌnjuː) *n.* a body of aides and retainers attending an important person. [C14: < OF *retenue,* < *retenir* to RETAIN]

retiral (rɪ'taɪərᵊl) *n. esp. Scot.* the act of retiring; retirement.

retire (rɪ'taɪə) *vb.* (*mainly intr.*) **1.** (*also tr.*) to give up or to cause (a person) to give up his work, esp. on reaching pensionable age. **2.** to go away, as into seclusion, for recuperation, etc. **3.** to go to bed. **4.** to recede or disappear: *the sun retired behind the clouds.* **5.** to withdraw from a sporting contest, esp. because of injury. **6.** (*also tr.*) to pull back (troops, etc.) from battle or (of troops, etc.) to fall back. **7.** (*tr.*) to remove (money, bonds, shares, etc.) from circulation. [C16: < F *retirer,* < OF RE- + *tirer* to pull, draw] —**re'tired** *adj.* —**re'tirement** *n.* —**re'tirer** *n.*

retirement pension *n. Brit.* a weekly payment made by the government to a retired man over 65 or a woman over 60.

retiring (rɪ'taɪərɪŋ) *adj.* shunning contact with others; shy; reserved. —**re'tiringly** *adv.*

retool (riː'tuːl) *vb.* **1.** to replace, re-equip, or rearrange the tools in (a factory, etc.). **2.** (*tr.*) *Chiefly U.S. & Canad.* to revise or reorganize.

retort[1] (rɪ'tɔːt) *vb.* **1.** (when *tr., takes a clause as object*) to utter (something) quickly, wittily, or angrily, in response. **2.** to use (an argument) against its originator. ~*n.* **3.** a sharp, angry, or witty reply. **4.** an argument used against its originator. [C16: < L *retorquēre,* < RE- + *torquēre* to twist, wrench] —**re'torter** *n.*

retort[2] (rɪ'tɔːt) *n.* **1.** a glass vessel with a long tapering neck that is bent down, used for distillation. **2.** a vessel used for heating ores in the production of metals or heating coal to produce gas. ~*vb.* **3.** (*tr.*) to heat in a retort. [C17: < F *retorte,* < Med. L *retorta,* < L *retorquēre* to twist back; see RETORT[1]]

retouch (riː'tʌtʃ) *vb.* (*tr.*) **1.** to restore, correct, or improve (a painting, make-up, etc.) with new touches. **2.** *Photog.* to alter (a negative or print) by painting over blemishes or adding details. ~*n.* **3.** the art or practice of retouching. **4.** a detail that is the result of retouching. **5.** a photograph, painting, etc., that has been retouched. —**re'toucher** *n.*

retrace (rɪ'treɪs) *vb.* (*tr.*) **1.** to go back over (one's steps, a route, etc.) again. **2.** to go over (a past event) in the mind; recall. **3.** to go over (a story, account, etc.) from the beginning.

re-trace (riː'treɪs) *vb.* (*tr.*) to trace (a map, etc.) again.

retract (rɪ'trækt) *vb.* **1.** (*tr.*) to draw in (a part or appendage): *a snail can retract its horns; to retract the landing gear of an aircraft.* **2.** to withdraw (a statement, opinion, charge, etc.) as invalid or unjustified. **3.** to go back on (a promise or agreement). [C16: < L *retractāre* to withdraw, < *tractāre,* < *trahere* to drag] —**re'tractable** *or* **re'tractible** *adj.* —**re'traction** *n.* —**re'tractive** *adj.*

retractile (rɪ'træktaɪl) *adj.* capable of being drawn in: *the retractile claws of a cat.* —**retractility** (ˌriːtræk'tɪlɪtɪ) *n.*

retractor (rɪ'træktə) *n.* **1.** *Anat.* any of various muscles that retract an organ or part. **2.** *Surgery.* an instrument for holding back an organ or part. **3.** a person or thing that retracts.

retral ('riːtrəl, 'rɛtrəl) *adj. Rare.* at, near, or towards the back. [C19: < L *retrō* backwards] —'**retrally** *adv.*

retread *vb.* (riː'trɛd), **-treading, -treaded. 1.** (*tr.*) another word for **remould** (sense 2). ~*n.* ('riːˌtrɛd). **2.** another word for **remould** (sense 3). **3.** *N.Z. sl.* a pensioner who has resumed

---

re'testi,fy *vb.*
re'think *vb.*
'**re,think** *n.*
re'tie *vb.*
re'title *vb.*
re'train *vb.*
ˌ**retrans'mission** *n.*

employment, esp. in the same profession as formerly.

re-tread (riːˈtrɛd) *vb.* **-treading, -trod, -trodden** *or* **-trod.** (*tr.*) to tread (one's steps, etc.) again.

retreat (rɪˈtriːt) *vb.* (*mainly intr.*) **1.** *Mil.* to withdraw or retire in the face of or from action with an enemy. **2.** to retire or withdraw, as to seclusion or shelter. **3.** (of a person's features) to slope back; recede. **4.** (*tr.*) *Chess.* to move (a piece) back. ~*n.* **5.** the act of retreating or withdrawing. **6.** *Mil.* **a.** a withdrawal or retirement in the face of the enemy. **b.** a bugle call signifying withdrawal or retirement. **7.** retirement or seclusion. **8.** a place to which one may retire for religious contemplation. **9.** a period of seclusion, esp. for religious contemplation. **10.** an institution for the care and treatment of the mentally ill, infirm, elderly, etc. [C14: < OF *retret,* < *retraire* to withdraw, < L *retrahere* to pull back]

retrench (rɪˈtrɛntʃ) *vb.* **1.** to reduce (costs); economize. **2.** (*tr.*) to shorten, delete, or abridge. [C17: < OF *retrenchier,* < RE- + *trenchier* to cut, < L *truncāre* to lop] **—reˈtrenchment** *n.*

retribution (ˌrɛtrɪˈbjuːʃən) *n.* **1.** the act of punishing or taking vengeance for wrongdoing, sin, or injury. **2.** punishment or vengeance. [C14: via OF < Church L *retribūtiō,* < L *retribuere,* < RE- + *tribuere* to pay] **—retributive** (rɪˈtrɪbjʊtɪv) *adj.* **—reˈtributively** *adv.*

retrieval (rɪˈtriːvᵊl) *n.* **1.** the act or process of retrieving. **2.** the possibility of recovery, restoration, or rectification. **3.** a computer operation that recalls data from a file.

retrieve (rɪˈtriːv) *vb.* (*mainly tr.*) **1.** to get or fetch back again; recover. **2.** to bring back to a more satisfactory state; revive. **3.** to rescue or save. **4.** to recover or make newly available (stored information) from a computer system. **5.** (*also intr.*) (of dogs) to find and fetch (shot game, etc.). **6.** *Tennis, etc.* to return successfully (a shot difficult to reach). **7.** to recall; remember. ~*n.* **8.** the act of retrieving. **9.** the chance of being retrieved. [C15: < OF *retrover,* < RE- + *trouver* to find, ? < Vulgar L *tropāre* (unattested) to compose] **—reˈtrievable** *adj.*

retriever (rɪˈtriːvə) *n.* **1.** one of a breed of large dogs that can be trained to retrieve game. **2.** any dog used to retrieve shot game. **3.** a person or thing that retrieves.

retro (ˈrɛtrəʊ) *n., pl.* **-ros. 1.** short for **retrorocket.** ~*adj.* **2.** denoting something associated with or revived from the past: *retro fashion.*

retro- *prefix.* **1.** back or backwards: *retroactive.* **2.** located behind: *retrochoir.* [< L *retrō* behind, backwards]

retroact (ˈrɛtrəʊˌækt) *vb.* (*intr.*) **1.** to act in opposition. **2.** to influence or have reference to past events. **—ˌretroˈaction** *n.*

retroactive (ˌrɛtrəʊˈæktɪv) *adj.* **1.** applying or referring to the past: *retroactive legislation.* **2.** effective from a date or for a period in the past. **—ˌretroˈactively** *adv.* **—ˌretroacˈtivity** *n.*

retrocede (ˌrɛtrəʊˈsiːd) *vb.* **1.** (*tr.*) to give back; return. **2.** (*intr.*) to go back; recede. **—retrocession** (ˌrɛtrəʊˈsɛʃən) *or* **ˌretroˈcedence** *n.* **—ˌretroˈcessive** *or* **ˌretroˈcedent** *adj.*

retrochoir (ˈrɛtrəʊˌkwaɪə) *n.* the space in a large church or cathedral behind the high altar.

retrofire (ˈrɛtrəʊˌfaɪə) *n.* **1.** the act of firing a retrorocket. **2.** the moment at which it is fired.

retrofit (ˈrɛtrəʊˌfɪt) *vb.* **-fitting, -fitted.** (*tr.*) to equip (a car, aircraft, etc.) with new parts, safety devices, etc., after manufacture.

retroflex (ˈrɛtrəʊˌflɛks) *or* **retroflexed** *adj.* **1.** bent or curved backwards. **2.** *Phonetics.* of or involving retroflexion. [C18: < L *retrōflexus,* < *retrōflectere,* < RETRO- + *flectere* to bend]

retroflexion *or* **retroflection** (ˌrɛtrəʊˈflɛkʃən) *n.* **1.** the act or condition of bending or being bent backwards. **2.** the act of turning the tip of the tongue upwards and backwards in the articulation of a vowel or a consonant.

retrograde (ˈrɛtrəʊˌgreɪd) *adj.* **1.** moving or bending backwards. **2.** (esp. of order) reverse or inverse. **3.** tending towards an earlier worse condition; declining or deteriorating. **4.** *Astron.* **a.** occurring or orbiting in a direction opposite to that of the earth's motion around the sun. Cf. **direct** (sense 18). **b.** occurring or orbiting in a direction around a planet opposite to the planet's rotational direction. **c.** appearing to move in a clockwise direction due to the rotational period exceeding the period of revolution around the sun: *Venus has retrograde rotation.* ~*vb.* (*intr.*) **5.** to move in a retrograde direction; retrogress. [C14: < L *retrōgradī,* < *gradi* to walk, go] **—ˌretrograˈdation** *n.* **—ˈretroˌgradely** *adv.*

retrogress (ˌrɛtrəʊˈgrɛs) *vb.* (*intr.*) **1.** to go back to an earlier, esp. worse, condition; degenerate or deteriorate. **2.** to move backwards; recede. [C19: < L *retrōgressus* having moved backwards; see RETROGRADE] **—ˌretroˈgression** *n.* **—ˌretroˈgressive** *adj.* **—ˌretroˈgressively** *adv.*

retrorocket (ˈrɛtrəʊˌrɒkɪt) *n.* a small auxiliary rocket engine on a larger rocket, missile, or spacecraft, that produces thrust in the opposite direction to the direction of flight in order to decelerate. Often shortened to **retro.**

retrorse (rɪˈtrɔːs) *adj.* (esp. of plant parts) pointing backwards. [C19: < L *retrōrsus,* < *retrōversus* turned back, < RETRO- + *vertere* to turn] **—reˈtrorsely** *adv.*

retrospect (ˈrɛtrəʊˌspɛkt) *n.* the act of surveying things past (often in **in retrospect**). [C17: < L *retrōspicere* to look back, < RETRO- + *specere* to look] **—ˌretroˈspection** *n.*

retrospective (ˌrɛtrəʊˈspɛktɪv) *adj.* **1.** looking or directed backwards, esp. in time; characterized by retrospection. **2.** applying to the past; retroactive. ~*n.* **3.** an exhibition of an artist's life's work. **—ˌretroˈspectively** *adv.*

retroussé (rəˈtruːseɪ) *adj.* (of a nose) turned up. [C19: < F *retrousser* to tuck up]

retroversion (ˌrɛtrəʊˈvɜːʃən) *n.* **1.** the act of turning or condition of being turned backwards. **2.** the condition of a part or organ, esp. the uterus, that is turned backwards. **—ˈretroˌverted** *adj.*

Retrovir (ˈrɛtrəʊˌvɪə) *n. Trademark.* the brand name for AZT.

retrovirus (ˈrɛtrəʊˌvaɪrəs) *n.* any of several viruses that are able to reverse the normal flow of genetic information from DNA to RNA by transcribing RNA into DNA: many retroviruses are known to cause cancer in animals.

retsina (rɛtˈsiːnə) *n.* a Greek wine flavoured with resin. [Mod. Gk, < It. *resina* RESIN]

return (rɪˈtɜːn) *vb.* **1.** (*intr.*) to come back to a former place or state. **2.** (*tr.*) to give, take, or carry back; replace or restore. **3.** (*tr.*) to repay or recompense, esp. with something of equivalent value: *return the compliment.* **4.** (*tr.*) to earn or yield (profit or interest) as an income from an investment or venture. **5.** (*intr.*) to come back or revert in thought or speech: *I'll return to that later.* **6.** (*intr.*) to recur or reappear: *the symptoms have returned.* **7.** to answer or reply. **8.** (*tr.*) to vote into office; elect. **9.** (*tr.*) *Law.* (of a jury) to deliver or render (a verdict). **10.** (*tr.*) to submit (a report, etc.) about (someone or something) to someone in authority. **11.** (*tr.*) *Cards.* to lead back (the suit led by one's partner). **12.** (*tr.*) *Ball games.* to hit, throw, or play (a ball) back. **13. return thanks.** (of Christians) to say grace before a meal. ~*n.* **14.** the act or an instance of coming back. **15.** something that is given or sent back, esp. unsatisfactory merchandise or a theatre ticket for resale. **16.** the act or an instance of putting, sending, or carrying back; replacement or restoration. **17.** (*often pl.*) the yield or profit from an investment or venture. **18.** the act or an instance of reciprocation or repayment (esp. in **in return for**). **19.** a

reˈtrial *n.* **reˈtry** *vb.* **reˈturf** *vb.*

recurrence or reappearance. **20.** an official report, esp. of the financial condition of a company. **21. a.** a form (a **tax return**) on which a statement of one's taxable income is made. **b.** the statement itself. **22.** (*often pl.*) a statement of the votes counted at an election. **23.** an answer or reply. **24.** *Brit.* short for **return ticket. 25.** *Archit.* a part of a building that forms an angle with the façade. **26.** *Law.* a report by a bailiff or other officer on the outcome of a formal document such as a writ, summons, etc. **27.** *Cards.* a lead of a card in the suit that one's partner has previously led. **28.** *Ball games.* the act of playing or throwing a ball, etc., back. **29.** (*modifier*) of, relating to, or characterized by a return: *a return visit.* **30. by return (of post).** *Brit.* by the next post back to the sender. **31. many happy returns (of the day).** a conventional birthday greeting. [C14: < OF *retorner;* see RE-, TURN] —**re'turnable** *adj.* —**re'turner** *n.*

returned soldier *n. Austral. & N.Z.* a soldier who has served abroad. Also (Austral. and Canad.): **returned man.**

returning officer *n.* (in Britain, Canada, Australia, etc.) an official in charge of conducting an election in a constituency, etc.

return ticket *n. Brit.* a ticket entitling a passenger to travel to his destination and back.

retuse (rɪ'tjuːs) *adj. Bot.* having a rounded apex and a central depression. [C18: < L *retundere* to make blunt, < RE- + *tundere* to pound]

reunify (riː'juːnɪˌfaɪ) *vb.* **-fying, -fied.** (*tr.*) to bring together again (something, esp. a country previously divided). —ˌ**reunifi'cation** *n.*

reunion (riː'juːnjən) *n.* **1.** the act of coming together again. **2.** the state or condition of having been brought together again. **3.** a gathering of relatives, friends, or former associates.

reunite (ˌriːjuː'naɪt) *vb.* to bring or come together again. —ˌ**reu'nitable** *adj.*

Reuters ('rɔɪtəz) *n.* a private news agency in London that distributes news to member newspapers. It was founded by Baron Paul Julius von Reuter, a 19th-century telegrapher.

rev (rɛv) *Inf.* ~*n.* **1.** revolution per minute. ~*vb.* **revving, revved. 2.** (often foll. by *up*) to increase the speed of revolution of (an engine).

rev. *abbrev. for:* **1.** revenue. **2.** reverse(d). **3.** review. **4.** revise(d). **5.** revision. **6.** revolution. **7.** revolving.

Rev. *abbrev. for:* **1.** *Bible.* Revelation (of Saint John the Divine). **2.** Reverend.

revalue (riː'væljuː) *or U.S.* **revaluate** *vb.* **1.** to adjust the exchange value of (a currency), esp. upwards. Cf. **devalue. 2.** (*tr.*) to make a fresh valuation of. —**re**ˌ**valu'ation** *n.*

revamp (riː'væmp) *vb.* (*tr.*) **1.** to patch up or renovate; repair or restore. ~*n.* **2.** something that has been renovated or revamped. **3.** the act or process of revamping. [C19: < RE- + VAMP[2]]

revanchism (rɪ'væntʃɪzəm) *n.* **1.** a foreign policy aimed at revenge or the regaining of lost territories. **2.** support for such a policy. [C20: < F *revanche* REVENGE] —**re'vanchist** *n., adj.*

rev counter *n. Brit.* an informal name for **tachometer.**

Revd *abbrev. for* Reverend.

reveal (rɪ'viːl) *vb.* (*tr.*) **1.** (*may take a clause as object or an infinitive*) to disclose (a secret); divulge. **2.** to expose to view or show (something concealed). **3.** (of God) to disclose (divine truths). ~*n.* **4.** *Archit.* the vertical side of an opening in a wall, esp. the side of a window or door between the frame and the front of the wall. [C14: < OF *reveler,* < L *revēlāre* to unveil, < RE- + *vēlum* a VEIL] —**re'vealable** *adj.* —**re'vealer** *n.* —**re'vealment** *n.*

revealed religion *n.* religion that is based on the revelation by God to man of ideas that he would not have arrived at by reason alone.

revealing (rɪ'viːlɪŋ) *adj.* **1.** of significance or import: *a very revealing experience.* **2.** showing more of the body than is usual: *a revealing costume.* —**re'vealingly** *adv.*

reveille (rɪ'vælɪ) *n.* **1.** a signal, given by a bugle, drum, etc., to awaken soldiers or sailors in the morning. **2.** the hour at which this takes place. [C17: < F *réveillez!* awake! < RE- + OF *esveillier* to be wakeful, ult. < L *vigilāre* to keep watch]

revel ('rɛvᵊl) *vb.* **-elling, -elled** *or U.S.* **-eling, -eled.** (*intr.*) **1.** (foll. by *in*) to take pleasure or wallow: *to revel in success.* **2.** to take part in noisy festivities; make merry. ~*n.* **3.** (*often pl.*) an occasion of noisy merrymaking. [C14: < OF *reveler* to be merry, noisy, < L *rebellāre* to revolt] —**'reveller** *n.*

revelation (ˌrɛvə'leɪʃən) *n.* **1.** the act or process of disclosing something previously secret or obscure, esp. something true. **2.** a fact disclosed or revealed, esp. in a dramatic or surprising way. **3.** *Christianity.* God's disclosure of his own nature and his purpose for mankind. [C14: < Church L *revēlātiō,* < L *revēlāre* to REVEAL] —ˌ**reve'lational** *adj.*

Revelation (ˌrɛvə'leɪʃən) *n.* (*popularly, often pl.*) the last book of the New Testament, containing visionary descriptions of heaven, and of the end of the world. Also called: the **Apocalypse,** the **Revelation of Saint John the Divine.**

revelationist (ˌrɛvə'leɪʃənɪst) *n.* a person who believes that God has revealed certain truths to man.

revelry ('rɛvᵊlrɪ) *n., pl.* **-ries.** noisy or unrestrained merrymaking.

revenant ('rɛvɪnənt) *n.* something, esp. a ghost, that returns. [C19: < F: ghost, < *revenir,* < L *revenīre,* < RE- + *venīre* to come]

revenge (rɪ'vɛndʒ) *n.* **1.** the act of retaliating for wrongs or injury received; vengeance. **2.** something done as a means of vengeance. **3.** the desire to take vengeance. **4.** a return match, regarded as a loser's opportunity to even the score. ~*vb.* (*tr.*) **5.** to inflict equivalent injury or damage for (injury received). **6.** to take vengeance for (oneself or another); avenge. [C14: < OF *revenger,* < LL *revindicāre,* < RE- + *vindicāre* to VINDICATE] —**re'venger** *n.* —**re'venging** *adj.* —**re'vengingly** *adv.*

revengeful (rɪ'vɛndʒfʊl) *adj.* full of or characterized by desire for vengeance; vindictive. —**re'vengefully** *adv.* —**re'vengefulness** *n.*

revenue ('rɛvɪˌnjuː) *n.* **1.** the income accruing from taxation to a government. **2. a.** a government department responsible for the collection of government revenue. **b.** (*as modifier*): *revenue men.* **3.** the gross income from a business enterprise, investment, etc. **4.** a particular item of income. **5.** a source of income. [C16: < OF, < *revenir* to return, < L *revenīre;* see REVENANT]

revenue cutter *n.* a small lightly armed boat used to enforce customs regulations and catch smugglers.

reverb (rɪ'vɜːb) *n.* an electronic device that creates artificial acoustics.

reverberate (rɪ'vɜːbəˌreɪt) *vb.* **1.** (*intr.*) to resound or re-echo. **2.** to reflect or be reflected many times. **3.** (*intr.*) to rebound or recoil. **4.** (*intr.*) (of the flame or heat in a reverberatory furnace) to be deflected onto the metal or ore on the hearth. **5.** (*tr.*) to heat, melt, or refine (a metal or ore) in a reverberatory furnace. [C16: < L *reverberāre,* < RE- + *verberāre* to beat, < *verber* a lash] —**re'verberantly** *adv.* —**re**ˌ**verber'ation** *n.* —**re'verberative** *adj.* —**re'verbe**ˌ**rator** *n.* —**re'verberatory** *adj.*

reverberation time *n.* a measure of the acoustic properties of a room, equal to the time taken for a sound to fall in intensity by 60 decibels. It is usually measured in seconds.

---

re'type *vb.*
ˌ**reup'holster** *vb.*
re'usable *adj.*
re'use *vb., n.*
ˌ**reutili'zation** *or* **-li'sation** *n.*
re'utiˌ**lize** *or* **-**ˌ**lise** *vb.*
re'varnish *vb.*

reverberatory furnace *n.* a metallurgical furnace having a curved roof that deflects heat onto the charge so that the fuel is not in direct contact with the ore.

revere (rɪˈvɪə) *vb.* (*tr.*) to be in awe of and respect deeply; venerate. [C17: < L *reverērī*, < RE- + *verērī* to fear, be in awe of]

reverence (ˈrɛvərəns) *n.* **1.** a feeling or attitude of profound respect, usually reserved for the sacred or divine. **2.** an outward manifestation of this feeling, esp. a bow or act of obeisance. **3.** the state of being revered or commanding profound respect. ~*vb.* **4.** (*tr.*) to revere or venerate.

Reverence (ˈrɛvərəns) *n.* (preceded by *Your* or *His*) a title sometimes used to address or refer to a Roman Catholic priest.

reverend (ˈrɛvərənd) *adj.* **1.** worthy of reverence. **2.** relating to or designating a clergyman. ~*n.* **3.** *Inf.* a clergyman. [C15: < L *reverendus* fit to be revered]

Reverend (ˈrɛvərənd) *adj.* a title of respect for a clergyman. Abbrev.: **Rev., Revd.**

▷ **Usage.** *Reverend* with a surname alone (*Reverend Smith*), as a term of address (*"Yes, Reverend"*), or in the salutation of a letter (*Dear Rev. Mr Smith*) are all considered to be wrong usage. Preferred are (*the*) *Reverend John Smith* or *Reverend Mr Smith* and *Dear Mr Smith.*

reverent (ˈrɛvərənt, ˈrɛvrənt) *adj.* feeling, expressing, or characterized by reverence. [C14: < L *reverēns* respectful] —ˈ**reverently** *adv.*

reverential (ˌrɛvəˈrɛnʃəl) *adj.* resulting from or showing reverence. —ˌ**reverˈentially** *adv.*

reverie (ˈrɛvərɪ) *n.* **1.** an act or state of absent-minded daydreaming: *to fall into a reverie.* **2.** a piece of instrumental music suggestive of a daydream. **3.** *Arch.* a fanciful or visionary notion; daydream. [C14: < OF *resverie* wildness, < *resver* to behave wildly, <?]

revers (rɪˈvɪə) *n., pl.* **-vers** (-ˈvɪəz). (*usually pl.*) the turned-back lining of part of a garment, esp. of a lapel or cuff. [C19: < F, lit.: REVERSE]

reversal (rɪˈvɜːsᵊl) *n.* **1.** the act or an instance of reversing. **2.** a change for the worse; reverse. **3.** the state of being reversed. **4.** the annulment of a judicial decision, esp. by an appeal court.

reverse (rɪˈvɜːs) *vb.* (*mainly tr.*) **1.** to turn or set in an opposite direction, order, or position. **2.** to change into something different or contrary; alter completely: *reverse one's policy.* **3.** (*also intr.*) to move or cause to move backwards or in an opposite direction: *to reverse a car.* **4.** to run (machinery, etc.) in the opposite direction to normal. **5.** to turn inside out. **6.** *Law.* to revoke or set aside (a judgment, decree, etc.); annul. **7.** **reverse the charge(s).** to make a telephone call at the recipient's expense. ~*n.* **8.** the opposite or contrary of something. **9.** the back or rear side of something. **10.** a change to an opposite position, state, or direction. **11.** a change for the worse; setback or defeat. **12. a.** the mechanism or gears by which machinery, a vehicle, etc., can be made to reverse its direction. **b.** (*as modifier*): *reverse gear.* **13.** the side of a coin bearing a secondary design. **14. a.** printed matter in which normally black or coloured areas, esp. lettering, appear white, and vice versa. **b.** (*as modifier*): *reverse plates.* **15.** **in reverse.** in an opposite or backward direction. **16.** **the reverse of.** emphatically not; not at all: *he was the reverse of polite when I called.* ~*adj.* **17.** opposite or contrary in direction, position, order, nature, etc.; turned backwards. **18.** back to front; inverted. **19.** operating or moving in a manner contrary to that which is usual. **20.** denoting or relating to a mirror image. [C14: < OF, < L *reversus*, < *revertere* to turn back] —**reˈversely** *adv.* —**reˈverser** *n.*

reverse-charge *adj.* (*prenominal*) (of a telephone call) made at the recipient's expense.

reverse transcriptase (trænˈskrɪpteɪz) *n.* an enzyme present in retroviruses that copies RNA into DNA, thus reversing the usual flow of genetic information in which DNA is copied into RNA.

reverse video *n. Computers.* highlighting by reversing the colours of normal characters and background on a visual display unit.

reversible (rɪˈvɜːsɪbᵊl) *adj.* **1.** capable of being reversed: *a reversible decision.* **2.** capable of returning to an original condition. **3.** *Chem., physics.* capable of assuming or producing either of two possible states and changing from one to the other: *a reversible reaction.* **4.** (of a fabric or garment) woven, printed, or finished so that either side may be used as the outer side. ~*n.* **5.** a reversible garment, esp. a coat. —**reˌversiˈbility** *n.* —**reˈversibly** *adv.*

reversing light *n.* a light on the rear of a motor vehicle to provide illumination when the vehicle is being reversed.

reversion (rɪˈvɜːʃən) *n.* **1.** a return to an earlier condition, practice, or belief; act of reverting. **2.** *Biol.* the return of individuals, organs, etc., to a more primitive condition or type. **3.** *Property law.* **a.** an interest in an estate that reverts to the grantor or his heirs at the end of a period, esp. at the end of the life of a grantee. **b.** an estate so reverting. **c.** the right to succeed to such an estate. **4.** the benefit payable on the death of a life-insurance policyholder. —**reˈversionary** *or* **reˈversional** *adj.*

revert (rɪˈvɜːt) *vb.* (*intr.*; foll. by *to*). **1.** to go back to a former practice, condition, belief, etc.: *he reverted to his old wicked ways.* **2.** to take up again or come back to a former topic. **3.** *Biol.* (of individuals, organs, etc.) to return to a more primitive, earlier, or simpler condition or type. **4.** *Property law.* (of an estate or interest in land) to return to its former owner or his heirs. **5.** **revert to type.** to resume characteristics that were thought to have disappeared. [C13: < L *revertere*, < RE- + *vertere* to turn] —**reˈverter** *n.* —**reˈvertible** *adj.*

revet (rɪˈvɛt) *vb.* **-vetting, -vetted.** to face (a wall or embankment) with stones. [C19: < F *revêt*, < OF *revestir* to reclothe; see REVETMENT]

revetment (rɪˈvɛtmənt) *n.* **1.** a facing of stones, sandbags, etc., to protect a wall, embankment, or earthworks. **2.** another name for **retaining wall.** [C18: < F *revêtement*, lit.: a reclothing, < *revêtir*; ult. < L RE- + *vestīre* to clothe]

review (rɪˈvjuː) *vb.* (*mainly tr.*) **1.** to look at or examine again: *to review a situation.* **2.** to look back upon (a period of time, sequence of events, etc.); remember: *he reviewed his achievements with pride.* **3.** to inspect, esp. formally or officially: *the general reviewed his troops.* **4.** *Law.* to re-examine (a decision) judicially. **5.** to write a critical assessment of (a book, film, play, concert, etc.), esp. as a profession. ~*n.* **6.** Also called: **reviewal.** the act or an instance of reviewing. **7.** a general survey or report: *a review of the political situation.* **8.** a critical assessment of a book, film, play, concert, etc., esp. one printed in a newspaper or periodical. **9.** a publication containing such articles. **10.** a second consideration; re-examination. **11.** a retrospective survey. **12.** a formal or official inspection. **13.** a U.S. and Canad. word for **revision** (sense 2). **14.** *Law.* judicial re-examination of a case, esp. by a superior court. **15.** a less common spelling of **revue.** [C16: < F, < *revoir* to see again, < L RE- + *vidēre* to see] —**reˈviewer** *n.*

revile (rɪˈvaɪl) *vb.* to use abusive or scornful language against (someone or something). [C14: < OF *reviler*, < RE- + *vil* VILE] —**reˈvilement** *n.* —**reˈviler** *n.*

revise (rɪˈvaɪz) *vb.* **1.** (*tr.*) to change or amend: *to revise one's opinion.* **2.** *Brit.* to reread (a subject or notes on it) so as to memorize it, esp. for an examination. **3.** (*tr.*) to prepare a new version or edition of (a previously printed work). ~*n.* **4.** the act, process, or result of revising; revision. [C16: < L *revīsere*, < RE- + *vīsere* to inspect, < *vidēre* to see] —**reˈvisal** *n.* —**reˈviser** *n.*

Revised Standard Version *n.* a revision by American scholars of the American Standard Version of the Bible. The New Testament was published in 1946 and the entire Bible in 1953.

Revised Version *n.* a revision of the Authorized

Version of the Bible by two committees of British scholars, the New Testament being published in 1881 and the Old in 1885.

revision (rɪˈvɪʒən) *n.* **1.** the act or process of revising. **2.** *Brit.* the process of rereading a subject or notes on it, esp. for an examination. **3.** a corrected or new version of a book, article, etc. —**reˈvisionary** *adj.*

revisionism (rɪˈvɪʒəˌnɪzəm) *n.* **1.** (*sometimes cap.*) **a.** a moderate, nonrevolutionary version of Marxism developed in Germany around 1900. **b.** (in Marxist-Leninist ideology) any dangerous departure from the true interpretation of Marx's teachings. **2.** the advocacy of revision of some political theory, etc. —**reˈvisionist** *n., adj.*

revisory (rɪˈvaɪzərɪ) *adj.* of, relating to, or having the power of revision.

revitalize *or* **-lise** (riːˈvaɪtᵊˌlaɪz) *vb.* (*tr.*) to restore vitality or animation to.

revival (rɪˈvaɪvᵊl) *n.* **1.** the act or an instance of reviving or the state of being revived. **2.** an instance of returning to life or consciousness; restoration of vigour or vitality. **3.** a renewed use, acceptance of, or interest in (past customs, styles, etc.): *the Gothic revival.* **4.** a new production of a play that has not been recently performed. **5.** a reawakening of faith. **6.** an evangelistic meeting or meetings intended to effect such a reawakening in those present.

revivalism (rɪˈvaɪvəˌlɪzəm) *n.* **1.** a movement that seeks to reawaken faith. **2.** the tendency or desire to revive former customs, styles, etc. —**reˈvivalist** *n.* —**reˌvivalˈistic** *adj.*

revive (rɪˈvaɪv) *vb.* **1.** to bring or be brought back to life, consciousness, or strength: *revived by a drop of whisky.* **2.** to give or assume new vitality; flourish again or cause to flourish again. **3.** to make or become operative or active again: *the youth movement was revived.* **4.** to bring or come back to mind. **5.** (*tr.*) *Theatre.* to mount a new production of (an old play). [C15: < OF *revivre* to live again, < L *revīvere,* < RE- + *vīvere* to live] —**reˈvivable** *adj.* —**reˌvivaˈbility** *n.* —**reˈviver** *n.* —**reˈviving** *adj.*

revivify (rɪˈvɪvɪˌfaɪ) *vb.* **-fying, -fied.** (*tr.*) to give new life or spirit to. —**reˌvivifiˈcation** *n.*

revocable (ˈrɛvəkəbᵊl) *or* **revokable** (rɪˈvəʊkəbᵊl) *adj.* capable of being revoked. —ˌ**revocaˈbility** *or* **reˌvokaˈbility** *n.* —ˈ**revocably** *or* **reˈvokably** *adv.*

revocation (ˌrɛvəˈkeɪʃən) *n.* **1.** the act of revoking or state of being revoked. **2. a.** the cancellation or annulment of a legal instrument. **b.** the withdrawal of an offer, power of attorney, etc. —**revocatory** (ˈrɛvəkətərɪ, -trɪ) *adj.*

revoice (riːˈvɔɪs) *vb.* (*tr.*) **1.** to utter again; echo. **2.** to adjust the design of (an organ pipe or wind instrument) as after disuse or to conform with modern pitch.

revoke (rɪˈvəʊk) *vb.* **1.** (*tr.*) to take back or withdraw; cancel; rescind. **2.** (*intr.*) *Cards.* to break a rule by failing to follow suit when able to do so. ~*n.* **3.** *Cards.* the act of revoking. [C14: < L *revocāre* to call back, withdraw, < RE- + *vocāre* to call] —**reˈvoker** *n.*

revolt (rɪˈvəʊlt) *n.* **1.** a rebellion or uprising against authority. **2. in revolt.** in the process or state of rebelling. ~*vb.* **3.** (*intr.*) to rise up in rebellion against authority. **4.** (*usually passive*) to feel or cause to feel revulsion, disgust, or abhorrence. [C16: < F *révolter,* < OIt. *rivoltare* to overturn, ult. < L *revolvere* to roll back]

revolting (rɪˈvəʊltɪŋ) *adj.* **1.** causing revulsion; nauseating, disgusting, or repulsive. **2.** *Inf.* unpleasant or nasty. —**reˈvoltingly** *adv.*

revolute (ˈrɛvəˌluːt) *adj.* (esp. of the margins of a leaf) rolled backwards and downwards. [C18: < L *revolūtus* rolled back; see REVOLVE]

revolution (ˌrɛvəˈluːʃən) *n.* **1.** the overthrow or repudiation of a regime or political system by the governed. **2.** (in Marxist theory) the inevitable, violent transition from one system of production in a society to the next. **3.** a far-reaching and drastic change, esp. in ideas, methods, etc. **4. a.** movement in or as if in a circle. **b.** one complete turn in such a circle: *33 revolutions per minute.* **5. a.** the orbital motion of one body, such as a planet, around another. **b.** one complete turn in such motion. **6.** a cycle of successive events or changes. [C14: via OF < LL *revolūtiō,* < L *revolvere* to REVOLVE]

revolutionary (ˌrɛvəˈluːʃənərɪ) *n., pl.* **-aries. 1.** a person who advocates or engages in revolution. ~*adj.* **2.** relating to or characteristic of a revolution. **3.** advocating or engaged in revolution. **4.** radically new or different: *a revolutionary method of making plastics.*

Revolutionary (ˌrɛvəˈluːʃənərɪ) *adj.* **1.** *Chiefly U.S.* of or relating to the War of American Independence (1775–83). **2.** of or relating to any of various other Revolutions, esp. the **Russian Revolution** (1917) or the **French Revolution** (1789).

revolutionist (ˌrɛvəˈluːʃənɪst) *n.* **1.** a less common word for a **revolutionary.** ~*adj.* **2.** of or relating to revolution or revolutionaries.

revolutionize *or* **-ise** (ˌrɛvəˈluːʃəˌnaɪz) *vb.* (*tr.*) **1.** to bring about a radical change in: *science has revolutionized civilization.* **2.** to inspire or infect with revolutionary ideas: *they revolutionized the common soldiers.* **3.** to cause a revolution in (a country, etc.). —ˌ**revoˈlutionˌizer** *or* -ˌ**iser** *n.*

revolve (rɪˈvɒlv) *vb.* **1.** to move or cause to move around a centre or axis; rotate. **2.** (*intr.*) to occur periodically or in cycles. **3.** to consider or be considered. **4.** (*intr.;* foll. by *around* or *about*) to be centred or focused (upon): *Juliet's thoughts revolved around Romeo.* ~*n.* **5.** *Theatre.* a circular section of a stage that can be rotated by electric power to provide a scene change. [C14: < L *revolvere,* < RE- + *volvere* to roll, wind] —**reˈvolvable** *adj.*

revolver (rɪˈvɒlvə) *n.* a pistol having a revolving multichambered cylinder that allows several shots to be discharged without reloading.

revolving (rɪˈvɒlvɪŋ) *adj.* denoting or relating to an engine, such as a radial aero engine, in which the cylinders revolve about a fixed shaft.

revolving credit *n.* a letter of credit for a fixed sum, specifying that the beneficiary may make repeated use of the credit provided that the fixed sum is never exceeded.

revolving door *n.* a door that rotates about a vertical axis, esp. one with four leaves at right angles to each other, thereby excluding draughts.

revue (rɪˈvjuː) *n.* a light entertainment consisting of topical sketches, songs, dancing, etc. [C20: < F; see REVIEW]

revulsion (rɪˈvʌlʃən) *n.* **1.** a sudden violent reaction in feeling, esp. one of extreme loathing. **2.** the act or an instance of drawing back or recoiling from something. **3.** the diversion of disease from one part of the body to another by cupping, counterirritants, etc. [C16: < L *revulsiō* a pulling away, < *revellere,* < RE- + *vellere* to pull, tear]

revulsive (rɪˈvʌlsɪv) *adj.* **1.** of or causing revulsion. ~*n.* **2.** *Med.* a counterirritant. —**reˈvulsively** *adv.*

reward (rɪˈwɔːd) *n.* **1.** something given in return for a deed or service rendered. **2.** a sum of money offered, esp. for help in finding a criminal or for the return of lost or stolen property. **3.** profit or return. **4.** something received in return for good or evil; deserts. ~*vb.* **5.** (*tr.*) to give something to (someone), esp. in gratitude for (a service rendered); recompense. [C14: < OF *rewarder,* < RE- + *warder* to care for, guard, of Gmc origin] —**reˈwardless** *adj.*

rewarding (rɪˈwɔːdɪŋ) *adj.* giving personal satisfaction; gratifying.

---

reˈvisit *vb.* **reˈwash** *vb.* **reˈweigh** *vb.*

rewa-rewa (ˈreɪwəˈreɪwə) *n.* a tall tree of New Zealand, yielding reddish timber. [C19: < Maori]

rewind *vb.* (riːˈwaɪnd), **-winding, -wound. 1.** (*tr.*) to wind back, esp. a film or tape onto the original reel. ~*n.* (ˈriːˌwaɪnd, riːˈwaɪnd). **2.** something rewound. **3.** the act of rewinding. —**reˈwinder** *n.*

rewire (riːˈwaɪə) *vb.* (*tr.*) to provide (a house, engine, etc.) with new wiring. —**reˈwirable** *adj.*

reword (riːˈwɜːd) *vb.* (*tr.*) to alter the wording of; express differently.

rework (riːˈwɜːk) *vb.* (*tr.*) **1.** to use again in altered form. **2.** to rewrite or revise. **3.** to reprocess for use again.

rewrite *vb.* (riːˈraɪt), **-writing, -wrote, -written.** (*tr.*) **1.** to write (material) again, esp. changing the words or form. ~*n.* (ˈriːˌraɪt). **2.** something rewritten.

Rex (rɛks) *n.* king: part of the official title of a king, now used chiefly in documents, legal proceedings, on coins, etc. Cf. **Regina.** [L]

Rexine (ˈrɛksiːn) *n. Trademark.* a form of artificial leather.

Reye's syndrome (raɪz, reɪz) *n.* a rare metabolic disease in children that can be fatal, involving damage to the brain, liver, and kidneys. [C20: after R.D.K. *Reye* (1912-78), Austral. paediatrician]

Reynard *or* **Renard** (ˈrɛnəd, ˈrɛnɑːd) *n.* a name for a fox, used in fables, etc.

RF *abbrev. for* radio frequency.

RFC *abbrev. for:* **1.** Royal Flying Corps. **2.** Rugby Football Club.

RGS *abbrev. for* Royal Geographical Society.

rh *or* **RH** *abbrev. for* right hand.

Rh 1. *the chemical symbol for* rhodium. ~ **2.** *abbrev. for* rhesus (esp. in **Rh factor**).

RHA *abbrev. for* Royal Horse Artillery.

rhabdomancy (ˈræbdəˌmænsɪ) *n.* divination for water or mineral ore by means of a rod or wand. [C17: via LL < LGk *rhabdomanteia,* < Gk *rhabdos* rod + *manteia* divination] —ˈ**rhabdoˌmantist** *or* ˈ**rhabdoˌmancer** *n.*

rhachis (ˈreɪkɪs) *n., pl.* **rhachises** *or* **rhachides** (ˈrækɪˌdiːz, ˈreɪ-). a variant spelling of **rachis.**

Rhadamanthine (ˌrædəˈmænθaɪn) *adj.* impartial; judicially strict. [C19: after *Rhadamanthus,* in Gk myth one of the judges of the dead in the underworld]

rhapsodic (ræpˈsɒdɪk) *adj.* **1.** of or like a rhapsody. **2.** lyrical or romantic.

rhapsodize *or* **-ise** (ˈræpsəˌdaɪz) *vb.* **1.** to speak or write (something) with extravagant enthusiasm. **2.** (*intr.*) to recite or write rhapsodies. —ˈ**rhapsodist** *n.*

rhapsody (ˈræpsədɪ) *n., pl.* **-dies. 1.** *Music.* a composition free in structure and highly emotional in character. **2.** an expression of ecstatic enthusiasm. **3.** (in ancient Greece) an epic poem or part of an epic recited by a rhapsodist. **4.** a literary work composed in an intense or exalted style. **5.** rapturous delight or ecstasy. [C16: via L < Gk *rhapsōidia,* < *rhaptein* to sew together + *ōidē* song]

rhatany (ˈrætənɪ) *n., pl.* **-nies. 1.** either of two South American leguminous shrubs that have thick fleshy roots. **2.** the dried roots used as an astringent. ~Also called: **krameria.** [C19: < NL *rhatānia,* ult. < Quechua *ratánya*]

rhea (rɪə) *n.* either of two large fast-running flightless birds inhabiting the open plains of S South America. They are similar to but smaller than the ostrich. [C19: NL; arbitrarily after *Rhea,* in Gk myth., mother of Zeus]

rhebuck *or* **rhebok** (ˈriːbʌk) *n., pl.* **-boks** *or* **-bok.** an antelope of southern Africa, having woolly brownish-grey hair. [C18: Afrik., < Du. *reebok* ROEBUCK]

Rhenish (ˈrɛnɪʃ, ˈriː-) *adj.* **1.** of or relating to the River Rhine or the lands adjacent to it. ~*n.* **2.** another word for **hock** (the wine).

rhenium (ˈriːnɪəm) *n.* a dense silvery-white metallic element that has a high melting point. Symbol: Re; atomic no.: 75; atomic wt.: 186.2. [C19: NL, < *Rhēnus* the Rhine]

rheo- *combining form.* indicating stream, flow, or current: *rheostat.* [< Gk *rheos* stream, anything flowing, < *rhein* to flow]

rheology (rɪˈɒlədʒɪ) *n.* the branch of physics concerned with the flow and change of shape of matter, esp. the viscosity of liquids. —**rheological** (ˌriːəˈlɒdʒɪkᵊl) *adj.* —**rheˈologist** *n.*

rheostat (ˈrɪəˌstæt) *n.* a variable resistance, usually a coil of wire with a terminal at one end and a sliding contact that moves along the coil to tap off the current. —ˌ**rheoˈstatic** *adj.*

rhesus baby (ˈriːsəs) *n.* a baby suffering from haemolytic disease at birth as its red blood cells (which are Rh positive) have been attacked in the womb by antibodies from its Rh negative mother. [C20: see RH FACTOR]

rhesus factor *n.* See **Rh factor.**

rhesus monkey *n.* a macaque monkey of S Asia. [C19: NL, arbitrarily < Gk *Rhesos,* mythical Thracian king]

rhetoric (ˈrɛtərɪk) *n.* **1.** the study of the technique of using language effectively. **2.** the art of using speech to persuade, influence, or please; oratory. **3.** excessive ornamentation and contrivance in spoken or written discourse; bombast. **4.** speech or discourse that pretends to significance but lacks true meaning: *mere rhetoric.* [C14: via L < Gk *rhētorikē* (*tekhnē*) (the art of) rhetoric, < *rhētōr* teacher of rhetoric, orator]

rhetorical (rɪˈtɒrɪkᵊl) *adj.* **1.** concerned with effect or style rather than content or meaning; bombastic. **2.** of or relating to rhetoric or oratory. —**rheˈtorically** *adv.*

rhetorical question *n.* a question to which no answer is required: used esp. for dramatic effect. An example is *Who knows?* (with the implication *Nobody knows*).

rhetorician (ˌrɛtəˈrɪʃən) *n.* **1.** a teacher of rhetoric. **2.** a stylish or eloquent writer or speaker. **3.** a pompous or extravagant speaker.

rheum (ruːm) *n.* a watery discharge from the eyes or nose. [C14: < OF *reume,* ult. < Gk *rheuma* bodily humour, stream, < *rhein* to flow] —ˈ**rheumy** *adj.*

rheumatic (ruːˈmætɪk) *adj.* **1.** of, relating to, or afflicted with rheumatism. ~*n.* **2.** a person afflicted with rheumatism. [C14: ult. < Gk *rheumatikos,* < *rheuma* a flow; see RHEUM] —**rheuˈmatically** *adv.*

rheumatic fever *n.* a disease characterized by inflammation and pain in the joints.

rheumatics (ruːˈmætɪks) *n.* (*functioning as sing.*) *Inf.* rheumatism.

rheumatism (ˈruːməˌtɪzəm) *n.* any painful disorder of joints, muscles, or connective tissue. [C17: < L *rheumatismus* catarrh, < Gk *rheumatismos;* see RHEUM]

rheumatoid (ˈruːməˌtɔɪd) *adj.* (of symptoms) resembling rheumatism.

rheumatoid arthritis *n.* a chronic disease characterized by inflammation and swelling of joints (esp. in the hands, wrists, knees, and feet), muscle weakness, and fatigue.

rheumatology (ˌruːməˈtɒlədʒɪ) *n.* the study of rheumatic diseases. —**rheumatological** (ˌruːmətəˈlɒdʒɪkᵊl) *adj.*

Rh factor *n.* an antigen commonly found in human blood: the terms **Rh positive** and **Rh negative** are used to indicate its presence or absence. It may cause a haemolytic reaction, esp. during pregnancy or following transfusion of blood that does not contain this antigen. Full name: **rhesus factor.** [after the rhesus monkey, in which it was first discovered]

rhinal (ˈraɪnᵊl) *adj.* of or relating to the nose.

rhinestone (ˈraɪnˌstəʊn) *n.* an imitation gem made of paste. [C19: translation of F *caillou du Rhin,* referring to Strasbourg, where such gems were made]

reˈweld *vb.* **reˈwrap** *vb.* **reˈzone** *vb.*

Rhine wine (raɪn) *n.* any wine produced along the Rhine, characteristically a white table wine.

rhinitis (raɪˈnaɪtɪs) *n.* inflammation of the mucous membrane that lines the nose. —**rhinitic** (raɪˈnɪtɪk) *adj.*

rhino[1] (ˈraɪnəʊ) *n., pl.* **-nos** *or* **-no.** short for **rhinoceros.**

rhino[2] (ˈraɪnəʊ) *n. Brit.* a slang word for **money.** [C17: <?]

rhino- *or before a vowel* **rhin-** *combining form.* the nose: *rhinology.* [< Gk *rhis, rhin*]

rhinoceros (raɪˈnɒsərəs, -ˈnɒsrəs) *n., pl.* **-oses** *or* **-os.** any of several mammals constituting a family of SE Asia and Africa and having either one horn on the nose, like the **Indian rhinoceros,** or two horns, like the African **white rhinoceros.** They have a very thick skin and a massive body. [C13: via L < Gk *rhinokerōs,* < *rhis* nose + *keras* horn] —**rhinocerotic** (ˌraɪnəʊsɪˈrɒtɪk) *adj.*

rhinology (raɪˈnɒlədʒɪ) *n.* the branch of medical science concerned with the nose. —**rhinological** (ˌraɪnəˈlɒdʒɪkəl) *adj.* —**rhiˈnologist** *n.*

rhinoplasty (ˈraɪnəʊˌplæstɪ) *n.* plastic surgery of the nose. —ˌ**rhinoˈplastic** *adj.*

rhinoscopy (raɪˈnɒskəpɪ) *n. Med.* examination of the nasal passages, esp. with a special instrument called a **rhinoscope** (ˈraɪnəʊˌskəʊp).

rhizo- *or before a vowel* **rhiz-** *combining form.* root: *rhizocarpous.* [< Gk *rhiza*]

rhizocarpous (ˌraɪzəʊˈkɑːpəs) *adj.* **1.** (of plants) producing subterranean flowers and fruit. **2.** (of plants) having perennial roots but stems and leaves that wither.

rhizoid (ˈraɪzɔɪd) *n.* any of various hairlike structures that function as roots in mosses, ferns, and fungi. —**rhiˈzoidal** *adj.*

rhizome (ˈraɪzəʊm) *n.* a thick horizontal underground stem whose buds develop into new plants. Also called: **rootstock, rootstalk.** [C19: < NL *rhizoma,* < Gk, < *rhiza* a root] —**rhizomatous** (raɪˈzɒmətəs, -ˈzəʊ-) *adj.*

rhizopod (ˈraɪzəʊˌpɒd) *n.* **1.** any of various protozoans characterized by naked protoplasmic processes (pseudopodia). ~*adj.* **2.** of, relating to, or belonging to rhizopods.

rho (rəʊ) *n., pl.* **rhos.** the 17th letter in the Greek alphabet (Ρ, ρ).

rhodamine (ˈrəʊdəˌmiːn, -mɪn) *n.* any one of a group of synthetic red or pink basic dyestuffs used for wool and silk. [C20: < RHODO- + AMINE]

Rhode Island Red (rəʊd) *n.* a breed of domestic fowl, originating in America, characterized by a dark reddish-brown plumage and brown eggs.

Rhodesian man (rəʊˈdiːʃən) *n.* a type of early man, occurring in Africa in late Pleistocene times and resembling Neanderthal man.

Rhodes scholarship (rəʊdz) *n.* one of 72 scholarships founded by Cecil Rhodes (1853-1902), English statesman, awarded annually to Commonwealth and U.S. students to study at Oxford University. —**Rhodes scholar** *n.*

rhodium (ˈrəʊdɪəm) *n.* a hard silvery-white element of the platinum metal group. Used as an alloying agent to harden platinum and palladium. Symbol: Rh; atomic no.: 45; atomic wt.: 102.90. [C19: NL, < Gk *rhodon* rose, from the pink colour of its compounds]

rhodo- *or before a vowel* **rhod-** *combining form.* rose or rose-coloured: *rhododendron; rhodolite.* [< Gk *rhodon* rose]

rhodochrosite (ˌrəʊdəʊˈkrəʊsaɪt) *n.* a pink, grey, or brown mineral that consists of manganese carbonate in hexagonal crystalline form. Formula: $MnCO_3$. [C19: < Gk *rhodokhrōs,* < *rhodon* rose + *khrōs* colour]

rhododendron (ˌrəʊdəˈdɛndrən) *n.* any of various shrubs native to S Asia but widely cultivated in N temperate regions. They are mostly evergreen and have clusters of showy red, purple, pink, or white flowers. [C17: < L: oleander, < Gk, < *rhodon* rose + *dendron* tree]

rhodolite (ˈrɒdəˌlaɪt) *n.* a pale violet or red variety of garnet, used as a gemstone.

rhodonite (ˈrɒdəˌnaɪt) *n.* a brownish translucent mineral consisting of manganese silicate in crystalline form with calcium, iron, or magnesium sometimes replacing the manganese. It is used as an ornamental stone, glaze, and pigment. [C19: < G *Rhodonit,* < Gk *rhodon* rose + -ITE[1]]

rhodopsin (rəʊˈdɒpsɪn) *n.* a red pigment in the rods of the retina in vertebrates. Also called: **visual purple.** See also **iodopsin.** [C20: < RHODO- + Gk *opsis* sight + -IN]

rhomb (rɒm) *n.* another name for **rhombus.**

rhombencephalon (ˌrɒmbɛnˈsɛfəˌlɒn) *n.* the part of the brain that develops from the posterior portion of the embryonic neural tube. Nontechnical name: **hindbrain.** [C20: < RHOMBUS + ENCEPHALON]

rhombic aerial *n.* a directional travelling-wave aerial, usually horizontal, consisting of two conductors forming a rhombus.

rhombohedral (ˌrɒmbəʊˈhiːdrəl) *adj.* **1.** of or relating to a rhombohedron. **2.** *Crystallog.* another term for **trigonal** (sense 2).

rhombohedron (ˌrɒmbəʊˈhiːdrən) *n., pl.* **-drons** *or* **-dra** (-drə). a six-sided prism whose sides are parallelograms. [C19: < RHOMBUS + -HEDRON]

rhomboid (ˈrɒmbɔɪd) *n.* **1.** a parallelogram having adjacent sides of unequal length. ~*adj.* *also* **rhomˈboidal. 2.** having such a shape. [C16: < LL, < Gk *rhomboeidēs* shaped like a RHOMBUS]

rhombus (ˈrɒmbəs) *n., pl.* **-buses** *or* **-bi** (-baɪ). an oblique-angled parallelogram having four equal sides. Also called: **rhomb.** [C16: < Gk *rhombos* something that spins; rel. to *rhembein* to whirl] —ˈ**rhombic** *adj.*

rhonchus (ˈrɒŋkəs) *n., pl.* **-chi** (-kaɪ). a rattling or whistling respiratory sound resembling snoring, caused by secretions in the trachea or bronchi. [C19: < L, < Gk *rhenkhos* snoring]

RHS *abbrev. for:* **1.** Royal Historical Society. **2.** Royal Horticultural Society. **3.** Royal Humane Society.

rhubarb (ˈruːbɑːb) *n.* **1.** any of several temperate and subtropical plants, esp. **common garden rhubarb,** which has long green and red acid-tasting edible leafstalks, usually eaten sweetened and cooked. **2.** the leafstalks of this plant. **3.** a related plant of central Asia, having a bitter-tasting underground stem that can be dried and used as a laxative or astringent. **4.** *U.S. & Canad. sl.* a heated discussion or quarrel. ~*interj., n., vb.* **5.** the noise made by actors to simulate conversation, esp. by repeating the word *rhubarb.* [C14: < OF *reubarbe,* < Med. L *reubarbum,* prob. var. of *rha barbarum,* < *rha* rhubarb (< Gk, ? < *Rha,* ancient name of the Volga) + L *barbarus* barbarian]

rhumb (rʌm) *n.* short for **rhumb line.**

rhumba (ˈrʌmbə, ˈrʊm-) *n., pl.* **-bas.** a variant spelling of **rumba.**

rhumb line *n.* **1.** an imaginary line on the surface of a sphere that intersects all meridians at the same angle. **2.** the course navigated by a vessel or aircraft that maintains a uniform compass heading. [C16: < OSp. *rumbo,* apparently < MDu. *ruum* space, ship's hold, infl. by RHOMBUS]

rhyme *or* (*Arch.*) **rime** (raɪm) *n.* **1.** identity of the terminal sounds in lines of verse or in words. **2.** a word that is identical to another in its terminal sound: *"while" is a rhyme for "mile".* **3.** a piece of poetry, esp. having corresponding sounds at the ends of the lines. **4. rhyme or reason.** sense, logic, or meaning. ~*vb.* **5.** to use (a word) or (of a word) to be used so as to form a rhyme. **6.** to render (a subject) into rhyme. **7.** to compose (verse) in a metrical structure. ~See also **eye rhyme.** [C12: < OF *rime,* ult. < OHG *rīm* a number; spelling infl. by RHYTHM]

rhymester, rimester (ˈraɪmstə), **rhymer,** *or* **rimer** *n.* a poet, esp. one considered to be mediocre; poetaster or versifier.

rhyming slang *n.* slang in which a word is replaced by another word or phrase that rhymes with it; e.g. *apples and pears* meaning *stairs.*

rhyolite (ˈraɪəˌlaɪt) *n.* a fine-grained igneous rock consisting of quartz, feldspars, and mica or amphibole. [C19: *rhyo-* < Gk *rhuax* a stream of lava + -LITE] —**rhyolitic** (ˌraɪəˈlɪtɪk) *adj.*

rhythm (ˈrɪðəm) *n.* **1. a.** the arrangement of the durations of and accents on the notes of a melody, usually laid out into regular groups (**bars**) of beats. **b.** any specific arrangement of such groupings; time: *quadruple rhythm.* **2.** (in poetry) **a.** the arrangement of words into a sequence of stressed and unstressed or long and short syllables. **b.** any specific such arrangement; metre. **3.** (in painting, sculpture, etc.) a harmonious sequence or pattern of masses alternating with voids, of light alternating with shade, of alternating colours, etc. **4.** any sequence of regularly recurring functions or events, such as certain physiological functions of the body. [C16: < L *rhythmus,* < Gk *rhuthmos;* rel. to *rhein* to flow]

rhythm and blues *n.* (*functioning as sing.*) any of various kinds of popular music derived from or influenced by the blues. Abbrev.: **R & B.**

rhythmical (ˈrɪðmɪkᵊl) *or* **rhythmic** *adj.* of, relating to, or characterized by rhythm, as in movement or sound; metrical, periodic, or regularly recurring. —ˈ**rhythmically** *adv.* —**rhythmicity** (rɪðˈmɪsɪtɪ) *n.*

rhythm method *n.* a method of contraception by restricting sexual intercourse to those days in a woman's menstrual cycle when conception is considered least likely to occur.

rhythm section *n.* those instruments in a band or group (usually piano, double bass, and drums) whose prime function is to supply the rhythm.

RI *abbrev. for:* **1.** Regina et Imperatrix. [L: Queen and Empress] **2.** Rex et Imperator. [L: King and Emperor] **3.** Royal Institution.

ria (rɪə) *n.* a long narrow inlet of the seacoast, being a former valley that was submerged by the sea. [C19: < Sp., < *río* river]

rialto (rɪˈæltəʊ) *n., pl.* **-tos.** a market or exchange. [C19: after the *Rialto,* the business centre of medieval and renaissance Venice]

riata *or* **reata** (rɪˈɑːtə) *n. South & West U.S.* a lariat or lasso. [C19: < American Sp., < Sp. *reatar* to tie together again, < RE- + *atar* to tie, < L *aptāre* to fit]

rib[1] (rɪb) *n.* **1.** any of the 24 elastic arches of bone that together form the chest wall in man. All are attached behind to the thoracic part of the spinal column. **2.** the corresponding bone in other vertebrates. **3.** a cut of meat including one or more ribs. **4.** a part or element similar in function or appearance to a rib, esp. a structural member or a ridge. **5.** a structural member in a wing that extends from the leading edge to the trailing edge. **6.** a projecting moulding or band on the underside of a vault or ceiling. **7.** one of a series of raised rows in knitted fabric. **8.** a raised ornamental line on the spine of a book where the stitching runs across it. **9.** any of the transverse stiffening timbers or joists forming the frame of a ship's hull. **10.** any of the larger veins of a leaf. **11.** a vein of ore in rock. **12.** a projecting ridge of a mountain; spur. ~*vb.* **ribbing, ribbed.** (*tr.*) **13.** to furnish or support with a rib or ribs. **14.** to mark with or form into ribs or ridges. **15.** to knit plain and purl stitches alternately in order to make raised rows in (knitting). [OE *ribb;* rel. to OHG *rippi,* ON *rif* REEF[1]] —ˈ**ribless** *adj.*

rib[2] (rɪb) *vb.* **ribbing, ribbed.** (*tr.*) *Inf.* to tease or ridicule. [C20: short for *rib-tickle* (vb.)]

RIBA *abbrev. for* Royal Institute of British Architects.

ribald (ˈrɪbᵊld) *adj.* **1.** coarse, obscene, or licentious, usually in a humorous or mocking way. ~*n.* **2.** a ribald person. [C13: < OF *ribauld,* < *riber* to live licentiously, of Gmc origin]

ribaldry (ˈrɪbᵊldrɪ) *n.* ribald language or behaviour.

riband *or* **ribband** (ˈrɪbənd) *n.* a ribbon, esp. one awarded for some achievement. [C14: var. of RIBBON]

ribbing (ˈrɪbɪŋ) *n.* **1.** a framework or structure of ribs. **2.** a pattern of ribs in woven or knitted material. **3.** *Inf.* teasing.

ribbon (ˈrɪbᵊn) *n.* **1.** a narrow strip of fine material, esp. silk, used for trimming, tying, etc. **2.** something resembling a ribbon; a long strip. **3.** a long thin flexible band of metal used as a graduated measure, spring, etc. **4.** a long narrow strip of ink-impregnated cloth for making the impression of type characters on paper in a typewriter, etc. **5.** (*pl.*) ragged strips or shreds (esp. in **torn to ribbons**). **6.** a small strip of coloured cloth signifying membership of an order or award of military decoration, prize, etc. ~*vb.* (*tr.*) **7.** to adorn with a ribbon or ribbons. **8.** to mark with narrow ribbon-like marks. [C14 *ryban,* < OF *riban,* apparently of Gmc origin]

ribbon development *n. Brit.* the building of houses in a continuous row along a main road.

ribbonfish (ˈrɪbᵊnˌfɪʃ) *n., pl.* **-fish** *or* **-fishes.** any of various soft-finned deep-sea fishes that have an elongated compressed body.

ribbonwood (ˈrɪbᵊnˌwʊd) *n.* a small evergreen malvaceous tree of New Zealand. Its wood is used in furniture-making. Also: **lacebark.**

ribcage (ˈrɪbˌkeɪdʒ) *n.* the bony structure of the ribs and their connective tissue that encloses the lungs, heart, etc.

riboflavin *or* **riboflavine** (ˌraɪbəʊˈfleɪvɪn) *n.* a vitamin of the B complex that occurs in green vegetables, milk, fish, egg yolk, liver, and kidney: used as a yellow or orange food colouring (**E 101**). Also called: **vitamin B$_2$.** [C20: < RIBOSE + FLAVIN]

ribonuclease (ˌraɪbəʊˈnjuːklɪˌeɪz) *n.* any of a group of enzymes that catalyse the hydrolysis of RNA. [C20: < RIBONUCLE(IC ACID) + -ASE]

ribonucleic acid (ˌraɪbəʊnjuːˈkliːɪk, -ˈkleɪ-) *n.* the full name of **RNA.** [C20: < RIBO(SE) + NUCLEIC ACID]

ribose (ˈraɪbəʊz, -bəʊs) *n.* a sugar that occurs in RNA and riboflavin. [C20: changed < *arabinose,* < (GUM) ARAB(IC) + -IN + -OSE[2]]

ribosomal RNA (ˌraɪbəˈsəʊməl) *n.* a type of RNA thought to form the component of ribosomes on which the translation of messenger RNA into protein chains is accomplished.

ribosome (ˈraɪbəˌsəʊm) *n.* any of numerous minute particles in the cytoplasm of cells that contain RNA and protein and are the site of protein synthesis. [C20: < RIBO(NUCLEIC ACID) + -SOME[3]] —ˌ**riboˈsomal** *adj.*

rib-tickler *n.* a very amusing joke or story. —ˈ**rib-**ˌ**tickling** *adj.*

ribwort (ˈrɪbˌwɜːt) *n.* a Eurasian plant that has lancelike ribbed leaves. Also called: **ribgrass.** See also **plantain**[1].

rice (raɪs) *n.* **1.** an erect grass that grows in East Asia on wet ground and has yellow oblong edible grains that become white when polished. **2.** the grain of this plant. ~*vb.* **3.** (*tr.*) *U.S. & Canad.* to sieve (potatoes or other vegetables) to a coarse mashed consistency. [C13 *rys,* via F, It., & L < Gk *orūza,* of Oriental origin]

rice bowl *n.* **1.** a small bowl used for eating rice. **2.** a fertile rice-producing region.

rice paper *n.* **1.** a thin edible paper made from the straw of rice, on which macaroons and similar cakes are baked. **2.** a thin delicate Chinese paper made from the **rice-paper plant**, the pith of which is pared and flattened into sheets.

rich (rɪtʃ) *adj.* **1. a.** well supplied with wealth, property, etc.; owning much. **b.** (*as collective n.;* preceded by *the*): *the rich.* **2.** (when *postpositive,* usually foll. by *in*) having an abundance of natural resources, minerals, etc.: *a land rich in metals.* **3.** producing abundantly; fertile: *rich soil.* **4.** (when *postpositive,* foll. by *in* or *with*) well supplied (with desirable qualities); abundant (in): *a country rich with cultural interest.* **5.** of great worth or quality: *a rich collection of antiques.* **6.** luxuriant or prolific: *a rich growth of weeds.* **7.** expensively elegant, elaborate, or fine; costly: *a rich display.* **8.** (of food) having a large proportion of flavoursome or fatty ingredients. **9.** having a full-bodied flavour: *a rich ruby port.* **10.** (of a smell) pungent or fragrant. **11.** (of colour) intense or vivid; deep: *a rich red.* **12.** (of sound or a voice) full, mellow, or resonant. **13.** (of a fuel-air mixture) containing a relatively high proportion of fuel. **14.** very amusing or ridiculous: *a rich joke.* ~*n.* **15.** See **riches.** [OE *rīce* (orig. of persons: great, mighty), of Gmc origin, ult. < Celtic] —ˈ**richness** *n.*

riches (ˈrɪtʃɪz) *pl. n.* wealth; an abundance of money, valuable possessions, or property.

richly (ˈrɪtʃlɪ) *adv.* **1.** in a rich or elaborate manner: *a richly decorated carving.* **2.** fully and appropriately: *he was richly rewarded.*

Richter scale (ˈrɪxtə) *n.* a scale for expressing the magnitude of an earthquake, ranging from 0 to over 8. [C20: after Charles *Richter* (1900–85), U.S. seismologist]

rick[1] (rɪk) *n.* **1.** a large stack of hay, corn, etc., built in a regular-shaped pile, esp. with a thatched top. ~*vb.* **2.** (*tr.*) to stack into ricks. [OE *hrēac*]

rick[2] (rɪk) *n.* **1.** a wrench or sprain, as of the back. ~*vb.* **2.** (*tr.*) to wrench or sprain (a joint, a limb, the back, etc.). [C18: var. of *wrick*]

rickets (ˈrɪkɪts) *n.* (*functioning as sing. or pl.*) a disease mainly of children, characterized by softening of developing bone, and hence bow legs, caused by a deficiency of vitamin D. [C17: <?]

rickettsia (rɪˈkɛtsɪə) *n., pl.* **-siae** (-sɪˌiː) *or* **-sias.** any of a group of parasitic microorganisms, that live in the tissues of ticks, mites, etc., and cause disease when transmitted to man. [C20: after Howard T. *Ricketts* (1871–1910), U.S. pathologist] —**rickˈettsial** *adj.*

rickettsial disease *n.* any of several acute infectious diseases, such as typhus, caused by ticks, mites, or body lice infected with rickettsiae.

rickety (ˈrɪkɪtɪ) *adj.* **1.** (of a structure, piece of furniture, etc.) likely to collapse or break. **2.** feeble. **3.** resembling or afflicted with rickets. [C17: < RICKETS] —ˈ**ricketiness** *n.*

rickrack *or* **ricrac** (ˈrɪkˌræk) *n.* a zigzag braid used for trimming. [C20: reduplication of RACK[1]]

rickshaw (ˈrɪkʃɔː) *or* **ricksha** (ˈrɪkʃə) *n.* **1.** Also called: **jinrikisha.** a small two-wheeled passenger vehicle drawn by one or two men, used in parts of Asia. **2.** Also called: **trishaw.** a similar vehicle with three wheels, propelled by a man pedalling as on a tricycle. [C19: shortened < JINRIKISHA]

ricochet (ˈrɪkəˌʃeɪ, ˈrɪkəˌʃɛt) *vb.* **-cheting** (-ˌʃeɪɪŋ), **-cheted** (-ˌʃeɪd) *or* **-chetting** (-ˌʃɛtɪŋ), **-chetted** (-ˌʃɛtɪd). **1.** (*intr.*) (esp. of a bullet) to rebound from a surface, usually with a whining or zipping sound. ~*n.* **2.** the motion or sound of a rebounding object, esp. a bullet. **3.** an object that ricochets. [C18: < F, <?]

ricotta (rɪˈkɒtə) *n.* a soft white unsalted cheese made from sheep's milk. [It., < L *recocta* recooked, < *recoquere*, < RE- + *coquere* to COOK]

RICS *abbrev. for* Royal Institution of Chartered Surveyors.

rictus (ˈrɪktəs) *n., pl.* **-tus** *or* **-tuses.** **1.** the gap or cleft of an open mouth or beak. **2.** a fixed or unnatural grin or grimace as in horror or death. [C18: < L, < *ringī* to gape] —ˈ**rictal** *adj.*

rid (rɪd) *vb.* **ridding, rid** *or* **ridded.** (*tr.*) **1.** (foll. by *of*) to relieve from something disagreeable or undesirable; make free (of). **2. get rid of.** to relieve or free oneself of (something unpleasant or undesirable). [C13 (meaning: to clear land): < ON *rythja*]

riddance (ˈrɪdᵊns) *n.* the act of getting rid of something; removal (esp. in **good riddance**).

ridden (ˈrɪdᵊn) *vb.* **1.** the past participle of **ride.** ~*adj.* **2.** (*in combination*) afflicted or dominated by something specified: *disease-ridden.*

riddle[1] (ˈrɪdᵊl) *n.* **1.** a question, puzzle, or verse so phrased that ingenuity is required for elucidation of the answer or meaning. **2.** a person or thing that puzzles, perplexes, or confuses. ~*vb.* **3.** to solve, explain, or interpret (a riddle). **4.** (*intr.*) to speak in riddles. [OE *rǣdelle, rǣdelse*, < *rǣd* counsel] —ˈ**riddler** *n.*

riddle[2] (ˈrɪdᵊl) *vb.* (*tr.*) **1.** (usually foll. by *with*) to pierce or perforate with numerous holes: *riddled with bullets.* **2.** to put through a sieve; sift. ~*n.* **3.** a sieve, esp. a coarse one used for sand, grain, etc. [OE *hriddel* a sieve] —ˈ**riddler** *n.*

ride (raɪd) *vb.* **riding, rode, ridden.** **1.** to sit on and control the movements of (a horse or other animal). **2.** (*tr.*) to sit on and propel (a bicycle or similar vehicle). **3.** (*intr.; often foll. by on or in*) to be carried along or travel on or in a vehicle: *she rides to work on the bus.* **4.** (*tr.*) to travel over or traverse: *they rode the countryside in search of shelter.* **5.** (*tr.*) to take part in by riding: *to ride a race.* **6.** to travel through or be carried across (sea, sky, etc.): *the small boat rode the waves; the moon was riding high.* **7.** (*tr.*) *U.S. & Canad.* to cause to be carried: *to ride someone out of town.* **8.** (*intr.*) to be supported as if floating: *the candidate rode to victory on his new policies.* **9.** (*intr.*) (of a vessel) to lie at anchor. **10.** (*tr.*) (of a vessel) to be attached to (an anchor). **11.** (*tr.*) (esp. of a male animal) to copulate with; mount. **12.** (*tr.; usually passive*) to tyrannize over or dominate: *ridden by fear.* **13.** (*tr.*) *Inf.* to persecute, esp. by constant or petty criticism: *don't ride me so hard.* **14.** (*intr.*) *Inf.* to continue undisturbed: *let it ride.* **15.** (*tr.*) to endure successfully; ride out. **16.** (*tr.*) to yield slightly to (a punch, etc.) to lessen its impact. **17.** (*intr.; often foll. by on*) (of a bet) to remain placed: *let your winnings ride on the same number.* **18. ride again.** *Inf.* to return to a former activity or scene. **19. ride for a fall.** to act in such a way as to invite disaster. **20. riding high.** confident, popular, and successful. ~*n.* **21.** a journey or outing on horseback or in a vehicle. **22.** a path specially made for riding on horseback. **23.** transport in a vehicle; lift: *can you give me a ride to the station?* **24.** a device or structure, such as a roller coaster at a fairground, in which people ride for pleasure or entertainment. **25. take for a ride.** *Inf.* **a.** to cheat, swindle, or deceive. **b.** to take (someone) away in a car and murder him. [OE *rīdan*] —ˈ**ridable** *or* ˈ**rideable** *adj.*

ride out *vb.* (*tr., adv.*) to endure successfully; survive (esp. in **ride out the storm**).

rider (ˈraɪdə) *n.* **1.** a person or thing that rides. **2.** an additional clause, amendment, or stipulation added to a document, esp. (in Britain) a legislative bill at its third reading. **3.** *Brit.* a statement made by a jury in addition to its verdict, such as a recommendation for mercy. **4.** any of various objects or devices resting on or strengthening something else. —ˈ**riderless** *adj.*

ride up *vb.* (*intr., adv.*) to work away from the proper position: *her new skirt rode up.*

ridge (rɪdʒ) *n.* **1.** a long narrow raised land formation with sloping sides. **2.** any long narrow raised strip or elevation, as on a fabric or in ploughed land. **3.** *Anat.* any elongated raised margin or border on a bone, tissue, etc. **4. a.** the top of a roof at the junction of two sloping sides. **b.** (*as modifier*): *a ridge tile.* **5.** *Meteorol.* an elongated area of high pressure, esp. an extension of an anticyclone. Cf. **trough** (sense 4). ~*vb.* **6.** to form into a ridge or ridges. [OE *hrycg*] —ˈ**ridgeˌlike** *adj.* —ˈ**ridgy** *adj.*

ridgepole (ˈrɪdʒˌpəʊl) *n.* **1.** a timber along the ridge of a roof, to which the rafters are attached. **2.** the horizontal pole at the apex of a tent.

ridgeway (ˈrɪdʒˌweɪ) *n. Brit.* a road or track along a ridge, esp. one of great antiquity.

ridicule (ˈrɪdɪˌkjuːl) *n.* **1.** language or behaviour intended to humiliate or mock. ~*vb.* **2.** (*tr.*) to make fun of or mock. [C17: < F, < L *rīdiculus*, < *rīdēre* to laugh]

ridiculous (rɪˈdɪkjʊləs) *adj.* worthy of or exciting ridicule; absurd, preposterous, laughable, or contemptible. [C16: < L *rīdiculōsus*, < *rīdēre* to laugh] —**riˈdiculousness** *n.*

riding[1] (ˈraɪdɪŋ) *n.* **1. a.** the art or practice of horsemanship. **b.** (*as modifier*): *a riding school.* **2.** a track for riding.

riding[2] (ˈraɪdɪŋ) *n.* (*cap. when part of a name*) any of the three former administrative divisions of Yorkshire: **North Riding, East Riding,** and **West Riding.** [< OE *thriding*, < ON *thrithjungr* a third]

riding crop *n.* a short whip with a handle at one end for opening gates.

riding lamp *or* **light** *n.* a light on a boat or ship showing that it is at anchor.

riempie (ˈrɪmpɪ) *n. S. African.* a leather thong or lace used mainly to make chair seats. [C19: Afrik., dim. of *riem*, < Du.: RIM]

riesling (ˈriːzlɪŋ, ˈraɪz-) *n.* **1.** a dry white wine from the Rhine valley in Germany and from certain districts in other countries. **2.** the grape used to make this wine. [C19: < G, < earlier *Rüssling*, <?]

rife (raɪf) *adj.* (*postpositive*) **1.** of widespread occurrence; current. **2.** very plentiful; abundant. **3.** (foll. by *with*) rich or abounding (in): *a garden rife with flowers.* [OE *rīfe*] —ˈ**rifely** *adv.* —ˈ**rifeness** *n.*

riff (rɪf) *Jazz, rock.* ~*n.* **1.** an ostinato played over changing harmonies. ~*vb.* **2.** (*intr.*) to play riffs. [C20: prob. altered from REFRAIN[2]]

riffle (ˈrɪfᵊl) *vb.* **1.** (when *intr.*, often foll. by *through*) to flick rapidly through (pages of a book, etc.). **2.** to shuffle (cards) by halving the pack and flicking the corners together. **3.** to make or become a riffle. ~*n.* **4.** *U.S. & Canad.* **a.** a rapid in a stream. **b.** a rocky shoal causing a rapid. **c.** a ripple on water. **5.** *Mining.* a contrivance on the bottom of a sluice, containing grooves for trapping particles of gold. **6.** the act or an instance of riffling. [C18: prob. < RUFFLE[1], infl. by RIPPLE[1]]

riffraff (ˈrɪfˌræf) *n.* (*sometimes functioning as pl.*) worthless people, esp. collectively; rabble. [C15 *rif and raf*, < OF *rif et raf*; rel. to *rifler* to plunder, and *rafle* a sweeping up]

rifle[1] (ˈraɪfᵊl) *n.* **1. a.** a firearm having a long barrel with a spirally grooved interior, which imparts to the bullet spinning motion and thus greater accuracy over a longer range. **b.** (*as modifier*): *rifle fire.* **2.** (formerly) a large cannon with a rifled bore. **3.** one of the grooves in a rifled bore. **4.** (*pl.*) **a.** a unit of soldiers equipped with rifles. **b.** (*cap. when part of a name*): *the King's Own Rifles.* ~*vb.* (*tr.*) **5.** to make spiral grooves inside the barrel of (a gun). [C18: < OF *rifler* to scratch; rel. to Low G *rifeln* < *riefe* groove]

rifle[2] (ˈraɪfᵊl) *vb.* (*tr.*) **1.** to search (a house, safe, etc.) and steal from it; ransack. **2.** to steal and carry off: *to rifle goods.* [C14: < OF *rifler* to plunder, scratch, of Gmc origin] —ˈ**rifler** *n.*

riflebird (ˈraɪfᵊlˌbɜːd) *n.* any of various Australian birds of paradise whose plumage has a metallic sheen.

rifleman (ˈraɪfᵊlmən) *n., pl.* **-men. 1.** a person skilled in the use of a rifle, esp. a soldier. **2.** a wren of New Zealand.

rifle range *n.* an area used for target practice with rifles.

rifling (ˈraɪflɪŋ) *n.* **1.** the cutting of spiral grooves on the inside of a firearm's barrel. **2.** the series of grooves so cut.

rift (rɪft) *n.* **1.** a gap or space made by cleaving or splitting. **2.** *Geol.* a fault produced by tension on either side of the fault plane. **3.** a gap between two cloud masses; break or chink. **4.** a break in friendly relations between people, nations, etc. ~*vb.* **5.** to burst or cause to burst open; split. [C13: < ON]

rift valley *n.* a long narrow valley resulting from the subsidence of land between two faults.

rig (rɪg) *vb.* **rigging, rigged.** (*tr.*) **1.** *Naut.* to equip (a vessel, mast, etc.) with (sails, rigging, etc.). **2.** *Naut.* to set up or prepare ready for use. **3.** to put the components of (an aircraft, etc.) into their correct positions. **4.** to manipulate in a fraudulent manner, esp. for profit: *to rig prices.* ~*n.* **5.** *Naut.* the distinctive arrangement of the sails, masts, etc., of a vessel. **6.** the installation used in drilling for and exploiting natural gas and oil deposits: *an oil rig.* **7.** apparatus or equipment. **8.** *U.S. & Canad.* an articulated lorry. ~See also **rig out, rig up.** [C15: of Scand. origin; rel. to Norwegian *rigga* to wrap]

rigadoon (ˌrɪgəˈduːn) *n.* **1.** an old Provençal couple dance, light and graceful, in lively duple time. **2.** a piece of music composed for or in the rhythm of this dance. [C17: < F, allegedly after *Rigaud*, a dancing master at Marseilles]

rigamarole (ˈrɪgəməˌrəʊl) *n.* a variant of **rigmarole.**

-rigged *adj.* (*in combination*) (of a sailing vessel) having a rig of a certain kind: *ketch-rigged; schooner-rigged.*

rigger (ˈrɪgə) *n.* **1.** a workman who rigs vessels, etc. **2.** *Rowing.* a bracket on a boat to support a projecting rowlock. **3.** a person skilled in the use of pulleys, cranes, etc.

rigging (ˈrɪgɪŋ) *n.* **1.** the shrouds, stays, etc., of a vessel. **2.** the bracing wires, struts, and lines of a biplane, etc. **3.** any form of lifting gear.

right (raɪt) *adj.* **1.** in accordance with accepted standards of moral or legal behaviour, justice, etc.: *right conduct.* **2.** correct or true: *the right answer.* **3.** appropriate, suitable, or proper: *the right man for the job.* **4.** most favourable or convenient: *the right time to act.* **5.** in a satisfactory condition: *things are right again now.* **6.** indicating or designating the correct time: *the clock is right.* **7.** correct in opinion or judgment. **8.** sound in mind or body. **9.** (*usually prenominal*) of, designating, or located near the side of something or someone that faces east when the front is turned towards the north. **10.** (*usually prenominal*) worn on a right hand, foot, etc. **11.** (*sometimes cap.*) of, designating, belonging to, or relating to the political or intellectual right (see sense 36). **12.** (*sometimes cap.*) conservative: *the right wing of the party.* **13.** *Geom.* **a.** formed by or containing a line or plane perpendicular to another line or plane. **b.** having the axis perpendicular to the base: *a right circular cone.* **c.** straight: *a right line.* **14.** relating to or designating the side of cloth worn or facing outwards. **15. in one's right mind.** sane. **16. she'll be right.** *Austral. & N.Z. inf.* that's all right; not to worry. **17. the right side of. a.** in favour with: *you'd better stay on the right side of him.* **b.** younger than: *she's still on the right side of fifty.* **18. too right.** *Austral. & N.Z. inf.* an exclamation of agreement. ~*adv.* **19.** in accordance with correctness or truth: *to guess right.* **20.** in the appropriate manner: *do it right next time!* **21.** in a straight line: *right to the top.* **22.** in the direction of the east from the point of view of a person or thing facing north. **23.** absolutely or completely: *he went right through the floor.* **24.** all the way: *the bus goes right into town.* **25.** without delay: *I'll be right over.* **26.** exactly or precisely: *right here.* **27.** in a manner consistent with a legal or moral code: *do right by me.* **28.** in accordance with propriety; fittingly: *it serves you right.* **29.** to good or favourable advantage: *it all came out right in the end.* **30.** (esp. in religious titles) most or very: *right reverend.* **31. right, left, and centre.** on all sides. ~*n.* **32.** any claim, title, etc., that is morally just or legally granted as allowable or due to a person: *I know my rights.* **33.** anything that accords with the principles of legal or moral justice. **34.** the fact or state of being in accordance with reason, truth, or accepted standards (esp. in **in the right**). **35.** the right side, direction, position, area, or part: *the right of the army.* **36.** (*often cap.* and preceded by *the*) the supporters or advocates of social, political, or economic conservatism or reaction. **37.** *Boxing.* **a.** a punch with the right hand. **b.** the right hand. **38.** (*often pl.*) *Finance.* the privilege of a company's shareholders to subscribe for new issues of the company's shares on advantageous terms. **39. by right** (*or* **rights**). properly: *by rights you should be in bed.* **40. in one's own right.** having a claim or title oneself rather than through marriage or other connection. **41. to rights.** consistent with justice or orderly arrangement: *he put the matter to rights.* ~*vb.* (*mainly tr.*) **42.** (*also intr.*) to restore to or attain a normal, esp. an upright, position: *the raft righted in a few seconds.* **43.** to make (something) accord with truth or facts. **44.** to restore to an orderly state or condition. **45.** to compensate for or redress (esp. in **right a wrong**). ~*interj.* **46.** an expression of agreement or compliance. [OE *riht, reoht*] —ˈ**rightable** *adj.* —ˈ**righter** *n.* —ˈ**rightness** *n.*

right about *n.* 1. a turn executed through 180°. ~*adj., adv.* 2. in the opposite direction.

right angle *n.* 1. the angle between radii of a circle that cut off on the circumference an arc equal in length to one quarter of the circumference; an angle of 90° or $\pi/2$ radians. 2. **at right angles.** perpendicular or perpendicularly. —ˈ**right-ˌangled** *adj.*

right-angled triangle *n.* a triangle one angle of which is a right angle. U.S. and Canad. name: **right triangle.**

right ascension *n. Astron.* the angular distance measured eastwards along the celestial equator from the vernal equinox to the point at which the celestial equator intersects a great circle passing through the celestial pole and the heavenly object in question.

right away *adv.* without delay.

righteous (ˈraɪtʃəs) *adj.* 1. a. characterized by, proceeding from, or in accordance with accepted standards of morality, justice, or uprightness: *a righteous man.* b. (*as collective n.;* preceded by *the*): *the righteous.* 2. morally justifiable or right: *righteous indignation.* [OE *rīhtwīs,* < RIGHT + WISE[2]] —ˈ**righteously** *adv.* —ˈ**righteousness** *n.*

rightful (ˈraɪtfʊl) *adj.* 1. in accordance with what is right. 2. (*prenominal*) having a legally or morally just claim: *the rightful owner.* 3. (*prenominal*) held by virtue of a legal or just claim: *my rightful property.* —ˈ**rightfully** *adv.*

right-hand *adj.* (*prenominal*) 1. of, located on, or moving towards the right: *a right-hand bend.* 2. for use by the right hand. 3. **right-hand man.** one's most valuable assistant.

right-handed *adj.* 1. using the right hand with greater skill or ease than the left. 2. performed with the right hand. 3. made for use by the right hand. 4. turning from left to right. —ˌ**right-ˈhandedness** *n.*

rightist (ˈraɪtɪst) *adj.* 1. of, tending towards, or relating to the political right or its principles. ~*n.* 2. a person who supports or belongs to the political right. —ˈ**rightism** *n.*

rightly (ˈraɪtlɪ) *adv.* 1. in accordance with the true facts. 2. in accordance with principles of justice or morality. 3. with good reason: *he was rightly annoyed with her.* 4. properly or suitably. 5. (*used with a negative*) *Inf.* with certainty (usually in **I don't rightly know**).

right-minded *adj.* holding opinions or principles that accord with what is right or with the opinions of the speaker.

righto *or* **right oh** (ˈraɪtˈəʊ) *sentence substitute. Brit. inf.* an expression of agreement or compliance.

right off *adv.* immediately; right away.

right of way *n., pl.* **rights of way.** 1. the right of one vehicle or vessel to take precedence over another, as laid down by law or custom. 2. a. the legal right of someone to pass over another's land, acquired by grant or by long usage. b. the path used by this right. 3. *U.S.* the strip of land over which a power line, road, etc., extends.

Right Reverend *adj.* (in Britain) a title of respect for an Anglican or Roman Catholic bishop.

rights issue *n. Stock Exchange.* an issue of new shares offered by a company to its existing shareholders on favourable terms.

right-thinking (ˈraɪtˌθɪŋkɪŋ) *adj.* possessing reasonable and generally acceptable opinions.

rightward (ˈraɪtwəd) *adj.* 1. situated on or directed towards the right. ~*adv.* 2. a variant of **rightwards.**

rightwards (ˈraɪtwədz) *or* **rightward** *adv.* towards or on the right.

right whale *n.* a large whalebone whale which is grey or black, has a large head and no dorsal fin, and is hunted as a source of whalebone and oil. [C19: ? because it was *right* for hunting]

right wing *n.* 1. (*often cap.*) the conservative faction of an assembly, party, etc. 2. the part of an army or field of battle on the right from the point of view of one facing the enemy. 3. a. the right-hand side of the field of play from the point of view of a team facing its opponent's goal. b. a player positioned in this area in any of various games. ~*adj.* **right-wing.** 4. of, belonging to, or relating to the right wing. —ˈ**right-ˈwinger** *n.*

rigid (ˈrɪdʒɪd) *adj.* 1. physically inflexible or stiff: *a rigid piece of plastic.* 2. rigorously strict: *rigid rules.* [C16: < L *rigidus,* < *rigēre* to be stiff] —**riˈgidity** *n.* —ˈ**rigidly** *adv.*

rigidify (rɪˈdʒɪdɪˌfaɪ) *vb.* **-fying, -fied.** to make or become rigid.

rigmarole (ˈrɪgməˌrəʊl) *or* **rigamarole** *n.* 1. any long complicated procedure. 2. a set of incoherent or pointless statements. [C18: < earlier *ragman roll* a list, prob. a roll used in a medieval game, wherein characters were described in verse, beginning with *Ragemon le bon* Ragman the good]

rigor (ˈraɪgɔː, ˈrɪgə) *n.* 1. *Med.* a sudden feeling of chilliness, often accompanied by shivering: it sometimes precedes a fever. 2. (ˈrɪgə). *Pathol.* rigidity of a muscle. 3. a state of rigidity assumed in reaction to shock. [see RIGOUR]

rigor mortis (ˈrɪgə ˈmɔːtɪs) *n. Pathol.* the stiffness of joints and muscular rigidity of a dead body. [C19: L, lit.: rigidity of death]

rigorous (ˈrɪgərəs) *adj.* 1. harsh, strict, or severe: *rigorous discipline.* 2. severely accurate: *rigorous book-keeping.* 3. (esp. of weather) extreme or harsh. 4. *Maths, logic.* (of a proof) making the validity of each step explicit. —ˈ**rigorously** *adv.*

rigour *or U.S.* **rigor** (ˈrɪgə) *n.* 1. harsh but just treatment or action. 2. a severe or cruel circumstance: *the rigours of famine.* 3. strictness, harshness, or severity of character. 4. strictness in judgment or conduct. [C14: < L *rigor*]

rig out *vb.* 1. (*tr., adv.;* often foll. by *with*) to equip or fit out (with): *his car is rigged out with gadgets.* 2. to dress or be dressed: *rigged out smartly.* ~*n.* **rigout.** 3. *Inf.* a person's clothing or costume, esp. a bizarre outfit.

rig up *vb.* (*tr., adv.*) to erect or construct, esp. as a temporary measure: *cameras were rigged up to televise the event.*

Rig-Veda (rɪgˈveɪdə) *n.* a compilation of Hindu poems dating from 2000 B.C. or earlier. [C18: < Sansk. *rigveda,* < *ric* song of praise + VEDA]

rile (raɪl) *vb.* (*tr.*) 1. to annoy or anger. 2. *U.S. & Canad.* to agitate (water, etc.). [C19: var. of ROIL]

rill (rɪl) *n.* 1. a brook or stream. 2. a small channel or gulley, such as one formed during soil erosion. 3. Also: **rille.** one of many winding cracks on the moon. [C15: < Low G *rille*]

rim (rɪm) *n.* 1. the raised edge of an object, esp. of something more or less circular such as a cup or crater. 2. the peripheral part of a wheel, to which the tyre is attached. 3. *Basketball.* the hoop from which the net is suspended. ~*vb.* **rimming, rimmed.** (*tr.*) 4. to put a rim on (a pot, cup, wheel, etc.). [OE *rima*]

rime[1] (raɪm) *n.* 1. frost formed by the freezing of water droplets in fog onto solid objects. ~*vb.* 2. (*tr.*) to cover with rime or something resembling rime. [OE *hrīm*]

rime[2] (raɪm) *n., vb.* an archaic spelling of **rhyme.**

rim-fire *adj.* 1. (of a cartridge) having the primer in the rim of the base. 2. (of a firearm) adapted for such cartridges.

rimose (raɪˈməʊs, -ˈməʊz) *adj.* (esp. of plant parts) having the surface marked by a network of cracks. [C18: < L *rīmōsus,* < *rīma* a split]

rimu (ˈriːmuː) *n.* a New Zealand tree. Also called: **red pine.** [< Maori]

rimy (ˈraɪmɪ) *adj.* **rimier, rimiest.** coated with rime.

rind (raɪnd) *n.* 1. a hard outer layer or skin on bacon, cheese, etc. 2. the outer layer of a fruit or of the spore-producing body of certain fungi. 3. the outer layer of the bark of a tree. [OE *rinde*]

rinderpest (ˈrɪndəˌpɛst) *n.* an acute contagious viral disease of cattle, characterized by severe inflammation of the intestinal tract and diarrhoea. [C19: < G *Rinderpest* cattle pest]

ring[1] (rɪŋ) *n.* 1. a circular band of a precious

metal often set with gems and worn upon the finger as an adornment or as a token of engagement or marriage. **2.** any object or mark that is circular in shape. **3.** a circular path or course: *to run around in a ring.* **4.** a group of people or things standing or arranged so as to form a circle: *a ring of spectators.* **5.** an enclosed space, usually circular in shape, where circus acts are performed. **6.** a square raised platform, marked off by ropes, in which contestants box or wrestle. **7. the ring.** the sport of boxing. **8. throw one's hat in the ring.** to announce one's intention to be a candidate or contestant. **9.** a group of people, usually illegal, cooperating for the purpose of controlling the market in antiques, etc. **10.** (esp. at country fairs) an enclosure where horses, cattle, and other livestock are paraded and auctioned. **11.** an area reserved for betting at a racecourse. **12.** a circular strip of bark cut from a tree or branch. **13.** a single turn in a spiral. **14.** *Geom.* the area of space lying between two concentric circles. **15.** *Maths.* a set that is subject to two binary operations, addition and multiplication, such that the set is a commutative group under addition and is closed under multiplication, this latter operation being associative. **16.** *Bot.* short for **annual ring.** **17.** *Chem.* a closed loop of atoms in a molecule. **18.** one of the systems of circular bands orbiting the planets Saturn and Uranus. **19. run rings around.** *Inf.* to outclass completely. ~*vb.* **ringing, ringed.** (*tr.*) **20.** to surround with, or as if with, or form a ring. **21.** to mark a bird with a ring or clip for subsequent identification. **22.** to fit a ring in the nose of (a bull, etc.) so that it can be led easily. **23.** to ringbark. [OE *hring*] —**ringed** *adj.*

ring[2] (rɪŋ) *vb.* **ringing, rang, rung.** **1.** to emit or cause to emit a resonant sound, characteristic of certain metals when struck. **2.** to cause (a bell, etc.) to emit a ringing sound by striking it once or repeatedly or (of a bell) to emit such a sound. **3. a.** (*tr.*) to cause (a large bell) to emit a ringing sound by pulling on a rope attached to a wheel on which the bell swings back and forth, being sounded by a clapper inside it. **b.** (*intr.*) (of a bell) to sound by being swung in this way. **4.** (*intr.*) (of a building, place, etc.) to be filled with sound: *the church rang with singing.* **5.** (*intr.*; foll. by *for*) to call by means of a bell, etc.: *to ring for the butler.* **6.** Also: **ring up.** *Chiefly Brit.* to call (a person) by telephone. **7.** (*tr.*) to strike or tap (a coin) in order to assess its genuineness by the sound produced. **8.** (*intr.*) (of the ears) to have or give the sensation of humming or ringing. **9. ring a bell.** to bring something to the mind or memory: *that rings a bell.* **10. ring down the curtain. a.** to lower the curtain at the end of a theatrical performance. **b.** (foll. by *on*) to put an end (to). **11. ring false.** to give the impression of being false. **12. ring true.** to give the impression of being true. ~*n.* **13.** the act of or a sound made by ringing. **14.** a sound produced by or suggestive of a bell. **15.** any resonant or metallic sound: *the ring of trumpets.* **16.** *Inf., chiefly Brit.* a telephone call. **17.** the complete set of bells in a tower or belfry: *a ring of eight bells.* **18.** an inherent quality or characteristic: *his explanation has the ring of sincerity.* ~See also **ring in, ring off,** etc. [OE *hringan*]

▷ **Usage.** *Rang* and *sang* are the correct forms of the past tenses of *ring* and *sing,* although *rung* and *sung* are still heard informally and dialectally: *he rung* (*rang*) *the bell.*

ringbark (ˈrɪŋˌbɑːk) *vb.* (*tr.*) to kill (a tree) by cutting away a strip of bark from around the trunk.

ring binder *n.* a loose-leaf binder with metal rings that can be opened to insert perforated paper.

ringbolt (ˈrɪŋˌbəʊlt) *n.* a bolt with a ring fitted through an eye attached to the bolt head.

ringdove (ˈrɪŋˌdʌv) *n.* **1.** another name for **wood pigeon.** **2.** an Old World turtledove, having a black band around the neck.

ringed plover *n.* a European shorebird with a greyish-brown back, white underparts, a black throat band, and orange legs.

ringer (ˈrɪŋə) *n.* **1.** a person or thing that rings a bell, etc. **2.** Also called: **dead ringer.** *Sl.* a person or thing that is almost identical to another. **3.** *Chiefly U.S.* a contestant, esp. a horse, entered in a competition under false representations of identity, record, or ability. **4.** *Austral.* a stockman; station hand. **5.** *Austral.* the fastest shearer in a shed. **6.** *Austral. inf.* the fastest or best at anything. **7.** a quoit thrown so as to encircle a peg. **8.** such a throw.

ring finger *n.* the third finger, esp. of the left hand, on which a wedding ring is worn.

ringhals (ˈrɪŋˌhæls) *or* **rinkhals** *n., pl.* **-hals** *or* **-halses.** a venomous snake of southern Africa, which spits venom at its enemies from a distance. [Afrik., lit.: ring neck]

ring in *vb.* (*adv.*) **1.** (*intr.*) *Chiefly Brit.* to report to someone by telephone. **2.** (*tr.*) to accompany the arrival of with bells (esp. in **ring in the new year**). ~*n.* **ring-in.** **3.** *Austral. & N.Z. sl.* a person or thing that is not normally a member of a particular group; outsider.

ringing tone *n. Brit.* a sequence of pairs of tones heard by the dialler on a telephone when the number dialled is ringing. Cf. **engaged tone, dialling tone.**

ringleader (ˈrɪŋˌliːdə) *n.* a person who leads others in unlawful or mischievous activity.

ringlet (ˈrɪŋlɪt) *n.* **1.** a lock of hair hanging down in a spiral curl. **2.** a butterfly that occurs in S Europe and has dark brown wings marked with small black-and-white eyespots. —**ˈringleted** *adj.*

ring main *n.* a domestic electrical supply in which outlet sockets are connected to the mains supply through a continuous closed circuit (**ring circuit**).

ringmaster (ˈrɪŋˌmɑːstə) *n.* the master of ceremonies in a circus.

ring-necked *adj.* (of animals, esp. certain birds and snakes) having a band of distinctive colour around the neck.

ring-necked pheasant *n.* a common pheasant originating in Asia. The male has a bright plumage with a band of white around the neck and the female is mottled brown.

ring off *vb.* (*intr., adv.*) *Chiefly Brit.* to terminate a telephone conversation by replacing the receiver; hang up.

ring out *vb.* (*adv.*) **1.** (*tr.*) to accompany the departure of with bells (esp. in **ring out the old year**). **2.** (*intr.*) to send forth a loud resounding noise.

ring ouzel *n.* a European thrush common in rocky areas. The male has a blackish plumage and the female is brown.

ring road *n.* a main road that bypasses a town or town centre. U.S. names: **belt, beltway.**

ringside (ˈrɪŋˌsaɪd) *n.* **1.** the row of seats nearest a boxing or wrestling ring. **2. a.** any place affording a close uninterrupted view. **b.** (*as modifier*): *a ringside seat.*

ringtail (ˈrɪŋˌteɪl) *n. Austral.* any of several tree-living phalangers having curling prehensile tails used to grasp branches while climbing.

ring up *vb.* (*adv.*) **1.** *Chiefly Brit.* to make a telephone call (to). **2.** (*tr.*) to record on a cash register. **3. ring up the curtain. a.** to begin a theatrical performance. **b.** (often foll. by *on*) to make a start (on).

ringworm (ˈrɪŋˌwɜːm) *n.* any of various fungal infections of the skin or nails, often appearing as itching circular patches. Also called: **tinea.**

rink (rɪŋk) *n.* **1.** an expanse of ice for skating on, esp. one that is artificially prepared and under cover. **2.** an area for roller-skating on. **3.** a building or enclosure for ice-skating or roller-skating. **4.** *Bowls.* a strip of the green on which a game is played. **5.** *Curling.* the strip of ice on which the game is played. **6.** (in bowls and curling) the players on one side in a game. [C14 (Scots): < OF *renc* row]

rinkhals (ˈrɪŋkˌhæls) *n.* a South African name for **ringhals.**

rink rat *n. Canad. sl.* a youth who helps with odd chores around an ice-hockey rink in return for free admission to games, etc.

rinse (rɪns) *vb.* (*tr.*) **1.** to remove soap from (clothes, etc.) by applying clean water in the final stage in washing. **2.** to wash lightly, esp. without using soap. **3.** to give a light tint to (hair). ~*n.* **4.** the act or an instance of rinsing. **5.** *Hairdressing.* a liquid preparation put on the hair when wet to give a tint to it: *a blue rinse.* [C14: < OF *rincer,* < L *recens* fresh] —ˈ**rinser** *n.*

riot (ˈraɪət) *n.* **1. a.** a disturbance made by an unruly mob or (in law) three or more persons. **b.** (*as modifier*): *a riot shield.* **2.** unrestrained revelry. **3.** an occasion of boisterous merriment. **4.** *Sl.* a person who occasions boisterous merriment. **5.** a dazzling display: *a riot of colour.* **6.** *Hunting.* the indiscriminate following of any scent by hounds. **7.** *Arch.* wanton lasciviousness. **8. run riot. a.** to behave without restraint. **b.** (of plants) to grow profusely. ~*vb.* **9.** (*intr.*) to take part in a riot. **10.** (*intr.*) to indulge in unrestrained revelry. **11.** (*tr.;* foll. by *away*) to spend (time or money) in wanton or loose living. [C13: < OF *riote* dispute, < *ruihoter* to quarrel, prob. < *ruir* to make a commotion, < L *rugīre* to roar] —ˈ**rioter** *n.*

Riot Act *n.* **1.** *Criminal law.* (formerly, in England) a statute of 1715 by which persons committing a riot had to disperse within an hour of the reading of the act by a magistrate. **2. read the riot act to.** to warn or reprimand severely.

riotous (ˈraɪətəs) *adj.* **1.** proceeding from or of the nature of riots or rioting. **2.** characterized by wanton revelry: *riotous living.* **3.** characterized by unrestrained merriment: *riotous laughter.* —ˈ**riotously** *adv.* —ˈ**riotousness** *n.*

riot shield *n.* (in Britain) a large oblong curved transparent shield used by police controlling crowds.

rip[1] (rɪp) *vb.* **ripping, ripped. 1.** to tear or be torn violently or roughly. **2.** (*tr.;* foll. by *off* or *out*) to remove hastily or roughly. **3.** (*intr.*) *Inf.* to move violently or precipitously. **4.** (*intr.;* foll. by *into*) *Inf.* to pour violent abuse (on). **5.** (*tr.*) to saw or split (wood) in the direction of the grain. **6. let rip.** to act or speak without restraint. ~*n.* **7.** a tear or split. **8.** short for **ripsaw.** ~See also **rip off.** [C15: ? < Flemish *rippen*]

rip[2] (rɪp) *n.* short for **riptide.** [C18: ? < RIP[1]]

rip[3] (rɪp) *n. Inf., arch.* **1.** a debauched person. **2.** an old worn-out horse. [C18: ? < *rep,* shortened < REPROBATE]

RIP *abbrev. for* requiescat *or* requiescant in pace. [L: may he, she, *or* they rest in peace]

riparian (raɪˈpɛərɪən) *adj.* **1.** of, inhabiting, or situated on the bank of a river. **2.** denoting or relating to the legal rights of the owner of land on a river bank, such as fishing. ~*n.* **3.** *Property law.* a person who owns land on a river bank. [C19: < L, < *rīpa* river bank]

ripcord (ˈrɪpˌkɔːd) *n.* **1.** a cord that when pulled opens a parachute from its pack. **2.** a cord on the gas bag of a balloon that when pulled enables gas to escape and the balloon to descend.

ripe (raɪp) *adj.* **1.** (of fruit, grain, etc.) mature and ready to be eaten or used. **2.** mature enough to be eaten or used: *ripe cheese.* **3.** fully developed in mind or body. **4.** resembling ripe fruit, esp. in redness or fullness: *a ripe complexion.* **5.** (*postpositive;* foll. by *for*) ready or eager (to undertake or undergo an action). **6.** (*postpositive;* foll. by *for*) suitable: *the time is not yet ripe.* **7.** mature in judgment or knowledge. **8.** advanced but healthy (esp. in **a ripe old age**). **9.** *Sl.* **a.** complete; thorough. **b.** excessive; exorbitant. **10.** *Sl.* slightly indecent; risqué. [OE *rīpe*] —ˈ**ripely** *adv.* —ˈ**ripeness** *n.*

ripen (ˈraɪpᵊn) *vb.* to make or become ripe.

ripieno (ˌrɪpɪˈeɪnəʊ) *n., pl.* **-ni** (-niː) *or* **-nos.** *Music.* a supplementary instrument or player. [It.]

rip off *vb.* (*tr.*) **1.** to tear roughly (from). **2.** (*adv.*) *Sl.* to steal from or cheat (someone). ~*n.* **rip-off. 3.** *Sl.* a grossly overpriced article. **4.** *Sl.* the act of stealing or cheating.

riposte (rɪˈpɒst, rɪˈpəʊst) *n.* **1.** a swift sharp reply in speech or action. **2.** *Fencing.* a counterattack made immediately after a successful parry. ~*vb.* **3.** (*intr.*) to make a riposte. [C18: < F, < It., < *rispondere* to reply]

ripper (ˈrɪpə) *n.* **1.** a person or thing that rips. **2.** a murderer who dissects or mutilates his victim's body. **3.** *Sl., chiefly Austral. & N.Z.* a fine or excellent person or thing.

ripping (ˈrɪpɪŋ) *adj. Arch. Brit. sl.* excellent; splendid. —ˈ**rippingly** *adv.*

ripple[1] (ˈrɪpᵊl) *n.* **1.** a slight wave or undulation on the surface of water. **2.** a small wave or undulation in fabric, hair, etc. **3.** a sound reminiscent of water flowing quietly in ripples: *a ripple of laughter.* **4.** *Electronics.* an oscillation of small amplitude superimposed on a steady value. **5.** *U.S. & Canad.* another word for **riffle** (sense 4). ~*vb.* **6.** (*intr.*) to form ripples or flow with an undulating motion. **7.** (*tr.*) to stir up (water) so as to form ripples. **8.** (*tr.*) to make ripple marks. **9.** (*intr.*) (of sounds) to rise and fall gently. [C17: ? < RIP[1]] —ˈ**rippler** *n.* —ˈ**rippling** *or* ˈ**ripply** *adj.*

ripple[2] (ˈrɪpᵊl) *n.* **1.** a special kind of comb designed to separate the seed from the stalks in flax or hemp. ~*vb.* **2.** (*tr.*) to comb with this tool. [C14: of Gmc origin] —ˈ**rippler** *n.*

ripple mark *n.* one of a series of small wavy ridges of sand formed by waves on a beach, by a current in a sandy riverbed, or by wind on land.

rip-roaring *adj. Inf.* characterized by excitement, intensity, or boisterous behaviour.

ripsaw (ˈrɪpˌsɔː) *n.* a handsaw for cutting along the grain of timber.

ripsnorter (ˈrɪpˌsnɔːtə) *n. Sl.* a person or thing noted for intensity or excellence. —ˈ**ripˌsnorting** *adj.*

riptide (ˈrɪpˌtaɪd) *n.* **1.** Also called: **rip.** a stretch of turbulent water in the sea, caused by the meeting of currents. **2.** Also called: **rip current.** a strong current, esp. one flowing outwards from the shore.

rise (raɪz) *vb.* **rising, rose, risen** (ˈrɪzᵊn). (*mainly intr.*) **1.** to get up from a lying, sitting, kneeling, or prone position. **2.** to get out of bed, esp. to begin one's day: *he always rises early.* **3.** to move from a lower to a higher position or place. **4.** to ascend or appear above the horizon: *the sun is rising.* **5.** to increase in height or level: *the water rose above the normal level.* **6.** to attain higher rank, status, or reputation: *he will rise in the world.* **7.** to be built or erected: *those blocks of flats are rising fast.* **8.** to appear: *new troubles rose to afflict her.* **9.** to increase in strength, degree, etc.: *the wind is rising.* **10.** to increase in amount or value: *house prices are always rising.* **11.** to swell up: *dough rises.* **12.** to become erect, stiff, or rigid: *the hairs on his neck rose in fear.* **13.** (of one's stomach or gorge) to manifest nausea. **14.** to revolt: *the people rose against their oppressors.* **15.** to slope upwards: *the ground rises beyond the lake.* **16.** to be resurrected. **17.** to originate: *that river rises in the mountains.* **18.** (of a session of a court, legislative assembly, etc.) to come to an end. **19.** *Angling.* (of fish) to come to the surface of the water. **20.** (often foll. by *to*) *Inf.* to respond (to teasing, etc.). ~*n.* **21.** the act or an instance of rising. **22.** an increase in height. **23.** an increase in rank, status, or position. **24.** an increase in amount, cost, or value. **25.** an increase in degree or intensity. **26.** *Brit.* an increase in salary or wages. U.S. and Canad. word: **raise. 27.** the vertical height of a step or of a flight of stairs. **28.** the vertical height of a roof above the walls or columns. **29.** *Angling.* the act or instance of fish coming to the surface of the water to take flies, etc. **30.** the beginning, origin, or source. **31.** a piece of rising ground; incline. **32. get** *or* **take a rise out of.** *Sl.* to provoke an angry or petulant reaction from. **33. give rise to.** to cause the development of. [OE *rīsan*]

riser (ˈraɪzə) *n.* **1.** a person who rises, esp. from bed: *an early riser.* **2.** the vertical part of a stair. **3.** a vertical pipe, esp. one within a building.

rise to *vb.* (*intr., prep.*) to respond adequately to (the demands of something, esp. a testing challenge).

risibility (ˌrɪzɪˈbɪlɪtɪ) *n., pl.* **-ties.** **1.** a tendency to laugh. **2.** hilarity; laughter.

risible (ˈrɪzɪbᵊl) *adj.* **1.** having a tendency to laugh. **2.** causing laughter; ridiculous. [C16: < LL *rīsibilis,* < L *rīdēre* to laugh] —ˈ**risibly** *adv.*

rising (ˈraɪzɪŋ) *n.* **1.** a rebellion; revolt. **2.** the leaven used to make dough rise in baking. ~*adj.* (*prenominal*) **3.** increasing in rank, status, or reputation: *a rising young politician.* **4.** growing up to adulthood: *the rising generation.* ~*adv.* **5.** *Inf.* approaching: *he's rising 50.*

rising damp *n.* capillary movement of moisture from the ground into the walls of buildings, resulting in damage up to a level of 3 feet.

rising trot *n.* a horse's trot in which the rider rises from the saddle every second beat.

risk (rɪsk) *n.* **1.** the possibility of incurring misfortune or loss. **2.** *Insurance.* **a.** chance of a loss or other event on which a claim may be filed. **b.** the type of such an event, such as fire or theft. **c.** the amount of the claim should such an event occur. **d.** a person or thing considered with respect to the characteristics that may cause an insured event to occur. **3. at risk.** vulnerable. **4. take** *or* **run a risk.** to proceed in an action without regard to the possibility of danger involved. ~*vb.* (*tr.*) **5.** to expose to danger or loss. **6.** to act in spite of the possibility of (injury or loss): *to risk a fall in climbing.* [C17: < F, < It., < *rischiare* to be in peril, < Gk *rhiza* cliff (from the hazards of sailing along rocky coasts)]

risk capital *n. Chiefly Brit.* capital invested in an issue of ordinary shares, esp. of a speculative enterprise. Also called: **venture capital.**

risky (ˈrɪskɪ) *adj.* **riskier, riskiest.** involving danger. —ˈ**riskily** *adv.* —ˈ**riskiness** *n.*

risotto (rɪˈzɒtəʊ) *n., pl.* **-tos.** a dish of rice cooked in stock and served variously with tomatoes, cheese, chicken, etc. [C19: < It., < *riso* RICE]

risqué (ˈrɪskeɪ) *adj.* bordering on impropriety or indecency: *a risqué joke.* [C19: < F *risquer* to hazard, RISK]

rissole (ˈrɪsəʊl) *n.* a mixture of minced cooked meat coated in egg and breadcrumbs and fried. [C18: < F, prob. ult. < L *russus* red]

risus sardonicus (ˈriːsəs sɑːˈdɒnɪkəs) *n. Pathol.* fixed contraction of the facial muscles resulting in a peculiar distorted grin, caused esp. by tetanus. Also called: **trismus cynicus** (ˈtrɪzməs ˈsɪnɪkəs). [C17: NL, lit.: sardonic laugh]

rit. *Music. abbrev. for:* **1.** ritardando. **2.** ritenuto.

ritardando (ˌrɪtɑːˈdændəʊ) *adj., adv.* another term for **rallentando.** Abbrev.: **rit.** [C19: < It., < *ritardare* to slow down]

rite (raɪt) *n.* **1.** a formal act prescribed or customary in religious ceremonies: *the rite of baptism.* **2.** a particular body of such acts, esp. of a particular Christian Church: *the Latin rite.* **3.** a Christian Church: *the Greek rite.* [C14: < L *rītus* religious ceremony]

ritenuto (ˌrɪtəˈnuːtəʊ) *adj., adv. Music.* **1.** held back momentarily. **2.** Abbrev.: **rit.** another term for **rallentando.** [C19: < It., < L *retinēre* to hold back]

rite of passage *n.* a ceremony performed in some cultures at times when an individual changes his status, as at puberty and marriage.

ritornello (ˌrɪtəˈnɛləʊ) *n., pl.* **-los** *or* **-li** (-liː). *Music.* a short piece of instrumental music interpolated in a song. [It., lit.: a little return]

ritual (ˈrɪtjʊəl) *n.* **1.** the prescribed or established form of a religious or other ceremony. **2.** such prescribed forms in general or collectively. **3.** stereotyped activity or behaviour. **4.** any formal act, institution, or procedure that is followed consistently: *the ritual of the law.* ~*adj.* **5.** of or characteristic of religious, social, or other rituals. [C16: < L *rītuālis,* < *rītus* RITE] —ˈ**ritually** *adv.*

ritualism (ˈrɪtjʊəˌlɪzəm) *n.* **1.** exaggerated emphasis on the importance of rites and ceremonies. **2.** the study of rites and ceremonies, esp. magical or religious ones. —ˈ**ritualist** *n.* —ˌ**ritualˈistic** *adj.* —ˌ**ritualˈistically** *adv.*

ritualize *or* **-ise** (ˈrɪtjʊəˌlaɪz) *vb.* **1.** (*intr.*) to engage in ritualism or devise rituals. **2.** (*tr.*) to make (something) into a ritual.

ritzy (ˈrɪtsɪ) *adj.* **ritzier, ritziest.** *Sl.* luxurious or elegant. [C20: after the hotels established by César *Ritz* (1850–1918), Swiss hotelier] —ˈ**ritzily** *adv.* —ˈ**ritziness** *n.*

rival (ˈraɪvᵊl) *n.* **1. a.** a person, organization, team, etc., that competes with another for the same object or in the same field. **b.** (*as modifier*): *rival suitors.* **2.** a person or thing that is considered the equal of another: *she is without rival in the field of physics.* ~*vb.* **-valling, -valled** *or U.S.* **-valing, -valed.** (*tr.*) **3.** to be the equal or near equal of: *an empire that rivalled Rome.* **4.** to try to equal or surpass. [C16: < L *rīvalis,* lit.: one who shares the same brook, < *rīvus* a brook]

rivalry (ˈraɪvəlrɪ) *n., pl.* **-ries.** **1.** the act of rivalling. **2.** the state of being a rival or rivals.

rive (raɪv) *vb.* **riving, rived, rived** *or* **riven** (ˈrɪvᵊn). (*usually passive*) **1.** to split asunder: *a tree riven by lightning.* **2.** to tear apart: *riven to shreds.* [C13: < ON *rīfa*]

river (ˈrɪvə) *n.* **1. a.** a large natural stream of fresh water flowing along a definite course, usually into the sea, being fed by tributary streams. **b.** (*as modifier*): *river traffic.* **c.** (*in combination*): *riverside; riverbed.* Related adj.: **fluvial.** **2.** any abundant stream or flow: *a river of blood.* [C13: < OF, < L *rīpārius* of a river bank, < *rīpa* bank] —ˈ**riverless** *adj.*

riverine (ˈrɪvəˌraɪn) *adj.* **1.** of, like, relating to, or produced by a river. **2.** located or dwelling near a river; riparian.

rivet (ˈrɪvɪt) *n.* **1.** a short metal pin for fastening two or more pieces together, having a head at one end, the other end being hammered flat after being passed through holes in the pieces. ~*vb.* (*tr.*) **2.** to join by riveting. **3.** to hammer in order to form into a head. **4.** (*often passive*) to cause to be fixed, as in fascinated attention, horror, etc.: *to be riveted to the spot.* [C14: < OF, < *river* to fasten, <?] —ˈ**riveter** *n.* —ˈ**riveting** *adj.*

riviera (ˌrɪvɪˈɛərə) *n.* a coastal region reminiscent of the Mediterranean coast of France and N Italy. [C20: < *Riviera,* < It., lit.: shore, ult. < L *ripa* shore]

rivière (ˌrɪvɪˈɛə) *n.* a necklace the diamonds or other precious stones of which gradually increase in size up to a large centre stone. [C19: < F: brook, RIVER]

rivulet (ˈrɪvjʊlɪt) *n.* a small stream. [C16: < It. *rivoletto,* < L *rīvulus,* < *rīvus* stream]

riyal (rɪˈjɑːl) *n.* the standard monetary and currency unit of Saudi Arabia, Yemen, or Dubai. [< Ar. *riyāl,* < Sp. *real*]

RL *abbrev. for* Rugby League.

rly *abbrev. for* railway.

rm *abbrev. for:* **1.** ream. **2.** room.

RM *abbrev. for:* **1.** Royal Mail. **2.** Royal Marines. **3.** (in Canada) Rural Municipality.

RMA *abbrev. for* Royal Military Academy (Sandhurst).

rms *abbrev. for* root mean square.

Rn *the chemical symbol for* radon.

RN *abbrev. for:* **1.** (in Canada) Registered Nurse. **2.** Royal Navy.

RNA *n. Biochem.* ribonucleic acid; any of a group of nucleic acids, present in all living cells, that play an essential role in the synthesis of proteins.

RNAS *abbrev. for:* **1.** Royal Naval Air Service(s). **2.** Royal Naval Air Station.

RNIB (in Britain) *abbrev. for* Royal National Institute for the Blind.

RNLI *abbrev. for* Royal National Lifeboat Institution.

RNZAF *abbrev. for* Royal New Zealand Air Force.

RNZN *abbrev. for* Royal New Zealand Navy.

roach[1] (rəʊtʃ) *n., pl.* **roaches** *or* **roach.** a European freshwater food fish having a deep compressed body and reddish ventral and tail fins. [C14: < OF *roche*, <?]

roach[2] (rəʊtʃ) *n.* **1.** short for **cockroach.** **2.** *Sl.* the butt of a cannabis cigarette.

roach[3] (rəʊtʃ) *n. Naut.* the curve at the foot of a square sail. [C18: <?]

road (rəʊd) *n.* **1. a.** an open way, usually surfaced with tarmac or concrete, providing passage from one place to another. **b.** (*as modifier*): *road traffic; a road sign.* **c.** (*in combination*): *the roadside.* **2. a.** a street. **b.** (*cap. when part of a name*): *London Road.* **3.** *Brit.* one of the tracks of a railway. **4.** a way, path, or course: *the road to fame.* **5.** (*often pl.*) *Naut.* Also called: **roadstead.** a partly sheltered anchorage. **6.** a drift or tunnel in a mine, esp. a level one. **7. hit the road.** *Sl.* to start or resume travelling. **8. one for the road.** *Inf.* a last alcoholic drink before leaving. **9. on the road. a.** travelling about; on tour. **b.** leading a wandering life. **10. take (to) the road.** to begin a journey or tour. [OE *rād;* rel. to *rīdan* to RIDE] —ˈ**roadless** *adj.*

roadblock (ˈrəʊdˌblɒk) *n.* a barrier set up across a road by the police or military, in order to stop a fugitive, inspect traffic, etc.

road-fund licence *n. Brit.* a licence showing that the tax payable in respect of a motor vehicle has been paid. [C20: < the former *road fund* for the maintenance of public highways]

road hog *n. Inf.* a selfish or aggressive driver.

roadholding (ˈrəʊdˌhəʊldɪŋ) *n.* the extent to which a motor vehicle is stable and does not skid, esp. on sharp bends or wet roads.

roadhouse (ˈrəʊdˌhaʊs) *n.* a pub, restaurant, etc., that is situated at the side of a road.

road hump *n.* the official name for **sleeping policeman.**

roadie (ˈrəʊdɪ) *n. Inf.* a person who transports and sets up equipment for a band or group. [C20: shortened < *road manager*]

road metal *n.* crushed rock, broken stone, etc., used to construct a road.

road movie *n.* a genre of film in which the chief character is travelling or on the run, often as it were, in search of, or to escape from, himself.

roadroller (ˈrəʊdˌrəʊlə) *n.* a motor vehicle with heavy rollers for compressing road surfaces during road-making.

road show *n.* **1.** *Radio.* **a.** a live programme, usually with some audience participation, transmitted from a radio van taking a particular show on the road. **b.** the personnel and equipment needed for such a show. **2.** a group of entertainers on tour. **3.** any occasion when an organization attracts publicity while touring or visiting: *the royal road show.*

roadstead (ˈrəʊdˌstɛd) *n. Naut.* another word for **road** (sense 5).

roadster (ˈrəʊdstə) *n.* **1.** *Arch.* an open car, esp. one seating only two. **2.** a kind of bicycle.

road test *n.* **1.** a test to ensure that a vehicle is roadworthy, esp. after repair or servicing, by driving it on roads. **2.** a test of something in actual use. ~*vb.* **road-test.** (*tr.*) **3.** to test (a vehicle, etc.) in this way.

road train *n. Austral.* a truck pulling one or more large trailers, esp. on western roads.

roadway (ˈrəʊdˌweɪ) *n.* **1.** the surface of a road. **2.** the part of a road that is used by vehicles.

roadwork (ˈrəʊdˌwɜːk) *n.* sports training by running along roads.

road works *pl. n.* repairs to a road or cable under a road, esp. when forming a hazard or obstruction to traffic.

roadworthy (ˈrəʊdˌwɜːðɪ) *adj.* (of a motor vehicle) mechanically sound; fit for use on the roads. —ˈ**roadˌworthiness** *n.*

roam (rəʊm) *vb.* **1.** to travel or walk about with no fixed purpose or direction. ~*n.* **2.** the act of roaming. [C13: <?] —ˈ**roamer** *n.*

roan (rəʊn) *adj.* **1.** (of a horse) having a bay (**red roan**), chestnut (**strawberry roan**), or black (**blue roan**) coat sprinkled with white hairs. ~*n.* **2.** a horse having such a coat. **3.** a soft sheepskin leather used in bookbinding, etc. [C16: < OF, < Sp. *roano*, prob. < Gothic *rauths* red]

roar (rɔː) *vb.* (*mainly intr.*) **1.** (of lions and other animals) to utter characteristic loud growling cries. **2.** (*also tr.*) (of people) to utter (something) with a loud deep cry, as in anger or triumph. **3.** to laugh in a loud hearty unrestrained manner. **4.** (of horses) to breathe with laboured rasping sounds. **5.** (of the wind, waves, etc.) to blow or break loudly and violently, as during a storm. **6.** (of a fire) to burn fiercely with a roaring sound. **7.** (*tr.*) to bring (oneself) into a certain condition by roaring: *to roar oneself hoarse.* ~*n.* **8.** a loud deep cry, uttered by a person or crowd, esp. in anger or triumph. **9.** a prolonged loud cry of certain animals, esp. lions. **10.** any similar noise made by a fire, the wind, waves, an engine, etc. [OE *rārian*] —ˈ**roarer** *n.*

roaring (ˈrɔːrɪŋ) *adj.* **1.** *Inf.* very brisk and profitable (esp. in **a roaring trade**). ~*adv.* **2.** noisily or boisterously (esp. in **roaring drunk**). ~*n.* **3.** a loud prolonged cry. —ˈ**roaringly** *adv.*

roast (rəʊst) *vb.* (*mainly tr.*) **1.** to cook (meat or other food) by dry heat, usually with added fat and esp. in an oven. **2.** to brown or dry (coffee, etc.) by exposure to heat. **3.** *Metallurgy.* to heat (an ore) in order to produce a concentrate that is easier to smelt. **4.** to heat (oneself or something) to an extreme degree, as when sunbathing, etc. **5.** (*intr.*) to be excessively and uncomfortably hot. **6.** (*tr.*) *Inf.* to criticize severely. ~*n.* **7.** something that has been roasted, esp. meat. [C13: < OF *rostir*, of Gmc origin] —ˈ**roaster** *n.*

roasting (ˈrəʊstɪŋ) *Inf.* ~*adj.* **1.** extremely hot. ~*n.* **2.** severe criticism.

rob (rɒb) *vb.* **robbing, robbed.** **1.** to take something from (someone) illegally, as by force. **2.** (*tr.*) to plunder (a house, etc.). **3.** (*tr.*) to deprive unjustly: *to be robbed of an opportunity.* [C13: < OF *rober*, of Gmc origin] —ˈ**robber** *n.*

robbery (ˈrɒbərɪ) *n., pl.* **-beries.** **1.** *Criminal law.* the stealing of property from a person by using or threatening to use force. **2.** the act or an instance of robbing.

robe (rəʊb) *n.* **1.** any loose flowing garment, esp. the official vestment of a peer, judge, or academic. **2.** a dressing gown or bathrobe. ~*vb.* **3.** to put a robe, etc., on (oneself or someone else). [C13: < OF; of Gmc origin]

robin (ˈrɒbɪn) *n.* **1.** Also called: **robin redbreast.** a small Old World songbird related to the thrushes. The male has a brown back, orange-red breast and face, and grey underparts. **2.** a North American thrush similar to but larger than the Old World robin. [C16: arbitrary use of given name]

Robin Hood *n.* a legendary English outlaw of the reign of Richard I, who lived in Sherwood Forest and robbed the rich to give to the poor.

robinia (rəˈbɪnɪə) *n.* any tree of the leguminous genus *Robinia*, esp. the locust tree.

roborant (ˈrəʊbərənt, ˈrɒb-) *adj.* **1.** tending to fortify or increase strength. ~*n.* **2.** a drug or agent that increases strength. [C17: < L *roborāre* to strengthen, < *rōbur* an oak]

robot (ˈrəʊbɒt) *n.* **1.** any automated machine programmed to perform specific mechanical functions in the manner of a man. **2.** (*modifier*) automatic: *a robot pilot.* **3.** a person who works or behaves like a machine. **4.** *S. African.* a set of traffic lights. [C20: (used in *R.U.R.*, a play by Karel Čapek (1890-1938), Czech writer) < Czech *robota* work] —**roˈbotic** *adj.* —ˈ**robot-ˌlike** *adj.*

robot bomb *n.* another name for the **V-1.**

robot dancing *or* **robotic dancing** (rəʊˈbɒtɪk) *n.* a dance of the 1980s, characterized by jerky, mechanical movements.

robust (rəʊˈbʌst, ˈrəʊbʌst) *adj.* **1.** strong in constitution. **2.** sturdily built: *a robust shelter.* **3.** requiring or suited to physical strength: *a robust sport.* **4.** (esp. of wines) having a full-bodied flavour. **5.** rough or boisterous. **6.** (of thought, intellect, etc.) straightforward. [C16: < L *rōbustus*, < *rōbur* an oak, strength] —**roˈbustly** *adv.* —**roˈbustness** *n.*

robustious (rəʊˈbʌstʃəs) *adj. Arch.* **1.** rough; boisterous. **2.** strong, robust, or stout. —**roˈbustiously** *adv.* —**roˈbustiousness** *n.*

roc (rɒk) *n.* (in Arabian legend) a bird of enormous size and power. [C16: < Ar., < Persian *rukh*]

ROC *abbrev. for* Royal Observer Corps.

rocaille (rɒˈkaɪ) *n.* decorative rock or shell work, esp. as ornamentation in a rococo fountain, grotto, or interior. [< F, < *roc* ROCK[1]]

rocambole (ˈrɒkəmˌbəʊl) *n.* a variety of alliaceous plant whose garlic-like bulb is used for seasoning. [C17: < F, < G *Rockenbolle,* lit.: distaff bulb (with reference to its shape)]

Rochelle salt (rɒˈʃɛl) *n.* a white crystalline double salt used in Seidlitz powder. [C18: after *La Rochelle* in France]

roche moutonnée (rəʊʃ ˌmuːtəˈneɪ) *n., pl.* **roches moutonnées** (rəʊʃ ˌmuːtəˈneɪz). a rounded mass of rock smoothed and striated by ice that has flowed over it. [C19: F, lit.: fleecy rock, < *mouton* sheep]

rochet (ˈrɒtʃɪt) *n.* a white surplice with tight sleeves, worn by bishops, abbots, and certain other Church dignitaries. [C14: < OF, < *roc* coat, of Gmc origin]

rock[1] (rɒk) *n.* **1.** *Geol.* any aggregate of minerals that makes up part of the earth's crust. It may be unconsolidated, such as a sand, clay, or mud, or consolidated, such as granite, limestone, or coal. **2.** any hard mass of consolidated mineral matter, such as a boulder. **3.** *U.S., Canad., & Austral.* a stone. **4.** a person or thing suggesting a rock, esp. in being dependable, unchanging, or providing firm foundation. **5.** *Brit.* a hard sweet, typically a long brightly coloured peppermint-flavoured stick, sold esp. in holiday resorts. **6.** *Sl.* a jewel, esp. a diamond. **7.** *Sl.* another name for **crack** (sense 28). **8. on the rocks. a.** in a state of ruin or destitution. **b.** (of drinks, esp. whisky) served with ice. [C14: < OF *roche,* <?]

rock[2] (rɒk) *vb.* **1.** to move or cause to move from side to side or backwards and forwards. **2.** to reel or sway or cause (someone) to reel or sway, as with a violent shock or emotion. **3.** (*tr.*) to shake or move (something) violently. **4.** (*intr.*) to dance in the rock-and-roll style. ~*n.* **5.** a rocking motion. **6.** short for **rock and roll. 7.** Also called: **rock music.** any of various styles of pop music having a heavy beat, derived from rock and roll. [OE *roccian*]

Rock (rɒk) *n.* **the.** an informal name for Gibraltar, a promontory at the Western end of the Mediterranean.

rockabilly (ˈrɒkəˌbɪlɪ) *n.* a fast, spare style of White rock music which originated in the mid-1950s in the U.S. South. [C20: < ROCK (AND ROLL) + (HILL)BILLY]

rock and roll *or* **rock'n'roll** *n.* **1. a.** a type of pop music originating in the 1950s as a blend of rhythm and blues and country and western. **b.** (*as modifier*): *the rock-and-roll era.* **2.** dancing performed to such music, with exaggerated body movements stressing the beat. ~*vb.* **3.** (*intr.*) to perform this dance. —**rock and roller** *or* **rock'n'roller** *n.*

rock bass (bæs) *n.* an eastern North American freshwater food fish, related to the sunfish family.

rock bottom *n.* **a.** the lowest possible level. **b.** (*as modifier*): *rock-bottom prices.*

rock-bound *adj.* hemmed in or encircled by rocks. Also (poetic): **rock-girt.**

rock cake *n.* a small cake containing dried fruit and spice, with a rough surface supposed to resemble a rock.

rock crystal *n.* a pure transparent colourless quartz, used in electronic and optical equipment.

rock dove *or* **pigeon** *n.* a common dove from which domestic and feral pigeons are descended.

rocker (ˈrɒkə) *n.* **1.** any of various devices that transmit or operate with a rocking motion. See also **rocker arm. 2.** another word for **rocking chair. 3.** either of two curved supports on the legs of a chair on which it may rock. **4. a.** an ice skate with a curved blade. **b.** the curve itself. **5.** *Brit.* an adherent of a youth movement rooted in the 1950s, characterized by motorcycle trappings. **6. off one's rocker.** *Sl.* crazy.

rocker arm *n.* a lever that rocks about a central pivot, esp. one in an internal-combustion engine that transmits the motion of a pushrod or cam to a valve.

rockery (ˈrɒkərɪ) *n., pl.* **-eries.** a garden constructed with rocks, esp. one where alpine plants are grown.

rocket (ˈrɒkɪt) *n.* **1.** a self-propelling device, esp. a cylinder containing a mixture of solid explosives, used as a firework, distress signal, etc. **2. a.** any vehicle propelled by a rocket engine, esp. one used to carry a spacecraft, etc. **b.** (*as modifier*): *rocket launcher.* **3.** *Brit. & N.Z. inf.* a severe reprimand (esp. in **get a rocket**). ~*vb.* **4.** (*tr.*) to propel (a missile, spacecraft, etc.) by means of a rocket. **5.** (*intr.;* foll. by *off, away,* etc.) to move off at high speed. **6.** (*intr.*) to rise rapidly: *he rocketed to the top.* [C17: < OF, < It. *rochetto,* dim. of *rocca* distaff, of Gmc origin]

rocket engine *n.* a reaction engine in which a fuel and oxidizer are burnt in a combustion chamber, the products of combustion expanding through a nozzle and producing thrust.

rocketry (ˈrɒkɪtrɪ) *n.* the science and technology of the design, operation, maintenance, and launching of rockets.

rockfish (ˈrɒkˌfɪʃ) *n., pl.* **-fish** *or* **-fishes. 1.** any of various fishes that live among rocks, such as the goby, bass, etc. **2.** *Brit.* any of several coarse fishes when used as food, esp. the dogfish or wolffish.

rock garden *n.* a garden featuring rocks or rockeries.

rocking chair *n.* a chair set on curving supports so that the sitter may rock backwards and forwards.

rocking horse *n.* a toy horse mounted on a pair of rockers on which a child can rock to and fro in a seesaw movement.

rocking stone *n.* a boulder so delicately poised that it can be rocked.

rockling (ˈrɒklɪŋ) *n., pl.* **-lings** *or* **-ling.** a small gadoid fish which has an elongated body with barbels around the mouth and occurs mainly in the North Atlantic Ocean. [C17: < ROCK[1] + -LING[1]]

rock lobster *n.* another name for the **spiny lobster.**

rock melon *n. U.S., Austral., & N.Z.* another name for **cantaloupe.**

rock pigeon *n.* another name for **rock dove.**

rock plant *n.* any plant that grows on rocks or in rocky ground.

rock rabbit *n. S. African.* another name for **dassie.** See **hyrax.**

rockrose (ˈrɒkˌrəʊz) *n.* any of various shrubs or herbaceous plants cultivated for their yellow-white or reddish roselike flowers.

rock salmon *n. Brit.* a former term for **rockfish** (sense 2).

rock salt *n.* another name for **halite.**

rock snake *or* **python** *n.* any large Australasian python of the genus *Liasis.*

rock tripe *n. Canad.* any of various edible lichens that grow on rocks and are used in the North as a survival food.

rock wool *n.* another name for **mineral wool.**

rocky[1] (ˈrɒkɪ) *adj.* **rockier, rockiest. 1.** consisting of or abounding in rocks: *a rocky shore.* **2.** unyielding: *rocky determination.* **3.** hard like rock: *rocky muscles.* —ˈ**rockiness** *n.*

rocky[2] (ˈrɒkɪ) *adj.* **rockier, rockiest. 1.** weak or unstable. **2.** *Inf.* (of a person) dizzy; nauseated. —ˈ**rockily** *adv.* —ˈ**rockiness** *n.*

Rocky Mountain spotted fever *n.* an acute rickettsial disease characterized by high fever, chills, pain in muscles and joints, etc. It is caused by the bite of an infected tick.

rococo (rəˈkəʊkəʊ) *n.* (*often cap.*) **1.** a style of architecture and decoration that originated in France in the early 18th century, characterized by elaborate but graceful ornamentation. **2.** an 18th-century style of music characterized by prettiness and extreme use of ornamentation. **3.** any florid or excessively ornamental style. ~*adj.* **4.** denoting, being in, or relating to the rococo. **5.** florid or excessively elaborate. [C19: < F, < ROCAILLE, < *roc* ROCK[1]]

rod (rɒd) *n.* **1.** a slim cylinder of metal, wood, etc. **2.** a switch or bundle of switches used to administer corporal punishment. **3.** any of various staffs of insignia or office. **4.** power, esp. of a tyrannical kind: *a dictator's iron rod.* **5.** a straight slender shoot, stem, or cane of a woody plant. **6.** See **fishing rod. 7.** Also called: **pole, perch. a.** a unit of length equal to 5½ yards. **b.** a unit of square measure equal to 30¼ square yards. **8.** *Surveying.* another name (esp. U.S.) for **staff**[1] (sense 8). **9.** Also called: **retinal rod.** any of the elongated cylindrical cells in the retina of the eye, which are sensitive to dim light but not to colour. **10.** any rod-shaped bacterium. **11.** *U.S.* a slang name for **pistol. 12.** short for **hot rod.** [OE *rodd*] —ˈ**rod**ˌ**like** *adj.*

rode (rəʊd) *vb.* the past tense of **ride.**

rodent (ˈrəʊdᵊnt) *n.* **a.** any of the relatively small placental mammals having constantly growing incisor teeth specialized for gnawing. The group includes rats, mice, squirrels, etc. **b.** (*as modifier*): *rodent characteristics.* [C19: < L *rōdere* to gnaw] —ˈ**rodent-**ˌ**like** *adj.*

rodent ulcer *n.* a slow-growing malignant tumour on the face, usually occurring at the edge of the eyelids, lips, or nostrils.

rodeo (ˈrəʊdɪˌəʊ) *n., pl.* **-deos.** *Chiefly U.S. & Canad.* **1.** a display of the skills of cowboys, including bareback riding. **2.** the rounding up of cattle for branding, etc. **3.** an enclosure for cattle that have been rounded up. [C19: < Sp., < *rodear* to go around, < *rueda* a wheel, < L *rota*]

rodomontade (ˌrɒdəmɒnˈteɪd, -ˈtɑːd) *Literary.* ~*n.* **1. a.** boastful words or behaviour. **b.** (*as modifier*): *rodomontade behaviour.* ~*vb.* **2.** (*intr.*) to boast or rant. [C17: < F, < It. *rodomonte* a boaster, < *Rodomonte,* the name of a braggart king of Algiers in epic poems]

roe[1] (rəʊ) *n.* **1.** Also called: **hard roe.** the ovary of a female fish filled with mature eggs. **2.** Also called: **soft roe.** the testis of a male fish filled with mature sperm. [C15: < MDu. *roge,* < OHG *roga*]

roe[2] (rəʊ) *n., pl.* **roes** *or* **roe.** short for **roe deer.** [OE *rā(ha)*]

roebuck (ˈrəʊˌbʌk) *n., pl.* **-bucks** *or* **-buck.** the male of the roe deer.

roe deer *n.* a small graceful deer of woodlands of Europe and Asia. The antlers are small and the summer coat is reddish-brown.

roentgen *or* **röntgen** (ˈrɒntgən, -tjən, ˈrɛnt-) *n.* a unit of dose of electromagnetic radiation equal to the dose that will produce in air a charge of 0.258 $\times 10^{-3}$ coulomb on all ions of one sign. [C19: after Wilhelm Konrad *Roentgen* (1845-1923), G physicist who discovered x-rays]

roentgen ray *n.* a former name for **x-ray.**

rogation (rəʊˈgeɪʃən) *n.* (*usually pl.*) *Christianity.* a solemn supplication, esp. in a form of ceremony prescribed by the Church. [C14: < L *rogātiō,* < *rogāre* to ask, make supplication]

Rogation Days *pl. n.* April 25 (the **Major Rogation**) and the Monday, Tuesday, and Wednesday before Ascension Day, observed by Christians as days of solemn supplication and marked by processions and special prayers.

roger (ˈrɒdʒə) *interj.* **1.** (used in signalling, telecommunications, etc.) message received and understood. **2.** an expression of agreement. [C20: < the name *Roger,* representing *R* for *received*]

rogue (rəʊg) *n.* **1.** a dishonest or unprincipled person, esp. a man. **2.** *Often jocular.* a mischievous or wayward person, often a child. **3.** any inferior or defective specimen, esp. a defective crop plant. **4.** *Arch.* a vagrant. **5. a.** an animal of vicious character that leads a solitary life. **b.** (*as modifier*): *a rogue elephant.* ~*vb.* **6.** (*tr.*) to rid (a field or crop) of plants that are inferior, diseased, etc. [C16: <?]

roguery (ˈrəʊgərɪ) *n., pl.* **-gueries. 1.** behaviour characteristic of a rogue. **2.** a roguish or mischievous act.

rogues' gallery *n.* a collection of portraits of known criminals kept by the police for identification purposes.

roguish (ˈrəʊgɪʃ) *adj.* **1.** dishonest or unprincipled. **2.** mischievous. —ˈ**roguishly** *adv.*

roil (rɔɪl) *vb.* **1.** (*tr.*) to make (a liquid) cloudy or turbid by stirring up dregs or sediment. **2.** (*intr.*) (esp. of a liquid) to be agitated. **3.** (*intr.*) *Dialect.* to be noisy. **4.** (*tr.*) *Now rare.* another word for **rile** (sense 1). [C16: <?]

roister (ˈrɔɪstə) *vb.* (*intr.*) **1.** to engage in noisy or unrestrained merrymaking. **2.** to brag, bluster, or swagger. [C16: < OF *rustre* lout, < *ruste* uncouth, < L *rusticus* rural] —ˈ**roisterer** *n.* —ˈ**roisterous** *adj.* —ˈ**roisterously** *adv.*

Roland (ˈrəʊlənd) *n.* **1.** the greatest of the legendary 12 peers or paladins (of whom Oliver was another) in attendance on Charlemagne. **2. a Roland for an Oliver.** an effective retort or retaliation.

role *or* **rôle** (rəʊl) *n.* **1.** a part or character in a play, film, etc., to be played by an actor or actress. **2.** *Psychol.* the part played by a person in a particular social setting, influenced by his expectation of what is appropriate. **3.** usual function: *what is his role in the organization?* [C17: < F *rôle* ROLL, an actor's script]

role-playing *n. Psychol.* activity in which a person imitates, consciously or unconsciously, a role uncharacteristic of himself. See also **psychodrama.**

roll (rəʊl) *vb.* **1.** to move or cause to move along by turning over and over. **2.** to move or cause to move along on wheels or rollers. **3.** to flow or cause to flow onwards in an undulating movement. **4.** (*intr.*) (of animals, etc.) to turn onto the back and kick. **5.** (*intr.*) to extend in undulations: *the hills roll down to the sea.* **6.** (*intr.;* usually foll. by *around*) to move or occur in cycles. **7.** (*intr.*) (of a planet, the moon, etc.) to revolve in an orbit. **8.** (*intr.;* foll. by *on, by,* etc.) to pass or elapse: *the years roll by.* **9.** to rotate or cause to rotate wholly or partially: *to roll one's eyes.* **10.** to curl, cause to curl, or admit of being curled, so as to form a ball, tube, or cylinder. **11.** to make or form by shaping into a ball, tube, or cylinder: *to roll a cigarette.* **12.** (often foll. by *out*) to spread or cause to spread out flat or smooth under or as if under a roller: *to roll pastry.* **13.** to emit or utter with a deep prolonged reverberating sound: *the thunder rolled continuously.* **14.** to trill or cause to be trilled: *to roll one's r's.* **15.** (*intr.*) (of a vessel, aircraft, rocket, etc.) to turn from side to side around the longitudinal axis. **16.** to cause (an aircraft) to execute a roll or (of an aircraft) to execute a roll (sense 34). **17.** (*intr.*) to walk with a swaying gait, as when drunk. **18.** *Chiefly U.S.* to throw (dice). **19.** (*intr.*) to operate or begin to operate: *the presses rolled.* **20.** (*intr.*) *Inf.* to make progress: *let the good times roll.* **21.** (*tr.*) *Inf., chiefly U.S. & N.Z.* to rob (a helpless person). ~*n.* **22.** the act or an instance of rolling. **23.** anything rolled up in a cylindrical form: *a roll of newspaper.* **24.** an official list or register, esp. of names: *an electoral roll.* **25.** a rounded mass: *rolls of flesh.* **26.** a cylinder used to flatten something; roller. **27.** a small cake of bread for one person. **28.** a flat pastry or cake rolled up with a meat (**sausage roll**), jam (**jam roll**), or other filling. **29.** a swell or undulation on a surface: *the roll of the hills.* **30.** a swaying, rolling, or unsteady movement or gait. **31.** a deep prolonged reverberating sound: *the roll of thunder.* **32.** a trilling sound; trill. **33.** a very rapid beating of the sticks on a drum. **34.** a flight manoeuvre in which an aircraft makes one complete rotation about its longitudinal axis without loss of height or change in direction. **35.** *Sl.* an act of sexual intercourse or petting (esp. in **a roll in the hay**). **36.** *U.S. sl.* an amount of money, esp. a wad of paper money. **37. strike off the roll(s). a.** to expel from membership. **b.** to debar (a solicitor) from practising, usually because of dishonesty. ~See also **roll in, roll on,** etc. [C14 *rollen*, < OF *roler*, < L *rotulus*, dim. of *rota* a wheel]

rollbar (ˈrəʊlˌbɑː) *n.* a bar that reinforces the frame of a car used for racing, rallying, etc., to protect the driver if the car should turn over.

roll call *n.* the reading aloud of an official list of names, those present responding when their names are read out.

rolled gold *n.* a metal, such as brass, coated with a thin layer of gold. Also (U.S.): **filled gold.**

rolled-steel joist *n.* a steel beam, esp. one with a cross section in the form of a letter *H* or *I*. Abbrev.: **RSJ.**

roller (ˈrəʊlə) *n.* **1.** a cylinder having an absorbent surface and a handle, used for spreading paint. **2.** Also called: **garden roller.** a heavy cast-iron cylinder on an axle to which a handle is attached; used for flattening lawns. **3.** a long heavy wave of the sea, advancing towards the shore. **4.** a hardened cylinder of precision-ground steel that forms one of the rolling components of a roller bearing or of a linked driving chain. **5.** a cylinder fitted on pivots, used to enable heavy objects to be easily moved. **6.** *Printing.* a cylinder, usually of hard rubber, used to ink a plate before impression. **7.** any of various other cylindrical devices that rotate about a cylinder, used for any of various purposes. **8.** a small cylinder onto which a woman's hair may be rolled to make it curl. **9.** *Med.* a bandage consisting of a long strip of muslin rolled tightly into a cylindrical form before application. **10.** any of various Old World birds, such as the **European roller**, that have a blue, green, and brown plumage, a slightly hooked bill, and an erratic flight. **11.** (*often cap.*) a variety of tumbler pigeon. **12.** a person or thing that rolls. **13.** short for **steamroller.**

rollerball (ˈrəʊləˌbɔːl) *n.* a pen having a small moving nylon, plastic, or metal ball as a writing point.

roller bearing *n.* a bearing in which a shaft runs on a number of hardened-steel rollers held within a cage.

roller coaster *n.* another term for **big dipper.**

roller derby *n.* a race on roller skates, esp. one involving aggressive tactics.

roller skate *n.* **1.** a device having straps for fastening to a shoe and four small wheels that enable the wearer to glide swiftly over a floor. ~*vb.* **roller-skate. 2.** (*intr.*) to move on roller skates. —**roller skater** *n.*

roller towel *n.* **1.** a towel with the two ends sewn together, hung on a roller. **2.** a towel wound inside a roller enabling a clean section to be pulled out when needed.

rollick (ˈrɒlɪk) *vb.* **1.** (*intr.*) to behave in a carefree or boisterous manner. ~*n.* **2.** a boisterous or carefree escapade. [C19: Scot. dialect, prob. < ROMP + FROLIC]

rollicking[1] (ˈrɒlɪkɪŋ) *adj.* boisterously carefree. [C19: < ROLLICK]

rollicking[2] (ˈrɒlɪkɪŋ) *n. Brit. inf.* a very severe telling-off. [C20: < ROLLICK (vb.) (in former sense: to be angry, make a fuss); ? infl. by BOLLOCKING]

roll in *vb.* (*mainly intr.*) **1.** (*adv.*) to arrive in abundance or in large numbers. **2.** (*adv.*) *Inf.* to arrive at one's destination. **3. be rolling in.** (*prep.*) *Sl.* to abound or luxuriate in (wealth, money, etc.).

rolling (ˈrəʊlɪŋ) *adj.* **1.** having gentle rising and falling slopes: *rolling country.* **2.** progressing by stages or by occurrences in different places in succession: *a rolling strike.* **3.** subject to regular review and updating: *a rolling plan for overseas development.* **4.** reverberating: *rolling thunder.* **5.** *Sl.* extremely rich. **6.** that may be turned up or down: *a rolling hat brim.* ~*adv.* **7.** *Sl.* swaying or staggering (in **rolling drunk**).

rolling mill *n.* **1.** a mill or factory where ingots of heated metal are passed between rollers to produce sheets or bars of a required cross section and form. **2.** a machine having rollers that may be used for this purpose.

rolling pin *n.* a cylinder with handles at both ends used for rolling dough, pastry, etc., out flat.

rolling stock *n.* the wheeled vehicles collectively used on a railway, including the locomotives, passenger coaches, etc.

rolling stone *n.* a restless or wandering person.

rollmop (ˈrəʊlˌmɒp) *n.* a herring fillet rolled, usually around onion slices, and pickled in spiced vinegar. [C20: < G *Rollmops*, < *rollen* to ROLL + *Mops* pug dog]

rollneck (ˈrəʊlˌnɛk) *adj.* **1.** (of a garment) having a high neck that may be rolled over. ~*n.* **2.** a rollneck sweater or other garment.

roll of honour *n.* a list of those who have died in war for their country.

roll on *vb.* **1.** *Brit.* used to express the wish that an eagerly anticipated event or date will come quickly: *roll on Saturday.* ~*adj.* **roll-on. 2.** (of a deodorant, etc.) dispensed by means of a revolving ball fitted into the neck of the container. ~*n.* **roll-on. 3.** a woman's foundation garment, made of elasticized material and having no fastenings.

roll-on/roll-off *adj.* denoting a cargo ship or ferry designed so that vehicles can be driven straight on and straight off.

roll out *vb.* (*tr., adv.*) **1.** to cause (pastry) to become flatter and thinner by pressure with a rolling pin. **2.** to show (a new type of aircraft) to the public for the first time. **3.** to launch (a new film, product, etc.) in a series of successive waves, as over the whole country. ~*n.* **roll-out. 4.** a presentation to the public of a new aircraft, product, etc.; a launch.

roll over *vb.* (*adv.*) **1.** (*intr.*) to overturn. **2.** (*intr.*) (of an animal, esp. a dog) to lie on its back while kicking its legs in the air. **3.** (*intr.*) to capitulate. **4.** (*tr.*) to continue (a loan, debt, etc.) in force for a further period. ~*n.* **roll-over. 5.** an instance of such continuance of a loan, debt, etc.

roll-top desk *n.* a desk having a slatted wooden panel that can be pulled down over the writing surface when not in use.

roll up *vb.* (*adv.*) **1.** to form or cause to form a cylindrical shape. **2.** (*tr.*) to wrap (an object) round on itself or on an axis: *to roll up a map.* **3.** (*intr.*) *Inf.* to arrive, esp. in a vehicle. **4.** (*intr.*) *Austral.* to assemble; congregate. ~*n.* **roll-up. 5.** *Brit. inf.* a cigarette made by hand from loose tobacco and cigarette papers. **6.** *Austral.* the number attending a meeting, etc.

roly-poly (ˈrəʊlɪˈpəʊlɪ) *adj.* **1.** plump, buxom, or rotund. ~*n., pl.* **-lies. 2.** *Brit.* a strip of suet pastry spread with jam, fruit, or a savoury mixture, rolled up, and baked or steamed. [C17: apparently by reduplication < *roly*, < ROLL]

ROM (rɒm) *n. Computers. acronym for* read only memory: a storage device that holds data permanently and cannot be altered by the programmer.

rom. *Printing. abbrev. for* roman (type).

Rom. *abbrev. for:* **1.** Roman. **2.** Romance (languages). **3.** Romania(n). **4.** *Bible.* Romans.

Romaic (rəʊˈmeɪɪk) *Obs.* ~*n.* **1.** the modern Greek vernacular. ~*adj.* **2.** of or relating to Greek. [C19: < Gk *Rhōmaikos* Roman, with reference to the Eastern Roman Empire]

roman (ˈrəʊmən) *adj.* **1.** of, relating to, or denoting a vertical style of printing type: the usual form of type for most printed matter. Cf. **italic.** ~*n.* **2.** roman type. [C16: so called because the style of letters is that used in ancient Roman inscriptions]

Roman (ˈrəʊmən) *adj.* **1.** of or relating to Rome or its inhabitants in ancient or modern times. **2.** of or relating to Roman Catholicism or the Roman Catholic Church. ~*n.* **3.** a citizen or inhabitant of ancient or modern Rome.

roman à clef *French.* (rɔmɑ̃ a kle) *n., pl.* ***romans à clef*** (rɔmɑ̃ a kle). a novel in which real people are depicted under fictitious names. [lit.: novel with a key]

Roman alphabet *n.* the alphabet evolved by the ancient Romans for the writing of Latin, derived ultimately from the Phoenicians. The alphabet serves for writing most of the languages of W Europe.

Roman candle *n.* a firework that produces a continuous shower of sparks punctuated by coloured balls of fire. [C19: it originated in Italy]

Roman Catholic *adj.* **1.** of or relating to the Roman Catholic Church. ~*n.* **2.** a member of this Church. ~Often shortened to **Catholic.** —**Roman Catholicism** *n.*

Roman Catholic Church *n.* the Christian Church over which the pope presides, with administrative headquarters in the Vatican. Also called: **Catholic Church, Church of Rome.**

romance *n.* (rəˈmæns, ˈrəʊmæns). **1.** a love affair. **2.** love, esp. romantic love idealized for its purity or beauty. **3.** a spirit of or inclination for adventure or mystery. **4.** a mysterious, exciting, sentimental, or nostalgic quality, esp. one associated with a place. **5.** a narrative in verse or prose, written in a vernacular language in the Middle Ages, dealing with adventures of chivalrous heroes. **6.** any similar narrative work dealing with events and characters remote from ordinary life. **7.** a story, novel, film, etc., dealing with love, usually in an idealized or sentimental way. **8.** an extravagant, absurd, or fantastic account. **9.** a lyrical song or short instrumental composition having a simple melody. ~*vb.* (rəˈmæns). **10.** (*intr.*) to tell, invent, or write extravagant or romantic fictions. **11.** (*intr.*) to tell extravagant or improbable lies. **12.** (*intr.*) to have romantic thoughts. **13.** (*intr.*) (of a couple) to indulge in romantic behaviour. **14.** (*tr.*) to be romantically involved with. [C13 *romauns,* < OF *romans,* ult. < L *Rōmānicus* Roman] —**roˈmancer** *n.*

Romance (rəˈmæns, ˈrəʊmæns) *adj.* **1.** denoting, relating to, or belonging to the languages derived from Latin, including Italian, Spanish, Portuguese, French, and Romanian. **2.** denoting a word borrowed from a Romance language. ~*n.* **3.** this group of languages.

Roman Empire *n.* **1.** the territories ruled by ancient Rome. At its height the Roman Empire included W and S Europe, N Africa, and SW Asia. In 395 A.D. it was divided into the **Eastern Roman Empire,** whose capital was Byzantium, and the **Western Roman Empire,** whose capital was Rome. **2.** the government of Rome and its dominions by the emperors from 27 B.C. **3.** the Byzantine Empire. **4.** the Holy Roman Empire.

Romanesque (ˌrəʊməˈnɛsk) *adj.* **1.** denoting or having the style of architecture used in W and S Europe from the 9th to the 12th century, characterized by the rounded arch and massive-masonry wall construction. **2.** denoting a corresponding style in painting, sculpture, etc. [C18: see ROMAN, -ESQUE]

Roman holiday *n.* entertainment or pleasure that depends on the suffering of others. [C19: < Byron's poem *Childe Harold* (IV, 141)]

Romanian (rəʊˈmeɪnɪən) *or* **Rumanian** *n.* **1.** the official language of Romania in SE Europe. **2.** a native, citizen, or inhabitant of Romania. ~*adj.* **3.** relating to, denoting, or characteristic of Romania, its people, or their language.

Romanic (rəʊˈmænɪk) *adj.* another word for **Roman** or **Romance.**

Romanism (ˈrəʊməˌnɪzəm) *n.* Roman Catholicism, esp. when regarded as excessively or superstitiously ritualistic. —ˈ**Romanist** *n.*

Romanize *or* **-nise** (ˈrəʊməˌnaɪz) *vb.* **1.** (*tr.*) to impart a Roman Catholic character to (a ceremony, etc.). **2.** (*intr.*) to be converted to Roman Catholicism. **3.** (*tr.*) to transcribe (a language) into the Roman alphabet. —ˌ**Romaniˈzation** *or* **-niˈsation** *n.*

Roman law *n.* the system of jurisprudence of ancient Rome, codified under Justinian and forming the basis of many modern legal systems.

Roman nose *n.* a nose having a high prominent bridge.

Roman numerals *pl. n.* the letters used by the Romans for the representation of cardinal numbers, still used occasionally today. The integers are represented by the following letters: I (= 1), V (= 5), X (= 10), L (= 50), C (= 100), D (= 500), and M (= 1000). VI = 6 (V + I) but IV = 4 (V - I).

Romansch *or* **Romansh** (rəʊˈmænʃ) *n.* a group of Romance dialects spoken in the Swiss canton of Grisons; an official language of Switzerland since 1938. [C17: < Romansch, lit.: Romance language]

romantic (rəʊˈmæntɪk) *adj.* **1.** of, relating to, imbued with, or characterized by romance. **2.** evoking or given to thoughts and feelings of love, esp. idealized or sentimental love: *a romantic setting.* **3.** impractical, visionary, or idealistic: *a romantic scheme.* **4.** *Often euphemistic.* imaginary or fictitious: *a romantic account of one's war service.* **5.** (*often cap.*) of or relating to a movement in European art, music, and literature in the late 18th and early 19th centuries, characterized by an emphasis on feeling and content rather than order and form. ~*n.* **6.** a person who is romantic, as in being idealistic, amorous, or soulful. **7.** a person whose tastes in art, literature, etc., lie mainly in romanticism. **8.** (*often cap.*) a poet, composer, etc., of the romantic period or whose main inspiration is romanticism. [C17: < F, < obs. *romant* story, romance, < OF *romans* ROMANCE] —**roˈmantically** *adv.*

romanticism (rəʊˈmæntɪˌsɪzəm) *n.* **1.** (*often cap.*) the theory, practice, and style of the romantic art, music, and literature of the late 18th and early 19th centuries, usually opposed to classicism. **2.** romantic attitudes, ideals, or qualities. —**roˈmanticist** *n.*

romanticize *or* **-cise** (rəʊˈmæntɪˌsaɪz) *vb.* **1.** (*intr.*) to think or act in a romantic way. **2.** (*tr.*) to interpret according to romantic precepts. **3.** to make or become romantic, as in style. —**roˌmanticiˈzation** *or* **-ciˈsation** *n.*

Romany *or* **Romani** (ˈrɒmənɪ, ˈrəʊ-) *n.* **1. a.** (*pl.* **-nies** *or* **-nis**) another name for a **Gypsy. b.** (*as modifier*): *Romany customs.* **2.** the language of the Gypsies, belonging to the Indic branch of the Indo-European family. [C19: < Romany *romani* (adj.) Gypsy, ult. < Sansk. *domba* man of a low caste of musicians, of Dravidian origin]

romanza (rəʊˈmænzə) *n.* a short instrumental piece of songlike character. [It.]

romaunt (rəˈmɔːnt) *n. Arch.* a verse romance. [C16: < OF; see ROMANTIC]

Romeo (ˈrəʊmɪəʊ) *n., pl.* **Romeos.** an ardent male lover. [after the hero of Shakespeare's *Romeo and Juliet*]

Romish (ˈrəʊmɪʃ) *adj. Usually derog.* of or resembling Roman Catholic beliefs or practices.

romp (rɒmp) *vb.* (*intr.*) **1.** to play or run about wildly, boisterously, or joyfully. **2. romp home** (*or* **in**). to win a race, etc., easily. ~*n.* **3.** a noisy or boisterous game or prank. **4.** *Arch.* a playful or boisterous child, esp. a girl. **5.** an easy victory. [C18: prob. var. of RAMP, < OF *ramper* to crawl, climb]

rompers (ˈrɒmpəz) *pl. n.* **1.** a one-piece baby garment consisting of trousers and a bib with straps. **2.** *N.Z.* a type of costume worn by schoolgirls for games and gymnastics.

rondavel (ˌrɒnˈdɑːvəl) *n. S. African.* a circular building, often thatched. [<?]

rondeau (ˈrɒndəʊ) *n., pl.* **-deaux** (-dəʊ, -dəʊz). a poem consisting of 13 or 10 lines with two rhymes and having the opening words of the first line used as an unrhymed refrain. [C16: < OF, < *rondel* a little round, < *rond* ROUND]

rondel (ˈrɒndᵊl) *n.* a rondeau consisting of three stanzas of 13 or 14 lines with a two-line refrain appearing twice or three times. [C14: < OF, lit.: a little circle, < *rond* ROUND]

rondo (ˈrɒndəʊ) *n., pl.* **-dos.** a piece of music in which a refrain is repeated between episodes: often constitutes the form of the last movement of a sonata or concerto. [C18: < It., < F RONDEAU]

rone (rəʊn) *or* **ronepipe** *n. Scot.* a drainpipe for carrying rainwater from a roof. [C19: <?]

röntgen (ˈrɒntgən, -tjən, ˈrɛnt-) *n.* a variant spelling of **roentgen.**

roo (ruː) *n. Austral. inf.* a kangaroo.

rood (ruːd) *n.* **1. a.** a crucifix, esp. one set on a beam or screen at the entrance to the chancel of a church. **b.** (*as modifier*): *rood screen.* **2.** the Cross on which Christ was crucified. **3.** a unit of area equal to one quarter of an acre or 0.10117 hectare. **4.** a unit of area equal to one square rod. [OE *rōd*]

roof (ruːf) *n., pl.* **roofs** (ruːfs, ruːvz). **1. a.** a structure that covers or forms the top of a building. **b.** (*in combination*): *the rooftop.* **c.** (*as modifier*): *a roof garden.* **2.** the top covering of a vehicle, oven, or other structure: *the roof of a car.* **3.** *Anat.* any structure that covers an organ or part: *the roof of the mouth.* **4.** a highest or topmost point or part: *Mount Everest is the roof of the world.* **5.** a house or other shelter: *a poor man's roof.* **6. hit** (*or* **raise** *or* **go through**) **the roof.** *Inf.* to get extremely angry. ~*vb.* **7.** (*tr.*) to provide or cover with a roof or rooflike part. [OE *hrōf*] —ˈ**roofer** *n.* —ˈ**roofless** *adj.*

roof garden *n.* a garden on a flat roof of a building.

roofing (ˈruːfɪŋ) *n.* **1.** material used to construct a roof. **2.** the act of constructing a roof.

roof rack *n.* a rack attached to the roof of a motor vehicle for carrying luggage, skis, etc.

rooftree (ˈruːfˌtriː) *n.* another name for **ridge-pole.**

rooibos (ˈrɔɪˌbɒs, ˈrʊɪˌbɒs) *n.* any of various South African trees with red leaves. [< Afrik. *rooi* red + *bos* bush]

rooibos tea *n. S. African.* a tealike drink made from the leaves of the rooibos.

rooikat (ˈrɔɪˌkæt, ˈrʊɪˌkæt) *n.* a South African lynx. [< Afrik. *rooi* red + *kat* cat]

rooinek (ˈrɔɪˌnɛk, ˈrʊɪˌnɛk) *n. S. African.* a facetious name for an **Englishman.** [C19: Afrik., lit.: red neck]

rook[1] (rʊk) *n.* **1.** a large Eurasian passerine bird, with a black plumage and a whitish base to its bill. **2.** *Sl.* a swindler or cheat, esp. one who cheats at cards. ~*vb.* **3.** (*tr.*) *Sl.* to overcharge, swindle, or cheat. [OE *hrōc*]

rook[2] (rʊk) *n.* a chesspiece that may move any number of unoccupied squares in a straight line, horizontally or vertically. Also called: **castle.** [C14: < OF *rok,* ult. < Ar. *rukhkh*]

rookery (ˈrʊkərɪ) *n., pl.* **-eries. 1.** a group of nesting rooks. **2.** a clump of trees containing rooks' nests. **3. a.** a breeding ground or communal living area of certain other birds or mammals, esp. penguins or seals. **b.** a colony of any such creatures. **4.** *Arch.* an overcrowded slum.

rookie (ˈrʊkɪ) *n. Inf.* a newcomer, esp. a raw recruit in the army. [C20: changed < RECRUIT]

room (ruːm, rʊm) *n.* **1.** space or extent, esp. unoccupied or unobstructed space for a particular purpose: *is there room to pass?* **2.** an area within a building enclosed by a floor, a ceiling, and walls or partitions. **3.** (*functioning as sing. or pl.*) the people present in a room: *the whole room was laughing.* **4.** (foll. by *for*) opportunity or scope: *room for manoeuvre.* **5.** (*pl.*) a part of a house, hotel, etc., that is rented out as separate accommodation: *living in dingy rooms in Dalry.* ~*vb.* **6.** (*intr.*) to occupy or share a room or lodging: *where does he room?* [OE *rūm*] —ˈ**roomer** *n.*

roomful (ˈruːmˌfʊl, ˈrʊm-) *n., pl.* **-fuls.** a number or quantity sufficient to fill a room: *a roomful of furniture.*

rooming house *n. U.S. & Canad.* a house having self-contained furnished rooms or flats for renting.

roommate (ˈruːmˌmeɪt, ˈrʊm-) *n.* a person with whom one shares a room or lodging.

room service *n.* service in a hotel providing meals, drinks, etc., in guests' rooms.

roomy (ˈruːmɪ, ˈrʊmɪ) *adj.* **roomier, roomiest.** spacious. —ˈ**roomily** *adv.* —ˈ**roominess** *n.*

roost (ruːst) *n.* **1.** a place, perch, branch, etc., where birds, esp. domestic fowl, rest or sleep. **2.** a temporary place to rest or stay. ~*vb.* **3.** (*intr.*) to rest or sleep on a roost. **4.** (*intr.*) to settle down or stay. **5. come home to roost.** to have unfavourable repercussions. [OE *hrōst*]

Roost (ruːst) *n.* **the.** a powerful current caused by conflicting tides around the Shetland and Orkney Islands. [C16: < ON *röst*]

rooster (ˈruːstə) *n. Chiefly U.S. & Canad.* the male of the domestic fowl; a cock.

root[1] (ruːt) *n.* **1. a.** the organ of a higher plant that anchors the rest of the plant in the ground and absorbs water and mineral salts from the soil. **b.** (loosely) any of the branches of such an organ. **2.** any plant part, such as a tuber, that is similar to a root in function or appearance. **3. a.** the essential part or nature of something: *your analysis strikes at the root of the problem.* **b.** (*as modifier*): *the root cause of the problem.* **4.** *Anat.* the embedded portion of a tooth, nail, hair, etc. **5.** origin or derivation. **6.** (*pl.*) a person's sense of belonging in a community, place, etc., esp. the one in which he was born or brought up. **7.** *Bible.* a descendant. **8.** *Linguistics.* the form of a word that remains after removal of all affixes. **9.** *Maths.* a quantity that when multiplied by itself a certain number of times equals a given quantity: *3 is a cube root of 27.* **10.** Also called: **solution.** *Maths.* a number that when substituted for the variable satisfies a given equation. **11.** *Music.* (in harmony) the note forming the foundation of a chord. **12.** *Austral. & N.Z. sl.* sexual intercourse. **13. root and branch.** (*adv.*) entirely; utterly. ~Related adj.: **radical.** ~*vb.* **14.** (*intr.*) Also: **take root.** to establish a root and begin to grow. **15.** (*intr.*) Also: **take root.** to become established, embedded, or effective. **16.** (*tr.*) to embed with or as if with a root or roots. **17.** *Austral. & N.Z. sl.* to have sexual intercourse (with). ~See also **root out, roots.** [OE *rōt,* < ON] —ˈ**rooter** *n.* —ˈ**root**ˌ**like** *adj.* —ˈ**rooty** *adj.* —ˈ**rootiness** *n.*

root[2] (ruːt) *vb.* (*intr.*) **1.** (of a pig) to burrow in or dig up the earth in search of food, using the snout. **2.** (foll. by *about, around, in,* etc.) *Inf.* to search vigorously but unsystematically. [C16: changed (through infl. of ROOT[1]) < earlier *wroot,* < OE *wrōtan;* rel. to OE *wrōt* snout] —ˈ**rooter** *n.*

root[3] (ruːt) *vb.* (*intr.;* usually foll. by *for*) *Inf.* to give support to (a contestant, team, etc.), as by cheering. [C19: ? var. of Scot. *rout* to make a loud noise, < ON *rauta* to roar]

root beer *n. U.S. & Canad.* an effervescent drink made from extracts of various roots and herbs.

root canal *n.* the passage in the root of a tooth through which its nerves and blood vessels enter the pulp cavity.

root climber *n.* any of various climbing plants, such as the ivy, that adhere to a supporting structure by means of small roots growing from the side of the stem.

root crop *n.* a crop, as of turnips or beets, cultivated for the food value of its roots.

rooted (ˈruːtɪd) *adj.* **1.** having roots. **2.** deeply felt: *rooted objections.*

root hair *n.* any of the hollow hairlike outgrowths of the outer cells of a root, just behind the tip, that absorb water and salts from the soil.

rootle (ˈruːtᵊl) *vb.* (*intr.*) *Brit.* another word for **root**[2].

rootless (ˈruːtlɪs) *adj.* having no roots, esp. (of a person) having no ties with a particular place.

rootlet (ˈruːtlɪt) *n.* a small root.

root mean square *n.* the square root of the average of the squares of a set of numbers or quantities: *the root mean square of* 1, 2, *and* 4 *is* $\sqrt{[(1^2 + 2^2 + 4^2)/3]} = \sqrt{7}$. Abbrev.: **rms.**

root nodule *n.* a swelling on the root of a leguminous plant, such as clover, that contains bacteria capable of nitrogen fixation.

root out *vb.* (*tr., adv.*) to remove or eliminate completely: *we must root out inefficiency.*

roots (ruːts) *adj.* (of popular music) going back to the origins of a style, esp. in being genuine and unpretentious: *roots rock.*

rootstock (ˈruːtˌstɒk) *n.* **1.** another name for **rhizome.** **2.** another name for **stock** (sense 7). **3.** *Biol.* a basic structure from which offshoots have developed.

ropable *or* **ropeable** (ˈrəʊpəbᵊl) *adj.* **1.** capable of being roped. **2.** *Austral. & N.Z. inf.* **a.** angry. **b.** wild or intractable: *a ropable beast.*

rope (rəʊp) *n.* **1. a.** a fairly thick cord made of intertwined hemp or other fibres or of wire or other strong material. **b.** (*as modifier*): *a rope ladder.* **2.** a row of objects fastened to form a line: *a rope of pearls.* **3.** a quantity of material wound in the form of a cord. **4.** a filament or strand, esp. of something viscous or glutinous: *a rope of slime.* **5. give (someone) enough** (*or* **plenty of**) **rope to hang himself.** to allow (someone) to accomplish his own downfall by his own foolish acts. **6. know the ropes.** to have a thorough understanding of a particular sphere of activity. **7. on the ropes. a.** *Boxing.* driven against the ropes enclosing the ring by an opponent's attack. **b.** in a hopeless position. **8. the rope. a.** a rope halter used for hanging. **b.** death by hanging. ~*vb.* **9.** (*tr.*) to bind or fasten with or as if with a rope. **10.** (*tr.; usually foll. by off*) to enclose or divide by means of a rope. **11.** (when *intr.*, foll. by *up*) *Mountaineering.* to tie (climbers) together with a rope. [OE *rāp*]

rope in *vb.* (*tr., adv.*) **1.** *Brit.* to persuade to take part in some activity. **2.** *U.S. & Canad.* to trick or entice into some activity.

rope's end *n.* a short piece of rope, esp. as formerly used for flogging sailors.

ropewalk (ˈrəʊpˌwɔːk) *n.* a long narrow usually covered path or shed where ropes are made.

ropy *or* **ropey** (ˈrəʊpɪ) *adj.* **ropier, ropiest. 1.** *Brit. inf.* **a.** inferior. **b.** slightly unwell. **2.** (of a viscous or sticky substance) forming strands. **3.** resembling a rope. —ˈ**ropily** *adv.* —ˈ**ropiness** *n.*

Roquefort (ˈrɒkfɔː) *n.* a blue-veined cheese with a strong flavour, made from ewe's and goat's milk. [C19: after *Roquefort*, village in S France]

roquet (ˈrəʊkɪ) *Croquet.* ~*vb.* **-queting** (-kɪɪŋ), **-queted** (-kɪd). **1.** to drive one's ball against (another person's ball) in order to be allowed to croquet. ~*n.* **2.** the act of roqueting. [C19: var. of CROQUET]

ro-ro (ˈrəʊrəʊ) *adj. acronym for* roll-on/roll-off.

rorqual (ˈrɔːkwəl) *n.* any of several whalebone whales that have a dorsal fin and a series of grooves along the throat and chest. Also called: **finback.** [C19: < F, < Norwegian *rörhval*, < ON *reytharhvalr*, < *reythr* (< *rauthr* red) + *hvalr* whale]

Rorschach test (ˈrɔːʃɑːk) *n. Psychol.* a personality test consisting of a number of unstructured inkblots presented for interpretation. [C20: after Hermann *Rorschach* (1884–1922), Swiss psychiatrist]

rort (rɔːt) *n. Austral. sl.* **1.** a rowdy party or celebration. **2.** a fraud; deception. [C20: back formation < E dialect *rorty* (in the sense: good, splendid)] —ˈ**rorty** *adj.*

rosace (ˈrəʊzeɪs) *n.* **1.** another name for **rose window. 2.** another name for **rosette.** [C19: < F, < L *rosāceus* ROSACEOUS]

rosaceous (rəʊˈzeɪʃəs) *adj.* **1.** of or belonging to the Rosaceae, a family of plants typically having white, yellow, pink, or red five-petalled flowers. The family includes the rose, strawberry, blackberry, and many fruit trees. **2.** like a rose, esp., rose-coloured. [C18: < L *rosāceus* composed of roses, < *rosa* ROSE[1]]

rosarian (rəʊˈzɛərɪən) *n.* a person who cultivates roses, esp. professionally.

rosarium (rəʊˈzɛərɪəm) *n., pl.* **-sariums** *or* **-saria** (-ˈzɛərɪə). a rose garden. [C19: NL]

rosary (ˈrəʊzərɪ) *n., pl.* **-saries. 1.** *R.C. Church.* **a.** a series of prayers counted on a string of beads, usually five or 15 decades of Aves, each decade beginning with a Paternoster and ending with a Gloria. **b.** a string of 55 or 165 beads used to count these prayers as they are recited. **2.** (in other religions) a similar string of beads used in praying. **3.** an archaic word for a **garland** (of flowers, etc.). [C14: < L *rosārium* rose garden, < *rosārius* of roses, < *rosa* ROSE[1]]

rose[1] (rəʊz) *n.* **1. a.** a shrub or climbing plant having prickly stems, compound leaves, and fragrant flowers. **b.** (*in combination*): *rosebush.* **2.** the flower of any of these plants. **3.** any of various similar plants, such as the Christmas rose. **4. a.** a purplish-pink colour. **b.** (*as adj.*): *rose paint.* **5.** a rose, or a representation of one, as the national emblem of England. **6. a.** a cut for a gemstone, having a hemispherical faceted crown and a flat base. **b.** a gem so cut. **7.** a perforated cap fitted to a watering can or hose, causing the water to issue in a spray. **8.** a design or decoration shaped like a rose; rosette. **9.** *History.* See **red rose, white rose. 10. bed of roses.** a situation of comfort or ease. **11. under the rose.** in secret; privately; sub rosa. ~*vb.* **12.** (*tr.*) to make rose-coloured; cause to blush or redden. [OE, < L *rosa*, prob. < Gk *rhodon* rose] —ˈ**roseˌlike** *adj.*

rose[2] (rəʊz) *vb.* the past tense of **rise.**

rosé (ˈrəʊzeɪ) *n.* any pink wine, made either by removing the skins of red grapes after only a little colour has been extracted or by mixing red and white wines. [C19: < F, lit.: pink, < L *rosa* ROSE[1]]

roseate (ˈrəʊzɪˌeɪt) *adj.* **1.** of the colour rose or pink. **2.** excessively or idealistically optimistic.

rosebay (ˈrəʊzˌbeɪ) *n.* **1.** any of several rhododendrons. **2. rosebay willowherb.** a perennial plant that has spikes of deep pink flowers and is widespread in N temperate regions. **3.** another name for **oleander.**

rosebud (ˈrəʊzˌbʌd) *n.* **1.** the bud of a rose. **2.** *Literary.* a pretty young woman.

rose campion *n.* a European plant widely cultivated for its pink flowers. Its stems and leaves are covered with white woolly down. Also called: **dusty miller.**

rose chafer *or* **beetle** *n.* a British beetle that has a greenish-golden body with a metallic lustre and feeds on plants.

rose-coloured *adj.* **1.** of the colour rose; rosy. **2.** excessively optimistic. **3. see through rose-coloured glasses** (*or* **spectacles**). to view in an excessively optimistic light.

rose-cut *adj.* (of a gemstone) cut with a hemispherical faceted crown and a flat base.

rosehip (ˈrəʊzˌhɪp) *n.* the berry-like fruit of a rose plant.

rosella (rəʊˈzɛlə) *n.* any of various Australian parrots. [C19: prob. alteration of *Rose-hiller*, after *Rose Hill*, Parramatta, near Sydney]

rosemary (ˈrəʊzmərɪ) *n., pl.* **-maries.** an aromatic European shrub widely cultivated for its grey-green evergreen leaves, which are used in cookery and in the manufacture of perfumes. It is the traditional flower of remembrance. [C15: earlier *rosmarine*, < L *rōs* dew + *marīnus* marine; modern form infl. by folk etymology, as if ROSE[1] + *Mary*]

rose of Sharon (ˈʃærən) *n.* a creeping shrub native to SE Europe but widely cultivated, having large yellow flowers. Also called: **Aaron's beard.**

roseola (rəʊˈziːələ) *n. Pathol.* **1.** any red skin rash. **2.** another name for **rubeola.** [C19: < NL, dim. of L *roseus* rosy] —**roˈseolar** *adj.*

rosery (ˈrəʊzərɪ) *n., pl.* **-series.** a bed or garden of roses.

Rosetta stone (rəʊˈzɛtə) *n.* a basalt slab discovered in 1799 at Rosetta, N Egypt, dating to the reign of Ptolemy V (196 B.C.) and carved with parallel inscriptions in hieroglyphics, Egyptian demotic, and Greek, which provided the key to the decipherment of ancient Egyptian texts.

rosette (rəʊˈzɛt) *n.* **1.** a decoration resembling a rose, esp. an arrangement of ribbons in a rose-shaped design worn as a badge or presented as a prize. **2.** another name for **rose window. 3.** *Bot.* a circular cluster of leaves growing from the base of a stem. [C18: < OF: a little ROSE[1]]

rose-water *n.* **1.** scented water made by the distillation of rose petals or by impregnation with oil of roses. **2.** (*modifier*) elegant or delicate, esp. excessively so.

rose window *n.* a circular window, esp. one that has ornamental tracery radiating from the centre to form a symmetrical roselike pattern. Also called: **wheel window, rosette.**

rosewood (ˈrəʊzˌwʊd) *n.* the hard dark wood of any of various tropical trees. It has a roselike scent and is used in cabinetwork.

Rosh Hashanah *or* **Rosh Hashana** (ˈrɒʃ həˈʃɑːnə; *Hebrew* ˈrɔʃ haʃaˈna) *n.* the Jewish New Year festival, celebrated on the first and second of Tishri. [< Heb., lit.: beginning of the year, < *rōsh* head + *hash-shānāh* year]

Rosicrucian (ˌrəʊzɪˈkruːʃən) *n.* **1.** a member of a society professing esoteric religious doctrines, venerating the rose and Cross as symbols of Christ's Resurrection and Redemption, and claiming various occult powers. ~*adj.* **2.** of or designating the Rosicrucians or Rosicrucianism. [C17: < L *Rosae Crucis* Rose of the Cross, translation of the G name Christian *Rosenkreuz,* supposed founder of the society]

rosin (ˈrɒzɪn) *n.* **1.** Also called: **colophony.** a translucent brittle amber substance produced in the distillation of crude turpentine oleoresin and used esp. in making varnishes, printing inks, and sealing waxes and for treating the bows of stringed instruments. **2.** another name for **resin** (sense 1). ~*vb.* **3.** (*tr.*) to treat or coat with rosin. [C14: var. of RESIN] —ˈ**rosiny** *adj.*

ROSPA (ˈrɒspə) *n.* (in Britain) *acronym for* Royal Society for the Prevention of Accidents.

roster (ˈrɒstə) *n.* **1.** a list or register, esp. one showing the order of people enrolled for duty. ~*vb.* **2.** (*tr.*) to place on a roster. [C18: < Du. *rooster* grating or list (the lined paper looking like a grid)]

rostrum (ˈrɒstrəm) *n., pl.* **-trums** *or* **-tra** (-trə). **1.** any platform on which public speakers stand to address an audience. **2.** a platform in front of an orchestra on which the conductor stands. **3.** another word for **ram** (sense 5). **4.** the prow of an ancient Roman ship. **5.** *Biol., zool.* a beak or beaklike part. [C16: < L *rōstrum* beak, ship's prow, < *rōdere* to nibble, gnaw; in pl., *rōstra* orator's platform, because this platform in the Roman forum was adorned with the prows of captured ships] —ˈ**rostral** *adj.*

rosy (ˈrəʊzɪ) *adj.* **rosier, rosiest. 1.** of the colour rose or pink. **2.** having a healthy pink complexion: *rosy cheeks.* **3.** optimistic, esp. excessively so: *a rosy view of social improvements.* **4.** resembling or abounding in roses. —ˈ**rosily** *adv.* —ˈ**rosiness** *n.*

rot (rɒt) *vb.* **rotting, rotted. 1.** to decay or cause to decay as a result of bacterial or fungal action. **2.** (*intr.;* usually foll. by *off* or *away*) to crumble (off) or break (away), as from decay or long use. **3.** (*intr.*) to become weak or depressed through inertia, confinement, etc.; languish: *rotting in prison.* **4.** to become or cause to become morally degenerate. ~*n.* **5.** the process of rotting or the state of being rotten. **6.** something decomposed. Related adj.: **putrid. 7.** short for **dry rot. 8.** *Pathol.* any putrefactive decomposition of tissues. **9.** a condition in plants characterized by decay of tissues, caused by bacteria, fungi, etc. **10.** *Vet. science.* a contagious fungal disease of sheep. **11.** (*also interj.*) nonsense; rubbish. [OE *rotian* (vb.); rel. to ON, *rotna;* C13 (n.), < ON]

rota (ˈrəʊtə) *n. Chiefly Brit.* a register of names showing the order in which people take their turn to perform certain duties. [C17: < L: a wheel]

Rota (ˈrəʊtə) *n. R.C. Church.* the supreme ecclesiastical tribunal.

rotary (ˈrəʊtərɪ) *adj.* **1.** operating by rotation. **2.** turning; revolving. ~*n., pl.* **-ries. 3.** a part of a machine that rotates about an axis. **4.** *U.S. & Canad.* another term for **roundabout** (sense 2). [C18: < Med. L *rotārius,* < L *rota* wheel]

Rotary Club *n.* any of the local clubs that form **Rotary International,** an international association of professional and business men founded in the U.S. in 1905 to promote community service. —**Rotarian** (rəʊˈtɛərɪən) *n., adj.*

rotary engine *n.* **1.** an internal-combustion engine having radial cylinders that rotate about a fixed crankshaft. **2.** an engine, such as a turbine or wankel engine, in which power is transmitted directly to rotating components.

rotary plough *or* **tiller** *n.* an implement with a series of blades mounted on a power-driven shaft which rotates so as to break up soil.

rotary press *n.* a machine for printing from a revolving cylindrical forme, usually onto a continuous strip of paper.

rotary table *n.* a chain or gear-driven unit, mounted in the derrick floor which rotates the drill pipe and bit.

rotate *vb.* (rəʊˈteɪt). **1.** to turn or cause to turn around an axis; revolve or spin. **2.** to follow or cause to follow a set sequence. **3.** to replace (one set of personnel) with another. ~*adj.* (ˈrəʊteɪt). **4.** *Bot.* designating a corolla the petals of which radiate like the spokes of a wheel. —**roˈtatable** *adj.*

rotation (rəʊˈteɪʃən) *n.* **1.** the act of rotating; rotary motion. **2.** a regular cycle of events in a set order or sequence. **3.** a planned sequence of cropping according to which the crops grown in successive seasons on the same land are varied so as to make a balanced demand on its resources of fertility. **4.** the spinning motion of a body, such as a planet, about an internal axis. **5.** *Maths.* **a.** a circular motion of a configuration about a given point, without a change in shape. **b.** a transformation in which the coordinate axes are rotated by a fixed angle about the origin. —**roˈtational** *adj.*

rotator (rəʊˈteɪtə) *n.* **1.** a person, device, or part that rotates or causes rotation. **2.** *Anat.* any of various muscles that revolve a part on its axis.

rotatory (ˈrəʊtətərɪ, -trɪ) *or* (*less commonly*) **rotative** *adj.* of, possessing, or causing rotation. —ˈ**rotatorily** *adv.*

rote (rəʊt) *n.* **1.** a habitual or mechanical routine or procedure. **2. by rote.** by repetition; by heart (often in **learn by rote**). [C14: <?]

rotenone (ˈrəʊtɪˌnəʊn) *n.* a white odourless crystalline substance extracted from the roots of derris: a powerful insecticide. [C20: < Japanese *rōten* derris + -ONE]

rotgut (ˈrɒtˌgʌt) *n. Facetious sl.* alcoholic drink, esp. spirits, of inferior quality.

rotifer (ˈrəʊtɪfə) *n.* a minute aquatic multicellular invertebrate having a ciliated wheel-like organ used in feeding and locomotion: common constituents of freshwater plankton. Also called: **wheel animalcule.** [C18: < NL *Rotifera,* < L *rota* wheel + *ferre* to bear] —**rotiferal** (rəʊˈtɪfərəl) *or* **roˈtiferous** *adj.*

rotisserie (rəʊˈtɪsərɪ) *n.* **1.** a rotating spit on which meat, poultry, etc., can be cooked. **2.** a shop or restaurant where meat is roasted to order. [C19: < F, < OF *rostir* to ROAST]

rotogravure (ˌrəʊtəʊgrəˈvjʊə) *n.* **1.** a printing process using cylinders with many small holes, from which ink is transferred to a moving web of paper, etc., in a rotary press. **2.** printed material produced in this way, esp. magazines. [C20: < L *rota* wheel + GRAVURE]

rotor (ˈrəʊtə) *n.* **1.** the rotating member of a machine or device, such as the revolving arm of the distributor of an internal-combustion engine. **2.** a rotating device having radiating blades projecting from a hub which produces thrust to lift and propel a helicopter. [C20: shortened form of ROTATOR]

Rotovator (ˈrəʊtəˌveɪtə) *n. Trademark.* a mechanical cultivator with rotary blades. [C20: *Rotavator* < ROTA(RY) + (CULTI)VATOR] —ˈ**Rotoˌvate** *vb.* (*tr.*)

rotten (ˈrɒtᵊn) *adj.* **1.** decomposing, decaying, or putrid. **2.** breaking up, esp. through age or hard use: *rotten ironwork.* **3.** morally corrupt. **4.** disloyal or treacherous. **5.** *Inf.* unpleasant: *rotten weather.* **6.** *Inf.* unsatisfactory or poor: *rotten workmanship.* **7.** *Inf.* miserably unwell. **8.** *Inf.* distressed and embarrassed: *I felt rotten breaking the bad news to him.* [C13: < ON *rottin;* rel. to OE *rotian* to ROT] —ˈ**rottenly** *adv.* —ˈ**rottenness** *n.*

rotten borough *n.* (before the Reform Act of 1832) any of certain English parliamentary constituencies with few or no electors.

rottenstone (ˈrɒtᵊnˌstəʊn) *n.* a much-weathered

limestone, rich in silica: used in powdered form for polishing metal.

rotter ('rɒtə) *n. Sl., chiefly Brit.* a worthless, unpleasant, or despicable person.

rotund (rəʊ'tʌnd) *adj.* **1.** rounded or spherical in shape. **2.** plump. **3.** sonorous or grandiloquent. [C18: < L *rotundus* round, < *rota* wheel] —**ro'tundity** *n.* —**ro'tundly** *adv.*

rotunda (rəʊ'tʌndə) *n.* a circular building or room, esp. one that has a dome. [C17: < It. *rotonda,* < L *rotundus* round, < *rota* a wheel]

rouble *or* **ruble** ('ru:bᵊl) *n.* the standard monetary unit of the Soviet Union. [C16: < Russian *rubl* silver bar, < ORussian *rublĭ* bar, block of wood, < *rubiti* to cut up]

roué ('ru:eɪ) *n.* a debauched or lecherous man; rake. [C19: < F, lit.: one broken on the wheel; with reference to the fate deserved by a debauchee]

rouge (ru:ʒ) *n.* **1.** a red powder or cream, used as a cosmetic for adding redness to the cheeks. **2.** short for **jeweller's rouge.** ~*vb.* **3.** (*tr.*) to apply rouge to. [C18: F: red, < L *rubeus*]

rouge et noir ('ru:ʒ eɪ 'nwɑ:) *n.* a card game in which the players put their stakes on any of two red and two black diamond-shaped spots marked on the table. [F, lit.: red and black]

rough (rʌf) *adj.* **1.** (of a surface) not smooth; uneven or irregular. **2.** (of ground) covered with scrub, boulders, etc. **3.** denoting or taking place on uncultivated ground: *rough grazing.* **4.** shaggy or hairy. **5.** turbulent: *a rough sea.* **6.** (of performance or motion) uneven; irregular: *a rough engine.* **7.** (of behaviour or character) rude, coarse, or violent. **8.** harsh or sharp: *rough words.* **9.** *Inf.* severe or unpleasant: *a rough lesson.* **10.** (of work, etc.) requiring physical rather than mental effort. **11.** *Inf.* ill: *he felt rough after an evening of heavy drinking.* **12.** unfair: *rough luck.* **13.** harsh or grating to the ear. **14.** without refinement, luxury, etc. **15.** not perfected in any detail; rudimentary: *rough workmanship; rough justice.* **16.** not prepared or dressed: *rough gemstones.* **17.** (of a guess, etc.) approximate. **18.** having the sound of *h;* aspirated. **19. rough on.** *Inf., chiefly Brit.* **a.** severe towards. **b.** unfortunate for (a person). **20. the rough side of one's tongue.** harsh words; a rebuke. ~*n.* **21.** rough ground. **22.** a sketch or preliminary piece of artwork. **23.** unfinished or crude state (esp. in **in the rough**). **24. the rough.** *Golf.* the part of the course bordering the fairways where the grass is untrimmed. **25.** *Inf.* a violent person; thug. **26.** the unpleasant side of something (esp. in **take the rough with the smooth**). ~*adv.* **27.** roughly. **28. sleep rough.** to spend the night in the open; be without shelter. ~*vb.* (*tr.*) **29.** to make rough; roughen. **30.** (foll. by *out, in,* etc.) to prepare (a sketch, report, etc.) in preliminary form. **31. rough it.** *Inf.* to live without the usual comforts of life. ~See also **rough up.** [OE *rūh*] —'**roughly** *adv.* —'**roughness** *n.*

roughage ('rʌfɪdʒ) *n.* **1.** the coarse indigestible constituents of food, which provide bulk to the diet and aid digestion. **2.** any rough material.

rough-and-ready *adj.* **1.** crude, unpolished, or hastily prepared, but sufficient for the purpose. **2.** (of a person) without formality or refinement.

rough-and-tumble *n.* **1.** a fight or scuffle without rules. ~*adj.* **2.** characterized by disorderliness and disregard for rules.

rough breathing *n.* (in Greek) the sign (ʽ) placed over an initial vowel, indicating that (in ancient Greek) it was pronounced with an *h.*

roughcast ('rʌf,kɑ:st) *n.* **1.** a coarse plaster used to cover the surface of an external wall. **2.** any rough or preliminary form, model, etc. ~*adj.* **3.** covered with roughcast. ~*vb.* **-casting, -cast. 4.** to apply roughcast to (a wall, etc.). **5.** to prepare in rough. —'**rough,caster** *n.*

rough-cut *n.* a first basic edited version of a film with the scenes in sequence and the soundtrack synchronized.

rough diamond *n.* **1.** an unpolished diamond. **2.** an intrinsically trustworthy or good person with uncouth manners or dress.

rough-dry *adj.* **1.** (of clothes or linen) dried ready for pressing. ~*vb.* **-drying, -dried. 2.** (*tr.*) to dry (clothes, etc.) without ironing them.

roughen ('rʌfᵊn) *vb.* to make or become rough.

rough-hew *vb.* **-hewing, -hewed; -hewed** *or* **-hewn.** (*tr.*) to cut or shape roughly without finishing the surface.

roughhouse ('rʌf,haʊs) *n. Sl.* rough, disorderly, or noisy behaviour.

roughish ('rʌfɪʃ) *adj.* somewhat rough.

roughneck ('rʌf,nɛk) *n. Sl.* **1.** a rough or violent person; thug. **2.** a worker in an oil-drilling operation.

rough puff pastry *n.* a rich flaky pastry.

roughrider ('rʌf,raɪdə) *n.* a rider of wild or unbroken horses.

roughshod ('rʌf,ʃɒd) *adj.* **1.** (of a horse) shod with rough-bottomed shoes to prevent sliding. ~*adv.* **2. ride roughshod over.** to domineer over or act with complete disregard for.

rough stuff *n. Inf.* violence.

rough trade *n. Sl.* (in homosexual use) a tough or violent sexual partner, esp. one casually picked up.

rough up *vb.* (*tr., adv.*) **1.** *Inf.* to treat violently; beat up. **2.** to cause (feathers, hair, etc.) to stand up by rubbing against the grain.

roulade (ru:'lɑ:d) *n.* **1.** something cooked in the shape of a roll, esp. a slice of meat. **2.** an elaborate run in vocal music. [C18: < F, lit.: a rolling, < *rouler* to ROLL]

roulette (ru:'lɛt) *n.* **1.** a gambling game in which a ball is dropped onto a spinning horizontal wheel divided into numbered slots, with players betting on the slot into which the ball will fall. **2.** a toothed wheel for making a line of perforations. **3.** a curve generated by a point on one curve rolling on another. ~*vb.* (*tr.*) **4.** to use a roulette on (something), as in engraving, making stationery, etc. [C18: < F, < *rouelle,* dim. of *roue* a wheel, < L *rota*]

round (raʊnd) *adj.* **1.** having a flat circular shape, as a hoop. **2.** having the shape of a ball. **3.** curved; not angular. **4.** involving or using circular motion. **5.** (*prenominal*) complete: *a round dozen.* **6.** *Maths.* **a.** forming or expressed by a whole number, with no fraction. **b.** expressed to the nearest ten, hundred, or thousand: *in round figures.* **7.** (of a sum of money) considerable. **8.** fully depicted or developed, as a character in a book. **9.** full and plump: *round cheeks.* **10.** (of sound) full and sonorous. **11.** (of pace) brisk; lively. **12.** (*prenominal*) (of speech) candid; unmodified: *a round assertion.* **13.** (of a vowel) pronounced with rounded lips. ~*n.* **14.** a round shape or object. **15. in the round. a.** in full detail. **b.** *Theatre.* with the audience all round the stage. **16.** a session, as of a negotiation: *a round of talks.* **17.** a series: *a giddy round of parties.* **18. the daily round.** the usual activities of one's day. **19.** a stage of a competition: *he was eliminated in the first round.* **20.** (*often pl.*) a series of calls: *a milkman's round.* **21.** a playing of all the holes on a golf course. **22.** a single turn of play by each player, as in a card game. **23.** one of a number of periods in a boxing, wrestling, or other match. **24.** a single discharge by a gun. **25.** a bullet or other charge of ammunition. **26.** a number of drinks bought at one time for a group of people. **27.** a single slice of bread. **28.** a general outburst of applause, etc. **29.** movement in a circle. **30.** *Music.* a part song in which the voices follow each other at equal intervals at the same pitch. **31.** a sequence of bells rung in order of treble to tenor. **32.** a cut of beef from the thigh. **33. go** *or* **make the rounds. a.** to go from place to place, as in making social calls. **b.** (of information, rumour, etc.) to be passed around, so as to be generally known. ~*prep.* **34.** surrounding, encircling, or enclosing: *a band round her head.* **35.** on all or most sides of: *to look round one.* **36.** on or outside the circumference or perimeter of. **37.** from place to place in: *driving round Ireland.* **38.**

reached by making a partial circuit about: *the shop round the corner.* **39.** revolving round (a centre or axis): *the earth's motion round its axis.* ~*adv.* **40.** on all or most sides. **41.** on or outside the circumference or perimeter: *the racing track is two miles round.* **42.** to all members of a group: *pass the food round.* **43.** in rotation or revolution: *the wheels turn round.* **44.** by a circuitous route: *the road to the farm goes round by the pond.* **45.** to a specific place: *she came round to see me.* **46. all year round.** throughout the year. ~*vb.* **47.** to make or become round. **48.** (*tr.*) to encircle; surround. **49.** to move or cause to move with turning motion: *to round a bend.* **50.** (*tr.*) **a.** to pronounce (a speech sound) with rounded lips. **b.** to purse (the lips). ~See also **round down, round off,** etc. [C13: < OF *ront,* < L *rotundus* round, < *rota* a wheel] —ˈ**roundish** *adj.* —ˈ**roundness** *n.*

▷ **Usage.** See at **around.**

roundabout (ˈraʊndəˌbaʊt) *n.* **1.** *Brit.* a revolving circular platform provided with wooden animals, seats, etc., on which people ride for amusement; merry-go-round. **2.** a road junction in which traffic streams circulate around a central island. U.S. and Canad. name: **traffic circle.** ~*adj.* **3.** indirect; devious. ~*adv., prep.* **round about. 4.** on all sides: *spectators standing round about.* **5.** approximately: *at round about 5 o'clock.*

round dance *n.* **1.** a dance in which the dancers form a circle. **2.** a ballroom dance, such as the waltz, in which couples revolve.

round down *vb.* (*tr., adv.*) to lower (a number) to the nearest whole number or ten, hundred, or thousand below it.

rounded (ˈraʊndɪd) *adj.* **1.** round or curved. **2.** mature or complete. **3.** (of the lips) pursed. **4.** (of a speech sound) articulated with rounded lips.

roundel (ˈraʊndᵊl) *n.* **1.** a form of rondeau consisting of three stanzas each of three lines with a refrain after the first and the third. **2.** a circular identifying mark in national colours on military aircraft. **3.** a small circular window, medallion, etc. **4.** a round plate of armour used to protect the armpit. **5.** another word for **roundelay.** [C13: < OF *rondel;* see RONDEL]

roundelay (ˈraʊndɪˌleɪ) *n.* **1.** Also called: **roundel.** a slow medieval dance performed in a circle. **2.** a song in which a line or phrase is repeated as a refrain. [C16: < OF *rondelet* a little rondel, < *rondel;* also infl. by LAY[4]]

rounders (ˈraʊndəz) *n.* (*functioning as sing.*) *Brit.* a ball game in which players run between posts after hitting the ball, scoring a **rounder** if they run round all four before the ball is retrieved.

Roundhead (ˈraʊndˌhɛd) *n. English history.* a supporter of Parliament against Charles I during the Civil War. [referring to their short-cut hair]

roundhouse (ˈraʊndˌhaʊs) *n.* **1.** *U.S.* a building in which railway locomotives are serviced, radial tracks being fed by a central turntable. **2.** *U.S. boxing sl.* a swinging punch or style of punching. **3.** an obsolete word for **jail.** **4.** *Obs.* a cabin on the quarterdeck of a sailing ship.

rounding (ˈraʊndɪŋ) *n. Computers.* a process in which a number is approximated as the closest number that can be expressed using the number of bits or digits available.

roundly (ˈraʊndlɪ) *adv.* **1.** frankly, bluntly, or thoroughly: *to be roundly criticized.* **2.** in a round manner or so as to be round.

round off *vb.* (*tr., adv.*) **1.** (often foll. by *with*) to complete, esp. agreeably: *we rounded off the evening with a brandy.* **2.** to make less jagged.

round on *vb.* (*intr., prep.*) to attack or reply to (someone) with sudden irritation or anger.

round robin *n.* **1.** a petition or protest having the signatures in a circle to disguise the order of signing. **2.** a tournament in which each player plays against every other player.

round-shouldered *adj.* denoting a faulty posture characterized by drooping shoulders and a slight forward bending of the back.

roundsman (ˈraʊndzmən) *n., pl.* **-men. 1.** *Brit.* a person who makes rounds, as for inspection or to deliver goods. **2.** *Austral. & N.Z.* a reporter covering a particular district or topic.

round table *n.* **a.** a meeting of parties or people on equal terms for discussion. **b.** (*as modifier*): *a round-table conference.*

Round Table *n.* **the. 1.** (in Arthurian legend) the table of King Arthur, shaped so that his knights could sit around it without any having precedence. **2.** Arthur and his knights collectively. **3.** one of an organization of clubs of young business and professional men who meet in order to further charitable work.

round-the-clock *adj.* (*or as adv.* **round the clock**) throughout the day and night.

round trip *n.* a trip to a place and back again, esp. returning by a different route.

round up *vb.* (*tr., adv.*) **1.** to gather together: *to round ponies up.* **2.** to raise (a number) to the nearest whole number or ten, hundred, or thousand above it. ~*n.* **roundup. 3.** the act of gathering together livestock, esp. cattle, so that they may be branded, counted, or sold. **4.** any similar act of bringing together: *a roundup of today's news.*

roundworm (ˈraʊndˌwɜːm) *n.* a nematode worm that is a common intestinal parasite of man and pigs.

roup (raʊp) *Scot. & N English dialect.* ~*vb.* (*tr.*) **1.** to sell by auction. ~*n.* **2.** an auction. [C16 (orig.: to shout): of Scand. origin]

rouse (raʊz) *vb.* **1.** to bring (oneself or another person) out of sleep, etc., or (of a person) to come to consciousness in this way. **2.** (*tr.*) to provoke: *to rouse someone's anger.* **3. rouse oneself.** to become energetic. **4.** to start or cause to start from cover: *to rouse game birds.* **5.** (*intr.;* foll. by *on*) *Austral.* to scold or rebuke. [C15 (in sense of hawks ruffling their feathers): <?] —ˈ**rouser** *n.*

rouseabout (ˈraʊzəˌbaʊt) *n.* **1.** *Austral. & N.Z.* an unskilled labourer in a shearing shed. **2.** a variant of **roustabout** (sense 1).

rousing (ˈraʊzɪŋ) *adj.* tending to excite; lively or vigorous: *a rousing chorus.* —ˈ**rousingly** *adv.*

roust (raʊst) *vb.* (*tr.;* often foll. by *out*) to rout or stir, as out of bed. [C17: ? < ROUSE]

roustabout (ˈraʊstəˌbaʊt) *n.* **1.** an unskilled labourer on an oil rig. **2.** *Austral. & N.Z.* a variant of **rouseabout** (sense 1).

rout[1] (raʊt) *n.* **1.** an overwhelming defeat. **2.** a disorderly retreat. **3.** a noisy rabble. **4.** *Law.* a group of three or more people proceeding to commit an illegal act. **5.** *Arch.* a large party or social gathering. ~*vb.* **6.** (*tr.*) to defeat and cause to flee in confusion. [C13: < Anglo-Norman *rute,* < OF: disorderly band, < L *ruptus,* < *rumpere* to burst]

rout[2] (raʊt) *vb.* **1.** to dig over or turn up (something), esp. (of an animal) with the snout; root. **2.** (*tr.;* usually foll. by *out* or *up*) to find by searching. **3.** (*tr.;* usually foll. by *out*) to drive out: *they routed him out of bed at midnight.* **4.** (*tr.;* often foll. by *out*) to hollow or gouge out. **5.** (*intr.*) to search, poke, or rummage. [C16: var. of ROOT[2]]

route (ruːt) *n.* **1.** the choice of roads taken to get to a place. **2.** a regular journey travelled. ~*vb.* (*tr.*) **3.** to plan the route of; send by a particular route. [C13: < OF *rute,* < Vulgar L *rupta via* (unattested), lit.: a broken (established) way, < L *ruptus,* < *rumpere* to break]

▷ **Usage.** When forming the present participle or verbal noun from the verb *to route* it is preferable to retain the *e* in order to distinguish the word from *routing,* the present participle or verbal noun from *rout*[1], to defeat or *rout*[2], to dig, rummage: *the routeing of buses from the city centre to the suburbs.* The spelling *routing* in this sense is, however, sometimes encountered, esp. in American English.

routemarch (ˈruːtˌmɑːtʃ) *n.* **1.** *Mil.* a long training march. **2.** *Inf.* any long exhausting walk.

router (ˈraʊtə) *n.* any of various tools or machines for hollowing out, cutting grooves, etc.

routine (ruːˈtiːn) *n.* **1.** a usual or regular method of procedure, esp. one that is unvarying. **2.** *Computers.* a program or part of a program performing a specific function: *an input routine.* **3.** a set sequence of dance steps. **4.** *Inf.* a hackneyed or insincere speech. ~*adj.* **5.** relating to or characteristic of routine. [C17: < OF, < *route* a customary way, ROUTE] —**rou'tinely** *adv.*

roux (ruː) *n.* a mixture of equal amounts of fat and flour, heated, blended, and used as a basis for sauces. [F: brownish, < L *russus* RUSSET]

rove[1] (rəʊv) *vb.* **1.** to wander about (a place) with no fixed direction; roam. **2.** (*intr.*) (of the eyes) to look around; wander. ~*n.* **3.** the act of roving. [C15 *roven* (in archery) to shoot at a target chosen at random (C16: to wander, stray), < ON]

rove[2] (rəʊv) *vb.* **1.** (*tr.*) to pull out and twist (fibres of wool, cotton, etc.) lightly, as before spinning. ~*n.* **2.** wool, cotton, etc., thus prepared. [C18: < ?]

rove[3] (rəʊv) *vb.* a past tense and past participle of **reeve**[2].

rover[1] ('rəʊvə) *n.* **1.** a person who roves. **2.** *Archery.* a mark selected at random for use as a target. **3.** *Australian Rules football.* a player without a fixed position who, with the ruckmen, forms the ruck. [C15: < ROVE[1]]

rover[2] ('rəʊvə) *n.* a pirate or pirate ship. [C14: prob. < MDu. or MLow G, < *roven* to rob]

Rover *or* **Rover Scout** ('rəʊvə) *n. Brit.* the former name for **Venture Scout.**

roving commission *n.* authority or power given in a general area, without precisely defined terms of reference.

row[1] (rəʊ) *n.* **1.** an arrangement of persons or things in a line: *a row of chairs.* **2.** *Chiefly Brit.* a street, esp. a narrow one lined with identical houses. **3.** a line of seats, as in a cinema, theatre, etc. **4.** *Maths.* a horizontal linear arrangement of numbers, quantities, or terms. **5.** a horizontal rank of squares on a chessboard or draughtboard. **6. a hard row to hoe.** a difficult task or assignment. **7. in a row.** in succession; one after the other: *he won two gold medals in a row.* [OE *rāw, rǣw*]

row[2] (rəʊ) *vb.* **1.** to propel (a boat) by using oars. **2.** (*tr.*) to carry (people, goods, etc.) in a rowing boat. **3.** to be propelled by means of (oars or oarsmen). **4.** (*intr.*) to take part in the racing of rowing boats as a sport. **5.** (*tr.*) to race against in a boat propelled by oars: *Oxford row Cambridge every year.* ~*n.* **6.** an act, instance, period, or distance of rowing. **7.** an excursion in a rowing boat. [OE *rōwan*] —'**rower** *n.*

row[3] (raʊ) *n.* **1.** a noisy quarrel. **2.** a noisy disturbance: *we couldn't hear the music for the row next door.* **3.** a reprimand. ~*vb.* **4.** (*intr.*; often foll. by *with*) to quarrel noisily. **5.** (*tr.*) *Arch.* to reprimand. [C18: < ?]

rowan ('rəʊən, 'raʊ-) *n.* another name for the (European) **mountain ash.** [C16: of Scand. origin]

rowdy ('raʊdɪ) *adj.* **-dier, -diest.** **1.** tending to create noisy disturbances; rough, loud, or disorderly: *a rowdy gang of football supporters.* ~*n., pl.* **-dies.** **2.** a person who behaves in such a fashion. [C19: orig. U.S. sl., ? rel. to ROW[3]] —'**rowdily** *adv.* —'**rowdiness** *or* '**rowdyism** *n.*

rowel ('raʊəl) *n.* **1.** a small spiked wheel attached to a spur. **2.** *Vet. science.* a piece of leather inserted under the skin of a horse to cause a discharge. ~*vb.* **-elling, -elled** *or U.S.* **-eling, -eled.** (*tr.*) **3.** to goad (a horse) using a rowel. **4.** *Vet. science.* to insert a rowel in (the skin of a horse) to cause a discharge. [C14: < OF *roel* a little wheel, < *roe* a wheel, < L *rota*]

rowing boat ('rəʊɪŋ) *n. Chiefly Brit.* a small pleasure boat propelled by one or more pairs of oars. Usual U.S. and Canad. word: **rowboat.**

rowing machine ('rəʊɪŋ) *n.* a device with oars and a sliding seat, resembling a sculling boat, used to provide exercise.

rowlock ('rɒlək) *n.* a swivelling device attached to the gunwale of a boat that holds an oar in place. Usual U.S. and Canad. word: **oarlock.**

royal ('rɔɪəl) *adj.* **1.** of, relating to, or befitting a king, queen, or other monarch; regal. **2.** (*prenominal; often cap.*) established by, chartered by, under the patronage of, or in the service of royalty: *the Royal Society of St George.* **3.** being a member of a royal family. **4.** above the usual or normal in standing, size, quality, etc. **5.** *Inf.* unusually good or impressive; first-rate. **6.** *Naut.* just above the topgallant (in **royal mast**). ~*n.* **7.** (*sometimes cap.*) a member of a royal family. **8.** Also: **royal stag.** a stag with antlers having 12 or more branches. **9.** *Naut.* a sail set next above the topgallant, on a royal mast. **10.** a size of printing paper, 20 by 25 inches. [C14: < OF *roial,* < L *rēgālis* fit for a king, < *rēx* king; cf. REGAL] —'**royally** *adv.*

Royal Air Force *n.* the air force of Great Britain. Abbrev.: **RAF.**

royal assent *n. Brit.* the formal signing of an act of Parliament by the sovereign, by which it becomes law.

royal blue *n.* **a.** a deep blue colour. **b.** (*as adj.*): *a royal-blue carpet.*

Royal Commission *n.* (in Britain) a body set up by the monarch on the recommendation of the prime minister to gather information about the operation of existing laws or to investigate any social, educational, or other matter.

royal fern *n.* a fern of damp regions, having large fronds up to 2 metres (7 feet) in height.

royal flush *n. Poker.* a hand made up of the five top honours of a suit.

royalist ('rɔɪəlɪst) *n.* **1.** a supporter of a monarch or monarchy, esp. during the English Civil War. **2.** *Inf.* an extreme reactionary: *an economic royalist.* ~*adj.* **3.** of or relating to royalists. —'**royalism** *n.*

royal jelly *n.* a substance secreted by the pharyngeal glands of worker bees and fed to all larvae when very young and to larvae destined to become queens throughout their development.

Royal Marines *pl. n. Brit.* a corps of soldiers specially trained in amphibious warfare.

Royal Navy *n.* the navy of Great Britain. Abbrev.: **RN.**

royal palm *n.* any of several palm trees of tropical America, having a tall trunk with a tuft of feathery pinnate leaves.

royal standard *n.* a flag bearing the arms of the British sovereign, flown only when she or he is present.

royal tennis *n.* another name for **real tennis.**

royalty ('rɔɪəltɪ) *n., pl.* **-ties.** **1.** the rank, power, or position of a king or queen. **2. a.** royal persons collectively. **b.** a person who belongs to a royal family. **3.** any quality characteristic of a monarch. **4.** a percentage of the revenue from the sale of a book, performance of a theatrical work, use of a patented invention or of land, etc., paid to the author, inventor, or proprietor.

royal warrant *n.* an authorization to a tradesman to supply goods to a royal household.

rozzer ('rɒzə) *n. Sl.* a policeman. [C19: < ?]

RPI (in Britain) *abbrev. for* retail price index.

rpm *abbrev. for:* **1.** resale price maintenance. **2.** revolutions per minute.

RR *abbrev. for:* **1.** Right Reverend. **2.** *Canad. & U.S.* rural route.

-rrhagia *n. combining form.* (in pathology) an abnormal discharge: *menorrhagia.* [< Gk *-rrhagia* a bursting forth, < *rhēgnunai* to burst]

-rrhoea *or esp. U.S.* **-rrhea** *n. combining form.* (in pathology) a flow: *diarrhoea.* [< NL, < Gk *-rrhoia,* < *rhein* to flow]

r-RNA *abbrev. for* ribosomal RNA.

Rs *symbol for* rupees.

RS (in Britain) *abbrev. for* Royal Society.

RSA *abbrev. for:* **1.** Republic of South Africa. **2.** (in New Zealand) Returned Services Association. **3.** Royal Scottish Academician. **4.** Royal Scottish Academy. **5.** Royal Society of Arts.

RSFSR *abbrev. for* Russian Soviet Federative Socialist Republic.

RSL (in Australia) *abbrev. for* Returned Services League.

RSM *abbrev. for:* **1.** regimental sergeant major. **2.** Royal School of Music. **3.** Royal Society of Medicine.

RSNZ *abbrev. for* Royal Society of New Zealand.
RSPB (in Britain) *abbrev. for* Royal Society for the Protection of Birds.
RSPCA (in Britain) *abbrev. for* Royal Society for the Prevention of Cruelty to Animals.
RSV *abbrev. for* Revised Standard Version (of the Bible).
RSVP *abbrev. for* répondez s'il vous plaît. [F: please reply]
rt *abbrev. for* right.
RTE *abbrev. for* Radio Telefis Éireann. [Irish Gaelic: Irish Radio and Television]
Rt Hon. *abbrev. for* Right Honourable.
Ru *the chemical symbol for* ruthenium.
RU *abbrev. for* Rugby Union.
rub (rʌb) *vb.* **rubbing, rubbed.** 1. to apply pressure and friction to (something) with a backward and forward motion. 2. to move (something) with pressure along, over, or against (a surface). 3. to chafe or fray. 4. (*tr.*) to bring into a certain condition by rubbing: *rub it clean.* 5. (*tr.*) to spread with pressure, esp. in order to cause to be absorbed: *she rubbed ointment into his back.* 6. (*tr.*) to mix (fat) into flour with the fingertips, as in making pastry. 7. (foll. by *off, out, away,* etc.) to remove or be removed by rubbing: *the mark would not rub off the chair.* 8. (*intr.*) *Bowls.* (of a bowl) to be slowed or deflected by an uneven patch on the green. 9. (*tr.*; often foll. by *together*) to move against each other with pressure and friction (esp. in **rub one's hands,** often a sign of glee, keen anticipation, or satisfaction, and **rub noses,** a greeting among Eskimos). 10. **rub (up) the wrong way.** to arouse anger in; annoy. ~*n.* 11. the act of rubbing. 12. (preceded by *the*) an obstacle or difficulty (esp. in **there's the rub**). 13. something that hurts the feelings or annoys; cut; rebuke. 14. *Bowls.* an uneven patch in the green. ~See also **rub along, rub down,** etc. [C15: ? < Low G *rubben,* <?]
rub along *vb.* (*intr., adv.*) *Brit.* 1. to continue in spite of difficulties. 2. to maintain an amicable relationship; not quarrel.
rubato (ruːˈbɑːtəʊ) *Music.* ~*n., pl.* **-tos.** 1. flexibility of tempo in performance. ~*adj., adv.* 2. to be played with a flexible tempo. [C19: < It. *tempo rubato,* lit.: stolen time, < *rubare* to ROB]
rubber[1] (ˈrʌbə) *n.* 1. Also called: **India rubber, gum elastic, caoutchouc.** a cream to dark brown elastic material obtained by coagulating and drying the latex from certain plants, esp. the rubber tree. 2. any of a large variety of elastomers produced from natural rubber or by synthetic means. 3. *Chiefly Brit.* a piece of rubber used for erasing something written; eraser. 4. a cloth, pad, etc., used for polishing. 5. a person who rubs something in order to smooth, polish, or massage. 6. (*often pl.*) *Chiefly U.S. & Canad.* a rubberized waterproof overshoe. 7. *Sl.* a condom. 8. (*modifier*) made of or producing rubber: a *rubber ball; a rubber factory.* [C17: < RUB + -ER[1]; the tree was so named because its product was used for rubbing out writing] —ˈ**rubbery** *adj.*
rubber[2] (ˈrʌbə) *n.* 1. *Bridge, whist, etc.* **a.** a match of three games. **b.** the deal that wins such a match. 2. a series of matches or games in any of various sports. [C16: <?]
rubber band *n.* a continuous loop of thin rubber, used to hold papers, etc., together. Also called: **elastic band.**
rubber cement *n.* any of a number of adhesives made by dissolving rubber in a solvent such as benzene.
rubberize *or* **-ise** (ˈrʌbəˌraɪz) *vb.* (*tr.*) to coat or impregnate with rubber.
rubberneck (ˈrʌbəˌnɛk) *Sl.* ~*n.* 1. a person who stares or gapes inquisitively. 2. a sightseer or tourist. ~*vb.* 3. (*intr.*) to stare in a naive or foolish manner.
rubber plant *n.* 1. a plant with glossy leathery leaves that grows as a tall tree in India and Malaya but is cultivated as a house plant in Europe and North America. 2. any of several tropical trees, the sap of which yields crude rubber.
rubber stamp *n.* 1. a device used for imprinting dates, etc., on forms, invoices, etc. 2. automatic authorization of a payment, proposal, etc. 3. a person who makes such automatic authorizations; a cipher or person of little account. ~*vb.* **rubber-stamp.** (*tr.*) 4. to imprint (forms, invoices, etc.) with a rubber stamp. 5. *Inf.* to approve automatically.
rubber tree *n.* a tropical American tree cultivated throughout the tropics, esp. in Malaya, for the latex of its stem, which is the major source of commercial rubber.
rubbing (ˈrʌbɪŋ) *n.* an impression taken of an incised or raised surface by laying paper over it and rubbing with wax, graphite, etc.
rubbish (ˈrʌbɪʃ) *n.* 1. worthless, useless, or unwanted matter. 2. discarded or waste matter; refuse. 3. foolish words or speech; nonsense. ~*vb.* 4. (*tr.*) *Inf.* to criticize; attack verbally. [C14 *robys,* <?] —ˈ**rubbishy** *adj.*
rubble (ˈrʌbᵊl) *n.* 1. fragments of broken stones, bricks, etc. 2. debris from ruined buildings. 3. Also called: **rubblework.** masonry constructed of broken pieces of rock, stone, etc. [C14 *robyl;* ? rel. to RUBBISH, or to ME *rubben* to rub] —ˈ**rubbly** *adj.*
rub down *vb.* (*adv.*) 1. to dry or clean (a horse, athlete, oneself, etc.) vigorously, esp. after exercise. 2. to make or become smooth by rubbing. 3. (*tr.*) to prepare (a surface) for painting by rubbing it with sandpaper. ~*n.* **rubdown.** 4. the act of rubbing down.
rube (ruːb) *n. U.S. sl.* an unsophisticated countryman. [C20: prob. < the name *Reuben*]
rubella (ruːˈbɛlə) *n.* a mild contagious viral disease, somewhat similar to measles, characterized by cough, sore throat, and skin rash. Also called: **German measles.** [C19: < NL, < L *rubellus* reddish, < *rubeus* red]
rubellite (ˈruːbɪˌlaɪt, ruːˈbɛl-) *n.* a red transparent variety of tourmaline, used as a gemstone. [C18: < L *rubellus* reddish]
rubeola (ruːˈbiːələ) *n.* the technical name for **measles.** [C17: < NL, < L *rubeus* reddish]
Rubicon (ˈruːbɪkən) *n.* 1. a stream in N Italy: in ancient times the boundary between Italy and Cisalpine Gaul. By leading his army across it and marching on Rome in 49 B.C., Julius Caesar committed himself to civil war with the senatorial party. 2. (*sometimes not cap.*) a point of no return. 3. a penalty in piquet by which the score of a player who fails to reach 100 points in six hands is added to his opponent's. 4. **cross** (*or* **pass**) **the Rubicon.** to commit oneself irrevocably to some course of action.
rubicund (ˈruːbɪkənd) *adj.* of a reddish colour; ruddy; rosy. [C16: < L *rubicundus,* < *rubēre* to be ruddy, < *ruber* red] —**rubicundity** (ˌruːbɪˈkʌndɪtɪ) *n.*
rubidium (ruːˈbɪdɪəm) *n.* a soft highly reactive radioactive element of the alkali metal group. It is used in electronic valves, photocells, and special glass. Symbol: Rb; atomic no.: 37; atomic wt.: 85.47; half-life of ^{87}Rb: 5×10^{11} years. [C19: < NL, < L *rubidus* dark red, with reference to the two red lines in its spectrum] —**ruˈbidic** *adj.*
rubidium-strontium dating *n.* a technique for determining the age of minerals based on the occurrence in natural rubidium of a fixed amount of the radioisotope ^{87}Rb which decays to the stable strontium isotope ^{87}Sr with a half-life of 5×10^{11} years.
rubiginous (ruːˈbɪdʒɪnəs) *adj.* rust-coloured. [C17: < L *rūbīginōsus,* < *rūbīgō* rust, < *ruber* red]
rub in *vb.* (*tr., adv.*) 1. to spread with pressure, esp. in order to cause to be absorbed. 2. **rub it in.** *Inf.* to harp on something distasteful to a person.
ruble (ˈruːbᵊl) *n.* a variant spelling of **rouble.**
rub off *vb.* 1. to remove or be removed by rubbing. 2. (*intr.*; often foll. by *on* or *onto*) to have an effect through close association or contact: *her crude manners have rubbed off on you.*
rub out *vb.* (*tr., adv.*) 1. to remove or be removed with a rubber. 2. *U.S. sl.* to murder.
rubric (ˈruːbrɪk) *n.* 1. a title, heading, or initial

letter in a book, manuscript, or section of a legal code, esp. one printed or painted in red ink or in some similarly distinguishing manner. **2.** a set of rules of conduct or procedure. **3.** a set of directions for the conduct of Christian church services, often printed in red in a prayer book or missal. [C15 *rubrike* red ochre, red lettering, < L *rubrīca* (*terra*) red (earth), ruddle, < *ruber* red] —ˈ**rubrical** *adj.* —ˈ**rubrically** *adv.*

ruby (ˈruːbɪ) *n., pl.* **-bies. 1.** a deep red transparent precious variety of corundum: used as a gemstone, in lasers, and for bearings and rollers in watchmaking. **2. a.** the deep-red colour of a ruby. **b.** (*as adj.*): *ruby lips.* **3. a.** something resembling, made of, or containing a ruby. **b.** (*as modifier*): *a ruby necklace.* **4.** (*modifier*) denoting a fortieth anniversary: *our ruby wedding.* [C14: < OF *rubi,* < L *rubeus,* < *ruber* red]

RUC *abbrev. for* Royal Ulster Constabulary.

ruche (ruːʃ) *n.* a strip of pleated or frilled lawn, lace, etc., used to decorate blouses, dresses, etc. [C19: < F, lit.: beehive, < Med. L *rūsca* bark of a tree, of Celtic origin]

ruching (ˈruːʃɪŋ) *n.* **1.** material used for a ruche. **2.** a ruche or ruches collectively.

ruck[1] (rʌk) *n.* **1.** a large number or quantity; mass, esp. of undistinguished people or things. **2.** (in a race) a group of competitors who are well behind the leaders. **3.** *Rugby.* a loose scrum that forms around the ball when it is on the ground. **4.** *Australian Rules football.* the three players who do not have fixed positions but follow the ball closely. ~*vb.* **5.** (*intr.*) *Rugby.* to try to win the ball by mauling and scrummaging. [C13 (meaning "heap of firewood"): ? < ON]

ruck[2] (rʌk) *n.* **1.** a wrinkle, crease, or fold. ~*vb.* **2.** (usually foll. by *up*) to become or make wrinkled, creased, or puckered. [C18: of Scand. origin; rel. to ON *hrukka*]

ruckman (ˈrʌkmən) *n., pl.* **-men.** *Australian Rules football.* either of two players who, with the rover, form the ruck.

ruck-rover *n. Australian Rules football.* a player playing a role midway between that of the rover and the ruckmen.

rucksack (ˈrʌkˌsæk) *n.* a large bag, usually having two straps, carried on the back and often used by climbers, campers, etc. Also called: **backpack.** [C19: < G, lit.: back sack]

ruction (ˈrʌkʃən) *n. Inf.* **1.** an uproar; noisy or quarrelsome disturbance. **2.** (*pl.*) an unpleasant row; trouble. [C19: ? changed < INSURRECTION]

rudaceous (ruːˈdeɪʃəs) *adj.* (of conglomerate, breccia, and similar rocks) composed of coarse-grained material. [C20: < L *rudis* coarse, rough + -ACEOUS]

rudbeckia (rʌdˈbɛkɪə) *n.* any of a genus of North American plants of the composite family, cultivated for their showy flowers, which have golden-yellow rays and green or black conical centres. See also **black-eyed Susan.** [C18: NL, after Olaus *Rudbeck* (1630–1702), Swedish botanist]

rudd (rʌd) *n.* a European freshwater fish, having a compressed dark greenish body and reddish ventral and tail fins. [C17: prob. < dialect *rud* red colour, < OE *rudu* redness]

rudder (ˈrʌdə) *n.* **1.** *Naut.* a pivoted vertical vane that projects into the water at the stern and can be used to steer a vessel. **2.** a vertical control surface attached to the rear of the fin used to steer an aircraft. **3.** anything that guides or directs. [OE *rōther*] —ˈ**rudderless** *adj.*

rudderpost (ˈrʌdəˌpəʊst) *n. Naut.* **1.** a postlike member at the forward edge of a rudder. **2.** the part of the stern frame of a vessel to which a rudder is fitted.

ruddle (ˈrʌdᵊl), **raddle,** *or* **reddle** *n.* **1.** a red ochre, used esp. to mark sheep. ~*vb.* **2.** (*tr.*) to mark (sheep) with ruddle. [C16: dim. formed < OE *rudu* redness; see RUDD]

ruddy (ˈrʌdɪ) *adj.* **-dier, -diest. 1.** (of the complexion) having a healthy reddish colour. **2.** coloured red or pink: *a ruddy sky.* ~*adv., adj. Inf., chiefly Brit.* **3.** (intensifier) bloody; damned: *a ruddy fool.* [OE *rudig,* < *rudu* redness] —ˈ**ruddily** *adv.* —ˈ**ruddiness** *n.*

rude (ruːd) *adj.* **1.** insulting or uncivil; discourteous; impolite. **2.** lacking refinement; coarse or uncouth. **3.** vulgar or obscene: *a rude joke.* **4.** roughly or crudely made: *we made a rude shelter on the island.* **5.** rough or harsh in sound, appearance, or behaviour. **6.** humble or lowly. **7.** (*prenominal*) robust or sturdy: *in rude health.* **8.** (*prenominal*) approximate or imprecise: *a rude estimate.* [C14: via OF < L *rudis* coarse, unformed] —ˈ**rudely** *adv.* —ˈ**rudeness** *or* (*inf.*) ˈ**rudery** *n.*

ruderal (ˈruːdərəl) *n.* **1.** a plant that grows on waste ground. ~*adj.* **2.** growing in waste places. [C19: < NL *rūderālis,* < L *rūdus* rubble]

rudiment (ˈruːdɪmənt) *n.* **1.** (*often pl.*) the first principles or elementary stages of a subject. **2.** (*often pl.*) a partially developed version of something. **3.** *Biol.* an organ or part in an embryonic or vestigial state. [C16: < L *rudīmentum* a beginning, < *rudis* unformed]

rudimentary (ˌruːdɪˈmɛntərɪ, -trɪ) *or* **rudimental** *adj.* **1.** basic; fundamental. **2.** incompletely developed; vestigial: *rudimentary leaves.* —ˌ**rudiˈmentarily** *or* (*less commonly*) ˌ**rudiˈmentally** *adv.*

rudish (ˈruːdɪʃ) *adj.* somewhat rude.

rue[1] (ruː) *vb.* **ruing, rued. 1.** to feel sorrow, remorse, or regret for (one's own wrongdoing, past events, etc.). ~*n.* **2.** *Arch.* sorrow, pity, or regret. [OE *hrēowan*] —ˈ**ruer** *n.*

rue[2] (ruː) *n.* an aromatic Eurasian shrub with small yellow flowers and evergreen leaves which yield an acrid volatile oil, formerly used medicinally as a narcotic and stimulant. Archaic name: **herb of grace.** [C14: < OF, < L *rūta,* < Gk *rhutē*]

rueful (ˈruːfʊl) *adj.* **1.** feeling or expressing sorrow or regret: *a rueful face.* **2.** inspiring sorrow or pity. —ˈ**ruefully** *adv.* —ˈ**ruefulness** *n.*

ruff[1] (rʌf) *n.* **1.** a circular pleated or fluted collar of lawn, muslin, etc., worn by both men and women in the 16th and 17th centuries. **2.** a natural growth of long or coloured hair or feathers around the necks of certain animals or birds. **3.** an Old World shore bird of the sandpiper family, the male of which has a large erectile ruff of feathers in the breeding season. [C16: back formation < RUFFLE[1]] —ˈ**ruffˌlike** *adj.*

ruff[2] (rʌf) *Cards.* ~*n., vb.* **1.** another word for **trump**[1]. ~*n.* **2.** an old card game similar to whist. [C16: < OF *roffle;* ? changed < It. *trionfa* TRUMP[1]]

ruffe *or* **ruff** (rʌf) *n.* a European freshwater teleost fish of the perch family, having a single spiny dorsal fin. [C15: ? alteration of ROUGH (referring to its scales)]

ruffian (ˈrʌfɪən) *n.* a violent or lawless person; hoodlum. [C16: < OF *rufien,* < It. *ruffiano* pander] —ˈ**ruffianism** *n.* —ˈ**ruffianly** *adj.*

ruffle[1] (ˈrʌfᵊl) *vb.* **1.** to make, be, or become irregular or rumpled: *a breeze ruffling the water.* **2.** to annoy, irritate, or be annoyed or irritated. **3.** (*tr.*) to make into a ruffle; pleat. **4.** (of a bird) to erect (its feathers) in anger, display, etc. **5.** (*tr.*) to flick (cards, pages, etc.) rapidly. ~*n.* **6.** an irregular or disturbed surface. **7.** a strip of pleated material used as a trim. **8.** *Zool.* another name for **ruff**[1] (sense 2). **9.** annoyance or irritation. [C13: of Gmc origin; cf. MLow G *ruffelen* to crumple, ON *hrufla* to scratch]

ruffle[2] (ˈrʌfᵊl) *n.* **1.** a low continuous drumbeat. ~*vb.* **2.** (*tr.*) to beat (a drum) with a low repetitive beat. [C18: < earlier *ruff,* imit.]

rufous (ˈruːfəs) *adj.* reddish-brown. [C18: < L *rūfus*]

rug (rʌg) *n.* **1.** a floor covering, smaller than a carpet and made of thick wool or of other material, such as an animal skin. **2.** *Chiefly Brit.* a blanket, esp. one used for travellers. **3. pull the rug out from under.** to betray, expose, or leave defenceless. [C16: of Scand. origin]

ruga (ˈruːgə) *n., pl.* **-gae** (-dʒiː). (*usually pl.*) *Anat.* a fold, wrinkle, or crease. [C18: L]

rugby *or* **rugby football** (ˈrʌgbɪ) *n.* a form of football played with an oval ball in which the handling and carrying of the ball is permitted. Also called: **rugger.** See also **rugby league, rugby union.** [after the public school at *Rugby*, where it was first played]

rugby league *n.* a form of rugby football played between teams of 13 players, professionalism being allowed.

rugby union *n.* a form of rugby football played only by amateurs, in teams of 15.

rugged (ˈrʌgɪd) *adj.* **1.** having an uneven or jagged surface. **2.** rocky or steep: *rugged scenery.* **3.** (of the face) strong-featured or furrowed. **4.** rough, severe, or stern in character. **5.** without refinement or culture; rude: *rugged manners.* **6.** involving hardship; harsh: *he leads a rugged life in the mountains.* **7.** difficult or hard: *a rugged test.* **8.** (of equipment, machines, etc.) designed to withstand rough treatment or use in rough conditions. **9.** *Chiefly U.S. & Canad.* sturdy or strong; robust. [C14: < ON] —ˈ**ruggedly** *adv.* —ˈ**ruggedness** *n.*

rugger (ˈrʌgə) *n. Chiefly Brit.* an informal name for **rugby.**

rugose (ˈruːgəʊs, -gəʊz) *adj.* wrinkled: *rugose leaves.* [C18: < L *rūgōsus*, < *rūga* wrinkle] —ˈ**rugosely** *adv.* —**rugosity** (ruːˈgɒsɪtɪ) *n.*

ruin (ˈruːɪn) *n.* **1.** a destroyed or decayed building or town. **2.** the state of being destroyed or decayed. **3.** loss of wealth, position, etc., or something that causes such loss; downfall. **4.** something that is severely damaged: *his life was a ruin.* **5.** a person who has suffered a downfall, bankruptcy, etc. **6.** *Arch.* loss of her virginity by a woman outside marriage. ~*vb.* **7.** (*tr.*) to bring to ruin; destroy. **8.** (*tr.*) to injure or spoil: *the town has been ruined with tower blocks.* **9.** (*intr.*) *Arch. or poetic.* to fall into ruins; collapse. **10.** (*tr.*) *Arch.* to seduce and abandon (a woman). [C14: < OF *ruine*, < L *ruīna* a falling down, < *ruere* to fall violently]

ruination (ˌruːɪˈneɪʃən) *n.* **1.** the act of ruining or the state of being ruined. **2.** something that causes ruin.

ruinous (ˈruːɪnəs) *adj.* causing, tending to cause, or characterized by ruin or destruction. —ˈ**ruinously** *adv.* —ˈ**ruinousness** *n.*

rule (ruːl) *n.* **1.** an authoritative regulation or direction concerning method or procedure, as for a court of law, legislative body, game, or other activity: *judges' rules; play according to the rules.* **2.** the exercise of governmental authority or control: *the rule of Caesar.* **3.** the period of time in which a monarch or government has power: *his rule lasted 100 days.* **4.** a customary form or procedure: *he made a morning swim his rule.* **5.** (usually preceded by *the*) the common order of things: *violence was the rule rather than the exception.* **6.** a prescribed method or procedure for solving a mathematical problem. **7.** any of various devices with a straight edge for guiding or measuring; ruler: *a carpenter's rule.* **8.** *Printing.* **a.** a printed or drawn character in the form of a long thin line. **b.** another name for **dash**[1] (sense 12): *en rule; em rule.* **c.** a strip of metal used to print such a line. **9.** *Christianity.* a systematic body of prescriptions followed by members of a religious order. **10.** *Law.* an order by a court or judge. **11. as a rule.** normally or ordinarily. ~*vb.* **12.** to exercise governing or controlling authority over (a people, political unit, individual, etc.). **13.** (when *tr., often takes a clause as object*) to decide authoritatively; decree: *the chairman ruled against the proposal.* **14.** (*tr.*) to mark with straight parallel lines or one straight line. **15.** (*tr.*) to restrain or control. **16.** (*intr.*) to be customary or prevalent: *chaos rules in this school.* **17.** (*intr.*) to be pre-eminent or superior: *football rules in the field of sport.* **18. rule the roost** (*or* **roast**). to be pre-eminent; be in charge. [C13: < OF *riule*, < L *rēgula* a straight edge] —ˈ**rulable** *adj.*

rule of three *n.* a mathematical rule asserting that the value of one unknown quantity in a proportion is found by multiplying the denominator of each ratio by the numerator of the other.

rule of thumb *n.* **a.** a rough and practical approach, based on experience, rather than theory. **b.** (*as modifier*): *a rule-of-thumb decision.*

rule out *vb.* (*tr., adv.*) **1.** to dismiss from consideration. **2.** to make impossible; preclude.

ruler (ˈruːlə) *n.* **1.** a person who rules or commands. **2.** Also called: **rule.** a strip of wood, metal, or other material, having straight edges, used for measuring and drawing straight lines.

Rules (ruːlz) *pl. n.* **1.** short for **Australian Rules** (football). **2. the Rules.** *English history.* the neighbourhood around certain prisons in which trusted prisoners were allowed to live under specified restrictions.

ruling (ˈruːlɪŋ) *n.* **1.** a decision of someone in authority, such as a judge. **2.** one or more parallel ruled lines. ~*adj.* **3.** controlling or exercising authority. **4.** predominant.

rum[1] (rʌm) *n.* spirit made from sugar cane. [C17: ? shortened < C16 *rumbullion*, <?]

rum[2] (rʌm) *adj.* **rummer, rummest.** *Brit. sl.* strange; peculiar; odd. [C19: ? < Romany *rom* man] —ˈ**rumly** *adv.* —ˈ**rumness** *n.*

Rumanian (ruːˈmeɪnɪən) *n., adj.* a variant of **Romanian.**

rumba *or* **rhumba** (ˈrʌmbə, ˈrʊm-) *n.* **1.** a rhythmic and syncopated Cuban dance in duple time. **2.** a ballroom dance derived from this. **3.** a piece of music composed for or in the rhythm of this dance. [C20: < Sp.: lavish display, <?]

rumble (ˈrʌmbᵊl) *vb.* **1.** to make or cause to make a deep resonant sound: *thunder rumbled in the sky.* **2.** (*intr.*) to move with such a sound: *the train rumbled along.* **3.** (*tr.*) to utter with a rumbling sound: *he rumbled an order.* **4.** (*tr.*) *Brit. sl.* to find out about (someone or something): *the police rumbled their plans.* **5.** (*intr.*) *U.S. sl.* to be involved in a gang fight. ~*n.* **6.** a deep resonant sound. **7.** a widespread murmur of discontent. **8.** *U.S. & N.Z. sl.* a gang fight. [C14: ? < MDu. *rummelen*] —ˈ**rumbler** *n.* —ˈ**rumbling** *adj.*

rumble seat *n. U.S. & Canad.* a folding outside seat at the rear of some early cars; dicky.

rumbustious (rʌmˈbʌstʃəs) *adj.* boisterous or unruly. [C18: prob. var. of ROBUSTIOUS] —**rumˈbustiously** *adv.* —**rumˈbustiousness** *n.*

rumen (ˈruːmɛn) *n., pl.* **-mens** *or* **-mina** (-mɪnə). the first compartment of the stomach of ruminants, in which food is partly digested before being regurgitated as cud. [C18: < L: gullet]

ruminant (ˈruːmɪnənt) *n.* **1.** any of a suborder of artiodactyl mammals which chew the cud and have a stomach of four compartments. The suborder includes deer, antelopes, cattle, sheep, and goats. **2.** any other animal that chews the cud, such as a camel. ~*adj.* **3.** of, relating to, or belonging to this suborder. **4.** (of members of this suborder and related animals, such as camels) chewing the cud; ruminating. **5.** meditating or contemplating in a slow quiet way.

ruminate (ˈruːmɪˌneɪt) *vb.* **1.** (of ruminants) to chew (the cud). **2.** (when *intr.*, often foll. by *upon*, *on*, etc.) to meditate or ponder (upon). [C16: < L *rūmināre* to chew the cud, < RUMEN] —ˌ**rumiˈnation** *n.* —ˈ**ruminative** *adj.* —ˈ**ruminatively** *adv.* —ˈ**rumiˌnator** *n.*

rummage (ˈrʌmɪdʒ) *vb.* **1.** (when *intr.*, often foll. by *through*) to search (through) while looking for something, often causing disorder. ~*n.* **2.** an act of rummaging. **3.** a jumble of articles. [C14 (in the sense: to pack a cargo): < OF *arrumage*, < *arrumer* to stow in a ship's hold, prob. of Gmc origin] —ˈ**rummager** *n.*

rummage sale *n.* **1.** the U.S. and Canad. term for **jumble sale.** **2.** *U.S.* a sale of unclaimed property.

rummer (ˈrʌmə) *n.* a drinking glass having an ovoid bowl on a short stem. [C17: < Du. *roemer* a glass for drinking toasts, < *roemen* to praise]

rummy (ˈrʌmɪ) *or* **rum** *n.* a card game based on collecting sets and sequences. [C20: ? < RUM[2]]

rumour *or U.S.* **rumor** (ˈruːmə) *n.* **1. a.**

information, often a mixture of truth and untruth, passed around verbally. **b.** (*in combination*): *a rumourmonger.* **2.** gossip or hearsay. ~*vb.* **3.** (*tr.; usually passive*) to pass around or circulate in the form of a rumour: *it is rumoured that the Queen is coming.* [C14: via OF < L *rūmor* common talk]

rump (rʌmp) *n.* **1.** the hindquarters of a mammal, not including the legs. **2.** the rear part of a bird's back, nearest to the tail. **3.** a person's buttocks. **4.** Also called: **rump steak.** a cut of beef from behind the loin. **5.** an inferior remnant. [C15: < ON] —ˈ**rumpless** *adj.*

rumple (ˈrʌmpᵊl) *vb.* **1.** to make or become crumpled or dishevelled. ~*n.* **2.** a wrinkle, fold, or crease. [C17: < MDu. *rompelen;* rel. to OE *gerumpen* wrinkled] —ˈ**rumply** *adj.*

Rump Parliament *or* **the Rump** *n. English history.* the remainder of the Long Parliament after Pride's Purge (the expulsion by Thomas Pride in 1648 of those members hostile to the army). It sat from 1648–53.

rumpus (ˈrʌmpəs) *n., pl.* **-puses.** a noisy, confused, or disruptive commotion. [C18: <?]

rumpus room *n. U.S., Canad., & N.Z.* a room used for noisy activities, such as parties or children's games.

run (rʌn) *vb.* **running, ran, run. 1.** (*intr.*) **a.** (of a two-legged creature) to move on foot at a rapid pace so that both feet are off the ground for part of each stride. **b.** (of a four-legged creature) to move at a rapid gait. **2.** (*tr.*) to pass over (a distance, route, etc.) in running: *to run a mile.* **3.** (*intr.*) to run in or finish a race as specified, esp. in a particular position: *John is running third.* **4.** (*tr.*) to perform as by running: *to run an errand.* **5.** (*intr.*) to flee; run away. **6.** (*tr.*) to bring into a specified state by running: *to run oneself to a standstill.* **7.** (*tr.*) to track down or hunt (an animal): *to run a fox to earth.* **8.** (*tr.*) to set (animals) loose on (a field or tract of land) so as to graze freely: *he ran stock on that pasture last year.* **9.** (*intr.;* often foll. by *over, round,* or *up*) to make a short trip or brief visit: *I'll run over this afternoon.* **10.** (*intr.*) to move quickly and easily on wheels by rolling, or in any of certain other ways: *a sledge running over snow.* **11.** to move or cause to move with a specified result: *to run a ship aground; run into a tree.* **12.** (often foll. by *over*) to move or pass or cause to move or pass quickly: *to run one's eyes over a page.* **13.** (*tr.;* foll. by *into, out of, through,* etc.) to force, thrust, or drive: *she ran a needle into her finger.* **14.** (*tr.*) to drive or maintain and operate (a vehicle). **15.** (*tr.*) to give a lift to (someone) in a vehicle: *he ran her to the station.* **16.** to ply or cause to ply between places on a route: *the bus runs from Piccadilly to Golders Green.* **17.** to function or cause to function: *the engine is running smoothly.* **18.** (*tr.*) to manage: *to run a company.* **19.** to extend or continue or cause to extend or continue in a particular direction, for a particular duration or distance, etc.: *the road runs north; the play ran for two years.* **20.** (*intr.*) *Law.* to have legal force or effect: *the lease runs for two more years.* **21.** (*tr.*) to be subjected to, be affected by, or incur: *to run a risk; run a temperature.* **22.** (*intr.;* often foll. by *to*) to be characterized (by); tend or incline: *to run to fat.* **23.** (*intr.*) to recur persistently or be inherent: *red hair runs in my family.* **24.** to cause or allow (liquids) to flow or (of liquids) to flow: *the well has run dry.* **25.** (*intr.*) to melt and flow: *the wax grew hot and began to run.* **26.** *Metallurgy.* **a.** to melt or fuse. **b.** (*tr.*) to cast (molten metal): *to run lead into ingots.* **27.** (*intr.*) (of waves, tides, rivers, etc.) to rise high, surge, or be at a specified height: *a high sea was running that night.* **28.** (*intr.*) to be diffused: *the colours in my dress ran when I washed it.* **29.** (*intr.*) (of stitches) to unravel or come undone or (of a garment) to have stitches unravel or come undone. **30.** (*intr.*) (of growing creepers, etc.) to trail, spread, or climb: *ivy running over a cottage wall.* **31.** (*intr.*) to spread or circulate quickly: *a rumour ran through the town.* **32.** (*intr.*) to be stated or reported: *his story runs as follows.* **33.** to publish or print or be published or printed in a newspaper, magazine, etc.: *they ran his story in the next issue.* **34.** (often foll. by *for*) *Chiefly U.S. & Canad.* to be a candidate or present as a candidate for political or other office: *Jones is running for president.* **35.** (*tr.*) to get past or through: *to run a blockade.* **36.** (*tr.*) to deal in (arms, etc.), esp. by importing illegally: *he runs guns for the rebels.* **37.** *Naut.* to sail (a vessel, esp. a sailing vessel) or (of such a vessel) to be sailed with the wind coming from astern. **38.** (*intr.*) (of fish) to migrate upstream from the sea, esp. in order to spawn. **39.** (*tr.*) *Cricket.* to score (a run or number of runs) by hitting the ball and running between the wickets. **40.** (*tr.*) *Billiards, etc.* to make (a number of successful shots) in sequence. **41.** (*tr.*) *Golf.* to hit (the ball) so that it rolls along the ground. **42.** (*tr.*) *Bridge.* to cash (all one's winning cards in a long suit) successively. ~*n.* **43.** an act, instance, or period of running. **44.** a gait, pace, or motion faster than a walk: *she went off at a run.* **45.** a distance covered by running or a period of running: *a run of ten miles.* **46.** an instance or period of travelling in a vehicle, esp. for pleasure: *to go for a run in the car.* **47.** free and unrestricted access: *we had the run of the house.* **48. a.** a period of time during which a machine, computer, etc., operates. **b.** the amount of work performed in such a period. **49.** a continuous or sustained period: *a run of good luck.* **50.** a continuous sequence of performances: *the play had a good run.* **51.** *Cards.* a sequence of winning cards in one suit: *a run of spades.* **52.** tendency or trend: *the run of the market.* **53.** type, class, or category: *the usual run of graduates.* **54.** (usually foll. by *on*) a continuous and urgent demand: *a run on the dollar.* **55.** a series of unravelled stitches, esp. in tights; ladder. **56.** the characteristic pattern or direction of something: *the run of the grain on wood.* **57. a.** a period during which water or other liquid flows. **b.** the amount of such a flow. **58.** a pipe, channel, etc., through which water or other liquid flows. **59.** *U.S.* a small stream. **60.** a steeply inclined course, esp. a snow-covered one used for skiing. **61.** an enclosure for domestic fowls or other animals: *a chicken run.* **62.** (esp. in Australia and New Zealand) a tract of land for grazing livestock. **63.** the migration of fish upstream in order to spawn. **64.** *Mil.* **a.** a mission in a warplane. **b.** Also called: **bombing run.** an approach by a bomber to a target. **65.** the movement of an aircraft along the ground during takeoff or landing. **66.** *Music.* a rapid scalelike passage of notes. **67.** *Cricket.* a score of one, normally achieved by both batsmen running from one end of the wicket to the other after one of them has hit the ball. **68.** *Baseball.* an instance of a batter touching all four bases safely, thereby scoring. **69.** *Golf.* the distance that a ball rolls after hitting the ground. **70. a run for (one's) money.** *Inf.* **a.** a close competition. **b.** pleasure derived from an activity. **71. in the long run.** as the eventual outcome of a series of events, etc. **72. in the short run.** as the immediate outcome of a series of events, etc. **73. on the run. a.** escaping from arrest; fugitive. **b.** in rapid flight; retreating: *the enemy is on the run.* **c.** hurrying from place to place. **74. the runs.** *Sl.* diarrhoea. ~See also **runabout, run across,** etc. [OE *runnen,* p.p. of (*ge*)*rinnan*]

runabout (ˈrʌnəˌbaʊt) *n.* **1.** a small light vehicle or aeroplane. ~*vb.* **run about. 2.** (*intr., adv.*) to move busily from place to place.

run across *vb.* (*intr., prep.*) to meet unexpectedly; encounter by chance.

run along *vb.* (*intr., adv.*) (often said patronizingly) to go away; leave.

run around *Inf.* ~*vb.* (*intr., adv.*) **1.** (often foll. by *with*) to associate habitually (with). **2.** to behave in a fickle or promiscuous manner. ~*n.* **run-around. 3.** deceitful or evasive treatment of a person (esp. in **give** *or* **get the run-around**).

run away *vb.* (*intr., adv.*) **1.** to take flight; escape. **2.** to go away; depart. **3.** (of a horse) to gallop away uncontrollably. **4. run away with. a.** to abscond or elope with: *he ran away with his boss's daughter.* **b.** to make off with; steal. **c.** to escape from the control of: *his enthusiasm ran away with him.* **d.** to win easily or be assured of victory in (a competition): *he ran away with the race.* ~*n.* **runaway. 5. a.** a person or animal that runs away. **b.** (*as modifier*): *a runaway horse.* **6.** the act or an instance of running away. **7.** (*modifier*) rising rapidly, as prices: *runaway inflation.* **8.** (*modifier*) (of a race, victory, etc.) easily won.

runcible spoon (ˈrʌnsɪbəl) *n.* a forklike utensil with two broad prongs and one sharp curved prong. [*runcible* coined by Edward Lear, E humorist, in a nonsense poem (1871)]

run down *vb.* (*mainly adv.*) **1.** to allow (an engine, etc.) to lose power gradually and cease to function or (of an engine, etc.) to do this. **2.** to decline or reduce in number or size: *the firm ran down its sales force.* **3.** (*tr.; usually passive*) to tire, sap the strength of, or exhaust: *he was thoroughly run down.* **4.** (*tr.*) to criticize adversely; decry. **5.** (*tr.*) to hit and knock to the ground with a moving vehicle. **6.** (*tr.*) *Naut.* to collide with and cause to sink. **7.** (*tr.*) to pursue and find or capture: *to run down a fugitive.* **8.** (*tr.*) to read swiftly or perfunctorily: *he ran down their list of complaints.* ~*adj.* **run-down. 9.** tired; exhausted. **10.** worn-out, shabby, or dilapidated. ~*n.* **rundown. 11.** a brief review, résumé, or summary. **12.** the process of a mechanism coming gradually to a standstill after the power is removed. **13.** a reduction in number or size.

rune (ruːn) *n.* **1.** any of the characters of an ancient Germanic alphabet, in use, esp. in Scandinavia, from the 3rd century A.D. to the end of the Middle Ages. **2.** any obscure piece of writing using mysterious symbols. **3.** a kind of Finnish poem or a stanza in such a poem. [OE *rūn*, < ON *rūn* secret] —ˈ**runic** *adj.*

rung[1] (rʌŋ) *n.* **1.** one of the bars or rods that form the steps of a ladder. **2.** a crosspiece between the legs of a chair, etc. **3.** *Naut.* a spoke on a ship's wheel or a handle projecting from the periphery. [OE *hrung*] —ˈ**rungless** *adj.*

rung[2] (rʌŋ) *vb.* the past participle of **ring**[2].

▷ **Usage.** See at **ring**[2].

run in *vb.* (*adv.*) **1.** to run (an engine) gently, usually when it is new. **2.** (*tr.*) to insert or include. **3.** (*intr.*) (of an aircraft) to approach a point or target. **4.** (*tr.*) *Inf.* to take into custody; arrest. ~*n.* **run-in. 5.** *Inf.* an argument or quarrel. **6.** *Printing.* matter inserted in an existing paragraph.

run into *vb.* (*prep., mainly intr.*) **1.** (*also tr.*) to collide with or cause to collide with: *her car ran into a tree.* **2.** to encounter unexpectedly. **3.** (*also tr.*) to be beset by: *the project ran into financial difficulties.* **4.** to extend to; be of the order of: *debts running into thousands.*

runnel (ˈrʌnəl) *n. Literary.* a small stream. [C16: < OE *rynele;* rel. to RUN]

runner (ˈrʌnə) *n.* **1.** a person who runs, esp. an athlete. **2.** a messenger for a bank, etc. **3.** a person engaged in the solicitation of business. **4.** a person on the run; fugitive. **5. a.** a person or vessel engaged in smuggling. **b.** (*in combination*): *a gunrunner.* **6.** a person who operates, manages, or controls something. **7. a.** either of the strips of metal or wood on which a sledge runs. **b.** the blade of an ice skate. **8.** a roller or guide for a sliding component. **9.** *Bot.* **a.** Also called: **stolon.** a slender horizontal stem, as of the strawberry, that grows along the surface of the soil and propagates by producing roots and shoots at the nodes or tip. **b.** a plant that propagates in this way. **10.** a strip of lace, linen, etc., placed across a table or dressing table for protection and decoration. **11.** another word for **rocker** (on a rocking chair).

runner bean *n.* another name for **scarlet runner.**

runner-up *n., pl.* **runners-up.** a contestant finishing a race or competition in second place.

running (ˈrʌnɪŋ) *adj.* **1.** maintained continuously; incessant: *running commentary.* **2.** (*postpositive*) without interruption; consecutive: *he lectured for two hours running.* **3.** denoting or relating to the scheduled operation of a public vehicle: *the running time of a train.* **4.** accomplished at a run: *a running jump.* **5.** moving or slipping easily, as a rope or a knot. **6.** (of a wound, etc.) discharging pus. **7.** prevalent; current: *running prices.* **8.** repeated or continuous: *a running design.* **9.** (of plants, plant stems, etc.) creeping along the ground. **10.** flowing: *running water.* **11.** (of handwriting) having the letters run together. ~*n.* **12.** management or organization: *the running of a company.* **13.** operation or maintenance: *the running of a machine.* **14.** competition or competitive situation (in **in the running, out of the running**). **15. make the running.** to set the pace in a competition or race.

running board *n.* a footboard along the side of a vehicle, esp. an early motorcar.

running head *or* **title** *n. Printing.* a heading printed at the top of every page of a book.

running light *n. Naut.* one of several lights displayed by vessels operating at night.

running mate *n.* **1.** *U.S.* a candidate for the subordinate of two linked positions, esp. a candidate for the vice-presidency. **2.** a horse that pairs another in a team.

running repairs *pl. n.* repairs that do not, or do not greatly, interrupt operations.

runny (ˈrʌnɪ) *adj.* **-nier, -niest. 1.** tending to flow; liquid. **2.** (of the nose) exuding mucus.

run off *vb.* (*adv.*) **1.** (*intr.*) to depart in haste. **2.** (*tr.*) to produce quickly, as copies on a duplicating machine. **3.** to drain (liquid) or (of liquid) to be drained. **4.** (*tr.*) to decide (a race) by a run-off. **5. run off with. a.** to steal; purloin. **b.** to elope with. ~*n.* **run-off. 6.** an extra race, contest, election, etc., to decide the winner after a tie. **7.** *N.Z.* grazing land for store cattle. **8.** that portion of rainfall that runs into streams as surface water rather than being absorbed by the soil. **9.** the overflow of a liquid from a container.

run-of-the-mill *adj.* ordinary, average, or undistinguished in quality, character, or nature.

run on *vb.* (*adv.*) **1.** (*intr.*) to continue without interruption. **2.** to write with linked-up characters. **3.** *Printing.* to compose text matter without indentation or paragraphing. ~*n.* **run-on. 4.** *Printing.* **a.** text matter composed without indenting. **b.** an additional quantity required in excess of the originally stated amount, whilst the job is being produced. **5. a.** a word added at the end of a dictionary entry whose meaning can be easily inferred from the definition of the headword. **b.** (*as modifier*): *a run-on entry.*

run out *vb.* (*adv.*) **1.** (*intr.;* often foll. by *of*) to exhaust (a supply of something) or (of a supply) to become exhausted. **2. run out on.** *Inf.* to desert or abandon. **3.** (*tr.*) *Cricket.* to dismiss (a running batsman) by breaking the wicket with the ball, or with the ball in the hand, while he is out of his ground. ~*n.* **run-out. 4.** *Cricket.* dismissal of a batsman by running him out.

run over *vb.* **1.** (*tr., adv.*) to knock down (a person) with a moving vehicle. **2.** (*intr.*) to overflow the capacity of (a container). **3.** (*intr., prep.*) to examine hastily or make a rapid survey of. **4.** (*intr., prep.*) to exceed (a limit): *we've run over our time.*

runt (rʌnt) *n.* **1.** the smallest and weakest young animal in a litter, esp. the smallest piglet in a litter. **2.** *Derog.* an undersized or inferior person. **3.** a large pigeon, originally bred for eating. [C16: <?] —ˈ**runtish** *or* ˈ**runty** *adj.* —ˈ**runtiness** *n.*

run through *vb.* **1.** (*tr., adv.*) to transfix with a sword or other weapon. **2.** (*intr., prep.*) to exhaust (money) by wasteful spending. **3.** (*intr., prep.*) to practise or rehearse: *let's run through the plan.* **4.** (*intr., prep.*) to examine hastily. ~*n.* **run-through. 5.** a practice or rehearsal. **6.** a brief survey.

run to *vb.* (*intr., prep.*) to be sufficient for: *my income doesn't run to luxuries.*

run up *vb.* (*tr., adv.*) **1.** to amass; incur: *to run up debts.* **2.** to make by sewing together quickly. **3.** to hoist: *to run up a flag.* ~*n.* **run-up. 4.** an approach run by an athlete for the long jump, pole vault, etc. **5.** a preliminary or preparatory period: *the run-up to the election.*

runway (ˈrʌnˌweɪ) *n.* **1.** a hard level roadway from which aircraft take off and on which they land. **2.** *Forestry, North American.* a chute for sliding logs down. **3.** a narrow ramp extending from the stage into the audience in a theatre, etc.

rupee (ruːˈpiː) *n.* the standard monetary unit of India, Pakistan, Sri Lanka, the Maldive Islands, Mauritius, the Seychelles, and Nepal. [C17: < Hindi *rupaīyā*, < Sansk. *rūpya* coined silver, < *rūpa* shape, beauty]

rupiah (ruːˈpiːə) *n., pl.* **-ah** *or* **-ahs.** the standard monetary unit of Indonesia. [< Hindi: RUPEE]

rupture (ˈrʌptʃə) *n.* **1.** the act of breaking or bursting or the state of being broken or burst. **2.** a breach of peaceful or friendly relations. **3.** *Pathol.* **a.** the breaking or tearing of a bodily structure or part. **b.** another word for **hernia.** ~*vb.* **4.** to break or burst. **5.** to affect or be affected with a rupture or hernia. **6.** to undergo or cause to undergo a breach in relations or friendship. [C15: < L *ruptūra*, < *rumpere* to burst forth] —ˈ**rupturable** *adj.*

rural (ˈrʊərəl) *adj.* **1.** of, relating to, or characteristic of the country or country life. **2.** living in the country. **3.** of, relating to, or associated with farming. ~Cf. **urban.** [C15: via OF < L *rūrālis*, < *rūs* the country] —ˈ**ruralism** *n.* —ˈ**ruralist** *n.* —**ruˈrality** *n.* —ˈ**rurally** *adv.*

rural dean *n. Chiefly Brit.* a clergyman having authority over a group of parishes.

rural district *n.* (formerly) a rural division of a county.

ruralize *or* **-ise** (ˈrʊərəˌlaɪz) *vb.* **1.** (*tr.*) to make rural in character, appearance, etc. **2.** (*intr.*) to go into the country to live. —ˌ**ruraliˈzation** *or* **-iˈsation** *n.*

rural route *n. U.S. & Canad.* a mail service or route in a rural area, the mail being delivered by car or van.

Ruritanian (ˌrʊərɪˈteɪnɪən) *adj.* of or characteristic of a romantic and idealistic setting in which adventure and intrigue occur. [C19: after the imaginary kingdom created by Anthony Hope (1863-1933), in *The Prisoner of Zenda*]

rusbank (ˈrʊsˌbæŋk) *n. S. African.* a wooden bench or settle without upholstery. [< Afrik., < Du. *rust* rest + *bank* bench]

ruse (ruːz) *n.* an action intended to mislead, deceive, or trick; stratagem. [C15: < OF: trick, esp. to evade capture, < *ruser* to retreat, < L *recūsāre* to refuse]

rush[1] (rʌʃ) *vb.* **1.** to hurry or cause to hurry; hasten. **2.** (*tr.*) to make a sudden attack upon (a fortress, position, person, etc.). **3.** (when *intr.*, often foll. by *at, in,* or *into*) to proceed or approach in a reckless manner. **4. rush one's fences.** to proceed with precipitate haste. **5.** (*intr.*) to come, flow, swell, etc., quickly or suddenly: *tears rushed to her eyes.* **6.** (*tr.*) *Sl.* to cheat, esp. by grossly overcharging. **7.** (*tr.*) *U.S. & Canad.* to make a concerted effort to secure the agreement, participation, etc., of (a person). **8.** (*tr.*) *Rugby.* (of a pack) to move (the ball) forwards by short kicks and runs. ~*n.* **9.** the act or condition of rushing. **10.** a sudden surge towards someone or something: *a gold rush.* **11.** a sudden surge of sensation, esp. from a drug. **12.** a sudden demand. **13.** (*usually pl.*) (in film-making) the initial prints of a scene before editing. ~*adj.* (*prenominal*) **14.** requiring speed or urgency: *a rush job.* **15.** characterized by much movement, business, etc.: *a rush period.* [C14 *ruschen*, < OF *ruser* to put to flight, < L *recūsāre* to refuse] —ˈ**rusher** *n.*

rush[2] (rʌʃ) *n.* **1.** an annual or perennial plant growing in wet places and typically having grasslike cylindrical leaves and small green or brown flowers. **2.** something valueless; a trifle; straw: *not worth a rush.* **3.** short for **rush light.** [OE *risce, rysce*] —ˈ**rushˌlike** *adj.* —ˈ**rushy** *adj.*

rush hour *n.* a period at the beginning and end of the working day when large numbers of people are travelling to or from work.

rush light *or* **candle** *n.* a narrow candle, formerly in use, made of the pith of various types of rush dipped in tallow.

rusk (rʌsk) *n.* a light bread dough, sweet or plain, baked twice until it is brown, hard, and crisp: often given to babies. [C16: < Sp. or Port. *rosca* screw, bread shaped in a twist, <?]

Russ. *abbrev. for* Russia(n).

russet (ˈrʌsɪt) *n.* **1.** brown with a yellowish or reddish tinge. **2.** a rough homespun fabric, reddish-brown in colour, formerly in use for clothing. **3.** any of various apples with rough brownish-red skins. ~*adj.* **4.** *Arch.* simple; homely; rustic: *a russet life.* **5.** of the colour russet: *russet hair.* [C13: < Anglo-Norman, < OF *rosset*, < *rous*, < L *russus*; rel. to L *ruber* red] —ˈ**russety** *adj.*

Russia leather (ˈrʌʃə) *n.* a smooth dyed leather made from calfskin and scented with birch-tar oil, originally produced in Russia.

Russian (ˈrʌʃən) *n.* **1.** the official language of the Soviet Union: an Indo-European language belonging to the East Slavonic branch. **2.** a native or inhabitant of Russia or the Soviet Union. ~*adj.* **3.** of, relating to, or characteristic of Russia or the Soviet Union, its people, or their language.

Russianize *or* **-ise** (ˈrʌʃəˌnaɪz) *vb.* to make or become Russian in style, etc. —ˌ**Russianiˈzation** *or* **-iˈsation** *n.*

Russian roulette *n.* **1.** an act of bravado in which each person in turn spins the cylinder of a revolver loaded with only one cartridge and presses the trigger with the barrel against his own head. **2.** any foolish or potentially suicidal undertaking.

Russian salad *n.* a salad of cold diced cooked vegetables mixed with mayonnaise and pickles.

Russo- (ˈrʌsəʊ) *combining form.* Russia or Russian: *Russo-Japanese.*

rust (rʌst) *n.* **1.** a reddish-brown oxide coating formed on iron or steel by the action of oxygen and moisture. **2.** Also called: **rust fungus.** *Plant pathol.* **a.** any of a group of fungi which are parasitic on cereal plants, conifers, etc. **b.** any of various plant diseases characterized by reddish-brown discoloration of the leaves and stem, esp. that caused by the rust fungi. **3. a.** a strong brown colour, sometimes with a reddish or yellowish tinge. **b.** (*as adj.*): *a rust carpet.* **4.** any corrosive or debilitating influence, esp. lack of use. ~*vb.* **5.** to become or cause to become coated with a layer of rust. **6.** to deteriorate or cause to deteriorate through some debilitating influence or lack of use: *he allowed his talent to rust over the years.* [OE *rūst*] —ˈ**rustless** *adj.*

rustic (ˈrʌstɪk) *adj.* **1.** of, characteristic of, or living in the country; rural. **2.** having qualities ascribed to country life or people; simple; unsophisticated: *rustic pleasures.* **3.** crude, awkward, or uncouth. **4.** made of untrimmed branches: *a rustic seat.* **5.** (of masonry, etc.) having a rusticated finish. ~*n.* **6.** a person who comes from or lives in the country. **7.** an unsophisticated, simple, or clownish person from the country. **8.** Also called: **rusticwork.** brick or stone having a rough finish. [C16: < OF *rustique*, < L *rūsticus*, < *rūs* the country] —ˈ**rustically** *adv.* —**rusticity** (rʌˈstɪsɪtɪ) *n.*

rusticate (ˈrʌstɪˌkeɪt) *vb.* **1.** to banish or retire to the country. **2.** to make or become rustic in style, etc. **3.** (*tr.*) *Architect.* to finish (an exterior wall) with large blocks of masonry separated by deep joints. **4.** (*tr.*) *Brit.* to send down from university for a specified time as a punishment. [C17: < L *rūsticārī*, < *rūs* the country] —ˌ**rustiˈcation** *n.* —ˈ**rustiˌcator** *n.*

rusticated (ˈrʌstɪˌkeɪtɪd) *or* **rusticating** (ˈrʌstɪˌkeɪtɪŋ) *n.* (in New Zealand) a wide type of weatherboarding used in older houses.

rustle[1] (ˈrʌsᵊl) *vb.* **1.** to make or cause to make a low crisp whispering or rubbing sound, as of dry leaves or paper. **2.** to move with such a sound. ~*n.* **3.** such a sound or sounds. [OE *hrūxlian*]

rustle[2] (ˈrʌsᵊl) *vb.* **1.** *Chiefly U.S. & Canad.* to steal (cattle, horses, etc.). **2.** *Inf., U.S. & Canad.* to move swiftly and energetically. [C19: prob. special use of RUSTLE[1] (in the sense: to move with a quiet sound)] —ˈ**rustler** *n.*

rustle up *vb.* (*tr., adv.*) *Inf.* **1.** to prepare (a meal, etc.) rapidly, esp. at short notice. **2.** to forage for and obtain.

rustproof (ˈrʌstˌpruːf) *adj.* treated against rusting.

rusty (ˈrʌstɪ) *adj.* **rustier, rustiest.** **1.** covered with, affected by, or consisting of rust: *a rusty machine.* **2.** of the colour rust. **3.** discoloured by age: *a rusty coat.* **4.** (of the voice) tending to croak. **5.** old-fashioned in appearance: *a rusty old gentleman.* **6.** impaired in skill or knowledge by inaction or neglect. **7.** (of plants) affected by the rust fungus. —ˈ**rustily** *adv.* —ˈ**rustiness** *n.*

rut[1] (rʌt) *n.* **1.** a groove or furrow in a soft road, caused by wheels. **2.** a narrow or predictable way of life; dreary or undeviating routine (esp. in **in a rut**). ~*vb.* **rutting, rutted.** **3.** (*tr.*) to make a rut in. [C16: prob. < F *route* road]

rut[2] (rʌt) *n.* **1.** a recurrent period of sexual excitement and reproductive activity in certain male ruminants. ~*vb.* **rutting, rutted.** **2.** (*intr.*) (of male ruminants) to be in a period of sexual excitement and activity. [C15: < OF *rut* noise, roar, < L *rugītus*, < *rugīre* to roar]

rutabaga (ˌruːtəˈbeɪgə) *n.* the U.S. and Canad. name for **swede.** [C18: < Swedish dialect *rotabagge*, lit.: root bag]

rutaceous (ruːˈteɪʃəs) *adj.* of, relating to, or belonging to a family of tropical and temperate flowering plants many of which have aromatic leaves. The family includes rue, citrus trees, and dittany. [C19: < NL *Rutaceae*, < L *rūta* RUE[2]]

ruth (ruːθ) *n. Arch.* **1.** pity; compassion. **2.** repentance; remorse. [C12: < *rewen* to RUE[1]]

ruthenium (ruːˈθiːnɪəm) *n.* a hard brittle white element of the platinum metal group. It is used to harden platinum and palladium. Symbol: Ru; atomic no.: 44; atomic wt.: 101.07. [C19: < Med. L *Ruthenia* Russia, where it was discovered]

rutherford (ˈrʌðəfəd) *n.* a unit of activity equal to the quantity of a radioactive nuclide required to produce one million disintegrations per second. Abbrev.: **rd.** [C20: after Ernest *Rutherford* (1871-1937), Brit. physicist who discovered the atomic nucleus]

rutherfordium (ˌrʌðəˈfɔːdɪəm) *n.* the U.S. name for the element with the atomic no. 104, known in the USSR as kurchatovium. Symbol: Rf [C20: after E. *Rutherford*]

ruthful (ˈruːθfʊl) *adj. Arch.* full of or causing sorrow or pity. —ˈ**ruthfully** *adv.* —ˈ**ruthfulness** *n.*

ruthless (ˈruːθlɪs) *adj.* feeling or showing no mercy; hardhearted. —ˈ**ruthlessly** *adv.* —ˈ**ruthlessness** *n.*

rutile (ˈruːtaɪl) *n.* a mineral consisting of titanium dioxide in tetragonal crystalline form. It is an important source of titanium. [C19: via F < G *Rutil*, < L *rutilus* red, glowing]

ruttish (ˈrʌtɪʃ) *adj.* **1.** (of an animal) in a condition of rut. **2.** lascivious or salacious. —ˈ**ruttishly** *adv.* —ˈ**ruttishness** *n.*

rutty (ˈrʌtɪ) *adj.* **-tier, -tiest.** full of ruts or holes: *a rutty track.* —ˈ**ruttily** *adv.* —ˈ**ruttiness** *n.*

RV *abbrev. for* Revised Version (of the Bible).

-ry *suffix forming nouns.* a variant of **-ery:** *dentistry.*

rye (raɪ) *n.* **1.** a tall hardy widely cultivated annual grass having bristly flower spikes and light brown grain. **2.** the grain of this grass, used in making flour and whisky, and as a livestock food. **3.** Also called: (esp. U.S.): **rye whiskey.** whisky distilled from rye. **4.** *U.S.* short for **rye bread.** [OE *ryge*]

rye bread *n.* any of various breads made entirely or partly from rye flour, often with caraway seeds.

rye-grass *n.* any of various grasses native to Europe, N Africa, and Asia, and widely cultivated as forage crops. They have flattened flower spikes and hairless leaves.

S

s *or* **S** (ɛs) *n., pl.* **s's, S's,** *or* **Ss. 1.** the 19th letter of the English alphabet. **2.** a speech sound represented by this letter, either voiceless, as in *sit*, or voiced, as in *dogs*. **3. a.** something shaped like an S. **b.** (*in combination*): *an S-bend in a road.*

s *symbol for* second (of time).

S *symbol for:* **1.** small. **2.** Society. **3.** South. **4.** *Chem.* sulphur. **5.** *Physics.* **a.** entropy. **b.** siemens. **c.** strangeness. **6.** *Currency.* Schilling.

s. *abbrev. for:* **1.** shilling. **2.** singular. **3.** son. **4.** succeeded.

s. *or* **S.** *Music. abbrev. for* soprano.

S. *abbrev. for:* **1.** sabbath. **2.** (*pl.* **SS**) Saint. **3.** Saturday. **4.** Saxon. **5.** school. **6.** September. **7.** Signor. **8.** Sunday.

-s[1] *or* **-es** *suffix.* forming the plural of most nouns: *boys; boxes.* [< OE *-as*, pl. nominative and accusative ending of some masc. nouns]

-s[2] *or* **-es** *suffix.* forming the third person singular present indicative tense of verbs: *he runs.* [< OE (northern dialect) *-es, -s*, orig. the ending of the second person singular]

-'s *suffix.* **1.** forming the possessive singular of nouns and some pronouns: *man's; one's.* **2.** forming the possessive plural of nouns whose plurals do not end in *-s: children's.* (The possessive plural of nouns ending in *s* and of some singular nouns is formed by the addition of an apostrophe after the final *s: girls'; for goodness' sake.*) **3.** forming the plural of numbers, letters, or symbols: *20's.* **4.** *Inf.* contraction of *is* or *has: it's gone.* **5.** *Inf.* contraction of *us* with *let: let's.* **6.** *Inf.* contraction of *does* in some questions: *what's he do?* [senses 1, 2: assimilated contraction < ME *-es*, < OE, masc. and neuter genitive sing.; sense 3, equivalent to *-s*[1]]

SA *abbrev. for:* **1.** Salvation Army. **2.** South Africa. **3.** South America. **4.** South Australia. **5.** *Sturmabteilung:* the Nazi terrorist militia.

sabadilla (ˌsæbəˈdɪlə) *n.* **1.** a tropical American liliaceous plant. **2.** the bitter brown seeds of this plant, which contain the alkaloid veratrine used in insecticides. [C19: < Sp. *cebadilla*, dim. of *cebada* barley, < L *cibāre* to feed, < *cibus* food]

sabbat (ˈsæbæt, -ət) *n.* another word for **Sabbath** (sense 4).

Sabbatarian (ˌsæbəˈtɛərɪən) *n.* **1.** a person advocating the strict religious observance of Sunday. **2.** a person who observes Saturday as the Sabbath. ~*adj.* **3.** of the Sabbath or its observance. [C17: < LL *sabbatārius* a Sabbath-keeper] —ˌ**Sabbaˈtarianism** *n.*

Sabbath (ˈsæbəθ) *n.* **1.** the seventh day of the week, Saturday, devoted to worship and rest from work in Judaism and in certain Christian Churches. **2.** Sunday, observed by Christians as the day of worship and rest. **3.** (*not cap.*) a period of rest. **4.** Also called: **sabbat, witches' Sabbath.** a midnight meeting for practitioners of witchcraft or devil worship. [OE *sabbat*, < L, < Gk *sabbaton*, < Heb., < *shābath* to rest]

sabbatical (səˈbætɪkᵊl) *adj.* **1.** denoting a period of leave granted to university staff, teachers, etc., esp. originally every seventh year: *a sabbatical year.* ~*n.* **2.** any sabbatical period. [C16: < Gk *sabbatikos;* see SABBATH]

Sabbatical (səˈbætɪkᵊl) *adj.* of, relating to, or appropriate to the Sabbath as a day of rest and religious observance.

SABC *abbrev. for* South African Broadcasting Corporation.

saber (ˈseɪbə) *n., vb.* the U.S. spelling of **sabre.**

sabin (ˈsæbɪn, ˈseɪ-) *n. Physics.* a unit of acoustic absorption. [C20: introduced by Wallace C. *Sabine* (1868–1919), U.S. physicist]

Sabine (ˈsæbaɪn) *n.* **1.** a member of an ancient people who lived in central Italy. ~*adj.* **2.** of or relating to this people or their language.

sable (ˈseɪbᵊl) *n., pl.* **-bles** *or* **-ble. 1.** a marten of N Asian forests, with dark brown luxuriant fur. **2. a.** the highly valued fur of this animal. **b.** (*as modifier*): *a sable coat.* **3. American sable.** the brown, slightly less valuable fur of the American marten. **4.** a dark brown to yellowish-brown colour. ~*adj.* **5.** of the colour of sable fur. **6.** black; dark. **7.** (*usually postpositive*) *Heraldry.* of the colour black. [C15: < OF, < OHG *zobel*, of Slavic origin]

sable antelope *n.* a large black E African antelope with long backward-curving horns.

sabot (ˈsæbəʊ) *n.* **1.** a shoe made from a single block of wood. **2.** a shoe with a wooden sole and a leather or cloth upper. **3.** *Austral.* a small sailing boat with a shortened bow. [C17: < F, prob. < OF *savate* an old shoe, also infl. by *bot* BOOT[1]]

sabotage (ˈsæbəˌtɑːʒ) *n.* **1.** the deliberate destruction, disruption, or damage of equipment, a public service, etc., as by enemy agents, dissatisfied employees, etc. **2.** any similar action. ~*vb.* **3.** (*tr.*) to destroy or disrupt, esp. by secret means. [C20: < F, < *saboter* to spoil through clumsiness (lit.: to clatter in sabots)]

saboteur (ˌsæbəˈtɜː) *n.* a person who commits sabotage. [C20: < F]

sabra (ˈsɑːbrə) *n.* a Jew born in Israel. [< Heb. *Sabēr* prickly pear, common plant in the coastal areas of the country]

sabre *or U.S.* **saber** (ˈseɪbə) *n.* **1.** a stout single-edged cavalry sword, having a curved blade. **2.** a sword used in fencing, having a narrow V-shaped blade. ~*vb.* **3.** (*tr.*) to injure or kill with a sabre. [C17: via F < G (dialect) *Sabel*, < MHG *sebel*, ? < Magyar *szablya*]

sabre-rattling *n., adj. Inf.* seeking to intimidate by an aggressive display of military power.

sabre-toothed tiger *or* **cat** *n.* any of various extinct felines with long curved upper canine teeth.

sac (sæk) *n.* a pouch, bag, or pouchlike part in an animal or plant. [C18: < F, < L *saccus;* see SACK[1]] —**saccate** (ˈsækɪt, -eɪt) *adj.* —ˈ**sac**ˌ**like** *adj.*

saccharide (ˈsækəˌraɪd) *n.* any sugar or other carbohydrate, esp. a simple sugar.

saccharimeter (ˌsækəˈrɪmɪtə) *n.* any instrument for measuring the strength of sugar solutions. —ˌ**sacchaˈrimetry** *n.*

saccharin (ˈsækərɪn) *n.* a very sweet white crystalline slightly soluble powder used as a nonfattening sweetener. [C19: < SACCHARO- + -IN]

saccharine (ˈsækəˌriːn) *adj.* **1.** excessively sweet; sugary: *a saccharine smile.* **2.** of the nature of or containing sugar or saccharin.

saccharo- *or before a vowel* **sacchar-** *combining form.* sugar. [via L < Gk *sakkharon*, ult. < Sansk. *śarkarā* sugar]

saccharose (ˈsækəˌrəʊz, -ˌrəʊs) *n.* a technical name for **sugar** (sense 1).

saccule (ˈsækjuːl) *or* **sacculus** (ˈsækjʊləs) *n.* **1.** a small sac. **2.** the smaller of the two parts of the membranous labyrinth of the internal ear. Cf. **utricle.** [C19: < L *sacculus* dim. of *saccus* SACK[1]]

sacerdotal (ˌsæsəˈdəʊtᵊl) *adj.* of, relating to, or characteristic of priests. [C14: < L *sacerdōtālis*, < *sacerdōs* priest, < *sacer* sacred] —ˌ**sacerˈdotaˌlism** *n.* —ˌ**sacerˈdotally** *adv.*

sachem (ˈseɪtʃəm) *n.* **1.** *U.S.* a leader of a political party or organization. **2.** another name for **sagamore.** [C17: < Amerind *sâchim* chief]

sachet (ˈsæʃeɪ) *n.* **1.** a small sealed envelope, usually made of plastic, for containing shampoo, etc. **2. a.** a small soft bag containing perfumed powder, placed in drawers to scent clothing. **b.** the powder contained in such a bag. [C19: < OF: a little bag, < *sac* bag; see SACK[1]]

sack[1] (sæk) *n.* **1.** a large bag made of coarse cloth, thick paper, etc., used as a container. **2.** Also called: **sackful.** the amount contained in a sack. **3. a.** a woman's loose tube-shaped dress. **b.**

Also called: **sacque** (sæk). a woman's full loose hip-length jacket. **4. the sack.** *Inf.* dismissal from employment. **5.** a slang word for **bed. 6. hit the sack.** *Sl.* to go to bed. ~*vb.* (*tr.*) **7.** *Inf.* to dismiss from employment. **8.** to put into a sack or sacks. [OE *sacc,* < L *saccus* bag, < Gk *sakkos*] —ˈ**sack**ˌ**like** *adj.*

sack[2] (sæk) *n.* **1.** the plundering of a place by an army or mob. ~*vb.* **2.** (*tr.*) to plunder and partially destroy (a place). [C16: < F *mettre à sac,* lit.: to put (loot) in a sack, < L *saccus* SACK[1]] —ˈ**sacker** *n.*

sack[3] (sæk) *n. Arch. except in trademarks.* any dry white wine from SW Europe. [C16 *wyne seck,* < F *vin sec* dry wine, < L *siccus* dry]

sackbut (ˈsækˌbʌt) *n.* a medieval form of trombone. [C16: < F *saqueboute,* < OF *saquer* to pull + *bouter* to push]

sackcloth (ˈsækˌklɒθ) *n.* **1.** coarse cloth such as sacking. **2.** garments made of such cloth, worn formerly to indicate mourning. **3. sackcloth and ashes.** a public display of extreme grief.

sacking (ˈsækɪŋ) *n.* coarse cloth used for making sacks, woven from flax, hemp, jute, etc.

sack race *n.* a race in which the competitors' legs and often bodies are enclosed in sacks.

sacral[1] (ˈseɪkrəl) *adj.* of or associated with sacred rites. [C19: < L *sacrum* sacred object]

sacral[2] (ˈseɪkrəl) *adj.* of or relating to the sacrum. [C18: < NL *sacrālis* of the SACRUM]

sacrament (ˈsækrəmənt) *n.* **1.** an outward sign combined with a prescribed form of words and regarded as conferring grace upon those who receive it. The Protestant sacraments are baptism and the Lord's Supper. In the Roman Catholic and Eastern Churches they are baptism, penance, confirmation, the Eucharist, holy orders, matrimony, and extreme unction. **2.** (*often cap.*) the Eucharist. **3.** the consecrated elements of the Eucharist, esp. the bread. **4.** something regarded as possessing a sacred significance. **5.** a pledge. [C12: < Church L *sacrāmentum* vow, < L *sacrāre* to consecrate]

sacramental (ˌsækrəˈmɛntᵊl) *adj.* **1.** of or having the nature of a sacrament. ~*n.* **2.** *R.C. Church.* a sacrament-like ritual action, such as the sign of the cross or the use of holy water. —ˌ**sacra**ˈ**menta**ˌ**lism** *n.* —**sacramentality** (ˌsækrəmɛnˈtælɪtɪ) *n.*

sacrarium (sæˈkrɛərɪəm) *n., pl.* **-craria** (-ˈkrɛərɪə). **1.** the sanctuary of a church. **2.** *R.C. Church.* a place near the altar of a church where materials used in the sacred rites are deposited or poured away. [C18: < L, < *sacer* sacred]

sacred (ˈseɪkrɪd) *adj.* **1.** exclusively devoted to a deity or to some religious ceremony or use. **2.** worthy of or regarded with reverence and awe. **3.** connected with or intended for religious use: *sacred music.* **4. sacred to.** dedicated to. [C14: < L *sacrāre* to set apart as holy, < *sacer* holy] —ˈ**sacredly** *adv.* —ˈ**sacredness** *n.*

sacred cow *n. Inf.* a person, custom, etc., held to be beyond criticism. [alluding to the Hindu belief that cattle are sacred]

sacred mushroom *n.* **1.** any of various hallucinogenic mushrooms that have been eaten in rituals in various parts of the world. **2.** a mescal button, used in a similar way.

sacrifice (ˈsækrɪˌfaɪs) *n.* **1.** a surrender of something of value as a means of gaining something more desirable or of preventing some evil. **2.** a ritual killing of a person or animal with the intention of propitiating or pleasing a deity. **3.** a symbolic offering of something to a deity. **4.** the person, animal, or object killed or offered. **5.** loss entailed by giving up or selling something at less than its value. **6.** *Chess.* the act or an instance of sacrificing a piece. ~*vb.* **7.** to make a sacrifice (of). **8.** *Chess.* to permit or force one's opponent to capture a piece freely, as in playing a gambit: *he sacrificed his queen and checkmated his opponent on the next move.* [C13: via OF < L *sacrificium,* < *sacer* holy + *facere* to make] —ˈ**sacri**ˌ**ficer** *n.*

sacrifice paddock *n. N.Z.* a grassed field which is allowed to be grazed completely, so that it can be cultivated and resown later.

sacrificial (ˌsækrɪˈfɪʃəl) *adj.* used in or connected with a sacrifice. —ˌ**sacri**ˈ**ficially** *adv.*

sacrilege (ˈsækrɪlɪdʒ) *n.* **1.** the misuse or desecration of anything regarded as sacred or as worthy of extreme respect. **2.** the act or an instance of taking anything sacred for secular use. [C13: < OF, < L, < *sacrilegus* temple-robber, < *sacra* sacred things + *legere* to take] —**sacrilegist** (ˌsækrɪˈliːdʒɪst) *n.*

sacrilegious (ˌsækrɪˈlɪdʒəs) *adj.* **1.** of, relating to, or involving sacrilege. **2.** guilty of sacrilege. —ˌ**sacri**ˈ**legiously** *adv.*

sacring bell (ˈseɪkrɪŋ) *n. Chiefly R.C. Church.* a small bell rung at the elevation of the Host and chalice during Mass.

sacristan (ˈsækrɪstən) *or* **sacrist** (ˈsækrɪst, ˈseɪ-) *n.* **1.** a person who has charge of the contents of a church. **2.** a less common word for **sexton** (sense 1). [C14: < Med. L *sacristānus,* ult. < L *sacer* holy]

sacristy (ˈsækrɪstɪ) *n., pl.* **-ties.** a room attached to a church or chapel where the sacred vessels, vestments, etc., are kept. [C17: < Med. L *sacristia;* see SACRISTAN]

sacroiliac (ˌseɪkrəʊˈɪlɪˌæk) *Anat.* ~*adj.* **1.** of or relating to the sacrum and ilium or their articulation. ~*n.* **2.** the joint where these bones meet.

sacrosanct (ˈsækrəʊˌsæŋkt) *adj.* very sacred or holy. [C17: < L *sacrōsanctus* made holy by sacred rite, < *sacer* holy + *sanctus,* < *sancīre* to hallow] —ˌ**sacro**ˈ**sanctity** *n.*

sacrum (ˈseɪkrəm) *n., pl.* **-cra** (-krə). the large wedge-shaped bone, consisting of five fused vertebrae, in the lower part of the back. [C18: < L *os sacrum* holy bone, because it was used in sacrifices, < *sacer* holy]

sad (sæd) *adj.* **sadder, saddest. 1.** feeling sorrow; unhappy. **2.** causing, suggestive, or expressive of such feelings: *a sad story.* **3.** unfortunate; shabby: *her clothes were in a sad state.* [OE *sæd* weary] —ˈ**sadly** *adv.* —ˈ**sadness** *n.*

sadden (ˈsædᵊn) *vb.* to make or become sad.

saddle (ˈsædᵊl) *n.* **1.** a seat for a rider, usually made of leather, placed on a horse's back and secured with a girth under the belly. **2.** a similar seat on a bicycle, tractor, etc. **3.** a back pad forming part of the harness of a packhorse. **4.** anything that resembles a saddle in shape, position, or function. **5.** a cut of meat, esp. mutton, consisting of both loins. **6.** the part of a horse or similar animal on which a saddle is placed. **7.** the part of the back of a domestic chicken that is nearest to the tail. **8.** another word for **col** (sense 1). **9. in the saddle.** in a position of control. ~*vb.* **10.** (sometimes foll. by *up*) to put a saddle on (a horse). **11.** (*intr.*) to mount into the saddle. **12.** (*tr.*) to burden: *I didn't ask to be saddled with this job.* [OE *sadol, sædel*] —ˈ**saddle-**ˌ**like** *adj.*

saddleback (ˈsædᵊlˌbæk) *n.* a marking resembling a saddle on the backs of various animals. —ˈ**saddle-**ˌ**backed** *adj.*

saddlebag (ˈsædᵊlˌbæg) *n.* a pouch or small bag attached to the saddle of a horse, bicycle, etc.

saddlebill (ˈsædᵊlˌbɪl) *n.* a large black-and-white stork of tropical Africa, having a heavy red bill with a black band around the middle. Also called: **jabiru.**

saddlebow (ˈsædᵊlˌbəʊ) *n.* the pommel of a saddle.

saddlecloth (ˈsædᵊlˌklɒθ) *n.* a light cloth put under a horse's saddle, so as to prevent rubbing.

saddle horse *n.* a lightweight horse kept for riding only.

saddler (ˈsædlə) *n.* a person who makes, deals in, or repairs saddles and other leather equipment for horses.

saddle roof *n.* a roof that has a ridge and two gables.

saddlery (ˈsædlərɪ) *n., pl.* **-dleries. 1.** saddles, harness, and other leather equipment for horses collectively. 2. the business, work, or place of work of a saddler.

saddle soap *n.* a soft soap containing neat's-foot oil used to preserve and clean leather.

saddletree (ˈsædᵊlˌtriː) *n.* the frame of a saddle.

Sadducee (ˈsædjʊˌsiː) *n. Judaism.* a member of an ancient Jewish sect that was opposed to the Pharisees, denying the resurrection of the dead and the validity of oral tradition. [OE *saddūcēas,* via L & Gk < LHeb. *ṣaddūqi,* prob. < *Sadoq* Zadok, high priest and supposed founder of the sect] —ˌ**Sadduˈcean** *adj.*

sadhu *or* **saddhu** (ˈsɑːduː) *n.* a Hindu wandering holy man. [Sansk., < *sādhu* good]

sadiron (ˈsædˌaɪən) *n.* a heavy iron, pointed at both ends for pressing clothes. [C19: < SAD (in the obs. sense: heavy) + IRON]

sadism (ˈseɪdɪzəm) *n.* the gaining of pleasure or sexual gratification from the infliction of pain and mental suffering on another person. Cf. **masochism.** [C19: < F, after the Marquis de *Sade* (1740–1814), F soldier & writer] —ˈ**sadist** *n.* —**sadistic** (səˈdɪstɪk) *adj.* —**saˈdistically** *adv.*

sadomasochism (ˌseɪdəʊˈmæsəˌkɪzəm) *n.* the combination of sadistic and masochistic elements in one person. —ˌ**sadomasoˈchistic** *adj.*

s.a.e. *abbrev. for* stamped addressed envelope.

safari (səˈfɑːrɪ) *n., pl.* **-ris.** 1. an overland journey or hunting expedition, esp. in Africa. 2. the people, animals, etc., that go on the expedition. [C19: < Swahili: journey, < Ar., < *safara* to travel]

safari park *n.* an enclosed park in which lions and other wild animals are kept uncaged in the open and can be viewed by the public from cars, etc.

safari suit *n.* an outfit made of tough cotton, denim, etc., consisting of a bush jacket with matching trousers, shorts, or skirt.

safe (seɪf) *adj.* 1. affording security or protection from harm: *a safe place.* 2. (*postpositive*) free from danger: *you'll be safe here.* 3. secure from risk: *a safe investment.* 4. worthy of trust: *a safe companion.* 5. tending to avoid controversy or risk: *a safe player.* 6. not dangerous: *water safe to drink.* 7. **on the safe side.** as a precaution. ~*adv.* 8. in a safe condition: *the children are safe in bed now.* 9. **play safe.** to act in a way least likely to cause danger, controversy, or defeat. ~*n.* 10. a strong container, usually of metal and provided with a secure lock, for storing money or valuables. 11. a small cupboard-like container for storing food. [C13: < OF *salf,* < L *salvus*] —ˈ**safely** *adv.* —ˈ**safeness** *n.*

safe-breaker *n.* a person who breaks open and robs safes. Also called: **safe-cracker.**

safe-conduct *n.* 1. a document giving official permission to travel through a region, esp. in time of war. 2. the protection afforded by such a document.

safe-deposit *or* **safety-deposit** *n.* **a.** a place with facilities for the safe storage of money. **b.** (*as modifier*): *a safe-deposit box.*

safeguard (ˈseɪfˌgɑːd) *n.* 1. a person or thing that ensures protection against danger, injury, etc. 2. a safe-conduct. ~*vb.* 3. (*tr.*) to protect.

safe house *n.* a place used secretly by undercover agents, terrorists, etc., as a refuge.

safekeeping (ˈseɪfˈkiːpɪŋ) *n.* the act of keeping or state of being kept in safety.

safe period *n. Inf.* the period during the menstrual cycle when conception is considered least likely to occur.

safe seat *n.* a Parliamentary seat that at an election is sure to be held by the same party as held it before.

safety (ˈseɪftɪ) *n., pl.* **-ties.** 1. the quality of being safe. 2. freedom from danger or risk of injury. 3. a contrivance designed to prevent injury. 4. *American football.* Also called: **safetyman.** the defensive player furthest back in the field.

safety belt *n.* 1. another name for **seat belt** (sense 1). 2. a belt or strap worn by a person working at a great height to prevent him from falling.

safety curtain *n.* a curtain made of fireproof material that can be lowered to separate the auditorium and stage in a theatre to prevent the spread of a fire.

safety factor *n.* the ratio of the breaking stress of a material to the calculated maximum stress in use. Also called: **factor of safety.**

safety glass *n.* glass that if broken will not shatter.

safety lamp *n.* an oil-burning miner's lamp in which the flame is surrounded by a metal gauze to prevent it from igniting combustible gas.

safety match *n.* a match that will light only when struck against a specially prepared surface.

safety net *n.* 1. a net used in a circus to catch high-wire and trapeze artistes if they fall. 2. any means of protection from hardship or loss.

safety pin *n.* a spring wire clasp with a covering catch, made so as to shield the point when closed.

safety razor *n.* a razor with a guard over the blade or blades to prevent deep cuts.

safety valve *n.* 1. a valve in a pressure vessel that allows fluid to escape at excess pressure. 2. a harmless outlet for emotion, etc.

saffian (ˈsæfɪən) *n.* leather tanned with sumach and usually dyed a bright colour. [C16: via Russian & Turkish < Persian *sakhtiyān* goatskin, < *sakht* hard]

safflower (ˈsæflaʊə) *n.* 1. a thistle-like Eurasian annual plant having large heads of orange-yellow flowers and yielding a dye and an oil used in paints, medicines, etc. 2. a red dye used for cotton and for colouring foods and cosmetics. [C16: via Du. *saffloer* or G *safflor* < OF *saffleur*]

saffron (ˈsæfrən) *n.* 1. an Old World crocus having purple or white flowers with orange stigmas. 2. the dried stigmas of this plant, used to flavour or colour food. 3. **meadow saffron.** another name for **autumn crocus.** 4. **a.** an orange to orange-yellow colour. **b.** (*as adj.*): *a saffron dress.* [C13: < OF *safran,* < Med. L *safranum,* < Ar. *za'farān*]

S.Afr. *abbrev. for* South Africa(n).

safranine *or* **safranin** (ˈsæfrənɪn) *n.* any of a class of azine dyes used for textiles. [C19: < F *safran* SAFFRON + -INE²]

sag (sæg) *vb.* **sagging, sagged.** (*mainly intr.*) 1. (*also tr.*) to sink or cause to sink in parts, as under weight or pressure: *the bed sags in the middle.* 2. to fall in value: *prices sagged to a new low.* 3. to hang unevenly. 4. (of courage, etc.) to weaken. ~*n.* 5. the act or an instance of sagging: *a sag in profits.* 6. *Naut.* the extent to which a vessel's keel sags at the centre. [C15: < ON] —ˈ**saggy** *adj.*

saga (ˈsɑːgə) *n.* 1. any of several medieval prose narratives written in Iceland and recounting the exploits of a hero or a family. 2. any similar heroic narrative. 3. a series of novels about several generations or members of a family. 4. *Inf.* a series of events or a story stretching over a long period. [C18: < ON: a narrative]

sagacious (səˈgeɪʃəs) *adj.* having or showing sagacity; wise. [C17: < L *sagāx,* < *sāgīre* to be astute] —**saˈgaciously** *adv.*

sagacity (səˈgæsɪtɪ) *n.* foresight, discernment, or keen perception; ability to make good judgments.

sagamore (ˈsægəˌmɔː) *n.* (among some North American Indians) a chief or eminent man. [C17: < Amerind *sāgimau,* lit.: he overcomes]

sage¹ (seɪdʒ) *n.* 1. a man revered for his profound wisdom. ~*adj.* 2. profoundly wise or prudent. [C13: < OF, < L *sapere* to be sensible] —ˈ**sagely** *adv.* —ˈ**sageness** *n.*

sage² (seɪdʒ) *n.* 1. a perennial Mediterranean plant having grey-green leaves and purple, blue, or white flowers. 2. the leaves of this plant, used in cooking for flavouring. 3. short for **sagebrush.** [C14: < OF *saulge,* < L *salvia,* < *salvus* in good health (from its curative properties)]

sagebrush (ˈseɪdʒˌbrʌʃ) *n.* any of a genus of aromatic plants of W North America, having silver-green leaves and large clusters of small white flowers.

saggar *or* **sagger** (ˈsægə) *n.* a clay box in which

ceramic wares are placed during firing. [C17: ? alteration of SAFEGUARD]

sagittal suture (ˈsædʒɪtᵊl) *n.* a serrated line on the top of the skull that marks the junction of the two parietal bones.

Sagittarius (ˌsædʒɪˈtɛərɪəs) *n., Latin genitive* **Sagittarii** (ˌsædʒɪˈtɛərɪˌaɪ). **1.** *Astron.* a S constellation. **2.** Also called: the **Archer.** *Astrol.* the ninth sign of the zodiac. The sun is in this sign between Nov. 22 and Dec. 21. [C14: < L: an archer, < *sagitta* an arrow] —**Sagittarian** (ˌsædʒɪˈtɛərɪən) *adj.*

sagittate (ˈsædʒɪˌteɪt) *adj.* (esp. of leaves) shaped like the head of an arrow. [C18: < NL *sagittātus,* < L *sagitta* arrow]

sago (ˈseɪgəʊ) *n.* a starchy cereal obtained from the powdered pith of a palm (**sago palm**), used for puddings and as a thickening agent. [C16: < Malay *sāgū*]

saguaro (səˈgwɑːrəʊ) *n., pl.* **-ros.** a giant cactus of desert regions of Arizona, S California, and Mexico. [Mexican Sp., var. of *sahuaro,* an Indian name]

sahib (ˈsɑːhɪb) *n.* (in India) a form of address placed after a man's name, used as a mark of respect. [C17: < Urdu, < Ar. *çāhib,* lit.: friend]

said[1] (sɛd) *adj.* **1.** (*prenominal*) (in contracts, etc.) aforesaid. ~*vb.* **2.** the past tense and past participle of **say.**

said[2] (ˈsɑːɪd) *n.* a variant of **sayyid.**

saiga (ˈsaɪgə) *n.* either of two antelopes of the plains of central Asia, having a slightly elongated nose. [C19: < Russian]

sail (seɪl) *n.* **1.** an area of fabric, usually Terylene or nylon (formerly canvas), with fittings for holding it in any suitable position to catch the wind, used for propelling certain kinds of vessels, esp. over water. **2.** a voyage on such a vessel: *a sail down the river.* **3.** a vessel with sails or such vessels collectively: *to travel by sail.* **4.** a ship's sails collectively. **5.** something resembling a sail in shape, position, or function, such as the part of a windmill that is turned by the wind. **6. in sail.** having the sail set. **7. make sail. a.** to run up the sail or to run up more sail. **b.** to begin a voyage. **8. set sail. a.** to embark on a voyage by ship. **b.** to hoist sail. **9. under sail. a.** with sail hoisted. **b.** under way. ~*vb.* (*mainly intr.*) **10.** to travel in a boat or ship: *we sailed to Le Havre.* **11.** to begin a voyage: *we sail at 5 o'clock.* **12.** (of a vessel) to move over the water. **13.** (*tr.*) to manoeuvre or navigate a vessel: *he sailed the schooner up the channel.* **14.** (*tr.*) to sail over: *she sailed the Atlantic single-handed.* **15.** (often foll. by *over, through,* etc.) to move fast or effortlessly: *we sailed through customs.* **16.** to move along smoothly; glide. **17.** (often foll. by *in* or *into*) *Inf.* **a.** to begin (something) with vigour. **b.** to make an attack (on) violently. [OE *segl*] —ˈ**sailable** *adj.* —ˈ**sailless** *adj.*

sailboard (ˈseɪlˌbɔːd) *n.* the craft used for windsurfing, consisting of a moulded board to which a mast bearing a single sail is attached.

sailcloth (ˈseɪlˌklɒθ) *n.* **1.** any of various fabrics from which sails are made. **2.** a canvas-like cloth used for clothing, etc.

sailer (ˈseɪlə) *n.* a vessel, with specified sailing characteristics: *a good sailer.*

sailfish (ˈseɪlˌfɪʃ) *n., pl.* **-fish** *or* **-fishes. 1.** any of several large game fishes of warm and tropical seas. They have an elongated upper jaw and a long sail-like dorsal fin. **2.** another name for **basking shark.**

sailing ship *n.* a large sailing vessel.

sailor (ˈseɪlə) *n.* **1.** any member of a ship's crew, esp. one below the rank of officer. **2.** a person who sails, esp. with reference to the likelihood of his becoming seasick: *a good sailor.*

sailplane (ˈseɪlˌpleɪn) *n.* a high-performance glider.

sainfoin (ˈsænfɔɪn) *n.* a Eurasian perennial plant, widely grown as a forage crop, having pale pink flowers and curved pods. [C17: < F, < Med. L *sānum faenum* wholesome hay, referring to its former use as a medicine]

saint (seɪnt; *unstressed* sənt) *n.* **1.** a person who after death is formally recognized by a Christian Church as having attained a specially exalted place in heaven and the right to veneration. **2.** a person of exceptional holiness. **3.** (*pl.*) *Bible.* the collective body of those who are righteous in God's sight. ~*vb.* **4.** (*tr.*) to recognize formally as a saint. [C12: < OF, < L *sanctus* holy, < *sancīre* to hallow] —ˈ**sainthood** *n.* —ˈ**saintlike** *adj.*

Saint Agnes' Eve (ˈægnɪs) *n., usually abbreviated to* **St Agnes' Eve.** the night of Jan. 20, when according to tradition a woman can discover the identity of her future husband by performing certain rites.

Saint Andrew's Cross (ˈændruːz) *n., usually abbreviated to* **St Andrew's Cross. 1.** a diagonal cross with equal arms. **2.** a white diagonal cross on a blue ground.

Saint Anthony's fire (ˈæntənɪz) *n., usually abbreviated to* **St Anthony's fire.** *Pathol.* another name for **ergotism** or **erysipelas.**

Saint Bernard (ˈbɜːnəd) *n., usually abbreviated to* **St Bernard.** a large breed of dog with a dense red-and-white coat, formerly used as a rescue dog in mountainous areas.

sainted (ˈseɪntɪd) *adj.* **1.** canonized. **2.** like a saint in character or nature. **3.** hallowed or holy.

Saint Elmo's fire (ˈɛlməʊz) *n., usually abbreviated to* **St Elmo's fire.** (not in technical usage) a luminous region that sometimes appears around church spires, the masts of ships, etc.

Saint John's wort (ˈdʒɒnz) *n., usually abbreviated to* **St John's wort.** any of a genus of shrubs or herbaceous plants, having yellow flowers.

Saint Leger (ˈlɛdʒə) *n., usually abbreviated to* **St Leger. the.** an annual horse race run at Doncaster, England, since 1776.

saintly (ˈseɪntlɪ) *adj.* like, relating to, or suitable for a saint. —ˈ**saintlily** *adv.* —ˈ**saintliness** *n.*

saintpaulia (səntˈpɔːlɪə) *n.* another name for **African violet.** [C20: NL, after Baron W. von *Saint Paul,* G soldier (died 1910), who discovered it]

saint's day *n. Christianity.* a day in the church calendar commemorating a saint.

Saint Vitus's dance (ˈvaɪtəsɪz) *n., usually abbreviated to* **St Vitus's dance.** *Pathol.* a nontechnical name for **chorea.**

saith (sɛθ) *vb.* (used with *he, she,* or *it*) *Arch.* a form of the present tense of **say.**

saithe (seɪθ) *n. Brit.* another name for **coalfish.** [C19: < ON]

sake[1] (seɪk) *n.* **1.** benefit or interest (esp. in **for (someone's** *or* **one's own) sake**). **2.** the purpose of obtaining or achieving (esp. in **for the sake of (something)**). **3.** used in various exclamations of impatience, urgency, etc.: *for heaven's sake.* [C13 (in the phrase *for the sake of,* prob. from legal usage): < OE *sacu* lawsuit (hence, a cause)]

sake[2], **saké,** *or* **saki** (ˈsækɪ) *n.* a Japanese alcoholic drink made from fermented rice. [C17: < Japanese]

saker (ˈseɪkə) *n.* a large falcon of E Europe and Asia. [C14 *sagre,* < OF *sacre,* < Ar. *saqr*]

saki (ˈsɑːkɪ) *n.* **1.** any of several small mostly arboreal New World monkeys having a long bushy tail. **2.** another name for **sake**[2]. [sense 1: C20: F, < Tupi *saqi*]

sal (sæl) *n.* a pharmacological term for **salt** (sense 3). [L: salt]

salaam (səˈlɑːm) *n.* **1.** a Muslim salutation consisting of a deep bow with the right palm on the forehead. **2.** a salutation signifying peace. ~*vb.* **3.** to make a salaam (to). [C17: < Ar. *salām* peace, < *assalām 'alaikum* peace be to you]

salable (ˈseɪləbᵊl) *adj.* the U.S. spelling of **saleable.**

salacious (səˈleɪʃəs) *adj.* **1.** having an excessive interest in sex. **2.** (of books, etc.) erotic, bawdy, or lewd. [C17: < L *salax* fond of leaping, < *salīre* to leap] —**sa'laciously** *adv.* —**sa'laciousness** *or* **salacity** (səˈlæsɪtɪ) *n.*

salad (ˈsæləd) *n.* **1.** a dish of raw vegetables, such as lettuce, tomatoes, etc., served as a separate course with cold meat, eggs, etc., or as part of a main course. **2.** any dish of cold vegetables or fruit served with a dressing: *potato salad.* **3.** any green vegetable or herb used in such a dish. [C15: < OF *salade,* < OProvençal *salada,* < *salar* to season with salt, < L *sal* salt]

salad days *pl. n.* a period of youth and inexperience.

salad dressing *n.* a sauce for salad, such as oil and vinegar or mayonnaise.

salade niçoise (sæˈlɑːd niːˈswɑːz) *n.* a cold dish consisting of a variety of ingredients, usually including hard-boiled eggs, anchovy fillets, olives, tomatoes, and sometimes tuna fish. [C20: < F, lit.: salad of or from *Nice,* S France]

salamander (ˈsæləˌmændə) *n.* **1.** any of various amphibians of central and S Europe. They have an elongated body, and only return to water to breed. **2.** *Chiefly U.S. & Canad.* any amphibian with a tail, as the newt. **3.** a mythical reptilian creature supposed to live in fire. **4.** an elemental fire-inhabiting being. [C14: < OF *salamandre,* < L *salamandra,* < Gk]

salami (səˈlɑːmɪ) *n.* a highly seasoned type of sausage, usually flavoured with garlic. [C19: < It., pl. of *salame,* < Vulgar L *salāre* (unattested) to salt, < L *sal* salt]

sal ammoniac *n.* another name for **ammonium chloride.**

salaried (ˈsælərɪd) *adj.* earning or yielding a salary: *a salaried worker; salaried employment.*

salary (ˈsælərɪ) *n., pl.* **-ries. 1.** a fixed payment made by an employer, often monthly, for professional or office work. Cf. **wage.** ~*vb.* **-rying, -ried. 2.** (*tr.*) to pay a salary to. [C14: < Anglo-Norman *salarie,* < L *salārium* the sum given to Roman soldiers to buy salt, < *sal* salt]

salchow (ˈsɔːlkəʊ) *n. Figure skating.* a jump from the inner backward edge of one foot with one, two, or three full turns in the air, returning to the outer backward edge of the opposite foot. [C20: after Ulrich *Salchow* (1877–1949), Swedish figure skater, who originated it]

sale (seɪl) *n.* **1.** the exchange of goods, property, or services for an agreed sum of money or credit. **2.** the amount sold. **3.** the opportunity to sell: *there was no sale for luxuries.* **4. a.** an event at which goods are sold at reduced prices, usually to clear old stocks. **b.** (*as modifier*): *sale bargains.* **5.** an auction. [OE *sala,* < ON *sala*]

saleable *or U.S.* **salable** (ˈseɪləbᵊl) *adj.* fit for selling or capable of being sold. —**ˌsaleaˈbility** *or U.S.* **ˌsalaˈbility** *n.*

sale of work *n.* a sale of articles, often handmade, the proceeds of which benefit a charity or charities.

sale or return *n.* an arrangement by which a retailer pays only for goods sold, returning those that are unsold.

saleroom (ˈseɪlˌruːm, -ˌrʊm) *n. Chiefly Brit.* a room where objects are displayed for sale, esp. by auction.

salesclerk (ˈseɪlzˌklɑːk) *n. U.S. & Canad.* a shop assistant.

salesman (ˈseɪlzmən) *n., pl.* **-men. 1.** Also called: **saleswoman** (*fem.*), **salesgirl** (*fem.*), *or* **salesperson.** a person who sells merchandise or services in a shop. **2.** short for **travelling salesman.**

salesmanship (ˈseɪlzmənʃɪp) *n.* **1.** the technique of, skill, or ability in selling. **2.** the work of a salesman.

sales resistance *n.* opposition of potential customers to selling, esp. aggressive selling.

sales talk *or* **pitch** *n.* an argument or other persuasion used in selling.

sales tax *n.* a tax levied on retail sales receipts and added to selling prices by retailers.

sales trader *n. Stock Exchange.* a person employed by a market maker, or his firm, to find clients.

Salian (ˈseɪlɪən) *adj.* **1.** denoting or relating to a group of Franks (the **Salii**) who settled in the Netherlands in the 4th century A.D. ~*n.* **2.** a member of this group.

salicin (ˈsælɪsɪn) *n.* a crystalline water-soluble glucoside obtained from the bark of poplar trees and used as a medical analgesic. [C19: < F, < L *salix* willow]

Salic law (ˈsælɪk) *n. History.* **1.** the code of laws of the Salian Franks and other Germanic tribes. **2.** a law excluding women from succession to the throne in certain countries, such as France.

salicylate (səˈlɪsɪˌleɪt) *n.* any salt or ester of salicylic acid.

salicylic acid (ˌsælɪˈsɪlɪk) *n.* a white crystalline substance with a sweet taste and bitter aftertaste, used in the manufacture of aspirin, and as a fungicide.

salient (ˈseɪlɪənt) *adj.* **1.** conspicuous or striking: *a salient feature.* **2.** projecting outwards at an angle of less than 180°. **3.** (esp. of animals) leaping. ~*n.* **4.** *Mil.* a projection of the forward line into enemy-held territory. **5.** a salient angle. [C16: < L *salīre* to leap] —**ˈsalience** *or* **ˈsaliency** *n.* —**ˈsaliently** *adv.*

salientian (ˌseɪlɪˈɛnʃɪən) *n.* **1.** any of an order of vertebrates with no tail and long hind legs adapted for hopping, as the frog or the toad. ~*adj.* **2.** of or belonging to this order. [C19: < NL *Salientia,* lit.: leapers, < L *salīre* to leap]

salina (səˈlaɪnə) *n.* a salt marsh or lake. [C17: < Sp., < Med. L: salt pit, < LL *salīnus* SALINE]

saline (ˈseɪlaɪn) *adj.* **1.** of, consisting of, or containing common salt: *a saline taste.* **2.** *Med.* of or relating to a saline. **3.** of, consisting of, or containing any chemical salt, esp. sodium chloride. ~*n.* **4.** *Med.* a solution of sodium chloride and water. [C15: < LL *salīnus,* < L *sal* salt] —**salinity** (səˈlɪnɪtɪ) *n.*

salinometer (ˌsælɪˈnɒmɪtə) *n.* a hydrometer for determining the amount of salt in a solution. —**ˌsaliˈnometry** *n.*

saliva (səˈlaɪvə) *n.* the secretion of salivary glands, consisting of a clear usually slightly acid aqueous fluid of variable composition. [C17: < L, <?] —**salivary** (səˈlaɪvərɪ) *adj.*

salivary gland *n.* any of the glands in mammals that secrete saliva.

salivate (ˈsælɪˌveɪt) *vb.* **1.** (*intr.*) to secrete saliva, esp. an excessive amount. **2.** (*tr.*) to cause (an animal, etc.) to produce saliva, as by the administration of mercury. —**ˌsaliˈvation** *n.*

Salk vaccine (sɔːlk) *n.* a vaccine against poliomyelitis. [C20: after Jonas *Salk* (born 1914), U.S. virologist, who developed it]

sallee (ˈsælɪ) *n. Austral.* **1.** a SE Australian eucalyptus tree with pale grey bark. **2.** any of various acacia trees. [prob. < Abor.]

sallow[1] (ˈsæləʊ) *adj.* **1.** (esp. of human skin) of an unhealthy pale or yellowish colour. ~*vb.* **2.** (*tr.*) to make sallow. [OE *salu*] —**ˈsallowish** *adj.* —**ˈsallowness** *n.*

sallow[2] (ˈsæləʊ) *n.* **1.** any of several small willow trees, esp. the common sallow, which has large catkins that appear before the leaves. **2.** a twig or the wood of any of these trees. [OE *sealh*] —**ˈsallowy** *adj.*

sally (ˈsælɪ) *n., pl.* **-lies. 1.** a sudden sortie, esp. by troops. **2.** a sudden outburst or emergence into action or expression. **3.** an excursion. **4.** a jocular retort. ~*vb.* **-lying, -lied.** (*intr.*) **5.** to make a sudden violent sortie. **6.** (often foll. by *forth*) to go out on an expedition, etc. **7.** to come or set out in an energetic manner. **8.** to rush out suddenly. [C16: < OF *saillie,* < *saillir* to dash forwards, < L *salīre* to leap]

Sally Lunn (lʌn) *n.* a flat round cake made from a sweet yeast dough. [C19: said to be after an 18th-century E baker who invented it]

salmagundi (ˌsælməˈgʌndɪ) *n.* **1.** a mixed salad dish of cooked meats, eggs, beetroot, etc., popular in 18th-century England. **2.** a miscellany. [C17: < F *salmigondis,* ? < It. *salami conditi* pickled salami]

salmon (ˈsæmən) *n., pl.* **-ons** *or* **-on. 1.** a soft-finned fish of the Atlantic and the Pacific, which is an important food fish. Salmon occur in cold and temperate waters and many species migrate to fresh water to spawn. **2.** *Austral.* any of several unrelated fish. [C13: < OF *saumon*, < L *salmō*] —**'salmo,noid** *adj.*

salmonella (ˌsælməˈnɛlə) *n., pl.* **-lae** (-ˌliː). any of a genus of rod-shaped aerobic bacteria including many species which cause food poisoning. [C19: NL, after Daniel E. *Salmon* (1850–1914), U.S. veterinary surgeon]

salmon ladder *n.* a series of steps designed to enable salmon to move upstream to their breeding grounds.

salon (ˈsælɒn) *n.* **1.** a room in a large house in which guests are received. **2.** an assembly of guests in a fashionable household, esp. a gathering of major literary, artistic, and political figures. **3.** a commercial establishment in which hairdressers, etc., carry on their businesses. **4. a.** a hall for exhibiting works of art. **b.** such an exhibition, esp. one showing the work of living artists. [C18: < F, < It. *salone*, augmented form of *sala* hall, of Gmc origin]

saloon (səˈluːn) *n.* **1.** Also called: **saloon bar.** *Brit.* another word for **lounge** (sense 5). **2.** a large public room on a passenger ship. **3.** any large public room used for a purpose: *a dancing saloon.* **4.** *Chiefly U.S. & Canad.* a place where alcoholic drink is sold and consumed. **5.** a closed two-door or four-door car with four to six seats. U.S., Canad., and N.Z. name: **sedan.** [C18: < F SALON]

salopettes (ˌsæləˈpɛts) *pl. n.* a garment worn for skiing, consisting of quilted trousers held up by shoulder straps. [C20: < F]

salpiglossis (ˌsælpɪˈglɒsɪs) *n.* any of a genus of plants, some species of which are cultivated for their bright funnel-shaped flowers. [C19: NL, < Gk *salpinx* trumpet + *glōssa* tongue]

salpinx (ˈsælpɪŋks) *n., pl.* **salpinges** (sælˈpɪndʒiːz). *Anat.* another name for **Fallopian tube** or **Eustachian tube.** [C19: < Gk: trumpet] —**salpingectomy** (ˌsælpɪnˈdʒɛktəmɪ) *n.* —**salpingitis** (ˌsælpɪnˈdʒaɪtɪs) *n.*

salsa (ˈsælsə) *n.* **1.** a type of Puerto Rican big-band dance music. **2.** a dance performed to this.

salsify (ˈsælsɪfɪ) *n., pl.* **-fies.** **1.** Also called: **oyster plant, vegetable oyster.** a Mediterranean plant having grasslike leaves, purple flower heads, and a long white edible taproot. **2.** the root of this plant, which tastes of oysters and is eaten as a vegetable. [C17: < F, < It. *sassefrica*, < LL, < L *saxum* rock + *fricāre* to rub]

sal soda *n.* the crystalline decahydrate of sodium carbonate.

salt (sɔːlt) *n.* **1.** a white powder or colourless crystalline solid, consisting mainly of sodium chloride and used for seasoning and preserving food. **2.** (*modifier*) preserved in, flooded with, containing, or growing in salt or salty water: *salt pork.* **3.** *Chem.* any of a class of crystalline solid compounds that are formed from, or can be regarded as formed from, an acid and a base. **4.** liveliness or pungency: *his wit added salt to the discussion.* **5.** dry or laconic wit. **6.** an experienced sailor. **7.** short for **saltcellar.** **8. rub salt into someone's wounds.** to make someone's pain, shame, etc., even worse. **9. salt of the earth.** a person or group of people regarded as the finest of their kind. **10. with a grain** (*or* **pinch**) **of salt.** with reservations. **11. worth one's salt.** worthy of one's pay. ~*vb.* (*tr.*) **12.** to season or preserve with salt. **13.** to scatter salt over (an iced road, etc.) to melt the ice. **14.** to add zest to. **15.** (often foll. by *down* or *away*) to preserve or cure with salt. **16.** *Chem.* to treat with salt. **17.** to give a false appearance of value to, esp. to introduce valuable ore fraudulently into (a mine, sample, etc.). ~*adj.* **18.** not sour, sweet, or bitter; salty. ~See also **salt away, salts.** [OE *sealt*] —**'salt,like** *adj.* —**'saltness** *n.*

SALT (sɔːlt) *n. acronym for* Strategic Arms Limitation Talks *or* Treaty.

saltation (sælˈteɪʃən) *n.* **1.** *Biol.* an abrupt variation in the appearance of an organism, species, etc. **2.** *Geol.* the leaping movement of sand or soil particles carried in water or by the wind. **3.** a sudden abrupt movement. [C17: < L *saltātiō* a dance, < *saltāre* to leap about] —**saltatorial** (ˌsæltəˈtɔːrɪəl) *or* **'saltatory** *adj.*

salt away *or* (*less commonly*) **down** *vb.* (*tr., adv.*) to hoard or save (money, valuables, etc.).

saltbush (ˈsɔːltˌbʊʃ) *n.* any of certain shrubs that grow in alkaline desert regions.

salt cake *n.* an impure form of sodium sulphate used in the manufacture of detergents, glass, and ceramic glazes.

saltcellar (ˈsɔːltˌsɛlə) *n.* **1.** a small container for salt used at the table. **2.** *Brit. inf.* either of the two hollows formed above the collarbones. [changed (through infl. of cellar) < C15 *salt saler; saler* < OF *saliere* container for salt, < L *salārius* belonging to salt, < *sal* salt]

salt dome *or* **plug** *n.* a domelike structure of stratified rocks containing a central core of salt.

salted (ˈsɔːltɪd) *adj.* seasoned, preserved, or treated with salt.

salt flat *n.* a flat expanse of salt left by the total evaporation of a body of water.

saltigrade (ˈsæltɪˌgreɪd) *adj.* (of animals) adapted for moving in a series of jumps. [C19: < NL *Saltigradae*, name formerly applied to jumping spiders, < L *saltus* a leap + *gradī* to move]

saltings (ˈsɔːltɪŋz) *pl. n.* meadow land or marsh that is periodically flooded by sea water.

saltire *or* **saltier** (ˈsɔːlˌtaɪə) *n. Heraldry.* an ordinary consisting of a diagonal cross on a shield. [C14 *sawturoure*, < OF *sauteour* cross-shaped barricade, < *saulter* to jump, < L *saltāre*]

salt lick *n.* **1.** a place where wild animals go to lick salt deposits. **2.** a block of salt given to domestic animals to lick. **3.** *Austral. & N.Z.* a soluble cake of minerals used to supplement the diet of farm animals.

saltpan (ˈsɔːltˌpæn) *n.* a shallow basin, usually in a desert region, containing salt, gypsum, etc., that was deposited from an evaporated salt lake.

saltpetre *or U.S.* **saltpeter** (ˌsɔːltˈpiːtə) *n.* **1.** another name for **potassium nitrate.** **2.** short for **Chile saltpetre.** [C16: < OF *salpetre*, < L *sal petrae* salt of rock]

salt pork *n.* pork, esp. taken from the back and belly, that has been cured with salt.

salts (sɔːlts) *pl. n.* **1.** *Med.* any of various mineral salts, such as magnesium sulphate, for use as a cathartic. **2.** short for **smelling salts.** **3. like a dose of salts.** *Inf.* very quickly.

saltus (ˈsæltəs) *n., pl.* **-tuses.** a break in the continuity of a sequence. [L: a leap]

saltwater (ˈsɔːltˌwɔːtə) *adj.* of or inhabiting salt water, esp. the sea: *saltwater fishes.*

saltworks (ˈsɔːltˌwɜːks) *n.* (*functioning as sing.*) a building or factory where salt is produced.

saltwort (ˈsɔːltˌwɜːt) *n.* any of various plants, of beaches and salt marshes, having prickly leaves, striped stems, and small green flowers. Also called: **glasswort, kali.**

salty (ˈsɔːltɪ) *adj.* **saltier, saltiest.** **1.** of, tasting of, or containing salt. **2.** (esp. of humour) sharp. **3.** relating to life at sea. —**'saltiness** *n.*

salubrious (səˈluːbrɪəs) *adj.* conducive or favourable to health. [C16: < L, < *salūs* health] —**sa'lubriously** *adv.* —**sa'lubrity** *n.*

Saluki (səˈluːkɪ) *n.* a tall breed of hound with a smooth coat and long fringes on the ears and tail. [C19: < Ar. *salūqīy* of Saluq, an ancient Arabian city]

salutary (ˈsæljʊtərɪ) *adj.* **1.** promoting or intended to promote an improvement: *a salutary warning.* **2.** promoting or intended to promote health. [C15: < L *salūtāris* wholesome, < *salūs* safety] —**'salutarily** *adv.*

salutation (ˌsæljʊˈteɪʃən) *n.* **1.** an act, phrase, gesture, etc., that serves as a greeting. **2.** a form of words used as an opening to a speech or letter, such as *Dear Sir.* [C14: < L *salūtātiō*, < *salūtāre* to greet; see SALUTE]

salutatory (səˈluːtətərɪ) *adj.* of, relating to, or resembling a salutation. —**sa'lutatorily** *adv.*

salute (səˈluːt) *vb.* **1.** (*tr.*) to address or welcome with friendly words or gestures of respect, such as bowing. **2.** (*tr.*) to acknowledge with praise: *we salute your gallantry.* **3.** *Mil.* to pay formal respect, as by raising the right arm. ~*n.* **4.** the act of saluting. **5.** a formal military gesture of respect. [C14: < L *salūtāre* to greet, < *salūs* wellbeing] —**sa'luter** *n.*

salvable ('sælvəbᵊl) *adj.* capable of or suitable for being saved or salvaged. [C17: < LL *salvāre* to save, < *salvus* safe]

salvage ('sælvɪdʒ) *n.* **1.** the act, process, or business of rescuing vessels or their cargoes from loss at sea. **2. a.** the act of saving any goods or property in danger of damage or destruction. **b.** (*as modifier*): *a salvage operation.* **3.** the goods or property so saved. **4.** compensation paid for the salvage of a vessel or its cargo. **5.** the proceeds from the sale of salvaged goods. ~*vb.* (*tr.*) **6.** to save or rescue (goods or property) from fire, shipwreck, etc. **7.** to gain (something beneficial) from a failure. [C17: < OF, < Med. L *salvāgium,* < *salvāre* to SAVE[1]] —**'salvageable** *adj.* —**'salvager** *n.*

salvation (sæl'veɪʃən) *n.* **1.** the act of preserving or the state of being preserved from harm. **2.** a person or thing that is the means of preserving from harm. **3.** *Christianity.* deliverance by redemption from the power of sin. [C13: < OF, < LL *salvātiō,* < L *salvātus* saved, < *salvāre* to SAVE[1]]

Salvation Army *n.* a Christian body founded in 1865 by William Booth and organized on quasi-military lines for evangelism and social work among the poor.

salvationist (sæl'veɪʃənɪst) *n.* **1.** a member of an evangelical sect emphasizing the doctrine of salvation. **2.** (*often cap.*) a member of the Salvation Army.

salve (sælv, sɑːv) *n.* **1.** an ointment for wounds, etc. **2.** anything that heals or soothes. ~*vb.* (*tr.*) **3.** to apply salve to (a wound, etc.). **4.** to soothe, comfort, or appease. [OE *sealf*]

salver ('sælvə) *n.* a tray, esp. one of silver, on which food, letters, visiting cards, etc., are presented. [C17: < F *salve,* < Sp. *salva* tray from which the king's taster sampled food, < L *salvāre* to SAVE[1]]

salvia ('sælvɪə) *n.* any of a genus of herbaceous plants or small shrubs, such as the sage, grown for their medicinal or culinary properties or for ornament. [C19: < L: SAGE[2]]

salvo ('sælvəʊ) *n., pl.* **-vos** *or* **-voes. 1.** a discharge of fire from weapons in unison, esp. on a ceremonial occasion. **2.** concentrated fire from many weapons, as in a naval battle. **3.** an outburst, as of applause. [C17: < It. *salva,* < OF *salve,* < L *salvē!* greetings!, ult. < *salvus* safe]

Salvo ('sælvəʊ) *n., pl.* **-vos.** *Austral. sl.* a member of the Salvation Army.

sal volatile (vɒ'lætɪlɪ) *n.* a solution of ammonium carbonate in alcohol and aqueous ammonia, used as smelling salts. Also called: **spirits of ammonia.** [C17: < NL: volatile salt]

SAM (sæm) *n. acronym for* surface-to-air missile.

Sam. *Bible. abbrev. for* Samuel.

samara (sə'mɑːrə) *n.* a dry winged one-seeded fruit: occurs in the ash, maple, etc. Also called: **key fruit.** [C16: < NL, < L: seed of an elm]

Samaritan (sə'mærɪtᵊn) *n.* **1.** a native or inhabitant of Samaria, a kingdom in ancient Palestine. **2.** short for **Good Samaritan. 3.** a member of a voluntary organization (**the Samaritans**) whose aim is to help people in distress or despair.

samarium (sə'mɛərɪəm) *n.* a silvery metallic element of the lanthanide series used in carbon-arc lighting, as a doping agent in laser crystals, and as a neutron-absorber. Symbol: Sm; atomic no.: 62; atomic wt.: 150.35. [C19: < NL, < mineral, *samarskite,* after Col. von *Samarski,* 19th-century Russian inspector of mines + -IUM]

samba ('sæmbə) *n., pl.* **-bas. 1.** a modern ballroom dance from Brazil in bouncy duple time. **2.** a piece of music composed for or in the rhythm of this dance. ~*vb.* **-baing, -baed. 3.** (*intr.*) to perform such a dance. [Port., of African origin]

sambar *or* **sambur** ('sæmbə) *n., pl.* **-bars, -bar** *or* **-burs, -bur.** a S Asian deer with three-tined antlers. [C17: < Hindi, < Sansk. *śambarra,* <?]

Sam Browne belt (ˌsæm 'braʊn) *n.* a military officer's wide belt supported by a strap passing from the left side of the belt over the right shoulder. [C20: after Sir *Samuel J. Browne* (1824–1901), British general, who invented it]

same (seɪm) *adj.* (usually preceded by *the*) **1.** being the very one: *she is wearing the same hat.* **2. a.** being the one previously referred to. **b.** (*as n.*): *a note received about same.* **3. a.** identical in kind, quantity, etc.: *two girls of the same age.* **b.** (*as n.*): *we'd like the same.* **4.** unchanged in character or nature: *his attitude is the same as ever.* **5. all the same. a.** Also: **just the same.** nevertheless; yet. **b.** immaterial: *it's all the same to me.* ~*adv.* **6.** in an identical manner. [C12: < ON *samr*] —**'sameness** *n.*

▷ **Usage.** The use of *same* exemplified in *if you send us your order for the materials, we will deliver same tomorrow* is common in business and official English. In general English, however, this use of the word is avoided: *may I borrow your book? I'll return it* (not *same*) *tomorrow.*

samfoo ('sæmfuː) *n.* a style of dress worn by Chinese women, consisting of a waisted blouse and trousers. [< Chinese *sam* dress + *foo* trousers]

Samian ('seɪmɪən) *adj.* **1.** of or relating to Samos, an island in the Aegean, or its inhabitants. ~*n.* **2.** a native or inhabitant of Samos.

Samian ware *n.* a fine earthenware pottery, reddish-brown or black in colour, found in large quantities on Roman sites. [C19: after the Gk island of *Samos,* source of a reddish earth similar to that from which the pottery was made]

samisen ('sæmɪˌsɛn) *n.* a Japanese plucked stringed instrument with a long neck and a rectangular soundbox. [Japanese, < Chinese *san-hsien,* < *san* three + *hsien* string]

samite ('sæmaɪt) *n.* a heavy fabric of silk, often woven with gold or silver threads, used in the Middle Ages. [C13: < OF *samit,* < Med. L *examitum,* < Gk, < *hexamitos* having six threads]

samizdat (*Russian* səmiz'dat) *n.* (in the Soviet Union) **a.** a system of clandestine printing and distribution of banned literature. **b.** (*as modifier*): *a samizdat publication.* [< Russian]

samosa (sə'məʊsə) *n., pl.* **-sas** *or* **-sa.** (in Indian cookery) a small, fried, triangular spiced meat or vegetable pasty. [C20: < Hindi]

samovar ('sæməˌvɑː) *n.* (esp. in Russia) a metal urn for making tea, in which the water is usually heated by an inner container. [C19: < Russian, < *samo-* self + *varit'* to boil]

Samoyed (ˌsæmə'jɛd) *n.* **1.** (*pl.* **-yed** *or* **-yeds**) a member of a group of peoples who live chiefly in the area of the N Urals: related to the Finns. **2.** the languages of these peoples. **3.** (sə'mɔɪɛd) a white or cream breed of dog having a dense coat and a tightly curled tail. [C17: < Russian *Samoed*]

samp (sæmp) *n. S. African.* crushed maize used for porridge. [< Amerind *nasaump* corn mush, soup]

sampan ('sæmpæn) *n.* a small skiff, widely used in the Orient, that is propelled by oars. [C17: < Chinese, < *san* three + *pan* board]

samphire ('sæmˌfaɪə) *n.* **1.** an umbelliferous plant of Eurasian coasts, having fleshy divided leaves and clusters of small white flowers. **2. golden samphire.** a Eurasian coastal plant with fleshy leaves and yellow flower heads. **3. marsh samphire.** another name for **glasswort** (sense 1). **4.** any of several other plants of coastal areas. [C16 *sampiere,* < F *herbe de Saint Pierre* Saint Peter's herb]

sample ('sɑːmpᵊl) *n.* **1. a.** a small part of anything, intended as representative of the whole. **b.** (*as modifier*): *a sample bottle.* **2.** Also called: **sampling.** *Statistics.* a set of individuals or items selected from a population and analysed to test hypotheses about or yield estimates of the population. ~*vb.* **3.** (*tr.*) to take a sample or samples of. [C13: < OF *essample,* < L *exemplum* EXAMPLE]

sampler (ˈsɑːmplə) *n.* **1.** a person who takes samples. **2.** a piece of embroidery done to show the embroiderer's skill in using many different stitches.

sampling (ˈsɑːmplɪŋ) *n.* **1.** the process of selecting a random sample. **2.** a variant of **sample** (sense 2).

sampling distribution *n. Statistics.* the distribution of a random, experimentally obtained sample.

Samson (ˈsæmsən) *n.* **1.** a judge of Israel, who performed herculean feats of strength until he was betrayed by his mistress Delilah (Judges 13–16). **2.** any man of outstanding physical strength.

samurai (ˈsæmʊˌraɪ) *n., pl.* **-rai. 1.** the Japanese warrior caste from the 11th to the 19th centuries. **2.** a member of this aristocratic caste. [C19: < Japanese]

sanative (ˈsænətɪv) *adj., n.* a less common word for **curative.** [C15: < Med. L *sānātīvus,* < L *sānāre* to heal, < *sānus* healthy]

sanatorium (ˌsænəˈtɔːrɪəm) *or U.S.* **sanitarium** *n., pl.* **-riums** *or* **-ria** (-rɪə). **1.** an institution for the medical care and recuperation of persons who are chronically ill. **2.** *Brit.* a room as in a boarding school where sick pupils may be treated. [C19: < NL, < L *sānāre* to heal]

sanctified (ˈsæŋktɪˌfaɪd) *adj.* **1.** consecrated or made holy. **2.** sanctimonious.

sanctify (ˈsæŋktɪˌfaɪ) *vb.* **-fying, -fied.** (*tr.*) **1.** to make holy. **2.** to free from sin. **3.** to sanction (an action or practice) as religiously binding: *to sanctify a marriage.* **4.** to declare or render (something) productive of or conductive to holiness or grace. [C14: < LL *sanctificāre,* < L *sanctus* holy + *facere* to make] —ˌ**sanctifiˈcation** *n.* —ˈ**sanctiˌfier** *n.*

sanctimonious (ˌsæŋktɪˈməʊnɪəs) *adj.* affecting piety or making a display of holiness. [C17: < L *sanctimonia* sanctity, < *sanctus* holy] —ˌ**sanctiˈmoniously** *adv.* —ˌ**sanctiˈmoniousness** *or* ˈ**sanctimony** *n.*

sanction (ˈsæŋkʃən) *n.* **1.** authorization. **2.** aid or encouragement. **3.** something, such as an ethical principle, that imparts binding force to a rule, oath, etc. **4.** the penalty laid down in a law for contravention of its provisions. **5.** (*often pl.*) a coercive measure, esp. one taken by one or more states against another guilty of violating international law. ~*vb.* (*tr.*) **6.** to give authority to. **7.** to confirm. [C16: < L *sanctiō* the establishment of an inviolable decree, < *sancīre* to decree]

sanctitude (ˈsæŋktɪˌtjuːd) *n.* saintliness; holiness.

sanctity (ˈsæŋktɪtɪ) *n., pl.* **-ties. 1.** the condition of being sanctified; holiness. **2.** anything regarded as sanctified or holy. **3.** the condition of being inviolable: *the sanctity of marriage.* [C14: < OF *saincteté,* < L *sanctitās,* < *sanctus* holy]

sanctuary (ˈsæŋktjʊərɪ) *n., pl.* **-aries. 1.** a holy place. **2.** a consecrated building or shrine. **3.** *Old Testament.* **a.** the Israelite temple at Jerusalem. **b.** the tabernacle in which the Ark was enshrined. **4.** the chancel, or that part of a sacred building surrounding the main altar. **5. a.** a sacred building where fugitives were formerly entitled to immunity from arrest or execution. **b.** the immunity so afforded. **6.** a place of refuge. **7.** a place, protected by law, where animals can live and breed without interference. [C14: < OF *sainctuarie,* < LL *sanctuārium* repository for holy things, < L *sanctus* holy]

sanctuary lamp *n. Christianity.* a lamp, usually red, placed in a prominent position in the sanctuary of a church, which, when lit, indicates the presence of the Blessed Sacrament.

sanctum (ˈsæŋktəm) *n., pl.* **-tums** *or* **-ta** (-tə). **1.** a sacred or holy place. **2.** a room or place of total privacy. [C16: < L, < *sanctus* holy]

sanctum sanctorum (sæŋkˈtɔːrəm) *n.* **1.** *Bible.* another term for the **holy of holies. 2.** *Often facetious.* an especially private place. [C14: < L, lit.: holy of holies, rendering Heb. *qōdesh haqqodāshīm*]

Sanctus (ˈsæŋktəs) *n.* **1.** *Liturgy.* the hymn that occurs immediately after the preface in the celebration of the Eucharist. **2.** a musical setting of this. [C14: < the hymn, *Sanctus sanctus sanctus* Holy, holy, holy, < L *sancīre* to consecrate]

Sanctus bell *n. Chiefly R.C. Church.* a bell rung as the opening words of the Sanctus are pronounced.

sand (sænd) *n.* **1.** loose material consisting of rock or mineral grains, esp. rounded grains of quartz. **2.** (*often pl.*) a sandy area, esp. on the seashore or in a desert. **3. a.** a greyish-yellow colour. **b.** (*as adj.*): *sand upholstery.* **4.** the grains of sandlike material in an hourglass. **5.** *U.S. inf.* courage. **6. the sands are running out.** there is not much time left before the end. ~*vb.* **7.** (*tr.*) to smooth or polish the surface of with sandpaper or sand. **8.** (*tr.*) to sprinkle or cover with or as if with sand. **9.** to fill or cause to fill with sand: *the channel sanded up.* [OE] —ˈ**sandˌlike** *adj.*

sandal (ˈsændᵊl) *n.* **1.** a light shoe consisting of a sole held on the foot by thongs, straps, etc. **2.** a strap passing over the instep or around the ankle to keep a low shoe on the foot. **3.** another name for **sandalwood.** [C14: < L *sandalium,* < Gk, < *sandalon* sandal] —ˈ**sandalled** *adj.*

sandalwood (ˈsændᵊlˌwʊd) *or* **sandal** *n.* **1.** any of a genus of evergreen trees, esp. the **white sandalwood,** of S Asia and Australia, having hard light-coloured heartwood. **2.** the wood of any of these trees, which is used for carving, is burned as incense, and yields an aromatic oil used in perfumery. **3.** any of various similar trees or their wood, esp. a leguminous tree of SE Asia having dark red wood used as a dye. [C14 *sandal,* < Med. L, < LGk *sandanon,* < Sansk. *candana* sandalwood]

sandarac *or* **sandarach** (ˈsændəˌræk) *n.* **1.** a pinaceous tree of NW Africa, having hard fragrant dark wood. **2.** a brittle pale yellow transparent resin obtained from the bark of this tree and used in making varnish and incense. [C16 *sandaracha,* < L *sandaraca* red pigment, < Gk *sandarakē*]

sandbag (ˈsændˌbæg) *n.* **1.** a sack filled with sand used for protection against gunfire, floodwater, etc., or as ballast in a balloon, etc. **2.** a bag filled with sand and used as a weapon. ~*vb.* **-bagging, -bagged.** (*tr.*) **3.** to protect or strengthen with sandbags. **4.** to hit with or as if with a sandbag. —ˈ**sandˌbagger** *n.*

sandbank (ˈsændˌbæŋk) *n.* a bank of sand in a sea or river, that may be exposed at low tide.

sand bar *n.* a ridge of sand in a river or sea, built up by the action of tides, currents, etc., and often exposed at low tide.

sandblast (ˈsændˌblɑːst) *n.* **1.** a jet of sand blown from a nozzle under air or steam pressure. ~*vb.* **2.** (*tr.*) to clean or decorate (a surface) with a sandblast. —ˈ**sandˌblaster** *n.*

sand-blind *adj.* not completely blind. Cf. **stone-blind.** [C15: changed (through infl. of SAND) < OE *samblind* (unattested), < *sam-* half, + BLIND] —ˈ**sand-ˌblindness** *n.*

sandbox (ˈsændˌbɒks) *n.* **1.** a container on a railway locomotive from which sand is released onto the rails to assist the traction. **2.** a container of sand for small children to play in.

sandboy (ˈsændˌbɔɪ) *n.* **happy** (*or* **jolly**) **as a sandboy.** very happy; high-spirited.

sand castle *n.* a mass of sand moulded into a castle-like shape, esp. by a child on the beach.

sand eel *or* **lance** *n.* a silvery eel-like marine spiny-finned fish found burrowing in sand or shingle. Popular name: **launce.**

sander (ˈsændə) *n.* **1.** a power-driven tool for smoothing surfaces by rubbing with an abrasive disc. **2.** a person who uses such a device.

sanderling (ˈsændəlɪŋ) *n.* a small sandpiper that frequents sandy shores. [C17: ? < SAND + OE *erthling, eorthling* inhabitant of earth]

sand flea *n.* another name for the **chigoe** or **sand hopper.**

sandfly (ˈsændˌflaɪ) *n., pl.* **-flies. 1.** any of various small mothlike dipterous flies: the bloodsucking females transmit diseases including leishmaniasis. **2.** any of various similar flies.

sandgrouse (ˈsændˌgraʊs) *n.* a bird of dry regions of the Old World, having very short feet, a short bill, and long pointed wings and tail.

sand hopper *n.* any of various small hopping crustaceans, common in intertidal regions of seashores. Also called: **beach flea, sand flea.**

sandman (ˈsændˌmæn) *n., pl.* **-men.** (in folklore) a magical person supposed to put children to sleep by sprinkling sand in their eyes.

sand martin *n.* a small brown European songbird with white underparts: it nests in tunnels bored in sand, river banks, etc.

sandpaper (ˈsændˌpeɪpə) *n.* **1.** a strong paper coated with sand or other abrasive material for smoothing and polishing. ~*vb.* **2.** (*tr.*) to polish or grind (a surface) with or as if with sandpaper.

sandpiper (ˈsændˌpaɪpə) *n.* **1.** any of numerous N hemisphere shore birds having a long slender bill and legs and cryptic plumage. **2.** any other bird of the family which includes snipes and woodcocks.

sandpit (ˈsændˌpɪt) *n.* **1.** a shallow pit or container holding sand for children to play in. **2.** a pit from which sand is extracted.

sandshoes (ˈsændˌʃuːz) *pl. n.* light canvas shoes with rubber soles.

sandstone (ˈsændˌstəʊn) *n.* any of a group of common sedimentary rocks consisting of sand grains consolidated with such materials as quartz, haematite, and clay minerals.

sandstorm (ˈsændˌstɔːm) *n.* a strong wind that whips up clouds of sand, esp. in a desert.

sand trap *n.* another name (esp. U.S.) for **bunker** (sense 2).

sand viper *n.* a S European viper having a yellowish-brown coloration with a zigzag pattern along the back.

sandwich (ˈsænwɪdʒ, -wɪtʃ) *n.* **1.** two or more slices of bread, usually buttered, with a filling of meat, cheese, etc. **2.** anything that resembles a sandwich in arrangement. ~*vb.* (*tr.*) **3.** to insert tightly between two other things. **4.** to put into a sandwich. **5.** to place between two dissimilar things. [C18: after 4th Earl of *Sandwich* (1718–92), who ate sandwiches rather than leave the gambling table for meals]

sandwich board *n.* one of two connected boards that are hung over the shoulders in front of and behind a person to display advertisements.

sandwich course *n.* any of several courses consisting of alternate periods of study and industrial work.

sandwich man *n.* a man who carries sandwich boards.

sandwort (ˈsændˌwɜːt) *n.* **1.** any of various plants which grow in dense tufts on sandy soil and have white or pink solitary flowers. **2.** any of various related plants.

sandy (ˈsændɪ) *adj.* **sandier, sandiest. 1.** consisting of, containing, or covered with sand. **2.** (esp. of hair) reddish-yellow. **3.** resembling sand in texture. —ˈ**sandiness** *n.*

sand yacht *n.* a wheeled boat with sails, built to be propelled over sand by the wind.

sandy blight *n. Austral. inf.* any inflammation and irritation of the eye.

sane (seɪn) *adj.* **1.** free from mental disturbance. **2.** having or showing reason or sound sense. [C17: < L *sānus* healthy] —ˈ**sanely** *adv.* —ˈ**saneness** *n.*

Sanforize *or* **-rise** (ˈsænfəˌraɪz) *vb.* (*tr.*) *Trademark.* to preshrink (a fabric) using a patented process.

sang (sæŋ) *vb.* the past tense of **sing.**

▷ Usage. See at **ring**[2].

sang-froid (*French* sɑ̃frwa) *n.* composure; self-possession. [C18: < F, lit.: cold blood]

sangoma (sæŋˈgəʊmə) *n., pl.* **-mas.** *S. African.* a witch doctor. [< Bantu]

Sangraal (sæŋˈgreɪl), **Sangrail,** *or* **Sangreal** (ˈsæŋgrɪəl) *n.* another name for the **Holy Grail.**

sangria (sæŋˈgriːə) *n.* a Spanish drink of red wine, sugar, and orange or lemon juice, sometimes laced with brandy. [Sp.: a bleeding]

sanguinary (ˈsæŋgwɪnərɪ) *adj.* **1.** accompanied by much bloodshed. **2.** bloodthirsty. **3.** consisting of or stained with blood. [C17: < L *sanguinārius*] —ˈ**sanguinarily** *adv.* —ˈ**sanguinariness** *n.*

sanguine (ˈsæŋgwɪn) *adj.* **1.** cheerful and confident; optimistic. **2.** (esp. of the complexion) ruddy in appearance. **3.** blood-red. ~*n.* **4.** a red pencil containing ferric oxide, used in drawing. [C14: < L *sanguineus* bloody, < *sanguis* blood] —ˈ**sanguinely** *adv.* —ˈ**sanguineness** *n.*

sanguineous (sæŋˈgwɪnɪəs) *adj.* **1.** of, containing, or associated with blood. **2.** a less common word for **sanguine.** —**sanˈguineousness** *n.*

Sanhedrin (ˈsænɪdrɪn) *n. Judaism.* the supreme judicial, ecclesiastical, and administrative council of the Jews in New Testament times. [C16: < LHeb., < Gk *sunedrion* council, < *sun-* SYN- + *hedra* seat]

sanies (ˈseɪnɪˌiːz) *n. Pathol.* a thin greenish foul-smelling discharge from a wound, ulcer, etc., containing pus and blood. [C16: < L, <?]

sanitarium (ˌsænɪˈtɛərɪəm) *n., pl.* **-riums** *or* **-ria** (-rɪə). the U.S. word for **sanatorium.** [C19: < L *sānitās* health]

sanitary (ˈsænɪtərɪ) *adj.* **1.** of or relating to health and measures for the protection of health. **2.** free from dirt, germs, etc.; hygienic. [C19: < F *sanitaire,* < L *sānitās* health] —**sanitarian** (ˌsænɪˈtɛərɪən) *n.* —ˈ**sanitariness** *n.*

sanitary engineering *n.* the branch of civil engineering associated with the supply of water, disposal of sewage, and other public health services. —**sanitary engineer** *n.*

sanitary towel *or esp. U.S.* **napkin** *n.* an absorbent pad worn externally by women during menstruation to absorb the menstrual flow.

sanitation (ˌsænɪˈteɪʃən) *n.* the study and use of practical measures for the preservation of public health.

sanitize *or* **-tise** (ˈsænɪˌtaɪz) *vb.* (*tr.*) *Chiefly U.S. & Canad.* to make hygienic, as by sterilizing. —ˌ**sanitiˈzation** *or* **-tiˈsation** *n.*

sanity (ˈsænɪtɪ) *n.* **1.** the state of being sane. **2.** good sense or soundness of judgment. [C15: < L *sānitās* health, < *sānus* healthy]

sank (sæŋk) *vb.* the past tense of **sink.**

sans (sænz) *prep.* an archaic word for **without.** [C13: < OF *sanz,* < L *sine* without, but prob. also infl. by L *absentiā* in the absence of]

Sans. *or* **Sansk.** *abbrev. for* Sanskrit.

sans-culotte (ˌsænzkjʊˈlɒt) *n.* **1.** (during the French Revolution) **a.** (originally) a revolutionary of the poorer class. **b.** (later) any revolutionary. **2.** any revolutionary extremist. [C18: < F, lit.: without knee breeches, because the revolutionaries wore pantaloons or trousers rather than knee breeches]

sansevieria (ˌsænsɪˈvɪərɪə) *n.* any of a genus of herbaceous perennial plants of Old World tropical regions: some are cultivated as house plants for their bayonet-like leaves; others yield a useful fibre. [NL, after Raimondo di Sangro (1710–71), It. scholar and prince of *San Seviero*]

Sanskrit (ˈsænskrɪt) *n.* an ancient language of India. It is the oldest recorded member of the Indic branch of the Indo-European family of languages. Although it is used only for religious purposes, it is one of the official languages of India. [C17: < Sansk. *samskrta* perfected, lit.: put together] —**Sanˈskritic** *adj.*

sans serif *or* **sanserif** (sænˈsɛrɪf) *n.* a style of printer's typeface in which the characters have no serifs.

Santa Claus (ˈsæntə ˌklɔːz) *n.* the legendary patron saint of children, commonly identified with Saint Nicholas, who brings presents to children on Christmas Eve. Often shortened to **Santa.** Also called: **Father Christmas.**

Santa Gertrudis (ˈsæntə gəˈtruːdɪs) *n.* one of a breed of red beef cattle developed in Texas.

santonica (sænˈtɒnɪkə) *n.* **1.** an oriental wormwood plant. **2.** the dried flower heads of this plant, formerly used as a vermifuge. ~Also called: **wormseed.** [C17: NL, < LL *herba* *santonica* herb of the *Santones* (prob. wormwood), < L *Santonī* a people of Aquitania]

santonin (ˈsæntənɪn) *n.* a white crystalline soluble substance extracted from the dried flower heads of santonica and used in medicine as an anthelmintic. [C19: < SANTONICA + -IN]

sap[1] (sæp) *n.* **1.** a solution of mineral salts, sugars, etc., that circulates in a plant. **2.** any vital body fluid. **3.** energy; vigour. **4.** *Sl.* a gullible person. **5.** another name for **sapwood.** ~*vb.* **sapping, sapped.** (*tr.*) **6.** to drain of sap. [OE *sæp*]

sap[2] (sæp) *n.* **1.** a deep and narrow trench used to approach or undermine an enemy position. ~*vb.* **sapping, sapped. 2.** to undermine (a fortification, etc.) by digging saps. **3.** (*tr.*) to weaken. [C16 *zappe,* < It. *zappa* spade, <?]

sapele (səˈpiːlɪ) *n.* **1.** any of various W African trees yielding a hard timber resembling mahogany. **2.** the timber of such a tree, used to make furniture. [C20: West African name]

sapid (ˈsæpɪd) *adj.* **1.** having a pleasant taste. **2.** agreeable or engaging. [C17: < L *sapidus,* < *sapere* to taste] —**sapidity** (səˈpɪdɪtɪ) *n.*

sapient (ˈseɪpɪənt) *adj. Often used ironically.* wise or sagacious. [C15: < L *sapere* to taste] —ˈ**sapience** *n.* —ˈ**sapiently** *adv.*

sapiential (ˌseɪpɪˈɛnʃəl) *adj.* showing, having, or providing wisdom.

sapling (ˈsæplɪŋ) *n.* **1.** a young tree. **2.** *Literary.* a youth.

sapodilla (ˌsæpəˈdɪlə) *n.* **1.** a large tropical American evergreen tree, the latex of which yields chicle. **2.** Also called: **sapodilla plum.** the edible brown rough-skinned fruit of this tree. [C17: < Sp. *zapotillo,* dim. of *zapote* sapodilla fruit, < Nahuatl *tsapotl*]

saponaceous (ˌsæpəʊˈneɪʃəs) *adj.* resembling soap. [C18: < NL, < L *sāpō* soap]

saponify (səˈpɒnɪˌfaɪ) *vb.* **-fying, -fied.** *Chem.* **1.** to undergo or cause to undergo a process in which a fat is converted into a soap by treatment with alkali. **2.** to undergo or cause to undergo a reaction in which an ester is hydrolysed to an acid and an alcohol as a result of treatment with an alkali. [C19: < F *saponifier,* < L *sāpō* soap] —**saˌponifiˈcation** *n.*

saponin (ˈsæpənɪn) *n.* any of a group of plant glycosides with a steroid structure that foam when shaken and are used in detergents. [C19: < F *saponine,* < L *sāpō* soap]

sappanwood *or* **sapanwood** (ˈsæpənˌwʊd) *n.* **1.** a small tree of S Asia producing wood that yields a red dye. **2.** the wood of this tree. [C16: *sapan,* via Du. < Malay *sapang*]

sapper (ˈsæpə) *n.* **1.** a soldier who digs trenches, etc. **2.** (in the British Army) a private of the Royal Engineers.

Sapphic (ˈsæfɪk) *adj.* **1.** *Prosody.* denoting a metre associated with Sappho, 6th-century B.C. Greek poetess. **2.** of or relating to Sappho or her poetry. **3.** lesbian. ~*n.* **4.** *Prosody.* a verse, line, or stanza written in the Sapphic form.

sapphire (ˈsæfaɪə) *n.* **1. a.** any precious corundum gemstone that is not red, esp. the highly valued transparent blue variety. **b.** (*as modifier*): *a sapphire ring.* **2. a.** the blue colour of sapphire. **b.** (*as adj.*): *sapphire eyes.* **3.** (*modifier*) denoting a forty-fifth anniversary: *our sapphire wedding.* [C13 *safir,* < OF, < L *sapphīrus,* < Gk *sappheiros,* ? < Sansk. *śanipriya,* lit.: beloved of the planet Saturn]

sappy (ˈsæpɪ) *adj.* **-pier, -piest. 1.** (of plants) full of sap. **2.** full of energy or vitality.

sapro- *or before a vowel* **sapr-** *combining form.* indicating dead or decaying matter: *saprogenic.* [< Gk *sapros* rotten]

saprogenic (ˌsæprəʊˈdʒɛnɪk) *or* **saprogenous** (sæˈprɒdʒɪnəs) *adj.* **1.** producing or resulting from decay. **2.** growing on decaying matter.

saprophyte (ˈsæprəʊˌfaɪt) *n.* any plant, esp. a fungus, that lives and feeds on dead organic matter. —**saprophytic** (ˌsæprəʊˈfɪtɪk) *adj.*

saprozoic (ˌsæprəʊˈzəʊɪk) *adj.* (of animals or plants) feeding on dead organic matter.

sapsucker (ˈsæpˌsʌkə) *n.* either of two North American woodpeckers that have white wing patches and feed on the sap from trees.

sapwood (ˈsæpˌwʊd) *n.* the soft wood, just beneath the bark in tree trunks, that consists of living tissue.

saraband *or* **sarabande** (ˈsærəˌbænd) *n.* **1.** a decorous 17th-century courtly dance. **2.** a piece of music composed for or in the rhythm of this dance, in slow triple time. [C17: < F *sarabande,* < Sp. *zarabanda,* <?]

Saracen (ˈsærəsən) *n.* **1.** *History.* a member of one of the nomadic Arabic tribes, esp. of the Syrian desert. **2. a.** a Muslim, esp. one who opposed the crusades. **b.** (in later use) any Arab. ~*adj.* **3.** of or relating to Arabs of either of these periods, regions, or types. [C13: < OF *Sarrazin,* < LL *Saracēnus,* < LGk *Sarakēnos,* ? < Ar. *sharq* sunrise] —**Saracenic** (ˌsærəˈsɛnɪk) *adj.*

sarcasm (ˈsɑːkæzəm) *n.* **1.** mocking or ironic language intended to convey scorn or insult. **2.** the use or tone of such language. [C16: < LL *sarcasmus,* < Gk, < *sarkazein* to rend the flesh, < *sarx* flesh]

sarcastic (sɑːˈkæstɪk) *adj.* **1.** characterized by sarcasm. **2.** given to the use of sarcasm. —**sarˈcastically** *adv.*

sarcenet *or* **sarsenet** (ˈsɑːsnɪt) *n.* a fine soft silk fabric used for clothing, ribbons, etc. [C15: < OF *sarzinet,* < *Sarrazin* SARACEN]

sarco- *or before a vowel* **sarc-** *combining form.* indicating flesh: *sarcoma.* [< Gk *sark-, sarx* flesh]

sarcocarp (ˈsɑːkəʊˌkɑːp) *n. Bot.* the fleshy mesocarp of such fruits as the peach or plum.

sarcoma (sɑːˈkəʊmə) *n., pl.* **-mata** (-mətə) *or* **-mas.** *Pathol.* a usually malignant tumour arising from connective tissue. [C17: via NL < Gk *sarkōma* fleshy growth] —**sarˈcomatous** *adj.*

sarcomatosis (sɑːˌkəʊməˈtəʊsɪs) *n. Pathol.* a condition characterized by the development of several sarcomas at various bodily sites. [C19: see SARCOMA, -OSIS]

sarcophagus (sɑːˈkɒfəgəs) *n., pl.* **-gi** (-ˌgaɪ) *or* **-guses.** a stone or marble coffin or tomb, esp. one bearing sculpture or inscriptions. [C17: via L < Gk *sarkophagos* flesh-devouring; from the type of stone used, which was believed to destroy the flesh of corpses]

sarcous (ˈsɑːkəs) *adj.* (of tissue) muscular or fleshy. [C19: < Gk *sarx* flesh]

sard (sɑːd) *or* **sardius** (ˈsɑːdɪəs) *n.* a red or brown variety of chalcedony. [C14: < L *sarda,* < Gk *sardios* stone from Sardis]

sardar *or* **sirdar** (səˈdɑː) *n.* (in India) **1.** a title used before the name of Sikh men. **2.** a leader. [Hindi, < Persian]

sardine[1] (sɑːˈdiːn) *n., pl.* **-dine** *or* **-dines. 1.** any of various small food fishes of the herring family, esp. a young pilchard. **2. like sardines.** very closely crowded together. [C15: via OF < L *sardīna,* dim. of *sarda* a fish suitable for pickling]

sardine[2] (ˈsɑːdiːn) *n.* another name for **sard.** [C14: < LL *sardinus,* < Gk *sardinos lithos* Sardian stone, < *Sardeis* Sardis]

sardonic (sɑːˈdɒnɪk) *adj.* characterized by irony, mockery, or derision. [C17: < F, < L, < Gk *sardonios* derisive, lit.: of Sardinia, alteration of Homeric *sardanios* scornful (laughter or smile)] —**sarˈdonically** *adv.*

sardonyx (ˈsɑːdənɪks) *n.* a variety of chalcedony with alternating reddish-brown and white parallel bands. [C14: via L < Gk *sardonux,* ? < *sardion* SARD + *onux* nail]

sargassum (sɑːˈgæsəm) *n.* a floating brown seaweed having ribbon-like fronds containing air sacs, esp. abundant in the **Sargasso Sea** in the N Atlantic. [C16: < Port. *sargaço* < ?]

sarge (sɑːdʒ) *n. Inf.* sergeant.

sari *or* **saree** (ˈsɑːrɪ) *n., pl.* **-ris** *or* **-rees.** the traditional dress of women of India, Pakistan, etc., consisting of a very long piece of cloth swathed around the body. [C18: < Hindi *sārī,* < Sansk. *śāṭī*]

sarking (ˈsɑːkɪŋ) *n. Scot., northern English, & N.Z.* flat planking supporting the roof cladding of a building. [C15 in England: < Scot. *sark* shirt]

sarky (ˈsɑːkɪ) *adj.* **-kier, -kiest.** *Brit. inf.* sarcastic.

sarmentose (sɑːˈmɛntəʊs) *or* **sarmentous** (sɑːˈmɛntəs) *adj.* (of plants such as the strawberry) having stems in the form of runners. [C18: < L *sarmentōsus* full of twigs, < *sarmentum* brushwood, < *sarpere* to prune]

sarod (sæˈrəʊd) *n.* an Indian stringed musical instrument that may be played with a bow or plucked. [C19: < Hindi]

sarong (səˈrɒŋ) *n.* a skirtlike garment worn by men and women in the Malay Archipelago, Sri Lanka, etc. [C19: < Malay, lit.: sheath]

saros (ˈseɪrɒs) *n.* a cycle of about 18 years 11 days (6585.32 days) in which eclipses of the sun and moon occur in the same sequence. [C19: < Gk, < Babylonian *šāru* 3600 (years); modern use apparently based on mistaken interpretation of *šāru* as a period of 18½ years]

sarrusophone (səˈruːzəˌfəʊn) *n.* a wind instrument resembling the oboe but made of brass. [C19: after *Sarrus*, F bandmaster, who invented it (1856)]

sarsaparilla (ˌsɑːsəpəˈrɪlə) *n.* **1.** any of a genus of tropical American prickly climbing plants having large aromatic roots and heart-shaped leaves. **2.** the dried roots of any of these plants, formerly used in medicine to treat psoriasis, etc. **3.** a nonalcoholic drink prepared from these roots. [C16: < Sp. *sarzaparrilla*, < *zarza* a bramble + *-parrilla*, < *parra* a climbing plant]

sarsen (ˈsɑːsᵊn) *n.* **1.** *Geol.* a boulder of silicified sandstone, probably of Tertiary age. **2.** such a stone used in a megalithic monument. [C17: prob. a var. of SARACEN]

sarsenet (ˈsɑːsnɪt) *n.* a variant spelling of **sarcenet.**

sartorial (sɑːˈtɔːrɪəl) *adj.* **1.** of or relating to a tailor or to tailoring. **2.** *Anat.* of the sartorius. [C19: < LL *sartōrius* < L *sartor* a patcher, < *sarcīre* to patch] —**sarˈtorially** *adv.*

sartorius (sɑːˈtɔːrɪəs) *n., pl.* **-torii** (-ˈtɔːrɪˌaɪ). *Anat.* a long ribbon-shaped muscle that aids in flexing the knee. [C18: NL, < *sartorius musculus*, lit.: tailor's muscle, because it is used when one sits in the cross-legged position in which tailors traditionally sat while sewing]

Sarum use (ˈsɛərəm) *n.* the distinctive local rites used at Salisbury Cathedral in late medieval times. [< *Sarum*, ancient name of Salisbury]

SAS *abbrev. for* Special Air Service.

sash[1] (sæʃ) *n.* a long piece of ribbon, etc., worn around the waist or over one shoulder, as a symbol of rank. [C16: < Ar. *shāsh* muslin]

sash[2] (sæʃ) *n.* **1.** a frame that contains the panes of a window or door. **2.** a complete frame together with panes of glass. ~*vb.* **3.** (*tr.*) to furnish with a sash, sashes, or sash windows. [C17: orig. pl. *sashes*, var. of *shashes*, < CHASSIS]

sashay (sæˈʃeɪ) *vb.* (*intr.*) *Inf., chiefly U.S. & Canad.* **1.** to move, walk, or glide along casually. **2.** to move or walk in a showy way; parade. [C19: < an alteration of *chassé*, a gliding dance step]

sash cord *n.* a strong cord connecting a sash weight to a sliding sash.

sashimi (ˈsæʃɪmɪ) *n.* a Japanese dish of thin fillets of raw fish. [C19: < Japanese *sashi* pierce + *mi* flesh]

sash weight *n.* a weight used to counterbalance the weight of a sliding sash in a sash window and thus hold it in position at any height.

sash window *n.* a window consisting of two sashes placed one above the other so that they can be slid past each other.

sasquatch (ˈsæsˌkwætʃ) *n.* (in Canadian folklore) in British Columbia, a hairy beast or manlike monster said to leave huge footprints. [< Amerind]

sass (sæs) *U.S. & Canad. inf.* ~*n.* **1.** impudent talk or behaviour. ~*vb.* (*intr.*) **2.** to talk or answer back in such a way. [C20: back formation < SASSY]

sassaby (ˈsæsəbɪ) *n., pl.* **-bies.** an African antelope of grasslands and semideserts, having angular curved horns. [C19: < Bantu *tshêsêbê*]

sassafras (ˈsæsəˌfræs) *n.* **1.** an aromatic deciduous tree of North America, having three-lobed leaves and dark blue fruits. **2.** the aromatic dried root bark of this tree, used as a flavouring, and yielding **sassafras oil.** **3.** *Austral.* any of several unrelated trees having a similar fragrant bark. [C16: < Sp. *sasafras*, <?]

Sassenach (ˈsæsəˌnæx) *n. Scot. & occasionally Irish.* an English person or Lowland Scot. [C18: < Gaelic *Sassunach*, < LL *saxonēs* Saxons]

sassy (ˈsæsɪ) *adj.* **-sier, -siest.** *U.S. & Canad. inf.* insolent; impertinent. [C19: var. of SAUCY] —**ˈsassily** *adv.* —**ˈsassiness** *n.*

sat (sæt) *vb.* the past tense and past participle of **sit.**

Sat. *abbrev. for:* **1.** Saturday. **2.** Saturn.

Satan (ˈseɪtᵊn) *n.* the devil, adversary of God, and tempter of mankind: sometimes identified with Lucifer (Luke 4:5–8). [OE, < LL, < Gk, < Heb.: plotter, < *sātan* to plot against]

satanic (səˈtænɪk) *adj.* **1.** of or relating to Satan. **2.** supremely evil or wicked. —**saˈtanically** *adv.*

Satanism (ˈseɪtᵊˌnɪzəm) *n.* **1.** the worship of Satan. **2.** a form of such worship which includes blasphemous parodies of Christian prayers, etc. **3.** a satanic disposition. —**ˈSatanist** *n., adj.*

SATB *abbrev. for* soprano, alto, tenor, bass: a combination of voices in choral music.

satchel (ˈsætʃəl) *n.* a rectangular bag, usually made of leather or cloth and provided with a shoulder strap, used for carrying school books. [C14: < OF *sachel*, < LL *saccellus*, < L *saccus* SACK[1]] —**ˈsatchelled** *adj.*

sate[1] (seɪt) *vb.* (*tr.*) **1.** to satisfy (a desire or appetite) fully. **2.** to supply beyond capacity or desire. [OE *sadian*]

sate[2] (sæt, seɪt) *vb. Arch.* a past tense and past participle of **sit.**

sateen (sæˈtiːn) *n.* a glossy linen or cotton fabric that resembles satin. [C19: changed < SATIN, on the model of VELVETEEN]

satellite (ˈsætᵊˌlaɪt) *n.* **1.** a celestial body orbiting around a planet or star: *the earth is a satellite of the sun.* **2.** a man-made device orbiting around the earth, moon, or another planet transmitting to earth scientific information or used for communication. **3.** a country or political unit under the domination of a foreign power. **4.** a subordinate area that is dependent upon a larger adjacent town. **5.** (*modifier*) **a.** of or relating to a satellite: *satellite communications.* **b.** dependent upon another: *a satellite nation.* [C16: < L *satelles* an attendant, prob. of Etruscan origin]

satiable (ˈseɪʃɪəbᵊl) *adj.* capable of being satiated. —ˌ**satiaˈbility** *n.* —**ˈsatiably** *adv.*

satiate (ˈseɪʃɪˌeɪt) *vb.* (*tr.*) **1.** to fill or supply beyond capacity or desire. **2.** to supply to capacity. [C16: < L *satiāre* to satisfy, < *satis* enough] —ˌ**satiˈation** *n.*

satiety (səˈtaɪɪtɪ) *n.* the state of being satiated. [C16: < L *satietās*, < *satis* enough]

satin (ˈsætɪn) *n.* **1.** a fabric of silk, rayon, etc., closely woven to show much of the warp, giving a smooth glossy appearance. **2.** (*modifier*) like satin in texture: *a satin finish.* [C14: via OF < Ar. *zaitūnī*, Ar. rendering of Chinese *Tseutung* (now *Tsinkiang*), port from which the cloth was prob. first exported] —**ˈsatiny** *adj.*

satinet *or* **satinette** (ˌsætɪˈnɛt) *n.* a thin satin or satin-like fabric. [C18: < F: small satin]

satinflower (ˈsætɪnˌflaʊə) *n.* another name for **greater stitchwort** (see **stitchwort**).

satinwood (ˈsætɪnˌwʊd) *n.* **1.** a tree that occurs in the East Indies and has hard wood with a satiny texture. **2.** the wood of this tree, used in veneering, marquetry, etc.

satire (ˈsætaɪə) *n.* **1.** a novel, play, etc., in which topical issues, folly, or evil are held up to scorn by means of ridicule. **2.** the genre constituted by such works. **3.** the use of ridicule, irony, etc., to create such an effect. [C16: < L *satira* a mixture, < *satur* sated, < *satis* enough]

satirical (səˈtɪrɪkᵊl) *or* **satiric** *adj.* **1.** of, relating to, or containing satire. **2.** given to the use of satire. —**saˈtirically** *adv.*

satirist ('sætərɪst) *n.* **1.** a person who writes satire. **2.** a person given to the use of satire.

satirize *or* **-rise** ('sætəˌraɪz) *vb.* to deride (a person or thing) by means of satire. —ˌ**satiri'zation** *or* **-ri'sation** *n.*

satisfaction (ˌsætɪs'fækʃən) *n.* **1.** the act of satisfying or state of being satisfied. **2.** the fulfilment of a desire. **3.** the pleasure obtained from such fulfilment. **4.** a source of fulfilment. **5.** compensation for a wrong done or received. **6.** *R.C. Church, Church of England.* the performance of a penance. **7.** *Christianity.* the atonement for sin by the death of Christ.

satisfactory (ˌsætɪs'fæktərɪ) *adj.* **1.** adequate or suitable; acceptable. **2.** giving satisfaction. **3.** constituting or involving atonement or expiation for sin. —ˌ**satis'factorily** *adv.*

satisfy ('sætɪsˌfaɪ) *vb.* **-fying, -fied.** (*mainly tr.*) **1.** (*also intr.*) to fulfil the desires or needs of (a person). **2.** to provide amply for (a need or desire). **3.** to convince. **4.** to dispel (a doubt). **5.** to make reparation to or for. **6.** to discharge or pay off (a debt) to (a creditor). **7.** to fulfil the requirements of; comply with: *you must satisfy the terms of your lease.* **8.** *Maths, logic.* to fulfil the conditions of (a theorem, assumption, etc.); to yield a truth by substitution of the given value. [C15: < OF *satisfier,* < L *satisfacere,* < *satis* enough + *facere* to make] —'**satisˌfiable** *adj.* —'**satisˌfying** *adj.* —'**satisˌfyingly** *adv.*

satori (sə'tɔːrɪ) *n. Zen Buddhism.* a state of sudden intuitive enlightenment. [< Japanese]

satrap ('sætrəp) *n.* **1.** (in ancient Persia) a provincial governor. **2.** a subordinate ruler. [C14: < L *satrapa,* < Gk *satrapēs,* < OPersian *khshathrapāvan,* lit.: protector of the land]

satrapy ('sætrəpɪ) *n., pl.* **-trapies.** the province, office, or period of rule of a satrap.

satsuma (sæt'suːmə) *n.* **1.** a small citrus tree cultivated, esp. in Japan, for its edible fruit. **2.** the fruit of this tree, which has easily separable segments. [< name of former province of Japan]

saturable ('sætʃərəb^{ə}l) *adj. Chem.* capable of being saturated. —ˌ**satura'bility** *n.*

saturate *vb.* ('sætʃəˌreɪt). **1.** to fill, soak, or imbue totally. **2.** to make (a chemical compound, solution, etc.) saturated or (of a compound, etc.) to become saturated. **3.** (*tr.*) *Mil.* to bomb or shell heavily. ~*adj.* ('sætʃərɪt, -ˌreɪt). **4.** saturated. [C16: < L *saturāre,* < *satur* sated, < *satis* enough]

saturated ('sætʃəˌreɪtɪd) *adj.* **1.** (of a solution or solvent) containing the maximum amount of solute that can normally be dissolved at a given temperature and pressure. **2.** (of a chemical compound) containing no multiple bonds: *a saturated hydrocarbon.* **3.** (of a fat) containing a high proportion of fatty acids having single bonds. **4.** (of a vapour) containing the maximum amount of gaseous material at a given temperature and pressure.

saturation (ˌsætʃə'reɪʃən) *n.* **1.** the act of saturating or the state of being saturated. **2.** *Chem.* the state of a chemical compound, solution, or vapour when it is saturated. **3.** *Meteorol.* the state of the atmosphere when it can hold no more water vapour at its particular temperature and pressure. **4.** the attribute of a colour that enables an observer to judge its proportion of pure chromatic colour. **5.** the level beyond which demand for a product or service is not expected to rise. ~*modifier.* **6.** denoting the maximum possible intensity of coverage of an area: *saturation bombing.*

saturation point *n.* the point at which no more can be absorbed, accommodated, used, etc.

Saturday ('sætədɪ) *n.* the seventh and last day of the week: the Jewish Sabbath. [OE *sæternes dæg,* translation of L *Saturnī diēs* day of Saturn]

Saturn[1] ('sætɜːn) *n.* the Roman god of agriculture and vegetation.

Saturn[2] ('sætɜːn) *n.* **1.** the sixth planet from the sun, around which revolve planar concentric rings (**Saturn's rings**) consisting of small frozen particles. **2.** the alchemical name for **lead**[2]. —**Saturnian** (sæ'tɜːnɪən) *adj.*

Saturnalia (ˌsætə'neɪlɪə) *n., pl.* **-lia** *or* **-lias. 1.** an ancient Roman festival celebrated in December: renowned for its general merrymaking. **2.** (*sometimes not cap.*) a period or occasion of wild revelry. [C16: < L *Sāturnālis* relating to SATURN[1]] —ˌ**Satur'nalian** *adj.*

saturnine ('sætəˌnaɪn) *adj.* **1.** having a gloomy temperament. **2.** *Arch.* **a.** of or relating to lead. **b.** having lead poisoning. [C15: < F *saturnin,* < Med. L *sāturnīnus* (unattested), < L *Sāturnus* Saturn, < the gloomy influence attributed to the planet Saturn] —'**saturˌninely** *adv.*

satyagraha ('sɔːtjɑːgrɔːhɑː) *n.* the policy of nonviolent resistance adopted by Mahatma Gandhi to oppose British rule in India. [via Hindi < Sansk., lit.: insistence on truth, < *satya* truth + *agraha* fervour]

satyr ('sætə) *n.* **1.** *Greek myth.* one of a class of sylvan deities, represented as goatlike men who drank and danced in the train of Dionysus and chased the nymphs. **2.** a man who has strong sexual desires. **3.** any of various butterflies, having dark wings often marked with eyespots. [C14: < L *satyrus,* < Gk *saturos*] —**satyric** (sə'tɪrɪk) *adj.*

satyriasis (ˌsætɪ'raɪəsɪs) *n.* a neurotic compulsion in men to have sexual intercourse with many women without being able to have lasting relationships with them. [C17: via NL < Gk *saturiasis*]

sauce (sɔːs) *n.* **1.** any liquid or semiliquid preparation eaten with food to enhance its flavour. **2.** anything that adds piquancy. **3.** *U.S. & Canad.* stewed fruit. **4.** *Inf.* impudent language or behaviour. ~*vb.* (*tr.*) **5.** to prepare (food) with sauce. **6.** to add zest to. **7.** *Inf.* to be saucy to. [C14: via OF < L *salsus* salted, < *sal* salt]

saucepan ('sɔːspən) *n.* a metal or enamel pan with a long handle and often a lid, used for cooking food.

saucer ('sɔːsə) *n.* **1.** a small round dish on which a cup is set. **2.** any similar dish. [C14: < OF *saussier* container for SAUCE] —'**saucerful** *n.*

saucy ('sɔːsɪ) *adj.* **saucier, sauciest. 1.** impertinent. **2.** pert; jaunty: *a saucy hat.* —'**saucily** *adv.* —'**sauciness** *n.*

sauerkraut ('saʊəˌkraʊt) *n.* finely shredded cabbage which has been fermented in brine. [G, < *sauer* sour + *Kraut* cabbage]

sauger ('sɔːgə) *n.* a small North American pikeperch with a spotted dorsal fin: valued as a food and game fish. [C19: < ?]

sault (suː) *n. Canad.* a waterfall or rapids. [C17: < Canad. F, < F *saut* a leap]

sauna ('sɔːnə) *n.* **1.** an invigorating bath originating in Finland in which the bather is subjected to hot steam, usually followed by a cold plunge. **2.** the place in which such a bath is taken. [C20: < Finnish]

saunter ('sɔːntə) *vb.* **1.** (*intr.*) to walk in a casual manner; stroll. ~*n.* **2.** a leisurely pace or stroll. [C17 (meaning: to wander aimlessly), C15 (to muse): < ?] —'**saunterer** *n.*

-saur *or* **-saurus** *n. combining form.* lizard: *dinosaur.* [< NL *saurus*]

saurian ('sɔːrɪən) *adj.* **1.** of or resembling a lizard. ~*n.* **2.** a former name for **lizard.** [C15: < NL *Sauria,* < Gk *sauros*]

saury ('sɔːrɪ) *n., pl.* **-ries.** a fish of tropical and temperate seas, having an elongated body and long toothed jaws. Also called: **skipper.** [C18: ? < LL *saurus,* < ?]

sausage ('sɒsɪdʒ) *n.* **1.** finely minced meat, esp. pork or beef, mixed with fat, cereal, and seasonings (**sausage meat**), and packed into a tube-shaped edible casing. **2.** *Scot.* sausage meat. **3.** an object shaped like a sausage. **4. not a sausage.** nothing at all. [C15: < OF *saussiche,* < LL *salsīcia,* < L *salsus* salted; see SAUCE]

sausage dog *n.* an informal name for **dachshund.**

sausage roll *n. Brit.* a roll of sausage meat in pastry.

sauté ('səʊteɪ) *vb.* **-téing** *or* **téeing, -téed. 1.** to fry (food) quickly in a little fat. ~*n.* **2.** a dish of sautéed food, esp. meat that is browned and then cooked in a sauce. *~adj.* **3.** sautéed until lightly brown: *sauté potatoes.* [C19: < F: tossed, < *sauter* to jump, < L, < *salīre* to spring]

savage (ˈsævɪdʒ) *adj.* **1.** wild; untamed: *savage beasts.* **2.** ferocious in temper: *a savage dog.* **3.** uncivilized; crude: *savage behaviour.* **4.** (of peoples) nonliterate or primitive: *a savage tribe.* **5.** (of terrain) rugged and uncultivated. *~n.* **6.** a member of a nonliterate society, esp. one regarded as primitive. **7.** a fierce or vicious person or animal. *~vb.* (*tr.*) **8.** to criticize violently. **9.** to attack ferociously and wound. [C13: < OF *sauvage*, < L *silvāticus* belonging to a wood, < *silva* a wood] —ˈ**savagely** *adv.* —ˈ**savageness** *n.*

savagery (ˈsævɪdʒrɪ) *n., pl.* **-ries. 1.** an uncivilized condition. **2.** a savage act or nature. **3.** savages collectively.

savanna *or* **savannah** (səˈvænə) *n.* open grasslands, usually with scattered bushes or trees, characteristic of much of tropical Africa. [C16: < Sp. *zavana*, < Amerind *zabana*]

savant (ˈsævənt) *n.* a man of great learning; sage. [C18: < F, < *savoir* to know, < L *sapere* to be wise] —ˈ**savante** *fem. n.*

savate (səˈvæt) *n.* a form of boxing in which blows may be delivered with the feet as well as the hands. [C19: < F, lit.: old worn-out shoe]

save[1] (seɪv) *vb.* **1.** (*tr.*) to rescue, preserve, or guard (a person or thing) from danger or harm. **2.** to avoid the spending, waste, or loss of (money, possessions, etc.). **3.** (*tr.*) to deliver from sin; redeem. **4.** (often foll. by *up*) to set aside or reserve (money, goods, etc.) for future use. **5.** (*tr.*) to treat with care so as to avoid or lessen wear or degeneration. **6.** (*tr.*) to prevent the necessity for; obviate the trouble of. **7.** (*tr.*) *Soccer, hockey, etc.* to prevent (a goal) by stopping (a struck ball or puck). *~n.* **8.** *Soccer, hockey, etc.* the act of saving a goal. **9.** *Computers.* an instruction to write information from the memory onto a tape or disk. [C13: < OF *salver*, via LL < L *salvus* safe] —ˈ**savable** *or* ˈ**saveable** *adj.* —ˈ**saver** *n.*

save[2] (seɪv) *Arch.* *~prep.* **1.** (often foll. by *for*) Also: **saving.** with the exception of. *~conj.* **2.** but. [C13 *sauf*, < OF, < L *salvō*, < *salvus* safe]

save as you earn *n.* (in Britain) a savings scheme operated by the government, in which monthly contributions earn tax-free interest. Abbrev.: **SAYE.**

saveloy (ˈsævɪˌlɔɪ) *n.* a smoked sausage made from salted pork, coloured red with saltpetre. [C19: prob. via F < It. *cervellato*, < *cervello* brain, < L, < *cerebrum* brain]

savin *or* **savine** (ˈsævɪn) *n.* **1.** a small spreading juniper bush of Europe, N Asia, and North America. **2.** the oil derived from the shoots and leaves of this plant, formerly used in medicine to treat rheumatism, etc. [C14: < OF *savine*, < L *herba Sabīna* the Sabine plant]

saving (ˈseɪvɪŋ) *adj.* **1.** tending to save or preserve. **2.** redeeming or compensating (esp. in **saving grace**). **3.** thrifty or economical. **4.** *Law.* denoting or relating to an exception or reservation: *a saving clause in an agreement.* *~n.* **5.** preservation or redemption. **6.** economy or avoidance of waste. **7.** reduction in cost or expenditure. **8.** anything saved. **9.** (*pl.*) money saved for future use. *~prep.* **10.** with the exception of. *~conj.* **11.** except. —ˈ**savingly** *adv.*

savings bank *n.* a bank that accepts the savings of depositors and pays interest on them.

saviour *or* *U.S.* **savior** (ˈseɪvjə) *n.* a person who rescues another person or a thing from danger or harm. [C13 *saveour*, < OF, < Church L *Salvātor* the Saviour]

Saviour *or* *U.S.* **Savior** (ˈseɪvjə) *n.* *Christianity.* Jesus Christ regarded as the saviour of men from sin.

savoir-faire (ˈsævwɑːˈfɛə) *n.* the ability to do the right thing in any situation. [F, lit.: a knowing how to do]

savory (ˈseɪvərɪ) *n., pl.* **-vories. 1.** any of numerous aromatic plants, including the **winter savory** and **summer savory**, of the Mediterranean region, having narrow leaves and white, pink, or purple flowers. **2.** the leaves of any of these plants, used as a potherb. [C14: prob. < OE *sætherie*, < L *saturēia*, <?]

savour *or* *U.S.* **savor** (ˈseɪvə) *n.* **1.** the quality in a substance that is perceived by the sense of taste or smell. **2.** a specific taste or smell: *the savour of lime.* **3.** a slight but distinctive quality or trace. **4.** the power to excite interest: *the savour of wit has been lost.* *~vb.* **5.** (*intr.*; often foll. by *of*) to possess the taste or smell (of). **6.** (*intr.*; often foll. by *of*) to have a suggestion (of). **7.** (*tr.*) to season. **8.** (*tr.*) to taste or smell, esp. appreciatively. **9.** (*tr.*) to relish or enjoy. [C13: < OF *savour*, < L *sapor* taste, < *sapere* to taste] —ˈ**savourless** *or* *U.S.* ˈ**savorless** *adj.*

savoury *or* *U.S.* **savory** (ˈseɪvərɪ) *adj.* **1.** attractive to the sense of taste or smell. **2.** salty or spicy: *a savoury dish.* **3.** pleasant. **4.** respectable. *~n., pl.* **-vouries. 5.** *Chiefly Brit.* a savoury dish served as an hors d'oeuvre or dessert. [C13 *savure*, < OF, < *savourer* to SAVOUR] —ˈ**savouriness** *or* *U.S.* ˈ**savoriness** *n.*

savoy (səˈvɔɪ) *n.* a cultivated variety of cabbage having a compact head and wrinkled leaves. [C16: after the *Savoy* region in France]

savvy (ˈsævɪ) *Sl.* *~vb.* **-vying, -vied. 1.** to understand or get the sense of (an idea, etc.). *~n.* **2.** comprehension. *~adj.* **-vier, -viest. 3.** *Chiefly U.S.* shrewd. [C18: corruption of Sp. *sabe* (*usted*) (you) know, < *saber* to know, < L *sapere* to be wise]

saw[1] (sɔː) *n.* **1.** any of various hand tools for cutting wood, metal, etc., having a blade with teeth along one edge. **2.** any of various machines or devices for cutting by use of a toothed blade, such as a power-driven toothed band of metal. *~vb.* **sawing, sawed; sawed** *or* **sawn. 3.** to cut with a saw. **4.** to form by sawing. **5.** to cut as if wielding a saw: *to saw the air.* **6.** to move (an object) from side to side as if moving a saw. [OE *sagu*: rel. to L *secare* to cut] —ˈ**sawer** *n.* —ˈ**sawˌlike** *adj.*

saw[2] (sɔː) *vb.* the past tense of **see**[1].

saw[3] (sɔː) *n.* a wise saying, maxim, or proverb. [OE *sagu* a saying]

sawbones (ˈsɔːˌbəʊnz) *n., pl.* **-bones** *or* **-boneses.** *Sl.* a surgeon or doctor.

sawdust (ˈsɔːˌdʌst) *n.* particles of wood formed by sawing.

sawfish (ˈsɔːˌfɪʃ) *n., pl.* **-fish** *or* **-fishes.** a sharklike ray of subtropical coastal waters, having a serrated bladelike mouth.

sawfly (ˈsɔːˌflaɪ) *n., pl.* **-flies.** any of various hymenopterous insects, the females of which have a sawlike ovipositor.

sawhorse (ˈsɔːˌhɔːs) *n.* a stand for timber during sawing.

sawmill (ˈsɔːˌmɪl) *n.* an industrial establishment where timber is sawn into planks, etc.

sawn (sɔːn) *vb.* a past participle of **saw**[1].

sawn-off *or* *esp. U.S.* **sawed-off** *adj.* (*prenominal*) (of a shotgun) having the barrel cut short, mainly to facilitate concealment of the weapon.

saw set *n.* a tool used for setting the teeth of a saw, consisting of a clamp used to bend each tooth at a slight angle to the plane of the saw, alternate teeth being bent in the same direction.

sawyer (ˈsɔːjə) *n.* a person who saws timber for a living. [C14 *sawier*, < SAW[1] + *-ier*, var. of -ER[1]]

sax (sæks) *n. Inf.* short for **saxophone.**

saxe blue (sæks) *n.* **a.** a light greyish-blue colour. **b.** (*as adj.*): *a saxe-blue dress.* [C19: < F *Saxe* Saxony, source of a dye of this colour]

saxhorn (ˈsæksˌhɔːn) *n.* a valved brass instrument used chiefly in brass and military bands, having a tube of conical bore. It resembles the tuba. [C19: after Adolphe *Sax* (see SAXOPHONE), who invented it (1845)]

saxicolous (sækˈsɪkələs) *adj.* living on or among rocks: *saxicolous plants.* Also: **saxatile** (ˈsæksə-

ˌtaɪl). [C19: < NL *saxicolus,* < L *saxum* rock + *colere* to dwell]

saxifrage (ˈsæksɪˌfreɪdʒ) *n.* a plant having small white, yellow, purple, or pink flowers. [C15: < LL *saxifraga,* lit.: rock-breaker, < L *saxum* rock + *frangere* to break]

Saxon (ˈsæksən) *n.* **1.** a member of a West Germanic people who raided and settled parts of S Britain in the fifth and sixth centuries A.D. **2.** a native or inhabitant of Saxony, in Germany. **3. a.** the Low German dialect of Saxony. **b.** any of the West Germanic dialects spoken by the ancient Saxons. ~*adj.* **4.** of or characteristic of the ancient Saxons, the Anglo-Saxons, or their descendants. **5.** of or characteristic of Saxony, its inhabitants, or their Low German dialect. [C13 (replacing OE *Seaxe*): via OF < LL *Saxon-, Saxo,* < Gk; of Gmc origin]

saxophone (ˈsæksəˌfəʊn) *n.* a keyed single-reed wind instrument of mellow tone colour, used mainly in jazz and dance music. Often shortened to **sax.** [C19: after Adolphe *Sax* (1814–94), Belgian musical-instrument maker, who invented it (1846)] —**saxophonic** (ˌsæksəˈfɒnɪk) *adj.* —**saxophonist** (sækˈsɒfənɪst) *n.*

say (seɪ) *vb.* **saying, said.** (*mainly tr.*) **1.** to speak, pronounce, or utter. **2.** (*also intr.*) to express (an idea, etc.) in words; tell. **3.** (*also intr.; may take a clause as object*) to state (an opinion, fact, etc.) positively. **4.** to recite: *to say grace.* **5.** (*may take a clause as object*) to report or allege: *they say we shall have rain today.* **6.** (*may take a clause as object*) to suppose: *let us say that he is lying.* **7.** (*may take a clause as object*) to convey by means of artistic expression. **8.** to make a case for: *there is much to be said for it.* **9. go without saying.** to be so obvious as to need no explanation. **10. I say!** *Inf., chiefly Brit.* an exclamation of surprise. **11. not to say.** even. **12. that is to say.** in other words. **13. to say the least.** at the very least. ~*adv.* **14.** approximately: *there were, say, 20 people present.* **15.** for example: *choose a number, say, four.* ~*n.* **16.** the right or chance to speak: *let him have his say.* **17.** authority, esp. to influence a decision: *he has a lot of say.* **18.** a statement of opinion: *you've had your say.* ~*interj.* **19.** *U.S. & Canad. inf.* an exclamation to attract attention or express surprise. [OE *secgan*] —ˈ**sayer** *n.*

SAYE (in Britain) *abbrev. for* save as you earn.

saying (ˈseɪɪŋ) *n.* a maxim, adage, or proverb.

say-so *n. Inf.* **1.** an arbitrary assertion. **2.** an authoritative decision. **3.** the authority to make a final decision.

sayyid (ˈsaɪɪd) *or* **said** *n.* **1.** a Muslim claiming descent from Mohammed's grandson Husain. **2.** a Muslim honorary title. [C17: < Ar.: lord]

Sb *the chemical symbol for* antimony. [< NL *stibium*]

sc *Printing. abbrev. for* small capitals.

Sc *the chemical symbol for* scandium.

SC *abbrev. for:* **1.** *Austral. & N.Z.* School Certificate. **2.** Signal Corps. **3.** *Canad.* Social Credit.

sc. *abbrev. for:* **1.** scale. **2.** scene. **3.** science. **4.** scilicet. **5.** screw. **6.** scruple (unit of weight).

scab (skæb) *n.* **1.** the dried crusty surface of a healing skin wound or sore. **2.** a contagious disease of sheep resembling mange, caused by a mite. **3.** a fungal disease of plants characterized by crusty spots on the fruits, leaves, etc. **4.** *Derog.* **a.** Also called: **blackleg.** a person who refuses to support a trade union's actions, esp. strikes. **b.** (*as modifier*)*: scab labour.* **5.** a despicable person. ~*vb.* **scabbing, scabbed.** (*intr.*) **6.** to become covered with a scab. **7.** to replace a striking worker. [OE *sceabb*]

scabbard (ˈskæbəd) *n.* a holder for a bladed weapon such as a sword or bayonet. [C13 *scauberc,* < Norman F *escaubers,* (pl.) of Gmc origin]

scabby (ˈskæbɪ) *adj.* **-bier, -biest.** **1.** *Pathol.* having an area of the skin covered with scabs. **2.** *Pathol.* having scabies. **3.** *Inf.* despicable. —ˈ**scabbily** *adv.* —ˈ**scabbiness** *n.*

scabies (ˈskeɪbiːz) *n.* a contagious skin infection caused by a mite, characterized by intense itching and inflammation. [C15: < L: scurf, < *scabere* to scratch]

scabious[1] (ˈskeɪbɪəs) *adj.* **1.** having or covered with scabs. **2.** of, relating to, or resembling scabies. [C17: < L *scabiōsus,* < SCABIES]

scabious[2] (ˈskeɪbɪəs) *n.* any of a genus of plants of the Mediterranean region, having blue, red, or whitish dome-shaped flower heads. [C14: < Med. L *scabiōsa herba* the scabies plant, referring to its use in treating scabies]

scabrous (ˈskeɪbrəs) *adj.* **1.** roughened because of small projections. **2.** indecent or salacious: *scabrous humour.* **3.** difficult to deal with. [C17: < L *scaber* rough] —ˈ**scabrously** *adv.*

scad (skæd) *n., pl.* **scad** *or* **scads.** any of various marine fishes having a deeply forked tail, such as the large mackerel. [C17: <?]

scads (skædz) *pl. n. Inf.* a large amount or number. [C19: <?]

scaffold (ˈskæfəld) *n.* **1.** a temporary framework that is used to support workmen and materials during the erection, repair, etc., of a building. **2.** a raised wooden platform on which plays are performed, tobacco, etc., is dried, or (esp. formerly) criminals are executed. ~*vb.* (*tr.*) **3.** to provide with a scaffold. **4.** to support by means of a scaffold. [C14: < OF *eschaffaut,* < Vulgar L *catafalicum* (unattested)] —ˈ**scaffolder** *n.*

scaffolding (ˈskæfəldɪŋ) *n.* **1.** a scaffold or system of scaffolds. **2.** the building materials used to make scaffolds.

scalable (ˈskeɪləbᵊl) *adj.* capable of being climbed. —ˈ**scalableness** *n.* —ˈ**scalably** *adv.*

scalar (ˈskeɪlə) *n.* **1.** a quantity, such as time or temperature, that has magnitude but not direction. ~*adj.* **2.** having magnitude but not direction. [C17 (meaning: resembling a ladder): < L *scālāris,* < *scāla* ladder]

scalar product *n.* the product of two vectors to form a scalar, whose value is the product of the magnitudes of the vectors and the cosine of the angle between them. Also called: **dot product.**

scalawag (ˈskæləˌwæg) *n.* a variant of **scallywag.**

scald[1] (skɔːld) *vb.* **1.** to burn or be burnt with or as if with hot liquid or steam. **2.** (*tr.*) to subject to the action of boiling water, esp. so as to sterilize. **3.** (*tr.*) to heat (a liquid) almost to boiling point. **4.** to plunge (tomatoes, etc.) into boiling water in order to skin them more easily. ~*n.* **5.** the act or result of scalding. **6.** an abnormal condition in plants, caused by exposure to excessive sunlight, gases, etc. [C13: via OF < LL *excaldāre* to wash in warm water, < *calida* (*aqua*) warm (water), < *calēre* to be warm] —ˈ**scalder** *n.*

scald[2] (skɔːld) *n.* a variant spelling of **skald.**

scaldfish (ˈskɔːldˌfɪʃ, ˈskɑːld-) *n., pl.* **-fish** *or* **-fishes.** a small European flatfish, covered with large fragile scales.

scale[1] (skeɪl) *n.* **1.** any of the numerous plates, made of various substances, covering the bodies of fishes. **2. a.** any of the horny or chitinous plates covering a part or the entire body of certain reptiles and mammals. **b.** any of the numerous minute structures covering the wings of lepidoptera. **3.** a thin flat piece or flake. **4.** a thin flake of dead epidermis shed from the skin. **5.** a specialized leaf or bract, esp. the protective covering of a bud or the dry membranous bract of a catkin. **6.** See **scale insect.** **7.** any oxide formed on a metal when heated. **8.** tartar formed on the teeth. ~*vb.* **9.** (*tr.*) to remove the scales or coating from. **10.** to peel off or cause to peel off in flakes or scales. **11.** (*intr.*) to shed scales. **12.** to cover or become covered with scales, incrustation, etc. [C14: < OF *escale,* of Gmc origin]

scale[2] (skeɪl) *n.* **1.** (*often pl.*) a machine or device for weighing. **2.** one of the pans of a balance. **3. tip the scales. a.** to exercise a decisive influence. **b.** (foll. by *at*) to amount in weight (to). ~*vb.* (*tr.*) **4.** to weigh with or as if with scales. [C13: < ON *skāl* bowl]

scale[3] (skeɪl) *n.* **1.** a sequence of marks either at regular intervals, or representing equal steps, used as a reference in making measurements. **2.** a measuring instrument having such a scale. **3. a.** the ratio between the size of something real and that of a representation of it. **b.** (*as modifier*): *a scale model.* **4.** a line, numerical ratio, etc., for showing this ratio. **5.** a progressive or graduated table of things, wages, etc.: *a wage scale for carpenters.* **6.** an established standard. **7.** a relative degree or extent: *he entertained on a grand scale.* **8.** *Music.* a group of notes taken in ascending or descending order, esp. within the compass of one octave. **9.** *Maths.* the notation of a given number system: *the decimal scale.* ~*vb.* **10.** to climb to the top of (a height) by or as if by a ladder. **11.** (*tr.*) to make or draw (a model, etc.) according to a particular ratio of proportionate reduction. **12.** (*tr.;* usually foll. by *up* or *down*) to increase or reduce proportionately in size, etc. **13.** (*intr.*) *Austral. inf.* to ride on public transport without paying a fare. [C15: via It. < L *scāla* ladder]

scaleboard (ˈskeɪlˌbɔːd) *n.* a very thin piece of board, used for backing a picture, etc.

scale insect *n.* a small insect which typically lives and feeds on plants and secretes a protective scale around itself. Many species are pests.

scalene (ˈskeɪliːn) *adj.* **1.** *Maths.* (of a triangle) having all sides of unequal length. **2.** *Anat.* of or relating to any of the scalenus muscles. [C17: < LL *scalēnus* with unequal sides, < Gk *skalēnos*]

scalenus (skəˈliːnəs) *n., pl.* **-ni** (-naɪ). *Anat.* any one of the three muscles situated on each side of the neck extending from the cervical vertebrae to the first or second pair of ribs. [C18: < NL; see SCALENE]

scaling ladder *n.* a ladder used to climb high walls, esp. one used formerly to enter a besieged town, fortress, etc.

scallion (ˈskæljən) *n.* any of various onions, such as the spring onion, that have a small bulb and long leaves and are eaten in salads. [C14: < Anglo-F *scalun,* < L *Ascalōnia* (*caepa*) Ascalonian (onion), < *Ascalo* Ascalon, a Palestinian port]

scallop (ˈskɒləp, ˈskæl-) *n.* **1.** any of various marine bivalves having a fluted fan-shaped shell. **2.** the edible adductor muscle of certain of these molluscs. **3.** either of the shell valves of any of these molluscs. **4.** a scallop shell in which fish, esp. shellfish, is cooked and served. **5.** one of a series of curves along an edge. **6.** the shape of a scallop shell used as the badge of a pilgrim, esp. in the Middle Ages. **7.** *Chiefly Austral.* a potato cake fried in batter. ~*vb.* **8.** (*tr.*) to decorate (an edge) with scallops. **9.** to bake (food) in a scallop shell or similar dish. [C14: < OF *escalope* shell, of Gmc origin] —ˈ**scalloper** *n.* —ˈ**scalloping** *n.*

scallywag (ˈskælɪˌwæg) *n. Inf.* a scamp; rascal. ~Also: **scalawag, scallawag.** [C19: (orig. undersized animal): <?]

scalp (skælp) *n.* **1.** *Anat.* the skin and subcutaneous tissue covering the top of the head. **2.** (among North American Indians) a part of this removed as a trophy from a slain enemy. **3.** a trophy or token signifying conquest. **4.** *Scot. dialect.* a projection of bare rock from vegetation. ~*vb.* (*tr.*) **5.** to cut the scalp from. **6.** *Inf., chiefly U.S.* to purchase and resell (securities) quickly so as to make several small profits. **7.** *Inf.* to buy (tickets) cheaply and resell at an inflated price. [C13: prob. < ON] —ˈ**scalper** *n.*

scalpel (ˈskælpᵊl) *n.* a surgical knife with a short thin blade. [C18: < L *scalpellum,* < *scalper* a knife, < *scalpere* to scrape]

scaly (ˈskeɪlɪ) *adj.* **scalier, scaliest. 1.** resembling or covered in scales. **2.** peeling off in scales. —ˈ**scaliness** *n.*

scaly anteater *n.* another name for **pangolin.**

scamp[1] (skæmp) *n.* **1.** an idle mischievous person. **2.** a mischievous child. [C18: < *scamp* (vb.) to be a highway robber, prob. < MDu. *schampen* to decamp, < OF *escamper,* < L *campus* field] —ˈ**scampish** *adj.*

scamp[2] (skæmp) *vb.* a less common word for **skimp.** —ˈ**scamper** *n.*

scamper (ˈskæmpə) *vb.* **1.** (*intr.*) to run about playfully. **2.** (often foll. by *through*) to hurry through (a place, task, etc.) ~*n.* **3.** the act of scampering. [C17: prob. < *scamp* (vb.); see SCAMP[1]]

scampi (ˈskæmpɪ) *n.* (*usually functioning as sing.*) large prawns, usually eaten fried in breadcrumbs. [It.: pl. of *scampo* shrimp, <?]

scan (skæn) *vb.* **scanning, scanned. 1.** (*tr.*) to scrutinize minutely. **2.** (*tr.*) to glance at quickly. **3.** (*tr.*) *Prosody.* to read or analyse (verse) according to the rules of metre and versification. **4.** (*intr.*) *Prosody.* to conform to the rules of metre and versification. **5.** (*tr.*) *Electronics.* to move a beam of light, electrons, etc., in a predetermined pattern over (a surface or region) to obtain information, esp. to reproduce a television image. **6.** (*tr.*) to examine data stored on (magnetic tape, etc.), usually in order to retrieve information. **7.** to examine or search (a prescribed region) by systematically varying the direction of a radar or sonar beam. **8.** *Med.* to obtain an image of (a part of the body) by means of ultrasound or a scanner. ~*n.* **9.** the act or an instance of scanning. [C14: < LL *scandere* to scan (verse), < L: to climb] —ˈ**scannable** *adj.*

Scand. *or* **Scan.** *abbrev. for* Scandinavia(n).

scandal (ˈskændᵊl) *n.* **1.** a disgraceful action or event: *his negligence was a scandal.* **2.** censure or outrage arising from an action or event. **3.** a person whose conduct causes reproach or disgrace. **4.** malicious talk, esp. gossip. **5.** *Law.* a libellous action or statement. [C16: < LL *scandalum* stumbling block, < Gk *skandalon* a trap] —ˈ**scandalous** *adj.* —ˈ**scandalously** *adv.*

scandalize *or* **-ise** (ˈskændəˌlaɪz) *vb.* (*tr.*) to shock, as by improper behaviour. —ˌ**scandaliˈzation** *or* **-iˈsation** *n.*

scandalmonger (ˈskændᵊlˌmʌŋgə) *n.* a person who spreads or enjoys scandal, gossip, etc.

Scandinavian (ˌskændɪˈneɪvɪən) *adj.* **1.** of or characteristic of Scandinavia (Norway, Sweden, Denmark, and Iceland), its inhabitants, or their languages. ~*n.* **2.** a native or inhabitant of Scandinavia. **3.** the group of Germanic languages, consisting of Swedish, Danish, Norwegian, Icelandic, and Faeroese.

scandium (ˈskændɪəm) *n.* a rare silvery-white metallic element occurring in minute quantities in numerous minerals. Symbol: Sc; atomic no.: 21; atomic wt.: 44.96. [C19: < NL, < L *Scandia* Scandinavia, where discovered]

scanner (ˈskænə) *n.* **1.** a person or thing that scans. **2.** a device, usually electronic, used to measure or sample the distribution of some quantity or condition in a particular system, region, or area. **3.** an aerial or similar device designed to transmit or receive signals, esp. radar signals, inside a given solid angle of space. **4.** any device used in medical diagnosis to obtain an image of an internal organ or part.

scanning electron microscope *n.* a type of electron microscope that produces a three-dimensional image.

scansion (ˈskænʃən) *n.* the analysis of the metrical structure of verse. [C17: < L: climbing up, < *scandere* to climb]

scant (skænt) *adj.* **1.** scarcely sufficient: *he paid her scant attention.* **2.** (*prenominal*) bare: *a scant ten inches.* **3.** (*postpositive;* foll. by *of*) having a short supply (of). ~*vb.* (*tr.*) **4.** to limit in size or quantity. **5.** to provide with a limited supply of. **6.** to treat in an inadequate manner. ~*adv.* **7.** scarcely; barely. [C14: < ON *skamt,* < *skammr* short] —ˈ**scantly** *adv.*

scantling (ˈskæntlɪŋ) *n.* **1.** a piece of sawn timber, such as a rafter, that has a small cross section. **2.** the dimensions of a piece of building material or the structural parts of a ship or aircraft. **3.** a building stone. **4.** a small quantity or amount. [C16: changed (through infl. of SCANT & -LING[1]) < earlier *scantillon* a carpenter's gauge, < OF *escantillon,* ult. < L *scandere* to climb]

scanty (ˈskæntɪ) *adj.* **scantier, scantiest. 1.**

limited; barely enough. **2.** inadequate. **3.** lacking fullness. —**ˈscantily** *adv.* —**ˈscantiness** *n.*

scape *or* **'scape** (skeɪp) *vb., n.* an archaic word for **escape.**

-scape *suffix forming nouns.* indicating a scene or view of something: *seascape.* [< LANDSCAPE]

scapegoat (ˈskeɪpˌgəʊt) *n.* **1.** a person made to bear the blame for others. **2.** *Bible.* a goat symbolically laden with the sins of the Israelites and sent into the wilderness. [C16: < ESCAPE + GOAT, coined by William Tyndale to translate Biblical Heb. *azāzēl* (prob.) goat for Azazel, mistakenly thought to mean "goat that escapes"]

scapegrace (ˈskeɪpˌgreɪs) *n.* a mischievous person. [C19: < SCAPE + GRACE, alluding to a person who lacks God's grace]

scaphoid (ˈskæfɔɪd) *adj. Anat.* an obsolete word for **navicular.** [C18: via NL < Gk *skaphoeidēs,* < *skaphē* boat]

scapula (ˈskæpjʊlə) *n., pl.* **-lae** (-liː) *or* **-las.** either of two large flat triangular bones, one on each side of the back part of the shoulder in man. Nontechnical name: **shoulder blade.** [C16: < LL: shoulder]

scapular (ˈskæpjʊlə) *adj.* **1.** *Anat.* of or relating to the scapula. ~*n.* **2.** part of the monastic habit worn by members of many Christian religious orders, consisting of a piece of woollen cloth worn over the shoulders, and hanging down to the ankles. **3.** two small rectangular pieces of cloth joined by tapes passing over the shoulders and worn in token of affiliation to a religious order. **4.** any of the small feathers of a bird that lie along the shoulder. ~Also called (for senses 2 and 3): **scapulary.**

scar[1] (skɑː) *n.* **1.** any mark left on the skin or other tissue following the healing of a wound, etc. **2.** a permanent change in a person's character resulting from emotional distress. **3.** the mark on a plant indicating the former point of attachment of a part. **4.** a mark of damage. ~*vb.* **scarring, scarred. 5.** to mark or become marked with a scar. **6.** (*intr.*) to heal leaving a scar. [C14: via LL < Gk *eskhara* scab]

scar[2] (skɑː) *n.* a bare craggy rock formation. [C14: < ON *sker* low reef]

scarab (ˈskærəb) *n.* **1.** any scarabaeid beetle, esp. the **sacred scarab,** regarded by the ancient Egyptians as divine. **2.** the scarab as represented on amulets, etc. [C16: < L *scarabaeus*]

scarabaeid (ˌskærəˈbiːɪd) *n.* **1.** any of a family of beetles including the sacred scarab and other dung beetles, the chafers, and rhinoceros beetles. ~*adj.* **2.** of or belonging to this family. [C19: < NL]

Scaramouch (ˈskærəˌmaʊtʃ) *n.* a stock character who appears as a boastful coward in commedia dell'arte. [C17: via F < It. *Scaramuccia,* < *scaramuccia* a SKIRMISH]

scarce (skɛəs) *adj.* **1.** rarely encountered. **2.** insufficient to meet the demand. **3. make oneself scarce.** *Inf.* to go away. ~*adv.* **4.** *Arch. or literary.* scarcely. [C13: < OF *scars,* < Vulgar L *excarpsus* (unattested) plucked out, < L *excerpere* to select] —**ˈscarceness** *n.*

scarcely (ˈskɛəslɪ) *adv.* **1.** hardly at all. **2.** *Often used ironically.* probably or definitely not: *that is scarcely justification for your actions.*

▷ **Usage.** See at **hardly.**

scarcity (ˈskɛəsɪtɪ) *n., pl.* **-ties. 1.** inadequate supply. **2.** rarity or infrequent occurrence.

scare (skɛə) *vb.* **1.** to fill or be filled with fear or alarm. **2.** (*tr.;* often foll. by *away* or *off*) to drive (away) by frightening. ~*n.* **3.** a sudden attack of fear or alarm. **4.** a period of general fear or alarm. ~*adj.* **5.** causing (needless) fear or alarm: *a scare story.* [C12: < ON *skirra*] —**ˈscarer** *n.*

scarecrow (ˈskɛəˌkrəʊ) *n.* **1.** an object, usually in the shape of a man, made out of sticks and old clothes to scare birds away from crops. **2.** a person or thing that appears frightening. **3.** *Inf.* an untidy-looking person.

scaremonger (ˈskɛəˌmʌŋgə) *n.* a person who delights in spreading rumours of disaster. —**ˈscareˌmongering** *n.*

scarf[1] (skɑːf) *n., pl.* **scarfs** *or* **scarves.** a rectangular, triangular, or long narrow piece of cloth worn around the head, neck, or shoulders for warmth or decoration. [C16: <?]

scarf[2] (skɑːf) *n., pl.* **scarfs. 1.** Also called: **scarf joint, scarfed joint.** a lapped joint between two pieces of timber made by notching the ends and strapping or gluing the two pieces together. **2.** the end of a piece of timber shaped to form such a joint. **3.** *Whaling.* an incision made along a whale before stripping off the blubber. ~*vb.* (*tr.*) **4.** to join (two pieces of timber) by means of a scarf. **5.** to make a scarf on (a piece of timber). **6.** to cut a scarf in (a whale). [C14: prob. < ON]

scarfskin (ˈskɑːfˌskɪn) *n.* the outermost layer of the skin; epidermis or cuticle. [C17: < SCARF[1] (in the sense: an outer covering)]

scarify (ˈskɛərɪˌfaɪ, ˈskærɪ-) *vb.* **-fying, -fied.** (*tr.*) **1.** *Surgery.* to make tiny punctures or superficial incisions in (the skin or other tissue), as for inoculating. **2.** *Agriculture.* to break up and loosen (soil) to a shallow depth. **3.** to wound with harsh criticism. [C15: via OF < L *scarīfāre* to scratch open, < Gk *skariphasthai* to draw, < *skariphos* a pencil] —**ˌscarifiˈcation** *n.* —**ˈscariˌfier** *n.*

scarlatina (ˌskɑːləˈtiːnə) *n.* the technical name for **scarlet fever.** [C19: < NL, < It. *scarlattina,* dim. of *scarlatto* scarlet]

scarlet (ˈskɑːlɪt) *n.* **1.** a vivid orange-red colour. **2.** cloth or clothing of this colour. ~*adj.* **3.** of the colour scarlet. **4.** sinful or immoral. [C13: < OF *escarlate* fine cloth, <?]

scarlet fever *n.* an acute communicable disease characterized by fever, strawberry-coloured tongue, and a rash starting on the neck and chest and spreading to the abdomen and limbs. Technical name: **scarlatina.**

scarlet letter *n.* (esp. among U.S. Puritans) a scarlet letter *A* formerly worn by a person convicted of adultery.

scarlet pimpernel *n.* a plant, related to the primrose, having small red, purple, or white star-shaped flowers that close in bad weather. Also called: **shepherd's** (or **poor man's**) **weatherglass.**

scarlet runner *n.* a climbing perennial bean plant of tropical America, having scarlet flowers: widely cultivated for its long green edible pods containing edible seeds. Also: **runner bean.**

scarlet woman *n.* **1.** a sinful woman described in the Bible (Rev. 17), interpreted as a symbol of pagan Rome or of the Roman Catholic Church. **2.** any sexually promiscuous woman.

scarp (skɑːp) *n.* **1.** a steep slope, esp. one formed by erosion or faulting. **2.** *Fortifications.* the side of a ditch cut nearest to a rampart. ~*vb.* **3.** (*tr.; often passive*) to wear or cut so as to form a steep slope. [C16: < It. *scarpa*]

scarper (ˈskɑːpə) *Brit. sl.* ~*vb.* **1.** (*intr.*) to depart in haste. ~*n.* **2.** a hasty departure. [<?]

scarves (skɑːvz) *n.* a plural of **scarf**[1].

scary (ˈskɛərɪ) *adj.* **scarier, scariest.** *Inf.* **1.** causing fear or alarm. **2.** timid.

scat[1] (skæt) *vb.* **scatting, scatted.** (*intr.; usually imperative*) *Inf.* to go away in haste. [C19: ? < a hiss + *cat,* used to frighten away cats]

scat[2] (skæt) *n.* **1.** a type of jazz singing characterized by improvised vocal sounds instead of words. ~*vb.* **scatting, scatted. 2.** (*intr.*) to sing jazz in this way. [C20: ? imit.]

scathe (skeɪð) *vb.* (*tr.*) **1.** *Rare.* to attack with severe criticism. **2.** *Arch. or dialect.* to injure. ~*n.* **3.** *Arch. or dialect.* harm. [OE *sceatha*]

scathing (ˈskeɪðɪŋ) *adj.* **1.** harshly critical; scornful. **2.** damaging. —**ˈscathingly** *adv.*

scatology (skæˈtɒlədʒɪ) *n.* **1.** the scientific study of excrement, esp. in medicine and in palaeontology. **2.** obscenity or preoccupation with obscenity, esp. in the form of references to excrement. [C19: < Gk *skat-* excrement + -LOGY] —**scatological** (ˌskætəˈlɒdʒɪkᵊl) *adj.*

scatter (ˈskætə) *vb.* **1.** (*tr.*) to throw about in various directions. **2.** to separate and move or cause to separate and move in various directions. **3.** to deviate or cause to deviate in many directions, as in the refraction of light. ~*n.* **4.** the act of scattering. **5.** a substance or a number of objects scattered about. [C13: prob. a var. of SHATTER] —ˈ**scatterer** *n.*

scatterbrain (ˈskætəˌbreɪn) *n.* a person who is incapable of serious thought or concentration. —ˈ**scatterˌbrained** *adj.*

scatter diagram *n. Statistics.* a representation by a Cartesian graph of the correlation between two quantities, such as height and weight.

scattering (ˈskætərɪŋ) *n.* **1.** a small amount. **2.** *Physics.* the process in which particles, atoms, etc., are deflected as a result of collision.

scatty (ˈskætɪ) *adj.* **-tier, -tiest.** *Brit. inf.* **1.** empty-headed or thoughtless. **2.** distracted (esp. in **drive someone scatty**). [C20: < SCATTERBRAINED] —ˈ**scattily** *adv.* —ˈ**scattiness** *n.*

scaup *or* **scaup duck** (skɔːp) *n.* either of two diving ducks, the **greater scaup** or the **lesser scaup**, of Europe and America, having a black-and-white plumage in the male. [C16: Scot. var. of SCALP]

scavenge (ˈskævɪndʒ) *vb.* **1.** to search for (anything usable) among discarded material. **2.** (*tr.*) to purify (a molten metal) by bubbling a suitable gas through it. **3.** to clean up filth from (streets, etc.).

scavenger (ˈskævɪndʒə) *n.* **1.** a person who collects things discarded by others. **2.** any animal that feeds on decaying organic matter. **3.** a person employed to clean the streets. [C16: < Anglo-Norman *scawager,* < OF *escauwage* examination, < *escauwer* to scrutinize, of Gmc origin] —ˈ**scavengery** *n.*

ScD *abbrev. for* Doctor of Science.

SCE (in Scotland) *abbrev. for* Scottish Certificate of Education: either of two public examinations in specific subjects taken as school-leaving qualifications or as qualifying examinations for entry into a university, college, etc.

scena (ˈʃeɪnə) *n., pl.* **-ne** (-ˌneɪ) a solo vocal piece of dramatic style and large scope, esp. in opera. [C19: It., < L *scēna* scene]

scenario (sɪˈnɑːrɪˌəʊ) *n., pl.* **-narios. 1.** a summary of the plot of a play, etc., including information about its characters, scenes, etc. **2.** a predicted sequence of events. [C19: via It. < L *scēnārium,* < *scēna;* see SCENE]

scene (siːn) *n.* **1.** the place where an action or event, real or imaginary, occurs. **2.** the setting for the action of a play, novel, etc. **3.** an incident or situation, real or imaginary, esp. as described or represented. **4. a.** a subdivision of an act of a play, in which the setting is fixed. **b.** a single event, esp. a significant one, in a play. **5.** *Films.* a shot or series of shots that constitutes a unit of the action. **6.** the backcloths, etc., for a play or film set. **7.** the prospect of a place, landscape, etc. **8.** a display of emotion. **9.** *Inf.* the environment for a specific activity: *the fashion scene.* **10.** *Inf.* interest or chosen occupation: *classical music is not my scene.* **11.** *Rare.* the stage. **12. behind the scenes.** out of public view. [C16: < L *scēna* theatrical stage, < Gk *skēnē* tent, stage]

scene dock *or* **bay** *n.* a place in a theatre where scenery is stored, usually near the stage.

scenery (ˈsiːnərɪ) *n., pl.* **-eries. 1.** the natural features of a landscape. **2.** *Theatre.* the painted backcloths, etc., used to represent a location in a theatre or studio. [C18: < It. SCENARIO]

scenic (ˈsiːnɪk) *adj.* **1.** of or relating to natural scenery. **2.** having beautiful natural scenery: *a scenic drive.* **3.** of or relating to the stage or stage scenery. **4.** (in painting, etc.) representing a scene. —ˈ**scenically** *adv.*

scenic railway *n.* a miniature railway used for amusement in a park, zoo, etc.

scenic reserve *n. N.Z.* an area of natural beauty, set aside for public recreation.

scent (sɛnt) *n.* **1.** a distinctive smell, esp. a pleasant one. **2.** a smell left in passing, by which a person or animal may be traced. **3.** a trail, clue, or guide. **4.** an instinctive ability for detecting. **5.** another word (esp. Brit.) for **perfume.** ~*vb.* **6.** (*tr.*) to recognize by or as if by the smell. **7.** (*tr.*) to have a suspicion of: *I scent foul play.* **8.** (*tr.*) to fill with odour or fragrance. **9.** (*intr.*) (of hounds, etc.) to hunt by the sense of smell. **10.** to smell (at): *the dog scented the air.* [C14: < OF *sentir* to sense, < L *sentīre* to feel] —ˈ**scented** *adj.*

sceptic *or arch. & U.S.* **skeptic** (ˈskɛptɪk) *n.* **1.** a person who habitually doubts the authenticity of accepted beliefs. **2.** a person who mistrusts people, ideas, etc., in general. **3.** a person who doubts the truth of religion. [C16: < L *scepticus,* < Gk *skeptikos* one who reflects upon, < *skeptesthai* to consider] —ˈ**sceptical** *or arch. & U.S.* ˈ**skeptical** *adj.* —ˈ**sceptically** *or arch. & U.S.* ˈ**skeptically** *adv.* —ˈ**scepticism** *or arch. & U.S.* ˈ**skepticism** *n.*

Sceptic *or arch. & U.S.* **Skeptic** (ˈskɛptɪk) *n.* **1.** a member of one of the ancient Greek schools of philosophy, esp. that of Pyrrho ?365–?275 B.C., who believed that real knowledge of things is impossible. ~*adj.* **2.** of or relating to the Sceptics. —ˈ**Scepticism** *or arch. & U.S.* ˈ**Skepticism** *n.*

sceptre *or U.S.* **scepter** (ˈsɛptə) *n.* **1.** a ceremonial staff held by a monarch as the symbol of authority. **2.** imperial authority; sovereignty. [C13: < OF *sceptre,* < L, < Gk *skeptron* staff] —ˈ**sceptred** *or U.S.* ˈ**sceptered** *adj.*

schedule (ˈʃɛdjuːl; *also, esp. U.S.* ˈskɛdʒʊəl) *n.* **1.** a plan of procedure for a project. **2.** a list of items: *a schedule of fixed prices.* **3.** a list of times; timetable. **4.** a list of tasks to be performed, esp. within a set period. **5.** *Law.* a list or inventory. ~*vb.* (*tr.*) **6.** to make a schedule of or place in a schedule. **7.** to plan to occur at a certain time. [C14: earlier *cedule, sedule* via OF < LL *schedula* small piece of paper, < L *scheda* sheet of paper]

scheduled castes *pl. n.* certain classes in Indian society officially granted special concessions. See **Harijan.**

scheduled territories *pl. n.* **the.** another name for **sterling area.**

scheelite (ˈʃiːlaɪt) *n.* a white, brownish, or greenish mineral, usually fluorescent, consisting of calcium tungstate with some tungsten often replaced by molybdenum. It is an important source of tungsten. [C19: < G *Scheelit,* after K. W. *Scheele* (1742–86), Swedish chemist]

schema (ˈskiːmə) *n., pl.* **-mata** (-mətə). **1.** a plan, diagram, or scheme. **2.** (in the philosophy of Kant) a rule or principle that enables the understanding to unify experience. **3.** *Logic.* **a.** a syllogistic figure. **b.** a representation of the form of an inference. [C19: < Gk: form]

schematic (skɪˈmætɪk) *adj.* **1.** of or relating to the nature of a diagram, plan, or schema. ~*n.* **2.** a schematic diagram, esp. of an electrical circuit, etc. —**scheˈmatically** *adv.*

schematize *or* **-ise** (ˈskiːməˌtaɪz) *vb.* (*tr.*) to form into or arrange in a scheme. —ˈ**schemaˌtism** *n.* —ˌ**schematiˈzation** *or* **-iˈsation** *n.*

scheme (skiːm) *n.* **1.** a systematic plan for a course of action. **2.** a systematic arrangement of parts. **3.** a secret plot. **4.** a chart, diagram, or outline. **5.** an astrological diagram giving the aspects of celestial bodies. **6.** *Chiefly Brit.* a plan formally adopted by a commercial enterprise or governmental body, as for pensions, etc. **7.** Short for **housing scheme.** ~*vb.* **8.** (*tr.*) to devise a system for. **9.** to form intrigues (for) in an underhand manner. [C16: < L *schema,* < Gk *skhēma* form] —ˈ**schemer** *n.*

scheming (ˈskiːmɪŋ) *adj.* **1.** given to making plots; cunning. ~*n.* **2.** intrigues.

scherzando (skɛəˈtsændəʊ) *Music.* ~*adj., adv.* **1.** to be performed in a light-hearted manner. ~*n., pl.* **-di** (-diː) *or* **-dos. 2.** a movement, passage, etc., directed to be performed in this way. [It., lit.: joking; see SCHERZO]

scherzo (ˈskɛətsəʊ) *n., pl.* **-zos** *or* **-zi** (-tsiː). a brisk lively movement, developed from the minuet, with a contrastive middle section (a trio). [It.: joke, of Gmc origin]

Schick test (ʃɪk) *n. Med.* a skin test to determine

immunity to diphtheria. [C20: after Bela *Schick* (1877–1967), U.S. paediatrician]

schilling (ˈʃɪlɪŋ) *n.* the standard monetary unit of Austria. [C18: < G: SHILLING]

schism (ˈsɪzəm, ˈskɪz-) *n.* **1.** the division of a group into opposing factions. **2.** the factions so formed. **3.** division within or separation from an established Church, not necessarily involving differences in doctrine. [C14: < Church L *schisma*, < Gk *skhisma* a cleft, < *skhizein* to split]

schismatic (sɪzˈmætɪk, skɪz-) *or* **schismatical** *adj.* **1.** of or promoting schism. ~*n.* **2.** a person who causes schism or belongs to a schismatic faction. —**schisˈmatically** *adv.*

schist (ʃɪst) *n.* any metamorphic rock that can be split into thin layers. [C18: < F *schiste*, < L *lapis schistos* stone that may be split, < Gk *skhizein* to split] —ˈ**schistose** *adj.*

schistosome (ˈʃɪstəˌsəʊm) *n.* any of a genus of blood flukes which cause disease in man and domestic animals. Also called: **bilharzia.** [C19: < NL *Schistosoma*; see SCHIST, -SOME[3]]

schistosomiasis (ˌʃɪstəsəʊˈmaɪəsɪs) *n.* a disease caused by infestation of the body with schistosomes. Also called: **bilharziasis.**

schizanthus (skɪzˈænθəs) *n.* a flowering annual plant, native to Chile, that has finely divided leaves. [C19: NL < Gk *skhizein* to cut + *anthos* flower]

schizo (ˈskɪtsəʊ) *Inf.* ~*adj.* **1.** schizophrenic. ~*n., pl.* **-os. 2.** a schizophrenic person.

schizo- *or before a vowel* **schiz-** *combining form.* indicating a cleavage, split, or division: *schizophrenia.* [< Gk *skhizein* to split]

schizocarp (ˈskɪzəˌkɑːp) *n. Bot.* a dry fruit that splits into two or more one-seeded portions at maturity. —ˌ**schizoˈcarpous** *adj.*

schizoid (ˈskɪtsɔɪd) *adj.* **1.** *Psychol.* denoting a personality disorder characterized by extreme shyness and oversensitivity. **2.** *Inf.* characterized by conflicting or contradictory ideas, attitudes, etc. ~*n.* **3.** a person who has a schizoid personality.

schizomycete (ˌskɪtsəʊmaɪˈsiːt) *n.* any microscopic organism of the class *Schizomycetes*, which includes the bacteria.

schizophrenia (ˌskɪtsəʊˈfriːnɪə) *n.* **1.** any of a group of psychotic disorders characterized by progressive deterioration of the personality, withdrawal from reality, hallucinations, emotional instability, etc. **2.** *Inf.* behaviour that seems to be motivated by contradictory or conflicting principles. [C20: < SCHIZO- + Gk *phrēn* mind] —ˌ**schizoˈphrenic** *adj., n.*

schizothymia (ˌskɪtsəʊˈθaɪmɪə) *n. Psychiatry.* the condition of being schizoid or introverted. It encompasses elements of schizophrenia. [C20: NL, < SCHIZO- + *-thymia*, < Gk *thumos* spirit] —ˌ**schizoˈthymic** *adj.*

schlieren (ˈʃlɪərən) *n.* **1.** *Physics.* visible streaks produced in a transparent fluid as a result of variations in the fluid's density. **2.** streaks or platelike masses of mineral in a rock mass. [G, pl. of *Schliere* streak]

schmaltz *or* **schmalz** (ʃmælts, ʃmɔːlts) *n.* excessive sentimentality, esp. in music. [C20: < G (*Schmalz*) & Yiddish: melted fat, < OHG *smalz*] —ˈ**schmaltzy** *or* ˈ**schmalzy** *adj.*

Schmidt telescope *or* **camera** (ʃmɪt) *n.* a type of reflecting telescope incorporating a camera. Wide areas of the sky can be photographed in one exposure. [C20: after B. *Schmidt* (1879–1935), Swedish-born G inventor]

schnapper (ˈʃnæpə) *n.* a variant spelling of **snapper** (senses 1, 2).

schnapps *or* **schnaps** (ʃnæps) *n.* **1.** a Dutch spirit distilled from potatoes. **2.** (in Germany) any strong spirit. [C19: < G *Schnaps*, < *schnappen* to SNAP]

schnauzer (ˈʃnaʊtsə) *n.* a wire-haired breed of dog of the terrier type, originally from Germany, with a greyish coat. [C19: < G *Schnauze* snout]

schnitzel (ˈʃnɪtsəl) *n.* a thin slice of meat, esp. veal. [G: cutlet, < *schnitzen* to carve, *schnitzeln* to whittle]

schnorkle (ˈʃnɔːkᵊl) *n., vb.* a less common variant of **snorkel.**

schnozzle (ˈʃnɒzᵊl) *n. Chiefly U.S.* a slang word for **nose.** [alteration of Yiddish *shnoitsl*, < G *Schnauze* snout]

scholar (ˈskɒlə) *n.* **1.** a learned person, esp. in the humanities. **2.** a person, esp. a child, who studies; pupil. **3.** a student receiving a scholarship. [C14: < OF *escoler*, via LL < L *schola* SCHOOL[1]] —ˈ**scholarly** *adj.* —ˈ**scholarliness** *n.*

scholarship (ˈskɒləʃɪp) *n.* **1.** academic achievement; learning. **2. a.** financial aid provided for a scholar because of academic merit. **b.** the position of a student who gains this financial aid. **c.** (*as modifier*): *a scholarship student.* **3.** the qualities of a scholar.

scholastic (skəˈlæstɪk) *adj.* **1.** of or befitting schools, scholars, or education. **2.** pedantic or precise. **3.** (*often cap.*) characteristic of or relating to the medieval Schoolmen. ~*n.* **4.** a student or pupil. **5.** a person who is given to logical subtleties. **6.** (*often cap.*) a disciple or adherent of scholasticism; Schoolman. **7.** a Jesuit student who is undergoing a period of probation prior to commencing his theological studies. [C16: via L < Gk *skholastikos* devoted to learning, ult. < *skholē* SCHOOL[1]] —**schoˈlastically** *adv.*

scholasticism (skəˈlæstɪˌsɪzəm) *n.* (*sometimes cap.*) the system of philosophy, theology, and teaching that dominated medieval western Europe and was based on the writings of the Church Fathers and Aristotle.

scholiast (ˈskəʊlɪˌæst) *n.* a medieval annotator, esp. of classical texts. [C16: < LGk, ult. < Gk *skholē* school] —ˌ**scholiˈastic** *adj.*

school[1] (skuːl) *n.* **1. a.** an institution or building at which children and young people receive education. **b.** (*as modifier*): *school day.* **c.** (*in combination*): *schoolwork.* **2.** any educational institution or building. **3.** a faculty or department specializing in a particular subject: *a law school.* **4.** the staff and pupils of a school. **5.** the period of instruction in a school or one session of this: *he stayed after school to do extra work.* **6.** a place or sphere of activity that instructs: *the school of hard knocks.* **7.** a body of people or pupils adhering to a certain set of principles, doctrines, or methods. **8.** a group of artists, writers, etc., linked by the same style, teachers, or aims. **9.** a style of life: *a gentleman of the old school.* **10.** *Inf.* a group assembled for a common purpose, esp. gambling or drinking. ~*vb.* (*tr.*) **11.** to train or educate in or as in a school. **12.** to discipline or control. [OE *scōl*, < L *schola* school, < Gk *skholē* leisure spent in the pursuit of knowledge]

school[2] (skuːl) *n.* **1.** a group of fish or other aquatic animals that swim together. ~*vb.* **2.** (*intr.*) to form such a group. [OE *scolu* SHOAL[2]]

school board *n.* **1.** *English History.* an elected board of ratepayers who provided elementary schools (**board schools**). **2.** (in the U.S. and Canada) a local board of education.

schoolboy (ˈskuːlˌbɔɪ) *or* (*fem.*) **schoolgirl** *n.* a child attending school.

schoolhouse (ˈskuːlˌhaʊs) *n.* **1.** a building used as a school. **2.** a house attached to a school.

schoolie (ˈskuːlɪ) *n. Austral. sl.* a schoolteacher.

schooling (ˈskuːlɪŋ) *n.* **1.** education, esp. when received at school. **2.** the process of teaching or being taught in a school. **3.** the training of an animal, esp. of a horse for dressage.

schoolman (ˈskuːlmən) *n., pl.* **-men.** (*sometimes cap.*) a scholar versed in the learning of the **Schoolmen**, the masters in the universities of the Middle Ages who were versed in scholasticism.

schoolmarm (ˈskuːlˌmɑːm) *n. Inf.* **1.** a woman schoolteacher. **2.** any woman considered to be prim or old-fashioned. —ˈ**schoolˌmarmish** *adj.*

schoolmaster (ˈskuːlˌmɑːstə) *or* (*fem.*) **schoolmistress** *n.* **1.** a person who teaches in or runs a school. **2.** a person or thing that acts as an instructor.

schoolmate (ˈskuːlˌmeɪt) *or* **schoolfellow** *n.* a companion at school; fellow pupil.

school of arts *n. Austral.* a public building in a small town: orig. one used for adult education.

Schools (skuːlz) *pl. n.* **1.** **the Schools.** the medieval Schoolmen collectively. **2.** (at Oxford University) **a.** the University building in which examinations are held. **b.** *Inf.* the Second Public Examination for the degree of Bachelor of Arts.

schoolteacher (ˈskuːlˌtiːtʃə) *n.* a person who teaches in a school. —**ˈschoolˌteaching** *n.*

school year *n.* **1.** a twelve-month period, usually of three terms, during which pupils remain in the same class. **2.** the time during this period when the school is open.

schooner (ˈskuːnə) *n.* **1.** a sailing vessel with at least two masts, with lower sails rigged fore-and-aft. **2.** *Brit.* a large glass for sherry. **3.** *U.S., Canad., Austral., & N.Z.* a large glass for beer. [C18: <?]

schottische (ʃɒˈtiːʃ) *n.* **1.** a 19th-century German dance resembling a slow polka. **2.** a piece of music composed for or in the manner of this dance. [C19: < G *der schottische Tanz* the Scottish dance]

Schrödinger equation (*German* ˈʃrøːdɪŋər) *n.* an equation used in wave mechanics to describe a physical system. Also called: **wave equation.** [C20: after Erwin *Schrödinger* (1887–1961), Austrian physicist]

schuss (ʃʊs) *Skiing.* ~*n.* **1.** a straight high-speed downhill run. ~*vb.* **2.** (*intr.*) to perform a schuss. [G: SHOT[1]]

schwa *or* **shwa** (ʃwɑː) *n.* **1.** a central vowel represented in the International Phonetic Alphabet by (ə). The sound occurs in unstressed syllables in English, as in *around* and *sofa.* **2.** the symbol (ə) used to represent this sound. [C19: via G < Heb. *shewā*, a diacritic indicating lack of a vowel sound]

sci. *abbrev. for:* **1.** science. **2.** scientific.

sciatic (saɪˈætɪk) *adj.* **1.** *Anat.* of or relating to the hip or the hipbone. **2.** of or afflicted with sciatica. [C16: < F, < LL, < L *ischiadicus* relating to pain in the hip, < Gk, < *iskhia* hip-joint]

sciatica (saɪˈætɪkə) *n.* a form of neuralgia characterized by intense pain along the body's longest nerve (**sciatic nerve**), extending from the back of the thigh down to the calf of the leg. [C15: < LL *sciatica;* see SCIATIC]

science (ˈsaɪəns) *n.* **1.** the systematic study of the nature and behaviour of the material and physical universe, based on observation, experiment, and measurement. **2.** the knowledge so obtained or the practice of obtaining it. **3.** any particular branch of this knowledge: *the applied sciences.* **4.** any body of knowledge organized in a systematic manner. **5.** skill or technique. **6.** *Arch.* knowledge. [C14: via OF < L *scientia* knowledge, < *scīre* to know]

science fiction *n.* **a.** a literary genre that makes imaginative use of scientific knowledge. **b.** (*as modifier*): *a science-fiction writer.*

science park *n.* an area where scientific research and commercial development are carried on in cooperation.

scienter (saɪˈɛntə) *adv. Law.* knowingly; wilfully. [< L]

sciential (saɪˈɛnʃəl) *adj.* **1.** of or relating to science. **2.** skilful or knowledgeable.

scientific (ˌsaɪənˈtɪfɪk) *adj.* **1.** (*prenominal*) of, derived from, or used in science: *scientific equipment.* **2.** (*prenominal*) occupied in science: *scientific manpower.* **3.** conforming with the methods used in science. —**ˌscienˈtifically** *adv.*

scientism (ˈsaɪənˌtɪzəm) *n.* **1.** the application of the scientific method. **2.** the uncritical application of scientific methods to inappropriate fields of study. —**ˌscienˈtistic** *adj.*

scientist (ˈsaɪəntɪst) *n.* a person who studies or practises any of the sciences or who uses scientific methods.

Scientology (ˌsaɪənˈtɒlədʒɪ) *n. Trademark.* a cult, founded in the early 1950s, based on the belief that self-awareness is paramount, that believes in reincarnation. [C20: < L *scient(ia)* SCIENCE + -LOGY] —**ˌScienˈtologist** *n.*

sci-fi (ˈsaɪˈfaɪ) *n.* short for **science fiction.**

scilicet (ˈsɪlɪˌsɛt) *adv.* namely: used esp. in explaining an obscure text or supplying a missing word. [L: < *scīre licet* it is permitted to know]

scilla (ˈsɪlə) *n.* any of a genus of liliaceous plants having small bell-shaped flowers. See also **squill** (sense 3). [C19: via L < Gk *skilla*]

scimitar (ˈsɪmɪtə) *n.* an oriental sword with a curved blade broadening towards the point. [C16: < OIt., prob. < Persian *shimshīr*, <?]

scintigraphy (ˌsɪnˈtɪgrəfɪ) *n. Med.* a diagnostic technique using a radioactive tracer and scintillation counter for producing pictures (**scintigrams**) of internal parts of the body. [C20: < SCINTI(LLATION) + -GRAPHY]

scintilla (sɪnˈtɪlə) *n. Rare.* a minute amount; hint, trace, or particle. [C17: < L: a spark]

scintillate (ˈsɪntɪˌleɪt) *vb.* (*mainly intr.*) **1.** (*also tr.*) to give off (sparks); sparkle. **2.** to be animated or brilliant. **3.** *Physics.* to give off flashes of light as a result of the impact of photons. [C17: < L *scintillāre*, < *scintilla* a spark] —**ˈscintillant** *adj.* —**ˈscintilˌlating** *adj.*

scintillation (ˌsɪntɪˈleɪʃən) *n.* **1.** the act of scintillating. **2.** a spark or flash. **3.** the twinkling of stars. **4.** *Physics.* a flash of light produced when a material scintillates.

scintillation counter *n.* an instrument for detecting and measuring the intensity of high-energy radiation. It consists of a phosphor with which particles collide producing flashes of light that are converted into pulses of electric current that are counted by electronic equipment.

sciolism (ˈsaɪəˌlɪzəm) *n. Rare.* the practice of opinionating on subjects of which one has only superficial knowledge. [C19: < LL *sciolus* someone with a smattering of knowledge, < L *scīre* to know] —**ˈsciolist** *n.* —**ˌscioˈlistic** *adj.*

scion (ˈsaɪən) *n.* **1.** a descendant or young member of a family. **2.** a shoot of a plant used to form a graft. [C14: < OF *cion,* of Gmc origin]

scirrhus (ˈsɪrəs) *n., pl.* **-rhi** (-raɪ) *or* **-rhuses.** *Pathol.* a firm cancerous growth composed of fibrous tissues. [C17: < NL, < L *scirros,* < Gk, < *skiros* hard] —**scirrhoid** (ˈsɪrɔɪd) *adj.*

scission (ˈsɪʃən) *n.* the act or an instance of cutting, splitting, or dividing. [C15: < LL *scissiō,* < *scindere* to split]

scissor (ˈsɪzə) *vb.* to cut (an object) with scissors.

scissors (ˈsɪzəz) *pl. n.* **1.** Also called: **pair of scissors.** a cutting instrument used for cloth, hair, etc., having two crossed pivoted blades that cut by a shearing action. **2.** a wrestling hold in which a wrestler wraps his legs round his opponent's body or head and squeezes. **3.** any gymnastic feat in which the legs cross and uncross in a scissor-like movement. [C14 *sisoures,* < OF *cisoires,* < Vulgar L *cīsōria* (unattested), ult. < L *caedere* to cut]

scissors kick *n.* a type of swimming kick in which one leg is moved forward and the other bent back and they are then brought together again in a scissor-like action.

sciurine (ˈsaɪjʊrɪn, -ˌraɪn) *adj.* of or belonging to a family of rodents inhabiting most parts of the world except Australia and southern South America: includes squirrels, marmots, and chipmunks. [C19: < L *sciūrus,* < Gk *skiouros* squirrel, < *skia* a shadow + *oura* a tail]

sclera (ˈsklɪərə) *n.* the firm white fibrous membrane that forms the outer covering of the eyeball. Also called: **sclerotic.** [C19: < NL, < Gk *sklēros* hard] —**scleˈritis** *n.*

sclerenchyma (sklɪəˈrɛŋkɪmə) *n.* a supporting tissue in plants consisting of dead cells with very thick lignified walls. [C19: < SCLERO- + PARENCHYMA]

sclero- *or before a vowel* **scler-** *combining form.* **1.** indicating hardness: *sclerosis.* **2.** of the sclera: *sclerotomy.* [< Gk *sklēros* hard]

scleroderma (ˌsklɪərəʊˈdɜːmə) *or* **sclerodermia** (ˌsklɪərəʊˈdɜːmɪə) *n.* a chronic disease common among women, characterized by thickening and hardening of the skin.

scleroma (sklɪəˈrəʊmə) *n., pl.* **-mata** (-mətə). *Pathol.* any small area of abnormally hard tissue, esp. in a mucous membrane. [C17: < NL, < Gk, < *sklēroun* to harden, < *sklēros* hard]

scleroprotein (ˌsklɪərəʊˈprəʊtiːn) *n.* any of a group of insoluble stable proteins such as keratin that occur in skeletal and connective tissues.

sclerosis (sklɪəˈrəʊsɪs) *n., pl.* **-ses** (-siːz). **1.** *Pathol.* a hardening or thickening of organs, tissues, or vessels from inflammation, degeneration, or (esp. on the inner walls of arteries) deposition of fatty plaques. **2.** the hardening of a plant cell wall or tissue. [C14: via Med. L < Gk *sklērōsis* a hardening]

sclerotic (sklɪəˈrɒtɪk) *adj.* **1.** of or relating to the sclera. **2.** of, relating to, or having sclerosis. ~*n.* **3.** another name for **sclera.** [C16: < Med. L *sclērōticus*, < Gk; see SCLEROMA]

sclerous (ˈsklɪərəs) *adj. Anat., pathol.* hard; bony; indurated. [C19: < Gk *sklēros* hard]

SCM (in Britain) *abbrev. for:* **1.** State Certified Midwife. **2.** Student Christian Movement.

scoff[1] (skɒf) *vb.* **1.** (*intr.;* often foll. by *at*) to speak contemptuously (about); mock. **2.** (*tr.*) *Obs.* to regard with derision. ~*n.* **3.** an expression of derision. **4.** an object of derision. [C14: prob. < ON] —ˈ**scoffer** *n.* —ˈ**scoffing** *adj., n.*

scoff[2] (skɒf) *Inf., chiefly Brit.* ~*vb.* **1.** to eat (food) fast and greedily. ~*n.* **2.** food or rations. [C19: var. of *scaff* food]

scold (skəʊld) *vb.* **1.** to find fault with or reprimand (a person) harshly. **2.** (*intr.*) to use harsh or abusive language. ~*n.* **3.** a person, esp. a woman, who constantly finds fault. [C13: < ON SKALD] —ˈ**scolder** *n.* —ˈ**scolding** *n.*

scoliosis (ˌskɒlɪˈəʊsɪs) *n. Pathol.* an abnormal lateral curvature of the spine. [C18: < NL, < Gk: a curving, < *skolios* bent] —**scoliotic** (ˌskɒlɪˈɒtɪk) *adj.*

scollop (ˈskɒləp) *n., vb.* a variant spelling of **scallop.**

scombroid (ˈskɒmbrɔɪd) *adj.* **1.** of, relating to, or belonging to the *Scombroidea*, a suborder of marine spiny-finned fishes having a forked powerful tail: includes the mackerels, tunnies, and sailfish. ~*n.* **2.** any fish belonging to the suborder *Scombroidea*. [C19: < Gk *skombros* a mackerel; see -OID]

sconce[1] (skɒns) *n.* **1.** a bracket fixed to a wall for holding candles or lights. **2.** a flat candlestick with a handle. [C14: < OF *esconse* hiding place, lantern, or < LL *sconsa*, < *absconsa* dark lantern]

sconce[2] (skɒns) *n.* a small protective fortification, such as an earthwork. [C16: < Du. *schans*, < MHG *schanze* bundle of brushwood]

scone (skəʊn, skɒn) *n.* a light plain doughy cake made from flour with very little fat, cooked in an oven or (esp. originally) on a griddle. [C16: Scot., ? < MDu. *schoonbrot* fine bread]

scoop (skuːp) *n.* **1.** a utensil used as a shovel or ladle, esp. a small shovel with deep sides and a short handle, used for taking up flour, etc. **2.** a utensil with a long handle and round bowl used for dispensing liquids, etc. **3.** anything that resembles a scoop in action, such as the bucket on a dredge. **4.** a utensil used for serving mashed potatoes, ice cream, etc. **5.** a spoonlike surgical instrument for extracting foreign matter, etc., from the body. **6.** the quantity taken up by a scoop. **7.** the act of scooping, dredging, etc. **8.** a hollow cavity. **9.** *Sl.* a large quick gain, as of money. **10.** a news story reported in one newspaper before all the others. ~*vb.* (*mainly tr.*) **11.** (often foll. by *up*) to take up and remove (an object or substance) with or as if with a scoop. **12.** (often foll. by *out*) to hollow out with or as if with a scoop. **13.** to make (a large sudden profit). **14.** to beat (rival newspapers) in uncovering a news item. [C14: via MDu. *schōpe* < Gmc] —ˈ**scooper** *n.* —ˈ**scoopˌful** *n.*

scoot (skuːt) *vb.* **1.** to go or cause to go quickly or hastily; dart or cause to dart off or away. ~*n.* **2.** the act of scooting. [C19 (U.S.): <?]

scooter (ˈskuːtə) *n.* **1.** a child's vehicle consisting of a low footboard mounted between two small wheels with a handlebar. **2.** See **motor scooter.**

scope (skəʊp) *n.* **1.** opportunity for exercising the faculties or abilities. **2.** range of view or grasp. **3.** the area covered by an activity, topic, etc.: *the scope of his thesis was vast.* **4.** *Naut.* slack left in an anchor cable. **5.** *Logic.* the part of a formula that follows a quantifier or an operator. **6.** *Inf.* short for **telescope, microscope, oscilloscope,** etc. **7.** *Arch.* purpose. [C16: < It. *scopo* goal, < L *scopus*, < Gk *skopos* target]

-scope *n. combining form.* indicating an instrument for observing or detecting: *microscope.* [< NL *-scopium*, < Gk *-skopion*, < *skopein* to look at] —**-scopic** *adj. combining form.*

scopolamine (skəˈpɒləˌmiːn) *n.* a colourless viscous liquid alkaloid extracted from certain plants, such as henbane: used in preventing travel sickness and as a sedative and truth serum. Also called: **hyoscine.** [C20: *scopol-* < NL *scopolia Japonica* Japanese belladonna (from which the alkaloid is extracted), after G. A. *Scopoli* (1723–88), It. naturalist, + AMINE]

-scopy *n. combining form.* indicating a viewing or observation: *microscopy.* [< Gk *-skopia*, < *skopein* to look at]

scorbutic (skɔːˈbjuːtɪk) *adj.* of or having scurvy. [C17: < NL *scorbūticus*, < Med. L *scorbūtus*, prob. of Gmc origin] —**scorˈbutically** *adv.*

scorch (skɔːtʃ) *vb.* **1.** to burn or become burnt, esp. so as to affect the colour, taste, etc. **2.** to wither or parch or cause to wither from exposure to heat. **3.** (*intr.*) *Inf.* to be very hot: *it is scorching outside.* **4.** (*tr.*) *Inf.* to criticize harshly. ~*n.* **5.** a slight burn. **6.** a mark caused by the application of too great heat. **7.** *Horticulture.* a mark on fruit, etc., caused by pests or insecticides. [C15: prob. < ON *skorpna* to shrivel up] —ˈ**scorching** *adj.*

scorched earth policy *n.* the policy in warfare of removing or destroying everything that might be useful to an invading enemy.

scorcher (ˈskɔːtʃə) *n.* **1.** a person or thing that scorches. **2.** something caustic. **3.** *Inf.* a very hot day. **4.** *Brit. inf.* something remarkable.

score (skɔː) *n.* **1.** a numerical record of a competitive game or match. **2.** the total number of points made by a side or individual in a game. **3.** the act of scoring, esp. a point or points. **4. the score.** *Inf.* the actual situation. **5.** a group or set of twenty: *three score years and ten.* **6.** (*usually pl.;* foll. by *of*) lots: *I have scores of things to do.* **7.** *Music.* **a.** the printed form of a composition in which the instrumental or vocal parts appear on separate staves vertically arranged on large pages (**full score**) or in a condensed version, usually for piano (**short score**) or voices and piano (**vocal score**). **b.** the incidental music for a film or play. **c.** the songs, music, etc., for a stage or film musical. **8.** a mark or notch, esp. one made in keeping a tally. **9.** an account of amounts due. **10.** an amount recorded as due. **11.** a reason: *the book was rejected on the score of length.* **12.** a grievance. **13. a.** a line marking a division or boundary. **b.** (*as modifier*): *score line.* **14. over the score.** *Inf.* excessive; unfair. **15. settle** *or* **pay off a score. a.** to avenge a wrong. **b.** to repay a debt. ~*vb.* **16.** to gain (a point or points) in a game or contest. **17.** (*tr.*) to make a total score of. **18.** to keep a record of the score (of). **19.** (*tr.*) to be worth (a certain amount) in a game. **20.** (*tr.*) to record by making notches in. **21.** to make (cuts, lines, etc.) in or on. **22.** (*intr.*) *Sl.* to obtain something desired, esp. to purchase an illegal drug. **23.** (*intr.*) *Sl.* (of men) to be successful in seducing a person. **24.** (*tr.*) **a.** to arrange (a piece of music) for specific instruments or voices. **b.** to write the music for (a film, play, etc.). **25.** to achieve (success or an advantage): *your idea scored with the boss.* [OE *scora*] —ˈ**scorer** *n.*

scoreboard (ˈskɔːˌbɔːd) *n. Sport, etc.* a board for displaying the score of a game or match.

scorecard (ˈskɔːˌkɑːd) *n.* **1.** a card on which scores are recorded, as in golf. **2.** a card identifying the players in a sports match, esp. cricket.

score off *vb.* (*intr., prep.*) to gain an advantage at someone else's expense.

scoria (ˈskɔːrɪə) *n., pl.* **-riae** (-rɪˌiː). **1.** a mass of solidified lava containing many cavities. **2.** refuse obtained from smelted ore. [C17: < L: dross, < Gk *skōria*, < *skōr* excrement]

scorify (ˈskɔːrɪˌfaɪ) *vb.* **-fying, -fied.** to remove (impurities) from metals by forming scoria. —ˌ**scorifiˈcation** *n.* —ˈ**scoriˌfier** *n.*

scoring (ˈskɔːrɪŋ) *n.* another name for **orchestration** (see **orchestrate**).

scorn (skɔːn) *n.* **1.** open contempt for a person or thing. **2.** an object of contempt or derision. ~*vb.* **3.** to treat with contempt or derision. **4.** (*tr.*) to reject with contempt. [C12 *schornen*, < OF *escharnir*, of Gmc origin] —ˈ**scorner** *n.* —ˈ**scornful** *adj.* —ˈ**scornfully** *adv.*

Scorpio (ˈskɔːpɪˌəʊ) *n.* **1.** Also called: **Scorpius.** *Astron.* a large S constellation. **2.** Also called: the **Scorpion.** *Astrol.* the eighth sign of the zodiac. The sun is in this sign between about Oct. 23 and Nov. 21. [L: SCORPION]

scorpion (ˈskɔːpɪən) *n.* **1.** an arachnid of warm dry regions, having a segmented body with a long tail terminating in a venomous sting. **2. false scorpion.** a small nonvenomous arachnid that superficially resembles the scorpion but lacks the long tail. **3.** *Bible.* a barbed scourge (I Kings 12:11). [C13: via OF < L *scorpiō*, < Gk *skorpios*, <?]

Scorpion (ˈskɔːpɪən) *n.* **the.** the constellation Scorpio, the eighth sign of the zodiac.

scorpion fish *n.* any of a genus of fish of temperate and tropical seas, having venomous spines on the dorsal and anal fins.

Scot (skɒt) *n.* **1.** a native or inhabitant of Scotland. **2.** a member of a tribe of Celtic raiders from northern Ireland who eventually settled in N Britain during the 5th and 6th centuries.

Scot. *abbrev. for:* **1.** Scotch (whisky). **2.** Scotland. **3.** Scottish.

scot and lot *n. Brit. history.* a municipal tax paid by burgesses that came to be regarded as a qualification for the borough franchise in parliamentary elections. [C13 *scot* tax, < Gmc]

scotch[1] (skɒtʃ) *vb.* (*tr.*) **1.** to put an end to; crush: *bad weather scotched our plans.* **2.** *Obs.* to cut or score. ~*n.* **3.** *Arch.* a gash. **4.** a line marked down, as for hopscotch. [C15: <?]

scotch[2] (skɒtʃ) *vb.* **1.** (*tr.*) to block, prop, or prevent from moving with or as if with a wedge. ~*n.* **2.** a block or wedge to prevent motion. [C17: <?]

Scotch[1] (skɒtʃ) *adj.* **1.** another word for **Scottish.** ~*n.* **2.** the Scots or their language.

▷ **Usage.** In the north of England and in Scotland, *Scotch* is not used outside fixed expressions such as *Scotch whisky.* The use of *Scotch* for *Scots* or *Scottish* is otherwise felt to be incorrect, esp. when applied to persons.

Scotch[2] (skɒtʃ) *n.* whisky distilled from fermented malted barley and made in Scotland. Also called: **Scotch whisky.**

Scotch broth *n. Brit.* a thick soup made from mutton or beef stock, vegetables, and pearl barley.

Scotch egg *n. Brit.* a hard-boiled egg enclosed in a layer of sausage meat, covered in egg and crumbs, and fried.

Scotchman (ˈskɒtʃmən) *or* (*fem.*) **Scotchwoman** *n., pl.* **-men** *or* **-women.** (*regarded as bad usage by the Scots*) another word for **Scotsman** or **Scotswoman.**

Scotch mist *n.* **1.** a heavy wet mist. **2.** drizzle.

Scotch snap *n. Music.* a rhythmical pattern consisting of a short note followed by a long one. Also called: **Scotch catch.**

Scotch terrier *n.* another name for **Scottish terrier.**

scoter (ˈskəʊtə) *n., pl.* **-ters** *or* **-ter.** a sea duck of northern regions. The male plumage is black with white patches around the head and eyes. [C17: <?]

scot-free *adv., adj.* (*predicative*) without harm, loss, or penalty. [C16: see SCOT AND LOT]

Scotland Yard (ˈskɒtlənd) *n.* the headquarters of the police force of metropolitan London. Official name: **New Scotland Yard.**

scotoma (skɒˈtəʊmə) *n., pl.* **-mas** *or* **-mata** (-mətə). **1.** *Pathol.* a blind spot. **2.** *Psychol.* a mental blind spot. [C16: via Med. L < Gk *skotōma* giddiness, < *skotoun* to make dark, < *skotos* darkness]

Scots (skɒts) *adj.* **1.** of or characteristic of Scotland, its people, their English dialects, or their Gaelic language. ~*n.* **2.** any of the English dialects spoken or written in Scotland.

Scotsman (ˈskɒtsmən) *or* (*fem.*) **Scotswoman** *n., pl.* **-men** *or* **-women.** a native or inhabitant of Scotland.

Scots pine *or* **Scotch pine** *n.* **1.** a coniferous tree of Europe and W and N Asia, having blue-green needle-like leaves and brown cones with a small prickle on each scale. **2.** the wood of this tree.

Scotticism (ˈskɒtɪˌsɪzəm) *n.* a Scottish idiom, word, etc.

Scottie *or* **Scotty** (ˈskɒtɪ) *n., pl.* **-ties.** **1.** See **Scottish terrier.** **2.** *Inf.* a Scotsman.

Scottish (ˈskɒtɪʃ) *adj.* of, relating to, or characteristic of Scotland, its people, their Gaelic language, or their English dialects.

Scottish Certificate of Education *n.* See **SCE.**

Scottish Gaelic *n.* the Goidelic language of the Celts of Scotland, used esp. in the Highlands and Western Isles.

Scottish National Party *n.* a political party advocating the independence of Scotland. Abbrev.: **SNP.**

Scottish terrier *n.* a small but sturdy long-haired breed of terrier, usually with a black coat.

scoundrel (ˈskaʊndrəl) *n.* a worthless or villainous person. [C16: <?]

scour[1] (ˈskaʊə) *vb.* **1.** to clean or polish (a surface) by washing and rubbing. **2.** to remove dirt from or have the dirt removed from. **3.** (*tr.*) to clear (a channel) by the force of water. **4.** (*tr.*) to remove by or as if by rubbing. **5.** (*tr.*) to cause (livestock) to purge their bowels. ~*n.* **6.** the act of scouring. **7.** the place scoured, esp. by running water. **8.** something that scours, such as a cleansing agent. **9.** (*often pl.*) prolonged diarrhoea in livestock, esp. cattle. [C13: via MLow G *schūren*, < OF *escurer*, < LL *excūrāre* to cleanse, < *cūrāre*; see CURE] —ˈ**scourer** *n.*

scour[2] (ˈskaʊə) *vb.* **1.** to range over (territory), as in making a search. **2.** to move swiftly or energetically over (territory). [C14: < ON *skūr*]

scourge (skɜːdʒ) *n.* **1.** a person who harasses or causes destruction. **2.** a means of inflicting punishment or suffering. **3.** a whip used for inflicting punishment or torture. ~*vb.* (*tr.*) **4.** to whip. **5.** to punish severely. [C13: < Anglo-F, < OF *escorgier* (unattested) to lash, < *es-* EX-[1] + L *corrigia* whip] —ˈ**scourger** *n.*

scourings (ˈskaʊərɪŋz) *pl. n.* **1.** the residue left after cleaning grain. **2.** residue that remains after scouring.

scouse (skaʊs) *n. Liverpool dialect.* a stew made from left-over meat. [C19: shortened < LOBSCOUSE]

Scouse (skaʊs) *Brit. inf.* ~*n.* **1.** a person who comes from Liverpool. **2.** the dialect spoken by such a person. ~*adj.* **3.** of or from Liverpool. [C20: < SCOUSE]

scout[1] (skaʊt) *n.* **1.** a person, ship, or aircraft sent out to gain information. **2.** *Mil.* a person or unit despatched to reconnoitre the position of the enemy, etc. **3.** the act or an instance of scouting. **4.** (esp. at Oxford University) a college servant. **5.** *Inf.* a fellow. ~*vb.* **6.** to examine or observe (anything) in order to obtain information. **7.** (*tr.;* sometimes foll. by *out* or *up*) to seek. **8.** (*intr.;* foll. by *about* or *around*) to go in search (for).

[C14: < OF *ascouter* to listen to, < L *auscultāre* to AUSCULTATE] —ˈ**scouter** *n.*

scout[2] (skaʊt) *vb.* to reject (a person, etc.) with contempt. [C17: < ON *skūta* derision]

Scout (skaʊt) *n.* (*sometimes not cap.*) a boy or (in the U.S.) a girl who is a member of a worldwide movement (the **Scout Association**) founded as the Boy Scouts in England in 1908 by Lord Baden-Powell. British female counterpart: **Guide.** —ˈ**Scouting** *n.*

Scouter (ˈskaʊtə) *n.* the leader of a troop of Scouts. Also called (esp. formerly): **Scoutmaster.**

scow (skaʊ) *n.* an unpowered barge used for freight, etc.; lighter. [C18: via Du. *schouw* < Low G *schalde*]

scowl (skaʊl) *vb.* **1.** (*intr.*) to contract the brows in a threatening or angry manner. ~*n.* **2.** a gloomy or threatening expression. [C14: prob. < ON] —ˈ**scowler** *n.*

SCPS (in Britain) *abbrev. for* Society of Civil and Public Servants.

scrabble (ˈskræbᵊl) *vb.* **1.** (*intr.; often* foll. by *about* or *at*) to scrape (at) or grope (for), as with hands or claws. **2.** to struggle (with). **3.** (*intr.;* often foll. by *for*) to struggle to gain possession. **4.** to scribble. ~*n.* **5.** the act or an instance of scrabbling. **6.** a scribble. **7.** a disorderly struggle. [C16: < MDu. *shrabbelen,* frequentative of *shrabben* to scrape] —ˈ**scrabbler** *n.*

Scrabble (ˈskræbᵊl) *n. Trademark.* a game in which words are formed by placing lettered tiles in a pattern similar to a crossword puzzle.

scrag (skræg) *n.* **1.** a thin or scrawny person or animal. **2.** the lean end of a neck of veal or mutton. **3.** *Inf.* the neck of a human being. ~*vb.* **scragging, scragged. 4.** (*tr.*) *Inf.* to wring the neck of. [C16: ? var. of CRAG]

scraggly (ˈskræglɪ) *adj.* **-glier, -gliest.** *Chiefly U.S.* untidy or irregular.

scraggy (ˈskrægɪ) *adj.* **-gier, -giest. 1.** lean or scrawny. **2.** rough; unkempt. —ˈ**scraggily** *adv.* —ˈ**scragginess** *n.*

scram[1] (skræm) *vb.* **scramming, scrammed.** (*intr.; often imperative*) *Inf.* to go away hastily. [C20: < SCRAMBLE]

scram[2] (skræm) *n.* **1.** an emergency shutdown of a nuclear reactor. ~*vb.* **2.** (of a nuclear reactor) to shut down or be shut down in an emergency. [C20: ? < SCRAM[1]]

scramble (ˈskræmbᵊl) *vb.* **1.** (*intr.*) to climb or crawl, esp. by using the hands to aid movement. **2.** to proceed hurriedly or in a disorderly fashion. **3.** (*intr.;* often foll. by *for*) to compete with others, esp. in a disordered manner. **4.** (*intr.;* foll. by *through*) to deal with hurriedly. **5.** (*tr.*) to throw together in a haphazard manner. **6.** (*tr.*) to collect in a hurried or disorganized manner. **7.** (*tr.*) to cook (eggs that have been whisked up with milk) in a pan containing a little melted butter. **8.** *Mil.* to order (a crew or aircraft) to take off immediately or (of a crew or aircraft) to take off immediately. **9.** (*tr.*) to render (speech) unintelligible during transmission by means of an electronic scrambler. ~*n.* **10.** the act of scrambling. **11.** a climb or trek over difficult ground. **12.** a disorderly struggle, esp. to gain possession. **13.** *Mil.* an immediate preparation for action, as of crew, aircraft, etc. **14.** *Brit.* a motorcycle rally in which competitors race across rough open ground. [C16: blend of SCRABBLE & RAMP]

scrambler (ˈskræmblə) *n.* an electronic device that renders speech unintelligible during transmission, by altering frequencies.

scrap[1] (skræp) *n.* **1.** a small piece of something larger; fragment. **2.** an extract from something written. **3. a.** waste material or used articles, esp. metal, often collected and reprocessed. **b.** (*as modifier*): *scrap iron.* **4.** (*pl.*) pieces of discarded food. ~*vb.* **scrapping, scrapped.** (*tr.*) **5.** to discard as useless. [C14: < ON *skrap*]

scrap[2] (skræp) *Inf.* ~*n.* **1.** a fight or argument. ~*vb.* **scrapping, scrapped. 2.** (*intr.*) to quarrel or fight. [C17: ? < SCRAPE]

scrapbook (ˈskræpˌbʊk) *n.* a book or album of blank pages in which to mount newspaper cuttings, pictures, etc.

scrape (skreɪp) *vb.* **1.** to move (a rough or sharp object) across (a surface), esp. to smooth or clean. **2.** (*tr.;* often foll. by *away* or *off*) to remove (a layer) by rubbing. **3.** to produce a harsh or grating sound by rubbing against (a surface, etc.). **4.** (*tr.*) to injure or damage by rough contact: *to scrape one's knee.* **5.** (*intr.*) to be very economical (esp. in **scrimp and scrape**). **6.** (*intr.*) to draw the foot backwards in making a bow. **7. scrape acquaintance with.** to contrive an acquaintance with. ~*n.* **8.** the act of scraping. **9.** a scraped place. **10.** a harsh or grating sound. **11.** *Inf.* an awkward or embarrassing predicament. **12.** *Inf.* a conflict or struggle. [OE *scrapian*] —ˈ**scraper** *n.*

scraperboard (ˈskreɪpəˌbɔːd) *n.* thin card covered with a layer of china clay and a top layer of Indian ink, which can be scraped away with a special tool to leave a white line.

scrape through *vb.* (*adv.*) **1.** (*intr.*) to manage or survive with difficulty. **2.** to succeed in with difficulty or by a narrow margin.

scrape together *or* **up** *vb.* (*tr., adv.*) to collect with difficulty: *to scrape together money for a new car.*

scrappy (ˈskræpɪ) *adj.* **-pier, -piest.** fragmentary; disjointed. —ˈ**scrappily** *adv.*

scratch (skrætʃ) *vb.* **1.** to mark or cut (the surface of something) with a rough or sharp instrument. **2.** (often foll. by *at, out, off,* etc.) to scrape (the surface of something), as with claws, nails, etc. **3.** to scrape (the surface of the skin) with the nails, as to relieve itching. **4.** to chafe or irritate (a surface, esp. the skin). **5.** to make or cause to make a grating sound. **6.** (*tr.;* sometimes foll. by *out*) to erase by or as if by scraping. **7.** (*tr.*) to write or draw awkwardly. **8.** (*intr.;* sometimes foll. by *along*) to earn a living, manage, etc., with difficulty. **9.** to withdraw (an entry) from a race, (U.S.) election, etc. ~*n.* **10.** the act of scratching. **11.** a slight injury. **12.** a mark made by scratching. **13.** a slight grating sound. **14.** (in a handicap sport) a competitor or the status of a competitor who has no allowance. **15. a.** the line from which competitors start in a race. **b.** (formerly) a line drawn on the floor of a prize ring at which the contestants stood to begin fighting. **16.** *Billiards, etc.* a lucky shot. **17. from scratch.** *Inf.* from the very beginning. **18. up to scratch.** (*usually used with a negative*) *Inf.* up to standard. ~*adj.* **19.** *Sport.* (of a team) assembled hastily. **20.** (in a handicap sport) with no allowance or penalty. **21.** *Inf.* rough or haphazard. [C15: via OF *escrater* < Gmc] —ˈ**scratcher** *n.* —ˈ**scratchy** *adj.*

scratching (ˈskrætʃɪŋ) *n.* a percussive effect obtained by rotating a gramophone record manually: a disc-jockey and dub technique.

scratch pad *n. Chiefly U.S.* a notebook, esp. one with detachable leaves.

scratch video *n.* the recycling of images from films or television to make collages.

scrawl (skrɔːl) *vb.* **1.** to write or draw (words, etc.) carelessly or hastily. ~*n.* **2.** careless or scribbled writing or drawing. [C17: ? a blend of SPRAWL & CRAWL[1]] —ˈ**scrawly** *adj.*

scrawny (ˈskrɔːnɪ) *adj.* **scrawnier, scrawniest. 1.** very thin and bony. **2.** meagre or stunted. [C19: var. of dialect *scranny*] —ˈ**scrawnily** *adv.* —ˈ**scrawniness** *n.*

scream (skriːm) *vb.* **1.** to utter or emit (a sharp piercing cry or similar sound), esp. as of fear, pain, etc. **2.** (*intr.*) to laugh wildly. **3.** (*intr.*) to speak, shout, or behave in a wild manner. **4.** (*tr.*) to bring (oneself) into a specified state by screaming: *she screamed herself hoarse.* **5.** (*intr.*) to be extremely conspicuous: *these orange curtains scream; you need something more restful.* ~*n.* **6.** a sharp piercing cry or sound, esp. one denoting fear or pain. **7.** *Inf.* a person or thing that causes great amusement. [C13: < Gmc]

screamer (ˈskriːmə) *n.* **1.** a person or thing that

screams. **2.** a goose-like aquatic bird, such as the **crested screamer** of tropical and subtropical South America. **3.** *Inf.* (in printing) an exclamation mark. **4.** someone or something that raises screams of laughter or astonishment. **5.** *U.S. & Canad. sl.* a sensational headline. **6.** *Austral. sl.* a person or thing that is excellent of its kind.

scree (skriː) *n.* an accumulation of rock fragments at the foot of a cliff or hillside, often forming a sloping heap. [OE *scrīthan* to slip; rel. to ON *skrītha* to slide]

screech[1] (skriːtʃ) *n.* **1.** a shrill or high-pitched sound or cry. ~*vb.* **2.** to utter with or produce a screech. [C16: var. of earlier *scritch*, imit.] —**'screecher** *n.* —**'screechy** *adj.*

screech[2] (skriːtʃ) *n. Canad. sl.* **1.** a dark rum. **2.** any strong cheap drink. [? < SCREECH[1]]

screech owl *n.* **1.** *Brit.* another name for **barn owl.** **2.** a small North American owl having a reddish-brown or grey plumage.

screed (skriːd) *n.* **1.** a long or prolonged speech or piece of writing. **2.** a strip of wood, plaster, or metal placed on a surface to act as a guide to the thickness of the cement or plaster coat to be applied. **3.** a mixture of cement, sand, and water applied to a concrete slab, etc., to give a smooth surface finish. [C14: prob. var. of OE *scrēade* shred]

screen (skriːn) *n.* **1.** a light movable frame, panel, or partition serving to shelter, divide, hide, etc. **2.** anything that serves to shelter, protect, or conceal. **3.** a frame containing a mesh that is placed over a window to keep out insects. **4.** a decorated partition, esp. in a church around the choir. **5.** a sieve. **6.** the wide end of a cathode-ray tube, esp. in a television set, on which a visible image is formed. **7.** a white or silvered surface, placed in front of a projector to receive the enlarged image of a film or of slides. **8. the screen.** the film industry or films collectively. **9.** *Photog.* a plate of ground glass in some types of camera on which the image of a subject is focused. **10.** men or ships deployed around and ahead of a larger military formation to warn of attack. **11.** *Electronics.* See **screen grid.** ~*vb.* (*tr.*) **12.** (sometimes foll. by *off*) to shelter, protect, or conceal. **13.** to sieve or sort. **14.** to test or check (an individual or group) so as to determine suitability for a task, etc. **15.** to examine for the presence of a disease, weapons, etc. **16.** to provide with a screen or screens. **17.** to project (a film) onto a screen, esp. for public viewing. [C15: < OF *escren* (F *écran*)] —**'screenable** *adj.* —**'screener** *n.*

screen grid *n. Electronics.* an electrode placed between the control grid and anode of a valve which acts as an electrostatic shield, thus increasing the stability of the device. Sometimes shortened to **screen.**

screenings ('skriːnɪŋz) *pl. n.* refuse separated by sifting.

screenplay ('skriːnˌpleɪ) *n.* the script for a film, including instructions for sets and camera work.

screen process *n.* a method of printing using a fine mesh of silk, nylon, etc., treated with an impermeable coating except in the areas through which ink is subsequently forced onto the paper behind. Also called: **silk-screen printing.**

screenwriter ('skriːnˌraɪtə) *n.* a person who writes screenplays.

screw (skruː) *n.* **1.** a device used for fastening materials together, consisting of a threaded shank that has a slotted head by which it may be rotated so as to cut its own thread. **2.** Also called: **screw-bolt.** a threaded cylindrical rod that engages with a similarly threaded cylindrical hole. **3.** a thread in a cylindrical hole corresponding with that on the screw with which it is designed to engage. **4.** anything resembling a screw in shape or spiral form. **5.** a twisting movement of or resembling that of a screw. **6.** Also called: **screw-back.** *Billiards, etc.* a stroke in which the cue ball moves backward after striking the object ball. **7.** another name for **propeller** (sense 1). **8.** *Sl.* a prison guard. **9.** *Brit. sl.* salary, wages, or earnings. **10.** *Brit.* a small amount of salt, tobacco, etc., in a twist of paper. **11.** *Sl.* a person who is mean with money. **12.** *Sl.* an old or worthless horse. **13.** (*often pl.*) *Sl.* force or compulsion (esp. in **put the screws on**). **14.** *Taboo sl.* sexual intercourse. **15. have a screw loose.** *Inf.* to be insane. ~*vb.* **16.** (*tr.*) to rotate (a screw or bolt) so as to drive it into or draw it out of a material. **17.** (*tr.*) to cut a screw thread in (a rod or hole) with a tap or die or on a lathe. **18.** to turn or cause to turn in the manner of a screw. **19.** (*tr.*) to attach or fasten with a screw or screws. **20.** (*tr.*) *Inf.* to take advantage of; cheat. **21.** (*tr.*; often foll. by *up*) *Inf.* to distort or contort: *he screwed his face into a scowl.* **22.** (*tr.*; often foll. by *from* or *out of*) *Inf.* to coerce or force out of; extort. **23.** *Taboo sl.* to have sexual intercourse (with). **24.** (*tr.*) *Sl.* to burgle. **25. have one's head screwed on the right way.** *Inf.* to be sensible. ~See also **screw up.** [C15: < F *escroe*, < Med. L *scrōfa* screw, < L: sow, presumably because the thread of the screw is like the spiral of the sow's tail] —**'screwer** *n.*

screwball ('skruːˌbɔːl) *Sl., chiefly U.S. & Canad.* ~*n.* **1.** an odd or eccentric person. ~*adj.* **2.** odd; eccentric.

screwdriver ('skruːˌdraɪvə) *n.* **1.** a tool used for turning screws, usually having a steel shank with a flattened square-cut tip that fits into a slot in the head of the screw. **2.** an alcoholic beverage consisting of orange juice and vodka.

screwed (skruːd) *adj.* **1.** fastened by a screw or screws. **2.** having spiral grooves like a screw. **3.** twisted or distorted. **4.** *Brit. sl.* drunk.

screw eye *n.* a wood screw with its shank bent into a ring.

screw pine *n.* any of various tropical Old World plants having a spiral mass of pineapple-like leaves and conelike fruits.

screw propeller *n.* an early form of ship's propeller in which an Archimedes' screw is used to produce thrust by accelerating a flow of water.

screw top *n.* **1.** a bottle top that screws onto the bottle, allowing the bottle to be resealed after use. **2.** a bottle with such a top. —**'screw-ˌtop** *adj.*

screw up *vb.* (*tr., adv.*) **1.** to twist out of shape or distort. **2.** to summon up: *to screw up one's courage.* **3.** *Inf.* to mishandle or bungle.

screwy ('skruːɪ) *adj.* **screwier, screwiest.** *Inf.* odd, crazy, or eccentric.

scribble ('skrɪbᵊl) *vb.* **1.** to write or draw in a hasty or illegible manner. **2.** to make meaningless or illegible marks (on). **3.** *Derog. or facetious.* to write poetry, novels, etc. ~*n.* **4.** hasty careless writing or drawing. **5.** meaningless or illegible marks. [C15: < Med. L *scrībillāre* to write hastily, < L *scrībere* to write] —**'scribbler** *n.* —**'scribbly** *adj.*

scribbly gum *n. Austral.* a eucalypt with smooth white bark, marked with random patterns made by wood-boring insects.

scribe (skraɪb) *n.* **1.** a person who copies documents, esp. a person who made handwritten copies before the invention of printing. **2.** a clerk or public copyist. **3.** *Bible.* a recognized scholar and teacher of the Jewish Law. ~*vb.* **4.** to score a line on (a surface) with a pointed instrument, as in metalworking. [(in the senses: writer, etc.) C14: < L *scrība* clerk, < *scrībere* to write; C17 (vb.): ? < INSCRIBE] —**'scribal** *adj.*

scriber ('skraɪbə) *n.* a pointed steel tool used to score materials as a guide to cutting, etc. Also called: **scribe.**

scrim (skrɪm) *n.* a fine open-weave fabric, used in upholstery, lining, building, and in the theatre to create the illusion of a solid wall. [C18: <?]

scrimmage ('skrɪmɪdʒ) *n.* **1.** a rough or disorderly struggle. **2.** *American football.* the period of a game from the time the ball goes into play to the time it is declared dead. ~*vb.* **3.** (*intr.*) to engage in a scrimmage. **4.** (*tr.*) to put (the ball) into a scrimmage. [C15: < earlier *scrimish*, var. of SKIRMISH] —**'scrimmager** *n.*

scrimp (skrɪmp) *vb.* **1.** (when *intr.*, sometimes

foll. by *on*) to be very sparing in the use (of) (esp. in **scrimp and scrape**). **2.** (*tr.*) to treat meanly: *he is scrimping his children.* [C18: Scot., <?] —**ˈscrimpy** *adj.* —**ˈscrimpiness** *n.*

scrimshank (ˈskrɪmˌʃæŋk) *vb.* (*intr.*) *Brit. mil. sl.* to shirk work. [C19: <?]

scrimshaw (ˈskrɪmˌʃɔː) *n.* **1.** the art of decorating or carving shells, bone, ivory, etc., done by sailors as a leisure activity. **2.** an article or articles made in this manner. [C19: <?]

scrip (skrɪp) *n.* **1.** a written certificate, list, etc. **2.** a small scrap, esp. of paper with writing on it. **3.** *Finance.* **a.** a certificate representing a claim to part of a share of stock. **b.** the shares issued by a company (**scrip** or **bonus issue**) without charge and distributed among existing shareholders. [C18: in some senses, prob. < SCRIPT; otherwise, short for *subscription receipt*]

script (skrɪpt) *n.* **1.** handwriting as distinguished from print. **2.** the letters, characters, or figures used in writing by hand. **3.** any system or style of writing. **4.** written copy for the use of performers in films and plays. **5.** *Law.* an original or principal document. **6.** an answer paper in an examination. ~*vb.* **7.** (*tr.*) to write a script for. [C14: < L *scriptum* something written, < *scrībere* to write]

Script. *abbrev. for* Scripture(s).

scriptorium (skrɪpˈtɔːrɪəm) *n., pl.* **-riums** *or* **-ria** (-rɪə). a room, esp. in a monastery, set apart for the copying of manuscripts. [< Med. L]

scripture (ˈskrɪptʃə) *n.* a sacred, solemn, or authoritative book or piece of writing. [C13: < L *scriptūra* written material, < *scrībere* to write] —**ˈscriptural** *adj.*

Scripture (ˈskrɪptʃə) *n.* **1.** Also called: **Holy Scripture, Holy Writ, the Scriptures.** *Christianity.* the Old and New Testaments. **2.** any book or body of writings, esp. when regarded as sacred by a particular religious group.

scriptwriter (ˈskrɪptˌraɪtə) *n.* a person who prepares scripts, esp. for a film. —**ˈscriptˌwriting** *n.*

scrivener (ˈskrɪvnə) *n. Arch.* **1.** a person who writes out deeds, etc. **2.** a notary. [C14: < *scrivein* clerk, < OF *escrivain*, ult. < L *scrība* SCRIBE]

scrod (skrɒd) *n. U.S.* a young cod or haddock. [C19: ? < obs. Du. *schrood*, < MDu. *schrode* SHRED (n.); the name perhaps refers to the method of preparing the fish for cooking]

scrofula (ˈskrɒfjʊlə) *n. Pathol.* (*no longer in technical use*) tuberculosis of the lymphatic glands. Also called (formerly): (the) **king's evil.** [C14: < Med. L, < LL *scrōfulae* swollen glands in the neck, lit.: little sows (sows were thought to be particularly prone to the disease), < L *scrōfa* sow] —**ˈscrofulous** *adj.*

scroll (skrəʊl) *n.* **1.** a roll of parchment, etc., usually inscribed with writing. **2.** an ancient book in the form of a roll of parchment, papyrus, etc. **3.** a decorative carving or moulding resembling a scroll. ~*vb.* **4.** (*tr.*) to saw into scrolls. **5.** to roll up like a scroll. **6.** *Computers.* to move (text) on a screen in order to view a section that cannot be fitted into a single display. [C15 *scrowle*, < *scrowe*, < OF *escroe* scrap of parchment, but also infl. by ROLL]

scroll saw *n.* a saw with a narrow blade for cutting intricate ornamental curves in wood.

scrollwork (ˈskrəʊlˌwɜːk) *n.* ornamental work in scroll-like patterns.

Scrooge (skruːdʒ) *n.* a mean or miserly person. [C19: after a character in Dickens' story *A Christmas Carol* (1843)]

scrophulariaceous (ˌskrɒfjʊˌlɛərɪˈeɪʃəs) *adj.* of or belonging to the *Scrophulariaceae*, a family of plants including figwort, snapdragon, foxglove, and mullein. [C19: < NL (*herba*) *scrophularia* scrofula (plant), from the use of such plants in treating scrofula]

scrotum (ˈskrəʊtəm) *n., pl.* **-ta** (-tə) *or* **-tums.** the pouch of skin containing the testes in most mammals. [C16: < L] —**ˈscrotal** *adj.*

scrounge (skraʊndʒ) *vb. Inf.* **1.** (when *intr.*, sometimes foll. by *around*) to search in order to acquire (something) without cost. **2.** to obtain or seek to obtain (something) by begging. [C20: var. of dialect *scrunge* to steal, <?] —**ˈscrounger** *n.*

scrub[1] (skrʌb) *vb.* **scrubbing, scrubbed. 1.** to rub (a surface, etc.) hard, with or as if with a brush, soap, and water, in order to clean it. **2.** to remove (dirt) by rubbing, esp. with a brush and water. **3.** (*intr.*; foll. by *up*) (of a surgeon) to wash the hands and arms thoroughly before operating. **4.** (*tr.*) to purify (a gas) by removing impurities. **5.** (*tr.*) *Inf.* to delete or cancel. ~*n.* **6.** the act of or an instance of scrubbing. [C14: < MLow G *schrubben*, or MDu. *schrobben*]

scrub[2] (skrʌb) *n.* **1. a.** vegetation consisting of stunted trees, bushes, and other plants growing in an arid area. **b.** (*as modifier*): *scrub vegetation.* **2.** an area of arid land covered with such vegetation. **3. a.** an animal of inferior breeding or condition. **b.** (*as modifier*): *a scrub bull.* **4.** a small person. **5.** anything stunted or inferior. **6.** *Sport, U.S.* **a.** a player not in the first team. **b.** a team composed of such players. **7. the scrub.** *Austral. inf.* a remote or uncivilized place. ~*adj.* (*prenominal*) **8.** small or inferior. **9.** *Sport, U.S.* **a.** (of a player) not in the first team. **b.** (of a team) composed of such players. [C16: var. of SHRUB[1]]

scrubber (ˈskrʌbə) *n.* **1.** a person or thing that scrubs. **2.** an apparatus for purifying a gas. **3.** *Derog. sl.* a promiscuous girl.

scrubby (ˈskrʌbɪ) *adj.* **-bier, -biest. 1.** covered with or consisting of scrub. **2.** (of trees, etc.) stunted in growth. **3.** *Brit. inf.* messy.

scrubland (ˈskrʌbˌlænd) *n.* an area of scrub vegetation.

scrub turkey *n.* another term for **megapode.**

scrub typhus *n.* a disease characterized by severe headache, skin rash, chills, and swelling of the lymph nodes, caused by the bite of mites infected with a microorganism: occurs mainly in Asia and Australia.

scruff[1] (skrʌf) *n.* the nape of the neck (esp. in **by the scruff of the neck**). [C18: var. of *scuft*, ? < ON *skoft* hair]

scruff[2] (skrʌf) *n. Inf.* **1.** an untidy scruffy person. **2.** a disreputable person; ruffian.

scruffy (ˈskrʌfɪ) *adj.* **scruffier, scruffiest.** unkempt or shabby.

scrum (skrʌm) *n.* **1.** *Rugby.* the act or method of restarting play when the two opposing packs of forwards group together with heads down and arms interlocked and push to gain ground while the scrum half throws the ball in and the hookers attempt to scoop it out to their own team. **2.** *Inf.* a disorderly struggle. ~*vb.* **scrumming, scrummed. 3.** (*intr.*; usually foll. by *down*) *Rugby.* to form a scrum. [C19: < SCRUMMAGE]

scrum half *n. Rugby.* **1.** a player who puts in the ball at scrums and tries to get it away to his three-quarter backs. **2.** this position in a team.

scrummage (ˈskrʌmɪdʒ) *n., vb.* **1.** *Rugby.* another word for **scrum. 2.** a variant of **scrimmage.** [C19: var. of SCRIMMAGE]

scrump (skrʌmp) *vb. Dialect.* to steal (apples) from an orchard or garden. [var. of SCRIMP]

scrumptious (ˈskrʌmpʃəs) *adj. Inf.* very pleasing; delicious. [C19: prob. changed < SUMPTUOUS] —**ˈscrumptiously** *adv.*

scrumpy (ˈskrʌmpɪ) *n.* a rough dry cider, brewed esp. in the West Country of England. [< *scrump*, var. of SCRIMP (in obs. sense: withered), referring to the apples used]

scrunch (skrʌntʃ) *vb.* **1.** to crumple or crunch or to be crumpled or crunched. ~*n.* **2.** the act or sound of scrunching. [C19: var. of CRUNCH]

scruple (ˈskruːpᵊl) *n.* **1.** (*often pl.*) a doubt or hesitation as to what is morally right in a certain situation. **2.** *Arch.* a very small amount. **3.** a unit of weight equal to 20 grains (1.296 grams). ~*vb.* **4.** (*obs. when tr.*) to have doubts (about), esp. from a moral compunction. [C16: < L *scrūpulus* a small weight, < *scrūpus* rough stone]

scrupulous (ˈskruːpjʊləs) *adj.* **1.** characterized by careful observation of what is morally right. **2.**

very careful or precise. [C15: < L *scrūpulōsus* punctilious] —ˈ**scrupulously** *adv.* —ˈ**scrupulousness** *n.*

scrutineer (ˌskruːtɪˈnɪə) *n.* a person who examines, esp. one who scrutinizes the conduct of an election poll.

scrutinize *or* **-nise** (ˈskruːtɪˌnaɪz) *vb.* (*tr.*) to examine carefully or in minute detail. —ˈ**scrutiˌnizer** *or* **-ˌniser** *n.*

scrutiny (ˈskruːtɪnɪ) *n., pl.* **-nies.** 1. close or minute examination. 2. a searching look. 3. (in the early Christian Church) a formal testing that catechumens had to undergo before being baptized. [C15: < LL *scrūtinium* an investigation, < *scrūtārī* to search (orig. referring to rag-and-bone men), < *scrūta* rubbish]

scry (skraɪ) *vb.* **scrying, scried.** (*intr.*) to divine, esp. by crystal gazing. [C16: < DESCRY]

scuba (ˈskjuːbə) *n.* an apparatus used in skin diving, consisting of a cylinder or cylinders containing compressed air attached to a breathing apparatus. [C20: < the initials of *self-contained underwater breathing apparatus*]

scud (skʌd) *vb.* **scudding, scudded.** (*intr.*) 1. (esp. of clouds) to move along swiftly and smoothly. 2. *Naut.* to run before a gale. ~*n.* 3. the act of scudding. 4. a. a formation of low ragged clouds driven by a strong wind beneath rain-bearing clouds. b. a sudden shower or gust of wind. [C16: prob. of Scand. origin]

scuff (skʌf) *vb.* 1. to drag (the feet) while walking. 2. to scratch (a surface) or (of a surface) to become scratched. 3. (*tr.*) *U.S.* to poke at (something) with the foot. ~*n.* 4. the act or sound of scuffing. 5. a rubbed place caused by scuffing. 6. a backless slipper. [C19: prob. imit.]

scuffle (ˈskʌfᵊl) *vb.* (*intr.*) 1. to fight in a disorderly manner. 2. to move by shuffling. ~*n.* 3. a disorderly struggle. 4. the sound made by scuffling. [C16: of Scand. origin; cf. Swedish *skuff, skuffa* to push]

scull (skʌl) *n.* 1. a single oar moved from side to side over the stern of a boat to propel it. 2. one of a pair of short-handled oars, both of which are pulled by one oarsman. 3. a racing shell propelled by a single oarsman pulling two oars. 4. an act, instance, period, or distance of sculling. ~*vb.* 5. to propel (a boat) with a scull. [C14: <?] —ˈ**sculler** *n.*

scullery (ˈskʌlərɪ) *n., pl.* **-leries.** *Chiefly Brit.* a small room or part of a kitchen where washing-up, vegetable preparation, etc., is done. [C15: < Anglo-Norman *squillerie,* < OF, < *escuele* a bowl, < L *scutella,* < *scutra* a flat tray]

scullion (ˈskʌljən) *n.* 1. a mean or despicable person. 2. *Arch.* a servant employed to work in a kitchen. [C15: < OF *escouillon* cleaning cloth, < *escouve* a broom, < L *scōpa* a broom, twig]

sculpt (skʌlpt) *vb.* 1. a variant of **sculpture.** 2. (*intr.*) to practise sculpture. ~Also: **sculp.** [C19: < F *sculpter,* < L *sculpere* to carve]

sculptor (ˈskʌlptə) *or* (*fem.*) **sculptress** *n.* a person who practises sculpture.

sculpture (ˈskʌlptʃə) *n.* 1. the art of making figures or designs in relief or the round by carving wood, moulding plaster, etc., or casting metals, etc. 2. works or a work made in this way. 3. ridges or indentations as on a shell, formed by natural processes. ~*vb.* (*mainly tr.*) 4. (*also intr.*) to carve, cast, or fashion (stone, bronze, etc.) three-dimensionally. 5. to portray (a person, etc.) by means of sculpture. 6. to form in the manner of sculpture. 7. to decorate with sculpture. [C14: < L *sculptūra* a carving] —ˈ**sculptural** *adj.*

sculpturesque (ˌskʌlptʃəˈrɛsk) *adj.* resembling sculpture. —ˌ**sculpturˈesquely** *adv.*

scum (skʌm) *n.* 1. a layer of impure matter that forms on the surface of a liquid, often as the result of boiling or fermentation. 2. the greenish film of algae and similar vegetation surface of a stagnant pond. 3. the skin of oxides or impurities on the surface of a molten metal. 4. waste matter. 5. a worthless person or group of people. ~*vb.* **scumming, scummed.** 6. (*tr.*) to remove scum from. 7. (*intr.*) *Rare.* to form a layer of or become covered with scum. [C13: of Gmc origin] —ˈ**scummy** *adj.*

scumble (ˈskʌmbᵊl) *vb.* 1. (in painting and drawing) to soften or blend (an outline or colour) with an upper coat of opaque colour, applied very thinly. 2. to produce an effect of broken colour on doors, panelling, etc., by exposing coats of paint below the top coat. ~*n.* 3. the upper layer of colour applied in this way. [C18: prob. < SCUM]

scuncheon (ˈskʌntʃən) *n.* the inner part of a door jamb or window frame. [C15: < OF *escoinson,* < *coin* angle]

scungy (ˈskʌndʒɪ) *adj.* **scungier, scungiest.** *Austral.* & *N.Z. sl.* miserable; sordid. [C20: <?]

scunner (ˈskʌnə) *Dialect, chiefly Scot.* ~*vb.* 1. (*intr.*) to feel aversion. 2. (*tr.*) to produce a feeling of aversion in. ~*n.* 3. a strong aversion (often in **take a scunner**). 4. an object of dislike; nuisance. [C14: < Scot. *skunner,* <?]

scup (skʌp) *n.* a common fish of American coastal regions of the Atlantic. [C19: < Amerind *mishcup,* < *mishe* big + *kuppe* close together; < the form of the scales]

scupper[1] (ˈskʌpə) *n. Naut.* a drain or spout allowing water on the deck of a vessel to flow overboard. [C15 *skopper,* <?]

scupper[2] (ˈskʌpə) *vb.* (*tr.*) *Brit. sl.* 1. to overwhelm, ruin, or disable. 2. to sink (one's ship) deliberately. [C19: <?]

scurf (skɜːf) *n.* 1. another name for **dandruff.** 2. flaky or scaly matter adhering to or peeling off a surface. [OE *scurf*] —ˈ**scurfy** *adj.*

scurrilous (ˈskʌrɪləs) *adj.* 1. grossly or obscenely abusive or defamatory. 2. characterized by gross or obscene humour. [C16: < L *scurrīlis* derisive, < *scurra* buffoon] —**scurrility** (skəˈrɪlɪtɪ) *n.* —ˈ**scurrilously** *adv.*

scurry (ˈskʌrɪ) *vb.* **-rying, -ried.** 1. to move about hurriedly. 2. (*intr.*) to whirl about. ~*n., pl.* **-ries.** 3. the act or sound of scurrying. 4. a brisk light whirling movement, as of snow. [C19: prob. < *hurry-scurry,* < HURRY]

scurvy (ˈskɜːvɪ) *n.* 1. a disease caused by a lack of vitamin C, characterized by anaemia, spongy gums, and bleeding beneath the skin. ~*adj.* **-vier, -viest.** 2. mean or despicable. [C16: see SCURF] —ˈ**scurvily** *adv.* —ˈ**scurviness** *n.*

scurvy grass *n.* any of various plants of Europe and North America, formerly used to treat scurvy.

scut (skʌt) *n.* the short tail of animals such as the deer and rabbit. [C15: prob. < ON]

scutage (ˈskjuːtɪdʒ) *n.* (in feudal society) a payment sometimes exacted by a lord from his vassal in lieu of military service. [C15: < Med. L *scūtāgium,* lit.: shield dues, < L *scūtum* a shield]

scutate (ˈskjuːteɪt) *adj.* 1. (of animals) covered with large bony or horny plates. 2. *Bot.* shaped like a round shield. [C19: < L *scūtātus* armed with a shield, < *scūtum* a shield]

scutcheon (ˈskʌtʃən) *n.* 1. a variant of **escutcheon.** 2. any rounded or shield-shaped structure.

scutch grass (skʌtʃ) *n.* another name for **couch grass.** [var. of COUCH GRASS]

scute (skjuːt) *n. Zool.* a horny plate that makes up part of the exoskeleton in armadillos, turtles, etc. [C14 (the name of a F coin; C19 in zoological sense): < L *scūtum* shield]

scutellum (skjuːˈtɛləm) *n., pl.* **-la** (-lə). *Biol.* 1. the last of three plates into which an insect's thorax is divided. 2. one of the scales on the tarsus of a bird's leg. 3. the cotyledon of a developing grass seed. [C18: < NL: a little shield, < L *scūtum* a shield] —**scutellate** (ˈskjuːtɪˌleɪt, -lɪt) *adj.*

scutter (ˈskʌtə) *vb., n. Brit. inf.* scurry. [C18: prob. < SCUTTLE[2], with -ER[1] as in SCATTER]

scuttle[1] (ˈskʌtᵊl) *n.* 1. See **coal scuttle.** 2. *Dialect, chiefly Brit.* a shallow basket, esp. for carrying vegetables. 3. the part of a motorcar body lying immediately behind the bonnet. [OE *scutel* trencher, < L *scutella* bowl, dim. of *scutra* platter]

scuttle[2] (ˈskʌtᵊl) *vb.* 1. (*intr.*) to run or move

about with short hasty steps. ~*n.* **2.** a hurried pace or run. [C15: ? < SCUD, infl. by SHUTTLE]

scuttle[3] ('skʌtᵊl) *vb.* (*tr.*) **1.** *Naut.* to cause (a vessel) to sink by opening the seacocks or making holes in the bottom. **2.** to give up (hopes, plans, etc.). ~*n.* **3.** *Naut.* a small hatch or its cover. [C15 (n.): via OF < Sp. *escotilla* a small opening, < *escote* opening in a piece of cloth, < *escotar* to cut out]

scuttlebutt ('skʌtᵊlˌbʌt) *n. Naut.* **1.** a drinking fountain. **2.** (formerly) a cask of drinking water aboard a ship. **3.** *Chiefly U.S. sl.* gossip.

scutum ('skjuːtəm) *n., pl.* **-ta** (-tə). **1.** the middle of three plates into which an insect's thorax is divided. **2.** another word for **scute.** [L: shield]

scuzzy ('skʌzɪ) *adj.* **-zier, -ziest.** *Sl., chiefly U.S.* unkempt, dirty, or squalid. [C20: ? < *disgusting* or ? < blend of *scum* & *fuzz*]

Scylla ('sɪlə) *n.* **1.** *Greek myth.* a sea nymph transformed into a sea monster believed to drown sailors navigating the Straits of Messina. Cf. **Charybdis.** **2. between Scylla and Charybdis.** in a predicament in which avoidance of either of two dangers means exposure to the other.

scythe (saɪð) *n.* **1.** a long-handled implement for cutting grass, etc., having a curved sharpened blade that moves in a plane parallel to the ground. ~*vb.* **2.** (*tr.*) to cut (grass, etc.) with a scythe. [OE *sigthe*]

Scythian ('sɪðɪən) *adj.* **1.** of or relating to ancient Scythia, in SE Europe, its inhabitants, or their language. ~*n.* **2.** a member of an ancient nomadic people of Scythia.

SDI *abbrev. for* Strategic Defense Initiative. See **Star Wars.**

SDLP *abbrev. for* Social and Democratic Labour Party (of Ulster).

SDP *abbrev. for* Social Democratic Party.

SDRs *Finance. abbrev. for* special drawing rights.

Se *the chemical symbol for* selenium.

SE *symbol for* southeast(ern).

sea (siː) *n.* **1. a.** (usually preceded by *the*) the mass of salt water on the earth's surface as differentiated from the land. Related adjs.: **marine, maritime. b.** (*as modifier*): *sea air.* **2.** (*cap. when part of place name*) **a.** one of the smaller areas of ocean: *the Irish Sea.* **b.** a large inland area of water: *the Caspian Sea.* **3.** turbulence or swell: *heavy seas.* **4.** (*cap. when part of a name*) *Astron.* any of many huge dry plains on the surface of the moon: *Sea of Serenity.* See also **mare**[2]. **5.** anything resembling the sea in size or apparent limitlessness. **6. at sea. a.** on the ocean. **b.** in a state of confusion. **7. go to sea.** to become a sailor. **8. put (out) to sea.** to embark on a sea voyage. [OE *sǣ*]

sea anchor *n. Naut.* any device, such as a bucket, dragged in the water to keep a vessel heading into the wind or reduce drifting.

sea anemone *n.* any of various coelenterates having a polypoid body with oral rings of tentacles.

sea bag *n.* a canvas bag used by a seaman for his belongings.

sea bass (bæs) *n.* any of various American coastal fishes having an elongated body with a long spiny dorsal fin almost divided into two.

sea bird *n.* a bird such as a gull, that lives on the sea.

seaboard ('siːˌbɔːd) *n.* land bordering on the sea.

seaborne ('siːˌbɔːn) *adj.* **1.** carried on or by the sea. **2.** transported by ship.

sea bream *n.* a fish of European seas, valued as a food fish.

sea breeze *n.* a wind blowing from the sea to the land, esp. during the day when the land surface is warmer.

sea change *n.* a seemingly magical change. [< Ariel's song "Full Fathom Five" in *The Tempest*]

seacoast ('siːˌkəʊst) *n.* land bordering on the sea; a coast.

seacock ('siːˌkɒk) *n. Naut.* a valve in the hull of a vessel below the water line for admitting sea water or for pumping out bilge water.

sea cow *n.* **1.** a dugong or manatee. **2.** an archaic name for the **walrus.**

sea cucumber *n.* an echinoderm having an elongated body covered with a leathery skin and a cluster of tentacles at the oral end.

sea dog *n.* an experienced or old sailor.

sea eagle *n.* any of various fish-eating eagles of coastal areas, esp. the **European sea eagle,** having a brown plumage and white tail.

seafarer ('siːˌfɛərə) *n.* **1.** a traveller who goes by sea. **2.** a sailor.

seafaring ('siːˌfɛərɪŋ) *adj.* (*prenominal*) **1.** travelling by sea. **2.** working as a sailor. ~*n.* **3.** the act of travelling by sea. **4.** the work of a sailor.

seafood ('siːˌfuːd) *n.* edible saltwater fish or shellfish.

seafront ('siːˌfrʌnt) *n.* a built-up area facing the sea.

sea-girt *adj. Literary.* surrounded by the sea.

seagoing ('siːˌgəʊɪŋ) *adj.* intended for or used at sea.

sea green *n.* **a.** a moderate green colour, sometimes with a bluish or yellowish tinge. **b.** (*as adj.*): *a sea-green carpet.*

sea gull *n.* **1.** a popular name for the **gull** (the bird). **2.** *Austral. & N.Z. inf.* a casual dock worker.

sea holly *n.* a European plant of sandy shores, having bluish-green stems and blue flowers.

sea horse *n.* **1.** a marine teleost fish of temperate and tropical waters, having a bony-plated body, a prehensile tail, and a horselike head and swimming in an upright position. **2.** an archaic name for the **walrus.** **3.** a fabled sea creature with the tail of a fish and the front parts of a horse.

sea-island cotton *n.* **1.** a cotton plant of the Sea Islands, off the Florida coast, widely cultivated for its fine long fibres. **2.** the fibre of this plant or the material woven from it.

sea kale *n.* a European coastal plant with broad fleshy leaves and white flowers: cultivated for its edible asparagus-like shoots. Cf. **kale.**

seal[1] (siːl) *n.* **1.** a device impressed on a piece of wax, etc., fixed to a letter, etc., as a mark of authentication. **2.** a stamp, ring, etc., engraved with a device to form such an impression. **3.** a substance, esp. wax, so placed over an envelope, etc., that it must be broken before the object can be opened or used. **4.** any substance or device used to close or fasten tightly. **5.** a small amount of water contained in the trap of a drain to prevent the passage of foul smells. **6.** anything that gives a pledge or confirmation. **7.** a token; sign: *seal of death.* **8.** a decorative stamp sold in aid of charity. **9.** *R.C. Church.* Also called: **seal of confession.** the obligation never to reveal anything said in confession. **10. set one's seal on** (*or* **to**). **a.** to mark with one's sign or seal. **b.** to endorse. ~*vb.* (*tr.*) **11.** to affix a seal to, as proof of authenticity, etc. **12.** to stamp with or as if with a seal. **13.** to approve or authorize. **14.** (sometimes foll. by *up*) to close or secure with or as if with a seal: *to seal one's lips.* **15.** (foll. by *off*) to enclose (a place) with a fence, etc. **16.** to decide irrevocably. **17.** to close tightly so as to render airtight or watertight. **18.** to subject (the outside of meat, etc.) to fierce heat so as to retain the juices during cooking. **19.** to paint (a porous material) with a nonporous coating. **20.** *Austral.* to cover (a road) with bitumen, asphalt, tarmac, etc. [C13 *seel,* < OF, < L *sigillum* little figure, < *signum* a sign] —**'sealable** *adj.*

seal[2] (siːl) *n.* **1.** a fish-eating mammal with four flippers which is aquatic but comes on shore to breed. **2.** sealskin. ~*vb.* **3.** (*intr.*) to hunt for seals. [OE *seolh*] —**'sealer** *n.* —**'seal-ˌlike** *adj.*

sea lane *n.* an established route for ships.

sealant ('siːlənt) *n.* **1.** any substance, such as wax, used for sealing documents, bottles, etc. **2.** any of a number of substances used for stopping leaks, waterproofing wood, etc.

sea lavender *n.* any of various plants found on temperate salt marshes, having spikes of white, pink, or mauve flowers.

sealed-beam *adj.* (esp. of a car headlight) having a lens and prefocused reflector sealed in the lamp vacuum.

sealed road *n. Austral. & N.Z.* a road surfaced with bitumen or some other hard material.

sea legs *pl. n. Inf.* **1.** the ability to maintain one's balance on board ship. **2.** the ability to resist seasickness.

sea level *n.* the level of the surface of the sea with respect to the land, taken to be the mean level between high and low tide.

sea lily *n.* any of various echinoderms in which the body consists of a long stalk bearing a central disc with delicate radiating arms.

sealing wax *n.* a hard material made of shellac, turpentine, and pigment that softens when heated.

sea lion *n.* any of various large eared seals, such as the **Californian sea lion,** of the N Pacific, often used as a performing animal.

Sea Lord *n.* (in Britain) either of the two serving naval officers (**First** and **Second Sea Lords**) who sit on the admiralty board of the Ministry of Defence.

seal ring *n.* another term for **signet ring.**

sealskin (ˈsiːlˌskɪn) *n.* **a.** the skin or pelt of a fur seal, esp. when dressed with the outer hair removed and the underfur dyed dark brown. **b.** (*as modifier*): *a sealskin coat.*

Sealyham terrier (ˈsiːlɪəm) *n.* a short-legged wire-haired breed of terrier with a medium-length white coat. [C19: after *Sealyham,* village in S Wales]

seam (siːm) *n.* **1.** the line along which pieces of fabric, etc., are joined, esp. by stitching. **2.** a ridge or line made by joining two edges. **3.** a stratum of coal, ore, etc. **4.** a linear indentation, such as a wrinkle or scar. **5.** (*modifier*) *Cricket.* of or relating to a style of bowling in which the bowler utilizes the stitched seam round the ball in order to make it swing in flight and after touching the ground: *a seam bowler.* **6. bursting at the seams.** full to overflowing. ~*vb.* **7.** (*tr.*) to join or sew together by or as if by a seam. **8.** to mark or become marked with or as if with a seam or wrinkle. [OE] —ˈ**seamer** *n.* —ˈ**seamless** *adj.*

seaman (ˈsiːmən) *n., pl.* **-men. 1.** a naval rating trained in seamanship. **2.** a man who serves as a sailor. **3.** a person skilled in seamanship. —ˈ**seamanly** *adj., adv.* —ˈ**seaman-**ˌ**like** *adj.*

seamanship (ˈsiːmənʃɪp) *n.* skill in and knowledge of the work of navigating, maintaining, and operating a vessel.

sea mile *n.* an Imperial unit of length, formerly used in navigation, equal to 6000 feet or 1000 fathoms. It is equivalent to 1828.8 metres.

sea mouse *n.* any of various large worms having a broad flattened body covered dorsally with a dense mat of iridescent hairlike setae.

seamstress (ˈsɛmstrɪs) *or* (*rarely*) **sempstress** (ˈsɛmpstrɪs) *n.* a woman who sews and makes clothes, esp. professionally.

seamy (ˈsiːmɪ) *adj.* **seamier, seamiest.** showing the least pleasant aspect; sordid. —ˈ**seaminess** *n.*

Seanad Eireann (ˈʃænəð ˈeːrən) *n.* (in the Republic of Ireland) the upper chamber of parliament. [< Irish, lit.: senate of Ireland]

seance *or* **séance** (ˈseɪɑ̃ns) *n.* a meeting at which spiritualists attempt to receive messages from the spirits of the dead. [C19: < F, lit.: a sitting, < OF *seoir* to sit, < L *sedēre*]

sea otter *n.* a large marine otter of N Pacific coasts, formerly hunted for its thick brown fur.

sea pink *n.* another name for **thrift** (the plant).

seaplane (ˈsiːˌpleɪn) *n.* any aircraft that lands on and takes off from water.

seaport (ˈsiːˌpɔːt) *n.* **1.** a port or harbour accessible to seagoing vessels. **2.** a town or city located at such a place.

SEAQ (ˈsiːˌæk) *n. acronym for* Stock Exchange Automated Quotations: an electronic system that collects and displays information needed to trade in equities.

sear (sɪə) *vb.* (*tr.*) **1.** to scorch or burn the surface of. **2.** to brand with a hot iron. **3.** to cause to wither. **4.** *Rare.* to make unfeeling. ~*adj.* **5.** *Poetic.* dried up. [OE *sēarian* to become withered, < *sēar* withered]

search (sɜːtʃ) *vb.* **1.** to look through (a place, etc.) thoroughly in order to find someone or something. **2.** (*tr.*) to examine (a person) for concealed objects. **3.** to look at or examine (something) closely: *to search one's conscience.* **4.** (*tr.;* foll. by *out*) to discover by investigation. **5.** *Surgery.* to probe (a wound, etc.). **6.** *Computers.* to review (a file) to locate specific information. **7.** *Arch.* to penetrate. **8. search me.** *Inf.* I don't know. ~*n.* **9.** the act or an instance of searching. **10.** the examination of a vessel by the right of search. **11. right of search.** *International law.* the right possessed by the warships of a belligerent state to search merchant vessels to ascertain whether ship or cargo is liable to seizure. [C14: < OF *cerchier,* < LL *circāre* to go around, < L *circus* circle] —ˈ**searchable** *adj.* —ˈ**searcher** *n.*

searching (ˈsɜːtʃɪŋ) *adj.* keenly penetrating: *a searching look.* —ˈ**searchingly** *adv.*

searchlight (ˈsɜːtʃˌlaɪt) *n.* **1.** a device that projects a powerful beam of light in a particular direction. **2.** the beam of light produced by such a device.

search party *n.* a group of people taking part in an organized search, as for a lost, missing, or wanted person.

search warrant *n.* a written order issued by a justice of the peace authorizing a constable to enter and search premises for stolen goods, etc.

seascape (ˈsiːˌskeɪp) *n.* a sketch, etc., of the sea.

sea scorpion *n.* any of various northern marine fishes having a tapering body and a large head covered with bony plates and spines.

Sea Scout *n.* a Scout belonging to any of a number of Scout troops whose main activities are canoeing, sailing, etc.

sea serpent *n.* a huge legendary creature of the sea resembling a snake or dragon.

seashell (ˈsiːˌʃɛl) *n.* the empty shell of a marine mollusc.

seashore (ˈsiːˌʃɔː) *n.* **1.** land bordering on the sea. **2.** *Law.* the land between the marks of high and low water.

seasick (ˈsiːˌsɪk) *adj.* suffering from nausea and dizziness caused by the motion of a ship at sea. —ˈ**sea**ˌ**sickness** *n.*

seaside (ˈsiːˌsaɪd) *n.* **a.** any area bordering on the sea, esp. one regarded as a resort. **b.** (*as modifier*): *a seaside hotel.*

sea snail *n.* a small spiny-finned fish of cold seas, having a soft scaleless tadpole-shaped body with the pelvic fins fused into a sucker.

sea snake *n.* a venomous snake of tropical seas that swims by means of a laterally compressed oarlike tail.

season (ˈsiːzᵊn) *n.* **1.** one of the four equal periods into which the year is divided by the equinoxes and solstices. These periods (spring, summer, autumn, and winter) have characteristic weather conditions, and occur at opposite times of the year in the N and S hemispheres. **2.** a period of the year characterized by particular conditions or activities: *the rainy season.* **3.** the period during which any particular species of animal, bird, or fish is legally permitted to be caught or killed: *open season on red deer.* **4.** a period during which a particular entertainment, sport, etc., takes place: *the football season.* **5.** any definite or indefinite period. **6.** any of the major periods into which the ecclesiastical calendar is divided, such as Lent or Easter. **7.** fitting or proper time. **8. in good season.** early enough. **9. in season. a.** (of game) permitted to be killed. **b.** (of fresh food) readily available. **c.** Also: **in** *or* **on heat.** (of some female mammals) sexually receptive. **d.** appropriate. ~*vb.* **10.** (*tr.*) to add herbs, salt, pepper, or spice to (food). **11.** (*tr.*) to add zest to. **12.** (in the preparation of timber) to undergo or cause to undergo drying. **13.** (*tr.; usually passive*) to make or become experienced: *seasoned troops.* **14.** (*tr.*) to mitigate or temper. [C13: < OF *seson,* < L *satiō* a sowing, < *serere* to sow] —ˈ**seasoned** *adj.* —ˈ**seasoner** *n.*

seasonable (ˈsiːzənəbᵊl) *adj.* **1.** suitable for the season: *a seasonable Christmas snow scene.* **2.** taking place at the appropriate time. —ˈ**seasonableness** *n.* —ˈ**seasonably** *adv.*

seasonal (ˈsiːzənᵊl) *adj.* of, relating to, or occurring at a certain season or certain seasons of the year: *seasonal labour.* —ˈ**seasonally** *adv.*

seasoning (ˈsiːzənɪŋ) *n.* **1.** something that enhances the flavour of food, such as salt or herbs. **2.** another term (not now in technical usage) for **drying.**

season ticket *n.* a ticket for a series of events, number of journeys, etc., within a limited time, usually obtained at a reduced rate.

sea squirt *n.* a minute primitive marine animal, most of which are sedentary, having a saclike body with openings through which water enters and leaves.

sea swallow *n.* a popular name for **tern.**

seat (siːt) *n.* **1.** a piece of furniture designed for sitting on, such as a chair or sofa. **2.** the part of a chair, bench, etc., on which one sits. **3.** a place to sit, esp. one that requires a ticket: *I have two seats for the film tonight.* **4.** the buttocks. **5.** the part of a garment covering the buttocks. **6.** the part or area serving as the base of an object. **7.** the part or surface on which the base of an object rests. **8.** the place or centre in which something is located: *a seat of government.* **9.** a place of abode, esp. a country mansion. **10.** a membership or the right to membership in a legislative or similar body. **11.** *Chiefly Brit.* a parliamentary constituency. **12.** the manner in which a rider sits on a horse. ~*vb.* **13.** (*tr.*) to bring to or place on a seat. **14.** (*tr.*) to provide with seats. **15.** (*tr.; often passive*) to place or centre: *the ministry is seated in the capital.* **16.** (*tr.*) to set firmly in place. **17.** (*tr.*) to fix or install in a position of power. **18.** (*intr.*) (of garments) to sag in the area covering the buttocks: *your skirt has seated badly.* [OE *gesete*]

seat belt *n.* **1.** Also called: **safety belt.** a belt or strap worn in a car to restrain forward motion in the event of a collision. **2.** a similar belt or strap worn in an aircraft at takeoff and landing.

seating (ˈsiːtɪŋ) *n.* **1.** the act of providing with a seat or seats. **2. a.** the provision of seats, as in a theatre, etc. **b.** (*as modifier*): *seating arrangements.* **3.** material used for covering seats. **4.** a surface on which a part, such as a valve, is supported.

SEATO (ˈsiːtəʊ) *n. acronym for* South East Asia Treaty Organization; a former anti-Communist defence association for the Far East and the W Pacific (1954–77).

sea trout *n.* a silvery marine variety of the brown trout that migrates to fresh water to spawn.

sea urchin *n.* any echinoderm such as the **edible sea urchin,** having a globular body enclosed in a rigid spiny test and occurring in shallow marine waters.

sea wall *n.* a wall or embankment built to prevent encroachment or erosion by the sea.

seaward (ˈsiːwəd) *adv.* **1.** Also called: **seawards.** towards the sea. ~*adj.* **2.** directed or moving towards the sea. **3.** (esp. of a wind) coming from the sea.

seaway (ˈsiːˌweɪ) *n.* **1.** a waterway giving access to an inland port. **2.** a vessel's progress. **3.** a route across the sea.

seaweed (ˈsiːˌwiːd) *n.* any of numerous multicellular marine algae that grow on the seashore, in salt marshes, in brackish water, or submerged in the ocean.

seaworthy (ˈsiːˌwɜːðɪ) *adj.* in a fit condition or ready for a sea voyage. —ˈ**seaˌworthiness** *n.*

sebaceous (sɪˈbeɪʃəs) *adj.* **1.** of or resembling sebum, fat, or tallow. **2.** secreting fat. [C18: < LL *sēbāceus,* < SEBUM]

sebaceous glands *pl. n.* the small glands in the skin that secrete sebum into hair follicles and onto most of the body surface except the soles of the feet and the palms of the hands.

seborrhoea *or esp. U.S.* **seborrhea** (ˌsɛbəˈrɪə) *n.* a disease of the sebaceous glands characterized by excessive secretion of sebum.

sebum (ˈsiːbəm) *n.* the oily secretion of the sebaceous glands that acts as a lubricant for the hair and skin and provides some protection against bacteria. [C19: < NL, < L: tallow]

sec[1] (sɛk) *adj.* **1.** (of wines) dry. **2.** (of champagne) of medium sweetness. [C19: < F, < L *siccus*]

sec[2] (sɛk) *n. Inf.* short for **second**[2]: *wait a sec.*

sec[3] (sɛk) *abbrev. for* secant.

sec. *abbrev. for:* **1.** second (of time). **2.** secondary. **3.** secretary. **4.** section. **5.** sector.

secant (ˈsiːkənt) *n.* **1.** (of an angle) a trigonometric function that in a right-angled triangle is the ratio of the length of the hypotenuse to that of the adjacent side; the reciprocal of cosine. Abbrev.: **sec.** **2.** a line that intersects a curve. [C16: < L *secāre* to cut]

secateurs (ˈsɛkətəz) *pl. n. Chiefly Brit.* a small pair of shears for pruning, having a pair of pivoted handles and usually a single cutting blade that closes against a flat surface. [C19: pl. of F *sécateur,* < L *secāre* to cut]

secede (sɪˈsiːd) *vb.* (*intr.;* often foll. by *from*) (of a person, section, etc.) to make a formal withdrawal of membership, as from a political alliance, etc. [C18: < L *sēcēdere* to withdraw, < *sē-* apart + *cēdere* to go] —**seˈceder** *n.*

secession (sɪˈsɛʃən) *n.* **1.** the act of seceding. **2.** (*often cap.*) *Chiefly U.S.* the withdrawal in 1860–61 of 11 Southern states from the Union to form the Confederacy, precipitating the American Civil War. [C17: < L *sēcessiō* a withdrawing, < *sēcēdere* to SECEDE] —**seˈcessionˌism** *n.* —**seˈcessionist** *n., adj.*

sech (ʃɛk, sɛtʃ, ˈsekˈeɪtʃ) *n.* hyperbolic secant.

seclude (sɪˈkluːd) *vb.* (*tr.*) **1.** to remove from contact with others. **2.** to shut off or screen from view. [C15: < L *sēclūdere* to shut off, < *sē-* + *claudere* to imprison]

secluded (sɪˈkluːdɪd) *adj.* **1.** kept apart from the company of others: *a secluded life.* **2.** private. —**seˈcludedly** *adv.* —**seˈcludedness** *n.*

seclusion (sɪˈkluːʒən) *n.* **1.** the act of secluding or the state of being secluded. **2.** a secluded place. [C17: < Med. L *sēclūsiō;* see SECLUDE]

second[1] (ˈsɛkənd) *adj.* (*usually prenominal*) **1. a.** coming directly after the first in numbering or counting order, position, time, etc.; being the ordinal number of *two:* often written 2nd. **b.** (*as n.*): *the second in line.* **2.** graded or ranked between the first and third levels. **3.** alternate: *every second Thursday.* **4.** extra: *a second opportunity.* **5.** resembling a person or event from an earlier period of history: *a second Wagner.* **6.** of lower quality; inferior. **7.** denoting the lowest but one forward ratio of a gearbox in a motor vehicle. **8.** *Music.* denoting a musical part, voice, or instrument subordinate to or lower in pitch than another (the first): *the second tenors.* **9. at second hand.** by hearsay. ~*n.* **10.** *Brit. education.* an honours degree of the second class, usually further divided into an upper and lower designation. Full term: **second-class honours degree.** **11.** the lowest but one forward ratio of a gearbox in a motor vehicle. **12.** (in boxing, duelling, etc.) an attendant who looks after a competitor. **13.** a speech seconding a motion or the person making it. **14.** *Music.* the interval between one note and another lying next above or below it in the diatonic scale. **15.** (*pl.*) goods of inferior quality. **16.** (*pl.*) *Inf.* a second helping of food. **17.** (*pl.*) the second course of a meal. ~*vb.* (*tr.*) **18.** to give aid or backing to. **19.** (in boxing, etc.) to act as second to (a competitor). **20.** to express formal support for (a motion already proposed). ~*adv.* **21.** Also: **secondly.** in the second place. ~*sentence connector.* **22.** Also: **secondly.** as the second point. [C13: via OF < L *secundus* coming next in order, < *sequī* to follow] —ˈ**seconder** *n.*

▷ **Usage.** See at **important.**

second[2] (ˈsɛkənd) *n.* **1. a.** 1/60 of a minute of

time. **b.** the basic SI unit of time: the duration of 9 192 631 770 periods of radiation corresponding to the transition between two hyperfine levels of the ground state of caesium-133. Symbol: s **2.** 1/60 of a minute of angle. Symbol: ″ **3.** a very short period of time. [C14: < OF, < Med. L *pars minūta secunda* the second small part (a minute being the first small part of an hour); see SECOND[1]]

second[2] (sɪˈkɒnd) *vb.* (*tr.*) *Brit.* **1.** to transfer (an employee) temporarily to another branch, etc. **2.** *Mil.* to transfer (an officer) to another post. [C19: < F *en second* in second rank (or position)] —**seˈcondment** *n.*

secondary (ˈsɛkəndərɪ) *adj.* **1.** one grade or step after the first. **2.** derived from or depending on what is primary or first: *a secondary source.* **3.** below the first in rank, importance, etc. **4.** (*prenominal*) of or relating to the education of young people between the ages of 11 and 18: *secondary education.* **5.** (of the flight feathers of a bird's wing) growing from the ulna. **6. a.** being the part of an electric circuit, such as a transformer or induction coil, in which a current is induced by a changing current in a neighbouring coil: *a secondary coil.* **b.** (of a current) flowing in such a circuit. **7.** *Chem.* **a.** (of an amine) containing the group NH. **b.** (of a salt) derived from a tribasic acid by replacement of two acidic hydrogen atoms with metal atoms. ~*n., pl.* **-aries. 8.** a person or thing that is secondary. **9.** a subordinate, deputy, or inferior. **10.** a secondary coil, winding, inductance, or current in an electric circuit. **11.** *Ornithol.* any of the flight feathers that grow from the ulna of a bird's wing. **12.** *Astron.* a celestial body that orbits around a specified primary body: *the moon is the secondary of the earth.* **13.** short for **secondary colour.** —**ˈsecondarily** *adv.* —**ˈsecondariness** *n.*

secondary cell *n.* an electric cell that can be recharged and can therefore be used to store electrical energy in the form of chemical energy.

secondary colour *n.* a colour formed by mixing two primary colours.

secondary emission *n. Physics.* the emission of electrons (**secondary electrons**) from a solid as a result of bombardment with a beam of electrons, ions, or metastable atoms.

secondary picketing *n.* the picketing by striking workers of a factory, distribution outlet, etc., that supplies goods to or distributes goods from their employer.

secondary sexual characteristic *n.* any of various features distinguishing individuals of different sex but not directly concerned in reproduction. Examples are the antlers of a stag and the beard of a man.

second ballot *n.* an electoral procedure in which, after a first ballot, candidates at the bottom of the poll are eliminated and another ballot is held among the remaining candidates.

second-best *adj.* **1.** next to the best. **2. come off second best.** *Inf.* to be worsted by someone. ~*n.* **3. second best.** an inferior alternative.

second chamber *n.* the upper house of a bicameral legislative assembly.

second childhood *n.* dotage; senility (esp. in **in his, her,** etc., **second childhood**).

second class *n.* **1.** the class or grade next in value, quality, etc., to the first. ~*adj.* (**second-class** *when prenominal*). **2.** of the class or grade next to the best in quality, etc. **3.** shoddy or inferior. **4.** of or denoting the class of accommodation in a hotel or on a train, etc., lower in quality and price than first class. **5.** (in Britain) of letters that are handled more slowly than first-class letters. **6.** *Education.* See **second**[1] (sense 10). ~*adv.* **7.** by second-class mail, transport, etc.

second-class citizen *n.* a person whose rights and opportunities are treated as less important than those of other people in the same society.

Second Coming *n.* the prophesied return of Christ to earth at the Last Judgment.

second cousin *n.* the child of a first cousin of either of one's parents.

second-degree burn *n. Pathol.* a burn in which blisters appear on the skin.

seconde (sɪˈkɒnd) *n.* the second of eight positions from which a parry or attack can be made in fencing. [C18: < F *seconde parade* the second parry]

Second Empire *n.* the style of furniture and decoration of the Second Empire in France (1852–70), reviving the Empire style, but with fussier ornamentation.

second fiddle *n. Inf.* **1. a.** the second violin in a string quartet or an orchestra. **b.** the musical part assigned to such an instrument. **2.** a person who has a secondary status.

second floor *n. Brit.* the storey of a building immediately above the first and two floors up from the ground. U.S. and Canad. term: **third floor.**

second generation *n.* **1.** offspring of parents born in a given country. **2.** (*modifier*) of a refined stage of development in manufacture: *a second-generation robot.*

second growth *n.* natural regrowth of a forest after fire, cutting, etc.

second hand *n.* a pointer on the face of a timepiece that indicates the seconds.

second-hand *adj.* **1.** previously owned or used. **2.** not from an original source or experience. **3.** dealing in or selling goods that are not new: *a second-hand car dealer.* ~*adv.* **4.** from a source of previously owned or used goods: *he prefers to buy second-hand.* **5.** not directly: *he got the news second-hand.*

Second International *n.* an international association of socialist parties and trade unions that began in Paris in 1889 and collapsed during World War I.

second language *n.* **1.** a language other than the mother tongue used for business transactions, teaching, debate, etc. **2.** a language that is officially recognized in a country, other than the main national language.

second lieutenant *n.* an officer holding the lowest commissioned rank in the armed forces of certain nations.

secondly (ˈsɛkəndlɪ) *adv.* another word for **second**[1], usually used to precede the second item in a list of topics.

second nature *n.* a habit, characteristic, etc., long practised or acquired so as to seem innate.

second person *n.* a grammatical category of pronouns and verbs used when referring to or describing the individual or individuals being addressed.

second-rate *adj.* **1.** not of the highest quality; mediocre. **2.** second in importance, etc.

second reading *n.* the second presentation of a bill in a legislative assembly, as to approve its general principles (in Britain), or to discuss a committee's report on it (in the U.S.).

second sight *n.* the alleged ability to foresee the future, see actions taking place elsewhere, etc. —**ˈsecond-ˈsighted** *adj.*

second string *n.* **1.** *Chiefly Brit.* an alternative course of action, etc., intended to come into use should the first fail (esp. in **a second string to one's bow**). **2.** *Chiefly U.S. & Canad.* a substitute or reserve player or team.

second thought *n.* (*usually pl.*) a revised opinion or idea on a matter already considered.

second wind (wɪnd) *n.* **1.** the return of the ability to breathe at a normal rate, esp. following a period of exertion. **2.** renewed ability to continue in an effort.

secrecy (ˈsiːkrɪsɪ) *n., pl.* **-cies. 1.** the state or quality of being secret. **2.** the state of keeping something secret. **3.** the ability or tendency to keep things secret.

secret (ˈsiːkrɪt) *adj.* **1.** kept hidden or separate from the knowledge of others. Related adj.: **cryptic. 2.** known only to initiates: *a secret password.* **3.** hidden from general view or use: *a secret garden.* **4.** able or tending to keep things private or to oneself. **5.** operating without the knowledge of outsiders: *a secret society.* ~*n.* **6.** something kept or to be kept hidden. **7.** something unrevealed; a mystery. **8.** an underlying explanation, reason, etc.: *the secret of success.* **9.** a method, plan, etc., known only to initiates. **10.** *Liturgy.* a prayer said by the celebrant of the Mass after the offertory and before the preface. [C14: via OF < L *sēcrētus* concealed, < *sēcernere* to sift] —**ˈsecretly** *adv.*

secret agent *n.* a person employed in espionage.

secretaire (ˌsɛkrɪˈtɛə) *n.* an enclosed writing desk, usually having an upper cabinet section. [C19: < F; see SECRETARY]

secretariat (ˌsɛkrɪˈtɛərɪət) *n.* **1. a.** an office responsible for the secretarial, clerical, and administrative affairs of a legislative body or international organization. **b.** the staff of such an office. **2.** a body of secretaries. **3.** a secretary's place of work; office. **4.** the position of a secretary. [C19: via F < Med. L *sēcrētāriātus*, < *sēcrētārius* SECRETARY]

secretary (ˈsɛkrətrɪ) *n., pl.* **-taries. 1.** a person who handles correspondence, keeps records, and does general clerical work for an individual, organization, etc. **2.** the official manager of the day-to-day business of a society or board. **3.** (in Britain) a senior civil servant who assists a government minister. **4.** (in the U.S.) the head of a government administrative department. **5.** (in Britain) See **secretary of state. 6.** another name for **secretaire.** [C14: < Med. L *sēcrētārius*, < L *sēcrētum* something hidden; see SECRET] —**secretarial** (ˌsɛkrɪˈtɛərɪəl) *adj.* —**ˈsecretaryship** *n.*

secretary bird *n.* a large African long-legged bird of prey having a crest and tail of long feathers and feeding chiefly on snakes.

secretary-general *n., pl.* **secretaries-general.** a chief administrative official, as of the United Nations.

secretary of state *n.* **1.** (in Britain) the head of any of several government departments. **2.** (in the U.S.) the head of the government department in charge of foreign affairs (**State Department**).

secrete[1] (sɪˈkriːt) *vb.* (of a cell, organ, etc.) to synthesize and release (a secretion). [C18: back formation < SECRETION] —**seˈcretor** *n.* —**seˈcretory** *adj.*

secrete[2] (sɪˈkriːt) *vb.* (*tr.*) to put in a hiding place. [C18: var. of obs. *secret* to hide away]

secretion (sɪˈkriːʃən) *n.* **1.** a substance that is released from a cell, esp. a glandular cell. **2.** the process involved in producing and releasing such a substance from the cell. [C17: < Med. L *sēcrētiō*, < L: a separation]

secretive (ˈsiːkrɪtɪv) *adj.* inclined to secrecy. —**ˈsecretively** *adv.* —**ˈsecretiveness** *n.*

secretory (sɪˈkriːtərɪ) *adj.* of, relating to, or producing a secretion: *secretory function.*

secret police *n.* a police force that operates relatively secretly to check subversion or political dissent.

secret service *n.* a government agency or department that conducts intelligence or counter-intelligence operations.

sect (sɛkt) *n.* **1.** a subdivision of a larger religious group (esp. the Christian Church as a whole) the members of which have to some extent diverged from the rest by developing deviating beliefs, practices, etc. **2.** *Often disparaging.* **a.** a schismatic religious body. **b.** a religious group regarded as extreme or heretical. **3.** a group of people with a common interest, doctrine, etc. [C14: < L *secta* faction, < *sequī* to follow]

-sect *vb. combining form.* to cut or divide, esp. into a specified number of parts: *trisect.* [< L *sectus* cut, < *secāre* to cut]

sectarian (sɛkˈtɛərɪən) *adj.* **1.** of, relating to, or characteristic of sects or sectaries. **2.** adhering to a particular sect, faction, or doctrine. **3.** narrow-minded, esp. as a result of adherence to a particular sect. ~*n.* **4.** a member of a sect or faction, esp. one who is intolerant towards other sects, etc. —**secˈtarianˌism** *n.*

sectary (ˈsɛktərɪ) *n., pl.* **-taries. 1.** a member of a sect, esp. a religous sect. **2.** a member of a Nonconformist denomination, esp. one that is small. [C16: < Med. L *sectārius*, < L *secta* SECT]

section (ˈsɛkʃən) *n.* **1.** a part cut off or separated from the main body of something. **2.** a part or subdivision of a piece of writing, book, etc.: *the sports section of the newspaper.* **3.** one of several component parts. **4.** a distinct part of a country, community, etc. **5.** *U.S. & Canad.* an area one mile square. **6.** *N.Z.* a plot of land for building, esp. in a suburban area. **7.** the section of a railway track that is controlled by a particular signal box. **8.** the act or process of cutting or separating by cutting. **9.** a representation of an object cut by an imaginary vertical plane so as to show its construction and interior. **10.** *Geom.* a plane surface formed by cutting through a solid. **11.** a thin slice of biological tissue, etc., prepared for examination by microscope. **12.** a segment of an orange or other citrus fruit. **13.** a small military formation. **14.** *Austral. & N.Z.* a fare stage on a bus, tram, etc. **15.** *Music.* **a.** an extended division of a composition or movement: *the development section.* **b.** a division in an orchestra, band, etc., containing instruments belonging to the same class: *the brass section.* **16.** Also called: **signature, gathering.** a folded printing sheet or sheets ready for gathering and binding. ~*vb.* (*tr.*) **17.** to cut or divide into sections. **18.** to cut through so as to reveal a section. **19.** (in drawing, esp. mechanical drawing) to shade so as to indicate sections. [C16: < L *sectiō*, < *secāre* to cut]

sectional (ˈsɛkʃənᵊl) *adj.* **1.** composed of several sections. **2.** of or relating to a section. —**ˈsectionaˌlize** *or* **-ise** *vb.* (*tr.*) —**ˈsectionally** *adv.*

sectionalism (ˈsɛkʃənəˌlɪzəm) *n.* excessive or narrow-minded concern for local or regional interests. —**ˈsectionalist** *n., adj.*

sector (ˈsɛktə) *n.* **1.** a part or subdivision, esp. of a society or an economy: *the private sector.* **2.** *Geom.* either portion of a circle included between two radii and an arc. **3.** a measuring instrument consisting of two graduated arms hinged at one end. **4.** a part or subdivision of an area of military operations. [C16: < LL: sector, < L: a cutter, < *secāre* to cut] —**ˈsectoral** *adj.*

sectorial (sɛkˈtɔːrɪəl) *adj.* **1.** of or relating to a sector. **2.** *Zool.* adapted for cutting: *the sectorial teeth of carnivores.*

secular (ˈsɛkjʊlə) *adj.* **1.** of or relating to worldly as opposed to sacred things. **2.** not concerned with or related to religion. **3.** not within the control of the Church. **4.** (of an education, etc.) having no particular religious affinities. **5.** (of clerics) not bound by religious vows to a monastic or other order. **6.** occurring or appearing once in an age or century. **7.** lasting for a long time. **8.** *Astron.* occurring slowly over a long period of time. ~*n.* **9.** a member of the secular clergy. [C13: < OF *seculer*, < LL *saeculāris* temporal, < L: concerning an age, < *saeculum* an age] —**secularity** (ˌsɛkjʊˈlærɪtɪ) *n.* —**ˈsecularly** *adv.*

secularism (ˈsɛkjʊləˌrɪzəm) *n.* **1.** *Philosophy.* a doctrine that rejects religion, esp. in ethics. **2.** the attitude that religion should have no place in civil affairs. —**ˈsecularist** *n., adj.*

secularize *or* **-rise** (ˈsɛkjʊləˌraɪz) *vb.* (*tr.*) **1.** to change from religious or sacred to secular functions, etc. **2.** to dispense from allegiance to a religious order. **3.** *Law.* to transfer (property) from ecclesiastical to civil possession or use. —ˌ**seculariˈzation** *or* **-riˈsation** *n.*

secund (sɪˈkʌnd) *adj. Bot.* having parts arranged on or turned to one side of the axis. [C18: < L *secundus* following, < *sequī* to follow]

secure (sɪˈkjʊə) *adj.* **1.** free from danger, damage, etc. **2.** free from fear, care, etc. **3.** in safe custody. **4.** not likely to fail, become loose, etc. **5.** able to be relied on: *a secure investment.* **6.** *Arch.* overconfident. ~*vb.* **7.** (*tr.*) to obtain: *I will secure some good seats.* **8.** (when *intr.*, often foll. by *against*) to make or become free from danger, fear, etc. **9.** (*tr.*) to make fast or firm. **10.** (when *intr.*, often foll. by *against*) to make or become certain: *this plan will secure your happiness.* **11.** (*tr.*) to assure (a creditor) of payment, as by giving security. **12.** (*tr.*) to make (a military position) safe from attack. **13.** *Naut.* to make (a vessel or its contents) safe or ready by battening down hatches, etc. [C16: < L *sēcūrus* free from care] **—se'curable** *adj.* **—se'curely** *adv.* **—se'curement** *n.* **—se'curer** *n.*

securitization *or* **-tisation** (sɪˌkjʊərɪtaɪˈzeɪʃən) *n. Stock Exchange.* the packaging of a number of instruments (stocks, bonds, debts, etc.) into one instrument that can be treated as a single security or bond.

security (sɪˈkjʊərɪtɪ) *n., pl.* **-ties. 1.** the state of being secure. **2.** assured freedom from poverty or want: *he needs the security of a permanent job.* **3.** a person or thing that secures, guarantees, etc. **4.** precautions taken to ensure against theft, espionage, etc. **5.** (*often pl.*) **a.** a certificate of creditorship or property carrying the right to receive interest or dividend, such as shares or bonds. **b.** the financial asset represented by such a certificate. **6.** the specific asset that a creditor can claim in the event of default on an obligation. **7.** something given or pledged to secure the fulfilment of a promise or obligation. **8.** the protection of data to ensure that only authorised personnel have access to computer files.

security blanket *n.* **1.** a policy of temporary secrecy by police or those in charge of security, in order to protect a person, place, etc., threatened with danger, from further risk. **2.** a baby's blanket, soft toy, etc., to which a baby or young child becomes very attached, using it as a comforter.

Security Council *n.* an organ of the United Nations established to maintain world peace.

security guard *n.* someone employed to protect buildings, people, etc., and to collect and deliver large sums of money.

security risk *n.* a person deemed to be a threat to state security in that he could be open to pressure, have subversive political beliefs, etc.

secy. *or* **sec'y.** *abbrev. for* secretary.

sedan (sɪˈdæn) *n.* **1.** *U.S., Canad., & N.Z.* a saloon car. **2.** short for **sedan chair.** [C17: <?]

sedan chair *n.* a closed chair for one passenger, carried on poles by two bearers, commonly used in the 17th and 18th centuries.

sedate[1] (sɪˈdeɪt) *adj.* **1.** habitually calm and composed in manner. **2.** sober or decorous. [C17: < L *sēdāre* to soothe] **—se'dately** *adv.* **—se'dateness** *n.*

sedate[2] (sɪˈdeɪt) *vb.* (*tr.*) to administer a sedative to. [C20: back formation < SEDATIVE]

sedation (sɪˈdeɪʃən) *n.* **1.** a state of calm or reduced nervous activity. **2.** the administration of a sedative.

sedative (ˈsɛdətɪv) *adj.* **1.** having a soothing or calming effect. **2.** of or relating to sedation. ~*n.* **3.** *Med.* a sedative drug or agent. [C15: < Med. L *sēdātīvus*, < L *sēdātus* assuaged; see SEDATE[1]]

sedentary (ˈsɛdəntərɪ) *adj.* **1.** characterized by or requiring a sitting position: *sedentary work.* **2.** tending to sit about without taking much exercise. **3.** (of animals) moving about very little. **4.** (of birds) not migratory. [C16: < L *sedentārius*, < *sedēre* to sit] **—'sedentarily** *adv.* **—'sedentariness** *n.*

Seder (ˈseɪdə) *n. Judaism.* a ceremonial meal on the first night or first two nights of Passover. [< Heb. *sēdher* order]

sedge (sɛdʒ) *n.* a grasslike plant growing on wet ground and having rhizomes, triangular stems, and minute flowers in spikelets. [OE *secg*] **—'sedgy** *adj.*

sedge warbler *n.* a European songbird of reed beds and swampy areas, having a streaked brownish plumage with white eye stripes.

sedilia (sɛˈdaɪlɪə) *n.* (*functioning as sing.*) the group of three seats, each called a **sedile** (sɛˈdaɪlɪ) on the south side of a sanctuary where the celebrant and ministers sit during High Mass. [C18: < L, < *sedīle* a chair, < *sedēre* to sit]

sediment (ˈsɛdɪmənt) *n.* **1.** matter that settles to the bottom of a liquid. **2.** material that has been deposited from water, ice, or wind. [C16: < L *sedimentum* a settling, < *sedēre* to sit] **—ˌsedimen'tation** *n.*

sedimentary (ˌsɛdɪˈmɛntərɪ) *adj.* **1.** characteristic of, resembling, or containing sediment. **2.** (of rocks) formed by the accumulation of mineral and organic fragments that have been deposited by water, ice, or wind. **—ˌsedi'mentarily** *adv.*

sedition (sɪˈdɪʃən) *n.* **1.** speech or behaviour directed against the peace of a state. **2.** an offence that tends to undermine the authority of a state. **3.** an incitement to public disorder. [C14: < L *sēditiō* discord, < *sēd-* apart + *itiō* a going, < *īre* to go] **—se'ditionary** *n., adj.*

seditious (sɪˈdɪʃəs) *adj.* **1.** of, like, or causing sedition. **2.** inclined to or taking part in sedition.

seduce (sɪˈdjuːs) *vb.* (*tr.*) **1.** to persuade to engage in sexual intercourse. **2.** to lead astray, as from the right action. **3.** to win over, attract, or lure. [C15: < L *sēdūcere* to lead apart] **—se'ducible** *adj.*

seducer (sɪˈdjuːsə) *or* (*fem.*) **seductress** (sɪˈdʌktrɪs) *n.* a person who entices, allures, or seduces, esp. one who entices another to engage in sexual intercourse.

seduction (sɪˈdʌkʃən) *n.* **1.** the act of seducing or the state of being seduced. **2.** a means of seduction.

seductive (sɪˈdʌktɪv) *adj.* tending to seduce or capable of seducing; enticing; alluring. **—se'ductively** *adv.* **—se'ductiveness** *n.*

sedulous (ˈsɛdjʊləs) *adj.* assiduous; diligent. [C16: < L *sēdulus*, <?] **—sedulity** (sɪˈdjuːlɪtɪ) *or* **'sedulousness** *n.* **—'sedulously** *adv.*

sedum (ˈsiːdəm) *n.* a rock plant having thick fleshy leaves and clusters of white, yellow, or pink flowers. [C15: < L: houseleek]

see[1] (siː) *vb.* **seeing, saw, seen. 1.** to perceive with the eyes. **2.** (when *tr., may take a clause as object*) to understand: *I explained the problem but he could not see it.* **3.** (*tr.*) to perceive with any or all of the senses: *I hate to see you so unhappy.* **4.** (*tr.; may take a clause as object*) to foresee: *I can see what will happen if you don't help.* **5.** (when *tr., may take a clause as object*) to ascertain or find out (a fact): *see who is at the door.* **6.** (when *tr., takes a clause as object;* when *intr.*, foll. by *to*) to make sure (of something) or take care (of something): *see that he gets to bed early.* **7.** (when *tr., may take a clause as object*) to consider, deliberate, or decide: *see if you can come next week.* **8.** (*tr.*) to have experience of: *he had seen much unhappiness in his life.* **9.** (*tr.*) to allow to be in a specified condition: *I cannot stand by and see a child in pain.* **10.** (*tr.*) to be characterized by: *this period of history has seen much unrest.* **11.** (*tr.*) to meet or pay a visit to: *to see one's solicitor.* **12.** (*tr.*) to receive: *the Prime Minister will see the deputation now.* **13.** (*tr.*) to frequent the company of: *she is seeing a married man.* **14.** (*tr.*) to accompany: *I saw her to the door.* **15.** (*tr.*) to refer to or look up: *for further information see the appendix.* **16.** (in gambling, esp. in poker) to match (another player's bet) or match the bet of (another player) by staking an equal sum. **17. as far as I can see.** to the best of my judgment. **18. see fit.** (*takes an infinitive*) to consider proper, etc.: *I don't see fit to allow her to come here.* **19. see (someone) hanged** *or* **damned first.** *Inf.* to refuse absolutely to do what one has been asked. **20. see you, see you later,** *or* **be seeing you.** an expression of farewell. ~See also **see about, see into,** etc. [OE *sēon*]

see[2] (siː) *n.* the diocese of a bishop, or the place within it where his cathedral is situated. [C13: < OF *sed*, < L *sēdēs* a seat]

see about *vb.* (*intr., prep.*) **1.** to take care of: *he couldn't see about the matter because he was ill.* **2.** to investigate: *to see about a new car.*

Seebeck effect (ˈsiːbɛk) *n.* the phenomenon in which a current is produced in a circuit containing two or more different metals when the junctions between the metals are maintained at different temperatures. Also called: **thermoelectric effect.** [C19: after Thomas *Seebeck* (1770–1831), G physicist]

seed (siːd) *n.* **1.** *Bot.* a mature fertilized plant ovule, consisting of an embryo and its food store surrounded by a protective seed coat (testa). Related adj.: **seminal. 2.** the small hard seedlike fruit of plants such as wheat. **3.** any propagative part of a plant, such as a tuber, spore, or bulb. **4.** the source, beginning, or germ of anything: *the seeds of revolt.* **5.** *Chiefly Bible.* descendants: *the seed of Abraham.* **6.** an archaic term for **sperm** or **semen. 7.** *Sport.* a seeded player. **8.** *Chem.* a small crystal added to a supersaturated solution to induce crystallization. **9. go** *or* **run to seed. a.** (of plants) to produce and shed seeds. **b.** to lose vigour, usefulness, etc. ~*vb.* **10.** to plant (seeds, grain, etc.) in (soil): *we seeded this field with oats.* **11.** (*intr.*) (of plants) to form or shed seeds. **12.** (*tr.*) to remove the seeds from (fruit, etc.). **13.** (*tr.*) *Chem.* to add a small crystal to (a supersaturated solution) in order to cause crystallization. **14.** (*tr.*) to scatter certain substances, such as silver iodide, in (clouds) in order to cause rain. **15.** (*tr.*) to arrange (the draw of a tournament) so that outstanding teams or players will not meet in the early rounds. [OE *sǣd*] —**'seeder** *n.* —**'seedless** *adj.*

seedbed ('siːdˌbɛd) *n.* **1.** a plot of land in which seedlings are grown before being transplanted. **2.** the place where something develops.

seedcake ('siːdˌkeɪk) *n.* a sweet cake flavoured with caraway seeds and lemon rind or essence.

seed coral *n.* small pieces of coral used in jewellery, etc.

seed corn *n.* **1.** the good quality ears or kernels of corn that are used as seed. **2.** assets that are expected to provide future benefits.

seed leaf *n.* the nontechnical name for **cotyledon.**

seedling ('siːdlɪŋ) *n.* a plant produced from a seed, esp. a very young plant.

seed money *n.* money used for the establishment of an enterprise.

seed oyster *n.* a young oyster, esp. a cultivated oyster, ready for transplantation.

seed pearl *n.* a tiny pearl weighing less than a quarter of a grain.

seed pod *n.* a carpel or pistil enclosing the seeds of a plant, esp. a flowering plant.

seed potato *n.* a potato tuber used for planting.

seed vessel *n. Bot.* a dry fruit, such as a capsule.

seedy ('siːdɪ) *adj.* **seedier, seediest. 1.** shabby in appearance: *seedy clothes.* **2.** (of a plant) at the stage of producing seeds. **3.** *Inf.* not physically fit. —**'seedily** *adv.* —**'seediness** *n.*

seeing ('siːɪŋ) *n.* **1.** the sense or faculty of sight. **2.** *Astron.* the condition of the atmosphere with respect to observation of stars, planets, etc. ~*conj.* **3.** (*subordinating;* often foll. by *that*) in light of the fact (that).

see into *vb.* (*intr., prep.*) to discover the true nature of: *I can't see into your thoughts.*

seek (siːk) *vb.* **seeking, sought.** (*mainly tr.*) **1.** (when *intr.*, often foll. by *for* or *after*) to try to find by searching: *to seek a solution.* **2.** (*also intr.*) to try to obtain or acquire: *to seek happiness.* **3.** to attempt (to do something): *I'm only seeking to help.* **4.** (*also intr.*) to inquire about or request (something). **5.** to resort to: *to seek the garden for peace.* [OE *sēcan*] —**'seeker** *n.*

seek out *vb.* (*tr., adv.*) to search hard for and find a specific person or thing: *she sought out her friend from amongst the crowd.*

seem (siːm) *vb.* (*may take an infinitive*) **1.** (*copula*) to appear to the mind or eye; look: *the car seems to be running well.* **2.** to appear to be: *there seems no need for all this nonsense.* **3.** used to diminish the force of a following infinitive to be polite, more noncommittal, etc.: *I can't seem to get through to you.* [C12: ? < ON *soma* to beseem, < *sœmr* befitting]

seeming ('siːmɪŋ) *adj.* **1.** (*prenominal*) apparent but not actual or genuine. ~*n.* **2.** outward or false appearance. —**'seemingly** *adv.*

seemly ('siːmlɪ) *adj.* **-lier, -liest. 1.** proper or fitting. **2.** *Obs.* pleasing in appearance. ~*adv.* **3.** *Arch.* decorously. [C13: < ON *sœmiligr*, < *sœmr* befitting]

seen (siːn) *vb.* the past participle of **see**[1].

see off *vb.* (*tr., adv.*) **1.** to be present at the departure of (a person making a journey). **2.** *Inf.* to cause to leave or depart, esp. by force.

seep (siːp) *vb.* **1.** (*intr.*) to pass gradually or leak as if through small openings. ~*n.* **2.** a small spring or place where water, oil, etc., has oozed through the ground. [OE *sīpian*] —**'seepage** *n.*

seer[1] (sɪə) *n.* **1.** a person who can supposedly see into the future. **2.** a person who professes supernatural powers. **3.** a person who sees.

seer[2] (sɪə) *n.* a varying unit of weight used in India, usually about two pounds or one kilogram. [< Hindi]

seersucker ('sɪəˌsʌkə) *n.* a light cotton, linen, or other fabric with a crinkled surface and often striped. [C18: < Hindi *śīrśakar*, < Persian *shīr o shakkar*, lit.: milk and sugar]

seesaw ('siːˌsɔː) *n.* **1.** a plank balanced in the middle so that two people seated on the ends can ride up and down by pushing on the ground with their feet. **2.** the pastime of riding up and down on a seesaw. **3.** an up-and-down or back-and-forth movement. ~*vb.* **4.** (*intr.*) to move up and down or back and forth in such a manner. [C17: reduplication of SAW[1], alluding to the movement from side to side, as in sawing]

seethe (siːð) *vb.* **1.** (*intr.*) to boil or to foam as if boiling. **2.** (*intr.*) to be in a state of extreme agitation, esp. through anger. **3.** (*tr.*) to soak in liquid. **4.** (*tr.*) *Arch.* to cook by boiling. [OE *sēothan*] —**'seething** *adj.* —**'seethingly** *adv.*

see through *vb.* **1.** (*tr.*) to help out in time of need or trouble. **2.** (*tr., adv.*) to remain with until the end or completion: *let's see the job through.* **3.** (*intr., prep.*) to perceive the true nature of: *I can see through your evasion.* ~*adj.* **see-through. 4.** partly or wholly transparent or translucent, esp. (of clothes) in a titillating way.

segment *n.* ('sɛgmənt). **1.** *Maths.* **a.** a part of a line or curve between two points. **b.** a part of a plane or solid figure cut off by an intersecting line, plane, or planes. **2.** one of several parts or sections into which an object is divided. **3.** *Zool.* any of the parts into which the body or appendages of an annelid or arthropod are divided. **4.** *Linguistics.* a speech sound considered in isolation. ~*vb.* (sɛg'mɛnt). **5.** to cut or divide (a whole object) into segments. [C16: < L *segmentum*, < *secāre* to cut] —**seg'mental** *adj.* —**segmentary** ('sɛgməntərɪ) *adj.*

segmentation (ˌsɛgmɛn'teɪʃən) *n.* **1.** the act or an instance of dividing into segments. **2.** *Embryol.* another name for **cleavage** (sense 4).

segregate ('sɛgrɪˌgeɪt) *vb.* **1.** to set or be set apart from others or from the main group. **2.** (*tr.*) to impose segregation on (a racial or minority group). **3.** *Genetics.* to undergo or cause to undergo segregation. [C16: < L *sēgregāre*, < *sē-* apart + *grex* a flock] —**'segreˌgative** *adj.* —**'segreˌgator** *n.*

segregation (ˌsɛgrɪ'geɪʃən) *n.* **1.** the act of segregating or state of being segregated. **2.** *Sociol.* the practice or policy of creating separate facilities within the same society for the use of a particular group. **3.** *Genetics.* the separation at meiosis of the two members of any pair of alleles into separate gametes. —**ˌsegre'gational** *adj.* —**ˌsegre'gationist** *n.*

segue ('seɪgwɪ) *vb.* (*intr.*) **segueing, segued. 1.** (often foll. by *into*) to proceed from one piece of music to another without a break. ~*n.* **2.** the practice or an instance of segueing. [< It.: follows, < *seguire* to follow, < L *sequī*]

seguidilla (ˌsɛgɪ'diːljə) *n.* **1.** a Spanish dance in a fast triple rhythm. **2.** a piece of music composed for or in the rhythm of this dance. [Sp.: a little dance, < *seguida* a dance, < *seguir* to follow, < L *sequī*]

seiche (seɪʃ) *n.* a tide-like movement of a body of

water caused by barometric pressure, earth tremors, etc. [C19: < Swiss F, <?]

Seidlitz powder *or* **powders** (ˈsɛdlɪts) *n.* a laxative consisting of two powders, tartaric acid and a mixture of sodium bicarbonate and Rochelle salt. [C19: after *Seidlitz,* a village in Bohemia with mineral springs having similar laxative effects]

seif dune (seɪf) *n.* (in deserts, esp. the Sahara) a long ridge of blown sand, often several miles long. [*seif,* < Ar.: sword, from the shape of the dune]

seigneur (sɛˈnjɜː; *French* sɛɲœr) *n.* a feudal lord, esp. in France. [C16: < OF, < Vulgar L *senior,* < L: an elderly man; see SENIOR] —**seiˈgneurial** *adj.*

seigneury (ˈseɪnjərɪ) *n., pl.* **-gneuries.** the estate of a seigneur.

seignior (ˈseɪnjə) *n.* **1.** a less common name for a **seigneur. 2.** (in England) the lord of a seigniory. [C14: < Anglo-F *segnour*] —**seigniorial** (seɪˈnjɔːrɪəl) *adj.*

seigniory (ˈseɪnjərɪ) *or* **signory** (ˈsiːnjərɪ) *n., pl.* **-gniories** *or* **-gnories. 1.** less common names for a **seigneury. 2.** (in England) the fee or manor of a seignior; a feudal domain. **3.** the authority of a seignior.

seine (seɪn) *n.* **1.** a large fishing net that hangs vertically in the water by means of floats at the top and weights at the bottom. ~*vb.* **2.** to catch (fish) using this net. [OE *segne,* < L *sagēna,* < Gk *sagēnē*]

seise *or U.S.* **seize** (siːz) *vb.* to put into legal possession of (property, etc.). —ˈ**seiser** *n.*

seisin *or U.S.* **seizin** (ˈsiːzɪn) *n. Property law.* feudal possession of an estate in land. [C13: < OF *seisine,* < *seisir* to SEIZE]

seismic (ˈsaɪzmɪk) *adj.* relating to or caused by earthquakes or artificially produced earth tremors.

seismo- *or before a vowel* **seism-** *combining form.* earthquake: *seismology.* [< Gk *seismos*]

seismograph (ˈsaɪzməˌgrɑːf) *n.* an instrument that registers and records earthquakes. A **seismogram** is the record from such an instrument. —**seismographic** (ˌsaɪzməˈgræfɪk) *adj.* —**seismographer** (saɪzˈmɒgrəfə) *n.* —**seisˈmography** *n.*

seismology (saɪzˈmɒlədʒɪ) *n.* the branch of geology concerned with the study of earthquakes. —**seismologic** (ˌsaɪzməˈlɒdʒɪk) *or* ˌ**seismoˈlogical** *adj.* —ˌ**seismoˈlogically** *adv.* —**seisˈmologist** *n.*

seize[1] (siːz) *vb.* (*mainly tr.*) **1.** (also *intr.,* foll. by *on*) to take hold of quickly; grab. **2.** (sometimes foll. by *on* or *upon*) to grasp mentally, esp. rapidly: *she immediately seized his idea.* **3.** to take mental possession of: *alarm seized the crowd.* **4.** to take possession of rapidly and forcibly: *the thief seized the woman's purse.* **5.** to take legal possession of. **6.** to take by force or capture: *the army seized the undefended town.* **7.** to take immediate advantage of: *to seize an opportunity.* **8.** *Naut.* to bind (two ropes together). **9.** (*intr.;* often foll. by *up*) (of mechanical parts) to become jammed, esp. because of excessive heat. [C13 *saisen,* < OF *saisir,* < Med. L *sacīre* to position, of Gmc origin] —ˈ**seizable** *adj.*

seize[2] (siːz) *vb.* the U.S. spelling of **seise.**

seizure (ˈsiːʒə) *n.* **1.** the act or an instance of seizing or the state of being seized. **2.** *Pathol.* a sudden manifestation or recurrence of a disease, such as an epileptic convulsion.

selachian (sɪˈleɪkɪən) *adj.* of or belonging to a large subclass of cartilaginous fishes including the sharks, rays, dogfish, and skates. [C19: < NL *Selachii,* < Gk *selakhē* a shark]

seldom (ˈsɛldəm) *adv.* rarely. [OE *seldon*]

select (sɪˈlɛkt) *vb.* **1.** to choose (someone or something) in preference to another or others. ~*adj. also* **selected. 2.** chosen in preference to others. **3.** of particular quality. **4.** limited as to membership or entry: *a select gathering.* ~*n. Austral. history.* **5.** a piece of land acquired by a free-selector. **6.** the process of free-selection. [C16: < L *sēligere* to sort, < *sē-* apart + *legere* to choose] —**seˈlectness** *n.* —**seˈlector** *n.*

select committee *n.* (in Britain) a small committee of members of parliament, set up to investigate and report on a specified matter.

selection (sɪˈlɛkʃən) *n.* **1.** the act or an instance of selecting or the state of being selected. **2.** a thing or number of things that have been selected. **3.** a range from which something may be selected: *a good selection of clothes.* **4.** *Biol.* the process by which certain organisms or characters are reproduced and perpetuated in the species in preference to others.

selective (sɪˈlɛktɪv) *adj.* **1.** of or characterized by selection. **2.** tending to choose carefully or characterized by careful choice. **3.** *Electronics.* occurring at or operating at a particular frequency or band of frequencies. —**seˈlectively** *adv.*

selectivity (sɪˌlɛkˈtɪvɪtɪ) *n.* **1.** the state or quality of being selective. **2.** the degree to which a radio receiver, etc., can respond to the frequency of a desired signal.

selenite (ˈsɛlɪˌnaɪt) *n.* a colourless glassy variety of gypsum.

selenium (sɪˈliːnɪəm) *n.* a nonmetallic element that exists in several allotropic forms. The common form is a grey crystalline solid that is photoconductive, photovoltaic, and semiconducting: used in photocells, solar cells, and in xerography. Symbol: Se; atomic no.: 34; atomic wt.: 78.96. [C19: < NL, < Gk *selēnē* moon; by analogy to TELLURIUM (< L *tellus* earth)]

seleno- *or before a vowel* **selen-** *combining form.* denoting the moon: *selenography.* [< Gk *selēnē* moon]

selenography (ˌsiːlɪˈnɒgrəfɪ) *n.* the branch of astronomy concerned with the description and mapping of the surface features of the moon. —ˌ**seleˈnographer** *n.* —**selenographic** (sɪˌliːnəʊˈgræfɪk) *adj.*

self (sɛlf) *n., pl.* **selves. 1.** the distinct individuality or identity of a person or thing. **2.** a person's typical bodily make-up or personal characteristics: *she's looking her old self again.* **3.** one's own welfare or interests: *he only thinks of self.* **4.** an individual's consciousness of his own identity or being. **5.** a bird, animal, etc., that is a single colour throughout. ~*pron.* **6.** *Not standard.* myself, yourself, etc.: *seats for self and wife.* ~*adj.* **7.** of the same colour or material. **8.** *Obs.* the same. [OE *seolf*]

self- *combining form.* **1.** of oneself or itself: *self-defence.* **2.** by, to, in, due to, for, or from the self: *self-employed; self-respect.* **3.** automatic or automatically: *self-propelled.*

self-abnegation *n.* the denial of one's own interests in favour of the interests of others.

self-absorption *n.* **1.** preoccupation with oneself to the exclusion of others. **2.** *Physics.* the process in which some of the radiation emitted by a material is absorbed by the material itself.

self-abuse *n.* **1.** disparagement or misuse of one's own abilities, etc. **2.** a censorious term for **masturbation.**

self-acting *adj.* not requiring an external influence or control to function; automatic.

self-addressed *adj.* **1.** addressed for return to the sender. **2.** directed to oneself: *a self-addressed remark.*

self-aggrandizement *n.* the act of increasing one's own power, importance, etc. —ˌ**self-agˈgranˌdizing** *adj.*

self-appointed *adj.* having assumed authority without the agreement of others: *a self-appointed critic.*

self-assertion *n.* the act or an instance of putting forward one's own opinions, etc., esp. in an

---

ˌ**self-aˈbasement** *n.*
ˌ**self-abˈhorrence** *n.*
ˌ**self-abˈsorbed** *adj.*
ˌ**self-adˈhesive** *adj.*
ˌ**self-adˈvancement** *n.*
ˌ**self-aˈnalysis** *n.*

aggressive or conceited manner. —ˌself-asˈserting *adj.* —ˌself-asˈsertive *adj.*

self-assurance *n.* confidence in the validity, value, etc., of one's own ideas, opinions, etc. —ˌ**self-asˈsured** *adj.* —ˌ**self-asˈsuredly** *adv.*

self-centred *adj.* totally preoccupied with one's own concerns. —ˌ**self-ˈcentredness** *n.*

self-certification *n.* (in Britain) a formal assertion by a worker to his employer that absence from work for up to seven days was due to sickness.

self-coloured *adj.* **1.** having only a single and uniform colour: *a self-coloured dress.* **2.** (of cloth, etc.) having the natural or original colour.

self-command *n.* another term for **self-control.**

self-confessed *adj.* according to one's own testimony or admission: *a self-confessed liar.*

self-confidence *n.* confidence in one's own powers, judgment, etc. —ˌ**self-ˈconfident** *adj.* —ˌ**self-ˈconfidently** *adv.*

self-conscious *adj.* **1.** unduly aware of oneself as the object of the attention of others. **2.** conscious of one's existence. —ˌ**self-ˈconsciously** *adv.* —ˌ**self-ˈconsciousness** *n.*

self-contained *adj.* **1.** containing within itself all parts necessary for completeness. **2.** (of a flat) having its own kitchen, bathroom, and lavatory not shared by others. **3.** able or tending to keep one's feelings, thoughts, etc., to oneself. —ˌ**self-conˈtainedness** *n.*

self-contradictory *adj. Logic.* (of a proposition) both asserting and denying a given proposition.

self-control *n.* the ability to exercise restraint or control over one's feelings, emotions, reactions, etc. —ˌ**self-conˈtrolled** *adj.*

self-deception *or* **self-deceit** *n.* the act or an instance of deceiving oneself. —ˌ**self-deˈceptive** *adj.*

self-defence *n.* **1.** the act of defending oneself, one's actions, ideas, etc. **2.** boxing as a means of defending the person (esp. in **noble art of self-defence**). **3.** *Law.* the right to defend one's person, family, or property against attack or threat of attack. —ˌ**self-deˈfensive** *adj.*

self-denial *n.* the denial or sacrifice of one's own desires. —ˌ**self-deˈnying** *adj.*

self-determination *n.* **1.** the ability to make a decision for oneself without influence from outside. **2.** the right of a nation or people to determine its own form of government. —ˌ**self-deˈtermined** *adj.* —ˌ**self-deˈtermining** *adj.*

self-discipline *n.* the act of disciplining or power to discipline one's own feelings, desires, etc. —ˌ**self-ˈdisciplined** *adj.*

self-drive *adj.* denoting or relating to a hired car that is driven by the hirer.

self-educated *adj.* **1.** educated through one's own efforts without formal instruction. **2.** educated at one's own expense.

self-effacement *n.* the act of making oneself, one's actions, etc., inconspicuous, esp. because of timidity. —ˌ**self-efˈfacing** *adj.*

self-employed *adj.* earning one's living in one's own business or through freelance work, rather than as the employee of another. —ˌ**self-emˈployment** *n.*

self-esteem *n.* **1.** respect for or a favourable opinion of oneself. **2.** an unduly high opinion of oneself.

self-evident *adj.* containing its own evidence or proof without need of further demonstration. —ˌ**self-ˈevidence** *n.* —ˌ**self-ˈevidently** *adv.*

self-existent *adj. Philosophy.* existing independently of any other being or cause.

self-explanatory *adj.* understandable without explanation; self-evident.

self-expression *n.* the expression of one's own personality, feelings, etc., as in painting or poetry. —ˌ**self-exˈpressive** *adj.*

self-government *n.* **1.** the government of a country, nation, etc., by its own people. **2.** the state of being self-controlled. —ˌ**self-ˈgoverned** *adj.* —ˌ**self-ˈgoverning** *adj.*

selfheal (ˈsɛlfˌhiːl) *n.* **1.** a low-growing European herbaceous plant with tightly clustered violet-blue flowers and reputedly having healing powers. **2.** any of several other plants thought to have healing powers.

self-help *n.* the act or state of providing the means to help oneself without relying on the assistance of others.

self-important *adj.* having or showing an unduly high opinion of one's own abilities, importance, etc. —ˌ**self-imˈportantly** *adv.* —ˌ**self-imˈportance** *n.*

self-improvement *n.* the improvement of one's status, position, education, etc., by one's own efforts.

self-induced *adj.* **1.** induced or brought on by oneself or itself. **2.** *Electronics.* produced by self-induction.

self-induction *n.* the production of an electromotive force in a circuit when the magnetic flux linked with the circuit changes as a result of a change in current in the same circuit.

self-indulgent *adj.* tending to indulge one's own desires, etc. —ˌ**self-inˈdulgence** *n.*

self-interest *n.* **1.** one's personal interest or advantage. **2.** the act or an instance of pursuing one's own interest. —ˌ**self-ˈinterested** *adj.*

selfish (ˈsɛlfɪʃ) *adj.* **1.** chiefly concerned with one's own interest, advantage, etc., esp. to the exclusion of the interests of others. **2.** relating to or characterized by self-interest. —ˈ**selfishly** *adv.* —ˈ**selfishness** *n.*

self-justification *n.* the act or an instance of justifying or providing excuses for one's own behaviour, etc.

selfless (ˈsɛlflɪs) *adj.* having little concern for one's own interests. —ˈ**selflessly** *adv.* —ˈ**selflessness** *n.*

self-loading *adj.* (of a firearm) utilizing some of the force of the explosion to eject the empty shell and replace it with a new one. —ˌ**self-ˈloader** *n.*

self-love *n.* the instinct to seek one's own well-being or to further one's own interest.

self-made *adj.* **1.** having achieved wealth, status, etc., by one's own efforts. **2.** made by oneself.

self-opinionated *adj.* **1.** having an unduly high regard for oneself or one's own opinions. **2.** clinging stubbornly to one's own opinions.

self-pity *n.* the act or state of pitying oneself, esp. in an exaggerated or self-indulgent manner. —ˌ**self-ˈpitying** *adj.* —ˌ**self-ˈpityingly** *adv.*

self-pollination *n.* the transfer of pollen from the anthers to the stigma of the same flower. —ˌ**self-ˈpolliˌnated** *adj.*

self-possessed *adj.* having control of one's emotions, etc. —ˌ**self-posˈsession** *n.*

self-preservation *n.* the preservation of oneself from danger or injury.

ˌ**self-aˈware** *adj.*
ˌ**self-ˈcatering** *adj.*
ˌ**self-ˈcensorship** *n.*
ˌ**self-ˈcleaning** *adj.*
ˌ**self-ˈclosing** *adj.*
ˌ**self-conˈceit** *n.*
ˌ**self-condemˈnation** *n.*
ˌ**self-conˌgratuˈlation** *n.*
ˌ**self-conˈsistency** *n.*
ˌ**self-conˈsistent** *adj.*
ˌ**self-deˈfeating** *adj.*
ˌ**self-degraˈdation** *n.*
ˌ**self-deˈlusion** *n.*
ˌ**self-deˈstruct** *vb.*
ˌ**self-ˈdoubt** *n.*
ˌ**self-exˌamiˈnation** *n.*
ˌ**self-ˌfertiliˈzation** *or* **-liˈsation** *n.*
ˌ**self-fiˈnancing** *adj.*
ˌ**self-ˈfocusing** *adj.*
ˌ**self-fulˈfilment** *n.*
ˌ**self-ˈgenerˌating** *adj.*
ˌ**self-hypˈnosis** *n.*
ˌ**self-imˈposed** *adj.*
ˌ**self-inˈflicted** *adj.*
ˌ**self-ˈknowledge** *n.*
ˌ**self-ˈmastery** *n.*
ˌ**self-ˈmockery** *n.*
ˌ**self-neˈglect** *n.*
ˌ**self-mutiˈlation** *n.*
ˌ**self-neˈglect** *n.*
ˌ**self-ˈparody** *n.*
ˌ**self-perˈpetuˌating** *adj.*
ˌ**self-ˈportrait** *n.*
ˌ**self-proˈclaimed** *adj.*

self-pronouncing *adj.* (in a phonetic transcription) of or denoting a word that, except for marks of stress, keeps the letters of its ordinary orthography to represent its pronunciation.

self-propelled *adj.* (of a vehicle) provided with its own source of tractive power rather than requiring an external means of propulsion. —ˌ**self-proˈpelling** *adj.*

self-raising *adj.* (of flour) having a raising agent, such as baking powder, already added.

self-realization *n.* the realization or fulfilment of one's own potential or abilities.

self-regard *n.* **1.** concern for one's own interest. **2.** proper esteem for oneself.

self-reliance *n.* reliance on one's own abilities, decisions, etc. —ˌ**self-reˈliant** *adj.*

self-reproach *n.* the act of finding fault with or blaming oneself. —ˌ**self-reˈproachful** *adj.*

self-respect *n.* a proper sense of one's own dignity and integrity. —ˌ**self-reˈspecting** *adj.*

self-restraint *n.* restraint imposed by oneself on one's own feelings, desires, etc.

self-righteous *adj.* having an exaggerated awareness of one's own virtuousness. —ˌ**self-ˈrighteously** *adv.* —ˌ**self-ˈrighteousness** *n.*

self-rule *n.* another term for **self-government** (sense 1).

self-sacrifice *n.* the sacrifice of one's own desires, etc., for the sake of duty or for the well-being of others. —ˌ**self-ˈsacriˌficing** *adj.*

selfsame (ˈsɛlfˌseɪm) *adj.* (*prenominal*) the very same.

self-satisfied *adj.* having or showing a complacent satisfaction with oneself, one's own actions, behaviour, etc. —ˌ**self-ˌsatisˈfaction** *n.*

self-sealing *adj.* (esp. of an envelope) designed to become sealed with the application of pressure only.

self-seeking *n.* **1.** the act or an instance of seeking one's own profit or interest. ~*adj.* **2.** having or showing an exclusive preoccupation with one's own profit or interest: *a self-seeking attitude.* —ˌ**self-ˈseeker** *n.*

self-service *adj.* **1.** of or denoting a shop, restaurant, etc., where the customer serves himself. ~*n.* **2.** the practice of serving oneself, as in a shop, etc.

self-serving *adj.* habitually seeking one's own advantage, esp. at the expense of others.

self-sown *adj.* (of plants) growing from seed dispersed by any means other than by the agency of man or animals. Also: **self-seeded.**

self-starter *n.* **1.** an electric motor used to start an internal-combustion engine. **2.** the switch that operates this motor. **3.** a person who is strongly motivated and shows initiative, esp. at work.

self-styled *adj.* (*prenominal*) claiming to be of a specified nature, quality, profession, etc.: *a self-styled expert.*

self-sufficient *or* **self-sufficing** *adj.* **1.** able to provide for or support oneself without the help of others. **2.** *Rare.* having undue confidence in oneself. —ˌ**self-sufˈficiency** *n.* —ˌ**self-sufˈficiently** *adv.*

self-supporting *adj.* **1.** able to support or maintain oneself without the help of others. **2.** able to stand up or hold firm without support, props, attachments, etc.

self-will *n.* stubborn adherence to one's own will, desires, etc., esp. at the expense of others. —ˌ**self-ˈwilled** *adj.*

self-winding *adj.* (of a wristwatch) having a mechanism in which a rotating or oscillating weight rewinds the mainspring.

Seljuk (sɛlˈdʒuːk) *n.* **1.** a member of any of the pre-Ottoman Turkish dynasties ruling over large parts of Asia in the 11th, 12th, and 13th centuries A.D. ~*adj.* **2.** of or relating to these dynasties. [C19: < Turkish]

sell (sɛl) *vb.* **selling, sold. 1.** to dispose of or transfer or be disposed of or transferred to a purchaser in exchange for money or other consideration. **2.** to deal in (objects, property, etc.): *he sells used cars.* **3.** (*tr.*) to give up or surrender for a price or reward: *to sell one's honour.* **4.** to promote or facilitate the sale of (objects, property, etc.): *publicity sells many products.* **5.** to gain acceptance of: *to sell an idea.* **6.** (*intr.*) to be in demand on the market: *these dresses sell well.* **7.** (*tr.*) *Inf.* to deceive. **8. sell down the river.** *Inf.* to betray. **9. sell oneself. a.** to convince someone else of one's potential or worth. **b.** to give up one's moral standards, etc. **10. sell short. a.** *Inf.* to belittle. **b.** *Finance.* to sell securities or goods without owning them in anticipation of buying them before delivery at a lower price. ~*n.* **11.** the act or an instance of selling: *a soft sell.* **12.** *Inf.* a hoax or deception. ~See also **sell off, sell out,** etc. [OE *sellan* to lend, deliver] —ˈ**sellable** *adj.* —ˈ**seller** *n.*

selling race *or* **plate** *n.* a horse race in which the winner must be offered for sale at auction.

sell off *vb.* (*tr., adv.*) to sell (remaining or unprofitable items), esp. at low prices.

Sellotape (ˈsɛləˌteɪp) *n.* **1.** *Trademark.* a type of transparent adhesive tape. ~*vb.* (*tr.*) **2.** to seal or stick using adhesive tape.

sell out *vb.* (*adv.*) **1.** Also (*chiefly Brit.*): **sell up.** to dispose of (something) completely by selling. **2.** (*tr.*) *Inf.* to betray. ~*n.* **sellout. 3.** *Inf.* a performance for which all tickets are sold. **4.** a commercial success. **5.** *Inf.* a betrayal.

sell up *vb.* (*adv.*) *Chiefly Brit.* **1.** (*tr.*) to sell all (the possessions) of (a bankrupt debtor) in order to discharge his debts. **2.** (*intr.*) to sell a business.

selsyn (ˈsɛlsɪn) *n.* another name for **synchro.** [< SEL(F-) + SYN(CHRONOUS)]

Seltzer (ˈsɛltsə) *n.* **1.** a natural effervescent water with a high content of minerals. **2.** a similar synthetic water, used as a beverage. [C18: changed < G *Selterser Wasser* water from (*Nieder*) *Selters,* district where mineral springs are located, near Wiesbaden, Germany]

selva (ˈsɛlvə) *n.* **1.** dense equatorial forest, esp. in the Amazon basin, characterized by tall broad-leaved evergreen trees. **2.** a tract of such forest. [C19: < Sp. & Port., < L *silva* forest]

selvage *or* **selvedge** (ˈsɛlvɪdʒ) *n.* **1.** the finished nonfraying edge of a length of woven fabric. **2.** a similar strip of material allowed in fabricating a metal or plastic article. [C15: < SELF + EDGE] —ˈ**selvaged** *adj.*

selves (sɛlvz) *n.* **a.** the plural of **self. b.** (*in combination*): *ourselves, yourselves, themselves.*

Sem. *abbrev. for:* **1.** Seminary. **2.** Semitic.

semantic (sɪˈmæntɪk) *adj.* **1.** of or relating to the meanings of different words or symbols. **2.** of or relating to semantics. [C19: < Gk *sēmantikos* having significance, < *sēmainein* to signify, < *sēma* a sign] —**seˈmantically** *adv.*

semantics (sɪˈmæntɪks) *n.* (*functioning as sing.*) **1.** the branch of linguistics that deals with the study of meaning. **2.** the study of the relationships between signs and symbols and what they represent. **3.** *Logic.* the principles that determine the truth-values of the formulas in a logical system. —**seˈmanticist** *n.*

semaphore (ˈsɛməˌfɔː) *n.* **1.** an apparatus for conveying information by means of visual signals, as with flags, etc. **2.** a system of signalling by holding a flag in each hand and moving the arms to designated positions for each letter of the alphabet. ~*vb.* **3.** to signal (information) by means of semaphore. [C19: via F, < Gk *sēma* a signal + -PHORE] —**semaphoric** (ˌsɛməˈfɒrɪk) *adj.*

semasiology (sɪˌmeɪsɪˈɒlədʒɪ) *n.* another name for **semantics.** [C19: < Gk *sēmasia* meaning, < *sēmainein* to signify + -LOGY]

ˌ**self-proˈmotion** *n.*
ˌ**self-reguˈlation** *n.*
ˌ**self-ˈregulatory** *adj.*
ˌ**self-reˌnunciˈation** *n.*
ˌ**self-reˈvealing** *adj.*
ˌ**self-ˈrighting** *adj.*
ˌ**self-ˈtaught** *adj.*

sematic (sɪˈmætɪk) *adj.* (of the conspicuous coloration of certain animals) acting as a warning. [C19: < Gk *sēma* a sign]

semblance (ˈsɛmbləns) *n.* **1.** outward appearance, esp. without any inner substance. **2.** a resemblance. [C13: < OF, < *sembler* to seem, < L *simulāre* to imitate, < *similis* like]

sememe (ˈsiːmiːm) *n. Linguistics.* the meaning of a morpheme. [C20 (coined in 1933 by L. Bloomfield, U.S. linguist): < Gk *sēma* a sign + -EME]

semen (ˈsiːmɛn) *n.* **1.** the thick whitish fluid containing spermatozoa that is ejaculated from the male genital tract. **2.** another name for **sperm**[1]. [C14: < L: seed]

semester (sɪˈmɛstə) *n.* **1.** *Chiefly U.S. & Canad.* either of two divisions of the academic year. **2.** (in German universities) a session of six months. [C19: via G < L *sēmestris* half-yearly, < *sex* six + *mensis* a month]

semi (ˈsɛmɪ) *n., pl.* **semis.** *Inf.* **1.** *Brit.* short for **semidetached (house)**. **2.** short for **semifinal.**

semi- *prefix.* **1.** half: *semicircle.* **2.** partially, partly, or almost: *semiprofessional.* **3.** occurring twice in a specified period of time: *semiweekly.* [< L]

▷ **Usage.** See at **bi-.**

semiannual (ˌsɛmɪˈænjʊəl) *adj.* **1.** occurring every half-year. **2.** lasting for half a year. —ˌ**semiˈannually** *adv.*

semiarid (ˌsɛmɪˈærɪd) *adj.* characterized by scanty rainfall and scrubby vegetation, often occurring in continental interiors.

semiautomatic (ˌsɛmɪˌɔːtəˈmætɪk) *adj.* **1.** partly automatic. **2.** (of a firearm) self-loading but firing only one shot at each pull of the trigger. ~*n.* **3.** a semiautomatic firearm. —ˌ**semiˌautoˈmatically** *adv.*

semibreve (ˈsɛmɪˌbriːv) *n. Music.* a note, now the longest in common use, having a time value that may be divided by any power of 2 to give all other notes. Usual U.S. and Canad. name: **whole note.**

semicircle (ˈsɛmɪˌsɜːkᵊl) *n.* **1. a.** one half of a circle. **b.** half the circumference of a circle. **2.** anything having the shape or form of half a circle. —**semicircular** (ˌsɛmɪˈsɜːkjʊlə) *adj.*

semicircular canal *n. Anat.* any of the three looped fluid-filled membranous tubes, at right angles to one another, that comprise the labyrinth of the ear.

semicolon (ˌsɛmɪˈkəʊlən) *n.* the punctuation mark (;) used to indicate a pause intermediate in value or length between that of a comma and that of a full stop.

semiconductor (ˌsɛmɪkənˈdʌktə) *n.* **1.** a substance, such as germanium or silicon, that has an electrical conductivity that increases with temperature. **2. a.** a device, such as a transistor or integrated circuit, that depends on the properties of such a substance. **b.** (*as modifier*): *a semiconductor diode.*

semiconscious (ˌsɛmɪˈkɒnʃəs) *adj.* not fully conscious. —ˌ**semiˈconsciously** *adv.* —ˌ**semiˈconsciousness** *n.*

semidetached (ˌsɛmɪdɪˈtætʃt) *adj.* **a.** (of a building) joined to another building on one side by a common wall. **b.** (*as n.*): *they live in a semidetached.*

semifinal (ˌsɛmɪˈfaɪnᵊl) *n.* **a.** the round before the final in a competition. **b.** (*as modifier*): *the semifinal draw.* —ˌ**semiˈfinalist** *n.*

semifluid (ˌsɛmɪˈfluːɪd) *adj.* **1.** having properties between those of a liquid and those of a solid. ~*n.* **2.** a substance that has such properties because of high viscosity: *tar is a semifluid.* ~Also: **semiliquid.**

semiliterate (ˌsɛmɪˈlɪtərɪt) *adj.* **1.** hardly able to read or write. **2.** able to read but not to write.

semilunar (ˌsɛmɪˈluːnə) *adj.* shaped like a crescent or half-moon.

semilunar valve *n. Anat.* either of two crescent-shaped valves, one in the aorta and one in the pulmonary artery, that prevent regurgitation of blood into the heart.

seminal (ˈsɛmɪnəl) *adj.* **1.** potentially capable of development. **2.** highly original and important. **3.** rudimentary or unformed. **4.** of or relating to semen: *seminal fluid.* **5.** *Biol.* of or relating to seed. [C14: < LL *sēminālis* belonging to seed, < L *sēmen* seed] —ˈ**seminally** *adv.*

seminar (ˈsɛmɪˌnɑː) *n.* **1.** a small group of students meeting regularly under the guidance of a tutor, professor, etc. **2.** one such meeting or the place in which it is held. **3.** a higher course for postgraduates. **4.** any group or meeting for holding discussions or exchanging information. [C19: via G < L *sēminārium* SEMINARY]

seminary (ˈsɛmɪnərɪ) *n., pl.* **-naries.** **1.** an academy for the training of priests, etc. **2.** *Arch.* a private secondary school, esp. for girls. [C15: < L *sēminārium* a nursery garden, < *sēmen* seed] —ˌ**semiˈnarial** *adj.* —**seminarian** (ˌsɛmɪˈnɛərɪən) *n.*

seminiferous (ˌsɛmɪˈnɪfərəs) *adj.* **1.** containing, conveying, or producing semen. **2.** (of plants) bearing or producing seeds.

semiotics (ˌsɛmɪˈɒtɪks) *n.* (*functioning as sing.*) **1.** the study of signs and symbols, esp. the relations between written or spoken signs and their referents in the physical world or the world of ideas. **2.** the scientific study of the symptoms of disease. ~Also called: **semiology.** [< Gk *sēmeiōtikos,* < *sēmeion* a sign] —ˌ**semiˈotic** *adj.*

semipermeable (ˌsɛmɪˈpɜːmɪəbᵊl) *adj.* (esp. of a cell membrane) selectively permeable. —ˌ**semiˌpermeaˈbility** *n.*

semiprecious (ˌsɛmɪˈprɛʃəs) *adj.* (of certain stones) having less value than a precious stone.

semiprofessional (ˌsɛmɪprəˈfɛʃənᵊl) *adj.* **1.** (of a person) engaged in an activity or sport part-time but for pay. **2.** (of an activity or sport) engaged in by semiprofessional people. **3.** of or relating to a person whose activities are professional in some respects. ~*n.* **4.** a semiprofessional person. —ˌ**semiproˈfessionally** *adv.*

semiquaver (ˈsɛmɪˌkweɪvə) *n. Music.* a note having the time value of one-sixteenth of a semibreve. Usual U.S. and Canad. name: **sixteenth note.**

semirigid (ˌsɛmɪˈrɪdʒɪd) *adj.* **1.** partly but not wholly rigid. **2.** (of an airship) maintaining shape by means of a main supporting keel and internal gas pressure.

semiskilled (ˌsɛmɪˈskɪld) *adj.* partly skilled or trained but not sufficiently so to perform specialized work.

semisolid (ˌsɛmɪˈsɒlɪd) *adj.* having a viscosity and rigidity intermediate between that of a solid and a liquid.

Semite (ˈsiːmaɪt) *n.* a member of the group of peoples who speak a Semitic language, including the Jews and Arabs as well as the ancient Babylonians, Assyrians, and Phoenicians. [C19: <

ˌ**semiˌagriˈcultural** *adj.*
ˌ**semiaˈquatic** *adj.*
ˌ**semiˌautobioˈgraphical** *adj.*
ˌ**semiauˈtonomous** *adj.*
ˌ**semiˈclassical** *adj.*
ˌ**semiˈdarkness** *n.*
ˌ**semidiˈrect** *adj.*
ˌ**semidiˈvine** *adj.*
ˌ**semiˌdocuˈmentary** *n., adj.*
ˈ**semiˌdome** *n.*
ˌ**semiˈdry** *adj.*
ˌ**semielˈliptical** *adj.*
ˌ**semiˈhard** *adj.*
ˌ**semi-ˌindeˈpendent** *adj.*
ˌ**semi-inˈdustrial** *adj.*
ˌ**semi-ˈinvalid** *n.*
ˌ**semiˈlegendary** *adj.*
ˌ**semimaˈture** *adj.*
ˌ**semiˈnude** *adj.*
ˌ**semiofˈficial** *adj.*
ˌ**semiˌparaˈsitic** *adj.*
ˌ**semiˈpermanent** *adj.*
ˌ**semiˈplastic** *adj.*
ˌ**semipoˈlitical** *adj.*
ˌ**semiˈporous** *adj.*
ˌ**semiˈprivate** *adj.*
ˌ**semiˈpublic** *adj.*
ˌ**semireˈtired** *adj.*
ˌ**semiˈrural** *adj.*
ˌ**semiˈserious** *adj.*
ˌ**semiˈsweet** *adj.*

NL *sēmīta* descendant of Shem, eldest of Noah's sons (Genesis 10:21)]

Semitic (sɪˈmɪtɪk) *n.* **1.** a branch or subfamily of the Afro-Asiatic family of languages that includes Arabic, Hebrew, Aramaic, and such ancient languages as Phoenician. *~adj.* **2.** denoting or belonging to this group of languages. **3.** denoting or characteristic of any of the peoples speaking a Semitic language, esp. the Jews or the Arabs. **4.** another word for **Jewish.**

semitone (ˈsɛmɪˌtəʊn) *n.* an interval denoting the pitch difference between certain adjacent degrees of the diatonic scale (**diatonic semitone**) or between one note and its sharpened or flattened equivalent (**chromatic semitone**); minor second. Also called (U.S. and Canad.): **half step.** Cf. **whole tone.** —**semitonic** (ˌsɛmɪˈtɒnɪk) *adj.*

semitrailer (ˌsɛmɪˈtreɪlə) *n.* a type of trailer or articulated lorry that has wheels only at the rear, the front end being supported by the towing vehicle.

semitropical (ˌsɛmɪˈtrɒpɪkᵊl) *adj.* partly tropical. —ˌ**semiˈtropics** *pl. n.*

semivowel (ˈsɛmɪˌvaʊəl) *n. Phonetics.* a vowel-like sound that acts like a consonant. In English and many other languages the chief semivowels are (w) in *well* and (j), represented as *y*, in *yell*. Also called: **glide.**

semiyearly (ˌsɛmɪˈjɪəlɪ) *adj.* another word for **semiannual.**

semolina (ˌsɛməˈliːnə) *n.* the large hard grains of wheat left after flour has been bolted, used for puddings, soups, etc. [C18: < It. *semolino*, dim. of *semola* bran, < L *simila* very fine wheat flour]

sempervivum (ˌsɛmpəˈvaɪvəm) *n.* any of a genus of hardy perennials including the houseleek. [C16 (used of the houseleek, adopted C18 by Linnaeus (1707-78), Swedish botanist, for the genus): L, < *sempervivus* everliving]

sempiternal (ˌsɛmpɪˈtɜːnᵊl) *adj. Literary.* everlasting; eternal. [C15: < OF, < LL *sempiternālis*, < L, < *semper* always + *aeternus* ETERNAL] —ˌ**sempiˈternally** *adv.*

semplice (ˈsɛmplɪtʃɪ) *adj., adv. Music.* to be performed in a simple manner. [It.: simple, < L *simplex*]

sempre (ˈsɛmprɪ) *adv. Music.* (preceding a tempo or dynamic marking) always; consistently. It is used to indicate that a specified volume, tempo, etc., is to be sustained throughout a piece or passage. [It.: always, < L *semper*]

sempstress (ˈsɛmpstrɪs) *n.* a rare word for **seamstress.**

SEN (in Britain) *abbrev. for* State Enrolled Nurse.

Sen. *or* **sen.** *abbrev. for:* **1.** senate. **2.** senator. **3.** senior.

senate (ˈsɛnɪt) *n.* **1.** any legislative body considered to resemble a Senate. **2.** the main governing body at some universities. [C13: < L *senātus* council of the elders, < *senex* an old man]

Senate (ˈsɛnɪt) *n.* (*sometimes not cap.*) **1.** the upper chamber of the legislatures of the U.S., Canada, Australia, and many other countries. **2.** the legislative council of ancient Rome.

senator (ˈsɛnətə) *n.* **1.** (*often cap.*) a member of a Senate or senate. **2.** any legislator. —**senatorial** (ˌsɛnəˈtɔːrɪəl) *adj.*

send (sɛnd) *vb.* **sending, sent. 1.** (*tr.*) to cause or order (a person or thing) to be taken, directed, or transmitted to another place: *to send a letter.* **2.** (when *intr.*, foll. by *for;* when *tr.*, *takes an infinitive*) to dispatch a request or command (for something or to do something): *he sent for a bottle of wine.* **3.** (*tr.*) to direct or cause to go to a place or point: *his blow sent the champion to the floor.* **4.** (*tr.*) to bring to a state or condition: *this noise will send me mad.* **5.** (*tr.;* often foll. by *forth, out,* etc.) to cause to issue: *his cooking sent forth a lovely smell.* **6.** (*tr.*) to cause to happen or come: *misery sent by fate.* **7.** to transmit (a message) by radio. **8.** (*tr.*) *Sl.* to move to excitement or rapture: *this music really sends me.* *~n.* **9.** another word for **swash** (sense 4). [OE *sendan*] —ˈ**sendable** *adj.* —ˈ**sender** *n.*

send down *vb.* (*tr., adv.*) **1.** *Brit.* to expel from a university. **2.** *Inf.* to send to prison.

sendoff (ˈsɛndˌɒf) *n. Inf.* **1.** a demonstration of good wishes to a person about to set off on a journey, etc. *~vb.* **send off.** (*tr., adv.*) **2.** to cause to depart. **3.** *Soccer, rugby, etc.* (of the referee) to dismiss (a player) from the field of play for some offence. **4.** *Inf.* to give a sendoff to.

send up *vb.* (*tr., adv.*) **1.** *Sl.* to send to prison. **2.** *Brit. inf.* to make fun of, esp. by doing an imitation or parody of. *~n.* **send-up. 3.** *Brit. inf.* a parody or imitation.

senescent (sɪˈnɛsᵊnt) *adj.* **1.** growing old. **2.** characteristic of old age. [C17: < L *senēscere* to grow old, < *senex* old] —**seˈnescence** *n.*

seneschal (ˈsɛnɪʃəl) *n.* **1.** a steward of the household of a medieval prince or nobleman. **2.** *Brit.* a cathedral official. [C14: < OF, < Med. L *siniscalcus*, of Gmc origin]

senile (ˈsiːnaɪl) *adj.* **1.** of or characteristic of old age. **2.** mentally or physically weak or infirm on account of old age. [C17: < L *senīlis*, < *senex* an old man] —**senility** (sɪˈnɪlɪtɪ) *n.*

senior (ˈsiːnjə) *adj.* **1.** higher in rank or length of service. **2.** older in years: *senior citizens.* **3.** of or relating to maturity or old age: *senior privileges.* **4.** *Education.* **a.** of or designating more advanced or older pupils. **b.** of or relating to a secondary school. **c.** *U.S.* denoting a student in the last year of school or university. *~n.* **5.** a senior person. **6.** a senior pupil, student, etc. [C14: < L: older, < *senex* old]

Senior (ˈsiːnjə) *adj. Chiefly U.S.* being the older: used to distinguish the father from the son: *Charles Parker, Senior.* Abbrevs.: **Sr., Sen.**

senior aircraftman *n.* a rank in the Royal Air Force comparable to that of a private in the army, though not the lowest rank in the Royal Air Force.

senior citizen *n. Euphemistic.* an old age pensioner.

senior common room *n.* (in British universities, colleges, etc.) a common room for the use of academic staff.

seniority (ˌsiːnɪˈɒrɪtɪ) *n., pl.* **-ties. 1.** the state of being senior. **2.** precedence in rank, etc., due to senior status.

senior service *n. Brit.* the Royal Navy.

senna (ˈsɛnə) *n.* **1.** any of a genus of tropical plants having typically yellow flowers and long pods. **2. senna leaf.** the dried leaflets of any of these plants, used as a cathartic and laxative. **3. senna pods.** the dried fruits of any of these plants, used as a cathartic and laxative. [C16: via NL < Ar. *sanā*]

sennight *or* **se'nnight** (ˈsɛnaɪt) *n.* an archaic word for **week.** [OE *seofan nihte;* see SEVEN, NIGHT]

señor (sɛˈnjɔː; *Spanish* seˈɲor) *n., pl.* **-ñors** *or* **-ñores** (*Spanish* -ˈɲores). a Spaniard: a title of address equivalent to *Mr* when placed before a name or *sir* when used alone. [Sp., < L *senior* an older man, SENIOR]

señora (sɛˈnjɔːrə; *Spanish* seˈɲora) *n., pl.* **-ras** (-rəz; *Spanish* -ras). a married Spanish woman: a title of address equivalent to *Mrs* when placed before a name or *madam* when used alone.

señorita (ˌsɛnjɔːˈriːtə; *Spanish* ˌseɲoˈrita) *n., pl.* **-tas** (-təz; *Spanish* -tas). an unmarried Spanish woman: a title of address equivalent to *Miss* when placed before a name or *madam* or *miss* when used alone.

sensation (sɛnˈseɪʃən) *n.* **1.** the power of perceiving through the senses. **2.** a physical experience resulting from the stimulation of one of the sense organs. **3.** a general feeling or awareness: *a sensation of fear.* **4.** a state of

---

ˌ**semiˈtrained** *adj.*
ˌ**semitransˈlucent** *adj.*
ˌ**semitransˈparent** *adj.*
ˌ**semiˈtruthful** *adj.*
ˌ**semiˈurban** *adj.*

widespread public excitement: *his announcement caused a sensation.* 5. anything that causes such a state: *your speech was a sensation.* [C17: < Med. L, < LL *sensātus* endowed with SENSE]

sensational (sɛnˈseɪʃənᵊl) *adj.* 1. causing or intended to cause intense feelings, esp. of curiosity, horror, etc.: *sensational disclosures in the press.* 2. *Inf.* extremely good: *a sensational skater.* 3. of or relating to the faculty of sensation. —**senˈsationally** *adv.*

sensationalism (sɛnˈseɪʃənᵊˌlɪzəm) *n.* 1. the use of sensational language, etc., to arouse an intense emotional response. 2. such sensational matter itself. 3. *Philosophy.* the doctrine that knowledge cannot go beyond the analysis of experience. —**senˈsationalist** *n.* —**senˌsationalˈistic** *adj.*

sense (sɛns) *n.* 1. any of the faculties by which the mind receives information about the external world or the state of the body. The five traditional senses are sight, hearing, touch, taste, and smell. 2. the ability to perceive. 3. a feeling perceived through one of the senses: *a sense of warmth.* 4. a mental perception or awareness: *a sense of happiness.* 5. moral discernment: *a sense of right and wrong.* 6. (*sometimes pl.*) sound practical judgment or intelligence. 7. reason or purpose: *what is the sense of going out?* 8. meaning: *what is the sense of this proverb?* 9. specific meaning; definition: *in what sense are you using the word?* 10. an opinion or consensus. 11. *Maths.* one of two opposite directions in which a vector can operate. 12. **make sense.** to be understandable. 13. **take leave of one's senses.** *Inf.* to go mad. ~*vb.* (*tr.*) 14. to perceive through one or more of the senses. 15. to apprehend or detect without or in advance of the evidence of the senses. 16. to understand. 17. *Computers.* a. to test or locate the position of (a part of computer hardware). b. to read (data). [C14: < L *sēnsus,* < *sentīre* to feel]

sense datum *n.* a unit of sensation, such as a sharp pain, detached both from any information it may convey and from its putative source in the external world.

senseless (ˈsɛnslɪs) *adj.* 1. foolish: *a senseless plan.* 2. lacking in feeling; unconscious. 3. lacking in perception. —**ˈsenselessly** *adv.* —**ˈsenselessness** *n.*

sense organ *n.* a structure in animals that is specialized for receiving external or internal stimuli and transmitting them in the form of nervous impulses to the brain.

sensibility (ˌsɛnsɪˈbɪlɪtɪ) *n., pl.* **-ties.** 1. the ability to perceive or feel. 2. (*often pl.*) the capacity for responding to emotion, etc. 3. (*often pl.*) the capacity for responding to aesthetic stimuli. 4. discernment; awareness. 5. (*usually pl.*) emotional or moral feelings: *cruelty offends most people's sensibilities.*

sensible (ˈsɛnsɪbᵊl) *adj.* 1. having or showing good sense or judgment. 2. (of clothing) serviceable; practical. 3. having the capacity for sensation; sensitive. 4. capable of being apprehended by the senses. 5. perceptible to the mind. 6. (sometimes foll. by *of*) having perception; aware: *sensible of your kindness.* 7. readily perceived: *a sensible difference.* [C14: < OF, < LL *sēnsibilis,* < L *sentīre* to sense] —**ˈsensibleness** *n.* —**ˈsensibly** *adv.*

sensitive (ˈsɛnsɪtɪv) *adj.* 1. having the power of sensation. 2. easily irritated; delicate. 3. affected by external conditions or stimuli. 4. easily offended. 5. of or relating to the senses or the power of sensation. 6. capable of registering small differences or changes in amounts, etc.: *a sensitive instrument.* 7. *Photog.* responding readily to light: *a sensitive emulsion.* 8. *Chiefly U.S.* connected with matters affecting national security. 9. (of a stock market or prices) quickly responsive to external influences. [C14: < Med. L *sēnsitīvus,* < L *sentīre* to feel] —**ˈsensitively** *adv.* —**ˌsensiˈtivity** *n.*

sensitive plant *n.* a tropical American mimosa plant, the leaflets and stems of which fold if touched.

sensitize *or* **-tise** (ˈsɛnsɪˌtaɪz) *vb.* 1. to make or become sensitive. 2. (*tr.*) to render (an individual) sensitive to a drug, etc. 3. (*tr.*) *Photog.* to make (a material) sensitive to light by coating it with a photographic emulsion often containing special chemicals, such as dyes. —**ˌsensitiˈzation** *or* **-tiˈsation** *n.* —**ˈsensiˌtizer** *or* **-ˌtiser** *n.*

sensitometer (ˌsɛnsɪˈtɒmɪtə) *n.* an instrument for measuring the sensitivity to light of a photographic material over a range of exposures.

sensor (ˈsɛnsə) *n.* anything, such as a photoelectric cell, that receives a signal or stimulus and responds to it. [C19: < L *sēnsus* perceived, < *sentīre* to observe]

sensorimotor (ˌsɛnsərɪˈməʊtə) *or* **sensomotor** (ˌsɛnsəˈməʊtə) *adj.* of or relating to both the sensory and motor functions of an organism or to the nerves controlling them.

sensorium (sɛnˈsɔːrɪəm) *n., pl.* **-riums** *or* **-ria** (-rɪə). 1. the area of the brain considered responsible for receiving and integrating sensations from the outside world. 2. *Physiol.* the entire sensory and intellectual apparatus of the body. [C17: < LL, < L *sēnsus* felt, < *sentīre* to perceive]

sensory (ˈsɛnsərɪ) *adj.* of or relating to the senses or the power of sensation. [C18: < L *sensōrius,* < *sentīre* to feel]

sensual (ˈsɛnsjʊəl) *adj.* 1. of or relating to any of the senses or sense organs; bodily. 2. strongly or unduly inclined to gratification of the senses. 3. tending to arouse the bodily appetites, esp. the sexual appetite. [C15: < LL *sensuālis,* < L *sēnsus* SENSE] —**ˈsensually** *adv.*

sensualism (ˈsɛnsjʊəˌlɪzəm) *n.* 1. the quality or state of being sensual. 2. the doctrine that the ability to gratify the senses is the only criterion of goodness.

sensuality (ˌsɛnsjʊˈælɪtɪ) *n., pl.* **-ties.** 1. the quality or state of being sensual. 2. excessive indulgence in sensual pleasures. —**sensualist** (ˈsɛnsjʊəlɪst) *n.*

sensuous (ˈsɛnsjʊəs) *adj.* 1. aesthetically pleasing to the senses. 2. appreciative of qualities perceived by the senses. 3. of or derived from the senses. [C17, but not common until C19: apparently coined by Milton to avoid the sexual overtones of SENSUAL] —**ˈsensuously** *adv.* —**ˈsensuousness** *n.*

sent (sɛnt) *vb.* the past tense and past participle of **send.**

sentence (ˈsɛntəns) *n.* 1. a sequence of words capable of standing alone to make an assertion, ask a question, or give a command, usually consisting of a subject and a predicate. 2. the judgment formally pronounced upon a person convicted in criminal proceedings, esp. the decision as to what punishment is to be imposed. 3. *Music.* a passage or division of a piece of music, usually consisting of two or more contrasting musical phrases and ending in a cadence. 4. *Arch.* a proverb, maxim, or aphorism. ~*vb.* 5. (*tr.*) to pronounce sentence on (a convicted person) in a court of law. [C13: via OF < L *sententia* a way of thinking, < *sentīre* to feel] —**sentential** (sɛnˈtɛnʃəl) *adj.*

sentence connector *n.* a word or phrase that introduces a clause or sentence and serves as a transition between it and a previous clause or sentence, as for example *also* in *I'm buying eggs and also I'm looking for a dessert for tonight.*

sentence substitute *n.* a word or phrase, esp. one traditionally classified as an adverb, that is used in place of a finite sentence, such as *yes, no, certainly,* and *never.*

sententious (sɛnˈtɛnʃəs) *adj.* 1. characterized by or full of aphorisms or axioms. 2. constantly using aphorisms, etc. 3. tending to indulge in pompous moralizing. [C15: < L *sententiōsus* full of meaning, < *sententia;* see SENTENCE] —**senˈtentiously** *adv.* —**senˈtentiousness** *n.*

sentient (ˈsɛntɪənt) *adj.* 1. having the power of sense perception or sensation; conscious. ~*n.* 2. *Rare.* a sentient person or thing. [C17: < L *sentiēns* feeling, < *sentīre* to perceive] —**sentience** (ˈsɛnʃəns) *n.*

sentiment (ˈsɛntɪmənt) *n.* 1. susceptibility to

tender or romantic emotion: *she has too much sentiment to be successful.* **2.** (*often pl.*) a thought, opinion, or attitude. **3.** exaggerated or mawkish feeling or emotion. **4.** an expression of response to deep feeling, esp. in art. **5.** a feeling or awareness: *a sentiment of pity.* **6.** a mental attitude determined by feeling: *there is a strong revolutionary sentiment in his country.* **7.** a feeling conveyed, or intended to be conveyed, in words. [C17: < Med. L *sentīmentum*, < L *sentīre* to feel]

sentimental (ˌsɛntɪˈmɛntᵊl) *adj.* **1.** tending to indulge the emotions excessively. **2.** making a direct appeal to the emotions, esp. to romantic feelings. **3.** relating to or characterized by sentiment. —ˌ**sentiˈmentaˌlism** *n.* —ˌ**sentiˈmentalist** *n.* —ˌ**sentiˈmentally** *adv.*

sentimentality (ˌsɛntɪmɛnˈtælɪtɪ) *n., pl.* **-ties.** **1.** the state, quality, or an instance of being sentimental. **2.** an act, statement, etc., that is sentimental.

sentimentalize *or* **-lise** (ˌsɛntɪˈmɛntᵊˌlaɪz) *vb.* to make sentimental or behave sentimentally. —ˌ**sentiˌmentaliˈzation** *or* **-liˈsation** *n.*

sentimental value *n.* the value of an article in terms of its sentimental associations for a particular person.

sentinel (ˈsɛntɪnᵊl) *n.* **1.** a person, such as a sentry, assigned to keep guard. ~*vb.* **-nelling, -nelled.** (*tr.*) **2.** to guard as a sentinel. **3.** to post as a sentinel. [C16: < OF *sentinelle*, < OIt., < *sentina* watchfulness, < *sentire* to notice, < L]

sentry (ˈsɛntrɪ) *n., pl.* **-tries.** a soldier who guards or prevents unauthorized access to a place, etc. [C17: ? shortened < obs. *centrinel*, C16 var. of SENTINEL]

sentry box *n.* a small shelter with an open front in which a sentry may stand to be sheltered from the weather.

senza (ˈsɛntsɑː) *prep. Music.* omitting. [It.]

Sep. *abbrev. for:* **1.** September. **2.** Septuagint.

sepal (ˈsɛpᵊl) *n.* any of the separate parts of the calyx of a flower. [C19: < NL *sepalum*: *sep-* < Gk *skepē* a covering + *-alum*, < NL *petalum* PETAL]

-sepalous *adj. combining form.* having sepals of a specified type or number: *polysepalous.* —**-sepaly** *n. combining form.*

separable (ˈsɛpərəbᵊl) *adj.* able to be separated, divided, or parted. —ˌ**separaˈbility** *or* ˈ**separableness** *n.* —ˈ**separably** *adv.*

separate *vb.* (ˈsɛpəˌreɪt). **1.** (*tr.*) to act as a barrier between: *a range of mountains separates the two countries.* **2.** to part or be parted from a mass or group. **3.** (*tr.*) to discriminate between: *to separate the men and the boys.* **4.** to divide or be divided into component parts. **5.** to sever or be severed. **6.** (*intr.*) (of a married couple) to cease living together. ~*adj.* (ˈsɛprɪt, ˈsɛpərɪt). **7.** existing or considered independently: *a separate problem.* **8.** disunited or apart. **9.** set apart from the main body or mass. **10.** distinct, individual, or particular. **11.** solitary or withdrawn. [C15: < L *sēparāre*, < *sē-* apart + *parāre* to obtain] —ˈ**separately** *adv.* —ˈ**separateness** *n.* —ˈ**separative** *adj.* —ˈ**sepaˌrator** *n.*

separates (ˈsɛprɪts, ˈsɛpərɪts) *pl. n.* women's outer garments that only cover part of the body; skirts, blouses, jackets, trousers, etc.

separate school *n.* **1.** (in certain Canadian provinces) a school for a large religious minority financed by provincial grants in addition to the education tax. **2.** a Roman Catholic school.

separation (ˌsɛpəˈreɪʃən) *n.* **1.** the act of separating or state of being separated. **2.** the place or line where a separation is made. **3.** a gap that separates. **4.** *Family law.* the cessation of cohabitation between a man and wife, either by mutual agreement or under a decree of a court.

separatist (ˈsɛpərətɪst) *n.* **a.** a person who advocates secession from an organization, federation, union, etc. **b.** (*as modifier*): *a separatist movement.* —ˈ**separaˌtism** *n.*

Sephardi (sɪˈfɑːdiː) *n., pl.* **-dim** (-dɪm). *Judaism.* **1.** a Jew of Spanish, Portuguese, or North African descent. **2.** the pronunciation of Hebrew used by these Jews, and of Modern Hebrew as spoken in Israel. ~Cf. **Ashkenazi.** [C19: < LHeb., < Heb. *sepharad* a region mentioned in Obadiah 20, thought to have been Spain] —**Seˈphardic** *adj.*

sepia (ˈsiːpɪə) *n.* **1.** a dark reddish-brown pigment obtained from the inky secretion of the cuttlefish. **2.** a brownish tone imparted to a photograph, esp. an early one. **3.** a brownish-grey to dark yellowish-brown colour. **4.** a drawing or photograph in sepia. ~*adj.* **5.** of the colour sepia or done in sepia: *a sepia print.* [C16: < L: a cuttlefish, < Gk]

sepoy (ˈsiːpɔɪ) *n.* (formerly) an Indian soldier in the service of the British. [C18: < Port. *sipaio*, < Urdu *sipāhī*, < Persian: horseman, < *sipāh* army]

seppuku (sɛˈpuːkuː) *n.* another word for **harakiri.** [< Japanese, < Chinese *ch'ieh* to cut + *fu* bowels]

sepsis (ˈsɛpsɪs) *n.* the presence of pus-forming bacteria in the body. [C19: via NL < Gk *sēpsis* a rotting]

sept (sɛpt) *n.* **1.** *Anthropol.* a clan that believes itself to be descended from a common ancestor. **2.** a branch of a tribe, esp. in Ireland or Scotland. [C16: ? a var. of SECT]

Sept. *abbrev. for:* **1.** September. **2.** Septuagint.

septa (ˈsɛptə) *n.* the plural of **septum.**

septal (ˈsɛptəl) *adj.* of or relating to a septum.

September (sɛpˈtɛmbə) *n.* the ninth month of the year, consisting of 30 days. [OE, < L: the seventh (month) according to the calendar of ancient Rome, < *septem* seven]

septenary (ˈsɛptɪnərɪ) *adj.* **1.** of or relating to the number seven. **2.** forming a group of seven. ~*n., pl.* **-naries.** **3.** the number seven. **4.** a group of seven things. **5.** a period of seven years. [C16: < L *septēnārius*, < *septēnī* seven each, < *septem* seven]

septennial (sɛpˈtɛnɪəl) *adj.* **1.** occurring every seven years. **2.** relating to or lasting seven years. [C17: < L, < *septem* seven + *annus* a year]

septet (sɛpˈtɛt) *n.* **1.** *Music.* a group of seven singers or instrumentalists or a piece of music composed for such a group. **2.** a group of seven people or things. [C19: < G, < L *septem* seven]

septic (ˈsɛptɪk) *adj.* **1.** of or caused by sepsis. **2.** of or caused by putrefaction. ~*n.* **3.** *Austral. & N.Z. inf.* short for **septic tank.** [C17: < L *sēpticus*, < Gk, < *sēptos* decayed, < *sēpein* to make rotten] —ˈ**septically** *adv.* —**septicity** (sɛpˈtɪsɪtɪ) *n.*

septicaemia *or* **septicemia** (ˌsɛptɪˈsiːmɪə) *n.* any of various diseases caused by microorganisms in the blood. Nontechnical name: **blood poisoning.** [C19: < NL, < Gk *sēptik(os)* SEPTIC + -AEMIA] —ˌ**septiˈcaemic** *or* ˌ**septiˈcemic** *adj.*

septic tank *n.* a tank, usually below ground, for containing sewage to be decomposed by anaerobic bacteria. Also called (Austral.): **septic system.**

septillion (sɛpˈtɪljən) *n., pl.* **-lions** *or* **-lion.** **1.** (in Britain, France, and Germany) the number represented as one followed by 42 zeros (10^{42}). **2.** (in the U.S. and Canada) the number represented as one followed by 24 zeros (10^{24}). Brit. word: **quadrillion.** [C17: < F, < *sept* seven + *-illion*, on the model of *million*] —**sepˈtillionth** *adj., n.*

septime (ˈsɛptiːm) *n.* the seventh of eight basic positions from which a parry or attack can be made in fencing. [C19: < L *septimus* seventh, < *septem* seven]

septuagenarian (ˌsɛptjʊədʒɪˈnɛərɪən) *n.* **1.** a person who is from 70 to 79 years old. ~*adj.* **2.** being between 70 and 79 years old. **3.** of or relating to a septuagenarian. [C18: < L, < *septuāgintā* seventy]

Septuagesima (ˌsɛptjʊəˈdʒɛsɪmə) *n.* the third Sunday before Lent. [C14: < Church L *septuāgēsima* (*dies*) the seventieth (day)]

Septuagint (ˈsɛptjʊəˌdʒɪnt) *n.* the principal Greek version of the Old Testament, including the Apocrypha, believed to have been translated by 70 or 72 scholars. [C16: < L *septuāgintā* seventy]

septum (ˈsɛptəm) *n., pl.* **-ta.** *Biol., anat.* a dividing partition between two tissues or cavities. [C18: < L *saeptum* wall, < *saepīre* to enclose]

septuple (ˈsɛptjʊpᵊl) *adj.* **1.** seven times as much or as many. **2.** consisting of seven parts or members. ~*vb.* **3.** (*tr.*) to multiply by seven. [C17: < LL *septuplus,* < *septem* seven] —**septuplicate** (sɛpˈtjuːplɪkət) *n., adj.*

sepulchral (sɪˈpʌlkrəl) *adj.* **1.** suggestive of a tomb; gloomy. **2.** of or relating to a sepulchre. —**seˈpulchrally** *adv.*

sepulchre *or U.S.* **sepulcher** (ˈsɛpəlkə) *n.* **1.** a burial vault, tomb, or grave. **2.** Also called: **Easter sepulchre.** an alcove in some churches in which the Eucharistic elements were kept from Good Friday until Easter. ~*vb.* **3.** (*tr.*) to bury in a sepulchre. [C12: < OF *sépulcre,* < L *sepulcrum,* < *sepelīre* to bury]

sepulture (ˈsɛpəltʃə) *n.* the act of placing in a sepulchre. [C13: via OF < L *sepultūra,* < *sepultus* buried, < *sepelīre* to bury]

seq. *abbrev. for:* **1.** sequel. **2.** sequens. [L: the following (one)]

sequel (ˈsiːkwəl) *n.* **1.** anything that follows from something else. **2.** a consequence. **3.** a novel, play, etc., that continues a previously related story. [C15: < LL *sequēla,* < L *sequī* to follow]

sequela (sɪˈkwiːlə) *n., pl.* **-lae** (-liː). (*often pl.*) *Med.* **1.** any abnormal bodily condition or disease arising from a pre-existing disease. **2.** any complication of a disease. [C18: < L: SEQUEL]

sequence (ˈsiːkwəns) *n.* **1.** an arrangement of two or more things in a successive order. **2.** the successive order of two or more things: *chronological sequence.* **3.** an action or event that follows another or others. **4. a.** *Cards.* a set of three or more consecutive cards, usually of the same suit. **b.** *Bridge.* a set of two or more consecutive cards. **5.** *Music.* an arrangement of notes or chords repeated several times at different pitches. **6.** *Maths.* an ordered set of numbers or other mathematical entities in one-to-one correspondence with the integers 1 to *n.* **7.** a section of a film constituting a single continuous uninterrupted episode. **8.** *Biochem.* the unique order of amino acids in a protein or of nucleotides in DNA or RNA. [C14: < Med. L *sequentia* that which follows, < L *sequī* to follow]

sequence of tenses *n. Grammar.* the sequence according to which the tense of a subordinate verb in a sentence is determined by the tense of the principal verb, as in *I believe he is lying, I believed he was lying,* etc.

sequent (ˈsiːkwənt) *adj.* **1.** following in order or succession. **2.** following as a result. ~*n.* **3.** something that follows. [C16: < L *sequēns,* < *sequī* to follow] —**ˈsequently** *adv.*

sequential (sɪˈkwɛnʃəl) *adj.* **1.** characterized by or having a regular sequence. **2.** another word for **sequent.** —**sequentiality** (sɪˌkwɛnʃɪˈælɪtɪ) *n.* —**seˈquentially** *adv.*

sequential access *n.* a method of reading data from a computer file by reading through the file from the beginning.

sequester (sɪˈkwɛstə) *vb.* (*tr.*) **1.** to remove or separate. **2.** (*usually passive*) to retire into seclusion. **3.** *Law.* to take (property) temporarily out of the possession of its owner, esp. until creditors are satisfied or a court order is complied with. **4.** *International law.* to appropriate (enemy property). [C14: < LL *sequestrāre* to surrender for safekeeping, < L *sequester* a trustee]

sequestrate (sɪˈkwɛstreɪt) *vb.* (*tr.*) *Law.* a variant of **sequester** (sense 3). [C16: < LL *sequestrāre* to SEQUESTER] —**sequestrator** (ˈsiːkwɛsˌtreɪtə) *n.*

sequestration (ˌsiːkwɛˈstreɪʃən) *n.* **1.** the act of sequestering or state of being sequestered. **2.** *Law.* the sequestering of property. **3.** *Chem.* the effective removal of ions from a solution by coordination with another type of ion or molecule to form complexes.

sequestrum (sɪˈkwɛstrəm) *n., pl.* **-tra** (-trə). *Pathol.* a detached piece of dead bone that often migrates to a wound, etc. [C19: < NL, < L: something deposited] —**seˈquestral** *adj.*

sequin (ˈsiːkwɪn) *n.* **1.** a small piece of shiny often coloured metal foil, usually round, used to decorate garments, etc. **2.** a gold coin formerly minted in Italy. [C17: via F < It. *zecchino,* < *zecca* mint, < Ar. *sikkah* die for striking coins] —**ˈsequined** *adj.*

sequoia (sɪˈkwɔɪə) *n.* either of two giant Californian coniferous trees, the **redwood,** or the **big tree** or **giant sequoia.** [C19: NL, after *Sequoya,* known also as George Guess, (?1770–1843), American Indian scholar and leader]

sérac (ˈsɛræk) *n.* a pinnacle of ice among crevasses on a glacier, usually on a steep slope. [C19: < Swiss F: a variety of white cheese (hence the ice that resembles it), < Med. L *serācium,* < L *serum* whey]

seraglio (sɛˈrɑːlɪˌəʊ) *or* **serail** (səˈraɪ) *n., pl.* **-raglios** *or* **-rails. 1.** the harem of a Muslim house or palace. **2.** a sultan's palace, esp. in the former Turkish empire. [C16: < It. *serraglio* animal cage, < Med. L *serrāculum* bolt, < L *sera* a door bar; associated also with Turkish *seray* palace]

seraph (ˈsɛrəf) *n., pl.* **-aphs** *or* **-aphim** (-əfɪm). *Theol.* a member of the highest order of angels in the celestial hierarchies, often depicted as the winged head of a child. [C17: back formation < pl. *seraphim,* via LL < Heb.] —**seraphic** (sɪˈræfɪk) *adj.*

Serb (sɜːb) *n., adj.* another word for **Serbian.** [C19: < Serbian *Srb*]

Serbian (ˈsɜːbɪən) *adj.* **1.** of, relating to, or characteristic of Serbia, in Yugoslavia, its people, or their dialect of Serbo-Croatian. ~*n.* **2.** the dialect of Serbo-Croatian spoken in Serbia. **3.** a native or inhabitant of Serbia.

Serbo-Croatian *or* **Serbo-Croat** *n.* **1.** the chief official language of Yugoslavia. The Serbian dialect is usually written in the Cyrillic alphabet, the Croatian in Roman. ~*adj.* **2.** of or relating to this language.

SERC (in Britain) *abbrev. for* Science and Engineering Research Council.

sere[1] (sɪə) *adj.* **1.** *Arch.* dried up. ~*vb., n.* **2.** a rare spelling of **sear.** [OE *sēar*]

sere[2] (sɪə) *n.* the series of changes occurring in the ecological succession of a particular community. [C20: < SERIES]

serenade (ˌsɛrɪˈneɪd) *n.* **1.** a piece of music characteristically played outside the house of a woman. **2.** a piece of music suggestive of this. **3.** an extended composition in several movements similar to the modern suite. ~*vb.* **4.** (*tr.*) to play a serenade for (someone). **5.** (*intr.*) to play a serenade. [C17: < F *sérénade,* < It. *serenata,* < *sereno* peaceful, < L *serēnus;* also infl. in meaning by It. *sera* evening, < L *sērus* late] —**ˌsereˈnader** *n.*

serendipity (ˌsɛrənˈdɪpɪtɪ) *n.* the faculty of making fortunate discoveries by accident. [C18: coined by Horace Walpole, from the Persian fairytale *The Three Princes of Serendip,* in which the heroes possess this gift] —**ˌserenˈdipitous** *adj.*

serene (sɪˈriːn) *adj.* **1.** peaceful or tranquil; calm. **2.** clear or bright: *a serene sky.* **3.** (*often cap.*) honoured: *His Serene Highness.* [C16: < L *serēnus*] —**seˈrenely** *adv.* —**serenity** (sɪˈrɛnɪtɪ) *n.*

serf (sɜːf) *n.* (esp. in medieval Europe) an unfree person, esp. one bound to the land. [C15: < OF, < L *servus* a slave] —**ˈserfdom** *or* **ˈserfhood** *n.*

serge (sɜːdʒ) *n.* **1.** a twill-weave woollen or worsted fabric used for clothing. **2.** a similar twilled cotton, silk, or rayon fabric. [C14: < OF *sarge,* < Vulgar L *sārica* (unattested), < L *sēricum,* < Gk *sērikon* silk, ult. < *sēr* silkworm]

sergeant (ˈsɑːdʒənt) *n.* **1.** a noncommissioned officer in certain armies, air forces, and marine corps, usually ranking immediately above a corporal. **2. a.** (in Britain) a police officer ranking between constable and inspector. **b.** (in the U.S.) a police officer ranking below a captain. **3.** a court or municipal officer who has ceremonial duties. ~Also: **serjeant.** [C12: < OF *sergent,* < L *serviēns,* lit.: serving, < *servīre* to SERVE]

sergeant at arms *n.* an officer of a legislative

or fraternal body responsible for maintaining internal order. Also: **sergeant, serjeant at arms.**

Sergeant Baker (ˈbeɪkə) *n.* a large brightly coloured Australian sea fish.

sergeant major *n.* the chief administrative noncommissioned officer of a military headquarters. See also **warrant officer.**

Sergt *abbrev. for* Sergeant.

serial (ˈsɪərɪəl) *n.* **1.** a novel, film, etc., presented in instalments at regular intervals. **2.** a publication, regularly issued and consecutively numbered. ~*adj.* **3.** of or resembling a series. **4.** published or presented as a serial. **5.** of or relating to such publication or presentation. **6.** *Computers.* of or operating on items of information, etc., in the order in which they occur. **7.** of or using the techniques of serialism. [C19: < NL *seriālis*, < L *seriēs* SERIES] —ˈ**serially** *adv.*

serialism (ˈsɪərɪəˌlɪzəm) *n.* (in 20th-century music) the use of a sequence of notes in a definite order as a thematic basis for a composition. See also **twelve-tone.**

serialize *or* **-lise** (ˈsɪərɪəˌlaɪz) *vb.* (*tr.*) to publish or present in the form of a serial. —ˌ**serialiˈzation** *or* **-liˈsation** *n.*

serial number *n.* any of the consecutive numbers assigned to machines, tools, books, etc.

seriate (ˈsɪərɪɪt) *adj.* forming a series.

seriatim (ˌsɪərɪˈætɪm) *adv.* one after another in order. [C17: < Med. L, < L *seriēs* SERIES]

sericeous (sɪˈrɪʃəs) *adj. Bot.* **1.** covered with a layer of small silky hairs: *a sericeous leaf.* **2.** silky. [C18: < LL *sēriceus* silken, < L *sēricus*; see SERGE]

sericulture (ˈsɛrɪˌkʌltʃə) *n.* the rearing of silkworms for the production of raw silk. [C19: via F; *seri-* < L *sēricum* silk, ult. < Gk *sēr* a silkworm] —ˌ**seriˈcultural** *adj.* —ˌ**seriˈculturist** *n.*

series (ˈsɪəriːz) *n., pl.* **-ries. 1.** a group or succession of related things, usually arranged in order. **2.** a set of radio or television programmes having the same characters but different stories. **3.** a set of books having the same format, related content, etc., published by one firm. **4.** a set of stamps, coins, etc., issued at a particular time. **5.** *Maths.* the sum of a finite or infinite sequence of numbers or quantities. **6.** *Electronics.* a configuration of two or more components connected in a circuit so that the same current flows in turn through each of them (esp. in **in series**). Cf. **parallel** (sense 10). **7.** *Geol.* a stratigraphical unit that represents the rocks formed during an epoch. [C17: < L: a row, < *serere* to link]

series-wound (ˈsɪəriːzˌwaʊnd) *adj.* (of a motor or generator) having the field and armature circuits connected in series.

serif (ˈsɛrɪf) *n. Printing.* a small line at the extremities of a main stroke in a type character. [C19: ? < Du. *schreef* dash, prob. of Gmc origin]

serigraph (ˈsɛrɪˌgrɑːf) *n.* a colour print made by an adaptation of the silk-screen process. [C19: < *seri-*, < L *sēricum* silk + -GRAPH] —**serigraphy** (səˈrɪgrəfɪ) *n.*

serin (ˈsɛrɪn) *n.* any of various small yellow-and-brown finches of parts of Europe. [C16: < F, ? < OProvençal *sirena* a bee-eater, < L *sīrēn*, a kind of bird, < SIREN]

seringa (səˈrɪŋgə) *n.* **1.** any of a Brazilian genus of trees that yield rubber. **2.** a deciduous tree of southern Africa with a graceful shape. [C18: < Port., var. of SYRINGA]

seriocomic (ˌsɪərɪəʊˈkɒmɪk) *adj.* mixing serious and comic elements. —ˌ**serioˈcomically** *adv.*

serious (ˈsɪərɪəs) *adj.* **1.** grave in nature or disposition: *a serious person.* **2.** marked by deep feeling; sincere: *is he serious or joking?* **3.** concerned with important matters: *a serious conversation.* **4.** requiring effort or concentration: *a serious book.* **5.** giving rise to fear or anxiety: *a serious illness.* [C15: < LL *sēriōsus*, < L *sērius*] —ˈ**seriously** *adv.* —ˈ**seriousness** *n.*

serjeant (ˈsɑːdʒənt) *n.* a variant spelling of **sergeant.**

serjeant at law *n.* (formerly, in England) a barrister of a special rank. Also: **serjeant, sergeant at law, sergeant.**

sermon (ˈsɜːmən) *n.* **1. a.** an address of religious instruction or exhortation, often based on a passage from the Bible, esp. one delivered during a church service. **b.** a written version of such an address. **2.** a serious speech, esp. one administering reproof. [C12: via OF < L *sermō* discourse, prob. < *serere* to join together]

sermonize *or* **-ise** (ˈsɜːməˌnaɪz) *vb.* to address (a person or audience) as if delivering a sermon. —ˈ**sermonˌizer** *or* **-ˌiser** *n.*

Sermon on the Mount *n. Bible.* the first major discourse delivered by Christ (Matthew 5–7).

sero- *combining form.* indicating a serum: *serology.*

serology (sɪˈrɒlədʒɪ) *n.* the branch of science concerned with serums. —**serologic** (ˌsɪərəˈlɒdʒɪk) *or* ˌ**seroˈlogical** *adj.*

seropositive (ˌsɪərəʊˈpɒzɪtɪv) *adj.* (of a person whose blood has been tested for a specific disease, such as AIDS) showing a serological reaction indicating the presence of the disease.

serotine (ˈsɛrəˌtaɪn) *adj.* **1.** *Biol.* produced, flowering, or developing late in the season. ~*n.* **2.** a reddish-coloured European insectivorous bat. [C16: < L *sērōtinus* late, < *sērus* late; applied to the bat because it flies late in the evening]

serotonin (ˌsɛrəˈtəʊnɪn) *n.* a compound that occurs in the brain, intestines, and blood platelets and induces vasoconstriction.

serous (ˈsɪərəs) *adj.* of, producing, or containing serum. [C16: < L *serōsus*] —**serosity** (sɪˈrɒsɪtɪ) *n.*

serous fluid *n.* a thin watery fluid found in many body cavities.

serous membrane *n.* any of the smooth moist delicate membranes, such as the pleura, that line the closed cavities of the body.

serow (ˈsɛrəʊ) *n.* either of two antelopes of mountainous regions of S and SE Asia, having a dark coat and conical backward-pointing horns. [C19: < native name *sǎ-ro* Tibetan goat]

serpent (ˈsɜːpənt) *n.* **1.** a literary word for **snake. 2.** *Bible.* a manifestation of Satan as a guileful tempter (Genesis 3:1–5). **3.** a sly or unscrupulous person. **4.** an obsolete wind instrument resembling a snake in shape. [C14: via OF < L *serpēns* a creeping thing, < *serpere* to creep]

serpentine[1] (ˈsɜːpənˌtaɪn) *adj.* **1.** of, relating to, or resembling a serpent. **2.** twisting; winding. [C14: < LL *serpentīnus*, < *serpēns* SERPENT]

serpentine[2] (ˈsɜːpənˌtaɪn) *n.* any of several secondary minerals, consisting of hydrated magnesium silicate, that are green to brown in colour and greasy to the touch. [C15 *serpentyn*, < Med. L *serpentīnum* SERPENTINE[1]; referring to the snakelike patterns of these minerals]

serpigo (sɜːˈpaɪgəʊ) *n. Pathol.* any progressive skin eruption, such as ringworm or herpes. [C14: < Med. L, < L *serpere* to creep]

SERPS *or* **Serps** (sɜːps) *n.* (in Britain) *acronym for* state earnings-related pension scheme.

serrate *adj.* (ˈsɛrɪt, -eɪt). **1.** (of leaves) having a margin of forward pointing teeth. **2.** having a notched or sawlike edge. ~*vb.* (sɛˈreɪt). **3.** (*tr.*) to make serrate. [C17: < L *serrātus* saw-shaped, < *serra* a saw] —**serˈrated** *adj.*

serration (sɛˈreɪʃən) *n.* **1.** the state or condition of being serrated. **2.** a row of toothlike projections on an edge. **3.** a single notch.

serried (ˈsɛrɪd) *adj.* in close or compact formation: *serried ranks of troops.* [C17: < OF *serré* close-packed, < *serrer* to shut up]

serriform (ˈsɛrɪˌfɔːm) *adj. Biol.* resembling a notched or sawlike edge. [*serri-*, < L *serra* saw]

serrulate (ˈsɛrʊˌleɪt, -lɪt) *adj.* (esp. of leaves) minutely serrate. [C18: < NL *serrulātus*, < L *serrula* dim. of *serra* a saw] —ˌ**serruˈlation** *n.*

serum (ˈsɪərəm) *n., pl.* **-rums** *or* **-ra** (-rə). **1.** Also called: **blood serum.** blood plasma from which the clotting factors have been removed. **2.** antitoxin obtained from the blood serum of immunized animals. **3.** *Physiol., zool.* clear watery fluid, esp.

that exuded by serous membranes. **4.** a less common word for **whey.** [C17: < L: whey]

serum albumin *n.* the principal protein of the blood. See also **albumin.**

serum hepatitis *n.* an acute infectious viral disease characterized by inflammation of the liver, fever, and jaundice: transmitted by means of injection with a contaminated needle or transfusion of contaminated blood.

serum sickness *n.* an allergic reaction, such as vomiting, skin rash, etc., that sometimes follows injection of a foreign serum.

serval ('sɜːvᵊl) *n., pl.* **-vals** *or* **-val.** a slender feline mammal of the African bush, having an orange-brown coat with black spots. [C18: via F < LL *cervālis* staglike, < L *cervus* a stag]

servant ('sɜːvᵊnt) *n.* **1.** a person employed to work for another, esp. one who performs household duties. **2.** See **public servant.** [C13: via OF < *servant* serving, < *servir* to SERVE]

serve (sɜːv) *vb.* **1.** to be in the service of (a person). **2.** to render or be of service to (a person, cause, etc.); help. **3.** to attend to (customers) in a shop, etc. **4.** (*tr.*) to provide (guests, etc.) with food, drink, etc.: *she served her guests with cocktails.* **5.** to distribute or provide (food, etc.) for guests, etc.: *do you serve coffee?* **6.** (*tr.;* sometimes foll. by *up*) to present (food, etc.) in a specified manner: *duck served with orange sauce.* **7.** (*tr.*) to provide with a regular supply of. **8.** (*tr.*) to work actively for: *to serve the government.* **9.** (*tr.*) to pay homage to: *to serve God.* **10.** to suit: *this will serve my purpose.* **11.** (*intr.; may take an infinitive*) to function: *this wood will serve to build a fire.* **12.** to go through (a period of service, enlistment, etc.). **13.** (*intr.*) (of weather, conditions, etc.) to be suitable. **14.** (*tr.*) Also: **service.** (of a male animal) to copulate with (a female animal). **15.** *Tennis, squash, etc.* to put (the ball) into play. **16.** (*tr.*) to deliver (a legal document) to (a person). **17.** (*tr.*) *Naut.* to bind (a rope, etc.) with fine cord to protect it from chafing, etc. **18. serve (a person) right.** *Inf.* to pay (a person) back, esp. for wrongful or foolish treatment or behaviour. ~*n.* **19.** *Tennis, squash, etc.* short for **service. 20.** *Austral. inf.* hostile or critical remarks. [C13: < OF *servir,* < L *servīre,* < *servus* a slave] —'**servable** *or* '**serveable** *adj.*

server ('sɜːvə) *n.* **1.** a person who serves. **2.** *R.C. Church.* a person who assists the priest at Mass. **3.** something that is used in serving food and drink. **4.** the player who serves in racket games.

service ('sɜːvɪs) *n.* **1.** an act of help or assistance. **2.** an organized system of labour and material aids used to supply the needs of the public: *telephone service.* **3.** the supply, installation, or maintenance of goods carried out by a dealer. **4.** the state of availability for use by the public (esp. in **into** *or* **out of service**). **5.** a periodic overhaul made on a car, etc. **6.** the act or manner of serving guests, customers, etc., in a shop, hotel, etc. **7.** a department of public employment and its employees: *civil service.* **8.** employment in or performance of work for another: *in the service of his firm.* **9. a.** one of the branches of the armed forces. **b.** (*as modifier*): *service life.* **10.** the state or duties of a domestic servant (esp. in **in service**). **11.** the act or manner of serving food. **12.** a set of dishes, cups, etc., for use at table. **13.** public worship carried out according to certain prescribed forms: *divine service.* **14.** the prescribed form according to which a specific kind of religious ceremony is to be carried out: *the burial service.* **15.** *Tennis, squash, etc.* **a.** the act, manner, or right of serving a ball. **b.** the game in which a particular player serves: *he has lost his service.* **16.** the serving of a writ, summons, etc., upon a person. **17.** (of male animals) the act of mating. **18.** (*modifier*) of or for the use of servants or employees. **19.** (*modifier*) serving the public rather than producing goods: *service industry.* ~*vb.* (*tr.*) **20.** to provide service or services to. **21.** to make fit for use. **22.** to supply with assistance. **23.** to overhaul (a car, machine, etc.). **24.** (of a male animal) to mate with (a female). **25.** *Brit.* to meet interest on (debt). ~See also **services.** [C12 *servise,* < OF, < L *servitium* condition of a slave, < *servus* a slave]

serviceable ('sɜːvɪsəbᵊl) *adj.* **1.** capable of or ready for service. **2.** capable of giving good service. —ˌ**servicea'bility** *n.* —'**serviceably** *adv.*

service area *n.* a place on a motorway providing garage services, restaurants, toilet facilities, etc.

service car *n. N.Z.* a bus operating on a long-distance route.

service charge *n.* a percentage of a bill, as at a hotel, added to the total to pay for service.

serviceman ('sɜːvɪsmən) *n., pl.* **-men. 1.** a person who serves in the armed services of a country. **2.** a man employed to service and maintain equipment. —'**service**ˌ**woman** *fem. n.*

service road *n. Brit.* a narrow road running parallel to a main road and providing access to houses, shops, etc., situated along its length.

services ('sɜːvɪsɪz) *pl. n.* **1.** work performed for remuneration. **2.** (usually preceded by *the*) the armed forces. **3.** (*sometimes sing.*) *Econ.* commodities, such as banking, that are mainly intangible and usually consumed concurrently with their production. **4.** a system of providing the public with gas, water, etc.

service station *n.* a place that supplies fuel, oil, etc., for motor vehicles and often carries out repairs, servicing, etc.

service tree *n.* **1.** Also called: **sorb.** a Eurasian rosaceous tree, cultivated for its white flowers and brown edible apple-like fruits. **2. wild service tree.** a similar and related Eurasian tree. [*service* < OE *syrfe,* < Vulgar L *sorbea* (unattested), < L *sorbus* sorb]

serviette (ˌsɜːvɪ'ɛt) *n. Chiefly Brit.* a small square of cloth or paper used while eating to protect the clothes, etc. [C15: < OF, < *servir* to SERVE; on the model of OUBLIETTE]

servile ('sɜːvaɪl) *adj.* **1.** obsequious or fawning in attitude or behaviour. **2.** of or suitable for a slave. **3.** existing in or relating to a state of slavery. **4.** (when *postpositive,* foll. by *to*) submitting or obedient. [C14: < L *servīlis,* < *servus* slave] —**servility** (sɜː'vɪlɪtɪ) *n.*

serving ('sɜːvɪŋ) *n.* a portion or helping of food or drink.

servitor ('sɜːvɪtə) *n. Arch.* a person who serves another. [C14: < OF, < LL, < L *servīre* to SERVE]

servitude ('sɜːvɪˌtjuːd) *n.* **1.** the state or condition of a slave. **2.** the state or condition of being subjected to or dominated by a person or thing. **3.** *Law.* a burden attaching to an estate for the benefit of an adjoining estate or of some definite person. See also **easement.** [C15: via OF < L *servitūdō,* < *servus* a slave]

servo ('sɜːvəʊ) *adj.* **1.** (*prenominal*) of or activated by a servomechanism: *servo brakes.* ~*n., pl.* **-vos. 2.** *Inf.* short for **servomechanism.** [< *servomotor* < F, < L *servus* slave + F *moteur* motor]

servomechanism ('sɜːvəʊˌmɛkəˌnɪzəm) *n.* a mechanical or electromechanical system for control of the position or speed of an output transducer.

servomotor ('sɜːvəʊˌməʊtə) *n.* any motor that supplies power to a servomechanism.

sesame ('sɛsəmɪ) *n.* **1.** a tropical herbaceous plant of the East Indies, cultivated, esp. in India, for its small oval seeds. **2.** the seeds of this plant, used in flavouring bread and yielding an edible oil (**benne oil** or **gingili**). [C15: < L *sēsamum,* < Gk *sēsamon, sēsamē,* of Semitic origin]

sesamoid ('sɛsəˌmɔɪd) *adj. Anat.* **1.** of or relating to various small bones formed in tendons, such as the patella. **2.** of or relating to any of various small cartilages, esp. those of the nose. [C17: < L *sēsamoīdēs* like sesame (seed), < Gk]

sesqui- *prefix.* **1.** indicating one and a half: *sesquicentennial.* **2.** (in a chemical compound) indicating a ratio of two to three. [< L, contraction of SEMI- + *as* AS[2] + *-que* and]

sesquicentennial (ˌsɛskwɪsɛn'tɛnɪəl) *adj.* **1.** of a

period of 150 years. ~*n.* **2.** a period of 150 years. **3.** a 150th anniversary or its celebration. —ˌ**sesquicen'tennially** *adv.*

sessile ('sɛsaɪl) *adj.* **1.** (of flowers or leaves) having no stalk. **2.** (of animals such as the barnacle) permanently attached. [C18: < L *sēssilis* concerning sitting, < *sedēre* to sit] —**sessility** (sɛ'sɪlɪtɪ) *n.*

sessile oak *n.* another name for the **durmast.**

session ('sɛʃən) *n.* **1.** the meeting of a court, legislature, judicial body, etc., for the execution of its function or the transaction of business. **2.** a single continuous meeting of such a body. **3.** a series or period of such meetings. **4.** *Education.* **a.** the time during which classes are held. **b.** a school or university year. **5.** *Presbyterian Church.* the body presiding over a local congregation and consisting of the minister and elders. **6.** any period devoted to an activity. [C14: < L *sessiō* a sitting, < *sedēre* to sit] —'**sessional** *adj.*

sesterce ('sɛstəs) *or* **sestertius** (sɛ'stɜːtɪəs) *n.* a silver or, later, bronze coin of ancient Rome worth a quarter of a denarius. [C16: < L *sēstertius* a coin worth two and a half asses, < *sēmis* half + *tertius* a third]

sestet (sɛ'stɛt) *n.* **1.** *Prosody.* the last six lines of a sonnet. **2.** another word for **sextet** (sense 1). [C19: < It., < *sesto* sixth, < L, < *sex* six]

sestina (sɛ'stiːnə) *n.* an elaborate verse form of Italian origin in which the six final words of the lines in the first stanza are repeated in a different order in each of the remaining five stanzas. [C19: < It., < *sesto* sixth, < L *sextus*]

set[1] (sɛt) *vb.* **setting, set.** (*mainly tr.*) **1.** to put or place in position or into a specified state or condition: *to set someone free.* **2.** (*also intr.;* foll. by *to* or *on*) to put or be put (to); apply or be applied: *he set fire to the house.* **3.** to put into order or readiness for use: *to set the table for dinner.* **4.** (*also intr.*) to put, form, or be formed into a jelled, firm, or rigid state: *the jelly set in three hours.* **5.** (*also intr.*) to put or be put into a position that will restore a normal state: *to set a broken bone.* **6.** to adjust (a clock or other instrument) to a position. **7.** to establish: *we have set the date for our wedding.* **8.** to prescribe (an undertaking, course of study, etc.): *the examiners have set "Paradise Lost".* **9.** to arrange in a particular fashion, esp. an attractive one: *she set her hair.* **10.** Also: **set to music.** to provide music for (a poem or other text to be sung). **11.** Also: **set up.** *Printing.* to arrange or produce (type, film, etc.) from (text or copy). **12.** to arrange (a stage, television studio, etc.) with scenery and props. **13.** to describe (a scene or the background to a literary work, etc.) in words: *his novel is set in Russia.* **14.** to present as a model of good or bad behaviour (esp. in **set an example**). **15.** (foll. by *on* or *by*) to value (something) at a specified price or estimation of worth: *he set a high price on his services.* **16.** (*also intr.*) to give or be given a particular direction: *his course was set to the East.* **17.** (*also intr.*) to rig (a sail) or (of a sail) to be rigged so as to catch the wind. **18.** (*intr.*) (of the sun, moon, etc.) to disappear beneath the horizon. **19.** to leave (dough, etc.) in one place so that it may prove. **20.** to sink (the head of a nail) below the surface surrounding it by using a nail set. **21.** *Computers.* to give (a binary circuit) the value 1. **22.** (of plants) to produce (fruits, seeds, etc.) after pollination or (of fruits or seeds) to develop after pollination. **23.** to plant (seeds, seedlings, etc.). **24.** to place (a hen) on (eggs) for the purpose of incubation. **25.** (*intr.*) (of a gun dog) to turn in the direction of game. **26.** *Bridge.* to defeat (one's opponents) in their attempt to make a contract. **27.** a dialect word for **sit.** ~*n.* **28.** the act of setting or the state of being set. **29.** a condition of firmness or hardness. **30.** bearing, carriage, or posture: *the set of a gun dog when pointing.* **31.** the scenery and other props used in a dramatic production, film, etc. **32.** Also called: **set width.** *Printing.* **a.** the width of the body of a piece of type. **b.** the width of the lines of type in a page or column. **33.** *Psychol.* a temporary bias disposing an organism to react to a stimulus in one way rather than in others. **34.** a seedling, cutting, or similar part that is ready for planting: *onion sets.* **35.** a variant spelling of **sett.** ~*adj.* **36.** fixed or established by authority or agreement: *set hours of work.* **37.** (*usually postpositive*) rigid or inflexible: *she is set in her ways.* **38.** unmoving; fixed: *a set expression on his face.* **39.** conventional, artificial, or stereotyped: *she made her apology in set phrases.* **40.** (*postpositive;* foll. by *on* or *upon*) resolute in intention: *he is set upon marrying.* **41.** (of a book, etc.) prescribed for students' preparation for an examination. ~See also **set about, set against,** etc. [OE *settan,* causative of *sittan* to SIT]

set[2] (sɛt) *n.* **1.** a number of objects or people grouped or belonging together, often having certain features or characteristics in common: *a set of coins.* **2.** a group of people who associate together, etc.: *he's part of the jet set.* **3.** *Maths.* a collection of numbers, objects, etc., that are treated as an entity: {3, the moon} is the set the two members of which are the number 3 and the moon. **4.** any apparatus that receives or transmits television or radio signals. **5.** *Tennis, squash, etc.* one of the units of a match, in tennis, one in which one player or pair of players must win at least six games. **6. a.** the number of couples required for a formation dance. **b.** a series of figures that make up a formation dance. **7. a.** a band's or performer's concert repertoire on a given occasion: *the set included no new songs.* **b.** a continuous performance: *the Who played two sets.* **8. make a dead set at. a.** to attack by arguing or ridiculing. **b.** (of a woman) to try to gain the affections of (a man). ~*vb.* **setting, set.** **9.** (*intr.*) (in square and country dancing) to perform a sequence of steps while facing towards another dancer. **10.** (*usually tr.*) to divide into sets: *in this school we set our older pupils for English.* [C14 (in the obs. sense: a religious sect): < OF *sette,* < L *secta* SECT; later sense infl. by the verb SET[1]]

seta ('siːtə) *n., pl.* **-tae** (-tiː). (in invertebrates and plants) any bristle or bristle-like appendage. [C18: < L] —**setaceous** (sɪ'teɪʃəs) *adj.*

set about *vb.* (*intr., prep.*) **1.** to start or begin. **2.** to attack physically or verbally.

set against *vb.* (*tr., prep.*) **1.** to balance or compare. **2.** to cause to be unfriendly to.

set aside *vb.* (*tr., adv.*) **1.** to reserve for a special purpose. **2.** to discard or quash.

set back *vb.* (*tr., adv.*) **1.** to hinder; impede. **2.** *Inf.* to cost (a person) a specified amount. ~*n.* **setback.** **3.** anything that serves to hinder or impede. **4.** a recession in the upper part of a high building. **5.** a steplike shelf where a wall is reduced in thickness.

set down *vb.* (*tr., adv.*) **1.** to record. **2.** to judge or regard: *he set him down as an idiot.* **3.** (foll. by *to*) to attribute: *his attitude was set down to his illness.* **4.** to rebuke. **5.** to snub. **6.** *Brit.* to allow (passengers) to alight from a bus, etc.

set forth *vb.* (*adv.*) *Formal or arch.* **1.** (*tr.*) to state, express, or utter. **2.** (*intr.*) to start out on a journey.

setiferous (sɪ'tɪfərəs) *or* **setigerous** (sɪ'tɪdʒərəs) *adj. Biol.* bearing bristles. [C19: see SETA, -FEROUS, -GEROUS]

set in *vb.* (*intr., adv.*) **1.** to become established: *the winter has set in.* **2.** (of wind) to blow or (of current) to move towards shore. ~*adj.* **set-in.** **3.** (of a part) made separately and then added to a larger whole: *a set-in sleeve.*

setline ('sɛtˌlaɪn) *n.* any of various types of fishing line that consist of a long suspended line having shorter hooked and baited lines attached.

set off *vb.* (*adv.*) **1.** (*intr.*) to embark on a journey. **2.** (*tr.*) to cause (a person) to act or do something, such as laugh. **3.** (*tr.*) to cause to explode. **4.** (*tr.*) to act as a foil or contrast to: *that brooch sets your dress off well.* **5.** (*tr.*) *Accounting.* to cancel a credit on (one account) against a debit on another. ~*n.* **setoff.** **6.**

anything that serves as a counterbalance. **7.** anything that serves to contrast with or enhance something else; foil. **8.** a cross claim brought by a debtor that partly offsets the creditor's claim.

set-off *n. Printing.* a fault in which ink is transferred from a heavily inked or undried printed sheet to the sheet next to it in a pile.

set on *vb.* **1.** (*prep.*) Also: **set upon.** to attack or cause to attack: *they set the dogs on him.* **2.** (*tr., adv.*) to instigate or incite; urge.

setose (ˈsiːtəʊs) *adj. Biol.* covered with setae; bristly. [C17: < L *saetōsus*, < *saeta* a bristle]

set out *vb.* (*adv., mainly tr.*) **1.** to present, arrange, or display. **2.** to give a full account of: *he set out the matter in full.* **3.** to plan or lay out (a garden, etc.). **4.** (*intr.*) to begin or embark on an undertaking, esp. a journey.

set piece *n.* **1.** a work of literature, music, etc., often having a conventional or prescribed theme, intended to create an impressive effect. **2.** a display of fireworks. **3.** *Sport.* a rehearsed team manoeuvre usually attempted at a restart of play.

setscrew (ˈsɛtˌskruː) *n.* a screw that fits into the boss or hub of a wheel, coupling, cam, etc., and prevents motion of the part relative to the shaft on which it is mounted.

set square *n.* a thin flat piece of plastic, metal, etc., in the shape of a right-angled triangle, used in technical drawing.

sett *or* **set** (sɛt) *n.* **1.** a small rectangular paving block made of stone. **2.** the burrow of a badger. **3. a.** a square in a pattern of tartan. **b.** the pattern itself. [C19: var. of SET[1] (n.)]

settee (sɛˈtiː) *n.* a seat, for two or more people, with a back and usually with arms. [C18: changed < SETTLE[2]]

setter (ˈsɛtə) *n.* any of various breeds of large long-haired gun dog trained to point out game by standing rigid.

set theory *n. Maths.* the branch of mathematics concerned with the properties and interrelationships of sets.

setting (ˈsɛtɪŋ) *n.* **1.** the surroundings in which something is set. **2.** the scenery, properties, or background used to create the location for a stage play, film, etc. **3.** *Music.* a composition consisting of a certain text and music arranged for it. **4.** the metal mounting and surround of a gem. **5.** the tableware, cutlery, etc., for a single place at table. **6.** any of a set of points on a scale or dial that can be selected to control the speed, temperature, etc., at which a machine operates.

settle[1] (ˈsɛtᵊl) *vb.* **1.** (*tr.*) to put in order: *he settled his affairs before he died.* **2.** to arrange or be arranged in a fixed or comfortable position: *he settled himself by the fire.* **3.** (*intr.*) to come to rest or a halt: *a bird settled on the hedge.* **4.** to take up or cause to take up residence: *the family settled in the country.* **5.** to establish or become established in a way of life, job, etc. **6.** (*tr.*) to migrate to and form a community; colonize. **7.** to make or become quiet, calm, or stable. **8.** to cause (sediment) to sink to the bottom, as in a liquid, or (of sediment) to sink thus. **9.** to subside or cause to subside: *the dust settled.* **10.** (sometimes foll. by *up*) to pay off or account for (a bill, debt, etc.). **11.** (*tr.*) to decide or dispose of: *to settle an argument.* **12.** (*intr.;* often foll. by *on* or *upon*) to agree or fix: *to settle upon a plan.* **13.** (*tr.;* usually foll. by *on* or *upon*) to secure (title, property, etc.) to a person: *he settled his property on his wife.* **14.** to determine (a legal dispute, etc.) by agreement of the parties without resort to court action (esp. in **settle out of court**). [OE *setlan*] —ˈ**settleable** *adj.*

settle[2] (ˈsɛtᵊl) *n.* a seat, for two or more people, usually made of wood with a high back and arms, and sometimes having a storage space in the boxlike seat. [OE *setl*]

settle down *vb.* (*adv., mainly intr.*) **1.** (*also tr.*) to make or become quiet and orderly. **2.** (often foll. by *to*) to apply oneself diligently: *please settle down to work.* **3.** to adopt an orderly and routine way of life, esp. after marriage.

settle for *vb.* (*intr., prep.*) to accept or agree to in spite of dispute or dissatisfaction.

settlement (ˈsɛtᵊlmənt) *n.* **1.** the act or state of settling or being settled. **2.** the establishment of a new region; colonization. **3.** a place newly settled; colony. **4.** a community formed by members of a group, esp. of a religious sect. **5.** a public building used to provide educational and general welfare facilities for persons living in deprived areas. **6.** a subsidence of all or part of a structure. **7.** an agreement reached in matters of finance, business, etc. **8.** *Law.* **a.** a conveyance, usually to trustees, of property to be enjoyed by several persons in succession. **b.** the deed conveying such property.

settler (ˈsɛtlə) *n.* a person who settles in a new country or a colony.

settlings (ˈsɛtlɪŋz) *pl. n.* any matter that has settled at the bottom of a liquid.

set to *vb.* (*intr., adv.*) **1.** to begin working. **2.** to start fighting. ~*n.* **set-to. 3.** *Inf.* a brief disagreement or fight.

set up *vb.* (*adv., mainly tr.*) **1.** (*also intr.*) to put into a position of power, etc. **2.** (*also intr.*) to begin or enable (someone) to begin (a new venture), as by acquiring or providing means, etc. **3.** to build or construct: *to set up a shed.* **4.** to raise or produce: *to set up a wail.* **5.** to advance or propose: *to set up a theory.* **6.** to restore the health of: *the sea air will set you up again.* **7.** to establish (a record). **8.** *Inf.* to cause (a person) to be blamed, accused, etc. ~*n.* **setup. 9.** *Inf.* the way in which anything is organized or arranged. **10.** *Sl., chiefly U.S. & Canad.* an event the result of which is prearranged: *it's a setup.* **11.** a prepared arrangement of materials, machines, etc., for a job or undertaking. ~*adj.* **set-up. 12.** physically well-built.

seven (ˈsɛvᵊn) *n.* **1.** the cardinal number that is the sum of six and one and is a prime number. **2.** a numeral, 7, VII, etc., representing this number. **3.** the amount or quantity that is one greater than six. **4.** anything representing, represented by, or consisting of seven units, such as a playing card with seven symbols on it. **5.** Also called: **seven o'clock.** seven hours after noon or midnight. ~*determiner.* **6. a.** amounting to seven: *seven swans a-swimming.* **b.** (*as pron.*): *you've eaten seven already.* ~See also **sevens.** [OE *seofon*]

seven deadly sins *pl. n.* a fuller name for the **deadly sins.**

sevenfold (ˈsɛvᵊnˌfəʊld) *adj.* **1.** equal to or having seven times as many or as much. **2.** composed of seven parts. ~*adv.* **3.** by or up to seven times as many or as much.

sevens (ˈsɛvᵊnz) *n.* (*functioning as sing.*) a rugby union match or competition played with seven players on each side.

seven seas *pl. n.* the oceans of the world considered as the N and S Pacific, the N and S Atlantic, and the Arctic, Antarctic, and Indian Oceans.

seventeen (ˈsɛvᵊnˈtiːn) *n.* **1.** the cardinal number that is the sum of ten and seven and is a prime number. **2.** a numeral, 17, XVII, etc., representing this number. **3.** the amount or quantity that is seven more than ten. **4.** something represented by, representing, or consisting of 17 units. ~*determiner.* **5. a.** amounting to seventeen: *seventeen attempts.* **b.** (*as pron.*): *seventeen were sold.* [OE *seofontīene*] —ˈ**seven**ˈ**teenth** *adj., n.*

seventh (ˈsɛvᵊnθ) *adj.* **1.** (*usually prenominal*) **a.** coming after the sixth and before the eighth in numbering, position, etc.; being the ordinal number of *seven:* often written 7th. **b.** (*as n.*): *she left on the seventh.* ~*n.* **2. a.** one of seven equal parts of an object, quantity, measurement, etc. **b.** (*as modifier*): *a seventh part.* **3.** the fraction equal to one divided by seven (1/7). **4.** *Music.* **a.** the interval between one note and another seven notes away from it in a diatonic scale. **b.** one of two notes constituting such an interval in relation to the other. ~*adv.* **5.** Also: **seventhly.** after the sixth person, event, etc.

Seventh-Day Adventist *n.* a member of that branch of the Adventists which constituted itself as a separate body after the expected Second Coming of Christ failed to be realized in 1844. They believe that Christ's coming is imminent and observe Saturday instead of Sunday as their Sabbath.

seventh heaven *n.* **1.** the final state of eternal bliss. **2.** a state of supreme happiness.

seventy (ˈsɛvᵊntɪ) *n., pl.* **-ties.** **1.** the cardinal number that is the product of ten and seven. **2.** a numeral, 70, LXX, etc., representing this number. **3.** (*pl.*) the numbers 70–79, esp. the 70th to the 79th year of a person's life or of a particular century. **4.** the amount or quantity that is seven times as big as ten. **5.** something represented by, representing, or consisting of 70 units. ~*determiner.* **6. a.** amounting to seventy: *the seventy varieties of fabric.* **b.** (*as pron.*): *to invite seventy to the wedding.* —ˈ**seventieth** *adj., n.*

sever (ˈsɛvə) *vb.* **1.** to put or be put apart. **2.** to divide or be divided into parts. **3.** (*tr.*) to break off or dissolve (a tie, relationship, etc.). [C14 *severen,* < OF, < L *sēparāre* to SEPARATE] —ˈ**severable** *adj.*

several (ˈsɛvrəl) *determiner.* **1. a.** more than a few: *several people objected.* **b.** (*as pronoun; functioning as pl.*): *several of them know.* ~*adj.* **2.** (*prenominal*) various; separate: *the members with their several occupations.* **3.** (*prenominal*) distinct; different: *three several times.* **4.** *Law.* capable of being dealt with separately. [C15: via Anglo-F < Med. L *sēparālis,* < L *sēpār,* < *sēparāre* to SEPARATE]

severally (ˈsɛvrəlɪ) *adv. Arch. or literary.* **1.** separately or distinctly. **2.** each in turn.

severalty (ˈsɛvrəltɪ) *n., pl.* **-ties.** **1.** the state of being several or separate. **2.** (usually preceded by *in*) *Property law.* the tenure of property, esp. land, in a person's own right.

severance (ˈsɛvərəns) *n.* **1.** the act of severing or state of being severed. **2.** a separation. **3.** *Law.* the division into separate parts of a joint estate, contract, etc.

severance pay *n.* compensation paid by a firm to employees for loss of employment.

severe (sɪˈvɪə) *adj.* **1.** rigorous or harsh in the treatment of others: *a severe parent.* **2.** serious in appearance or manner. **3.** critical or dangerous: *a severe illness.* **4.** causing discomfort by its harshness: *severe weather.* **5.** strictly restrained in appearance: *a severe way of dressing.* **6.** hard to perform or accomplish: *a severe test.* [C16: < L *sevērus*] —**seˈverely** *adv.* —**severity** (sɪˈvɛrɪtɪ) *n.*

Seville orange (səˈvɪl) *n.* **1.** an orange tree of tropical and semitropical regions: grown for its bitter fruit, which is used to make marmalade. **2.** the fruit of this tree. [C16: after *Seville* in Spain]

Sèvres (*French* sɛvrə) *n.* porcelain ware manufactured at Sèvres, near Paris, from 1756, characterized by the use of clear colours and elaborate decorative detail.

sew (səʊ) *vb.* **sewing, sewed; sewn** *or* **sewed.** **1.** to join or decorate (pieces of fabric, etc.) by means of a thread repeatedly passed through with a needle. **2.** (*tr.;* often foll. by *on* or *up*) to attach, fasten, or close by sewing. **3.** (*tr.*) to make (a garment, etc.) by sewing. ~See also **sew up.** [OE *sēowan*]

sewage (ˈsuːɪdʒ) *n.* waste matter from domestic or industrial establishments that is carried away in sewers or drains. [C19: back formation < SEWER[1]]

sewage farm *n.* a place where sewage is treated, esp. for use as manure.

sewer[1] (sʊə) *n.* **1.** a drain or pipe, esp. one that is underground, used to carry away surface water or sewage. ~*vb.* **2.** (*tr.*) to provide with sewers. [C15: < OF, < *essever* to drain, < Vulgar L *exaquāre* (unattested), < L EX-[1] + *aqua* water]

sewer[2] (ˈsəʊə) *n.* a person or thing that sews.

sewerage (ˈsʊərɪdʒ) *n.* **1.** an arrangement of sewers. **2.** the removal of surface water or sewage by means of sewers. **3.** another word for **sewage.**

sewing (ˈsəʊɪŋ) *n.* **a.** a piece of cloth, etc., that is sewn or to be sewn. **b.** (*as modifier*): *sewing basket.*

sewing machine *n.* any machine designed to sew material. It is now usually driven by electric motor but is sometimes operated by a foot treadle or by hand.

sewn (səʊn) *vb.* a past participle of **sew.**

sew up *vb.* (*tr., adv.*) **1.** to fasten or mend completely by sewing. **2.** *U.S.* to acquire sole use or control of. **3.** *Inf.* to complete or negotiate successfully: *to sew up a deal.*

sex (sɛks) *n.* **1.** the sum of the characteristics that distinguish organisms on the basis of their reproductive function. **2.** either of the two categories, male or female, into which organisms are placed on this basis. **3.** short for **sexual intercourse.** **4.** feelings or behaviour resulting from the urge to gratify the sexual instinct. **5.** sexual matters in general. ~*modifier.* **6.** of or concerning sexual matters: *sex education.* **7.** based on or arising from the difference between the sexes: *sex discrimination.* ~*vb.* **8.** (*tr.*) to ascertain the sex of. [C14: < L *sexus*]

sex- *combining form.* six: *sexcentenary.* [< L]

sexagenarian (ˌsɛksədʒɪˈnɛərɪən) *n.* **1.** a person from 60 to 69 years old. ~*adj.* **2.** being from 60 to 69 years old. **3.** of or relating to a sexagenarian. [C18: < L, < *sexāgēnī* sixty each, < *sexāgintā* sixty]

Sexagesima (ˌsɛksəˈdʒɛsɪmə) *n.* the second Sunday before Lent. [C16: < L: sixtieth, < *sexāgintā* sixty]

sexagesimal (ˌsɛksəˈdʒɛsɪməl) *adj.* **1.** relating to or based on the number 60: *sexagesimal measurement of angles.* ~*n.* **2.** a fraction in which the denominator is some power of 60.

sex appeal *n.* the quality or power of attracting the opposite sex.

sexcentenary (ˌsɛksɛnˈtiːnərɪ) *adj.* **1.** of or relating to 600 or a period of 600 years. **2.** of or celebrating a 600th anniversary. ~*n., pl.* **-naries.** **3.** a 600th anniversary or its celebration. [C18: < L *sexcentēnī* six hundred each]

sex chromosome *n.* either of the chromosomes determining the sex of animals.

sexed (sɛkst) *adj.* **1.** (*in combination*) having a specified degree of sexuality: *undersexed.* **2.** of, relating to, or having sexual differentiation.

sex hormone *n.* an animal hormone affecting development and growth of reproductive organs and related parts.

sexism (ˈsɛksɪzəm) *n.* discrimination on the basis of sex, esp. the oppression of women by men. —ˈ**sexist** *n., adj.*

sexless (ˈsɛkslɪs) *adj.* **1.** having or showing no sexual differentiation. **2.** having no sexual desires. **3.** sexually unattractive.

sex linkage *n. Genetics.* the condition in which a gene is located on a sex chromosome so that the character controlled by the gene is associated with either of the sexes. —ˈ**sex-ˌlinked** *adj.*

sex object *n.* someone, esp. a woman, regarded only from the point of view of someone else's sexual desires.

sexology (sɛkˈsɒlədʒɪ) *n.* the study of sexual behaviour in human beings. —**sexˈologist** *n.* —**sexological** (ˌsɛksəˈlɒdʒɪkᵊl) *adj.*

sexpartite (sɛksˈpɑːtaɪt) *adj.* **1.** (esp. of vaults, arches, etc.) divided into or composed of six parts. **2.** involving six participants.

sex shop *n.* a shop selling aids to sexual activity, pornographic material, etc.

sext (sɛkst) *n. Chiefly R.C. Church.* the fourth of the seven canonical hours of the divine office or the prayers prescribed for it. [C15: < Church L *sexta hōra* the sixth hour]

sextan (ˈsɛkstən) *adj.* (of a fever) marked by paroxysms that recur every fifth day. [C17: < Med. L *sextana* (*febris*) (fever) of the sixth (day)]

sextant (ˈsɛkstənt) *n.* **1.** an instrument used in navigation and consisting of a telescope through which a sighting of a heavenly body is taken, with protractors for determining its angular distance above the horizon. **2.** a sixth part of a circle. [C17: < L *sextāns* one sixth of a unit]

sextet *or* **sextette** (sɛksˈtɛt) *n.* **1.** *Music.* a group of six singers or instrumentalists or a piece of music composed for such a group. **2.** a group of six people or things. [C19: var. of SESTET]

sextillion (sɛksˈtɪljən) *n., pl.* **-lions** *or* **-lion.** **1.** (in Britain, France, and Germany) the number represented as one followed by 36 zeros (10^{36}). **2.** (in the U.S. and Canada) the number represented as one followed by 21 zeros (10^{21}). [C17: < F, < SEX- + *-illion,* on the model of SEPTILLION]

sexton (ˈsɛkstən) *n.* **1.** a man employed to act as caretaker of a church and often also as a bell-ringer, grave-digger, etc. **2.** another name for the **burying beetle.** [C14: < OF, < Med. L *sacristānus* SACRISTAN]

sextuple (ˈsɛkstjʊpᵊl) *n.* **1.** a quantity or number six times as great as another. ~*adj.* **2.** six times as much or as many. **3.** consisting of six parts or members. [C17: L *sextus* sixth + *-uple,* as in QUADRUPLE]

sextuplet (ˈsɛkstjʊplɪt) *n.* **1.** one of six offspring at one birth. **2.** a group of six. **3.** *Music.* a group of six notes played in a time value of four.

sexual (ˈsɛksjʊəl) *adj.* **1.** of or characterized by sex. **2.** (of reproduction) characterized by the union of male and female gametes. Cf. **asexual** (sense 2). [C17: < LL *sexuālis*] —**sexuality** (ˌsɛksjʊˈælɪtɪ) *n.* —ˈ**sexually** *adv.*

sexual harassment *n.* the persistent unwelcome directing of sexual remarks, looks, etc., at a woman, esp. in the workplace.

sexual intercourse *n.* the sexual act in which the male's erect penis is inserted into the female's vagina; copulation; coitus.

sexually transmitted disease *n.* any of various diseases, such as syphilis or gonorrhoea, transmitted by sexual intercourse. Also called: **venereal disease.**

sexual selection *n.* an evolutionary process in animals, in which selection by females of males with certain characters results in the preservation of these characters in the species.

sexy (ˈsɛksɪ) *adj.* **sexier, sexiest.** *Inf.* **1.** provoking or intended to provoke sexual interest: *a sexy dress.* **2.** feeling sexual interest; aroused. —ˈ**sexily** *adv.* —ˈ**sexiness** *n.*

sf *or* **sfz** *Music. abbrev. for* sforzando.

SF *or* **sf** *abbrev. for* science fiction.

SFA *abbrev. for:* **1.** Scottish Football Association. **2.** sweet Fanny Adams. See **fanny adams.**

sforzando (sfɔːˈtsɑːndəʊ) *or* **sforzato** (sfɔːˈtsɑːtəʊ) *Music.* ~*adj., adv.* **1.** to be played with strong initial attack. Abbrevs.: **sf, sfz.** ~*n.* **2.** a symbol, mark, etc., indicating this. [C19: < It., < *sforzare* to force, < Vulgar L *fortiāre* (unattested) to FORCE]

SG *abbrev. for* solicitor general.

sgd *abbrev. for* signed.

S. Glam *abbrev. for* South Glamorgan.

sgraffito (sgræˈfiːtəʊ) *n., pl.* **-ti** (-tɪ). **1.** a technique in mural or ceramic decoration in which the top layer of glaze, plaster, etc., is incised with a design to reveal parts of the ground. **2.** such a decoration. [C18: < It., < *sgraffire* to scratch]

Sgt *abbrev. for* Sergeant.

sh (*spelling pron.* ʃʃʃ) *interj.* an exclamation to request silence or quiet.

sh. *abbrev. for:* **1.** *Stock Exchange.* share. **2.** sheep. **3.** *Bookbinding.* sheet.

shabby (ˈʃæbɪ) *adj.* **-bier, -biest. 1.** threadbare or dilapidated in appearance. **2.** wearing worn and dirty clothes. **3.** mean or unworthy: *shabby treatment.* **4.** dirty or squalid. [C17: < OE *sceabb* scab] —ˈ**shabbily** *adv.* —ˈ**shabbiness** *n.*

shack (ʃæk) *n.* **1.** a roughly built hut. ~*vb.* **2.** See **shack up.** [C19: ? < dialect *shackly* ramshackle, < dialect *shack* to shake]

shackle (ˈʃækᵊl) *n.* **1.** (*often pl.*) a metal ring or fastening, usually part of a pair used to secure a person's wrists or ankles. **2.** (*often pl.*) anything that confines or restricts freedom. **3.** a U-shaped bracket, the open end of which is closed by a bolt (**shackle pin**), used for securing ropes, chains, etc. ~*vb.* (*tr.*) **4.** to confine with or as if with shackles. **5.** to fasten or connect with a shackle. [OE *sceacel*] —ˈ**shackler** *n.*

shack up *vb.* (*intr., adv.;* usually foll. by *with*) *Sl.* to live, esp. with a lover.

shad (ʃæd) *n., pl.* **shad** *or* **shads.** any of various herring-like food fishes that migrate from the sea to fresh water to spawn. [OE *sceadd*]

shaddock (ˈʃædək) *n.* another name for **pomelo** (sense 1). [C17: after Captain *Shaddock,* who brought its seed from the East Indies to Jamaica in 1696]

shade (ʃeɪd) *n.* **1.** relative darkness produced by the blocking out of light. **2.** a place made relatively darker or cooler than other areas by the blocking of light, esp. sunlight. **3.** a position of relative obscurity. **4.** something used to provide a shield or protection from a direct source of light, such as a lampshade. **5.** a darker area indicated in a painting, drawing, etc., by shading. **6.** a colour that varies slightly from a standard colour: *a darker shade of green.* **7.** a slight amount: *a shade of difference.* **8.** *Literary.* a ghost. ~*vb.* (*mainly tr.*) **9.** to screen or protect from heat, light, view, etc. **10.** to make darker or dimmer. **11.** to represent (a darker area) in (a painting, etc.), by means of hatching, etc. **12.** (*also intr.*) to change or cause to change slightly. **13.** to lower (a price) slightly. [OE *sceadu*] —ˈ**shadeless** *adj.*

shades (ʃeɪdz) *pl. n.* **1.** gathering darkness at nightfall. **2.** *Sl.* sunglasses. **3.** (*often cap.;* preceded by *the*) a literary term for **Hades. 4.** (foll. by *of*) undertones: *shades of my father!*

shading (ˈʃeɪdɪŋ) *n.* the graded areas of tone, lines, dots, etc., indicating light and dark in a painting or drawing.

shadoof (ʃəˈduːf) *n.* a mechanism for raising water, consisting of a pivoted pole with a bucket at one end and a counterweight at the other, esp. as used in Egypt. [C19: < Egyptian Ar.]

shadow (ˈʃædəʊ) *n.* **1.** a dark image or shape cast on a surface by the interception of light rays by an opaque body. **2.** an area of relative darkness. **3.** the dark portions of a picture. **4.** a hint or faint semblance: *beyond a shadow of a doubt.* **5.** a remnant or vestige: *a shadow of one's past self.* **6.** a reflection. **7.** a threatening influence: *a shadow over one's happiness.* **8.** a spectre. **9.** an inseparable companion. **10.** a person who trails another in secret, such as a detective. **11.** *Med.* a dark area on an x-ray film representing an opaque structure or part. **12.** *Arch.* shelter. **13.** (*modifier*) *Brit.* designating a member or members of the main opposition party in Parliament who would hold ministerial office if their party were in power: *shadow cabinet.* ~*vb.* (*tr.*) **14.** to cast a shadow over. **15.** to make dark or gloomy. **16.** to shade from light. **17.** to follow or trail secretly. **18.** (often foll. by *forth*) to represent vaguely. [OE *sceadwe,* oblique case of *sceadu* shade] —ˈ**shadower** *n.*

shadow-box *vb.* (*intr.*) *Boxing.* to practise blows and footwork against an imaginary opponent. —ˈ**shadow-ˌboxing** *n.*

shadowgraph (ˈʃædəʊˌgrɑːf) *n.* **1.** a silhouette made by casting a shadow on a lighted surface. **2.** another name for **radiograph.**

shadow play *n.* a theatrical entertainment using shadows thrown by puppets or actors onto a lighted screen.

shadowy (ˈʃædəʊɪ) *adj.* **1.** dark; shady. **2.** resembling a shadow in faintness. **3.** illusory or imaginary. —ˈ**shadowiness** *n.*

shady (ˈʃeɪdɪ) *adj.* **shadier, shadiest. 1.** shaded. **2.** affording or casting a shade. **3.** quiet or concealed. **4.** *Inf.* questionable as to honesty or legality. —ˈ**shadily** *adv.* —ˈ**shadiness** *n.*

SHAEF (ʃeɪf) *n. acronym for* Supreme Headquarters Allied Expeditionary Forces.

shaft (ʃɑːft) *n.* **1.** the long narrow pole that forms the body of a spear, arrow, etc. **2.** something directed at a person in the manner of a missile. **3.** a ray or streak, esp. of light. **4.** a rod or pole forming the handle of a hammer, golf club, etc. **5.** a revolving rod that transmits motion or power. **6.** one of the two wooden poles by which an animal is harnessed to a vehicle. **7.** *Anat.* the middle part of a long bone. **8.** the middle part of a column or pier, between the base and the capital. **9.** *Archit.* a column that supports a vaulting rib, sometimes one of a set. **10.** a vertical passageway through a building, as for a lift. **11.** a vertical passageway into a mine. **12.** *Ornithol.* the central rib of a feather. **13.** an archaic or literary word for **arrow.** ~*vb.* **14.** *U.S. & Canad. sl.* to trick or cheat. [OE *sceaft*]

shag[1] (ʃæg) *n.* **1.** a matted tangle, esp. of hair, etc. **2.** a napped fabric, usually a rough wool. **3.** shredded coarse tobacco. [OE *sceacga*]

shag[2] (ʃæg) *n.* another name for **cormorant,** esp. (in Britain) the **green cormorant.** [C16: special use of SHAG[1], with reference to its crest]

shag[3] (ʃæg) *Brit. sl.* ~*vb.* **shagging, shagged. 1.** *Taboo.* to have sexual intercourse with (a person). **2.** (*tr.; often foll. by out; usually passive*) to exhaust. ~*n.* **3.** *Taboo.* an act of sexual intercourse. [C20: <?]

shaggy (ˈʃægɪ) *adj.* **-gier, -giest. 1.** having or covered with rough unkempt fur, hair, wool, etc.: *a shaggy dog.* **2.** rough or unkempt. —**ˈshaggily** *adv.* —**ˈshagginess** *n.*

shaggy dog story *n. Inf.* a long rambling joke ending in a deliberate anticlimax, such as a pointless punch line.

shagreen (ʃæˈgriːn) *n.* **1.** the rough skin of certain sharks and rays, used as an abrasive. **2.** a rough grainy leather made from certain animal hides. [C17: < F *chagrin,* < Turkish *çagri* rump]

shah (ʃɑː) *n.* a ruler of certain Middle Eastern countries, esp. (formerly) Iran. [C16: < Persian: king] —**ˈshahdom** *n.*

shake (ʃeɪk) *vb.* **shaking, shook, shaken. 1.** to move or cause to move up and down or back and forth with short quick movements. **2.** to sway or totter or cause to sway or totter. **3.** to clasp or grasp (the hand) of (a person) in greeting, agreement, etc.: *he shook John's hand.* **4. shake hands.** to clasp hands in greeting, agreement, etc. **5. shake on it.** *Inf.* to shake hands in agreement, reconciliation, etc. **6.** to bring or come to a specified condition by or as if by shaking: *he shook free and ran.* **7.** (*tr.*) to wave or brandish: *he shook his sword.* **8.** (*tr.;* often foll. by *up*) to rouse or agitate. **9.** (*tr.*) to shock, disturb, or upset: *he was shaken by the news.* **10.** (*tr.*) to undermine or weaken: *the crisis shook his faith.* **11.** to mix (dice) by rattling in a cup or the hand before throwing. **12.** *Austral. sl.* to steal. **13.** (*tr.*) *U.S. & Canad. inf.* to get rid of. **14.** *Music.* to perform a trill on (a note). **15. shake in one's shoes.** to tremble with fear or apprehension. **16. shake one's head.** to indicate disagreement or disapproval by moving the head from side to side. ~*n.* **17.** the act or an instance of shaking. **18.** a tremor or vibration. **19. the shakes.** *Inf.* a state of uncontrollable trembling or a condition that causes it, such as a fever. **20.** *Inf.* a very short period of time: *in half a shake.* **21.** a fissure or crack in timber or rock. **22.** an instance of shaking dice before casting. **23.** *Music.* another word for **trill**[1] (sense 1). **24.** an informal name for **earthquake. 25.** short for **milk shake. 26. no great shakes.** *Inf.* of no great merit or value. ~See also **shake down, shake off, shake up.** [OE *sceacan*] —**ˈshakable** *or* **ˈshakeable** *adj.*

shake down *vb.* (*adv.*) **1.** to fall or settle or cause to fall or settle by shaking. **2.** (*tr.*) *U.S. sl.* to extort money from, esp. by blackmail. **3.** (*tr.*) *Inf., chiefly U.S.* to submit (a vessel, etc.) to a shakedown test. **4.** (*intr.*) to go to bed, esp. to a makeshift bed. ~*n.* **shakedown. 5.** *U.S. sl.* a swindle or act of extortion. **6.** a makeshift bed, esp. of straw, blankets, etc. **7.** *Inf., chiefly U.S.* **a.** a voyage to test the performance of a ship or aircraft or to familiarize the crew with their duties. **b.** (*as modifier*): *a shakedown run.*

shake off *vb.* (*adv.*) **1.** to remove or be removed with or as if with a quick movement: *she shook off her depression.* **2.** (*tr.*) to escape from; elude: *they shook off the police.*

shaker (ˈʃeɪkə) *n.* **1.** a person or thing that shakes. **2.** a container from which a condiment is shaken. **3.** a container in which the ingredients of alcoholic drinks are shaken together.

Shakers (ˈʃeɪkəz) *pl. n.* **the.** an American millenarian sect, founded in 1747 as an offshoot of the Quakers, given to ecstatic shaking and practising common ownership of property.

Shakespearean *or* **Shakespearian** (ʃeɪkˈspɪərɪən) *adj.* **1.** of, relating to, or characteristic of William Shakespeare (1564–1616), English dramatist and poet, or his works. ~*n.* **2.** a student of or specialist in Shakespeare's works.

Shakespearean sonnet *n.* a sonnet form developed in 16th-century England and employed by Shakespeare, having the rhyme scheme a b a b c d c d e f e f g g.

shake up *vb.* (*tr., adv.*) **1.** to shake in order to mix. **2.** to reorganize drastically. **3.** to stir. **4.** to restore the shape of (a pillow, etc.). **5.** *Inf.* to shock mentally or physically. ~*n.* **shake-up. 6.** *Inf.* a radical reorganization.

shako (ˈʃækəʊ) *n., pl.* **shakos** *or* **shakoes.** a tall usually cylindrical military headdress, having a plume and often a peak. [C19: via F < Hungarian *csákó,* < MHG *zacke* a sharp point]

shaky (ˈʃeɪkɪ) *adj.* **shakier, shakiest. 1.** tending to shake or tremble. **2.** liable to prove defective. **3.** uncertain or questionable: *your arguments are very shaky.* —**ˈshakily** *adv.* —**ˈshakiness** *n.*

shale (ʃeɪl) *n.* a dark fine-grained sedimentary rock formed by compression of successive layers of clay. [OE *scealu* shell] —**ˈshaly** *adj.*

shale oil *n.* an oil distilled from shales and used as fuel.

shall (ʃæl; *unstressed* ʃəl) *vb. past* **should.** (takes an infinitive without *to* or an implied infinitive) used as an auxiliary: **1.** (esp. with *I* or *we* as subject) to make the future tense: *we shall see you tomorrow.* Cf. **will**[1] (sense 1). **2.** (with *you, he, she, it, they,* or a noun as subject) **a.** to indicate determination on the part of the speaker, as in issuing a threat: *you shall pay for this!* **b.** to indicate compulsion, now esp. in official documents. **c.** to indicate certainty or inevitability: *our day shall come.* **3.** (*with any noun or pronoun as subject, esp. in conditional clauses or clauses expressing doubt*) to indicate nonspecific futurity: *I don't think I shall ever see her again.* [OE *sceal*]

▷ **Usage.** The usual rule given for the use of *shall* and *will* is that where the meaning is one of simple futurity, *shall* is used for the first person of the verb and *will* for the second and third: *I shall go tomorrow; they will be there now.* Where the meaning involves command, obligation, or determination, the positions are reversed: *it shall be done; I will definitely go.* However, *shall* has come to be largely neglected in favour of *will.*

shallop (ˈʃæləp) *n.* a light boat used for rowing in shallow water. [C16: < F *chaloupe,* < Du. *sloep* sloop]

shallot (ʃəˈlɒt) *n.* **1.** an alliaceous plant cultivated for its edible bulb. **2.** the bulb of this plant, which divides into small sections and is used in cooking for flavouring. [C17: < OF, < *eschaloigne,* < L *Ascalōnia caepa* Ascalonian onion, < *Ascalon,* a Palestinian town]

shallow (ˈʃæləʊ) *adj.* **1.** having little depth. **2.** lacking intellectual or mental depth or subtlety. ~*n.* **3.** (*often pl.*) a shallow place in a body of water. ~*vb.* **4.** to make or become shallow. [C15: rel. to OE *sceald* shallow] —**ˈshallowly** *adv.* —**ˈshallowness** *n.*

shalom aleichem *Hebrew.* (ʃaˈlɔm aˈlexɛm) *sentence substitute.* peace be to you: used by Jews as a greeting or farewell. Often shortened to **shalom.**

shalt (ʃælt) *vb. Arch. or dialect.* (used with the pronoun *thou*) a singular form of the present tense (indicative mood) of **shall.**

sham (ʃæm) *n.* **1.** anything that is not what it appears to be. **2.** something false or fictitious that purports to be genuine. **3.** a person who pretends to be something other than he is. ~*adj.* **4.** counterfeit or false. ~*vb.* **shamming, shammed.** **5.** to assume the appearance of (something); counterfeit: *to sham illness.* [C17: ? a N English dialect var. of SHAME]

shaman (ˈʃæmən) *n.* **1.** a priest of shamanism. **2.** a medicine man of a similar religion, esp. among certain tribes of North American Indians. [C17: < Russian *shaman,* ult. < Sansk. *śrama* religious exercise]

shamanism (ˈʃæməˌnɪzəm) *n.* **1.** the religion of certain peoples of northern Asia, based on the belief that the world is pervaded by good and evil spirits who can be influenced or controlled only by the shamans. **2.** any similar religion involving forms of spiritualism. —ˈ**shamanist** *n., adj.*

shamateur (ˈʃæmətə) *n.* a sportsperson who is officially an amateur but accepts payment. [C20: < *sham* + *amateur*]

shamble (ˈʃæmbᵊl) *vb.* **1.** (*intr.*) to walk or move along in an awkward or unsteady way. ~*n.* **2.** an awkward or unsteady walk. [C17: < *shamble* (adj.) ungainly, ? < *shamble legs* legs resembling those of a meat vendor's table; see SHAMBLES] —ˈ**shambling** *adj., n.*

shambles (ˈʃæmbᵊlz) *n.* (*functioning as sing. or pl.*) **1.** a place of great disorder: *the room was a shambles after the party.* **2.** a place where animals are brought to be slaughtered. **3.** any place of slaughter or execution. [C14 *shamble* table used by meat vendors, < OE *sceamel* stool, < LL *scamellum* a small bench, < L *scamnum* stool]

shambolic (ʃæmˈbɒlɪk) *adj. Inf.* completely disorganized; chaotic. [C20: < SHAMBLES]

shame (ʃeɪm) *n.* **1.** a painful emotion resulting from an awareness of having done something dishonourable, unworthy, etc. **2.** capacity to feel such an emotion. **3.** ignominy or disgrace. **4.** a person or thing that causes this. **5.** an occasion for regret, disappointment, etc.: *it's a shame you can't come with us.* **6. put to shame. a.** to disgrace. **b.** to surpass totally. ~*vb.* (*tr.*) **7.** to cause to feel shame. **8.** to bring shame on. **9.** (often foll. by *into*) to compel through a sense of shame. ~*interj.* **10.** *S. African sl.* a general exclamation of delight, sympathy, etc. [OE *scamu*] —ˈ**shamable** *or* ˈ**shameable** *adj.*

shamefaced (ˈʃeɪmˌfeɪst) *adj.* **1.** bashful or modest. **2.** showing a sense of shame. [C16: alteration of earlier *shamefast,* < OE *sceamfaest*] —**shamefacedly** (ʃeɪmˈfeɪsɪdlɪ) *adv.*

shameful (ˈʃeɪmfʊl) *adj.* causing or deserving shame. —ˈ**shamefully** *adv.* —ˈ**shamefulness** *n.*

shameless (ˈʃeɪmlɪs) *adj.* **1.** having no sense of shame. **2.** without decency or modesty. —ˈ**shamelessly** *adv.* —ˈ**shamelessness** *n.*

shammy (ˈʃæmɪ) *n., pl.* **-mies.** *Inf.* another word for **chamois** (sense 3). Also called: **shammy leather.** [C18: variant of CHAMOIS]

shampoo (ʃæmˈpuː) *n.* **1.** a preparation of soap or detergent to wash the hair. **2.** a similar preparation for washing carpets, etc. **3.** the process of shampooing. ~*vb.* **-pooing, -pooed.** (*tr.*) **4.** to wash (the hair, etc.) with such a preparation. [C18: < Hindi, < *chāmpnā* to knead]

shamrock (ˈʃæmˌrɒk) *n.* a plant having leaves divided into three leaflets: the national emblem of Ireland. [C16: < Irish Gaelic *seamrōg,* dim. of *seamar* clover]

shamus (ˈʃɑːməs, ˈʃeɪ-) *n., pl.* **-muses.** *U.S. sl.* a police or private detective. [prob. < *shammes* caretaker of a synagogue, infl. by Irish *Séamas* James]

shandy (ˈʃændɪ) *n., pl.* **-dies.** an alcoholic drink made of beer and ginger beer or lemonade. [C19: <?]

shanghai (ˈʃæŋhaɪ, ʃæŋˈhaɪ) *Sl.* ~*vb.* **-haiing, -haied.** (*tr.*) **1.** to kidnap (a man or seaman) for enforced service at sea. **2.** to force or trick (someone) into doing something, etc. **3.** *Austral. & N.Z.* to shoot with a catapult. ~*n.* **4.** *Austral. & N.Z.* a catapult. [C19: < the city of *Shanghai;* < the forceful methods formerly used to collect crews for voyages to the Orient]

Shangri-la (ˌʃæŋgrɪˈlɑː) *n.* a remote or imaginary utopia. [C20: < the name of an imaginary valley in the Himalayas, < *Lost Horizon* (1933), a novel by James Hilton]

shank (ʃæŋk) *n.* **1.** *Anat.* the shin. **2.** the corresponding part of the leg in vertebrates other than man. **3.** a cut of meat from the top part of an animal's shank. **4.** the main part of a tool, between the working part and the handle. **5.** the part of a bolt between the thread and the head. **6.** the ring or stem on the back of some buttons. **7.** the stem or long narrow part of a key, hook, spoon handle, nail, etc. **8.** the band of a ring as distinguished from the setting. **9.** the part of a shoe connecting the wide part of the sole with the heel. **10.** *Printing.* the body of a piece of type. ~*vb.* **11.** (*intr.*) (of fruits, roots, etc.) to show disease symptoms, esp. discoloration. **12.** (*tr.*) *Golf.* to mishit (the ball) with the foot of the shaft. [OE *scanca*]

shanks's pony *or U.S.* **shanks's mare** (ˈʃæŋksɪz) *n. Inf.* one's own legs as a means of transportation.

shanny (ˈʃænɪ) *n., pl.* **-nies.** a European blenny of rocky coastal waters. [C19: <?]

shan't (ʃɑːnt) *contraction of* shall not.

shantung (ˌʃænˈtʌŋ) *n.* **1.** a heavy silk fabric with a knobbly surface. **2.** a cotton or rayon imitation of this. [C19: after province of NE China]

shanty[1] (ˈʃæntɪ) *n., pl.* **-ties.** **1.** a ramshackle hut; crude dwelling. **2.** *Austral. & N.Z.* a public house, esp. an unlicensed one. [C19: < Canad. F *chantier* cabin built in a lumber camp, < OF *gantier* GANTRY]

shanty[2] (ˈʃæntɪ) *or* **chanty** *n., pl.* **-ties.** a song originally sung by sailors, esp. a rhythmical one forming an accompaniment to work. [C19: < F *chanter* to sing; see CHANT]

shantytown (ˈʃæntɪˌtaʊn) *n.* a town or section of a town or city inhabited by very poor people living in shanties.

shape (ʃeɪp) *n.* **1.** the outward form of an object defined by outline. **2.** the figure or outline of the body of a person. **3.** a phantom. **4.** organized or definite form: *my plans are taking shape.* **5.** the form that anything assumes. **6.** pattern; mould. **7.** condition or state of efficiency: *to be in good shape.* **8. out of shape. a.** in bad physical condition. **b.** bent, twisted, or deformed. **9. take shape.** to assume a definite form. ~*vb.* **10.** (when *intr.,* often foll. by *into* or *up*) to receive or cause to receive shape or form. **11.** (*tr.*) to mould into a particular pattern or form. **12.** (*tr.*) to plan, devise, or prepare: *to shape a plan of action.* ~See also **shape up.** [OE *gesceap,* lit.: that which is created, < *sceippan* to create] —ˈ**shapable** *or* ˈ**shapeable** *adj.* —ˈ**shaper** *n.*

SHAPE (ʃeɪp) *n. acronym for* Supreme Headquarters Allied Powers Europe.

-shaped (ʃeɪpt) *adj. combining form.* having the shape of: *an L-shaped room; a pear-shaped figure.*

shapeless (ˈʃeɪplɪs) *adj.* **1.** having no definite shape or form: *a shapeless mass.* **2.** lacking a symmetrical or aesthetically pleasing shape: *a shapeless figure.* —ˈ**shapelessness** *n.*

shapely (ˈʃeɪplɪ) *adj.* **-lier, -liest.** (esp. of a woman's body or legs) pleasing or attractive in shape. —ˈ**shapeliness** *n.*

shape up *vb.* (*intr., adv.*) *Inf.* **1.** to proceed or develop satisfactorily. **2.** to develop a definite or proper form.

shard (ʃɑːd) *or* **sherd** *n.* **1.** a broken piece or fragment of a brittle substance, esp. of pottery. **2.** *Zool.* a tough sheath, scale, or shell, esp. the elytra of a beetle. [OE *sceard*]

share[1] (ʃɛə) *n.* **1.** a part or portion of something owned or contributed by a person or group. **2.** (*often pl.*) any of the equal parts, usually of low par value, into which the capital stock of a company is divided. **3. go shares.** *Inf.* to share (something) with another or others. ~*vb.* **4.** (*tr.; often foll. by out*) to divide or apportion, esp. equally. **5.** (when *intr.,* often foll. by *in*) to receive or contribute a portion of: *we can share the cost* *of the petrol.* **6.** to join with another or others in the use of (something): *can I share your umbrella?* [OE *scearu*] —**ˈsharable** *or* **ˈshareable** *adj.* —**ˈsharer** *n.*

share[2] (ʃɛə) *n.* short for **ploughshare.** [OE *scear*]

sharecrop (ˈʃɛəˌkrɒp) *vb.* **-cropping, -cropped.** *Chiefly U.S.* to cultivate (farmland) as a sharecropper.

sharecropper (ˈʃɛəˌkrɒpə) *n. Chiefly U.S.* a farmer, esp. a tenant farmer, who pays over a proportion of a crop or crops as rent.

shared ownership *n.* (in Britain) a form of house purchase whereby the purchaser buys a proportion of the dwelling, usually from a local authority or housing association, and rents the rest.

share-farmer *n. Chiefly Austral.* a farmer who pays a fee to another in return for use of land to raise crops, etc.

shareholder (ˈʃɛəˌhəʊldə) *n.* the owner of one or more shares in a company.

share-milker *n.* (in New Zealand) a person who lives on a dairy farm and milks the farmer's herd in return for an agreed share of the profits.

share option *n.* a scheme whereby employees may take out an option to buy, at a favourable price, shares in the company they work for.

share premium *n. Brit.* the excess of the amount actually subscribed for an issue of corporate capital over its par value.

share shop *n.* a high-street shop or a department within a store that is run by a stockbroking firm, where the public can buy and sell shares quickly, with little formality and no investment advice.

sharia *or* **sheria** (ʃəˈriːə) *n.* the body of doctrines that regulate the lives of those who profess Islam. [Ar.]

shark[1] (ʃɑːk) *n.* any of various usually ferocious fishes, with a long body, two dorsal fins, and rows of sharp teeth. [C16: <?] —**ˈsharkˌlike** *adj.*

shark[2] (ʃɑːk) *n.* a person who preys on or victimizes others, esp. by swindling or extortion. [C18: prob. < G *Schurke* rogue]

sharkskin (ˈʃɑːkˌskɪn) *n.* a smooth glossy fabric of acetate rayon, used for sportswear, etc.

sharp (ʃɑːp) *adj.* **1.** having a keen edge suitable for cutting. **2.** having an edge or point. **3.** involving a sudden change, esp. in direction: *a sharp bend.* **4.** moving, acting, or reacting quickly, etc.: *sharp reflexes.* **5.** clearly defined. **6.** mentally acute; keen-witted; attentive. **7.** sly or artful: *sharp practice.* **8.** bitter or harsh: *sharp words.* **9.** shrill or penetrating: *a sharp cry.* **10.** having an acrid taste. **11.** keen; biting: *a sharp wind.* **12.** *Music.* **a.** (*immediately postpositive*) denoting a note that has been raised in pitch by one chromatic semitone: *B sharp.* **b.** (of an instrument, voice, etc.) out of tune by being too high in pitch. Cf. **flat**[1] (sense 19). **13.** *Inf.* **a.** stylish. **b.** too smart. **14. at the sharp end.** involved in the most competitive or difficult aspect of any activity. ~*adv.* **15.** in a sharp manner. **16.** exactly: *six o'clock sharp.* **17.** *Music.* **a.** higher than a standard pitch. **b.** out of tune by being too high in pitch: *she sings sharp.* Cf. **flat**[1] (sense 24). ~*n.* **18.** *Music.* **a.** an accidental that raises the pitch of a note by one chromatic semitone. Usual symbol: # **b.** a note affected by this accidental. Cf. **flat**[1] (sense 30). **19.** a thin needle with a sharp point. **20.** *Inf.* a sharper. ~*vb.* **21.** (*tr.*) *Music.* the usual U.S. and Canad. word for **sharpen.** [OE *scearp*] —**ˈsharply** *adv.* —**ˈsharpness** *n.*

sharpen (ˈʃɑːpᵊn) *vb.* **1.** to make or become sharp or sharper. **2.** *Music.* to raise the pitch of (a note), esp. by one semitone. —**ˈsharpener** *n.*

sharper (ˈʃɑːpə) *n.* a person who cheats or swindles; fraud.

sharpish (ˈʃɑːpɪʃ) *adj.* **1.** rather sharp. ~*adv.* **2.** *Inf.* quickly; fairly sharply: *quick sharpish.*

sharp-set *adj.* **1.** set to give an acute cutting angle. **2.** keenly hungry. **3.** keen or eager.

sharpshooter (ˈʃɑːpˌʃuːtə) *n.* an expert marksman. —**ˈsharpˌshooting** *n.*

sharp-tongued *adj.* bitter or critical in speech; sarcastic.

sharp-witted *adj.* having or showing a keen intelligence; perceptive. —**ˌsharp-ˈwittedly** *adv.* —**ˌsharp-ˈwittedness** *n.*

Shasta daisy (ˈʃæstə) *n.* a plant widely cultivated for its large white daisy-like flowers.

shastra (ˈʃɑːstrə), **shaster** (ˈʃɑːstə), *or* **sastra** (ˈʃɑːstrə) *n.* any of the sacred writings of Hinduism. [C17: < Sansk. *śāstra,* < *śās* to teach]

shatter (ˈʃætə) *vb.* **1.** to break or be broken into many small pieces. **2.** (*tr.*) to impair or destroy: *his nerves were shattered by the torture.* **3.** (*tr.*) to dumbfound or thoroughly upset: *she was shattered by the news.* **4.** (*tr.*) *Inf.* to cause to be tired out or exhausted. [C12: ? obscurely rel. to SCATTER] —**ˈshattered** *adj.* —**ˈshattering** *adj.* —**ˈshatteringly** *adv.*

shatterproof (ˈʃætəˌpruːf) *adj.* designed to resist shattering.

shave (ʃeɪv) *vb.* **shaving, shaved; shaved** *or* **shaven.** (*mainly tr.*) **1.** (*also intr.*) to remove (the beard, hair, etc.) from (the face, head, or body) by scraping the skin with a razor. **2.** to cut or trim very closely. **3.** to reduce to shavings. **4.** to remove thin slices from (wood, etc.) with a sharp cutting tool. **5.** to touch or graze in passing. **6.** *Inf.* to reduce (a price) by a slight amount. ~*n.* **7.** the act or an instance of shaving. **8.** any tool for scraping. **9.** a thin slice or shaving. [OE *sceafan*] —**ˈshavable** *or* **ˈshaveable** *adj.*

shaveling (ˈʃeɪvlɪŋ) *n. Arch.* **1.** *Derog.* a priest or clergyman with a shaven head. **2.** a young fellow; youth.

shaven (ˈʃeɪvᵊn) *adj.* **a.** closely shaved or tonsured. **b.** (*in combination*): *clean-shaven.*

shaver (ˈʃeɪvə) *n.* **1.** a person or thing that shaves. **2.** Also called: **electric razor, electric shaver.** an electrically powered implement for shaving, having rotating blades behind a fine metal comb. **3.** *Inf.* a youngster, esp. a young boy.

Shavian (ˈʃeɪvɪən) *adj.* **1.** of or like George Bernard Shaw (1856–1950), Irish dramatist, his works, ideas, etc. ~*n.* **2.** an admirer of Shaw or his works.

shaving (ˈʃeɪvɪŋ) *n.* **1.** a thin paring or slice, esp. of wood, that has been shaved from something. ~*modifier.* **2.** used when shaving the face, etc.: *shaving cream.*

shawl (ʃɔːl) *n.* a piece of fabric or knitted or crocheted material worn around the shoulders by women or wrapped around a baby. [C17: < Persian *shāl*]

shawm (ʃɔːm) *n. Music.* a medieval form of the oboe with a conical bore and flaring bell. [C14 *shalmye,* < OF *chalemie,* ult. < L *calamus* a reed, < Gk *kalamos*]

shay (ʃeɪ) *n.* a dialect word for **chaise.** [C18: back formation < CHAISE, mistaken for pl.]

she (ʃiː) *pron.* (*subjective*) **1.** refers to a female person or animal: *she is an actress.* **2.** refers to things personified as feminine, such as cars, ships, and nations. **3.** *Austral. & N.Z.* a pronoun often used instead of *it,* as in **she'll be right** (it will be all right). ~*n.* **4. a.** a female person or animal. **b.** (*in combination*): *she-cat.* [OE *sīe,* accusative of *sēo,* fem. demonstrative pron.]

shea (ʃɪə) *n.* **1.** a tropical African tree with oily seeds. **2. shea butter.** the white butter-like fat obtained from the seeds of this plant and used as food, etc. [C18: < W African *si*]

sheading (ˈʃiːdɪŋ) *n.* any of the six subdivisions of the Isle of Man. [var. of *shedding*]

sheaf (ʃiːf) *n., pl.* **sheaves. 1.** a bundle of reaped but unthreshed corn tied with one or two bonds. **2.** a bundle of objects tied together. **3.** the arrows contained in a quiver. ~*vb.* **4.** (*tr.*) to bind or tie into a sheaf. [OE *sceaf*]

shear (ʃɪə) *vb.* **shearing, sheared** *or arch., Austral., & N.Z. sometimes* **shore; sheared** *or* **shorn. 1.** (*tr.*) to remove (the fleece or hair) of (sheep, etc.) by cutting or clipping. **2.** to cut or cut through (something) with shears or a sharp instrument. **3.** *Engineering.* to cause (a part, member, etc.) to deform or fracture or (of a part, etc.) to deform or fracture as a result of excess torsion. **4.** (*tr.; often foll. by of*) to strip or divest: *to shear someone of his power.* **5.** (when *intr.*, foll. by *through*) to move through (something) by or as if by cutting. ~*n.* **6.** the act, process, or an instance of shearing. **7.** a shearing of a sheep or flock of sheep: *a sheep of two shears.* **8.** a form of deformation or fracture in which parallel planes in a body slide over one another. **9.** *Physics.* the deformation of a body, part, etc., expressed as the lateral displacement between two points in parallel planes divided by the distance between the planes. **10.** either one of the blades of a pair of shears, scissors, etc. ~See also **shears.** [OE *sceran*] —ˈ**shearer** *n.*

shearling (ˈʃɪəlɪŋ) *n.* **1.** a young sheep after its first shearing. **2.** the skin of such an animal.

shear pin *n.* an easily replaceable pin in a machine designed to break and stop the machine if the stress becomes too great.

shears (ʃɪəz) *pl. n.* **1. a.** large scissors, as for cutting cloth, jointing poultry, etc. **b.** a large scissor-like and usually hand-held cutting tool with flat blades, as for cutting hedges. **2.** any of various analogous cutting implements.

shearwater (ˈʃɪəˌwɔːtə) *n.* any of several oceanic birds specialized for an aerial or aquatic existence.

sheatfish (ˈʃiːtˌfɪʃ) *n., pl.* **-fish** *or* **-fishes.** another name for **European catfish** (see **silurid** (sense 1)). [C16: var. of *sheathfish;* ? infl. by G *Schaid* sheatfish]

sheath (ʃiːθ) *n., pl.* **sheaths** (ʃiːðz). **1.** a case or covering for the blade of a knife, sword, etc. **2.** any similar close-fitting case. **3.** *Biol.* an enclosing or protective structure. **4.** the protective covering on an electric cable. **5.** a figure-hugging dress with a narrow tapering skirt. **6.** another name for **condom.** [OE *scēath*]

sheathe (ʃiːð) *vb.* (*tr.*) **1.** to insert (a knife, sword, etc.) into a sheath. **2.** (esp. of cats) to retract (the claws). **3.** to surface with or encase in a sheath or sheathing.

sheathing (ˈʃiːðɪŋ) *n.* **1.** any material used as an outer layer, as on a ship's hull. **2.** boarding, etc., used to cover a timber frame.

sheath knife *n.* a knife carried in or protected by a sheath.

sheave[1] (ʃiːv) *vb.* (*tr.*) to gather or bind into sheaves.

sheave[2] (ʃiːv) *n.* a wheel with a grooved rim, esp. one used as a pulley. [C14: of Gmc origin]

sheaves (ʃiːvz) *n.* the plural of **sheaf.**

shebang (ʃɪˈbæŋ) *n. Sl., chiefly U.S. & Canad.* a situation or affair (esp. in **the whole shebang**). [C19: <?]

shebeen *or* **shebean** (ʃəˈbiːn) *n.* **1.** *Irish, Scot., & S. African.* a place where alcoholic drink is sold illegally. **2.** (in Ireland) alcohol, esp. home-distilled whiskey, sold without a licence. **3.** (in South Africa) a place where Black African men engage in social drinking. [C18: < Irish Gaelic *sībīn* beer of poor quality]

shebeen king *or* (*fem.*) **shebeen queen** *n.* (in South Africa) the proprietor of a shebeen.

shed[1] (ʃɛd) *n.* **1.** a small building or lean-to of light construction, used for storage, shelter, etc. **2.** a large roofed structure, esp. one with open sides, used for storage, repairing locomotives, etc. **3.** *Austral. & N.Z.* the building in which sheep are shorn. [OE *sced;* prob. var. of *scead* shelter]

shed[2] (ʃɛd) *vb.* **shedding, shed.** (*mainly tr.*) **1.** to pour forth or cause to pour forth: *to shed tears.* **2.** **shed light on** *or* **upon.** to clarify (a problem, etc.). **3.** to cast off or lose: *the snake shed its skin.* **4.** to repel: *this coat sheds water.* **5.** *N.Z.* to separate or divide a group of sheep: *a good dog can shed his sheep in minutes.* **6.** *Dialect.* to make a parting in (the hair). ~*n.* **7.** short for **watershed.** **8.** *N.Z.* the action of separating or dividing a group of sheep: *the old dog was better at the shed than the young one.* [OE *sceadan*] —ˈ**shedable** *or* ˈ**sheddable** *adj.*

she'd (ʃiːd) *contraction of* she had *or* she would.

shedder[1] (ˈʃɛdə) *n.* **1.** a person or thing that sheds. **2.** an animal, such as a llama, snake, or lobster, that moults.

shedder[2] (ˈʃɛdə) *n. N.Z.* a person who milks cows in a cow shed.

shed hand *n. Chiefly Austral.* an unskilled worker in a sheepshearing shed.

shed out *vb.* (*tr., adv.*) *N.Z.* to separate off (sheep that have lambed) and move them to better pasture.

sheen (ʃiːn) *n.* **1.** a gleaming or glistening brightness; lustre. **2.** *Poetic.* splendid clothing. ~*adj.* **3.** *Rare.* beautiful. [OE *sciene*] —ˈ**sheeny** *adj.*

sheep (ʃiːp) *n., pl.* **sheep.** **1.** any of a genus of ruminant mammals having transversely ribbed horns and a narrow face. **2.** **Barbary sheep.** another name for **aoudad.** **3.** a meek or timid person. **4. separate the sheep from the goats.** to pick out the members of a group who are superior in some respects. [OE *sceap*] —ˈ**sheepˌlike** *adj.*

sheepcote (ˈʃiːpˌkəʊt) *n. Chiefly Brit.* another word for **sheepfold.**

sheep-dip *n.* **1.** any of several liquid disinfectants and insecticides in which sheep are immersed. **2.** a deep trough containing such a liquid.

sheepdog (ˈʃiːpˌdɒg) *n.* **1.** a dog used for herding sheep. **2.** any of various breeds of dog reared originally for herding sheep. See **Old English sheepdog, Shetland sheepdog.**

sheepdog trial *n.* (*often pl.*) a competition in which sheepdogs are tested in their tasks.

sheepfold (ˈʃiːpˌfəʊld) *n.* a pen or enclosure for sheep.

sheepish (ˈʃiːpɪʃ) *adj.* **1.** abashed or embarrassed, esp. through looking foolish. **2.** resembling a sheep in timidity. —ˈ**sheepishly** *adv.* —ˈ**sheepishness** *n.*

sheepo (ˈʃiːpəʊ) *n., pl.* **sheepos.** *N.Z.* a person employed to bring sheep to the catching pen in a shearing shed.

sheep's eyes *pl. n. Old-fashioned.* amorous or inviting glances.

sheepshank (ˈʃiːpˌʃæŋk) *n.* a knot made in a rope to shorten it temporarily.

sheepskin (ˈʃiːpˌskɪn) *n.* **a.** the skin of a sheep, esp. when used for clothing, etc. **b.** (*as modifier*): *a sheepskin coat.*

sheepwalk (ˈʃiːpˌwɔːk) *n. Chiefly Brit.* a tract of land for grazing sheep.

sheer[1] (ʃɪə) *adj.* **1.** perpendicular; very steep: *a sheer cliff.* **2.** (of textiles) so fine as to be transparent. **3.** (*prenominal*) absolute: *sheer folly.* **4.** *Obs.* bright. ~*adv.* **5.** steeply. **6.** completely or absolutely. [OE *scīr*] —ˈ**sheerly** *adv.* —ˈ**sheerness** *n.*

sheer[2] (ʃɪə) *vb.* (foll. by *off* or *away* (*from*)). **1.** to deviate or cause to deviate from a course. **2.** (*intr.*) to avoid an unpleasant person, thing, topic, etc. ~*n.* **3.** *Naut.* the position of a vessel relative to its mooring. [C17: ? var. of SHEAR]

sheerlegs *or* **shearlegs** (ˈʃɪəˌlɛgz) *n.* (*functioning as sing.*) a device for lifting weights consisting of two spars lashed together at the upper ends from which a lifting tackle is suspended. Also called: **shears.** [C19: var. of *shear legs*]

sheet[1] (ʃiːt) *n.* **1.** a large rectangular piece of cloth, generally one of a pair used as inner bedclothes. **2. a.** a thin piece of a substance such as paper or glass, usually rectangular in form. **b.** (*as modifier*): *sheet iron.* **3.** a broad continuous surface: *a sheet of water.* **4.** a newspaper, esp. a tabloid. **5.** a piece of printed paper to be folded into a section for a book. ~*vb.* **6.** (*tr.*) to provide with, cover, or wrap in a sheet. [OE *sciete*]

sheet[2] (ʃiːt) *n. Naut.* a line or rope for controlling the position of a sail relative to the wind. [OE *scēata* corner of a sail]

sheet anchor *n.* **1.** *Naut.* a large strong anchor for use in emergency. **2.** a person or thing to be relied on in an emergency. [C17: < earlier *shute anker,* < *shoot* (obs.) the sheet of a sail]

sheet bend *n.* a knot used esp. for joining ropes of different sizes.

sheeting (ˈʃiːtɪŋ) *n.* fabric from which sheets are made.

sheet lightning *n.* lightning that appears as a broad sheet, caused by the reflection of more distant lightning.

sheet metal *n.* metal in the form of a sheet, the thickness being intermediate between that of plate and that of foil.

sheet music *n.* **1.** the printed or written copy of a short composition or piece. **2.** music in its written or printed form.

sheik *or* **sheikh** (ʃeɪk) *n.* (in Muslim countries) **a.** the head of an Arab tribe, village, etc. **b.** a religious leader. [C16: < Ar. *shaykh* old man] —ˈ**sheikdom** *or* ˈ**sheikhdom** *n.*

sheila (ˈʃiːlə) *n. Austral. & N.Z.* an informal word for **girl** or **woman.** [C19: < the girl's name *Sheila*]

shekel (ˈʃɛkᵊl) *n.* **1.** any of several former coins and units of weight of the Near East. **2.** (*often pl.*) *Inf.* any coin or money. [C16: < Heb. *sheqel*]

shelduck (ˈʃɛlˌdʌk) *or* (*masc.*) **sheldrake** (ˈʃɛlˌdreɪk) *n., pl.* **-ducks, -duck** *or* **-drakes, -drake.** any of various large usually brightly coloured gooselike ducks of the Old World. [C14: *shel*, prob. < dialect *sheld* pied]

shelf (ʃɛlf) *n., pl.* **shelves. 1.** a thin flat plank of wood, metal, etc., fixed horizontally against a wall, etc., for the purpose of supporting objects. **2.** something resembling this in shape or function. **3.** the objects placed on a shelf: *a shelf of books.* **4.** a projecting layer of ice, rock, etc., on land or in the sea. **5. off the shelf.** readily available from existing stock. **6. on the shelf.** put aside or abandoned; used esp. of unmarried women considered to be past the age of marriage. [OE *scylfe* ship's deck] —ˈ**shelfˌlike** *adj.*

shelf life *n.* the length of time a packaged food, etc., will last without deteriorating.

shell (ʃɛl) *n.* **1.** the protective outer layer of an egg, esp. a bird's egg. **2.** the hard outer covering of many molluscs. **3.** any other hard outer layer, such as the exoskeleton of many arthropods. **4.** the hard outer layer of some fruits, esp. of nuts. **5.** any hard outer case. **6.** a hollow artillery projectile filled with explosive primed to explode either during flight or on impact. **7.** a small-arms cartridge. **8.** a pyrotechnic cartridge designed to explode in the air. **9.** *Rowing.* a very light narrow racing boat. **10.** the external structure of a building, esp. one that is unfinished. **11.** *Physics.* a class of electron orbits in an atom in which the electrons have the same principal quantum number and little difference in their energy levels. **12. come** (*or* **bring**) **out of one's shell.** to become (or help to become) less shy and reserved. ~*vb.* **13.** to divest or be divested of a shell, husk, etc. **14.** to separate or be separated from an ear, husk, etc. **15.** (*tr.*) to bombard with artillery shells. ~See also **shell out.** [OE *sciell*] —ˈ**shell-less** *adj.* —ˈ**shell-ˌlike** *adj.* —ˈ**shelly** *adj.*

she'll (ʃiːl; *unstressed* ʃɪl) *contraction of* she will *or* she shall.

shellac (ʃəˈlæk, ˈʃɛlæk) *n.* **1.** a yellowish resin secreted by the lac insect, esp. a commercial preparation of this used in varnishes, polishes, etc. **2.** Also called: **shellac varnish.** a varnish made by dissolving shellac in ethanol or a similar solvent. ~*vb.* **-lacking, -lacked.** (*tr.*) **3.** to coat (an article) with a shellac varnish. [C18: SHELL + LAC[1], translation of F *laque en écailles*, lit.: lac in scales, that is, in thin plates]

shellback (ˈʃɛlˌbæk) *n.* an experienced or old sailor.

shellfire (ˈʃɛlˌfaɪə) *n.* the firing of artillery shells.

shellfish (ˈʃɛlˌfɪʃ) *n., pl.* **-fish** *or* **-fishes.** any aquatic invertebrate having a shell or shell-like carapace, esp. such an animal used as human food. Examples are crustaceans such as crabs and lobsters and molluscs such as oysters.

shell out *vb.* (*adv.*) *Inf.* to pay out or hand over (money).

shell program *n. Computers.* a basic low-cost computer program that provides a framework within which the user can develop the program to suit his personal requirements.

shellproof (ˈʃɛlˌpruːf) *adj.* designed, intended, or able to resist shellfire.

shell shock *n.* loss of sight, etc., resulting from psychological strain during prolonged engagement in warfare. —ˈ**shell-ˌshocked** *adj.*

Shelta (ˈʃɛltə) *n.* a secret language used by some itinerant tinkers in Ireland and parts of Britain, based on Gaelic. [C19: < earlier *sheldrū*, ? an arbitrary alteration of OIrish *bēlre* speech]

shelter (ˈʃɛltə) *n.* **1.** something that provides cover or protection, as from weather or danger. **2.** the protection afforded by such a cover. **3.** the state of being sheltered. ~*vb.* **4.** (*tr.*) to provide with or protect by a shelter. **5.** (*intr.*) to take cover, as from rain. **6.** (*tr.*) to act as a shelter for. [C16: <?] —ˈ**shelterer** *n.*

sheltered (ˈʃɛltəd) *adj.* **1.** protected from wind or weather. **2.** protected from outside influences: *a sheltered upbringing.* **3.** specially designed to provide a safe environment for the elderly, handicapped, or disabled: *sheltered housing.*

sheltie *or* **shelty** (ˈʃɛltɪ) *n., pl.* **-ties.** another name for **Shetland pony** or **Shetland sheepdog.** [C17: prob. < Orkney dialect *sjalti*, < ON *Hjalti* Shetlander, < *Hjaltland* Shetland]

shelve[1] (ʃɛlv) *vb.* (*tr.*) **1.** to place on a shelf. **2.** to provide with shelves. **3.** to put aside or postpone from consideration. **4.** to dismiss or cause to retire. —ˈ**shelver** *n.*

shelve[2] (ʃɛlv) *vb.* (*intr.*) to slope away gradually.

shelves (ʃɛlvz) *n.* the plural of **shelf.**

shelving (ˈʃɛlvɪŋ) *n.* **1.** material for making shelves. **2.** a set of shelves; shelves collectively.

shemozzle (ʃɪˈmɒzᵊl) *n. Inf.* a noisy confusion or dispute; uproar. [C19: ? < Yiddish *shlimazl* misfortune]

shenanigan (ʃɪˈnænɪgən) *n. Inf.* **1.** (*usually pl.*) roguishness; mischief. **2.** an act of treachery; deception. [C19: <?]

she-oak *n.* any of various Australian trees of the genus *Casuarina.* See **casuarina.** [C18: *she* (in the sense: inferior) + OAK]

Sheol (ˈʃiːəʊl, -ɒl) *n. Bible.* **1.** the abode of the dead. **2.** (*often not cap.*) hell. [C16: < Heb. *she'ōl*]

shepherd (ˈʃɛpəd) *n.* **1.** a person employed to tend sheep. Fem. equivalent: **shepherdess. 2.** a person, such as a clergyman, who watches over a group of people. ~*vb.* (*tr.*) **3.** to guide or watch over in the manner of a shepherd. **4.** *Australian Rules football, rugby, etc.* to prevent opponents from tackling (a member of one's own team) by blocking their path: illegal in rugby.

shepherd dog *n.* another term for **sheepdog** (sense 1).

shepherd's pie *n. Chiefly Brit.* a baked dish of minced meat covered with mashed potato.

shepherd's-purse *n.* a plant having small white flowers and flattened triangular seed pods.

shepherd's weatherglass *n. Brit.* another name for the **scarlet pimpernel.**

Sheraton (ˈʃɛrətən) *adj.* denoting furniture made by or in the style of Thomas Sheraton (1751–1806), English furniture maker, characterized by lightness and elegance.

sherbet (ˈʃɜːbət) *n.* **1.** a fruit-flavoured slightly effervescent powder, eaten as a sweet or used to make a drink. **2.** another word (esp. U.S. and Canad.) for **sorbet** (sense 1). [C17: < Turkish, < Persian, < Ar. *sharbah* drink, < *shariba* to drink]

sherd (ʃɜːd) *n.* another word for **shard.**

sherif *or* **shereef** (ʃɛˈriːf) *n. Islam.* **1.** a descendant of Mohammed through his daughter Fatima. **2.** an honorific title accorded to any Muslim ruler. [C16: < Ar. *sharīf* noble]

sheriff (ˈʃɛrɪf) *n.* **1.** (in the U.S.) the chief elected law-enforcement officer in a county. **2.** (in Canada) a municipal official who enforces court orders, escorts convicted criminals to prison, etc. **3.** (in England and Wales) the chief executive officer of the Crown in a county, having chiefly ceremonial duties. **4.** (in Scotland) a judge in any of the sheriff courts. [OE *scīrgerēfa*, < *scīr* SHIRE + *gerēfa* REEVE[1]] —ˈ**sheriffdom** *n.*

sheriff court *n.* (in Scotland) a court having jurisdiction to try all but the most serious crimes and to deal with most civil actions.

Sherpa (ˈʃɜːpə) *n., pl.* **-pas** *or* **-pa.** a member of a people of Mongolian origin living on the southern slopes of the Himalayas in Nepal, noted as mountaineers.

sherry (ˈʃɛrɪ) *n., pl.* **-ries.** a fortified wine, originally only from the Jerez region of southern Spain. [C16: < earlier *sherris* (assumed to be pl.), < Sp. *Xeres*, now *Jerez*]

sherwani (ʃɛəˈwɑːnɪ) *n.* a long coat closed up to the neck, worn by men in India. [Hindi]

she's (ʃiːz) *contraction of* she is *or* she has.

Shetland pony (ˈʃɛtlənd) *n.* a very small sturdy breed of pony with a long shaggy mane and tail.

Shetland sheepdog *n.* a small dog similar in appearance to a collie.

shew (ʃəʊ) *vb.* **shewing, shewed; shewn** *or* **shewed.** an archaic spelling of **show.**

shewbread *or* **showbread** (ˈʃəʊˌbrɛd) *n. Bible.* the loaves of bread placed every Sabbath on the table beside the altar of incense in the tabernacle or temple of ancient Israel.

SHF *or* **shf** *Radio. abbrev. for* superhigh frequency.

Shiah *or* **Shia** (ˈʃiːə) *n.* **1.** one of the two main branches of Islam, now mainly in Iran, which regards Mohammed's cousin Ali and his successors as the true imams. *~adj.* **2.** designating or characteristic of this sect or its beliefs and practices. [C17: < Ar. *shīʿah* sect, < *shāʿa* to follow]

shibboleth (ˈʃɪbəˌlɛθ) *n.* **1.** a slogan or catch phrase, usually considered outworn, characteristic of a particular party or sect. **2.** a custom, phrase, or use of language that acts as a test of belonging to, or as a stumbling block to joining a particular social class, profession, etc. [C14: < Heb., lit.: ear of grain; the word is used in the Old Testament by the Gileadites as a test word for the Ephraimites, who could not pronounce the sound *sh*]

shickered (ˈʃɪkəd) *adj. Austral. & N.Z. sl.* drunk; intoxicated. [via Yiddish < Heb.]

shied (ʃaɪd) *vb.* the past tense and past participle of **shy**[1] and **shy**[2].

shield (ʃiːld) *n.* **1.** any protection used to intercept blows, missiles, etc., such as a tough piece of armour carried on the arm. **2.** any similar protective device. **3.** *Heraldry.* a pointed stylized shield used for displaying armorial bearings. **4.** anything that resembles a shield in shape, such as a prize in a sports competition. **5.** *Physics.* a structure of concrete, lead, etc., placed around a nuclear reactor. **6.** a broad stable plateau of ancient Precambrian rocks forming the rigid nucleus of a particular continent. **7. the shield.** *N.Z.* the Ranfurly Shield, a trophy competed for by provincial rugby teams. *~vb.* (*tr.*) **8.** to protect, hide, or conceal (something) from danger or harm. [OE *scield*] —**ˈshieldˌlike** *adj.*

Shield (ʃiːld) *n.* **the.** *Canad.* another term for the **Canadian Shield.**

Shield cricket *n. Austral.* the interstate cricket competition held for the Sheffield Shield.

Shield rugby *n. N.Z.* the rugby competition held between provinces for the Ranfurly Shield.

shieling (ˈʃiːlɪŋ) *or* **shiel** (ʃiːl) *n. Chiefly Scot.* **1.** a temporary shelter used by people tending cattle on high or remote ground. **2.** pasture land for the grazing of cattle in summer. [C16: < earlier *shiel*, < ME *shale* hut, <?]

shier (ˈʃaɪə) *adj.* a comparative of **shy**[1].

shiest (ˈʃaɪɪst) *adj.* a superlative of **shy**[1].

shift (ʃɪft) *vb.* **1.** to move or cause to move from one place or position to another. **2.** (*tr.*) to change for another or others. **3.** to change (gear) in a motor vehicle. **4.** (*intr.*) (of a sound or set of sounds) to alter in a systematic way. **5.** (*intr.*) to provide for one's needs (esp. in **shift for oneself**). **6.** to remove or be removed, esp. with difficulty: *no detergent can shift these stains.* **7.** (*intr.*) *Sl.* to move quickly. *~n.* **8.** the act or an instance of shifting. **9.** a group of workers who work for a specific period. **10.** the period of time worked by such a group. **11.** an expedient, contrivance, or artifice. **12.** an underskirt or dress with little shaping. [OE *sciftan*] —**ˈshifter** *n.*

shiftless (ˈʃɪftlɪs) *adj.* lacking in ambition or initiative. —**ˈshiftlessness** *n.*

shifty (ˈʃɪftɪ) *adj.* **shiftier, shiftiest.** **1.** given to evasions. **2.** furtive in character or appearance. —**ˈshiftily** *adv.* —**ˈshiftiness** *n.*

shigella (ʃɪˈgɛlə) *n.* any of a genus of rod-shaped bacteria, some species of which cause dysentery. [C20: after K. *Shiga* (1870–1957), Japanese bacteriologist, who discovered them]

Shiite (ˈʃiːaɪt) *or* **Shiah** *Islam.* *~n.* **1.** an adherent of Shiah. *~adj.* **2.** of or relating to Shiah. —**Shiism** (ˈʃiːɪzəm) *n.* —**Shiitic** (ʃiːˈɪtɪk) *adj.*

shillelagh *or* **shillala** (ʃəˈleɪlə, -lɪ) *n.* (in Ireland) a stout club or cudgel. [C18: < Irish Gaelic *sail* cudgel + *éille* leash, thong]

shilling (ˈʃɪlɪŋ) *n.* **1.** a British silver or (later) cupronickel coin worth one twentieth of a pound, replaced by the 5p piece in 1970. Abbrev.: **s., sh.** **2.** the standard monetary unit of Kenya, Uganda, the Somali Republic, and Tanzania. [OE *scilling*]

shillyshally (ˈʃɪlɪˌʃælɪ) *Inf.* *~vb.* **-lying, -lied.** **1.** (*intr.*) to be indecisive, esp. over unimportant matters. *~adv.* **2.** in an indecisive manner. *~adj.* **3.** indecisive or hesitant. *~n., pl.* **-lies.** **4.** vacillation. [C18: < *shill I shall I*, by reduplication of *shall I*] —**ˈshillyˌshallier** *n.*

shily (ˈʃaɪlɪ) *adv.* a less common spelling of **shyly.** See **shy**[1].

shim (ʃɪm) *n.* **1.** a thin washer or strip often used with a number of similar washers or strips to adjust a clearance for gears, etc. *~vb.* **shimming, shimmed.** **2.** (*tr.*) to modify clearance on (a gear, etc.) by use of shims. [C18: <?]

shimmer (ˈʃɪmə) *vb.* **1.** (*intr.*) to shine with a glistening or tremulous light. *~n.* **2.** a faint, glistening, or tremulous light. [OE *scimerian*] —**ˈshimmering** *or* **ˈshimmery** *adj.*

shimmy (ˈʃɪmɪ) *n., pl.* **-mies.** **1.** an American ragtime dance with much shaking of the hips and shoulders. **2.** abnormal wobbling motion in a motor vehicle, esp. in the front wheels or steering. *~vb.* **-mying, -mied.** (*intr.*) **3.** to dance the shimmy. **4.** to vibrate or wobble. [C19: changed < CHEMISE, mistaken for pl.]

shin (ʃɪn) *n.* **1.** the front part of the lower leg. **2.** the front edge of the tibia. **3.** *Chiefly Brit.* a cut of beef, the lower foreleg. *~vb.* **shinning, shinned.** **4.** (when *intr.*, often foll. by *up*) to climb (a pole, tree, etc.) by gripping with the hands or arms and the legs and hauling oneself up. **5.** (*tr.*) to kick (a person) in the shins. [OE *scinu*]

shinbone (ˈʃɪnˌbəʊn) *n.* the nontechnical name for **tibia** (sense 1).

shindig (ˈʃɪnˌdɪg) *or* **shindy** (ˈʃɪndɪ) *n., pl.* **-digs** *or* **-dies.** *Sl.* **1.** a noisy party, dance, etc. **2.** a quarrel or commotion. [C19: var. of SHINTY]

shine (ʃaɪn) *vb.* **shining, shone.** **1.** (*intr.*) to emit light. **2.** (*intr.*) to glow or be bright with reflected light. **3.** (*tr.*) to direct the light of (a lamp, etc.): *he shone the torch in my eyes.* **4.** (*tr.; p.t. & p.p.* **shined**) to cause to gleam by polishing: *to shine shoes.* **5.** (*intr.*) to excel: *she shines at tennis.* **6.** (*intr.*) to appear clearly. *~n.* **7.** the state or quality of shining; sheen; lustre. **8.** *Inf.* a liking or fancy (esp. in **take a shine to**). [OE *scīnan*]

shiner (ˈʃaɪnə) *n.* **1.** something that shines, such as a polishing device. **2.** any of numerous small North American freshwater cyprinid fishes. **3.** *Inf.* a black eye. **4.** *N.Z. old-fashioned inf.* a tramp.

shingle[1] (ˈʃɪŋgᵊl) *n.* **1.** a thin rectangular tile, esp. one made of wood, that is laid with others in overlapping rows to cover a roof or a wall. **2.** a woman's short-cropped hairstyle. **3.** *U.S. & Canad.* a small signboard fixed outside the office of a doctor, lawyer, etc. *~vb.* (*tr.*) **4.** to cover (a roof or a wall) with shingles. **5.** to cut (the hair) in a short-cropped style. [C12 *scingle*, < LL *scindula* a split piece of wood, < L *scindere* to split] —ˈ**shingler** *n.*

shingle[2] (ˈʃɪŋgᵊl) *n.* **1.** coarse gravel, esp. the pebbles found on beaches. **2.** a place or area strewn with shingle. [C16: of Scand. origin] —ˈ**shingly** *adj.*

shingles (ˈʃɪŋgᵊlz) *n.* (*functioning as sing.*) an acute viral disease characterized by inflammation, pain, and skin eruptions along the course of affected nerves. Technical names: **herpes zoster, zoster.** [C14: < Med. L *cingulum* girdle, rendering Gk *zōnē* zone]

Shinto (ˈʃɪntəʊ) *n.* the indigenous religion of Japan, incorporating the worship of a number of ethnic divinities. [C18: < Japanese: the way of the gods, < Chinese *shên* gods + *tao* way] —ˈ**Shintoism** *n.* —ˈ**Shintoist** *n., adj.*

shinty (ˈʃɪntɪ) *n.* **1.** a game resembling hockey played with a ball and sticks curved at the lower end. **2.** (*pl.* **-ties**) the stick used in this game. [C17: prob. < the cry *shin ye* in the game]

shiny (ˈʃaɪnɪ) *adj.* **shinier, shiniest. 1.** glossy or polished; bright. **2.** (of clothes or material) worn to a smooth and glossy state, as by continual rubbing. —ˈ**shininess** *n.*

ship (ʃɪp) *n.* **1.** a vessel propelled by engines or sails for navigating on the water, esp. a large vessel. **2.** *Naut.* a large sailing vessel with three or more square-rigged masts. **3.** the crew of a ship. **4.** short for **airship** or **spaceship. 5. when one's ship comes in** (*or* **home**). when one has become successful. ~*vb.* **shipping, shipped. 6.** to place, transport, or travel on any conveyance, esp. aboard a ship. **7.** (*tr.*) *Naut.* to take (water) over the side. **8.** to bring or go aboard a vessel: *to ship oars.* **9.** (*tr.; often foll. by off*) *Inf.* to send away: *they shipped the children off to boarding school.* **10.** (*intr.*) to engage to serve aboard a ship: *I shipped aboard a Liverpool liner.* [OE *scip*] —ˈ**shippable** *adj.*

-ship *suffix forming nouns.* **1.** indicating state or condition: *fellowship.* **2.** indicating rank, office, or position: *lordship.* **3.** indicating craft or skill: *scholarship.* [OE *-scipe*]

shipboard (ˈʃɪpˌbɔːd) *n.* (*modifier*) taking place, used, or intended for use aboard a ship: *a shipboard encounter.*

shipbuilder (ˈʃɪpˌbɪldə) *n.* a person or business engaged in building ships. —ˈ**shipˌbuilding** *n.*

ship chandler *n.* a person or business dealing in supplies for ships. —**ship chandlery** *n.*

shipload (ˈʃɪpˌləʊd) *n.* the quantity carried by a ship.

shipmaster (ˈʃɪpˌmɑːstə) *n.* the master or captain of a ship.

shipmate (ˈʃɪpˌmeɪt) *n.* a sailor who serves on the same ship as another.

shipment (ˈʃɪpmənt) *n.* **1. a.** goods shipped together as part of the same lot: *a shipment of grain.* **b.** (*as modifier*): *a shipment schedule.* **2.** the act of shipping cargo.

ship money *n. English history.* a tax levied to finance the fitting out of warships: abolished 1640.

ship of the line *n. Naut.* (formerly) a warship large enough to fight in the first line of battle.

shipowner (ˈʃɪpˌəʊnə) *n.* a person who owns or has shares in a ship or ships.

shipper (ˈʃɪpə) *n.* a person or company in the business of shipping freight.

shipping (ˈʃɪpɪŋ) *n.* **1. a.** the business of transporting freight, esp. by ship. **b.** (*as modifier*): *a shipping magnate.* **2.** ships collectively: *there is a lot of shipping in the Channel.*

ship's biscuit *n.* another name for **hardtack.**

shipshape (ˈʃɪpˌʃeɪp) *adj.* **1.** neat; orderly. ~*adv.* **2.** in a neat and orderly manner.

shipworm (ˈʃɪpˌwɜːm) *n.* any of a genus of wormlike marine bivalve molluscs that bore into wooden piers, ships, etc., by means of drill-like shell valves.

shipwreck (ˈʃɪpˌrɛk) *n.* **1.** the partial or total destruction of a ship at sea. **2.** a wrecked ship or part of such a ship. **3.** ruin or destruction: *the shipwreck of all my hopes.* ~*vb.* (*tr.*) **4.** to wreck or destroy (a ship). **5.** to bring to ruin or destruction. [OE *scipwræc,* < SHIP + *wræc* something driven by the sea]

shipwright (ˈʃɪpˌraɪt) *n.* an artisan skilled in one or more of the tasks required to build vessels.

shipyard (ˈʃɪpˌjɑːd) *n.* a place or facility for the building, maintenance, and repair of ships.

shiralee (ˌʃɪrəˈliː) *n. Austral. sl.* a swagman's bundle. [<?]

shire (ˈʃaɪə) *n.* **1. a.** one of the British counties. **b.** (*in combination*): *Yorkshire.* **2.** (in Australia) a rural district having its own local council. **3.** See **shire horse. 4. the Shires.** the Midland counties of England, famous for hunting, etc. [OE *scīr* office]

shire horse *n.* a large heavy breed of carthorse with long hair on the fetlocks.

shirk (ʃɜːk) *vb.* **1.** to avoid discharging (work, a duty, etc.); evade. ~*n. also* **shirker. 2.** a person who shirks. [C17: prob. < G *Schurke* rogue]

shirr (ʃɜː) *vb.* **1.** to gather (fabric) into two or more parallel rows to decorate a dress, blouse, etc., often using elastic thread. **2.** (*tr.*) to bake (eggs) out of their shells. ~*n. also* **shirring. 3.** a series of gathered rows decorating a dress, blouse, etc. [C19: <?]

shirt (ʃɜːt) *n.* **1.** a garment worn on the upper part of the body, esp. by men, usually having a collar and sleeves and buttoning up the front. **2.** short for **nightshirt. 3. keep your shirt on.** *Inf.* refrain from losing your temper. **4. put** *or* **lose one's shirt on.** *Inf.* to bet or lose all one has on (a horse, etc.). [OE *scyrte*]

shirting (ˈʃɜːtɪŋ) *n.* fabric used in making men's shirts.

shirtsleeve (ˈʃɜːtˌsliːv) *n.* **1.** the sleeve of a shirt. **2. in one's shirtsleeves.** not wearing a jacket.

shirt-tail *n.* the part of a shirt that extends below the waist.

shirtwaister (ˈʃɜːtˌweɪstə) *or U.S.* **shirtwaist** *n.* a woman's dress with a tailored bodice resembling a shirt.

shirty (ˈʃɜːtɪ) *adj.* **shirtier, shirtiest.** *Sl., chiefly Brit.* bad-tempered or annoyed. [C19: ? based on such phrases as *to get someone's shirt out* to annoy someone] —ˈ**shirtily** *adv.*

shish kebab (ˈʃiːʃ kəˈbæb) *n.* the full term for **kebab.** [< Turkish *şiş kebab,* < *şiş* skewer; see KEBAB]

shit (ʃɪt) *Taboo.* ~*vb.* **shitting; shitted** *or* **shit. 1.** to defecate. ~*n.* **2.** faeces; excrement. **3.** *Sl.* rubbish; nonsense. **4.** *Sl.* an obnoxious or worthless person. ~*interj.* **5.** *Sl.* an exclamation expressing anger, disgust, etc. [OE *scite* (unattested) dung, *scītan* to defecate, of Gmc origin] —ˈ**shitty** *adj.*

shiv (ʃɪv) *n.* a variant of **chiv.**

Shiva (ˈʃiːvə, ˈʃɪvə) *n.* a variant spelling of **Siva.**

shivaree (ˌʃɪvəˈriː) *n.* a variant spelling (esp. U.S. and Canad.) of **charivari.**

shiver[1] (ˈʃɪvə) *vb.* (*intr.*) **1.** to shake or tremble, as from cold or fear. ~*n.* **2.** the act of shivering; a tremulous motion. **3. the shivers.** an attack of shivering, esp. through fear or illness. [C13 *chiveren,* ? var. of *chevelen* to chatter (used of teeth), < OE *ceafl* jowl] —ˈ**shiverer** *n.* —ˈ**shivering** *n., adj.* —ˈ**shivery** *adj.*

shiver[2] (ˈʃɪvə) *vb.* **1.** to break or cause to break into fragments. ~*n.* **2.** a splintered piece. [C13: of Gmc origin]

shivoo (ʃɪˈvuː) *n., pl.* **shivoos.** *Austral. sl.* a party or celebration. [C19: < E dialect]

shoal[1] (ʃəʊl) *n.* **1.** a stretch of shallow water. **2.** a sandbank or rocky area, esp. one that is visible at low water. ~*vb.* **3.** to make or become shallow. **4.** (*intr.*) *Naut.* to sail into shallower water. ~*adj. also* **shoaly. 5.** a less common word for **shallow.** [OE *sceald* shallow]

shoal[2] (ʃəʊl) *n.* **1.** a large group of fish. **2.** a large group of people or things. ~*vb.* **3.** (*intr.*) to collect together in such a group. [OE *scolu*]

shock[1] (ʃɒk) *vb.* **1.** to experience or cause to experience extreme horror, disgust, surprise, etc.: *the atrocities shocked us.* **2.** to cause a state of shock in (a person). **3.** to come or cause to come into violent contact. ~*n.* **4.** a sudden and violent jarring blow or impact. **5.** something that causes a sudden and violent disturbance in the emotions. **6.** *Pathol.* a state of bodily collapse, as from severe bleeding, burns, fright, etc. **7.** Also: **electric shock.** pain and muscular spasm as the physical reaction to an electric current passing through the body. [C16: < OF *choc.* < *choquier* to make violent contact with] —ˈ**shockable** *adj.*

shock[2] (ʃɒk) *n.* **1.** a number of sheaves set on end in a field to dry. **2.** a pile or stack of unthreshed corn. ~*vb.* **3.** (*tr.*) to set up (sheaves) in shocks. [C14: prob. of Gmc origin]

shock[3] (ʃɒk) *n.* a thick bushy mass, esp. of hair. [C19: ? < SHOCK[2]]

shock absorber *n.* any device designed to absorb mechanical shock, esp. one fitted to a motor vehicle to damp the recoil of the road springs.

shocker (ˈʃɒkə) *n. Inf.* **1.** a person or thing that shocks. **2.** a sensational novel, film, or play.

shockheaded (ˈʃɒkˌhɛdɪd) *adj.* having a head of bushy or tousled hair.

shocking (ˈʃɒkɪŋ) *adj.* **1.** causing shock, horror, or disgust. **2. shocking pink. a.** of a garish shade of pink. **b.** (*as n.*): *dressed in shocking pink.* **3.** *Inf.* very bad or terrible: *shocking weather.* —ˈ**shockingly** *adv.*

shockproof (ˈʃɒkˌpruːf) *adj.* capable of absorbing shock without damage.

shock therapy *or* **treatment** *n.* the treatment of certain psychotic conditions by injecting drugs or by passing an electric current through the brain (**electroconvulsive therapy**) to produce convulsions or coma.

shock troops *pl. n.* soldiers specially trained and equipped to carry out an assault.

shock wave *n.* a region across which there is a rapid pressure, temperature, and density rise caused by a body moving supersonically in a gas or by a detonation. See also **sonic boom.**

shod (ʃɒd) *vb.* the past participle of **shoe.**

shoddy (ˈʃɒdɪ) *adj.* **-dier, -diest. 1.** imitating something of better quality. **2.** of poor quality. ~*n., pl.* **-dies. 3.** a yarn or fabric made from wool waste or clippings. **4.** anything of inferior quality that is designed to simulate superior quality. [C19: <?] —ˈ**shoddily** *adv.* —ˈ**shoddiness** *n.*

shoe (ʃuː) *n.* **1. a.** one of a matching pair of coverings shaped to fit the foot, esp. one ending below the ankle, having an upper of leather, plastic, etc., on a sole and heel of heavier material. **b.** (*as modifier*): *shoe cleaner.* **2.** anything resembling a shoe in shape, function, position, etc., such as a horseshoe. **3.** a band of metal or wood on the bottom of the runner of a sledge. **4.** *Engineering.* a lining to protect from wear: see **brake shoe. 5. be in (a person's) shoes.** *Inf.* to be in (another person's) situation. ~*vb.* **shoeing, shod.** (*tr.*) **6.** to furnish with shoes. **7.** to fit (a horse) with horseshoes. **8.** to furnish with a hard cover, such as a metal plate, for protection against friction or bruising. [OE *scōh*]

shoeblack (ˈʃuːˌblæk) *n.* (esp. formerly) a person who shines boots and shoes.

shoehorn (ˈʃuːˌhɔːn) *n.* **1.** a smooth curved implement of horn, metal, plastic, etc., inserted at the heel of a shoe to ease the foot into it. ~*vb.* (*tr.*) **2.** to cram (people or things) into a small space.

shoelace (ˈʃuːˌleɪs) *n.* a cord for fastening shoes.

shoe leather *n.* **1.** leather used to make shoes. **2. save shoe leather.** to avoid wearing out shoes, as by taking a bus rather than walking.

shoemaker (ˈʃuːˌmeɪkə) *n.* a person who makes or repairs shoes or boots. —ˈ**shoeˌmaking** *n.*

shoer (ˈʃuːə) *n. Rare.* a person who shoes horses.

shoeshine (ˈʃuːˌʃaɪn) *n.* the act or an instance of polishing a pair of shoes.

shoestring (ˈʃuːˌstrɪŋ) *n.* **1.** another word for **shoelace. 2.** *Inf.* a very small or petty amount of money (esp. in **on a shoestring**).

shoetree (ˈʃuːˌtriː) *n.* a wooden or metal form inserted into a shoe or boot to stretch it or preserve its shape.

shofar *or* **shophar** (*Hebrew* ʃɔˈfar) *n., pl.* **-fars, -phars** *or* **-froth, -phroth** (*Hebrew* -ˈfrɔt). *Judaism.* a ram's horn sounded on certain religious occasions. [< Heb. *shōphār* ram's horn]

shogun (ˈʃəʊˌguːn) *n. Japanese history.* (from about 1192 to 1867) any of a line of hereditary military dictators who relegated the emperors to a position of purely theoretical supremacy. [C17: < Japanese, < Chinese *chiang chün* general, < *chiang* to lead + *chün* army] —ˈ**shogunate** *n.*

shone (ʃɒn; *U.S.* ʃəʊn) *vb.* a past tense and past participle of **shine.**

shoo (ʃuː) *sentence substitute.* **1.** go away!: used to drive away unwanted or annoying people, animals, etc. ~*vb.* **shooing, shooed. 2.** (*tr.*) to drive away by or as if by crying "shoo". **3.** (*intr.*) to cry "shoo". [C15: imit.]

shoo-in *n. U.S. & Canad.* a person or thing that is certain to win or succeed.

shook[1] (ʃʊk) *n.* **1.** a set of parts ready for assembly, esp. of a barrel. **2.** a group of sheaves piled together on end; shock. [C18: <?]

shook[2] (ʃʊk) *vb.* the past tense of **shake.**

shoon (ʃuːn) *n. Dialect, chiefly Scot.* a plural of **shoe.**

shoot (ʃuːt) *vb.* **shooting, shot. 1.** (*tr.*) to hit, wound, damage, or kill with a missile discharged from a weapon. **2.** to discharge (a missile or missiles) from a weapon. **3.** to fire (a weapon) or (of a weapon) to be fired. **4.** to send out or be sent out as if from a weapon: *he shot questions at her.* **5.** (*intr.*) to move very rapidly. **6.** (*tr.*) to slide or push into or out of a fastening: *to shoot a bolt.* **7.** to emit (a ray of light) or (of a ray of light) to be emitted. **8.** (*tr.*) to go or pass quickly over or through: *to shoot rapids.* **9.** (*intr.*) to hunt game with a gun for sport. **10.** (*tr.*) to pass over (an area) in hunting game. **11.** (*intr.*) (of a plant) to produce (buds, branches, etc.). **12.** to photograph or record (a sequence, etc.). **13.** (*tr.; usually passive*) to variegate or streak, as with colour. **14.** *Soccer, hockey, etc.* to hit or propel (the ball, etc.) towards the goal. **15.** (*tr.*) *Sport, chiefly U.S. & Canad.* to score (strokes, etc.): *he shot 72 on the first round.* **16.** (*tr.*) to measure the altitude of (a celestial body). **17.** (often foll. by *up*) *Sl.* to inject (someone, esp. oneself) with (a drug, esp. heroin). **18. shoot a line.** *Sl.* **a.** to boast. **b.** to tell a lie. **19. shoot oneself in the foot.** *Inf.* to damage one's own cause inadvertently. ~*n.* **20.** the act of shooting. **21.** the action or motion of something that is shot. **22.** the first aerial part of a plant to develop from a germinating seed. **23.** any new growth of a plant, such as a bud, etc. **24.** *Chiefly Brit.* a meeting or party organized for hunting game with guns. **25.** an area where game can be hunted with guns. **26.** a steep descent in a stream; rapid. **27. the whole shoot.** *Sl.* everything. ~*interj.* **28.** *U.S. & Canad.* an exclamation expressing disbelief, scepticism, etc. ~See also **shoot down, shoot through.** [OE *sceōtan*] —ˈ**shooter** *n.*

shoot down *vb.* (*tr., adv.*) **1.** to shoot callously. **2.** to defeat or disprove: *he shot down her argument.*

shooting box *n.* a small country house providing accommodation for a shooting party. Also called: **shooting lodge.**

shooting brake *n. Brit.* another name for **estate car.**

shooting star *n. Inf.* a meteor.

shooting stick *n.* a device that resembles a walking stick, having a spike at one end and a folding seat at the other.

shoot through *vb.* (*intr., adv.*) *Austral. inf.* to leave; go away.

shop (ʃɒp) *n.* **1.** a place, esp. a small building, for the retail sale of goods and services. **2.** an act or instance of shopping. **3.** a place for the performance of a specified type of work; workshop. **4. all over the shop.** *Inf.* **a.** in disarray: *his papers were all over the shop.* **b.** in every direction: *I've searched for it all over the shop.* **5. shut up shop.** to close business at the end of the day or permanently. **6. talk shop.** *Inf.* to discuss one's business, profession, etc., esp. on a social occasion. ~*vb.* **shopping, shopped.** **7.** (*intr.;* often foll. by *for*) to visit a shop or shops in search of (goods) with the intention of buying them. **8.** (*tr.*) *Sl., chiefly Brit.* to inform on (someone), esp. to the police. [OE *sceoppa* stall] —**'shopping** *n.*

shop around *vb.* (*intr., adv.*) *Inf.* **1.** to visit a number of shops or stores to compare goods and prices. **2.** to consider a number of possibilities before making a choice.

shop assistant *n.* a person who serves in a shop.

shop floor *n.* **1.** the part of a factory housing the machines and men directly involved in production. **2.** workers, esp. factory workers organized in a union.

shopkeeper ('ʃɒpˌkiːpə) *n.* a person who owns or manages a shop or small store. —**'shop-ˌkeeping** *n.*

shoplifter ('ʃɒpˌlɪftə) *n.* a customer who steals goods from a shop. —**'shopˌlifting** *n.*

shopper ('ʃɒpə) *n.* **1.** a person who buys goods in a shop. **2.** a bag for shopping.

shopping centre *n.* **1.** the area of a town where most of the shops are situated. **2.** a complex of stores, restaurants, etc., with an adjoining car park.

shopping mall *n. U.S., Canad., & Austral.* a large enclosed shopping centre, often with central heating and air conditioning.

shopping plaza *n. Chiefly U.S. & Canad.* a shopping centre, esp. a small group of stores built as a strip.

shopsoiled ('ʃɒpˌsɔɪld) *adj.* worn, faded, etc., from being displayed in a shop or store.

shop steward *n.* an elected representative of the union workers in a shop, factory, etc.

shoptalk ('ʃɒpˌtɔːk) *n.* conversation concerning one's work, esp. when carried on outside business hours.

shopwalker ('ʃɒpˌwɔːkə) *n. Brit.* a person employed by a departmental store to supervise sales personnel, assist customers, etc.

shoran ('ʃɔːræn) *n.* a short-range radar system by which an aircraft, ship, etc., can accurately determine its position. [C20: *sho(rt-)ra(nge) n(avigation)*]

shore[1] (ʃɔː) *n.* **1.** the land along the edge of a sea, lake, or wide river. Related adj.: **littoral.** **2. a.** land, as opposed to water. **b.** (*as modifier*): *shore duty.* **3.** *Law.* the tract of coastland lying between the ordinary marks of high and low water. **4.** (*often pl.*) a country: *his native shores.* [C14: prob. < MLow G, MDu. *schōre*]

shore[2] (ʃɔː) *n.* **1.** a prop or beam used to support a wall, building, etc. ~*vb.* **2.** (*tr.;* often foll. by *up*) to make safe with or as if with a shore. [C15: < MDu. *schōre*] —**'shoring** *n.*

shore[3] (ʃɔː) *vb. Arch., Austral., & N.Z.* a past tense of **shear.**

shore bird *n.* any of various birds that live close to water, esp. plovers, sandpipers, etc. Also called (Brit.): **wader.**

shore leave *n. Naval.* **1.** permission to go ashore, esp. when granted to an officer. **2.** time spent ashore during leave.

shoreless ('ʃɔːlɪs) *adj.* **1.** without a shore suitable for landing. **2.** *Poetic.* boundless; vast.

shoreline ('ʃɔːˌlaɪn) *n.* the edge of a body of water.

shoreward ('ʃɔːwəd) *adj.* **1.** near or facing the shore. ~*adv. also* **shorewards. 2.** towards the shore.

shorn (ʃɔːn) *vb.* a past participle of **shear.**

short (ʃɔːt) *adj.* **1.** of little length; not long. **2.** of little height; not tall. **3.** of limited duration. **4.** deficient: *the number of places laid at the table was short by four.* **5.** (*postpositive;* often foll. by *of* or *on*) lacking (in) or needful (of): *I'm always short of money.* **6.** concise; succinct. **7.** (of drinks) consisting chiefly of a spirit, such as whisky. **8.** *Cricket.* (of a fielding position) near the batsman: *short leg.* **9.** lacking in the power of retentiveness: *a short memory.* **10.** abrupt to the point of rudeness: *the salesgirl was very short with him.* **11.** (of betting odds) almost even. **12.** *Finance.* **a.** not possessing the securities or commodities that have been sold under contract and therefore obliged to make a purchase before the delivery date. **b.** of or relating to such sales, which depend on falling prices for profit. **13.** *Phonetics.* **a.** denoting a vowel of relatively brief temporal duration. **b.** (in popular usage) denoting the qualities of the five English vowels represented orthographically in the words *pat, pet, pit, pot, put,* and *putt.* **14.** *Prosody.* **a.** denoting a vowel that is phonetically short or a syllable containing such a vowel. **b.** (of a vowel or syllable in verse) not carrying emphasis or accent. **15.** (of pastry) crumbly in texture. **16. in short supply.** scarce. **17. short and sweet.** unexpectedly brief. **18. short for.** an abbreviation for. ~*adv.* **19.** abruptly: *to stop short.* **20.** briefly or concisely. **21.** rudely or curtly. **22.** *Finance.* without possessing the securities or commodities at the time of their contractual sale: *to sell short.* **23. caught** *or* **taken short.** having a sudden need to urinate or defecate. **24. go short.** not to have a sufficient amount, etc. **25. short of.** except: *nothing short of a miracle can save him now.* ~*n.* **26.** anything that is short. **27.** a drink of spirits. **28.** *Phonetics, prosody.* a short vowel or syllable. **29.** *Finance.* **a.** a short contract or sale. **b.** a short seller. **30.** a short film, usually of a factual nature. **31.** See **short circuit. 32. for short.** *Inf.* as an abbreviation: *he is called J.R. for short.* **33. in short. a.** as a summary. **b.** in a few words. ~*vb.* **34.** See **short circuit** (sense 2). ~See also **shorts.** [OE *scort*] —**'shortness** *n.*

shortage ('ʃɔːtɪdʒ) *n.* a deficiency or lack in the amount needed, expected, or due; deficit.

shortbread ('ʃɔːtˌbrɛd) *n.* a rich crumbly biscuit made with a large proportion of butter.

shortcake ('ʃɔːtˌkeɪk) *n.* **1.** shortbread. **2.** a dessert made of layers of biscuit or cake filled with fruit and cream.

short-change *vb.* (*tr.*) **1.** to give less than correct change to. **2.** *Sl.* to cheat or swindle.

short circuit *n.* **1.** a faulty or accidental connection between two points of different potential in an electric circuit, establishing a path of low resistance through which an excessive current can flow. ~*vb.* **short-circuit. 2.** to develop or cause to develop a short circuit. **3.** (*tr.*) to bypass (a procedure, etc.). **4.** (*tr.*) to hinder or frustrate (plans, etc.). ~Sometimes (for senses 1, 2) shortened to **short.**

shortcoming ('ʃɔːtˌkʌmɪŋ) *n.* a failing, defect, or deficiency.

short covering *n.* the purchase of securities or commodities by a short seller to meet delivery requirements.

shortcrust pastry ('ʃɔːtˌkrʌst) *n.* a basic type of pastry that has a crisp but crumbly texture. Also: **short pastry.**

short cut *n.* **1.** a route that is shorter than the usual one. **2.** a means of saving time or effort. ~*vb.* **short-cut, -cutting, -cut. 3.** (*intr.*) to use a short cut.

short-dated *adj.* (of a gilt-edged security) having less than five years to run before redemption. Cf. **medium-dated, long-dated.**

short-day *adj.* (of plants) able to flower only if exposed to short periods of daylight, each followed by a long dark period. Cf. **long-day.**

shorten ('ʃɔːtᵊn) *vb.* **1.** to make or become short or shorter. **2.** (*tr.*) *Naut.* to reduce the area of (sail). **3.** (*tr.*) to make (pastry, etc.) short, by adding fat. **4.** *Gambling.* to cause (the odds) to lessen or (of odds) to become less.

shortening ('ʃɔːtᵊnɪŋ) *n.* butter or other fat, used in a dough, etc., to make the mixture short.

Shorter Catechism *n. Chiefly Presbyterian Church.* the more widely used of two catechisms of religious instruction drawn up in 1647.

shortfall ('ʃɔːtˌfɔːl) *n.* **1.** failure to meet a goal or a requirement. **2.** the amount of such a failure.

shorthand ('ʃɔːtˌhænd) *n.* **a.** a system of rapid handwriting employing simple strokes and other symbols to represent words or phrases. **b.** (*as modifier*): *a shorthand typist.*

short-handed *adj.* lacking the usual or necessary number of assistants, workers, etc.

shorthand typist *n. Brit.* a person skilled in the use of shorthand and in typing. U.S. and Canad. name: **stenographer.**

short head *n. Horse racing.* a distance shorter than the length of a horse's head.

shorthorn (ˈʃɔːtˌhɔːn) *n.* a short-horned breed of cattle with several regional varieties.

shortie *or* **shorty** (ˈʃɔːtɪ) *n., pl.* **shorties.** *Inf.* **a.** a person or thing that is extremely short. **b.** (*as modifier*): *a shortie nightdress.*

short list *Chiefly Brit.* ~*n.* **1.** Also called (Scot.): **short leet.** a list of suitable applicants for a job, post, etc., from which the successful candidate will be selected. ~*vb.* **short-list.** (*tr.*) **2.** to put (someone) on a short list.

short-lived *adj.* living or lasting only for a short time.

shortly (ˈʃɔːtlɪ) *adv.* **1.** in a short time; soon. **2.** briefly. **3.** in a curt or rude manner.

short-order *adj. Chiefly U.S.* of or connected with food that is easily and quickly prepared.

short-range *adj.* of small or limited extent in time or distance: *a short-range forecast.*

shorts (ʃɔːts) *pl. n.* **1.** trousers reaching the top of the thigh or partway to the knee, worn by both sexes for sport, etc. **2.** *Chiefly U.S. & Canad.* men's underpants that usually reach mid-thigh. **3.** short-dated gilt-edged securities. **4.** short-term bonds. **5.** a livestock feed containing a large proportion of bran and wheat germ.

short shrift *n.* **1.** brief and unsympathetic treatment. **2.** (formerly) a brief period allowed to a condemned prisoner to make confession. **3.** **make short shrift of.** to dispose of quickly.

short-sighted *adj.* **1.** relating to or suffering from myopia. **2.** lacking foresight: *a short-sighted plan.* —ˌ**short-ˈsightedly** *adv.* —ˌ**short-ˈsightedness** *n.*

short-spoken *adj.* tending to be abrupt in speech.

short story *n.* a prose narrative of shorter length than the novel.

short-tempered *adj.* easily moved to anger.

short-term *adj.* **1.** of, for, or extending over a limited period. **2.** *Finance.* extending over or maturing within a short period of time, usually twelve months: *short-term credit.*

short time *n.* the state or condition of working less than the normal working week, esp. because of a business recession.

short ton *n.* the full name for **ton**[1] (sense 2).

short-waisted *adj.* unusually short from the shoulders to the waist.

short wave *n.* **a.** a radio wave with a wavelength in the range 10–100 metres. **b.** (*as modifier*): *a short-wave broadcast.*

short-winded *adj.* **1.** tending to run out of breath, esp. after exertion. **2.** (of speech or writing) terse or abrupt.

shot[1] (ʃɒt) *n.* **1.** the act or an instance of discharging a projectile. **2.** (*pl.* **shot**) a solid missile, such as an iron ball or a lead pellet, discharged from a firearm. **3.** **a.** small round pellets of lead collectively, as used in cartridges. **b.** metal in the form of coarse powder or small pellets. **4.** the distance that a discharged projectile travels or is capable of travelling. **5.** a person who shoots, esp. with regard to his ability: *he is a good shot.* **6.** *Inf.* an attempt. **7.** *Inf.* a guess. **8.** any act of throwing or hitting something, as in certain sports. **9.** the launching of a rocket, etc., esp. to a specified destination: *a moon shot.* **10.** **a.** a single photograph. **b.** a length of film taken by a single camera without breaks. **11.** *Inf.* an injection, as of a vaccine or narcotic drug. **12.** *Inf.* a glass of alcoholic drink, esp. spirits. **13.** *Sport.* a heavy metal ball used in the shot put. **14.** **call the shots.** *Sl.* to have control over an organization, etc. **15.** **have a shot at.** *Inf.* to attempt. **16.** **like a shot.** very quickly, esp. willingly. **17.** **shot in the arm.** *Inf.* anything that regenerates, increases confidence or efficiency, etc. **18.** **shot in the dark.** a wild guess. [OE *scot*]

shot[2] (ʃɒt) *vb.* **1.** the past tense and past participle of **shoot.** ~*adj.* **2.** (of textiles) woven to give a changing colour effect. **3.** streaked with colour.

shotgun (ˈʃɒtˌgʌn) *n.* **1.** a shoulder firearm with unrifled bore used mainly for hunting small game. ~*adj.* **2.** *Chiefly U.S.* involving coercion or duress: *a shotgun merger.*

shotgun wedding *n. Inf.* a wedding into which one or both partners are coerced, usually because the woman is pregnant.

shot put *n.* an athletic event in which contestants hurl or put a heavy metal ball or shot as far as possible. —ˈ**shot-**ˌ**putter** *n.*

shotten (ˈʃɒtᵊn) *adj.* **1.** (of fish, esp. herring) having recently spawned. **2.** *Arch.* worthless. [C15: < obs. p.p. of SHOOT]

shot tower *n.* a building formerly used in the production of shot, in which molten lead was graded and dropped into water, thus cooling it and forming the shot.

should (ʃʊd) *vb.* the past tense of **shall:** used as an auxiliary verb to indicate that an action is considered by the speaker to be obligatory (*you should go*) or to form the subjunctive mood with *I* or *we* (*I should like to see you*). [OE *sceold*]

▷ **Usage.** *Should* has, as its most common meaning in modern English, the sense *ought to* as in *I should go to the graduation, but I don't see how I can.* However, the older sense of the subjunctive of *shall* is often used with *I* or *we* to indicate a more polite form than *would*: *I should like to go, but I can't.* In much speech and writing, *should* has been replaced by *would* in contexts of this kind, but it remains in conditional subjunctives: *should* (never *would*) *I go, I should* (or *would*) *wear my black dress.*

shoulder (ˈʃəʊldə) *n.* **1.** the part of the vertebrate body where the arm or a corresponding forelimb joins the trunk. **2.** the joint at the junction of the forelimb with the pectoral girdle. **3.** a cut of meat including the upper part of the foreleg. **4.** *Printing.* the flat surface of a piece of type from which the face rises. **5.** the part of a garment that covers the shoulder. **6.** anything that resembles a shoulder in shape or position. **7.** the strip of unpaved land that borders a road. **8.** **a shoulder to cry on.** a person one turns to for sympathy with one's troubles. **9.** **give (someone) the cold shoulder.** *Inf.* **a.** to treat in a cold manner; snub. **b.** to ignore or shun. **10.** **put one's shoulder to the wheel.** *Inf.* to work very hard. **11.** **rub shoulders with.** *Inf.* to mix with socially or associate with. **12.** **shoulder to shoulder.** **a.** side by side. **b.** in a corporate effort. ~*vb.* **13.** (*tr.*) to bear or carry (a burden, etc.) as if on one's shoulders. **14.** to push (something) with or as if with the shoulder. **15.** (*tr.*) to lift or carry on the shoulders. **16.** **shoulder arms.** *Mil.* to bring the rifle vertically close to the right side with the muzzle uppermost. [OE *sculdor*]

shoulder blade *n.* the nontechnical name for **scapula.**

shoulder strap *n.* a strap over the shoulders, as to hold up a garment or to support a bag, etc.

shouldn't (ˈʃʊdᵊnt) *contraction of* should not.

shouldst (ʃʊdst) *or* **shouldest** (ˈʃʊdɪst) *vb. Arch. or dialect.* (used with the pronoun *thou*) a form of the past tense of **shall.**

shout (ʃaʊt) *n.* **1.** a loud cry, esp. to convey emotion or a command. **2.** *Inf.* **a.** a round, esp. of drinks. **b.** one's turn to buy a round of drinks. ~*vb.* **3.** to utter (something) in a loud cry. **4.** (*intr.*) to make a loud noise. **5.** (*tr.*) *Austral. & N.Z. inf.* to treat (someone) to (something), esp. a round of drinks. [C14: prob. < ON *skūta* taunt] —ˈ**shouter** *n.*

shout down *vb.* (*tr., adv.*) to drown, overwhelm, or silence by talking loudly.

shove (ʃʌv) *vb.* **1.** to give a thrust or push to (a person or thing). **2.** (*tr.*) to give a violent push to. **3.** (*intr.*) to push one's way roughly. **4.** (*tr.*) *Inf.* to put (something) somewhere: *shove it in the bin.* ~*n.* **5.** the act or an instance of shoving. ~See also **shove off.** [OE *scūfan*] —ˈ**shover** *n.*

shove-halfpenny *n. Brit.* a game in which

players try to propel coins, originally old halfpennies, with the hand into lined sections of a wooden board.

shovel (ˈʃʌvᵊl) *n.* **1.** an instrument for lifting or scooping loose material, such as earth, coal, etc., consisting of a curved blade or a scoop attached to a handle. **2.** any machine or part resembling a shovel in action. **3.** Also called: **shovelful.** the amount that can be contained in a shovel. ~*vb.* **-elling, -elled** *or U.S.* **-eling, -eled. 4.** to lift (earth, etc.) with a shovel. **5.** (*tr.*) to clear or dig (a path) with or as if with a shovel. **6.** (*tr.*) to gather, load, or unload in a hurried or careless way. [OE *scofl*] —ˈ**shoveller** *or U.S.* ˈ**shoveler** *n.*

shoveler (ˈʃʌvələ) *n.* a duck of ponds and marshes, having a spoon-shaped bill, a blue patch on each wing, and in the male a green head, white breast, and reddish-brown body.

shovelhead (ˈʃʌvᵊlˌhɛd) *n.* a common shark of the Atlantic and Pacific Oceans, having a shovel-shaped head.

shove off *vb.* (*intr., adv.; often imperative*) **1.** to move from the shore in a boat. **2.** *Inf.* to go away; depart.

show (ʃəʊ) *vb.* **showing, showed; shown** *or* **showed. 1.** to make, be, or become visible or noticeable: *to show one's dislike.* **2.** (*tr.*) to exhibit: *he showed me a picture.* **3.** (*tr.*) to indicate or explain; prove: *to show that the earth moves round the sun.* **4.** (*tr.*) to present (oneself or itself) in a specific character: *to show oneself to be trustworthy.* **5.** (*tr.;* foll. by *how* and an infinitive) to instruct by demonstration: *show me how to swim.* **6.** (*tr.*) to indicate: *a barometer shows changes in the weather.* **7.** (*tr.*) to grant or bestow: *to show favour to someone.* **8.** (*intr.*) to appear: *to show to advantage.* **9.** to exhibit, display, or offer (goods, etc.) for sale: *three artists were showing at the gallery.* **10.** (*tr.*) to allege, as in a legal document: *to show cause.* **11.** to present (a film, etc.) or (of a play, etc.) to be presented, as at a theatre or cinema. **12.** (*tr.*) to guide or escort: *please show me to my room.* **13. show in** *or* **out.** to conduct a person into or out of a room or building by opening the door for him. **14.** (*intr.*) *Inf.* to arrive. ~*n.* **15.** a display or exhibition. **16.** a public spectacle. **17.** an ostentatious display. **18.** a theatrical or other entertainment. **19.** a trace or indication. **20.** *Obstetrics.* a discharge of blood at the onset of labour. **21.** *U.S., Austral., & N.Z. inf.* a chance (esp. in **give someone a show**). **22.** *Sl., chiefly Brit.* a thing or affair (esp. in **good show, bad show,** etc.). **23. for show.** in order to attract attention. **24. run the show.** *Inf.* to take charge of or manage an affair, business, etc. **25. steal the show.** *Inf.* to be looked upon as the most interesting, popular, etc., esp. unexpectedly. ~See also **show off, show up.** [OE *scēawian*]

showboat (ˈʃəʊˌbəʊt) *n.* a paddle-wheel river steamer with a theatre and a repertory company.

showbread (ˈʃəʊˌbrɛd) *n.* a variant spelling of **shewbread.**

show business *n.* the entertainment industry, including theatre, films, television, and radio. Informal term: **show biz.**

show card *n. Commerce.* a card containing a tradesman's advertisement; poster.

showcase (ˈʃəʊˌkeɪs) *n.* **1.** a glass case used to display objects in a museum or shop. **2.** a setting in which anything may be displayed to best advantage. ~*vb.* **3.** (*tr.*) *Chiefly U.S. & Canad.* to display or exhibit.

showdown (ˈʃəʊˌdaʊn) *n.* **1.** *Inf.* an action that brings matters to a head or acts as a conclusion. **2.** *Poker.* the exposing of the cards in the players' hands at the end of the game.

shower[1] (ˈʃaʊə) *n.* **1.** a brief period of rain, hail, sleet, or snow. **2.** a sudden abundant fall or downpour, as of tears, sparks, or light. **3.** a rush: *a shower of praise.* **4. a.** a kind of bath in which a person stands upright and is sprayed with water from a nozzle. **b.** the room, booth, etc., containing such a bath. Full name: **shower bath. 5.** *Brit. sl.* a derogatory term applied to a person or group. **6.** *U.S., Canad., Austral., & N.Z.* a party held to honour and present gifts to a person, as to a prospective bride. **7.** a large number of particles formed by the collision of a cosmic-ray particle with a particle in the atmosphere. **8.** *N.Z.* a light fabric put over a tea table to protect the food from flies, etc. ~*vb.* **9.** (*tr.*) to sprinkle or spray with or as if with a shower. **10.** (often with *it* as subject) to fall or cause to fall in the form of a shower. **11.** (*tr.*) to give (gifts, etc.) in abundance or present (a person) with (gifts, etc.): *they showered gifts on him.* **12.** (*intr.*) to take a shower. [OE *scūr*] —ˈ**showery** *adj.*

shower[2] (ˈʃəʊə) *n.* a person or thing that shows.

showgirl (ˈʃəʊˌgɜːl) *n.* a girl who appears in variety shows, nightclub acts, etc.

show house *n.* a house on a newly built estate that is decorated and furnished for prospective buyers to view.

showing (ˈʃəʊɪŋ) *n.* **1.** a presentation, exhibition, or display. **2.** manner of presentation.

showjumping (ˈʃəʊˌdʒʌmpɪŋ) *n.* the riding of horses in competitions to demonstrate skill in jumping over or between various obstacles. —ˈ**show-ˌjumper** *n.*

showman (ˈʃəʊmən) *n., pl.* **-men. 1.** a person who presents or produces a theatrical show, etc. **2.** a person skilled at presenting anything in an effective manner. —ˈ**showmanship** *n.*

shown (ʃəʊn) *vb.* a past participle of **show.**

show off *vb.* (*adv.*) **1.** (*tr.*) to exhibit or display so as to invite admiration. **2.** (*intr.*) *Inf.* to behave in such a manner as to make an impression. ~*n.* **show-off. 3.** *Inf.* a person who makes a vain display of himself.

showpiece (ˈʃəʊˌpiːs) *n.* **1.** anything displayed or exhibited. **2.** anything prized as a very fine example of its type.

showplace (ˈʃəʊˌpleɪs) *n.* a place exhibited or visited for its beauty, historic interest, etc.

showroom (ˈʃəʊˌruːm, -ˌrʊm) *n.* a room in which goods for sale, such as cars, are on display.

show up *vb.* (*adv.*) **1.** to reveal or be revealed clearly. **2.** (*tr.*) to expose or reveal the faults or defects of by comparison. **3.** (*tr.*) *Inf.* to put to shame; embarrass. **4.** (*intr.*) *Inf.* to appear or arrive.

showy (ˈʃəʊɪ) *adj.* **showier, showiest. 1.** gaudy or ostentatious. **2.** making an imposing display. —ˈ**showily** *adv.* —ˈ**showiness** *n.*

shrank (ʃræŋk) *vb.* a past tense of **shrink.**

shrapnel (ˈʃræpnᵊl) *n.* **1.** a projectile containing a number of small pellets or bullets exploded before impact. **2.** fragments from this type of shell. [C19: after H. *Shrapnel* (1761–1842), E army officer, who invented it]

shred (ʃrɛd) *n.* **1.** a long narrow strip or fragment torn or cut off. **2.** a very small piece or amount. ~*vb.* **shredding, shredded** *or* **shred. 3.** (*tr.*) to tear or cut into shreds. [OE *scread*] —ˈ**shredder** *n.*

shrew (ʃruː) *n.* **1.** Also called: **shrewmouse.** a small mouselike long-snouted insectivorous mammal. **2.** a bad-tempered or mean-spirited woman. [OE *scrēawa*]

shrewd (ʃruːd) *adj.* **1.** astute and penetrating, often with regard to business. **2.** artful: *a shrewd politician.* **3.** *Obs.* piercing: *a shrewd wind.* [C14: < *shrew* (obs. vb.) to curse, < SHREW] —ˈ**shrewdly** *adv.* —ˈ**shrewdness** *n.*

shrewish (ˈʃruːɪʃ) *adj.* (esp. of a woman) bad-tempered and nagging.

shriek (ʃriːk) *n.* **1.** a shrill and piercing cry. ~*vb.* **2.** to produce or utter (words, sounds, etc.) in a shrill piercing tone. [C16: prob. < ON *skrækja* to screech] —ˈ**shrieker** *n.*

shrieval (ˈʃriːvᵊl) *adj.* of or relating to a sheriff.

shrievalty (ˈʃriːvəltɪ) *n., pl.* **-ties. 1.** the office or term of office of a sheriff. **2.** the jurisdiction of a sheriff. [C16: < arch. *shrieve* sheriff, on the model of *mayoralty*]

shrift (ʃrɪft) *n. Arch.* the act or an instance of shriving or being shriven. See also **short shrift.** [OE *scrift,* < L *scriptum* SCRIPT]

shrike (ʃraɪk) *n.* an Old World songbird having a

heavy hooked bill and feeding on smaller animals which it sometimes impales on thorns, etc. Also called: **butcherbird.** [OE *scrīc* thrush]

shrill (ʃrɪl) *adj.* **1.** sharp and high-pitched in quality. **2.** emitting a sharp high-pitched sound. ~*vb.* **3.** to utter (words, sounds, etc.) in a shrill tone. [C14: prob. < OE *scralletan*] —ˈ**shrillness** *n.* —ˈ**shrilly** *adv.*

shrimp (ʃrɪmp) *n.* **1.** any of a genus of chiefly marine decapod crustaceans having a slender flattened body with a long tail and a single pair of pincers. **2.** *Inf.* a diminutive person, esp. a child. ~*vb.* **3.** (*intr.*) to fish for shrimps. [C14: prob. of Gmc origin] —ˈ**shrimper** *n.*

shrine (ʃraɪn) *n.* **1.** a place of worship hallowed by association with a sacred person or object. **2.** a container for sacred relics. **3.** the tomb of a saint or other holy person. **4.** a place or site venerated for its association with a famous person or event. **5.** *R.C. Church.* a building, alcove, or shelf arranged as a setting for a statue, picture, etc., of Christ, the Virgin Mary, or a saint. ~*vb.* **6.** short for **enshrine.** [OE *scrīn*, < L *scrīnium* bookcase] —ˈ**shrine**ˌ**like** *adj.*

shrink (ʃrɪŋk) *vb.* **shrinking; shrank** *or* **shrunk; shrunk** *or* **shrunken. 1.** to contract or cause to contract as from wetness, heat, cold, etc. **2.** to become or cause to become smaller in size. **3.** (*intr.;* often foll. by *from*) **a.** to recoil or withdraw: *to shrink from the sight of blood.* **b.** to feel great reluctance (at). ~*n.* **4.** the act or an instance of shrinking. **5.** a slang word for **psychiatrist.** [OE *scrincan*] —ˈ**shrinkable** *adj.* —ˈ**shrinker** *n.* —ˈ**shrinking** *adj.*

shrinkage (ˈʃrɪŋkɪdʒ) *n.* **1.** the act or fact of shrinking. **2.** the amount by which anything decreases in size, value, weight, etc.

shrinking violet *n. Inf.* a shy person.

shrink-wrap *vb.* **-wrapping, -wrapped.** (*tr.*) to package a product in a flexible plastic wrapping designed to shrink about its contours to protect and seal it.

shrive (ʃraɪv) *vb.* **shriving; shrove** *or* **shrived; shriven** (ˈʃrɪvᵊn) *or* **shrived.** *Chiefly R.C. Church.* **1.** to hear the confession of (a penitent). **2.** (*tr.*) to impose a penance upon (a penitent) and grant him absolution. **3.** (*intr.*) to confess one's sins to a priest in order to obtain forgiveness. [OE *scrīfan*, < L *scrībere* to write] —ˈ**shriver** *n.*

shrivel (ˈʃrɪvᵊl) *vb.* **-elling, -elled** *or U.S.* **-eling, -eled. 1.** to make or become shrunken and withered. **2.** to lose or cause to lose vitality. [C16: prob. of Scand. origin]

shroud (ʃraʊd) *n.* **1.** a garment or piece of cloth used to wrap a dead body. **2.** anything that envelops like a garment: *a shroud of mist.* **3.** a protective covering for a piece of equipment. **4.** *Naut.* one of a pattern of ropes or cables used to stay a mast. ~*vb.* (*tr.*) **5.** to wrap in a shroud. **6.** to cover, envelop, or hide. [OE *scrūd* garment] —ˈ**shroudless** *adj.*

shrove (ʃrəʊv) *vb.* a past tense of **shrive.**

Shrovetide (ˈʃrəʊvˌtaɪd) *n.* the Sunday, Monday, and Tuesday before Ash Wednesday, formerly a time when confessions were made for Lent.

shrub[1] (ʃrʌb) *n.* a woody perennial plant, smaller than a tree, with several major branches arising from near the base of the main stem. [OE *scrybb*] —ˈ**shrub**ˌ**like** *adj.*

shrub[2] (ʃrʌb) *n.* a mixed drink of rum, fruit juice, sugar, and spice. [C18: < Ar. *sharāb*, var. of *shurb* drink; see SHERBET]

shrubbery (ˈʃrʌbərɪ) *n., pl.* **-beries. 1.** a place where a number of shrubs are planted. **2.** shrubs collectively.

shrubby (ˈʃrʌbɪ) *adj.* **-bier, -biest. 1.** consisting of, planted with, or abounding in shrubs. **2.** resembling a shrub. —ˈ**shrubbiness** *n.*

shrug (ʃrʌg) *vb.* **shrugging, shrugged. 1.** to draw up and drop (the shoulders) abruptly in a gesture expressing indifference, ignorance, etc. ~*n.* **2.** the gesture so made. [C14: <?]

shrug off *vb.* (*tr., adv.*) **1.** to minimize the importance of; dismiss. **2.** to get rid of.

shrunk (ʃrʌŋk) *vb.* a past participle and past tense of **shrink.**

shrunken (ˈʃrʌŋkᵊn) *vb.* **1.** a past participle of **shrink.** ~*adj.* **2.** (*usually prenominal*) reduced in size.

shtoom (ʃtʊm) *adj. Sl.* silent, dumb (esp. in **keep shtoom**). [< Yiddish, < G *stumm* silent]

shuck (ʃʌk) *n.* **1.** the outer covering of something, such as the husk of a grain of maize, a pea pod, or an oyster shell. ~*vb.* (*tr.*) **2.** to remove the shucks from. [C17: U.S. dialect, <?] —ˈ**shucker** *n.*

shucks (ʃʌks) *interj. U.S. & Canad. inf.* an exclamation of disappointment, annoyance, etc.

shudder (ˈʃʌdə) *vb.* **1.** (*intr.*) to shake or tremble suddenly and violently, as from horror, fear, aversion, etc. ~*n.* **2.** a convulsive shiver. [C18: < MLow G *schōderen*] —ˈ**shuddering** *adj.* —ˈ**shudderingly** *adv.* —ˈ**shuddery** *adj.*

shuffle (ˈʃʌfᵊl) *vb.* **1.** to walk or move (the feet) with a slow dragging motion. **2.** to change the position of (something), esp. in order to deceive others. **3.** (*tr.*) to mix together in a careless manner: *he shuffled the papers nervously.* **4.** to mix up (cards in a pack) to change their order. **5.** (*intr.*) to behave in an evasive or underhand manner. **6.** (when *intr.*, often foll. by *into* or *out of*) to move or cause to move clumsily: *he shuffled out of the door.* ~*n.* **7.** the act or an instance of shuffling. **8.** a rearrangement: *a Cabinet shuffle.* **9.** a dance or dance step with short dragging movements of the feet. [C16: prob. < Low G *schüffeln*] —ˈ**shuffler** *n.*

shuffleboard (ˈʃʌfᵊlˌbɔːd) *n.* a game in which players push wooden or plastic discs with a long cue towards numbered scoring sections marked on a floor, esp. a ship's deck.

shuffle off *vb.* (*tr., adv.*) to thrust off or put aside.

shufty *or* **shufti** (ˈʃʊftɪ, ˈʃʌftɪ) *n., pl.* **-ties.** *Brit. sl.* a look; peep. [C20: < Ar.]

shun (ʃʌn) *vb.* **shunning, shunned.** (*tr.*) to avoid deliberately. [OE *scunian*, <?]

shunt (ʃʌnt) *vb.* **1.** to turn or cause to turn to one side. **2.** *Railways.* to transfer (rolling stock) from track to track. **3.** *Electronics.* to divert or be diverted through a shunt. **4.** (*tr.*) to evade by putting off onto someone else. ~*n.* **5.** the act or an instance of shunting. **6.** a railway point. **7.** *Electronics.* a low-resistance conductor connected in parallel across a part of a circuit to provide an alternative path for a known fraction of the current. **8.** *Med.* a channel that bypasses the normal circulation of the blood. **9.** *Sl.* a car crash. [C13: ? < *shunen* to SHUN]

shunt-wound (ˈʃʌntˌwaʊnd) *adj. Electrical engineering.* (of a motor or generator) having the field and armature circuits connected in parallel.

shush (ʃʊʃ) *interj.* **1.** be quiet! hush! ~*vb.* **2.** to silence or calm (someone) by or as if by saying "shush". [C20: reduplication of SH, infl. by HUSH]

shut (ʃʌt) *vb.* **shutting, shut. 1.** to move (something) so as to cover an aperture: *to shut a door.* **2.** to close (something) by bringing together the parts: *to shut a book.* **3.** (*tr.;* often foll. by *up*) to close or lock the doors of: *to shut up a house.* **4.** (*tr.;* foll. by *in, out,* etc.) to confine, enclose, or exclude. **5.** (*tr.*) to prevent (a business, etc.) from operating. **6. shut the door on. a.** to refuse to think about. **b.** to render impossible. ~*adj.* **7.** closed or fastened. ~*n.* **8.** the act or time of shutting. ~See also **shutdown, shut-off,** etc. [OE *scyttan*]

shutdown (ˈʃʌtˌdaʊn) *n.* **1.** the closing of a factory, shop, etc. ~*vb.* **shut down.** (*adv.*) **2.** to cease or cause to cease operation. **3.** (*tr.*) to close by lowering.

shuteye (ˈʃʌtˌaɪ) *n.* a slang term for **sleep.**

shut-in *n.* **a.** *Chiefly U.S.* a person confined indoors by illness. **b.** (*as modifier*): *a shut-in patient.*

shut-off *n.* **1.** a device that shuts something off, esp. a machine control. **2.** a stoppage or cessation. ~*vb.* **shut off.** (*tr., adv.*) **3.** to stem the flow of. **4.** to block off the passage through. **5.** to isolate or separate.

shutout (ˈʃʌtˌaʊt) *n.* **1.** a less common word for a **lockout.** **2.** *Sport.* a match in which the opposition does not score. ~*vb.* **shut out.** (*tr., adv.*) **3.** to keep out or exclude. **4.** to conceal from sight: *we planted trees to shut out the view of the road.*

shutter (ˈʃʌtə) *n.* **1.** a hinged doorlike cover, often louvred and usually one of a pair, for closing off a window. **2. put up the shutters.** to close business at the end of the day or permanently. **3.** *Photog.* an opaque shield in a camera that, when tripped, admits light to expose the film or plate for a predetermined period, usually a fraction of a second. **4.** *Music.* one of the louvred covers over the mouths of organ pipes, operated by the swell pedal. **5.** a person or thing that shuts. ~*vb.* (*tr.*) **6.** to close with a shutter or shutters. **7.** to equip with a shutter or shutters.

shuttering (ˈʃʌtərɪŋ) *n.* another word (esp. Brit.) for **formwork.**

shuttle (ˈʃʌtᵊl) *n.* **1.** a bobbin-like device used in weaving for passing the weft thread between the warp threads. **2.** a small bobbin-like device used to hold the thread in a sewing machine, etc. **3.** a bus, train, aircraft, etc., that plies between two points. **4. a.** the movement between various countries of a diplomat in order to negotiate with rulers who refuse to meet each other. **b.** (*as modifier*): *shuttle diplomacy.* **5.** *Badminton, etc.* short for **shuttlecock.** ~*vb.* **6.** to move or cause to move by or as if by a shuttle. [OE *scytel* bolt]

shuttlecock (ˈʃʌtᵊlˌkɒk) *n.* **1.** a light cone consisting of a cork stub with feathered flights, struck to and fro in badminton and battledore. **2.** anything moved to and fro, as in an argument.

shut up *vb.* (*adv.*) **1.** (*tr.*) to prevent all access to. **2.** (*tr.*) to confine or imprison. **3.** *Inf.* to cease to talk or make a noise or cause to cease to talk or make a noise: often used in commands.

shwa (ʃwɑː) *n.* a variant spelling of **schwa.**

shy[1] (ʃaɪ) *adj.* **shyer, shyest** *or* **shier, shiest. 1.** not at ease in the company of others. **2.** easily frightened; timid. **3.** (often foll. by *of*) watchful or wary. **4.** (foll. by *of*) *Inf., chiefly U.S. & Canad.* short (of). **5.** (*in combination*) showing reluctance or disinclination: *workshy.* ~*vb.* **shying, shied.** (*intr.*) **6.** to move suddenly, as from fear: *the horse shied at the snake in the road.* **7.** (usually foll. by *off* or *away*) to draw back. ~*n., pl.* **shies. 8.** a sudden movement, as from fear. [OE *sceoh*] —ˈ**shyer** *n.* —ˈ**shyly** *adv.* —ˈ**shyness** *n.*

shy[2] (ʃaɪ) *vb.* **shying, shied. 1.** to throw (something) with a sideways motion. ~*n., pl.* **shies. 2.** a quick throw. **3.** *Inf.* a gibe. **4.** *Inf.* an attempt. [C18: of Gmc origin] —ˈ**shyer** *n.*

Shylock (ˈʃaɪˌlɒk) *n.* a heartless or demanding creditor. [C19: after *Shylock*, the heartless usurer in Shakespeare's *The Merchant of Venice* (1595)]

shyster (ˈʃaɪstə) *n. Sl., chiefly U.S.* a person, esp. a lawyer or politician, who uses discreditable methods. [C19: prob. based on *Scheuster*, a disreputable 19th-cent. New York lawyer]

si (siː) *n. Music.* a variant of **te.**

Si *the chemical symbol for* silicon.

SI See **SI unit.**

sial (ˈsaɪəl) *n.* the silicon-rich and aluminium-rich rocks of the earth's continental upper crust. [C20: *si*(*licon*) + *al*(*uminium*)] —**sialic** (saɪˈælɪk) *adj.*

siamang (ˈsaɪəˌmæŋ) *n.* a large black gibbon of Sumatra and the Malay Peninsula, having the second and third toes united. [C19: < Malay]

Siamese (ˌsaɪəˈmiːz) *n., pl.* **-mese. 1.** See **Siamese cat.** ~*adj.* **2.** characteristic of, relating to, or being a Siamese twin. ~*adj., n., pl.* **-mese. 3.** another word for **Thai.**

Siamese cat *n.* a short-haired breed of cat with a tapering tail, blue eyes, and dark ears, mask, tail, and paws.

Siamese fighting fish *n.* a brightly coloured labyrinth fish of Thailand and Malaysia: the males are very pugnacious.

Siamese twins *pl. n.* twin babies born joined together at some point, such as at the hips.

sib (sɪb) *n.* **1.** a blood relative. **2.** kinsmen collectively; kindred. [OE *sibb*]

SIB (in Britain) *abbrev. for* Securities and Investments Board: a body that regulates financial dealings in the City of London.

Siberian (saɪˈbɪərɪən) *adj.* **1.** of or relating to Siberia, a vast region of the Soviet Union, or to its peoples. ~*n.* **2.** a native or inhabitant of Siberia.

sibilant (ˈsɪbɪlənt) *adj.* **1.** *Phonetics.* relating to or denoting the consonants (s, z, ʃ, ʒ), all pronounced with a characteristic hissing sound. **2.** having a hissing sound. ~*n.* **3.** a sibilant consonant. [C17: < L *sībilāre* to hiss, imit.] —ˈ**sibilance** *or* ˈ**sibilancy** *n.* —ˈ**sibilantly** *adv.*

sibilate (ˈsɪbɪˌleɪt) *vb.* to pronounce or utter (words or speech) with a hissing sound. —ˌ**sibiˈlation** *n.*

sibling (ˈsɪblɪŋ) *n.* **a.** a person's brother or sister. **b.** (*as modifier*): *sibling rivalry.* [C19: specialized modern use of OE *sibling* relative, < SIB]

sibyl (ˈsɪbɪl) *n.* **1.** (in ancient Greece and Rome) any of a number of women believed to be oracles or prophetesses. **2.** a witch, fortune-teller, or sorceress. [C13: ult. < Gk *Sibulla*, <?] —**sibylline** (ˈsɪbɪˌlaɪn) *adj.*

sic[1] (sɪk) *adv.* so or thus: inserted in brackets in a text to indicate that an odd or questionable reading is in fact accurate. [L]

sic[2] (sɪk) *vb.* **sicking, sicked.** (*tr.*) **1.** to attack: used only in commands, as to a dog. **2.** to urge (a dog) to attack. [C19: dialect var. of SEEK]

siccative (ˈsɪkətɪv) *n.* a substance added to a liquid to promote drying: used in paints and some medicines. [C16: < LL *siccātīvus*, < L *siccāre* to dry up, < *siccus* dry]

Sicilian (sɪˈsɪlɪən) *adj.* **1.** of or relating to the island of Sicily, in the Mediterranean. ~*n.* **2.** a native or inhabitant of Sicily.

siciliano (ˌsiːtʃiːˈljɑːnəʊ) *n., pl.* **-lianos. 1.** an old dance in six-beat or twelve-beat time. **2.** a piece of music composed for or in the rhythm of this dance. [It.]

sick[1] (sɪk) *adj.* **1.** inclined or likely to vomit. **2. a.** suffering from ill health. **b.** (*as collective n.; preceded by the*): *the sick.* **3. a.** of or used by people who are unwell: *sick benefits.* **b.** (*in combination*): *a sickroom.* **4.** deeply affected with a mental or spiritual feeling akin to physical sickness: *sick at heart.* **5.** mentally or spiritually disturbed. **6.** *Inf.* delighting in or catering for the macabre: *sick humour.* **7.** Also: **sick and tired.** (often foll. by *of*) *Inf.* disgusted or weary: *I am sick of his everlasting laughter.* **8.** (often foll. by *for*) weary with longing: *I am sick for my own country.* **9.** pallid or sickly. **10.** not in working order. ~*n., vb.* **11.** an informal word for **vomit.** [OE *sēoc*] —ˈ**sickish** *adj.*

sick[2] (sɪk) *vb.* a variant spelling of **sic**[2].

sickbay (ˈsɪkˌbeɪ) *n.* a room for the treatment of the sick or injured, as on board a ship.

sick building syndrome *n.* a group of symptoms, such as headaches, eye irritation, and lethargy, that may be experienced by workers in offices that are totally air-conditioned.

sicken (ˈsɪkən) *vb.* **1.** to make or become nauseated or disgusted. **2.** (*intr.;* often foll. by *for*) to show symptoms (of an illness). —ˈ**sickener** *n.*

sickening (ˈsɪkənɪŋ) *adj.* **1.** causing sickness or revulsion. **2.** *Inf.* extremely annoying. —ˈ**sickeningly** *adv.*

sick headache *n.* **1.** a headache accompanied by nausea. **2.** a nontechnical name for **migraine.**

sickie (ˈsɪkɪ) *n. Austral. & N.Z. inf.* a day of sick leave from work. [C20: < SICK[1] + -IE]

sickle (ˈsɪkᵊl) *n.* an implement for cutting grass, corn, etc., having a curved blade and a short handle. [OE *sicol*, < L *sēcula*]

sick leave *n.* leave of absence from work through illness.

sicklebill (ˈsɪkᵊlˌbɪl) *n.* any of various birds having a markedly curved bill, such as certain hummingbirds and birds of paradise.

sickle-cell anaemia *n.* a hereditary form of anaemia occurring mainly in Black populations, in which a large number of red blood cells become sickle-shaped.

sick list *n.* **1.** a list of the sick, esp. in the army or navy. **2. on the sick list.** ill.

sickly (ˈsɪklɪ) *adj.* **-lier, -liest.** **1.** disposed to frequent ailments; not healthy; weak. **2.** of or caused by sickness. **3.** (of a smell, taste, etc.) causing revulsion or nausea. **4.** (of light or colour) faint or feeble. **5.** mawkish; insipid. ~*adv.* **6.** in a sick or sickly manner. —ˈ**sickliness** *n.*

sick-making *adj. Inf.* galling; sickening.

sickness (ˈsɪknɪs) *n.* **1.** an illness or disease. **2.** nausea or queasiness. **3.** the state or an instance of being sick.

sick pay *n.* wages paid to an employee while he is on sick leave.

sic transit gloria mundi *Latin.* (ˈsɪk ˈtrænsɪt ˈglɔːrɪˌɑː ˈmʊndiː) thus passes the glory of the world.

sidalcea (sɪˈdælsɪə) *n.* any of a genus of hardy perennial plants with pink flowers. Also called: **Greek mallow.** [< NL]

side (saɪd) *n.* **1.** a line or surface that borders anything. **2.** *Geom.* **a.** any line segment forming part of the perimeter of a plane geometric figure. **b.** another name for **face** (sense 13). **3.** either of two parts into which an object, surface, area, etc., can be divided: *the right side and the left side.* **4.** either of the two surfaces of a flat object: *the right and wrong side of the cloth.* **5.** a surface or part of an object that extends vertically: *the side of a cliff.* **6.** either half of a human or animal body, esp. the area around the waist: *I have a pain in my side.* **7.** the area immediately next to a person or thing: *he stood at her side.* **8.** a district, point, or direction within an area identified by reference to a central point: *the south side of the city.* **9.** the area at the edge of a room, road, etc. **10.** aspect or part: *look on the bright side.* **11.** one of two or more contesting factions, teams, etc. **12.** a page in an essay, etc. **13.** a position, opinion, etc., held in opposition to another in a dispute. **14.** line of descent: *he gets his brains from his mother's side.* **15.** *Inf.* a television channel. **16.** *Billiards, etc.* spin imparted to a ball by striking it off-centre with the cue. **17.** *Brit. sl.* insolence or pretentiousness: *to put on side.* **18. on one side.** set apart from the rest, as provision for emergencies, etc. **19. on the side. a.** apart from or in addition to the main object. **b.** as a sideline. **c.** *U.S.* as a side dish. **20. take sides.** to support one group, opinion, etc., as against another. ~*adj.* **21.** being on one side; lateral. **22.** from or viewed as if from one side. **23.** directed towards one side. **24.** subordinate or incidental: *side road.* ~*vb.* **25.** (*intr.;* usually foll. by *with*) to support or associate oneself (with a faction, interest, etc.). [OE *sīde*]

side arms *pl. n.* weapons carried on the person, by belt or holster, such as a sword, pistol, etc.

sideband (ˈsaɪdˌbænd) *n.* the frequency band either above (**upper sideband**) or below (**lower sideband**) the carrier frequency, within which fall the components produced by modulation of a carrier wave.

sideboard (ˈsaɪdˌbɔːd) *n.* a piece of furniture intended to stand at the side of a dining room, with drawers, cupboards, and shelves to hold silver, china, linen, etc.

sideboards (ˈsaɪdˌbɔːdz) *pl. n. Brit.* a man's whiskers grown down either side of the face in front of the ears. U.S. and Canad. term: **sideburns.**

sideburns (ˈsaɪdˌbɜːnz) *pl. n.* another term (esp. U.S. and Canad.) for **sideboards.**

sidecar (ˈsaɪdˌkɑː) *n.* a small car attached on one side to a motorcycle, the other side being supported by a single wheel.

side chain *n. Chem.* a group of atoms bound to an atom, usually a carbon, that forms part of a larger chain or ring in a molecule.

-sided *adj.* (*in combination*) having a side or sides as specified: *three-sided; many-sided.*

side dish *n.* a portion of food served in addition to the main dish.

side drum *n.* a small double-headed drum carried at the side with snares that produce a rattling effect.

side effect *n.* **1.** any unwanted nontherapeutic effect caused by a drug. **2.** any secondary effect, esp. an undesirable one.

sidekick (ˈsaɪdˌkɪk) *n. Inf.* a close friend or follower who accompanies another on adventures, etc.

sidelight (ˈsaɪdˌlaɪt) *n.* **1.** light coming from the side. **2.** a side window. **3.** either of the two navigational running lights used by vessels at night, a red light on the port and a green on the starboard. **4.** *Brit.* either of two small lights on the front of a motor vehicle. **5.** additional or incidental information.

sideline (ˈsaɪdˌlaɪn) *n.* **1.** *Sport.* a line that marks the side boundary of a playing area. **2.** a subsidiary interest or source of income. **3.** an auxiliary business activity or line of merchandise. ~*vb.* **4.** (*tr.*) *Chiefly U.S. & Canad.* to prevent (a player) from taking part in a game.

sidelines (ˈsaɪdˌlaɪnz) *pl. n.* **1.** *Sport.* the area immediately outside the playing area, where substitute players sit. **2.** the peripheral areas of any region, organization, etc.

sidelong (ˈsaɪdˌlɒŋ) *adj.* (*prenominal*) **1.** directed or inclining to one side. **2.** indirect or oblique. ~*adv.* **3.** from the side; obliquely.

sidereal (saɪˈdɪərɪəl) *adj.* **1.** of or involving the stars. **2.** determined with reference to one or more stars: *the sidereal day.* [C17: < L *sīdereus,* < *sīdus* a star] —**siˈdereally** *adv.*

sidereal day *n.* See **day** (sense 5).

sidereal time *n.* time based upon the rotation of the earth with respect to a particular star, the **sidereal day** being the unit of measurement.

sidereal year *n.* See **year** (sense 5).

siderite (ˈsaɪdəˌraɪt) *n.* **1.** a pale yellow to brownish-black mineral consisting chiefly of iron carbonate. It occurs mainly in ore veins and sedimentary rocks and is an important source of iron. Formula: $FeCO_3$. **2.** a meteorite consisting principally of metallic iron.

sidero- *or before a vowel* **sider-** *combining form.* indicating iron: *siderolite.* [< Gk *sidēros*]

siderolite (ˈsaɪdərəˌlaɪt) *n.* a meteorite consisting of a mixture of iron, nickel, and such ferromagnesian minerals as olivine.

siderosis (ˌsaɪdəˈrəʊsɪs) *n.* a lung disease caused by breathing in fine particles of iron or other metallic dust.

siderostat (ˈsaɪdərəʊˌstæt) *n.* an astronomical instrument consisting of a plane mirror rotated by a clock mechanism about two axes so that light from a celestial body, esp. the sun, is reflected along a constant direction for a long period of time. [C19: < *sidero-,* < L *sidus* a star + -STAT]

side-saddle *n.* **1.** a riding saddle originally designed for women riders in skirts who sit with both legs on the near side of the horse. ~*adv.* **2.** on or as if on a side-saddle.

sideshow (ˈsaɪdˌʃəʊ) *n.* **1.** a small show or entertainment offered in conjunction with a larger attraction, as at a circus or fair. **2.** a subordinate event or incident.

sideslip (ˈsaɪdˌslɪp) *n.* **1.** a sideways skid, as of a motor vehicle. ~*vb.* **-slipping, -slipped.** **2.** another name for **slip**[1] (sense 11).

sidesman (ˈsaɪdzmən) *n., pl.* **-men.** *Church of England.* a man elected to help the parish church-warden.

side-splitting *adj.* **1.** producing great mirth. **2.** (of laughter) uproarious or very hearty.

sidestep (ˈsaɪdˌstɛp) *vb.* **-stepping, -stepped.** **1.** to step aside from or out of the way of (something). **2.** (*tr.*) to dodge or circumvent. ~*n.* **side step.** **3.** a movement to one side, as in dancing, boxing, etc. —ˈ**sideˌstepper** *n.*

sidestroke (ˈsaɪdˌstrəʊk) *n.* a type of swimming stroke in which the swimmer lies sideways in the water making a scissors kick with his legs.

sideswipe (ˈsaɪdˌswaɪp) *n.* **1.** a glancing blow or hit along or from the side. ~*vb.* **2.** to strike (someone) with such a blow. —ˈ**sideˌswiper** *n.*

sidetrack (ˈsaɪdˌtræk) *vb.* **1.** to distract or be

distracted from a main subject or topic. ~*n.* **2.** *U.S. & Canad.* a railway siding. **3.** a digression.

side-valve engine *n.* a type of internal-combustion engine in which the inlet and exhaust valves are in the cylinder block at the side of the pistons.

sidewalk (ˈsaɪdˌwɔːk) *n.* the U.S. and Canad. word for **pavement.**

sidewall (ˈsaɪdˌwɔːl) *n.* either of the sides of a pneumatic tyre between the tread and the rim.

sideward (ˈsaɪdwəd) *adj.* **1.** directed or moving towards one side. ~*adv. also* **sidewards. 2.** towards one side.

sideways (ˈsaɪdˌweɪz) *adv.* **1.** moving, facing, or inclining towards one side. **2.** from one side; obliquely. **3.** with one side forward. ~*adj.* (*prenominal*) **4.** moving or directed to or from one side. **5.** towards or from one side.

side whiskers *pl. n.* another name for **sideboards.**

sidewinder (ˈsaɪdˌwaɪndə) *n.* **1.** a North American rattlesnake that moves forwards by a sideways looping motion. **2.** *Boxing, U.S.* a heavy swinging blow from the side.

siding (ˈsaɪdɪŋ) *n.* **1.** a short stretch of railway track connected to a main line, used for storing rolling stock. **2.** a short railway line giving access to the main line for freight from a factory, etc. **3.** *U.S. & Canad.* material attached to the outside of a building to make it weatherproof.

sidle (ˈsaɪdᵊl) *vb.* (*intr.*) **1.** to move in a furtive or stealthy manner. **2.** to move along sideways. [C17: back formation < obs. *sideling* sideways]

SIDS *abbrev. for* sudden infant death syndrome. See **cot death.**

siege (siːdʒ) *n.* **1. a.** the offensive operations carried out to capture a fortified place by surrounding it and deploying weapons against it. **b.** (*as modifier*): *siege warfare.* **2.** a persistent attempt to gain something. **3.** *Obs.* a seat or throne. **4. lay siege to. a.** to besiege. **b.** to importune. [C13: < OF *sege* a seat, < Vulgar L *sēdicāre* (unattested) to sit down, < L *sedēre*]

siemens (ˈsiːmənz) *n., pl.* **siemens.** the derived SI unit of electrical conductance equal to 1 reciprocal ohm. Symbol: S Formerly called: **mho.** [C20: after Ernst Werner von *Siemens* (1816–92), G engineer]

sienna (sɪˈɛnə) *n.* **1.** a natural earth containing ferric oxide used as a yellowish-brown pigment when untreated (**raw sienna**) or a reddish-brown pigment when roasted (**burnt sienna**). **2.** the colour of this pigment. [C18: < It. *terra di Siena* earth of Siena, It. city]

sierra (sɪˈɛərə) *n.* a range of mountains with jagged peaks, esp. in Spain or America. [C17: < Sp., lit.: saw, < L *serra*] —**siˈerran** *adj.*

siesta (sɪˈɛstə) *n.* a rest or nap, usually taken in the early afternoon, as in hot countries. [C17: < Sp., < L *sexta hōra* the sixth hour, i.e. noon]

sieve (sɪv) *n.* **1.** a device for separating lumps from powdered material, straining liquids, etc., consisting of a container with a mesh or perforated bottom through which the material is shaken or poured. ~*vb.* **2.** to pass or cause to pass through a sieve. **3.** (*tr.;* often foll. by *out*) to separate or remove (lumps, materials, etc.) by use of a sieve. [OE *sife*] —**ˈsieveˌlike** *adj.*

sift (sɪft) *vb.* **1.** (*tr.*) to sieve (sand, flour, etc.) in order to remove the coarser particles. **2.** to scatter (something) over a surface through a sieve. **3.** (*tr.*) to separate with or as if with a sieve. **4.** (*tr.*) to examine minutely: *to sift evidence.* **5.** (*intr.*) to move as if through a sieve. [OE *siftan*] —**ˈsifter** *n.*

siftings (ˈsɪftɪŋz) *pl. n.* material or particles separated out by or as if by a sieve.

sigh (saɪ) *vb.* **1.** (*intr.*) to draw in and exhale audibly a deep breath as an expression of weariness, relief, etc. **2.** (*intr.*) to make a sound resembling this. **3.** (*intr.;* often foll. by *for*) to yearn, long, or pine. **4.** (*tr.*) to utter or express with sighing. ~*n.* **5.** the act or sound of sighing. [OE *sīcan,* <?] —**ˈsigher** *n.*

sight (saɪt) *n.* **1.** the power or faculty of seeing; vision. Related adj.: **visual. 2.** the act or an instance of seeing. **3.** the range of vision: *within sight of land.* **4.** point of view; judgment: *in his sight she could do no wrong.* **5.** a glimpse or view (esp. in **catch** *or* **lose sight of**). **6.** anything that is seen. **7.** (*often pl.*) anything worth seeing: *the sights of London.* **8.** *Inf.* anything unpleasant or undesirable to see: *his room was a sight!* **9.** any of various devices or instruments used to assist the eye in making alignments or directional observations, esp. such a device used in aiming a gun. **10.** an observation or alignment made with such a device. **11. a sight.** *Inf.* a great deal: *she's a sight too good for him.* **12. a sight for sore eyes.** a person or thing that one is pleased or relieved to see. **13. at** *or* **on sight. a.** as soon as seen. **b.** on presentation: *a bill payable at sight.* **14. know by sight.** to be familiar with the appearance of without having personal acquaintance. **15. not by a long sight.** *Inf.* on no account. **16. set one's sights on.** to have (a specified goal) in mind. **17. sight unseen.** without having seen the object at issue: *to buy a car sight unseen.* ~*vb.* **18.** (*tr.*) to see, view, or glimpse. **19.** (*tr.*) **a.** to furnish with a sight or sights. **b.** to adjust the sight of. **20.** to aim (a firearm) using the sight. [OE *sihth*] —**ˈsightable** *adj.*

sighted (ˈsaɪtɪd) *adj.* **1.** not blind. **2.** (*in combination*) having sight of a specified kind: *short-sighted.*

sightless (ˈsaɪtlɪs) *adj.* **1.** blind. **2.** invisible. —**ˈsightlessly** *adv.* —**ˈsightlessness** *n.*

sightly (ˈsaɪtlɪ) *adj.* **-lier, -liest.** pleasing or attractive to see. —**ˈsightliness** *n.*

sight-read (ˈsaɪtˌriːd) *vb.* **-reading, -read** (-ˌrɛd). to sing or play (music in a printed or written form) without previous preparation. —**ˈsight-ˌreader** *n.* —**ˈsight-ˌreading** *n.*

sightscreen (ˈsaɪtˌskriːn) *n. Cricket.* a large white screen placed near the boundary behind the bowler to help the batsman see the ball.

sightsee (ˈsaɪtˌsiː) *vb.* **-seeing, -saw, -seen.** *Inf.* to visit the famous or interesting sights of (a place). —**ˈsightˌseeing** *n.* —**ˈsightˌseer** *n.*

sigla (ˈsɪglə) *n.* the list of symbols used in a book, usually collected together as part of the preliminaries. [L: pl. of *siglum,* dim. of *signum* sign]

sigma (ˈsɪgmə) *n.* **1.** the 18th letter in the Greek alphabet (Σ, σ, or, when final, ς), a consonant, transliterated as *S.* **2.** *Maths.* the symbol Σ, indicating summation. [C17: < Gk]

sigma notation *n.* an algebraic notation in which a capital Greek sigma (Σ) is used to indicate that all values of the expression following the sigma are to be added together (usually for values of a variable between specified limits).

sigmoid (ˈsɪgmɔɪd) *adj. also* **sigmoidal. 1.** shaped like the letter S. **2.** of or relating to the sigmoid flexure of the large intestine. ~*n.* **3. sigmoid flexure.** the S-shaped bend in the final portion of the large intestine. [C17: < Gk *sigmoeidēs* sigma-shaped]

sign (saɪn) *n.* **1.** something that indicates a fact, condition, etc., that is not immediately or outwardly observable. **2.** an action or gesture intended to convey information, a command, etc. **3. a.** a board, placard, etc., displayed in public and intended to inform, warn, etc. **b.** (*as modifier*): *a sign painter.* **4.** an arbitrary mark or device that stands for a word, phrase, etc. **5.** *Maths, logic.* **a.** any symbol used to indicate an operation: *a plus sign.* **b.** the positivity or negativity of a number, expression, etc. **6.** an indication or vestige: *the house showed no signs of being occupied.* **7.** a portentous or significant event. **8.** the scent or spoor of an animal. **9.** *Med.* any objective evidence of the presence of a disease or disorder. **10.** *Astrol.* See **sign of the zodiac.** ~*vb.* **11.** to write (one's name) as a signature to (a document, etc.) in attestation, confirmation, etc. **12.** (*intr.;* often foll. by *to*) to make a sign. **13.** to engage or be engaged by written agreement, as a player for a team, etc. **14.** (*tr.*) to outline in gestures a sign over, esp. the sign of the cross. **15.** (*tr.*) to indicate by or as if by a sign; betoken. ~See also **sign away, sign in,** etc. [C13: < OF, < L *signum* a sign] —**'signable** *adj.* —**'signer** *n.*

signal ('sɪgnᵊl) *n.* **1.** any sign, gesture, etc., that serves to communicate information. **2.** anything that acts as an incitement to action: *the rise in prices was a signal for rebellion.* **3. a.** a variable parameter, such as a current or electromagnetic wave, by which information is conveyed through an electronic circuit, etc. **b.** the information so conveyed. **c.** (*as modifier*): *a signal generator.* ~*adj.* **4.** distinguished or conspicuous. **5.** used to give or act as a signal. ~*vb.* **-nalling, -nalled** *or U.S.* **-naling, -naled. 6.** to communicate (a message, etc.) to (a person). [C16: < OF *seignal,* < Med. L *signāle,* < L *signum* sign] —**'signaller** *or U.S.* **'signaler** *n.*

signal box *n.* **1.** a building containing signal levers for all the railway lines in its section. **2.** a control point for a large area of a railway system.

signalize *or* **-lise** ('sɪgnəˌlaɪz) *vb.* (*tr.*) **1.** to make noteworthy. **2.** to point out carefully.

signally ('sɪgnəlɪ) *adv.* conspicuously or especially.

signalman ('sɪgnᵊlmən) *n., pl.* **-men.** a railway employee in charge of the signals and points within a section.

signal-to-noise ratio *n.* the ratio of one parameter, such as power of a wanted signal, to the same parameter of the noise at a specified point in an electronic circuit, etc.

signatory ('sɪgnətərɪ, -trɪ) *n., pl.* **-ries. 1.** a person who has signed a document such as a treaty or an organization, state, etc., on whose behalf such a document has been signed. ~*adj.* **2.** having signed a document, treaty, etc. [C17: < L *signātōrius* concerning sealing, < *signāre* to seal, < *signum* a mark]

signature ('sɪgnɪtʃə) *n.* **1.** the name of a person or a mark or sign representing his name. **2.** the act of signing one's name. **3.** a distinctive mark, characteristic, etc., that identifies a person or thing. **4.** *Music.* See **key signature, time signature. 5.** *Printing.* **a.** a sheet of paper printed with several pages that upon folding will become a section or sections of a book. **b.** such a sheet so folded. **c.** a mark, esp. a letter, printed on the first page of a signature. [C16: < OF, < Med. L *signātura,* < L *signāre* to sign]

signature tune *n. Brit.* a melody used to introduce or identify a television or radio programme, a dance band, a performer, etc.

sign away *vb.* (*tr., adv.*) to dispose of by or as if by signing a document.

signboard ('saɪnˌbɔːd) *n.* a board carrying a sign or notice, esp. one used to advertise a product, event, etc.

signet ('sɪgnɪt) *n.* **1.** a small seal, esp. one as part of a finger ring. **2.** a seal used to stamp or authenticate documents. **3.** the impression made by such a seal. [C14: < Med. L *signētum* a little seal, < L *signum* a sign]

signet ring *n.* a finger ring bearing a signet.

significance (sɪg'nɪfɪkəns) *n.* **1.** consequence or importance. **2.** something expressed or intended. **3.** the state or quality of being significant. **4.** *Statistics.* a measure of the confidence that can be placed in a result as not being merely a matter of chance.

significant (sɪg'nɪfɪkənt) *adj.* **1.** having or expressing a meaning. **2.** having a covert or implied meaning. **3.** important or momentous. **4.** *Statistics.* of or relating to a difference between a result derived from a hypothesis and its observed value that is too large to be attributed to chance. [C16: < L *significāre* to SIGNIFY] —**sig'nificantly** *adv.*

significant figures *pl. n.* **1.** the figures of a number that express a magnitude to a specified degree of accuracy: *3.141 59 to four significant figures is 3.142.* **2.** the number of such figures: *3.142 has four significant figures.*

signification (ˌsɪgnɪfɪ'keɪʃən) *n.* **1.** meaning or sense. **2.** the act of signifying.

signify ('sɪgnɪˌfaɪ) *vb.* **-fying, -fied.** (when *tr., may take a clause as object*) **1.** (*tr.*) to indicate or suggest. **2.** (*tr.*) to imply or portend: *the clouds signified the coming storm.* **3.** (*tr.*) to stand as a symbol, sign, etc. (for). **4.** (*intr.*) to be important. [C13: < OF, < L *significāre,* < *signum* a mark + *facere* to make] —**sig'nificative** *adj.* —**'signiˌfier** *n.*

sign in *vb.* (*adv.*) **1.** to sign or cause to sign a register, as at a hotel, club, etc. **2.** to make or become a member, as of a club.

sign language *n.* any system of communication by manual signs or gestures, such as one used by the deaf.

sign off *vb.* (*adv.*) **1.** (*intr.*) to announce the end of a radio or television programme, esp. at the end of a day. **2.** (*tr.*) (of a doctor) to declare unfit for work, because of illness.

sign of the zodiac *n.* any of the 12 equal areas into which the zodiac can be divided, named after the 12 zodiacal constellations. In astrology, it is thought that a person's attitudes to life can be correlated with the sign in which the sun lay at the moment of his birth.

sign on *vb.* (*adv.*) **1.** (*tr.*) to hire or employ. **2.** (*intr.*) to commit oneself to a job, activity, etc. **3.** (*intr.*) *Brit.* to register and report regularly at an unemployment benefit office.

signor *or* **signior** ('siːnjɔː; *Italian* siɲ'ɲor) *n., pl.* **-gnors** *or* **-gnori** (*Italian* -'ɲori). an Italian man: usually used before a name as a title equivalent to *Mr.*

signora (siːn'jɔːrə; *Italian* siɲ'ɲora) *n., pl.* **-ras** *or* **-re** (*Italian* -re). a married Italian woman: a title of address equivalent to *Mrs* when placed before a name or *madam* when used alone. [It., fem. of SIGNORE]

signore (siːn'jɔːreɪ; *Italian* siɲ'ɲore) *n., pl.* **-ri** (-rɪ; *Italian* -ri). an Italian man: a title of respect equivalent to *sir* when used alone. [It., ult. < L *senior* an elder, < *senex* an old man]

signorina (ˌsiːnjɔː'riːnə; *Italian* siɲɲo'rina) *n., pl.* **-nas** *or* **-ne** (*Italian* -ne). an unmarried Italian woman: a title of address equivalent to *Miss* when placed before a name or *madam* or *miss* when used alone. [It., dim. of SIGNORA]

signory ('siːnjərɪ) *n., pl.* **-gnories.** a variant spelling of **seigniory.**

sign out *vb.* (*adv.*) to sign (one's name) to indicate that one is leaving a place: *he signed out for the evening.*

signpost ('saɪnˌpəʊst) *n.* **1.** a post bearing a sign that shows the way, as at a roadside. **2.** something that serves as a clue or indication. ~*vb.* (*tr.; usually passive*) **3.** to mark with signposts. **4.** to indicate direction towards.

sign up *vb.* (*adv.*) to enlist or cause to enlist, as for military service.

sika ('siːkə) *n.* a Japanese forest-dwelling deer, now introduced into Britain, having a brown coat and a large white patch on the rump. [< Japanese *shika*]

Sikh (siːk) *n.* **1.** a member of a Hindu sect, founded in the 16th century, that teaches monotheism and rejects the authority of the Vedas. ~*adj.* **2.** of or relating to the Sikhs or their religious beliefs. [C18: < Hindi, lit.: disciple, < Sansk. *śiksati* he studies] —**'Sikhˌism** *n.*

silage ('saɪlɪdʒ) *n.* any crop harvested while green for fodder and kept succulent by partial fermentation in a silo. Also called: **ensilage.** [C19: alteration (infl. by SILO) of ENSILAGE]

sild (sɪld) *n.* any of various small young herrings, esp. when prepared and canned in Norway. [Norwegian]

silence ('saɪləns) *n.* **1.** the state or quality of being silent. **2.** the absence of sound or noise. **3.** refusal or failure to speak, etc., when expected: *his silence on their promotion was alarming.* **4.** a period of time without noise. **5.** oblivion or obscurity. ~*vb.* (*tr.*) **6.** to bring to silence. **7.** to put a stop to: *to silence all complaint.*

silencer ('saɪlənsə) *n.* **1.** any device designed to reduce noise, esp. the device in the exhaust system of a motor vehicle. U.S. and Canad. name: **muffler. 2.** a device fitted to the muzzle of a firearm to deaden the report. **3.** a person or thing that silences.

silene (saɪˈliːnɪ) *n.* any of a genus of plants with pink or white flowers and slender leaves. [C18: NL, < L]

silent (ˈsaɪlənt) *adj.* **1.** characterized by an absence or near absence of noise or sound: *a silent house.* **2.** tending to speak very little or not at all. **3.** unable to speak. **4.** failing to speak, communicate, etc., when expected: *the witness chose to remain silent.* **5.** not spoken or expressed. **6.** (of a letter) used in the orthography of a word but no longer pronounced in that word: *the "k" in "know" is silent.* **7.** denoting a film that has no accompanying soundtrack. [C16: < L *silēns*, < *silēre* to be quiet] —ˈ**silently** *adv.* —ˈ**silentness** *n.*

silent cop *n. Austral. sl.* a small raised hemispherical marker in the middle of a crossroads.

silent majority *n.* a presumed moderate majority of the citizens who are too passive to make their views known.

Silenus (saɪˈliːnəs) *n. Greek myth.* **1.** chief of the satyrs and foster father to Dionysus. **2.** (*often not cap.*) one of a class of woodland deities, closely similar to the satyrs.

silex (ˈsaɪlɛks) *n.* a type of heat-resistant glass made from fused quartz. [C16: < L: hard stone]

silhouette (ˌsɪluːˈɛt) *n.* **1.** the outline of a solid figure as cast by its shadow. **2.** an outline drawing filled in with black, often a profile portrait cut out of black paper and mounted on a light ground. ~*vb.* **3.** (*tr.*) to cause to appear in silhouette. [C18: after Etienne de *Silhouette* (1709–67), F politician]

silica (ˈsɪlɪkə) *n.* the dioxide of silicon, occurring naturally as quartz. It is a refractory insoluble material used in the manufacture of glass, ceramics, and abrasives. [C19: NL, < L *silex* hard stone]

silica gel *n.* an amorphous form of silica capable of absorbing large quantities of water: used esp. in drying gases and oils.

silicate (ˈsɪlɪkɪt, -ˌkeɪt) *n.* a salt or ester of silicic acid. Silicates constitute a large proportion of the earth's minerals and are present in cement and glass.

siliceous *or* **silicious** (sɪˈlɪʃəs) *adj.* **1.** of, relating to, or containing silica: *a siliceous clay.* **2.** (of plants) growing in soil rich in silica.

silicic (sɪˈlɪsɪk) *adj.* of or containing silicon or an acid obtained from silicon.

silicic acid *n.* a white gelatinous substance obtained by adding an acid to a solution of sodium silicate. It is best regarded as hydrated silica.

silicify (sɪˈlɪsɪˌfaɪ) *vb.* **-fying, -fied.** to convert or be converted into silica: *silicified wood.* —**siˌlicifiˈcation** *n.*

silicon (ˈsɪlɪkən) *n.* **a.** a brittle metalloid element that exists in two allotropic forms; occurs principally in sand, quartz, granite, feldspar, and clay. It is usually a grey crystalline solid but is also found as a brown amorphous powder. It is used in transistors, solar cells, and alloys. Its compounds are widely used in glass manufacture and the building industry. Symbol: Si; atomic no.: 14; atomic wt.: 28.09. **b.** (*modifier; sometimes cap.*) denoting an area of a country that contains much high-technology industry. [C19: < SILICA, on the model of *boron, carbon*]

silicon carbide *n.* an extremely hard bluish-black insoluble crystalline substance produced by heating carbon with sand at a high temperature and used as an abrasive and refractory material. Very pure crystals are used as semiconductors. Formula: SiC.

silicon chip *n.* another term for **chip** (sense 7).

silicon controlled rectifier *n.* a semiconductor rectifier whose forward current between two electrodes, the anode and cathode, is initiated by means of a signal applied to a third electrode, the gate. The current subsequently becomes independent of the signal. Also called: **thyristor.**

silicone (ˈsɪlɪˌkəʊn) *n. Chem.* **a.** any of a large class of polymeric synthetic materials that usually have resistance to temperature, water, and chemicals, and good insulating and lubricating properties, making them suitable for wide use as oils, water repellents, resins, etc. **b.** (*as modifier*): *silicone rubber.*

Silicon Valley *n.* any area in which industries associated with information technology are concentrated.

silicosis (ˌsɪlɪˈkəʊsɪs) *n. Pathol.* a form of pneumoconiosis caused by breathing in tiny particles of silica, quartz, or slate, and characterized by shortness of breath.

siliqua (sɪˈliːkwə, ˈsɪlɪkwə) *or* **silique** (sɪˈliːk, ˈsɪlɪk) *n., pl.* **-liquae** (-ˈliːkwiː), **-liquas,** *or* **-liques.** the long dry dehiscent fruit of cruciferous plants, such as the wallflower. [C18: via F < L *siliqua* a pod] —**siliquose** (ˈsɪlɪˌkwəʊs) *or* **siliquous** (ˈsɪlɪkwəs) *adj.*

silk (sɪlk) *n.* **1.** the very fine soft lustrous fibre produced by a silkworm to make its cocoon. **2. a.** thread or fabric made from this fibre. **b.** (*as modifier*): *a silk dress.* **3.** a garment made of this. **4.** a very fine fibre produced by a spider to build its web, nest, or cocoon. **5.** the tuft of long fine styles on an ear of maize. **6.** *Brit.* **a.** the gown worn by a Queen's (or King's) Counsel. **b.** *Inf.* a Queen's (or King's) Counsel. **c. take silk.** to become a Queen's (or King's) Counsel. [OE *sioluc;* ult. < Chinese *ssŭ* silk] —ˈ**silkˌlike** *adj.*

silk cotton *n.* another name for **kapok.**

silk-cotton tree *n.* any of a genus of tropical trees having seeds covered with silky hairs from which kapok is obtained. Also called: **kapok tree.**

silken (ˈsɪlkən) *adj.* **1.** made of silk. **2.** resembling silk in smoothness or gloss. **3.** dressed in silk. **4.** soft and delicate.

silk hat *n.* a man's top hat covered with silk.

silkworm (ˈsɪlkˌwɜːm) *n.* **1.** the larva of the Chinese moth that feeds on the leaves of the mulberry tree: widely cultivated as a source of silk. **2.** any of various similar or related larvae.

silky (ˈsɪlkɪ) *adj.* **silkier, silkiest. 1.** resembling silk in texture; glossy. **2.** made of silk. **3.** (of a voice, manner, etc.) suave; smooth. **4.** *Bot.* covered with long fine soft hairs: *silky leaves.* —ˈ**silkily** *adv.* —ˈ**silkiness** *n.*

silky oak *n.* any of an Australian genus of trees having divided leaves and showy clusters of orange, red, or white flowers: cultivated in the tropics as shade trees.

sill (sɪl) *n.* **1.** a shelf at the bottom of a window inside a room. **2.** a horizontal piece along the outside lower member of a window, that throws water clear of the wall below. **3.** the lower horizontal member of a window or door frame. **4.** a horizontal member placed on top of a foundation wall in order to carry a timber framework. **5.** a mass of igneous rock, situated between two layers of older sedimentary rock. [OE *syll*]

sillabub (ˈsɪləˌbʌb) *n.* a variant spelling of **syllabub.**

silly (ˈsɪlɪ) *adj.* **-lier, -liest. 1.** lacking in good sense; absurd. **2.** frivolous, trivial, or superficial. **3.** feeble-minded. **4.** dazed, as from a blow. ~*n.* **5.** (*modifier*) *Cricket.* (of a fielding position) near the batsman's wicket: *silly mid-on.* **6.** (*pl.* **lies**) Also called: **silly-billy.** *Inf.* a foolish person. [C15 (in the sense: pitiable, hence the later senses: foolish): < OE *sǣlig* (unattested) happy, < *sǣl* happiness] —ˈ**silliness** *n.*

silly season *n. Brit.* a period, usually during the summer months, when journalists fill space reporting on frivolous events and activities.

silo (ˈsaɪləʊ) *n., pl.* **-los. 1.** a pit, trench, or tower, often cylindrical in shape, in which silage is made and stored. **2.** an underground position in which missile systems are sited for protection. [C19: < Sp., ? of Celtic origin]

silt (sɪlt) *n.* **1.** a fine deposit of mud, clay, etc., esp. one in a river or lake. ~*vb.* **2.** (usually foll. by *up*) to fill or become filled with silt; choke. [C15: < ON] —**silˈtation** *n.* —ˈ**silty** *adj.*

Silurian (saɪˈlʊərɪən) *adj.* **1.** of or formed in the third period of the Palaeozoic era, during which fishes first appeared. ~*n.* **2. the.** the Silurian period or rock system. [C19: < *Silures* a Welsh tribe who opposed the Romans]

silurid (saɪˈlʊərɪd) *n.* **1.** any freshwater teleost fish of the family Siluridae, such as the European catfish, which has an elongated body, naked skin, and a long anal fin. ~*adj.* **2.** of, relating to, or belonging to the family Siluridae. [C19: < L *silūrus*, < Gk *silouros* a river fish]

silva (ˈsɪlvə) *n.* a variant spelling of **sylva.**

silvan (ˈsɪlvən) *adj.* a variant spelling of **sylvan.**

silver (ˈsɪlvə) *n.* **1. a.** a ductile malleable brilliant greyish-white element having the highest electrical and thermal conductivity of any metal. It occurs free and in argentite and other ores: used in jewellery, tableware, coinage, electrical contacts, and electroplating. Symbol: Ag; atomic no.: 47; atomic wt.: 107.870. **b.** (*as modifier*): *a silver coin.* Related adj.: **argent. 2.** coin made of this metal. **3.** cutlery, whether made of silver or not. **4.** any household articles made of silver. **5.** short for **silver medal. 6. a.** a brilliant or light greyish-white colour. **b.** (*as adj.*): *silver hair.* ~*adj.* **7.** well-articulated: *silver speech.* **8.** (*prenominal*) denoting the 25th in a series: *a silver wedding anniversary.* ~*vb.* **9.** (*tr.*) to coat with silver or a silvery substance: *to silver a spoon.* **10.** to become or cause to become silvery in colour. [OE *siolfor*] —ˈ**silvering** *n.*

silver age *n.* **1.** (in Greek and Roman mythology) the second of the world's major epochs, inferior to the preceding golden age. **2.** the postclassical period of Latin literature, occupying the early part of the Roman imperial era.

silver beet *n.* an Australian and New Zealand variety of beet, cultivated for its edible spinach-like leaves with white stems.

silver bell *n.* any of various deciduous trees of North America and China, having white bell-shaped flowers. Also called: **snowdrop tree.**

silver birch *n.* a tree of N temperate regions of the Old World, having silvery-white peeling bark.

silver bromide *n.* a yellowish powder that darkens when exposed to light: used in making photographic emulsions. Formula: AgBr.

silver chloride *n.* a white powder that darkens on exposure to light: used in making photographic emulsions and papers. Formula: AgCl.

silver-eye *n. Austral. & N.Z.* another name for **waxeye** or **white-eye.**

silver fern *n. N.Z.* **1.** another name for **ponga. 2.** a formalized spray of fern leaf, silver on a black background: the symbol of New Zealand sporting teams.

silver fir *n.* any of various fir trees the leaves of which have a silvery undersurface.

silverfish (ˈsɪlvəˌfɪʃ) *n., pl.* **-fish** *or* **-fishes. 1.** a silver variety of the goldfish. **2.** any of various other silvery fishes, such as the moonfish. **3.** any of various small primitive wingless insects that have long antennae and tail appendages and occur in buildings, feeding on food scraps, book-bindings, etc.

silver fox *n.* **1.** an American red fox in a colour phase in which the fur is black with long silver-tipped hairs. **2.** the valuable fur or pelt of this animal.

silver-gilt *n.* silver covered with a thin film of gold.

silver iodide *n.* a yellow powder that darkens on exposure to light: used in photography and artificial rainmaking. Formula: AgI.

silver lining *n.* a hopeful aspect of an otherwise desperate or unhappy situation.

silver medal *n.* a medal of silver awarded to a competitor who comes second in a contest or race.

silver nitrate *n.* a white crystalline soluble poisonous substance used in making photographic emulsions and as a medical antiseptic and astringent. Formula: $AgNO_3$.

silver plate *n.* **1.** a thin layer of silver deposited on a base metal. **2.** articles, esp. tableware, made of silver plate. ~*vb.* **silver-plate. 3.** (*tr.*) to coat (a metal, object, etc.) with silver, as by electroplating.

silver screen *n.* **the.** *Inf.* **1.** films collectively or the film industry. **2.** the screen onto which films are projected.

silver service *n.* (in restaurants) a style of serving food using a spoon and fork in one hand like a pair of tongs.

silverside (ˈsɪlvəˌsaɪd) *n.* **1.** *Brit. & N.Z.* a cut of beef below the aitchbone and above the leg. **2.** a small marine or freshwater teleost fish related to the grey mullets.

silversmith (ˈsɪlvəˌsmɪθ) *n.* a craftsman who makes or repairs articles of silver. —ˈ**silver-ˌsmithing** *n.*

silverware (ˈsɪlvəˌwɛə) *n.* articles, esp. table-ware, made of or plated with silver.

silverweed (ˈsɪlvəˌwiːd) *n.* **1.** a rosaceous perennial creeping plant with silvery pinnate leaves and yellow flowers. **2.** any of various twining shrubs of SE Asia and Australia, having silvery leaves and showy purple flowers.

silvery (ˈsɪlvərɪ) *adj.* **1.** of or having the appearance of silver: *the silvery moon.* **2.** containing or covered with silver. **3.** having a clear ringing sound. —ˈ**silveriness** *n.*

silviculture (ˈsɪlvɪˌkʌltʃə) *n.* the branch of forestry that is concerned with the cultivation of trees. [C20: *silvi-*, < L *silva* woodland + CULTURE] —ˌ**silviˈcultural** *adj.* —ˌ**silviˈculturist** *n.*

sima (ˈsaɪmə) *n.* **1.** the silicon-rich and magnesium-rich rocks of the earth's oceanic crust. **2.** the earth's continental lower crust. [C20: < SI(LICA) + MA(GNESIA)]

simian (ˈsɪmɪən) *adj.* **1.** of or resembling a monkey or ape. ~*n.* **2.** a monkey or ape. [C17: < L *sīmia* an ape, prob. < Gk *sīmos* flat-nosed]

similar (ˈsɪmɪlə) *adj.* **1.** showing resemblance in qualities, characteristics, or appearance. **2.** *Geom.* (of two or more figures) having corresponding angles equal and all corresponding sides in the same ratio. [C17: < OF, < L *similis*] —**similarity** (ˌsɪmɪˈlærɪtɪ) *n.* —ˈ**similarly** *adv.*

▷ **Usage.** Careful writers prefer not to use *similarly* where *correspondingly* would be appropriate: *if our competitors raise their prices, we must correspondingly* (not *similarly*) *make increases in ours.*

simile (ˈsɪmɪlɪ) *n.* a figure of speech that expresses the resemblance of one thing to another of a different category, usually introduced by *as* or *like.* Cf. **metaphor.** [C14: < L *simile* something similar, < *similis* like]

similitude (sɪˈmɪlɪˌtjuːd) *n.* **1.** likeness. **2.** a thing or sometimes a person that is like or the counterpart of another. **3.** *Arch.* a simile or parable. [C14: < L *similitūdō*, < *similis* like]

simmer (ˈsɪmə) *vb.* **1.** to cook (food) gently at or just below the boiling point. **2.** (*intr.*) to be about to break out in rage or excitement. ~*n.* **3.** the act, sound, or state of simmering. [C17: ? imit.]

simmer down *vb.* (*adv.*) **1.** (*intr.*) *Inf.* to grow calmer, as after intense rage. **2.** (*tr.*) to reduce the volume of (a liquid) by boiling slowly.

simnel cake (ˈsɪmnᵊl) *n. Brit.* a fruit cake covered with a layer of marzipan, traditionally eaten during Lent or at Easter. [C13 *simenel*, < OF, < L *simila* fine flour, prob. of Semitic origin]

simon-pure (ˈsaɪmən-) *adj. Rare.* real; authentic. [C19: < *the real Simon Pure*, a character in the play *A Bold Stroke for a Wife* (1717) by Susannah Centlivre (1669-1723), who is impersonated by another character in some scenes]

simony (ˈsaɪmənɪ) *n. Christianity.* the practice, now usually regarded as a sin, of buying or selling spiritual or Church benefits such as pardons, relics, etc. [C13: < OF *simonie*, < LL *sīmōnia*, < *Simon Magus*, a biblical sorcerer who tried to buy magical powers] —ˈ**simonist** *n.*

simoom (sɪˈmuːm) *or* **simoon** (sɪˈmuːn) *n.* a strong suffocating sand-laden wind of the deserts of Arabia and North Africa. [< Ar. *samūm* poisonous, < Aramaic *sammā* poison]

simpatico (sɪmˈpɑːtɪˌkəʊ) *adj. Inf.* **1.** pleasant or congenial. **2.** of similar mind or temperament. [It.: < *simpatia* SYMPATHY]

simper ('sɪmpə) *vb.* **1.** (*intr.*) to smile coyly, affectedly, or in a silly self-conscious way. **2.** (*tr.*) to utter (something) in such a manner. ~*n.* **3.** a simpering smile; smirk. [C16: prob. < Du. *simper* affected] —'**simpering** *adj.* —'**simperingly** *adv.*

simple ('sɪmpᵊl) *adj.* **1.** easy to understand or do: *a simple problem.* **2.** plain; unadorned: *a simple dress.* **3.** not combined or complex: *a simple mechanism.* **4.** unaffected or unpretentious: *although he became famous, he remained a simple man.* **5.** sincere; frank: *her simple explanation was readily accepted.* **6.** of humble condition or rank: *the peasant was of simple birth.* **7.** feeble-minded. **8.** (*prenominal*) without additions or modifications: *the witness told the simple truth.* **9.** (*prenominal*) straightforward: *a simple case of mumps.* **10.** *Chem.* (of a substance) consisting of only one chemical compound. **11.** *Maths.* (of an equation) containing variables to the first power only. **12.** *Biol.* **a.** not divided into parts: *a simple leaf.* **b.** formed from only one ovary: *simple fruit.* **13.** *Music.* relating to or denoting a time where the number of beats per bar may be two, three, or four. ~*n. Arch.* **14.** a simpleton. **15.** a plant having medicinal properties. [C13: via OF < L *simplex* plain] —**simplicity** (sɪm'plɪsɪtɪ) *n.*

simple fraction *n.* a fraction in which the numerator and denominator are both integers. Also called: **common fraction, vulgar fraction.**

simple fracture *n.* a fracture in which the broken bone does not pierce the skin.

simple harmonic motion *n.* a form of periodic motion of a particle, etc., in which the acceleration is always directed towards some equilibrium point and is proportional to the displacement from this point. Abbrev.: **SHM.**

simple-hearted *adj.* free from deceit; frank.

simple interest *n.* interest paid on the principal alone. Cf. **compound interest.**

simple machine *n.* a simple device for altering the magnitude or direction of a force. The six basic types are the lever, wheel and axle, pulley, screw, wedge, and inclined plane.

simple-minded *adj.* **1.** stupid; foolish; feeble-minded. **2.** mentally defective. **3.** unsophisticated; artless. —ˌ**simple-'mindedly** *adv.* —ˌ**simple-'mindedness** *n.*

simple sentence *n.* a sentence consisting of a single main clause.

simpleton ('sɪmpᵊltən) *n.* a foolish or ignorant person.

simplify ('sɪmplɪˌfaɪ) *vb.* **-fying, -fied.** (*tr.*) **1.** to make less complicated or easier. **2.** *Maths.* to reduce (an equation, fraction, etc.) to its simplest form. [C17: via F < Med. L *simplificāre*, < L *simplus* simple + *facere* to make] —ˌ**simplifi'cation** *n.*

simplistic (sɪm'plɪstɪk) *adj.* **1.** characterized by extreme simplicity. **2.** making unrealistically simple judgments or analyses. —'**simplism** *n.* —**sim'plistically** *adv.*

simply ('sɪmplɪ) *adv.* **1.** in a simple manner. **2.** merely. **3.** absolutely; altogether: *a simply wonderful holiday.* **4.** (*sentence modifier*) frankly.

simulacrum (ˌsɪmjʊ'leɪkrəm) *n., pl.* **-cra** (-krə). *Arch.* **1.** any image or representation of something. **2.** a superficial likeness. [C16: < L: likeness, < *simulāre* to imitate, < *similis* like]

simulate *vb.* ('sɪmjʊˌleɪt). (*tr.*) **1.** to make a pretence of: *to simulate anxiety.* **2.** to reproduce the conditions of (a situation, etc.), as in carrying out an experiment: *to simulate weightlessness.* **3.** to have the appearance of. ~*adj.* ('sɪmjʊlɪt, -ˌleɪt). **4.** *Arch.* assumed. [C17: < L *simulāre* to copy, < *similis* like] —ˌ**simu'lation** *n.* —'**simulative** *adj.*

simulated ('sɪmjʊˌleɪtɪd) *adj.* **1.** (of fur, leather, pearls, etc.) being an imitation of the genuine article, usually made from cheaper material. **2.** (of actions, emotions, etc.) imitated; feigned.

simulator ('sɪmjʊˌleɪtə) *n.* **1.** any device that simulates specific conditions for the purposes of research or operator training: *space simulator.* **2.** a person who simulates.

simulcast ('sɪməlˌkɑːst) *vb.* **1.** (*tr.*) to broadcast (a programme, etc.) simultaneously on radio and television. ~*n.* **2.** a programme, etc., so broadcast. [C20: < SIMUL(TANEOUS) + (BROAD)CAST]

simultaneous (ˌsɪməl'teɪnɪəs) *adj.* occurring, existing, or operating at the same time. [C17: on the model of INSTANTANEOUS < L *simul* at the same time] —ˌ**simul'taneously** *adv.* —ˌ**simul'taneousness** *or* **simultaneity** (ˌsɪməltə'niːɪtɪ) *n.*

▷ **Usage.** See at **unique.**

simultaneous equations *pl. n.* a set of equations that are all satisfied by the same values of the variables, the number of variables being equal to the number of equations.

sin[1] (sɪn) *n.* **1. a.** transgression of God's known will or any principle or law regarded as embodying this. **b.** the condition of estrangement from God arising from such transgression. **2.** any serious offence, as against a religious or moral principle. **3.** any offence against a principle or standard. **4.** **live in sin.** *Inf.* (of an unmarried couple) to live together. ~*vb.* (*intr.*) **sinning, sinned. 5.** to commit a sin. **6.** (usually foll. by *against*) to commit an offence (against a person, etc.). [OE *synn*] —'**sinner** *n.*

sin[2] (saɪn) *Maths. abbrev. for* sine.

SIN (in Canada) *abbrev. for* Social Insurance Number.

sinanthropus (sɪn'ænθrəpəs) *n.* a primitive apelike man of the genus *Sinanthropus,* now considered a subspecies of *Homo erectus.* [C20: < NL, < LL *Sīnae* the Chinese + *-anthropus,* < Gk *anthrōpos* man]

sin bin *n.* **1.** *Sl.* (in ice hockey, etc.) an area off the field of play where a player who has committed a foul can be sent to sit for a specified period. **2.** *Inf.* a separate unit for disruptive schoolchildren.

since (sɪns) *prep.* **1.** during or throughout the period of time after: *since May it has only rained once.* ~*conj.* (*subordinating*) **2.** (sometimes preceded by *ever*) continuously from or starting from the time when. **3.** seeing that; because. ~*adv.* **4.** since that time: *I haven't seen him since.* [OE *sīththan*, lit.: after that]

▷ **Usage.** See at **ago.**

sincere (sɪn'sɪə) *adj.* **1.** not hypocritical or deceitful; genuine: *sincere regret.* **2.** *Arch.* pure; unmixed. [C16: < L *sincērus*] —**sin'cerely** *adv.* —**sincerity** (sɪn'sɛrɪtɪ) *or* **sin'cereness** *n.*

sinciput ('sɪnsɪˌpʌt) *n., pl.* **sinciputs** *or* **sincipita** (sɪn'sɪpɪtə). *Anat.* the forward upper part of the skull. [C16: < L: half a head, < SEMI- + *caput* head] —**sin'cipital** *adj.*

sine[1] (saɪn) *n.* (of an angle) a trigonometric function that in a right-angled triangle is the ratio of the length of the opposite side to that of the hypotenuse. [C16: < L *sinus* a bend; in NL, *sinus* was mistaken as a translation of Ar. *jiba* sine (< Sansk. *jīva*, lit.: bowstring) because of confusion with Ar. *jaib* curve]

sine[2] ('saɪnɪ) *prep.* (esp. in Latin phrases or legal terms) lacking; without.

sinecure ('saɪnɪˌkjʊə) *n.* **1.** a paid office or post involving minimal duties. **2.** a Church benefice to which no spiritual charge is attached. [C17: < Med. L (*beneficium*) *sine cūrā* (benefice) without cure (of souls), < L *sine* without + *cūra* cure] —'**sineˌcurism** *n.* —'**sineˌcurist** *n.*

sine curve (saɪn) *n.* a curve of the equation $y = \sin x$. Also called: **sinusoid.**

sine die *Latin.* ('saɪnɪ 'daɪɪ) *adv., adj.* without a day fixed. [lit.: without a day]

sine qua non *Latin.* ('saɪnɪ kweɪ 'nɒn) *n.* an essential requirement. [lit.: without which not]

sinew ('sɪnjuː) *n.* **1.** *Anat.* another name for **tendon. 2.** (*often pl.*) **a.** a source of strength or power. **b.** a literary word for **muscle.** [OE *sionu*] —'**sinewless** *adj.*

sine wave (saɪn) *n.* any oscillation, such as an

alternating current, whose waveform is that of a sine curve.

sinewy (ˈsɪnjuɪ) *adj.* **1.** consisting of or resembling a tendon or tendons. **2.** muscular. **3.** (esp. of language, style, etc.) forceful. **4.** (of meat, etc.) tough. —ˈ**sinewiness** *n.*

sinfonia (ˌsɪnfəˈnɪə) *n., pl.* **-nie** (-ˈniːeɪ) *or* **-nias.** **1.** another word for **symphony** (senses 2, 3). **2.** (*cap. when part of a name*) a symphony orchestra. [It.]

sinfonietta (ˌsɪnfənˈjɛtə) *n.* **1.** a short or light symphony. **2.** (*cap. when part of a name*) a small symphony orchestra. [It.: a little symphony]

sinful (ˈsɪnfʊl) *adj.* **1.** having committed or tending to commit sin: *a sinful person.* **2.** characterized by or being a sin: *a sinful act.* —ˈ**sinfully** *adv.* —ˈ**sinfulness** *n.*

sing (sɪŋ) *vb.* **singing, sang, sung.** **1.** to produce or articulate (sounds, words, a song, etc.) with musical intonation. **2.** (when *intr.*, often foll. by *to*) to perform (a song) to the accompaniment (of): *to sing to a guitar.* **3.** (*intr.;* foll. by *of*) to tell a story in song (about): *I sing of a maiden.* **4.** (*intr.*) to perform songs for a living. **5.** (*intr.*) (esp. of certain birds and insects) to utter calls or sounds reminiscent of music. **6.** (when *intr.*, usually foll. by *of*) to tell (something), esp. in verse: *the poet who sings of the Trojan dead.* **7.** (*intr.*) to make a whining, ringing, or whistling sound: *the arrow sang past his ear.* **8.** (*intr.*) (of the ears) to experience a continuous ringing. **9.** (*tr.*) to bring to a given state by singing: *to sing a child to sleep.* **10.** (*intr.*) *Sl., chiefly U.S.* to confess or act as an informer. ~*n.* **11.** *Inf.* an act or performance of singing. ~See also **sing out.** [OE *singan*] —ˈ**singable** *adj.* —ˈ**singer** *n.* —ˈ**singing** *adj., n.*

▷ **Usage.** See at **ring**[2].

sing. *abbrev. for* singular.

singe (sɪndʒ) *vb.* **1.** to burn or be burnt superficially; scorch: *to singe one's clothes.* **2.** (*tr.*) to burn the ends of (hair, etc.). **3.** (*tr.*) to expose (a carcass) to flame to remove bristles or hair. ~*n.* **4.** a superficial burn. [OE *sengan*]

Singh (sɪŋ) *n.* a title assumed by a Sikh when he becomes a full member of the community. [< Hindi, < Sansk. *sinhá* a lion]

Singhalese (ˌsɪŋəˈliːz) *n., pl.* **-leses** *or* **-lese,** *adj.* a variant spelling of **Sinhalese.**

singing telegram *n.* a service by which a person is employed to present greetings or congratulations by singing.

single (ˈsɪŋgᵊl) *adj.* (*usually prenominal*) **1.** existing alone; solitary: *upon the hill stood a single tower.* **2.** distinct from other things. **3.** composed of one part. **4.** designed or sufficient for one user: *a single bed.* **5.** (*also postpositive*) unmarried. **6.** connected with the condition of being unmarried: *he led a single life.* **7.** (esp. of combat) involving two individuals. **8.** even one: *there wasn't a single person on the beach.* **9.** (of a flower) having only one set or whorl of petals. **10.** single-minded: *a single devotion to duty.* **11.** *Rare.* honest or sincere. ~*n.* **12.** something forming one individual unit. **13.** (*often pl.*) **a.** an unmarried person. **b.** (*as modifier*): *singles bar.* **14.** a gramophone record with a short recording, usually of pop music, on each side. **15.** *Cricket.* a hit from which one run is scored. **16. a.** *Brit.* a pound note. **b.** *U.S. & Canad.* a dollar note. **17.** See **single ticket.** ~*vb.* **18.** (*tr.;* usually foll. by *out*) to select from a group of people or things: *he singled him out for special mention.* ~See also **singles.** [C14: < OF *sengle,* < L *singulus* individual] —ˈ**singleness** *n.*

single-acting *adj.* (of a reciprocating engine or pump) having a piston or pistons pressurized on one side only.

single-breasted *adj.* (of a garment) having the fronts overlapping only slightly and with one row of fastenings.

single cream *n.* cream having a low fat content that does not thicken with beating.

single-decker *n. Brit. inf.* a bus with only one passenger deck.

single-end *n. Scot.* accommodation consisting of a single room.

single entry *n.* **a.** a book-keeping system in which transactions are entered in one account only. **b.** (*as modifier*): *a single-entry account.*

single file *n.* a line of persons, animals, or things ranged one behind the other.

single-foot *n.* **1.** a rapid showy gait of a horse in which each foot strikes the ground separately. ~*vb.* **2.** to move or cause to move at this gait.

single-handed *adj., adv.* **1.** unaided or working alone: *a single-handed crossing of the Atlantic.* **2.** having or operated by one hand or one person only. —ˌ**single-**ˈ**handedly** *adv.* —ˌ**single-**ˈ**handedness** *n.*

single-lens reflex *n.* See **reflex camera.**

single-minded *adj.* having but one aim or purpose; dedicated. —ˌ**single-**ˈ**mindedly** *adv.* —ˌ**single-**ˈ**mindedness** *n.*

single-parent family *n.* another term for **one-parent family.**

singles (ˈsɪŋgᵊlz) *pl. n. Tennis, etc.* a match played with one person on each side.

singles bar *n.* a bar or club that is a social meeting place for single people.

single-sex *adj.* (of schools, etc.) admitting members of one sex only.

single sideband transmission *n.* a method of transmitting radio waves in which either the upper or the lower sideband is transmitted, the carrier being either wholly or partially suppressed.

singlestick (ˈsɪŋgᵊlˌstɪk) *n.* **1.** a wooden stick used instead of a sword for fencing. **2.** fencing with such a stick. **3.** any short heavy stick.

singlet (ˈsɪŋglɪt) *n. Chiefly Brit.* **1.** a man's sleeveless vest. **2.** a garment worn with shorts by athletes, boxers, etc. [C18: < SINGLE, on the model of *doublet*]

single ticket *n. Brit.* a ticket entitling a passenger to travel only to his destination, without returning.

singleton (ˈsɪŋgᵊltən) *n.* **1.** *Bridge, etc.* an original holding of one card only in a suit. **2.** a single object, etc., distinguished from a pair or group. **3.** *Maths.* a set containing only one member. [C19: < SINGLE, on the model of SIMPLETON]

single-track *adj.* **1.** (of a railway) having only a single pair of lines, so that trains can travel in only one direction at a time. **2.** (of a road) only wide enough for one vehicle.

singletree (ˈsɪŋgᵊlˌtriː) *n. U.S. & Austral.* another word for **swingletree.**

singly (ˈsɪŋglɪ) *adv.* **1.** one at a time; one by one. **2.** apart from others; separately; alone.

sing out *vb.* (*tr., adv.*) to call out in a loud voice; shout.

singsong (ˈsɪŋˌsɒŋ) *n.* **1.** an accent or intonation that is characterized by an alternately rising and falling rhythm, such as in a person's voice. **2.** *Brit.* an informal session of singing, esp. of popular songs. ~*adj.* **3.** having a monotonous rhythm: *a singsong accent.*

singular (ˈsɪŋgjʊlə) *adj.* **1.** remarkable; extraordinary: *a singular feat.* **2.** unusual; odd: *a singular character.* **3.** unique. **4.** denoting a word or an inflected form of a word indicating that one referent is being referred to or described. **5.** *Logic.* (of a proposition) referring to a specific thing or person. ~*n.* **6.** *Grammar.* **a.** the singular number. **b.** a singular form of a word. [C14: < L *singulāris* single] —ˈ**singularly** *adv.*

singularity (ˌsɪŋgjʊˈlærɪtɪ) *n., pl.* **-ties.** **1.** the state or quality of being singular. **2.** something distinguishing a person or thing from others. **3.** something unusual. **4.** *Maths.* a point at which a function is not differentiable although it is differentiable in a neighbourhood of that point. **5.** *Astron.* a hypothetical point in space at which matter is infinitely compressed to infinitesimal volume. Cf. **black hole.**

singularize *or* **-rise** (ˈsɪŋgjʊləˌraɪz) *vb.* (*tr.*) **1.** to make (a word, etc.) singular. **2.** to make conspicuous. —ˌ**singulari**ˈ**zation** *or* **-ri**ˈ**sation** *n.*

singultus (sɪŋˈgʌltəs) *n.* a technical name for **hiccup.** [C18: < L, lit.: a sob]

sinh (ʃaɪn, sɪnʃ) *n.* hyperbolic sine. [C20: < SIN(E)¹ + H(YPERBOLIC)]

Sinhalese (ˌsɪnhəˈliːz) *or* **Singhalese** *n.* **1.** (*pl.* **-leses** *or* **-lese**) a member of a people living chiefly in Sri Lanka, where they constitute the majority of the population. **2.** the language of this people: the official language of Sri Lanka. ~*adj.* **3.** of or relating to this people or their language. ~See also **Sri Lankan.**

sinister (ˈsɪnɪstə) *adj.* **1.** threatening or suggesting evil or harm: *a sinister glance.* **2.** evil or treacherous. **3.** (*usually postpositive*) *Heraldry.* of, on, or starting from the left side from the bearer's point of view. **4.** *Arch.* located on the left side. [C15: < L *sinister* on the left-hand side, considered by Roman augurers to be the unlucky one] —ˈ**sinisterly** *adv.* —ˈ**sinisterness** *n.*

sinistral (ˈsɪnɪstrəl) *adj.* **1.** of or located on the left side, esp. the left side of the body. **2.** a technical term for **left-handed.** **3.** (of the shells of certain molluscs) coiling in a clockwise direction from the apex. —ˈ**sinistrally** *adv.*

sinistrorse (ˈsɪnɪˌstrɔːs, ˌsɪnɪˈstrɔːs) *adj.* (of some climbing plants) growing upwards in a spiral from right to left. [C19: < L *sinistrōrsus* turned towards the left, < *sinister* on the left + *vertere* to turn] —ˌ**sinisˈtrorsal** *adj.*

Sinitic (sɪˈnɪtɪk) *n.* **1.** a branch of the Sino-Tibetan family of languages, consisting of the various dialects of Chinese. ~*adj.* **2.** belonging to this group of languages.

sink (sɪŋk) *vb.* **sinking, sank** *or* **sunk; sunk** *or* **sunken.** **1.** to descend or cause to descend, esp. beneath the surface of a liquid. **2.** (*intr.*) to appear to move down towards or descend below the horizon. **3.** (*intr.*) to slope downwards. **4.** (*intr.;* often foll. by *in* or *into*) to pass into a specified lower state or condition: *to sink into apathy.* **5.** to make or become lower in volume, pitch, etc. **6.** to make or become lower in value, price, etc. **7.** (*intr.*) to become weaker in health, strength, etc. **8.** (*intr.*) to seep or penetrate. **9.** (*tr.*) to dig, cut, drill, bore, or excavate (a hole, shaft, etc.). **10.** (*tr.*) to drive into the ground: *to sink a stake.* **11.** (*tr.;* usually foll. by *in* or *into*) **a.** to invest (money). **b.** to lose (money) in an unwise investment. **12.** (*tr.*) to pay (a debt). **13.** (*intr.*) to become hollow: *his cheeks had sunk during his illness.* **14.** (*tr.*) to hit or propel (a ball) into a hole, pocket, etc.: *he sank a 15-foot putt.* **15.** (*tr.*) *Brit. inf.* to drink, esp. quickly: *he sank three pints in half an hour.* **16. sink or swim.** to take risks where the alternatives are loss or success. ~*n.* **17.** a fixed basin, esp. in a kitchen, made of stone, metal, etc., used for washing. **18.** a place of vice or corruption. **19.** an area of ground below that of the surrounding land, where water collects. **20.** *Physics.* a device by which energy is removed from a system: *a heat sink.* [OE *sincan*] —ˈ**sinkable** *adj.*

sinker (ˈsɪŋkə) *n.* **1.** a weight attached to a fishing line, net, etc., to cause it to sink in water. **2.** a person who sinks shafts, etc.

sinkhole (ˈsɪŋkˌhəʊl) *n.* **1.** Also called (esp. in Britain): **swallow hole.** a depression in the ground surface, esp. in limestone, where a surface stream disappears underground. **2.** a place into which foul matter runs.

sink in *vb.* (*intr., adv.*) to enter or penetrate the mind: *eventually the news sank in.*

sinking (ˈsɪŋkɪŋ) *n.* **a.** a feeling in the stomach caused by hunger or uneasiness. **b.** (*as modifier*): *a sinking feeling.*

sinking fund *n.* a fund accumulated out of a business enterprise's earnings or a government's revenue and invested to repay a long-term debt.

sinless (ˈsɪnlɪs) *adj.* free from sin or guilt; pure. —ˈ**sinlessly** *adv.* —ˈ**sinlessness** *n.*

Sinn Féin (ˈʃɪn ˈfeɪn) *n.* an Irish republican political movement founded about 1905 and linked to the revolutionary Irish Republican Army. [C20: < Irish Gaelic: we ourselves] —**Sinn** ˈ**Feiner** *n.* —**Sinn** ˈ**Feinism** *n.*

Sino- *combining form.* Chinese: *Sino-Tibetan; Sinology.* [< F, < LL *Sīnae* the Chinese, < LGk, < Ar. *Sīn* China, prob. < Chinese *Ch'in*]

Sinology (saɪˈnɒlədʒɪ) *n.* the study of Chinese history, language, culture, etc. —**Sinological** (ˌsaɪnəˈlɒdʒɪkᵊl) *adj.* —**Si**ˈ**nologist** *n.* —**Sinologue** (ˈsaɪnəˌlɒg) *n.*

Sino-Tibetan (ˈsaɪnəʊ-) *n.* **1.** a family of languages that includes most of the languages of China, as well as Tibetan, Burmese, and possibly Thai. ~*adj.* **2.** belonging or relating to this family of languages.

sinsemilla (ˌsɪnsəˈmiːljə) *n.* **1.** a type of marijuana with a very high narcotic content. **2.** the plant from which it is obtained, a strain of *Cannabis sativa.* [C20: < American Sp., lit.: without seed]

sinter (ˈsɪntə) *n.* **1.** a whitish porous incrustation, usually consisting of silica, that is deposited from hot springs. **2.** the product of a sintering process. ~*vb.* **3.** (*tr.*) to form large particles, lumps, or masses from (metal powders) by heating or pressure or both. [C18: < G *Sinter* CINDER]

sinuate (ˈsɪnjʊɪt, -ˌeɪt) *adj.* **1.** Also: **sinuous.** (of leaves) having a strongly waved margin. **2.** another word for **sinuous.** [C17: < L *sinuātus* curved] —ˈ**sinuately** *adv.*

sinuous (ˈsɪnjʊəs) *adj.* **1.** full of turns or curves. **2.** devious; not straightforward. **3.** supple. [C16: < L *sinuōsus* winding, < *sinus* a curve] —ˈ**sinuously** *adv.* —**sinuosity** (ˌsɪnjʊˈɒsɪtɪ) *n.*

sinus (ˈsaɪnəs) *n., pl.* **-nuses.** **1.** *Anat.* **a.** any bodily cavity or hollow space. **b.** a large channel for venous blood, esp. between the brain and the skull. **c.** any of the air cavities in the cranial bones. **2.** *Pathol.* a passage leading to a cavity containing pus. [C16: < L: a curve]

sinusitis (ˌsaɪnəˈsaɪtɪs) *n.* inflammation of the membrane lining a sinus, esp. a nasal sinus.

sinusoid (ˈsaɪnəˌsɔɪd) *n.* another name for **sine curve.** —ˌ**sinu**ˈ**soidal** *adj.*

sinusoidal projection *n.* an equal-area map projection on which all parallels are straight lines and all except the prime meridian are sine curves, often used to show tropical latitudes.

Sion (ˈsaɪən) *n.* a variant spelling of **Zion.**

Siouan (ˈsuːən) *n.* a family of North American Indian languages, including Sioux.

Sioux (suː) *n.* **1.** (*pl.* **Sioux** (suː, suːz)) a member of a group of North American Indian peoples. **2.** any of the languages of the Sioux. [< F, shortened < *Nadowessioux*]

sip (sɪp) *vb.* **sipping, sipped.** **1.** to drink (a liquid) by taking small mouthfuls. ~*n.* **2.** a small quantity of a liquid taken into the mouth and swallowed. **3.** an act of sipping. [C14: prob. < Low G *sippen*] —ˈ**sipper** *n.*

siphon *or* **syphon** (ˈsaɪfᵊn) *n.* **1.** a tube placed with one end at a certain level in a vessel of liquid and the other end outside the vessel below this level, so that atmospheric pressure forces the liquid through the tube and out of the vessel. **2.** See **soda siphon.** **3.** *Zool.* any of various tubular organs in different aquatic animals, such as molluscs, through which water passes. ~*vb.* **4.** (often foll. by *off*) to draw off through or as if through a siphon. [C17: < L *sīphō,* < Gk *siphōn*] —ˈ**siphonal** *or* **siphonic** (saɪˈfɒnɪk) *adj.*

siphon bottle *n.* another name (esp. U.S.) for **soda siphon.**

siphonophore (ˈsaɪfənəˌfɔː) *n.* any of an order of marine colonial hydrozoans, including the Portuguese man-of-war. [C19: < NL, < Gk *siphōnophoros* tube-bearing]

sippet (ˈsɪpɪt) *n.* a small piece of something, esp. a piece of toast or fried bread eaten with soup or gravy. [C16: used as dim. of SOP]

sir (sɜː) *n.* **1.** a polite term of address for a man. **2.** *Arch.* a gentleman of high social status. [C13: var. of SIRE]

Sir (sɜː) *n.* **1.** a title of honour placed before the name of a knight or baronet: *Sir Walter Raleigh.* **2.** *Arch.* a title placed before the name of a figure from ancient history.

sirdar (ˈsɜːdɑː) *n.* **1.** a general or military leader in Pakistan and India. **2.** (formerly) the title of the British commander in chief of the Egyptian Army. **3.** a variant of **sardar.** [< Hindi *sardār,* < Persian, < *sar* head + *dār* possession]

sire ('saɪə) *n.* **1.** a male parent, esp. of a horse or other domestic animal. **2.** a respectful term of address, now used only in addressing a male monarch. ~*vb.* **3.** (*tr.*) (esp. of a domestic animal) to father. [C13: < OF, < L *senior* an elder, < *senex* an old man]

siren ('saɪərən) *n.* **1.** a device for emitting a loud wailing sound, esp. as a warning or signal, consisting of a rotating perforated metal drum through which air or steam is passed under pressure. **2.** (*sometimes cap.*) *Greek myth.* one of several sea nymphs whose singing was believed to lure sailors to destruction on the rocks the nymphs inhabited. **3.** a woman considered to be dangerously alluring or seductive. **4.** an aquatic eel-like salamander of North America, having external gills, no hind limbs, and reduced forelimbs. [C14: < OF *sereine,* < L *sīrēn,* < Gk *seirēn*]

sirenian (saɪ'riːnɪən) *adj.* **1.** of or belonging to the *Sirenia,* an order of aquatic herbivorous placental mammals having forelimbs modified as paddles and a horizontally flattened tail: contains only the dugong and manatees. ~*n.* **2.** an animal belonging to this order; sea cow.

Sirius ('sɪrɪəs) *n.* the brightest star in the sky, lying in the constellation Canis Major. Also called: the **Dog Star.** [C14: via L < Gk *Seirios,* <?]

sirloin ('sɜːˌlɔɪn) *n.* a prime cut of beef from the loin, esp. the upper part. [C16 *surloyn,* < OF *surlonge,* < *sur* above + *longe,* < *loigne* LOIN]

sirocco (sɪ'rɒkəʊ) *n., pl.* **-cos.** a hot oppressive and often dusty wind usually occurring in spring, beginning in N Africa and reaching S Europe. [C17: < It., < Ar. *sharq* east wind]

sironize *or* **-ise** ('saɪrəˌnaɪz) *vb.* (*tr.*) *Austral.* to treat (a woollen fabric) chemically to prevent it wrinkling after being washed. [C20: < (C)SIRO + *-n-* + -IZE]

siroset ('saɪrəʊˌsɛt) *adj. Austral.* of or relating to the chemical treatment of woollen fabrics to give a permanent-press effect, or a garment so treated.

sirrah ('sɪrə) *n. Arch.* a contemptuous term used in addressing a man or boy. [C16: prob. var. of SIRE]

sirree (sə'riː) *interj.* (*sometimes cap.*) *U.S. inf.* an exclamation used with *yes* or *no.*

sirup ('sɪrəp) *n. U.S.* a less common spelling of **syrup.**

sis (sɪs) *n. Inf.* short for **sister.**

sisal ('saɪsᵊl) *n.* **1.** a Mexican agave plant cultivated for its large fleshy leaves, which yield a stiff fibre used for making rope. **2.** the fibre of this plant. ~Also called: **sisal hemp.** [C19: < Mexican Sp., after *Sisal,* a port in Yucatán, Mexico]

siskin ('sɪskɪn) *n.* **1.** a yellow-and-black Eurasian finch. **2. pine siskin.** a North American finch, having a streaked yellowish-brown plumage. [C16: < MDu. *sīseken,* < MLow G *sīsek*]

sissy *or* **cissy** ('sɪsɪ) *n., pl.* **-sies.** **1.** an effeminate, weak, or cowardly boy or man. ~*adj.* **2.** effeminate, weak, or cowardly.

sister ('sɪstə) *n.* **1.** a female person having the same parents as another person. **2.** a female person who belongs to the same group, trade union, etc., as another or others. **3.** a senior nurse. **4.** *Chiefly R.C. Church.* a nun or a title given to a nun. **5.** a woman fellow member of a religious body. **6.** (*modifier*) belonging to the same class, fleet, etc., as another or others: *a sister ship.* [OE *sweostor*]

sisterhood ('sɪstəˌhʊd) *n.* **1.** the state of being related as a sister or sisters. **2.** a religious body or society of sisters.

sister-in-law *n., pl.* **sisters-in-law.** **1.** the sister of one's husband or wife. **2.** the wife of one's brother. **3.** the wife of the brother of one's husband or wife.

sisterly ('sɪstəlɪ) *adj.* of or suitable to a sister, esp. in showing kindness. —'**sisterliness** *n.*

sistrum ('sɪstrəm) *n., pl.* **-tra** (-trə). a musical instrument of ancient Egypt consisting of a metal rattle. [C14: via L < Gk *seistron,* < *seiein* to shake]

Sisyphean (ˌsɪsɪ'fiːən) *adj.* **1.** relating to Sisyphus, in Greek myth doomed to roll a stone uphill eternally. **2.** actually or seemingly endless and futile.

sit (sɪt) *vb.* **sitting, sat.** (*mainly intr.*) **1.** (*also tr.;* when *intr.,* often foll. by *down, in,* or *on*) to adopt a posture in which the body is supported on the buttocks and the torso is more or less upright: *to sit on a chair.* **2.** (*tr.*) to cause to adopt such a posture. **3.** (of an animal) to adopt or rest in a posture with the hindquarters lowered to the ground. **4.** (of a bird) to perch or roost. **5.** (of a hen or other bird) to cover eggs to hatch them. **6.** to be situated or located. **7.** (of the wind) to blow from the direction specified. **8.** to adopt and maintain a posture for one's portrait to be painted, etc. **9.** to occupy or be entitled to a seat in some official capacity, as a judge, etc. **10.** (of a deliberative body) to be in session. **11.** to remain inactive or unused: *his car sat in the garage.* **12.** (of a garment) to fit or hang as specified: *that dress sits well on you.* **13.** to weigh, rest, or lie as specified: *greatness sits easily on him.* **14.** (*tr.*) *Chiefly Brit.* to take (an examination): *he's sitting his bar finals.* **15.** (usually foll. by *for*) *Chiefly Brit.* to be a candidate (for a qualification): *he's sitting for a BA.* **16.** to keep watch over an invalid, a baby, etc. **17.** (*tr.*) to have seating capacity for. **18. sit tight.** *Inf.* **a.** to wait patiently. **b.** to maintain one's stand, opinion, etc., firmly. ~See also **sit back, sit down,** etc. [OE *sittan*]

sitar (sɪ'tɑː) *n.* a stringed musical instrument, esp. of India, having a long neck, a rounded body, and movable frets. [< Hindi *sitār,* lit.: three-stringed] —**si'tarist** *n.*

sit back *vb.* (*intr., adv.*) to relax, as when action should be taken: *many people just sit back and ignore the problems of today.*

sitcom ('sɪtˌkɒm) *n.* an informal term for **situation comedy.**

sit down *vb.* (*adv.*) **1.** to adopt or cause (oneself or another) to adopt a sitting posture. **2.** (*intr.;* foll. by *under*) to suffer (insults, etc.) without protests or resistance. ~*n.* **sit-down.** **3.** a form of civil disobedience in which demonstrators sit down in a public place. **4.** See **sit-down strike.** ~*adj.* **sit-down.** **5.** (of a meal, etc.) eaten while sitting down at a table.

sit-down strike *n.* a strike in which workers refuse to leave their place of employment until a settlement is reached.

site (saɪt) *n.* **1. a.** the piece of land where something was, is, or is intended to be located: *a building site.* **b.** (*as modifier*): *site office.* ~*vb.* **2.** (*tr.*) to locate or install (something) in a specific place. [C14: < L, < *sinere* to be placed]

sith (sɪθ) *adv., conj., prep.* an archaic word for **since.** [OE *siththa*]

sit-in *n.* **1.** a form of civil disobedience in which demonstrators occupy seats in a public place and refuse to move. **2.** another term for **sit-down strike.** ~*vb.* **sit in.** (*intr., adv.*) **3.** (often foll. by *for*) to deputize (for). **4.** (foll. by *on*) to take part (in) as a visitor or guest. **5.** to organize or take part in a sit-in.

sitkamer ('sɪtˌkɑːmə) *n. S. African.* a sitting room. [< Afrik.]

sitka spruce ('sɪtkə) *n.* a tall North American spruce tree having yellowish-green needle-like leaves. [< *Sitka,* a town in SE Alaska]

sit on *vb.* (*intr., prep.*) **1.** to be a member of (a committee, etc.). **2.** *Inf.* to suppress. **3.** *Inf.* to check or rebuke.

sit out *vb.* (*tr., adv.*) **1.** to endure to the end: *I sat out the play although it was terrible.* **2.** to remain seated throughout (a dance, etc.).

sitter ('sɪtə) *n.* **1.** a person or animal that sits. **2.** a person who is posing for his or her portrait to be painted, etc. **3.** a broody hen that is sitting on its eggs to hatch them. **4.** See **baby-sitter.** **5.**

anything that is extremely easy, such as an easy catch in cricket.

sitting (ˈsɪtɪŋ) *n.* **1.** a continuous period of being seated: *I read his novel at one sitting.* **2.** such a period in a restaurant, canteen, etc.: *dinner will be served in two sittings.* **3.** the act or period of posing for one's portrait to be painted, etc. **4.** a meeting, esp. of an official body, to conduct business. **5.** the incubation period of a bird's eggs during which the mother sits on them. ~*adj.* **6.** in office: *a sitting councillor.* **7.** seated: *in a sitting position.*

sitting duck *n. Inf.* a person or thing in a defenceless or vulnerable position. Also called: **sitting target.**

sitting room *n.* a room in a private house or flat used for relaxation and entertainment of guests.

sitting tenant *n.* a tenant occupying a house, flat, etc.

situate (ˈsɪtjʊˌeɪt) *vb.* **1.** (*tr.; often passive*) to place. ~*adj.* **2.** (now used esp. in legal contexts) situated. [C16: < LL *situāre* to position, < L *situs* a SITE]

situation (ˌsɪtjʊˈeɪʃən) *n.* **1.** physical placement, esp. with regard to the surroundings. **2. a.** state of affairs. **b.** a complex or critical state of affairs in a novel, play, etc. **3.** social or financial status, position, or circumstances. **4.** a position of employment. —ˌ**situˈational** *adj.*

situation comedy *n.* (on television or radio) a comedy series involving the same characters in various day-to-day situations which are developed as separate stories for each episode. Also called: **sitcom.**

sit up *vb.* (*adv.*) **1.** to raise (oneself or another) from a recumbent to an upright posture. **2.** (*intr.*) to remain out of bed and awake, esp. until a late hour. **3.** (*intr.*) *Inf.* to become suddenly interested: *devaluation of the dollar made the money market sit up.* ~*n.* **sit-up. 4.** *Gymnastics.* another name for **trunk curl.**

sitz bath (sɪts, zɪts) *n.* a bath in which the buttocks and hips are immersed in hot water. [half translation of G *Sitzbad,* < *Sitz* seat + *Bad* bath]

SI unit *n.* any of the units adopted for international use under the Système International d'Unités, now employed for all scientific and most technical purposes. There are seven fundamental units: the metre, kilogram, second, ampere, kelvin, candela, and mole; and two supplementary units: the radian and the steradian. All other units are derived by multiplication or division of these units.

Siva (ˈsiːvə) *n. Hinduism.* the destroyer, one of the three chief divinities of the later Hindu pantheon. [< Sansk. *Śiva,* lit.: the auspicious (one)] —ˈ**Sivaˌism** *n.*

six (sɪks) *n.* **1.** the cardinal number that is the sum of five and one. **2.** a numeral, 6, VI, etc., representing this number. **3.** something representing, represented by, or consisting of six units, such as a playing card with six symbols on it. **4.** Also: **six o'clock.** six hours after noon or midnight. **5.** *Cricket.* **a.** a stroke from which the ball crosses the boundary without bouncing. **b.** the six runs scored for such a shot. **6.** a division of a Brownie Guide or Cub Scout pack. **7. at sixes and sevens. a.** in disagreement. **b.** in a state of confusion. **8. knock (someone) for six.** *Inf.* to upset or overwhelm (someone) completely. **9. six of one and half a dozen of the other.** a situation in which the alternatives are considered equivalent. ~*determiner.* **10. a.** amounting to six: *six nations.* **b.** (*as pron.*): *set the table for six.* [OE *siex*]

Six Counties *pl. n.* the counties of Northern Ireland.

sixer (ˈsɪksə) *n.* the leader of a group of six Cub Scouts or Brownie Guides.

sixfold (ˈsɪksˌfəʊld) *adj.* **1.** equal to or having six times as many or as much. **2.** composed of six parts. ~*adv.* **3.** by or up to six times as many or as much.

sixmo (ˈsɪksməʊ) *n., pl.* **-mos.** a book size resulting from folding a sheet of paper into six leaves or twelve pages, each one sixth the size of the sheet. Often written: **6mo, 6°.** Also called: **sexto.**

sixpence (ˈsɪkspəns) *n.* (formerly) a small British cupronickel coin with a face value of six old pennies, worth 2½ pence.

six-shooter *n. U.S. inf.* a revolver with six chambers. Also called: **six-gun.**

sixte (sɪkst) *n.* the sixth of eight basic positions from which a parry or attack can be made in fencing. [< F: (the) sixth (parrying position), < L *sextus* sixth]

sixteen (ˈsɪksˈtiːn) *n.* **1.** the cardinal number that is the sum of ten and six. **2.** a numeral, 16, XVI, etc., representing this number. **3.** something represented by, representing, or consisting of 16 units. ~*determiner.* **4. a.** amounting to sixteen: *sixteen tons.* **b.** (*as pron.*): *sixteen are known to the police.* —ˈ**sixˈteenth** *adj., n.*

sixteenmo (ˈsɪksˈtiːnməʊ) *n., pl.* **-mos.** a book size resulting from folding a sheet of paper into 16 leaves or 32 pages. Often written: **16mo, 16°.** Also called: **sextodecimo.**

sixteenth note *n.* the usual U.S. and Canad. name for **semiquaver.**

sixth (sɪksθ) *adj.* **1.** (*usually prenominal*) **a.** coming after the fifth and before the seventh in numbering, position, time, etc.; being the ordinal number of *six:* often written 6th. **b.** (*as n.*)*: the sixth to go.* ~*n.* **2. a.** one of six parts of an object, quantity, measurement, etc. **b.** (*as modifier*)*: a sixth part.* **3.** the fraction equal to one divided by six (1/6). **4.** *Music.* **a.** the interval between one note and another six notes away from it in the diatonic scale. **b.** one of two notes constituting such an interval in relation to the other. ~*adv.* **5.** Also: **sixthly.** after the fifth person, position, etc. ~*sentence connector.* **6.** Also: **sixthly.** as the sixth point.

sixth form *n.* **a.** (in England and Wales) the most senior level in a secondary school to which pupils, usually above the legal leaving age, may proceed to take A levels, retake O levels, etc. **b.** (*as modifier*)*: a sixth-form college.* —ˈ**sixth-ˌformer** *n.*

sixth sense *n.* any supposed means of perception, such as intuition, other than the five senses of sight, hearing, touch, taste, and smell.

sixty (ˈsɪkstɪ) *n., pl.* **-ties. 1.** the cardinal number that is the product of ten and six. **2.** a numeral, 60, LX, etc., representing sixty. **3.** something represented by, representing, or consisting of 60 units. ~*determiner.* **4. a.** amounting to sixty: *sixty soldiers.* **b.** (*as pron.*)*: sixty are dead.* [OE *sixtig*] —ˈ**sixtieth** *adj., n.*

sixty-fourmo (ˌsɪkstɪˈfɔːməʊ) *n., pl.* **-mos.** a book size resulting from folding a sheet of paper into 64 leaves or 128 pages, each one sixty-fourth the size of the sheet. Often written **64mo, 64°.**

sixty-fourth note *n.* the usual U.S. and Canad. name for **hemidemisemiquaver.**

sixty-nine *n.* another term for **soixante-neuf.**

sizable *or* **sizeable** (ˈsaɪzəbᵊl) *adj.* quite large. —ˈ**sizably** *or* ˈ**sizeably** *adv.*

size[1] (saɪz) *n.* **1.** the dimensions, amount, or extent of something. **2.** large dimensions, etc. **3.** one of a series of graduated measurements, as of clothing: *she takes size 4 shoes.* **4.** *Inf.* state of affairs as summarized: *he's bankrupt, that's the size of it.* ~*vb.* **5.** to sort according to size. **6.** (*tr.*) to cut to a particular size or sizes. [C13: < OF *sise,* shortened < *assise* ASSIZE] —ˈ**sizer** *n.*

size[2] (saɪz) *n.* **1.** Also called: **sizing.** a thin gelatinous mixture, made from glue, clay, or wax, that is used as a sealer on paper or plaster surfaces. ~*vb.* **2.** (*tr.*) to treat or coat (a surface) with size. [C15: ? < OF *sise;* see SIZE[1]]

sized (saɪzd) *adj.* of a specified size: *medium-sized.*

size up *vb.* (*adv.*) **1.** (*tr.*) *Inf.* to make an assessment of (a person, problem, etc.). **2.** to conform to or make so as to conform to certain specifications of dimension.

sizzle (ˈsɪzᵊl) *vb.* (*intr.*) **1.** to make the hissing sound characteristic of frying fat. **2.** *Inf.* to be very hot. **3.** *Inf.* to be very angry. ~*n.* **4.** a hissing sound. [C17: imit.] —ˈ**sizzler** *n.* —ˈ**sizzling** *adj.*

SJ *abbrev. for* Society of Jesus.

SJA *abbrev. for* Saint John's Ambulance (Brigade *or* Association).

sjambok (ˈʃæmbʌk) *n.* (in South Africa) a heavy whip of rhinoceros or hippopotamus hide. [C19: < Afrik., ult. < Urdu *chābuk* horsewhip]

ska (skɑː) *n.* a type of West Indian pop music: a precursor of reggae. [C20: <?]

skaapsteker (ˈskɑːpˌstɪəkə) *n.* any of several back-fanged venomous South African snakes. [< Afrik. *skaap* sheep + *steek* to pierce]

skald *or* **scald** (skɔːld) *n.* (in ancient Scandinavia) a bard or minstrel. [< ON, <?] —ˈ**skaldic** *or* ˈ**scaldic** *adj.*

skat (skæt) *n.* a three-handed card game using 32 cards, popular in German-speaking communities. [C19: < G, < It. *scarto* played cards, < *scartare* to discard, < L *charta* CARD[1]]

skate[1] (skeɪt) *n.* **1.** See **roller skate, ice skate. 2.** the steel blade or runner of an ice skate. **3.** such a blade fitted with straps for fastening to a shoe. **4. get one's skates on.** to hurry. ~*vb.* (*intr.*) **5.** to glide swiftly on skates. **6.** to slide smoothly over a surface. **7. skate on thin ice.** to place oneself in a dangerous situation. [C17: via Du. < OF *éschasse* stilt, prob. of Gmc origin] —ˈ**skater** *n.*

skate[2] (skeɪt) *n., pl.* **skate** *or* **skates.** any of a family of large rays of temperate and tropical seas, having two dorsal fins, a short spineless tail, and a long snout. [C14: < ON *skata*]

skateboard (ˈskeɪtˌbɔːd) *n.* **1.** a plank mounted on roller-skate wheels, usually ridden while standing up. ~*vb.* **2.** (*intr.*) to ride on a skateboard. —ˈ**skateˌboarder** *n.* —ˈ**skateˌboarding** *n.*

skate over *vb.* (*intr., prep.*) **1.** to cross on or as if on skates. **2.** to avoid dealing with (a matter) fully.

skean-dhu (ˌskiːənˈduː) *n.* a dirk worn in the stocking as part of Highland dress. [C19: < Gaelic *sgian dubh* black knife]

skedaddle (skɪˈdædᵊl) *Inf.* ~*vb.* **1.** (*intr.*) to run off hastily. ~*n.* **2.** a hasty retreat. [C19: <?]

skeet (skiːt) *n.* a form of clay-pigeon shooting in which targets are hurled from two traps at varying speeds and angles. [C20: changed < ON *skeyti* a thrown object, < *skjōta* to shoot]

skein (skeɪn) *n.* **1.** a length of yarn, etc., wound in a long coil. **2.** something resembling this, such as a lock of hair. **3.** a flock of geese flying. [C15: < OF *escaigne*, <?]

skeleton (ˈskɛlɪtən) *n.* **1.** a hard framework consisting of inorganic material that supports and protects the soft parts of an animal's body: may be internal, as in vertebrates, or external, as in arthropods. **2.** *Inf.* a very thin emaciated person or animal. **3.** the essential framework of any structure, such as a building or leaf. **4.** an outline consisting of bare essentials: *the skeleton of a novel.* **5.** (*modifier*) reduced to a minimum: *a skeleton staff.* **6. skeleton in the cupboard** *or U.S. & Canad.* **closet.** a scandalous fact or event in the past that is kept secret. [C16: via NL < Gk: something desiccated, < *skellein* to dry up] —ˈ**skeletal** *or* ˈ**skeleton-ˌlike** *adj.*

skeletonize *or* **-nise** (ˈskɛlɪtəˌnaɪz) *vb.* (*tr.*) **1.** to reduce to a minimum framework or outline. **2.** to create the essential framework of.

skeleton key *n.* a key with the serrated edge filed down so that it can open numerous locks. Also called: **passkey.**

skep (skɛp) *n.* **1.** a beehive, esp. one constructed of straw. **2.** *Now chiefly dialect.* a large basket of wickerwork or straw. [OE *sceppe*]

skeptic (ˈskɛptɪk) *n., adj.* an archaic and the usual U.S. spelling of **sceptic.**

skerrick (ˈskɛrɪk) *n. U.S., Austral., & N.Z. inf.* a small fragment or amount (esp. in **not a skerrick**). [C20: N English dialect, prob. of Scand. origin]

skerry (ˈskɛrɪ) *n., pl.* **-ries.** *Chiefly Scot.* **1.** a small rocky island. **2.** a reef. [C17: Orkney dialect, < ON *sker* scar (rock formation)]

sketch (skɛtʃ) *n.* **1.** a rapid drawing or painting. **2.** a brief usually descriptive essay or other literary composition. **3.** a short play, often comic, forming part of a revue. **4.** a short evocative piece of instrumental music. **5.** any brief outline. ~*vb.* **6.** to make a rough drawing (of). **7.** (*tr.*; often foll. by *out*) to make a brief description of. [C17: < Du. *schets*, via It. < L *schedius* hastily made, < Gk *skhedios* unprepared] —ˈ**sketcher** *n.*

sketchbook (ˈskɛtʃˌbʊk) *n.* **1.** a book of plain paper containing sketches or for making sketches in. **2.** a book of literary sketches.

sketchy (ˈskɛtʃɪ) *adj.* **sketchier, sketchiest. 1.** existing only in outline. **2.** superficial or slight. —ˈ**sketchily** *adv.* —ˈ**sketchiness** *n.*

skew (skjuː) *adj.* **1.** placed in or turning into an oblique position or course. **2.** *Machinery.* having a component that is at an angle to the main axis of an assembly: *a skew bevel gear.* **3.** *Maths.* composed of or being elements that are neither parallel nor intersecting. **4.** (of a statistical distribution) not having equal probabilities above and below the mean. **5.** distorted or biased. ~*n.* **6.** an oblique, slanting, or indirect course or position. ~*vb.* **7.** to take or cause to take an oblique course or direction. **8.** (*intr.*) to look sideways. **9.** (*tr.*) to distort. [C14: < OF *escuer* to shun, of Gmc origin] —ˈ**skewness** *n.*

skewback (ˈskjuːˌbæk) *n. Archit.* the sloping surface on both sides of a segmental arch that takes the thrust.

skewbald (ˈskjuːˌbɔːld) *adj.* **1.** marked or spotted in white and any colour except black. ~*n.* **2.** a horse with this marking. [C17: see SKEW, PIEBALD]

skewer (skjʊə) *n.* **1.** a long pin for holding meat in position while being cooked, etc. **2.** a similar pin having some other function. ~*vb.* **3.** (*tr.*) to drive a skewer through or fasten with a skewer. [C17: prob. < dialect *skiver*]

skewwhiff (ˈskjuːˈwɪf) *adj.* (*postpositive*) *Brit. inf.* not straight. [C18: prob. infl. by ASKEW]

ski (skiː) *n., pl.* **skis** *or* **ski. 1. a.** one of a pair of wood, metal, or plastic runners that are used for gliding over snow. **b.** (*as modifier*): *a ski boot.* **2.** a water-ski. ~*vb.* **skiing; skied** *or* **ski'd. 3.** (*intr.*) to travel on skis. [C19: < Norwegian, < ON *skith* snowshoes] —ˈ**skier** *n.* —ˈ**skiing** *n.*

skibob (ˈskiːbɒb) *n.* a vehicle made of two short skis, the forward one having a steering handle and the rear one supporting a low seat, for gliding down snow slopes. —ˈ**skibobber** *n.*

skid (skɪd) *vb.* **skidding, skidded. 1.** to cause (a vehicle) to slide sideways or (of a vehicle) to slide sideways while in motion, esp. out of control. **2.** (*intr.*) to slide without revolving, as the wheel of a moving vehicle after sudden braking. ~*n.* **3.** an instance of sliding, esp. sideways. **4.** a support on which heavy objects may be stored and moved short distances by sliding. **5.** a shoe or drag used to apply pressure to the metal rim of a wheel to act as a brake. [C17: ? of Scand. origin]

skidoo (ˈskɪduː) *Canad.* ~*n., pl.* **-doos. 1.** a snowmobile. ~*vb.* (*intr.*) **2.** to travel using a snowmobile. [C20: < *Ski-Doo*, orig. a trademark]

skid row (rəʊ) *or* **skid road** *n. Sl., chiefly U.S. & Canad.* a dilapidated section of a city inhabited by vagrants, etc.

skied[1] (skaɪd) *vb.* the past tense and past participle of **sky.**

skied[2] (skiːd) *vb.* a past tense and past participle of **ski.**

skiff (skɪf) *n.* any of various small boats propelled by oars, sail, or motor. [C18: < F *esquif*, < OIt. *schifo* a boat, of Gmc origin]

skiffle (ˈskɪfᵊl) *n.* a style of popular music of the 1950s, played chiefly on guitars and improvised percussion instruments. [C20: <?]

skijoring (skiːˈdʒɔːrɪŋ, -ˈjɔːrɪŋ) *n.* a sport in which a skier is pulled over snow or ice, usually by a horse. [Norwegian *skikjöring*, lit.: ski-driving] —**ski**ˈ**jorer** *n.*

ski jump *n.* **1.** a high ramp overhanging a slope from which skiers compete to make the longest jump. ~*vb.* **ski-jump. 2.** (*intr.*) to perform a ski jump. —**ski jumper** *n.*

skilful *or U.S.* **skillful** (ˈskɪlfʊl) *adj.* 1. possessing or displaying accomplishment or skill. 2. involving or requiring accomplishment or skill. —ˈ**skilfully** *or U.S.* ˈ**skillfully** *adv.*

ski lift *n.* any device for carrying skiers up a slope, such as a chair lift.

skill (skɪl) *n.* 1. special ability in a sport, etc., esp. ability acquired by training. 2. something, esp. a trade or technique, requiring special training or manual proficiency. [C12: < ON *skil* distinction] —ˈ**skill-less** *or* ˈ**skilless** *adj.*

skilled (skɪld) *adj.* 1. demonstrating accomplishment or special training. 2. (*prenominal*) involving skill or special training: *a skilled job.*

skillet (ˈskɪlɪt) *n.* 1. a small frying pan. 2. *Chiefly Brit.* a saucepan. [C15: prob. < *skele* bucket, < ON]

skilly (ˈskɪlɪ) *n. Chiefly Brit.* a thin soup or gruel. [C19: < *skilligallee*, <?]

skim (skɪm) *vb.* **skimming, skimmed.** 1. (*tr.*) to remove floating material from the surface of (a liquid), as with a spoon: *to skim milk.* 2. to glide smoothly or lightly over (a surface). 3. (*tr.*) to throw (something) in a path over a surface, so as to bounce or ricochet: *to skim stones over water.* 4. (when *intr.*, usually foll. by *through*) to read (a book) in a superficial manner. ~*n.* 5. the act or process of skimming. 6. material skimmed off a liquid, esp. off milk. 7. any thin layer covering a surface. [C15 *skimmen*, prob. < *scumen* to skim]

skimmer (ˈskɪmə) *n.* 1. a person or thing that skims. 2. any of several mainly tropical coastal aquatic birds having a bill with an elongated lower mandible for skimming food from the surface of the water. 3. a flat perforated spoon used for skimming fat from liquids.

skimmia (ˈskɪmɪə) *n.* any of a genus of rutaceous shrubs grown for their ornamental red berries and evergreen foliage. [C18: NL < Japanese (*mijama-*)*shikimi*, a native name of the plant]

skim milk *n.* milk from which the cream has been removed. Also called: **skimmed milk.**

skimp (skɪmp) *vb.* 1. to be extremely sparing or supply (someone) sparingly. 2. to perform (work, etc.) carelessly or with inadequate materials. [C17: ? a combination of SCANT & SCRIMP]

skimpy (ˈskɪmpɪ) *adj.* **skimpier, skimpiest.** 1. made of too little material. 2. excessively thrifty; mean. —ˈ**skimpily** *adv.* —ˈ**skimpiness** *n.*

skin (skɪn) *n.* 1. the tissue forming the outer covering of the vertebrate body: it consists of two layers, the outermost of which may be covered with hair, scales, feathers, etc. 2. a person's complexion: *a fair skin.* 3. any similar covering in a plant or lower animal. 4. any coating or film, such as one that forms on the surface of a liquid. 5. the outer covering of a fur-bearing animal, dressed and finished with the hair on. 6. a container made from animal skin. 7. the outer covering surface of a vessel, rocket, etc. 8. a person's skin regarded as his life: *to save one's skin.* 9. (*often pl.*) *Inf.* (in jazz or pop use) a drum. 10. *Inf.* short for **skinhead.** 11. **by the skin of one's teeth.** only just. 12. **get under one's skin.** *Inf.* to irritate. 13. **no skin off one's nose.** *Inf.* not a matter that affects one adversely. 14. **skin and bone.** extremely thin. 15. **thick** (*or* **thin**) **skin.** an insensitive (*or* sensitive) nature. ~*vb.* **skinning, skinned.** 16. (*tr.*) to remove the outer covering from (fruit, etc.). 17. (*tr.*) to scrape a small piece of skin from (a part of oneself) in falling, etc.: *he skinned his knee.* 18. (often foll. by *over*) to cover (something) with skin or a skinlike substance or (of something) to become covered in this way. 19. (*tr.*) *Sl.* to swindle. ~*adj.* 20. of or for the skin: *skin cream.* [OE *scinn*] —ˈ**skinless** *adj.* —ˈ**skin,like** *adj.*

skin-deep *adj.* 1. superficial; shallow. ~*adv.* 2. superficially.

skin diving *n.* the sport or activity of underwater swimming using breathing apparatus. —ˈ**skin-,diver** *n.*

skin flick *n. Sl.* a film containing much nudity and explicit sex for sensational purposes.

skinflint (ˈskɪn,flɪnt) *n.* an ungenerous or niggardly person. [C18: referring to a person so avaricious that he would skin (swindle) a flint]

skinful (ˈskɪn,fʊl) *n., pl.* **-fuls.** *Sl.* sufficient alcoholic drink to make one drunk.

skin graft *n.* a piece of skin removed from one part of the body and surgically grafted at the site of a severe burn or similar injury.

skinhead (ˈskɪn,hɛd) *n. Brit.* one of a gang of White boys characterized by closely cropped hair, heavy boots, and braces.

skink (skɪŋk) *n.* any of a family of lizards commonest in tropical Africa and Asia, having an elongated body covered with smooth scales. [C16: < L *scincus* a lizard, < Gk *skinkos*]

skinned (skɪnd) *adj.* 1. stripped of the skin. 2. a. having a skin as specified. b. (*in combination*): *thick-skinned.*

skinny (ˈskɪnɪ) *adj.* **-nier, -niest.** 1. lacking in flesh; thin. 2. consisting of or resembling skin.

skint (skɪnt) *adj.* (*usually postpositive*) *Brit. sl.* without money. [var. of *skinned*, p.p. of SKIN]

skin test *n. Med.* any test to determine immunity to a disease or hypersensitivity by introducing a small amount of the test substance beneath the skin.

skintight (ˈskɪnˈtaɪt) *adj.* (of garments) fitting tightly over the body; clinging.

skip[1] (skɪp) *vb.* **skipping, skipped.** 1. (when *intr.*, often foll. by *over, into*, etc.) to spring or move lightly, esp. to move by hopping from one foot to the other. 2. (*intr.*) to jump over a skipping-rope. 3. to cause (a stone, etc.) to skim over a surface or (of a stone) to move in this way. 4. to omit (intervening matter): *he skipped a chapter of the book.* 5. (*intr.*; foll. by *through*) *Inf.* to read or deal with quickly or superficially. 6. **skip it!** *Inf.* it doesn't matter! 7. (*tr.*) *Inf.* to miss deliberately: *to skip school.* 8. (*tr.*) *Inf.*, *chiefly U.S. & Canad.* to leave (a place) in haste: *to skip town.* ~*n.* 9. a skipping movement or gait. 10. the act of passing over or omitting. [C13: prob. < ON]

skip[2] (skɪp) *n., vb.* **skipping, skipped.** *Inf.* short for **skipper**[1].

skip[3] (skɪp) *n.* 1. a large open container for transporting building materials, etc. 2. a cage used as a lift in mines, etc. [C19: var. of SKEP]

ski pants *pl. n.* stretch trousers, worn for skiing or as a fashion garment, kept taut by a strap under the foot.

skip distance *n.* the shortest distance between a transmitter and a receiver that will permit reception of radio waves of a specified frequency by one reflection from the ionosphere.

skipjack (ˈskɪp,dʒæk) *n., pl.* **-jack** *or* **-jacks.** 1. Also called: **skipjack tuna.** an important food fish that has a striped abdomen and occurs in all tropical seas. 2. **black skipjack.** a small spotted tuna of Indo-Pacific seas.

skiplane (ˈski:,pleɪn) *n.* an aircraft fitted with skis to enable it to land on and take off from snow.

skipper[1] (ˈskɪpə) *n.* 1. the captain of any vessel. 2. the captain of an aircraft. 3. a leader, as of a sporting team. ~*vb.* 4. to act as skipper (of). [C14: < MLow G, MDu. *schipper* shipper]

skipper[2] (ˈskɪpə) *n.* 1. a person or thing that skips. 2. a small butterfly having a hairy mothlike body and erratic darting flight.

skipping (ˈskɪpɪŋ) *n.* the act of jumping over a rope that is held either by the person jumping or by two other people, as a game or for exercise.

skipping-rope *n. Brit.* a cord, usually having handles at each end, that is held in the hands and swung round and down so that the holder or others can jump over it.

skip zone *n.* a region surrounding a broadcasting station that cannot receive transmissions either directly or by reflection off the ionosphere.

skirl (skɜ:l) *Scot. & N English dialect.* ~*vb.* 1. (*intr.*) (esp. of bagpipes) to emit a shrill sound. ~*n.* 2. the sound of bagpipes. [C14: prob. < ON]

skirmish (ˈskɜ:mɪʃ) *n.* 1. a minor short-lived military engagement. 2. any brisk clash or encounter. ~*vb.* 3. (*intr.*; often foll. by *with*) to engage in a skirmish. [C14: < OF *eskirmir*, of Gmc origin] —ˈ**skirmisher** *n.*

skirt (skɜːt) *n.* 1. a garment hanging from the waist, worn chiefly by women and girls. 2. the part of a dress below the waist. 3. Also called: **apron.** a circular flap, as round the base of a hovercraft. 4. the flaps on a saddle. 5. *Brit.* a cut of beef from the flank. 6. (*often pl.*) an outlying area. 7. **bit of skirt.** *Sl.* a girl or woman. ~*vb.* 8. (*tr.*) to form the edge of. 9. (*tr.*) to provide with a border. 10. (when *intr.*, foll. by *around, along,* etc.) to pass (by) or be situated (near) the outer edge of (an area, etc.). 11. (*tr.*) to avoid (a difficulty, etc.): *he skirted the issue.* 12. *Chiefly Austral. & N.Z.* to trim the ragged edges from (a fleece). [C13: < ON *skyrta* shirt] —ˈ**skirted** *adj.*

skirting (ˈskɜːtɪŋ) *n.* 1. a border, esp. of wood or tiles, fixed round the base of an interior wall to protect it. 2. material used for skirts.

skirting board *n.* a skirting made of wood.

skirtings (ˈskɜːtɪŋz) *pl. n. Austral. & N.Z.* ragged edges trimmed from the fleece of a sheep.

ski stick *or* **pole** *n.* a stick, usually with a metal point, used by skiers to gain momentum and maintain balance.

skit (skɪt) *n.* 1. a brief satirical theatrical sketch. 2. a short satirical piece of writing. [C18: rel. to earlier verb *skit* to move rapidly, hence to score a satirical hit, prob. of Scand. origin]

skite[1] (skaɪt) *Scot. dialect.* ~*vb.* 1. (*intr.*) to slide or slip, as on ice. 2. (*tr.*) to strike with a sharp blow. ~*n.* 3. an instance of slipping or sliding. 4. a sharp blow. [C18: <?]

skite[2] (skaɪt) *Austral. & N.Z. inf.* ~*vb.* (*intr.*) 1. to boast. ~*n.* 2. boastful talk. 3. a person who boasts. [C19: < Scot. & N English dialect]

ski tow *n.* a device for pulling skiers uphill, usually a motor-driven rope grasped by the skier while riding on his skis.

skitter (ˈskɪtə) *vb.* 1. (*intr.*; often foll. by *off*) to move or run rapidly or lightly. 2. to skim or cause to skim lightly and rapidly. 3. (*intr.*) *Angling.* to draw a bait lightly over the surface of water. [C19: prob. < dialect *skite* to dash about]

skittish (ˈskɪtɪʃ) *adj.* 1. playful, lively, or frivolous. 2. difficult to handle or predict. [C15: prob. < ON] —ˈ**skittishly** *adv.* —ˈ**skittishness** *n.*

skittle (ˈskɪtᵊl) *n.* 1. a wooden or plastic pin, typically widest just above the base. 2. (*pl.; functioning as sing.*) Also called (esp. U.S.): **ninepins.** a bowling game in which players knock over as many skittles as possible by rolling a wooden ball at them. [C17: <?]

skive[1] (skaɪv) *vb.* (*tr.*) to shave or remove the surface of (leather). [C19: of Scand. origin, < *skifa*] —ˈ**skiver** *n.*

skive[2] (skaɪv) *vb.* (when *intr.*, often foll. by *off*) *Brit. inf.* to evade (work or responsibility). [C20: <?] —ˈ**skiver** *n.*

skivvy[1] (ˈskɪvɪ) *n., pl.* **-vies.** 1. *Chiefly Brit., often contemptuous.* a servant, esp. a female; drudge. ~*vb.* **-vying, -vied.** 2. (*intr.*) *Brit.* to work as a skivvy. [C20: <?]

skivvy[2] (ˈskɪvɪ) *n., pl.* **-vies.** *Austral. & N.Z.* a lightweight sweater-like garment with long sleeves and a polo neck. [<?]

skol (skɒl) *or* **skoal** (skəʊl) *sentence substitute* good health! (a drinking toast). [C16: < Danish *skaal* bowl, of Scand. origin, < *skal*]

skookum (ˈskuːkəm) *adj. W Canad.* large or big. [< Chinook Jargon]

Skt, Skt., Skr, *or* **Skr.** *abbrev. for* Sanskrit.

skua (ˈskjuːə) *n.* any of various predatory aquatic gull-like birds having a dark plumage and long tail. [C17: < NL, < Faeroese *skūgvur,* of Scand. origin, < *skūfr*]

skulduggery *or U.S.* **skullduggery** (skʌlˈdʌgərɪ) *n. Inf.* underhand dealing; trickery. [C18: < earlier Scot. *skulduddery,* <?]

skulk (skʌlk) *vb.* (*intr.*) 1. to move stealthily so as to avoid notice. 2. to lie in hiding; lurk. 3. to shirk duty or evade responsibilities. ~*n.* 4. a person who skulks. 5. *Obs.* a pack of foxes. [C13: < ON] —ˈ**skulker** *n.*

skull (skʌl) *n.* 1. the bony skeleton of the head of vertebrates. 2. *Often derog.* the head regarded as the mind or intelligence: *to have a dense skull.* 3. a picture of a skull used to represent death or danger. [C13: < ON]

skull and crossbones *n.* a picture of the human skull above two crossed thighbones, formerly on the pirate flag, now used as a warning of danger or death.

skullcap (ˈskʌlˌkæp) *n.* 1. a rounded brimless hat fitting the crown of the head. 2. the top part of the skull. 3. any of a genus of perennial plants, that have helmet-shaped flowers.

skunk (skʌŋk) *n., pl.* **skunk** *or* **skunks.** 1. any of various American mammals having a black-and-white coat and bushy tail: they eject an unpleasant-smelling fluid from the anal gland when attacked. 2. *Inf.* a despicable person. [C17: of Amerind origin]

skunk cabbage *n.* a low-growing fetid aroid swamp plant of E North America, having broad leaves and minute flowers enclosed in a greenish spathe.

sky (skaɪ) *n., pl.* **skies.** 1. (*sometimes pl.*) the apparently dome-shaped expanse extending upwards from the horizon that is blue or grey during the day and black at night. 2. outer space, as seen from the earth. 3. (*often pl.*) weather, as described by the appearance of the upper air: *sunny skies.* 4. heaven. 5. *Inf.* the highest level of attainment: *the sky's the limit.* 6. **to the skies.** extravagantly. ~*vb.* **skying, skied.** 7. *Rowing.* to lift (the blade of an oar) too high before a stroke. 8. (*tr.*) *Inf.* to hit (a ball) high in the air. [C13: < ON *sky̅*]

sky blue *n., adj.* (of) a light or pale blue colour.

skydiving (ˈskaɪˌdaɪvɪŋ) *n.* the sport of parachute jumping, in which participants perform manoeuvres before opening the parachute. —ˈ**sky,dive** *vb.* (*intr.*) —ˈ**sky,diver** *n.*

Skye terrier (skaɪ) *n.* a short-legged long-bodied breed of terrier with long wiry hair and erect ears. [C19: after *Skye,* Scot. island]

sky-high *adj., adv.* 1. at or to an unprecedented level: *prices rocketed sky-high.* ~*adv.* 2. high into the air. 3. **blow sky-high.** to destroy.

skyjack (ˈskaɪˌdʒæk) *vb.* (*tr.*) to hijack (an aircraft). [C20: < SKY + HIJACK]

skylark (ˈskaɪˌlɑːk) *n.* 1. an Old World lark, noted for singing while hovering at a great height. ~*vb.* 2. (*intr.*) *Inf.* to romp or play jokes.

skylight (ˈskaɪˌlaɪt) *n.* a window placed in a roof or ceiling to admit daylight. Also called: **fanlight.**

skyline (ˈskaɪˌlaɪn) *n.* 1. the line at which the earth and sky appear to meet. 2. the outline of buildings, trees, etc., seen against the sky.

sky pilot *n. Sl.* a clergyman, esp. a chaplain.

skyrocket (ˈskaɪˌrɒkɪt) *n.* 1. another word for **rocket** (sense 1). ~*vb.* 2. (*intr.*) *Inf.* to rise rapidly, as in price.

skysail (ˈskaɪˌseɪl) *n. Naut.* a square sail set above the royal on a square-rigger.

skyscraper (ˈskaɪˌskreɪpə) *n.* a very tall multistorey building.

skyward (ˈskaɪwəd) *adj.* 1. directed or moving towards the sky. ~*adv.* 2. Also: **skywards.** towards the sky.

skywriting (ˈskaɪˌraɪtɪŋ) *n.* 1. the forming of words in the sky by the release of smoke or vapour from an aircraft. 2. the words so formed. —ˈ**sky,writer** *n.*

slab (slæb) *n.* 1. a broad flat thick piece of wood, stone, or other material. 2. a thick slice of cake, etc. 3. any of the outside parts of a log that are sawn off while the log is being made into planks. 4. *Austral. & N.Z.* **a.** a rough-hewn wooden plank. **b.** (*as modifier*): *a slab hut.* 5. *Inf., chiefly Brit.* an operating or mortuary table. ~*vb.* **slabbing, slabbed.** (*tr.*) 6. to cut or make into a slab or slabs. 7. to saw slabs from (a log). [C13: <?]

slack[1] (slæk) *adj.* 1. not tight, tense, or taut. 2. negligent or careless. 3. (esp. of water, etc.) moving slowly. 4. (of trade, etc.) not busy. 5. *Phonetics.* another term for **lax** (sense 4). ~*adv.* 6. in a slack manner. ~*n.* 7. a part of a rope, etc., that is slack: *take in the slack.* 8. a period of decreased activity. ~*vb.* 9. to neglect (one's duty, etc.). 10. (often foll. by *off*) to loosen. ~See also **slacks.** [OE *slæc, sleac*] —'**slackly** *adv.* —'**slackness** *n.*

slack[2] (slæk) *n.* small pieces of coal with a high ash content. [C15: prob. < MLow G *slecke*]

slacken ('slækən) *vb.* (often foll. by *off*) **1.** to make or become looser. **2.** to make or become slower, less intense, etc.

slacker ('slækə) *n.* a person who evades work or duty; shirker.

slacks (slæks) *pl. n.* informal trousers worn by both sexes.

slack water *n.* the period of still water around the turn of the tide, esp. at low tide.

slag (slæg) *n.* **1.** Also called: **cinder.** the fused material formed during the smelting or refining of metals. It usually consists of a mixture of silicates with calcium, phosphorus, sulphur, etc. **2.** the mass of rough fragments of rock derived from volcanic lava. **3.** a mixture of shale, clay, coal dust, etc., produced during coal mining. ~*vb.* **slagging, slagged. 4.** to convert into or become slag. **5.** (*tr.;* sometimes foll. by *off*) *Sl.* to make disparaging comments about; slander. [C16: < MLow G *slagge,* ? < *slagen* to slay] —'**slagging** *n.* —'**slaggy** *adj.*

slag heap *n.* a hillock of waste matter from coal mining, etc.

slain (sleɪn) *vb.* the past participle of **slay.**

slake (sleɪk) *vb.* **1.** (*tr.*) *Literary.* to satisfy (thirst, desire, etc.). **2.** (*tr.*) *Poetic.* to cool or refresh. **3.** to undergo or cause to undergo the process in which lime reacts with water to produce calcium hydroxide. [OE *slacian,* < *slæc* SLACK[1]] —'**slakable** *or* '**slakeable** *adj.*

slaked lime *n.* another name for **calcium hydroxide.**

slalom ('slɑːləm) *n. Skiing, canoeing, etc.* a race over a winding course marked by artificial obstacles. [Norwegian, < *slad* sloping + *lom* path]

slam[1] (slæm) *vb.* **slamming, slammed. 1.** to cause (a door or window) to close noisily or (of a door, etc.) to close in this way. **2.** (*tr.*) to throw (something) down violently. **3.** (*tr.*) *Sl.* to criticize harshly. **4.** (*intr.;* usually foll. by *into* or *out of*) *Inf.* to go (into or out of a room, etc.) in violent haste or anger. **5.** (*tr.*) to strike with violent force. **6.** (*tr.*) *Inf.* to defeat easily. ~*n.* **7.** the act or noise of slamming. [C17: of Scand. origin]

slam[2] (slæm) *n.* **a.** the winning of all (**grand slam**) or all but one (**little** *or* **small slam**) of the 13 tricks at bridge or whist. **b.** the bid to do so in bridge. [C17: <?]

slammer ('slæmə) *n.* **the.** *Sl.* prison.

slander ('slɑːndə) *n.* **1.** *Law.* **a.** defamation in some transient form, as by spoken words, gestures, etc. **b.** a slanderous statement, etc. **2.** any defamatory words spoken about a person. ~*vb.* **3.** to utter or circulate slander (about). [C13: via Anglo-F < OF *escandle,* < LL *scandalum* a cause of offence; see SCANDAL] —'**slanderer** *n.* —'**slanderous** *adj.*

slang (slæŋ) *n.* **1. a.** vocabulary, idiom, etc., that is not appropriate to the standard form of a language or to formal contexts and may be restricted as to social status or distribution. **b.** (*as modifier*): *a slang word.* ~*vb.* **2.** to abuse (someone) with vituperative language. [C18: <?] —'**slangy** *adj.* —'**slangily** *adv.* —'**slanginess** *n.*

slant (slɑːnt) *vb.* **1.** to incline or be inclined at an oblique or sloping angle. **2.** (*tr.*) to write or present (news, etc.) with a bias. **3.** (*intr.;* foll. by *towards*) (of a person's opinions) to be biased. ~*n.* **4.** an inclined or oblique line or direction. **5.** a way of looking at something. **6.** a bias or opinion, as in an article. **7. on a** (*or* **the**) **slant.** sloping. ~*adj.* **8.** oblique; sloping. [C17: short for ASLANT, prob. of Scand. origin] —'**slanting** *adj.*

slantwise ('slɑːnt,waɪz) *or* **slantways** *adv., adj.* (*prenominal*) in a slanting or oblique direction.

slap (slæp) *n.* **1.** a sharp blow or smack, as with the open hand, something flat, etc. **2.** the sound made by or as if by such a blow. **3. (a bit of) slap and tickle.** *Brit. inf.* sexual play. **4. a slap in the face.** an insult or rebuff. **5. a slap on the back.** congratulation. ~*vb.* **slapping, slapped. 6.** (*tr.*) to strike (a person or thing) sharply, as with the open hand or something flat. **7.** (*tr.*) to bring down (the hand, etc.) sharply. **8.** (when *intr.,* usually foll. by *against*) to strike (something) with or as if with a slap. **9.** (*tr.*) *Inf., chiefly Brit.* to apply in large quantities, haphazardly, etc.: *she slapped butter on the bread.* **10. slap on the back.** to congratulate. ~*adv. Inf.* **11.** exactly: *slap on time.* **12.** forcibly or abruptly: *to fall slap on the floor.* [C17: < Low G *slapp,* G *Schlappe,* imit.]

slapdash ('slæp,dæʃ) *adv.* **1.** in a careless, hasty, or haphazard manner. ~*adj.* **2.** careless, hasty, or haphazard. ~*n.* **3.** slapdash activity or work.

slaphappy ('slæp,hæpɪ) *adj.* **-pier, -piest.** *Inf.* **1.** cheerfully irresponsible or careless. **2.** dazed or giddy from or as if from repeated blows.

slapstick ('slæp,stɪk) *n.* **1. a.** comedy characterized by horseplay and physical action. **b.** (*as modifier*): *slapstick humour.* **2.** a pair of paddles formerly used in pantomime to strike a blow with a loud sound but without injury.

slap-up *adj.* (*prenominal*) *Brit. inf.* (esp. of meals) lavish; excellent; first-class.

slash (slæʃ) *vb.* (*tr.*) **1.** to cut or lay about (a person or thing) with sharp sweeping strokes, as with a sword, etc. **2.** to lash with a whip. **3.** to make large gashes in: *to slash tyres.* **4.** to reduce (prices, etc.) drastically. **5.** to criticize harshly. **6.** to slit (the outer fabric of a garment) so that the lining material is revealed. ~*n.* **7.** a sharp sweeping stroke, as with a sword or whip. **8.** a cut or rent made by such a stroke. **9.** a decorative slit in a garment revealing the lining material. **10.** *North American.* littered wood chips that remain after trees have been cut down. **11.** another name for **solidus. 12.** *Brit. sl.* the act of urinating. [C14 *slaschen,* ? < OF *esclachier* to break]

slasher ('slæʃə) *n.* **1.** a person or thing that slashes. **2.** *N.Z.* a tool used for cutting scrub or undergrowth in the bush.

slashing ('slæʃɪŋ) *adj.* aggressively or harshly critical (esp. in **slashing attack**).

slat (slæt) *n.* **1.** a narrow thin strip of wood or metal, as used in a Venetian blind, etc. **2.** a movable or fixed aerofoil attached to the leading edge of an aircraft wing to increase lift. [C14: < OF *esclat* splinter, < *esclater* to shatter]

slate[1] (sleɪt) *n.* **1. a.** a compact fine-grained metamorphic rock that can be split into thin layers and is used as a roofing and paving material. **b.** (*as modifier*): *a slate tile.* **2.** a roofing tile of slate. **3.** (formerly) a writing tablet of slate. **4.** a dark grey colour. **5.** *Chiefly U.S. & Canad.* a list of candidates in an election. **6. clean slate.** a record without dishonour. **7. on the slate.** *Brit. inf.* on credit. ~*vb.* (*tr.*) **8.** to cover (a roof) with slates. **9.** *Chiefly U.S.* to enter (a person's name) on a list, esp. on a political slate. ~*adj.* **10.** of the colour slate. [C14: < OF *esclate,* < *esclat* a fragment] —'**slaty** *adj.*

slate[2] (sleɪt) *vb.* (*tr.*) *Inf., chiefly Brit.* to criticize harshly. [C19: prob. < SLATE[1]] —'**slating** *n.*

slater ('sleɪtə) *n.* **1.** a person trained in laying roof slates. **2.** another name for **woodlouse.**

slather ('slɑːðə) *n.* **1.** (*usually pl.*) *Inf., chiefly U.S. & Canad.* a large quantity. **2. open slather.** *Austral. & N.Z. sl.* a free-for-all. [C19: <?]

slattern ('slætən) *n.* a slovenly woman or girl. [C17: prob. < *slattering,* < dialect *slatter* to slop] —'**slatternly** *adj.* —'**slatternliness** *n.*

slaughter ('slɔːtə) *n.* **1.** the killing of animals, esp. for food. **2.** the savage killing of a person. **3.** the indiscriminate or brutal killing of large numbers of people, as in war. ~*vb.* (*tr.*) **4.** to kill (animals), esp. for food. **5.** to kill in a brutal manner. **6.** to kill indiscriminately or in large numbers. [OE *sleaht*] —'**slaughterer** *n.* —'**slaughterous** *adj.*

slaughterhouse ('slɔːtə,haʊs) *n.* a place where animals are butchered for food; abattoir.

Slav (slɑːv) *n.* a member of any of the peoples of E Europe or Soviet Asia who speak a Slavonic language. [C14: < Med. L *Sclāvus* a captive Slav; see SLAVE]

slave (sleɪv) *n.* **1.** a person legally owned by another and having no freedom of action or right to property. **2.** a person who is forced to work for another against his will. **3.** a person under the domination of another person or some habit or influence. **4.** a drudge. **5.** a device that is controlled by or that duplicates the action of another similar device. ~*vb.* **6.** (*intr.;* often foll. by *away*) to work like a slave. [C13: via OF < Med. L *Sclāvus* a Slav, one held in bondage (the Slavonic races were frequently conquered in the Middle Ages), < LGk *Sklabos* a Slav]

slave cylinder *n.* a small cylinder containing a piston that operates the brake shoes or pads in hydraulic brakes or the working part in any other hydraulically operated system.

slave-driver *n.* **1.** (esp. formerly) a person forcing slaves to work. **2.** an employer who demands excessively hard work from his employees.

slaveholder (ˈsleɪvˌhəʊldə) *n.* a person who owns slaves. —ˈ**slaveˌholding** *n.*

slaver[1] (ˈsleɪvə) *n.* **1.** an owner of or dealer in slaves. **2.** another name for **slave ship.**

slaver[2] (ˈslævə) *vb.* (*intr.*) **1.** to dribble saliva. **2.** (often foll. by *over*) **a.** to fawn or drool (over someone). **b.** to show great desire (for). ~*n.* **3.** saliva dribbling from the mouth. **4.** *Inf.* drivel. [C14: prob. < Low Du.] —ˈ**slaverer** *n.*

slavery (ˈsleɪvərɪ) *n.* **1.** the state or condition of being a slave. **2.** the subjection of a person to another person, esp. in being forced into work. **3.** the condition of being subject to some influence or habit. **4.** work done in harsh conditions for low pay.

slave ship *n.* a ship used to transport slaves, esp. formerly from Africa to the New World.

Slave State *n. U.S. history.* any of the 15 Southern states in which slavery was legal until the Civil War.

slave trade *n.* the business of trading in slaves, esp. the transportation of Black Africans to America from the 16th to 19th centuries. —ˈ**slave-ˌtrader** *n.* —ˈ**slave-ˌtrading** *n.*

slavey (ˈsleɪvɪ) *n. Brit. inf.* a female general servant.

Slavic (ˈslɑːvɪk) *n., adj.* another word (esp. U.S.) for **Slavonic.**

slavish (ˈsleɪvɪʃ) *adj.* **1.** of or befitting a slave. **2.** being or resembling a slave. **3.** unoriginal; imitative. —ˈ**slavishly** *adv.*

Slavonic (sləˈvɒnɪk) *or esp. U.S.* **Slavic** *n.* **1.** a branch of the Indo-European family of languages, usually divided into three subbranches: **South Slavonic** (including Bulgarian), **East Slavonic** (including Russian), and **West Slavonic** (including Polish and Czech). ~*adj.* **2.** of or relating to this group of languages. **3.** of or relating to the people who speak these languages.

slaw (slɔː) *n. Chiefly U.S. & Canad.* short for **coleslaw.** [C19: < Danish *sla,* short for *salade* SALAD]

slay (sleɪ) *vb.* **slaying, slew, slain.** (*tr.*) **1.** *Arch. or literary.* to kill, esp. violently. **2.** *Sl.* to impress (someone of the opposite sex). [OE *slēan*] —ˈ**slayer** *n.*

sleaze (sliːz) *n. Inf.* sleaziness.

sleazy (ˈsliːzɪ) *adj.* **-zier, -ziest. 1.** disreputable: *a sleazy nightclub.* **2.** flimsy, as cloth. [C17: <?] —ˈ**sleazily** *adv.* —ˈ**sleaziness** *n.*

sledge[1] (slɛdʒ) *or esp. U.S. & Canad.* **sled** (slɛd) *n.* **1.** a vehicle mounted on runners, drawn by horses or dogs, for transporting people or goods, esp. over snow. **2.** a light wooden frame used, esp. by children, for sliding over snow. ~*vb.* **3.** to convey, travel, or go by sledge. [C17: < MDu. *sleedse;* C14 *sled,* < MLow G, < ON *slethi*] —ˈ**sledger** *n.*

sledge[2] (slɛdʒ) *n.* short for **sledgehammer.**

sledge[3] (slɛdʒ) *vb.* (*tr.*) *Austral.* to bait (an opponent, esp. a batsman in cricket) in order to upset his concentration. [<?]

sledgehammer (ˈslɛdʒˌhæmə) *n.* **1.** a large heavy hammer with a long handle used with both hands for heavy work such as breaking rocks, etc. **2.** (*modifier*) resembling the action of a sledgehammer in power, etc.: *a sledgehammer blow.* [C15: *sledge,* < OE *slecg* a large hammer]

sleek (sliːk) *adj.* **1.** smooth and shiny. **2.** polished in speech or behaviour. **3.** (of an animal or bird) having a shiny healthy coat or feathers. **4.** (of a person) having a prosperous appearance. ~*vb.* (*tr.*) **5.** to make smooth and glossy, as by grooming, etc. **6.** (usually foll. by *over*) to gloss (over). [C16: var. of SLICK] —ˈ**sleekly** *adv.* —ˈ**sleekness** *n.* —ˈ**sleeky** *adj.*

sleep (sliːp) *n.* **1.** a periodic state of physiological rest during which consciousness is suspended. **2.** *Bot.* the nontechnical name for **nyctitropism. 3.** a period spent sleeping. **4.** a state of quiescence or dormancy. **5.** a poetic word for **death.** ~*vb.* **sleeping, slept. 6.** (*intr.*) to be in or as in the state of sleep. **7.** (*intr.*) (of plants) to show nyctitropism. **8.** (*intr.*) to be inactive or quiescent. **9.** (*tr.*) to have sleeping accommodation for (a certain number): *the boat could sleep six.* **10.** (*tr.;* foll. by *away*) to pass (time) sleeping. **11.** (*intr.*) *Poetic.* to be dead. **12. sleep on it.** to give (something) extended consideration, esp. overnight. ~See also **sleep around, sleep in,** etc. [OE *slǣpan*]

sleep around *vb.* (*intr., adv.*) *Inf.* to be sexually promiscuous.

sleeper (ˈsliːpə) *n.* **1.** a person, animal, or thing that sleeps. **2.** a railway sleeping car or compartment. **3.** *Brit.* one of the blocks supporting the rails on a railway track. **4.** a heavy timber beam, esp. one that is laid horizontally on the ground. **5.** *Chiefly Brit.* a small plain gold circle worn in a pierced ear lobe to prevent the hole from closing up. **6.** *Inf., chiefly U.S. & Canad.* a person or thing that achieves unexpected success. **7.** a spy planted in advance for future use.

sleep in *vb.* (*intr., adv.*) **1.** *Brit.* to sleep longer than usual. **2.** to sleep at the place of one's employment.

sleeping bag *n.* a large well-padded bag designed for sleeping in, esp. outdoors.

sleeping car *n.* a railway carriage fitted with compartments containing bunks for people to sleep in.

sleeping partner *n.* a partner in a business who does not play an active role. Also called: **silent partner.**

sleeping pill *n.* a pill or tablet containing a sedative drug, such as a barbiturate, used to induce sleep.

sleeping policeman *n.* a bump built across a road to deter motorists from speeding. Official name: **road hump.**

sleeping sickness *n.* **1.** Also called: **African sleeping sickness.** an African disease transmitted by the bite of tsetse fly, characterized by fever and sluggishness. **2.** Also called: **sleepy sickness.** an epidemic viral form of encephalitis characterized by extreme drowsiness. Technical name: **encephalitis lethargica.**

sleepless (ˈsliːplɪs) *adj.* **1.** without sleep or rest: *a sleepless journey.* **2.** unable to sleep. **3.** always alert. **4.** *Chiefly poetic.* always active or moving. —ˈ**sleeplessly** *adv.* —ˈ**sleeplessness** *n.*

sleep off *vb.* (*tr., adv.*) *Inf.* to lose by sleeping: *to sleep off a hangover.*

sleep out *vb.* (*intr., adv.*) **1.** (esp. of a tramp) to sleep in the open air. **2.** to sleep away from the place of one's employment. ~*n.* **sleep-out. 3.** *Austral. & N.Z.* an area of a veranda partitioned off so that it may be used as a bedroom.

sleepwalk (ˈsliːpˌwɔːk) *vb.* (*intr.*) to walk while asleep. —ˈ**sleepˌwalker** *n.* —ˈ**sleepˌwalking** *n., adj.*

sleep with *vb.* (*intr., prep.*) to have sexual intercourse and (usually) spend the night with. Also: **sleep together.**

sleepy (ˈsliːpɪ) *adj.* **sleepier, sleepiest. 1.** inclined to or needing sleep. **2.** characterized by or exhibiting drowsiness, etc. **3.** conducive to sleep.

4. without activity or bustle: *a sleepy town.* —**'sleepily** *adv.* —**'sleepiness** *n.*

sleet (sliːt) *n.* 1. partly melted falling snow or hail or (esp. U.S.) partly frozen rain. 2. *Chiefly U.S.* the thin coat of ice that forms when sleet or rain freezes on cold surfaces. ~*vb.* 3. (*intr.*) to fall as sleet. [C13: of Gmc origin] —**'sleety** *adj.*

sleeve (sliːv) *n.* 1. the part of a garment covering the arm. 2. a tubular piece that is shrunk into a cylindrical bore to reduce its bore or to line it with a different material. 3. a tube fitted externally over two cylindrical parts in order to join them. 4. a flat cardboard container to protect a gramophone record. U.S. name: **jacket.** 5. (**have a few tricks**) **up one's sleeve.** (to have options, etc.) secretly ready. 6. **roll up one's sleeves.** to prepare oneself for work, a fight, etc. ~*vb.* 7. (*tr.*) to provide with a sleeve or sleeves. [OE *slīf, slēf*] —**'sleeveless** *adj.* —**'sleeve,like** *adj.*

sleeve board *n.* a small ironing board for pressing sleeves, fitted onto an ironing board or table.

sleeving ('sliːvɪŋ) *n.* *Electronics, chiefly Brit.* tubular flexible insulation into which bare wire can be inserted.

sleigh (sleɪ) *n.* 1. another name for **sledge**[1] (sense 1). ~*vb.* 2. (*intr.*) to travel by sleigh. [C18: < Du. *slee,* var. of *slede* SLEDGE[1]]

sleight (slaɪt) *n. Arch.* 1. skill; dexterity. 2. a trick or stratagem. 3. cunning. [C14: < ON *slægth,* < *slǣgr* SLY]

sleight of hand *n.* 1. manual dexterity used in performing conjuring tricks. 2. the performance of such tricks.

slender ('slɛndə) *adj.* 1. of small width relative to length or height. 2. (esp. of a person's figure) slim and well-formed. 3. small or inadequate in amount, size, etc.: *slender resources.* 4. (of hopes, etc.) feeble. 5. very small: *a slender margin.* [C14 *slendre,* <?] —**'slenderly** *adv.* —**'slenderness** *n.*

slenderize *or* **-rise** ('slɛndə,raɪz) *vb. Chiefly U.S. & Canad.* to make or become slender.

slept (slɛpt) *vb.* the past tense and past participle of **sleep.**

sleuth (sluːθ) *n.* 1. an informal word for **detective.** 2. short for **sleuthhound** (sense 1). ~*vb.* 3. (*tr.*) to track or follow. [C19: short for *sleuthhound,* < C12 *sleuth* trail, < ON *sloth*]

sleuthhound ('sluːθ,haʊnd) *n.* 1. a dog trained to track people, esp. a bloodhound. 2. an informal word for **detective.**

slew[1] (sluː) *vb.* the past tense of **slay.**

slew[2] *or esp. U.S.* **slue** (sluː) *vb.* 1. to twist or be twisted sideways, esp. awkwardly. 2. *Naut.* to cause (a mast) to rotate in its step or (of a mast) to rotate in its step. ~*n.* 3. the act of slewing. [C18: <?]

slew[3] (sluː) *n.* a variant spelling (esp. U.S.) of **slough**[1] (sense 2).

slew[4] *or* **slue** (sluː) *n. U.S. & Canad. inf.* a great number. [C20: < Irish Gaelic *sluagh*]

slice (slaɪs) *n.* 1. a thin flat piece cut from something having bulk: *a slice of pork.* 2. a share or portion: *a slice of the company's revenue.* 3. any of various utensils having a broad flat blade and resembling a spatula. 4. (in golf, tennis, etc.) a. the flight of a ball that travels obliquely. b. the action of hitting such a shot. c. the shot so hit. ~*vb.* 5. to divide or cut (something) into parts or slices. 6. (when *intr.,* usually foll. by *through*) to cut in a clean and effortless manner. 7. (when *intr.,* foll. by *into* or *through*) to move or go (through something) like a knife. 8. (usually foll. by *off, from, away,* etc.) to cut or be cut (from) a larger piece. 9. (*tr.*) to remove by use of a slicing implement. 10. to hit (a ball) with a slice. [C14: < OF *esclice* a piece split off, < *esclicier* to splinter] —**'sliceable** *adj.* —**'slicer** *n.*

slick (slɪk) *adj.* 1. flattering and glib: *a slick salesman.* 2. adroitly devised or executed: *a slick show.* 3. *Inf., chiefly U.S. & Canad.* shrewd; sly. 4. *Inf.* superficially attractive: *a slick publication.* 5. *Chiefly U.S. & Canad.* slippery. ~*n.* 6. a slippery area, esp. a patch of oil floating on water. ~*vb.* (*tr.*) 7. *Chiefly U.S. & Canad.* to make smooth or sleek. [C14: prob. < ON] —**'slickly** *adv.* —**'slickness** *n.*

slicker ('slɪkə) *n.* 1. *Inf.* a sly or untrustworthy person (esp. in **city slicker**). 2. *U.S. & Canad.* a shiny raincoat, esp. an oilskin.

slide (slaɪd) *vb.* **sliding, slid** (slɪd); **slid** *or* **slidden** ('slɪdᵊn). 1. to move or cause to move smoothly along a surface in continual contact with it: *doors that slide open.* 2. (*intr.*) to lose grip or balance: *he slid on his back.* 3. (*intr.;* usually foll. by *into, out of, away from,* etc.) to pass or move unobtrusively: *she slid into the room.* 4. (*intr.;* usually foll. by *into*) to go (into a specified condition) by degrees, etc.: *he slid into loose living.* 5. (foll. by *in, into,* etc.) to move (an object) unobtrusively or (of an object) to move in this way: *he slid the gun into his pocket.* 6. **let slide.** to allow to deteriorate: *to let things slide.* ~*n.* 7. the act or an instance of sliding. 8. a smooth surface, as of ice or mud, for sliding on. 9. a construction incorporating an inclined smooth slope for sliding down in playgrounds, etc. 10. a small glass plate on which specimens are mounted for microscopical study. 11. Also called: **transparency.** a positive photograph on a transparent base, mounted in a frame, that can be viewed by means of a slide projector. 12. Also called: **hair slide.** *Chiefly Brit.* an ornamental clip to hold hair in place. 13. *Machinery.* a sliding part or member. 14. *Music.* a portamento. 15. *Music.* the sliding curved tube of a trombone that is moved in or out. 16. a. a tube placed over a finger held against the frets of a guitar to produce a portamento. b. the style of guitar playing using a slide. 17. *Geol.* a. the downward movement of a large mass of earth, rocks, etc. b. the mass of material involved in this descent. See also **landslide.** [OE *slīdan*] —**'slidable** *adj.* —**'slider** *n.*

slide over *vb.* (*intr., prep.*) 1. to cross as if by sliding. 2. to avoid dealing with (a matter) fully.

slide rule *n.* a mechanical calculating device consisting of two strips, one sliding along a central groove in the other, each strip graduated in two or more logarithmic scales of numbers, trigonometric functions, etc.

sliding scale *n.* a variable scale according to which specified wages, prices, etc., fluctuate in response to changes in some other factor.

slier ('slaɪə) *adj.* a comparative of **sly.**

sliest ('slaɪɪst) *adj.* a superlative of **sly.**

slight (slaɪt) *adj.* 1. small in quantity or extent. 2. of small importance. 3. slim and delicate. 4. lacking in strength or substance. ~*vb.* (*tr.*) 5. to show disregard for (someone); snub. 6. to treat as unimportant or trifling. 7. *U.S.* to devote inadequate attention to (work, duties, etc.). ~*n.* 8. an act or omission indicating supercilious neglect. [C13: < ON *slēttr* smooth] —**'slightingly** *adv.* —**'slightly** *adv.* —**'slightness** *n.*

slily ('slaɪlɪ) *adv.* a variant spelling of **slyly.**

slim (slɪm) *adj.* **slimmer, slimmest.** 1. small in width relative to height or length. 2. poor; meagre: *slim chances of success.* ~*vb.* 3. to make or become slim, esp. by diets and exercise. 4. (*tr.*) to reduce in size: *the workforce was slimmed.* [C17: < Du.: crafty, < MDu. *slimp* slanting] —**'slimmer** *n.* —**'slimming** *n.* —**'slimness** *n.*

Slim (slɪm) *n.* the E African name for **AIDS.** [< its wasting effects]

slime (slaɪm) *n.* 1. soft thin runny mud or filth. 2. any moist viscous fluid, esp. when noxious or unpleasant. 3. a mucous substance produced by various organisms, such as fish, slugs, and fungi. ~*vb.* (*tr.*) 4. to cover with slime. [OE *slīm*]

slimline ('slɪm,laɪn) *adj.* slim or conducive to slimness.

slimy ('slaɪmɪ) *adj.* **slimier, slimiest.** 1. characterized by, covered with, secreting, or resembling slime. 2. offensive or repulsive. 3. *Chiefly Brit.* characterized by servility.

sling[1] (slɪŋ) *n.* 1. a simple weapon consisting of a

loop of leather, etc., in which a stone is whirled and then let fly. **2.** a rope or strap by which something may be secured or lifted. **3.** *Med.* a wide piece of cloth suspended from the neck for supporting an injured hand or arm. **4.** a loop or band attached to an object for carrying. **5.** the act of slinging. ~*vb.* **slinging, slung.** **6.** (*tr.*) to hurl with or as if with a sling. **7.** to attach a sling or slings to (a load, etc.). **8.** (*tr.*) to carry or hang loosely from or as if from a sling: *to sling washing from the line.* **9.** (*tr.*) *Inf.* to throw. [C13: ? < ON] —ˈ**slinger** *n.*

sling[2] (slɪŋ) *n.* a mixed drink with a spirit base, usually sweetened. [C19: <?]

slingback (ˈslɪŋˌbæk) *n.* a shoe with a strap instead of a full covering for the heel.

sling off *vb.* (*intr., adv.;* often foll. by *at*) *Austral. & N.Z. inf.* to mock; deride; jeer (at).

slingshot (ˈslɪŋˌʃɒt) *n.* **1.** the U.S. and Canad. name for **catapult** (sense 1). **2.** another name for **sling**[1] (sense 1).

slink (slɪŋk) *vb.* **slinking, slunk.** **1.** (*intr.*) to move or act in a furtive manner from or as if from fear, guilt, etc. **2.** (*intr.*) to move in a sinuous alluring manner. **3.** (*tr.*) (of animals, esp. cows) to give birth to prematurely. ~*n.* **4.** an animal, esp. a calf, born prematurely. [OE *slincan*]

slinky (ˈslɪŋkɪ) *adj.* **slinkier, slinkiest.** *Inf.* **1.** moving in a sinuously graceful or provocative way. **2.** (of clothes) figure-hugging. —ˈ**slinkily** *adv.* —ˈ**slinkiness** *n.*

slip[1] (slɪp) *vb.* **slipping, slipped.** **1.** to move or cause to move smoothly and easily. **2.** (*tr.*) to place, insert, or convey quickly or stealthily. **3.** (*tr.*) to put on or take off easily or quickly: *to slip on a sweater.* **4.** (*intr.*) to lose balance and slide unexpectedly: *he slipped on the ice.* **5.** to let loose or be let loose. **6.** to be released from (something). **7.** (*tr.*) to let go (mooring or anchor lines) over the side. **8.** (when *intr.*, often foll. by *from* or *out of*) to pass out of (the mind or memory). **9.** (*intr.*) to move or pass swiftly or unperceived: *to slip quietly out of the room.* **10.** (*intr.;* sometimes foll. by *up*) to make a mistake. **11.** Also: **sideslip.** to cause (an aircraft) to slide sideways or (of an aircraft) to slide sideways. **12.** (*intr.*) to decline in health, mental ability, etc. **13.** (*intr.*) (of an intervertebral disc) to become displaced from the normal position. **14.** (*tr.*) to dislocate (a bone). **15.** (of animals) to give birth to (offspring) prematurely. **16.** (*tr.*) to pass (a stitch) from one needle to another without knitting it. **17. a.** (*tr.*) to operate (the clutch of a motor vehicle) so that it partially disengages. **b.** (*intr.*) (of the clutch of a motor vehicle) to fail to engage, esp. as a result of wear. **18. let slip. a.** to allow to escape. **b.** to say unintentionally. ~*n.* **19.** the act or an instance of slipping. **20.** a mistake or oversight: *a slip of the pen.* **21.** a moral lapse or failing. **22.** a woman's sleeveless undergarment, worn as a lining for a dress. **23.** a pillowcase. **24.** See **slipway.** **25.** *Cricket.* **a.** the position of the fielder who stands a little way behind and to the offside of the wicketkeeper. **b.** the fielder himself. **26.** the relative movement of rocks along a fault plane. **27.** *Metallurgy, crystallog.* the deformation of a metallic crystal caused when one part glides over another part along a plane. **28.** a landslide. **29.** the deviation of a propeller from its helical path through a fluid. **30.** another name for **sideslip** (sense 1). **31. give someone the slip.** to elude or escape from someone. ~See also **slip up.** [C13: < MLow G or Du. *slippen*] —ˈ**slipless** *adj.*

slip[2] (slɪp) *n.* **1.** a narrow piece; strip. **2.** a small piece of paper: *a receipt slip.* **3.** a part of a plant that, when detached from the parent, will grow into a new plant; cutting. **4.** a young slender person: *a slip of a child.* **5.** *Printing.* **a.** a long galley. **b.** a galley proof. ~*vb.* **slipping, slipped.** **6.** (*tr.*) to detach (portions of stem, etc.) from (a plant) for propagation. [C15: prob. < MLow G, MDu. *slippe* to cut, strip]

slip[3] (slɪp) *n.* clay mixed with water to a creamy consistency, used for decorating or patching a ceramic piece. [OE *slyppe* slime]

slipcase (ˈslɪpˌkeɪs) *n.* a protective case for a book or set of books that is open at one end so that only the spines of the books are visible.

slipcover (ˈslɪpˌkʌvə) *n. U.S. & Canad.* **1.** a loose cover. **2.** a book jacket; dust cover.

slipe (slaɪp) *n. N.Z.* **a.** wool removed from the pelt of a slaughtered sheep by immersion in a chemical bath. **b.** (*as modifier*): *slipe wool.* [C14 in England: < *slype* to strip, skin]

slipknot (ˈslɪpˌnɒt) *n.* **1.** Also called: **running knot.** a nooselike knot tied so that it will slip along the rope round which it is made. **2.** a knot that can be easily untied by pulling one free end.

slip-on *adj.* **1.** (of a garment or shoe) made so as to be easily and quickly put on or taken off. ~*n.* **2.** a slip-on garment or shoe.

slipover (ˈslɪpˌəʊvə) *adj.* **1.** of or denoting a garment that can be put on easily over the head. ~*n.* **2.** such a garment, esp. a sleeveless pullover.

slippage (ˈslɪpɪdʒ) *n.* **1.** the act or an instance of slipping. **2.** the amount of slipping or the extent to which slipping occurs. **3. a.** an instance of not reaching a target, etc. **b.** the extent of this.

slipped disc *n. Pathol.* a herniated intervertebral disc, often resulting in pain because of pressure on the spinal nerves.

slipper (ˈslɪpə) *n.* **1.** a light shoe of some soft material, for wearing around the house. **2.** a woman's evening shoe. ~*vb.* **3.** (*tr.*) *Inf.* to hit or beat with a slipper. —ˈ**slippered** *adj.*

slipper bath *n.* a bath in the shape of a slipper, with a covered end.

slipperwort (ˈslɪpəˌwɜːt) *n.* another name for **calceolaria.**

slippery (ˈslɪpərɪ, -prɪ) *adj.* **1.** causing or tending to cause objects to slip: *a slippery road.* **2.** liable to slip from the grasp, etc. **3.** not to be relied upon: *a slippery character.* **4.** (esp. of a situation) unstable. [C16: prob. coined by Coverdale to translate G *schlipfferig* in Luther's Bible (Psalm 35:6)] —ˈ**slipperiness** *n.*

slippery elm *n.* **1.** a North American tree, having notched winged fruits and a mucilaginous inner bark. **2.** the bark of this tree, used medicinally as a demulcent. ~Also called: **red elm.**

slippy (ˈslɪpɪ) *adj.* **-pier, -piest.** **1.** *Inf. or dialect.* another word for **slippery** (senses 1, 2). **2.** *Brit. inf.* alert; quick. —ˈ**slippiness** *n.*

slip rail *n. Austral. & N.Z.* a rail in a fence that can be slipped out of place to make an opening.

slip road *n. Brit.* a short road connecting a motorway to another road.

slipshod (ˈslɪpˌʃɒd) *adj.* **1.** (of an action) negligent; careless. **2.** (of a person's appearance) slovenly; down-at-heel. [C16: < SLIP[1] + SHOD]

slip-slop *n. S. African.* the usual name for **flip-flop** (sense 5).

slipstream (ˈslɪpˌstriːm) *n.* Also called: **airstream. a.** the stream of air forced backwards by an aircraft propeller. **b.** a stream of air behind any moving object.

slip up *Inf.* ~*vb.* (*intr., adv.*) **1.** to make a blunder or mistake. ~*n.* **slip-up.** **2.** a mistake or mishap.

slipware (ˈslɪpˌwɛə) *n.* pottery that has been decorated with slip and glazed.

slipway (ˈslɪpˌweɪ) *n.* **1.** the sloping area in a shipyard, containing the ways. **2.** the ways on which a vessel is launched.

slit (slɪt) *vb.* **slitting, slit.** (*tr.*) **1.** to make a straight long incision in. **2.** to cut into strips lengthwise. ~*n.* **3.** a long narrow cut. **4.** a long narrow opening. [OE *slītan* to slice] —ˈ**slitter** *n.*

slither (ˈslɪðə) *vb.* **1.** to move or slide or cause to move or slide unsteadily, as on a slippery surface. **2.** (*intr.*) to travel with a sliding motion. ~*n.* **3.** a slithering motion. [OE *slidrian*, < *slīdan* to slide] —ˈ**slithery** *adj.*

slit trench *n. Mil.* a narrow trench dug for the protection of a small number of people.

sliver (ˈslɪvə) *n.* **1.** a thin piece that is cut or broken off lengthwise. **2.** a loose fibre obtained by carding. ~*vb.* **3.** to divide or be divided into splinters. **4.** (*tr.*) to form (wool, etc.) into slivers. [C14: < *sliven* to split]

Sloane Ranger (sləʊn) *n.* (in Britain) *Inf.* a young upper-class person having a home in London and in the country, characterized as wearing expensive informal clothes. Also called: **Sloane.** [C20: pun on *Sloane* Square, London, and *Lone Ranger,* cowboy cartoon character]

slob (slɒb) *n.* **1.** *Inf.* a stupid or coarse person. **2.** *Irish.* mire. [C19: < Irish Gaelic *slab* mud]

slobber (ˈslɒbə) *or* **slabber** *vb.* **1.** to dribble (saliva, food, etc.) from the mouth. **2.** (*intr.*) to speak or write mawkishly. **3.** (*tr.*) to smear with matter dribbling from the mouth. ~*n.* **4.** liquid or saliva spilt from the mouth. **5.** maudlin language or behaviour. [C15: < MLow G, MDu. *slubberen*] —ˈ**slobberer** *or* ˈ**slabberer** *n.* —ˈ**slobbery** *or* ˈ**slabbery** *adj.*

sloe (sləʊ) *n.* **1.** the small sour blue-black fruit of the blackthorn. **2.** another name for **blackthorn.** [OE *slāh*]

sloe-eyed *adj.* having dark slanted or almond-shaped eyes.

sloe gin *n.* gin flavoured with sloe juice.

slog (slɒg) *vb.* **slogging, slogged.** **1.** to hit with heavy blows, as in boxing. **2.** (*intr.*) to work hard; toil. **3.** (*intr.;* foll. by *down, up, along,* etc.) to move with difficulty. **4.** *Cricket.* to take large swipes at the ball. ~*n.* **5.** a tiring walk. **6.** long exhausting work. **7.** a heavy blow or swipe. [C19: <?] —ˈ**slogger** *n.*

slogan (ˈsləʊgən) *n.* **1.** a distinctive or topical phrase used in politics, advertising, etc. **2.** *Scot. history.* a Highland battle cry. [C16: < Gaelic *sluagh-ghairm* war cry]

sloop (sluːp) *n.* a single-masted sailing vessel, rigged fore-and-aft. [C17: < Du. *sloep*]

sloot (sluːt) *n. S. African.* a ditch for irrigation or drainage. [< Afrik., < Du. *sluit, sluis* SLUICE]

slop[1] (slɒp) *vb.* **slopping, slopped.** **1.** (when *intr.,* often foll. by *about*) to cause (liquid) to splash or spill or (of liquid) to splash or spill. **2.** (*intr.;* foll. by *along, through,* etc.) to tramp (through) mud or slush. **3.** (*tr.*) to feed slop or swill to: *to slop the pigs.* **4.** (*tr.*) to ladle or serve, esp. clumsily. **5.** (*intr.;* foll. by *over*) *Inf., chiefly U.S. & Canad.* to be unpleasantly effusive. ~*n.* **6.** a puddle of spilt liquid. **7.** (*pl.*) wet feed, esp. for pigs, made from kitchen waste, etc. **8.** (*pl.*) waste food or liquid refuse. **9.** (*often pl.*) *Inf.* liquid or semiliquid food of low quality. **10.** soft mud, snow, etc. [C14: prob. < OE *-sloppe* in *cūsloppe* COWSLIP]

slop[2] (slɒp) *n.* **1.** (*pl.*) sailors' clothing and bedding issued from a ship's stores. **2.** any loose article of clothing, esp. a smock. **3.** (*pl.*) shoddy manufactured clothing. [OE *oferslop* surplice]

slop basin *n.* a bowl or basin into which the dregs from teacups are emptied at the table.

slope (sləʊp) *vb.* **1.** to lie or cause to lie at a slanting or oblique angle. **2.** (*intr.*) (esp. of natural features) to follow an inclined course: *many paths sloped down the hillside.* **3.** (*intr.;* foll. by *off, away,* etc.) to go furtively. **4.** (*tr.*) *Mil.* (formerly) to hold (a rifle) in the slope position. ~*n.* **5.** an inclined portion of ground. **6.** (*pl.*) hills or foothills. **7.** any inclined surface or line. **8.** the degree or amount of such inclination. **9.** *Maths.* (of a line) the tangent of the angle between the line and another line parallel to the *x*-axis. **10.** (formerly) the position adopted for military drill when the rifle is rested on the shoulder. [C15: short for *aslope,* ? < the p.p. of OE *āslūpan* to slip away] —ˈ**sloper** *n.* —ˈ**sloping** *adj.*

slop out *vb.* (*intr., adv.*) (of prisoners) to empty chamber pots and collect water for washing.

sloppy (ˈslɒpɪ) *adj.* **-pier, -piest.** **1.** (esp. of the ground, etc.) wet; slushy. **2.** *Inf.* careless; untidy. **3.** *Inf.* mawkishly sentimental. **4.** (of food or drink) watery and unappetizing. **5.** splashed with slops. **6.** (of clothes) loose; baggy. —ˈ**sloppily** *adv.* —ˈ**sloppiness** *n.*

slosh (slɒʃ) *n.* **1.** watery mud, snow, etc. **2.** *Brit. sl.* a heavy blow. **3.** the sound of splashing liquid. ~*vb.* **4.** (*tr.;* foll. by *around, on, in,* etc.) *Inf.* to throw or pour (liquid). **5.** (when *intr.,* often foll. by *about* or *around*) *Inf.* **a.** to shake or stir (something) in a liquid. **b.** (of a person) to splash (around) in water, etc. **6.** (*tr.*) *Brit. sl.* to deal a heavy blow to. **7.** (usually foll. by *about* or *around*) *Inf.* to shake (a container of liquid) or (of liquid within a container) to be shaken. [C19: var. of SLUSH, infl. by SLOP[1]] —ˈ**sloshy** *adj.*

sloshed (slɒʃt) *adj. Chiefly Brit. sl.* drunk.

slot[1] (slɒt) *n.* **1.** an elongated aperture or groove, such as one in a vending machine for inserting a coin. **2.** *Inf.* a place in a series or scheme. ~*vb.* **slotting, slotted.** **3.** (*tr.*) to furnish with a slot or slots. **4.** (usually foll. by *in* or *into*) to fit or adjust in a slot. **5.** *Inf.* to situate or be situated in a series. [C13: < OF *esclot* the depression of the breastbone, <?] —ˈ**slotter** *n.*

slot[2] (slɒt) *n.* the trail of an animal, esp. a deer. [C16: < OF *esclot* horse's hoofprint, prob. of Scand. origin]

sloth (sləʊθ) *n.* **1.** any of a family of shaggy-coated arboreal edentate mammals, such as the three-toed sloth or ai or the two-toed sloth or unau, of Central and South America. They are slow-moving, hanging upside down by their long arms and feeding on vegetation. **2.** reluctance to exert oneself. [OE *slǣwth,* < *slǣw,* var. of *slāw* slow]

sloth bear *n.* a bear of forests of S India and Sri Lanka, having an elongated snout specialized for feeding on termites.

slothful (ˈsləʊθfʊl) *adj.* lazy; indolent. —ˈ**slothfully** *adv.* —ˈ**slothfulness** *n.*

slot machine *n.* a machine, esp. one for gambling, activated by placing a coin in a slot.

slouch (slaʊtʃ) *vb.* **1.** (*intr.*) to sit or stand with a drooping bearing. **2.** (*intr.*) to walk or move with an awkward slovenly gait. **3.** (*tr.*) to cause (the shoulders) to droop. ~*n.* **4.** a drooping carriage. **5.** (*usually used in negative constructions*) *Inf.* an incompetent or slovenly person: *he's no slouch at football.* [C16: <?] —ˈ**slouching** *adj.*

slouch hat *n.* any soft hat with a brim that can be pulled down over the ears, esp. an Australian army hat with the left side of the brim turned up.

slough[1] (slaʊ) *n.* **1.** a hollow filled with mud; bog. **2.** (sluː) *North American.* a large hole where water collects or a marshy inlet. **3.** despair or degradation. [OE *slōh*] —ˈ**sloughy** *adj.*

slough[2] (slʌf) *n.* **1.** any outer covering that is shed, such as the dead outer layer of the skin of a snake, the cellular debris in a wound, etc. ~*vb.* **2.** (often foll. by *off*) to shed (a skin, etc.) or (of a skin, etc.) to be shed. [C13: of Gmc origin] —ˈ**sloughy** *adj.*

slough off (slʌf) *vb.* (*tr., adv.*) to cast off (cares, etc.).

Slovak (ˈsləʊvæk) *adj.* **1.** of or characteristic of Slovakia in Czechoslovakia, its people, or their language. ~*n.* **2.** one of the two official languages of Czechoslovakia. Czech and Slovak are closely related and mutually intelligible. **3.** a native or inhabitant of Slovakia.

sloven (ˈslʌvᵊn) *n.* a person who is habitually negligent in appearance, hygiene, or work. [C15: prob. rel. to Flemish *sloef* dirty, Du. *slof* negligent]

Slovene (sləʊˈviːn) *adj.* **1.** of or characteristic of Slovenia, in Yugoslavia, its people, or their language. ~*n.* **2.** the Slavonic language spoken in Slovenia. **3.** a native or inhabitant of Slovenia.

slovenly (ˈslʌvənlɪ) *adj.* **1.** frequently or habitually unclean or untidy. **2.** negligent and careless: *slovenly manners.* ~*adv.* **3.** in a negligent or slovenly manner. —ˈ**slovenliness** *n.*

slow (sləʊ) *adj.* **1.** performed or occurring during a comparatively long interval of time. **2.** lasting a comparatively long time: *a slow journey.* **3.** characterized by lack of speed: *a slow walker.* **4.** (*prenominal*) adapted to or productive of slow movement: *the slow lane of a motorway.* **5.** (of a clock, etc.) indicating a time earlier than the correct time. **6.** not readily responsive to stimulation: *a slow mind.* **7.** dull or uninteresting: *the play was very slow.* **8.** not easily aroused: *a slow temperament.* **9.** lacking promptness or immediacy: *a slow answer.* **10.** unwilling to perform an action or enter into a state: *slow to anger.* **11.** behind the times. **12.** (of trade, etc.) unproductive; slack. **13.** (of a fire) burning weakly. **14.** (of an oven) cool. **15.** *Photog.* requiring a relatively long time of exposure to produce a given density: *a slow lens.* **16.** *Sport.* (of a court, track, etc.) tending to reduce the speed of the ball or the competitors. **17.** *Cricket.* (of a bowler, etc.) delivering the ball slowly, usually with spin. *~adv.* **18.** in a manner characterized by lack of speed; slowly. *~vb.* **19.** (often foll. by *up, down,* etc.) to decrease or cause to decrease in speed, efficiency, etc. [OE *slāw* sluggish] —ˈ**slowly** *adv.* —ˈ**slowness** *n.*

slowcoach (ˈsləʊˌkəʊtʃ) *n. Brit. inf.* a person who moves or works slowly. U.S. and Canad. equivalent: **slowpoke.**

slow handclap *n. Brit.* slow rhythmic clapping, esp. used by an audience to indicate dissatisfaction or impatience.

slow march *n. Mil.* a march in **slow time,** usually 65 or 75 paces to the minute.

slow match *or* **fuse** *n.* a match or fuse that burns slowly without flame.

slow motion *n.* **1.** *Films, television, etc.* action that is made to appear slower than normal by passing the film through the camera at a faster rate or by replaying a video recording more slowly. *~adj.* **slow-motion. 2.** of or relating to such action. **3.** moving or functioning at considerably less than usual speed.

slow virus *n.* a type of virus that is present in the body for a long time before it becomes active or infectious.

slowworm (ˈsləʊˌwɜːm) *n.* a Eurasian legless lizard with a brownish-grey snakelike body. Also called: **blindworm.**

SLR *abbrev. for* single-lens reflex: see **reflex camera.**

slub (slʌb) *n.* **1.** a lump in yarn or fabric, often made intentionally to give a knobbly effect. **2.** a loosely twisted roll of fibre prepared for spinning. *~vb.* **slubbing, slubbed. 3.** (*tr.*) to draw out and twist (a sliver of fibre). *~adj.* **4.** (of material) having an irregular appearance. [C18: <?]

sludge (slʌdʒ) *n.* **1.** soft mud, snow, etc. **2.** any deposit or sediment. **3.** a surface layer of ice that is not frozen solid but has a slushy appearance. **4.** (in sewage disposal) the solid constituents of sewage that are removed for purification. [C17: prob. rel. to SLUSH] —ˈ**sludgy** *adj.*

slue[1] (sluː) *n., vb.* a variant spelling (esp. U.S.) of **slew**[2].

slue[2] (sluː) *n.* a variant spelling of **slough**[1] (sense 2).

slug[1] (slʌg) *n.* **1.** any of various terrestrial gastropod molluscs in which the body is elongated and the shell is absent or very much reduced. **2.** any of various other invertebrates having a soft slimy body, esp. the larvae of certain sawflies. [C15 (in the sense: a slow person or animal): prob. < ON]

slug[2] (slʌg) *n.* **1.** an fps unit of mass; the mass that will acquire an acceleration of 1 foot per second per second when acted upon by a force of 1 pound. **2.** *Metallurgy.* a metal blank from which small forgings are worked. **3.** a bullet. **4.** *Chiefly U.S. & Canad.* a metal token for use in slot machines, etc. **5.** *Printing.* **a.** a thick strip of type metal that is used for spacing. **b.** a metal strip containing a line of characters as produced by a Linotype machine. **6.** a draught of alcoholic drink, esp. spirits. [C17 (bullet), C19 (printing): ? < SLUG[1], with allusion to the shape of the animal]

slug[3] (slʌg) *vb.* **slugging, slugged. 1.** *Chiefly U.S. & Canad.* to hit very hard and solidly. **2.** (*tr.*) *Austral. & N.Z. inf.* to charge (someone) an exorbitant price. *~n.* **3.** *U.S. & Canad.* a heavy blow. **4.** *Austral. & N.Z. inf.* an exorbitant price. [C19: ? < SLUG[2] (bullet)]

sluggard (ˈslʌgəd) *n.* **1.** a person who is habitually indolent. *~adj.* **2.** lazy. [C14 *slogarde*] —ˈ**sluggardly** *adj.*

sluggish (ˈslʌgɪʃ) *adj.* **1.** lacking energy; inactive. **2.** functioning at below normal rate or level. **3.** exhibiting poor response to stimulation. —ˈ**sluggishly** *adv.* —ˈ**sluggishness** *n.*

sluice (sluːs) *n.* **1.** Also called: **sluiceway.** a channel that carries a rapid current of water, esp. one that has a sluicegate to control the flow. **2.** the body of water controlled by a sluicegate. **3.** See **sluicegate. 4.** *Mining.* an inclined trough for washing ore. **5.** an artificial channel through which logs can be floated. *~vb.* **6.** (*tr.*) to draw out or drain (water, etc.) from (a pond, etc.) by means of a sluice. **7.** (*tr.*) to wash or irrigate with a stream of water. **8.** (*tr.*) *Mining.* to wash in a sluice. **9.** (*tr.*) to send (logs, etc.) down a sluice. **10.** (*intr.;* often foll. by *away* or *out*) (of water, etc.) to run or flow from or as if from a sluice. **11.** (*tr.*) to provide with a sluice. [C14: < OF *escluse,* < LL *exclūsa aqua* water shut out, < L *exclūdere* to shut out] —ˈ**sluiceˌlike** *adj.*

sluicegate (ˈsluːsˌgeɪt) *n.* a valve or gate fitted to a sluice to control the rate of flow of water. See also **floodgate** (sense 1).

slum (slʌm) *n.* **1.** a squalid overcrowded house, etc. **2.** (*often pl.*) a squalid section of a city, characterized by inferior living conditions. **3.** (*modifier*) of or characteristic of slums: *slum conditions.* *~vb.* **slumming, slummed.** (*intr.*) **4.** to visit slums, esp. for curiosity. **5.** Also: **slum it.** to suffer conditions below those to which one is accustomed. [C19: orig. sl., <?] —ˈ**slummy** *adj.*

slumber (ˈslʌmbə) *vb.* **1.** (*intr.*) to sleep, esp. peacefully. **2.** (*intr.*) to be quiescent or dormant. **3.** (*tr.;* foll. by *away*) to spend (time) sleeping. *~n.* **4.** (*sometimes pl.*) sleep. **5.** a dormant or quiescent state. [OE *slūma* sleep (n.)] —ˈ**slumberer** *n.* —ˈ**slumbering** *adj.*

slumberous (ˈslʌmbərəs) *adj. Chiefly poetic.* **1.** sleepy; drowsy. **2.** inducing sleep. —ˈ**slumberously** *adv.* —ˈ**slumberousness** *n.*

slump (slʌmp) *vb.* (*intr.*) **1.** to sink or fall heavily and suddenly. **2.** to relax ungracefully. **3.** (of business activity, etc.) to decline suddenly. **4.** (of health, interest, etc.) to deteriorate or decline suddenly. *~n.* **5.** a sudden or marked decline or failure, as in progress or achievement. **6.** a decline in commercial activity, prices, etc.; depression. **7.** the act of slumping. [C17: prob. of Scand. origin]

slung (slʌŋ) *vb.* the past tense and past participle of **sling**[1].

slunk (slʌŋk) *vb.* the past tense and past participle of **slink.**

slur (slɜː) *vb.* **slurring, slurred.** (*mainly tr.*) **1.** (often foll. by *over*) to treat superficially, hastily, or without due deliberation. **2.** (*also intr.*) to pronounce or utter (words, etc.) indistinctly. **3.** to speak disparagingly of. **4.** *Music.* to execute (a melodic interval of two or more notes) smoothly, as in legato performance. *~n.* **5.** an indistinct sound or utterance. **6.** a slighting remark. **7.** a stain or disgrace, as upon one's reputation. **8.** *Music.* **a.** a performance or execution of a melodic interval of two or more notes in a part. **b.** the curved line (⌒ or ‿) indicating this. [C15: prob. < MLow G]

slurp (slɜːp) *Inf.* *~vb.* **1.** to eat or drink (something) noisily. *~n.* **2.** a sound produced in this way. [C17: < MDu. *slorpen* to sip]

slurry (ˈslʌrɪ) *n., pl.* **-ries.** a suspension of solid particles in a liquid, as in a mixture of cement, manure, or coal dust with water. [C15 *slory*]

slush (slʌʃ) *n.* **1.** any watery muddy substance, esp. melting snow. **2.** *Inf.* sloppily sentimental language. *~vb.* **3.** (*intr.;* often foll. by *along*) to make one's way through or as if through slush. [C17: rel. to Danish *slus* sleet, Norwegian *slusk* slops] —ˈ**slushiness** *n.* —ˈ**slushy** *adj.*

slush fund *n.* a fund for financing political or commercial corruption.

slushy (ˈslʌʃɪ) *adj.* **slushier, slushiest.** of, resembling, or consisting of slush.

slut (slʌt) *n.* **1.** a dirty slatternly woman. **2.** an immoral woman. [C14: <?] —ˈ**sluttish** *adj.* —ˈ**sluttishness** *n.*

sly (slaɪ) *adj.* **slyer, slyest** *or* **slier, sliest. 1.**

crafty; artful: *a sly dodge.* **2.** insidious; furtive: *a sly manner.* **3.** roguish: *sly humour.* ~*n.* **4. on the sly.** in a secretive manner. [C12: < ON *slǣgr* clever, lit.: able to strike, < *slā* to slay] —ˈ**slyly** *or* ˈ**slily** *adv.* —ˈ**slyness** *n.*

slype (slaɪp) *n.* a covered passage in a church that connects the transept to the chapterhouse. [C19: prob. < MFlemish *slijpen* to slip]

Sm *the chemical symbol for* samarium.

SM *abbrev. for* sergeant major.

smack[1] (smæk) *n.* **1.** a smell or flavour that is distinctive though faint. **2.** a distinctive trace: *the smack of corruption.* **3.** a small quantity, esp. a taste. **4.** a slang word for **heroin.** ~*vb.* (*intr.*; foll. by *of*) **5.** to have the characteristic smell or flavour (of something): *to smack of the sea.* **6.** to have an element suggestive (of something): *his speeches smacked of bigotry.* [OE *smæc*]

smack[2] (smæk) *vb.* **1.** (*tr.*) to strike or slap smartly, with or as if with the open hand. **2.** to strike or send forcibly or loudly or to be struck or sent forcibly or loudly. **3.** to open and close (the lips) loudly, esp. to show pleasure. ~*n.* **4.** a sharp resounding slap or blow with something flat, or the sound of such a blow. **5.** a loud kiss. **6.** a sharp sound made by the lips, as in enjoyment. **7. have a smack at.** *Inf., chiefly Brit.* to attempt. **8. smack in the eye.** *Inf., chiefly Brit.* a snub or setback. ~*adv. Inf.* **9.** directly; squarely. **10.** sharply and unexpectedly. [C16: < MLow G or MDu. *smacken*, prob. imit.]

smack[3] (smæk) *n.* a sailing vessel, usually sloop-rigged, used in coasting and fishing along the British coast. [C17: < Low G *smack* or Du. *smak*, <?]

smacker (ˈsmækə) *n. Sl.* **1.** a loud kiss; smack. **2.** a pound note or dollar bill.

small (smɔːl) *adj.* **1.** limited in size, number, importance, etc. **2.** of little importance or on a minor scale: *a small business.* **3.** lacking in moral or mental breadth or depth: *a small mind.* **4.** modest or humble: *small beginnings.* **5.** of low or inferior status, esp. socially. **6. feel small.** to be humiliated. **7.** (of a child or animal) young; not mature. **8.** unimportant; trivial: *a small matter.* **9.** of or designating the ordinary modern minuscule letter used in printing and cursive writing. **10.** lacking great strength or force: *a small effort.* **11.** in fine particles: *small gravel.* ~*adv.* **12.** into small pieces: *cut it small.* **13.** in a small or soft manner. ~*n.* **14.** (often preceded by *the*) an object, person, or group considered to be small: *the small or the large?* **15.** a small slender part, esp. of the back. **16.** (*pl.*) *Inf., chiefly Brit.* items of personal laundry, such as underwear. [OE *smæl*] —ˈ**smallish** *adj.* —ˈ**smallness** *n.*

small arms *pl. n.* portable firearms of relatively small calibre.

small beer *n.* **1.** *Inf., chiefly Brit.* people or things of no importance. **2.** *Now rare.* weak beer.

small change *n.* **1.** coins, esp. those of low value. **2.** a person or thing that is not outstanding or important.

small circle *n.* a circular section of a sphere that does not contain the centre of the sphere.

small claims court *n. Brit.* a local court administered by the county court with jurisdiction to try civil actions involving small claims.

small fry *pl. n.* **1.** people or things regarded as unimportant. **2.** young children. **3.** young or small fishes.

small goods *pl. n. Austral. & N.Z.* meats bought from a delicatessen, such as sausages.

smallholding (ˈsmɔːlˌhəʊldɪŋ) *n.* a holding of agricultural land smaller than a small farm. —ˈ**smallˌholder** *n.*

small hours *pl. n.* **the.** the early hours of the morning, after midnight and before dawn.

small intestine *n.* the longest part of the alimentary canal, in which digestion is completed. Cf. **large intestine.**

small-minded *adj.* narrow-minded; intolerant. —ˌ**small-ˈmindedly** *adv.* —ˌ**small-ˈmindedness** *n.*

smallpox (ˈsmɔːlˌpɒks) *n.* a highly contagious viral disease characterized by high fever and a rash changing to pustules, which dry up and form scabs that are cast off, leaving pitted depressions. Technical name: **variola.**

small print *n.* matter in a contract, etc., printed in small type, esp. when considered to be a trap for the unwary.

small-scale *adj.* **1.** of limited size or scope. **2.** (of a map, model, etc.) giving a relatively small representation of something.

small screen *n.* an informal name for **television.**

small slam *n. Bridge.* another name for **little slam.**

small talk *n.* light conversation for social occasions.

small-time *adj. Inf.* insignificant; minor: *a small-time criminal.* —ˈ**small-ˈtimer** *n.*

smalt (smɔːlt) *n.* **1.** a type of silica glass coloured deep blue with cobalt oxide. **2.** a pigment made by crushing this glass, used in colouring enamels. [C16: via F < It. *smalto* coloured glass, of Gmc origin]

smarm (smɑːm) *vb. Brit. inf.* **1.** (*tr.*; often foll. by *down*) to flatten (the hair, etc.) with grease. **2.** (when *intr.*, foll. by *up to*) to ingratiate oneself (with). [C19: <?]

smarmy (ˈsmɑːmɪ) *adj.* **smarmier, smarmiest.** *Brit. inf.* obsequiously flattering or unpleasantly suave. —ˈ**smarmily** *adv.* —ˈ**smarminess** *n.*

smart (smɑːt) *adj.* **1.** astute, as in business. **2.** quick, witty, and often impertinent in speech: *a smart talker.* **3.** fashionable; chic: *a smart hotel.* **4.** well-kept; neat. **5.** causing a sharp stinging pain. **6.** vigorous or brisk. **7.** (of systems) operating as if by human intelligence by using automatic computer control. **8.** *U.S.* (of a bomb, etc.) containing a device which enables it to be guided to its target. ~*vb.* (*mainly intr.*) **9.** to feel, cause, or be the source of a sharp stinging physical pain or keen mental distress: *he smarted under their abuse.* **10.** (often foll. by *for*) to suffer a harsh penalty. ~*n.* **11.** a stinging pain or feeling. ~*adv.* **12.** in a smart manner. ~See also **smarts.** [OE *smeortan*] —ˈ**smartly** *adv.* —ˈ**smartness** *n.*

smart aleck (ˈælɪk) *n. Inf.* **a.** an irritatingly oversmart person. **b.** (*as modifier*): *a smart-aleck remark.* [C19: < *Aleck, Alec*, short for *Alexander*] —ˈ**smart-ˌalecky** *adj.*

smart card *n.* another name for **intelligent card.**

smarten (ˈsmɑːtᵊn) *vb.* (usually foll. by *up*) **1.** (*intr.*) to make oneself neater. **2.** (*tr.*) to make quicker or livelier.

smart money *n. U.S.* **1.** money bet or invested by experienced gamblers or investors. **2.** money paid in order to extricate oneself from an unpleasant situation or agreement, esp. from military service. **3.** *Law.* damages awarded to a plaintiff where the wrong was aggravated by fraud, malice, etc.

smarts (smɑːts) *pl. n. Sl., chiefly U.S.* know-how, intelligence, or wits: *street smarts.*

smart set *n.* (*functioning as sing. or pl.*) fashionable people considered as a group.

smash (smæʃ) *vb.* **1.** to break into pieces violently and usually noisily. **2.** (when *intr.*, foll. by *against, through, into*, etc.) to throw or crash (against) vigorously, causing shattering: *he smashed the equipment.* **3.** (*tr.*) to hit forcefully and suddenly. **4.** (*tr.*) *Tennis, etc.* to hit (the ball) fast and powerfully, esp. with an overhead stroke. **5.** (*tr.*) to defeat (persons, theories, etc.). **6.** to make or become bankrupt. **7.** (*intr.*) to collide violently; crash. ~*n.* **8.** an act, instance, or sound of smashing or the state of being smashed. **9.** a violent collision, esp. of vehicles. **10.** a total failure or collapse, as of a business. **11.** *Tennis, etc.* a fast and powerful overhead stroke. **12.** *Inf.* **a.** something having popular success. **b.** (*in combination*): *smash-hit.* ~*adv.* **13.** with a smash. ~See also **smash-up.** [C18: prob. < SM(ACK[2] + M)ASH] —ˈ**smashable** *adj.*

smash-and-grab *adj. Inf.* of or relating to a

robbery in which a shop window is broken and the contents removed.

smashed (smæʃt) *adj. Sl.* drunk or under the influence of a drug.

smasher (ˈsmæʃə) *n. Inf., chiefly Brit.* a person or thing that is very attractive or outstanding.

smashing (ˈsmæʃɪŋ) *adj. Inf., chiefly Brit.* excellent or first-rate: *we had a smashing time.*

smash-up *Inf.* ~*n.* **1.** a bad collision, esp of cars. ~*vb.* **smash up. 2.** (*tr., adv.*) to damage to the point of complete destruction: *they smashed the place up.*

smatter (ˈsmætə) *n.* **1.** a smattering. ~*vb.* **2.** (*tr.*) *Arch.* to dabble in. [C14 (in the sense: to prattle): <?] —**ˈsmatterer** *n.*

smattering (ˈsmætərɪŋ) *n.* **1.** a slight or superficial knowledge. **2.** a small amount.

smear (smɪə) *vb.* (*mainly tr.*) **1.** to bedaub or cover with oil, grease, etc. **2.** to rub over or apply thickly. **3.** to rub so as to produce a smudge. **4.** to slander. **5.** (*intr.*) to be or become smeared or dirtied. ~*n.* **6.** a dirty mark or smudge. **7. a.** a slanderous attack. **b.** (*as modifier*): *smear tactics.* **8.** a preparation of blood, secretions, etc., smeared onto a glass slide for examination under a microscope. [OE *smeoru* (n.)] —**ˈsmeary** *adj.* —**ˈsmearily** *adv.* —**ˈsmeariness** *n.*

smear test *n. Med.* another name for **Pap test.**

smectic (ˈsmɛktɪk) *adj. Chem.* (of a substance) existing in or having a mesomorphic state in which the molecules are oriented in layers. [C17: via L < Gk *smēktikos,* < *smēkhein* to wash; from the soaplike consistency of a smectic substance]

smegma (ˈsmɛgmə) *n. Physiol.* sebum. [C19: via L < Gk *smēgma* detergent, < *smekhein* to wash]

smell (smɛl) *vb.* **smelling, smelt** *or* **smelled. 1.** (*tr.*) to perceive the scent of (a substance) by means of the olfactory nerves. **2.** (*copula*) to have a specified smell: *the curry smells very spicy.* **3.** (*intr.;* often foll. by *of*) to emit an odour (of): *the park smells of flowers.* **4.** (*intr.*) to emit an unpleasant odour. **5.** (*tr.;* often foll. by *out*) to detect through shrewdness or instinct. **6.** (*intr.*) to have or use the sense of smell; sniff. **7.** (*intr.;* foll. by *of*) to give indications (of): *he smells of money.* **8.** (*intr.;* foll. by *around, about,* etc.) to search, investigate, or pry. **9.** (*copula*) to be or seem to be untrustworthy. ~*n.* **10.** that sense (olfaction) by which scents or odours are perceived. Related adj.: **olfactory. 11.** anything detected by the sense of smell. **12.** a trace or indication. **13.** the act or an instance of smelling. [C12: <?] —**ˈsmeller** *n.*

▷ **Usage.** *Smell* in its neutral sense of emitting an odour is followed by an adjective rather than by an adverb: *this flower smells good* (rather than *well*). *Smell* in the sense of emitting an unpleasant odour is followed by an adverb.

smelling salts *pl. n.* a pungent preparation containing crystals of ammonium carbonate that has a stimulant action when sniffed in cases of faintness, headache, etc.

smelly (ˈsmɛlɪ) *adj.* **smellier, smelliest.** having a strong or nasty smell. —**ˈsmelliness** *n.*

smelt[1] (smɛlt) *vb.* (*tr.*) to extract (a metal) from (an ore) by heating. [C15: < MLow G, MDu. *smelten*]

smelt[2] (smɛlt) *n., pl.* **smelt** *or* **smelts.** a marine or freshwater salmonoid food fish having a long silvery body and occurring in temperate and cold northern waters. [OE *smylt*]

smelt[3] (smɛlt) *vb.* a past tense and past participle of **smell.**

smelter (ˈsmɛltə) *n.* **1.** a person engaged in smelting. **2.** Also called: **smeltery.** an industrial plant in which smelting is carried out.

smew (smjuː) *n.* a merganser of N Europe and Asia, having a male plumage of white with black markings. [C17: <?]

smidgen *or* **smidgin** (ˈsmɪdʒən) *n. Inf., chiefly U.S.* a very small amount. [C20: <?]

smilax (ˈsmaɪlæks) *n.* **1.** any of a genus of climbing shrubs having slightly lobed leaves, small greenish or yellow flowers, and berry-like fruits: includes the sarsaparilla plant and greenbrier. **2.** a fragile, much branched vine of southern Africa: cultivated for its glossy green foliage. [C17: via L < Gk: bindweed]

smile (smaɪl) *n.* **1.** a facial expression characterized by an upturning of the corners of the mouth, usually showing amusement, friendliness, etc. **2.** favour or blessing: *the smile of fortune.* ~*vb.* **3.** (*intr.*) to wear or assume a smile. **4.** (*intr.;* foll. by *at*) **a.** to look (at) with a kindly expression. **b.** to look derisively (at). **c.** to bear (troubles, etc.) patiently. **5.** (*intr.;* foll. by *on* or *upon*) to show approval. **6.** (*tr.*) to express by means of a smile: *she smiled a welcome.* **7.** (*tr.;* often foll. by *away*) to drive away or change by smiling. **8. come up smiling.** to recover cheerfully from misfortune. [C13: prob. < ON] —**ˈsmiler** *n.* —**ˈsmiling** *adj.* —**ˈsmilingly** *adv.*

smirch (smɜːtʃ) *vb.* (*tr.*) **1.** to dirty; soil. ~*n.* **2.** the act of smirching or state of being smirched. **3.** a smear or stain. [C15 *smorchen,* <?]

smirk (smɜːk) *n.* **1.** a smile expressing scorn, smugness, etc., rather than pleasure. ~*vb.* **2.** (*intr.*) to give such a smile. **3.** (*tr.*) to express with such a smile. [OE *smearcian*] —**ˈsmirker** *n.* —**ˈsmirking** *adj.* —**ˈsmirkingly** *adv.*

smite (smaɪt) *vb.* **smiting, smote; smitten** *or* **smit** (smɪt). (*mainly tr.*) *Now arch. in most senses.* **1.** to strike with a heavy blow. **2.** to damage with or as if with blows. **3.** to affect severely: *smitten with flu.* **4.** to afflict in order to punish. **5.** (*intr.;* foll. by *on*) to strike forcibly or abruptly: *the sun smote down on him.* [OE *smītan*] —**ˈsmiter** *n.*

smith (smɪθ) *n.* **1. a.** a person who works in metal. **b.** (*in combination*): *a silversmith.* **2.** See **blacksmith.** [OE]

smithereens (ˌsmɪðəˈriːnz) *pl. n.* little shattered pieces or fragments. [C19: < Irish Gaelic *smidirīn,* < *smiodar*]

smithery (ˈsmɪθərɪ) *n., pl.* **-eries. 1.** the trade or craft of a blacksmith. **2.** a rare word for **smithy.**

smithy (ˈsmɪðɪ) *n., pl.* **smithies.** a place in which metal, usually iron or steel, is worked by heating and hammering; forge. [OE *smiththe*]

smitten (ˈsmɪtᵊn) *vb.* **1.** a past participle of **smite.** ~*adj.* **2.** (*postpositive*) affected by love (for).

smock (smɒk) *n.* **1.** any loose protective garment, worn by artists, laboratory technicians, etc. **2.** a woman's loose blouselike garment, reaching to below the waist, worn over slacks, etc. **3.** Also called: **smock frock.** a loose protective overgarment decorated with smocking, worn formerly esp. by farm workers. **4.** *Arch.* a woman's loose undergarment. ~*vb.* **5.** to ornament (a garment) with smocking. [OE *smocc*] —**ˈsmockˌlike** *adj.*

smocking (ˈsmɒkɪŋ) *n.* ornamental needlework used to gather and stitch material in a honeycomb pattern so that the part below the gathers hangs in even folds.

smog (smɒg) *n.* a mixture of smoke, fog, and chemical fumes. [C20: < SM(OKE + F)OG[1]] —**ˈsmoggy** *adj.*

smoke (sməʊk) *n.* **1.** the product of combustion, consisting of fine particles of carbon carried by hot gases and air. **2.** any cloud of fine particles suspended in a gas. **3. a.** the act of smoking tobacco, esp. as a cigarette. **b.** the duration of smoking such substances. **4.** *Inf.* a cigarette or cigar. **5.** something with no concrete or lasting substance: *everything turned to smoke.* **6.** a thing or condition that obscures. **7. go** *or* **end up in smoke. a.** to come to nothing. **b.** to burn up vigorously. **c.** to flare up in anger. ~*vb.* **8.** (*intr.*) to emit smoke or the like, sometimes excessively or in the wrong place. **9.** to draw in on (a burning cigarette, etc.) and exhale the smoke. **10.** (*tr.*) to bring (oneself) into a specified state by smoking. **11.** (*tr.*) to subject or expose to smoke. **12.** (*tr.*) to cure (meat, fish, etc.) by treating with smoke. **13.** (*tr.*) to fumigate or purify the air of (rooms, etc.). **14.** (*tr.*) to darken (glass, etc.) by exposure to smoke. ~See also **smoke out.** [OE *smoca* (n.)] —**ˈsmokable** *or* **ˈsmokeable** *adj.*

Smoke (smәʊk) *n.* **the.** *Brit. & Austral. sl.* a big city, esp. (in Britain) London. Also called: **the big smoke.**

smoke-dried *adj.* (of fish, etc.) cured in smoke.

smoked rubber *n.* a type of crude natural rubber in the form of brown sheets obtained by coagulating latex with an acid, rolling it into sheets, and drying over open wood fires. It is the main raw material for natural rubber products.

smokeho (ˈsmәʊkәʊ) *n.* a variant spelling of **smoko.**

smokehouse (ˈsmәʊkˌhaʊs) *n.* a building or special construction for curing meat, fish, etc., by smoking.

smokeless (ˈsmәʊklɪs) *adj.* having or producing little or no smoke: *smokeless fuel.*

smokeless zone *n.* an area where only smokeless fuels are permitted to be used.

smoke out *vb.* (*tr., adv.*) **1.** to subject to smoke in order to drive out of hiding. **2.** to bring into the open: *they smoked out the plot.*

smoker (ˈsmәʊkә) *n.* **1.** a person who habitually smokes tobacco. **2.** Also called: **smoking compartment.** a compartment of a train where smoking is permitted. **3.** an informal social gathering, as at a club.

smoke screen *n.* **1.** *Mil.* a cloud of smoke produced to obscure movements. **2.** something said or done in order to hide the truth.

smokestack (ˈsmәʊkˌstæk) *n.* **1.** a tall chimney that conveys smoke into the air. **2.** (*modifier*) relating to heavy industry.

smoking jacket *n.* (formerly) a man's comfortable jacket of velvet, etc., closed by a tie belt or fastenings, worn at home.

smoko *or* **smokeho** (ˈsmәʊkәʊ) *n., pl.* **-kos** *or* **-hos.** *Austral. & N.Z. inf.* **1.** a short break from work for tea, a cigarette, etc. **2.** refreshment taken during this break.

smoky (ˈsmәʊkɪ) *adj.* **smokier, smokiest. 1.** emitting or resembling smoke. **2.** emitting smoke excessively or in the wrong place: *a smoky fireplace.* **3.** having the flavour of having been cured by smoking. **4.** made dirty or hazy by smoke. —ˈ**smokily** *adv.* —ˈ**smokiness** *n.*

smolder (ˈsmәʊldә) *vb., n.* the U.S. spelling of **smoulder.**

smolt (smәʊlt) *n.* a young salmon at the stage when it migrates from fresh water to the sea. [C14: Scot., <?]

smooch (smuːtʃ) *Sl.* ~*vb.* (*intr.*) **1.** Also (Austral. and N.Z.): **smoodge, smooge.** (of two people) to kiss and cuddle. **2.** *Brit.* to dance very slowly and amorously with one's arms around another person or (of two people) to dance together in such a way. ~*n.* **3.** the act of smooching. [C20: var. of dialect *smouch,* imit.]

smoodge *or* **smooge** (smuːdʒ) *vb.* (*intr.*) *Austral. & N.Z.* **1.** another word for **smooch** (sense 1). **2.** to seek to ingratiate oneself.

smooth (smuːð) *adj.* **1.** without bends or irregularities. **2.** silky to the touch: *smooth velvet.* **3.** lacking roughness of surface; flat. **4.** tranquil or unruffled: *smooth temper.* **5.** lacking obstructions or difficulties. **6. a.** suave or persuasive, esp. as suggestive of insincerity. **b.** (*in combination*): *smooth-tongued.* **7.** (of the skin) free from hair. **8.** of uniform consistency: *smooth batter.* **9.** free from jolts: *smooth driving.* **10.** not harsh or astringent: *a smooth wine.* **11.** having all projections worn away: *smooth tyres.* **12.** *Phonetics.* without preliminary aspiration. **13.** *Physics.* (of a plane, etc.) regarded as being frictionless. ~*adv.* **14.** in a calm or even manner. ~*vb.* (*mainly tr.*) **15.** (*also intr.; often* foll. by *down*) to make or become flattened or without roughness. **16.** (often foll. by *out* or *away*) to take or rub (away) in order to make smooth: *she smoothed out the creases in her dress.* **17.** to make calm; soothe. **18.** to make easier: *smooth his path.* ~*n.* **19.** the smooth part of something. **20.** the act of smoothing. **21.** *Tennis, etc.* the side of a racket on which the binding strings form a continuous line. ~See also **smooth over.** [OE *smōth*] —ˈ**smoother** *n.* —ˈ**smoothly** *adv.* —ˈ**smoothness** *n.*

smoothbore (ˈsmuːðˌbɔː) *n.* (*modifier*) (of a firearm) having an unrifled bore: *a smoothbore shotgun.* —ˈ**smoothˌbored** *adj.*

smooth breathing *n.* (in Greek) the sign (ʼ) placed over an initial vowel, indicating that (in ancient Greek) it was not pronounced with an *h.*

smoothen (ˈsmuːðәn) *vb.* to make or become smooth.

smooth hound *n.* any of several small sharks of North Atlantic coastal regions.

smoothie *or* **smoothy** (ˈsmuːðɪ) *n., pl.* **smoothies.** *Sl., usually derog.* a person, esp. a man, who is suave or slick, esp. in speech, dress, or manner.

smoothing iron *n.* a former name for **iron** (sense 3).

smooth muscle *n.* muscle that is capable of slow rhythmic involuntary contractions: occurs in the walls of the blood vessels, etc.

smooth over *vb.* (*tr.*) to ease or gloss over: *to smooth over a difficulty.*

smooth snake *n.* any of several slender nonvenomous European snakes having very smooth scales and a reddish-brown coloration.

smooth-spoken *adj.* speaking or spoken in a gently persuasive or competent manner.

smooth-tongued *adj.* suave or persuasive in speech.

smorgasbord (ˈsmɔːgәsˌbɔːd) *n.* a variety of cold or hot savoury dishes served in Scandinavia as hors d'oeuvres or as a buffet meal. [Swedish, < *smörgås* sandwich + *bord* table]

smote (smәʊt) *vb.* the past tense of **smite.**

smother (ˈsmʌðә) *vb.* **1.** to suffocate or stifle by cutting off or being cut off from the air. **2.** (*tr.*) to surround (with) or envelop (in): *he smothered her with love.* **3.** (*tr.*) to extinguish (a fire) by covering so as to cut it off from the air. **4.** to be or cause to be suppressed or stifled: *smother a giggle.* **5.** (*tr.*) to cook or serve (food) thickly covered with sauce, etc. ~*n.* **6.** anything, such as a cloud of smoke, that stifles. **7.** a profusion or turmoil. [OE *smorian* to suffocate] —ˈ**smothery** *adj.*

smothered mate *n. Chess.* checkmate given by a knight when the king is prevented from moving by surrounding men.

smoulder *or U.S.* **smolder** (ˈsmәʊldә) *vb.* (*intr.*) **1.** to burn slowly without flame, usually emitting smoke. **2.** (esp. of anger, etc.) to exist in a suppressed state. **3.** to have strong repressed feelings, esp. anger. ~*n.* **4.** a smouldering fire. [C14: < *smolder* (n.), <?]

smudge (smʌdʒ) *vb.* **1.** to smear or soil or cause to do so. **2.** (*tr.*) *Chiefly U.S. & Canad.* to fill (an area) with smoke in order to drive insects away. ~*n.* **3.** a smear or dirty mark. **4.** a blurred form or area: *that smudge in the distance is a quarry.* **5.** *Chiefly U.S. & Canad.* a smoky fire for driving insects away or protecting plants from frost. [C15: <?] —ˈ**smudgy** *adj.* —ˈ**smudgily** *adv.* —ˈ**smudginess** *n.*

smug (smʌg) *adj.* **smugger, smuggest.** excessively self-satisfied or complacent. [C16: of Gmc origin] —ˈ**smugly** *adv.* —ˈ**smugness** *n.*

smuggle (ˈsmʌgᵊl) *vb.* **1.** to import or export (prohibited or dutiable goods) secretly. **2.** (*tr.; often* foll. by *into* or *out of*) to bring or take secretly, as against the law or rules. [C17: < Low G *smukkelen* & Du. *smokkelen,* ? < OE *smūgen* to creep] —ˈ**smuggler** *n.* —ˈ**smuggling** *n.*

smut (smʌt) *n.* **1.** a small dark smudge or stain, esp. one caused by soot. **2.** a speck of soot or dirt. **3.** something obscene or indecent. **4. a.** any of various fungal diseases of flowering plants, esp. cereals, in which black sooty masses of spores cover the affected parts. **b.** any parasitic fungus that causes such a disease. ~*vb.* **smutting, smutted. 5.** to mark or become marked or smudged, as with soot. **6.** to affect (grain, etc.) or (of grain) to be affected with smut. [OE *smitte;* associated with SMUDGE, SMUTCH] —ˈ**smutty** *adj.* —ˈ**smuttily** *adv.* —ˈ**smuttiness** *n.*

smutch (smʌtʃ) *vb.* **1.** (*tr.*) to smudge; mark.

~*n.* **2.** a mark; smudge. **3.** soot; dirt. [C16: prob. < MHG *smutzen* to soil] —ˈ**smutchy** *adj.*

Sn *the chemical symbol for* tin. [< NL *stannum*]

snack (snæk) *n.* **1.** a light quick meal eaten between or in place of main meals. **2.** a sip or bite. ~*vb.* **3.** (*intr.*) to eat a snack. [C15: prob. < MDu. *snacken*, var. of *snappen* to snap]

snack bar *n.* a place where light meals or snacks can be obtained, often with a self-service system.

snaffle (ˈsnæfˀl) *n.* **1.** Also called: **snaffle bit.** a simple jointed bit for a horse. ~*vb.* (*tr.*) **2.** *Brit. inf.* to steal or take for oneself. **3.** to equip or control with a snaffle. [C16: <?]

snafu (snæˈfuː) *Sl., chiefly mil.* ~*n.* **1.** confusion or chaos regarded as the normal state. ~*adj.* **2.** (*postpositive*) confused or muddled up, as usual. ~*vb.* **-fuing, -fued.** **3.** (*tr.*) *U.S. & Canad.* to throw into chaos. [C20: < *s*(*ituation*) *n*(*ormal*): *a*(*ll*) *f*(*ucked*) *u*(*p*)]

snag[1] (snæg) *n.* **1.** a difficulty or disadvantage: *the snag is that I have nothing suitable to wear.* **2.** a sharp protuberance, such as a tree stump. **3.** a small loop or hole in a fabric caused by a sharp object. **4.** a tree stump in a riverbed that is dangerous to navigation. ~*vb.* **snagging, snagged.** **5.** (*tr.*) to hinder or impede. **6.** (*tr.*) to tear or catch (fabric). **7.** (*intr.*) to develop a snag. **8.** (*intr.*) *Chiefly U.S. & Canad.* (of a boat) to strike a snag. **9.** (*tr.*) *Chiefly U.S. & Canad.* to clear (a stretch of water) of snags. **10.** (*tr.*) *U.S.* to seize (an opportunity, etc.). [C16: of Scand. origin] —ˈ**snaggy** *adj.*

snag[2] (snæg) *n.* (*usually pl.*) *Austral. sl.* a sausage. [<?]

snaggletooth (ˈsnægˀlˌtuːθ) *n., pl.* **-teeth.** a tooth that is broken or projecting.

snail (sneɪl) *n.* **1.** any of numerous terrestrial or freshwater gastropod molluscs with a spirally coiled shell, esp. the **garden snail.** **2.** any other gastropod with a spirally coiled shell, such as a whelk. **3.** a slow-moving person or animal. [OE *snægl*] —ˈ**snail-ˌlike** *adj.*

snail's pace *n.* a very slow speed or rate.

snake (sneɪk) *n.* **1.** a reptile having a scaly cylindrical limbless body, fused eyelids, and a jaw modified for swallowing large prey: includes venomous forms such as cobras and rattlesnakes, large nonvenomous constrictors (boas and pythons), and small harmless types such as the grass snake. **2.** Also: **snake in the grass.** a deceitful or treacherous person. **3.** anything resembling a snake in appearance or action. **4.** a group of currencies, any one of which can only fluctuate within narrow limits, but each can fluctuate more against other currencies. **5.** a tool in the form of a long flexible wire for unblocking drains. ~*vb.* **6.** (*intr.*) to glide or move like a snake. **7.** (*tr.*) to move in or follow (a sinuous course). [OE *snaca*] —ˈ**snakeˌlike** *adj.*

snakebite (ˈsneɪkˌbaɪt) *n.* **1.** a bite inflicted by a snake, esp. a venomous one. **2.** the condition resulting from being bitten by a poisonous snake.

snakebird (ˈsneɪkˌbɜːd) *n.* another name for **darter** (the bird).

snake charmer *n.* an entertainer, esp. in Asia, who charms or appears to charm snakes by playing music.

snakeroot (ˈsneɪkˌruːt) *n.* **1.** any of various North American plants the roots or rhizomes of which have been used as a remedy for snakebite. **2.** the rhizome or root of any such plant.

snakes and ladders *n.* (*functioning as sing.*) a board game in which players move counters along a series of squares by means of dice. A ladder provides a short cut to a square nearer the finish and a snake obliges a player to return to a square nearer the start.

snake's head *n.* a European fritillary plant of damp meadows, having purple-and-white flowers.

snakeskin (ˈsneɪkˌskɪn) *n.* the skin of a snake, esp. when made into a leather valued for handbags, shoes, etc.

snaky (ˈsneɪkɪ) *adj.* **snakier, snakiest.** **1.** of or like a snake. **2.** treacherous or insidious. **3.** infested with snakes. **4.** *Austral. & N.Z. sl.* angry or bad-tempered. —ˈ**snakily** *adv.* —ˈ**snakiness** *n.*

snap (snæp) *vb.* **snapping, snapped.** **1.** to break or cause to break suddenly, esp. with a sharp sound. **2.** to make or cause to make a sudden sharp cracking sound. **3.** (*intr.*) to give way or collapse suddenly, esp. from strain. **4.** to move, close, etc., or cause to move, close, etc., with a sudden sharp sound. **5.** to move or cause to move in a sudden or abrupt way. **6.** (*intr.*; often foll. by *at* or *up*) to seize something suddenly or quickly. **7.** (when *intr.*, often foll. by *at*) to bite at (something) bringing the jaws rapidly together. **8.** to speak (words) sharply or abruptly. **9.** to take a snapshot of (something). **10.** (*tr.*) *American football.* to put (the ball) into play by sending it back from the line of scrimmage. **11. snap one's fingers at.** *Inf.* **a.** to dismiss with contempt. **b.** to defy. **12. snap out of it.** *Inf.* to recover quickly, esp. from depression or anger. ~*n.* **13.** the act of breaking suddenly or the sound produced by a sudden breakage. **14.** a sudden sharp sound, esp. of bursting, popping, or cracking. **15.** a catch, clasp, or fastener that operates with a snapping sound. **16.** a sudden grab or bite. **17.** a thin crisp biscuit: *ginger snaps.* **18.** *Inf.* See **snapshot.** **19.** *Inf.* vigour, liveliness, or energy. **20.** *Inf.* a task or job that is easy or profitable to do. **21.** a short spell or period, esp. of cold weather. **22.** *Brit.* a card game in which the word *snap* is called when two cards of equal value are turned up on the separate piles dealt by each player. **23.** (*modifier*) done on the spur of the moment: *a snap decision.* **24.** (*modifier*) closed or fastened with a snap. ~*adv.* **25.** with a snap. ~*interj.* **26. a.** *Cards.* the word called while playing snap. **b.** an exclamation used to draw attention to the similarity of two things. ~See also **snap up.** [C15: < MLow G or MDu. *snappen* to seize] —ˈ**snapless** *adj.* —ˈ**snappingly** *adv.*

snapdragon (ˈsnæpˌdrægən) *n.* any of several plants of the genus *Antirrhinum* having spikes of showy white, yellow, pink, red, or purplish flowers. Also called: **antirrhinum.**

snap fastener *n.* another name for **press stud.**

snapper (ˈsnæpə) *n., pl.* **-per** *or* **-pers.** **1.** any large sharp-toothed percoid food fish of warm and tropical coastal regions. See also **red snapper.** **2.** a food fish of Australia and New Zealand that has a pinkish body covered with blue spots. **3.** another name for the **snapping turtle.** **4.** a person or thing that snaps. ~Also (for sense 1, 2): **schnapper.**

snapping turtle *n.* any large aggressive North American river turtle having powerful hooked jaws and a rough shell. Also called: **snapper.**

snappy (ˈsnæpɪ) *adj.* **-pier, -piest.** **1.** Also: **snappish.** apt to speak sharply or irritably. **2.** Also: **snappish.** apt to snap or bite. **3.** crackling in sound: *a snappy fire.* **4.** brisk, sharp, or chilly: *a snappy pace.* **5.** smart and fashionable: *a snappy dresser.* **6. make it snappy.** *Sl.* hurry up! —ˈ**snappily** *adv.* —ˈ**snappiness** *n.*

snap ring *n. Mountaineering.* another name for **karabiner.**

snapshot (ˈsnæpˌʃɒt) *n.* an informal photograph taken with a simple camera. Often shortened to **snap.**

snap up *vb.* (*tr., adv.*) **1.** to avail oneself of eagerly and quickly: *she snapped up the bargains.* **2.** to interrupt abruptly.

snare[1] (snɛə) *n.* **1.** a device for trapping birds or small animals, esp. a flexible loop that is drawn tight around the prey. **2.** a surgical instrument for removing certain tumours, consisting of a wire loop that may be drawn tight around their base to sever them. **3.** anything that traps or entangles someone or something unawares. ~*vb.* (*tr.*) **4.** to catch (birds or small animals) with a snare. **5.** to catch or trap in or as if in a snare. [OE *sneare*] —ˈ**snarer** *n.*

snare[2] (snɛə) *n. Music.* a set of gut strings wound with wire fitted against the lower drumhead of a snare drum. They produce a rattling sound when the drum is beaten. [C17: < MDu. *snaer* or MLow G *snare* string]

snare drum *n. Music.* a cylindrical drum with two drumheads, the upper of which is struck and the lower fitted with a snare. See **snare**[2].

snarl[1] (snɑːl) *vb.* **1.** (*intr.*) (of an animal) to growl viciously, baring the teeth. **2.** to speak or express (something) viciously. ~*n.* **3.** a vicious growl or facial expression. **4.** the act of snarling. [C16: of Gmc origin] —'**snarler** *n.* —'**snarling** *adj.* —'**snarly** *adj.*

snarl[2] (snɑːl) *n.* **1.** a tangled mass of thread, hair, etc. **2.** a complicated or confused state or situation. **3.** a knot in wood. ~*vb.* **4.** (often foll. by *up*) to be, become, or make tangled or complicated. **5.** (*tr.;* often foll. by *up*) to confuse mentally. **6.** (*tr.*) to emboss (metal) by hammering on a tool held against the under surface. [C14: < ON] —'**snarler** *n.* —'**snarly** *adj.*

snarl-up *n. Inf., chiefly Brit.* a confusion, obstruction, or tangle, esp. a traffic jam.

snatch (snætʃ) *vb.* **1.** (*tr.*) to seize or grasp (something) suddenly or peremptorily: *he snatched the chocolate.* **2.** (*intr.;* usually foll. by *at*) to seize or attempt to seize suddenly. **3.** (*tr.*) to take hurriedly: *to snatch some sleep.* **4.** (*tr.*) to remove suddenly: *she snatched her hand away.* **5.** (*tr.*) to gain, win, or rescue, esp. narrowly: *they snatched victory in the closing seconds.* ~*n.* **6.** an act of snatching. **7.** a fragment or incomplete part: *snatches of conversation.* **8.** a brief spell: *snatches of time off.* **9.** *Weightlifting.* a lift in which the weight is raised in one quick motion from the floor to an overhead position. **10.** *Sl., chiefly U.S.* an act of kidnapping. **11.** *Brit. sl.* a robbery: *a diamond snatch.* [C13 *snacchen*] —'**snatcher** *n.*

snatchy ('snætʃɪ) *adj.* **snatchier, snatchiest.** disconnected or spasmodic. —'**snatchily** *adv.*

snazzy ('snæzɪ) *adj.* **-zier, -ziest.** *Inf.* (esp. of clothes) stylishly and often flashily attractive. [C20: ? < SN(APPY + J)AZZY] —'**snazzily** *adv.* —'**snazziness** *n.*

sneak (sniːk) *vb.* **1.** (*intr.;* often foll. by *along, off, in,* etc.) to move furtively. **2.** (*intr.*) to behave in a cowardly or underhand manner. **3.** (*tr.*) to bring, take, or put stealthily. **4.** (*intr.*) *Inf., chiefly Brit.* to tell tales (esp. in schools). **5.** (*tr.*) *Inf.* to steal. **6.** (*intr.;* foll. by *off, out, away,* etc.) *Inf.* to leave unobtrusively. ~*n.* **7.** a person who acts in an underhand or cowardly manner, esp. as an informer. **8. a.** a stealthy act. **b.** (*as modifier*): *a sneak attack.* [OE *snīcan* to creep] —'**sneaky** *adj.* —'**sneakily** *adv.* —'**sneakiness** *n.*

sneakers ('sniːkəz) *pl. n. Chiefly U.S. & Canad.* canvas shoes with rubber soles worn informally.

sneaking ('sniːkɪŋ) *adj.* **1.** acting in a furtive or cowardly way. **2.** secret: *a sneaking desire to marry a millionaire.* **3.** slight but nagging (esp. in **a sneaking suspicion**). —'**sneakingly** *adv.*

sneak thief *n.* a person who steals paltry articles from premises, which he enters through open doors, windows, etc.

sneer (snɪə) *n.* **1.** a facial expression of scorn or contempt, typically with the upper lip curled. **2.** a scornful or contemptuous remark or utterance. ~*vb.* **3.** (*intr.*) to assume a facial expression of scorn or contempt. **4.** to say or utter (something) in a scornful manner. [C16: ? < Low Du.] —'**sneerer** *n.* —'**sneering** *adj., n.*

sneeze (sniːz) *vb.* **1.** (*intr.*) to expel air from the nose involuntarily, esp. as the result of irritation of the nasal mucous membrane. ~*n.* **2.** the act or sound of sneezing. [OE *fnēosan* (unattested)] —'**sneezer** *n.* —'**sneezy** *adj.*

sneeze at *vb.* (*intr., prep.;* usually with a negative) *Inf.* to dismiss lightly: *his offer is not to be sneezed at.*

sneezewood ('sniːzˌwʊd) *n.* **1.** a South African tree. **2.** its exceptionally hard wood, used for furniture, gateposts and railway sleepers.

sneezewort ('sniːzˌwɜːt) *n.* a Eurasian plant having daisy-like flowers and long grey-green leaves, which cause sneezing when powdered.

snick (snɪk) *n.* **1.** a small cut; notch. **2.** *Cricket.* **a.** a glancing blow off the edge of the bat. **b.** the ball so hit. ~*vb.* (*tr.*) **3.** to cut a small corner or notch in (material, etc.). **4.** *Cricket.* to hit (the ball) with a snick. [C18: prob. of Scand. origin]

snicker ('snɪkə) *n., vb.* **1.** another word (esp. U.S. and Canad.) for **snigger.** ~*vb.* **2.** (*intr.*) (of a horse) to whinny. [C17: prob. imit.]

snide (snaɪd) *adj.* **1.** (of a remark, etc.) maliciously derogatory. **2.** counterfeit. ~*n.* **3.** *Sl.* sham jewellery. [C19: <?] —'**snidely** *adv.* —'**snideness** *n.*

sniff (snɪf) *vb.* **1.** to inhale through the nose, usually in short rapid audible inspirations, as for clearing a congested nasal passage or for taking a drug. **2.** (when *intr.*, often foll. by *at*) to perceive or attempt to perceive (a smell) by inhaling through the nose. ~*n.* **3.** the act or sound of sniffing. **4.** a smell perceived by sniffing, esp. a faint scent. ~See also **sniff at, sniff out.** [C14: prob. rel. to *snivelen* to snivel] —'**sniffer** *n.* —'**sniffing** *n., adj.*

sniff at *vb.* (*intr., prep.*) to express contempt or dislike for.

sniffer dog *n.* a police dog trained to detect drugs or explosives by smell.

sniffle ('snɪf°l) *vb.* **1.** (*intr.*) to breathe audibly through the nose, as when the nasal passages are congested. ~*n.* **2.** the act, sound, or an instance of sniffling. —'**sniffler** *n.* —'**sniffly** *adj.*

sniffles ('snɪf°lz) *or* **snuffles** *pl. n. Inf.* **the.** a cold in the head.

sniff out *vb.* (*tr., adv.*) to detect through shrewdness or instinct.

sniffy ('snɪfɪ) *adj.* **-fier, -fiest.** *Inf.* contemptuous or disdainful. —'**sniffily** *adv.* —'**sniffiness** *n.*

snifter ('snɪftə) *n.* **1.** a pear-shaped glass with a bowl that narrows towards the top so that the aroma of brandy or a liqueur is retained. **2.** *Inf.* a small quantity of alcoholic drink. [C19: ? < dialect *snifter* to sniff, ? of Scand. origin]

snig *vb.* **snigging, snigged.** (*tr.*) *N.Z.* to drag (a felled log) by a chain or cable. [< E dialect]

snigger ('snɪgə) *n.* **1.** a sly or disrespectful laugh, esp. one partly stifled. ~*vb.* (*intr.*) **2.** to utter such a laugh. [C18: var. of SNICKER] —'**sniggering** *n., adj.*

snigging chain *Austral. & N.Z.* a chain attached to a log when being hauled out of the bush.

snip (snɪp) *vb.* **snipping, snipped.** **1.** to cut or clip with a small quick stroke or a succession of small quick strokes, esp. with scissors or shears. ~*n.* **2.** the act of snipping. **3.** the sound of scissors or shears closing. **4.** Also called: **snipping.** a small piece of anything. **5.** a small cut made by snipping. **6.** *Chiefly Brit.* an informal word for **bargain.** **7.** *Inf.* something easily done; cinch. ~See also **snips.** [C16: < Low G, Du. *snippen*]

snipe (snaɪp) *n., pl.* **snipe** *or* **snipes.** **1.** any of a genus of birds, such as the common snipe, of marshes and river banks, having a long straight bill. **2.** a shot, esp. a gunshot, fired from a place of concealment. ~*vb.* **3.** (when *intr.*, often foll. by *at*) to attack (a person or persons) with a rifle from a place of concealment. **4.** (*intr.;* often foll. by *at*) to criticize a person or persons from a position of security. **5.** (*intr.*) to hunt or shoot snipe. [C14: < ON *snīpa*] —'**sniper** *n.*

snipefish ('snaɪpˌfɪʃ) *n., pl.* **-fish** *or* **fishes.** a teleost fish of tropical and temperate seas, having a deep body, long snout, and a single long dorsal fin. Also called: **bellows fish.**

snippet ('snɪpɪt) *n.* a small scrap or fragment of fabric, news, etc. —'**snippetiness** *n.* —'**snippety** *adj.*

snips (snɪps) *pl. n.* a small pair of shears used for cutting sheet metal.

snitch (snɪtʃ) *Sl.* ~*vb.* **1.** (*tr.*) to steal; take, esp. in an underhand way. **2.** (*intr.*) to act as an informer. ~*n.* **3.** an informer. **4.** the nose. [C17: <?]

snitchy ('snɪtʃɪ) *adj.* **snitchier, snitchiest.** *N.Z. inf.* bad-tempered or irritable.

snivel ('snɪv°l) *vb.* **-elling, -elled** *or U.S.* **-eling, -eled.** **1.** (*intr.*) to sniffle as a sign of distress. **2.**

to utter (something) tearfully; whine. **3.** (*intr.*) to have a runny nose. ~*n.* **4.** an instance of snivelling. [C14 *snivelen*] —ˈ**sniveller** *n.* —ˈ**snivelling** *adj., n.*

SNO *abbrev. for* Scottish National Orchestra.

snob (snɒb) *n.* **1. a.** a person who strives to associate with those of higher social status and who behaves condescendingly to others. **b.** (*as modifier*): *snob appeal.* **2.** a person having similar pretensions with regard to his tastes, etc.: *an intellectual snob.* [C18 (in the sense: shoemaker; hence, C19: a person who flatters those of higher station, etc.): <?] —ˈ**snobbery** *n.* —ˈ**snobbish** *adj.* —ˈ**snobbishly** *adv.*

SNOBOL (ˈsnəʊbɒl) *n.* String Oriented Symbolic Language: a computer-programming language for handling strings of symbols.

Sno-Cat (ˈsnəʊˌkæt) *n. Trademark.* a type of snowmobile.

snoek (snʊk) *n.* a South African edible marine fish. [< Afrik., < Du. *snoek* pike]

snog (snɒg) *Brit. sl.* ~*vb.* **snogging, snogged. 1.** (*intr.*) to kiss and cuddle. ~*n.* **2.** the act of kissing and cuddling. [<?]

snood (snuːd) *n.* **1.** a pouchlike hat, often of net, loosely holding a woman's hair at the back. **2.** a headband, esp. one formerly worn by young unmarried women in Scotland. [OE *snōd*; <?]

snook[1] (snuːk) *n., pl.* **snook** *or* **snooks. 1.** any of a genus of large game fishes of tropical American marine and fresh waters. **2.** *Austral.* the sea pike. [C17: < Du. *snoek* pike]

snook[2] (snuːk) *n. Brit.* a rude gesture, made by putting one thumb to the nose with the fingers of the hand outstretched (esp. in **cock a snook**). [C19: <?]

snooker (ˈsnuːkə) *n.* **1.** a game played on a billiard table with 15 red balls, six balls of other colours, and a white cue ball. The object is to pot the balls in a certain order. **2.** a shot in which the cue ball is left in a position such that another ball blocks the target ball. ~*vb.* (*tr.*) **3.** to leave (an opponent) in an unfavourable position by playing a snooker. **4.** to place (someone) in a difficult situation. **5.** (*often passive*) to thwart; defeat. [C19: <?]

snoop (snuːp) *Inf.* ~*vb.* **1.** (*intr.*; often foll. by *about* or *around*) to pry into the private business of others. ~*n.* **2.** a person who pries into the business of others. **3.** an act or instance of snooping. [C19: < Du. *snoepen* to eat furtively] —ˈ**snooper** *n.* —ˈ**snoopy** *adj.*

snooperscope (ˈsnuːpəˌskəʊp) *n. Mil., U.S.* an instrument that enables the user to see objects in the dark by illuminating the object with infrared radiation.

snoot (snuːt) *n. Sl.* the nose. [C20: var. of SNOUT]

snooty (ˈsnuːtɪ) *adj.* **snootier, snootiest.** *Inf.* **1.** aloof or supercilious. **2.** snobbish: *a snooty restaurant.* —ˈ**snootily** *adv.* —ˈ**snootiness** *n.*

snooze (snuːz) *Inf.* ~*vb.* **1.** (*intr.*) to take a brief light sleep. ~*n.* **2.** a nap. [C18: <?] —ˈ**snoozer** *n.* —ˈ**snoozy** *adj.*

snore (snɔː) *vb.* **1.** (*intr.*) to breathe through the mouth and nose while asleep with snorting sounds caused by the soft palate vibrating. ~*n.* **2.** the act or sound of snoring. [C14: imit.] —ˈ**snorer** *n.*

snorkel (ˈsnɔːkᵊl) *n.* **1.** a device allowing a swimmer to breathe while face down on the surface of the water, consisting of a bent tube fitting into the mouth and projecting above the surface. **2.** (on a submarine) a retractable vertical device containing air-intake and exhaust pipes for the engines and general ventilation. ~*vb.* **-kelling, -kelled** *or U.S.* **-keling, -keled. 3.** (*intr.*) to swim with a snorkel. [C20: < G *Schnorchel*]

snort (snɔːt) *vb.* **1.** (*intr.*) to exhale forcibly through the nostrils, making a characteristic noise. **2.** (*intr.*) (of a person) to express contempt or annoyance by such an exhalation. **3.** (*tr.*) to utter in a contemptuous or annoyed manner. **4.** *Sl.* to inhale (a powdered drug) through the nostrils. ~*n.* **5.** a forcible exhalation of air through the nostrils, esp. (of persons) as a noise of contempt. **6.** *Sl.* an instance of snorting a drug. [C14 *snorten*] —ˈ**snorting** *n., adj.* —ˈ**snortingly** *adv.*

snorter (ˈsnɔːtə) *n.* **1.** a person or animal that snorts. **2.** *Brit. sl.* something outstandingly impressive or difficult.

snot (snɒt) *n.* (*usually considered vulgar*) **1.** nasal mucus or discharge. **2.** *Sl.* a contemptible person. [OE *gesnot*]

snotty (ˈsnɒtɪ) *adj.* **-tier, -tiest.** (*considered vulgar*) **1.** dirty with nasal discharge. **2.** *Sl.* contemptible; nasty. **3.** snobbish; conceited. —ˈ**snottily** *adv.* —ˈ**snottiness** *n.*

snout (snaʊt) *n.* **1.** the part of the head of a vertebrate, esp. a mammal, consisting of the nose, jaws, and surrounding region. **2.** the corresponding part of the head of such insects as weevils. **3.** anything projecting like a snout, such as a nozzle. **4.** *Sl.* a person's nose. **5.** *Brit. sl.* a cigarette or tobacco. **6.** *Sl.* an informer. [C13: of Gmc origin] —ˈ**snouted** *adj.* —ˈ**snoutless** *adj.* —ˈ**snoutˌlike** *adj.*

snout beetle *n.* another name for **weevil.**

snow (snəʊ) *n.* **1.** precipitation from clouds in the form of flakes of ice crystals formed in the upper atmosphere. **2.** a layer of snowflakes on the ground. **3.** a fall of such precipitation. **4.** anything resembling snow in whiteness, softness, etc. **5.** the random pattern of white spots on a television or radar screen, occurring when the signal is weak. **6.** *Sl.* cocaine. ~*vb.* **7.** (*intr.*, with *it* as subject) to be the case that snow is falling. **8.** (*tr.*; usually passive, foll. by *over, under, in,* or *up*) to cover or confine with a heavy fall of snow. **9.** (often with *it* as subject) to fall or cause to fall as or like snow. **10.** (*tr.*) *U.S. & Canad. sl.* to overwhelm with elaborate often insincere talk. **11. be snowed under.** to be overwhelmed, esp. with paperwork. [OE *snāw*] —ˈ**snowless** *adj.* —ˈ**snowˌlike** *adj.*

snowball (ˈsnəʊˌbɔːl) *n.* **1.** snow pressed into a ball for throwing, as in play. **2.** a drink made of advocaat and lemonade. ~*vb.* **3.** (*intr.*) to increase rapidly in size, importance, etc. **4.** (*tr.*) to throw snowballs at.

snowball tree *n.* any of several shrubs of the genus *Viburnum,* with spherical clusters of white or pinkish flowers.

snowberry (ˈsnəʊbərɪ) *n., pl.* **-ries. 1.** a shrub cultivated for its small pink flowers and white berries. **2.** Also called: **waxberry.** any of the berries of such a plant.

snow-blind *adj.* having temporarily impaired vision because of the intense reflection of sunlight from snow. —**snow blindness** *n.*

snowblower (ˈsnəʊˌbləʊə) *n.* a snow-clearing machine that draws the snow in and blows it away.

snowbound (ˈsnəʊˌbaʊnd) *adj.* confined to one place by heavy falls or drifts of snow; snowed in.

snow bunting *n.* a bunting of northern and arctic regions, having a white plumage with dark markings on the wings, back, and tail.

snowcap (ˈsnəʊˌkæp) *n.* a cap of snow, as on top of a mountain. —ˈ**snowˌcapped** *adj.*

snowdrift (ˈsnəʊˌdrɪft) *n.* a bank of deep snow driven together by the wind.

snowdrop (ˈsnəʊˌdrɒp) *n.* a Eurasian plant having drooping white bell-shaped flowers that bloom in early spring.

snowfall (ˈsnəʊˌfɔːl) *n.* **1.** a fall of snow. **2.** *Meteorol.* the amount of snow received in a specified place and time.

snow fence *n.* a lath-and-wire fence put up in winter beside windy roads to prevent snowdrifts.

snowfield (ˈsnəʊˌfiːld) *n.* a large area of permanent snow.

snowflake (ˈsnəʊˌfleɪk) *n.* **1.** one of the mass of small thin delicate arrangements of ice crystals that fall as snow. **2.** any of various European plants that have white nodding bell-shaped flowers.

snow goose *n.* a North American goose having a white plumage with black wing tips.

snow gum *n.* any of several eucalypts of mountainous regions of SE Australia.

snow-in-summer *n.* a plant of SE Europe and Asia having white flowers and downy stems and leaves: cultivated as a rock plant.

snow leopard *n.* a large feline mammal of mountainous regions of central Asia, closely related to the leopard but having a long pale brown coat marked with black rosettes.

snow lily *n. Canad.* another name for **dogtooth violet.**

snow line *n.* the altitudinal or latitudinal limit of permanent snow.

snowman (ˈsnəʊˌmæn) *n., pl.* **-men.** a figure resembling a man, made of packed snow.

snowmobile (ˈsnəʊməˌbiːl) *n.* a motor vehicle for travelling on snow, esp. one with caterpillar tracks and front skis.

snowplough *or esp. U.S.* **snowplow** (ˈsnəʊˌplaʊ) *n.* an implement or vehicle for clearing away snow.

snowshoe (ˈsnəʊˌʃuː) *n.* **1.** a device to facilitate walking on snow, esp. a racket-shaped frame with a network of thongs stretched across it. ~*vb.* **-shoeing, -shoed. 2.** (*intr.*) to walk or go using snowshoes. —ˈ**snowˌshoer** *n.*

snowstorm (ˈsnəʊˌstɔːm) *n.* a storm with heavy snow.

snow tyre *n.* a motor-vehicle tyre with deep treads to give improved grip on snow and ice.

snow-white *adj.* **1.** white as snow. **2.** pure as white snow.

snowy (ˈsnəʊɪ) *adj.* **snowier, snowiest. 1.** covered with or abounding in snow: *snowy hills.* **2.** characterized by snow: *snowy weather.* **3.** resembling snow in whiteness, purity, etc. —ˈ**snowily** *adv.* —ˈ**snowiness** *n.*

snowy owl *n.* a large owl of tundra regions, having a white plumage flecked with brown.

SNP *abbrev. for* Scottish National Party.

Snr *or* **snr** *abbrev. for* senior.

snub (snʌb) *vb.* **snubbing, snubbed.** (*tr.*) **1.** to insult (someone) deliberately. **2.** to stop or check the motion of (a boat, horse, etc.) by taking turns of a rope around a post. ~*n.* **3.** a deliberately insulting act or remark. **4.** *Naut.* an elastic shock absorber attached to a mooring line. ~*adj.* **5.** short and blunt. See also **snub-nosed.** [C14: < ON *snubba* to scold] —ˈ**snubber** *n.* —ˈ**snubby** *adj.*

snub-nosed *adj.* **1.** having a short turned-up nose. **2.** (of a pistol) having an extremely short barrel.

snuff[1] (snʌf) *vb.* **1.** (*tr.*) to inhale through the nose. **2.** (when *intr.*, often foll. by *at*) (esp. of an animal) to examine by sniffing. ~*n.* **3.** an act or the sound of snuffing. [C16: prob. < MDu. *snuffen* to snuffle, ult. imit.] —ˈ**snuffer** *n.*

snuff[2] (snʌf) *n.* **1.** finely powdered tobacco, esp. for sniffing up the nostrils. **2.** a small amount of this. **3. up to snuff.** *Inf.* **a.** in good health or in good condition. **b.** *Chiefly Brit.* not easily deceived. ~*vb.* **4.** (*intr.*) to use or inhale snuff. [C17: < Du. *snuf*, shortened < *snuftabale*, lit.: tobacco for snuffing]

snuff[3] (snʌf) *vb.* (*tr.*) **1.** (often foll. by *out*) to extinguish (a light from a candle). **2.** to cut off the charred part of (the wick of a candle, etc.). **3.** (usually foll. by *out*) *Inf.* to put an end to. **4. snuff it.** *Brit. inf.* to die. ~*n.* **5.** the burned portion of the wick of a candle. [C14 *snoffe*, <?]

snuffbox (ˈsnʌfˌbɒks) *n.* a container, often of elaborate ornamental design, for holding small quantities of snuff.

snuff-dipping *n.* the practice of absorbing nicotine by holding in one's mouth, between the cheek and the gum, a small amount of tobacco.

snuffer (ˈsnʌfə) *n.* **1.** a cone-shaped implement for extinguishing candles. **2.** (*pl.*) an instrument resembling a pair of scissors for trimming the wick or extinguishing the flame of a candle.

snuffle (ˈsnʌfᵊl) *vb.* **1.** (*intr.*) to breathe noisily or with difficulty. **2.** to say or speak in a nasal tone. **3.** (*intr.*) to snivel. ~*n.* **4.** an act or the sound of snuffling. **5.** a nasal voice. **6. the snuffles.** a condition characterized by snuffling. [C16: < Low G or Du. *snuffelen*] —ˈ**snuffly** *adj.*

snuff movie *or* **film** *n. Sl.* a pornographic film in which an unsuspecting actress or actor is murdered as the climax of the film.

snuffy (ˈsnʌfɪ) *adj.* **snuffier, snuffiest. 1.** of or resembling snuff. **2.** covered with or smelling of snuff. **3.** disagreeable. —ˈ**snuffiness** *n.*

snug (snʌg) *adj.* **snugger, snuggest. 1.** comfortably warm and well protected; cosy: *the children were snug in bed.* **2.** small but comfortable: *a snug cottage.* **3.** well ordered; compact: *a snug boat.* **4.** sheltered and secure: *a snug anchorage.* **5.** fitting closely and comfortably. **6.** offering safe concealment. ~*n.* **7.** (in Britain and Ireland) one of the bars in certain pubs, offering intimate seating for only a few persons. ~*vb.* **snugging, snugged. 8.** to make or become comfortable and warm. [C16 (in the sense: prepared for storms (used of a ship))] —ˈ**snugly** *adv.* —ˈ**snugness** *n.*

snuggery (ˈsnʌgərɪ) *n., pl.* **-geries. 1.** a cosy and comfortable place or room. **2.** another name for **snug** (sense 7).

snuggle (ˈsnʌgᵊl) *vb.* **1.** (usually *intr.;* usually foll. by *down, up,* or *together*) to nestle into or draw close to (somebody or something) for warmth or from affection. ~*n.* **2.** the act of snuggling. [C17: frequentative of SNUG (vb.)]

so[1] (səʊ) *adv.* **1.** (foll. by an adjective or adverb and a correlative clause often introduced by *that*) to such an extent: *the river is so dirty that it smells.* **2.** (*used with a negative;* it replaces the first *as* in an equative comparison) to the same extent as: *she is not so old as you.* **3.** (intensifier): *it's so lovely.* **4.** in the state or manner expressed or implied: *they're happy and will remain so.* **5.** (*not used with a negative;* foll. by an auxiliary verb or *do, have,* or *be* used as main verbs) also: *I can speak Spanish and so can you.* **6.** *Dialect.* indeed: used to contradict a negative statement: *"you didn't phone her." "I did so!"* **7.** *Arch.* provided that. **8. and so on** *or* **forth.** and continuing similarly. **9. or so.** approximately: *fifty or so people came to see me.* **10. so be it.** used to express agreement or resignation. **11. so much. a.** a certain degree or amount (of). **b.** a lot (of): *it's just so much nonsense.* **12. so much for. a.** no more can or need be said about. **b.** used to express contempt for something that has failed. ~*conj.* (*subordinating;* often foll. by *that*) **13.** in order (that): *to die so that you might live.* **14.** with the consequence (that): *he was late home, so that there was trouble.* **15. so as.** (*takes an infinitive*) in order (to): *to diet so as to lose weight.* ~*sentence connector.* **16.** in consequence: *she wasn't needed, so she left.* **17.** thereupon: *and so we ended up in France.* **18. so what!** *Inf.* what importance does that have? ~*pron.* **19.** used to substitute for a clause or sentence, which may be understood: *you'll stop because I said so.* ~*adj.* **20.** (used with *is, was,* etc.) factual: *it can't be so.* ~*interj.* **21.** an exclamation of surprise, etc. [OE swā]

▷ **Usage.** Careful writers of formal English consider it poor style to use *so* as a conjunction, to indicate either purpose (*he did it so he could feel happier*) or result (*he could not do it so he did not try*). In the former case *in order to* should be used instead and in the latter case *and so* or *and therefore* would be more acceptable.

so[2] (səʊ) *n. Music.* a variant spelling of **soh.**

So. *abbrev. for* south(ern).

soak (səʊk) *vb.* **1.** to make, become, or be thoroughly wet or saturated, esp. by immersion in a liquid. **2.** (when *intr.*, usually foll. by *in* or *into*) (of a liquid) to penetrate or permeate. **3.** (*tr.;* usually foll. by *in* or *up*) (of a permeable solid) to take in (a liquid) by absorption: *the earth soaks up rainwater.* **4.** (*tr.;* foll. by *out* or *out of*) to remove by immersion in a liquid: *she soaked the stains out of the dress.* **5.** *Inf.* to drink excessively or make or become drunk. **6.** (*tr.*) *Sl.* to overcharge. ~*n.* **7.** the act of immersing in a liquid or the period of immersion. **8.** the liquid in which something may be soaked. **9.** *Austral.* a natural depression holding rainwater, esp. just beneath the surface of the ground. **10.** *Sl.* a person who drinks to excess. [OE *sōcian* to cook] —ˈ**soaker** *n.* —ˈ**soaking** *n., adj.* —ˈ**soakingly** *adv.*

soakaway (ˈsəʊkəˌweɪ) *n.* a pit filled with rubble, etc., into which waste water drains.

so-and-so *n., pl.* **so-and-sos.** *Inf.* **1.** a person whose name is forgotten or ignored. **2.** *Euphemistic.* a person or thing regarded as unpleasant: *which so-and-so broke my razor?*

soap (səʊp) *n.* **1.** a cleaning agent made by reacting animal or vegetable fats or oils with potassium or sodium hydroxide. Soaps act by emulsifying grease and lowering the surface tension of water, so that it more readily penetrates open materials such as textiles. **2.** any metallic salt of a fatty acid, such as palmitic or stearic acid. **3.** *Sl.* flattery or persuasive talk (esp. in **soft soap**). **4.** *Inf.* short for **soap opera. 5. no soap.** *Sl.* not possible. ~*vb.* (*tr.*) **6.** to apply soap to. **7.** (often foll. by *up*) *Sl.* to flatter. [OE *sāpe*] —ˈ**soapless** *adj.* —ˈ**soapˌlike** *adj.*

soapberry (ˈsəʊpˌbɛrɪ) *n., pl.* **-ries. 1.** any of various chiefly tropical American trees having pulpy fruit containing saponin. **2.** the fruit of any of these trees.

soapbox (ˈsəʊpˌbɒks) *n.* **1.** a box or crate for packing soap. **2.** a crate used as a platform for speech-making. **3.** a child's home-made racing cart.

soap opera *n.* a serialized drama, usually dealing with domestic themes, broadcast on radio or television. [C20: so called because manufacturers of soap were typical sponsors]

soapstone (ˈsəʊpˌstəʊn) *n.* a massive compact soft variety of talc, used for making table tops, hearths, ornaments, etc. Also called: **steatite.**

soapsuds (ˈsəʊpˌsʌdz) *pl. n.* foam or lather made from soap. —ˈ**soapˌsudsy** *adj.*

soapwort (ˈsəʊpˌwɜːt) *n.* a Eurasian plant having rounded clusters of fragrant pink or white flowers and leaves that were formerly used as a soap substitute. Also called: **bouncing Bet.**

soapy (ˈsəʊpɪ) *adj.* **soapier, soapiest. 1.** containing or covered with soap: *soapy water.* **2.** resembling or characteristic of soap. **3.** *Sl.* flattering. —ˈ**soapily** *adv.* —ˈ**soapiness** *n.*

soar (sɔː) *vb.* (*intr.*) **1.** to rise or fly upwards into the air. **2.** (of a bird, aircraft, etc.) to glide while maintaining altitude by the use of ascending air currents. **3.** to rise or increase in volume, size, etc.: *soaring prices.* [C14: < OF *essorer,* < Vulgar L *exaurāre* (unattested) to expose to the breezes, < L EX-[1] + *aura* breeze] —ˈ**soarer** *n.* —ˈ**soaring** *n., adj.* —ˈ**soaringly** *adv.*

sob (sɒb) *vb.* **sobbing, sobbed. 1.** (*intr.*) to weep with convulsive gasps. **2.** (*tr.*) to utter with sobs. **3.** to cause (oneself) to be in a specified state by sobbing: *to sob oneself to sleep.* ~*n.* **4.** a convulsive gasp made in weeping. [C12: prob. < Low G] —ˈ**sobbing** *adj.*

sober (ˈsəʊbə) *adj.* **1.** not drunk. **2.** not given to excessive indulgence in drink or any other activity. **3.** sedate and rational: *a sober attitude to a problem.* **4.** (of colours) plain and dull or subdued. **5.** free from exaggeration or speculation: *he told us the sober truth.* ~*vb.* **6.** (usually foll. by *up*) to make or become less intoxicated. [C14 *sobre,* < OF, < L *sōbrius*] —ˈ**sobering** *n., adj.* —ˈ**soberly** *adv.*

sobriety (səʊˈbraɪətɪ) *n.* **1.** the state or quality of being sober. **2.** the quality of refraining from excess. **3.** the quality of being serious or sedate.

sobriquet *or* **soubriquet** (ˈsəʊbrɪˌkeɪ) *n.* a humorous epithet, assumed name, or nickname. [C17: < F *soubriquet,* <?]

sob story *n.* a tale of personal distress intended to arouse sympathy.

Soc. *or* **soc.** *abbrev. for:* **1.** socialist. **2.** society.

soca (ˈsəʊkə) *n.* a mixture of soul and calypso music typical of the E Caribbean. [C20: a blend of *soul + calypso*]

socage (ˈsɒkɪdʒ) *n. English legal history.* the tenure of land by certain services, esp. of an agricultural nature. [C14: < Anglo-F, < *soc* SOKE]

so-called *adj.* **a.** (*prenominal*) designated or styled by the name or word mentioned, esp. (in the speaker's opinion) incorrectly: *a so-called genius.* **b.** (also used parenthetically after a noun): *these experts, so-called, are no help.*

soccer (ˈsɒkə) *n.* **a.** a game in which two teams of eleven players try to kick or head a ball into their opponents' goal, only the goalkeeper on either side being allowed to touch the ball with his hands and arms, except in the case of throw-ins. **b.** (*as modifier*): *a soccer player.* ~Also called: **Association Football.** [C19: < *Assoc*(*iation Football*) + -ER[1]]

socceroo (ˌsɒkəˈruː) *n., pl.* **-ceroos.** *Austral. sl.* a member of the Australian national soccer team. [C20: < SOCCER + (KANGAR)OO]

sociable (ˈsəʊʃəbᵊl) *adj.* **1.** friendly or companionable. **2.** (of an occasion) providing the opportunity for friendliness and conviviality. ~*n.* **3.** *Chiefly U.S.* a social. **4.** a type of open carriage with two seats facing each other. [C16: via F < L, < *sociāre* to unite, < *socius* an associate] —ˌ**sociaˈbility** *n.* —ˈ**sociably** *adv.*

social (ˈsəʊʃəl) *adj.* **1.** living or preferring to live in a community rather than alone. **2.** denoting or relating to human society or any of its subdivisions. **3.** of or characteristic of the behaviour and interaction of persons forming groups. **4.** relating to or having the purpose of promoting companionship, communal activities, etc.: *a social club.* **5.** relating to or engaged in social services: *a social worker.* **6.** relating to or considered appropriate to a certain class of society. **7.** (esp. of certain species of insects) living together in organized colonies: *social bees.* **8.** (of plant species) growing in clumps. ~*n.* **9.** an informal gathering, esp. of an organized group. [C16: < L *sociālis* companionable, < *socius* a comrade] —ˈ**socially** *adv.*

social anthropology *n.* the branch of anthropology that deals with cultural and social phenomena such as kinship systems or beliefs.

social climber *n.* a person who seeks advancement to a higher social class, esp. by obsequious behaviour. —**social climbing** *n.*

social contract *or* **compact** *n.* (in the theories of Rousseau and others) an agreement, entered into by individuals, that results in the formation of the state, the prime motive being the desire for protection, which entails the surrender of some personal liberties.

Social Credit *n.* **1.** (esp. in Canada) a right-wing Populist political party, movement, or doctrine. **2. Social Credit League.** (in New Zealand) a middle-of-the-road political party, in favour of free enterprise. **3. Social Credit Rally.** (in Canada) a political party formed in 1963 from a splinter group of the Social Credit Party.

social democrat *n.* **1.** any socialist who believes in the gradual transformation of capitalism into democratic socialism. **2.** (*usually cap.*) a member of a Social Democratic Party. —**social democracy** *n.*

Social Democratic Party *n.* **1.** (in Britain) a centre party formed in 1981 by ex-members of the Labour Party. See also **Alliance. 2.** one of the two major political parties in West Germany, favouring gradual reform. **3.** any of the similar parties in other countries.

social insurance *n.* government insurance providing coverage for the unemployed, the injured, the old, etc.: usually financed by contributions from employers and employees.

Social Insurance Number *n. Canad.* an identification number issued to individuals by the government in connection with income tax and social insurance.

socialism (ˈsəʊʃəˌlɪzəm) *n.* **1.** an economic theory or system in which the means of production, distribution, and exchange are owned by the community collectively, usually through the state. Cf. **capitalism. 2.** any of various social or political theories or movements in which the common welfare is to be achieved through the establishment of a socialist economic system. **3.**

(in Marxist theory) a transitional stage in the development of a society from capitalism to communism: characterized by the distribution of income according to work rather than need.

socialist (ˈsəʊʃəlɪst) *n.* **1.** a supporter or advocate of socialism or any party promoting socialism (**socialist party**). ~*adj.* **2.** of, implementing, or relating to socialism. **3.** (*sometimes cap.*) of or relating to socialists or a socialist party. —ˌ**sociaˈlistic** *adj.*

Socialist International *n.* an international association of largely anti-Communist Social Democratic Parties founded in Frankfurt in 1951.

socialite (ˈsəʊʃəˌlaɪt) *n.* a person who is or seeks to be prominent in fashionable society.

sociality (ˌsəʊʃɪˈælɪtɪ) *n., pl.* **-ties. 1.** the tendency of groups and persons to develop social links and live in communities. **2.** the quality or state of being social.

socialize *or* **-lise** (ˈsəʊʃəˌlaɪz) *vb.* **1.** (*intr.*) to behave in a friendly or sociable manner. **2.** (*tr.*) to prepare for life in society. **3.** (*tr.*) *Chiefly U.S.* to alter or create so as to be in accordance with socialist principles.

social science *n.* **1.** the study of society and of the relationship of individual members within society, including economics, history, political science, psychology, anthropology, and sociology. **2.** any of these subjects studied individually. —**social scientist** *n.*

social secretary *n.* **1.** a member of an organization who arranges its social events. **2.** a personal secretary who deals with private correspondence, etc.

social security *n.* **1.** public provision for the economic welfare of the aged, unemployed, etc., esp. through pensions and other monetary assistance. **2.** (*often cap.*) a government programme designed to provide such assistance.

social services *pl. n.* welfare activities organized by the state or a local authority and carried out by trained personnel.

social studies *n.* (*functioning as sing.*) the study of how people live and organize themselves in society, embracing geography, history, economics, and other subjects.

social welfare *n.* **1.** social services provided by a state for the benefit of its citizens. **2.** (*caps.*) (in New Zealand) a government department concerned with pensions and benefits for the elderly, the sick, etc.

social work *n.* any of various social services designed to alleviate the conditions of the poor and aged and to increase the welfare of children. —**social worker** *n.*

societal (səˈsaɪətᵊl) *adj.* of or relating to society, esp. human society. —**soˈcietally** *adv.*

society (səˈsaɪətɪ) *n., pl.* **-ties. 1.** the totality of social relationships among organized groups of human beings or animals. **2.** a system of human organizations generating distinctive cultural patterns and institutions. **3.** such a system with reference to its mode of social and economic organization or its dominant class: *middle-class society.* **4.** those with whom one has companionship. **5.** an organized group of people associated for some specific purpose or on account of some common interest: *a learned society.* **6. a.** the privileged class of people in a community, esp. as considered superior or fashionable. **b.** (*as modifier*): *a society woman.* **7.** the social life and intercourse of such people: *to enter society.* **8.** companionship: *I enjoy her society.* **9.** *Ecology.* a small community of plants within a larger association. [C16: via OF *societé* < L *societās*, < *socius* a comrade]

Society of Friends *n.* the official name for the **Quakers.**

Society of Jesus *n.* the religious order of the Jesuits, founded by Ignatius Loyola.

socio- *combining form.* denoting social or society: *socioeconomic; sociopolitical; sociology.*

sociobiology (ˌsəʊsɪəʊbaɪˈɒlədʒɪ) *n.* the study of social behaviour in animals and humans.

socioeconomic (ˌsəʊsɪəʊˌiːkəˈnɒmɪk, -ˌɛkə-) *adj.* of, relating to, or involving both economic and social factors. —ˌ**socioˌecoˈnomically** *adv.*

sociolinguistics (ˌsəʊsɪəʊlɪŋˈgwɪstɪks) *n.* (*functioning as sing.*) the study of language in relation to its social context. —ˌ**socioˈlinguist** *n.*

sociology (ˌsəʊsɪˈɒlədʒɪ) *n.* the study of the development, organization, functioning, and classification of human societies. —**sociological** (ˌsəʊsɪəˈlɒdʒɪkᵊl) *adj.* —ˌ**sociˈologist** *n.*

sociometry (ˌsəʊsɪˈɒmɪtrɪ) *n.* the study of sociological relationships within groups. —**sociometric** (ˌsəʊsɪəˈmɛtrɪk) *adj.* —ˌ**sociˈometrist** *n.*

sociopath (ˈsəʊsɪəˌpæθ) *n.* *Psychiatry.* another term for **psychopath.** —ˌ**socioˈpathic** *adj.* —**sociopathy** (ˌsəʊsɪˈɒpəθɪ) *n.*

sociopolitical (ˌsəʊsɪəʊpəˈlɪtɪkᵊl) *adj.* of or involving both political and social factors.

sock[1] (sɒk) *n.* **1.** a cloth covering for the foot, reaching to between the ankle and knee and worn inside a shoe. **2.** an insole put in a shoe, as to make it fit better. **3.** a light shoe worn by actors in ancient Greek and Roman comedy. **4. pull one's socks up.** *Brit. inf.* to make a determined effort, esp. in order to regain control of a situation. **5. put a sock in it.** *Brit. sl.* be quiet! [OE *socc* a light shoe, < L *soccus*, < Gk *sukkhos*]

sock[2] (sɒk) *Sl.* ~*vb.* **1.** (*usually tr.*) to hit with force. **2. sock it to.** *Sl.* to make a forceful impression on. ~*n.* **3.** a forceful blow. [C17: <?]

socket (ˈsɒkɪt) *n.* **1.** a device into which an electric plug can be inserted in order to make a connection in a circuit. **2.** *Chiefly Brit.* such a device mounted on a wall and connected to the electricity supply; power point. **3.** a part with an opening or hollow into which some other part can be fitted. **4.** *Anat.* **a.** a bony hollow into which a part or structure fits: *an eye socket.* **b.** the receptacle of a ball-and-socket joint. ~*vb.* **5.** (*tr.*) to furnish with or place into a socket. [C13: < Anglo-Norman *soket* a little ploughshare, < *soc*, of Celtic origin]

sockeye (ˈsɒkˌaɪ) *n.* a Pacific salmon having red flesh and valued as a food fish. Also called: **red salmon.** [by folk etymology < *sukkegh*, of Amerind origin]

socle (ˈsəʊkᵊl) *n.* another name for **plinth** (sense 1). [C18: via F < It. *zoccolo*, < L *socculus* a little shoe, < *soccus* a SOCK[1]]

Socratic (sɒˈkrætɪk) *adj.* **1.** of Socrates (?470-399 B.C.), the Greek philosopher, his methods, etc. ~*n.* **2.** a person who follows the teachings of Socrates. —**Soˈcratically** *adv.*

Socratic irony *n.* *Philosophy.* a means by which the feigned ignorance of a questioner leads the person answering to expose his own ignorance.

Socratic method *n.* *Philosophy.* the method of instruction by question and answer used by Socrates in order to elicit from his pupils truths he considered to be implicitly known by all rational beings.

sod[1] (sɒd) *n.* **1.** a piece of grass-covered surface soil held together by the roots of the grass; turf. **2.** *Poetic.* the ground. ~*vb.* **sodding, sodded. 3.** (*tr.*) to cover with sods. [C15: < Low G]

sod[2] (sɒd) *Sl., chiefly Brit.* ~*n.* **1.** a person considered to be obnoxious. **2.** a jocular word for a **person. 3. sod all.** *Sl.* nothing. ~*interj.* **4.** a strong exclamation of annoyance. [C19: shortened < SODOMITE] —**ˈsodding** *adj.*

soda (ˈsəʊdə) *n.* **1.** any of a number of simple inorganic compounds of sodium, such as sodium carbonate (**washing soda**), sodium bicarbonate (**baking soda**), and sodium hydroxide (**caustic soda**). **2.** See **soda water. 3.** *U.S. & Canad.* a fizzy drink. [C16: < Med. L, < *sodanum* barilla, a plant that was burned to obtain a type of sodium carbonate, ? < Ar.]

soda ash *n.* the anhydrous commercial form of sodium carbonate.

soda bread *n.* a type of bread leavened with sodium bicarbonate combined with milk and cream of tartar.

soda fountain *n.* *U.S. & Canad.* **1.** a counter that serves drinks, snacks, etc. **2.** an apparatus dispensing soda water.

sodality (səʊˈdælɪtɪ) *n., pl.* **-ties.** **1.** *R.C. Church.* a religious society. **2.** fellowship. [C16: < L *sodālitās* fellowship, < *sodālis* a comrade]

sodamide (ˈsəʊdəˌmaɪd) *n.* a white crystalline compound used as a dehydrating agent and in making sodium cyanide. Formula: $NaNH_2$.

soda siphon *n.* a sealed bottle containing and dispensing soda water. The water is forced up a tube reaching to the bottom of the bottle by the pressure of gas above the water.

soda water *n.* an effervescent beverage made by charging water with carbon dioxide under pressure. Sometimes shortened to **soda.**

sodden (ˈsɒdᵊn) *adj.* **1.** completely saturated. **2. a.** dulled, esp. by excessive drinking. **b.** (*in combination*): *a drink-sodden mind.* **3.** doughy, as bread is when improperly cooked. ~*vb.* **4.** to make or become sodden. [C13 *soden,* p.p. of SEETHE] —ˈ**soddenness** *n.*

sodium (ˈsəʊdɪəm) *n.* **a.** a very reactive soft silvery-white element of the alkali metal group occurring principally in common salt, Chile saltpetre, and cryolite. It is used in the production of chemicals, in metallurgy, and, alloyed with potassium, as a cooling medium in nuclear reactors. Symbol: Na; atomic no.: 11; atomic wt.: 22.99. **b.** (*as modifier*): *sodium light.* [C19: NL, < SODA + -IUM]

sodium amytal *n.* another name for **Amytal.**

sodium benzoate *n.* a white crystalline soluble compound used in preserving food (**E 211**), as an antiseptic, and in making dyes.

sodium bicarbonate *n.* a white crystalline soluble compound used in effervescent drinks, baking powders, fire-extinguishers, and in medicine as an antacid; sodium hydrogen carbonate. Formula: $NaHCO_3$. Also called: **bicarbonate of soda, baking soda.**

sodium carbonate *n.* a colourless or white odourless soluble crystalline compound used in the manufacture of glass, ceramics, soap, and paper, and as a cleansing agent. Formula: Na_2CO_3.

sodium chlorate *n.* a colourless crystalline soluble compound used as a bleaching agent, antiseptic, and weedkiller. Formula: $NaClO_3$.

sodium chloride *n.* common table salt; a soluble colourless crystalline compound widely used as a seasoning and preservative for food and in the manufacture of chemicals, glass, and soap. Formula: NaCl. Also called: **salt.**

sodium cyanide *n.* a white odourless crystalline soluble poisonous compound used for extracting gold and silver from their ores and for case-hardening steel. Formula: NaCN.

sodium glutamate (ˈgluːtəˌmeɪt) *n.* another name for **monosodium glutamate.**

sodium hydroxide *n.* a white strongly alkaline solid used in the manufacture of rayon, paper, aluminium, soap, and sodium compounds. Formula: NaOH. Also called: **caustic soda.**

sodium hyposulphite *n.* another name (not in technical usage) for **sodium thiosulphate.**

sodium lamp *n.* another name for **sodium-vapour lamp.**

sodium nitrate *n.* a white crystalline soluble solid compound used in matches, explosives, and rocket propellants, as a fertilizer, and as a curing salt for preserving food (**E 251**). Formula: $NaNO_3$.

Sodium Pentothal *n. Trademark.* another name for **thiopentone sodium.**

sodium silicate *n.* **1.** Also called: **soluble glass.** See **water glass. 2.** any sodium salt of silicic acid.

sodium sulphate *n.* a solid white substance used in making glass, detergents, and pulp. Formula: Na_2SO_4. See **salt cake** and **Glauber's salt.**

sodium thiosulphate *n.* a white soluble substance used in photography as a fixer to dissolve unchanged silver halides and also to remove excess chlorine from chlorinated water. Formula: $Na_2S_2O_3$. Also called (not in technical usage): **sodium hyposulphite, hypo.**

sodium-vapour lamp *n.* a type of electric lamp consisting of a glass tube containing neon and sodium vapour at low pressure through which an electric current is passed to give an orange light: used in street lighting.

sod' off *Brit. taboo sl.* ~*interj.* **1.** a forceful expression of dismissal. ~*vb.* **sodding, sodded. 2.** (*intr., adv.*) to go away.

Sodom (ˈsɒdəm) *n.* **1.** *Old Testament.* a city destroyed by God for its wickedness that, with Gomorrah, traditionally typifies depravity (Genesis 19:24). **2.** this city as representing homosexuality. **3.** any place notorious for depravity.

sodomite (ˈsɒdəˌmaɪt) *n.* a person who practises sodomy.

sodomy (ˈsɒdəmɪ) *n.* anal intercourse committed by a man with another man or a woman. [C13: via OF *sodomie* < L (Vulgate) *Sodoma* Sodom]

Sod's law (sɒdz) *n. Inf.* a facetious precept stating that if something can go wrong or turn out inconveniently it will.

soever (səʊˈɛvə) *adv.* in any way at all: used to emphasize or make less precise a word or phrase, usually in combination with *what, where, when, how,* etc., or else separated by intervening words. Cf. **whatsoever.**

sofa (ˈsəʊfə) *n.* an upholstered seat with back and arms for two or more people. [C17 (in the sense: dais upholstered as a seat): < Ar. *suffah*]

soffit (ˈsɒfɪt) *n.* the underside of a part of a building or a structural component, such as an arch, beam, stair, etc. [C17: via F < It. *soffitto,* < L *suffixus* something fixed underneath, < *suffigere,* < *sub-* under + *figere* to fasten]

S. of Sol. *Bible. abbrev. for* Song of Solomon.

soft (sɒft) *adj.* **1.** easy to dent, work, or cut without shattering; malleable. **2.** not hard; giving little or no resistance to pressure or weight. **3.** fine, light, smooth, or fluffy to the touch. **4.** gentle; tranquil. **5.** (of music, sounds, etc.) low and pleasing. **6.** (of light, colour, etc.) not excessively bright or harsh. **7.** (of a breeze, climate, etc.) temperate, mild, or pleasant. **8.** slightly blurred; not sharply outlined: *soft focus.* **9.** (of a diet) consisting of easily digestible foods. **10.** kind or lenient, often excessively so. **11.** easy to influence or impose upon. **12.** prepared to compromise; not doctrinaire: *the soft left.* **13.** *Inf.* feeble or silly; simple (often in **soft in the head**). **14.** unable to endure hardship, esp. through pampering. **15.** physically out of condition; flabby: *soft muscles.* **16.** loving; tender: *soft words.* **17.** *Inf.* requiring little exertion; easy: *a soft job.* **18.** *Chem.* (of water) relatively free of mineral salts and therefore easily able to make soap lather. **19.** (of a drug such as cannabis) nonaddictive. **20.** *Phonetics.* (not in technical usage) denoting the consonants *c* and *g* in English when they are pronounced as palatal or alveolar fricatives or affricates (s, dʒ, ʃ, ð, tʃ) before *e* and *i,* rather than as velar stops (k, g). **21.** *Finance, chiefly U.S.* (of prices, a market, etc.) unstable and tending to decline. **22.** (of currency) relatively unstable in exchange value. **23.** (of radiation, such as x-rays and ultraviolet radiation) having low energy and not capable of deep penetration of materials. **24. soft on** *or* **about. a.** gentle, sympathetic, or lenient towards. **b.** feeling affection or infatuation for. ~*adv.* **25.** in a soft manner: *to speak soft.* ~*n.* **26.** a soft object, part, or piece. **27.** *Inf.* See **softy.** ~*sentence substitute. Arch.* **28.** quiet! **29.** wait! [OE *sōfte*] —ˈ**softly** *adv.* —ˈ**softness** *n.*

softa (ˈsɒftə) *n.* a Muslim student of divinity and jurisprudence, esp. in Turkey. [C17: < Turkish, < Persian *sōkhtah* aflame (with love of learning)]

softball (ˈsɒftˌbɔːl) *n.* a variation of baseball using a larger softer ball, pitched underhand.

soft ball *n. Cookery.* a term used for sugar syrup boiled to a consistency at which it may be rubbed into balls after dipping in cold water.

soft-boiled *adj.* (of an egg) boiled for a short time so that the yolk is still soft.

soft coal *n.* another name for **bituminous coal.**

soft-core *adj.* (of pornography) suggestive and titillating through not being totally explicit.

soft-cover *adj.* a less common word for **paperback.**

soft drink *n.* a nonalcoholic drink.

soften (ˈsɒfᵊn) *vb.* **1.** to make or become soft or softer. **2.** to make or become more gentle. —ˈ**softener** *n.*

softening of the brain *n.* an abnormal softening of the tissues of the cerebrum characterized by mental impairment.

soft-focus lens *n. Photog.* a lens designed to produce an image that is slightly out of focus: typically used for portrait work.

soft furnishings *pl. n. Brit.* curtains, hangings, rugs, etc.

soft goods *pl. n.* textile fabrics and related merchandise.

soft-headed *adj.* **1.** *Inf.* feeble-minded; stupid; simple. **2.** (of a stick or hammer for playing a percussion instrument) having a soft head. —ˌ**soft-ˈheadedness** *n.*

softhearted (ˌsɒftˈhɑːtɪd) *adj.* easily moved to pity. —ˌ**softˈheartedly** *adv.* —ˌ**softˈheartedness** *n.*

soft landing *n.* a landing by a spacecraft on the moon or a planet at a sufficiently low velocity for the equipment or occupants to remain unharmed.

soft option *n.* in a number of choices, the one involving the least difficulty or exertion.

soft palate *n.* the posterior fleshy portion of the roof of the mouth.

soft paste *n.* **a.** artificial porcelain made from clay, bone ash, etc. **b.** (*as modifier*): *softpaste porcelain.*

soft-pedal *vb.* **-alling, -alled** *or U.S.* **-aling, -aled.** (*tr.*) **1.** to mute the tone of (a piano) by depressing the soft pedal. **2.** *Inf.* to make (something, esp. something unpleasant) less obvious by deliberately failing to emphasize or allude to it. ~*n.* **soft pedal. 3.** a foot-operated lever on a piano, the left one of two, that either moves the whole action closer to the strings so that the hammers strike with less force or causes fewer of the strings to sound.

soft porn *n. Inf.* soft-core pornography.

soft sell *n.* a method of selling based on indirect suggestion or inducement.

soft shoulder *or* **verge** *n.* a soft edge along the side of a road that is unsuitable for vehicles to drive on.

soft soap *n.* **1.** *Med.* Also called: **green soap.** a soft or liquid alkaline soap used in treating certain skin disorders. **2.** *Inf.* flattering, persuasive, or cajoling talk. ~*vb.* **soft-soap. 3.** *Inf.* to use such talk on (a person).

soft-spoken *adj.* **1.** speaking or said with a soft gentle voice. **2.** able to persuade or impress by glibness of tongue.

soft spot *n.* a sentimental fondness (esp. in **have a soft spot for**).

soft touch *n. Inf.* a person easily persuaded or imposed on, esp. to lend money.

software (ˈsɒftˌwɛə) *n. Computers.* the programs that can be used with a particular computer system. Cf. **hardware** (sense 2).

softwood (ˈsɒftˌwʊd) *n.* **1.** the open-grained wood of any of numerous coniferous trees, such as pine and cedar. **2.** any tree yielding this wood.

softy *or* **softie** (ˈsɒftɪ) *n., pl.* **softies.** *Inf.* a person who is sentimental, weakly foolish, or lacking in physical endurance.

SOGAT (ˈsəʊgæt) *n.* (in Britain) *acronym for* Society of Graphical and Allied Trades.

soggy (ˈsɒgɪ) *adj.* **-gier, -giest. 1.** soaked with liquid. **2.** (of bread, pastry, etc.) moist and heavy. **3.** *Inf.* lacking in spirit or positiveness. [C18: prob. < dialect *sog* marsh, <?] —ˈ**soggily** *adv.* —ˈ**sogginess** *n.*

soh *or* **so** (səʊ) *n. Music.* (in tonic sol-fa) the name used for the fifth note or dominant of any scale. [C13: see GAMUT]

soi-disant *French.* (swadizɑ̃) *adj.* so-called; self-styled. [lit.: calling oneself]

soigné *or* (*fem.*) **soignée** (ˈswɑːnjeɪ) *adj.* well-groomed; elegant. [F, < *soigner* to take good care of, of Gmc origin]

soil[1] (sɔɪl) *n.* **1.** the top layer of the land surface of the earth that is composed of disintegrated rock particles, humus, water, and air. **2.** a type of this material having specific characteristics: *loamy soil.* **3.** land, country, or region: *one's native soil.* **4. the soil.** life and work on a farm; land: *he belonged to the soil.* **5.** any place or thing encouraging growth or development. [C14: < Anglo-Norman, < L *solium* a seat, but confused with L *solum* the ground]

soil[2] (sɔɪl) *vb.* **1.** to make or become dirty or stained. **2.** (*tr.*) to pollute with sin or disgrace; sully; defile. ~*n.* **3.** the state or result of soiling. **4.** refuse, manure, or excrement. [C13: < OF *soillier* to defile, < *soil* pigsty, prob. < L *sūs* a swine]

soil[3] (sɔɪl) *vb.* (*tr.*) to feed (livestock) green fodder to fatten or purge them. [C17: ? < obs. vb. (C16) *soil* to manure, < SOIL[2] (n.)]

soil pipe *n.* a pipe that conveys sewage or waste water from a toilet, etc., to a soil drain or sewer.

soiree (ˈswɑːreɪ) *n.* an evening party or gathering, usually at a private house, esp. where guests listen to, play, or dance to music. [C19: < F, < OF *soir* evening, < L *sērum* a late time, < *sērus* late]

soixante-neuf *French.* (swasɑ̃tnœf) *n.* a sexual activity in which two people simultaneously stimulate each other's genitalia with their mouths. Also called: **sixty-nine.** [lit.: sixty-nine, from the position adopted by the participants]

sojourn (ˈsɒdʒɜːn, ˈsʌdʒ-) *n.* **1.** a temporary stay. ~*vb.* **2.** (*intr.*) to stay or reside temporarily. [C13: < OF *sojorner,* < Vulgar L *subdiurnāre* (unattested) to spend a day, < L *sub-* during + LL *diurnum* day] —ˈ**sojourner** *n.*

soke (səʊk) *n. English legal history.* **1.** the right to hold a local court. **2.** the territory under the jurisdiction of a particular court. [C14: < Med. L *sōca,* < OE *sōcn* a seeking]

sol[1] (sɒl) *n. Music.* another name for **soh.** [C14: see GAMUT]

sol[2] (sɒl) *n.* a colloid that has a continuous liquid phase, esp. one in which a solid is suspended in a liquid. [C20: shortened < SOLUTION]

Sol (sɒl) *n.* **1.** the Roman god personifying the sun. **2.** a poetic word for the **sun.**

sol. *abbrev. for:* **1.** soluble. **2.** solution.

Sol. *Bible abbrev. for* Solomon.

sola *Latin.* (ˈsəʊlə) *adj.* the feminine form of ***solus.***

solace (ˈsɒlɪs) *n.* **1.** comfort in misery, disappointment, etc. **2.** something that gives comfort or consolation. ~*vb.* (*tr.*) **3.** to give comfort or cheer to (a person) in time of sorrow, distress, etc. **4.** to alleviate (sorrow, misery, etc.). [C13: < OF *solas,* < L *sōlātium* comfort, < *sōlārī* to console] —ˈ**solacer** *n.*

solan *or* **solan goose** (ˈsəʊlən) *n.* an archaic name for the **gannet.** [C15 *soland,* < ON]

solanaceous (ˌsɒləˈneɪʃəs) *adj.* of or relating to the Solanaceae, a family of plants having typically tubular flowers, protruding anthers, and often poisonous or narcotic properties: includes the potato, tobacco, and several nightshades. [C19: < NL *Sōlānāceae,* < L *sōlānum* nightshade]

solanum (səʊˈleɪnəm) *n.* any tree, shrub, or herbaceous plant of the mainly tropical solanaceous genus *Solanum:* includes the potato and certain nightshades. [C16: < L: nightshade]

solar (ˈsəʊlə) *adj.* **1.** of or relating to the sun. **2.** operating by or utilizing the energy of the sun: *solar cell.* **3.** *Astron.* determined from the motion of the earth relative to the sun: *solar year.* **4.** *Astrol.* subject to the influence of the sun. [C15: < L *sōlāris,* < *sōl* the sun]

solar cell *n.* a cell that produces electricity from the sun's rays, used esp. in spacecraft.

solar constant *n.* the rate at which the sun's energy is received per unit area on the earth's surface when the sun is at its mean distance from the earth and atmospheric absorption has been corrected for.

solar day *n.* See under **day** (sense 6).

solar flare *n.* a brief powerful eruption of intense high-energy radiation from the sun's surface, associated with sunspots and causing radio and magnetic disturbances on earth.

solarium (səʊˈlɛərɪəm) *n., pl.* **-laria** (-ˈlɛərɪə) *or* **-lariums.** **1.** a room built largely of glass to afford exposure to the sun. **2.** a bed equipped with ultraviolet lights used for acquiring an artificial suntan. **3.** an establishment offering such facilities. [C19: < L: a terrace, < *sōl* sun]

solar month *n.* See under **month** (sense 4).

solar plexus *n.* **1.** *Anat.* the network of nerves situated behind the stomach that supply the abdominal organs. **2.** (not in technical usage) the part of the stomach beneath the diaphragm; pit of the stomach. [C18: referring to resemblance between the radial network of nerves & ganglia & the rays of the sun]

solar system *n.* the system containing the sun and the bodies held in its gravitational field, including the planets (Mercury, Venus, earth, Mars, Jupiter, Saturn, Uranus, Neptune, Pluto), the asteroids, and comets.

solar wind (wɪnd) *n.* the stream of charged particles, such as protons, emitted by the sun at high velocities, its intensity increasing during periods of solar activity.

solar year *n.* See under **year** (sense 4).

solatium (səʊˈleɪʃɪəm) *n., pl.* **-tia** (-ʃɪə). compensation awarded for injury to the feelings as distinct from physical suffering and pecuniary loss. [C19: < L: see SOLACE]

sold (səʊld) *vb.* **1.** the past tense and past participle of **sell.** ~*adj.* **2.** **sold on.** *Sl.* uncritically attached to or enthusiastic about.

solder (ˈsɒldə; *U.S.* ˈsɒdər) *n.* **1.** an alloy for joining two metal surfaces by melting the alloy so that it forms a thin layer between the surfaces. **2.** something that joins things together firmly; a bond. ~*vb.* **3.** to join or mend or be joined or mended with or as if with solder. [C14: via OF < L *solidāre* to strengthen, < *solidus* solid] —ˈ**solderable** *adj.* —ˈ**solderer** *n.*

soldering iron *n.* a hand tool consisting of a handle fixed to an iron or copper tip that is heated and used to melt and apply solder.

soldier (ˈsəʊldʒə) *n.* **1. a.** a person who serves or has served in an army. **b.** Also called: **common soldier.** a noncommissioned member of an army as opposed to a commissioned officer. **2.** a person who works diligently for a cause. **3.** *Zool.* an individual in a colony of social insects, esp. ants, that has powerful jaws adapted for defending the colony, crushing food, etc. ~*vb.* **5.** (*intr.*) to serve as a soldier. [C13: < OF *soudier,* < *soude* (army) pay, < LL *solidus* a gold coin, < L: firm] —ˈ**soldierly** *adj.*

soldier of fortune *n.* a man who seeks money or adventure as a soldier; mercenary.

soldier on *vb.* (*intr., adv.*) to persist in one's efforts in spite of difficulties, pressure, etc.

soldiery (ˈsəʊldʒərɪ) *n., pl.* **-dieries.** **1.** soldiers collectively. **2.** a group of soldiers. **3.** the profession of being a soldier.

sole[1] (səʊl) *adj.* **1.** (*prenominal*) being the only one; only. **2.** (*prenominal*) of or relating to one individual or group and no other: *sole rights.* **3.** *Law.* having no wife or husband. **4.** an archaic word for **solitary.** [C14: < OF *soule,* < L *sōlus* alone] —ˈ**soleness** *n.*

sole[2] (səʊl) *n.* **1.** the underside of the foot. **2.** the underside of a shoe. **3. a.** the bottom of a furrow. **b.** the bottom of a plough. **4.** the underside of a golf-club head. ~*vb.* (*tr.*) **5.** to provide (a shoe) with a sole. [C14: via OF < L *solea* sandal]

sole[3] (səʊl) *n., pl.* **sole** *or* **soles.** any of various tongue-shaped flatfishes, esp. the **European sole:** most common in warm seas and highly valued as food fishes. [C14: via OF < Vulgar L *sola* (unattested), < L *solea* a sandal (< the fish's shape)]

solecism (ˈsɒlɪˌsɪzəm) *n.* **1. a.** the nonstandard use of a grammatical construction. **b.** any mistake, incongruity, or absurdity. **2.** a violation of good manners. [C16: < L *soloecismus,* < Gk, < *soloikos* speaking incorrectly, < *Soloi* an Athenian colony of Cilicia where the inhabitants spoke a corrupt form of Greek] —ˈ**solecist** *n.* —ˌ**soleˈcistic** *adj.* —ˌ**soleˈcistically** *adv.*

solely (ˈsəʊllɪ) *adv.* **1.** only; completely. **2.** without others; singly. **3.** for one thing only.

solemn (ˈsɒləm) *adj.* **1.** characterized or marked by seriousness or sincerity: *a solemn vow.* **2.** characterized by pomp, ceremony, or formality. **3.** serious, glum, or pompous. **4.** inspiring awe: *a solemn occasion.* **5.** performed with religious ceremony. **6.** gloomy or sombre: *solemn colours.* [C14: < OF *solempne,* < L *sōllemnis* appointed, ? < *sollus* whole] —ˈ**solemnly** *adv.* —ˈ**solemnness** *or* ˈ**solemness** *n.*

solemnify (səˈlɛmnɪˌfaɪ) *vb.* **-fying, -fied.** (*tr.*) to make serious or grave. —**soˌlemnifiˈcation** *n.*

solemnity (səˈlɛmnɪtɪ) *n., pl.* **-ties.** **1.** the state or quality of being solemn. **2.** (*often pl.*) solemn ceremony, observance, etc. **3.** *Law.* a formality necessary to validate a deed, contract, etc.

solemnize *or* **-ise** (ˈsɒləmˌnaɪz) *vb.* (*tr.*) **1.** to celebrate or observe with rites or formal ceremonies, as a religious occasion. **2.** to celebrate or perform the ceremony of (marriage). **3.** to make solemn or serious. **4.** to perform or hold (ceremonies, etc.) in due manner. —ˌ**solemniˈzation** *or* **-iˈsation** *n.* —ˈ**solemˌnizer** *or* **-iser** *n.*

solenodon (səˈlɛnədən) *n.* either of two rare shrewlike nocturnal mammals of the West Indies having a long hairless tail and an elongated snout. [C19: < NL, < L *sōlēn* sea mussel (< Gk: pipe) + Gk *odōn* tooth]

solenoid (ˈsəʊlɪˌnɔɪd) *n.* **1.** a coil of wire, usually cylindrical, in which a magnetic field is set up by passing a current through it. **2.** a coil of wire, partially surrounding an iron core, that is made to move inside the coil by the magnetic field set up by a current: used to convert electrical to mechanical energy, as in the operation of a switch. [C19: < F *solénoïde,* < Gk *sōlēn* a tube] —ˌ**soleˈnoidal** *adj.*

sol-fa (ˈsɒlˈfɑː) *n.* **1.** short for **tonic sol-fa.** ~*vb.* **-faing, -faed.** **2.** *U.S.* to use tonic sol-fa syllables in singing (a tune). [C16: see GAMUT]

solfatara (ˌsɒlfəˈtɑːrə) *n.* a volcanic vent emitting only sulphurous gases and water vapour or sometimes hot mud. [C18: < It.: a sulphurous volcano near Naples, < *solfo* sulphur]

solfeggio (sɒlˈfɛdʒɪəʊ) *or* **solfège** (sɒlˈfɛʒ) *n., pl.* **-feggi** (-ˈfɛdʒiː), **-feggios,** *or* **-fèges.** *Music.* **1.** a voice exercise in which runs, scales, etc., are sung to the same syllable or syllables. **2.** solmization, esp. the French or Italian system, in which the names correspond to the notes of the scale of C major. [C18: < It. *solfeggiare* to use the syllables sol-fa; see GAMUT]

soli (ˈsəʊlɪ) *adj., adv. Music.* (of a piece or passage) (to be performed) by or with soloists.

solicit (səˈlɪsɪt) *vb.* **1.** (when *intr.,* foll. by *for*) to make a request, application, etc., to (a person for business, support, etc.). **2.** to accost (a person) with an offer of sexual relations in return for money. **3.** to provoke or incite (a person) to do something wrong or illegal. [C15: < OF *solliciter* to disturb, < L *sollicitāre* to harass, < *sollus* whole + *ciēre* to excite] —**soˌliciˈtation** *n.*

solicitor (səˈlɪsɪtə) *n.* **1.** (in Britain) a lawyer who advises clients on matters of law, draws up legal documents, prepares cases for barristers, etc. **2.** (in the U.S.) an officer responsible for the legal affairs of a town, city, etc. **3.** a person who solicits. —**soˈlicitorˌship** *n.*

Solicitor General *n., pl.* **Solicitors General.** **1.** (in Britain) the law officer of the Crown ranking next to the Attorney General (in Scotland to the Lord Advocate) and acting as his assistant. **2.** (in New Zealand) the government's chief lawyer.

solicitous (səˈlɪsɪtəs) *adj.* **1.** showing consideration, concern, attention, etc. **2.** keenly anxious or willing; eager. [C16: < L *sollicitus* anxious; see SOLICIT] —**soˈlicitousness** *n.*

solicitude (səˈlɪsɪˌtjuːd) *n.* **1.** the state or quality of being solicitous. **2.** (*often pl.*) something that causes anxiety or concern. **3.** anxiety or concern.

solid (ˈsɒlɪd) *adj.* **1.** of, concerned with, or being a substance in a physical state in which it resists changes in size and shape. **2.** consisting of matter all through. **3.** of the same substance all through: *solid rock.* **4.** sound; proved or provable: *solid facts.* **5.** reliable or sensible; upstanding: *a solid citizen.* **6.** firm, strong, compact, or substantial: *a solid table; solid ground.* **7.** (of a meal or food) substantial. **8.** (*often postpositive*) without interruption or respite: *solid bombardment.* **9.** financially sound or solvent: *a solid institution.* **10.** strongly linked or consolidated: *a solid relationship.* **11. solid for.** unanimously in favour of. **12.** *Geom.* having or relating to three dimensions. **13.** (of a word composed of two or more elements) written or printed as a single word without a hyphen. **14.** *Printing.* with no space or leads between lines of type. **15.** (of a writer, work, etc.) adequate; sensible. **16.** of or having a single uniform colour or tone. **17.** *Austral. & N.Z. inf.* excessively severe or unreasonable. ~*n.* **18.** *Geom.* **a.** a closed surface in three-dimensional space. **b.** such a surface together with the volume enclosed by it. **19.** a solid substance, such as wood, iron, or diamond. [C14: < OF *solide,* < L *solidus* firm] —**solidity** (səˈlɪdɪtɪ) *n.* —**ˈsolidly** *adv.* —**ˈsolidness** *n.*

solidago (ˌsɒlɪˈdeɪgəʊ) *n., pl.* **-gos.** any plant of a chiefly American genus, which includes the goldenrods. [C18: via NL < Med. L *soldago* a plant reputed to have healing properties, < *soldāre* to strengthen, < L *solidāre,* < *solidus* solid]

solid angle *n.* an area subtended in three dimensions by lines intersecting at a point on a sphere whose radius is the distance to the point. See also **steradian.**

solidarity (ˌsɒlɪˈdærɪtɪ) *n., pl.* **-ties.** unity of interests, sympathies, etc., as among members of the same class.

solid fuel *n.* **1.** a fuel, such as coal or coke, that is a solid rather than an oil or gas. **2.** Also called: **solid propellant.** a rocket fuel that is a solid rather than a liquid or a gas.

solid geometry *n.* the branch of geometry concerned with three-dimensional geometric figures.

solidify (səˈlɪdɪˌfaɪ) *vb.* **-fying, -fied. 1.** to make or become solid or hard. **2.** to make or become strong, united, determined, etc. —**soˌlidifiˈcation** *n.* —**soˈlidiˌfier** *n.*

solid-state *n.* (*modifier*) **1.** (of an electronic device) activated by a semiconductor component in which current flow is through solid material rather than in a vacuum. **2.** of, concerned with, characteristic of, or consisting of solid matter.

solid-state physics *n.* (*functioning as sing.*) the branch of physics concerned with the properties of solids, such as superconductivity, photoconductivity, and ferromagnetism.

solidus (ˈsɒlɪdəs) *n., pl.* **-di** (-ˌdaɪ). **1.** Also called: **diagonal, separatrix, shilling mark, slash, stroke, virgule.** a short oblique stroke used in text to separate items of information, such as days, months, and years in dates (*18/7/80*), alternative words (*and/or*), numerator from denominator in fractions (*55/103*), etc. **2.** a gold coin of the Byzantine empire. [C14: < LL *solidus* (*nummus*) a gold coin (< *solidus* solid); in Med. L, *solidus* referred to a shilling and was indicated by a long *s,* which ult. became the virgule]

solifluction *or* **solifluxion** (ˈsɒlɪˌflʌkʃən, ˈsəʊlɪ-) *n.* slow downhill movement of soil, saturated with meltwater, over a permanently frozen subsoil in tundra regions. [C20: < L *solum* soil + *fluctio* act of flowing]

soliloquize *or* **-ise** (səˈlɪləˌkwaɪz) *vb.* to utter (something) in soliloquy. —**soˈliloquist** *n.* —**soˈliloˌquizer** *or* **-iser** *n.*

soliloquy (səˈlɪləkwɪ) *n., pl.* **-quies. 1.** the act of speaking alone or to oneself, esp. as a theatrical device. **2.** a speech in a play that is spoken in soliloquy. [C17: via LL *sōliloquium,* < L *sōlus* sole + *loquī* to speak]

solipsism (ˈsɒlɪpˌsɪzəm) *n. Philosophy.* the extreme form of scepticism which denies the possibility of any knowledge other than of one's own existence. [C19: < L *sōlus* alone + *ipse* self] —**ˈsolipsist** *n., adj.* —**ˌsolipˈsistic** *adj.*

solitaire (ˈsɒlɪˌtɛə, ˌsɒlɪˈtɛə) *n.* **1.** Also called: **pegboard.** a game played by one person, esp. one involving moving and taking pegs in a pegboard with the object of being left with only one. **2.** the U.S. name for **patience** (the card game). **3.** a gem, esp. a diamond, set alone in a ring. **4.** any of several extinct birds related to the dodo. **5.** any of several dull grey North American songbirds. [C18: < OF: SOLITARY]

solitary (ˈsɒlɪtərɪ, -trɪ) *adj.* **1.** following or enjoying a life of solitude: *a solitary disposition.* **2.** experienced or performed alone: *a solitary walk.* **3.** (of a place) unfrequented. **4.** (*prenominal*) single; sole: *a solitary cloud.* **5.** having few companions; lonely. **6.** (of animals) not living in organized colonies or large groups: *solitary bees.* **7.** (of flowers) growing singly. ~*n., pl.* **-taries. 8.** a person who lives in seclusion; hermit. **9.** *Inf.* short for **solitary confinement.** [C14: < L *sōlitārius,* < *sōlus* SOLE[1]] —**ˈsolitarily** *adv.* —**ˈsolitariness** *n.*

solitary confinement *n.* isolation imposed on a prisoner, as by confinement in a special cell.

solitude (ˈsɒlɪˌtjuːd) *n.* **1.** the state of being solitary or secluded. **2.** *Poetic.* a solitary place. [C14: < L *sōlitūdō,* < *sōlus* alone, SOLE[1]] —**ˌsoliˈtudinous** *adj.*

solmization *or* **-isation** (ˌsɒlmɪˈzeɪʃən) *n. Music.* a system of naming the notes of a scale by syllables instead of letters, which assigns the names *ut* (or *do*), *re, mi, fa, sol, la, si* (or *ti*) to the degrees of the major scale of C (**fixed system**) or (excluding the syllables *ut* and *si*) to the major scale in any key (**movable system**). See also **tonic sol-fa.** [C18: < F *solmisation,* < *solmiser* to use the sol-fa syllables, < SOL[1] + MI]

solo (ˈsəʊləʊ) *n., pl.* **-los. 1.** (*pl.* **-los** *or* **-li** (-liː)). a musical composition for one performer with or without accompaniment. **2.** any of various card games in which each person plays on his own, such as solo whist. **3.** a flight in which an aircraft pilot is unaccompanied. **4. a.** any performance carried out by an individual without assistance. **b.** (*as modifier*)*: a solo attempt.* ~*adj.* **5.** *Music.* unaccompanied: *a sonata for cello solo.* ~*adv.* **6.** by oneself; alone: *to fly solo.* ~*vb.* **7.** (*intr.*) to operate an aircraft alone. [C17: via It. < L *sōlus* alone] —**soloist** (ˈsəʊləʊɪst) *n.*

Solomon (ˈsɒləmən) *n.* any person credited with great wisdom. [after 10th-cent. B.C. king of Israel] —**Solomonic** (ˌsɒləˈmɒnɪk) *adj.*

Solomon's seal *n.* **1.** another name for **Star of David. 2.** any of several plants of N temperate regions, having greenish or yellow paired flowers, long narrow waxy leaves, and prominent leaf scars. [C16: translation of Med. L *sigillum Solomonis,* ? < resemblance of the leaf scars to seals]

Solon (ˈsəʊlən) *n.* a wise lawmaker. [after Athenian statesman (?638–?559 B.C.), who introduced economic, political, and legal reforms]

so long *sentence substitute.* **1.** *Inf.* farewell; goodbye. ~*adv.* **2.** *S. African sl.* for the time being; meanwhile.

solo whist *n.* a version of whist for four players acting independently, each of whom may bid to win or lose a fixed number of tricks.

solstice (ˈsɒlstɪs) *n.* **1.** either the shortest day of the year (**winter solstice**) or the longest day of the year (**summer solstice**). **2.** either of the two points on the ecliptic at which the sun is overhead at the tropic of Cancer or Capricorn at the summer and winter solstices. [C13: via OF < L *sōlstitium,* lit.: the (apparent) standing still of the sun, < *sōl* sun + *sistere* to stand still] —**solstitial** (sɒlˈstɪʃəl) *adj.*

soluble (ˈsɒljʊbᵊl) *adj.* **1.** (of a substance) capable of being dissolved, esp. easily dissolved. **2.** capable of being solved or answered. [C14: < LL *solūbilis,* < L *solvere* to dissolve] —**ˌsoluˈbility** *n.* —**ˈsolubly** *adv.*

solus *Latin.* ('səʊlʊs) *or* (*fem.*) **sola** *adj.* alone; by oneself (formerly used in stage directions).

solute (sɒ'ljuːt) *n.* **1.** the substance in a solution that is dissolved. *~adj.* **2.** *Bot.* loose or unattached; free. [C16: < L *solūtus* free, < *solvere* to release]

solution (sə'luːʃən) *n.* **1.** a homogeneous mixture of two or more substances in which the molecules or atoms of the substances are completely dispersed. **2.** the act or process of forming a solution. **3.** the state of being dissolved (esp. in **in solution**). **4.** a mixture of substances in which one or more components are present as small particles with colloidal dimension: *a colloidal solution.* **5.** a specific answer to or way of answering a problem. **6.** the act or process of solving a problem. **7.** *Maths.* **a.** the unique set of values that yield a true statement when substituted for the variables in an equation. **b.** a member of a set of assignments of values to variables under which a given statement is satisfied; a member of a solution set. [C14: < L *solūtiō* an unloosing, < *solūtus*; see SOLUTE]

solution set *n.* another name for **truth set.**

Solutrean (sə'luːtrɪən) *adj.* of or relating to an Upper Palaeolithic culture of Europe. [C19: after *Solutré*, village in central France where traces of this culture were orig. found]

solvation (sɒl'veɪʃən) *n.* the process in which there is some chemical association between the molecules of a solute and those of the solvent.

Solvay process ('sɒlveɪ) *n.* an industrial process for manufacturing sodium carbonate. Carbon dioxide is passed into a solution of sodium chloride saturated with ammonia. Sodium bicarbonate is precipitated and heated to form the carbonate. [C19: after Ernest *Solvay* (1838–1922), Belgian chemist who invented it]

solve (sɒlv) *vb.* (*tr.*) **1.** to find the explanation for or solution to (a mystery, problem, etc.). **2.** *Maths.* **a.** to work out the answer to (a problem). **b.** to obtain the roots of (an equation). [C15: < L *solvere* to loosen] —'**solvable** *adj.*

solvent ('sɒlvənt) *adj.* **1.** capable of meeting financial obligations. **2.** (of a substance, esp. a liquid) capable of dissolving another substance. *~n.* **3.** a liquid capable of dissolving another substance. **4.** something that solves. [C17: < L *solvēns* releasing, < *solvere* to free] —'**solvency** *n.*

solvent abuse *n.* the deliberate inhaling of intoxicating fumes given off by certain solvents.

Som. *abbrev. for* Somerset.

soma[1] ('səʊmə) *n., pl.* **-mata** (-mətə) *or* **-mas.** the body of an organism, as distinct from the germ cells. [C19: via NL < Gk *sōma* the body]

soma[2] ('səʊmə) *n.* an intoxicating plant juice drink used in Vedic rituals. [< Sansk.]

Somali (səʊ'mɑːlɪ) *n.* **1.** (*pl.* **-lis** *or* **-li**) a member of a tall dark-skinned people inhabiting Somalia in NE Africa. **2.** the Cushitic language of this people. *~adj.* **3.** of, relating to, or characteristic of Somalia, the Somalis, or their language.

somatic (səʊ'mætɪk) *adj.* **1.** of or relating to the soma: *somatic cells.* **2.** of or relating to an animal body or body wall as distinct from the viscera, limbs, and head. **3.** of or relating to the human body as distinct from the mind: *a somatic disease.* [C18: < Gk *sōmatikos* concerning the body, < *sōma* the body] —**so'matically** *adv.*

somato- *or before a vowel* **somat-** *combining form.* body: *somatotype.* [< Gk *sōma, sōmat-* body]

somatotype ('səʊmətəˌtaɪp) *n.* a type or classification of physique or body build. See **endomorph, mesomorph, ectomorph.**

sombre *or U.S.* **somber** ('sɒmbə) *adj.* **1.** dismal; melancholy: *a sombre mood.* **2.** dim, gloomy, or shadowy. **3.** (of colour, clothes, etc.) sober, dull, or dark. [C18: < F, < Vulgar L *subumbrāre* (unattested) to shade, < L *sub* beneath + *umbra* shade] —'**sombrely** *or U.S.* '**somberly** *adv.* —'**sombreness** *or U.S.* '**somberness** *n.* —**sombrous** ('sɒmbrəs) *adj.*

sombrero (sɒm'brɛərəʊ) *n., pl.* **-ros.** a hat with a wide brim, as worn in Mexico. [C16: < Sp., < *sombrero de sol* shade from the sun]

some (sʌm; *unstressed* səm) *determiner.* **1. a.** (a) certain unknown or unspecified: *some people never learn.* **b.** (*as pron.; functioning as sing. or pl.*): *some can teach and others can't.* **2. a.** an unknown or unspecified quantity or amount of: *there's some rice on the table; he owns some horses.* **b.** (*as pron.; functioning as sing. or pl.*): *we'll buy some.* **3. a.** a considerable number or amount of: *he lived some years afterwards.* **b.** a little: *show him some respect.* **4.** (*usually stressed*) *Inf.* an impressive or remarkable: *that was some game!* *~adv.* **5.** about; approximately: *some thirty pounds.* **6.** a certain amount (more) (in **some more** and (*inf.*) **and then some**). **7.** *U.S., not standard.* to a certain degree or extent: *I like him some.* [OE *sum*]

-some[1] *suffix forming adjectives.* characterized by; tending to: *awesome; tiresome.* [OE *-sum*]

-some[2] *suffix forming nouns.* indicating a group of a specified number of members: *threesome.* [OE *sum*, special use of SOME (determiner)]

-some[3] (-səʊm) *n. combining form.* a body: *chromosome.* [< Gk *sōma* body]

somebody ('sʌmbədɪ) *pron.* **1.** some person; someone. *~n., pl.* **-bodies. 2.** a person of great importance: *he is somebody in this town.*

▷ **Usage.** See at **everyone.**

someday ('sʌmˌdeɪ) *adv.* at some unspecified time in the (distant) future.

somehow ('sʌmˌhaʊ) *adv.* **1.** in some unspecified way. **2.** Also: **somehow or other.** by any means that are necessary.

someone ('sʌmˌwʌn, -wən) *pron.* some person; somebody.

▷ **Usage.** See at **everyone.**

someplace ('sʌmˌpleɪs) *adv. U.S. & Canad inf.* in, at, or to some unspecified place or region.

somersault *or* **summersault** ('sʌməˌsɔːlt) *n.* **1. a.** a forward roll in which the head is placed on the ground and the trunk and legs are turned over it. **b.** a similar roll in a backward direction. **2.** an acrobatic feat in which either of these rolls is performed in midair, as in diving or gymnastics. **3.** a complete reversal of opinion, policy, etc. *~vb.* **4.** (*intr.*) to perform a somersault. [C16: < OF *soubresault*, prob. < OProvençal *sobresaut*, < *sobre* over (< L *super*) + *saut* a jump, leap (< L *saltus*)]

something ('sʌmθɪŋ) *pron.* **1.** an unspecified or unknown thing; some thing: *take something warm with you.* **2. something or other.** one unspecified thing or an alternative thing. **3.** an unspecified or unknown amount: *something less than a hundred.* **4.** an impressive or important person, thing, or event: *isn't that something?* *~adv.* **5.** to some degree; a little; somewhat: *to look something like me.* **6.** (foll. by an *adj.*) *Inf.* (intensifier): *it hurts something awful.* **7. something else.** *Sl., chiefly U.S.* a remarkable person or thing.

sometime ('sʌmˌtaɪm) *adv.* **1.** at some unspecified point of time. *~adj.* **2.** (*prenominal*) having been at one time; former: *the sometime President.*

sometimes ('sʌmˌtaɪmz) *adv.* **1.** now and then; from time to time. **2.** *Obs.* formerly; sometime.

someway ('sʌmˌweɪ) *adv.* in some unspecified manner.

somewhat ('sʌmˌwɒt) *adv.* (*not used with a negative*) rather; a bit: *she found it somewhat odd.*

somewhere ('sʌmˌwɛə) *adv.* **1.** in, to, or at some unknown or unspecified place or point: *somewhere in England; somewhere between 3 and 4 o'clock.* **2. get somewhere.** *Inf.* to make progress.

sommelier ('sʌməlˌjeɪ) *n.* a wine waiter. [F: butler, via OF < OProvençal *saumalier* pack-animal driver, < LL *sagma* a packsaddle, < Gk]

somnambulate (sɒm'næmbjʊˌleɪt) *vb.* (*intr.*) to walk while asleep. [C19: < L *somnus* sleep + *ambulāre* to walk] —**som'nambulance** *n.* —**som'nambulant** *adj., n.* —**somˌnambu'lation** *n.* —**som'nambuˌlator** *n.*

somnambulism (sɒm'næmbjʊˌlɪzəm) *n.* a condition characterized by walking while asleep or in a hypnotic trance. Also called: **noctambulism.** —**somˈnambulist** *n.*

somniferous (sɒmˈnɪfərəs) *or* **somnific** *adj. Rare.* tending to induce sleep.

somnolent (ˈsɒmnələnt) *adj.* **1.** drowsy; sleepy. **2.** causing drowsiness. [C15: < L *somnus* sleep] —ˈ**somnolence** *or* ˈ**somnolency** *n.* —ˈ**somnolently** *adv.*

son (sʌn) *n.* **1.** a male offspring; a boy or man in relation to his parents. **2.** a male descendant. **3.** (*often cap.*) a familiar term of address for a boy or man. **4.** a male from a certain country, environment, etc.: *a son of the circus.* ~Related adj.: **filial.** [OE *sunu*] —ˈ**sonless** *adj.*

Son (sʌn) *n. Christianity.* the second person of the Trinity, Jesus Christ.

sonant (ˈsəʊnənt) *adj.* **1.** *Phonetics.* denoting a voiced sound capable of forming a syllable or syllable nucleus. **2.** inherently possessing, exhibiting, or producing a sound. **3.** *Rare.* resonant; sounding. ~*n.* **4.** *Phonetics.* a voiced sound belonging to the class of frictionless continuants or nasals (l, r, m, n, ŋ) considered from the point of view of being a vowel and, in this capacity, able to form a syllable or syllable nucleus. [C19: < L *sonāns* sounding, < *sonāre* to make a noise, resound] —ˈ**sonance** *n.*

sonar (ˈsəʊnɑː) *n.* a communication and position-finding device used in underwater navigation and target detection using echolocation. [C20: < *so*(*und*) *na*(*vigation and*) *r*(*anging*)]

sonata (səˈnɑːtə) *n.* **1.** an instrumental composition, usually in three or more movements, for piano alone (**piano sonata**) or for any other instrument with or without piano accompaniment (**violin sonata, cello sonata,** etc.). See also **sonata form. 2.** a one-movement keyboard composition of the baroque period. [C17: < It., < *sonare* to sound, < L]

sonata form *n.* a musical structure consisting of an expanded ternary form whose three sections (exposition, development, and recapitulation), followed by a coda, are characteristic of the first movement in a sonata, symphony, string quartet, concerto, etc.

sondage (sɒnˈdɑːʒ) *n., pl.* **-dages** (-ˈdɑːʒɪz, -ˈdɑːʒ). *Archaeol.* a deep trial trench for inspecting stratigraphy. [C20: < F: a sounding, < *sonder* to sound]

sonde (sɒnd) *n.* a rocket, balloon, or probe used for observing in the upper atmosphere. [C20: < F: plummet, plumb line; see SOUND[3]]

sone (səʊn) *n.* a unit of loudness equal to 40 phons. [C20: < L *sonus* a sound]

son et lumière (ˈsɒn eɪ ˈluːmɪˌɛə) *n.* an entertainment staged at night at a famous building, historical site, etc., whereby the history of the location is presented by means of lighting effects, sound effects, and narration. [F, lit.: sound and light]

song (sɒŋ) *n.* **1. a.** a piece of music, usually employing a verbal text, composed for the voice, esp. one intended for performance by a soloist. **b.** the whole repertory of such pieces. **c.** (*as modifier*): *a song book.* **2.** poetical composition; poetry. **3.** the characteristic tuneful call or sound made by certain birds or insects. **4.** the act or process of singing: *they raised their voices in song.* **5. for a song.** at a bargain price. **6. on song.** *Brit. inf.* performing at peak efficiency or ability. [OE *sang*]

song and dance *n. Inf.* **1.** *Brit.* a fuss, esp. one that is unnecessary. **2.** *U.S. & Canad.* a long or elaborate story or explanation.

songbird (ˈsɒŋˌbɜːd) *n.* **1.** any of a suborder of passerine birds having highly developed vocal organs and, in most, a musical call. **2.** any bird having a musical call.

song cycle *n.* any of several groups of songs written during and after the Romantic period, each series relating a story or grouped around a central motif.

songololo (ˌsɒŋgɒˈlɒlɒ) *n., pl.* **-los.** *S. African.* a millipede. [< Bantu, < *ukusonga* to roll up]

songster (ˈsɒŋstə) *n.* **1.** a singer or poet. **2.** a singing bird; songbird. —ˈ**songstress** *fem. n.*

song thrush *n.* a common Old World thrush with a spotted breast, noted for its song.

songwriter (ˈsɒŋˌraɪtə) *n.* a person who composes songs in a popular idiom.

sonic (ˈsɒnɪk) *adj.* **1.** of, involving, or producing sound. **2.** having a speed about equal to that of sound in air. [C20: < L *sonus* sound]

sonic barrier *n.* another name for **sound barrier.**

sonic boom *n.* a loud explosive sound caused by the shock wave of an aircraft, etc., travelling at supersonic speed.

sonic depth finder *n.* an instrument for detecting the depth of water or of a submerged object by means of sound waves; Fathometer.

son-in-law *n., pl.* **sons-in-law.** the husband of one's daughter.

sonnet (ˈsɒnɪt) *Prosody.* ~*n.* **1.** a verse form consisting of 14 lines in iambic pentameter with a fixed rhyme scheme, usually divided into octave and sestet or, in the English form, into three quatrains and a couplet. ~*vb.* **2.** (*intr.*) to compose sonnets. **3.** (*tr.*) to celebrate in a sonnet. [C16: via It. < OProvençal *sonet* a little poem, < *son* song, < L *sonus* a sound]

sonneteer (ˌsɒnɪˈtɪə) *n.* a writer of sonnets.

sonny (ˈsʌnɪ) *n., pl.* **-nies.** *Often patronizing.* a familiar term of address to a boy or man.

sonobuoy (ˈsəʊnəˌbɔɪ) *n.* a buoy equipped to detect underwater noises and transmit them by radio. [SONIC + BUOY]

sonorant (ˈsɒnərənt) *n. Phonetics.* **1.** one of the frictionless continuants or nasals (l, r, m, n, ŋ) having consonantal or vocalic functions depending on its situation within the syllable. **2.** either of the two consonants represented in English orthography by *w* or *y* and regarded as either consonantal or vocalic articulations of the vowels (iː) and (uː).

sonorous (səˈnɔːrəs, ˈsɒnərəs) *adj.* **1.** producing or capable of producing sound. **2.** (of language, sound, etc.) deep or resonant. **3.** (esp. of speech) high-flown; grandiloquent. [C17: < L *sonōrus* loud, < *sonor* a noise] —**sonority** (səˈnɒrɪtɪ) *n.* —**soˈnorously** *adv.* —**soˈnorousness** *n.*

sonsy *or* **sonsie** (ˈsɒnsɪ) *adj.* **-sier, -siest.** *Scot., Irish, & English dialect.* **1.** plump; buxom. **2.** cheerful; good-natured. **3.** lucky. [C16: < Gaelic *sonas* good fortune]

sook (sʊk) *n.* **1.** *SW English dialect.* a baby. **2.** *Derog.* a coward. [? < OE *sūcan* to suck, infl. by Welsh *swci swead* tame]

sool (suːl) *vb.* (*tr.*) *Austral. & N.Z. sl.* **1.** to incite (esp. a dog) to attack. **2.** to attack. —ˈ**sooler** *n.*

soon (suːn) *adv.* **1.** in or after a short time; in a little while; before long. **2. as soon as.** at the very moment that: *as soon as she saw him.* **3. as soon . . . as.** used to indicate that the second alternative is not preferable to the first: *I'd just as soon go by train as drive.* [OE *sōna*]

sooner (ˈsuːnə) *adv.* **1.** the comparative of **soon:** *he came sooner than I thought.* **2.** rather; in preference: *I'd sooner die than give up.* **3. no sooner . . . than.** immediately after or when: *no sooner had he got home than the rain stopped.* **4. sooner or later.** eventually; inevitably.

soot (sʊt) *n.* **1.** finely divided carbon deposited from flames during the incomplete combustion of organic substances such as coal. ~*vb.* **2.** (*tr.*) to cover with soot. [OE *sōt*]

sooth (suːθ) *Arch. or poetic.* ~*n.* **1.** truth or reality (esp. in **in sooth**). ~*adj.* **2.** true or real. [OE *sōth*]

soothe (suːð) *vb.* **1.** (*tr.*) to make calm or tranquil. **2.** (*tr.*) to relieve or assuage (pain, longing, etc.). **3.** (*intr.*) to bring tranquillity or relief. [C16 (in the sense: to mollify): < OE *sōthian* to prove] —ˈ**soother** *n.* —ˈ**soothing** *adj.* —ˈ**soothingly** *adv.* —ˈ**soothingness** *n.*

soothsayer (ˈsuːθˌseɪə) *n.* a seer or prophet.

sooty (ˈsʊtɪ) *adj.* **sootier, sootiest. 1.** covered with soot. **2.** resembling or consisting of soot. —ˈ**sootily** *adv.* —ˈ**sootiness** *n.*

sop (sɒp) *n.* **1.** (*often pl.*) food soaked in a liquid before being eaten. **2.** a concession, bribe, etc., given to placate or mollify: *a sop to one's feelings.* **3.** *Inf.* a stupid or weak person. ~*vb.* **sopping, sopped. 4.** (*tr.*) to dip or soak (food) in liquid. **5.** (when *intr.*, often foll. by *in*) to soak or be soaked. **6.** (*tr.*; often foll. by *up*) to mop or absorb (liquid) as with a sponge. [OE *sopp*]

SOP *abbrev. for* standard operating procedure.

sop. *abbrev. for* soprano.

sophism (ˈsɒfɪzəm) *n.* an instance of sophistry. Cf. **paralogism.** [C14: < L *sophisma*, < Gk: ingenious trick, < *sophizesthai* to use clever deceit, < *sophos* wise]

sophist (ˈsɒfɪst) *n.* **1.** a person who uses clever or quibbling but unsound arguments. **2.** one of the pre-Socratic philosophers who were prepared to enter into debate on any subject however specious. [C16: < L *sophista*, < Gk *sophistēs* a wise man, < *sophizesthai* to act craftily]

sophistic (səˈfɪstɪk) *or* **sophistical** *adj.* **1.** of or relating to sophists or sophistry. **2.** consisting of sophisms or sophistry; specious. —**soˈphistically** *adv.*

sophisticate *vb.* (səˈfɪstɪˌkeɪt). **1.** (*tr.*) to make (someone) less natural or innocent, as by education. **2.** to pervert or corrupt (an argument, etc.) by sophistry. **3.** (*tr.*) to make more complex or refined. **4.** *Rare.* to falsify (a text, etc.) by alterations. ~*n.* (səˈfɪstɪˌkeɪt, -kɪt). **5.** a sophisticated person. [C14: < Med. L *sophisticāre*, < L *sophisticus* sophistic] —**soˌphistiˈcation** *n.* —**soˈphistiˌcator** *n.*

sophisticated (səˈfɪstɪˌkeɪtɪd) *adj.* **1.** having refined or cultured tastes and habits. **2.** appealing to sophisticates: *a sophisticated restaurant.* **3.** unduly refined or cultured. **4.** pretentiously or superficially wise. **5.** (of machines, methods, etc.) complex and refined.

sophistry (ˈsɒfɪstrɪ) *n., pl.* **-ries. 1. a.** a method of argument that is seemingly plausible though actually invalid and misleading. **b.** the art of using such arguments. **2.** subtle but unsound or fallacious reasoning. **3.** an instance of this.

sophomore (ˈsɒfəˌmɔː) *n. Chiefly U.S. & Canad.* a second-year student. [C17: ? < earlier *sophumer*, < *sophum*, var. of SOPHISM, + -ER[1]]

Sophy *or* **Sophi** (ˈsəʊfɪ) *n., pl.* **-phies.** (formerly) a title of the Persian monarchs. [C16: < L *sophī* wise men, < Gk *sophos* wise]

-sophy *n. combining form.* indicating knowledge or an intellectual system: *philosophy.* [< Gk, < *sophia* wisdom, < *sophos* wise] —**-sophic** *or* **-sophical** *adj. combining form.*

soporific (ˌsɒpəˈrɪfɪk) *adj. also* (*arch.*) ˌ**soporˈiferous. 1.** inducing sleep. **2.** drowsy; sleepy. ~*n.* **3.** a drug or other agent that induces sleep. [C17: < F, < L *sopor* sleep + -FIC]

sopping (ˈsɒpɪŋ) *adj.* completely soaked; wet through. Also: **sopping wet.**

soppy (ˈsɒpɪ) *adj.* **-pier, -piest. 1.** wet or soggy. **2.** *Brit. inf.* silly or sentimental. **3. soppy on.** *Brit. inf.* foolishly charmed or affected by. —ˈ**soppily** *adv.* —ˈ**soppiness** *n.*

sopranino (ˌsɒprəˈniːnəʊ) *n., pl.* **-nos. a.** the instrument with the highest possible pitch in a family of instruments. **b.** (*as modifier*): *a sopranino recorder.* [It., dim. of SOPRANO]

soprano (səˈprɑːnəʊ) *n., pl.* **-pranos** *or* **-prani** (-ˈprɑːniː). **1.** the highest adult female voice. **2.** the voice of a young boy before puberty. **3.** a singer with such a voice. **4.** the highest part of a piece of harmony. **5. a.** the highest or second highest instrument in a family of instruments. **b.** (*as modifier*): *a soprano saxophone.* ~See also **treble.** [C18: < It., < *sopra* above, < L *suprā*]

soprano clef *n.* the clef that establishes middle C as being on the bottom line of the staff.

sorb (sɔːb) *n.* **1.** another name for **service tree. 2.** any of various related trees, esp. the mountain ash. **3.** Also called: **sorb apple.** the fruit of any of these trees. [C16: < L *sorbus*]

sorbefacient (ˌsɔːbɪˈfeɪʃənt) *adj.* **1.** inducing absorption. ~*n.* **2.** a sorbefacient drug. [C19: < L *sorbē(re)* to absorb + -FACIENT]

sorbet (ˈsɔːbɪt, -beɪ) *n.* **1.** a water ice made from fruit juice, egg whites, etc. **2.** a U.S. word for **sherbet** (sense 1). [C16: < F, < OIt. *sorbetto*, < Turkish *şerbet*, < Ar. *sharbah* a drink]

sorbic acid (ˈsɔːbɪk) *n.* a white crystalline carboxylic acid found in berries of the mountain ash and used to inhibit the growth of moulds and as an additive (**E 200**) for certain synthetic coatings. [C19: < SORB (the tree), < its discovery in berries of the mountain ash]

sorbitol (ˈsɔːbɪˌtɒl) *n.* a white crystalline alcohol, found in certain fruits and berries and manufactured by the catalytic hydrogenation of sucrose: used as a sweetener (**E 420**) and in the manufacture of ascorbic acid and synthetic resins. [C19: < SORB + -ITOL]

sorbo rubber (ˈsɔːbəʊ) *n. Brit.* a spongy form of rubber. [C20: < ABSORB]

sorcerer (ˈsɔːsərə) *or* (*fem.*) **sorceress** (ˈsɔːsərɪs) *n.* a person who seeks to control and use magic powers; a wizard or magician. [C16: < OF *sorcier*, < Vulgar L *sortiārius* (unattested) caster of lots, < L *sors* lot]

sorcery (ˈsɔːsərɪ) *n., pl.* **-ceries.** the art, practices, or spells of magic, esp. black magic. [C13: < OF *sorcerie*, < *sorcier* SORCERER]

sordid (ˈsɔːdɪd) *adj.* **1.** dirty, foul, or squalid. **2.** degraded; vile; base. **3.** selfish and grasping: *sordid avarice.* [C16: < L *sordidus*, < *sordēre* to be dirty] —ˈ**sordidly** *adv.* —ˈ**sordidness** *n.*

sordino (sɔːˈdiːnəʊ) *n., pl.* **-ni** (-niː). **1.** a mute for a stringed or brass musical instrument. **2.** any of the dampers in a piano. **3. con sordino** *or* **sordini.** a musical direction to play with a mute. **4. senza sordino** *or* **sordini.** a musical direction to remove or play without the mute or (on the piano) with the sustaining pedal pressed down. [It.: < *sordo* deaf, < L *surdus*]

sore (sɔː) *adj.* **1.** (esp. of a wound, injury, etc.) painfully sensitive; tender. **2.** causing annoyance: *a sore point.* **3.** resentful; irked. **4.** urgent; pressing: *in sore need.* **5.** (*postpositive*) grieved; distressed. **6.** causing grief or sorrow. ~*n.* **7.** a painful or sensitive wound, injury, etc. **8.** any cause of distress or vexation. ~*adv.* **9.** *Arch.* direly; sorely (now only in such phrases as **sore afraid**). [OE *sār*] —ˈ**soreness** *n.*

sorehead (ˈsɔːˌhɛd) *n. Inf., chiefly U.S. & Canad.* a peevish or disgruntled person.

sorely (ˈsɔːlɪ) *adv.* **1.** painfully or grievously: *sorely wounded.* **2.** pressingly or greatly: *to be sorely taxed.*

sorghum (ˈsɔːgəm) *n.* any grass of the Old World genus *Sorghum*, having glossy seeds: cultivated for grain, hay, and as a source of syrup. [C16: < NL, < It. *sorgo*, prob. < Vulgar L *Syricum grānum* (unattested) Syrian grain]

soroptimist (səˈrɒptɪmɪst) *n.* a member of Soroptimist International, an organization of clubs for professional and executive businesswomen.

sorority (səˈrɒrɪtɪ) *n., pl.* **-ties.** *Chiefly U.S.* a social club or society for university women. [C16: < Med. L *sorōritās*, < L *soror* sister]

sorption (ˈsɔːpʃən) *n.* the process in which one substance takes up or holds another; adsorption or absorption. [C20: back formation < ABSORPTION, ADSORPTION]

sorrel[1] (ˈsɒrəl) *n.* **1. a.** a light brown to brownish-orange colour. **b.** (*as adj.*): *a sorrel carpet.* **2.** a horse of this colour. [C15: < OF *sorel*, < *sor* a reddish brown, of Gmc origin]

sorrel[2] (ˈsɒrəl) *n.* **1.** any of several plants of Eurasia and North America, having acid-tasting leaves used in salads and sauces. **2.** short for **wood sorrel.** [C14: < OF *surele*, < *sur* sour, of Gmc origin]

sorrow (ˈsɒrəʊ) *n.* **1.** the feeling of sadness, grief, or regret associated with loss, bereavement, sympathy for another's suffering, etc. **2.** a particular cause or source of this. **3.** Also called: **sorrowing.** the outward expression of grief or sadness. ~*vb.* **4.** (*intr.*) to mourn or grieve. [OE *sorg*] —ˈ**sorrowful** *adj.* —ˈ**sorrowfully** *adv.* —ˈ**sorrowfulness** *n.*

sorry (ˈsɒrɪ) *adj.* **-rier, -riest. 1.** (*usually*

postpositive; often foll. by *for*) feeling or expressing pity, sympathy, grief, or regret: *I feel sorry for him.* **2.** pitiful, wretched, or deplorable: *a sorry sight.* **3.** poor; paltry: *a sorry excuse.* **4.** affected by sorrow; sad. **5.** causing sorrow or sadness. *~interj.* **6.** an exclamation expressing apology. [OE *sārig*] —'**sorrily** *adv.* —'**sorriness** *n.*

sort (sɔːt) *n.* **1.** a class, group, kind, etc., as distinguished by some common quality or characteristic. **2.** *Inf.* a type of character, nature, etc.: *he's a good sort.* **3.** *Austral. sl.* a person, esp. a girl. **4.** a more or less definable or adequate example: *it's a sort of review.* **5.** (*often pl.*) *Printing.* any of the individual characters making up a fount of type. **6.** *Arch.* manner; way: *in this sort we struggled home.* **7. after a sort.** to some extent. **8. of sorts** *or* **of a sort. a.** of an inferior kind. **b.** of an indefinite kind. **9. out of sorts.** not in normal good health, temper, etc. **10. sort of.** in some way or other; as it were; rather. *~vb.* **11.** (*tr.*) to arrange according to class, type, etc. **12.** (*tr.*) to put (something) into working order. **13.** to arrange (computer information) by machine in an order convenient to the user. **14.** (*intr.*) *Arch.* to agree; accord. [C14: < OF, < Med. L *sors* kind, < L: fate] —'**sortable** *adj.* —'**sorter** *n.*

▷ **Usage.** See at **kind**[2].

sortie ('sɔːtɪ) *n.* **1. a.** (of troops, etc.) the act of attacking from a contained or besieged position. **b.** the troops doing this. **2.** an operational flight made by one aircraft. *~vb.* **-tieing, -tied. 3.** (*intr.*) to make a sortie. [C17: < F: a going out, < *sortir* to go out]

sortilege ('sɔːtɪlɪdʒ) *n.* the act or practice of divination by drawing lots. [C14: via OF < Med. L *sortilegium,* < L *sortilegus* a soothsayer, < *sors* fate + *legere* to select]

sort out *vb.* (*tr., adv.*) **1.** to find a solution to (a problem, etc.), esp. to make clear or tidy: *to sort out the mess.* **2.** to take or separate, as from a larger group: *to sort out the likely ones.* **3.** to organize into an orderly and disciplined group. **4.** *Inf.* to beat or punish.

SOS *n.* **1.** an internationally recognized distress signal in which the letters SOS are repeatedly spelt out, as by radiotelegraphy: used esp. by ships and aircraft. **2.** a message broadcast in an emergency for people otherwise unobtainable. **3.** *Inf.* a call for help.

sosatie (sə'sɑːtɪ) *n. S. African.* curried meat on skewers. [< Afrik., < Du.]

so-so *Inf.* *~adj.* **1.** (*postpositive*) neither good nor bad. *~adv.* **2.** in an average or indifferent manner.

sostenuto (ˌsɒstə'nuːtəʊ) *adj., adv. Music.* to be performed in a smooth sustained manner. [C18: < It., < *sostenere* to sustain, < L *sustinēre*]

sot (sɒt) *n.* **1.** a habitual or chronic drunkard. **2.** a person stupefied by or as if by drink. [OE, < Med. L *sottus*] —'**sottish** *adj.*

soteriology (sɒˌtɪərɪ'ɒlədʒɪ) *n. Christian theol.* the doctrine of salvation. [C19: < Gk *sōtēria* deliverance (< *sōtēr* a saviour) + -LOGY]

sotto voce ('sɒtəʊ 'vəʊtʃɪ) *adv.* in an undertone. [C18: < It.: under (one's) voice]

sou (suː) *n.* **1.** a former French coin of low denomination. **2.** a very small amount of money: *I haven't a sou.* [C19: < F, < OF *sol,* < L: SOLIDUS]

soubrette (suː'brɛt) *n.* **1.** a minor female role in comedy, often that of a pert lady's maid. **2.** any pert or flirtatious girl. [C18: < F: maidservant, < Provençal, < *soubret* conceited, < *soubra* to exceed, < L *superāre* to surmount]

soubriquet ('səʊbrɪˌkeɪ) *n.* a variant spelling of **sobriquet.**

soufflé ('suːfleɪ) *n.* **1.** a light fluffy dish made with beaten egg whites combined with cheese, fish, etc. **2.** a similar sweet or savoury cold dish, set with gelatin. *~adj. also* **souffléed. 3.** made light and puffy, as by beating and cooking. [C19: < F, < *souffler* to blow, < L *sufflāre*]

sough (saʊ) *vb.* **1.** (*intr.*) (esp. of the wind) to make a sighing sound. *~n.* **2.** a soft continuous murmuring sound. [OE *swōgan* to resound]

sought (sɔːt) *vb.* the past tense and past participle of **seek.**

souk (suːk) *n.* an open-air marketplace in Muslim countries, esp. North Africa and the Middle East. [< Ar.]

soul (səʊl) *n.* **1.** the spirit or immaterial part of man, the seat of human personality, intellect, will, and emotions: regarded as an entity that survives the body after death. **2.** *Christianity.* the spiritual part of a person, capable of redemption from sin through divine grace. **3.** the essential part or fundamental nature of anything. **4.** a person's feelings or moral nature. **5. a.** Also called: **soul music.** a type of Black music resulting from the addition of jazz, gospel, and pop elements to the urban blues style. **b.** (*as modifier*): *a soul singer.* **6.** (*modifier*) of or relating to Black Americans and their culture: *soul food.* **7.** nobility of spirit or temperament: *a man of great soul.* **8.** an inspiring or leading figure, as of a movement. **9. the life and soul.** *Inf.* a person regarded as the main source of gaiety, merriment, etc.: *the life and soul of the party.* **10.** a person regarded as typifying some characteristic or quality: *the soul of discretion.* **11.** a person; individual: *an honest soul.* **12. upon my soul!** an exclamation of surprise. [OE *sāwol*]

soul-destroying *adj.* (of an occupation, situation, etc.) unremittingly monotonous.

soul food *n. Inf.* food, such as chitterlings, yams, etc., traditionally eaten by U.S. Blacks.

soulful ('səʊlfʊl) *adj.* expressing profound thoughts or feelings. —'**soulfully** *adv.* —'**soulfulness** *n.*

soulless ('səʊllɪs) *adj.* **1.** lacking humanizing qualities or influences; mechanical: *soulless work.* **2.** (of a person) lacking in sensitivity or nobility. —'**soullessness** *n.*

soul mate *n.* a person for whom one has a deep affinity, esp. a lover, wife, husband, etc.

soul-searching *n.* **1.** deep or critical examination of one's motives, actions, beliefs, etc. *~adj.* **2.** displaying the characteristics of this.

sound[1] (saʊnd) *n.* **1. a.** a periodic disturbance in the pressure or density of a fluid or in the elastic strain of a solid, produced by a vibrating object. It travels as longitudinal waves. **b.** (*as modifier*): *a sound wave.* **2.** the sensation produced by such a periodic disturbance in the organs of hearing. **3.** anything that can be heard. **4.** (*modifier*) of or relating to radio as distinguished from television: *sound broadcasting.* **5.** a particular instance or type of sound: *the sound of running water.* **6.** volume or quality of sound: *a radio with poor sound.* **7.** the area or distance over which something can be heard: *within the sound of Big Ben.* **8.** impression or implication: *I don't like the sound of that.* **9.** (*often pl.*) *Sl.* music, esp. rock, jazz, or pop. *~vb.* **10.** to cause (an instrument, etc.) to make a sound or (of an instrument, etc.) to emit a sound. **11.** to announce or be announced by a sound: *to sound the alarm.* **12.** (*intr.*) (of a sound) to be heard. **13.** (*intr.*) to resonate with a certain quality or intensity: *to sound loud.* **14.** (*copula*) to give the impression of being as specified: *to sound reasonable.* **15.** (*tr.*) to pronounce distinctly or audibly: *to sound one's consonants.* [C13: < OF *soner* to make a sound, < L *sonāre,* < *sonus* a sound] —'**soundable** *adj.*

sound[2] (saʊnd) *adj.* **1.** free from damage, injury, decay, etc. **2.** firm; substantial: *a sound basis.* **3.** financially safe or stable: *a sound investment.* **4.** showing good judgment or reasoning; wise: *sound advice.* **5.** valid, logical, or justifiable: *a sound argument.* **6.** holding approved beliefs; ethically correct; honest. **7.** (of sleep) deep; peaceful; unbroken. **8.** thorough: *a sound examination.* *~adv.* **9.** soundly; deeply: now archaic except when applied to sleep. [OE *sund*] —'**soundly** *adv.* —'**soundness** *n.*

sound[3] (saʊnd) *vb.* **1.** to measure the depth of (a well, the sea, etc.) by plumb line, sonar, etc. **2.** to seek to discover (someone's views, etc.), as by questioning. **3.** (*intr.*) (of a whale, etc.) to dive downwards swiftly and deeply. **4.** *Med.* **a.** to probe or explore (a bodily cavity or passage) by means of a sound. **b.** to examine (a patient) by means of percussion and auscultation. ~*n.* **5.** *Med.* an instrument for insertion into a bodily cavity or passage to dilate strictures, dislodge foreign material, etc. ~See also **sound out.** [C14: < OF *sonder,* < *sonde* sounding line, prob. of Gmc origin] —ˈ**sounder** *n.*

sound[4] (saʊnd) *n.* **1.** a relatively narrow channel between two larger areas of sea or between an island and the mainland. **2.** an inlet or deep bay of the sea. **3.** the air bladder of a fish. [OE *sund* swimming, narrow sea]

sound barrier *n.* (not in technical usage) a hypothetical barrier to flight at or above the speed of sound, when a sudden large increase in drag occurs. Also called: **sonic barrier.**

soundbox (ˈsaʊndˌbɒks) *n.* the resonating chamber of the hollow body of a violin, guitar, etc.

sound effect *n.* any sound artificially produced, reproduced from a recording, etc., to create a theatrical effect, as in plays, films, etc.

sounding[1] (ˈsaʊndɪŋ) *adj.* **1.** resounding; resonant. **2.** having an imposing sound and little content; pompous: *sounding phrases.*

sounding[2] (ˈsaʊndɪŋ) *n.* **1.** (*sometimes pl.*) the act or process of measuring depth of water or examining the bottom of a river, lake, etc., as with a sounding line. **2.** an observation or measurement of atmospheric conditions, as made using a sonde. **3.** (*often pl.*) measurements taken by sounding. **4.** (*pl.*) a place where a sounding line will reach the bottom, esp. less than 100 fathoms in depth.

sounding board *n.* **1.** Also called: **soundboard.** a thin wooden board in a violin, piano, etc., serving to amplify the vibrations produced by the strings passing across it. **2.** Also called: **soundboard.** a thin screen suspended over a pulpit, stage, etc., to reflect sound towards an audience. **3.** a person, group, experiment, etc., used to test a new idea, policy, etc.

sounding line *n.* a line marked off to indicate its length and having a **sounding lead** at one end. It is dropped over the side of a vessel to determine the depth of the water.

soundless (ˈsaʊndlɪs) *adj.* extremely still or silent. —ˈ**soundlessness** *n.*

sound out *vb.* (*tr., adv.*) to question (someone) in order to discover (opinions, facts, etc.).

soundpost (ˈsaʊndˌpəʊst) *n. Music.* a small wooden post in guitars, violins, etc., that joins the front to the back and helps support the bridge.

soundproof (ˈsaʊndˌpruːf) *adj.* **1.** not penetrable by sound. ~*vb.* **2.** (*tr.*) to render soundproof.

sound spectrograph *n.* an electronic instrument that produces a record (**sound spectrogram**) of the frequencies and intensities of the components of a sound.

soundtrack (ˈsaʊndˌtræk) *n.* **1.** the recorded sound accompaniment to a film. **2.** a narrow strip along the side of a spool of film, which carries the sound accompaniment.

sound wave *n.* a wave that propagates sound.

soup (suːp) *n.* **1.** a liquid food made by boiling or simmering meat, fish, vegetables, etc. **2.** *Inf.* a photographic developer. **3.** *Inf.* anything resembling soup, esp. thick fog. **4.** a slang name for **nitroglycerin. 5. in the soup.** *Sl.* in trouble or difficulties. [C17: < OF *soupe,* < LL *suppa,* of Gmc origin] —ˈ**soupy** *adj.*

soupçon *French.* (supsɔ̃) *n.* a slight amount; dash. [C18: < F, ult. < L *suspicio* SUSPICION]

soup kitchen *n.* **1.** a place or mobile stall where food and drink, esp. soup, is served to destitute people. **2.** *Mil.* a mobile kitchen.

soup plate *n.* a deep plate with a wide rim, used esp. for drinking soup.

soup up *vb.* (*tr., adv.*) *Sl.* to modify (a car or motorcycle engine) in order to increase its power. Also: **hot up,** (esp. U.S. and Canad.) **hop up.**

sour (ˈsaʊə) *adj.* **1.** having or denoting a sharp biting taste like that of lemon juice or vinegar. **2.** made acid or bad, as in the case of milk, by the action of microorganisms. **3.** having a rancid or unwholesome smell. **4.** (of a person's temperament) sullen, morose, or disagreeable. **5.** (esp. of the weather) harsh and unpleasant. **6.** disagreeable; distasteful: *a sour experience.* **7.** (of land, etc.) lacking in fertility, esp. due to excessive acidity. **8.** (of petrol, gas, etc.) containing a relatively large amount of sulphur compounds. **9. go** *or* **turn sour.** to become unfavourable or inharmonious: *his marriage went sour.* ~*n.* **10.** something sour. **11.** *Chiefly U.S.* an iced drink usually made with spirits, lemon juice, and ice: *a whiskey sour.* **12.** an acid used in bleaching clothes or in curing skins. ~*vb.* **13.** to make or become sour. [OE *sūr*] —ˈ**sourish** *adj.* —ˈ**sourly** *adv.* —ˈ**sourness** *n.*

source (sɔːs) *n.* **1.** the point or place from which something originates. **2. a.** a spring that forms the starting point of a stream. **b.** the area where the headwaters of a river rise. **3.** a person, group, etc., that creates, issues, or originates something: *the source of a complaint.* **4. a.** any person, book, organization, etc., from which information, evidence, etc., is obtained. **b.** (*as modifier*): *source material.* **5.** anything, such as a story or work of art, that provides a model or inspiration for a later work. **6. at source.** at the point of origin. ~*vb.* **7.** (*tr.*) to establish an originator or source of (a product, etc.). [C14: < OF *sors,* < *sourdre* to spring forth, < L *surgere* to rise]

source program *n.* an original computer program written by a programmer that is converted into the equivalent object program, written in machine language.

sour cherry *n.* **1.** a Eurasian tree with white flowers: cultivated for its tart red fruits. **2.** the fruit.

sour cream *n.* cream soured by lactic acid bacteria, used in making salads, dips, etc.

sourdough (ˈsaʊəˌdəʊ) *Dialect.* ~*adj.* **1.** (of bread) made with fermented dough used as leaven. ~*n.* **2.** (in the Western U.S., Canada, and Alaska) an old-time prospector or pioneer.

sour gourd *n.* **1.** a large tree of N Australia, having gourdlike fruit. **2.** the acid-tasting fruit. **3.** the fruit of the baobab tree.

sour grapes *n.* (*functioning as sing.*) the attitude of affecting to despise something because one cannot have it oneself.

sourpuss (ˈsaʊəˌpʊs) *n. Inf.* a person who is habitually gloomy or sullen.

sourveld (ˈsaʊəˌfɛlt) *n.* (in South Africa) a type of grazing characterized by long coarse grass. [< Afrik. *suur* sour + *veld* grassland]

sousaphone (ˈsuːzəˌfəʊn) *n.* a large tuba that encircles the player's body and has a bell facing forwards. [C20: after J. P. *Sousa* (1854–1932), U.S. composer & bandmaster] —ˈ**sousaˌphonist** *n.*

souse (saʊs) *vb.* **1.** to plunge (something) into water or other liquid. **2.** to drench or be drenched. **3.** (*tr.*) to pour or dash (liquid) over (a person or thing). **4.** to steep or cook (food) in a marinade. **5.** (*tr.*) *Sl.* to make drunk. ~*n.* **6.** the liquid used in pickling. **7.** the act or process of sousing. **8.** *Sl.* a drunkard. [C14: < OF *sous,* of Gmc origin]

soutane (suːˈtæn) *n. R.C. Church.* a priest's cassock. [C19: < F, < OIt. *sottana,* < Med. L *subtanus* (adj.) (worn) beneath, < L *subtus* below]

souterrain (ˈsuːtəˌreɪn) *n. Archaeol.* an underground chamber or passage. [C18: < F]

south (saʊθ) *n.* **1.** one of the four cardinal points of the compass, at 180° from north and 90° clockwise from east and anticlockwise from west. **2.** the direction along a meridian towards the South Pole. **3. the south.** (*often cap.*) any area lying in or towards the south. **4.** (*usually cap.*) *Cards.* the player or position corresponding to south on the compass. ~*adj.* **5.** in, towards, or facing the south. **6.** (esp. of the wind) from the south. ~*adv.* **7.** in, to, or towards the south. [OE *sūth*]

South (saʊθ) *n.* **the. 1.** the southern part of England, generally regarded as lying to the south of an imaginary line between the Wash and the Severn. **2.** (in the U.S.) **a.** the states south of the

Mason-Dixon Line that formed the Confederacy during the Civil War. **b.** the Confederacy itself. **3.** the countries of the world that are not economically and technically advanced. *~adj.* **4.** of or denoting the southern part of a specified country, area, etc.

South African *adj.* **1.** of or relating to the Republic of South Africa, its inhabitants, or any of their languages. *~n.* **2.** a native or inhabitant of the Republic of South Africa.

southbound (ˈsaʊθˌbaʊnd) *adj.* going or leading towards the south.

south by east *n.* **1.** one point on the compass east of south. *~adj., adv.* **2.** in, from, or towards this direction.

south by west *n.* **1.** one point on the compass west of south. *~adj., adv.* **2.** in, from, or towards this direction.

Southdown (ˈsaʊθˌdaʊn) *n.* an English breed of sheep with short wool and a greyish-brown face.

southeast (ˌsaʊθˈiːst; *Naut.* ˌsaʊˈiːst) *n.* **1.** the point of the compass or the direction midway between south and east. *~adj. also* **ˌsouthˈeastern. 2.** (*sometimes cap.*) of or denoting the southeastern part of a specified country, area, etc. **3.** in, towards, or facing the southeast. **4.** (esp. of the wind) from the southeast. *~adv.* **5.** in, to, or towards the southeast. —**ˌsouthˈeasternmost** *adj.*

Southeast (ˌsaʊθˈiːst) *n.* (usually preceded by *the*) the southeastern part of Britain, esp. the London area.

southeast by east *n.* **1.** one point on the compass north of southeast. *~adj., adv.* **2.** in, from, or towards this direction.

southeast by south *n.* **1.** one point on the compass south of southeast. *~adj., adv.* **2.** in, from, or towards this direction.

southeaster (ˌsaʊθˈiːstə; *Naut.* ˌsaʊˈiːstə) *n.* a strong wind or storm from the southeast.

southeasterly (ˌsaʊθˈiːstəlɪ; *Naut.* ˌsaʊˈiːstəlɪ) *adj., adv.* **1.** in, towards, or (esp. of the wind) from the southeast. *~n., pl.* **-lies. 2.** a strong wind or storm from the southeast.

southeastward (ˌsaʊθˈiːstwəd; *Naut.* ˌsaʊˈiːstwəd) *adj.* **1.** towards or (esp. of a wind) from the southeast. *~n.* **2.** a direction towards or area in the southeast. *~adv.* **3.** Also: **southeastwards.** towards the southeast.

souther (ˈsaʊðə) *n.* a strong wind or storm from the south.

southerly (ˈsʌðəlɪ) *adj.* **1.** of or situated in the south. *~adv., adj.* **2.** towards the south. **3.** from the south. *~n., pl.* **-lies. 4.** a wind from the south. —**ˈsoutherliness** *n.*

southern (ˈsʌðən) *adj.* **1.** in or towards the south. **2.** (of a wind, etc.) coming from the south. **3.** native to or inhabiting the south. —**ˈsouthernˌmost** *adj.*

Southern (ˈsʌðən) *adj.* of, relating to, or characteristic of the south of a particular region or country.

Southern Cross *n.* a small constellation in the S hemisphere whose four brightest stars form a cross. It is represented on the national flags of Australia and New Zealand.

Southerner (ˈsʌðənə) *n.* (*sometimes not cap.*) a native or inhabitant of the south of any specified region, esp. the South of England or the Southern states of the U.S.

southern hemisphere *n.* (*often caps.*) that half of the earth lying south of the equator.

southern lights *pl. n.* another name for **aurora australis.**

southing (ˈsaʊðɪŋ) *n.* **1.** *Navigation.* movement, deviation, or distance covered in a southerly direction. **2.** *Astron.* a south or negative declination.

southpaw (ˈsaʊθˌpɔː) *Inf.* *~n.* **1.** a left-handed boxer. **2.** any left-handed person. *~adj.* **3.** of or relating to a southpaw.

South Pole *n.* **1.** the southernmost point on the earth's axis, at the latitude of 90°S. **2.** *Astron.* the point of intersection of the earth's extended axis and the southern half of the celestial sphere. **3.** (*usually not caps.*) the south-seeking pole of a freely suspended magnet.

South Sea Bubble *n. Brit. history.* the financial crash that occurred in 1720 after the **South Sea Company** had taken over the national debt in return for a monopoly of trade with the South Seas, causing feverish speculation in their stocks.

South Sea Islands *pl. n.* the islands in the S Pacific.

South Seas *pl. n.* the seas south of the equator.

south-southeast *n.* **1.** the point on the compass or the direction midway between southeast and south. *~adj., adv.* **2.** in, from, or towards this direction.

south-southwest *n.* **1.** the point on the compass or the direction midway between south and southwest. *~adj., adv.* **2.** in, from, or towards this direction.

southward (ˈsaʊθwəd; *Naut.* ˈsʌðəd) *adj.* **1.** situated, directed, or moving towards the south. *~n.* **2.** the southward part, direction, etc. *~adv.* **3.** Also: **southwards.** towards the south.

southwest (ˌsaʊθˈwɛst; *Naut.* ˌsaʊˈwɛst) *n.* **1.** the point of the compass or the direction midway between west and south. *~adj. also* **ˌsouthˈwestern. 2.** (*sometimes cap.*) of or denoting the southwestern part of a specified country, area, etc.: *southwest Italy.* **3.** in or towards the southwest. **4.** (esp. of the wind) from the southwest. *~adv.* **5.** in, to, or towards the southwest. —**ˌsouthˈwesternmost** *adj.*

Southwest (ˌsaʊθˈwɛst) *n.* (usually preceded by *the*) the southwestern part of Britain, esp. Cornwall, Devon, and Somerset.

southwest by south *n.* **1.** one point on the compass south of southwest. *~adj., adv.* **2.** in, from, or towards this direction.

southwest by west *n.* **1.** one point on the compass north of southwest. *~adj., adv.* **2.** in, from, or towards this direction.

southwester (ˌsaʊθˈwɛstə; *Naut.* ˌsaʊˈwɛstə) *n.* a strong wind or storm from the southwest.

southwesterly (ˌsaʊθˈwɛstəlɪ; *Naut.* ˌsaʊˈwɛstəlɪ) *adj., adv.* **1.** in, towards, or (esp. of a wind) from the southwest. *~n., pl.* **-lies. 2.** a wind or storm from the southwest.

southwestward (ˌsaʊθˈwɛstwəd; *Naut.* ˌsaʊˈwɛstwəd) *adj.* **1.** from or towards the southwest. *~adv.* **2.** Also: **southwestwards.** towards the southwest. *~n.* **3.** a direction towards or area in the southwest.

souvenir (ˌsuːvəˈnɪə, ˈsuːvəˌnɪə) *n.* **1.** an object that recalls a certain place, occasion, or person; memento. **2.** *Rare.* a thing recalled. *~vb.* **3.** (*tr.*) *Austral. & N.Z., sl.* to steal or keep for one's own use; purloin. [C18: < F, < (*se*) *souvenir* to remember, < L *subvenīre* to come to mind]

sou'wester (saʊˈwɛstə) *n.* a waterproof hat having a very broad rim behind, worn esp. by seamen. [C19: a contraction of SOUTHWESTER]

sovereign (ˈsɒvrɪn) *n.* **1.** a person exercising supreme authority, esp. a monarch. **2.** a former British gold coin worth one pound sterling. *~adj.* **3.** supreme in rank or authority: *a sovereign lord.* **4.** excellent or outstanding: *a sovereign remedy.* **5.** of or relating to a sovereign. **6.** independent of outside authority: *a sovereign state.* [C13: < OF *soverain,* < Vulgar L *superānus* (unattested), < L *super* above; also infl. by REIGN] —**ˈsovereignly** *adv.*

sovereignty (ˈsɒvrəntɪ) *n., pl.* **-ties. 1.** supreme and unrestricted power, as of a state. **2.** the position, dominion, or authority of a sovereign. **3.** an independent state.

soviet (ˈsəʊvɪət, ˈsɒv-) *n.* **1.** (in the Soviet Union) an elected government council at the local, regional, and national levels, culminating in the Supreme Soviet. *~adj.* **2.** of or relating to a soviet. [C20: < Russian *sovyet* council, < ORussian *sŭvětŭ*] —**ˈsovieˌtism** *n.*

Soviet (ˈsəʊvɪət, ˈsɒv-) *adj.* of or relating to the Soviet Union, its people, or its government.

sovietize *or* **-ise** (ˈsəʊvɪɪˌtaɪz, ˈsɒv-) *vb.* (*tr.*) (*often cap.*) **1.** to bring (a country, person, etc.) under Soviet control or influence. **2.** to cause (a country) to conform to the Soviet model in its social, political, and economic structure. —ˌ**sovietiˈzation** *or* **-iˈsation** *n.*

Soviets (ˈsəʊvɪəts, ˈsɒv-) *pl. n.* the people or government of the Soviet Union.

sow[1] (səʊ) *vb.* **sowing, sowed; sown** *or* **sowed. 1.** to scatter or place (seed, a crop, etc.) in or on (a piece of ground, field, etc.) so that it may grow: *to sow wheat; to sow a strip of land.* **2.** (*tr.*) to implant or introduce: *to sow a doubt in someone's mind.* [OE *sāwan*] —ˈ**sower** *n.*

sow[2] (saʊ) *n.* **1.** a female adult pig. **2.** the female of certain other animals, such as the mink. **3.** *Metallurgy.* **a.** the channels for leading molten metal to the moulds in casting pig iron. **b.** iron that has solidified in these channels. [OE *sugu;* rel. to ON *sȳr,* OHG *sū,* L *sūs,* Norwegian *sugga,* Du. *zeug:* see SWINE]

sown (səʊn) *vb.* a past participle of **sow**[1].

sow thistle (saʊ) *n.* any of various plants of an Old World genus, having milky juice, prickly leaves, and heads of yellow flowers.

soya bean (ˈsɔɪə) *or U.S. & Canad.* **soybean** (ˈsɔɪˌbiːn) *n.* **1.** an Asian bean plant cultivated for its nutritious seeds, for forage, and to improve the soil. **2.** the seed, used as food, forage, and as the source of an oil. [C17 *soya,* via Du. < Japanese *shōyu,* < Chinese *chiang yu,* < *chiang* paste + *yu* sauce]

soy sauce (sɔɪ) *n.* a salty dark brown sauce made from fermented soya beans, used esp. in Chinese cookery. Also called: **soya sauce.**

sozzled (ˈsɒzəld) *adj.* an informal word for **drunk.** [C19: ? < obs. *sozzle* stupor]

SP *abbrev. for* starting price.

sp. *abbrev. for:* **1.** special. **2.** (*pl.* **spp.**) species. **3.** specific. **4.** specimen. **5.** spelling.

Sp. *abbrev. for:* **1.** Spain. **2.** Spaniard. **3.** Spanish.

spa (spɑː) *n.* a mineral spring or a place or resort where such a spring is found. [C17: after *Spa,* a watering place in Belgium]

space (speɪs) *n.* **1.** the unlimited three-dimensional expanse in which all material objects are located. Related adj.: **spatial. 2.** an interval of distance or time between two points, objects, or events. **3.** a blank portion or area. **4. a.** unoccupied area or room: *there is no space for a table.* **b.** (*in combination*): *space-saving.* Related adj.: **spacious. 5. a.** the region beyond the earth's atmosphere containing other planets, stars, galaxies, etc.; universe. **b.** (*as modifier*): *a space probe.* **6.** a seat or place, as on a train, aircraft, etc. **7.** *Printing.* a piece of metal, less than type-high, used to separate letters or words. **8.** *Music.* any of the gaps between the lines that make up the staff. **9.** Also called: **spacing.** *Telegraphy.* the period of time that separates characters in Morse code. ~*vb.* (*tr.*) **10.** to place or arrange at intervals or with spaces between. **11.** to divide into or by spaces: *to space one's time evenly.* **12.** *Printing.* to separate (letters, words, or lines) by the insertion of spaces. [C13: < OF *espace,* < L *spatium*] —ˈ**spacer** *n.*

space age *n.* **1.** the period in which the exploration of space has become possible. ~*adj.* **space-age. 2.** (*usually prenominal*) futuristic or ultramodern.

space-bar *n.* a horizontal bar on a typewriter that is depressed in order to leave a space between words, letters, etc.

space capsule *n.* a vehicle, sometimes carrying men or animals, designed to obtain scientific information from space, planets, etc., and be recovered on returning to earth.

spacecraft (ˈspeɪsˌkrɑːft) *n.* a manned or unmanned vehicle designed to orbit the earth or travel to celestial objects.

spaced out *adj. Sl.* intoxicated through taking a drug. Often shortened to **spaced.**

Space Invaders *n. Trademark.* a video game, the object of which is to obliterate a series of symbols moving down a television screen by operating levers or buttons.

spaceman (ˈspeɪsˌmæn) *or* (*fem.*) **spacewoman** *n., pl.* **-men** *or* (*fem.*) **-women.** a person who travels in outer space.

space platform *n.* another name for **space station.**

spaceport (ˈspeɪsˌpɔːt) *n.* a base equipped to launch, maintain, and test spacecraft.

space probe *n.* a vehicle, such as a satellite, equipped to obtain scientific information, normally transmitted back to earth by radio, about a planet, conditions in space, etc.

spaceship (ˈspeɪsˌʃɪp) *n.* a manned spacecraft.

space shuttle *n.* a manned reusable spacecraft designed for making regular orbital flights.

space station *n.* any large manned artificial satellite designed to orbit the earth during a long period of time thus providing a base for scientific research in space and a construction site, launching pad, and docking arrangements for spacecraft.

spacesuit (ˈspeɪsˌsuːt, -ˌsjuːt) *n.* a sealed and pressurized suit worn by astronauts providing an artificial atmosphere, acceptable temperature, radiocommunication link, and protection from radiation.

space-time *or* **space-time continuum** *n. Physics.* the four-dimensional continuum having three spatial coordinates and one time coordinate that together completely specify the location of a particle or an event.

spacewalk (ˈspeɪsˌwɔːk) *n.* **1.** the act or an instance of floating and manoeuvring in space, outside but attached by a lifeline to a spacecraft. Technical name: **extravehicular activity.** ~*vb.* **2.** (*intr.*) to engage in this activity.

spacial (ˈspeɪʃəl) *adj.* a variant spelling of **spatial.**

spacing (ˈspeɪsɪŋ) *n.* **1.** the arrangement of letters, words, spaces, etc., on a page. **2.** the arrangement of objects in a space.

spacious (ˈspeɪʃəs) *adj.* having a large capacity or area. —ˈ**spaciously** *adv.* —ˈ**spaciousness** *n.*

spade[1] (speɪd) *n.* **1.** a tool for digging, typically consisting of a flat rectangular steel blade attached to a long wooden handle. **2.** something resembling a spade. **3.** a cutting tool for stripping the blubber from a whale or skin from a carcass. **4. call a spade a spade.** to speak plainly and frankly. ~*vb.* **5.** (*tr.*) to use a spade on. [OE *spadu*] —ˈ**spader** *n.*

spade[2] (speɪd) *n.* **1. a.** the black symbol on a playing card resembling a heart-shaped leaf with a stem. **b.** a card with one or more of these symbols or (*when pl.*) the suit of cards so marked, usually the highest ranking of the four. **2.** a derogatory word for a **Negro. 3. in spades.** *Inf.* in an extreme or emphatic way. [C16: < It. *spada* sword, used as an emblem on playing cards, < L *spatha,* < Gk *spathē* blade]

spadework (ˈspeɪdˌwɜːk) *n.* dull or routine preparatory work.

spadix (ˈspeɪdɪks) *n., pl.* **spadices** (speɪˈdaɪsiːz). a spike of small flowers on a fleshy stem, the whole being enclosed in a spathe. [C18: < L: pulled-off branch of a palm, with its fruit, < Gk: torn-off frond]

spaghetti (spəˈgetɪ) *n.* pasta in the form of long strings. [C19: < It.: little cords, < *spago* a cord]

spaghetti junction *n.* a junction, usually between motorways, in which there are a large number of intersecting roads used by a large volume of high-speed traffic. [C20: < the nickname given to the Gravelly Hill Interchange, Birmingham, where the M6, A38M, A38, and A5127 intersect]

spaghetti western *n.* a cowboy film made in Europe, esp. by an Italian director.

spahi *or* **spahee** (ˈspɑːhiː, ˈspɑːiː) *n., pl.* **-his** *or* **-hees. 1.** (formerly) an irregular cavalryman in the Turkish army. **2.** (formerly) a member of a body of native Algerian cavalry in the French army. [C16: < OF, < Turkish *sipahi,* < Persian *sipāhī* soldier]

spake (speɪk) *vb. Arch.* a past tense of **speak.**

Spam (spæm) *n. Trademark.* a kind of tinned luncheon meat, made largely from pork.

span[1] (spæn) *n.* **1.** the interval, space, or distance between two points, such as the ends of a bridge or arch. **2.** the complete duration or extent: *the span of his life.* **3.** *Psychol.* the amount of material that can be processed in a single mental act: *span of attention.* **4.** short for **wingspan.** **5.** a unit of length based on the width of an expanded hand, usually taken as nine inches. ~*vb.* **spanning, spanned.** (*tr.*) **6.** to stretch or extend across, over, or around. **7.** to provide with something that spans: *to span a river with a bridge.* **8.** to measure or cover, esp. with the extended hand. [OE *spann*]

span[2] (spæn) *n.* a team of horses or oxen, esp. two matched animals. [C16 (in the sense: yoke): < MDu.: something stretched, < *spannen* to stretch]

span[3] (spæn) *vb. Arch. or dialect.* a past tense of **spin.**

Span. *abbrev. for* Spanish.

spandrel *or* **spandril** (ˈspændrəl) *n. Archit.* **1.** an approximately triangular surface bounded by the outer curve of an arch and the adjacent wall. **2.** the surface area between two adjacent arches and the horizontal cornice above them. [C15 *spaundrell,* < Anglo-F *spaundre,* < OF *spandre* to spread]

spangle (ˈspæŋgᵊl) *n.* **1.** a small thin piece of metal or other shiny material used as a decoration, esp. on clothes; sequin. **2.** any glittering or shiny spot or object. ~*vb.* **3.** (*intr.*) to glitter or shine with or like spangles. **4.** (*tr.*) to cover with spangles. [C15: dim. of *spange,* ? < MDu.: clasp] —ˈ**spangly** *adj.*

Spaniard (ˈspænjəd) *n.* a native or inhabitant of Spain.

spaniel (ˈspænjəl) *n.* **1.** any of several breeds of gundog with long drooping ears and a silky coat. **2.** an obsequiously devoted person. [C14: < OF *espaigneul* Spanish (dog), < OProvençal *espanhol,* ult. < L *Hispāniolus* Spanish]

Spanish (ˈspænɪʃ) *n.* **1.** the official language of Spain, Mexico, and most countries of South and Central America except Brazil. Spanish is an Indo-European language belonging to the Romance group. **2. the Spanish.** (*functioning as pl.*) the natives, citizens, or inhabitants of Spain. ~*adj.* **3.** of or relating to the Spanish language or its speakers. **4.** of or relating to Spain or Spaniards.

Spanish America *n.* the parts of America colonized by Spaniards and now chiefly Spanish-speaking: includes most of South and Central America, Mexico, and much of the West Indies.

Spanish-American *adj.* **1.** of or relating to any of the Spanish-speaking countries or peoples of the Americas. ~*n.* **2.** a native or inhabitant of Spanish America. **3.** a Spanish-speaking person in the U.S.

Spanish fly *n.* **1.** a European blister beetle, the dried body of which yields cantharides. **2.** another name for **cantharides.**

Spanish guitar *n.* the classic form of the guitar; a six-stringed instrument with a waisted body and a central sound hole.

Spanish Main *n.* **1.** the mainland of Spanish America, esp. the N coast of South America. **2.** the Caribbean Sea, the S part of which in colonial times was the haunt of pirates.

Spanish moss *n.* **1.** an epiphytic plant growing in tropical and subtropical regions as long bluish-grey strands suspended from the branches of trees. **2.** a tropical lichen growing as long trailing green threads from the branches of trees.

Spanish omelette *n.* an omelette containing green peppers, onions, tomato, etc.

Spanish rice *n.* rice cooked with tomatoes, onions, green peppers, etc.

spank[1] (spæŋk) *vb.* **1.** (*tr.*) to slap with the open hand, esp. on the buttocks. ~*n.* **2.** one or a series of these slaps. [C18: prob. imit.]

spank[2] (spæŋk) *vb.* (*intr.*) to go at a quick and lively pace. [C19: back formation < SPANKING[2]]

spanker (ˈspæŋkə) *n.* **1.** a person or thing that spanks. **2.** *Naut.* a fore-and-aft sail or a mast that is aftermost in a sailing vessel. **3.** *Inf.* something outstandingly fine or large.

spanking[1] (ˈspæŋkɪŋ) *n.* a series of spanks, usually as a punishment for children.

spanking[2] (ˈspæŋkɪŋ) *adj.* (*prenominal*) **1.** *Inf.* outstandingly fine, smart, large, etc. **2.** quick and energetic. **3.** (esp. of a breeze) fresh and brisk.

spanner (ˈspænə) *n.* **1.** a steel hand tool with jaws or a hole, designed to grip a nut or bolt head. **2. spanner in the works.** *Brit. inf.* an impediment or annoyance. [C17: < G, < *spannen* to stretch]

span roof *n.* a roof consisting of two equal sloping sides.

spanspek (ˈspænˌspɛk) *n. S. African.* the sweet melon. [< Afrik., < early Du.]

spar[1] (spɑː) *n.* **1.** any piece of nautical gear resembling a pole and used as a mast, boom, gaff, etc. **2.** a principal supporting structural member of an aerofoil that runs from tip to tip or root to tip. [C13: < ON *sperra* beam]

spar[2] (spɑː) *vb.* **sparring, sparred.** (*intr.*) **1.** *Boxing.* to box using light blows, as in training. **2.** to dispute or argue. **3.** (of gamecocks, etc.) to fight with the feet or spurs. ~*n.* **4.** an unaggressive fight. **5.** an argument or wrangle. [OE, ? < SPUR]

spar[3] (spɑː) *n.* any of various minerals, such as feldspar, that are light-coloured, crystalline, and easily cleavable. [C16: < MLow G *spar*]

sparaxis (spərˈæksɪs) *n.* a South African plant of the iris family, having lacerated spathes and showy flowers. [C19: NL, < Gk, < *sparassō* to tear]

spare (spɛə) *vb.* **1.** (*tr.*) to refrain from killing, punishing, or injuring. **2.** (*tr.*) to release or relieve, as from pain, suffering, etc. **3.** (*tr.*) to refrain from using: *spare the rod, spoil the child.* **4.** (*tr.*) to be able to afford or give: *I can't spare the time.* **5.** (*usually passive*) (esp. of Providence) to allow to survive: *I'll see you next year if we are spared.* **6.** (*intr.*) *Now rare.* to act or live frugally. **7. not spare oneself.** to exert oneself to the full. **8. to spare.** more than is required: *two minutes to spare.* ~*adj.* **9.** (*often immediately postpositive*) in excess of what is needed; additional. **10.** able to be used when needed: *a spare part.* **11.** (of a person) thin and lean. **12.** scanty or meagre. **13.** (*postpositive*) *Brit. sl.* upset, angry, or distracted (esp. in **go spare**). ~*n.* **14.** a duplicate kept as a replacement in case of damage or loss. **15.** a spare tyre. **16.** *Tenpin bowling.* **a.** the act of knocking down all the pins with the two bowls of a single frame. **b.** the score thus made. [OE *sparian* to refrain from injuring] —ˈ**sparely** *adv.* —ˈ**spareness** *n.* —ˈ**sparer** *n.*

spare-part surgery *n.* surgical replacement of defective or damaged organs by transplant or insertion of artficial devices.

sparerib (ˌspɛəˈrɪb) *n.* a cut of pork ribs with most of the meat trimmed off.

spare tyre *n.* **1.** an additional tyre carried by a motor vehicle in case of puncture. **2.** *Brit. sl.* a deposit of fat just above the waist.

sparing (ˈspɛərɪŋ) *adj.* **1.** (sometimes foll. by *of*) economical or frugal (with). **2.** scanty; meagre. **3.** merciful or lenient. —ˈ**sparingly** *adv.* —ˈ**sparingness** *n.*

spark[1] (spɑːk) *n.* **1.** a fiery particle thrown out or left by burning material or caused by the friction of two hard surfaces. **2. a.** a momentary flash of light accompanied by a sharp crackling noise, produced by a sudden electrical discharge through the air or some other insulating medium between two points. **b.** the electrical discharge itself. **c.** (*as modifier*): *a spark gap.* **3.** anything that serves to animate or kindle. **4.** a trace or hint: *a spark of interest.* **5.** vivacity, enthusiasm, or humour. **6.** a small piece of diamond, as used in cutting glass. ~*vb.* **7.** (*intr.*) to give off sparks. **8.** (*intr.*) (of the sparking plug or ignition system of an internal-combustion engine) to produce a spark. **9.** (*tr.*; often foll. by *off*) to kindle or animate. ~See also **sparks.** [OE *spearca*]

spark[2] (spɑːk) *n.* **1.** *Rare.* a fashionable or gallant young man. **2. bright spark.** *Brit., usually ironic.* a person who appears clever or witty. [C16 (in the sense: beautiful or witty woman): ? of Scand. origin] —ˈ**sparkish** *adj.*

spark gap *n.* the space between two electrodes across which a spark can jump.

sparking plug *n.* a device screwed into the cylinder head of an internal-combustion engine to ignite the explosive mixture by means of an electric spark. Also called: **spark plug.**

sparkle (ˈspɑːkᵊl) *vb.* **1.** to issue or reflect or cause to issue or reflect bright points of light. **2.** (*intr.*) (of wine, mineral water, etc.) to effervesce. **3.** (*intr.*) to be vivacious or witty. ~*n.* **4.** a point of light, spark, or gleam. **5.** vivacity or wit. [C12 *sparklen,* frequentative of *sparken* to SPARK¹]

sparkler (ˈspɑːklə) *n.* **1.** a type of firework that throws out sparks. **2.** *Inf.* a sparkling gem.

sparkling wine *n.* a wine made effervescent by carbon dioxide gas added artificially or produced naturally by secondary fermentation.

spark plug *n.* another name for **sparking plug.**

sparks (spɑːks) *n.* (*functioning as sing.*) *Inf.* **1.** an electrician. **2.** a radio officer, esp. on a ship.

sparky (ˈspɑːkɪ) *adj.* **sparkier, sparkiest.** lively, vivacious, spirited.

sparring partner (ˈspɑːrɪŋ) *n.* **1.** a person who practises with a boxer during training. **2.** a person with whom one has friendly arguments.

sparrow (ˈspærəʊ) *n.* **1.** any of various weaverbirds, esp. the house sparrow, having a brown or grey plumage and feeding on seeds or insects. **2.** *U.S. & Canad.* any of various North American finches, such as the chipping sparrow, that have a dullish streaked plumage. ~See also **hedge sparrow, tree sparrow.** [OE *spearwa*]

sparrowgrass (ˈspærəʊˌgrɑːs) *n.* a dialect or popular name for **asparagus.**

sparrowhawk (ˈspærəʊˌhɔːk) *n.* any of several small hawks of Eurasia and N Africa that prey on smaller birds.

sparrow hawk *n.* a very small North American falcon, closely related to the kestrels.

sparse (spɑːs) *adj.* scattered or scanty; not dense. [C18: < L *sparsus,* < *spargere* to scatter] —ˈ**sparsely** *adv.* —ˈ**sparseness** *or* ˈ**sparsity** *n.*

Spartan (ˈspɑːtᵊn) *adj.* **1.** of or relating to the ancient Greek city of Sparta or its citizens. **2.** (*sometimes not cap.*) very strict or austere: *a Spartan upbringing.* **3.** (*sometimes not cap.*) possessing courage and resolve. ~*n.* **4.** a citizen of Sparta. **5.** (*sometimes not cap.*) a disciplined or brave person.

spasm (ˈspæzəm) *n.* **1.** an involuntary muscular contraction, esp. one resulting in cramp or convulsion. **2.** a sudden burst of activity, emotion, etc. [C14: < L *spasmus,* < Gk *spasmos* a cramp, < *span* to tear]

spasmodic (spæzˈmɒdɪk) *or* (*rarely*) **spasmodical** *adj.* **1.** taking place in sudden brief spells. **2.** of or characterized by spasms. [C17: NL, < Gk *spasmos* SPASM] —**spasˈmodically** *adv.*

spastic (ˈspæstɪk) *adj.* **1.** affected by or resembling spasms. **2.** *Derog. sl.* clumsy, incapable, or incompetent. ~*n.* **3.** a person who has cerebral palsy. **4.** *Derog. sl.* a clumsy, incapable, or incompetent person. [C18: < L *spasticus,* < Gk, < *spasmos* SPASM] —ˈ**spastically** *adv.*

spat¹ (spæt) *n.* **1.** *Now rare.* a slap or smack. **2.** a slight quarrel. ~*vb.* **spatting, spatted. 3.** *Rare.* to slap (someone). **4.** (*intr.*) *U.S., Canad., & N.Z.* to have a slight quarrel. [C19: prob. imit.]

spat² (spæt) *vb.* a past tense and past participle of **spit**¹.

spat³ (spæt) *n.* another name for **gaiter** (sense 2). [C19: short for SPATTERDASH]

spat⁴ (spæt) *n.* **1.** a larval oyster or similar bivalve mollusc. **2.** such oysters or other molluscs collectively. [C17: < Anglo-Norman *spat*]

spatchcock (ˈspætʃˌkɒk) *n.* **1.** a chicken or game bird split down the back and grilled. ~*vb.* (*tr.*) **2.** to interpolate (words, a story, etc.) into a sentence, narrative, etc., esp. inappropriately. [C18: ? var. of *spitchcock* eel when prepared & cooked]

spate (speɪt) *n.* **1.** a fast flow, rush, or outpouring: *a spate of words.* **2.** *Chiefly Brit.* a sudden flood: *the rivers were in spate.* **3.** *Chiefly Brit.* a sudden heavy downpour. [C15 (Scot. & N English): <?]

spathe (speɪð) *n.* a large bract that encloses the inflorescence of several members of the lily family. [C18: < L *spatha,* < Gk *spathē* a blade] —**spathaceous** (spəˈθeɪʃəs) *adj.*

spathic (ˈspæθɪk) *or* **spathose** (ˈspæθəʊs) *adj.* (of minerals) resembling spar, esp. in having good cleavage. [C18: < G *Spat* SPAR²]

spatial *or* **spacial** (ˈspeɪʃəl) *adj.* **1.** of or relating to space. **2.** existing or happening in space. —**spatiality** (ˌspeɪʃɪˈælɪtɪ) *n.* —ˈ**spatially** *adv.*

spatiotemporal (ˌspeɪʃɪəʊˈtɛmpərəl) *adj.* **1.** of or existing in both space and time. **2.** of or concerned with space-time. —ˌ**spatioˈtemporally** *adv.*

spatter (ˈspætə) *vb.* **1.** to scatter or splash (a substance, esp. a liquid) or (of a substance) to splash (something) in scattered drops: *to spatter mud on the car; mud spattered in her face.* **2.** (*tr.*) to sprinkle, cover, or spot (with a liquid). **3.** (*tr.*) to slander or defame. **4.** (*intr.*) to shower or rain down: *bullets spattered around them.* ~*n.* **5.** the sound of spattering. **6.** something spattered, such as a spot or splash. **7.** the act or an instance of spattering. [C16: imit.]

spatterdash (ˈspætəˌdæʃ) *n.* **1.** *U.S.* another name for **roughcast. 2.** (*pl.*) long leather leggings worn in the 18th century, as to protect from mud when riding. [C17: see SPATTER, DASH¹]

spatula (ˈspætjʊlə) *n.* a utensil with a broad flat blade, used for lifting, spreading, or stirring foods, etc. [C16: < L: a broad piece, < *spatha* a flat wooden implement; see SPATHE] —ˈ**spatular** *adj.*

spatulate (ˈspætjʊlɪt) *adj.* **1.** shaped like a spatula; having thickened rounded ends: *spatulate fingers.* **2.** Also: **spathulate.** *Bot.* having a narrow base and a broad rounded apex.

spavin (ˈspævɪn) *n.* enlargement of the hock of a horse by a bony growth (**bony spavin**) or distension of the ligament (**bog spavin**), often resulting in lameness. [C15: < OF *espavin,* <?] —ˈ**spavined** *adj.*

spawn (spɔːn) *n.* **1.** the mass of eggs deposited by fish, amphibians, or molluscs. **2.** *Often derog.* offspring, product, or yield. **3.** *Bot.* the nontechnical name for **mycelium.** ~*vb.* **4.** (of fish, amphibians, etc.) to produce or deposit (eggs). **5.** *Often derog.* (of people) to produce (offspring). **6.** (*tr.*) to produce or engender. [C14: < Anglo-Norman *espaundre,* < OF *spandre* to spread out] —ˈ**spawner** *n.*

spay (speɪ) *vb.* (*tr.*) to remove the ovaries from (a female animal). [C15: < OF *espeer* to cut with the sword, < *espee* sword, < L *spatha*]

SPCK (in Britain) *abbrev. for* Society for Promoting Christian Knowledge.

speak (spiːk) *vb.* **speaking, spoke, spoken. 1.** to make (verbal utterances); utter (words). **2.** to communicate or express (something) in or as if in words. **3.** (*intr.*) to deliver a speech, discourse, etc. **4.** (*tr.*) to know how to talk in (a language or dialect): *he does not speak German.* **5.** (*intr.*) to make a characteristic sound: *the clock spoke.* **6.** (*intr.*) (of hounds used in hunting) to give tongue; bark. **7.** (*tr.*) *Naut.* to hail and communicate with (another vessel) at sea. **8.** (*intr.*) (of a musical instrument) to produce a sound. **9.** (*intr.; foll. by for*) to be a representative or advocate (of). **10. on speaking terms.** on good terms; friendly. **11. so to speak.** in a manner of speaking; as it were. **12. speak one's mind.** to express one's opinions frankly and plainly. **13. to speak of.** of a significant or worthwhile nature: *no support to speak of.* ~See also **speak for, speak out, speak to.** [OE *specan*] —ˈ**speakable** *adj.*

speakeasy (ˈspiːkˌiːzɪ) *n., pl.* **-easies.** *U.S.* a place where alcoholic drink was sold illicitly during Prohibition.

speaker (ˈspiːkə) *n.* **1.** a person who speaks, esp. at a formal occasion. **2.** See **loudspeaker.** —ˈ**speakership** *n.*

Speaker (ˈspiːkə) *n.* the presiding officer in any of numerous legislative bodies.

speak for *vb.* (*intr., prep.*) **1.** to speak as a representative of (other people). **2. speak for itself.** to be so evident that no further comment is necessary. **3. speak for yourself.** *Inf.* (used as an imperative) do not presume that other people agree with you.

speaking (ˈspiːkɪŋ) *adj.* **1.** (*prenominal*) eloquent, impressive, or striking. **2. a.** able to speak. **b.** (*in combination*) able to speak a particular language: *French-speaking.*

speaking clock *n. Brit.* a telephone service that gives a verbal statement of the time.

speaking in tongues *n.* another term for **gift of tongues.**

speaking tube *n.* a tube for conveying a person's voice from one room or building to another.

speak out *or* **up** *vb.* (*intr., adv.*) **1.** to state one's beliefs, objections, etc., bravely and firmly. **2.** to speak more loudly and clearly.

speak to *vb.* (*intr., prep.*) **1.** to address (a person). **2.** to reprimand. **3.** *Formal.* to give evidence of or comments on (a subject).

spear[1] (spɪə) *n.* **1.** a weapon consisting of a long shaft with a sharp pointed end of metal, stone, or wood that may be thrown or thrust. **2.** a similar implement used to catch fish. **3.** another name for **spearman.** ~*vb.* **4.** to pierce (something) with or as if with a spear. [OE *spere*]

spear[2] (spɪə) *n.* a shoot, stalk, or blade, as of grass. [C16: prob. var. of SPIRE[1], infl. by SPEAR[1]]

spear grass *n.* **1.** Also called: **wild Spaniard.** a New Zealand grass with sharp leaves that grows on mountains. **2.** any of various other grasses with sharp stiff blades or seeds.

spear gun *n.* a device for shooting spears underwater.

spearhead (ˈspɪəˌhɛd) *n.* **1.** the pointed head of a spear. **2.** the leading force in a military attack. **3.** any person or thing that leads or initiates an attack, campaign, etc. ~*vb.* **4.** (*tr.*) to lead or initiate (an attack, campaign, etc.).

spearman (ˈspɪəmən) *n., pl.* **-men.** a soldier armed with a spear.

spearmint (ˈspɪəmɪnt) *n.* a purple-flowered mint plant of Europe, having leaves that yield an oil used for flavouring.

spec (spɛk) *n.* **1. on spec.** *Inf.* as a speculation or gamble: *all the tickets were sold so I went to the theatre on spec.* ~*adj.* **2.** (*prenominal*) *Austral. & N.Z. inf.* speculative: *a spec developer.*

spec. *abbrev. for:* **1.** special. **2.** specification. **3.** speculation.

special (ˈspɛʃəl) *adj.* **1.** distinguished from, set apart from, or excelling others of its kind. **2.** (*prenominal*) designed or reserved for a particular purpose. **3.** not usual or commonplace. **4.** (*prenominal*) particular or primary: *his special interest was music.* **5.** of or relating to the education of handicapped children: *a special school.* ~*n.* **6.** a special person or thing, such as an extra edition of a newspaper or a train reserved for a particular purpose. **7.** a dish or meal given prominence, esp. at a low price, in a café, etc. **8.** short for **special constable.** **9.** *U.S., Canad., Austral., & N.Z. inf.* an item in a store advertised at a reduce price. ~*vb.* **-cialling, -cialled.** (*tr.*) **10.** (of a nurse) to give (a gravely ill patient) constant individual care. **11.** *N.Z. inf.* to advertise and sell (an item) at a reduced price. [C13: < OF *especial,* < L *speciālis* individual, special, < *speciēs* appearance] —**ˈspecially** *adv.* —**ˈspecialness** *n.*

▷ **Usage.** See at **especial.**

Special Branch *n.* (in Britain) the department of the police force that is concerned with political security.

special constable *n.* a person recruited for temporary or occasional police duties, esp. in time of emergency.

special delivery *n.* the delivery of a piece of mail outside the time of a scheduled delivery.

special drawing rights *pl. n.* (*sometimes caps.*) the reserve assets of the International Monetary Fund on which member nations may draw.

specialist (ˈspɛʃəlɪst) *n.* a person who specializes in a particular activity, field of research, etc. —**ˈspecialˌism** *n.* —**ˌspecialˈistic** *adj.*

speciality (ˌspɛʃɪˈælɪtɪ) *or esp. U.S. & Canad.* **specialty** *n., pl.* **-ties.** **1.** a special interest or skill. **2. a.** a service or product specialized in, as at a restaurant. **b.** (*as modifier*)*: a speciality dish.* **3.** a special feature or characteristic.

specialize *or* **-ise** (ˈspɛʃəˌlaɪz) *vb.* **1.** (*intr.*) to train in or devote oneself to a particular area of study, occupation, or activity. **2.** (*usually passive*) to cause (organisms or parts) to develop in a way most suited to a particular environment or way of life or (of organisms, etc.) to develop in this way. **3.** (*tr.*) to modify for a special use or purpose. —**ˌspecialiˈzation** *or* **-iˈsation** *n.*

special licence *n. Brit.* a licence permitting a marriage to take place by dispensing with the usual legal conditions.

special pleading *n. Law.* **1.** a pleading that alleges new facts that offset those put forward by the other side rather than directly admitting or denying those facts. **2.** a pleading that emphasizes the favourable aspects of a case while omitting the unfavourable.

special school *n. Brit.* a school for children who are unable to benefit from ordinary schooling because they are educationally subnormal, handicapped, etc.

specialty (ˈspɛʃəltɪ) *n., pl.* **-ties.** **1.** *Law.* a formal contract or obligation expressed in a deed. **2.** a variant (esp. U.S. and Canad.) of **speciality.**

speciation (ˌspiːʃɪˈeɪʃən) *n.* the evolutionary development of a biological species.

specie (ˈspiːʃiː) *n.* **1.** coin money, as distinguished from bullion or paper money. **2. in specie. a.** (of money) in coin. **b.** in kind. [C16: < L *in speciē* in kind]

species (ˈspiːʃiːz; *Latin* ˈspiːʃɪˌiːz) *n., pl.* **-cies.** **1.** *Biol.* **a.** any of the taxonomic groups into which a genus is divided, the members of which are capable of interbreeding. **b.** the animals of such a group. **c.** any group of related animals or plants not necessarily of this taxonomic rank. **2.** (*modifier*) denoting a plant that is a natural member of a species rather than a hybrid or cultivar: *a species clematis.* **3.** *Logic.* a group of objects or individuals, all sharing common attributes, that forms a subdivision of a genus. **4.** a kind, sort, or variety: *a species of treachery.* **5.** *Chiefly R.C. Church.* the outward form of the bread and wine in the Eucharist. **6.** *Obs.* an outward appearance or form. [C16: < L: appearance, < *specere* to look]

specif. *abbrev. for* specifically.

specific (spɪˈsɪfɪk) *adj.* **1.** explicit, particular, or definite. **2.** relating to a specified or particular thing: *a specific treatment for arthritis.* **3.** of or relating to a biological species. **4.** (of a disease) caused by a particular pathogenic agent. **5.** *Physics.* **a.** characteristic of a property of a substance, esp. in relation to the same property of a standard reference substance: *specific gravity.* **b.** characteristic of a property of a substance per unit mass, length, area, etc.: *specific heat.* **c.** (of an extensive physical quantity) divided by mass: *specific volume.* **6.** denoting a tariff levied at a fixed sum per unit of weight, quantity, volume, etc., irrespective of value. ~*n.* **7.** (*sometimes pl.*) a designated quality, thing, etc. **8.** *Med.* any drug used to treat a particular disease. [C17: < Med. L *specificus,* < L SPECIES] —**speˈcifically** *adv.* —**specificity** (ˌspɛsɪˈfɪsɪtɪ) *n.*

specification (ˌspɛsɪfɪˈkeɪʃən) *n.* **1.** the act or an instance of specifying. **2.** (in patent law) a written statement accompanying an application for a patent that describes the nature of an invention. **3.** a detailed description of the criteria for the constituents, construction, appearance, performance, etc., of a material, apparatus, etc., or of the standard of workmanship required in its manufacture. **4.** an item, detail, etc., specified.

specific gravity *n.* the ratio of the density of a substance to that of water.

specific heat capacity *n.* the heat required to raise unit mass of a substance by unit temperature interval under specified conditions, such as constant pressure. Also called: **specific heat.**

specific volume *n. Physics.* the volume of matter per unit mass.

specify (ˈspɛsɪˌfaɪ) *vb.* **-fying, -fied.** (*tr.; may take a clause as object*) **1.** to refer to or state specifically. **2.** to state as a condition. **3.** to state or include in the specification of. [C13: < Med. L *specificāre* to describe] —**ˈspeciˌfiable** *adj.* —**specificative** (ˈspɛsɪfɪˌkeɪtɪv) *adj.*

specimen (ˈspɛsɪmɪn) *n.* **1. a.** an individual, object, or part regarded as typical of its group or class. **b.** (*as modifier*): *a specimen page.* **2.** *Med.* a sample of tissue, blood, urine, etc., taken for diagnostic examination or evaluation. **3.** the whole or a part of an organism, plant, rock, etc., collected and preserved as an example of its class, species, etc. **4.** *Inf., often derog.* a person. [C17: < L: mark, proof, < *specere* to look at]

specious (ˈspiːʃəs) *adj.* **1.** apparently correct or true, but actually wrong or false. **2.** deceptively attractive in appearance. [C14 (orig.: fair): < L *speciōsus* plausible, < *speciēs* outward appearance, < *specere* to look at] —**ˈspeciously** *adv.* —**ˌspeciˈosity** (ˌspiːʃɪˈɒsɪtɪ) *or* **ˈspeciousness** *n.*

speck (spɛk) *n.* **1.** a very small mark or spot. **2.** a small or tiny piece of something. ~*vb.* **3.** (*tr.*) to mark with specks or spots. [OE *specca*]

speckle (ˈspɛkᵊl) *n.* **1.** a small mark usually of a contrasting colour, as on the skin, eggs, etc. ~*vb.* **2.** (*tr.*) to mark with or as if with speckles. [C15: < MDu. *spekkel*] —**ˈspeckled** *adj.*

specs (spɛks) *pl. n. Inf.* **1.** short for **spectacles. 2.** short for **specifications.**

spectacle (ˈspɛktəkᵊl) *n.* **1.** a public display or performance, esp. a showy or ceremonial one. **2.** a thing or person seen, esp. an unusual or ridiculous one: *he makes a spectacle of himself.* **3.** a strange or interesting object or phenomenon. [C14: via OF < L *spectaculum* a show, < *spectāre* to watch, < *specere* to look at]

spectacles (ˈspɛktəkᵊlz) *pl. n.* a pair of glasses for correcting defective vision. Often (informal) shortened to **specs.** —**ˈspectacled** *adj.*

spectacular (spɛkˈtækjʊlə) *adj.* **1.** of or resembling a spectacle; impressive, grand, or dramatic. **2.** unusually marked or great: *a spectacular increase.* ~*n.* **3.** a lavishly produced performance. —**specˈtacularly** *adv.*

spectate (spɛkˈteɪt) *vb.* (*intr.*) to be a spectator; watch. [C20: back formation < SPECTATOR]

spectator (spɛkˈteɪtə) *n.* a person viewing anything; onlooker; observer. [C16: < L, < *spectāre* to watch; see SPECTACLE]

spectator sport *n.* a sport that attracts people as spectators rather than as participants.

spectra (ˈspɛktrə) *n.* the plural of **spectrum.**

spectral (ˈspɛktrəl) *adj.* **1.** of or like a spectre. **2.** of or relating to a spectrum. —**spectrality** (spɛkˈtrælɪtɪ) *n.* —**ˈspectrally** *adv.*

spectral type *or* **class** *n.* any of various groups into which stars are classified according to characteristic spectral lines and bands.

spectre *or U.S.* **specter** (ˈspɛktə) *n.* **1.** a ghost; phantom; apparition. **2.** an unpleasant or menacing mental image: *the spectre of redundancy.* [C17: < L *spectrum*, < *specere* to look at]

spectro- *combining form.* indicating a spectrum: *spectrogram.*

spectrograph (ˈspɛktrəʊˌgrɑːf) *n.* a spectroscope or spectrometer that produces a photographic record (**spectrogram**) of a spectrum. See also **sound spectrograph.** —**ˌspectroˈgraphic** *adj.* —**ˌspectroˈgraphically** *adv.* —**spectrography** (spɛkˈtrɒgrəfɪ) *n.*

spectroheliograph (ˌspɛktrəʊˈhiːlɪəˌgrɑːf) *n.* an instrument used to take a photograph (**spectroheliogram**) of the sun in light of a particular wavelength, usually that of calcium or hydrogen, to show the distribution of the element over the surface and in the atmosphere. —**ˌspectroˌhelioˈgraphic** *adj.*

spectrometer (spɛkˈtrɒmɪtə) *n.* any instrument for producing a spectrum, esp. one in which wavelength, energy, intensity, etc., can be measured. See also **mass spectrometer.** —**spectrometric** (ˌspɛktrəʊˈmɛtrɪk) *adj.* —**specˈtrometry** *n.*

spectrophotometer (ˌspɛktrəʊfəʊˈtɒmɪtə) *n.* an instrument for producing or recording a spectrum and measuring the photometric intensity of each wavelength present. —**spectrophotometric** (ˌspɛktrəʊˌfəʊtəˈmɛtrɪk) *adj.* —**ˌspectrophoˈtometry** *n.*

spectroscope (ˈspɛktrəˌskəʊp) *n.* any of a number of instruments for dispersing electromagnetic radiation and thus forming or recording a spectrum. —**spectroscopic** (ˌspɛktrəˈskɒpɪk) *or* **ˌspectroˈscopical** *adj.*

spectroscopy (spɛkˈtrɒskəpɪ) *n.* the science and practice of using spectrometers and spectroscopes and of analysing spectra. —**specˈtroscopist** *n.*

spectrum (ˈspɛktrəm) *n., pl* **-tra. 1.** the distribution of colours produced when white light is dispersed by a prism or diffraction grating. There is a continuous change in wavelength from red, the longest wavelength, to violet, the shortest. Seven colours are usually distinguished: violet, indigo, blue, green, yellow, orange, and red. **2.** the whole range of electromagnetic radiation with respect to its wavelength or frequency. **3.** any particular distribution of electromagnetic radiation often showing lines or bands characteristic of the substance emitting the radiation or absorbing it. **4.** any similar distribution or record of the energies, velocities, masses, etc., of atoms, ions, electrons, etc.: *a mass spectrum.* **5.** any range or scale, as of capabilities, emotions, or moods. **6.** another name for an **afterimage.** [C17: < L: image, < *spectāre* to observe, < *specere* to look at]

spectrum analysis *n.* the analysis of a spectrum to determine the properties of its source.

specular (ˈspɛkjʊlə) *adj.* **1.** of, relating to, or having the properties of a mirror. **2.** of or relating to a speculum. [C16: < L *speculāris*, < *speculum* a mirror, < *specere* to look at]

speculate (ˈspɛkjʊˌleɪt) *vb.* **1.** (when *tr., takes a clause as object*) to conjecture without knowing the complete facts. **2.** (*intr.*) to buy or sell securities, property, etc., in the hope of deriving capital gains. **3.** (*intr.*) to risk loss for the possibility of considerable gain. **4.** (*intr.*) *N.Z.* in rugby football, to make an emergency undirected forward kick at the ball. [C16: < L *speculārī* to spy out, < *specula* a watchtower, < *specere* to look at]

speculation (ˌspɛkjʊˈleɪʃən) *n.* **1.** the act or an instance of speculating. **2.** a supposition, theory, or opinion arrived at through speculating. **3.** investment involving high risk but also possible high profits. —**ˈspeculative** *adj.*

speculator (ˈspɛkjʊˌleɪtə) *n.* **1.** a person who speculates. **2.** *N.Z. rugby.* an undirected kick of the ball.

speculum (ˈspɛkjʊləm) *n., pl.* **-la** (-lə) *or* **-lums. 1.** a mirror, esp. one made of polished metal for use in a telescope, etc. **2.** *Med.* an instrument for dilating a bodily cavity or passage to permit examination of its interior. **3.** a patch of distinctive colour on the wing of a bird. [C16: < L: mirror, < *specere* to look at]

sped (spɛd) *vb.* a past tense and past participle of **speed.**

speech (spiːtʃ) *n.* **1. a.** the act or faculty of speaking. **b.** (*as modifier*): *speech therapy.* **2.** that which is spoken; utterance. **3.** a talk or address delivered to an audience. **4.** a person's characteristic manner of speaking. **5.** a national or regional language or dialect. **6.** *Linguistics.* another word for **parole.** [OE *spēc*]

speech day *n. Brit.* (in schools) an annual day

on which prizes are presented, speeches are made by guest speakers, etc.

speechify (ˈspiːtʃɪˌfaɪ) *vb.* **-fying, -fied.** (*intr.*) **1.** to make a speech or speeches. **2.** to talk pompously and boringly. —ˈ**speechiˌfier** *n.*

speechless (ˈspiːtʃlɪs) *adj.* **1.** not able to speak. **2.** temporarily deprived of speech. **3.** not expressed or able to be expressed in words: *speechless fear.* —ˈ**speechlessly** *adv.* —ˈ**speechlessness** *n.*

speed (spiːd) *n.* **1.** the act or quality of acting or moving fast; rapidity. **2.** the rate at which something moves, is done, or acts. **3.** *Physics.* **a.** a scalar measure of the rate of movement of a body expressed either as the distance travelled divided by the time taken (**average speed**) or the rate of change of position with respect to time at a particular point (**instantaneous speed**). **b.** another word for **velocity** (sense 2). **4.** a rate of rotation, usually expressed in revolutions per unit time. **5. a.** a gear ratio in a motor vehicle, bicycle, etc. **b.** (*in combination*): *a three-speed gear.* **6.** *Photog.* a numerical expression of the sensitivity to light of a particular type of film, paper, or plate. **7.** *Photog.* a measure of the ability of a lens to pass light from an object to the image position. **8.** a slang word for **amphetamine.** **9.** *Arch.* prosperity or success. **10. at speed.** quickly. ~*vb.* **speeding; sped** *or* **speeded.** **11.** to move or go or cause to move or go quickly. **12.** (*intr.*) to drive (a motor vehicle) at a high speed, esp. above legal limits. **13.** (*tr.*) to help further the success or completion of. **14.** (*intr.*) *Sl.* to take or be under the influence of amphetamines. **15.** (*intr.*) to operate or run at a high speed. **16.** *Arch.* **a.** (*intr.*) to prosper or succeed. **b.** (*tr.*) to wish success to. ~See also **speed up.** [OE *spēd* (orig. in the sense: success)] —ˈ**speeder** *n.*

speedball (ˈspiːdˌbɔːl) *n. Sl.* a mixture of heroin with amphetamine or cocaine.

speedboat (ˈspiːdˌbəʊt) *n.* a high-speed motorboat.

speed chess *n.* a form of chess in which each player's game is limited to a total stipulated time, usually half an hour; the first player to exceed the time limit loses.

speed limit *n.* the maximum permitted speed at which a vehicle may travel on certain roads.

speedo (ˈspiːdəʊ) *n., pl.* **speedos.** an informal name for **speedometer.**

speedometer (spɪˈdɒmɪtə) *n.* a device fitted to a vehicle to measure and display the speed of travel. See also **mileometer.**

speed up *vb.* (*adv.*) **1.** to increase or cause to increase in speed or rate; accelerate. ~*n.* **speedup.** **2.** an instance of this; acceleration.

speedway (ˈspiːdˌweɪ) *n.* **1.** the sport of racing on light powerful motorcycles round cinder tracks. **2.** the track or stadium where such races are held. **3.** *U.S. & Canad.* **a.** a racetrack for cars. **b.** a road on which fast driving is allowed.

speedwell (ˈspiːdˌwɛl) *n.* any of various temperate plants, such as the **common speedwell** and the **germander speedwell,** having small blue or pinkish-white flowers.

speedy (ˈspiːdɪ) *adj.* **speedier, speediest.** **1.** characterized by speed. **2.** done or decided without delay. —ˈ**speedily** *adv.* —ˈ**speediness** *n.*

spek (spɛk) *n. S. African.* bacon. [< Afrik., < Du.]

speleology *or* **spelaeology** (ˌspiːlɪˈɒlədʒɪ) *n.* **1.** the scientific study of caves. **2.** the sport or pastime of exploring caves. [C19: < L *spēlaeum* cave] —**speleological** *or* **spelaeological** (ˌspiːlɪəˈlɒdʒɪkᵊl) *adj.* —ˌ**speleˈologist** *or* ˌ**spelaeˈologist** *n.*

spell[1] (spɛl) *vb.* **spelling; spelt** *or* **spelled.** **1.** to write or name in correct order the letters that comprise the conventionally accepted form of (a word). **2.** (*tr.*) (of letters) to go to make up the conventionally established form of (a word) when arranged correctly: *d-o-g spells dog.* **3.** (*tr.*) to indicate or signify: *such actions spell disaster.* ~See also **spell out.** [C13: < OF *espeller,* of Gmc origin] —ˈ**spellable** *adj.*

spell[2] (spɛl) *n.* **1.** a verbal formula considered as having magical force. **2.** any influence that can control the mind or character; fascination. **3.** a state induced as by the pronouncing of a spell; trance: *to break the spell.* **4. under a spell.** held in or as if in a spell. [OE *spell* speech]

spell[3] (spɛl) *n.* **1.** an indeterminate, usually short, period of time: *a spell of cold weather.* **2.** a period or tour of duty after which one person or group relieves another. **3.** *Scot., Austral., & N.Z.* a period or interval of rest. ~*vb.* **4.** (*tr.*) to take over from (a person) for an interval of time; relieve temporarily. [OE *spelian* to take the place of, <?]

spellbind (ˈspɛlˌbaɪnd) *vb.* **-binding, -bound.** (*tr.*) to cause to be spellbound; entrance or enthral. —ˈ**spellˌbinder** *n.*

spellbound (ˈspɛlˌbaʊnd) *adj.* having one's attention held as though one is bound by a spell.

speller (ˈspɛlə) *n.* **1.** a person who spells words in the manner specified: *a bad speller.* **2.** a book designed to teach or improve spelling.

spelling (ˈspɛlɪŋ) *n.* **1.** the act or process of writing words by using the letters conventionally accepted for their formation; orthography. **2.** the art or study of orthography. **3.** the way in which a word is spelt. **4.** the ability of a person to spell.

spelling bee *n.* a contest in which players are required to spell words.

spell out *vb.* (*tr., adv.*) **1.** to make clear, distinct, or explicit; clarify in detail: *let me spell out the implications.* **2.** to read laboriously or with difficulty, working out each word letter by letter. **3.** to discern by study; puzzle out.

spelt[1] (spɛlt) *vb.* a past tense and past participle of **spell**[1].

spelt[2] (spɛlt) *n.* a species of wheat that was formerly much cultivated and was used to develop present-day cultivated wheats. [OE]

spelter (ˈspɛltə) *n.* impure zinc. [C17: prob. < MDu. *speauter,* <?]

spelunker (spɪˈlʌŋkə) *n.* a person whose hobby is the exploration of caves. [C20: < L *spēlunca,* < Gk *spēlunx* a cave] —**speˈlunking** *n.*

spencer[1] (ˈspɛnsə) *n.* **1.** a short fitted coat or jacket. **2.** a woman's knitted vest. [C18: after Earl *Spencer* (1758–1834)]

spencer[2] (ˈspɛnsə) *n. Naut.* a large loose-footed gaffsail on a square-rigger or barque. [C19: ? < a proper name]

spend (spɛnd) *vb.* **spending, spent.** **1.** to pay out (money, wealth, etc.). **2.** (*tr.*) to concentrate (time, effort, etc.) upon an object, activity, etc. **3.** (*tr.*) to pass (time) in a specific way, place, etc. **4.** (*tr.*) to use up completely: *the hurricane spent its force.* **5.** (*tr.*) to give up (one's blood, life, etc.) in a cause. [OE *spendan,* < L *expendere;* infl. also by OF *despendre* to spend; see EXPEND, DISPENSE] —ˈ**spendable** *adj.* —ˈ**spender** *n.*

spendthrift (ˈspɛndˌθrɪft) *n.* **1.** a person who spends money in an extravagant manner. ~*adj.* **2.** (*usually prenominal*) of or like a spendthrift.

Spenserian (spɛnˈsɪərɪən) *adj.* **1.** relating to or characteristic of the 16th-century English poet Edmund Spenser or his poetry. ~*n.* **2.** a student or imitator of Edmund Spenser.

Spenserian stanza *n. Prosody.* the stanza form used by the poet Spenser in his poem *The Faerie Queene,* consisting of eight lines in iambic pentameter and a concluding Alexandrine, rhyming a b a b b c b c c.

spent (spɛnt) *vb.* **1.** the past tense and past participle of **spend.** ~*adj.* **2.** used up or exhausted; consumed. **3.** (of a fish) exhausted by spawning.

sperm[1] (spɜːm) *n.* **1.** another name for **semen.** **2.** a male reproductive cell; male gamete. [C14: < LL *sperma,* < Gk]

sperm[2] (spɜːm) *n.* short for **sperm whale, spermaceti,** or **sperm oil.**

-sperm *n. combining form.* (in botany) a seed: *gymnosperm.* —**-spermous** *or* **-spermal** *adj. combining form.*

spermaceti (ˌspɜːməˈsɛtɪ, -ˈsiːtɪ) *n.* a white waxy substance obtained from oil from the head of the sperm whale. [C15: < Med. L *sperma cētī* whale's sperm, < *sperma* SPERM[1] + L *cētus* whale, < Gk *kētos*]

spermatic (spɜːˈmætɪk), **spermic** (ˈspɜːmɪk), *or* **spermous** (ˈspɜːməs) *adj.* **1.** of or relating to spermatozoa: *spermatic fluid.* **2.** of or relating to the testis: *the spermatic artery.* [C16: < LL *spermaticus,* < Gk *spermatikos* concerning seed, < *sperma* seed] —**sperˈmatically** *adv.*

spermatid (ˈspɜːmətɪd) *n. Zool.* any of four immature male gametes that are formed from a spermatocyte, each of which develops into a spermatozoon.

spermato-, spermo- *or before a vowel* **spermat-, sperm-** *combining form.* **1.** indicating sperm: *spermatozoon.* **2.** indicating seed: *spermatophyte.* [< Gk *sperma, spermat-* seed]

spermatocyte (ˈspɜːmətəʊˌsaɪt) *n.* an immature male germ cell.

spermatogenesis (ˌspɜːmətəʊˈdʒɛnɪsɪs) *n.* the formation and maturation of spermatozoa in the testis. —**spermatogenetic** (ˌspɜːmətəʊdʒɪˈnɛtɪk) *adj.*

spermatogonium (ˌspɜːmətəˈgəʊnɪəm) *n., pl.* **-nia** (-nɪə). *Zool.* an immature male germ cell that divides to form many spermatocytes.

spermatophyte (ˈspɜːmətəʊˌfaɪt) *or* **spermophyte** *n.* any seed-bearing plant. Former name: **phanerogam.** —**spermatophytic** (ˌspɜːmətəʊˈfɪtɪk) *adj.*

spermatozoon (ˌspɜːmətəʊˈzəʊɒn) *n., pl.* **-zoa** (-ˈzəʊə). any of the male reproductive cells released in the semen during ejaculation. Also called: **sperm, zoosperm.** —ˌ**spermatoˈzoal,** ˌ**spermatoˈzoan,** *or* ˌ**spermatoˈzoic** *adj.*

spermicide (ˈspɜːmɪˌsaɪd) *n.* any agent that kills spermatozoa. —ˌ**spermiˈcidal** *adj.*

sperm oil *n.* an oil obtained from the head of the sperm whale, used as a lubricant.

spermous (ˈspɜːməs) *adj.* **1.** of or relating to the sperm whale or its products. **2.** another word for **spermatic.**

sperm whale *n.* a large toothed whale, having a square-shaped head and hunted for sperm oil, spermaceti, and ambergris. Also called: **cachalot.** [C19: short for SPERMACETI *whale*]

spew (spjuː) *vb.* **1.** to eject (the contents of the stomach) involuntarily through the mouth; vomit. **2.** to spit (spittle, phlegm, etc.) out of the mouth. **3.** (usually foll. by *out*) to send or be sent out in a stream: *flames spewed out.* ~*n.* **4.** something ejected from the mouth. ~Also (archaic): **spue.** [OE *spīwan*] —ˈ**spewer** *n.*

sp. gr. *abbrev. for* specific gravity.

sphagnum (ˈsfægnəm) *n.* any moss of the genus *Sphagnum,* of temperate bogs: layers of these mosses decay to form peat. Also called: **peat moss, bog moss.** [C18: < NL, < Gk *sphagnos* a variety of moss] —ˈ**sphagnous** *adj.*

sphairee (sfaɪˈriː) *n. Austral.* a game resembling tennis played with wooden bats and a perforated plastic ball. [< Gk *sphaira* a ball]

sphalerite (ˈsfæləˌraɪt, ˈsfeɪlə-) *n.* a yellow to brownish-black mineral consisting mainly of zinc sulphide in cubic crystalline form: the chief source of zinc. Formula: ZnS. Also called: **zinc blende.** [C19: < Gk *sphaleros* deceitful, < *sphallein* to cause to stumble]

sphene (sfiːn) *n.* a brown, yellow, green, or grey lustrous mineral consisting of calcium titanium silicate in monoclinic crystalline form. Also called: **titanite.** [C19: < F *sphène,* < Gk *sphēn* a wedge, alluding to its crystals]

sphenoid (ˈsfiːnɔɪd) *adj. also* **sphenoidal. 1.** wedge-shaped. **2.** of or relating to the sphenoid bone. ~*n.* **3.** See **sphenoid bone.**

sphenoid bone *n.* the large butterfly-shaped compound bone at the base of the skull.

sphere (sfɪə) *n.* **1.** *Maths.* **a.** a three-dimensional closed surface such that every point on the surface is equidistant from a given point, the centre. **b.** the solid figure bounded by this surface or the space enclosed by it. **2.** any object having approximately this shape; a globe. **3.** the night sky considered as a vaulted roof; firmament. **4.** any heavenly object such as a planet, natural satellite, or star. **5.** (in the Ptolemaic or Copernican systems of astronomy) one of a series of revolving hollow globes, arranged concentrically, on whose transparent surfaces the sun, the moon, the planets, and fixed stars were thought to be set. **6.** a particular field of activity; environment. **7.** a social class or stratum of society. ~*vb.* (*tr.*) *Chiefly poetic.* **8.** to surround or encircle. **9.** to place aloft or in the heavens. [C14: < LL *sphēra,* < L *sphaera* globe, < Gk *sphaira*] —ˈ**spheral** *adj.*

-sphere *n. combining form.* **1.** having the shape or form of a sphere: *bathysphere.* **2.** indicating a spherelike enveloping mass: *atmosphere.* —**-spheric** *adj. combining form.*

spherical (ˈsfɛrɪkᵊl) *or* **spheric** *adj.* **1.** shaped like a sphere. **2.** of or relating to a sphere: *spherical geometry.* **3.** *Geom.* formed on the surface of or inside a sphere: *a spherical triangle.* **4. a.** of or relating to heavenly bodies. **b.** of or relating to the spheres of the Ptolemaic or the Copernican system. —ˈ**spherically** *adv.* —ˈ**sphericalness** *n.*

spherical aberration *n. Physics.* a defect of optical systems that arises when light striking a mirror or lens near its edge is focused at different points on the axis to the light striking near the centre. The effect occurs when the mirror or lens has spherical surfaces.

spherical angle *n.* an angle formed at the intersection of two great circles of a sphere.

spherical coordinates *pl. n.* three coordinates that define the location of a point in space in terms of its radius vector, r, the angle, θ, which this vector makes with one axis, and the angle, ϕ, which the plane of this vector makes with a mutually perpendicular axis.

spherical trigonometry *n.* the branch of trigonometry concerned with the measurement of the angles and sides of spherical triangles.

spheroid (ˈsfɪərɔɪd) *n.* **1.** another name for **ellipsoid of revolution.** ~*adj.* **2.** shaped like but not exactly a sphere. —**spherˈoidal** *adj.* —ˌ**spheroidˈicity** *n.*

spherometer (sfɪəˈrɒmɪtə) *n.* an instrument for measuring the curvature of a surface.

spherule (ˈsfɛruːl) *n.* a very small sphere. [C17: < LL *sphaerula*] —ˈ**spherular** *adj.*

spherulite (ˈsfɛrʊˌlaɪt) *n.* any of several spherical masses of radiating needle-like crystals of one or more minerals occurring in rocks such as obsidian. —**spherulitic** (ˌsfɛrʊˈlɪtɪk) *adj.*

sphincter (ˈsfɪŋktə) *n. Anat.* a ring of muscle surrounding the opening of a hollow organ or body and contracting to close it. [C16: < LL, < Gk *sphinkter,* < *sphingein* to grip tightly] —ˈ**sphincteral** *adj.*

sphinx (sfɪŋks) *n., pl.* **sphinxes** *or* **sphinges** (ˈsfɪndʒiːz). **1.** any of a number of huge stone statues built by the ancient Egyptians, having the body of a lion and the head of a man. **2.** an inscrutable person.

Sphinx (sfɪŋks) *n.* **the. 1.** *Greek myth.* a monster with a woman's head and a lion's body. She lay outside Thebes, asking travellers a riddle and killing them when they failed to answer it. Oedipus answered the riddle and the Sphinx then killed herself. **2.** the huge statue of a sphinx near the pyramids at El Gîza in Egypt. [C16: via L < Gk, apparently < *sphingein* to hold fast]

sphragistics (sfrəˈdʒɪstɪks) *n.* (*functioning as sing.*) the study of seals and signet rings. [C19: < Gk *sphragistikos,* < *sphragizein* to seal, < *sphragis* a seal] —**sphraˈgistic** *adj.*

sphygmo- *or before a vowel* **sphygm-** *combining form.* indicating the pulse: *sphygmograph.* [< Gk *sphugmos* pulsation, < *sphuzein* to throb]

sphygmograph (ˈsfɪgməʊˌgrɑːf) *n. Med.* an instrument for making a recording (**sphygmogram**) of variations in blood pressure and pulse. —**sphygmographic** (ˌsfɪgməʊˈgræfɪk) *adj.* —**sphygmography** (sfɪgˈmɒgrəfɪ) *n.*

sphygmomanometer (ˌsfɪgməʊməˈnɒmɪtə) *n.*

Med. an instrument for measuring arterial blood pressure.

spicate (ˈspaɪkeɪt) *adj. Bot.* having, arranged in, or relating to spikes: *a spicate inflorescence.* [C17: < L *spīcātus* having spikes, < *spīca* a point]

spiccato (spɪˈkɑːtəʊ) *Music.* ~*n.* **1.** a style of playing a bowed stringed instrument in which the bow bounces lightly off the strings. ~*adj., adv.* **2.** (to be played) in this manner. [It.: detached]

spice (spaɪs) *n.* **1. a.** any of a variety of aromatic vegetable substances, such as ginger, cinnamon, or nutmeg, used as flavourings. **b.** these substances collectively. **2.** something that represents or introduces zest, charm, or gusto. **3.** *Rare.* a small amount. ~*vb.* (*tr.*) **4.** to prepare or flavour (food) with spices. **5.** to introduce charm or zest into. [C13: < OF *espice,* < LL *speciēs* (pl.) spices, < L *speciēs* (sing.) kind; also associated with LL *spīcea* (unattested) fragrant herb, < L *spīceus* having spikes of foliage]

spicebush (ˈspaɪsˌbʊʃ) *n.* a North American shrub having aromatic leaves and bark.

spick-and-span *or* **spic-and-span** (ˈspɪkənˈspæn) *adj.* **1.** extremely neat and clean. **2.** new and fresh. [C17: shortened < *spick-and-span-new,* < obs. *spick* spike + *span-new,* < ON *spānnȳr* absolutely new]

spicule (ˈspɪkjuːl) *n.* **1.** Also called: **spiculum.** a small slender pointed structure or crystal, esp. any of the calcareous or siliceous elements of the skeleton of sponges, corals, etc. **2.** *Astron.* a spiked ejection of hot gas above the sun's surface. [C18: < L *spiculum* small, sharp point] —**spiculate** (ˈspɪkjʊˌleɪt, -lɪt) *adj.*

spicy (ˈspaɪsɪ) *adj.* **spicier, spiciest. 1.** seasoned with or containing spice. **2.** highly flavoured; pungent. **3.** *Inf.* suggestive of scandal or sensation. —ˈ**spicily** *adv.* —ˈ**spiciness** *n.*

spider (ˈspaɪdə) *n.* **1.** any of various predatory silk-producing arachnids, having four pairs of legs and a rounded unsegmented body. **2.** any of various similar or related arachnids. **3.** any implement or tool having the shape of a spider. **4.** any part of a machine having a number of radiating spokes, tines, or arms. **5.** Also called: **octopus.** *Brit.* a cluster of elastic straps fastened at a central point and used to hold a load on a car rack, motorcycle, etc. **6.** *Snooker, etc.* a rest having long legs, used to raise the cue above the level of the height of the ball. [OE *spīthra*] —ˈ**spidery** *adj.*

spider crab *n.* any of various crabs having a small triangular body and very long legs.

spiderman (ˈspaɪdəˌmæn) *n., pl.* **-men.** *Inf., chiefly Brit.* a person who erects the steel structure of a building.

spider mite *n.* any of various plant-feeding mites, esp. the **red spider mite,** which is a serious orchard pest.

spider monkey *n.* **1.** any of several arboreal New World monkeys of Central and South America, having very long legs, a long prehensile tail, and a small head. **2. woolly spider monkey.** a rare related monkey of SE Brazil.

spider plant *n.* a house plant having long narrow leaves with a light central stripe.

spiderwort (ˈspaɪdəˌwɜːt) *n.* **1.** any of various American plants having blue, purplish, or pink flowers and widely grown as house plants. See also **tradescantia. 2.** any of various similar or related plants.

spiel (ʃpiːl) *n.* **1.** glib plausible talk, associated esp. with salesmen. ~*vb.* **2.** (*intr.*) to deliver a prepared spiel. **3.** (*tr.;* usually foll. by *off*) to recite (a prepared oration). [C19: < G *Spiel* play] —ˈ**spieler** *n.*

spier (ˈspaɪə) *n. Arch.* a person who spies or scouts.

spiffing (ˈspɪfɪŋ) *adj. Brit. sl., old-fashioned.* excellent; splendid. [C19: prob. < dialect *spiff* spruce, smart]

spiffy (ˈspɪfɪ) *adj.* **-fier, -fiest.** *U.S. & Canad. sl.* smart; stylish. [C19: < dialect *spiff* smartly dressed] —ˈ**spiffily** *adv.*

spigot (ˈspɪgət) *n.* **1.** a stopper for the vent hole of a cask. **2.** a tap, usually of wood, fitted to a cask. **3.** a U.S. name for **tap**[2] (sense 1). **4.** a short projection on one component designed to fit into a hole on another, esp. the male part of a joint between two pipes. [C14: prob. < OProvençal *espiga* a head of grain, < L *spīca* a point]

spike[1] (spaɪk) *n.* **1.** a sharp point. **2.** any sharp-pointed object, esp. one made of metal. **3.** a long metal nail. **4.** (*pl.*) shoes with metal projections on the sole and heel for greater traction, as used by athletes. **5.** *Brit. sl.* another word for **dosshouse.** ~*vb.* (*tr.*) **6.** to secure or supply with or as with spikes. **7.** to render ineffective or block the intentions of; thwart. **8.** to impale on a spike. **9.** to add alcohol to (a drink). **10.** *Volleyball.* to hit (a ball) sharply downwards with an overarm motion from the front of one's own court into the opposing court. **11.** (formerly) to render (a cannon) ineffective by blocking its vent with a spike. **12. spike (someone's) guns.** to thwart (someone's) purpose. [C13 *spyk*] —ˈ**spiky** *adj.*

spike[2] (spaɪk) *n. Bot.* **1.** an inflorescence consisting of a raceme of sessile flowers. **2.** an ear of wheat, etc. [C14: < L *spīca* ear of corn]

spikelet (ˈspaɪklɪt) *n. Bot.* a small spike, esp. the inflorescence of most grasses and sedges.

spikenard (ˈspaɪknɑːd, ˈspaɪkəˌnɑːd) *n.* **1.** an aromatic Indian plant, having rose-purple flowers. **2.** an aromatic ointment obtained from this plant. **3.** any of various similar or related plants. **4.** a North American plant having small green flowers and an aromatic root. ~Also called (for senses 1, 2): **nard.** [C14: < Med. L *spīca nardī;* see SPIKE[2], NARD]

spile (spaɪl) *n.* **1.** a heavy timber stake or pile. **2.** *U.S.* a spout for tapping sap from the sugar maple tree. **3.** a plug or spigot. ~*vb.* (*tr.*) **4.** to provide or support with a spile. **5.** *U.S.* to tap (a tree) with a spile. [C16: prob. < MDu. *spile* peg]

spill[1] (spɪl) *vb.* **spilling; spilt** *or* **spilled.** (*mainly tr.*) **1.** (when *intr.,* usually foll. by *from, out of,* etc.) to fall or cause to fall from or as from a container, esp. unintentionally. **2.** to disgorge (contents, occupants, etc.) or (of contents, occupants, etc.) to be disgorged. **3.** to shed (blood). **4.** Also: **spill the beans.** *Inf.* to divulge something confidential. **5.** *Naut.* to let (wind) escape from a sail or (of the wind) to escape from a sail. ~*n.* **6.** *Inf.* a fall or tumble. **7.** short for **spillway. 8.** a spilling of liquid, etc., or the amount spilt. **9.** *Austral.* the declaring of several political jobs vacant when one higher up becomes so. [OE *spillan* to destroy] —ˈ**spillage** *n.* —ˈ**spiller** *n.*

spill[2] (spɪl) *n.* a splinter of wood or strip of twisted paper with which pipes, fires, etc., are lit. [C13: of Gmc origin]

spillikin, spilikin (ˈspɪlɪkɪn), *or* **spellican** (ˈspɛlɪkən) *n.* a thin strip of wood, cardboard, or plastic, esp. one used in spillikins.

spillikins (ˈspɪlɪkɪnz) *n.* (*functioning as sing.*) *Brit.* a game in which players try to pick each spillikin from a heap without moving any of the others. Also called: **jackstraws.**

spill over *vb.* **1.** (*intr., adv.*) to overflow or be forced out of an area, container, etc. ~*n.* **spillover.** *Chiefly U.S. & Canad.* **2.** the act of spilling over. **3.** the excess part of something.

spillway (ˈspɪlˌweɪ) *n.* a channel that carries away surplus water, as from a dam.

spilt (spɪlt) *vb.* a past tense and past participle of **spill**[1].

spin (spɪn) *vb.* **spinning, spun. 1.** to rotate or cause to rotate rapidly, as on an axis. **2. a.** to draw out and twist (natural fibres, as of silk or cotton) into a long continuous thread. **b.** to make such a thread or filament from (synthetic resins, etc.), usually by forcing through a nozzle. **3.** (of spiders, silkworms, etc.) to form (webs, cocoons, etc.) from a silky fibre exuded from the body. **4.** (*tr.*) to shape (metal) into a rounded form on a lathe. **5.** (*tr.*) *Inf.* to tell (a tale, story, etc.) by drawing it out at great length (esp. in **spin a yarn**). **6.** to bowl, pitch, hit, or kick (a ball) so that it rotates in the air and changes direction or speed on bouncing, or (of a ball) to be projected in this way. **7.** (*intr.*) (of wheels) to revolve rapidly without causing propulsion. **8.** to cause (an aircraft) to dive in a spiral descent or (of an aircraft) to dive in a spiral descent. **9.** (*intr.*; foll. by *along*) to drive or travel swiftly. **10.** (*tr.*) Also: **spin-dry.** to rotate (clothes) in a washing machine in order to extract surplus water. **11.** (*intr.*) to reel or grow dizzy, as from turning around: *my head is spinning.* **12.** (*intr.*) to fish by drawing a revolving lure through the water. ~*n.* **13.** a swift rotating motion; instance of spinning. **14.** *Physics.* **a.** the intrinsic angular momentum of an elementary particle or atomic nucleus. **b.** a quantum number determining values of this angular momentum. **15.** a condition of loss of control of an aircraft or an intentional flight manoeuvre in which the aircraft performs a continuous spiral descent. **16.** a spinning motion imparted to a ball, etc. **17.** *Inf.* a short or fast drive, ride, etc., esp. in a car, for pleasure. **18.** **flat spin.** *Inf., chiefly Brit.* a state of agitation or confusion. **19.** *Austral. & N.Z. inf.* a period of a specified kind of fortune: *a bad spin.* ~See also **spin out.** [OE *spinnan*]

spina bifida (ˈspaɪnə ˈbɪfɪdə) *n.* a congenital condition in which the meninges of the spinal cord protrude through a gap in the backbone, sometimes causing enlargement of the skull and paralysis. [NL; see SPINE, BIFID]

spinach (ˈspɪnɪdʒ, -ɪtʃ) *n.* **1.** an annual plant cultivated for its dark green edible leaves. **2.** the leaves, eaten as a vegetable. [C16: < OF *espinache,* < OSp., < Ar. *isfānākh,* < Persian]

spinal (ˈspaɪnᵊl) *adj.* **1.** of or relating to the spine or the spinal cord. ~*n.* **2.** short for **spinal anaesthesia.** —ˈ**spinally** *adv.*

spinal anaesthesia *n.* **1.** anaesthesia of the lower half of the body produced by injecting an anaesthetic beneath the arachnoid membrane. **2.** loss of sensation in part of the body as the result of injury of the spinal cord.

spinal canal *n.* the passage through the spinal column that contains the spinal cord.

spinal column *n.* a series of contiguous or interconnecting bony or cartilaginous segments that surround and protect the spinal cord. Also called: **spine, vertebral column.** Nontechnical name: **backbone.**

spinal cord *n.* the thick cord of nerve tissue within the spinal canal, which together with the brain forms the central nervous system.

spin bowler *n.* another name for **spinner** (sense 2).

spindle (ˈspɪndᵊl) *n.* **1.** a rod or stick that has a notch in the top, used to draw out natural fibres for spinning into thread, and a long narrow body around which the thread is wound when spun. **2.** one of the thin rods or pins bearing bobbins upon which spun thread is wound in a spinning machine. **3.** any of various parts in the form of a rod, esp. a rotating rod that acts as an axle, etc. **4.** a piece of wood that has been turned, such as a table leg. **5.** a small square metal shaft that passes through the lock of a door and to which the door knobs or handles are fixed. **6.** *Biol.* a spindle-shaped structure formed in a cell during mitosis or meiosis which draws the duplicated chromosomes apart during cell division. **7.** a device consisting of a sharp upright spike on a pedestal on which bills, order forms, etc., are impaled. ~*vb.* **8.** (*tr.*) to form into a spindle or equip with spindles. **9.** (*intr.*) *Rare.* (of a plant, stem, shoot, etc.) to grow rapidly and become elongated and thin. [OE *spinel*]

spindlelegs (ˈspɪndᵊlˌlɛgz) *or* **spindleshanks** *n.* **1.** (*functioning as pl.*) long thin legs. **2.** (*functioning as sing.*) a person who has such legs.

spindle tree *n.* any of various shrubs or trees of Europe and W Asia, typically having red fruits and yielding a hard wood formerly used in making spindles.

spindly (ˈspɪndlɪ) *adj.* **-dlier, -dliest.** tall, slender, and frail; attenuated.

spindrift (ˈspɪnˌdrɪft) *n.* spray blown up from the sea. Also: **spoondrift.** [C16: Scot. var. of *spoondrift,* < *spoon* to scud + DRIFT]

spin-dry *vb.* **-drying, -dried.** (*tr.*) to dry (clothes, etc.) in a spin-dryer.

spin-dryer *n.* a device that extracts water from clothes, etc., by spinning them in a perforated drum.

spine (spaɪn) *n.* **1.** the spinal column. **2.** the sharply pointed tip or outgrowth of a leaf, stem, etc. **3.** *Zool.* a hard pointed process or structure, such as the quill of a porcupine. **4.** the back of a book, record sleeve, etc. **5.** a ridge, esp. of a hill. **6.** strength of endurance, will, etc. **7.** anything resembling the spinal column in function or importance; main support or feature. [C14: < OF *espine* spine, < L *spīna* thorn, backbone] —**spined** *adj.*

spine-chiller *n.* a book, film, etc., that arouses terror. —ˈ**spine-**ˌ**chilling** *adj.*

spinel (spɪˈnɛl) *n.* any of a group of hard glassy minerals of variable colour consisting of oxides of aluminium, magnesium, iron, zinc, or manganese: used as gemstones. [C16: < F *spinelle,* < It. *spinella,* dim. of *spina* a thorn, < L; so called from the shape of the crystals]

spineless (ˈspaɪnlɪs) *adj.* **1.** lacking a backbone. **2.** having no spiny processes: *spineless stems.* **3.** lacking character, resolution, or courage. —ˈ**spinelessly** *adv.* —ˈ**spinelessness** *n.*

spinet (spɪˈnɛt, ˈspɪnɪt) *n.* a small type of harpsichord having one manual. [C17: < It. *spinetta,* ? < Giovanni *Spinetti,* 16th-cent. It. maker of musical instruments & its supposed inventor]

spinifex (ˈspɪnɪˌfɛks) *n.* **1.** any of various Australian grasses having pointed leaves and spiny seed heads. **2.** Also called: **porcupine grass.** *Austral.* any of various coarse spiny-leaved inland grasses. [C19: < NL, < L *spīna* a thorn + *-fex* maker, < *facere* to make]

spinnaker (ˈspɪnəkə; *Naut.* ˈspæŋkə) *n.* a large light triangular racing sail set from the foremast of a yacht. [C19: prob. < SPIN + (MO)NIKER, but traditionally < *Sphinx,* the yacht that first adopted this type of sail]

spinner (ˈspɪnə) *n.* **1.** a person or thing that spins. **2.** *Cricket.* **a.** a ball that is bowled with a spinning motion. **b.** a bowler who specializes in bowling such balls. **3.** a streamlined fairing that fits over the hub of an aircraft propeller. **4.** a fishing lure with a fin or wing that revolves.

spinneret (ˈspɪnəˌrɛt) *n.* **1.** any of several organs in spiders and certain insects through which silk threads are exuded. **2.** a finely perforated dispenser through which a liquid is extruded in the production of synthetic fibres.

spinney (ˈspɪnɪ) *n. Chiefly Brit.* a small wood or copse. [C16: < OF *espinei,* < *espine* thorn, < L *spīna*]

spinning (ˈspɪnɪŋ) *n.* **1.** the act or process of spinning. **2.** the act or technique of casting and drawing a revolving lure through the water so as to imitate a live fish, etc.

spinning jenny *n.* an early type of spinning frame with several spindles, invented in 1764.

spinning wheel *n.* a wheel-like machine for spinning at home, having one hand- or foot-operated spindle.

spin-off *n.* any product or development derived incidentally from the application of existing knowledge or enterprise.

spinose (ˈspaɪnəʊs, spaɪˈnəʊs) *adj.* (esp. of plants) bearing many spines. [C17: < L *spīnōsus* prickly, < *spīna* a thorn]

spin out *vb.* (*tr., adv.*) **1.** to extend or protract (a story, etc.) by including superfluous detail. **2.** to spend or pass (time). **3.** to contrive to cause (money, etc.) to last as long as possible.

spinster (ˈspɪnstə) *n.* **1.** an unmarried woman. **2.** a woman regarded as being beyond the age of marriage. **3.** (formerly) a woman who spins thread for her living. [C14 (in the sense: a person, esp. a woman, whose occupation is spinning; C17: a woman still unmarried): < SPIN + -STER] —ˈ**spinster**ˌ**hood** *n.* —ˈ**spinsterish** *adj.*

spiny (ˈspaɪnɪ) *adj.* **spinier, spiniest.** **1.** (of animals) having or covered with quills or spines. **2.** (of plants) covered with spines; thorny. **3.** troublesome; puzzling. —ˈ**spininess** *n.*

spiny anteater *n.* another name for **echidna.**

spiny-finned *adj.* (of certain fishes) having fins that are supported by stiff bony spines.

spiny lobster *n.* any of various large edible marine decapod crustaceans having a very tough spiny carapace. Also called: **rock lobster, crawfish, langouste.**

spiracle (ˈspaɪərəkᵊl, ˈspaɪrə-) *n.* **1.** any of several paired apertures in the cuticle of an insect, by which air enters and leaves the trachea. **2.** a small paired rudimentary gill slit in skates, rays, and related fishes. **3.** any similar respiratory aperture, such as the blowhole in whales. [C14 (orig.: breath): < L *spīrāculum* vent, < *spīrāre* to breathe] —**spiracular** (spɪˈrækjʊlə) *adj.* —**spiˈraculate** *adj.*

spiraea *or esp. U.S.* **spirea** (spaɪˈrɪə) *n.* any of various rosaceous plants having sprays of small white or pink flowers. See also **meadowsweet** (sense 2). [C17: via L < Gk *speiraia*, < *speira* SPIRE[2]]

spiral (ˈspaɪərəl) *n.* **1.** *Geom.* one of several plane curves formed by a point winding about a fixed point at an ever-increasing distance from it. **2.** a curve that lies on a cylinder or cone, at a constant angle to the line segments making up the surface; helix. **3.** something that pursues a winding, usually upward, course or that displays a twisting form or shape. **4.** a flight manoeuvre in which an aircraft descends describing a helix of comparatively large radius with the angle of attack within the normal flight range. **5.** *Econ.* a continuous upward or downward movement in economic activity or prices, caused by interaction between prices, wages, demand, and production. ~*adj.* **6.** having the shape of a spiral. ~*vb.* **-ralling, -ralled** *or U.S.* **-raling, -raled. 7.** to assume or cause to assume a spiral course or shape. **8.** (*intr.*) to increase or decrease with steady acceleration: *prices continue to spiral.* [C16: via F < Med. L *spīrālis*, < L *spīra* a coil; see SPIRE[2]] —ˈ**spirally** *adv.*

spiral galaxy *n.* a galaxy consisting of an ellipsoidal nucleus of old stars from opposite sides of which arms, containing younger stars, spiral outwards around the nucleus.

spirant (ˈspaɪrənt) *adj.* **1.** *Phonetics.* another word for **fricative.** ~*n.* **2.** a fricative consonant. [C19: < L *spīrāns* breathing, < *spīrāre* to breathe]

spire[1] (ˈspaɪə) *n.* **1.** Also called: **steeple.** a tall structure that tapers upwards to a point, esp. one on a tower or roof or one that forms the upper part of a steeple. **2.** a slender tapering shoot or stem, such as a blade of grass. **3.** the apical part of any tapering formation; summit. ~*vb.* **4.** (*intr.*) to assume the shape of a spire; point up. **5.** (*tr.*) to furnish with a spire or spires. [OE *spīr* blade] —ˈ**spiry** *adj.*

spire[2] (ˈspaɪə) *n.* **1.** any of the coils or turns in a spiral structure. **2.** the apical part of a spiral shell. [C16: < L *spīra* a coil, < Gk *speira*]

spirillum (spaɪˈrɪləm) *n., pl.* **-la** (-lə). **1.** any bacterium having a curved or spirally twisted rodlike body. **2.** any bacterium of the genus *Spirillum*, such as *S. minus*, which causes ratbite fever. [C19: < NL, lit.: a little coil, < *spīra* a coil]

spirit[1] (ˈspɪrɪt) *n.* **1.** the force or principle of life that animates the body of living things. **2.** temperament or disposition: *truculent in spirit.* **3.** liveliness; mettle: *they set to it with spirit.* **4.** the fundamental, emotional, and activating principle of a person; will: *the experience broke his spirit.* **5.** a sense of loyalty or dedication: *team spirit.* **6.** the prevailing element; feeling: *a spirit of joy pervaded the atmosphere.* **7.** state of mind or mood; attitude: *he did it in the wrong spirit.* **8.** (*pl.*) an emotional state, esp. with regard to exaltation or dejection: *in high spirits.* **9.** a person characterized by some activity, quality, or disposition: *a leading spirit of the movement.* **10.** the deeper more significant meaning as opposed to a pedantic interpretation: *the spirit of the law.* **11.** a person's intangible being as contrasted with his physical presence: *I shall be with you in spirit.* **12. a.** an incorporeal being, esp. the soul of a dead person. **b.** (*as modifier*): *spirit world.* ~*vb.* (*tr.*) **13.** (usually foll. by *away* or *off*) to carry off mysteriously or secretly. **14.** (often foll. by *up*) to impart animation or determination to. [C13: < OF *esperit*, < L *spīritus* breath, spirit] —ˈ**spiritless** *adj.*

spirit[2] (ˈspɪrɪt) *n.* **1.** (*often pl.*) any distilled alcoholic liquor, such as whisky or gin. **2.** *Chem.* **a.** an aqueous solution of ethanol, esp. one obtained by distillation. **b.** the active principle or essence of a substance, extracted as a liquid, esp. by distillation. **3.** *Pharmacol.* a solution of a volatile substance, esp. a volatile oil, in alcohol. **4.** *Alchemy.* any of the four substances sulphur, mercury, sal ammoniac, or arsenic. [C14: special use of SPIRIT[1], name applied to alchemical substances (as in sense 4), hence extended to distilled liquids]

Spirit (ˈspɪrɪt) *n.* **the. a.** another name for the **Holy Spirit. b.** God, esp. when regarded as transcending material limitations.

spirited (ˈspɪrɪtɪd) *adj.* **1.** displaying animation, vigour, or liveliness. **2.** (*in combination*) characterized by mood, temper, or disposition as specified: *high-spirited; public-spirited.* —ˈ**spiritedly** *adv.* —ˈ**spiritedness** *n.*

spirit gum *n.* a glue made from gum dissolved in ether used to affix a false beard, etc.

spiritism (ˈspɪrɪˌtɪzəm) *n.* a less common word for **spiritualism.** —ˈ**spiritist** *n.* —ˌ**spiritˈistic** *adj.*

spirit lamp *n.* a lamp that burns methylated or other spirits instead of oil.

spirit level *n.* a device for setting horizontal surfaces, consisting of a block of material in which a sealed tube partially filled with liquid is set so that the air bubble rests between two marks on the tube when the block is horizontal.

spiritous (ˈspɪrɪtəs) *adj.* a variant spelling of **spirituous.**

spirits of ammonia *n.* (*functioning as sing. or pl.*) another name for **sal volatile.**

spirits of hartshorn *n.* (*functioning as sing. or pl.*) a solution of ammonia gas in water. See **ammonium hydroxide.** Also called: **aqueous ammonia.**

spirits of salt *n.* (*functioning as sing. or pl.*) a solution of hydrochloric acid in water.

spiritual (ˈspɪrɪtjʊəl) *adj.* **1.** relating to the spirit or soul and not to physical nature or matter; intangible. **2.** of or relating to sacred things, the Church, religion, etc. **3.** standing in a relationship based on communication between souls or minds: *a spiritual father.* **4.** having a mind or emotions of a high and delicately refined quality. ~*n.* **5.** Also called: **Negro spiritual.** a type of religious song originating among Black slaves in the American South. **6.** (*often pl.*) the sphere of religious, spiritual, or ecclesiastical matters, or such matters in themselves. —ˌ**spirituˈality** *n.* —ˈ**spiritually** *adv.*

spiritualism (ˈspɪrɪtjʊəˌlɪzəm) *n.* **1.** the belief that the disembodied spirits of the dead, surviving in another world, can communicate with the living in this world, esp. through mediums. **2.** the doctrines and practices associated with this belief. **3.** *Philosophy.* the belief that because reality is to some extent immaterial it is therefore spiritual. **4.** any doctrine that prefers the spiritual to the material. —ˈ**spiritualist** *n.*

spiritualize *or* **-ise** (ˈspɪrɪtjʊəˌlaɪz) *vb.* (*tr.*) to make spiritual or infuse with spiritual content. —ˌ**spiritualiˈzation** *or* **-iˈsation** *n.* —ˈ**spiritualˌizer** *or* **-ˌiser** *n.*

spirituel (ˌspɪrɪtjʊˈɛl) *adj.* having a refined and lively mind or wit. Also (fem.): **spirituelle.** [C17: < F]

spirituous (ˈspɪrɪtjʊəs) *adj.* **1.** characterized by or containing alcohol. **2.** (of a drink) being a spirit. —**spirituosity** (ˌspɪrɪtjʊˈɒsɪtɪ) *or* ˈ**spirituousness** *n.*

spirochaete *or U.S.* **spirochete** (ˈspaɪrəʊˌkiːt) *n.*

any of a group of spirally coiled rodlike bacteria that includes the causative agent of syphilis. [C19: < NL, < *spiro-*, < L *spira*, < Gk *speira* a coil + *chaeta*, < Gk *khaitē* long hair]

spirograph (ˈspaɪrəˌgrɑːf) *n. Med.* an instrument for recording the movements of breathing. [C20: NL, < *spiro-*, < L *spīrāre* to breathe + -GRAPH] —ˌ**spiroˈgraphic** *adj.*

spirogyra (ˌspaɪrəˈdʒaɪrə) *n.* any of various green freshwater multicellular algae containing spirally coiled chloroplasts. [C20: < NL, < *spiro-*, < L *spīra*, < Gk *speira* a coil + Gk *guros* a circle]

spirt (spɜːt) *n.* a variant spelling of **spurt.**

spiry (ˈspaɪərɪ) *adj. Poetic.* of spiral form; helical.

spit[1] (spɪt) *vb.* **spitting, spat** *or* **spit. 1.** (*intr.*) to expel saliva from the mouth; expectorate. **2.** (*intr.*) *Inf.* to show disdain or hatred by spitting. **3.** (of a fire, hot fat, etc.) to eject (sparks, etc.) violently and with an explosive sound. **4.** (*intr.*) to rain very lightly. **5.** (*tr.*; often foll. by *out*) to eject or discharge (something) from the mouth: *he spat the food out.* **6.** (*tr.*; often foll. by *out*) to utter (short sharp words or syllables), esp. in a violent manner. **7. spit it out!** *Brit. inf.* a command given to someone that he should speak forthwith. ~*n.* **8.** another name for **spittle. 9.** a light or brief fall of rain, snow, etc. **10.** the act or an instance of spitting. **11.** *Inf., chiefly Brit.* another word for **spitting image.** [OE *spittan*] —ˈ**spitter** *n.*

spit[2] (spɪt) *n.* **1.** a pointed rod on which meat is skewered and roasted before or over an open fire. **2.** Also called: **rotisserie, rotating spit.** a similar device fitted onto a cooker. **3.** an elongated often hooked strip of sand or shingle projecting from a shore. ~*vb.* **spitting, spitted. 4.** (*tr.*) to impale on or transfix with or as if with a spit. [OE *spitu*]

spit and polish *n. Inf.* punctilious attention to neatness, discipline, etc., esp. in the armed forces.

spite (spaɪt) *n.* **1.** maliciousness; venomous ill will. **2.** an instance of such malice; grudge. **3. in spite of.** (*prep.*) in defiance of; regardless of; notwithstanding. ~*vb.* (*tr.*) **4.** to annoy in order to vent spite. [C13: var. of DESPITE] —ˈ**spiteful** *adj.*

spitfire (ˈspɪtˌfaɪə) *n.* a person given to outbursts of spiteful temper, esp. a woman or girl.

spitting image *n. Inf.* a person who bears a strong physical resemblance to another. Also called: **spit, spit and image.** [C19: modification of *spit and image*, < SPIT[1] (as in *the very spit of* the exact likeness of)]

spitting snake *n.* another name for the **ringhals.**

spittle (ˈspɪtᵊl) *n.* **1.** the fluid secreted in the mouth; saliva. **2.** Also called: **cuckoo spit, frog spit.** the frothy substance secreted on plants by the larvae of certain froghoppers. [OE *spǣtl* saliva]

spittoon (spɪˈtuːn) *n.* a receptacle for spittle, usually in a public place.

spitz (spɪts) *n.* any of various breeds of dog characterized by a stocky build, a pointed muzzle, erect ears, and a tightly-curled tail. [C19: < G *Spitz*, < *spitz* pointed]

spiv (spɪv) *n. Brit. sl.* a person who makes a living by underhand dealings or swindling; black marketeer. [C20: back formation < dialect *spiving* smart] —ˈ**spivvy** *adj.*

splake (spleɪk) *n.* a type of hybrid trout bred by Canadian zoologists. [< *sp(eckled)* + *lake (trout)*]

splanchnic (ˈsplæŋknɪk) *adj.* of or relating to the viscera: *a splanchnic nerve.* [C17: < NL *splanchnicus*, < Gk, < *splankhna* the entrails]

splash (splæʃ) *vb.* **1.** to scatter (liquid) about in blobs; spatter. **2.** to descend or cause to descend upon in scattered blobs: *he splashed his jacket; rain splashed against the window.* **3.** to make (one's way) by or as if by splashing: *he splashed through the puddle.* **4.** (*tr.*) to print (a story or photograph) prominently in a newspaper. ~*n.* **5.** an instance or sound of splashing. **6.** an amount splashed. **7.** a mark or patch created by or as if by splashing. **8.** *Inf.* an extravagant display, usually for effect (esp. in **make a splash**). **9.** a small amount of soda water, etc., added to an alcoholic drink. [C18: alteration of PLASH] —ˈ**splashy** *adj.*

splashdown (ˈsplæʃˌdaʊn) *n.* **1.** the controlled landing of a spacecraft on water at the end of a space flight. **2.** the time scheduled for this event. ~*vb.* **splash down. 3.** (*intr., adv.*) (of a spacecraft) to make a splashdown.

splat[1] (splæt) *n.* a wet slapping sound. [C19: imit.]

splat[2] (splæt) *n.* a wide flat piece of wood, esp. one that is the upright central part of a chair back. [C19: ? rel. to OE *splātan* to split]

splatter (ˈsplætə) *vb.* **1.** to splash with small blobs. ~*n.* **2.** a splash of liquid, mud, etc.

splay (spleɪ) *adj.* **1.** spread out; broad and flat. **2.** turned outwards in an awkward manner. ~*vb.* **3.** to spread out; turn out or expand. ~*n.* **4.** a surface of a wall that forms an oblique angle to the main flat surfaces, esp. at a doorway or window opening. [C14: short for DISPLAY]

splayfoot (ˈspleɪˌfʊt) *n., pl.* **-feet.** *Pathol.* another word for **flatfoot.** —ˈ**splayˌfooted** *adj.*

spleen (spliːn) *n.* **1.** a spongy highly vascular organ situated near the stomach in man. It forms lymphocytes, produces antibodies, and filters bacteria and foreign particles from the blood. **2.** the corresponding organ in other animals. **3.** spitefulness or ill humour: *to vent one's spleen.* **4.** *Arch.* the organ in the human body considered to be the seat of the emotions. **5.** *Arch.* another word for **melancholy.** [C13: < OF *esplen*, < L *splēn*, < Gk] —ˈ**spleenish** *or* ˈ**spleeny** *adj.*

spleenwort (ˈspliːnˌwɜːt) *n.* any of various ferns that often grow on walls.

splendent (ˈsplɛndənt) *adj. Arch.* **1.** shining brightly; lustrous: *a splendent sun.* **2.** famous; illustrious. [C15: < L *splendēns* brilliant, < *splendēre* to shine]

splendid (ˈsplɛndɪd) *adj.* **1.** brilliant or fine, esp. in appearance. **2.** characterized by magnificence. **3.** glorious or illustrious: *a splendid reputation.* **4.** brightly gleaming; radiant: *splendid colours.* **5.** very good or satisfactory: *a splendid time.* [C17: < L *splendidus*, < *splendēre* to shine] —ˈ**splendidly** *adv.* —ˈ**splendidness** *n.*

splendiferous (splɛnˈdɪfərəs) *adj. Facetious.* grand; splendid: *a really splendiferous meal.* [C15: < Med. L *splendiferus*, < L *splendor* radiance + *ferre* to bring]

splendour *or U.S.* **splendor** (ˈsplɛndə) *n.* **1.** the state or quality of being splendid. **2. sun in splendour.** *Heraldry.* a representation of the sun with rays and a human face.

splenetic (splɪˈnɛtɪk) *adj.* **1.** of or relating to the spleen. **2.** spiteful or irritable; peevish. ~*n.* **3.** a spiteful or irritable person. —**spleˈnetically** *adv.*

splenic (ˈsplɛnɪk, ˈspliː-) *adj.* **1.** of, relating to, or in the spleen. **2.** having a disease or disorder of the spleen.

splenius (ˈspliːnɪəs) *n., pl.* **-nii** (-nɪˌaɪ). either of two muscles at the back of the neck that rotate, flex, and extend the head and neck. [C18: via NL < Gk *splēnion* a plaster] —ˈ**splenial** *adj.*

splenomegaly (ˌspliːnəʊˈmɛgəlɪ) *n.* abnormal enlargement of the spleen. [C20: NL, < Gk *splēn* spleen + *megal-*, stem of *megas* big]

splice (splaɪs) *vb.* (*tr.*) **1.** to join (two ropes) by intertwining the strands. **2.** to join up the trimmed ends of (two pieces of wire, film, etc.) with solder or an adhesive material. **3.** to join (timbers) by overlapping and binding or bolting the ends together. **4.** (*passive*) *Inf.* to enter into marriage: *the couple got spliced.* **5. splice the mainbrace.** *Naut.* to issue and partake of an extra allocation of alcoholic spirits. ~*n.* **6.** a join made by splicing. **7.** the place where such a join occurs. **8.** the wedge-shaped end of a cricket-bat handle that fits into the blade. [C16: prob. < MDu. *splissen*] —ˈ**splicer** *n.*

spline (splaɪn) *n.* **1.** any one of a series of narrow keys formed longitudinally around a shaft that fit into corresponding grooves in a mating part: used to prevent movement between two parts, esp. in transmitting torque. **2.** a long narrow strip of wood, metal, etc.; slat. **3.** a thin narrow strip made of wood, metal, or plastic fitted into a groove in the edge of a board, tile, etc., to connect it to another. ~*vb.* **4.** (*tr.*) to provide (a shaft, part, etc.) with splines. [C18: East Anglian dialect; ? rel. to OE *splin* spindle]

splint (splɪnt) *n.* **1.** a rigid support for restricting movement of an injured part, esp. a broken bone. **2.** a thin sliver of wood, esp. one used to light cigars, a fire, etc. **3.** a thin strip of wood woven with others to form a chair seat, basket, etc. **4.** *Vet. science.* a bony enlargement of the cannon bone of a horse. ~*vb.* **5.** to apply a splint to (a broken arm, etc.). [C13: < MLow G *splinte*]

splinter (ˈsplɪntə) *n.* **1.** a small thin sharp piece of wood, glass, etc., broken off from a whole. **2.** a metal fragment from a shell, bomb, etc., thrown out during an explosion. ~*vb.* **3.** to reduce or be reduced to sharp fragments. **4.** to break or be broken off in small sharp fragments. [C14: < MDu. *splinter;* see SPLINT] —ˈ**splintery** *adj.*

splinter group *n.* a number of members of an organization, political party, etc., who split from the main body and form an independent association of their own.

split (splɪt) *vb.* **splitting, split. 1.** to break or cause to break, esp. forcibly, by cleaving into separate pieces, often into two roughly equal pieces. **2.** to separate or be separated from a whole: *he split a piece of wood from the block.* **3.** to separate or be separated into factions, usually through discord. **4.** (often foll. by *up*) to separate or cause to separate through a disagreement. **5.** (when *tr.*, often foll. by *up*) to divide or be divided among two or more persons: *split up the pie among us.* **6.** *Sl.* to depart; leave: *let's split.* **7.** (*tr.*) to separate (something) into its components by interposing something else: *to split a word with hyphens.* **8.** (*intr.;* usually foll. by *on*) *Sl.* to betray; inform: *he split on me to the cops.* **9.** (*tr.*) *U.S. politics.* to mark (a ballot, etc.) so as to vote for the candidates of more than one party: *he split the ticket.* **10. split one's sides.** to laugh very heartily. ~*n.* **11.** the act or process of splitting. **12.** a gap or rift caused or a piece removed by the process of splitting. **13.** a breach or schism in a group or the faction resulting from such a breach. **14.** a dessert of sliced fruit and ice cream, covered with whipped cream, nuts, etc.: *banana split.* **15.** See **Devonshire split. 16.** *Tenpin bowling.* a formation of the pins after the first bowl in which there is a large gap between two pins or groups of pins. **17.** *Inf.* an arrangement or process of dividing up loot or money. ~*adj.* **18.** having been split; divided: *split logs.* **19.** having a split or splits: *hair with split ends.* ~See also **splits, split up.** [C16: < MDu. *splitten* to cleave] —ˈ**splitter** *n.*

split infinitive *n.* (in English grammar) an infinitive used with another word between *to* and the verb itself, as in *to really finish it.*

▷ **Usage.** The traditional rule against placing an adverb between *to* and its verb is gradually disappearing. Although it is true that a split infinitive may result in a clumsy sentence, this is not enough to justify the absolute condemnation that this practice has attracted. Indeed, very often the most natural position of the adverb is between *to* and the verb (*he decided to really try*) and to change it would result in an artificial and awkward construction (*he really decided to try*). The current view is therefore that the split infinitive is not a grammatical error. Nevertheless, many writers prefer to avoid splitting infinitives in formal English, since readers with a more traditional point of view are likely to interpret this as incorrect.

split-level *adj.* (of a house, room, etc.) having the floor level of one part about half a storey above the floor level of an adjoining part.

split pea *n.* a pea dried and split and used in soups, pease pudding, or as a vegetable.

split personality *n.* **1.** the tendency to change rapidly in mood or temperament. **2.** a nontechnical term for **multiple personality.**

splits (splɪts) *n.* (*functioning as sing.*) (in gymnastics, etc.) the act of sinking to the floor to achieve a sitting position in which both legs are straight, pointing in opposite directions, and at right angles to the body.

split-screen technique *n.* a cinematic device by which two or more complete images are projected simultaneously onto separate parts of the screen. Also called: **split screen.**

split second *n.* **1.** an infinitely small period of time; instant. ~*adj.* **split-second.** (*prenominal*) **2.** made or arrived at in an infinitely short time: *a split-second decision.* **3.** depending upon minute precision: *split-second timing.*

split shift *n.* a work period divided into two parts that are separated by an interval longer than a normal rest period.

splitting (ˈsplɪtɪŋ) *adj.* **1.** (of a headache) intolerably painful; acute. **2.** (of the head) assailed by an overpowering unbearable pain.

split up *vb.* (*adv.*) **1.** (*tr.*) to separate out into parts; divide. **2.** (*intr.*) to become parted through disagreement: *they split up after years of marriage.* **3.** to break down or be capable of being broken down into constituent parts. ~*n.* **split-up. 4.** the act or an instance of separating.

splodge (splɒdʒ) *n.* **1.** a large irregular spot or blot. ~*vb.* **2.** (*tr.*) to mark (something) with such a blot or blots. [C19: alteration of earlier SPLOTCH] —ˈ**splodgy** *adj.*

splotch (splɒtʃ) *n., vb.* the usual U.S. word for **splodge.** [C17: ? a blend of SPOT + BLOTCH] —ˈ**splotchy** *adj.*

splurge (splɜːdʒ) *n.* **1.** an ostentatious display, esp. of wealth. **2.** a bout of unrestrained extravagance. ~*vb.* **3.** (often foll. by *on*) to spend (money) extravagantly. [C19: <?]

splutter (ˈsplʌtə) *vb.* **1.** to spit out (saliva, food particles, etc.) from the mouth in an explosive manner, as through choking or laughing. **2.** to utter (words) with spitting sounds, as through rage or choking. **3.** to eject or be ejected in an explosive manner: *sparks spluttered from the fire.* **4.** (*tr.*) to bespatter (a person) with tiny particles explosively ejected. ~*n.* **5.** the process or noise of spluttering. **6.** spluttering incoherent speech. **7.** anything ejected through spluttering. [C17: var. of SPUTTER, infl. by SPLASH] —ˈ**splutterer** *n.*

spode (spəʊd) *n.* (*sometimes cap.*) china or porcelain manufactured by Josiah Spode (1754–1827), English potter, or his company.

spoil (spɔɪl) *vb.* **spoiling, spoilt** *or* **spoiled. 1.** (*tr.*) to cause damage to (something), in regard to its value, beauty, usefulness, etc. **2.** (*tr.*) to weaken the character of (a child) by complying unrestrainedly with its desires. **3.** (*intr.*) (of perishable substances) to become unfit for consumption or use. **4.** (*intr.*) *Sport.* to disrupt the play or style of an opponent, as to prevent him from settling into a rhythm. **5.** *Arch.* to strip (a person or place) of (property) by force. **6. be spoiling for.** to have an aggressive desire for (a fight, etc.). ~*n.* **7.** waste material thrown up by an excavation. **8.** any treasure accumulated by a person. **9.** *Obs.* the act of plundering. ~See **spoils.** [C13: < OF *espoillier,* < L *spoliāre* to strip, < *spolium* booty]

spoilage (ˈspɔɪlɪdʒ) *n.* **1.** the act or an instance of spoiling or the state or condition of being spoilt. **2.** an amount of material that has been wasted by being spoilt: *considerable spoilage.*

spoiler (ˈspɔɪlə) *n.* **1.** a plunderer or robber. **2.** a person or thing that causes spoilage or corruption. **3.** a device fitted to an aircraft wing to increase drag and reduce lift. **4.** a similar device fitted to a car. **5.** *Sport.* a competitor who adopts spoiling tactics.

spoils (spɔɪlz) *pl. n.* **1.** (*sometimes sing.*) valuables seized by violence, esp. in war. **2.** *Chiefly U.S.* the rewards and benefits of public office regarded as plunder for the winning party or candidate. See also **spoils system.**

spoilsport (ˈspɔɪlˌspɔːt) *n. Inf.* a person who spoils the pleasure of other people.

spoils system *n. Chiefly U.S.* the practice of filling appointive public offices with friends and supporters of the ruling political party.

spoilt (spɔɪlt) *vb.* a past tense and past participle of **spoil.**

spoke[1] (spəʊk) *vb.* **1.** the past tense of **speak. 2.** *Arch. or dialect.* a past participle of **speak.**

spoke[2] (spəʊk) *n.* **1.** a radial member of a wheel, joining the hub to the rim. **2.** a radial projection from the rim of a wheel, as in a ship's wheel. **3.** a rung of a ladder. **4. put a spoke in someone's wheel.** *Brit.* to thwart someone's plans. ~*vb.* **5.** (*tr.*) to equip with or as if with spokes. [OE *spaca*]

spoken (ˈspəʊkən) *vb.* **1.** the past participle of **speak.** ~*adj.* **2.** uttered in speech. **3.** (*in combination*) having speech as specified: *soft-spoken.* **4. spoken for.** engaged or reserved.

spokeshave (ˈspəʊkˌʃeɪv) *n.* a small plane with two handles, one on each side of its blade, used for shaping or smoothing cylindrical wooden surfaces, such as spokes.

spokesman (ˈspəʊksmən), **spokesperson** (ˈspəʊksˌpɜːsᵊn), *or* **spokeswoman** (ˈspəʊksˌwʊmən) *n., pl.* **-men, -persons** *or* **-people,** *or* **-women.** a person authorized to speak on behalf of another person or group.

spoliation (ˌspəʊlɪˈeɪʃən) *n.* **1.** the act or an instance of despoiling or plundering. **2.** the authorized plundering of neutral vessels on the seas by a belligerent state in time of war. **3.** *Law.* the material alteration of a document so as to render it invalid. **4.** *English ecclesiastical law.* the taking of the fruits of a benefice by a person not entitled to them. [C14: < L *spoliātiō,* < *spoliāre* to SPOIL] **—spoliatory** (ˈspəʊlɪətərɪ, -trɪ) *adj.*

spondee (ˈspɒndiː) *n. Prosody.* a metrical foot consisting of two long syllables (¯¯). [C14: < OF *spondée,* < L *spondēus,* < Gk, < *spondē* ritual libation; < use of spondee in the music for such ceremonies] **—spondaic** (spɒnˈdeɪɪk) *adj.*

spondylitis (ˌspɒndɪˈlaɪtɪs) *n.* inflammation of the vertebrae. [C19: < NL, < Gk *spondulos* vertebra; see -ITIS]

sponge (spʌndʒ) *n.* **1.** any of various multicellular typically marine animals, usually occurring in complex sessile colonies, in which the porous body is supported by a fibrous, calcareous, or siliceous skeletal framework. **2.** a piece of the light porous highly absorbent elastic skeleton of certain sponges, used in bathing, cleaning, etc. **3.** any of a number of materials resembling a sponge. **4.** another word for **sponger** (sense 1). **5.** *Inf.* a person who indulges in heavy drinking. **6.** leavened dough, esp. before kneading. **7.** See **sponge cake. 8.** Also called: **sponge pudding.** *Brit.* a light steamed or baked spongy pudding. **9.** porous metal capable of absorbing large quantities of gas: *platinum sponge.* **10.** a rub with a sponge. **11. throw in** (*or* **up**) **the sponge** (*or* **towel**). **See throw in** (sense 3). ~*vb.* **12.** (*tr.;* often foll. by *off* or *down*) to clean (something) by wiping or rubbing with a damp or wet sponge. **13.** (*tr.;* usually foll. by *off, away, out,* etc.) to remove (marks, etc.) by rubbing with a damp or wet sponge or cloth. **14.** (when *tr.,* often foll. by *up*) to absorb (liquids, esp. when spilt) in the manner of a sponge. **15.** (*intr.*) to go collecting sponges. **16.** (foll. by *off*) to get something from (someone) by presuming on his generosity: *to sponge a meal off someone.* **17.** (foll. by *off* or *on*) to obtain one's subsistence, etc., unjustifiably (from): *he sponges off his friends.* [OE, < L *spongia,* < Gk] **—ˈspongy** *adj.*

sponge bag *n.* a small waterproof bag made of plastic, etc., that holds toilet articles, used esp. when travelling.

sponge bath *n.* a washing of the body with a wet sponge or cloth, without immersion in water.

sponge cake *n.* a light porous cake, made of eggs, sugar, flour, and flavourings, without any fat.

sponger (ˈspʌndʒə) *n.* **1.** *Inf.* a person who lives off other people by continually taking advantage of their generosity; parasite or scrounger. **2.** a person or ship employed in collecting sponges.

sponsion (ˈspɒnʃən) *n.* **1.** the act or process of becoming surety; sponsorship. **2.** (*often pl.*) *International law.* an unauthorized agreement made by a public officer, requiring ratification by his government. **3.** any act or promise, esp. one made on behalf of someone else. [C17: < L *sponsiō,* < *spondēre* to pledge]

sponson (ˈspɒnsən) *n.* **1.** *Naval.* an outboard support for a gun, etc. **2.** a structural projection from the side of a paddle steamer for supporting a paddle wheel. **3.** a structural unit attached to a helicopter fuselage by struts, housing the landing gear and flotation bags. [C19: ? < EXPANSION]

sponsor (ˈspɒnsə) *n.* **1.** a person or group that promotes either another person or group in an activity or the activity itself, either for profit or charity. **2.** *Chiefly U.S. & Canad.* a person or business firm that pays the costs of a radio or television programme in return for advertising time. **3.** a legislator who presents and supports a bill, motion, etc. **4.** Also called: **godparent. a.** an authorized witness who makes the required promises on behalf of a person to be baptized and thereafter assumes responsibility for his Christian upbringing. **b.** a person who presents a candidate for confirmation. ~*vb.* **5.** (*tr.*) to act as a sponsor for. [C17: < L, < *spondēre* to promise solemnly] **—sponsorial** (spɒnˈsɔːrɪəl) *adj.* **—ˈsponsorˌship** *n.*

sponsored (ˈspɒnsəd) *adj.* denoting an activity organized to raise money for a charity in which sponsors agree to donate money on completion of the activity by participants.

spontaneity (ˌspɒntəˈniːɪtɪ, -ˈneɪ-) *n., pl.* **-ties. 1.** the state or quality of being spontaneous. **2.** (*often pl.*) the exhibiting of spontaneous actions, impulses, or behaviour.

spontaneous (spɒnˈteɪnɪəs) *adj.* **1.** occurring, produced, or performed through natural processes without external influence. **2.** arising from an unforced personal impulse; voluntary; unpremeditated. **3.** (of plants) growing naturally; indigenous. [C17: < LL *spontāneus,* < L *sponte* voluntarily] **—sponˈtaneously** *adv.* **—sponˈtaneousness** *n.*

spontaneous combustion *n.* the ignition of a substance or body as a result of internal oxidation processes, without the application of an external source of heat.

spontaneous generation *n.* another name for **abiogenesis.**

spoof (spuːf) *Inf.* ~*n.* **1.** a mildly satirical mockery or parody; lampoon. **2.** a good-humoured deception or trick. ~*vb.* **3.** to indulge in a spoof of (a person or thing). [C19: coined by A. Roberts (1852–1933), E comedian] **—ˈspoofer** *n.*

spook (spuːk) *Inf.* ~*n.* **1.** a ghost or a person suggestive of this. **2.** *U.S. & Canad.* a spy. ~*vb.* (*tr.*) *U.S. & Canad.* **3.** to frighten: *to spook horses; to spook a person.* **4.** (of a ghost) to haunt. [C19: Du. *spook,* < MLow G *spōk* ghost] **—ˈspooky** *adj.*

spool (spuːl) *n.* **1.** a device around which magnetic tape, film, cotton, etc., can be wound, with plates at top and bottom to prevent it from slipping off. **2.** anything round which other materials, esp. thread, are wound. ~*vb.* **3.** (sometimes foll. by *up*) to wind or be wound onto a spool. [C14: of Gmc origin]

spoon (spuːn) *n.* **1.** a utensil having a shallow concave part, usually elliptical in shape, attached to a handle, used in eating or serving food, stirring, etc. **2.** Also called: **spoonbait.** an angling lure consisting of a bright piece of metal which swivels on a trace to which are attached a hook or hooks. **3.** a golf club with a shorter shaft and shallower face than a brassie. **4. be born with a silver spoon in one's mouth.** to inherit wealth or social standing. **5.** *Rowing.* a type of oar blade that is curved at the edges and tip. ~*vb.* **6.** (*tr.*) to scoop up or transfer (food, liquid, etc.) from one container to another with or as if with a spoon. **7.** (*intr.*) *Old-fashioned sl.* to kiss and cuddle. **8.** *Sport.* to hit (a ball) with a weak lifting motion, as in golf, cricket, etc. [OE *spōn* splinter]

spoonbill (ˈspuːnˌbɪl) *n.* any of several wading birds of warm regions, having a long horizontally flattened bill.

spoondrift (ˈspuːnˌdrɪft) *n.* a less common spelling of **spindrift.**

spoonerism (ˈspuːnəˌrɪzəm) *n.* the transposition of the initial consonants or consonant clusters of a pair of words, often resulting in an amusing ambiguity, such as *hush my brat* for *brush my hat.* [C20: after W. A. *Spooner* (1844–1930), E clergyman renowned for this]

spoon-feed *vb.* **-feeding, -fed.** (*tr.*) **1.** to feed with a spoon. **2.** to overindulge or spoil. **3.** to provide (a person) with ready-made opinions, judgments, etc.

spoonful (ˈspuːnˌfʊl) *n., pl.* **-fuls. 1.** the amount that a spoon is able to hold. **2.** a small quantity.

spoony *or* **spooney** (ˈspuːnɪ) *Sl., rare old-fashioned.* ~*adj.* **spoonier, spooniest. 1.** foolishly or stupidly amorous. ~*n., pl.* **spoonies. 2.** a fool or silly person, esp. one in love.

spoor (spʊə, spɔː) *n.* **1.** the trail of an animal or person, esp. as discernible to the eye. ~*vb.* **2.** to track (an animal) by following its trail. [C19: < Afrik., < MDu. *spor;* rel. to OE *spor* track]

sporadic (spəˈrædɪk) *adj.* **1.** occurring at irregular points in time; intermittent: *sporadic firing.* **2.** scattered; isolated: *a sporadic disease.* [C17: < Med. L *sporadicus,* < Gk, < *sporas* scattered] —**spoˈradically** *adv.*

sporangium (spəˈrændʒɪəm) *n., pl.* **-gia** (-dʒɪə). any organ, esp. in fungi, in which asexual spores are produced. [C19: < NL, < SPORO- + Gk *angeion* receptacle] —**spoˈrangial** *adj.*

spore (spɔː) *n.* **1.** a reproductive body, produced by some protozoans and many plants, that develops into a new individual. A **sexual spore** is formed after the fusion of gametes and an **asexual spore** is the result of asexual reproduction. **2.** a germ cell, seed, dormant bacterium, or similar body. ~*vb.* **3.** (*intr.*) to produce, carry, or release spores. [C19: < NL *spora,* < Gk: a sowing; rel. to Gk *speirein* to sow]

spore case *n.* the nontechnical name for **sporangium.**

sporo- *or before a vowel* **spor-** *combining form.* spore: *sporophyte.* [< NL *spora*]

sporogenesis (ˌspɔːrəʊˈdʒɛnɪsɪs, ˌspɒ-) *n.* the process of spore formation in plants and animals. —**sporogenous** (spɔːˈrɒdʒɪnəs, spɒ-) *adj.*

sporogonium (ˌspɔːrəʊˈgəʊnɪəm, ˌspɒ-) *n., pl.* **-nia** (-nɪə). a structure in mosses and liverworts consisting of a spore-bearing capsule on a short stalk that arises from the parent plant.

sporophyll *or* **sporophyl** (ˈspɔːrəʊfɪl, ˈspɒ-) *n.* a leaf in mosses, ferns, and related plants that bears the sporangia.

sporophyte (ˈspɔːrəʊˌfaɪt, ˈspɒ-) *n.* the diploid form of plants that have alternation of generations. It produces asexual spores. —**sporophytic** (ˌspɔːrəˈfɪtɪk, ˌspɒ-) *adj.*

-sporous *adj. combining form.* (in botany) having a specified type or number of spores.

sporozoan (ˌspɔːrəˈzəʊən, ˌspɒ-) *n.* **1.** any parasitic protozoan of a class that includes the malaria parasite. ~*adj.* **2.** of or relating to the sporozoans.

sporran (ˈspɒrən) *n.* a large pouch, usually of fur, worn hanging from a belt in front of the kilt in Scottish Highland dress. [C19: < Scot. Gaelic *sporan* purse]

sport (spɔːt) *n.* **1.** an individual or group activity pursued for exercise or pleasure, often taking a competitive form. **2.** such activities considered collectively. **3.** any pastime indulged in for pleasure. **4.** the pleasure derived from a pastime, esp. hunting, shooting, or fishing. **5.** playful or good-humoured joking: *to say a thing in sport.* **6.** derisive mockery or the object of such mockery: *to make sport of someone.* **7.** someone or something that is controlled by external influences: *the sport of fate.* **8.** *Inf.* (sometimes qualified by *good, bad,* etc.) a person who reacts cheerfully in the face of adversity, esp. a good loser. **9.** *Inf.* a person noted for being scrupulously fair and abiding by the rules of a game. **10.** *Inf.* a person who leads a merry existence, esp. a gambler: *he's a bit of a sport.* **11.** *Austral. & N.Z. inf.* a form of address used esp. between males. **12.** *Biol.* **a.** an animal or plant that differs conspicuously from other organisms of the same species, usually because of a mutation. **b.** an anomalous characteristic of such an organism. ~*vb.* **13.** (*tr.*) *Inf.* to wear or display in an ostentatious or proud manner: *she was sporting a new hat.* **14.** (*intr.*) to skip about or frolic happily. **15.** to amuse (oneself), esp. in outdoor physical recreation. **16.** (*intr.; often foll. by with*) *Arch.* to make fun (of). **17.** (*intr.*) *Biol.* to produce or undergo a mutation. ~See also **sports.** [C15 *sporten,* var. of *disporten* to DISPORT] —**ˈsporter** *n.* —**ˈsportful** *adj.* —**ˈsportfully** *adv.* —**ˈsportfulness** *n.*

sporting (ˈspɔːtɪŋ) *adj.* **1.** (*prenominal*) of, relating to, or used or engaged in a sport or sports. **2.** relating or conforming to sportsmanship; fair. **3.** of or relating to gambling. **4.** willing to take a risk. —**ˈsportingly** *adv.*

sportive (ˈspɔːtɪv) *adj.* **1.** playful or joyous. **2.** done in jest rather than seriously. —**ˈsportively** *adv.* —**ˈsportiveness** *n.*

sports (spɔːts) *n.* **1.** (*modifier*) relating to, concerned with, or used in sports: *sports equipment.* **2.** Also called: **sports day.** *Brit.* a meeting held at a school or college for competitions in various athletic events.

sports car *n.* a production car designed for speed and manoeuvrability, having a low body and usually seating only two persons.

sportscast (ˈspɔːtsˌkɑːst) *n. U.S.* a broadcast consisting of sports news. —**ˈsportsˌcaster** *n.*

sports jacket *n.* a man's informal jacket, made esp. of tweed. Also called (U.S., Austral. & N.Z.): **sports coat.**

sportsman (ˈspɔːtsmən) *n., pl.* **-men. 1.** a man who takes part in sports, esp. of the outdoor type. **2.** a person who exhibits fairness, generosity, observance of the rules, and good humour when losing. —**ˈsportsman-ˌlike** *or* **ˈsportsmanly** *adj.* —**ˈsportsmanˌship** *n.*

sports medicine *n.* the branch of medicine concerned with injuries sustained through sport.

sportswear (ˈspɔːtsˌwɛə) *n.* clothes worn for sport or outdoor leisure wear.

sportswoman (ˈspɔːtsˌwʊmən) *n., pl.* **-women.** a woman who takes part in sports, esp. of the outdoor type.

sporty (ˈspɔːtɪ) *adj.* **sportier, sportiest. 1.** vulgarly ostentatious; stylish, loud, or gay. **2.** relating to or appropriate to a sportsman or sportswoman. **3.** (of women) amorous or wanton; lusty. —**ˈsportily** *adv.* —**ˈsportiness** *n.*

sporule (ˈspɒruːl) *n.* a very small spore. [C19: < NL *sporula*]

spot (spɒt) *n.* **1.** a small mark on a surface, such as a circular patch or stain, differing in colour or texture from its surroundings. **2.** a location: *this is the exact spot.* **3.** a blemish of the skin, esp. a pimple or one occurring through some disease. **4.** a blemish on the character of a person; moral flaw. **5.** *Inf.* a place of entertainment: *a night spot.* **6.** *Inf., chiefly Brit.* a small quantity or amount: *a spot of lunch.* **7.** *Inf.* an awkward situation: *that puts me in a spot.* **8.** a short period between regular television or radio programmes that is used for advertising. **9.** a position or length of time in a show assigned to a specific performer. **10.** short for **spotlight. 11.** (in billiards) **a.** Also called: **spot ball.** the white ball that is distinguished from the plain by a mark or spot. **b.** the player using this ball. **12.** *Billiards, snooker, etc.* one of the marked places where the ball is placed. **13.** (*modifier*) **a.** to be paid or delivered immediately: *spot cash.* **b.** involving immediate cash payment: *spot sales.* **14. change one's spots.** (*used mainly in negative constructions*) to reform one's character. **15. high spot.** an outstanding event: *the high spot of the holiday.* **16. knock spots off.** to outstrip or outdo with ease. **17. on the spot. a.** immediately. **b.** at the place in question. **c.** in the best position to deal with a situation. **d.** in an awkward predicament. **e.** (*as modifier*): *our on-the-spot reporter.* **18. soft spot.**

a special sympathetic affection or weakness for a person or thing. **19. tight spot.** a serious, difficult, or dangerous situation. **20. weak spot. a.** some aspect of a character or situation that is susceptible to criticism. **b.** a flaw in a person's knowledge. ~*vb.* **spotting, spotted. 21.** (*tr.*) to observe or perceive suddenly; discern. **22.** to put stains or spots upon (something). **23.** (*intr.*) (of some fabrics) to be susceptible to spotting by or as if by water: *silk spots easily.* **24.** *Billiards.* to place (a ball) on one of the spots. **25.** to look out for and note (trains, talent, etc.). **26.** (*intr.*) to rain slightly; spit. [C12 (in the sense: moral blemish): < G] —**'spotless** *adj.* —**'spotlessly** *adv.* —**'spotlessness** *n.*

spot check *n.* **1.** a quick random examination. **2.** a check made without prior warning. ~*vb.* **spot-check. 3.** (*tr.*) to perform a spot check on.

spot height *n.* a mark on a map indicating the height of a hill, mountain, etc.

spotlight ('spɒtˌlaɪt) *n.* **1.** a powerful light focused so as to illuminate a small area. **2. the.** the focus of attention. ~*vb.* **-lighting, -lit** *or* **-lighted.** (*tr.*) **3.** to direct a spotlight on. **4.** to focus attention on.

spot-on *adj. Brit. inf.* absolutely correct; very accurate.

spotted ('spɒtɪd) *adj.* **1.** characterized by spots or marks, esp. in having a pattern of spots. **2.** stained or blemished; soiled or bespattered.

spotted dick *or* **dog** *n. Brit.* a steamed or boiled suet pudding containing dried fruit and shaped into a roll.

spotted fever *n.* any of various severe febrile diseases characterized by small irregular spots on the skin.

spotter ('spɒtə) *n.* **1. a.** a person or thing that watches or observes. **b.** (*as modifier*): *a spotter plane.* **2.** a person who makes a hobby of watching for and noting numbers or types of trains, buses, etc.: *a train spotter.* **3.** *Mil.* a person who advises adjustment of fire on a target by observations. **4.** a person, esp. one engaged in civil defence, who watches for enemy aircraft.

spottie ('spɒtɪ) *n. N.Z.* a young deer of up to three months of age.

spotty ('spɒtɪ) *adj.* **-tier, -tiest. 1.** abounding in or characterized by spots or marks, esp. on the skin. **2.** not consistent or uniform; irregular or uneven. —**'spottily** *adv.* —**'spottiness** *n.*

spot-weld *vb.* **1.** (*tr.*) to join (two pieces of metal) by small circular welds by means of heat, usually electrically generated, and pressure. ~*n.* **2.** a weld so formed. —**'spot-ˌwelder** *n.*

spousal ('spaʊzəl) *n.* **1.** (*often pl.*) **a.** the marriage ceremony. **b.** a wedding. ~*adj.* **2.** of or relating to marriage. —**'spousally** *adv.*

spouse *n.* (spaʊs, spaʊz). **1.** a person's partner in marriage. Related adj.: **spousal.** ~*vb.* (spaʊz, spaʊs). **2.** (*tr.*) *Obs.* to marry. [C12: < OF *spus* (masc.), *spuse* (fem.), < L *sponsus, sponsa* betrothed man or woman, < *spondēre* to promise solemnly]

spout (spaʊt) *vb.* **1.** to discharge (a liquid) in a continuous jet or in spurts, esp. through a narrow gap or under pressure, or (of a liquid) to gush thus. **2.** (of a whale, etc.) to discharge air through the blowhole in a spray at the surface of the water. **3.** *Inf.* to utter (a stream of words) on a subject. ~*n.* **4.** a tube, pipe, chute, etc., allowing the passage or pouring of liquids, grain, etc. **5.** a continuous stream or jet of liquid. **6.** short for **waterspout. 7. up the spout.** *Sl.* **a.** ruined or lost: *any hope of rescue is right up the spout.* **b.** pregnant. [C14: ? < MDu. *spouten,* < ON *spyta* to spit] —**'spouter** *n.*

spouting ('spaʊtɪŋ) *n. N.Z.* **a.** a rainwater downpipe on the exterior of a building. **b.** such pipes collectively.

SPQR *abbrev. for* Senatus Populusque Romanus. [L: the Senate and People of Rome]

sprag (spræg) *n.* **1.** a chock or steel bar used to prevent a vehicle from running backwards on an incline. **2.** a support or post used in mining. [C19: <?]

sprain (spreɪn) *vb.* **1.** (*tr.*) to injure (a joint) by a sudden twisting or wrenching of its ligaments. ~*n.* **2.** the injury, characterized by swelling and temporary disability. [C17: <?]

sprang (spræŋ) *vb.* a past tense of **spring.**

sprat (spræt) *n.* **1.** Also called: **brisling.** a small marine food fish of the herring family. **2.** any of various small or young herrings. [C16: var. of OE *sprott*]

sprawl (sprɔːl) *vb.* **1.** (*intr.*) to sit or lie in an ungainly manner with one's limbs spread out. **2.** to fall down or knock down with the limbs spread out in an ungainly way. **3.** to spread out or cause to spread out in a straggling fashion: *his handwriting sprawled all over the paper.* ~*n.* **4.** the act or an instance of sprawling. **5.** a sprawling posture or arrangement of items. [OE *spreawlian*] —**'sprawling** *or* **'sprawly** *adj.*

spray[1] (spreɪ) *n.* **1.** fine particles of a liquid. **2. a.** a liquid, such as perfume, paint, etc., designed to be discharged from an aerosol or atomizer: *hair spray.* **b.** the aerosol or atomizer itself. **3.** a quantity of small objects flying through the air: *a spray of bullets.* ~*vb.* **4.** to scatter (liquid) in the form of fine particles. **5.** to discharge (a liquid) from an aerosol or atomizer. **6.** (*tr.*) to treat or bombard with a spray: *to spray the lawn.* [C17: < MDu. *spräien*] —**'sprayer** *n.*

spray[2] (spreɪ) *n.* **1.** a single slender shoot, twig, or branch that bears buds, leaves, flowers, or berries. **2.** an ornament or floral design like this. [C13: of Gmc origin]

spray gun *n.* a device that sprays a fluid in a finely divided form by atomizing it in an air jet.

spread (sprɛd) *vb.* **spreading, spread. 1.** to extend or unfold or be extended or unfolded to the fullest width: *she spread the map.* **2.** to extend or cause to extend over a larger expanse: *the milk spread all over the floor; the political unrest spread over several years.* **3.** to apply or be applied in a coating: *butter does not spread very well when cold.* **4.** to distribute or be distributed over an area or region. **5.** to display or be displayed in its fullest extent: *the landscape spread before us.* **6.** (*tr.*) to prepare (a table) for a meal. **7.** (*tr.*) to lay out (a meal) on a table. **8.** to send or be sent out in all directions; disseminate or be disseminated: *someone was spreading rumours; the disease spread quickly.* **9.** (of rails, wires, etc.) to force or be forced apart. **10.** to increase the breadth of (a part), esp. to flatten the head of a rivet by pressing, hammering, or forging. **11.** (*tr.*) *Agriculture.* **a.** to lay out (hay) in a relatively thin layer to dry. **b.** to scatter (seed, manure, etc.) over an area. **12.** (*tr.; often foll. by around*) *Inf.* to make (oneself) agreeable to a large number of people. ~*n.* **13.** the act or process of spreading; diffusion, dispersion, expansion, etc. **14.** *Inf.* the wingspan of an aircraft. **15.** an extent of space or time; stretch: *a spread of 50 years.* **16.** *Inf., chiefly U.S. & Canad.* a ranch or large tract of land. **17.** the limit of something fully extended: *the spread of a bird's wings.* **18.** a covering for a table or bed. **19.** *Inf.* a large meal or feast, esp. when it is laid out on a table. **20.** a food which can be spread on bread, etc.: *salmon spread.* **21.** two facing pages in a book or other publication. **22.** a widening of the hips and waist: *middle-age spread.* ~*adj.* **23.** extended or stretched out, esp. to the fullest extent. [OE *sprǣdan*] —**'spreadable** *adj.* —**'spreader** *n.*

spread eagle *n.* **1.** the representation of an eagle with outstretched wings, used as an emblem of the U.S. **2.** an acrobatic skating figure.

spread-eagle *adj. also* **spread-eagled. 1.** lying or standing with arms and legs outstretched. ~*vb.* **2.** to assume or cause to assume the shape of a spread eagle. **3.** (*intr.*) *Skating.* to execute a spread eagle.

spreadsheet ('sprɛdˌʃiːt) *n.* a computer program that allows easy entry and manipulation of text: used esp. for financial planning.

sprechgesang (*German* 'ʃprɛçgəzaŋ) *n. Music.* a type of vocalization between singing and recitation. [C20: < G *Sprechgesang,* lit.: speaking-song]

spree (spriː) *n.* **1.** a session of considerable overindulgence, esp. in drinking, squandering money, etc. **2.** a romp. [C19: ? changed < Scot. *spreath* plundered cattle, ult. < L *praeda* booty]

sprig (sprɪg) *n.* **1.** a shoot, twig, or sprout of a tree, shrub, etc.; spray. **2.** an ornamental device resembling a spray of leaves or flowers. **3.** Also called: **dowel pin.** a small wire nail without a head. **4.** *Inf., rare.* a youth. **5.** *Inf., rare.* a person considered as the descendant of an established family, social class, etc. **6.** *N.Z.* another word for **stud**[1] (sense 5). *~vb.* **sprigging, sprigged.** (*tr.*) **7.** to fasten or secure with sprigs. **8.** to ornament (fabric, etc.) with a design of sprigs. [C15: prob. of Gmc origin] —**ˈsprigger** *n.* —**ˈspriggy** *adj.*

sprightly (ˈspraɪtlɪ) *adj.* **-lier, -liest. 1.** full of vitality; lively and gay. *~adv.* **2.** *Obs.* in a gay or lively manner. [C16: < *spright,* var. of SPRITE + -LY[1]] —**ˈsprightliness** *n.*

spring (sprɪŋ) *vb.* **springing, sprang** *or* **sprung; sprung. 1.** to move or cause to move suddenly upwards or forwards in a single motion. **2.** to release or be released from a forced position by elastic force: *the bolt sprang back.* **3.** (*tr.*) to leap or jump over. **4.** (*intr.*) to come or arise suddenly. **5.** (*intr.*) (of a part of a mechanism, etc.) to jump out of place. **6.** to make (wood, etc.) warped or split or (of wood, etc.) to become warped or split. **7.** to happen or cause to happen unexpectedly: *to spring a surprise.* **8.** (*intr.;* usually foll. by *from*) to originate; be descended: *the idea sprang from a chance meeting; he sprang from peasant stock.* **9.** (*intr.;* often foll. by *up*) to come into being or appear suddenly: *factories springing up.* **10.** (*tr.*) (of a gundog) to rouse (game) from cover. **11.** (*intr.*) (of game or quarry) to start or rise suddenly from cover. **12.** to explode (a mine) or (of a mine) to explode. **13.** (*tr.*) to provide with a spring or springs. **14.** (*tr.*) *Inf.* to arrange the escape of (someone) from prison. **15.** (*intr.*) *Arch. or poetic.* (of daylight or dawn) to begin to appear. *~n.* **16.** the act or an instance of springing. **17.** a leap, jump, or bound. **18. a.** the quality of resilience; elasticity. **b.** (*as modifier*): *spring steel.* **19.** the act or an instance of moving rapidly back from a position of tension. **20. a.** a natural outflow of ground water, as forming the source of a stream. **b.** (*as modifier*): *spring water.* **21. a.** a device, such as a coil or strip of steel, that stores potential energy when it is compressed, stretched, or bent and releases it when the restraining force is removed. **b.** (*as modifier*): *a spring mattress.* **22.** a structural defect such as a warp or bend. **23. a.** (*sometimes cap.*) the season of the year between winter and summer, astronomically from the March equinox to the June solstice in the N hemisphere and from the September equinox to the December solstice in the S hemisphere. **b.** (*as modifier*): *spring showers.* Related adj.: **vernal. 24.** the earliest or freshest time of something. **25.** a source or origin. **26.** Also called: **spring line.** *Naut.* a mooring line, usually one of a pair that cross amidships. [OE *springan*] —**ˈspringless** *adj.* —**ˈspringˌlike** *adj.*

spring balance *or esp. U.S.* **spring scale** *n.* a device in which an object to be weighed is attached to the end of a helical spring, the extension of which indicates the weight of the object on a calibrated scale.

springboard (ˈsprɪŋˌbɔːd) *n.* **1.** a flexible board, usually projecting low over the water, used for diving. **2.** a similar board used for gaining height or momentum in gymnastics. **3.** *Austral. & N.Z.* a board inserted into the trunk of a tree at some height above the ground on which a lumberjack stands to chop down the tree. **4.** anything that serves as a point of departure or initiation.

springbok (ˈsprɪŋˌbʌk) *n., pl.* **-bok** *or* **-boks.** an antelope of semidesert regions of southern Africa, which moves in leaps. [C18: < Afrik., < Du. *springen* to spring + *bok* goat]

Springbok (ˈsprɪŋˌbʌk, -ˌbɒk) *n.* an amateur athlete who has represented South Africa in international competitions.

spring chicken *n.* **1.** *Chiefly U.S.* a young chicken, tender for cooking, esp. one from two to ten months old. **2.** *Inf.* a young, inexperienced, or unsophisticated person (esp. in **no spring chicken**).

spring-clean *vb.* **1.** to clean (a house) thoroughly: traditionally at the end of winter. *~n.* **2.** an instance of this. —**ˌspring-ˈcleaning** *n.*

springe (sprɪndʒ) *n.* **1.** a snare set to catch small wild animals or birds and consisting of a loop attached to a bent twig or branch under tension. *~vb.* **2.** (*tr.*) to catch (animals or birds) with this. [C13: rel. to OE *springan* to spring]

springer (ˈsprɪŋə) *n.* **1.** a person or thing that springs. **2.** short for **springer spaniel. 3.** *Archit.* **a.** the first and lowest stone of an arch. **b.** the impost of an arch.

springer spaniel *n.* either of two breeds of spaniel with a slightly domed head and ears of medium length.

springhaas (ˈsprɪŋˌhɑːs) *n., pl.* **-haas** *or* **-hase** (-ˌhɑːzə). a small S and E African nocturnal kangaroo-like rodent. [< Afrik.: spring hare]

springing (ˈsprɪŋɪŋ) *n. Archit.* the level where an arch or vault rises from a support.

spring lock *n.* a type of lock having a spring-loaded bolt, a key being required only to unlock it.

spring onion *n.* an immature form of the onion, widely cultivated for its tiny bulb and long green leaves which are eaten in salads, etc. Also called: **scallion.**

spring roll *n.* a Chinese dish consisting of a savoury mixture rolled up in a thin pancake and fried.

springtail (ˈsprɪŋˌteɪl) *n.* any of various primitive wingless insects having a forked springing organ.

spring tide *n.* **1.** either of the two tides that occur at or just after new moon and full moon: the greatest rise and fall in tidal level. Cf. **neap tide. 2.** any great rush or flood.

springtime (ˈsprɪŋˌtaɪm) *n.* **1.** Also called: **springtide.** the season of spring. **2.** the earliest, usually the most attractive, period of the existence of something.

springy (ˈsprɪŋɪ) *adj.* **springier, springiest. 1.** possessing or characterized by resilience or bounce. **2.** (of a place) having many springs of water. —**ˈspringily** *adv.* —**ˈspringiness** *n.*

sprinkle (ˈsprɪŋkᵊl) *vb.* **1.** to scatter (liquid, powder, etc.) in tiny particles or droplets over (something). **2.** (*tr.*) to distribute over (something): *the field was sprinkled with flowers.* **3.** (*intr.*) to drizzle slightly. *~n.* **4.** the act or an instance of sprinkling or a quantity that is sprinkled. **5.** a slight drizzle. [C14: prob. < MDu. *sprenkelen*] —**ˈsprinkler** *n.*

sprinkler system *n.* a fire-extinguishing system that releases water from overhead nozzles opened automatically by a temperature rise.

sprinkling (ˈsprɪŋklɪŋ) *n.* a small quantity or amount: *a sprinkling of common sense.*

sprint (sprɪnt) *n.* **1.** *Athletics.* **a.** a short race run at top speed. **b.** a fast finishing run at the end of a longer race. **2.** any quick run. *~vb.* **3.** (*intr.*) to go at top speed, as in running, cycling, etc. [C16: of Scand. origin] —**ˈsprinter** *n.*

sprit (sprɪt) *n. Naut.* a light spar pivoted at the mast and crossing a fore-and-aft quadrilateral sail diagonally to the peak. [OE *spreot*]

sprite (spraɪt) *n.* **1.** (in folklore) a nimble elflike creature, esp. one associated with water. **2.** a small dainty person. [C13: < OF *esprit,* < L *spīritus* SPIRIT[1]]

spritsail (ˈsprɪtˌseɪl; *Naut.* ˈsprɪtsəl) *n. Naut.* a sail mounted on a sprit or bowsprit.

spritzer (ˈsprɪtsə) *n.* a drink, usually white wine, with soda water added. [< G *spritzen* to splash]

sprocket (ˈsprɒkɪt) *n.* **1.** Also called: **sprocket wheel.** a relatively thin wheel having teeth projecting radially from the rim, esp. one that drives or is driven by a chain. **2.** an individual tooth on such a wheel. **3.** a cylindrical wheel with teeth on one or both rims for pulling film through a camera or projector. [C16: <?]

sprout (spraʊt) *vb.* **1.** (of a plant, seed, etc.) to produce (new leaves, shoots, etc.). **2.** (*intr.;* often foll. by *up*) to begin to grow or develop. ~*n.* **3.** a new shoot or bud. **4.** something that grows like a sprout. **5.** See **Brussels sprout.** [OE *sprūtan*]

spruce[1] (spruːs) *n.* **1.** any coniferous tree of a N temperate genus, cultivated for timber and for ornament. They grow in a pyramidal shape and have needle-like leaves and light-coloured wood. See also **Norway spruce. 2.** the wood of any of these trees. [C17: short for *Spruce fir,* < C14 *Spruce* Prussia, changed < *Pruce,* via OF < L *Prussia*]

spruce[2] (spruːs) *adj.* neat, smart, and trim. [C16: ? < *Spruce leather,* a fashionable leather imported from Prussia; see SPRUCE[1]] —**ˈsprucely** *adv.* —**ˈspruceness** *n.*

spruce beer *n.* an alcoholic drink made of fermented molasses flavoured with spruce twigs and cones.

spruce up *vb.* (*adv.*) to make (oneself, a person, or thing) smart and neat.

sprue[1] (spruː) *n.* **1.** a vertical channel in a mould through which plastic or molten metal is introduced or out of which it flows when the mould is filled. **2.** plastic or metal that solidifies in a sprue. [C19: <?]

sprue[2] (spruː) *n.* a chronic disease, esp. of tropical climates, characterized by diarrhoea and emaciation. [C19: < Du. *spruw*]

spruik (ˈspruːɪk) *vb.* (*intr.*) *Austral. sl.* to describe or hold forth like a salesman; spiel or advertise loudly. [C20: <?] —**ˈspruiker** *n.*

spruit (spreɪt) *n. S. African.* a small tributary stream or watercourse. [Afrik.]

sprung (sprʌŋ) *vb.* a past tense and past participle of **spring.**

sprung rhythm *n. Prosody.* a type of poetic rhythm characterized by metrical feet of irregular composition, each having one strongly stressed syllable, often the first, and an indefinite number of unstressed syllables.

spry (spraɪ) *adj.* **spryer, spryest** *or* **sprier, spriest.** active and brisk; nimble. [C18: ? of Scand. origin] —**ˈspryly** *adv.* —**ˈspryness** *n.*

spud (spʌd) *n.* **1.** an informal word for **potato. 2.** a narrow-bladed spade for cutting roots, digging up weeds, etc. ~*vb.* **spudding, spudded. 3.** (*tr.*) to eradicate (weeds) with a spud. **4.** (*intr.*) to drill the first foot of an oil well. [C15 *spudde* short knife, <?; applied later to a digging tool, & hence to a potato]

spue (spjuː) *vb.* **spuing, spued.** an archaic spelling of **spew.** —**ˈspuer** *n.*

spume (spjuːm) *n.* **1.** foam or surf, esp. on the sea; froth. ~*vb.* **2.** (*intr.*) to foam or froth. [C14: < OF *espume,* < L *spūma*] —**ˈspumous** *or* **ˈspumy** *adj.*

spun (spʌn) *vb.* **1.** the past tense and past participle of **spin.** ~*adj.* **2.** formed or manufactured by spinning: *spun gold; spun glass.*

spunk (spʌŋk) *n.* **1.** *Inf.* courage or spirit. **2.** *Brit. taboo sl.* semen. **3.** touchwood or tinder. [C16 (in the sense: a spark): < Scot. Gaelic *spong* tinder, sponge, < L *spongia* sponge] —**ˈspunky** *adj.* —**ˈspunkily** *adv.*

spun silk *n.* shiny yarn or fabric made from silk waste.

spur (spɜː) *n.* **1.** a pointed device or sharp spiked wheel fixed to the heel of a rider's boot to enable him to urge his horse on. **2.** anything serving to urge or encourage. **3.** a sharp horny projection from the leg in male birds, such as the domestic cock. **4.** a pointed process in any of various animals. **5.** a tubular extension at the base of the corolla in flowers such as larkspur. **6.** a short or stunted branch of a tree. **7.** a ridge projecting laterally from a mountain or mountain range. **8.** another name for **groyne. 9.** Also called: **spur track.** a railway branch line or siding. **10.** a short side road leading off a main road. **11.** a sharp cutting instrument attached to the leg of a gamecock. **12. on the spur of the moment.** on impulse. **13. win one's spurs. a.** to prove one's ability; gain distinction. **b.** *History.* to earn knighthood. ~*vb.* **spurring, spurred. 14.** (*tr.*) to goad or urge with or as if with spurs. **15.** (*intr.*) to go or ride quickly; press on. **16.** (*tr.*) to provide with a spur or spurs. [OE *spura*]

spurge (spɜːdʒ) *n.* any of various plants that have milky sap and small flowers typically surrounded by conspicuous bracts. [C14: < OF *espurge,* < *espurgier* to purge, < L *expurgāre* to cleanse]

spur gear *or* **wheel** *n.* a gear having involuted teeth either straight or helically cut on a cylindrical surface.

spurious (ˈspjʊərɪəs) *adj.* **1.** not genuine or real. **2.** (of a plant part or organ) resembling another part in appearance only; false: *a spurious fruit.* **3.** *Rare.* illegitimate. [C17: < L *spurius* of illegitimate birth] —**ˈspuriously** *adv.* —**ˈspuriousness** *n.*

spurn (spɜːn) *vb.* **1.** to reject (a person or thing) with contempt. **2.** (when *intr.,* often foll. by *against*) *Arch.* to kick (at). ~*n.* **3.** an instance of spurning. **4.** *Arch.* a kick or thrust. [OE *spurnan*] —**ˈspurner** *n.*

spurt *or* **spirt** (spɜːt) *vb.* **1.** to gush or cause to gush forth in a sudden stream or jet. **2.** (*intr.*) to make a sudden effort. ~*n.* **3.** a sudden stream or jet. **4.** a short burst of activity, speed, or energy. [C16: ? rel. to MHG *sprützen* to squirt]

sputnik (ˈspʊtnɪk, ˈspʌt-) *n.* any of a series of Soviet artificial satellites, **Sputnik 1** (launched in 1957) being the first man-made satellite to orbit the earth. [C20: < Russian, lit.: fellow traveller, < *s-* with + *put* path + *-nik,* suffix indicating agent]

sputter (ˈspʌtə) *vb.* **1.** another word for **splutter** (senses 1-3). **2.** *Physics.* **a.** to undergo or cause to undergo a process in which atoms of a solid are removed from its surface by the impact of high-energy ions. **b.** to coat (a metal) onto (a solid surface) by this process. ~*n.* **3.** the process or noise of sputtering. **4.** incoherent stammering speech. **5.** something ejected while sputtering. [C16: < Du. *sputteren,* imit.] —**ˈsputterer** *n.*

sputum (ˈspjuːtəm) *n., pl.* **-ta** (-tə). saliva ejected from the mouth, esp. mixed with mucus. [C17: < L: spittle, < *spuere* to spit out]

spy (spaɪ) *n., pl.* **spies. 1.** a person employed by a state or institution to obtain secret information from rival countries, organizations, companies, etc. **2.** a person who keeps secret watch on others. **3.** *Obs.* a close view. ~*vb.* **spying, spied. 4.** (*intr.;* usually foll. by *on*) to keep a secret or furtive watch (on). **5.** (*intr.*) to engage in espionage. **6.** (*tr.*) to catch sight of; descry. [C13 *spien,* < OF *espier,* of Gmc origin]

spyglass (ˈspaɪˌglɑːs) *n.* a small telescope.

spy out *vb.* (*tr., adv.*) **1.** to discover by careful observation. **2.** to make a close scrutiny of.

sq. *abbrev. for:* **1.** sequence. **2.** square. **3.** (*pl.* **sqq.**) the following one. [< L *sequens*]

Sq. *abbrev. for:* **1.** Squadron. **2.** Square.

squab (skwɒb) *n., pl.* **squabs** *or* **squab. 1.** a young unfledged bird, esp. a pigeon. **2.** a short fat person. **3. a.** a well-stuffed bolster or cushion. **b.** a sofa. ~*adj.* **4.** (of birds) unfledged. **5.** short and fat. [C17: prob. of Gmc origin] —**ˈsquabby** *adj.*

squabble (ˈskwɒbᵊl) *vb.* **1.** (*intr.*) to quarrel over a small matter. ~*n.* **2.** a petty quarrel. [C17: prob. of Scand. origin] —**ˈsquabbler** *n.*

squad (skwɒd) *n.* **1.** the smallest military formation, typically a dozen soldiers, esp. a drill formation. **2.** any small group of people engaged in a common pursuit. **3.** *Sport.* a number of players from which a team is to be selected. [C17: < OF *esquade,* < OSp. *escuadra,* < *escuadrar* to SQUARE, from the square formations used]

squaddie *or* **squaddy** (ˈskwɒdɪ) *n., pl.* **-dies.** *Brit. sl.* a private soldier. [C20: < SQUAD]

squadron (ˈskwɒdrən) *n.* **1.** a subdivision of a naval fleet detached for a particular task. **2.** a cavalry unit comprising two or more troops. **3.** the basic tactical and administrative air force unit comprising two or more flights. [C16: < It.

squadrone soldiers drawn up in square formation, < *squadro* square]

squadron leader *n.* an officer holding commissioned rank, between flight lieutenant and wing commander in the air forces of Britain and certain other countries.

squalene (ˈskweɪˌliːn) *n. Biochemistry.* a terpene first found in the liver of sharks but also present in the livers of most higher animals. [C20: < NL *squalus,* genus name of the shark]

squalid (ˈskwɒlɪd) *adj.* **1.** dirty and repulsive, esp. as a result of neglect or poverty. **2.** sordid. [C16: < L *squālidus,* < *squālēre* to be stiff with dirt] —**squaˈlidity** *or* **ˈsqualidness** *n.* —**ˈsqualidly** *adv.*

squall[1] (skwɔːl) *n.* **1.** a sudden strong wind or brief turbulent storm. **2.** any sudden commotion. ~*vb.* **3.** (*intr.*) to blow in a squall. [C18: ? a special use of SQUALL[2]] —**ˈsqually** *adj.*

squall[2] (skwɔːl) *vb.* **1.** (*intr.*) to cry noisily; yell. ~*n.* **2.** a shrill or noisy yell or howl. [C17: prob. of Scand. origin] —**ˈsqualler** *n.*

squalor (ˈskwɒlə) *n.* the condition or quality of being squalid; disgusting filth. [C17: < L]

squama (ˈskweɪmə) *n., pl.* **-mae** (-miː). *Biol.* a scale or scalelike structure. [C18: < L] —**squamate** (ˈskweɪmeɪt) *adj.* —**squaˈmation** *n.* —**ˈsquamose** *or* **ˈsquamous** *adj.*

squander (ˈskwɒndə) *vb.* (*tr.*) to spend wastefully or extravagantly; dissipate. [C16: <?] —**ˈsquanderer** *n.*

square (skwɛə) *n.* **1.** a plane geometric figure having four equal sides and four right angles. **2.** any object, part, or arrangement having this or a similar shape. **3.** an open area in a town, sometimes including the surrounding buildings, which may form a square. **4.** *Maths.* the product of two equal factors; the second power: *9 is the square of 3, written* 3^2. **5.** an instrument having two strips of wood, metal, etc., set in the shape of a T or L, used for constructing or testing right angles. **6.** *Inf.* a person who is old-fashioned in views, customs, appearance, etc. **7.** *Obs.* a standard, pattern, or rule. **8. back to square one.** indicating a return to the starting point because of failure, lack of progress, etc. **9. on the square. a.** at right angles. **b.** *Inf.* honestly and openly. **10. out of square. a.** not at right angles or not having a right angle. **b.** not in order or agreement. ~*adj.* **11.** being a square in shape or section. **12.** having or forming one or more right angles or being at right angles to something. **13. a.** (*prenominal*) denoting a measure of area of any shape: *a circle of four square feet.* **b.** (*immediately postpositive*) denoting a square having a specified length on each side: *a board four feet square.* **14.** fair and honest (esp. in **a square deal**). **15.** straight, even, or level: *a square surface.* **16.** *Cricket.* at right angles to the wicket: *square leg.* **17.** *Soccer, hockey, etc.* in a straight line across the pitch: *a square pass.* **18.** *Naut.* (of the sails of a square-rigged ship) set at right angles to the keel. **19.** *Inf.* old-fashioned. **20.** stocky or sturdy: *square shoulders.* **21.** (*postpositive*) having no remaining debts or accounts to be settled. **22.** (*prenominal*) unequivocal or straightforward: *a square contradiction.* **23.** (*postpositive*) neat and tidy. **24.** *Maths.* (of a matrix) having the same number of rows and columns. **25. all square.** on equal terms; even in score. **26. square peg (in a round hole).** *Inf.* a person or thing that is a misfit. ~*vb.* (*mainly tr.*) **27.** to make into a square or similar shape. **28.** *Maths.* to raise (a number or quantity) to the second power. **29.** to test or adjust for deviation with respect to a right angle, plane surface, etc. **30.** (sometimes foll. by *off*) to divide into squares. **31.** to position so as to be rectangular, straight, or level: *to square the shoulders.* **32.** (sometimes foll. by *up*) to settle (debts, accounts, etc.). **33.** to level (the score) in a game, etc. **34.** (*also intr.;* often foll. by *with*) to agree or cause to agree: *your ideas don't square with mine.* **35.** to arrange (something) or come to an arrangement with (someone) as by bribery. **36. square the circle.** to attempt the impossible (in reference to the insoluble problem of constructing a square having exactly the same area as a given circle). ~*adv.* **37.** in order to be square. **38.** at right angles. **39.** *Soccer, hockey, etc.* in a straight line across the pitch: *to pass the ball square.* **40.** *Inf.* squarely. ~See also **square away, square off, square up.** [C13: < OF *esquare,* < Vulgar L *exquadra* (unattested), < L *quadrāre* to make square] —**ˈsquareness** *n.* —**ˈsquarer** *n.*

square away *vb.* (*adv.*) **1.** to set the sails of (a square-rigged ship) at right angles to the keel. **2.** (*tr.*) *U.S. & Canad.* to make neat and tidy.

square-bashing *n. Brit. mil. sl.* drill on a barracks square.

square bracket *n.* **1.** either of a pair of characters [ ], used to enclose a section of writing or printing to separate it from the main text. **2.** Also called: **bracket.** either of these characters used as a sign of aggregation in mathematical or logical expressions.

square dance *n.* **1.** any of various formation dances in which the couples form squares. ~*vb.* **square-dance. 2.** (*intr.*) to perform such a dance. —**ˈsquare-ˌdancer** *n.*

square knot *n.* another name for **reef knot.**

square leg *n. Cricket.* **1.** a fielding position on the on side approximately at right angles to the batsman. **2.** a person who fields in this position.

squarely (ˈskwɛəlɪ) *adv.* **1.** in a direct way; straight: *he hit me squarely on the nose.* **2.** in an honest, frank, and just manner. **3.** at right angles.

square meal *n.* a substantial meal consisting of enough to satisfy.

square measure *n.* a unit or system of units for measuring areas.

square number *n.* an integer, such as 1, 4, 9, or 16, that is the square of an integer.

square off *vb.* (*intr., adv.*) to assume a posture of offence or defence, as in boxing.

square of opposition *n. Logic.* the diagrammatic representation of the relationships between the four types of proposition found in the syllogism.

square-rigged *adj. Naut.* rigged with square sails. See **square sail.**

square root *n.* a number or quantity that when multiplied by itself gives a given number or quantity: *the square roots of 4 are 2 and* -2.

square sail *n. Naut.* a rectangular or square sail set on a horizontal yard rigged more or less at right angles to the keel.

square shooter *n. Inf., chiefly U.S.* an honest or frank person. —**square shooting** *adj.*

square up *vb.* (*adv.*) **1.** to pay or settle (bills, debts, etc.). **2.** *Inf.* to arrange or be arranged satisfactorily. **3.** (*intr.;* foll. by *to*) to prepare to be confronted (with), esp. courageously. **4.** (*tr.;* foll. by *to*) to adopt a position of readiness to fight (an opponent). **5.** *Scot.* to tidy up.

squarrose (ˈskwærəʊz, ˈskwɒ-) *adj.* **1.** *Biol.* having a rough surface, caused by projecting hairs, scales, etc. **2.** *Bot.* having or relating to overlapping parts that are pointed or recurved. [C18: < L *squarrōsus* scabby]

squash[1] (skwɒʃ) *vb.* **1.** to press or squeeze or be pressed or squeezed in or down so as to crush, distort, or pulp. **2.** (*tr.*) to suppress or overcome. **3.** (*tr.*) to humiliate or crush (a person), esp. with a disconcerting retort. **4.** (*intr.*) to make a sucking, splashing, or squelching sound. **5.** (often foll. by *in* or *into*) to enter or insert in a confined space. ~*n.* **6.** *Brit.* a still drink made from fruit juice or fruit syrup diluted with water. **7.** a crush, esp. of people in a confined space. **8.** something squashed. **9.** the act or sound of squashing or the state of being squashed. **10.** Also called: **squash rackets.** a game for two or four players played in an enclosed court with a small rubber ball and light long-handled rackets. **11.** Also called: **squash tennis.** a similar game played with larger rackets and a larger pneumatic ball. [C16: < OF *esquasser,* < Vulgar L *exquassāre* (unattested), < L EX-[1] + *quassāre* to shatter] —**ˈsquasher** *n.*

squash[2] (skwɒʃ) *n., pl.* **squashes** *or* **squash.** *U.S. &*

Canad. **1.** any of various marrow-like plants, the fruits of which have a hard rind surrounding edible flesh. **2.** the fruit, eaten as a vegetable. [C17: of Amerind origin, < *askutasquash,* lit.: green vegetable eaten green]

squashy (ˈskwɒʃɪ) *adj.* **squashier, squashiest. 1.** easily squashed; pulpy: *a squashy peach.* **2.** soft and wet; marshy: *squashy ground.* —ˈ**squashily** *adv.* —ˈ**squashiness** *n.*

squat (skwɒt) *vb.* **squatting, squatted.** (*intr.*) **1.** to rest in a crouching position with the knees bent and the weight on the feet. **2.** to crouch down, esp. in order to hide. **3.** *Law.* to occupy land or property to which the occupant has no legal title. ~*adj.* **4.** Also: **squatty.** short and broad. ~*n.* **5.** a squatting position. **6.** a house occupied by squatters. [C13: < OF *esquater,* < *es-* EX-[1] + *catir* to press together, < Vulgar L *coactīre* (unattested), < L *cōgere* to compress] —ˈ**squatly** *adv.* —ˈ**squatness** *n.*

squatter (ˈskwɒtə) *n.* **1.** (in Britain) a person who occupies land or property wrongfully. **2.** (in Australia) **a.** a grazier with extensive holdings. **b.** *History.* a person occupying land as tenant of the Crown. **3.** (in New Zealand) a 19th-century settler who took up large acreage on a crown lease.

squattocracy (skwɒˈtɒkrəsɪ) *n. Austral.* squatters collectively, regarded as rich and influential. See **squatter** (sense 2a). [C19: < SQUATTER + -CRACY]

squaw (skwɔː) *n.* **1.** *Offens.* a North American Indian woman. **2.** *Sl., usually facetious.* a woman or wife. [C17: of Amerind origin]

squawk (skwɔːk) *n.* **1.** a loud raucous cry; screech. **2.** *Inf.* a loud complaint. ~*vb.* **3.** to utter (with) a squawk. **4.** (*intr.*) *Inf.* to complain loudly. [C19: imit.] —ˈ**squawker** *n.*

squaw man *n. Derog.* a White man married to a North American Indian woman.

squeak (skwiːk) *n.* **1.** a short shrill cry or high-pitched sound. **2.** *Inf.* an escape (esp. in **narrow squeak, near squeak**). **3.** *Inf.* (*usually used with a negative*) a word; a slight sound. ~*vb.* **4.** to make or cause to make a squeak. **5.** (*intr.;* usually foll. by *through* or *by*) to pass with only a narrow margin: *to squeak through an examination.* **6.** (*intr.*) *Inf.* to confess information about oneself or another. **7.** (*tr.*) to utter with a squeak. [C17: prob. of Scand. origin] —ˈ**squeaky** *adj.* —ˈ**squeakily** *adv.* —ˈ**squeakiness** *n.*

squeaky-clean *adj.* **1.** (of hair) washed so clean that wet strands squeak when rubbed. **2.** completely clean. **3.** above reproach: *his squeaky-clean image.*

squeal (skwiːl) *n.* **1.** a high shrill yelp, as of pain. **2.** a screaming sound. ~*vb.* **3.** to utter (with) a squeal. **4.** (*intr.*) *Sl.* to confess information about another. **5.** (*intr.*) *Inf., chiefly Brit.* to complain loudly. [C13 *squelen,* imit.] —ˈ**squealer** *n.*

squeamish (ˈskwiːmɪʃ) *adj.* **1.** easily sickened or nauseated. **2.** easily shocked; prudish. **3.** easily frightened: *squeamish about spiders.* [C15: < Anglo-F *escoymous,* <?] —ˈ**squeamishly** *adv.* —ˈ**squeamishness** *n.*

squeegee (ˈskwiːdʒiː) *n.* **1.** an implement with a rubber blade used for wiping away surplus water from a surface, such as a windowpane. **2.** any of various similar devices used in photography for pressing water out of wet prints or negatives or for squeezing prints onto a glazing surface. ~*vb.* **-geeing, -geed. 3.** to remove (liquid) from (something) by use of a squeegee. [C19: prob. imit., infl. by SQUEEZE]

squeeze (skwiːz) *vb.* (*mainly tr.*) **1.** to grip or press firmly, esp. so as to crush or distort. **2.** to crush or press (something) so as to extract (a liquid): *to squeeze juice from an orange; to squeeze an orange.* **3.** to apply gentle pressure to, as in affection or reassurance: *he squeezed her hand.* **4.** to push or force in a confined space: *to squeeze six lettuces into one box; to squeeze through a crowd.* **5.** to hug closely. **6.** to oppress with exacting demands, such as excessive taxes. **7.** to exert pressure on (someone) in order to extort (something): *to squeeze money out of a victim by blackmail.* **8.** *Bridge, whist.* to lead a card that forces (opponents) to discard potentially winning cards. ~*n.* **9.** the act or an instance of squeezing or of being squeezed. **10.** a hug or handclasp. **11.** a crush of people in a confined space. **12.** *Chiefly Brit.* a condition of restricted credit imposed by a government to counteract price inflation. **13.** an amount extracted by squeezing: *a squeeze of lemon juice.* **14.** *Inf.* pressure brought to bear in order to extort something (esp. in **put the squeeze on**). **15.** Also called: **squeeze play.** *Bridge, whist.* a manoeuvre that forces opponents to discard potentially winning cards. [C16: < ME *queysen* to press, < OE *cwȳsan*] —ˈ**squeezable** *adj.* —ˈ**squeezer** *n.*

squelch (skwɛltʃ) *vb.* **1.** (*intr.*) to walk laboriously through soft wet material or with wet shoes, making a sucking noise. **2.** (*intr.*) to make such a noise. **3.** (*tr.*) to crush completely; squash. **4.** (*tr.*) *Inf.* to silence, as by a crushing retort. ~*n.* **5.** a squelching sound. **6.** something that has been squelched. **7.** *Inf.* a crushing remark. [C17: imit.] —ˈ**squelcher** *n.* —ˈ**squelchy** *adj.*

squib (skwɪb) *n.* **1.** a firework that burns with a hissing noise and culminates in a small explosion. **2.** a short witty attack; lampoon. **3. damp squib.** something intended but failing to impress. ~*vb.* **squibbing, squibbed. 4.** (*intr.*) to sound, move, or explode like a squib. **5.** (*intr.*) to let off or shoot a squib. **6.** to write a squib against (someone). [C16: prob. imit. of a light explosion]

squid (skwɪd) *n., pl.* **squid** *or* **squids.** any of various ten-limbed pelagic cephalopod molluscs of most seas, having a torpedo-shaped body ranging from about 10 centimetres to 16.5 metres long. See also **cuttlefish.** [C17: <?]

squiffy (ˈskwɪfɪ) *adj.* **-fier, -fiest.** *Brit. inf.* slightly drunk. [C19: <?]

squiggle (ˈskwɪgᵊl) *n.* **1.** a mark or movement in the form of a wavy line; curlicue. **2.** an illegible scrawl. ~*vb.* **3.** (*intr.*) to wriggle. **4.** (*intr.*) to form or draw squiggles. **5.** (*tr.*) to make into squiggles. [C19: ? a blend of SQUIRM + WIGGLE] —ˈ**squiggler** *n.* —ˈ**squiggly** *adj.*

squilgee (ˈskwɪldʒiː) *n.* a variant spelling of **squeegee.** [C19: ? < SQUEEGEE, infl. by SQUELCH]

squill (skwɪl) *n.* **1.** Also called: **sea squill.** a Mediterranean plant of the lily family. **2.** any of various related Old World plants. **3.** the bulb of the sea squill, which is sliced, dried, and used medicinally, as an expectorant. [C14: < L *squilla* sea onion, < Gk *skilla,* <?]

squinch (skwɪntʃ) *n.* a small arch, corbelling, etc., across an internal corner of a tower, used to support a spire, etc. Also called: **squinch arch.** [C15: < obs. *scunch,* < ME *sconcheon,* < OF *escoinson,* < *es-* EX-[1] + *coin* corner]

squint (skwɪnt) *vb.* **1.** (*usually intr.*) to cross or partly close (the eyes). **2.** (*intr.*) to have a squint. **3.** (*intr.*) to look or glance sideways or askance. ~*n.* **4.** the nontechnical name for **strabismus. 5.** the act or an instance of squinting; glimpse. **6.** a narrow oblique opening in a wall or pillar of a church to permit a view of the main altar from a side aisle or transept. **7.** *Inf.* a quick look; glance. ~*adj.* **8.** having a squint. **9.** *Inf.* askew; crooked. [C14: short for ASQUINT] —ˈ**squinter** *n.* —ˈ**squinty** *adj.*

squire (ˈskwaɪə) *n.* **1.** a country gentleman in England, esp. the main landowner in a rural community. **2.** *Feudal history.* a young man of noble birth, who attended upon a knight. **3.** *Rare.* a man who courts or escorts a woman. **4.** *Inf., chiefly Brit.* a term of address used by one man to another. ~*vb.* **5.** (*tr.*) (of a man) to escort a woman. [C13: < OF *esquier;* see ESQUIRE]

squirearchy *or* **squirarchy** (ˈskwaɪəˌrɑːkɪ) *n., pl.* **-chies. 1.** government by squires. **2.** squires collectively, esp. as a political or social force. —**squireˈarchal, squirˈarchal** *or* **squireˈarchical, squirˈarchical** *adj.*

squireen (skwaɪˈriːn) *or* **squireling** (ˈskwaɪəlɪŋ) *n. Rare.* a petty squire. [C19: < SQUIRE + *-een,* Anglo-Irish dim. suffix]

squirm (skwɜːm) *vb.* (*intr.*) **1.** to move with a

wriggling motion; writhe. **2.** to feel deep mental discomfort, guilt, embarrassment, etc. *~n.* **3.** a squirming movement. [C17: imit. (? infl. by WORM)] —**ˈsquirmer** *n.* —**ˈsquirmy** *adj.*

squirrel (ˈskwɪrəl) *n., pl.* **-rels** *or* **-rel.** **1.** any of various arboreal rodents having a bushy tail and feeding on nuts, seeds, etc. **2.** any of various related rodents, such as a ground squirrel or a marmot. **3.** the fur of such an animal. **4.** *Inf.* a person who hoards things. *~vb.* **-relling, -relled** *or (esp. U.S.)* **-reling, -reled.** **5.** (*tr.;* usually foll. by *away*) *Inf.* to store for future use; hoard. [C14: < OF *esquireul,* < LL *sciūrus,* < Gk *skiouros,* < *skia* shadow + *oura* tail]

squirrel cage *n.* **1.** a cage consisting of a cylindrical framework that is made to rotate by a small animal running inside the framework. **2.** a repetitive purposeless task, way of life, etc. **3.** Also called: **squirrel-cage motor.** *Electrical engineering.* the rotor of an induction motor with a cylindrical winding having copper bars around the periphery parallel to the axis.

squirt (skwɜːt) *vb.* **1.** to force (a liquid) or (of a liquid) to be forced out of a narrow opening. **2.** (*tr.*) to cover or spatter with liquid so ejected. *~n.* **3.** a jet or amount of liquid so ejected. **4.** the act or an instance of squirting. **5.** an instrument used for squirting. **6.** *Inf.* **a.** a person regarded as insignificant or contemptible. **b.** a short person. [C15: imit.] —**ˈsquirter** *n.*

squirting cucumber *n.* a hairy plant of the Mediterranean region, having a fruit that discharges seeds explosively when ripe.

squish (skwɪʃ) *vb.* **1.** (*tr.*) to crush, esp. so as to make a soft splashing noise. **2.** (*intr.*) (of mud, etc.) to make a splashing noise. *~n.* **3.** a soft squashing sound. [C17: imit.] —**ˈsquishy** *adj.*

squit (skwɪt) *n. Brit. sl.* **1.** an insignificant person. **2.** nonsense. [C19: var. of SQUIRT]

squiz (skwɪz) *n., pl.* **squizzes.** *Austral. & N.Z. sl.* a look or glance, esp. an inquisitive one. [C20: ? blend of SQUINT + QUIZ]

sr *Maths. abbrev. for* steradian.

Sr *abbrev. for:* **1.** (after a name) senior. **2.** Señor. **3.** Sir. **4.** Sister (religious). *~***5.** *the chemical symbol for* strontium.

Sra *abbrev. for* Señora.

SRC (in Britain) *abbrev. for* Science Research Council.

Sri Lankan (srɪ ˈlæŋkən) *adj.* **1.** of Sri Lanka, a republic in S Asia, or its inhabitants. *~n.* **2.** an inhabitant of Sri Lanka.

SRN (in Britain) *abbrev. for* State Registered Nurse.

SRO *abbrev. for:* **1.** standing room only. **2.** (in Britain) Statutory Rules and Orders.

Srta *abbrev. for* Señorita.

SS *abbrev. for:* **1.** Saints. **2.** a paramilitary organization within the Nazi party that provided Hitler's bodyguard, security forces, concentration-camp guards, etc. [G *Schutzstaffel* protection squad] **3.** steamship.

SSE *symbol for* south-southeast.

SSR *abbrev. for* Soviet Socialist Republic.

SSRC (in Britain, formerly) *abbrev. for* Social Science Research Council.

SST *abbrev. for* supersonic transport.

SSW *symbol for* south-southwest.

St *abbrev. for:* **1.** Saint (all entries that are usually preceded by *St* are in this dictionary listed alphabetically under **Saint**). **2.** statute. **3.** Strait. **4.** Street.

st. *abbrev. for:* **1.** stanza. **2.** statute. **3.** stone. **4.** *Cricket.* stumped by.

s.t. *abbrev. for* short ton.

-st *suffix.* a variant of **-est**[2].

stab (stæb) *vb.* **stabbing, stabbed.** **1.** (*tr.*) to pierce or injure with a sharp pointed instrument. **2.** (*tr.*) (of a sharp pointed instrument) to pierce or wound. **3.** (when *intr.,* often foll. by *at*) to make a thrust (at); jab. **4.** (*tr.*) to inflict with a sharp pain. **5. stab in the back. a.** (*vb.*) to damage the reputation of (a person, esp. a friend) in a surreptitious way. **b.** (*n.*) a treacherous action or remark that causes the downfall of or injury to a person. *~n.* **6.** the act or an instance of stabbing. **7.** an injury or rift made by stabbing. **8.** a sudden sensation, esp. an unpleasant one: *a stab of pity.* **9.** *Inf.* an attempt (esp. in **make a stab at**). [C14: < *stabbe* stab wound] —**ˈstabber** *n.*

Stabat Mater (ˈstɑːbæt ˈmɑːtə) *n.* **1.** *R.C. Church.* a Latin hymn commemorating the sorrows of the Virgin Mary at the crucifixion. **2.** a musical setting of this hymn. [< opening words, lit.: the mother was standing]

stabile (ˈsteɪbaɪl) *n.* **1.** *Arts.* a stationary abstract construction, usually of wire, metal, wood, etc. *~adj.* **2.** fixed; stable. **3.** resistant to chemical change. [C18: < L *stabilis*]

stability (stəˈbɪlɪtɪ) *n., pl.* **-ties.** **1.** the quality of being stable. **2.** the ability of an aircraft to resume its original flight path after inadvertent displacement.

stabilize *or* **-ise** (ˈsteɪbɪˌlaɪz) *vb.* **1.** to make or become stable or more stable. **2.** to keep or be kept stable. **3.** (*tr.*) to put or keep (an aircraft, vessel, etc.) in equilibrium by one or more special devices or (of an aircraft, etc.) to become stable. —ˌ**stabiliˈzation** *or* **-iˈsation** *n.*

stabilizer *or* **-iser** (ˈsteɪbɪˌlaɪzə) *n.* **1.** any device for stabilizing an aircraft. **2.** a substance added to something to maintain it in a stable or unchanging state, such as an additive that preserves the texture of food. **3.** *Naut.* **a.** a system of pairs of fins projecting from the hull of a ship and controllable to counteract roll. **b.** See **gyrostabilizer.** **4.** a person or thing that stabilizes. **5.** either of a pair of small wheels fitted to the back wheel of a bicycle to help a beginner to maintain balance.

stable[1] (ˈsteɪbᵊl) *n.* **1.** a building, usually consisting of stalls, for the lodging of horses or other livestock. **2.** the animals lodged in such a building, collectively. **3. a.** the racehorses belonging to a particular establishment or owner. **b.** the establishment itself. **c.** (*as modifier*): *stable companion.* **4.** *Inf.* a source of training, such as a school, theatre, etc.: *the two athletes were out of the same stable.* **5.** a number of people considered as a source of a particular talent: *a stable of writers.* **6.** (*modifier*) of, relating to, or suitable for a stable: *stable door.* *~vb.* **7.** to put, keep, or be kept in a stable. [C13: < OF *estable* cowshed, < L *stabulum* shed, < *stāre* to stand]

stable[2] (ˈsteɪbᵊl) *adj.* **1.** steady in position or balance; firm. **2.** lasting: *a stable relationship.* **3.** steadfast or firm of purpose. **4.** (of an elementary particle, etc.) not undergoing decay; not radioactive. **5.** (of a chemical compound) not readily partaking in a chemical change. [C13: < OF *estable,* < L *stabilis* steady, < *stāre* to stand] —**ˈstableness** *n.* —**ˈstably** *adv.*

stableboy (ˈsteɪbᵊlˌbɔɪ), **stablegirl** (ˈsteɪbᵊlˌgɜːl), *or* **stableman** (ˈsteɪbᵊlˌmæn, -mən) *n., pl.* **-boys, -girls,** *or* **-men.** a boy, girl, or man who works in a stable.

stable door *n.* a door with an upper and lower leaf that may be opened separately. U.S. and Canad. equivalent: **Dutch door.**

stable lad *n.* a person who looks after the horses in a racing stable.

stabling (ˈsteɪblɪŋ) *n.* stable buildings or accommodation.

stablish (ˈstæblɪʃ) *vb.* an archaic variant of **establish.**

staccato (stəˈkɑːtəʊ) *adj.* **1.** *Music.* (of notes) short, clipped, and separate. **2.** characterized by short abrupt sounds, as in speech: *a staccato command.* *~adv.* **3.** (esp. used as a musical direction) in a staccato manner. [C18: < It., < *staccare* to detach, shortened < *distaccare*]

stachys (ˈstækɪs) *n.* any plant of the herbaceous genus *Stachys.* See also **woundwort.** [C16: < L, < Gk: ear of corn]

stack (stæk) *n.* **1.** an ordered pile or heap. **2.** a large orderly pile of hay, straw, etc., for storage in the open air. **3.** (*often pl.*) compactly spaced bookshelves, used to house collections of books in an area usually prohibited to library users. **4.** a number of aircraft circling an airport at different altitudes, awaiting their signal to land. **5.** a large amount. **6.** *Mil.* a pile of rifles or muskets in the shape of a cone. **7.** *Brit.* a measure of coal or wood equal to 108 cubic feet. **8.** See **chimney stack, smokestack. 9.** a vertical pipe, such as the funnel of a ship or the soil pipe attached to the side of a building. **10.** a high column of rock, esp. one isolated from the mainland by the erosive action of the sea. **11.** an area in a computer memory for temporary storage. ~*vb.* (*tr.*) **12.** to place in a stack; pile. **13.** to load or fill up with piles of something: *to stack a lorry with bricks.* **14.** to control a number of aircraft waiting to land at an airport so that each flies at a different altitude. **15. stack the cards.** to prearrange the order of a pack of cards secretly so as to cheat. [C13: < ON *stakkr* haystack, of Gmc origin] —ˈ**stacker** *n.*

stacked (stækt) *adj. Sl.* a variant of **well-stacked.**

stadholder *or* **stadtholder** (ˈstædˌhəʊldə) *n.* **1.** the chief magistrate of the former Dutch republic or any of its provinces (from about 1580 to 1802). **2.** a viceroy or governor of a province. [C16: < Du. *stad houder,* < *stad* city + *houder* holder]

stadia[1] (ˈsteɪdɪə) *n.* **1.** measurement of distance using a telescopic surveying instrument and a graduated staff calibrated to correspond with the distance from the observer. **2.** the two parallel cross hairs or **stadia hairs** in the eyepiece of the instrument used. **3.** the staff used. [C19: prob. < STADIA[2]]

stadia[2] (ˈsteɪdɪə) *n.* a plural of **stadium.**

stadium (ˈsteɪdɪəm) *n., pl.* **-diums** *or* **-dia. 1.** a sports arena with tiered seats for spectators. **2.** (in ancient Greece) a course for races, usually located between two hills providing slopes for tiers of seats. **3.** an ancient Greek measure of length equivalent to about 607 feet or 184 metres. [C16: via L < Gk *stadion,* changed < *spadion* racecourse, < *spān* to pull; infl. by Gk *stadios* steady]

staff[1] (stɑːf) *n., pl.* **staffs** *for senses 1-4;* **staffs** *or* **staves** *for senses 5-9.* **1.** a group of people employed by a company, individual, etc., for executive, clerical, sales work, etc. **2.** (*modifier*) attached to or provided for the staff of an establishment: *a staff doctor.* **3.** the body of teachers or lecturers of an educational institution. **4.** *Mil.* the officers appointed to assist a commander, service, or central headquarters organization. **5.** a stick with some special use, such as a walking stick or an emblem of authority. **6.** something that sustains or supports: *bread is the staff of life.* **7.** a pole on which a flag is hung. **8.** *Chiefly Brit.* a graduated rod used in surveying, esp. for sighting to with a levelling instrument. **9.** Also called: **stave.** *Music.* **a.** the system of horizontal lines grouped into sets of five (four in plainsong) upon which music is written. The spaces between them are employed in conjunction with a clef in order to give a graphic indication of pitch. **b.** any set of five lines in this system together with its clef: *the treble staff.* ~*vb.* **10.** (*tr.*) to provide with a staff. [OE *stæf*]

staff[2] (stɑːf) *n. U.S.* a mixture of plaster and hair used to cover the external surface of temporary structures and for decoration. [C19: <?]

staff corporal *n.* a noncommissioned rank in the British Army above that of staff sergeant and below that of warrant officer.

staff nurse *n.* a qualified nurse ranking immediately below a sister.

staff officer *n.* a commissioned officer serving on the staff of a commander, service, or central headquarters.

Staffordshire bull terrier (ˈstæfədˌʃɪə) *n.* a breed of smooth-coated terrier with a stocky frame and generally a pied or brindled coat.

Staffs. (stæfs) *abbrev. for* Staffordshire.

staff sergeant *n. Mil.* **1.** *Brit.* a noncommissioned officer holding a rank between sergeant and warrant officer and employed on administrative duties. **2.** *U.S.* a noncommissioned officer who ranks: **a.** (in the Army) above sergeant and below sergeant first class. **b.** (in the Air Force) above airman first class and below technical sergeant. **c.** (in the Marine Corps) above sergeant and below gunnery sergeant.

stag (stæg) *n.* **1.** the adult male of a deer. **2.** a man unaccompanied by a woman at a social gathering. **3.** *Stock Exchange, Brit.* a speculator who buys heavily on a new share issue in anticipation of a rise in its price and thus a quick profit on its resale. **4.** (*modifier*) (of a social gathering) attended by men only. ~*adv.* **5.** without a female escort. [OE *stagga* (unattested); rel. to ON *steggr* male bird]

stag beetle *n.* any of various beetles, the males of which have large branched mandibles.

stage (steɪdʒ) *n.* **1.** a distinct step or period of development, growth, or progress. **2.** a raised area or platform. **3.** the platform in a theatre where actors perform. **4. the.** the theatre as a profession. **5.** any scene regarded as a setting for an event or action. **6.** a portion of a journey or a stopping place after such a portion. **7.** short for **stagecoach. 8.** *Brit.* a division of a bus route for which there is a fixed fare. **9.** one of the separate propulsion units of a rocket that can be jettisoned when it has burnt out. **10.** a small stratigraphical unit; a subdivision of a rock series or system. **11.** the platform on a microscope on which the specimen is mounted for examination. **12.** *Electronics.* a part of a complex circuit, esp. a transistor with the associated elements required to amplify a signal in an amplifier. **13. by** *or* **in easy stages.** not hurriedly: *he learnt French by easy stages.* ~*vb.* (*tr.*) **14.** to perform (a play), esp. on a stage: *to stage "Hamlet".* **15.** to set the action of (a play) in a particular time or place. **16.** to plan, organize, and carry out (an event). [C13: < OF *estage* position, < Vulgar L *staticum* (unattested), < L *stāre* to stand]

stagecoach (ˈsteɪdʒˌkəʊtʃ) *n.* a large four-wheeled horse-drawn vehicle formerly used to carry passengers, mail, etc., on a regular route.

stagecraft (ˈsteɪdʒˌkrɑːft) *n.* skill in or the art of writing or staging plays.

stage direction *n.* an instruction to an actor or director, written into the script of a play.

stage door *n.* a door at a theatre leading backstage.

stage fright *n.* nervousness or panic that may beset a person about to appear in front of an audience.

stagehand (ˈsteɪdʒˌhænd) *n.* a person who sets the stage, moves props, etc., in a theatrical production.

stage left *n.* the part of the stage to the left of a performer facing the audience.

stage-manage *vb.* **1.** to work as stage manager (for a play, etc.). **2.** (*tr.*) to arrange, present, or supervise from behind the scenes.

stage manager *n.* a person who supervises the stage arrangements of a theatrical production.

stager (ˈsteɪdʒə) *n.* **1.** a person of experience; veteran (esp. in **old stager**). **2.** an archaic word for **actor.**

stage right *n.* the part of the stage to the right of a performer facing the audience.

stage-struck *adj.* infatuated with the glamour of theatrical life, esp. with the desire to act.

stage whisper *n.* **1.** a loud whisper from one actor to another onstage intended to be heard by the audience. **2.** any loud whisper that is intended to be overheard.

stagflation (stægˈfleɪʃən) *n.* a situation in which inflation is combined with stagnant or falling output and employment. [C20: blend of *stagnation* + *inflation*]

stagger (ˈstægə) *vb.* **1.** (*usually intr.*) to walk or cause to walk unsteadily as if about to fall. **2.** (*tr.*) to astound or overwhelm, as with shock: *I am staggered by his ruthlessness.* **3.** (*tr.*) to place or arrange in alternating or overlapping positions or time periods to prevent confusion or congestion: *a staggered junction; to stagger holidays.* **4.** (*intr.*) to falter or hesitate: *his courage staggered in the face of the battle.* ~*n.* **5.** the act or an instance of staggering. [C13: < dialect *stacker,* < ON *staka* to push] —**ˈstaggerer** *n.* —**ˈstaggering** *adj.* —**ˈstaggeringly** *adv.*

staggers (ˈstægəz) *n.* (*functioning as sing. or pl.*) **1.** a form of vertigo associated with decompression sickness. **2.** Also called: **blind staggers.** a disease of horses and some other domestic animals characterized by a swaying unsteady gait, caused by infection or lesions of the central nervous system.

staging (ˈsteɪdʒɪŋ) *n.* any temporary structure used in the process of building, esp. the horizontal platforms supported by scaffolding.

staging area *n.* a checkpoint or regrouping area for military formations in transit.

staging post *n.* a place where a journey is usually broken, esp. a stopover on a flight.

stagnant (ˈstægnənt) *adj.* **1.** (of water, etc.) standing still; without flow or current. **2.** brackish and foul from standing still. **3.** stale, sluggish, or dull from inaction. **4.** not growing or developing; static. [C17: < L *stagnāns*, < *stagnāre* to be stagnant, < *stagnum* a pool] —**ˈstagnancy** *n.*

stagnate (stægˈneɪt) *vb.* (*intr.*) to be or become stagnant. —**stagˈnation** *n.*

stag party *n.* a party for men only, esp. one held for a man just before he is married.

stagy *or U.S.* **stagey** (ˈsteɪdʒɪ) *adj.* **stagier, stagiest.** excessively theatrical or dramatic. —**ˈstagily** *adv.* —**ˈstaginess** *n.*

staid (steɪd) *adj.* of a settled, sedate, and steady character. [C16: obs. p.p. of STAY[1]] —**ˈstaidly** *adv.* —**ˈstaidness** *n.*

stain (steɪn) *vb.* (*mainly tr.*) **1.** to mark or discolour with patches of something that dirties. **2.** to dye with a penetrating dyestuff or pigment. **3.** to bring disgrace or shame on: *to stain one's honour.* **4.** to colour (specimens) for microscopic study by treatment with a dye or similar reagent. **5.** (*intr.*) to produce indelible marks or discoloration: *does ink stain?* ~*n.* **6.** a spot, mark, or discoloration. **7.** a moral taint; blemish or slur. **8.** a dye or similar reagent, used to colour specimens for microscopic study. **9.** a solution or liquid used to penetrate the surface of a material, esp. wood, and impart a rich colour without covering up the surface or grain. **10.** any dye used to colour textiles and hides. [C14 *steynen* (vb.), shortened < *disteynen* to remove colour from, < OF *desteindre* to discolour, ult. < L *tingere* to tinge] —**ˈstainable** *adj.* —**ˌstainaˈbility** *n.* —**ˈstainer** *n.*

stained glass *n.* **a.** glass that has been coloured, as by fusing with a film of metallic oxide or burning pigment into the surface. **b.** (*as modifier*): *a stained-glass window.*

stainless (ˈsteɪnlɪs) *adj.* **1.** resistant to discoloration, esp. that resulting from corrosion; rust-resistant: *stainless steel.* **2.** having no blemish: *stainless reputation.* —**ˈstainlessly** *adv.*

stainless steel *n.* **a.** a type of steel resistant to corrosion as a result of the presence of large amounts of chromium. **b.** (*as modifier*): *stainless-steel cutlery.*

stair (stɛə) *n.* **1.** one of a flight of stairs. **2.** a series of steps: *a narrow stair.* ~See also **stairs.** [OE *stæger*]

staircase (ˈstɛəˌkeɪs) *n.* a flight of stairs, its supporting framework, and, usually, a handrail or banisters.

stairs (stɛəz) *pl. n.* **1.** a flight of steps leading from one storey or level to another, esp. indoors. **2. below stairs.** *Brit.* in the servants' quarters.

stairway (ˈstɛəˌweɪ) *n.* a means of access consisting of stairs; staircase or flight of steps.

stairwell (ˈstɛəˌwɛl) *n.* a vertical shaft or opening that contains a staircase.

stake[1] (steɪk) *n.* **1.** a stick or metal bar driven into the ground as a marker, part of a fence, support for a plant, etc. **2.** one of a number of vertical posts that fit into sockets around a flat truck or railway wagon to hold the load in place. **3.** a method or the practice of executing a person by binding him to a stake in the centre of a pile of wood that is then set on fire. **4. pull up stakes.** to leave one's home or resting place and move on. ~*vb.* (*tr.*) **5.** to tie, fasten, or tether with or to a stake. **6.** (often foll. by *out* or *off*) to fence or surround with stakes. **7.** (often foll. by *out*) to lay (a claim) to land, rights, etc. **8.** to support with a stake. [OE *staca* pin]

stake[2] (steɪk) *n.* **1.** the money or valuables that a player must hazard in order to buy into a gambling game or make a bet. **2.** an interest, often financial, held in something: *a stake in the company's future.* **3.** (*often pl.*) the money that a player has available for gambling. **4.** (*often pl.*) a prize in a race, etc., esp. one made up of contributions from contestants or owners. **5.** (*pl.*) a horse race in which all owners of competing horses contribute to the prize. **6.** *U.S. & Canad. inf.* short for **grubstake. 7. at stake.** at risk: *lives are at stake.* ~*vb.* (*tr.*) **8.** to hazard (money, etc.) on a result. **9.** to invest in or support with money, etc.: *to stake a business.* [C16: <?]

stakeout (ˈsteɪkaʊt) *Chiefly U.S. & Canad. sl.* ~*n.* **1.** a police surveillance. **2.** an area or house kept under such surveillance. ~*vb.* **stake out. 3.** (*tr., adv.*) to keep under surveillance.

Stakhanovism (stæˈkænəˌvɪzəm) *n.* (in the Soviet Union) a system designed to raise production by offering incentives to efficient workers. [C20: after A. G. *Stakhanov* (1906–77), Soviet miner, the worker first rewarded under the system in 1935] —**Staˈkhanovˌite** *n., adj.*

stalactite (ˈstæləkˌtaɪt) *n.* a cylindrical mass of calcium carbonate hanging from the roof of a limestone cave: formed by precipitation from continually dripping water. Cf. **stalagmite.** [C17: < NL *stalactites*, < Gk *stalaktos* dripping, < *stalassein* to drip] —**stalactiform** (stəˈlæktɪˌfɔːm) *adj.* —**stalactitic** (ˌstæləkˈtɪtɪk) *or* **ˌstalacˈtitical** *adj.*

stalag (ˈstælæg) *n.* a German prisoner-of-war camp in World War II, esp. for men from the ranks. [short for *Stammlager* base camp]

stalagmite (ˈstæləgˌmaɪt) *n.* a cylindrical mass of calcium carbonate projecting upwards from the floor of a limestone cave: formed by precipitation from continually dripping water. Cf. **stalactite.** [C17: < NL *stalagmites*, < Gk *stalagmos* dripping; rel. to Gk *stalassein* to drip] —**stalagmitic** (ˌstæləgˈmɪtɪk) *or* **ˌstalagˈmitical** *adj.*

stale[1] (steɪl) *adj.* **1.** (esp. of food) hard, musty, or dry from being kept too long. **2.** (of beer, etc.) flat and tasteless from being kept open too long. **3.** (of air) stagnant; foul. **4.** uninteresting from overuse: *stale clichés.* **5.** no longer new: *stale news.* **6.** lacking in energy or ideas through overwork or lack of variety. **7.** *Law.* (of a claim, etc.) having lost its effectiveness or force, as by failure to act or by the lapse of time. ~*vb.* **8.** to make or become stale. [C13 (orig. applied to liquor in the sense: well matured): prob. < OF *estale* (unattested) motionless, of Frankish origin] —**ˈstaleness** *n.*

stale[2] (steɪl) *vb.* **1.** (*intr.*) (of livestock) to urinate. ~*n.* **2.** the urine of horses or cattle. [C15: ? < OF *estaler* to stand in one position]

stalemate (ˈsteɪlˌmeɪt) *n.* **1.** a chess position in which any of a player's possible moves would place his king in check: in this position the game ends in a draw. **2.** a situation in which two opposing forces find that further action is impossible or futile; deadlock. ~*vb.* **3.** (*tr.*) to subject to a stalemate. [C18: < obs. *stale*, < OF *estal* STALL[1] + (CHECK)MATE]

Stalinism (ˈstɑːlɪˌnɪzəm) *n.* the theory and form of government associated with Joseph Stalin (1879–1953), general secretary of the Communist Party of the Soviet Union 1922–53: a variant of Marxism-Leninism characterized by totalitarianism, rigid bureaucracy, and loyalty to the Soviet state. —**ˈStalinist** *n., adj.*

stalk[1] (stɔːk) *n.* **1.** the main stem of a herbaceous plant. **2.** any of various subsidiary plant stems, such as a leafstalk or flower stalk. **3.** a slender supporting structure in animals such as crinoids and barnacles. **4.** any long slender supporting shaft or column. [C14: prob. dim. < OE *stalu* upright piece of wood] —**stalked** *adj.* —**ˈstalkˌlike** *adj.*

stalk[2] (stɔːk) *vb.* **1.** to follow or approach (game, prey, etc.) stealthily and quietly. **2.** to spread over (a place) in a menacing or grim manner: *fever stalked the camp.* **3.** (*intr.*) to walk in a haughty, stiff, or threatening way. **4.** to search (a piece of land) for prey. ~*n.* **5.** the act of stalking. **6.** a stiff or threatening stride. [OE *bestealcian* to walk stealthily] —ˈ**stalker** *n.*

stalking-horse *n.* **1.** a horse or an imitation one used by a hunter to hide behind while stalking. **2.** something serving as a means of concealing plans; pretext. **3.** *Chiefly U.S.* a candidate put forward to divide the opposition or mask the candidacy of another person for whom the stalking-horse would then withdraw.

stalky (ˈstɔːkɪ) *adj.* **stalkier, stalkiest.** **1.** like a stalk; slender and tall. **2.** having or abounding in stalks. —ˈ**stalkily** *adv.* —ˈ**stalkiness** *n.*

stall[1] (stɔːl) *n.* **1. a.** a compartment in a stable or shed for a single animal. **b.** another name for **stable**[1]. **2.** a small often temporary stand or booth for the sale of goods. **3.** (in a church) **a.** one of a row of seats usually divided by armrests or a small screen, for the choir or clergy. **b.** a pen. **4.** an instance of an engine stalling. **5.** a condition of an aircraft in flight in which a reduction in speed or an increase in the aircraft's angle of attack causes a sudden loss of lift resulting in a downward plunge. **6.** any small room or compartment. **7.** *Brit.* **a.** a seat in a theatre or cinema, usually fixed to the floor. **b.** (*pl.*) the area of seats on the ground floor of a theatre or cinema nearest to the stage or screen. **8.** a tubelike covering for a finger. **9.** (*pl.*) short for **starting stalls.** ~*vb.* **10.** to cause (a motor vehicle or its engine) to stop, usually by incorrect use of the clutch or incorrect adjustment of the fuel mixture, or (of an engine or motor vehicle) to stop, usually for these reasons. **11.** to cause (an aircraft) to go into a stall or (of an aircraft) to go into a stall. **12.** to stick or cause to stick fast, as in mud or snow. **13.** (*tr.*) to confine (an animal) in a stall. [OE *steall* a place for standing]

stall[2] (stɔːl) *vb.* **1.** to employ delaying tactics towards (someone); be evasive. ~*n.* **2.** an evasive move; pretext. [C16: < Anglo-F *estale* bird used as a decoy, infl. by STALL[1]]

stall-feed *vb.* **-feeding, -fed.** (*tr.*) to keep and feed (an animal) in a stall, esp. as an intensive method of fattening it for slaughter.

stallion (ˈstæljən) *n.* an uncastrated male horse, esp. one used for breeding. [C14 *staloun,* < OF *estalon,* of Gmc origin]

stalwart (ˈstɔːlwət) *adj.* **1.** strong and sturdy; robust. **2.** solid, dependable, and courageous. **3.** resolute and firm. ~*n.* **4.** a stalwart person, esp. a supporter. [OE *stǣlwirthe* serviceable, < *stǣl,* < *stathol* support + *wierthe* worth] —ˈ**stalwartly** *adv.* —ˈ**stalwartness** *n.*

stamen (ˈsteɪmɛn) *n., pl.* **stamens** *or* **stamina.** the male reproductive organ of a flower, consisting of a stalk (filament) bearing an anther in which pollen is produced. [C17: < L: the warp in an upright loom, < *stāre* to stand] —**staminiferous** (ˌstæmɪˈnɪfərəs) *adj.*

stamina[1] (ˈstæmɪnə) *n.* enduring energy, strength, and resilience. [C19: identical with STAMINA[2], < L *stāmen* thread, hence the threads of life spun out by the Fates, hence energy, etc.]

stamina[2] (ˈstæmɪnə) *n.* a plural of **stamen.**

staminate (ˈstæmɪnɪt, -ˌneɪt) *adj.* (of plants) having stamens, esp. having stamens but no carpels; male.

stammer (ˈstæmə) *vb.* **1.** to speak or say (something) in a hesitant way, esp. as a result of a speech disorder or through fear, stress, etc. ~*n.* **2.** a speech disorder characterized by involuntary repetitions and hesitations. [OE *stamerian*] —ˈ**stammerer** *n.* —ˈ**stammering** *n., adj.*

stamp (stæmp) *vb.* **1.** (when *intr.,* often foll. by *on*) to bring (the foot) down heavily (on the ground, etc.). **2.** (*intr.*) to walk with heavy or noisy footsteps. **3.** (*intr.;* foll. by *on*) to repress or extinguish: *he stamped on criticism.* **4.** (*tr.*) to impress or mark (a device or sign) on (something). **5.** to mark (something) with an official seal or device: *to stamp a passport.* **6.** (*tr.*) to fix or impress permanently: *the date was stamped on her memory.* **7.** (*tr.*) to affix a postage stamp to. **8.** (*tr.*) to distinguish or reveal: *that behaviour stamps him as a cheat.* **9.** to pound or crush (ores, etc.). ~*n.* **10.** the act or an instance of stamping. **11. a.** See **postage stamp. b.** a mark applied to postage stamps for cancellation. **12.** a similar piece of gummed paper used for commercial or trading purposes. **13.** a block, die, etc., used for imprinting a design or device. **14.** a design, device, or mark that has been stamped. **15.** a characteristic feature or trait; hallmark: *the stamp of authenticity.* **16.** a piece of gummed paper or other mark applied to official documents to indicate payment, validity, ownership, etc. **17.** *Brit. inf.* a national insurance contribution, formerly recorded by means of a stamp on an official card. **18.** type or class: *men of his stamp.* **19.** an instrument or machine for crushing or pounding ores, etc., or the pestle in such a device. ~See also **stamp out.** [OE *stampe*] —ˈ**stamper** *n.*

stamp duty *or* **tax** *n.* a tax on legal documents, publications, etc., the payment of which is certified by the attaching or impressing of official stamps.

stampede (stæmˈpiːd) *n.* **1.** an impulsive headlong rush of startled cattle or horses. **2.** headlong rush of a crowd. **3.** any sudden large-scale action, such as a rush of people to support a candidate. **4.** *Canad.* a rodeo. ~*vb.* **5.** to run away or cause to run away in a stampede. [C19: < American Sp. *estampida,* < Sp.: a din, < *estampar* to stamp, of Gmc origin] —**stamˈpeder** *n.*

stamping ground *n.* a habitual or favourite meeting or gathering place.

stamp mill *n.* a machine for crushing ore.

stamp out *vb.* (*tr., adv.*) **1.** to put out or extinguish by stamping: *to stamp out a fire.* **2.** to suppress by force: *to stamp out a rebellion.*

stance (stæns, stɑːns) *n.* **1.** the manner and position in which a person or animal stands. **2.** *Sport.* the posture assumed when about to play the ball, as in golf, cricket, etc. **3.** emotional or intellectual attitude: *a leftist stance.* **4.** *Chiefly Scot.* a place where a vehicle waits: *taxi stance.* [C16: via F < It. *stanza* place for standing, < L *stāns,* < *stāre* to stand]

stanch (stɑːntʃ) *or* **staunch** (stɔːntʃ) *vb.* **1.** to stem the flow of (a liquid, esp. blood) or (of a liquid) to stop flowing. **2.** to prevent the flow of a liquid, esp. blood, from (a hole, wound, etc.). [C14: < OF *estanchier,* < Vulgar L *stanticāre* (unattested) to cause to stand, < L *stāre* to halt] —ˈ**stanchable** *or* ˈ**staunchable** *adj.* —ˈ**stancher** *or* ˈ**stauncher** *n.*

stanchion (ˈstɑːnʃən) *n.* **1.** any vertical pole, beam, rod, etc., used as a support. ~*vb.* **2.** (*tr.*) to provide or support with a stanchion or stanchions. [C15: < OF *estanchon,* < *estance,* < Vulgar L *stantia* (unattested) a standing, < L *stāre* to stand]

stand (stænd) *vb.* **standing, stood.** (*mainly intr.*) **1.** (*also tr.*) to be or cause to be in an erect or upright position. **2.** to rise to, assume, or maintain an upright position. **3.** (*copula*) to have a specified height when standing: *to stand six feet tall.* **4.** to be situated or located: *the house stands in the square.* **5.** to be in a specified state or condition: *to stand in awe of someone.* **6.** to adopt or remain in a resolute position or attitude. **7.** (*may take an infinitive*) to be in a specified position: *I stand to lose money in this venture.* **8.** to remain in force or continue in effect: *my orders stand.* **9.** to come to a stop or halt, esp. temporarily. **10.** (of water, etc.) to collect and remain without flowing. **11.** (often foll. by *at*) (of a score, account, etc.) to indicate the specified position: *the score stands at 20 to 1.* **12.** (*also tr.;* when *intr.,* foll. by *for*) to tolerate or bear: *I won't stand for your nonsense; I can't stand spiders.* **13.** (*tr.*) to resist; survive: *to stand the test of time.*

14. (*tr.*) to submit to: *to stand trial.* **15.** (often foll. by *for*) *Chiefly Brit.* to be or become a candidate: *stand for Parliament.* **16.** to navigate in a specified direction: *we were standing for Madeira.* **17.** (of a gun dog) to point at game. **18.** to halt, esp. to give action, repel attack, or disrupt an enemy advance when retreating. **19.** (*tr.*) *Inf.* to bear the cost of; pay for: *to stand someone a drink.* **20. stand a chance.** to have a hope or likelihood of winning, succeeding, etc. **21. stand fast.** to maintain one's position firmly. **22. stand one's ground.** to maintain a stance or position in the face of opposition. **23. stand still. a.** to remain motionless. **b.** (foll. by *for*) *U.S.* to tolerate: *I won't stand still for your threats.* ~*n.* **24.** the act or an instance of standing. **25.** an opinion, esp. a resolutely held one: *he took a stand on capital punishment.* **26.** a halt or standstill. **27.** a place where a person or thing stands. **28.** *Austral. & N.Z.* **a.** a position on the floor of a shearing shed allocated to one shearer. **b.** the shearer's equipment. **29.** a structure on which people can sit or stand. **30.** a frame or rack on which such articles as coats and hats may be hung. **31.** a small table or piece of furniture where articles may be placed or stored: *a music stand.* **32.** a supporting framework, esp. for a tool or instrument. **33.** a stall, booth, or counter from which goods may be sold. **34.** a halt to give action, etc., esp. during a retreat and having some duration or success. **35.** *Cricket.* an extended period at the wicket by two batsmen. **36.** a growth of plants in a particular area, esp. trees in a forest or a crop in a field. **37.** a stop made by a touring theatrical company, pop group, etc., to give a performance (esp. in **one-night stand**). **38.** (of a gun dog) the act of pointing at game. ~See also **stand by, stand down,** etc. [OE *standan*] —ˈ**stander** *n.*

standard (ˈstændəd) *n.* **1.** an accepted or approved example of something against which others are judged or measured. **2.** (*often pl.*) a principle of propriety, honesty, and integrity. **3.** a level of excellence or quality. **4.** any distinctive flag or device, etc., as of a nation, sovereign, or special cause, etc., or the colours of a cavalry regiment. **5.** a flag or emblem formerly used to show the central or rallying point of an army in battle. **6.** the commodity or commodities in which is stated the value of a basic monetary unit: *the gold standard; the silver standard.* **7.** an authorized model of a unit of measure or weight. **8.** a unit of board measure equal to 1980 board feet. **9.** (in coinage) the prescribed proportion by weight of precious metal and base metal that each coin must contain. **10.** an upright pole or beam, esp. one used as a support. **11. a.** a piece of furniture consisting of an upright pole or beam on a base or support. **b.** (*as modifier*): *a standard lamp.* **12. a.** a plant, esp. a fruit tree, that is trained so that it has an upright stem free of branches. **b.** (*as modifier*): *a standard cherry.* **13.** a song or piece of music that has remained popular for many years. **14.** a form or grade in an elementary school. ~*adj.* **15.** of the usual, regularized, medium, or accepted kind: *a standard size.* **16.** of recognized authority, competence, or excellence: *the standard work on Greece.* **17.** denoting or characterized by idiom, vocabulary, etc., that is regarded as correct and acceptable by educated native speakers. **18.** *Brit.* (formerly) (of eggs) of a size that is smaller than *large* and larger than *medium.* [C12: < OF *estandart* gathering place, flag to mark such a place, prob. of Gmc origin]

standard-bearer *n.* **1.** a man who carries a standard. **2.** a leader of a cause or party.

standard cell *n.* a voltaic cell producing a constant and accurately known electromotive force that can be used to calibrate voltage-measuring instruments.

standard cost *n.* the predetermined budgeted cost of a manufacturing process against which actual costs are compared.

standard deviation *n. Statistics.* a measure of dispersion obtained by extracting the square root of the mean of the squared deviations of the observed values from their mean in a frequency distribution.

standard error of the mean *n. Statistics.* the standard deviation of the distribution of means of samples chosen from a larger population; equal to the standard deviation of the whole population divided by the square root of the sample size.

standard gauge *n.* **1.** a railway track with a distance of 4 ft. 8½ in. (1.435 m) between the lines; used on most railways. ~*adj.* **standard-gauge** *or* **standard-gauged.** **2.** of, relating to, or denoting a railway with a standard gauge.

Standard Grade *n.* (in Scotland) a new type of examination designed to test skills and the application of knowledge, which will gradually replace O grade.

standardize *or* **-ise** (ˈstændəˌdaɪz) *vb.* **1.** to make or become standard. **2.** (*tr.*) to test by or compare with a standard. —ˌ**standardiˈzation** *or* **-iˈsation** *n.* —ˈ**standardˌizer** *or* **-ˌiser** *n.*

standard of living *n.* a level of subsistence or material welfare of a community, class, or person.

standard time *n.* the official local time of a region or country determined by the distance from Greenwich of a line of longitude passing through the area.

stand by *vb.* (*intr.*) **1.** (*adv.*) to be available and ready to act if needed. **2.** (*adv.*) to be present as an onlooker or without taking any action: *he stood by at the accident.* **3.** (*prep.*) to be faithful to: *to stand by one's principles.* ~*n.* **stand-by.** **4. a.** a person or thing that is ready for use or can be relied on in an emergency. **b.** (*as modifier*): *stand-by provisions.* **5. on stand-by.** in a state of readiness for action or use. ~*adj.* **stand-by.** **6.** not booked in advance but awaiting or subject to availability: *a stand-by ticket.*

stand down *vb.* (*adv.*) **1.** (*intr.*) to resign or withdraw, esp. in favour of another. **2.** (*intr.*) to leave the witness box in a court of law after giving evidence. **3.** *Chiefly Brit.* to go or be taken off duty.

stand for *vb.* (*intr., prep.*) **1.** to represent or mean. **2.** *Chiefly Brit.* to be or become a candidate for. **3.** to support or recommend. **4.** *Inf.* to tolerate or bear: *he won't stand for it.*

stand in *vb.* **1.** (*intr., adv.;* usually foll. by *for*) to act as a substitute. **2. stand (someone) in good stead.** to be of benefit or advantage to (someone). ~*n.* **stand-in.** **3. a.** a person or thing that serves as a substitute. **b.** (*as modifier*): *a stand-in teacher.* **4.** a person who substitutes for an actor during intervals of waiting or in dangerous stunts.

standing (ˈstændɪŋ) *n.* **1.** social or financial position, status, or reputation: *a man of some standing.* **2.** length of existence, experience, etc. **3.** (*modifier*) used to stand in or on: *standing room.* ~*adj.* **4.** *Athletics.* **a.** (of the start of a race) begun from a standing position. **b.** (of a jump, leap, etc.) performed from a stationary position without a run-up. **5.** (*prenominal*) permanent, fixed, or lasting. **6.** (*prenominal*) still or stagnant: *a standing pond.* **7.** *Printing.* (of type) set and stored for future use.

standing army *n.* a permanent army of paid soldiers maintained by a nation.

standing order *n.* **1.** Also called: **banker's order.** an instruction to a bank by a depositor to pay a stated sum at regular intervals. **2.** a rule or order governing the procedure, conduct, etc., of an organization. **3.** *Mil.* one of a number of orders which have long-term validity.

standing rigging *n.* the stays, shrouds, and other more or less fixed, though adjustable, ropes that support the masts of a sailing vessel.

standing wave *n. Physics.* a wave that has unchanging amplitude at each point along its axis. Also called: **stationary wave.**

standoff (ˈstændˌɒf) *n.* **1.** *U.S. & Canad.* the act or an instance of standing off or apart. **2.** a deadlock or stalemate. **3.** *Rugby.* short for **stand-off half.** ~*vb.* **stand off.** (*adv.*) **4.** (*intr.*) to navigate a vessel so as to avoid the shore, an obstruction, etc. **5.** (*tr.*) to keep or cause to keep at a distance. **6.** (*intr.*) to reach a deadlock or stalemate. **7.** (*tr.*) to dismiss (workers), esp. temporarily.

stand-off half *n. Rugby.* **1.** a player who acts as a link between his scrum half and three-quarter backs and who marks the opposing scrum half. **2.** this position. ~Also called: **fly half.**

standoffish (ˌstændˈɒfɪʃ) *adj.* reserved, haughty, or aloof. —ˌ**standˈoffishness** *n.*

stand on *vb.* (*intr.*) **1.** (*adv.*) to continue to navigate a vessel on the same heading. **2.** (*prep.*) to insist on: *to stand on ceremony.*

stand out *vb.* (*intr., adv.*) **1.** to be distinctive or conspicuous. **2.** to refuse to agree or comply: *they stood out for a better price.* **3.** to protrude or project. **4.** to navigate a vessel away from a port, harbour, etc. ~*n.* **standout. 5.** *U.S. & Canad. inf.* a person or thing that is distinctive or outstanding.

stand over *vb.* (*tr. prep.*) **1.** to supervise closely. **2.** *Austral. & N.Z. inf.* to threaten or intimidate.

standpipe (ˈstændˌpaɪp) *n.* **1.** a vertical pipe, open at the upper end, attached to a pipeline or tank serving to limit the pressure head to that of the height of the pipe. **2.** a temporary freshwater outlet installed in a street when household water supplies are cut off.

standpoint (ˈstændˌpɔɪnt) *n.* a physical or mental position from which things are viewed.

standstill (ˈstændˌstɪl) *n.* a complete cessation of movement; halt: *come to a standstill.*

stand to *vb.* **1.** (*adv.*) *Mil.* to assume positions or cause to assume positions to resist a possible attack. **2. stand to reason.** to conform with the dictates of reason: *it stands to reason.*

stand up *vb.* (*adv.*) **1.** (*intr.*) to rise to the feet. **2.** (*intr.*) to resist or withstand wear, criticism, etc. **3.** (*tr.*) *Inf.* to fail to keep an appointment with, esp. intentionally. **4. stand up for.** to support, side with, or defend. **5. stand up to. a.** to confront or resist courageously. **b.** to withstand or endure (wear, criticism, etc.). ~*adj.* **stand-up.** (*prenominal*) **6.** having or being in an erect position: *a stand-up collar.* **7.** done, taken, etc., while standing: *a stand-up meal.* **8.** (of a comedian) telling jokes, stories, etc., directly to the audience.

Stanford-Binet test (ˈstænfədbɪˈneɪ) *n. Psychol.* a revision, esp. for U.S. use, of the Binet-Simon scale designed to measure mental ability by comparing the performance of an individual with the average performance for his age group. See also **Binet-Simon scale, intelligence test.** [C20: after *Stanford University,* California, & Alfred *Binet* (1857–1911), F psychologist]

stanhope (ˈstænəp) *n.* a light one-seater carriage with two or four wheels. [C18: after Fitzroy *Stanhope* (1787–1864), E clergyman for whom it was first built]

stank (stæŋk) *vb.* a past tense of **stink.**

stann- *combining form.* denoting tin: *stannite.* [< LL *stannum* tin]

Stannaries (ˈstænərɪz) *n.* (*sometimes functioning as sing.*) **the.** a tin-mining district of Devon and Cornwall, under the jurisdiction of special courts.

stannary (ˈstænərɪ) *n., pl.* **-ries.** a place or region where tin is mined or worked. [C15: < Med. L *stannāria,* < LL *stannum* tin]

stannic (ˈstænɪk) *adj.* of or containing tin, esp. in the tetravalent state. [C18: < LL *stannum* tin]

stannite (ˈstænaɪt) *n.* a grey metallic mineral that consists of a sulphide of tin, copper, and iron and is a source of tin. Formula: Cu_2FeSnS_4. [C19: < LL *stannum* tin + -ITE[1]]

stannous (ˈstænəs) *adj.* of or containing tin, esp. in the divalent state.

stanza (ˈstænzə) *n.* **1.** *Prosody.* a fixed number of verse lines arranged in a definite metrical pattern, forming a unit of a poem. **2.** *U.S. & Austral.* a half or a quarter in a football match. [C16: < It.: halting place, < Vulgar L *stantia* (unattested) station, < L *stāre* to stand] —ˈ**stanzaed** *adj.* —**stanzaic** (stænˈzeɪɪk) *adj.*

stapelia (stəˈpiːlɪə) *n.* any of various fleshy cactus-like leafless African plants having large fetid flowers. [C18: < NL, after J. B. van *Stapel* (died 1636), Du. botanist]

stapes (ˈsteɪpiːz) *n., pl.* **stapes** *or* **stapedes** (stæˈpiːdiːz). the stirrup-shaped bone that is the innermost of three small bones in the middle ear of mammals. Nontechnical name: **stirrup bone.** Cf. **incus, malleus.** [C17: via NL < Med. L, ? var. of *stapeda* stirrup, infl. by L *stāre* to stand + *pēs* a foot]

staphylo- *combining form.* **1.** uvula: *staphyloplasty.* **2.** resembling a bunch of grapes: *staphylococcus.* [< Gk *staphulē* bunch of grapes, uvula]

staphylococcus (ˌstæfɪləʊˈkɒkəs) *n., pl.* **-cocci** (-ˈkɒksaɪ). any spherical Gram-positive bacterium of the genus *Staphylococcus,* typically occurring in clusters and causing boils, infection in wounds, and septicaemia. Often shortened to **staph.** —ˌ**staphyloˈcoccal** *adj.*

staphyloplasty (ˈstæfɪləʊˌplæstɪ) *n.* plastic surgery or surgical repair involving the soft palate or the uvula. —ˌ**staphyloˈplastic** *adj.*

staple[1] (ˈsteɪpᵊl) *n.* **1.** a short length of thin wire bent into a square U-shape, used to fasten papers, cloth, etc. **2.** a short length of stiff wire formed into a U-shape with pointed ends, used for holding a hasp to a post, securing electric cables, etc. ~*vb.* **3.** (*tr.*) to secure (papers, wire, etc.) with staples. [OE *stapol* prop, of Gmc origin] —ˈ**stapler** *n.*

staple[2] (ˈsteɪpᵊl) *adj.* **1.** of prime importance; principal: *staple foods.* **2.** (of a commodity) forming a predominant element in the product, consumption, or trade of a nation, region, etc. ~*n.* **3.** a staple commodity. **4.** a main constituent; integral part. **5.** *Chiefly U.S. & Canad.* a principal raw material produced or grown in a region. **6.** the fibre of wool, cotton, etc., graded as to length and degree of fineness. ~*vb.* **7.** (*tr.*) to arrange or sort (wool, cotton, etc.) according to length and fineness. [C15: < MDu. *stapel* warehouse]

staple gun *n.* a mechanism that fixes staples to a surface.

star (stɑː) *n.* **1.** any of a vast number of celestial objects visible in the clear night sky as points of light. **2. a.** a hot gaseous mass, such as the sun, that radiates energy, esp. as heat and light, and in some cases as radio waves and x-rays. **b.** (*as modifier*): *a star catalogue.* Related adjs.: **astral, sidereal, stellar. 3.** *Astrol.* **a.** a celestial body, esp. a planet, supposed to influence events, personalities, etc. **b.** (*pl.*) another name for **horoscope** (sense 1). **4.** an emblem shaped like a conventionalized star, often used as a symbol of rank, an award, etc. **5.** a small white blaze on the forehead of an animal, esp. a horse. **6. a.** a distinguished or glamorous celebrity, often from the entertainment world. **b.** (*as modifier*): *star quality.* **7.** another word for **asterisk. 8. see stars.** to see or seem to see bright moving pinpoints of light, as from a blow on the head, increased blood pressure, etc. ~*vb.* **starring, starred. 9.** (*tr.*) to mark or decorate with a star or stars. **10.** to feature or be featured as a star: *"Greed" starred Erich von Stroheim; Olivier starred in "Hamlet".* [OE *steorra*] —ˈ**starless** *adj.* —ˈ**star**ˌ**like** *adj.*

starboard (ˈstɑːbəd, -ˌbɔːd) *n.* **1.** the right side of an aeroplane or vessel when facing the nose or bow. Cf. **port**[2]. ~*adj.* **2.** relating to or on the starboard. ~*vb.* **3.** to turn or be turned towards the starboard. [OE *stēorbord,* lit.: steering side, < *stēor* steering paddle + *bord* side; < the fact that boats were formerly steered by a paddle held over the right-hand side]

starch (stɑːtʃ) *n.* **1.** a polysaccharide composed of glucose units that occurs widely in plant tissues in the form of storage granules. **2.** a starch obtained from potatoes and some grain: it is fine white powder that, in solution with water, is used to stiffen fabric. **3.** any food containing a large amount of starch, such as rice and potatoes. **4.** stiff or pompous formality. ~*vb.* **5.** (*tr.*) to stiffen with or soak in starch. [OE *stercan* (unattested except by the p.p. *sterced*) to stiffen] —ˈ**starcher** *n.*

Star Chamber *n.* **1.** *English history.* the Privy Council sitting as a court of equity; abolished 1641. **2.** (*sometimes not caps.*) any arbitrary tribunal dispensing summary justice. **3.** (*sometimes not caps.*) (in Britain, in a Conservative government) a group of senior ministers who make the final decision on the public spending of each government department.

starch-reduced *adj.* (of food, esp. bread) having the starch content reduced, as in proprietary slimming products.

starchy (ˈstɑːtʃɪ) *adj.* **starchier, starchiest. 1.** of or containing starch. **2.** extremely formal, stiff, or conventional: *a starchy manner.* **3.** stiffened with starch. —ˈ**starchily** *adv.* —ˈ**starchiness** *n.*

star connection *n.* a connection used in a polyphase electrical device or system of devices in which the windings each have one end connected to a common junction, the **star point,** and the other end to a separate terminal.

star-crossed *adj.* dogged by ill luck; destined to misfortune.

stardom (ˈstɑːdəm) *n.* **1.** the fame and prestige of being a star in films, sport, etc. **2.** the world of celebrities.

stardust (ˈstɑːˌdʌst) *n.* **1.** a large number of distant stars appearing to the observer as a cloud of dust. **2.** a dreamy romantic or sentimental quality or feeling.

stare (stɛə) *vb.* **1.** (*intr.*) (often foll. by *at*) to look or gaze fixedly, often with hostility or rudeness. **2.** (*intr.*) to stand out as obvious; glare. **3. stare one in the face.** to be glaringly obvious or imminent. ~*n.* **4.** the act or an instance of staring. [OE *starian*] —ˈ**starer** *n.*

starfish (ˈstɑːˌfɪʃ) *n., pl.* **-fish** *or* **-fishes.** any of various echinoderms, typically having a flattened body covered with a flexible test and five arms radiating from a central disc.

stargaze (ˈstɑːˌgeɪz) *vb.* (*intr.*) **1.** to observe the stars. **2.** to daydream. —ˈ**starˌgazer** *n.* —ˈ**starˌgazing** *n., adj.*

stark (stɑːk) *adj.* **1.** (*usually prenominal*) devoid of any elaboration; blunt: *the stark facts.* **2.** grim; desolate: *a stark landscape.* **3.** (*usually prenominal*) utter; absolute: *stark folly.* **4.** *Arch.* severe; violent. **5.** *Arch. or poetic.* rigid, as in death (esp. in **stiff and stark, stark dead**). **6.** short for **stark-naked.** ~*adv.* **7.** completely: *stark mad.* **8.** *Rare.* starkly. [OE *stearc* stiff] —ˈ**starkly** *adv.* —ˈ**starkness** *n.*

stark-naked *adj.* completely naked. Informal word (*postpositive*): **starkers.** [C13 *stert naket,* lit.: tail naked; *stert,* < OE *steort* tail]

starlet (ˈstɑːlɪt) *n.* **1.** a young actress who is projected as a potential star. **2.** a small star.

starlight (ˈstɑːˌlaɪt) *n.* **1.** the light emanating from the stars. ~*adj. also* **starlighted. 2.** of or like starlight. **3.** Also: **starlit** (ˈstɑːˌlɪt). illuminated by starlight.

starling (ˈstɑːlɪŋ) *n.* any gregarious passerine songbird of an Old World family, esp. the **common starling,** which has a blackish iridescent plumage and a short tail. [OE *stærlinc,* < *stær* starling + *-line* -LING[1]]

star-of-Bethlehem *n.* **1.** Also: **starflower.** a Eurasian liliaceous plant having narrow leaves and starlike white flowers. **2.** any of several similar and related plants.

Star of David *n.* an emblem symbolizing Judaism and consisting of a six-pointed star formed by superimposing one inverted equilateral triangle upon another of equal size.

starry (ˈstɑːrɪ) *adj.* **-rier, -riest. 1.** filled, covered with, or illuminated by stars. **2.** of, like, or relating to a star or stars. —ˈ**starriness** *n.*

starry-eyed *adj.* given to naive wishes, judgments, etc.; full of unsophisticated optimism.

Stars and Stripes *n.* (*functioning as sing.*) **the.** the national flag of the United States of America, consisting of 50 white stars representing the present states on a blue field and seven red and six white horizontal stripes representing the original states. Also called: the **Star-Spangled Banner.**

star sapphire *n.* a sapphire showing a starlike figure in reflected light because of its crystalline structure.

Star-Spangled Banner *n.* **the. 1.** the national anthem of the United States of America. **2.** another term for the **Stars and Stripes.**

star stream *n.* one of two main streams of stars that, because of the rotation of the Milky Way, appear to move in opposite directions.

star-studded *adj.* featuring a large proportion of well-known performers: *a star-studded cast.*

start (stɑːt) *vb.* **1.** to begin or cause to begin (something or to do something); come or cause to come into being, operation, etc.: *he started a quarrel; they started to work.* **2.** (when *intr.,* sometimes foll. by *on*) to make or cause to make a beginning of (a process, series of actions, etc.): *they started on the project.* **3.** (sometimes foll. by *up*) to set or be set in motion: *he started up the machine.* **4.** (*intr.*) to make a sudden involuntary movement, as from fright; jump. **5.** (*intr.;* sometimes foll. by *up, away,* etc.) to spring or jump suddenly from a position or place. **6.** to establish or be established; set up: *to start a business.* **7.** (*tr.*) to support (someone) in the first part of a venture, career, etc. **8.** to work or cause to work loose. **9.** to enter or be entered in a race. **10.** (*intr.*) to flow violently from a source: *wine started from a hole in the cask.* **11.** (*tr.*) to rouse (game) from a hiding place, lair, etc. **12.** (*intr.*) (esp. of eyes) to bulge; pop. **13.** (*intr.*) *Brit. inf.* to commence quarrelling or causing a disturbance. **14. to start with.** in the first place. ~*n.* **15.** the first or first part of a series of actions, a journey, etc. **16.** the place or time of starting, as of a race or performance. **17.** a signal to proceed, as in a race. **18.** a lead or advantage, either in time or distance, in a competitive activity: *he had an hour's start on me.* **19.** a slight involuntary movement, as through fright, surprise, etc.: *she gave a start as I entered.* **20.** an opportunity to enter a career, undertake a project, etc. **21.** *Inf.* a surprising incident. **22. for a start.** in the first place. ~See also **start in, start off,** etc. [OE *styrtan*]

starter (ˈstɑːtə) *n.* **1.** Also called: **self-starter.** a device for starting an internal-combustion engine, usually consisting of a powerful electric motor that engages with the flywheel. **2.** a person who supervises and signals the start of a race. **3.** a competitor who starts in a race or contest. **4.** *Austral. inf.* an acceptable or practicable proposition, plan, idea, etc. **5.** *Chiefly Brit.* the first course of a meal. **6. for starters.** *Sl.* in the first place. **7. under starter's orders. a.** (of horses in a race) awaiting the start signal. **b.** (of a person) eager or ready to begin.

start in *vb.* (*adv.*) to undertake (something or doing something); commence or begin.

starting block *n.* one of a pair of adjustable devices with pads or blocks against which a sprinter braces his feet in crouch starts.

starting gate *n.* **1.** a movable barrier so placed on the starting line of a racecourse that the raising of it releases all the contestants simultaneously. **2.** the U.S. name for **starting stalls.**

starting grid *n. Motor racing.* a marked section of the track at the start where the cars line up according to their times in practice, the fastest occupying the front position.

starting price *n.* (esp. in horse racing) the latest odds offered by bookmakers at the start of a race.

starting stalls *pl. n. Brit.* a line of stalls in which horses are enclosed at the start of a race and from which they are released by the simultaneous springing open of retaining barriers at the front of each stall.

startle (ˈstɑːtᵊl) *vb.* to be or cause to be surprised or frightened, esp. so as to start involuntarily. [OE *steartlian* to stumble] —ˈ**startler** *n.* —ˈ**startling** *adj.*

start off *vb.* (*adv.*) **1.** (*intr.*) to set out on a journey. **2.** to be or make the first step in (an activity); initiate: *he started the show off with a lively song.* **3.** (*tr.*) to cause (a person) to act or do something, such as to laugh, to tell stories, etc.

start on *vb.* (*intr., prep.*) *Brit. inf.* to pick a quarrel with; upbraid.

start out *vb.* (*intr., adv.*) **1.** to set out on a journey. **2.** to take the first steps, as in life, one's career, etc.: *he started out as a salesman.* **3.** to take the first actions in an activity in a particular way or with a specified aim: *they started out wanting a house, but eventually bought a flat.*

start up *vb.* (*adv.*) **1.** to come or cause to come into being for the first time; originate. **2.** (*intr.*) to spring or jump suddenly. **3.** to set in or go into motion, activity, etc.: *he started up the engine.* ~*n.* **start-up.** **4.** the setting up of a new business.

starve (stɑːv) *vb.* **1.** to die or cause to die from lack of food. **2.** to deprive (a person or animal) or (of a person, etc.) to be deprived of food. **3.** (*intr.*) *Inf.* to be very hungry. **4.** (foll. by *of* or *for*) to deprive or be deprived (of something), esp. so as to cause suffering or malfunctioning: *the engine was starved of fuel.* **5.** (*tr.;* foll. by *into*) to bring (to) a specified condition by starving: *to starve someone into submission.* **6.** *Arch. or dialect.* to be or cause to be extremely cold. [OE *steorfan* to die] —**starˈvation** *n.*

starveling (ˈstɑːvlɪŋ) *Arch.* ~*n.* **1. a.** a starving or poorly fed person, animal, etc. **b.** (*as modifier*): *a starveling child.* ~*adj.* **2.** insufficient; meagre; scant.

Star Wars *n.* (*functioning as sing.*) (in the U.S.) a proposed system of artificial satellites armed with lasers to destroy enemy missiles in space. [C20: popularly named after the science-fiction film *Star Wars* (1977)]

starwort (ˈstɑːˌwɜːt) *n.* **1.** any of several plants with star-shaped flowers, esp. the stitchwort. **2.** any of several aquatic plants having a star-shaped rosette of floating leaves.

stash (stæʃ) *vb.* **1.** (*tr.;* often foll. by *away*) *Inf.* to put or store (money, valuables, etc.) in a secret place, as for safekeeping. ~*n.* **2.** *Inf., chiefly U.S. & Canad.* a secret store or the place where this is hidden. **3.** *Sl.* drugs kept for personal consumption. [C20: <?]

stasis (ˈsteɪsɪs) *n.* **1.** *Pathol.* a stagnation in the normal flow of bodily fluids, such as the blood or urine. **2.** a state or condition in which there is no action or progress. [C18: via NL < Gk: a standing, < *histanai* to cause to stand]

-stat *n. combining form.* indicating a device that causes something to remain stationary or constant: *thermostat.* [< Gk *-statēs,* < *histanai* to cause to stand]

state (steɪt) *n.* **1.** the condition of a person, thing, etc., with regard to main attributes. **2.** the structure or form of something: *a solid state.* **3.** any mode of existence. **4.** position in life or society; estate. **5.** ceremonious style, as befitting wealth or dignity: *to live in state.* **6.** a sovereign political power or community. **7.** the territory occupied by such a community. **8.** the sphere of power in such a community: *affairs of state.* **9.** (*often cap.*) one of a number of areas or communities having their own governments and forming a federation under a sovereign government, as in the U.S. **10.** (*often cap.*) the body politic of a particular sovereign power, esp. as contrasted with a rival authority such as the Church. **11.** *Obs.* a class or order; estate. **12.** *Inf.* a nervous, upset, or excited condition (esp. in **in a state**). **13. lie in state.** (of a body) to be placed on public view before burial. **14. state of affairs.** a situation; circumstances or condition. ~*modifier.* **15.** controlled or financed by a state: *state university.* **16.** of, relating to, or concerning the State: *State trial.* **17.** involving ceremony or concerned with a ceremonious occasion: *state visit.* ~*vb.* (*tr.; may take a clause as object*) **18.** to articulate in words; utter. **19.** to declare formally or publicly. [C13: < OF *estat,* < L *status* a standing, < *stāre* to stand] —ˈ**statable** *or* ˈ**stateable** *adj.* —ˈ**statehood** *n.*

state bank *n.* (in the U.S.) a commercial bank incorporated under a State charter and not required to be a member of the Federal Reserve System.

statecraft (ˈsteɪtˌkrɑːft) *n.* the art of conducting public affairs; statesmanship.

State Enrolled Nurse *n.* a nurse who has trained and is qualified to perform many nursing services.

Statehouse (ˈsteɪtˌhaʊs) *n.* (in the U.S.) the building which houses a state legislature.

state house *n. N.Z.* a house built by the government and rented to a **state tenant.** Brit. equivalent: **council house.**

stateless (ˈsteɪtlɪs) *adj.* **1.** without nationality: *stateless persons.* **2.** without a state or states. —ˈ**statelessness** *n.*

stately (ˈsteɪtlɪ) *adj.* **-lier, -liest.** **1.** characterized by a graceful, dignified, and imposing appearance or manner. ~*adv.* **2.** in a stately manner. —ˈ**stateliness** *n.*

stately home *n. Brit.* a large mansion, esp. one open to the public.

statement (ˈsteɪtmənt) *n.* **1.** the act of stating. **2.** something that is stated, esp. a formal prepared announcement or reply. **3.** *Law.* a declaration of matters of fact. **4.** an account containing a summary of bills or invoices and displaying the total amount due. **5.** an account prepared by a bank for a client, usually at regular intervals, to show all credits and debits and the balance at the end of the period. **6.** a computer instruction written in a source language, such as FORTRAN, which is converted into one or more machine-code instructions by a compiler. **7.** *Logic.* the content of a sentence that affirms or denies something and may be true or false.

statement of claim *n. Law.* (in England) the first pleading made by the plaintiff in a High Court action.

state of the art *n.* **1.** the level of knowledge and development achieved in a technique, science, etc., esp. at present. ~*adj.* **state-of-the-art.** (*prenominal*) **2.** the most recent and therefore considered the best; up-to-the-minute: *a state-of-the-art amplifier.*

State Registered Nurse *n.* a nurse who has had extensive training and is qualified to perform all nursing services.

stateroom (ˈsteɪtˌruːm, -ˌrʊm) *n.* **1.** a private cabin or room on a ship, train, etc. **2.** *Chiefly Brit.* a large room in a palace or other building for use on state occasions.

States (steɪts) *n.* (*functioning as sing. or pl.*) **the.** an informal name for the **United States of America.**

state school *n.* any school maintained by the state, in which education is free.

stateside (ˈsteɪtˌsaɪd) *adj., adv. U.S.* of, in, to, or towards the U.S.

statesman (ˈsteɪtsmən) *n., pl.* **-men.** **1.** a political leader whose wisdom, integrity, etc., win great respect. **2.** a person active and influential in the formulation of high government policy. —ˈ**statesman-ˌlike** *or* ˈ**statesmanly** *adj.* —ˈ**statesmanship** *n.* —ˈ**statesˌwoman** *fem. n.*

state socialism *n.* a variant of socialism in which the power of the state is employed for the purpose of creating an egalitarian society by means of public control of major industries, banks, etc. —**state socialist** *n.*

state trooper *n. U.S.* a state policeman.

static (ˈstætɪk) *adj. also* **statical.** **1.** not active or moving; stationary. **2.** (of a weight, force, or pressure) acting but causing no movement. **3.** of or concerned with forces that do not produce movement. **4.** relating to or causing stationary electric charges; electrostatic. **5.** of or relating to interference in the reception of radio or television transmissions. **6.** of or concerned with statics. **7.** *Computers.* (of a memory) not needing its contents refreshed periodically. ~*n.* **8.** random hissing or crackling or a speckled picture caused by interference in the reception of radio or television transmissions. **9.** electric sparks or crackling produced by friction. [C16: < NL *staticus,* < Gk *statikos* causing to stand, < *histanai* to stand] —ˈ**statically** *adv.*

statice (ˈstætɪsɪ) *n.* another name for **sea lavender.**

static electricity *n.* electricity that is not dynamic or flowing as a current.

statics (ˈstætɪks) *n.* (*functioning as sing.*) the branch of mechanics concerned with the forces that produce a state of equilibrium in a system.

station (ˈsteɪʃən) *n.* **1.** the place or position at which a thing or person stands. **2. a.** a place along a route or line at which a bus, train, etc., stops for fuel or to pick up or let off passengers or goods, esp. one with ancillary buildings and services. **b.** (*as modifier*): *a station buffet.* **3. a.** the headquarters or local offices of an organization such as the police or fire services. **b.** (*as modifier*): *a station sergeant.* See **police station, fire station. 4.** a building, depot, etc., with special equipment for some particular purpose: *power station; petrol station.* **5.** *Mil.* a place of duty: *an action station.* **6.** *Navy.* **a.** a location to which a ship or fleet is assigned for duty. **b.** an assigned location for a member of a ship's crew. **7.** a television or radio channel. **8.** a position or standing, as in a particular society or organization. **9.** the type of one's occupation; calling. **10.** (in British India) a place where the British district officials or garrison officers resided. **11.** *Biol.* the habitat occupied by a particular animal or plant. **12.** *Austral. & N.Z.* a large sheep or cattle farm. **13.** (*sometimes cap.*) *R.C. Church.* **a.** one of the stations of the Cross. **b.** any of the churches (**station churches**) in Rome used as points of assembly for religious processions and ceremonies on particular days (**station days**). ~*vb.* **14.** (*tr.*) to place in or assign to a station. [C14: via OF < L *statiō* a standing still, < *stāre* to stand]

stationary (ˈsteɪʃənərɪ) *adj.* **1.** not moving; standing still. **2.** not able to be moved. **3.** showing no change: *the doctors said his condition was stationary.* **4.** tending to remain in one place. [C15: < L *statiōnārius,* < *statiō* STATION]

stationary orbit *n. Astronautics.* a synchronous orbit lying in or approximately in the plane of the equator.

stationary wave *n.* another name for **standing wave.**

stationer (ˈsteɪʃənə) *n.* a person who sells stationery or a shop where stationery is sold. [C14: < Med. L *stationarius* a person having a regular station, hence a shopkeeper (esp. a bookseller) as distinguished from an itinerant tradesman; see STATION]

stationery (ˈsteɪʃənərɪ) *n.* any writing materials, such as paper, envelopes, pens, ink, rulers, etc.

station house *n. Chiefly U.S.* a house that is situated by or serves as a station, esp. as a police or fire station.

stationmaster (ˈsteɪʃənˌmɑːstə) *n.* the senior official in charge of a railway station.

stations of the Cross *pl. n. R.C. Church.* **1.** a series of 14 crosses, often accompanied by 14 pictures or carvings, arranged around the walls of a church, to commemorate 14 stages in Christ's journey to Calvary. **2.** a devotion of 14 prayers relating to each of these stages.

station wagon *n.* another name (less common in Britain) for **estate car.**

statism (ˈsteɪtɪzəm) *n.* the theory or practice of concentrating economic and political power in the state. —ˈ**statist** *n.*

statistic (stəˈtɪstɪk) *n.* a datum capable of exact numerical representation, such as the correlation coefficient of two series or the standard deviation of a sample. —**staˈtistical** *adj.* —**staˈtistically** *adv.* —**statistician** (ˌstætɪˈstɪʃən) *n.*

statistical mechanics *n.* (*functioning as sing.*) the study of the properties of physical systems as predicted by the statistical behaviour of their constituent particles.

statistics (stəˈtɪstɪks) *n.* **1.** (*functioning as sing.*) a science concerned with the collection, classification, and interpretation of quantitative data and with the application of probability theory to the analysis and estimation of population parameters. **2.** the quantitative data themselves. [C18 (orig. "science dealing with facts of a state"): via G *Statistik,* < NL *statisticus* concerning state affairs, < L *status* STATE]

stator (ˈsteɪtə) *n.* the stationary part of a rotary machine or device, esp. of a motor or generator. [C20: < L: one who stands (by), < *stāre* to stand]

statoscope (ˈstætəˌskəʊp) *n.* a very sensitive form of aneroid barometer used to detect and measure small variations in atmospheric pressure, such as one used in an aircraft to indicate small changes in altitude.

statuary (ˈstætjʊərɪ) *n.* **1.** statues collectively. **2.** the art of making statues. ~*adj.* **3.** of or for statues. [C16: < L *statuārius*]

statue (ˈstætjuː) *n.* a wooden, stone, metal, plaster, or other sculpture of a human or animal figure, usually life-size or larger. [C14: via OF < L *statua,* < *statuere* to set up; cf. STATUTE]

statuesque (ˌstætjʊˈɛsk) *adj.* like a statue, esp. in possessing great formal beauty or dignity. —ˌ**statuˈesquely** *adv.* —ˌ**statuˈesqueness** *n.*

statuette (ˌstætjʊˈɛt) *n.* a small statue.

stature (ˈstætʃə) *n.* **1.** height, esp. of a person or animal when standing. **2.** the degree of development of a person: *the stature of a champion.* **3.** intellectual or moral greatness: *a man of stature.* [C13: via OF < L *statūra,* < *stāre* to stand]

status (ˈsteɪtəs) *n., pl.* **-tuses. 1.** a social or professional position, condition, or standing. **2.** the relative position or standing of a person or thing. **3.** a high position or standing: *he has acquired a new status in that job.* **4.** the legal standing or condition of a person. **5.** a state of affairs. [C17: < L: posture, < *stāre* to stand]

status quo (kwəʊ) *n.* (usually preceded by *the*) the existing state of affairs. [lit.: the state in which]

status symbol *n.* a possession which is regarded as proof of the owner's social position, wealth, prestige, etc.

statute (ˈstætjuːt) *n.* **1. a.** an enactment of a legislative body expressed in a formal document. **b.** this document. **2.** a permanent rule made by a body or institution. [C13: < OF *estatut,* < LL *statūtum,* < L *statuere* to set up, decree, ult. < *stāre* to stand]

statute book *n. Chiefly Brit.* a register of enactments passed by the legislative body of a state: *not on the statute book.*

statute law *n.* **1.** a law enacted by a legislative body. **2.** a particular example of this. ~Cf. **common law, equity.**

statute mile *n.* a legal or formal name for **mile** (sense 1).

statute of limitations *n.* a legislative enactment prescribing the period of time within which proceedings must be instituted to enforce a right or bring an action at law.

statutory (ˈstætjʊtərɪ, -trɪ) *adj.* **1.** of, relating to, or having the nature of a statute. **2.** prescribed or authorized by statute. **3.** (of an offence) **a.** recognized by statute. **b.** subject to a punishment or penalty prescribed by statute. —ˈ**statutorily** *adv.*

staunch[1] (stɔːntʃ) *adj.* **1.** loyal, firm, and dependable: *a staunch supporter.* **2.** solid or substantial in construction. **3.** *Rare.* (of a ship, etc.) watertight; seaworthy. [C15 (orig.: watertight): < OF *estanche,* < *estanchier* to STANCH] —ˈ**staunchly** *adv.* —ˈ**staunchness** *n.*

staunch[2] (stɔːntʃ) *vb., n.* a variant spelling of **stanch.**

stave (steɪv) *n.* **1.** any one of a number of long strips of wood joined together to form a barrel, bucket, boat hull, etc. **2.** any of various bars, slats, or rods, usually of wood, such as a rung of a ladder. **3.** any stick, staff, etc. **4.** a stanza or verse of a poem. **5.** *Music.* **a.** *Brit.* an individual group of five lines and four spaces used in staff notation. **b.** another word for **staff**[1] (sense 9). ~*vb.* **staving, staved** *or* **stove. 6.** (often foll. by *in*) to break or crush (the staves of a boat, barrel, etc.) or (of the staves of a boat) to be broken or crushed. **7.** (*tr.;* usually foll. by *in*) to burst or force (a hole in something). **8.** (*tr.*) to provide (a ladder, chair, etc.) with staves. [C14: back formation < *staves*, pl. of STAFF[1]]

stave off *vb.* (*tr., adv.*) to avert or hold off, esp. temporarily: *to stave off hunger.*

staves (steɪvz) *n.* a plural of **staff**[1] or **stave.**

stavesacre (ˈsteɪvzˌeɪkə) *n.* **1.** a Eurasian ranunculaceous plant having poisonous seeds. **2.** the seeds, which have strong emetic and cathartic properties. [C14 *staphisagre,* < L *staphis agria,* < Gk, < *staphis* raisin + *agria* wild]

stay[1] (steɪ) *vb.* **1.** (*intr.*) to continue or remain in a certain place, position, etc.: *to stay outside.* **2.** (*copula*) to continue to be; remain: *to stay awake.* **3.** (*intr.;* often foll. by *at*) to reside temporarily: *to stay at a hotel.* **4.** (*tr.*) to remain for a specified period: *to stay the weekend.* **5.** (*intr.*) *Scot. & S. African.* to reside permanently or habitually; live. **6.** *Arch.* to stop or cause to stop. **7.** (*intr.*) to wait, pause, or tarry. **8.** (*tr.*) to delay or hinder. **9.** (*tr.*) **a.** to discontinue or suspend (a judicial proceeding). **b.** to hold in abeyance or restrain from enforcing (an order, decree, etc.). **10.** to endure (something testing or difficult, such as a race): *stay the course.* **11.** (*tr.*) to hold back or restrain: *to stay one's anger.* **12.** (*tr.*) to satisfy or appease (an appetite, etc.) temporarily. ~*n.* **13.** the act of staying or sojourning in a place or the period during which one stays. **14.** the act of stopping or restraining or state of being stopped, etc. **15.** the suspension of a judicial proceeding, etc.: *stay of execution.* [C15 *staien,* < Anglo-F *estaier* to stay, < OF *ester* to stay, < L *stāre* to stand] —ˈ**stayer** *n.*

stay[2] (steɪ) *n.* **1.** anything that supports or steadies, such as a prop or buttress. **2.** a thin strip of metal, plastic, bone, etc., used to stiffen corsets, etc. See also **stays** (sense 1). ~*vb.* (*tr.*) *Arch.* **3.** (often foll. by *up*) to prop or hold. **4.** (often foll. by *up*) to comfort or sustain. **5.** (foll. by *on* or *upon*) to cause to rely or depend. [C16: < OF *estaye,* of Gmc origin]

stay[3] (steɪ) *n.* a rope, cable, or chain, usually one of a set, used for bracing uprights, such as masts, funnels, flagpoles, chimneys, etc.; guy. ~See also **stays** (senses 2, 3). [OE *stæg*]

stay-at-home *adj.* **1.** (of a person) enjoying a quiet, settled, and unadventurous use of leisure. ~*n.* **2.** a stay-at-home person.

staying power *n.* endurance; stamina.

stays (steɪz) *pl. n.* **1.** old-fashioned corsets with bones in them. **2.** a position of a sailing vessel relative to the wind so that the sails are luffing or aback. **3. miss** *or* **refuse stays.** (of a sailing vessel) to fail to come about.

staysail (ˈsteɪˌseɪl; *Naut.* ˈsteɪsᵊl) *n.* an auxiliary sail, often triangular, set on a stay.

STD *abbrev. for:* **1.** Doctor of Sacred Theology. **2.** sexually transmitted disease. **3.** subscriber trunk dialling.

STD code *n. Brit.* a code of two or more digits, other than those comprising a subscriber's local telephone number, that determines the routing of a call. [C20: *s*(*ubscriber*) *t*(*runk*) *d*(*ialling*)]

Ste *abbrev. for* Saint (female). [F *Sainte*]

stead (stɛd) *n.* **1.** (preceded by *in*) *Rare.* the place, function, or position that should be taken by another: *to come in someone's stead.* **2. stand (someone) in good stead.** to be useful or of good service to (someone). ~*vb.* **3.** (*tr.*) *Arch.* to help or benefit. [OE *stede*]

steadfast *or* **stedfast** (ˈstɛdfəst, -ˌfɑːst) *adj.* **1.** (esp. of a person's gaze) fixed in intensity or direction; steady. **2.** unwavering or determined in purpose, loyalty, etc.: *steadfast resolve.* —ˈ**steadfastly** *or* ˈ**stedfastly** *adv.* —ˈ**steadfastness** *or* ˈ**stedfastness** *n.*

steading (ˈstɛdɪŋ) *n.* another name for **farmstead.**

steady (ˈstɛdɪ) *adj.* **steadier, steadiest. 1.** not able to be moved or disturbed easily; stable. **2.** free from fluctuation. **3.** not easily excited; imperturbable. **4.** staid; sober. **5.** regular; habitual: *a steady drinker.* **6.** continuous: *a steady flow.* **7.** *Naut.* (of a vessel) keeping upright, as in heavy seas. ~*vb.* **steadying, steadied. 8.** to make or become steady. ~*adv.* **9.** in a steady manner. **10. go steady.** *Inf.* to date one person regularly. ~*n., pl.* **steadies. 11.** *Inf.* one's regular boyfriend or girlfriend. ~*interj.* **12.** *Naut.* an order to the helmsman to stay on a steady course. **13.** a warning to keep calm, be careful, etc. **14.** *Brit.* a command to get set to start, as in a race: *ready, steady, go!* [C16: < STEAD + -Y[1]] —ˈ**steadily** *adv.* —ˈ**steadiness** *n.* —ˈ**steadying** *adj.*

steady state *n. Physics.* the condition of a system when some or all of the quantities describing it are independent of time but not necessarily in thermodynamic or chemical equilibrium.

steady-state theory *n.* a theory postulating that the universe exists throughout time in a steady state such that the average density of matter does not vary with distance or time. Matter is continuously created in the space left by the receding stars and galaxies of the expanding universe. Cf. **big-bang theory.**

steak (steɪk) *n.* **1.** See **beefsteak. 2.** any of various cuts of beef, for braising, stewing, etc. **3.** a thick slice of pork, veal, cod, salmon, etc. **4.** minced meat prepared in the same way as steak: *hamburger steak.* [C15: < ON *steik* roast]

steakhouse (ˈsteɪkˌhaʊs) *n.* a restaurant that has steaks as its speciality.

steak tartare (tɑːˈtɑː) *or* **tartar** *n.* raw minced steak, mixed with onion, seasonings, and raw egg. Also called: **tartare steak, tartar steak.**

steal (stiːl) *vb.* **stealing, stole, stolen. 1.** to take (something) from someone, etc. without permission or unlawfully, esp. in a secret manner. **2.** (*tr.*) to obtain surreptitiously. **3.** (*tr.*) to appropriate (ideas, etc.) without acknowledgment, as in plagiarism. **4.** to move or convey stealthily: *they stole along the corridor.* **5.** (*intr.*) to pass unnoticed: *the hours stole by.* **6.** (*tr.*) to win or gain by strategy or luck, as in various sports: *to steal a few yards.* ~*n. Inf.* **7.** the act of stealing. **8.** *U.S. & Canad.* something stolen or acquired easily or at little cost. [OE *stelan*] —ˈ**stealer** *n.*

stealth (stɛlθ) *n.* **1.** the act or characteristic of moving with extreme care and quietness, esp. so as to avoid detection. **2.** cunning or underhand procedure or dealing. [C13 *stelthe;* see STEAL, -TH[1]] —ˈ**stealthy** *adj.*

steam (stiːm) *n.* **1.** the gas or vapour into which water is changed when boiled. **2.** the mist formed when such gas or vapour condenses in the atmosphere. **3.** any vaporous exhalation. **4.** *Inf.* power, energy, or speed. **5. get up steam. a.** (of a ship, etc.) to work up a sufficient head of steam in a boiler to drive an engine. **b.** *Inf.* to go quickly. **6. let off steam.** *Inf.* to release pent-up energy, feelings, etc. **7. under one's own steam.** without the assistance of others. **8.** (*modifier*) driven, operated, heated, powered, etc., by steam: *a steam radiator.* **9.** (*modifier*) treated by steam: *steam-ironed.* **10.** (*modifier*) *Humorous.* old-fashioned; outmoded: *steam radio.* ~*vb.* **11.** to emit or be emitted as steam. **12.** (*intr.*) to generate steam, as a boiler, etc. **13.** (*intr.*) to move or travel by steam power, as a ship, etc. **14.** (*intr.*) *Inf.* to proceed quickly and sometimes forcefully. **15.** to cook or be cooked in steam. **16.** (*tr.*) to treat with steam or apply steam to, as in cleaning, pressing clothes, etc. ~See also **steam up.** [OE]

steam bath *n.* **1.** a room or enclosure that can be filled with steam in which people bathe to induce sweating and refresh or cleanse themselves. **2.** an act of taking such a bath.

steamboat (ˈstiːmˌbəʊt) *n.* a boat powered by a steam engine.

steam boiler *n.* a vessel in which water is boiled to generate steam.

steam engine *n.* an engine that uses steam to

produce mechanical work, esp. one in which steam from a boiler is expanded in a cylinder to drive a reciprocating piston.

steamer (ˈstiːmə) *n.* **1.** a boat or ship driven by steam engines. **2.** a vessel used to cook food by steam. **3.** *Austral. sl.* a rough clash between sports teams.

steam iron *n.* an electric iron that emits steam from channels in the iron face to facilitate pressing and ironing, the steam being produced from water contained within the iron.

steam jacket *n. Engineering.* a jacket containing steam that surrounds and heats a cylinder.

steam organ *n.* a type of organ powered by steam, once common at fairgrounds, played either by a keyboard or by a moving punched card. U.S. name: **calliope.**

steam point *n.* the temperature at which the maximum vapour pressure of water is equal to one atmosphere (1.01325×10^5 N/m^2). It has the value of 100° on the Celsius scale.

steamroller (ˈstiːmˌrəʊlə) *n.* **1. a.** a steam-powered vehicle with heavy rollers used for compressing road surfaces during road-making. **b.** another word for **roadroller. 2. a.** an overpowering force or person that overcomes all opposition. **b.** (*as modifier*): *steamroller tactics.* ~*vb.* **3.** (*tr.*) to crush (opposition, etc.) by overpowering force.

steamship (ˈstiːmˌʃɪp) *n.* a ship powered by one or more steam engines.

steam shovel *n.* a steam-driven mechanical excavator.

steam turbine *n.* a turbine driven by steam.

steam up *vb.* (*adv.*) **1.** to cover (windows, etc.) or (of windows, etc.) to become covered with a film of condensed steam. **2.** (*tr.; usually passive*) *Sl.* to excite or make angry: *he's all steamed up about the delay.*

steamy (ˈstiːmɪ) *adj.* **steamier, steamiest. 1.** of, resembling, full of, or covered with steam. **2.** *Inf.* lustful or erotic: *steamy nightlife.* —ˈ**steaminess** *n.*

steapsin (stɪˈæpsɪn) *n. Biochem.* a pancreatic lipase. [C19: < Gk *stear* fat + PEPSIN]

stearic (stɪˈærɪk) *adj.* **1.** of or relating to suet or fat. **2.** of, consisting of, containing, or derived from stearic acid.

stearic acid *n.* a colourless odourless insoluble waxy carboxylic acid used for making candles and suppositories.

stearin *or* **stearine** (ˈstɪərɪn) *n.* **1.** Also called: **tristearin.** a colourless crystalline ester of glycerol and stearic acid, present in fats and used in soap and candles. **2.** another name for **stearic acid. 3.** fat in its solid form. [C19: < F *stéarine,* < Gk *stear* fat + -IN]

steatite (ˈstɪəˌtaɪt) *n.* another name for **soapstone.** [C18: < L *steatitēs,* < Gk *stear* fat + -ITE[1]] —**steatitic** (ˌstɪəˈtɪtɪk) *adj.*

steato- *combining form.* denoting fat. [< Gk *stear, steat-* fat, tallow]

steatolysis (ˌstɪəˈtɒlɪsɪs) *n. Physiol.* **1.** the digestive process whereby fats are emulsified and then hydrolysed to fatty acids and glycerin. **2.** the breaking down of fat.

steatopygia (ˌstɪətəʊˈpɪdʒɪə, -ˈpaɪ-) *or* **steatopyga** (ˌstɪətəʊˈpaɪgə) *n.* excessive fatness of the buttocks. [C19: < NL, < STEATO- + Gk *pugē* the buttocks] —ˌ**steatoˈpygic** *or* **steatopygous** (ˌstɪəˈtɒpɪgəs) *adj.*

stedfast (ˈstɛdfəst, -ˌfɑːst) *adj.* a less common spelling of **steadfast.**

steed (stiːd) *n. Arch. or literary.* a horse, esp. one that is spirited or swift. [OE *stēda* stallion]

steel (stiːl) *n.* **1. a.** any of various alloys based on iron containing carbon and often small quantities of other elements such as sulphur, manganese, chromium, and nickel. Steels exhibit a variety of properties, such as strength, malleability, etc., depending on their composition and the way they have been treated. **b.** (*as modifier*): *steel girders.* See also **stainless steel. 2.** something that is made of steel. **3.** a steel stiffener in a corset, etc. **4.** a ridged steel rod used for sharpening knives. **5.** the quality of hardness, esp. with regard to a person's character or attitudes. **6.** *Canad.* a railway track or line. **7. cold steel.** bladed weapons. ~*vb.* (*tr.*) **8.** to fit, plate, edge, or point with steel. **9.** to make hard and unfeeling: *he steeled his heart against her sorrow; he steeled himself for the blow.* [OE *stēli*] —ˈ**steely** *adj.* —ˈ**steeliness** *n.*

steel band *n. Music.* a type of band, popular in the Caribbean Islands, consisting mainly of percussion instruments made from oil drums, hammered or embossed to obtain different notes.

steel blue *n.* **a.** a dark bluish-grey colour. **b.** (*as adj.*): *steel-blue eyes.*

steel engraving *n.* **a.** a method or art of engraving (letters, etc.) on a steel plate. **b.** a print made from such a plate.

steel grey *n.* **a.** a dark grey colour, usually slightly purple. **b.** (*as adj.*): *a steel-grey suit.*

steelhead (ˈstiːlˌhɛd) *n., pl.* **-heads** *or* **-head.** a silvery North Pacific variety of the rainbow trout.

steel wool *n.* a tangled or woven mass of fine steel fibres, used for cleaning or polishing.

steelworks (ˈstiːlˌwɜːks) *n.* (*functioning as sing. or pl.*) a plant in which steel is made from iron ore and rolled or forged into bars, sheets, etc. —ˈ**steelˌworker** *n.*

steelyard (ˈstiːlˌjɑːd) *n.* a portable balance consisting of a pivoted bar with two unequal arms. The load is suspended from the shorter one and the bar is returned to the horizontal by sliding a weight along the longer, graduated arm.

steenbok (ˈstiːnˌbɒk) *n., pl.* **-boks** *or* **-bok.** a small antelope of central and southern Africa, having a reddish-brown coat and straight horns. [C18: < Afrik., < Du. *steen* stone + *bok* BUCK[1]]

steep[1] (stiːp) *adj.* **1. a.** having or being a slope or gradient approaching the perpendicular. **b.** (*as n.*): *the steep.* **2.** *Inf.* (of a fee, price, demand, etc.) unduly high; unreasonable (esp. in **that's a bit steep**). **3.** *Inf.* excessively demanding or ambitious: *a steep task.* **4.** *Brit. inf.* (of a statement) extreme or far-fetched. [OE *steap*] —ˈ**steeply** *adv.* —ˈ**steepness** *n.*

steep[2] (stiːp) *vb.* **1.** to soak or be soaked in a liquid in order to soften, cleanse, extract an element, etc. **2.** (*tr.; usually passive*) to saturate; imbue: *steeped in ideology.* ~*n.* **3.** an instance or the process of steeping or the condition of being steeped. **4.** a liquid or solution used for the purpose of steeping something. [OE *stēpan*] —ˈ**steeper** *n.*

steepen (ˈstiːpᵊn) *vb.* to become or cause to become steep or steeper.

steeple (ˈstiːpᵊl) *n.* **1.** a tall ornamental tower that forms the superstructure of a church, temple, etc. **2.** such a tower with the spire above it. **3.** any spire or pointed structure. [OE *stēpel*] —ˈ**steepled** *adj.*

steeplechase (ˈstiːpᵊlˌtʃeɪs) *n.* **1.** a horse race over a course equipped with obstacles to be jumped. **2.** a track race in which the runners have to leap hurdles, a water jump, etc. **3.** *Arch.* **a.** a horse race across a stretch of open countryside including obstacles to be jumped. **b.** a rare word for **point-to-point.** ~*vb.* **4.** (*intr.*) to take part in a steeplechase. —ˈ**steepleˌchaser** *n.* —ˈ**steepleˌchasing** *n.*

steeplejack (ˈstiːpᵊlˌdʒæk) *n.* a person trained and skilled in the construction and repair of steeples, chimneys, etc.

steer[1] (stɪə) *vb.* **1.** to direct the course of (a vehicle or vessel) with a steering wheel, rudder, etc. **2.** (*tr.*) to guide with tuition: *his teachers steered him through his exams.* **3.** (*tr.*) to direct the movements or course of (a person, conversation, etc.). **4.** to pursue (a specified course). **5.** (*intr.*) (of a vessel, vehicle, etc.) to admit of being guided in a specified fashion: *this boat does not steer properly.* **6. steer clear of.** to keep away from; shun. ~*n.* **7.** *Chiefly U.S.* guidance; information (esp. in **a bum steer**). [OE *stieran*] —ˈ**steerable** *adj.* —ˈ**steerer** *n.*

steer[2] (stɪə) *n.* a castrated male ox or bull; bullock. [OE *stēor*]

steerage (ˈstɪərɪdʒ) *n.* **1.** the cheapest accommodation on a passenger ship, originally the compartments containing steering apparatus. **2.** an instance or the practice of steering and its effect on a vessel or vehicle.

steerageway (ˈstɪərɪdʒˌweɪ) *n. Naut.* enough forward movement to allow a vessel to be steered.

steering committee *n.* a committee set up to prepare and arrange topics to be discussed, the order of business, etc., for a legislative assembly or other body.

steering wheel *n.* a wheel turned by the driver of a motor vehicle, ship, etc., when he wishes to change direction.

steersman (ˈstɪəzmən) *n., pl.* **-men.** the helmsman of a vessel.

stegosaur (ˈstɛgəˌsɔː) *or* **stegosaurus** (ˌstɛgəˈsɔːrəs) *n.* any of various quadrupedal herbivorous dinosaurs of Jurassic and early Cretaceous times, having an armour of bony plates. [C19: < Gk *stegos* roof + -SAUR]

stein (staɪn) *n.* an earthenware beer mug, esp. of a German design. [< G *Stein*, lit.: stone]

steinbok (ˈstaɪnˌbɒk) *n., pl.* **-boks** *or* **-bok.** a variant of **steenbok.**

stele (ˈstiːlɪ, stiːl) *n., pl.* **stelae** (ˈstiːliː) *or* **steles. 1.** an upright stone slab or column decorated with figures or inscriptions, common in prehistoric times. **2.** a prepared vertical surface that has a commemorative inscription or design, esp. one on the face of a building. **3.** the conducting tissue of the stems and roots of plants, which is in the form of a cylinder. ~Also called (for senses 1, 2): **stela.** [C19: < Gk *stēlē*] —ˈ**stelar** *adj.*

stellar (ˈstɛlə) *adj.* **1.** of, relating to, or resembling a star or stars. **2.** of or relating to star entertainers. [C17: < LL *stellāris*, < L *stella* star]

stellate (ˈstɛlɪt, -eɪt) *or* **stellated** *adj.* resembling a star in shape; radiating from the centre: *a stellate arrangement of petals.* [C16: < L *stellātus* starry, < *stellāre* to stud with stars, < *stella* a star] —ˈ**stellately** *adv.*

stellular (ˈstɛljʊlə) *adj.* **1.** displaying or abounding in small stars: *a stellular pattern.* **2.** resembling a little star or little stars. [C18: < LL *stellula*, dim. of L *stella* star] —ˈ**stellularly** *adv.*

stem[1] (stɛm) *n.* **1.** the main axis of a plant, which bears the leaves, axillary buds, and flowers and contains a hollow cylinder of vascular tissue. **2.** any similar subsidiary structure in such plants that bears a flower, fruit, or leaf. **3.** a corresponding structure in algae and fungi. **4.** any long slender part, such as the hollow part of a tobacco pipe between the bit and the bowl. **5.** the main line of descent or branch of a family. **6.** any shank or cylindrical pin or rod, such as the pin that carries the winding knob on a watch. **7.** *Linguistics.* the form of a word that remains after removal of all inflectional affixes. **8.** the main, usually vertical, stroke of a letter or of a musical note such as a minim. **9. a.** the main upright timber or structure at the bow of a vessel. **b.** the very forward end of a vessel (esp. in **from stem to stern**). ~*vb.* **stemming, stemmed. 10.** (*intr.*; usually foll. by *from*) to be derived; originate. **11.** (*tr.*) to make headway against (a tide, wind, etc.). **12.** (*tr.*) to remove or disengage the stem or stems from. [OE *stemn*] —ˈ**stem**ˌ**like** *adj.*

stem[2] (stɛm) *vb.* **stemming, stemmed. 1.** (*tr.*) to restrain or stop (the flow of something) by or as if by damming up. **2.** (*tr.*) to pack tightly or stop up. **3.** *Skiing.* to manoeuvre (a ski or skis), as in performing a stem. ~*n.* **4.** *Skiing.* a technique in which the heel of one ski or both skis is forced outwards from the direction of movement in order to slow down or turn. [C15 *stemmen*, < ON *stemma*]

stem cell *n. Histology.* an undifferentiated cell that gives rise to specialized cells, such as blood cells.

stemma (ˈstɛmə) *n.* a family tree; pedigree. [C19: via L < Gk *stema* garland, wreath, < *stephein* to crown, wreathe]

stemmed (stɛmd) *adj.* **1. a.** having a stem. **b.** (*in combination*): *a long-stemmed glass.* **2.** having had the stem or stems removed.

stem turn *n. Skiing.* a turn in which the heel of one ski is stemmed and the other ski is brought parallel. Also called: **stem.**

stench (stɛntʃ) *n.* a strong and extremely offensive odour; stink. [OE *stenc*]

stencil (ˈstɛnsᵊl) *n.* **1.** a device for applying a design, characters, etc., to a surface, consisting of a thin sheet of plastic, metal, etc., in which the design or characters have been cut so that ink or paint can be applied through the incisions onto the surface. **2.** a design or characters produced in this way. ~*vb.* **-cilling, -cilled** *or U.S.* **-ciling, -ciled.** (*tr.*) **3.** to mark (a surface) with a stencil. **4.** to produce (characters or a design) with a stencil. [C14 *stanselen* to decorate with bright colours, < OF *estenceler*, < *estencele* a spark, < L *scintilla*]

Sten gun (stɛn) *n.* a light 9mm sub-machine-gun formerly used in the British Army. [C20: < *S* & *T* (initials of Shepherd & Turpin, the inventors) + *-en*, as in BREN GUN]

steno- *or before a vowel* **sten-** *combining form.* indicating narrowness or contraction: *stenography; stenosis.* [< Gk *stenos* narrow]

stenograph (ˈstɛnəˌgrɑːf) *n.* **1.** any of various keyboard machines for writing in shorthand. **2.** any character used in shorthand. ~*vb.* **3.** (*tr.*) to record (minutes, letters, etc.) in shorthand.

stenographer (stəˈnɒgrəfə) *n.* the U.S. & Canad. name for **shorthand typist.**

stenography (stəˈnɒgrəfɪ) *n.* **1.** the act or process of writing in shorthand by hand or machine. **2.** matter written in shorthand. —**stenographic** (ˌstɛnəˈgræfɪk) *adj.*

stenosis (stɪˈnəʊsɪs) *n., pl.* **-ses** (-siːz). *Pathol.* an abnormal narrowing of a bodily canal or passage. [C19: via NL < Gk *stenōsis*, ult. < *stenos* narrow] —**stenotic** (stɪˈnɒtɪk) *adj.*

Stenotype (ˈstɛnəˌtaɪp) *n.* **1.** *Trademark.* a machine with a keyboard for recording speeches, etc., in a phonetic shorthand. **2.** any machine resembling this. **3.** the phonetic symbol typed in one stroke of such a machine.

stenotypy (ˈstɛnəˌtaɪpɪ) *n.* a form of shorthand in which alphabetic combinations are used to represent groups of sounds or short common words. —ˈ**steno**ˌ**typist** *n.*

Stentor (ˈstɛntɔː) *n.* **1.** *Greek myth.* a Greek herald with a powerful voice who died after he lost a shouting contest with Hermes, herald of the gods. **2.** (*not cap.*) any person with an unusually loud voice.

stentorian (stɛnˈtɔːrɪən) *adj.* (of the voice, etc.) uncommonly loud: *stentorian tones.* [C17: after STENTOR]

step (stɛp) *n.* **1.** the act of raising the foot and setting it down again in coordination with the transference of the weight of the body. **2.** the distance or space covered by such a motion. **3.** the sound made by such a movement. **4.** the impression made by such movement of the foot; footprint. **5.** the manner of walking or moving the feet; gait: *a proud step.* **6.** a sequence of foot movements that make up a particular dance or part of a dance: *the steps of the waltz.* **7.** any of several paces or rhythmic movements in marching, dancing, etc.: *the goose step.* **8.** (*pl.*) a course followed by a person in walking or as walking: *they followed in their leader's steps.* **9.** one of a sequence of separate consecutive stages in the progression towards some goal. **10.** a rank or grade in a series or scale. **11.** an object or device that offers support for the foot when ascending or descending. **12.** (*pl.*) a flight of stairs, esp. out of doors. **13.** (*pl.*) another name for **stepladder. 14.** a very short easily walked distance: *it is only a step.* **15.** *Music.* a melodic interval of a second. **16.** an offset or change in the level of a surface similar to the step of a stair. **17.** a strong block or frame bolted onto the keel of a vessel and fitted to receive the base of a mast. **18.** a ledge cut in mining or quarrying excavations. **19. break step.** to cease to march in step. **20. in step. a.** marching, dancing, etc., in conformity with a specified pace or moving in unison with others. **b.** *Inf.* in agreement or harmony. **21. keep step.** to remain walking, marching, dancing, etc., in unison or in a specified rhythm. **22. out of step. a.** not moving in conformity with a specified pace or in accordance with others. **b.** *Inf.* not in agreement; out of harmony. **23. step by step.** with care and deliberation; gradually. **24. take steps.** to undertake measures (to do something). **25. watch one's step. a.** *Inf.* to conduct oneself with caution and good behaviour. **b.** to walk or move carefully. ~*vb.* **stepping, stepped. 26.** (*intr.*) to move by raising the foot and then setting it down in a different position, transferring the weight of the body to this foot and repeating the process with the other foot. **27.** (*intr.;* often foll. by *in, out,* etc.) to move or go on foot, esp. for a short distance: *step this way.* **28.** (*intr.*) *Inf., chiefly U.S.* to move, often in an attractive graceful manner, as in dancing: *he can really step around.* **29.** (*intr.;* usually foll. by *on* or *upon*) to place or press the foot; tread: *to step on the accelerator.* **30.** (*intr.;* usually foll. by *into*) to enter (into a situation) apparently with ease: *she stepped into a life of luxury.* **31.** (*tr.*) to walk or take (a number of paces, etc.): *to step ten paces.* **32.** (*tr.*) to perform the steps of: *they step the tango well.* **33.** (*tr.*) to set or place (the foot). **34.** (*tr.;* usually foll. by *off* or *out*) to measure (some distance of ground) by stepping. **35.** (*tr.*) to arrange in or supply with a series of steps so as to avoid coincidence or symmetry. **36.** (*tr.*) to raise (a mast) and fit it into its step. ~See also **step down, step in,** etc. [OE *stepe, stæpe*] —**ˈstepˌlike** *adj.*

step- *combining form.* indicating relationship through the previous marriage of a spouse or parent: *stepson; stepfather.* [OE *stēop-*]

stepbrother (ˈstɛpˌbrʌðə) *n.* a son of one's stepmother or stepfather by a union with someone other than one's father or mother.

stepchild (ˈstɛpˌtʃaɪld) *n., pl.* **-children.** a stepson or stepdaughter.

stepdaughter (ˈstɛpˌdɔːtə) *n.* a daughter of one's husband or wife by a former union.

step down *vb.* (*adv.*) **1.** (*tr.*) to reduce gradually. **2.** (*intr.*) *Inf.* to resign or abdicate (from a position). **3.** (*intr.*) *Inf.* to assume an inferior or less senior position. ~*adj.* **step-down.** (*prenominal*) **4.** (of a transformer) reducing a high voltage to a lower voltage. Cf. **step-up** (sense 3). ~*n.* **step-down. 5.** *Inf.* a decrease in quantity or size.

stepfather (ˈstɛpˌfɑːðə) *n.* a man who has married one's mother after the death or divorce of one's father.

stephanotis (ˌstɛfəˈnəʊtɪs) *n.* any of various climbing shrubs of Madagascar and Malaya, cultivated for their fragrant white waxy flowers. [C19: via NL < Gk: fit for a crown, < *stephanos* a crown]

step in *vb.* **1.** (*intr., adv.*) *Inf.* to intervene or involve oneself. ~*adj.* **step-in. 2.** (*prenominal*) (of garments, etc.) put on by being stepped into; without fastenings. **3.** (of a ski binding) engaging automatically when the boot is positioned on the ski. ~*n.* **step-in. 4.** (*often pl.*) a step-in garment, esp. underwear.

stepladder (ˈstɛpˌlædə) *n.* a folding portable ladder that is made of broad flat steps fixed to a supporting frame hinged at the top to another supporting frame.

stepmother (ˈstɛpˌmʌðə) *n.* a woman who has married one's father after the death or divorce of one's mother.

step on *vb.* (*intr., prep.*) **1.** to place or press the foot on. **2.** *Inf.* to behave harshly or contemptuously towards. **3. step on it.** *Inf.* to go more quickly; hurry up.

step out *vb.* (*intr., adv.*) **1.** to go outside or leave a room, etc., esp. briefly. **2.** to begin to walk more quickly and take longer strides. **3.** *U.S. & Canad. inf.* to withdraw from involvement.

step-parent (ˈstɛpˌpɛərənt) *n.* a stepfather or stepmother. —**ˈstep-ˌparenting** *n.*

steppe (stɛp) *n.* (*often pl.*) an extensive grassy plain usually without trees. [C17: < ORussian *step* lowland]

stepper (ˈstɛpə) *n.* a person who or animal that steps, esp. a horse or a dancer.

Steppes (stɛps) *pl. n.* **the.** the huge grasslands of Eurasia, chiefly in the Soviet Union.

stepping stone *n.* **1.** one of a series of stones acting as footrests for crossing streams, marshes, etc. **2.** a circumstance that assists progress towards some goal.

stepsister (ˈstɛpˌsɪstə) *n.* a daughter of one's stepmother or stepfather by a union with someone other than one's father or mother.

stepson (ˈstɛpˌsʌn) *n.* a son of one's husband or wife by a former union.

step up *vb.* (*adv.*) *Inf.* **1.** (*tr.*) to increase or raise by stages; accelerate. **2.** (*intr.*) to make progress or effect an advancement; be promoted. ~*adj.* **step-up.** (*prenominal*) **3.** (of a transformer) increasing a low voltage to a higher voltage. Cf. **step-down** (sense 4). ~*n.* **step-up. 4.** *Inf.* an increment in quantity, size, etc.

-ster *suffix forming nouns.* **1.** indicating a person who is engaged in a certain activity: *prankster; songster.* **2.** indicating a person associated with or being something specified: *mobster; youngster.* [OE *-estre*]

steradian (stəˈreɪdɪən) *n.* an SI unit of solid angle; the angle that, having its vertex in the centre of a sphere, cuts off an area of the surface of the sphere equal to the square of the length of the radius. Symbol: sr [C19: < STEREO- + RADIAN]

stercoraceous (ˌstɜːkəˈreɪʃəs) *adj.* of, relating to, or consisting of dung or excrement. [C18: < L *stercus* dung + -ACEOUS]

stere (stɪə) *n.* a unit used to measure volumes of stacked timber equal to one cubic metre (35.315 cubic feet). [C18: < F *stère,* < Gk *stereos* solid]

stereo (ˈstɛrɪəʊ, ˈstɪər-) *adj.* **1.** short for **stereophonic** or **stereoscopic.** ~*n., pl.* **stereos. 2.** stereophonic sound: *to broadcast in stereo.* **3.** a stereophonic record player, tape recorder, etc. **4.** *Photog.* **a.** stereoscopic photography. **b.** a stereoscopic photograph. **5.** *Printing.* short for **stereotype.** [C20: shortened form]

stereo- *or sometimes before a vowel* **stere-** *combining form.* indicating three-dimensional quality or solidity: *stereoscope.* [< Gk *stereos* solid]

stereochemistry (ˌstɛrɪəʊˈkɛmɪstrɪ, ˌstɪər-) *n.* the study of the spatial arrangement of atoms in molecules and its effect on chemical properties.

stereograph (ˈstɛrɪəˌgrɑːf, ˈstɪər-) *n.* two almost identical pictures, or one special picture, that when viewed through special glasses or a stereoscope form a single three-dimensional image. Also called: **stereogram.**

stereoisomer (ˌstɛrɪəʊˈaɪsəmə, ˌstɪər-) *n. Chem.* an isomer that exhibits stereoisomerism.

stereoisomerism (ˌstɛrɪəʊaɪˈsɒməˌrɪzəm, ˌstɪər-) *n. Chem.* isomerism caused by differences in the spatial arrangement of atoms in molecules.

stereophonic (ˌstɛrɪəˈfɒnɪk, ˌstɪər-) *adj.* (of a system for recording, reproducing, or broadcasting sound) using two or more separate microphones to feed two or more loudspeakers through separate channels in order to give a spatial effect to the sound. Often shortened to **stereo.** —**ˌstereoˈphonically** *adv.* —**stereophony** (ˌstɛrɪˈɒfənɪ, ˌstɪər-) *n.*

stereoscope (ˈstɛrɪəˌskəʊp, ˈstɪər-) *n.* an optical instrument for viewing two-dimensional pictures, giving an illusion of depth and relief. It has a binocular eyepiece through which two slightly different pictures of an object are viewed, one with each eye. —**stereoscopic** (ˌstɛrɪəˈskɒpɪk, ˌstɪər-) *adj.*

stereoscopy (ˌstɛrɪˈɒskəpɪ, ˌstɪər-) *n.* **1.** the viewing or appearance of objects in or as if in three dimensions. **2.** the study and use of the stereoscope. —**ˌstereoˈscopic** *adj.*

stereospecific (ˌstɛrɪəʊspɪˈsɪfɪk, ˌstɪər-) *adj.*

Chem. relating to or having fixed position in space, as in the spatial arrangements of atoms in certain polymers.

stereotype (ˈstɛrɪəˌtaɪp, ˈstɪər-) *n.* **1. a.** a method of producing cast-metal printing plates from a mould made from a forme of type. **b.** the plate so made. **2.** another word for **stereotypy. 3.** an idea, convention, etc., that has grown stale through fixed usage. **4.** a standardized image or conception of a type of person, etc. ~*vb.* (*tr.*) **5. a.** to make a stereotype of. **b.** to print from a stereotype. **6.** to impart a fixed usage or convention to. —ˈ**stereoˌtyper** *or* ˈ**stereoˌtypist** *n.*

stereotyped (ˈstɛrɪəˌtaɪpt, ˈstɪər-) *adj.* **1.** lacking originality or individuality; conventional; trite. **2.** reproduced from or on a stereotype printing plate.

stereotypy (ˈstɛrɪəˌtaɪpɪ, ˈstɪər-) *n.* **1.** the act or process of making stereotype printing plates. **2.** a tendency to think or act in rigid, repetitive, and often meaningless patterns.

stereovision (ˈstɛrɪəʊˌvɪʒən, ˈstɪər-) *n.* the perception or exhibition of three-dimensional objects in three dimensions.

steric (ˈstɛrɪk, ˈstɪər-) *or* **sterical** *adj. Chem.* of or caused by the spatial arrangement of atoms in a molecule. [C19: < STEREO- + -IC]

sterile (ˈstɛraɪl) *adj.* **1.** unable to produce offspring; permanently infertile. **2.** free from living, esp. pathogenic, microorganisms. **3.** (of plants or their parts) not producing or bearing seeds, fruit, spores, stamens, or pistils. **4.** lacking inspiration or vitality; fruitless. [C16: < L *sterilis*] —ˈ**sterilely** *adv.* —**sterility** (stɛˈrɪlɪtɪ) *n.*

sterilize *or* **-ise** (ˈstɛrɪˌlaɪz) *vb.* (*tr.*) to render sterile; make infertile or barren. —ˌ**steriliˈzation** *or* **-iˈsation** *n.* —ˈ**steriˌlizer** *or* **-iser** *n.*

sterling (ˈstɜːlɪŋ) *n.* **1. a.** British money: *pound sterling.* **b.** (*as modifier*): *sterling reserves.* **2.** the official standard of purity of British coins. **3. a.** short for **sterling silver. b.** (*as modifier*): *a sterling bracelet.* **4.** an article or articles manufactured from sterling silver. ~*adj.* **5.** (*prenominal*) genuine and reliable: first-class: *sterling quality.* [C13: prob. < OE *steorra* star + -LING[1]; referring to a small star on early Norman pennies]

sterling area *n.* a group of countries that use sterling as a medium of international payments. Also called: **scheduled territories.**

sterling silver *n.* **1.** an alloy containing not less than 92.5 per cent of silver. **2.** sterling-silver articles collectively.

stern[1] (stɜːn) *adj.* **1.** showing uncompromising or inflexible resolve; firm or authoritarian. **2.** lacking leniency or clemency. **3.** relentless; unyielding: *the stern demands of parenthood.* **4.** having an austere or forbidding appearance or nature. [OE *styrne*] —ˈ**sternly** *adv.* —ˈ**sternness** *n.*

stern[2] (stɜːn) *n.* **1.** the rear or after part of a vessel, opposite the bow or stem. **2.** the rear part of any object. ~*adj.* **3.** relating to or located at the stern. [C13: < ON *stjörn* steering]

sternforemost (ˈstɜːnˈfɔːməʊst) *adv. Naut.* backwards.

sternmost (ˈstɜːnˌməʊst) *adj. Naut.* **1.** farthest to the stern; aftmost. **2.** nearest the stern.

sternpost (ˈstɜːnˌpəʊst) *n. Naut.* the main upright timber or structure at the stern of a vessel.

stern sheets *pl. n. Naut.* the part of an open boat near the stern.

sternum (ˈstɜːnəm) *n., pl.* **-na** (-nə) *or* **-nums. 1.** (in man) a long flat vertical bone in front of the thorax, to which are attached the collarbone and the first seven pairs of ribs. Nontechnical name: **breastbone. 2.** the corresponding part in many other vertebrates. [C17: via NL < Gk *sternon* breastbone] —ˈ**sternal** *adj.*

sternutation (ˌstɜːnjʊˈteɪʃən) *n.* a sneeze or the act of sneezing. [C16: < LL *sternūtāre* to sneeze, < *sternuere* to sputter (of a light)]

sternutator (ˈstɜːnjʊˌteɪtə) *n.* a substance that causes sneezing, coughing, and tears; used in chemical warfare. —**sternutatory** (stɜːˈnjuːtətərɪ, -trɪ) *adj., n.*

sternwards (ˈstɜːnwədz) *or* **sternward** *adv. Naut.* towards the stern; astern.

sternway (ˈstɜːnˌweɪ) *n. Naut.* movement of a vessel sternforemost.

stern-wheeler *n.* a vessel, esp. a river boat, propelled by a large paddle wheel at the stern.

steroid (ˈstɪərɔɪd) *n. Biochem.* any of a large group of organic compounds containing a characteristic chemical ring system, including sterols, bile acids, many hormones, and the D vitamins. [C20: < STEROL + -OID] —**steˈroidal** *adj.*

sterol (ˈstɛrɒl) *n. Biochem.* any of a group of natural steroid alcohols, such as cholesterol and ergosterol, that are waxy insoluble substances. [C20: shortened < CHOLESTEROL, ERGOSTEROL, etc.]

stertorous (ˈstɜːtərəs) *adj.* **1.** marked by heavy snoring. **2.** breathing in this way. [C19: < L *stertere* to snore] —ˈ**stertorously** *adv.* —ˈ**stertorousness** *n.*

stet (stɛt) *n.* **1.** a word or mark indicating that certain deleted typeset or written matter is to be retained. ~*vb.* **stetting, stetted. 2.** (*tr.*) to mark (matter) thus. [L, lit.: let it stand]

stethoscope (ˈstɛθəˌskəʊp) *n. Med.* an instrument for listening to the sounds made within the body, typically consisting of a hollow disc that transmits the sound through hollow tubes to earpieces. [C19: < F, < Gk *stēthos* breast + -SCOPE] —**stethoscopic** (ˌstɛθəˈskɒpɪk) *adj.* —**stethoscopy** (stɛˈθɒskəpɪ) *n.*

stetson (ˈstɛtsᵊn) *n.* a man's felt slouch hat with a broad brim and high crown. [C20: after John *Stetson* (1830–1906), American hat-maker]

stevedore (ˈstiːvɪˌdɔː) *n.* **1.** a person employed to load or unload ships. ~*vb.* **2.** to load or unload (a ship, ship's cargo, etc.). [C18: < Sp. *estibador* a packer, < *estibar* to load (a ship), < L *stīpāre* to pack full]

stew[1] (stjuː) *n.* **1. a.** a dish of meat, fish, or other food, cooked by stewing. **b.** (*as modifier*): *stew pot.* **2.** *Inf.* a difficult or worrying situation or a troubled state (esp. in **in a stew**). **3.** a heterogeneous mixture: *a stew of people of every race.* **4.** (*usually pl.*) *Arch.* a brothel. ~*vb.* **5.** to cook or cause to cook by long slow simmering. **6.** (*intr.*) *Inf.* to be troubled or agitated. **7.** (*intr.*) *Inf.* to be oppressed with heat or crowding. **8.** to cause (tea) to become bitter or (of tea) to become bitter through infusing for too long. **9. stew in one's own juice.** to suffer unaided the consequences of one's actions. [C14 *stuen* to take a very hot bath, < OF *estuver,* < Vulgar L *extūfāre* (unattested), < EX-[1] + (unattested) *tūfus* vapour, < Gk *tuphos*]

stew[2] (stjuː) *n. Brit.* **1.** a fishpond or fishtank. **2.** an artificial oyster bed. [C14: < OF *estui,* < *estoier* to confine, ult. < L *studium* STUDY]

steward (stjʊəd) *n.* **1.** a person who administers the property, house, finances, etc., of another. **2.** a person who manages the eating arrangements, staff, or service at a club, hotel, etc. **3.** a waiter on a ship or aircraft. **4.** a mess attendant in a naval mess. **5.** a person who helps to supervise some event or proceedings in an official capacity. **6.** short for **shop steward.** ~*vb.* **7.** to act or serve as a steward (of something). [OE *stigweard,* < *stig* hall + *weard* WARD] —ˈ**stewardship** *n.*

stewardess (ˈstjʊədɪs, ˌstjʊəˈdɛs) *n.* a woman steward on an aircraft or ship.

stewed (stjuːd) *adj.* **1.** (of meat, fish, etc.) cooked by stewing. **2.** *Brit.* (of tea) bitter through having been left to infuse for too long. **3.** a slang word for **drunk** (sense 1).

stg *abbrev. for* sterling.

sthenic (ˈsθɛnɪk) *adj.* abounding in energy or bodily strength; active or strong. [C18: < NL *sthenicus,* < Gk *sthenos* force, on the model of *asthenic*]

stibine (ˈstɪbaɪn) *n.* **1.** a colourless poisonous gas with an offensive odour: made by the action of hydrochloric acid on an alloy of antimony and zinc. **2.** any one of a class of stibine derivatives in which one or more hydrogen atoms have been replaced by organic groups. [C19: < L *stibium* antimony + -INE[2]]

stibnite ('stɪbnaɪt) *n.* a soft greyish mineral consisting of antimony sulphide in crystalline form: the chief ore of antimony. [C19: < obs. *stibine* stibnite + -ITE[1]]

-stichous *adj. combining form.* having a certain number of rows. [< LL *-stichus*, < Gk *-stikhos*, < *stikhos* row]

stick[1] (stɪk) *n.* **1.** a small thin branch of a tree. **2. a.** any long thin piece of wood. **b.** such a piece of wood having a characteristic shape for a special purpose: *a walking stick; a hockey stick.* **c.** a baton, wand, staff, or rod. **3.** an object or piece shaped like a stick: *a stick of celery.* **4.** In full: **control stick.** the lever by which a pilot controls the movements of an aircraft. **5.** *Inf.* the lever used to change gear in a motor vehicle. **6.** *Naut.* a mast or yard. **7. a.** a group of bombs arranged to fall at intervals across a target. **b.** a number of paratroops jumping in sequence. **8.** *Sl.* **a.** verbal abuse, criticism: *I got some stick for that blunder.* **b.** physical power, force (esp. in **give it some stick**). **9.** (*usually pl.*) a piece of furniture: *these few sticks are all I have.* **10.** (*pl.*) *Inf.* a rural area considered remote or backward (esp. in **in the sticks**). **11.** (*pl.*) *Hockey.* a declaration made by the umpire if a player's stick is above the shoulders. **12.** (*pl.*) *Austral.* goal posts. **13.** *Inf.* a dull boring person. **14.** (usually preceded by *old*) *Inf.* a familiar name for a person: *not a bad old stick.* **15.** punishment; beating. **16. in a cleft stick.** in a difficult position. **17. wrong end of the stick.** a complete misunderstanding of a situation, explanation, etc. ~*vb.* **sticking, sticked. 18.** to support (a plant) with sticks; stake. [OE *sticca*]

stick[2] (stɪk) *vb.* **sticking, stuck. 1.** (*tr.*) to pierce or stab with or as if with something pointed. **2.** to thrust or push (a sharp or pointed object) or (of a sharp or pointed object) to be pushed into or through another object. **3.** (*tr.*) to fasten in position by pushing or forcing a point into something: *to stick a peg in a hole.* **4.** (*tr.*) to fasten in position by or as if by pins, nails, etc.: *to stick a picture on the wall.* **5.** (*tr.*) to transfix or impale on a pointed object. **6.** (*tr.*) to cover with objects piercing or set in the surface. **7.** (when *intr.*, foll. by *out, up, through*, etc.) to put forward or be put forward; protrude or cause to protrude: *to stick one's head out.* **8.** (*tr.*) *Inf.* to place or put in a specified position: *stick your coat on this chair.* **9.** to fasten or be fastened by or as if by an adhesive substance: *stick the pages together; they won't stick.* **10.** (*tr.*) *Inf.* to cause to become sticky. **11.** (when *tr.*, *usually passive*) to come or cause to come to a standstill: *stuck in a traffic jam; the wheels stuck.* **12.** (*intr.*) to remain for a long time: *the memory sticks in my mind.* **13.** (*tr.*) *Sl., chiefly Brit.* to tolerate; abide: *I can't stick that man.* **14.** (*intr.*) to be reluctant. **15.** (*tr.; usually passive*) *Inf.* to cause to be at a loss; baffle or puzzle: *I was totally stuck for an answer.* **16.** (*tr.*) *Sl.* to force or impose something unpleasant on: *they stuck me with the bill.* **17.** (*tr.*) to kill by piercing or stabbing. **18. stick to the ribs.** *Inf.* (of food) to be hearty and satisfying. ~*n.* **19.** the state or condition of adhering. **20.** *Inf.* a substance causing adhesion. **21.** *Obs.* something that causes delay or stoppage. ~See also **stick around, stick by,** etc. [OE *stician*]

stick around *or* **about** *vb.* (*intr., adv.*) *Inf.* to remain in a place, esp. awaiting something.

stick by *vb.* (*intr., prep.*) to remain faithful to; adhere to.

sticker ('stɪkə) *n.* **1.** an adhesive label, poster, or paper. **2.** a person or thing that sticks. **3.** a persevering or industrious person. **4.** something prickly, such as a thorn, that clings to one's clothing, etc. **5.** *Inf.* something that perplexes. **6.** *Inf.* a knife used for stabbing or piercing.

sticking plaster *n.* a thin cloth with an adhesive substance on one side, used for covering slight or superficial wounds.

stick insect *n.* any of various mostly tropical insects that have an elongated cylindrical body and long legs and resemble twigs.

stick-in-the-mud *n. Inf.* a conservative person who lacks initiative or imagination.

stickle ('stɪkəl) *vb.* (*intr.*) **1.** to dispute stubbornly, esp. about minor points. **2.** to refuse to agree or concur, esp. by making petty stipulations. [C16 *stightle* (in the sense: to arbitrate): frequentative of OE *stihtan* to arrange]

stickleback ('stɪkəlˌbæk) *n.* any of various small fishes that have a series of spines along the back and occur in cold and temperate northern regions. [C15: < OE *stickel* prick, sting + BACK[1]]

stickler ('stɪklə) *n.* **1.** (usually foll. by *for*) a person who makes insistent demands: *a stickler for accuracy.* **2.** a problem or puzzle.

stick out *vb.* (*adv.*) **1.** to project or cause to project. **2.** (*tr.*) *Inf.* to endure (something disagreeable) (esp. in **stick it out**). **3. stick out a mile** *or* **like a sore thumb.** *Inf.* to be extremely obvious. **4. stick out for.** to insist on (a demand), refusing to yield until it is met.

stick to *vb.* (*prep., mainly intr.*) **1.** (*also tr.*) to adhere or cause to adhere to. **2.** to continue constantly at. **3.** to remain faithful to. **4.** not to move or digress from: *the speaker stuck closely to his subject.* **5. stick to someone's fingers.** *Inf.* to be stolen by someone.

stick-up *n.* **1.** *Sl., chiefly U.S.* a robbery at gunpoint; hold-up. ~*vb.* **stick up.** (*adv.*) **2.** (*tr.*) *Sl., chiefly U.S.* to rob, esp. at gunpoint. **3.** (*intr.;* foll. by *for*) *Inf.* to support or defend: *stick up for oneself.*

sticky ('stɪkɪ) *adj.* **stickier, stickiest. 1.** covered or daubed with an adhesive or viscous substance: *sticky fingers.* **2.** having the property of sticking to a surface. **3.** (of weather or atmosphere) warm and humid; muggy. **4.** *Inf.* difficult, awkward, or painful: *a sticky business.* ~*vb.* **stickying, stickied. 5.** (*tr.*) *Inf.* to make sticky. —'**stickily** *adv.* —'**stickiness** *n.*

stickybeak ('stɪkɪˌbiːk) *Austral. & N.Z. inf.* ~*n.* **1.** an inquisitive person. ~*vb.* **2.** (*intr.*) to pry.

sticky end *n. Inf.* an unpleasant finish or death (esp. in **come to** *or* **meet a sticky end**).

sticky wicket *n.* **1.** a cricket pitch that is rapidly being dried by the sun after rain and is particularly conducive to spin. **2.** *Inf.* a difficult or awkward situation.

stiff (stɪf) *adj.* **1.** not easily bent; rigid; inflexible. **2.** not working or moving easily or smoothly: *a stiff handle.* **3.** difficult to accept in its severity or harshness: *a stiff punishment.* **4.** moving with pain or difficulty; not supple: *a stiff neck.* **5.** difficult; arduous: *a stiff climb.* **6.** unrelaxed or awkward; formal. **7.** firmer than liquid in consistency; thick or viscous. **8.** powerful; strong: *a stiff breeze; a stiff drink.* **9.** excessively high: *a stiff price.* **10.** lacking grace or attractiveness. **11.** stubborn or stubbornly maintained: *a stiff fight.* **12.** *Obs.* tightly stretched; taut. **13.** *Sl.* intoxicated. **14. stiff with.** *Inf.* amply provided with. ~*n.* **15.** *Sl.* a corpse. ~*adv.* **16.** completely or utterly: *bored stiff; frozen stiff.* [OE *stif*] —'**stiffish** *adj.* —'**stiffly** *adv.* —'**stiffness** *n.*

stiffen ('stɪfən) *vb.* **1.** to make or become stiff or stiffer. **2.** (*intr.*) to become suddenly tense or unyielding. —'**stiffener** *n.*

stiff-necked *adj.* haughtily stubborn or obstinate.

stifle ('staɪfəl) *vb.* **1.** (*tr.*) to smother or suppress: *stifle a cough.* **2.** to feel or cause to feel discomfort and difficulty in breathing. **3.** to prevent or be prevented from breathing so as to cause death. **4.** (*tr.*) to crush or stamp out. [C14: var. of *stuflen*, prob. < OF *estouffer* to smother]

stigma ('stɪgmə) *n., pl.* **stigmas** *or* **stigmata** ('stɪgmətə, stɪg'mɑːtə). **1.** a distinguishing mark of social disgrace: *the stigma of having been in prison.* **2.** a small scar or mark such as a birthmark. **3.** *Pathol.* any mark on the skin, such as one characteristic of a specific disease. **4.** *Bot.* the terminal part of the ovary, at the end of the style, where deposited pollen enters the gynoecium. **5.** *Zool.* **a.** a pigmented eyespot in some invertebrates. **b.** the spiracle of an insect. **6.** *Arch.* a mark branded on the skin. **7.** (*pl.*) *Christianity.* marks resembling the wounds of the crucified Christ, believed to appear on the bodies of certain individuals. [C16: via L < Gk: brand, < *stizein* to tattoo]

stigmatic (stɪgˈmætɪk) *adj.* **1.** relating to or having a stigma or stigmata. **2.** another word for **anastigmatic.** ~*n. also* **stigmatist** (ˈstɪgmətɪst). **3.** *Chiefly R.C. Church.* a person marked with the stigmata.

stigmatism (ˈstɪgməˌtɪzəm) *n.* **1.** *Physics.* the state or condition of being anastigmatic. **2.** *Pathol.* the condition resulting from or characterized by stigmata.

stigmatize *or* **-ise** (ˈstɪgməˌtaɪz) *vb.* (*tr.*) **1.** to mark out or describe (as something bad). **2.** to mark with a stigma or stigmata. —ˌ**stigmatiˈzation** *or* **-iˈsation** *n.* —ˈ**stigmaˌtizer** *or* **-iser** *n.*

stilbene (ˈstɪlbiːn) *n.* a colourless or slightly yellow crystalline unsaturated hydrocarbon used in the manufacture of dyes. [C19: < Gk *stilbos* glittering + -ENE]

stilboestrol *or U.S.* **stilbestrol** (stɪlˈbiːstrəl) *n.* a synthetic hormone having derivatives with oestrogenic properties. Also called: **diethylstilboestrol.** [C20: < STILBENE + OESTRUS + -OL[1]]

stile[1] (staɪl) *n.* **1.** a set of steps or rungs in a wall or fence to allow people, but not animals, to pass over. **2.** short for **turnstile.** [OE *stigel*]

stile[2] (staɪl) *n.* a vertical framing member in a door, window frame, etc. [C17: prob. < Du. *stijl* pillar, ult. < L *stilus* writing instrument]

stiletto (stɪˈlɛtəʊ) *n., pl.* **-tos.** **1.** a small dagger with a slender tapered blade. **2.** a sharply pointed tool used to make holes in leather, cloth, etc. **3.** Also called: **spike heel, stiletto heel.** a very high heel on a woman's shoe, tapering to a very narrow tip. ~*vb.* **-toeing, -toed.** **4.** (*tr.*) to stab with a stiletto. [C17: < It., < *stilo* a dagger, < L *stilus* a stake, pen]

still[1] (stɪl) *adj.* **1.** (*usually predicative*) motionless; stationary. **2.** undisturbed or tranquil; silent and calm. **3.** not sparkling or effervescent. **4.** gentle or quiet; subdued. **5.** *Obs.* (of a child) dead at birth. ~*adv.* **6.** continuing now or in the future as in the past: *do you still love me?* **7.** up to this or that time; yet: *I still don't know your name.* **8.** (often used with a comparative) even or yet: *still more insults.* **9.** quiet or without movement: *sit still.* **10.** *Poetic & dialect.* always. ~*n.* **11.** *Poetic.* silence or tranquillity: *the still of the night.* **12. a.** a still photograph, esp. of a scene from a film. **b.** (*as modifier*): *a still camera.* ~*vb.* **13.** to make or become still, quiet, or calm. **14.** (*tr.*) to allay or relieve: *her fears were stilled.* ~*sentence connector.* **15.** even then; nevertheless: *the child has some new toys and still cries.* [OE *stille*] —ˈ**stillness** *n.*

still[2] (stɪl) *n.* an apparatus for carrying out distillation, used esp. in the manufacture of spirits. [C16: < OF *stiller* to drip, < L *stillāre*, < *stilla* a drip]

stillborn (ˈstɪlˌbɔːn) *adj.* **1.** (of a fetus) dead at birth. **2.** (of an idea, plan, etc.) fruitless; abortive; unsuccessful. —ˈ**stillˌbirth** *n.*

still life *n., pl.* **still lifes.** **1. a.** a painting or drawing of inanimate objects, such as fruit, flowers, etc. **b.** (*as modifier*): *a still-life painting.* **2.** the genre of such paintings.

still room *n. Brit.* **1.** a room in which distilling is carried out. **2.** a pantry or storeroom, as in a large house.

Stillson wrench (ˈstɪlsᵊn) *n. Trademark.* a large wrench having jaws that tighten as the pressure on the handle is increased.

stilly *adv.* (ˈstɪllɪ). **1.** *Arch. or literary.* quietly or calmly. ~*adj.* (ˈstɪlɪ). **2.** *Poetic.* still, quiet, or calm.

stilt (stɪlt) *n.* **1.** either of a pair of two long poles with footrests on which a person stands and walks, as used by circus clowns. **2.** a long post or column that is used with others to support a building above ground level. **3.** any of several shore birds similar to the avocets but having a straight bill. ~*vb.* **4.** (*tr.*) to raise or place on or as if on stilts. [C14 (in the sense: crutch, handle of a plough): rel. to Low G *stilte* pole]

stilted (ˈstɪltɪd) *adj.* **1.** (of speech, writing, etc.) formal, pompous, or bombastic. **2.** not flowing continuously or naturally: *stilted conversation.* **3.** *Archit.* (of an arch) having vertical piers between the impost and the springing. —ˈ**stiltedly** *adv.* —ˈ**stiltedness** *n.*

Stilton (ˈstɪltən) *n. Trademark.* either of two rich cheeses, blue-veined (**blue Stilton**) or white (**white Stilton**), both very strong in flavour. [C18: named after *Stilton*, Cambridgeshire, where it was orig. sold]

stimulant (ˈstɪmjʊlənt) *n.* **1.** a drug or similar substance that increases physiological activity, esp. of a particular organ. **2.** any stimulating agent or thing. ~*adj.* **3.** stimulating. [C18: < L *stimulāns* goading, < *stimulāre* to urge on]

stimulate (ˈstɪmjʊˌleɪt) *vb.* **1.** (*tr.*) to arouse or quicken the activity or senses of. **2.** (*tr.*) *Physiol.* to excite (a nerve, organ, etc.) with a stimulus. **3.** (*intr.*) to act as a stimulant or stimulus. [C16: < L *stimulāre*] —ˈ**stimuˌlating** *adj.* —ˌ**stimuˈlation** *n.* —ˈ**stimulative** *adj., n.* —ˈ**stimuˌlator** *n.*

stimulus (ˈstɪmjʊləs) *n., pl.* **-li** (-ˌlaɪ, -ˌliː). **1.** something that stimulates or acts as an incentive. **2.** any drug, agent, electrical impulse, or other factor able to cause a response in an organism. [C17: < L: a cattle goad]

sting (stɪŋ) *vb.* **stinging, stung.** **1.** (of certain animals and plants) to inflict a wound on (an organism) by the injection of poison. **2.** to feel or cause to feel a sharp mental or physical pain. **3.** (*tr.*) to goad or incite (esp. in **sting into action**). **4.** (*tr.*) *Inf.* to cheat, esp. by overcharging. ~*n.* **5.** a skin wound caused by the poison injected by certain insects or plants. **6.** pain caused by or as if by the sting of a plant or animal. **7.** a mental pain or pang: *a sting of conscience.* **8.** a sharp pointed organ, such as the ovipositor of a wasp, by which poison can be injected. **9.** the ability to sting: *a sharp sting in his criticism.* **10.** something as painful or swift of action as a sting: *the sting of death.* **11.** a sharp stimulus or incitement. **12.** *Sl.* a deceptive ruse. [OE *stingan*] —ˈ**stinger** *n.* —ˈ**stinging** *adj.*

stinging nettle *n.* See **nettle** (sense 1).

stingray (ˈstɪŋˌreɪ) *n.* any of various rays having a whiplike tail bearing a serrated venomous spine capable of inflicting painful weals.

stingy[1] (ˈstɪndʒɪ) *adj.* **-gier, -giest.** **1.** unwilling to spend or give. **2.** insufficient or scanty. [C17 (? in the sense: ill-tempered): ? < *stinge*, dialect var. of STING] —ˈ**stingily** *adv.* —ˈ**stinginess** *n.*

stingy[2] (ˈstɪŋɪ) *adj.* **stingier, stingiest.** *Inf.* stinging or capable of stinging.

stink (stɪŋk) *n.* **1.** a strong foul smell; stench. **2.** *Sl.* a great deal of trouble (esp. in **make** *or* **raise a stink**). **3. like stink.** intensely; furiously. ~*vb.* **stinking, stank** *or* **stunk; stunk.** (*mainly intr.*) **4.** to emit a foul smell. **5.** *Sl.* to be thoroughly bad or abhorrent: *this town stinks.* **6.** *Inf.* to have a very bad reputation: *his name stinks.* **7.** to be of poor quality. **8.** (foll. by *of* or *with*) *Sl.* to have or appear to have an excessive amount (of money). **9.** (*tr.*; usually foll. by *up*) *Inf.* to cause to stink. ~See also **stink out.** [OE *stincan*]

stink bomb *n.* a small glass globe used by practical jokers: it releases a liquid with an offensive smell when broken.

stinker (ˈstɪŋkə) *n.* **1.** a person or thing that stinks. **2.** *Sl.* a difficult or very unpleasant person or thing. **3.** *Sl.* something of very poor quality. **4.** *Inf.* any of several fulmars or related birds that feed on carrion.

stinkhorn (ˈstɪŋkˌhɔːn) *n.* any of various fungi having an offensive odour.

stinking (ˈstɪŋkɪŋ) *adj.* **1.** having a foul smell. **2.** *Inf.* unpleasant or disgusting. **3.** (*postpositive*) *Sl.* very drunk. **4. cry stinking fish.** to decry something, esp. one's own products. ~*adv.* **5.** *Inf.* (intensifier, expressing contempt): *stinking rich.* —ˈ**stinkingly** *adv.* —ˈ**stinkingness** *n.*

stinko (ˈstɪŋkəʊ) *adj.* (*postpositive*) *Sl.* drunk.

stink out *vb.* (*tr., adv.*) **1.** to drive out or away by a foul smell. **2.** *Brit.* to cause to stink: *the smell of orange peel stinks out the room.*

stinkweed (ˈstɪŋkˌwiːd) *n.* **1.** Also called: **wall mustard.** a cruciferous plant, naturalized in Britain and S and central Europe, having pale yellow flowers and a disagreeable smell when bruised. **2.** any of various other ill-smelling plants.

stinkwood (ˈstɪŋkˌwʊd) *n.* **1.** any of various trees having offensive-smelling wood, esp. a southern African lauraceous tree yielding a hard wood used for furniture. **2.** the heavy durable wood of any of these trees.

stint[1] (stɪnt) *vb.* **1.** to be frugal or miserly towards (someone) with (something). **2.** *Arch.* to stop or check (something). ~*n.* **3.** an allotted or fixed amount of work. **4.** a limitation or check. [OE *styntan* to blunt] —ˈ**stinter** *n.*

stint[2] (stɪnt) *n.* any of various small sandpipers of a chiefly northern genus. [OE]

stipe (staɪp) *n.* **1.** a stalk in plants that bears reproductive structures, esp. the stalk bearing the cap of a mushroom. **2.** the stalk that bears the leaflets of a fern or the thallus of a seaweed. **3.** *Zool.* any stalklike part; stipes. [C18: via F < L *stīpes* tree trunk]

stipel (ˈstaɪpᵊl) *n.* a small paired leaflike structure at the base of certain leaflets; secondary stipule. [C19: via NL < L *stipula*, dim. of *stīpes* a log] —**stipellate** (staɪˈpɛlɪt, -eɪt) *adj.*

stipend (ˈstaɪpɛnd) *n.* a fixed or regular amount of money paid as a salary or allowance, as to a clergyman. [C15: < OF *stipende*, < L *stīpendium* tax, < *stips* a contribution + *pendere* to pay out]

stipendiary (staɪˈpɛndɪərɪ) *adj.* **1.** receiving or working for regular pay: *a stipendiary magistrate.* **2.** paid for by a stipend. ~*n., pl.* **-aries. 3.** a person who receives regular payment. [C16: < L *stīpendiārius* concerning tribute, < *stīpendium* STIPEND]

stipes (ˈstaɪpiːz) *n., pl.* **stipites** (ˈstɪpɪˌtiːz). *Zool.* **1.** the second maxillary segment in insects and crustaceans. **2.** the eyestalk of a crab or similar crustacean. **3.** any similar stemlike structure. [C18: < L; see STIPE] —**stipiform** (ˈstaɪpɪˌfɔːm) *or* **stipitiform** (ˈstɪpɪtɪˌfɔːm) *adj.*

stipple (ˈstɪpᵊl) *vb.* (*tr.*) **1.** to draw, engrave, or paint using dots or flecks. **2.** to apply paint, powder, etc., to (something) with many light dabs. ~*n. also* **stippling. 3.** the technique of stippling or a picture produced by or using stippling. [C18: < Du. *stippelen*, < *stippen* to prick, < *stip* point] —ˈ**stippler** *n.*

stipulate (ˈstɪpjʊˌleɪt) *vb.* **1.** (*tr.; may take a clause as object*) to specify, often as a condition of an agreement. **2.** (*intr.;* foll. by *for*) to insist (on) as a term of an agreement. **3.** (*tr.; may take a clause as object*) to guarantee or promise. [C17: < L *stipulārī*, prob. < OL *stipulus* firm] —ˌ**stipuˈlation** *n.* —ˈ**stipuˌlator** *n.*

stipule (ˈstɪpjuːl) *n.* a small paired usually leaflike outgrowth occurring at the base of a leaf or its stalk. [C18: < L; see STIPE] —**stipular** (ˈstɪpjʊlə) *adj.*

stir[1] (stɜː) *vb.* **stirring, stirred. 1.** to move an implement such as a spoon around in (a liquid) so as to mix up the constituents. **2.** to change or cause to change position; disturb or be disturbed. **3.** (*intr.;* often foll. by *from*) to venture or depart (from one's usual or preferred place). **4.** (*intr.*) to be active after a rest; be up and about. **5.** (*tr.*) to excite or stimulate, esp. emotionally. **6.** to move (oneself) briskly or vigorously; exert (oneself). **7.** (*tr.*) to rouse or awaken: *to stir someone from sleep; to stir memories.* **8.** (when *tr.*, foll. by *up*) to cause or incite others to cause (trouble, arguments, etc.). **9. stir one's stumps.** to move or become active. ~*n.* **10.** the act or an instance of stirring or the state of being stirred. **11.** a strong reaction, esp. of excitement: *his publication caused a stir.* **12.** a slight movement. **13.** *N.Z. inf.* a noisy party. ~See also **stir up.** [OE *styrian*]

stir[2] (stɜː) *n.* **1.** a slang word for **prison:** *in stir.* **2. stir-crazy.** *Sl., chiefly U.S. & Canad.* mentally disturbed as a result of being in prison. [C19: <?]

stir-fry (ˈstɜːˈfraɪ) *vb.* **-frying, -fried. 1.** to cook (chopped meat, vegetables, etc.) rapidly by stirring them in a wok or frying pan over a high heat. ~*n., pl.* **-fries. 2.** a dish cooked in this way.

stirk (stɜːk) *n.* **1.** a heifer of 6 to 12 months old. **2.** a yearling heifer or bullock. [OE *stierc*]

stirps (stɜːps) *n., pl.* **stirpes** (ˈstɜːpiːz). **1.** *Genealogy.* a line of descendants from an ancestor. **2.** *Bot.* a race or variety. [C17: < L: root, family origin]

stirrer (ˈstɜːrə) *n.* **1.** a person or thing that stirs. **2.** *Inf.* a person who deliberately causes trouble. **3.** *Austral. & N.Z. inf.* a political activist or agitator.

stirring (ˈstɜːrɪŋ) *adj.* **1.** exciting the emotions; stimulating. **2.** active, lively, or busy. —ˈ**stirringly** *adv.*

stirrup (ˈstɪrəp) *n.* **1.** Also called: **stirrup iron.** either of two metal loops on a riding saddle, with a flat footpiece through which a rider puts his foot for support. They are attached to the saddle by **stirrup leathers. 2.** a U-shaped support or clamp. **3.** *Naut.* one of a set of ropes fastened to a yard at one end and having a thimble at the other through which a footrope is reeved for support. [OE *stigrāp*, < *stīg* step + *rāp* rope]

stirrup cup *n.* a cup containing an alcoholic drink offered to a horseman ready to ride away.

stirrup pump *n.* a hand-operated pump, the base of the cylinder of which is placed in a bucket of water: used in fighting fires.

stir up *vb.* (*tr., adv.*) to set in motion; instigate or be instigated: *he stirred up trouble.*

stitch (stɪtʃ) *n.* **1.** a link made by drawing a thread through material by means of a needle. **2.** a loop of yarn formed around an implement used in knitting, crocheting, etc. **3.** a particular method of stitching or shape of stitch. **4.** a sharp spasmodic pain in the side resulting from running or exercising. **5.** (*usually used with a negative*) *Inf.* the least fragment of clothing: *he wasn't wearing a stitch.* **6.** *Agriculture.* the ridge between two furrows. **7. drop a stitch.** to allow a loop of wool to fall off a knitting needle accidentally while knitting. **8. in stitches.** *Inf.* laughing uncontrollably. ~*vb.* **9.** (*tr.*) to sew, fasten, etc., with stitches. **10.** (*intr.*) to be engaged in sewing. **11.** (*tr.*) to bind together (the leaves of a book, pamphlet, etc.) with wire staples or thread. ~*n., vb.* **12.** an informal word for **suture** (senses 1b, 5). [OE *stice* sting] —ˈ**stitcher** *n.*

stitchwort (ˈstɪtʃˌwɜːt) *n.* any of several low-growing N temperate herbaceous plants having small white star-shaped flowers.

stiver (ˈstaɪvə) *n.* **1.** a former Dutch coin worth one twentieth of a guilder. **2.** a small amount, esp. of money. [C16: < Du. *stuiver*]

stoa (ˈstəʊə) *n., pl.* **stoae** (ˈstəʊiː) *or* **stoas.** a covered walk that has a colonnade on one or both sides, esp. as in ancient Greece. [C17: < Gk]

stoat (stəʊt) *n.* a small Eurasian mammal, closely related to the weasels, having a brown coat and a black-tipped tail: in the northern parts of its range it has a white winter coat and is then known as an ermine. [C15: <?]

stochastic (stɒˈkæstɪk) *adj.* **1.** *Statistics.* **a.** (of a random variable) having a probability distribution, usually with finite variance. **b.** (of a process) involving a random variable the successive values of which are not independent. **c.** (of a matrix) square with non-negative elements that add to unity in each row. **2.** *Rare.* involving conjecture. [C17: < Gk *stokhastikos* capable of guessing, < *stokhazesthai* to aim at, conjecture, < *stokhos* a target]

stock (stɒk) *n.* **1. a.** (*sometimes pl.*) the total goods or raw material kept on the premises of a shop or business. **b.** (*as modifier*): *a stock book.* **2.** a supply of something stored for future use. **3.** *Finance.* **a.** the capital raised by a company through the issue and subscription of shares entitling their holders to dividends, partial ownership, and usually voting rights. **b.** the proportion of such capital held by an individual shareholder. **c.** the shares of a specified company or industry. **4.** standing or status. **5. a.** farm animals, such as cattle and sheep, bred and kept for their meat, skins, etc. **b.** (*as modifier*): *stock farming.* **6.** the trunk or main stem of a tree or other plant. **7.** *Horticulture.* **a.** a rooted plant into which a scion is inserted during grafting. **b.** a plant or stem from which cuttings are taken. **8.** the original type from which a particular race, family, group, etc., is derived. **9.** a race, breed, or variety of animals or plants. **10.** (*often pl.*) a small pen in which a single animal can be confined. **11.** a line of descent. **12.** any of the major subdivisions of the human species; race or ethnic group. **13.** the part of a rifle, etc., into which the barrel is set: held by the firer against the shoulder. **14.** the handle of something, such as a whip or fishing rod. **15.** the main body of a tool, such as the block of a plane. **16.** short for **diestock, gunstock,** or **rolling stock. 17.** (formerly) the part of a plough to which the irons and handles were attached. **18.** the main upright part of a supporting structure. **19.** a liquid or broth in which meat, fish, bones, or vegetables have been simmered for a long time. **20.** film material before exposure and processing. **21.** Also called: **gillyflower.** any of several cruciferous plants such as **evening** or **night-scented stock**, of the Mediterranean region: cultivated for their brightly coloured flowers. **22. Virginian stock.** a similar and related North American plant. **23.** a long usually white neckcloth wrapped around the neck, worn in the 18th century and as part of modern riding dress. **24. a.** the repertoire of plays available to a repertory company. **b.** (*as modifier*): *a stock play.* **25.** a log or block of wood. **26.** See **laughing stock. 27. in stock. a.** stored on the premises or available for sale or use. **b.** supplied with goods of a specified kind. **28. out of stock. a.** not immediately available for sale or use. **b.** not having goods of a specified kind immediately available. **29. take stock. a.** to make an inventory. **b.** to make a general appraisal, esp. of prospects, resources, etc. **30. take stock in.** to attach importance to. ~*adj.* **31.** staple; standard: *stock sizes in clothes.* **32.** (*prenominal*) being a cliché; hackneyed: *a stock phrase.* ~*vb.* **33.** (*tr.*) to keep (goods) for sale. **34.** (*intr.*; usually foll. by *up* or *up on*) to obtain a store of (something) for future use or sale: *to stock up on beer.* **35.** (*tr.*) to supply with live animals, fish, etc.: *to stock a farm.* **36.** (*intr.*) (of a plant) to put forth new shoots. **37.** (*tr.*) *Obs.* to punish by putting in the stocks. ~See also **stocks.** [OE *stocc* trunk (of a tree), stem, stick (the various senses developed from these meanings, as trunk of a tree, hence line of descent; structures made of timber; a store of timber or other goods for future use, hence an aggregate of goods, animals, etc.)] —**ˈstocker** *n.*

stockade (stɒˈkeɪd) *n.* **1.** an enclosure or barrier of stakes and timbers. ~*vb.* **2.** (*tr.*) to surround with a stockade. [C17: < Sp. *estacada*, < *estaca* a stake, of Gmc origin]

stockbreeder (ˈstɒkˌbriːdə) *n.* a person who breeds or rears livestock as an occupation. —**ˈstockˌbreeding** *n.*

stockbroker (ˈstɒkˌbrəʊkə) *n.* a person who buys and sells securities on a commission basis for customers. —**ˈstockˌbrokerage** *or* **ˈstockˌbroking** *n.*

stockbroker belt *n. Brit. inf.* the area outside a city, esp. London, in which rich commuters live.

stock car *n.* **1.** a car, usually a production saloon, strengthened and modified for a form of racing in which the cars often collide. **2.** *U.S. & Canad.* a railway wagon for carrying livestock.

stock dove *n.* a European dove, smaller than the wood pigeon and having a grey plumage.

stock exchange *n.* **1.** Also called: **stock market. a.** a highly organized market facilitating the purchase and sale of securities and operated by professional stockbrokers and stockjobbers according to fixed rules. **b.** a place where securities are regularly traded. **c.** (*as modifier*): *a stock-exchange operator; stock-exchange prices.* **2.** the prices or trading activity of a stock exchange: *the stock exchange fell heavily today.*

stockfish (ˈstɒkˌfɪʃ) *n., pl.* **-fish** *or* **-fishes.** fish cured by splitting and drying in the air.

stockholder (ˈstɒkˌhəʊldə) *n.* **1.** an owner of corporate capital stock. **2.** *Austral.* a person who keeps livestock. —**ˈstockˌholding** *n.*

stockhorse (ˈstɒkˌhɔːs) *n. Austral.* a stockman's horse.

stockinet (ˌstɒkɪˈnɛt) *n.* a machine-knitted elastic fabric used, esp. formerly, for stockings, underwear, etc. [C19: ? < earlier *stocking-net*]

stocking (ˈstɒkɪŋ) *n.* **1.** one of a pair of close-fitting garments made of knitted yarn to cover the foot and part or all of the leg. **2.** something resembling this in position, function, etc. **3. in (one's) stocking** *or* **stockinged feet.** wearing stockings or socks but no shoes. [C16: < dialect *stock* stocking + -ING[1]] —**ˈstockinged** *adj.*

stocking cap *n.* a conical knitted cap, often with a tassel.

stocking filler *n. Brit.* a present of a size suitable for inclusion in a Christmas stocking.

stock in trade *n.* **1.** goods in stock necessary for carrying on a business. **2.** anything constantly used by someone as a part of his profession, occupation, or trade: *friendliness is the salesman's stock in trade.*

stockist (ˈstɒkɪst) *n. Commerce, Brit.* a dealer who undertakes to maintain stocks of a specified product at or above a certain minimum in return for favourable buying terms granted by the manufacturer of the product.

stockjobber (ˈstɒkˌdʒɒbə) *n.* **1.** *Brit.* before Big Bang, a wholesale dealer on a stock exchange who operates as an intermediary between brokers without transacting directly with the public and derives his income from the spread between the bid and offered prices. See **market maker. 2.** *U.S., disparaging.* a stockbroker, esp. one dealing in worthless securities. —**ˈstockˌjobbery** *or* **ˈstockˌjobbing** *n.*

stockman (ˈstɒkmən, -ˌmæn) *n., pl.* **-men. 1. a.** a man engaged in the rearing or care of farm livestock, esp. cattle. **b.** an owner of cattle or other livestock. **2.** *U.S. & Canad.* a man employed in a warehouse or stockroom.

stock market *n.* another name for **stock exchange.**

stockpile (ˈstɒkˌpaɪl) *vb.* **1.** to acquire and store a large quantity of (something). ~*n.* **2.** a large store or supply accumulated for future use. —**ˈstockˌpiler** *n.*

stockpot (ˈstɒkˌpɒt) *n. Chiefly Brit.* a pot in which stock for soup, etc., is made or kept.

stockroom (ˈstɒkˌruːm, -ˌrʊm) *n.* a room in which a stock of goods is kept, as in a shop or factory.

stock route *n. Austral. & N.Z.* a route designated for droving stock, avoiding traffic.

stocks (stɒks) *pl. n.* **1.** *History.* an instrument of punishment consisting of a heavy wooden frame with holes in which the feet, hands, or head of an offender were locked. **2.** a frame used to support a boat while under construction. **3.** *Naut.* a vertical post or shaft at the forward edge of a rudder, extended upwards for attachment to the steering controls. **4. on the stocks.** in preparation or under construction.

stock-still *adv.* absolutely still; motionless.

stocktaking (ˈstɒkˌteɪkɪŋ) *n.* **1.** the examination, counting, and valuing of goods on hand in a shop or business. **2.** a reassessment of one's current situation, progress, prospects, etc.

stock whip *n.* a whip with a long lash and a short handle, used to herd cattle, etc.

stocky (ˈstɒkɪ) *adj.* **stockier, stockiest.** (usually of a person) thickset; sturdy. —**ˈstockily** *adv.* —**ˈstockiness** *n.*

stockyard (ˈstɒkˌjɑːd) *n.* a large yard with pens or covered buildings where farm animals are assembled, sold, etc.

stodge (stɒdʒ) *Inf.* ~*n.* **1.** heavy filling starchy food. **2.** a dull person or subject. ~*vb.* **3.** to stuff (oneself or another) with food. [C17: ? blend of STUFF + *podge*, < *podgy* fat]

stodgy (ˈstɒdʒɪ) *adj.* **stodgier, stodgiest.** **1.** (of food) heavy or uninteresting. **2.** excessively formal and conventional. [C19: < STODGE] —ˈ**stodgily** *adv.* —ˈ**stodginess** *n.*

stoep (stuːp) *n.* (in South Africa) a veranda. [< Afrik., < Du.]

stoic (ˈstəʊɪk) *n.* **1.** a person who maintains stoical qualities. ~*adj.* **2.** a variant of **stoical.**

Stoic (ˈstəʊɪk) *n.* **1.** a member of the ancient Greek school of philosophy founded by Zeno of Citium (?336–?264 B.C.), holding that virtue and happiness can be attained only by submission to destiny and the natural law. ~*adj.* **2.** of or relating to the doctrines of the Stoics. [C16: via L < Gk *stōikos*, < *stoa*, the porch in Athens where Zeno taught]

stoical (ˈstəʊɪkᵊl) *adj.* characterized by impassivity or resignation. —ˈ**stoically** *adv.*

stoichiometry *or* **stoicheiometry** (ˌstɔɪkɪˈɒmɪtrɪ) *n.* the branch of chemistry concerned with the proportions in which elements are combined in compounds and the quantitative relationships between reactants and products in chemical reactions. [C19: < Gk *stoikheion* element + -METRY] —ˌ**stoichioˈmetric** *or* ˌ**stoicheioˈmetric** *adj.*

stoicism (ˈstəʊɪˌsɪzəm) *n.* **1.** indifference to pleasure and pain. **2.** (*cap.*) the philosophy of the Stoics.

stoke (stəʊk) *vb.* **1.** to feed, stir, and tend (a fire, furnace, etc.). **2.** (*tr.*) to tend the furnace of; act as a stoker for. [C17: back formation < STOKER]

stokehold (ˈstəʊkˌhəʊld) *n. Naut.* **1.** a coal bunker for a ship's furnace. **2.** the hold for a ship's boilers; fire room.

stokehole (ˈstəʊkˌhəʊl) *n.* **1.** another word for **stokehold.** **2.** a hole in a furnace through which it is stoked.

stoker (ˈstəʊkə) *n.* a person employed to tend a furnace, as on a steamship. [C17: < Du., < *stoken* to stoke]

stoke up *vb.* (*adv.*) **1.** to feed and tend (a fire, etc.) with fuel. **2.** (*intr.*) to fill oneself with food.

STOL (stɒl) *n.* **1.** a system in which an aircraft can take off and land in a short distance. **2.** an aircraft using this system. Cf. **VTOL** [C20: *s*(*hort*) *t*(*ake*)*o*(*ff and*) *l*(*anding*)]

stole[1] (stəʊl) *vb.* the past tense of **steal.**

stole[2] (stəʊl) *n.* **1.** a long scarf or shawl, worn by women. **2.** a long narrow scarf worn by various officiating clergymen. [OE *stole*, < L *stola*, < Gk *stolē* clothing]

stolen (ˈstəʊlən) *vb.* the past participle of **steal.**

stolid (ˈstɒlɪd) *adj.* showing little or no emotion or interest. [C17: < L *stolidus* dull] —**stolidity** (stɒˈlɪdɪtɪ) *or* ˈ**stolidness** *n.* —ˈ**stolidly** *adv.*

stolon (ˈstəʊlən) *n.* **1.** another name for **runner** (sense 9). **2.** a branching structure in lower animals, esp. the anchoring rootlike part of colonial organisms. [C17: < L *stolō* shoot] —**stoloniferous** (ˌstəʊləˈnɪfərəs) *adj.*

stoma (ˈstəʊmə) *n., pl.* **stomata.** **1.** *Bot.* an epidermal pore in plant leaves, that controls the passage of gases into and out of a plant. **2.** *Zool., anat.* a mouth or mouthlike part. [C17: via NL < Gk: mouth]

stomach (ˈstʌmək) *n.* **1.** (in vertebrates) the enlarged muscular saclike part of the alimentary canal in which food is stored until it has been partially digested. Related adj.: **gastric.** **2.** the corresponding organ in invertebrates. **3.** the abdominal region. **4.** desire, appetite, or inclination: *I have no stomach for arguments.* ~*vb.* (*tr.; used mainly in negative constructions*) **5.** to tolerate; bear: *I can't stomach his bragging.* **6.** to eat or digest: *he cannot stomach oysters.* [C14: < OF *stomaque*, < L *stomachus*, < Gk *stomakhos*, < *stoma* mouth]

stomachache (ˈstʌməkˌeɪk) *n.* pain in the stomach, as from acute indigestion. Also called: **stomach upset, upset stomach.**

stomacher (ˈstʌməkə) *n.* a decorative V-shaped panel of stiff material worn over the chest and stomach by men and women in the 16th century, later only by women.

stomachic (stəˈmækɪk) *adj. also* **stomachical.** **1.** stimulating gastric activity. **2.** of or relating to the stomach. ~*n.* **3.** a stomachic medicine.

stomach pump *n. Med.* a suction device for removing stomach contents via an orally inserted tube.

stomata (ˈstəʊmətə, ˈstɒm-, stəʊˈmɑːtə) *n.* the plural of **stoma.**

stomatitis (ˌstəʊməˈtaɪtɪs, ˌstɒm-) *n.* inflammation of the mouth. —**stomatitic** (ˌstəʊməˈtɪtɪk, ˌstɒm-) *adj.*

stomato- *or before a vowel* **stomat-** *combining form.* indicating the mouth or a mouthlike part: *stomatology.* [< Gk *stoma, stomat-*]

stomatology (ˌstəʊməˈtɒlədʒɪ) *n.* the branch of medicine concerned with the mouth. —**stomatological** (ˌstəʊmətəˈlɒdʒɪkᵊl) *adj.*

-stome *n. combining form.* indicating a mouth or opening resembling a mouth: *peristome.* [< Gk *stoma* mouth, & *stomion* little mouth]

-stomous *adj. combining form.* having a specified type of mouth.

stomp (stɒmp) *vb.* **1.** (*intr.*) to tread or stamp heavily. ~*n.* **2.** a rhythmical stamping jazz dance. [var. of STAMP] —ˈ**stomper** *n.*

-stomy *n. combining form.* indicating a surgical operation performed to make an artificial opening into or for a specified part: *cytostomy.* [< Gk *-stomia*, < *stoma* mouth]

stone (stəʊn) *n.* **1.** the hard compact nonmetallic material of which rocks are made. **2.** a small lump of rock; pebble. **3.** short for **gemstone.** **4. a.** a piece of rock designed or shaped for some particular purpose. **b.** (*in combination*): *gravestone; millstone.* **5. a.** something that resembles a stone. **b.** (*in combination*): *hailstone.* **6.** the woody central part of such fruits as the peach and plum, that contains the seed; endocarp. **7.** any similar hard part of a fruit, such as the stony seed of a date. **8.** (*pl.* **stone**) *Brit.* a unit of weight, used esp. to express human body weight, equal to 14 pounds or 6.350 kilograms. **9.** Also called: **granite.** the rounded heavy mass of granite or iron used in the game of curling. **10.** *Pathol.* a nontechnical name for **calculus.** **11.** *Printing.* a table with a very flat iron or stone surface upon which pages are composed. **12.** (*modifier*) relating to or made of stone: *a stone house.* **13.** (*modifier*) made of stoneware: *a stone jar.* **14. cast a stone (at).** cast aspersions (upon). **15. heart of stone.** an obdurate or unemotional nature. **16. leave no stone unturned.** to do everything possible to achieve an end. ~*vb.* (*tr.*) **17.** to throw stones at, esp. to kill. **18.** to remove the stones from. **19.** to furnish or provide with stones. [OE *stān*] —ˈ**stoner** *n.*

stone- *prefix.* very, completely: *stone-blind, stone-cold.* [< STONE in sense of "like a stone"]

Stone Age *n.* **1.** a period in human culture identified by the use of stone implements. ~*modifier.* **Stone-Age.** **2.** (*sometimes not caps.*) of or relating to this period.

stone-blind *adj.* completely blind. Cf. **sand-blind.**

stonechat (ˈstəʊnˌtʃæt) *n.* an Old World songbird having a black plumage with a reddish-brown breast. [C18: < its cry, which sounds like clattering pebbles]

stone-cold *adj.* **1.** completely cold. **2. stone-cold sober.** completely sober.

stonecrop (ˈstəʊnˌkrɒp) *n.* any of various N temperate plants having fleshy leaves and typically red, yellow, or white flowers.

stone curlew *n.* any of several brownish shore birds having a large head and eyes. Also called: **thick-knee.**

stonecutter (ˈstəʊnˌkʌtə) *n.* **1.** a person who is skilled in cutting and carving stone. **2.** a machine used to dress stone. —ˈ**stoneˌcutting** *n.*

stoned (stəʊnd) *adj. Sl.* under the influence of drugs or alcohol.

stone-deaf *adj.* completely deaf.

stonefish (ˈstəʊnˌfɪʃ) *n., pl.* **-fish** *or* **-fishes.** a venomous tropical marine fish that resembles a piece of rock on the seabed.

stonefly (ˈstəʊnˌflaɪ) *n., pl.* **-flies.** any of various insects, in which the larvae are aquatic, living beneath stones.

stone fruit *n.* the nontechnical name for **drupe.**

stonemason (ˈstəʊnˌmeɪsᵊn) *n.* a person who is skilled in preparing stone for building. —ˈ**stone**ˌ**masonry** *n.*

stone pine *n.* a pine tree with a short bole and radiating branches forming an umbrella shape.

stone's throw *n.* a short distance.

stonewall (ˌstəʊnˈwɔːl) *vb.* **1.** (*intr.*) *Cricket.* (of a batsman) to play defensively. **2.** to obstruct or hinder (parliamentary business). —ˌ**stone**ˈ**waller** *n.*

stoneware (ˈstəʊnˌwɛə) *n.* **1.** a hard opaque pottery, fired at a very high temperature. ~*adj.* **2.** made of stoneware.

stonewashed (ˈstəʊnˌwɒʃt) *adj.* (of clothes or fabric) given a worn faded look by being subjected to the abrasive action of many small pieces of pumice.

stonework (ˈstəʊnˌwɜːk) *n.* **1.** any structure or part of a building made of stone. **2.** the process of dressing or setting stones. —ˈ**stone**ˌ**worker** *n.*

stonkered (ˈstɒŋkəd) *adj. Sl.* completely exhausted or beaten. [C20: < *stonker* to beat, <?]

stony *or* **stoney** (ˈstəʊnɪ) *adj.* **stonier, stoniest. 1.** of or resembling stone. **2.** abounding in stone or stones. **3.** unfeeling or obdurate. **4.** short for **stony-broke.** —ˈ**stonily** *adv.* —ˈ**stoniness** *n.*

stony-broke *adj. Brit. sl.* completely without money; penniless.

stony-hearted *adj.* unfeeling; hardhearted. —ˌ**stony**-ˈ**heartedness** *n.*

stood (stʊd) *vb.* the past tense and past participle of **stand.**

stooge (stuːdʒ) *n.* **1.** an actor who feeds lines to a comedian or acts as his butt. **2.** *Sl.* someone who is taken advantage of by another. ~*vb.* **3.** (*intr.*) *Sl.* to act as a stooge. [C20: <?]

stook (stuːk) *n.* **1.** a number of sheaves set upright in a field to dry with their heads together. ~*vb.* **2.** (*tr.*) to set up (sheaves) in stooks. [C15: var. of *stouk,* of Gmc origin] —ˈ**stooker** *n.*

stool (stuːl) *n.* **1.** a simple seat or footrest consisting of a small flat piece of wood, etc., resting on three or four legs, a pedestal, etc. **2.** a rootstock or base of a plant from which shoots, etc., are produced. **3.** a cluster of shoots growing from such a base. **4.** *Chiefly U.S.* a decoy used in hunting. **5.** waste matter evacuated from the bowels. **6.** a lavatory seat. **7.** (in W Africa, esp. Ghana) a chief's throne. **8. fall between two stools.** to fail through vacillation between two alternatives. ~*vb.* (*intr.*) **9.** (of a plant) to send up shoots from the base of the stem, rootstock, etc. **10.** to lure wildfowl with a decoy. [OE *stōl*]

stool ball *n.* a game resembling cricket, still played by girls and women in Sussex, England.

stool pigeon *n.* **1.** an informer for the police. **2.** *U.S. sl.* a person acting as a decoy. [C19: < use of pigeon fixed to a stool as a decoy]

stoop[1] (stuːp) *vb.* (*mainly intr.*) **1.** (*also tr.*) to bend (the body) forward and downward. **2.** to carry oneself with head and shoulders habitually bent forward. **3.** (often foll. by *to*) to abase or degrade oneself. **4.** (often foll. by *to*) to condescend; deign. **5.** (of a bird of prey) to swoop down. ~*n.* **6.** the act, position, or characteristic of stooping. **7.** a lowering from a position of dignity or superiority. **8.** a downward swoop, esp. of a bird of prey. [OE *stūpan*] —ˈ**stooping** *adj.*

stoop[2] (stuːp) *n. U.S.* an open porch or small platform with steps leading up to it at the entrance to a building. [C18: < Du. *stoep,* of Gmc origin]

stop (stɒp) *vb.* **stopping, stopped. 1.** to cease from doing or being (something); discontinue. **2.** to cause (something moving) to halt or (of something moving) to come to a halt. **3.** (*tr.*) to prevent the continuance or completion of. **4.** (*tr.;* often foll. by *from*) to prevent or restrain: *to stop George from fighting.* **5.** (*tr.*) to keep back: *to stop supplies.* **6.** (*tr.*) to intercept or hinder in transit: *to stop a letter.* **7.** (*tr.;* often foll. by *up*) to block or plug, esp. so as to close: *to stop up a pipe.* **8.** (*tr.;* often foll. by *up*) to fill a hole or opening in: *to stop up a wall.* **9.** (*tr.*) to staunch or stem: *to stop a wound.* **10.** (*tr.*) to instruct a bank not to honour (a cheque). **11.** (*tr.*) to deduct (money) from pay. **12.** (*tr.*) *Brit.* to provide with punctuation. **13.** (*tr.*) *Boxing.* to beat (an opponent) by a knockout. **14.** (*tr.*) *Inf.* to receive (a blow, hit, etc.). **15.** (*intr.*) to stay or rest: *we stopped at the Robinsons'.* **16.** (*tr.*) *Rare.* to defeat, beat, or kill. **17.** (*tr.*) *Music.* **a.** to alter the vibrating length of (a string on a violin, guitar, etc.) by pressing down on it at some point with the finger. **b.** to alter the vibrating length of an air column in a wind instrument by closing (a finger hole, etc.). **c.** to produce (a note) in this manner. **18.** *Bridge.* to have a protecting card or winner in (a suit in which one's opponents are strong). **19. stop at nothing.** to be prepared to do anything; be unscrupulous or ruthless. ~*n.* **20.** an arrest of movement or progress. **21.** the act of stopping or the state of being stopped. **22.** a place where something halts or pauses: *a bus stop.* **23.** a stay in or as if in the course of a journey. **24.** the act or an instance of blocking or obstructing. **25.** a plug or stopper. **26.** a block, screw, etc., that prevents, limits, or terminates the motion of a mechanism or moving part. **27.** *Brit.* a punctuation mark, esp. a full stop. **28.** *Music.* **a.** the act of stopping the string, finger hole, etc., of an instrument. **b.** a set of organ pipes or harpsichord strings that may be allowed to sound as a group by muffling or silencing all other such sets. **c.** a knob, lever, or handle on an organ, etc., that is operated to allow sets of pipes to sound. **d.** an analogous device on a harpsichord or other instrument with variable registers, such as an electronic instrument. **29. pull out all the stops. a.** to play at full volume. **b.** to spare no effort. **30.** Also called: **stop consonant.** *Phonetics.* any of a class of consonants articulated by first making a complete closure at some point of the vocal tract and then releasing it abruptly with audible plosion. **31.** Also called: **f-stop.** *Photog.* **a.** a setting of the aperture of a camera lens, calibrated to the corresponding f-number. **b.** another name for **diaphragm** (sense 4). **32.** Also called: **stopper.** *Bridge.* a protecting card or winner in a suit in which one's opponents are strong. ~See also **stop off, stop out, stopover.** [C14: < OE *stoppian* (unattested), as in *forstoppian* to plug the ear, ult. < LL *stuppāre* to stop with tow, < L *stuppa* tow, < Gk *stuppē*] —ˈ**stoppable** *adj.*

stopbank (ˈstɒpbæŋk) *n. N.Z.* an embankment to prevent flooding.

stop bath *n.* a weakly acidic solution used to stop the action of a developer on a film, plate, or paper before the material is immersed in fixer.

stopcock (ˈstɒpˌkɒk) *n.* a valve used to control or stop the flow of a fluid in a pipe.

stope (stəʊp) *n.* **1.** a steplike excavation made in a mine to extract ore. ~*vb.* **2.** to mine (ore, etc.) in stopes. [C18: prob. < Low G *stope*]

stopgap (ˈstɒpˌgæp) *n.* **a.** a temporary substitute. **b.** (*as modifier*): *a stopgap programme.*

stop-go *adj. Brit.* (of economic policy) characterized by deliberate alternate expansion and contraction of aggregate demand in an effort to curb inflation and eliminate balance-of-payments deficits, and yet maintain full employment.

stoplight (ˈstɒpˌlaɪt) *n.* **1.** a red light on a traffic signal indicating that vehicles or pedestrians coming towards it should stop. **2.** another word for **brake light.**

stop off *vb. also* **stop in,** (esp. U.S.) **stop by. 1.** (*intr., adv.;* often foll. by *at*) to halt and call somewhere, as on a visit or errand, esp. en route to another place. ~*n.* **stopoff. 2. a.** a break in a journey. **b.** (*as modifier*): *stopoff point.*

stop out *vb.* (*adv.*) **1.** (*tr.*) to cover (part of the area) of a piece of cloth, printing plate, etc., to prevent it from being dyed, etched, etc. **2.** (*intr.*) to remain out of a house, esp. overnight.

stopover (ˈstɒpˌəʊvə) *n.* **1.** a stopping place on a journey. ~*vb.* **stop over. 2.** (*intr., adv.*) to make a stopover.

stoppage (ˈstɒpɪdʒ) *n.* **1.** the act of stopping or the state of being stopped. **2.** something that stops or blocks. **3.** a deduction of money, as from pay. **4.** an organized cessation of work, as during a strike.

stopped (stɒpt) *adj.* (of a pipe, esp. an organ pipe) closed at one end and thus sounding an octave lower than an open pipe of the same length.

stopper (ˈstɒpə) *n.* **1.** Also called: **stopple.** a plug or bung for closing a bottle, pipe, duct, etc. **2.** a person or thing that stops or puts an end to something. **3.** *Bridge.* another name for **stop** (sense 32). ~*vb.* **4.** (*tr.*) Also: **stopple.** to close or fit with a stopper.

stopping (ˈstɒpɪŋ) *n.* **1.** *Brit. inf.* a dental filling. ~*adj.* **2.** *Chiefly Brit.* making many stops in a journey: *a stopping train.*

stop press *n. Brit.* **1.** news items inserted into a newspaper after the printing has been started. **2.** the space regularly left blank for this.

stopwatch (ˈstɒpˌwɒtʃ) *n.* a type of watch used for timing sporting events, etc., accurately, having a device for stopping the hands instantly.

storage (ˈstɔːrɪdʒ) *n.* **1.** the act of storing or the state of being stored. **2.** space or an area reserved for storing. **3.** a charge made for storing. **4.** *Computers.* **a.** the act or process of storing information in a computer memory or on a disk, etc. **b.** (*as modifier*): *storage capacity.*

storage battery *n.* another name (esp. U.S.) for **accumulator** (sense 1).

storage capacity *n.* the maximum number of bits, bytes, words, etc., that can be held in a memory system such as that of a computer or of the brain.

storage device *n.* a piece of computer equipment, such as a magnetic tape, disk, drum, etc., in or on which information can be stored.

storage heater *n.* an electric device capable of accumulating and radiating heat generated by off-peak electricity.

storax (ˈstɔːræks) *n.* **1.** any of numerous trees or shrubs of tropical and subtropical regions, having drooping showy white flowers. **2.** a vanilla-scented solid resin obtained from one of these trees, formerly used as incense and in perfumery and medicine. **3.** a liquid aromatic balsam obtained from liquidambar trees and used in perfumery and medicine. [C14: via LL < Gk *sturax*]

store (stɔː) *vb.* **1.** (*tr.*) to keep, set aside, or accumulate for future use. **2.** (*tr.*) to place in a warehouse, depository, etc., for safekeeping. **3.** (*tr.*) to supply, provide, or stock. **4.** (*intr.*) to be put into storage. **5.** *Computers.* to enter or retain (information) in a storage device. ~*n.* **6. a.** an establishment for the retail sale of goods and services. **b.** (*in combination*): *storefront.* **7.** a large supply or stock kept for future use. **8.** short for **department store. 9. a.** a storage place such as a warehouse or depository. **b.** (*in combination*): *storeman.* **10.** the state of being stored (esp. in **in store**). **11.** a large amount or quantity. **12.** *Computers, chiefly Brit.* another name for **memory** (sense 7). **13. in store.** forthcoming or imminent. **14. lay, put,** *or* **set store by.** to value or reckon as important. ~*adj.* **15.** (of cattle, sheep, etc.) bought lean to be fattened up for market. ~See also **stores.** [C13: < OF *estor,* < *estorer* to restore, < L *instaurāre* to refresh] —ˈ**storable** *adj.*

storehouse (ˈstɔːˌhaʊs) *n.* a place where things are stored.

storekeeper (ˈstɔːˌkiːpə) *n.* a manager, owner, or keeper of a store. —ˈ**storeˌkeeping** *n.*

storeroom (ˈstɔːˌruːm, -ˌrʊm) *n.* **1.** a room in which things are stored. **2.** room for storing.

stores (stɔːz) *pl. n.* supply or stock of something, esp. essentials, for a specific purpose.

storey *or U.S.* **story** (ˈstɔːrɪ) *n., pl.* **-reys** *or* **-ries.** **1.** a floor or level of a building. **2.** a set of rooms on one level. [C14: < Anglo-L *historia,* picture, < L: narrative, prob. < the pictures on medieval windows]

storeyed *or U.S.* **storied** (ˈstɔːrɪd) *adj.* **a.** having a storey or storeys. **b.** (*in combination*): *a two-storeyed house.*

storied (ˈstɔːrɪd) *adj.* **1.** recorded in history or in a story. **2.** decorated with narrative scenes.

stork (stɔːk) *n.* any of a family of large wading birds, chiefly of warm regions of the Old World, having very long legs and a long stout pointed bill, and typically having a white-and-black plumage. [OE *storc*]

storksbill (ˈstɔːksˌbɪl) *n.* a plant related to the geranium, having pink or reddish-purple flowers and fruits with a beaklike process.

storm (stɔːm) *n.* **1. a.** a violent weather condition of strong winds, rain, hail, thunder, lightning, blowing sand, snow, etc. **b.** (*as modifier*): *storm cloud.* **c.** (*in combination*): *stormproof.* **2.** *Meteorol.* a wind of force 10 on the Beaufort scale, reaching speeds of 55 to 63 mph. **3.** a violent disturbance or quarrel. **4.** a direct assault on a stronghold. **5.** a heavy discharge or rain, as of bullets or missiles. **6.** short for **storm window. 7. storm in a teacup.** *Brit.* a violent fuss or disturbance over a trivial matter. **8. take by storm. a.** to capture or overrun by a violent assault. **b.** to overwhelm and enthral. ~*vb.* **9.** to attack or capture (something) suddenly and violently. **10.** (*intr.*) to be vociferously angry. **11.** (*intr.*) to move or rush violently or angrily. **12.** (*intr.;* with *it* as subject) to rain, hail, or snow hard and be very windy, often with thunder and lightning. [OE]

stormbound (ˈstɔːmˌbaʊnd) *adj.* detained or harassed by storms.

storm centre *n.* **1.** the centre of a cyclonic storm, etc., where pressure is lowest. **2.** the centre of any disturbance or trouble.

storm cloud *n.* **1.** a heavy dark cloud presaging rain or a storm. **2.** a herald of disturbance, anger, etc.: *the storm clouds of war.*

storm-cock *n.* another name for **mistle thrush.**

storm cone *n. Brit.* a canvas cone hoisted as a warning of high winds.

storm door *n.* an additional door outside an ordinary door, providing extra insulation against wind, cold, rain, etc.

storm lantern *n.* another name for **hurricane lamp.**

storm trooper *n.* **1.** a member of the Nazi SA. **2.** a member of a force of shock troops.

storm window *n.* **1.** an additional window fitted outside an ordinary window to provide insulation against wind, cold, rain, etc. **2.** a type of dormer window.

stormy (ˈstɔːmɪ) *adj.* **stormier, stormiest. 1.** characterized by storms. **2.** involving or characterized by violent disturbance or emotional outburst. —ˈ**stormily** *adv.* —ˈ**storminess** *n.*

stormy petrel *n.* **1.** Also called: **storm petrel.** any of various small petrels typically having dark plumage and paler underparts. **2.** a person who brings or portends trouble.

Storting *or* **Storthing** (ˈstɔːtɪŋ) *n.* the parliament of Norway. [C19: Norwegian, < *stor* great + *thing* assembly]

story[1] (ˈstɔːrɪ) *n., pl.* **-ries. 1.** a narration of a chain of events told or written in prose or verse. **2.** Also called: **short story.** a piece of fiction, briefer and usually less detailed than a novel. **3.** Also called: **story line.** the plot of a book, film, etc. **4.** an event that could be the subject of a narrative. **5.** a report or statement on a matter or event. **6.** the event or material for such a report. **7.** *Inf.* a lie, fib, or untruth. **8. cut** (*or* **make**) **a long story short.** to leave out details in a narration. **9. the same old story.** *Inf.* the familiar or regular course of events. **10. the story goes.** it is commonly said or believed. ~*vb.* **-rying, -ried.** (*tr.*) **11.** to decorate (a pot, wall, etc.) with scenes from history or legends. [C13: < Anglo-F *estorie,* < L *historia;* see HISTORY]

story[2] (ˈstɔːrɪ) *n., pl.* **-ries.** another spelling (esp. U.S.) of **storey.**

storyboard (ˈstɔːrɪˌbɔːd) *n.* (in films, television, etc.) a series of sketches or photographs showing the sequence of shots or images planned for a film.

storybook (ˈstɔːrɪˌbʊk) *n.* **1.** a book containing stories, esp. for children. *~adj.* **2.** unreal or fantastic: *a storybook world.*

storyteller (ˈstɔːrɪˌtɛlə) *n.* **1.** a person who tells stories. **2.** *Inf.* a liar. —ˈ**storyˌtelling** *n.*

stoup *or* **stoop** (stuːp) *n.* **1.** a small basin for holy water. **2.** *Dialect.* a bucket or cup. [C14 (in the sense: bucket): < ON]

stoush (staʊʃ) *Austral. & N.Z. sl.* *~vb.* **1.** (*tr.*) to hit or punch. *~n.* **2.** fighting, violence, or a fight. [C19: <?]

stout (staʊt) *adj.* **1.** solidly built or corpulent. **2.** (*prenominal*) resolute or valiant: *stout fellow.* **3.** strong, substantial, and robust. **4. a stout heart.** courage; resolution. *~n.* **5.** strong porter highly flavoured with malt. [C14: < OF *estout* bold, of Gmc origin] —ˈ**stoutly** *adv.* —ˈ**stoutness** *n.*

stouthearted (ˌstaʊtˈhɑːtɪd) *adj.* valiant; brave. —ˌ**stoutˈheartedly** *adv.* —ˌ**stoutˈheartedness** *n.*

stove[1] (stəʊv) *n.* **1.** another word for **cooker** (sense 1). **2.** any heating apparatus, such as a kiln. [OE *stofa* bathroom]

stove[2] (stəʊv) *vb.* a past tense and past participle of **stave.**

stove enamel *n.* a type of enamel made heatproof by treatment in a stove.

stovepipe (ˈstəʊvˌpaɪp) *n.* **1.** a pipe that serves as a flue to a stove. **2.** Also called: **stovepipe hat.** a man's tall silk hat.

stow (stəʊ) *vb.* (*tr.*) **1.** (often foll. by *away*) to pack or store. **2.** to fill by packing. **3.** *Naut.* to pack or put away (cargo, sails, etc.). **4.** to have enough room for. **5.** (*usually imperative*) *Brit. sl.* to cease from: *stow your noise!* [OE *stōwian* to keep, < *stōw* a place]

stowage (ˈstəʊɪdʒ) *n.* **1.** space, room, or a charge for stowing goods. **2.** the act or an instance of stowing or the state of being stowed. **3.** something that is stowed.

stowaway (ˈstəʊəˌweɪ) *n.* **1.** a person who hides aboard a vehicle, ship, or aircraft in order to gain free passage. *~vb.* **stow away. 2.** (*intr., adv.*) to travel in such a way.

STP *abbrev. for:* **1.** Professor of Sacred Theology. [< L: *Sanctae Theologiae Professor*] **2.** *Trademark.* scientifically treated petroleum: an oil substitute promising renewed power for an internal-combustion engine. **3.** standard temperature and pressure. *~n.* **4.** a synthetic hallucinogenic drug related to mescaline. [< humorous reference to the extra power resulting from scientifically treated petroleum]

strabismus (strəˈbɪzməs) *n.* abnormal alignment of one or both eyes, characterized by a turning inwards or outwards from the nose: caused by paralysis of an eye muscle, etc. Also called: **squint.** [C17: via NL < Gk *strabismos,* < *strabizein* to squint, < *strabos* cross-eyed] —**straˈbismal, straˈbismic,** *or* **straˈbismical** *adj.*

straddle (ˈstræd³l) *vb.* **1.** (*tr.*) to have one leg, part, or support on each side of. **2.** (*tr.*) *U.S. & Canad. inf.* to be in favour of both sides of (something). **3.** (*intr.*) to stand, walk, or sit with the legs apart. **4.** (*tr.*) to spread (the legs) apart. **5.** *Gunnery.* to fire a number of shots slightly beyond and slightly short of (a target) to determine the correct range. **6.** (*intr.*) (in poker, of the second player after the dealer) to double the ante before looking at one's cards. *~n.* **7.** the act or position of straddling. **8.** a noncommittal attitude or stand. **9.** *Stock Exchange.* a contract or option permitting its purchaser either to sell securities to or buy securities from the maker of the contract within a specified period of time. **10.** *Athletics.* a high-jumping technique in which the body is parallel with the bar and the legs straddle it at the highest point of the jump. **11.** (in poker) the stake put up after the ante in poker by the second player after the dealer. [C16: < obs. *strad-* (OE *strode*), past stem of STRIDE] —ˈ**straddler** *n.*

Stradivarius (ˌstrædɪˈvɛərɪəs) *n.* any of a number of violins manufactured in Italy by Antonio Stradivari (?1644–1737) or his family. Often shortened to (informal): **Strad.**

strafe (streɪf, strɑːf) *vb.* (*tr.*) **1.** to machine-gun (troops, etc.) from the air. **2.** *Sl.* to punish harshly. *~n.* **3.** an act or instance of strafing. [C20: < G *strafen* to punish] —ˈ**strafer** *n.*

straggle (ˈstræg³l) *vb.* (*intr.*) **1.** to go, come, or spread in a rambling or irregular way. **2.** to linger behind or wander from a main line or part. [C14: <?] —ˈ**straggler** *n.* —ˈ**straggly** *adj.*

straight (streɪt) *adj.* **1.** not curved or crooked; continuing in the same direction without deviating. **2.** straightforward, outright, or candid: *a straight rejection.* **3.** even, level, or upright. **4.** in keeping with the facts; accurate. **5.** honest, respectable, or reliable. **6.** accurate or logical: *straight reasoning.* **7.** continuous; uninterrupted. **8.** (esp. of an alcoholic drink) undiluted; neat. **9.** not crisp, kinked, or curly: *straight hair.* **10.** correctly arranged; orderly. **11.** (of a play, acting style, etc.) straightforward or serious. **12.** *Boxing.* (of a blow) delivered with an unbent arm: *a straight left.* **13.** (of the cylinders of an internal-combustion engine) in line, rather than in a V-formation or in some other arrangement: *a straight eight.* **14.** a slang word for **heterosexual. 15.** *Inf.* no longer owing or being owed something: *if you buy the next round we'll be straight.* **16.** *Sl.* conventional in views, customs, appearance, etc. **17.** *Sl.* not using narcotics. *~adv.* **18.** in a straight line or direct course. **19.** immediately; at once: *he came straight back.* **20.** in an even, level, or upright position. **21.** without cheating, lying, or unreliability: *tell it to me straight.* **22.** continuously; uninterruptedly. **23.** (often foll. by *out*) frankly; candidly: *he told me straight out.* **24. go straight.** *Inf.* to reform after having been dishonest or a criminal. *~n.* **25.** the state of being straight. **26.** a straight line, form, part, or position. **27.** *Brit.* a straight part of a racetrack. **28.** *Poker.* **a.** five cards that are in sequence irrespective of suit. **b.** a hand containing such a sequence. **c.** (*as modifier*): *a straight flush.* **29.** *Sl.* a conventional person. **30.** a slang word for a **heterosexual. 31.** *Sl.* a cigarette containing only tobacco, without marijuana, etc. [C14: < p.p. of OE *streccan* to stretch] —ˈ**straightly** *adv.* —ˈ**straightness** *n.*

straight and narrow *n. Inf.* the proper, honest, and moral path of behaviour.

straight angle *n.* an angle of 180°.

straightaway *adv.* (ˌstreɪtəˈweɪ). *also* **straight away. 1.** at once. *~n.* (ˈstreɪtəˌweɪ). **2.** the U.S. word for **straight** (sense 27).

straight chair *n.* a straight-backed side chair.

straightedge (ˈstreɪtˌɛdʒ) *n.* a stiff strip of wood or metal with one edge straight, used for ruling and testing straight lines.

straighten (ˈstreɪt³n) *vb.* (sometimes foll. by *up* or *out*) **1.** to make or become straight. **2.** (*tr.*) to make neat or tidy. —ˈ**straightener** *n.*

straighten out *vb.* (*adv.*) **1.** to make or become less complicated or confused. **2.** *U.S. & Canad.* to reform or become reformed.

straight face *n.* a serious facial expression, esp. one that conceals the impulse to laugh. —ˈ**straight-ˈfaced** *adj.*

straight fight *n.* a contest between two candidates only.

straight flush *n.* (in poker) five consecutive cards of the same suit.

straightforward (ˌstreɪtˈfɔːwəd) *adj.* **1.** (of a person) honest, frank, or simple. **2.** *Chiefly Brit.* (of a task, etc.) simple; easy. *~adv., adj.* **3.** in a straight course. —ˌ**straightˈforwardly** *adv.* —ˌ**straightˈforwardness** *n.*

straightjacket (ˈstreɪtˌdʒækɪt) *n.* a less common spelling of **straitjacket.**

straight-laced *adj.* a variant spelling of **strait-laced.**

straight man *n.* a subsidiary actor who acts as stooge to a comedian.

straight-out *adj. U.S. inf.* **1.** complete; thoroughgoing. **2.** frank or honest.

straight razor *n.* another name for **cutthroat** (sense 2).

straightway (ˈstreɪtˌweɪ) *adv. Arch.* at once.

strain[1] (streɪn) *vb.* **1.** to draw or be drawn taut; stretch tight. **2.** to exert, tax, or use (resources) to the utmost extent. **3.** to injure or damage or be injured or damaged by overexertion: *he strained himself.* **4.** to deform or be deformed as a result of a stress. **5.** (*intr.*) to make intense or violent efforts; strive. **6.** to subject or be subjected to mental tension or stress. **7.** to pour or pass (a substance) or (of a substance) to be poured or passed through a sieve, filter, or strainer. **8.** (*tr.*) to draw off or remove (one part of a substance or mixture from another) by or as if by filtering. **9.** (*tr.*) to clasp tightly; hug. **10.** (*intr.;* foll. by *at*) to push, pull, or work with violent exertion (upon). ~*n.* **11.** the act or an instance of straining. **12.** the damage resulting from excessive exertion. **13.** an intense physical or mental effort. **14.** (*often pl.*) *Music.* a theme, melody, or tune. **15.** a great demand on the emotions, resources, etc. **16.** a way of speaking; tone of voice: *don't go on in that strain.* **17.** tension or tiredness resulting from overwork, worry, etc.; stress. **18.** *Physics.* the change in dimension of a body under load expressed as the ratio of the total deflection or change in dimension to the original unloaded dimension. [C13: < OF *estreindre* to press together, < L *stringere* to bind tightly]

strain[2] (streɪn) *n.* **1.** the main body of descendants from one ancestor. **2.** a group of organisms within a species or variety, distinguished by one or more minor characteristics. **3.** a variety of bacterium or fungus, esp. one used for a culture. **4.** a streak; trace. **5.** *Arch.* a kind, type, or sort. [OE *strēon*]

strained (streɪnd) *adj.* **1.** (of an action, expression, etc.) not natural or spontaneous. **2.** (of an atmosphere, relationship, etc.) not relaxed; tense.

strainer (ˈstreɪnə) *n.* **1.** a sieve used for straining sauces, vegetables, tea, etc. **2.** a gauze or simple filter used to strain liquids.

strait (streɪt) *n.* **1.** (*often pl.*) a narrow channel of the sea linking two larger areas of sea. **2.** (*often pl.*) a position of acute difficulty (often in **in dire** *or* **desperate straits**). **3.** *Arch.* a narrow place or passage. ~*adj.* **4.** *Arch.* (of spaces, etc.) affording little room. [C13: < OF *estreit* narrow, < L *strictus* constricted, < *stringere* to bind tightly] —ˈ**straitly** *adv.* —ˈ**straitness** *n.*

straiten (ˈstreɪtᵊn) *vb.* **1.** (*tr.; usually passive*) to embarrass or distress, esp. financially. **2.** (*tr.*) to limit, confine, or restrict. **3.** *Arch.* to make or become narrow.

straitjacket (ˈstreɪtˌdʒækɪt) *n.* **1.** Also: **straightjacket.** a jacket made of strong canvas material with long sleeves for binding the arms of violent prisoners or mental patients. **2.** a restriction or limitation. ~*vb.* **3.** (*tr.*) to confine in or as if in a straitjacket.

strait-laced *or* **straight-laced** *adj.* prudish or puritanical.

strake (streɪk) *n.* **1. a.** a curved metal plate forming part of the metal rim on a wooden wheel. **b.** any metal plate let into a rubber tyre. **2.** Also called: **streak.** *Naut.* one of a continuous range of planks or plates forming the side of a vessel. [C14: rel. to OE *streccan* to stretch]

stramonium (strəˈməʊnɪəm) *n.* **1.** a preparation of the dried leaves and flowers of the thorn apple, containing hyoscyamine and used as a drug to treat nervous disorders. **2.** another name for **thorn apple** (sense 1). [C17: < NL, <?]

strand[1] (strænd) *vb.* **1.** to leave or drive (ships, fish, etc.) aground or ashore or (of ships, etc.) to be left or driven ashore. **2.** (*tr.; usually passive*) to leave helpless, as without transport, money, etc. ~*n.* **3.** *Chiefly poetic.* a shore or beach. [OE]

strand[2] (strænd) *n.* **1.** a set of or one of the individual fibres or threads of string, wire, etc., that form a rope, cable, etc. **2.** a single length of string, hair, wool, wire, etc. **3.** a string of pearls or beads. **4.** a constituent element of something. ~*vb.* **5.** (*tr.*) to form (a rope, cable, etc.) by winding strands together. [C15: <?]

strange (streɪndʒ) *adj.* **1.** odd, unusual, or extraordinary; peculiar. **2.** not known, seen, or experienced before; unfamiliar. **3.** not easily explained. **4.** (usually foll. by *to*) inexperienced (in) or unaccustomed (to): *strange to a task.* **5.** not of one's own kind, locality, etc.; alien; foreign. **6.** shy; distant; reserved. **7. strange to say.** it is unusual or surprising (that). ~*adv.* **8.** *Not standard.* in a strange manner. [C13: < OF *estrange,* < L *extrāneus* foreign; see EXTRANEOUS] —ˈ**strangely** *adv.*

strangeness (ˈstreɪndʒnɪs) *n.* **1.** the state or quality of being strange. **2.** *Physics.* a property of certain elementary particles characterized by a quantum number (**strangeness number**) conserved in strong but not in weak interactions.

strange particle *n. Physics.* an elementary particle having a nonzero strangeness number.

stranger (ˈstreɪndʒə) *n.* **1.** any person whom one does not know. **2.** a person who is new to a particular locality, from another region, town, etc. **3.** a guest or visitor. **4.** (foll. by *to*) a person who is unfamiliar (with) or new (to) something: *he is no stranger to computers.*

strangle (ˈstræŋgᵊl) *vb.* (*tr.*) **1.** to kill by compressing the windpipe; throttle. **2.** to prevent or inhibit the growth or development of: *to strangle originality.* **3.** to suppress (an utterance) by or as if by swallowing suddenly: *to strangle a cry.* ~See also **strangles.** [C13: via OF, ult. < Gk *strangalē* a halter] —ˈ**strangler** *n.*

stranglehold (ˈstræŋgᵊlˌhəʊld) *n.* **1.** a wrestling hold in which a wrestler's arms are pressed against his opponent's windpipe. **2.** complete power or control over a person or situation.

strangles (ˈstræŋgᵊlz) *n.* (*functioning as sing.*) an acute infectious bacterial disease of horses, characterized by inflammation of the respiratory tract. Also called: **equine distemper.**

strangulate (ˈstræŋgjʊˌleɪt) *vb.* (*tr.*) **1.** to constrict (a hollow organ, vessel, etc.) so as to stop the flow of air, blood, etc., through it. **2.** another word for **strangle.** —ˌ**stranguˈlation** *n.*

strangury (ˈstræŋgjʊrɪ) *n. Pathol.* painful excretion of urine, drop by drop. [C14: < L *strangūria,* < Gk, < *stranx* a drop squeezed out + *ouron* urine]

strap (stræp) *n.* **1.** a long strip of leather or similar material, for binding trunks, baggage, etc. **2.** a strip of leather or similar material used for carrying, lifting, or holding. **3.** a loop of leather, rubber, etc., suspended from the roof in a bus or train for standing passengers to hold on to. **4.** a razor strop. **5.** short for **shoulder strap.** **6. the strap.** a beating with a strap as a punishment. ~*vb.* **strapping, strapped.** (*tr.*) **7.** to tie or bind with a strap. **8.** to beat with a strap. **9.** to sharpen with a strap or strop. [C16: var. of STROP]

straphanger (ˈstræpˌhæŋə) *n. Inf.* a passenger in a bus, train, etc., who has to travel standing, esp. holding on to a strap. —ˈ**strapˌhanging** *n.*

strapping (ˈstræpɪŋ) *adj.* (*prenominal*) tall and sturdy. [C17: from STRAP (in the arch. sense: to work vigorously)]

strap work *n. Archit.* decorative work resembling interlacing straps.

strata (ˈstrɑːtə) *n.* a plural of **stratum.**

▷ **Usage.** In careful usage, *strata* is the standard plural of *stratum* and is not treated as singular.

stratagem (ˈstrætɪdʒəm) *n.* a plan or trick, esp. to deceive an enemy. [C15: ult. < Gk *stratēgos* a general, < *stratos* an army + *agein* to lead]

strategic (strəˈtiːdʒɪk) *or* **strategical** *adj.* **1.** of or characteristic of strategy. **2.** important to strategy. **3.** (of weapons, esp. missiles) directed against an enemy's homeland rather than used on a battlefield. Cf. **tactical.** —**straˈtegically** *adv.*

strategics (strəˈtiːdʒɪks) *n.* (*functioning as sing.*) strategy, esp. in a military sense.

strategist (ˈstrætɪdʒɪst) *n.* a specialist or expert in strategy.

strategy (ˈstrætɪdʒɪ) *n., pl.* **-gies.** **1.** the art or science of the planning and conduct of a war. **2.** a particular long-term plan for success, esp. in politics, business, etc. **3.** a plan or stratagem. [C17: < F *stratégie*, < Gk *stratēgia* function of a general; see STRATAGEM]

strath (stræθ) *n. Scot.* a flat river valley. [C16: < Scot. & Irish Gaelic *srath*]

strathspey (ˌstræθˈspeɪ) *n.* **1.** a Scottish dance with gliding steps, slower than a reel. **2.** a piece of music composed for or in the rhythm of this dance. [after *Strathspey*, valley of the river Spey]

strati- *combining form.* indicating stratum or strata: *stratigraphy.*

straticulate (strəˈtɪkjʊlɪt, -ˌleɪt) *adj.* (of a rock formation) composed of very thin even strata. [C19: < NL *strāticulum* (unattested), dim. of L *strātum* something strewn; see STRATUS] —**straˌticuˈlation** *n.*

stratify (ˈstrætɪˌfaɪ) *vb.* **-fying, -fied.** **1.** to form or be formed in layers or strata. **2.** *Sociol.* to divide (a society) into status groups or (of a society) to develop such groups. [C17: < F *stratifier*, < NL *stratificāre*, < L STRATUM] —ˌ**stratifiˈcation** *n.* —ˈ**stratiˌfied** *adj.*

stratigraphy (strəˈtɪgrəfɪ) *n.* **1.** the study of the composition, relative positions, etc., of rock strata in order to determine their geological history. **2.** *Archaeol.* a vertical section through the earth showing the relative positions of the human artefacts and therefore the chronology of successive levels of occupation. —**stratigraphic** (ˌstrætɪˈgræfɪk) *or* ˌ**stratiˈgraphical** *adj.*

stratocumulus (ˌstrætəʊˈkjuːmjʊləs) *n., pl.* **-li** (-ˌlaɪ). *Meteorol.* a uniform stretch of cloud containing dark grey globular masses.

stratopause (ˈstrætəˌpɔːz) *n. Meteorol.* the transitional zone of maximum temperature between the stratosphere and the mesosphere.

stratosphere (ˈstrætəˌsfɪə) *n.* the atmospheric layer lying between the troposphere and the mesosphere, in which temperature generally increases with height. —**stratospheric** (ˌstrætəˈsfɛrɪk) *or* ˌ**stratoˈspherical** *adj.*

stratum (ˈstrɑːtəm) *n., pl.* **-ta** *or* **-tums.** **1.** (*usually pl.*) any of the distinct layers into which sedimentary rocks are divided. **2.** *Biol.* a single layer of tissue or cells. **3.** a layer of any material, esp. one of several parallel layers. **4.** a layer of ocean or atmosphere either naturally or arbitrarily demarcated. **5.** a level of a social hierarchy. [C16: via NL < L: something strewn, < *sternere* to scatter] —ˈ**stratal** *adj.*

stratus (ˈstreɪtəs) *n., pl.* **-ti** (-taɪ). a grey layer cloud. [C19: via NL < L: strewn, < *sternere* to extend]

straw (strɔː) *n.* **1. a.** stalks of threshed grain, esp. of wheat, rye, oats, or barley, used in plaiting hats, baskets, etc., or as fodder. **b.** (*as modifier*): *a straw hat.* **2.** a single dry or ripened stalk, esp. of a grass. **3.** a long thin hollow paper or plastic tube, used for sucking up liquids into the mouth. **4.** (*usually used with a negative*) anything of little value or importance: *I wouldn't give a straw for our chances.* **5.** a measure or remedy that one turns to in desperation (esp. in **clutch** *or* **grasp at a straw** *or* **straws**). **6. a.** a pale yellow colour. **b.** (*as adj.*): *straw hair.* **7. draw the short straw.** to be the person to whom an unpleasant task falls. **8. straw in the wind.** a hint or indication. **9. the last straw.** a small incident, setback, etc., that coming after others proves insufferable. [OE *streaw*] —ˈ**strawy** *adj.*

strawberry (ˈstrɔːbərɪ, -brɪ) *n., pl.* **-ries.** **1.** any of various low-growing rosaceous plants which have red edible fruits and spread by runners. **2. a.** the fruit of any of these plants, consisting of a sweet fleshy receptacle bearing small seedlike parts (the true fruits). **b.** (*as modifier*): *strawberry ice cream.* **3. a.** a purplish-red colour. **b.** (*as adj.*): *strawberry shoes.* [OE *streawberige*; ? < the strawlike appearance of the runners]

strawberry blonde *adj.* **1.** (of hair) reddish blonde. ~*n.* **2.** a woman with such hair.

strawberry mark *n.* a soft vascular red birthmark. Also called: **strawberry.**

strawberry tomato *n.* **1.** a tropical annual plant having bell-shaped whitish-yellow flowers and small edible round yellow berries. **2.** the fruit of this plant, eaten fresh or made into preserves or pickles. ~Also called: **Cape gooseberry.**

strawberry tree *n.* a S European evergreen tree having white or pink flowers and red strawberry-like berries. See also **arbutus.**

strawboard (ˈstrɔːˌbɔːd) *n.* a board made of compressed straw and adhesive.

strawflower (ˈstrɔːˌflaʊə) *n.* an Australian plant in which the coloured bracts retain their colour when the plant is dried. See also **immortelle.**

straw man *n. Chiefly U.S.* **1.** a figure of a man made from straw. **2.** a person of little substance. **3.** a person used as a cover for some dubious plan or enterprise.

straw poll *or esp. U.S., Canad., & N.Z.* **vote** *n.* an unofficial poll or vote taken to determine the opinion of a group or the public on some issue.

stray (streɪ) *vb.* (*intr.*) **1.** to wander away, as from the correct path or from a given area. **2.** to wander haphazardly. **3.** to digress from the point, lose concentration, etc. **4.** to deviate from certain moral standards. ~*n.* **5. a.** a domestic animal, fowl, etc., that has wandered away from its place of keeping and is lost. **b.** (*as modifier*): *stray dogs.* **6.** a lost or homeless person, esp. a child: *waifs and strays.* **7.** an occurrence, specimen, etc., that is out of place or outside the usual pattern. ~*adj.* **8.** scattered, random, or haphazard. [C14: < OF *estraier*, < Vulgar L *estragāre* (unattested), < L *extrā-* outside + *vagāri* to roam] —ˈ**strayer** *n.*

strays (streɪz) *pl. n.* **1.** Also called: **stray capacitance.** *Electronics.* undesired capacitance in equipment. **2.** another word for **static** (sense 8).

streak (striːk) *n.* **1.** a long thin mark, stripe, or trace of some contrasting colour. **2.** (of lightning) a sudden flash. **3.** an element or trace, as of some quality or characteristic. **4.** a strip, vein, or layer. **5.** a short stretch or run, esp. of good or bad luck. **6.** *Inf.* an act or the practice of running naked through a public place. ~*vb.* **7.** (*tr.*) to mark or daub with a streak or streaks. **8.** (*intr.*) to form streaks or become streaked. **9.** (*intr.*) to move rapidly in a straight line. **10.** (*intr.*) *Inf.* to run naked through a public place in order to shock or amuse. [OE *strica*] —**streaked** *adj.* —ˈ**streaker** *n.* —ˈ**streakˌlike** *adj.*

streaky (ˈstriːkɪ) *adj.* **streakier, streakiest.** **1.** marked with streaks. **2.** occurring in streaks. **3.** (of bacon) having alternate layers of meat and fat. **4.** of varying or uneven quality. —ˈ**streakiness** *n.*

stream (striːm) *n.* **1.** a small river; brook. **2.** any steady flow of water or other fluid. **3.** something that resembles a stream in moving continuously in a line or particular direction. **4.** a rapid or unbroken flow of speech, etc.: *a stream of abuse.* **5.** *Brit.* any of several parallel classes of schoolchildren, or divisions of children within a class, grouped together because of similar ability. **6. go** (*or* **drift**) **with the stream.** to conform to the accepted standards. **7. on** (*or* **off**) **stream.** (of an industrial plant, manufacturing process, etc.) in (*or* not in) operation or production. ~*vb.* **8.** to emit or be emitted in a continuous flow: *his nose streamed blood.* **9.** (*intr.*) to move in unbroken succession, as a crowd of people, vehicles, etc. **10.** (*intr.*) to float freely or with a waving motion: *bunting streamed in the wind.* **11.** (*tr.*) to unfurl (a flag, etc.). **12.** *Brit. education.* to group or divide (children) in streams. [OE] —ˈ**streamlet** *n.*

streamer (ˈstriːmə) *n.* **1.** a long narrow flag or part of a flag. **2.** a long narrow coiled ribbon of coloured paper that becomes unrolled when tossed. **3.** a stream of light, esp. one appearing in some forms of the aurora. **4.** *Journalism.* a large heavy headline printed across the width of a page. **5.** *Computers.* an electromechanical device that enables a hard disk to copy data byte by byte onto magnetic tape for security or storage.

streamline (ˈstriːmˌlaɪn) *n.* **1.** a contour on a body that offers the minimum resistance to a gas or liquid flowing around it. ~*vb.* **2.** (*tr.*) to make streamlined.

streamlined (ˈstriːmˌlaɪnd) *adj.* **1.** offering or designed to offer the minimum resistance to the flow of a gas or liquid. **2.** made more efficient, esp. by simplifying.

stream of consciousness *n.* **1.** *Psychol.* the continuous flow of ideas, thoughts, and feelings forming the content of an individual's consciousness. **2.** a literary technique that reveals the flow of thoughts and feelings of characters through long passages of soliloquy.

streamy (ˈstriːmɪ) *adj.* **streamier, streamiest.** *Chiefly poetic.* **1.** (of an area, land, etc.) having many streams. **2.** flowing or streaming.

street (striːt) *n.* **1. a.** a public road that is usually lined with buildings, esp. in a town: *Oxford Street.* **b.** (*as modifier*): *a street directory.* **2.** the buildings lining a street. **3.** the part of the road between the pavements, used by vehicles. **4.** the people living, working, etc., in a particular street. **5.** (*modifier*) of or relating to the urban counterculture. **6. man in the street.** an ordinary or average citizen. **7. on the streets. a.** earning a living as a prostitute. **b.** homeless. **8. (right) up one's street.** *Inf.* (just) what one knows or likes best. **9. streets ahead of.** *Inf.* superior to, more advanced than, etc. **10. streets apart.** *Inf.* markedly different. [OE *strǣt,* < L *via strāta* paved way (*strāta,* < *strātus,* p.p. of *sternere* to stretch out)]

street Arab *n.* a homeless child, esp. one who survives by begging and stealing; urchin.

streetcar (ˈstriːtˌkɑː) *n.* the usual U.S. and Canad. name for **tram** (sense 1).

street credibility *n.* a command of the style, knowledge, etc., associated with urban counterculture. Sometimes shortened to **street cred.** —ˌ**street-**ˈ**credible** *adj.*

street cry *n.* (*often pl.*) the cry of a street hawker.

street value *n.* the monetary worth of a commodity, usually an illicit one, considered as the price it would fetch when sold to the ultimate user.

streetwalker (ˈstriːtˌwɔːkə) *n.* a prostitute who solicits on the streets. —ˈ**street**ˌ**walking** *n., adj.*

streetwise (ˈstriːtˌwaɪz) *adj.* adept at surviving in an urban, poor, and often criminal environment.

strelitzia (strɛˈlɪtsɪə) *n.* any of various southern African perennial herbaceous plants, cultivated for their showy flowers: includes the bird-of-paradise flower. [C18: after Charlotte of Mecklenburg-*Strelitz* (1744–1818), queen of Great Britain & Ireland]

strength (strɛŋθ) *n.* **1.** the state or quality of being physically or mentally strong. **2.** the ability to withstand or exert great force, stress, or pressure. **3.** something regarded as beneficial or a source of power: *their chief strength is technology.* **4.** potency, as of a drink, drug, etc. **5.** power to convince; cogency: *the strength of an argument.* **6.** degree of intensity or concentration of colour, light, sound, flavour, etc. **7.** the full or part of the full complement as specified: *at full strength; below strength.* **8. from strength to strength.** with ever-increasing success. **9. in strength.** in large numbers. **10. on the strength of.** on the basis of or relying upon. **11. the strength of.** *Austral. & N.Z. inf.* the essential facts about. [OE *strengthu*]

strengthen (ˈstrɛŋθən) *vb.* to make or become stronger. —ˈ**strengthener** *n.*

strenuous (ˈstrɛnjʊəs) *adj.* **1.** requiring or involving the use of great energy or effort. **2.** characterized by great activity, effort, or endeavour. [C16: < L *strēnuus* brisk] —ˈ**strenuously** *adv.* —ˈ**strenuousness** *n.*

strep (strɛp) *n. Inf.* short for **streptococcus.**

strepitoso (ˌstrɛpɪˈtəʊsəʊ) *adv. Music.* boisterously. [It.]

strepto- *combining form.* **1.** indicating a shape resembling a twisted chain: *streptococcus.* **2.** indicating streptococcus. [< Gk *streptos* twisted, < *strephein* to twist]

streptocarpus (ˌstrɛptəʊˈkɑːpəs) *n.* any of various mostly African plants having spirally-twisted capsules. [C19: < NL, < Gk *streptos* twisted + *karpos* fruit]

streptococcus (ˌstrɛptəʊˈkɒkəs) *n., pl.* **-cocci** (-ˈkɒkaɪ). any spherical bacterium of the genus *Streptococcus,* typically occurring in chains and including many pathogenic species. Often shortened to **strep.** —**streptococcal** (ˌstrɛptəʊˈkɒkᵊl) *or* **streptococcic** (ˌstrɛptəʊˈkɒksɪk) *adj.*

streptomycin (ˌstrɛptəʊˈmaɪsɪn) *n.* an antibiotic obtained from the bacterium *Streptomyces griseus:* used in the treatment of tuberculosis and other bacterial infections.

streptothricin (ˌstrɛptəʊˈθraɪsɪn) *n.* an antibiotic produced by the bacterium *Streptomyces lavendulae.*

stress (strɛs) *n.* **1.** special emphasis or significance. **2.** mental, emotional, or physical strain or tension. **3.** emphasis placed upon a syllable by pronouncing it more loudly than those that surround it. **4.** such emphasis as part of a rhythm in music or poetry. **5.** a syllable so emphasized. **6.** *Physics.* **a.** force or a system of forces producing deformation or strain. **b.** the force acting per unit area. ~*vb.* (*tr.*) **7.** to give emphasis or prominence to. **8.** to pronounce (a word or syllable) more loudly than those that surround it. **9.** to subject to stress. [C14 *stresse,* shortened < DISTRESS] —ˈ**stressful** *adj.*

-stress *suffix forming nouns.* indicating a woman who performs or is engaged in a certain activity: *songstress; seamstress.* [< -ST(E)R + -ESS]

stretch (strɛtʃ) *vb.* **1.** to draw out or extend or be drawn out or extended in length, area, etc. **2.** to extend or be extended to an undue degree, esp. so as to distort or lengthen permanently. **3.** to extend (the limbs, body, etc.). **4.** (*tr.*) to reach or suspend (a rope, etc.) from one place to another. **5.** (*tr.*) to draw tight; tighten. **6.** (often foll. by *out, forward,* etc.) to reach or hold (out); extend. **7.** (*intr.;* usually foll. by *over*) to extend in time: *the course stretched over three months.* **8.** (*intr.;* foll. by *for, over,* etc.) (of a region, etc.) to extend in length or area. **9.** (*intr.*) (esp. of a garment) to be capable of expanding, as to a larger size: *socks that will stretch.* **10.** (*tr.*) to put a great strain upon or extend to the limit. **11.** to injure (a muscle, tendon, etc.) by means of a strain or sprain. **12.** (*tr.;* often foll. by *out*) to make do with (limited resources): *to stretch one's budget.* **13.** (*tr.*) *Inf.* to expand or elaborate (a story, etc.) beyond what is credible or acceptable. **14.** (*tr.; often passive*) to extend, as to the limit of one's abilities or talents. **15.** *Arch. or sl.* to hang or be hanged by the neck. **16. stretch a point. a.** to make a concession or exception not usually made. **b.** to exaggerate. ~*n.* **17.** the act of stretching or state of being stretched. **18.** a large or continuous expanse or distance: *a stretch of water.* **19.** extent in time, length, area, etc. **20. a.** capacity for being stretched, as in some garments. **b.** (*as modifier*): *stretch pants.* **21.** the section or sections of a racecourse that are straight, esp. the final section leading to the finishing line. **22.** *Sl.* a term of imprisonment. **23. at a stretch.** *Chiefly Brit.* **a.** with some difficulty; by making a special effort. **b.** if really necessary or in extreme circumstances. **c.** at one time: *he sometimes read for hours at a stretch.* [OE *streccan*] —ˈ**stretchable** *adj.* —ˌ**stretcha**ˈ**bility** *n.*

stretcher (ˈstrɛtʃə) *n.* **1.** a device for transporting the ill, wounded, or dead, consisting of a frame covered by canvas or other material. **2.** a strengthening often decorative member joining the legs of a chair, table, etc. **3.** the wooden frame on which canvas is stretched and fixed for oil painting. **4.** a tie beam or brace used in a structural framework. **5.** a brick or stone laid horizontally with its length parallel to the length of a wall. **6.** *Rowing.* a fixed board across a boat on which an oarsman braces his feet. **7.** *Austral. & N.Z.* a camp bed. ~*vb.* (*tr.*) **8.** to transport (a sick or injured person) on a stretcher.

stretcher-bearer *n.* a person who helps to carry a stretcher, esp. in wartime.

stretchmarks (ˈstrɛtʃˌmɑːks) *pl. n.* marks that remain visible on the abdomen after its distension in pregnancy.

stretchy (ˈstrɛtʃɪ) *adj.* **stretchier, stretchiest.** characterized by elasticity. —ˈ**stretchiness** *n.*

stretto (ˈstrɛtəʊ) *n., pl.* **-tos** *or* **-ti** (-tiː). **1.** (in a fugue) the close overlapping of two parts or voices, the second one entering before the first has completed its statement. **2.** Also called: **stretta.** a concluding passage, played at a faster speed than earlier material. [C17: < It., < L *strictus* tightly bound; see STRICT]

strew (struː) *vb.* **strewing, strewed; strewn** *or* **strewed.** to spread or scatter or be spread or scattered, as over a surface or area. [OE *streowian*] —ˈ**strewer** *n.*

strewth (struːθ) *interj.* an expression of surprise or dismay. [C19: alteration of *God's truth*]

stria (ˈstraɪə) *n., pl.* **striae** (ˈstraɪiː). (*often pl.*) **1.** Also called: **striation.** *Geol.* any of the parallel scratches or grooves on the surface of a rock over which a glacier has flowed or on the surface of a crystal. **2.** *Biol., anat.* a narrow band of colour or a ridge, groove, or similar linear mark. **3.** *Archit.* a narrow channel, such as a flute on the shaft of a column. [C16: < L: a groove]

striate *adj.* (ˈstraɪɪt), *also* **striated. 1.** marked with striae; striped. ~*vb.* (ˈstraɪeɪt). **2.** (*tr.*) to mark with striae. [C17: < L *striāre* to make grooves]

striation (straɪˈeɪʃən) *n.* **1.** an arrangement or pattern of striae. **2.** the condition of being striate. **3.** another word for **stria** (sense 1).

stricken (ˈstrɪkən) *adj.* **1.** laid low, as by disease or sickness. **2.** deeply affected, as by grief, love, etc. **3.** *Arch.* wounded or injured. **4. stricken in years.** made feeble by age. [C14: p.p. of STRIKE] —ˈ**strickenly** *adv.*

strict (strɪkt) *adj.* **1.** adhering closely to specified rules, ordinances, etc. **2.** complied with or enforced stringently; rigorous: *a strict code of conduct.* **3.** severely correct in attention to conduct or morality: *a strict teacher.* **4.** (of a punishment, etc.) harsh; severe. **5.** (*prenominal*) complete; absolute: *strict secrecy.* [C16: < L *strictus,* < *stringere* to draw tight] —ˈ**strictly** *adv.* —ˈ**strictness** *n.*

strict implication *n. Logic.* a form of implication in which the proposition "if A then B" is true only when B is deducible from A.

stricture (ˈstrɪktʃə) *n.* **1.** a severe criticism; censure. **2.** *Pathol.* an abnormal constriction of a tubular organ or part. [C14: < L *strictūra* contraction; see STRICT] —ˈ**strictured** *adj.*

stride (straɪd) *n.* **1.** a long step or pace. **2.** the space measured by such a step. **3.** a striding gait. **4.** an act of forward movement by an animal. **5.** progress or development (esp. in **make rapid strides**). **6.** a regular pace or rate of progress: *to get into one's stride; to be put off one's stride.* **7.** Also: **stride piano.** *Jazz.* a piano style characterized by single bass notes on the first and third beats and chords on the second and fourth. **8.** (*pl.*) *Inf., chiefly Austral.* men's trousers. **9. take (something) in one's stride.** to do (something) without difficulty or effort. ~*vb.* **striding, strode, stridden. 10.** (*intr.*) to walk with long regular or measured paces, as in haste, etc. **11.** (*tr.*) to cover or traverse by striding: *he strode thirty miles.* **12.** (often foll. by *over, across,* etc.) to cross (over a space, obstacle, etc.) with a stride. **13.** *Arch. or poetic.* to straddle or bestride. [OE *strīdan*] —ˈ**strider** *n.*

strident (ˈstraɪdᵊnt) *adj.* **1.** (of a shout, voice, etc.) loud or harsh. **2.** urgent, clamorous, or vociferous: *strident demands.* [C17: < L *strīdēns,* < *strīdēre* to make a grating sound] —ˈ**stridence** *or* ˈ**stridency** *n.* —ˈ**stridently** *adv.*

stridor (ˈstraɪdɔː) *n.* **1.** *Pathol.* a high-pitched whistling sound made during respiration, caused by obstruction of the air passages. **2.** *Chiefly literary.* a harsh or shrill sound. [C17: < L; see STRIDENT]

stridulate (ˈstrɪdjʊˌleɪt) *vb.* (*intr.*) (of insects such as the cricket) to produce sounds by rubbing one part of the body against another. [C19: back formation < *stridulation,* < L *strīdulus* creaking, < *strīdēre* to make a harsh noise] —ˌ**striduˈlation** *n.* —ˈ**striduˌlator** *n.*

stridulous (ˈstrɪdjʊləs) *or* **stridulant** *adj.* **1.** making a harsh, shrill, or grating noise. **2.** *Pathol.* of, relating to, or characterized by stridor. —ˈ**stridulousness** *or* ˈ**stridulance** *n.*

strife (straɪf) *n.* **1.** angry or violent struggle; conflict. **2.** rivalry or contention, esp. of a bitter kind. **3.** *Austral. & N.Z. inf.* trouble or discord of any kind. **4.** *Arch.* striving. [C13: < OF *estrif,* prob. < *estriver* to STRIVE]

strigil (ˈstrɪdʒɪl) *n.* a curved blade used by the ancient Romans and Greeks to scrape the body after bathing. [C16: < L *strigilis,* < *stringere* to graze]

strigose (ˈstraɪgəʊs) *adj.* **1.** *Bot.* bearing stiff hairs or bristles. **2.** *Zool.* marked with fine closely set grooves or ridges. [C18: via NL *strigōsus,* < *striga* a bristle, < L: grain cut down]

strike (straɪk) *vb.* **striking, struck. 1.** to deliver (a blow or stroke) to (a person). **2.** to come or cause to come into sudden or violent contact (with). **3.** (*tr.*) to make an attack on. **4.** to produce (fire, sparks, etc.) or (of fire, sparks, etc.) to be produced by ignition. **5.** to cause (a match) to light by friction or (of a match) to be lighted. **6.** to press (the key of a piano, organ, etc.) or to sound (a specific note) in this or a similar way. **7.** to indicate (a specific time) by the sound of a hammer striking a bell or by any other percussive sound. **8.** (of a venomous snake) to cause injury by biting. **9.** (*tr.*) to affect or cause to affect deeply, suddenly, or radically: *her appearance struck him as strange.* **10.** (*past participle* **struck** *or* **stricken**) (*tr.; passive;* usually foll. by *with*) to render incapable or nearly so: *stricken with grief.* **11.** (*tr.*) to enter the mind of: *it struck me that he had become very quiet.* **12.** (*past participle* **struck** *or* **stricken**) to render: *struck dumb.* **13.** (*tr.*) to be perceived by; catch: *the glint of metal struck his eye.* **14.** to arrive at or come upon (something), esp. suddenly or unexpectedly: *to strike the path for home; to strike upon a solution.* **15.** (*intr.;* sometimes foll. by *out*) to set (out) or proceed, esp. upon a new course: *to strike out for the coast.* **16.** (*tr.; usually passive*) to afflict with a disease, esp. unexpectedly: *he was struck with polio.* **17.** (*tr.*) to discover or come upon a source of (ore, petroleum, etc.). **18.** (*tr.*) (of a plant) to produce or send down (a root or roots). **19.** (*tr.*) to take apart or pack up; break (esp. in **strike camp**). **20.** (*tr.*) to take down or dismantle (a stage set, etc.). **21.** (*tr.*) *Naut.* **a.** to lower or remove (a specified piece of gear). **b.** to haul down or dip (a flag, sail, etc.) in salute or in surrender. **22.** to attack (an objective). **23.** to impale the hook in the mouth of (a fish) by suddenly tightening or jerking the line after the bait has been taken. **24.** (*tr.*) to form or impress (a coin, metal, etc.) by or as if by stamping. **25.** to level (a surface) by use of a flat board. **26.** (*tr.*) to assume or take up (an attitude, posture, etc.). **27.** (*intr.*) (of workers in a factory, etc.) to cease work collectively as a protest against working conditions, low pay, etc. **28.** (*tr.*) to reach by agreement: *to strike a bargain.* **29.** (*tr.*) to form (a jury, esp. a special jury) by cancelling certain names among those nominated for jury service until only the requisite number remains. **30. strike home. a.** to deliver an effective blow. **b.** to achieve the intended effect. **31. strike it rich.** *Inf.* **a.** to discover an extensive deposit of a mineral, petroleum, etc. **b.** to have an unexpected financial success. ~*n.* **32.** an act or instance of striking. **33.** a cessation of work, as a protest against working conditions or low pay: *on strike.* **34.** a military attack, esp. an air attack on a surface target: *air strike.* **35.** *Baseball.* a pitched ball judged good but missed or not swung at, three of which cause a batter to be out. **36.** Also called: **ten-strike.** *Tenpin bowling.* **a.** the act or an instance of knocking down all the pins with the first bowl of a single frame. **b.** the score thus made. **37.** a sound made by striking. **38.** the mechanism that makes a clock strike. **39.** the discovery of a source of ore, petroleum, etc. **40.** the horizontal direction of a fault, rock stratum, etc. **41.** *Angling.* the act or an instance of striking. **42.** *Inf.* an unexpected or complete success, esp. one that brings financial gain. **43. take strike.** *Cricket.* (of a batsman) to prepare to play a ball delivered by the bowler. ~See also **strike down, strike off,** etc. [OE *strīcan*]

strikebound (ˈstraɪkˌbaʊnd) *adj.* (of a factory, etc.) closed or made inoperative by a strike.

strikebreaker (ˈstraɪkˌbreɪkə) *n.* a person who tries to make a strike ineffectual by working or by taking the place of those on strike. —**ˈstrikeˌbreaking** *n., adj.*

strike down *vb.* (*tr., adv.*) to cause to die, esp. suddenly: *he was struck down in his prime.*

strike off *vb.* (*tr.*) **1.** to remove or erase from (a list, record, etc.) by or as if by a stroke of the pen. **2.** (*adv.*) to cut off or separate by or as if by a blow: *she was struck off from the inheritance.*

strike out *vb.* (*adv.*) **1.** (*tr.*) to remove or erase. **2.** (*intr.*) to start out or begin: *to strike out on one's own.* **3.** *Baseball.* to put out or be put out on strikes. **4.** (*intr.*) *U.S. inf.* to fail utterly.

strike pay *n.* money paid to strikers from the funds of a trade union.

striker (ˈstraɪkə) *n.* **1.** a person who is on strike. **2.** the hammer in a timepiece that rings a bell or alarm. **3.** any part in a mechanical device that strikes something, such as the firing pin of a gun. **4.** *Soccer, inf.* an attacking player, esp. one who generally positions himself near his opponent's goal in the hope of scoring. **5.** *Cricket.* the batsman who is about to play a ball.

strike up *vb.* (*adv.*) **1.** (of a band, orchestra, etc.) to begin to play or sing. **2.** (*tr.*) to bring about; cause to begin: *to strike up a friendship.*

striking (ˈstraɪkɪŋ) *adj.* **1.** attracting attention; fine; impressive: *a striking beauty.* **2.** conspicuous; noticeable: *a striking difference.* —**ˈstrikingly** *adv.* —**ˈstrikingness** *n.*

striking circle *n. Hockey.* the semicircular area in front of each goal, which an attacking player must have entered before scoring a goal.

Strine (straɪn) *n.* a humorous transliteration of Australian pronunciation, as in *Gloria Soame* for *glorious home.* [C20: a jocular rendering of the Australian pronunciation of *Australian*]

string (strɪŋ) *n.* **1.** a thin length of cord, twine, fibre, or similar material used for tying, hanging, binding, etc. **2.** a group of objects threaded on a single strand: *a string of beads.* **3.** a series or succession of things, events, etc.: *a string of oaths.* **4.** a number, chain, or group of similar things, animals, etc., owned by or associated with one person or body: *a string of girlfriends.* **5.** a tough fibre or cord in a plant. **6.** *Music.* a tightly stretched wire, cord, etc., found on stringed instruments, such as the violin, guitar, and piano. **7.** short for **bowstring. 8.** *Archit.* short for **string-course** or **stringer** (sense 1). **9.** (*pl.; usually preceded by the*) **a.** violins, violas, cellos, and double basses collectively. **b.** the section of a symphony orchestra constituted by such instruments. **10.** a group of characters that can be treated as a unit by a computer program. **11.** (*pl.*) complications or conditions (esp. in **no strings attached**). **12.** (*modifier*) composed of string-like strands woven in a large mesh: *a string bag; a string vest.* **13. first (second, *etc.*) string.** a person or thing regarded as a primary (secondary, etc.) source of strength. **14. keep on a string.** to have control or a hold over (a person), esp. emotionally. **15. pull strings.** *Inf.* to exert power or influence, esp. secretly or unofficially. **16. pull the strings.** to have real or ultimate control of something. ~*vb.* **stringing, strung. 17.** (*tr.*) to provide with a string or strings. **18.** (*tr.*) to suspend or stretch from one point to another. **19.** (*tr.*) to thread on a string. **20.** (*tr.*) to form or extend in a line or series. **21.** (foll. by *out*) to space or spread out at intervals. **22.** (*tr.; usually foll. by up*) *Inf.* to kill (a person) by hanging. **23.** (*tr.*) to remove the stringy parts from (vegetables, esp. beans). **24.** (*intr.*) (esp. of viscous liquids) to become stringy or ropy. **25.** (*tr.; often foll. by up*) to cause to be tense or nervous. [OE *streng*] —**ˈstringˌlike** *adj.*

string along *vb.* (*adv.*) *Inf.* **1.** (*intr.; often foll. by with*) to agree or appear to be in agreement (with). **2.** (*intr.; often foll. by with*) to accompany. **3.** to deceive or hoax, esp. in order to gain time.

stringboard (ˈstrɪŋˌbɔːd) *n.* a skirting that covers the ends of the steps in a staircase. Also called: **stringer.**

string course *n. Archit.* an ornamental projecting band or continuous moulding along a wall. Also called: **cordon.**

stringed (strɪŋd) *adj.* (of musical instruments) having or provided with strings.

stringendo (strɪnˈdʒɛndəʊ) *adj., adv. Music.* to be performed with increasing speed. [It., < *stringere* to compress, < L: to draw tight]

stringent (ˈstrɪndʒənt) *adj.* **1.** requiring strict attention to rules, procedure, detail, etc. **2.** *Finance.* characterized by or causing a shortage of credit, loan capital, etc. [C17: < L *stringere* to bind] —**ˈstringency** *n.* —**ˈstringently** *adv.*

stringer (ˈstrɪŋə) *n.* **1.** *Archit.* **a.** a long horizontal timber beam that is used for structural purposes. **b.** another name for **stringboard. 2.** *Naut.* a longitudinal structural brace for strengthening the hull of a vessel. **3.** a journalist retained by a newspaper or news service on a part-time basis to cover a particular town or area.

stringhalt (ˈstrɪŋˌhɔːlt) *n. Vet. science.* a sudden spasmodic lifting of the hind leg of a horse. Also called: **springhalt.** [C16: prob. STRING + HALT[2]]

stringpiece (ˈstrɪŋˌpiːs) *n.* a long horizontal timber beam used to strengthen or support a framework.

string quartet *n. Music.* **1.** an instrumental ensemble consisting of two violins, one viola, and one cello. **2.** a piece of music for such a group.

string tie *n.* a very narrow tie.

stringy (ˈstrɪŋɪ) *adj.* **stringier, stringiest. 1.** made of strings or resembling strings. **2.** (of meat, etc.) fibrous. **3.** (of a person's build) wiry; sinewy. **4.** (of liquids) forming in strings. —**ˈstringily** *adv.* —**ˈstringiness** *n.*

stringy-bark *n. Austral.* any of several eucalyptus trees having fibrous bark.

strip[1] (strɪp) *vb.* **stripping, stripped. 1.** to take or pull (the covering, clothes, etc.) off (oneself, another person, or thing). **2.** (*intr.*) **a.** to remove all one's clothes. **b.** to perform a striptease. **3.** (*tr.*) to denude or empty completely. **4.** (*tr.*) to deprive: *he was stripped of his pride.* **5.** (*tr.*) to rob or plunder. **6.** (*tr.*) to remove (paint, etc.) from (a surface, furniture, etc.): *stripped pine.* **7.** (*tr.*) to pull out the old coat of hair from (dogs of certain long- and wire-haired breeds). **8. a.** to remove the leaves from the stalks of (tobacco, etc.). **b.** to separate the leaves from the stems of (tobacco, etc.). **9.** (*tr.*) *Agriculture.* to draw the last milk from (a cow). **10.** to dismantle (an engine, mechanism, etc.). **11.** to tear off or break (the thread) from (a screw, bolt, etc.) or (the teeth) from (a gear). **12.** (often foll. by *down*) to remove the accessories from (a motor vehicle): *his car was stripped down.* ~*n.* **13.** the act or an instance of undressing or of performing a striptease. [OE *bestriepan* to plunder]

strip[2] (strɪp) *n.* **1.** a relatively long, flat, narrow piece of something. **2.** short for **airstrip. 3.** the clothes worn by the members of a team, esp. a football team. **4. tear (someone) off a strip.** *Inf.* to rebuke (someone) angrily. ~*vb.* **stripping, stripped. 5.** to cut or divide into strips. [C15: < MDu. *strīpe* STRIPE[1]]

strip cartoon *n.* a sequence of drawings in a

newspaper, magazine, etc., relating a humorous story or an adventure. Also called: **comic strip.**

strip club *n.* a small club in which striptease performances take place.

stripe[1] (straɪp) *n.* **1.** a relatively long band of colour or texture that differs from the surrounding material or background. **2.** a fabric having such bands. **3.** a strip, band, or chevron worn on a uniform, etc., esp. to indicate rank. **4.** *Chiefly U.S. & Canad.* kind; type: *a man of a certain stripe.* ~*vb.* **5.** (*tr.*) to mark with stripes. [C17: prob. < MDu. *strīpe*] **—striped** *adj.*

stripe[2] (straɪp) *n.* a stroke from a whip, rod, cane, etc. [C15: ? < MLow G *strippe*]

striped muscle *n.* a type of contractile tissue that is marked by transverse striations. Also called: **striated muscle.**

strip lighting *n.* electric lighting by means of long glass tubes that are fluorescent lamps or that contain long filaments.

stripling (ˈstrɪplɪŋ) *n.* a lad. [C13: < STRIP[2] + -LING[1]]

strip mining *n.* another term (esp. U.S.) for **opencast mining.**

stripper (ˈstrɪpə) *n.* **1.** a striptease artiste. **2.** a person or thing that strips. **3.** a device or substance for removing paint, varnish, etc.

strip-searching *n.* the practice by police or customs officials of stripping a prisoner or suspect naked and searching him or her for contraband, narcotics, etc. **—ˈstrip-ˌsearch** *n., vb.*

striptease (ˈstrɪpˌtiːz) *n.* **a.** a form of erotic entertainment in which a person gradually undresses to music. **b.** (*as modifier*): *a striptease club.* **—ˈstripˌteaser** *n.*

stripy (ˈstraɪpɪ) *adj.* **stripier, stripiest.** marked by or with stripes; striped.

strive (straɪv) *vb.* **striving, strove, striven. 1.** (*may take a clause as object or an infinitive*) to make a great and tenacious effort. **2.** (*intr.*) to fight; contend. [C13: < OF *estriver,* of Gmc origin] **—ˈstriver** *n.*

strobe (strəʊb) *n.* short for **strobe lighting** or **stroboscope.**

strobe lighting *n.* **1.** a high-intensity flashing beam of light produced by rapid electrical discharges in a tube or by a perforated disc rotating in front of an intense light source. **2.** the use of or the apparatus for producing such light. Sometimes shortened to **strobe.**

strobilus (ˈstrəʊbɪləs) *or* **strobile** (ˈstrəʊbaɪl) *n., pl.* **-biluses, -bili** (-bɪlaɪ), *or* **-biles.** *Bot.* the technical name for **cone** (sense 3). [C18: via LL < Gk *strobilos* a fir cone]

stroboscope (ˈstrəʊbəˌskəʊp) *n.* **1.** an instrument producing an intense flashing light, the frequency of which can be synchronized with some multiple of the frequency of rotation, vibration, or operation of an object, etc., making it appear stationary. Sometimes shortened to **strobe. 2.** a similar device synchronized with the shutter of a camera so that a series of still photographs can be taken of a moving object. [C19: < *strobo-,* < Gk *strobos* a whirling + -SCOPE] **—stroboscopic** (ˌstrəʊbəˈskɒpɪk) *or* **ˌstroboˈscopical** *adj.* **—ˌstroboˈscopically** *adv.*

strode (strəʊd) *vb.* the past tense of **stride.**

stroganoff (ˈstrɒgəˌnɒf) *n.* a dish of sliced beef cooked with onions and mushrooms, served in a sour-cream sauce. Also called: **beef stroganoff.** [C19: after Count *Stroganoff,* 19th-century Russian diplomat]

stroke (strəʊk) *n.* **1.** the act or an instance of striking; a blow, knock, or hit. **2.** a sudden action, movement, or occurrence: *a stroke of luck.* **3.** a brilliant or inspired act or feat: *a stroke of genius.* **4.** *Pathol.* apoplexy; rupture of a blood vessel in the brain resulting in loss of consciousness, often followed by paralysis, or embolism or thrombosis affecting a cerebral vessel. **5. a.** the striking of a clock. **b.** the hour registered by this: *on the stroke of three.* **6.** a mark made by a writing implement. **7.** another name for **solidus** (sense 1), used esp. when dictating or reading aloud. **8.** a light touch or caress, as with the fingers. **9.** a pulsation, esp. of the heart. **10.** a single complete movement or one of a series of complete movements. **11.** *Sport.* the act or manner of striking the ball with a club, bat, etc. **12.** any one of the repeated movements used by a swimmer. **13.** a manner of swimming, esp. one of several named styles such as the crawl. **14. a.** any one of a series of linear movements of a reciprocating part, such as a piston. **b.** the distance travelled by such a part from one end of its movement to the other. **15.** a single pull on an oar or oars in rowing. **16.** manner or style of rowing. **17.** the oarsman who sits nearest the stern of a shell, facing the cox, and sets the rate of rowing. **18. a stroke (of work).** (*usually used with a negative*) a small amount of work. **19. at a stroke.** with one action. **20. off one's stroke.** performing or working less well than usual. **21. on the stroke.** punctually. ~*vb.* **22.** (*tr.*) to touch, brush, etc. lightly or gently. **23.** (*tr.*) to mark a line or a stroke on or through. **24.** to act as the stroke of (a racing shell). **25.** (*tr.*) *Sport.* to strike (a ball) with a smooth swinging blow. [OE *strācian*]

stroke play *n. Golf.* **a.** scoring by counting the strokes taken. **b.** (*as modifier*): *a strokeplay tournament.* ~Also called: **medal play.** Cf. **match play.**

stroll (strəʊl) *vb.* **1.** to walk about in a leisurely manner. **2.** (*intr.*) to wander about. ~*n.* **3.** a leisurely walk. [C17: prob. < dialect G *strollen,* <?]

stroller (ˈstrəʊlə) *n.* the usual U.S., Canad., and Austral. word for **pushchair.**

stroma (ˈstrəʊmə) *n., pl.* **-mata** (-mətə). *Biol.* **1.** the dense colourless framework of a chloroplast and certain cells. **2.** the fibrous connective tissue forming the matrix of the mammalian ovary and testis. **3.** a dense mass of hyphae that is produced by certain fungi and gives rise to spore-producing bodies. [C19: via NL < LL: a mattress, < Gk] **—stromatic** (strəʊˈmætɪk) *or* **ˈstromatous** *adj.*

strong (strɒŋ) *adj.* **stronger** (ˈstrɒŋgə), **strongest** (ˈstrɒŋgɪst). **1.** involving or possessing strength. **2.** solid or robust; not easily broken or injured. **3.** resolute or morally firm. **4.** intense in quality; not faint or feeble: *a strong voice; a strong smell.* **5.** easily defensible; incontestable or formidable. **6.** concentrated; not weak or diluted. **7. a.** (*postpositive*) containing or having a specified number: *a navy 40 000 strong.* **b.** (*in combination*): *a 40 000-strong navy.* **8.** having an unpleasantly powerful taste or smell. **9.** having an extreme or drastic effect: *strong discipline.* **10.** emphatic or immoderate: *strong language.* **11.** convincing, effective, or cogent. **12.** (of a colour) having a high degree of saturation or purity; produced by a concentrated quantity of colouring agent. **13.** *Grammar.* **a.** of or denoting a class of verbs, in certain languages including the Germanic languages, whose conjugation shows vowel gradation, as *sing, sang, sung.* **b.** belonging to any part-of-speech class, in various languages, whose inflections follow the less regular of two possible patterns. Cf. **weak** (sense 10). **14.** (of a wind, current, etc.) moving fast. **15.** (of a syllable) accented or stressed. **16.** (of an industry, etc.) firm in price or characterized by firm or increasing prices. **17.** (of certain acids and bases) producing high concentrations of hydrogen or hydroxide ions in aqueous solution. **18. have a strong stomach.** not to be prone to nausea. ~*adv.* **19.** *Inf.* in a strong way; effectively: *going strong.* **20. come on strong.** to make a forceful or exaggerated impression. [OE *strang*] **—ˈstrongly** *adv.* **—ˈstrongness** *n.*

strong-arm *Inf.* ~*n.* **1.** (*modifier*) of or involving physical force or violence: *strong-arm tactics.* ~*vb.* **2.** (*tr.*) to show violence towards.

strongbox (ˈstrɒŋˌbɒks) *n.* a box or safe in which valuables are locked for safety.

strong breeze *n. Meteorol.* a wind of force 6 on the Beaufort scale, reaching speeds of 25 to 31 mph.

strong drink *n.* alcoholic drink.

strong-eye dog *n. N.Z.* See **eye dog.**

strong gale *n. Meteorol.* a wind of force 9 on the Beaufort scale, reaching speeds of 47 to 54 mph.

stronghold ('strɒŋ,həʊld) *n.* **1.** a defensible place; fortress. **2.** a major centre or area of predominance.

strong interaction *n. Physics.* an interaction between elementary particles responsible for the forces between nucleons in the nucleus. Cf. **weak interaction.**

strong-minded *adj.* having strength of mind; firm, resolute, and determined. —,**strong-'mindedly** *adv.* —,**strong-'mindedness** *n.*

strong point *n.* something at which one excels; forte.

strongroom ('strɒŋ,ru:m, -,rʊm) *n.* a specially designed room in which valuables are locked for safety.

strong-willed *adj.* having strength of will.

strontium ('strɒntɪəm) *n.* a soft silvery-white element of the alkaline earth group of metals. The radioisotope **strontium-90,** with a half-life of 28.1 years, is used in nuclear power sources and is a hazardous nuclear fallout product. Symbol: Sr; atomic no.: 38; atomic wt.: 87.62. [C19: < NL, after *Strontian,* in the Highlands of Scotland where discovered]

strontium unit *n.* a unit expressing the concentration of strontium-90 in an organic medium, such as soil, bone, etc., relative to the concentration of calcium in the medium.

strop (strɒp) *n.* **1.** a leather strap or an abrasive strip for sharpening razors. **2.** a rope or metal band around a block or deadeye for support. ~*vb.* **stropping, stropped. 3.** (*tr.*) to sharpen (a razor, etc.) on a strop. [C14 (in nautical use: a strip of rope): via MLow G or MDu. *strop,* ult. < L *stroppus,* < Gk *strophos* cord]

strophanthin (strəʊ'fænθɪn) *n.* a toxic glycoside or mixture of glycosides obtained from the ripe seeds of certain species of strophanthus. [C19: NL, < STROPHANTH(US) + -IN]

strophanthus (strəʊ'fænθəs) *n.* **1.** any of various small trees or shrubs of tropical Africa and Asia, having strap-shaped twisted petals. **2.** the seeds of any of these plants. [C19: NL, < Gk *strophos* twisted cord + *anthos* flower]

strophe ('strəʊfɪ) *n. Prosody.* (in ancient Greek drama) **a.** the first of two movements made by a chorus during the performance of a choral ode. **b.** the first part of a choral ode sung during this movement. ~See **antistrophe, epode.** [C17: < Gk: a verse, lit.: a turning, < *strephein* to twist] —**strophic** ('strɒfɪk, 'strəʊ-) *adj.*

stroppy ('strɒpɪ) *adj.* **-pier, -piest.** *Brit. inf.* angry or awkward. [C20: changed & shortened < OBSTREPEROUS] —'**stroppily** *adv.* —'**stroppiness** *n.*

strove (strəʊv) *vb.* the past tense of **strive.**

strow (strəʊ) *vb.* **strowing, strowed; strown** *or* **strowed.** an archaic variant of **strew.**

struck (strʌk) *vb.* **1.** the past tense and past participle of **strike.** ~*adj.* **2.** *Chiefly U.S. & Canad.* (of an industry, factory, etc.) shut down or otherwise affected by a labour strike.

structural ('strʌktʃərəl) *adj.* **1.** of, relating to, or having structure or a structure. **2.** of, relating to, or forming part of the structure of a building. **3.** of or relating to the structure of the earth's crust. **4.** of or relating to the structure of organisms. **5.** *Chem.* of or involving the arrangement of atoms in molecules. —'**structurally** *adv.*

structural formula *n.* a chemical formula showing the composition and structure of a molecule.

structuralism ('strʌktʃərə,lɪzəm) *n.* **1.** an approach to social sciences and to literature in terms of oppositions, contrasts, and hierarchical structures, esp. as they might reflect universal mental characteristics or organizing principles. **2.** an approach to linguistics that analyses and describes the structure of language, as distinguished from its comparative and historical aspects. —'**structuralist** *n., adj.*

structural linguistics *n.* (*functioning as sing.*) a descriptive approach to an analysis of language on the basis of its structure as reflected by irreducible units of phonological, morphological, and semantic features.

structure ('strʌktʃə) *n.* **1.** a complex construction or entity. **2.** the arrangement and interrelationship of parts in a construction. **3.** the manner of construction or organization. **4.** *Chem.* the arrangement of atoms in a molecule of a chemical compound. **5.** *Geol.* the way in which a mineral, rock, etc., is made up of its component parts. ~*vb.* (*tr.*) **6.** to impart a structure to. [C15: < L *structūra,* < *struere* to build]

strudel ('stru:dəl) *n.* a thin sheet of filled dough rolled up and baked: *apple strudel.* [G, < MHG *strodel* whirlpool, < the way the pastry is rolled]

struggle ('strʌgᵊl) *vb.* **1.** (*intr.; usually foll. by for* or *against; may take an infinitive*) to exert strength, energy, and force; work or strive. **2.** (*intr.*) to move about strenuously so as to escape from something confining. **3.** (*intr.*) to contend, battle, or fight. **4.** (*intr.*) to go or progress with difficulty. ~*n.* **5.** a laboured or strenuous exertion or effort. **6.** a fight or battle. **7.** the act of struggling. [C14: <?] —'**struggling** *adj.*

strum (strʌm) *vb.* **strumming, strummed. 1.** to sound (the strings of a guitar, etc.) with a downward or upward sweep of the thumb or of a plectrum. **2.** to play (chords, a tune, etc.) in this way. [C18: prob. imit.] —'**strummer** *n.*

struma ('stru:mə) *n., pl.* **-mae** (-mi:). **1.** an abnormal enlargement of the thyroid gland; goitre. **2.** *Bot.* a swelling, esp. at the base of a moss capsule. **3.** another word for **scrofula.** [C16: < L: scrofulous tumour, < *struere* to heap up] —**strumous** ('stru:məs) *or* **strumose** ('stru:məʊs) *adj.*

strumpet ('strʌmpɪt) *n. Arch.* a prostitute or promiscuous woman. [C14: <?]

strung (strʌŋ) *vb.* **1.** a past tense and past participle of **string.** ~*adj.* **2. a.** (of a piano, etc.) provided with strings. **b.** (*in combination*): *gut-strung.* **3. highly strung.** very nervous or volatile in character.

strung up *adj.* (*postpositive*) *Inf.* tense or nervous.

strut (strʌt) *vb.* **strutting, strutted. 1.** (*intr.*) to walk in a pompous manner; swagger. **2.** (*tr.*) to support or provide with struts. ~*n.* **3.** a structural member, esp. as part of a framework. **4.** an affected, proud, or stiff walk. [C14 *strouten* (in the sense: swell, stand out; C16: to walk stiffly), < OE *strūtian* to stand stiffly] —'**strutter** *n.* —'**strutting** *adj.* —'**struttingly** *adv.*

struthious ('stru:θɪəs) *adj.* **1.** (of birds) related to or resembling the ostrich. **2.** of, relating to, or designating all flightless birds. [C18: < LL *strūthiō,* < Gk *strouthiōn,* < *strouthos* ostrich]

strychnine ('strɪkni:n) *n.* a white crystalline very poisonous alkaloid, obtained from the plant nux vomica: used in small quantities as a stimulant. [C19: via F < NL *Strychnos,* < Gk *strukhnos* nightshade]

Stuart ('stjʊət) *adj.* of or relating to the royal house that ruled Scotland from 1371 to 1714 and England from 1603 to 1714.

stub (stʌb) *n.* **1.** a short piece remaining after something has been cut, removed, etc.: *a cigar stub.* **2.** the residual piece or section of a receipt, ticket, cheque, etc. **3.** the usual U.S. and Canad. word for **counterfoil. 4.** any short projection or blunted end. **5.** the stump of a tree or plant. ~*vb.* **stubbing, stubbed.** (*tr.*) **6.** to strike (one's toe, foot, etc.) painfully against a hard surface. **7.** (usually foll. by *out*) to put (out a cigarette or cigar) by pressing the end against a surface. **8.** to clear (land) of stubs. **9.** to dig up (the roots) of (a tree or bush). [OE *stubb*]

stub axle *n.* a short axle that carries one of the front steered wheels of a motor vehicle.

stubble ('stʌbᵊl) *n.* **1. a.** the stubs of stalks left in a field where a crop has been harvested. **b.** (*as modifier*): *a stubble field.* **2.** any bristly growth. [C13: < OF *estuble,* < L *stupula,* var. of *stipula* stalk] —'**stubbled** *or* '**stubbly** *adj.*

stubble-jumper *n. Canad. sl.* a prairie grain farmer.

stubborn (ˈstʌbᵊn) *adj.* **1.** refusing to comply, agree, or give in. **2.** difficult to handle, treat, or overcome. **3.** persistent and dogged. [C14 *stoborne,* <?] —ˈ**stubbornly** *adv.* —ˈ**stubbornness** *n.*

stubby (ˈstʌbɪ) *adj.* **-bier, -biest. 1.** short and broad; stumpy or thickset. **2.** bristling and stiff. ~*n.* **3.** *Austral. sl.* a small bottle of beer. —ˈ**stubbily** *adv.* —ˈ**stubbiness** *n.*

stucco (ˈstʌkəʊ) *n., pl.* **-coes** *or* **-cos. 1.** a weather-resistant mixture of dehydrated lime, powdered marble, and glue, used in decorative mouldings on buildings. **2.** any of various types of cement or plaster used for coating outside walls. **3.** Also called: **stuccowork.** decorative work moulded in stucco. ~*vb.* **-coing, -coed. 4.** (*tr.*) to apply stucco to. [C16: < It., of Gmc origin]

stuck (stʌk) *vb.* **1.** the past tense and past participle of **stick**[2]. ~*adj.* **2.** *Inf.* baffled or nonplussed. **3.** (foll. by *on*) *Sl.* keen (on) or infatuated (with). **4. get stuck in** *or* **into.** *Inf.* **a.** to perform (a task) with determination. **b.** to attack (a person).

stuck-up *adj. Inf.* conceited, arrogant, or snobbish. —ˈ**stuck-**ˈ**upness** *n.*

stud[1] (stʌd) *n.* **1.** a large-headed nail or other projection protruding from a surface, usually as decoration. **2.** a type of fastener consisting of two discs at either end of a short shank, used to fasten shirtfronts, collars, etc. **3.** a vertical member used with others to construct the framework of a wall. **4.** the crossbar in the centre of a link of a heavy chain. **5.** one of a number of rounded projections on the sole of a boot or shoe to give better grip, as on a football boot. ~*vb.* **studding, studded.** (*tr.*) **6.** to provide, ornament, or make with studs. **7.** to dot or cover with: *the park was studded with daisies.* **8.** to provide or support (a wall, partition, etc.) with studs. [OE *studu*]

stud[2] (stʌd) *n.* **1.** a group of pedigree animals, esp. horses, kept for breeding purposes. **2.** any male animal kept principally for breeding purposes, esp. a stallion. **3.** a farm or stable where a stud is kept. **4.** the state or condition of being kept for breeding purposes: *at stud; put to stud.* **5.** (*modifier*) of or relating to such animals or the place where they are kept: *a stud farm; a stud horse.* **6.** *Sl.* a virile or sexually active man. **7.** short for **stud poker.** [OE *stōd*]

studbook (ˈstʌdˌbʊk) *n.* a written record of the pedigree of a purebred stock, esp. of racehorses.

studding (ˈstʌdɪŋ) *n.* **1.** studs collectively, esp. as used to form a wall or partition. **2.** material used to form or serve as studs.

studdingsail (ˈstʌdɪŋˌseɪl; *Naut.* ˈstʌnsᵊl) *n. Naut.* a light auxiliary sail set outboard on spars on either side of a square sail. Also called: **stunsail, stuns'l.** [C16: *studding,* ? < MLow G, MDu. *stōtinge,* < *stōten* to thrust]

student (ˈstjuːdᵊnt) *n.* **1. a.** a person following a course of study, as in a school, college, university, etc. **b.** (*as modifier*): *student teacher.* **2.** a person who makes a thorough study of a subject. [C15: < L *studēns* diligent, < *studēre* to be zealous]

Student's t *n.* a statistic often used to test the hypothesis that a random sample of normally distributed observations has a given mean. [after *Student,* pen name of W. S. Gosset (1876–1937), E mathematician]

studhorse (ˈstʌdˌhɔːs) *n.* another word for **stallion.**

studied (ˈstʌdɪd) *adj.* carefully practised, designed, or premeditated: *a studied reply.* —ˈ**studiedly** *adv.* —ˈ**studiedness** *n.*

studio (ˈstjuːdɪəʊ) *n., pl.* **-dios. 1.** a room in which an artist, photographer, or musician works. **2.** a room used to record television or radio programmes, make films, etc. **3.** (*pl.*) the premises of a radio, television, or film company. [C19: < It., lit.: study, < L *studium* diligence]

studio couch *n.* an upholstered couch, usually backless, convertible into a double bed.

studio flat *n.* a flat with one main room.

studious (ˈstjuːdɪəs) *adj.* **1.** given to study. **2.** of a serious, thoughtful, and hard-working character. **3.** showing deliberation, care, or precision. [C14: < L *studiōsus* devoted to, < *studium* assiduity] —ˈ**studiously** *adv.* —ˈ**studiousness** *n.*

stud poker *n.* a variety of poker in which the first card is dealt face down before each player and the next four are dealt face up (**five-card stud**) or in which the first two cards and the last card are dealt face down and the intervening four cards are dealt face up (**seven-card stud**).

study (ˈstʌdɪ) *vb.* **studying, studied. 1.** to apply the mind to the learning or understanding of (a subject), esp. by reading. **2.** (*tr.*) to investigate or examine, as by observation, research, etc. **3.** (*tr.*) to look at minutely; scrutinize. **4.** (*tr.*) to give much careful or critical thought to. **5.** to take a course in (a subject), as at a college. **6.** (*tr.*) to try to memorize: *to study a part for a play.* **7.** (*intr.*) to meditate or contemplate; reflect. ~*n., pl.* **studies. 8. a.** the act or process of studying. **b.** (*as modifier*): *study group.* **9.** a room used for studying, reading, writing, etc. **10.** (*often pl.*) work relating to a particular discipline: *environmental studies.* **11.** an investigation and analysis of a subject, institution etc. **12.** a product of studying, such as a written paper or book. **13.** a drawing, sculpture, etc., executed for practice or in preparation for another work. **14.** a musical composition intended to develop one aspect of performing technique. **15. in a brown study.** in a reverie or daydream. [C13: < OF *estudie,* < L *studium* zeal, < *studēre* to be diligent]

stuff (stʌf) *vb.* (*mainly tr.*) **1.** to pack or fill completely; cram. **2.** (*intr.*) to eat large quantities. **3.** to force, shove, or squeeze: *to stuff money into a pocket.* **4.** to fill (food such as poultry or tomatoes) with a stuffing. **5.** to fill (an animal's skin) with material so as to restore the shape of the live animal. **6.** *Taboo sl.* to have sexual intercourse with (a woman). **7.** *U.S. & Canad.* to fill (a ballot box) with fraudulent votes. ~*n.* **8.** the raw material or fabric of something. **9.** woollen cloth or fabric. **10.** any general or unspecified substance or accumulation of objects. **11.** stupid or worthless actions, speech, etc. **12.** subject matter, skill, etc.: *he knows his stuff.* **13.** a slang word for **money. 14.** *Sl.* a drug, esp. cannabis. **15.** *Inf.* **do one's stuff.** to do what is expected of one. **16. that's the stuff.** that is what is needed. **17.** *Brit. sl.* a girl or woman considered sexually (esp. in **bit of stuff**). [C14: < OF *estoffe,* < *estoffer* to furnish, of Gmc origin] —ˈ**stuffer** *n.*

stuffed (stʌft) *adj.* **1.** filled with something, esp. (of poultry and other food) filled with stuffing. **2.** (foll. by *up*) (of the nasal passages) blocked with mucus. **3. get stuffed!** *Brit. taboo sl.* an exclamation of contemptuous anger or annoyance against another person.

stuffed shirt *n. Inf.* a pompous person.

stuff gown *n. Brit.* a woollen gown worn by a barrister who has not taken silk.

stuffing (ˈstʌfɪŋ) *n.* **1.** the material with which something is stuffed. **2.** a mixture of ingredients with which poultry, meat, etc., is stuffed before cooking. **3. knock the stuffing out of (someone).** to defeat (someone) utterly.

stuffing box *n.* a small chamber in which packing is compressed around a reciprocating or rotating rod or shaft to form a seal.

stuffy (ˈstʌfɪ) *adj.* **-ier, -iest. 1.** lacking fresh air. **2.** excessively dull, staid, or conventional. **3.** (of the nasal passages) blocked with mucus. —ˈ**stuffily** *adv.* —ˈ**stuffiness** *n.*

stultify (ˈstʌltɪˌfaɪ) *vb.* **-fying, -fied.** (*tr.*) **1.** to make useless, futile, or ineffectual, esp. by routine. **2.** to cause to appear absurd or inconsistent. [C18: < L *stultus* stupid + *facere* to make] —ˌ**stultifi**ˈ**cation** *n.* —ˈ**stultiˌfier** *n.*

stum (stʌm) (in wine-making) ~*n.* **1.** a less common word for **must**[2]. **2.** partly fermented wine added to fermented wine as a preservative. ~*vb.* **stumming, stummed. 3.** to preserve (wine) by adding stum. [C17: < Du. *stom* dumb]

stumble (ˈstʌmbᵊl) *vb.* (*intr.*) **1.** to trip or fall while walking or running. **2.** to walk in an awkward, unsteady, or unsure way. **3.** to make mistakes or hesitate in speech or actions. **4.** (foll. by *across* or *upon*) to come (across) by accident. ~*n.* **5.** a false step, trip, or blunder. **6.** the act of stumbling. [C14: rel. to Norwegian *stumla*, Danish dialect *stumle*] —ˈ**stumbler** *n.* —ˈ**stumbling** *adj.* —ˈ**stumblingly** *adv.*

stumbling block *n.* any impediment or obstacle.

stumer (ˈstjuːmə) *n.* **1.** *Sl.* a forgery or cheat. **2.** *Irish dialect.* a poor bargain. **3.** *Scot.* a stupid person. **4. come a stumer.** *Austral. sl.* to crash financially. [<?]

stump (stʌmp) *n.* **1.** the base of a tree trunk left standing after the tree has been felled or has fallen. **2.** the part of something, such as a tooth, limb, or blade, that remains after a larger part has been removed. **3.** (*often pl.*) *Inf., facetious.* a leg (esp. in **stir one's stumps**). **4.** *Cricket.* any of three upright wooden sticks that, with two bails laid across them, form a wicket (the **stumps**). **5.** Also called: **tortillon.** a short sharply-pointed stick of cork or rolled paper or leather, used in drawing and shading. **6.** a heavy tread or the sound of heavy footsteps. **7.** a platform used by an orator when addressing a meeting. ~*vb.* **8.** (*tr.*) to stop, confuse, or puzzle. **9.** (*intr.*) to plod or trudge heavily. **10.** (*tr.*) *Cricket.* to dismiss (a batsman) by breaking his wicket with the ball or with the ball in the hand while he is out of his crease. **11.** *Chiefly U.S. & Canad.* to campaign or canvass (an area), esp. by political speech-making. [C14: < MLow G *stump*] —ˈ**stumper** *n.*

stump up *vb.* (*adv.*) *Brit. inf.* to give (the money required).

stumpy (ˈstʌmpɪ) *adj.* **stumpier, stumpiest. 1.** short and thickset like a stump; stubby. **2.** full of stumps. —ˈ**stumpiness** *n.*

stun (stʌn) *vb.* **stunning, stunned.** (*tr.*) **1.** to render unconscious, as by a heavy blow or fall. **2.** to shock or overwhelm. **3.** to surprise or astound. ~*n.* **4.** the state or effect of being stunned. [C13 *stunen*, < OF *estoner* to daze, ult. < L EX-[1] + *tonāre* to thunder]

stung (stʌŋ) *vb.* the past tense and past participle of **sting.**

stunk (stʌŋk) *vb.* a past tense and past participle of **stink.**

stunner (ˈstʌnə) *n. Inf.* a person or thing of great beauty, quality, size, etc.

stunning (ˈstʌnɪŋ) *adj. Inf.* very attractive, impressive, astonishing, etc. —ˈ**stunningly** *adv.*

stunsail *or* **stuns'l** (ˈstʌnsᵊl) *n.* another word for **studdingsail.**

stunt[1] (stʌnt) *vb.* **1.** (*tr.*) to prevent or impede (the growth or development) of (a plant, animal, etc.). ~*n.* **2.** the act or an instance of stunting. **3.** a person, animal, or plant that has been stunted. [C17 (as vb.: to check the growth of): ? < C15 *stont* of short duration, < OE *stunt* foolish; sense prob. infl. by ON *stuttr* dwarfed] —ˈ**stunted** *adj.* —ˈ**stuntedness** *n.*

stunt[2] (stʌnt) *n.* **1.** a feat of daring or skill. **2. a.** an acrobatic or dangerous piece of action in a film, etc. **b.** (*as modifier*): *a stunt man.* **3.** anything spectacular or unusual done for attention. ~*vb.* **4.** (*intr.*) to perform a stunt or stunts. [C19: U.S. student slang, <?]

stupa (ˈstuːpə) *n.* a domed edifice housing Buddhist or Jain relics. [C19: < Sansk.: dome]

stupe (stjuːp) *n. Med.* a hot damp cloth, usually sprinkled with an irritant, applied to the body to relieve pain by counterirritation. [C14: < L *stuppa* flax, < Gk *stuppē*]

stupefacient (ˌstjuːpɪˈfeɪʃɪənt) *n.* **1.** a drug that causes stupor. ~*adj.* **2.** of, relating to, or designating this type of drug. [C17: < L *stupefaciēns*, < *stupēre* to be stunned + *facere* to make]

stupefaction (ˌstjuːpɪˈfækʃən) *n.* **1.** astonishment. **2.** the act of stupefying or the state of being stupefied.

stupefy (ˈstjuːpɪˌfaɪ) *vb.* **-fying, -fied.** (*tr.*) **1.** to render insensitive or lethargic. **2.** to confuse or astound. [C16: < OF *stupefier*, < L *stupefacere*; see STUPEFACIENT] —ˈ**stupeˌfying** *adj.*

stupendous (stjuːˈpɛndəs) *adj.* astounding, wonderful, huge, etc. [C17: < L *stupēre* to be amazed] —**stuˈpendously** *adv.* —**stuˈpendousness** *n.*

stupid (ˈstjuːpɪd) *adj.* **1.** lacking in common sense, perception, or intelligence. **2.** (*usually postpositive*) dazed or stupefied: *stupid from lack of sleep.* **3.** slow-witted. **4.** trivial, silly, or frivolous. ~*n.* **5.** *Inf.* a stupid person. [C16: < F *stupide*, < L *stupidus* silly, < *stupēre* to be amazed] —**stuˈpidity** *or* ˈ**stupidness** *n.*

stupor (ˈstjuːpə) *n.* **1.** a state of unconsciousness. **2.** mental dullness; torpor. [C17: < L, < *stupēre* to be aghast] —ˈ**stuporous** *adj.*

sturdy (ˈstɜːdɪ) *adj.* **-dier, -diest. 1.** healthy, strong, and vigorous. **2.** strongly built; stalwart. [C13 (in the sense: rash, harsh): < OF *estordi* dazed, < *estordir* to stun] —ˈ**sturdily** *adv.* —ˈ**sturdiness** *n.*

sturgeon (ˈstɜːdʒən) *n.* any of various primitive bony fishes of temperate waters of the N hemisphere, having an elongated snout and rows of spines along the body. [C13: < OF *estourgeon*, of Gmc origin]

Sturt's desert pea (stɜːts) *n.* another name for **desert pea.**

stutter (ˈstʌtə) *vb.* **1.** to speak (a word, phrase, etc.) with recurring repetition of consonants, esp. initial ones. **2.** to make (an abrupt sound) repeatedly: *the gun stuttered.* ~*n.* **3.** the act or habit of stuttering. **4.** a stuttering sound. [C16] —ˈ**stutterer** *n.* —ˈ**stuttering** *n., adj.* —ˈ**stutteringly** *adv.*

sty[1] (staɪ) *n., pl.* **sties. 1.** a pen in which pigs are housed. **2.** any filthy or corrupt place. ~*vb.* **stying, stied. 3.** to enclose or be enclosed in a sty. [OE *stig*]

sty[2] *or* **stye** (staɪ) *n., pl.* **sties** *or* **styes.** inflammation of a sebaceous gland of the eyelid. [C15 *styanye* (mistaken as *sty on eye*), < OE *stīgend* rising, hence swelling, + *ye* eye]

Stygian (ˈstɪdʒɪən) *adj.* **1.** of or relating to the Styx, a river in Hades. **2.** *Chiefly literary.* dark, gloomy, or hellish. [C16: < L *Stygius*, < Gk *Stugios*, < *Stux* Styx]

style (staɪl) *n.* **1.** a form of appearance, design, or production; type or make. **2.** the way in which something is done: *good style.* **3.** the manner in which something is expressed or performed, considered as separate from its intrinsic content, meaning, etc. **4.** a distinctive, formal, or characteristic manner of expression in words, music, painting, etc. **5.** elegance or refinement of manners, dress, etc. **6.** prevailing fashion in dress, looks, etc. **7.** a fashionable or ostentatious mode of existence: *to live in style.* **8.** the particular mode of orthography, punctuation, design, etc., followed in a book, journal, etc., or in a printing or publishing house. **9.** *Chiefly Brit.* the distinguishing title or form of address of a person or firm. **10.** *Bot.* the long slender extension of the ovary, bearing the stigma. **11.** a method of expressing or calculating dates. See **Old Style, New Style. 12.** another word for **stylus** (sense 1). **13.** the arm of a sundial. ~*vb.* (*mainly tr.*) **14.** to design, shape, or tailor: *to style hair.* **15.** to adapt or make suitable for. **16.** to make consistent or correct according to a printing or publishing style. **17.** to name or call; designate: *to style a man a fool.* [C13: < L *stylus*, *stilus* writing implement, hence characteristics of the writing, style] —ˈ**stylar** *adj.* —ˈ**styler** *n.*

stylebook (ˈstaɪlˌbʊk) *n.* a book containing rules and examples of punctuation, typography, etc., for the use of writers, editors, and printers.

stylet (ˈstaɪlɪt) *n. Surgery.* **1.** a wire for insertion into a catheter, etc., to maintain its rigidity during passage. **2.** a slender probe. [C17: < F *stilet*, < OIt. STILETTO; infl. by L *stylus* style]

styling mousse *n.* a light foamy substance applied to the hair before styling in order to retain the style.

stylish (ˈstaɪlɪʃ) *adj.* having style; smart; fashionable. —ˈ**stylishly** *adv.* —ˈ**stylishness** *n.*

stylist (ˈstaɪlɪst) *n.* **1.** a person who performs, writes, or acts with attention to style. **2.** a designer of clothes, décor, etc. **3.** a hairdresser who styles hair.

stylistic (staɪˈlɪstɪk) *adj.* of or relating to style, esp. artistic or literary style. —**styˈlistically** *adv.*

stylite (ˈstaɪlaɪt) *n. Christianity.* one of a class of recluses who in ancient times lived on the top of high pillars. [C17: < LGk *stulitēs*, < Gk *stulos* a pillar] —**stylitic** (staɪˈlɪtɪk) *adj.*

stylize *or* **-ise** (ˈstaɪlaɪz) *vb.* (*tr.*) to give a conventional or established stylistic form to. —ˌ**styliˈzation** *or* **-iˈsation** *n.*

stylo- *or before a vowel* **styl-** *combining form.* **1.** (in biology) a style. **2.** indicating a column or point: *stylobate; stylograph.* [< Gk *stulos* column]

stylobate (ˈstaɪləˌbeɪt) *n.* a continuous horizontal course of masonry that supports a colonnade. [C17: < L *stylobatēs*, < Gk *stulos* pillar + *-batēs*, < *bainein* to walk]

stylograph (ˈstaɪləˌgrɑːf) *n.* a fountain pen having a fine hollow tube as the writing point instead of a nib. [C19: < STYL(US) + -GRAPH]

styloid (ˈstaɪlɔɪd) *adj.* **1.** resembling a stylus. **2.** *Anat.* of or relating to a projecting process of the temporal bone. [C18: < NL *styloides*, < Gk *stuloeidēs* like a stylus; infl. by Gk *stulos* pillar]

stylops (ˈstaɪlɒps) *n., pl.* **-lopes** (-ləˌpiːz). any of various insects living as a parasite in other insects, esp. bees and wasps. [C19: NL, < Gk, < *stulos* a pillar + *ōps* an eye, from the fact that the male has stalked eyes]

stylus (ˈstaɪləs) *n., pl.* **-li** (-laɪ) *or* **-luses.** **1.** Also called: **style.** a pointed instrument for engraving, drawing, or writing. **2.** a tool used in ancient times for writing on wax tablets, which was pointed at one end and blunt at the other for erasing. **3.** a device attached to the cartridge in the pick-up arm of a record player that rests in the groove in the record, transmitting the vibrations to the sensing device in the cartridge. [C18: < L, var. of *stilus* writing implement]

stymie *or* **stymy** (ˈstaɪmɪ) *vb.* **-mieing, -mied** *or* **-mying, -mied.** (*tr.; often passive*) **1.** to hinder or thwart. **2.** *Golf.* to impede with a stymie. ~*n., pl.* **-mies.** **3.** *Golf.* (formerly) a situation in which an opponent's ball is blocking the line between the hole and the ball about to be played. **4.** a situation of obstruction. [C19: <?]

styptic (ˈstɪptɪk) *adj.* **1.** contracting the blood vessels or tissues. ~*n.* **2.** a styptic drug. [C14: via LL, < Gk *stuptikos* capable of contracting, < *stuphein* to contract]

styrene (ˈstaɪriːn) *n.* a colourless oily volatile flammable liquid made from ethylene and benzene. It readily polymerizes and is used in making synthetic plastics and rubbers. [C20: < Gk *sturax* tree of the genus *Styrax* + -ENE]

suable (ˈsjuːəbᵊl) *adj.* liable to be sued in a court. —ˌ**suaˈbility** *n.*

suasion (ˈsweɪʒən) *n.* a rare word for **persuasion.** [C14: < L *suāsiō*, < *suādēre* to PERSUADE] —ˈ**suasive** *adj.*

suave (swɑːv) *adj.* (esp. of a man) displaying smoothness and sophistication in manner; urbane. [C16: < L *suāvis* sweet] —ˈ**suavely** *adv.* —**suavity** (ˈswɑːvɪtɪ) *or* ˈ**suaveness** *n.*

sub (sʌb) *n.* **1.** short for several words beginning with *sub-*, such as **subeditor, submarine, subordinate, subscription,** and **substitute.** **2.** *Brit. inf.* an advance payment of wages or salary. Formal term: **subsistence allowance.** ~*vb.* **subbing, subbed.** **3.** (*intr.*) to serve or act as a substitute. **4.** *Brit. inf.* to grant or receive (an advance payment of wages or salary). **5.** (*tr.*) *Inf.* short for **subedit.**

sub. *abbrev. for:* **1.** subeditor. **2.** *Music.* subito. **3.** subscription. **4.** substitute.

sub- *prefix.* **1.** situated under or beneath: *subterranean.* **2.** secondary in rank; subordinate: *subeditor.* **3.** falling short of; less than or imperfectly: *subarctic; subhuman.* **4.** forming a subdivision or subordinate part: *subcommittee.* **5.** (in chemistry) **a.** indicating that a compound contains a relatively small proportion of a specified element: *suboxide.* **b.** indicating that a salt is basic salt: *subacetate.* [< L *sub*]

subacid (sʌbˈæsɪd) *adj.* (esp. of some fruits) moderately acid or sour. —**subacidity** (ˌsʌbəˈsɪdɪtɪ) *or* **subˈacidness** *n.*

subadar *or* **subahdar** (ˈsuːbəˌdɑː) *n.* (formerly) the chief native officer of a company of Indian soldiers in the British service. [C17: via Urdu < Persian, < *sūba* province + *-dār* holding]

subalpine (sʌbˈælpaɪn) *adj.* **1.** situated in or relating to the regions at the foot of mountains. **2.** (of plants) growing below the tree line in mountainous regions.

subaltern (ˈsʌbᵊltən) *n.* **1.** a commissioned officer below the rank of captain in certain armies, esp. the British. ~*adj.* **2.** of inferior position or rank. **3.** *Logic.* (of a proposition) particular, esp. in relation to a universal of the same quality. [C16: < LL *subalternus*, < L SUB- + *alternus* alternate, < *alter* the other]

subalternation (ˌsʌbɔːltəˈneɪʃən) *n. Logic.* the relation between a universal and a particular proposition of the same quality where the universal proposition implies the particular proposition.

subantarctic (ˌsʌbæntˈɑːktɪk) *adj.* of or relating to latitudes immediately north of the Antarctic Circle.

subaqua (ˌsʌbˈækwə) *adj.* of or relating to underwater sport: *subaqua swimming.*

subaqueous (sʌbˈeɪkwɪəs, -ˈækwɪ-) *adj.* occurring, formed, or used under water.

subarctic (sʌbˈɑːktɪk) *adj.* of or relating to latitudes immediately south of the Arctic Circle.

subatomic (ˌsʌbəˈtɒmɪk) *adj.* **1.** of, relating to, or being a particle making up an atom or a process occurring within atoms. **2.** having dimensions smaller than atomic dimensions.

subbasement (ˈsʌbˌbeɪsmənt) *n.* a storey of a building beneath the main basement.

subclass (ˈsʌbˌklɑːs) *n.* **1.** a principal subdivision of a class. **2.** *Biol.* a taxonomic group that is a subdivision of a class. **3.** *Maths.* another name for **subset.**

subclavian (sʌbˈkleɪvɪən) *adj. Anat.* (of an artery, vein, etc.) below the clavicle. [C17: < NL *subclāvius*, < L SUB- + *clavis* key]

subclinical (sʌbˈklɪnɪkᵊl) *adj. Med.* of or relating to the stage in the course of a disease before the symptoms are first noted. —**subˈclinically** *adv.*

subconscious (sʌbˈkɒnʃəs) *adj.* **1.** acting or existing without one's awareness. ~*n.* **2.** *Psychol.* that part of the mind on the fringe of consciousness which contains material it is possible to become aware of by redirecting attention. —**subˈconsciously** *adv.* —**subˈconsciousness** *n.*

subcontinent (sʌbˈkɒntɪnənt) *n.* a large land mass that is a distinct part of a continent, such as India is of Asia. —**subcontinental** (ˌsʌbkɒntɪˈnɛntᵊl) *adj.*

subcontract *n.* (sʌbˈkɒntrækt). **1.** a subordinate contract under which the supply of materials, labour, etc. is let out to someone other than a party to the main contract. ~*vb.* (ˌsʌbkənˈtrækt). **2.** (*intr.; often foll. by for*) to enter into or

---

ˌ**subabˈdominal** *adj.*
ˌ**subaˈcute** *adj.*
subˈagent *n.*
ˌ**subaˈquatic** *adj.*
ˈ**subˌarticle** *n.*
subˈaverage *adj.*
ˌ**subaxˈillary** *adj.*
ˈ**subˌbranch** *n.*
subˈcategory *n.*
ˈ**subˌcell** *n.*
ˈ**subˌchapter** *n.*
ˈ**subˌchief** *n.*
ˌ**subclassifiˈcation** *n.*
subˈclassiˌfy *vb.*
ˈ**subˌclause** *n.*
ˈ**subcomˌmission** *n.*
ˌ**subcomˈmissioner** *n.*
ˈ**subcomˌmittee** *n.*

make a subcontract. **3.** (*tr.*) to let out (work) on a subcontract. —ˌ**subconˈtractor** *n.*

subcontrary (sʌbˈkɒntrərɪ) *Logic.* ~*adj.* **1.** (of a pair of propositions) related such that they cannot both be false at once, although they may be true together. ~*n., pl.* **-ries. 2.** a statement which cannot be false when a given statement is false.

subcritical (sʌbˈkrɪtɪkᵊl) *adj. Physics.* (of a nuclear reaction, power station, etc.) having or involving a chain reaction that is not self-sustaining; not yet critical.

subculture (ˈsʌbˌkʌltʃə) *n.* a subdivision of a national culture or an enclave within it with a distinct integrated network of behaviour, beliefs, and attitudes. —**subˈcultural** *adj.*

subcutaneous (ˌsʌbkjuːˈteɪnɪəs) *adj. Med.* situated, used, or introduced beneath the skin. —ˌ**subcuˈtaneously** *adv.*

subdeacon (ˌsʌbˈdiːkən) *n. Chiefly R.C. Church.* **1.** a cleric who assists at High Mass. **2.** (formerly) a person ordained to the lowest of the major orders. —**subdeaconate** (sʌbˈdiːkənɪt) *n.*

subdivide (ˌsʌbdɪˈvaɪd, ˈsʌbdɪˌvaɪd) *vb.* to divide (something) resulting from an earlier division. —ˈ**subdiˌvision** *n.*

subdominant (sʌbˈdɒmɪnənt) *Music.* ~*n.* **1.** the fourth degree of a major or minor scale. **2.** a key or chord based on this. ~*adj.* **3.** of or relating to the subdominant.

subdue (səbˈdjuː) *vb.* **-duing, -dued.** (*tr.*) **1.** to establish ascendancy over by force. **2.** to overcome and bring under control, as by intimidation or persuasion. **3.** to hold in check or repress (feelings, etc.). **4.** to render less intense or less conspicuous. [C14 *sobdue,* < OF *soduire* to mislead, < L *subdūcere* to remove; infl. by L *subdere* to subject] —**subˈduable** *adj.* —**subˈdual** *n.*

subdued (səbˈdjuːd) *adj.* **1.** cowed, passive, or shy. **2.** gentle or quiet: *a subdued whisper.* **3.** (of colours, lighting, etc.) not harsh or bright.

subedit (sʌbˈɛdɪt) *vb.* to edit and correct (written or printed material).

subeditor (sʌbˈɛdɪtə) *n.* a person who checks and edits copy, esp. on a newspaper.

subequatorial (sʌbˌɛkwəˈtɔːrɪəl) *adj.* in or characteristic of regions immediately north or south of equatorial regions.

suberose (ˈsjuːbəˌrəʊs), **subereous** (sjuːˈbɛrɪəs), *or* **suberic** (sjuːˈbɛrɪk) *adj. Bot.* relating to, resembling, or consisting of cork; corky. [C19: < L *sūber* cork + -OSE[1]]

subfamily (ˈsʌbˌfæmɪlɪ) *n., pl.* **-lies. 1.** *Biol.* a taxonomic group that is a subdivision of a family. **2.** a subdivision of a family of languages.

subfusc (ˈsʌbfʌsk) *adj.* **1.** devoid of brightness or appeal; drab, dull, or dark. ~*n.* **2.** (at Oxford University) formal academic dress. [C18: < L *subfuscus* dusky, < *fuscus* dark]

subgenus (ˈsʌbˌdʒiːnəs, -ˌdʒɛn-) *n., pl.* **-genera** (-ˌdʒɛnərə) *or* **-genuses.** *Biol.* a subdivision of a genus that is of higher rank than a species. —**subgeneric** (ˌsʌbdʒəˈnɛrɪk) *adj.*

subheading (ˈsʌbˌhɛdɪŋ) *or* **subhead** *n.* **1.** the heading or title of a subdivision or subsection of a printed work. **2.** a division subordinate to a main heading or title.

subhuman (sʌbˈhjuːmən) *adj.* **1.** of or designating animals below man (*Homo sapiens*) in evolutionary development. **2.** less than human.

subindex (sʌbˈɪndɛks) *n., pl.* **-dices** (-dɪˌsiːz) *or* **-dexes.** another word for **subscript** (sense 2).

subito (ˈsuːbɪˌtəʊ) *adv. Music.* suddenly; immediately. [C18: via It. < L: suddenly, < *subitus* sudden, < *subīre* to approach]

subj. *abbrev. for:* **1.** subject. **2.** subjective(ly). **3.** subjunctive.

subjacent (sʌbˈdʒeɪsᵊnt) *adj.* **1.** forming a foundation; underlying. **2.** lower than. [C16: < L *subjacēre* to lie close, be under] —**subˈjacency** *n.* —**subˈjacently** *adv.*

subject *n.* (ˈsʌbdʒɪkt). **1.** the predominant theme or topic, as of a book, discussion, etc. **2.** any branch of learning considered as a course of study. **3.** *Grammar, logic.* a word, phrase, etc., about which something is predicated or stated in a sentence; for example, *the cat* in the sentence *The cat catches mice.* **4.** a person or thing that undergoes experiment, treatment, etc. **5.** a person under the rule of a monarch, government, etc. **6.** an object, figure, scene, etc., as portrayed by an artist or photographer. **7.** *Philosophy.* **a.** that which thinks or feels as opposed to the object of thinking and feeling; the self or the mind. **b.** a substance as opposed to its attributes. **8.** Also called: **theme.** *Music.* the principal motif of a fugue, the basis from which the musical material is derived in a sonata-form movement, or the recurrent figure in a rondo. **9.** *Logic.* the term of a proposition about which something is asserted. **10.** an originating motive. **11. change the subject.** to select a new topic of conversation. ~*adj.* (ˈsʌbdʒɪkt). (*usually postpositive;* foll. by *to*) **12.** being under the power or sovereignty of a ruler, government, etc.: *subject peoples.* **13.** showing a tendency (towards): *a child subject to indiscipline.* **14.** exposed or vulnerable: *subject to ribaldry.* **15.** conditional upon: *the results are subject to correction.* ~*adv.* (ˈsʌbdʒɪkt). **16. subject to.** (*prep.*) under the condition that: *we accept, subject to her agreement.* ~*vb.* (səbˈdʒɛkt). (*tr.*) **17.** (foll. by *to*) to cause to undergo: *they subjected him to torture.* **18.** (*often passive;* foll. by *to*) to expose or render vulnerable or liable (to some experience): *he was subjected to great danger.* **19.** (foll. by *to*) to bring under the control or authority (of): *to subject a soldier to discipline.* **20.** *Rare.* to present for consideration; submit. [C14: < L *subjectus* brought under, < *subicere* to place under, < SUB- + *jacere* to throw] —**subˈjectable** *adj.* —**subˈjection** *n.*

subjective (səbˈdʒɛktɪv) *adj.* **1.** of, proceeding from, or relating to the mind of the thinking subject and not the nature of the object being considered. **2.** of, relating to, or emanating from a person's emotions, prejudices, etc. **3.** relating to the inherent nature of a person or thing; essential. **4.** existing only as perceived and not as a thing in itself. **5.** *Med.* (of a symptom, condition, etc.) experienced only by the patient and incapable of being recognized or studied by anyone else. **6.** *Grammar.* denoting a case of nouns and pronouns, esp. in languages having only two cases, that identifies the subject of a finite verb and (in formal use in English) is selected for predicate complements, as in *It is I.* ~*n.* **7.** *Grammar.* **a.** the subjective case. **b.** a subjective word or speech element. Cf. **objective.** —**subˈjectively** *adv.* —ˌ**subjecˈtivity** *or* **subˈjectiveness** *n.*

subjectivism (səbˈdʒɛktɪˌvɪzəm) *n. Philosophy.* the doctrine that there are no absolute moral values but that these are variable in the same way that taste is. —**subˈjectivist** *n.*

subjoin (sʌbˈdʒɔɪn) *vb.* (*tr.*) to add or attach at the end of something spoken, written, etc. [C16: < F *subjoindre,* < L *subjungere* to add to, < *sub-* in addition + *jungere* to join] —**subˈjoinder** *n.*

sub judice (ˈdʒuːdɪsɪ) *adj.* (*usually postpositive*) before a court of law or a judge; under judicial consideration. [L]

subjugate (ˈsʌbdʒʊˌgeɪt) *vb.* (*tr.*) **1.** to bring into subjection. **2.** to make subservient or submissive. [C15: < LL *subjugāre* to subdue, < L SUB- + *jugum* yoke] —**subjugable** (ˈsʌbdʒəgəbᵊl) *adj.* —ˌ**subjuˈgation** *n.* —ˈ**subjuˌgator** *n.*

subjunctive (səbˈdʒʌŋktɪv) *Grammar.* ~*adj.* **1.** denoting a mood of verbs used when the content of the clause is being doubted, supposed, feared true, etc., rather than being asserted. In the

---

subˈcranial *adj.*
ˈ**subˌdepot** *n.*
subˈentry *n.*
ˈ**subˌfile** *n.*
ˈ**subˌfloor** *n.*
subˈforeman *n.*
subˈfreezing *adj.*
ˈ**subˌfunction** *n.*
ˈ**subˌgroup** *n.*

following sentence, *were* is in the subjunctive: *I'd think seriously about it if I were you.* Cf. **indicative.** ~*n.* **2. a.** the subjunctive mood. **b.** a verb in this mood. [C16: via LL *subjunctīvus,* < L *subjungere* to SUBJOIN] —**sub'junctively** *adv.*

sublease *n.* ('sʌbˌliːs). **1.** a lease of property made by a lessee or tenant of that property. ~*vb.* (sʌb'liːs). **2.** to grant a sublease of (property); sublet. **3.** (*tr.*) to obtain or hold by sublease. —**sublessee** (ˌsʌblɛ'siː) *n.* —**sublessor** (ˌsʌblɛ'sɔː) *n.*

sublet (sʌb'lɛt) *vb.* **-letting, -let. 1.** to grant a sublease of (property). **2.** to let out (work, etc.) under a subcontract.

sublieutenant (ˌsʌblə'tɛnənt) *n.* the most junior commissioned officer in the Royal Navy and certain other navies. —ˌ**sublieu'tenancy** *n.*

sublimate ('sʌblɪˌmeɪt) *vb.* **1.** *Psychol.* to direct the energy of (a primitive impulse) into activities that are socially more acceptable. **2.** (*tr.*) to make purer; refine. ~*n.* **3.** *Chem.* the material obtained when a substance is sublimed. [C16: < L *sublīmāre* to elevate, < *sublīmis* lofty; see SUBLIME] —ˌ**subli'mation** *n.*

sublime (sə'blaɪm) *adj.* **1.** of high moral, intellectual, or spiritual value; noble; exalted. **2.** inspiring deep veneration or awe. **3.** unparalleled; supreme. **4.** *Poetic.* of proud bearing or aspect. **5.** *Arch.* raised up. ~*n.* **the sublime. 6.** something that is sublime. **7.** the ultimate degree or perfect example: *the sublime of folly.* ~*vb.* **8.** (*tr.*) to make higher or purer. **9.** to change or cause to change directly from a solid to a vapour or gas without first melting. **10.** to undergo or cause to undergo this process followed by a reverse change directly from a vapour to a solid: *to sublime iodine onto glass.* [C14: < L *sublīmis* lofty, ? < *sub-* up to + *līmen* lintel] —**sub'limely** *adv.* —**sublimity** (sə'blɪmɪtɪ) *n.*

subliminal (sʌb'lɪmɪnᵊl) *adj.* **1.** resulting from processes of which the individual is not aware. **2.** (of stimuli) less than the minimum intensity or duration required to elicit a response. [C19: < L *sub-* below + *līmen* threshold] —**sub'liminally** *adv.*

subliminal advertising *n.* advertising on film or television that employs subliminal images to influence the viewer unconsciously.

sublingual (sʌb'lɪŋgwəl) *adj. Anat.* situated beneath the tongue.

sublunary (sʌb'luːnərɪ) *adj.* **1.** between the moon and the earth. **2.** of or relating to the earth. [C16: via LL, < L SUB- + *lūna* moon]

sub-machine-gun *n.* a portable automatic or semiautomatic light gun with a short barrel, designed to be fired from the hip or shoulder.

submarginal (sʌb'mɑːdʒɪnᵊl) *adj.* **1.** below the minimum requirements. **2.** (of land) infertile and unprofitable. —**sub'marginally** *adv.*

submarine ('sʌbməˌriːn, ˌsʌbmə'riːn) *n.* **1.** a vessel, esp. a warship, capable of operating below the surface of the sea. **2.** (*modifier*) **a.** of or relating to a submarine: *a submarine captain.* **b.** below the surface of the sea: *a submarine cable.* —**submariner** (sʌb'mærɪnə) *n.*

submaxillary gland (ˌsʌbmæk'sɪlərɪ) *n.* (in mammals) either of a pair of salivary glands situated on each side behind the lower jaw.

submediant (sʌb'miːdɪənt) *Music.* ~*n.* **1.** the sixth degree of a major or minor scale. **2.** a key or chord based on this. ~*adj.* **3.** of or relating to the submediant.

submerge (səb'mɜːdʒ) *or* **submerse** (səb'mɜːs) *vb.* **1.** to plunge, sink, or dive or cause to plunge, sink, or dive below the surface of water, etc. **2.** (*tr.*) to cover with water or other liquid. **3.** (*tr.*) to hide; suppress. **4.** (*tr.*) to overwhelm, as with work, etc. [C17: < L *submergere*] —**sub'mergence** *or* **sub'mersion** *n.*

submersible (səb'mɜːsɪbᵊl) *or* **submergible** (səb'mɜːdʒɪbᵊl) *adj.* **1.** able to be submerged. **2.** capable of operating under water, etc. ~*n.* **3.** a vessel designed to operate under water for short periods. **4.** a submarine designed and equipped to carry out work below the level that divers can work. —**subˌmersi'bility** *or* **subˌmergi'bility** *n.*

subminiature (sʌb'mɪnɪətʃə) *adj.* smaller than miniature.

subminiature camera *n.* a pocket-sized camera, usually using 16 millimetre film.

submission (səb'mɪʃən) *n.* **1.** an act or instance of submitting. **2.** something submitted; a proposal, etc. **3.** the quality or condition of being submissive. **4.** the act of referring a document, etc., for the consideration of someone else.

submissive (səb'mɪsɪv) *adj.* of, tending towards, or indicating submission, humility, or servility. —**sub'missively** *adv.* —**sub'missiveness** *n.*

submit (səb'mɪt) *vb.* **-mitting, -mitted. 1.** (often foll. by *to*) to yield (oneself), as to the will of another person, a superior force, etc. **2.** (foll. by *to*) to subject or be voluntarily subjected (to analysis, treatment, etc.). **3.** (*tr.;* often foll. by *to*) to refer (something to someone) for judgment or consideration. **4.** (*tr.; may take a clause as object*) to state, contend, or propose deferentially. **5.** (*intr.;* often foll. by *to*) to defer or accede (to the decision, etc., of another). [C14: < L *submittere* to place under] —**sub'mittable** *or* **sub'missible** *adj.* —**sub'mittal** *n.* —**sub'mitter** *n.*

submultiple (sʌb'mʌltɪpᵊl) *n.* **1.** a number that can be divided into another number an integral number of times without a remainder: *three is a submultiple of nine.* ~*adj.* **2.** being a submultiple of a quantity or number.

subnormal (sʌb'nɔːməl) *adj.* **1.** less than the normal. **2.** having a low intelligence. ~*n.* **3.** a subnormal person. —**subnormality** (ˌsʌbnɔː'mælɪtɪ) *n.*

subnuclear (sʌb'njuːklɪə) *adj.* in or smaller than the nucleus of an atom.

suborbital (sʌb'ɔːbɪtᵊl) *adj.* **1.** (of a rocket, missile, etc.) having a flight path that is less than an orbit of the earth or other celestial body. **2.** *Anat.* situated beneath the orbit of the eye.

suborder ('sʌbˌɔːdə) *n. Biol.* a subdivision of an order. —**sub'ordinal** *adj.*

subordinate *adj.* (sə'bɔːdɪnɪt). **1.** of lesser order or importance. **2.** under the authority or control of another: *a subordinate functionary.* ~*n.* (sə'bɔːdɪnɪt). **3.** a person or thing that is subordinate. ~*vb.* (sə'bɔːdɪˌneɪt). (*tr.;* usually foll. by *to*) **4.** to put in a lower rank or position (than). **5.** to make subservient: *to subordinate mind to heart.* [C15: < Med. L *subordināre,* < L SUB- + *ordō* rank] —**sub'ordinately** *adv.* —**subˌordi'nation** *n.* —**sub'ordinative** *adj.*

subordinate clause *n. Grammar.* a clause with an adjectival, adverbial, or nominal function, rather than one that functions as a separate sentence in its own right.

subordinating conjunction *n.* a conjunction that introduces subordinate clauses, such as *if, because, although,* and *until.*

suborn (sə'bɔːn) *vb.* (*tr.*) **1.** to bribe, incite, or instigate (a person) to commit a wrongful act. **2.** *Law.* to induce (a witness) to commit perjury. [C16: < L *subornāre,* < *sub-* secretly + *ornāre* to furnish] —**subornation** (ˌsʌbɔː'neɪʃən) *n.* —**subornative** (sʌ'bɔːnətɪv) *adj.* —**sub'orner** *n.*

suboxide (sʌb'ɒksaɪd) *n.* an oxide of an element containing less oxygen than the common oxide formed by the element: *carbon suboxide,* C_3O_2.

subplot ('sʌbˌplɒt) *n.* a subordinate or auxiliary plot in a novel, play, film, etc.

subpoena (səb'piːnə) *n.* **1.** a writ issued by a court of justice requiring a person to appear before the court at a specified time. ~*vb.* **-naing, -naed. 2.** (*tr.*) to serve with a subpoena. [C15: < L: under penalty]

subrogate ('sʌbrəˌgeɪt) *vb.* (*tr.*) *Law.* to put (one person or thing) in the place of another in respect

---

ˌ**submicro'scopic** *adj.*
ˌ**submo'lecular** *adj.*
sub'paraˌgraph *n.*
sub'phylum *n.*
sub'region *n.*

of a right or claim. [C16: < L *subrogāre,* < *sub-* in place of + *rogāre* to ask] —ˌ**subro'gation** *n.*

sub rosa ('rəʊzə) *adv.* in secret. [L, lit.: under the rose; < use of the rose in ancient times as a token of secrecy]

subroutine ('sʌbruːˌtiːn) *n.* a section of a computer program that is stored only once but can be used at several different points in the program. Also called: **procedure.**

subscribe (səb'skraɪb) *vb.* **1.** (usually foll. by *to*) to pay or promise to pay (money) as a contribution (to a fund, for a magazine, etc.), esp. at regular intervals. **2.** to sign (one's name, etc.) at the end of a document. **3.** (*intr.;* foll. by *to*) to give support or approval: *to subscribe to the theory of reincarnation.* [C15: < L *subscrībere* to write underneath] —**sub'scriber** *n.*

subscriber trunk dialling *n. Brit.* a service by which telephone subscribers can obtain trunk calls by dialling direct without the aid of an operator. Abbrev.: **STD.**

subscript ('sʌbskrɪpt) *adj.* **1.** *Printing.* (of a character) written or printed below the base line. Cf. **superscript.** ~*n.* **2.** Also called: **subindex.** a subscript character.

subscription (səb'skrɪpʃən) *n.* **1.** a payment or promise of payment for consecutive issues of a magazine, newspaper, book, etc., over a specified period of time. **2. a.** the advance purchase of tickets for a series of concerts, etc. **b.** (*as modifier*): *a subscription concert.* **3.** money paid or promised, as to a charity, or the fund raised in this way. **4.** an offer to buy shares or bonds issued by a company. **5.** the act of signing one's name to a document, etc. **6.** a signature or other appendage attached to the bottom of a document, etc. **7.** agreement or acceptance expressed by or as if by signing one's name. **8.** a signed document, statement, etc. **9.** *Chiefly Brit.* the membership dues or fees paid to a society or club. **10.** an advance order for a new product. **11. a.** the sale of books, etc., prior to publishing. **b.** (*as modifier*): *a subscription edition.* —**sub'scriptive** *adj.* —**sub'scriptively** *adv.*

subsequence ('sʌbsɪkwəns) *n.* **1.** the fact or state of being subsequent. **2.** a subsequent incident or occurrence.

subsequent ('sʌbsɪkwənt) *adj.* occurring after; succeeding. [C15: < L *subsequēns* following on, < *subsequī,* < *sub-* near + *sequī* to follow] —'**subsequently** *adv.* —'**subsequentness** *n.*

subserve (səb'sɜːv) *vb.* (*tr.*) to be helpful or useful to. [C17: < L *subservīre* to be subject to, < SUB- + *servīre* to serve]

subservient (səb'sɜːvɪənt) *adj.* **1.** obsequious. **2.** serving as a means to an end. **3.** a less common word for **subordinate** (sense 2). [C17: < L *subserviēns* complying with, < *subservīre* to SUBSERVE] —**sub'serviently** *adv.* —**sub'servience** *or* **sub'serviency** *n.*

subset ('sʌbˌsɛt) *n.* a mathematical set contained within a larger set.

subshrub ('sʌbˌʃrʌb) *n.* a small bushy plant that is woody except for the tips of the branches.

subside (səb'saɪd) *vb.* (*intr.*) **1.** to become less loud, excited, violent, etc.; abate. **2.** to sink or fall to a lower level. **3.** (of the surface of the earth, etc.) to cave in; collapse. **4.** (of sediment, etc.) to sink or descend to the bottom; settle. [C17: < L *subsīdere* to settle down] —**sub'sider** *n.*

subsidence (səb'saɪdᵊns, 'sʌbsɪdᵊns) *n.* **1.** the act or process of subsiding or the condition of having subsided. **2.** *Geol.* the gradual sinking of landforms to a lower level.

subsidiary (səb'sɪdɪərɪ) *adj.* **1.** serving to aid or supplement; auxiliary. **2.** of lesser importance; subordinate. ~*n., pl.* **-aries. 3.** a subsidiary person or thing. **4.** Also called: **subsidiary company.** a company with at least half of its capital stock owned by another company. [C16: < L *subsidiārius* supporting, < *subsidium* SUBSIDY] —**sub'sidiarily** *adv.* —**sub'sidiariness** *n.*

subsidize *or* **-ise** ('sʌbsɪˌdaɪz) *vb.* (*tr.*) **1.** to aid or support with a subsidy. **2.** to obtain the aid of by means of a subsidy. —ˌ**subsidi'zation** *or* **-i'sation** *n.* —'**subsiˌdizer** *or* **-iser** *n.*

subsidy ('sʌbsɪdɪ) *n., pl.* **-dies. 1.** a financial aid supplied by a government, as to industry, for public welfare, the balance of payments, etc. **2.** *English history.* a financial grant made originally for special purposes by Parliament to the Crown. **3.** any monetary aid, grant, or contribution. [C14: < Anglo-Norman *subsidie,* < L *subsidium* assistance, < *subsidēre* to remain, < *sub-* down + *sedēre* to sit]

subsist (səb'sɪst) *vb.* (*mainly intr.*) **1.** (often foll. by *on*) to be sustained; manage to live: *to subsist on milk.* **2.** to continue in existence. **3.** (foll. by *in*) to lie or reside by virtue (of); consist. **4.** (*tr.*) *Obs.* to provide with support. [C16: < L *subsistere* to stand firm] —**sub'sistent** *adj.*

subsistence (səb'sɪstəns) *n.* **1.** the means by which one maintains life. **2.** the act or condition of subsisting.

subsistence farming *n.* a type of farming in which most of the produce is consumed by the farmer and his family.

subsistence level *n.* a standard of living barely adequate to support life.

subsoil ('sʌbˌsɔɪl) *n.* **1.** Also called: **undersoil.** the layer of soil beneath the surface soil and overlying the bedrock. ~*vb.* **2.** (*tr.*) to plough (land) to a depth so as to break up the subsoil.

subsonic (sʌb'sɒnɪk) *adj.* being, having, or travelling at a velocity below that of sound.

subspecies ('sʌbˌspiːʃiːz) *n., pl.* **-cies.** *Biol.* a subdivision of a species: usually occurs because of isolation within a species.

substance ('sʌbstəns) *n.* **1.** the tangible basic matter of which a thing consists. **2.** a specific type of matter, esp. a homogeneous material with definite or fairly definite chemical composition. **3.** the essence, meaning, etc., of a discourse, thought, or written article. **4.** solid or meaningful quality: *an education of substance.* **5.** material density or body: *free space has no substance.* **6.** material possessions or wealth: *a man of substance.* **7.** *Philosophy.* the supposed immaterial substratum of anything that can receive modifications and in which attributes and accidents inhere. **8. in substance.** with regard to the salient points. [C13: via OF < L *substantia,* < *substāre,* < SUB- + *stāre* to stand]

substandard (sʌb'stændəd) *adj.* **1.** below an established or required standard. **2.** another word for **nonstandard.**

substantial (səb'stænʃəl) *adj.* **1.** of a considerable size or value: *substantial funds.* **2.** worthwhile; important; telling: *a substantial reform.* **3.** having wealth or importance: *a substantial member of the community.* **4.** (of food or a meal) sufficient and nourishing. **5.** solid or strong: *a substantial door.* **6.** real; actual; true: *substantial evidence.* **7.** of or relating to the basic or fundamental substance or aspects of a thing. ~*n.* **8.** (*often pl.*) *Rare.* an essential or important element. —**substantiality** (səbˌstænʃɪ'ælɪtɪ) *or* **sub'stantialness** *n.* —**sub'stantially** *adv.*

substantialism (səb'stænʃəˌlɪzəm) *n. Philosophy.* the doctrine that a substantial reality underlies phenomena. —**sub'stantialist** *n.*

substantiate (səb'stænʃɪˌeɪt) *vb.* (*tr.*) **1.** to establish as valid or genuine. **2.** to give form or real existence to. [C17: < NL *substantiāre,* < L *substantia* SUBSTANCE] —**subˌstanti'ation** *n.*

substantive ('sʌbstəntɪv) *n.* **1.** *Grammar.* a noun or pronoun used in place of a noun. ~*adj.* **2.** of, relating to, containing, or being the essential element of a thing. **3.** having independent function, resources, or existence. **4.** of substantial quantity. **5.** solid in foundation or basis. **6.**

ˌ**subsatu'ration** *n.*
sub'scapular *adj., n.*
sub'section *n.*
sub'series *n.*

Grammar. denoting, relating to, or standing in place of a noun. **7.** (səbˈstæntɪv). (of a dye or colour) staining the material directly without use of a mordant. [C15: < LL *substantīvus,* < L *substāre* to stand beneath] —**substantival** (ˌsʌbstənˈtaɪvᵊl) *adj.* —ˌ**substanˈtivally** *adv.* —ˈ**substantively** *adv.*

substantive rank *n.* a permanent rank in the armed services.

substation (ˈsʌbˌsteɪʃən) *n.* **1.** a subsidiary station. **2.** an installation at which electrical energy is received from one or more power stations for conversion from alternating to direct current, stepping down the voltage, or switching before distribution by a low-tension network.

substituent (sʌbˈstɪtjʊənt) *n.* **1.** *Chem.* an atom or group that replaces another atom or group in a molecule or can be regarded as replacing an atom in a parent compound. ~*adj.* **2.** substituted or substitutable. [C19: < L *substituere* to SUBSTITUTE]

substitute (ˈsʌbstɪˌtjuːt) *vb.* **1.** (often foll. by *for*) to serve or cause to serve in place of another person or thing. **2.** *Chem.* to replace (an atom or group in a molecule) with (another atom or group). ~*n.* **3. a.** a person or thing that serves in place of another, such as a player in a game who takes the place of an injured colleague. **b.** (*as modifier*): *a substitute goalkeeper.* [C16: < L *substituere,* < *sub-* in place of + *statuere* to set up] —ˌ**substiˈtutable** *adj.* —ˈ**substiˌtutive** *adj.*

substitution (ˌsʌbstɪˈtjuːʃən) *n.* **1.** the act of substituting or state of being substituted. **2.** something or someone substituted.

substrate (ˈsʌbstreɪt) *n.* **1.** *Biochem.* the substance upon which an enzyme acts. **2.** another word for **substratum.**

substratum (sʌbˈstrɑːtəm, -ˈstreɪ-) *n., pl.* **-strata** (-ˈstrɑːtə, -ˈstreɪtə). **1.** any layer or stratum lying underneath another. **2.** a basis or foundation; groundwork. [C17: < NL, < L *substrātus* strewn beneath, < *substernere* to spread under] —**subˈstrative** *or* **subˈstratal** *adj.*

substructure (ˈsʌbˌstrʌktʃə) *n.* **1.** a structure, pattern, etc., that forms the basis of anything. **2.** a structure forming a foundation or framework for a building or other construction. —**subˈstructural** *adj.*

subsume (səbˈsjuːm) *vb.* (*tr.*) **1.** to incorporate (an idea, case, etc.) under a comprehensive or inclusive classification. **2.** to consider (an instance of something) as part of a general rule. [C16: < NL *subsumere,* < L SUB- + *sumere* to take] —**subˈsumable** *adj.* —**subsumption** (səbˈsʌmpʃən) *n.*

subtemperate (sʌbˈtɛmpərɪt) *adj.* of or relating to the colder temperate regions.

subtenant (sʌbˈtɛnənt) *n.* a person who rents or leases property from a tenant. —**subˈtenancy** *n.*

subtend (səbˈtɛnd) *vb.* (*tr.*) **1.** *Geom.* to be opposite to and delimit (an angle or side). **2.** (of a bract, stem, etc.) to have (a bud or similar part) growing in its axil. [C16: < L *subtendere* to extend beneath]

subterfuge (ˈsʌbtəˌfjuːdʒ) *n.* a stratagem employed to conceal something, evade an argument, etc. [C16: < LL *subterfugium,* < L *subterfugere* to escape by stealth, < *subter* secretly + *fugere* to flee]

subterminal (sʌbˈtɜːmɪnᵊl) *adj.* almost at an end.

subterranean (ˌsʌbtəˈreɪnɪən) *adj.* **1.** Also: **subterraneous, subterrestrial.** situated, living, or operating below the surface of the earth. **2.** existing or operating in concealment. [C17: < L *subterrāneus,* < SUB- + *terra* earth] —ˌ**subterˈraneanly** *or* ˌ**subterˈraneously** *adv.*

subtile (ˈsʌtᵊl) *adj.* a rare spelling of **subtle.** —ˈ**subtilely** *adv.* —**subtility** (sʌbˈtɪlɪtɪ) *or* ˈ**subtileness** *n.* —ˈ**subtilty** *n.*

subtilize *or* **-ise** (ˈsʌtɪˌlaɪz) *vb.* **1.** (*tr.*) to bring to a purer state; refine. **2.** to debate subtly. **3.** (*tr.*) to make (the mind, etc.) keener. —ˌ**subtiliˈzation** *or* **-iˈsation** *n.*

subtitle (ˈsʌbˌtaɪtᵊl) *n.* **1.** an additional subordinate title given to a literary or other work. **2.** (*often pl.*) Also called: **caption.** *Films.* **a.** a written translation superimposed on a film that has foreign dialogue. **b.** explanatory text on a silent film. ~*vb.* **3.** (*tr.; usually passive*) to provide a subtitle for.

subtle (ˈsʌtᵊl) *adj.* **1.** not immediately obvious or comprehensible. **2.** difficult to detect or analyse, often through being delicate or highly refined: *a subtle scent.* **3.** showing or making or capable of showing or making fine distinctions of meaning. **4.** marked by or requiring mental acuteness or ingenuity; discriminating. **5.** delicate or faint: *a subtle shade.* **6.** cunning or wily: *a subtle rogue.* **7.** operating or executed in secret: *a subtle intrigue.* [C14: < OF *soutil,* < L *subtīlis* finely woven] —ˈ**subtleness** *n.* —ˈ**subtly** *adv.*

subtlety (ˈsʌtᵊltɪ) *n., pl.* **-ties. 1.** the state or quality of being subtle; delicacy. **2.** a fine distinction. **3.** something subtle.

subtonic (sʌbˈtɒnɪk) *n. Music.* the seventh degree of a major or minor scale.

subtotal (sʌbˈtəʊtᵊl, ˈsʌbˌtəʊtᵊl) *n.* **1.** the total made up by a column of figures, etc., forming part of the total made up by a larger column. ~*vb.* **-talling, -talled** *or U.S.* **-taling, -taled. 2.** to work out a subtotal for (a column, etc.).

subtract (səbˈtrækt) *vb.* **1.** to calculate the difference between (two numbers or quantities) by subtraction. **2.** to remove (a part of a thing, quantity, etc.) from the whole. [C16: < L *subtractus* withdrawn, < *subtrahere* to draw away from beneath] —**subˈtracter** *n.* —**subˈtractive** *adj.*

subtraction (səbˈtrækʃən) *n.* **1.** the act or process of subtracting. **2.** a mathematical operation in which the difference between two numbers or quantities is calculated.

subtrahend (ˈsʌbtrəˌhɛnd) *n.* the number to be subtracted from another number (the **minuend**). [C17: < L *subtrahendus,* < *subtrahere* to SUBTRACT]

subtropics (sʌbˈtrɒpɪks) *pl. n.* the region lying between the tropics and temperate lands. —**subˈtropical** *adj.*

subulate (ˈsuːbjʊlɪt, -ˌleɪt) *adj.* (esp. of plant parts) tapering to a point; awl-shaped. [C18: < NL *subulatus* like an awl, < L *sūbula* awl]

suburb (ˈsʌbɜːb) *n.* a residential district situated on the outskirts of a city or town. [C14: < L *suburbium,* < *sub-* close to + *urbs* a city]

suburban (səˈbɜːbᵊn) *adj.* **1.** of, in, or inhabiting a suburb or the suburbs. **2.** characteristic of a suburb or the suburbs. **3.** *Mildly derog.* narrow or unadventurous in outlook. ~*n.* **4.** Also called: **suburbanite.** a person who lives in a suburb. —**suˈburbaˌnize** *or* **-ise** *vb.*(*tr.*)

suburbia (səˈbɜːbɪə) *n.* **1.** suburbs or the people living in them considered as an identifiable community or class in society. **2.** the life, customs, etc., of suburbanites.

subvention (səbˈvɛnʃən) *n.* a grant, aid, or subsidy, as from a government. [C15: < LL *subventiō* assistance, < L *subvenīre,* < *sub-* under + *venīre* to come]

subversion (səbˈvɜːʃən) *n.* **1.** the act or an instance of subverting a legally constituted government, institution, etc. **2.** the state of being subverted; destruction or ruin. [C14: < LL *subversiō* destruction, < L *subvertere* to overturn]

subversive (səbˈvɜːsɪv) *adj.* **1.** liable to subvert or overthrow a government, legally constituted institution, etc. ~*n.* **2.** a person engaged in subversive activities, etc. —**subˈversively** *adv.* —**subˈversiveness** *n.*

subvert (səbˈvɜːt) *vb.* (*tr.*) **1.** to bring about the complete downfall or ruin of (something existing by a system of law, etc.). **2.** to undermine the moral principles of (a person, etc.). [C14: < L *subvertere* to overturn] —**subˈverter** *n.*

subway (ˈsʌbˌweɪ) *n.* **1.** *Brit.* an underground tunnel enabling pedestrians to cross a road,

---

subˈsurface *n., adj.* ˈ**subˌsystem** *n.*

railway, etc. **2.** an underground tunnel for traffic, power supplies, etc. **3.** an underground railway.

succedaneum (ˌsʌksɪˈdeɪnɪəm) *n., pl.* **-nea** (-nɪə). something that is used as a substitute, esp. any medical drug or agent that may be taken or prescribed in place of another. [C17: < L *succēdāneus* following after; see SUCCEED] —ˌ**succeˈdaneous** *adj.*

succeed (səkˈsiːd) *vb.* **1.** (*intr.*) to accomplish an aim, esp. in the manner desired. **2.** (*intr.*) to happen in the manner desired: *the plan succeeded.* **3.** (*intr.*) to acquit oneself satisfactorily or do well, as in a specified field. **4.** (when *intr.*, often foll. by *to*) to come next in order (after someone or something). **5.** (when *intr.*, often foll. by *to*) to take over an office, post, etc. (from a person). **6.** (*intr.;* usually foll. by *to*) to come into possession (of property, etc.); inherit. **7.** (*intr.*) to have a result according to a specified manner: *the plan succeeded badly.* [C15: < L *succēdere* to follow after] —**sucˈceeder** *n.* —**sucˈceedingly** *adv.*

success (səkˈsɛs) *n.* **1.** the favourable outcome of something attempted. **2.** the attainment of wealth, fame, etc. **3.** an action, performance, etc., that is characterized by success. **4.** a person or thing that is successful. [C16: < L *successus* an outcome; see SUCCEED]

successful (səkˈsɛsful) *adj.* **1.** having succeeded in one's endeavours. **2.** marked by a favourable outcome. **3.** having obtained fame, wealth, etc. —**sucˈcessfully** *adv.* —**sucˈcessfulness** *n.*

succession (səkˈsɛʃən) *n.* **1.** the act or an instance of one person or thing following another. **2.** a number of people or things following one another in order. **3.** the act, process, or right by which one person succeeds to the office, etc., of another. **4.** the order that determines how one person or thing follows another. **5.** a line of descent to a title, etc. **6. in succession.** in a manner such that one thing is followed uninterruptedly by another. [C14: < L *successio;* see SUCCEED] —**sucˈcessional** *adj.*

successive (səkˈsɛsɪv) *adj.* **1.** following another without interruption. **2.** of or involving succession: *a successive process.* —**sucˈcessively** *adv.* —**sucˈcessiveness** *n.*

successor (səkˈsɛsə) *n.* a person or thing that follows, esp. a person who succeeds another.

succinct (səkˈsɪŋkt) *adj.* marked by brevity and clarity; concise. [C15: < L *succinctus* girt about, < *succingere* to gird from below] —**sucˈcinctly** *adv.* —**sucˈcinctness** *n.*

succinic acid (sʌkˈsɪnɪk) *n.* a colourless odourless water-soluble acid found in plant and animal tissues, deriving from amber. [C19: < L *succinum* amber]

succotash (ˈsʌkəˌtæʃ) *n. U.S. & Canad.* a mixture of cooked sweet corn kernels and lima beans, served as a vegetable. [C18: of Amerind origin, < *msiquatash,* lit.: broken pieces]

succour *or U.S.* **succor** (ˈsʌkə) *n.* **1.** help or assistance, esp. in time of difficulty. **2.** a person or thing that provides help. ~*vb.* **3.** (*tr.*) to give aid to. [C13: < OF *sucurir,* < L *succurrere* to hurry to help]

succubus (ˈsʌkjʊbəs) *n., pl.* **-bi** (-ˌbaɪ). **1.** Also called: **succuba.** a female demon fabled to have sexual intercourse with sleeping men. Cf. **incubus. 2.** any evil demon. [C16: < Med. L, < LL *succuba* harlot, < L *succubāre* to lie beneath]

succulent (ˈsʌkjʊlənt) *adj.* **1.** juicy. **2.** (of plants) having thick fleshy leaves or stems. ~*n.* **3.** a plant that can exist in arid conditions by using water stored in its fleshy tissues. [C17: < L *succulentus,* < *sūcus* juice] —ˈ**succulence** *or* ˈ**succulency** *n.* —ˈ**succulently** *adv.*

succumb (səˈkʌm) *vb.* (*intr.;* often foll. by *to*) **1.** to give way to the force (of) or desire (for). **2.** to be fatally overwhelmed (by disease, etc.); die (of). [C15: < L *succumbere* to be overcome, < SUB- + *-cumbere,* < *cubāre* to lie down]

succursal (sʌˈkɜːsᵊl) *adj.* **1.** (esp. of a religious establishment) subsidiary. ~*n.* **2.** a subsidiary establishment. [C19: < F, < Med. L *succursus,* < L *succurrere* to SUCCOUR]

such (sʌtʃ) (often foll. by a corresponding subordinate clause introduced by *that* or *as*) ~*determiner.* **1. a.** of the sort specified or understood: *such books.* **b.** (*as pronoun*): *such is life; robbers, rapists, and such.* **2.** so great; so much: *such a help.* **3. a. as such.** in the capacity previously specified or understood: *a judge as such hasn't so much power.* **b.** in itself or themselves: *intelligence as such can't guarantee success.* **4. such and such.** specific, but not known or named: *at such and such a time.* **5. such as. a.** for example: *animals, such as tigers.* **b.** of a similar kind as; like: *people such as your friend.* **c.** of the (usually small) amount, etc.: *the food, such as there was, was excellent.* **6. such that.** so that: used to express purpose or result: *power such that it was effortless.* ~*adv.* **7.** (intensifier): *such a nice person.* [OE *swilc*]

suchlike (ˈsʌtʃˌlaɪk) *adj.* **1.** (*prenominal*) of such a kind; similar: *John, Ken, and other suchlike idiots.* ~*n.* **2.** such or similar persons or things: *hyenas, jackals, and suchlike.*

suck (sʌk) *vb.* **1.** to draw (a liquid or other substance) into the mouth by creating a partial vacuum in the mouth. **2.** to draw in (fluid, etc.) by or as if by a similar action: *plants suck moisture from the soil.* **3.** to drink milk from (a mother's breast); suckle. **4.** (*tr.*) to extract fluid content from (a solid food): *to suck a lemon.* **5.** (*tr.*) to take into the mouth and moisten, dissolve, or roll around with the tongue: *to suck one's thumb.* **6.** (*tr.;* often foll. by *down, in,* etc.) to draw by using irresistible force. **7.** (*intr.*) (of a pump) to draw in air because of a low supply level or leaking valves, etc. **8.** (*tr.*) to assimilate or acquire (knowledge, comfort, etc.). ~*n.* **9.** the act or an instance of sucking. **10.** something that is sucked, esp. milk from the mother's breast. **11. give suck to.** to give (a baby or young animal) milk from the breast or udder. **12.** an attracting or sucking force. **13.** a sound caused by sucking. ~See also **suck in, sucks, suck up to.** [OE *sūcan*]

sucker (ˈsʌkə) *n.* **1.** a person or thing that sucks. **2.** *Sl.* a person who is easily deceived or swindled. **3.** *Sl.* a person who cannot resist the attractions of a particular type of person or thing: *he's a sucker for blondes.* **4.** a young animal that is not yet weaned. **5.** *Zool.* an organ specialized for sucking or adhering. **6.** a cup-shaped device, generally made of rubber, that may be attached to articles allowing them to adhere to a surface by suction. **7.** *Bot.* **a.** a strong shoot that arises in a mature plant from a root, rhizome, or the base of the main stem. **b.** a short branch of a parasitic plant that absorbs nutrients from the host. **8.** a pipe or tube through which a fluid is drawn by suction. **9.** any of various small mainly North American cyprinoid fishes having a large sucking mouth. **10.** any of certain fishes that have sucking discs, esp. the sea snail. **11.** a piston in a suction pump or the valve in such a piston. ~*vb.* **12.** (*tr.*) to strip the suckers from (a plant). **13.** (*intr.*) (of a plant) to produce suckers.

suck in *vb.* (*adv.*) **1.** (*tr.*) to attract by using an inexorable force, inducement, etc. **2.** to draw in (one's breath) sharply.

suckle (ˈsʌkᵊl) *vb.* **1.** to give (a baby or young animal) milk from the breast or (of a baby, etc.) to suck milk from the breast. **2.** (*tr.*) to bring up; nurture. [C15: prob. back formation < SUCKLING] —ˈ**suckler** *n.*

suckling (ˈsʌklɪŋ) *n.* **1.** an infant or young animal that is still taking milk from the mother. **2.** a very young child. [C15: see SUCK, -LING[1]]

sucks (sʌks) *interj. Sl.* **1.** an expression of disappointment. **2.** an exclamation of defiance or derision (esp. in **yah boo sucks to you**).

---

subˈzero *adj.*

suck up to *vb.* (*intr., adv.* + *prep.*) *Inf.* to flatter for one's own profit; toady.

sucrase (ˈsjuːkreɪz) *n.* another name for **invertase.** [C19: < F *sucre* sugar + -ASE]

sucre (*Spanish* ˈsukre) *n.* the standard monetary unit of Ecuador. [C19: after Antonio José de *Sucre* (1795–1830), S American liberator]

sucrose (ˈsjuːkrəʊz, -krəʊs) *n.* the technical name for **sugar** (sense 1). [C19: F *sucre* sugar + -OSE[2]]

suction (ˈsʌkʃən) *n.* **1.** the act or process of sucking. **2.** the force produced by a pressure difference, as the force holding a suction cap onto a surface. **3.** the act or process of producing such a force. [C17: < LL *suctiō* a sucking, < L *sūgere* to suck] —ˈ**suctional** *adj.*

suction pump *n.* a pump for raising water or a similar fluid by suction. It usually consists of a cylinder containing a piston fitted with a flap valve.

suctorial (sʌkˈtɔːrɪəl) *adj.* **1.** specialized for sucking or adhering. **2.** relating to or possessing suckers or suction. [C19: < NL *suctōrius,* < L *sūgere* to suck]

Sudanese (ˌsuːdᵊˈniːz) *adj.* **1.** of or relating to the Sudan, in NE Africa. ~*n.* **2.** a native or inhabitant of the Sudan.

sudarium (sjʊˈdɛərɪəm) *n., pl.* **-daria** (-ˈdɛərɪə). another word for **sudatorium.** [C17: < L, < *sūdāre* to sweat]

sudatorium (ˌsjuːdəˈtɔːrɪəm) *or* **sudatory** *n., pl.* **-toria** (-ˈtɔːrɪə) *or* **-tories.** a room, esp. in a Roman bathhouse, where sweating is induced by heat. [C18: < L, < *sūdāre* to sweat]

sudatory (ˈsjuːdətərɪ, -trɪ) *adj.* **1.** relating to or producing sweating. ~*n., pl.* **-ries. 2.** a sudatory agent. **3.** another word for **sudatorium.**

sudd (sʌd) *n.* floating masses of reeds and weeds that occur on the White Nile and obstruct navigation. [C19: < Ar., lit.: obstruction]

sudden (ˈsʌdᵊn) *adj.* **1.** occurring or performed quickly and without warning. **2.** marked by haste; abrupt. **3.** *Rare.* rash; precipitate. ~*n.* **4.** *Arch.* an abrupt occurrence (in **on a sudden**). **5. all of a sudden.** without warning; unexpectedly. [C13: via F < LL *subitāneus,* < L *subitus* unexpected, < *subīre* to happen unexpectedly, < *sub-* secretly + *īre* to go] —ˈ**suddenly** *adv.* —ˈ**suddenness** *n.*

sudden death *n.* **1.** (in sports, etc.) an extra game or contest to decide the winner of a tied competition. **2.** an unexpected or quick death.

sudden infant death syndrome *n.* a technical name for **cot death.**

sudor (ˈsjuːdɔː) *n.* a technical name for **sweat.** [L] —**sudoral** (ˈsjuːdərəl) *adj.*

sudoriferous (ˌsjuːdəˈrɪfərəs) *adj.* producing or conveying sweat. [C16: via NL < SUDOR + L *ferre* to bear] —ˌ**sudorˈiferousness** *n.*

sudorific (ˌsjuːdəˈrɪfɪk) *adj.* **1.** producing or causing sweating. ~*n.* **2.** a sudorific agent. [C17: < NL *sūdōrificus,* < SUDOR + L *facere* to make]

suds (sʌdz) *pl. n.* **1.** the bubbles on the surface of water in which soap, detergents, etc., have been dissolved; lather. **2.** soapy water. [C16: prob. < MDu. *sudse* marsh] —ˈ**sudsy** *adj.*

sue (sjuː, suː) *vb.* **suing, sued. 1.** to institute legal proceedings (against). **2.** to make suppliant requests of (someone for something). [C13: < OF *sivre,* < L *sequī* to follow] —ˈ**suer** *n.*

suede (sweɪd) *n.* **a.** a leather with a fine velvet-like nap on the flesh side, produced by abrasive action. **b.** (*as modifier*): *a suede coat.* [C19: < F *gants de Suède,* lit.: gloves from Sweden]

suet (ˈsuːɪt, ˈsjuːɪt) *n.* a hard waxy fat around the kidneys and loins in sheep, cattle, etc., used in cooking and making tallow. [C14: < OF *seu,* < L *sēbum*] —ˈ**suety** *adj.*

suet pudding *n. Brit.* any of a variety of puddings made with suet and steamed or boiled.

suffer (ˈsʌfə) *vb.* **1.** to undergo or be subjected to (pain, punishment, etc.). **2.** (*tr.*) to undergo or experience (anything): *to suffer a change of management.* **3.** (*intr.*) to be set at a disadvantage: *this author suffers in translation.* **4.** (*tr.*) *Arch.* to tolerate; permit (someone to do something): *suffer the little children to come unto me.* **5. suffer from. a.** to be ill with, esp. recurrently. **b.** to be given to: *he suffers from a tendency to exaggerate.* [C13: < OF *soffrir,* < L *sufferre,* < SUB- + *ferre* to bear] —ˈ**sufferer** *n.* —ˈ**suffering** *n.*

sufferable (ˈsʌfərəbᵊl, ˈsʌfrə-) *adj.* able to be tolerated or suffered; endurable.

sufferance (ˈsʌfərəns, ˈsʌfrəns) *n.* **1.** tolerance arising from failure to prohibit; tacit permission. **2.** capacity to endure pain, injury, etc. **3.** the state or condition of suffering. **4. on sufferance.** tolerated with reluctance. [C13: via OF < LL *sufferentia* endurance, < L *sufferre* to SUFFER]

suffice (səˈfaɪs) *vb.* **1.** to be adequate or satisfactory for (something). **2. suffice it to say that.** (*takes a clause as object*) let us say no more than that; I shall just say that. [C14: < OF *suffire,* < L *sufficere* < *sub-* below + *facere* to make]

sufficiency (səˈfɪʃənsɪ) *n., pl.* **-cies. 1.** the quality or condition of being sufficient. **2.** an adequate amount. **3.** *Arch.* efficiency.

sufficient (səˈfɪʃənt) *adj.* **1.** enough to meet a need or purpose; adequate. **2.** *Logic.* (of a condition) assuring the truth of a statement; requiring but not necessarily caused by some other state of affairs. Cf. **necessary** (sense 3b). **3.** *Arch.* competent; capable. ~*n.* **4.** a sufficient quantity. [C14: < L *sufficiens* supplying the needs of, < *sufficere* to SUFFICE] —**sufˈficiently** *adv.*

suffix *n.* (ˈsʌfɪks). **1.** *Grammar.* an affix that follows the stem to which it is attached, as for example *-s* and *-ness* in *dogs* and *softness.* Cf. **prefix** (sense 1). **2.** anything added at the end of something else. ~*vb.* (ˈsʌfɪks, səˈfɪks). **3.** (*tr.*) *Grammar.* to add (a morpheme) as a suffix to a word. [C18: < NL *suffixum,* < L *suffixus* fastened below, < *suffigere* to fasten below]

suffocate (ˈsʌfəˌkeɪt) *vb.* **1.** to kill or be killed by the deprivation of oxygen, as by obstruction of the air passage. **2.** to block the air passages or have the air passages blocked. **3.** to feel or cause to feel discomfort from heat and lack of air. [C16: < L *suffōcāre,* < SUB- + *faucēs* throat] —ˈ**suffoˌcating** *adj.* —ˌ**suffoˈcation** *n.*

Suffolk punch (ˈsʌfək) *n.* a breed of draught horse with a chestnut coat and short legs.

suffragan (ˈsʌfrəgən) *adj.* **1. a.** (of any bishop of a diocese) subordinate to and assisting his superior archbishop or metropolitan. **b.** (of any assistant bishop) assisting the bishop of his diocese but having no ordinary jurisdiction in that diocese. ~*n.* **2.** a suffragan bishop. [C14: < Med. L *suffragāneus,* < *suffrāgium* assistance, < L: suffrage] —ˈ**suffraganship** *n.*

suffrage (ˈsʌfrɪdʒ) *n.* **1.** the right to vote, esp. in public elections; franchise. **2.** the exercise of such a right; casting a vote. **3.** a short intercessory prayer. [C14: < L *suffrāgium*]

suffragette (ˌsʌfrəˈdʒɛt) *n.* a female advocate of the extension of the franchise to women, esp. a militant one, as in Britain at the beginning of the 20th century. [C20: < SUFFRAG(E) + -ETTE]

suffragist (ˈsʌfrədʒɪst) *n.* an advocate of the extension of the franchise, esp. to women. —ˈ**suffragism** *n.*

suffruticose (səˈfruːtɪˌkəʊz) *adj.* (of a plant) having a permanent woody base and herbaceous branches. [C18: < NL *suffruticōsus,* < L SUB- + *frutex* shrub]

suffuse (səˈfjuːz) *vb.* (*tr.; usually passive*) to spread or flood through or over (something). [C16: < L *suffūsus* overspread with, < *suffundere,* < SUB- + *fundere* to pour] —**suffusion** (səˈfjuːʒən) *n.* —**sufˈfusive** *adj.*

sug (sʌg) *vb.* **sugging, sugged.** (*intr.*) to use the pretence of conducting a survey in order to try to sell something to a person. [C20: < selling under the guise (of market research)] —ˈ**sugging** *n.*

sugar (ˈʃʊgə) *n.* **1.** Also called: **sucrose, saccharose.** a white crystalline sweet carbohydrate, a disaccharide, found in many plants: used esp. as a sweetening agent in food and drinks. Related adj.: **saccharine. 2.** any of a class of simple water-soluble carbohydrates, such as sucrose, lactose, and fructose. **3.** *Inf., chiefly U.S. & Canad.* a term of affection, esp. for one's sweetheart. ~*vb.* **4.** (*tr.*) to add sugar to; make sweet. **5.** (*tr.*) to cover or sprinkle with sugar. **6.** (*intr.*) to produce sugar. **7. sugar the pill** *or* **medicine.** to make something unpleasant more agreeable by adding something pleasant. [C13 *suker,* < OF *çucre,* < Med. L *zuccārum,* ult. < Sansk. *śarkarā*] —ˈ**sugared** *adj.*

sugar beet *n.* a variety of beet cultivated for its white roots from which sugar is obtained.

sugar candy *n.* **1.** Also called: **rock candy.** large crystals of sugar formed by suspending strings in a strong sugar solution that hardens on the strings, used chiefly for sweetening coffee. **2.** *Chiefly U.S.* confectionery; sweets.

sugar cane *n.* a coarse perennial grass of Old World tropical regions, having tall stout canes that yield sugar: cultivated chiefly in the West Indies and the southern U.S.

sugar-coat *vb.* (*tr.*) **1.** to coat or cover with sugar. **2.** to cause to appear more attractive.

sugar diabetes *n.* an informal name for **diabetes mellitus** (see **diabetes**).

sugar glider *n.* a common Australian possum that glides from tree to tree feeding on insects and nectar.

sugaring off *n. Canad.* the boiling down of maple sap to produce sugar, traditionally a social event in early spring.

sugar loaf *n.* **1.** a large conical mass of hard refined sugar. **2.** something resembling this.

sugar maple *n.* a North American maple tree, grown as a source of sugar, which is extracted from the sap, and for its hard wood.

sugar of lead (lɛd) *n.* another name for **lead acetate.**

sugarplum (ˈʃʊgəˌplʌm) *n.* a crystallized plum.

sugary (ˈʃʊgərɪ) *adj.* **1.** of, like, or containing sugar. **2.** excessively sweet. **3.** deceptively pleasant; insincere. —ˈ**sugariness** *n.*

suggest (səˈdʒɛst) *vb.* (*tr.; may take a clause as object*) **1.** to put forward (a plan, idea, etc.) for consideration: *I suggest Smith for the post; a plan suggested itself.* **2.** to evoke (a person, thing, etc.) in the mind by the association of ideas: *that painting suggests home to me.* **3.** to give an indirect or vague hint of: *his face always suggests his peace of mind.* [C16: < L *suggerere* to bring up] —**sugˈgester** *n.*

suggestible (səˈdʒɛstɪbəl) *adj.* **1.** easily influenced by ideas provided by other persons. **2.** characteristic of something that can be suggested. —**sugˌgestiˈbility** *n.*

suggestion (səˈdʒɛstʃən) *n.* **1.** something that is suggested. **2.** a hint or indication: *a suggestion of the odour of violets.* **3.** *Psychol.* the process whereby the mere presentation of an idea to a receptive individual leads to the acceptance of that idea. See also **autosuggestion.**

suggestive (səˈdʒɛstɪv) *adj.* **1.** (*postpositive;* foll. by *of*) conveying a hint (of something). **2.** tending to suggest something improper or indecent. —**sugˈgestively** *adv.* —**sugˈgestiveness** *n.*

suicidal (ˌsuːɪˈsaɪdəl, ˌsjuː-) *adj.* **1.** involving, indicating, or tending towards suicide. **2.** liable to result in suicide: *a suicidal attempt.* **3.** liable to destroy one's own interests or prospects; dangerously rash. —ˌ**suiˈcidally** *adv.*

suicide (ˈsuːɪˌsaɪd, ˈsjuː-) *n.* **1.** the act or an instance of killing oneself intentionally. **2.** the self-inflicted ruin of one's own prospects or interests: *a merger would be financial suicide.* **3.** a person who kills himself intentionally. **4.** (*modifier*) reckless; extremely dangerous: *a suicide mission.* **5.** (*modifier*) (of an action) undertaken or (of a person) undertaking an action in the knowledge that it will result in the death of the person performing it in order that maximum damage may be inflicted: *suicide bomber.* [C17: < NL *suīcīdium,* < L *suī* of oneself + *-cīdium,* < *caedere* to kill]

sui generis (ˌsuːaɪ ˈdʒɛnərɪs) *adj.* unique. [L, lit.: of its own kind]

suint (ˈsuːɪnt, swɪnt) *n.* a water-soluble substance found in the fleece of sheep, formed from dried perspiration. [C18: < F *suer* to sweat, < L *sūdāre*]

suit (suːt, sjuːt) *n.* **1.** any set of clothes of the same or similar material designed to be worn together, now usually (for men) a jacket with matching trousers or (for women) a jacket with matching or contrasting skirt or trousers. **2.** (*in combination*) any outfit worn for a specific purpose: *a spacesuit.* **3.** any set of items, such as parts of personal armour. **4.** any of the four sets of 13 cards in a pack of playing cards, being spades, hearts, diamonds, and clubs. **5.** a civil proceeding; lawsuit. **6.** the act or process of suing in a court of law. **7.** a petition or appeal made to a person of superior rank or status or the act of making such a petition. **8.** a man's courting of a woman. **9. follow suit. a.** to play a card of the same suit as the card played immediately before it. **b.** to act in the same way as someone else. **10. strong** *or* **strongest suit.** something that one excels in. ~*vb.* **11.** to make or be fit or appropriate for: *that dress suits your figure.* **12.** to meet the requirements or standards (of). **13.** to be agreeable or acceptable to (someone). **14. suit oneself.** to pursue one's own intentions without reference to others. [C13: < OF *sieute* set of things, < *sivre* to follow]

suitable (ˈsuːtəbəl, ˈsjuːt-) *adj.* appropriate; proper; fit. —ˌ**suitaˈbility** *or* ˈ**suitableness** *n.* —ˈ**suitably** *adv.*

suitcase (ˈsuːtˌkeɪs, ˈsjuːt-) *n.* a portable rectangular travelling case for clothing, etc.

suite (swiːt) *n.* **1.** a series of items intended to be used together; set. **2.** a set of connected rooms in a hotel. **3.** a matching set of furniture, esp. of two armchairs and a settee. **4.** a number of attendants or followers. **5.** *Music.* **a.** an instrumental composition consisting of several movements in the same key based on or derived from dance rhythms, esp. in the baroque period. **b.** an instrumental composition in several movements less closely connected than a sonata. [C17: < F, < OF *sieute;* see SUIT]

suiting (ˈsuːtɪŋ, ˈsjuːt-) *n.* a fabric used for suits.

suitor (ˈsuːtə, ˈsjuːt-) *n.* **1.** a man who courts a woman; wooer. **2.** *Law.* a person who brings a suit in a court of law; plaintiff. [C13: < Anglo-Norman *suter,* < L *secūtor* follower, < *sequī* to follow]

sukiyaki (ˌsuːkɪˈjɑːkɪ) *n.* a Japanese dish consisting of very thinly sliced beef or other meat, vegetables, and seasonings cooked together quickly, usually at the table. [< Japanese]

sulcate (ˈsʌlkeɪt) *adj. Biol.* marked with longitudinal parallel grooves. [C18: via L *sulcātus* < *sulcāre* to plough, < *sulcus* a furrow]

sulcus (ˈsʌlkəs) *n., pl.* **-ci** (-saɪ). **1.** a linear groove, furrow, or slight depression. **2.** any of the narrow grooves on the surface of the brain that mark the cerebral convolutions. [C17: < L]

sulf- *combining form.* a U.S. variant of **sulph-.**

sulfur (ˈsʌlfə) *n.* the U.S. spelling of **sulphur.**

sulk (sʌlk) *vb.* **1.** (*intr.*) to be silent and resentful because of a wrong done to one; brood sullenly: *the child sulked after being slapped.* ~*n.* **2.** (*often pl.*) a state or mood of feeling resentful or sullen: *he's in a sulk; he's got the sulks.* **3.** Also: **sulker.** a person who sulks. [C18: ? back formation < SULKY[1]]

sulky[1] (ˈsʌlkɪ) *adj.* **sulkier, sulkiest. 1.** sullen, withdrawn, or moody, through or as if through resentment. **2.** dull or dismal: *sulky weather.* [C18: ? < obs. *sulke* sluggish] —ˈ**sulkily** *adv.* —ˈ**sulkiness** *n.*

sulky[2] (ˈsʌlkɪ) *n., pl.* **sulkies.** a light two-wheeled vehicle for one person, usually drawn by one horse. [C18: < SULKY[1]]

sullage (ˈsʌlɪdʒ) *n.* **1.** filth or waste, esp. sewage. **2.** sediment deposited by running water. [C16: ? < F *souiller* to sully]

sullen (ˈsʌlən) *adj.* **1.** unwilling to talk or be sociable; sulky; morose. **2.** sombre; gloomy: *a sullen day.* ~*n.* **3.** (*pl.*) *Arch.* a sullen mood.

[C16: ? < Anglo-F *solain* (unattested), ult. rel. to L *sōlus* alone] —ˈ**sullenly** *adv.* —ˈ**sullenness** *n.*

sully (ˈsʌlɪ) *vb.* **-lying, -lied.** (*tr.*) to stain or tarnish (a reputation, etc.) or (of a reputation) to become stained or tarnished. [C16: prob. < F *souiller* to soil]

sulph- *or U.S.* **sulf-** *combining form.* containing sulphur: *sulphate.*

sulphadiazine *or U.S.* **sulfadiazine** (ˌsʌlfəˈdaɪəˌziːn) *n.* an important sulpha drug used chiefly in combination with an antibiotic. [< SULPH- + DIAZ(O) + -INE[2]]

sulpha *or U.S.* **sulfa drug** (ˈsʌlfə) *n.* any of a group of sulphonamides that inhibit the activity of bacteria and are used to treat bacterial infections.

sulphanilamide *or U.S.* **sulfanilamide** (ˌsʌlfəˈnɪləˌmaɪd) *n.* a white crystalline compound formerly used in the treatment of bacterial infections. [< SULPH- + ANIL(INE) + AMIDE]

sulphate *or U.S.* **sulfate** (ˈsʌlfeɪt) *n.* **1.** any salt or ester of sulphuric acid. ~*vb.* **2.** (*tr.*) to treat with a sulphate or convert into a sulphate. **3.** to undergo or cause to undergo the formation of a layer of lead sulphate on the plates of an accumulator. [C18: < NL *sulfātum*] —**sulˈphation** *or U.S.* **sulˈfation** *n.*

sulphide *or U.S.* **sulfide** (ˈsʌlfaɪd) *n.* a compound of sulphur with a more electropositive element.

sulphite *or U.S.* **sulfite** (ˈsʌlfaɪt) *n.* any salt or ester of sulphurous acid. —**sulphitic** *or U.S.* **sulfitic** (sʌlˈfɪtɪk) *adj.*

sulphonamide *or U.S.* **sulfonamide** (sʌlˈfɒnəˌmaɪd) *n.* any of a class of organic compounds that are amides of sulphonic acids containing the group $-SO_2NH_2$ or a group derived from this. An important class of sulphonamides are the sulpha drugs.

sulphone *or U.S.* **sulfone** (ˈsʌlfəʊn) *n.* any of a class of organic compounds containing the divalent group SO_2 linked to two other organic groups.

sulphonic *or U.S.* **sulfonic acid** (sʌlˈfɒnɪk) *n.* any of a large group of strong organic acids that contain the group $-SO_2OH$ and are used in the manufacture of dyes and drugs.

sulphonmethane *or U.S.* **sulfonmethane** (ˌsʌlfɒnˈmiːθeɪn) *n.* a colourless crystalline compound used medicinally as a hypnotic. Formula: $C_7H_{16}O_4S_2$.

sulphur *or U.S.* **sulfur** (ˈsʌlfə) *n.* **a.** an allotropic nonmetallic element, occurring free in volcanic regions and in combined state in gypsum, pyrite, and galena. It is used in the production of sulphuric acid, in the vulcanization of rubber, and in fungicides. Symbol: S; atomic no.: 16; atomic wt.: 32.064. **b.** (*as modifier*): *sulphur springs.* [C14 *soufre,* < OF, < L *sulfur*] —**sulphuric** *or U.S.* **sulfuric** (sʌlˈfjʊərɪk) *adj.*

sulphurate *or U.S.* **sulfurate** (ˈsʌlfjʊˌreɪt) *vb.* (*tr.*) to combine or treat with sulphur or a sulphur compound. —ˌ**sulphuˈration** *or U.S.* ˌ**sulfuˈration** *n.*

sulphur-bottom *n.* another name for **blue whale.**

sulphur dioxide *n.* a colourless soluble pungent gas. It is both an oxidizing and a reducing agent and is used in the manufacture of sulphuric acid, the preservation of foodstuffs (**E 220**), bleaching, and disinfecting. Formula: SO_2.

sulphureous *or U.S.* **sulfureous** (sʌlˈfjʊərɪəs) *adj.* **1.** another word for **sulphurous** (sense 1). **2.** of the yellow colour of sulphur.

sulphuretted *or U.S.* **sulfureted hydrogen** (ˈsʌlfjʊˌrɛtɪd) *n.* another name for **hydrogen sulphide.**

sulphuric acid *n.* a colourless dense oily corrosive liquid used in accumulators and in the manufacture of fertilizers, dyes, and explosives. Formula: H_2SO_4.

sulphurize, -ise, *or U.S.* **sulfurize** (ˈsʌlfjʊˌraɪz) *vb.* (*tr.*) to combine or treat with sulphur or a sulphur compound. —ˌ**sulphuriˈzation, -iˈsation,** *or U.S.* ˌ**sulfuriˈzation** *n.*

sulphurous *or U.S.* **sulfurous** (ˈsʌlfərəs) *adj.* **1.** Also: **sulphureous.** of, relating to, or resembling sulphur: *a sulphurous colour.* **2.** of or containing sulphur in the divalent state: *sulphurous acid.* **3.** of or relating to hellfire. **4.** hot-tempered. —ˈ**sulphurously** *or U.S.* ˈ**sulfurously** *adv.* —ˈ**sulphurousness** *or U.S.* ˈ**sulfurousness** *n.*

sulphurous acid *n.* an unstable acid produced when sulphur dioxide dissolves in water: used as a preservative for food and a bleaching agent. Formula: H_2SO_3.

sultan (ˈsʌltən) *n.* **1.** the sovereign of a Muslim country, esp. of the former Ottoman Empire. **2.** a small domestic fowl with a white crest and heavily feathered legs and feet: originated in Turkey. [C16: < Med. L *sultānus,* < Ar. *sultān* rule, < Aramaic *salita* to rule]

sultana (sʌlˈtɑːnə) *n.* **1. a.** the dried fruit of a small white seedless grape, originally produced in SW Asia; seedless raisin. **b.** the grape itself. **2.** Also called: **sultaness.** a wife, concubine, or female relative of a sultan. **3.** a mistress; concubine. [C16: < It., fem. of *sultano* SULTAN]

sultanate (ˈsʌltəˌneɪt) *n.* **1.** the territory or a country ruled by a sultan. **2.** the office, rank, or jurisdiction of a sultan.

sultry (ˈsʌltrɪ) *adj.* **-trier, -triest. 1.** (of weather or climate) oppressively hot and humid. **2.** characterized by or emitting oppressive heat. **3.** displaying or suggesting passion; sensual: *sultry eyes.* [C16: < obs. *sulter* to swelter + -Y[1]] —ˈ**sultrily** *adv.* —ˈ**sultriness** *n.*

sum (sʌm) *n.* **1.** the result of the addition of numbers, quantities, objects, etc. **2.** one or more columns or rows of numbers to be added, subtracted, multiplied, or divided. **3.** *Maths.* the limit of the first *n* terms of a converging infinite series as *n* tends to infinity. **4.** a quantity, esp. of money: *he borrows enormous sums.* **5.** the essence or gist of a matter (esp. in **in sum, in sum and substance**). **6.** a less common word for **summary. 7.** (*modifier*) complete or final (esp. in **sum total**). ~*vb.* **summing, summed. 8.** (often foll. by *up*) to add or form a total of (something). **9.** (*tr.*) to calculate the sum of (the terms in a sequence). ~See also **sum up.** [C13 *summe,* < OF, < L *summa* the top, sum, < *summus* highest, < *super* above]

sumach *or U.S.* **sumac** (ˈsuːmæk, ˈʃuː-) *n.* **1.** any of various temperate or subtropical shrubs or small trees, having compound leaves and red hairy fruits. See also **poison sumach. 2.** a preparation of powdered leaves of certain species of sumach, used in dyeing and tanning. **3.** the wood of any of these plants. [C14: via OF < Ar. *summāq*]

Sumerian (suːˈmɪərɪən, -ˈmɛər-) *n.* **1.** a member of a people who established a civilization in Sumer, in SW Asia, during the 4th millennium B.C. **2.** the extinct language of this people. ~*adj.* **3.** of or relating to ancient Sumer, its inhabitants, or their language or civilization.

summa cum laude (ˈsʊmɑː kʊm ˈlaʊdeɪ) *adv., adj. Chiefly U.S.* with the utmost praise: the highest designation for achievement in examinations. In Britain it is sometimes used to designate a first-class honours degree. [< L]

summarize *or* **-ise** (ˈsʌməˌraɪz) *vb.* (*tr.*) to make or be a summary of; express concisely. —ˌ**summariˈzation** *or* **-iˈsation** *n.* —ˈ**summaˌrizer, -iser,** *or* ˈ**summarist** *n.*

summary (ˈsʌmərɪ) *n., pl.* **-maries. 1.** a brief account giving the main points of something. ~*adj.* (*usually prenominal*). **2.** performed arbitrarily and quickly, without formality: *a summary execution.* **3.** (of legal proceedings) short and free from the complexities and delays of a full trial. **4. summary jurisdiction.** the right a court has to adjudicate immediately upon some matter. **5.** giving the gist or essence. [C15: < L *summārium,* < *summa* SUM] —ˈ**summarily** *adv.* —ˈ**summariness** *n.*

summary offence *n.* an offence that is triable in a magistrates' court.

summation (sʌˈmeɪʃən) *n.* **1.** the act or process of determining a sum; addition. **2.** the result of such an act or process. **3.** a summary. **4.** *U.S.*

law. the concluding statements made by opposing counsel in a case before a court. [C18: < Med. L *summātiō,* < *summāre* to total, < L *summa* SUM] **—sum'mational** *adj.*

summer (ˈsʌmə) *n.* **1.** (*sometimes cap.*) **a.** the warmest season of the year, between spring and autumn, astronomically from the June solstice to the September equinox in the N hemisphere and at the opposite time of year in the S hemisphere. **b.** (*as modifier*): *summer flowers.* Related adj.: **aestival. 2.** the period of hot weather associated with the summer. **3.** a time of blossoming, greatest happiness, etc. **4.** *Chiefly poetic.* a year represented by this season: *a child of nine summers.* ~*vb.* **5.** (*intr.*) to spend the summer (at a place). **6.** (*tr.*) to keep or feed (farm animals) during the summer: *they summered their cattle on the mountain slopes.* [OE *sumor*] **—ˈsummerly** *adj.* **—ˈsummery** *adj.*

summerhouse (ˈsʌmə͵haʊs) *n.* a small building in a garden or park, used for shade or recreation in the summer.

summer pudding *n. Brit.* a pudding made by filling a bread-lined basin with a purée of fruit.

summersault (ˈsʌmə͵sɔːlt) *n., vb.* a variant spelling of **somersault.**

summer school *n.* a school, academic course, etc., held during the summer.

summer solstice *n.* **1.** the time at which the sun is at its northernmost point in the sky (southernmost point in the S hemisphere). It occurs about June 21 (December 22 in the S hemisphere). **2.** *Astron.* the point on the celestial sphere, opposite the **winter solstice,** at which the ecliptic is furthest north from the celestial equator.

summertime (ˈsʌmə͵taɪm) *n.* the period or season of summer.

summer time *n. Brit.* any daylight-saving time, esp. British Summer Time.

summerweight (ˈsʌmə͵weɪt) *adj.* (of clothes) suitable in weight for wear in the summer.

summing-up *n.* **1.** a review or summary of the main points of an argument, speech, etc. **2.** concluding statements made by a judge to the jury before they retire to consider their verdict.

summit (ˈsʌmɪt) *n.* **1.** the highest point or part, esp. of a mountain; top. **2.** the highest possible degree or state; peak or climax: *the summit of ambition.* **3.** the highest level, importance, or rank: *a meeting at the summit.* **4. a.** a meeting of chiefs of governments or other high officials. **b.** (*as modifier*): *a summit conference.* [C15: < OF *somet,* dim. of *som,* < L *summum;* see SUM]

summon (ˈsʌmən) *vb.* (*tr.*) **1.** to order to come; send for, esp. to attend court, by issuing a summons. **2.** to order or instruct (to do something) or call (to something): *the bell summoned them to their work.* **3.** to call upon to meet or convene. **4.** (often foll. by *up*) to muster or gather (one's strength, courage, etc.). **5.** *Arch.* to call upon to surrender. [C13: < L *summonēre* to give a discreet reminder, < *monēre* to advise]

summons (ˈsʌmənz) *n., pl.* **-monses. 1.** a call, signal, or order to do something, esp. to attend at a specified place or time. **2. a.** an official order requiring a person to attend court, either to answer a charge or to give evidence. **b.** the writ making such an order. **3.** a call or command given to the members of an assembly to convene a meeting. ~*vb.* **4.** to take out a summons against (a person). [C13: < OF *somonse,* < *somondre* to SUMMON]

summum bonum *Latin.* (ˈsʊmʊm ˈbɒnʊm) *n.* the principle of goodness in which all moral values are included or from which they are derived; highest or supreme good.

sumo (ˈsuːməʊ) *n.* the national style of wrestling of Japan, the object of which is to force one's opponent to touch the ground with any part of his body except the soles of his feet or to step out of the ring. [< Japanese *sumō*]

sump (sʌmp) *n.* **1.** a receptacle, as in the crankcase of an internal-combustion engine, into which liquids, esp. lubricants, can drain to form a reservoir. **2.** another name for **cesspool** (sense 1). **3.** *Mining.* a depression at the bottom of a shaft where water collects. [C17: < MDu. *somp* marsh]

sumpter (ˈsʌmptə) *n. Arch.* a packhorse, mule, or other beast of burden. [C14: < OF *sometier* driver of a baggage horse, < Vulgar L *sagmatārius* (unattested), < LL *sagma* pack-saddle]

sumptuary (ˈsʌmptjʊərɪ) *adj.* relating to or controlling expenditure or extravagance. [C17: < L *sumptuārius* concerning expense, < *sumptus* expense, < *sūmere* to spend]

sumptuous (ˈsʌmptjʊəs) *adj.* **1.** expensive or extravagant: *sumptuous costumes.* **2.** magnificent; splendid: *a sumptuous scene.* [C16: < OF *somptueux,* < L *sumptuōsus* costly, < *sumptus;* see SUMPTUARY] **—ˈsumptuously** *adv.* **—ˈsumptuousness** *n.*

sum up *vb.* (*adv.*) **1.** to summarize (the main points of an argument, etc.). **2.** (*tr.*) to form a quick opinion of: *I summed him up in five minutes.*

sun (sʌn) *n.* **1.** the star that is the source of heat and light for the planets in the solar system. Related adj.: **solar. 2.** any star around which a planetary system revolves. **3.** the sun as it appears at a particular time or place: *the winter sun.* **4.** the radiant energy, esp. heat and light, received from the sun; sunshine. **5.** a person or thing considered as a source of radiant warmth, glory, etc. **6.** a pictorial representation of the sun, often depicted with a human face. **7.** *Poetic.* a year or a day. **8.** *Poetic.* a climate. **9.** *Arch.* sunrise or sunset (esp. in **from sun to sun**). **10. catch the sun.** to become slightly sunburnt. **11. place in the sun.** a prominent or favourable position. **12. take** *or* **shoot the sun.** *Naut.* to measure the altitude of the sun in order to determine latitude. **13. touch of the sun.** slight sunstroke. **14. under** *or* **beneath the sun.** on earth; at all: *nobody under the sun eats more than you.* ~*vb.* **sunning, sunned. 15.** to expose (oneself) to the sunshine. **16.** (*tr.*) to expose to the sunshine in order to warm, etc. [OE *sunne*]

Sun. *abbrev. for* Sunday.

sunbaked (ˈsʌn͵beɪkt) *adj.* **1.** (esp. of roads, etc.) dried or cracked by the sun's heat. **2.** baked hard by the heat of the sun: *sunbaked bricks.*

sun bath *n.* the exposure of the body to the rays of the sun or a sun lamp, esp. in order to get a suntan.

sunbathe (ˈsʌn͵beɪð) *vb.* (*intr.*) to bask in the sunshine, esp. in order to get a suntan. **—ˈsun͵bather** *n.*

sunbeam (ˈsʌn͵biːm) *n.* a beam, ray, or stream of sunlight.

sunbird (ˈsʌn͵bɜːd) *n.* any of various small songbirds of tropical regions of the Old World, esp. Africa, having a long slender curved bill and a bright plumage in the males.

sunbonnet (ˈsʌn͵bɒnɪt) *n.* a hat that shades the face and neck from the sun, esp. one of cotton with a projecting brim, now worn esp. by babies.

sunburn (ˈsʌn͵bɜːn) *n.* **1.** inflammation of the skin caused by overexposure to the sun. **2.** another word for **suntan. —ˈsun͵burnt** *or* **ˈsun͵burned** *adj.*

sunburst (ˈsʌn͵bɜːst) *n.* **1.** a burst of sunshine, as through a break in the clouds. **2.** a pattern or design resembling that of the sun. **3.** a jewelled brooch with this pattern.

sun-cured *adj.* cured or preserved by exposure to the sun.

sundae (ˈsʌndɪ, -deɪ) *n.* ice cream topped with a sweet sauce, nuts, whipped cream, etc. [C20: <?]

Sunday (ˈsʌndɪ) *n.* the first day of the week and the Christian day of worship. [OE *sunnandæg,* translation of L *diēs sōlis* day of the sun, translation of Gk *hēmera hēliou*]

Sunday best *n.* one's best clothes, esp. regarded as those most suitable for churchgoing.

Sunday school *n.* **1. a.** a school for the religious instruction of children on Sundays, usually held in a church. **b.** (*as modifier*): *a Sunday-school outing.* **2.** the members of such a school.

sunder (ˈsʌndə) *Arch. or literary.* ~*vb.* **1.** to break or cause to break apart or in pieces. ~*n.* **2. in sunder.** into pieces; apart. [OE *sundrian*]

sundew (ˈsʌnˌdjuː) *n.* any of several bog plants having leaves covered with sticky hairs that trap and digest insects. [C16: translation of L *ros solis*]

sundial (ˈsʌnˌdaɪəl) *n.* a device indicating the time during the hours of sunlight by means of a stationary arm (the **gnomon**) that casts a shadow onto a plate or surface marked in hours.

sun disc *n.* a disc symbolizing the sun, esp. one flanked by two serpents and the extended wings of a vulture: a religious figure in ancient Egypt.

sundog (ˈsʌnˌdɒg) *n.* another word for **parhelion.**

sundown (ˈsʌnˌdaʊn) *n.* another name for **sunset.**

sundowner (ˈsʌnˌdaʊnə) *n.* **1.** *Austral. sl.* a tramp, esp. one who seeks food and lodging at sundown when it is too late to work. **2.** *Inf., chiefly Brit.* an alcoholic drink taken at sunset.

sundress (ˈsʌnˌdrɛs) *n.* a dress for hot weather that exposes the shoulders, arms, and back.

sun-dried *adj.* dried or preserved by exposure to the sun.

sundry (ˈsʌndrɪ) *determiner.* **1.** several or various; miscellaneous. ~*pron.* **2. all and sundry.** everybody, individually and collectively. ~*n., pl.* **-dries. 3.** (*pl.*) miscellaneous unspecified items. **4.** the Austral. term for **extra** (sense 6). [OE *syndrig* separate]

sunfast (ˈsʌnˌfɑːst) *adj. Chiefly U.S. & Canad.* not fading in sunlight.

sunfish (ˈsʌnˌfɪʃ) *n., pl.* **-fish** *or* **-fishes. 1.** any of various large fishes of temperate and tropical seas, esp. one which has a large rounded compressed body, long pointed dorsal and anal fins, and a fringelike tail fin. **2.** any of various small predatory North American freshwater percoid fishes, typically having a compressed brightly coloured body.

sunflower (ˈsʌnˌflaʊə) *n.* **1.** any of several American plants having very tall thick stems, large flower heads with yellow rays, and seeds used as food, esp. for poultry. See also **Jerusalem artichoke. 2. sunflower seed oil.** the oil extracted from sunflower seeds, used as a salad oil, in margarine, etc.

sung (sʌŋ) *vb.* **1.** the past participle of **sing.** ~*adj.* **2.** produced by singing: *a sung syllable.*

▷ **Usage.** See at **ring**[2].

sunglass (ˈsʌnˌglɑːs) *n.* another name for **burning glass.**

sunglasses (ˈsʌnˌglɑːsɪz) *pl. n.* glasses with darkened or polarizing lenses that protect the eyes from the sun's glare.

sun-god *n.* **1.** the sun considered as a personal deity. **2.** a deity associated with the sun or controlling its movements.

sunk (sʌŋk) *vb.* **1.** a past tense and past participle of **sink.** ~*adj.* **2.** *Inf.* with all hopes dashed; ruined.

sunken (ˈsʌŋkən) *vb.* **1.** a past participle of **sink.** ~*adj.* **2.** unhealthily hollow: *sunken cheeks.* **3.** situated at a lower level than the surrounding or usual one: *a sunken bath.* **4.** situated under water; submerged. **5.** depressed; low: *sunken spirits.*

sunk fence *n.* a ditch, one side of which is made into a retaining wall so as to enclose an area of land while remaining hidden in the total landscape. Also called: **ha-ha.**

sun lamp *n.* **1.** a lamp that generates ultraviolet rays, used for obtaining an artificial suntan, for muscular therapy, etc. **2.** a lamp used in film studios, etc., to give an intense beam of light by means of parabolic mirrors.

sunless (ˈsʌnlɪs) *adj.* **1.** without sun or sunshine. **2.** gloomy; depressing. —ˈ**sunlessly** *adv.*

sunlight (ˈsʌnlaɪt) *n.* **1.** the light emanating from the sun. **2.** an area or the time characterized by sunshine. —ˈ**sunlit** *adj.*

sun lounge *or U.S.* **sun parlor** *n.* a room with large windows positioned to receive as much sunlight as possible.

Sunna (ˈsʌnə) *n.* the body of traditional Islamic law accepted by most orthodox Muslims as based on the words and acts of Mohammed. [C18: < Ar. *sunnah* rule]

Sunni (ˈsʌnɪ) *n.* **1.** one of the two main branches of orthodox Islam (the other being the Shiah), consisting of those who acknowledge the authority of the Sunna. **2.** (*pl.* **-ni**) a less common word for **Sunnite.**

Sunnite (ˈsʌnaɪt) *n.* an adherent of the Sunni.

sunny (ˈsʌnɪ) *adj.* **-nier, -niest. 1.** full of or exposed to sunlight. **2.** radiating good humour. **3.** of or resembling the sun. —ˈ**sunnily** *adv.* —ˈ**sunniness** *n.*

sunrise (ˈsʌnˌraɪz) *n.* **1.** the daily appearance of the sun above the horizon. **2.** the atmospheric phenomena accompanying this appearance. **3.** Also called (esp. U.S.): **sunup.** the time at which the sun rises at a particular locality.

sunrise industry *n.* any of the high-technology industries, such as electronics, that hold promise of future development.

sunset (ˈsʌnˌsɛt) *n.* **1.** the daily disappearance of the sun below the horizon. **2.** the atmospheric phenomena accompanying this disappearance. **3.** Also called: **sundown.** the time at which the sun sets at a particular locality. **4.** the final stage or closing period, as of a person's life.

sunshade (ˈsʌnˌʃeɪd) *n.* a device, esp. a parasol or awning, serving to shade from the sun.

sunshine (ˈsʌnˌʃaɪn) *n.* **1.** the light received directly from the sun. **2.** the warmth from the sun. **3.** a sunny area. **4.** a light-hearted or ironic term of address. —ˈ**sunˌshiny** *adj.*

sunshine roof *or* **sunroof** (ˈsʌnˌruːf) *n.* a panel in the roof of a car that may be opened by sliding it back.

sunspot (ˈsʌnˌspɒt) *n.* **1.** any of the dark cool patches that appear on the surface of the sun and last about a week. **2.** *Inf.* a sunny holiday resort. **3.** *Austral.* a small cancerous spot produced by overexposure to the sun.

sunstroke (ˈsʌnˌstrəʊk) *n.* heatstroke caused by prolonged exposure to intensely hot sunlight.

sunsuit (ˈsʌnˌsuːt, -ˌsjuːt) *n.* a child's outfit consisting of a brief top and shorts or skirt.

suntan (ˈsʌnˌtæn) *n.* **a.** a brownish colouring of the skin caused by the formation of the pigment melanin within the skin on exposure to the ultraviolet rays of the sun or a sunlamp. Often shortened to **tan. b.** (*as modifier*): *suntan oil.* —ˈ**sunˌtanned** *adj.*

suntrap (ˈsʌnˌtræp) *n.* a very sunny sheltered place.

sunward (ˈsʌnwəd) *adj.* **1.** directed or moving towards the sun. ~*adv.* **2.** Also: **sunwards.** towards the sun.

sup[1] (sʌp) *vb.* **supping, supped.** (*intr.*) *Arch.* to have supper. [C13: < OF *soper*]

sup[2] (sʌp) *vb.* **supping, supped. 1.** to partake of (liquid) by swallowing a little at a time. **2.** *Scot. & N English dialect.* to drink. ~*n.* **3.** a sip. [OE *sūpan*]

sup. *abbrev. for:* **1.** above. [< L *supra*] **2.** superior. **3.** *Grammar.* superlative. **4.** supplement. **5.** supplementary. **6.** supply.

super (suːpə) *adj.* **1.** *Inf.* outstanding; exceptional. ~*n.* **2.** petrol with a high octane rating. **3.** *Inf.* a supervisor. **4.** *Austral. & N.Z. inf.* superannuation benefits. **5.** *Austral & N.Z. inf.* superphosphate. ~*interj.* **6.** *Brit. inf.* an enthusiastic expression of approval. [< L: above]

super. *abbrev. for:* **1.** superfine. **2.** superior.

super- *prefix.* **1.** placed above or over: *superscript.* **2.** surpassing others; outstanding: *superstar.* **3.** of greater size, extent, quality, etc.: *supermarket.* **4.** beyond a standard or norm: *supersonic.* **5.** indicating that a chemical compound contains a specified element in a higher proportion than usual: *superphosphate.* [< L *super* above]

superable (ˈsuːpərəbᵊl) *adj.* able to be surmounted or overcome. [C17: < L *superābilis*, < *superāre* to overcome] —ˌ**superaˈbility** *or* ˈ**superableness** *n.* —ˈ**superably** *adv.*

ˌ**superaˈbound** *vb.*

superannuate (ˌsuːpərˈænjʊˌeɪt) *vb.* (*tr.*) **1.** to pension off. **2.** to discard as obsolete or old-fashioned.

superannuated (ˌsuːpərˈænjʊˌeɪtɪd) *adj.* **1.** discharged, esp. with a pension, owing to age or illness. **2.** too old to serve usefully. **3.** obsolete. [C17: < Med. L *superannātus* aged more than one year, < L SUPER- + *annus* a year]

superannuation (ˌsuːpərˌænjʊˈeɪʃən) *n.* **1. a.** the amount deducted regularly from employees' incomes in a contributory pension scheme. **b.** the pension finally paid. **2.** the act or process of superannuating or the condition of being superannuated.

superb (sʊˈpɜːb, sjʊ-) *adj.* **1.** surpassingly good; excellent. **2.** majestic or imposing. **3.** magnificently rich; luxurious. [C16: < OF *superbe*, < L *superbus* distinguished, < *super* above] **—suˈperbly** *adv.* **—suˈperbness** *n.*

supercalender (ˌsuːpəˈkæləndə) *n.* **1.** a calender that gives a high gloss to paper. ~*vb.* **2.** (*tr.*) to finish (paper) in this way. **—ˌsuperˈcalendered** *adj.*

supercargo (ˌsuːpəˈkɑːgəʊ) *n., pl.* **-goes.** an officer on a merchant ship who supervises commercial matters and is in charge of the cargo. [C17: changed < Sp. *sobrecargo*, < *sobre* over + *cargo* CARGO]

supercharge (ˈsuːpəˌtʃɑːdʒ) *vb.* (*tr.*) **1.** to increase the intake pressure of (an internal-combustion engine) with a supercharger; boost. **2.** to charge (the atmosphere, a remark, etc.) with an excess amount of (tension, emotion, etc.). **3.** to apply pressure to (a fluid); pressurize.

supercharger (ˈsuːpəˌtʃɑːdʒə) *n.* a device that increases the mass of air drawn into an internal-combustion engine by raising the intake pressure. Also called: **blower, booster.**

superciliary (ˌsuːpəˈsɪlɪərɪ) *adj.* over the eyebrow or a corresponding region in lower animals. [C18: < NL *superciliaris*, < L, < SUPER- + *cilium* eyelid]

supercilious (ˌsuːpəˈsɪlɪəs) *adj.* displaying arrogant pride, scorn, or indifference. [C16: < L, < *supercilium* eyebrow] **—ˌsuperˈciliously** *adv.* **—ˌsuperˈciliousness** *n.*

superclass (ˈsuːpəˌklɑːs) *n.* a taxonomic group that is a subdivision of a subphylum.

supercolumnar (ˌsuːpəkəˈlʌmnə) *adj. Archit.* **1.** having one colonnade above another. **2.** placed above a colonnade or a column. **—ˌsupercolˌumniˈation** *n.*

superconductivity (ˌsuːpəˌkɒndʌkˈtɪvɪtɪ) *n. Physics.* the property of certain substances that have almost no electrical resistance at very low temperatures. **—superconduction** (ˌsuːpəkənˈdʌkʃən) *n.* **—ˌsuperconˈductive** *or* **ˌsuperconˈducting** *adj.* **—ˌsuperconˈductor** *n.*

supercool (ˌsuːpəˈkuːl) *vb. Chem.* to cool or be cooled without freezing or crystallization to a temperature below that at which freezing or crystallization should occur.

superdense theory (ˌsuːpəˈdɛns) *n. Astron.* another name for the **big-bang theory.**

super-duper (ˈsuːpəˈduːpə) *adj. Inf.* extremely pleasing, impressive, etc.: often used as an exclamation.

superego (ˌsuːpərˈiːgəʊ, -ˈɛgəʊ) *n., pl.* **-gos.** *Psychoanal.* that part of the unconscious mind that acts as a conscience for the ego.

superelevation (ˌsuːpərˌɛlɪˈveɪʃən) *n.* **1.** another name for **bank**[2] (sense 8). **2.** the difference between the heights of the sides of a road or railway track on a bend.

supereminent (ˌsuːpərˈɛmɪnənt) *adj.* of distinction, dignity, or rank superior to that of others; pre-eminent. **—ˌsuperˈeminence** *n.* **—ˌsuperˈeminently** *adv.*

supererogation (ˌsuːpərˌɛrəˈgeɪʃən) *n.* **1.** the performance of work in excess of that required or expected. **2.** *R.C. Church.* supererogatory prayers, devotions, etc.

supererogatory (ˌsuːpərɛˈrɒgətərɪ, -trɪ) *adj.* **1.** performed to an extent exceeding that required or expected. **2.** exceeding what is needed; superfluous. **3.** *R.C. Church.* of or relating to prayers, good works, etc., performed over and above those prescribed as obligatory. [C16: < Med. L *superērogātōrius*, < L *supererogāre* to spend over and above]

superfamily (ˈsuːpəˌfæmɪlɪ) *n., pl.* **-lies.** **1.** *Biol.* a subdivision of a suborder. **2.** any analogous group, such as a group of related languages.

superfecundation (ˌsuːpəˌfiːkənˈdeɪʃən) *n. Physiol.* the fertilization of two or more ova, produced during the same menstrual cycle, by sperm ejaculated during two or more acts of sexual intercourse.

superfetation (ˌsuːpəfiːˈteɪʃən) *n. Physiol.* the presence in the uterus of two fetuses developing from ova fertilized at different times. [C17 *superfetate*, < L *superfētāre* to fertilize when already pregnant, < *fētus* offspring]

superficial (ˌsuːpəˈfɪʃəl) *adj.* **1.** of, near, or forming the surface: *superficial bruising.* **2.** displaying a lack of thoroughness or care: a *superficial inspection.* **3.** only outwardly apparent rather than genuine or actual: *the similarity was merely superficial.* **4.** of little substance or significance: *superficial differences.* **5.** lacking profundity: *the film's plot was quite superficial.* **6.** (of measurements) involving only the surface area. [C14: < LL *superficiālis* of the surface, < L SUPERFICIES] **—superficiality** (ˌsuːpəˌfɪʃɪˈælɪtɪ) *n.* **—ˌsuperˈficially** *adv.*

superficies (ˌsuːpəˈfɪʃiːz) *n., pl.* **-cies.** **1.** a surface or outer face. **2.** the outward form of a thing. [C16: < L: upper side]

superfine (ˌsuːpəˈfaɪn) *adj.* **1.** of exceptional fineness or quality. **2.** excessively refined. **—ˌsuperˈfineness** *n.*

superfix (ˈsuːpəˌfɪks) *n. Linguistics.* a type of feature distinguishing the meaning or grammatical function of one word or phrase from that of another, as stress does for example between the noun *conduct* and the verb *conduct.*

superfluid (ˌsuːpəˈfluːɪd) *n.* **1.** *Physics.* a fluid in a state characterized by a very low viscosity, high thermal conductivity, high capillarity, etc. The only known example is that of liquid helium at temperatures close to absolute zero. ~*adj.* **2.** being or relating to a superfluid. **—ˌsuperfluˈidity** *n.*

superfluity (ˌsuːpəˈfluːɪtɪ) *n.* **1.** the condition of being superfluous. **2.** a quantity or thing that is in excess of what is needed. **3.** a thing that is not needed. [C14: < OF *superfluité*, via LL < L *superfluus* SUPERFLUOUS]

superfluous (suːˈpɜːfluəs) *adj.* **1.** exceeding what is sufficient or required. **2.** not necessary or relevant; uncalled for. [C15: < L *superfluus* overflowing, < *fluere* to flow] **—suˈperfluously** *adv.* **—suˈperfluousness** *n.*

supergiant (ˈsuːpəˌdʒaɪənt) *n.* any of a class of extremely bright stars which have expanded to a diameter hundreds or thousands of times greater than that of the sun and have an extremely low mean density.

superglue (ˈsuːpəˌgluː) *n.* any of various adhesives that quickly make an exceptionally strong bond.

supergrass (ˈsuːpəˌgrɑːs) *n.* an informer whose information implicates a large number of people.

superheat (ˌsuːpəˈhiːt) *vb.* (*tr.*) **1.** to heat (a vapour, esp. steam) to a temperature above its saturation point for a given pressure. **2.** to heat (a liquid) to a temperature above its boiling point without boiling occurring. **3.** to heat excessively; overheat. **—ˌsuperˈheater** *n.*

superheterodyne receiver (ˌsuːpəˈhɛtərə-

ˌsuperaˈbundant *adj.*
ˌsuperceˈlestial *adj.*
ˌsuperˈconfident *adj.*
ˌsuperˈcritical *adj.*
ˌsuperˈdose *n.*
ˌsuperefˈficient *adj.*
ˌsuperˈfatted *adj.*

ˌdaɪn) *n.* a radio receiver that combines two radio-frequency signals by heterodyne action, to produce a signal above the audible frequency limit. Sometimes shortened to **superhet.** [C20: < SUPER(SONIC) + HETERODYNE]

superhigh frequency (ˈsuːpəˌhaɪ) *n.* a radio-frequency band or radio frequency lying between 30 000 and 3000 megahertz.

superhuman (ˌsuːpəˈhjuːmən) *adj.* **1.** having powers above and beyond those of mankind. **2.** exceeding normal human ability or experience. —ˌ**superˈhumanly** *adv.*

superimpose (ˌsuːpərɪmˈpəʊz) *vb.* (*tr.*) **1.** to set or place on or over something else. **2.** (usually foll. by *on* or *upon*) to add (to). —ˌ**superˌimpoˈsition** *n.*

superinduce (ˌsuːpərɪnˈdjuːs) *vb.* (*tr.*) to introduce as an additional feature, factor, etc. —**superinduction** (ˌsuːpərɪnˈdʌkʃən) *n.*

superintend (ˌsuːpərɪnˈtɛnd) *vb.* to undertake the direction or supervision (of); manage. [C17: < Church L *superintendere*, < L SUPER- + *intendere* to give attention to] —ˌ**superinˈtendence** *n.*

superintendent (ˌsuːpərɪnˈtɛndənt) *n.* **1.** a person who directs and manages an organization, office, etc. **2.** (in Britain) a senior police officer higher in rank than an inspector but lower than a chief superintendent. **3.** (in the U.S.) the head of a police department. **4.** *Chiefly U.S. & Canad.* a caretaker, esp. of a block of apartments. ~*adj.* **5.** of or relating to supervision; superintending. [C16: < Church L *superintendens* overseeing] —ˌ**superinˈtendency** *n.*

superior (suːˈpɪərɪə) *adj.* **1.** greater in quality, quantity, etc. **2.** of high or extraordinary worth, merit, etc. **3.** higher in rank or status. **4.** displaying a conscious sense of being above or better than others; supercilious. **5.** (*often postpositive;* foll. by *to*) not susceptible (to) or influenced (by). **6.** placed higher up; further from the base. **7.** *Astron.* (of a planet) having an orbit further from the sun than the orbit of the earth. **8.** (of a plant ovary) situated above the calyx and other floral parts. **9.** *Printing.* (of a character) written or printed above the line; superscript. ~*n.* **10.** a person or thing of greater rank or quality. **11.** *Printing.* a character set in a superior position. **12.** (*often cap.*) the head of a community in a religious order. [C14: < L, < *superus* placed above, < *super* above] —**suˈperioress** *fem. n.* —**superiority** (suːˌpɪərɪˈɒrɪtɪ) *n.*

superior court *n.* **1.** (in England) a higher court not subject to control by any other court except by way of appeal. See also **Supreme Court of Judicature.** **2.** (in several states of the U.S.) a court of general jurisdiction ranking above the inferior courts and below courts of last resort.

superiority complex *n. Inf.* an inflated estimate of one's own merit, usually manifested in arrogance.

superior planet *n.* any of the six planets (Mars, Jupiter, Saturn, Uranus, Neptune, and Pluto) whose orbit lies outside that of the earth.

superl. *abbrev. for* superlative.

superlative (suːˈpɜːlətɪv) *adj.* **1.** of outstanding quality, degree, etc.; supreme. **2.** *Grammar.* denoting the form of an adjective or adverb that expresses the highest or a very high degree of quality. In English this is usually marked by the suffix *-est* or the word *most,* as in *loudest* or *most loudly.* **3.** (of language or style) excessive; exaggerated. ~*n.* **4.** a thing that excels all others or is of the highest quality. **5.** *Grammar.* the superlative form of an adjective. **6.** the highest degree; peak. [C14: < OF *superlatif,* via LL < L *superlātus* extravagant, < *superferre* to carry beyond] —**suˈperlatively** *adv.* —**suˈperlativeness** *n.*

superlunar (ˌsuːpəˈluːnə) *adj.* beyond the moon; celestial. —ˌ**superˈlunary** *adj.*

superman (ˈsuːpəˌmæn) *n., pl.* **-men.** **1.** (in the philosophy of Nietzsche) an ideal man who would rise above good and evil and who represents the goal of human evolution. **2.** any man of apparently superhuman powers.

supermarket (ˈsuːpəˌmɑːkɪt) *n.* a large self-service store selling food and household supplies.

supermundane (ˌsuːpəˈmʌndeɪn) *adj.* elevated above earthly things.

supernal (suːˈpɜːnᵊl, sjuː-) *adj. Literary.* **1.** divine; celestial. **2.** of, from above, or from the sky. [C15: < Med. L *supernālis,* < L *supernus* that is on high, < *super* above] —**suˈpernally** *adv.*

supernatant (ˌsuːpəˈneɪtᵊnt) *adj.* **1.** floating on the surface or over something. **2.** *Chem.* (of a liquid) lying above a sediment or settled precipitate. [C17: < L *supernatāre* to float, < SUPER- + *natāre* to swim] —ˌ**supernaˈtation** *n.*

supernatural (ˌsuːpəˈnætʃərəl) *adj.* **1.** of or relating to things that cannot be explained according to natural laws. **2.** of or caused as if by a god; miraculous. **3.** of or involving occult beings. **4.** exceeding the ordinary; abnormal. ~*n.* **5. the supernatural.** supernatural forces, occurrences, and beings collectively. —ˌ**superˈnaturally** *adv.* —ˌ**superˈnaturalness** *n.*

supernaturalism (ˌsuːpəˈnætʃərəlɪzəm) *n.* **1.** the quality or condition of being supernatural. **2.** belief in supernatural forces or agencies as producing effects in this world. —ˌ**superˈnaturalist** *n., adj.* —ˌ**superˌnaturalˈistic** *adj.*

supernormal (ˌsuːpəˈnɔːməl) *adj.* greatly exceeding the normal. —**supernormality** (ˌsuːpənɔːˈmælɪtɪ) *n.* —ˌ**superˈnormally** *adv.*

supernova (ˌsuːpəˈnəʊvə) *n., pl.* **-vae** (-viː) *or* **-vas.** a star that explodes owing to instabilities following the exhaustion of its nuclear fuel, becoming for a few days up to one hundred million times brighter than the sun. Cf. **nova.**

supernumerary (ˌsuːpəˈnjuːmərərɪ) *adj.* **1.** exceeding a regular or proper number; extra. **2.** functioning as a substitute or assistant with regard to a regular body or staff. ~*n., pl.* **-aries.** **3.** a person or thing that exceeds the required or regular number. **4.** a substitute or assistant. **5.** an actor who has no lines, esp. a nonprofessional one. [C17: < LL *supernumerārius,* < L SUPER- + *numerus* number]

superorder (ˈsuːpərˌɔːdə) *n. Biol.* a subdivision of a subclass.

superordinate *adj.* (ˌsuːpərˈɔːdənɪt). **1.** of higher status or condition. ~*n.* (ˌsuːpərˈɔːdɪnɪt) **2.** a person or thing that is superordinate. **3.** a word the meaning of which includes the meaning of another word or words: *"red" is the superordinate of "scarlet" and "crimson".*

superphosphate (ˌsuːpəˈfɒsfeɪt) *n.* **1.** a mixture of the diacid calcium salt of orthophosphoric acid with calcium sulphate and small quantities of other phosphates: used as a fertilizer. **2.** a salt of phosphoric acid formed by incompletely replacing its acidic hydrogen atoms.

superpose (ˌsuːpəˈpəʊz) *vb.* (*tr.*) *Geom.* to transpose (the coordinates of one geometric figure) to coincide with those of another. [C19: < F *superposer,* < L *superpōnere,* < *pōnere* to place]

superposition (ˌsuːpəpəˈzɪʃən) *n.* **1.** the act of superposing or state of being superposed. **2.** *Geol.* the principle that in any sequence of sedimentary rocks that has not been disturbed the lowest strata are the oldest.

superpower (ˈsuːpəˌpaʊə) *n.* **1.** an extremely powerful state, such as the U.S. **2.** extremely high power, esp. electrical or mechanical. —ˈ**superˌpowered** *adj.*

supersaturated (ˌsuːpəˈsætʃəˌreɪtɪd) *adj.* **1.** (of a solution) containing more solute than a saturated solution. **2.** (of a vapour) containing more material than a saturated vapour. —ˌ**superˌsatuˈration** *n.*

superscribe (ˌsuːpəˈskraɪb) *vb.* (*tr.*) to write (an

ˌ**superinˈtelligent** *adj.*
ˌ**superˈpolymer** *n.*
ˌ**superˈpure** *adj.*
ˌ**superreˈfine** *vb.*
ˌ**superˈrich** *adj.*

inscription, name, etc.) above, on top of, or outside. [C16: < L *superscrībere*, < *scrībere* to write] —**superscription** (ˌsuːpəˈskrɪpʃən) *n.*

superscript (ˈsuːpəˌskrɪpt) *adj.* **1.** *Printing.* (of a character) written or printed above the line; superior. Cf. **subscript.** ~*n.* **2.** a superscript or superior character. [C16: < L *superscriptus*]

supersede (ˌsuːpəˈsiːd) *vb.* (*tr.*) **1.** to take the place of (something old-fashioned or less appropriate); supplant. **2.** to replace in function, office, etc.; succeed. **3.** to discard or set aside or cause to be set aside as obsolete or inferior. [C15: via OF < L *supersedēre* to sit above] —ˌ**superˈsedence** *n.* —**supersedure** (ˌsuːpəˈsiːdʒə) *n.* —**supersession** (ˌsuːpəˈsɛʃən) *n.*

supersex (ˈsuːpəˌsɛks) *n. Genetics.* a sterile organism in which the ratio between the sex chromosomes is disturbed.

supersonic (ˌsuːpəˈsɒnɪk) *adj.* being, having, or capable of a velocity in excess of the velocity of sound. —ˌ**superˈsonically** *adv.*

supersonics (ˌsuːpəˈsɒnɪks) *n.* (*functioning as sing.*) **1.** the study of supersonic motion. **2.** a less common name for **ultrasonics.**

superstar (ˈsuːpəˌstɑː) *n.* an extremely popular film star, pop star, etc.

superstition (ˌsuːpəˈstɪʃən) *n.* **1.** irrational belief usually founded on ignorance or fear and characterized by obsessive reverence for omens, charms, etc. **2.** a notion, act, or ritual that derives from such belief. **3.** any irrational belief, esp. with regard to the unknown. [C15: < L *superstitiō*, < *superstāre* to stand still by something (as in amazement)]

superstitious (ˌsuːpəˈstɪʃəs) *adj.* **1.** disposed to believe in superstition. **2.** of or relating to superstition. —ˌ**superˈstitiously** *adv.* —ˌ**superˈstitiousness** *n.*

superstore (ˈsuːpəˌstɔː) *n.* a large supermarket.

superstratum (ˌsuːpəˈstrɑːtəm, -ˈstreɪ-) *n., pl.* **-ta** (-tə) *or* **-tums.** *Geol.* a layer or stratum overlying another layer or similar structure.

superstructure (ˈsuːpəˌstrʌktʃə) *n.* **1.** the part of a building above its foundation. **2.** any structure or concept erected on something else. **3.** *Naut.* any structure above the main deck of a ship with sides flush with the sides of the hull. **4.** the part of a bridge supported by the piers and abutments. —ˈ**superˌstructural** *adj.*

supertanker (ˈsuːpəˌtæŋkə) *n.* a large fast tanker of more than 275 000 tons capacity.

supertax (ˈsuːpəˌtæks) *n.* a tax levied in addition to the basic or normal tax, esp. a surtax on incomes above a certain level.

supertonic (ˌsuːpəˈtɒnɪk) *n. Music.* **1.** the second degree of a major or minor scale. **2.** a key or chord based on this.

supervene (ˌsuːpəˈviːn) *vb.* (*intr.*) **1.** to follow closely; ensue. **2.** to occur as an unexpected or extraneous development. [C17: < L *supervenīre* to come upon] —ˌ**superˈvenience** *or* **supervention** (ˌsuːpəˈvɛnʃən) *n.* —ˌ**superˈvenient** *adj.*

supervise (ˈsuːpəˌvaɪz) *vb.* (*tr.*) **1.** to direct or oversee the performance or operation of. **2.** to watch over so as to maintain order, etc. [C16: < Med. L *supervidēre*, < L SUPER- + *vidēre* to see] —**supervision** (ˌsuːpəˈvɪʒən) *n.*

supervisor (ˈsuːpəˌvaɪzə) *n.* **1.** a person who manages or supervises. **2.** a foreman or forewoman. **3.** (in some British universities) a tutor supervising the work, esp. research work, of a student. **4.** (in some U.S. schools) an administrator running a department of teachers. —ˈ**superˌvisorship** *n.* —ˈ**superˌvisory** *adj.*

supinate (ˈsuːpɪˌneɪt, ˈsjuː-) *vb.* to turn (the hand and forearm) so that the palm faces up or forwards. [C19: < L *supīnāre* to lay on the back, < *supīnus* supine] —ˌ**supiˈnation** *n.*

supine *adj.* (suːˈpaɪn, sjuː-; ˈsuːpaɪn, ˈsjuː-). **1.** lying or resting on the back with the face, palm, etc., upwards. **2.** displaying no interest or animation; lethargic. ~*n.* (ˈsuːpaɪn, ˈsjuː-). **3.** *Grammar.* a noun form derived from a verb in Latin, often used to express purpose with verbs of motion. [C15: < L *supīnus* rel. to *sub* under, up; (in grammatical sense) < L *verbum supīnum* supine word (<?)] —**suˈpinely** *adv.* —**suˈpineness** *n.*

supp. *or* **suppl.** *abbrev. for* supplement(ary).

supper (ˈsʌpə) *n.* **1.** an evening meal, esp. a light one. **2.** an evening social event featuring a supper. **3. sing for one's supper.** to obtain something by performing a service. [C13: < OF *soper*] —ˈ**supperless** *adj.*

supplant (səˈplɑːnt) *vb.* (*tr.*) to take the place of, often by trickery or force. [C13: via OF < L *supplantāre* to trip up, < *sub-* from below + *planta* sole of the foot] —**supˈplanter** *n.*

supple (ˈsʌpᵊl) *adj.* **1.** bending easily without damage. **2.** capable of or showing easy or graceful movement; lithe. **3.** mentally flexible; responding readily. **4.** disposed to agree, sometimes to the point of servility. ~*vb.* **5.** *Rare.* to make or become supple. [C13: < OF *souple*, < L *supplex* bowed] —ˈ**suppleness** *n.*

supplejack (ˈsʌpᵊlˌdʒæk) *n.* **1.** a North American twining woody vine that has greenish-white flowers and purple fruits. **2.** a bush plant of New Zealand having tough climbing vines. **3.** a tropical American woody vine having strong supple wood. **4.** any of various other vines with strong supple stems. **5.** *U.S.* a walking stick made from the wood of the tropical supplejack.

supplement *n.* (ˈsʌplɪmənt). **1.** an addition designed to complete, make up for a deficiency, etc. **2.** a section appended to a publication to supply further information, correct errors, etc. **3.** a magazine or section inserted into a newspaper or periodical, such as one issued every week. **4.** *Geom.* **a.** either of a pair of angles whose sum is 180°. **b.** an arc of a circle that when added to another arc forms a semicircle. ~*vb.* (ˈsʌplɪˌmɛnt). **5.** (*tr.*) to provide a supplement to, esp. in order to remedy a deficiency. [C14: < L *supplēmentum*, < *supplēre* to SUPPLY] —ˌ**supplemenˈtation** *n.*

supplementary (ˌsʌplɪˈmɛntərɪ) *adj.* **1.** Also (*less commonly*): **supplemental** (ˌsʌpləˈmɛntᵊl). forming or acting as a supplement. ~*n., pl.* **-ries. 2.** a person or thing that is a supplement. —ˌ**suppleˈmentarily** *or* (*less commonly*) ˌ**suppleˈmentally** *adv.*

supplementary angle *n.* either of two angles whose sum is 180°.

supplementary benefit *n.* (in Britain) a weekly allowance paid to various groups of people by the state to bring their incomes up to minimum levels established by law.

suppliant (ˈsʌplɪənt) *adj.* **1.** expressing entreaty or supplication. ~*n., adj.* **2.** another word for **supplicant.** [C15: < F *supplier* to beseech, < L *supplicāre* to kneel in entreaty] —ˈ**suppliantly** *adv.*

supplicant (ˈsʌplɪkənt) *or* **suppliant** *n.* **1.** a person who supplicates. ~*adj.* **2.** entreating humbly; supplicating. [C16: < L *supplicāns* beseeching]

supplicate (ˈsʌplɪˌkeɪt) *vb.* **1.** to make a humble request to (someone); plead. **2.** (*tr.*) to ask for or seek humbly. [C15: < L *supplicāre* to beg on one's knees] —ˌ**suppliˈcation** *n.* —ˈ**suppliˌcatory** *adj.*

supply[1] (səˈplaɪ) *vb.* **-plying, -plied. 1.** (*tr.; often foll. by with*) to furnish with something required. **2.** (*tr.; often foll. by to or for*) to make available or provide (something desired or lacking): *to supply books to the library.* **3.** (*tr.*) to provide for adequately; satisfy: *who will supply their needs?* **4.** to serve as a substitute, usually temporary, in (another's position, etc.): *there are no clergymen to supply the pulpit.* **5.** (*tr.*) *Brit.* to fill (a vacancy, position, etc.). ~*n., pl.* **-plies. 6. a.** the act of providing or something provided. **b.** (*as modifier*): *a supply dump.* **7.** (*often pl.*) an amount

ˌ**superˈsensitive** *adj.* ˌ**supersufˈficiency** *n.*

available for use; stock. **8.** (*pl.*) food, equipment, etc., needed for a campaign or trip. **9.** *Econ.* **a.** willingness and ability to offer goods and services for sale. **b.** the amount of a commodity that producers are willing and able to offer for sale at a specified price. Cf. **demand** (sense 9). **10.** *Mil.* **a.** the management and disposal of food and equipment. **b.** (*as modifier*): *supply routes.* **11.** (*often pl.*) a grant of money voted by a legislature for government expenses. **12.** (in Parliament and similar legislatures) the money voted annually for the expenses of the civil service and armed forces. **13. a.** a person who acts as a temporary substitute, esp. a clergyman. **b.** (*as modifier*): *a supply teacher.* **14.** a source of electricity, gas, etc. [C14: < OF *souppleier,* < L *supplēre* to complete, < *sub-* up + *plēre* to fill] **—supˈpliable** *adj.* **—supˈplier** *n.*

supply[2] (ˈsʌplɪ) *or* **supplely** (ˈsʌpᵊlɪ) *adv.* in a supple manner.

supply-side economics *n.* (*functioning as sing.*) the theory that reductions in taxation lead to greater investment in industry, which is seen as the driving force of the economy, rather than to demand for consumer goods and services.

support (səˈpɔːt) *vb.* (*tr.*) **1.** to carry the weight of. **2.** to bear (pressure, weight, etc.). **3.** to provide the necessities of life for (a family, person, etc.). **4.** to tend to establish (a theory, statement, etc.) by providing new facts. **5.** to speak in favour of (a motion). **6.** to give aid or courage to. **7.** to give approval to (a cause, principle, etc.); subscribe to. **8.** to endure with forbearance: *I will no longer support bad behaviour.* **9.** to give strength to; maintain: *to support a business.* **10.** (*tr.*) (in a concert) to perform earlier than (the main attraction). **11.** *Films, theatre.* **a.** to play a subordinate role to. **b.** to accompany (the feature) in a film programme. **12.** to act or perform (a role or character). *~n.* **13.** the act of supporting or the condition of being supported. **14.** a thing that bears the weight or part of the weight of a construction. **15.** a person who or thing that furnishes aid. **16.** the means of maintenance of a family, person, etc. **17.** a band or entertainer not topping the bill. **18.** (often preceded by *the*) an actor or group of actors playing subordinate roles. **19.** *Med.* an appliance worn to ease the strain on an injured bodily structure or part. **20.** Also: **athletic support.** a more formal term for **jockstrap.** [C14: < OF *supporter,* < L *supportāre* to bring, < *sub-* up + *portāre* to carry] **—supˈportable** *adj.* **—supˈportive** *adj.*

supporter (səˈpɔːtə) *n.* **1.** a person who or thing that acts as a support. **2.** a person who backs a sports team, politician, etc. **3.** a garment or device worn to ease the strain on or restrict the movement of a bodily structure or part. **4.** *Heraldry.* a figure or beast in a coat of arms depicted as holding up the shield.

supporting (səˈpɔːtɪŋ) *adj.* **1.** (of a role) being a fairly important but not leading part. **2.** (of an actor or actress) playing a supporting role.

suppose (səˈpəʊz) *vb.* (*tr.; may take a clause as object*) **1.** to presume (something) to be true without certain knowledge: *I suppose he meant to kill her.* **2.** to consider as a possible suggestion for the sake of discussion, etc.: *suppose that he wins.* **3.** (of theories, etc.) to imply the inference or assumption (of): *your policy supposes full employment.* [C14: < OF *supposer,* < Med. L *suppōnere,* < L: to substitute, < SUB- + *pōnere* to put] **—supˈposable** *adj.* **—supˈposer** *n.*

supposed (səˈpəʊzd, -ˈpəʊzɪd) *adj.* **1.** (*prenominal*) presumed to be true without certain knowledge. **2.** (*prenominal*) believed to be true on slight grounds; highly doubtful. **3.** (səˈpəʊzd). (*postpositive; foll. by to*) expected or obliged (to): *I'm supposed to be there.* **4.** (*postpositive; used in negative;* foll. by *to*) expected or obliged not (to): *you're not supposed to walk on the grass.* **—supposedly** (səˈpəʊzɪdlɪ) *adv.*

supposition (ˌsʌpəˈzɪʃən) *n.* **1.** the act of supposing. **2.** a fact, theory, etc., that is supposed. **—ˌsuppoˈsitional** *adj.* **—ˌsuppoˈsitionally** *adv.*

suppositious (ˌsʌpəˈzɪʃəs) *or* **supposititious** (səˌpɒzɪˈtɪʃəs) *adj.* **1.** deduced from supposition; hypothetical. **2.** substituted with intent to mislead or deceive. **—ˌsuppoˈsitiously** *or* **supˌposiˈtitiously** *adv.* **—ˌsuppoˈsitiousness** *or* **supˌposiˈtitiousness** *n.*

suppositive (səˈpɒzɪtɪv) *adj.* **1.** of, involving, or arising out of supposition. **2.** *Grammar.* denoting a conjunction introducing a clause expressing a supposition, as for example *if, supposing,* or *provided that.* *~n.* **3.** *Grammar.* a suppositive conjunction. **—supˈpositively** *adv.*

suppository (səˈpɒzɪtərɪ, -trɪ) *n., pl.* **-ries.** *Med.* a solid medication for insertion into the vagina, rectum, or urethra, where it melts and releases the active substance. [C14: < Med. L *suppositōrium,* < L *suppositus* placed beneath]

suppress (səˈprɛs) *vb.* (*tr.*) **1.** to put an end to; prohibit. **2.** to hold in check; restrain: *I was obliged to suppress a smile.* **3.** to withhold from circulation or publication: *to suppress seditious pamphlets.* **4.** to stop the activities of; crush: *to suppress a rebellion.* **5.** *Electronics.* **a.** to reduce or eliminate (unwanted oscillations) in a circuit. **b.** to eliminate (a particular frequency or frequencies) in a signal. **6.** *Psychiatry.* to resist consciously (an idea or a desire entering one's mind). [C14: < L *suppressus* held down, < *supprimere* to restrain, < *sub-* down + *premere* to press] **—supˈpressible** *adj.* **—supˈpressive** *adj.* **—supˈpressor** *or* **supˈpresser** *n.*

suppression (səˈprɛʃən) *n.* **1.** the act or process of suppressing or the condition of being suppressed. **2.** *Psychiatry.* the conscious avoidance of unpleasant thoughts.

suppurate (ˈsʌpjʊˌreɪt) *vb.* (*intr.*) *Pathol.* (of a wound, sore, etc.) to discharge pus; fester. [C16: < L *suppūrāre,* < SUB- + *pūs* pus] **—ˌsuppuˈration** *n.* **—ˈsuppurative** *adj.*

supra- *prefix.* over, above, beyond, or greater than: *supranational.* [< L *suprā* above]

supraliminal (ˌsuːprəˈlɪmɪnᵊl, ˌsjuː-) *adj.* of or relating to any stimulus that is above the threshold of sensory awareness. **—ˌsupraˈliminally** *adv.*

supramolecular (ˌsuːprəməˈlɛkjʊlə, ˌsjuː-) *adj.* **1.** more complex than a molecule. **2.** consisting of more than one molecule.

supranational (ˌsuːprəˈnæʃnᵊl, ˌsjuː-) *adj.* involving or relating to more than one nation. **—ˌsupraˈnationalism** *n.*

supraorbital (ˌsuːprəˈɔːbɪtᵊl, ˌsjuː-) *adj.* *Anat.* situated above the orbit.

suprarenal (ˌsuːprəˈriːnᵊl, ˌsjuː-) *adj.* *Anat.* situated above a kidney.

suprarenal gland *n.* another name for **adrenal gland.**

supremacist (sʊˈprɛməsɪst, sjʊ-) *n.* **1.** a person who promotes or advocates the supremacy of any particular group. *~adj.* **2.** characterized by belief in the supremacy of any particular group. **—suˈprematism** *n.*

supremacy (sʊˈprɛməsɪ, sjʊ-) *n.* **1.** supreme power; authority. **2.** the quality or condition of being supreme.

supreme (sʊˈpriːm, sjʊ-) *adj.* **1.** of highest status or power. **2.** (*usually prenominal*) of highest quality, importance, etc. **3.** greatest in degree; extreme: *supreme folly.* **4.** (*prenominal*) final or last, ultimate: *the supreme judgment.* [C16: < L *suprēmus* highest, < *superus* that is above, < *super* above] **—suˈpremely** *adv.*

Supreme Being *n.* God.

Supreme Court *n.* (in the U.S.) **1.** the highest Federal court. **2.** (in many states) the highest state court.

Supreme Court of Judicature *n.* (in England) a court formed in 1873 by the amalgamation of several superior courts into two divisions, the High Court of Justice and the Court of Appeal.

supreme sacrifice *n.* **the.** the sacrifice of one's life.

Supreme Soviet *n.* (in the Soviet Union) **1.** the

bicameral legislature, comprising the **Soviet of the Union** and the **Soviet of the Nationalities.** **2.** a similar legislature in each republic.

supremo (sʊˈpriːməʊ, sjʊ-) *n., pl.* **-mos.** *Brit. inf.* a person in overall authority. [C20: < SUPREME]

Supt *or* **supt** *abbrev. for* superintendent.

sur-[1] *prefix.* over; above; beyond: *surcharge; surrealism.* Cf. **super-.** [< OF, < L SUPER-]

sur-[2] *prefix.* a variant of **sub-** before *r: surrogate.*

sura (ˈsʊərə) *n.* any of the 114 chapters of the Koran. [C17: < Ar. *sūrah* section]

surah (ˈsʊərə) *n.* a twill-weave fabric of silk or rayon. [C19: < F pronunciation of *Surat,* a port in W India where orig. made]

sural (ˈsjʊərəl) *adj. Anat.* of or relating to the calf of the leg. [C17: via NL < L *sūra* calf]

surbase (ˈsɜːˌbeɪs) *n.* the uppermost part, such as a moulding, of a pedestal, base, or skirting.

surcease (sɜːˈsiːs) *Arch.* ~*n.* **1.** cessation or intermission. ~*vb.* **2.** to desist from (some action). **3.** to cease or cause to cease. [C16: < earlier *sursesen,* < OF *surseoir,* < L *supersedēre* to sit above]

surcharge *n.* (ˈsɜːˌtʃɑːdʒ). **1.** a charge in addition to the usual payment, tax, etc. **2.** an excessive sum charged, esp. when unlawful. **3.** an extra and usually excessive burden or supply. **4.** an overprint that alters the face value of a postage stamp. ~*vb.* (sɜːˈtʃɑːdʒ, ˈsɜːˌtʃɑːdʒ). (*tr.*) **5.** to charge an additional sum, tax, etc. **6.** to overcharge (a person) for something. **7.** to put an extra physical burden upon; overload. **8.** to fill to excess; overwhelm. **9.** *Law.* to insert credits that have been omitted in (an account). **10.** to overprint a surcharge on (a stamp).

surcingle (ˈsɜːˌsɪŋɡᵊl) *n.* a girth for a horse which goes around the body, used esp. with a racing saddle. [C14: < OF *surcengle,* < *sur-* over + *cengle* a belt, < L *cingulum*]

surcoat (ˈsɜːˌkəʊt) *n.* **1.** a tunic, often embroidered with heraldic arms, worn by a knight over his armour during the Middle Ages. **2.** (formerly) an outer coat or other garment.

surculose (ˈsɜːkjʊˌləʊs) *adj.* (of a plant) bearing suckers. [C19: < L *surculōsus* woody, < *surculus* twig, < *sūrus* a branch]

surd (sɜːd) *n.* **1.** *Maths.* a number containing an irrational root, such as $2\sqrt{3}$; irrational number. **2.** *Phonetics.* a voiceless consonant, such as (t). ~*adj.* **3.** of or relating to a surd. [C16: < L *surdus* muffled]

sure (ʃʊə, ʃɔː) *adj.* **1.** (sometimes foll. by *of*) free from hesitancy or uncertainty (with regard to a belief, conviction, etc.): *we are sure of the accuracy of the data; I am sure that he is lying.* **2.** (foll. by *of*) having no doubt, as of the occurrence of a future state or event: *sure of success.* **3.** always effective; unfailing: *a sure remedy.* **4.** reliable in indication or accuracy: *a sure criterion.* **5.** (of persons) worthy of trust or confidence: *a sure friend.* **6.** not open to doubt: *sure proof.* **7.** admitting of no vacillation or doubt: *he is sure in his beliefs.* **8.** bound to be or occur; inevitable: *victory is sure.* **9.** (*postpositive*) bound inevitably (to be or do something); certain: *she is sure to be there.* **10.** physically secure or dependable: *a sure footing.* **11. be sure.** (*usually imperative or dependent imperative; takes a clause as object or an infinitive,* sometimes with *to* replaced by *and*) to be careful or certain: *be sure and shut the door; be sure to shut the door.* **12. for sure.** without a doubt; surely. **13. make sure. a.** (*takes a clause as object*) to make certain; ensure. **b.** (foll. by *of*) to establish or confirm power or possession (over). **14. sure enough.** *Inf.* as might have been confidently expected; definitely: often used as a sentence substitute. **15. to be sure. a.** without doubt; certainly. **b.** it has to be acknowledged; admittedly. ~*adv.* **16.** (*sentence modifier*) *U.S. & Canad inf.* without question; certainly. **17.** (*sentence substitute*) *U.S. & Canad. inf.* willingly; yes. [C14: < OF *seur,* < L *sēcūrus* SECURE] —ˈ**sureness** *n.*

sure-fire *adj.* (*usually prenominal*) *Inf.* certain to succeed or meet expectations; assured.

sure-footed *adj.* **1.** unlikely to fall, slip, or stumble. **2.** not likely to err or fail. —ˌ**sure-ˈfootedly** *adv.* —ˌ**sure-ˈfootedness** *n.*

surely (ˈʃʊəlɪ, ˈʃɔː-) *adv.* **1.** without doubt; assuredly. **2.** without fail; inexorably (esp. in **slowly but surely**). **3.** (*sentence modifier*) am I not right in thinking that?; I am sure that: *surely you don't mean it?* **4.** *Rare.* in a sure manner. **5.** *Arch.* safely; securely. **6.** (*sentence substitute*) *Chiefly U.S. & Canad.* willingly; yes.

sure thing *Inf.* **1.** (*sentence substitute*) *Chiefly U.S.* used to express enthusiastic assent. ~*n.* **2.** something guaranteed to be successful.

surety (ˈʃʊətɪ, ˈʃʊərɪtɪ) *n., pl.* **-ties.** **1.** a person who assumes legal responsibility for the fulfilment of another's debt or obligation and himself becomes liable if the other defaults. **2.** security given against loss or damage or as a guarantee that an obligation will be met. **3.** *Obs.* the quality or condition of being sure. **4. stand surety.** to act as a surety. [C14: < OF *seurte,* < L *sēcūritās* security] —ˈ**suretyship** *n.*

surf (sɜːf) *n.* **1.** waves breaking on the shore or on a reef. **2.** foam caused by the breaking of waves. ~*vb.* **3.** (*intr.*) to take part in surfing. [C17: prob. var. of SOUGH] —ˈ**surfy** *adj.*

surface (ˈsɜːfɪs) *n.* **1. a.** the exterior face of an object or one such face. **b.** (*as modifier*): *surface gloss.* **2.** the area or size of such a face. **3.** material resembling such a face, with length and width but without depth. **4. a.** the superficial appearance as opposed to the real nature. **b.** (*as modifier*): *a surface resemblance.* **5.** *Geom.* **a.** the complete boundary of a solid figure. **b.** a continuous two-dimensional configuration. **6. a.** the uppermost level of the land or sea. **b.** (*as modifier*): *surface transportation.* **7. come to the surface.** to emerge; become apparent. **8. on the surface.** to all appearances. ~*vb.* **9.** to rise or cause to rise to or as if to the surface (of water, etc.). **10.** (*tr.*) to treat the surface of, as by polishing, smoothing, etc. **11.** (*tr.*) to furnish with a surface. **12.** (*intr.*) to become apparent; emerge. **13.** (*intr.*) *Inf.* **a.** to wake up. **b.** to get up. [C17: < F, < *sur* on + *face* FACE] —ˈ**surfacer** *n.*

surface-active *adj.* (of a substance, esp. a detergent) capable of lowering the surface tension of a liquid. See also **surfactant.**

surface mail *n.* mail transported by land or sea. Cf. **air mail.**

surface structure *n. Generative grammar.* a representation of a string of words or morphemes as they occur in a sentence, together with labels and brackets that represent syntactic structure. Cf. **deep structure.**

surface tension *n.* **1.** a property of liquids caused by intermolecular forces near the surface leading to the apparent presence of a surface film and to capillarity, etc. **2.** a measure of this.

surface-to-air *adj.* of or relating to a missile launched from the surface of the earth against airborne targets.

surfactant (sɜːˈfæktənt) *n.* a substance, such as a detergent, that can reduce the surface tension of a liquid and thus allow it to foam or penetrate solids; a wetting agent. Also called: **surface-active agent.** [C20: *surf*(*ace*)-*act*(*ive*) *a*(*ge*)*nt*]

surfboard (ˈsɜːfˌbɔːd) *n.* a long narrow board used in surfing.

surfboat (ˈsɜːfˌbəʊt) *n.* a boat with a high bow and stern and flotation chambers, equipped for use in rough surf.

surfcasting (ˈsɜːfˌkɑːstɪŋ) *n.* fishing from the shore by casting into the surf. —ˈ**surfˌcaster** *n.*

surfeit (ˈsɜːfɪt) *n.* **1.** (usually foll. by *of*) an excessive amount. **2.** overindulgence, esp. in eating or drinking. **3.** disgust, nausea, etc., caused by such overindulgence. ~*vb.* **4.** (*tr.*) to supply or feed excessively; satiate. **5.** (*intr.*) *Arch.* to eat, drink, or be supplied to excess. [C13: < F *sourfait,* < *sourfaire* to overdo, < SUR-[1] + *faire,* < L *facere* to do]

surfie (ˈsɜːfɪ) *n. Austral. & N.Z. sl.* a young person whose main interest in life is surfing.

surfing (ˈsɜːfɪŋ) *n.* the sport of riding towards shore on the crest of a wave by standing or lying on a surfboard. —**ˈsurfer** *or* **ˈsurfˌrider** *n.*

surg. *abbrev. for:* **1.** surgeon. **2.** surgery. **3.** surgical.

surge (sɜːdʒ) *n.* **1.** a strong rush or sweep; sudden increase: *a surge of anger.* **2.** the rolling swell of the sea. **3.** a heavy rolling motion or sound: *the surge of the trumpets.* **4.** an undulating rolling surface, as of hills. **5.** a billowing cloud or volume. **6.** *Naut.* a temporary release or slackening of a rope or cable. **7.** a large momentary increase in the voltage or current in an electric circuit. **8.** an instability or unevenness in the power output of an engine. ~*vb.* **9.** (*intr.*) (of waves, the sea, etc.) to rise or roll with a heavy swelling motion. **10.** (*intr.*) to move like a heavy sea. **11.** *Naut.* to slacken or temporarily release (a rope or cable) from a capstan or (of a rope, etc.) to be slackened or released and slip back. **12.** (*intr.*) (of an electric current or voltage) to undergo a large momentary increase. **13.** (*tr.*) *Rare.* to cause to move in or as if in a wave or waves. [C15: < L *surgere* to rise, < *sub-* up + *regere* to lead] —**ˈsurger** *n.*

surgeon (ˈsɜːdʒən) *n.* **1.** a medical practitioner who specializes in surgery. **2.** a medical officer in the Royal Navy. [C14: < Anglo-Norman *surgien,* < OF *cirurgien;* see SURGERY]

surgeonfish (ˈsɜːdʒənˌfɪʃ) *n., pl.* **-fish** *or* **-fishes.** any of various tropical marine spiny-finned fishes, having a compressed brightly coloured body with knifelike spines at the base of the tail.

surgeon general *n., pl.* **surgeons general. 1.** (esp. in the British and U.S. armies and navies) the senior officer of the medical service. **2.** the head of the U.S. public health service.

surgery (ˈsɜːdʒərɪ) *n., pl.* **-geries. 1.** the branch of medicine concerned with manual or operative procedures, esp. incision into the body. **2.** the performance of such procedures by a surgeon. **3.** *Brit.* a place where, or time when, a doctor, dentist, etc., can be consulted. **4.** *Brit.* an occasion when an MP, lawyer, etc. is available for consultation. **5.** *U.S. & Canad.* an operating theatre. [C14: via OF < L *chirurgia,* < Gk *kheirurgia,* < *kheir* hand + *ergon* work]

surgical (ˈsɜːdʒɪkᵊl) *adj.* of, relating to, involving, or used in surgery. —**ˈsurgically** *adv.*

surgical boot *n.* a specially designed boot or shoe that compensates for deformities of the foot or leg.

surgical spirit *n.* methylated spirit used medically for sterilizing.

suricate (ˈsjʊərɪˌkeɪt) *n.* another name for **slender-tailed meerkat** (see **meerkat**). [C18: < F *surikate,* prob. < a native South African word]

surly (ˈsɜːlɪ) *adj.* **-lier, -liest. 1.** sullenly ill-tempered or rude. **2.** (of an animal) ill-tempered or refractory. [C16: < obs. *sirly* haughty] —**ˈsurlily** *adv.* —**ˈsurliness** *n.*

surmise *vb.* (sɜːˈmaɪz). **1.** (when *tr., may take a clause as object*) to infer (something) from incomplete or uncertain evidence. ~*n.* (sɜːˈmaɪz, ˈsɜːmaɪz). **2.** an idea inferred from inconclusive evidence. [C15: < OF, < *surmettre* to accuse, < L *supermittere* to throw over] —**surmisedly** (sɜːˈmaɪzɪdlɪ) *adv.*

surmount (sɜːˈmaʊnt) *vb.* (*tr.*) **1.** to prevail over; overcome. **2.** to ascend and cross to the opposite side of. **3.** to lie on top of or rise above. **4.** to put something on top of or above. [C14: < OF *surmonter,* < SUR-[1] + *monter* to mount] —**surˈmountable** *adj.*

surname (ˈsɜːˌneɪm) *n.* **1.** Also called: **last name, second name.** a family name as opposed to a Christian name. **2.** (formerly) a descriptive epithet attached to a person's name to denote a personal characteristic, profession, etc.; nickname. ~*vb.* **3.** (*tr.*) to furnish with or call by a surname. —**ˈsurˌnamer** *n.*

surpass (sɜːˈpɑːs) *vb.* (*tr.*) **1.** to be greater than in degree, extent, etc. **2.** to be superior to in achievement or excellence. **3.** to overstep the limit or range of: *the theory surpasses my comprehension.* [C16: < F *surpasser,* < SUR-[1] + *passer* to PASS] —**surˈpassable** *adj.*

surpassing (sɜːˈpɑːsɪŋ) *adj.* **1.** exceptional; extraordinary. ~*adv.* **2.** *Obs. or poetic.* (intensifier): *surpassing fair.* —**surˈpassingly** *adv.*

surplice (ˈsɜːplɪs) *n.* a loose wide-sleeved liturgical vestment of linen, reaching to the knees, worn over the cassock by clergymen, choristers, and acolytes. [C13: < OF *sourpelis,* < Med. L *superpellicium,* < SUPER- + *pellicium* coat made of skins, < L *pellis* a skin]

surplus (ˈsɜːpləs) *n., pl.* **-pluses. 1.** a quantity or amount in excess of what is required. **2.** *Accounting.* **a.** an excess of total assets over total liabilities. **b.** an excess of actual net assets over the nominal value of capital stock. **c.** an excess of revenues over expenditures. **3.** *Econ.* **a.** an excess of government revenues over expenditures. **b.** an excess of receipts over payments on the balance of payments. ~*adj.* **4.** being in excess; extra. [C14: < OF, < Med. L *superplūs,* < L SUPER- + *plūs* more]

surprise (səˈpraɪz) *vb.* (*tr.*) **1.** to cause to feel amazement or wonder. **2.** to encounter or discover unexpectedly or suddenly. **3.** to capture or assault suddenly and without warning. **4.** to present with something unexpected, such as a gift. **5.** (foll. by *into*) to provoke (someone) to unintended action by a trick, etc. **6.** (often foll. by *from*) to elicit by unexpected behaviour or by a trick: *to surprise information from a prisoner.* ~*n.* **7.** the act or an instance of surprising; the act of taking unawares. **8.** a sudden or unexpected event, gift, etc. **9.** the feeling or condition of being surprised; astonishment. **10.** (*modifier*) causing, characterized by, or relying upon surprise: *a surprise move.* **11. take by surprise. a.** to come upon suddenly and without warning. **b.** to capture unexpectedly or catch unprepared. **c.** to astonish; amaze. [C15: < OF, < *surprendre* to overtake, < SUR-[1] + L *prehendere* to grasp] —**surˈprisal** *n.* —**surˈprised** *adj.* —**surprisedly** (səˈpraɪzɪdlɪ) *adv.*

surprising (səˈpraɪzɪŋ) *adj.* causing surprise; unexpected or amazing. —**surˈprisingly** *adv.*

surra (ˈsʊərə) *n.* a tropical febrile disease of cattle, horses, camels, and dogs. [< Marathi, a language of India]

surrealism (səˈrɪəˌlɪzəm) *n.* (*sometimes cap.*) a movement in art and literature in the 1920s, which developed esp. from Dada, characterized by the evocative juxtaposition of incongruous images in order to include unconscious and dream elements. [C20: < F *surréalisme,* < SUR-[1] + *réalisme* realism] —**surˈreal** *adj.* —**surˈrealist** *n., adj.* —**surˌrealˈistic** *adj.*

surrebutter (ˌsɜːrɪˈbʌtə) *n. Law.* (in pleading) the plaintiff's reply to the defendant's rebutter. —ˌ**surreˈbuttal** *n.*

surrejoinder (ˌsɜːrɪˈdʒɔɪndə) *n. Law.* (in pleading) the plaintiff's reply to the defendant's rejoinder.

surrender (səˈrɛndə) *vb.* **1.** (*tr.*) to relinquish to another under duress or on demand: *to surrender a city.* **2.** (*tr.*) to relinquish or forego (an office, position, etc.), esp. as a voluntary concession to another: *he surrendered his place to a lady.* **3.** to give (oneself) up physically, as to an enemy. **4.** to allow (oneself) to yield, as to a temptation, influence, etc. **5.** (*tr.*) to give up (hope, etc.) **6.** (*tr.*) *Law.* to give up or restore (an estate), esp. to give up a lease before expiration of the term. **7. surrender to bail.** to present oneself at court at the appointed time after having been on bail. ~*n.* **8.** the act or instance of surrendering. **9.** *Insurance.* the voluntary discontinuation of a life policy by its holder in return for a consideration (the **surrender value**). **10.** *Law.* **a.** the yielding up or restoring of an estate, esp. the giving up of a lease before its term has expired. **b.** the giving up to the appropriate authority of a fugitive from justice. **c.** the act of surrendering or being surrendered to bail. **d.** the deed by which a legal surrender is effected. [C15: < OF *surrendre* to yield]

surreptitious (ˌsʌrəpˈtɪʃəs) *adj.* **1.** done, acquired, etc., in secret or by improper means. **2.** operating by stealth. [C15: < L *surreptīcius* furtive, < *surripere* to steal, < *sub-* secretly + *rapere* to snatch] —ˌ**surrepˈtitiously** *adv.* —ˌ**surrepˈtitiousness** *n.*

surrey (ˈsʌrɪ) *n.* a light four-wheeled horse-drawn carriage having two or four seats. [C19: < *Surrey cart*, after *Surrey* where orig. made]

surrogate *n.* (ˈsʌrəgɪt). **1.** a person or thing acting as a substitute. **2.** *Chiefly Brit.* a deputy, such as a clergyman appointed to deputize for a bishop in granting marriage licences. **3.** (in some U.S. states) a judge with jurisdiction over the probate of wills, etc. **4.** (*modifier*) of, relating to, or acting as a surrogate: *a surrogate pleasure.* ~*vb.* (ˈsʌrəˌgeɪt). (*tr.*) **5.** to put in another's position as a deputy, substitute, etc. [C17: < L *surrogāre* to substitute] —ˈ**surrogateship** *n.* —ˌ**surroˈgation** *n.*

surrogate motherhood *or* **surrogacy** (ˈsʌrəgəsɪ) *n.* the role of a woman who bears a child on behalf of a childless couple, either by artificial insemination or implantation of an embryo. —**surrogate mother** *n.*

surround (səˈraʊnd) *vb.* (*tr.*) **1.** to encircle or enclose or cause to be encircled or enclosed. **2.** to deploy forces on all sides of (a place or military formation), so preventing access or retreat. **3.** to exist around: *the people who surround her.* ~*n.* **4.** *Chiefly Brit.* a border, esp. the area of uncovered floor between the walls of a room and the carpet or around an opening or panel. **5.** *Chiefly U.S.* **a.** a method of capturing wild beasts by encircling the area in which they are believed to be. **b.** the area so encircled. [C15 *surrounden* to overflow, < OF *suronder*, < LL, < L SUPER- + *undāre* to abound, < *unda* a wave] —**surˈrounding** *adj.*

surroundings (səˈraʊndɪŋz) *pl. n.* the conditions, scenery, etc., around a person, place, or thing; environment.

sursum corda (ˈsɜːsəm ˈkɔːdə) *n.* **1.** *R.C. Church.* a Latin versicle meaning *Lift up your hearts,* said by the priest at Mass. **2.** a cry of exhortation, hope, etc.

surtax (ˈsɜːˌtæks) *n.* **1.** a tax, usually highly progressive, levied on the amount by which a person's income exceeds a specific level. **2.** an additional tax on something that has already been taxed. ~*vb.* **3.** (*tr.*) to assess for liability to surtax; charge with an extra tax.

surtitles (ˈsɜːˌtaɪtᵊlz) *pl. n.* brief translations of the text of an opera that is being sung in a foreign language, projected above the stage.

surtout (ˈsɜːtuː) *n.* a man's overcoat resembling a frock coat, popular in the late 19th century. [C17: < F, < *sur* over + *tout* all]

surveillance (sɜːˈveɪləns) *n.* close observation or supervision over a person, group, etc., esp. one in custody or under suspicion. [C19: < F, < *surveiller* to watch over, < SUR-¹ + *veiller* to keep watch (< L *vigilāre;* see VIGIL)] —**surˈveillant** *adj., n.*

survey *vb.* (sɜːˈveɪ, ˈsɜːveɪ). **1.** (*tr.*) to view or consider in a comprehensive or general way. **2.** (*tr.*) to examine carefully, as or as if to appraise value. **3.** to plot a detailed map of (an area of land) by measuring or calculating distances and height. **4.** *Brit.* to inspect a building to determine its condition and value. **5.** to examine a vessel thoroughly in order to determine its seaworthiness. **6.** (*tr.*) to run a statistical survey on (incomes, opinions, etc.). ~*n.* (ˈsɜːveɪ). **7.** a comprehensive or general view. **8.** a critical, detailed, and formal inspection. **9.** *Brit.* an inspection of a building to determine its condition and value. **10.** a report incorporating the results of such an inspection. **11. a.** a body of surveyors. **b.** an area surveyed. [C15: < F *surveoir,* < SUR-¹ + *veoir* to see, < L *vidēre*]

surveying (sɜːˈveɪɪŋ) *n.* **1.** the study or practice of making surveys of land. **2.** the setting out on the ground of the positions of proposed construction or engineering works.

surveyor (sɜːˈveɪə) *n.* **1.** a person whose occupation is to survey land or buildings. See also **quantity surveyor. 2.** *Chiefly Brit.* a person concerned with the official inspection of something for purposes of measurement and valuation. **3.** a person who carries out surveys, esp. of ships (**marine surveyor**) to determine seaworthiness, etc. **4.** a customs official. **5.** *Arch.* a supervisor. —**surˈveyorship** *n.*

surveyor's measure *n.* the system of measurement based on the **surveyor's chain** (66 feet) as a unit.

survival (səˈvaɪvᵊl) *n.* **1.** a person or thing that survives, such as a custom. **2. a.** the act or fact of surviving or condition of having survived. **b.** (*as modifier*): *survival kit.*

survival bag *n.* a large plastic bag carried by climbers for use in an emergency as protection against exposure.

survival of the fittest *n.* a popular term for **natural selection.**

survive (səˈvaɪv) *vb.* **1.** (*tr.*) to live after the death of (another). **2.** to continue in existence or use after (a passage of time, adversity, etc.). **3.** *Inf.* to endure (something): *I don't know how I survive such an awful job.* [C15: < OF *sourvivre,* < L *supervīvere,* < SUPER- + *vīvere* to live] —**surˈvivor** *n.*

sus (sʌs) *Brit. sl.* ~*n.* **1.** short for **suspicion,** with reference to police powers (**sus laws**) of detaining for questioning, searching, etc. any person suspected of criminal intent: *he was picked up on sus.* ~*vb.* **2.** a variant spelling of **suss.**

susceptance (səˈsɛptəns) *n. Physics.* the imaginary component of the admittance. [C19: < *suscept(ibility)* + -ANCE]

susceptibility (səˌsɛptəˈbɪlɪtɪ) *n., pl.* **-ties. 1.** the quality or condition of being susceptible. **2.** the ability or tendency to be impressed by emotional feelings. **3.** (*pl.*) emotional sensibilities; feelings. **4.** *Physics.* **a.** Also called: **electric susceptibility.** (of a dielectric) the amount by which the relative permittivity differs from unity. **b.** Also called: **magnetic susceptibility.** (of a magnetic medium) the amount by which the relative permeability differs from unity.

susceptible (səˈsɛptəbᵊl) *adj.* **1.** (*postpositive;* foll. by *of* or *to*) yielding readily (to); capable (of): *hypotheses susceptible of refutation; susceptible to control.* **2.** (*postpositive;* foll. by *to*) liable to be afflicted (by): *susceptible to colds.* **3.** easily impressed emotionally. [C17: < LL *susceptibilis,* < L *suscipere* to take up] —**susˈceptibly** *adv.*

suslik (ˈsʌslɪk) *or* **souslik** *n.* a central Eurasian ground squirrel having large eyes and small ears. [< Russian]

suspect *vb.* (səˈspɛkt). **1.** (*tr.*) to believe guilty of a specified offence without proof. **2.** (*tr.*) to think false, questionable, etc.: *she suspected his sincerity.* **3.** (*tr.; may take a clause as object*) to surmise to be the case; think probable: *to suspect fraud.* **4.** (*intr.*) to have suspicion. ~*n.* (ˈsʌspɛkt). **5.** a person under suspicion. ~*adj.* (ˈsʌspɛkt). **6.** causing or open to suspicion. [C14: < L *suspicere* to mistrust, < SUB- + *specere* to look]

suspend (səˈspɛnd) *vb.* **1.** (*tr.*) to hang from above. **2.** (*tr.; passive*) to cause to remain floating or hanging: *a cloud of smoke was suspended over the town.* **3.** (*tr.*) to render inoperative or cause to cease, esp. temporarily. **4.** (*tr.*) to hold in abeyance; postpone action on. **5.** (*tr.*) to debar temporarily from privilege, office, etc., as a punishment. **6.** (*tr.*) *Chem.* to cause (particles) to be held in suspension in a fluid. **7.** (*tr.*) *Music.* to continue (a note) until the next chord is sounded, with which it usually forms a dissonance. See **suspension** (sense 11). **8.** (*intr.*) to cease payment, as from incapacity to meet financial obligations. [C13: < L *suspendere* < SUB- + *pendere* to hang] —**susˈpendible** *or* **susˈpensible** *adj.* —**susˌpendiˈbility** *n.*

suspended animation *n.* a temporary cessation of the vital functions, as by freezing an organism.

suspended sentence *n.* a sentence of imprisonment that is not served by an offender unless he commits a further offence during its currency.

suspender (səˈspɛndə) *n.* **1.** (*often pl.*) *Brit.* **a.** an elastic strap attached to a belt or corset having a fastener at the end, for holding up women's stockings. **b.** a similar fastener attached to a garter worn by men in order to support socks. **2.** (*pl.*) the U.S. and Canad. name for **braces. 3.** a person or thing that suspends, such as one of the vertical cables in a suspension bridge.

suspender belt *n.* a belt with suspenders hanging from it to hold up women's stockings.

suspense (səˈspɛns) *n.* **1.** the condition of being insecure or uncertain. **2.** mental uncertainty; anxiety: *their father's illness kept them in a state of suspense.* **3.** excitement felt at the approach of the climax: *a play of terrifying suspense.* **4.** the condition of being suspended. [C15: < Med. L *suspensum* delay, < L *suspendere* to hang up] —**susˈpenseful** *adj.*

suspense account *n.* an account in which entries are made until determination of their proper disposition.

suspension (səˈspɛnʃən) *n.* **1.** an interruption or temporary revocation: *the suspension of a law.* **2.** a temporary debarment, as from position, privilege, etc. **3.** a deferment, esp. of a decision, judgment, etc. **4.** *Law.* a postponement of execution of a sentence or the deferring of a judgment, etc. **5.** cessation of payment of business debts, esp. as a result of insolvency. **6.** the act of suspending or the state of being suspended. **7.** a system of springs, shock absorbers, etc., that supports the body of a wheeled or tracked vehicle and insulates it from shocks transmitted by the wheels. **8.** a device or structure, usually a wire or spring, that serves to suspend or support something, such as the pendulum of a clock. **9.** *Chem.* a dispersion of fine solid or liquid particles in a fluid, the particles being supported by buoyancy. See also **colloid. 10.** the process by which eroded particles of rock are transported in a river. **11.** *Music.* one or more notes of a chord that are prolonged until a subsequent chord is sounded, usually to form a dissonance.

suspension bridge *n.* a bridge suspended from cables or chains that hang between two towers and are anchored at both ends.

suspensive (səˈspɛnsɪv) *adj.* **1.** having the power of deferment; effecting suspension. **2.** causing, characterized by, or relating to suspense. —**susˈpensively** *adv.* —**susˈpensiveness** *n.*

suspensory (səˈspɛnsərɪ) *n., pl.* **-ries. 1.** Also called: **suspensor.** *Anat.* a ligament or muscle that holds a structure or part in position. **2.** *Med.* a bandage, sling, etc., for supporting a dependent part. ~*adj.* **3.** suspending or supporting. **4.** *Anat.* (of a ligament or muscle) supporting or holding a structure or part in position.

suspicion (səˈspɪʃən) *n.* **1.** the act or an instance of suspecting; belief without sure proof, esp. that something is wrong. **2.** the feeling of mistrust of a person who suspects. **3.** the state of being suspected: *to be shielded from suspicion.* **4.** a slight trace. **5. above suspicion.** in such a position that no guilt may be thought or implied, esp. through having an unblemished reputation. **6. on suspicion.** as a suspect. **7. under suspicion.** regarded with distrust. [C14: < OF *sospeçon,* < L *suspīciō* distrust, < *suspicere;* see SUSPECT] —**susˈpicional** *adj.*

suspicious (səˈspɪʃəs) *adj.* **1.** exciting or liable to excite suspicion; questionable. **2.** disposed to suspect something wrong. **3.** indicative or expressive of suspicion. —**susˈpiciously** *adv.* —**susˈpiciousness** *n.*

suss (sʌs) *vb.* (*tr.*) *Brit. & N.Z. sl.* **1.** (often foll. by *out*) to attempt to work out (a situation, person's character, etc.), esp. using one's intuition. **2.** Also: **sus.** to become aware of; suspect (esp. in **suss it**). [C20: shortened < SUSPECT]

sustain (səˈsteɪn) *vb.* (*tr.*) **1.** to hold up under; withstand: *to sustain great provocation.* **2.** to undergo (an injury, loss, etc.); suffer: *to sustain a broken arm.* **3.** to maintain or prolong: *to sustain a discussion.* **4.** to support physically from below. **5.** to provide for or give support to, esp. by supplying necessities: *to sustain one's family.* **6.** to keep up the vitality or courage of. **7.** to uphold or affirm the justice or validity of: *to sustain a decision.* **8.** to establish the truth of; confirm. ~*n.* **9.** *Music.* the prolongation of a note, by playing technique or electronics. [C13: via OF < L *sustinēre* to hold up] —**susˈtainable** *adj.* —**susˈtained** *adj.* —**sustainedly** (səˈsteɪnɪdlɪ) *adv.* —**susˈtainer** *n.* —**susˈtaining** *adj.* —**susˈtainment** *n.*

sustaining pedal *n. Music.* a foot-operated lever on a piano that keeps the dampers raised from the strings when keys are released, allowing them to continue to vibrate.

sustenance (ˈsʌstənəns) *n.* **1.** means of sustaining health or life; nourishment. **2.** means of maintenance; livelihood. **3.** Also: **sustention** (səˈstɛnʃən). the act or process of sustaining or the quality of being sustained. [C13: < OF *sostenance,* < *sustenir* to SUSTAIN]

sustentation (ˌsʌstɛnˈteɪʃən) *n.* a less common word for **sustenance.** [C14: < L *sustentātio,* < *sustentāre,* frequentative of *sustinēre* to SUSTAIN]

susurrate (ˈsjuːsəˌreɪt) *vb.* (*intr.*) *Literary.* to make a soft rustling sound; whisper; murmur. [C17: < L *susurrāre* to whisper] —ˌ**susurˈration** *or* ˈ**susurrus** *n.*

sutler (ˈsʌtlə) *n.* (formerly) a merchant who accompanied an army in order to sell provisions to the soldiers. [C16: < obs. Du. *soeteler,* ult. < MHG *sudelen* to do dirty work]

sutra (ˈsuːtrə) *n.* **1.** *Hinduism.* Sanskrit sayings or collections of sayings on Vedic doctrine dating from about 200 A.D. onwards. **2.** (*modifier*) *Hinduism.* **a.** of or relating to the last of the Vedic literary periods, from about 500 to 100 B.C.: *the sutra period.* **b.** of or relating to the sutras or compilations of sutras of about 200 A.D. onwards. **3.** *Buddhism.* collections of dialogues and discourses of classic Mahayana Buddhism dating from the 2nd to the 6th century A.D. [C19: < Sansk.: list of rules]

suttee (sʌˈtiː, ˈsʌtiː) *n.* **1.** the former Hindu custom whereby a widow burnt herself to death on her husband's funeral pyre. **2.** a widow performing this. [C18: < Sansk. *satī* virtuous woman, < *sat* good] —**sutˈteeism** *n.*

suture (ˈsuːtʃə) *n.* **1.** *Surgery.* **a.** catgut, silk thread, or wire used to stitch together two bodily surfaces. **b.** the surgical seam formed after stitching. **2.** *Anat.* a type of immovable joint, esp. between the bones of the skull (**cranial suture**). **3.** a seam or joining, as in sewing. **4.** *Zool.* a line of junction in a mollusc shell. ~*vb.* **5.** (*tr.*) *Surgery.* to join (the edges of a wound, etc.) by means of sutures. [C16: < L *sūtūra,* < *suere* to sew] —ˈ**sutural** *adj.*

suzerain (ˈsuːzəˌreɪn) *n.* **1. a.** a state or sovereign exercising some degree of dominion over a dependent state, usually controlling its foreign affairs. **b.** (*as modifier*): *a suzerain power.* **2. a.** a feudal overlord. **b.** (*as modifier*): *suzerain lord.* [C19: < F, < *sus* above (< L *sursum* turned upwards) + *-erain,* as in *souverain* sovereign]

suzerainty (ˈsuːzərəntɪ) *n., pl.* **-ties. 1.** the position, power, or dignity of a suzerain. **2.** the relationship between suzerain and subject.

sv *abbrev. for:* **1.** sailing vessel. **2.** side valve. **3.** sub verbo *or* voce. [L: under the word]

svelte (svɛlt, sfɛlt) *adj.* attractively or gracefully slim; slender. [C19: < F, < It. *svelto,* < *svellere* to pull out, < L *ēvellere*]

SW 1. *symbol for* southwest(ern). **2.** *abbrev. for* short wave.

Sw. *abbrev. for:* **1.** Sweden. **2.** Swedish.

swab (swɒb) *n.* **1.** *Med.* **a.** a small piece of cotton, gauze, etc., for use in applying medication, cleansing a wound, or obtaining a specimen of a secretion, etc. **b.** the specimen so obtained. **2.** a mop for cleaning floors, decks, etc. **3.** a brush used to clean a firearm's bore. **4.** *Sl.* an uncouth or worthless fellow. ~*vb.* **swabbing, swabbed.** **5.** (*tr.*) to clean or medicate with or as if with a swab. **6.** (*tr.;* foll. by *up*) to take up with a swab. [C16: prob. < MDu. *swabbe* mop] —**'swabber** *n.*

swaddle ('swɒdᵊl) *vb.* (*tr.*) **1.** to wind a bandage round. **2.** to wrap (a baby) in swaddling clothes. **3.** to restrain as if by wrapping with bandages; smother. ~*n.* **4.** *Chiefly U.S.* swaddling clothes. [C15: < OE *swæthel* swaddling clothes]

swaddling clothes *pl. n.* **1.** long strips of linen or other cloth formerly wrapped round a newly born baby. **2.** restrictions or supervision imposed on the immature.

swaddy *or* **swaddie** ('swɒdɪ) *n. Brit. sl., old-fashioned.* a soldier. [C19: < E dialect *swad* country bumpkin, soldier]

swag (swæg) *n.* **1.** *Sl.* property obtained by theft or other illicit means. **2.** *Sl.* goods; valuables. **3.** an ornamental festoon of fruit, flowers, or drapery or a representation of this. **4.** a swaying movement; lurch. **5.** *Austral. & N.Z. inf.* a swagman's pack containing personal belongings, etc. **6. swags of.** *Austral. & N.Z. inf.* lots of. ~*vb.* **swagging, swagged.** **7.** *Chiefly Brit.* to lurch or sag or cause to lurch or sag. **8.** (*tr.*) to adorn or arrange with swags. [C17: ? of Scand. origin]

swage (sweɪdʒ) *n.* **1.** a shaped tool or die used in forming cold metal by hammering, pressing, etc. ~*vb.* **2.** (*tr.*) to form (metal) with a swage. [C19: < F *souage,* <?] —**'swager** *n.*

swage block *n.* an iron block with holes, grooves, etc., to assist in the cold-working of metal.

swagger ('swægə) *vb.* **1.** (*intr.*) to walk or behave in an arrogant manner. **2.** (*intr.;* often foll. by *about*) to brag loudly. ~*n.* **3.** an arrogant gait or manner. ~*adj.* **4.** *Brit. inf., rare.* elegantly fashionable. [C16: prob. < SWAG] —**'swaggerer** *n.* —**'swaggering** *adj.* —**'swaggeringly** *adv.*

swagger stick *or esp. Brit.* **swagger cane** *n.* a short cane or stick carried on occasion mainly by army officers.

swaggie ('swægɪ) *n. Austral. sl.* short for **swagman.**

swagman ('swæg,mæn, -mən) *n., pl.* **-men.** *Austral. & N.Z. inf.* a tramp or vagrant worker who carries his possessions on his back. Also called: **swaggie.**

Swahili (swɑː'hiːlɪ) *n.* **1.** a language of E Africa that is an official language of Kenya and Tanzania and is widely used as a lingua franca throughout E and central Africa. **2.** (*pl.* **-lis** *or* **-li**) a member of a people speaking this language, living chiefly in Zanzibar. ~*adj.* **3.** of or relating to the Swahilis or their language. [C19: < Ar. *sawāhil* coasts] —**Swa'hilian** *adj.*

swain (sweɪn) *n. Arch. or poetic.* **1.** a male lover or admirer. **2.** a country youth. [OE *swān* swineherd]

swallow[1] ('swɒləʊ) *vb.* (*mainly tr.*) **1.** to pass (food, drink, etc.) through the mouth to the stomach by means of the muscular action of the oesophagus. **2.** (often foll. by *up*) to engulf or destroy as if by ingestion. **3.** *Inf.* to believe gullibly: *he will never swallow such an excuse.* **4.** to refrain from uttering or manifesting: *to swallow one's disappointment.* **5.** to endure without retaliation. **6.** to enunciate (words, etc.) indistinctly; mutter. **7.** (often foll. by *down*) to eat or drink reluctantly. **8.** (*intr.*) to perform or simulate the act of swallowing, as in gulping. ~*n.* **9.** the act of swallowing. **10.** the amount swallowed at any single time; mouthful. **11.** *Rare.* another word for **throat** or **gullet.** [OE *swelgan*] —**'swallowable** *adj.* —**'swallower** *n.*

swallow[2] ('swɒləʊ) *n.* any of various passerine songbirds having long pointed wings, a forked tail, short legs, and a rapid flight. [OE *swealwe*]

swallow dive *n.* a type of dive in which the diver arches back while in the air, keeping his legs straight and together and his arms outstretched, finally entering the water headfirst. U.S. and Canad. equivalent: **swan dive.**

swallow hole *n. Chiefly Brit.* another word for **sinkhole** (sense 1).

swallowtail ('swɒləʊ,teɪl) *n.* **1.** any of various butterflies of Europe, having a tail-like extension of each hind wing. **2.** the forked tail of a swallow or similar bird. **3.** short for **swallow-tailed coat.** —**'swallow-,tailed** *adj.*

swallow-tailed coat *n.* another name for **tail coat.**

swam (swæm) *vb.* the past tense of **swim.**

swami ('swɑːmɪ) *n., pl.* **-mies** *or* **-mis.** (in India) a title of respect for a Hindu saint or religious teacher. [C18: < Hindi *svāmī,* < Sansk. *svāmin* master, < *sva* one's own]

swamp (swɒmp) *n.* **1.** permanently waterlogged ground that is usually overgrown and sometimes partly forested. Cf. **marsh.** ~*vb.* **2.** to drench or submerge or be drenched or submerged. **3.** *Naut.* to cause (a boat) to sink or fill with water or (of a boat) to sink or fill with water. **4.** to overburden or overwhelm or be overburdened or overwhelmed, as by excess work or great numbers. **5.** (*tr.*) to render helpless. [C17: prob. < MDu. *somp*] —**'swampy** *adj.*

swamp boat *n.* a shallow-draught boat powered by an aeroplane engine mounted on a raised structure for use in swamps. Also called: **airboat.**

swamp cypress *n.* a North American deciduous coniferous tree that grows in swamps. Also called: **bald cypress.**

swamp fever *n.* **1.** Also called: **equine infectious anaemia.** a viral disease of horses. **2.** *U.S.* another name for **malaria.**

swampland ('swɒmp,lænd) *n.* a permanently waterlogged area; marshland.

swan (swɒn) *n.* **1.** any of various large aquatic birds having a long neck and usually a white plumage. **2.** *Rare, literary.* **a.** a poet. **b.** (*cap. when part of a title or epithet*): *the Swan of Avon* (Shakespeare). ~*vb.* **swanning, swanned.** **3.** (*intr.;* usually foll. by *around* or *about*) *Inf.* to wander idly. [OE] —**'swan,like** *adj.*

swan dive *n.* the U.S. and Canad. name for **swallow dive.**

swank (swæŋk) *Inf.* ~*vb.* **1.** (*intr.*) to show off or swagger. ~*n.* **2.** Also called: **swankpot.** *Brit.* a swaggering or conceited person. **3.** *Chiefly U.S.* showy elegance or style. **4.** swagger; ostentation. ~*adj.* **5.** another word (esp. U.S.) for **swanky.** [C19: ? < MHG *swanken* to sway]

swanky ('swæŋkɪ) *adj.* **swankier, swankiest.** *Inf.* **1.** expensive and showy; stylish: *a swanky hotel.* **2.** boastful or conceited. —**'swankily** *adv.* —**'swankiness** *n.*

swan neck *n.* a tube, rail, etc., curved like a swan's neck.

swannery ('swɒnərɪ) *n., pl.* **-neries.** a place where swans are kept and bred.

swan's-down *n.* **1.** the fine soft down feathers of a swan, used to trim powder puffs, clothes, etc. **2.** a thick soft fabric of wool with silk, cotton, or rayon, used for infants' clothing, etc. **3.** a cotton fabric with a heavy nap.

swan song *n.* **1.** the last act, publication, etc., of a person before retirement or death. **2.** the song that a dying swan is said to sing.

swan-upping *n. Brit.* **1.** the practice or action of marking nicks in swans' beaks as a sign of ownership. **2.** the annual swan-upping of royal cygnets on the River Thames.

swap *or* **swop** (swɒp) *vb.* **swapping, swapped** *or* **swopping, swopped.** **1.** to trade or exchange (something or someone) for another. ~*n.* **2.** an exchange. **3.** something that is exchanged. [C14 (in the sense: to shake hands on a bargain, strike): prob. imit.] —**'swapper** *or* **'swopper** *n.*

SWAPO *or* **Swapo** ('swɑːpəʊ) *n. acronym for* South-West Africa People's Organization.

swaraj (swə'rɑːdʒ) *n.* (in British India) self-government; independence. [C20: < Sansk.

svarāj, < *sva* self + *rājya* rule] —**swa'rajism** *n.* —**swa'rajist** *n., adj.*

sward (swɔːd) *n.* **1.** turf or grass or a stretch of turf or grass. ~*vb.* **2.** to cover or become covered with grass. [OE *sweard* skin]

swarf (swɔːf, swɑːf) *n.* material removed by cutting or grinding tools in the machining of metals, stone, etc. [C16: of Scand. origin]

swarm[1] (swɔːm) *n.* **1.** a group of bees, led by a queen, that has left the parent hive to start a new colony. **2.** a large mass of small animals, esp. insects. **3.** a throng or mass, esp. when moving or in turmoil. ~*vb.* **4.** (*intr.*) (of small animals, esp. bees) to move in or form a swarm. **5.** (*intr.*) to congregate, move about or proceed in large numbers. **6.** (when *intr.*, often foll. by *with*) to overrun or be overrun (with): *swarming with rats.* **7.** (*tr.*) to cause to swarm. [OE *swearm*]

swarm[2] (swɔːm) *vb.* (when *intr.*, usually foll. by *up*) to climb (a ladder, etc.) by gripping with the hands and feet: *the boys swarmed up the rigging.* [C16: <?]

swart (swɔːt) *or* **swarth** (swɔːθ) *adj. Arch. or dialect.* swarthy. [OE *sweart*]

swarthy ('swɔːðɪ) *adj.* **swarthier, swarthiest.** dark-hued or dark-complexioned. [C16: < obs. *swarty*] —'**swarthily** *adv.* —'**swarthiness** *n.*

swash (swɒʃ) *vb.* **1.** (*intr.*) (esp. of water or things in water) to wash or move with noisy splashing. **2.** (*tr.*) to dash (a liquid, esp. water) against or upon. **3.** (*intr.*) *Arch.* to swagger. ~*n.* **4.** Also called: **send.** the dashing movement or sound of water, as of waves on a beach. **5.** Also called: **swash channel.** a channel of moving water cutting through or running behind a sandbank. **6.** *Arch.* swagger or bluster. [C16: prob. imit.]

swashbuckler ('swɒʃˌbʌklə) *n.* a swaggering or daredevil adventurer or bully. [C16: < SWASH (in archaic sense: to make the noise of a sword striking a shield) + BUCKLER]

swashbuckling ('swɒʃˌbʌklɪŋ) *adj.* (*usually prenominal*) **1.** of or characteristic of a swashbuckler. **2.** (esp. of films in period costume) full of adventure and excitement.

swash letter *n. Printing.* a decorative letter, esp. an ornamental italic capital. [C17: < *aswash* aslant]

swastika ('swɒstɪkə) *n.* **1.** a primitive religious symbol or ornament in the shape of a Greek cross, usually having the ends of the arms bent at right angles. **2.** this symbol with clockwise arms, the emblem of Nazi Germany. [C19: < Sansk. *svastika*, < *svasti* prosperity; < belief that it brings good luck]

swat (swɒt) *vb.* **swatting, swatted.** (*tr.*) **1.** to strike or hit sharply: *to swat a fly.* ~*n.* **2.** a sharp or violent blow. ~Also: **swot.** [C17: N English dialect & U.S. var. of SQUAT] —'**swatter** *n.*

swatch (swɒtʃ) *n.* **1.** a sample of cloth or other material. **2.** a number of such samples, usually fastened together in book form. [C16: Scot. & N English, <?]

swath (swɔːθ) *or* **swathe** (sweɪð) *n., pl.* **swaths** (swɔːðz) *or* **swathes. 1.** the width of one sweep of a scythe or of the blade of a mowing machine. **2.** the strip cut by these in one course. **3.** the quantity of cut grass, hay, etc., left in one such course. **4.** a long narrow strip or belt. [OE *swæth*]

swathe (sweɪð) *vb.* (*tr.*) **1.** to bandage (a wound, limb, etc.), esp. completely. **2.** to wrap a band, garment, etc., around, esp. so as to cover completely; swaddle. **3.** to envelop. ~*n.* **4.** a bandage or wrapping. **5.** a variant spelling of **swath.** [OE *swathian*]

sway (sweɪ) *vb.* **1.** (*usually intr.*) to swing or cause to swing to and fro: *the door swayed in the wind.* **2.** (*usually intr.*) to lean or incline or cause to lean or incline to one side or in different directions in turn. **3.** (*usually intr.*) to vacillate or cause to vacillate between two or more opinions. **4.** to be influenced or swerve or influence or cause to swerve to or from a purpose or opinion. **5.** *Arch. or poetic.* to rule or wield power (over). ~*n.* **6.** control; power. **7.** a swinging or leaning movement. **8.** *Arch.* dominion; governing authority. **9. hold sway.** to be master; reign. [C16: prob. < ON *sveigja* to bend]

sway-back *n.* an abnormal sagging or concavity of the spine in horses. —'**sway-ˌbacked** *adj.*

swear (swɛə) *vb.* **swearing, swore, sworn. 1.** to declare or affirm (a statement) as true, esp. by invoking a deity, etc., as witness. **2.** (foll. by *by*) **a.** to invoke (a deity, etc.) by name as a witness or guarantee to an oath. **b.** to trust implicitly; have complete confidence (in). **3.** (*intr.*; often foll. by *at*) to curse, blaspheme, or use swearwords. **4.** (when *tr.*, *may take a clause as object or an infinitive*) to promise solemnly on oath; vow. **5.** (*tr.*) to assert or affirm with great emphasis or earnestness. **6.** (*intr.*) to give evidence or make any statement or solemn declaration on oath. **7.** to take an oath in order to add force or solemnity to (a statement or declaration). ~*n.* **8.** a period of swearing. [OE *swerian*] —'**swearer** *n.*

swear in *vb.* (*tr., adv.*) to administer an oath to (a person) on his assuming office, entering the witness box to give evidence, etc.

swear off *vb.* (*intr., prep.*) to promise to abstain from something: *to swear off drink.*

swearword ('swɛəˌwɜːd) *n.* a socially taboo word of a profane, obscene, or insulting character.

sweat (swɛt) *n.* **1.** the secretion from the sweat glands, esp. when profuse and visible, as during strenuous activity, from excessive heat, etc.; perspiration. **2.** the act or process of secreting this fluid. **3.** the act of inducing the exudation of moisture. **4.** drops of moisture given forth or gathered on the surface of something. **5.** *Inf.* a state or condition of worry or eagerness (esp. in **in a sweat**). **6.** *Sl.* drudgery or hard labour: *mowing lawns is a real sweat!* **7.** *Sl., chiefly Brit.* a soldier, esp. one who is old and experienced. **8. no sweat!** *Sl.* an expression conveying consent or assurance. ~*vb.* **sweating; sweat** *or* **sweated. 9.** to secrete (sweat) through the pores of the skin, esp. profusely; perspire. **10.** (*tr.*) to make wet or stain with perspiration. **11.** to give forth or cause to give forth (moisture) in droplets: *the maple sweats sap.* **12.** (*intr.*) to collect and condense moisture on an outer surface: *a glass of beer sweating.* **13.** (*intr.*) (of a liquid) to pass through a porous surface in droplets. **14.** (of tobacco leaves, hay, etc.) to exude moisture and, sometimes, begin to ferment or to cause (tobacco leaves, etc.) to exude moisture. **15.** (*tr.*) to heat (food, esp. vegetables) slowly in butter in a tightly closed saucepan. **16.** (*tr.*) to join (pieces of metal) by pressing together and heating. **17.** (*tr.*) to heat (solder) until it melts. **18.** (*tr.*) to heat (partially fused metal) to extract an easily fusible constituent. **19.** *Inf.* to suffer anxiety, impatience, or distress. **20.** *Inf.* to overwork or be overworked. **21.** (*tr.*) *Inf.* to employ at very low wages and under bad conditions. **22.** (*tr.*) *Inf.* to extort, esp. by torture: *to sweat information out of a captive.* **23.** (*intr.*) *Inf.* to suffer punishment: *you'll sweat for this!* **24. sweat blood.** *Inf.* **a.** to work very hard. **b.** to be filled with anxiety or impatience. ~See also **sweat off, sweat out, sweats.** [OE *swætan* to sweat, < *swāt* sweat]

sweatband ('swɛtˌbænd) *n.* **1.** a band of material set in a hat or cap to protect it from sweat. **2.** a piece of cloth tied around the forehead to keep sweat out of the eyes or around the wrist to keep the hands dry, as in sports.

sweated ('swɛtɪd) *adj.* **1.** made by exploited labour: *sweated goods.* **2.** (of workers, etc.) forced to work in poor conditions for low pay.

sweater ('swɛtə) *n.* **1.** a garment made of knitted or crocheted material covering the upper part of the body, esp. a heavy one worn for warmth. **2.** a person or thing that sweats. **3.** an employer who overworks and underpays his employees.

sweat gland *n.* any of the coiled tubular subcutaneous glands that secrete sweat.

sweating sickness *n.* an acute infectious febrile disease that was widespread in Europe during the late 15th century, characterized by profuse sweating.

sweat off *or* **away** *vb.* (*tr., adv.*) *Inf.* to get rid of (weight) by strenuous exercise or sweating.

sweat out *vb.* (*tr., adv.*) **1.** to cure or lessen the effects of (a cold, respiratory infection, etc.) by sweating. **2.** *Inf.* to endure (hardships) for a time (often in **sweat it out**). **3. sweat one's guts out.** *Inf.* to work extremely hard.

sweats (swɛts) *pl. n.* sweat shirts and sweat-suit trousers: *jeans and sweats.*

sweat shirt *n.* a long-sleeved knitted cotton sweater worn by athletes, etc.

sweatshop (ˈswɛtˌʃɒp) *n.* a workshop where employees work long hours under bad conditions for low wages.

sweat suit *n.* a suit worn by athletes for training comprising knitted cotton trousers and a light cotton sweater.

sweaty (ˈswɛtɪ) *adj.* **sweatier, sweatiest. 1.** covered with perspiration; sweating. **2.** smelling of or like sweat. **3.** causing sweat. —ˈ**sweatily** *adv.* —ˈ**sweatiness** *n.*

swede (swiːd) *n.* **1.** a Eurasian plant cultivated for its bulbous edible root, which is used as a vegetable and as cattle fodder. **2.** the root of this plant. ~Also called: **Swedish turnip.** [C19: so called after being introduced into Scotland from Sweden in the 18th century]

Swede (swiːd) *n.* a native, citizen, or inhabitant of Sweden, a kingdom in E Scandinavia.

Swedish (ˈswiːdɪʃ) *adj.* **1.** of, relating to, or characteristic of Sweden, its people, or their language. ~*n.* **2.** the official language of Sweden.

sweep (swiːp) *vb.* **sweeping, swept. 1.** to clean or clear (a space, chimney, etc.) with a brush, broom, etc. **2.** (often foll. by *up*) to remove or collect (dirt, rubbish, etc.) with a brush, broom, etc. **3.** to move in a smooth or continuous manner, esp. quickly or forcibly: *cars swept along the road.* **4.** to move in a proud or dignified fashion: *she swept past.* **5.** to spread or pass rapidly across, through, or along (a region, area, etc.): *the news swept through the town.* **6.** (*tr.*) to direct (the gaze, line of fire, etc.) over; survey. **7.** (*tr.;* foll. by *away* or *off*) to overwhelm emotionally: *she was swept away by his charm.* **8.** (*tr.*) to brush or lightly touch (a surface, etc.): *the dress swept along the ground.* **9.** (*tr.;* often foll. by *away*) to convey, clear, or abolish, esp. with strong or continuous movements: *the sea swept the sandcastle away; secondary modern schools were swept away.* **10.** (*intr.*) to extend gracefully or majestically, esp. in a wide circle: *the plains sweep down to the sea.* **11.** to search (a body of water) for mines, etc., by dragging. **12.** (*tr.*) to win overwhelmingly, esp. in an election: *Labour swept the country.* **13.** (*tr.*) to propel (a boat) with sweeps. **14. sweep the board. a.** (in gambling) to win all the cards or money. **b.** to win every event or prize in a contest. **15. sweep (something) under the carpet.** to conceal (something, esp. a problem) in the hope that it will be overlooked by others. ~*n.* **16.** the act or an instance of sweeping; removal by or as if by a brush or broom. **17.** a swift or steady movement, esp. in an arc. **18.** the distance, arc, etc., through which something, such as a pendulum, moves. **19.** a wide expanse or scope: *the sweep of the plains.* **20.** any curving line or contour. **21.** short for **sweepstake. 22. a.** a long oar used on an open boat. **b.** *Austral.* a person steering a surf boat with such an oar at the stern. **23.** any of the sails of a windmill. **24.** *Electronics.* a steady horizontal or circular movement of an electron beam across or around the fluorescent screen of a cathode-ray tube. **25.** a curving driveway. **26.** *Chiefly Brit.* See **chimney sweep. 27.** another name for **swipe** (sense 4). **28. clean sweep. a.** an overwhelming victory or success. **b.** a complete change; purge: *to make a clean sweep.* [C13 *swepen*] —ˈ**sweepy** *adj.*

sweeper (ˈswiːpə) *n.* **1.** a person employed to sweep, such as a roadsweeper. **2.** any device for sweeping: *a carpet sweeper.* **3.** *Inf., soccer.* a player who supports the main defenders, as by intercepting loose balls, etc.

sweep hand *n. Horology.* a long hand that registers seconds or fractions of seconds on the perimeter of the dial.

sweeping (ˈswiːpɪŋ) *adj.* **1.** comprehensive and wide-ranging: *sweeping reforms.* **2.** indiscriminate or without reservations: *sweeping statements.* **3.** decisive or overwhelming: *a sweeping victory.* **4.** taking in a wide area: *a sweeping glance.* **5.** driving steadily onwards, esp. over a large area: *a sweeping attack.* —ˈ**sweepingly** *adv.* —ˈ**sweepingness** *n.*

sweepstake (ˈswiːpˌsteɪk) *or esp. U.S.* **sweepstakes** *n.* **1. a.** a lottery in which the stakes of the participants constitute the prize. **b.** the prize itself. **2.** any event involving such a lottery, esp. a horse race. ~Often shortened to **sweep.** [C15: orig. referring to someone who *sweeps* or takes all the stakes in a game]

sweet (swiːt) *adj.* **1.** having or denoting a pleasant taste like that of sugar. **2.** agreeable to the senses or the mind: *sweet music.* **3.** having pleasant manners; gentle: *a sweet child.* **4.** (of wine, etc.) having a relatively high sugar content; not dry. **5.** (of foods) not decaying or rancid: *sweet milk.* **6.** not salty: *sweet water.* **7.** free from unpleasant odours: *sweet air.* **8.** containing no corrosive substances: *sweet soil.* **9.** (of petrol) containing no sulphur compounds. **10.** sentimental or unrealistic. **11.** *Jazz.* performed with a regular beat, with the emphasis on clearly outlined melody and little improvisation. **12.** *Arch.* respected; dear (used in polite forms of address): *sweet sir.* **13.** smooth and precise; perfectly executed: *a sweet shot.* **14. at one's own sweet will.** as it suits oneself alone. **15. keep (someone) sweet.** to ingratiate oneself in order to ensure cooperation. **16. sweet on.** fond of or infatuated with. ~*adv.* **17.** *Inf.* in a sweet manner. ~*n.* **18.** a sweet taste or smell; sweetness in general. **19.** (*often pl.*) *Brit.* any of numerous kinds of confectionery consisting wholly or partly of sugar, esp. of sugar boiled and crystallized (**boiled sweets**). **20.** *Brit.* any sweet dish served as a dessert. **21.** dear; sweetheart (used as a form of address). **22.** anything that is sweet. **23.** (*often pl.*) a pleasurable experience, state, etc.: *the sweets of success.* [OE *swēte*] —ˈ**sweetish** *adj.* —ˈ**sweetly** *adv.* —ˈ**sweetness** *n.*

sweet alyssum *n.* a Mediterranean plant having clusters of small fragrant white or violet flowers. See also **alyssum.**

sweet-and-sour *adj.* (of food) cooked in a sauce made from sugar and vinegar and other ingredients.

sweet bay *n.* **1.** a small tree of SE North America, belonging to the magnolia family and having large fragrant white flowers. **2.** another name for **bay**[4] (sense 1).

sweetbread (ˈswiːtˌbrɛd) *n.* the pancreas or the thymus gland of an animal, used for food. [C16: SWEET + BREAD, ? < OE *brǣd* meat]

sweetbrier (ˈswiːtˌbraɪə) *n.* a Eurasian rose having a tall bristly stem, fragrant leaves, and single pink flowers. Also called: **eglantine.**

sweet cherry *n.* either of two types of cherry tree that are cultivated for their edible sweet fruit.

sweet chestnut *n.* See **chestnut** (sense 1).

sweet cicely *n.* **1.** Also called: **myrrh.** an aromatic European plant, having compound leaves and clusters of small white flowers. **2.** the leaves, formerly used in cookery for their flavour of aniseed. **3.** any of various related plants of Asia and America, having aromatic roots.

sweet corn *n.* **1.** a variety of maize whose kernels are rich in sugar and eaten as a vegetable when young. **2.** the unripe ears of maize, esp. the sweet kernels removed from the cob, cooked as a vegetable.

sweeten (ˈswiːtᵊn) *vb.* (*mainly tr.*) **1.** (*also intr.*) to make or become sweet or sweeter. **2.** to mollify or soften (a person). **3.** to make more agreeable. **4.** (*also intr.*) *Chem.* to free or be freed from unpleasant odours, acidic or corrosive substances, or the like.

sweetener (ˈswiːtᵊnə) *n.* **1.** a sweetening agent, esp. one that does not contain sugar. **2.** a slang word for **bribe.**

sweetening (ˈswiːtᵊnɪŋ) *n.* something that sweetens.

sweet flag *n.* an aroid marsh plant, having swordlike leaves, small greenish flowers, and aromatic roots. Also called: **calamus.**

sweet gale *n.* a shrub of northern swamp regions, having yellow catkin-like flowers and aromatic leaves. Also called: **bog myrtle.** Often shortened to **gale.**

sweet gum *n.* **1.** a North American liquidambar tree, having prickly spherical fruit clusters and fragrant sap: the wood is used to make furniture. **2.** the wood or sap of this tree.

sweetheart (ˈswiːtˌhɑːt) *n.* **1.** a person loved by another. **2.** *Inf.* a lovable, generous, or obliging person. **3.** a term of endearment.

sweetheart agreement *n. Austral. inf.* an industrial agreement on pay and conditions concluded without resort to arbitration.

sweetie (ˈswiːtɪ) *n. Inf.* **1.** sweetheart; darling: used as a term of endearment. **2.** *Brit.* another word for **sweet** (sense 19). **3.** *Chiefly Brit.* an endearing person.

sweeting (ˈswiːtɪŋ) *n.* **1.** a variety of sweet apple. **2.** an archaic word for **sweetheart.**

sweet marjoram *n.* another name for **marjoram** (sense 1).

sweetmeat (ˈswiːtˌmiːt) *n.* a sweetened delicacy, such as a preserve, sweet, or, formerly, a cake or pastry.

sweet pea *n.* a climbing plant of S Europe, widely cultivated for its butterfly-shaped fragrant flowers of delicate pastel colours.

sweet pepper *n.* **1.** a pepper plant with large bell-shaped fruits that are eaten unripe (**green pepper**) or ripe (**red pepper**). **2.** the fruit of this plant.

sweet potato *n.* **1.** a twining plant of tropical America, cultivated in the tropics for its edible fleshy yellow root. **2.** the root of this plant.

sweet shop *n. Chiefly Brit.* a shop solely or largely selling sweets, esp. boiled sweets.

sweetsop (ˈswiːtˌsɒp) *n.* **1.** a small West Indian tree, having yellowish-green fruit. **2.** the fruit, which has a sweet edible pulp. ~Also called: **custard apple.**

sweet-talk *Inf.* ~*vb.* **1.** to coax, flatter, or cajole (someone). ~*n.* **sweet talk. 2.** cajolery; coaxing.

sweet tooth *n.* a strong liking for sweet foods.

sweetveld (ˈswiːtˌfɛlt) *n.* (in South Africa) a type of grazing characterized by high-quality grass. [pron. < Afrik. *soetveld*]

sweet william *n.* a widely cultivated Eurasian plant with flat clusters of white, pink, red, or purple flowers.

swell (swɛl) *vb.* **swelling, swelled; swollen** *or* **swelled. 1.** to grow or cause to grow in size, esp. as a result of internal pressure. **2.** to expand or cause to expand at a particular point or above the surrounding level; protrude. **3.** to grow or cause to grow in size, amount, intensity, or degree: *the party is swelling with new recruits.* **4.** to puff or be puffed up with pride or another emotion. **5.** (*intr.*) (of seas or lakes) to rise in waves. **6.** (*intr.*) to well up or overflow. **7.** (*tr.*) to make (a musical phrase) increase gradually in volume and then diminish. ~*n.* **8. a.** the undulating movement of the surface of the open sea. **b.** a succession of waves or a single large wave. **9.** a swelling or being swollen; expansion. **10.** an increase in quantity or degree; inflation. **11.** a bulge; protuberance. **12.** a gentle hill. **13.** *Inf.* a person very fashionably dressed. **14.** *Inf.* a man of high social or political standing. **15.** *Music.* a crescendo followed by an immediate diminuendo. **16.** Also called: **swell organ.** *Music.* **a.** a set of pipes on an organ housed in a box (**swell box**) fitted with a shutter operated by a pedal, which can be opened or closed to control the volume. **b.** the manual on an organ controlling this. ~*adj.* **17.** *Inf.* stylish or grand. **18.** *Sl.* excellent; first-class. [OE *swellan*]

swelled head *or* **swollen head** *Inf. n.* **1.** an inflated view of one's own worth, often caused by sudden success. ~*adj.* **swelled-headed, swell-headed,** *or* **swollen-headed. 2.** conceited.

swelling (ˈswɛlɪŋ) *n.* **1.** the act of expansion or inflation. **2.** the state of being or becoming swollen. **3.** a swollen or inflated part or area. **4.** an abnormal enlargement of a bodily structure or part, esp. as the result of injury. ~ Related adj.: **tumescent.**

swelter (ˈswɛltə) *vb.* **1.** (*intr.*) to suffer under oppressive heat, esp. to perspire and feel faint. **2.** (*tr.*) *Rare.* to cause to suffer under oppressive heat. ~*n.* **3.** a sweltering condition (esp. in **in a swelter**). **4.** oppressive humid heat. [C15 *swelten*, < OE *sweltan* to die]

sweltering (ˈswɛltərɪŋ) *adj.* oppressively hot and humid: *a sweltering day.* —ˈ**swelteringly** *adv.*

swept (swɛpt) *vb.* the past tense of **sweep.**

sweptback (ˈswɛptˌbæk) *adj.* (of an aircraft wing) inclined backwards towards the rear of the fuselage.

sweptwing (ˈswɛptˌwɪŋ) *adj.* (of an aircraft, etc.) having wings swept (usually) backwards.

swerve (swɜːv) *vb.* **1.** to turn or cause to turn aside, usually sharply or suddenly, from a course. ~*n.* **2.** the act, instance, or degree of swerving. [OE *sweorfan* to scour] —ˈ**swervable** *adj.* —ˈ**swerver** *n.* —ˈ**swerving** *adj.*

SWG *abbrev. for* Standard Wire Gauge; a notation for the diameters of metal rods or thickness of metal sheet ranging from 16 mm to 0.02 mm or from 0.5 inch to 0.001 inch.

swift (swɪft) *adj.* **1.** moving or able to move quickly; fast. **2.** occurring or performed quickly or suddenly; instant. **3.** (*postpositive;* foll. by *to*) prompt to act or respond: *swift to take revenge.* ~*adv.* **4. a.** swiftly or quickly. **b.** (*in combination*): *swift-moving.* ~*n.* **5.** any of various insectivorous birds of the Old World. They have long narrow wings and spend most of the time on the wing. **6.** any of certain North American lizards of the iguana family that can run very rapidly. **7.** the main cylinder in a carding machine. **8.** an expanding circular frame used to hold skeins of silk, wool, etc. [OE, < *swīfan* to turn] —ˈ**swiftly** *adv.* —ˈ**swiftness** *n.*

swiftlet (ˈswɪftlɪt) *n.* any of various small swifts of an Asian genus that often live in caves and use echolocation.

swig (swɪg) *Inf.* ~*n.* **1.** a large swallow or deep drink, esp. from a bottle. ~*vb.* **swigging, swigged. 2.** to drink (some liquid) deeply, esp. from a bottle. [C16: <?] —ˈ**swigger** *n.*

swill (swɪl) *vb.* **1.** to drink large quantities of (liquid, esp. alcoholic drink); guzzle. **2.** (*tr.;* often foll. by *out*) *Chiefly Brit.* to drench or rinse in large amounts of water. **3.** (*tr.*) to feed swill to (pigs, etc.). ~*n.* **4.** wet feed, esp. for pigs, consisting of kitchen waste, skim milk, etc. **5.** refuse, esp. from a kitchen. **6.** a deep drink, esp. beer. **7.** any liquid mess. **8.** the act of swilling. [OE *swilian* to wash out] —ˈ**swiller** *n.*

swim (swɪm) *vb.* **swimming, swam, swum. 1.** (*intr.*) to move along in water, etc., by means of movements of the body, esp. the arms and legs, or (in the case of fish) tail and fins. **2.** (*tr.*) to cover (a distance or stretch of water) in this way. **3.** (*tr.*) to compete in (a race) in this way. **4.** (*intr.*) to be supported by and on a liquid; float. **5.** (*tr.*) to use (a particular stroke) in swimming. **6.** (*intr.*) to move smoothly, usually through air or over a surface. **7.** (*intr.*) to reel or seem to reel: *my head swam; the room swam around me.* **8.** (*intr.;* often foll. by *in* or *with*) to be covered or flooded with water or other liquid. **9.** (*intr.;* often foll. by *in*) to be liberally supplied (with): *he's swimming in money.* **10.** (*tr.*) to cause to float or swim. **11. swim with** (*or* **against**) **the stream** *or* **tide.** to conform to (or resist) prevailing opinion. ~*n.* **12.** the act, an instance, or period of swimming. **13.** any graceful gliding motion. **14.** a condition of dizziness; swoon. **15.** a pool in a river good for fishing. **16. in the swim.** *Inf.* fashionable or active in social or political activities. [OE *swimman*] —ˈ**swimmable** *adj.* —ˈ**swimmer** *n.* —ˈ**swimming** *n., adj.*

swim bladder *n. Ichthyol.* another name for **air bladder** (sense 1).

swimmeret (ˈswɪməˌrɛt) *n.* any of the small paired appendages on the abdomen of crustaceans, used chiefly in locomotion.

swimming bath *n.* (*often pl.*) an indoor swimming pool.

swimming costume *or* **bathing costume** *n. Chiefly Brit.* any garment worn for swimming or sunbathing, such as a woman's one-piece garment covering most of the torso but not the limbs.

swimmingly (ˈswɪmɪŋlɪ) *adv.* successfully, effortlessly, or well (esp. in **go swimmingly**).

swimming pool *n.* an artificial pool for swimming.

swimsuit (ˈswɪmˌsuːt, -ˌsjuːt) *n.* a woman's one-piece swimming garment that leaves the arms and legs bare.

swindle (ˈswɪndᵊl) *vb.* **1.** to cheat (someone) of money, etc.; defraud. **2.** (*tr.*) to obtain (money, etc.) by fraud. ~*n.* **3.** a fraudulent scheme or transaction. [C18: back formation < G *Schwindler*, < *schwindeln*, < OHG *swintilōn*, < *swintan* to disappear] —ˈ**swindler** *n.*

swindle sheet *n.* a slang term for **expense account.**

swine (swaɪn) *n., pl.* **swine.** **1.** a coarse or contemptible person. **2.** another name for a **pig.** [OE *swīn*] —ˈ**swinish** *adj.* —ˈ**swinishly** *adv.* —ˈ**swinishness** *n.*

swine fever *n.* an infectious viral disease of pigs, characterized by fever and diarrhoea.

swineherd (ˈswaɪnˌhɜːd) *n.* a person who looks after pigs.

swing (swɪŋ) *vb.* **swinging, swung.** **1.** to move or cause to move rhythmically to and fro, as a free-hanging object; sway. **2.** (*intr.*) to move, walk, etc., with a relaxed and swaying motion. **3.** to pivot or cause to pivot, as on a hinge. **4.** to move or cause to move in a curve: *the car swung around the bend.* **5.** to move or cause to move by suspending or being suspended. **6.** to hang or be hung so as to be able to turn freely. **7.** (*intr.*) *Sl.* to be hanged: *he'll swing for it.* **8.** to alter or cause to alter habits, a course, etc. **9.** (*tr.*) *Inf.* to influence or manipulate successfully: *I hope he can swing the deal.* **10.** (*tr.; foll. by up*) to raise or hoist, esp. in a sweeping motion. **11.** (*intr.; often foll. by at*) to hit out or strike (at), esp. with a sweeping motion. **12.** (*tr.*) to wave (a weapon, etc.) in a sweeping motion; flourish. **13.** to arrange or play (music) with the rhythmically flexible and compulsive quality associated with jazz. **14.** (*intr.*) (of popular music, esp. jazz, or of the musicians who play it) to have this quality. **15.** *Sl.* to be lively and modern. **16.** (*intr.*) *Cricket.* to bowl (a ball) with swing or (of a ball) to move with a swing. **17. swing the lead.** *Inf.* to malinger or make up excuses. ~*n.* **18.** the act or manner of swinging or the distance covered while swinging: *a wide swing.* **19.** a sweeping stroke or blow. **20.** *Boxing.* a wide punch from the side similar to but longer than a hook. **21.** *Cricket.* the lateral movement of a bowled ball through the air. **22.** any free swaying motion. **23.** any curving movement; sweep. **24.** something that swings or is swung, esp. a suspended seat on which a person may swing back and forth. **25.** a kind of popular dance music influenced by jazz, usually played by big bands and originating in the 1930s. **26.** *Prosody.* a steady distinct rhythm or cadence in prose or verse. **27.** *Inf.* the normal round or pace: *the swing of things.* **28.** a fluctuation, as in some business activity, voting pattern, etc. **29.** *Canad.* (in the North) a train of freight sleighs or canoes. **30.** *Chiefly U.S.* a circular tour. **31. go with a swing.** to go well; be successful. **32. in full swing.** at the height of activity. [OE *swingan*]

swingboat (ˈswɪŋˌbəʊt) *n.* a piece of fairground equipment consisting of a boat-shaped carriage for swinging in.

swing bridge *n.* a low bridge that can be rotated about a vertical axis to permit the passage of ships, etc.

swinge (swɪndʒ) *vb.* **swingeing** *or* **swinging, swinged.** (*tr.*) *Arch.* to beat, flog, or punish. [OE *swengan*]

swingeing (ˈswɪndʒɪŋ) *adj. Chiefly Brit.* punishing; severe.

swinger (ˈswɪŋə) *n. Sl.* a person regarded as being modern and lively. —ˈ**swinging** *adj.* —ˈ**swingingly** *adv.*

swingle (ˈswɪŋgᵊl) *n.* **1.** a flat-bladed wooden instrument used for beating and scraping flax or hemp to remove coarse matter from it. ~*vb.* **2.** to use a swingle on. [OE *swingel* stroke]

swingletree (ˈswɪŋgᵊlˌtriː) *n.* a crossbar in a horse's harness to which the ends of the traces are attached. Also called: **whippletree.**

swing shift *n. U.S. & Canad. inf.* the evening work shift, usually from mid-afternoon until midnight. —**swing shifter** *n.*

swing-wing *adj.* **1.** of or relating to an aircraft equipped with wings that are automatically swept back close to the fuselage when flying at high speed and are brought forward for landing and takeoff. ~*n.* **2. a.** an aircraft fitted with such wings. **b.** either of the two wings of such an aircraft.

swingy (ˈswɪŋɪ) *adj.* **swingier, swingiest.** (of a garment, esp. a skirt) styled so that it swings as the wearer moves.

swipe (swaɪp) *vb.* **1.** (when *intr.*, usually foll. by *at*) *Inf.* to hit hard with a sweeping blow. **2.** (*tr.*) *Sl.* to steal. ~*n.* **3.** *Inf.* a hard blow. **4.** Also called: **sweep.** a type of lever for raising and lowering a weight, such as a bucket in a well. [C19: ? rel. to SWEEP]

swirl (swɜːl) *vb.* **1.** to turn or cause to turn in a twisting spinning fashion. **2.** (*intr.*) to be dizzy; swim: *my head was swirling.* ~*n.* **3.** a whirling or spinning motion, esp. in water. **4.** a whorl; curl. **5.** the act of swirling or stirring. **6.** dizzy confusion or disorder. [C15: prob. < Du. *zwirrelen*] —ˈ**swirling** *adj.* —ˈ**swirly** *adj.*

swish (swɪʃ) *vb.* **1.** to move with or make or cause to move with or make a whistling or hissing sound. **2.** (*intr.*) (esp. of fabrics) to rustle. **3.** (*tr.*) *Sl., now rare.* to whip; flog. **4.** (*tr.; foll. by off*) to cut with a swishing blow. ~*n.* **5.** a hissing or rustling sound or movement. **6.** a rod for flogging or a blow from this. ~*adj.* **7.** *Inf., chiefly Brit.* fashionable; smart. [C18: imit.] —ˈ**swishy** *adj.*

Swiss (swɪs) *adj.* **1.** of, relating to, or characteristic of Switzerland, a republic in W central Europe, its inhabitants, or their dialects of German, French, and Italian. ~*n.* **2.** a native or inhabitant of Switzerland.

Swiss chard *n.* another name for **chard.**

Swiss cheese plant *n.* See **monstera.**

swiss roll *n.* a sponge cake spread with jam, cream, or some other filling, and rolled up.

switch (swɪtʃ) *n.* **1.** a mechanical, electrical, or electronic device for opening or closing a circuit or for diverting a current from one part of a circuit to another. **2.** a swift and usually sudden shift or change. **3.** an exchange or swap. **4.** a flexible rod or twig, used esp. for punishment. **5.** the sharp movement or blow of such an instrument. **6.** a tress of false hair used to give added length or bulk to a woman's own hair-style. **7.** the tassel-like tip of the tail of cattle and certain other animals. **8.** any of various card games in which the suit is changed during play. **9.** *U.S. & Canad.* a railway siding. **10.** *U.S. & Canad.* a railway point. **11.** *Austral. inf.* short for **switchboard** (sense 1). ~*vb.* **12.** to shift, change, turn aside, or change the direction of (something). **13.** to exchange (places); replace (something by something else). **14.** *Chiefly U.S. & Canad.* to transfer (rolling stock) from one railway track to another. **15.** (*tr.*) to cause (an electric current) to start or stop flowing or to change its path by operating a switch. **16.** (*tr.*) to lash or whip with or as if with a switch. ~See also **switch off, switch on.** [C16: ? < MDu. *swijch* twig] —ˈ**switcher** *n.*

switchback (ˈswɪtʃˌbæk) *n.* **1.** a steep mountain road, railway, or track with hairpin bends or a hairpin bend on such a road, etc. **2.** another word (esp. Brit.) for **big dipper.**

switchblade *or* **switchblade knife** (ˈswɪtʃˌbleɪd) *n.* another name (esp. U.S. and Canad.) for **flick knife.**

switchboard (ˈswɪtʃˌbɔːd) *n.* **1.** an installation in a telephone exchange, office, etc., at which the interconnection of telephone lines is manually controlled. **2.** a similar installation by which certain electrical equipment is operated.

switchman (ˈswɪtʃmən) *n., pl.* **-men.** the U.S. and Canad. name for **pointsman.**

switch off *vb. (adv.)* **1.** to cause (a device) to stop operating as by moving a switch, knob, or lever. **2.** *Inf.* to cease to interest or be interested; make or become bored, alienated, etc.

switch on *vb. (adv.)* **1.** to cause (a device) to operate as by moving a switch, knob, or lever. **2.** *(tr.) Inf.* to produce (charm, tears, etc.) suddenly or automatically. **3.** *(tr.) Inf.* (now dated) to make up-to-date, esp. in outlook, dress, etc.

swither (ˈswɪðə) *Scot.* ~*vb. (intr.)* **1.** to hesitate; vacillate; be perplexed. ~*n.* **2.** hesitation; perplexity; agitation. [C16: <?]

Switzer (ˈswɪtsə) *n.* a less common word for **Swiss.** [C16: < MHG, < *Swīz* Switzerland]

swivel (ˈswɪvᵊl) *n.* **1.** a coupling device which allows an attached object to turn freely. **2.** such a device made of two parts which turn independently, such as a compound link of a chain. **3. a.** a pivot on which is mounted a gun that may be swung horizontally from side to side. **b.** Also called: **swivel gun.** the gun itself. ~*vb.* **-elling, -elled** *or U.S.* **-eling, -eled.** **4.** to turn or swing on or as if on a pivot. **5.** *(tr.)* to provide with, secure by, or support with a swivel. [C14: < OE *swīfan* to turn]

swivel chair *n.* a chair, the seat of which is joined to the legs by a swivel and which thus may be spun round.

swivel pin *n.* another name for **kingpin** (sense 2).

swizzle (ˈswɪzᵊl) *n.* **1.** an alcoholic drink containing gin or rum. **2.** Also called: **swizz.** *Brit. inf.* a swindle or disappointment. ~*vb.* **3.** *(tr.)* to stir a swizzle stick in (a drink). **4.** *Brit. inf.* to swindle; cheat. [C19: <?]

swizzle stick *n.* a small rod used to agitate an effervescent drink to facilitate the escape of carbon dioxide.

swob (swɒb) *n., vb.,* **swobbing, swobbed.** a less common word for **swab.**

swollen (ˈswəʊlən) *vb.* **1.** a past participle of **swell.** ~*adj.* **2.** tumid or enlarged as by swelling. **3.** turgid or bombastic. —ˈ**swollenness** *n.*

swoon (swuːn) *vb. (intr.)* **1.** a literary word for **faint.** **2.** to become ecstatic. ~*n.* **3.** an instance of fainting. ~Also (archaic or dialect): **swound** (swaʊnd). [OE *geswōgen* insensible, p.p. of *swōgan* (unattested except in compounds) suffocate] —ˈ**swooning** *adj.*

swoop (swuːp) *vb.* **1.** *(intr.;* usually foll. by *down, on,* or *upon)* to sweep or pounce suddenly. **2.** *(tr.;* often foll. by *up, away,* or *off)* to seize or scoop suddenly. ~*n.* **3.** the act of swooping. **4.** a swift descent. [OE *swāpan* to sweep]

swoosh (swʊʃ) *vb.* **1.** to make or cause to make a rustling or swirling sound, esp. when moving or pouring out. ~*n.* **2.** a swirling or rustling sound or movement. [C20: imit.]

swop (swɒp) *n., vb.,* **swopping, swopped.** a variant spelling of **swap.**

sword (sɔːd) *n.* **1.** a thrusting, striking, or cutting weapon with a long blade having one or two cutting edges, a hilt, and usually a crosspiece or guard. **2.** such a weapon worn on ceremonial occasions as a symbol of authority. **3.** something resembling a sword, such as the snout of a swordfish. **4. the sword. a.** violence or power, esp. military power. **b.** death; destruction: *to put to the sword.* [OE *sweord*]

swordbearer (ˈsɔːdˌbɛərə) *n.* an official who carries a ceremonial sword.

sword dance *n.* a dance in which the performers dance nimbly over swords on the ground or brandish them in the air. —**sword dancer** *n.* —**sword dancing** *n.*

swordfish (ˈsɔːdˌfɪʃ) *n., pl.* **-fish** *or* **-fishes.** a large fish with a very long upper jaw: valued as a food and game fish.

sword grass *n.* any of various grasses and other plants having sword-shaped sharp leaves.

sword knot *n.* a loop on the hilt of a sword by which it was attached to the wrist, now purely decorative.

sword lily *n.* another name for **gladiolus.**

Sword of Damocles (ˈdæməˌkliːz) *n.* a closely impending disaster. [after a sycophant forced by Dionysius, tyrant of ancient Syracuse, to sit under a sword suspended by a hair]

swordplay (ˈsɔːdˌpleɪ) *n.* **1.** the action or art of fighting with a sword. **2.** verbal sparring.

swordsman (ˈsɔːdzmən) *n., pl.* **-men.** one who uses or is skilled in the use of a sword. —ˈ**swordsmanship** *n.*

swordstick (ˈsɔːdˌstɪk) *n.* a hollow walking stick containing a short sword or dagger.

swordtail (ˈsɔːdˌteɪl) *n.* any of several small freshwater fishes of Central America having a long swordlike tail.

swore (swɔː) *vb.* the past tense of **swear.**

sworn (swɔːn) *vb.* **1.** the past participle of **swear.** ~*adj.* **2.** bound, pledged, or made inveterate, by or as if by an oath: *a sworn statement; he was sworn to God.*

swot[1] (swɒt) *Brit. inf.* ~*vb.* **swotting, swotted.** **1.** (often foll. by *up*) to study (a subject) intensively, as for an examination; cram. ~*n.* **2.** Also called: **swotter.** a person who works or studies hard. **3.** hard work or grind. ~Also: **swat.** [C19: var. of SWEAT (n.)]

swot[2] (swɒt) *vb.* **swotting, swotted,** *n.* a variant of **swat.**

swounds *or* **'swounds** (zwaʊndz, zaʊndz) *interj. Arch.* less common spellings of **zounds.**

swum (swʌm) *vb.* the past participle of **swim.**

swung (swʌŋ) *vb.* the past tense and past participle of **swing.**

swy (swaɪ) *n. Austral.* another name for **two-up.** [C20: < G *zwei* two]

sybarite (ˈsɪbəˌraɪt) *n.* **1.** *(sometimes cap.)* a devotee of luxury and the sensual vices. ~*adj.* **2.** luxurious; sensuous. [C16: < L *Sybarīta,* < Gk *Subaritēs* inhabitant of *Sybaris,* Gk colony in S Italy, famed for its luxury] —**sybaritic** (ˌsɪbəˈrɪtɪk) *adj.* —ˌ**sybaˈritically** *adv.* —ˈ**sybaritism** *n.*

sycamore (ˈsɪkəˌmɔː) *n.* **1.** a Eurasian maple tree, naturalized in Britain and North America, having five-lobed leaves and two-winged fruits. **2.** *U.S. & Canad.* an American plane tree. See **plane tree.** **3.** a tree of N Africa and W Asia, having an edible figlike fruit. [C14: < OF *sicamor,* < L *sȳcomorus,* < Gk, < *sukon* fig + *moron* mulberry]

syconium (saɪˈkəʊnɪəm) *n., pl.* **-nia** (-nɪə). *Bot.* the fleshy fruit of the fig, consisting of an enlarged receptacle. [C19: < NL, < Gk *sukon* fig]

sycophant (ˈsɪkəfənt) *n.* a person who uses flattery to win favour from individuals wielding influence; toady. [C16: < L *sȳcophanta,* < Gk *sukophantēs,* lit.: person showing a fig, apparently referring to the fig sign used in accusation, < *sukon* fig + *phainein* to show; sense prob. developed from "accuser" to "informer, flatterer"] —ˈ**sycophancy** *n.* —**sycophantic** (ˌsɪkəˈfæntɪk) *adj.* —ˌ**sycoˈphantically** *adv.*

sycosis (saɪˈkəʊsɪs) *n.* chronic inflammation of the hair follicles, esp. those of the beard. [C16: via NL < Gk *sukōsis,* < *sukon* fig]

syenite (ˈsaɪəˌnaɪt) *n.* a light-coloured coarse-grained igneous rock consisting of feldspars with hornblende. [C18: < F, < L *syēnītēs lapis* stone from *Syene,* Egypt where orig. quarried] —**syenitic** (ˌsaɪəˈnɪtɪk) *adj.*

syllabary (ˈsɪləbərɪ) *n., pl.* **-baries.** **1.** a table or list of syllables. **2.** a set of symbols used in certain writing systems, such as one used for Japanese, in which each symbol represents a spoken syllable. [C16: < NL *syllabārium*, < L *syllaba* SYLLABLE]

syllabi (ˈsɪləˌbaɪ) *n.* a plural of **syllabus.**

syllabic (sɪˈlæbɪk) *adj.* **1.** of or relating to syllables or the division of a word into syllables. **2.** denoting a kind of verse line based on a specific number of syllables rather than being regulated by stresses or quantities. **3.** (of a consonant) constituting a syllable. ~*n.* **4.** a syllabic consonant. **—sylˈlabically** *adv.*

syllabify (sɪˈlæbɪˌfaɪ) *or* **syllabicate** *vb.* **-fying, -fied** *or* **-cating, -cated.** (*tr.*) to divide (a word) into its constituent syllables. **—sylˌlabifiˈcation** *or* **sylˌlabiˈcation** *n.*

syllable (ˈsɪləbᵊl) *n.* **1.** a combination or set of one or more units of sound in a language that must consist of a sonorous element (a sonant or vowel) and may or may not contain less sonorous elements (consonants or semivowels) flanking it: for example "paper" has two syllables. **2.** (in the writing systems of certain languages, esp. ancient ones) a symbol or set of symbols standing for a syllable. **3.** the least mention: *don't breathe a syllable of it.* **4. in words of one syllable.** simply; bluntly. ~*vb.* **5.** to pronounce syllables of (a text); articulate. **6.** (*tr.*) to write down in syllables. [C14: via OF < L *syllaba*, < Gk *sullabē*, < *sullambanein* to collect together]

syllabub *or* **sillabub** (ˈsɪləˌbʌb) *n.* **1.** a spiced drink made of milk with rum, port, brandy, or wine, often hot. **2.** *Brit.* a cold dessert made from milk or cream beaten with sugar, wine, and lemon juice. [C16: <?]

syllabus (ˈsɪləbəs) *n., pl.* **-buses** *or* **-bi** (-ˌbaɪ). **1.** an outline of a course of studies, text, etc. **2.** *Brit.* **a.** the subjects studied for a particular course. **b.** a list of these subjects. [C17: < LL, erroneously < L *sittybus* parchment strip giving title and author, < Gk *sittuba*]

syllepsis (sɪˈlɛpsɪs) *n., pl.* **-ses** (-siːz). **1.** (in grammar or rhetoric) the use of a single sentence construction in which a verb, adjective, etc., is made to cover two syntactical functions, as *have* in *she and they have promised to come.* **2.** another word for **zeugma.** [C16: < LL, < Gk *sullēpsis*, < *sul-* SYN- + *lēpsis*, < *lambanein* to take] **—sylˈleptic** *adj.* **—sylˈleptically** *adv.*

syllogism (ˈsɪləˌdʒɪzəm) *n.* **1.** a deductive inference consisting of two premises and a conclusion, all of which are categorical propositions. The subject of the conclusion is the **minor term** and its predicate the **major term;** the **middle term** occurs in both premises but not the conclusion. There are 256 such arguments but only 24 are valid. *Some men are mortal; some men are angelic; so some mortals are angelic* is invalid, while *some temples are in ruins; all ruins are fascinating; so some temples are fascinating* is valid. Here *fascinating, in ruins,* and *temples* are respectively major, middle, and minor terms. **2.** a piece of deductive reasoning from the general to the particular. [C14: via L < Gk *sullogismos*, < *sullogizesthai* to reckon together, < *logos* a discourse] **—ˌsylloˈgistic** *adj.* **—ˈsylloˌgize** *or* **-ise** *vb.*

sylph (sɪlf) *n.* **1.** a slender graceful girl or young woman. **2.** any of a class of imaginary beings assumed to inhabit the air. [C17: < NL *sylphus*, prob. coined from L *silva* wood + Gk *numphē* nymph] **—ˈsylphˌlike** *adj.*

sylva *or* **silva** (ˈsɪlvə) *n., pl.* **-vas** *or* **-vae** (-viː). the trees growing in a particular region. [C17: < L *silva* a wood]

sylvan *or* **silvan** (ˈsɪlvən) *Chiefly poetic.* ~*adj.* **1.** of or consisting of woods or forests. **2.** in woods or forests. **3.** idyllically rural or rustic. ~*n.* **4.** an inhabitant of the woods, esp. a spirit. [C16: < L *silvānus*, < *silva* forest]

sylvanite (ˈsɪlvəˌnaɪt) *n.* a silver-white mineral consisting of a compound of tellurium with gold and silver in the form of elongated crystals. [C18: < (*Tran*)*sylvan*(*ia*), Romania, + -ITE[1], with reference to the region where first found]

sylviculture (ˈsɪlvɪˌkʌltʃə) *n.* a variant spelling of **silviculture.**

sym- *prefix.* a variant of **syn-** before *b, p,* and *m.*

symbiont (ˈsɪmbɪˌɒnt) *n.* an organism living in a state of symbiosis. [C19: < Gk *sumbioun* to live together, < *bioun* to live] **—ˌsymbiˈontic** *adj.* **—ˌsymbiˈontically** *adv.*

symbiosis (ˌsɪmbɪˈəʊsɪs) *n.* **1.** a close association of two interdependent animal or plant species. **2.** a similar relationship between persons or groups. [C19: via NL < Gk: a living together] **—ˌsymbiˈotic** *adj.*

symbol (ˈsɪmbᵊl) *n.* **1.** something that represents or stands for something else, usually by convention or association, esp. a material object used to represent something abstract. **2.** an object, person, etc., used in a literary work, film, etc., to stand for or suggest something else with which it is associated. **3.** a letter, figure, or sign used in mathematics, music, etc., to represent a quantity, phenomenon, operation, function, etc. ~*vb.* **-bolling, -bolled** *or U.S.* **-boling, -boled. 4.** (*tr.*) another word for **symbolize.** [C15: < Church L *symbolum*, < Gk *sumbolon* sign, < *sumballein* to throw together, < SYN- + *ballein* to throw]

symbolic (sɪmˈbɒlɪk) *or* **symbolical** *adj.* **1.** of or relating to a symbol or symbols. **2.** serving as a symbol. **3.** characterized by the use of symbols or symbolism. **—symˈbolically** *adv.*

symbolic logic *n.* another name for **formal logic.**

symbolism (ˈsɪmbəˌlɪzəm) *n.* **1.** the representation of something in symbolic form or the attribution of symbolic character to something. **2.** a system of symbols or symbolic representation. **3.** a symbolic significance or quality. **4.** (*often cap.*) a late 19th-century movement in art that sought to express mystical or abstract ideas through the symbolic use of images.

symbolist (ˈsɪmbəlɪst) *n.* **1.** a person who uses or can interpret symbols, esp. as a means to revealing aspects of truth and reality. **2.** an artist or writer who practises symbolism in his work. **3.** (*usually cap.*) a writer associated with the symbolist movement. **4.** (*often cap.*) an artist associated with the symbolism movement. ~*adj.* **5.** of, relating to, or characterizing symbolism or symbolists. **—ˌsymbolˈistic** *adj.* **—ˌsymbolˈistically** *adv.*

symbolist movement *n.* (*usually cap.*) a movement beginning in French and Belgian poetry towards the end of the 19th century with Mallarmé, Valéry, Verlaine, Rimbaud, and others, and seeking to express states of mind rather than objective reality by the power of words and images to suggest as well as denote.

symbolize *or* **-ise** (ˈsɪmbəˌlaɪz) *vb.* **1.** (*tr.*) to serve as or be a symbol of. **2.** (*tr.;* usually foll. by *by*) to represent by a symbol or symbols. **3.** (*intr.*) to use symbols. **4.** (*tr.*) to treat or regard as symbolic. **—ˌsymboliˈzation** *or* **-iˈsation** *n.*

symmetrical (sɪˈmɛtrɪkᵊl) *adj.* possessing or displaying symmetry.

symmetry (ˈsɪmɪtrɪ) *n., pl.* **-tries.** **1.** similarity, correspondence, or balance among systems or parts of a system. **2.** *Maths.* an exact correspondence in position or form about a given point, line, or plane. **3.** beauty or harmony of form based on a proportionate arrangement of parts. [C16: < L *symmetria*, < Gk *summetria* proportion, < SYN- + *metron* measure]

sympathectomy (ˌsɪmpəˈθɛktəmɪ) *n., pl.* **-mies.** the surgical excision or chemical destruction (**chemical sympathectomy**) of one or more parts of the sympathetic nervous system. [C20: < SYMPATHETIC + -ECTOMY]

sympathetic (ˌsɪmpəˈθɛtɪk) *adj.* **1.** characterized by, feeling, or showing sympathy; understanding. **2.** in accord with the subject's personality or mood; congenial: *a sympathetic atmosphere.* **3.** (when *postpositive,* often foll. by *to* or *towards*) showing agreement (with) or favour (towards). **4.**

Anat., physiol. of or relating to the division of the autonomic nervous system that acts in opposition to the parasympathetic system accelerating the heartbeat, dilating the bronchi, inhibiting the smooth muscles of the digestive tract, etc. Cf. **parasympathetic.** **5.** relating to vibrations occurring as a result of similar vibrations in a neighbouring body: *sympathetic strings on a sitar.* —ˌ**sympaˈthetically** *adv.*

sympathetic magic *n.* a type of magic in which it is sought to produce a large-scale effect, often at a distance, by performing some small-scale ceremony resembling it, such as the pouring of water on an altar to induce rainfall.

sympathize *or* **-ise** (ˈsɪmpəˌθaɪz) *vb.* (*intr.; often foll. by* *with*) **1.** to feel or express compassion or sympathy (for); commiserate: *he sympathized with my troubles.* **2.** to share or understand the sentiments or ideas (of); be in sympathy (with). —ˈ**sympaˌthizer** *or* **-iser** *n.*

sympatholytic (ˌsɪmpəθəʊˈlɪtɪk) *Med.* ~*adj.* **1. a.** inhibiting or antagonistic to nerve impulses of the sympathetic nervous system. **b.** of or relating to such inhibition. ~*n.* **2.** a sympatholytic drug. Cf. **sympathomimetic.** [C20: < SYMPATH(ETIC) + -LYTIC]

sympathomimetic (ˌsɪmpəθəʊmɪˈmɛtɪk) *Med.* ~*adj.* **1.** causing a physiological effect similar to that produced by stimulation of the sympathetic nervous system. ~*n.* **2.** a sympathomimetic drug. Cf. **sympatholytic.** [C20: < SYMPATH(ETIC) + MIMETIC]

sympathy (ˈsɪmpəθɪ) *n., pl.* **-thies. 1.** the sharing of another's emotions, esp. of sorrow or anguish; compassion. **2.** affinity or harmony, usually of feelings or interests, between persons or things: *to be in sympathy with someone.* **3.** mutual affection or understanding arising from such a relationship. **4.** the condition of a physical system or body when its behaviour is similar or corresponds to that of a different system that influences it, such as the vibration of sympathetic strings. **5.** (*sometimes pl.*) a feeling of loyalty, support, or accord, as for an idea, cause, etc. **6.** *Physiol.* the relationship between two organs or parts whereby a change in one affects the other. [C16: < L *sympathīa,* < Gk, < *sumpathēs,* < SYN- + *pathos* suffering]

sympathy strike *n.* a strike organized in support of another strike or cause. Also called: **sympathetic strike.**

symphonic poem *n. Music.* an extended orchestral composition, originated by Liszt, (1811–86), Hungarian composer, based on nonmusical material, such as a work of literature or folk tale. Also called: **tone poem.**

symphony (ˈsɪmfənɪ) *n., pl.* **-nies. 1.** an extended large-scale orchestral composition, usually with several movements, at least one of which is in sonata form. **2.** a piece of instrumental music in up to three very short movements, used as an overture to or interlude in a baroque opera. **3.** any purely orchestral movement in a vocal work, such as a cantata or oratorio. **4.** short for **symphony orchestra. 5.** anything distinguished by a harmonious composition: *the picture was a symphony of green.* **6.** *Arch.* harmony in general; concord. [C13: < OF *symphonie,* < L *symphōnia* concord, < Gk, < SYN- + *phōnē* sound] —**symphonic** (sɪmˈfɒnɪk) *adj.* —**symˈphonically** *adv.*

symphony orchestra *n. Music.* an orchestra capable of performing symphonies, esp. a large orchestra comprising strings, brass, woodwind, harp and percussion.

symphysis (ˈsɪmfɪsɪs) *n., pl.* **-ses** (-ˌsiːz). **1.** *Anat., bot.* a growing together of parts or structures, such as two bony surfaces joined by an intermediate layer of fibrous cartilage. **2.** a line marking this growing together. **3.** *Pathol.* an abnormal adhesion of two or more parts or structures. [C16: via NL < Gk *sumphusis,* < *sumphuein,* < SYN- + *phuein* to grow] —**symphysial** *or* **symphyseal** (sɪmˈfɪzɪəl) *adj.*

sympodium (sɪmˈpəʊdɪəm) *n., pl.* **-dia** (-dɪə). the main axis of growth in the grapevine and similar plants: a number of lateral branches that arise from just behind the apex of the main stem, which ceases to grow. [C19: < NL, < SYN- + Gk *podion* a little foot] —**symˈpodial** *adj.* —**symˈpodially** *adv.*

symposium (sɪmˈpəʊzɪəm) *n., pl.* **-siums** *or* **-sia** (-zɪə). **1.** a conference or meeting for the discussion of some subject, esp. an academic topic or social problem. **2.** a collection of scholarly contributions on a given subject. **3.** (in classical Greece) a drinking party with intellectual conversation, music, etc. [C16: via L < Gk *sumposion,* < *sumpinein* to drink together]

symptom (ˈsɪmptəm) *n.* **1.** *Med.* any sensation or change in bodily function experienced by a patient that is associated with a particular disease. **2.** any phenomenon or circumstance accompanying something and regarded as evidence of its existence; indication. [C16: < LL *symptōma,* < Gk *sumptōma* chance, < *sumpiptein* to occur, < SYN- + *piptein* to fall]

symptomatic (ˌsɪmptəˈmætɪk) *adj.* **1.** (often foll. by *of*) being a symptom; indicative: *symptomatic of insanity.* **2.** of, relating to, or according to symptoms: *a symptomatic analysis.* —ˌ**symptoˈmatically** *adv.*

symptomatology (ˌsɪmptəməˈtɒlədʒɪ) *n.* the branch of medicine concerned with the study and classification of the symptoms of disease.

syn. *abbrev. for* synonym(ous).

syn- *prefix.* **1.** with or together: *synecology.* **2.** fusion: *syngamy.* [< Gk *sun* together]

synaeresis (sɪˈnɪərɪsɪs) *n.* a variant spelling of **syneresis.**

synaesthesia *or U.S.* **synesthesia** (ˌsɪniːsˈθiːzɪə) *n.* **1.** *Physiol.* a sensation experienced in a part of the body other than the part stimulated. **2.** *Psychol.* the subjective sensation of a sense other than the one being stimulated. [C19: < NL, < SYN- + *-esthesia,* < Gk *aisthēsis* sensation] —**synaesthetic** *or U.S.* **synesthetic** (ˌsɪniːsˈθɛtɪk) *adj.*

synagogue (ˈsɪnəˌgɒg) *n.* **1. a.** a building for Jewish religious services and religious instruction. **b.** (*as modifier*): *synagogue services.* **2.** a congregation of Jews who assemble for worship or religious study. **3.** the religion of Judaism as organized in such congregations. [C12: < OF, < LL *synagōga,* < Gk *sunagōgē* a gathering, < *sunagein* to bring together] —**synagogical** (ˌsɪnəˈgɒdʒɪkᵊl) *or* **synagogal** (ˈsɪnəˌgɒgᵊl) *adj.*

synapse (ˈsaɪnæps) *n.* the point at which a nerve impulse is relayed from the terminal portion of an axon to the dendrites of an adjacent neuron.

synapsis (sɪˈnæpsɪs) *n., pl.* **-ses** (-siːz). **1.** *Cytology.* the association in pairs of homologous chromosomes at the start of meiosis. **2.** another word for **synapse.** [C19: < NL, < Gk *sunapsis* junction, < *sunaptein* to join together] —**synaptic** (sɪˈnæptɪk) *adj.* —**synˈaptically** *adv.*

synarthrosis (ˌsɪnɑːˈθrəʊsɪs) *n., pl.* **-ses** (-siːz). *Anat.* any of various joints which lack a synovial cavity and are virtually immovable; a fixed joint. [C16: via NL < Gk *sunarthrōsis,* < *sunarthrousthai* to be connected by joints, < *sun-* SYN- + *arthron* a joint] —ˌ**synarˈthrodial** *adj.*

sync *or* **synch** (sɪŋk) *Films, television, computers.* ~*vb.* **1.** an informal word for **synchronize.** ~*n.* **2.** an informal word for **synchronization** (esp. in **in** *or* **out of sync**).

syncarp (ˈsɪnkɑːp) *n. Bot.* a fleshy multiple fruit, formed from two or more carpels of one flower or the aggregated fruits of several flowers. [C19: < NL *syncarpium,* < SYN- + Gk *karpos* fruit]

syncarpous (sɪnˈkɑːpəs) *adj.* **1.** (of the ovaries of certain flowering plants) consisting of united carpels. **2.** of or relating to a syncarp.

synchro (ˈsɪŋkrəʊ) *n., pl.* **-chros.** any of a number of electrical devices in which the angular position of a rotating part is transformed into a voltage, or vice versa. Also called: **selsyn.**

synchro- *combining form.* indicating synchronization: *synchromesh.*

synchrocyclotron (ˌsɪŋkrəʊˈsaɪkləˌtrɒn) *n.* a

cyclotron in which the frequency of the electric field is modulated to allow for relativistic effects at high velocities and thus produce higher energies.

synchromesh (ˈsɪŋkrəʊˌmɛʃ) *adj.* **1.** (of a gearbox, etc.) having a system of clutches that synchronizes the speeds of the driving and driven members before engagement to avoid shock in gear changing and to reduce noise and wear. ~*n.* **2.** a gear system having these features. [C20: shortened < *synchronized mesh*]

synchronic (sɪnˈkrɒnɪk) *adj.* **1.** concerned with the events or phenomena at a particular period without considering historical antecedents: *synchronic linguistics.* Cf. **diachronic. 2.** synchronous. —**synˈchronically** *adv.* —**synchronicity** (ˌsɪnkrəˈnɪsɪtɪ) *n.*

synchronism (ˈsɪŋkrəˌnɪzəm) *n.* **1.** the quality or condition of being synchronous. **2.** a chronological list of historical persons and events, arranged to show parallel or synchronous occurrence. **3.** the representation in a work of art of one or more incidents that occurred at separate times. [C16: < Gk *sunkhronismos*] —ˌ**synchroˈnistic** *or* ˌ**synchroˈnistical** *adj.* —ˌ**synchroˈnistically** *adv.*

synchronize *or* **-ise** (ˈsɪŋkrəˌnaɪz) *vb.* **1.** (when *intr.*, usually foll. by *with*) to occur or recur or cause to occur or recur at the same time or in unison. **2.** to indicate or cause to indicate the same time: *synchronize your watches.* **3.** (*tr.*) *Films.* to establish (the picture and soundtrack records) in their correct relative position. **4.** (*tr.*) to designate (events) as simultaneous. —ˌ**synchroniˈzation** *or* **-iˈsation** *n.* —ˈ**synchroˌnizer** *or* **-iser** *n.*

synchronized swimming *n.* a sport in which swimmers move in patterns in time to music.

synchronous (ˈsɪŋkrənəs) *adj.* **1.** occurring at the same time. **2.** *Physics.* (of periodic phenomena, such as voltages) having the same frequency and phase. **3.** occurring or recurring exactly together and at the same rate. [C17: < LL *synchronus*, < Gk *sunkhronos*, < SYN- + *khronos* time] —ˈ**synchronously** *adv.* —ˈ**synchronousness** *n.* —ˈ**synchrony** *n.*

synchronous machine *n.* an electrical machine whose rotating speed is proportional to the frequency of the alternating-current supply and independent of the load.

synchronous motor *n.* an alternating-current motor that runs at a speed that is equal to or is a multiple of the frequency of the supply.

synchrotron (ˈsɪŋkrəˌtrɒn) *n.* a particle accelerator having an electric field of fixed frequency and a changing magnetic field. [C20: < SYNCHRO- + (ELEC)TRON]

syncline (ˈsɪŋklaɪn) *n.* a downward fold of stratified rock in which the strata slope towards a vertical axis. [C19: < SYN- + Gk *klīnein* to lean] —**synˈclinal** *adj.*

Syncom (ˈsɪnˌkɒm) *n.* a communications satellite in stationary orbit. [C20: < *syn*(*chronous*) *com*(*munication*)]

syncopate (ˈsɪŋkəˌpeɪt) *vb.* (*tr.*) **1.** *Music.* to modify or treat (a beat, rhythm, note, etc.) by syncopation. **2.** to shorten (a word) by omitting sounds or letters from the middle. [C17: < Med. L *syncopāre* to omit a letter or syllable, < LL *syncopa* SYNCOPE] —ˈ**syncoˌpator** *n.*

syncopation (ˌsɪŋkəˈpeɪʃən) *n.* **1.** *Music.* **a.** the displacement of the usual rhythmical accent away from a strong beat onto a weak beat. **b.** a note, beat, rhythm, etc., produced by syncopation. **2.** another word for **syncope** (sense 2).

syncope (ˈsɪŋkəpɪ) *n.* **1.** a technical word for a **faint. 2.** the omission of sounds or letters from the middle of a word. [C16: < LL *syncopa*, < Gk *sunkopē* a cutting off, < SYN- + *koptein* to cut] —**syncopic** (sɪŋˈkɒpɪk) *or* ˈ**syncopal** *adj.*

syncretism (ˈsɪŋkrɪˌtɪzəm) *n.* **1.** the tendency to syncretize. **2.** the historical tendency of languages to reduce their use of inflection, as in the development of Old English into Modern English. [C17: < NL *syncrētismus*, < Gk *sunkrētismos* alliance of Cretans, < *sunkrētizein* to join forces (in the manner of the Cretan towns), < SYN- + *Krēs* a Cretan] —**syncretic** (sɪŋˈkrɛtɪk) *or* ˌ**syncreˈtistic** *adj.* —ˈ**syncretist** *n.*

syncretize *or* **-ise** (ˈsɪŋkrɪˌtaɪz) *vb.* to attempt to combine the characteristic teachings, beliefs, or practices of (differing systems of religion or philosophy). —ˌ**syncretiˈzation** *or* **-iˈsation** *n.*

syndactyl (sɪnˈdæktɪl) *adj.* **1.** (of certain animals) having two or more digits growing fused together. ~*n.* **2.** an animal with this arrangement of digits. —**synˈdactylism** *n.*

syndesmosis (ˌsɪndɛsˈməʊsɪs) *n., pl.* **-ses** (-siːz). *Anat.* a type of joint in which the articulating bones are held together by a ligament of connective tissue. [C18: NL, < Gk *sundein* to bind together] —**syndesmotic** (ˌsɪndɛsˈmɒtɪk) *adj.*

syndetic (sɪnˈdɛtɪk) *adj.* denoting a grammatical construction in which two clauses are connected by a conjunction. [C17: < Gk *sundetikos*, < *sundetos* bound together] —**syndesis** (sɪnˈdiːsɪs) *n.* —**synˈdetically** *adv.*

syndic (ˈsɪndɪk) *n.* **1.** *Brit.* a business agent of some universities or other bodies. **2.** (in several countries) a government administrator or magistrate with varying powers. [C17: via OF < LL *syndicus*, < Gk *sundikos* defendant's advocate, < SYN- + *dikē* justice] —ˈ**syndical** *adj.*

syndicalism (ˈsɪndɪkəˌlɪzəm) *n.* **1.** a revolutionary movement and theory advocating seizure of the means of production and distribution by syndicates of workers, esp. by a general strike. **2.** an economic system resulting from such action. —ˈ**syndical** *adj.* —ˈ**syndicalist** *adj., n.* —ˌ**syndicalˈ istic** *adj.*

syndicate *n.* (ˈsɪndɪkɪt). **1.** an association of business enterprises or individuals organized to undertake a joint project. **2.** a news agency that sells articles, photographs, etc., to a number of newspapers for simultaneous publication. **3.** any association formed to carry out an enterprise of common interest to its members. **4.** a board of syndics or the office of syndic. ~*vb.* (ˈsɪndɪˌkeɪt). **5.** (*tr.*) to sell (articles, photographs, etc.) to several newspapers for simultaneous publication. **6.** (*tr.*) *U.S.* to sell (a programme or programmes) to several local commercial stations. **7.** to form a syndicate of (people). [C17: < OF *syndicat* office of a SYNDIC] —ˌ**syndiˈcation** *n.*

syndrome (ˈsɪndrəʊm) *n.* **1.** *Med.* any combination of signs and symptoms that are indicative of a particular disease or disorder. **2.** a symptom, characteristic, or set of symptoms or characteristics indicating the existence of a condition, problem, etc. [C16: via NL < Gk *sundromē*, lit.: a running together, < SYN- + *dramein* to run] —**syndromic** (sɪnˈdrɒmɪk) *adj.*

syne *or* **syn** (saɪn) *adv., prep., conj.* a Scottish word for **since.** [C14: prob. rel. to OE *sīth* since]

synecdoche (sɪnˈɛkdəkɪ) *n.* a figure of speech in which a part is substituted for a whole or a whole for a part, as in *50 head of cattle* for *50 cows*, or *the army* for *a soldier.* [C14: via L < Gk *sunekdokhē*, < SYN- + *ekdokhē* interpretation, < *dekhesthai* to accept] —**synecdochic** (ˌsɪnɛkˈdɒkɪk) *or* ˌ**synecˈdochical** *adj.*

synecious (sɪˈniːʃəs) *adj.* a variant spelling of **synoecious.**

synecology (ˌsɪnɪˈkɒlədʒɪ) *n.* the ecological study of communities of plants and animals. —**synecologic** (sɪnˌɛkəˈlɒdʒɪk) *or* **synˌecoˈlogical** *adj.* —**synˌecoˈlogically** *adv.*

syneresis *or* **synaeresis** (sɪˈnɪərɪsɪs) *n.* **1.** *Chem.* the process in which a gel contracts on standing and exudes liquid, as in the separation of whey in cheese-making. **2.** the contraction of two vowels into a diphthong. [C16: via LL < Gk *sunairesis* a shortening, < *sunairein* to draw together, < SYN- + *hairein* to take]

synergism (ˈsɪnəˌdʒɪzəm, sɪˈnɜː-) *n.* the working together of two or more drugs, muscles, etc., to produce an effect greater than the sum of their individual effects. Also called: **synergy.** [C18: < NL *synergismus*, < Gk *sunergos*, < SYN- + *ergon* work] —ˌsyner'getic *adj.* —syn'ergic *adj.* —synergist ('sɪnədʒɪst, sɪ'nɜː-) *n., adj.*

synesis ('sɪnɪsɪs) *n.* a grammatical construction in which the inflection or form of a word is conditioned by the meaning rather than the syntax, as for example the plural form *have* with the singular noun *group* in the sentence *the group have already assembled.* [via NL < Gk *sunesis* union, < *sunienai* to bring together, < SYN- + *hienai* to send]

synesthesia (ˌsɪniːs'θiːzɪə) *n.* the usual U.S. spelling of **synaesthesia.**

syngamy ('sɪŋgəmɪ) *or* **syngenesis** (sɪn'dʒɛnɪsɪs) *n.* reproduction involving the fusion of a male and female haploid gamete. Also called: **sexual reproduction.** —**syngamic** (sɪŋ'gæmɪk) *or* **syngamous** ('sɪŋgəməs) *adj.*

synod ('sɪnəd, 'sɪnɒd) *n.* **1.** a local or special ecclesiastical council, esp. of a diocese, formally convened to discuss ecclesiastical affairs. **2.** *Rare.* any council, esp. for discussion. [C14: < LL *synodus,* < Gk *sunodos,* < SYN- + *hodos* a way] —'**synodal** *adj.*

synodic (sɪ'nɒdɪk) *adj.* relating to or involving a conjunction or two successive conjunctions of the same star, planet, or satellite: *the synodic month.*

synoecious *or* **synecious** (sɪ'niːʃəs) *adj.* (of plants) having male and female organs on the same flower or structure. [C19: SYN- + *-oecious,* < Gk *oikion* dim. of *oikos* house]

synonym ('sɪnənɪm) *n.* **1.** a word that means the same or nearly the same as another word, such as *bucket* and *pail.* **2.** a word or phrase used as another name for something, such as *Hellene* for a *Greek.* —ˌ**syno'nymic** *or* ˌ**syno'nymical** *adj.* —ˌ**syno'nymity** *n.*

synonymous (sɪ'nɒnɪməs) *adj.* **1.** (often foll. by *with*) being a synonym (of). **2.** (*postpositive;* foll. by *with*) closely associated (with) or suggestive (of): *his name was synonymous with greed.* —**syn'onymously** *adv.* —**syn'onymousness** *n.*

synonymy (sɪ'nɒnɪmɪ) *n., pl.* **-mies. 1.** the study of synonyms. **2.** the character of being synonymous; equivalence. **3.** a list or collection of synonyms, esp. one in which their meanings are discriminated.

synopsis (sɪ'nɒpsɪs) *n., pl.* **-ses** (-siːz). a brief review of a subject; summary. [C17: via LL < Gk *sunopsis,* < SYN- + *opsis* view]

synopsize *or* **-ise** (sɪ'nɒpsaɪz) *vb.* (*tr.*) **1.** *U.S.* variants of **epitomize. 2.** *U.S. & Canad.* to make a synopsis of.

synoptic (sɪ'nɒptɪk) *adj.* **1.** of or relating to a synopsis. **2.** (*often cap.*) *Bible.* **a.** (of the Gospels of Matthew, Mark, and Luke) presenting the narrative of Christ's life, ministry, etc., from a point of view held in common by all three, and with close similarities in content, order, etc. **b.** of or relating to these three Gospels. **3.** *Meteorol.* concerned with the distribution of meteorological conditions over a wide area at a given time: *a synoptic chart.* ~*n.* **4.** (*often cap.*) *Bible.* **a.** any of the three synoptic Gospels. **b.** any of the authors of these. [C18: < Gk *sunoptikos*] —**syn'optically** *adv.* —**syn'optist** *n.*

synovia (saɪ'nəʊvɪə, sɪ-) *n.* a transparent viscid lubricating fluid, secreted by the membrane lining joints, tendon sheaths, etc. [C17: < NL, prob. < SYN- + L *ōvum* egg] —**syn'ovial** *adj.*

synovitis (ˌsaɪnəʊ'vaɪtɪs, ˌsɪn-) *n.* inflammation of the membrane surrounding a joint. —**synovitic** (ˌsaɪnəʊ'vɪtɪk, ˌsɪn-) *adj.*

synroc ('sɪnˌrɒk) *n.* a titanium-ceramic substance that can incorporate nuclear waste in its crystals. [< *syn*(*thetic*) + *roc*(*k*)]

syntactics (sɪn'tæktɪks) *n.* (*functioning as sing.*) the branch of semiotics that deals with the formal properties of symbol systems; proof theory.

syntagma (sɪn'tægmə) *or* **syntagm** ('sɪnˌtæm) *n., pl.* **-tagmata** (-'tægmətə) *or* **-tagms. 1.** a word or phrase forming a syntactic unit. **2.** a systematic collection of statements or propositions. [C17: < LL, < Gk, < *suntassein* to put in order; see SYNTAX] —ˌ**syntag'matic** *adj.*

syntax ('sɪntæks) *n.* **1.** the branch of linguistics that deals with the grammatical arrangement of words and morphemes in sentences. **2.** the totality of facts about the grammatical arrangement of words in a language. **3.** a systematic statement of the rules governing the grammatical arrangement of words and morphemes in a language. **4.** a systematic statement of the rules governing the properly formed formulas of a logical system. [C17: < LL *syntaxis,* < Gk *suntaxis,* < *suntassein* to put in order, < SYN- + *tassein* to arrange] —**syn'tactic** *or* **syn'tactical** *adj.* —**syn'tactically** *adv.*

synth (sɪnθ) *n.* short for **synthesizer.**

synthesis ('sɪnθɪsɪs) *n., pl.* **-ses** (-ˌsiːz). **1.** the process of combining objects or ideas into a complex whole. **2.** the combination or whole produced by such a process. **3.** the process of producing a compound by a chemical reaction or series of reactions, usually from simpler starting materials. **4.** *Linguistics.* the use of inflections rather than word order and function words to express the syntactic relations in a language. [C17: via L < Gk *sunthesis,* < *suntithenai* to put together, < SYN- + *tithenai* to place] —'**synthesist** *n.*

synthesize ('sɪnθɪˌsaɪz), **synthetize** *or* **-sise, -tise** *vb.* **1.** to combine or cause to combine into a whole. **2.** (*tr.*) to produce by synthesis. —ˌ**synthesi'zation,** ˌ**syntheti'zation** *or* **-si'sation, -ti'sation** *n.*

synthesizer ('sɪnθɪˌsaɪzə) *n.* **1.** an electronic musical instrument, usually operated by means of a keyboard, in which sounds are produced by oscillators, filters, and amplifiers. **2.** a person or thing that synthesizes.

synthetic (sɪn'θɛtɪk) *adj. also* **synthetical. 1.** (of a substance or material) made artificially by chemical reaction. **2.** not genuine; insincere: *synthetic compassion.* **3.** denoting languages, such as Latin, whose morphology is characterized by synthesis. **4.** *Philosophy.* **a.** (of a proposition) having a truth-value that is not determined solely by virtue of the meanings of the words, as in *all men are arrogant.* **b.** contingent. ~*n.* **5.** a synthetic substance or material. [C17: < NL *syntheticus,* < Gk *sunthetikos* expert in putting together, < *suntithenai* to put together; see SYNTHESIS] —**syn'thetically** *adv.*

syphilis ('sɪfɪlɪs) *n.* a venereal disease caused by infection with the microorganism *Treponema pallidum:* characterized by an ulcerating chancre, usually on the genitals and progressing through the lymphatic system to nearly all tissues of the body, producing serious clinical manifestations. [C18: < NL *Syphilis* (*sive Morbus Gallicus*) "Syphilis (or the French disease)", title of a poem (1530) by G. Fracastoro, It. physician and poet, in which a shepherd *Syphilus* is portrayed as the first victim of the disease] —**syphilitic** (ˌsɪfɪ'lɪtɪk) *adj.* —'**syphiˌloid** *adj.*

syphon ('saɪfᵊn) *n.* a variant spelling of **siphon.**

Syriac ('sɪrɪˌæk) *n.* a dialect of Aramaic spoken in Syria until about the 13th century A.D.

Syrian ('sɪrɪən) *adj.* **1.** of or relating to Syria, a republic in W Asia, its people, or their dialect of Arabic. ~*n.* **2.** a native or inhabitant of Syria.

syringa (sɪ'rɪŋgə) *n.* another name for **mock orange** (sense 1) or **lilac** (sense 1). [C17: < NL, < Gk *surinx* tube, < use of its hollow stems for pipes]

syringe ('sɪrɪndʒ, sɪ'rɪndʒ) *n.* **1.** *Med.* a hypodermic syringe or a rubber ball with a slender nozzle, for use in withdrawing or injecting fluids, cleaning wounds, etc. **2.** any similar device for injecting, spraying, or extracting liquids by means of pressure or suction. ~*vb.* **3.** (*tr.*) to cleanse, inject, or spray with a syringe. [C15: < LL, < L: SYRINX]

syringomyelia (səˌrɪŋgəʊmaɪ'iːlɪə) *n.* a chronic progressive disease of the spinal cord in which cavities form in the grey matter: characterized by loss of the sense of pain and temperature. [C19: *syringo-,* < Gk: SYRINX + *-myelia* < Gk *muelos* marrow] —**syringomyelic** (səˌrɪŋgəʊmaɪ'ɛlɪk) *adj.*

syrinx (ˈsɪrɪŋks) *n., pl.* **syringes** (sɪˈrɪndʒiːz) *or* **syrinxes. 1.** the vocal organ of a bird, situated in the lower part of the trachea. **2.** (in classical Greek music) a panpipe or set of panpipes. [C17: via L < Gk *surinx* pipe] —**syringeal** (sɪˈrɪndʒɪəl) *adj.*

syrup (ˈsɪrəp) *n.* **1.** a solution of sugar dissolved in water and often flavoured with fruit juice: used for sweetening fruit, etc. **2.** any of various thick sweet liquids prepared for cooking or table use from molasses, sugars, etc. **3.** *Inf.* cloying sentimentality. **4.** a liquid medicine containing a sugar solution for flavouring or preservation. ~Also: **sirup.** [C15: < Med. L *syrupus,* < Ar. *sharāb* a drink, < *shariba* to drink] —ˈ**syrupy** *adj.*

syssarcosis (ˌsɪsɑːˈkəʊsɪs) *n., pl.* **-ses** (-siːz). *Anat.* the union or articulation of bones by muscle. [C17: < NL, < Gk *sussarkōsis,* < *sus-* SYN- + *sarkoun* to become fleshy, < *sarx* flesh] —**syssarcotic** (ˌsɪsɑːˈkɒtɪk) *adj.*

systaltic (sɪˈstæltɪk) *adj.* (esp. of the action of the heart) of, relating to, or characterized by alternate contractions and dilations; pulsating. [C17: < LL *systalticus,* < Gk, < *sustellein* to contract, < SYN- + *stellein* to place]

system (ˈsɪstəm) *n.* **1.** a group or combination of interrelated, interdependent, or interacting elements forming a collective entity; a methodical or coordinated assemblage of parts, facts, etc. **2.** any scheme of classification or arrangement. **3.** a network of communications, transportation, or distribution. **4.** a method or complex of methods: *he has a perfect system at roulette.* **5.** orderliness; an ordered manner. **6. the system.** (*often cap.*) society seen as an environment exploiting, restricting, and repressing individuals. **7.** an organism considered as a functioning entity. **8.** any of various bodily parts or structures that are anatomically or physiologically related: *the digestive system.* **9.** one's physiological or psychological constitution: *get it out of your system.* **10.** any assembly of electronic, mechanical, etc., components with interdependent functions, usually forming a self-contained unit: *a brake system.* **11.** a group of celestial bodies that are associated as a result of natural laws, esp. gravitational attraction: *the solar system.* **12.** a point of view or doctrine used to interpret a branch of knowledge. **13.** *Mineralogy.* one of a group of divisions into which crystals may be placed on the basis of the lengths and inclinations of their axes. **14.** *Geol.* a stratigraphical unit for the rock strata formed during a period of geological time. [C17: < F, < LL *systēma,* < Gk *sustēma,* < SYN- + *histanai* to cause to stand]

systematic (ˌsɪstɪˈmætɪk) *adj.* **1.** characterized by the use of order and planning; methodical: *a systematic administrator.* **2.** comprising or resembling a system: *systematic theology.* **3.** Also: **systematical.** *Biol.* of or relating to taxonomic classification. —ˌ**systemˈatically** *adv.* —ˈ**systemaˌtism** *n.* —ˈ**systematist** *n.*

systematics (ˌsɪstɪˈmætɪks) *n.* (*functioning as sing.*) the study of systems and the principles of classification and nomenclature.

systematize (ˈsɪstɪməˌtaɪz), **systemize** *or* **-tise, -mise** *vb.* (*tr.*) to arrange in a system. —ˌ**systematiˈzation, -iˈsation** *or* ˌ**systemiˈzation, -iˈsation** *n.* —ˈ**systemaˌtizer, -iser** *or* ˈ**systemˌizer, -ˌiser** *n.*

Système International d'Unités (*French* sistɛm ɛ̃tɛrnasjɔnal dynite) *n.* the International System of units. See **SI unit.**

systemic (sɪˈstɛmɪk, -ˈstiː-) *adj.* **1.** another word for **systematic** (senses 1, 2). **2.** *Physiol.* (of a poison, disease, etc.) affecting the entire body. **3.** (of an insecticide, fungicide, etc.) designed to be absorbed by a plant into its tissues. ~*n.* **4.** a systemic insecticide, fungicide, etc. —**sysˈtemically** *adv.*

systems analysis *n.* the analysis of the requirements of a task and the expression of these in a form that permits the assembly of computer hardware and software to perform the task. —**systems analyst** *n.*

systems engineering *n.* the branch of engineering, based on systems analysis and information theory, concerned with the design of integrated systems.

systole (ˈsɪstəlɪ) *n.* contraction of the heart, during which blood is pumped into the aorta and the arteries. Cf. **diastole.** [C16: via LL < Gk *sustolē,* < *sustellein* to contract; see SYSTALTIC] —**systolic** (sɪˈstɒlɪk) *adj.*

syzygy (ˈsɪzɪdʒɪ) *n., pl.* **-gies. 1.** either of the two positions (conjunction or opposition) of a celestial body when sun, earth, and the body lie in a straight line: *the moon is at syzygy when full.* **2.** *Rare.* any pair, usually of opposites. [C17: < LL, < Gk *suzugia,* < *suzugos* yoked together, < SYN- + *zugon* a yoke] —**syzygial** (sɪˈzɪdʒɪəl), **syzygetic** (ˌsɪzɪˈdʒɛtɪk), *or* **syzygal** (ˈsɪzɪgᵊl) *adj.* —ˌ**syzyˈgetically** *adv.*

T

t *or* **T** (tiː) *n., pl.* **t's, T's,** *or* **Ts.** **1.** the 20th letter of the English alphabet. **2.** a speech sound represented by this letter. **3.** something shaped like a T. **4. to a T.** in every detail; perfectly.

t *symbol for:* **1.** *Statistics.* distribution. **2.** tonne(s). **3.** troy (weight).

T *symbol for:* **1.** absolute temperature. **2.** surface tension. **3.** tera-. **4.** tesla. **5.** *Chem.* tritium.

t. *abbrev. for:* **1.** *Commerce.* tare. **2.** teaspoon(ful). **3.** temperature. **4.** *Music.* tempo. **5.** *Music.* Also: **T.** tenor. **6.** *Grammar.* tense. **7.** ton(s). **8.** transitive.

't *contraction of* it.

ta (tɑː) *interj. Brit. inf.* thank you. [C18: imit. of baby talk]

Ta *the chemical symbol for* tantalum.

TA (in Britain) *abbrev. for* Territorial Army (now superseded by **TAVR**).

TAA *abbrev. for* Trans-Australia Airlines.

Taal (tɑːl) *n.* **the.** another name for **Afrikaans.** [Du.: speech]

tab[1] (tæb) *n.* **1.** a small flap of material, esp. one on a garment for decoration or for fastening to a button. **2.** any similar flap, such as a piece of paper attached to a file for identification. **3.** *Brit. mil.* the insignia on the collar of a staff officer. **4.** *Chiefly U.S. & Canad.* a bill, esp. for a meal or drinks. **5. keep tabs on.** *Inf.* to keep a watchful eye on. ~*vb.* **tabbing, tabbed. 6.** (*tr.*) to supply with a tab or tabs. [C17: <?]

tab[2] (tæb) *n.* short for **tabulator** or **tablet.**

TAB *abbrev. for:* **1.** *Austral. & N.Z.* Totalizator Agency Board. **2.** typhoid-paratyphoid A and B (vaccine).

tabard (ˈtæbəd) *n.* a sleeveless or short-sleeved jacket, esp. one worn by a herald, bearing a coat of arms, or by a knight over his armour. [C13: < OF *tabart,* <?]

tabaret (ˈtæbərɪt) *n.* a hard-wearing fabric of silk or similar cloth with stripes of satin or moire, used esp. for upholstery. [C19: ? < TABBY]

Tabasco (təˈbæskəʊ) *n. Trademark.* a very hot red sauce made from matured capsicums.

tabby (ˈtæbɪ) *adj.* **1.** (esp. of cats) brindled with dark stripes or wavy markings on a lighter background. **2.** having a wavy or striped pattern, particularly in colours of grey and brown. ~*n., pl.* **-bies. 3.** a tabby cat. **4.** any female domestic cat. **5.** a fabric with a watered pattern, esp. silk or taffeta. [C17: < OF *tabis* silk cloth, < Ar. *al-'attabiya,* lit.: the quarter of (Prince) 'Attab, the part of Baghdad where the fabric was first made]

tabernacle (ˈtæbəˌnækᵊl) *n.* **1.** (*often cap.*) *Old Testament.* **a.** the portable sanctuary in which the ancient Israelites carried the Ark of the Covenant. **b.** the Jewish Temple. **2.** any place of worship that is not called a church. **3.** *R.C. Church.* a receptacle in which the Blessed Sacrament is kept. **4.** *Chiefly R.C. Church.* a canopied niche. **5.** *Naut.* a strong framework for holding the foot of a mast, allowing it to be swung down to pass under low bridges, etc. [C13: < L *tabernāculum* a tent, < *taberna* a hut] —ˌ**taberˈnacular** *adj.*

tabes (ˈteɪbiːz) *n., pl.* **tabes. 1.** a wasting of a bodily organ or part. **2.** short for **tabes dorsalis.** [C17: < L: a wasting away] —**tabetic** (təˈbɛtɪk) *adj.*

tabescent (təˈbɛsᵊnt) *adj.* **1.** progressively emaciating; wasting away. **2.** of, relating to, or having tabes. [C19: < L *tābēscere,* < TABES] —**taˈbescence** *n.*

tabes dorsalis (dɔːˈsɑːlɪs) *n.* a form of late syphilis that attacks the spinal cord causing degeneration of the nerve fibres, paralysis of the leg muscles, acute abdominal pain, etc. [NL, lit.: tabes of the back]

tabla (ˈtʌblə, ˈtɑːblɑː) *n.* a musical instrument of India consisting of a pair of drums whose pitches can be varied. [Hindu, < Ar. *tabla* drum]

tablature (ˈtæblətʃə) *n. Music.* any of a number of forms of musical notation, esp. for playing the lute, consisting of letters and signs indicating rhythm and fingering. [C16: < F, ult. < L *tabulātum* wooden floor, < *tabula* a plank]

table (ˈteɪbᵊl) *n.* **1.** a flat horizontal slab or board supported by one or more legs. **2. a.** such a slab or board on which food is served. **b.** (*as modifier*): *table linen.* **3.** food as served in a particular household, etc.: *a good table.* **4.** such a piece of furniture specially designed for any of various purposes: *a bird table.* **5. a.** a company of persons assembled for a meal, game, etc. **b.** (*as modifier*): *table talk.* **6.** any flat or level area, such as a plateau. **7.** a rectangular panel set below or above the face of a wall. **8.** *Archit.* another name for **string course. 9.** any of various flat surfaces, as an upper horizontal facet of a cut gem. **10.** *Music.* the sounding board of a violin, guitar, etc. **11. a.** an arrangement of words, numbers, or signs, usually in parallel columns. **b.** See **multiplication table. 12.** a tablet on which laws were inscribed by the ancient Romans, the Hebrews, etc. **13. turn the tables.** to cause a complete reversal of circumstances. **14. under the table. a.** (**under-the-table** *when prenominal*) done illicitly and secretly. **b.** *Sl.* drunk. ~*vb.* (*tr.*) **15.** to place on a table. **16.** *Brit.* to submit (a bill, etc.) for consideration by a legislative body. **17.** *U.S.* to suspend discussion of (a bill, etc.) indefinitely. **18.** to enter in or form into a list. [C12: via OF < L *tabula* a writing tablet]

tableau (ˈtæbləʊ) *n., pl.* **-leaux** (-ləʊ, -ləʊz) *or* **-leaus. 1.** See ***tableau vivant.*** **2.** a pause on stage when all the performers briefly freeze in position. **3.** any dramatic group or scene. [C17: < F, < OF *tablel* a picture, dim. of TABLE]

tableau vivant *French.* (tablo vivɑ̃) *n., pl.* ***tableaux vivants*** (tablo vivɑ̃). a representation of a scene by a person or group posed silent and motionless. [C19, lit.: living picture]

tablecloth (ˈteɪbᵊlˌklɒθ) *n.* a cloth for covering the top of a table, esp. during meals.

table d'hôte (ˈtɑːbᵊl ˈdəʊt) *adj.* **1.** (of a meal) consisting of a set number of courses with limited choice of dishes offered at a fixed price. Cf. **à la carte.** ~*n., pl.* **tables d'hôte** (ˈtɑːbᵊlz ˈdəʊt). **2.** a table d'hôte meal or menu. [C17: < F, lit.: the host's table]

tableland (ˈteɪbᵊlˌlænd) *n.* flat elevated land.

table licence *n.* a licence authorizing the sale of alcoholic drinks with meals only.

tablespoon (ˈteɪbᵊlˌspuːn) *n.* **1.** a spoon, larger than a dessertspoon, used for serving food, etc. **2.** Also called: **tablespoonful.** the amount contained in such a spoon. **3.** a unit of capacity used in cooking, etc., equal to half a fluid ounce.

tablet (ˈtæblɪt) *n.* **1.** a pill made of a compressed medicinal substance. **2.** a flattish cake of some substance, such as soap. **3.** a slab of stone, wood, etc., esp. one used for inscriptions. **4. a.** a rigid sheet, as of bark, etc., used for similar purposes. **b.** (*often pl.*) a set of these fastened together. **5.** a pad of writing paper. **6.** *Scot.* a sweet made from butter, sugar, and condensed milk, usually shaped into flat oblong cakes. [C14: < OF *tablete* a little table, < L *tabula* a board]

table tennis *n.* a miniature form of tennis played on a table with bats and a hollow ball.

table-turning *n.* the movement of a table attributed by spiritualists to the power of spirits.

tableware (ˈteɪbᵊlˌwɛə) *n.* articles such as dishes, plates, knives, forks, etc., used at meals.

tabloid (ˈtæblɔɪd) *n.* **1.** a newspaper with pages about 30 cm (12 inches) by 40 cm (16 inches), usually with many photographs and a concise and often sensational style. **2.** something in a condensed or summarized form. [C20: < earlier *Tabloid*, a trademark for a medicine in tablet form]

taboo *or* **tabu** (tə'buː) *adj.* **1.** forbidden or disapproved of: *taboo words.* **2.** (in Polynesia) marked off as sacred and forbidden. *~n., pl.* **-boos** *or* **-bus. 3.** any prohibition resulting from social or other conventions. **4.** ritual restriction or prohibition, esp. of something that is considered holy or unclean. *~vb.* **5.** (*tr.*) to place under a taboo. [C18: < Tongan *tabu*]

tabor *or* **tabour** ('teɪbə) *n.* a small drum used esp. in the Middle Ages, struck with one hand while the other held a pipe. [C13: < OF *tabour,* ? < Persian *tabīr*]

taboret *or* **tabouret** ('tæbərɪt) *n.* **1.** a low stool. **2.** a frame for stretching out cloth while it is being embroidered. **3.** a small tabor. [C17: < F *tabouret,* dim. of TABOR]

tabular ('tæbjʊlə) *adj.* **1.** arranged in systematic or table form. **2.** calculated from or by means of a table. **3.** like a table in form; flat. [C17: < L *tabulāris* concerning boards, < *tabula* a board] **—'tabularly** *adv.*

tabula rasa ('tæbjʊlə 'rɑːsə) *n., pl.* **tabulae rasae** ('tæbjʊliː 'rɑːsiː). **1.** the mind in its uninformed original state. **2.** an opportunity for a fresh start; clean slate. [L: a scraped tablet]

tabulate *vb.* ('tæbjʊˌleɪt). (*tr.*) **1.** to set out, arrange, or write in tabular form. **2.** to form or cut with a flat surface. *~adj.* ('tæbjʊlɪt, -ˌleɪt). **3.** having a flat surface. [C18: < L *tabula* a board] **—'tabulable** *adj.* **—ˌtabu'lation** *n.*

tabulator ('tæbjʊˌleɪtə) *n.* **1.** a device for setting the stops that locate the column margins on a typewriter. **2.** *Computers.* a machine that reads data from one medium, such as punched cards, producing lists, tabulations, or totals.

tacamahac ('tækəməˌhæk) *or* **tacmahack** *n.* **1.** any of several strong-smelling resinous gums used in ointments, incense, etc. **2.** any tree yielding this resin. [C16: < Sp. *tacamahaca,* < Nahuatl *tecomahca* aromatic resin]

tacet ('teɪsɛt, 'tæs-) *vb.* (*intr.*) (on a musical score) a direction indicating that a particular instrument or singer does not take part. [C18: < L: it is silent, < *tacēre* to be quiet]

tacheometer (ˌtækɪ'ɒmɪtə) *or* **tachymeter** *n.* *Surveying.* a type of theodolite designed for the rapid measurement of distances, elevations, and directions. **—ˌtache'ometry** *n.*

tachisme ('tɑːʃɪzəm) *n.* a type of action painting in which haphazard dabs and blots of colour are treated as a means of unconscious expression. [C20: F, < *tache* stain]

tachistoscope (tæ'kɪstəˌskəʊp) *n.* an instrument for displaying visual images for very brief intervals, usually a fraction of a second. [C20: < Gk *takhistos* swiftest + -SCOPE] **—tachistoscopic** (tæˌkɪstə'skɒpɪk) *adj.*

tacho- *combining form.* speed: *tachograph; tachometer.* [< Gk *takhos*]

tachograph ('tækəˌgrɑːf) *n.* a tachometer that produces a record (**tachogram**) of its readings, esp. a device for recording the speed of and distance covered by a vehicle.

tachometer (tæ'kɒmɪtə) *n.* any device for measuring speed, esp. the rate of revolution of a shaft. Tachometers are often fitted to cars to indicate the number of revolutions per minute of the engine. **—ta'chometry** *n.*

tachy- *or* **tacheo-** *combining form.* swift or accelerated: *tachyon.* [< Gk *takhus* swift]

tachycardia (ˌtækɪ'kɑːdɪə) *n.* abnormally rapid beating of the heart.

tachygraphy (tæ'kɪgrəfɪ) *n.* shorthand, esp. as used in ancient Rome or Greece.

tachymeter (tæ'kɪmɪtə) *n.* another name for **tacheometer.**

tachyon ('tækɪˌɒn) *n.* *Physics.* a hypothetical elementary particle capable of travelling faster than the velocity of light. [C20: < TACHY- + -ON]

tachyphylaxis (ˌtækɪfɪ'læksɪs) *n.* very rapid development of tolerance or immunity to the effects of a drug. [NL, < TACHY- + *phylaxis* on the model of *prophylaxis;* see PROPHYLACTIC]

tacit ('tæsɪt) *adj.* implied or inferred without direct expression; understood: *a tacit agreement.* [C17: < L *tacitus,* p.p. of *tacēre* to be silent] **—'tacitly** *adv.*

taciturn ('tæsɪˌtɜːn) *adj.* habitually silent, reserved, or uncommunicative. [C18: < L *taciturnus,* < *tacēre* to be silent] **—ˌtaci'turnity** *n.* **—'taciˌturnly** *adv.*

tack[1] (tæk) *n.* **1.** a short sharp-pointed nail, with a large flat head. **2.** *Brit.* a long loose temporary stitch used in dressmaking, etc. **3.** See **tailor's-tack. 4.** a temporary fastening. **5.** stickiness. **6.** *Naut.* the heading of a vessel sailing to windward, stated in terms of the side of the sail against which the wind is pressing. **7.** *Naut.* **a.** a course sailed with the wind blowing from forward of the beam. **b.** one such course or a zigzag pattern of such courses. **8.** *Naut.* **a.** a sheet for controlling the weather clew of a course. **b.** the weather clew itself. **9.** *Naut.* the forward lower clew of a fore-and-aft sail. **10.** a course of action or policy. **11. on the wrong tack.** under a false impression. *~vb.* **12.** (*tr.*) to secure by a tack or tacks. **13.** *Brit.* to sew (something) with long loose temporary stitches. **14.** (*tr.*) to attach or append. **15.** *Naut.* to change the heading of (a sailing vessel) to the opposite tack. **16.** *Naut.* to steer (a sailing vessel) on alternate tacks. **17.** (*intr.*) *Naut.* (of a sailing vessel) to proceed on a different tack or to alternate tacks. **18.** (*intr.*) to follow a zigzag route; keep changing one's course of action. [C14 *tak* fastening, nail] **—'tacker** *n.*

tack[2] (tæk) *n.* riding harness for horses, such as saddles, bridles, etc. [C20: shortened < TACKLE]

tack hammer *n.* a light hammer for driving tacks.

tackies ('tækɪz) *pl. n., sing.* **tacky.** *S. African inf.* tennis shoes or plimsolls. [C20: prob. < TACKY[1], from their nonslip rubber soles]

tackle ('tæk'l) *n.* **1.** an arrangement of ropes and pulleys designed to lift heavy weights. **2.** the equipment required for a particular occupation, etc. **3.** *Naut.* the halyards and other running rigging aboard a vessel. **4.** *Sport.* a physical challenge to an opponent, as to prevent his progress with the ball. *~vb.* **5.** (*tr.*) to undertake (a task, etc.). **6.** (*tr.*) to confront (esp. an opponent) with a difficult proposition. **7.** *Sport.* to challenge (an opponent) with a tackle. [C13: rel. to MLow G *takel* ship's rigging] **—'tackler** *n.*

tacky[1] ('tækɪ) *adj.* **tackier, tackiest.** slightly sticky or adhesive. [C18: < TACK[1] (in the sense: stickiness)] **—'tackily** *adv.* **—'tackiness** *n.*

tacky[2] ('tækɪ) *adj.* **tackier, tackiest.** *Inf.* **1.** shabby or shoddy. **2.** ostentatious and vulgar. **3.** *U.S.* (of a person) dowdy; seedy. [C19: < dialect *tacky* an inferior horse, <?] **—'tackiness** *n.*

tacnode ('tækˌnəʊd) *n.* another name for **osculation** (sense 1). [C19: < L *tactus* touch (< *tangere* to touch) + NODE]

tact (tækt) *n.* **1.** a sense of what is fitting and considerate in dealing with others, so as to avoid giving offence. **2.** skill in handling difficult situations; diplomacy. [C17: < L *tactus* a touching, < *tangere* to touch] **—'tactful** *adj.* **—'tactfulness** *n.* **—'tactless** *adj.* **—'tactlessness** *n.*

tactic ('tæktɪk) *n.* a piece of tactics; tactical move. See also **tactics.**

-tactic *adj. combining form.* having a specified kind of pattern or arrangement or having an orientation determined by a specified force: *syndiotactic; phototactic.* [< Gk *taktikos* relating to order; see TACTICS]

tactical ('tæktɪk'l) *adj.* **1.** of, relating to, or employing tactics: *a tactical error.* **2.** (of missiles, bombing, etc.) for use in or supporting limited military operations; short-range. **3.** skilful, adroit, or diplomatic. **—'tactically** *adv.*

tactical voting *n.* (in an election) the practice of casting one's vote not for the party of one's choice but for the second strongest contender in a constituency in order to defeat the likeliest winner.

tactics (ˈtæktɪks) *pl. n.* **1.** (*functioning as sing.*) *Mil.* the art and science of the detailed direction and control of movement of forces in battle to achieve an aim or task. **2.** the manoeuvres used to achieve an aim or task. **3.** plans followed to achieve a particular short-term aim. [C17: < NL *tactica*, < Gk, < *taktikos* concerning arrangement, < *taktos* arranged (for battle), < *tassein* to arrange] —**tacˈtician** *n.*

tactile (ˈtæktaɪl) *adj.* **1.** of, relating to, affecting, or having a sense of touch. **2.** *Now rare.* capable of being touched; tangible. [C17: < L *tactilis*, < *tangere* to touch] —**tactility** (tækˈtɪlɪtɪ) *n.*

tadpole (ˈtædˌpəʊl) *n.* the aquatic larva of frogs, toads, etc., which develops from a limbless tailed form with external gills into a form with internal gills, limbs, and a reduced tail. [C15 *taddepol*, < *tadde* toad + *pol* head]

taedium vitae (ˈtiːdɪəm ˈviːtaɪ, ˈvaɪtiː) *n.* the feeling that life is boring and dull. [L, lit.: weariness of life]

tael (teɪl) *n.* **1.** a unit of weight, used in the Far East. **2.** (formerly) a Chinese monetary unit. [C16: < Port., < Malay *tahil* weight, ? < Sansk.]

ta'en (teɪn) *vb.* a Scot. or poetic contraction of **taken.**

taenia *or U.S.* **tenia** (ˈtiːnɪə) *n., pl.* **-niae** (-nɪˌiː). **1.** (in ancient Greece) a headband. **2.** *Archit.* the fillet between the architrave and frieze of a Doric entablature. **3.** *Anat.* any bandlike structure or part. **4.** any of a genus of tapeworms. [C16: via L < Gk *tainia* narrow strip]

taeniasis *or U.S.* **teniasis** (tiːˈnaɪəsɪs) *n. Pathol.* infestation with tapeworms of the genus *Taenia*.

taffeta (ˈtæfɪtə) *n.* a thin crisp lustrous plain-weave fabric of silk, rayon, etc., used esp. for women's clothes. [C14: < Med. L *taffata*, < Persian *tāftah* spun, < *tāftan* to spin]

taffrail (ˈtæfˌreɪl) *n. Naut.* a rail at the stern of a vessel. [C19: changed < earlier *tafferel*, < Du. *taffereel* panel (hence applied to the part of a vessel decorated with carved panels), < *tafel* table]

Taffy (ˈtæfɪ) *n., pl.* **-fies.** a slang word or nickname for a **Welshman.** [C17: < the supposed Welsh pronunciation of *Davy* (< *David*, Welsh *Dafydd*), a common Welsh Christian name]

tafia *or* **taffia** (ˈtæfɪə) *n.* a type of rum, esp. from Guyana or the West Indies. [C18: < F, < West Indian Creole, prob. < RATAFIA]

tag[1] (tæg) *n.* **1.** a piece of paper, leather, etc., for attaching to something as a mark or label: *a price tag.* **2.** a small piece of material hanging from a part or piece. **3.** a point of metal, etc., at the end of a cord or lace. **4.** an epithet or verbal appendage, the refrain of a song, the moral of a fable, etc. **5.** a brief quotation. **6.** an ornamental flourish. **7.** the tip of an animal's tail. **8.** a matted lock of wool or hair. ~*vb.* **tagging, tagged.** (*mainly tr.*) **9.** to mark with a tag. **10.** to add or append as a tag. **11.** to supply (prose or blank verse) with rhymes. **12.** (*intr.;* usually foll. by *on* or *along*) to trail (behind). **13.** to name or call (someone something). **14.** to cut the tags of wool or hair from (an animal). [C15: <?]

tag[2] (tæg) *n.* **1.** Also called: **tig.** a children's game in which one player chases the others in an attempt to catch one of them who will then become the chaser. **2.** the act of tagging one's partner in tag wrestling. **3.** (*modifier*) denoting a wrestling contest between two teams of two wrestlers, in which only one from each team may be in the ring at one time. The contestant outside the ring may change places with his team-mate inside the ring after touching his hand. ~*vb.* **tagging, tagged.** (*tr.*) **4.** to catch (another child) in the game of tag. **5.** (in tag wrestling) to touch the hand of (one's partner). [C18: ? < TAG[1]]

Tagalog (təˈgɑːlɒg) *n.* **1.** (*pl.* **-logs** *or* **-log**) a member of a people of the Philippines. **2.** the language of this people. ~*adj.* **3.** of or relating to this people or their language.

tag end *n.* **1.** *Chiefly U.S. & Canad.* the last part of something. **2.** a loose end of cloth, thread, etc.

tagetes (tæˈdʒiːtiːz) *n., pl.* **-tes.** any of a genus of plants with yellow or orange flowers, including the French and African marigolds. [< NL, < *Tages*, an Etruscan god]

tagliatelle (ˌtæljəˈtelɪ) *n.* a form of pasta made in narrow strips. [It., < *tagliare* to cut]

tahr *or* **thar** (tɑː) *n.* any of several goatlike mammals of S and SW Asia, having a shaggy coat and curved horns. [< Nepali *thār*]

tahsil (təˈsiːl) *n.* an administrative division in certain states in India. [Urdu, < Ar.: collection]

taiaha (ˈtaɪəˌhɑː) *n. N.Z.* a carved weapon in the form of a staff, now used in Maori ceremonial oratory. [< Maori]

t'ai chi ch'uan (ˈtaɪ dʒiː ˈtʃwɑːn) *n.* a Chinese system of callisthenics characterized by coordinated and rhythmic movements. Often shortened to **t'ai chi** (ˈtaɪ ˈdʒiː). [Chinese, lit.: great art of boxing]

taiga (ˈtaɪgɑː) *n.* the coniferous forests extending across much of subarctic North America and Eurasia. [< Russian, of Turkic origin]

taihoa (ˈtaɪhəʊə) *sentence substitute. N.Z.* hold on! no hurry!

tail[1] (teɪl) *n.* **1.** the rear part of the vertebrate body that contains an elongation of the vertebral column, esp. forming a flexible appendage. **2.** anything resembling such an appendage; the bottom, lowest, or rear part. **3.** the last part or parts: *the tail of the storm.* **4.** the rear part of an aircraft including the fin, tailplane, and control surfaces. **5.** *Astron.* the luminous stream of gas and dust particles driven from the head of a comet when close to the sun. **6.** the rear portion of a bomb, rocket, missile, etc., usually fitted with guiding or stabilizing vanes. **7.** a line of people or things. **8.** a long braid or tress of hair: *a pigtail.* **9.** a final short line in a stanza. **10.** *Inf.* a person employed to follow and spy upon another. **11.** an informal word for **buttocks. 12.** *Taboo sl.* **a.** the female genitals. **b.** a woman considered sexually (esp. in **piece of tail, bit of tail**). **13.** the foot of a page. **14.** the lower end of a pool or part of a stream. **15.** *Inf.* the course or track of a fleeing person or animal. **16.** (*modifier*) coming from or situated in the rear: *a tail wind.* **17. turn tail.** to run away; escape. **18. with one's tail between one's legs.** in a state of utter defeat or confusion. ~*vb.* **19.** to form or cause to form the tail. **20.** to remove the tail of (an animal). **21.** (*tr.*) to remove the stalk of. **22.** (*tr.*) to connect (objects, ideas, etc.) together by or as if by the tail. **23.** (*tr.*) *Inf.* to follow stealthily. **24.** (*intr.*) (of a vessel) to assume a specified position, as when at a mooring. **25.** to build the end of (a brick, joist, etc.) into a wall or (of a brick, etc.) to have one end built into a wall. ~See also **tail off, tail out, tails.** [OE *tægel*] —ˈ**tailless** *adj.*

tail[2] (teɪl) *Law.* ~*n.* **1.** the limitation of an estate or interest to a person and the heirs of his body. ~*adj.* **2.** (*immediately postpositive*) limited in this way. [C15: < OF *taille* a division; see TAILOR] —ˈ**tailless** *adj.*

tailback (ˈteɪlˌbæk) *n.* a queue of traffic stretching back from an obstruction.

tailboard (ˈteɪlˌbɔːd) *n.* a board at the rear of a lorry, etc., that can be removed or let down.

tail coat *n.* **1.** a man's black coat having a horizontal cut over the hips and a tapering tail with a vertical slit up to the waist. **2.** a cutaway frock coat, part of morning dress.

tail covert *n.* any of the covert feathers of a bird covering the bases of the tail feathers.

tail end *n.* the last, endmost, or final part.

tailgate (ˈteɪlˌgeɪt) *n.* **1.** another name for **tailboard.** ~*vb.* **2.** to drive very close behind (a vehicle).

tail gate *n.* a gate that is used to control the flow of water at the lower end of a lock.

tailing (ˈteɪlɪŋ) *n.* the part of a beam, rafter, projecting brick, etc., embedded in a wall.

tailings (ˈteɪlɪŋz) *pl. n.* waste left over after

certain processes, such as from an ore-crushing plant or in milling grain.

taillight (ˈteɪlˌlaɪt) *or* **taillamp** *n.* the U.S. and Canad. names for **rear light.**

tail off *or* **away** *vb.* (*adv.; usually intr.*) to decrease or cause to decrease in quantity, degree, etc., esp. gradually.

tailor (ˈteɪlə) *n.* **1.** a person who makes, repairs, or alters outer garments, esp. menswear. Related adj.: **sartorial. 2.** a voracious and active marine food fish of Australia. ~*vb.* **3.** to cut or style (material, etc.) to satisfy certain requirements. **4.** (*tr.*) to adapt so as to make suitable. **5.** (*intr.*) to work as a tailor. [C13: < Anglo-Norman *taillour,* < OF *taillier* to cut, < L *tālea* a cutting] —ˈ**tailored** *adj.*

tailorbird (ˈteɪləˌbɜːd) *n.* any of several tropical Asian warblers that build nests by sewing together large leaves using plant fibres.

tailor-made *adj.* **1.** made by a tailor to fit exactly. **2.** perfectly meeting a particular purpose. ~*n.* **3.** a tailor-made garment. **4.** *Inf.* a factory-made cigarette.

tailor's chalk *n.* pipeclay used by tailors and dressmakers to mark seams, darts, etc., on material.

tailor's-tack *n.* one of a series of loose looped stitches used to transfer markings for seams, darts, etc., from a paper pattern to material.

tail out *vb.* (*tr., adv.*) *N.Z.* to guide (timber) as it emerges from a circular saw.

tailpiece (ˈteɪlˌpiːs) *n.* **1.** an extension or appendage that lengthens or completes something. **2.** a decorative design at the foot of a page or end of a chapter. **3.** *Music.* a piece of wood to which the strings of a violin, etc., are attached at their lower end. **4.** a short beam or rafter that has one end embedded in a wall.

tailpipe (ˈteɪlˌpaɪp) *n.* a pipe from which exhaust gases are discharged, esp. the terminal pipe of the exhaust system of a motor vehicle.

tailplane (ˈteɪlˌpleɪn) *n.* a small horizontal wing at the tail of an aircraft to provide longitudinal stability. Also called (esp. U.S.): **horizontal stabilizer.**

tailrace (ˈteɪlˌreɪs) *n.* a channel that carries water away from a water wheel, turbine, etc.

tail rotor *n.* a small propeller fitted to the rear of a helicopter to counteract the torque reaction of the main rotor and thus prevent the body of the helicopter from rotating in an opposite direction.

tails (teɪlz) *pl. n.* **1.** an informal name for **tail coat.** ~*interj., adv.* **2.** with the reverse side of a coin uppermost.

tailskid (ˈteɪlˌskɪd) *n.* **1.** a runner under the tail of an aircraft. **2.** a rear-wheel skid of a motor vehicle.

tailspin (ˈteɪlˌspɪn) *n.* **1.** *Aeronautics.* another name for **spin** (sense 15). **2.** *Inf.* a state of confusion or panic.

tailstock (ˈteɪlˌstɒk) *n.* a casting that slides on the bed of a lathe and is locked in position to support the free end of a workpiece.

tailwind (ˈteɪlˌwɪnd) *n.* a wind blowing in the same direction as the course of an aircraft or ship.

Taino (ˈtaɪnəʊ) *n.* **1.** (*pl.* **-nos** *or* **-no**) a member of an extinct American Indian people of the West Indies. **2.** the language of this people.

taint (teɪnt) *vb.* **1.** to affect or be affected by pollution or contamination. **2.** to tarnish (someone's reputation, etc.). ~*n.* **3.** a defect or flaw. **4.** a trace of contamination or infection. [C14: (infl. by *attaint* infected, < ATTAIN) < OF *teindre* to dye, < L *tingere*] —ˈ**taintless** *adj.*

taipan (ˈtaɪˌpæn) *n.* a large highly venomous Australian snake. [C20: < Abor.]

taj (tɑːdʒ) *n.* a tall conical cap worn as a mark of distinction by Muslims. [via Ar. < Persian: crown]

takahe (ˈtɑːkəˌhiː) *n.* a rare flightless New Zealand rail. Also called: **notornis.** [< Maori]

take (teɪk) *vb.* **taking, took, taken.** (*mainly tr.*) **1.** (*also intr.*) to gain possession of (something) by force or effort. **2.** to appropriate or steal. **3.** to receive or accept into a relationship with oneself: *to take a wife.* **4.** to pay for or buy. **5.** to rent or lease. **6.** to obtain by regular payment. **7.** to win. **8.** to obtain or derive from a source. **9.** to assume the obligations of: *to take office.* **10.** to endure, esp. with fortitude: *to take punishment.* **11.** to adopt as a symbol of duty, etc.: *to take the veil.* **12.** to receive in a specified way: *she took the news very well.* **13.** to adopt as one's own: *to take someone's part in a quarrel.* **14.** to receive and make use of: *to take advice.* **15.** to receive into the body, as by eating, inhaling, etc. **16.** to eat, drink, etc., esp. habitually. **17.** to have or be engaged in for one's benefit or use: *to take a rest.* **18.** to work at or study: *to take economics at college.* **19.** to make, do, or perform (an action). **20.** to make use of: *to take an opportunity.* **21.** to put into effect: *to take measures.* **22.** (*also intr.*) to make a photograph of or admit of being photographed. **23.** to act or perform. **24.** to write down or copy: *to take notes.* **25.** to experience or feel: *to take offence.* **26.** to consider or regard: *I take him to be honest.* **27.** to accept as valid: *I take your point.* **28.** to hold or maintain in the mind: *his father took a dim view of his career.* **29.** to deal or contend with. **30.** to use as a particular case: *take hotels for example.* **31.** (*intr.;* often foll. by *from*) to diminish or detract: *the actor's bad performance took from the effect of the play.* **32.** to confront successfully: *the horse took the jump at the third attempt.* **33.** (*intr.*) to have or produce the intended effect: *her vaccination took.* **34.** (*intr.*) (of plants, etc.) to start growing successfully. **35.** to aim or direct: *he took a swipe at his opponent.* **36.** to deal a blow to in a specified place. **37.** *Arch.* to have sexual intercourse with (a woman). **38.** to remove from a place. **39.** to carry along or have in one's possession. **40.** to convey or transport. **41.** to use as a means of transport: *I shall take the bus.* **42.** to conduct or lead. **43.** to escort or accompany. **44.** to bring or deliver to a state, position, etc.: *his ability took him to the forefront.* **45.** to seek: *to take cover.* **46.** to ascertain by measuring, etc.: *to take a pulse.* **47.** (*intr.*) (of a mechanism) to catch or engage (a part). **48.** to put an end to: *she took her own life.* **49.** to come upon unexpectedly. **50.** to contract: *he took a chill.* **51.** to affect or attack: *the fever took him one night.* **52.** (*copula*) to become suddenly or be rendered (ill): *he was taken sick.* **53.** (*also intr.*) to absorb or become absorbed by something: *to take a polish.* **54.** (*usually passive*) to charm: *she was very taken with the puppy.* **55.** (*intr.*) to be or become popular; win favour. **56.** to require: *that task will take all your time.* **57.** to subtract or deduct. **58.** to hold: *the suitcase won't take all your clothes.* **59.** to quote or copy. **60.** to proceed to occupy: *to take a seat.* **61.** (often foll. by *to*) to use or employ: *to take steps to ascertain the answer.* **62.** to win or capture (a trick, piece, etc.). **63.** *Sl.* to cheat, deceive, or victimize. **64. take five** (*or* **ten**). *Inf., chiefly U.S. & Canad.* to take a break of five (or ten) minutes. **65. take it. a.** to assume; believe. **b.** *Inf.* to stand up to or endure criticism, harsh treatment, etc. **66. take one's time.** to use as much time as is needed. **67. take (someone's) name in vain. a.** to use a name, esp. of God, disrespectfully or irreverently. **b.** *Jocular.* to say (someone's) name. **68. take upon oneself.** to assume the right to do or responsibility for something. ~*n.* **69.** the act of taking. **70.** the number of quarry killed or captured. **71.** *Inf., chiefly U.S.* the amount of anything taken, esp. money. **72.** *Films, music.* **a.** one of a series of recordings from which the best will be selected. **b.** the process of taking one such recording. **c.** a scene photographed without interruption. ~See also **take after, take apart,** etc. [OE *tacan*] —ˈ**takable** *or* ˈ**takeable** *adj.* —ˈ**taker** *n.*

take after *vb.* (*intr., prep.*) to resemble in appearance, character, behaviour, etc.

take apart *vb.* (*tr., adv.*) **1.** to separate (something) into component parts. **2.** to criticize severely.

take away *vb.* (*tr., adv.*) **1.** to subtract: *take away four from nine to leave five.* ~*prep.* **2.**

minus: *nine take away four is five.* ~*adj.* **takeaway.** *Brit., Austral., & N.Z.* **3.** sold for consumption away from the premises: *a takeaway meal.* **4.** selling food for consumption away from the premises: *a takeaway Indian restaurant.* ~*n.* **takeaway.** *Brit., Austral., & N.Z.* **5.** a shop or restaurant that sells such food. **6.** a meal bought at such a shop or restaurant: *we'll have a Chinese takeaway tonight.* ~Scot. word (for senses 3-6): **carry out.** U.S. and Canad. word (for senses 3-6): **takeout.**

take back *vb.* (*adv., mainly tr.*) **1.** to retract or withdraw (something said, promised, etc.). **2.** to regain possession of. **3.** to return for exchange. **4.** to accept (someone) back (into one's home, affections, etc.). **5.** to remind one of the past: *that tune really takes me back.* **6.** (*also intr.*) *Printing.* to move (copy) to the previous line.

take down *vb.* (*tr., adv.*) **1.** to record in writing. **2.** to dismantle or tear down. **3.** to lower or reduce in power, arrogance, etc. (esp. in **take down a peg**). ~*adj.* **take-down. 4.** made or intended to be disassembled.

take for *vb.* (*tr., prep.*) **1.** *Inf.* to consider or suppose to be, esp. mistakenly: *the fake coins were taken for genuine; who do you take me for?* **2. take for granted. a.** to accept or assume without question. **b.** to fail to appreciate the value, merit, etc., of.

take-home pay *n.* the remainder of one's pay after all income tax and other compulsory deductions have been made.

take in *vb.* (*tr., adv.*) **1.** to understand. **2.** to include. **3.** to receive into one's house in exchange for payment: *to take in lodgers.* **4.** to make (clothing, etc.) smaller by altering seams. **5.** *Inf.* to cheat or deceive. **6.** *U.S.* to go to: *let's take in a movie tonight.*

taken (ˈteɪkən) *vb.* **1.** the past participle of **take.** ~*adj.* **2.** (*postpositive;* foll. by *with*) enthusiastically impressed (by); infatuated (with).

take off *vb.* (*adv.*) **1.** (*tr.*) to remove (a garment). **2.** (*intr.*) (of an aircraft) to become airborne. **3.** *Inf.* to set out or cause to set out on a journey: *they took off for Spain.* **4.** (*tr.*) (of a disease) to kill. **5.** (*tr.*) *Inf.* to mimic. **6.** (*intr.*) *Inf.* to become successful or popular. ~*n.* **takeoff. 7.** the act or process of making an aircraft airborne. **8.** the stage of a country's economic development when rapid and sustained economic growth is first achieved. **9.** *Inf.* an act of mimicry.

take on *vb.* (*adv., mainly tr.*) **1.** to employ or hire. **2.** to assume or acquire: *his voice took on a plaintive note.* **3.** to agree to do; undertake. **4.** to compete against; fight. **5.** (*intr.*) *Inf.* to exhibit great emotion, esp. grief.

take out *vb.* (*tr., adv.*) **1.** to extract or remove. **2.** to obtain or secure (a licence, patent, etc.). **3.** to go out with; escort. **4.** *Bridge.* to bid a different suit from (one's partner) in order to rescue him from a difficult contract. **5.** *Sl.* to kill or destroy. **6.** *Austral. inf.* to win, esp. in sport. **7. take it** *or* **a lot out of.** *Inf.* to sap the energy or vitality of. **8. take out on.** *Inf.* to vent (anger, etc.) on. **9. take someone out of himself.** *Inf.* to make someone forget his anxieties, problems, etc. ~*adj.* **takeout. 10.** *Bridge.* of or designating a conventional informatory bid, asking one's partner to bid another suit. ~*adj., n.* **11.** the U.S. and Canad. word for **takeaway** (senses 3–6).

take over *vb.* (*adv.*) **1.** to assume the control or management of. **2.** *Printing.* to move (copy) to the next line. ~*n.* **takeover. 3.** the act of seizing or assuming power, control, etc.

take to *vb.* (*intr., prep.*) **1.** to make for; flee to: *to take to the hills.* **2.** to form a liking for. **3.** to have recourse to: *to take to the bottle.*

take up *vb.* (*adv., mainly tr.*) **1.** to adopt the study, practice, or activity of: *to take up gardening.* **2.** to shorten (a garment). **3.** to pay off (a note, mortgage, etc.). **4.** to agree to or accept (an invitation, etc.). **5.** to pursue further or resume (something): *he took up French where he left off.* **6.** to absorb (a liquid). **7.** to act as a patron to. **8.** to occupy or fill (space or time). **9.** to interrupt, esp. in order to contradict or criticize. **10.** *Austral. & N.Z.* to occupy and break in (uncultivated land): *he took up some hundreds of acres in the back country.* **11. take up on. a.** to argue with (someone): *can I take you up on two points in your talk?* **b.** to accept what is offered by (someone): *let me take you up on your invitation.* **12. take up with. a.** to discuss with (someone); refer to. **b.** (*intr.*) to begin to keep company or associate with. ~*n.* **take-up. 13. a.** the claiming of something, esp. a state benefit. **b.** (*as modifier*): *take-up rate.*

takin (ˈtɑːkiːn) *n.* a massive bovid mammal of S Asia, having a shaggy coat, short legs, and horns. [C19: < Tibetan native name]

taking (ˈteɪkɪŋ) *adj.* **1.** charming, fascinating, or intriguing. **2.** *Inf.* infectious; catching. ~*n.* **3.** something taken. **4.** (*pl.*) receipts; earnings. —ˈ**takingly** *adv.* —ˈ**takingness** *n.*

talapoin (ˈtæləˌpɔɪn) *n.* **1.** a small W African monkey. **2.** (in Burma and Thailand) a Buddhist monk. [C16: < F, lit.: Buddhist monk, < Port. *talapão;* orig. jocular, < the appearance of the monkey]

talaria (təˈlɛərɪə) *pl. n. Greek myth.* winged sandals. [C16: < L, < *tālāris* belonging to the ankle, < *tālus* ankle]

talc (tælk) *n. also* **talcum. 1.** See **talcum powder. 2.** a soft mineral, consisting of magnesium silicate, used in the manufacture of ceramics and paints and as a filler in talcum powder, etc. ~*vb.* **talcking, talcked** *or* **talcing, talced. 3.** (*tr.*) to apply talc to. [C16: < Med. L *talcum,* < Ar. *talq* mica, < Persian *talk*] —ˈ**talcose** *or* ˈ**talcous** *adj.*

talcum powder (ˈtælkəm) *n.* a powder made of purified talc, usually scented, used for perfuming the body and for absorbing excess moisture. Often shortened to **talcum** or **talc.**

tale (teɪl) *n.* **1.** a report, narrative, or story. **2.** one of a group of short stories. **3. a.** a malicious or meddlesome rumour or piece of gossip. **b.** (*in combination*): *talebearer; taleteller.* **4.** a fictitious or false statement. **5. tell tales. a.** to tell fanciful lies. **b.** to report malicious stories, trivial complaints, etc., esp. to someone in authority. **6. tell a tale.** to reveal something important. **7. tell its own tale.** to be self-evident. **8.** *Arch.* a number; amount. [OE *talu* list]

talent (ˈtælənt) *n.* **1.** innate ability, aptitude, or faculty; above average ability: *a talent for cooking; a child with talent.* **2.** a person or persons possessing such ability. **3.** any of various ancient units of weight and money. **4.** *Inf.* members of the opposite sex collectively: *the local talent.* [OE *talente,* < L *talenta,* pl. of *talentum* sum of money, < Gk *talanton* unit of money; in Med. L the sense was extended to ability through the infl. of the parable of the talents (Matthew 25:14–30)] —ˈ**talented** *adj.*

talent scout *n.* a person whose occupation is the search for talented sportsmen, performers, etc., for engagements as professionals.

tales (ˈteɪliːz) *n. Law.* **1.** (*functioning as pl.*) a group of persons summoned to fill vacancies on a jury panel. **2.** (*functioning as sing.*) the writ summoning such jurors. [C15: < Med. L *tālēs dē circumstantibus* such men from among the bystanders, < L *tālis* such] —ˈ**talesman** *n.*

taligrade (ˈtælɪˌgreɪd) *adj.* (of mammals) walking on the outer side of the foot. [C20: < NL, < L *tālus* ankle, heel + -GRADE]

talion (ˈtælɪən) *n.* the system or legal principle of making the punishment correspond to the crime; retaliation. [C15: via OF < L *tāliō,* < *tālis* such]

talipes (ˈtælɪˌpiːz) *n.* **1.** a congenital deformity of the foot by which it is twisted in any of various positions. **2.** a technical name for **club foot.** [C19: NL, < L *tālus* ankle + *pēs* foot]

talipot *or* **talipot palm** (ˈtælɪˌpɒt) *n.* a palm tree of the East Indies, having large leaves that are used for fans, thatching houses, etc. [C17: < Bengali: palm leaf, < Sansk. *tālī* fan palm + *pattra* leaf]

talisman (ˈtælɪzmən) *n., pl.* **-mans. 1.** a stone or

other small object, usually inscribed or carved, believed to protect the wearer from evil influences. **2.** anything thought to have magical or protective powers. [C17: via F or Sp. < Ar. *tilsam,* < Med. Gk *telesma* ritual, < Gk: consecration, < *telein* to perform a rite, complete] —**talismanic** (ˌtælɪzˈmænɪk) *adj.*

talk (tɔːk) *vb.* **1.** (*intr.;* often foll. by *to* or *with*) to express one's thoughts, feelings, or desires by means of words (to). **2.** (*intr.*) to communicate by other means: *lovers talk with their eyes.* **3.** (*intr.;* usually foll. by *about*) to exchange ideas or opinions (about). **4.** (*intr.*) to articulate words. **5.** (*tr.*) to give voice to; utter: *to talk rubbish.* **6.** (*tr.*) to discuss: *to talk business.* **7.** (*intr.*) to reveal information. **8.** (*tr.*) to know how to communicate in (a language or idiom): *he talks English.* **9.** (*intr.*) to spread rumours or gossip. **10.** (*intr.*) to make sounds suggestive of talking. **11.** (*intr.*) to be effective or persuasive: *money talks.* **12. now you're talking.** *Inf.* at last you're saying something agreeable. **13. talk big.** to boast. **14. you can talk.** *Inf.* **a.** you don't have to worry about doing a particular thing yourself. **b.** Also: **you can't talk.** you yourself are guilty of offending in the very matter you are upholding or decrying. ~*n.* **15.** a speech or lecture. **16.** an exchange of ideas or thoughts. **17.** idle chatter, gossip, or rumour. **18.** a subject of conversation; theme. **19.** (*often pl.*) a conference, discussion, or negotiation. **20.** a specific manner of speaking: *children's talk.* ~See also **talk about, talk back,** etc. [C13 *talkien*] —ˈ**talker** *n.*

talk about *vb.* (*intr., prep.*) **1.** to discuss. **2.** used informally and often ironically to add emphasis to a statement: *all his plays have such ridiculous plots—talk about good drama!*

talkative (ˈtɔːkətɪv) *adj.* given to talking a great deal. —ˈ**talkatively** *adv.* —ˈ**talkativeness** *n.*

talk back *vb.* (*intr., adv.*) **1.** to answer boldly or impudently. **2.** *N.Z.* to conduct a telephone dialogue for immediate transmission over the air. ~*n.* **talkback. 3.** *Television, radio.* a system of telephone links enabling spoken directions to be given during the production of a programme. **4.** *N.Z.* a broadcast telephone dialogue.

talk down *vb.* (*adv.*) **1.** (*intr.;* often foll. by *to*) to behave (towards) in a superior manner. **2.** (*tr.*) to override (a person) by continuous or loud talking. **3.** (*tr.*) to give instructions to (an aircraft) by radio to enable it to land.

talkie (ˈtɔːkɪ) *n. Inf.* an early film with a soundtrack. Full name: **talking picture.**

talking book *n.* a recording of a book, designed to be used by the blind.

talking head *n.* (on television) a person, shown only from the shoulders up, who speaks without illustrative material.

talking-to *n. Inf.* a session of criticism, as of a subordinate by a person in authority.

talk into *vb.* (*tr., prep.*) to persuade to by talking: *I talked him into buying the house.*

talk out *vb.* (*tr., adv.*) **1.** to resolve or eliminate by talking. **2.** *Brit.* to block (a bill, etc.) in a legislative body by lengthy discussion. **3. talk out of.** to dissuade from by talking.

talk round *vb.* **1.** (*tr., adv.*) Also: **talk over.** to persuade to one's opinion. **2.** (*intr., prep.*) to discuss (a subject), esp. without coming to a conclusion.

talk show *n.* another name for **chat show.**

tall (tɔːl) *adj.* **1.** of more than average height. **2.** (*postpositive*) having a specified height: *five feet tall.* [C14 (in the sense: big, comely, valiant)] —ˈ**tallness** *n.*

tallage (ˈtælɪdʒ) *n. English history.* **a.** a tax levied by kings on Crown lands and royal towns. **b.** a toll levied by a lord upon his tenants or by a feudal lord upon his vassals. [C13: < OF *taillage,* < *taillier* to cut; see TAILOR]

tallboy (ˈtɔːlˌbɔɪ) *n.* a high chest of drawers made in two sections placed one on top of the other.

tallith (ˈtælɪθ) *n.* a shawl with fringed corners worn by Jewish males, esp. during religious services. [C17: < Heb. *tallīt*]

tall order *n. Inf.* a difficult or unreasonable request.

tallow (ˈtæləʊ) *n.* **1.** a fatty substance extracted chiefly from the suet of sheep and cattle: used for making soap, candles, food, etc. ~*vb.* **2.** (*tr.*) to cover or smear with tallow. [OE *tælg,* a dye] —ˈ**tallowy** *adj.*

tallowwood (ˈtæləʊˌwʊd) *n. Austral.* a tall eucalyptus tree having soft fibrous bark and a greasy timber.

tall poppy *n. Austral. inf.* a prominent or highly paid person.

tall ship *n.* any square-rigged sailing ship.

tall story *n. Inf.* an exaggerated or incredible account.

tally (ˈtælɪ) *vb.* **-lying, -lied. 1.** (*intr.*) to correspond one with the other: *the two stories don't tally.* **2.** (*tr.*) to supply with an identifying tag. **3.** (*intr.*) to keep score. **4.** (*tr.*) *Obs.* to record or mark. ~*n., pl.* **-lies. 5.** any record of debit, credit, the score in a game, etc. **6.** *Austral. & N.Z.* the number of sheep shorn in a specified period. **7.** an identifying label or mark. **8.** a counterpart or duplicate of something. **9.** a stick used (esp. formerly) as a record of the amount of a debt according to the notches cut in it. **10.** a notch or mark made on such a stick. **11.** a mark used to represent a certain number in counting. [C15: < Med. L *tālea,* < L: cutting]

tally clerk *n. Austral. & N.Z.* a person, esp. on a wharf, who checks the count of goods being loaded or unloaded.

tally-ho (ˌtælɪˈhəʊ) *interj.* **1.** the cry of a participant at a hunt when the quarry is sighted. ~*n., pl.* **-hos. 2.** an instance of crying tally-ho. **3.** another name for a **four-in-hand** (sense 1). ~*vb.* **-hoing, -hoed** *or* **-ho'd. 4.** (*intr.*) to make the cry of tally-ho. [C18: ? < F *taïaut* cry used in hunting]

tallyman (ˈtælɪmən) *n., pl.* **-men. 1.** a scorekeeper or recorder. **2.** *Dialect.* a travelling salesman for a firm specializing in hire-purchase. —ˈ**tallyˌwoman** *fem. n.*

Talmud (ˈtælmʊd) *n. Judaism.* the primary source of Jewish religious law, consisting of the Mishnah and the Gemara. [C16: < Heb. *talmūdh,* lit.: instruction, < *lāmadh* to learn] —**Talˈmudic** *or* **Talˈmudical** *adj.* —ˈ**Talmudism** *n.* —ˈ**Talmudist** *n.*

talon (ˈtælən) *n.* **1.** a sharply hooked claw, esp. of a bird of prey. **2.** anything resembling this. **3.** the part of a lock that the key presses on when it is turned. **4.** *Piquet, etc.* the pile of cards left after the deal. **5.** *Archit.* another name for **ogee.** [C14: < OF: heel, < L *tālus*] —ˈ**taloned** *adj.*

talus[1] (ˈteɪləs) *n., pl.* **-li** (-laɪ). the bone of the ankle that articulates with the leg bones to form the ankle joint; anklebone. [C18: < L: ankle]

talus[2] (ˈteɪləs) *n., pl.* **-luses. 1.** *Geol.* another name for **scree. 2.** *Fortifications.* the sloping side of a wall. [C17: < F, < L *talūtium* slope, ? of Iberian origin]

tam (tæm) *n.* short for **tam-o'-shanter.**

tamale (təˈmɑːlɪ) *n.* a Mexican dish made of minced meat mixed with crushed maize and seasonings, wrapped in maize husks and steamed. [C19: erroneously for *tamal,* < Mexican Sp., < Nahuatl *tamalli*]

tamandua (ˌtæmənˈduə) *n.* a small arboreal mammal of Central and South America, having a tubular mouth specialized for feeding on termites. Also called: **lesser anteater.** [C17: via Port. < Tupi: ant trapper, < *taixi* ant + *mondê* to catch]

tamarack (ˈtæməˌræk) *n.* **1.** any of several North American larches. **2.** the wood of any of these trees. [C19: of Amerind origin]

tamarillo (ˌtæməˈrɪləʊ) *n., pl.* **-los.** *N.Z.* another name for **tree tomato.**

tamarin (ˈtæmərɪn) *n.* any of numerous small monkeys of South and Central American forests; similar to the marmosets. [C18: via F, of Amerind origin]

tamarind (ˈtæmərɪnd) *n.* **1.** a tropical evergreen tree having yellow flowers and brown pods. **2.** the fruit of this tree, used as a food and to make beverages and medicines. **3.** the wood of this tree. [C16: < Med. L *tamarindus*, ult. < Ar. *tamr hindī* Indian date]

tamarisk (ˈtæmərɪsk) *n.* any of a genus of trees and shrubs of the Mediterranean region and S and SE Asia, having scalelike leaves, slender branches, and feathery flower clusters. [C15: < LL *tamariscus*, < L *tamarix*]

tambour (ˈtæmbʊə) *n.* **1.** *Real Tennis.* the sloping buttress on one side of the receiver's end of the court. **2.** a small embroidery frame, consisting of two hoops over which the fabric is stretched while being worked. **3.** embroidered work done on such a frame. **4.** a sliding door on desks, cabinets, etc., made of thin strips of wood glued onto a canvas backing. **5.** *Archit.* a wall that is circular in plan, esp. one that supports a dome or one that is surrounded by a colonnade. **6.** a drum. ~*vb.* **7.** to embroider on a tambour. [C15: < F, < *tabour* TABOR]

tamboura (tæmˈbʊərə) *n.* a stringed instrument with a long neck used in Indian music to provide a drone. [< Persian *tanbūr*, < Ar. *tunbūr*]

tambourin (ˈtæmbʊrɪn) *n.* **1.** an 18th-century Provençal folk dance. **2.** a piece of music composed for or in the rhythm of this dance. **3.** a small drum. [C18: < F: a little drum]

tambourine (ˌtæmbəˈriːn) *n. Music.* a percussion instrument consisting of a single drumhead of skin stretched over a circular wooden frame hung with pairs of metal discs that jingle when it is struck or shaken. [C16: < MFlemish *tamborijn* a little drum, < OF: TAMBOURIN] —ˌ**tambouˈrinist** *n.*

tame (teɪm) *adj.* **1.** changed by man from a wild state into a domesticated or cultivated condition. **2.** (of animals) not fearful of human contact. **3.** meek or submissive. **4.** flat, insipid, or uninspiring. ~*vb.* (*tr.*) **5.** to make tame; domesticate. **6.** to break the spirit of, subdue, or curb. **7.** to tone down, soften, or mitigate. [OE *tam*] —ˈ**tamable** *or* ˈ**tameable** *adj.* —ˈ**tamely** *adv.* —ˈ**tameness** *n.* —ˈ**tamer** *n.*

Tamil (ˈtæmɪl) *n.* **1.** (*pl.* **-ils** *or* **-il**) a member of a mixed Dravidian and Caucasoid people of S India and Sri Lanka. **2.** the language of this people. ~*adj.* **3.** of or relating to this people or their language.

tammy[1] (ˈtæmɪ) *n., pl.* **-mies.** another word for **tam-o'-shanter.**

tammy[2] (ˈtæmɪ) *n., pl.* **-mies.** (esp. formerly) a woollen cloth used for straining sauces, soups, etc. [C18: changed < F *tamis*, ? of Celtic origin]

tam-o'-shanter (ˌtæməˈʃæntə) *n.* a Scottish brimless wool or cloth cap with a bobble in the centre. [C19: after the hero of Burns's poem *Tam o' Shanter* (1790)]

tamp (tæmp) *vb.* (*tr.*) **1.** to force or pack down firmly by repeated blows. **2.** to pack sand, earth, etc., into (a drill hole) over an explosive. [C17: prob. back formation < *tampin* (obs. var. of TAMPION), taken as a present participle *tamping*]

tamper[1] (ˈtæmpə) *vb.* (*intr.*) **1.** (usually foll. by *with*) to interfere or meddle. **2.** to use bribery or blackmail. **3.** (usually foll. by *with*) to attempt to influence, esp. by bribery. [C16: alteration of TEMPER (vb.)] —ˈ**tamperer** *n.*

tamper[2] (ˈtæmpə) *n.* **1.** a person or thing that tamps, esp. an instrument for packing down tobacco in a pipe. **2.** a casing around the core of a nuclear weapon to increase its efficiency by reflecting neutrons and delaying the expansion.

tampion (ˈtæmpɪən) *or* **tompion** *n.* a plug placed in a gun's muzzle when the gun is not in use. [C15: < F: TAMPON]

tampon (ˈtæmpɒn) *n.* **1.** a plug of lint, cotton wool, etc., inserted into a wound or body cavity to stop the flow of blood, absorb secretions, etc. ~*vb.* **2.** (*tr.*) to plug (a wound, etc.) with a tampon. [C19: via F < OF *tapon* a little plug, of Gmc origin] —**tamponage** (ˈtæmpənɪdʒ) *n.*

tam-tam *n.* another name for **gong** (sense 1). [< Hindi; see TOM-TOM]

tan[1] (tæn) *n.* **1.** the brown colour produced by the skin after exposure to ultraviolet rays, esp. those of the sun. **2.** a yellowish-brown colour. **3.** short for **tanbark.** ~*vb.* **tanning, tanned.** **4.** to go brown or cause to go brown after exposure to ultraviolet rays. **5.** to convert (a skin or hide) into leather by treating it with a tanning agent. **6.** (*tr.*) *Sl.* to beat or flog. ~*adj.* **tanner, tannest. 7.** of the colour tan. [OE *tannian* (unattested as infinitive, attested as *getanned*, p.p.), < Med. L *tannāre*, < *tannum* tanbark, ? of Celtic origin] —ˈ**tannable** *adj.* —ˈ**tannish** *adj.*

tan[2] (tæn) *abbrev. for* tangent (sense 2).

tanager (ˈtænədʒə) *n.* any of a family of American songbirds having a short thick bill and, in the male, a brilliantly coloured plumage. [C19: < NL *tanagra*, based on Amerind *tangara*]

tanbark (ˈtænˌbɑːk) *n.* the bark of certain trees, esp. the oak, used as a source of tannin.

T & E *abbrev. for* tired and emotional.

tandem (ˈtændəm) *n.* **1.** a bicycle with two sets of pedals and two saddles, arranged one behind the other for two riders. **2.** a two-wheeled carriage drawn by two horses harnessed one behind the other. **3.** a team of two horses so harnessed. **4.** any arrangement of two things in which one is placed behind the other. ~*adj.* **5.** *Brit.* used as, used in, or routed through an intermediate automatic telephone exchange. ~*adv.* **6.** one behind the other. [C18: whimsical use of L *tandem* at length, to indicate a long vehicle]

tandoori (tænˈdʊərɪ) *n.* an Indian method of cooking meat or vegetables on a spit in a clay oven. [< Urdu, < *tandoor* an oven]

tang (tæŋ) *n.* **1.** a strong taste or flavour. **2.** a pungent or characteristic smell. **3.** a trace, touch, or hint of something. **4.** the pointed end of a tool, such as a chisel, file, knife, etc., which is fitted into a handle, shaft, or stock. [C14: < ON *tangi* point]

tangent (ˈtændʒənt) *n.* **1.** a geometric line, curve, plane, or curved surface that touches another curve or surface at one point but does not intersect it. **2.** (of an angle) a trigonometric function that in a right-angled triangle is the ratio of the length of the opposite side to that of the adjacent side; the ratio of sine to cosine. Abbrev.: **tan. 3.** *Music.* a small piece of metal that strikes the string of a clavichord. **4. on** *or* **at a tangent.** on a completely different or divergent course, esp. of thought. ~*adj.* **5. a.** of or involving a tangent. **b.** touching at a single point. **6.** touching. [C16: < L *līnea tangēns* the touching line, < *tangere* to touch] —ˈ**tangency** *n.*

tangent galvanometer *n.* a galvanometer having a vertical coil of wire with a horizontal magnetic needle at its centre. The current to be measured is passed through the coil and produces a proportional magnetic field which deflects the needle.

tangential (tænˈdʒɛnʃəl) *adj.* **1.** of, being, or in the direction of a tangent. **2.** *Astron.* (of velocity) in a direction perpendicular to the line of sight of a celestial object. **3.** of superficial relevance only; digressive. —**tanˌgentiˈality** *n.* —**tanˈgentially** *adv.*

tangerine (ˌtændʒəˈriːn) *n.* **1.** an Asian citrus tree cultivated for its small orange-like fruits. **2.** the fruit of this tree, having sweet spicy flesh. **3. a.** a reddish-orange colour. **b.** (*as adj.*): *a tangerine door.* [C19: < *Tangier*, a port in N Morocco]

tangi (ˈtæŋiː) *n. N.Z.* **1.** a Maori funeral ceremony. **2.** *Inf.* a lamentation.

tangible (ˈtændʒɪbᵊl) *adj.* **1.** capable of being touched or felt. **2.** capable of being clearly grasped by the mind. **3.** having a physical existence: *tangible property.* [C16: < LL *tangibilis*, < L *tangere* to touch] —ˌ**tangiˈbility** *or* ˈ**tangibleness** *n.* —ˈ**tangibly** *adv.*

tangle (ˈtæŋgᵊl) *n.* **1.** a confused or complicated mass of hairs, lines, fibres, etc., knotted or coiled together. **2.** a complicated problem, condition, or situation. ~*vb.* **3.** to become or cause to become twisted together in a confused mass. **4.** (*intr.*; often foll. by *with*) to come into conflict; contend. **5.** (*tr.*) to involve in matters which hinder or confuse. **6.** (*tr.*) to ensnare or trap, as in a net.

[C14 *tangilen,* var. of *tagilen,* prob. < ON] —ˈ**tangled** *or* ˈ**tangly** *adj.*

tango (ˈtæŋgəʊ) *n., pl.* **-gos.** **1.** a Latin-American dance characterized by long gliding steps and sudden pauses. **2.** a piece of music composed for or in the rhythm of this dance. ~*vb.* **-going, -goed.** **3.** (*intr.*) to perform this dance. [C20: < American Sp., prob. of Niger-Congo origin]

tangram (ˈtæŋgræm) *n.* a Chinese puzzle in which a square, cut into a parallelogram, a square, and five triangles, is formed into figures. [C19: ? < Chinese *t'ang* Chinese + -GRAM]

tangy (ˈtæŋɪ) *adj.* **tangier, tangiest.** having a pungent, fresh, or briny flavour or aroma.

tanh (θæn, tænʃ) *n.* hyperbolic tangent; a hyperbolic function that is the ratio of sinh to cosh. [C20: < TAN(GENT) + H(YPERBOLIC)]

tank (tæŋk) *n.* **1.** a large container or reservoir for liquids or gases. **2.** an armoured combat vehicle moving on tracks and armed with guns, etc. **3.** *Brit. or U.S. dialect.* a reservoir, lake, or pond. **4.** *Sl., chiefly U.S.* a jail. **5.** Also called: **tankful.** the quantity contained in a tank. **6.** *Austral.* a reservoir formed by excavation and damming. ~*vb.* **7.** (*tr.*) to put or keep in a tank. ~See also **tank up.** [C17: < Gujarati (a language of W India) *tānkh* artificial lake, but infl. also by Port. *tanque,* < *estanque* pond, ult. < Vulgar L *stanticāre* (unattested) to block]

tanka (ˈtɑːŋkə) *n., pl.* **-kas** *or* **-ka.** a Japanese verse form consisting of five lines, the first and third having five syllables, the others seven. [C19: < Japanese, < *tan* short + *ka* verse]

tankage (ˈtæŋkɪdʒ) *n.* **1.** the capacity or contents of a tank or tanks. **2.** the act of storing in a tank or tanks, or a fee charged for this. **3.** *Agriculture.* **a.** fertilizer consisting of the dried and ground residues of animal carcasses. **b.** a protein supplement feed for livestock.

tankard (ˈtæŋkəd) *n.* a large one-handled drinking vessel sometimes fitted with a hinged lid. [C14]

tank engine *or* **locomotive** *n.* a steam locomotive that carries its water supply in tanks mounted around its boiler.

tanker (ˈtæŋkə) *n.* a ship, lorry, or aeroplane designed to carry liquid in bulk, such as oil.

tank farming *n.* another name for **hydroponics.** —**tank farmer** *n.*

tank top *n.* a sleeveless upper garment with wide shoulder straps and a low neck. [C20: after *tank suits,* one-piece bathing costumes of the 1920s worn in tanks or swimming pools]

tank up *vb.* (*adv.*) *Chiefly Brit.* **1.** to fill the tank of (a vehicle) with petrol. **2.** *Sl.* to imbibe or cause to imbibe a large quantity of alcoholic drink.

tank wagon *or esp. U.S. & Canad.* **tank car** *n.* a form of railway wagon carrying a tank for the transport of liquids.

tanner[1] (ˈtænə) *n.* a person who tans skins and hides.

tanner[2] (ˈtænə) *n. Brit.* an informal word for **sixpence.** [C19: <?]

tannery (ˈtænərɪ) *n., pl.* **-neries.** a place or building where skins and hides are tanned.

tannic (ˈtænɪk) *adj.* of, relating to, containing, or produced from tan, tannin, or tannic acid.

tannin (ˈtænɪn) *n.* any of a class of yellowish compounds found in many plants and used as tanning agents, mordants, medical astringents, etc. Also called: **tannic acid.** [C19: < F *tanin,* < TAN[1]]

Tannoy (ˈtænɔɪ) *n. Trademark.* a type of public-address system.

tansy (ˈtænzɪ) *n., pl.* **-sies.** any of numerous plants having yellow flowers in flat-topped clusters and formerly used in medicine and for seasoning. [C15: < OF *tanesie,* < Med. L *athanasia* (< its alleged power to prolong life) < Gk: immortality]

tantalite (ˈtæntəˌlaɪt) *n.* a heavy brownish mineral: it occurs in coarse granite and is an ore of tantalum. [C19: < TANTALUM + -ITE[1]]

tantalize *or* **-ise** (ˈtæntəˌlaɪz) *vb.* (*tr.*) to tease or make frustrated, as by tormenting with the sight of something desired but inaccessible. [C16: < *Tantalus,* a king in Gk mythology condemned to stand in water that receded when he tried to drink it and under fruit that moved away when he tried to reach for it] —ˌ**tantaliˈzation** *or* **-iˈsation** *n.* —ˈ**tantaˌlizing** *or* **ising** *adj.* —ˈ**tantaˌlizingly** *or* **-isingly** *adv.*

tantalum (ˈtæntələm) *n.* a hard greyish-white metallic element: used in electrolytic rectifiers and in alloys to increase hardness and chemical resistance, esp. in surgical instruments. Symbol: Ta; atomic no.: 73; atomic wt.: 180.95. [C19: after *Tantalus* (see TANTALIZE), < the metal's incapacity to absorb acids]

tantalus (ˈtæntələs) *n. Brit.* a case in which bottles may be locked with their contents tantalizingly visible.

tantamount (ˈtæntəˌmaʊnt) *adj.* (*postpositive;* foll. by *to*) as good (as); equivalent in effect (to). [C17: < Anglo-F *tant amunter* to amount to as much]

tantara (ˈtæntərə, tænˈtɑːrə) *n.* a fanfare or blast, as on a trumpet or horn. [C16: < L *taratantara,* imit. of the sound of the tuba]

tantivy (tænˈtɪvɪ) *adv.* **1.** at full speed; rapidly. ~*n., pl.* **-tivies,** *sentence substitute.* **2.** a hunting cry, esp. at full gallop. [C17: ? imit. of galloping hooves]

tant mieux *French.* (tɑ̃ mjø) so much the better.

tanto (ˈtæntəʊ) *adv. Music.* too much; excessively. [It.]

tant pis *French.* (tɑ̃ pi) so much the worse.

Tantrism (ˈtæntrɪzəm) *n.* **1.** a movement within Hinduism combining magical and mystical elements and with sacred writings of its own (**the Tantra**). **2.** a similar movement within Buddhism. [C18: < Sansk. *tantra,* lit.: warp, hence doctrine] —ˈ**Tantric** *adj.* —ˈ**Tantrist** *n.*

tantrum (ˈtæntrəm) *n.* (*often pl.*) a childish fit of rage; outburst of bad temper. [C18: <?]

Tao (taʊ) *n.* (in the philosophy of Taoism) **1.** that in virtue of which all things happen or exist. **2.** the rational basis of human conduct. **3.** the course of life and its relation to eternal truth. [Chinese, lit.: path, way]

Taoiseach (ˈtiːʃæx) *n.* the prime mininster of the Irish Republic. [< Irish, lit.: leader]

Taoism (ˈtaʊɪzəm) *n.* a system of religion and philosophy based on the teachings of Lao Zi, 6th-century B.C. Chinese philosopher, and advocating a simple honest life and noninterference with the course of natural events. —ˈ**Taoist** *n., adj.* —ˌ**Taoˈistic** *adj.*

tap[1] (tæp) *vb.* **tapping, tapped.** **1.** to strike (something) lightly and usually repeatedly. **2.** (*tr.*) to produce by striking in this way: *to tap a rhythm.* **3.** (*tr.*) to strike lightly with (something): *to tap one's finger on the desk.* **4.** (*intr.*) to walk with a tapping sound. **5.** (*tr.*) to attach reinforcing pieces to (the toe or heel of a shoe). ~*n.* **6.** a light blow or knock, or the sound made by it. **7.** the metal piece attached to the toe or heel of a shoe used for tap-dancing. **8.** short for **tap-dancing.** ~See also **taps.** [C13 *tappen,* prob. < OF *taper,* of Gmc origin]

tap[2] (tæp) *n.* **1.** a valve by which a fluid flow from a pipe can be controlled. U.S. names: **faucet, spigot.** **2.** a stopper to plug a cask or barrel. **3.** a particular quality of alcoholic drink, esp. when contained in casks: *an excellent tap.* **4.** *Brit.* short for **taproom.** **5.** the withdrawal of fluid from a bodily cavity. **6.** a tool for cutting female screw threads. **7.** *Electronics, chiefly U.S. & Canad.* a connection made at some point between the end terminals of an inductor, resistor, etc. Usual Brit. name: **tapping.** **8.** a concealed listening or recording device connected to a telephone or telegraph wire. **9. on tap. a.** *Inf.* ready for use. **b.** (of drinks) on draught. ~*vb.* **tapping, tapped.** (*tr.*) **10.** to furnish with a tap. **11.** to draw off with or as if with a tap. **12.** to cut into (a tree) and draw off sap from it. **13.** *Brit. inf.* **a.** to ask (someone) for money: *he tapped me for a fiver.* **b.** to obtain (money) from someone. **14.** to connect a tap to (a telephone or telegraph wire).

15. to make a connection to (a pipe, drain, etc.). **16.** to cut a female screw thread in (an object or material) by use of a tap. [OE *tæppa*] —ˈ**tapper** *n.*

tapa (ˈtɑːpə) *n.* **1.** the inner bark of the paper mulberry. **2.** a cloth made from this in the Pacific islands. [C19: < native Polynesian name]

tap dance *n.* **1.** a step dance in which the performer wears shoes equipped with taps that make a rhythmic sound on the stage as he dances. ~*vb.* **tap-dance.** (*intr.*) **2.** to perform a tap dance. —ˈ**tap-ˌdancer** *n.* —ˈ**tap-ˌdancing** *n.*

tape (teɪp) *n.* **1.** a long thin strip of cotton, linen, etc., used for binding, fastening, etc. **2.** a long narrow strip of paper, metal, etc. **3.** a string stretched across the track at the end of a race course. **4.** See **magnetic tape, ticker tape, paper tape, tape recording.** ~*vb.* (*mainly tr.*) **5.** to furnish with tapes. **6.** to bind, measure, secure, or wrap with tape. **7.** (*usually passive*) *Brit. inf.* to take stock of (a person or situation). **8.** (*also intr.*) Also: **tape-record.** to record (speech, music, etc.). [OE *tæppe*] —ˈ**tapeˌlike** *adj.* —ˈ**taper** *n.*

tape deck *n.* the platform supporting the spools, cassettes, or cartridges of a tape recorder, incorporating the motor and the playback, recording, and erasing heads.

tape machine *n.* a telegraphic device that records current stock quotations electronically or on ticker tape. U.S. equivalent: **ticker.**

tape measure *n.* a tape or length of metal marked off in inches, centimetres, etc., used for measuring. Also called (esp. U.S.): **tapeline.**

taper (ˈteɪpə) *vb.* **1.** to become or cause to become narrower towards one end. **2.** (often foll. by *off*) to become or cause to become smaller or less significant. ~*n.* **3.** a thin candle. **4.** a thin wooden or waxed strip for transferring a flame; spill. **5.** a narrowing. **6.** any feeble light. [OE *tapor,* prob. < L *papȳrus* papyrus (< its use as a wick)] —ˈ**taperer** *n.* —ˈ**tapering** *adj.*

tape recorder *n.* an electrical device used for recording sounds on magnetic tape and usually also for reproducing them.

tape recording *n.* **1.** the act of recording on magnetic tape. **2.** the magnetized tape used for this. **3.** the speech, music, etc., so recorded.

tapestry (ˈtæpɪstrɪ) *n., pl.* **-tries. 1.** a heavy woven fabric, often in the form of a picture, used for wall hangings, furnishings, etc. **2.** another word for **needlepoint** (sense 1). [C15: < OF *tapisserie* carpeting, < OF *tapiz;* see TAPIS] —ˈ**tapestried** *adj.*

tapeworm (ˈteɪpˌwɜːm) *n.* any of a class of parasitic ribbon-like flatworms. The adults inhabit the intestines of vertebrates.

taphole (ˈtæpˌhəʊl) *n.* a hole in a furnace for running off molten metal or slag.

taphouse (ˈtæpˌhaʊs) *n. Now rare.* an inn.

tapioca (ˌtæpɪˈəʊkə) *n.* a beadlike starch obtained from cassava root, used in cooking as a thickening agent, esp. in puddings. [C18: via Port. < Tupi *tipioca* pressed-out juice, < *tipi* residue + *ok* to squeeze out]

tapir (ˈteɪpə) *n., pl.* **-pirs** *or* **-pir.** any of various mammals of South and Central America and SE Asia, having an elongated snout, three-toed hind legs, and four-toed forelegs. [C18: < Tupi *tapiira*]

tapis (ˈtæpiː) *n., pl.* **tapis. 1.** tapestry or carpeting, esp. as formerly used to cover a table. **2. on the tapis.** currently under consideration. [C17: < F, < OF *tapiz,* < Gk *tapētion* rug, < *tapēs* carpet]

tappet (ˈtæpɪt) *n.* a mechanical part that reciprocates to receive or transmit intermittent motion. [C18: < TAP[1] + -ET]

taproom (ˈtæpˌruːm, -ˌrʊm) *n.* a bar, as in a hotel or pub.

taproot (ˈtæpˌruːt) *n.* the main root of plants such as the dandelion, which grows vertically downwards and bears smaller lateral roots.

taps (tæps) *n.* (*functioning as sing.*) **1.** *Chiefly U.S.* **a.** (in army camps, etc.) a signal given on a bugle, drum, etc., indicating that lights are to be put out. **b.** any similar signal, as at a military funeral. **2.** (in the Guide movement) a closing song sung at an evening camp fire or at the end of a meeting.

tapster (ˈtæpstə) *n.* **1.** *Rare.* a barman. **2.** (in W Africa) a man who taps palm trees. [OE *tæppestre,* fem. of *tæppere,* < *tappian* to TAP[2]]

tap water *n.* water drawn off through taps from pipes in a house, as distinguished from distilled water, mineral water, etc.

tar[1] (tɑː) *n.* **1.** any of various dark viscid substances obtained by the destructive distillation of organic matter such as coal, wood, or peat. **2.** another name for **coal tar.** ~*vb.* **tarring, tarred.** (*tr.*) **3.** to coat with tar. **4. tar and feather.** to punish by smearing tar and feathers over (someone). **5. tarred with the same brush.** having the same faults. [OE *teoru*] —ˈ**tarry** *adj.* —ˈ**tarriness** *n.*

tar[2] (tɑː) *n.* an informal word for **seaman.** [C17: short for TARPAULIN]

taradiddle (ˈtærəˌdɪdᵊl) *n.* a variant spelling of **tarradiddle.**

tarakihi *or* **terakihi** (ˈtærəˌkiːhiː) *n., pl.* **-kihis.** a common edible sea fish of New Zealand waters. [< Maori]

taramasalata (ˌtærəməsəˈlɑːtə) *n.* a creamy pale pink pâté, made from the roe of grey mullet or smoked cod and served as an hors d'oeuvre. [C20: < Mod. Gk, < *tarama* cod's roe]

tarantass (ˌtɑːrənˈtæs) *n.* a four-wheeled Russian carriage without springs. [C19: < Russian *tarantas*]

tarantella (ˌtærənˈtɛlə) *n.* **1.** a peasant dance from S Italy. **2.** a piece of music composed for or in the rhythm of this dance. [C18: < It., < *Taranto,* port in SE Italy]

tarantism (ˈtærənˌtɪzəm) *n.* a nervous disorder marked by uncontrollable bodily movement, widespread in S Italy during the 15th to 17th centuries: popularly thought to be caused by the bite of a tarantula. [C17: < NL *tarantismus,* < *Taranto;* see TARANTULA, TARANTELLA]

tarantula (təˈræntjʊlə) *n., pl.* **-las** *or* **-lae** (-ˌliː). **1.** any of various large hairy spiders of tropical America. **2.** a large hairy spider of S Europe. [C16: < Med. L, < OIt. *tarantola,* < *Taranto;* see TARANTELLA]

taraxacum (təˈræksəkəm) *n.* **1.** any of a genus of perennial plants of the composite family, such as the dandelion. **2.** the dried root of the dandelion, used as a laxative, diuretic, and tonic. [C18: < Med. L, < Ar. *tarakhshaqūn* wild chicory, ? of Persian origin]

tarboosh (tɑːˈbuːʃ) *n.* a felt or cloth brimless cap, usually red and often with a silk tassel, worn by Muslim men. [C18: < Ar. *tarbūsh*]

tarboy (ˈtɑːˌbɔɪ) *n. Austral. & N.Z. inf.* a boy who applies tar to the skin of sheep cut during shearing.

Tardenoisian (ˌtɑːdəˈnɔɪzɪən) *adj.* of or referring to a Mesolithic culture characterized by small flint instruments. [C20: after *Tardenois,* France, where implements were found]

tardigrade (ˈtɑːdɪˌgreɪd) *n.* any of various minute aquatic segmented eight-legged invertebrates occurring in soil, ditches, etc. Popular name: **water bear.** [C17: via L *tardigradus,* < *tardus* sluggish + *gradī* to walk]

tardy (ˈtɑːdɪ) *adj.* **-dier, -diest. 1.** occurring later than expected. **2.** slow in progress, growth, etc. [C15: < OF *tardif,* < L *tardus* slow] —ˈ**tardily** *adv.* —ˈ**tardiness** *n.*

tare[1] (tɛə) *n.* **1.** any of various vetch plants of Eurasia and N Africa. **2.** the seed of any of these plants. **3.** *Bible.* a weed, thought to be the darnel. [C14: <?]

tare[2] (tɛə) *n.* **1.** the weight of the wrapping or container in which goods are packed. **2.** a deduction from gross weight to compensate for this. **3.** the weight of an unladen vehicle. ~*vb.* **4.** (*tr.*) to weigh (a package, etc.) in order to calculate the amount of tare. [C15: < OF: waste, < Med. L *tara,* < Ar. *tarhah* something discarded, < *taraha* to reject]

targe (tɑːdʒ) *n.* an archaic word for **shield.** [C13: < OF, of Gmc origin]

target (ˈtɑːgɪt) *n.* **1. a.** an object or area at which an archer or marksman aims, usually a round flat surface marked with concentric rings. **b.** (*as modifier*): *target practice.* **2. a.** any point or area aimed at. **b.** (*as modifier*): *target area.* **3.** a fixed goal or objective. **4.** a person or thing at which an action or remark is directed or the object of a person's feelings. **5.** a joint of lamb consisting of the breast and neck. **6.** (formerly) a small round shield. **7.** *Physics, electronics.* **a.** a substance subjected to bombardment by electrons or other particles, or to irradiation. **b.** an electrode in a television camera tube whose surface is scanned by the electron beam. **8.** *Electronics.* an object detected by the reflection of a radar or sonar signal, etc. ~*vb.* (*tr.*) **9.** to make a target of. **10.** to direct or aim: *to target benefits at those most in need.* [C14: < OF *targette* a little shield, < OF TARGE]

tariff (ˈtærɪf) *n.* **1. a.** a tax levied by a government on imports or occasionally exports. **b.** a system or list of such taxes. **2.** any schedule of prices, fees, fares, etc. **3.** *Chiefly Brit.* **a.** a method of charging for the supply of services such as gas and electricity. **b.** a schedule of such charges. **4.** *Chiefly Brit.* a bill of fare with prices listed; menu. ~*vb.* (*tr.*) **5.** to set a tariff on. **6.** to price according to a schedule of tariffs. [C16: < It. *tariffa,* < Ar. *ta'rīfa* to inform]

tarlatan (ˈtɑːlətən) *n.* an open-weave cotton fabric, used for stiffening garments. [C18: < F *tarlatane,* var. of *tarnatane* type of muslin, ? of Indian origin]

Tarmac (ˈtɑːmæk) *n.* **1.** *Trademark.* (*often not cap.*) a paving material that consists of crushed stone rolled and bound with a mixture of tar and bitumen, esp. as used for a road, airport runway, etc. Full name: **Tarmacadam** (ˌtɑːməˈkædəm). See also **macadam.** ~*vb.* **-macking, -macked.** (*tr.*) **2.** (*usually not cap.*) to apply tarmac to.

tarn (tɑːn) *n.* a small mountain lake or pool. [C14: < ON]

tarnation (tɑːˈneɪʃən) *n.* a euphemism for **damnation.**

tarnish (ˈtɑːnɪʃ) *vb.* **1.** to lose or cause to lose the shine, esp. by exposure to air or moisture resulting in surface oxidation; discolour. **2.** to stain or become stained; taint. ~*n.* **3.** a tarnished condition, surface, or film. [C16: < OF *ternir* to make dull, < *terne* lustreless of Gmc origin] —**ˈtarnishable** *adj.*

taro (ˈtɑːrəʊ) *n., pl.* **-ros. 1.** an Asian plant, cultivated in the tropics for its large edible rootstock. **2.** the rootstock of this plant. [C18: < Tahitian & Maori]

tarot (ˈtærəʊ) *n.* **1.** one of a special pack of cards, now used mainly for fortune-telling. **2.** a card in a tarot pack with distinctive symbolic design. ~*adj.* **3.** relating to tarot cards. [C16: < F, < OIt. *tarocco,* <?]

tarpan (ˈtɑːpæn) *n.* a European wild horse, now extinct. [< Tatar]

tarpaulin (tɑːˈpɔːlɪn) *n.* **1.** a heavy waterproof fabric made of canvas or similar material coated with tar, wax, or paint. **2.** a sheet of this fabric. **3.** a hat made of or covered with this fabric, esp. a sailor's hat. **4.** a rare word for **seaman.** [C17: prob. < TAR[1] + PALL[1] + -ING[1]]

tarpon (ˈtɑːpən) *n., pl.* **-pons** *or* **-pon.** a large silvery game fish of warm oceans. [C17: ? < Du. *tarpoen,* <?]

tarradiddle (ˈtærəˌdɪdəl) *n.* **1.** a trifling lie. **2.** nonsense; twaddle. [C18: <?]

tarragon (ˈtærəgən) *n.* **1.** an aromatic plant of the Old World, having leaves which are used as seasoning. **2.** the leaves of this plant. [C16: < OF *targon,* < Med. L *tarcon,* ? ult. < Gk *drakontion* adderwort]

tarry (ˈtærɪ) *vb.* **-rying, -ried. 1.** (*intr.*) to delay; linger. **2.** (*intr.*) to remain temporarily or briefly. **3.** (*intr.*) to wait or stay. **4.** (*tr.*) *Arch. or poetic.* to await. [C14 *tarien,* <?] —**ˈtarrier** *n.*

tarsal (ˈtɑːsəl) *adj.* **1.** of the tarsus or tarsi. ~*n.* **2.** a tarsal bone.

tarseal (ˈtɑːˌsiːl) *n. N.Z.* **1.** the bitumen surface of a road. **2. the tarseal.** the main highway.

tarsia (ˈtɑːsɪə) *n.* another term for **intarsia.** [C17: < It., < Ar. *tarsī'*]

tarsier (ˈtɑːsɪə) *n.* any of several nocturnal arboreal primates of Indonesia and the Philippines, having huge eyes, long hind legs, and digits ending in pads to facilitate climbing. [C18: < F, < *tarse* the flat of the foot; see TARSUS]

tarsus (ˈtɑːsəs) *n., pl.* **-si** (-saɪ). **1.** the bones of the ankle and heel, collectively. **2.** the corresponding part in other mammals and in amphibians and reptiles. **3.** the connective tissue supporting the free edge of each eyelid. **4.** the part of an insect's leg that lies distal to the tibia. [C17: < NL, < Gk *tarsos* flat surface, instep]

tart[1] (tɑːt) *n.* **1.** *Chiefly Brit.* a pastry case often having no top crust, with a filling of fruit, jam, custard, etc. **2.** *Chiefly U.S.* a small open pie with a fruit filling. [C14: < OF *tarte,* <?]

tart[2] (tɑːt) *adj.* **1.** (of a flavour, etc.) sour; acid. **2.** cutting; sharp: *a tart remark.* [OE *teart* rough] —**ˈtartly** *adv.* —**ˈtartness** *n.*

tart[3] (tɑːt) *n. Inf.* a promiscuous woman, esp. a prostitute. See also **tart up.** [C19: shortened < SWEETHEART] —**ˈtarty** *adj.*

tartan (ˈtɑːtən) *n.* **1. a.** a design of straight lines, crossing at right angles to give a chequered appearance, esp. the distinctive design or designs associated with each Scottish clan. **b.** (*as modifier*): *a tartan kilt.* **2.** a fabric or garment with this design. [C16: ? < OF *tertaine* linsey-woolsey, < OSp. *tiritaña* a fine silk fabric, < *tiritar* to rustle] —**ˈtartaned** *adj.*

tartar[1] (ˈtɑːtə) *n.* **1.** a hard deposit on the teeth, consisting of food, cellular debris, and mineral salts. **2.** a brownish-red substance consisting mainly of potassium hydrogen tartrate, deposited during the fermentation of wine. [C14: < Med. L *tartarum,* < Med. Gk *tartaron*]

tartar[2] (ˈtɑːtə) *n.* (*sometimes cap.*) a fearsome or formidable person. [C16: special use of TARTAR]

Tartar (ˈtɑːtə) *n., adj.* a variant spelling of **Tatar.**

Tartarean (tɑːˈtɛərɪən) *adj. Literary.* of or relating to Tartarus, in Greek mythology an abyss below Hades; infernal.

tartar emetic *n.* antimony potassium tartrate, a poisonous, crystalline salt used as a mordant and in medicine.

tartaric (tɑːˈtærɪk) *adj.* of, containing, or derived from tartar or tartaric acid.

tartaric acid *n.* a colourless crystalline acid which is found in many fruits: used as a food additive (**E 334**) in soft drinks, confectionery, and baking powders, and in tanning and photography.

tartar sauce *n.* a mayonnaise sauce mixed with hard-boiled egg yolks, chopped herbs, capers, etc. [< F *sauce tartare,* < TARTAR]

tartlet (ˈtɑːtlɪt) *n. Brit.* an individual pastry case with a sweet or savoury filling.

tartrate (ˈtɑːtreɪt) *n.* any salt or ester of tartaric acid.

tartrated (ˈtɑːtreɪtɪd) *adj.* being in the form of a tartrate.

tartrazine (ˈtɑːtrəˌziːn, -zɪn) *n.* an azo dye that produces a yellow colour: used as a food additive (**E102**), in drugs, and to dye textiles.

tart up *vb.* (*tr.; adv.*) *Brit. inf.* **1.** to dress and make (oneself) up in a provocative or promiscuous way. **2.** to reissue or decorate in a cheap and flashy way: *to tart up a bar.*

tarwhine (ˈtɑːˌwaɪn) *n.* any of various Australian marine food fishes, esp. the sea bream. [? < Abor.]

Tarzan (ˈtɑːzən) *n.* (*sometimes not cap.*) *Inf., often ironical.* a man with great physical strength, agility, and virility. [C20: after the hero of a series of stories by E. R. Burroughs]

Tas. *abbrev. for* Tasmania.

tasimeter (təˈsɪmɪtə) *n.* a device for measuring small temperature changes. It depends on the changes of pressure resulting from expanding or contracting solids. [C19 *tasi-,* < Gk *tasis* tension + -METER] —**tasimetric** (ˌtæsɪˈmɛtrɪk) *adj.* —**taˈsimetry** *n.*

task (tɑːsk) *n.* **1.** a specific piece of work required to be done. **2.** an unpleasant or difficult job or duty. **3.** any piece of work. **4. take to task.** to criticize or reprove. ~*vb.* (*tr.*) **5.** to assign a task to. **6.** to subject to severe strain; tax. [C13: < OF *tasche,* < Med. L *tasca,* < *taxa* tax, < L *taxāre* to TAX]

task force *n.* **1.** a temporary grouping of military units formed to undertake a specific mission. **2.** any organization set up to carry out a continuing task.

taskmaster (ˈtɑːskˌmɑːstə) *n.* a person, discipline, etc., that enforces work, esp. hard or continuous work. —ˈ**taskˌmistress** *fem. n.*

taskwork (ˈtɑːskˌwɜːk) *n.* **1.** hard or unpleasant work. **2.** a rare word for **piecework.**

Tasmanian devil (tæzˈmeɪnɪən) *n.* a small ferocious carnivorous marsupial of Tasmania.

Tasmanian wolf *or* **tiger** *n.* other names for **thylacine.**

tass (tæs) *or* **tassie** (ˈtæsɪ) *n. Scot. & N English dialect.* **1.** a cup or glass. **2.** its contents. [C15: < OF *tasse* cup, < Ar. *tassah* basin, < Persian *tast*]

Tass (tæs) *n.* the principal news agency of the Soviet Union. [*T*(*elegrafnoye*) *a*(*gentstvo*) *S*(*ovetskogo*) *S*(*oyuza*) Telegraphic Agency of the Soviet Union]

TASS (tæs) *n.* (in Britain) *acronym for* Technical, Administrative, and Supervisory Section (of the AEU).

tassel (ˈtæsᵊl) *n.* **1.** a tuft of loose threads secured by a knot or knob, used to decorate soft furnishings, clothes, etc. **2.** anything resembling this, esp. the tuft of stamens at the tip of a maize inflorescence. ~*vb.* **-selling, -selled** *or U.S.* **-seling, -seled. 3.** (*tr.*) to adorn with tassels. **4.** (*intr.*) (of maize) to produce stamens in a tuft. [C13: < OF, < Vulgar L *tassellus* (unattested), changed < L *taxillus* a small die]

taste (teɪst) *n.* **1.** the sense by which the qualities and flavour of a substance are distinguished by the taste buds. **2.** the sensation experienced by means of the taste buds. **3.** the act of tasting. **4.** a small amount eaten, drunk, or tried on the tongue. **5.** a brief experience of something: *a taste of the whip.* **6.** a preference or liking for something. **7.** the ability to make discerning judgments about aesthetic, artistic, and intellectual matters. **8.** judgment of aesthetic or social matters according to a generally accepted standard: *bad taste.* **9.** discretion; delicacy: *that remark lacks taste.* ~*vb.* **10.** to distinguish the taste of (a substance) by means of the taste buds. **11.** (*usually tr.*) to take a small amount of (a food, liquid, etc.) into the mouth, esp. in order to test the quality. **12.** (often foll. by *of*) to have a specific flavour or taste. **13.** (when *intr.,* usually foll. by *of*) to have an experience of (something): *to taste success.* **14.** (*tr.*) an archaic word for **enjoy.** [C13: < OF *taster,* ult. < L *taxāre* to appraise] —ˈ**tastable** *adj.*

taste bud *n.* any of the elevated sensory organs on the surface of the tongue, by means of which the sensation of taste is experienced.

tasteful (ˈteɪstfʊl) *adj.* indicating good taste: *a tasteful design.* —ˈ**tastefully** *adv.* —ˈ**tastefulness** *n.*

tasteless (ˈteɪstlɪs) *adj.* **1.** lacking in flavour; insipid. **2.** lacking social or aesthetic taste. —ˈ**tastelessly** *adv.* —ˈ**tastelessness** *n.*

taster (ˈteɪstə) *n.* **1.** a person who samples food or drink for quality. **2.** any device used in tasting or sampling. **3.** a person employed, esp. formerly, to taste food and drink prepared for a king, etc., to test for poison.

tasty (ˈteɪstɪ) *adj.* **tastier, tastiest.** having a pleasant flavour. —ˈ**tastily** *adv.* —ˈ**tastiness** *n.*

tat[1] (tæt) *vb.* **tatting, tatted.** to make (something) by tatting. [C19: <?]

tat[2] (tæt) *n.* **1.** tatty articles or a tatty condition. **2.** tasteless articles. **3.** a tangled mass. [C20: back formation < TATTY]

tat[3] (tæt) *n.* See **tit for tat.**

ta-ta (tæˈtɑː) *sentence substitute. Brit. inf.* goodbye; farewell. [C19: <?]

Tatar *or* **Tartar** (ˈtɑːtə) *n.* **1. a.** a member of a Mongoloid people who established a powerful state in central Asia in the 13th century. **b.** a descendant of this people, now scattered throughout the Soviet Union. **2.** any of the Turkic languages spoken by the present-day Tatars. ~*adj.* **3.** of or relating to the Tatars. [C14: < OF *Tartare,* < Med. L *Tartarus* (associated with L *Tartarus* the underworld), < Persian *Tātār*] —**Tatarian** (tɑːˈtɛərɪən), **Tarˈtarian** *or* **Tataric** (tɑːˈtærɪk), **Tarˈtaric** *adj.*

tater (ˈteɪtə) *n.* a dialect word for **potato.**

tatouay (ˈtætʊˌeɪ) *n.* a large armadillo of South America. [C16: < Sp. *tatuay,* < Guarani, < *tatu* armadillo + *ai* worthless (because inedible)]

tatter (ˈtætə) *vb.* **1.** to make or become ragged or worn to shreds. ~*n.* **2.** a torn or ragged piece, esp. of material. [C14: < ON]

tatterdemalion (ˌtætədɪˈmeɪljən) *n. Rare.* a person dressed in ragged clothes. [C17: < TATTER + *-demalion,* <?]

tattersall (ˈtætəˌsɔːl) *n.* a fabric having stripes or bars in a checked or squared pattern. [C19: after *Tattersall's,* a horse market in London founded by Richard *Tattersall* (died 1795), E horseman; the horse blankets at the market orig. had this pattern]

Tattersall's (ˈtætəˌsɔːlz) *n. Austral.* **1.** Also called (inf.): **Tatt's.** a lottery now based in Melbourne. **2.** a name used for sportsmen's clubs. [< Richard *Tattersall;* see TATTERSALL]

tatting (ˈtætɪŋ) *n.* **1.** an intricate type of lace made by looping a thread of cotton or linen by means of a hand shuttle. **2.** the act or work of producing this. [C19: <?]

tattle (ˈtætᵊl) *vb.* **1.** (*intr.*) to gossip about another's personal matters. **2.** (*tr.*) to reveal by gossiping. **3.** (*intr.*) to talk idly; chat. ~*n.* **4.** the act or an instance of tattling. **5.** a scandalmonger; gossip. [C15 (in the sense: to stammer, hesitate): < MDu. *tatelen* to prate, imit.] —ˈ**tattler** *n.*

tattletale (ˈtætᵊlˌteɪl) *Chiefly U.S. & Canad.* ~*n.* **1.** a scandalmonger or gossip. ~*adj.* **2.** telltale.

tattoo[1] (tæˈtuː) *n., pl.* **-toos. 1.** (formerly) a signal by drum or bugle ordering the military to return to their quarters. **2.** a military display or pageant. **3.** any similar beating on a drum, etc. [C17: < Du. *taptoe,* < *tap toe!* turn off the taps! < *tap* tap of a barrel + *toe* to shut]

tattoo[2] (tæˈtuː) *vb.* **-tooing, -tooed. 1.** to make (pictures or designs) on (the skin) by pricking and staining with indelible colours. ~*n., pl.* **-toos. 2.** a design made by this process. **3.** the practice of tattooing. [C18: < Tahitian *tatau*] —**tatˈtooer** *or* **tatˈtooist** *n.*

tatty (ˈtætɪ) *adj.* **-tier, -tiest.** *Chiefly Brit.* worn out, shabby, or unkempt. [C16: of Scot. origin] —ˈ**tattily** *adv.* —ˈ**tattiness** *n.*

tau (tɔː, taʊ) *n.* the 19th letter in the Greek alphabet (Τ or τ). [C13: < Gk]

tau cross *n.* a cross shaped like the Greek letter tau. Also called: **Saint Anthony's cross.**

taught (tɔːt) *vb.* the past tense and past participle of **teach.**

taunt (tɔːnt) *vb.* (*tr.*) **1.** to provoke or deride with mockery, contempt, or criticism. **2.** to tease; tantalize. ~*n.* **3.** a jeering remark. [C16: < F *tant pour tant* like for like] —ˈ**taunting** *adj.*

taupe (təʊp) *n.* **a.** a brownish-grey colour. **b.** (*as adj.*): *a taupe coat.* [C20: < F, lit.: mole, < L *talpa*]

taurine (ˈtɔːraɪn) *adj.* of or resembling a bull. [C17: < L *taurīnus,* < *taurus* a bull]

tauromachy (tɔːˈrɒməkɪ) *n.* the art or act of bullfighting. [C19: Gk *tauromakhia,* < *tauros* bull + *makhē* fight]

Taurus (ˈtɔːrəs) *n.* **1.** *Astron.* a constellation in the N hemisphere. **2.** *Astrol.* Also called: the **Bull.** the second sign of the zodiac. The sun is in this sign between about April 20 and May 20. [C14: < L: bull]

taut (tɔːt) *adj.* **1.** tightly stretched; tense. **2.** showing nervous strain; stressed. **3.** *Chiefly naut.* in good order; neat. [C14 *tought*] —ˈ**tautly** *adv.* —ˈ**tautness** *n.*

tauten (ˈtɔːtᵊn) *vb.* to make or become taut.

tauto- *or before a vowel* **taut-** *combining form.* identical or same: *tautology.* [< Gk *tauto,* < *to auto*]

tautog (tɔːˈtɒg) *n.* a large dark-coloured food fish of the North American coast of the Atlantic Ocean. [C17: < Narraganset *tautauog,* pl. of *tautau* sheepshead]

tautology (tɔːˈtɒlədʒɪ) *n., pl.* **-gies.** **1.** the use of words that merely repeat elements of the meaning already conveyed, as in *Will these supplies be adequate enough?* in place of *Will these supplies be adequate?* **2.** *Logic.* a statement that is always true, as in *either the sun is out or the sun is not out.* [C16: < LL *tautologia,* < Gk, < *tautologos*] —**tautological** (ˌtɔːtəˈlɒdʒɪkəl) *or* **tauˈtologous** *adj.*

tautomerism (tɔːˈtɒməˌrɪzəm) *n.* the ability of certain chemical compounds to exist as a mixture of two interconvertible isomers in equilibrium. [C19: < TAUTO- + ISOMERISM] —**tautomer** (ˈtɔːtəmə) *n.* —**tautomeric** (ˌtɔːtəˈmɛrɪk) *adj.*

tautonym (ˈtɔːtənɪm) *n. Biol.* a taxonomic name in which the generic and specific components are the same, as in *Rattus rattus* (black rat). —ˌ**tautoˈnymic** *or* **tautonymous** (tɔːˈtɒnəməs) *adj.* —**tauˈtonymy** *n.*

tavern (ˈtævən) *n.* **1.** a less common word for **pub.** **2.** *U.S., Canad., & N.Z.* a place licensed for the sale and consumption of alcoholic drink. [C13: < OF *taverne,* < L *taberna* hut]

taverna (təˈvɜːnə) *n.* **1.** (in Greece) a guesthouse that has its own bar. **2.** a Greek restaurant. [C20: Mod. Gk, < L *taberna*]

TAVR *abbrev. for* Territorial and Army Volunteer Reserve.

taw[1] (tɔː) *n.* **1.** a large marble used for shooting. **2.** a game of marbles. **3.** the line from which the players shoot in marbles. **4. back to taws.** *Austral. inf.* back to the beginning. [C18: <?]

taw[2] (tɔː) *vb.* (*tr.*) to convert (skins) into leather by treatment with alum and salt rather than by normal tanning processes. [OE *tawian*] —ˈ**tawer** *n.*

tawa (ˈtɑːwə) *n.* a New Zealand timber tree with edible berries. [< Maori]

tawdry (ˈtɔːdrɪ) *adj.* **-drier, -driest.** cheap, showy, and of poor quality: *tawdry jewellery.* [C16 *tawdry lace,* shortened & altered < *Seynt Audries lace,* finery sold at the fair of St *Audrey* (Etheldrida), 7th-century queen of Northumbria] —ˈ**tawdrily** *adv.* —ˈ**tawdriness** *n.*

tawny (ˈtɔːnɪ) *n.* **a.** a light brown to brownish-orange colour. **b.** (*as adj.*)*: tawny port.* [C14: < OF *tané,* < *taner* to tan] —ˈ**tawniness** *n.*

tawny owl *n.* a European owl having a reddish-brown plumage and a round head.

tawse *or* **taws** (tɔːz) *n. Chiefly Scot.* a leather strap having one end cut into thongs, formerly used as an instrument of punishment by a schoolteacher. [C16: prob. pl. of obs. *taw* strip of leather; see TAW[2]]

tax (tæks) *n.* **1.** a compulsory financial contribution imposed by a government to raise revenue, levied on income or property, on the prices of goods and services, etc. **2.** a heavy demand on something; strain. ~*vb.* (*tr.*) **3.** to levy a tax on (persons, companies, etc.). **4.** to make heavy demands on; strain. **5.** to accuse or blame. **6.** *Law.* to determine (the amount legally chargeable or allowable to a party to a legal action): *to tax costs.* [C13: < OF *taxer,* < L *taxāre* to appraise, < *tangere* to touch] —ˈ**taxable** *adj.* —ˈ**taxer** *n.*

taxation (tækˈseɪʃən) *n.* **1.** the act or principle of levying taxes or the condition of being taxed. **2. a.** an amount assessed as tax. **b.** a tax rate. **3.** revenue from taxes. —**taxˈational** *adj.*

tax avoidance *n.* reduction or minimization of tax liability by lawful methods.

tax-deductible *adj.* legally deductible from income or wealth before tax assessment.

tax disc *n.* a paper disc displayed on the windscreen of a motor vehicle showing that the tax due on it has been paid.

taxeme (ˈtæksiːm) *n. Linguistics.* any element of speech that may differentiate one utterance from another with a different meaning, such as the occurrence of a particular phoneme, the presence of a certain intonation, or a distinctive word order. [C20: < Gk *taxis* order, arrangement + -EME] —**taxˈemic** *adj.*

tax evasion *n.* reduction or minimization of tax liability by illegal methods.

tax exile *n.* a person having a high income who chooses to live abroad so as to avoid paying high taxes.

tax haven *n.* a country or state having a lower rate of taxation than elsewhere.

taxi (ˈtæksɪ) *n., pl.* **taxis** *or* **taxies.** **1.** Also called: **cab, taxicab.** a car, usually fitted with a taximeter, that may be hired to carry passengers to any specified destination. ~*vb.* **taxiing** *or* **taxying, taxied.** **2.** to cause (an aircraft) to move along the ground, esp. before takeoff and after landing, or (of an aircraft) to move along the ground in this way. **3.** (*intr.*) to travel in a taxi. [C20: shortened < *taximeter cab*]

taxidermy (ˈtæksɪˌdɜːmɪ) *n.* the art or process of preparing, stuffing, and mounting animal skins so that they have a lifelike appearance. [C19: < Gk *taxis* arrangement + *-dermy,* < Gk *derma* skin] —ˌ**taxiˈdermal** *or* ˌ**taxiˈdermic** *adj.* —ˈ**taxiˌdermist** *n.*

taximeter (ˈtæksɪˌmiːtə) *n.* a meter fitted to a taxi to register the fare, based on the length of the journey. [C19: < F *taximètre;* see TAX, -METER]

taxing (ˈtæksɪŋ) *adj.* demanding, onerous, and wearing. —ˈ**taxingly** *adv.*

taxi rank *n.* a place where taxis wait to be hired.

taxis (ˈtæksɪs) *n.* **1.** the movement of an organism in response to an external stimulus. **2.** *Surgery.* the repositioning of a displaced part by manual manipulation only. [C18: via NL < Gk: arrangement, < *tassein* to place in order]

-taxis *or* **-taxy** *n. combining form.* **1.** indicating movement towards or away from a specified stimulus: *thermotaxis.* **2.** order or arrangement: *phyllotaxis.* [< NL, < Gk *taxis* order] —**-tactic** *or* **-taxic** *adj. combining form.*

taxiway (ˈtæksɪˌweɪ) *n.* a marked path along which aircraft taxi to or from a runway, parking area, etc.

taxon (ˈtæksɒn) *n., pl.* **taxa** (ˈtæksə). *Biol.* any taxonomic group or rank. [C20: back formation < TAXONOMY]

taxonomy (tækˈsɒnəmɪ) *n.* **1.** the branch of biology concerned with the classification of organisms into groups based on similarities of structure, origin, etc. **2.** the science or practice of classification. [C19: < F *taxonomie,* < Gk *taxis* order + -NOMY] —**taxonomic** (ˌtæksəˈnɒmɪk) *or* ˌ**taxoˈnomical** *adj.* —ˌ**taxoˈnomically** *adv.* —**taxˈonomist** *n.*

taxpayer (ˈtæksˌpeɪə) *n.* a person or organization that pays taxes.

tax return *n.* a declaration of personal income used as a basis for assessing an individual's liability for taxation.

tax shelter *n.* a form into which business activities may be organized to minimize taxation.

-taxy *n. combining form.* a variant of **-taxis.**

tazza (ˈtætsə) *n.* a wine cup with a shallow bowl and a circular foot. [C19: < It., prob. < Ar. *tassah* bowl]

Tb *the chemical symbol for* terbium.

TB *abbrev. for:* **1.** torpedo boat. **2.** Also: **tb.** tuberculosis.

T-bar *n.* **1.** a T-shaped wrench for use with a socket. **2.** a T-shaped bar on a ski tow which skiers hold on to while being pulled up slopes.

T-bone steak *n.* a large choice steak cut from the sirloin of beef, containing a T-shaped bone.

tbs. *or* **tbsp.** *abbrev. for* tablespoon(ful).

TBT *abbrev. for* tri-*n*-butyl tin: a biocide used in marine paints to prevent fouling.

Tc *the chemical symbol for* technetium.

T-cell *n.* a type of lymphocyte that matures in the thymus gland and is responsible for killing cells infected by a virus. Also called: **T-lymphocyte.**

t distribution *n.* See **Student's t.**

te *or* **ti** (tiː) *n. Music.* (in tonic sol-fa) the syllable used for the seventh note or subtonic of any scale. [see GAMUT]

Te *the chemical symbol for* tellurium.

tea (tiː) *n.* **1.** an evergreen shrub of tropical and subtropical Asia, having white fragrant flowers: family *Theaceae.* **2. a.** the dried leaves of this shrub, used to make a beverage by infusion in boiling water. **b.** such a beverage, served hot or iced. **3. a.** any of various similar plants or any plants that are used to make a tealike beverage. **b.** any such beverage. **4.** Also called: **afternoon tea.** *Chiefly Brit.* a light meal eaten in midafternoon, usually consisting of tea and cakes, etc. **5.** Also called (Brit.): **high tea.** *Brit., Austral., & N.Z.* the main evening meal. **6.** *U.S. & Canad. dated sl.* marijuana. [C17: < Chinese (Amoy) *t'e,* < Ancient Chinese *d'a*]

tea bag *n.* a small bag containing tea leaves, infused in boiling water to make tea.

tea ball *n. Chiefly U.S.* a perforated metal ball filled with tea leaves and used to make tea.

teacake (ˈtiːˌkeɪk) *n. Brit.* a flat bun, usually eaten toasted and buttered.

teach (tiːtʃ) *vb.* **teaching, taught. 1.** (*tr.; may take a clause as object or an infinitive;* often foll. by *how*) to help to learn; tell or show (how). **2.** to give instruction or lessons in (a subject) to (a person or animal). **3.** (*tr.; may take a clause as object or an infinitive*) to cause to learn or understand: *experience taught him that he could not be a journalist.* [OE *tǣcan*] —ˈ**teachable** *adj.*

teacher (ˈtiːtʃə) *n.* a person whose occupation is teaching others, esp. children.

teach-in *n.* an informal conference, esp. on a topical subject, usually held at a university or college and involving a panel of visiting speakers, lecturers, students, etc.

teaching (ˈtiːtʃɪŋ) *n.* **1.** the art or profession of a teacher. **2.** (*sometimes pl.*) something taught; precept. **3.** (*modifier*) denoting a person or institution that teaches: *a teaching hospital.* **4.** (*modifier*) used in teaching: *teaching aids.*

teaching machine *n.* a machine that presents information and questions to the user, registers the answers, and indicates whether these are correct or acceptable.

tea cloth *n.* another name for **tea towel.**

tea cosy *n.* a covering for a teapot to keep the contents hot.

teacup (ˈtiːˌkʌp) *n.* **1.** a cup out of which tea may be drunk. **2.** Also called: **teacupful.** the amount a teacup will hold, about four fluid ounces.

teahouse (ˈtiːˌhaʊs) *n.* a restaurant, esp. in Japan or China, where tea and light refreshments are served.

teak (tiːk) *n.* **1.** a large tree of the East Indies. **2.** the hard resinous yellowish-brown wood of this tree, used for furniture making, etc. [C17: < Port. *teca,* < Malayalam *tēkka*]

teakettle (ˈtiːˌketᵊl) *n.* a kettle for boiling water to make tea.

teal (tiːl) *n., pl.* **teals** *or* **teal. 1.** any of various small freshwater ducks that are related to the mallard. **2.** a greenish-blue colour. [C14]

tea leaf *n.* **1.** the dried leaf of the tea shrub, used to make tea. **2.** (*usually pl.*) shredded parts of these leaves, esp. after infusion.

team (tiːm) *n.* (*sometimes functioning as pl.*) **1.** a group of people organized to work together. **2.** a group of players forming one of the sides in a sporting contest. **3.** two or more animals working together, as to pull a vehicle. **4.** such animals and the vehicle. ~*vb.* **5.** (when *intr.,* often foll. by *up*) to make or cause to make a team. **6.** (*tr.*) *U.S. & Canad.* to drag or transport in or by a team. **7.** (*intr.*) *U.S. & Canad.* to drive a team. [OE *team* offspring]

tea-maker *n.* a spoon with a perforated cover used to infuse tea in a cup of boiling water.

team-mate *n.* a fellow member of a team.

team spirit *n.* willingness to cooperate as part of a team.

teamster (ˈtiːmstə) *n.* **1.** a driver of a team of horses. **2.** *U.S. & Canad.* the driver of a lorry.

team teaching *n.* a system whereby two or more teachers pool their skills, knowledge, etc., to teach combined classes.

teamwork (ˈtiːmˌwɜːk) *n.* **1.** the cooperative work done by a team. **2.** the ability to work efficiently as a team.

teapot (ˈtiːˌpɒt) *n.* a container with a lid, spout, and handle, in which tea is made and from which it is served.

teapoy (ˈtiːpɔɪ) *n.* a small table with a tripod base. [C19: < Hindi *tipāī,* < Sansk. *tri* three + *pāda* foot]

tear[1] (tɪə) *n.* **1.** a drop of the secretion of the lacrimal glands. See **tears. 2.** something shaped like a falling drop: *a tear of amber.* ~Also called: **teardrop.** [OE *tēar*] —ˈ**tearless** *adj.*

tear[2] (tɛə) *vb.* **tearing, tore, torn. 1.** to cause to come apart or to come apart; rip. **2.** (*tr.*) to make (a hole or split) in (something). **3.** (*intr.;* often foll. by *along*) to hurry or rush. **4.** (*tr.;* usually foll. by *away* or *from*) to remove or take by force. **5.** (when *intr.,* often foll. by *at*) to cause pain, distress, or anguish (to). **6. tear one's hair.** *Inf.* to be angry, frustrated, very worried, etc. ~*n.* **7.** a hole, cut, or split. **8.** the act of tearing. ~See also **tear away, tear down,** etc. [OE *teran*] —ˈ**tearable** *adj.* —ˈ**tearer** *n.*

tear away (tɛə) *vb.* **1.** (*tr., adv.*) to persuade (oneself or someone else) to leave. ~*n.* **tearaway. 2.** *Brit.* a reckless impetuous unruly person.

tear down (tɛə) *vb.* (*tr., adv.*) to destroy or demolish: *to tear down an argument.*

tear duct (tɪə) *n.* a short tube in the inner corner of the eyelid through which tears drain into the nose. Technical name: **lacrimal duct.**

tearful (ˈtɪəfʊl) *adj.* **1.** crying or about to cry. **2.** tending to produce tears; sad. —ˈ**tearfully** *adv.* —ˈ**tearfulness** *n.*

tear gas (tɪə) *n.* a gas that makes the eyes smart and water, causing temporary blindness; used in warfare and to control riots.

tearing (ˈtɛərɪŋ) *adj.* violent or furious (esp. in **tearing hurry** *or* **rush**).

tear into (tɛə) *vb.* (*intr., prep.*) *Inf.* to attack vigorously and damagingly.

tear-jerker (ˈtɪəˌdʒɜːkə) *n. Inf.* an excessively sentimental film, play, book, etc.

tearoom (ˈtiːˌruːm, -ˌrʊm) *n. Brit.* a restaurant where tea and light refreshments are served. Also called: **teashop.**

tea rose *n.* any of several varieties of hybrid rose that have pink or yellow flowers with a scent resembling that of tea.

tears (tɪəz) *pl. n.* **1.** the clear salty solution secreted by the lacrimal glands that lubricates and cleanses the surface of the eyeball. **2.** a state of intense frustration (esp. in **bored to tears**). **3. in tears.** weeping.

tear sheet (tɛə) *n.* a page in a newspaper or periodical that is cut or perforated so that it can be easily torn out.

tease (tiːz) *vb.* **1.** to annoy (someone) by deliberately offering something with the intention of delaying or withdrawing the offer. **2.** to vex (someone) maliciously or playfully. **3.** (*tr.*) to separate the fibres of; comb; card. **4.** (*tr.*) to raise the nap of (a fabric) with a teasel. **5.** another word (esp. U.S. and Canad.) for **backcomb. 6.** (*tr.*) to loosen or pull apart (biological tissues, etc.). ~*n.* **7.** a person or thing that teases. **8.** the act of teasing. [OE *tǣsan*] —ˈ**teaser** *n.* —ˈ**teasing** *adj.* —ˈ**teasingly** *adv.*

teasel, teazel, *or* **teazle** (ˈtiːzəl) *n.* **1.** any of various plants (esp. the **fuller's teasel**) of Eurasia and N Africa, having prickly leaves and prickly heads of yellow or purple flowers. **2. a.** the dried flower head of the fuller's teasel, used for teasing. **b.** any implement used for the same purpose. ~*vb.* **-selling, -selled** *or U.S.* **-seling, -seled. 3.** (*tr.*) to tease (a fabric). [OE *tǣsel*] —ˈ**teaseller** *n.*

tea service *or* **set** *n.* the china or pottery articles used in serving tea, including a teapot, cups, saucers, etc.

teashop (ˈtiːˌʃɒp) *n. Brit.* another name for **tearoom.**

teaspoon (ˈtiːˌspuːn) *n.* **1.** a small spoon used for stirring tea, etc. **2.** Also called: **teaspoonful.** the amount contained in such a spoon. **3.** a unit of capacity used in cooking, medicine, etc., equal to about one fluid dram.

teat (tiːt) *n.* **1. a.** the nipple of a mammary gland. **b.** (in cows, etc.) any of the projections from the udder. **2.** something resembling a teat such as the rubber mouthpiece of a feeding bottle. [C13: < OF *tete,* of Gmc origin]

tea towel *or* **cloth** *n.* a towel for drying dishes, etc. U.S. name: **dishtowel.**

tea tree *n.* any of various trees of Australia and New Zealand, the leaves of which were formerly used to make tea.

tea trolley *n. Brit.* a trolley from which tea is served.

tech (tɛk) *n. Inf.* a technical college.

tech. *abbrev. for:* **1.** technical. **2.** technology.

technetium (tɛkˈniːʃɪəm) *n.* a silvery-grey metallic element, artificially produced by bombardment of molybdenum by deuterons. The radioisotope **technetium-99m** is used in radiotherapy. Symbol: Tc; atomic no.: 43; half-life of most stable isotope, ^{97}Tc: 2.6 × 10^{6} years. [C20: NL, < Gk *tekhnētos* manmade, < *tekhnasthai* to devise artificially, < *tekhnē* skill]

technic *n.* **1.** (tɛkˈniːk). another word for **technique.** **2.** (ˈtɛknɪk). another word for **technics.** [C17: < L *technicus,* < Gk *tekhnikos,* < *tekhnē* skill]

technical (ˈtɛknɪkᵊl) *adj.* **1.** of or specializing in industrial, practical, or mechanical arts and applied sciences: *a technical institute.* **2.** skilled in practical arts rather than abstract thinking. **3.** relating to a particular field of activity: *the technical jargon of linguistics.* **4.** existing by virtue of a strict application of the rules or a strict interpretation of the wording: *a technical loophole in the law.* **5.** of or showing technique: *technical brilliance.* —ˈ**technically** *adv.* —ˈ**technicalness** *n.*

technical college *n. Brit.* an institution for further education that provides courses in technology, art, secretarial skills, agriculture, etc.

technical drawing *n.* the study and practice of the basic techniques of draughtsmanship, as employed in mechanical drawing, architecture, etc.

technicality (ˌtɛknɪˈkælɪtɪ) *n., pl.* **-ties. 1.** a petty formal point arising from a strict interpretation of rules, etc. **2.** the state or quality of being technical. **3.** technical methods and vocabulary.

technical knockout *n. Boxing.* a judgment of a knockout given when a boxer is in the referee's opinion too badly beaten to continue without risk of serious injury.

technician (tɛkˈnɪʃən) *n.* **1.** a person skilled in mechanical or industrial techniques or in a particular technical field. **2.** a person employed in a laboratory, etc., to do mechanical and practical work. **3.** a person having specific artistic or mechanical skill, esp. if lacking flair.

Technicolor (ˈtɛknɪˌkʌlə) *n. Trademark.* the process of producing colour film by means of superimposing synchronized films of the same scene, each of which has a different colour filter.

technics (ˈtɛknɪks) *n.* (*functioning as sing.*) the study or theory of industry and industrial arts; technology.

technique (tɛkˈniːk) *n.* **1.** a practical method, skill, or art applied to a particular task. **2.** proficiency in a practical or mechanical skill. **3.** special facility; knack. [C19: < F, < *technique* (adj.): see TECHNIC]

techno- *combining form.* **1.** craft or art: *technology; technography.* **2.** technological or technical: *technocracy.* [< Gk *tekhnē* skill]

technocracy (tɛkˈnɒkrəsɪ) *n., pl.* **-cies.** government by scientists, engineers, and other such experts. —**technocrat** (ˈtɛknəˌkræt) *n.* —ˌ**technoˈcratic** *adj.*

technology (tɛkˈnɒlədʒɪ) *n., pl.* **-gies. 1.** the application of practical or mechanical sciences to industry or commerce. **2.** the methods, theory, and practices governing such application. **3.** the total knowledge and skills available to any human society. [C17: < Gk *tekhnologia* systematic treatment, < *tekhnē* skill] —**technological** (ˌtɛknəˈlɒdʒɪkᵊl) *adj.* —**techˈnologist** *n.*

techy (ˈtɛtʃɪ) *adj.* **techier, techiest.** a variant spelling of **tetchy.** —ˈ**techily** *adv.* —ˈ**techiness** *n.*

tectonic (tɛkˈtɒnɪk) *adj.* **1.** denoting or relating to building. **2.** *Geol.* **a.** (of landforms, etc.) resulting from distortion of the earth's crust due to forces within it. **b.** (of processes, movements, etc.) occurring within the earth's crust and causing structural deformation. [C17: < LL *tectonicus,* < Gk *tektonikos* belonging to carpentry, < *tektōn* a builder]

tectonics (tɛkˈtɒnɪks) *n.* (*functioning as sing.*) **1.** the art and science of construction or building. **2.** the study of the processes by which the earth's surface has attained its present structure.

tectrix (ˈtɛktrɪks) *n., pl.* **tectrices** (ˈtɛktrɪˌsiːz). (*usually pl.*) *Ornithol.* another name for **covert** (sense 5). [C19: NL, < L *tector* plasterer, < *tegere* to cover] —**tectricial** (tɛkˈtrɪʃəl) *adj.*

ted[1] (tɛd) *vb.* **tedding, tedded.** to shake out (hay), so as to dry it. [C15: < ON *tethja*]

ted[2] (tɛd) *n. Inf.* short for **teddy boy.**

tedder (ˈtɛdə) *n.* **1.** a machine equipped with a series of small rotating forks for tedding hay. **2.** a person who teds.

teddy (ˈtɛdɪ) *n., pl.* **-dies.** a woman's one-piece undergarment, incorporating a chemise top and panties.

teddy bear *n.* a stuffed toy bear. Often shortened to **teddy.** [C20: < *Teddy,* < *Theodore,* after Theodore Roosevelt (1858–1919), U.S. president, well known as a hunter of bears]

teddy boy *n.* **1.** (in Britain, esp. in the mid-1950s) one of a cult of youths who wore mock Edwardian fashions. **2.** any tough or delinquent youth. [C20: < *Teddy,* < *Edward,* referring to the Edwardian dress]

Te Deum (ˌtiː ˈdiːəm) *n.* **1.** an ancient Latin hymn in rhythmic prose. **2.** a musical setting of this hymn. **3.** a service of thanksgiving in which the recital of this hymn forms a central part. [< the L canticle beginning *Tē Deum laudāmus,* lit.: Thee, God, we praise]

tedious (ˈtiːdɪəs) *adj.* causing fatigue or tedium; monotonous. —ˈ**tediousness** *n.*

tedium (ˈtiːdɪəm) *n.* the state of being bored or the quality of being boring; monotony. [C17: < L *taedium,* < *taedēre* to weary]

tee[1] (tiː) *n.* **1.** a pipe fitting in the form of a letter *T,* used to join three pipes. **2.** a metal section with a cross section in the form of a letter *T.*

tee[2] (tiː) *Golf.* ~*n.* **1.** an area from which the first stroke of a hole is made. **2.** a support for a golf ball, usually a small wooden or plastic peg, used when teeing off or in long grass, etc. ~*vb.* **teeing, teed. 3.** (when *intr.,* often foll. by *up*) to position (the ball) ready for striking, on or as if on a tee. ~See also **tee off.** [C17 *teaz,* <?]

tee[3] (tiː) *n.* a mark used as a target in certain games such as curling and quoits. [C18: ? < T-shaped marks, which may have orig. been used in curling]

tee-hee *or* **te-hee** (ˈtiːˈhiː) *interj.* **1.** an exclamation of laughter, esp. when mocking. ~*n.* **2.** a chuckle. ~*vb.* **-heeing, -heed. 3.** (*intr.*) to snigger or laugh, esp. derisively. [C14: imit.]

teem[1] (tiːm) *vb.* (*intr.;* usually foll. by *with*) to be prolific or abundant (in). [OE *tēman* to produce offspring; rel. to West Saxon *tīeman;* see TEAM]

teem[2] (tiːm) *vb.* **1.** (*intr.;* often foll. by *down* or *with rain*) to pour in torrents. **2.** (*tr.*) to pour or empty out. [C15 *temen* to empty, < ON *tœma*]

teen (tiːn) *adj. Inf.* another word for **teenage.**

teenage (ˈtiːnˌeɪdʒ) *adj. also* **teenaged.** (*prenominal*) of or relating to the time in a person's life between the ages of 13 and 19.

teenager (ˈtiːnˌeɪdʒə) *n.* a person between the ages of 13 and 19 inclusive.

teens (tiːnz) *pl. n.* **1.** the years of a person's life between the ages of 13 and 19 inclusive. **2.** all the numbers that end in *-teen.*

teeny (ˈtiːnɪ) *adj.* **-nier, -niest.** extremely small; tiny. Also: **teeny-weeny** (ˈtiːnɪˈwiːnɪ) *or* **teensy-weensy** (ˈtiːnzɪˈwiːnzɪ). [C19: var. of TINY]

teenybopper (ˈtiːnɪˌbɒpə) *n. Sl.* a young teenager, usually a girl, who avidly follows fashions in clothes and pop music. [C20: *teeny*, < teenage + *-bopper*; see BOP]

tee off *vb. (adv.)* **1.** *Golf.* to strike (the ball) from a tee. **2.** *Inf.* to begin; start.

teepee (ˈtiːpiː) *n.* a variant spelling of **tepee.**

tee shirt *n.* a variant of **T-shirt.**

teeter (ˈtiːtə) *vb.* **1.** to move or cause to move unsteadily; wobble. ~*n., vb.* **2.** another word for **seesaw.** [C19: < ME *titeren*]

teeth (tiːθ) *n.* **1.** the plural of **tooth. 2.** the most violent part: *the teeth of the gale.* **3.** the power to produce a desired effect: *that law has no teeth.* **4. get one's teeth into.** to become engrossed in. **5. in the teeth of.** in direct opposition to; against. **6. to the teeth.** to the greatest possible degree: *armed to the teeth.* **7. show one's teeth.** to threaten.

teethe (tiːð) *vb. (intr.)* to cut one's baby (deciduous) teeth.

teething ring *n.* a hard ring on which babies may bite while teething.

teething troubles *pl. n.* the problems that arise during the initial stages of a project, etc.

teetotal (tiːˈtəʊtᵊl) *adj.* **1.** of or practising abstinence from alcoholic drink. **2.** *Dialect.* complete. [C19: allegedly coined in 1833 by Richard Turner, E advocate of total abstinence from alcohol; prob. < TOTAL, with emphatic reduplication] —**teeˈtotaller** *n.* —**teeˈtotalism** *n.*

teetotum (tiːˈtəʊtəm) *n. Arch.* a spinning top bearing letters of the alphabet on its four sides. [C18: < *T totum*, < *T* initial on one of the faces + *totum* the name of the toy, < L *tōtum* the whole]

teff (tɛf) *n.* an annual grass of NE Africa, grown for its grain. [C18: < Amharic *tēf*]

TEFL *abbrev. for* Teaching (of) English as a Foreign Language.

Teflon (ˈtɛflɒn) *n.* a trademark for **polytetrafluoroethylene.**

teg (tɛg) *n.* **1.** a two-year-old sheep. **2.** the fleece of a two-year-old sheep. [C16: <?]

tegmen (ˈtɛgmən) *n., pl.* **-mina** (-mənə). **1.** either of the leathery forewings of the cockroach and related insects. **2.** the delicate inner covering of a seed. **3.** any similar covering or layer. [C19: < L: a cover, < *tegere* to cover] —ˈ**tegminal** *adj.*

tegument (ˈtɛgjʊmənt) *n.* a less common word for **integument.** [C15: < L *tegumentum* a covering, < *tegere* to cover]

te-hee (tiːˈhiː) *interj., n., vb.* a variant of **tee-hee.**

te igitur *Latin.* (teɪ ˈɪgɪˌtʊə; *English* teɪ ˈɪdʒɪtʊə) *n. R.C. Church.* the first prayer of the canon of the Mass, which begins *Te igitur clementissime Pater* (Thee, therefore, most merciful Father).

tektite (ˈtɛktaɪt) *n.* a small dark glassy object found in several areas around the world, thought to be a product of meteorite impact. [C20: < Gk *tēktos* molten]

tel. *abbrev. for:* **1.** telegram. **2.** telegraph(ic). **3.** telephone.

tel- *combining form.* a variant of **tele-** and **telo-** before a vowel.

telaesthesia *or U.S.* **telesthesia** (ˌtɛlɪsˈθiːzɪə) *n.* the alleged perception of events that are beyond the normal range of perceptual processes. —**telaesthetic** *or U.S.* **telesthetic** (ˌtɛlɪsˈθɛtɪk) *adj.*

telamon (ˈtɛləmən) *n., pl.* **-mones** (-ˈməʊniːz) *or* **-mons.** a column in the form of a male figure, used to support an entablature. [C18: via L < Gk, < *tlēnai* to bear]

telangiectasis (tɪˌlændʒɪˈɛktəsɪs) *or* **telangiectasia** (tɪˌlændʒɪɛkˈteɪzɪə) *n., pl.* **-ses** (-ˌsiːz). *Pathol.* an abnormal dilation of the capillaries or terminal arteries producing blotched red spots, esp. on the face or thighs. [C19: NL, < Gk *telos* end + *angeion* vessel + *ektasis* dilation] —**telangiectatic** (tɪˌlændʒɪɛkˈtætɪk) *adj.*

tele- *combining form.* **1.** at or over a distance; distant: *telescope; telekinesis.* **2.** television: *telecast.* **3.** by means of or via telephone or television: *teleshopping.* [< Gk *tele* far]

telecast (ˈtɛləˌkɑːst) *vb.* **-casting, -cast** *or* **-casted. 1.** to broadcast by television. ~*n.* **2.** a television broadcast. —ˈ**teleˌcaster** *n.*

telecom (ˈtɛlɪˌkɒm) *or* **telecoms** (ˈtɛlɪˌkɒmz) *n. (functioning as sing.)* short for **telecommunications.**

telecommunications (ˌtɛlɪkəˌmjuːnɪˈkeɪʃənz) *n. (functioning as sing.)* the science and technology of communications by telephony, radio, television, etc.

teledu (ˈtɛlɪˌduː) *n.* a badger of SE Asia and Indonesia, having dark brown hair with a white stripe along the back and producing a fetid secretion when attacked. [C19: < Malay]

telegenic (ˌtɛlɪˈdʒɛnɪk) *adj.* having or showing a pleasant television image. [C20: < TELE(VISION) + (PHOTO)GENIC] —ˌ**teleˈgenically** *adv.*

telegnosis (ˌtɛləˈnəʊsɪs, ˌtɛləg-) *n.* knowledge about distant events alleged to have been obtained without the use of any normal sensory mechanism. [C20: < TELE- + *-gnosis*, < Gk *gnōsis* knowledge]

telegony (tɪˈlɛgənɪ) *n. Genetics.* the supposed influence of a previous sire on offspring borne by a female to other sires. —**telegonic** (ˌtɛlɪˈgɒnɪk) *or* **teˈlegonous** *adj.*

telegram (ˈtɛlɪˌgræm) *n.* a communication transmitted by telegraph.

telegraph (ˈtɛlɪˌgrɑːf) *n.* **1. a.** a device, system, or process by which information can be transmitted over a distance, esp. using radio signals or coded electrical signals sent along a transmission line. **b.** *(as modifier): telegraph pole.* ~*vb.* **2.** to send a telegram to (a person or place); wire. **3.** *(tr.)* to transmit or send by telegraph. **4.** *(tr.)* to give advance notice of (anything), esp. unintentionally. **5.** *(tr.) Canad. inf.* to cast (votes) illegally by impersonating registered voters. —**telegrapher** (tɪˈlɛgrəfə) *or* **teˈlegraphist** *n.* —ˌ**teleˈgraphic** *adj.*

telegraph plant *n.* a small tropical Asian shrub having small leaflets that turn in various directions during the day and droop at night.

telegraphy (tɪˈlɛgrəfɪ) *n.* **1.** a system of telecommunications involving any process providing reproduction at a distance of written, printed, or pictorial matter. **2.** the skill or process of operating a telegraph.

telekinesis (ˌtɛlɪkaɪˈniːsɪs) *n.* **1.** the movement of a body caused by thought or willpower without the application of a physical force. **2.** the ability to cause such movement. —**telekinetic** (ˌtɛlɪkɪˈnɛtɪk) *adj.*

telemark (ˈtɛlɪˌmɑːk) *n. Skiing.* a turn in which one ski is placed far forward of the other and turned gradually inwards. [C20: after *Telemark*, county in Norway]

telemeter (tɪˈlɛmɪtə) *n.* **1.** any device for recording or measuring a distant event and transmitting the data to a receiver. **2.** any device used to measure a distance without directly comparing it with a measuring rod, etc. ~*vb.* **3.** *(tr.)* to obtain and transmit (data) from a distant source. —**telemetric** (ˌtɛlɪˈmɛtrɪk) *adj.*

telemetry (tɪˈlɛmɪtrɪ) *n.* **1.** the use of radio waves, telephone lines, etc., to transmit the readings of measuring instruments to a device on which the readings can be indicated or recorded. **2.** the measurement of linear distance using a tellurometer.

telencephalon (ˌtɛlɛnˈsɛfəˌlɒn) *n.* the cerebrum together with related parts of the hypothalamus and the third ventricle. —**telencephalic** (ˌtɛlɛnsɪˈfælɪk) *adj.*

teleology (ˌtɛlɪˈɒlədʒɪ, ˌtiːlɪ-) *n.* **1.** *Philosophy.* **a.** the doctrine that there is evidence of purpose or design in the universe, and esp. that this provides proof of the existence of a Designer. **b.** the belief that certain phenomena are best explained in terms of purpose rather than cause. **2.** *Biol.* the belief that natural phenomena have a predetermined purpose and are not determined by mechanical laws. [C18: < NL *teleologia*, < Gk *telos* end + -LOGY] —**teleological** (ˌtɛlɪəˈlɒdʒɪkᵊl, ˌtiːlɪ-) *adj.* —ˌ**teleˈologist** *n.*

teleost (ˈtɛlɪˌɒst, ˈtiːlɪ-) *n.* any of a subclass of bony fishes having rayed fins and a swim bladder, as herrings, carps, eels, cod, perches, etc. [C19: < NL *teleosteī* (pl.) creatures having complete skeletons, < Gk *teleos* complete + *osteon* bone]

telepathy (tɪˈlɛpəθɪ) *n.* the communication between people of thoughts, feelings, etc., involving mechanisms that cannot be understood in terms of known scientific laws. —**telepathic** (ˌtɛlɪˈpæθɪk) *adj.* —**teˈlepathist** *n.* —**teˈlepaˌthize** *or* **-ise** *vb.* (*intr.*)

telephone (ˈtɛlɪˌfəʊn) *n.* **1.** an electrical device for transmitting speech, consisting of a microphone and receiver mounted on a handset. **2. a.** a worldwide system of communications using telephones. The microphone in one telephone converts sound waves into electrical oscillations that are transmitted along a telephone wire or by radio to one or more distant sets. **b.** (*as modifier*): *a telephone exchange.* ~*vb.* **3.** to call or talk to (a person) by telephone. **4.** to transmit (a message, etc.) by telephone. —ˈ**teleˌphoner** *n.* —**telephonic** (ˌtɛlɪˈfɒnɪk) *adj.*

telephone box *n.* a soundproof enclosure from which a paid telephone call can be made. Also called: **telephone kiosk, telephone booth.**

telephone directory *n.* a book listing the names, addresses, and telephone numbers of subscribers in a particular area.

telephone number *n.* a set of figures identifying the telephone of a particular subscriber, and used in making connections to that telephone.

telephonist (tɪˈlɛfənɪst) *n. Brit.* a person who operates a telephone switchboard. Also called (esp. U.S.): **telephone operator.**

telephony (tɪˈlɛfənɪ) *n.* a system of telecommunications for the transmission of speech or other sounds.

telephotography (ˌtɛlɪfəˈtɒgrəfɪ) *n.* the process or technique of photographing distant objects using a telephoto lens.

telephoto lens (ˈtɛlɪˌfəʊtəʊ) *n.* a compound camera lens in which the focal length is greater than that of a simple lens and thus produces a magnified image of a distant object.

teleprinter (ˈtɛlɪˌprɪntə) *n.* **1.** a telegraph apparatus consisting of a keyboard transmitter, which converts a typed message into coded pulses for transmission along a wire or cable, and a printing receiver, which converts incoming signals and prints out the message. U.S. name: **teletypewriter. 2.** a network of such devices. **3.** a similar device used for direct input/output of data into a computer at a distant location.

Teleprompter (ˈtɛlɪˌprɒmptə) *n. Trademark.* a device for displaying a television script so that the speaker can read it while appearing to look at the camera.

Teleran (ˈtɛləˌræn) *n. Trademark.* an electronic navigational aid in which the image of a ground-based radar system is televised to aircraft. [C20: < *Tele*(*vision*) *R*(*adar*) *A*(*ir*) *N*(*avigation*)]

telesales (ˈtɛlɪˌseɪlz) *pl. n.* the selling of a commodity or service by a salesperson who makes an initial approach by telephone.

telescope (ˈtɛlɪˌskəʊp) *n.* **1.** an optical instrument for making distant objects appear closer by use of a combination of lenses (**refracting telescope**) or lenses and curved mirrors (**reflecting telescope**). **2.** any instrument, such as a radio telescope, for collecting, focusing, and detecting electromagnetic radiation from space. ~*vb.* **3.** to crush together or be crushed together, as in a collision. **4.** to fit together like a set of cylinders that slide into one another, thus allowing extension and shortening. **5.** to make or become smaller or shorter. [C17: < It. *telescopio* or NL *telescopium,* lit.: far-seeing instrument]

telescopic (ˌtɛlɪˈskɒpɪk) *adj.* **1.** of or relating to a telescope. **2.** seen through or obtained by means of a telescope. **3.** visible only with a telescope. **4.** able to see far. **5.** having parts that telescope. —ˌ**teleˈscopically** *adv.*

telescopic sight *n.* a telescope mounted on a rifle, etc., used for sighting.

telescopy (tɪˈlɛskəpɪ) *n.* the branch of astronomy concerned with the use and design of telescopes.

telespectroscope (ˌtɛlɪˈspɛktrəˌskəʊp) *n.* a combination of a telescope and a spectroscope, used for spectroscopic analysis of radiation from stars and other celestial bodies.

telestereoscope (ˌtɛlɪˈstɪərɪəˌskəʊp, -ˈstɛrɪə-) *n.* an optical instrument for obtaining stereoscopic images of distant objects.

telestich (tɪˈlɛstɪk, ˈtɛlɪˌstɪk) *n.* a short poem in which the last letters of each successive line form a word. [C17: < Gk *telos* end + *stikhos* row]

teletext (ˈtɛlɪˌtɛkst) *n.* a videotext service in which the consumer is not able to interact with the computer. Cf. **viewdata.**

telethon (ˈtɛləˌθɒn) *n. U.S.* a lengthy television programme to raise charity funds, etc. [C20: < TELE- + MARATHON]

Teletype (ˈtɛlɪˌtaɪp) *n.* **1.** *Trademark.* a type of teleprinter. **2.** (*sometimes not cap.*) a network of such devices. ~*vb.* **3.** (*sometimes not cap.*) to transmit (a message) by Teletype.

teletypewriter (ˌtɛlɪˈtaɪpˌraɪtə, ˈtɛlɪˌtaɪp-) *n.* a U.S. name for **teleprinter.**

televise (ˈtɛlɪˌvaɪz) *vb.* **1.** to put on television. **2.** (*tr.*) to transmit by television.

television (ˈtɛlɪˌvɪʒən) *n.* **1.** the system or process of producing on a distant screen a series of transient visible images, usually with an accompanying sound signal. Electrical signals, converted from optical images by a camera tube, are transmitted by radio waves or by cable and reconverted into optical images by means of a television tube inside a television set. **2.** Also called: **television set.** a device designed to receive and convert incoming electrical signals into a series of visible images on a screen together with accompanying sound. **3.** the content, etc., of television programmes. **4.** the occupation or profession concerned with any aspect of the broadcasting of television programmes. **5.** (*modifier*) of, relating to, or used in the transmission or reception of video and audio UHF or VHF radio signals: *a television transmitter.* ~Abbrev.: **TV.**

television tube *n.* a cathode-ray tube designed for the reproduction of television pictures. Sometimes shortened to **tube.**

televisual (ˌtɛlɪˈvɪʒʊəl, -zjʊ-) *adj.* relating to or suitable for production on television.

telex (ˈtɛlɛks) *n.* **1.** an international telegraph service in which teleprinters are rented out to subscribers. **2.** a teleprinter used in such a service. **3.** a message transmitted or received by telex. ~*vb.* **4.** to transmit (a message) to (a person, etc.) by telex. [C20: < *tel*(*eprinter*) *ex*(*change*)]

Telidon (ˈtɛlɪˌdɒn) *n. Trademark.* a Canadian interactive viewdata service.

tell[1] (tɛl) *vb.* **telling, told. 1.** (when *tr., may take a clause as object*) to let know or notify. **2.** (*tr.*) to order or instruct. **3.** (when *intr.,* usually foll. by *of*) to give an account or narration (of). **4.** (*tr.*) to communicate by words; utter: *to tell the truth.* **5.** (*tr.*) to make known: *to tell fortunes.* **6.** (*intr.;* often foll. by *of*) to serve as an indication: *her blush told of her embarrassment.* **7.** (*tr.;* used with *can,* etc.; *may take a clause as object*) to discover or discern: *I can tell what is wrong.* **8.** (*tr.;* used with *can,* etc.) to distinguish or discriminate: *he couldn't tell chalk from cheese.* **9.** (*intr.*) to have or produce an impact, effect, or strain: *every step told on his bruised feet.* **10.** (*intr.;* sometimes foll. by *on*) *Inf.* to reveal secrets or gossip (about). **11.** (*tr.*) to assure: *I tell you, I've had enough!* **12.** (*tr.*) to count (votes). **13. tell the time.** to read the time from a clock. **14. you're telling me.** *Sl.* I know that very well. ~See also **tell apart, tell off.** [OE *tellan*] —ˈ**tellable** *adj.*

tell[2] (tɛl) *n.* a large mound resulting from the accumulation of rubbish on a long-settled site, esp. in the Middle East. [C19: < Ar. *tall*]

tell apart *vb.* (*tr., adv.*) to distinguish between.

teller (ˈtɛlə) *n.* **1.** a bank cashier. **2.** a person appointed to count votes. **3.** a person who tells; narrator.

telling (ˈtɛlɪŋ) *adj.* **1.** having a marked effect or impact. **2.** revealing. —ˈ**tellingly** *adv.*

tell off *vb.* (*tr., adv.*) **1.** *Inf.* to reprimand; scold. **2.** to count and select for duty.

telltale (ˈtɛlˌteɪl) *n.* **1.** a person who tells tales about others. **2. a.** an outward indication of something concealed. **b.** (*as modifier*): *a telltale paw mark.* **3.** a device used to monitor a process, machine, etc.

tellurian (tɛˈlʊərɪən) *adj.* **1.** of the earth. ~*n.* **2.** (esp. in science fiction) an inhabitant of the earth. [C19: < L *tellūs* the earth]

telluric[1] (tɛˈlʊərɪk) *adj.* of or originating on or in the earth or soil; terrestrial. [C19: < L *tellūs* the earth]

telluric[2] (tɛˈlʊərɪk) *adj.* of or containing tellurium, esp. in a high valence state. [C20: < TELLUR(IUM) + -IC]

tellurion *or* **tellurian** (tɛˈlʊərɪən) *n.* an instrument that shows how day and night and the seasons result from the earth's rotation on its axis, etc. [C19: < L *tellūs* the earth]

tellurium (tɛˈlʊərɪəm) *n.* a brittle silvery-white nonmetallic element. Symbol: Te; atomic no.: 52; atomic wt.: 127.60. [C19: NL, < L *tellūs* the earth, by analogy with URANIUM]

tellurometer (ˌtɛljʊˈrɒmɪtə) *n. Surveying.* an electronic instrument for measuring distances by the transmission of radio waves. [C20: < L *tellūs* the earth + -METER]

telly (ˈtɛlɪ) *n., pl.* **-lies.** *Inf., chiefly Brit.* short for **television.**

telo- *or before a vowel* **tel-** *combining form.* **1.** complete; final; perfect. **2.** end; at the end. [< Gk *telos* end]

telpherage (ˈtɛlfərɪdʒ) *n.* an overhead transport system in which an electrically driven truck runs along a rail or cable, the load being suspended in a car beneath. Also called: **telpher.** [C19: changed < *telephore,* < TELE- + -PHORE + -AGE]

telson (ˈtɛlsən) *n.* the last segment or an appendage on the last segment of the body of crustaceans and arachnids. [C19: < Gk: a boundary]

Telugu *or* **Telegu** (ˈtɛləˌguː) *n.* **1.** a language of SE India, belonging to the Dravidian family of languages. **2.** (*pl.* **-gus** *or* **-gu**) a member of the people who speak this language. ~*adj.* **3.** of or relating to this people or their language.

temerity (tɪˈmɛrɪtɪ) *n.* rashness or boldness. [C15: < L *temeritās* accident, < *temere* at random] —**temerarious** (ˌtɛməˈrɛərɪəs) *adj.*

temp (tɛmp) *Inf.* ~*n.* **1.** a person, esp. a typist or other office worker, employed on a temporary basis. ~*vb.* (*intr.*) **2.** to work as a temp.

temp. *abbrev. for:* **1.** temperature. **2.** temporary. **3.** tempore. [L: in the time of]

temper (ˈtɛmpə) *n.* **1.** a frame of mind; mood or humour. **2.** a sudden outburst of anger. **3.** a tendency to exhibit anger; irritability. **4.** a mental condition of moderation and calm (esp. in **keep one's temper** *or* **lose one's temper**). **5.** the degree of hardness, elasticity, etc., of a metal. ~*vb.* (*tr.*) **6.** to make more acceptable or suitable by adding something else; moderate: *he tempered his criticism with sympathy.* **7.** to strengthen or toughen (a metal), as by heating and quenching. **8.** *Music.* **a.** to adjust the frequency differences between the notes of a scale on (a keyboard instrument). **b.** to make such an adjustment to the pitches of notes in (a scale). [OE *temprian* to mingle, < L *temperāre* to mix, prob. < *tempus* time] —ˈ**temperable** *adj.* —ˈ**temperer** *n.*

tempera (ˈtɛmpərə) *n.* **1.** a painting medium for powdered pigments, consisting usually of egg yolk and water. **2. a.** any emulsion used as a painting medium, with casein, glue, wax, etc., as a base. **b.** the paint made from this. **3.** the technique of painting with tempera. [C19: < It. *pingere a tempera* painting in tempera, < *temperare* to mingle; see TEMPER]

temperament (ˈtɛmpərəmənt) *n.* **1.** a person's character, disposition, and tendencies. **2.** excitability, moodiness, or anger. **3.** the characteristic way an individual behaves, esp. towards other people. **4. a.** an adjustment made to the frequency differences between notes on a keyboard instrument to allow modulation to other keys. **b.** any of several systems of such adjustment, esp. **equal temperament,** a system giving a scale based on an octave divided into twelve exactly equal semitones. **5.** *Obs.* the characteristic way an individual behaves, viewed as the result of the influence of the four humours. [C15: < L *temperāmentum* a mixing in proportion, < *temperāre* to TEMPER]

temperamental (ˌtɛmpərəˈmɛntᵊl) *adj.* **1.** easily upset or irritated; excitable. **2.** of or caused by temperament. **3.** *Inf.* working erratically and inconsistently; unreliable. —ˌ**temperaˈmentally** *adv.*

temperance (ˈtɛmpərəns) *n.* **1.** restraint or moderation, esp. in yielding to one's appetites or desires. **2.** abstinence from alcoholic drink. [C14: < L *temperantia,* < *temperāre* to regulate]

temperate (ˈtɛmpərɪt) *adj.* **1.** having a climate intermediate between tropical and polar; moderate or mild in temperature. **2.** mild in quality or character; exhibiting temperance. [C14: < L *temperātus*] —ˈ**temperately** *adv.* —ˈ**temperateness** *n.*

Temperate Zone *n.* those parts of the earth's surface lying between the Arctic Circle and the tropic of Cancer and between the Antarctic Circle and the tropic of Capricorn.

temperature (ˈtɛmprɪtʃə) *n.* **1.** the degree of hotness of a body, substance, or medium, esp. as measured on a scale that has one or more fixed reference points. **2.** *Inf.* a body temperature in excess of the normal. [C16 (orig.: a mingling): < L *temperātūra* proportion, < *temperāre* to TEMPER]

temperature gradient *n.* the rate of change in temperature in a given direction.

temperature-humidity index *n.* an index of the effect on human comfort of temperature and humidity levels, 65 being the highest comfortable level.

tempered (ˈtɛmpəd) *adj.* **1.** *Music.* adjusted in accordance with a system of temperament. **2.** (*in combination*) having a temper or temperament as specified: *ill-tempered.*

tempest (ˈtɛmpɪst) *n.* **1.** *Chiefly literary.* a violent wind or storm. **2.** a violent commotion, uproar, or disturbance. [C13: < OF *tempeste,* < L *tempestās* storm, < *tempus* time]

tempestuous (tɛmˈpɛstjʊəs) *adj.* **1.** of or relating to a tempest. **2.** violent or stormy. —**temˈpestuously** *adv.* —**temˈpestuousness** *n.*

tempi (ˈtɛmpiː) *n.* (in musical senses) the plural of **tempo.**

Templar (ˈtɛmplə) *n.* **1.** a member of a military religious order (**Knights of the Temple of Solomon**) founded by Crusaders in Jerusalem around 1118; suppressed in 1312. **2.** (*sometimes not cap.*) *Brit.* a lawyer who has chambers in the Temple in London. [C13: < Med. L *templārius* of the temple, < L *templum* temple; first applied to the knightly order because their house was near the site of the Temple of Solomon]

template *or* **templet** (ˈtɛmplɪt) *n.* **1.** a gauge or pattern, cut out in wood or metal, used in woodwork, etc., to help shape something accurately. **2.** a pattern cut out in card or plastic, used to reproduce shapes. **3.** a short beam that is used to spread a load, as over a doorway. **4.** *Biochem.* the molecular structure of a compound that serves as a pattern for the production of another compound. [C17 *templet* (later spelling infl. by PLATE), prob. < F, dim. of TEMPLE[2]]

temple[1] (ˈtɛmpᵊl) *n.* **1.** a building or place dedicated to the worship of a deity or deities. **2.** a Mormon church. **3.** *U.S.* another name for a **synagogue.** **4.** a Christian church. **5.** any place or object regarded as a shrine where God makes himself present. **6.** a building regarded as the focus of an activity, interest, or practice: *a temple of the arts.* [OE *tempel,* < L *templum*]

temple[2] (ˈtɛmpᵊl) *n.* the region on each side of the head in front of the ear and above the cheek bone. [C14: < OF *temple,* < L *tempora* the temples, < *tempus* temple of the head]

temple[3] (ˈtɛmpᵊl) *n.* the part of a loom that keeps the cloth being woven stretched to the correct width. [C15: < F, < L *templum* a small timber]

Temple (ˈtɛmpᵊl) *n.* **1.** a building in London that belonged to the Templars: it now houses two law societies. **2.** any of three buildings erected by the Jews in ancient Jerusalem for the worship of Jehovah.

tempo (ˈtɛmpəʊ) *n., pl.* **-pos** *or* **-pi** (-piː). **1.** the speed at which a piece of music is meant to be played. **2.** rate or pace. [C18: < It., < L *tempus* time]

temporal[1] (ˈtɛmpərəl) *adj.* **1.** of or relating to time. **2.** of secular as opposed to spiritual or religious affairs. **3.** lasting for a relatively short time. **4.** *Grammar.* of or relating to tense or the linguistic expression of time. [C14: < L *temporālis,* < *tempus* time] —ˈ**temporally** *adv.*

temporal[2] (ˈtɛmpərəl) *adj. Anat.* of or near the temple or temples. [C16: < LL *temporālis* belonging to the temples; see TEMPLE[2]]

temporal bone *n.* either of two compound bones forming the sides of the skull.

temporality (ˌtɛmpəˈrælɪtɪ) *n., pl.* **-ties. 1.** the state or quality of being temporal. **2.** something temporal. **3.** (*often pl.*) a secular possession or revenue belonging to a Church.

temporal lobe *n.* the laterally protruding portion of each cerebral hemisphere, situated below the parietal lobe and associated with sound perception and interpretation.

temporary (ˈtɛmpərərɪ) *adj.* **1.** not permanent; provisional. **2.** lasting only a short time. ~*n., pl.* **-raries. 3.** a person employed on a temporary basis. [C16: < L *temporārius,* < *tempus* time] —ˈ**temporarily** *adv.* —ˈ**temporariness** *n.*

temporize *or* **-ise** (ˈtɛmpəˌraɪz) *vb.* (*intr.*) **1.** to delay, act evasively, or protract a negotiation, etc., esp. in order to gain time or effect a compromise. **2.** to adapt oneself to the circumstances, as by temporary or apparent agreement. [C16: < F *temporiser,* < Med. L *temporizāre,* < L *tempus* time] —ˌ**temporiˈzation** *or* **-iˈsation** *n.* —ˈ**tempoˌrizer** *or* **-iser** *n.*

tempt (tɛmpt) *vb.* (*tr.*) **1.** to entice to do something, esp. something morally wrong or unwise. **2.** to allure or attract. **3.** to give rise to a desire in (someone) to do something; dispose. **4.** to risk provoking (esp. in **tempt fate**). [C13: < OF *tempter,* < L *temptāre* to test] —ˈ**temptable** *adj.* —ˈ**tempter** *n.* —ˈ**temptress** *fem. n.*

temptation (tɛmpˈteɪʃən) *n.* **1.** the act of tempting or the state of being tempted. **2.** a person or thing that tempts.

tempting (ˈtɛmptɪŋ) *adj.* attractive or inviting: *a tempting meal.* —ˈ**temptingly** *adv.*

tempus fugit *Latin.* (ˈtɛmpəs ˈfjuːdʒɪt) time flies.

ten (tɛn) *n.* **1.** the cardinal number that is the sum of nine and one. It is the base of the decimal number system and the base of the common logarithm. **2.** a numeral, 10, X, etc., representing this number. **3.** something representing or consisting of ten units. **4.** Also called: **ten o'clock.** ten hours after noon or midnight. ~*determiner.* **5.** amounting to ten. ~Related adj.: **decimal.** [OE *tēn*]

ten. *Music. abbrev. for:* **1.** tenor. **2.** tenuto.

tenable (ˈtɛnəbᵊl) *adj.* able to be upheld, believed, maintained, or defended. [C16: < OF, < *tenir* to hold, < L *tenēre*] —ˌ**tenaˈbility** *or* ˈ**tenableness** *n.* —ˈ**tenably** *adv.*

tenace (ˈtɛneɪs) *n. Bridge, whist.* a holding of two nonconsecutive high cards of a suit, such as the ace and queen. [C17: < F, < Sp. *tenaza* forceps, ult. < L *tenāx* holding fast, < *tenēre* to hold]

tenacious (tɪˈneɪʃəs) *adj.* **1.** holding firmly: *a tenacious grip.* **2.** retentive: *a tenacious memory.* **3.** stubborn or persistent. **4.** holding together firmly; cohesive. **5.** tending to stick or adhere. [C16: < L *tenāx,* < *tenēre* to hold] —**teˈnaciously** *adv.* —**teˈnaciousness** *or* **tenacity** (tɪˈnæsɪtɪ) *n.*

tenaculum (tɪˈnækjʊləm) *n., pl.* **-la** (-lə). a hooked surgical instrument for grasping and holding parts. [C17: < LL, < L *tenēre* to hold]

tenancy (ˈtɛnənsɪ) *n., pl.* **-cies. 1.** the temporary possession or holding by a tenant of lands or property owned by another. **2.** the period of holding or occupying such property. **3.** the period of holding office, a position, etc.

tenant (ˈtɛnənt) *n.* **1.** a person who holds, occupies, or possesses land or property, esp. from a landlord. **2.** a person who has the use of a house, etc., subject to the payment of rent. **3.** any holder or occupant. ~*vb.* **4.** (*tr.*) to hold as a tenant. [C14: < OF, lit.: (one who is) holding, < *tenir* to hold, < L *tenēre*] —ˈ**tenantable** *adj.* —ˈ**tenantless** *adj.*

tenant farmer *n.* a person who farms land rented from another, the rent usually taking the form of crops or livestock.

tenantry (ˈtɛnəntrɪ) *n.* **1.** tenants collectively. **2.** the status or condition of being a tenant.

tench (tɛntʃ) *n.* a European freshwater game fish of the carp family. [C14: < OF *tenche,* < LL *tinca*]

Ten Commandments *pl. n.* **the.** *Old Testament.* the commandments summarizing the basic obligations of man towards God and his fellow men, delivered to Moses on Mount Sinai engraved on two tables of stone (Exodus 20:1–17).

tend[1] (tɛnd) *vb.* (when *intr.,* usually foll. by *to* or *towards*) **1.** (when *tr., takes an infinitive*) to have a general disposition (to do something); be inclined: *children tend to prefer sweets to meat.* **2.** (*intr.*) to have or be an influence (towards a specific result). **3.** (*intr.*) to go or move (in a particular direction): *to tend to the south.* [C14: < OF *tendre,* < L *tendere* to stretch]

tend[2] (tɛnd) *vb.* **1.** (*tr.*) to care for. **2.** (when *intr.,* often foll. by *on* or *to*) to attend (to). **3.** (*tr.*) to handle or control. **4.** (*intr.;* often foll. by *to*) *Inf., chiefly U.S. & Canad.* to pay attention. [C14: var. of ATTEND]

tendency (ˈtɛndənsɪ) *n., pl.* **-cies. 1.** (often foll. by *to*) an inclination, predisposition, propensity, or leaning. **2.** the general course, purport, or drift of something, esp. a written work. [C17: < Med. L *tendentia,* < L *tendere* to TEND[1]]

tendentious *or* **tendencious** (tɛnˈdɛnʃəs) *adj.* having or showing an intentional tendency or bias, esp. a controversial one. [C20: < TENDENCY] —**tenˈdentiously** *or* **tenˈdenciously** *adv.* —**tenˈdentiousness** *or* **tenˈdenciousness** *n.*

tender[1] (ˈtɛndə) *adj.* **1.** easily broken, cut, or crushed; soft. **2.** easily damaged; vulnerable or sensitive: *at a tender age.* **3.** having or expressing warm feelings. **4.** kind or sympathetic: *a tender heart.* **5.** arousing warm feelings; touching. **6.** gentle and delicate: *a tender breeze.* **7.** requiring care in handling: *a tender question.* **8.** painful or sore. **9.** sensitive to moral or spiritual feelings. **10.** (*postpositive;* foll. by *of*) protective: *tender of one's emotions.* [C13: < OF *tendre,* < L *tener* delicate] —ˈ**tenderly** *adv.* —ˈ**tenderness** *n.*

tender[2] (ˈtɛndə) *vb.* **1.** (*tr.*) to give, present, or offer: *to tender a bid.* **2.** (*intr.;* foll. by *for*) to make a formal offer or estimate (for a job or contract). **3.** (*tr.*) *Law.* to offer (money or goods) in settlement of a debt or claim. ~*n.* **4.** the act or an instance of tendering; offer. **5.** a formal offer to supply specified goods or services at a stated cost or rate. **6.** something, esp. money, used as an official medium of payment: *legal tender.* [C16: < Anglo-F *tendre,* < L *tendere* to extend] —ˈ**tenderer** *n.*

tender[3] (ˈtɛndə) *n.* **1.** a small boat towed or carried by a ship. **2.** a vehicle drawn behind a steam locomotive to carry the fuel and water. **3.** a person who tends. [C15: var. of *attender*]

tenderfoot (ˈtɛndəˌfʊt) *n., pl.* **-foots** *or* **-feet. 1.** a newcomer, esp. to the mines or ranches of the southwestern U.S. **2.** (formerly) a beginner in the Scouts or Guides.

tenderhearted (ˌtɛndəˈhɑːtɪd) *adj.* having a compassionate, kindly, or sensitive disposition.

tenderize *or* **-ise** (ˈtɛndəˌraɪz) *vb.* (*tr.*) to make (meat) tender, as by pounding it or adding a substance to break down the fibres. —ˌ**tenderiˈzation** *or* **-iˈsation** *n.* —ˈ**tenderˌizer** *or* **-ˌiser** *n.*

tenderloin (ˈtɛndəˌlɔɪn) *n.* a tender cut of pork or other meat from between the sirloin and ribs.

tendon (ˈtɛndən) *n.* a cord or band of tough tissue that attaches a muscle to a bone or some other part; sinew. [C16: < Med. L *tendō*, < L *tendere* to stretch]

tendril (ˈtɛndrɪl) *n.* a threadlike leaf or stem that attaches climbing plants to a support by twining or adhering. [C16: ? < OF *tendron* tendril (confused with OF *tendron* bud), < Med. L *tendō* TENDON]

tenebrism (ˈtɛnəˌbrɪzəm) *n.* (*sometimes cap.*) a school, style, or method of painting, adopted chiefly by 17th-century Spanish and Neapolitan painters, characterized by large areas of dark colours, usually relieved with a shaft of light. —ˈ**tenebrist** *n., adj.*

tenebrous (ˈtɛnəbrəs) *or* **tenebrious** (təˈnɛbrɪəs) *adj.* gloomy, shadowy, or dark. [C15: < L *tenebrōsus* < *tenebrae* darkness]

tenement (ˈtɛnəmənt) *n.* **1.** Also called: **tenement building.** a large building divided into rooms or flats. **2.** a dwelling place or residence. **3.** *Chiefly Brit.* a room or flat for rent. **4.** *Property law.* any form of permanent property, such as land, dwellings, offices, etc. [C14: < Med. L *tenementum*, < L *tenēre* to hold] —**tenemental** (ˌtɛnəˈmɛntˀl) *adj.*

tenesmus (tɪˈnɛzməs) *n.* an ineffective painful straining to empty the bowels or bladder. [C16: < Med. L, < L *tēnesmos*, < Gk, < *teinein* to strain] —**teˈnesmic** *adj.*

tenet (ˈtɛnɪt, ˈtiːnɪt) *n.* a belief, opinion, or dogma. [C17: < L, lit.: he (it) holds, < *tenēre* to hold]

tenfold (ˈtɛnˌfəʊld) *adj.* **1.** equal to or having 10 times as many or as much. **2.** composed of 10 parts. ~*adv.* **3.** by or up to 10 times as many or as much.

ten-gallon hat *n.* (in the U.S.) a cowboy's broad-brimmed felt hat with a very high crown.

tenner (ˈtɛnə) *n. Inf.* **1.** *Brit.* **a.** a ten-pound note. **b.** the sum of ten pounds. **2.** *U.S.* a ten-dollar bill.

tennis (ˈtɛnɪs) *n.* **a.** a racket game played between two players or pairs of players who hit a ball to and fro over a net on a rectangular court of grass, asphalt, clay, etc. See also **lawn tennis, real tennis, table tennis.** **b.** (*as modifier*): *tennis court; tennis racket.* [C14: prob. < Anglo-F *tenetz* hold (imperative), < OF *tenir* to hold, < L *tenēre*]

tennis elbow *n.* inflammation of the elbow caused by exertion in playing tennis, etc.

tennis shoe *n.* a rubber-soled canvas shoe tied with laces.

Tennysonian (ˌtɛnɪˈsəʊnɪən) *adj.* of or in the style of Alfred, Lord Tennyson (1809-92), English poet.

teno- *or before a vowel* **ten-** *combining form.* tendon: *tenosynovitis.* [< Gk *tenōn*]

tenon (ˈtɛnən) *n.* **1.** the projecting end of a piece of wood formed to fit into a corresponding mortise in another piece. ~*vb.* (*tr.*) **2.** to form a tenon on (a piece of wood). **3.** to join with a tenon and mortise. [C15: < OF, < *tenir* to hold, < L *tenēre*] —ˈ**tenoner** *n.*

tenon saw *n.* a small fine-toothed saw with a strong back, used esp. for cutting tenons.

tenor (ˈtɛnə) *n.* **1.** *Music.* **a.** the male voice intermediate between alto and baritone. **b.** a singer with such a voice. **c.** a saxophone, horn, etc., intermediate between the alto and baritone or bass. **2.** general drift of thought; purpose. **3.** a settled course of progress. **4.** *Arch.* general tendency. **5.** *Law.* **a.** the exact words of a deed, etc. **b.** an exact copy. [C13 (orig.: general sense): < OF *tenour*, < L *tenor* a holding to a course, < *tenēre* to hold; musical sense via It. *tenore*, referring to the voice part that was continuous, that is, to which the melody was assigned]

tenor clef *n.* the clef that establishes middle C as being on the fourth line of the staff.

tenorrhaphy (tɪˈnɒrəfɪ) *n., pl.* **-phies.** *Surgery.* the union of torn or divided tendons by means of sutures. [C19: < TENO- + Gk *raphē* a sewing]

tenosynovitis (ˈtɛnəʊˌsaɪnəʊˈvaɪtɪs) *n.* painful swelling and inflammation of tendons, usually of the wrist, often the result of repetitive movements such as typing.

tenotomy (təˈnɒtəmɪ) *n., pl.* **-mies.** surgical incision into a tendon. —**teˈnotomist** *n.*

tenpin bowling (ˈtɛnˌpɪn) *n.* a bowling game in which bowls are rolled down a lane to knock over the ten target pins. Also called (esp. U.S. and Canad.): **tenpins.**

tenrec (ˈtɛnrɛk) *n.* any of a family of small mammals of Madagascar resembling hedgehogs or shrews. [C18: via F < Malagasy *trandraka*]

tense[1] (tɛns) *adj.* **1.** stretched or stressed tightly; taut or rigid. **2.** under mental or emotional strain. **3.** producing mental or emotional strain: *a tense day.* **4.** *Phonetics.* pronounced with considerable muscular effort, as the vowel (iː) *in "beam".* ~*vb.* (often foll. by *up*) **5.** to make or become tense. [C17: < L *tensus* taut, < *tendere* to stretch] —ˈ**tensely** *adv.* —ˈ**tenseness** *n.*

tense[2] (tɛns) *n. Grammar.* a category of the verb or verbal inflections, such as present, past, and future, that expresses the temporal relations between what is reported in a sentence and the time of its utterance. [C14: < OF *tens* time, < L *tempus*] —ˈ**tenseless** *adj.*

tense logic *n. Logic.* the study of temporal relations between propositions, usually pursued by considering the logical properties of symbols representing the tenses of natural languages.

tensile (ˈtɛnsaɪl) *adj.* **1.** of or relating to tension. **2.** sufficiently ductile to be stretched or drawn out. [C17: < NL *tensilis*, < L *tendere* to stretch] —**tensility** (tɛnˈsɪlɪtɪ) *or* ˈ**tensileness** *n.*

tensile strength *n.* a measure of the ability of a material to withstand a longitudinal stress, expressed as the greatest stress that the material can stand without breaking.

tensimeter (tɛnˈsɪmɪtə) *n.* a device that measures differences in vapour pressures. [C20: < TENSI(ON) + -METER]

tensiometer (ˌtɛnsɪˈɒmɪtə) *n.* **1.** an instrument for measuring the tensile strength of a wire, beam, etc. **2.** an instrument used to compare the vapour pressures of two liquids. **3.** an instrument for measuring the surface tension of a liquid. **4.** an instrument for measuring the moisture content of soil.

tension (ˈtɛnʃən) *n.* **1.** the act of stretching or the state or degree of being stretched. **2.** mental or emotional strain; stress. **3.** a situation or condition of hostility, suspense, or uneasiness. **4.** *Physics.* a force that tends to produce an elongation of a body or structure. **5.** *Physics.* voltage, electromotive force, or potential difference. **6.** a device for regulating the tension in a part, string, thread, etc., as in a sewing machine. **7.** the degree of tightness or looseness with which a person knits. [C16: < L *tensiō*, < *tendere* to strain] —ˈ**tensional** *adj.* —ˈ**tensionless** *adj.*

tensor (ˈtɛnsə, -sɔː) *n.* **1.** *Anat.* any muscle that can cause a part to become firm or tense. **2.** *Maths.* a set of components, functions of the coordinates of any point in space, that transform linearly between coordinate systems. [C18: < NL, lit.: a stretcher] —**tensorial** (tɛnˈsɔːrɪəl) *adj.*

tent (tɛnt) *n.* **1.** a portable shelter of canvas, plastic, etc., supported on poles and fastened to the ground by pegs and ropes. **2.** something resembling this in function or shape. ~*vb.* **3.** (*intr.*) to camp in a tent. **4.** (*tr.*) to cover with or as if with a tent or tents. **5.** (*tr.*) to provide with a tent as shelter. [C13: < OF *tente*, < L *tentōrium* something stretched out, < *tendere* to stretch] —ˈ**tentage** *n.* —ˈ**tented** *adj.*

tentacle (ˈtɛntəkˀl) *n.* **1.** any of various elongated flexible organs that occur near the mouth in many invertebrates and are used for feeding, grasping, etc. **2.** any of the hairs on the leaf of an insectivorous plant that are used to capture prey. [C18: < NL *tentāculum,* < L *tentāre,* var. of *temptāre* to feel] —**ˈtentacled** *adj.* —**tentacular** (tɛnˈtækjʊlə) *adj.*

tentation (tɛnˈteɪʃən) *n.* a method of achieving the correct adjustment of a mechanical device by a series of trials. [C14: < L *tentātiō,* variant of *temptātiō* TEMPTATION]

tentative (ˈtɛntətɪv) *adj.* **1.** provisional or experimental. **2.** hesitant, uncertain, or cautious. [C16: < Med. L *tentātīvus,* < L *tentāre* to test] —**ˈtentatively** *adv.* —**ˈtentativeness** *n.*

tenter (ˈtɛntə) *n.* **1.** a frame on which cloth is stretched in order that it may retain its shape while drying. **2.** a person who stretches cloth on a tenter. ~*vb.* **3.** (*tr.*) to stretch (cloth) on a tenter. [C14: < Med. L *tentōrium,* < L *tentus* stretched, < *tendere* to stretch]

tenterhook (ˈtɛntəˌhʊk) *n.* **1.** one of a series of hooks used to hold cloth on a tenter. **2. on tenterhooks.** in a state of tension or suspense.

tenth (tɛnθ) *adj.* **1.** (*usually prenominal*) **a.** coming after the ninth in numbering, position, etc.; being the ordinal number of *ten:* often written 10th. **b.** (*as n.*)*: see you on the tenth.* ~*n.* **2. a.** one of 10 equal parts of something. **b.** (*as modifier*)*: a tenth part.* **3.** the fraction equal to one divided by ten (1/10). ~*adv.* **4.** Also: **tenthly.** after the ninth person, position, event, etc. [C12 *tenthe,* < OE *tēotha*]

tent stitch *n.* another term for **petit point.** [C17: <?]

tenuis (ˈtɛnjʊɪs) *n., pl.* **tenues** (ˈtɛnjʊˌiːz). (in classical Greek) a voiceless stop (k, p, t). [C17: < L: thin]

tenuous (ˈtɛnjʊəs) *adj.* **1.** insignificant or flimsy: *a tenuous argument.* **2.** slim, fine, or delicate: *a tenuous thread.* **3.** diluted or rarefied in consistency or density: *a tenuous fluid.* [C16: < L *tenuis*] —**tenuity** (tɛˈnjuːɪtɪ) *or* **ˈtenuousness** *n.* —**ˈtenuously** *adv.*

tenure (ˈtɛnjʊə, ˈtɛnjə) *n.* **1.** the possession or holding of an office or position. **2.** the length of time an office, position, etc., lasts. **3.** *U.S. & Canad.* the improved security status of a person after having been in the employ of the same company or institution for a specified period. **4. a.** the holding of property, esp. realty, in return for services rendered, etc. **b.** the duration of such holding. [C15: < OF, < Med. L *tenitūra,* ult. < L *tenēre* to hold] —**tenˈurial** *adj.*

tenuto (tɪˈnjuːtəʊ) *adj., adv. Music.* (of a note) to be held for or beyond its full time value. [< It., lit.: held, < *tenere* to hold, < L *tenēre*]

teocalli (ˌtiːəʊˈkælɪ) *n., pl.* **-lis.** any of various truncated pyramids built by the Aztecs as bases for their temples. [C17: < Nahuatl, < *teotl* god + *calli* house]

tepee *or* **teepee** (ˈtiːpiː) *n.* a cone-shaped tent of animal skins used by American Indians. [C19: < Siouan *tīpī,* < *ti* to dwell + *pi* used for]

tephra (ˈtɛfrə) *n. Chiefly U.S.* solid matter ejected during a volcanic eruption. [C20: Gk, lit.: ashes]

tepid (ˈtɛpɪd) *adj.* **1.** slightly warm; lukewarm. **2.** relatively unenthusiastic or apathetic. [C14: < L *tepidus,* < *tepēre* to be lukewarm] —**tepidity** (tɛˈpɪdɪtɪ) *or* **ˈtepidness** *n.* —**ˈtepidly** *adv.*

tequila (tɪˈkiːlə) *n.* **1.** a spirit that is distilled in Mexico from an agave plant and forms the basis of many mixed drinks. **2.** the plant from which this drink is made. [C19: < Mexican Sp., < *Tequila,* district in Mexico]

ter. *abbrev. for:* **1.** terrace. **2.** territory.

ter- *combining form.* three, third, or three times. [< L *ter* thrice]

tera- *prefix.* denoting 10^{12}: *terameter.* Symbol: T [< Gk *teras* monster]

terat- *or* **terato-** *combining form.* indicating a monster or something abnormal: *teratism.* [< Gk *terat-, teras* monster, prodigy]

teratism (ˈtɛrəˌtɪzəm) *n.* a malformed animal or human, esp. in the fetal stage; monster.

teratogenic (ˌtɛrətəʊˈdʒɛnɪk) *adj.* producing malformation in a fetus.

teratoid (ˈtɛrəˌtɔɪd) *adj. Biol.* resembling a monster.

teratology (ˌtɛrəˈtɒlədʒɪ) *n.* **1.** the branch of biology concerned with the structure, development, etc., of monsters. **2.** a collection of tales about mythical or fantastic creatures, monsters, etc. —**ˌteraˈtologist** *n.*

teratoma (ˌtɛrəˈtəʊmə) *n., pl.* **mata** (-mətə) *or* **mas.** a tumour composed of tissue foreign to the site of growth.

terbium (ˈtɜːbɪəm) *n.* a soft malleable silvery-grey element of the lanthanide series of metals. Symbol: Tb; atomic no.: 65; atomic wt.: 158.925. [C19: < NL, after *Ytterby,* Sweden, village where discovered] —**ˈterbic** *adj.*

terbium metal *n. Chem.* any of a group of related lanthanides, including terbium, europium, and gadolinium.

terce (tɜːs) *or* **tierce** *n. Chiefly R.C. Church.* the third of the seven canonical hours, originally fixed at the third hour of the day, about 9 a.m. [C14: var. of TIERCE]

tercel (ˈtɜːsᵊl) *or* **tiercel** *n.* a male falcon or hawk, esp. as used in falconry. [C14: < OF, < Vulgar L *tertiolus* (unattested), < L *tertius* third, < the tradition that only one egg in three hatched a male chick]

tercentenary (ˌtɜːsɛnˈtiːnərɪ) *or* **tercentennial** *adj.* **1.** of a period of 300 years. **2.** of a 300th anniversary. ~*n., pl.* **-tenaries** *or* **-tennials. 3.** an anniversary of 300 years.

tercet (ˈtɜːsɪt, tɜːˈsɛt) *n.* a group of three lines of verse that rhyme together or are connected by rhyme with adjacent groups of three lines. [C16: < F, < It. *terzetto,* dim. of *terzo* third, < L *tertius*]

terebene (ˈtɛrəˌbiːn) *n.* a mixture of hydrocarbons prepared from oil of turpentine and sulphuric acid, used to make paints and varnishes and medicinally as an expectorant and antiseptic. [C19: < TEREB(INTH) + -ENE]

terebinth (ˈtɛrɪbɪnθ) *n.* a small Mediterranean tree that yields a turpentine. [C14: < L *terebinthus,* < Gk *terebinthos* turpentine tree]

terebinthine (ˌtɛrɪˈbɪnθaɪn) *adj.* **1.** of or relating to terebinth or related plants. **2.** of, consisting of, or resembling turpentine.

teredo (tɛˈriːdəʊ) *n., pl.* **-dos** *or* **-dines** (-dɪˌniːz). any of a genus of marine bivalve molluscs. See **shipworm.** [C17: via L < Gk *terēdōn* wood-boring worm]

terete (ˈtɛriːt) *adj.* (esp. of plant parts) cylindrical and tapering. [C17: < L *teres* smooth, < *terere* to rub]

tergiversate (ˈtɜːdʒɪvəˌseɪt) *vb.* (*intr.*) **1.** to change sides or loyalties. **2.** to be evasive or ambiguous. [C17: < L *tergiversārī* to turn one's back, < *tergum* back + *vertere* to turn] —**ˌtergiverˈsation** *n.* —**ˈtergiverˌsator** *n.*

tergum (ˈtɜːgəm) *n., pl.* **-ga** (-gə). a cuticular plate covering the dorsal surface of a body segment of an arthropod. [C19: < L: the back] —**ˈtergal** *adj.*

term (tɜːm) *n.* **1.** a name, expression, or word used for some particular thing, esp. in a specialized field of knowledge: *a medical term.* **2.** any word or expression. **3.** a limited period of time: *a prison term.* **4.** any of the divisions of the academic year during which a school, college, etc., is in session. **5.** a point in time determined for an event or for the end of a period. **6.** the period at which childbirth is imminent. **7.** *Law.* **a.** an estate or interest in land limited to run for a specified period. **b.** the duration of an estate, etc. **c.** a period of time during which sessions of courts of law are held. **d.** time allowed to a debtor to settle. **8.** *Maths.* any distinct quantity making up a fraction or proportion, or contained in a polynominal, sequence, series, etc. **9.** *Logic.* **a.** the word or phrase that forms either the subject or predicate of a proposition. **b.** a name or variable, as opposed to a predicate. **c.** any of the three subjects or predicates occurring in a syllogism. **10.** *Archit.* a sculptured post, esp. one in the form of an armless bust or an animal on the top of a square pillar. ~*vb.* **11.** (*tr.*) to designate; call: *he was termed a thief.* ~See also **terms.**

[C13: < OF *terme*, < L *terminus* end] —ˈ**termly** *adj., adv.*

termagant (ˈtɜːməgənt) *n. Rare.* a shrewish woman; scold. [C13: < earlier *Tervagaunt*, < OF *Tervagan*, < It. *Trivigante;* after an arrogant character in medieval mystery plays who was supposed to be a Muslim deity]

-termer *n.* (*in combination*) a person serving a specified length of time in prison: *a short-termer.*

terminable (ˈtɜːmɪnəbᵊl) *adj.* **1.** able to be terminated. **2.** terminating after a specific period or event. —ˌ**terminaˈbility** *or* ˈ**terminableness** *n.* —ˈ**terminably** *adv.*

terminal (ˈtɜːmɪnᵊl) *adj.* **1.** of, being, or situated at an end, terminus, or boundary. **2.** of or occurring after or in a term: *terminal examinations.* **3.** (of a disease) terminating in death. **4.** *Inf.* extreme: *terminal boredom.* **5.** of or relating to the storage or delivery of freight at a warehouse. ~*n.* **6.** a terminating point, part, or place. **7. a.** a point at which current enters or leaves an electrical device, such as a battery or a circuit. **b.** a conductor by which current enters or leaves at such a point. **8.** *Computers.* a device having input/output links with a computer. **9.** *Archit.* **a.** an ornamental carving at the end of a structure. **b.** another name for **term** (sense 10). **10. a.** a point or station at the end of the line of a railway or at an airport, serving as an important access point for passengers or freight. **b.** a less common name for **terminus** (sense 2). **11.** a reception and departure building at the terminus of a bus, sea, or air transport route. **11.** a site where raw material is unloaded and processed, esp. an onshore installation designed to receive offshore oil or gas. [C15: < L *terminālis*, < *terminus* end] —ˈ**terminally** *adv.*

terminal velocity *n.* **1.** the constant maximum velocity reached by a body falling under gravity through a fluid, esp. the atmosphere. **2.** the velocity of a missile or projectile when it reaches its target. **3.** the maximum velocity attained by a rocket, missile, or shell flying in a parabolic flight path. **4.** the maximum velocity that an aircraft can attain.

terminate (ˈtɜːmɪˌneɪt) *vb.* (when *intr.*, often foll. by *in* or *with*) to form, be, or put an end (to); conclude. [C16: < L *terminātus* limited, < *termināre* to set boundaries, < *terminus* end] —ˈ**terminative** *adj.* —ˈ**termiˌnator** *n.*

termination (ˌtɜːmɪˈneɪʃən) *n.* **1.** the act of terminating or the state of being terminated. **2.** something that terminates. **3.** a final result.

terminology (ˌtɜːmɪˈnɒlədʒɪ) *n., pl.* **-gies. 1.** the body of specialized words relating to a particular subject. **2.** the study of terms. [C19: < Med. L *terminus* term < L: end] —**terminological** (ˌtɜːmɪnəˈlɒdʒɪkᵊl) *adj.* —ˌ**termiˈnologist** *n.*

term insurance *n.* life assurance, usually low in cost and offering no cash value, that provides for the payment of a specified sum of money only if the insured dies within a stipulated time.

terminus (ˈtɜːmɪnəs) *n., pl.* **-ni** (-naɪ) *or* **-nuses. 1.** the last or final part or point. **2.** either end of a railway, bus route, etc., or a station or town at such a point. **3.** a goal aimed for. **4.** a boundary or boundary marker. **5.** *Archit.* another name for **term** (sense 10). [C16: < L: end]

terminus ad quem *Latin.* (ˈtɜːmɪˌnʊs æd ˈkwɛm) *n.* the aim or terminal point. [lit.: the end to which]

terminus a quo *Latin.* (ˈtɜːmɪˌnʊs ɑː ˈkwəʊ) *n.* the starting point; beginning. [lit.: the end from which]

termitarium (ˌtɜːmɪˈtɛərɪəm) *n., pl.* **-ia** (-ɪə). the nest of a termite colony. [C20: < TERMITE + -ARIUM]

termite (ˈtɜːmaɪt) *n.* any of an order of whitish antlike social insects of warm and tropical regions. Some species feed on wood, causing damage to buildings, trees, etc. [C18: < NL *termitēs* white ants, pl. of *termes*, < L: a woodworm] —**termitic** (tɜːˈmɪtɪk) *adj.*

termless (ˈtɜːmlɪs) *adj.* **1.** without limit or boundary. **2.** unconditional. **3.** an archaic word for **indescribable.**

termor *or* **termer** (ˈtɜːmə) *n. Property law.* a person who holds an estate for a term of years or until he dies.

terms (tɜːmz) *pl. n.* **1.** (usually specified prenominally) the actual language or mode of presentation used: *he described the project in loose terms.* **2.** conditions of an agreement. **3.** a sum of money paid for a service. **4.** (usually preceded by *on*) mutual relationship or standing: *they are on affectionate terms.* **5. bring to terms.** to cause to agree or submit. **6. come to terms.** to reach acceptance or agreement. **7. in terms of.** as expressed by; regarding: *in terms of money he was no better off.*

terms of trade *pl. n. Economics, Brit.* the ratio of export prices to import prices.

tern (tɜːn) *n.* any of several aquatic birds related to the gulls, having a forked tail, long narrow wings, and a typically black-and-white plumage. [C18: < ON *therna*]

ternary (ˈtɜːnərɪ) *adj.* **1.** consisting of three or groups of three. **2.** *Maths.* (of a number system) to the base three. [C14: < L *ternārius*, < *ternī* three each]

ternary form *n.* a musical structure consisting of two contrasting sections followed by a repetition of the first; the form *aba.*

ternate (ˈtɜːnɪt, -neɪt) *adj.* **1.** (esp. of a leaf) consisting of three leaflets or other parts. **2.** (esp. of plants) having groups of three members. [C18: < NL *ternātus*, < Med. L *ternāre* to increase threefold] —ˈ**ternately** *adv.*

terne (tɜːn) *n.* **1.** an alloy of lead containing tin and antimony. **2.** Also called: **terne plate.** steel plate coated with this alloy. [C16: ? < F *terne* dull, < OF *ternir* to TARNISH]

terotechnology (ˌtɪərəʊtɛkˈnɒlədʒɪ, ˌtɛr-) *n.* a branch of technology that utilizes management, financial, and engineering expertise in the installation, efficient operation, and maintenance of equipment and machinery. [C20: < Gk *tērein* to care for + TECHNOLOGY]

terpene (ˈtɜːpiːn) *n.* any one of a class of unsaturated hydrocarbons, such as pinene and the carotenes, that are found in the essential oils of many plants, esp. conifers. [C19: *terp-* < obs. *terpentine* turpentine + -ENE]

terpineol (tɜːˈpɪnɪˌɒl) *n.* a terpene alcohol with an odour of lilac, existing in three isomeric forms that occur in several essential oils. [C20: < TERPENE + -INE² + -OL¹]

Terpsichore (tɜːpˈsɪkərɪ) *n.* the Muse of the dance and of choral song. [C18: via L < Gk, < *terpsikhoros* delighting in the dance, < *terpein* to delight + *khoros* dance]

Terpsichorean (ˌtɜːpsɪkəˈrɪən, -ˈkɔːrɪən) *Often used facetiously.* ~*adj. also* **Terpsichoreal. 1.** of or relating to dancing. ~*n.* **2.** a dancer.

terra (ˈtɛrə) *n.* (in legal contexts) earth or land. [< L]

terra alba (ˈælbə) *n.* **1.** a white finely powdered form of gypsum, used to make paints, paper, etc. **2.** any of various other white earthy substances, such as kaolin, pipeclay, and magnesia. [< L, lit.: white earth]

terrace (ˈtɛrəs) *n.* **1.** a horizontal flat area of ground, often one of a series in a slope. **2. a.** a row of houses, usually identical and having common dividing walls, or the street onto which they face. **b.** (*cap. when part of a street name*): *Grosvenor Terrace.* **3.** a paved area alongside a building, serving partly as a garden. **4.** a balcony or patio. **5.** the flat roof of a house built in a Spanish or Oriental style. **6.** a flat area bounded by a short steep slope formed by the down-cutting of a river or by erosion. **7.** (*usually pl.*) unroofed tiers around a football pitch on which the spectators stand. ~*vb.* (*tr.*) **8.** to make into or provide with a terrace or terraces. [C16: < OF *terrasse*, < OProvençal *terrassa* pile of earth, < *terra* earth, < L]

terraced house *n. Brit.* a house that is part of a terrace. U.S. and Canad. name: **row house.**

terra cotta (ˈkɒtə) *n.* **1.** a hard unglazed brownish-red earthenware, or the clay from which it is made. **2.** something made of terra cotta, such as a sculpture. **3.** a strong reddish-brown to brownish-orange colour. [C18: < It., lit.: baked earth] —**ˈterra-ˈcotta** *adj.*

terra firma (ˈfɜːmə) *n.* the solid earth; firm ground. [C17: < L]

terrain (təˈreɪn) *n.* a piece of ground, esp. with reference to its physical character or military potential: *a rocky terrain.* [C18: < F, ult. < L *terrēnum* ground, < *terra* earth]

terra incognita *Latin.* (ˈtɛrə ɪnˈkɒgnɪtə) *n.* an unexplored or unknown land, region, or area.

Terramycin (ˌtɛrəˈmaɪsɪn) *n. Trademark.* a broad-spectrum antibiotic used in treating various infections.

terrapin (ˈtɛrəpɪn) *n.* any of various web-footed reptiles that live on land and in fresh water and feed on small aquatic animals. Also called: **water tortoise.** [C17: of Amerind origin]

terrarium (tɛˈrɛərɪəm) *n., pl.* **-rariums** *or* **-raria** (-ˈrɛərɪə). **1.** an enclosure for small land animals. **2.** a glass container, often a globe, in which plants are grown. [C19: NL, < L *terra* earth]

terra sigillata (ˌsɪdʒɪˈlɑːtə) *n.* **1.** a reddish-brown clayey earth found on the Aegean island of Lemnos: formerly used as an astringent and in the making of earthenware pottery. **2.** earthenware pottery made from this or a similar earth, esp. Samian ware. [< L: sealed earth]

terrazzo (tɛˈrætsəʊ) *n., pl.* **-zos.** a floor made by setting marble chips into a layer of mortar and polishing the surface. [C20: < It.: TERRACE]

terrene (tɛˈriːn) *adj.* **1.** of the earth; worldly; mundane. **2.** *Rare.* of earth; earthy. ~*n.* **3.** a land. **4.** a rare word for **earth.** [C14: < Anglo-Norman, < L *terrēnus,* < *terra* earth]

terreplein (ˈtɛəˌpleɪn) *n.* the top of a rampart where guns are placed behind the parapet. [C16: < F, < Med. L *terrā plēnus* filled with earth]

terrestrial (təˈrɛstrɪəl) *adj.* **1.** of the earth. **2.** of the land as opposed to the sea or air. **3.** (of animals and plants) living or growing on the land. **4.** earthly, worldly, or mundane. ~*n.* **5.** an inhabitant of the earth. [C15: < L *terrestris,* < *terra* earth] —**terˈrestrially** *adv.*

terrestrial telescope *n.* a telescope for use on earth rather than for making astronomical observations. Such telescopes contain an additional lens or prism system to produce an erect image.

terret (ˈtɛrɪt) *n.* **1.** either of the two rings on a harness through which the reins are passed. **2.** the ring on a dog's collar for attaching the lead. [C15: var. of *toret,* < OF, dim. of *tor* loop]

terre-verte (ˈtɛəˌvɜːt) *n.* **1.** a greyish-green pigment used in paints. It is made from a mineral found in greensand and similar rocks. ~*adj.* **2.** of a greyish-green colour. [C17: < F, lit.: green earth]

terrible (ˈtɛrəbᵊl) *adj.* **1.** very serious or extreme. **2.** *Inf.* of poor quality; unpleasant or bad. **3.** causing terror. **4.** causing awe. [C15: < L *terribilis,* < *terrēre* to terrify] —**ˈterribleness** *n.* —**ˈterribly** *adv.*

terricolous (tɛˈrɪkələs) *adj.* living on or in the soil. [C19: < L *terricola,* < *terra* earth + *colere* to inhabit]

terrier[1] (ˈtɛrɪə) *n.* any of several usually small, active, and short-bodied breeds of dog, originally trained to hunt animals living underground. [C15: < OF *chien terrier* earth dog, < Med. L *terrārius* belonging to the earth, < L *terra* earth]

terrier[2] (ˈtɛrɪə) *n. English legal history.* a register or survey of land. [C15: < OF, < Med. L *terrārius* of the land, < L *terra* land]

terrific (təˈrɪfɪk) *adj.* **1.** very great or intense. **2.** *Inf.* very good; excellent. **3.** very frightening. [C17: < L *terrificus,* < *terrēre* to frighten] —**terˈrifically** *adv.*

terrify (ˈtɛrɪˌfaɪ) *vb.* **-fying, -fied.** (*tr.*) to inspire fear or dread in; frighten greatly. [C16: < L *terrificāre,* < *terrēre* to alarm + *facere* to cause] —**ˈterriˌfying** *adj.* —**ˈterriˌfyingly** *adv.*

terrigenous (tɛˈrɪdʒɪnəs) *adj.* **1.** of or produced by the earth. **2.** (of geological deposits) formed in the sea from material derived from the land by erosion. [C17: < L *terrigenus,* < *terra* earth + *gignere* to beget]

terrine (tɛˈriːn) *n.* **1.** an oval earthenware cooking dish with a tightly fitting lid used for pâtés, etc. **2.** the food cooked or served in such a dish, esp. pâté. [C18: earlier form of TUREEN]

territorial (ˌtɛrɪˈtɔːrɪəl) *adj.* **1.** of or relating to a territory or territories. **2.** restricted to or owned by a particular territory. **3.** local or regional. **4.** *Zool.* establishing and defending a territory. **5.** pertaining to a territorial army, providing a reserve of trained men for use in emergency. —**ˌterriˌtoriˈality** *n.* —**ˌterriˈtorially** *adv.*

Territorial (ˌtɛrɪˈtɔːrɪəl) *n.* a member of a Territorial Army.

Territorial Army *n.* (in Britain) a standing reserve army originally organized between 1907 and 1908. Full name: **Territorial and Volunteer Reserve.**

Territorial Council *n.* (in Canada) an elected body responsible for local government in the Northwest Territories or the Yukon.

territorial waters *pl. n.* the waters over which a nation exercises jurisdiction and control.

territory (ˈtɛrɪtərɪ) *n., pl.* **-ries. 1.** any tract of land; district. **2.** the geographical domain under the jurisdiction of a political unit, esp. of a sovereign state. **3.** the district for which an agent, etc., is responsible. **4.** an area inhabited and defended by an animal or a pair of animals. **5.** an area of knowledge. **6.** (in football, hockey, etc.) the area defended by a team. **7.** (*often cap.*) a region of a country, esp. of a federal state, that enjoys less autonomy and a lower status than most constituent parts of the state. **8.** (*often cap.*) a protectorate or other dependency of a country. [C15: < L *territōrium* land surrounding a town, < *terra* land]

Territory (ˈtɛrɪtərɪ) *n.* **the.** *Austral.* the Northern Territory of Australia.

terror (ˈtɛrə) *n.* **1.** great fear, panic, or dread. **2.** a person or thing that inspires great dread. **3.** *Inf.* a troublesome person or thing, esp. a child. **4.** terrorism. [C14: < OF *terreur,* < L *terror,* < *terrēre* to frighten] —**ˈterrorful** *adj.* —**ˈterrorless** *adj.*

terrorism (ˈtɛrəˌrɪzəm) *n.* **1.** the systematic use of violence and intimidation to achieve some goal. **2.** the act of terrorizing. **3.** the state of being terrorized. —**ˈterrorist** *n., adj.*

terrorize *or* **-ise** (ˈtɛrəˌraɪz) *vb.* (*tr.*) **1.** to coerce or control by violence, fear, threats, etc. **2.** to inspire with dread; terrify. —**ˌterroriˈzation** *or* **-iˈsation** *n.* —**ˈterrorˌizer** *or* **-ˌiser** *n.*

terror-stricken *or* **terror-struck** *adj.* in a state of terror.

terry (ˈtɛrɪ) *n., pl.* **-ries. 1.** an uncut loop in the pile of towelling or a similar fabric. **2.** a fabric with such a pile. [C18: ? var. of TERRET]

terse (tɜːs) *adj.* **1.** neatly brief and concise. **2.** curt; abrupt. [C17: < L *tersus* precise, < *tergēre* to polish] —**ˈtersely** *adv.* —**ˈterseness** *n.*

tertial (ˈtɜːʃəl) *adj., n.* another word for **tertiary** (senses 5, 6). [C19: < L *tertius* third, < *ter* thrice, < *trēs* three]

tertian (ˈtɜːʃən) *adj.* **1.** (of a fever) occurring every other day. ~*n.* **2.** a tertian fever. [C14: < L *febris tertiāna* fever occurring every third day, < *tertius* third]

tertiary (ˈtɜːʃərɪ) *adj.* **1.** third in degree, order, etc. **2.** (of an industry) involving services as opposed to extraction or manufacture, such as transport, finance, etc. **3.** *R.C. Church.* of or relating to a Third Order. **4.** *Chem.* **a.** (of an organic compound) having a functional group attached to a carbon atom that is attached to three other groups. **b.** (of an amine) having three organic groups attached to a nitrogen atom. **c.** (of a salt) derived from a tribasic acid by replacement of all its acidic hydrogen atoms with metal atoms or electropositive groups. **5.** *Ornithol., rare.* of or designating any of the small flight feathers attached to the part of the humerus nearest to the body. ~*n., pl.* **-tiaries.** **6.** *Ornithol., rare.* any of the tertiary feathers. **7.** *R.C. Church.* a member of a Third Order. [C16: < L *tertiārius* containing one third, < *tertius* third]

Tertiary (ˈtɜːʃərɪ) *adj.* **1.** of, denoting, or formed in the first period of the Cenozoic era. ~*n.* **2.** **the.** the Tertiary period or rock system.

tertiary college *n. Brit.* a college system incorporating the secondary school sixth form and vocational courses.

tertium quid (ˈtɜːtɪəm) *n.* an unknown or indefinite thing related in some way to two known or definite things, but distinct from both. [C18: < LL, rendering Gk *triton ti* some third thing]

tervalent (tɜːˈveɪlənt) *adj. Chem.* another word for **trivalent.** —**terˈvalency** *n.*

Terylene (ˈtɛrɪˌliːn) *n. Trademark.* a synthetic polyester fibre or fabric. U.S. name (trademark): **Dacron.**

terza rima (ˈtɛətsə ˈriːmə) *n., pl.* **terze rime** (ˈtɛətseɪ ˈriːmeɪ). a verse form consisting of a series of tercets in which the middle line of one tercet rhymes with the first and third lines of the next. [C19: < It., lit.: third rhyme]

TESL *abbrev. for* Teaching (of) English as a Second Language.

tesla (ˈtɛslə) *n.* the derived SI unit of magnetic flux density equal to a flux of 1 weber in an area of 1 square metre. Symbol: T [C20: after Nikola *Tesla* (1857-1943), U.S. electrical engineer & inventor]

tesla coil *n.* a step-up transformer with an air core, used for producing high voltages at high frequencies.

tessellate (ˈtɛsɪˌleɪt) *vb.* **1.** (*tr.*) to construct, pave, or inlay with a mosaic of small tiles. **2.** (*intr.*) (of identical shapes) to fit together exactly. [C18: < L *tessellātus* checked, < *tessella* small stone cube, < TESSERA]

tessera (ˈtɛsərə) *n., pl.* **-serae** (-səˌriː). **1.** a small square tile of stone, glass, etc., used in mosaics. **2.** a die, tally, etc., used in classical times, made of bone or wood. [C17: < L, < Ionic Gk *tesseres* four] —ˈ**tesseral** *adj.*

tessitura (ˌtɛsɪˈtʊərə) *n. Music.* the general pitch level of a piece of vocal music. [It.: texture, < L *textura;* see TEXTURE]

test[1] (tɛst) *vb.* **1.** to ascertain (the worth, capability, or endurance) of (a person or thing) by subjection to certain examinations, etc.; try. **2.** (often foll. by *for*) to carry out an examination on (a substance, material, or system) to indicate the presence of a substance or the possession of a property: *to test food for arsenic.* ~*n.* **3.** a method, practice, or examination designed to test a person or thing. **4.** a series of questions or problems designed to test a specific skill or knowledge. **5.** a standard of judgment; criterion. **6. a.** a chemical reaction or physical procedure for testing a substance, material, etc. **b.** a chemical reagent used in such a procedure. **c.** the result of the procedure or the evidence gained from it. **7.** *Sport.* See **test match.** **8.** *Arch.* a declaration of truth, loyalty, etc. **9.** (*modifier*) performed as a test: *test drive.* [C14 (in the sense: vessel used in treating metals): < L *testum* earthen vessel] —ˈ**testable** *adj.* —ˈ**testing** *adj.*

test[2] (tɛst) *n.* the hard outer covering of certain invertebrates and tunicates. [C19: < L *testa* shell]

testa (ˈtɛstə) *n., pl.* **-tae** (-tiː). the hard outer layer of a seed. [C18: < L: shell]

testaceous (tɛˈsteɪʃəs) *adj. Biol.* **1.** of or possessing a test or testa. **2.** of the reddish-brown colour of terra cotta. [C17: < L *testācens,* < TESTA]

testament (ˈtɛstəmənt) *n.* **1.** *Law.* a will (esp. in **last will and testament**). **2.** a proof, attestation, or tribute. **3. a.** a covenant instituted between God and man. **b.** a copy of either the Old or the New Testament, or of the complete Bible. [C14: < L: a will, < *testārī* to bear witness, < *testis* a witness] —ˌ**testaˈmental** *adj.* —ˌ**testaˈmentary** *adj.*

Testament (ˈtɛstəmənt) *n.* **1.** either of the two main parts of the Bible; the Old Testament or the New Testament. **2.** the New Testament as distinct from the Old.

testate (ˈtɛsteɪt, ˈtɛstɪt) *adj.* **1.** having left a legally valid will at death. ~*n.* **2.** a person who dies testate. [C15: < L *testārī* to make a will; see TESTAMENT] —**testacy** (ˈtɛstəsɪ) *n.*

testator (tɛˈsteɪtə) *or* (*fem.*) **testatrix** (tɛˈsteɪtrɪks) *n.* a person who makes a will, esp. one who dies testate. [C15: < Anglo-F *testatour,* < LL *testātor,* < L *testārī* to make a will]

test ban *n.* an agreement among nations to forgo tests of nuclear weapons.

test-bed *n. Engineering.* an area used for testing machinery, etc., under working conditions.

test case *n.* a legal action that serves as a precedent in deciding similar succeeding cases.

test-drive *vb.* (*tr.*) **-driving, -drove, -driven.** to drive (a car or other motor vehicle) for a limited period in order to assess it.

tester[1] (ˈtɛstə) *n.* a person or thing that tests.

tester[2] (ˈtɛstə) *n.* a canopy over a bed. [C14: < Med. L *testerium,* < LL *testa* a skull, < L: shell]

testes (ˈtɛstiːz) *n.* the plural of **testis.**

testicle (ˈtɛstɪkᵊl) *n.* either of the two male reproductive glands, in most mammals enclosed within the scrotum, that produce spermatozoa. [C15: < L *testiculus,* dim. of *testis*] —**testicular** (tɛˈstɪkjʊlə) *adj.*

testiculate (tɛˈstɪkjʊlɪt) *adj. Bot.* having an oval shape: *the testiculate tubers of certain orchids.* [C18: < LL *testiculātus;* see TESTICLE]

testify (ˈtɛstɪˌfaɪ) *vb.* **-fying, -fied.** **1.** (when *tr.*, *may take a clause as object*) to state (something) formally as a declaration of fact. **2.** *Law.* to declare or give (evidence) under oath, esp. in court. **3.** (when *intr.*, often foll. by *to*) to be evidence (of); serve as witness (to). **4.** (*tr.*) to declare or acknowledge openly. [C14: < L *testificārī,* < *testis* witness] —ˌ**testifiˈcation** *n.* —ˈ**testiˌfier** *n.*

testimonial (ˌtɛstɪˈməʊnɪəl) *n.* **1.** a recommendation of the character, ability, etc., of a person or of the quality of a product or service. **2.** a formal statement of truth or fact. **3.** a tribute given for services or achievements. ~*adj.* **4.** of or relating to a testimony or testimonial.

testimony (ˈtɛstɪmənɪ) *n., pl.* **-nies.** **1.** a declaration of truth or fact. **2.** *Law.* evidence given by a witness, esp. in court under oath. **3.** evidence testifying to something: *her success was a testimony to her good luck.* **4.** *Old Testament.* the Ten Commandments. [C15: < L *testimōnium,* < *testis* witness]

testis (ˈtɛstɪs) *n., pl.* **-tes.** another word for **testicle.** [C17: < L, lit.: witness (to masculinity)]

test match *n.* (in various sports, esp. cricket) any of a series of international matches.

testosterone (tɛˈstɒstəˌrəʊn) *n.* a potent steroid hormone secreted mainly by the testes. [C20: < TESTIS + STEROL + -ONE]

test paper *n.* **1.** *Chem.* paper impregnated with an indicator for use in chemical tests. **2. a.** the question sheet of a test. **b.** the paper completed by a test candidate.

test pilot *n.* a pilot who flies aircraft of new design to test their performance in the air.

test tube *n.* **1.** a cylindrical round-bottomed glass tube open at one end: used in scientific experiments. **2.** (*modifier*) made synthetically in, or as if in, a test tube: *a test-tube product.*

test-tube baby *n.* **1.** a fetus that has developed from an ovum fertilized in an artificial womb. **2.** a baby conceived by artificial insemination.

testudinal (tɛˈstjuːdɪnᵊl) *adj.* of or resembling a tortoise. [C19: < L TESTUDO]

testudo (tɛˈstjuːdəʊ) *n., pl.* **-dines** (-dɪˌniːz). a form of shelter used by the ancient Roman Army as protection against attack from above, consisting of a mobile arched structure or of overlapping shields held by the soldiers over their heads. [C17: < L: a tortoise, < *testa* a shell]

testy (ˈtɛstɪ) *adj.* **-tier, -tiest.** irritable or touchy. [C14: < Anglo-Norman *testif* headstrong, < OF *teste* head, < LL *testa* skull, < L: shell] —ˈ**testily** *adv.* —ˈ**testiness** *n.*

tetanus (ˈtɛtənəs) *n.* **1.** Also called: **lockjaw.** an acute infectious disease in which sustained muscular spasm, contraction, and convulsion are caused by the release of toxins from a bacterium. **2.** *Physiol.* any tense contraction of a muscle. [C16: via L < Gk *tetanos*, ult. < *teinein* to stretch] —ˈ**tetanal** *adj.* —ˈ**teta**ˌ**noid** *adj.*

tetany (ˈtɛtənɪ) *n.* an abnormal increase in the excitability of nerves and muscles caused by a deficiency of parathyroid secretion. [C19: < F; see TETANUS]

tetchy (ˈtɛtʃɪ) *adj.* **tetchier, tetchiest.** being or inclined to be cross, irritable, or touchy. [C16: prob. < obs. *tetch* defect, < OF *tache* spot, of Gmc origin] —ˈ**tetchily** *adv.* —ˈ**tetchiness** *n.*

tête-à-tête (ˌteɪtəˈteɪt) *n., pl.* **-têtes** *or* **-tête. 1. a.** a private conversation between two people. **b.** (*as modifier*): *a tête-à-tête conversation.* **2.** a small sofa for two people, esp. one that is S-shaped in plan so that the sitters are almost face to face. ~*adv.* **3.** intimately; in private. [C17: < F, lit.: head to head]

tête-bêche (tɛtˈbɛʃ) *adj. Philately.* (of an unseparated pair of stamps) printed so that one is inverted in relation to the other. [C19: < F, < *tête* head + *bêche*, < obs. *béchevet* double-headed (orig. of a bed)]

tether (ˈtɛðə) *n.* **1.** a rope, chain, etc., by which an animal is tied to a particular spot. **2.** the range of one's endurance, etc. **3. at the end of one's tether.** distressed or exasperated to the limit of one's endurance. ~*vb.* **4.** (*tr.*) to tie with or as if with a tether. [C14: < ON *tjothr*]

Tethys (ˈtiːθɪs, ˈtɛθ-) *n.* the sea that lay between the two ancient supercontinents, Laurasia and Gondwanaland, and which can be regarded as the predecessor of today's smaller Mediterranean.

tetra- *or before a vowel* **tetr-** *combining form.* four: *tetrameter.* [< Gk]

tetrabasic (ˌtɛtrəˈbeɪsɪk) *adj.* (of an acid) containing four replaceable hydrogen atoms. —**tetrabasicity** (ˌtɛtrəbeɪˈsɪsɪtɪ) *n.*

tetrachord (ˈtɛtrəˌkɔːd) *n. Music.* any of several groups of four notes in descending order, in which the first and last notes form a perfect fourth. [C17: < Gk *tetrakhordos* four-stringed] —ˌ**tetra**ˈ**chordal** *adj.*

tetracyclic (ˌtɛtrəˈsaɪklɪk) *adj. Chem.* containing four rings in its molecular structure.

tetracycline (ˌtɛtrəˈsaɪklaɪn, -klɪn) *n.* an antibiotic synthesized from chlortetracycline or derived from a bacterium. [C20: < TETRA- + CYCL(IC) + -INE[2]]

tetrad (ˈtɛtræd) *n.* a group or series of four. [C17: < Gk *tetras*, < *tettares* four]

tetraethyl lead (ˌtɛtrəˈiːθaɪl lɛd) *n.* a colourless oily insoluble liquid used in petrol to prevent knocking.

tetrafluoroethylene (ˈtɛtrəˌfluərəʊˈɛθɪˌliːn) *n. Chem.* a dense colourless gas that is polymerized to make plastics. [C20: < TETRA- + FLUORO- + ETHYLENE]

tetragon (ˈtɛtrəˌgɒn) *n.* a less common name for **quadrilateral** (sense 2). [C17: < Gk *tetragōnon*]

tetragonal (tɛˈtrægənᵊl) *adj.* **1.** *Crystallog.* relating or belonging to the crystal system characterized by three mutually perpendicular axes of which only two are equal. **2.** of or shaped like a quadrilateral. —**te**ˈ**tragonally** *adv.*

Tetragrammaton (ˌtɛtrəˈgræmətᵊn) *n. Bible.* the Hebrew name for God consisting of the four consonants Y H V H (or Y H W H). It is usually transliterated as *Jehovah* or *Yahweh.* Sometimes shortened to **Tetragram.** [C14: < Gk, < *tetragrammatos* having four letters]

tetrahedron (ˌtɛtrəˈhiːdrən) *n., pl.* **-drons** *or* **-dra** (-drə). a solid figure having four plane faces. A **regular tetrahedron** has faces that are equilateral triangles. [C16: < NL, < LGk *tetraedron*] —ˌ**tetra**ˈ**hedral** *adj.*

tetralogy (tɛˈtrælədʒɪ) *n., pl.* **-gies.** a series of four related works, as in drama or opera. [C17: < Gk *tetralogia*]

tetramerous (tɛˈtræmərəs) *adj. Biol.* having or consisting of four parts. [C19: < NL *tetramerus*, < Gk *tetramerēs*]

tetrameter (tɛˈtræmɪtə) *n. Prosody.* **1.** a line of verse consisting of four metrical feet. **2.** a verse composed of such lines.

tetraplegia (ˌtɛtrəˈpliːdʒɪə) *n.* another name for **quadriplegia.** —ˌ**tetra**ˈ**plegic** *adj.*

tetraploid (ˈtɛtrəˌplɔɪd) *Genetics.* ~*adj.* **1.** having four times the haploid number of chromosomes in the nucleus. ~*n.* **2.** a tetraploid organism, nucleus, or cell.

tetrapod (ˈtɛtrəˌpɒd) *n.* **1.** any vertebrate that has four limbs. **2.** a device consisting of four arms radiating from a central point: three arms form a supporting tripod and the fourth is vertical.

tetrapterous (tɛˈtræptərəs) *adj.* having four wings. [C19: < NL *tetrapterus*, < Gk *tetrapteros*, < TETRA- + *pteron* wing]

tetrarch (ˈtɛtrɑːk) *n.* **1.** the ruler of one fourth of a country. **2.** a subordinate ruler. **3.** any of four joint rulers. [C14: < Gk *tetrarkhēs*; see TETRA-, -ARCH] —**tetrarchate** (tɛˈtrɑːˌkeɪt, -kɪt) *n.* —**te**ˈ**trarchic** *adj.* —ˈ**tetrarchy** *n.*

tetrastich (ˈtɛtrəˌstɪk) *n.* a poem, stanza, or strophe that consists of four lines. [C16: via L < Gk *tetrastikhon*, < TETRA- + *stikhos* row] —**tetrastichic** (ˌtɛtrəˈstɪkɪk) *or* **tetrastichal** (tɛˈtræstɪkᵊl) *adj.*

tetravalent (ˌtɛtrəˈveɪlənt) *adj. Chem.* **1.** having a valency of four. **2.** Also: **quadrivalent.** having four valencies. —ˌ**tetra**ˈ**valency** *n.*

tetrode (ˈtɛtrəʊd) *n.* an electronic valve having four electrodes.

tetroxide (tɛˈtrɒksaɪd) *n.* any oxide that contains four oxygen atoms per molecule.

tetryl (ˈtɛtrɪl) *n.* a yellow crystalline explosive solid, trinitrophenylmethylnitramine used in detonators.

Teut. *abbrev. for* Teuton(ic).

Teuton (ˈtjuːtən) *n.* **1.** a member of an ancient Germanic people from Jutland who migrated to S Gaul in the 2nd century B.C. **2.** a member of any people speaking a Germanic language, esp. a German. ~*adj.* **3.** Teutonic. [C18: < L *Teutonī* the Teutons, of Gmc origin]

Teutonic (tjuːˈtɒnɪk) *adj.* **1.** characteristic of or relating to the German people. **2.** of the ancient Teutons. **3.** (not used in linguistics) of or relating to the Germanic languages.

Tex-Mex (ˈtɛksˌmɛks) *adj.* of, relating to, or denoting the Texan version of something Mexican, such as music, food, or language.

text (tɛkst) *n.* **1.** the main body of a printed or written work as distinct from commentary, notes, illustrations, etc. **2.** the words of something printed, written, or displayed on a visual display unit. **3.** the original exact wording of a work as distinct from a revision or translation. **4.** a short passage of the Bible used as a starting point for a sermon. **5.** the topic or subject of a discussion or work. **6.** short for **textbook. 7.** any novel, play, etc., prescribed as part of a course of study. [C14: < Med. L *textus* version, < L *textus* texture, < *texere* to compose]

textbook (ˈtɛkstˌbʊk) *n.* a book used as a standard source of information on a particular subject. —ˈ**text**ˌ**bookish** *adj.*

textile (ˈtɛkstaɪl) *n.* **1.** any fabric or cloth, esp. woven. **2.** raw material suitable to be made into cloth. ~*adj.* **3.** of or relating to fabrics. [C17: < L *textilis* woven, < *texere* to weave]

textual (ˈtɛkstjʊəl) *adj.* **1.** of or relating to a text or texts. **2.** based on a text. —ˈ**textually** *adv.*

textual criticism *n.* **1.** the scholarly study of manuscripts, esp. of the Bible, in an effort to establish the original text. **2.** literary criticism emphasizing a close analysis of the text.

textualism (ˈtɛkstjʊəˌlɪzəm) *n.* **1.** doctrinaire adherence to a text, esp. of the Bible. **2.** textual criticism, esp. of the Bible. —ˈ**textualist** *n., adj.*

texture (ˈtɛkstʃə) *n.* **1.** the surface of a material, esp. as perceived by the sense of touch. **2.** the structure, appearance, and feel of a woven fabric. **3.** the general structure and disposition of the constituent parts of something: *the texture of a cake.* **4.** the distinctive character or quality of something: *the texture of life in America.* ~*vb.* **5.** (*tr.*) to give a distinctive texture to. [C15: < L *textūra* web, < *texere* to weave] —ˈ**textural** *adj.* —ˈ**texturally** *adv.*

TGWU (in Britain) *abbrev. for* Transport and General Workers' Union.

Th *the chemical symbol for* thorium.

Th. *abbrev. for* Thursday.

-th[1] *suffix forming nouns.* **1.** (*from verbs*) indicating an action or its consequence: *growth.* **2.** (*from adjectives*) indicating a quality: *width.* [< OE *-thu, -tho*]

-th[2] *or* **-eth** *suffix.* forming ordinal numbers: *fourth; thousandth.* [< OE *-(o)tha, -(o)the*]

Thai (taɪ) *adj.* **1.** of Thailand, its people, or their language. ~*n.* **2.** (*pl.* **Thais** *or* **Thai**) a native or inhabitant of Thailand. **3.** the language of Thailand, sometimes classified as belonging to the Sino-Tibetan family.

thalamus (ˈθæləməs) *n., pl.* **-mi** (-ˌmaɪ). **1.** either of the two contiguous egg-shaped masses of grey matter at the base of the brain. **2.** both of these masses considered as a functional unit. **3.** the receptacle or torus of a flower. [C18: < L, < Gk *thalamos* inner room] —**thalamic** (θəˈlæmɪk) *adj.*

thalassaemia *or U.S.* **thalassemia** (ˌθæləˈsiː-mɪə) *n.* a hereditary disease resulting from defects in the synthesis of the red blood pigment haemoglobin. [NL, < Gk *thalassa* sea + -AEMIA, it being esp. prevalent round the eastern Mediterranean]

thalassic (θəˈlæsɪk) *adj.* of or relating to the sea, esp. to small or inland seas. [C19: < F *thalassique,* < Gk *thalassa* sea]

thaler (ˈtɑːlə) *n., pl.* **-ler** *or* **-lers.** a former German, Austrian, or Swiss silver coin. [< G; see DOLLAR]

Thalia (θəˈlaɪə) *n. Greek myth.* **1.** the Muse of comedy and pastoral poetry. **2.** one of the three Graces. [C17: via L < Gk, < *thaleia* blooming]

thalidomide (θəˈlɪdəˌmaɪd) *n.* **a.** a drug formerly used as a sedative and hypnotic but withdrawn from use when found to cause abnormalities in developing fetuses. **b.** (*as modifier*): *a thalidomide baby.* [C20: < *thali(mi)do(glutari)mide*]

thallium (ˈθælɪəm) *n.* a soft malleable highly toxic white metallic element. Symbol: Tl; atomic no.: 81; atomic wt.: 204.37. [C19: < NL, < Gk *thallos* a green shoot; < the green line in its spectrum]

thallophyte (ˈθæləˌfaɪt) *n.* any of a group of plants lacking true stems, leaves, and roots: includes the algae, fungi, lichens, and bacteria. [C19: < NL *thallophyta,* < Gk *thallos* a young shoot + *phuton* a plant] —**thallophytic** (ˌθæləˈfɪtɪk) *adj.*

thallus (ˈθæləs) *n., pl.* **thalli** (ˈθælaɪ) *or* **thalluses.** the undifferentiated plant body of algae, fungi, and lichens. [C19: < L, < Gk *thallos* green shoot, < *thallein* to bloom] —ˈ**thalloid** *adj.*

thalweg *or* **talweg** (ˈtɑːlvɛg) *n. Geog., rare.* **1.** the longitudinal outline of a riverbed from source to mouth. **2.** the line of steepest descent from any point on the land surface. [C19: < G *thal* or *tal* valley + *weg* way]

than (ðæn; *unstressed* ðən) *conj.* (*coordinating*), *prep.* **1.** used to introduce the second element of a comparison, the first element of which expresses difference: *shorter than you.* **2.** used after adverbs such as *rather* or *sooner* to introduce a rejected alternative in an expression of preference: *rather than be imprisoned, I shall die.* [OE *thanne*]

▷ **Usage.** In sentences such as *he does it far better than I, than* is usually regarded in careful usage as a conjunction governing an unexpressed verb: *he does it far better than I (do it).* The case of any pronoun therefore depends on whether it is the subject or the object of that unexpressed verb: *she likes him more than I (like him); she likes him more than (she likes) me.* However, in informal usage *than* is often treated as a preposition and any pronoun is therefore used in its objective form, so that *she likes him more than me* is ambiguous.

thanatology (ˌθænəˈtɒlədʒɪ) *n.* the scientific study of death and its related phenomena. [C19: < Gk *thanatos* death + -LOGY]

thanatopsis (ˌθænəˈtɒpsɪs) *n.* a meditation on death, as in a poem. [C19: < Gk *thanatos* death + *opsis* a view]

thane *or* (*less commonly*) **thegn** (θeɪn) *n.* **1.** (in Anglo-Saxon England) a member of an aristocratic class who held land from the king or from another nobleman in return for certain services. **2.** (in medieval Scotland) a person of rank holding land from the king. [OE *thegn*] —**thanage** (ˈθeɪnɪdʒ) *n.*

thank (θæŋk) *vb.* (*tr.*) **1.** to convey feelings of gratitude to. **2.** to hold responsible: *he has his creditors to thank for his bankruptcy.* [OE *thancian*]

thankful (ˈθæŋkfʊl) *adj.* grateful and appreciative. —ˈ**thankfully** *adv.* —ˈ**thankfulness** *n.*

thankless (ˈθæŋklɪs) *adj.* **1.** receiving no thanks or appreciation. **2.** ungrateful. —ˈ**thanklessly** *adv.* —ˈ**thanklessness** *n.*

thanks (θæŋks) *pl. n.* **1.** an expression of appreciation or gratitude. **2. thanks to.** because of: *thanks to him we lost the match.* ~*interj.* **3.** *Inf.* an exclamation expressing gratitude.

thanksgiving (ˈθæŋksˌgɪvɪŋ; *U.S.* θæŋksˈgɪv-) *n.* **1.** the act of giving thanks. **2.** a formal public expression of thanks to God.

Thanksgiving Day *n.* an annual day of holiday celebrated in thanksgiving to God on the fourth Thursday of November in the United States, and on the second Monday of October in Canada. Often shortened to **Thanksgiving.**

thar (tɑː) *n.* a variant spelling of **tahr.**

that (ðæt; *unstressed* ðət) *determiner.* (*used before a sing. n.*) **1. a.** used preceding a noun that has been mentioned or is understood: *that idea of yours.* **b.** (*as pronoun*): *don't eat that.* **2. a.** used preceding a noun that denotes something more remote or removed: *that building over there is for sale.* **b.** (*as pronoun*): *that is John and this is his wife.* **3.** used to refer to something that is familiar: *that old chap from across the street.* **4. and (all) that.** *Inf.* everything connected with the subject mentioned: *he knows a lot about building and that.* **5. at that.** (*completive-intensive*) additionally, all things considered, or nevertheless: *I might decide to go at that.* **6. like that. a.** effortlessly: *he gave me the answer just like that.* **b.** of such a nature, character, etc.: *he paid for all our tickets—he's like that.* **7. that is. a.** to be precise. **b.** in other words. **c.** for example. **8. that's that.** there is no more to be done, discussed, etc. ~*conj.* (*subordinating*) **9.** used to introduce a noun clause: *I believe that you'll come.* **10.** used to introduce: **a.** a clause of purpose: *they fought that others might have peace.* **b.** a clause of result: *he laughed so hard that he cried.* **c.** a clause after an understood sentence expressing desire, indignation, or amazement: *oh, that I had never lived!* ~*adv.* **11.** used to reinforce the specification of a precise degree already mentioned: *go just that fast and you should be safe.* **12.** Also: **all that.** (*usually used with a negative*) *Inf.* (intensifier): *he wasn't that upset at the news.* **13.** *Dialect.* (intensifier): *the cat was that weak after the fight.* ~*pron.* **14.** used to introduce a restrictive relative clause: *the book that we want.* **15.** used to introduce a clause with the verb *to be* to emphasize the extent to which the preceding noun is applicable: *genius that she is, she outwitted the computer.* [OE *thæt*]

▷ **Usage.** Precise stylists maintain a distinction between *that* and *which: that* is used as a relative pronoun in restrictive clauses and *which* in nonrestrictive clauses. In *the book that is on the table is mine,* the clause *that is on the table* is used to distinguish one particular book (the one on the table) from another or others (which may be anywhere, but not on the table). In *the book, which is on the table, is mine,* the *which* clause is merely descriptive or incidental. The more formal the level of language, the more important it is to preserve the distinction between the two relative pronouns; but in informal or colloquial usage, the words are often used interchangeably.

thatch (θætʃ) *n.* **1. a.** Also called: **thatching.** a roofing material that consists of straw, reed, etc. **b.** a roof made of such a material. **2.** anything resembling this, such as the hair of the head. **3.** Also called: **thatch palm.** any of various palms with leaves suitable for thatching. ~*vb.* **4.** to cover with thatch. [OE *theccan* to cover] —ˈ**thatcher** *n.*

thaumatology (ˌθɔːməˈtɒlədʒɪ) *n.* the study of or a treatise on miracles. [C19: < Gk *thaumato-* combining form of *thauma* a wonder, marvel + -LOGY]

thaumatrope (ˈθɔːməˌtrəʊp) *n.* a toy in which partial pictures on the two sides of a card appear to merge when the card is twirled rapidly. [C19: < Gk *thaumato-* (see THAUMATOLOGY) + -TROPE] —**thaumatropical** (ˌθɔːməˈtrɒpɪkᵊl) *adj.*

thaumaturge (ˈθɔːməˌtɜːdʒ) *n. Rare.* a performer of miracles; magician. [C18: < Med. L *thaumaturgus,* < Gk *thaumatourgos* miracle-working] —ˌ**thaumaˈturgic** *adj.* —ˈ**thaumaˌturgy** *n.*

thaw (θɔː) *vb.* **1.** to melt or cause to melt: *the snow thawed.* **2.** to become or cause to become unfrozen; defrost. **3.** (*intr.*) to be the case that the ice or snow is melting: *it's thawing fast.* **4.** (*intr.*) to become more relaxed or friendly. ~*n.* **5.** the act or process of thawing. **6.** a spell of relatively warm weather, causing snow or ice to melt. **7.** an increase in relaxation or friendliness. [OE *thawian*]

ThD *abbrev. for* Doctor of Theology.

the[1] (*stressed or emphatic* ðiː; *unstressed before a consonant* ðə; *unstressed before a vowel* ðɪ) *determiner.* (*article*) **1.** used preceding a noun that has been previously specified: *the pain should disappear soon.* Cf. **a**[1]. **2.** used to indicate a particular person, object, etc.: *ask the man standing outside.* Cf. **a**[1]. **3.** used preceding certain nouns associated with one's culture, society, or community: *to go to the doctor; to listen to the news.* **4.** used preceding present participles and adjectives when they function as nouns: *the singing is awful.* **5.** used preceding titles and certain uniquely specific or proper nouns: *the United States; the Chairman.* **6.** used preceding a qualifying adjective or noun in certain names or titles: *Edward the First.* **7.** used preceding a noun to make it refer to its class generically: *the white seal is hunted for its fur.* **8.** used instead of *my, your, her,* etc., with parts of the body: *take me by the hand.* **9.** (usually stressed) the best, only, or most remarkable: *Harry's is* the *club in this town.* **10.** used with proper nouns when qualified: *written by the young Hardy.* **11.** another word for **per:** *fifty pence the pound.* **12.** *Often facetious or derog.* my; our: *the wife goes out on Thursdays.* **13.** used preceding a unit of time in phrases or titles indicating an outstanding person, event, etc.: *housewife of the year.* [ME, < OE *thē,* a demonstrative adjective that later superseded *sē* (masculine singular) and *sēo, sio* (feminine singular)]

the[2] (ðə, ðɪ) *adv.* **1.** (often foll. by *for*) used before comparative adjectives or adverbs for emphasis: *she looks the happier for her trip.* **2.** used correlatively before each of two comparative adjectives or adverbs to indicate equality: *the sooner you come, the better; the more I see you, the more I love you.* [OE *thī, thȳ*]

theanthropism (θiːˈænθrəˌpɪzəm) *n.* **1.** the ascription of human traits or characteristics to a god or gods. **2.** *Christian theol.* the doctrine of the union of the divine and human natures in the single person of Christ. [C19: < Ecclesiastical Gk *theanthrōpos* (< *theos* god + *anthrōpos* man) + -ISM] —**theanthropic** (ˌθiːænˈθrɒpɪk) *adj.*

thearchy (ˈθiːɑːkɪ) *n., pl.* **-chies.** rule or government by God or gods; theocracy. [C17: < Church Gk *thearkhia;* see THEO-, -ARCHY]

theatre *or U.S.* **theater** (ˈθɪətə) *n.* **1.** a building designed for the performance of plays, operas, etc. **2.** a large room or hall, usually with a raised platform and tiered seats for an audience. **3.** a room in a hospital equipped for surgical operations. **4.** plays regarded collectively as a form of art. **5. the theatre.** the world of actors, theatrical companies, etc. **6.** a setting for dramatic or important events. **7.** writing that is suitable for dramatic presentation: *a good piece of theatre.* **8.** *U.S., Austral., & N.Z.* the usual word for **cinema** (sense 1). **9.** a major area of military activity. **10.** a circular or semicircular open-air building with tiers of seats. [C14: < L *theātrum,* < Gk *theatron* place for viewing, < *theasthai* to look at]

theatre-in-the-round *n., pl.* **theatres-in-the-round.** a theatre with seats arranged around a central acting area.

theatre of cruelty *n.* a type of theatre that seeks to communicate a sense of pain, suffering, and evil, using gesture, movement, sound, and symbolism rather than language.

theatre of the absurd *n.* drama in which normal conventions and dramatic structure are modified in order to present life as irrational.

theatrical (θɪˈætrɪkᵊl) *adj.* **1.** of or relating to the theatre or dramatic performances. **2.** exaggerated and affected in manner or behaviour; histrionic. —**theˌatriˈcality** *or* **theˈatricalness** *n.* —**theˈatrically** *adv.*

theatricals (θɪˈætrɪkᵊlz) *pl. n.* dramatic performances, esp. as given by amateurs.

theatrics (θɪˈætrɪks) *n.* (*functioning as sing.*) **1.** the art of staging plays. **2.** exaggerated mannerisms or displays of emotions.

thebaine (ˈθiːbəˌiːn) *n.* a poisonous white crystalline alkaloid, extracted from opium. [C19: < NL *thebaia* opium of Thebes (with reference to Egypt as a chief source of opium) + -INE[2]]

Theban (ˈθiːbən) *adj.* **1.** of or relating to Thebes, (in ancient Greece) the chief city of Boeotia, or (in ancient Egypt) a city on the Nile, at various times the capital. ~*n.* **2.** a native or inhabitant of either of these cities.

theca (ˈθiːkə) *n., pl.* **-cae** (-siː). **1.** *Bot.* an enclosing organ, cell, or spore case. **2.** *Zool.* a hard outer covering, such as the container of a coral polyp. [C17: < L *thēca,* < Gk *thēkē* case] —ˈ**thecate** *adj.*

thecodont (ˈθiːkəˌdɒnt) *adj.* **1.** (of mammals and certain reptiles) having teeth that grow in sockets. **2.** of or relating to teeth of this type. ~*n.* **3.** any of various extinct reptiles of Triassic times, having teeth set in sockets: they gave rise to the dinosaurs, crocodiles, pterodactyls, and birds. [C20: NL *Thecodontia,* < Gk *thēkē* case + -ODONT]

thé dansant *French.* (te dɑ̃sɑ̃) *n., pl.* ***thés dansant*** (te dɑ̃sɑ̃). a dance held while afternoon tea is served, popular in the 1920s and 1930s. [lit.: dancing tea]

thee (ðiː) *pron.* **1.** the objective form of **thou**[1]. **2.** (*subjective*) *Rare.* refers to the person addressed: used mainly by members of the Society of Friends. [OE *thē*]

theft (θɛft) *n.* **1.** the dishonest taking of property belonging to another person with the intention of depriving the owner permanently of its possession. **2.** *Rare.* something stolen. [OE *thēofth*]

thegn (θeɪn) *n.* a less common variant of **thane.**

theine (ˈθiːiːn, -ɪn) *n.* caffeine, esp. when present in tea. [C19: < NL *thea* tea + -INE[2]]

their (ðɛə) *determiner.* **1.** of or associated in some way with them: *their own clothes; she tried to combat their mocking her.* **2.** belonging to or associated with people in general: *in many countries they wash their clothes in the river.* **3.** belonging to or associated with an indefinite antecedent such as *one, whoever,* or *anybody: everyone should bring their own lunch.* [C12: < ON *theira*]

▷ **Usage.** The use of *their* and similar plural forms as in sense 3 is sometimes regarded as unacceptable in formal contexts, though it has existed in the language for at least five centuries and is common in informal contexts.

theirs (ðɛəz) *pron.* **1.** something or someone belonging to or associated with them: *theirs is difficult.* **2.** something or someone belonging to or associated with an indefinite antecedent such as *one, whoever,* or *anybody: everyone thinks theirs is best.* **3. of theirs.** belonging to or associated with them.

▷ **Usage.** See at **their.**

theism (ˈθiːɪzəm) *n.* **1.** the belief in one God as the creator and ruler of the universe. **2.** the belief in the existence of a God or gods. —ˈ**theist** *n., adj.* —**theˈistic** *or* **theˈistical** *adj.*

them (ðɛm; *unstressed* ðəm) *pron.* **1.** (*objective*) refers to things or people other than the speaker or people addressed: *I'll kill them; what happened to them?* ~*determiner.* **2.** a nonstandard word for **those:** *three of them oranges.* [OE *thǣm,* infl. by ON *theim*]

▷ **Usage.** See at **me.**

theme (θiːm) *n.* **1.** an idea or topic expanded in a discourse, discussion, etc. **2.** (in literature, music, art, etc.) a unifying idea, image, or motif, repeated or developed throughout a work. **3.** *Music.* **a.** a group of notes forming a recognizable melodic unit, often used as the basis of the musical material in a composition. **4.** a short essay, esp. one set as an exercise for a student. **5.** *Grammar.* another word for **root**[1] or **stem**[1] (sense 7). **6.** (*modifier*) planned or designed round one unifying subject, image, etc.: *a theme holiday.* ~*vb.* (*tr.*) **7.** to design, decorate, etc., in accordance with a theme. [C13: < L *thema,* < Gk: deposit, < *tithenai* to lay down] —**thematic** (θɪˈmætɪk) *adj.*

theme park *n.* an area planned as a leisure attraction, in which all the displays, buildings, activities, etc., are based on one subject.

theme song *n.* **1.** a melody used, esp. in a film score, to set a mood, introduce a character, etc. **2.** another term for **signature tune.**

themselves (ðəmˈsɛlvz) *pron.* **1. a.** the reflexive form of *they* or *them.* **b.** (intensifier): *the team themselves voted on it.* **2.** (*preceded by a copula*) their normal or usual selves: *they don't seem themselves any more.* **3.** Also: **themself.** *Not standard.* a reflexive form of an indefinite antecedent such as *one, whoever,* or *anybody: everyone has to look after themselves.*

▷ **Usage.** See at **myself.**

then (ðɛn) *adv.* **1.** at that time; over that period of time. **2.** (*sentence modifier*) in that case; that being so: *then why don't you ask her? go on then, take it.* ~*sentence connector.* **3.** after that; with that: *then John left the room.* ~*n.* **4.** that time: *from then on.* ~*adj.* **5.** (*prenominal*) existing, functioning, etc., at that time: *the then prime minister.* [OE *thenne*]

thenar (ˈθiːnɑː) *n.* **1.** the palm of the hand. **2.** the fleshy area of the palm at the base of the thumb. [C17: via NL < Gk]

thence (ðɛns) *adv.* **1.** from that place. **2.** Also: **thenceforth** (ˈðɛnsˈfɔːθ). from that time or event; thereafter. **3.** therefore. [C13 *thannes,* < *thanne,* < OE *thanon*]

thenceforward (ˈðɛnsˈfɔːwəd) *or* **thenceforwards** *adv.* from that time or place on.

theo- *or before a vowel* **the-** *combining form.* indicating God or gods: *theology.* [< Gk *theos* god]

theobromine (ˌθiːəʊˈbrəʊmiːn, -mɪn) *n.* a white crystalline alkaloid that occurs in tea and cacao: used to treat coronary heart disease and headaches. [C18: < NL *theobroma* genus of trees, lit.: food of the gods]

theocentric (ˌθɪəˈsɛntrɪk) *adj. Theol.* having God as the focal point of attention.

theocracy (θɪˈɒkrəsɪ) *n., pl.* **-cies. 1.** government by a deity or by a priesthood. **2.** a community under such government. —ˈ**theoˌcrat** *n.* —ˌ**theoˈcratic** *adj.*

theocrasy (θɪˈɒkrəsɪ) *n.* **1.** a mingling into one of deities or divine attributes previously regarded as distinct. **2.** the union of the soul with God in mysticism. [C19: < Gk *theokrasia,* < THEO- + *-krasia* < *krasis* a blending]

theodicy (θɪˈɒdɪsɪ) *n., pl.* **-cies.** the branch of theology concerned with defending the attributes of God against objections resulting from the existence of physical and moral evil. [C18: coined by Leibnitz in F as *théodicée,* < THEO- + Gk *dikē* justice] —**theˌodiˈcean** *adj.*

theodolite (θɪˈɒdəˌlaɪt) *n.* a surveying instrument for measuring horizontal and vertical angles, consisting of a small tripod-mounted telescope. Also called (in the U.S. and Canada): **transit.** [C16: < NL *theodolitus,* <?] —**theodolitic** (θɪˌɒdəˈlɪtɪk) *adj.*

theogony (θɪˈɒgənɪ) *n., pl.* **-nies. 1.** the origin and descent of the gods. **2.** an account of this. [C17: < Gk *theogonia*] —**theogonic** (ˌθɪəˈgɒnɪk) *adj.* —**theˈogonist** *n.*

theol. *abbrev. for:* **1.** theologian. **2.** theological. **3.** theology.

theologian (ˌθɪəˈləʊdʒɪən) *n.* a person versed in or engaged in the study of theology.

theological (ˌθɪəˈlɒdʒɪkəl) *adj.* of, relating to, or based on theology. —ˌ**theoˈlogically** *adv.*

theological virtues *pl. n.* those virtues that are infused into man by a special grace of God, specifically faith, hope, and charity.

theologize *or* **-ise** (θɪˈɒləˌdʒaɪz) *vb.* **1.** (*intr.*) to speculate upon theological subjects or engage in theological study or discussion. **2.** (*tr.*) to render theological or treat from a theological point of view. —**theˌologiˈzation** *or* **-iˈsation** *n.* —**theˈoloˌgizer** *or* **-iser** *n.*

theology (θɪˈɒlədʒɪ) *n., pl.* **-gies. 1.** the systematic study of the existence and nature of the divine and its relationship to other beings. **2.** the systematic study of Christian revelation concerning God's nature and purpose. **3.** a specific system, form, or branch of this study. [C14: < LL *theologia,* < L] —**theˈologist** *n.*

theomachy (θɪˈɒməkɪ) *n., pl.* **-chies.** a battle among the gods or against them. [C16: < Gk *theomakhia,* < THEO- + *makhē* battle]

theomancy (ˈθiːəʊmænsɪ) *n.* divination or prophecy by an oracle or by people directly inspired by a god.

theomania (ˌθɪəˈmeɪnɪə) *n.* religious madness, esp. when it takes the form of believing oneself to be a god. —ˌ**theoˈmaniˌac** *n.*

theophany (θɪˈɒfənɪ) *n., pl.* **-nies.** a visible manifestation of a deity to man. [C17: < LL *theophania,* < LGk, < THEO- + *phainein* to show] —**theophanic** (ˌθɪəˈfænɪk) *adj.*

theophylline (ˌθɪəˈfɪliːn, -ɪn) *n.* a white crystalline alkaloid that is an isomer of theobromine: it occurs in plants such as tea. [C19: < THEO(BROMINE) + PHYLLO- + -INE[2]]

theorem (ˈθɪərəm) *n.* a statement or formula that can be deduced from the axioms of a formal system by means of its rules of inference. [C16: < LL *theōrēma,* < Gk: something to be viewed, < *theōrein* to view] —**theorematic** (ˌθɪərəˈmætɪk) *or* **theoremic** (ˌθɪəˈrɛmɪk) *adj.*

theoretical (ˌθɪəˈrɛtɪkəl) *or* **theoretic** *adj.* **1.** of or based on theory. **2.** lacking practical application or actual existence; hypothetical. **3.** using or dealing in theory; impractical. —ˌ**theoˈretically** *adv.*

theoretician (ˌθɪərɪˈtɪʃən) *n.* a student or user of the theory rather than the practical aspects of a subject.

theoretics (ˌθɪəˈrɛtɪks) *n.* (*functioning as sing. or pl.*) the theory of a particular subject.

theorize *or* **-ise** (ˈθɪəˌraɪz) *vb.* (*intr.*) to produce or use theories; speculate. —ˈ**theorist** *n.* —ˌ**theoriˈzation** *or* **-iˈsation** *n.* —ˈ**theoˌrizer** *or* **-iser** *n.*

theory (ˈθɪərɪ) *n., pl.* **-ries. 1.** a system of rules, procedures, and assumptions used to produce a result. **2.** abstract knowledge or reasoning. **3.** a conjectural view or idea: *I have a theory about that.* **4.** an ideal or hypothetical situation (esp. in **in theory**). **5.** a set of hypotheses related by logical or mathematical arguments to explain a wide variety of connected phenomena in general terms: *the theory of relativity.* **6.** a nontechnical name for **hypothesis.** [C16: < LL *theōria,* < Gk: a sight, < *theōrein* to gaze upon]

theory of games *n.* a mathematical theory concerned with the optimum choice of strategy in situations involving a conflict of interest. Also called: **game theory.**

theosophy (θɪˈɒsəfɪ) *n.* **1.** any of various religious or philosophical systems claiming to be based on or to express an intuitive insight into the divine nature. **2.** the system of beliefs of the Theosophical Society founded in 1875, claiming to be derived from the sacred writings of Brahmanism and Buddhism. [C17: < Med. L *theosophia,* < LGk; see THEO-, -SOPHY] —**theosophical** (ˌθɪəˈsɒfɪkᵊl) *or* ˌ**theoˈsophic** *adj.* —**theˈosophist** *n.*

therapeutic (ˌθɛrəˈpjuːtɪk) *adj.* **1.** of or relating to the treatment of disease; curative. **2.** serving or performed to maintain health: *therapeutic abortion.* [C17: < NL *therapeuticus,* < Gk, < *therapeuein* to minister to, < *theraps* an attendant] —ˌ**theraˈpeutically** *adv.*

therapeutics (ˌθɛrəˈpjuːtɪks) *n.* (*functioning as sing.*) the branch of medicine concerned with the treatment of disease.

therapy (ˈθɛrəpɪ) *n., pl.* **-pies.** **a.** the treatment of physical, mental, or social disorders or disease. **b.** (*in combination*): *physiotherapy.* [C19: < NL *therapia,* < Gk *therapeia* attendance; see THERAPEUTIC] —ˈ**therapist** *n.*

Theravada (ˌθɛrəˈvɑːdə) *n.* the southern school of Buddhism, the name preferred by Hinayana Buddhists for their doctrines. [< Pali: doctrine of the elders]

there (ðɛə) *adv.* **1.** in, at, or to that place, point, case, or respect: *we never go there; I agree with you there.* ~*pron.* **2.** used as a grammatical subject with some verbs, esp. *be,* when the true subject follows the verb: *there is a girl in that office.* ~*adj.* **3.** (*postpositive*) who or which is in that place or position: *that boy there did it.* **4. all there.** (*predicative*) of normal intelligence. **5. so there.** an exclamation that usually follows a declaration of refusal or defiance. **6. there you are. a.** an expression used when handing a person something requested or desired. **b.** an exclamation of triumph. ~*n.* **7.** that place: *near there.* ~*interj.* **8.** an expression of sympathy, as in consoling a child: *there, there, dear.* [OE *thǣr*]

▷ **Usage.** Careful writers and speakers ensure that the verb agrees with the number of the subject in such constructions as *there is a man waiting* and *there are several people waiting.* However, where the subject is compound even careful speakers frequently use the singular as in *there is a pen and a book on the table.*

thereabouts (ˈðɛərəˌbaʊts) *or U.S.* **thereabout** *adv.* near that place, time, amount, etc.

thereafter (ˌðɛərˈɑːftə) *adv.* from that time on or after that time.

thereat (ˌðɛərˈæt) *adv. Rare.* **1.** at that point or time. **2.** for that reason.

thereby (ˌðɛəˈbaɪ, ˈðɛəˌbaɪ) *adv.* **1.** by that means; because of that. **2.** *Arch.* thereabouts.

therefor (ˌðɛəˈfɔː) *adv. Arch.* for this, that, or it.

therefore (ˈðɛəˌfɔː) *sentence connector.* **1.** thus; hence: *those people have their umbrellas up; therefore, it must be raining.* **2.** consequently; as a result.

therefrom (ˌðɛəˈfrɒm) *adv. Arch.* from that or there: *the roads that lead therefrom.*

therein (ˌðɛərˈɪn) *adv. Formal or law.* in or into that place, thing, etc.

thereinto (ˌðɛərˈɪntuː) *adv. Formal or law.* into that place, circumstance, etc.

thereof (ˌðɛərˈɒv) *adv. Formal or law.* **1.** of or concerning that or it. **2.** from or because of that.

thereon (ˌðɛərˈɒn) *adv. Arch.* thereupon.

thereto (ˌðɛəˈtuː) *adv.* **1.** *Formal or law.* to that or it. **2.** *Obs.* in addition to that.

theretofore (ˌðɛətʊˈfɔː) *adv. Formal or law.* before that time; previous to that.

thereunder (ˌðɛərˈʌndə) *adv. Formal or law.* **1.** (in documents, etc.) below that or it; subsequently in that; thereafter. **2.** under the terms or authority of that.

thereupon (ˌðɛərəˈpɒn) *adv.* **1.** immediately after that; at that point. **2.** *Formal or law.* upon that thing, point, subject, etc.

therewith (ˌðɛəˈwɪθ, -ˈwɪð) *or* **therewithal** *adv.* **1.** *Formal or law.* with or in addition to that. **2.** a less common word for **thereupon** (sense 1). **3.** *Arch.* by means of or on account of that.

therianthropic (ˌθɪərɪənˈθrɒpɪk) *adj.* **1.** (of certain mythical creatures or deities) having a partly animal, partly human form. **2.** of or relating to such creatures or deities. [C19: < Gk *thērion* wild animal + *anthrōpos* man] —**therianthropism** (ˌθɪərɪˈænθrəˌpɪzəm) *n.*

theriomorphic (ˌθɪərɪəʊˈmɔːfɪk) *adj.* (esp. of a deity) possessing or depicted in the form of a beast. [C19: < Gk *thēriomorphos,* < *thērion* wild animal + *morphē* shape]

therm (θɜːm) *n. Brit.* a unit of heat equal to 100000 British thermal units. One therm is equal to $1.055\,056 \times 10^8$ joules. [C19: < Gk *thermē* heat]

thermae (ˈθɜːmiː) *pl. n.* public baths or hot springs, esp. in ancient Greece or Rome. [C17: < L, < Gk *thermai,* pl. of *thermē* heat]

thermal (ˈθɜːməl) *adj.* **1.** Also: **thermic.** of, caused by, or generating heat. **2.** hot or warm: *thermal baths.* **3.** (of garments) specially made so as to have exceptional heat-retaining qualities: *thermal underwear.* ~*n.* **4.** a column of rising air caused by local unequal heating of the land surface, and used by gliders and birds to gain height. **5.** (*pl.*) thermal garments, esp. underclothes. —ˈ**thermally** *adv.*

thermal barrier *n.* an obstacle to flight at very high speeds as a result of the heating effect of air friction. Also called: **heat barrier.**

thermal conductivity *n.* a measure of the ability of a substance to conduct heat.

thermal efficiency *n.* the ratio of the work done by a heat engine to the energy supplied to it.

thermal equator *n.* an imaginary line round the earth running through the point on each meridian with the highest average temperature.

thermalize *or* **-ise** (ˈθɜːməˌlaɪz) *vb. Physics.* to undergo or cause to undergo a process in which neutrons lose energy in a moderator and become thermal neutrons. —ˌ**thermaliˈzation** *or* **-iˈsation** *n.*

thermal neutrons *pl. n.* slow neutrons that are approximately in thermal equilibrium with a moderator.

thermal reactor *n.* a nuclear reactor in which most of the fission is caused by thermal neutrons.

thermal shock *n.* a fluctuation in temperature causing stress in a material. It often results in fracture, esp. in brittle materials such as ceramics.

thermion (ˈθɜːmɪən) *n. Physics.* an electron or ion emitted by a body at high temperature.

thermionic (ˌθɜːmɪˈɒnɪk) *adj.* of, relating to, or operated by electrons emitted from materials at high temperatures: *a thermionic valve.*

thermionic current *n.* an electric current produced between two electrodes as a result of electrons emitted by thermionic emission.

thermionic emission *n.* the emission of electrons from very hot solids or liquids.

thermionics (ˌθɜːmɪˈɒnɪks) *n.* (*functioning as sing.*) the branch of electronics concerned with the emission of electrons by hot bodies and with devices based on this effect.

thermionic valve *or esp. U.S. & Canad.* **tube** *n.* an electronic valve in which electrons are emitted from a heated rather than a cold cathode.

thermistor (θɜːˈmɪstə) *n.* a semiconductor device having a resistance that decreases rapidly with an increase in temperature. It is used for temperature measurement and control. [C20: < THERMO- + (RES)ISTOR]

Thermit (ˈθɜːmɪt) *or* **Thermite** (ˈθɜːmaɪt) *n. Trademark.* a mixture of aluminium powder and a metal oxide, which when ignited produces great heat: used for welding and in incendiary bombs.

thermo- *or before a vowel* **therm-** *combining*

form. related to, caused by, or measuring heat: *thermodynamics; thermophile.* [< Gk *thermos* hot, *thermē* heat]

thermobarograph (ˌθɜːməʊˈbærəˌgrɑːf) *n.* a device that simultaneously records the temperature and pressure of the atmosphere.

thermobarometer (ˌθɜːməʊbəˈrɒmɪtə) *n.* an apparatus that provides an accurate measurement of pressure by observation of the change in the boiling point of a fluid.

thermochemistry (ˌθɜːməʊˈkɛmɪstrɪ) *n.* the branch of chemistry concerned with the study and measurement of the heat evolved or absorbed during chemical reactions. —ˌ**thermoˈchemical** *adj.* —ˌ**thermoˈchemist** *n.*

thermocline (ˈθɜːməʊˌklaɪn) *n.* a temperature gradient in a thermally stratified body of water, such as a lake.

thermocouple (ˈθɜːməʊˌkʌpᵊl) *n.* **1.** a device for measuring temperature consisting of a pair of wires of different metals or semiconductors joined at both ends. One junction is at the temperature to be measured, the second at a fixed temperature. The electromotive force generated depends upon the temperature difference. **2.** a similar device with only one junction between two dissimilar metals or semiconductors.

thermodynamic (ˌθɜːməʊdaɪˈnæmɪk) *or* **thermodynamical** *adj.* **1.** of or concerned with thermodynamics. **2.** determined by or obeying the laws of thermodynamics.

thermodynamic equilibrium *n.* the condition of a system in which the quantities that specify its properties, such as pressure, temperature, etc., all remain unchanged.

thermodynamics (ˌθɜːməʊdaɪˈnæmɪks) *n.* (*functioning as sing.*) the branch of physical science concerned with the interrelationship and interconversion of different forms of energy.

thermodynamic temperature *n.* temperature defined in terms of the laws of thermodynamics and not in terms of the properties of any real material: usually expressed in the Kelvin scale.

thermoelectric (ˌθɜːməʊɪˈlɛktrɪk) *or* **thermoelectrical** *adj.* **1.** of, relating to, used in, or operated by the conversion of heat energy to electrical energy. **2.** of, relating to, used in, or operated by the conversion of electrical energy.

thermoelectric effect *n.* another name for the **Seebeck effect.**

thermoelectricity (ˌθɜːməʊɪlɛkˈtrɪsɪtɪ) *n.* **1.** electricity generated by a thermocouple. **2.** the study of the relationship between heat and electrical energy.

thermoelectron (ˌθɜːməʊɪˈlɛktrɒn) *n.* an electron emitted at high temperature, such as one produced in a thermionic valve.

thermogenesis (ˌθɜːməʊˈdʒɛnɪsɪs) *n.* the production of heat by metabolic processes.

thermograph (ˈθɜːməʊˌgrɑːf) *n.* a type of thermometer that produces a continuous record (**thermogram**) of a fluctuating temperature.

thermojunction (ˌθɜːməʊˈdʒʌŋkʃən) *n.* a point of electrical contact between two dissimilar metals across which a voltage appears, the magnitude of which depends on the temperature of the contact and the nature of the metals.

thermolabile (ˌθɜːməʊˈleɪbɪl) *adj.* easily decomposed or subject to a loss of characteristic properties by the action of heat.

thermoluminescence (ˌθɜːməʊˌluːmɪˈnɛsəns) *n.* phosphorescence of certain materials or objects as a result of heating.

thermolysis (θɜːˈmɒlɪsɪs) *n.* **1.** *Physiol.* loss of heat from the body. **2.** the dissociation of a substance as a result of heating. —**thermolytic** (ˌθɜːməʊˈlɪtɪk) *adj.*

thermomagnetic (ˌθɜːməʊmægˈnɛtɪk) *adj.* of or concerned with the relationship between heat and magnetism, esp. the change in temperature of a body when it is magnetized or demagnetized.

thermometer (θəˈmɒmɪtə) *n.* an instrument used to measure temperature, esp. one in which a thin column of liquid, such as mercury, expands and contracts within a graduated sealed tube. —**therˈmometry** *n.*

thermonuclear (ˌθɜːməʊˈnjuːklɪə) *adj.* **1.** involving nuclear fusion. **2.** involving thermonuclear weapons.

thermonuclear reaction *n.* a nuclear fusion reaction occurring at a very high temperature: responsible for the energy produced in the sun, nuclear weapons, and fusion reactors.

thermophile (ˈθɜːməʊˌfaɪl) *or* **thermophil** (ˈθɜːməʊˌfɪl) *n.* **1.** an organism, esp. a bacterium or plant, that thrives under warm conditions. ~*adj.* **2.** thriving under warm conditions. —ˌ**thermoˈphilic** *adj.*

thermopile (ˈθɜːməʊˌpaɪl) *n.* an instrument for detecting and measuring heat radiation or for generating a thermoelectric current. It consists of a number of thermocouple junctions.

thermoplastic (ˌθɜːməʊˈplæstɪk) *adj.* **1.** (of a material, esp. a synthetic plastic) becoming soft when heated and rehardening on cooling without appreciable change of properties. ~*n.* **2.** a synthetic plastic or resin, such as polystyrene, with these properties.

Thermos *or* **Thermos flask** (ˈθɜːməs) *n.* *Trademark.* a type of stoppered vacuum flask used to preserve the temperature of its contents.

thermosetting (ˌθɜːməʊˈsɛtɪŋ) *adj.* (of a material, esp. a synthetic plastic) hardening permanently after one application of heat and pressure.

thermosiphon (ˌθɜːməʊˈsaɪfən) *n.* a system in which a coolant is circulated by convection caused by a difference in density between the hot and cold portions of the liquid.

thermosphere (ˈθɜːməˌsfɪə) *n.* an atmospheric layer lying between the mesosphere and the exosphere.

thermostable (ˌθɜːməʊˈsteɪbᵊl) *adj.* capable of withstanding moderate heat without loss of characteristic properties.

thermostat (ˈθɜːməˌstæt) *n.* **1.** a device that maintains a system at a constant temperature. **2.** a device that sets off a sprinkler, etc., at a certain temperature. —ˌ**thermoˈstatic** *adj.* —ˌ**thermoˈstatically** *adv.*

thermostatics (ˌθɜːməˈstætɪks) *n.* (*functioning as sing.*) the branch of science concerned with thermal equilibrium.

thermotaxis (ˌθɜːməʊˈtæksɪs) *n.* the directional movement of an organism in response to the stimulus of heat. —ˌ**thermoˈtaxic** *adj.*

thermotropism (ˌθɜːməʊˈtrəʊpɪzəm) *n.* the directional growth of a plant in response to the stimulus of heat. —ˌ**thermoˈtropic** *adj.*

-thermy *n. combining form.* indicating heat: *diathermy.* [< NL *-thermia,* < Gk *thermē*] —**-thermic** *or* **-thermal** *adj. combining form.*

theroid (ˈθɪərɔɪd) *adj.* of, relating to, or resembling a beast. [C19: < Gk *thēroeidēs,* < *thēr* wild animal; see -OID]

thesaurus (θɪˈsɔːrəs) *n., pl.* **-ri** (-raɪ) *or* **-ruses. 1.** a book containing systematized lists of synonyms and related words. **2.** a dictionary of selected words or topics. **3.** *Rare.* a treasury. [C18: < L, Gk: TREASURE]

these (ðiːz) *determiner.* **a.** the form of **this** used before a plural noun: *these men.* **b.** (*as pronoun*): *I don't much care for these.*

thesis (ˈθiːsɪs) *n., pl.* **-ses** (-siːz). **1.** a dissertation resulting from original research, esp. when submitted for a degree or diploma. **2.** a doctrine maintained in argument. **3.** a subject for a discussion or essay. **4.** an unproved statement put forward as a premise in an argument. [C16: via LL < Gk: a placing, < *tithenai* to place]

Thespian (ˈθɛspɪən) *adj.* **1.** of or relating to Thespis, 6th-century B.C. Greek poet. **2.** of or relating to drama and the theatre; dramatic. ~*n.* **3.** *Often facetious.* an actor or actress.

Thess. *Bible. abbrev. for* Thessalonians.

theta (ˈθiːtə) *n.* the eighth letter of the Greek alphabet (Θ, θ). [C17: < Gk]

theurgy (ˈθiːˌɜːdʒɪ) *n., pl.* **-gies. 1.** the intervention of a divine or supernatural agency in the affairs of man. **2.** beneficent magic as taught by Egyptian Neoplatonists. [C16: < LL *theūrgia*, < LGk *theourgia* the practice of magic, < *theo-* THEO- + *-urgia*, < *ergon* work] —**the'urgic** *or* **the'urgical** *adj.* —**'theurgist** *n.*

thew (θjuː) *n.* **1.** muscle, esp. if strong or well-developed. **2.** (*pl.*) muscular strength. [OE *thēaw*] —**'thewless** *adj.* —**'thewy** *adj.*

they (ðeɪ) *pron.* (*subjective*) **1.** refers to people or things other than the speaker or people addressed: *they fight among themselves.* **2.** refers to people in general: *in Australia they have Christmas in the summer.* **3.** refers to an indefinite antecedent such as *one*, *whoever*, or *anybody*: *if anyone objects, they can go.* [C12 *thei* < ON *their*, masc. nominative pl., equivalent to OE *thā*]

▷ **Usage.** See at **their.**

they'd (ðeɪd) *contraction of* they would *or* they had.

they'll (ðeɪl) *contraction of* they will *or* they shall.

they're (ðɛə, 'ðeɪə) *contraction of* they are.

they've (ðeɪv) *contraction of* they have.

thi- *combining form.* a variant of **thio-.**

thiamine ('θaɪəˌmiːn, -mɪn) *or* **thiamin** ('θaɪəmɪn) *n.* a white crystalline vitamin that occurs in the outer coat of rice and other grains. It forms part of the vitamin B complex: deficiency leads to nervous disorders and to the disease beriberi. Also called: **vitamin B_1, aneurin.** [C20: THIO- + (VIT)AMIN]

thiazine ('θaɪəˌziːn, -ˌzaɪn) *n.* any of a group of organic compounds containing a ring system composed of four carbon atoms, a sulphur atom, and a nitrogen atom.

thiazole ('θaɪəˌzəʊl) *n.* **1.** a colourless liquid that contains a ring system composed of three carbon atoms, a sulphur atom, and a nitrogen atom. **2.** any of a group of compounds derived from this substance that are used in dyes.

thick (θɪk) *adj.* **1.** of relatively great extent from one surface to the other: *a thick slice of bread.* **2. a.** (*postpositive*) of specific fatness: *ten centimetres thick.* **b.** (*in combination*): *a six-inch-thick wall.* **3.** having a dense consistency: *thick soup.* **4.** abundantly covered or filled: *a piano thick with dust.* **5.** impenetrable; dense: *a thick fog.* **6.** stupid, slow, or insensitive. **7.** throaty or badly articulated: *a voice thick with emotion.* **8.** (of accents, etc.) pronounced. **9.** *Inf.* very friendly (esp. in **thick as thieves**). **10. a bit thick.** *Brit.* unfair or excessive. ~*adv.* **11.** in order to produce something thick: *to slice bread thick.* **12.** profusely; in quick succession (esp. in **thick and fast**). **13. lay it on thick.** *Inf.* **a.** to exaggerate a story, etc. **b.** to flatter excessively. ~*n.* **14.** a thick piece or part. **15. the thick.** the most intense or active part. **16. through thick and thin.** in good times and bad. [OE *thicce*] —**'thickish** *adj.* —**'thickly** *adv.*

thicken ('θɪkən) *vb.* **1.** to make or become thick or thicker. **2.** (*intr.*) to become more involved: *the plot thickened.* —**'thickener** *n.*

thickening ('θɪkənɪŋ) *n.* **1.** something added to a liquid to thicken it. **2.** a thickened part or piece.

thicket ('θɪkɪt) *n.* a dense growth of small trees, shrubs, and similar plants. [OE *thiccet*]

thickhead ('θɪkˌhɛd) *n.* **1.** a stupid or ignorant person; fool. **2.** any of a family of Australian and SE Asian songbirds. —ˌ**thick'headed** *adj.*

thickie *or* **thicky** ('θɪkɪ) *n., pl.* **-ies.** *Brit. sl.* a slow-witted unintelligent person.

thick-knee *n.* another name for **stone curlew.**

thickness ('θɪknɪs) *n.* **1.** the state or quality of being thick. **2.** the dimension through an object, as opposed to length or width. **3.** a layer.

thickset (ˌθɪk'sɛt) *adj.* **1.** stocky in build; sturdy. **2.** densely planted or placed. ~*n.* **3.** a rare word for **thicket.**

thick-skinned *adj.* insensitive to criticism or hints; not easily upset or affected.

thick-witted *or* **thick-skulled** *adj.* stupid, dull, or slow to learn. —ˌ**thick-'wittedly** *adv.* —ˌ**thick-'wittedness** *n.*

thief (θiːf) *n., pl.* **thieves** (θiːvz). a person who steals something from another. [OE *thēof*] —**'thievish** *adj.*

thieve (θiːv) *vb.* to steal (someone's possessions). [OE *thēofian*, < *thēof* thief] —**'thievery** *n.* —**'thieving** *adj.*

thigh (θaɪ) *n.* **1.** the part of the leg between the hip and the knee in man. **2.** the corresponding part in other vertebrates and insects. ~Related adj.: **femoral.** [OE *thēh*]

thighbone ('θaɪˌbəʊn) *n.* a nontechnical name for the **femur.**

thimble ('θɪmbᵊl) *n.* **1.** a cap of metal, plastic, etc., used to protect the end of the finger when sewing. **2.** any small metal cap resembling this. **3.** *Naut.* a loop of metal having a groove at its outer edge for a rope or cable. [OE *thӯmel* thumbstall, < *thūma* thumb]

thimbleful ('θɪmbᵊlˌfʊl) *n.* a very small amount, esp. of a liquid.

thimblerig ('θɪmbᵊlˌrɪg) *n.* a game in which the operator rapidly moves about three inverted thimbles, often with sleight of hand, one of which conceals a token, the other player betting on which thimble the token is under. [C19: < THIMBLE + RIG (in obs. sense meaning a trick, scheme)] —**'thimbleˌrigger** *n.*

thin (θɪn) *adj.* **thinner, thinnest.** **1.** of relatively small extent from one side or surface to the other. **2.** slim or lean. **3.** sparsely placed; meagre: *thin hair.* **4.** of low density: *a thin liquid.* **5.** weak; poor: *a thin disguise.* **6. thin on the ground.** few in number; scarce. ~*adv.* **7.** in order to produce something thin: *to cut bread thin.* ~*vb.* **thinning, thinned.** **8.** to make or become thin or sparse. [OE *thynne*] —**'thinly** *adv.* —**'thinness** *n.*

thine (ðaɪn) *determiner. Arch.* **a.** (*preceding a vowel*) of or associated with you (thou): *thine eyes.* **b.** (*as pronoun*): *thine is the greatest burden.* [OE *thīn*]

thin-film *adj.* (of an electronic component, etc.) composed of one or more extremely thin layers of metal, semiconductor, etc.

thing (θɪŋ) *n.* **1.** an object, fact, affair, circumstance, or concept considered as being a separate entity. **2.** any inanimate object. **3.** an object or entity that cannot or need not be precisely named. **4.** *Inf.* a person or animal: *you poor thing.* **5.** an event or act. **6.** a thought or statement. **7.** *Law.* property. **8.** a device, means, or instrument. **9.** (*often pl.*) a possession, article of clothing, etc. **10.** *Inf.* a preoccupation or obsession (esp. in **have a thing about**). **11.** an activity or mode of behaviour satisfying to one's personality (esp. in **do one's (own) thing**). **12. make a thing of.** exaggerate the importance of. **13. the thing.** the latest fashion. [OE *thing* assembly]

thing-in-itself *n.* (in the philosophy of Immanuel Kant (1724–1804), German idealist philosopher) reality regarded apart from human knowledge and perception.

thingumabob *or* **thingamabob** ('θɪŋəməˌbɒb) *n. Inf.* a person or thing the name of which is unknown, temporarily forgotten, or deliberately overlooked. Also: **thingumajig, thingamajig,** *or* **thingummy.** [C18: < THING, with humorous suffix]

think (θɪŋk) *vb.* **thinking, thought.** **1.** (*tr.; may take a clause as object*) to consider, judge, or believe: *he thinks my ideas impractical.* **2.** (*intr.; often foll. by about*) to exercise the mind as in order to make a decision; ponder. **3.** (*intr.*) to be capable of conscious thought: *man is the only animal that thinks.* **4.** to remember; recollect. **5.** (*intr.; foll. by of*) to make the mental choice (of): *think of a number.* **6.** (*may take a clause as object or an infinitive*) **a.** to expect; suppose. **b.** to be considerate enough (to do something): *he did not think to thank them.* **7.** (*intr.*) to focus the attention on being: *think big.* **8. think twice.** to consider carefully before deciding. ~*n.* **9.** *Inf.* a careful, open-minded assessment. **10.** (*modifier*) *Inf.* characterized by or involving thinkers, thinking, or thought. ~See also **think over, think up.** [OE *thencan*] —**'thinkable** *adj.* —**'thinker** *n.*

thinking ('θɪŋkɪŋ) *n.* **1.** opinion or judgment. **2.**

the process of thought. ~*adj.* **3.** (*prenominal*) using or capable of using intelligent thought: *thinking people.* **4. put on one's thinking cap.** to ponder a matter or problem.

think over *vb.* (*tr., adv.*) to ponder or consider.

think-tank *n. Inf.* a group of specialists commissioned to undertake intensive study and research into specified problems.

think up *vb.* (*tr., adv.*) to invent or devise.

thinner ('θɪnə) *n.* (*often pl., functioning as sing.*) a solvent, such as turpentine, added to paint or varnish to dilute it, reduce its opacity or viscosity, or increase its penetration.

thin-skinned *adj.* sensitive to criticism or hints; easily upset or affected.

thio- *or before a vowel* **thi-** *combining form.* sulphur, esp. denoting the replacement of an oxygen atom with a sulphur atom: *thiol; thiosulphate.* [< Gk *theion* sulphur]

thiol ('θaɪɒl) *n.* any of a class of sulphur-containing organic compounds with the formula RSH, where R is an organic group.

thionine ('θaɪəʊˌniːn, -ˌnaɪn) *or* **thionin** ('θaɪənɪn) *n.* **1.** a crystalline derivative of thiazine used as a violet dye to stain microscope specimens. **2.** any of a class of related dyes. [C19: by shortening, < *ergothioneine*]

thiopentone sodium (ˌθaɪəʊ'pɛntəʊn) *or* **thiopental sodium** (ˌθaɪəʊ'pɛntæl) *n.* a barbiturate drug used as an intravenous general anaesthetic. Also called: **Sodium Pentothal.**

thiophen ('θaɪəʊˌfɛn) *or* **thiophene** ('θaɪəʊˌfiːn) *n.* a colourless liquid heterocyclic compound found in the benzene fraction of coal tar and manufactured from butane and sulphur.

thiosulphate (ˌθaɪəʊ'sʌlfeɪt) *n.* any salt of thiosulphuric acid.

thiosulphuric acid (ˌθaɪəʊsʌl'fjʊərɪk) *n.* an unstable acid known only in solutions and in the form of its salts. Formula: $H_2S_2O_3$.

thiouracil (ˌθaɪəʊ'jʊərəsɪl) *n.* a white crystalline water-insoluble substance with an intensely bitter taste, used in medicine to treat hyperthyroidism. [< THIO- + *uracil* (URO- + AC(ETIC) + -IL(E)]

thiourea (ˌθaɪəʊ'jʊərɪə) *n.* a white crystalline substance used in photographic fixing, rubber vulcanization, and the manufacture of synthetic resins.

third (θɜːd) *adj.* (*usually prenominal*) **1. a.** coming after the second in numbering, position, etc.; being the ordinal number of *three:* often written 3rd. **b.** (*as n.*): *the third got a prize.* **2.** rated, graded, or ranked below the second level. **3.** denoting the third from lowest forward ratio of a gearbox in a motor vehicle. ~*n.* **4. a.** one of three equal parts of an object, quantity, etc. **b.** (*as modifier*): *a third part.* **5.** the fraction equal to one divided by three (1/3). **6.** the forward ratio above second of a gearbox in a motor vehicle. **7. a.** the interval between one note and another three notes away from it counting inclusively along the diatonic scale. **b.** one of two notes constituting such an interval in relation to the other. **8.** *Brit.* an honours degree of the third and usually the lowest class. Full term: **third class honours degree.** ~*adv.* **9.** Also: **thirdly.** in the third place. [OE *thirda,* var. of *thridda;* rel. to OFrisian *thredda,* OSaxon *thriddio*] —'**thirdly** *adv.*

Third Age *n.* **the.** old age, esp. when viewed as a period of opportunity for learning something new or for other new developments.

third class *n.* **1.** the class or grade next in value, quality, etc., to the second. ~*adj.* (**third-class** *when prenominal*). **2.** of the class or grade next in value, quality, etc., to the second. ~*adv.* **3.** by third-class transport, etc.

third degree *n. Inf.* torture or bullying, esp. used to extort confessions or information.

third-degree burn *n. Pathol.* the most severe type of burn, involving the destruction of both epidermis and dermis.

third dimension *n.* the dimension of depth by which a solid object may be distinguished from a two-dimensional drawing or picture of it.

third eyelid *n.* another name for **nictitating membrane.**

Third International *n.* another name for **Comintern.**

third man *n. Cricket.* a fielding position on the off side near the boundary behind the batsman's wicket.

Third Market *n. Stock Exchange.* a new small market designed to meet the needs of young growing British companies for raising capital.

third party *n.* **1.** a person who is involved by chance or only incidentally in a legal proceeding, agreement, or other transaction. ~*adj.* **2.** *Insurance.* providing protection against liability caused by accidental injury or death of other persons.

third person *n.* a grammatical category of pronouns and verbs used when referring to objects or individuals other than the speaker or his addressee or addressees.

third-rate *adj.* mediocre or inferior.

third reading *n.* (in a legislative assembly) **1.** *Brit.* the process of discussing the committee's report on a bill. **2.** *U.S.* the final consideration of a bill.

Third World *n.* the countries of Africa, Asia, and Latin America collectively, esp. when viewed as underdeveloped.

thirst (θɜːst) *n.* **1.** a craving to drink, accompanied by a feeling of dryness in the mouth and throat. **2.** an eager longing, craving, or yearning. ~*vb.* (*intr.*) **3.** to feel a thirst. [OE *thyrstan,* < *thurst*]

thirsty ('θɜːstɪ) *adj.* **thirstier, thirstiest. 1.** feeling a desire to drink. **2.** dry; arid. **3.** (foll. by *for*) feeling an eager desire. **4.** causing thirst. —'**thirstily** *adv.* —'**thirstiness** *n.*

thirteen ('θɜː'tiːn) *n.* **1.** the cardinal number that is the sum of ten and three and is a prime number. **2.** a numeral, 13, XIII, etc., representing this number. **3.** something representing or consisting of 13 units. ~*determiner.* **4. a.** amounting to thirteen. **b.** (*as pronoun*): *thirteen of them fell.* [OE *threotēne*] —'**thir'teenth** *adj., n.*

thirteenth chord *n.* a chord much used in jazz and pop, consisting of a major or minor triad upon which are superimposed the seventh, ninth, eleventh, and thirteenth above the root. Often shortened to **thirteenth.**

thirty ('θɜːtɪ) *n., pl.* **-ties. 1.** the cardinal number that is the product of ten and three. **2.** a numeral, 30, XXX, etc., representing this number. **3.** (*pl.*) the numbers 30-39, esp. the 30th to the 39th year of a person's life or of a century. **4.** the amount or quantity that is three times as big as ten. **5.** something representing or consisting of 30 units. ~*determiner.* **6. a.** amounting to thirty. **b.** (*as pronoun*): *thirty are broken.* [OE *thritig*] —'**thirtieth** *adj., n.*

Thirty-nine Articles *pl. n.* a set of formulas defining the doctrinal position of the Church of England, drawn up in the 16th century.

thirty-second note *n.* the usual U.S. and Canad. name for **demisemiquaver.**

thirty-twomo (ˌθɜːtɪ'tuːməʊ) *n., pl.* **-mos.** a book size resulting from folding a sheet of paper into 32 leaves or 64 pages.

this (ðɪs) *determiner.* (*used before a sing. n.*) **1. a.** used preceding a noun referring to something or someone that is closer: *look at this picture.* **b.** (*as pronoun*): *take this.* **2. a.** used preceding a noun that has just been mentioned or is understood: *this plan of yours won't work.* **b.** (*as pronoun*): *I first saw this on Sunday.* **3. a.** used to refer to something about to be said, read, etc.: *consider this argument.* **b.** (*as pronoun*): *listen to this.* **4. a.** the present or immediate: *this time you'll know better.* **b.** (*as pronoun*): *before this, I was mistaken.* **5.** *Inf.* an emphatic form of **a** or **the**[1]: *I saw this big brown bear.* **6. this and that.** various unspecified and trivial actions, matters, objects, etc. **7. with** (*or* **at**) **this.** after this. ~*adv.* **8.** used with adjectives and adverbs to specify a precise degree that is about to be mentioned: *go* *just this fast and you'll be safe.* [OE *thēs, thēos, this* (masc., fem., neuter sing.).

thistle ('θɪsᵊl) *n.* **1.** any of a genus of plants of the composite family, having prickly-edged leaves, dense flower heads, and feathery hairs on the seeds: the national emblem of Scotland. **2.** any of various similar or related plants. [OE *thīstel*] —'**thistly** *adj.*

thistledown ('θɪsᵊlˌdaʊn) *n.* the mass of feathery plumed seeds produced by a thistle.

thither ('ðɪðə) *or* **thitherward** *adv. Obs. or formal.* to or towards that place; in that direction. [OE *thider,* var. of *thæder,* infl. by *hider* hither]

thitherto (ˌðɪðə'tuː, 'ðɪðəˌtuː) *adv. Obs. or formal.* until that time.

thixotropic (ˌθɪksə'trɒpɪk) *adj.* (of fluids and gels) having a reduced viscosity when stress is applied, as when stirred: *thixotropic paints.* [< Gk *thixis* the act of touching + -TROPIC] —**thixotropy** (θɪk'sɒtrəpɪ) *n.*

tho *or* **tho'** (ðəʊ) *conj., adv. U.S. or poetic.* a variant spelling of **though.**

thole[1] (θəʊl) *or* **tholepin** ('θəʊlˌpɪn) *n.* a wooden pin or one of a pair, set upright in the gunwales of a rowing boat to serve as a fulcrum in rowing. [OE *tholl*]

thole[2] (θəʊl) *vb.* **1.** (*tr.*) *Scot. & N English dialect.* to put up with; bear. **2.** an archaic word for **suffer.** [OE *tholian*]

tholos ('θəʊlɒs) *n., pl.* **-loi** (-lɔɪ). a dry-stone beehive-shaped tomb associated with the Mycenaean culture of Greece from the 16th to the 12th centuries B.C. [C17: < Gk]

Thomism ('təʊmɪzəm) *n.* the system of philosophy and theology developed by Saint Thomas Aquinas in the 13th century.

Thompson sub-machine-gun ('tɒmsən) *n. Trademark.* a .45 calibre sub-machine-gun.

-thon *suffix forming nouns.* indicating a large-scale event or operation of a specified kind: *telethon.* [C20: on the pattern of MARATHON]

thong (θɒŋ) *n.* **1.** a thin strip of leather or other material. **2.** a whip or whiplash, esp. one made of leather. **3.** *U.S., Canad., Austral., & N.Z.* the usual name for **flip-flop** (sense 5). [OE *thwang*]

thoracic (θɔː'ræsɪk) *adj.* of, near, or relating to the thorax.

thoracic duct *n.* the major duct of the lymphatic system, beginning below the diaphragm and ascending in front of the spinal column to the base of the neck.

thoraco- *or before a vowel* **thorac-** *combining form.* thorax: *thoracotomy.*

thoracoplasty ('θɔːrəkəʊˌplæstɪ) *n., pl.* **-ties. 1.** plastic surgery of the thorax. **2.** surgical removal of several ribs or a part of them to permit the collapse of a diseased lung.

thorax ('θɔːræks) *n., pl.* **thoraxes** *or* **thoraces** ('θɔːrəˌsiːz, θɔː'reɪsiːz). **1.** the part of the human body enclosed by the ribs. **2.** the corresponding part in other vertebrates. **3.** the part of an insect's body between the head and abdomen. [C16: via L < Gk *thōrax* breastplate, chest]

thorium ('θɔːrɪəm) *n.* a silvery-white radioactive metallic element. It is used in electronic equipment and as a nuclear power source. Symbol: Th; atomic no.: 90; atomic wt.: 232.04. [C19: NL, *Thor* Norse god of thunder + -IUM] —'**thoric** *adj.*

thorium dioxide *n.* a white powder used in incandescent mantles. Also called: **thoria.**

thorium series *n.* a radioactive series that starts with thorium-232 and ends with lead-208.

thorn (θɔːn) *n.* **1.** a sharp pointed woody extension of a stem or leaf. Cf. **prickle** (sense 1). **2.** any of various trees or shrubs having thorns, esp. the hawthorn. **3.** a Germanic character of runic origin (þ) used in Icelandic to represent the sound of *th,* as in *thin, bath.* **4.** this same character as used in Old and Middle English to represent this sound. **5.** a source of irritation (esp. in **a thorn in one's side** *or* **flesh**). [OE] —'**thornless** *adj.*

thorn apple *n.* **1.** a poisonous plant of the N hemisphere, having white funnel-shaped flowers and spiny fruits. U.S. name: **jimson weed. 2.** the fruit of certain types of hawthorn.

thornbill ('θɔːnˌbɪl) *n.* **1.** any of various South American hummingbirds having a thornlike bill. **2.** Also called: **thornbill warbler.** any of various Australasian wrens. **3.** any of various other birds with thornlike bills.

thorny ('θɔːnɪ) *adj.* **thornier, thorniest. 1.** bearing or covered with thorns. **2.** difficult or unpleasant. **3.** sharp. —'**thornily** *adv.* —'**thorniness** *n.*

thoron ('θɔːrɒn) *n.* a radioisotope of radon that is a decay product of thorium. Symbol: Tn or ^{220}Rn; atomic no.: 86; half-life: 54.5s. [C20: < THORIUM + -ON]

thorough ('θʌrə) *adj.* **1.** carried out completely and carefully. **2.** (*prenominal*) utter: *a thorough bore.* **3.** painstakingly careful. [OE *thurh*] —'**thoroughly** *adv.* —'**thoroughness** *n.*

thorough bass (beɪs) *n.* a bass part underlying a piece of concerted music. Also called: **basso continuo, continuo.** See also **figured bass.**

thoroughbred ('θʌrəˌbrɛd) *adj.* **1.** purebred. ~*n.* **2.** a pedigree animal; purebred. **3.** a person regarded as being of good breeding.

Thoroughbred ('θʌrəˌbrɛd) *n.* a British breed of horse the ancestry of which can be traced to English mares and Arab sires.

thoroughfare ('θʌrəˌfɛə) *n.* **1.** a road from one place to another, esp. a main road. **2.** way through, access, or passage: *no thoroughfare.*

thoroughgoing ('θʌrəˌgəʊɪŋ) *adj.* **1.** extremely thorough. **2.** (*usually prenominal*) absolute; complete: *thoroughgoing incompetence.*

thoroughpaced ('θʌrəˌpeɪst) *adj.* **1.** (of a horse) showing performing ability in all paces. **2.** thoroughgoing.

thorp *or* **thorpe** (θɔːp) *n. Obs. except in place names.* a small village. [OE]

those (ðəʊz) *determiner.* the form of **that** used before a plural noun. [OE *thās,* pl. of THIS]

thou[1] (ðaʊ) *pron.* (*subjective*) **1.** *Arch. or dialect.* refers to the person addressed: used mainly in familiar address. **2.** (*usually cap.*) refers to God when addressed in prayer, etc. [OE *thū*]

▷ **Usage.** Although *thou* has now disappeared from general use in English and is restricted to certain dialects, it was part of standard English until the 18th century. *Thou* was a form of address reserved for God, friends, family, and those inferior in age and status and was therefore similar in meaning and use to the modern French *tu. You* was the more formal mode of address until the disappearance of *thou.*

thou[2] (θaʊ) *n., pl.* **thous** *or* **thou. 1.** one thousandth of an inch. **2.** *Inf.* short for **thousand.**

though (ðəʊ) *conj.* (*subordinating*) **1.** (sometimes preceded by *even*) despite the fact that: *though he tries hard, he always fails.* ~*adv.* **2.** nevertheless; however: *he can't dance; he sings well, though.* [OE *theah*]

thought (θɔːt) *vb.* **1.** the past tense and past participle of **think.** ~*n.* **2.** the act or process of thinking. **3.** a concept, opinion, or idea. **4.** ideas typical of a particular time or place: *German thought in the 19th century.* **5.** application of mental attention; consideration. **6.** purpose or intention: *I have no thought of giving up.* **7.** expectation: *no thought of reward.* **8.** a small amount; trifle: *you could be a thought more enthusiastic.* **9.** kindness or regard. [OE *thōht*]

thoughtful ('θɔːtfʊl) *adj.* **1.** considerate in the treatment of other people. **2.** showing careful thought. **3.** pensive; reflective. —'**thoughtfully** *adv.* —'**thoughtfulness** *n.*

thoughtless ('θɔːtlɪs) *adj.* **1.** inconsiderate. **2.** having or showing lack of thought. —'**thoughtlessly** *adv.* —'**thoughtlessness** *n.*

thought-out *adj.* conceived and developed by careful thought: *a well thought-out scheme.*

thought transference *n. Psychol.* another name for **telepathy.**

thousand ('θaʊzənd) *n.* **1.** the cardinal number that is the product of 10 and 100. **2.** a numeral, 1000, 10^3, M, etc., representing this number. **3.**

(*often pl.*) a very large but unspecified number, amount, or quantity. **4.** something representing or consisting of 1000 units. ~*determiner.* **5. a.** amounting to a thousand. **b.** (*as pronoun*): *a thousand is hardly enough.* ~Related adj.: **millenary.** [OE *thūsend*] —ˈ**thousandth** *adj., n*

Thousand Guineas *n.* (*functioning as sing.*), usually written **1,000 Guineas.** an annual horse race, restricted to fillies, run at Newmarket in England since 1814.

Thousand Island dressing *n.* a salad dressing made from mayonnaise with ketchup, chopped gherkins, etc.

Thracian (ˈθreɪʃɪən) *n.* **1.** a member of an ancient Indo-European people who lived in Thrace, an ancient country in the SE corner of the Balkan Peninsula. **2.** the ancient language spoken by this people. ~*adj.* **3.** of or relating to Thrace, its inhabitants, or the extinct Thracian language.

thrall (θrɔːl) *n.* **1.** Also: **thraldom** *or U.S.* **thralldom** (ˈθrɔːldəm). the state or condition of being in the power of another person. **2.** a person who is in such a state. **3.** a person totally subject to some need, desire, appetite, etc. ~*vb.* **4.** (*tr.*) to enslave or dominate. [OE *thrǣl* slave]

thrash (θræʃ) *vb.* **1.** (*tr.*) to beat soundly, as with a whip or stick. **2.** (*tr.*) to defeat totally; overwhelm. **3.** (*intr.*) to beat or plunge about in a wild manner. **4.** to sail (a boat) against the wind or tide or (of a boat) to sail in this way. **5.** another word for **thresh.** ~*n.* **6.** the act of thrashing; beating. **7.** *Inf.* a party. ~See also **thrash out.** [OE *threscan*]

thrasher[1] (ˈθræʃə) *n.* another name for **thresher** (the shark).

thrasher[2] (ˈθræʃə) *n.* any of various brown thrushlike American songbirds.

thrashing (ˈθræʃɪŋ) *n.* a physical assault; flogging.

thrash out *vb.* (*tr., adv.*) to discuss fully or vehemently, esp. in order to come to an agreement.

thrasonical (θrəˈsɒnɪkᵊl) *adj. Rare.* bragging; boastful. [C16: < L *Thrasō* name of boastful soldier in *Eunuchus,* a play by Terence, < Gk *Thrasōn,* < *thrasus* forceful] —**thraˈsonically** *adv.*

thrawn (θrɔːn) *adj. Scot. & N English dialect.* **1.** crooked or twisted. **2.** stubborn; perverse. [N English dialect, var. of *thrown,* < OE *thrāwan* to twist about, throw]

thread (θrɛd) *n.* **1.** a fine strand, filament, or fibre of some material. **2.** a fine cord of twisted filaments, esp. of cotton, used in sewing, etc. **3.** any of the filaments of which a spider's web is made. **4.** any fine line, stream, mark, or piece. **5.** the helical ridge on a screw, bolt, nut, etc. **6.** a very thin seam of coal or vein of ore. **7.** something acting as the continuous link or theme of a whole: *the thread of the story.* **8.** the course of an individual's life believed in Greek mythology to be spun, measured, and cut by the Fates. ~*vb.* **9.** (*tr.*) to pass (thread, film, tape, etc.) through (something). **10.** (*tr.*) to string on a thread: *she threaded the beads.* **11.** to make (one's way) through or over (something). **12.** (*tr.*) to produce a screw thread. **13.** (*tr.*) to pervade: *hysteria threaded his account.* **14.** (*intr.*) (of boiling syrup) to form a fine thread when poured from a spoon. [OE *thrǣd*] —ˈ**threader** *n.* —ˈ**thread͵like** *adj.*

threadbare (ˈθrɛd͵bɛə) *adj.* **1.** (of cloth, clothing, etc.) having the nap worn off so that the threads are exposed; worn out. **2.** meagre or poor. **3.** hackneyed: *a threadbare argument.* **4.** wearing threadbare clothes; shabby.

thread mark *n.* a mark put into paper money to prevent counterfeiting, consisting of a pattern of silk fibres.

threadworm (ˈθrɛd͵wɜːm) *n.* any of various nematodes, esp. the pinworm.

thready (ˈθrɛdɪ) *adj.* **threadier, threadiest. 1.** of or resembling a thread. **2.** (of the pulse) barely perceptible; weak. **3.** sounding thin, weak, or reedy. —ˈ**threadiness** *n.*

threat (θrɛt) *n.* **1.** a declaration of the intention to inflict harm, pain, or misery. **2.** an indication of imminent harm, danger, or pain. **3.** a person or thing that is regarded as dangerous or likely to inflict pain or misery. [OE]

threaten (ˈθrɛtᵊn) *vb.* **1.** (*tr.*) to be a threat to. **2.** to be a menacing indication of (something); portend. **3.** (when *tr., may take a clause as object*) to express a threat to (a person or people). —ˈ**threatening** *adj.* —ˈ**threateningly** *adv.*

three (θriː) *n.* **1.** the cardinal number that is the sum of two and one and is a prime number. **2.** a numeral, 3, III, (iii), representing this number. **3.** something representing or consisting of three units. **4.** Also called: **three o'clock.** three hours after noon or midnight. ~*determiner.* **5. a.** amounting to three. **b.** (*as pronoun*): *three were killed.* ~Related adjs.: **ternary, tertiary, treble, triple.** [OE *thrēo*]

three-card trick *n.* a game in which players bet on which of three playing cards is the queen.

three-colour *adj.* of or comprising a colour print or a photomechanical process in which a picture is reproduced by superimposing three prints from half-tone plates in inks corresponding to the three primary colours.

three-D *or* **3-D** *n.* a three-dimensional effect.

three-decker *n.* **1. a.** anything having three levels or layers. **b.** (*as modifier*): *a three-decker sandwich.* **2.** a warship with guns on three decks.

three-dimensional *adj.* **1.** of, having, or relating to three dimensions. **2.** simulating the effect of depth. **3.** having volume. **4.** lifelike.

threefold (ˈθriː͵fəʊld) *adj.* **1.** equal to or having three times as many or as much; triple. **2.** composed of three parts. ~*adv.* **3.** by or up to three times as many or as much.

three-legged race *n.* a race in which pairs of competitors run with their adjacent legs tied together.

threepenny bit *or* **thrupenny bit** (ˈθrʌpnɪ, -ənɪ, ˈθrɛp-) *n.* a twelve-sided British coin valued at three old pence, obsolete since 1971.

three-phase *adj.* (of an electrical circuit, etc.) having or using three alternating voltages of the same frequency, displaced in phase by 120°.

three-ply *adj.* **1.** having three layers or thicknesses. **2.** (of wool, etc.) three-stranded.

three-point landing *n.* an aircraft landing in which the main wheels and the nose or tail wheel touch the ground simultaneously.

three-point turn *n.* a complete turn of a motor vehicle using forward and reverse gears alternately, and completed after only three movements.

three-quarter *adj.* **1.** being three quarters of something. **2.** being of three quarters the normal length. ~*n.* **3.** *Rugby.* any of the players between the fullback and the forwards.

three-ring circus *n. U.S.* **1.** a circus with three rings for simultaneous performances. **2.** a situation of confusion, characterized by a bewildering variety of events or activities.

three Rs *pl. n.* **the.** the three skills regarded as the fundamentals of education; reading, writing, and arithmetic. [< the humorous spelling *reading, 'riting,* and *'rithmetic*]

threescore (ˈθriːˈskɔː) *determiner.* an archaic word for **sixty.**

threesome (ˈθriːsəm) *n.* **1.** a group of three. **2.** *Golf.* a match in which a single player playing his own ball competes against two others playing on the same ball. **3.** any game, etc., for three people. **4.** (*modifier*) performed by three.

thremmatology (͵θrɛməˈtɒlədʒɪ) *n.* the science of breeding domesticated animals and plants. [C19: < Gk *thremma* nursling + -LOGY]

threnody (ˈθrɛnədɪ, ˈθriː-) *or* **threnode** (ˈθriːnəʊd, ˈθrɛn-) *n., pl.* **threnodies** *or* **threnodes.** an ode, song, or speech of lamentation, esp. for the dead. [C17: < Gk *thrēnōidia,* < *thrēnos* dirge + *ōidē* song] —**threnodic** (θrɪˈnɒdɪk) *adj.* —**threnodist** (ˈθrɛnədɪst, ˈθriː-) *n.*

thresh (θrɛʃ) *vb.* **1.** to beat stalks of ripe corn, etc., either with a hand implement or a machine to separate the grain from the husks and straw.

2. (*tr.*) to beat or strike. **3.** (*intr.; often foll. by about*) to toss and turn; thrash. [OE *threscan*]

thresher (ˈθrɛʃə) *n.* **1.** a person who threshes. **2.** short for **threshing machine. 3.** any of a genus of large sharks occurring in tropical and temperate seas. They have a very long whiplike tail.

threshing machine *n.* a machine for threshing crops.

threshold (ˈθrɛʃəʊld, ˈθrɛʃˌhəʊld) *n.* **1.** a sill, esp. one made of stone or hardwood, placed at a doorway. **2.** any doorway or entrance. **3.** the starting point of an experience, event, or venture. **4.** *Psychol.* the strength at which a stimulus is just perceived: *the threshold of consciousness.* **5.** a point at which something would stop, take effect, etc. **6.** the minimum intensity or value of a signal, etc., that will produce a response or specified effect. **7.** (*modifier*) of a pay agreement, clause, etc., that raises wages to compensate for increases in the cost of living. ~Related adj.: **liminal.** [OE *therscold*]

threw (θruː) *vb.* the past tense of **throw.**

thrice (θraɪs) *adv.* **1.** three times. **2.** threefold. **3.** *Arch.* greatly. [OE *thrīwa, thrīga*]

thrift (θrɪft) *n.* **1.** wisdom and caution in the management of money. **2.** Also called: **sea pink.** any of a genus of perennial low-growing plants of Europe, W Asia, and North America, having narrow leaves and round heads of pink or white flowers. [C13: < ON: success; see THRIVE] —ˈ**thriftless** *adj.* —ˈ**thriftlessly** *adv.*

thrifty (ˈθrɪftɪ) *adj.* **thriftier, thriftiest. 1.** showing thrift; economical or frugal. **2.** *Rare.* thriving or prospering. —ˈ**thriftily** *adv.* —ˈ**thriftiness** *n.*

thrill (θrɪl) *n.* **1.** a sudden sensation of excitement and pleasure. **2.** a situation producing such a sensation. **3.** a trembling sensation caused by fear or emotional shock. **4.** *Pathol.* an abnormal slight tremor. ~*vb.* **5.** to feel or cause to feel a thrill. **6.** to tremble or cause to tremble; vibrate or quiver. [OE *thȳrlian* to pierce, < *thyrel* hole] —ˈ**thrilling** *adj.*

thriller (ˈθrɪlə) *n.* a book, film, play, etc., depicting crime, mystery, or espionage in an atmosphere of excitement and suspense.

thrips (θrɪps) *n., pl.* **thrips.** any of various small slender-bodied insects typically having piercing mouthparts and feeding on plant sap. [C18: via NL < Gk: woodworm]

thrive (θraɪv) *vb.* **thriving; thrived** *or* **throve; thrived** *or* **thriven** (ˈθrɪvᵊn). (*intr.*) **1.** to grow strongly and vigorously. **2.** to do well; prosper. [C13: < ON *thrīfask* to grasp for oneself, <?]

thro' *or* **thro** (θruː) *prep., adv. Inf. or poetic.* variant spellings of **through.**

throat (θrəʊt) *n.* **1. a.** that part of the alimentary and respiratory tracts extending from the back of the mouth to just below the larynx. **b.** the front part of the neck. **2.** something resembling a throat, esp. in shape or function: *the throat of a chimney.* **3. cut one's (own) throat.** to bring about one's own ruin. **4. ram** *or* **force (something) down someone's throat.** to insist that someone listen to or accept (something). ~Related adjs.: **guttural, laryngeal.** [OE *throtu*]

throaty (ˈθrəʊtɪ) *adj.* **throatier, throatiest. 1.** indicating a sore throat; hoarse: *a throaty cough.* **2.** of or produced in the throat. **3.** deep, husky, or guttural. —ˈ**throatily** *adv.*

throb (θrɒb) *vb.* **throbbing, throbbed.** (*intr.*) **1.** to pulsate or beat repeatedly, esp. with increased force. **2.** (of engines, drums, etc.) to have a strong rhythmic vibration or beat. ~*n.* **3.** a throbbing, esp. a rapid pulsation as of the heart: *a throb of pleasure.* [C14: ? imit.]

throes (θrəʊz) *pl. n.* **1.** a condition of violent pangs, pain, or convulsions: *death throes.* **2. in the throes of.** struggling with great effort with. [OE *thrāwu* threat]

thrombin (ˈθrɒmbɪn) *n. Biochem.* an enzyme that acts on fibrinogen in blood causing it to clot. [C19: < THROMB(US) + -IN]

thrombocyte (ˈθrɒmbəˌsaɪt) *n.* another name for **platelet.** —**thrombocytic** (ˌθrɒmbəˈsɪtɪk) *adj.*

thromboembolism (ˌθrɒmbəʊˈɛmbəˌlɪzəm) *n.* the obstruction of a blood vessel by a thrombus that has become detached from its original site.

thrombose (ˈθrɒmbəʊz) *vb.* to become or affect with a thrombus. [C19: back formation < THROMBOSIS]

thrombosis (θrɒmˈbəʊsɪs) *n., pl.* **-ses** (-siːz). **1.** the formation or presence of a thrombus. **2.** *Inf.* short for **coronary thrombosis.** [C18: < NL, < Gk: curdling, < *thrombousthai* to clot, < *thrombos* THROMBUS] —**thrombotic** (θrɒmˈbɒtɪk) *adj.*

thrombus (ˈθrɒmbəs) *n., pl.* **-bi** (-baɪ). a clot of coagulated blood that forms within a blood vessel or inside the heart, often impeding the flow of blood. [C17: < NL, < Gk *thrombos* lump, <?]

throne (θrəʊn) *n.* **1.** the ceremonial seat occupied by a monarch, bishop, etc., on occasions of state. **2.** the power or rank ascribed to a royal person. **3.** a person holding royal rank. **4.** (*pl.; often cap.*) the third of the nine orders into which the angels are divided in medieval angelology. ~*vb.* **5.** to place or be placed on a throne. [C13: < OF *trone,* < L *thronus,* < Gk *thronos*]

throng (θrɒŋ) *n.* **1.** a great number of people or things crowded together. ~*vb.* **2.** to gather in or fill (a place) in large numbers; crowd. **3.** (*tr.*) to hem in (a person); jostle. [OE *gethrang*]

throstle (ˈθrɒsᵊl) *n.* **1.** a poetic name for the **song thrush. 2.** a spinning machine for wool or cotton in which the fibres are twisted and wound continuously. [OE]

throttle (ˈθrɒtᵊl) *n.* **1.** Also called: **throttle valve.** any device that controls the quantity of fuel or fuel and air mixture entering an engine. **2.** an informal or dialect word for **throat.** ~*vb.* (*tr.*) **3.** to kill or injure by squeezing the throat. **4.** to suppress. **5.** to control or restrict (a flow of fluid) by means of a throttle valve. [C14: *throtelen,* < *throte* THROAT] —ˈ**throttler** *n.*

through (θruː) *prep.* **1.** going in at one side and coming out at the other side of: *a path through the wood.* **2.** occupying or visiting several points scattered around in (an area). **3.** as a result of; by means of. **4.** *Chiefly U.S.* up to and including: *Monday through Friday.* **5.** during: *through the night.* **6.** at the end of; having completed. **7. through with.** having finished with (esp. when dissatisfied with). ~*adj.* **8.** (*postpositive*) having successfully completed some specified activity. **9.** (on a telephone line) connected. **10.** (*postpositive*) no longer able to function successfully in some specified capacity: *as a journalist, you're through.* **11.** (*prenominal*) (of a route, journey, etc.) continuous or unbroken: *a through train.* ~*adv.* **12.** through some specified thing, place, or period of time. **13. through and through.** thoroughly; completely. [OE *thurh*]

throughout (θruːˈaʊt) *prep.* **1.** right through; through the whole of (a place or a period of time): *throughout the day.* ~*adv.* **2.** throughout some specified period or area.

throughput (ˈθruːˌpʊt) *n.* the quantity of raw material processed in a given period, esp. by a computer.

throughway (ˈθruːˌweɪ) *n. U.S.* a thoroughfare, esp. a motorway.

throve (θrəʊv) *vb.* a past tense of **thrive.**

throw (θrəʊ) *vb.* **throwing, threw, thrown.** (*mainly tr.*) **1.** (*also intr.*) to project (something) through the air, esp. with a rapid motion of the arm. **2.** (foll. by *in, on, onto,* etc.) to put or move suddenly, carelessly, or violently. **3.** to bring to or cause to be in a specified state or condition, esp. suddenly: *the news threw them into a panic.* **4.** to direct or cast (a shadow, light, etc.). **5.** to project (the voice) so as to make it appear to come from other than its source. **6.** to give or hold (a party). **7.** to cause to fall or be upset: *the horse threw his rider.* **8. a.** to tip (dice) out onto a flat surface. **b.** to obtain (a specified number) in this way. **9.** to shape on a potter's wheel. **10.** to move (a switch or lever) to engage or disengage a mechanism. **11.** to be subjected to (a fit). **12.** to turn (wood, etc.) on a lathe. **13.** *Inf.* to baffle or astonish;

confuse: *the question threw me.* **14.** *Boxing.* to deliver (a punch). **15.** *Wrestling.* to hurl (an opponent) to the ground. **16.** *Inf.* to lose (a contest, etc.) deliberately. **17. a.** to play (a card). **b.** to discard (a card). **18.** (of an animal) to give birth to (young). **19.** to twist or spin (filaments) into thread. **20.** *Austral. inf.* (often foll. by *at*) to mock or poke fun. **21. throw oneself at.** to strive actively to attract the attention or affection of. **22. throw oneself into.** to involve oneself enthusiastically in. **23. throw oneself on.** to rely entirely upon. ~*n.* **24.** the act or an instance of throwing. **25.** the distance over which anything may be thrown: *a stone's throw.* **26.** *Inf.* a chance or try. **27.** an act or result of throwing dice. **28. a.** the eccentricity of a cam. **b.** the radial distance between the central axis of a crankshaft and the axis of a crankpin forming part of the shaft. **29.** *Chiefly U.S. & Canad.* a decorative blanket or cover. **30.** *Geol.* the vertical displacement of rock strata at a fault. **31.** *Physics.* the deflection of a measuring instrument as a result of a fluctuation. ~See also **throwaway, throwback, throw in,** etc. [OE *thrāwan* to turn, torment] —ˈ**thrower** *n.*

throwaway (ˈθrəʊəˌweɪ) *adj.* **1.** (*prenominal*) *Chiefly Brit.* said or done incidentally, esp. for rhetorical effect; casual: *a throwaway remark.* **2.** designed to be discarded after use rather than reused, refilled, etc.: *a throwaway carton.* ~*n.* **3.** *Chiefly U.S. & Canad.* a handbill. ~*vb.* **throw away.** (*tr., adv.*) **4.** to get rid of; discard. **5.** to fail to make good use of; waste.

throwback (ˈθrəʊˌbæk) *n.* **1. a.** a person, animal, or plant that has the characteristics of an earlier or more primitive type. **b.** a reversion to such an organism. ~*vb.* **throw back.** (*adv.*) **2.** (*intr.*) to revert to an earlier or more primitive type. **3.** (*tr.;* foll. by *on*) to force to depend (on): *the crisis threw her back on her faith in God.*

throw in *vb.* (*tr., adv.*) **1.** to add at no additional cost. **2.** to contribute or interpose (a remark, argument, etc.). **3. throw in the towel** (*or* **sponge**). to give in; accept defeat. ~*n.* **throw-in. 4.** *Soccer.* the method of putting the ball into play after it has gone into touch by throwing it to a team-mate.

thrown (θrəʊn) *vb.* the past participle of **throw.**

throw off *vb.* (*adv., mainly tr.*) **1.** to free oneself of; discard. **2.** to produce or utter in a casual manner. **3.** to escape from or elude. **4.** to confuse or disconcert. **5.** (*intr.;* often foll. by **at**) *Austral. & N.Z. inf.* to deride or ridicule.

throw out *vb.* (*tr., adv.*) **1.** to discard or reject. **2.** to expel or dismiss, esp. forcibly. **3.** to construct (something projecting or prominent). **4.** to put forward or offer. **5.** to utter in a casual or indirect manner. **6.** to confuse or disconcert. **7.** to give off or emit. **8.** *Cricket.* (of a fielder) to put (the batsman) out by throwing the ball to hit the wicket. **9.** *Baseball.* to make a throw to a team-mate who in turn puts out (a base runner).

throw over *vb.* (*tr., adv.*) to forsake or abandon; jilt.

throw together *vb.* (*tr., adv.*) **1.** to assemble hurriedly. **2.** to cause to become casually acquainted.

throw up *vb.* (*adv., mainly tr.*) **1.** to give up; abandon. **2.** to construct hastily. **3.** to reveal; produce. **4.** (*also intr.*) *Inf.* to vomit.

thru (θruː) *prep., adv., adj. Chiefly U.S.* a variant spelling of **through.**

thrum[1] (θrʌm) *vb.* **thrumming, thrummed. 1.** to strum rhythmically but without expression on (a musical instrument). **2.** (*intr.*) to drum incessantly: *rain thrummed on the roof.* ~*n.* **3.** a repetitive strumming. [C16: imit.]

thrum[2] (θrʌm) *n.* **1. a.** any of the unwoven ends of warp thread remaining on the loom when the web has been removed. **b.** such ends of thread collectively. **2.** a fringe or tassel of short unwoven threads. ~*vb.* **thrumming, thrummed. 3.** (*tr.*) to trim with thrums. [C14: < OE]

thrush[1] (θrʌʃ) *n.* any of a subfamily of songbirds, esp. those having a brown plumage with a spotted breast, such as the mistle thrush and song thrush. [OE *thrȳsce*]

thrush[2] (θrʌʃ) *n.* **1.** a fungal disease, esp. of infants, characterized by the formation of whitish spots. **2.** a vaginal infection caused by the same fungus. **3.** a softening of the frog of a horse's hoof characterized by inflammation and a thick foul discharge. [C17: <?]

thrust (θrʌst) *vb.* **1.** (*tr.*) to push (someone or something) with force. **2.** (*tr.*) to force upon (someone) or into (some condition or situation): *they thrust responsibilities upon her.* **3.** (*tr.;* foll. by *through*) to pierce; stab. **4.** (*intr.;* usually foll. by *through* or *into*) to force a passage. **5.** to make a stab or lunge at. ~*n.* **6.** a forceful drive, push, stab, or lunge. **7.** a force, esp. one that produces motion. **8. a.** a propulsive force produced by the fluid pressure or the change of momentum of the fluid in a jet engine, rocket engine, etc. **b.** a similar force produced by a propeller. **9.** a continuous pressure exerted by one part of an object, structure, etc., against another. **10.** force, impetus, or drive. **11.** the essential or most forceful part: *the thrust of the argument.* [C12: < ON *thrysta*]

thruster (ˈθrʌstə) *n.* **1.** a person or thing that thrusts. **2.** a small rocket engine, esp. one used to correct the altitude or course of a spacecraft.

thrust fault *n.* a fault in which the rocks on the lower side of an inclined fault plane have been displaced downwards; a reverse fault.

thud (θʌd) *n.* **1.** a dull heavy sound. **2.** a blow or fall that causes such a sound. ~*vb.* **thudding, thudded. 3.** to make or cause to make such a sound. [OE *thyddan* to strike]

thug (θʌg) *n.* **1.** a tough and violent man, esp. a criminal. **2.** (*sometimes cap.*) (formerly) a member of an organization of robbers and assassins in India. [C19: < Hindi *thag* thief, < Sansk. *sthaga* scoundrel, < *sthagati* to conceal] —ˈ**thuggery** *n.* —ˈ**thuggish** *adj.*

thuja *or* **thuya** (ˈθuːjə) *n.* any of a genus of coniferous trees of North America and East Asia, having scalelike leaves, small cones, and an aromatic wood. [C18: < NL, < Med. L *thuia*, ult. < Gk *thua* an African tree]

thulium (ˈθjuːlɪəm) *n.* a malleable ductile silvery-grey element. The radioisotope **thulium-170** is used as an electron source in portable x-ray units. Symbol: Tm; atomic no.: 69; atomic wt.: 168.93. [C19: NL, < *Thule* a region thought, by ancient geographers, to be northernmost in the world + -IUM]

thumb (θʌm) *n.* **1.** the first and usually shortest and thickest of the digits of the hand. **2.** the corresponding digit in other vertebrates. **3.** the part of a glove shaped to fit the thumb. **4. all thumbs.** clumsy. **5. thumbs down.** an indication of refusal or disapproval. **6. thumbs up.** an indication of encouragement or approval. **7. under someone's thumb.** at someone's mercy or command. ~*vb.* **8.** (*tr.*) to touch, mark, or move with the thumb. **9.** to attempt to obtain (a lift or ride) by signalling with the thumb. **10.** (when *intr.*, often foll. by *through*) to flip the pages of (a book, etc.) in order to glance at the contents. **11. thumb one's nose at.** to deride or mock, esp. by placing the thumb on the nose with fingers extended. [OE *thūma*]

thumb index *n.* **1.** a series of indentations cut into the fore-edge of a book to facilitate quick reference. ~*vb.* **thumb-index. 2.** (*tr.*) to furnish with a thumb index.

thumbnail (ˈθʌmˌneɪl) *n.* **1.** the nail of the thumb. **2.** (*modifier*) concise and brief: *a thumbnail sketch.*

thumbnut (ˈθʌmˌnʌt) *n.* a wing nut.

thumbscrew (ˈθʌmˌskruː) *n.* **1.** an instrument of torture that pinches or crushes the thumbs. **2.** a screw with projections on its head enabling it to be turned by the thumb and forefinger.

thumbtack (ˈθʌmˌtæk) *n.* the U.S. and Canad. name for **drawing pin.**

thump (θʌmp) *n.* **1.** the sound of a heavy solid body hitting a comparatively soft surface. **2.** a heavy blow with the hand. ~*vb.* **3.** (*tr.*) to strike or beat heavily; pound. **4.** (*intr.*) to throb, beat, or pound violently. [C16] —ˈ**thumper** *n.*

thumping (ˈθʌmpɪŋ) *adj.* (*prenominal*) *Sl.* huge or excessive: *a thumping loss.*

thunbergia (θʌnˈbɜːdʒɪə) *n.* any of various climbing or dwarf plants of tropical and subtropical Africa and Asia. [C19: after K. P. *Thunberg* (1743-1822), Swedish botanist]

thunder (ˈθʌndə) *n.* **1.** a loud cracking or deep rumbling noise caused by the rapid expansion of atmospheric gases which are suddenly heated by lightning. **2.** any loud booming sound. **3.** *Rare.* a violent threat or denunciation. **4. steal someone's thunder.** to lessen the effect of someone's idea or action by anticipating it. ~*vb.* **5.** to make (a loud sound) or utter (words) in a manner suggesting thunder. **6.** (*intr.;* with *it* as subject) to be the case that thunder is being heard. **7.** (*intr.*) to move fast and heavily: *the bus thundered downhill.* **8.** (*intr.*) to utter vehement threats or denunciation; rail. [OE *thunor*] —ˈ**thundery** *adj.* —ˈ**thunderer** *n.*

thunderbolt (ˈθʌndəˌbəʊlt) *n.* **1.** a flash of lightning accompanying thunder. **2.** the imagined agency of destruction produced by a flash of lightning. **3.** (in mythology) the destructive weapon wielded by several gods, esp. the Greek god Zeus. **4.** something very startling.

thunderclap (ˈθʌndəˌklæp) *n.* **1.** a loud outburst of thunder. **2.** something as violent or unexpected as a clap of thunder.

thundercloud (ˈθʌndəˌklaʊd) *n.* a towering electrically charged cumulonimbus cloud associated with thunderstorms.

thunderhead (ˈθʌndəˌhɛd) *n. Chiefly U.S.* the anvil-shaped top of a cumulonimbus cloud.

thundering (ˈθʌndərɪŋ) *adj.* (*prenominal*) *Sl.* very great or excessive: *a thundering idiot.*

thunderous (ˈθʌndərəs) *adj.* **1.** threatening; angry. **2.** resembling thunder, esp. in loudness.

thunderstorm (ˈθʌndəˌstɔːm) *n.* a storm with thunder and lightning and usually heavy rain or hail.

thunderstruck (ˈθʌndəˌstrʌk) *or* **thunderstricken** (ˈθʌndəˌstrɪkən) *adj.* **1.** completely taken aback; amazed or shocked. **2.** *Rare.* struck by lightning.

thurible (ˈθjʊərɪbᵊl) *n.* another word for **censer.** [C15: < L *tūribulum* censer, < *tūs* incense]

Thurs. *abbrev. for* Thursday.

Thursday (ˈθɜːzdɪ) *n.* the fifth day of the week; fourth day of the working week. [OE *Thursdæg,* lit.: Thor's day]

thus (ðʌs) *adv.* **1.** in this manner: *do it thus.* **2.** to such a degree: *thus far and no further.* ~*sentence connector.* **3.** therefore: *We have failed. Thus we have to take the consequences.* [OE]

thuya (ˈθuːjə) *n.* a variant spelling of **thuja.**

thwack (θwæk) *vb.* **1.** to beat, esp. with something flat. ~*n.* **2. a.** a blow with something flat. **b.** the sound made by it. [C16: imit.]

thwart (θwɔːt) *vb.* **1.** to oppose successfully or prevent; frustrate. **2.** *Obs.* to be or move across. ~*n.* **3.** an oarsman's seat lying across a boat. ~*adj.* **4.** passing or being situated across. ~*prep., adv.* **5.** *Obs.* across. [C13: < ON *thvert,* < *thverr* transverse]

thy (ðaɪ) *determiner.* (*usually preceding a consonant*) *Arch. or Brit. dialect.* belonging to or associated in some way with you (thou): *thy goodness and mercy.* [C12: var. of THINE]

thylacine (ˈθaɪləˌsaɪn) *n.* an extinct or very rare doglike carnivorous marsupial of Tasmania. Also called: **Tasmanian wolf.** [C19: < NL *thȳlacīnus,* < Gk *thulakos* pouch]

thyme (taɪm) *n.* any of various small shrubs having a strong odour, small leaves, and white, pink, or red flowers. [C14: < OF *thym,* < L *thymum,* < Gk, < *thuein* to make a burnt offering] —ˈ**thymy** *adj.*

-thymia *n. combining form.* indicating a certain emotional condition, mood, or state of mind: *cyclothymia.* [NL, < Gk *thumos* temper]

thymine (ˈθaɪmiːn) *n.* a white crystalline base found in DNA. [C19: < THYMIC + -INE[2]]

thymol (ˈθaɪmɒl) *n.* a white crystalline substance obtained from thyme and used as a fungicide, antiseptic, etc. [C19: < THYME + -OL[2]]

thymus (ˈθaɪməs) *n., pl.* **-muses** *or* **-mi** (-maɪ). a glandular organ of vertebrates, consisting in man of two lobes situated below the thyroid. It atrophies with age and is almost nonexistent in the adult. [C17: < NL, < Gk *thumos* sweetbread]

thyratron (ˈθaɪrəˌtrɒn) *n.* an electronic relay consisting of a gas-filled tube, usually a triode, in which a signal applied to the control grid initiates a transient anode current but subsequently loses control over it. [C20: orig. a trademark, < Gk *thura* door, valve + -TRON]

thyristor (θaɪˈrɪstə) *n.* another name for **silicon controlled rectifier.** [C20: < THYR(ATRON) + (TRANS)ISTOR]

thyroid (ˈθaɪrɔɪd) *adj.* **1.** of or relating to the thyroid gland. **2.** of or relating to the largest cartilage of the larynx. ~*n.* **3.** See **thyroid gland.** **4.** a preparation of the thyroid gland of certain animals, used to treat hypothyroidism. [C18: < NL *thyroidēs,* < Gk *thureoeidēs,* < *thureos* oblong (lit.: door-shaped), < *thura* door]

thyroid gland *n.* an endocrine gland of vertebrates, consisting in man of two lobes near the base of the neck. It secretes hormones that control metabolism and body growth.

thyrotropin (ˌθaɪrəʊˈtrəʊpɪn) *or* **thyrotrophin** *n.* a hormone secreted by the pituitary gland: it stimulates the activity of the thyroid gland. [C20: < *thyro-* thyroid + -TROPE + -IN]

thyroxine (θaɪˈrɒksiːn, -sɪn) *or* **thyroxin** (θaɪˈrɒksɪn) *n.* the principal hormone produced by the thyroid gland. [C19: < *thyro-* thyroid + OXY-[2] + -INE[2]]

thyrse (θɜːs) *or* **thyrsus** (ˈθɜːsəs) *n., pl.* **thyrses** *or* **thyrsi** (ˈθɜːsaɪ). *Bot.* a type of inflorescence, occurring in the lilac and grape, in which the main branch is racemose and the lateral branches cymose. [C17: < F: THYRSUS]

thyrsus (ˈθɜːsəs) *n., pl.* **-si** (-saɪ). **1.** *Greek myth.* a staff, usually one tipped with a pine cone, borne by Dionysus (Bacchus) and his followers. **2.** a variant spelling of **thyrse.** [C18: < L, < Gk *thursos* stalk]

thyself (ðaɪˈsɛlf) *pron. Arch.* **a.** the reflexive form of *thou* or *thee.* **b.** (intensifier): *thou, thyself, wouldst know.*

ti (tiː) *n. Music.* a variant spelling of **te.**

Ti *the chemical symbol for* titanium.

tiara (tɪˈɑːrə) *n.* **1.** a woman's semicircular jewelled headdress for formal occasions. **2.** a high headdress worn by Persian kings in ancient times. **3.** a headdress worn by the pope, consisting of a beehive-shaped diadem surrounded by three coronets. [C16: via L < Gk, of Oriental origin] —**tiˈaraed** *adj.*

Tibetan (tɪˈbɛtᵊn) *adj.* **1.** of or characteristic of Tibet, its people, or their language. ~*n.* **2.** a native or inhabitant of Tibet. **3.** the language of Tibet.

tibia (ˈtɪbɪə) *n., pl.* **tibiae** (ˈtɪbɪˌiː) *or* **tibias. 1.** the inner and thicker of the two bones of the human leg below the knee; shinbone. **2.** the corresponding bone in other vertebrates. **3.** the fourth segment of an insect's leg. [C16: < L: leg, pipe] —ˈ**tibial** *adj.*

tic (tɪk) *n.* spasmodic twitching of a particular group of muscles. [C19: < F, <?]

tic douloureux (ˈtɪk ˌduːləˈruː) *n.* a condition of momentary stabbing pain along the trigeminal nerve. [C19: < F, lit.: painful tic]

tick[1] (tɪk) *n.* **1.** a recurrent metallic tapping or clicking sound, such as that made by a clock. **2.** *Brit. inf.* a moment or instant. **3.** a mark (√) used to check off or indicate the correctness of something. ~*vb.* **4.** to produce a recurrent tapping sound or indicate by such a sound: *the clock ticked the minutes away.* **5.** (when *tr.,* often foll. by *off*) to mark or check with a tick. **6. what makes someone tick.** *Inf.* the basic drive or motivation of a person. ~See also **tick off, tick over.** [C13: < Low G *tikk* touch]

tick² (tɪk) *n.* any of a large group of small parasitic arachnids typically living on the skin of warm-blooded animals and feeding on the blood and tissues of their hosts. [OE *ticca*]

tick³ (tɪk) *n.* **1.** the strong covering of a pillow, mattress, etc. **2.** *Inf.* short for **ticking.** [C15: prob. < MDu. *tīke*]

tick⁴ (tɪk) *n. Brit. inf.* account or credit (esp. in **on tick).** [C17: shortened < TICKET]

tick bird *n.* another name for **oxpecker.**

ticker (ˈtɪkə) *n.* **1.** *Sl.* **a.** the heart. **b.** a watch. **2.** a person or thing that ticks. **3.** the U.S. word for **tape machine.**

ticker tape *n.* a continuous paper ribbon on which a tape machine prints current stock quotations.

ticket (ˈtɪkɪt) *n.* **1. a.** a piece of paper, cardboard, etc., showing that the holder is entitled to certain rights, such as travel on a train or bus, entry to a place of public entertainment, etc. **b.** (*modifier*) concerned with the issue, sale, or checking of tickets: *a ticket collector.* **2.** a piece of card, cloth, etc., attached to an article showing information such as its price, size, etc. **3.** a summons served for a parking or traffic offence. **4.** *Inf.* the certificate of competence issued to a ship's captain or an aircraft pilot. **5.** *U.S. & N.Z.* the group of candidates nominated by one party in an election; slate. **6.** *Chiefly U.S.* the declared policy of a political party at an election. **7.** *Brit. inf.* a certificate of discharge from the armed forces. **8.** *Inf.* the right or appropriate thing: *that's the ticket.* **9. have (got) tickets on oneself.** *Austral. inf.* to be conceited. ~*vb.* (*tr.*) **10.** to issue or attach a ticket or tickets to. [C17: < OF *etiquet,* < *estiquier* to stick on, < MDu. *steken* to stick]

ticket day *n. Stock Exchange.* the day before settling day, when the stockbrokers are given the names of the purchasers.

ticket of leave *n.* (formerly, in Britain) a permit allowing a convict (**ticket-of-leave man**) to leave prison, after serving only part of his sentence, with certain restrictions placed on him.

tick fever *n.* any acute infectious febrile disease caused by the bite of an infected tick.

ticking (ˈtɪkɪŋ) *n.* a strong cotton fabric, often striped, used esp. for mattress and pillow covers. [C17: < TICK³]

tickle (ˈtɪkᵊl) *vb.* **1.** to touch or stroke, so as to produce pleasure, laughter, or a twitching sensation. **2.** (*tr.*) to excite pleasurably; gratify. **3.** (*tr.*) to delight or entertain (often in **tickle one's fancy**). **4.** (*intr.*) to itch or tingle. **5.** (*tr.*) to catch (a fish, esp. a trout) with the hands. **6. tickle pink** *or* **to death.** *Inf.* to please greatly. ~*n.* **7.** a sensation of light stroking or itching. **8.** the act of tickling. **9.** *Canad.* (in the Atlantic Provinces) a narrow strait. [C14]

tickler (ˈtɪklə) *n.* **1.** *Inf., chiefly Brit.* a difficult problem. **2.** Also called: **tickler file.** *U.S.* a memorandum book. **3.** a person or thing that tickles.

ticklish (ˈtɪklɪʃ) *adj.* **1.** sensitive to being tickled. **2.** delicate or difficult. **3.** easily upset or offended. —ˈ**ticklishly** *adv.* —ˈ**ticklishness** *n.*

tick off *vb.* (*tr., adv.*) **1.** to mark with a tick. **2.** *Inf., chiefly Brit.* to scold; reprimand.

tick over *vb.* (*intr., adv.*) **1.** Also: **idle.** *Brit.* (of an engine) to run at low speed with the throttle control closed and the transmission disengaged. **2.** to run smoothly without any major changes.

ticktack (ˈtɪkˌtæk) *n.* **1.** *Brit.* a system of sign language, mainly using the hands, by which bookmakers transmit their odds to each other at race courses. **2.** *U.S.* a ticking sound. [< TICK¹]

ticktock (ˈtɪkˌtɒk) *n.* **1.** a ticking sound as made by a clock. ~*vb.* **2.** (*intr.*) to make a ticking sound.

tidal (ˈtaɪdᵊl) *adj.* **1.** relating to, characterized by, or affected by tides. **2.** dependent on the tide: *a tidal ferry.* —ˈ**tidally** *adv.*

tidal wave *n.* **1.** a name (not in technical usage) for **tsunami.** **2.** an unusually large incoming wave, often caused by high winds and spring tides. **3.** a forceful and widespread movement in public opinion, action, etc.

tidbit (ˈtɪdˌbɪt) *n.* the usual U.S. spelling of **titbit.**

tiddler (ˈtɪdlə) *n. Brit. inf.* **1.** a very small fish, esp. a stickleback. **2.** a small child. [C19: < *tittlebat,* childish var. of STICKLEBACK, infl. by TIDDLY¹]

tiddly¹ (ˈtɪdlɪ) *adj.* **dlier, dliest.** *Brit.* small; tiny. [C19: childish var. of LITTLE]

tiddly² (ˈtɪdlɪ) *adj. Sl., chiefly Brit.* slightly drunk. [C19 (meaning: a drink): <?]

tiddlywinks (ˈtɪdlɪˌwɪŋks) *n.* (*functioning as sing.*) a game in which players try to flick discs of plastic into a cup by pressing them with other larger discs. [C19: prob. < TIDDLY¹ + dialect *wink,* var. of WINCH¹]

tide (taɪd) *n.* **1.** the cyclic rise and fall of sea level caused by the gravitational pull of the sun and moon. There are usually two high tides and two low tides in each lunar day. **2.** the current, ebb, or flow of water at a specified place resulting from these changes in level. **3.** See **ebb** (sense 3) and **flood** (sense 3). **4.** a widespread tendency or movement. **5.** a critical point in time; turning point. **6.** *Arch. except in combination.* a season or time: *Christmastide.* **7.** *Arch.* a favourable opportunity. **8. the tide is in** (*or* **out**). the sea has reached its highest (*or* lowest) level. ~*vb.* **9.** to carry or be carried with or as if with the tide. **10.** (*intr.*) to ebb and flow like the tide. [OE *tīd* time] —ˈ**tideless** *adj.*

tideland (ˈtaɪdˌlænd) *n. U.S.* land between high-water and low-water marks.

tidemark (ˈtaɪdˌmɑːk) *n.* **1.** a mark left by the highest or lowest point of a tide. **2.** *Chiefly Brit.* a mark showing a level reached by a liquid: *a tidemark on the bath.* **3.** *Inf., chiefly Brit.* a dirty mark on the skin, indicating the extent to which someone has washed.

tide over *vb.* (*tr., adv.*) to help to get through (a period of difficulty, distress, etc.).

tide-rip *n.* another word for **riptide** (sense 1).

tidewaiter (ˈtaɪdˌweɪtə) *n.* (formerly) a customs officer who boarded and inspected incoming ships.

tidewater (ˈtaɪdˌwɔːtə) *n.* **1.** water that advances and recedes with the tide. **2.** *U.S.* coastal land drained by tidal streams.

tideway (ˈtaɪdˌweɪ) *n.* a strong tidal current or its channel, esp. the tidal part of a river.

tidings (ˈtaɪdɪŋz) *pl. n.* information or news. [OE *tīdung*]

tidy (ˈtaɪdɪ) *adj.* **-dier, -diest.** **1.** characterized by or indicating neatness and order. **2.** *Inf.* considerable: *a tidy sum of money.* ~*vb.* **-dying, -died.** **3.** (when *intr.,* usually foll. by *up*) to put (things) in order; neaten. ~*n., pl.* **-dies.** **4. a.** a small container for odds and ends. **b. sink tidy.** a container to retain rubbish that might clog the plughole. **5.** *Chiefly U.S. & Canad.* an ornamental protective covering for the back or arms of a chair. [C13 (in the sense: timely, excellent): < TIDE + -Y¹] —ˈ**tidily** *adv.* —ˈ**tidiness** *n.*

tie (taɪ) *vb.* **tying, tied.** **1.** (when *tr.,* often foll. by *up*) to fasten or be fastened with string, thread, etc. **2.** to make (a knot or bow) in (something). **3.** (*tr.*) to restrict or secure. **4.** to equal (the score) of a competitor, etc. **5.** (*tr.*) *Inf.* to unite in marriage. **6.** *Music.* **a.** to execute (two successive notes) as though they formed one note. **b.** to connect (two printed notes) with a tie. ~*n.* **7.** a bond, link, or fastening. **8.** a restriction or restraint. **9.** a string, wire, etc., with which something is tied. **10.** a long narrow piece of material worn, esp. by men, under the collar of a shirt, tied in a knot close to the throat with the ends hanging down the front. U.S. name: **necktie.** **11. a.** an equality in score, attainment, etc., in a contest. **b.** the match or competition in which such a result is attained. **12.** a structural member such as a tie beam or tie rod. **13.** *Sport, Brit.* a match or game in an eliminating competition: *a cup tie.* **14.** (*usually pl.*) a shoe fastened by means of laces. **15.** the U.S. and Canad. name for **sleeper** (on a railway track). **16.** *Music.* a slur connecting two notes of the same pitch indicating that the sound is to be prolonged for their joint time value. ~See also **tie in, tie up.** [OE *tīgan* to tie]

tie beam *n.* a horizontal beam that serves to prevent two other structural members from separating, esp. one that connects two corresponding rafters in a roof or roof truss.

tiebreaker (ˈtaɪˌbreɪkə) *n.* any method of deciding quickly the result of a drawn contest, esp. an extra game, question, etc.

tie clasp *n.* a clip which holds a tie in place against a shirt. Also called: **tie clip.**

tied (taɪd) *adj. Brit.* **1.** (of a public house) obliged to sell only the beer of a particular brewery. **2.** (of a house) rented out to the tenant for as long as he is employed by the owner.

tie-dyeing, tie-dye *or* **tie and dye** *n.* a method of dyeing textiles to produce patterns by tying sections of the cloth together so that they will not absorb the dye. —**ˈtie-ˌdyed** *adj.*

tie in *vb.* (*adv.*) **1.** to come or bring into a certain relationship; coordinate. ~*n.* **tie-in. 2.** a link, relationship, or coordination. **3.** publicity material, a book, etc., linked to a film, etc. **4.** *U.S.* **a.** a sale or advertisement offering products of which a purchaser must buy one or more in addition to his purchase. **b.** an item sold or advertised in this way. **c.** (*as modifier*): *a tie-in sale.*

tie line *n.* a telephone line between two private branch exchanges or private exchanges that may or may not pass through a main exchange.

tiepin (ˈtaɪˌpɪn) *n.* an ornamental pin of various shapes used to pin the two ends of a tie to a shirt.

tier[1] (tɪə) *n.* **1.** one of a set of rows placed one above and behind the other, such as theatre seats. **2. a.** a layer or level. **b.** (*in combination*): *a three-tier cake.* ~*vb.* **3.** to be or arrange in tiers. [C16: < OF *tire* rank, of Gmc origin]

tier[2] (ˈtaɪə) *n.* a person or thing that ties.

tierce (tɪəs) *n.* **1.** a variant of **terce. 2.** the third of eight positions from which a parry or attack can be made in fencing. **3.** (tɜːs). a sequence of three cards. **4.** an obsolete measure of capacity equal to 42 wine gallons. [C15: < OF, fem. of *tiers* third, < L *tertius*]

tiercel (ˈtɪəsᵊl) *n.* a variant of **tercel.**

tie up *vb.* (*adv.*) **1.** (*tr.*) to bind securely with or as if with string, rope, etc. **2.** to moor (a vessel). **3.** (*tr.; often passive*) to engage the attentions of. **4.** (*tr.; often passive*) to conclude (the organization of something). **5.** to come or bring to a complete standstill. **6.** (*tr.*) to commit (funds, etc.) and so make unavailable for other uses. **7.** (*tr.*) to subject (property) to conditions that prevent sale, alienation, etc. ~*n.* **tie-up. 8.** a link or connection. **9.** *Chiefly U.S. & Canad.* a standstill. **10.** *Chiefly U.S. & Canad.* an informal term for **traffic jam.**

tiff (tɪf) *n.* **1.** a petty quarrel. **2.** a fit of ill humour. ~*vb.* **3.** (*intr.*) to have or be in a tiff. [C18: <?]

tiffany (ˈtɪfənɪ) *n., pl.* **-nies.** a sheer fine gauzy fabric. [C17 (in the sense: a fine dress worn on Twelfth Night): < OF *tifanie,* < ecclesiastical L *theophania* Epiphany]

tiffin (ˈtɪfɪn) *n.* (in India) a light meal, esp. at midday. [C18: prob. < obs. *tiffing,* < *tiff* to sip]

tig (tɪg) *n., vb.* **tigging, tigged.** another word for **tag**[2] (senses 1, 4).

tiger (ˈtaɪgə) *n.* **1.** a large feline mammal of forests in most of Asia, having a tawny yellow coat with black stripes. **2.** a dynamic, forceful, or cruel person. [C13: < OF *tigre,* < L *tigris,* < Gk, of Iranian origin] —**ˈtigerish** *or* **ˈtigrish** *adj.*

tiger beetle *n.* any of a family of active predatory beetles, chiefly of warm dry regions, having powerful mandibles and long legs.

tiger cat *n.* a medium-sized feline mammal of Central and South America, having a dark-striped coat.

tiger lily *n.* a lily plant of China and Japan cultivated for its flowers, which have black-spotted orange petals.

tiger moth *n.* any of various moths having wings that are conspicuously marked with stripes and spots.

tiger's-eye *or* **tigereye** (ˈtaɪgərˌaɪ) *n.* a semiprecious golden-brown stone.

tiger shark *n.* a voracious omnivorous requiem shark of tropical waters, having a striped or spotted body.

tiger snake *n.* a highly venomous and aggressive Australian snake, usually with dark bands on the back.

tight (taɪt) *adj.* **1.** stretched or drawn so as not to be loose; taut. **2.** fitting in a close manner. **3.** held, made, fixed, or closed firmly and securely: *a tight knot.* **4. a.** of close and compact construction or organization, esp. so as to be impervious to water, air, etc. **b.** (*in combination*): *airtight.* **5.** unyielding or stringent. **6.** cramped or constricted: *a tight fit.* **7.** mean or miserly. **8.** difficult and problematic: *a tight situation.* **9.** hardly profitable: *a tight bargain.* **10.** *Econ.* **a.** (of a commodity) difficult to obtain. **b.** (of funds, money, etc.) difficult and expensive to borrow. **c.** (of markets) characterized by excess demand or scarcity. **11.** (of a match or game) very close or even. **12.** (of a team or group, esp. of a pop group) playing well together, in a disciplined coordinated way. **13.** *Inf.* drunk. **14.** *Inf.* (of a person) showing tension. ~*adv.* **15.** in a close, firm, or secure way. [C14: prob. var. of *thight,* < ON *thēttr* close] —**ˈtightly** *adv.* —**ˈtightness** *n.*

tighten (ˈtaɪtᵊn) *vb.* to make or become tight or tighter.

tightfisted (ˌtaɪtˈfɪstɪd) *adj.* mean; miserly.

tightknit (ˌtaɪtˈnɪt) *adj.* **1.** closely integrated: *a tightknit community.* **2.** organized carefully.

tight-lipped *adj.* **1.** secretive or taciturn. **2.** with the lips pressed tightly together, as through anger.

tightrope (ˈtaɪtˌrəʊp) *n.* a rope stretched taut on which acrobats walk or perform balancing feats. —**tightrope walker** *n.*

tights (taɪts) *pl. n.* **1.** Also called: (U.S.) **panty hose,** (Canad. and N.Z.) **pantyhose,** (Austral. and N.Z.) **pantihose.** a one-piece clinging garment covering the body from the waist to the feet, worn by women and also by acrobats, dancers, etc. **2.** a similar garment formerly worn by men, as in the 16th century with a doublet.

tiglic acid (ˈtɪglɪk) *n.* a syrupy liquid or crystalline unsaturated carboxylic acid, found in croton oil and used in perfumery. [C19 *tiglic,* < NL *Croton tiglium* (the croton plant), <?]

tigon (ˈtaɪgən) *or* **tiglon** (ˈtɪglɒn) *n.* the hybrid offspring of a male tiger and a female lion.

tigress (ˈtaɪgrɪs) *n.* **1.** a female tiger. **2.** a fierce, cruel, or wildly passionate woman.

tigridia (taɪˈgrɪdɪə) *n.* any of various bulbous plants of Mexico, Central America, and tropical S America. [C19: < Mod. L, < Gk *tigris* tiger (alluding to the spotted flowers of these plants)]

tike (taɪk) *n.* a variant spelling of **tyke.**

tiki (ˈtiːkiː) *n.* a Maori greenstone neck ornament in the form of a fetus. Also called: **heitiki.** [< Maori *heitiki* figure worn round neck]

tilbury (ˈtɪlbərɪ, -brɪ) *n., pl.* **-buries.** a light two-wheeled horse-drawn open carriage, seating two people. [C19: prob. after the inventor]

tilde (ˈtɪldə) *n.* the diacritical mark (˜) placed over a letter to indicate a nasal sound, as in Spanish *señor.* [C19: < Sp., < L *titulus* title]

tile (taɪl) *n.* **1.** a flat thin slab of fired clay, rubber, linoleum, etc., used with others to cover a roof, floor, wall, etc. **2.** a short pipe made of earthenware, plastic, etc., used with others to form a drain. **3.** tiles collectively. **4.** a rectangular block used as a playing piece in mahjong and other games. **5. on the tiles.** *Inf.* on a spree, esp. of drinking or debauchery. ~*vb.* **6.** (*tr.*) to cover with tiles. [OE *tīgele,* < L *tēgula*] —**ˈtiler** *n.*

tiling (ˈtaɪlɪŋ) *n.* **1.** tiles collectively. **2.** something made of or surfaced with tiles.

till[1] (tɪl) *conj., prep.* short for **until.** Also (not standard): **'til.** [OE *til*]

▸ **Usage.** *Till* is a variant of *until* that is acceptable at all levels of language. *Until* is, however, often preferred at the beginning of a sentence in formal writing.

till[2] (tɪl) *vb.* (*tr.*) **1.** to cultivate and work (land) for the raising of crops. **2.** to plough. [OE *tilian* to try, obtain] —**'tillable** *adj.* —**'tiller** *n.*

till[3] (tɪl) *n.* a box, case, or drawer into which money taken from customers is put, now usually part of a cash register. [C15 *tylle*, <?]

till[4] (tɪl) *n.* a glacial deposit consisting of rock fragments of various sizes. The most common is boulder clay. [C17: <?]

tillage ('tɪlɪdʒ) *n.* **1.** the act, process, or art of tilling. **2.** tilled land.

tiller[1] ('tɪlə) *n. Naut.* a handle fixed to the top of a rudderpost to serve as a lever in steering it. [C14: < Anglo-F *teiler* beam of a loom, < Med. L *tēlārium*, < L *tēla* web] —**'tillerless** *adj.*

tiller[2] ('tɪlə) *n.* **1.** a shoot that arises from the base of the stem in grasses. **2.** a less common name for **sapling.** ~*vb.* **3.** (*intr.*) (of a plant) to produce tillers. [OE *telgor* twig]

tilt (tɪlt) *vb.* **1.** to incline or cause to incline at an angle. **2.** (*usually intr.*) to attack or overthrow (a person) in a tilt or joust. **3.** (when *intr.*, often foll. by *at*) to aim or thrust: *to tilt a lance.* **4.** (*tr.*) to forge with a tilt hammer. ~*n.* **5.** a slope or angle: *at a tilt.* **6.** the act of tilting. **7.** (esp. in medieval Europe) **a.** a jousting contest. **b.** a thrust with a lance or pole delivered during a tournament. **8.** any dispute or contest. **9.** See **tilt hammer. 10. (at) full tilt.** at full speed or force. [OE *tealtian*] —**'tilter** *n.*

tilth (tɪlθ) *n.* **1.** the act or process of tilling land. **2.** the condition of soil or land that has been tilled. [OE *tilthe*]

tilt hammer *n.* a drop hammer with a heavy head; used in forging.

tiltyard ('tɪltˌjɑːd) *n.* (formerly) an enclosed area for tilting.

Tim. *Bible. abbrev. for* Timothy.

timbal *or* **tymbal** ('tɪmbᵊl) *n. Music.* a type of kettledrum. [C17: < F *timbale*, < OF *tamballe*, (associated also with *cymbale* cymbal), < OSp. *atabal*, < Ar. *at-tabl* the drum]

timbale (tæm'bɑːl) *n.* **1.** a mixture of meat, fish, etc., cooked in a mould lined with potato or pastry. **2.** a straight-sided mould in which such a dish is prepared. [C19: < F: kettledrum]

timber ('tɪmbə) *n.* **1. a.** wood, esp. when regarded as a construction material. **b.** (*as modifier*): *a timber cottage.* Usual U.S. and Canad. word: **lumber. 2. a.** trees collectively. **b.** *Chiefly U.S.* woodland. **3.** a piece of wood used in a structure. **4.** *Naut.* a frame in a wooden vessel. ~*vb.* **5.** (*tr.*) to provide with timbers. ~*sentence substitute.* **6.** a lumberjack's shouted warning when a tree is about to fall. [OE] —**'timbered** *adj.* —**'timbering** *n.*

timber hitch *n.* a knot used for tying a rope round a spar, log, etc., for haulage.

timber limit *n. Canad.* **1.** the area to which rights of cutting timber, granted by a government licence, are limited. **2.** another term for **timber line.**

timber line *n.* the altitudinal or latitudinal limit of tree growth. Also called: **tree line.**

timber wolf *n.* a wolf with a grey brindled coat found in forested northern regions, esp. of North America.

timberyard ('tɪmbəˌjɑːd) *n. Brit.* an establishment where timber, etc., is stored or sold. U.S. and Canad. word: **lumberyard.**

timbre ('tɪmbə, 'tæmbə) *n.* **1.** *Phonetics.* the distinctive tone quality differentiating one vowel or sonant from another. **2.** *Music.* tone colour or quality of sound. [C19: < F: note of a bell, < OF: drum, < Med. Gk *timbanon*, < Gk *tumpanon*]

timbrel ('tɪmbrəl) *n. Chiefly biblical.* a tambourine. [C16: < OF; see TIMBRE]

Timbuktu (ˌtɪmbʌk'tuː) *n.* any distant or outlandish place: *from here to Timbuktu.* [< *Timbuktu*, town in Africa: terminus of a trans-Saharan caravan route]

time (taɪm) *n.* **1.** the continuous passage of existence in which events pass from a state of potentiality in the future, through the present, to a state of finality in the past. Related adj.: **temporal. 2.** *Physics.* a quantity measuring duration, usually with reference to a periodic process such as the rotation of the earth or the vibration of electromagnetic radiation emitted from certain atoms. Time is considered as a fourth coordinate required to specify an event. See **space-time continuum. 3.** a specific point on this continuum expressed in hours and minutes: *the time is four o'clock.* **4.** a system of reckoning for expressing time: *Greenwich Mean Time.* **5. a.** a definite and measurable portion of this continuum. **b.** (*as modifier*): *time limit.* **6. a.** an accepted period such as a day, season, etc. **b.** (*in combination*): *springtime.* **7.** an unspecified interval; a while. **8.** (*often pl.*) a period or point marked by specific attributes or events: *the Victorian times.* **9.** a sufficient interval or period: *have you got time to help me?* **10.** an instance or occasion: *I called you three times.* **11.** an occasion or period of specified quality: *have a good time.* **12.** the duration of human existence. **13.** the heyday of human life: *in her time she was a great star.* **14.** a suitable moment: *it's time I told you.* **15.** the expected interval in which something is done. **16.** a particularly important moment, esp. childbirth or death: *her time had come.* **17.** (*pl.*) indicating a degree or amount calculated by multiplication with the number specified: *ten times three is thirty.* **18.** (*often pl.*) the fashions, thought, etc., of the present age (esp. in **ahead of one's time, behind the times**). **19.** *Brit.* Also: **closing time.** the time at which bars, pubs, etc., are legally obliged to stop selling alcoholic drinks. **20.** *Inf.* a term in jail (esp. in **do time**). **21. a.** a customary or full period of work. **b.** the rate of pay for this period. **22.** Also (esp. U.S.): **metre. a.** the system of combining beats or pulses in music into successive groupings by which the rhythm of the music is established. **b.** a specific system having a specific number of beats in each grouping or bar: *duple time.* **23.** *Music.* short for **time value. 24. against time.** in an effort to complete something in a limited period. **25. ahead of time.** before the deadline. **26. at one time. a.** once; formerly. **b.** simultaneously. **27. at the same time. a.** simultaneously. **b.** nevertheless; however. **28. at times.** sometimes. **29. beat time.** to indicate the tempo of a piece of music by waving a baton, hand, etc. **30. for the time being.** for the moment; temporarily. **31. from time to time.** at intervals; occasionally. **32. have no time for.** to have no patience with; not tolerate. **33. in good time. a.** early. **b.** quickly. **34. in no time.** very quickly. **35. in one's own time. a.** outside paid working hours. **b.** at one's own rate. **36. in time. a.** early or at the appointed time. **b.** eventually. **c.** *Music.* at a correct metrical or rhythmical pulse. **37. keep time.** to observe correctly the accent or rhythmical pulse of a piece of music in relation to tempo. **38. make time. a.** to find an opportunity. **b.** (often foll. by *with*) *U.S. inf.* to succeed in seducing. **39. on time. a.** at the expected or scheduled time. **b.** *U.S.* payable in instalments. **40. pass the time of day.** to exchange casual greetings (with an acquaintance). **41. time and again.** frequently. **42. time off.** a period when one is absent from work for a holiday, through sickness, etc. **43. time of one's life.** a memorably enjoyable time. **44. time out of mind.** from time immemorial. **45.** (*modifier*) operating automatically at or for a set time: *time lock; time switch.* ~*vb.* (*tr.*) **46.** to ascertain the duration or speed of. **47.** to set a time for. **48.** to adjust to keep accurate time. **49.** to pick a suitable time for. **50.** *Sport.* to control the execution or speed of (an action). ~*sentence substitute.* **51.** the word called out by a publican signalling that it is closing time. [OE *tīma*]

time and a half *n.* the rate of pay equalling one

and a half times the normal rate, often offered for overtime work.

time and motion study *n.* the analysis of industrial or work procedures to determine the most efficient methods of operation. Also: **time and motion, time study, motion study.**

time bomb *n.* a bomb containing a timing mechanism that determines the time at which it will detonate.

time capsule *n.* a container holding articles, documents, etc., representative of the current age, buried for discovery in the future.

time clock *n.* a clock which records, by punching or stamping **timecards** inserted into it, the time of arrival or departure of people, such as employees in a factory.

time-consuming *adj.* taking up or involving a great deal of time.

time exposure *n.* **1.** an exposure of a photographic film for a relatively long period, usually a few seconds. **2.** a photograph produced by such an exposure.

time-honoured *adj.* having been observed for a long time and sanctioned by custom.

time immemorial *n.* the distant past beyond memory or record.

timekeeper (ˈtaɪmˌkiːpə) *n.* **1.** a person or thing that keeps or records time. **2.** an employee who maintains a record of the hours worked by the other employees. **3.** an employee whose record of punctuality is of a specified nature: *a bad timekeeper.* —ˈ**timeˌkeeping** *n.*

time-lag *n.* an interval between two connected events.

time-lapse photography *n.* the technique of recording a very slow process on film by exposing single frames at regular intervals. The film is then projected at normal speed.

timeless (ˈtaɪmlɪs) *adj.* **1.** unaffected or unchanged by time; ageless. **2.** eternal. —ˈ**timelessly** *adv.* —ˈ**timelessness** *n.*

timely (ˈtaɪmlɪ) *adj.* **-lier, -liest,** *adv.* at the right or an opportune or appropriate time.

time machine *n.* (in science fiction) a machine in which people or objects can be transported into the past or the future.

time-out *n. Chiefly U.S. & Canad.* **1.** *Sport.* an interruption in play during which players rest, discuss tactics, etc. **2.** a period of rest; break.

timepiece (ˈtaɪmˌpiːs) *n.* any of various devices, such as a clock, watch, or chronometer, which measure and indicate time.

timer (ˈtaɪmə) *n.* **1.** a device for measuring, recording, or indicating time. **2.** a switch or regulator that causes a mechanism to operate at a specific time. **3.** a person or thing that times.

timesaving (ˈtaɪmˌseɪvɪŋ) *adj.* shortening the length of time required for an operation, activity, etc. —ˈ**timeˌsaver** *n.*

timescale (ˈtaɪmˌskeɪl) *n.* the span of time within which certain events occur or are scheduled in relation to any broader period of time.

time-served *adj.* (of a craftsman or tradesman) having completed an apprenticeship; fully trained and competent.

timeserver (ˈtaɪmˌsɜːvə) *n.* a person who compromises and changes his opinions, way of life, etc., to suit the current fashions.

time sharing *n.* **1.** a system of part ownership of a property for use as a holiday home whereby each participant owns the property for a particular period every year. **2.** a system by which users at different terminals of a computer can, because of its high speed, apparently communicate with it at the same time.

time signal *n.* an announcement of the correct time, esp. on radio or television.

time signature *n. Music.* a sign usually consisting of two figures, one above the other, the upper figure representing the number of beats per bar and the lower one the time value of each beat: it is placed after the key signature.

timetable (ˈtaɪmˌteɪbᵊl) *n.* **1.** a list or table of events arranged according to the time when they take place; schedule. ~*vb.* (*tr.*) **2.** to include in or arrange according to a timetable.

time value *n. Music.* the duration of a note relative to other notes in a composition and considered in relation to the basic tempo.

time warp *n.* an imagined distortion of the progress of time so that, for instance, events from the past may appear to be happening in the present.

timeworn (ˈtaɪmˌwɔːn) *adj.* **1.** showing the adverse effects of overlong use or of old age. **2.** hackneyed; trite.

time zone *n.* a region throughout which the same standard time is used. There are 24 time zones in the world, demarcated approximately by meridians at 15° intervals, an hour apart.

timid (ˈtɪmɪd) *adj.* **1.** easily frightened or upset, esp. by human contact; shy. **2.** indicating shyness or fear. [C16: < L *timidus,* < *timēre* to fear] —**tiˈmidity** *or* ˈ**timidness** *n.* —ˈ**timidly** *adv.*

timing (ˈtaɪmɪŋ) *n.* the regulation of actions or remarks in relation to others to produce the best effect, as in music, the theatre, etc.

timocracy (taɪˈmɒkrəsɪ) *n., pl.* **-cies. 1.** a political system in which possession of property is a requirement for participation in government. **2.** a political system in which love of honour is deemed the guiding principle of government. [C16: < OF *tymocracie,* ult. < Gk *timokratia,* < *timē* worth, honour, + -CRACY]

timorous (ˈtɪmərəs) *adj.* **1.** fearful or timid. **2.** indicating fear or timidity. [C15: < OF *temoros,* < Med. L, < L *timor* fear, < *timēre* to be afraid] —ˈ**timorously** *adv.* —ˈ**timorousness** *n.*

timothy grass *or* **timothy** (ˈtɪməθɪ) *n.* a perennial grass of temperate regions having erect stiff stems: grown for hay and pasture. [C18: apparently after a *Timothy Hanson,* who brought it to colonial Carolina]

timpani *or* **tympani** (ˈtɪmpənɪ) *pl. n.* (*sometimes functioning as sing.*) a set of kettledrums. [< It., pl. of *timpano* kettledrum, < L: TYMPANUM] —ˈ**timpanist** *or* ˈ**tympanist** *n.*

tin (tɪn) *n.* **1.** a malleable silvery-white metallic element. It is used extensively in alloys, esp. bronze and pewter, and as a noncorroding coating for steel. Symbol: Sn; atomic no.: 50; atomic wt.: 118.69. **2.** Also called (esp. U.S. and Canad.): **can.** an airtight sealed container of thin sheet metal coated with tin, used for preserving and storing food or drink. **3.** any container made of metallic tin. **4.** Also called: **tinful.** the contents of a tin. **5.** *Brit., Austral., & N.Z.* galvanized iron: *a tin roof.* **6.** any metal regarded as cheap or flimsy. **7.** *Brit.* a loaf of bread with a rectangular shape. **8.** *N.Z.* a receptacle for home-baked biscuits, etc. (esp. in **to fill her tins** to bake a supply of biscuits, etc.). ~*vb.* **tinning, tinned.** (*tr.*) **9.** to put (food, etc.) into a tin or tins; preserve in a tin. **10.** to plate or coat with tin. **11.** to prepare (a metal) for soldering or brazing by applying a thin layer of solder to the surface. ~Related adjs.: **stannic, stannous.** [OE]

tinamou (ˈtɪnəˌmuː) *n.* any of various birds of Central and South America, having small wings and a heavy body. [C18: via F < Carib *tinamu*]

tin can *n.* a metal food container, esp. when empty.

tinctorial (tɪŋkˈtɔːrɪəl) *adj.* of or relating to colouring, staining, or dyeing. [C17: < L *tinctōrius,* < *tingere* to tinge]

tincture (ˈtɪŋktʃə) *n.* **1.** a medicinal extract in a solution of alcohol. **2.** a tint, colour, or tinge. **3.** a slight flavour, aroma, or trace. **4.** a colour or metal used on heraldic arms. **5.** *Obs.* a dye. ~*vb.* **6.** (*tr.*) to give a tint or colour to. [C14: < L *tinctūra* a dyeing, < *tingere* to dye]

tinder (ˈtɪndə) *n.* **1.** dry wood or other easily combustible material used for lighting a fire. **2.** anything inflammatory or dangerous. [OE *tynder*] —ˈ**tindery** *adj.*

tinderbox (ˈtɪndəˌbɒks) *n.* **1.** a box used formerly for holding tinder, esp. one fitted with a flint and steel. **2.** a person or thing that is particularly touchy or explosive.

tine (taɪn) *n.* **1.** a slender prong, esp. of a fork. **2.** any of the sharp terminal branches of a deer's antler. [OE *tind*] —**tined** *adj.*

tinea (ˈtɪnɪə) *n.* any fungal skin disease, esp. ringworm. [C17: < L: worm] —ˈ**tineal** *adj.*

tinfoil (ˈtɪnˌfɔɪl) *n.* **1.** thin foil made of tin or an alloy of tin and lead. **2.** thin foil made of aluminium; used for wrapping foodstuffs.

ting (tɪŋ) *n.* **1.** a high metallic sound such as that made by a small bell. ~*vb.* **2.** to make or cause to make such a sound. [C15: imit.]

ting-a-ling (ˈtɪŋəˈlɪŋ) *n.* the sound of a small bell.

tinge (tɪndʒ) *n.* **1.** a slight tint or colouring. **2.** any slight addition. ~*vb.* **tingeing** *or* **tinging, tinged.** (*tr.*) **3.** to colour or tint faintly. **4.** to impart a slight trace to: *her thoughts were tinged with nostalgia.* [C15: < L *tingere* to colour]

tingle (ˈtɪŋgᵊl) *vb.* **1.** (*usually intr.*) to feel or cause to feel a prickling, itching, or stinging sensation of the flesh, as from a cold plunge. ~*n.* **2.** a sensation of tingling. [C14: ? a var. of TINKLE] —ˈ**tingler** *n.* —ˈ**tingling** *adj.* —ˈ**tingly** *adj.*

tin god *n.* **1.** a self-important person. **2.** a person erroneously regarded as holy or venerable.

tin hat *n. Inf.* a steel helmet worn by military personnel.

tinker (ˈtɪŋkə) *n.* **1.** (esp. formerly) a travelling mender of pots and pans. **2.** a clumsy worker. **3.** the act of tinkering. **4.** *Scot. & Irish.* a Gypsy. ~*vb.* **5.** (*intr.;* foll. by *with*) to play, fiddle, or meddle (with machinery, etc.), esp. while undertaking repairs. **6.** to mend (pots and pans) as a tinker. [C13 *tinkere,* ? < *tink* tinkle, imit.] —ˈ**tinkerer** *n.*

tinker's damn *or* **cuss** *n. Sl.* the slightest heed (esp. in **not give a tinker's damn** *or* **cuss).**

tinkle (ˈtɪŋkᵊl) *vb.* **1.** to ring with a high tinny sound like a small bell. **2.** (*tr.*) to announce or summon by such a ringing. **3.** (*intr.*) *Brit. inf.* to urinate. ~*n.* **4.** a high clear ringing sound. **5.** the act of tinkling. **6.** *Brit. inf.* a telephone call. [C14: imit.] —ˈ**tinkly** *adj.*

tin lizzie (ˈlɪzɪ) *n. Inf.* an old or decrepit car.

tinned (tɪnd) *adj.* **1.** plated, coated, or treated with tin. **2.** *Chiefly Brit.* preserved or stored in airtight tins. **3.** coated with a layer of solder.

tinned dog *n. Sl., chiefly Austral.* tinned meat.

tinnitus (tɪˈnaɪtəs) *n. Pathol.* a ringing, hissing, or booming sensation in one or both ears, caused by infection of the ear, a side effect of certain drugs, etc. [C19: < L, < *tinnīre* to ring]

tinny (ˈtɪnɪ) *adj.* **-nier, -niest.** **1.** of or resembling tin. **2.** cheap or shoddy. **3.** (of a sound) high, thin, and metallic. **4.** (of food or drink) flavoured with metal, as from a container. **5.** *Austral. inf.* lucky. ~*n., pl.* **-nies.** **6.** *Austral. sl.* a can of beer. —ˈ**tinnily** *adv.* —ˈ**tinniness** *n.*

tin-opener *n.* a small tool for opening tins.

Tin Pan Alley *n.* **1.** originally, a district in New York concerned with the production of popular music. **2.** the commercial side of show business and pop music.

tin plate *n.* **1.** thin steel sheet coated with a layer of tin that protects the steel from corrosion. ~*vb.* **tin-plate.** **2.** (*tr.*) to coat with a layer of tin.

tinpot (ˈtɪnˌpɒt) *adj.* (*prenominal*) *Brit. inf.* **1.** inferior, cheap, or worthless. **2.** petty; unimportant.

tinsel (ˈtɪnsəl) *n.* **1.** a decoration consisting of a piece of string with thin strips of metal foil attached along its length. **2.** a yarn or fabric interwoven with strands of glittering thread. **3.** anything cheap, showy, and gaudy. ~*vb.* **-selling, -selled** *or U.S.* **-seling, -seled.** (*tr.*) **4.** to decorate with or as if with tinsel: *snow tinsels the trees.* **5.** to give a gaudy appearance to. ~*adj.* **6.** made of or decorated with tinsel. **7.** showily but cheaply attractive; gaudy. [C16: < OF *estincele* a spark, < L *scintilla*] —ˈ**tinselly** *adj.*

Tinseltown (ˈtɪnsəlˌtaʊn) *n.* an informal name for **Hollywood,** esp. as the home of the film industry. [C20: < the insubstantial glitter of the film world]

tinsmith (ˈtɪnˌsmɪθ) *n.* a person who works with tin or tin plate.

tin soldier *n.* a miniature toy soldier, usually made of lead.

tinstone (ˈtɪnˌstəʊn) *n.* another name for **cassiterite.**

tint (tɪnt) *n.* **1.** a shade of a colour, esp. a pale one. **2.** a colour that is softened by the addition of white. **3.** a tinge. **4.** a dye for the hair. **5.** a trace or hint. **6.** *Engraving.* uniform shading, produced esp. by hatching. ~*vb.* **7.** (*tr.*) to colour or tinge. **8.** (*intr.*) to acquire a tint. [C18: < earlier *tinct,* < L *tingere* to colour] —ˈ**tinter** *n.*

tintinnabulation (ˌtɪntɪˌnæbjʊˈleɪʃən) *n.* the act or an instance of the ringing or pealing of bells. [< L, < *tintinnāre* to tinkle, < *tinnīre* to ring]

tinware (ˈtɪnˌwɛə) *n.* objects made of tin plate.

tin whistle *n.* another name for **penny whistle.**

tinworks (ˈtɪnˌwɜːks) *n.* (*functioning as sing. or pl.*) a place where tin is mined, smelted, or rolled.

tiny (ˈtaɪnɪ) *adj.* **tinier, tiniest.** very small. [C16 *tine,* <?] —ˈ**tinily** *adv.* —ˈ**tininess** *n.*

-tion *suffix forming nouns.* indicating state, condition, action, process, or result: *election; prohibition.* [< OF, < L *-tiō, -tiōn-*]

tip[1] (tɪp) *n.* **1.** a narrow or pointed end of something. **2.** the top or summit. **3.** a small piece forming an end: *a metal tip on a cane.* ~*vb.* **tipping, tipped.** (*tr.*) **4.** to adorn or mark the tip of. **5.** to cause to form a tip. [C15: < ON *typpa*] —ˈ**tipless** *adj.*

tip[2] (tɪp) *vb.* **tipping, tipped.** **1.** to tilt or cause to tilt. **2.** (usually foll. by *over* or *up*) to tilt or cause to tilt, so as to overturn or fall. **3.** *Brit.* to dump (rubbish, etc.). **4. tip one's hat.** to raise one's hat in salutation. ~*n.* **5.** a tipping or being tipped. **6.** *Brit.* a dump for refuse, etc. [C14: <?] —ˈ**tipper** *n.*

tip[3] (tɪp) *n.* **1.** a payment given for services in excess of the standard charge; gratuity. **2.** a helpful hint or warning. **3.** a piece of inside information, esp. in betting or investing. ~*vb.* **tipping, tipped.** **4.** to give a tip to. [C18: ? < TIP[4]] —ˈ**tipper** *n.*

tip[4] (tɪp) *vb.* **tipping, tipped.** (*tr.*) **1.** to hit or strike lightly. ~*n.* **2.** a light blow. [C13: ? < Low G *tippen*]

tip-off *n.* **1.** a warning or hint, esp. given confidentially and based on inside information. **2.** *Basketball.* the act or an instance of putting the ball in play by the referee throwing it high between two opposing players. ~*vb.* **tip off.** **3.** (*tr., adv.*) to give a hint or warning to.

tipper truck *or* **lorry** *n.* a truck or lorry the rear platform of which can be raised at the front end to enable the load to be discharged.

tippet (ˈtɪpɪt) *n.* **1.** a woman's fur cape for the shoulders. **2.** the long stole of Anglican clergy worn during a service. **3.** a long streamer-like part to a sleeve, hood, etc., esp. in the 16th century. [C14: ? < TIP[1]]

tipple (ˈtɪpᵊl) *vb.* **1.** to make a habit of taking (alcoholic drink), esp. in small quantities. ~*n.* **2.** alcoholic drink. [C15: back formation < obs. *tippler* tapster, <?] —ˈ**tippler** *n.*

tipstaff (ˈtɪpˌstɑːf) *n.* **1.** a court official. **2.** a metal-tipped staff formerly used as a symbol of office. [C16 *tipped staff*]

tipster (ˈtɪpstə) *n.* a person who sells tips on horse racing, the stock market, etc.

tipsy (ˈtɪpsɪ) *adj.* **-sier, -siest.** **1.** slightly drunk. **2.** slightly tilted or tipped; askew. [C16: < TIP[2]] —ˈ**tipsily** *adv.* —ˈ**tipsiness** *n.*

tipsy cake *n. Brit.* a kind of trifle made from a sponge cake soaked with wine or sherry and decorated with almonds and crystallized fruit.

tiptoe (ˈtɪpˌtəʊ) *vb.* **-toeing, -toed.** (*intr.*) **1.** to walk with the heels off the ground. **2.** to walk silently or stealthily. ~*n.* **3. on tiptoe. a.** on the tips of the toes or on the ball of the foot and the toes. **b.** eagerly anticipating something. **c.** stealthily or silently. ~*adv.* **4.** on tiptoe. ~*adj.* **5.** walking or standing on tiptoe.

tiptop (ˌtɪpˈtɒp) *adj., adv.* **1.** at the highest point of health, excellence, etc. **2.** at the topmost point. ~*n.* **3.** the best in quality. **4.** the topmost point.

tip-up *adj.* (*prenominal*) able to be turned upwards around a hinge or pivot: *a tip-up seat.*

TIR *abbrev. for* Transports Internationaux Routiers. [F: International Road Transport]

tirade (taɪˈreɪd) *n.* a long angry speech or denunciation. [C19: < F, lit.: a pulling, < It. *tirata*, < *tirare* to pull, <?]

tire[1] (ˈtaɪə) *vb.* **1.** (*tr.*) to reduce the energy of, esp. by exertion; weary. **2.** (*tr.; often passive*) to reduce the tolerance of; bore or irritate: *I'm tired of the children's chatter.* **3.** (*intr.*) to become wearied or bored; flag. [OE *tēorian*, <?] —ˈ**tiring** *adj.*

tire[2] (ˈtaɪə) *n., vb.* the U.S. spelling of **tyre.**

tired (ˈtaɪəd) *adj.* **1.** weary; fatigued. **2.** no longer fresh; hackneyed. **3. tired and emotional.** *Euphemistic.* drunk.

tireless (ˈtaɪəlɪs) *adj.* unable to be tired. —ˈ**tirelessly** *adv.* —ˈ**tirelessness** *n.*

tiresome (ˈtaɪəsəm) *adj.* boring and irritating. —ˈ**tiresomely** *adv.* —ˈ**tiresomeness** *n.*

tirewoman (ˈtaɪəˌwʊmən) *n., pl.* **-women.** an obsolete term for a lady's maid. [C17: < *tire* (obs.) to ATTIRE]

tiring room (ˈtaɪərɪŋ) *n. Arch.* a dressing room.

tiro (ˈtaɪrəʊ) *n., pl.* **-ros.** a variant spelling of **tyro.**

'tis (tɪz) *Poetic or dialect. contraction of* it is.

tisane (tɪˈzæn) *n.* an infusion of leaves or flowers. [C19: < F, < L *ptisana* barley water]

Tishri *Hebrew.* (tɪʃˈriː) *n.* (in the Jewish calendar) the seventh month of the year according to biblical reckoning and the first month of the civil year, falling in September and October. [C19: < Heb.]

tissue (ˈtɪsjuː, ˈtɪʃuː) *n.* **1.** a part of an organism consisting of a large number of cells having a similar structure and function: nerve tissue. **2.** a thin piece of soft absorbent paper used as a disposable handkerchief, towel, etc. **3.** See **tissue paper. 4.** an interwoven series: *a tissue of lies.* **5.** a woven cloth, esp. of a light gauzy nature. ~*vb.* (*tr.*) **6.** to decorate or clothe with tissue or tissue paper. [C14: < OF *tissu* woven cloth, < *tistre* to weave, < L *texere*]

tissue culture *n.* **1.** the growth of small pieces of animal or plant tissue in a sterile controlled medium. **2.** the tissue produced.

tissue paper *n.* very thin soft delicate paper used to wrap breakable goods, as decoration, etc.

tit[1] (tɪt) *n.* any of numerous small active Old World songbirds, esp. the bluetit, great tit, etc. They have a short bill and feed on insects and seeds. [C16: ? imit., applied to small animate or inanimate objects]

tit[2] (tɪt) *n.* **1.** *Sl.* a female breast. **2.** a teat or nipple. **3.** *Derog.* a young woman. **4.** *Taboo sl.* a despicable or unpleasant person. [OE *titt*]

Tit. *Bible. abbrev. for* Titus.

titan (ˈtaɪtᵊn) *n.* a person of great strength or size. [after *Titans*, a family of gods in Gk myth.]

titanic (taɪˈtænɪk) *adj.* possessing or requiring colossal strength: *a titanic battle.*

titanium (taɪˈteɪnɪəm) *n.* a strong malleable white metallic element, which is very corrosion-resistant. It is used in the manufacture of strong lightweight alloys, esp. aircraft parts. Symbol: Ti; atomic no.: 22; atomic wt.: 47.90. [C18: NL; see TITAN, -IUM]

titanium dioxide *n.* a white powder used chiefly as a pigment. Formula: TiO_2. Also called: **titanium oxide, titanic oxide, titania.**

titbit (ˈtɪtˌbɪt) *or esp. U.S.* **tidbit** *n.* **1.** a tasty small piece of food; dainty. **2.** a pleasing scrap of anything, such as scandal. [C17: ? < dialect *tid* tender, <?]

titchy *or* **tichy** (ˈtɪtʃɪ) *adj.* **-chier, -chiest.** *Brit. sl.* very small; tiny. [C20: < *tich* or *titch* a small person, < *Little Tich*, stage name of Harry Relph (1867-1928), E actor noted for his small stature]

titfer (ˈtɪtfə) *n. Brit. sl.* a hat. [< rhyming slang *tit for tat*]

tit for tat *n.* an equivalent given in return or retaliation; blow for blow. [C16: < earlier *tip for tap*]

tithe (taɪð) *n.* **1.** (*often pl.*) a tenth part of produce, income, or profits, contributed for the support of the church or clergy. **2.** any levy, esp. of one tenth. **3.** a tenth or very small part of anything. ~*vb.* **4.** (*tr.*) **a.** to exact or demand a tithe from. **b.** to levy a tithe upon. **5.** (*intr.*) to pay a tithe or tithes. [OE *teogoth*] —ˈ**tithable** *adj.*

tithe barn *n.* a large barn where, formerly, the agricultural tithe of a parish was stored.

titi (ˈtiːtiː) *n., pl.* **-tis.** any of a genus of small New World monkeys of South America, having beautifully coloured fur and a long tail. [via Sp. < Aymara, lit.: little cat]

Titian red (ˈtɪʃən) *n.* a reddish-yellow colour, as in the hair colour in many of the works of Titian (?1490-1576), Italian painter.

titillate (ˈtɪtɪˌleɪt) *vb.* (*tr.*) **1.** to arouse or excite pleasurably. **2.** to cause a tickling or tingling sensation in, esp. by touching. [C17: < L *tītillāre*] —ˈ**titilˌlating** *adj.* —ˌ**titilˈlation** *n.*

titivate *or* **tittivate** (ˈtɪtɪˌveɪt) *vb.* to smarten up; spruce up. [C19: earlier *tidivate*, ? based on TIDY & CULTIVATE] —ˌ**titiˈvation** *or* ˌ**tittiˈvation** *n.*

titlark (ˈtɪtˌlɑːk) *n.* another name for **pipit,** esp. the meadow pipit. [C17: < TIT[1] + LARK[1]]

title (ˈtaɪtᵊl) *n.* **1.** the distinctive name of a work of art, musical or literary composition, etc. **2.** a descriptive name or heading of a section of a book, speech, etc. **3.** See **title page. 4.** a name or epithet signifying rank, office, or function. **5.** a formal designation, such as *Mr.* **6.** an appellation designating nobility. **7.** *Films.* **a.** short for **subtitle. b.** written material giving credits in a film or television programme. **8.** *Sport.* a championship. **9.** *Law.* **a.** the legal right to possession of property, esp. real property. **b.** the basis of such right. **c.** the documentary evidence of such right: *title deeds.* **10. a.** any customary or established right. **b.** a claim based on such a right. **11.** a definite spiritual charge or office in the church as a prerequisite for ordination. **12.** *R.C. Church.* a titular church. ~*vb.* **13.** (*tr.*) to give a title to. [C13: < OF, < L *titulus*]

title deed *n.* a document evidencing a person's legal right or title to property, esp. real property.

titleholder (ˈtaɪtᵊlˌhəʊldə) *n.* a person who holds a title, esp. a sporting championship.

title page *n.* the page in a book that gives the title, author, publisher, etc.

title role *n.* the role of the character after whom a play, etc., is named.

titmouse (ˈtɪtˌmaʊs) *n., pl.* **-mice.** another name for **tit**[1]. [C14 *titemous*, < *tite* (see TIT[1]) + MOUSE]

titrate (ˈtaɪtreɪt) *vb.* (*tr.*) to measure the volume or concentration of (a solution) by titration. [C19: < F *titrer;* see TITRE] —**tiˈtratable** *adj.*

titration (taɪˈtreɪʃən) *n.* an operation in which a measured amount of one solution is added to a known quantity of another solution until the reaction between the two is complete. If the concentration of one solution is known, that of the other can be calculated.

titre *or U.S.* **titer** (ˈtaɪtə) *n.* the concentration of a solution as determined by titration. [C19: < F *titre* proportion of gold or silver in an alloy, < OF *title* TITLE]

titter (ˈtɪtə) *vb.* (*intr.*) **1.** to snigger, esp. derisively or in a suppressed way. ~*n.* **2.** a suppressed laugh, chuckle, or snigger. [C17: imit.] —ˈ**titterer** *n.* —ˈ**tittering** *adj.*

tittle (ˈtɪtᵊl) *n.* **1.** a small mark in printing or writing, esp. a diacritic. **2.** a jot; particle. [C14: < Med. L *titulus* label, < L: title]

tittle-tattle *n.* **1.** idle chat or gossip. ~*vb.* **2.** (*intr.*) to chatter or gossip. —ˈ**tittle-ˌtattler** *n.*

tittup (ˈtɪtəp) *vb.* **-tupping, -tupped** *or U.S.* **-tuping, -tuped. 1.** (*intr.*) to prance or frolic. ~*n.* **2.** a caper. [C18 (in the sense: a horse's gallop): prob. imit.]

titubation (ˌtɪtjʊˈbeɪʃən) *n. Pathol.* a disordered gait characterized by stumbling or staggering, often caused by a lesion of the cerebellum. [C17: < L *titubātiō*, < *titubāre* to reel]

titular (ˈtɪtjʊlə) *adj.* **1.** of, relating to, or of the nature of a title. **2.** in name only. **3.** bearing a title. **4.** *R.C. Church.* designating any of certain churches in Rome to whom cardinals or bishops are attached as their nominal incumbents. ~*n.* **5.** the bearer of a title. **6.** the bearer of a nominal office. [C18: < F *titulaire,* < L *titulus* title]

tizzy (ˈtɪzɪ) *n., pl.* **-zies.** *Inf.* a state of confusion or excitement. Also called: **tizz, tiz-woz.** [C19: <?]

T-junction *n.* a road junction in which one road joins another at right angles but does not cross it.

TKO *Boxing. abbrev. for* technical knockout.

Tl *the chemical symbol for* thallium.

Tm *the chemical symbol for* thulium.

TM *abbrev. for* transcendental meditation.

tmesis (təˈmiːsɪs) *n.* interpolation of a word or words between the parts of a compound word, as in *every-blooming-where.* [C16: via L < Gk, lit.: a cutting, < *temnein* to cut]

TNT *n.* 2,4,6-trinitrotoluene; a yellow solid: used chiefly as a high explosive.

T-number *or* **T number** *n. Photog.* a function of the f-number of a lens that takes into account the light transmitted by the lens. [< *T(otal Light Transmission) Number*]

to (tuː; *unstressed* tʊ, tə) *prep.* **1.** used to indicate the destination of the subject or object of an action: *he climbed to the top.* **2.** used to mark the indirect object of a verb: *telling stories to children.* **3.** used to mark the infinitive of a verb: *he wanted to go.* **4.** as far as; until: *working from Monday to Friday.* **5.** used to indicate equality: *16 ounces to the pound.* **6.** against; upon; onto: *put your ear to the wall.* **7.** before the hour of: *five to four.* **8.** accompanied by: *dancing to loud music.* **9.** as compared with, as against: *the score was eight to three.* **10.** used to indicate a resulting condition: *they starved to death.* ~*adv.* **11.** towards a fixed position, esp. (of a door) closed. [OE *tō*]

▷ **Usage.** In formal usage, *to* is always used with an infinitive and never omitted as in *come see the show.* The use of *and* instead of *to* (*try and come*) is very common in informal speech but is avoided by careful writers.

toad (təʊd) *n.* **1.** any of a group of amphibians similar to frogs but more terrestrial, having a drier warty skin. **2.** a loathsome person. [OE *tādige,* <?] —ˈ**toadish** *adj.*

toadfish (ˈtəʊdˌfɪʃ) *n., pl.* **-fish** *or* **-fishes.** any of various spiny-finned marine fishes of tropical and temperate seas.

toadflax (ˈtəʊdˌflæks) *n.* a perennial plant having narrow leaves and spurred two-lipped yellow-orange flowers. Also called: **butter-and-eggs.**

toad-in-the-hole *n. Brit.* a dish made of sausages baked in a batter.

toadstone (ˈtəʊdˌstəʊn) *n.* an intrusive volcanic rock occurring in limestone. [C18: ? < a supposed resemblance to a toad's spotted skin]

toadstool (ˈtəʊdˌstuːl) *n.* (*not in technical use*) any basidiomycetous fungus with a capped spore-producing body that is poisonous. Cf. **mushroom.**

toady (ˈtəʊdɪ) *n., pl.* **toadies.** **1.** Also: **toadeater.** a person who flatters and ingratiates himself in a servile way; sycophant. ~*vb.* **toadying, toadied.** **2.** to fawn on and flatter (someone). [C19: shortened < *toadeater,* orig. a quack's assistant who pretended to eat toads, hence a flatterer] —ˈ**toadyish** *adj.* —ˈ**toadyism** *n.*

to and fro *adj.,* **to-and-fro** *adv.* **1.** back and forth. **2.** here and there. —ˈ**toing and** ˈ**froing** *n.*

toast[1] (təʊst) *n.* **1. a.** sliced bread browned by exposure to heat. **b.** (*as modifier*): *a toast rack.* ~*vb.* **2.** (*tr.*) to brown under a grill or over a fire: *to toast cheese.* **3.** to warm or be warmed: *to toast one's hands by the fire.* [C14: < OF *toster,* < L *tōstus* parched, < *torrēre* to dry with heat]

toast[2] (təʊst) *n.* **1.** a tribute or proposal of health, success, etc., given to a person or thing and marked by people raising glasses and drinking together. **2.** a person or thing honoured by such a tribute or proposal. **3.** (esp. formerly) an attractive woman to whom such tributes are frequently made. ~*vb.* **4.** to propose or drink a toast to (a person or thing). **5.** (*intr.*) to add vocal effects to a prerecorded track: a disc-jockey technique. [C17 (in the sense: a lady to whom the company is asked to drink): < TOAST[1], < the idea that the name of the lady would flavour the drink like a piece of spiced toast] —ˈ**toaster** *n.*

toaster (ˈtəʊstə) *n.* a device, esp. an electrical device, for toasting bread.

toastmaster (ˈtəʊstˌmɑːstə) *n.* a person who introduces speakers, proposes toasts, etc., at public dinners. —ˈ**toastˌmistress** *fem. n.*

toasty *or* **toastie** (ˈtəʊstɪ) *n., pl.* **toasties.** a toasted sandwich.

Tob. *abbrev. for* Tobit.

tobacco (təˈbækəʊ) *n., pl.* **-cos** *or* **-coes.** **1.** any of a genus of plants having mildly narcotic properties, one species of which is cultivated as the chief source of commercial tobacco. **2.** the leaves of certain of these plants dried and prepared for snuff, chewing, or smoking. [C16: < Sp. *tabaco,* ? < Taino: leaves rolled for smoking, assumed by the Spaniards to be the name of the plant]

tobacco mosaic virus *n.* the virus that causes mosaic disease in tobacco and related plants: its discovery provided the first evidence of the existence of viruses. Abbrev.: **TMV.**

tobacconist (təˈbækənɪst) *n. Chiefly Brit.* a person or shop that sells tobacco, cigarettes, pipes, etc.

-to-be *adj.* (*in combination*) about to be; future: *a mother-to-be; the bride-to-be.*

toboggan (təˈbɒgən) *n.* **1.** a light wooden frame on runners used for sliding over snow and ice. **2.** a long narrow sledge made of a thin board curved upwards at the front. ~*vb.* (*intr.*) **3.** to ride on a toboggan. [C19: < Canad. F, of Amerind origin] —**toˈbogganer** *or* **toˈbogganist** *n.*

toby (ˈtəʊbɪ) *n., pl.* **-bies.** *N.Z.* a water stopcock at the boundary of a street and house section.

toby jug (ˈtəʊbɪ) *n.* a beer mug or jug in the form of a stout seated man wearing a three-cornered hat and smoking a pipe. Also called: **toby.** [C19: < the familiar form of the name *Tobias*]

toccata (təˈkɑːtə) *n.* a rapid keyboard composition for organ, harpsichord, etc., usually in a rhythmically free style. [C18: < It., lit.: touched, < *toccare* to play (an instrument)]

Toc H (ˈtɒk ˈeɪtʃ) *n.* a society formed after World War I to encourage Christian comradeship. [C20: < the obs. telegraphic code for *T.H.,* initials of *Talbot House,* Poperinge, Belgium, the original headquarters of the society]

Tocharian *or* **Tokharian** (tɒˈkɑːrɪən) *n.* **1.** a member of an Asian people who lived in the Tarim Basin until around 800 A.D. **2.** the language of this people, known from records in a N Indian script of the 7th and 8th centuries A.D. [C20: ult. < Gk *Tokharoi,* <?]

tocopherol (tɒˈkɒfəˌrɒl) *n.* any of a group of fat-soluble alcohols that occur in wheat-germ oil, lettuce, egg yolk, etc. Also called: **vitamin E.** [C20: < *toco-,* < Gk *tokos* offspring + *-pher-,* < *pherein* to bear + -OL[1]]

tocsin (ˈtɒksɪn) *n.* **1.** an alarm or warning signal, esp. one sounded on a bell. **2.** an alarm bell. [C16: < F, < OF *toquassen,* < OProvençal, < *tocar* to touch + *senh* bell, < L *signum*]

tod (tɒd) *n.* **on one's tod.** *Brit. sl.* on one's own. [C19: rhyming sl. *Tod Sloan/alone,* after *Tod* Sloan, a jockey]

today (təˈdeɪ) *n.* **1.** this day, as distinct from yesterday or tomorrow. **2.** the present age. ~*adv.* **3.** during or on this day. **4.** nowadays. [OE *tō dæge,* lit.: on this day]

toddle (ˈtɒdᵊl) *vb.* (*intr.*) **1.** to walk with short unsteady steps, as a child. **2.** (foll. by *off*) *Jocular.* to depart. **3.** (foll. by *round, over,* etc.) *Jocular.* to stroll. ~*n.* **4.** the act or an instance of toddling. [C16 (Scot. & N English): <?]

toddler (ˈtɒdlə) *n.* a young child, usually between the ages of one and two and a half.

toddy (ˈtɒdɪ) *n., pl.* **-dies.** **1.** a drink made from spirits, esp. whisky, hot water, sugar, and usually lemon juice. **2.** the sap of various palm trees used as a beverage. [C17: < Hindi *tārī* juice of the palmyra palm, < *tār* palmyra palm, < Sansk. *tāra*]

to-do (tə'duː) *n., pl.* **-dos.** a commotion, fuss, or quarrel.

toe (təʊ) *n.* **1.** any one of the digits of the foot. **2.** the corresponding part in other vertebrates. **3.** the part of a shoe, etc., covering the toes. **4.** anything resembling a toe in shape or position. **5. on one's toes.** alert. **6. tread on someone's toes.** to offend a person, esp. by trespassing on his field of responsibility. ~*vb.* **toeing, toed. 7.** (*tr.*) to touch, kick, or mark with the toe. **8.** (*tr.*) to drive (a nail, etc.) obliquely. **9.** (*intr.*) to walk with the toes pointing in a specified direction: *to toe inwards.* **10. toe the line** *or* **mark.** to conform to expected attitudes, standards, etc. [OE *tā*]

toe and heel *n.* a technique used by racing drivers on sharp bends, in which the brake and accelerator are operated simultaneously by the toe and heel of the right foot.

toecap ('təʊˌkæp) *n.* a reinforced covering for the toe of a boot or shoe.

toed (təʊd) *adj.* **1.** having a part resembling a toe. **2.** fixed by nails driven in at the foot. **3.** (*in combination*) having a toe or toes as specified: *five-toed; thick-toed.*

toehold ('təʊˌhəʊld) *n.* **1.** a small foothold to facilitate climbing. **2.** any means of gaining access, support, etc. **3.** a wrestling hold in which the opponent's toe is held and his leg twisted.

toe-in *n.* a slight forward convergence given to the wheels of motor vehicles to improve steering.

toenail ('təʊˌneɪl) *n.* **1.** a thin horny translucent plate covering part of the surface of the end joint of each toe. **2.** *Carpentry.* a nail driven obliquely. ~*vb.* **3.** (*tr.*) *Carpentry.* to join (beams) by driving nails obliquely.

toerag ('təʊˌræg) *n. Brit. sl.* a contemptible or despicable person. [C20: orig., a beggar, tramp: < the rags wrapped round their feet]

toey ('təʊɪ) *adj. Austral. sl.* nervous and restless; anxious.

toff (tɒf) *n. Brit. sl.* a well-dressed or upper-class person, esp. a man. [C19: ? var. of TUFT, nickname for a commoner at Oxford University]

toffee *or* **toffy** ('tɒfɪ) *n., pl.* **-fees** *or* **-fies. 1.** a sweet made from sugar or treacle boiled with butter, nuts, etc. **2. for toffee.** (preceded by *can't*) *Inf.* to be incompetent at: *he can't sing for toffee.* [C19: var. of earlier *taffy*]

toffee-apple *n.* an apple fixed on a stick and coated with a thin layer of toffee.

toffee-nosed *adj. Sl., chiefly Brit.* pretentious or supercilious; used esp. of snobbish people.

toft (tɒft) *n. British history.* **1.** a homestead. **2.** a homestead and its arable land. [OE]

tofu ('təʊˌfuː) *n.* unfermented soya-bean curd, a food with a soft cheeselike consistency. [< Japanese]

tog[1] (tɒg) *Inf.* ~*vb.* **togging, togged. 1.** (often foll. by *up* or *out*) to dress oneself, esp. in smart clothes. ~*n.* **2.** See **togs.** [C18: ? < obs. cant *togemans* coat, < L *toga* TOGA + *-mans*, < ?]

tog[2] (tɒg) *n.* **a.** a unit of thermal resistance used to measure the power of insulation of a fabric, garment, quilt, etc. **b.** (*as modifier*): *tog-rating.* [C20: arbitrary coinage < TOG[1] (n.)]

toga ('təʊgə) *n.* **1.** a garment worn by citizens of ancient Rome, consisting of a piece of cloth draped around the body. **2.** a robe of office. [C16: < L] —**togaed** ('təʊgəd) *adj.*

together (tə'gɛðə) *adv.* **1.** with cooperation and interchange between constituent elements, members, etc.: *we worked together.* **2.** in or into contact with each other: *to stick papers together.* **3.** in or into one place; with each other: *the people are gathered together.* **4.** at the same time. **5.** considered collectively: *all our wages put together couldn't buy that car.* **6.** continuously: *working for eight hours together.* **7.** closely or compactly united or held: *water will hold the dough together.* **8.** mutually or reciprocally: *to multiply seven and eight together.* **9.** *Inf.* organized: *to get things together.* ~*adj.* **10.** *Sl.* self-possessed, competent, and well-organized. **11. together with.** in addition to. [OE *tōgædre*]

▷ **Usage.** See at **plus.**

togetherness (tə'gɛðənɪs) *n.* a feeling of closeness or affection from being united with other people.

toggery ('tɒgərɪ) *n. Inf.* clothes; togs.

toggle ('tɒgᵊl) *n.* **1.** a peg or rod at the end of a rope, chain, or cable, for fastening by insertion through an eye in another rope, chain, etc. **2.** a bar-shaped button inserted through a loop for fastening. **3.** a toggle joint or a device having such a joint. ~*vb.* **4.** (*tr.*) to supply or fasten with a toggle. [C18: <?]

toggle joint *n.* a device consisting of two arms pivoted at a common joint and at their outer ends and used to apply pressure by straightening the angle between the two arms.

toggle switch *n.* **1.** an electric switch having a projecting lever that is manipulated in a particular way to open or close a circuit. **2.** a computer device used to turn a feature on or off.

togs (tɒgz) *pl. n. Inf.* **1.** clothes. **2.** *Austral. & N.Z.* a swimming costume. [< TOG[1]]

toheroa (ˌtəʊə'rəʊə) *n.* a large edible bivalve mollusc of New Zealand with a distinctive flavour. [< Maori]

tohunga ('tɒhʊŋə) *n. N.Z.* a Maori priest, the repository of traditional lore.

toil[1] (tɔɪl) *n.* **1.** hard or exhausting work. ~*vb.* (*intr.*) **2.** to labour. **3.** to progress with slow painful movements. [C13: < Anglo-F *toiler* to struggle, < OF *toeillier* to confuse, < L *tudiculāre* to stir, ult. < *tundere* to beat] —'**toiler** *n.*

toil[2] (tɔɪl) *n.* **1.** (*often pl.*) a net or snare. **2.** *Arch.* a trap for wild beasts. [C16: < OF *toile*, < L *tēla* loom]

toile (twɑːl) *n.* **1.** a transparent linen or cotton fabric. **2.** a garment of exclusive design made up in cheap cloth so that alterations can be made. [C19: < F, < L *tēla* a loom]

toilet ('tɔɪlɪt) *n.* **1.** another word for **lavatory. 2.** the act of dressing and preparing oneself. **3.** a dressing table. **4.** *Rare.* costume. **5.** the cleansing of a wound, etc., after an operation or childbirth. [C16: < F *toilette* dress, < TOILE]

toilet paper *or* **tissue** *n.* thin absorbent paper, often wound in a roll round a cardboard cylinder (**toilet roll**), used for cleaning oneself after defecation or urination.

toiletry ('tɔɪlɪtrɪ) *n., pl.* **-ries.** an object or cosmetic used in making up, dressing, etc.

toilet set *n.* a matching set consisting of a hairbrush, comb, mirror, and clothes brush.

toilette (twɑː'lɛt) *n.* another word for **toilet** (sense 2). [C16: < F; see TOILET]

toilet water *n.* a form of liquid perfume lighter than cologne.

toilsome ('tɔɪlsəm) *or* **toilful** *adj.* laborious. —'**toilsomely** *adv.* —'**toilsomeness** *n.*

toitoi ('tɔɪtɔɪ) *n.* a tall New Zealand grass with feathery seed-heads. [< Maori]

tokamak ('təʊkəˌmæk) *n. Physics.* a toroidal-shaped thermonuclear reactor designed for nuclear fusion in which strong magnetic fields keep the plasma from contacting the container walls. [C20: < Russian acronym, < *to*roidalnaya *ka*mera s *ma*gnitnym polem, toroidal chamber with magnetic field]

Tokay (təʊ'keɪ) *n.* **1.** a sweet wine made near Tokaj, Hungary. **2.** a variety of grape used to make this. **3.** a similar wine made elsewhere.

token ('təʊkən) *n.* **1.** an indication, warning, or sign of something. **2.** a symbol or visible representation of something. **3.** something that indicates authority, proof, etc. **4.** a metal or plastic disc, such as a substitute for currency for use in slot machines. **5.** a memento. **6.** a gift voucher that can be used as payment for goods of a specified value. **7.** (*modifier*) as a matter of form only; nominal: *a token increase in salary.* ~*vb.* **8.** (*tr.*) to act or serve as a warning or symbol of; betoken. [OE *tācen*]

tokenism ('təʊkəˌnɪzəm) *n.* the practice of making only a token effort or doing no more than

the minimum, esp. in order to comply with a law. —ˈ**tokenist** *adj.*
token money *n.* coins having greater face value than the value of their metal content.
token strike *n.* a brief strike intended to convey strength of feeling on a disputed issue.
token vote *n.* a Parliamentary vote of money in which the amount quoted is not binding.
tokoloshe (ˌtɒkɒˈlɒʃ, -ˈlɒʃɪ) *n.* (in Bantu folklore) a malevolent mythical manlike animal. Also called: **tikoloshe.** [< Xhosa *uthikoloshe*]
toktokkie (ˈtɒkˌtɒkɪ) *n.* a large S. African beetle. [< Afrik., < Du. *tokken* to tap]
tolbooth (ˈtəʊlˌbuːθ, -ˌbuːð, ˈtɒl-) *n.* **1.** *Chiefly Scot.* a town hall. **2.** a variant spelling of **tollbooth.**
tolbutamide (tɒlˈbjuːtəˌmaɪd) *n.* a synthetic crystalline compound used in the treatment of diabetes to lower blood glucose levels. [C20: < TOL(UENE) + BUT(YRIC ACID) + AMIDE]
told (təʊld) *vb.* **1.** the past tense and past participle of **tell**[1]. ~*adj.* **2.** See **all told.**
tole (təʊl) *n.* enamelled or lacquered metal ware, popular in the 18th century. [< F *tôle* sheet metal, < F (dialect): table, < L *tabula* table]
Toledo (tɒˈleɪdəʊ) *n.* a fine-tapered sword or sword blade. [C16: < *Toledo* city in Spain]
tolerable (ˈtɒlərəbᵊl) *adj.* **1.** able to be tolerated; endurable. **2.** permissible. **3.** *Inf.* fairly good. —ˌ**toleraˈbility** *n.* —ˈ**tolerably** *adv.*
tolerance (ˈtɒlərəns) *n.* **1.** the state or quality of being tolerant. **2.** capacity to endure something, esp. pain or hardship. **3.** the permitted variation in some characteristic of an object or workpiece. **4.** the capacity to endure the effects of a poison or other substance, esp. after it has been taken over a prolonged period.
tolerant (ˈtɒlərənt) *adj.* **1.** able to tolerate the beliefs, actions, etc., of others. **2.** permissive. **3.** able to withstand extremes. **4.** exhibiting tolerance to a drug. —ˈ**tolerantly** *adv.*
tolerate (ˈtɒləˌreɪt) *vb.* (*tr.*) **1.** to treat with indulgence or forbearance. **2.** to permit. **3.** to be able to bear; put up with. **4.** to have tolerance for (a drug, etc.). [C16: < L *tolerāre* to sustain]
toleration (ˌtɒləˈreɪʃən) *n.* **1.** the act or practice of tolerating. **2.** freedom to hold religious opinions that differ from the established religion of a country. —ˌ**tolerˈationist** *n.*
toll[1] (təʊl) *vb.* **1.** to ring slowly and recurrently. **2.** (*tr.*) to summon or announce by tolling. **3.** *U.S. & Canad.* to decoy (game, esp. ducks). ~*n.* **4.** the act or sound of tolling. [C15: ? rel. to OE *-tyllan*, as in *fortyllan* to attract]
toll[2] (təʊl, tɒl) *n.* **1. a.** an amount of money levied, esp. for the use of certain roads, bridges, etc. **b.** (*as modifier*): *toll road; toll bridge.* **2.** loss or damage incurred through a disaster, etc.: *the war took its toll of the inhabitants.* **3.** (formerly) the right to levy a toll. [OE *toln*]
tollbooth *or* **tolbooth** (ˈtəʊlˌbuːθ, -ˌbuːð, ˈtɒl-) *n.* a booth or kiosk at which a toll is collected.
tollgate (ˈtəʊlˌgeɪt, ˈtɒl-) *n.* a gate across a toll road or bridge at which travellers must pay.
tollhouse (ˈtəʊlˌhaʊs, ˈtɒl-) *n.* a small house at a tollgate occupied by a toll collector.
tollie (ˈtɒlɪ) *n., pl.* **-lies.** *S. African.* a castrated calf. [C19: < Xhosa *ithole* calf on which the horns have begun to appear]
Toltec (ˈtɒltɛk) *n., pl.* **-tecs** *or* **-tec. 1.** a member of a Central American Indian people who dominated the valley of Mexico until they were overrun by the Aztecs. ~*adj. also* **Toltecan. 2.** of or relating to this people.
tolu (tɒˈluː) *n.* an aromatic balsam obtained from a South American tree. [C17: after *Santiago de Tolu,* Colombia, from which it was exported]
toluene (ˈtɒljʊˌiːn) *n.* a colourless volatile flammable liquid obtained from petroleum and coal tar and used as a solvent and in the manufacture of many organic chemicals. [C19: < TOLU + -ENE, since it was previously obtained from tolu]
toluic acid (tɒˈluːɪk) *n.* a white crystalline derivative of toluene used in synthetic resins and as an insect repellent. [C19: < TOLU(ENE) + -IC]
toluidine (tɒˈljuːɪˌdiːn) *n.* an amine derived from toluene, used in making dyes. [C19: < TOLU(ENE) + -IDE + -INE[2]]
tom (tɒm) *n.* **a.** the male of various animals, esp. the cat. **b.** (*as modifier*): *a tom turkey.* **c.** (*in combination*): *a tomcat.* [C16: special use of the short form of *Thomas,* applied to any male, often implying a common or ordinary type of person, etc.]
tomahawk (ˈtɒməˌhɔːk) *n.* a fighting axe with a stone or iron head, used by the North American Indians. [C17: < Algonquian *tamahaac*]
tomato (təˈmɑːtəʊ) *n., pl.* **-toes. 1.** a South American plant widely cultivated for its red fleshy many-seeded fruits. **2.** the fruit of this plant, eaten in salads, as a vegetable, etc. [C17 *tomate,* < Sp., < Nahuatl *tomatl*]
tomb (tuːm) *n.* **1.** a place, esp. a vault beneath the ground, for the burial of a corpse. **2.** a monument to the dead. **3. the tomb.** a poetic term for death. [C13: < OF *tombe,* < LL *tumba* burial mound, < Gk *tumbos*]
tombac (ˈtɒmbæk) *n.* any of various alloys containing copper and zinc: used for making cheap jewellery, etc. [C17: < F, < Du. *tombak,* < Malay *tambâga* copper, apparently < Sansk. *tāmraka,* < *tāmra* dark coppery red]
tombola (tɒmˈbəʊlə) *n. Brit.* a type of lottery, esp. at a fête, in which tickets are drawn from a revolving drum. [C19: < It., < *tombolare* to somersault]
tomboy (ˈtɒmˌbɔɪ) *n.* a girl who acts or dresses in a boyish way, liking rough outdoor activities. —ˈ**tomˌboyish** *adj.* —ˈ**tomˌboyishly** *adv.*
tombstone (ˈtuːmˌstəʊn) *n.* another word for **gravestone.**
Tom Collins *n.* a long drink consisting of gin, lime or lemon juice, sugar, and soda water.
Tom, Dick, and (or) Harry *n.* an ordinary, undistinguished, or common person (esp. in **every Tom, Dick, and Harry; any Tom, Dick, or Harry**).
tome (təʊm) *n.* **1.** a large weighty book. **2.** one of the several volumes of a work. [C16: < F, < L *tomus* section of larger work, < Gk *tomos* a slice, < *temnein* to cut]
-tome *n. combining form.* indicating an instrument for cutting: *osteotome.* [< Gk *tomē* a cutting, *tomos* a slice, < *temnein* to cut]
tomentum (təˈmɛntəm) *n., pl.* **-ta** (-tə). **1.** a covering of downy hairs on leaves and other plant parts. **2.** a network of minute blood vessels occurring in the human brain. [C17: NL, < L: stuffing for cushions] —**toˈmentose** *adj.*
tomfool (ˌtɒmˈfuːl) *n.* **a.** a fool. **b.** (*as modifier*): *tomfool ideas.* —ˌ**tomˈfoolishness** *n.*
tomfoolery (ˌtɒmˈfuːlərɪ) *n., pl.* **-eries. 1.** foolish behaviour. **2.** utter nonsense; rubbish.
tommy (ˈtɒmɪ) *n., pl.* **-mies.** (*often cap.*) *Brit. inf.* a private in the British Army. [C19: orig. *Thomas Atkins,* name representing typical private in specimen forms]
Tommy gun *n.* an informal name for **Thompson sub-machine-gun.**
tommyrot (ˈtɒmɪˌrɒt) *n.* utter nonsense.
tomography (təˈmɒgrəfɪ) *n.* a technique used to obtain an x-ray photograph of a plane section of the human body or some other object. [C20: < Gk *tomē* a cutting + -GRAPHY]
tomorrow (təˈmɒrəʊ) *n.* **1.** the day after today. **2.** the future. ~*adv.* **3.** on the day after today. **4.** at some time in the future. [OE *tō morgenne,* < *to* on + *morgenne,* dative of *morgen* morning]
Tom Thumb *n.* a dwarf; midget. [after *Tom Thumb,* the tiny hero of several E folk tales]
tomtit (ˈtɒmˌtɪt) *n. Brit.* any of various tits, esp. the bluetit.
tom-tom *n.* a drum usually beaten with the hands as a signalling instrument. [C17: < Hindi *tamtam,* imit.]
-tomy *n. combining form.* indicating a surgical cutting of a specified part or tissue: *lobotomy.* [< Gk *-tomia*]
ton[1] (tʌn) *n.* **1.** Also called: **long ton.** *Brit.* a unit of

weight equal to 2240 pounds or 1016.046 909 kilograms. **2.** Also called: **short ton, net ton.** *U.S. & Canad.* a unit of weight equal to 2000 pounds or 907.184 kilograms. **3.** See **metric ton, tonne.** a unit of weight equal to 1000 kilograms. **4.** Also called: **freight ton, measurement ton.** a unit of volume or weight used for charging or measuring freight in shipping. It is usually equal to 40 cubic feet, 1 cubic metre, or 1000 kilograms. **5.** Also called: **displacement ton.** a unit used for measuring the displacement of a ship, equal to 35 cubic feet of sea water or 2240 pounds. **6.** Also called: **register ton.** a unit of internal capacity of ships equal to 100 cubic feet. ~*adv.* **7. tons.** (intensifier): *the new flat is tons better than the old one.* [C14: var. of TUN]

ton[2] (tʌn) *n. Sl., chiefly Brit.* a score or achievement of a hundred, esp. a hundred miles per hour, as on a motorcycle. [C20: special use of TON[1] applied to quantities of one hundred]

tonal (ˈtəʊnᵊl) *adj.* **1.** of or relating to tone. **2.** of or utilizing the diatonic system; having an established key. **3.** (of an answer in a fugue) not having the same melodic intervals as the subject, so as to remain in the original key. —ˈ**tonally** *adv.*

tonality (təʊˈnælɪtɪ) *n., pl.* **-ties. 1.** *Music.* **a.** the presence of a musical key in a composition. **b.** the system of major and minor keys prevalent in Western music. **2.** the overall scheme of colours and tones in a painting.

tondo (ˈtɒndəʊ) *n., pl.* **-di** (-diː). a circular easel painting or relief carving. [C19: < It.: a circle, shortened < *rotondo* round]

tone (təʊn) *n.* **1.** sound with reference to quality, pitch, or volume. **2.** short for **tone colour. 3.** *U.S. & Canad.* another word for **note** (sense 10). **4.** an interval of a major second; whole tone. **5.** Also called: **Gregorian tone.** any of several plainsong melodies or other chants used in the singing of psalms. **6.** *Linguistics.* any of the pitch levels or pitch contours at which a syllable may be pronounced, such as high tone, falling tone, etc. **7.** the quality or character of a sound: *a nervous tone of voice.* **8.** general aspect, quality, or style. **9.** high quality or style: *to lower the tone of a place.* **10.** the quality of a given colour, as modified by mixture with white or black; shade; tint. **11.** *Physiol.* **a.** the normal tension of a muscle at rest. **b.** the natural firmness of the tissues and normal functioning of bodily organs in health. **12.** the overall effect of the colour values and gradations of light and dark in a picture. **13.** *Photog.* a colour of a particular area on a negative or positive that can be distinguished from surrounding areas. ~*vb.* **14.** (*intr.;* often foll. by *with*) to be of a matching or similar tone (to). **15.** (*tr.*) to give a tone to or correct the tone of. **16.** (*tr.*) *Photog.* to soften or change the colour of the tones of (a photographic image). ~See also **tone down, tone up.** [C14: < L *tonus*, < Gk *tonos* tension, tone, < *teinein* to stretch] —ˈ**toneless** *adj.* —ˈ**tonelessly** *adv.*

tone arm *n.* another name for **pick-up.**

tone colour *n.* the quality of a musical sound that is conditioned or distinguished by the upper partials or overtones present in it.

tone-deaf *adj.* unable to distinguish subtle differences in musical pitch. —**tone deafness** *n.*

tone down *vb.* (*adv.*) to moderate or become moderated in tone: *to tone down an argument.*

tone language *n.* a language, such as Chinese, in which differences in tone may make differences in meaning.

toneme (ˈtəʊniːm) *n. Linguistics.* a phoneme that is distinguished from another phoneme only by its tone. [C20] —**to**ˈ**nemic** *adj.*

tone poem *n.* another term for **symphonic poem.**

toner (ˈtəʊnə) *n.* **1.** a person or thing that tones. **2.** a cosmetic preparation that is applied to produce a desired effect, such as to reduce the oiliness of the skin. **3.** *Photog.* a chemical solution that softens or alters the tones of a photographic image.

tone row *or* **series** *n. Music.* a group of notes having a characteristic pattern that forms the basis of the musical material in a serial composition, esp. one consisting of the twelve notes of the chromatic scale.

tone up *vb.* (*adv.*) to make or become more vigorous, healthy, etc.

tong (tɒŋ) *n.* (formerly) a secret society of Chinese Americans. [C20: < Chinese (Cantonese) *t'ong* meeting place]

tonga (ˈtɒŋgə) *n.* a light two-wheeled vehicle used in rural areas of India. [C19: < Hindi *tāngā*]

Tongan (ˈtɒŋən) *adj.* **1.** of or relating to Tonga, a kingdom occupying an archipelago in the SW Pacific. ~*n.* **2.** a native or inhabitant of Tonga. **3.** the Polynesian language of the Tongans.

tongs (tɒŋz) *pl. n.* a tool for grasping or lifting, consisting of a hinged, sprung, or pivoted pair of arms or levers, joined at one end. Also called: **pair of tongs.** [pl. of OE *tange*]

tongue (tʌŋ) *n.* **1.** a movable mass of muscular tissue attached to the floor of the mouth in most vertebrates. It is used in tasting, eating, and (in man) speaking. Related adj.: **lingual. 2.** an analogous organ in invertebrates. **3.** the tongue of certain animals used as food. **4.** a language, dialect, or idiom: *the English tongue.* **5.** the ability to speak: *to lose one's tongue.* **6.** a manner of speaking: *a glib tongue.* **7.** utterance or voice (esp. in **give tongue**). **8.** anything which resembles a tongue in shape or function. **9.** a promontory or spit of land. **10.** a flap of leather on a shoe. **11.** *Music.* the reed of an oboe or similar instrument. **12.** the clapper of a bell. **13.** the harnessing pole of a horse-drawn vehicle. **14.** a projection on a machine part that serves as a guide for assembly, etc. **15.** a projecting strip along an edge of a board that is made to fit a groove in another board. **16. hold one's tongue.** to keep quiet. **17. on the tip of one's tongue.** about to come to mind. **18. with (one's) tongue in (one's) cheek.** Also: **tongue in cheek.** with insincere or ironical intent. ~*vb.* **tonguing, tongued. 19.** to articulate (notes on a wind instrument) by tonguing. **20.** (*tr.*) to lick, feel, or touch with the tongue. **21.** (*tr.*) to provide (a board) with a tongue. **22.** (*intr.*) (of a piece of land) to project into a body of water. [OE *tunge*] —ˈ**tongueless** *adj.* —ˈ**tongue**ˌ**like** *adj.*

tongue-and-groove joint *n.* a joint made between two boards by means of a tongue along the edge of one board that fits into a groove along the edge of the other board.

tongued (tʌŋd) *adj.* **1.** having a tongue or tongues. **2.** (*in combination*) having a manner of speech as specified: *sharp-tongued.*

tongue-lash *vb.* (*tr.*) to reprimand severely; scold. —ˈ**tongue-**ˌ**lashing** *n., adj.*

tongue-tie *n.* a congenital condition in which the tongue has restricted mobility as the result of an abnormally short fraenum.

tongue-tied *adj.* **1.** speechless, esp. with embarrassment or shyness. **2.** having a condition of tongue-tie.

tongue twister *n.* a sentence or phrase that is difficult to articulate clearly and quickly, such as *Peter Piper picked a peck of pickled pepper.*

tonguing (ˈtʌŋɪŋ) *n.* a technique of playing (any nonlegato passage) on a wind instrument by obstructing and uncovering the air passage through the lips with the tongue.

tonic (ˈtɒnɪk) *n.* **1.** a medicinal preparation that improves the functioning of the body or increases the feeling of wellbeing. **2.** anything that enlivens or strengthens. **3.** Also called: **tonic water.** a mineral water, usually carbonated and containing quinine and often mixed with gin or other alcoholic drinks. **4.** *Music.* **a.** the first degree of a major or minor scale and the tonal centre of a piece composed in a particular key. **b.** a key or chord based on this. ~*adj.* **5.** serving to enliven and invigorate: *a tonic wine.* **6.** of or relating to a tone or tones. **7.** *Music.* of the first degree of a major or minor scale. **8.** of or denoting the general effect of colour and light and shade in a picture. **9.** *Physiol.* of or affecting normal muscular or bodily tone: *a tonic spasm.* [C17: < NL *tonicus,* < Gk *tonikos* concerning tone, < *tonos* TONE] —**ˈtonically** *adv.*

tonic accent *n.* **1.** emphasis imparted to a note by virtue of its having a higher pitch. **2.** (in some languages) an accent in which emphatic syllables are pronounced on a higher musical pitch.

tonicity (təʊˈnɪsɪtɪ) *n.* **1.** the condition or quality of being tonic. **2.** another name for **tonus.**

tonic sol-fa *n.* a method of teaching music, by which syllables are used as names for the notes of the major scale in any key.

tonight (təˈnaɪt) *n.* **1.** the night or evening of this present day. ~*adv.* **2.** in or during the night or evening of this day. **3.** *Obs.* last night. [OE *tōniht*]

tonka bean (ˈtɒŋkə) *n.* **1.** a tall tree of tropical America. **2.** the seeds of this tree, used in the manufacture of perfumes, snuff, etc. [C18: prob. < Tupi *tonka*]

tonnage *or* **tunnage** (ˈtʌnɪdʒ) *n.* **1.** the capacity of a merchant ship expressed in tons. **2.** the weight of the cargo of a merchant ship. **3.** the total amount of shipping of a port or nation. **4.** a duty on ships based either on their capacity or their register tonnage. [C15: < OF, < *tonne* barrel]

tonne (tʌn) *n.* a unit of mass equal to 1000 kg or 2204.6 pounds. Also called (not in technical use): **metric ton.** [< F]

tonneau (ˈtɒnəʊ) *n., pl.* **-neaus** *or* **-neaux** (-nəʊ, -nəʊz). **1.** a detachable cover to protect empty passenger seats in an open vehicle. **2.** *Rare.* the part of an open car in which the rear passengers sit. [C20: < F: special type of vehicle body, < OF *tonnel* cask, < *tonne* tun]

tonometer (təʊˈnɒmɪtə) *n.* **1.** an instrument for measuring the pitch of a sound, esp. one consisting of a set of tuning forks. **2.** any of various types of instrument for measuring pressure or tension, such as the blood pressure, vapour pressure, etc. [C18: < Gk *tonos* TONE + -METER] —**tonometric** (ˌtɒnəˈmɛtrɪk, ˌtəʊ-) *adj.*

tonsil (ˈtɒnsəl) *n.* either of two small masses of lymphatic tissue situated one on each side of the back of the mouth. [C17: < L *tōnsillae* (pl.) tonsils, <?] —**ˈtonsillar** *adj.*

tonsillectomy (ˌtɒnsɪˈlɛktəmɪ) *n., pl.* **-mies.** surgical removal of the tonsils.

tonsillitis (ˌtɒnsɪˈlaɪtɪs) *n.* inflammation of the tonsils. —**tonsillitic** (ˌtɒnsɪˈlɪtɪk) *adj.*

tonsorial (tɒnˈsɔːrɪəl) *adj. Often facetious.* of barbering or hairdressing. [C19: < L *tōnsōrius* concerning shaving, < *tondēre* to shave]

tonsure (ˈtɒnʃə) *n.* **1.** (in certain religions and monastic orders) **a.** the shaving of the head or the crown of the head only. **b.** the part of the head left bare by shaving. ~*vb.* **2.** (*tr.*) to shave the head of. [C14: < L *tōnsūra* a clipping, < *tondēre* to shave] —**ˈtonsured** *adj.*

tontine (ˈtɒntiːn, tɒnˈtiːn) *n.* an annuity scheme by which several subscribers accumulate and invest a common fund out of which they receive an annuity that increases as subscribers die until the last survivor takes the whole. [C18: < F, after Lorenzo *Tonti,* Neapolitan banker who devised the scheme]

ton-up *Brit. inf.* ~*adj.* (*prenominal*) **1.** (esp. of a motorcycle) capable of speeds of a hundred miles per hour or more. **2.** liking to travel at such speeds: *a ton-up boy.* ~*n.* **3.** a person who habitually rides at such speeds.

tonus (ˈtəʊnəs) *n.* the normal tension of a muscle at rest; tone. [C19: < L, < Gk *tonos* TONE]

too (tuː) *adv.* **1.** as well; in addition; also: *can I come too?* **2.** in or to an excessive degree: *I have too many things to do.* **3.** extremely: *you're too kind.* **4.** *U.S. & Canad. inf.* indeed: used to reinforce a command: *you will too do it!* [OE *tō*]

▷ **Usage.** See at **very.**

took (tʊk) *vb.* the past tense of **take.**

tool (tuːl) *n.* **1. a.** an implement, such as a hammer, saw, or spade, that is used by hand. **b.** a power-driven instrument; machine tool. **c.** (*in combination*): *a toolkit.* **2.** the cutting part of such an instrument. **3.** any of the instruments used by a bookbinder to impress a design on a book cover. **4.** anything used as a means of achieving an end. **5.** a person used to perform dishonourable or unpleasant tasks for another. **6.** a necessary medium for or adjunct to one's profession: *numbers are the tools of the mathematician's trade.* ~*vb.* **7.** to work, cut, or form (something) with a tool. **8.** (*tr.*) to decorate (a book cover) with a bookbinder's tool. **9.** (*tr.; often foll. by up*) to furnish with tools. [OE *tōl*] —**ˈtooler** *n.*

tooling (ˈtuːlɪŋ) *n.* **1.** any decorative work done with a tool, esp. a design stamped onto a book cover, etc. **2.** the selection, provision, and setting up of tools for a machining operation.

tool-maker *n.* a person who specializes in the production or reconditioning of precision tools, cutters, etc. —**ˈtool-ˌmaking** *n.*

toolroom (ˈtuːlruːm, -rʊm) *n.* a room, such as in a machine shop, where tools are made, stored, etc.

toot (tuːt) *vb.* **1.** to give or cause to give (a short blast, hoot, or whistle). ~*n.* **2.** the sound made by or as if by a horn, whistle, etc. **3.** *Sl.* any drug for snorting, esp. cocaine. **4.** *U.S. & Canad. sl.* a drinking spree. **5.** *Austral. sl.* a lavatory. [C16: < MLow G *tuten,* imit.] —**ˈtooter** *n.*

tooth (tuːθ) *n., pl.* **teeth** (tiːθ). **1.** any of various bonelike structures set in the jaws of most vertebrates and used for biting, tearing, or chewing. Related adj.: **dental. 2.** any of various similar structures in invertebrates. **3.** anything resembling a tooth in shape, prominence, or function: *the tooth of a comb.* **4.** any of the indentations on the margin of a leaf, petal, etc. **5.** any of the projections on a gear, sprocket, rack, etc. **6.** taste or appetite (esp. in **sweet tooth**). **7. long in the tooth.** old or ageing. **8. tooth and nail.** with ferocity and force. ~*vb.* (tuːð, tuːθ). **9.** (*tr.*) to provide with a tooth or teeth. **10.** (*intr.*) (of two gearwheels) to engage. [OE *tōth*] —**ˈtoothless** *adj.* —**ˈtoothˌlike** *adj.*

toothache (ˈtuːθˌeɪk) *n.* a pain in or about a tooth. Technical name: **odontalgia.**

toothbrush (ˈtuːθˌbrʌʃ) *n.* a small brush, usually with a long handle, for cleaning the teeth.

toothed (tuːθt) *adj.* **a.** having a tooth or teeth. **b.** (*in combination*): *sabre-toothed; six-toothed.*

toothed whale *n.* any of a suborder of whales having simple teeth and feeding on fish, smaller mammals, etc.: includes dolphins and porpoises.

toothpaste (ˈtuːθˌpeɪst) *n.* a paste used for cleaning the teeth, applied with a toothbrush.

toothpick (ˈtuːθˌpɪk) *n.* a small sharp sliver of wood, plastic, etc., used for extracting pieces of food from between the teeth.

tooth powder *n.* a powder used for cleaning the teeth, applied with a toothbrush.

tooth shell *n.* another name for the **tusk shell.**

toothsome (ˈtuːθsəm) *adj.* of delicious or appetizing appearance, flavour, or smell.

toothwort (ˈtuːθˌwɜːt) *n.* **1.** a European plant having scaly stems and pinkish flowers and a rhizome covered with toothlike scales. **2.** any of a genus of North American or Eurasian plants having rhizomes covered with toothlike projections.

toothy (ˈtuːθɪ) *adj.* **toothier, toothiest.** having or showing numerous, large, or projecting teeth: *a toothy grin.* —**ˈtoothily** *adv.* —**ˈtoothiness** *n.*

tootle (ˈtuːtᵊl) *vb.* **1.** to toot or hoot softly or repeatedly. ~*n.* **2.** a soft hoot or series of hoots. [C19: < TOOT] —**ˈtootler** *n.*

top[1] (tɒp) *n.* **1.** the highest or uppermost part of anything: *the top of a hill.* **2.** the most important or successful position: *the top of the class.* **3.** the part of a plant that is above ground: *carrot tops.* **4.** a thing that forms or covers the uppermost part of anything, esp. a lid or cap. **5.** the highest degree or point: *at the top of his career.* **6.** the most important person. **7.** the best part of anything. **8.** the loudest or highest pitch (esp. in **top of one's voice**). **9.** another name for **top gear** (sense 1). **10.** *Cards.* the highest card of a suit in a player's hand. **11.** *Sport.* **a.** a stroke that hits the ball above its centre. **b.** short for **topspin. 12.** a platform around the head of a lower mast of a sailing vessel. **13.** a garment, esp. for a woman, that extends from the shoulders to the waist or hips. **14. off the top of one's head.** with no previous preparation; extempore. **15. on top of. a.** in addition to. **b.** *Inf.* in complete control of (a difficult situation, etc.). **16. over the top. a.** over the parapet or leading edge of a trench. **b.** over the limit; lacking restraint or a sense of proportion. **17. the top of the morning.** a morning greeting regarded as characteristic of Irishmen. ~*adj.* **18.** of, relating to, serving as, or situated on the top. ~*vb.* **topping, topped.** (*mainly tr.*) **19.** to form a top on (something): *to top a cake with cream.* **20.** to remove the top of or from. **21.** to reach or pass the top of. **22.** to be at the top of: *he tops the team.* **23.** to exceed or surpass. **24.** *Sl.* to kill, esp. by hanging. **25.** (*also intr.*) *Sport.* **a.** to hit (a ball) above the centre. **b.** to make (a stroke) by hitting the ball in this way. ~See also **top off, top out, tops, top up.** [OE *topp*]

top[2] (tɒp) *n.* **1.** a toy that is spun on its pointed base. **2. sleep like a top.** to sleep very soundly. [OE, <?]

topaz (ˈtəʊpæz) *n.* **1.** a hard glassy mineral consisting of a silicate of aluminium and fluorine in crystalline form. It is yellow, pink, or colourless, and is a valuable gemstone. **2. oriental topaz.** a yellowish-brown variety of sapphire. **3. false topaz.** another name for **citrine. 4.** either of two South American hummingbirds. [C13: < OF *topaze*, < L *topazus*, < Gk *topazos*]

top boot *n.* a high boot, often with a decorative or contrasting upper section.

top brass *n.* (*functioning as pl.*) *Inf.* the most important or high-ranking officials or leaders.

topcoat (ˈtɒpˌkəʊt) *n.* an outdoor coat worn over a suit, etc.

top dog *n. Inf.* the leader or chief of a group.

top drawer *n.* people of the highest standing, esp. socially (esp. in **out of the top drawer**).

top dressing *n.* a surface application of some material, such as fertilizer. —**ˈtop-ˌdress** *vb.* (*tr.*)

tope[1] (təʊp) *vb.* to consume (alcoholic drink) as a regular habit, usually in large quantities. [C17: < F *toper* to keep an agreement, < Sp. *topar* to take a bet; prob. because a wager was generally followed by a drink] —**ˈtoper** *n.*

tope[2] (təʊp) *n.* a small grey shark of European coastal waters. [C17: <?]

topee *or* **topi** (ˈtəʊpiː, -pɪ) *n., pl.* **-pees** *or* **-pis.** another name for **pith helmet.** [C19: < Hindi *topī* hat]

top-flight *adj.* of superior or excellent quality.

topgallant (ˌtɒpˈgælənt; *Naut.* təˈgælənt) *n.* **1.** a mast on a square-rigger above a topmast or an extension of a topmast. **2.** a sail set on a yard of a topgallant mast. **3.** (*modifier*) of or relating to a topgallant.

top gear *n.* **1.** Also called: **top.** the highest forward ratio of a gearbox in a motor vehicle. **2.** the highest speed, greatest energy, etc.

top hat *n.* a man's hat with a tall cylindrical crown and narrow brim, often made of silk, now worn for some formal occasions.

top-heavy *adj.* **1.** unstable through being overloaded at the top. **2.** *Finance.* characterized by too much debt capital in relation to revenue or profit; overcapitalized.

top-hole *interj., adj. Brit. old-fashioned inf.* excellent; splendid.

tophus (ˈtəʊfəs) *n., pl.* **-phi** (-faɪ). a deposit of sodium urate in the ear or surrounding a joint: a diagnostic of gout. [C16: < L, var. of *tōfus* TUFA, TUFF]

topi *n., pl.* **-pis. 1.** (ˈtəʊpɪ). an African antelope. **2.** (ˈtəʊpiː, -pɪ). another name for **pith helmet.** [C19: < Hindi: hat]

topiary (ˈtəʊpɪərɪ) *adj.* **1.** of, relating to, or characterized by the trimming or training of trees or bushes into artificial decorative shapes. **2.** (*pl.* **-aries**) **a.** topiary work. **b.** a topiary garden. **3.** the art of topiary. [C16: < F *topiaire*, < L *topia* decorative garden work, < Gk *topion* little place, < *topos* place] —**ˈtopiarist** *n.*

topic (ˈtɒpɪk) *n.* **1.** a subject or theme of a speech, book, etc. **2.** a subject of conversation. [C16: < L *topica* translating Gk *ta topika*, lit.: matters relating to commonplaces, title of a treatise by Aristotle, < *topoi*, pl. of *topos* place]

topical (ˈtɒpɪkᵊl) *adj.* **1.** of, relating to, or constituting current affairs. **2.** relating to a particular place; local. **3.** of or relating to a topic or topics. **4.** (of a drug, ointment, etc.) for application to the body surface; local. —**topicality** (ˌtɒpɪˈkælɪtɪ) *n.* —**ˈtopically** *adv.*

topknot (ˈtɒpˌnɒt) *n.* **1.** a crest, tuft, decorative bow, chignon, etc., on the top of the head. **2.** any of several European flatfishes.

topless (ˈtɒplɪs) *adj.* **1.** having no top. **2. a.** denoting a costume which has no covering for the breasts. **b.** wearing such a costume.

top-level *n.* (*modifier*) of, involving, or by those on the highest level of influence or authority: *top-level talks.*

toplofty (ˈtɒpˌlɒftɪ) *adj. Inf.* haughty or pretentious. —**ˈtopˌloftiness** *n.*

topmast (ˈtɒpˌmɑːst; *Naut.* ˈtɒpməst) *n.* the mast next above a lower mast on a sailing vessel.

topmost (ˈtɒpˌməʊst) *adj.* at or nearest the top.

topnotch (ˈtɒpˈnɒtʃ) *adj. Inf.* excellent; superb. —**ˈtopˈnotcher** *n.*

topo- *or before a vowel* **top-** *combining form.* indicating place or region: *topography; topology.* [< Gk *topos* a place]

top off *vb.* (*tr., adv.*) to finish or complete, esp. with some decisive action.

topography (təˈpɒgrəfɪ) *n., pl.* **-phies. 1.** the study or detailed description of the surface features of a region. **2.** the detailed mapping of the configuration of a region. **3.** the land forms or surface configuration of a region. **4.** the surveying of a region's surface features. **5.** the study or description of the configuration of any object. —**toˈpographer** *n.* —**topographic** (ˌtɒpəˈgræfɪk) *or* **ˌtopoˈgraphical** *adj.*

topological group *n. Maths.* a group, such as the set of all real numbers, that constitutes a topological space and in which multiplication and inversion are continuous.

topological space *n. Maths.* a set *S* with an associated family of subsets τ that is closed under set union and finite intersection.

topology (təˈpɒlədʒɪ) *n.* **1.** the branch of mathematics concerned with generalization of the concepts of continuity, limit, etc. **2.** a branch of geometry describing the properties of a figure that are unaffected by continuous distortion. **3.** *Maths.* a family of subsets of a given set *S*, such that *S* is a topological space. **4.** the study of the topography of a given place. **5.** the anatomy of any specific bodily area, structure, or part. —**topologic** (ˌtɒpəˈlɒdʒɪk) *or* **ˌtopoˈlogical** *adj.* —**ˌtopoˈlogically** *adv.* —**toˈpologist** *n.*

top out *vb.* (*adv.*) to place the highest part of a building in position.

topper (ˈtɒpə) *n.* **1.** an informal name for **top hat. 2.** a person or thing that tops or excels.

topping (ˈtɒpɪŋ) *n.* **1.** something that tops something else, esp. a sauce or garnish for food. ~*adj.* **2.** high or superior in rank, degree, etc. **3.** *Brit. sl.* excellent; splendid.

topple (ˈtɒpᵊl) *vb.* **1.** to tip over or cause to tip over, esp. from a height. **2.** (*intr.*) to lean precariously or totter. [C16: frequentative of TOP[1] (vb.)]

tops (tɒps) *Sl.* ~*n.* **1. the tops.** a person or thing of top quality. ~*adj.* **2.** (*postpositive*) excellent.

topsail (ˈtɒpˌseɪl; *Naut.* ˈtɒpsəl) *n.* a square sail carried on a yard set on a topmast.

top-secret *adj.* classified as needing the highest level of secrecy and security.

topside (ˈtɒpˌsaɪd) *n.* **1.** the uppermost side of anything. **2.** *Brit. & N.Z.* a lean cut of beef from the thigh containing no bone. **3.** (*often pl.*) **a.** the part of a ship's sides above the water line. **b.** the parts of a ship above decks.

topsoil (ˈtɒpˌsɔɪl) *n.* the surface layer of soil.

topspin (ˈtɒpˌspɪn) *n. Tennis, etc.* a spin imparted to make a ball bounce or travel exceptionally far, high, or quickly.

topsy-turvy (ˈtɒpsɪˈtɜːvɪ) *adj.* **1.** upside down. **2.** in a state of confusion. *~adv.* **3.** in a topsy-turvy manner. *~n.* **4.** a topsy-turvy state. [C16: prob. < *tops,* pl. of TOP[1] + obs. *tervy* to turn upside down]

top up *vb.* (*tr., adv.*) *Brit.* to raise the level of (a liquid, powder, etc.) in (a container), usually bringing it to the brim of the container.

toque (təʊk) *n.* **1.** a woman's small round brimless hat. **2.** a chef's tall white hat. **3.** *Canad.* a knitted cap with a round tassel on top. **4.** a small plumed hat popular in the 16th century. [C16: < F, < OSp. *toca* headdress, prob. < Basque *tauka* hat]

tor (tɔː) *n.* a high hill, esp. a bare rocky one. [OE *torr*]

Torah (ˈtəʊrə) *n.* **1. a.** the Pentateuch. **b.** the scroll on which this is written. **2.** the whole body of traditional Jewish teaching, including the Oral Law. [C16: < Heb.: precept, < *yārāh* to instruct]

torc (tɔːk) *n.* a variant of **torque** (sense 1).

torch (tɔːtʃ) *n.* **1.** a small portable electric lamp powered by batteries. U.S. and Canad. word: **flashlight. 2.** a wooden or tow shaft dipped in wax or tallow and set alight. **3.** anything regarded as a source of enlightenment, guidance, etc. **4.** any apparatus with a hot flame for welding, brazing, etc. **5. carry a torch for.** to be in love with, esp. unrequitedly. [C13: < OF *torche* handful of twisted straw, < Vulgar L *torca* (unattested), < L *torquēre* to twist]

torchbearer (ˈtɔːtʃˌbɛərə) *n.* **1.** a person or thing that carries a torch. **2.** a person who leads or inspires.

torchère (tɔːˈʃɛə) *n.* a tall stand for holding a candelabrum. [C20: < F, < *torche* TORCH]

torchier *or* **torchiere** (ˈtɔːtʃɪə) *n.* a standing lamp with a bowl for casting light upwards. [C20: < TORCHÈRE]

torch song *n.* a sentimental song, usually sung by a woman. [C20: < *to carry a torch for (someone)*] **—torch singer** *n.*

tore (tɔː) *vb.* the past tense of **tear**[2].

toreador (ˈtɒrɪəˌdɔː) *n.* a bullfighter. [C17: < Sp., < *torear* to take part in bullfighting, < *toro* a bull, < L *taurus*]

torero (tɒˈrɛərəʊ) *n., pl.* **-ros.** a bullfighter, esp. one who fights on foot. [C18: < Sp., < LL *taurārius,* < L *taurus* a bull]

toric lens (ˈtɒrɪk) *n.* a lens used to correct astigmatism, having one of its surfaces shaped like part of a torus so that its focal lengths are different in different meridians.

torii (ˈtɔːrɪˌiː) *n., pl.* **-rii.** a gateway at the entrance to a Shinto temple. [C19: < Japanese, lit.: a perch for birds]

torment *vb.* (tɔːˈmɛnt). (*tr.*) **1.** to afflict with great pain, suffering, or anguish; torture. **2.** to tease or pester in an annoying way. *~n.* (ˈtɔːmɛnt). **3.** physical or mental pain. **4.** a source of pain, worry, annoyance, etc. [C13: < OF, < L *tormentum,* < *torquēre*] **—torˈmented** *adj.* **—torˈmenting** *adj., n.* **—torˈmentor** *n.*

tormentil (ˈtɔːməntɪl) *n.* a perennial plant of Europe and W Asia, having yellow flowers, and an astringent root used in medicine, tanning, and dyeing. [C15: < OF *tormentille,* < Med. L *tormentilla,* < L *tormentum* agony; from its use in relieving pain]

torn (tɔːn) *vb.* **1.** the past participle of **tear**[2]. **2. that's torn it.** *Brit. sl.* an unexpected event or circumstance has upset one's plans. *~adj.* **3.** split or cut. **4.** divided or undecided, as in preference: *torn between staying and leaving.*

tornado (tɔːˈneɪdəʊ) *n., pl.* **-does** *or* **-dos. 1.** a violent storm with winds whirling around a small area of extremely low pressure, usually characterized by a dark funnel-shaped cloud causing damage along its path. **2.** a small but violent squall or whirlwind. **3.** any violently active or destructive person or thing. [C16: prob. alteration of Sp. *tronada* thunderstorm (< *tronar* to thunder, < L *tonāre*) through infl. of *tornar* to turn, < L *tornāre* to turn in a lathe] **—tornadic** (tɔːˈnædɪk) *adj.*

toroid (ˈtɔːrɔɪd) *n.* **1.** *Geom.* a surface generated by rotating a closed plane curve about a coplanar line that does not intersect the curve. **2.** the solid enclosed by such a surface. See also **torus. —toˈroidal** *adj.*

torpedo (tɔːˈpiːdəʊ) *n., pl.* **-does. 1.** a cylindrical self-propelled weapon carrying explosives that is launched from aircraft, ships, or submarines and follows an underwater path to hit its target. **2.** *Obs.* a submarine mine. **3.** *U.S. & Canad.* a firework with a percussion cap. **4.** an electric ray. *~vb.* **doing, doed.** (*tr.*) **5.** to attack or hit (a ship, etc.) with one or a number of torpedoes. **6.** to destroy or wreck: *to torpedo the administration's plan.* [C16: < L: crampfish (whose electric discharges can cause numbness), < *torpēre* to be inactive] **—torˈpedo-ˌlike** *adj.*

torpedo boat *n.* (formerly) a small high-speed warship designed to carry out torpedo attacks.

torpedo tube *n.* the tube from which a torpedo is discharged from submarines or ships.

torpid (ˈtɔːpɪd) *adj.* **1.** apathetic; sluggish. **2.** (of a hibernating animal) dormant. **3.** unable to move or feel. [C17: < L *torpidus,* < *torpēre* to be numb] **—torˈpidity** *n.* **—ˈtorpidly** *adv.*

torpor (ˈtɔːpə) *n.* a state of torpidity. [C17: < L: inactivity, < *torpēre* to be motionless]

torque (tɔːk) *n.* **1.** a necklace or armband made of twisted metal. **2.** any force that causes rotation. [C19: < L *torquēs* necklace & *torquēre* to twist]

torque converter *n.* a device for the transmission of power in which an engine-driven impeller transmits its momentum to a fluid held in a sealed container, which in turn drives a rotor.

torques (ˈtɔːkwiːz) *n.* a distinctive band of hair, feathers, skin, or colour around the neck of an animal; a collar. [C17: < L: necklace, < *torquēre* to twist] **—torquate** (ˈtɔːkwɪt, -kweɪt) *adj.*

torque wrench *n.* a type of wrench with a gauge attached to indicate the torque applied.

torr (tɔː) *n., pl.* **torr.** a unit of pressure equal to one millimetre of mercury (133.322 newtons per square metre). [C20: after E. *Torricelli* (1608-47), It. physicist]

torrefy (ˈtɒrɪˌfaɪ) *vb.* **-fying, -fied.** (*tr.*) to dry (drugs, ores, etc.) by heat. [C17: < F *torréfier,* < L *torrefacere,* < *torrēre* to parch + *facere* to make] **—torrefaction** (ˌtɒrɪˈfækʃən) *n.*

Torrens title (ˈtɒrənz) *n. Austral.* legal title to land based on record of registration rather than on title deeds. [< Sir Robert Richard *Torrens* (1814–84), who introduced the system as premier of South Australia in 1857]

torrent (ˈtɒrənt) *n.* **1.** a fast or violent stream, esp. of water. **2.** an overwhelming flow of thoughts, words, sound, etc. [C17: < F, < L *torrēns* (n.), < *torrēns* (adj.) burning, < *torrēre* to burn] **—torrential** (tɒˈrɛnʃəl) *adj.*

Torricellian tube (ˌtɒrɪˈsɛlɪən) *n.* a vertical glass tube partly evacuated and partly filled with mercury, used to measure atmospheric pressure. [C17: after E. *Torricelli;* see TORR]

torrid (ˈtɒrɪd) *adj.* **1.** so hot and dry as to parch or scorch. **2.** arid or parched. **3.** highly charged emotionally: *a torrid love scene.* [C16: < L *torridus,* < *torrēre* to scorch] **—torˈridity** *or* **ˈtorridness** *n.* **—ˈtorridly** *adv.*

Torrid Zone *n. Rare.* that part of the earth's surface lying between the tropics of Cancer and Capricorn.

torsion (ˈtɔːʃən) *n.* **1. a.** the twisting of a part by application of equal and opposite torques. **b.** the condition of twist and shear stress produced by a torque on a part or component. **2.** a twisting or being twisted. [C15: < OF, < Medical L *torsiō* griping pains, < L *torquēre* to twist, torture] **—ˈtorsional** *adj.* **—ˈtorsionally** *adv.*

torsion balance *n.* an instrument used to measure small forces, esp. electric or magnetic forces, by the torsion they produce in a thin wire.

torsion bar *n.* a metal bar acting as a torsional spring.

torsk (tɔːsk) *n., pl.* **torsks** *or* **torsk.** a food fish of northern coastal waters. Usual U.S. name: **cusk.** [C17: of Scand. origin]

torso (ˈtɔːsəʊ) *n., pl.* **-sos** *or* **-si** (-sɪ). **1.** the trunk of the human body. **2.** a statue of a nude human trunk, esp. without the head or limbs. [C18: < It.: stalk, stump, < L: THYRSUS]

tort (tɔːt) *n. Law.* a civil wrong or injury arising out of an act or failure to act, independently of any contract, for which an action for damages may be brought. [C14: < OF, < Med. L *tortum,* lit.: something twisted, < L *torquēre* to twist]

torte (tɔːt) *n.* a rich cake usually decorated or filled with cream, fruit, etc. [C16: ult. ? < LL *tōrta* a round loaf, <?]

torticollis (ˌtɔːtɪˈkɒlɪs) *n. Pathol.* an abnormal position of the head, usually with the neck bent to one side. [C19: NL, < L *tortus* twisted (< *torquēre* to twist) + *collum* neck]

tortilla (tɔːˈtiːə) *n. Mexican cookery.* a kind of thin pancake made from corn meal. [C17: < Sp.: a little cake, < *torta* a round cake, < LL]

tortoise (ˈtɔːtəs) *n.* **1.** any of a family of herbivorous reptiles having a heavy dome-shaped shell and clawed limbs. **2.** a slow-moving person. **3.** another word for **testudo.** [C15: prob. < OF *tortue* (infl. by L *tortus* twisted), < Med. L *tortūca,* < LL *tartarūcha* coming from Tartarus (in the underworld), < Gk *tartaroukhos;* < belief that the tortoise originated in the underworld]

tortoiseshell (ˈtɔːtəsˌʃɛl) *n.* **1.** the horny yellow-and-brown mottled shell of the hawksbill turtle: used for making ornaments, jewellery, etc. **2.** a similar synthetic substance. **3.** a breed of domestic cat having black, cream, and brownish markings. **4.** any of several butterflies having orange-brown wings with black markings. **5. a.** a yellowish-brown mottled colour. **b.** (*as adj.*): *a tortoiseshell décor.* **6.** (*modifier*) made of tortoiseshell.

tortricid (ˈtɔːtrɪsɪd) *n.* any of a family of moths, the larvae of which live in leaves, which they roll or tie together. [C19: < NL *Tortrīcidae,* < *tortrix,* fem. of *tortor,* lit.: twister, < the leaf-rolling of the larvae, < *torquēre* to twist]

tortuous (ˈtɔːtjʊəs) *adj.* **1.** twisted or winding. **2.** devious or cunning. **3.** intricate. —**tortuosity** (ˌtɔːtjʊˈɒsɪtɪ) *n.* —ˈ**tortuously** *adv.* —ˈ**tortuousness** *n.*

torture (ˈtɔːtʃə) *vb.* (*tr.*) **1.** to cause extreme physical pain to, esp. to extract information, etc.: *to torture prisoners.* **2.** to give mental anguish to. **3.** to twist into a grotesque form. ~*n.* **4.** physical or mental anguish. **5.** the practice of torturing a person. **6.** a cause of mental agony. [C16: < LL *tortūra* a twisting, < *torquēre* to twist] —ˈ**torturer** *n.* —ˈ**torturous** *adj.* —ˈ**torturously** *adv.*

torus (ˈtɔːrəs) *n., pl.* **-ri** (-raɪ). **1.** a large convex moulding semicircular in cross section, esp. one used on the base of a column. **2.** *Geom.* a ring-shaped surface generated by rotating a circle about a coplanar line that does not intersect the circle. **3.** *Bot.* another name for **receptacle** (sense 2). [C16: < L: a swelling, <?] —**toric** (ˈtɒrɪk) *adj.*

Tory (ˈtɔːrɪ) *n., pl.* **-ries. 1.** a member of the Conservative Party in Great Britain or Canada. **2.** a member of the English political party that opposed the exclusion of James, Duke of York from the royal succession (1679–80). Tory remained the label for conservative interests until they gave birth to the Conservative Party in the 1830s. **3.** an American supporter of the British cause; loyalist. Cf. **Whig. 4.** (*sometimes not cap.*) an ultraconservative or reactionary. ~*adj.* **5.** of, characteristic of, or relating to Tories. **6.** (*sometimes not cap.*) ultraconservative or reactionary. [C17: < Irish *tōraidhe* outlaw, < MIrish *tōir* pursuit] —ˈ**Toryish** *adj.* —ˈ**Toryism** *n.*

tosh (tɒʃ) *n. Sl., chiefly Brit.* nonsense; rubbish. [C19: <?]

toss (tɒs) *vb.* **1.** (*tr.*) to throw lightly, esp. with the palm of the hand upwards. **2.** to fling or be flung about, esp. in an agitated or violent way: *a ship tosses in a storm.* **3.** to discuss or put forward for discussion in an informal way. **4.** (*tr.*) (of a horse, etc.) to throw (its rider). **5.** (*tr.*) (of an animal) to butt with the head or the horns and throw into the air. **6.** (*tr.*) to shake or disturb. **7.** to toss up a coin with (someone) in order to decide something. **8.** (*intr.*) to move away angrily or impatiently. ~*n.* **9.** an abrupt movement. **10.** a rolling or pitching motion. **11.** the act or an instance of tossing. **12.** the act of tossing up a coin. See **toss up. 13.** a fall from a horse. [C16: of Scand. origin] —ˈ**tosser** *n.*

toss off *vb.* (*adv.*) **1.** (*tr.*) to perform, write, etc., quickly and easily. **2.** (*tr.*) to drink at one draught. **3.** (*intr.*) *Brit. taboo.* to masturbate.

toss up *vb.* (*adv.*) **1.** to spin (a coin) in the air in order to decide between alternatives by guessing which side will fall uppermost. ~*n.* **toss-up. 2.** an instance of tossing up a coin. **3.** *Inf.* an even chance or risk.

tot[1] (tɒt) *n.* **1.** a young child; toddler. **2.** *Chiefly Brit.* a small amount of anything. **3.** a small measure of spirits. [C18: ? short for *totterer;* see TOTTER]

tot[2] (tɒt) *vb.* **totting, totted.** (usually foll. by *up*) *Chiefly Brit.* to total; add. [C17: shortened < TOTAL or < L *totum* all]

total (ˈtəʊtᵊl) *n.* **1.** the whole, esp. regarded as the complete sum of a number of parts. ~*adj.* **2.** complete; absolute. **3.** (*prenominal*) being or related to a total. ~*vb.* **-talling, -talled** *or U.S.* **-taling, -taled. 4.** (when *intr.*, sometimes foll. by *to*) to amount: *to total six pounds.* **5.** (*tr.*) to add up. **6.** (*tr.*) *Sl.* to kill or destroy. [C14: < OF, < Med. L *tōtālis,* < L *tōtus* all] —ˈ**totally** *adv.*

total internal reflection *n. Physics.* the complete reflection of a light ray at the boundary of two media, when the ray is in the medium with greater refractive index.

totalitarian (təʊˌtælɪˈtɛərɪən) *adj.* of, denoting, relating to, or characteristic of a dictatorial one-party state that regulates every realm of life. —**toˌtaliˈtarianism** *n.*

totality (təʊˈtælɪtɪ) *n., pl.* **-ties. 1.** the whole amount. **2.** the state of being total.

totalizator (ˈtəʊtᵊlaɪˌzeɪtə), **totalizer** *or* **totalisator, totaliser** *n.* **1.** a system of betting on horse races in which the aggregate stake, less tax, etc., is paid out to winners in proportion to their stake. **2.** the machine that records bets in this system and works out odds, pays out winnings, etc. ~U.S. and Canad. term: **pari-mutuel.**

totaquine (ˈtəʊtəˌkwiːn, -kwɪn) *n.* a mixture of quinine and other alkaloids derived from cinchona bark, used as a substitute for quinine in treating malaria. [C20: < NL *tōtaquīna,* < TOTA(L) + Sp. *quina* cinchona bark; see QUININE]

totara (ˈtəʊtərə) *n.* a tall coniferous forest tree of New Zealand with durable wood.

tote[1] (təʊt) *Inf.* ~*vb.* **1.** (*tr.*) to carry, convey, or drag. ~*n.* **2.** the act of or an instance of toting. **3.** something toted. [C17: <?] —ˈ**toter** *n.*

tote[2] (təʊt) *n.* (usually preceded by *the*) *Inf.* short for **totalizator.**

tote bag *n.* a large handbag or shopping bag.

totem (ˈtəʊtəm) *n.* **1.** (in some societies, esp. among North American Indians) an object, animal, plant, etc., symbolizing a clan, family, etc., often having ritual associations. **2.** a representation of such an object. [C18: < Ojibwa *nintōtēm* mark of my family] —**totemic** (təʊˈtɛmɪk) *adj.* —ˈ**totemˌism** *n.*

totem pole *n.* a pole carved or painted with totemic figures set up by certain North American Indians as a tribal symbol, etc.

tother *or* **t'other** (ˈtʌðə) *adj., n. Arch. or dialect.* the other. [C13 *the tother,* by mistaken division < *thet other* (*thet,* < OE *thæt,* neuter of THE[1])]

totipalmate (ˌtəʊtɪˈpælmɪt, -ˌmeɪt) *adj.* (of certain birds) having all four toes webbed. [C19: < L *tōtus* entire + *palmate,* < *palmātus* shaped like a hand, < *palma* PALM[1]]

totter (ˈtɒtə) *vb.* (*intr.*) **1.** to move in an unsteady manner. **2.** to sway or shake as if about to fall. **3.**

to be failing, unstable, or precarious. ~*n.* **4.** the act or an instance of tottering. [C12: ? < OE *tealtrian* to waver, & MDu. *touteren* to stagger] —**'totterer** *n.* —**'tottery** *adj.*

totting ('tɒtɪŋ) *n. Brit.* the practice of searching through rubbish for usable or saleable items. [C19: <?]

toucan ('tuːkən) *n.* any of a family of tropical American fruit-eating birds having a large brightly coloured bill and a bright plumage. [C16: < F, < Port. *tucano*, < Tupi *tucana*, prob. imit. of its cry]

touch (tʌtʃ) *n.* **1.** the sense by which the texture and other qualities of objects can be experienced when they come in contact with a part of the body surface, esp. the tips of the fingers. Related adj.: **tactile. 2.** the quality of an object as perceived by this sense; feel; feeling. **3.** the act or an instance of something coming into contact with the body. **4.** a gentle push, tap, or caress. **5.** a small amount; hint: *a touch of sarcasm.* **6.** a noticeable effect; influence: *the house needed a woman's touch.* **7.** any slight stroke or mark. **8.** characteristic manner or style. **9.** a detail of some work: *she added a few finishing touches to the book.* **10.** a slight attack, as of a disease. **11.** a specific ability or facility. **12.** the state of being aware of a situation or in contact with someone. **13.** the state of being in physical contact. **14.** a trial or test (esp. in **put to the touch**). **15.** *Rugby, soccer, etc.* the area outside the touchlines, beyond which the ball is out of play (esp. in **in touch**). **16.** a scoring hit in fencing. **17.** an estimate of the amount of gold in an alloy as obtained by use of a touchstone. **18.** the technique of fingering a keyboard instrument. **19.** the quality of the action of a keyboard instrument with regard to the ease with which the keys may be depressed. **20.** *Sl.* **a.** the act of asking for money, often by devious means. **b.** the money received. **c.** a person asked for money in this way. ~*vb.* **21.** (*tr.*) to cause or permit a part of the body to come into contact with. **22.** (*tr.*) to tap, feel, or strike. **23.** to come or cause to come into contact with. **24.** (*intr.*) to be in contact. **25.** (*tr.; usually used with a negative*) to take hold of (a person or thing), esp. in violence. **26.** to be adjacent to (each other). **27.** (*tr.*) to move or disturb by handling. **28.** (*tr.*) to have an effect on. **29.** (*tr.*) to produce an emotional response in. **30.** (*tr.*) to affect; concern. **31.** (*tr.; usually used with a negative*) to partake of, eat, or drink. **32.** (*tr.; usually used with a negative*) to handle or deal with: *I wouldn't touch that business.* **33.** (when *intr.*, often foll. by *on*) to allude (to) briefly or in passing. **34.** (*tr.*) to tinge or tint slightly: *brown hair touched with gold.* **35.** (*tr.*) to spoil slightly: *blackfly touched the flowers.* **36.** (*tr.*) to mark, as with a brush or pen. **37.** (*tr.*) to compare to in quality or attainment. **38.** (*tr.*) to reach or attain: *he touched the high point in his career.* **39.** (*intr.*) to dock or stop briefly: *the ship touches at Tenerife.* **40.** (*tr.*) *Sl.* to ask for a loan or gift of money from. ~See also **touchdown, touch off, touch up.** [C13: < OF *tochier*, < Vulgar L *toccāre* (unattested) to strike, prob. imit. of a tapping sound] —**'touchable** *adj.* —**'toucher** *n.*

touch and go *adj.* (**touch-and-go** *when prenominal*) risky or critical.

touchdown ('tʌtʃˌdaʊn) *n.* **1.** the moment at which a landing aircraft or spacecraft comes into contact with the landing surface. **2.** *Rugby.* the act of placing or touching the ball on the ground behind the goal line, as in scoring a try. **3.** *American football.* a scoring play for six points achieved by being in possession of the ball in the opponents' end zone. Abbrev.: **TD.** ~*vb.* **touch down.** (*intr., adv.*) **4.** (of an aircraft, etc.) to land. **5.** *Rugby.* to place the ball behind the goal line, as when scoring a try.

touché (tuː'ʃeɪ) *interj.* **1.** an acknowledgment of a scoring hit in fencing. **2.** an acknowledgment of the striking home of a remark, witty reply, etc. [< F, lit.: touched]

touched (tʌtʃt) *adj.* (*postpositive*) **1.** moved to sympathy or emotion. **2.** showing slight insanity.

touchhole ('tʌtʃˌhəʊl) *n.* a hole in the breech of early cannon and firearms through which the charge was ignited.

touching ('tʌtʃɪŋ) *adj.* **1.** evoking or eliciting tender feelings. ~*prep.* **2.** on the subject of; relating to. —**'touchingly** *adv.*

touch judge *n.* one of the two linesmen in rugby.

touchline ('tʌtʃˌlaɪn) *n.* either of the lines marking the side of the playing area in certain games, such as rugby.

touchmark ('tʌtʃˌmɑːk) *n.* a maker's mark stamped on pewter objects.

touch-me-not *n.* an impatiens with yellow spurred flowers and seed pods that burst open at a touch when ripe. Also called: **noli-me-tangere.**

touch off *vb.* (*tr., adv.*) **1.** to cause to explode, as by touching with a match. **2.** to cause (a disturbance, violence, etc.) to begin.

touchpaper ('tʌtʃˌpeɪpə) *n.* paper soaked in saltpetre for firing gunpowder.

touchstone ('tʌtʃˌstəʊn) *n.* **1.** a criterion or standard. **2.** a hard dark stone that is used to test gold and silver from the streak they produce on it.

touch-type *vb.* (*intr.*) to type without looking at the keyboard. —**'touch-ˌtypist** *n.*

touch up *vb.* (*tr., adv.*) **1.** to put extra or finishing touches to. **2.** to enhance, renovate, or falsify by putting extra touches to. **3.** *Brit. sl.* to touch or caress (someone).

touchwood ('tʌtʃˌwʊd) *n.* something, esp. dry wood or fungus material, used as tinder. [C16: TOUCH (in the sense: to kindle) + WOOD]

touchy ('tʌtʃɪ) *adj.* **touchier, touchiest. 1.** easily upset or irritated. **2.** extremely risky. **3.** easily ignited. —**'touchily** *adv.* —**'touchiness** *n.*

tough (tʌf) *adj.* **1.** strong or resilient; durable. **2.** not tender. **3.** hardy and fit. **4.** rough or pugnacious. **5.** resolute or intractable. **6.** difficult or troublesome to do or deal with: *a tough problem.* **7.** *Inf.* unfortunate or unlucky: *it's tough on him.* ~*n.* **8.** a rough, vicious, or pugnacious person. ~*adv.* **9.** *Inf.* violently, aggressively, or intractably: *to treat someone tough.* ~*vb.* (*tr.*) **10.** *Sl.* to stand firm, hold out against (a difficulty or difficult situation) (esp. in **tough it out**). [OE *tōh*] —**'toughly** *adv.* —**'toughness** *n.*

toughen ('tʌfən) *vb.* to make or become tough or tougher. —**'toughener** *n.*

tough-minded *adj.* practical, unsentimental, or intractable. —ˌ**tough-'mindedness** *n.*

toupee ('tuːpeɪ) *n.* a hairpiece worn by men to cover a bald place. [C18: apparently < F *toupet* forelock, < OF *toup* top, of Gmc origin]

tour (tʊə) *n.* **1.** an extended journey visiting places of interest along the route. **2.** *Mil.* a period of service, esp. in one place. **3.** a short trip, as for inspection. **4.** a trip made by a theatre company, orchestra, etc., to perform in several places. **5.** an overseas trip made by a cricket or rugby team, etc., to play in several places. ~*vb.* **6.** to make a tour of (a place). [C14: < OF: a turn, < L *tornus* a lathe, < Gk *tornos*]

touraco *or* **turaco** ('tʊərəˌkəʊ) *n., pl.* **-cos.** any of a family of brightly coloured crested African birds. [C18: of West African origin]

tour de force *French.* (tur də fɔrs) *n., pl.* ***tours de force*** (tur). a masterly or brilliant stroke, creation, effect, or accomplishment. [lit.: feat of skill or strength]

tourer ('tʊərə) *n.* a large open car with a folding top, usually seating a driver and four passengers. Also called (esp. U.S.): **touring car.**

tourism ('tʊərɪzəm) *n.* tourist travel, esp. when regarded as an industry.

tourist ('tʊərɪst) *n.* **1. a.** a person who travels for pleasure, usually sightseeing and staying in hotels. **b.** (*as modifier*): *tourist attractions.* **2.** a person on an excursion or sightseeing tour. **3.** a member of a touring team. **4.** Also called: **tourist class.** the lowest class of accommodation on a passenger ship. ~*adj.* **5.** of or relating to tourist accommodation. —**tour'istic** *adj.*

touristy (ˈtʊərɪstɪ) *adj. Inf., often derog.* abounding in or designed for tourists.

tourmaline (ˈtʊəməˌliːn) *n.* any of a group of hard glassy minerals of variable colour consisting of a complex silicate of boron and aluminium in crystalline form: used in jewellery and optical and electrical equipment. [C18: < G *Turmalin,* < Sinhalese *toramalli* carnelian]

tournament (ˈtʊənəmənt) *n.* **1.** a sporting competition in which contestants play a series of games to determine an overall winner. **2.** a meeting for athletic or other sporting contestants: *an archery tournament.* **3.** *Medieval history.* a martial sport or contest in which mounted combatants fought for a prize. [C13: < OF *torneiement,* < *torneier* to fight on horseback, lit.: to turn, from the constant wheeling round of the combatants; see TOURNEY]

tournedos (ˈtʊənəˌdəʊ) *n., pl.* **-dos** (-ˌdəʊz). a thick round steak of beef. [< F, < *tourner* to TURN + *dos* back]

tourney (ˈtʊənɪ, ˈtɔː-) *Medieval history.* ~*n.* **1.** a knightly tournament. ~*vb.* **2.** (*intr.*) to engage in a tourney. [C13: < OF *torneier,* < Vulgar L *tornidiāre* (unattested) to turn constantly, < L *tornāre* to TURN (in a lathe); see TOURNAMENT].

tourniquet (ˈtʊənɪˌkeɪ) *n. Med.* any device for constricting an artery of the arm or leg to control bleeding. [C17: < F: device that operates by turning, < *tourner* to TURN]

tour operator *n.* a person or company that specializes in providing package holidays.

tousle (ˈtaʊzᵊl) *vb.* (*tr.*) **1.** to tangle, ruffle, or disarrange. **2.** to treat roughly. ~*n.* **3.** a disorderly, tangled, or rumpled state. **4.** a dishevelled or disordered mass, esp. of hair. [C15: < Low G *tūsen* to shake]

tout (taʊt) *vb.* **1.** to solicit (business, customers, etc.) or hawk (merchandise), esp. in a brazen way. **2.** (*intr.*) **a.** to spy on racehorses being trained in order to obtain information for betting purposes. **b.** to sell such information or to take bets, esp. in public places. ~*n.* **3.** a person who touts. **4.** Also: **ticket tout.** a person who sells tickets for a heavily booked event at inflated prices. [C14 (in the sense: to peer, look out): rel. to OE *tȳtan* to peep out] —ˈ**touter** *n.*

tout à fait *French.* (tut a fɛ) *adv.* completely.

tout de suite *French.* (tud sɥit) *adv.* at once.

tout le monde *French.* (tu lə mɔ̃d) *n.* all the world; everyone.

tovarisch, tovarich, *or* **tovarish** (təˈvɑːrɪʃ) *n.* comrade: a term of address. [< Russian]

tow[1] (təʊ) *vb.* **1.** (*tr.*) to pull or drag (a vehicle, boat, etc.), esp. by means of a rope or cable. ~*n.* **2.** the act or an instance of towing. **3.** the state of being towed (esp. in **in tow, on tow**). **4.** something towed. **5.** something used for towing. **6. in tow.** in one's charge or under one's influence. **7.** short for **ski tow.** [OE *togian*] —ˈ**towable** *adj.* —ˈ**towage** *n.*

tow[2] (təʊ) *n.* the coarse and broken fibres of hemp, flax, jute, etc., preparatory to spinning. [OE *tōw*] —ˈ**towy** *adj.*

toward *adj.* (ˈtəʊəd). **1.** *Now rare.* in progress; afoot. **2.** *Obs.* about to happen; imminent. **3.** *Obs.* promising or favourable. ~*prep.* (təˈwɔːd, tɔːd). **4.** a variant of **towards.** [OE *tōweard*]

towards (təˈwɔːdz, tɔːdz) *prep.* **1.** in the direction or vicinity of: *towards London.* **2.** with regard to: *her feelings towards me.* **3.** as a contribution or help to: *money towards a new car.* **4.** just before: *towards noon.* ~Also: **toward.**

towbar (ˈtəʊˌbɑː) *n.* a rigid metal bar or frame used for towing vehicles.

towboat (ˈtəʊˌbəʊt) *n.* another word for **tug** (sense 4).

tow-coloured *adj.* pale yellow; flaxen.

towel (ˈtaʊəl) *n.* **1.** a piece of absorbent cloth or paper used for drying things. **2. throw in the towel.** See **throw in** (sense 3). ~*vb.* **-elling, -elled** *or U.S.* **-eling, -eled. 3.** (*tr.*) to dry or wipe with a towel. **4.** (*tr.;* often foll. by *up*) *Austral. sl.* to assault or beat (a person). [C13: < OF *toaille,* of Gmc origin]

towelling (ˈtaʊəlɪŋ) *n.* an absorbent fabric used for making towels, bathrobes, etc.

tower (ˈtaʊə) *n.* **1.** a tall, usually square or circular structure, sometimes part of a larger building and usually built for a specific purpose. **2.** a place of defence or retreat. **3. tower of strength.** a person who gives support, comfort, etc. ~*vb.* **4.** (*intr.*) to be or rise like a tower; loom. [C12: < OF *tur,* < L *turris,* < Gk]

towering (ˈtaʊərɪŋ) *adj.* **1.** very tall; lofty. **2.** outstanding, as in importance or stature. **3.** (*prenominal*) very intense: *a towering rage.*

towhead (ˈtəʊ hɛd) *n.* **1.** a person with blond or yellowish hair. **2.** a head of such hair. [< TOW[2] (flax)] —ˌ**tow**ˈ**headed** *adj.*

towhee (ˈtaʊˌhiː, ˈtəʊ-) *n.* any of various North American brownish-coloured sparrows. [C18: imit.]

towline (ˈtəʊˌlaɪn) *n.* another name for **towrope.**

town (taʊn) *n.* **1.** a densely populated urban area, typically smaller than a city and larger than a village. **2.** a city, borough, or other urban area. **3.** (in the U.S.) a territorial unit of local government that is smaller than a county; township. **4.** the nearest town or commercial district. **5.** London or the chief city of an area. **6.** the inhabitants of a town. **7. go to town. a.** to make a supreme or unrestricted effort. **b.** *Austral. & N.Z. inf.* to lose one's temper. **8. on the town.** seeking out entertainments and amusements. [OE *tūn* village] —ˈ**townish** *adj.*

town clerk *n.* **1.** (in Britain until 1974) the secretary and chief administrative officer of a town or city. **2.** (in the U.S.) the official who keeps the records of a town.

town crier *n.* (formerly) a person employed to make public announcements in the streets.

townee (taʊˈniː) *or U.S.* **townie** *or* **towny** (ˈtaʊnɪ) *n. Inf., often disparaging.* a permanent resident in a town, esp. as distinct from country dwellers or students.

town gas *n.* coal gas manufactured for domestic and industrial use.

town hall *n.* the chief building in which municipal business is transacted, often with a hall for public meetings.

town house *n.* **1.** a terraced house in an urban area, esp. a fashionable one. **2.** a person's town residence as distinct from his country residence.

town planning *n.* the comprehensive planning of the physical and social development of a town. U.S. term: **city planning.**

townscape (ˈtaʊnskeɪp) *n.* **1.** a view of an urban scene. **2.** an extensive area of urban development.

township (ˈtaʊnʃɪp) *n.* **1.** a small town. **2.** (in the Scottish Highlands) a small crofting community. **3.** (in the U.S. and Canada) a territorial area, esp. a subdivision of a county: often organized as a unit of local government. **4.** (in Canada) a land-survey area, usually 36 square miles (93 square kilometres). **5.** (in South Africa) a planned urban settlement of Black Africans or Coloureds. **6.** *English history.* **a.** any of the local districts of a large parish. **b.** the parish itself.

townsman (ˈtaʊnzmən) *n., pl.* **-men. 1.** an inhabitant of a town. **2.** a person from the same town as oneself. —ˈ**towns**ˌ**woman** *fem. n.*

townspeople (ˈtaʊnzˌpiːpᵊl) *or* **townsfolk** (ˈtaʊnzˌfəʊk) *pl. n.* the inhabitants of a town; citizens.

towpath (ˈtəʊˌpɑːθ) *n.* a path beside a canal or river, used by people or animals towing boats. Also called: **towing path.**

towrope (ˈtəʊˌrəʊp) *n.* a rope or cable used for towing a vehicle or vessel. Also called: **towline.**

tox-, toxic- *or before a consonant* **toxo-, toxico-** *combining form.* indicating poison: *toxaemia.* [< L *toxicum*]

toxaemia *or U.S.* **toxemia** (tɒkˈsiːmɪə) *n.* **1.** a condition characterized by the presence of bacterial toxins in the blood. **2.** the condition in pregnancy of pre-eclampsia or eclampsia. —**tox**ˈ**aemic** *or U.S.* **tox**ˈ**emic** *adj.*

toxic (ˈtɒksɪk) *adj.* **1.** of or caused by a toxin or poison. **2.** harmful or deadly. [C17: < Medical L *toxicus,* < L *toxicum* poison, < Gk *toxikon* (*pharmakon*) (poison) used on arrows, < *toxon* arrow] —ˈ**toxically** *adv.* —**toxicity** (tɒkˈsɪsɪtɪ) *n.*

toxicant (ˈtɒksɪkənt) *n.* **1.** a toxic substance; poison. ~*adj.* **2.** poisonous; toxic. [C19: < Med. L *toxicāre* to poison]

toxicology (ˌtɒksɪˈkɒlədʒɪ) *n.* the branch of science concerned with poisons, their effects, antidotes, etc. —**toxicological** (ˌtɒksɪkəˈlɒdʒɪkᵊl) *or* ˌ**toxicoˈlogic** *adj.* —ˌ**toxiˈcologist** *n.*

toxin (ˈtɒksɪn) *n.* **1.** any of various poisonous substances produced by microorganisms that stimulate the production of neutralizing substances (antitoxins) in the body. **2.** any other poisonous substance of plant or animal origin.

toxin-antitoxin *n.* a mixture of a toxin and antitoxin. The diphtheria toxin-antitoxin was formerly used for immunization.

toxocariasis (ˌtɒksəkəˈraɪəsɪs) *n.* the infection of humans with the larvae of a genus of roundworms, *Toxocara,* of dogs and cats.

toxoid (ˈtɒksɔɪd) *n.* a toxin that has been treated to reduce its toxicity and is used in immunization to stimulate production of antitoxins.

toxophilite (tɒkˈsɒfɪˌlaɪt) *Formal.* ~*n.* **1.** an archer. ~*adj.* **2.** of archery. [C18: < *Toxophilus,* the title of a book (1545) by Ascham, designed to mean: a lover of the bow, < Gk *toxon* bow + *philos* loving] —**toxˈophily** *n.*

toxoplasmosis (ˌtɒksəʊplæzˈməʊsɪs) *n.* a protozoal disease characterized by jaundice and convulsions. —ˌ**toxoˈplasmic** *adj.*

toy (tɔɪ) *n.* **1.** an object designed to be played with. **2. a.** something that is a nonfunctioning replica of something else, esp. a miniature one. **b.** (*as modifier*): *a toy guitar.* **3.** any small thing of little value; trifle. **4. a.** something small or miniature, esp. a miniature variety of a breed of dog. **b.** (*as modifier*): *a toy poodle.* ~*vb.* **5.** (*intr.;* usually foll. by *with*) to play, fiddle, or flirt. [C16 (in the sense: amorous dalliance): <?]

toy boy *n.* the much younger male lover of an older woman.

tr *abbrev. for* treasurer.

tr. *abbrev. for:* **1.** transitive. **2.** translated. **3.** translator. **4.** *Music.* trill. **5.** trustee.

trabeated (ˈtreɪbɪˌeɪtɪd) *or* **trabeate** (ˈtreɪbɪɪt, -ˌeɪt) *adj. Archit.* constructed with horizontal beams as opposed to arches. [C19: back formation < *trabeation,* < L *trabs* a beam]

trabecula (trəˈbɛkjʊlə) *n., pl.* **-lae** (-ˌliː). *Anat., bot.* any of various rod-shaped structures that support other organs. [C19: via NL < L: a little beam, < *trabs* a beam] —**traˈbecular** *or* **traˈbeculate** *adj.*

trace[1] (treɪs) *n.* **1.** a mark or other sign that something has been in a place. **2.** a scarcely detectable amount or characteristic. **3.** a footprint or other indication of the passage of an animal or person. **4.** any line drawn by a recording instrument or a record consisting of a number of such lines. **5.** something drawn, such as a tracing. **6.** *Chiefly U.S.* a beaten track or path. ~*vb.* **7.** (*tr.*) to follow, discover, or ascertain the course or development of (something). **8.** (*tr.*) to track down and find, as by following a trail. **9.** to copy (a design, map, etc.) by drawing over the lines visible through a superimposed sheet of transparent paper. **10.** (*tr.;* often foll. by *out*) **a.** to draw or delineate a plan or diagram of. **b.** to outline or sketch (an idea, etc.). **11.** (*tr.*) to decorate with tracery. **12.** (usually foll. by *back*) to follow or be followed to source; date back: *his ancestors trace back to the 16th century.* [C13: < F *tracier,* < Vulgar L *tractiāre* (unattested) to drag, < L *tractus,* < *trahere*] —ˈ**traceable** *adj.* —ˌ**traceaˈbility** *or* ˈ**traceableness** *n.* —ˈ**traceably** *adv.*

trace[2] (treɪs) *n.* **1.** either of the two side straps that connect a horse's harness to the swingletree. **2.** *Angling.* a length of nylon or, formerly, gut attaching a hook or fly to a line. **3. kick over the traces.** to escape or defy control. [C14 *trais,* < OF *trait,* ult. < L *trahere* to drag]

trace element *n.* any of various chemical elements that occur in very small amounts in organisms and are essential for many physiological and biochemical processes.

tracer (ˈtreɪsə) *n.* **1.** a person or thing that traces. **2.** a projectile that can be observed when in flight by the burning of chemical substances in its base. **3.** *Med.* any radioactive isotope introduced into the body to study metabolic processes, etc., by following its progress with a Geiger counter or other detector. **4.** an investigation to trace missing cargo, mail, etc.

tracer bullet *n.* a round of small arms ammunition containing a tracer.

tracery (ˈtreɪsərɪ) *n., pl.* **-eries. 1.** a pattern of interlacing ribs, esp. as used in the upper part of a Gothic window, etc. **2.** any fine pattern resembling this. —ˈ**traceried** *adj.*

trachea (trəˈkiːə) *n., pl.* **-cheae** (-ˈkiːiː). **1.** *Anat., zool.* the tube that conveys inhaled air from the larynx to the bronchi. **2.** any of the tubes in insects and related animals that convey air from the spiracles to the tissues. [C16: < Med. L, < Gk *trakheia,* shortened < (*artēria*) *trakheia* rough (artery), < *trakhus* rough] —**traˈcheal** *or* **traˈcheate** *adj.*

tracheitis (ˌtreɪkɪˈaɪtɪs) *n.* inflammation of the trachea.

tracheo- *or before a vowel* **trache-** *combining form.* denoting the trachea.

tracheotomy (ˌtrækɪˈɒtəmɪ) *n., pl.* **-mies.** surgical incision into the trachea, as performed when the air passage has been blocked.

trachoma (trəˈkəʊmə) *n.* a chronic contagious disease of the eye caused by a virus-like organism characterized by inflammation of the conjunctiva and cornea and the formation of scar tissue. [C17: < NL, < Gk *trakhōma* roughness, < *trakhus* rough] —**trachomatous** (trəˈkɒmətəs) *adj.*

trachyte (ˈtreɪkaɪt, ˈtræ-) *n.* a light-coloured fine-grained volcanic rock. [C19: < F, < Gk *trakhutēs,* < *trakhus* rough]

tracing (ˈtreɪsɪŋ) *n.* **1.** a copy made by tracing. **2.** the act of making a trace. **3.** a record made by an instrument.

track (træk) *n.* **1.** the mark or trail left by something that has passed by. **2.** any road or path, esp. a rough one. **3.** a rail or pair of parallel rails on which a vehicle, such as a locomotive, runs. **4.** a course of action, thought, etc.: *don't start on that track again!* **5.** a line of motion or travel, such as flight. **6.** an endless band on the wheels of a tank, tractor, etc., to enable it to move across rough ground. **7. a.** a course for running or racing. **b.** (*as modifier*): *track events.* **8.** *U.S. & Canad.* **a.** sports performed on a track. **b.** track and field events as a whole. **9.** a path on a magnetic recording medium, esp. magnetic tape, on which music or speech is recorded. **10.** Also called: **band.** any of a number of separate sections in the recording on either side of a gramophone record. **11.** the distance between the points of contact with the ground of a pair of wheels, as of a motor vehicle. **12. keep** (*or* **lose**) **track of.** to follow (or fail to follow) the passage, course, or progress of. **13. off the track.** away from what is correct or true. **14. on the track of.** on the scent or trail of; pursuing. ~*vb.* **15.** to follow the trail of (a person, animal, etc.). **16.** to follow the flight path of (a satellite, etc.) by picking up signals transmitted or reflected by it. **17.** *U.S. railways.* **a.** to provide with a track. **b.** to run on a track of (a certain width). **18.** (of a camera or camera-operator) to follow (a moving object) while operating. **19.** to follow a track through (a place): *to track the jungles.* **20.** (*intr.*) (of the pick-up, stylus, etc., of a record player) to follow the groove of a record. ~See also **tracks.** [C15: < OF *trac,* prob. of Gmc origin] —ˈ**tracker** *n.*

track down *vb.* (*tr., adv.*) to find by tracking or pursuing.

tracker dog *n.* a dog specially trained to search for missing people.

track event *n.* a competition in athletics, such as

relay running or sprinting, that takes place on a running track.

tracking station *n.* a station that can use a radio or radar beam to follow the path of an object in space or in the atmosphere.

tracklaying (ˈtræk,leɪɪŋ) *adj. also* **tracked.** (of a vehicle) having an endless jointed metal band around the wheels.

track record *n. Inf.* the past record of the accomplishments and failures of a person, business, etc.

track rod *n.* the rod connecting the two front wheels of a motor vehicle.

tracks (træks) *pl. n.* **1.** (*sometimes sing.*) marks, such as footprints, etc., left by someone or something that has passed. **2. in one's tracks.** on the very spot where one is standing. **3. make tracks.** to leave or depart. **4. make tracks for.** to go or head towards.

track shoe *n.* either of a pair of light running shoes fitted with steel spikes for better grip.

tracksuit (ˈtræk,suːt) *n.* a warm suit worn by athletes, etc., esp. during training.

tract[1] (trækt) *n.* **1.** an extended area, as of land. **2.** *Anat.* a system of organs, glands, etc., that has a particular function: *the digestive tract.* **3.** *Arch.* an extended period of time. [C15: < L *tractus* a stretching out, < *trahere* to drag]

tract[2] (trækt) *n.* a treatise or pamphlet, esp. a religious or moralistic one. [C15: < L *tractātus* TRACTATE]

tractable (ˈtræktəbᵊl) *adj.* **1.** easily controlled or persuaded. **2.** readily worked; malleable. [C16: < L *tractābilis*, < *tractāre* to manage, < *trahere* to draw] —,**tractaˈbility** *or* ˈ**tractableness** *n.* —ˈ**tractably** *adv.*

Tractarianism (trækˈtɛərɪə,nɪzəm) *n.* another name for the **Oxford Movement.** [after the series of tracts, *Tracts for the Times* published between 1833 and 1841, in which the principles of the movement were presented] —**Tracˈtarian** *n., adj.*

tractate (ˈtrækteɪt) *n.* a treatise. [C15: < L *tractātus*, < *tractāre* to handle; see TRACTABLE]

traction (ˈtrækʃən) *n.* **1.** the act of drawing or pulling, esp. by motive power. **2.** the state of being drawn or pulled. **3.** *Med.* the application of a steady pull on a limb, etc., using a system of weights and pulleys or splints. **4.** adhesive friction, as between a wheel of a motor vehicle and the road. [C17: < Med. L *tractiō*, < L *tractus* dragged, < *trahere* to drag] —ˈ**tractional** *adj.* —**tractive** (ˈtræktɪv) *adj.*

traction engine *n.* a steam-powered locomotive used, esp. formerly, for drawing heavy loads along roads or over rough ground.

tractor (ˈtræktə) *n.* **1.** a motor vehicle with large rear wheels or endless belt treads, used to pull heavy loads, esp. farm machinery. **2.** a short vehicle with a driver's cab, used to pull a trailer, as in an articulated lorry. [C18: < LL: one who pulls, < *trahere* to drag]

trad (træd) *n.* **1.** *Chiefly Brit.* traditional jazz. ~*adj.* **2.** short for **traditional.**

trade (treɪd) *n.* **1.** the act or an instance of buying and selling goods and services. **2.** a personal occupation, esp. a craft requiring skill. **3.** the people and practices of an industry, craft, or business. **4.** exchange of one thing for something else. **5.** the regular clientele of a firm or industry. **6.** amount of custom or commercial dealings; business. **7.** a specified market or business: *the tailoring trade.* **8.** an occupation in commerce, as opposed to a profession. ~*vb.* **9.** (*tr.*) to buy and sell (merchandise). **10.** to exchange (one thing) for another. **11.** (*intr.*) to engage in trade. **12.** (*intr.*) to deal or do business (with). ~See also **trade-in, trade on.** [C14 (in the sense: track, hence, a regular business)] —ˈ**tradable** *or* ˈ**tradeable** *adj.*

trade cycle *n.* the recurrent fluctuation between boom and depression in the economic activity of a capitalist country.

trade discount *n.* a sum or percentage deducted from the list price of a commodity allowed to a retailer or by one enterprise to another in the same trade.

trade gap *n.* the amount by which the value of a country's visible imports exceeds that of visible exports; an unfavourable balance of trade.

trade-in *n.* **1. a.** a used article given in part payment for the purchase of a new article. **b.** a transaction involving such part payment. **c.** the valuation put on the article traded in. ~*vb.* **trade in. 2.** (*tr., adv.*) to give (a used article) as part payment for a new article.

trademark (ˈtreɪd,mɑːk) *n.* **1. a.** the name or other symbol used by a manufacturer or dealer to distinguish his products from those of competitors. **b. Registered Trademark.** one that is officially registered and legally protected. **2.** any distinctive sign or mark of the presence of a person or animal. ~*vb.* (*tr.*) **3.** to label with a trademark. **4.** to register as a trademark.

trade name *n.* **1.** the name used by a trade to refer to a commodity, service, etc. **2.** the name under which a commercial enterprise operates in business.

trade-off *n.* an exchange, esp. as a compromise.

trade on *vb.* (*intr., prep.*) to exploit or take advantage of: *he traded on her endless patience.*

trade plate *n.* a numberplate attached temporarily to a vehicle by a dealer, etc., before the vehicle has been registered.

trader (ˈtreɪdə) *n.* **1.** a person who engages in trade. **2.** a vessel regularly employed in trade. **3.** *Stock Exchange, U.S.* a member who operates mainly on his own account.

tradescantia (,trædɛsˈkænʃɪə) *n.* any of a genus of plants widely cultivated for their striped variegated leaves. [C18: NL, after John *Tradescant* (1608–62), E botanist]

trade secret *n.* a secret formula, technique, process, etc., known and used to advantage by only one manufacturer.

tradesman (ˈtreɪdzmən) *n., pl.* **-men. 1.** a man engaged in trade, esp. a retail dealer. **2.** a skilled worker. —ˈ**trades,woman** *fem. n.*

tradespeople (ˈtreɪdz,piːpᵊl) *or* **tradesfolk** (ˈtreɪdz,fəʊk) *pl. n. Chiefly Brit.* people engaged in trade, esp. shopkeepers.

Trades Union Congress *n.* the major association of British trade unions, which includes all the larger unions. Abbrev.: **TUC**

trade union *or* **trades union** *n.* an association of employees formed to improve their incomes and working conditions by collective bargaining. —**trade unionism** *or* **trades unionism** *n.* —**trade unionist** *or* **trades unionist** *n.*

trade wind (wɪnd) *n.* a wind blowing obliquely towards the equator either from the northeast in the N hemisphere or the southeast in the S hemisphere, between latitudes 30° N and S. [C17: < *to blow trade* to blow steadily in one direction, < *trade* in the obs. sense: a track]

trading estate *n. Chiefly Brit.* a large area in which a number of commercial or industrial firms are situated.

trading post *n.* a general store in an unsettled or thinly populated region.

tradition (trəˈdɪʃən) *n.* **1.** the handing down from generation to generation of customs, beliefs, etc. **2.** the body of customs, thought, etc., belonging to a particular country, people, family, or institution over a long period. **3.** a specific custom or practice of long standing. **4.** *Christianity.* a doctrine regarded as having been established by Christ or the apostles though not contained in Scripture. **5.** (*often cap.*) *Judaism.* a body of laws regarded as having been handed down from Moses orally. **6.** the beliefs and customs of Islam supplementing the Koran. **7.** *Law, chiefly Roman & Scots.* the act of formally transferring ownership of movable property. [C14: < L *trāditiō* a handing down, surrender, < *trādere* to give up, transmit, < TRANS- + *dāre* to give] —**traˈditionless** *adj.*

traditional (trəˈdɪʃənᵊl) *adj.* **1.** of, relating to, or being a tradition. **2.** of the style of jazz originating in New Orleans, characterized by collective improvisation by a front line of trumpet, trombone, and clarinet. —**tra'ditionally** *adv.*

traditionalism (trə'dɪʃən°ˌlɪzəm) *n.* **1.** the doctrine that all knowledge originates in divine revelation and is perpetuated by tradition. **2.** adherence to tradition, esp. in religion. —**tra'ditionalist** *n., adj.* —**traˌditional'istic** *adj.*

traditional logic *n.* the logic of the late Middle Ages, derived from Aristotelian logic, and concerned esp. with the study of the syllogism.

traduce (trə'djuːs) *vb.* (*tr.*) to speak badly or maliciously of. [C16: < L *trādūcere* to lead over, disgrace] —**tra'ducement** *n.* —**tra'ducer** *n.*

traffic ('træfɪk) *n.* **1. a.** the vehicles coming and going in a street, town, etc. **b.** (*as modifier*): *traffic lights.* **2.** the movement of vehicles, people, etc., in a particular place or for a particular purpose: *sea traffic.* **3.** (usually foll. by *with*) dealings or business. **4.** trade, esp. of an illicit kind: *drug traffic.* **5.** the aggregate volume of messages transmitted through a communications system in a given period. **6.** *Chiefly U.S.* the number of customers patronizing a commercial establishment in a given time period. ~*vb.* **-ficking, -ficked.** (*intr.*) **7.** (often foll. by *in*) to carry on trade or business, esp. of an illicit kind. **8.** (usually foll. by *with*) to have dealings. [C16: < OF *trafique,* < OIt. *traffico,* < *trafficare* to engage in trade] —'**trafficker** *n.*

trafficator ('træfɪˌkeɪtə) *n.* (formerly) an illuminated arm on a motor vehicle that was raised to indicate a left or right turn.

traffic island *n.* a raised area in the middle of a road designed as a guide for traffic flow and to provide a stopping place for pedestrians crossing.

traffic light *or* **signal** *n.* one of a set of coloured lights placed at crossroads, junctions, etc., to control the flow of traffic.

traffic pattern *n.* a pattern of permitted lanes in the air around an airport to which an aircraft is restricted.

traffic warden *n. Brit.* a person who is appointed to supervise road traffic and report traffic offences.

tragacanth ('trægəˌkænθ) *n.* **1.** any of various spiny plants that yield a substance that is made into a gum. **2.** the gum obtained from these plants, used in the manufacture of pills and lozenges and in calico printing. [C16: < F *tragacante,* < L *tragacantha* goat's thorn, < Gk, < *tragos* goat + *akantha* thorn]

tragedian (trə'dʒiːdɪən) *or* (*fem.*) **tragedienne** (trəˌdʒiːdɪ'ɛn) *n.* **1.** an actor who specializes in tragic roles. **2.** a writer of tragedy.

tragedy ('trædʒɪdɪ) *n., pl.* **-dies. 1.** a play in which the protagonist falls to disaster through the combination of a personal failing and circumstances with which he cannot deal. **2.** any dramatic or literary composition dealing with serious or sombre themes and ending with disaster. **3.** the branch of drama dealing with such themes. **4.** the unfortunate aspect of something. **5.** a shocking or sad event; disaster. [C14: < OF *tragédie,* < L *tragoedia,* < Gk, < *tragos* goat + *ōidē* song; ? < the goat-satyrs of Peloponnesian plays]

tragic ('trædʒɪk) *or* (*less commonly*) **tragical** *adj.* **1.** of, relating to, or characteristic of tragedy. **2.** mournful or pitiable. —'**tragically** *adv.*

tragic flaw *n.* the failing of character in a tragic hero.

tragic irony *n.* the use of dramatic irony in a tragedy so that the audience is aware that a character's words or actions will bring about a tragic or fatal result, while the character himself is not.

tragicomedy (ˌtrædʒɪ'kɒmɪdɪ) *n., pl.* **-dies. 1.** a drama in which aspects of both tragedy and comedy are found. **2.** an event or incident having both comic and tragic aspects. [C16: < F, ult. < LL *tragicōmoedia*] —ˌ**tragi'comic** *or* ˌ**tragi'comical** *adj.*

tragopan ('trægəˌpæn) *n.* any of a genus of pheasants of S and SE Asia, having brightly coloured fleshy processes on the head. [C19: via L < Gk, < *tragos* goat + *Pan,* ancient Gk god, represented as a man with goat's legs, horns, and ears]

tragus ('treɪgəs) *n., pl.* **-gi** (-dʒaɪ). the fleshy projection that partially covers the entrance to the external ear. [C17: < LL, < Gk *tragos* hairy projection of the ear, lit.: goat]

trail (treɪl) *vb.* **1.** to drag, stream, or permit to drag or stream along a surface, esp. the ground. **2.** to make (a track) through (a place). **3.** to follow or hunt (an animal or person) by following marks or tracks. **4.** (when *intr.,* often foll. by *behind*) to lag or linger behind (a person or thing). **5.** (*intr.*) (esp. of plants) to extend or droop over or along a surface. **6.** (*intr.*) to be falling behind in a race: *the favourite is trailing at the last fence.* **7.** (*tr.*) to tow (a caravan, etc.) behind a motor vehicle. **8.** (*tr.*) to carry (a rifle) at the full length of the right arm in a horizontal position, with the muzzle to the fore. **9.** (*intr.*) to move wearily or slowly. **10.** (*tr.*) (on television or radio) to advertise (a future programme) with short extracts. ~*n.* **11.** a print, mark, or scent made by a person, animal, or object. **12.** the act or an instance of trailing. **13.** a path, track, or road, esp. one roughly blazed. **14.** something that trails behind or trails in loops or strands. **15.** the part of a towed gun carriage and limber that connects the two when in movement and rests on the ground as a partial support when unlimbered. [C14: < OF *trailler* to tow, < Vulgar L *tragulāre* (unattested), < L *trāgula* dragnet, < *trahere* to drag]

trail away *or* **off** *vb.* (*intr., adv.*) to make or become fainter, quieter, or weaker.

trailblazer ('treɪlˌbleɪzə) *n.* **1.** a leader or pioneer in a particular field. **2.** a person who blazes a trail. —'**trailˌblazing** *adj., n.*

trailer ('treɪlə) *n.* **1.** a road vehicle, usually two-wheeled, towed by a motor vehicle: used for transporting boats, etc. **2.** the rear section of an articulated lorry. **3.** a series of short extracts from a film, used to advertise it in a cinema or on television. **4.** a person or thing that trails. **5.** the U.S. and Canad. name for **caravan** (sense 1).

trailing edge *n.* the rear edge of a propeller blade or aerofoil. Cf. **leading edge.**

trail mix *n.* a mixture of nuts, dried fruits, and seeds, eaten as a snack, esp. originally by hikers.

train (treɪn) *vb.* **1.** (*tr.*) to guide or teach (to do something), as by subjecting to various exercises or experiences. **2.** (*tr.*) to control or guide towards a specific goal: *to train a plant up a wall.* **3.** (*intr.*) to do exercises and prepare for a specific purpose. **4.** (*tr.*) to improve or curb by subjecting to discipline: *to train the mind.* **5.** (*tr.*) to focus or bring to bear (on something): *to train a telescope on the moon.* ~*n.* **6.** a line of coaches or wagons coupled together and drawn by a railway locomotive. **7.** a sequence or series: *a train of disasters.* **8.** a procession of people, vehicles, etc., travelling together, such as one carrying equipment in support of a military operation. **9.** a series of interacting parts through which motion is transmitted: *a train of gears.* **10.** a fuse or line of gunpowder to an explosive charge, etc. **11.** something drawn along, such as the long back section of a dress that trails along the floor. **12.** a retinue or suite. [C14: < OF *trahiner,* < Vulgar L *tragīnāre* (unattested) to draw] —'**trainable** *adj.*

trainband ('treɪnˌbænd) *n.* a company of English militia from the 16th to the 18th century. [C17: altered < *trained band*]

trainbearer ('treɪnˌbɛərə) *n.* an attendant who holds up the train of a dignitary's robe or bride's gown.

trainee (treɪ'niː) *n.* **a.** a person undergoing training. **b.** (*as modifier*): *a trainee journalist.*

trainer ('treɪnə) *n.* **1.** a person who trains athletes. **2.** a piece of equipment employed in training, such as a simulated aircraft cockpit. **3.** a person who schools racehorses. **4.** (*pl.*) **a.** running shoes for sports training. **b.** casual shoes like these.

training ('treɪnɪŋ) *n.* **1. a.** the process of bringing a person, etc., to an agreed standard of proficiency, etc., by practice and instruction. **b.** (*as modifier*): *training college.* **2. in training. a.** undergoing physical training. **b.** physically fit. **3. out of training.** physically unfit.

train oil *n.* whale oil obtained from blubber. [C16: < earlier *train* or *trane,* < MLow G *trān,* or MDu. *traen* tear, drop]

train spotter *n.* a person who collects the numbers of railway locomotives.

traipse *or* **trapes** (treɪps) *Inf.* ~*vb.* **1.** (*intr.*) to walk heavily or tiredly. ~*n.* **2.** a long or tiring walk; trudge. [C16: <?]

trait (treɪt, treɪ) *n.* **1.** a characteristic feature or quality distinguishing a particular person or thing. **2.** *Rare.* a touch or stroke. [C16: < F, < OF: a pulling, < L *tractus,* < *trahere* to drag]

traitor (ˈtreɪtə) *n.* a person who is guilty of treason or treachery, in betraying friends, country, a cause, etc. [C13: < OF *traitour,* < L *trāditor,* < *trādere* to hand over] —ˈ**traitorous** *adj.* —ˈ**traitress** *fem. n.*

trajectory (trəˈdʒɛktərɪ) *n., pl.* **-ries. 1.** the path described by an object moving in air or space, esp. the curved path of a projectile. **2.** *Geom.* a curve that cuts a family of curves or surfaces at a constant angle. [C17: < L *trājectus* cast over, < *trāicere* to throw across]

tram (træm) *n.* **1.** Also called: **tramcar.** an electrically driven public transport vehicle that runs on rails let into the surface of the road. U.S. and Canad. names: **streetcar, trolley car. 2.** a small vehicle on rails for carrying loads in a mine; tub. [C16 (in the sense: shaft of a cart): prob. < Low G *traam* beam] —ˈ**tramless** *adj.*

tramline (ˈtræmˌlaɪn) *n.* **1.** (*often pl.*) Also called: **tramway.** the tracks on which a tram runs. **2.** the route taken by a tram. **3.** (*often pl.*) the outer markings along the sides of a tennis or badminton court.

trammel (ˈtræməl) *n.* **1.** (*often pl.*) a hindrance to free action or movement. **2.** Also called: **trammel net.** a fishing net in three sections, the two outer nets having a large mesh and the middle one a fine mesh. **3.** *Rare.* a fowling net. **4.** *U.S.* a shackle for a horse. **5.** a device for drawing ellipses consisting of a flat sheet having a cruciform slot in which run two pegs attached to a beam. **6.** (*sometimes pl.*) a beam compass. **7.** a device set in a fireplace to support cooking pots. ~*vb.* **-elling, -elled** *or U.S.* **-eling, -eled.** (*tr.*) **8.** to hinder or restrain. **9.** to catch or ensnare. [C14: < OF *tramail* three-mesh net, < LL *trēmaculum,* < L *trēs* three + *macula* mesh in a net]

tramontane (trəˈmɒnteɪn) *adj.* **1.** being or coming from the far side of the mountains, esp. from the other side of the Alps as seen from Italy. ~*n.* **2.** an inhabitant of a tramontane country. **3.** Also called: **tramontana.** a cold dry wind blowing south or southwest from the mountains in Italy and the W Mediterranean. [C16: < It. *tramontano,* < L *trānsmontānus,* < TRANS- + *montānus,* < *mōns* mountain]

tramp (træmp) *vb.* **1.** (*intr.*) to walk long and far; hike. **2.** to walk heavily or firmly across or through (a place). **3.** (*intr.*) to wander about as a vagabond or tramp. **4.** (*tr.*) to traverse on foot, esp. laboriously or wearily. **5.** (*intr.*) to tread or trample. ~*n.* **6.** a person who travels about on foot, living by begging or doing casual work. **7.** a long hard walk; hike. **8.** a heavy or rhythmic tread. **9.** the sound of heavy treading. **10.** a merchant ship that does not run on a regular schedule but carries cargo wherever the shippers desire. **11.** *Sl., chiefly U.S. & Canad.* a prostitute or promiscuous girl or woman. [C14: prob. < MLow G *trampen*] —ˈ**trampish** *adj.*

tramper (ˈtræmpə) *n. N.Z.* a person who tramps, or walks long distances, in the bush.

tramping (ˈtræmpɪŋ) *n. N.Z.* **1.** the leisure activity of walking in the bush. **2.** (*as modifier*): *tramping boots.*

trample (ˈtræmpᵊl) *vb.* (when *intr.,* usually foll. by *on, upon,* or *over*) **1.** to stamp or walk roughly (on). **2.** to encroach (upon) so as to violate or hurt. ~*n.* **3.** the action or sound of trampling. [C14: frequentative of TRAMP] —ˈ**trampler** *n.*

trampoline (ˈtræmpəlɪn, -ˌliːn) *n.* **1.** a tough canvas sheet suspended by springs or cords from a frame, used by acrobats, gymnasts, etc. ~*vb.* **2.** (*intr.*) to exercise on a trampoline. [C18: via Sp. < It. *trampolino,* < *trampoli* stilts, of Gmc origin] —ˈ**trampoliner** *or* ˈ**trampolinist** *n.*

trance (trɑːns) *n.* **1.** a hypnotic state resembling sleep. **2.** any mental state in which a person is unaware of the environment, characterized by loss of voluntary movement, rigidity, and lack of sensitivity to external stimuli. **3.** a dazed or stunned state. **4.** a state of ecstasy or mystic absorption so intense as to cause a temporary loss of consciousness at the earthly level. **5.** *Spiritualism.* a state in which a medium can supposedly be controlled by an intelligence from without as a means of communication with the dead. ~*vb.* **6.** (*tr.*) to put into or as into a trance. [C14: < OF *transe,* < *transir* to faint, < L *trānsīre* to go over] —ˈ**trance**ˌ**like** *adj.*

tranche (trɑːnʃ) *n.* an instalment or portion of a large sum of money, such as a loan to a government or an issue of shares. [F, lit.: slice]

trannie *or* **tranny** (ˈtrænɪ) *n., pl.* **-nies.** *Inf., chiefly Brit.* a transistor radio.

tranquil (ˈtræŋkwɪl) *adj.* calm, peaceful, or quiet. [C17: < L *tranquillus*] —ˈ**tranquilly** *adv.*

tranquillity *or U.S.* (*sometimes*) **tranquility** (træŋˈkwɪlɪtɪ) *n.* a state of calm or quietude.

tranquillize, -ise, *or U.S.* **tranquilize** (ˈtræŋkwɪˌlaɪz) *vb.* to make or become calm or calmer. —ˌ**tranquilliˈzation, -iˈsation,** *or U.S.* ˌ**tranquiliˈzation** *n.*

tranquillizer, -iser *or U.S.* **tranquilizer** (ˈtræŋkwɪˌlaɪzə) *n.* **1.** a drug that calms a person. **2.** anything that tranquillizes.

tranquillo (ˌtræŋˈkwiːləʊ) *adj. Music.* calm; tranquil. [It.]

trans. *abbrev. for:* **1.** transaction. **2.** transferred. **3.** transitive. **4.** translated. **5.** translator. **6.** transport(ation). **7.** transverse.

trans- *prefix.* **1.** across, beyond, crossing, on the other side: *transatlantic.* **2.** changing thoroughly: *transliterate.* **3.** transcending: *transubstantiation.* **4.** transversely: *transect.* **5.** (*often in italics*) indicating that a chemical compound has a molecular structure in which two identical groups or atoms are on opposite sides of a double bond: *trans*-butadiene. [< L *trāns* across, through, beyond]

transact (trænˈzækt) *vb.* to do, conduct, or negotiate (business, a deal, etc.). [C16: < L *trānsactus,* < *trānsigere,* lit.: to drive through] —**transˈactor** *n.*

transactinide (trænsˈæktɪˌnaɪd) *n.* any artificially produced element with an atomic number greater than 103. [C20]

transaction (trænˈzækʃən) *n.* **1.** something that is transacted, esp. a business deal. **2.** a transacting or being transacted. **3.** (*pl.*) the records of the proceedings of a society, etc. —**transˈactional** *adj.*

transalpine (trænzˈælpaɪn) *adj.* (*prenominal*) **1.** situated in or relating to places beyond the Alps, esp. from Italy. **2.** passing over the Alps.

transatlantic (ˌtrænzətˈlæntɪk) *adj.* **1.** on or from the other side of the Atlantic. **2.** crossing the Atlantic.

transceiver (trænˈsiːvə) *n.* a combined radio transmitter and receiver. [C20: < TRANS(MITTER) + (RE)CEIVER]

transcend (trænˈsɛnd) *vb.* **1.** to go above or beyond (a limit, expectation, etc.), as in degree or excellence. **2.** (*tr.*) to be superior to. [C14: < L *trānscendere* to climb over]

transcendent (trænˈsɛndənt) *adj.* **1.** exceeding or surpassing in degree or excellence. **2.** (in the philosophy of Kant) beyond or before experience. **3.** *Theol.* (of God) having existence outside the created world. **4.** free from the limitations inherent in matter. ~*n.* **5.** *Philosophy.* a transcendent thing. **—tranˈscendence** *or* **tranˈscendency** *n.* **—tranˈscendently** *adv.*

transcendental (ˌtrænsɛnˈdɛntᵊl) *adj.* **1.** transcendent, superior, or surpassing. **2.** (in the philosophy of Kant) **a.** (of a judgment or logical deduction) being both synthetic and a priori. **b.** of or relating to knowledge of the presuppositions of thought. **3.** *Philosophy.* beyond our experience of phenomena, although not beyond potential knowledge. **4.** *Theol.* supernatural or mystical. **5.** *Maths.* **a.** (of a number or quantity) not being a root of any polynomial with rational coefficients. **b.** (of a function) not capable of expression in terms of a finite number of arithmetical operations. **—ˌtranscenˈdentally** *adv.*

transcendentalism (ˌtrænsɛnˈdɛntəˌlɪzəm) *n.* **1. a.** any system of philosophy, esp. that of Kant, holding that the key to knowledge of the nature of reality lies in the critical examination of the processes of reason on which depends the nature of experience. **b.** any system of philosophy, esp. that of Emerson, that emphasizes intuition as a means to knowledge or the importance of the search for the divine. **2.** vague philosophical speculation. **3.** the state of being transcendental. **4.** something, such as thought or language, that is transcendental. **—ˌtranscenˈdentalist** *n., adj.*

transcendental meditation *n.* a technique, based on Hindu traditions, for relaxing and refreshing the mind and body through the silent repetition of a mantra.

transcontinental (ˌtrænzkɒntɪˈnɛntᵊl) *adj.* **1.** crossing a continent. **2.** on or from the far side of a continent. **—ˌtranscontiˈnentally** *adv.*

transcribe (trænˈskraɪb) *vb.* (*tr.*) **1.** to write, type, or print out fully from speech, notes, etc. **2.** to transliterate or translate. **3.** to make an electrical recording of (a programme or speech) for a later broadcast. **4.** *Music.* to rewrite (a piece of music) for an instrument or medium other than that originally intended; arrange. **5.** *Computers.* **a.** to transfer (information) from one storage device to another. **b.** to transfer (information) from a computer to an external storage device. [C16: < L *trānscrībere*] **—tranˈscribable** *adj.* **—tranˈscriber** *n.*

transcript (ˈtrænskrɪpt) *n.* **1.** a written, typed, or printed copy or manuscript made by transcribing. **2.** *Chiefly U.S. & Canad.* an official record of a student's school progress. **3.** any reproduction or copy. [C13: < L *trānscriptum*, < *trānscrībere* to transcribe]

transcription (trænˈskrɪpʃən) *n.* **1.** the act or an instance of transcribing or the state of being transcribed. **2.** something transcribed. **3.** a representation in writing of the actual pronunciation of a speech sound, word, etc., using phonetic symbols. **—tranˈscriptional** *or* **tranˈscriptive** *adj.*

transducer (trænzˈdjuːsə) *n.* any device, such as a microphone or electric motor, that converts one form of energy into another. [C20: < L *trānsducere* to lead across]

transect *vb.* (trænˈsɛkt). (*tr.*) **1.** to cut or divide crossways. ~*n.* (ˈtrænsɛkt). **2.** a sample strip of land used to monitor plant distribution, animal populations, or some other feature, within a given area. [C17: < L TRANS- + *secāre* to cut] **—tranˈsection** *n.*

transept (ˈtrænsɛpt) *n.* either of the two wings of a cruciform church at right angles to the nave. [C16: < Anglo-L *trānseptum*, < L TRANS- + *saeptum* enclosure] **—tranˈseptal** *adj.*

transfer *vb.* (trænsˈfɜː), **-ferring, -ferred. 1.** to change or go or cause to change or go from one thing, person, or point to another. **2.** to change (buses, trains, etc.). **3.** *Law.* to make over (property, etc.) to another; convey. **4.** to displace (a drawing, design, etc.) from one surface to another. **5.** (of a football player) to change clubs or (of a club, manager, etc.) to sell or release (a player) to another club. **6.** to leave one school, college, etc., and enrol at another. **7.** to change (the meaning of a word, etc.), esp. by metaphorical extension. ~*n.* (ˈtrænsfɜː). **8.** the act, process, or system of transferring, or the state of being transferred. **9.** a person or thing that transfers or is transferred. **10.** a design or drawing that is transferred from one surface to another. **11.** *Law.* the passing of title to property or other right from one person to another; conveyance. **12.** any document or form effecting or regulating a transfer. **13.** *Chiefly U.S. & Canad.* a ticket that allows a passenger to change routes. [C14: < L *trānsferre*, < TRANS- + *ferre* to carry] **—transˈferable** *or* **transˈferrable** *adj.* **—transference** (ˈtrænsfərəns) *n.*

transferable vote *n.* a vote that is transferred to a second candidate indicated by the voter if the first is eliminated from the ballot.

transferee (ˌtrænsfəˈriː) *n.* **1.** *Property law.* a person to whom property is transferred. **2.** a person who is transferred.

transfer fee *n.* a sum of money paid by one football club to another for a transferred player.

transferrin (trænsˈfɜːrɪn) *n. Biochem.* any of a group of blood proteins that transport iron. [C20: < TRANS- + FERRO- + -IN]

transfer RNA *n. Biochem.* any of several soluble forms of RNA of low molecular weight, each of which transports a specific amino acid to a ribosome during protein synthesis.

transfiguration (ˌtrænsfɪgjʊˈreɪʃən) *n.* a transfiguring or being transfigured.

Transfiguration (ˌtrænsfɪgjʊˈreɪʃən) *n.* **1.** *New Testament.* the change in the appearance of Christ that took place before three disciples (Matthew 17:1–9). **2.** the Church festival held in commemoration of this on Aug. 6.

transfigure (trænsˈfɪgə) *vb.* (*usually tr.*) **1.** to change or cause to change in appearance. **2.** to become or cause to become more exalted. [C13: < L *trānsfigūrāre*, < TRANS- + *figūra* appearance] **—transˈfigurement** *n.*

transfinite number (trænsˈfaɪnaɪt) *n.* a cardinal or ordinal number used in the comparison of infinite sets for which several types of infinity can be classified.

transfix (trænsˈfɪks) *vb.* **-fixing, -fixed** *or* **-fixt.** (*tr.*) **1.** to render motionless, esp. with horror or shock. **2.** to impale or fix with a sharp weapon or other device. [C16: < L *trānsfigere* to pierce through] **—transfixion** (trænsˈfɪkʃən) *n.*

transform *vb.* (trænsˈfɔːm). **1.** to alter or be altered in form, function, etc. **2.** (*tr.*) to convert (one form of energy) to another form. **3.** (*tr.*) *Maths.* to change the form of (an equation, etc.) by a mathematical transformation. **4.** (*tr.*) to change (an alternating current or voltage) using a transformer. ~*n.* (ˈtrænsˌfɔːm). **5.** *Maths.* the result of a mathematical transformation. [C14: < L *trānsformāre*] **—transˈformable** *adj.* **—transˈformative** *adj.*

transformation (ˌtrænsfəˈmeɪʃən) *n.* **1.** a change or alteration, esp. a radical one. **2.** a transforming or being transformed. **3.** *Maths.* **a.** a change in position or direction of the reference axes in a coordinate system without an alteration in their relative angle. **b.** an equivalent change in an expression or equation resulting from the substitution of one set of variables by another. **4.** *Physics.* a change in an atomic nucleus to a different nuclide as the result of the emission of either an alpha-particle or a beta-particle. **5.** *Linguistics.* another word for **transformational rule. 6.** an apparently miraculous change in the appearance of a stage set. **—ˌtransforˈmational** *adj.*

transformational grammar *n.* a grammatical description of a language making essential use of transformational rules.

transformational rule *n. Generative grammar.* a rule that converts one phrase marker into another. Taken together, these rules convert the deep structures of sentences into their surface structures.

transformer (trænsˈfɔːmə) *n.* **1.** a device that transfers an alternating current from one circuit to one or more other circuits, usually with a change of voltage. **2.** a person or thing that transforms.

transfuse (træns'fjuːz) *vb.* (*tr.*) **1.** to permeate or infuse. **2.** **a.** to inject (blood, etc.) into a blood vessel. **b.** to give a transfusion to (a patient). [C15: < L *trānsfundere* to pour out] —**trans'fuser** *n.* —**trans'fusible** *or* **trans'fusable** *adj.* —**trans'fusive** *adj.*

transfusion (træns'fjuːʒən) *n.* **1.** a transfusing. **2.** the injection of blood, blood plasma, etc., into the blood vessels of a patient.

transgress (trænz'grɛs) *vb.* **1.** to break (a law, etc.). **2.** to go beyond or overstep (a limit). [C16: < L *trānsgredī*, < TRANS- + *gradī* to step] —**trans'gressive** *adj.* —**trans'gressor** *n.*

transgression (trænz'grɛʃən) *n.* **1.** a breach of a law, etc.; sin or crime. **2.** a transgressing.

tranship (træn'ʃɪp) *vb.* **-shipping, -shipped.** a variant spelling of **transship.**

transhumance (træns'hjuːməns) *n.* the seasonal migration of livestock to suitable grazing grounds. [C20: < F, < *transhumer* to change one's pastures, < Sp. *trashumar*, < L TRANS- + *humus* ground] —**trans'humant** *adj.*

transient ('trænzɪənt) *adj.* **1.** for a short time only; temporary or transitory. ~*n.* **2.** a transient person or thing. [C17: < L *trānsiēns* going over, < *trānsīre* to pass over] —**'transiently** *adv.* —**'transience** *or* **'transiency** *n.*

transistor (træn'zɪstə) *n.* **1.** a semiconductor device, having three or more terminals attached to electrode regions, in which current flowing between two electrodes is controlled by a voltage or current applied to one or more specified electrodes. The device has replaced the valve in most circuits since it is much smaller and works at a much lower voltage. **2.** *Inf.* a transistor radio. [C20: orig. a trademark, < TRANSFER + RESISTOR, < the transfer of electric signals across a resistor]

transistorize *or* **-ise** (træn'zɪstəˌraɪz) *vb.* **1.** to convert to the use or manufacture of transistors and other solid-state components. **2.** (*tr.*) to equip with transistors and other solid-state components.

transit ('trænsɪt, 'trænz-) *n.* **1. a.** the passage or conveyance of goods or people. **b.** (*as modifier*): *a transit visa.* **2.** a change or transition. **3.** a route. **4.** *Astron.* **a.** the passage of a celestial body or satellite across the face of a larger body as seen from the earth. **b.** the apparent passage of a celestial body across the meridian. **5. in transit.** while being conveyed; during passage. ~*vb.* **6.** to make a transit through or over (something). [C15: < L *trānsitus* a going over, < *trānsīre* to pass over]

transit camp *n.* a camp in which refugees, soldiers, etc., live temporarily.

transit instrument *n.* an astronomical instrument used to time the transit of a star, etc., across the meridian.

transition (træn'zɪʃən) *n.* **1.** change or passage from one state or stage to another. **2.** the period of time during which something changes. **3.** *Music.* **a.** a movement from one key to another; modulation. **b.** a linking passage between two divisions in a composition; bridge. **4.** a style of architecture in the late 11th and early 12th centuries, characterized by late Romanesque forms combined with early Gothic details. **5.** *Physics.* a change in the configuration of an atomic nucleus, involving either a change in energy level or a transformation to another element or isotope. **6.** a sentence, passage, etc., that links sections of a written work. [C16: < L *transitio*; see TRANSIENT] —**tran'sitional** *adj.* —**tran'sitionally** *adv.*

transition element *n. Chem.* any element belonging to one of three series of elements with atomic numbers between 21 and 30, 39 and 48, and 57 and 80. They have an incomplete penultimate electron shell and tend to form complexes.

transition temperature *n.* the temperature at which a sudden change of physical properties occurs.

transitive ('trænsɪtɪv) *adj.* **1.** *Grammar.* **a.** denoting an occurrence of a verb when it requires a direct object or denoting a verb that customarily requires a direct object. **b.** (*as n.*): *these verbs are transitives.* **2.** *Logic, maths.* having the property that if one object bears a relationship to a second object that also bears the same relationship to a third object, then the first object bears this relationship to the third object: *if* $x = y$ *and* $y = z$ *then* $x = z$. ~Cf. **intransitive.** [C16: < LL *trānsitīvus*, < L *trānsitus* a going over; see TRANSIENT] —**'transitively** *adv.* —ˌ**transi'tivity** *or* **'transitiveness** *n.*

transitory ('trænsɪtərɪ, -trɪ) *adj.* of short duration; transient or ephemeral. [C14: < Church L *trānsitōrius* passing, < L *trānsitus* a crossing over] —**'transitoriness** *n.*

transit theodolite *n.* a theodolite the telescope of which can be rotated completely about its horizontal axis.

transl. *abbrev. for:* **1.** translated. **2.** translator.

translate (træns'leɪt, trænz-) *vb.* **1.** to express or be capable of being expressed in another language. **2.** (*intr.*) to act as translator. **3.** (*tr.*) to express or explain in simple or less technical language. **4.** (*tr.*) to interpret or infer the significance of (gestures, symbols, etc.). **5.** (*tr.*) to transform or convert: *to translate hope into reality.* **6.** to transfer from one place or position to another. **7.** (*tr.*) *Theol.* to transfer (a person) from one place or plane of existence to another, as from earth to heaven. **8.** (*tr.*) *Maths, physics.* to move (a figure or body) laterally, without rotation, dilation, or angular displacement. [C13: < L *trānslātus* carried over, < *trānsferre* to TRANSFER] —**trans'latable** *adj.* —**trans'lator** *n.*

translation (træns'leɪʃən, trænz-) *n.* **1.** something that is or has been translated. **2.** a translating or being translated. **3.** *Maths.* a transformation in which the origin of a coordinate system is moved to another position so that each axis retains the same direction. —**trans'lational** *adj.*

transliterate (trænz'lɪtəˌreɪt) *vb.* (*tr.*) to transcribe (a word, etc.) into corresponding letters of another alphabet. [C19: TRANS- + *-literate*, < L *līttera* letter] —ˌ**transliter'ation** *n.* —**trans'literˌator** *n.*

translocation (ˌtrænzləʊ'keɪʃən) *n.* **1.** *Genetics.* the transfer of one part of a chromosome to another part of the same or a different chromosome. **2.** *Bot.* the transport of minerals, sugars, etc., in solution within a plant. **3.** a movement from one position or place to another.

translucent (trænz'luːsᵊnt) *adj.* allowing light to pass through partially or diffusely; semitransparent. [C16: < L *trānslūcēre* to shine through] —**trans'lucence** *or* **trans'lucency** *n.* —**trans'lucently** *adv.*

translunar (trænz'luːnə) *or* **translunary** (trænz'luːnərɪ) *adj.* **1.** lying beyond the moon. **2.** unworldly or ethereal.

transmigrate (ˌtrænzmaɪ'greɪt) *vb.* (*intr.*) **1.** to move from one place, state, or stage to another. **2.** (of souls) to pass from one body into another at death. —ˌ**transmi'gration** *n.* —**trans'migratory** *adj.*

transmission (trænz'mɪʃən) *n.* **1.** the act or process of transmitting. **2.** something that is transmitted. **3.** the extent to which a body or medium transmits light, sound, etc. **4.** the transference of motive force or power. **5.** a system of shafts, gears, etc., that transmits power, esp. the arrangement of such parts that transmits the power of the engine to the driving wheels of a motor vehicle. **6.** the act or process of sending a message, picture, or other information by means of radio waves, electrical signals, light signals, etc. **7.** a radio or television broadcast. [C17: < L *trānsmissiō* a sending across] —**trans'missible** *adj.* —**trans'missive** *adj.*

transmission density *n. Physics.* a measure of the extent to which a substance transmits light or other electromagnetic radiation.

transmission line *n.* a coaxial cable, waveguide, etc., that transfers electrical signals from one location to another.

transmissivity (ˌtrænzmɪˈsɪvɪtɪ) *n. Physics.* a measure of the ability of a material to transmit radiation.

transmit (trænzˈmɪt) *vb.* **-mitting, -mitted. 1.** (*tr.*) to pass or cause to go from one place or person to another; transfer. **2.** (*tr.*) to pass on or impart (a disease, etc.). **3.** (*tr.*) to hand down to posterity. **4.** (*tr.; usually passive*) to pass (an inheritable characteristic) from parent to offspring. **5.** to allow the passage of (particles, energy, etc.): *radio waves are transmitted through the atmosphere.* **6. a.** to send out (signals) by means of radio waves or along a transmission line. **b.** to broadcast (a radio or television programme). **7.** (*tr.*) to transfer (a force, motion, etc.) from one part of a mechanical system to another. [C14: < L *trānsmittere* to send across] —**transˈmittable** *adj.* —**transˈmittal** *n.*

transmittance (trænzˈmɪtᵊns) *n.* **1.** the act of transmitting. **2.** Also called: **transmission factor.** *Physics.* a measure of the ability of anything to transmit radiation, equal to the ratio of the transmitted flux to the incident flux.

transmitter (trænzˈmɪtə) *n.* **1.** a person or thing that transmits. **2.** the equipment used for generating and amplifying a radio-frequency carrier, modulating the carrier with information, and feeding it to an aerial for transmission. **3.** the microphone in a telephone that converts sound waves into audio-frequency electrical signals. **4.** a device that converts mechanical movements into coded electrical signals transmitted along a telegraph circuit. **5.** a substance released by nerve endings that transmits impulses across synapses.

transmogrify (trænzˈmɒgrɪˌfaɪ) *vb.* **-fying, -fied.** (*tr.*) *Jocular.* to change or transform into a different shape, esp. a grotesque or bizarre one. [C17: <?] —**transˌmogrifiˈcation** *n.*

transmontane (ˌtrænzmɒnˈteɪn) *adj., n.* another word for **tramontane.**

transmutation (ˌtrænzmjuːˈteɪʃən) *n.* **1.** the act or an instance of transmuting. **2.** the change of one chemical element into another by a nuclear reaction. **3.** the attempted conversion, by alchemists, of base metals into gold or silver. —ˌ**transmuˈtational** *or* **transˈmutative** *adj.*

transmute (trænzˈmjuːt) *vb.* (*tr.*) **1.** to change the form, character, or substance of. **2.** to alter (an element, metal, etc.) by alchemy. [C15: via OF < L *trānsmūtāre* to shift, < TRANS- + *mūtāre* to change] —**transˌmutaˈbility** *n.* —**transˈmutable** *adj.*

transnational (trænzˈnæʃənəl) *adj.* extending beyond the boundaries, etc., of a single nation.

transoceanic (trænzˌəʊʃɪˈænɪk) *adj.* **1.** on or from the other side of an ocean. **2.** crossing an ocean.

transom (ˈtrænsəm) *n.* **1.** a horizontal member across a window. **2.** a horizontal member that separates a door from a window over it. **3.** the usual U.S. name for **fanlight. 4.** *Naut.* **a.** a surface forming the stern of a vessel. **b.** any of several transverse beams used for strengthening the stern of a vessel. [C14: earlier *traversayn,* < OF *traversin,* < TRAVERSE] —ˈ**transomed** *adj.*

transonic (trænˈsɒnɪk) *adj.* of or relating to conditions when travelling at or near the speed of sound.

transparency (trænsˈpærənsɪ) *n., pl.* **-cies. 1.** Also called: **transparence.** the state of being transparent. **2.** Also called: **slide.** a positive photograph on a transparent base, usually mounted in a frame or between glass plates. It can be viewed by means of a slide projector.

transparent (trænsˈpærənt) *adj.* **1.** permitting the uninterrupted passage of light; clear. **2.** easy to see through, understand, or recognize; obvious. **3.** permitting the free passage of electromagnetic radiation. **4.** candid, open, or frank. [C15: < Med. L *trānspārēre* to show through, < L TRANS- + *pārēre* to appear] —**transˈparently** *adv.* —**transˈparentness** *n.*

transpire (trænˈspaɪə) *vb.* **1.** (*intr.*) to come to light; be known. **2.** (*intr.*) *Inf.* to happen or occur. **3.** *Physiol.* to give off or exhale (water or vapour) through the skin, a mucous membrane, etc. **4.** (of plants) to lose (water), esp. through the stomata of the leaves. [C16: < Med. L *trānspīrāre,* < L TRANS- + *spīrāre* to breathe] —**transpiration** (ˌtrænspəˈreɪʃən) *n.* —**tranˈspiratory** *adj.*

▷ **Usage.** It is often maintained that *transpire* should not be used to mean happen or occur, as in *the event transpired late in the evening,* and that the word is properly used to mean become known, as in *it transpired later that the thief had been caught.* The word is, however, widely used in the former sense, esp. in spoken English.

transplant *vb.* (trænsˈplɑːnt). **1.** (*tr.*) to remove or transfer (esp. a plant) from one place to another. **2.** (*intr.*) to be capable of being transplanted. **3.** *Surgery.* to transfer (an organ or tissue) from one part of the body or from one person to another. ~*n.* (ˈtrænsˌplɑːnt). **4.** *Surgery.* **a.** the procedure involved in such a transfer. **b.** the organ or tissue transplanted. —**transˈplantable** *adj.* —ˌ**transplanˈtation** *n.*

transponder (trænˈspɒndə) *n.* **1.** a type of radio or radar transmitter-receiver that transmits signals automatically when it receives predetermined signals. **2.** the receiver and transmitter in a communications satellite, relaying signals back to earth. [C20: < TRANSMITTER + RESPONDER]

transport *vb.* (trænsˈpɔːt). (*tr.*) **1.** to carry or cause to go from one place to another, esp. over some distance. **2.** to deport or exile to a penal colony. **3.** (*usually passive*) to have a strong emotional effect on. ~*n.* (ˈtrænsˌpɔːt). **4. a.** the business or system of transporting goods or people. **b.** (*as modifier*)*: a modernized transport system.* **5.** *Brit.* freight vehicles generally. **6. a.** a vehicle used to transport goods or people, esp. troops. **b.** (*as modifier*)*: a transport plane.* **7.** a transporting or being transported. **8.** ecstasy, rapture, or any powerful emotion. **9.** a convict sentenced to be transported. [C14: < L *trānsportāre,* < TRANS- + *portāre* to carry] —**transˈportable** *adj.* —**transˈporter** *n.*

transportation (ˌtrænspɔːˈteɪʃən) *n.* **1.** a means or system of transporting. **2.** the act of transporting or the state of being transported. **3.** (esp. formerly) deportation to a penal colony.

transport café (ˈtrænsˌpɔːt) *n. Brit.* an inexpensive eating place on a main route, used mainly by long-distance lorry drivers.

transpose (trænsˈpəʊz) *vb.* **1.** (*tr.*) to alter the positions of; interchange, as words in a sentence. **2.** *Music.* to play (notes, music, etc.) in a different key from that originally intended. **3.** (*tr.*) *Maths.* to move (a term) from one side of an equation to the other with a corresponding reversal in sign. [C14: < OF *transposer,* < L *trānspōnere* to remove] —**transˈposable** *adj.* —**transˈposal** *n.* —**transˈposer** *n.* —**transposition** (ˌtrænspəˈzɪʃən) *n.*

transposing instrument *n.* a musical instrument, esp. a horn or clarinet, pitched in a key other than C major, but whose music is written down as if its basic scale were C major.

transputer (trænzˈpjuːtə) *n. Computers.* a type of fast powerful microchip that is the equivaient of a 32-bit microprocessor with its own RAM facility. [C20: < TRANS- + (COM)PUTER]

transsexual (trænzˈsɛksjʊəl) *n.* **1.** a person who is completely identified with the opposite sex. **2.** a person who has undergone medical procedures to alter sexual characteristics to those of the opposite sex.

transship (trænsˈʃɪp) *or* **tranship** *vb.* **-shipping, -shipped.** to transfer or be transferred from one vessel or vehicle to another. —**transˈshipment** *or* **tranˈshipment** *n.*

transubstantiation (ˌtrænsəbˌstænʃɪˈeɪʃən) *n.* **1.** (esp. in Roman Catholic theology) **a.** the doctrine that the whole substance of the bread and wine changes into the substance of the body and blood of Christ when consecrated in the Eucharist. **b.** the mystical process by which this is believed to take place during consecration. Cf. **consubstan-**

tiation. **2.** a substantial change; transmutation. —ˌ**transubˌstantiˈationalist** *n.*

transude (trænˈsjuːd) *vb.* (of a fluid) to ooze or pass through interstices, pores, or small holes. [C17: < NL *trānsūdāre,* < L TRANS- + *sūdāre* to sweat] —**transudation** (ˌtrænsjʊˈdeɪʃən) *n.*

transuranic (ˌtrænzjʊˈrænɪk), **transuranian** (ˌtrænzjʊˈreɪnɪən), *or* **transuranium** *adj.* **1.** (of an element) having an atomic number greater than that of uranium. **2.** of or having the behaviour of transuranic elements. [C20]

transversal (trænzˈvɜːsᵊl) *n.* **1.** *Geom.* a line intersecting two or more other lines. ~*adj.* **2.** a less common word for **transverse.** —**transˈversally** *adv.*

transverse (trænzˈvɜːs) *adj.* **1.** crossing from side to side; athwart; crossways. ~*n.* **2.** a transverse piece or object. [C16: < L *trānsversus,* < *trānsvertere* to turn across] —**transˈversely** *adv.*

transverse colon *n. Anat.* the part of the large intestine passing transversely in front of the liver and stomach.

transverse wave *n.* a wave, such as an electromagnetic wave, that is propagated in a direction perpendicular to the direction of displacement of the transmitting field or medium.

transvestite (trænzˈvɛstaɪt) *n.* a person who seeks sexual pleasure from wearing clothes of the opposite sex. [C19: < G *Transvestit,* < TRANS- + L *vestītus* clothed, < *vestīre* to clothe] —**transˈvestism** *or* **transˈvestitism** *n.*

trap[1] (træp) *n.* **1.** a mechanical device or enclosed place or pit in which something, esp. an animal, is caught or penned. **2.** any device or plan for tricking a person or thing into being caught unawares. **3.** anything resembling a trap or prison. **4.** a fitting for a pipe in the form of a U-shaped or S-shaped bend that contains standing water to prevent the passage of gases. **5.** any similar device. **6.** a device that hurls clay pigeons into the air to be fired at by trapshooters. **7.** *Greyhound racing.* any one of a line of boxlike stalls in which greyhounds are enclosed before the start of a race. **8.** See **trap door.** **9.** a light two-wheeled carriage. **10.** a slang word for **mouth.** **11.** *Golf.* an obstacle or hazard, esp. a bunker. **12.** (*pl.*) *Jazz sl.* percussion instruments. **13.** (*usually pl.*) *Austral. sl.* a policeman. ~*vb.* **trapping, trapped.** **14.** to catch, take, or pen in a trap. **15.** (*tr.*) to ensnare by trickery; trick. **16.** (*tr.*) to provide (a pipe) with a trap. **17.** to set traps in (a place), esp. for animals. [OE *træppe*] —ˈ**trapˌlike** *adj.*

trap[2] (træp) *vb.* **trapping, trapped.** (*tr.;* often foll. by *out*) to dress or adorn. ~See also **traps.** [C11: prob. < OF *drap* cloth]

trap[3] (træp) *or* **traprock** (ˈtræpˌrɒk) *n.* **1.** any fine-grained often columnar dark igneous rock, esp. basalt. **2.** any rock in which oil or gas has accumulated. [C18: < Swedish *trappa* stair (< its steplike formation)]

trap door *n.* a door or flap flush with and covering an opening, esp. in a ceiling.

trap-door spider *n.* any of various spiders that construct a silk-lined hole in the ground closed by a hinged door of earth and silk.

trapes (treɪps) *vb., n.* a less common spelling of **traipse.**

trapeze (trəˈpiːz) *n.* a free-swinging bar attached to two ropes, used by circus acrobats, etc. [C19: < F *trapèze,* < NL; see TRAPEZIUM]

trapezium (trəˈpiːzɪəm) *n., pl.* **-ziums** *or* **-zia** (-zɪə). **1.** *Chiefly Brit.* a quadrilateral having two parallel sides of unequal length. Usual U.S. and Canad. name: **trapezoid.** **2.** *Chiefly U.S. & Canad.* a quadrilateral having neither pair of sides parallel. [C16: via LL < Gk *trapezion,* < *trapeza* table] —**traˈpezial** *adj.*

trapezius (trəˈpiːzɪəs) *n., pl.* **-uses.** either of two flat triangular muscles that rotate the shoulder blades. [C18: < NL *trapezius* (*musculus*) trapezium-shaped (muscle)]

trapezoid (ˈtræpɪˌzɔɪd) *n.* **1.** a quadrilateral having neither pair of sides parallel. **2.** the usual U.S. and Canad. name for **trapezium.** [C18: < NL *trapezoidēs,* < LGk *trapezoeidēs* trapezium-shaped, < *trapeza* table]

trapper (ˈtræpə) *n.* a person who traps animals, esp. for their furs or skins.

trappings (ˈtræpɪŋz) *pl. n.* **1.** the accessories and adornments that symbolize a condition, office, etc.: *the trappings of success.* **2.** ceremonial harness for a horse or other animal. [C16: < TRAP[2]]

Trappist (ˈtræpɪst) *n.* **a.** a member of a branch of the Cistercian order of Christian monks, which originated at La Trappe in France in 1664. They are noted for their rule of silence. **b.** (*as modifier*): *a Trappist monk.*

traps (træps) *pl. n.* belongings; luggage. [C19: prob. shortened < TRAPPINGS]

trapshooting (ˈtræpˌʃuːtɪŋ) *n.* the sport of shooting at clay pigeons thrown up by a trap. —ˈ**trapˌshooter** *n.*

trash (træʃ) *n.* **1.** foolish ideas or talk; nonsense. **2.** *Chiefly U.S. & Canad.* useless or unwanted matter or objects; rubbish. **3.** a literary or artistic production of poor quality. **4.** *Chiefly U.S. & Canad.* a poor or worthless person or a group of such people. **5.** bits that are broken or lopped off, esp. the trimmings from trees or plants. **6.** the dry remains of sugar cane after the juice has been extracted. ~*vb.* **7.** to remove the outer leaves and branches from (growing plants, esp. sugar cane). [C16: <?]

trashy (ˈtræʃɪ) *adj.* **trashier, trashiest.** cheap, worthless, or badly made. —ˈ**trashily** *adv.* —ˈ**trashiness** *n.*

trass (træs) *n.* a volcanic rock used to make a hydraulic cement. [C18: < Du. *tras, tarasse,* < It. *terrazza* worthless earth; see TERRACE]

trattoria (ˌtrætəˈrɪə) *n.* an Italian restaurant. [C19: < It., < *trattore* innkeeper, < F *traiteur,* < OF *tretier* to TREAT]

trauma (ˈtrɔːmə) *n., pl.* **-mata** (-mətə) *or* **-mas.** **1.** *Psychol.* a powerful shock that may have long-lasting effects. **2.** *Pathol.* any bodily injury or wound. [C18: < Gk: a wound] —**traumatic** (trɔːˈmætɪk) *adj.* —**trauˈmatically** *adv.*

traumatize *or* **-ise** (ˈtrɔːməˌtaɪz) *vb.* **1.** (*tr.*) to wound or injure (the body). **2.** to subject or be subjected to mental trauma. —ˌ**traumatiˈzation** *or* **-iˈsation** *n.*

travail (ˈtræveɪl) *Literary.* ~*n.* **1.** painful or excessive labour or exertion. **2.** the pangs of childbirth; labour. ~*vb.* **3.** (*intr.*) to suffer or labour painfully, esp. in childbirth. [C13: < OF *travaillier,* < Vulgar L *tripaliāre* (unattested) to torture, < LL *trepālium* instrument of torture, < L *tripālis* having three stakes]

travel (ˈtrævᵊl) *vb.* **-elling, -elled** *or U.S.* **-eling, -eled.** (*mainly intr.*) **1.** to go, move, or journey from one place to another. **2.** (*tr.*) to go, move, or journey through or across (an area, region, etc.). **3.** to go, move, or cover a distance. **4.** to go from place to place as a salesman. **5.** (esp. of perishable goods) to withstand a journey. **6.** (of light, sound, etc.) to be transmitted or move. **7.** to progress or advance. **8.** *Basketball.* to take an excessive number of steps while holding the ball. **9.** (of part of a mechanism) to move in a fixed path. **10.** *Inf.* to move rapidly. ~*n.* **11. a.** the act of travelling. **b.** (*as modifier*): *a travel brochure.* Related adj.: **itinerant.** **12.** (*usually pl.*) a tour or journey. **13.** the distance moved by a mechanical part, such as the stroke of a piston. **14.** movement or passage. [C14 *travaillen* to make a journey, < OF *travaillier* to TRAVAIL]

travel agency *or* **bureau** *n.* an agency that arranges and negotiates flights, holidays, etc., for travellers. —**travel agent** *n.*

travelled *or U.S.* **traveled** (ˈtrævəld) *adj.* having experienced or undergone much travelling.

traveller (ˈtrævələ, ˈtrævlə) *n.* **1.** a person who travels, esp. habitually. **2.** See **travelling salesman.** **3.** a part of a mechanism that moves in a fixed course. **4.** *Austral.* a swagman.

traveller's cheque *n.* a cheque sold by a bank,

etc., to the bearer, who signs it on purchase and can cash it abroad by signing it again.

traveller's joy *n.* a ranunculaceous Old World climbing plant having white flowers and heads of feathery plumed fruits; wild clematis.

travelling people *or* **folk** *pl. n.* (*sometimes caps.*) *Brit.* Gypsies or other itinerant people: a term used esp. by such people of themselves.

travelling salesman *n.* a salesman who travels within an assigned territory in order to sell merchandise or to solicit orders for the commercial enterprise he represents by direct personal contact with customers.

travelling wave *n.* **a.** a wave carrying energy away from its source. **b.** (*as modifier*): *a travelling-wave aerial.*

travelogue *or U.S.* (*sometimes*) **travelog** ('træv^{ə}lɒg) *n.* a film, lecture, or brochure on travels and travelling.

traverse ('trævɜːs, trə'vɜːs) *vb.* **1.** to pass or go over or back and forth over (something); cross. **2.** (*tr.*) to go against; oppose. **3.** to move sideways or crosswise. **4.** (*tr.*) to extend or reach across. **5.** to turn (an artillery gun) laterally or (of an artillery gun) to turn laterally. **6.** (*tr.*) to examine carefully. **7.** (*tr.*) *Law.* to deny (an allegation). **8.** *Mountaineering.* to move across (a face) horizontally. ~*n.* **9.** something being or lying across, such as a transom. **10.** a gallery or loft inside a building that crosses it. **11.** an obstruction. **12.** a protective bank or other barrier across a trench or rampart. **13.** a railing, screen, or curtain. **14.** the act or an instance of traversing or crossing. **15.** *Mountaineering.* the act or an instance of moving horizontally across a face. **16.** a path or road across. **17.** *Naut.* the zigzag course of a vessel tacking frequently. **18.** *Law.* the formal denial of a fact alleged in the opposite party's pleading. **19.** *Surveying.* a survey consisting of a series of straight lines, the length of each and the angle between them being measured. ~*adj.* **20.** being or lying across; transverse. [C14: < OF *traverser,* < LL *trānsversāre,* < L *trānsversus* TRANSVERSE] —**tra'versal** *n.* —**'traverser** *n.*

travertine ('trævətɪn) *n.* a porous rock consisting of calcium carbonate, used for building. [C18: < It. *travertino* (infl. by *tra-* TRANS-), < L *lapis Tīburtīnus* Tiburtine stone, < *Tibur*s the district around Tibur (now Tivoli)]

travesty ('trævɪstɪ) *n., pl.* **-ties.** **1.** a farcical or grotesque imitation; mockery. ~*vb.* **-tying, -tied.** (*tr.*) **2.** to make or be a travesty of. [C17: < F *travesti* disguised, < *travestir* to disguise, < It. *travestire,* < *tra-* TRANS- + *vestire* to clothe]

travois (trə'vɔɪ) *n., pl.* **-vois** (-'vɔɪz). **1.** *History.* a sled formerly used by the Plains Indians of North America, consisting of two poles joined by a frame and pulled by an animal. **2.** *Canad.* a similar sled used for dragging logs. [< Canad. F, < F *travail* beam, < L *trabs*]

trawl (trɔːl) *n.* **1.** Also called: **trawl net.** a large net, usually in the shape of a sock or bag, drawn at deep levels behind special boats (trawlers). **2.** Also called: **trawl line.** a long line to which numerous shorter hooked lines are attached, suspended between buoys. **3.** the act of trawling. ~*vb.* **4.** to catch (fish) with a trawl net or trawl line. **5.** (*intr.;* foll. by *for*) to seek or gather (information, etc.) from a wide variety of sources. [C17: < MDu. *traghelen* to drag, < L *trāgula* dragnet; see TRAIL]

trawler ('trɔːlə) *n.* **1.** a vessel used for trawling. **2.** a person who trawls.

tray (treɪ) *n.* **1.** a thin flat board or plate of metal, plastic, etc., usually with a raised edge, on which things can be carried. **2.** a shallow receptacle for papers, etc., sometimes forming a drawer in a cabinet or box. [OE *trieg*]

treacherous ('trɛtʃərəs) *adj.* **1.** betraying or likely to betray faith or confidence. **2.** unstable, unreliable, or dangerous. —**'treacherously** *adv.* —**'treacherousness** *n.*

treachery ('trɛtʃərɪ) *n., pl.* **-eries.** **1.** the act or an instance of wilful betrayal. **2.** the disposition to betray. [C13: < OF *trecherie,* < *trechier* to cheat]

treacle ('triːk^{ə}l) *n.* **1.** Also called: **black treacle.** *Brit.* a dark viscous syrup obtained during the refining of sugar. **2.** *Brit.* another name for **golden syrup.** **3.** anything sweet and cloying. [C14: < OF *triacle,* < L *thēriaca* antidote to poison] —**'treacly** *adj.*

tread (trɛd) *vb.* **treading, trod, trodden** *or* **trod.** **1.** to walk or trample in, on, over, or across (something). **2.** (when *intr.,* foll. by *on*) to crush or squash by or as if by treading. **3.** (*intr.;* sometimes foll. by *on*) to subdue or repress. **4.** (*tr.*) to do by walking or dancing: *to tread a measure.* **5.** (*tr.*) (of a male bird) to copulate with (a female bird). **6. tread lightly.** to proceed with delicacy or tact. **7. tread water.** to stay afloat in an upright position by moving the legs in a walking motion. ~*n.* **8.** a manner or style of walking, dancing, etc.: *a light tread.* **9.** the act of treading. **10.** the top surface of a step in a staircase. **11.** the outer part of a tyre or wheel that makes contact with the road, esp. the grooved surface of a pneumatic tyre. **12.** the part of a rail that wheels touch. **13.** the part of a shoe that is generally in contact with the ground. [OE *tredan*] —**'treader** *n.*

treadle ('trɛd^{ə}l) *n.* **1.** a lever operated by the foot to drive a machine. ~*vb.* **2.** to work (a machine) with a treadle. [OE *tredel,* < *trǣde* something firm, < *tredan* to tread]

treadmill ('trɛd,mɪl) *n.* **1.** Also called: **treadwheel.** (formerly) an apparatus turned by the weight of men or animals climbing steps on the periphery of a cylinder or wheel. **2.** a dreary round or routine.

treas. *abbrev. for:* **1.** treasurer. **2.** treasury.

treason ('triːz^{ə}n) *n.* **1.** betrayal of one's sovereign or country, esp. by attempting to overthrow the government. **2.** any treachery or betrayal. [C13: < OF *traïson,* < L *trāditiō* a handing over; see TRADITION] —**'treasonable** *or* **'treasonous** *adj.* —**'treasonably** *adv.*

treasure ('trɛʒə) *n.* **1.** wealth and riches, usually hoarded, esp. in the form of money, precious metals, or gems. **2.** a thing or person that is highly prized or valued. ~*vb.* (*tr.*) **3.** to prize highly as valuable, rare, or costly. **4.** to store up and save; hoard. [C12: < OF *tresor,* < L *thēsaurus* anything hoarded, < Gk *thēsauros*]

treasure hunt *n.* a game in which players act upon successive clues to find a hidden prize.

treasurer ('trɛʒərə) *n.* a person appointed to look after the funds of a society, company, city, or other governing body. —**'treasurership** *n.*

Treasurer ('trɛʒərə) *n.* (in Australia) the minister of finance.

treasure-trove *n.* **1.** *Law.* any articles, such as coins, etc., found hidden and of unknown ownership. **2.** any valuable discovery. [C16: < Anglo-F *tresor trové* treasure found, < OF *tresor* TREASURE + *trover* to find]

treasury ('trɛʒərɪ) *n., pl.* **-uries.** **1.** a storage place for treasure. **2.** the revenues or funds of a government, private organization, or individual. **3.** a place where funds are kept and disbursed. **4.** a person or thing regarded as a valuable source of information. **5.** a collection of highly valued poems, etc.; anthology. **6.** Also: **treasure house.** a source of valuable items: *a treasury of information.* [C13: < OF *tresorie,* < *tresor* TREASURE]

Treasury ('trɛʒərɪ) *n.* (in various countries) the government department in charge of finance.

Treasury Bench *n.* (in Britain) the front bench to the right of the Speaker in the House of Commons, traditionally reserved for members of the Government.

treasury note *n.* a note issued by a government treasury and generally receivable as legal tender for any debt.

treat (triːt) *n.* **1.** a celebration, entertainment, gift, or feast given for or to someone and paid for by another. **2.** any delightful surprise or specially pleasant occasion. **3.** the act of treating. ~*vb.* **4.** (*tr.*) to deal with or regard in a certain manner:

she treats school as a joke. **5.** (*tr.*) to apply treatment to. **6.** (*tr.*) to subject to a process or to the application of a substance. **7.** (often foll. by *to*) to provide (someone) (with) as a treat. **8.** (*intr.*; usually foll. by *of*) to deal (with), as in writing or speaking. **9.** (*intr.*) to discuss settlement; negotiate. [C13: < OF *tretier,* < L *tractāre* to manage, < *trahere* to drag] —**ˈtreatable** *adj.* —**ˈtreater** *n.*

treatise (ˈtriːtɪz) *n.* a formal work on a subject, esp. one that deals systematically with its principles and conclusions. [C14: < Anglo-F *tretiz,* < OF *tretier* to TREAT]

treatment (ˈtriːtmənt) *n.* **1.** the application of medicines, surgery, etc., to a patient. **2.** the manner of handling a person or thing, as in a literary or artistic work. **3.** the act, practice, or manner of treating. **4. the treatment.** *Sl.* the usual manner of dealing with a particular type of person (esp. in **give someone the (full) treatment**).

treaty (ˈtriːtɪ) *n., pl.* **-ties. 1. a.** a formal agreement between two or more states, such as an alliance or trade arrangement. **b.** the document in which such a contract is written. **2.** any pact or agreement. **3.** an agreement between two parties concerning the purchase of property at a price privately agreed between them. [C14: < OF *traité,* < Med. L *tractātus,* < L: discussion, < *tractāre* to manage; see TREAT]

treaty port *n. History.* (in China, Japan, and Korea) a city, esp. a port, in which foreigners, esp. Westerners, were allowed by treaty to conduct trade.

treble (ˈtrɛbᵊl) *adj.* **1.** threefold; triple. **2.** of or denoting a soprano voice or part or a high-pitched instrument. ~*n.* **3.** treble the amount, size, etc. **4.** a soprano voice or part or a high-pitched instrument. **5.** the highest register of a musical instrument. **6.** the high-frequency response of an audio amplifier, esp. in a record player or tape recorder. **7. a.** the narrow inner ring on a dartboard. **b.** a hit on this ring. ~*vb.* **8.** to make or become three times as much. [C14: < OF, < L *triplus* threefold] —**ˈtrebly** *adv., adj.*

treble chance *n.* a method of betting in football pools in which the chances of winning are related to the number of draws and the number of home and away wins forecast by the competitor.

treble clef *n. Music.* the clef that establishes G a fifth above middle C as being on the second line of the staff. Symbol: 𝄞

trebuchet (ˈtrɛbjʊˌʃɛt) *or* **trebucket** (ˈtriːˌbʌkɪt) *n.* a large medieval siege engine consisting of a sling on a pivoted wooden arm set in motion by the fall of a weight. [C13: < OF, < *trebuchier* to stumble, < *tre-* TRANS- + *-buchier,* < *buc* trunk of the body, of Gmc origin]

trecento (treɪˈtʃɛntəʊ) *n.* the 14th century, esp. with reference to Italian art and literature. [C19: shortened < It. *mille trecento* one thousand three hundred] —**treˈcentist** *n.*

tree (triː) *n.* **1.** any large woody perennial plant with a distinct trunk giving rise to branches. Related adj.: **arboreal. 2.** any plant that resembles this. **3.** a wooden post, bar, etc. **4.** See **family tree, shoetree, saddletree. 5.** *Chem.* a treelike crystal growth. **6.** a branching diagrammatic representation of something. **7. at the top of the tree.** in the highest position of a profession, etc. **8. up a tree.** *U.S. & Canad. inf.* in a difficult situation; trapped or stumped. ~*vb.* **treeing, treed.** (*tr.*) **9.** to drive or force up a tree. **10.** *U.S. & Canad. inf.* to force into a difficult situation. **11.** to stretch on a shoetree. [OE *treo*] —**ˈtreeless** *adj.* —**ˈtreelessness** *n.* —**ˈtreeˌlike** *adj.*

tree creeper *n.* any of a family of small songbirds of the N hemisphere, having a slender downward-curving bill. They creep up trees to feed on insects.

tree diagram *n.* a diagram in which relationships are represented by lines and nodes having other lines branching off from them.

tree fern *n.* any of numerous large tropical ferns having a trunklike stem.

tree frog *n.* any of various arboreal frogs of SE Asia, Australia, and America.

treehopper (ˈtriːˌhɒpə) *n.* any of a family of insects which live among trees and have a large hoodlike thoracic process curving backwards over the body.

tree kangaroo *n.* any of several arboreal kangaroos of New Guinea and N Australia, having hind legs and forelegs of a similar length.

tree line *n.* another name for **timber line.**

treen (ˈtriːən) *adj.* **1.** made of wood; wooden. ~*n.* **2.** dishes and other utensils made of wood. [OE *trēowen,* < *trēow* tree] —**ˈtreenˌware** *n.*

treenail *or* **trenail** (ˈtriːneɪl, ˈtrɛnᵊl) *n.* a dowel used for pinning planks or timbers together.

tree of heaven *n.* another name for **ailanthus.**

tree shrew *n.* any of a family of small arboreal primates of SE Asia having large eyes and resembling squirrels.

tree sparrow *n.* **1.** a small European weaverbird similar to the house sparrow but having a brown head. **2.** a small North American finch.

tree surgery *n.* the treatment of damaged trees by filling cavities, applying braces, etc. —**tree surgeon** *n.*

tree toad *n.* a less common name for **tree frog.**

tree tomato *n.* **1.** an arborescent shrub of South America widely cultivated in New Zealand, bearing red egg-shaped edible fruit. **2.** the fruit of this plant. ~Also called: **tamarillo.**

tref (treɪf) *adj. Judaism.* ritually unfit to be eaten. [Yiddish, < Heb. *terēphāh,* lit.: torn (i.e., animal meat torn by beasts), < *tāraf* to tear]

trefoil (ˈtrɛfɔɪl) *n.* **1.** any of a genus of leguminous plants having leaves divided into three leaflets. **2.** any of various related plants having similar leaves. **3.** a flower or leaf having three lobes. **4.** *Archit.* an ornament in the form of three arcs arranged in a circle. [C14: < Anglo-F *trifoil,* < L *trifolium* three-leaved herb] —**ˈtrefoiled** *adj.*

trek (trɛk) *n.* **1.** a long and often difficult journey. **2.** *S. African.* a journey or stage of a journey, esp. a migration by ox wagon. ~*vb.* **trekking, trekked. 3.** (*intr.*) to make a trek. [C19: < Afrik., < MDu. *trekken* to travel]

trellis (ˈtrɛlɪs) *n.* **1.** a structure of latticework, esp. one used to support climbing plants. ~*vb.* (*tr.*) **2.** to interweave (strips of wood, etc.) to make a trellis. **3.** to provide or support with a trellis. [C14: < OF *treliz* fabric of open texture, < LL *trilīcius* woven with three threads, < L TRI- + *līcium* thread] —**ˈtrellisˌwork** *n.*

trematode (ˈtrɛməˌtəʊd, ˈtriː-) *n.* any of a class of parasitic flatworms, which includes the flukes. [C19: < NL *Trematoda,* < Gk *trēmatōdēs* full of holes, < *trēma* hole]

tremble (ˈtrɛmbᵊl) *vb.* (*intr.*) **1.** to vibrate with short slight movements; quiver. **2.** to shake involuntarily, as with cold or fear; shiver. **3.** to experience fear or anxiety. ~*n.* **4.** the act or an instance of trembling. [C14: < OF *trembler,* < Med. L *tremulāre,* < L *tremulus* quivering, < *tremere* to quake] —**ˈtrembling** *adj.* —**ˈtrembly** *adj.*

trembler (ˈtrɛmblə) *n.* a device that vibrates to make or break an electrical circuit.

trembles (ˈtrɛmbᵊlz) *n.* (*functioning as sing.*) a disease of cattle and sheep characterized by trembling.

trembling poplar *n.* another name for **aspen.**

tremendous (trɪˈmɛndəs) *adj.* **1.** vast; huge. **2.** *Inf.* very exciting or unusual. **3.** *Inf.* (intensifier): *a tremendous help.* **4.** *Arch.* terrible or dreadful. [C17: < L *tremendus* terrible, lit.: that is to be trembled at, < *tremere* to quake] —**treˈmendously** *adv.* —**treˈmendousness** *n.*

tremolo (ˈtrɛməˌləʊ) *n., pl.* **-los.** *Music.* **1.** (in playing the violin, cello, etc.) the rapid reiteration of a note or notes to produce a trembling effect. **2.** (in singing) a fluctuation in pitch. **3.** a device, as on an organ, that produces a tremolo effect. [C19: < It.: quavering, < Med. L *tremulāre* to TREMBLE]

tremor (ˈtrɛmə) *n.* **1.** an involuntary shudder or

vibration. 2. any trembling movement. 3. a vibrating or trembling effect, as of sound or light. 4. a minor earthquake. ~*vb.* 5. (*intr.*) to tremble. [C14: < L: a shaking, < *tremere* to tremble] —ˈ**tremorous** *adj.*

tremulous (ˈtrɛmjʊləs) *adj.* 1. vibrating slightly; quavering; trembling. 2. showing or characterized by fear, anxiety, excitement, etc. [C17: < L *tremulus*, < *tremere* to shake] —ˈ**tremulously** *adv.* —ˈ**tremulousness** *n.*

trenail (ˈtriːneɪl, ˈtrɛnᵊl) *n.* a variant spelling of **treenail.**

trench (trɛntʃ) *n.* 1. a deep ditch. 2. a ditch dug as a fortification, having a parapet of earth. ~*vb.* 3. to make a trench in (a place). 4. (*tr.*) to fortify with a trench. 5. to slash or be slashed. 6. (*intr.*; foll. by *on* or *upon*) to encroach or verge. [C14: < OF *trenche* something cut, < *trenchier* to cut, < L *truncāre* to cut off]

trenchant (ˈtrɛntʃənt) *adj.* 1. keen or incisive: *trenchant criticism.* 2. vigorous and effective: *a trenchant foreign policy.* 3. distinctly defined. 4. *Arch. or poetic.* sharp. [C14: < OF *trenchant* cutting, < *trenchier* to cut; see TRENCH] —ˈ**trenchancy** *n.* —ˈ**trenchantly** *adv.*

trench coat *n.* a belted waterproof coat resembling a military officer's coat.

trencher (ˈtrɛntʃə) *n.* 1. (esp. formerly) a wooden board on which food was served or cut. 2. Also called: **trencher cap.** a mortarboard. [C14 *trenchour* knife, plate for carving on, < OF *trencheoir*, < *trenchier* to cut; see TRENCH]

trencherman (ˈtrɛntʃəmən) *n., pl.* **-men.** a person who enjoys food; hearty eater.

trench fever *n.* an acute infectious disease characterized by fever and muscular aches and pains and transmitted by lice.

trench foot *n.* a form of frostbite affecting persons standing for long periods in cold water.

trench mortar *or* **gun** *n.* a portable mortar used in trench warfare to shoot projectiles at a high trajectory over a short range.

trench warfare *n.* a type of warfare in which opposing armies face each other in entrenched positions.

trend (trɛnd) *n.* 1. general tendency or direction. 2. fashion; mode. ~*vb.* 3. (*intr.*) to take a certain trend. [OE *trendan* to turn]

trendsetter (ˈtrɛndˌsɛtə) *n.* a person or thing that creates, or may create, a new fashion. —ˈ**trendˌsetting** *adj.*

trendy (ˈtrɛndɪ) *Brit. inf.* ~*adj.* **trendier, trendiest.** 1. consciously fashionable. ~*n., pl.* **trendies.** 2. a trendy person. —ˈ**trendily** *adv.* —ˈ**trendiness** *n.*

trente et quarante (*French* trɑ̃t e karɑ̃t) *n. Cards.* another name for **rouge et noir.** [C17: F, lit.: thirty and forty; < the rule that forty is the maximum number that may be dealt and the winning colour is the one closest to thirty-one]

trepan (trɪˈpæn) *n.* 1. *Surgery.* an instrument resembling a carpenter's brace and bit formerly used to remove circular sections of bone from the skull. 2. a tool for cutting out circular blanks or for making grooves around a fixed centre. ~*vb.* **-panning, -panned.** (*tr.*) 3. to cut (a hole or groove) with a trepan. 4. *Surgery.* another word for **trephine.** [C14: < Med. L *trepanum* rotary saw, < Gk *trupanon* auger, < *trupan* to bore, < *trupa* a hole] —**trepanation** (ˌtrɛpəˈneɪʃən) *n.*

trepang (trɪˈpæŋ) *n.* any of various large sea cucumbers of tropical Oriental seas, the dried body walls of which are used as food by the Chinese. [C18: < Malay *tĕripang*]

trephine (trɪˈfiːn) *n.* 1. a surgical sawlike instrument for removing circular sections of bone esp. from the skull. ~*vb.* 2. (*tr.*) to remove a circular section of bone from (esp. the skull). [C17: < F *tréphine*, < obs. E *trefine* TREPAN, allegedly < L *trēs fīnēs*, lit.: three ends] —**trephination** (ˌtrɛfɪˈneɪʃən) *n.*

trepidation (ˌtrɛpɪˈdeɪʃən) *n.* 1. a state of fear or anxiety. 2. a condition of quaking or palpitation, esp. one caused by anxiety. [C17: < L *trepidātiō*, < *trepidāre* to be in a state of alarm]

trespass (ˈtrɛspəs) *vb.* (*intr.*) 1. (often foll. by *on* or *upon*) to go or intrude (on the property, privacy, or preserves of another) with no right or permission. 2. *Law.* to commit trespass. 3. *Arch.* (often foll. by *against*) to sin or transgress. ~*n.* 4. *Law.* **a.** any unlawful act committed with force, which causes injury to another person, his property or his rights. **b.** a wrongful entry upon another's land. 5. an intrusion on another's privacy or preserves. 6. a sin or offence. [C13: < OF *trespas* a passage, < *trespasser* to pass through, ult. < L *passus* a PACE[1]] —ˈ**trespasser** *n.*

tress (trɛs) *n.* 1. (*often pl.*) a lock of hair, esp. a long lock of woman's hair. 2. a plait or braid of hair. ~*vb.* (*tr.*) 3. to arrange in tresses. [C13: < OF *trece*, <?] —ˈ**tressy** *adj.*

trestle (ˈtrɛsᵊl) *n.* 1. a framework in the form of a horizontal member supported at each end by a pair of splayed legs, used to carry scaffold boards, a table top, etc. 2. **a.** a framework of timber, metal, or reinforced concrete that is used to support a bridge or ropeway. **b.** a bridge constructed of such frameworks. [C14: < OF *trestel*, ult. < L *trānstrum* transom]

trestlework (ˈtrɛsᵊlˌwɜːk) *n.* an arrangement of trestles, esp. one that supports a bridge.

trevally (trɪˈvælɪ) *n., pl.* **-lies.** *Austral. & N.Z.* any of various food and game fishes of the genus *Caranx.* [C19: prob. alteration of *cavally*, < *cavalla* species of tropical fish, < Sp. *caballa* horse]

trews (truːz) *pl. n. Chiefly Brit.* close-fitting trousers of tartan cloth. [C16: < Scot. Gaelic *triubhas*, < OF *trebus*]

trey (treɪ) *n.* any card or dice throw with three spots. [C14: < OF *treis* three, < L *trēs*]

tri- *prefix.* 1. three or thrice: *triaxial; trigon; trisect.* 2. occurring every three: *trimonthly.* [< L *trēs*, Gk *treis*]

triable (ˈtraɪəbᵊl) *adj.* 1. subject to trial in a court of law. 2. *Rare.* able to be tested.

triacid (traɪˈæsɪd) *adj.* capable of reacting with three molecules of a monobasic acid.

triad (ˈtraɪæd) *n.* 1. a group of three; trio. 2. *Chem.* an atom, element, group, or ion that has a valency of three. 3. *Music.* a three-note chord consisting of a note and the third and fifth above it. 4. an aphoristic literary form used in medieval Welsh and Irish literature. [C16: < LL *trias*, < Gk] —**triˈadic** *adj.* —ˈ**triadism** *n.*

triage (ˈtraɪɪdʒ) *n.* 1. the action of sorting casualties, etc. according to priority. 2. the allocating of limited resources on a basis of expediency rather than moral principles. [C18: < F; see TRY, -AGE]

trial (ˈtraɪəl, traɪl) *n.* 1. **a.** the act or an instance of trying or proving; test or experiment. **b.** (*as modifier*): *a trial run.* 2. *Law.* **a.** the judicial examination and determination of the issues in a civil or criminal cause by a competent tribunal. **b.** the determination of an accused person's guilt or innocence after hearing evidence and the judicial examination of the issues involved. **c.** (*as modifier*): *trial proceedings.* 3. an effort or attempt to do something. 4. trouble or grief. 5. an annoying or frustrating person or thing. 6. (*often pl.*) a competition for individuals: *sheepdog trials.* 7. **on trial. a.** undergoing trial, esp. before a court of law. **b.** being tested, as before a commitment to purchase. [C16: < Anglo-F, < *trier* to TRY]

trial and error *n.* a method of discovery, solving problems, etc., based on practical experiment and experience rather than on theory: *he learnt to cook by trial and error.*

trial balance *n. Book-keeping.* a statement of all the debit and credit balances in the ledger of a double-entry system, drawn up to test their equality.

triangle (ˈtraɪˌæŋgᵊl) *n.* 1. *Geom.* a three-sided polygon that can be classified by angle, as in an acute triangle, or by side, as in an equilateral triangle. 2. any object shaped like a triangle. 3. any situation involving three parties or points of view. 4. *Music.* a percussion instrument consisting of a sonorous metal bar bent into a triangular shape, beaten with a metal stick. **5.** a group of three. [C14: < L *triangulum* (n.), < *triangulus* (adj.), < TRI- + *angulus* corner] —**triangular** (traɪˈæŋgjʊlə) *adj.*

triangle of forces *n. Physics.* a triangle whose sides represent the magnitudes and directions of three forces in equilibrium.

triangulate *vb.* (traɪˈæŋgjʊˌleɪt). (*tr.*) **1. a.** to survey by the method of triangulation. **b.** to calculate trigonometrically. **2.** to divide into triangles. **3.** to make triangular. ~*adj.* (traɪˈæŋgjʊlɪt, -ˌleɪt). **4.** marked with or composed of triangles. —**triˈangulately** *adv.*

triangulation (traɪˌæŋgjʊˈleɪʃən) *n.* a method of surveying in which an area is divided into triangles, one side (the base line) and all angles of which are measured and the lengths of the other lines calculated trigonometrically.

triangulation station *n.* a point on a hilltop, etc., used for triangulation by a surveyor.

Triassic (traɪˈæsɪk) *adj.* **1.** of or formed in the first period of the Mesozoic era. ~*n.* **2. the.** Also called: **Trias.** the Triassic period or rock system. [C19: < L *trias* triad, from the three subdivisions]

triatomic (ˌtraɪəˈtɒmɪk) *adj. Chem.* having three atoms in the molecule.

tribade (ˈtrɪbɑːd) *n.* a lesbian who practises tribadism. [C17: < L *tribas,* < Gk *tribein* to rub]

tribadism (ˈtrɪbədɪzəm) *n.* a lesbian practice in which one partner lies on top of the other and simulates the male role in heterosexual intercourse.

tribalism (ˈtraɪbəˌlɪzəm) *n.* **1.** the state of existing as a tribe. **2.** the customs and beliefs of a tribal society. **3.** loyalty to a tribe. —**ˈtribalist** *n., adj.* —**ˌtribalˈistic** *adj.*

tribasic (traɪˈbeɪsɪk) *adj.* **1.** (of an acid) containing three replaceable hydrogen atoms in the molecule. **2.** (of a molecule) containing three monovalent basic atoms or groups.

tribe (traɪb) *n.* **1.** a social division of a people, esp. of a preliterate people, defined in terms of common descent, territory, culture, etc. **2.** an ethnic or ancestral division of ancient cultures, esp.: **a.** one of the political divisions of the Roman people. **b.** any of the 12 divisions of ancient Israel, each of which was believed to be descended from one of the 12 patriarchs. **3.** *Inf.* **a.** a large number of persons, animals, etc. **b.** a specific class or group of persons. **c.** a family, esp. a large one. **4.** *Biol.* a taxonomic group that is a subdivision of a subfamily. [C13: < L *tribus*] —**ˈtribal** *adj.*

tribesman (ˈtraɪbzmən) *n., pl.* **-men.** a member of a tribe.

tribo- *combining form.* indicating friction: *triboelectricity.* [< Gk *tribein* to rub]

triboelectricity (ˌtraɪbəʊɪlɛkˈtrɪsɪtɪ, -ˌiːlɛk-) *n.* electricity generated by friction.

tribology (traɪˈbɒlədʒɪ) *n.* the study of friction, lubrication, and wear between moving surfaces.

triboluminescence (ˌtraɪbəʊˌluːmɪˈnɛsəns) *n.* luminescence produced by friction, such as the emission of light when certain crystals are crushed. —**ˌtriboˌlumiˈnescent** *adj.*

tribrach (ˈtraɪbræk, ˈtrɪb-) *n.* a metrical foot of three short syllables. [C16: < L *tribrachys,* < Gk, < TRI- + *brakhus* short]

tribromoethanol (traɪˌbrəʊməʊˈɛθəˌnɒl) *n.* a soluble white crystalline compound with a slight aromatic odour, used as a general anaesthetic.

tribulation (ˌtrɪbjʊˈleɪʃən) *n.* **1.** a cause of distress. **2.** a state of suffering or distress. [C13: < OF, < Church L *trībulātiō,* < L *trībulāre* to afflict, < *trībulum* a threshing board, < *terere* to rub]

tribunal (traɪˈbjuːnᵊl, trɪ-) *n.* **1.** a court of justice. **2.** (in England) a special court, convened by the government to inquire into a specific matter. **3.** a raised platform containing the seat of a judge. [C16: < L *tribūnus* TRIBUNE¹]

tribune¹ (ˈtrɪbjuːn) *n.* **1.** (in ancient Rome) **a.** an officer elected by the plebs to protect their interests. **b.** a senior military officer. **2.** a person who upholds public rights. [C14: < L *tribunus,* prob. < *tribus* tribe] —**tribunate** (ˈtrɪbjʊnɪt) *or* **ˈtribuneship** *n.*

tribune² (ˈtrɪbjuːn) *n.* **1. a.** the apse of a Christian basilica that contains the bishop's throne. **b.** the throne itself. **2.** a gallery or raised area in a church. **3.** *Rare.* a raised platform; dais. [C17: via F < It. *tribuna,* < Med. L *tribūna,* var. of L *tribūnal* TRIBUNAL]

tributary (ˈtrɪbjʊtərɪ) *n., pl.* **-taries. 1.** a stream, river, or glacier that feeds another larger one. **2.** a person, nation, or people that pays tribute. ~*adj.* **3.** (of a stream, etc.) feeding a larger stream. **4.** given or owed as a tribute. **5.** paying tribute. —**ˈtributarily** *adv.*

tribute (ˈtrɪbjuːt) *n.* **1.** a gift or statement made in acknowledgment, gratitude, or admiration. **2.** a payment by one ruler or state to another, usually as an acknowledgment of submission. **3.** the obligation to pay tribute. [C14: < L *tribūtum,* < *tribuere* to grant (orig.: to distribute among the tribes), < *tribus* tribe]

trice (traɪs) *n.* a moment; instant (esp. in **in a trice**). [C15 (in *at* or *in a trice,* in the sense: at one tug): apparent substantive use of *trice* to haul up, < MDu. *trīse* pulley]

tricentenary (ˌtraɪsɛnˈtiːnərɪ) *or* **tricentennial** (ˌtraɪsɛnˈtɛnɪəl) *adj.* **1.** of a period of 300 years. **2.** of a 300th anniversary. ~*n., pl.* **-naries. 3.** an anniversary of 300 years.

triceps (ˈtraɪsɛps) *n., pl.* **-cepses** (-sɛpsɪz) *or* **-ceps.** any muscle having three heads, esp. the one that extends the forearm. [C16: < L, < TRI- + *caput* head]

trichiasis (trɪˈkaɪəsɪs) *n. Pathol.* an abnormal position of the eyelashes that causes irritation when they rub against the eyeball. [C17: via LL < Gk *trikhiasis,* < *thrix* a hair]

trichina (trɪˈkaɪnə) *n., pl.* **-nae** (-niː). a parasitic nematode worm occurring in the intestines of pigs, rats, and man and producing larvae that form cysts in skeletal muscle. [C19: < NL, < Gk *trikhinos* relating to hair, < *thrix* a hair] —**trichinous** (ˈtrɪkɪnəs) *adj.*

trichinosis (ˌtrɪkɪˈnəʊsɪs) *n.* a disease characterized by nausea, fever, diarrhoea, and swelling of the muscles, caused by ingestion of pork infected with trichina larvae. [C19: < NL TRICHINA]

trichloride (traɪˈklɔːraɪd) *n.* any compound that contains three chlorine atoms per molecule.

tricho- *or before a vowel* **trich-** *combining form.* indicating hair or a part resembling hair: *trichocyst.* [< Gk *thrix* (genitive *thrikhos*) hair]

trichology (trɪˈkɒlədʒɪ) *n.* the branch of medicine concerned with the hair and its diseases. —**triˈchologist** *n.*

trichomoniasis (ˌtrɪkəʊməˈnaɪəsɪs) *n.* inflammation of the vagina caused by infection with parasitic protozoa. [C19: NL]

trichopteran (traɪˈkɒptərən) *n.* **1.** any insect of the order *Trichoptera,* which comprises the caddis flies. ~*adj.* **2.** Also: **trichopterous** (trɪˈkɒptərəs). of or belonging to the order *Trichoptera.* [C19: < NL *Trichoptera,* lit.: having hairy wings, < Gk *thrix* a hair + *pteron* wing]

trichosis (trɪˈkəʊsɪs) *n.* any abnormal condition or disease of the hair. [C19: via NL < Gk *trikhōsis* growth of hair]

trichotomy (traɪˈkɒtəmɪ) *n., pl.* **-mies. 1.** division into three categories. **2.** *Theol.* the division of man into body, spirit, and soul. [C17: prob. < NL *trichotomia,* < Gk *trikhotomein* to divide into three] —**trichotomic** (ˌtrɪkəˈtɒmɪk) *or* **triˈchotomous** *adj.*

trichroism (ˈtraɪkrəʊˌɪzəm) *n.* a property of biaxial crystals as a result of which they show a difference in colour when viewed along three different axes. [C19: < Gk *trikhroos* three-coloured, < TRI- + *khrōma* colour]

trichromatic (ˌtraɪkrəʊˈmætɪk) *or* **trichromic** (traɪˈkrəʊmɪk) *adj.* **1.** involving the combination of three primary colours. **2.** of or having normal colour vision. **3.** having or involving three colours. —**triˈchromaˌtism** *n.*

trick (trɪk) *n.* **1.** a deceitful or cunning action or plan. **2. a.** a mischievous, malicious, or humorous action or plan; joke. **b.** (*as modifier*): *a trick spider.* **3.** an illusory or magical feat. **4.** a simple feat learned by an animal or person. **5.** an adroit or ingenious device; knack: *a trick of the trade.* **6.** a habit or mannerism. **7.** a turn of duty. **8.** *Cards.* a batch of cards containing one from each player, usually played in turn and won by the player or side that plays the card with the highest value. **9. do the trick.** *Inf.* to produce the desired result. **10. how's tricks?** *Sl.* how are you? ~*vb.* **11.** (*tr.*) to defraud, deceive, or cheat (someone). ~See also **trick out.** [C15: < OF *trique,* < *trikier* to deceive, ult. < L *trīcārī* to play tricks]

trick cyclist *n.* **1.** a cyclist who performs tricks, such as in a circus. **2.** a slang term for **psychiatrist.**

trickery (ˈtrɪkərɪ) *n., pl.* **-eries.** the practice or an instance of using tricks.

trickle (ˈtrɪkᵊl) *vb.* **1.** to run or cause to run in thin or slow streams. **2.** (*intr.*) to move gradually: *the crowd trickled away.* ~*n.* **3.** a thin, irregular, or slow flow of something. **4.** the act of trickling. [C14: ? imit.] —**ˈtrickling** *adj.*

trickle charger *n.* a small mains-operated battery charger, esp. one used by car owners.

trick or treat *n. Chiefly U.S. & Canad.* a customary cry used at Hallowe'en by children dressed in disguises calling at houses, by which they imply that they want a present of sweets, apples, or money and, if refused, will play a trick on the householder.

trick out *or* **up** *vb.* (*tr., adv.*) to dress up; deck out: *tricked out in frilly dresses.*

trickster (ˈtrɪkstə) *n.* a person who deceives or plays tricks.

tricksy (ˈtrɪksɪ) *adj.* **-sier, -siest. 1.** playing tricks habitually; mischievous. **2.** crafty or difficult to deal with. —**ˈtricksiness** *n.*

tricky (ˈtrɪkɪ) *adj.* **trickier, trickiest. 1.** involving snags or difficulties. **2.** needing careful handling. **3.** sly; wily: *a tricky dealer.* —**ˈtrickily** *adv.* —**ˈtrickiness** *n.*

triclinic (traɪˈklɪnɪk) *adj.* of the crystal system characterized by three unequal axes, no pair of which are perpendicular.

triclinium (traɪˈklɪnɪəm) *n., pl.* **-ia** (-ɪə). (in ancient Rome) **1.** an arrangement of three couches around a table for reclining upon while dining. **2.** a dining room. [C17: < L, < Gk *triklinion,* < TRI- + *klinē* a couch]

tricolour *or U.S.* **tricolor** (ˈtrɪkələ, ˈtraɪˌkʌlə) *adj. also* **tricoloured** *or U.S.* **tricolored** (ˈtraɪˌkʌləd). **1.** having or involving three colours. ~*n.* **2.** (*often cap.*) the French flag, having three stripes in blue, white, and red. **3.** any flag, badge, etc., with three colours.

tricorn (ˈtraɪˌkɔːn) *n. also* **tricorne. 1.** a cocked hat with opposing brims turned back and caught in three places. ~*adj. also* **tricornered. 2.** having three horns or corners. [C18: < L *tricornis,* < TRI- + *cornu* horn]

tricot (ˈtrɪkəʊ, ˈtriː-) *n.* **1.** a thin rayon or nylon fabric knitted or resembling knitting, used for dresses, etc. **2.** a type of ribbed dress fabric. [C19: < F, < *tricoter* to knit, <?]

tricuspid (traɪˈkʌspɪd) *Anat.* ~*adj. also* **tricuspidal. 1.** having three points, cusps, or segments: *a tricuspid tooth; a tricuspid valve.* ~*n.* **2.** a tooth having three cusps.

tricycle (ˈtraɪsɪkᵊl) *n.* a three-wheeled cycle, esp. one driven by pedals. —**ˈtricyclist** *n.*

trident (ˈtraɪdᵊnt) *n.* a three-pronged spear. [C16: < L *tridēns* three-pronged, < TRI- + *dēns* tooth]

Trident (ˈtraɪdᵊnt) *n.* a type of U.S. submarine-launched ballistic missile with independently targetable warheads.

tridentate (traɪˈdenteɪt) *or* **tridental** *adj.* having three prongs, teeth, or points.

Tridentine (traɪˈdentaɪn) *adj.* **1. a.** *History.* of the Council of Trent in the 16th century. **b.** in accord with Tridentine doctrine: *Tridentine mass.* ~*n.* **2.** an orthodox Roman Catholic. [C16: < Med. L *Tridentīnus,* < *Tridentum* Trent]

tried (traɪd) *vb.* the past tense and past participle of **try.**

triella (traɪˈɛlə) *n.* a cumulative bet on horses in three specified races.

triennial (traɪˈɛnɪəl) *adj.* **1.** relating to, lasting for, or occurring every three years. ~*n.* **2.** a third anniversary. **3.** a triennial period, thing, or occurrence. [C17: < L TRIENNIUM] —**triˈennially** *adv.*

triennium (traɪˈɛnɪəm) *n., pl.* **-niums** *or* **-nia** (-nɪə). a period or cycle of three years. [C19: < L, < TRI- + *annus* a year]

trier (ˈtraɪə) *n.* a person or thing that tries.

trifacial (traɪˈfeɪʃəl) *adj.* another word for **trigeminal.**

trifecta (traɪˈfɛktə) *n. Austral.* a form of betting in which punters select first-, second-, and third-place winners in the correct order.

trifid (ˈtraɪfɪd) *adj.* divided or split into three parts or lobes. [C18: < L *trifidus,* < TRI- + *findere* to split]

trifle (ˈtraɪfᵊl) *n.* **1.** a thing of little or no value or significance. **2.** a small amount; bit: *a trifle more enthusiasm.* **3.** *Brit.* a cold dessert made with sponge cake spread with jam or fruit, soaked in sherry, covered with custard and cream. ~*vb.* **4.** (*intr.; usually foll. by with*) to deal (with) as if worthless; dally: *to trifle with a person's affections.* **5.** to waste (time) frivolously. [C13: < OF *trufle* mockery, < *trufler* to cheat] —**ˈtrifler** *n.*

trifling (ˈtraɪflɪŋ) *adj.* **1.** insignificant or petty. **2.** frivolous or idle. —**ˈtriflingly** *adv.*

trifocal *adj.* (traɪˈfəʊkᵊl). **1.** having three focuses. **2.** having three focal lengths. ~*n.* (traɪˈfəʊkᵊl, ˈtraɪˌfəʊkᵊl). **3.** (*pl.*) glasses that have trifocal lenses.

triforium (traɪˈfɔːrɪəm) *n., pl.* **-ria** (-rɪə). an arcade above the arches of the nave, choir, or transept of a church. [C18: < Anglo-L, apparently < L TRI- + *foris* a doorway; < the fact that each bay had three openings]

trifurcate (ˈtraɪfɜːkɪt, -ˌkeɪt) *or* **trifurcated** *adj.* having three branches or forks. [C19: < L *trifurcus,* < TRI- + *furca* a fork]

trig (trɪg) *Arch. or dialect.* ~*adj.* **1.** neat or spruce. ~*vb.* **trigging, trigged. 2.** to make or become trim or spruce. [C12 (orig.: trusty): < ON] —**ˈtrigly** *adv.* —**ˈtrigness** *n.*

trig. *abbrev. for:* **1.** trigonometrical. **2.** trigonometry.

trigeminal (traɪˈdʒɛmɪnᵊl) *adj. Anat.* of or relating to the trigeminal nerve. [C19: < L *trigeminus* triplet, < TRI- + *geminus* twin]

trigeminal nerve *n.* either one of the fifth pair of cranial nerves, which supply the muscles of the mandible and maxilla. Their ophthalmic branches supply the area around the orbit of the eye, the nasal cavity, and the forehead.

trigeminal neuralgia *n. Pathol.* another name for **tic douloureux.**

trigger (ˈtrɪgə) *n.* **1.** a small lever that activates the firing mechanism of a firearm. **2.** a device that releases a spring-loaded mechanism. **3.** any event that sets a course of action in motion. ~*vb.* (*tr.*) **4.** (usually foll. by *off*) to give rise (to); set off. **5.** to fire or set in motion by or as by pulling a trigger. [C17 *tricker,* < Du. *trekker,* < *trekken* to pull]

triggerfish (ˈtrɪgəˌfɪʃ) *n., pl.* **-fish** *or* **-fishes.** any of a family of fishes of tropical and temperate seas. They have erectile spines in the first dorsal fin.

trigger-happy *adj. Inf.* **1.** tending to resort to the use of firearms or violence irresponsibly. **2.** tending to act rashly.

triglyceride (traɪˈglɪsəˌraɪd) *n.* any ester of glycerol and one or more carboxylic acids, in which each glycerol molecule has combined with three carboxylic acid molecules.

triglyph (ˈtraɪˌglɪf) *n. Archit.* a stone block in a Doric frieze, having three vertical channels. [C16: via L < Gk *trigluphos,* < TRI- + *gluphē* carving]

trigonal (ˈtrɪgənᵊl) *adj.* **1.** triangular. **2.** of the crystal system characterized by three equal axes that are equally inclined and not perpendicular to each other. [C16: via L < Gk *trigōnon* triangle]

trigonometric function *n.* any of a group of functions of an angle expressed as a ratio of two of the sides of a right-angled triangle containing the angle. The group includes sine, cosine, tangent, etc.

trigonometry (ˌtrɪgəˈnɒmɪtrɪ) *n.* the branch of mathematics concerned with the properties of trigonometric functions and their application to the determination of the angles and sides of triangles: used in surveying, navigation, etc. [C17: < NL *trigōnometria,* < Gk *trigōnon* triangle] —**trigonometric** (ˌtrɪgənəˈmɛtrɪk) *or* ˌ**trigonoˈmetrical** *adj.*

trig point *n.* an informal name for **triangulation station.** [< *trigonometric*]

trigraph (ˈtraɪˌgrɑːf) *n.* a combination of three letters used to represent a single speech sound or phoneme, such as *eau* in French *beau.*

trihedral (traɪˈhiːdrəl) *adj.* **1.** having three plane faces. ~*n.* **2.** a figure formed by the intersection of three lines in different planes.

trihedron (traɪˈhiːdrən) *n., pl.* **-drons** *or* **-dra** (-drə). a figure determined by the intersection of three planes.

trike (traɪk) *n.* short for **tricycle.**

trilateral (traɪˈlætərəl) *adj.* having three sides.

trilby (ˈtrɪlbɪ) *n., pl.* **-bies.** a man's soft felt hat with an indented crown. [C19: after *Trilby,* the heroine of a dramatized novel (1893) of that title by George Du Maurier]

trilingual (traɪˈlɪŋgwəl) *adj.* **1.** able to speak three languages fluently. **2.** expressed or written in three languages. —**triˈlingualism** *n.*

trilithon (traɪˈlɪθɒn) *or* **trilith** (ˈtraɪlɪθ) *n.* a structure consisting of two upright stones with a third placed across the top, as at Stonehenge. [C18: < Gk] —**trilithic** (traɪˈlɪθɪk) *adj.*

trill (trɪl) *n.* **1.** *Music.* a rapid alternation between a principal note and the note above it. **2.** a shrill warbling sound, esp. as made by some birds. **3.** the articulation of an (r) sound produced by the rapid vibration of the tongue or the uvula. ~*vb.* **4.** to sound, sing, or play (a trill or with a trill). **5.** (*tr.*) to pronounce (an (r) sound) by the production of a trill. [C17: < It. *trillo,* < *trillare,* apparently < MDu. *trillen* to vibrate]

trillion (ˈtrɪljən) *n.* **1.** (in Britain, France, and Germany) the number represented as one followed by eighteen zeros (10^{18}); a million million million. U.S. and Canad. word: **quintillion. 2.** (in the U.S. and Canada) the number represented as one followed by twelve zeros (10^{12}); a million million. Brit. word: **billion.** ~*determiner.* **3.** (preceded by *a* or a numeral) amounting to a trillion. [C17: < F, on the model of *million*] —ˈ**trillionth** *n., adj.*

trillium (ˈtrɪljəm) *n.* any of a genus of herbaceous plants of Asia and North America, having a whorl of three leaves at the top of the stem with a single white, pink, or purple three-petalled flower. [C18: < NL, modification by Linnaeus of Swedish *trilling* triplet]

trilobate (traɪˈləʊbeɪt, ˈtraɪləˌbeɪt) *adj.* (esp. of a leaf) consisting of or having three lobes or parts.

trilobite (ˈtraɪləˌbaɪt) *n.* any of various extinct marine arthropods abundant in Palaeozoic times, having a segmented exoskeleton divided into three parts. [C19: < NL *Trilobītēs,* < Gk *trilobos* having three lobes] —**trilobitic** (ˌtraɪləˈbɪtɪk) *adj.*

trilogy (ˈtrɪlədʒɪ) *n., pl.* **-gies. 1.** a series of three related works, esp. in literature, etc. **2.** (in ancient Greece) a series of three tragedies performed together. [C19: < Gk *trilogia*]

trim (trɪm) *adj.* **trimmer, trimmest. 1.** neat and spruce in appearance. **2.** slim; slender. **3.** in good condition. ~*vb.* **trimming, trimmed.** (*mainly tr.*) **4.** to put in good order, esp. by cutting or pruning. **5.** to shape and finish (timber). **6.** to adorn or decorate. **7.** (sometimes foll. by *off* or *away*) to cut so as to remove: *to trim off a branch.* **8.** to cut down to the desired size or shape. **9.** *Naut.* **a.** (*also intr.*) to adjust the balance of (a vessel) or (of a vessel) to maintain an even balance, by distribution of ballast, cargo, etc. **b.** (*also intr.*) to adjust (a vessel's sails) to take advantage of the wind. **10.** to balance (an aircraft) before flight by adjusting the position of the load or in flight by the use of trim tabs, fuel transfer, etc. **11.** (*also intr.*) to modify (one's opinions, etc.) for expediency. **12.** *Inf.* to thrash or beat. **13.** *Inf.* to rebuke. ~*n.* **14.** a decoration or adornment. **15.** the upholstery and decorative facings of a car's interior. **16.** proper order or fitness; good shape. **17.** a haircut that neatens but does not alter the existing hairstyle. **18.** *Naut.* **a.** the general set and appearance of a vessel. **b.** the difference between the draught of a vessel at the bow and at the stern. **c.** the fitness of a vessel. **d.** the position of a vessel's sails relative to the wind. **19.** dress or equipment. **20.** *U.S.* window-dressing. **21.** the attitude of an aircraft in flight when the pilot allows the main control surfaces to take up their own positions. **22.** material that is trimmed off. **23.** decorative mouldings, such as architraves, picture rails, etc. [OE *trymman* to strengthen] —ˈ**trimly** *adv.* —ˈ**trimness** *n.*

trimaran (ˈtraɪməˌræn) *n.* a vessel, usually of shallow draught, with two hulls flanking the main hull. [C20: < TRI- + (CATA)MARAN]

trimer (ˈtraɪmə) *n.* a polymer or a molecule of a polymer consisting of three identical monomers.

trimerous (ˈtrɪmərəs) *adj.* **1.** having parts in groups of three. **2.** having three parts.

trimester (traɪˈmɛstə) *n.* **1.** a period of three months. **2.** (in some U.S. and Canad. universities or schools) any of the three academic sessions. [C19: < F *trimestre,* < L *trimēstris* of three months] —**triˈmestral** *or* **triˈmestrial** *adj.*

trimeter (ˈtrɪmɪtə) *Prosody.* ~*n.* **1.** a verse line consisting of three metrical feet. ~*adj.* **2.** designating such a line.

trimethadione (ˌtraɪmɛθəˈdaɪəʊn) *n.* a crystalline compound with a camphor-like odour, used in the treatment of epilepsy.

trimetric projection (traɪˈmɛtrɪk) *n.* a geometric projection, used in mechanical drawing, in which the three axes are at arbitrary angles, often using different linear scales.

trimmer (ˈtrɪmə) *n.* **1.** a beam attached to truncated joists in order to leave an opening for a staircase, chimney, etc. **2.** a machine for trimming timber. **3.** a variable capacitor of small capacitance used for making fine adjustments, etc. **4.** a person who alters his opinions on the grounds of expediency. **5.** a person who fits out motor vehicles.

trimming (ˈtrɪmɪŋ) *n.* **1.** an extra piece used to decorate or complete. **2.** (*pl.*) usual or traditional accompaniments: *roast turkey with all the trimmings.* **3.** (*pl.*) parts that are cut off.

trimolecular (ˌtraɪməˈlɛkjʊlə) *adj. Chem.* of, formed from, or involving three molecules.

trimonthly (traɪˈmʌnθlɪ) *adj., adv.* every three months.

trimorphism (traɪˈmɔːfɪzəm) *n.* **1.** *Biol.* the property exhibited by certain species of having or occurring in three different forms. **2.** the property of certain minerals of existing in three crystalline forms.

trinary (ˈtraɪnərɪ) *adj.* **1.** made up of three parts; ternary. **2.** going in threes. [C15: < LL *trīnārius* of three sorts, < L *trīnī* three each, < *trēs* three]

trine (traɪn) *n.* **1.** *Astrol.* an aspect of 120° between two planets. **2.** anything comprising three parts. ~*adj.* **3.** of or relating to a trine. **4.** threefold; triple. [C14: < OF *trin,* < L *trīnus* triple, < *trēs* three] —ˈ**trinal** *adj.*

Trinitarian (ˌtrɪnɪˈtɛərɪən) *n.* **1.** a person who believes in the doctrine of the Trinity. ~*adj.* **2.** of or relating to the doctrine of the Trinity or those who uphold it. —ˌ**Triniˈtarianˌism** *n.*

trinitroglycerin (traɪˌnaɪtrəʊˈglɪsərɪn) *n.* the full name for **nitroglycerin.**

trinitrotoluene (traɪˌnaɪtrəʊˈtɒljʊˌiːn) *or* **trinitrotoluol** (traɪˌnaɪtrəʊˈtɒljʊˌɒl) *n.* the full name for **TNT.**

trinity (ˈtrɪnɪtɪ) *n., pl.* **-ties. 1.** a group of three.

2. the state of being threefold. [C13: < OF *trinite*, < LL *trīnitās*, < L *trīnus* triple]

Trinity (ˈtrɪnɪtɪ) *n. Christian theol.* the union of three persons, the Father, Son, and Holy Spirit, in one Godhead.

Trinity Brethren *pl. n.* the members of Trinity House.

Trinity House *n.* an association that provides lighthouses, buoys, etc., around the British coast.

Trinity Sunday *n.* the Sunday after Whit Sunday.

Trinity term *n.* the summer term at certain universities.

trinket (ˈtrɪŋkɪt) *n.* **1.** a small or worthless ornament or piece of jewellery. **2.** a trivial object; trifle. [C16: ? < earlier *trenket* little knife, via OF, < L *truncāre* to lop]

trinomial (traɪˈnəʊmɪəl) *adj.* **1.** consisting of three terms. ~*n.* **2.** *Maths.* a polynomial consisting of three terms, such as $ax^2 + bx + c$. **3.** *Biol.* the three-part name of an organism that incorporates its genus, species, and subspecies. [C18: TRI- + *-nomial* on the model of *binomial*]

trio (ˈtriːəʊ) *n., pl.* **trios. 1.** a group of three. **2.** *Music.* **a.** a group of three singers or instrumentalists or a piece of music composed for such a group. **b.** a subordinate section in a scherzo, minuet, etc. [C18: < It., ult. < L *trēs* three]

triode (ˈtraɪəʊd) *n.* **1.** an electronic valve having three electrodes, a cathode, an anode, and a grid. **2.** any electronic device having three electrodes. [C20: TRI- + ELECTRODE]

trioecious *or* **triecious** (traɪˈiːʃəs) *adj.* (of a plant species) having male, female, and hermaphrodite flowers in three different plants. [C18: < NL *trioecia*, < Gk TRI- + *oikos* house]

triolein (traɪˈəʊlɪɪn) *n.* a naturally occurring glyceride of oleic acid, found in fats and oils.

triolet (ˈtriːəʊˌlɛt) *n.* a verse form of eight lines, having the first line repeated as the fourth and seventh and the second line as the eighth, rhyming a b a a a b a b. [C17: < F: a little TRIO]

trioxide (traɪˈɒksaɪd) *n.* any oxide that contains three oxygen atoms per molecule.

trip (trɪp) *n.* **1.** an outward and return journey, often for a specific purpose. **2.** any journey. **3.** a false step; stumble. **4.** any slip or blunder. **5.** a light step or tread. **6.** a manoeuvre or device to cause someone to trip. **7.** Also called: **tripper.** any catch on a mechanism that acts as a switch. **8.** *Inf.* a hallucinogenic drug experience. **9.** *Inf.* any stimulating, profound, etc., experience. ~*vb.* **tripping, tripped. 10.** (often foll. by *up*, or when *intr.*, by *on* or *over*) to stumble or cause to stumble. **11.** to make or cause to make a mistake. **12.** (*tr.*; often foll. by *up*) to trap or catch in a mistake. **13.** (*intr.*) to go on a short journey. **14.** (*intr.*) to move or tread lightly. **15.** (*intr.*) *Inf.* to experience the effects of a hallucinogenic drug. **16.** (*tr.*) to activate a mechanical trip. [C14: < OF *triper* to tread, of Gmc origin]

tripartite (traɪˈpɑːtaɪt) *adj.* **1.** divided into or composed of three parts. **2.** involving three participants. **3.** (esp. of leaves) consisting of three parts formed by divisions extending almost to the base. —**triˈpartitely** *adv.*

tripe (traɪp) *n.* **1.** the stomach lining of an ox, cow, etc., prepared for cooking. **2.** *Inf.* something silly; rubbish. [C13: < OF, <?]

triphammer (ˈtrɪpˌhæmə) *n.* a power hammer that is raised or tilted by a cam and allowed to fall under gravity.

triphibious (traɪˈfɪbɪəs) *adj.* (esp. of military operations) occurring on land, at sea, and in the air. [C20: < TRI- + (AM)PHIBIOUS]

triphthong (ˈtrɪfθɒŋ, ˈtrɪp-) *n.* **1.** a composite vowel sound during the articulation of which the vocal organs move from one position through a second, ending in a third. **2.** a trigraph representing such a composite vowel sound. [C16: via NL < Med. Gk *triphthongos*, < TRI- + *phthongos* sound] —**triphˈthongal** *adj.*

tripinnate (traɪˈpɪnɪt, -eɪt) *adj.* (of a leaf) having pinnate leaflets that are bipinnately arranged.

triplane (ˈtraɪˌpleɪn) *n.* an aeroplane having three wings arranged one above the other.

triple (ˈtrɪpᵊl) *adj.* **1.** consisting of three parts; threefold. **2.** (of musical time or rhythm) having three beats in each bar. **3.** three times as great or as much. ~*n.* **4.** a threefold amount. **5.** a group of three. ~*vb.* **6.** to increase threefold; treble. [C16: < L *triplus*] —ˈ**triply** *adv.*

triple jump *n.* an athletic event in which the competitor has to perform successively a hop, a step, and a jump in continuous movement.

triple point *n. Chem.* the temperature and pressure at which the three phases of a substance are in equilibrium.

triplet (ˈtrɪplɪt) *n.* **1.** a group or set of three similar things. **2.** one of three offspring born at one birth. **3.** *Music.* a group of three notes played in a time value of two, four, etc. [C17: < TRIPLE, on the model of *doublet*]

Triplex (ˈtrɪplɛks) *n. Brit. trademark.* a laminated safety glass, as used in car windows.

triplicate *adj.* (ˈtrɪplɪkɪt). **1.** triple. ~*vb.* (ˈtrɪplɪˌkeɪt). **2.** to multiply or be multiplied by three. ~*n.* (ˈtrɪplɪkɪt). **3. a.** a group of three things. **b.** one of such a group. **4. in triplicate.** written out three times. [C15: < L *triplicāre* to triple] —ˌ**tripliˈcation** *n.*

triploid (ˈtrɪplɔɪd) *adj.* **1.** having or relating to three times the haploid number of chromosomes: *a triploid organism.* ~*n.* **2.** a triploid organism. [C19: < Gk *tripl(oos)* triple + (HAPL)OID]

tripod (ˈtraɪpɒd) *n.* **1.** a three-legged stand to which a camera, etc., can be attached to hold it steady. **2.** a stand or table having three legs. —**tripodal** (ˈtrɪpədᵊl) *adj.*

tripoli (ˈtrɪpəlɪ) *n.* a lightweight porous siliceous rock used in a powdered form as a polish. [C17: after *Tripoli*, in Libya or in Lebanon]

tripos (ˈtraɪpɒs) *n. Brit.* the final honours degree examinations at Cambridge University. [C16: < L *tripūs*, infl. by Gk noun ending *-os*]

tripper (ˈtrɪpə) *n.* **1.** *Chiefly Brit.* a tourist. **2.** another word for **trip** (sense 7). **3.** any device that causes a trip to operate.

triptane (ˈtrɪpteɪn) *n.* a liquid hydrocarbon used in aviation fuel. [C20: shortened & altered < *trimethylbutane*]

triptych (ˈtrɪptɪk) *n.* **1.** a set of three pictures or panels, usually hinged so that the two wing panels fold over the larger central one: often used as an altarpiece. **2.** a set of three hinged writing tablets. [C18: < Gk *triptukhos*, < TRI- + *ptux* plate]

triptyque (trɪpˈtiːk) *n.* a customs permit for the temporary importation of a motor vehicle. [C20: < F: TRIPTYCH (from its three sections)]

tripwire (ˈtrɪpˌwaɪə) *n.* a wire that activates a trap, mine, etc., when tripped over.

trireme (ˈtraɪriːm) *n.* an ancient Greek galley with three banks of oars on each side. [C17: < L *trirēmis*, < TRI- + *rēmus* oar]

trisect (traɪˈsɛkt) *vb.* (*tr.*) to divide into three parts, esp. three equal parts. [C17: TRI- + *-sect* < L *secāre* to cut] —**trisection** (traɪˈsɛkʃən) *n.*

trishaw (ˈtraɪˌʃɔː) *n.* another name for **rickshaw** (sense 2). [C20: < TRI- + RICKSHAW]

triskelion (trɪˈskɛlɪˌɒn) *n., pl.* **triskelia** (trɪˈskɛlɪə). a symbol consisting of three bent limbs or lines radiating from a centre. [C19: < Gk *triskelēs* three-legged]

trismus (ˈtrɪzməs) *n. Pathol.* the state of being unable to open the mouth because of sustained contractions of the jaw muscles, caused by tetanus. Nontechnical name: **lockjaw.** [C17: < NL, < Gk *trismos* a grinding]

triste (triːst) *adj.* an archaic word for **sad.** [< F]

trisyllable (traɪˈsɪləbᵊl) *n.* a word of three syllables. —**trisyllabic** (ˌtraɪsɪˈlæbɪk) *adj.*

trite (traɪt) *adj.* hackneyed; dull: *a trite comment.* [C16: < L *trītus* worn down, < *terere* to rub] —ˈ**tritely** *adv.* —ˈ**triteness** *n.*

tritheism (ˈtraɪθɪˌɪzəm) *n. Theol.* belief in three gods, esp. in the Trinity as consisting of three distinct gods. —ˈ**tritheist** *n., adj.*

triticum (ˈtrɪtɪkəm) *n.* any of a genus of cereal

grasses which includes the wheats. [C19: L, lit.: wheat, prob. < *tritum,* supine of *terere* to grind]

tritium (ˈtrɪtɪəm) *n.* a radioactive isotope of hydrogen. Symbol: T or ^{3}H; half-life: 12.5 years. [C20: NL, < Gk *tritos* third]

triton[1] (ˈtraɪtᵊn) *n.* any of various chiefly tropical marine gastropod molluscs having large spiral shells. [C16: via L < Gk *tritōn*]

triton[2] (ˈtraɪtɒn) *n. Physics.* a nucleus of an atom of tritium, containing two neutrons and one proton. [C20: < TRIT(IUM) + -ON]

Triton (ˈtraɪtᵊn) *n. Greek myth.* a sea god depicted as having the upper parts of a man with a fish's tail.

tritone (ˈtraɪˌtəʊn) *n.* a musical interval consisting of three whole tones.

triturate (ˈtrɪtjʊˌreɪt) *vb.* **1.** (*tr.*) to grind or rub into a fine powder or pulp. ~*n.* **2.** the powder or pulp resulting from this. [C17: < LL *trītūrāre* to thresh, < L *trītūra* a threshing, < *terere* to grind] —ˌ**trituˈration** *n.*

triumph (ˈtraɪəmf) *n.* **1.** the feeling of exultation and happiness derived from a victory or major achievement. **2.** the act or condition of being victorious; victory. **3.** (in ancient Rome) a procession held in honour of a victorious general. ~*vb.* (*intr.*) **4.** (often foll. by *over*) to win a victory or control: *to triumph over one's weaknesses.* **5.** to rejoice over a victory. **6.** to celebrate a Roman triumph. [C14: < OF *triumphe,* < L *triumphus,* < OL *triumpus*] —**triumphal** (traɪˈʌmfəl) *adj.*

triumphant (traɪˈʌmfənt) *adj.* **1.** experiencing or displaying triumph. **2.** exultant through triumph. —**triˈumphantly** *adv.*

triumvir (traɪˈʌmvə) *n., pl.* **-virs** *or* **-viri** (-vɪˌriː). (esp. in ancient Rome) a member of a triumvirate. [C16: < L: one of three administrators, < *trium virōrum* of three men, < *trēs* three + *vir* man] —**triˈumviral** *adj.*

triumvirate (traɪˈʌmvɪrɪt) *n.* **1.** (in ancient Rome) a board of three officials jointly responsible for some task. **2.** joint rule by three men. **3.** any group of three men associated in some way. **4.** the office of a triumvir.

triune (ˈtraɪjuːn) *adj.* constituting three in one, esp. the three persons in one God of the Trinity. [C17: TRI- + *-une,* < L *ūnus* one] —**triˈunity** *n.*

trivalent (traɪˈveɪlənt, ˈtrɪvələnt) *adj. Chem.* **1.** having a valency of three. **2.** having three valencies. ~Also: **tervalent.** —**triˈvalency** *n.*

trivet (ˈtrɪvɪt) *n.* **1.** a stand, usually three-legged and metal, on which cooking vessels are placed over a fire. **2.** a short metal stand on which hot dishes are placed on a table. **3. as right as a trivet.** in perfect health. [OE *trefet* (infl. by OE *thrifēte* having three feet), < L *tripēs* having three feet]

trivia (ˈtrɪvɪə) *n.* (*functioning as sing. or pl.*) petty details or considerations; trifles; trivialities. [< NL, pl. of L *trivium* junction of three roads]

trivial (ˈtrɪvɪəl) *adj.* **1.** of little importance; petty or frivolous: *trivial complaints.* **2.** ordinary or commonplace; trite: *trivial conversation.* **3.** *Biol., chem.* denoting the common name of an organism or substance. **4.** *Biol.* denoting the specific name of an organism in binomial nomenclature. [C15: < L *triviālis* belonging to the public streets, common, < *trivium* junction of three roads] —ˈ**trivially** *adv.* —ˈ**trivialness** *n.*

triviality (ˌtrɪvɪˈælɪtɪ) *n., pl.* **-ties. 1.** the state or quality of being trivial. **2.** something, such as a remark, that is trivial.

trivialize *or* **-ise** (ˈtrɪvɪəˌlaɪz) *vb.* (*tr.*) to cause to seem trivial or more trivial; minimize. —ˌ**triviaIiˈzation** *or* **-iˈsation** *n.*

trivium (ˈtrɪvɪəm) *n., pl.* **-ia** (-ɪə). (in medieval learning) the arts of grammar, rhetoric, and logic. Cf. **quadrivium.** [C19: < Med. L, < L: crossroads]

-trix *suffix forming nouns.* indicating a feminine agent, corresponding to nouns ending in *-tor: executrix.* [< L]

t-RNA *abbrev. for* transfer RNA.

trocar (ˈtrəʊkɑː) *n.* a surgical instrument for removing fluid from bodily cavities. [C18: < F *trocart,* lit.: with three sides, < *trois* three + *carre* side]

trochal (ˈtrəʊkᵊl) *adj. Zool.* shaped like a wheel. [C19: < Gk *trokhos* wheel]

trochanter (trəʊˈkæntə) *n.* **1.** any of several processes on the upper part of the vertebrate femur, to which muscles are attached. **2.** the third segment of an insect's leg. [C17: via F < Gk *trokhantēr,* < *trekhein* to run]

troche (trəʊʃ) *n. Med.* another name for **lozenge** (sense 1). [C16: < F *trochisque,* < LL *trochiscus,* < Gk *trokhiskos* little wheel, < *trokhos* wheel]

trochee (ˈtrəʊkiː) *n.* a metrical foot of two syllables, the first long and the second short. [C16: via L < Gk *trokhaios pous,* lit.: a running foot, < *trekhein* to run] —**trochaic** (trəʊˈkeɪɪk) *adj.*

trochlea (ˈtrɒklɪə) *n., pl.* **-leae** (-lɪˌiː). any bony or cartilaginous part with a grooved surface over which a bone, etc., may slide or articulate. [C17: < L, < Gk *trokhileia* a sheaf of pulleys]

trochlear nerve (ˈtrɒklɪə) *n.* either one of the fourth pair of cranial nerves, which supply the superior oblique muscle of the eye.

trochoid (ˈtrəʊkɔɪd) *n.* **1.** the curve described by a fixed point on the radius of a circle as the circle rolls along a straight line. ~*adj. also* **trochoidal. 2.** rotating about a central axis. **3.** *Anat.* (of a structure or part) resembling or functioning as a pivot or pulley. [C18: < Gk *trokhoeidēs* circular, < *trokhos* wheel]

trod (trɒd) *vb.* the past tense and a past participle of **tread.**

trodden (ˈtrɒdᵊn) *vb.* a past participle of **tread.**

trode (trəʊd) *vb. Arch.* a past tense of **tread.**

troglodyte (ˈtrɒgləˌdaɪt) *n.* **1.** a cave dweller, esp. of prehistoric times. **2.** *Inf.* a person who lives alone and appears eccentric. [C16: via L < Gk *trōglodutēs* one who enters caves, < *trōglē* hole + *duein* to enter] —**troglodytic** (ˌtrɒgləˈdɪtɪk) *adj.*

trogon (ˈtrəʊgɒn) *n.* any of an order of birds of tropical regions of America, Africa, and Asia, having a brilliant plumage and long tail. See also **quetzal** (sense 1). [C18: < NL, < Gk *trōgōn,* < *trōgein* to gnaw]

troika (ˈtrɔɪkə) *n.* **1.** a Russian vehicle drawn by three horses abreast. **2.** three horses harnessed abreast. **3.** a triumvirate. [C19: < Russian, < *troe* three]

Trojan (ˈtrəʊdʒən) *n.* **1.** a native or inhabitant of ancient Troy. **2.** a person who is hard-working and determined. ~*adj.* **3.** of or relating to ancient Troy or its inhabitants.

Trojan Horse *n.* **1.** *Greek myth.* the huge wooden hollow figure of a horse left outside Troy by the Greeks and dragged inside by the Trojans. The men concealed inside it opened the city to the final Greek assault. **2.** a trap intended to undermine an enemy.

troll[1] (trəʊl) *vb.* **1.** *Angling.* **a.** to draw (a baited line, etc.) through the water. **b.** to fish (a stretch of water) by trolling. **c.** to fish (for) by trolling. **2.** to roll or cause to roll. **3.** *Arch.* to sing (a refrain, chorus, etc.) in a loud hearty voice. **4.** (*intr.*) *Brit. inf.* to walk or stroll. ~*n.* **5.** a trolling. **6.** *Angling.* a bait or lure used in trolling. [C14: < OF *troller* to run about] —ˈ**troller** *n.*

troll[2] (trəʊl) *n.* (in Scandinavian folklore) one of a class of supernatural creatures that dwell in caves or mountains and are depicted either as dwarfs or as giants. [C19: < ON: demon]

trolley (ˈtrɒlɪ) *n.* **1.** *Brit.* a small table on casters used for conveying food, etc. **2.** *Brit.* a wheeled cart or stand used for moving heavy items, such as shopping in a supermarket or luggage at a railway station. **3.** *Brit.* (in a hospital) a bed mounted on casters and used for moving patients who are unconscious, etc. **4.** *Brit.* See **trolley bus. 5.** *U.S. & Canad.* See **trolley car. 6.** a device that collects the current from an overhead wire, third rail, etc., to drive the motor of an electric vehicle. **7.** a pulley or truck that travels along an overhead wire in order to support a suspended load. **8.** *Chiefly Brit.* a low truck running on rails, used in factories, mines, etc. **9.** a truck, cage, or basket suspended from an overhead track or cable for carrying loads in a mine, etc. [C19: prob. < TROLL[1]]

trolley bus *n.* an electrically driven public-transport vehicle that does not run on rails but takes its power from an overhead wire.

trolley car *n.* a U.S. and Canad. name for **tram**[1] (sense 1).

trollius (ˈtrəʊlɪəs) *n.* another name for **globe-flower.** [< G *Trollblume* globeflower]

trollop (ˈtrɒləp) *n.* **1.** a promiscuous woman, esp. a prostitute. **2.** an untidy woman; slattern. [C17: ? < G dialect *Trolle* prostitute] —ˈ**trollopy** *adj.*

trombone (trɒmˈbəʊn) *n.* a brass instrument, a low-pitched counterpart of the trumpet, consisting of a tube the effective length of which is varied by means of a U-shaped slide. [C18: < It., < *tromba* a trumpet, < OHG *trumba*] —**tromˈbonist** *n.*

trommel (ˈtrɒməl) *n.* a revolving cylindrical sieve used to screen crushed ore. [C19: < G: a drum]

trompe (trɒmp) *n.* an apparatus for supplying the blast of air in a forge, consisting of a thin column down which water falls, drawing in air through side openings. [C19: < F, lit.: trumpet]

trompe l'oeil (*French* trɔ̃p lœj) *n., pl.* **trompe l'oeils** (trɔ̃p lœj). **1.** a painting, etc., giving a convincing illusion of reality. **2.** an effect of this kind. [< F, lit.: deception of the eye]

-tron *suffix forming nouns.* **1.** indicating a vacuum tube. **2.** indicating an instrument for accelerating atomic particles. [< Gk, suffix indicating instrument]

tronk (trɒŋk) *n. S. African sl.* a prison. [< Afrik., prob. < Malay *trungku* to imprison]

troop (truːp) *n.* **1.** a large group or assembly. **2.** a subdivision of a cavalry squadron or artillery battery of about platoon size. **3.** (*pl.*) armed forces; soldiers. **4.** a large group of Scouts comprising several patrols. ~*vb.* **5.** (*intr.*) to gather, move, or march in or as if in a crowd. **6.** (*tr.*) *Mil., chiefly Brit.* to parade (the colour or flag) ceremonially. [C16: < F *troupe,* < *troupeau* flock, of Gmc origin]

trooper (ˈtruːpə) *n.* **1.** a soldier in a cavalry regiment. **2.** *U.S. & Austral.* a mounted policeman. **3.** *U.S.* a state policeman. **4.** a cavalry horse. **5.** *Inf., chiefly Brit.* a troopship.

troopship (ˈtruːpˌʃɪp) *n.* a ship used to transport military personnel.

tropaeolum (trəʊˈpiːələm) *n., pl.* **-lums** *or* **-la** (-lə). any of a genus of garden plants, esp. the nasturtium. [C18: < NL, < L *tropaeum* TROPHY; < the shield-shaped leaves and helmet-shaped flowers]

trope (trəʊp) *n.* a word or expression used in a figurative sense. [C16: < L *tropus* figurative use of a word, < Gk *tropos* style, turn]

-trope *n. combining form.* indicating a turning towards, development in the direction of, or affinity to: *heliotrope.* [< Gk *tropos* a turn]

trophic (ˈtrɒfɪk) *adj.* of nutrition. [C19: < Gk *trophikos,* < *trophē* food, < *trephein* to feed]

tropho- *or before a vowel* **troph-** *combining form.* indicating nourishment or nutrition: *trophozoite.* [< Gk *trophē* food, < *trephein* to feed]

trophoblast (ˈtrɒfəˌblæst) *n.* a membrane that encloses the embryo of mammals and absorbs nourishment from the uterine fluids.

trophozoite (ˌtrɒfəˈzəʊaɪt) *n.* the form of a protozoan, esp. of certain parasites, in the feeding stage.

trophy (ˈtrəʊfɪ) *n., pl.* **-phies.** **1.** an object such as a silver cup that is symbolic of victory in a contest, esp. a sporting contest; prize. **2.** a memento of success, esp. one taken in war or hunting. **3.** (in ancient Greece and Rome) a memorial to a victory, usually consisting of captured arms raised on the battlefield or in a public place. **4.** an ornamental carving that represents a group of weapons, etc. [C16: < F *trophée,* < L *tropaeum,* < Gk *tropaion,* < *tropē* a turning, defeat of the enemy]

-trophy *n. combining form.* indicating a certain type of nourishment or growth: *dystrophy.* [< Gk *-trophia,* < *trophē* nourishment] —**-trophic** *adj. combining form.*

tropic (ˈtrɒpɪk) *n.* **1.** (*sometimes cap.*) either of the parallel lines of latitude at about 23½°N (**tropic of Cancer**) and 23½°S (**tropic of Capricorn**) of the equator. **2. the tropics.** (*often cap.*) that part of the earth's surface between the tropics of Cancer and Capricorn. **3.** *Astron.* either of the two parallel circles on the celestial sphere having the same latitudes and names as the lines on the earth. ~*adj.* **4.** tropical. [C14: < LL *tropicus* belonging to a turn, < Gk *tropikos,* < *tropos* a turn; < the belief that the sun turned back at the solstices]

-tropic *adj. combining form.* turning or developing in response to a certain stimulus: *heliotropic.* [< Gk *tropos* a turn]

tropical (ˈtrɒpɪkᵊl) *adj.* **1.** situated in, used in, characteristic of, or relating to the tropics. **2.** (of weather) very hot, esp. when humid. **3.** of a trope. —ˌ**tropiˈcality** *n.* —ˈ**tropically** *adv.*

tropicbird (ˈtrɒpɪkˌbɜːd) *n.* any of various tropical aquatic birds having long tail feathers and a white plumage with black markings.

tropism (ˈtrəʊpɪzəm) *n.* the response of an organism, esp. a plant, to an external stimulus by growth in a direction determined by the stimulus. [< Gk *tropos* a turn] —ˌ**tropisˈmatic** *adj.*

-tropism *or* **-tropy** *n. combining form.* indicating a tendency to turn or develop in response to a stimulus: *phototropism.* [< Gk *tropos* a turn]

tropo- *combining form.* indicating change or a turning: *tropophyte.* [< Gk *tropos* a turn]

tropopause (ˈtrɒpəˌpɔːz) *n. Meteorol.* the plane of discontinuity between the troposphere and the stratosphere, characterized by a sharp change in the lapse rate.

troposphere (ˈtrɒpəˌsfɪə) *n.* the lowest atmospheric layer, about 18 kilometres (11 miles) thick at the equator to about 6 km (4 miles) at the Poles, in which air temperature decreases normally with height at about 6.5°C per km.

-tropous *adj. combining form.* indicating a turning away: *anatropous.* [< Gk *-tropos* concerning a turn]

troppo[1] (ˈtrɒpəʊ) *adv. Music.* too much; excessively. See **non troppo.** [It.]

troppo[2] (ˈtrɒpəʊ) *adj. Austral. sl.* mentally affected by a tropical climate.

trot (trɒt) *vb.* **trotting, trotted.** **1.** to move or cause to move at a trot. ~*n.* **2.** a gait of a horse in which diagonally opposite legs come down together. **3.** a steady brisk pace. **4.** (in harness racing) a race for horses that have been trained to trot fast. **5.** *Chiefly Brit.* a small child. **6.** *U.S. sl.* a student's crib. **7. on the trot.** *Inf.* **a.** one after the other: *to read two books on the trot.* **b.** busy, esp. on one's feet. **8. the trots.** *Inf.* **a.** diarrhoea. **b.** *N.Z.* trotting races. ~See also **trot out.** [C13: < OF *trot,* < *troter* to trot, of Gmc origin]

Trot (trɒt) *n. Inf.* a follower of Trotsky; Trotskyite.

troth (trəʊθ) *n. Arch.* **1.** a pledge of fidelity, esp. a betrothal. **2.** truth (esp. in **in troth**). **3.** loyalty; fidelity. [OE *trēowth*]

trotline (ˈtrɒtˌlaɪn) *n. Angling.* a long line suspended across a stream, river, etc., to which shorter hooked and baited lines are attached.

trot out *vb.* (*tr., adv.*) *Inf.* to bring forward, as for approbation or admiration, esp. repeatedly.

Trotskyism (ˈtrɒtskɪˌɪzəm) *n.* the theory of communism of Leon Trotsky (1879–1940), Russian revolutionary and writer, in which he called for immediate worldwide revolution by the proletariat. —ˈ**Trotskyite** *or* ˈ**Trotskyist** *n., adj.*

trotter (ˈtrɒtə) *n.* **1.** a horse that is specially trained to trot fast. **2.** (*usually pl.*) the foot of certain animals, esp. of pigs.

troubadour (ˈtruːbəˌdʊə) *n.* any of a class of lyric poets who flourished principally in Provence and N Italy from the 11th to the 13th century, writing chiefly on courtly love. [C18: < F, < OProvençal *trobador*, < *trobar* to write verses, ? ult. < L *tropus* TROPE]

trouble (ˈtrʌbᵊl) *n.* **1.** a state of mental distress or anxiety. **2.** a state of disorder or unrest: *industrial trouble.* **3.** a condition of disease, pain, or malfunctioning: *liver trouble.* **4.** a cause of distress, disturbance, or pain. **5.** effort or exertion taken to do something. **6.** liability to suffer punishment or misfortune (esp. in **be in trouble**): *he's in trouble with the police.* **7.** a personal weakness or cause of annoyance: *his trouble is he's too soft.* **8.** political unrest. **9.** the condition of an unmarried girl who becomes pregnant (esp. in **in trouble**). ~*vb.* **10.** (*tr.*) to cause trouble to. **11.** (*intr.;* usually with a negative and foll. by *about*) to put oneself to inconvenience; be concerned: *don't trouble about me.* **12.** (*intr.;* usually with a negative) to take pains; exert oneself. **13.** (*tr.*) to cause inconvenience or discomfort to. **14.** (*tr.; usually passive*) to agitate or make rough: *the seas were troubled.* **15.** (*tr.*) *Caribbean.* to interfere with. [C13: < OF *troubler,* < Vulgar L *turbulāre* (unattested), < LL *turbidāre,* ult. < *turba* commotion] —ˈ**troubler** *n.*

troublemaker (ˈtrʌbᵊlˌmeɪkə) *n.* a person who makes trouble, esp. between people. —ˈ**troubleˌmaking** *adj., n.*

troubleshooter (ˈtrʌbᵊlˌʃuːtə) *n.* a person who locates the cause of trouble and removes or treats it. —ˈ**troubleˌshooting** *n., adj.*

troublesome (ˈtrʌbᵊlsəm) *adj.* **1.** causing trouble. **2.** characterized by violence; turbulent. —ˈ**troublesomeness** *n.*

troublous (ˈtrʌbləs) *adj. Arch. or literary.* unsettled; agitated. —ˈ**troublously** *adv.*

trough (trɒf) *n.* **1.** a narrow open container, esp. one in which food or water for animals is put. **2.** a narrow channel, gutter, or gulley. **3.** a narrow depression, as between two waves. **4.** *Meteorol.* an elongated area of low pressure. **5.** a single or temporary low point; depression. **6.** *Physics.* the portion of a wave in which the amplitude lies below its average value. **7.** *Econ.* the lowest point of the trade cycle. [OE *trōh*]

trounce (traʊns) *vb.* (*tr.*) to beat or defeat utterly; thrash. [C16: <?]

troupe (truːp) *n.* **1.** a company of actors or other performers, esp. one that travels. ~*vb.* **2.** (*intr.*) (esp. of actors) to move or travel in a group. [C19: < F; see TROOP]

trouper (ˈtruːpə) *n.* **1.** a member of a troupe. **2.** a dependable worker or associate.

trouser (ˈtraʊzə) *n.* (*modifier*) of or relating to trousers: *trouser buttons.*

trousers (ˈtraʊzəz) *pl. n.* a garment shaped to cover the body from the waist to the ankles or knees with separate tube-shaped sections for both legs. [C17: < earlier *trouse,* var. of TREWS, infl. by DRAWERS]

trousseau (ˈtruːsəʊ) *n., pl.* **-seaux** *or* **-seaus** (-səʊz). the clothes, linen, etc., collected by a bride for her marriage. [C19: < OF, lit.: a little bundle; see TRUSS]

trout (traʊt) *n., pl.* **trout** *or* **trouts.** any of various game fishes, mostly of fresh water in northern regions. They are related to the salmon but are smaller and spotted. [OE *trūht,* < LL *tructa,* < Gk *troktēs* sharp-toothed fish]

trouvère (truːˈvɛə) *n.* any of a group of poets of N France during the 12th and 13th centuries who composed chiefly narrative works. [C19: < F, < OF *troveor,* < *trover* to compose]

trove (trəʊv) *n.* See **treasure-trove.**

trow (trəʊ) *vb. Arch.* to think, believe, or trust. [OE *treow*]

trowel (ˈtraʊəl) *n.* **1.** any of various small hand tools having a flat metal blade attached to a handle, used for scooping or spreading plaster or similar materials. **2.** a similar tool with a curved blade used by gardeners for lifting plants, etc. ~*vb.* **-elling, -elled** *or U.S.* **-eling, -eled. 3.** (*tr.*) to use a trowel on. [C14: < OF *truele,* < L *trulla* a scoop, < *trua* a stirring spoon]

troy weight *or* **troy** (trɔɪ) *n.* a system of weights used for precious metals and gemstones, based on the grain. 24 grains = 1 pennyweight; 20 pennyweights = 1 (troy) ounce; 12 ounces = 1 (troy) pound. [C14: after the city of *Troyes,* France, where first used]

truant (ˈtruːənt) *n.* **1.** a person who is absent without leave, esp. from school. ~*adj.* **2.** being or relating to a truant. ~*vb.* **3.** (*intr.*) to play truant. [C13: < OF: vagabond, prob. of Celtic origin] —ˈ**truancy** *n.*

truce (truːs) *n.* **1.** an agreement to stop fighting, esp. temporarily. **2.** temporary cessation of something unpleasant. [C13: < pl. of OE *treow* trow]

truck[1] (trʌk) *n.* **1.** *Brit.* a vehicle for carrying freight on a railway; wagon. **2.** another name (esp. U.S. and Canad.) for **lorry. 3.** Also called: **truckload.** the amount carried by a truck. **4.** a frame carrying two or more pairs of wheels attached under an end of a railway coach, etc. **5.** *Naut.* a disc-shaped block fixed to the head of a mast having holes for receiving halyards. **6.** any wheeled vehicle used to move goods. ~*vb.* **7.** to convey (goods) in a truck. **8.** (*intr.*) *Chiefly U.S. & Canad.* to drive a truck. [C17: ? shortened < *truckle* a small wheel]

truck[2] (trʌk) *n.* **1.** commercial goods. **2.** dealings (esp. in **have no truck with**). **3.** commercial exchange. **4.** payment of wages in kind. **5.** miscellaneous articles. **6.** *Inf.* rubbish. **7.** *U.S. & Canad* vegetables grown for market. ~*vb.* **8.** to exchange (goods); barter. **9.** (*intr.*) to traffic or negotiate. [C13: < OF *troquer* (unattested) to barter, equivalent to Med. L *trocare,* <?]

trucker (ˈtrʌkə) *n. Chiefly U.S.& Canad.* **1.** a lorry driver. **2.** a person who arranges for the transport of goods by lorry.

truck farm *n. U.S. & Canad.* a market garden. —**truck farmer** *n.* —**truck farming** *n.*

truckie (ˈtrʌkɪ) *n. Austral. inf.* a truck driver.

trucking (ˈtrʌkɪŋ) *n. Chiefly U.S. & Canad.* the transportation of goods by lorry.

truckle (ˈtrʌkᵊl) *vb.* (*intr.;* usually foll. by *to*) to yield weakly; give in. [C17: < obs. *truckle* to sleep in a truckle bed] —ˈ**truckler** *n.*

truckle bed *n.* a low bed on wheels, stored under a larger bed. [C17: < *truckle* small wheel, ult. < L *trochlea* sheaf of a pulley]

truck system *n.* a system during the early years of the Industrial Revolution of forcing workers to accept payment of wages in kind.

truculent (ˈtrʌkjʊlənt) *adj.* **1.** defiantly aggressive, sullen, or obstreperous. **2.** *Arch.* savage, fierce, or harsh. [C16: < L *truculentus,* < *trux* fierce] —ˈ**truculence** *or* ˈ**truculency** *n.* —ˈ**truculently** *adv.*

trudge (trʌdʒ) *vb.* **1.** (*intr.*) to walk or plod heavily or wearily. **2.** (*tr.*) to pass through or over by trudging. ~*n.* **3.** a long tiring walk. [C16: <?] —ˈ**trudger** *n.*

trudgen (ˈtrʌdʒən) *n.* a type of swimming stroke that uses overarm action, as in the crawl, and a scissors kick. [C19: after John *Trudgen,* E swimmer, who introduced it]

true (truː) *adj.* **truer, truest. 1.** not false, fictional, or illusory; factual; conforming with reality. **2.** (*prenominal*) real; not synthetic. **3.** faithful and loyal. **4.** conforming to a required standard, law, or pattern: *a true aim.* **5.** exactly in tune. **6.** (of a compass bearing) according to the earth's geographical rather than magnetic poles: *true north.* **7.** *Biol.* conforming to the typical structure of a designated type. **8.** *Physics.* not apparent or relative. ~*n.* **9.** correct alignment (esp. in **in true, out of true**). ~*adv.* **10.** truthfully; rightly. **11.** precisely or unswervingly. ~*vb.* **truing, trued. 12.** (*tr.*) to adjust so as to make true. [OE *triewe*] —ˈ**trueness** *n.*

true bill *n.* (formerly in Britain; now U.S.) the endorsement made on a bill of indictment by a grand jury certifying it to be supported by sufficient evidence to warrant a trial.

true-blue *adj.* **1.** unwaveringly or staunchly loyal. ~*n.* **true blue. 2.** *Chiefly Brit.* a staunch royalist or Conservative.

true-life *adj.* directly comparable to reality: *a true-life story.*

truelove (ˈtruːˌlʌv) *n.* **1.** someone truly loved; sweetheart. **2.** another name for **herb Paris.**

truelove knot *or* **true-lovers' knot** *n.* a complicated bowknot that is hard to untie, symbolizing ties of love.

true north *n.* the direction from any point along a meridian towards the North Pole. Also called: **geographic north.** Cf. **magnetic north.**

true rib *n.* any of the upper seven pairs of ribs in man.

true time *n.* the time shown by a sundial.

truffle (ˈtrʌfᵊl) *n.* **1.** any of various edible subterranean European fungi. They have a tuberous appearance and are regarded as a delicacy. **2.** Also called: **rum truffle.** *Chiefly Brit.* a sweet resembling this fungus in shape, flavoured with chocolate or rum. [C16: < F *truffe,* < OProvençal *trufa,* ult. < L *tūber*]

trug (trʌg) *n.* a long shallow basket for carrying flowers, fruit, etc. [C16: ? var. of TROUGH]

trugo (ˈtruːgəʊ) *n. Austral.* a game similar to croquet, originally improvised in Victoria from the rubber discs used as buffers on railway carriages. [< *true go,* when the wheel is hit between the goal posts]

truism (ˈtruːɪzəm) *n.* an obvious truth; platitude. —**truˈistic** *adj.*

trull (trʌl) *n. Arch.* a prostitute; harlot. [C16: < G *Trulle*]

truly (ˈtruːlɪ) *adv.* **1.** in a true, just, or faithful manner. **2.** (intensifier): *a truly great man.* **3.** indeed; really.

trumeau (truˈməʊ) *n., pl.* **-meaux** (-məʊz). *Archit.* a section of a wall or pillar between two openings. [< F]

trump[1] (trʌmp) *n.* **1.** Also called: **trump card. a.** any card from the suit chosen as trumps. **b.** this suit itself; trumps. **2.** a decisive or advantageous move, resource, action, etc. **3.** *Inf.* a fine or reliable person. ~*vb.* **4.** to play a trump card on a suit or a particular card of a suit that is not trumps. **5.** (*tr.*) to outdo or surpass. ~See also **trumps, trump up.** [C16: var. of TRIUMPH]

trump[2] (trʌmp) *n. Arch. or literary.* **1.** a trumpet or the sound produced by one. **2. the last trump.** the final trumpet call on the Day of Judgment. [C13: < OF *trompe,* < OHG *trumpa* trumpet]

trumpery (ˈtrʌmpərɪ) *n., pl.* **-eries. 1.** foolish talk or actions. **2.** a useless or worthless article; trinket. ~*adj.* **3.** useless or worthless. [C15: < OF *tromperie* deceit, < *tromper* to cheat]

trumpet (ˈtrʌmpɪt) *n.* **1.** a valved brass instrument of brilliant tone consisting of a narrow tube ending in a flared bell. **2.** any similar instrument, esp. a straight instrument used for fanfares, signals, etc. **3.** a loud sound such as that of a trumpet, esp. when made by an animal. **4.** an eight-foot reed stop on an organ. **5.** something resembling a trumpet in shape. **6.** short for **ear trumpet. 7. blow one's own trumpet.** to boast about one's own skills or good qualities. ~*vb.* **8.** to proclaim or sound loudly. [C13: < OF *trompette* a little TRUMP[2]]

trumpeter (ˈtrʌmpɪtə) *n.* **1.** a person who plays the trumpet, esp. one whose duty it is to play fanfares, signals, etc. **2.** any of three birds of South America, having a rounded body, long legs, and a glossy blackish plumage. **3.** (*sometimes cap.*) a breed of domestic fancy pigeon with a long ruff. **4.** a large silvery-grey Australian marine food and game fish that grunts when taken from the water.

trumpeter swan *n.* a large swan of W North America, having a white plumage and black bill.

trumps (trʌmps) *pl. n.* **1.** (*sometimes sing.*) *Cards.* any one of the four suits that outranks all the other suits for the duration of a deal or game. **2. turn up trumps.** (of a person) to bring about a happy or successful conclusion, esp. unexpectedly.

trump up *vb.* (*tr., adv.*) to invent (a charge, accusation, etc.) so as to deceive.

truncate *vb.* (trʌŋˈkeɪt, ˈtrʌŋkeɪt). **1.** (*tr.*) to shorten by cutting. ~*adj.* (ˈtrʌŋkeɪt). **2.** cut short; truncated. **3.** *Biol.* having a blunt end. [C15: < L *truncāre* to lop] —**trunˈcation** *n.*

truncated (trʌŋˈkeɪtɪd) *adj.* **1.** (of a cone, prism, etc.) having an apex or end removed by a plane intersection. **2.** shortened by or as if by cutting off; truncate.

truncheon (ˈtrʌntʃən) *n.* **1.** *Chiefly Brit.* a short thick club or cudgel carried by a policeman. **2.** a baton of office. [C16: < OF *tronchon* stump, < L *truncus* trunk; see TRUNCATE]

trundle (ˈtrʌndᵊl) *vb.* **1.** to move heavily on or as if on wheels: *the bus trundled by.* ~*n.* **2.** a trundling. **3.** a small wheel or roller. [OE *tryndel*]

trundle bed *n.* a less common word for **truckle bed.**

trundler (ˈtrʌndlə) *n. N.Z.* **1.** a trolley for shopping or one for golf clubs. **2.** a child's pushchair.

trunk (trʌŋk) *n.* **1.** the main stem of a tree. **2.** a large strong case or box used to contain clothes, etc., when travelling and for storage. **3.** the body excluding the head, neck, and limbs; torso. **4.** the elongated nasal part of an elephant. **5.** the U.S. name for **boot**[1] (sense 2). **6.** the main stem of a nerve, blood vessel, etc. **7.** *Naut.* a watertight boxlike cover within a vessel, such as one used to enclose a centreboard. **8.** an enclosed duct or passageway for ventilation, etc. **9.** (*modifier*) of a main road, railway, etc., in a network: *a trunk line.* ~See also **trunks.** [C15: < OF *tronc,* < L *truncus,* < *truncus* (adj.) lopped]

trunk call *n. Chiefly Brit.* a long-distance telephone call.

trunk curl *n.* a physical exercise in which the body is brought into a sitting position from one of lying on the back. Also called: **sit-up.**

trunkfish (ˈtrʌŋkˌfɪʃ) *n., pl.* **-fish** *or* **-fishes.** any of a family of fishes having the body encased in bony plates.

trunk hose *n.* a man's puffed-out breeches reaching to the thighs and worn with tights in the 16th century.

trunk line *n.* **1.** a direct link between two telephone exchanges or switchboards that are a considerable distance apart. **2.** the main route or routes on a railway.

trunk road *n. Brit.* a main road, esp. one that is suitable for heavy vehicles.

trunks (trʌŋks) *pl. n.* **1.** a man's garment worn for swimming, extending from the waist to the thigh. **2.** shorts worn for some sports. **3.** *Chiefly Brit.* men's underpants with legs that reach midthigh.

trunnion (ˈtrʌnjən) *n.* one of a pair of coaxial projections attached to opposite sides of a container, cannon, etc., to provide a support about which it can turn. [C17: < OF *trognon* trunk]

truss (trʌs) *vb.* (*tr.*) **1.** (sometimes foll. by *up*) to tie, bind, or bundle. **2.** to bind the wings and legs of (a fowl) before cooking. **3.** to support or stiffen (a roof, bridge, etc.) with structural members. **4.** *Med.* to supply or support with a truss. ~*n.* **5.** a structural framework of wood or metal used to support a roof, bridge, etc. **6.** *Med.* a device for holding a hernia in place, typically consisting of a pad held in position by a belt. **7.** a cluster of flowers or fruit growing at the end of a single stalk. **8.** *Naut.* a metal fitting fixed to a yard at its centre for holding it to a mast. **9.** another name for **corbel. 10.** a bundle or pack. **11.** *Chiefly Brit.* a bundle of hay or straw, esp. one having a fixed weight of 36, 56, or 60 pounds. [C13: < OF *trousse,* < *trousser,* apparently < Vulgar L *torciāre* (unattested), < *torca* (unattested) a bundle]

trust (trʌst) *n.* **1.** reliance on and confidence in the truth, worth, reliability, etc., of a person or thing; faith. Related adj.: **fiducial. 2.** a group of commercial enterprises combined to control the market for any commodity. **3.** the obligation of someone in a responsible position. **4.** custody, charge, or care. **5.** a person or thing in which confidence or faith is placed. **6.** commercial credit. **7. a.** an arrangement whereby a person to whom the legal title to property is conveyed (the trustee) holds such property for the benefit of those entitled to the beneficial interest. **b.** property that is the subject of such an arrangement. Related adj.: **fiduciary.** **8.** (*modifier*) of or relating to a trust or trusts. ~*vb.* **9.** (*tr.; may take a clause as object*) to expect, hope, or suppose. **10.** (when *tr., may take an infinitive;* when *intr.*, often foll. by *in* or *to*) to place confidence in (someone to do something); rely (upon). **11.** (*tr.*) to consign for care. **12.** (*tr.*) to allow (someone to do something) with confidence in his or her good sense or honesty. **13.** (*tr.*) to extend business credit to. [C13: < ON *traust*] —ˈ**trustable** *adj.* —ˈ**truster** *n.*

trust account *n.* **1.** Also called: **trustee account.** a savings account deposited in the name of a trustee who controls it during his lifetime, after which the balance is payable to a prenominated beneficiary. **2.** property under the control of a trustee or trustees.

trustee (trʌˈstiː) *n.* **1.** a person to whom the legal title to property is entrusted. **2.** a member of a board that manages the affairs of an institution or organization.

trusteeship (trʌˈstiːʃɪp) *n.* **1.** the office or function of a trustee. **2. a.** the administration or government of a territory by a foreign country under the supervision of the **Trusteeship Council** of the United Nations. **b.** (*often cap.*) any such dependent territory; trust territory.

trustful (ˈtrʌstfʊl) *or* **trusting** *adj.* characterized by a tendency or readiness to trust others. —ˈ**trustfully** *or* ˈ**trustingly** *adv.*

trust fund *n.* money, securities, etc., held in trust.

trust territory *n.* (*sometimes cap.*) another name for a **trusteeship** (sense 2).

trustworthy (ˈtrʌstˌwɜːðɪ) *adj.* worthy of being trusted; honest, reliable, or dependable. —ˈ**trustˌworthily** *adv.* —ˈ**trustˌworthiness** *n.*

trusty (ˈtrʌstɪ) *adj.* **trustier, trustiest.** **1.** faithful or reliable. ~*n., pl.* **trusties.** **2.** a trustworthy convict to whom special privileges are granted. —ˈ**trustily** *adv.* —ˈ**trustiness** *n.*

truth (truːθ) *n.* **1.** the quality of being true, genuine, actual, or factual. **2.** something that is true as opposed to false. **3.** a proven or verified fact, principle, etc.: *the truths of astronomy.* **4.** (*usually pl.*) a system of concepts purporting to represent some aspect of the world: *the truths of ancient religions.* **5.** fidelity to a standard or law. **6.** faithful reproduction or portrayal. **7.** honesty. **8.** accuracy, as in the setting of a mechanical instrument. **9.** loyalty. ~Related adjs.: **veritable, veracious.** [OE *triewth*] —ˈ**truthless** *adj.*

truth drug *or* **serum** *n. Inf.* any of various drugs supposed to have the property of making people tell the truth, as by relaxing them.

truthful (ˈtruːθfʊl) *adj.* **1.** telling the truth; honest. **2.** realistic: *a truthful portrayal of the king.* —ˈ**truthfully** *adv.* —ˈ**truthfulness** *n.*

truth-function *n. Logic.* a function that determines the truth-value of a complex sentence solely in terms of the truth-values of the component sentences without reference to their meaning.

truth set *n. Logic, maths.* the set of values that satisfy an open sentence, equation, inequality, etc., having no unique solution. Also called: **solution set.**

truth table *n.* **1.** a table, used in logic, indicating the truth-value of a compound statement for every truth-value of its component propositions. **2.** a similar table, used in transistor technology, to indicate the value of the output signal of a logic circuit for every value of input signal.

truth-value *n. Logic.* either of the values, true or false, that may be taken by a statement.

try (traɪ) *vb.* **trying, tried.** **1.** (when *tr., may take an infinitive,* sometimes with *to* replaced by *and*) to make an effort or attempt. **2.** (*tr.;* often foll. by *out*) to sample, test, or give experimental use to (something). **3.** (*tr.*) to put strain or stress on: *he tries my patience.* **4.** (*tr.; often passive*) to give pain, affliction, or vexation to. **5. a.** to examine and determine the issues involved in (a cause) in a court of law. **b.** to hear evidence in order to determine the guilt or innocence of (an accused). **6.** (*tr.*) to melt (fat, lard, etc.) in order to separate out impurities. ~*n., pl.* **tries.** **7.** an experiment or trial. **8.** an attempt or effort. **9.** *Rugby.* the act of an attacking player touching the ball down behind the opposing team's goal line. **10.** *American football.* an attempt made after a touchdown to score an extra point, as by kicking a goal. ~See also **try on, try out.** [C13: < OF *trier* to sort, <?]

trying (ˈtraɪɪŋ) *adj.* upsetting, difficult, or annoying. —ˈ**tryingly** *adv.*

trying plane *n.* a plane with a long body for planing the edges of long boards. Also called: **try plane.**

try on *vb.* (*tr., adv.*) **1.** to put on (a garment) to find out whether it fits, etc. **2. try it on.** *Inf.* to attempt to deceive or fool someone. ~*n.* **try-on.** **3.** *Brit. inf.* something done to test out a person's tolerance, etc.

try out *vb.* (*adv.*) **1.** (*tr.*) to test or put to experimental use. **2.** (when *intr.*, usually foll. by *for*) *U.S. & Canad.* (of an athlete, actor, etc.) to undergo a test or to submit (an athlete, actor, etc.) to a test to determine suitability for a place in a team, an acting role, etc. ~*n.* **tryout.** **3.** *Chiefly U.S. & Canad.* a trial or test, as of an athlete or actor.

trypanosome (ˈtrɪpənəˌsəʊm) *n.* any of a genus of parasitic protozoa which live in the blood of vertebrates and cause sleeping sickness and certain other diseases. [C19: < NL *Trypanosoma,* < Gk *trupanon* borer + *sōma* body]

trypanosomiasis (ˌtrɪpənəsəˈmaɪəsɪs) *n.* any infection of an animal or human with a trypanosome.

trypsin (ˈtrɪpsɪn) *n.* a digestive enzyme in the pancreatic juice: it catalyses the hydrolysis of proteins to peptides. [C19 *tryp-,* < Gk *tripsis* a rubbing, < *tribein* to rub + -IN; < the fact that it was orig. produced by rubbing the pancreas with glycerin] —**tryptic** (ˈtrɪptɪk) *adj.*

tryptophan (ˈtrɪptəˌfæn) *n.* an essential amino acid; a component of proteins necessary for growth. [C20: < *trypt(ic),* < TRYPSIN + -O- + *-phan,* var. of -PHANE]

trysail (ˈtraɪˌseɪl; *Naut.* ˈtraɪsᵊl) *n.* a small fore-and-aft sail set on a sailing vessel in foul weather to help keep her head to the wind.

try square *n.* a device for testing or laying out right angles, consisting of a grooved metal ruler along which a frame runs, one edge of the frame always being perpendicular to the ruler.

tryst (trɪst, traɪst) *n. Arch. or literary.* **1.** an appointment to meet, esp. secretly. **2.** the place of such a meeting or the meeting itself. [C14: < OF *triste* lookout post, apparently < ON]

tsar *or* **czar** (zɑː) *n.* **1.** (until 1917) the emperor of Russia. **2.** a tyrant; autocrat. **3.** *Inf.* a person in authority. [C17: < Russian *tsar,* via Gothic *kaisar* < L: CAESAR] —ˈ**tsardom** *or* ˈ**czardom** *n.*

tsarevitch *or* **czarevitch** (ˈzɑːrəvɪtʃ) *n.* a son of a Russian tsar, esp. the eldest son. [< Russian *tsarevich,* < TSAR + *-evich,* masc. patronymic suffix]

tsarevna *or* **czarevna** (zɑːˈrɛvnə) *n.* **1.** a daughter of a Russian tsar. **2.** the wife of a Russian tsarevitch. [< Russian, < TSAR + *-evna,* fem. patronymic suffix]

tsarina, czarina (zɑːˈriːnə) *or* **tsaritsa, czaritza** (zɑːˈrɪtsə) *n.* the wife of a Russian tsar; Russian empress. [< Russian, < TSAR + *-ina,* fem. suffix]

tsarism *or* **czarism** (ˈzɑːrɪzəm) *n.* a system of government by a tsar. —ˈ**tsarist** *or* ˈ**czarist** *n., adj.*

TSE (in Canada) *abbrev.* for Toronto Stock Exchange.

tsetse fly *or* **tzetze fly** (ˈtsetsɪ) *n.* any of various bloodsucking African dipterous flies which transmit various diseases, esp. sleeping sickness. [C19: via Afrik. < Tswana]

T-shirt *or* **tee-shirt** *n.* a lightweight simple

garment for the upper body, usually short-sleeved. [< T-shape formed when laid out flat]

tsotsi (ˈtsɒtsɪ) *n., pl.* **-tsis.** *S. African inf.* a violent usually young criminal who operates mainly in Black African townships and lives by his wits. [C20: <?]

tsp. *abbrev. for* teaspoon.

T-square *n.* a T-shaped ruler used for drawing horizontal lines and to support set squares when drawing vertical and inclined lines.

T-stop *n.* a setting of the lens aperture on a camera calibrated photometrically and assigned a T-number.

tsunami (tsʊˈnɑːmɪ) *n., pl.* **-mis** *or* **-mi.** a large, often destructive sea wave produced by a submarine earthquake, subsidence, or volcanic eruption. [< Japanese, < *tsu* port + *nami* wave]

tsutsugamushi disease (ˌtsʊtsʊgəˈmʊʃɪ) *n.* one of the five major groups of acute infectious rickettsial diseases affecting man, common in Asia. It is transmitted by the bite of mites. [< Japanese, < *tsutsuga* disease + *mushi* insect]

Tswana (ˈtswɑːnə) *n.* **1.** (*pl.* **-na** *or* **-nas**) a member of a mixed Negroid and Bushman people of southern Africa, living chiefly in Botswana. **2.** the language of this people.

TT *abbrev. for:* **1.** teetotal. **2.** teetotaller. **3.** Tourist Trophy (annual motorcycle races held in the Isle of Man). **4.** tuberculin-tested.

TTL *abbrev. for:* **1.** transistor transistor logic: a method of constructing electronic logic circuits. **2.** through-the-lens: denoting a system of light metering in cameras.

TU *abbrev. for* trade union.

Tu. *abbrev. for* Tuesday.

tuatara (ˌtuːəˈtɑːrə) *n.* a lizard-like reptile occurring on certain islands near New Zealand. [C19: < Maori, < *tua* back + *tara* spine]

tub (tʌb) *n.* **1.** a low wide open container, typically round: used in a variety of domestic and industrial situations. **2.** a small plastic or cardboard container of similar shape for ice cream, margarine, etc. **3.** another word (esp. U.S.) for **bath**[1] (sense 1). **4.** Also called: **tubful.** the amount a tub will hold. **5.** a clumsy slow boat or ship. **6. a.** a small vehicle on rails for carrying loads in a mine. **b.** a container for lifting coal or ore up a mine shaft. ~*vb.* **tubbing, tubbed. 7.** *Brit. inf.* to wash (oneself) in a tub. **8.** (*tr.*) to keep or put in a tub. [C14: < MDu. *tubbe*] —ˈ**tubbable** *adj.* —ˈ**tubber** *n.*

tuba (ˈtjuːbə) *n., pl.* **-bas** *or* **-bae** (-biː). **1.** a valved brass instrument of bass pitch, in which the bell points upwards and the mouthpiece projects at right angles. **2.** a powerful reed stop on an organ. [L]

tubal (ˈtjuːbᵊl) *adj.* **1.** of or relating to a tube. **2.** of, relating to, or developing in a Fallopian tube.

tubby (ˈtʌbɪ) *adj.* **-bier, -biest. 1.** plump. **2.** shaped like a tub. —ˈ**tubbiness** *n.*

tube (tjuːb) *n.* **1.** a long hollow cylindrical object, used for the passage of fluids or as a container. **2.** a collapsible cylindrical container of soft metal or plastic closed with a cap, used to hold viscous liquids or pastes. **3.** *Anat.* short for **Eustachian tube** or **Fallopian tube. 4.** any hollow structure. **5.** (*sometimes cap.*) *Brit.* **a. the tube.** an underground railway system, esp. that in London. U.S. and Canad. equivalent: **subway. b.** the tunnels through which the railway runs. **6.** *Electronics.* **a.** another name for **valve** (sense 3). **b.** See **electron tube, cathode-ray tube, television tube. 7.** *Sl., chiefly U.S.* a television set. **8.** *Austral. sl.* a bottle or can of beer. ~*vb.* (*tr.*) **9.** to supply with a tube. **10.** to convey in a tube. **11.** to shape like a tube. [C17: < L *tubus*] —ˈ**tubeless** *adj.*

tube foot *n.* any of numerous tubular outgrowths of most echinoderms that are used for locomotion, to aid ingestion of food, etc.

tubeless tyre *n.* a pneumatic tyre in which the outer casing makes an airtight seal with the rim of the wheel so that an inner tube is unnecessary.

tuber (ˈtjuːbə) *n.* **1.** a fleshy underground stem or root. **2.** *Anat.* a raised area; swelling. [C17: < L *tūber* hump]

tubercle (ˈtjuːbəkᵊl) *n.* **1.** any small rounded nodule or elevation, esp. on the skin, on a bone, or on a plant. **2.** any small rounded pathological lesion, esp. one characteristic of tuberculosis. [C16: < L *tūberculum* a little swelling]

tubercle bacillus *n.* a rodlike bacterium that causes tuberculosis.

tubercular (tjʊˈbɜːkjʊlə) *adj. also* **tuberculous. 1.** of or symptomatic of tuberculosis. **2.** of or relating to a tubercle. **3.** characterized by the presence of tubercles. ~*n.* **4.** a person with tuberculosis.

tuberculate (tjʊˈbɜːkjʊlɪt) *adj.* covered with tubercles. —**tuˌbercuˈlation** *n.*

tuberculin (tjʊˈbɜːkjʊlɪn) *n.* a sterile liquid prepared from cultures of attenuated tubercle bacillus and used in the diagnosis of tuberculosis.

tuberculin-tested *adj.* (of milk) produced by cows that have been certified as free of tuberculosis.

tuberculosis (tjʊˌbɜːkjʊˈləʊsɪs) *n.* a communicable disease caused by infection with the tubercle bacillus, most frequently affecting the lungs. [C19: < NL]

tuberose (ˈtjuːbəˌrəʊz) *n.* a perennial Mexican agave plant having a tuberous root and fragrant white flowers. [C17: < L *tūberōsus* full of lumps; from its root]

tuberous (ˈtjuːbərəs) *or* **tuberose** (ˈtjuːbəˌrəʊs) *adj.* **1.** (of plants) forming, bearing, or resembling a tuber or tubers. **2.** *Anat.* of or having warty protuberances or tubers. [C17: < L *tūberōsus* full of knobs]

tube worm *n.* any of various worms that construct and live in a tube of sand, lime, etc.

tubifex (ˈtjuːbɪˌfɛks) *n., pl.* **-fex** *or* **-fexes.** any of a genus of small reddish freshwater worms. [C19: < NL, < L *tubus* tube + *facere* to make]

tubing (ˈtjuːbɪŋ) *n.* **1.** tubes collectively. **2.** a length of tube. **3.** a system of tubes. **4.** fabric in the form of a tube.

tub-thumper *n.* a noisy, violent, or ranting public speaker. —ˈ**tub-ˌthumping** *adj., n.*

tubular (ˈtjuːbjʊlə) *adj.* **1.** Also: **tubiform** (ˈtjuːbɪˌfɔːm). having the form of a tube or tubes. **2.** of or relating to a tube or tubing.

tubular bells *pl. n.* a set of long tubes of brass tuned for use in an orchestra and struck with a mallet to simulate the sound of bells.

tubule (ˈtjuːbjuːl) *n.* any small tubular structure. [C17: < L *tubulus* a little TUBE]

TUC (in Britain) *abbrev. for* Trades Union Congress.

tuck (tʌk) *vb.* **1.** (*tr.*) to push or fold into a small confined space or concealed place or between two surfaces. **2.** (*tr.*) to thrust the loose ends or sides of (something) into a confining space, so as to make neat and secure. **3.** to make a tuck or tucks in (a garment). **4.** (*usually tr.*) to draw together, contract, or pucker. ~*n.* **5.** a tucked object or part. **6.** a pleat or fold in a part of a garment, usually stitched down. **7.** the part of a vessel where the planks meet at the sternpost. **8.** *Brit. inf.* **a.** food, esp. cakes and sweets. **b.** (*as modifier*): *a tuck box.* **9.** a position of the body, as in certain dives, in which the legs are bent with the knees drawn up against the chest and tightly clasped. ~See also **tuck away, tuck in.** [C14: < OE *tūcian* to torment]

tuck away *vb.* (*tr., adv.*) *Inf.* **1.** to eat (a large amount of food). **2.** to store, esp. in a place difficult to find.

tucker[1] (ˈtʌkə) *n.* **1.** a person or thing that tucks. **2.** a detachable yoke of lace, linen, etc., often white, worn over the breast, as of a low-cut dress. **3.** *Austral. & N.Z.* an informal word for **food.**

tucker[2] (ˈtʌkə) *vb.* (*tr.; often passive;* usually foll. by *out*) *Inf., chiefly U.S. & Canad.* to weary or tire.

tucker-bag *or* **tuckerbox** (ˈtʌkəˌbɒks) *n.* *Austral. sl.* a bag in which food is carried or stored.

tucket (ˈtʌkɪt) *n. Arch.* a flourish on a trumpet. [C16: < OF *toquer* to sound (on a drum)]

tuck in *vb.* (*adv.*) **1.** (*tr.*) Also: **tuck into.** to put to bed and make snug. **2.** (*tr.*) to thrust the loose ends or sides of (something) into a confining space: *tuck the blankets in.* **3.** (*intr.*) Also: **tuck into.** *Inf.* to eat, esp. heartily. ~*n.* **tuck-in. 4.** *Brit. inf.* a meal, esp. a large one.

tuck shop *n. Chiefly Brit.* a shop, esp. one near a school, where cakes and sweets are sold.

-tude *suffix forming nouns.* indicating state or condition: *plenitude.* [< L *-tūdō*]

Tudor (ˈtjuːdə) *adj.* **1.** of or relating to the English royal house ruling from 1485 to 1603. **2.** characteristic of or happening in this period. **3.** denoting a style of architecture characterized by half-timbered houses.

Tues. *abbrev. for* Tuesday.

Tuesday (ˈtjuːzdɪ) *n.* the third day of the week; second day of the working week. [OE *tīwesdæg*]

tufa (ˈtjuːfə) *n.* a porous rock formed of calcium carbonate deposited from springs. [C18: < It. *tufo,* < LL *tōfus*] **—tufaceous** (tjuːˈfeɪʃəs) *adj.*

tuff (tʌf) *n.* a hard volcanic rock consisting of consolidated fragments of lava. [C16: < OF *tuf,* < It. *tufo;* see TUFA] **—tuffaceous** (tʌˈfeɪʃəs) *adj.*

tuffet (ˈtʌfɪt) *n.* a small mound or low seat. [C16: alteration of TUFT]

tuft (tʌft) *n.* **1.** a bunch of feathers, grass, hair, etc., held together at the base. **2.** a cluster of threads drawn tightly through upholstery, a quilt, etc., to secure the padding. **3.** a small clump of trees or bushes. **4.** (formerly) a gold tassel on the cap worn by titled undergraduates at English universities. ~*vb.* **5.** (*tr.*) to provide or decorate with a tuft or tufts. **6.** to form or be formed into tufts. **7.** to secure with tufts. [C14: ? < OF *tufe,* of Gmc origin] **—ˈtufted** *adj.* **—ˈtufty** *adj.*

tug (tʌg) *vb.* **tugging, tugged. 1.** (when *intr.,* sometimes foll. by *at*) to pull or drag with sharp or powerful movements. **2.** (*tr.*) to tow (a vessel) by means of a tug. ~*n.* **3.** a strong pull or jerk. **4.** Also called: **tugboat.** a boat with a powerful engine, used for towing barges, ships, etc. **5.** a hard struggle or fight. [C13: rel. to OE *tēon* to TOW[1]] **—ˈtugger** *n.*

tug of love *n.* a conflict over custody of a child between divorced parents or between natural parents and foster or adoptive parents.

tug of war *n.* **1.** a contest in which two people or teams pull opposite ends of a rope in an attempt to drag the opposition over a central line. **2.** any hard struggle between two factions.

tui (ˈtuːiː) *n., pl.* **tuis.** a New Zealand songbird with white feathers at the throat. Also called: **parson bird.** [< Maori]

tuition (tjuːˈɪʃən) *n.* **1.** instruction, esp. that received individually or in a small group. **2.** the payment for instruction, esp. in colleges or universities. [C15: < OF *tuicion,* < L *tuitiō* a guarding, < *tuērī* to watch over] **—tuˈitional** *adj.*

tularaemia *or U.S.* **tularemia** (ˌtuːləˈriːmɪə) *n.* an infectious disease of rodents, transmitted to man by infected ticks or flies or by handling contaminated flesh. [C19/20: < NL, < *Tulare,* county in California where first observed] **—ˌtulaˈraemic** *or U.S.* **ˌtulaˈremic** *adj.*

tulip (ˈtjuːlɪp) *n.* **1.** any of various spring-blooming bulb plants having long broad pointed leaves and single showy bell-shaped flowers. **2.** the flower or bulb. [C17: < NL *tulipa,* < Turkish *tülbend* turban, which the opened bloom was thought to resemble]

tulip tree *n.* **1.** Also called: **tulip poplar.** a North American tree having tulip-shaped greenish-yellow flowers and long conelike fruits. **2.** any of various other trees with tulip-shaped flowers, such as the magnolia.

tulipwood (ˈtjuːlɪpˌwʊd) *n.* **1.** the light soft wood of the tulip tree, used in making furniture and veneer. **2.** any of several woods having streaks of colour.

tulle (tjuːl) *n.* a fine net fabric of silk, rayon, etc. [C19: < F, < *Tulle,* city in S central France, where first manufactured]

tumble (ˈtʌmbᵊl) *vb.* **1.** to fall or cause to fall, esp. awkwardly, precipitately, or violently. **2.** (*intr.;* usually foll. by *about*) to roll or twist, esp. in playing. **3.** (*intr.*) to perform leaps, somersaults, etc. **4.** to move in a heedless or hasty way. **5.** (*tr.*) to polish (gemstones) in a tumbler. **6.** (*tr.*) to disturb, rumple, or toss around. ~*n.* **7.** a tumbling. **8.** a fall or toss. **9.** an acrobatic feat, esp. a somersault. **10.** a state of confusion. **11.** a confused heap or pile. ~See also **tumble to.** [OE *tumbian*]

tumbledown (ˈtʌmbᵊlˌdaʊn) *adj.* falling to pieces; dilapidated; crumbling.

tumble dryer *n.* a machine that dries wet laundry by rotating it in warmed air inside a metal drum. Also called: **tumbler dryer, tumbler.**

tumbler (ˈtʌmblə) *n.* **1. a.** a flat-bottomed drinking glass with no handle or stem. **b.** Also called: **tumblerful.** its contents. **2.** a person who performs somersaults and other acrobatic feats. **3.** another name for **tumble dryer. 4.** a box or drum rotated so that the contents (usually gemstones) become smooth and polished. **5.** the part of a lock that retains or releases the bolt and is moved by the action of a key. **6.** a lever in a gunlock that receives the action of the mainspring when the trigger is pressed and thus forces the hammer forwards. **7.** a part that moves a gear in a train of gears into and out of engagement.

tumbler switch *n.* a small electrical switch incorporating a spring, widely used in lighting.

tumble to *vb.* (*intr., prep.*) *Inf.* to understand; become aware of: *she tumbled to his plan quickly.*

tumbleweed (ˈtʌmbᵊlˌwiːd) *n.* any of various densely branched American and Australian plants that break off near the ground on withering and are rolled about by the wind.

tumbrel *or* **tumbril** (ˈtʌmbrəl) *n.* **1.** a farm cart, esp. one that tilts backwards to deposit its load. A cart of this type was used to take condemned prisoners to the guillotine during the French Revolution. **2.** (formerly) a covered cart used to carry ammunition, tools, etc. [C14 *tumberell* ducking stool, < Med. L *tumbrellum,* < OF *tumberel* dump cart, ult. of Gmc origin]

tumefacient (ˌtjuːmɪˈfeɪʃɪənt) *adj.* producing or capable of producing swelling: *a tumefacient drug.* [C16: < L *tumefacere* to cause to swell]

tumefy (ˈtjuːmɪˌfaɪ) *vb.* **-fying, -fied.** to make or become tumid; swell or puff up. [C16: < F *tuméfier,* < L *tumefacere*] **—ˌtumeˈfaction** *n.*

tumescent (tjuːˈmɛsənt) *adj.* swollen or becoming swollen. [C19: < L *tumescere* to begin to swell, < *tumēre*] **—tuˈmescence** *n.*

tumid (ˈtjuːmɪd) *adj.* **1.** enlarged or swollen. **2.** bulging. **3.** pompous or fulsome in style. [C16: < L *tumidus,* < *tumēre* to swell] **—tuˈmidity** *or* **ˈtumidness** *n.* **—ˈtumidly** *adv.*

tummy (ˈtʌmɪ) *n., pl.* **-mies.** an informal or childish word for **stomach.** Also called: **tum.**

tumour *or U.S.* **tumor** (ˈtjuːmə) *n. Pathol.* **a.** any abnormal swelling. **b.** a mass of tissue formed by a new growth of cells. [C16: < L, < *tumēre* to swell] **—ˈtumorous** *adj.*

tumult (ˈtjuːmʌlt) *n.* **1.** a loud confused noise, as of a crowd; commotion. **2.** violent agitation or disturbance. **3.** great emotional agitation. [C15: < L *tumultus,* < *tumēre* to swell up]

tumultuous (tjuːˈmʌltjʊəs) *adj.* **1.** uproarious, riotous, or turbulent. **2.** greatly agitated, confused, or disturbed. **3.** making a loud or unruly disturbance. **—tuˈmultuously** *adv.* **—tuˈmultuousness** *n.*

tumulus (ˈtjuːmjʊləs) *n., pl.* **-li** (-liː). *Archaeol.* (*no longer in technical usage*) another word for **barrow**[2]. [C17: < L: a hillock, < *tumēre* to swell up]

tun (tʌn) *n.* **1.** a large beer cask. **2.** a measure of capacity, usually equal to 252 wine gallons. ~*vb.* **tunning, tunned. 3.** (*tr.*) to put into or keep in tuns. [OE *tunne*]

tuna[1] (ˈtjuːnə) *n., pl.* **-na** *or* **-nas.** another name for **tunny** (sense 1). [C20: < American Sp., < Sp. *atún,* < Ar. *tūn,* < L *thunnus* tunny, < Gk]

tuna[2] (ˈtjuːnə) *n.* any of various tropical American prickly pear cacti. [C16: via Sp. < Taino]

tunable *or* **tuneable** (ˈtjuːnəbᵊl) *adj.* able to be tuned.

tundra (ˈtʌndrə) *n.* a vast treeless zone lying between the ice cap and the timber line of North America and Eurasia and having a permanently frozen subsoil. [C19: < Russian, < Lapp *tundar* hill]

tune (tjuːn) *n.* **1.** a melody, esp. one for which harmony is not essential. **2.** the condition of producing accurately pitched notes, intervals, etc. (esp. in **in tune, out of tune**). **3.** accurate correspondence of pitch and intonation between instruments (esp. in **in tune, out of tune**). **4.** the correct adjustment of a radio, television, etc., with respect to the required frequency. **5.** a frame of mind; mood. **6. call the tune.** to be in control of the proceedings. **7. change one's tune.** to alter one's attitude or tone of speech. **8. to the tune of.** *Inf.* to the amount or extent of. ~*vb.* **9.** to adjust (a musical instrument) to a certain pitch. **10.** to adjust (a note, etc.) so as to bring it into harmony or concord. **11.** (*tr.*) to adapt or adjust (oneself); attune. **12.** (*tr.; often foll. by up*) to make fine adjustments to (an engine, machine, etc.) to obtain optimum performance. **13.** *Electronics.* to adjust (one or more circuits) for resonance at a desired frequency. ~See also **tune in, tune up.** [C14: var. of TONE] —ˈ**tuner** *n.*

tuneful (ˈtjuːnfʊl) *adj.* **1.** having a pleasant tune; melodious. **2.** producing a melody or music. —ˈ**tunefully** *adv.* —ˈ**tunefulness** *n.*

tune in *vb.* (*adv.; often foll. by to*) **1.** to adjust (a radio or television) to receive (a station or programme). **2.** *Sl.* to make or become more aware, knowledgeable, etc. (about).

tuneless (ˈtjuːnlɪs) *adj.* having no melody or tune. —ˈ**tunelessly** *adv.* —ˈ**tunelessness** *n.*

tune up *vb.* (*adv.*) **1.** to adjust (a musical instrument) to a particular pitch. **2.** to tune (instruments) to a common pitch. **3.** (*tr.*) to adjust (an engine) in (a car, etc.) to improve performance. ~*n.* **tune-up. 4.** adjustments made to an engine to improve its performance.

tung oil (tʌŋ) *n.* a fast-drying oil obtained from the seeds of an Asian tree, used in paints, varnishes, etc. [partial translation of Chinese *yu t'ung* tung tree oil, < *yu* oil + *t'ung* tung tree]

tungsten (ˈtʌŋstən) *n.* a hard malleable ductile greyish-white element. It is used in lamp filaments, electrical contact points, x-ray targets, and, alloyed with steel, in high-speed cutting tools. Symbol: W; atomic no.: 74; atomic wt.: 183.85. [C18: < Swedish *tung* heavy + *sten* stone]

tungsten lamp *n.* a lamp in which light is produced by a tungsten filament heated to incandescence by an electric current.

tungsten steel *n.* any of various hard steels containing tungsten and traces of carbon.

Tungusic (tʊŋˈgʊsɪk) *n.* a branch or subfamily of the Altaic family of languages, some of which are spoken in NE Asia.

tunic (ˈtjuːnɪk) *n.* **1.** any of various hip-length or knee-length garments, such as the loose sleeveless garb worn in ancient Greece or Rome, the jacket of some soldiers, or a woman's hip-length garment, worn with a skirt or trousers. **2.** a covering, lining, or enveloping membrane of an organ or part. **3.** Also called: **tunicle.** a short vestment worn by a bishop or subdeacon. [OE *tunice* (unattested except in the accusative case), < L *tunica*]

tunicate (ˈtjuːnɪkɪt, -ˌkeɪt) *n.* **1.** any of various minute primitive marine animals having a saclike unsegmented body enclosed in a cellulose-like outer covering. ~*adj. also* **tunicated. 2.** (esp. of a bulb) having concentric layers of tissue. [C18: < L *tunicātus* clad in a TUNIC]

tuning (ˈtjuːnɪŋ) *n. Music.* **1.** a set of pitches to which the open strings of a guitar, violin, etc., are tuned. **2.** the accurate pitching of notes and intervals by a choir, orchestra, etc.; intonation.

tuning fork *n.* a two-pronged metal fork that when struck produces a pure note of constant specified pitch. It is used to tune musical instruments and in acoustics.

tunnage (ˈtʌnɪdʒ) *n.* a variant spelling of **tonnage.**

tunnel (ˈtʌnᵊl) *n.* **1.** an underground passageway, esp. one for trains or cars. **2.** any passage or channel through or under something. ~*vb.* **-nelling, -nelled** *or U.S.* **-neling, -neled. 3.** (*tr.*) to make or force (a way) through or under (something). **4.** (*intr.; foll. by through, under,* etc.) to make or force a way (through or under something). [C15: < OF *tonel* cask, < *tonne* tun, < Med. L *tonna* barrel, of Celtic origin] —ˈ**tunneller** *or U.S.* ˈ**tunneler** *n.*

tunnel diode *n.* an extremely stable semiconductor diode, having a very narrow highly doped p-n junction, in which electrons travel across the junction by means of the tunnel effect. Also called: **Esaki diode.**

tunnel effect *n. Physics.* the phenomenon in which an object, usually an elementary particle, tunnels through a potential barrier even though it does not have sufficient energy to surmount it.

tunnel vision *n.* **1.** a condition in which peripheral vision is greatly restricted. **2.** narrowness of viewpoint resulting from concentration on a single idea, opinion, etc.

tunny (ˈtʌnɪ) *n., pl.* **-nies** *or* **-ny. 1.** Also called: **tuna.** any of a genus of large marine spiny-finned fishes, chiefly of warm waters. They are important food fishes. **2.** any of various similar and related fishes. [C16: < OF *thon,* < OProvençal *ton,* < L *thunnus,* < Gk]

tup (tʌp) *n.* **1.** *Chiefly Brit.* a male sheep; ram. **2.** the head of a pile-driver or steam hammer. ~*vb.* **tupping, tupped. 3.** (*tr.*) (of a ram) to mate with (a ewe). [C14: <?]

Tupamaro (ˌtuːpəˈmɑːrəʊ) *n., pl.* **-ros.** any of a group of Marxist urban guerrillas in Uruguay. [C20: after *Tupac Amaru,* 18th-century Peruvian Indian who led a rebellion against the Spaniards]

tupelo (ˈtjuːpɪˌləʊ) *n., pl.* **-los. 1.** any of several gum trees of the southern U.S. **2.** the light strong wood of any of these trees. [C18: < Creek *ito opilwa,* < *ito* tree + *opilwa* swamp]

Tupi (tuːˈpiː) *n.* **1.** (*pl.* **-pis** *or* **-pi**) a member of a South American Indian people of Brazil and Paraguay. **2.** their language. —**Tuˈpian** *adj.*

tupik (ˈtuːpək) *n. Canad.* a tent of seal or caribou skin used for shelter by the Inuit in summer. [< Eskimo]

tuppence (ˈtʌpəns) *n. Brit.* a variant spelling of **twopence.** —ˈ**tuppenny** *adj.*

tuque (tuːk) *n.* (in Canada) a knitted cap with a long tapering end. [C19: < Canad. F, < F: TOQUE]

turaco (ˈtʊərəˌkəʊ) *n., pl.* **-cos.** a variant spelling of **touraco.**

Turanian (tjʊˈreɪnɪən) *n., adj.* another name for **Ural-Altaic.**

turban (ˈtɜːbᵊn) *n.* **1.** a man's headdress, worn esp. by Muslims, Hindus, and Sikhs, made by swathing a length of linen, silk, etc., around the head or around a caplike base. **2.** a woman's brimless hat resembling this. **3.** any headdress resembling this. [C16: < Turkish *tülbend,* < Persian *dulband*] —ˈ**turbaned** *adj.*

turbary (ˈtɜːbərɪ) *n., pl.* **-ries. 1.** land where peat or turf is cut. **2.** the legal right to cut peat for fuel on a common. [C14: < OF *turbarie,* < Med. L *turbāria,* < *turba* peat]

turbellarian (ˌtɜːbɪˈlɛərɪən) *n.* **1.** any of a class of flatworms having a ciliated epidermis and a simple life cycle. ~*adj.* **2.** of or belonging to this class of flatworms. [C19: < NL *Turbellāria,* < L *turbellae* (pl.) bustle, < *turba* brawl, referring to the swirling motion created in the water]

turbid (ˈtɜːbɪd) *adj.* **1.** muddy or opaque, as a liquid clouded with a suspension of particles. **2.** dense, thick, or cloudy: *turbid fog.* **3.** in turmoil or confusion. [C17: < L *turbidus,* < *turbāre* to agitate, < *turba* crowd] —**turˈbidity** *or* ˈ**turbidness** *n.* —ˈ**turbidly** *adv.*

turbinate (ˈtɜːbɪnɪt, -ˌneɪt) *or* **turbinal** (ˈtɜːbɪnᵊl) *adj. also* **turbinated. 1.** *Anat.* of any of the scroll-shaped bones on the walls of the nasal passages. **2.** shaped like a spiral or scroll. **3.** shaped like an inverted cone. ~*n.* **4.** a turbinate bone. **5.** a turbinate shell. [C17: < L *turbō* spinning top] —ˌ**turbiˈnation** *n.*

turbine (ˈtɜːbɪn, -baɪn) *n.* any of various types of machine in which the kinetic energy of a moving fluid, as water, steam, air, etc., is converted into mechanical energy by causing a bladed rotor to rotate. [C19: < F, < L *turbō* whirlwind, < *turbāre* to throw into confusion]

turbit (ˈtɜːbɪt) *n.* a crested breed of domestic pigeon. [C17: < L *turbō* top, < the bird's shape]

turbo- *combining form.* of, relating to, or driven by a turbine: *turbofan.*

turbofan (ˌtɜːbəʊˈfæn) *n.* **1.** a type of bypass engine in which a large fan driven by a turbine forces air rearwards around the exhaust gases in order to increase the propulsive thrust. **2.** an aircraft driven by turbofans. **3.** the fan in such an engine.

turbogenerator (ˌtɜːbəʊˈdʒɛnəˌreɪtə) *n.* an electrical generator driven by a steam turbine.

turbojet (ˌtɜːbəʊˈdʒɛt) *n.* **1.** a turbojet engine. **2.** an aircraft powered by turbojet engines.

turbojet engine *n.* a gas turbine in which the exhaust gases provide the propulsive thrust to drive an aircraft.

turboprop (ˌtɜːbəʊˈprɒp) *n.* **1.** a gas turbine for driving an aircraft propeller. **2.** an aircraft powered by turboprops.

turbosupercharger (ˌtɜːbəʊˈsuːpəˌtʃɑːdʒə) *n.* a supercharging device for an internal-combustion engine, consisting of a turbine driven by the exhaust gases.

turbot (ˈtɜːbət) *n., pl.* **-bot** *or* **-bots. 1.** a European flatfish having a speckled scaleless body covered with tubercles. It is highly valued as a food fish. **2.** any of various similar or related fishes. [C13: < OF *tourbot,* < Med. L *turbō,* < L: top, < a fancied similarity in shape]

turbulence (ˈtɜːbjʊləns) *n* **1.** a state or condition of confusion, movement, or agitation. **2.** *Meteorol.* instability in the atmosphere causing gusty air currents and cumulonimbus clouds.

turbulent (ˈtɜːbjʊlənt) *adj.* **1.** being in a state of turbulence. **2.** wild or insubordinate; unruly. [C16: < L *turbulentus,* < *turba* confusion] —ˈ**turbulently** *adv.*

turd (tɜːd) *n. Taboo.* **1.** a piece of excrement. **2.** *Sl.* a contemptible person or thing. [OE *tord*]

tureen (təˈriːn) *n.* a large deep usually rounded dish with a cover, used for serving soups, stews, etc. [C18: < F *terrine* earthenware vessel, < *terrin* made of earthenware, < Vulgar L *terrīnus* (unattested), < L *terra* earth]

turf (tɜːf) *n., pl.* **turfs** *or* **turves. 1.** the surface layer of fields and pastures, consisting of earth containing a dense growth of grasses with their roots; sod. **2.** a piece cut from this layer. **3. the turf. a.** a track where horse races are run. **b.** horse racing as a sport or industry. **4.** another word for **peat.** ~*vb.* **5.** (*tr.*) to cover with pieces of turf. ~See also **turf out.** [OE]

turf accountant *n. Brit.* a formal name for a **bookmaker.**

turfman (ˈtɜːfmən) *n., pl.* **-men.** *Chiefly U.S.* a person devoted to horse racing.

turf out *vb.* (*tr., adv.*) *Brit. inf.* to throw out or dismiss; eject.

turgescent (tɜːˈdʒɛsᵊnt) *adj.* becoming or being swollen; inflated; tumid. —**turˈgescence** *n.*

turgid (ˈtɜːdʒɪd) *adj.* **1.** swollen and distended. **2.** (of language) pompous; bombastic. [C17: < L *turgidus,* < *turgēre* to swell] —**turˈgidity** *or* ˈ**turgidness** *n.* —ˈ**turgidly** *adv.*

turgor (ˈtɜːgə) *n.* the normal rigid state of a cell, caused by pressure of the cell contents against the cell wall or membrane. [C19: < LL: a swelling, < L *turgēre* to swell]

Turing machine (ˈtjʊərɪŋ) *n.* a hypothetical universal computing machine able to modify its original instructions by reading, erasing, or writing a new symbol on a moving tape that acts as its program. [C20: after Alan Mathison *Turing* (1912–54), E mathematician]

turion (ˈtʊərɪən) *n.* a scaly shoot produced by many aquatic plants: it detaches from the parent plant and remains dormant until the following spring. [C17: < F *turion,* < L *turio*]

Turk (tɜːk) *n.* **1.** a native, inhabitant, or citizen of Turkey. **2.** a native speaker of any Turkic language. **3.** a brutal or domineering person.

Turk. *abbrev. for:* **1.** Turkey. **2.** Turkish.

turkey (ˈtɜːkɪ) *n., pl.* **-keys** *or* **-key. 1.** a large bird of North America, having a bare wattled head and neck and a brownish plumage. The male has a fan-shaped tail. A domesticated variety is bred for its flesh. **2.** *U.S. & Canad. inf.* something, esp. a theatrical production, that fails. **3.** See **cold turkey. 4. talk turkey.** *Inf., chiefly U.S. and Canad.* to discuss frankly and practically. [C16: shortened < *Turkey cock* (*hen*), used at first to designate the African guinea fowl (apparently because the bird was brought through Turkish territory), later applied by mistake to the American bird]

turkey buzzard *or* **vulture** *n.* a New World vulture having a naked red head.

turkey cock *n.* **1.** a male turkey. **2.** an arrogant person.

Turkey red *n.* **1. a.** a moderate or bright red colour. **b.** (*as adj.*)*: a Turkey-red fabric.* **2.** a cotton fabric of a bright red colour.

Turki (ˈtɜːkɪ) *adj.* **1.** of or relating to the Turkic languages. **2.** of or relating to speakers of these languages. ~*n.* **3.** these languages collectively.

Turkic (ˈtɜːkɪk) *n.* a branch of the Altaic family of languages, including Turkish, Tatar, etc., members of which are found from Turkey to NE China, esp. in Soviet central Asia.

Turkish (ˈtɜːkɪʃ) *adj.* **1.** of Turkey, its people, or their language. ~*n.* **2.** the official language of Turkey, belonging to the Turkic branch of the Altaic family.

Turkish bath *n.* **1.** a type of bath in which the bather sweats freely in a steam room, is then washed, often massaged, and has a cold plunge or shower. **2.** (*sometimes pl.*) an establishment where such a bath is obtainable.

Turkish coffee *n.* very strong black coffee.

Turkish delight *n.* a jelly-like sweet flavoured with flower essences, usually cut into cubes and covered in icing sugar.

Turkish towel *n.* a rough loose-piled towel.

Turk's-cap lily *n.* any of several cultivated lilies that have brightly coloured flowers with reflexed petals.

Turk's-head *n.* an ornamental turban-like knot.

turmeric (ˈtɜːmərɪk) *n.* **1.** a tropical Asian plant, *Curcuma longa,* having yellow flowers and an aromatic underground stem. **2.** the powdered stem of this plant, used as a condiment and as a yellow dye. [C16: < OF *terre merite,* < Med. L *terra merita,* lit.: meritorious earth, name applied for obscure reasons to curcuma]

turmeric paper *n. Chem.* paper impregnated with turmeric used as a test for alkalis and for boric acid.

turmoil (ˈtɜːmɔɪl) *n.* violent or confused movement; agitation; tumult. [C16: ? < TURN + MOIL]

turn (tɜːn) *vb.* **1.** to move around an axis: *to turn a knob.* **2.** (sometimes foll. by *round*) to change or cause to change positions by moving through an arc of a circle: *he turned the chair to face the light.* **3.** to change or cause to change in course, direction, etc. **4.** to go or pass to the other side of (a corner, etc.). **5.** to assume or cause to assume a rounded, curved, or folded form: *the road turns here.* **6.** to reverse or cause to reverse position. **7.** (*tr.*) to perform or do by a rotating movement: *to turn a somersault.* **8.** (*tr.*) to shape or cut a thread in (a workpiece) by rotating it on a lathe against a cutting tool. **9.** (when *intr.,* foll. by *into* or *to*) to change or convert or be changed or converted. **10.** (foll. by *into*) to change or cause to change in nature, character, etc.: *the frog turned into a prince.* **11.** (*copula*) to change so as to become: *he turned nasty.* **12.** to cause (foliage, etc.) to change colour or (of foliage, etc.) to change colour. **13.** to cause (milk, etc.) to become rancid or sour or (of milk, etc.) to become rancid or sour. **14.** to change or cause to change in subject, trend, etc.: *the conversation turned to fishing.* **15.** to direct or apply or be directed or applied: *he turned his attention to the problem.* **16.** (*intr.;* usually foll. by *to*) to appeal or apply (to) for help, advice, etc. **17.** to reach, pass, or progress beyond in age, time, etc.: *she has just turned twenty.* **18.** (*tr.*) to cause or allow to go: *to turn an animal loose.* **19.** to affect or be affected with nausea. **20.** to affect or be affected with giddiness: *my head is turning.* **21.** (*tr.*) to affect the mental or emotional stability of (esp. in **turn (someone's) head**). **22.** (*tr.*) to release from a container. **23.** (*tr.*) to render into another language. **24.** (usually foll. by *against* or *from*) to transfer or reverse (one's loyalties, affections, etc.). **25.** (*tr.*) to cause (an enemy agent) to become a double agent working for one's own side. **26.** (*tr.*) to bring (soil) from lower layers to the surface. **27.** to blunt (an edge) or (of an edge) to become blunted. **28.** (*tr.*) to give a graceful form to: *to turn a compliment.* **29.** (*tr.*) to reverse (a cuff, collar, etc.). **30.** (*intr.*) *U.S.* to be merchandised as specified: *shirts are turning well this week.* **31.** *Cricket.* to spin (the ball) or (of the ball) to spin. **32. turn a trick.** *Sl.* (of a prostitute) to gain a customer. **33. turn one's hand to.** to undertake (something practical). ~*n.* **34.** a turning or being turned. **35.** a movement of complete or partial rotation. **36.** a change of direction or position. **37.** direction or drift: *his thoughts took a new turn.* **38.** a deviation from a course or tendency. **39.** the place, point, or time at which a deviation or change occurs. **40.** another word for **turning** (sense 1). **41.** the right or opportunity to do something in an agreed order or succession: *now it's George's turn.* **42.** a change in nature, condition, etc.: *his illness took a turn for the worse.* **43.** a period of action, work, etc. **44.** a short walk, ride, or excursion. **45.** natural inclination: *a speculative turn of mind.* **46.** distinctive form or style: *a neat turn of phrase.* **47.** requirement, need, or advantage: *to serve someone's turn.* **48.** a deed that helps or hinders someone. **49.** a twist, bend, or distortion in shape. **50.** *Music.* a melodic ornament that makes a turn around a note, beginning with the note above, in a variety of sequences. **51.** a short theatrical act. **52.** *Stock Exchange, Brit.* the difference between a market maker's bid and offer prices, representing the market maker's income. **53.** *Inf.* a shock or surprise. **54. by turns.** one after another; alternately. **55. turn and turn about.** one after another; alternately. **56. to a turn.** to the proper amount; perfectly. ~See also **turn down, turn in,** etc. [OE *tyrnian,* < OF *torner,* < L *tornāre* to turn in a lathe, < *tornus* lathe, < Gk *tornos* dividers] —ˈ**turner** *n.*

turnabout (ˈtɜːnəˌbaʊt) *n.* **1.** the act of turning so as to face a different direction. **2.** a change or reversal of opinion, attitude, etc.

turnaround (ˈtɜːnəˌraʊnd) *n.* another word (esp. U.S. and Canad.) for **turnround.**

turnbuckle (ˈtɜːnˌbʌkᵊl) *n.* an open mechanical sleeve usually having a swivel at one end and a thread at the other to enable a threaded wire or rope to be tightened.

turncoat (ˈtɜːnˌkəʊt) *n.* a person who deserts one cause or party for the opposite faction.

turncock (ˈtɜːnˌkɒk) *n.* an official employed to turn on the water for the mains supply.

turn down *vb.* (*tr., adv.*) **1.** to reduce (the volume or brightness) of (something). **2.** to reject or refuse. **3.** to fold down (a collar, sheets, etc.). ~*adj.* **turndown. 4.** (*prenominal*) designed to be folded down.

turn in *vb.* (*adv.*) *Inf.* **1.** (*intr.*) to go to bed for the night. **2.** (*tr.*) to hand in; deliver. **3.** to give up or conclude (something). **4.** (*tr.*) to record (a score, etc.). **5. turn in on oneself.** to become preoccupied with one's own problems.

turning (ˈtɜːnɪŋ) *n.* **1.** a road, river, or path that turns off the main way. **2.** the point where such a way turns off. **3.** a bend in a straight course. **4.** an object made on a lathe. **5.** the process or skill of turning objects on a lathe. **6.** (*pl.*) the waste produced in turning on a lathe.

turning circle *n.* the smallest circle in which a vehicle can turn.

turning point *n.* **1.** a moment when the course of events is changed. **2.** a point at which there is a change in direction or motion.

turnip (ˈtɜːnɪp) *n.* **1.** a widely cultivated plant of the cabbage family with a large yellow or white edible root. **2.** the root of this plant, which is eaten as a vegetable. [C16: < earlier *turnepe,* ? < turn (indicating its rounded shape) + *nepe,* < L *nāpus* turnip]

turnkey (ˈtɜːnˌkiː) *n.* **1.** *Arch.* a keeper of the keys, esp. in a prison; warder or jailer. ~*adj.* **2.** denoting a project, as in civil engineering, in which a single contractor has responsibility for the complete job from the start to the time of installation or occupancy.

turn off *vb.* **1.** (*intr.*) to leave (a road, etc.). **2.** (*intr.*) (of a road, etc.) to deviate from (another road, etc.). **3.** (*tr., adv.*) to cause (something) to cease operating by turning a knob, pushing a button, etc. **4.** (*tr.*) *Inf.* to cause (a person, etc.) to feel dislike or distaste for (something): *this music turns me off.* **5.** (*tr., adv.*) *Brit. inf.* to dismiss from employment. ~*n.* **turn-off. 6.** a road or other way branching off from the main thoroughfare. **7.** *Inf.* a person or thing that elicits dislike or distaste.

turn on *vb.* **1.** (*tr., adv.*) to cause (something) to operate by turning a knob, etc. **2.** (*intr., prep.*) to depend or hinge on: *the success of the party turns on you.* **3.** (*prep.*) to become hostile or to retaliate: *the dog turned on the children.* **4.** (*tr., adv.*) *Inf.* to produce (charm, tears, etc.) suddenly or automatically. **5.** (*tr., adv.*) *Sl.* to arouse emotionally or sexually. **6.** (*intr., adv.*) *Sl.* to take or become intoxicated by drugs. **7.** (*tr., adv.*) *Sl.* to introduce (someone) to drugs. ~*n.* **turn-on. 8.** *Sl.* a person or thing that causes emotional or sexual arousal.

turn out *vb.* (*adv.*) **1.** (*tr.*) to cause (something, esp. a light) to cease operating by or as if by turning a knob, etc. **2.** (*tr.*) to produce by an effort or process. **3.** (*tr.*) to dismiss, discharge, or expel. **4.** (*tr.*) to empty the contents of, esp. in order to clean, tidy, or rearrange. **5.** (*copula*) to prove to be as specified. **6.** to end up; result: *it all turned out well.* **7.** (*tr.*) to fit as with clothes: *that woman turns her children out well.* **8.** (*intr.*) to assemble or gather. **9.** (of a soldier) to parade or to call (a soldier) to parade. **10.** (*intr.*) *Inf.* to get out of bed. ~*n.* **turnout. 11.** the body of people appearing together at a gathering. **12.** the quantity or amount produced. **13.** an array of clothing or equipment.

turn over *vb.* (*adv.*) **1.** to change or cause to change position, esp. so as to reverse top and bottom. **2.** to start (an engine), esp. with a starting handle, or (of an engine) to start or function correctly. **3.** to shift or cause to shift position, as by rolling from side to side. **4.** (*tr.*) to deliver; transfer. **5.** (*tr.*) to consider carefully. **6.** (*tr.*) **a.** to sell and replenish (stock in trade). **b.** to transact business and so generate gross revenue of (a specified sum). **7.** (*tr.*) to invest and recover (capital). **8.** (*tr.*) *Sl.* to rob. ~*n.* **turnover. 9. a.** the amount of business transacted during a specified period. **b.** the rate at which stock in trade is sold and replenished. **10.** a change or reversal of position. **11.** a small pastry case filled with fruit, jam, etc. **12. a.** the number of workers employed by a firm in a given period to replace those who have left. **b.** the ratio between this number and the average number of employees during the same period. **13.** *Banking.* the amount of capital funds loaned on call during a specified period. ~*adj.* **turnover. 14.** (*prenominal*) designed to be turned over.

turnpike (ˈtɜːnˌpaɪk) *n.* **1.** *History.* **a.** a barrier set across a road to prevent passage until a toll had been paid. **b.** a road on which a turnpike was operated. **2.** an obsolete word for **turnstile. 3.**

U.S. a motorway for use of which a toll is charged. [C15: < TURN + PIKE[2]]

turnround (ˈtɜːnˌraʊnd) *n.* **1. a.** the act or process in which a ship, aircraft, etc., unloads at the end of a trip and reloads for the next trip. **b.** the time taken for this. **2.** the total time taken by a vehicle in a round trip. **3.** a complete reversal of a situation.

turnspit (ˈtɜːnˌspɪt) *n.* **1.** (formerly) a servant or small dog whose job was to turn a spit. **2.** a spit that can be so turned.

turnstile (ˈtɜːnˌstaɪl) *n.* a mechanical barrier with metal arms that are turned to admit one person at a time.

turnstone (ˈtɜːnˌstəʊn) *n.* a shore bird, related to the plovers and sandpipers, that lifts up stones in search of food.

turntable (ˈtɜːnˌteɪbᵊl) *n.* **1.** the circular platform that rotates a gramophone record while it is being played. **2.** a circular platform used for turning locomotives and cars. **3.** the revolvable platform on a microscope on which specimens are examined.

turntable ladder *n. Brit.* a power-operated extending ladder mounted on a fire engine. U.S. and Canad. name: **aerial ladder.**

turn to *vb.* (*intr., adv.*) to set about a task.

turn up *vb.* (*adv.*) **1.** (*intr.*) to arrive or appear. **2.** to find or be found, esp. by accident. **3.** (*tr.*) to increase the flow, volume, etc., of. ~*n.* **turn-up. 4.** (*often pl.*) *Brit.* the turned-up fold at the bottom of some trouser legs. U.S. and Canad. name: **cuff. 5.** *Inf.* an unexpected or chance occurrence.

turpentine (ˈtɜːpᵊnˌtaɪn) *n.* **1.** Also called: **gum turpentine.** any of various oleoresins obtained from various coniferous trees and used as the main source of commercial turpentine. **2.** a sticky oleoresin that exudes from the terebinth tree. **3.** Also called: **oil of turpentine, spirits of turpentine.** a colourless volatile oil distilled from turpentine oleoresin. It is used as a solvent for paints and in medicine. **4.** Also called: **turpentine substitute, white spirit.** (*not in technical usage*) any one of a number of thinners for paints and varnishes, consisting of fractions of petroleum. Related adj.: **terebinthine.** ~*vb.* (*tr.*) **5.** to treat or saturate with turpentine. [C14 *terebentyne,* < Med. L, < L *terebinthīna* turpentine, < *terebinthus* the turpentine tree]

turpentine tree *n.* **1.** a tropical African tree yielding a hard dark wood and a useful resin. **2.** either of two Australian evergreen trees that yield resin.

turpeth (ˈtɜːpɪθ) *n.* **1.** an East Indian plant having roots with purgative properties. **2.** the root of this plant or the drug obtained from it. [C14: < Med. L *turbithum,* ult. < Ar. *turbid*]

turpitude (ˈtɜːpɪˌtjuːd) *n.* base character or action; depravity. [C15: < L *turpitūdō* ugliness, < *turpis* base]

turps (tɜːps) *n.* (*functioning as sing.*) *Brit.* short for **turpentine** (sense 3).

turquoise (ˈtɜːkwɔɪz, -kwɑːz) *n.* **1.** a greenish-blue fine-grained mineral consisting of hydrated copper aluminium phosphate. It is used as a gemstone. **2. a.** the colour of turquoise. **b.** (*as adj.*): *a turquoise dress.* [C14: < OF *turqueise* Turkish (stone)]

turret (ˈtʌrɪt) *n.* **1.** a small tower that projects from the wall of a building, esp. a castle. **2. a.** a self-contained structure, capable of rotation, in which weapons are mounted, esp. in tanks and warships. **b.** a similar structure on an aircraft. **3.** (on a machine tool) a turret-like steel structure with tools projecting radially that can be indexed round to bring each tool to bear on the work. [C14: < OF *torete,* < *tor* tower, < L *turris*] —ˈ**turreted** *adj.*

turret lathe *n.* another name for **capstan lathe.**

turtle[1] (ˈtɜːtᵊl) *n.* **1.** any of various aquatic reptiles, esp. those having a flattened shell enclosing the body and flipper-like limbs adapted for swimming. **2. turn turtle.** to capsize. [C17: < F *tortue* TORTOISE (infl. by TURTLE[2])]

turtle[2] (ˈtɜːtᵊl) *n.* an archaic name for **turtledove.** [OE *turtla,* < L *turtur,* imit.]

turtleback (ˈtɜːtᵊlˌbæk) *n.* an arched projection over the upper deck of a ship for protection in heavy seas.

turtledove (ˈtɜːtᵊlˌdʌv) *n.* **1.** any of several Old World doves having a brown plumage with speckled wings and a long dark tail. **2.** a gentle or loving person. [see TURTLE[2]]

turtleneck (ˈtɜːtᵊlˌnɛk) *n.* a round high close-fitting neck on a sweater or the sweater itself.

turves (tɜːvz) *n.* a plural of **turf.**

Tuscan (ˈtʌskən) *adj.* **1.** of or relating to Tuscany, a region of central Italy, its inhabitants, or their dialect of Italian. **2.** of or denoting one of the five classical orders of architecture: characterized by a column with an unfluted shaft and a capital and base with mouldings but no decoration. ~*n.* **3.** a native or inhabitant of Tuscany. **4.** any of the dialects of Italian spoken in Tuscany.

tusche (tʊʃ) *n.* a substance used in lithography for drawing the design and as a resist in silk-screen printing and lithography. [< G, < *tuschen* to touch up with colour, < F *toucher* to touch]

tush (tʌʃ) *interj. Arch.* an exclamation of disapproval or contempt. [C15: imit.]

tusk (tʌsk) *n.* **1.** a pointed elongated usually paired tooth in the elephant, walrus, and certain other mammals. **2.** a tusklike tooth or part. **3.** a sharp pointed projection. ~*vb.* **4.** to stab, tear, or gore with the tusks. [OE *tūsc*] —**tusked** *adj.*

tusker (ˈtʌskə) *n.* any animal with long tusks.

tusk shell *n.* any of various burrowing seashore molluscs that have a long narrow tubular shell open at both ends.

tussis (ˈtʌsɪs) *n.* the technical name for a **cough.** See **pertussis.** [L: cough] —ˈ**tussive** *adj.*

tussle (ˈtʌsᵊl) *vb.* **1.** (*intr.*) to fight or wrestle in a vigorous way. ~*n.* **2.** a vigorous fight; scuffle; struggle. [C15]

tussock (ˈtʌsək) *n.* **1.** a dense tuft of vegetation, esp. of grass. **2.** *Austral. & N.Z.* **a.** short for **tussock grass** (sense 1). **b. the.** country where tussock grass grows. [C16: <?] —ˈ**tussocky** *adj.*

tussock grass *n. Austral. & N.Z.* **1.** any of several pasture grasses. **2.** a tough grass that is unpalatable to stock.

tussore (tʊˈsɔː, ˈtʌsə), **tusser** (ˈtʌsə), *or* (*Chiefly U.S.*) **tussah** (ˈtʌsə) *n.* **1.** Also called: **wild silk.** a coarse silk obtained from an oriental silkworm. **2.** the silkworm producing this. [C17: < Hindi *tasar* shuttle, < Sansk. *tasara* a wild silkworm]

tut (tʌt) *interj., n., vb.* **tutting, tutted.** short for **tut-tut.**

tutelage (ˈtjuːtɪlɪdʒ) *n.* **1.** the act or office of a guardian or tutor. **2.** instruction or guidance, esp. by a tutor. **3.** the condition of being under the supervision of a guardian or tutor. [C17: < L *tūtēla* a caring for, < *tuērī* to watch over]

tutelary (ˈtjuːtɪlərɪ) *or* **tutelar** (ˈtjuːtɪlə) *adj.* **1.** invested with the role of guardian or protector. **2.** of or relating to a guardian. ~*n., pl.* **-laries** *or* **-lars. 3.** a tutelary person, deity, etc.

tutor (ˈtjuːtə) *n.* **1.** a teacher, usually instructing individual pupils. **2.** (at universities, colleges, etc.) a member of staff responsible for the teaching and supervision of a certain number of students. ~*vb.* **3.** to act as a tutor to (someone). **4.** (*tr.*) to act as guardian to. [C14: < L: a watcher, < *tuērī* to watch over] —ˈ**tutorage** *or* ˈ**tutorship** *n.*

tutorial (tjuːˈtɔːrɪəl) *n.* **1.** a period of intensive tuition given by a tutor to an individual student or to a small group of students. ~*adj.* **2.** of or relating to a tutor.

tutsan (ˈtʌtsən) *n.* a woodland shrub of Europe and W Asia, having yellow flowers and reddish-purple fruits. [C15: < OF *toute-saine* (unattested), lit.: all healthy]

tutti (ˈtʊtɪ) *adj., adv. Music.* to be performed by the whole orchestra, choir, etc. [C18: < It., pl. of *tutto* all, < L *tōtus*]

tutti-frutti (ˈtuːtɪˈfruːtɪ) *n.* **1.** (*pl.* **-fruttis**) an ice cream or a confection containing small pieces of candied or fresh fruits. **2.** a preserve of chopped mixed fruits. **3.** a flavour like that of many fruits combined. [< It., lit.: all the fruits]

tut-tut (ˈtʌtˈtʌt) *interj.* **1.** an exclamation of mild reprimand, disapproval, or surprise. ~*vb.* **-tutting, -tutted. 2.** (*intr.*) to express disapproval by the exclamation of "tut-tut". ~*n.* **3.** the act of tut-tutting.

tutty (ˈtʌtɪ) *n.* impure zinc oxide used as a polishing powder. [C14: < OF *tutie*, < Ar. *tūtiyā*, prob. < Persian, < Sansk. *tuttha*]

tutu (ˈtuːtuː) *n.* a very short skirt worn by ballerinas, made of projecting layers of stiffened material. [< F, changed < the nursery word *cucu* backside, < L *cūlus* the buttocks]

tu-whit tu-whoo (təˈwɪt təˈwuː) *interj.* an imitation of the sound made by an owl.

tuxedo (tʌkˈsiːdəʊ) *n., pl.* **-dos.** the usual U.S. and Canad. name for **dinner jacket.** [C19: after a country club in *Tuxedo Park*, New York]

tuyère (ˈtwiːɛə, ˈtwaɪə) *or* **twyer** (ˈtwaɪə) *n.* a water-cooled nozzle through which air is blown into a cupola, blast furnace, or forge. [C18: < F, < *tuyau* pipe, < OF *tuel*, prob. of Gmc origin]

TV *abbrev. for* television.

TVP *abbrev. for* textured vegetable protein: protein from soya beans or other vegetables spun into fibres and flavoured: used esp. as a substitute for meat.

twaddle (ˈtwɒdᵊl) *n.* **1.** silly, trivial, or pretentious talk or writing. ~*vb.* **2.** (*intr.*) to talk or write in a silly or pretentious way. [C16 *twattle*, var. of *twittle* or *tittle*] —**ˈtwaddler** *n.*

twain (tweɪn) *determiner, n.* an archaic word for **two.** [OE *twēgen*]

twang (twæŋ) *n.* **1.** a sharp ringing sound produced by or as if by the plucking of a taut string. **2.** the act of plucking a string to produce such a sound. **3.** a strongly nasal quality in a person's speech. ~*vb.* **4.** to make or cause to make a twang. **5.** to strum (music, a tune, etc.). **6.** to speak with a nasal voice. **7.** (*intr.*) to be released or move with a twang: *the arrow twanged away.* [C16: imit.] —**ˈtwangy** *adj.*

'twas (twɒz; *unstressed* twəz) *Poetic or dialect. contraction of* it was.

twat (twæt, twɒt) *n. Taboo sl.* **1.** the female genitals. **2.** a foolish person. [<?]

twayblade (ˈtweɪˌbleɪd) *n.* any of various orchids having a basal pair of unstalked leaves arranged opposite each other. [C16: translation of Med. L *bifolium* having two leaves, < obs. *tway* two + BLADE]

tweak (twiːk) *vb.* **1.** (*tr.*) to twist or pinch with a sharp or sudden movement. ~*n.* **2.** a tweaking. [OE *twiccian*]

twee (twiː) *adj. Brit. inf.* excessively sentimental, sweet, or pretty. [C19: < *tweet*, mincing or affected pronunciation of *sweet*]

tweed (twiːd) *n.* **1.** a thick woollen cloth produced originally in Scotland. **2.** (*pl.*) clothes made of this. [C19: prob. < *tweel*, Scot. var. of TWILL, infl. by *Tweed*, a Scot. river]

Tweedledum and Tweedledee (ˌtwiːdᵊlˈdʌm; ˌtwiːdᵊlˈdiː) *n.* any two persons or things that differ only slightly from each other; two of a kind. [C19: < the proverbial names of two musicians who were rivals]

tweedy (ˈtwiːdɪ) *adj.* **tweedier, tweediest. 1.** of, made of, or resembling tweed. **2.** showing a fondness for a hearty outdoor life, usually associated with wearers of tweeds.

'tween (twiːn) *Poetic or dialect. contraction of* between.

'tween deck *or* **decks** *n. Naut.* a space between two continuous decks of a vessel.

tweet (twiːt) *interj.* **1.** an imitation of the thin chirping sound made by small birds. ~*vb.* **2.** (*intr.*) to make this sound. [C19: imit.]

tweeter (ˈtwiːtə) *n.* a loudspeaker used in high-fidelity systems for the reproduction of high audio frequencies. It is usually employed in conjunction with a woofer. [C20: < TWEET]

tweezers (ˈtwiːzəz) *pl. n.* a small pincer-like instrument for handling small objects, plucking out hairs, etc. Also called: **pair of tweezers, tweezer** (esp. U.S.). [C17: pl. of *tweezer* (on the model of *scissors*, etc.), < *tweeze* case of instruments, < F *étuis*, < OF *estuier* to preserve, ult. < L *studēre* to care about]

Twelfth Day *n.* Jan. 6, the twelfth day after Christmas and the feast of the Epiphany.

twelfth man *n.* a reserve player in a cricket team.

Twelfth Night *n.* **a.** the evening of Jan. 5, the eve of Twelfth Day. **b.** the evening of Twelfth Day itself.

twelve (twɛlv) *n.* **1.** the cardinal number that is the sum of ten and two. **2.** a numeral, 12, XII, etc., representing this number. **3.** something representing or consisting of 12 units. **4.** Also called: **twelve o'clock.** noon or midnight. ~*determiner.* **5. a.** amounting to twelve. **b.** (*as pronoun*): *twelve have arrived.* ~Related adj.: **duodecimal.** [OE *twelf*] —**twelfth** *adj., n.*

twelvemo (ˈtwɛlvməʊ) *n., pl.* **-mos.** *Bookbinding.* another word for **duodecimo.**

twelvemonth (ˈtwɛlvˌmʌnθ) *n. Chiefly Brit.* an archaic or dialect word for a **year.**

twelve-tone *adj.* of or denoting the type of serial music which uses as musical material a tone row formed by the 12 semitones of the chromatic scale. See **serialism.**

twenty (ˈtwɛntɪ) *n., pl.* **-ties. 1.** the cardinal number that is the product of ten and two. **2.** a numeral, 20, XX, etc., representing this number. **3.** something representing or consisting of 20 units. ~*determiner.* **4. a.** amounting to twenty: *twenty questions.* **b.** (*as pronoun*): *to order twenty.* —**ˈtwentieth** *adj., n.* [OE *twēntig*]

twenty-twenty *adj. Med.* (of vision) being of normal acuity: usually written 20/20.

'twere (twɜː; *unstressed* twə) *Poetic or dialect. contraction of* it were.

twerp *or* **twirp** (twɜːp) *n. Inf.* a silly, weak-minded, or contemptible person. [C20: <?]

twibill *or* **twibil** (ˈtwaɪˌbɪl) *n.* **1.** a mattock with a blade shaped like an adze at one end and like an axe at the other. **2.** *Arch.* a double-bladed battle-axe. [OE, < *twi-* double + *bill* sword]

twice (twaɪs) *adv.* **1.** two times; on two occasions or in two cases. **2.** double in degree or quantity: *twice as long.* [OE *twiwa*]

twiddle (ˈtwɪdᵊl) *vb.* **1.** (when *intr.*, often foll. by *with*) to twirl or fiddle (with), often in an idle way. **2. twiddle one's thumbs.** to do nothing; be unoccupied. **3.** (*intr.*) to turn, twirl, or rotate. **4.** (*intr.*) *Rare.* to be occupied with trifles. ~*n.* **5.** an act or instance of twiddling. [C16: prob. a blend of TWIRL + FIDDLE] —**ˈtwiddler** *n.*

twig[1] (twɪg) *n.* **1.** any small branch or shoot of a tree. **2.** something resembling this, esp. a minute branch of a blood vessel. [OE *twigge*] —**ˈtwiggy** *adj.*

twig[2] (twɪg) *vb.* **twigging, twigged.** *Brit. inf.* **1.** to understand (something). **2.** to find out or suddenly comprehend (something): *he hasn't twigged yet.* [C18: ? < Scot. Gaelic *tuig* I understand]

twilight (ˈtwaɪˌlaɪt) *n.* **1.** the soft diffused light occurring when the sun is just below the horizon, esp. following sunset. **2.** the period in which this light occurs. **3.** any faint light. **4.** a period in which strength, importance, etc., are waning. **5.** (*modifier*) of or relating to twilight; dim. [C15: lit.: half light (between day and night), < OE *twi-* half + LIGHT[1]] —**twilit** (ˈtwaɪˌlɪt) *adj.*

Twilight of the Gods *n.* another term for **Götterdämmerung.**

twilight sleep *n. Med.* a state of partial anaesthesia in which the patient retains a slight degree of consciousness.

twilight zone *n.* **1.** an inner-city area where houses have become dilapidated. **2.** any indefinite or transitional condition or area.

twill (twɪl) *adj.* **1.** (in textiles) of a weave in which the yarns are worked to produce an effect of parallel diagonal lines or ribs. ~*n.* **2.** any fabric so woven. ~*vb.* **3.** (*tr.*) to weave in this fashion. [OE *twilic* having a double thread]

'twill (twɪl) *Poetic or dialect. contraction of* it will.

twin (twɪn) *n.* **1. a.** either of two persons or animals conceived at the same time. **b.** (*as modifier*): *a twin brother.* See also **identical** (sense 3), **fraternal** (sense 3). **2. a.** either of two persons or things that are identical or very similar. **b.** (*as modifier*): *twin carburettors.* **3.** Also called: **macle.** a crystal consisting of two parts each of which has a definite orientation to the other. ~*vb.* **twinning, twinned. 4.** to pair or be paired together; couple. **5.** (*intr.*) to bear twins. **6.** (*intr.*) (of a crystal) to form into a twin. [OE *twinn*]

twin bed *n.* one of a pair of matching single beds.

twine (twaɪn) *n.* **1.** string made by twisting together fibres of hemp, cotton, etc. **2.** a twining. **3.** something produced or characterized by twining. **4.** a twist, coil, or convolution. **5.** a knot or tangle. ~*vb.* **6.** (*tr.*) to twist together; interweave. **7.** (*tr.*) to form by or as if by twining. **8.** (when *intr.*, often foll. by *around*) to wind or cause to wind, esp. in spirals. [OE *twīn*] —**'twiner** *n.*

twin-engined *adj.* (of an aeroplane) having two engines.

twinge (twɪndʒ) *n.* **1.** a sudden brief darting or stabbing pain. **2.** a sharp emotional pang. ~*vb.* **3.** to have or cause to have a twinge. [OE *twengan* to pinch]

twinkle (ˈtwɪŋkᵊl) *vb.* (*mainly intr.*) **1.** to emit or reflect light in a flickering manner; shine brightly and intermittently; sparkle. **2.** (of the eyes) to sparkle, esp. with amusement or delight. **3.** *Rare.* to move about quickly. ~*n.* **4.** a flickering brightness; sparkle. **5.** an instant. [OE *twinclian*] —**'twinkler** *n.*

twinkling (ˈtwɪŋklɪŋ) *or* **twink** (twɪŋk) *n.* a very short time; instant; moment. Also called: **twinkling of an eye.**

Twins (twɪnz) *pl. n.* **the.** the constellation Gemini, the third sign of the zodiac.

twin-screw *adj.* (of a vessel) having two propellers.

twinset (ˈtwɪnˌsɛt) *n. Brit.* a matching jumper and cardigan.

twin town *n. Brit.* a town that has civic associations, such as reciprocal visits and cultural exchanges, with a foreign town.

twin-tub *n.* a type of washing machine that has two revolving drums, one for washing and the other for spin-drying.

twirl (twɜːl) *vb.* **1.** to move around rapidly and repeatedly in a circle. **2.** (*tr.*) to twist, wind, or twiddle, often idly: *she twirled her hair around her finger.* **3.** (*intr.*; often foll. by *around* or *about*) to turn suddenly to face another way. ~*n.* **4.** a rotating or being rotated; whirl or twist. **5.** something wound around or twirled; coil. **6.** a written flourish. [C16: ? a blend of TWIST + WHIRL] —**'twirler** *n.*

twirp (twɜːp) *n.* a variant spelling of **twerp.**

twist (twɪst) *vb.* **1.** to cause (one end or part) to turn or (of one end or part) to turn in the opposite direction from another; coil or spin. **2.** to distort or be distorted. **3.** to wind or twine. **4.** to force or be forced out of the natural form or position. **5.** to change for the worse in character, meaning, etc.; pervert: *she twisted the statement.* **6.** to revolve; rotate. **7.** (*tr.*) to wrench with a turning action. **8.** (*intr.*) to follow a winding course. **9.** (*intr.*) to squirm, as with pain. **10.** (*intr.*) to dance the twist. **11.** (*tr.*) *Brit. inf.* to cheat; swindle. **12. twist someone's arm.** to persuade or coerce someone. ~*n.* **13.** a twisting. **14.** something formed by or as if by twisting. **15.** a decisive change of direction, aim, meaning, or character. **16.** (in a novel, play, etc.) an unexpected event, revelation, etc. **17.** a bend: *a twist in the road.* **18.** a distortion of the original shape or form. **19.** a jerky pull, wrench, or turn. **20.** a strange personal characteristic, esp. a bad one. **21.** a confused tangle made by twisting. **22.** a twisted thread used in sewing where extra strength is needed. **23. the twist.** a dance popular in the 1960s, in which dancers vigorously twist the hips. **24.** a loaf or roll made of pieces of twisted dough. **25.** a thin sliver of peel from a lemon, lime, etc., twisted and added to a drink. **26. a.** a cigar made by twisting three cigars around one another. **b.** chewing tobacco made in the form of a roll by twisting the leaves together. **27.** *Physics.* torsional deformation or shear stress or strain. **28.** *Sport, chiefly U.S. & Canad.* spin given to a ball in various games. **29. round the twist.** *Brit. sl.* mad; eccentric. [OE]

twist drill *n.* a drill bit having two helical grooves running from the point along the shank to clear swarf and cuttings.

twister (ˈtwɪstə) *n.* **1.** *Brit.* a swindling or dishonest person. **2.** a person or thing that twists. **3.** *U.S. & Canad.* an informal name for **tornado. 4.** a ball moving with a twisting motion.

twist grip *n.* a handlebar control in the form of a ratchet-controlled rotating grip.

twit[1] (twɪt) *vb.* **twitting, twitted. 1.** (*tr.*) to tease, taunt, or reproach, often in jest. ~*n.* **2.** *U.S. & Canad. inf.* a nervous or excitable state. **3.** *Rare.* a reproach; taunt. [OE *ætwītan*, < *æt* against + *wītan* to accuse]

twit[2] (twɪt) *n. Inf., chiefly Brit.* a foolish or stupid person; idiot. [C19: < TWIT[1] (orig. in the sense: a person given to twitting)]

twitch (twɪtʃ) *vb.* **1.** to move in a jerky spasmodic way. **2.** (*tr.*) to pull (something) with a quick jerky movement. **3.** (*intr.*) to hurt with a sharp spasmodic pain. ~*n.* **4.** a sharp jerking movement. **5.** a mental or physical twinge. **6.** a sudden muscular spasm, esp. one caused by a nervous condition. **7.** a loop of cord used to control a horse by drawing it tight about its upper lip. [OE *twiccian* to pluck]

twitcher (ˈtwɪtʃə) *n.* **1.** a person or thing that twitches. **2.** *Inf.* a bird-watcher who tries to spot as many rare varieties as possible.

twitch grass *n.* another name for **couch grass.** Sometimes shortened to **twitch.** [C16: var. of QUITCH GRASS]

twite (twaɪt) *n.* a N European finch with a brown streaked plumage. [C16: imit. of its cry]

twitter (ˈtwɪtə) *vb.* **1.** (*intr.*) (esp. of a bird) to utter a succession of chirping sounds. **2.** (*intr.*) to talk or move rapidly and tremulously. **3.** (*intr.*) to giggle. **4.** (*tr.*) to utter in a chirping way. ~*n.* **5.** a twittering sound. **6.** the act of twittering. **7.** a state of nervous excitement (esp. in **in a twitter**). [C14: imit.] —**'twitterer** *n.* —**'twittery** *adj.*

'twixt *or* **twixt** (twɪkst) *Poetic or dialect. contraction of* betwixt.

two (tuː) *n.* **1.** the cardinal number that is the sum of one and one. **2.** a numeral, 2, II, (ii), etc., representing this number. **3.** something representing or consisting of two units. **4.** Also called: **two o'clock.** two hours after noon or midnight. **5. in two.** in or into two parts. **6. put two and two together.** to make an inference from available evidence, esp. an obvious inference. **7. that makes two of us.** the same applies to me. ~*determiner.* **8. a.** amounting to two: *two nails.* **b.** (*as pronoun*): *he bought two.* ~Related adjs.: **binary, double, dual.** [OE *twā* (fem.)]

two-by-four *n.* **1.** a length of untrimmed timber with a cross section that measures 2 inches by 4 inches. **2.** a trimmed timber joist with a cross section that measures 1½ inches by 3½ inches.

two-dimensional *adj.* **1.** of or having two dimensions. **2.** having an area but not enclosing any volume. **3.** lacking in depth.

two-edged *adj.* **1.** having two cutting edges. **2.** (esp. of a remark) having two interpretations, such as *she looks nice when she smiles.*

two-faced *adj.* deceitful; hypocritical.

twofold (ˈtuːˌfəʊld) *adj.* **1.** equal to twice as many or twice as much. **2.** composed of two parts. ~*adv.* **3.** doubly.

two-handed *adj.* **1.** requiring the use of both hands. **2.** ambidextrous. **3.** requiring the participation or cooperation of two people.

twopence *or* **tuppence** (ˈtʌpəns) *n. Brit.* **1.** the sum of two pennies. **2.** (*used with a negative*) something of little value (in **not care** *or* **give twopence**). **3.** a former British silver coin.

twopenny *or* **tuppenny** (ˈtʌpənɪ) *adj. Chiefly Brit.* **1.** Also: **twopenny-halfpenny.** cheap or tawdry. **2.** (intensifier): *a twopenny damn.* **3.** worth two pence.

two-phase *adj.* (of an electrical circuit, device, etc.) generating or using two alternating voltages of the same frequency, displaced in phase by 90°.

two-piece *adj.* **1.** consisting of two separate parts, usually matching, as of a garment. ~*n.* **2.** such an outfit.

two-ply *adj.* **1.** made of two thicknesses, layers, or strands. ~*n., pl.* **-plies. 2.** a two-ply wood, knitting yarn, etc.

two-sided *adj.* **1.** having two sides or aspects. **2.** controversial; debatable.

twosome (ˈtuːsəm) *n.* **1.** two together, esp. two people. **2.** a match between two people.

two-step *n.* **1.** an old-time dance in duple time. **2.** a piece of music composed for or in the rhythm of this dance.

two-stroke *adj.* of an internal-combustion engine whose piston makes two strokes for every explosion. U.S. and Canad. word: **two-cycle.**

Two Thousand Guineas *n., (functioning as sing.), usually written* **2000 Guineas. the.** an annual horse race run at Newmarket since 1809.

two-time *vb. Inf.* to deceive (someone, esp. a lover) by carrying on a relationship with another. —ˌ**two-**ˈ**timer** *n.*

two-tone *adj.* **1.** of two colours or two shades of the same colour. **2.** (esp. of sirens, car horns, etc.) producing or consisting of two notes.

'twould (twʊd) *Poetic or dialect. contraction of* it would.

two-up *n. Chiefly Austral.* a illegal gambling game in which two coins are tossed or spun.

two-way *adj.* **1.** moving, permitting movement, or operating in either of two opposite directions. **2.** involving two participants. **3.** involving reciprocal obligation or mutual action. **4.** (of a radio, telephone, etc.) allowing communications in two directions using both transmitting and receiving equipment.

two-way mirror *n.* a half-silvered sheet of glass that functions as a mirror when viewed from one side but is translucent from the other.

-ty[1] *suffix of numerals.* denoting a multiple of ten: *sixty; seventy.* [< OE *-tig*]

-ty[2] *suffix forming nouns.* indicating state, condition, or quality: *cruelty.* [< OF *-te, -tet,* < L *-tās, -tāt-*]

Tyburn (ˈtaɪbɜːn) *n.* (formerly) a place of execution in London, on the River Tyburn.

tychism (ˈtaɪkɪzəm) *n. Philosophy.* the theory that chance is an objective reality at work in the universe. [< Gk *tukhē* chance]

tycoon (taɪˈkuːn) *n.* **1.** a businessman of great wealth and power. **2.** an archaic name for a **shogun.** [C19: < Japanese *taikun,* < Chinese *ta* great + *chün* ruler]

tyke *or* **tike** (taɪk) *n.* **1.** a dog, esp. a mongrel. **2.** *Inf.* a small or cheeky child. **3.** *Brit. dialect.* a rough ill-mannered person. **4.** *Brit. sl. often offens.* a person from Yorkshire. **5.** *Austral. sl., offens.* a Roman Catholic. [C14: < ON *tīk* bitch]

tylopod (ˈtaɪləʊˌpɒd) *n.* a mammal having padded, rather than hoofed, digits, such as camels and llamas. [C19: < NL, < Gk *tulos* knob or *tulē* cushion + -POD]

tympan (ˈtɪmpən) *n.* **1.** a membrane stretched over a frame or cylinder. **2.** *Printing.* packing interposed between the platen and the paper to be printed in order to provide an even impression. **3.** *Archit.* another name for **tympanum.** [OE *timpana,* < L; see TYMPANUM]

tympani (ˈtɪmpənɪ) *pl. n.* a variant spelling of **timpani.**

tympanic bone (tɪmˈpænɪk) *n.* the part of the temporal bone that surrounds the auditory canal.

tympanic membrane *n.* the thin membrane separating the external ear from the middle ear. It transmits vibrations, produced by sound waves, to the cochlea. Nontechnical name: **eardrum.**

tympanites (ˌtɪmpəˈnaɪtiːz) *n.* distension of the abdomen caused by an accumulation of gas in the intestinal or peritoneal cavity. [C14: < LL, < Gk *tumpanitēs* concerning a drum, < *tumpanon* drum] —**tympanitic** (ˌtɪmpəˈnɪtɪk) *adj.*

tympanitis (ˌtɪmpəˈnaɪtɪs) *n.* inflammation of the eardrum.

tympanum (ˈtɪmpənəm) *n., pl.* **-nums** *or* **-na** (-nə). **1. a.** the cavity of the middle ear. **b.** another name for **tympanic membrane. 2.** any diaphragm resembling that in the middle ear in function. **3.** *Archit.* **a.** the recessed space bounded by the cornices of a pediment, esp. one that is triangular in shape. **b.** the recessed space bounded by an arch and the lintel of a doorway or window below it. **4.** *Music.* a tympan or drum. **5.** a scoop wheel for raising water. [C17: < L, < Gk *tumpanon* drum] —**tympanic** (tɪmˈpænɪk) *adj.*

Tyndall effect (ˈtɪndᵊl) *n.* the phenomenon in which light is scattered by particles of matter in its path. [C19: after John *Tyndall* (1820-93), Irish physicist]

Tynwald (ˈtɪnwəld, ˈtaɪn-) *n.* **the.** the Parliament of the Isle of Man. [C15: < ON *thingvollr,* < *thing* assembly + *vollr* field]

typ., typo., *or* **typog.** *abbrev. for:* **1.** typographer. **2.** typographic(al). **3.** typography.

typal (ˈtaɪpᵊl) *adj.* a rare word for **typical.**

type (taɪp) *n.* **1.** a kind, class, or category, the constituents of which share similar characteristics. **2.** a subdivision of a particular class; sort: *what type of shampoo do you use?* **3.** the general form, plan, or design distinguishing a particular group. **4.** *Inf.* a person who typifies a particular quality: *he's the administrative type.* **5.** *Inf.* a person, esp. of a specified kind: *he's a strange type.* **6. a.** a small block of metal or more rarely wood bearing a letter or character in relief for use in printing. **b.** such pieces collectively. **7.** characters printed from type; print. **8.** *Biol.* **a.** the taxonomic group the characteristics of which are used for defining the next highest group. **b.** (*as modifier*): *a type genus.* **9.** See **type specimen. 10.** the characteristic device on a coin. **11.** *Chiefly Christian theol.* a figure, episode, or symbolic factor resembling some future reality in such a way as to foreshadow or prefigure it. ~*vb.* **12.** to write (copy) on a typewriter. **13.** (*tr.*) to be a symbol of; typify. **14.** (*tr.*) to decide the type of. **15.** (*tr.*) *Med.* to determine the blood group of (a blood sample). **16.** (*tr.*) *Chiefly Christian theol.* to foreshadow or serve as a symbol of (some future reality). [C15: < L *typus* figure, < Gk *tupos* image, < *tuptein* to strike]

-type *n. combining form.* **1.** type or form: *archetype.* **2.** printing type or photographic process: *collotype.* [< L *-typus,* < Gk *-typos,* < *tupos* TYPE]

typecast (ˈtaɪpˌkɑːst) *vb.* **-casting, -cast.** (*tr.*) to cast (an actor) in the same kind of role continually, esp. because of his physical appearance or previous success in such roles.

typeface (ˈtaɪpˌfeɪs) *n.* another name for **face** (sense 14).

type founder *n.* a person who casts metallic printer's type. —**type foundry** *n.*

type metal *n. Printing.* an alloy of tin, lead, and antimony, from which type is cast.

typescript (ˈtaɪpˌskrɪpt) *n.* **1.** a typed copy of a document, etc. **2.** any typewritten material.

typeset (ˈtaɪpˌsɛt) *vb.* **-setting, -set.** (*tr.*) *Printing.* to set (textual matter) in type.

typesetter (ˈtaɪpˌsɛtə) *n.* **1.** a person who sets type; compositor. **2.** a typesetting machine.

type specimen *n. Biol.* the original specimen from which a description of a new species is made.

typewrite (ˈtaɪpˌraɪt) *vb.* **-writing, -wrote, -written.** to write by means of a typewriter; type. —ˈ**type**ˌ**writing** *n.*

typewriter (ˈtaɪpˌraɪtə) *n.* a keyboard machine for writing mechanically in characters resembling print.

typhlitis (tɪfˈlaɪtɪs) *n.* inflammation of the

caecum. [C19: < NL, < Gk *tuphlon* the caecum, < *tuphlos* blind] —**typhlitic** (tɪf'lɪtɪk) *adj.*

typhoid ('taɪfɔɪd) *Pathol.* ~*adj. also* **typhoidal.** 1. resembling typhus. ~*n.* 2. short for **typhoid fever.** [C19: < TYPHUS + -OID]

typhoid fever *n.* an acute infectious disease characterized by high fever, spots, abdominal pain, etc. It is caused by a bacillus ingested with food or water.

typhoon (taɪ'fuːn) *n.* a violent tropical storm or cyclone, esp. in the China Seas and W Pacific. [C16: < Chinese *tai fung* great wind; infl. by Gk *tuphōn* whirlwind] —**typhonic** (taɪ'fɒnɪk) *adj.*

typhus ('taɪfəs) *n.* any one of a group of acute infectious rickettsial diseases characterized by high fever, skin rash, and severe headache. Also called: **typhus fever.** [C18: < NL *tȳphus,* < Gk *tuphos* fever] —'**typhous** *adj.*

typical ('tɪpɪkᵊl) *adj.* 1. being or serving as a representative example of a particular type; characteristic. 2. considered to be an example of some undesirable trait: *that is typical of you!* 3. of or relating to a representative specimen or type. 4. conforming to a type. 5. *Biol.* having most of the characteristics of a particular taxonomic group. [C17: < Med. L *typicālis,* < LL *typicus* figurative, < Gk *tupikos,* < *tupos* TYPE] —'**typically** *adv.* —'**typicalness** *or* ˌ**typi'cality** *n.*

typify ('tɪpɪˌfaɪ) *vb.* **-fying, -fied.** (*tr.*) 1. to be typical of; characterize. 2. to symbolize or represent completely, by or as if by a type. [C17: < L *typus* TYPE] —ˌ**typifi'cation** *n.*

typist ('taɪpɪst) *n.* a person who types, esp. for a living.

typo ('taɪpəʊ) *n., pl.* **-pos.** *Inf.* a typographical error. Also called (Brit.): **literal.**

typographer (taɪ'pɒgrəfə) *n.* 1. a person skilled in typography. 2. a compositor.

typography (taɪ'pɒgrəfɪ) *n.* 1. the art, craft, or process of composing type and printing from it. 2. the planning, selection, and setting of type for a printed work. —**typographical** (ˌtaɪpə'græfɪkᵊl) *or* ˌ**typo'graphic** *adj.* —ˌ**typo'graphically** *adv.*

typology (taɪ'pɒlədʒɪ) *n.* 1. the study of types in archaeology, biology, etc. 2. *Christian theol.* the doctrine that symbols for events, figures, etc., in the New Testament can be found in the Old Testament. —**typological** (ˌtaɪpə'lɒdʒɪkᵊl) *adj.* —**ty'pologist** *n.*

tyrannical (tɪ'rænɪkᵊl) *or* **tyrannic** *adj.* characteristic of or relating to a tyrant or to tyranny; oppressive. —**ty'rannically** *adv.*

tyrannicide (tɪ'rænɪˌsaɪd) *n.* 1. the killing of a tyrant. 2. a person who kills a tyrant.

tyrannize *or* **-ise** ('tɪrəˌnaɪz) *vb.* (when *intr.,* often foll. by *over*) to rule or exercise power (over) in a cruel or oppressive manner. —'**tyranˌnizer** *or* **-iser** *n.*

tyrannosaur (tɪ'rænəˌsɔː) *or* **tyrannosaurus** (tɪˌrænə'sɔːrəs) *n.* any of various large carnivorous two-footed dinosaurs common in North America in Upper Jurassic and Cretaceous times. [C19: < NL *Tyrannosaurus,* < Gk *turannos* tyrant + -SAUR]

tyranny ('tɪrənɪ) *n., pl.* **-nies.** 1. a. government by a tyrant; despotism. b. oppressive and unjust government by more than one person. 2. arbitrary, unreasonable, or despotic behaviour or use of authority. 3. a tyrannical act. [C14: < OF *tyrannie,* < Med. L *tyrannia,* < L *tyrannus* TYRANT] —'**tyrannous** *adj.*

tyrant ('taɪrənt) *n.* 1. a person who governs oppressively, unjustly, and arbitrarily; despot. 2. any person who exercises authority in a tyrannical manner. [C13: < OF *tyrant,* < L *tyrannus,* < Gk *turannos*]

tyre *or U.S.* **tire** ('taɪə) *n.* 1. a rubber ring placed over the rim of a wheel of a road vehicle to provide traction and reduce road shocks, esp. a hollow inflated ring (**pneumatic tyre**) consisting of a reinforced outer casing enclosing an inner tube. 2. a metal band or hoop attached to the rim of a wooden cartwheel. [C18: var. of C15 *tire,* prob. < archaic var. of ATTIRE]

Tyrian ('tɪrɪən) *n.* 1. a native or inhabitant of ancient Tyre, a port in S Lebanon and centre of ancient Phoenician culture. ~*adj.* 2. of or relating to ancient Tyre.

Tyrian purple *n.* 1. a deep purple dye obtained from certain molluscs and highly prized in antiquity. 2. a. a vivid purplish-red colour. b. (*as adj.*): *a Tyrian-purple robe.*

tyro *or* **tiro** ('taɪrəʊ) *n., pl.* **-ros.** a novice or beginner. [C17: < L *tīrō* recruit]

tyrosinase (ˌtaɪrəʊsɪ'neɪz) *n.* an enzyme that is a catalyst in the conversion of tyrosine to the pigment melanin.

tyrosine ('taɪrəˌsiːn, -sɪn, 'tɪrə-) *n.* an amino acid that is a precursor of the hormones adrenaline and thyroxine and of the pigment melanin. [C19: < Gk *turos* cheese + -INE²]

tyrothricin (ˌtaɪrəʊ'θraɪsɪn) *n.* an antibiotic, obtained from a soil bacterium: applied locally for the treatment of ulcers and abscesses. [C20: < NL *Tyrothrix* (genus name), < Gk *turos* cheese + *thrix* hair]

tzar (zɑː) *n.* a less common spelling of **tsar.**

tzatziki (tsæt'sɪkɪ) *n.* a Greek dip made from yoghurt, chopped cucumber, and mint. [C20: < Mod. Gk]

tzetze fly ('tsɛtsɪ) *n.* a variant spelling of **tsetse fly.**

Tzigane (tsɪ'gɑːn, sɪ-) *n.* a. a Gypsy, esp. a Hungarian one. b. (*as modifier*): *Tzigane music.* [C19: via F < Hungarian *czigány* Gypsy, <?]

U

u *or* **U** (juː) *n., pl.* **u's, U's,** *or* **Us. 1.** the 21st letter and fifth vowel of the English alphabet. **2.** any of several speech sounds represented by this letter, as in *mute, cut,* or *minus.* **3. a.** something shaped like a U. **b.** (*in combination*): *a U-bolt.*

U *symbol for:* **1.** united. **2.** unionist. **3.** university. **4.** (in Britain) **a.** universal (used to describe a category of film certified as suitable for viewing by anyone). **b.** (*as modifier*): *a U certificate film.* **5.** *Chem.* uranium. ~*adj.* **6.** *Brit. inf.* (esp. of language habits) characteristic of or appropriate to the upper class.

U. *abbrev. for:* **1.** *Maths.* union. **2.** unit. **3.** united. **4.** university. **5.** upper.

UAE *abbrev. for* United Arab Emirates.

UB40 *n.* (in Britain) **1.** a registration card issued by the Department of Employment to a person registering as unemployed **2.** *Inf.* a person registered as unemployed.

U-bend *n.* a U-shaped bend in a pipe that traps water in the lower part of the U and prevents the escape of noxious fumes; trap.

ubiety (juːˈbaɪɪtɪ) *n.* the condition of being in a particular place. [C17: < L *ubī* where + *-ety,* on the model of *society*]

ubiquitarian (juːˌbɪkwɪˈtɛərɪən) *n.* **1.** a member of the Lutheran church who holds that Christ is no more present in the elements of the Eucharist than elsewhere, as he is present in all places at all times. ~*adj.* **2.** denoting or holding this belief. [C17: < L *ubīque* everywhere] —**uˌbiquiˈtarianˌism** *n.*

ubiquitous (juːˈbɪkwɪtəs) *adj.* having or seeming to have the ability to be everywhere at once. [C14: < L *ubīque* everywhere, < *ubī* where] —**uˈbiquitously** *adv.* —**uˈbiquity** *n.*

U-boat *n.* a German submarine, esp. in World Wars I and II. [< G *U-Boot,* short for *Unterseeboot,* lit.: undersea boat]

u.c. *Printing. abbrev. for* upper case.

UCATT (in Britain) *abbrev. for* Union of Construction, Allied Trades and Technicians.

UCCA (ˈʌkə) *n.* (in Britain) *acronym for* Universities Central Council on Admissions.

UCW (in Britain) *abbrev. for* Union of Communication Workers.

UDA *abbrev. for* Ulster Defence Association.

udal (ˈjuːdᵊl) *n. Law.* a form of freehold possession of land existing in northern Europe before the introduction of the feudal system and still used in Orkney and Shetland. [C16: Orkney & Shetland dialect, < ON *othal*]

UDC (in Britain) *abbrev. for* Urban District Council.

udder (ˈʌdə) *n.* the large baglike mammary gland of cows, sheep, etc., having two or more teats. [OE *ūder*]

UDF *abbrev. for* United Democratic Front: a federation of South African anti-apartheid groups.

UDI *abbrev. for* Unilateral Declaration of Independence.

UDM (in Britain) *abbrev. for* Union of Democratic Mineworkers.

udometer (juːˈdɒmɪtə) *n.* another term for **rain gauge.** [C19: < F, < L *ūdus* damp]

UDR *abbrev. for* Ulster Defence Regiment.

UEFA (juːˈeɪfə,ˈjuːfə) *n. acronym for* Union of European Football Associations.

uey (ˈjuːɪ) *n., pl.* **ueys.** *Austral. sl.* a U-turn.

UFO (*sometimes* ˈjuːfəʊ) *abbrev. for* unidentified flying object.

ufology (ˌjuːˈfɒlədʒɪ) *n.* the study of UFOs. —**uˈfologist** *n.*

Ugaritic (ˌuːgəˈrɪtɪk) *n.* **1.** an extinct Semitic language of N Syria. ~*adj.* **2.** of or relating to this language. [C19: after *Ugarit* (modern name: Ras Shamra), an ancient Syrian city-state]

UGC (in Britain) *abbrev. for* University Grants Committee.

ugh (ʊx, ʊh, ʌx) *interj.* an exclamation of disgust, annoyance, or dislike.

ugli (ˈʌglɪ) *n., pl.* **-lis** *or* **-lies.** a large juicy yellow-skinned citrus fruit of the West Indies: a cross between a tangerine, grapefruit, and orange. Also called: **ugli fruit.** [C20: prob. an alteration of UGLY, from its wrinkled skin]

uglify (ˈʌglɪˌfaɪ) *vb.* **-fying, -fied.** to make or become ugly or more ugly. —ˌ**uglifiˈcation** *n.*

ugly (ˈʌglɪ) *adj.* **uglier, ugliest. 1.** of unpleasant or unsightly appearance. **2.** repulsive or displeasing in any way: *war is ugly.* **3.** ominous or menacing: *an ugly situation.* **4.** bad-tempered or sullen: *an ugly mood.* [C13: < ON *uggligr* dreadful, < *ugga* fear] —**ˈuglily** *adv.* —**ˈugliness** *n.*

ugly duckling *n.* a person or thing, initially ugly or unpromising, that changes into something beautiful or admirable. [< *The Ugly Duckling* by Hans Christian Andersen]

Ugrian (ˈuːgrɪən, ˈjuː-) *adj.* **1.** of or relating to a subdivision of the Turanian people, who include the Samoyeds and Magyars. ~*n.* **2.** a member of this group of peoples. **3.** another word for **Ugric.** [C19: < ORussian *Ugre* Hungarians]

Ugric (ˈuːgrɪk, ˈjuː-) *n.* **1.** one of the two branches of the Finno-Ugric family of languages, including Hungarian and some languages of NW Siberia. ~*adj.* **2.** of or relating to this group of languages or their speakers.

UHF *Radio. abbrev. for* ultrahigh frequency.

uh-huh *sentence substitute. Inf.* a less emphatic variant of **yes.**

uhlan (ˈuːlɑːn) *n. History.* a member of a body of lancers first employed in the Polish army and later in W European armies. [C18: via G < Polish *ulan,* < Turkish *ōlan* young man]

UHT *abbrev. for* ultra-heat-treated (milk or cream).

uhuru (uːˈhuːruː) *n.* (esp. in E Africa) **1.** national independence. **2.** freedom. [C20: < Swahili]

uitlander (ˈeɪtˌlandə, -ˌlæn-) *n.* (*sometimes cap.*) *S. African.* a foreigner. [C19: Afrik.: outlander]

UK *abbrev. for* United Kingdom.

ukase (juːˈkeɪz) *n.* **1.** (in imperial Russia) an edict of the tsar. **2.** a rare word for **edict.** [C18: < Russian *ukaz,* < *ukazat* to command]

Ukrainian (juːˈkreɪnɪən) *adj.* **1.** of or relating to the Ukraine, its people, or their language. ~*n.* **2.** the official language of the Ukrainian SSR: an East Slavonic language closely related to Russian. **3.** a native or inhabitant of the Ukraine.

ukulele *or* **ukelele** (ˌjuːkəˈleɪlɪ) *n.* a small four-stringed guitar, esp. of Hawaii. [C19: < Hawaiian, lit.: jumping flea]

ulcer (ˈʌlsə) *n.* **1.** a disintegration of the surface of the skin or a mucous membrane resulting in an open sore that heals very slowly. **2.** a source or element of corruption or evil. [C14: < L *ulcus*]

ulcerate (ˈʌlsəˌreɪt) *vb.* to make or become ulcerous. —ˌ**ulceˈration** *n.* —**ˈulcerative** *adj.*

ulcerous (ˈʌlsərəs) *adj.* **1.** relating to or characterized by ulcers. **2.** being or having a corrupting influence. —**ˈulcerously** *adv.*

-ule *suffix forming nouns.* indicating smallness: *globule.* [< L *-ulus,* dim. suffix]

ulema (ˈuːlɪmə) *n.* **1.** a body of Muslim scholars or religious leaders. **2.** a member of this body. [C17: < Ar. *'ulamā* scholars, < *'alama* to know]

-ulent *suffix forming adjectives.* abundant or full of: *fraudulent.* [< L *-ulentus*]

ullage (ˈʌlɪdʒ) *n.* **1.** the volume by which a liquid container falls short of being full. **2. a.** the quantity of liquid lost from a container due to leakage or evaporation. **b.** (in customs terminology) the amount of liquid remaining in a container after such loss. [C15: < OF *ouillage* filling of a cask, < *ouil* eye, < L *oculus* eye]

ulna (ˈʌlnə) *n., pl.* **-nae** (-niː) *or* **-nas. 1.** the inner and longer of the two bones of the human forearm. **2.** the corresponding bone in other vertebrates. [C16: < L: elbow] —**'ulnar** *adj.*

ulnar nerve *n.* a nerve situated along the inner side of the arm and passing close to the surface of the skin near the elbow.

ulotrichous (juːˈlɒtrɪkəs) *adj.* having woolly or curly hair. [C19: < NL *Ulotrichī* (classification applied to humans having this type of hair), < Gk *oulothrix*, < *oulos* curly + *thrix* hair]

ulster (ˈʌlstə) *n.* a man's heavy double-breasted overcoat with a belt or half-belt. [C19: < *Ulster*, the northernmost province of Ireland]

Ulster Defence Association *n.* (in Northern Ireland) a Loyalist paramilitary organization. Abbrev.: **UDA.**

Ulsterman (ˈʌlstəmən) *n., pl.* **-men.** a native or inhabitant of Ulster. —**'Ulster,woman** *fem. n.*

ult. *abbrev. for:* **1.** ultimate(ly). **2.** ultimo.

ulterior (ʌlˈtɪərɪə) *adj.* **1.** lying beneath or beyond what is revealed or supposed: *ulterior motives.* **2.** succeeding, subsequent, or later. **3.** lying beyond a certain line or point. [C17: < L: further, < *ulter* beyond] —**ul'teriorly** *adv.*

ultima (ˈʌltɪmə) *n.* the final syllable of a word. [< L: the last]

ultimate (ˈʌltɪmɪt) *adj.* **1.** conclusive in a series or process; final: *an ultimate question.* **2.** the highest or most significant: *the ultimate goal.* **3.** elemental, fundamental, or essential. *~n.* **4.** the most significant, highest, or greatest thing. [C17: < LL *ultimāre* to come to an end, < L *ultimus* last, < *ulter* distant] —**'ultimately** *adv.* —**'ultimateness** *n.*

ultima Thule (ˈθjuːlɪ) *n.* **1.** a region believed by ancient geographers to be the northernmost land. **2.** any distant or unknown region. **3.** a remote goal or aim. [L: the most distant Thule]

ultimatum (ˌʌltɪˈmeɪtəm) *n., pl.* **-tums** *or* **-ta** (-tə). **1.** a final communication by a party setting forth conditions on which it insists, as during negotiations on some topic. **2.** any final or peremptory demand or proposal. [C18: < NL, neuter of *ultimatus* ULTIMATE]

ultimo (ˈʌltɪˌməʊ) *adv. Now rare except when abbreviated in formal correspondence.* in or during the previous month: *a letter of the 7th ultimo.* Abbrev.: **ult.** [C16: < L *ultimō* on the last]

ultimogeniture (ˌʌltɪməʊˈdʒɛnɪtʃə) *n. Law.* a principle of inheritance whereby the youngest son succeeds to the estate of his ancestor. [C19: *ultimo-* < L *ultimus* last + LL *genitūra* a birth]

ultra (ˈʌltrə) *adj.* **1.** extreme or immoderate, esp. in beliefs or opinions. *~n.* **2.** an extremist. [C19: < L: beyond, < *ulter* distant]

ultra- *prefix.* **1.** beyond or surpassing a specified extent, range, or limit: *ultramicroscopic.* **2.** extreme or extremely: *ultramodern.* [< L *ultrā* beyond]

ultracentrifuge (ˌʌltrəˈsɛntrɪˌfjuːdʒ) *n. Chem.* a high-speed centrifuge used to separate colloidal solutions.

ultraconservative (ˌʌltrəkənˈsɜːvətɪv) *adj.* **1.** highly reactionary. *~n.* **2.** a reactionary person.

ultrafiche (ˈʌltrəˌfiːʃ) *n.* a sheet of film, usually the size of a filing card, that is similar to a microfiche but has a much larger number of microcopies. [C20: < ULTRA- + F *fiche* small card]

ultrahigh frequency (ˈʌltrəˌhaɪ) *n.* a radio-frequency band or radio frequency lying between 3000 and 300 megahertz. Abbrev.: **UHF.**

ultraism (ˈʌltrəˌɪzəm) *n.* extreme philosophy, belief, or action. —**'ultraist** *n., adj.*

ultramarine (ˌʌltrəməˈriːn) *n.* **1.** a blue pigment obtained by powdering natural lapis lazuli or made synthetically: used in paints, printing ink, plastics, etc. **2.** a vivid blue colour. *~adj.* **3.** of the colour ultramarine. **4.** from across the seas. [C17: < Med. L *ultramarinus*, < *ultrā* beyond + *mare* sea; so called because the lapis lazuli from which the pigment was made was imported from Asia]

ultramicroscope (ˌʌltrəˈmaɪkrəˌskəʊp) *n.* a microscope used for studying colloids, in which the sample is illuminated from the side and colloidal particles are seen as bright points on a dark background.

ultramicroscopic (ˌʌltrəˌmaɪkrəˈskɒpɪk) *adj.* **1.** too small to be seen with an optical microscope. **2.** of or relating to an ultramicroscope.

ultramodern (ˌʌltrəˈmɒdən) *adj.* extremely modern. —ˌ**ultra'modernism** *n.* —ˌ**ultra'modernist** *n.* —ˌ**ultra**ˌ**modern'istic** *adj.*

ultramontane (ˌʌltrəmɒnˈteɪn) *adj.* **1.** on the other side of the mountains, esp. the Alps, from the speaker or writer. **2.** of or relating to a movement in the Roman Catholic Church which favours the centralized authority and influence of the pope as opposed to local independence. *~n.* **3.** a person from beyond the mountains, esp. the Alps. **4.** a member of the ultramontane party of the Roman Catholic Church.

ultramundane (ˌʌltrəˈmʌndeɪn) *adj.* extending beyond the world, this life, or the universe.

ultranationalism (ˌʌltrəˈnæʃnəˌlɪzəm) *n.* extreme devotion to one's own nation. —ˌ**ultra'national** *adj.* —ˌ**ultra'nationalist** *adj., n.*

ultrashort (ˌʌltrəˈʃɔːt) *adj.* (of a radio wave) having a wavelength shorter than 10 metres.

ultrasonic (ˌʌltrəˈsɒnɪk) *adj.* of, concerned with, or producing waves with the same nature as sound waves but frequencies above audio frequencies. —ˌ**ultra'sonically** *adv.*

ultrasonics (ˌʌltrəˈsɒnɪks) *n.* (*functioning as sing.*) the branch of physics concerned with ultrasonic waves. Also called: **supersonics.**

ultrasound (ˌʌltrəˈsaʊnd) *n.* ultrasonic waves at frequencies above the audible range (above about 20 kHz), used in cleaning metallic parts, echo sounding, medical diagnosis and therapy, etc.

ultrasound scan *n.* an examination of an internal bodily structure by the use of ultrasonic waves, esp. for the diagnosis of abnormality in a fetus.

ultrastructure (ˈʌltrəˌstrʌktʃə) *n.* the minute structure of an organ, tissue, or cell, as revealed by microscopy.

ultraviolet (ˌʌltrəˈvaɪəlɪt) *n.* **1.** the part of the electromagnetic spectrum with wavelengths shorter than light but longer than x-rays; in the range 0.4×10^{-6} and 1×10^{-8} metres. *~adj.* **2.** of, relating to, or consisting of radiation lying in the ultraviolet: *ultraviolet radiation.*

ultra vires (ˈvaɪriːz) *adv., adj.* (*predicative*) *Law.* beyond the legal power of a person, corporation, agent, etc. [L, lit.: beyond strength]

ultravirus (ˌʌltrəˈvaɪrəs) *n.* a virus small enough to pass through the panes of the finest filter.

ululate (ˈjuːljʊˌleɪt) *vb.* (*intr.*) to howl or wail, as with grief. [C17: < L *ululāre* to howl, < *ulula* screech owl] —**'ululant** *adj.* —ˌ**ulu'lation** *n.*

umbel (ˈʌmbᵊl) *n.* a racemose inflorescence, characteristic of umbelliferous plants, in which the flowers arise from the same point in the main stem and have stalks of the same length, to give a cluster with the youngest flowers at the centre. [C16: < L *umbella* a sunshade, < *umbra* shade] —**umbellate** (ˈʌmbɪlɪt, -ˌleɪt) *or* **umbellar** (ʌmˈbɛlə) *adj.* —**umbellule** (ʌmˈbɛljuːl) *n.*

umbelliferous (ˌʌmbɪˈlɪfərəs) *adj.* of or belonging to a family of herbaceous plants and shrubs, typically having hollow stems, divided or compound leaves, and flowers in umbels: includes fennel, parsley, carrot, and parsnip. [C17: < NL, < L *umbella* sunshade + *ferre* to bear] —**um'bellifer** *n.*

umber (ˈʌmbə) *n.* **1.** any of various natural brown earths containing ferric oxide together with lime and oxides of aluminium, manganese, and silicon. **2.** any of the dark brown to greenish-brown colours produced by this pigment. **3.** *Obs.* shade. *~adj.* **4.** of, relating to, or stained with umber. [C16: < F (*terre d'*)*ombre* or It. (*terra di*) *ombra* shadow (earth), < L *umbra* shade]

umbilical (ʌmˈbɪlɪkᵊl, ˌʌmbɪˈlaɪkᵊl) *adj.* **1.** of, relating to, or resembling the umbilicus or the umbilical cord. **2.** in the region of the umbilicus: *an umbilical hernia.*

umbilical cord *n.* **1.** the long flexible tubelike

structure connecting a fetus with the placenta. **2.** any flexible cord, tube, or cable, as between an astronaut walking in space and his spacecraft.

umbilicate (ʌmˈbɪlɪkɪt, -ˌkeɪt) *adj.* **1.** having an umbilicus. **2.** having a central depression: *an umbilicate leaf.* **3.** shaped like a navel, as some bacterial colonies. **—umˌbiliˈcation** *n.*

umbilicus (ʌmˈbɪlɪkəs, ˌʌmbɪˈlaɪkəs) *n., pl.* **-bilici** (-ˈbɪlɪˌsaɪ, -bɪˈlaɪsaɪ). **1.** *Biol.* a hollow or navel-like structure, such as the cavity at the base of a gastropod shell. **2.** *Anat.* a technical name for the **navel.** [C18: < L: navel, centre]

umble pie (ˈʌmbᵊl) *n.* See **humble pie** (sense 1).

umbles (ˈʌmbᵊlz) *pl. n.* See **numbles.**

umbo (ˈʌmbəʊ) *n., pl.* **umbones** (ʌmˈbəʊniːz) *or* **umbos.** **1.** *Bot., anat.* a small hump, prominence, or convex area, as in certain mushrooms, bivalve molluscs, and the outer surface of the eardrum. **2.** a large projecting central boss on a shield, esp. on a Saxon shield. [C18: < L: projecting piece] **—umbonate** (ˈʌmbənɪt, -ˌneɪt), **umbonal** (ˈʌmbənᵊl), *or* **umbonic** (ʌmˈbɒnɪk) *adj.*

umbra (ˈʌmbrə) *n., pl.* **-brae** (-briː) *or* **-bras.** **1.** a region of complete shadow resulting from the obstruction of light by an opaque object, esp. the shadow cast by the moon onto the earth during a solar eclipse. **2.** the darker inner region of a sunspot. [C16: < L: shade] **—ˈumbral** *adj.*

umbrage (ˈʌmbrɪdʒ) *n.* **1.** displeasure or resentment; offence (in **give** *or* **take umbrage**). **2.** the foliage of trees, considered as providing shade. **3.** *Rare.* shadow or shade. [C15: < OF, < L *umbrāticus* relating to shade, < *umbra* shade]

umbrageous (ʌmˈbreɪdʒəs) *adj.* **1.** shady or shading. **2.** *Rare.* easily offended.

umbrella (ʌmˈbrɛlə) *n.* **1.** a portable device used for protection against rain, snow, etc., and consisting of a light canopy supported on a collapsible metal frame mounted on a central rod. **2.** the flattened cone-shaped body of a jellyfish. **3.** a protective shield or screen, esp. of aircraft or gunfire. **4.** anything that has the effect of a protective screen, general cover, or organizing agency. [C17: < It. *ombrella*, dim. of *ombra* shade; see UMBRA] **—umˈbrella-ˌlike** *adj.*

umbrella pine *n.* another name for **stone pine.**

umbrella stand *n.* an upright rack or stand for umbrellas.

umbrella tree *n.* **1.** a North American magnolia having long leaves clustered into an umbrella formation at the ends of the branches and having unpleasant-smelling white flowers. **2.** Also called: **umbrella bush.** any of various trees or shrubs having umbrella-shaped leaves or growing in an umbrella-like cluster.

Umbrian (ˈʌmbrɪən) *adj.* **1.** of or relating to Umbria, in Italy, its inhabitants, or the ancient language once spoken there. **2.** of or relating to a Renaissance school of painting that included Raphael. ~*n.* **3.** a native or inhabitant of Umbria. **4.** an extinct language of ancient S Italy.

umfazi (ˌʊmˈfɑːʒɪ) *n. S. African.* a Black married woman. [< Bantu]

umiak *or* **oomiak** (ˈuːmɪˌæk) *n.* a large open boat made of stretched skins, used by Eskimos. [C18: < Eskimo: boat for the use of women]

umlaut (ˈʊmlaʊt) *n.* **1.** the mark (¨) placed over a vowel in some languages, such as German, indicating modification in the quality of the vowel. **2.** (esp. in Germanic languages) the change of a vowel within a word brought about by the assimilating influence of a vowel or semivowel in a preceding or following syllable. [C19: G, < *um* around (in the sense of changing places) + *Laut* sound]

umlungu (ˌʊmˈlʊŋgʊ) *n. S. African.* a White man: used esp. as a term of address. [< Bantu]

umpire (ˈʌmpaɪə) *n.* **1.** an official who rules on the playing of a game, as in cricket. **2.** a person who rules on or judges disputes between contesting parties. ~*vb.* **3.** to act as umpire in (a game, dispute, or controversy). [C15: by mistaken division < *a noumpere*, < OF *nomper* not one of a pair, < *nom-, non-* not + *per* equal]

umpteen (ˌʌmpˈtiːn) *determiner. Inf.* **a.** very many: *umpteen things to do.* **b.** (*as pronoun*): *umpteen of them came.* [C20: < *umpty* a great deal (? < *-enty* as in *twenty*) + *-teen* ten] **—ˌumpˈteenth** *n., adj.*

UN *abbrev. for* United Nations.

un-[1] *prefix.* (*freely used with adjectives, participles, and their derivative adverbs and nouns: less frequently used with certain other nouns*) not; contrary to; opposite of: *uncertain; untidiness; unbelief; untruth.* [< OE *on-, un-*]

un-[2] *prefix forming verbs.* **1.** denoting reversal of an action or state: *uncover; untangle.* **2.** denoting removal from, release, or deprivation: *unharness; unthrone.* **3.** (intensifier): *unloose.* [< OE *un-, on-*]

'un *or* **un** (ən) *pron.* a spelling of **one** intended to reflect a dialectal or informal pronunciation: *that's a big 'un.*

unable (ʌnˈeɪbᵊl) *adj.* (*postpositive;* foll. by *to*) lacking the necessary power, ability, or authority (to do something); not able.

unaccountable (ˌʌnəˈkaʊntəbᵊl) *adj.* **1.** allowing of no explanation; inexplicable. **2.** extraordinary: *an unaccountable fear of heights.* **3.** not accountable or answerable to. **—ˌunacˌcountaˈbility** *n.* **—ˌunacˈcountably** *adv.*

unaccustomed (ˌʌnəˈkʌstəmd) *adj.* **1.** (foll. by *to*) not used (to): *unaccustomed to pain.* **2.** not familiar. **—ˌunacˈcustomedness** *n.*

una corda (ˈuːnə ˈkɔːdə) *adj., adv. Music.* (of the piano) to be played with the soft pedal depressed. [It., lit.: one string; the pedal moves the mechanism so that only one string of the three tuned to each note is struck by the hammer]

unadopted (ˌʌnəˈdɒptɪd) *adj.* **1.** (of a child) not adopted. **2.** *Brit.* (of a road, etc.) not maintained by a local authority.

unadvised (ˌʌnədˈvaɪzd) *adj.* **1.** rash or unwise. **2.** not having received advice. **—unadvisedly** (ˌʌnədˈvaɪzɪdlɪ) *adv.* **—ˌunadˈvisedness** *n.*

unaffected[1] (ˌʌnəˈfɛktɪd) *adj.* unpretentious, natural, or sincere. **—ˌunafˈfectedly** *adv.* **—ˌunafˈfectedness** *n.*

unaffected[2] (ˌʌnəˈfɛktɪd) *adj.* not affected.

unalienable (ʌnˈeɪljənəbᵊl) *adj. Law.* a variant of **inalienable.**

un-American *adj.* **1.** not in accordance with the aims, ideals, customs, etc., of the U.S. **2.** against the interests of the U.S. **—ˌunAˈmericanism** *n.*

unanimous (juːˈnænɪməs) *adj.* **1.** in complete agreement. **2.** characterized by complete agreement: *a unanimous decision.* [C17: < L, < *ūnus* one + *animus* mind] **—uˈnanimously** *adv.* **—unanimity** (ˌjuːnəˈnɪmɪtɪ) *n.*

ˌunaˈbashed *adj.*
ˌunaˈbated *adj.*
ˌunabˈbreviˌated *adj.*
ˌunaˈbridged *adj.*
ˌunacˈcented *adj.*
ˌunacˈceptable *adj.*
ˌunacˈcommoˌdating *adj.*
ˌunacˈcompanied *adj.*
ˌunacˈcomplished *adj.*
ˌunacˈcounted *adj.*
ˌunacˈcounted-for *adj.*
ˌunacˈknowledged *adj.*
ˌunacˈquainted *adj.*
unˈacted *adj.*
unˈactionable *adj.*
ˌunaˈdaptable *adj.*
ˌunaˈdapted *adj.*
ˌunadˈdressed *adj.*
ˌunaˈdorned *adj.*
ˌunaˈdulterˌated *adj.*
ˌunadˈventurous *adj.*
ˌunˈadverˌtised *adj.*
ˌunadˈvisable *adj.*
ˌunafˈfiliˌated *adj.*
ˌunaˈfraid *adj.*
unˈaided *adj.*
ˌunaˈligned *adj.*
ˌunalˈlayed *adj.*
ˌunalˈleviˌated *adj.*
ˌunalˈlied *adj.*
ˌunalˈlowable *adj.*
ˌunalˈloyed *adj.*
unˈalterable *adj.*
ˌunamˈbiguous *adj.*
unˈamiable *adj.*
unˈampliˌfied *adj.*
ˌunaˈmused *adj.*
ˌunanˈnounced *adj.*
unˈanswerable *adj.*
unˈanswered *adj.*

unapproachable (ˌʌnəˈprəʊtʃəbᵊl) *adj.* **1.** discouraging intimacy, friendliness, etc.; aloof. **2.** inaccessible. **3.** not to be rivalled. —ˌ**unapˈproachableness** *n.* —ˌ**unapˈproachably** *adv.*

unappropriated (ˌʌnəˈprəʊprɪˌeɪtɪd) *adj.* **1.** not set aside for specific use. **2.** *Accounting.* designating that portion of the profits of a business enterprise that is retained in the business and not withdrawn by the proprietor. **3.** (of property) not having been taken into any person's possession or control.

unapt (ʌnˈæpt) *adj.* **1.** (*usually postpositive;* often foll. by *for*) not suitable or qualified; unfitted. **2.** mentally slow. **3.** (*postpositive; may take an infinitive*) not disposed or likely (to). —**unˈaptly** *adv.* —**unˈaptness** *n.*

unarm (ʌnˈɑːm) *vb.* a less common word for **disarm.**

unarmed (ʌnˈɑːmd) *adj.* **1.** without weapons. **2.** (of animals and plants) having no claws, prickles, spines, thorns, or similar structures.

unassailable (ˌʌnəˈseɪləbᵊl) *adj.* **1.** not able to be attacked. **2.** undeniable or irrefutable. —ˌ**unasˈsailableness** *n.* —ˌ**unasˈsailably** *adv.*

unassuming (ˌʌnəˈsjuːmɪŋ) *adj.* modest or unpretentious. —ˌ**unasˈsumingly** *adv.* —ˌ**unasˈsumingness** *n.*

unattached (ˌʌnəˈtætʃt) *adj.* **1.** not connected with any specific thing, body, group, etc. **2.** not engaged or married. **3.** (of property) not seized or held as security.

unavailing (ˌʌnəˈveɪlɪŋ) *adj.* useless or futile. —ˌ**unaˈvailingly** *adv.*

unavoidable (ˌʌnəˈvɔɪdəbᵊl) *adj.* **1.** unable to be avoided. **2.** *Law.* not capable of being declared null and void. —ˌ**unaˌvoidaˈbility** *or* ˌ**unaˈvoidableness** *n.* —ˌ**unaˈvoidably** *adv.*

unaware (ˌʌnəˈwɛə) *adj.* **1.** (*postpositive*) not aware or conscious (of): *unaware of the danger he ran across the road.* ~*adv.* **2.** a variant of **unawares.** —ˌ**unaˈwareness** *n.*

▷ **Usage.** Careful users of English distinguish between the adjective *unaware* (to be ignorant of) and the adverb *unawares* (by surprise): *they were unaware of the danger; the danger caught them unawares.*

unawares (ˌʌnəˈwɛəz) *adv.* **1.** without prior warning or plan: *she caught him unawares.* **2.** without knowing: *he lost it unawares.*

▷ **Usage.** See at **unaware.**

unbacked (ʌnˈbækt) *adj.* **1.** (of a book, chair, etc.) not having a back. **2.** bereft of support, esp. on a financial basis. **3.** not supported by bets.

unbalance (ʌnˈbæləns) *vb.* (*tr.*) **1.** to upset the equilibrium or balance of. **2.** to disturb the mental stability of (a person or his mind). ~*n.* **3.** imbalance or instability.

unbalanced (ʌnˈbælənst) *adj.* **1.** lacking balance. **2.** irrational or unsound; erratic. **3.** mentally disordered or deranged. **4.** biased; one-sided: *unbalanced reporting.* **5.** (in double-entry bookkeeping) not having total debit balances equal to total credit balances.

unbar (ʌnˈbɑː) *vb.* **-barring, -barred.** (*tr.*) **1.** to take away a bar or bars from. **2.** to unfasten bars, locks, etc., from (a door); open.

unbearable (ʌnˈbɛərəbᵊl) *adj.* not able to be borne or endured. —**unˈbearably** *adv.*

unbeatable (ʌnˈbiːtəbᵊl) *adj.* unable to be defeated or outclassed; surpassingly excellent.

unbeaten (ʌnˈbiːtᵊn) *adj.* **1.** having suffered no defeat. **2.** not worn down; untrodden. **3.** not mixed or stirred by beating: *unbeaten eggs.*

unbecoming (ˌʌnbɪˈkʌmɪŋ) *adj.* **1.** unsuitable or inappropriate, esp. through being unattractive: *an unbecoming hat.* **2.** (when *postpositive,* usually foll. by *of* or an object) not proper or seemly (for): *manners unbecoming a lady.* —ˌ**unbeˈcomingly** *adv.* —ˌ**unbeˈcomingness** *n.*

unbeknown (ˌʌnbɪˈnəʊn) *adv.* (*sentence modifier;* foll. by *to*) without the knowledge (of a person): *unbeknown to him she had left the country.* Also (esp. Brit.): **unbeknownst.** [C17: < arch. *beknown* known]

unbelief (ˌʌnbɪˈliːf) *n.* disbelief or rejection of belief.

unbelievable (ˌʌnbɪˈliːvəbᵊl) *adj.* unable to be believed; incredible. —ˌ**unbeˌlievaˈbility** *n.* —ˌ**unbeˈlievably** *adv.*

unbeliever (ˌʌnbɪˈliːvə) *n.* a person who does not believe, esp. in religious matters.

unbelieving (ˌʌnbɪˈliːvɪŋ) *adj.* **1.** not believing; sceptical. **2.** proceeding from or characterized by scepticism. —ˌ**unbeˈlievingly** *adv.*

unbend (ʌnˈbɛnd) *vb.* **-bending, -bent. 1.** to release or be released from the restraints of formality and ceremony. **2.** *Inf.* to relax (the mind) or (of the mind) to become relaxed. **3.** to straighten out from an originally bent shape. **4.** (*tr.*) *Naut.* **a.** to remove (a sail) from a stay, mast, etc. **b.** to untie (a rope, etc.) or cast (a cable) loose.

unbending (ʌnˈbɛndɪŋ) *adj.* **1.** rigid or inflexible. **2.** characterized by sternness or severity: *an unbending rule.* —**unˈbendingly** *adv.* —**unˈbendingness** *n.*

unbent (ʌnˈbɛnt) *vb.* **1.** the past tense and past participle of **unbend.** ~*adj.* **2.** not bent or bowed. **3.** not compelled to give way by force.

unbidden (ʌnˈbɪdᵊn) *adj.* **1.** not ordered or commanded; voluntary or spontaneous. **2.** not invited or asked.

unbind (ʌnˈbaɪnd) *vb.* **-binding, -bound.** (*tr.*) **1.** to set free from restraining bonds or chains. **2.** to unfasten or make loose (a bond, etc.).

unblessed (ʌnˈblɛst) *adj.* **1.** deprived of blessing. **2.** cursed or evil. **3.** unhappy or wretched. —**unblessedness** (ʌnˈblɛsɪdnɪs) *n.*

unblushing (ʌnˈblʌʃɪŋ) *adj.* immodest or shameless. —**unˈblushingly** *adv.*

unbolt (ʌnˈbəʊlt) *vb.* (*tr.*) **1.** to unfasten a bolt of (a door). **2.** to undo (the nut) on a bolt.

unbolted (ʌnˈbəʊltɪd) *adj.* (of grain, meal, or flour) not sifted.

unborn (ʌnˈbɔːn) *adj.* **1.** not yet born or brought to birth. **2.** still to come in the future: *the unborn world.*

unbosom (ʌnˈbʊzəm) *vb.* (*tr.*) to relieve (oneself) of (secrets, etc.) by telling someone. [C16: < UN-[2] + BOSOM (in the sense: seat of the emotions)]

unbounded (ʌnˈbaʊndɪd) *adj.* having no boundaries or limits. —**unˈboundedly** *adv.* —**unˈboundedness** *n.*

unbowed (ʌnˈbaʊd) *adj.* **1.** not bowed or bent. **2.** free or unconquered.

unbridled (ʌnˈbraɪdᵊld) *adj.* **1.** with all restraints

ˌ**unapˈparent** *adj.*
ˌ**unapˈpealable** *adj.*
ˌ**unapˈpealing** *adj.*
unˈappeˌtizing *or* **-ˌtising** *adj.*
ˌ**unapˈplied** *adj.*
ˌ**unapˈpreciˌated** *adj.*
ˌ**unapˈproved** *adj.*
unˈarguable *adj.*
unˈarguably *adv.*
ˌ**unarˈticuˌlated** *adj.*
ˌ**unarˈtistic** *adj.*
ˌ**unaˈshamed** *adj.*
unˈasked *adj.*
unˈaspiˌrated *adj.*
ˌ**unasˈpiring** *adj.*
ˌ**unasˈsertive** *adj.*
ˌ**unasˈsisted** *adj.*
ˌ**unasˈsorted** *adj.*
ˌ**unasˈsumed** *adj.*
ˌ**unaˈtoned** *adj.*
ˌ**unatˈtainable** *adj.*
ˌ**unatˈtended** *adj.*
ˌ**unatˈtractive** *adj.*
ˌ**unausˈpicious** *adj.*
ˌ**unauˈthentic** *adj.*
unˈauthorˌized *or* **-ˌised** *adj.*
ˌ**unaˈvailable** *adj.*
ˌ**unbeˈfitting** *adj.*
ˌ**unbeˈgotten** *adj.*
ˌ**unbeˈholden** *adj.*
unˈbelt *vb.*
unˈbiased *adj.*
unˈbiblical *adj.*
unˈbleached *adj.*
unˈblemished *adj.*
unˈblinking *adj.*
unˈblock *vb.*
unˈbound *adj.*
unˈbrace *vb.*
unˈbreakable *adj.*
unˈbridle *vb.*

removed. **2.** (of a horse) wearing no bridle. —**un'bridledly** *adv.* —**un'bridledness** *n.*

unbroken (ʌn'brəukən) *adj.* **1.** complete or whole. **2.** continuous or incessant. **3.** undaunted in spirit. **4.** (of animals, esp. horses) not tamed; wild. **5.** not disturbed or upset: *the unbroken quiet of the afternoon.* **6.** (of a record, esp. at sport) not improved upon. —**un'brokenly** *adv.* —**un'brokenness** *n.*

unburden (ʌn'bɜːdᵊn) *vb.* (*tr.*) **1.** to remove a load or burden from. **2.** to relieve or make free (one's mind, oneself, etc.) of a worry, trouble, etc., by revelation or confession.

unbutton (ʌn'bʌtᵊn) *vb.* to undo by unfastening (the buttons) of (a garment).

unbuttoned (ʌn'bʌtᵊnd) *adj.* **1.** with buttons not fastened. **2.** *Inf.* uninhibited; unrestrained: *hours of unbuttoned self-revelation.*

uncalled-for (ˌʌn'kɔːldfɔː) *adj.* unnecessary or unwarranted.

uncanny (ʌn'kænɪ) *adj.* **1.** characterized by apparently supernatural wonder, horror, etc. **2.** beyond what is normal: *uncanny accuracy.* —**un'cannily** *adv.* —**un'canniness** *n.*

uncap (ʌn'kæp) *vb.* **-capping, -capped. 1.** (*tr.*) to remove a cap or top from (a container): *to uncap a bottle.* **2.** to remove a cap from (the head).

uncared-for (ˌʌn'kɛədfɔː) *adj.* not cared for; neglected.

unceremonious (ˌʌnsɛrɪ'məunɪəs) *adj.* without ceremony; informal, abrupt, rude, or undignified. —**ˌuncere'moniously** *adv.* —**ˌuncere'moniousness** *n.*

uncertain (ʌn'sɜːtᵊn) *adj.* **1.** not able to be accurately known or predicted: *the issue is uncertain.* **2.** (when *postpositive,* often foll. by *of*) not sure or confident (about): *he was uncertain of the date.* **3.** not precisely determined or decided: *uncertain plans.* **4.** not to be depended upon: *an uncertain vote.* **5.** liable to variation; changeable: *the weather is uncertain.* **6. in no uncertain terms. a.** unambiguously. **b.** forcefully. —**un'certainly** *adv.*

uncertainty (ʌn'sɜːtᵊntɪ) *n., pl.* **-ties. 1.** Also: **uncertainness.** the state or condition of being uncertain. **2.** an uncertain matter, contingency, etc.

uncertainty principle *n.* **the.** the principle that energy and time or position and momentum, cannot both be accurately measured simultaneously. Also called: **Heisenberg uncertainty principle, indeterminacy principle.**

uncharted (ʌn'tʃɑːtɪd) *adj.* (of a physical or nonphysical region or area) not yet mapped, surveyed, or investigated: *uncharted waters; the uncharted depths of the mind.*

unchristian (ʌn'krɪstʃən) *adj.* **1.** not in accordance with the principles or ethics of Christianity. **2.** non-Christian or pagan. —**un'christianly** *adv.*

unchurch (ʌn'tʃɜːtʃ) *vb.* (*tr.*) **1.** to excommunicate. **2.** to remove church status from (a building).

uncial ('ʌnsɪəl) *adj.* **1.** of, relating to, or written in majuscule letters, as used in Greek and Latin manuscripts of the third to ninth centuries, that resemble modern capitals, but are characterized by much greater curvature. ~*n.* **2.** an uncial letter or manuscript. [C17: < LL *unciāles litterae* letters an inch long, < L *unciālis,* < *uncia* one twelfth, inch] —**'uncially** *adv.*

uncinate ('ʌnsɪnɪt, -ˌneɪt) *adj. Biol.* shaped like a hook: *the uncinate process of the ribs of certain vertebrates.* [C18: < L *uncīnātus,* < *uncīnus* a hook, < *uncus*]

uncircumcised (ʌn'sɜːkəmˌsaɪzd) *adj.* **1.** not circumcised. **2.** not Jewish; gentile. **3.** spiritually unpurified. —**ˌuncircum'cision** *n.*

uncivil (ʌn'sɪvəl) *adj.* **1.** lacking civility or good manners. **2.** an obsolete word for **uncivilized.** —**uncivility** (ˌʌnsɪ'vɪlɪtɪ) *n.* —**un'civilly** *adv.*

uncivilized *or* **-ised** (ʌn'sɪvɪˌlaɪzd) *adj.* **1.** (of a tribe or people) not yet civilized, esp. not having developed a written language. **2.** lacking culture or sophistication. —**un'civiˌlizedness** *or* **-isedness** *n.*

unclad (ʌn'klæd) *adj.* having no clothes on; naked.

unclasp (ʌn'klɑːsp) *vb.* **1.** (*tr.*) to unfasten the clasp of (something). **2.** to release one's grip (upon an object).

uncle ('ʌŋkᵊl) *n.* **1.** a brother of one's father or mother. **2.** the husband of one's aunt. **3.** a term of address sometimes used by children for a male friend of their parents. **4.** *Sl.* a pawnbroker. ~Related adj.: **avuncular.** [C13: < OF *oncle,* < L *avunculus*]

unclean (ʌn'kliːn) *adj.* lacking moral, spiritual, or physical cleanliness. —**un'cleanness** *n.*

uncleanly[1] (ʌn'kliːnlɪ) *adv.* in an unclean manner.

uncleanly[2] (ʌn'klɛnlɪ) *adj.* characterized by an absence of cleanliness. —**un'cleanliness** *n.*

Uncle Sam (sæm) *n.* a personification of the government of the United States. [C19: apparently a humorous interpretation of the letters stamped on army supply boxes during the War of 1812: *U.S.*]

Uncle Tom (tɒm) *n. Inf., derog.* a Black person whose behaviour towards White people is regarded as servile. [C20: after the main character of H. B. Stowe's novel *Uncle Tom's Cabin* (1852)] —**'Uncle 'Tomˌism** *n.*

unclose (ʌn'kləuz) *vb.* **1.** to open or cause to open. **2.** to come or bring to light.

unclothe (ʌn'kləuð) *vb.* **-clothing, -clothed** *or* **-clad.** (*tr.*) **1.** to take off garments from; strip. **2.** to uncover or lay bare.

uncoil (ʌn'kɔɪl) *vb.* to unwind or become unwound; untwist.

uncomfortable (ʌn'kʌmftəbᵊl) *adj.* **1.** not comfortable. **2.** feeling or causing discomfort or unease; disquieting. —**un'comfortableness** *n.* —**un'comfortably** *adv.*

uncommitted (ˌʌnkə'mɪtɪd) *adj.* not bound or pledged to a specific opinion, course of action, or cause.

uncommon (ʌn'kɒmən) *adj.* **1.** outside or beyond normal experience, etc. **2.** in excess of what is normal: *an uncommon liking for honey.* ~*adv.* **3.** an archaic word for **uncommonly** (sense 2). —**un'commonness** *n.*

uncommonly (ʌn'kɒmənlɪ) *adv.* **1.** in an uncommon or unusual manner or degree; rarely. **2.** (intensifier): *you're uncommonly friendly.*

uncommunicative (ˌʌnkə'mjuːnɪkətɪv) *adj.* disinclined to talk or give information or opinions. —**ˌuncom'municatively** *adv.* —**ˌuncom'municativeness** *n.*

uncompromising (ʌn'kɒmprəˌmaɪzɪŋ) *adj.* not prepared to give ground or to compromise. —**un'comproˌmisingly** *adv.*

---

un'bruised *adj.*
un'buckle *vb.*
un'built *adj.*
un'buried *adj.*
un'caged *adj.*
un'caring *adj.*
un'cashed *adj.*
un'caught *adj.*
un'ceasing *adj.*
un'censored *adj.*
un'censured *adj.*
un'chain *vb.*
un'challenged *adj.*
un'changed *adj.*
un'changing *adj.*
un'chaperˌoned *adj.*
ˌuncharacter'istic *adj.*
un'charged *adj.*
un'charitable *adj.*
un'chartered *adj.*
un'chaste *adj.*
un'checked *adj.*
un'chosen *adj.*
un'claimed *adj.*
un'classiˌfied *adj.*
un'clear *adj.*
un'clog *vb.*
un'clouded *adj.*
un'cluttered *adj.*
un'coloured *adj.*
un'combed *adj.*
ˌuncom'mercial *adj.*
un'compenˌsated *adj.*
ˌuncom'petitive *adj.*
ˌuncom'plaining *adj.*
ˌuncom'pleted *adj.*
un'compliˌcated *adj.*
ˌuncompli'mentary *adj.*
ˌuncom'pounded *adj.*
ˌuncompre'hending *adj.*
ˌuncon'cealed *adj.*

unconcern (ˌʌnkənˈsɜːn) *n.* apathy or indifference.

unconcerned (ˌʌnkənˈsɜːnd) *adj.* **1.** lacking in concern or involvement. **2.** untroubled. —**unconcernedly** (ˌʌnkənˈsɜːnɪdlɪ) *adv.*

unconditional (ˌʌnkənˈdɪʃənᵊl) *adj.* without conditions or limitations; total: *unconditional surrender.* —ˌ**unconˈditionally** *adv.*

unconditioned (ˌʌnkənˈdɪʃənd) *adj.* **1.** *Psychol.* characterizing an innate reflex and the stimulus and response that form parts of it. **2.** *Metaphysics.* unrestricted by conditions; absolute. **3.** without limitations. —ˌ**unconˈditionedness** *n.*

unconformable (ˌʌnkənˈfɔːməbᵊl) *adj.* **1.** not conformable or conforming. **2.** (of rock strata) consisting of a series of recent strata resting on different, much older rocks. —ˌ**unconˌformaˈbility** *or* ˌ**unconˈformableness** *n.* —ˌ**unconˈformably** *adv.* —ˌ**unconˈformity** *n.*

unconscionable (ʌnˈkɒnʃənəbᵊl) *adj.* **1.** unscrupulous or unprincipled: *an unconscionable liar.* **2.** immoderate or excessive: *unconscionable demands.* —**unˈconscionably** *adv.*

unconscious (ʌnˈkɒnʃəs) *adj.* **1.** lacking normal sensory awareness of the environment; insensible. **2.** not aware of one's actions, behaviour, etc.: *unconscious of his bad manners.* **3.** characterized by lack of awareness or intention: *an unconscious blunder.* **4.** coming from or produced by the unconscious: *unconscious resentment.* ~*n.* **5.** *Psychoanal.* the part of the mind containing instincts, impulses, images, and ideas that are not available for direct examination. —**unˈconsciously** *adv.* —**unˈconsciousness** *n.*

unconstitutional (ˌʌnkɒnstɪˈtjuːʃənᵊl) *adj.* at variance with or not permitted by a constitution. —ˌ**unconstiˌtutionˈality** *n.*

unconventional (ˌʌnkənˈvɛnʃənᵊl) *adj.* not conforming to accepted rules or standards. —ˌ**unconˌventionˈality** *n.* —ˌ**unconˈventionally** *adv.*

uncool (ʌnˈkuːl) *adj. Sl.* **1.** unsophisticated; unfashionable. **2.** excitable; tense; not cool.

uncork (ʌnˈkɔːk) *vb.* (*tr.*) **1.** to draw the cork from (a bottle, etc.). **2.** to release or unleash (emotions, etc.).

uncountable (ʌnˈkauntəbᵊl) *adj.* **1.** too many to be counted; innumerable. **2.** *Linguistics.* denoting a noun that does not refer to an isolable object. See **mass noun.**

uncounted (ʌnˈkauntɪd) *adj.* **1.** unable to be counted; innumerable. **2.** not counted.

uncouple (ʌnˈkʌpᵊl) *vb.* **1.** to disconnect or unfasten or become disconnected or unfastened. **2.** (*tr.*) to set loose; release.

uncouth (ʌnˈkuːθ) *adj.* lacking in good manners, refinement, or grace. [OE *uncūth,* < UN-¹ + *cūth* familiar] —**unˈcouthly** *adv.* —**unˈcouthness** *n.*

uncover (ʌnˈkʌvə) *vb.* **1.** (*tr.*) to remove the cover, cap, top, etc., from. **2.** (*tr.*) to reveal or disclose: *to uncover a plot.* **3.** to take off (one's head covering), esp. as a mark of respect.

uncovered (ʌnˈkʌvəd) *adj.* **1.** not covered; revealed or bare. **2.** not protected by insurance, security, etc. **3.** with hat off, as a mark of respect.

UNCTAD *abbrev. for* United Nations Conference on Trade and Development.

unction (ˈʌŋkʃən) *n.* **1.** *Chiefly R.C. & Eastern Churches.* the act of anointing with oil in sacramental ceremonies, in the conferring of holy orders. **2.** excessive suavity or affected charm. **3.** an ointment or unguent. **4.** anything soothing. [C14: < L *unctiō* an anointing, < *ungere* to anoint] —**ˈunctionless** *adj.*

unctuous (ˈʌŋktjʊəs) *adj.* **1.** slippery or greasy. **2.** affecting an oily charm. [C14: < Med. L *unctuōsus,* < L *unctum* ointment, < *ungere* to anoint] —**unctuosity** (ˌʌŋktjʊˈɒsɪtɪ) *or* **ˈunctuousness** *n.* —**ˈunctuously** *adv.*

uncut (ʌnˈkʌt) *adj.* **1.** (of a book) not having the edges of its pages trimmed or slit. **2.** (of a gemstone) not cut and faceted. **3.** not abridged.

undamped (ʌnˈdæmpt) *adj.* **1.** (of an oscillating system) having unrestricted motion; not damped. **2.** not repressed, discouraged, or subdued.

undaunted (ʌnˈdɔːntɪd) *adj.* not put off, discouraged, or beaten. —**unˈdauntedly** *adv.* —**unˈdauntedness** *n.*

undecagon (ʌnˈdɛkəˌgɒn) *n.* a polygon having eleven sides. [C18: < L *undecim* eleven + -GON]

undeceive (ˌʌndɪˈsiːv) *vb.* (*tr.*) to reveal the truth to (someone previously misled or deceived). —ˌ**undeˈceivable** *adj.* —ˌ**undeˈceiver** *n.*

undecidability (ˌʌndɪˌsaɪdəˈbɪlɪtɪ) *n., pl.* **-ties.** *Maths, logic.* the condition of not being open to formal proof or disproof by logical deduction from the axioms of a system.

undecided (ˌʌndɪˈsaɪdɪd) *adj.* **1.** not having made up one's mind. **2.** (of an issue, problem, etc.) not agreed or decided upon. —ˌ**undeˈcidedly** *adv.* —ˌ**undeˈcidedness** *n.*

undeniable (ˌʌndɪˈnaɪəbᵊl) *adj.* **1.** unquestionably or obviously true. **2.** of unquestionable excellence: *a man of undeniable character.* **3.** unable to be resisted or denied. —ˌ**undeˈniableness** *n.* —ˌ**undeˈniably** *adv.*

under (ˈʌndə) *prep.* **1.** directly below; on, to, or beneath the underside or base of: *under one's feet.* **2.** less than: *under forty years.* **3.** lower in rank than: *under a corporal.* **4.** subject to the supervision, jurisdiction, control, or influence of. **5.** subject to (conditions); in (certain circumstances). **6.** within a classification of: *a book under theology.* **7.** known by: *under an assumed name.* **8.** planted with: *a field under corn.* **9.** powered by: *under sail.* **10.** *Astrol.* during the period that the sun is in (a sign of the zodiac): *born under Aries.* ~*adv.* **11.** below; to a position underneath something. [OE]

under- *prefix.* **1.** below or beneath: *underarm; underground.* **2.** of lesser importance or lower rank: *undersecretary.* **3.** insufficient or insufficiently: *underemployed.* **4.** indicating secrecy or deception: *underhand.*

underachieve (ˌʌndərəˈtʃiːv) *vb.* (*intr.*) to fail to achieve a performance appropriate to one's age or talents. —ˌ**underaˈchievement** *n.* —ˌ**underaˈchiever** *n.*

underact (ˌʌndərˈækt) *vb. Theatre.* to play (a role) without adequate emphasis.

underage (ˌʌndərˈeɪdʒ) *adj.* below the required or standard age, esp. below the legal age for voting or drinking.

underarm (ˈʌndərˌɑːm) *adj.* **1.** (of a measurement) extending along the arm from wrist to armpit. **2.** *Cricket, tennis, etc.* denoting a style of

---

ˌ**unconˈcluded** *adj.*
ˌ**unconˈdemned** *adj.*
ˌ**unconˈfined** *adj.*
ˌ**unconˈfirmed** *adj.*
ˌ**unconˈnected** *adj.*
unˈconquered *adj.*
unˈconseˌcrated *adj.*
ˌ**unconˈsenting** *adj.*
ˌ**unconˈsidered** *adj.*
ˌ**unconˈstricted** *adj.*
unˈconsumˌmated *adj.*
ˌ**unconˈtamiˌnated** *adj.*
ˌ**unconˈtested** *adj.*
ˌ**unconˈtrollable** *adj.*
ˌ**unconˈtrolled** *adj.*
ˌ**uncontroˈversial** *adj.*
ˌ**unconˈverted** *adj.*
ˌ**unconˈvincing** *adj.*
ˌ**uncoˈoperative** *adj.*
ˌ**uncoˈordiˌnated** *adj.*
ˌ**uncorˈroboˌrated** *adj.*
unˈcovenanted *adj.*
ˌ**uncreˈative** *adj.*
unˈcritical *adj.*
unˈcrowned *adj.*
unˈcultiˌvated *adj.*
unˈcultured *adj.*
unˈcurbed *adj.*
unˈcured *adj.*
unˈcurl *vb.*
unˈdamaged *adj.*
unˈdated *adj.*
ˌ**undeˈclared** *adj.*
unˈdecoˌrated *adj.*
ˌ**undeˈfeated** *adj.*
ˌ**undeˈfended** *adj.*
ˌ**undeˈfiled** *adj.*
ˌ**undeˈfinable** *adj.*
ˌ**undeˈmanding** *adj.*
ˌ**undemoˈcratic** *adj.*
ˌ**undeˈmonstrative** *adj.*
ˌ**undeˈnied** *adj.*
ˌ**undeˈpendable** *adj.*
ˌ**underˈactive** *adj.*

throwing, bowling, or serving in which the hand is swung below shoulder level. **3.** below the arm. ~*adv.* **4.** in an underarm style.

underbelly (ˈʌndəˌbɛlɪ) *n., pl.* **-lies. 1.** the part of an animal's belly nearest to the ground. **2.** a vulnerable or unprotected part, aspect, or region.

underbid (ˌʌndəˈbɪd) *vb.* **-bidding, -bid. 1.** (*tr.*) to submit a bid lower than that of (others): *Irena underbid the other dealers.* **2.** (*tr.*) to submit an excessively low bid for. **3.** *Bridge.* to bid (one's hand) at a lower level than the strength of the hand warrants: *he underbid his hand.* —ˈ**underˌbidder** *n.*

underbody (ˈʌndəˌbɒdɪ) *n., pl.* **-bodies.** the underpart of a body, as of an animal or motor vehicle.

underbred (ˌʌndəˈbrɛd) *adj.* of impure stock; not thoroughbred. —ˌ**underˈbreeding** *n.*

underbuy (ˌʌndəˈbaɪ) *vb.* **-buying, -bought. 1.** to buy (stock in trade) in amounts lower than required. **2.** (*tr.*) to buy at a price below that paid by (others). **3.** (*tr.*) to pay a price less than the true value for.

undercapitalize *or* **-ise** (ˌʌndəˈkæpɪtəˌlaɪz) *vb.* to provide or issue capital for (a commercial enterprise) in an amount insufficient for efficient operation.

undercarriage (ˈʌndəˌkærɪdʒ) *n.* **1.** Also called: **landing gear.** the assembly of wheels, shock absorbers, struts, etc., that supports an aircraft on the ground and enables it to take off and land. **2.** the framework that supports the body of a vehicle, carriage, etc.

undercharge (ˌʌndəˈtʃɑːdʒ) *vb.* **1.** to charge too little for something. **2.** (*tr.*) to load (a gun, cannon, etc.) with an inadequate charge.

underclass (ˈʌndəˌklɑːs) *n.* a class beneath the usual social scale consisting of the most disadvantaged people, such as the long-term unemployed.

underclothes (ˈʌndəˌkləʊðz) *pl. n.* a variant of **underwear.** Also called: **underclothing.**

undercoat (ˈʌndəˌkəʊt) *n.* **1.** a coat of paint or other substance applied before the top coat. **2.** a coat worn under an overcoat. **3.** *Zool.* another name for **underfur.** ~*vb.* **4.** (*tr.*) to apply an undercoat to (a surface).

undercover (ˌʌndəˈkʌvə) *adj.* done or acting in secret: *undercover operations.*

undercroft (ˈʌndəˌkrɒft) *n.* an underground chamber, such as a church crypt, often with a vaulted ceiling. [C14: < *croft* a vault, cavern, ult. < L *crypta* CRYPT]

undercurrent (ˈʌndəˌkʌrənt) *n.* **1.** a current that is not apparent at the surface or lies beneath another current. **2.** an opinion, emotion, etc., lying beneath apparent feeling or meaning. ~Also called: **underflow.**

undercut *vb.* (ˌʌndəˈkʌt), **-cutting, -cut. 1.** to charge less than (a competitor) in order to obtain trade. **2.** to cut away the under part of (something). **3.** *Golf, tennis, etc.* to hit (a ball) in such a way as to impart backspin. ~*n.* (ˈʌndəˌkʌt). **4.** the act of cutting underneath. **5.** a part that is cut away underneath. **6.** a tenderloin of beef. **7.** *Forestry, chiefly U.S. & Canad.* a notch cut in a tree trunk, to ensure a clean break in felling. **8.** *Tennis, golf, etc.* a stroke that imparts backspin to the ball.

underdevelop (ˌʌndədɪˈvɛləp) *vb.* (*tr.*) *Photog.* to process (a film, plate, or paper) in developer for less than the required time, or at too low a temperature, or in an exhausted solution.

underdeveloped (ˌʌndədɪˈvɛləpt) *adj.* **1.** immature or undersized. **2.** relating to societies in which both the surplus capital and the social organization necessary to advance are lacking. **3.** *Photog.* (of a film, etc.) processed in developer for less than the required time.

underdog (ˈʌndəˌdɒg) *n.* **1.** the losing competitor in a fight or contest. **2.** a person in adversity or a position of inferiority.

underdone (ˌʌndəˈdʌn) *adj.* insufficiently or lightly cooked.

underdressed (ˌʌndəˈdrɛst) *adj.* wearing clothes that are not elaborate or formal enough for a particular occasion.

underemployed (ˌʌndərɪmˈplɔɪd) *adj.* not fully or adequately employed.

underestimate *vb.* (ˌʌndərˈɛstɪˌmeɪt). (*tr.*) **1.** to make too low an estimate of: *he underestimated the cost.* **2.** to think insufficiently highly of: *to underestimate a person.* ~*n.* (ˌʌndərˈɛstɪmɪt). **3.** too low an estimate. —ˌ**underˌestiˈmation** *n.*

underexpose (ˌʌndərɪkˈspəʊz) *vb.* (*tr.*) **1.** *Photog.* to expose (a film, plate, or paper) for too short a period or with insufficient light so as not to produce the required effect. **2.** (*often passive*) to fail to subject to appropriate or expected publicity. —ˌ**underexˈposure** *n.*

underfeed (ˌʌndəˈfiːd) *vb.* **-feeding, -fed.** (*tr.*) **1.** to give too little food to. **2.** to supply (a furnace, engine, etc.) with fuel from beneath.

underfelt (ˈʌndəˌfɛlt) *n.* thick felt laid between floorboards and carpet to increase insulation.

underfloor (ˈʌndəˌflɔː) *adj.* situated beneath the floor: *underfloor heating.*

underfoot (ˌʌndəˈfʊt) *adv.* **1.** underneath the feet; on the ground. **2.** in a position of subjugation. **3.** in the way.

underfur (ˈʌndəˌfɜː) *n.* the layer of dense soft fur occurring beneath the outer coarser fur in certain mammals, such as the otter and seal. Also called: **undercoat.**

undergarment (ˈʌndəˌgɑːmənt) *n.* any garment worn under the visible outer clothes, usually next to the skin.

undergird (ˌʌndəˈgɜːd) *vb.* **-girding, -girded** *or* **-girt.** (*tr.*) to strengthen or reinforce by passing a rope, cable, or chain around the underside of (an object, load, etc.). [C16: < UNDER- + GIRD[1]]

underglaze (ˈʌndəˌgleɪz) *adj.* **1.** *Ceramics.* applied to pottery or porcelain before the application of glaze. ~*n.* **2.** a pigment, etc., applied in this way.

undergo (ˌʌndəˈgəʊ) *vb.* **-going, -went, -gone.** (*tr.*) to experience, endure, or sustain: *to undergo a change of feelings.* [OE] —ˈ**underˌgoer** *n.*

undergraduate (ˌʌndəˈgrædjʊɪt) *n.* a person studying in a university for a first degree. Sometimes shortened to **undergrad.**

underground *adj.* (ˈʌndəˌgraʊnd), *adv.* (ˌʌndəˈgraʊnd). **1.** occurring, situated, used, or going below ground level: *an underground explosion.* **2.** secret; hidden: *underground activities.* ~*n.* (ˈʌndəˌgraʊnd). **3.** a space or region below ground level. **4. a.** a movement dedicated to overthrowing a government or occupation forces, as in the European countries occupied by the German army in World War II. **b.** (*as modifier*): *an underground group.* **5.** (often preceded by *the*) an electric passenger railway operated in underground tunnels. U.S. and Canad. equivalent: **subway. 6.** (usually preceded by *the*) **a.** any avant-garde, experimental, or subversive movement in popular art, films, music, etc. **b.** (*as modifier*): *the underground press.*

underground railroad *n.* (*often cap.*) (in the pre-Civil War U.S.) the system established by abolitionists to aid escaping slaves.

undergrowth (ˈʌndəˌgrəʊθ) *n.* small trees, bushes, ferns, etc., growing beneath taller trees in a wood or forest.

underhand (ˈʌndəˌhænd) *adj. also* **underhanded. 1.** clandestine, deceptive, or secretive. **2.** *Sport.* another word for **underarm.** ~*adv.* **3.** in an underhand manner or style.

underhanded (ˌʌndəˈhændɪd) *adj.* another word for **underhand** or **short-handed.**

underhung (ˌʌndəˈhʌŋ) *adj.* **1.** (of the lower jaw)

ˌ**underˈclad** *adj.*
ˌ**underˈclothed** *adj.*
ˌ**underˈcook** *vb.*
ˌ**underˈdo** *vb.*
ˌ**underˈeat** *vb.*
ˌ**underˈeduˌcated** *adj.*
ˌ**underˈemphaˌsize** *or* **-ise** *vb.*
ˌ**underˈexerˌcise** *vb.*
ˈ**underˌgrown** *adj.*

projecting beyond the upper jaw; undershot. **2.** (of a sliding door, etc.) supported at its lower edge by a track or rail.

underlay *vb.* (ˌʌndəˈleɪ), **-laying, -laid.** (*tr.*) **1.** to place (something) under or beneath. **2.** to support by something laid beneath. **3.** to achieve the correct printing pressure all over (a forme block) or to bring (a block) up to type height by adding material, such as paper, beneath it. ~*n.* (ˈʌndəˌleɪ). **4.** a lining, support, etc., laid underneath something else. **5.** *Printing.* material, such as paper, used to underlay a forme or block. **6.** felt, rubber, etc., laid beneath a carpet to increase insulation and resilience.

underlie (ˌʌndəˈlaɪ) *vb.* **-lying, -lay, -lain.** (*tr.*) **1.** to lie or be placed under or beneath. **2.** to be the foundation, cause, or basis of: *careful planning underlies all our decisions.* **3.** to be the root or stem from which (a word) is derived: *"happy" underlies "happiest".* —**ˈunderˌlier** *n.*

underline (ˌʌndəˈlaɪn) *vb.* (*tr.*) **1.** to put a line under. **2.** to state forcibly; emphasize.

underlinen (ˈʌndəˌlɪnən) *n.* underclothes, esp. when made of linen.

underling (ˈʌndəlɪŋ) *n.* a subordinate or lackey.

underlying (ˌʌndəˈlaɪɪŋ) *adj.* **1.** concealed but detectable: *underlying guilt.* **2.** fundamental; basic. **3.** lying under. **4.** *Finance.* (of a claim, liability, etc.) taking precedence; prior.

undermentioned (ˈʌndəˌmɛnʃənd) *adj.* mentioned below or subsequently.

undermine (ˌʌndəˈmaɪn) *vb.* (*tr.*) **1.** (of the sea, wind, etc.) to wear away the bottom or base of (land, cliffs, etc.). **2.** to weaken gradually or insidiously: *insults undermined her confidence.* **3.** to tunnel or dig beneath. —**ˌunderˈminer** *n.*

undermost (ˈʌndəˌməʊst) *adj.* **1.** being the furthest under; lowest. ~*adv.* **2.** in the lowest place.

underneath (ˌʌndəˈniːθ) *prep., adv.* **1.** under; beneath. ~*adj.* **2.** lower. ~*n.* **3.** a lower part, surface, etc. [OE *underneothan,* < UNDER + *neothan* below]

undernourish (ˌʌndəˈnʌrɪʃ) *vb.* (*tr.*) to deprive of or fail to provide with nutrients essential for health and growth. —**ˌunderˈnourishment** *n.*

underpants (ˈʌndəˌpænts) *pl. n.* a man's undergarment covering the body from the waist or hips to the thighs or ankles. Often shortened to **pants.**

underpass (ˈʌndəˌpɑːs) *n.* **1.** a section of a road that passes under another road, railway line, etc. **2.** another word for **subway** (sense 1).

underpay (ˌʌndəˈpeɪ) *vb.* **-paying, -paid.** to pay (someone) insufficiently. —**ˌunderˈpayment** *n.*

underpin (ˌʌndəˈpɪn) *vb.* **-pinning, -pinned.** (*tr.*) **1.** to support from beneath, esp. by a prop, while avoiding damaging or weakening the superstructure: *to underpin a wall.* **2.** to give corroboration, strength, or support to.

underpinning (ˈʌndəˌpɪnɪŋ) *n.* a structure of masonry, concrete, etc., placed beneath a wall to provide support.

underplay (ˌʌndəˈpleɪ) *vb.* **1.** to play (a role) with restraint or subtlety. **2.** to achieve (an effect) by deliberate lack of emphasis. **3.** (*intr.*) *Cards.* to lead or follow suit with a lower card when holding a higher one.

underprivileged (ˌʌndəˈprɪvɪlɪdʒd) *adj.* lacking the rights and advantages of other members of society; deprived.

underproduction (ˌʌndəprəˈdʌkʃən) *n. Commerce.* production below full capacity or below demand.

underproof (ˌʌndəˈpruːf) *adj.* (of a spirit) containing less than 57.1 per cent alcohol by volume.

underquote (ˌʌndəˈkwəʊt) *vb.* **1.** to offer for sale (securities, goods, or services) at a price lower than the market price. **2.** (*tr.*) to quote a price lower than that quoted by (another).

underrate (ˌʌndəˈreɪt) *vb.* (*tr.*) to underestimate.

underscore (ˌʌndəˈskɔː) *vb.* (*tr.*) **1.** to draw or score a line or mark under. **2.** to stress or reinforce.

undersea (ˈʌndəˌsiː) *adj., adv. also* **underseas** (ˌʌndəˈsiːz). below the surface of the sea.

underseal (ˈʌndəˌsiːl) *Brit.* ~*n.* **1.** a coating of a tar, etc., applied to the underside of a motor vehicle to retard corrosion. ~*vb.* **2.** (*tr.*) to apply a coating of underseal to (a vehicle).

undersecretary (ˌʌndəˈsɛkrətrɪ) *n., pl.* **-taries.** **1.** (in Britain) **a.** any of various senior civil servants in certain government departments. **b.** short for **undersecretary of state:** any of various high officials subordinate only to the minister in charge of a department. **2.** (in the U.S.) a high government official subordinate only to the secretary in charge of a department.

undersell (ˌʌndəˈsɛl) *vb.* **-selling, -sold.** **1.** to sell for less than the usual price. **2.** (*tr.*) to sell at a price lower than that of (another seller). **3.** (*tr.*) to advertise (merchandise) with moderation or restraint. —**ˌunderˈseller** *n.*

undersexed (ˌʌndəˈsɛkst) *adj.* having weaker sex urges or responses than is considered normal.

undershirt (ˈʌndəˌʃɜːt) *n.* the U.S. and Canad. name for **vest** (sense 1).

undershoot (ˌʌndəˈʃuːt) *vb.* **-shooting, -shot.** **1.** (of a pilot) to cause (an aircraft) to land short of (a runway) or (of an aircraft) to land in this way. **2.** to shoot a projectile so that it falls short of (a target).

undershorts (ˈʌndəˌʃɔːts) *pl. n.* another word for **shorts** (sense 2).

undershot (ˈʌndəˌʃɒt) *adj.* **1.** (of the lower jaw) projecting beyond the upper jaw; underhung. **2.** (of a water wheel) driven by a flow of water that passes under the wheel rather than over it.

underside (ˈʌndəˌsaɪd) *n.* the bottom or lower surface.

undersigned (ˈʌndəˌsaɪnd) *n.* **1. the.** the person or persons who have signed at the foot of a document, statement, etc. ~*adj.* **2.** having signed one's name at the foot of a document, statement, etc.

undersized (ˌʌndəˈsaɪzd) *adj.* of less than usual size.

underskirt (ˈʌndəˌskɜːt) *n.* any skirtlike garment worn under a skirt or dress; petticoat.

underslung (ˌʌndəˈslʌŋ) *adj.* suspended below a supporting member, esp. (of a motor vehicle chassis) suspended below the axles.

understand (ˌʌndəˈstænd) *vb.* **-standing, -stood.** **1.** (*may take a clause as object*) to know and comprehend the nature or meaning of: *I understand you.* **2.** (*may take a clause as object*) to realize or grasp (something): *he understands your position.* **3.** (*tr.; may take a clause as object*) to assume, infer, or believe: *I understand you are thinking of marrying.* **4.** (*tr.*) to know how to translate or read: *can you understand Spanish?* **5.** (*tr.; may take a clause as object; often passive*) to accept as a condition or proviso: *it is understood that children must be kept quiet.* **6.** (*tr.*) to be sympathetic to or compatible with: *we understand each other.* [OE *understandan*] —**ˌunderˈstandable** *adj.* —**ˌunderˈstandably** *adv.*

understanding (ˌʌndəˈstændɪŋ) *n.* **1.** the ability to learn, judge, make decisions, etc. **2.** personal opinion or interpretation of a subject: *my understanding of your predicament.* **3.** a mutual agreement or compact, esp. an informal or private one. **4.** *Chiefly Brit.* an unofficial engagement to be married. **5. on the understanding that.** providing. ~*adj.* **6.** sympathetic, tolerant, or wise towards people. **7.** possessing judgment and intelligence. —**ˌunderˈstandingly** *adv.*

ˌunderinˈsured *adj.*
ˌunderˈmanned *adj.*
ˈunderˌnamed *adj.*
ˌunderˈpaid *adj.*
ˈunderˌpart *n.*
ˌunderˈpopuˌlated *adj.*
ˌunderˈprice *vb.*
ˌunderproˈduce *vb.*
ˌunderˈstaffed *adj.*

understate (ˌʌndəˈsteɪt) *vb.* 1. to state (something) in restrained terms, often to obtain an ironic effect. 2. to state that (something, such as a number) is less than it is. —ˌ**underˈstatement** *n.*

understood (ˌʌndəˈstʊd) *vb.* 1. the past tense and past participle of **understand.** ~*adj.* 2. implied or inferred. 3. taken for granted.

understudy (ˈʌndəˌstʌdɪ) *vb.* **-studying, -studied.** 1. (*tr.*) to study (a role or part) so as to be able to replace the usual actor or actress if necessary. 2. to act as understudy to (an actor or actress). ~*n., pl.* **-studies.** 3. an actor or actress who studies a part so as to be able to replace the usual actor or actress if necessary. 4. anyone who is trained to take the place of another in case of need.

undertake (ˌʌndəˈteɪk) *vb.* **-taking, -took, -taken.** (*tr.*) 1. to contract to or commit oneself to (something) or (to do something): *to undertake a job.* 2. to attempt to; agree to start. 3. to take (someone) in charge. 4. to promise.

undertaker (ˈʌndəˌteɪkə) *n.* a person whose profession is the preparation of the dead for burial or cremation and the management of funerals; funeral director.

undertaking (ˈʌndəˌteɪkɪŋ) *n.* 1. a task, venture, or enterprise. 2. an agreement to do something. 3. the business of an undertaker.

underthings (ˈʌndəθɪŋz) *pl. n.* girls' or women's underwear.

underthrust (ˈʌndəˌθrʌst) *n. Geol.* a reverse fault in which the rocks on the lower surface of a fault plane have moved under the relatively static rocks on the upper surface.

undertone (ˈʌndəˌtəʊn) *n.* 1. a quiet or hushed tone of voice. 2. an underlying suggestion in words or actions: *his offer has undertones of dishonesty.*

undertow (ˈʌndəˌtəʊ) *n.* 1. the seaward undercurrent following the breaking of a wave on the beach. 2. any strong undercurrent flowing in a different direction from the surface current.

undertrick (ˈʌndəˌtrɪk) *n. Bridge.* a trick by which a declarer falls short of making his or her contract.

undervalue (ˌʌndəˈvæljuː) *vb.* **-valuing, -valued.** (*tr.*) to value at too low a level or price. —ˌ**underˌvaluˈation** *n.* —ˌ**underˈvaluer** *n.*

undervest (ˈʌndəˌvɛst) *n. Brit.* another name for **vest** (sense 1).

underwater (ˈʌndəˈwɔːtə) *adj.* 1. being, occurring, or going under the surface of the water, esp. the sea: *underwater exploration.* 2. *Naut.* below the water line of a vessel. ~*adv.* 3. beneath the surface of the water.

under way *adj.* (*postpositive*) 1. in progress; in operation: *the show was under way.* 2. *Naut.* in motion in the direction headed.

underwear (ˈʌndəˌwɛə) *n.* clothing worn under the outer garments, usually next to the skin.

underweight (ˌʌndəˈweɪt) *adj.* weighing less than is average, expected, or healthy.

underwent (ˌʌndəˈwɛnt) *vb.* the past tense of **undergo.**

underwhelm (ˌʌndəˈwɛlm) *vb.* (*tr.*) to make no positive impact on; disappoint. [C20: orig. a humorous coinage based on *overwhelm*] —ˌ**underˈwhelming** *adj.*

underwing (ˈʌndəˌwɪŋ) *n.* 1. the hind wing of an insect. 2. See **red underwing, yellow underwing.**

underwood (ˈʌndəˌwʊd) *n.* a less common word for **undergrowth.**

underworld (ˈʌndəˌwɜːld) *n.* 1. a. criminals and their associates. b. (*as modifier*): *underworld connections.* 2. *Greek & Roman myth.* the regions below the earth's surface regarded as the abode of the dead. 3. the antipodes.

underwrite (ˈʌndəˌraɪt, ˌʌndəˈraɪt) *vb.* **-writing, -wrote, -written.** (*tr.*) 1. *Finance.* to undertake to purchase at an agreed price any unsold portion of (a public issue of shares, etc.). 2. to accept financial responsibility for (a commercial project or enterprise). 3. *Insurance.* a. to sign and issue (an insurance policy) thus accepting liability. b. to insure (a property or risk). c. to accept liability up to (a specified amount) in an insurance policy. 4. to write (words, a signature, etc.) beneath (other written matter). 5. to support.

underwriter (ˈʌndəˌraɪtə) *n.* 1. a person or enterprise that underwrites public issues of shares, bonds, etc. 2. a. a person or enterprise that underwrites insurance policies. b. an employee or agent of an insurance company who determines the premiums payable.

undesirable (ˌʌndɪˈzaɪərəbᵊl) *adj.* 1. not desirable or pleasant; objectionable. ~*n.* 2. a person or thing considered undesirable. —ˌ**undeˌsiraˈbility** *or* ˌ**undeˈsirableness** *n.* —ˌ**undeˈsirably** *adv.*

undetermined (ˌʌndɪˈtɜːmɪnd) *adj.* 1. not yet resolved; undecided. 2. not known or discovered.

undies (ˈʌndɪz) *pl. n. Inf.* women's underwear.

undine (ˈʌndiːn) *n.* any of various female water spirits. [C17: < NL *undina*, < L *unda* a wave]

undistributed (ˌʌndɪˈstrɪbjʊtɪd) *adj. Logic.* 1. (of a term) referring only to some members of the class designated by the term, as *doctors* in *some doctors are overworked.* 2. **undistributed middle.** the fallacy arising from the failure of the middle term of a syllogism to apply to all members of a class.

undo (ʌnˈduː) *vb.* **-doing, -did, -done.** (*mainly tr.*) 1. (*also intr.*) to untie, unwrap, or open or become untied, unwrapped, etc. 2. to reverse the effects of. 3. to cause the downfall of.

undoing (ʌnˈduːɪŋ) *n.* 1. ruin; downfall. 2. the cause of downfall: *drink was his undoing.*

undone[1] (ʌnˈdʌn) *adj.* not done or completed; unfinished.

undone[2] (ʌnˈdʌn) *adj.* 1. ruined; destroyed. 2. unfastened; untied.

undoubted (ʌnˈdaʊtɪd) *adj.* beyond doubt; certain or indisputable. —**unˈdoubtedly** *adv.*

undreamed (ʌnˈdriːmd) *or* **undreamt** (ʌnˈdrɛmt) *adj.* (often foll. by *of*) not thought of, conceived, or imagined.

undress (ʌnˈdrɛs) *vb.* 1. to take off clothes from (oneself or another). 2. (*tr.*) to strip of ornamentation. 3. (*tr.*) to remove the dressing from (a wound). ~*n.* 4. partial or complete nakedness. 5. informal or normal working clothes or uniform.

undressed (ʌnˈdrɛst) *adj.* 1. partially or completely naked. 2. (of an animal hide) not fully processed. 3. (of food, esp. salad) not prepared with sauce or dressing.

undue (ʌnˈdjuː) *adj.* 1. excessive or unwarranted. 2. unjust, improper, or illegal. 3. (of a debt, bond, etc.) not yet payable.

undulant (ˈʌndjʊlənt) *adj. Rare.* resembling waves; undulating. —ˈ**undulance** *n.*

undulant fever *n.* another name for **brucellosis.** [C19: so called because the fever symptoms are intermittent]

undulate *vb.* (ˈʌndjʊˌleɪt). 1. to move or cause to move in waves or as if in waves. 2. to have or provide with a wavy form or appearance. ~*adj.*

ˌ**undersubˈscribe** *vb.*
ˌ**undersupˈply** *vb.*
ˈ**underˌsurface** *n.*
ˌ**underˈtrained** *adj.*
ˌ**undeˈserved** *adj.*
ˌ**undeˈserving** *adj.*
ˌ**undeˈsigning** *adj.*
ˌ**undeˈtected** *adj.*
ˌ**undeˈterred** *adj.*
ˌ**undeˈveloped** *adj.*
unˈdiagˌnosed *adj.*
ˌ**undifferˈentiˌated** *adj.*
unˈdigniˌfied *adj.*
ˌ**undiˈluted** *adj.*
ˌ**undiˈminished** *adj.*
ˌ**undiploˈmatic** *adj.*
ˌ**undiˈrected** *adj.*
unˈdisciplined *adj.*
ˌ**undisˈcovered** *adj.*
ˌ**undisˈcrimiˌnating** *adj.*
ˌ**undisˈmayed** *adj.*
ˌ**undisˈposed** *adj.*
ˌ**undisˈputed** *adj.*
ˌ**undisˈtinguishable** *adj.*
ˌ**undisˈtinguished** *adj.*
ˌ**undisˈturbed** *adj.*
ˌ**undiˈvided** *adj.*
unˈdoubtable *adj.*
unˈdrained *adj.*
unˈdrinkable *adj.*

('ʌndjʊlɪt, -ˌleɪt). **3.** having a wavy or rippled appearance, margin, or form: *an undulate leaf.* [C17: < L < *unda* a wave] —**'unduˌlator** *n.* —**'undulatory** *adj.*

undulation (ˌʌndjʊ'leɪʃən) *n.* **1.** the act or an instance of undulating. **2.** any wave or wavelike form, line, etc.

unduly (ʌn'dju:lɪ) *adv.* excessively.

undying (ʌn'daɪɪŋ) *adj.* unending; eternal. —**un'dyingly** *adv.*

unearned (ʌn'ɜ:nd) *adj.* **1.** not deserved. **2.** not yet earned.

unearned income *n.* income from property, investment, etc., comprising rent, interest, and dividends.

unearth (ʌn'ɜ:θ) *vb.* (*tr.*) **1.** to dig up out of the earth. **2.** to reveal or discover, esp. by exhaustive searching.

unearthly (ʌn'ɜ:θlɪ) *adj.* **1.** ghostly; eerie: *unearthly screams.* **2.** heavenly; sublime: *unearthly music.* **3.** ridiculous or unreasonable (esp. in **unearthly hour**). —**un'earthliness** *n.*

uneasy (ʌn'i:zɪ) *adj.* **1.** (of a person) anxious; apprehensive. **2.** (of a condition) precarious: *an uneasy truce.* **3.** (of a thought, etc.) disquieting. —**un'ease** *n.* —**un'easily** *adv.* —**un'easiness** *n.*

uneatable (ʌn'i:təbᵊl) *adj.* (of food) not fit or suitable for eating, esp. because it is rotten or unattractive.

▷ **Usage.** See at **inedible.**

uneconomic (ˌʌni:kə'nɒmɪk, ˌʌnɛkə-) *adj.* not economic; not profitable.

uneconomical (ˌʌni:kə'nɒmɪkᵊl, -ɛkə-) *adj.* not economical; wasteful.

unemployable (ˌʌnɪm'plɔɪəbᵊl) *adj.* unable or unfit to keep a job. —ˌ**unemˌployaˈbility** *n.*

unemployed (ˌʌnɪm'plɔɪd) *adj.* **1. a.** without remunerative employment; out of work. **b.** (*as collective n.;* preceded by *the*)*: the unemployed.* **2.** not being used; idle.

unemployment (ˌʌnɪm'plɔɪmənt) *n.* **1.** the condition of being unemployed. **2.** the number of unemployed workers, often as a percentage of the total labour force.

unemployment benefit *n.* (in the British National Insurance scheme) a regular payment to a person who is out of work and has usually paid a fixed number of insurance contributions. Informal term: **dole.**

unequal (ʌn'i:kwəl) *adj.* **1.** not equal in quantity, size, rank, value, etc. **2.** (foll. by *to*) inadequate; insufficient. **3.** not evenly balanced. **4.** (of character, quality, etc.) irregular; inconsistent. **5.** (of a contest, etc.) having competitors of different ability.

unequalled *or U.S.* **unequaled** (ʌn'i:kwəld) *adj.* not equalled; unrivalled; supreme.

unequivocal (ˌʌnɪ'kwɪvəkᵊl) *adj.* not ambiguous; plain. —ˌ**uneˈquivocally** *adv.* —ˌ**uneˈquivocalness** *n.*

unerring (ʌn'ɜ:rɪŋ) *adj.* **1.** not missing the mark or target. **2.** consistently accurate; certain. —**un'erringly** *adv.* —**un'erringness** *n.*

UNESCO (ju:'nɛskəʊ) *n. acronym for* United Nations Educational, Scientific, and Cultural Organization.

uneven (ʌn'i:vən) *adj.* **1.** (of a surface, etc.) not level or flat. **2.** spasmodic or variable. **3.** not parallel, straight, or horizontal. **4.** not fairly matched: *an uneven race.* **5.** *Arch.* not equal. —**un'evenly** *adv.* —**un'evenness** *n.*

uneventful (ˌʌnɪ'vɛntfʊl) *adj.* ordinary, routine, or quiet. —ˌ**uneˈventfully** *adv.* —ˌ**uneˈventfulness** *n.*

unexampled (ˌʌnɪg'zɑ:mpᵊld) *adj.* without precedent or parallel.

unexceptionable (ˌʌnɪk'sɛpʃənəbᵊl) *adj.* beyond criticism or objection. —ˌ**unexˈceptionably** *adv.*

unexceptional (ˌʌnɪk'sɛpʃənᵊl) *adj.* **1.** usual, ordinary, or normal. **2.** subject to or allowing no exceptions. —ˌ**unexˈceptionally** *adv.*

unexpected (ˌʌnɪk'spɛktɪd) *adj.* surprising or unforeseen. —ˌ**unexˈpectedly** *adv.* —ˌ**unexˈpectedness** *n.*

unfailing (ʌn'feɪlɪŋ) *adj.* **1.** not failing; unflagging. **2.** continuous. **3.** sure; certain. —**un'failingly** *adv.* —**un'failingness** *n.*

unfair (ʌn'fɛə) *adj.* **1.** characterized by inequality or injustice. **2.** dishonest or unethical. —**un'fairly** *adv.* —**un'fairness** *n.*

unfaithful (ʌn'feɪθfʊl) *adj.* **1.** not true to a promise, vow, etc. **2.** not true to a wife, husband, lover, etc., esp. in having sexual intercourse with someone else. **3.** inaccurate; untrustworthy: *unfaithful copy.* **4.** *Obs.* not having religious faith. —**un'faithfully** *adv.* —**un'faithfulness** *n.*

unfamiliar (ˌʌnfə'mɪljə) *adj.* **1.** not known or experienced; strange. **2.** (*postpositive;* foll. by *with*) not familiar. —**unfamiliarity** (ˌʌnfəˌmɪlɪ'ærɪtɪ) *n.* —ˌ**unfaˈmiliarly** *adv.*

unfasten (ʌn'fɑ:sᵊn) *vb.* to undo, untie, or open or become undone, untied, or opened.

unfathered (ʌn'fɑ:ðəd) *adj.* **1.** having no known father. **2.** of unknown or uncertain origin.

unfathomable (ʌn'fæðəməbᵊl) *adj.* **1.** incapable of being fathomed; immeasurable. **2.** incomprehensible. —**un'fathomableness** *n.* —**un'fathomably** *adv.*

unfavourable *or U.S.* **unfavorable** (ʌn'feɪvərəbᵊl) *adj.* not favourable; adverse or inauspicious. —**un'favourably** *or U.S.* **un'favorably** *adv.*

unfeeling (ʌn'fi:lɪŋ) *adj.* **1.** without sympathy; callous. **2.** without physical feeling or sensation. —**un'feelingly** *adv.* —**un'feelingness** *n.*

unfinished (ʌn'fɪnɪʃt) *adj.* **1.** incomplete or imperfect. **2.** (of paint, polish, varnish, etc.) without an applied finish; rough. **3.** (of fabric) unbleached or not processed.

unfit (ʌn'fɪt) *adj.* **1.** (*postpositive;* often foll. by *for*) unqualified, incapable, or incompetent: *unfit for military service.* **2.** (*postpositive;* often foll. by *for*) unsuitable or inappropriate: *the ground was unfit for football.* **3.** in poor physical condition. ~*vb.* **-fitting, -fitted. 4.** (*tr.*) *Rare.* to render unfit. —**un'fitly** *adv.* —**un'fitness** *n.*

unfix (ʌn'fɪks) *vb.* (*tr.*) **1.** to unfasten, detach, or loosen. **2.** to unsettle or disturb.

unflappable (ʌn'flæpəbᵊl) *adj. Inf.* hard to upset; calm; composed. —**unˌflappaˈbility** *n.* —**un'flappably** *adv.*

unfledged (ʌn'flɛdʒd) *adj.* **1.** (of a young bird) not having developed adult feathers. **2.** immature and undeveloped.

---

un'dutiful *adj.*
un'dyed *adj.*
un'eaten *adj.*
un'edited *adj.*
un'educable *adj.*
un'eduˌcated *adj.*
ˌ**une'manciˌpated** *adj.*
ˌ**unem'bellished** *adj.*
ˌ**une'motional** *adj.*
ˌ**unen'cumbered** *adj.*
un'ending *adj.*
ˌ**unen'dowed** *adj.*
ˌ**unen'durable** *adj.*
ˌ**unen'gaged** *adj.*
ˌ**unen'lightened** *adj.*
un'enterˌprising *adj.*
ˌ**unenˌthusi'astic** *adj.*
un'enviable *adj.*
ˌ**une'quipped** *adj.*
ˌ**unes'capable** *adj.*
ˌ**unes'corted** *adj.*
ˌ**unes'sential** *adj.*
un'ethical *adj.*
ˌ**unex'aggerˌated** *adj.*
ˌ**unex'cused** *adj.*
ˌ**unex'perienced** *adj.*
ˌ**unex'pired** *adj.*
ˌ**unex'plainable** *adj.*
ˌ**unex'plained** *adj.*
ˌ**unex'ploited** *adj.*
ˌ**unex'plored** *adj.*
ˌ**unex'pressed** *adj.*
un'expurˌgated *adj.*
un'fading *adj.*
un'fashionable *adj.*
un'fathomed *adj.*
un'favoured *adj.*
un'fed *adj.*
un'federˌated *adj.*
un'feigned *adj.*
ˌ**unfer'mented** *adj.*
un'fertiˌlized *or* **-ˌlised** *adj.*
un'fetter *vb.*
un'fettered *adj.*
un'fitting *adj.*
un'flattering *adj.*

unflinching (ʌnˈflɪntʃɪŋ) *adj.* not shrinking from danger, difficulty, etc. —**unˈflinchingly** *adv.*
unfold (ʌnˈfəʊld) *vb.* **1.** to open or spread out or be opened or spread out from a folded state. **2.** to reveal or be revealed: *the truth unfolds.* **3.** to develop or expand or be developed or expanded. —**unˈfolder** *n.*
unfortunate (ʌnˈfɔːtʃənɪt) *adj.* **1.** causing or attended by misfortune. **2.** unlucky or unhappy: *an unfortunate character.* **3.** regrettable or unsuitable: *an unfortunate speech.* ~*n.* **4.** an unlucky person. —**unˈfortunately** *adv.*
unfounded (ʌnˈfaʊndɪd) *adj.* **1.** (of ideas, allegations, etc.) baseless; groundless. **2.** not yet founded or established. —**unˈfoundedly** *adv.* —**unˈfoundedness** *n.*
unfreeze (ʌnˈfriːz) *vb.* **-freezing, -froze, -frozen.** **1.** to thaw or cause to thaw. **2.** (*tr.*) to relax governmental restrictions on (wages, prices, credit, etc.) or on the manufacture or sale of (goods, etc.).
unfriended (ʌnˈfrɛndɪd) *adj. Now rare.* without a friend or friends; friendless.
unfriendly (ʌnˈfrɛndlɪ) *adj.* **-lier, -liest.** **1.** not friendly; hostile. **2.** unfavourable or disagreeable. ~*adv.* **3.** *Rare.* in an unfriendly manner. —**unˈfriendliness** *n.*
unfrock (ʌnˈfrɒk) *vb.* (*tr.*) to deprive (a person in holy orders) of ecclesiastical status.
unfunded debt (ʌnˈfʌndɪd) *n.* a short-term floating debt not represented by bonds.
unfurl (ʌnˈfɜːl) *vb.* to unroll, unfold, or spread out or be unrolled, unfolded, or spread out from a furled state.
ungainly (ʌnˈgeɪnlɪ) *adj.* **-lier, -liest.** **1.** lacking grace when moving. **2.** difficult to move or use; unwieldy. [C17: < UN-¹ + obs. or dialect GAINLY graceful] —**unˈgainliness** *n.*
ungodly (ʌnˈgɒdlɪ) *adj.* **-lier, -liest.** **1. a.** wicked, sinful. **b.** (*as collective n.;* preceded by *the*)*: the ungodly.* **2.** *Inf.* unseemly; outrageous (esp. in **an ungodly hour**). —**unˈgodliness** *n.*
ungovernable (ʌnˈgʌvənəbᵊl) *adj.* not able to be disciplined, restrained, etc.: *an ungovernable temper.* —**unˈgovernableness** *n.* —**unˈgovernably** *adv.*
ungual (ˈʌŋgwəl) *adj.* **1.** of, relating to, or affecting the fingernails or toenails. **2.** of or relating to an unguis. [C19: < L *unguis* nail]
unguarded (ʌnˈgɑːdɪd) *adj.* **1.** unprotected; vulnerable. **2.** open; frank. **3.** incautious. —**unˈguardedly** *adv.* —**unˈguardedness** *n.*
unguent (ˈʌŋgwənt) *n.* a less common name for an **ointment.** [C15: < L, < *unguere* to anoint]
unguiculate (ʌŋˈgwɪkjʊlɪt, -ˌleɪt) *adj.* **1.** (of mammals) having claws or nails. **2.** (of petals) having a clawlike base. ~*n.* **3.** an unguiculate mammal. [C19: < NL *unguiculātus,* < L *unguiculus,* dim. of *unguis* nail]
unguis (ˈʌŋgwɪs) *n., pl.* **-gues** (-gwiːz). **1.** a nail, claw, or hoof, or the part of the digit giving rise to it. **2.** the clawlike base of a petal. [C18: < L]
ungulate (ˈʌŋgjʊlɪt, -ˌleɪt) *n.* any of a large group of mammals all of which have hooves: divided into odd-toed ungulates (see **perissodactyl**) and even-toed ungulates (see **artiodactyl**). [C19: < LL *ungulātus* having hooves, < *ungula* hoof]
unhallowed (ʌnˈhæləʊd) *adj.* **1.** not consecrated or holy: *unhallowed ground.* **2.** sinful.
unhand (ʌnˈhænd) *vb.* (*tr.*) *Arch. or literary.* to release from the grasp.
unhappy (ʌnˈhæpɪ) *adj.* **-pier, -piest.** **1.** not joyful; sad or depressed. **2.** unfortunate or wretched: *an unhappy fellow.* **3.** tactless or inappropriate: *an unhappy remark.* —**unˈhappily** *adv.* —**unˈhappiness** *n.*
unhealthy (ʌnˈhɛlθɪ) *adj.* **-healthier, -healthiest.** **1.** characterized by ill health; sick. **2.** characteristic of, conducive to, or resulting from ill health: *an unhealthy complexion.* **3.** morbid or unwholesome. **4.** *Inf.* dangerous; risky. —**unˈhealthily** *adv.* —**unˈhealthiness** *n.*
unheard (ʌnˈhɜːd) *adj.* **1.** not heard; not perceived by the ear. **2.** not listened to: *his warning went unheard.* **3.** *Arch.* unheard-of.
unheard-of *adj.* **1.** previously unknown: *an unheard-of actress.* **2.** without precedent: *an unheard-of treatment.* **3.** highly offensive: *unheard-of behaviour.*
unhinge (ʌnˈhɪndʒ) *vb.* (*tr.*) **1.** to remove (a door, etc.) from its hinges. **2.** to derange or unbalance (a person, his mind, etc.). **3.** to disrupt or unsettle (a process or state of affairs).
unholy (ʌnˈhəʊlɪ) *adj.* **-lier, -liest.** **1.** not holy or sacred. **2.** immoral or depraved. **3.** *Inf.* outrageous or unnatural: *an unholy alliance.* —**unˈholiness** *n.*
unhook (ʌnˈhʊk) *vb.* **1.** (*tr.*) to remove (something) from a hook. **2.** (*tr.*) to unfasten the hook of (a dress, etc.). **3.** (*intr.*) to become unfastened or be capable of unfastening: *the dress wouldn't unhook.*
unhorse (ʌnˈhɔːs) *vb.* (*tr.*) **1.** (*usually passive*) to knock or throw from a horse. **2.** to overthrow or dislodge, as from a powerful position.
unhouseled (ʌnˈhaʊzəld) *adj. Arch.* not having received the Eucharist. [C16: < *un-* + obs. *housel* to administer the sacrament, < OE *hūsl* (n.), *hūslian* (vb.), <?]
uni (ˈjuːnɪ) *n. Inf.* short for **university.**
uni- *combining form.* consisting of, relating to, or having only one: *unilateral.* [< L *ūnus* one]
Uniat (ˈjuːnɪˌæt) *or* **Uniate** (ˈjuːnɪɪt, -ˌeɪt) *adj.* **1.** designating any of the Eastern Churches that retain their own liturgy but submit to papal authority. ~*n.* **2.** a member of one of these Churches. [C19: < Russian *uniyat,* < Polish *unja* union, < LL *ūniō;* see UNION] —ˈ**Uniˌatism** *n.*
uniaxial (ˌjuːnɪˈæksɪəl) *adj.* **1.** (esp. of plants) having an unbranched main axis. **2.** (of a crystal) having only one direction along which double refraction of light does not occur.
unicameral (ˌjuːnɪˈkæmərəl) *adj.* of or characterized by a single legislative chamber. —ˌ**uniˈcameralism** *n.* —ˌ**uniˈcameralist** *n.* —ˌ**uniˈcamerally** *adv.*

ˌ**unforˈbearing** *adj.*
unˈforceable *adj.*
unˈforced *adj.*
ˌ**unforeˈseeable** *adj.*
ˌ**unforeˈseen** *adj.*
ˌ**unforeˈtold** *adj.*
ˌ**unforˈgettable** *adj.*
ˌ**unforˈgivable** *adj.*
ˌ**unforˈgiven** *adj.*
ˌ**unforˈgiving** *adj.*
ˌ**unforˈgotten** *adj.*
unˈformed *adj.*
ˌ**unforˈsaken** *adj.*
ˌ**unforthˈcoming** *adj.*
unˈfortiˌfied *adj.*
unˈfound *adj.*
unˈframed *adj.*
ˌ**unfreˈquented** *adj.*
unˈfruitful *adj.*
ˌ**unfulˈfilled** *adj.*
unˈfurnished *adj.*
unˈgenerous *adj.*
unˈgentlemanly *adj.*
unˈgifted *adj.*
unˈgird *vb.*
unˈglazed *adj.*
unˈgracious *adj.*
ˌ**ungramˈmatical** *adj.*
unˈgrateful *adj.*
unˈgrounded *adj.*
unˈgrudging *adj.*
unˈguided *adj.*
unˈhampered *adj.*
unˈhandy *adj.*
unˈhardened *adj.*
unˈharmed *adj.*
unˈharmful *adj.*
ˌ**unharˈmonious** *adj.*
unˈharness *vb.*
unˈharrowed *adj.*
unˈhatched *adj.*
unˈhealed *adj.*
unˈheated *adj.*
unˈheeded *adj.*
unˈheeding *adj.*
unˈhelpful *adj.*
unˈheralded *adj.*
ˌ**unheˈroic** *adj.*
unˈhesiˌtating *adj.*
unˈhindered *adj.*
ˌ**unhisˈtoric** *adj.*
unˈhitch *vb.*
unˈhoped-for *adj.*
unˈhoused *adj.*
unˈhuman *adj.*
unˈhurried *adj.*
unˈhurt *adj.*
ˌ**unhyˈgienic** *adj.*
unˈhyphenˌated *adj.*

UNICEF (ˈjuːnɪˌsɛf) *n. acronym for* United Nations Children's Fund (formerly, United Nations International Children's Emergency Fund).

unicellular (ˌjuːnɪˈsɛljʊlə) *adj.* (of organisms, such as protozoans and certain algae) consisting of a single cell. —ˌ**uniˌcelluˈlarity** *n.*

unicorn (ˈjuːnɪˌkɔːn) *n.* **1.** an imaginary creature usually depicted as a white horse with one long spiralled horn growing from its forehead. **2.** *Old Testament.* a two-horned animal: mistranslation in the Authorized Version of the original Hebrew. [C13: < OF, < L *ūnicornis* one-horned, < *ūnus* one + *cornu* a horn]

unicycle (ˈjuːnɪˌsaɪkᵊl) *n.* a one-wheeled vehicle driven by pedals, esp. one used in a circus, etc. Also called: **monocycle.** [< UNI- + CYCLE, on the model of TRICYCLE] —ˈ**uniˌcyclist** *n.*

unidirectional (ˌjuːnɪdɪˈrɛkʃənᵊl) *adj.* having, moving in, or operating in only one direction.

UNIDO (juːˈniːdəʊ) *n. acronym for* United Nations Industrial Development Organization.

Unification Church *n.* a religious sect founded by the Rev. Sun Myung Moon (born 1920), S Korean industrialist and religious leader.

unified field theory *n.* any theory capable of describing in one set of equations the properties of gravitational fields, electromagnetic fields, and strong and weak nuclear interactions. No satisfactory theory has yet been found.

uniform (ˈjuːnɪˌfɔːm) *n.* **1.** a prescribed identifying set of clothes for the members of an organization, such as soldiers or schoolchildren. **2.** a single set of such clothes. **3.** a characteristic feature of some class or group. ~*adj.* **4.** unchanging in form, quality, etc.: *a uniform surface.* **5.** alike or like: *a line of uniform toys.* ~*vb.* (*tr.*) **6.** to fit out (a body of soldiers, etc.) with uniforms. **7.** to make uniform. [C16: < L *ūniformis,* < *ūnus* one + *forma* shape] —ˈ**uniˌformly** *adv.* —ˈ**uniˌformness** *n.*

uniformitarianism (ˌjuːnɪˌfɔːmɪˈtɛərɪəˌnɪzəm) *n.* the concept that the earth's surface was shaped in the past by gradual processes, such as erosion, and by small sudden changes, such as earthquakes, rather than by sudden divine acts, such as Noah's flood. —ˌ**uniˌformiˈtarian** *n., adj.*

uniformity (ˌjuːnɪˈfɔːmɪtɪ) *n., pl.* **-ties. 1.** a state or condition in which everything is regular, homogeneous, or unvarying. **2.** lack of diversity or variation.

unify (ˈjuːnɪˌfaɪ) *vb.* **-fying, -fied.** to make or become one; unite. [C16: < Med. L *ūnificāre,* < L *ūnus* one + *facere* to make] —ˈ**uniˌfiable** *adj.* —ˌ**unifiˈcation** *n.* —ˈ**uniˌfier** *n.*

unilateral (ˌjuːnɪˈlætərəl) *adj.* **1.** of, having, affecting, or occurring on only one side. **2.** involving or performed by only one party of several: *unilateral disarmament.* **3.** *Law.* (of contracts, obligations, etc.) made by, affecting, or binding one party only. **4.** *Bot.* having or designating parts situated or turned to one side of an axis. —ˌ**uniˈlateralism** *n.* —ˌ**uniˈlaterally** *adv.*

Unilateral Declaration of Independence *n.* a declaration of independence made by a dependent state without the assent of the protecting state. Abbrev.: **UDI.**

unimpeachable (ˌʌnɪmˈpiːtʃəbᵊl) *adj.* unquestionable as to honesty, truth, etc. —ˌ**unimˈpeachably** *adv.*

unimproved (ˌʌnɪmˈpruːvd) *adj.* **1.** not improved or made better. **2.** (of land) not cleared, drained, cultivated, etc. **3.** neglected; unused: *unimproved resources.*

uninterested (ʌnˈɪntrɪstɪd) *adj.* indifferent. —**unˈinterestedly** *adv.* —**unˈinterestedness** *n.*
▷ **Usage.** See at **disinterested.**

union (ˈjuːnjən) *n.* **1.** the condition of being united, the act of uniting, or a conjunction formed by such an act. **2.** an association, alliance, or confederation of individuals or groups for a common purpose, esp. political. **3.** agreement or harmony. **4.** short for **trade union. 5.** the act or state of marriage or sexual intercourse. **6.** a device on a flag representing union, such as another flag depicted in the top left corner. **7.** a device for coupling pipes. **8.** (*often cap.*) **a.** an association of students at a university or college formed to look after the students' interests. **b.** the building or buildings housing the facilities of such an organization. **9.** *Maths.* a set containing all members of two given sets. Symbol: ∪ **10.** (in 19th-century England) a number of parishes united for the administration of poor relief. **11.** *Textiles.* a piece of cloth or fabric consisting of two different kinds of yarn. **12.** (*modifier*) of or related to a union, esp. a trade union. [C15: < Church L *ūniō* oneness, < L *ūnus* one]

Union (ˈjuːnjən) *n.* **the. 1.** *Brit.* **a.** the union of the English and Scottish crowns (1603–1707). **b.** the union of England and Scotland from 1707. **c.** the political union of Great Britain and Ireland (1801–1920). **d.** the union of Great Britain and Northern Ireland from 1920. **2.** *U.S.* **a.** the United States of America. **b.** the northern states of the U.S. during the Civil War. **c.** (*as modifier*): *Union supporters.*

union catalogue *n.* a catalogue listing every publication held at cooperating libraries.

unionism (ˈjuːnjəˌnɪzəm) *n.* **1.** the principles of trade unions. **2.** adherence to the principles of trade unions. **3.** the principle or theory of any union. —ˈ**unionist** *n., adj.*

Unionist (ˈjuːnjənɪst) *n.* **1.** a member or supporter of the Unionist Party. **2.** a supporter of the U.S. federal Union, esp. during the Civil War. **3.** (*sometimes not cap.*) **a.** (before 1920) a supporter of the union of all Ireland and Great Britain. **b.** (since 1920) a supporter of union between Britain and Northern Ireland. ~*adj.* **4.** of, resembling, or relating to Unionists. —ˈ**Unionˌism** *n.*

Unionist Party *n.* (in Northern Ireland) formerly, the major Protestant political party, closely identified with the Union with Britain.

unionize *or* **-nise** (ˈjuːnjəˌnaɪz) *vb.* **1.** to organize (workers) into a trade union. **2.** to join or cause to join a trade union. **3.** (*tr.*) to subject to the rules or codes of a trade union. —ˌ**unioniˈzation** *or* **-niˈsation** *n.*

Union Jack *n.* the national flag of the United Kingdom, being a composite design composed of Saint George's Cross (England), Saint Andrew's Cross (Scotland), and Saint Patrick's Cross (Ireland). Also called: **Union flag.**

union shop *n.* an establishment whose employment policy is governed by a contract between

---

ˌ**uniˈdentiˌfiable** *adj.*
ˌ**uniˈdentiˌfied** *adj.*
ˌ**unilˈlumiˌnated** *adj.*
ˌ**unilˈlumiˌnating** *adj.*
unˈillusˌtrated *adj.*
ˌ**unimˈaginable** *adj.*
ˌ**unimˈaginably** *adv.*
ˌ**unimˈaginative** *adj.*
ˌ**unimˈaginatively** *adv.*
ˌ**unimˈpaired** *adj.*
ˌ**unimˈpeded** *adj.*
ˌ**unimˈportant** *adj.*
ˌ**unimˈposing** *adj.*
ˌ**unimˈpressed** *adj.*
ˌ**uninˈclosed** *adj.*
ˌ**uninˈcorpoˌrated** *adj.*
ˌ**uninˈcumbered** *adj.*
ˌ**uninˈfected** *adj.*
ˌ**uninfluˈential** *adj.*
ˌ**uninˈformative** *adj.*
ˌ**uninˈformed** *adj.*
ˌ**uninˈhabitable** *adj.*
ˌ**uninˈhabited** *adj.*
ˌ**uninˈhibited** *adj.*
ˌ**uninˈitiˌated** *adj.*
unˈinjured *adj.*
ˌ**uninˈspired** *adj.*
ˌ**uninˈspiring** *adj.*
ˌ**uninˈstructed** *adj.*
ˌ**uninˈstructive** *adj.*
ˌ**uninˈsured** *adj.*
ˌ**uninˈtelligent** *adj.*
ˌ**uninˈtelligible** *adj.*
ˌ**uninˈtended** *adj.*
ˌ**uninˈtentional** *adj.*
unˈinteresting *adj.*
ˌ**uninterˈrupted** *adj.*
ˌ**uninˈvested** *adj.*
ˌ**uninˈvited** *adj.*
ˌ**uninˈviting** *adj.*
ˌ**uninˈvoked** *adj.*

employer and a trade union permitting the employment of nonunion labour only on the condition that such labour joins the union within a specified time period.

unipolar (ˌjuːnɪˈpəʊlə) *adj.* **1.** of, concerned with, or having a single magnetic or electric pole. **2.** (of a nerve cell) having a single process. **3.** (of a transistor) utilizing charge carriers of one polarity only, as in a field-effect transistor. —**unipolarity** (ˌjuːnɪpəʊˈlærɪtɪ) *n.*

unique (juːˈniːk) *adj.* **1.** being the only one of a particular type. **2.** without equal or like. **3.** *Inf.* very remarkable. **4.** *Maths.* **a.** leading to only one result: *the sum of two integers is unique.* **b.** having precisely one value: *the unique positive square root of 4 is 2.* [C17: via F < L *ūnicus* unparalleled, < *ūnus* one] —**uˈniquely** *adv.* —**uˈniqueness** *n.*

▷ **Usage.** Certain words in English, such as *unique, perfect,* and *simultaneous,* describe absolute states, that is to say, states that cannot be qualified; something is either *unique* or it is *not unique,* but it cannot be, for example, *rather unique.* Careful users of English therefore avoid the use of comparatives or intensifiers where absolute states are concerned: *that is very exceptional* (not *very unique*); *this one comes nearer to perfection* (not *is more perfect*).

unisex (ˈjuːnɪˌsɛks) *adj.* of or relating to clothing, a hairstyle, hairdressers, etc., that can be worn or used by either sex. [C20: < UNI- + SEX]

unisexual (ˌjuːnɪˈsɛksjʊəl) *adj.* **1.** of one sex only. **2.** (of some organisms) having either male or female reproductive organs but not both. —ˌ**uniˌsexuˈality** *n.* —ˌ**uniˈsexually** *adv.*

unison (ˈjuːnɪsᵊn) *n.* **1.** *Music.* **a.** the interval between two notes of identical pitch. **b.** (*modifier*) played or sung at the same pitch: *unison singing.* **2.** complete agreement (esp. in **in unison**). [C16: < LL *ūnisonus,* < UNI- + *sonus* sound] —**uˈnisonous, uˈnisonal,** *or* **uˈnisonant** *adj.*

unit (ˈjuːnɪt) *n.* **1.** a single undivided entity or whole. **2.** any group or individual, esp. when regarded as a basic element of a larger whole. **3.** a mechanical part or assembly of parts that performs a subsidiary function: *a filter unit.* **4.** a complete system or establishment that performs a specific function: *a production unit.* **5.** a subdivision of a larger military formation. **6.** a standard amount of a physical quantity, such as length, mass, energy, etc., specified multiples of which are used to express magnitudes of that physical quantity: *the second is a unit of time.* **7.** the amount of a drug, vaccine, etc., needed to produce a particular effect. **8.** the digit or position immediately to the left of the decimal point. **9.** (*modifier*) having or relating to a value of one: *a unit vector.* **10.** *N.Z.* a self-propelled railcar. **11.** *Austral. & N.Z.* short for **home unit.** [C16: back formation from UNITY, ? on the model of *digit*]

unitarian (ˌjuːnɪˈtɛərɪən) *n.* **1.** a supporter of unity or centralization in politics. ~*adj.* **2.** of or relating to unity or centralization.

Unitarian (ˌjuːnɪˈtɛərɪən) *n.* **1.** a person who believes that God is one being and rejects the doctrine of the Trinity. **2.** a member of the Church (**Unitarian Church**) that embodies this system of belief. ~*adj.* **3.** of or relating to Unitarians or Unitarianism. —ˌ**UniˈtariaˌnIsm** *n.*

unitary (ˈjuːnɪtərɪ, -trɪ) *adj.* **1.** of a unit or units. **2.** based on or characterized by unity. **3.** individual; whole.

unit character *n. Genetics.* a character inherited as a single unit and dependent on a single gene.

unit cost *n.* the actual cost of producing one article.

unite[1] (juːˈnaɪt) *vb.* **1.** to make or become an integrated whole or a unity. **2.** to join, unify or be unified in purpose, action, beliefs, etc. **3.** to enter or cause to enter into an association or alliance. **4.** to adhere or cause to adhere; fuse. **5.** (*tr.*) to possess (qualities) in combination or at the same time: *he united charm with severity.* [C15: < LL *ūnīre,* < *ūnus* one]

unite[2] (ˈjuːnaɪt, juːˈnaɪt) *n.* an English gold coin minted in the Stuart period, originally worth 20 shillings. [C17: < obs. *unite* joined, from the union of England & Scotland (1603)]

united (juːˈnaɪtɪd) *adj.* **1.** produced by two or more persons or things in combination or from their union or amalgamation: *a united effort.* **2.** in agreement. **3.** in association or alliance. —**uˈnitedly** *adv.* —**uˈnitedness** *n.*

United Empire Loyalist *n. Canad. history.* an American colonist who settled in Canada during or after the War of American Independence because of loyalty to the British Crown.

United Kingdom *n.* a kingdom of NW Europe, consisting chiefly of the island of Great Britain together with Northern Ireland. It became the **United Kingdom of Great Britain and Northern Ireland** in 1921, after the rest of Ireland became autonomous. Abbrev.: **UK.**

United Nations *n.* (*functioning as sing. or pl.*) an international organization of independent states, with its headquarters in New York City, that was formed in 1945 to promote peace and international cooperation and security. Abbrev.: **UN.**

United States of America *n.* (*functioning as sing. or pl.*) a federal republic, mainly in North America, consisting of 50 states and the District of Columbia. Often shortened to **United States.** Abbrev.: **U.S., U.S.A.**

unitive (ˈjuːnɪtɪv) *adj.* **1.** tending to unite or capable of uniting. **2.** characterized by unity.

unit-linked policy *n.* a life-assurance policy the benefits of which are directly in proportion to the number of units held by the policyholder.

unit of account *n.* a standard monetary denomination used for keeping accounts in Britain and to express loans and subsidies in the European Economic Community.

unit price *n.* a price for foodstuffs, etc., stated or shown as the cost per unit, as per pound, per kilogram, per dozen, etc.

unit trust *n. Brit.* an investment trust that issues units for public sale, the holders of which are creditors and not shareholders with their interests represented by a trust company independent of the issuing agency. U.S. and Canad. equivalent: **mutual fund.**

unity (ˈjuːnɪtɪ) *n., pl.* **-ties. 1.** the state or quality of being one; oneness. **2.** the act, state, or quality of forming a whole from separate parts. **3.** something whole or complete that is composed of separate parts. **4.** mutual agreement; harmony or concord: *the participants were no longer in unity.* **5.** uniformity or constancy: *unity of purpose.* **6.** *Maths.* **a.** the number or numeral one. **b.** a quantity assuming the value of one: *the area of the triangle was regarded as unity.* **c.** the element of a set producing no change in a number following multiplication. **7.** any one of the three principles of dramatic structure by which the action of a play should be limited to a single plot (unity of action), a single location (unity of place), and a single day (unity of time). [C13: < OF *unité,* < L *ūnitās,* < *ūnus* one]

Univ. *abbrev. for* University.

univalent (ˌjuːnɪˈveɪlənt, juːˈnɪvələnt) *adj.* **1.** (of a chromosome during meiosis) not paired with its homologue. **2.** *Chem.* another word for **monovalent.** —ˌ**uniˈvalency** *n.*

univalve (ˈjuːnɪˌvælv) *Zool.* ~*adj.* **1.** relating to or possessing a mollusc shell that consists of a single piece (valve). ~*n.* **2.** a gastropod mollusc.

universal (ˌjuːnɪˈvɜːsᵊl) *adj.* **1.** of or typical of the whole of mankind or of nature. **2.** common to or proceeding from all in a particular group. **3.** applicable to or affecting many individuals,

---

unˈironed *adj.*

conditions, or cases. **4.** existing or prevailing everywhere. **5.** applicable or occurring throughout or relating to the universe: *a universal constant.* **6.** (esp. of a language) capable of being used and understood by all. **7.** embracing or versed in many fields of knowledge, activity, interest, etc. **8.** *Machinery.* designed or adapted for a range of sizes, fittings, or uses. **9.** *Logic.* (of a statement or proposition) affirming or denying something about every member of a class, as in *all men are wicked.* Cf. **particular** (sense 6). **10.** *Arch.* entire; whole. ~*n.* **11.** *Philosophy.* a general term or concept or the type such a term signifies. **12.** *Logic.* a universal proposition, statement, or formula. **13.** a characteristic common to every member of a particular culture or to every human being.

universal class *or* **set** *n.* (in Boolean algebra) the class containing all points and including all other classes.

universalism (ˌjuːnɪˈvɜːsəˌlɪzəm) *n.* **1.** a universal feature or characteristic. **2.** another word for **universality.**

Universalism (ˌjuːnɪˈvɜːsəˌlɪzəm) *n.* a system of religious beliefs maintaining that all men are predestined for salvation. —ˌ**Uniˈversalist** *n., adj.*

universality (ˌjuːnɪvɜːˈsælɪtɪ) *n.* the state or quality of being universal.

universalize *or* **-ise** (ˌjuːnɪˈvɜːsəˌlaɪz) *vb.* (*tr.*) to make universal. —ˌ**uniˌversaliˈzation** *or* **-iˈsation** *n.*

universal joint *or* **coupling** *n.* a form of coupling between two rotating shafts allowing freedom of movement in all directions.

universally (ˌjuːnɪˈvɜːsəlɪ) *adv.* everywhere or in every case: *this principle applies universally.*

universal motor *n.* an electric motor capable of working on either direct current or single-phase alternating current at approximately the same speed and output.

universal time *n.* another name for **Greenwich Mean Time.**

universe (ˈjuːnɪˌvɜːs) *n.* **1.** *Astron.* the aggregate of all existing matter, energy, and space. **2.** human beings collectively. **3.** a province or sphere of thought or activity. [C16: < F, < L *ūniversum* the whole world, < *ūniversus* all together, < UNI- + *vertere* to turn]

universe of discourse *n. Logic.* the complete range of objects, relations, ideas, etc., that are expressed or implied in a discussion.

university (ˌjuːnɪˈvɜːsɪtɪ) *n., pl.* **-ties. 1.** an institution of higher education having authority to award bachelors' and higher degrees, usually having research facilities. **2.** the buildings, members, staff, or campus of a university. [C14: < OF, < Med. L *universitās* group of scholars, < LL: guild, body of men, < L: whole]

unjust (ʌnˈdʒʌst) *adj.* not in accordance with accepted standards of fairness or justice; unfair. —**unˈjustly** *adv.* —**unˈjustness** *n.*

unkempt (ʌnˈkɛmpt) *adj.* **1.** (of the hair) uncombed; dishevelled. **2.** ungroomed; slovenly: *unkempt appearance.* [OE *uncembed;* < UN-[1] + *cembed,* p.p. of *cemban* to comb] —**unˈkemptly** *adv.* —**unˈkemptness** *n.*

unkind (ʌnˈkaɪnd) *adj.* lacking kindness; unsympathetic or cruel. —**unˈkindly** *adv.* —**unˈkindness** *n.*

unknowing (ʌnˈnəʊɪŋ) *adj.* **1.** not knowing; ignorant. **2.** (*postpositive;* often foll. by *of*) unaware (of). —**unˈknowingly** *adv.*

unknown (ʌnˈnəʊn) *adj.* **1.** not known, understood, or recognized. **2.** not established, identified, or discovered: *an unknown island.* **3.** not famous: *some unknown artist.* ~*n.* **4.** an unknown person, quantity, or thing. **5.** *Maths.* a variable the value of which is to be discovered by solving an equation; a variable in a conditional equation. —**unˈknownness** *n.*

Unknown Soldier *or* **Warrior** *n.* (in various countries) an unidentified soldier who has died in battle and for whom a tomb is established as a memorial to the other unidentified dead of the nation's armed forces.

unlace (ʌnˈleɪs) *vb.* (*tr.*) **1.** to loosen or undo the lacing of (shoes, etc.). **2.** to unfasten or remove garments, etc., of (oneself or another) by or as if by undoing lacing.

unlawful assembly (ʌnˈlɔːfʊl) *n. Law.* a meeting of three or more people with the intent of carrying out any unlawful purpose.

unlay (ʌnˈleɪ) *vb.* **-laying, -laid.** (*tr.*) to untwist (a rope or cable) to separate its strands.

unleaded (ʌnˈlɛdɪd) *adj.* (of petrol) containing a reduced amount of tetraethyl lead, in order to reduce environmental pollution.

unlearn (ʌnˈlɜːn) *vb.* **-learning, -learnt** *or* **-learned** (-ˈlɜːnd). to try to forget (something learnt) or to discard (accumulated knowledge).

unlearned (ʌnˈlɜːnɪd) *adj.* ignorant or untaught. —**unˈlearnedly** *adv.*

unlearnt (ʌnˈlɜːnt) *or* **unlearned** (ʌnˈlɜːnd) *adj.* **1.** denoting knowledge or skills innately present and therefore not learnt. **2.** not learnt or taken notice of: *unlearnt lessons.*

unleash (ʌnˈliːʃ) *vb.* (*tr.*) **1.** to release from or as if from a leash. **2.** to free from restraint.

unleavened (ʌnˈlɛvənd) *adj.* (of bread, etc.) made from a dough containing no yeast or leavening.

unless (ʌnˈlɛs) *conj.* (*subordinating*) except under the circumstances that; except on the condition that: *they'll sell it unless he hears otherwise.* [C14 *onlesse,* < *on* ON + *lesse* LESS]

▷ **Usage.** Careful writers of English who wish to keep their style clear and concise avoid the use of the expressions *unless and until* and *unless or until.* The difference in meaning of these two words is, in this context, not sufficient to make mentioning them both worthwhile; either would be adequate alone: *Unless* (or *until,* but not *unless and until*) *a candidate is nominated, the election cannot take place.*

unlettered (ʌnˈlɛtəd) *adj.* uneducated; illiterate.

unlike (ʌnˈlaɪk) *adj.* **1.** not alike; dissimilar or unequal; different. ~*prep.* **2.** not like; not typical of: *unlike his father he lacks intelligence.* —**unˈlikeness** *n.*

unlikely (ʌnˈlaɪklɪ) *adj.* not likely; improbable. —**unˈlikeliness** *or* **unˈlikeliˌhood** *n.*

unlimber (ʌnˈlɪmbə) *vb.* **1.** (*tr.*) to disengage (a gun) from its limber. **2.** to prepare (something) for use.

unlimited (ʌnˈlɪmɪtɪd) *adj.* **1.** without limits or bounds: *unlimited knowledge.* **2.** not restricted, limited, or qualified: *unlimited power.* —**unˈlimitedly** *adv.* —**unˈlimitedness** *n.*

unlisted (ʌnˈlɪstɪd) *adj.* **1.** not entered on a list. **2.** the U.S. and Canad. word for **ex-directory. 3.** (of securities) not quoted on a stock exchange.

unload (ʌnˈləʊd) *vb.* **1.** to remove a load or cargo from (a ship, lorry, etc.). **2.** to discharge (cargo, freight, etc.). **3.** (*tr.*) to relieve of a burden or troubles. **4.** (*tr.*) to give vent to (anxiety, troubles, etc.). **5.** (*tr.*) to get rid of or dispose of (esp. surplus goods). **6.** (*tr.*) to remove the charge of ammunition from (a firearm). —**unˈloader** *n.*

unlock (ʌnˈlɒk) *vb.* **1.** (*tr.*) to unfasten (a lock, door, etc.). **2.** (*tr.*) to release or let loose. **3.** (*tr.*) to provide the key to: *unlock a puzzle.* **4.** (*intr.*) to become unlocked. —**unˈlockable** *adj.*

---

unˈjoint *vb.*
unˈjustiˌfiable *adj.*
unˈjustiˌfied *adj.*
unˈkept *adj.*
unˈkissed *adj.*
unˈknit *vb.*
unˈknowable *adj.*
unˈlabelled *adj.*
unˈlade *vb.*
unˈladen *adj.*
unˈladyˌlike *adj.*
unˈlaid *adj.*
ˌ**unlaˈmented** *adj.*
unˈlatch *vb.*
unˈlawful *adj.*
unˈliberˌated *adj.*
unˈlicensed *adj.*
unˈlighted *adj.*
unˈlikable *adj.*
unˈlined *adj.*
unˈlit *adj.*
unˈlocked *adj.*

unlooked-for (ˌʌnˈlʊktfɔː) *adj.* unexpected; unforeseen.
unloose (ʌnˈluːs) *or* **unloosen** *vb. (tr.)* **1.** to set free; release. **2.** to loosen or relax (a hold, grip, etc.). **3.** to unfasten or untie.
unlovely (ʌnˈlʌvlɪ) *adj.* unpleasant in appearance or character. —**unˈloveliness** *n.*
unlucky (ʌnˈlʌkɪ) *adj.* **1.** characterized by misfortune or failure: *an unlucky chance.* **2.** ill-omened; inauspicious: *an unlucky date.* **3.** regrettable; disappointing. —**unˈluckily** *adv.* —**unˈluckiness** *n.*
unmake (ʌnˈmeɪk) *vb.* **-making, -made.** *(tr.)* **1.** to undo or destroy. **2.** to depose from office or authority. **3.** to alter the nature of.
unman (ʌnˈmæn) *vb.* **-manning, -manned.** *(tr.)* **1.** to cause to lose courage or nerve. **2.** to make effeminate. **3.** to remove the men from.
unmanly (ʌnˈmænlɪ) *adj.* **1.** not masculine or virile. **2.** ignoble, cowardly, or dishonourable. ~*adv.* **3.** *Arch.* in an unmanly manner. —**unˈmanliness** *n.*
unmanned (ʌnˈmænd) *adj.* **1.** lacking personnel or crew: *an unmanned ship.* **2.** (of aircraft, spacecraft, etc.) operated by automatic or remote control. **3.** uninhabited.
unmannered (ʌnˈmænəd) *adj.* **1.** without good manners; rude. **2.** without mannerisms.
unmannerly (ʌnˈmænəlɪ) *adj.* **1.** lacking manners; discourteous. ~*adv.* **2.** *Arch.* rudely; discourteously. —**unˈmannerliness** *n.*
unmask (ʌnˈmɑːsk) *vb.* **1.** to remove (the mask or disguise) from (someone or oneself). **2.** to appear or cause to appear in true character. —**unˈmasker** *n.*
unmeaning (ʌnˈmiːnɪŋ) *adj.* **1.** having no meaning. **2.** showing no intelligence; vacant: *an unmeaning face.* —**unˈmeaningly** *adv.* —**unˈmeaningness** *n.*
unmeet (ʌnˈmiːt) *adj. Literary or arch.* unsuitable. —**unˈmeetly** *adv.* —**unˈmeetness** *n.*
unmentionable (ʌnˈmɛnʃənəbᵊl) *adj.* **a.** unsuitable or forbidden as a topic of conversation. **b.** *(as n.): the unmentionable.* —**unˈmentionableness** *n.* —**unˈmentionably** *adv.*
unmentionables (ʌnˈmɛnʃənəbᵊlz) *pl. n. Chiefly humorous.* underwear.
unmerciful (ʌnˈmɜːsɪfʊl) *adj.* **1.** showing no mercy; relentless. **2.** extreme or excessive. —**unˈmercifully** *adv.* —**unˈmercifulness** *n.*
unmindful (ʌnˈmaɪndfʊl) *adj.* *(usually postpositive* and foll. by *of)* careless or forgetful. —**unˈmindfully** *adv.* —**unˈmindfulness** *n.*
unmistakable *or* **unmistakeable** (ˌʌnmɪsˈteɪkəbᵊl) *adj.* not mistakable; clear or unambiguous. —ˌ**unmisˈtakably** *or* ˌ**unmisˈtakeably** *adv.*
unmitigated (ʌnˈmɪtɪˌgeɪtɪd) *adj.* **1.** not diminished in intensity, severity, etc. **2.** *(prenominal)* (intensifier): *an unmitigated disaster.* —**unˈmitiˌgatedly** *adv.*
unmoral (ʌnˈmɒrəl) *adj.* outside morality; amoral. —**unmorality** (ˌʌnməˈrælɪtɪ) *n.* —**unˈmorally** *adv.*
unmurmuring (ʌnˈmɜːmərɪŋ) *adj.* not complaining.
unmuzzle (ʌnˈmʌzᵊl) *vb.* *(tr.)* **1.** to take the muzzle off (a dog, etc.). **2.** to free from control or censorship.
unnatural (ʌnˈnætʃərəl) *adj.* **1.** contrary to nature; abnormal. **2.** not in accordance with accepted standards of behaviour or right and wrong: *unnatural love.* **3.** uncanny; supernatural: *unnatural phenomena.* **4.** affected or forced: *an unnatural manner.* **5.** inhuman or monstrous: *an unnatural crime.* —**unˈnaturally** *adv.* —**unˈnaturalness** *n.*
unnecessary (ʌnˈnɛsɪsərɪ) *adj.* not necessary. —**unˈnecessarily** *adv.* —**unˈnecessariness** *n.*
unnerve (ʌnˈnɜːv) *vb.* *(tr.)* to cause to lose courage, strength, confidence, self-control, etc.
unnumbered (ʌnˈnʌmbəd) *adj.* **1.** countless; innumerable. **2.** not counted or assigned a number.
UNO *abbrev. for* United Nations Organization.
unoccupied (ʌnˈɒkjʊˌpaɪd) *adj.* **1.** (of a building) without occupants. **2.** unemployed or idle. **3.** (of an area or country) not overrun by foreign troops.
unofficial (ˌʌnəˈfɪʃəl) *adj.* **1.** not official or formal: *an unofficial engagement.* **2.** not confirmed officially: *an unofficial report.* **3.** (of a strike) not approved by the strikers' trade union. —ˌ**unofˈficially** *adv.*
unorganized *or* **-nised** (ʌnˈɔːgəˌnaɪzd) *adj.* **1.** not arranged into an organized system, structure, or unity. **2.** (of workers) not unionized. **3.** nonliving; inorganic.
unpack (ʌnˈpæk) *vb.* **1.** to remove the packed contents of (a case, trunk, etc.). **2.** *(tr.)* to take (something) out of a packed container. **3.** *(tr.)* to unload: *to unpack a mule.* —**unˈpacker** *n.*
unpaged (ʌnˈpeɪdʒd) *adj.* (of a book) having no page numbers.
unparalleled (ʌnˈpærəˌlɛld) *adj.* unmatched; unequalled.
unparliamentary (ˌʌnpɑːləˈmɛntərɪ) *adj.* not consistent with parliamentary procedure or practice. —ˌ**unparliaˈmentarily** *adv.* —ˌ**unparliaˈmentariness** *n.*
unpeg (ʌnˈpɛg) *vb.* **-pegging, -pegged.** *(tr.)* **1.** to remove the peg from, esp. to unfasten. **2.** to allow (prices, etc.) to rise and fall freely.
unpeople (ʌnˈpiːpᵊl) *vb.* *(tr.)* to empty of people.
unperson (ˈʌnpɜːsᵊn) *n.* a person whose existence is officially denied or ignored.
unpick (ʌnˈpɪk) *vb.* *(tr.)* **1.** to undo (the stitches) of (a piece of sewing). **2.** to unravel or undo (a garment, etc.).

---

unˈlovable *adj.*
unˈloved *adj.*
unˈmade *adj.*
unˈmagniˌfied *adj.*
unˈmanageable *adj.*
unˈmarked *adj.*
unˈmarketable *adj.*
unˈmarried *adj.*
unˈmatched *adj.*
ˌ**unmaˈtured** *adj.*
unˈmeant *adj.*
unˈmeasured *adj.*
ˌ**unmeˈlodious** *adj.*
unˈmelted *adj.*
unˈmemorable *adj.*
unˈmentioned *adj.*
unˈmerchantable *adj.*
unˈmerited *adj.*
unˈmetrical *adj.*
ˌ**unmisˈtaken** *adj.*
unˈmixed *adj.*
unˈmodiˌfied *adj.*
unˈmoor *vb.*
unˈmotiˌvated *adj.*
unˈmounted *adj.*
unˈmourned *adj.*
unˈmovable *adj.*
unˈmoved *adj.*
unˈmusical *adj.*
unˈmystiˌfied *adj.*
unˈnamable *adj.*
unˈnamed *adj.*
unˈnavigable *adj.*
unˈnaviˌgated *adj.*
unˈneeded *adj.*
ˌ**unneˈgotiable** *adj.*
unˈneighbourly *adj.*
unˈnoticed *adj.*
ˌ**unobˈjectionable** *adj.*
ˌ**unoˈbliging** *adj.*
ˌ**unobˈserved** *adj.*
ˌ**unobˈstructed** *adj.*
ˌ**unobˈtainable** *adj.*
ˌ**unobˈtained** *adj.*
ˌ**unobˈtrusive** *adj.*
ˌ**unofˈfended** *adj.*
ˌ**unofˈfensive** *adj.*
ˌ**unofˈficious** *adj.*
unˈopened *adj.*
ˌ**unopˈposed** *adj.*
ˌ**unorˈdained** *adj.*
unoˈriginal *adj.*
unˈorthoˌdox *adj.*
ˌ**unostenˈtatious** *adj.*
unˈpaid *adj.*
unˈpaired *adj.*
unˈpalatable *adj.*
unˈpardonable *adj.*
unˈpasteurˌized *or* **-ˌised** *adj.*
unˈpatented *adj.*
ˌ**unpatriˈotic** *adj.*
ˌ**unperˈceived** *adj.*
ˌ**unperˈceptive** *adj.*
ˌ**unperˈfected** *adj.*
unˈperfoˌrated *adj.*
ˌ**unperˈformed** *adj.*
ˌ**unperˈsuaded** *adj.*
ˌ**unperˈturbable** *adj.*
ˌ**unperˈturbed** *adj.*
ˌ**unphiloˈsophical** *adj.*

unpin (ʌnˈpɪn) *vb.* **-pinning, -pinned.** (*tr.*) **1.** to remove a pin or pins from. **2.** to unfasten by removing pins.

unpleasant (ʌnˈplɛzᵊnt) *adj.* not pleasant or agreeable. —**unˈpleasantly** *adv.* —**unˈpleasantness** *n.*

unplumbed (ʌnˈplʌmd) *adj.* **1.** unfathomed; unsounded. **2.** not understood in depth. **3.** (of a building) having no plumbing.

unpolled (ʌnˈpəʊld) *adj.* **1.** not included in an opinion poll. **2.** not having voted. **3.** *Arch.* unshorn.

unpopular (ʌnˈpɒpjʊlə) *adj.* not popular with an individual or group of people. —**unpopularity** (ˌʌnpɒpjʊˈlærɪtɪ) *n.* —**unˈpopularly** *adv.*

unpractical (ʌnˈpræktɪkᵊl) *adj.* another word for **impractical.** —ˌ**unpractiˈcality** *n.* —**unˈpractically** *adv.*

unpractised *or U.S.* **unpracticed** (ʌnˈpræktɪst) *adj.* **1.** without skill, training, or experience. **2.** not used or done often or repeatedly. **3.** not yet tested.

unprecedented (ʌnˈprɛsɪˌdɛntɪd) *adj.* having no precedent; unparalleled. —**unˈpreceˌdentedly** *adv.*

unprejudiced (ʌnˈprɛdʒʊdɪst) *adj.* not prejudiced or biased; impartial. —**unˈprejudicedly** *adv.*

unprincipled (ʌnˈprɪnsɪpᵊld) *adj.* lacking moral principles; unscrupulous. —**unˈprincipledness** *n.*

unprintable (ʌnˈprɪntəbᵊl) *adj.* unsuitable for printing for reasons of obscenity, libel, etc. —**unˈprintableness** *n.* —**unˈprintably** *adv.*

unprofessional (ˌʌnprəˈfɛʃənᵊl) *adj.* **1.** contrary to the accepted code of conduct of a profession. **2.** amateur. **3.** not belonging to or having the required qualifications for a profession. —ˌ**unproˈfessionally** *adv.*

unputdownable (ˌʌnpʊtˈdaʊnəbᵊl) *adj.* (esp. of a novel) so gripping as to be read at one sitting.

unqualified (ʌnˈkwɒlɪˌfaɪd) *adj.* **1.** lacking the necessary qualifications. **2.** not restricted or modified: *an unqualified criticism.* **3.** (*usually prenominal*) (intensifier): *an unqualified success.* —**unˈqualiˌfiable** *adj.*

unquestionable (ʌnˈkwɛstʃənəbᵊl) *adj.* **1.** indubitable or indisputable. **2.** not admitting of exception: *an unquestionable ruling.* —**unˌquestionaˈbility** *n.* —**unˈquestionably** *adv.*

unquestioned (ʌnˈkwɛstʃənd) *adj.* **1.** accepted without question. **2.** not admitting of doubt or question: *unquestioned power.* **3.** not questioned or interrogated.

unquiet (ʌnˈkwaɪət) *Chiefly literary.* ~*adj.* **1.** characterized by disorder or tumult: *unquiet times.* **2.** anxious; uneasy. ~*n.* **3.** a state of unrest. —**unˈquietly** *adv.* —**unˈquietness** *n.*

unquote (ʌnˈkwəʊt) *interj.* **1.** an expression used parenthetically to indicate that the preceding quotation is finished. ~*vb.* **2.** to close (a quotation), esp. in printing.

unravel (ʌnˈrævᵊl) *vb.* **-elling, -elled** *or U.S.* **-eling, -eled. 1.** (*tr.*) to reduce (something knitted or woven) to separate strands. **2.** (*tr.*) to explain or solve: *the mystery was unravelled.* **3.** (*intr.*) to become unravelled.

unread (ʌnˈrɛd) *adj.* **1.** (of a book, etc.) not yet read. **2.** (of a person) having read little.

unreadable (ʌnˈriːdəbᵊl) *adj.* **1.** illegible; undecipherable. **2.** difficult or tedious to read. —**unˌreadaˈbility** *or* **unˈreadableness** *n.*

unready (ʌnˈrɛdɪ) *adj.* **1.** not ready or prepared. **2.** slow or hesitant to see or act. —**unˈreadily** *adv.* —**unˈreadiness** *n.*

unreal (ʌnˈrɪəl) *adj.* **1.** imaginary or fanciful or seemingly so: *an unreal situation.* **2.** having no actual existence or substance. **3.** insincere or artificial. —**unreality** (ˌʌnrɪˈælɪtɪ) *n.* —**unˈreally** *adv.*

unreason (ʌnˈriːzᵊn) *n.* **1.** irrationality or madness. **2.** something that lacks or is contrary to reason. **3.** lack of order; chaos.

unreasonable (ʌnˈriːznəbᵊl) *adj.* **1.** immoderate: *unreasonable demands.* **2.** refusing to listen to reason. **3.** lacking judgment. —**unˈreasonableness** *n.* —**unˈreasonably** *adv.*

unreasoning (ʌnˈriːzənɪŋ) *adj.* not controlled by reason; irrational. —**unˈreasoningly** *adv.*

unregenerate (ˌʌnrɪˈdʒɛnərɪt) *adj. also* **unregenerated. 1.** unrepentant; unreformed. **2.** obstinately adhering to one's own views. ~*n.* **3.** an unregenerate person. —ˌ**unreˈgeneracy** *n.* —ˌ**unreˈgenerately** *adv.*

unrelenting (ˌʌnrɪˈlɛntɪŋ) *adj.* **1.** refusing to relent or take pity. **2.** not diminishing in determination, speed, effort, force, etc. —ˌ**unreˈlentingly** *adv.* —ˌ**unreˈlentingness** *n.*

unreligious (ˌʌnrɪˈlɪdʒəs) *adj.* **1.** another word for **irreligious. 2.** secular. —ˌ**unreˈligiously** *adv.*

unremitting (ˌʌnrɪˈmɪtɪŋ) *adj.* never slackening or stopping; unceasing; constant. —ˌ**unreˈmittingly** *adv.* —ˌ**unreˈmittingness** *n.*

unreserved (ˌʌnrɪˈzɜːvd) *adj.* **1.** without reserve; having an open manner. **2.** without reservation. **3.** not booked or bookable. —**unreservedly** (ˌʌnrɪˈzɜːvɪdlɪ) *adv.* —ˌ**unreˈservedness** *n.*

---

unˈpitied *adj.*
unˈpitying *adj.*
unˈplaced *adj.*
unˈplanned *adj.*
unˈplayable *adj.*
unˈpleasing *adj.*
unˈplug *vb.*
unˈpointed *adj.*
unˈpolarˌized *or* **-ˌised** *adj.*
unˈpolished *adj.*
unˈpolitic *adj.*
ˌ**unpolˈluted** *adj.*
unˈpopuˌlated *adj.*
unˈposed *adj.*
unˈpracticable *adj.*
ˌ**unpreˌdictaˈbility** *or* ˌ**unpreˈdictableness** *n.*
ˌ**unpreˈdictable** *adj.*
ˌ**unpreˈdicted** *adj.*
ˌ**unpreˈmediˌtated** *adj.*
ˌ**unpreˈpared** *adj.*
ˌ**unpreposˈsessing** *adj.*
ˌ**unpreˈscribed** *adj.*
ˌ**unpreˈsentable** *adj.*
unˈpressed *adj.*
ˌ**unpreˈsumptuous** *adj.*
ˌ**unpreˈtending** *adj.*
ˌ**unpreˈtentious** *adj.*
unˈpriced *adj.*
ˌ**unproˈclaimed** *adj.*
ˌ**unproˈductive** *adj.*
ˌ**unproˈfessed** *adj.*
unˈprofitable *adj.*
ˌ**unproˈhibited** *adj.*
unˈpromising *adj.*
unˈprompted *adj.*
ˌ**unproˈnounceable** *adj.*
ˌ**unproˈnounced** *adj.*
ˌ**unproˈpitious** *adj.*
ˌ**unproˈtected** *adj.*
ˌ**unproˈtesting** *adj.*
unˈproved *adj.*
unˈproven *adj.*
ˌ**unproˈvided** *adj.*
ˌ**unproˈvoked** *adj.*
unˈpublished *adj.*
unˈpunished *adj.*
unˈquestioning *adj.*
unˈquotable *adj.*
ˌ**unrealˈistic** *adj.*
unˈrealˌized *or* **-ˌised** *adj.*
ˌ**unreˈceptive** *adj.*
unˈrecogˌnizable *or* **-ˌnisable** *adj.*
unˈrecogˌnized *or* **-ˌnised** *adj.*
ˌ**unrecomˈmended** *adj.*
unˈrecomˌpensed *adj.*
unˈreconˌciled *adj.*
ˌ**unreconˈstructed** *adj.*
ˌ**unreˈcorded** *adj.*
ˌ**unreˈdeemable** *adj.*
ˌ**unreˈdeemed** *adj.*
unˈreel *vb.*
ˌ**unreˈfined** *adj.*
ˌ**unreˈflected** *adj.*
ˌ**unreˈflecting** *adj.*
ˌ**unreˈfreshed** *adj.*
unˈregistered *adj.*
unˈreguˌlated *adj.*
ˌ**unreˈhearsed** *adj.*
ˌ**unreˈlated** *adj.*
ˌ**unreˈliable** *adj.*
ˌ**unreˈmarkable** *adj.*
ˌ**unreˈmembered** *adj.*
ˌ**unreˈmorseful** *adj.*
ˌ**unreˈnewed** *adj.*
ˌ**unreˈnowned** *adj.*
ˌ**unreˈpealed** *adj.*
ˌ**unreˈpeatable** *adj.*
ˌ**unreˈpentant** *adj.*
ˌ**unreˈported** *adj.*
ˌ**unrepreˈsentative** *adj.*
ˌ**unrepreˈsented** *adj.*
ˌ**unreˈproved** *adj.*
ˌ**unreˈquested** *adj.*
ˌ**unreˈquited** *adj.*
ˌ**unreˈsisting** *adj.*
ˌ**unreˈsolved** *adj.*
ˌ**unreˈsponsive** *adj.*

unrest (ʌnˈrɛst) *n.* **1.** a troubled or rebellious state of discontent. **2.** an uneasy or troubled state.

unriddle (ʌnˈrɪdᵊl) *vb.* (*tr.*) to solve or puzzle out. [C16: < UN-^{2} + RIDDLE^{1}] —**unˈriddler** *n.*

unrig (ʌnˈrɪg) *vb.* **-rigging, -rigged. 1.** (*tr.*) to strip (a vessel) of standing and running rigging. **2.** *Arch. or dialect.* to undress (someone or oneself).

unrighteous (ʌnˈraɪtʃəs) *adj.* **1. a.** sinful; wicked. **b.** (*as collective n.; preceded by* the): *the unrighteous.* **2.** not fair or right; unjust. —**unˈrighteously** *adv.* —**unˈrighteousness** *n.*

unrip (ʌnˈrɪp) *vb.* **-ripping, -ripped.** (*tr.*) **1.** to rip open. **2.** *Obs.* to reveal; disclose.

unripe (ʌnˈraɪp) *or* **unripened** *adj.* **1.** not fully matured. **2.** not fully prepared or developed; not ready. —**unˈripeness** *n.*

unrivalled *or U.S.* **unrivaled** (ʌnˈraɪvᵊld) *adj.* having no equal; matchless.

unroll (ʌnˈrəʊl) *vb.* **1.** to open out or unwind (something rolled, folded, or coiled) or (of something rolled, etc.) to become opened out or unwound. **2.** to make or become visible or apparent, esp. gradually; unfold.

unruffled (ʌnˈrʌfᵊld) *adj.* **1.** unmoved; calm. **2.** still: *the unruffled seas.* —**unˈruffledness** *n.*

unruly (ʌnˈruːlɪ) *adj.* **-lier, -liest.** disposed to disobedience or indiscipline. —**unˈruliness** *n.*

UNRWA (ˈʌnrə) *n. acronym for* United Nations Relief and Works Agency.

unsaddle (ʌnˈsædᵊl) *vb.* **1.** to remove the saddle from (a horse, mule, etc.). **2.** (*tr.*) to unhorse.

unsaddling enclosure *n.* the area at a racecourse where horses are unsaddled after a race and often where awards are given to owners, trainers, and jockeys.

unsaid (ʌnˈsɛd) *adj.* not said or expressed; unspoken.

unsaturated (ʌnˈsætʃəˌreɪtɪd) *adj.* **1.** not saturated. **2.** (of a chemical compound, esp. an organic compound) containing one or more double or triple bonds and thus capable of undergoing addition reactions. **3.** (of a fat, esp. a vegetable fat) containing a high proportion of fatty acids having double bonds. —**ˌunsatuˈration** *n.*

unsavoury *or U.S.* **unsavory** (ʌnˈseɪvərɪ) *adj.* **1.** objectionable or distasteful: *an unsavoury character.* **2.** disagreeable in odour or taste. —**unˈsavourily** *or U.S.* **unˈsavorily** *adv.* —**unˈsavouriness** *or U.S.* **unˈsavoriness** *n.*

unsay (ʌnˈseɪ) *vb.* **-saying, -said.** (*tr.*) to retract or withdraw (something said or written).

unscathed (ʌnˈskeɪðd) *adj.* not harmed or injured.

unscramble (ʌnˈskræmbᵊl) *vb.* (*tr.*) **1.** to resolve from confusion or disorderliness. **2.** to restore (a scrambled message) to an intelligible form. —**unˈscrambler** *n.*

unscrew (ʌnˈskruː) *vb.* **1.** (*tr.*) to remove a screw from (an object). **2.** (*tr.*) to loosen (a screw, lid, etc.) by rotating, usually in an anticlockwise direction. **3.** (*intr.*) (esp. of an engaged threaded part) to become loosened or separated.

unscripted (ʌnˈskrɪptɪd) *adj.* (of a speech, play, etc.) not using or based on a script.

unscrupulous (ʌnˈskruːpjʊləs) *adj.* without scruples; unprincipled. —**unˈscrupulously** *adv.* —**unˈscrupulousness** *n.*

unseal (ʌnˈsiːl) *vb.* (*tr.*) **1.** to remove or break the seal of. **2.** to free (something concealed or closed as if sealed): *to unseal one's lips.*

unsealed (ʌnˈsiːld) *adj. Austral. & N.Z.* (of a road) surfaced with road metal not bound by bitumen or other sealant.

unseam (ʌnˈsiːm) *vb.* (*tr.*) to open or undo the seam of.

unseasonable (ʌnˈsiːzənəbᵊl) *adj.* **1.** (esp. of the weather) inappropriate for the season. **2.** untimely; inopportune. —**unˈseasonableness** *n.* —**unˈseasonably** *adv.*

unseat (ʌnˈsiːt) *vb.* (*tr.*) **1.** to throw or displace from a seat, saddle, etc. **2.** to depose from office or position.

unseeded (ʌnˈsiːdɪd) *adj.* (of players in various sports) not assigned to a preferential position in the preliminary rounds of a tournament.

unseemly (ʌnˈsiːmlɪ) *adj.* **1.** not in good style or taste. **2.** *Obs.* unattractive. ~*adv.* **3.** *Rare.* in an unseemly manner. —**unˈseemliness** *n.*

unseen (ʌnˈsiːn) *adj.* **1.** not observed or perceived; invisible. **2.** (of passages of writing) not previously seen or prepared. ~*n.* **3.** *Chiefly Brit.* a passage, not previously seen, that is presented to students for translation.

unselfish (ʌnˈsɛlfɪʃ) *adj.* not selfish; generous. —**unˈselfishly** *adv.* —**unˈselfishness** *n.*

unsettle (ʌnˈsɛtᵊl) *vb.* **1.** (*usually tr.*) to change or become changed from a fixed or settled condition. **2.** (*tr.*) to confuse or agitate (emotions, the mind, etc.). —**unˈsettlement** *n.*

unsettled (ʌnˈsɛtᵊld) *adj.* **1.** lacking order or stability: *an unsettled era.* **2.** unpredictable: *an unsettled climate.* **3.** constantly changing or moving from place to place: *an unsettled life.* **4.** (of controversy, etc.) not brought to an agreed conclusion. **5.** (of debts, law cases, etc.) not disposed of. —**unˈsettledness** *n.*

unsex (ʌnˈsɛks) *vb.* (*tr.*) *Chiefly literary.* to deprive (a person) of the attributes of his or her sex, esp. to make a woman more callous.

unshapen (ʌnˈʃeɪpᵊn) *adj.* **1.** having no definite shape; shapeless. **2.** deformed; misshapen.

unsheathe (ʌnˈʃiːð) *vb.* (*tr.*) to draw or pull out (something, esp. a weapon) from a sheath.

unship (ʌnˈʃɪp) *vb.* **-shipping, -shipped. 1.** to be or cause to be unloaded, discharged, or disembarked from a ship. **2.** (*tr.*) *Naut.* to remove from a regular place: *to unship oars.*

unsighted (ʌnˈsaɪtɪd) *adj.* **1.** not sighted. **2.** not having a clear view. **3.** (of a gun) not equipped with a sight. —**unˈsightedly** *adv.*

unsightly (ʌnˈsaɪtlɪ) *adj.* unpleasant or unattractive to look at; ugly. —**unˈsightliness** *n.*

unskilful *or U.S.* **unskillful** (ʌnˈskɪlfʊl) *adj.* lacking dexterity or proficiency. —**unˈskilfully** *or U.S.* **unˈskillfully** *adv.* —**unˈskilfulness** *or U.S.* **unˈskillfulness** *n.*

unskilled (ʌnˈskɪld) *adj.* **1.** not having or

---

unˈrested *adj.*
ˌunreˈstrained *adj.*
ˌunreˈstricted *adj.*
ˌunreˈvealed *adj.*
ˌunreˈvealing *adj.*
ˌunreˈvised *adj.*
ˌunreˈwarded *adj.*
ˌunreˈwarding *adj.*
unˈridden *adj.*
unˈripened *adj.*
ˌunroˈmantic *adj.*
unˈrounded *adj.*
unˈruled *adj.*
unˈsafe *adj.*
unˈsalaried *adj.*
unˈsalted *adj.*
unˈsanctioned *adj.*
unˈsanitary *adj.*
ˌunsatisˈfactory *adj.*
unˈsatisˌfied *adj.*
unˈsatisˌfying *adj.*
unˈsaved *adj.*
unˈsayable *adj.*
unˈscented *adj.*
unˈscheduled *adj.*
unˈschooled *adj.*
ˌunscienˈtific *adj.*
unˈscratched *adj.*
unˈscreened *adj.*
unˈseasoned *adj.*
unˈseaˌworthy *adj.*
ˌunseˈcluded *adj.*
ˌunseˈcured *adj.*
unˈseeing *adj.*
unˈsegreˌgated *adj.*
ˌunseˈlected *adj.*
ˌunseˈlective *adj.*
ˌunselfˈconscious *adj.*
ˌunsentiˈmental *adj.*
unˈset *adj.*
unˈshackle *vb.*
unˈshakable *adj.*
unˈshaken *adj.*
unˈshared *adj.*
unˈshaved *adj.*
unˈshaven *adj.*
unˈshed *adj.*
unˈshielded *adj.*
unˈshockable *adj.*
unˈshod *adj.*
unˈshrinkable *adj.*
unˈsigned *adj.*
unˈsinkable *adj.*
unˈsized *adj.*

requiring any special skill or training: *an unskilled job.* **2.** having no skill; inexpert.

unsling (ʌnˈslɪŋ) *vb.* **-slinging, -slung.** (*tr.*) **1.** to remove or release from a slung position. **2.** to remove slings from.

unsnap (ʌnˈsnæp) *vb.* **-snapping, -snapped.** (*tr.*) to unfasten (the snap or catch) of (something).

unsnarl (ʌnˈsnɑːl) *vb.* (*tr.*) to free from a snarl or tangle.

unsociable (ʌnˈsəʊʃəbᵊl) *adj.* **1.** (of a person) disinclined to associate or fraternize with others. **2.** unconducive to social intercourse: *an unsociable neighbourhood.* **—unˌsociaˈbility** *or* **unˈsociableness** *n.*

unsocial (ʌnˈsəʊʃəl) *adj.* **1.** not social; antisocial. **2.** (of the hours of work of certain jobs) falling outside the normal working day.

unsophisticated (ˌʌnsəˈfɪstɪˌkeɪtɪd) *adj.* **1.** lacking experience or worldly wisdom. **2.** marked by a lack of refinement or complexity: *an unsophisticated machine.* **3.** unadulterated or genuine. **—ˌunsoˈphistiˌcatedly** *adv.* **—ˌunsoˈphistiˌcatedness** *or* **ˌunsoˌphistiˈcation** *n.*

unsound (ʌnˈsaʊnd) *adj.* **1.** diseased or unstable: *of unsound mind.* **2.** unreliable or fallacious: *unsound advice.* **3.** lacking strength or firmness: *unsound foundations.* **4.** of doubtful financial or commercial viability: *an unsound enterprise.* **—unˈsoundly** *adv.* **—unˈsoundness** *n.*

unsparing (ʌnˈspɛərɪŋ) *adj.* **1.** not sparing or frugal; lavish. **2.** showing harshness or severity. **—unˈsparingly** *adv.* **—unˈsparingness** *n.*

unspeakable (ʌnˈspiːkəbᵊl) *adj.* **1.** incapable of expression in words: *unspeakable ecstasy.* **2.** indescribably bad or evil. **3.** not to be uttered: *unspeakable thoughts.* **—unˈspeakableness** *n.* **—unˈspeakably** *adv.*

unstable (ʌnˈsteɪbᵊl) *adj.* **1.** lacking stability, fixity, or firmness. **2.** disposed to temperamental or psychological variability. **3.** (of a chemical compound) readily decomposing. **4.** *Physics.* **a.** (of an elementary particle) having a very short lifetime. **b.** spontaneously decomposing by nuclear decay: *an unstable nuclide.* **5.** *Electronics.* (of an electrical circuit, etc.) having a tendency to self-oscillation. **—unˈstableness** *n.* **—unˈstably** *adv.*

unsteady (ʌnˈstɛdɪ) *adj.* **1.** not securely fixed: *an unsteady foothold.* **2.** (of behaviour, etc.) erratic. **3.** without regularity: *an unsteady rhythm.* **4.** (of a manner of walking, etc.) precarious or staggering, as from intoxication. **—unˈsteadily** *adv.* **—unˈsteadiness** *n.*

unstep (ʌnˈstɛp) *vb.* **-stepping, -stepped.** (*tr.*) *Naut.* to remove (a mast) from its step.

unstick (ʌnˈstɪk) *vb.* **-sticking, -stuck.** (*tr.*) to free or loosen (something stuck).

unstop (ʌnˈstɒp) *vb.* **-stopping, -stopped.** (*tr.*) **1.** to remove the stop or stopper from. **2.** to free from any stoppage or obstruction. **3.** to draw out the stops on (an organ). **—unˈstoppable** *adj.* **—unˈstoppably** *adv.*

unstopped (ʌnˈstɒpt) *adj.* **1.** not obstructed or stopped up. **2.** *Phonetics.* denoting a speech sound for whose articulation the closure is not complete. **3.** *Prosody.* (of verse) having the sense of the line carried over into the next. **4.** (of an organ pipe or a string on a musical instrument) not stopped.

unstriated (ʌnˈstraɪˌeɪtɪd) *adj.* (of muscle) composed of elongated cells that do not have striations; smooth.

unstring (ʌnˈstrɪŋ) *vb.* **-stringing, -strung.** (*tr.*) **1.** to remove the strings of. **2.** (of beads, etc.) to remove from a string. **3.** to weaken emotionally (a person or his nerves).

unstriped (ʌnˈstraɪpt) *adj.* (esp. of smooth muscle) not having stripes; unstriated.

unstructured (ʌnˈstrʌktʃəd) *adj.* **1.** without formal structure or systematic organization. **2.** without a preformed shape; (esp. of clothes) loose; untailored.

unstrung (ʌnˈstrʌŋ) *adj.* **1.** emotionally distressed; unnerved. **2.** (of a stringed instrument) with the strings detached.

unstuck (ʌnˈstʌk) *adj.* **1.** freed from being stuck, glued, fastened, etc. **2. come unstuck.** to suffer failure or disaster.

unstudied (ʌnˈstʌdɪd) *adj.* **1.** natural. **2.** (foll. by *in*) without knowledge or training.

unsubstantial (ˌʌnsəbˈstænʃəl) *adj.* **1.** lacking weight or firmness. **2.** (of an argument) of doubtful validity. **3.** of no material existence. **—ˌunsubˌstantiˈality** *n.* **—ˌunsubˈstantially** *adv.*

unsung (ʌnˈsʌŋ) *adj.* **1.** not acclaimed or honoured: *unsung deeds.* **2.** not yet sung.

unsuspected (ˌʌnsəˈspɛktɪd) *adj.* **1.** not under suspicion. **2.** not known to exist. **—ˌunsusˈpectedly** *adv.* **—ˌunsusˈpectedness** *n.*

unswerving (ʌnˈswɜːvɪŋ) *adj.* not turning aside; constant.

untangle (ʌnˈtæŋgᵊl) *vb.* (*tr.*) **1.** to free from a tangled condition. **2.** to free from confusion.

untaught (ʌnˈtɔːt) *adj.* **1.** without training or education. **2.** attained or achieved without instruction.

untenable (ʌnˈtɛnəbᵊl) *adj.* **1.** (of theories, etc.) incapable of being maintained or vindicated. **2.** unable to be maintained against attack. **—unˌtenaˈbility** *or* **unˈtenableness** *n.* **—unˈtenably** *adv.*

unthinkable (ʌnˈθɪŋkəbᵊl) *adj.* **1.** not to be contemplated; out of the question. **2.** unimaginable; inconceivable. **3.** unreasonable; improbable. **—unˈthinkably** *adv.*

unthinking (ʌnˈθɪŋkɪŋ) *adj.* **1.** lacking thoughtfulness; inconsiderate. **2.** heedless; inadvertent. **3.** not thinking or able to think. **—unˈthinkingly** *adv.* **—unˈthinkingness** *n.*

unthread (ʌnˈθrɛd) *vb.* (*tr.*) **1.** to draw out the thread or threads from (a needle, etc.). **2.** to disentangle.

unthrone (ʌnˈθrəʊn) *vb.* (*tr.*) a less common word for **dethrone.**

untidy (ʌnˈtaɪdɪ) *adj.* **-dier, -diest.** **1.** not neat; slovenly. ~*vb.* **-dying, -died.** **2.** (*tr.*) to make untidy. **—unˈtidily** *adv.* **—unˈtidiness** *n.*

untie (ʌnˈtaɪ) *vb.* **-tying, -tied.** **1.** to unfasten or free (a knot or something that is tied) or (of a knot, etc.) to become unfastened. **2.** (*tr.*) to free from constraint or restriction.

until (ʌnˈtɪl) *conj.* (*subordinating*) **1.** up to (a time) that: *he laughed until he cried.* **2.** (*used with a negative*) before (a time or event): *until*

---

unˈsmiling *adj.*
unˈsold *adj.*
ˌunsoˈlicited *adj.*
unˈsolved *adj.*
unˈsought *adj.*
unˈspecialˌized *or* **-ˌised** *adj.*
unˈspeciˌfied *adj.*
ˌunspecˈtacular *adj.*
unˈspoiled *adj.*
unˈspoken *adj.*
unˈsporting *adj.*
unˈspotted *adj.*
unˈstatesmanˌlike *adj.*
unˈstinted *adj.*
unˈstrained *adj.*
unˈstrap *vb.*
ˌunsubˈdued *adj.*
ˌunsubˈstantiˌated *adj.*
ˌunsucˈcessful *adj.*
unˈsuitable *adj.*
unˈsuited *adj.*
unˈsullied *adj.*
unˈsuperˌvised *adj.*
ˌunsupˈportable *adj.*
ˌunsupˈported *adj.*
unˈsure *adj.*
ˌunsurˈpassable *adj.*
ˌunsurˈpassed *adj.*
ˌunsusˈceptible *adj.*
ˌunsusˈpecting *adj.*
ˌunsusˈtained *adj.*
unˈsweetened *adj.*
ˌunsympaˈthetic *adj.*
unˈtainted *adj.*
unˈtamed *adj.*
unˈtapped *adj.*
unˈtasted *adj.*
unˈtaxed *adj.*
unˈtended *adj.*
unˈtested *adj.*
unˈtethered *adj.*
unˈthanked *adj.*
unˈthankful *adj.*
unˈthoughtful *adj.*
unˈthought-of *adj.*

you change, you can't go out. ~*prep.* **3.** (often preceded by *up*) in or throughout the period before: *he waited until six.* **4.** (*used with a negative*) earlier than; before: *he won't come until tomorrow.* [C13 *untill*; see TILL[1]]

▷ **Usage.** See at **till**[1].

untimely (ʌnˈtaɪmlɪ) *adj.* **1.** occurring before the expected, normal, or proper time: *an untimely death.* **2.** inappropriate to the occasion, time, or season: *his joking at the funeral was most untimely.* ~*adv.* **3.** prematurely or inopportunely. —**unˈtimeliness** *n.*

unto (ˈʌntuː) *prep. Arch.* to. [C13: < ON]

untold (ʌnˈtəʊld) *adj.* **1.** incapable of description: *untold suffering.* **2.** incalculably great in number or quantity: *untold thousands.* **3.** not told.

untouchable (ʌnˈtʌtʃəbᵊl) *adj.* **1.** lying beyond reach. **2.** above reproach, suspicion, or impeachment. **3.** unable to be touched. ~*n.* **4.** a member of the lowest class in India, whom those of the four main castes were formerly forbidden to touch. —**un͵touchaˈbility** *n.*

untoward (͵ʌntəˈwɔːd) *adj.* **1.** characterized by misfortune or annoyance. **2.** not auspicious; unfavourable. **3.** unseemly. **4.** out of the ordinary; out of the way. **5.** *Arch.* perverse. **6.** *Obs.* awkward. —͵**untoˈwardly** *adv.* —͵**untoˈwardness** *n.*

untrue (ʌnˈtruː) *adj.* **1.** incorrect or false. **2.** disloyal. **3.** diverging from a rule, standard, or measure; inaccurate. —**unˈtruly** *adv.*

untruss (ʌnˈtrʌs) *vb.* **1.** (*tr.*) to release from or as if from a truss; unfasten. **2.** *Obs.* to undress.

untruth (ʌnˈtruːθ) *n.* **1.** the state or quality of being untrue. **2.** a statement, etc., that is not true.

untruthful (ʌnˈtruːθfʊl) *adj.* **1.** (of a person) given to lying. **2.** diverging from the truth. —**unˈtruthfully** *adv.* —**unˈtruthfulness** *n.*

untuck (ʌnˈtʌk) *vb.* to become or cause to become loose or not tucked in: *to untuck the blankets.*

untutored (ʌnˈtjuːtəd) *adj.* **1.** without formal education. **2.** lacking sophistication or refinement.

unused *adj.* **1.** (ʌnˈjuːzd). not being or never having been made use of. **2.** (ʌnˈjuːst). (*postpositive;* foll. by *to*) not accustomed or used (to something).

unusual (ʌnˈjuːʒʊəl) *adj.* uncommon; extraordinary: *an unusual design.* —**unˈusually** *adv.*

unutterable (ʌnˈʌtərəbᵊl) *adj.* incapable of being expressed in words. —**unˈutterableness** *n.* —**unˈutterably** *adv.*

unvarnished (ʌnˈvɑːnɪʃt) *adj.* not elaborated upon or glossed; plain and direct: *the unvarnished truth.*

unveil (ʌnˈveɪl) *vb.* **1.** (*tr.*) to remove the cover from, esp. in the ceremonial unveiling of a monument, etc. **2.** to remove the veil from (one's own or another person's face). **3.** (*tr.*) to make (something concealed) known or public.

unveiling (ʌnˈveɪlɪŋ) *n.* **1.** a ceremony involving the removal of a veil covering a statue, etc., for the first time. **2.** the presentation of something, esp. for the first time.

unvoice (ʌnˈvɔɪs) *vb.* (*tr.*) *Phonetics.* **1.** to pronounce without vibration of the vocal cords. **2.** Also: **devoice.** to make (a voiced speech sound) voiceless.

unvoiced (ʌnˈvɔɪst) *adj.* **1.** not expressed or spoken. **2.** articulated without vibration of the vocal cords; voiceless.

unwaged (ʌnˈweɪdʒd) *adj.* of or denoting a person who is not receiving pay because of being unemployed or working in the home.

unwarrantable (ʌnˈwɒrəntəbᵊl) *adj.* incapable of vindication or justification. —**unˈwarrantableness** *n.* —**unˈwarrantably** *adv.*

unwarranted (ʌnˈwɒrəntɪd) *adj.* **1.** lacking justification or authorization. **2.** another word for **unwarrantable.**

unwary (ʌnˈwɛərɪ) *adj.* lacking caution or prudence. —**unˈwarily** *adv.* —**unˈwariness** *n.*

unwearied (ʌnˈwɪərɪd) *adj.* **1.** not abating or tiring. **2.** not fatigued; fresh. —**unˈweariedly** *adv.* —**unˈweariedness** *n.*

unweighed (ʌnˈweɪd) *adj.* **1.** (of quantities purchased, etc.) not measured for weight. **2.** (of statements, etc.) not carefully considered.

unwell (ʌnˈwɛl) *adj.* (*postpositive*) not well; ill.

unwept (ʌnˈwɛpt) *adj.* **1.** not wept for or lamented. **2.** *Rare.* (of tears) not shed.

unwholesome (ʌnˈhəʊlsəm) *adj.* **1.** detrimental to physical or mental health: *an unwholesome climate.* **2.** morally harmful: *unwholesome practices.* **3.** indicative of illness, esp. in appearance. **4.** (esp. of food) of inferior quality. —**unˈwholesomeness** *n.*

unwieldy (ʌnˈwiːldɪ) *adj.* **1.** too heavy, large, or awkwardly shaped to be easily handled. **2.** ungainly; clumsy. —**unˈwieldily** *adv.* —**unˈwieldiness** *n.*

unwilled (ʌnˈwɪld) *adj.* not intentional; involuntary.

unwilling (ʌnˈwɪlɪŋ) *adj.* **1.** reluctant. **2.** performed or said with reluctance. —**unˈwillingly** *adv.* —**unˈwillingness** *n.*

unwind (ʌnˈwaɪnd) *vb.* **-winding, -wound.** **1.** to slacken, undo, or unravel or cause to slacken, undo, or unravel. **2.** (*tr.*) to disentangle. **3.** to make or become relaxed: *he finds it hard to unwind.* —**unˈwindable** *adj.*

unwise (ʌnˈwaɪz) *adj.* lacking wisdom or prudence. —**unˈwisely** *adv.* —**unˈwiseness** *n.*

unwish (ʌnˈwɪʃ) *vb.* (*tr.*) **1.** to retract or revoke (a wish). **2.** to desire (something) not to be or take place.

unwitting (ʌnˈwɪtɪŋ) *adj.* (*usually prenominal*) **1.** not knowing or conscious. **2.** not intentional; inadvertent. [OE *unwitende,* < UN-[1] + *witting,* present participle of *witan* to know] —**unˈwittingly** *adv.* —**unˈwittingness** *n.*

unwonted (ʌnˈwəʊntɪd) *adj.* **1.** out of the ordinary; unusual. **2.** (usually foll. by *to*) *Arch.* unaccustomed; unused. —**unˈwontedly** *adv.*

unworldly (ʌnˈwɜːldlɪ) *adj.* **1.** not concerned with material values or pursuits. **2.** lacking sophistication; naive. **3.** not of this earth or world. —**unˈworldliness** *n.*

unworthy (ʌnˈwɜːðɪ) *adj.* **1.** (often foll. by *of*) not deserving or worthy. **2.** (often foll. by *of*) beneath the level considered befitting (to): *that remark is unworthy of you.* **3.** lacking merit or value. **4.** (of

---

unˈtinged *adj.*
unˈtiring *adj.*
unˈtitled *adj.*
unˈtouched *adj.*
unˈtrained *adj.*
unˈtrammelled *adj.*
͵**untransˈferable** *adj.*
unˈtravelled *adj.*
unˈtreated *adj.*
unˈtried *adj.*
unˈtrodden *adj.*
unˈtroubled *adj.*
unˈtrust͵worthy *adj.*
unˈtucked *adj.*
unˈtwine *vb.*
unˈtwist *vb.*
unˈusable *adj.*
unˈuti͵lized *or* **-͵lised** *adj.*
unˈuttered *adj.*
unˈvalued *adj.*
unˈvanquished *adj.*
unˈvaried *adj.*
unˈvarying *adj.*
unˈveri͵fiable *adj.*
unˈveri͵fied *adj.*
unˈversed *adj.*
unˈviable *adj.*
unˈwanted *adj.*
unˈwarmed *adj.*
unˈwarned *adj.*
unˈwashed *adj.*
unˈwatched *adj.*
unˈwavering *adj.*
unˈweary *adj.*
unˈwearying *adj.*
unˈwedded *or* **unˈwed** *adj.*
unˈwelcome *adj.*
unˈwinking *adj.*
unˈwished *adj.*
unˈwished-for *adj.*
unˈwithered *adj.*
unˈwitnessed *adj.*
unˈworkable *adj.*
unˈworkman͵like *adj.*
unˈworn *adj.*
unˈworried *adj.*

treatment) not warranted. **—unˈworthily** *adv.* **—unˈworthiness** *n.*

unwound (ʌnˈwaʊnd) *vb.* the past tense and past participle of **unwind.**

unwrap (ʌnˈræp) *vb.* **-wrapping, -wrapped.** to remove the covering or wrapping from (something) or (of something wrapped) to have the covering come off.

unwritten (ʌnˈrɪtᵊn) *adj.* **1.** not printed or in writing. **2.** effective only through custom.

unwritten law *n.* the law based upon custom, usage, and judicial decisions, as distinguished from the enactments of a legislature, orders or decrees in writing, etc.

unyoke (ʌnˈjəʊk) *vb.* **1.** to release (an animal, etc.) from a yoke. **2.** (*tr.*) to set free; liberate. **3.** (*tr.*) to disconnect or separate.

unzip (ʌnˈzɪp) *vb.* **-zipping, -zipped.** to unfasten the zip of (a garment, etc.) or (of a zip or garment with a zip) to become unfastened: *her skirt unzipped as she sat down.*

up (ʌp) *prep.* **1.** indicating movement from a lower to a higher position: *climbing up a mountain.* **2.** at a higher or further level or position in or on: *a shop up the road.* ~*adv.* **3.** (*often particle*) to an upward, higher, or erect position, esp. indicating readiness for an activity: *up and doing something.* **4.** (*particle*) indicating intensity or completion of an action: *he tore up the cheque.* **5.** to the place referred to or where the speaker is: *the man came up and asked the way.* **6. a.** to a more important place: *up to London.* **b.** to a more northerly place: *up to Scotland.* **c.** (of a member of some British universities) to or at university. **d.** in a particular part of the country: *up north.* **7.** above the horizon: *the sun is up.* **8.** appearing for trial: *up before the magistrate.* **9.** having gained: *ten pounds up on the deal.* **10.** higher in price: *coffee is up again.* **11.** raised (for discussion, etc.): *the plan was up for consideration.* **12.** taught: *well up in physics.* **13.** (*functioning as imperative*) get, stand, etc., up: *up with you!* **14. all up with.** *Inf.* **a.** over; finished. **b.** doomed to die. **15. up with.** (*functioning as imperative*) wanting the beginning or continuation of: *up with the monarchy!* **16. something's up.** *Inf.* something strange is happening. **17. up against. a.** touching. **b.** having to cope with: *look what we're up against now.* **18. up for.** as a candidate or applicant for: *he's up for re-election again.* **19. up to. a.** devising or scheming: *she's up to no good.* **b.** dependent or incumbent upon: *the decision is up to you.* **c.** equal to (a challenge, etc.) or capable of (doing, etc.): *are you up to playing in the final?* **d.** as far as: *up to his waist in mud.* **e.** as many as: *up to two years' waiting time.* **f.** comparable with: *not up to your normal standard.* **20. up top.** *Inf.* in the head or mind. **21. up yours.** *Sl.* a vulgar expression of contempt or refusal. **22. what's up?** *Inf.* **a.** what is the matter? **b.** what is happening? ~*adj.* **23.** (*predicative*) of a high or higher position. **24.** (*predicative*) out of bed: *the children aren't up yet.* **25.** (*prenominal*) of or relating to a train or trains to a more important place or one regarded as higher: *the up platform.* ~*vb.* **upping, upped. 26.** (*tr.*) to increase or raise. **27.** (*intr.*; foll. by *and* with a verb) *Inf.* to do (something) suddenly, etc.: *she upped and married someone else.* ~*n.* **28.** a high point (esp. in **ups and downs**). **29.** *Sl.* another word (esp. U.S.) for **upper** (sense 8). **30. on the up and up. a.** trustworthy or honest. **b.** *Brit.* on the upward trend or movement: *our firm's on the up and up.* [OE *upp*]

up- *prefix.* up, upper, or upwards: *uproot; upmost; upthrust; upgrade; uplift.*

up-anchor *vb.* (*intr.*) *Naut.* to weigh anchor.

up-and-coming *adj.* promising continued or future success; enterprising.

up-and-down *adj.* **1.** moving or formed alternately upwards and downwards. ~*adv.*, *prep.* **up and down. 2.** backwards and forwards (along).

up-and-over *adj.* (of a door, etc.) opened by being lifted and moved into a horizontal position.

up-and-under *n. Rugby League.* a high kick forwards followed by a charge to the place where the ball lands.

Upanishad (uːˈpʌnɪʃəd) *n. Hinduism.* any of a class of the Sanskrit sacred books probably composed between 400 and 200 B.C. and embodying the mystical and esoteric doctrines of ancient Hindu philosophy. [C19: < Sansk. *upanisad* a sitting down near something]

upas (ˈjuːpəs) *n.* **1.** a large tree of Java having whitish bark and poisonous milky sap. **2.** the sap of this tree, used as an arrow poison. ~Also called: **antiar.** [C19: < Malay: poison]

upbeat (ˈʌpˌbiːt) *n.* **1.** *Music.* **a.** a usually unaccented beat, esp. the last in a bar. **b.** the upward gesture of a conductor's baton indicating this. ~*adj.* **2.** *Inf.* marked by cheerfulness or optimism.

upbraid (ʌpˈbreɪd) *vb.* (*tr.*) **1.** to reprove or reproach angrily. **2.** to find fault with. [OE *upbregdan*] **—upˈbraider** *n.* **—upˈbraiding** *n.*

upbringing (ˈʌpˌbrɪŋɪŋ) *n.* the education of a person during his formative years.

upcast (ˈʌpˌkɑːst) *n.* **1.** material cast or thrown up. **2.** a ventilation shaft through which air leaves a mine. **3.** *Geol.* (in a fault) the section of strata that has been displaced upwards. ~*adj.* **4.** directed or thrown upwards. ~*vb.* **-casting, -cast. 5.** (*tr.*) to throw or cast up.

upcountry (ʌpˈkʌntrɪ) *adj.* **1.** of or coming from the interior of a country or region. ~*n.* **2.** the interior part of a region or country. ~*adv.* **3.** towards, in, or into the interior part of a country or region.

update *vb.* (ʌpˈdeɪt). (*tr.*) **1.** to bring up to date. ~*n.* (ˈʌpˌdeɪt). **2.** the act of updating or something that is updated. **—upˈdateable** *adj.* **—upˈdater** *n.*

updraught *or U.S.* **updraft** (ˈʌpˌdrɑːft) *n.* an upward movement of air or other gas.

upend (ʌpˈɛnd) *vb.* **1.** to turn or set or become turned or set on end. **2.** (*tr.*) to affect or upset drastically.

upfront (ˈʌpˈfrʌnt) *adj.* **1.** open and frank. ~*adv.*, *adj.* **2.** (of money) paid out at the beginning of a business arrangement.

upgrade *vb.* (ʌpˈgreɪd). (*tr.*) **1.** to assign or promote (a person or job) to a higher professional rank or position. **2.** to raise in value, importance, esteem, etc. **3.** to improve (a breed of livestock) by crossing with a better strain. ~*n.* (ˈʌpˌgreɪd). **4.** *U.S. & Canad.* an upward slope. **5. on the upgrade.** improving or progressing, as in importance, status, health, etc. **—upˈgrader** *n.*

upheaval (ʌpˈhiːvᵊl) *n.* **1.** a strong, sudden, or violent disturbance, as in politics. **2.** *Geol.* another word for **uplift** (sense 7).

upheave (ʌpˈhiːv) *vb.* **-heaving, -heaved** *or* **-hove. 1.** to heave or rise upwards. **2.** *Geol.* to thrust (land) upwards or (of land) to be thrust upwards. **3.** (*tr.*) to throw into disorder.

upheld (ʌpˈhɛld) *vb.* the past tense and past participle of **uphold.**

uphill (ˈʌpˈhɪl) *adj.* **1.** inclining, sloping, or leading upwards. **2.** requiring protracted effort: *an uphill task.* ~*adv.* **3.** up an incline or slope. **4.** against difficulties. ~*n.* **5.** a rising incline.

uphold (ʌpˈhəʊld) *vb.* **-holding, -held.** (*tr.*) **1.** to maintain or defend against opposition. **2.** to give moral support to. **3.** *Rare.* to support physically. **4.** to lift up. **—upˈholder** *n.*

upholster (ʌpˈhəʊlstə) *vb.* (*tr.*) to fit (chairs, sofas, etc.) with padding, springs, webbing, and covering. **—upˈholstery** *n.*

upholsterer (ʌpˈhəʊlstərə) *n.* a person who upholsters furniture as a profession. [C17: < *upholster* small furniture dealer]

upkeep (ˈʌpˌkiːp) *n.* **1.** the act or process of

unˈwounded *adj.* **unˈyielding** *adj.*

keeping something in good repair, esp. over a long period. **2.** the cost of maintenance.

upland (ˈʌplənd) *n.* **1.** an area of high or relatively high ground. *~adj.* **2.** relating to or situated in an upland.

uplift *vb.* (ʌpˈlɪft). (*tr.*) **1.** to raise; lift up. **2.** to raise morally, spiritually, etc. **3.** *Scot. & N.Z.* to collect; pick up (goods, documents, etc.). *~n.* (ˈʌpˌlɪft). **4.** the act, process, or result of lifting up. **5.** the act or process of bettering moral, social, or cultural conditions, etc. **6.** (*modifier*) designating a brassiere for lifting and supporting the breasts: *an uplift bra.* **7.** the process or result of land being raised to a higher level, as during a period of mountain building. —**upˈlifter** *n.* —**upˈlifting** *adj.*

uplighter (ˈʌpˌlaɪtə) *n.* a lamp or wall light designed or positioned to cast its light upwards.

up-market *adj.* relating to commercial products, services, etc., that are relatively expensive and of superior quality.

upmost (ˈʌpˌməʊst) *adj.* another word for **uppermost.**

upon (əˈpɒn) *prep.* **1.** another word for **on. 2.** indicating a position reached by going up: *climb upon my knee.* **3.** imminent for: *the weekend was upon us again.* [C13: < UP + ON]

upper (ˈʌpə) *adj.* **1.** higher or highest in relation to physical position, wealth, rank, status, etc. **2.** (*cap. when part of a name*) lying farther upstream, inland, or farther north: *the upper valley of the Loire.* **3.** (*cap. when part of a name*) *Geol., archaeol.* denoting the late part or division of a period, system, etc.: *Upper Palaeolithic.* **4.** *Maths.* (of a limit or bound) greater than or equal to one or more numbers or variables. *~n.* **5.** the higher of two objects, people, etc. **6.** the part of a shoe above the sole, covering the upper surface of the foot. **7. on one's uppers.** destitute. **8.** *Sl.* any of various drugs having a stimulant effect.

upper atmosphere *n. Meteorol.* that part of the atmosphere above the troposphere, esp. at heights that cannot be reached by balloon.

Upper Canada *n.* (from 1791–1841) the official name of the region of Canada lying southwest of the Ottawa River and north of the lower Great Lakes.

upper case *Printing.* *~n.* **1.** the top half of a compositor's type case in which capital letters, reference marks, and accents are kept. *~adj.* (**upper-case** *when prenominal*). **2.** of or relating to capital letters kept in this case and used in the setting or production of printed or typed matter.

upper chamber *n.* another name for an **upper house.**

upper class *n.* **1.** the class occupying the highest position in the social hierarchy, esp. the aristocracy. *~adj.* (**upper-class** *when prenominal*). **2.** of or relating to the upper class.

upper crust *n. Inf.* the upper class.

uppercut (ˈʌpəˌkʌt) *n.* **1.** a short swinging upward blow with the fist delivered at an opponent's chin. *~vb.* **-cutting, -cut. 2.** to hit (an opponent) with an uppercut.

upper hand *n.* **the.** the position of control (esp. in **have** *or* **get the upper hand**).

upper house *n.* (*often cap.*) one of the two houses of a bicameral legislature.

uppermost (ˈʌpəˌməʊst) *adj. also* **upmost. 1.** highest in position, power, importance, etc. *~adv.* **2.** in or into the highest position, etc.

upper regions *pl. n.* **the.** *Chiefly literary.* the sky; heavens.

upper works *pl. n. Naut.* the parts of a vessel above the water line when fully laden.

uppish (ˈʌpɪʃ) *adj. Brit. inf.* another word for **uppity** (sense 1). [C18: < UP + -ISH] —**ˈuppishly** *adv.* —**ˈuppishness** *n.*

uppity (ˈʌpɪtɪ) *adj. Inf.* **1.** snobbish, arrogant, or presumptuous. **2.** offensively self-assertive. [< UP + fanciful ending, ? infl. by -ITY]

upraise (ʌpˈreɪz) *vb.* (*tr.*) *Chiefly literary.* to lift up; elevate. —**upˈraiser** *n.*

uprear (ʌpˈrɪə) *vb.* (*tr.*) to lift up; raise.

upright (ˈʌpˌraɪt) *adj.* **1.** vertical or erect. **2.** honest or just. *~adv.* **3.** vertically. *~n.* **4.** a vertical support, such as a stake or post. **5.** short for **upright piano. 6.** the state of being vertical. —**ˈupˌrightly** *adv.* —**ˈupˌrightness** *n.*

upright piano *n.* a piano which has a rectangular vertical case.

uprise *vb.* (ʌpˈraɪz), **-rising, -rose, -risen. 1.** (*tr.*) to rise up. *~n.* (ˈʌpˌraɪz). **2.** another word for **rise** (senses 23, 24). —**upˈriser** *n.*

uprising (ˈʌpˌraɪzɪŋ, ʌpˈraɪzɪŋ) *n.* **1.** a revolt or rebellion. **2.** *Arch.* an ascent.

uproar (ˈʌpˌrɔː) *n.* a commotion or disturbance characterized by loud noise and confusion.

uproarious (ʌpˈrɔːrɪəs) *adj.* **1.** causing or characterized by an uproar. **2.** extremely funny. **3.** (of laughter, etc.) loud and boisterous. —**upˈroariously** *adv.* —**upˈroariousness** *n.*

uproot (ʌpˈruːt) *vb.* (*tr.*) **1.** to pull up by or as if by the roots. **2.** to displace (a person or persons) from native or habitual surroundings. **3.** to remove or destroy utterly. —**upˈrooter** *n.*

uprush (ˈʌpˌrʌʃ) *n* an upward rush, as of consciousness.

upsadaisy (ˈʌpsəˈdeɪzɪ) *interj.* a variant spelling of **upsy-daisy.**

ups and downs *pl. n.* alternating periods of good and bad fortune, high and low spirits, etc.

upset *vb.* (ʌpˈsɛt), **-setting, -set.** (*mainly tr.*) **1.** (*also intr.*) to tip or be tipped over; overturn or spill. **2.** to disturb the normal state or stability of: *to upset the balance of nature.* **3.** to disturb mentally or emotionally. **4.** to defeat or overthrow, usually unexpectedly. **5.** to make physically ill: *seafood always upsets my stomach.* **6.** to thicken or spread (the end of a bar, etc.) by hammering. *~n.* (ˈʌpˌsɛt). **7.** an unexpected defeat or reversal, as in a contest or plans. **8.** a disturbance or disorder of the emotions, body, etc. *~adj.* (ʌpˈsɛt). **9.** overturned or capsized. **10.** emotionally or physically disturbed or distressed. **11.** disordered; confused. **12.** defeated or overthrown. [C14 (in the sense: to erect; C19 in the sense: to overthrow)] —**upˈsetter** *n.* —**upˈsetting** *adj.* —**upˈsettingly** *adv.*

upset price *n. Chiefly Scot., U.S., & Canad.* the lowest price acceptable for something that is for sale, esp. a house. Cf. **reserve price.**

upshot (ˈʌpˌʃɒt) *n.* **1.** the final result; conclusion; outcome. **2.** *Archery.* the final shot in a match. [C16: < UP + SHOT[1]]

upside (ˈʌpˌsaɪd) *n.* the upper surface or part.

upside down *adj.* **1.** (*usually postpositive;* **upside-down** *when prenominal*) turned over completely; inverted. **2.** (**upside-down** *when prenominal*) *Inf.* confused; topsy-turvy: *an upside-down world.* *~adv.* **3.** in an inverted fashion. **4.** in a chaotic manner. [C16: var., by folk etymology, of earlier *upsodown*]

upside-down cake *n.* a sponge cake baked with fruit at the bottom, and inverted before serving.

upsides (ˌʌpˈsaɪdz) *adv. Inf., chiefly Brit.* (foll. by *with*) equal or level (with), as through revenge.

upsilon (ˈʌpsɪˌlɒn) *n.* **1.** the 20th letter in the Greek alphabet (Υ or υ), a vowel transliterated as *y* or *u.* **2.** a heavy short-lived subatomic particle produced by bombarding beryllium nuclei with high-energy protons. [C17: < Med. Gk *u psilon* simple *u,* name adopted for graphic *u* to avoid confusion with graphic *oi,* since pronunciation was the same for both in LGk]

upstage (ˈʌpˈsteɪdʒ) *adv.* **1.** on, at, or to the rear of the stage. *~adj.* **2.** of or relating to the back half of the stage. **3.** *Inf.* haughty. *~vb.* (*tr.*) **4.** to move upstage of (another actor), thus forcing him to turn away from the audience. **5.** *Inf.* to draw attention to oneself from (someone else). **6.** *Inf.* to treat haughtily.

upstairs (ˈʌpˈstɛəz) *adv.* **1.** up the stairs; to or on an upper floor. **2.** *Inf.* to or into a higher rank or office. *~n.* (*functioning as sing. or pl.*) **3. a.** an upper floor. **b.** (*as modifier*): *an upstairs room.* **4.** *Brit. inf.* the masters of a household collectively, esp. of a large house.

upstanding (ʌpˈstændɪŋ) *adj.* **1.** of good character. **2.** upright and vigorous in build. **3. be**

upstanding. **a.** (in a court of law) a direction to all persons present to rise to their feet before the judge enters or leaves the court. **b.** (at a formal dinner) a direction to all persons present to rise to their feet for a toast.

upstart (ˈʌpˌstɑːt) *n.* **1. a.** a person, group, etc., that has risen suddenly to a position of power. **b.** (*as modifier*): *an upstart family.* **2. a.** an arrogant person. **b.** (*as modifier*): *his upstart ambition.*

upstate (ˈʌpˈsteɪt) *U.S.* ~*adj., adv.* **1.** towards, in, or relating to the outlying or northern sections of a state. ~*n.* **2.** the outlying, esp. northern, sections of a state. —ˈ**upˈstater** *n.*

upstream (ˈʌpˈstriːm) *adv., adj.* in or towards the higher part of a stream; against the current.

upstretched (ʌpˈstretʃt) *adj.* (esp. of the arms) stretched or raised up.

upstroke (ˈʌpˌstrəʊk) *n.* **1. a.** an upward stroke or movement, as of a pen or brush. **b.** the mark produced by such a stroke. **2.** the upward movement of a piston in a reciprocating engine.

upsurge *vb.* (ʌpˈsɜːdʒ). **1.** (*intr.*) *Chiefly literary.* to surge up. ~*n.* (ˈʌpˌsɜːdʒ). **2.** a rapid rise or swell.

upsweep *n.* (ˈʌpˌswiːp). **1.** a curve or sweep upwards. ~*vb.* (ʌpˈswiːp), **-sweeping, -swept. 2.** to sweep, curve, or brush or be swept, curved, or brushed upwards.

upswing (ˈʌpˌswɪŋ) *n.* **1.** *Econ.* a recovery period in the trade cycle. **2.** an upward swing or movement or any increase or improvement.

upsy-daisy (ˈʌpsɪˈdeɪzɪ) *or* **upsadaisy** *interj.* an expression, usually of reassurance, uttered as when someone, esp. a child, stumbles or is being lifted up. [C18 *up-a-daisy,* irregularly formed < UP (adv.)]

uptake (ˈʌpˌteɪk) *n.* **1.** a pipe, shaft, etc., that is used to convey smoke or gases, esp. one that connects a furnace to a chimney. **2.** lifting up. **3.** the act of accepting something on offer. **4. quick** (*or* **slow**) **on the uptake.** *Inf.* quick (or slow) to understand or learn.

upthrow (ˈʌpˌθrəʊ) *n. Geol.* the upward movement of rocks on one side of a fault plane relative to rocks on the other side.

upthrust (ˈʌpˌθrʌst) *n.* **1.** an upward push or thrust. **2.** *Geol.* a violent upheaval of the earth's surface.

uptight (ʌpˈtaɪt) *adj. Inf.* **1.** displaying tense repressed nervousness, irritability, or anger. **2.** unable to give expression to one's feelings.

uptime (ˈʌpˌtaɪm) *n. Commerce.* time during which a machine, such as a computer, actually operates.

up-to-date *adj.* **a.** modern or fashionable: *an up-to-date magazine.* **b.** (*predicative*): *the magazine is up to date.* —ˈ**up-to-ˈdateness** *n.*

uptown (ˈʌpˈtaʊn) *U.S. & Canad.* ~*adj., adv.* **1.** towards, in, or relating to some part of a town that is away from the centre. ~*n.* **2.** such a part of a town, esp. a residential part. —ˈ**upˈtowner** *n.*

upturn *vb.* (ʌpˈtɜːn). **1.** to turn or cause to turn over or upside down. **2.** (*tr.*) to create disorder. **3.** (*tr.*) to direct upwards. ~*n.* (ˈʌpˌtɜːn). **4.** an upward trend or improvement. **5.** an upheaval.

UPU *abbrev. for* Universal Postal Union.

upward (ˈʌpwəd) *adj.* **1.** directed or moving towards a higher point or level. ~*adv.* **2.** a variant of **upwards.** —ˈ**upwardly** *adv.* —ˈ**upwardness** *n.*

upwardly mobile *adj.* (of a person or social group) moving or aspiring to move to a higher social class or status.

upward mobility *n.* movement from a lower to a higher economic and social status.

upwards (ˈʌpwədz) *or* **upward** *adv.* **1.** from a lower to a higher place, level, condition, etc. **2.** towards a higher level, standing, etc.

upwind (ˈʌpˈwɪnd) *adv.* **1.** into or against the wind. **2.** towards or on the side where the wind is blowing; windward. ~*adj.* **3.** going against the wind: *the upwind leg of the course.* **4.** on the windward side.

uracil (ˈjʊərəsɪl) *n. Biochem.* a pyrimidine present in all living cells, usually in a combined form, as in RNA. [C20: < URO- + ACETIC + -ILE]

uraemia *or U.S.* **uremia** (jʊˈriːmɪə) *n. Pathol.* the accumulation of waste products, normally excreted in the urine, in the blood. [C19: < NL, < Gk *ouron* urine + *haima* blood] —**uˈraemic** *or U.S.* **uˈremic** *adj.*

uraeus (jʊˈriːəs) *n., pl.* **-uses.** the sacred serpent represented on the headdresses of ancient Egyptian kings and gods. [C19: < NL, < Gk *ouraios,* < Egyptian *uro* asp]

Ural-Altaic (ˈjʊərəl-) *n.* **1.** a postulated group of related languages consisting of the Uralic and Altaic families of languages. ~*adj.* **2.** of or relating to this group of languages, characterized by agglutination and vowel harmony.

Uralic (jʊˈrælɪk) *or* **Uralian** (jʊˈreɪlɪən) *n.* **1.** a superfamily of languages consisting of the Finno-Ugric family together with Samoyed. See also **Ural-Altaic.** ~*adj.* **2.** of or relating to these languages.

uranalysis (ˌjʊərəˈnælɪsɪs) *n., pl.* **-ses** (-ˌsiːz). *Med.* a variant spelling of **urinalysis.**

Urania (jʊˈreɪnɪə) *n. Greek myth.* the Muse of astronomy. [C17: < L, < Gk *Ourania,* < *ouranios* heavenly, < *ouranos* heaven]

uranide (ˈjʊərəˌnaɪd) *n.* any element having an atomic number greater than that of protactinium.

uranism (ˈjʊərænɪzəm) *n. Rare.* homosexuality (esp. male homosexuality). [C20: < G *Uranismus,* < Gk *ouranios* heavenly, i.e. spiritual]

uranium (jʊˈreɪnɪəm) *n.* a radioactive silvery-white metallic element of the actinide series. It occurs in several minerals including pitchblende and is used chiefly as a source of nuclear energy by fission of the radioisotope **uranium-235.** Symbol: U; atomic no.: 92; atomic wt.: 238.03; half-life of most stable isotope, ^{238}U: 4.51 × 10^9 years. [C18: < NL, < URANUS[2]; from the fact that the element was discovered soon after the planet]

uranium series *n. Physics.* a radioactive series that starts with uranium-238 and proceeds by radioactive decay to lead-206.

urano- *combining form.* denoting the heavens: *uranography.* [< Gk *ouranos*]

uranography (ˌjʊərəˈnɒgrəfɪ) *n.* the branch of astronomy concerned with the description and mapping of the stars, galaxies, etc. —ˌ**uraˈnographer** *n.* —**uranographic** (ˌjʊərənəˈgræfɪk) *adj.*

Uranus[1] (jʊˈreɪnəs, ˈjʊərənəs) *n. Greek myth.* the personification of the sky, who, as a god, ruled the universe and fathered the Titans and Cyclopes; overthrown by his son Cronus.

Uranus[2] (jʊˈreɪnəs, ˈjʊərənəs) *n.* the seventh planet from the sun, sometimes visible to the naked eye. [C19: < L *Ūranus,* < Gk *Ouranos* heaven]

urate (ˈjʊəreɪt) *n.* any salt or ester of uric acid. —**uratic** (jʊˈrætɪk) *adj.*

urban (ˈɜːbᵊn) *adj.* **1.** of, relating to, or constituting a city or town. **2.** living in a city or town. ~Cf. **rural.** [C17: < L *urbānus,* < *urbs* city]

urban area *n.* (in population censuses) a city area considered as the inner city plus built-up environs, irrespective of local body administrative boundaries.

urban district *n.* **1.** (in England and Wales from 1888 to 1974 and Northern Ireland from 1898 to 1973) an urban division of an administrative county with an elected council in charge of housing and environmental services. **2.** (in the Republic of Ireland) any of 49 medium-sized towns with their own elected councils.

urbane (ɜːˈbeɪn) *adj.* characterized by elegance or sophistication. [C16: < L *urbānus* of the town; see URBAN] —**urˈbanely** *adv.* —**urˈbaneness** *n.*

urban guerrilla *n.* a guerrilla who operates in a town or city, engaging in terrorism, kidnapping, etc.

urbanism (ˈɜːbəˌnɪzəm) *n. Chiefly U.S.* **a.** the character of city life. **b.** the study of this.

urbanite (ˈɜːbəˌnaɪt) *n.* a resident of an urban community; city dweller.

urbanity (ɜːˈbænɪtɪ) *n., pl.* **-ties. 1.** the quality of being urbane. **2.** (*usually pl.*) civilities or courtesies.

urbanize *or* **-nise** (ˈɜːbəˌnaɪz) *vb.* (*tr.*) (*usually passive*) **a.** to make (esp. a predominantly rural area or country) more industrialized and urban. **b.** to cause the migration of an increasing proportion of (rural dwellers) into cities. —ˌ**urbaniˈzation** *or* **-niˈsation** *n.*

urban renewal *n.* the process of redeveloping dilapidated or no longer functional urban areas.

urbi et orbi *Latin.* (ˈɜːbɪ ɛt ˈɔːbɪ) *adv. R.C. Church.* to the city and the world: a phrase qualifying the solemn papal blessing.

urceolate (ˈɜːsɪəlɪt, -ˌleɪt) *adj. Biol.* shaped like an urn or pitcher: *an urceolate corolla.* [C18: via NL < L *urceolus,* dim. of *urceus* a pitcher]

urchin (ˈɜːtʃɪn) *n.* **1.** a mischievous roguish child, esp. one who is young, small, or raggedly dressed. **2.** See **sea urchin.** **3.** *Arch., dialect.* a hedgehog. **4.** *Obs.* an elf or sprite. [C13 *urchon,* < OF *heriçon,* < L *ēricius* hedgehog]

Urdu (ˈʊəduː, ˈɜː-) *n.* an official language of Pakistan, also spoken in India. The script derives primarily from Persia. It belongs to the Indic branch of the Indo-European family of languages, being closely related to Hindi. [C18: < Hindustani (*zabānī*) *urdū* (language of the) camp, < Persian *urdū* camp, < Turkish *ordū*]

-ure *suffix forming nouns.* **1.** indicating act, process, or result: *seizure.* **2.** indicating function or office: *legislature; prefecture.* [< F, < L *-ūra*]

urea (ˈjʊərɪə) *n.* a white water-soluble crystalline compound, produced by protein metabolism and excreted in urine. A synthetic form is used as a fertilizer and animal feed. Formula: $CO(NH_2)_2$. [C19: < NL, < F *urée,* < Gk *ouron* urine] —**uˈreal** *or* **uˈreic** *adj.*

urea-formaldehyde resin *n.* any one of a class of rigid odourless synthetic materials that are made from urea and formaldehyde and are used in electrical fittings, adhesives, laminates, and finishes for textiles.

ureide (ˈjʊərɪˌaɪd) *n. Chem.* **1.** any of a class of organic compounds derived from urea by replacing one or more of its hydrogen atoms by organic groups. **2.** any of a class of derivatives of urea and carboxylic acids, in which one or more of the hydrogen atoms have been replaced by acid radical groups.

-uret *suffix of nouns.* formerly used to form the names of binary chemical compounds. [< NL *-uretum*]

ureter (jʊˈriːtə) *n.* the tube that conveys urine from the kidney to the urinary bladder or cloaca. [C16: via NL < Gk *ourētēr,* < *ourein* to urinate] —**uˈreteral** *or* **ureteric** (ˌjʊərɪˈtɛrɪk) *adj.*

urethane (ˈjʊərɪˌθeɪn) *or* **urethan** (ˈjʊərɪˌθæn) *n.* short for **polyurethane.** [C19: < URO- + ETHYL + -ANE]

urethra (jʊˈriːθrə) *n., pl.* **-thrae** (-θriː) *or* **-thras.** the canal that in most mammals conveys urine from the bladder out of the body. In human males it also conveys semen. [C17: via LL < Gk *ourēthra,* < *ourein* to urinate] —**uˈrethral** *adj.*

urethritis (ˌjʊərɪˈθraɪtɪs) *n.* inflammation of the urethra. [C19: < NL, < LL URETHRA] —**urethritic** (ˌjʊərɪˈθrɪtɪk) *adj.*

urethroscope (jʊˈriːθrəˌskəʊp) *n.* a medical instrument for examining the urethra. [C20: see URETHRA, -SCOPE] —**urethroscopic** (jʊˌriːθrəˈskɒpɪk) *adj.* —**urethroscopy** (ˌjʊərɪˈθrɒskəpɪ) *n.*

uretic (jʊˈrɛtɪk) *adj.* of or relating to the urine. [C19: via LL < Gk *ourētikos,* < *ouron* urine]

urge (ɜːdʒ) *vb.* (*tr.*) **1.** to plead, press, or move (someone to do something): *we urged him to surrender.* **2.** (*may take a clause as object*) to advocate or recommend earnestly and persistently: *to urge the need for safety.* **3.** to impel, drive, or hasten onwards: *he urged the horses on.* ~*n.* **4.** a strong impulse, inner drive, or yearning. [C16: < L *urgēre*]

urgent (ˈɜːdʒənt) *adj.* **1.** requiring or compelling speedy action or attention: *the matter is urgent.* **2.** earnest and persistent. [C15: via F < L *urgent-, urgens,* present participle of *urgēre* to URGE] —**urgency** (ˈɜːdʒənsɪ) *n.* —ˈ**urgently** *adv.*

-urgy *n. combining form.* indicating technology concerned with a specified material: *metallurgy.* [< Gk *-urgia,* < *ergon* work]

-uria *n. combining form.* indicating a diseased or abnormal condition of the urine: *pyuria.* [< Gk *-ouria,* < *ouron* urine] —**-uric** *adj. combining form.*

uric (ˈjʊərɪk) *adj.* of, concerning, or derived from urine. [C18: < URO- + -IC]

uric acid *n.* a white odourless tasteless crystalline product of protein metabolism, present in the blood and urine. Formula: $C_5H_4N_4O_3$.

uridine (ˈjʊərɪˌdiːn) *n. Biochem.* a nucleoside present in all living cells in a combined form, esp. in RNA. [C20: < URO- + -IDE + -INE[2]]

urinal (jʊˈraɪnᵊl, ˈjʊərɪ-) *n.* **1.** a sanitary fitting, esp. one fixed to a wall, used by men for urination. **2.** a room containing urinals. **3.** any vessel for holding urine prior to its disposal.

urinalysis (ˌjʊərɪˈnælɪsɪs) *n., pl.* **-ses** (-ˌsiːz). *Med.* chemical analysis of the urine to test for the presence of disease.

urinary (ˈjʊərɪnərɪ) *adj.* **1.** *Anat.* of or relating to urine or to the organs and structures that secrete and pass urine. ~*n., pl.* **-naries.** **2.** a reservoir for urine.

urinary bladder *n.* a distensible membranous sac in which the urine excreted from the kidneys is stored.

urinate (ˈjʊərɪˌneɪt) *vb.* (*intr.*) to excrete or void urine. —ˌ**uriˈnation** *n.* —ˈ**urinative** *adj.*

urine (ˈjʊərɪn) *n.* the pale yellow slightly acid fluid excreted by the kidneys, containing waste products removed from the blood. It is stored in the urinary bladder and discharged through the urethra. [C14: via OF < L *ūrīna*]

urinogenital (ˌjʊərɪnəʊˈdʒɛnɪtᵊl) *adj.* another word for **urogenital.**

urn (ɜːn) *n.* **1.** a vaselike receptacle or vessel, esp. a large bulbous one with a foot. **2.** a vase used as a receptacle for the ashes of the dead. **3.** a large vessel, usually of metal, with a tap, used for making and holding tea, coffee, etc. [C14: < L *ūrna*] —ˈ**urnˌlike** *adj.*

urnfield (ˈɜːnˌfiːld) *n.* **1.** a cemetery full of individual cremation urns. ~*adj.* **2.** (of a number of Bronze Age cultures) characterized by cremation in urns, which began in E Europe about the second millennium B.C.

uro- *or before a vowel* **ur-** *combining form.* indicating urine or the urinary tract: *urogenital; urology.* [< Gk *ouron* urine]

urogenital (ˌjʊərəʊˈdʒɛnɪtᵊl) *or* **urinogenital** *adj.* of or relating to the urinary and genital organs and their functions. Also: **genitourinary.**

urogenital system *or* **tract** *n. Anat.* the urinary tract and reproductive organs.

urolith (ˈjʊərəʊlɪθ) *n. Pathol.* a calculus in the urinary tract. —ˌ**uroˈlithic** *adj.*

urology (jʊˈrɒlədʒɪ) *n.* the branch of medicine concerned with the study and treatment of diseases of the urogenital tract. —**urologic** (ˌjʊərəˈlɒdʒɪk) *adj.* —**uˈrologist** *n.*

uropygial gland (ˌjʊərəˈpɪdʒɪəl) *n.* a gland, situated at the base of the tail in most birds, that secretes oil used in preening.

uropygium (ˌjʊərəˈpɪdʒɪəm) *n.* the hindmost part of a bird's body, from which the tail feathers grow. [C19: via NL < Gk *ouropugion,* < *oura* tail + *pugē* rump] —ˌ**uroˈpygial** *adj.*

uroscopy (jʊˈrɒskəpɪ) *n. Med.* examination of the urine. See also **urinalysis.** —**uroscopic** (ˌjʊərəˈskɒpɪk) *adj.* —**uˈroscopist** *n.*

Ursa Major (ˈɜːsə ˈmeɪdʒə) *n., Latin genitive* **Ursae Majoris** (ˈɜːsiː məˈdʒɔːrɪs). an extensive conspicuous constellation in the N hemisphere. The seven brightest stars form the **Plough.** Also called: the **Great Bear,** the **Bear.** [L: greater bear]

Ursa Minor (ˈɜːsə ˈmaɪnə) *n., Latin genitive* **Ursae Minoris** (ˈɜːsiː mɪˈnɔːrɪs). a small faint constellation, the brightest star of which is the

Pole Star. Also called: the **Little Bear,** the **Bear.** [L: lesser bear]

ursine (ˈɜːsaɪn) *adj.* of, relating to, or resembling a bear or bears. [C16: < L *ursus* a bear]

Ursprache *German.* (ˈuːrʃpraːxə) *n.* any hypothetical extinct and unrecorded language reconstructed from groups of related recorded languages. For example, Indo-European is an Ursprache reconstructed by comparison of the Germanic group, Latin, Sanskrit, etc. [< *ur-* primeval + *Sprache* language]

Ursuline (ˈɜːsjʊˌlaɪn) *n.* **1.** a member of an order of nuns devoted to teaching in the Roman Catholic Church: founded in 1537 at Brescia. ~*adj.* **2.** of or relating to this order. [C16: after St *Ursula,* patron saint of St Angela Merici, who founded the order]

Urtext *German.* (ˈuːrtɛkst) *n.* **1.** the earliest form of a text as established by linguistic scholars as a basis for variants in later texts still in existence. **2.** an edition of a musical score showing the composer's intentions without later editorial interpolation. [< *ur-* original + TEXT]

urticaceous (ˌɜːtɪˈkeɪʃəs) *adj.* of or belonging to a family of plants having small flowers and, in many species, stinging hairs: includes the nettles and pellitory. [C18: via NL < L *urtīca* nettle, < *ūrere* to burn]

urticaria (ˌɜːtɪˈkɛərɪə) *n.* a skin condition characterized by the formation of itchy red or whitish raised patches, usually caused by an allergy. Nontechnical names: **hives, nettle rash.** [C18: < NL, < L *urtīca* nettle]

urtication (ˌɜːtɪˈkeɪʃən) *n.* **1.** a burning or itching sensation. **2.** another name for **urticaria.**

urus (ˈjʊərəs) *n., pl.* **uruses.** another name for the **aurochs.** [C17: < *ūrus,* of Gmc origin]

urushiol (ˈuːrʊʃɪˌɒl, uːˈruː-) *n.* a poisonous pale yellow liquid occurring in poison ivy and the lacquer tree. [< Japanese *urushi* lacquer + -OL[2]]

us (ʌs) *pron.* (*objective*) **1.** refers to the speaker or writer and another person or other people: *don't hurt us.* **2.** refers to all people or people in general: *this table shows us the tides.* **3.** an informal word for **me:** *give us a kiss!* **4.** a formal word for **me** used by editors, monarchs, etc. [OE *ūs*]

▷ **Usage.** See at **me.**

U.S. *or* **US** *abbrev. for* United States.

USA *abbrev. for* United States Army.

U.S.A. *or* **USA** *abbrev. for* United States of America.

usable *or* **useable** (ˈjuːzəbᵊl) *adj.* able to be used. —ˌ**usaˈbility** *or* ˌ**useaˈbility** *n.*

USAF *abbrev. for* United States Air Force.

usage (ˈjuːsɪdʒ, -zɪdʒ) *n.* **1.** the act or a manner of using; use; employment. **2.** constant use, custom, or habit. **3.** something permitted or established by custom or practice. **4.** what is actually said in a language, esp. as contrasted with what is prescribed. [C14: via OF < L *ūsus* USE (n.)]

usance (ˈjuːzəns) *n. Commerce.* the period of time permitted by commercial usage for the redemption of foreign bills of exchange. [C14: < OF, < Med. L *ūsantia,* < *ūsāre* to USE]

USDAW (ˈʌsdɔː) *n.* (in Britain) *acronym for* Union of Shop, Distributive, and Allied Workers.

use *vb.* (juːz). (*tr.*) **1.** to put into service or action; employ for a given purpose: *to use a spoon to stir with.* **2.** to make a practice or habit of employing; exercise: *he uses his brain.* **3.** to behave towards in a particular way, esp. for one's own ends: *he uses people.* **4.** to consume, expend, or exhaust: *the engine uses very little oil.* **5.** to partake of (alcoholic drink, drugs, etc.) or smoke (tobacco, marijuana, etc.). ~*n.* (juːs). **6.** the act of using or the state of being used: *the carpet wore out through constant use.* **7.** the ability or permission to use. **8.** the occasion to use: *I have no use for this paper.* **9.** an instance or manner of using. **10.** usefulness; advantage: *it is of no use to complain.* **11.** custom; habit: *long use has inured him to it.* **12.** the purpose for which something is used; end. **13.** *Christianity.* a distinctive form of liturgical or ritual observance, esp. one that is traditional. **14.** the enjoyment of property, land, etc., by occupation or by deriving revenue from it. **15.** *Law.* the beneficial enjoyment of property the legal title to which is held by another person as trustee. **16. have no use for. a.** to have no need of. **b.** to have a contemptuous dislike for. **17. make use of. a.** to employ; use. **b.** to exploit (a person). ~See also **use up.** [C13: < OF *user,* < L *ūsus* having used, < *ūtī* to use]

used (juːzd) *adj.* second-hand: *used cars.*

used to (juːst) *adj.* **1.** accustomed to: *I am used to hitchhiking.* ~*vb.* (*tr.*) **2.** (*takes an infinitive or implied infinitive*) used as an auxiliary to express habitual or accustomed actions, states, etc., taking place in the past but not continuing into the present: *I used to fish here every day.*

useful (ˈjuːsfʊl) *adj.* **1.** able to be used advantageously, beneficially, or for several purposes. **2.** *Inf.* commendable or capable: *a useful term's work.* —ˈ**usefully** *adv.* —ˈ**usefulness** *n.*

useless (ˈjuːslɪs) *adj.* **1.** having no practical use or advantage. **2.** *Inf.* ineffectual, weak, or stupid: *he's useless at history.* —ˈ**uselessly** *adv.* —ˈ**uselessness** *n.*

user (ˈjuːzə) *n.* **1.** *Law.* **a.** the continued exercise, use, or enjoyment of a right, esp. in property. **b.** a presumptive right based on long-continued use: *right of user.* **2.** (*often in combination*) a person or thing that uses: *a road-user.* **3.** *Inf.* a drug addict.

user-friendly *adj.* (**user friendly** *when postpositive*) easy to familiarize oneself with, understand, or use.

use up *vb.* (*tr., adv.*) **1.** to finish (a supply); consume completely. **2.** to exhaust; wear out.

usher (ˈʌʃə) *n.* **1.** an official who shows people to their seats, as in a church or theatre. **2.** a person who acts as doorkeeper, esp. in a court of law. **3.** (in England) a minor official charged with maintaining order in a court of law. **4.** an officer responsible for preceding persons of rank in a procession. **5.** *Brit., obs.* a teacher. ~*vb.* (*tr.*) **6.** to conduct or escort, esp. in a courteous or obsequious way. **7.** (usually foll. by *in*) to be a precursor or herald (of). [C14: < OF *huissier* doorkeeper, < Vulgar L *ustiārius* (unattested), < L *ostium* door]

usherette (ˌʌʃəˈrɛt) *n.* a woman assistant in a cinema, etc., who shows people to their seats.

USM *Stock Exchange. abbrev. for* unlisted securities market.

USN *abbrev. for* United States Navy.

usquebaugh (ˈʌskwɪˌbɔː) *n.* **1.** *Irish.* the former name for **whiskey.** **2.** *Scot.* the former name for **whisky.** [C16: < Irish Gaelic *uisce beathadh* or Scot. Gaelic *uisge beatha* water of life]

USS *abbrev. for:* **1.** United States Senate. **2.** United States Ship.

USSR *abbrev. for* Union of Soviet Socialist Republics.

usual (ˈjuːʒʊəl) *adj.* **1.** of the most normal, frequent, or regular type: *that's the usual sort of application to send.* ~*n.* **2.** ordinary or commonplace events (esp. in **out of the usual**). **3. the usual.** *Inf.* the habitual or usual drink, etc. [C14: < LL *ūsuālis* ordinary, < L *ūsus* USE] —ˈ**usually** *adv.* —ˈ**usualness** *n.*

usufruct (ˈjuːsjʊˌfrʌkt) *n.* the right to use and derive profit from a piece of property belonging to another, provided the property itself remains undiminished and uninjured in any way. [C17: < LL *ūsūfrūctus,* < L *ūsus* use + *frūctus* enjoyment] —ˌ**usuˈfructuary** *n., adj.*

usurer (ˈjuːʒərə) *n.* a person who lends funds at an exorbitant rate of interest.

usurp (juːˈzɜːp) *vb.* to seize or appropriate (land, a throne, etc.) without authority. [C14: < OF, < L *ūsūrpāre* to take into use, prob. < *ūsus* use + *rapere* to seize] —ˌ**usurˈpation** *n.* —**uˈsurper** *n.*

usury (ˈjuːʒərɪ) *n., pl.* **-ries.** **1.** the practice of loaning money at an exorbitant rate of interest. **2.** an unlawfully high rate of interest. **3.** *Obs.* moneylending. [C14: < Med. L, < L *ūsūra* usage, < *ūsus* USE] —**usurious** (juːˈʒʊərɪəs) *adj.*

USW *Radio. abbrev. for* ultrashort wave.
ut (ʌt, uːt) *n. Music.* the syllable used in the fixed system of solmization for the note C. [C14: < L *ut;* see GAMUT]
UT *abbrev. for:* **1.** universal time. **2.** Utah.
ute (juːt) *n. Austral. & N.Z. inf.* short for **utility truck.**
utensil (juːˈtɛnsəl) *n.* an implement, tool, or container for practical use: *writing utensils.* [C14 *utensele,* via OF < L *ūtēnsilia* necessaries, < *ūtēnsilis* available for use, < *ūtī* to use]
uterine (ˈjuːtəˌraɪn) *adj.* **1.** of, relating to, or affecting the uterus. **2.** (of offspring) born of the same mother but not the same father.
uterus (ˈjuːtərəs) *n., pl.* **uteri** (ˈjuːtəˌraɪ). **1.** *Anat.* a hollow muscular organ lying within the pelvic cavity of female mammals. It houses the developing fetus. Nontechnical name: **womb. 2.** the corresponding organ in other animals. [C17: < L]
utilidor (juːˈtɪlədə; *Canad.* -ˌdɒr) *n. Canad.* aboveground insulated casing for pipes carrying water, etc., in permafrost regions.
utilitarian (juːˌtɪlɪˈtɛərɪən) *adj.* **1.** of or relating to utilitarianism. **2.** designed for use rather than beauty. ~*n.* **3.** a person who believes in utilitarianism.
utilitarianism (juːˌtɪlɪˈtɛərɪəˌnɪzəm) *n. Ethics.* **1.** the doctrine that right action consists in the greatest good for the greatest number, that is, in maximizing the total benefit resulting, without regard to the distribution of benefits and burdens. **2.** the theory that the criterion of virtue is utility.
utility (juːˈtɪlɪtɪ) *n., pl.* **-ties. 1. a.** the quality of practical use; usefulness. **b.** (*as modifier*): *a utility fabric.* **2.** something useful. **3. a.** a public service, such as the bus system. **b.** (*as modifier*): *utility vehicle.* **4.** *Econ.* the ability of a commodity to satisfy human wants. **5.** *Austral.* short for **utility truck.** [C14: < OF *utelite,* < L *ūtilitās* usefulness, < *ūtī* to use]
utility room *n.* a room, esp. in a private house, used for storage, laundry, etc.
utility truck *n. Austral. & N.Z.* a small truck with an open body and low sides, often with a removable tarpaulin cover; pick-up truck.
utilize *or* **-lise** (ˈjuːtɪˌlaɪz) *vb.* (*tr.*) to make practical or worthwhile use of. —**ˈutiˌlizable** *or* **-ˌlisable** *adj.* —**ˌutiliˈzation** *or* **-liˈsation** *n.* —**ˈutiˌlizer** *or* **-ˌliser** *n.*
utmost (ˈʌtˌməʊst) *or* **uttermost** *adj.* (*prenominal*) **1.** of the greatest possible degree or amount: *the utmost degree.* **2.** at the furthest limit: *the utmost town on the peninsula.* ~*n.* **3.** the greatest possible degree, extent, or amount: *he tried his utmost.* [OE *ūtemest,* < *ūte* out + *-mest* MOST]
Utopia (juːˈtəʊpɪə) *n.* (*sometimes not cap.*) any real or imaginary society, place, state, etc., considered to be perfect or ideal. [C16: < NL *Utopia* (coined by Sir Thomas More in 1516 as the title of his book that described an imaginary island representing the perfect society), lit.: no place, < Gk *ou* not + *topos* a place]
Utopian (juːˈtəʊpɪən) (*sometimes not cap.*) ~*adj.* **1.** of or relating to a perfect or ideal existence. ~*n.* **2.** an idealistic social reformer. —**Uˈtopianism** *n.*
utricle (ˈjuːtrɪkˀl) *n.* **1.** *Anat.* the larger of the two parts of the membranous labyrinth of the internal ear. Cf. **saccule. 2.** *Bot.* the bladder-like one-seeded indehiscent fruit of certain plants. [C18: < L *ūtriculus,* dim. of *ūter* bag] —**uˈtricular** *adj.*
utriculitis (juːˌtrɪkjʊˈlaɪtɪs) *n.* inflammation of the inner ear.
utter[1] (ˈʌtə) *vb.* **1.** to give audible expression to (something): *to utter a growl.* **2.** *Criminal law.* to put into circulation (counterfeit coin, forged banknotes, etc.). **3.** (*tr.*) to make publicly known; publish: *to utter slander.* [C14: prob. orig. a commercial term, < MDu. *ūteren* (modern Du. *uiteren*) to make known] —**ˈutterable** *adj.* —**ˈutterableness** *n.* —**ˈutterer** *n.*
utter[2] (ˈʌtə) *adj.* (*prenominal*) (intensifier): *an utter fool; the utter limit.* [C15: < OE *utera* outer, comp. of *ūte* out (adv.)] —**ˈutterly** *adv.*
utterance (ˈʌtərəns) *n.* **1.** something uttered, such as a statement. **2.** the act or power of uttering or ability to utter.
utter barrister *n. Law.* the full title of a barrister who is not a Queen's Counsel.
uttermost (ˈʌtəˌməʊst) *adj., n.* a variant of **utmost.**
U-turn *n.* **1.** a turn made by a vehicle in the shape of a U, resulting in a reversal of direction. **2.** a complete change in direction of political policy, etc.
UV *abbrev. for* ultraviolet.
UV-A *or* **UVA** *abbrev. for* ultraviolet radiation with a range of 320-380 nanometres.
uvarovite (uːˈvɑːrəˌvaɪt) *n.* an emerald-green garnet found in chromium deposits. [C19: < G *Uvarovit;* after Count Sergei *Uvarov* (1785–1855), Russian author & statesman]
UV-B *or* **UVB** *abbrev. for* ultraviolet radiation with a range of 280-320 nanometres.
uvea (ˈjuːvɪə) *n.* the part of the eyeball consisting of the iris, ciliary body, and choroid. [C16: < Med. L *ūvea,* < L *ūva* grape] —**ˈuveal** *adj.*
UVF *abbrev. for* Ulster Volunteer Force.
uvula (ˈjuːvjʊlə) *n., pl.* **-las** *or* **-lae** (-ˌliː). a small fleshy flap of tissue that hangs in the back of the throat and is an extension of the soft palate. [C14: < Med. L, lit.: a little grape, < L *ūva* a grape]
uvular (ˈjuːvjʊlə) *adj.* **1.** of or relating to the uvula. **2.** *Phonetics.* articulated with the uvula and the back of the tongue, such as the (r) sound of Parisian French. ~*n.* **3.** a uvular consonant.
uxorial (ʌkˈsɔːrɪəl) *adj.* of or relating to a wife: *uxorial influence.* [C19: < L *uxor* wife] —**uxˈorially** *adv.*
uxoricide (ʌkˈsɔːrɪˌsaɪd) *n.* **1.** the act of killing one's wife. **2.** a man who kills his wife. [C19: < L *uxor* wife + -CIDE] —**uxˌoriˈcidal** *adj.*
uxorious (ʌkˈsɔːrɪəs) *adj.* excessively attached to or dependent on one's wife. [C16: < L *uxōrius* concerning a wife, < *uxor* wife] —**uxˈoriously** *adv.* —**uxˈoriousness** *n.*
Uzbek (ˈʊzbɛk, ˈʌz-) *n.* **1.** (*pl.* **-beks** *or* **-bek**) a member of a Mongoloid people of Uzbekistan in the SE central Soviet Union. **2.** the language of this people.

V

v *or* **V** (viː) *n., pl.* **v's, V's,** *or* **Vs. 1.** the 22nd letter of the English alphabet. **2.** a speech sound represented by this letter, usually a voiced fricative, as in *vote*. **3. a.** something shaped like a V. **b.** (*in combination*): *a V neck.*

v *symbol. for:* **1.** *Physics.* velocity. **2.** specific volume (of a gas).

V *symbol for:* **1.** *Chem.* vanadium. **2.** (in transformational grammar) verb. **3.** volume (capacity). **4.** volt. **5.** victory. **~6.** *the Roman numeral for* five.

v. *abbrev. for:* **1.** ventral. **2.** verb. **3.** verse. **4.** verso. **5.** (*usually italic*) versus. **6.** very. **7.** vide [L: see]. **8.** volume.

V. *abbrev. for:* **1.** Venerable. **2.** (in titles) Very. **3.** (in titles) Vice. **4.** Viscount.

V-1 *n.* a robot bomb invented by the Germans in World War II: used esp. to bombard London. Also called: **doodlebug, buzz bomb, flying bomb.** [< G *Vergeltungswaffe* revenge weapon]

V-2 *n.* a rocket-powered ballistic missile invented by the Germans in World War II: used esp. to bombard London. [see V-1]

V6 *n.* a car or internal-combustion engine having six cylinders arranged in the form of a V.

V8 *n.* a car or internal-combustion engine having eight cylinders arranged in the form of a V.

VA *abbrev. for:* **1.** Vicar Apostolic. **2.** (Order of) Victoria and Albert.

vac (væk) *n. Brit. inf.* short for **vacation.**

vacancy (ˈveɪkənsɪ) *n., pl.* **-cies. 1.** the state or condition of being vacant or unoccupied; emptiness. **2.** an unoccupied post or office: *we have a vacancy in the accounts department.* **3.** an unoccupied room in a hotel, etc.: *put up the "No Vacancies" sign.* **4.** lack of thought or intelligent awareness. **5.** *Obs.* idleness or a period spent in idleness.

vacant (ˈveɪkənt) *adj.* **1.** without any contents; empty. **2.** (*postpositive;* foll. by *of*) devoid (of something specified). **3.** having no incumbent: *a vacant post.* **4.** having no tenant or occupant: *a vacant house.* **5.** characterized by or resulting from lack of thought or intelligent awareness. **6.** (of time, etc.) not allocated to any activity: *a vacant hour in one's day.* **7.** spent in idleness or inactivity: *a vacant life.* [C13: < L *vacāre* to be empty] —ˈ**vacantly** *adv.*

vacant possession *n.* ownership of an unoccupied house or property, any previous owner or tenant having departed.

vacate (vəˈkeɪt) *vb.* (*mainly tr.*) **1.** to cause (something) to be empty, esp. by departing from or abandoning it: *to vacate a room.* **2.** (*also intr.*) to give up the tenure, possession, or occupancy of (a place, post, etc.). **3.** *Law.* **a.** to cancel. **b.** to annul. —**vaˈcatable** *adj.*

vacation (vəˈkeɪʃən) *n.* **1.** *Chiefly Brit.* a period of the year when the law courts or universities are closed. **2.** another word (esp. U.S. and Canad.) for **holiday** (sense 1). **3.** the act of departing from or abandoning property, etc. *~vb.* **4.** (*intr.*) *U.S. & Canad.* to take a holiday. [C14: < L *vacātiō* freedom, < *vacāre* to be empty] —**vaˈcationer** *or* **vaˈcationist** *n.*

vaccinate (ˈvæksɪˌneɪt) *vb.* to inoculate (a person) with vaccine so as to produce immunity against a specific disease. —ˈ**vacciˌnator** *n.*

vaccination (ˌvæksɪˈneɪʃən) *n.* **1.** the act of vaccinating. **2.** the scar left following inoculation with a vaccine.

vaccine (ˈvæksiːn) *n. Med.* **1.** a suspension of dead, attenuated, or otherwise modified microorganisms for inoculation to produce immunity to a disease by stimulating the production of antibodies. **2.** a preparation of the virus of cowpox inoculated in humans to produce immunity to smallpox. **3.** (*modifier*) of or relating to vaccination or vaccinia. [C18: < NL *variolae vaccīnae* cowpox, title of medical treatise (1798) by Edward Jenner, < L *vacca* a cow] —ˈ**vaccinal** *adj.*

vaccinia (vækˈsɪnɪə) *n.* a technical name for **cowpox.** [C19: NL, < L *vaccīnus* of cows]

vacherin *French.* (vaʃrɛ̃) *n.* a dessert consisting of a meringue shell filled with whipped cream, ice cream, fruit, etc. [also in France a kind of cheese, < F *vache* cow, < L *vacca*]

vacillate (ˈvæsɪˌleɪt) *vb.* (*intr.*) **1.** to fluctuate in one's opinions. **2.** to sway from side to side physically. [C16: < L *vacillāre* to sway, <?] —ˌ**vacilˈlation** *n.* —ˈ**vacilˌlator** *n.*

vacua (ˈvækjʊə) *n.* a plural of **vacuum.**

vacuity (væˈkjuːɪtɪ) *n., pl.* **-ties. 1.** the state or quality of being vacuous. **2.** an empty space or void. **3.** a lack or absence of something specified: *a vacuity of wind.* **4.** lack of normal intelligence or awareness. **5.** a statement, saying, etc., that is inane or pointless. [C16: < L *vacuitās* empty space, < *vacuus* empty]

vacuole (ˈvækjʊˌəʊl) *n. Biol.* a fluid-filled cavity in a cell. [C19: < F, lit.: little vacuum, < L VACUUM] —**vacuolar** (ˌvækjʊˈəʊlə) *adj.*

vacuous (ˈvækjʊəs) *adj.* **1.** empty. **2.** bereft of ideas or intelligence. **3.** characterized by or resulting from vacancy of mind: *a vacuous gaze.* **4.** indulging in no useful mental or physical activity. [C17: < L *vacuus* empty] —ˈ**vacuously** *adv.*

vacuum (ˈvækjʊəm) *n., pl.* **vacuums** *or* **vacua. 1.** a region containing no free matter; in technical contexts now often called: **free space. 2.** a region in which gas is present at a low pressure. **3.** the degree of exhaustion of gas within an enclosed space: *a perfect vacuum.* **4.** a feeling of emptiness: *his death left a vacuum in her life.* **5.** short for **vacuum cleaner. 6.** (*modifier*) of, containing, producing, or operated by a low gas pressure: *a vacuum brake.* *~vb.* **7.** to clean (something) with a vacuum cleaner. [C16: < L: empty space, < *vacuus* empty]

vacuum cleaner *n.* an electrical household appliance used for cleaning floors, carpets, etc., by suction. —**vacuum cleaning** *n.*

vacuum distillation *n.* distillation in which the liquid distilled is enclosed at a low pressure in order to reduce its boiling point.

vacuum flask *n.* an insulating flask that has double walls, usually of silvered glass, with an evacuated space between them. It is used for maintaining substances at high or low temperatures. Also called: **Thermos.**

vacuum gauge *n.* any of a number of instruments for measuring pressures below atmospheric pressure.

vacuum-packed *adj.* packed in an airtight container or packet under low pressure in order to maintain freshness, prevent corrosion, etc.

vacuum pump *n.* a pump for producing a low gas pressure.

vacuum tube *or* **valve** *n.* the U.S. and Canad. name for **valve** (sense 3).

VAD 1. *abbrev. for* Voluntary Aid Detachment. **2.** a member of this organization.

vade mecum (ˈvɑːdɪ ˈmeɪkʊm) *n.* a handbook or other aid carried on the person for immediate use when needed. [C17: < L, lit.: go with me]

vadose (ˈveɪdəʊs) *adj.* of, designating, or derived from water occurring above the water table: *vadose deposits.* [C19: < L *vadōsus* full of shallows, < *vadum* a ford]

vagabond (ˈvægəˌbɒnd) *n.* **1.** a person with no fixed home. **2.** an idle wandering beggar or thief. **3.** (*modifier*) of or like a vagabond. [C15: < L *vagābundus* wandering, < *vagārī* to roam, < *vagus* VAGUE] —ˈ**vagaˌbondage** *n.*

vagal (ˈveɪgᵊl) *adj. Anat.* of, relating to, or affecting the vagus nerve: *vagal inhibition.*

vagary (ˈveɪgərɪ, vəˈgɛərɪ) *n., pl.* **-garies.** an erratic notion or action. [C16: prob. < L *vagārī* to roam; cf. L *vagus* VAGUE]

vagina (vəˈdʒaɪnə) *n., pl.* **-nas** *or* **-nae** (-niː). **1.** the canal in most female mammals that extends from the cervix of the uterus to an external opening between the labia minora. **2.** *Anat., biol.* any sheath or sheathlike structure. [C17: < L: sheath] —**vagˈinal** *adj.*

vaginate (ˈvædʒɪnɪt, -ˌneɪt) *adj.* (esp. of plant parts) sheathed: *a vaginate leaf.*

vaginectomy (ˌvædʒɪˈnɛktəmɪ) *n., pl.* **-mies. 1.** surgical removal of all or part of the vagina. **2.** surgical removal of part of the serous sheath surrounding the testis and epididymis.

vaginismus (ˌvædʒɪˈnɪzməs) *n.* painful spasm of the vagina. [C19: < NL, < VAGINA, + *-ismus*; see -ISM]

vaginitis (ˌvædʒɪˈnaɪtɪs) *n.* inflammation of the vagina.

vagotomy (væˈgɒtəmɪ) *n., pl.* **-mies.** surgical division of the vagus nerve, performed to limit gastric secretion in patients with severe peptic ulcers. [C19: < VAG(US) + -TOMY]

vagotonia (ˌveɪgəˈtəʊnɪə) *n.* pathological overactivity of the vagus nerve, affecting various bodily functions controlled by this nerve. [C19: < VAG(US) + *-tonia*, < L *tonus* tension, TONE]

vagrancy (ˈveɪgrənsɪ) *n., pl.* **-cies. 1.** the state or condition of being a vagrant. **2.** the conduct or mode of living of a vagrant.

vagrant (ˈveɪgrənt) *n.* **1.** a person of no settled abode, income, or job; tramp. ~*adj.* **2.** wandering about. **3.** of or characteristic of a vagrant or vagabond. **4.** moving in an erratic fashion; wayward. **5.** (of plants) showing straggling growth. [C15: prob. < OF *waucrant* (< *wancrer* to roam, of Gmc origin), but also infl. by OF *vagant* vagabond, < L *vagārī* to wander] —ˈ**vagrantly** *adv.*

vague (veɪg) *adj.* **1.** (of statements, meaning, etc.) imprecise: *vague promises.* **2.** not clearly perceptible or discernible: *a vague idea.* **3.** not clearly or definitely established or known: *a vague rumour.* **4.** (of a person or his expression) absent-minded. [C16: via F < L *vagus* wandering, <?] —ˈ**vaguely** *adv.* —ˈ**vagueness** *n.*

vagus *or* **vagus nerve** (ˈveɪgəs) *n., pl.* **-gi** (-dʒaɪ). the tenth cranial nerve, which supplies the heart, lungs, and viscera. [C19: < L *vagus* wandering] —ˈ**vagal** *adj.*

vail (veɪl) *Obs.* ~*vb.* (*tr.*) **1.** to lower (something, such as a weapon), esp. as a sign of deference. **2.** to remove (the hat, etc.) as a mark of respect. ~*n.* **3.** a tip. [C14 *valen*, < obs. *avalen*, < OF *avaler* to let fall, < L *ad vallem*, lit.: to the valley, i.e., down]

vain (veɪn) *adj.* **1.** inordinately proud of one's appearance, possessions, or achievements. **2.** given to ostentatious display. **3.** worthless. **4.** senseless or futile. ~*n.* **5. in vain.** fruitlessly. [C13: via OF < L *vānus*] —ˈ**vainly** *adv.* —ˈ**vainness** *n.*

vainglory (ˌveɪnˈglɔːrɪ) *n.* **1.** boastfulness or vanity. **2.** ostentation. —ˌ**vainˈglorious** *adj.*

vair (vɛə) *n.* **1.** a fur, probably Russian squirrel, used to trim robes in the Middle Ages. **2.** a fur used on heraldic shields, conventionally represented by white and blue skins in alternate lines. [C13: < OF: of more than one colour, < L *varius* variegated]

Vaisya (ˈvaɪsjə, ˈvaɪʃjə) *n.* the third of the four main Hindu castes, the traders. [C18: < Sansk., lit.: settler, < *viś* settlement]

valance (ˈvæləns) *n.* a short piece of drapery hung along a shelf or bed to hide structural detail. [C15: ? after *Valence*, SE France, town noted for its textiles] —ˈ**valanced** *adj.*

vale[1] (veɪl) *n.* a literary word for **valley.** [C13: < OF *val*, < L *vallis* valley]

vale[2] *Latin.* (ˈvɑːleɪ) *sentence substitute.* farewell; goodbye.

valediction (ˌvælɪˈdɪkʃən) *n.* **1.** the act or an instance of saying goodbye. **2.** any valedictory statement, speech, etc. [C17: < L *valedīcere*, < *valē* farewell + *dīcere* to say]

valedictory (ˌvælɪˈdɪktərɪ) *adj.* **1.** saying goodbye. **2.** of or relating to a farewell or an occasion of farewell. ~*n., pl.* **-ries. 3.** a farewell address or speech.

valence (ˈveɪləns) *n. Chem.* **1.** another name (esp. U.S. and Canad.) for **valency. 2.** the phenomenon of forming chemical bonds.

Valenciennes (ˌvælənsɪˈɛn) *n.* a flat bobbin lace typically having scroll and floral designs and originally made of linen. [after *Valenciennes*, N France, where orig. made]

valency (ˈveɪlənsɪ) *or esp. U.S. & Canad.* **valence** *n., pl.* **-cies** *or* **-ces.** *Chem.* a property of atoms or groups equal to the number of atoms of hydrogen that the atom or group could combine with or displace in forming compounds. [C19: < L *valentia* strength, < *valēre* to be strong]

valency electron *n. Chem.* an electron in the outer shell of an atom, responsible for forming chemical bonds.

valentine (ˈvælənˌtaɪn) *n.* **1.** a card or gift expressing love or affection, sent, often anonymously, on Saint Valentine's Day. **2.** a sweetheart selected for such a greeting. [C15: after *St Valentine*, 3rd-century A.D. Christian martyr]

valerian (vəˈlɛərɪən) *n.* **1.** Also called: **allheal.** a Eurasian plant having small white or pinkish flowers and a medicinal root. **2.** a sedative drug made from the dried roots of this plant. [C14: via OF < Med. L *valeriana* (*herba*) (herb) of *Valerius*, unexplained L personal name]

valeric (vəˈlɛrɪk, -ˈlɪərɪk) *adj.* of, relating to, or derived from valerian.

valeric acid *n.* another name for **pentanoic acid.**

valet (ˈvælɪt, ˈvæleɪ) *n.* **1.** a manservant who acts as personal attendant to his employer, looking after his clothing, serving his meals, etc. **2.** a manservant who attends to the requirements of patrons in a hotel, etc.; steward. [C16: < OF *vaslet* page, < Med. L *vassus* servant]

valeta (vəˈliːtə) *n.* a variant spelling of **veleta.**

valet de chambre *French.* (valɛ də ʃɑ̃brə) *n., pl.* ***valets de chambre*** (valɛ də ʃɑ̃brə). the full French term for **valet** (sense 1).

valetudinarian (ˌvælɪˌtjuːdɪˈnɛərɪən) *or* **valetudinary** (ˌvælɪˈtjuːdɪnərɪ) *n., pl.* **-narians** *or* **-naries. 1.** a person who is chronically sick. **2.** a hypochondriac. **3.** an old person who is in good health. ~*adj.* **4.** relating to or resulting from poor health. **5.** being a valetudinarian. [C18: < L *valētūdō* state of health, < *valēre* to be well] —ˌ**valeˌtudiˈnarianism** *n.*

valgus (ˈvælgəs) *adj. Pathol.* twisted away from the midline of the body. [C19: < L: bow-legged]

Valhalla (vælˈhælə) *n. Norse myth.* the great hall of Odin where warriors who die as heroes in battle dwell eternally. [C18: < ON, < *valr* slain warriors + *höll* HALL]

valiant (ˈvæljənt) *adj.* **1.** courageous or intrepid. **2.** marked by bravery or courage: *a valiant deed.* [C14: < OF, < *valoir* to be of value, < L *valēre* to be strong] —ˈ**valiantly** *adv.*

valid (ˈvælɪd) *adj.* **1.** having some foundation; based on truth. **2.** legally acceptable: *a valid licence.* **3. a.** having legal force. **b.** having legal authority. **4.** having some force or cogency: *a valid point in a debate.* **5.** *Logic.* (of an inference or argument) having premises and a conclusion so related that if the premises are true, the conclusion must be true. [C16: < L *validus* robust, < *valēre* to be strong] —**validity** (vəˈlɪdɪtɪ) *n.* —ˈ**validly** *adv.*

validate (ˈvælɪˌdeɪt) *vb.* (*tr.*) **1.** to confirm or corroborate. **2.** to give legal force or official confirmation to. —ˌ**valiˈdation** *n.*

valine (ˈveɪliːn) *n.* an essential amino acid: a component of proteins. [C19: < VAL(ERIC ACID) + -INE[2]]

valise (vəˈliːz) *n.* a small overnight travelling case. [C17: via F < It. *valigia*, <?]

Valium (ˈvælɪəm) *n. Trademark.* a preparation of the drug diazepam used as a tranquillizer.

Valkyrie (vælˈkɪərɪ, ˈvælkɪərɪ) *n. Norse myth.* any of the beautiful maidens who serve Odin and ride over battlefields to claim the dead heroes and take them to Valhalla. [C18: < ON *Valkyrja,* < *valr* slain warriors + *kōri* to CHOOSE]

vallation (vəˈleɪʃən) *n.* **1.** the act or process of building fortifications. **2.** a wall or rampart. [C17: < LL *vallātiō,* < L *vallum* rampart]

vallecula (vəˈlɛkjʊlə) *n., pl.* **-lae** (-ˌliː). **1.** *Anat.* any of various natural depressions or crevices. **2.** *Bot.* a groove or furrow. [C19: < LL: little valley, < L *vallis* valley]

valley (ˈvælɪ) *n.* **1.** a long depression in the land surface, usually containing a river, formed by erosion or by movements in the earth's crust. **2.** the broad area drained by a single river system: *the Thames valley.* **3.** any elongated depression resembling a valley. [C13: < OF *valee,* < L *vallis*]

vallum (ˈvæləm) *n. Archaeol.* a Roman rampart or earthwork.

valonia (vəˈləʊnɪə) *n.* the acorn cups and unripe acorns of the Eurasian oak, used in tanning, dyeing, and making ink. [C18: < It. *vallonia,* ult. < Gk *balanos* acorn]

valorize *or* **-rise** (ˈvæləˌraɪz) *vb.* (*tr.*) to fix an artificial price for (a commodity) by governmental action. [C20: back formation < *valorization;* see VALOUR] —**ˌvaloriˈzation** *or* **-riˈsation** *n.*

valour *or U.S.* **valor** (ˈvælə) *n.* courage or bravery, esp. in battle. [C15: < LL *valor,* < *valēre* to be strong] —**ˈvalorous** *adj.*

valse French. (vals) *n.* the French word for **waltz.**

valuable (ˈvæljʊəbᵊl) *adj.* **1.** having considerable monetary worth. **2.** of considerable importance or quality: *valuable information.* **3.** able to be valued. ~*n.* **4.** (*usually pl.*) a valuable article of personal property, esp. jewellery. —**ˈvaluably** *adv.*

valuate (ˈvæljʊˌeɪt) *vb. U.S.* another word for **value** (senses 10, 12) or **evaluate.** —**ˈvaluˌator** *n.*

valuation (ˌvæljʊˈeɪʃən) *n.* **1.** the act of valuing, esp. a formal assessment of the worth of property, jewellery, etc. **2.** the price arrived at by the process of valuing: *I set a high valuation on technical ability.* —**ˌvaluˈational** *adj.*

value (ˈvæljuː) *n.* **1.** the desirability of a thing, often in respect of some property such as usefulness or exchangeability. **2.** an amount, esp. a material or monetary one, considered to be a fair exchange in return for a thing: *the value of the picture is £10 000.* **3.** satisfaction: *value for money.* **4.** precise meaning or significance. **5.** (*pl.*) the moral principles or accepted standards of a person or group. **6.** *Maths.* a particular magnitude, number, or amount: *the value of the variable was 7.* **7.** *Music.* short for **time value. 8.** (in painting, drawing, etc.) **a.** a gradation of tone from light to dark. **b.** the relation of one of these elements to another or to the whole picture. **9.** *Phonetics.* the quality of the speech sound associated with a written character representing it: *"g" has the value* (dʒ) *in English "gem".* ~*vb.* **-uing, -ued.** (*tr.*) **10.** to assess or estimate the worth, merit, or desirability of. **11.** to have a high regard for, esp. in respect of worth, usefulness, merit, etc. **12.** (foll. by *at*) to fix the financial or material worth of (a unit of currency, work of art, etc.). [C14: < OF, < *valoir,* < L *valēre* to be worth] —**ˈvalued** *adj.* —**ˈvalueless** *adj.* —**ˈvaluer** *n.*

value added *n.* the difference between the total revenues of a firm, industry, etc., and its total purchases from other firms, industries, etc.

value-added tax *n.* (in Britain) the full name for **VAT.**

valued policy *n.* an insurance policy in which the amount payable in the event of a valid claim is agreed upon between the company and the policyholder when the policy is issued and is not related to the actual value of a loss.

value judgment *n.* a subjective assessment based on one's own values or those of one's class.

Valuer General *n. Austral.* a state official who values properties for rating purposes.

valuta (vəˈluːtə) *n. Rare.* the value of one currency in terms of its exchange rate with another. [C20: < It., lit.: VALUE]

valvate (ˈvælveɪt) *adj.* **1.** furnished with a valve or valves. **2.** *Bot.* **a.** taking place by means of valves: *valvate dehiscence.* **b.** (of petals) having the margins touching but not overlapping.

valve (vælv) *n.* **1.** any device that shuts off, starts, regulates, or controls the flow of a fluid. **2.** *Anat.* a flaplike structure in a hollow organ, such as the heart, that controls the one-way passage of fluid through that organ. **3.** Also called: **tube.** an evacuated electron tube containing a cathode, anode, and, usually, one or more additional control electrodes. When a positive potential is applied to the anode, it produces a one-way flow of current. **4.** *Zool.* any of the separable pieces that make up the shell of a mollusc. **5.** *Music.* a device on some brass instruments by which the effective length of the tube may be varied to enable a chromatic scale to be produced. **6.** *Bot.* any of the several parts that make up a dry dehiscent fruit, esp. a capsule. [C14: < L *valva* a folding door] —**ˈvalveless** *adj.* —**ˈvalveˌlike** *adj.*

valve-in-head engine *n.* the U.S. name for **overhead-valve engine.**

valvular (ˈvælvjʊlə) *adj.* **1.** of, relating to, operated by, or having a valve or valves. **2.** having the shape or function of a valve.

valvulitis (ˌvælvjʊˈlaɪtɪs) *n.* inflammation of a bodily valve, esp. a heart valve. [C19: < NL *valvula* dim. of VALVE + -ITIS]

vamoose (vəˈmuːs) *vb.* (*intr.*) *Sl., chiefly U.S.* to leave a place hurriedly; decamp. [C19: < Sp. *vamos* let us go, < L *vādere* to go, walk rapidly]

vamp[1] (væmp) *Inf.* ~*n.* **1.** a seductive woman who exploits men by use of her sexual charms. ~*vb.* **2.** to exploit (a man) in the fashion of a vamp. [C20: short for VAMPIRE]

vamp[2] (væmp) *n.* **1.** something patched up to make it look new. **2.** the reworking of a story, etc. **3.** an improvised accompaniment. **4.** the front part of the upper of a shoe. ~*vb.* **5.** (*tr.; often* foll. by *up*) to make a renovation of. **6.** to improvise (an accompaniment) to (a tune). [C13: < OF *avantpié* the front part of a shoe (hence, something patched, < *avant-* fore- + *pié* foot, < L *pēs*]

vampire (ˈvæmpaɪə) *n.* **1.** (in European folklore) a corpse that rises nightly from its grave to drink the blood of the living. **2.** See **vampire bat. 3.** a person who preys mercilessly upon others. [C18: < F, < G, < Magyar] —**vampiric** (væmˈpɪrɪk) *adj.* —**ˈvampirism** *n.*

vampire bat *n.* a bat of tropical regions of Central and South America, having sharp incisor and canine teeth and feeding on the blood of birds and mammals.

van[1] (væn) *n.* **1.** short for **caravan** (sense 1). **2.** a motor vehicle for transporting goods, etc., by road. **3.** *Brit.* a closed railway wagon in which the guard travels, for transporting goods, etc.

van[2] (væn) *n.* short for **vanguard.**

van[3] (væn) *n. Tennis, chiefly Brit.* short for **advantage** (sense 3).

van[4] (væn) *n.* **1.** any device for winnowing corn. **2.** *Arch.* a wing. [C17: var. of FAN[1]]

vanadium (vəˈneɪdɪəm) *n.* a toxic silvery-white metallic element used in steel alloys and as a catalyst. Symbol: V; atomic no.: 23; atomic wt.: 50.94. [C19: NL, < ON *Vanadis,* epithet of the goddess Freya + -IUM]

Van Allen belt (væn ˈælən) *n.* either of two regions of charged particles above the earth, the inner one extending from 2400 to 5600 kilometres above the earth and the outer one from 13 000 to 19 000 kilometres. [C20: after its discoverer, J. A. *Van Allen* (born 1914), U.S. physicist]

V and A (in Britain) *abbrev. for* Victoria and Albert Museum.

vandal (ˈvændᵊl) *n.* a person who deliberately causes damage to personal or public property. [C17: < VANDAL, < L *Vandallus,* of Gmc origin]

Vandal (ˈvændᵊl) *n.* a member of a Germanic people that raided Roman provinces in the 3rd and 4th centuries A.D. before devastating Gaul, conquering Spain and N Africa, and sacking Rome. —**Vandalic** (vænˈdælɪk) *adj.*

vandalism (ˈvændəˌlɪzəm) *n.* the deliberate destruction caused by a vandal or an instance of such destruction. —ˌ**vandalˈistic** *adj.*

vandalize *or* **-lise** (ˈvændəˌlaɪz) *vb.* (*tr.*) to destroy or damage (something) by an act of vandalism.

Van de Graaff generator (ˈvæn də ˌgrɑːf) *n.* a device for producing high electrostatic potentials, consisting of a hollow metal sphere on which a charge is accumulated from a continuous moving belt of insulating material: used in particle accelerators. [C20: after R. J. *Van de Graaff* (1901–67), U.S. physicist]

Vandyke beard (ˈvændaɪk) *n.* a short pointed beard. Often shortened to **Vandyke.** [C18: after Sir Anthony *Van Dyck* (1599-1641), Flemish painter]

Vandyke collar *or* **cape** *n.* a large white collar with several very deep points. Often shortened to **Vandyke.**

vane (veɪn) *n.* **1.** Also called: **weather vane.** a flat plate or blade of metal mounted on a vertical axis in an exposed position to indicate wind direction. **2.** any one of the flat blades or sails forming part of the wheel of a windmill. **3.** any flat or shaped plate used to direct fluid flow, esp. in a turbine, etc. **4.** a fin or plate fitted to a projectile or missile to provide stabilization or guidance. **5.** *Ornithol.* the flat part of a feather. **6.** *Surveying.* **a.** a sight on a quadrant or compass. **b.** the movable marker on a levelling staff. [OE *fana*] —**vaned** *adj.*

vanguard (ˈvænˌgɑːd) *n.* **1.** the leading division or units of a military force. **2.** the leading position in any movement or field, or the people who occupy such a position. [C15: < OF *avant-garde,* < *avant-* fore- + *garde* GUARD]

vanilla (vəˈnɪlə) *n.* **1.** any of a genus of tropical climbing orchids having spikes of large fragrant flowers and long fleshy pods containing the seeds (beans). **2.** the pod or bean of certain of these plants, used to flavour food, etc. **3.** a flavouring extract prepared from vanilla beans and used in cooking. ~*adj.* **4.** flavoured with or as with vanilla: *vanilla ice cream.* **5.** *Computers sl.* ordinary. [C17: < NL, < Sp. *vainilla* pod, < *vaina,* < L *vāgīna* sheath] —**vaˈnillic** *adj.*

vanillin (ˈvænɪlɪn, vəˈnɪlɪn) *n.* a white crystalline aldehyde found in vanilla and many natural balsams and resins. It is a by-product of paper manufacture and is used as a flavouring and in perfumes.

vanish (ˈvænɪʃ) *vb.* (*intr.*) **1.** to disappear, esp. suddenly or mysteriously. **2.** to cease to exist. **3.** *Maths.* to become zero. [C14 *vanissen,* < OF *esvanir,* < L *ēvānēscere* to evaporate, < *ē-* EX-[1] + *vānēscere,* < *vānus* empty] —ˈ**vanisher** *n.*

vanishing cream *n.* a cosmetic cream that is colourless once applied, used as a foundation for powder or as a cleansing cream.

vanishing point *n.* **1.** the point to which parallel lines appear to converge in the rendering of perspective, usually on the horizon. **2.** a point at which something disappears.

vanity (ˈvænɪtɪ) *n., pl.* **-ties.** **1.** the state or quality of being vain. **2.** ostentation occasioned by ambition or pride. **3.** an instance of being vain or something about which one is vain. **4.** the state or quality of being valueless or futile. [C13: < OF, < L *vānitās* emptiness, < *vānus* empty]

vanity bag, case, *or* **box** *n.* a woman's small bag or hand case used to carry cosmetics, etc.

vanity unit *n.* a hand basin built into a wooden Formica-covered or tiled top, usually with a built-in cupboard below it. Also called (trademark): **Vanitory unit.**

vanquish (ˈvæŋkwɪʃ) *vb.* (*tr.*) **1.** to defeat or overcome in a battle, contest, etc. **2.** to defeat in argument or debate. **3.** to conquer (an emotion). [C14 *vanquisshen,* < OF *venquis,* < *veintre* to overcome, < L *vincere*] —ˈ**vanquishable** *adj.* —ˈ**vanquisher** *n.*

vantage (ˈvɑːntɪdʒ) *n.* **1.** a state, position, or opportunity affording superiority or advantage. **2.** superiority or benefit accruing from such a position, etc. **3.** *Tennis.* short for **advantage** (sense 3). [C13: < OF *avantage* ADVANTAGE]

vantage point *n.* a position or place that allows one an overall view of a scene or situation.

vanward (ˈvænwəd) *adj., adv.* in or towards the front.

vapid (ˈvæpɪd) *adj.* **1.** bereft of strength, sharpness, flavour, etc. **2.** boring or dull: *vapid talk.* [C17: < L *vapidus*] —**vaˈpidity** *n.* —ˈ**vapidly** *adv.*

vapor (ˈveɪpə) *n.* the U.S. spelling of **vapour.**

vaporescence (ˌveɪpəˈrɛsəns) *n.* the production or formation of vapour. —ˌ**vaporˈescent** *adj.*

vaporetto (ˌveɪpəˈrɛtəʊ) *n., pl.* **-ti** (-tɪ) *or* **-tos.** a steam-powered passenger boat, as used on the canals in Venice. [It., < *vapore* a steamboat]

vaporific (ˌveɪpəˈrɪfɪk) *adj.* **1.** producing, causing, or tending to produce vapour. **2.** of, concerned with, or having the nature of vapour. **3.** tending to become vapour; volatile. [C18: < NL *vaporificus,* < L *vapor* steam + *facere* to make]

vaporimeter (ˌveɪpəˈrɪmɪtə) *n.* an instrument for measuring vapour pressure, used to determine the volatility of oils.

vaporize *or* **-rise** (ˈveɪpəˌraɪz) *vb.* **1.** to change or cause to change into vapour or into the gaseous state. **2.** to evaporate or disappear or cause to evaporate or disappear, esp. suddenly. **3.** to destroy or be destroyed by turning into a gas as a result of the extreme heat generated by a nuclear explosion. —ˌ**vaporiˈzation** *or* **-riˈsation** *n.*

vaporizer *or* **-riser** (ˈveɪpəˌraɪzə) *n.* **1.** a substance that vaporizes or a device that causes vaporization. **2.** *Med.* a device that produces steam or atomizes medication for inhalation.

vaporous (ˈveɪpərəs) *adj.* **1.** resembling or full of vapour. **2.** lacking permanence or substance. **3.** given to foolish imaginings. —**vaporosity** (ˌveɪpəˈrɒsɪtɪ) *n.* —ˈ**vaporously** *adv.*

vapour *or U.S.* **vapor** (ˈveɪpə) *n.* **1.** particles of moisture or other substance suspended in air and visible as clouds, smoke, etc. **2.** a gaseous substance at a temperature below its critical temperature. **3.** a substance that is in a gaseous state at a temperature below its boiling point. **4.** **the vapours.** *Arch.* a depressed mental condition believed originally to be the result of vaporous exhalations from the stomach. ~*vb.* **5.** to evaporate or cause to evaporate. **6.** (*intr.*) to make vain empty boasts. [C14: < L *vapor*] —ˈ**vapourer** *or U.S.* ˈ**vaporer** *n.* —ˈ**vapourish** *or U.S.* ˈ**vaporish** *adj.* —ˈ**vapour-**ˌ**like** *or U.S.* ˈ**vapor-**ˌ**like** *adj.* —ˈ**vapoury** *or U.S.* ˈ**vapory** *adj.*

vapour density *n.* the ratio of the density of a gas or vapour to that of hydrogen at the same temperature and pressure.

vapour lock *n.* a stoppage in a pipe carrying a liquid caused by a bubble of gas, esp. in the pipe feeding the carburettor of an internal-combustion engine.

vapour pressure *n. Physics.* the pressure exerted by a vapour in equilibrium with its solid or liquid phase at a particular temperature.

vapour trail *n.* a visible trail left by an aircraft flying at high altitude or through supercold air caused by the deposition of water vapour in the engine exhaust as minute ice crystals.

var. *abbrev. for:* **1.** variable. **2.** variant. **3.** variation. **4.** variety. **5.** various.

varactor (ˈvɛəˌræktə) *n.* a semiconductor diode that acts as a voltage-dependent capacitor, being operated with a reverse bias. [C20: prob. a blend of *variable reactor*]

varec (ˈværɛk) *n.* **1.** another name for **kelp.** **2.** the ash obtained from kelp. [C17: < F, < ON *wrek* (unattested); see WRECK]

variable (ˈvɛərɪəbᵊl) *adj.* **1.** liable to or capable of change: *variable weather.* **2.** (of behaviour, emotions, etc.) lacking constancy. **3.** *Maths.* having a range of possible values. **4.** (of a species, etc.) liable to deviate from the established type. **5.** (of a wind) varying in direction and intensity. **6.** (of an electrical component or device) designed so that a characteristic property, such as resistance, can be varied. ~*n.* 7. something that is subject to variation. 8. *Maths.* a. an expression that can be assigned any of a set of values. b. a symbol, esp. *x*, *y*, or *z*, representing an unspecified member of a class of objects, numbers, etc. 9. *Logic.* a symbol, esp. *x*, *y*, or *z*, representing any member of a class of entities. 10. *Astron.* See **variable star.** 11. a variable wind. 12. (*pl.*) a region where variable winds occur. [C14: < L *variābilis* changeable, < *variāre* to diversify] —ˌ**varia'bility** *or* '**variableness** *n.* —'**variably** *adv.*

variable cost *n.* a cost that varies directly with output.

variable star *n.* any star that varies considerably in brightness, either irregularly or in regular periods. **Intrinsic variables,** in which the variation is a result of internal changes, include novae and pulsating stars.

variance ('vɛərɪəns) *n.* 1. the act of varying or the quality, state, or degree of being divergent. 2. an instance of diverging; dissension. 3. **at variance.** a. (often foll. by *with*) (of facts, etc.) not in accord. b. (of persons) in a state of dissension. 4. *Statistics.* a measure of dispersion; the square of the standard deviations. 5. a difference or discrepancy between two steps in a legal proceeding, esp. between a statement and the evidence given to support it. 6. *Chem.* the number of degrees of freedom of a system, used in the phase rule.

variant ('vɛərɪənt) *adj.* 1. liable to or displaying variation. 2. differing from a standard or type: *a variant spelling.* ~*n.* 3. something that differs from a standard or type. 4. *Statistics.* another word for **variate.** [C14: via OF < L, < *variāre* to diversify, < *varius* VARIOUS]

variate ('vɛərɪɪt) *n. Statistics.* a random variable or a numerical value taken by it. [C16: < L *variāre* to VARY]

variation (ˌvɛərɪ'eɪʃən) *n.* 1. the act, process, condition, or result of changing or varying. 2. an instance of varying or the amount, rate, or degree of such change. 3. something that differs from a standard or convention. 4. *Music.* a repetition of a musical theme in which the rhythm, harmony, or melody is altered or embellished. 5. *Biol.* a marked deviation from the typical form or function. 6. *Astron.* any change in or deviation from the mean motion or orbit of a planet, satellite, etc. 7. another word for **magnetic declination.** 8. *Ballet.* a solo dance. —ˌ**vari'ational** *adj.*

varicella (ˌværɪ'sɛlə) *n.* the technical name for **chickenpox.** [C18: NL, irregular dim. of VARIOLA]

varices ('værɪˌsiːz) *pl. n.* the plural of **varix.**

varico- *or before a vowel* **varic-** *combining form.* indicating a varix or varicose veins: *varicotomy.* [< L *varix*, *varic-* distended vein]

varicoloured *or U.S.* **varicolored** ('vɛərɪˌkʌləd) *adj.* having many colours.

varicose ('værɪˌkəʊs) *adj.* of or resulting from varicose veins: *a varicose ulcer.* [C18: < L *varicōsus*, < VARIX]

varicose veins *pl. n.* a condition in which the superficial veins, esp. of the legs, become tortuous, knotted, and swollen.

varicosis (ˌværɪ'kəʊsɪs) *n. Pathol.* any condition characterized by distension of the veins. [C18: < NL, < L: VARIX]

varicosity (ˌværɪ'kɒsɪtɪ) *n., pl.* **-ties.** *Pathol.* 1. the state, condition, or quality of being varicose. 2. an abnormally distended vein.

varicotomy (ˌværɪ'kɒtəmɪ) *n., pl.* **-mies.** surgical excision of a varicose vein.

varied ('vɛərɪd) *adj.* 1. displaying or characterized by variety; diverse. 2. modified or altered: *the amount may be varied without notice.* 3. varicoloured; variegated. —'**variedly** *adv.*

variegate ('vɛərɪˌgeɪt) *vb.* (*tr.*) to alter the appearance of, esp. by adding different colours. [C17: < LL, < L *varius* diverse, VARIOUS + *agere* to make] —ˌ**varie'gation** *n.*

variegated ('vɛərɪˌgeɪtɪd) *adj.* 1. displaying differently coloured spots., streaks, etc. 2. (of foliage) having pale patches.

varietal (və'raɪɪtᵊl) *adj.* 1. of, characteristic of, designating, or forming a variety, esp. a biological variety. ~*n.* 2. a wine labelled with the name of the grape from which it is pressed. —**va'rietally** *adv.*

variety (və'raɪɪtɪ) *n., pl.* **-ties.** 1. the quality or condition of being diversified or various. 2. a collection of unlike things, esp. of the same general group. 3. a different form or kind within a general category: *varieties of behaviour.* 4. a. *Taxonomy.* a race whose distinct characters do not justify classification as a separate species. b. *Horticulture, stockbreeding.* a strain of animal or plant produced by artificial breeding. 5. a. entertainment consisting of a series of short unrelated acts, such as comedy turns, songs, etc. b. (*as modifier*): *a variety show.* [C16: < L *varietās*, < VARIOUS]

variform ('vɛərɪˌfɔːm) *adj.* varying in form or shape. —'**variˌformly** *adv.*

variola (və'raɪələ) *n.* the technical name for **smallpox.** [C18: < Med. L: disease marked by little spots, < L *varius* spotted] —**va'riolar** *adj.*

variole ('vɛərɪˌəʊl) *n.* any of the rounded masses that make up the rock variolite. [C19: < F, < Med. L; see VARIOLA]

variolite ('vɛərɪəˌlaɪt) *n.* any basic igneous rock containing rounded bodies (varioles). [C18: < VARIOLA, referring to the pockmarked appearance of the rock] —**variolitic** (ˌvɛərɪə'lɪtɪk) *adj.*

variometer (ˌvɛərɪ'ɒmɪtə) *n.* 1. an instrument for measuring variations in a magnetic field. 2. *Electronics.* a variable inductor consisting of a movable coil mounted inside and connected in series with a fixed coil.

variorum (ˌvɛərɪ'ɔːrəm) *adj.* 1. containing notes by various scholars or various versions of the text. ~*n.* 2. an edition or text of this kind. [C18: < L *ēditiō cum notīs variōrum* edition with the notes of various commentators]

various ('vɛərɪəs) *determiner.* 1. several different: *he is an authority on various subjects.* ~*adj.* 2. of different kinds, though often within the same general category: *his disguises are many and various.* 3. (*prenominal*) relating to a collection of separate persons or things: *the various members of the club.* 4. displaying variety; many-sided: *his various achievements.* [C16: < L *varius* changing] —'**variously** *adv.* —'**variousness** *n.*

▷ **Usage.** *Various of,* as in *he wrote to various of his friends,* is not current in good usage. Careful writers prefer *various* or *several of* to *various of: he wrote to various friends; he wrote to several of his friends.*

varistor (və'rɪstə) *n.* a two-electrode semiconductor device having a voltage-dependent nonlinear resistance. [C20: a blend of *variable resistor*]

Varityper ('vɛərɪˌtaɪpə) *n. Trademark.* a justifying typewriter used to produce copy in various type styles.

varix ('vɛərɪks) *n., pl.* **varices.** *Pathol.* a. a tortuous dilated vein. b. a similar condition affecting an artery or lymphatic vessel. [C15: < L]

varlet ('vɑːlɪt) *n. Arch.* 1. a menial servant. 2. a knight's page. 3. a rascal. [C15: < OF, var. of *vallet* VALET] —'**varletry** *n.*

varmint ('vɑːmɪnt) *n. Inf.* an irritating or obnoxious person or animal. [C16: dialect var. of *varmin* VERMIN]

varna ('vɑːnə) *n.* any of the four Hindu castes; Brahman, Kshatriya, Vaisya, or Sudra. [< Sansk.: class]

varnish ('vɑːnɪʃ) *n.* 1. a preparation consisting of a solvent, a drying oil, and usually resin, rubber, etc., for application to a surface where it yields a hard glossy, usually transparent, coating. 2. a similar preparation consisting of a substance, such as shellac, dissolved in a volatile solvent, such as alcohol. It hardens to a film on evaporation of the solvent. 3. the sap of certain trees used to produce such a coating. 4. a smooth surface, coated with or as with varnish. 5. an artificial, superficial, or deceptively pleasing manner, covering, etc. **6.** *Chiefly Brit.* another word for **nail polish.** ~*vb.* (*tr.*) **7.** to cover with varnish. **8.** to give a smooth surface to, as if by painting with varnish. **9.** to impart a more attractive appearance to. [C14: < OF, < Med. L *veronix* sandarac, resin, < Med. Gk *berenikē*, ? < Gk *Berenikē*, city in Cyrenaica, Libya where varnishes were used] —ˈ**varnisher** *n.*

varnish tree *n.* any of various trees, such as the lacquer tree, yielding substances used to make varnish or lacquer.

varsity (ˈvɑːsɪtɪ) *n., pl.* **-ties.** *Brit. & N.Z. inf.* short for **university.**

varus (ˈvɛərəs) *adj. Pathol.* turned inwards towards the midline of the body. [C19: < L: crooked, bent]

varve (vɑːv) *n. Geol.* a band of sediment deposited in glacial lakes, consisting of a light layer and a dark layer deposited at different seasons. [C20: < Swedish *varv* layer, < *varva*, < ON *hverfa* to turn]

vary (ˈvɛərɪ) *vb.* **varying, varied. 1.** to undergo or cause to undergo change or modification in appearance, character, form, etc. **2.** to be different or cause to be different; be subject to change. **3.** (*tr.*) to give variety to. **4.** (*intr.;* foll. by *from*) to differ, as from a convention, standard, etc. **5.** (*intr.*) to change in accordance with another variable: *her mood varies with the weather.* [C14: < L, < *varius* VARIOUS] —ˈ**varying** *adj.*

vas (væs) *n., pl.* **vasa** (ˈveɪsə). *Anat., zool.* a vessel or tube that carries a fluid. [C17: < L: vessel]

vascular (ˈvæskjʊlə) *adj. Biol., anat.* of, relating to, or having vessels that conduct and circulate liquids: *a vascular bundle.* [C17: < NL *vāsculāris*, < L *vāsculum*, dim. of *vās* vessel] —**vascularity** (ˌvæskjʊˈlærɪtɪ) *n.* —ˈ**vascularly** *adv.*

vascular bundle *n.* a longitudinal strand of vascular tissue in the stems and leaves of higher plants.

vascular tissue *n.* tissue of plants occurring as a continuous system throughout the plant: it conducts water, mineral salts, and synthesized food, and provides mechanical support.

vas deferens (ˈvæs ˈdɛfəˌrɛnz) *n., pl.* **vasa deferentia** (ˈveɪsə ˌdɛfəˈrɛnʃɪə). *Anat.* the duct within each testis that conveys spermatozoa to the ejaculatory duct. [C16: < NL, < L *vās* vessel + *deferēns*, present participle of *deferre* to bear away]

vase (vɑːz) *n.* a vessel used as an ornament or for holding cut flowers. [C17: via F < L *vās* vessel]

vasectomy (væˈsɛktəmɪ) *n., pl.* **-mies.** surgical removal of all or part of the vas deferens, esp. as a method of contraception.

Vaseline (ˈvæsɪˌliːn) *n.* a trademark for **petrolatum.**

vaso- *or before a vowel* **vas-** *combining form.* **1.** indicating a blood vessel: *vasodilator.* **2.** indicating the vas deferens: *vasectomy.* [< L *vās* vessel]

vasoconstrictor (ˌveɪzəʊkənˈstrɪktə) *n.* a drug, agent, or nerve that causes narrowing of the walls of blood vessels.

vasodilator (ˌveɪzəʊdaɪˈleɪtə) *n.* a drug, agent, or nerve that can cause dilation of the walls of blood vessels.

vasoinhibitor (ˌveɪzəʊɪnˈhɪbɪtə) *n.* any of a group of drugs that reduce or inhibit the action of the vasomotor nerves.

vasomotor (ˌveɪzəʊˈməʊtə) *adj.* (of a drug, agent, nerve, etc.) relating to or affecting the diameter of blood vessels.

vasopressin (ˌveɪzəʊˈprɛsɪn) *n.* a hormone secreted by the pituitary gland. It increases the reabsorption of water by the kidney tubules and increases blood pressure by constricting the arteries. [< *Vasopressin*, a trademark]

vassal (ˈvæsəl) *n.* **1.** (in feudal society) a man who entered into a relationship with a lord to whom he paid homage and fealty in return for protection and often a fief. **2. a.** a person, nation, etc., in a subordinate or dependent position relative to another. **b.** (*as modifier*): *vassal status.* ~*adj.* **3.** of or relating to a vassal. [C14: via OF < Med. L *vassallus*, < *vassus* servant, of Celtic origin] —ˈ**vassalage** *n.*

vast (vɑːst) *adj.* **1.** unusually large in size, degree, or number. **2.** (*prenominal*) (intensifier): *in vast haste.* ~*n.* **3. the vast.** *Chiefly poetic.* immense or boundless space. [C16: < L *vastus* deserted] —ˈ**vastly** *adv.* —ˈ**vastness** *n.*

vasty (ˈvɑːstɪ) *adj.* **vastier, vastiest.** an archaic or poetic word for **vast.**

vat (væt) *n.* **1.** a large container for holding or storing liquids. **2.** *Chem.* a preparation of reduced vat dye. ~*vb.* **vatting, vatted. 3.** (*tr.*) to place, store, or treat in a vat. [OE *fæt*]

VAT (*sometimes* væt) (in Britain) *abbrev. for* value-added tax: a tax levied on the difference between the cost of materials and the selling price of a commodity or service.

vat dye *n.* a dye, such as indigo, that is applied by first reducing it to its base, which is soluble in alkali, and then regenerating the insoluble dye by oxidation in the fibres of the material. —ˈ**vat-**ˌ**dyed** *adj.*

vatic (ˈvætɪk) *adj. Rare.* of, relating to, or characteristic of a prophet; oracular. [C16: < L *vātēs* prophet]

Vatican (ˈvætɪkən) *n.* **1. a.** the palace of the popes in Rome, which includes administrative offices and is attached to the basilica of St Peter's. **b.** (*as modifier*): *the Vatican Council.* **2. a.** the authority of the Pope and the papal curia. **b.** (*as modifier*): *a Vatican edict.* [C16: < L *Vāticānus mons* Vatican hill, on the western bank of the Tiber, of Etruscan origin]

vaudeville (ˈvəʊdəvɪl, ˈvɔː-) *n.* **1.** *Chiefly U.S. & Canad.* variety entertainment consisting of short acts such as acrobatic turns, song-and-dance routines, etc. **2.** a light or comic theatrical piece interspersed with songs and dances. [C18: < F, < *vaudevire* satirical folk song, shortened < *chanson du vau de Vire* song of the valley of Vire, a district in Normandy] —ˌ**vaude**ˈ**villian** *n., adj.*

Vaudois (ˈvəʊdwɑː) *pl. n., sing.* **-dois. 1.** another name for the **Waldenses. 2.** the inhabitants of Vaud, in Switzerland.

vault[1] (vɔːlt) *n.* **1.** an arched structure that forms a roof or ceiling. **2.** a room, esp. a cellar, having an arched roof down to floor level. **3.** a burial chamber, esp. when underground. **4.** a strongroom for the storage of valuables. **5.** an underground room used for the storage of wine, food, etc. **6.** *Anat.* any arched or domed bodily cavity or space: *the cranial vault.* **7.** something suggestive of an arched structure, as the sky. ~*vb.* **8.** (*tr.*) to furnish with or as if with an arched roof. **9.** (*tr.*) to construct in the shape of a vault. **10.** (*intr.*) to curve in the shape of a vault. [C14 *vaute*, < OF, < Vulgar L *volvita* (unattested) a turn, prob. < L *volvere* to roll]

vault[2] (vɔːlt) *vb.* **1.** to spring over (an object), esp. with the aid of a long pole or with the hands resting on the object. **2.** (*intr.*) to do, achieve, or attain something as if by a leap: *he vaulted to fame.* ~*n.* **3.** the act of vaulting. [C16: < OF *voulter* to turn < It. *voltare*, < Vulgar L *volvitāre* (unattested) to turn, leap; see VAULT[1]] —ˈ**vaulter** *n.*

vaulting[1] (ˈvɔːltɪŋ) *n.* one or more vaults in a building or such structures considered collectively.

vaulting[2] (ˈvɔːltɪŋ) *adj.* (*prenominal*) **1.** excessively confident: *vaulting arrogance.* **2.** used to vault: *a vaulting pole.*

vaunt (vɔːnt) *vb.* **1.** (*tr.*) to describe, praise, or display (one's success, possessions, etc.) boastfully. **2.** (*intr.*) *Rare or literary.* to brag. ~*n.* **3.** a boast. [C14: < OF, < LL *vānitāre*, < L *vānus* VAIN] —ˈ**vaunter** *n.*

vavasor (ˈvævəˌsɔː) *or* **vavasour** (ˈvævəˌsʊə) *n.* (in feudal society) the noble or knightly vassal of a baron or great lord who also has vassals himself. [C13: < OF *vavasour*, ? < Med. L *vassus vassōrum* vassal of vassals]

vb *abbrev. for* verb.

VC *abbrev. for:* **1.** Vice-chairman. **2.** Vice Chancellor. **3.** Vice Consul. **4.** Victoria Cross.

VCR *abbrev. for* video cassette recorder.
VD *abbrev. for* venereal disease.
V-Day *n.* a day nominated to celebrate victory, as in V-E Day or V-J Day in World War II.
VDU *Computers. abbrev. for* visual display unit.
've *contraction of* have: *I've; you've.*
veal (viːl) *n.* the flesh of the calf used as food. [C14: < OF *veel*, < L *vitellus*, dim. of *vitulus* calf]
vealer (ˈviːlə) *n. U.S., Canad., & Austral.* a calf bred for veal.
vector (ˈvɛktə) *n.* **1.** *Maths.* a variable quantity, such as force, that has magnitude and direction and can be resolved into components that are odd functions of the coordinates. **2.** Also called: **carrier.** *Pathol.* an organism, esp. an insect, that carries a disease-producing microorganism from one host to another. **3.** the course or compass direction of an aircraft. ~*vb.* (*tr.*) **4.** to direct or guide (a pilot, aircraft, etc.) by directions transmitted by radio. **5.** to alter the direction of (the thrust of a jet engine) as a means of steering an aircraft. [C18: < L: carrier, < *vehere* to convey] —**vectorial** (vɛkˈtɔːrɪəl) *adj.*
vector field *n.* a region of space under the influence of some vector quantity, such as magnetic field strength, in which each point can be described by a vector.
vector product *n.* the product of two vectors that is a pseudovector, whose magnitude is the product of the magnitudes of the given vectors and the sine of the angle between them. Its axis is perpendicular to the plane of the given vectors.
vector sum *n.* a vector whose length and direction are represented by the diagonal of a parallelogram whose sides represent the given vectors.
Veda (ˈveɪdə) *n.* any or all of the most ancient sacred writings of Hinduism, esp. the Rig-Veda, Yajur-Veda, Sama-Veda, and Atharva-Veda. [C18: < Sansk.: knowledge]
vedalia (vɪˈdeɪlɪə) *n.* an Australian ladybird introduced elsewhere to control the scale insect, which is a pest of citrus fruits. [C20: < NL]
Vedanta (vɪˈdɑːntə) *n.* one of the six main philosophical schools of Hinduism, expounding the monism regarded as implicit in the Veda in accordance with the doctrines of the Upanishads. [C19: < Sansk., < VEDA + *ánta* end] —**Veˈdantic** *adj.* —**Veˈdantist** *n.*
V-E Day *n.* the day marking the Allied victory in Europe in World War II (May 8, 1945).
vedette (vɪˈdɛt) *n.* **1.** *Naval.* a small patrol vessel. **2.** *Mil.* a mounted sentry posted forward of a formation's position. [C17: < F, < It. *vedetta* (infl. by *vedere* to see), < earlier *veletta*, ? < Sp., < L *vigilāre*]
Vedic (ˈveɪdɪk) *adj.* **1.** of or relating to the Vedas or the ancient form of Sanskrit in which they are written. ~*n.* **2.** the classical form of Sanskrit; the language of the Vedas.
veer (vɪə) *vb.* **1.** to alter direction (of). **2.** (*intr.*) to change from one position, opinion, etc., to another. **3.** (*intr.*) (of the wind) to change direction clockwise in the northern hemisphere and anticlockwise in the southern. ~*n.* **4.** a change of course or direction. [C16: < OF *virer*, prob. of Celtic origin]
veg (vɛdʒ) *n. Inf.* a vegetable or vegetables.
Vega (ˈviːgə) *n.* the brightest star in the constellation Lyra and one of the most conspicuous in the N hemisphere. [C17: < Med. L, < Ar. (*al nasr*) *al wāqi*, lit.: the falling (vulture), i.e. the constellation Lyra]
vegan (ˈviːgən) *n.* a person who uses no animal products.
Vegemite (ˈvɛdʒɪˌmaɪt) *n. Austral. trademark.* a yeast extract used as a spread, flavouring for stews, etc.
vegetable (ˈvɛdʒtəbᵊl) *n.* **1.** any of various herbaceous plants having parts that are used as food, such as peas, potatoes, cauliflower, and onions. **2.** *Inf.* a person who has lost control of his mental faculties, limbs, etc., as from an injury, mental disease, etc. **3.** a dull inactive person. **4.** (*modifier*) consisting of or made from edible vegetables: *a vegetable diet.* **5.** (*modifier*) of, characteristic of, derived from, or consisting of plants or plant material: *the vegetable kingdom.* **6.** *Rare.* any member of the plant kingdom. [C14 (adj.): < LL *vegetābilis*, < *vegetāre* to enliven, < L *vegēre* to excite]
vegetable butter *n.* any of a group of vegetable fats having the consistency of butter.
vegetable ivory *n.* the hard whitish material obtained from the endosperm of the ivory nut: used to make buttons, ornaments, etc.
vegetable marrow *n.* **1.** a plant, probably native to America but widely cultivated for its oblong green striped fruit which is eaten as a vegetable. **2.** the fruit of this plant. Often shortened to **marrow.**
vegetable oil *n.* any of a group of oils that are obtained from plants.
vegetable oyster *n.* another name for **salsify** (sense 1).
vegetable silk *n.* any of various silky fibres obtained from the seed pods of certain plants.
vegetable wax *n.* any of various waxes that occur on parts of certain plants, esp. the trunks of certain palms, and prevent loss of water.
vegetal (ˈvɛdʒɪtᵊl) *adj.* **1.** of or characteristic of vegetables or plant life. **2.** vegetative. [C15: < LL *vegetāre* to quicken]
vegetarian (ˌvɛdʒɪˈtɛərɪən) *n.* **1.** a person who advocates or practises the exclusion of meat and fish, and sometimes eggs, milk, and cheese from the diet. ~*adj.* **2.** *Cookery.* strictly, consisting of vegetables and fruit only, but often including milk, cheese, eggs, etc. —ˌ**vegeˈtarianism** *n.*
vegetate (ˈvɛdʒɪˌteɪt) *vb.* (*intr.*) **1.** to grow like a plant. **2.** to lead a life characterized by monotony, passivity, or mental inactivity. [C17: < LL *vegetāre* to invigorate]
vegetation (ˌvɛdʒɪˈteɪʃən) *n.* **1.** plant life as a whole, esp. the plant life of a particular region. **2.** the process of vegetating. —ˌ**vegeˈtational** *adj.*
vegetative (ˈvɛdʒɪtətɪv) *adj.* **1.** of or concerned with plant life or plant growth. **2.** (of reproduction) characterized by asexual processes. **3.** of or relating to functions such as digestion and circulation rather than sexual reproduction. **4.** (of a style of living, etc.) unthinking or passive. —ˈ**vegetatively** *adv.*
veggie (ˈvɛdʒɪ) *n., adj.* an informal word for **vegetarian.**
veg out *vb.* **vegging, vegged.** (*intr., adv.*) *Sl., chiefly U.S.* to relax in an inert, passive way; vegetate: *vegging out in front of the television set.*
vehement (ˈviːɪmənt) *adj.* **1.** marked by intensity of feeling or conviction. **2.** (of actions, gestures, etc.) characterized by great energy, vigour, or force. [C15: < L *vehemēns* ardent] —ˈ**vehemence** *n.* —ˈ**vehemently** *adv.*
vehicle (ˈviːɪkᵊl) *n.* **1.** any conveyance in or by which people or objects are transported, esp. one fitted with wheels. **2.** a medium for the expression or communication of ideas, power, etc. **3.** *Pharmacol.* a therapeutically inactive substance mixed with the active ingredient to give bulk to a medicine. **4.** Also called: **base.** a painting medium, such as oil, in which pigments are suspended. **5.** (in the performing arts) a play, etc., that enables a particular performer to display his talents. [C17: < L *vehiculum*, < *vehere* to carry] —**vehicular** (vɪˈhɪkjʊlə) *adj.*
veil (veɪl) *n.* **1.** a piece of more or less transparent material, usually attached to a hat or headdress, used to conceal or protect a woman's face and head. **2.** part of a nun's headdress falling round the face onto the shoulders. **3.** something that covers, conceals, or separates: *a veil of reticence.* **4. the veil.** the life of a nun in a religious order. **5. take the veil.** to become a nun. **6.** Also called: **velum.** *Bot.* a membranous structure, esp. the thin layer of cells covering a young mushroom. ~*vb.* **7.** (*tr.*) to cover, conceal, or separate with or as if with a veil. **8.** (*intr.*) to wear or put on a veil. [C13: < Norman F *veile*, < L *vēla*, pl. of *vēlum* a covering] —ˈ**veiler** *n.* —ˈ**veil-**ˌ**like** *adj.*

veiled (veɪld) *adj.* **1.** disguised: *a veiled insult.* **2.** (of sound, tone, the voice, etc.) not distinct. **—veiledly** (ˈveɪlɪdlɪ) *adv.*

veiling (ˈveɪlɪŋ) *n.* a veil or the fabric used for veils.

vein (veɪn) *n.* **1.** any of the tubular vessels that convey oxygen-depleted blood to the heart. Cf. **pulmonary vein, artery** (sense 1). **2.** any of the hollow branching tubes that form the supporting framework of an insect's wing. **3.** any of the vascular bundles of a leaf. **4.** a clearly defined mass of ore, mineral, etc. **5.** an irregular streak of colour or alien substance in marble, wood, or other material. **6.** a distinctive trait or quality in speech, writing, character, etc.: *a vein of humour.* **7.** a temporary attitude or temper: *the debate entered a frivolous vein.* ~*vb.* (*tr.*) **8.** to diffuse over or cause to diffuse over in streaked patterns. **9.** to fill, furnish, or mark with or as if with veins. [C13: < OF, < L *vēna*] **—ˈveinless** *adj.* **—ˈvein-ˌlike** *adj.* **—ˈveiny** *adj.*

veining (ˈveɪnɪŋ) *n.* a pattern or network of veins or streaks.

veinlet (ˈveɪnlɪt) *n.* any small vein or venule.

velamen (vəˈleɪmɛn) *n., pl.* **-lamina** (-ˈlæmɪnə). **1.** the thick layer of dead cells that covers the aerial roots of certain orchids. **2.** *Anat.* another word for **velum.** [C19: < L: veil, < *vēlāre* to cover]

velar (ˈviːlə) *adj.* **1.** of or attached to a velum: *velar tentacles.* **2.** *Phonetics.* articulated with the soft palate and the back of the tongue, as in (k) or (ŋ). [C18: < L, < *vēlum* VEIL]

Velcro (ˈvɛlkrəʊ) *n. Trademark.* a fastening consisting of two strips of nylon fabric, one having tiny hooked threads and the other a coarse surface, that form a strong bond when pressed together.

veld *or* **veldt** (fɛlt, vɛlt) *n.* elevated open grassland in Southern Africa. [C19: < Afrik., < earlier Du. *veldt* FIELD]

veldskoen (ˈfɛltˌskʊn, ˈvɛlt-) *n.* an ankle-length boot of soft but strong rawhide. [< Afrik., lit.: field shoe]

veleta *or* **valeta** (vəˈliːtə) *n.* a ballroom dance in triple time. [< Sp.: weather vane]

veliger (ˈvɛlɪdʒə) *n.* the free-swimming larva of many molluscs, having a rudimentary shell and a ciliated velum used for feeding and locomotion. [C19: < NL, < VEL(UM) + -GER(OUS)]

vellum (ˈvɛləm) *n.* **1.** a fine parchment prepared from the skin of a calf, kid, or lamb. **2.** a work printed or written on vellum. **3.** a creamy coloured heavy paper resembling vellum. ~*adj.* **4.** made of or resembling vellum. [C15: < OF, < *velin* of a calf, < *veel* VEAL]

veloce (vɪˈləʊtʃɪ) *adj., adv. Music.* to be played rapidly. [< It., < L *vēlōx* quick]

velocipede (vɪˈlɒsɪˌpiːd) *n.* an early form of bicycle, esp. one propelled by pushing along the ground with the feet. [C19: < F, < L *vēlōx* swift + *pēs* foot] **—veˈlociˌpedist** *n.*

velocity (vɪˈlɒsɪtɪ) *n., pl.* **-ties.** **1.** speed of motion or operation; swiftness. **2.** *Physics.* a measure of the rate of motion of a body expressed as the rate of change of its position in a particular direction with time. **3.** *Physics.* (not in technical usage) another word for **speed** (sense 3). [C16: < L *vēlōcitās,* < *vēlōx* swift]

velodrome (ˈviːləˌdrəʊm, ˈvɛl-) *n.* an arena with a banked track for cycle racing. [C20: < F *vélodrome,* < *vélo-* (< L *vēlōx* swift) + -DROME]

velours *or* **velour** (vɛˈlʊə) *n.* any of various fabrics with a velvet-like finish, used for upholstery, clothing, etc. [C18: < OF, < OProvençal *velos* velvet, < L, < *villus* shaggy hair]

velouté (vəˈluːteɪ) *n.* a rich white sauce or soup made from stock, egg yolks, and cream. [< F, lit.: velvety, < OF *velous;* see VELOURS]

velum (ˈviːləm) *n., pl.* **-la** (-lə). **1.** *Zool.* any of various membranous structures. **2.** *Anat.* any of various veil-like bodily structures, esp. the soft palate. **3.** *Bot.* another word for **veil** (sense 6). [C18: < L: veil]

velure (vəˈlʊə) *n.* velvet or a similar fabric. [C16: < OF, < *velous;* see VELOURS]

velutinous (vəˈluːtɪnəs) *adj.* covered with short dense soft hairs: *velutinous leaves.* [C19: < NL *velūtīnus* like velvet]

velvet (ˈvɛlvɪt) *n.* **1. a.** a fabric of silk, cotton, nylon, etc., with a thick close soft pile. **b.** (*as modifier*): *velvet curtains.* **2.** anything with a smooth soft surface. **3. a.** smoothness. **b.** (*as modifier*): *a velvet night.* **4.** the furry covering of the newly formed antlers of a deer. **5.** *Sl., chiefly U.S.* **a.** gambling winnings. **b.** a gain. **6. on velvet.** *Sl.* in a condition of ease, advantage, or wealth. **7. velvet glove.** gentleness, often concealing strength or determination (esp. in **an iron hand in a velvet glove**). [C14 *veluet,* < OF, < *velu* hairy, < Vulgar L *villutus* (unattested), < L *villus* shaggy hair] **—ˈvelvet-ˌlike** *adj.* **—ˈvelvety** *adj.*

velveteen (ˌvɛlvɪˈtiːn) *n.* **1.** a cotton fabric resembling velvet with a short thick pile, used for clothing, etc. **2.** (*pl.*) trousers made of velveteen.

Ven. *abbrev. for* Venerable.

vena (ˈviːnə) *n., pl.* **-nae** (-niː). *Anat.* a technical word for **vein.** [C15: < L *vēna* VEIN]

vena cava (ˈkeɪvə) *n., pl.* **venae cavae** (ˈkeɪviː). either one of two large veins that convey oxygen-depleted blood to the heart. [L: hollow vein]

venal (ˈviːnᵊl) *adj.* **1.** easily bribed or corrupted: *a venal magistrate.* **2.** characterized by corruption or bribery. [C17: < L *vēnālis,* < *vēnum* sale] **—veˈnality** *n.* **—ˈvenally** *adv.*

venation (viːˈneɪʃən) *n.* **1.** the arrangement of the veins in a leaf or in the wing of an insect. **2.** such veins collectively. **—veˈnational** *adj.*

vend (vɛnd) *vb.* **1.** to sell or be sold. **2.** to sell (goods) for a living. [C17: < L *vendere,* < *vēnum dare* to offer for sale]

vendace (ˈvɛndeɪs) *n., pl.* **-daces** *or* **-dace.** either of two small whitefish occurring in lakes in Scotland and NW England. [C18: < NL *vandēsius,* < OF *vandoise,* prob. of Celtic origin]

vendee (vɛnˈdiː) *n. Chiefly law.* a person to whom something, esp. real property, is sold.

vendetta (vɛnˈdɛtə) *n.* **1.** a private feud, originally between Corsican or Sicilian families, in which the relatives of a murdered person seek vengeance by killing the murderer or some member of his family. **2.** any prolonged feud. [C19: < It., < L *vindicta,* < *vindicāre* to avenge] **—venˈdettist** *n.*

vendible (ˈvɛndəbᵊl) *adj.* **1.** saleable or marketable. ~*n.* **2.** (*usually pl.*) *Rare.* a saleable object. **—ˌvendiˈbility** *n.*

vending machine *n.* a machine that automatically dispenses consumer goods such as cigarettes or food, when money is inserted.

vendor (ˈvɛndɔː) *or* **vender** (ˈvɛndə) *n.* **1.** *Chiefly law.* a person who sells something, esp. real property. **2.** another name for **vending machine.**

veneer (vɪˈnɪə) *n.* **1.** a thin layer of wood, plastic, etc., with a decorative or fine finish that is bonded to the surface of a less expensive material, usually wood. **2.** a superficial appearance: *a veneer of gentility.* **3.** any facing material that is applied to a different backing material. ~*vb.* (*tr.*) **4.** to cover (a surface) with a veneer. **5.** to conceal (something) under a superficially pleasant surface. [C17: < G *furnieren* to veneer, < OF *fournir* to FURNISH] **—veˈneerer** *n.*

veneering (vɪˈnɪərɪŋ) *n.* material used as veneer or a veneered surface.

venepuncture (ˈvɛnɪˌpʌŋktʃə) *n.* a variant spelling of **venipuncture.**

venerable (ˈvɛnərəbᵊl) *adj.* **1.** (esp. of a person) worthy of reverence on account of great age, religious associations, character, etc. **2.** (of inanimate objects) hallowed on account of age or historical or religious association. **3.** *R.C. Church.* a title bestowed on a deceased person when the first stage of his canonization has been accomplished. **4.** *Church of England.* a title given to an archdeacon. [C15: < L *venerābilis,* <

venerārī to venerate] —ˌ**venera'bility** *or* '**venerableness** *n.* —'**venerably** *adv.*

venerate (ˈvɛnəˌreɪt) *vb.* (*tr.*) **1.** to hold in deep respect. **2.** to honour in recognition of qualities of holiness, excellence, etc. [C17: < L *venerārī*, < *venus* love] —ˈ**venerˌator** *n.*

veneration (ˌvɛnəˈreɪʃən) *n.* **1.** a feeling or expression of awe or reverence. **2.** the act of venerating or the state of being venerated.

venereal (vɪˈnɪərɪəl) *adj.* **1.** of or infected with venereal disease. **2.** (of a disease) transmitted by sexual intercourse. **3.** of or involving the genitals. **4.** of or relating to sexual intercourse or erotic desire. [C15: < L *venereus*, < *venus* sexual love, < VENUS[1]]

venereal disease *n.* another name for **sexually transmitted disease.** Abbrev.: **VD.**

venereology (vɪˌnɪərɪˈɒlədʒɪ) *n.* the branch of medicine concerned with the study and treatment of venereal disease. —**veˌnereˈologist** *n.*

venery[1] (ˈvɛnərɪ, ˈviː-) *n. Arch.* the pursuit of sexual gratification. [C15: < Med. L *veneria*, < L *venus* love, VENUS[1]]

venery[2] (ˈvɛnərɪ, ˈviː-) *n.* the art, sport, lore, or practice of hunting, esp. with hounds; the chase. [C14: < OF *venerie*, < *vener* to hunt, < L *vēnārī*]

venesection (ˈvɛnɪˌsɛkʃən) *n.* surgical incision into a vein. [C17: < NL *vēnae sectiō*; see VEIN, SECTION]

Venetian (vɪˈniːʃən) *adj.* **1.** of, relating to, or characteristic of Venice, a port in NE Italy or its inhabitants. ~*n.* **2.** a native or inhabitant of Venice. **3.** See **Venetian blind.**

Venetian blind *n.* a window blind consisting of a number of horizontal slats whose angle may be altered to let in more or less light.

Venetian red *n.* **1.** natural or synthetic ferric oxide used as a red pigment. **2. a.** a moderate to strong reddish-brown colour. **b.** (*as adj.*): *a Venetian-red coat.*

vengeance (ˈvɛndʒəns) *n.* **1.** the act of or desire for taking revenge. **2. with a vengeance.** (intensifier): *he's a coward with a vengeance.* [C13: < OF, < *venger* to avenge, < L *vindicāre* to punish]

vengeful (ˈvɛndʒfʊl) *adj.* **1.** desiring revenge. **2.** characterized by or indicating a desire for revenge. **3.** inflicting or taking revenge: *with vengeful blows.* —ˈ**vengefully** *adv.*

venial (ˈviːnɪəl) *adj.* easily excused or forgiven: *a venial error.* [C13: via OF < LL *veniālis*, < L *venia* forgiveness] —ˌ**veniˈality** *n.* —ˈ**venially** *adv.*

venial sin *n. Christian theol.* a sin regarded as involving only a partial loss of grace.

venin (ˈvɛnɪn) *n.* any of the poisonous constituents of animal venoms. [C20: < F *ven(in)* poison + -IN]

venipuncture *or* **venepuncture** (ˈvɛnɪˌpʌŋktʃə) *n. Med.* the puncturing of a vein, esp. to take a sample of venous blood or inject a drug.

venison (ˈvɛnɪzᵊn, -sᵊn) *n.* the flesh of a deer, used as food. [C13: < OF *venaison*, < L *vēnātiō* hunting, < *vēnārī* to hunt]

Venite (vɪˈnaɪtɪ) *n.* **1.** the opening word of the 95th psalm, an invitatory prayer at matins. **2.** a musical setting of this. [L: come ye]

Venn diagram (vɛn) *n. Maths, logic.* a diagram in which mathematical sets or terms of a categorial statement are represented by overlapping circles within a boundary representing the universal set, so that all possible combinations of the relevant properties are represented by the various distinct areas in the diagram. [C19: after John *Venn* (1834–1923), E logician]

venom (ˈvɛnəm) *n.* **1.** a poisonous fluid secreted by such animals as certain snakes and scorpions and usually transmitted by a bite or sting. **2.** malice; spite. [C13: < OF, < L *venēnum* poison, love potion] —ˈ**venomous** *adj.* —ˈ**venomously** *adv.* —ˈ**venomousness** *n.*

venose (ˈviːnəʊs) *adj.* **1.** having veins; venous. **2.** (of a plant) covered with veins or similar ridges. [C17: via L *vēnōsus*, < *vēna* a VEIN]

venosity (vɪˈnɒsɪtɪ) *n.* **1.** an excessive quantity of blood in the venous system or in an organ or part. **2.** an unusually large number of blood vessels in an organ or part.

venous (ˈviːnəs) *adj.* **1.** *Physiol.* of or relating to the blood circulating in the veins. **2.** of or relating to the veins. [C17: see VENOSE]

vent[1] (vɛnt) *n.* **1.** a small opening for the escape of fumes, liquids, etc. **2.** the shaft of a volcano through which lava and gases erupt. **3.** the external opening of the urinary or genital systems of lower vertebrates. **4.** a small aperture at the breech of old guns through which the charge was ignited. **5. give vent to.** to release (an emotion, idea, etc.) in an outburst. ~*vb.* (*mainly tr.*) **6.** to release or give expression or utterance to (an emotion, etc.): *he vents his anger on his wife.* **7.** to provide a vent for or make vents in. **8.** to let out (steam, etc.) through a vent. [C14: < OF *esventer* to blow out, < EX-[1] + *venter*, < Vulgar L *ventāre* (unattested), < L *ventus* wind]

vent[2] (vɛnt) *n.* **1.** a vertical slit at the back or both sides of a jacket. ~*vb.* **2.** (*tr.*) to make a vent or vents in (a jacket). [C15: < OF *fente* slit, < *fendre* to split, < L *findere* to cleave]

venter (ˈvɛntə) *n.* **1.** *Anat., zool.* **a.** the belly or abdomen of vertebrates. **b.** a protuberant structure or part, such as the belly of a muscle. **2.** *Bot.* the swollen basal region of an archegonium. **3.** *Law.* the womb. [C16: < L]

ventilate (ˈvɛntɪˌleɪt) *vb.* (*tr.*) **1.** to drive foul air out of (an enclosed area). **2.** to provide with a means of airing. **3.** to expose (a question, grievance, etc.) to public discussion. **4.** *Physiol.* to oxygenate (the blood). [C15: < L *ventilāre* to fan, < *ventulus*, dim. of *ventus* wind] —ˈ**ventilable** *adj.* —ˌ**ventiˈlation** *n.*

ventilator (ˈvɛntɪˌleɪtə) *n.* **1.** an opening or device, such as a fan, used to ventilate a room, building, etc. **2.** *Med.* a machine that maintains a flow of air into and out of the lungs of a patient unable to breathe normally.

ventral (ˈvɛntrəl) *adj.* **1.** relating to the front part of the body. **2.** of or situated on the upper or inner side of a plant organ, esp. a leaf, that is facing the axis. [C18: < L *ventrālis*, < *venter* abdomen] —ˈ**ventrally** *adv.*

ventral fin *n.* **1.** another name for **pelvic fin. 2.** any unpaired median fin situated on the undersurface of fishes.

ventricle (ˈvɛntrɪkᵊl) *n. Anat.* **1.** a chamber of the heart that receives blood from the atrium and pumps it to the arteries. **2.** any one of the four main cavities of the vertebrate brain. **3.** any of various other small cavities in the body. [C14: < L *ventriculus*, dim. of *venter* belly] —**venˈtricular** *adj.*

ventricose (ˈvɛntrɪˌkəʊs) *adj.* **1.** *Bot., zool., anat.* having a swelling on one side: *the ventricose corolla of many labiate plants.* **2.** another word for **corpulent.** [C18: < NL, < L *venter* belly]

ventriculus (vɛnˈtrɪkjʊləs) *n., pl.* **-li** (-ˌlaɪ). **1.** *Zool.* **a.** the midgut of an insect, where digestion takes place. **b.** the gizzard of a bird. **2.** another word for **ventricle.** [C18: < L, dim. of *venter* belly]

ventriloquism (vɛnˈtrɪləˌkwɪzəm) *or* **ventriloquy** *n.* the art of producing vocal sounds that appear to come from another source. [C18: < L *venter* belly + *loquī* to speak] —**ventriloquial** (ˌvɛntrɪˈləʊkwɪəl) *adj.* —ˌ**ventriˈloquially** *adv.* —**venˈtriloquist** *n.* —**venˈtriloˌquize** *or* **-ˌquise** *vb.*

venture (ˈvɛntʃə) *vb.* **1.** (*tr.*) to expose to danger: *he ventured his life.* **2.** (*tr.*) to brave the dangers of (something): *I'll venture the seas.* **3.** (*tr.*) to dare (to do something): *does he venture to object?* **4.** (*tr.; may take a clause as object*) to express in spite of possible criticism: *I venture that he is not that honest.* **5.** (*intr.;* often foll. by *out, forth,* etc.) to embark on a possibly hazardous journey, etc.: *to venture forth upon the high seas.* ~*n.* **6.** an undertaking that is risky or of uncertain outcome. **7.** a commercial undertaking characterized by risk of loss as well as opportunity for profit. **8.** something hazarded or risked in an adventure. **9.**

at a venture. at random. [C15: var. of *aventure* ADVENTURE] —ˈ**venturer** *n.*

venture capital *n.* another name for **risk capital.**

Venture Scout *or* **Venturer** *n. Brit.* a person aged 16–20 who is a member of the senior branch of the Scouts.

venturesome (ˈvɛntʃəsəm) *or* **venturous** (ˈvɛntʃərəs) *adj.* **1.** willing to take risks; daring. **2.** hazardous.

Venturi tube (vɛnˈtjʊərɪ) *n. Physics.* a device for measuring or controlling fluid flow, consisting of a tube so constricted that the pressure differential produced by fluid flowing through the constriction gives a measure of the rate of flow. [C19: after G. B. *Venturi* (1746–1822), It. physicist]

venue (ˈvɛnjuː) *n.* **1.** *Law.* **a.** the place in which a cause of action arises. **b.** the place fixed for the trial of a cause. **c.** the locality from which the jurors must be summoned. **2.** a meeting place. **3.** any place where an organized gathering, such as a rock concert, is held. [C14: < OF, < *venir* to come, < L *venīre*]

venule (ˈvɛnjuːl) *n.* **1.** *Anat.* any of the small branches of a vein that receives oxygen-depleted blood from the capillaries and returns it to the heart via the venous system. **2.** any of the branches of a vein in an insect's wing. [C19: < L *vēnula*, dim. of *vēna* VEIN]

Venus[1] (ˈviːnəs) *n.* the Roman goddess of love. Greek counterpart: **Aphrodite.**

Venus[2] (ˈviːnəs) *n.* one of the inferior planets and the second nearest to the sun, visible as a bright morning or evening star. —**Venusian** (vɪˈnjuːzɪən) *n., adj.*

Venus's-flytrap *or* **Venus flytrap** *n.* an insectivorous plant having hinged two-lobed leaves that snap closed when the sensitive hairs on the surface are touched.

Venus's looking glass *n.* a purple-flowered campanulaceous plant of Europe, W Asia, and N Africa.

veracious (vɛˈreɪʃəs) *adj.* **1.** habitually truthful or honest. **2.** accurate. [C17: < L *vērax*, < *vērus* true] —**veˈraciously** *adv.* —**veˈraciousness** *n.*

veracity (vɛˈræsɪtɪ) *n., pl.* **-ties. 1.** truthfulness or honesty, esp. when consistent or habitual. **2.** accuracy. **3.** a truth. [C17: < Med. L *vērācitās*, < L *vērax*; see VERACIOUS]

veranda *or* **verandah** (vəˈrændə) *n.* **1.** a porch or portico, sometimes partly enclosed, along the outside of a building. **2.** *N.Z.* a continuous overhead canopy that gives shelter to pedestrians. [C18: < Port. *varanda* railing]

veratrine (ˈvɛrəˌtriːn) *or* **veratrin** (ˈvɛrətrɪn) *n.* a white poisonous mixture obtained from sabadilla, consisting of various alkaloids: formerly used in medicine as a counterirritant. [C19: < L *vērātrum* hellebore + -INE[2]]

verb (vɜːb) *n.* **1.** (in traditional grammar) any of a large class of words that serve to indicate the occurrence or performance of an action, the existence of a state, etc. Such words as *run, make, do,* etc., are verbs. **2.** (in modern descriptive linguistic analysis) **a.** a word or group of words that functions as the predicate of a sentence or introduces the predicate. **b.** (*as modifier*): *a verb phrase.* ~Abbrev.: **vb, v.** [C14: < L *verbum* word]

verbal (ˈvɜːbᵊl) *adj.* **1.** of, relating to, or using words: *merely verbal concessions.* **2.** oral rather than written: *a verbal agreement.* **3.** verbatim; literal: *an almost verbal copy.* **4.** *Grammar.* of or relating to verbs or a verb. ~See also **verbals.** —ˈ**verbally** *adv.*

verbalism (ˈvɜːbəˌlɪzəm) *n.* **1.** a verbal expression; phrase or word. **2.** an exaggerated emphasis on the importance of words. **3.** a statement lacking real content.

verbalist (ˈvɜːbəlɪst) *n.* **1.** a person who deals with words alone, rather than facts, ideas, etc. **2.** a person skilled in the use of words.

verbalize *or* **-lise** (ˈvɜːbəˌlaɪz) *vb.* **1.** to express (an idea, etc.) in words. **2.** to change (any word) into a verb or derive a verb from (any word). **3.** (*intr.*) to be verbose. —ˌ**verbaliˈzation** *or* **-liˈsation** *n.*

verbal noun *n.* a noun derived from a verb, such as *smoking* in the sentence *smoking is bad for you.*

verbals (ˈvɜːbᵊlz) *pl. n. Sl.* a criminal's admission of guilt on arrest.

verbascum (vɜːˈbæskəm) *n.* any of a genus of hairy plants, mostly biennial, having spikes of yellow, purple, or red flowers. [L: mullein]

verbatim (vɜːˈbeɪtɪm) *adv., adj.* using exactly the same words; word for word. [C15: < Med. L: word by word, < L *verbum* word]

verbena (vɜːˈbiːnə) *n.* **1.** any of a genus of plants of tropical and temperate America, having red, white, or purple fragrant flowers: much cultivated as garden plants. **2.** any of various similar plants, esp. the lemon verbena. [C16: via Med. L, < L: sacred bough used by the priest in religious acts]

verbiage (ˈvɜːbɪɪdʒ) *n.* the excessive and often meaningless use of words. [C18: < F, < OF *verbier* to chatter, < *verbe* word, < L *verbum*]

verbose (vɜːˈbəʊs) *adj.* using or containing an excess of words, so as to be pedantic or boring. [C17: < L, < *verbum* word] —**verˈbosely** *adv.* —**verbosity** (vɜːˈbɒsɪtɪ) *n.*

verboten *German.* (fɛrˈboːtən) *adj.* forbidden.

verb phrase *n. Grammar.* a constituent of a sentence that contains the verb and any direct and indirect objects but not the subject.

verdant (ˈvɜːdᵊnt) *adj.* **1.** covered with green vegetation. **2.** (of plants, etc.) green in colour. **3.** unsophisticated; green. [C16: < OF, < *verdoyer* to become green, < OF *verd* green, < L *viridis*] —ˈ**verdancy** *n.* —ˈ**verdantly** *adv.*

verd antique (vɜːd) *n.* **1.** a dark green mottled impure variety of serpentine marble. **2.** any of various similar marbles or stones. [C18: < F, < It. *verde antico* ancient green]

verdict (ˈvɜːdɪkt) *n.* **1.** the findings of a jury on the issues of fact submitted to it for examination and trial. **2.** any decision or conclusion. [C13: < Med. L *vērdictum*, < L *vērē dictum* truly spoken, < *vērus* true + *dīcere* to say]

verdigris (ˈvɜːdɪgrɪs) *n.* **1.** a green or bluish patina formed on copper, brass, or bronze. **2.** a green or blue crystalline substance obtained by the action of acetic acid on copper and used as a fungicide and pigment. [C14: < OF *vert de Grice* green of Greece]

verdure (ˈvɜːdʒə) *n.* **1.** flourishing green vegetation or its colour. **2.** a condition of freshness or healthy growth. [C14: < OF *verd* green, < L *viridis*] —ˈ**verdured** *adj.*

verge[1] (vɜːdʒ) *n.* **1.** an edge or rim; margin. **2.** a limit beyond which something occurs: *on the verge of ecstasy.* **3.** *Brit.* a grass border along a road. **4.** *Archit.* the edge of the roof tiles projecting over a gable. **5.** *English legal history.* **a.** the area encompassing the royal court that is subject to the jurisdiction of the Lord High Steward. **b.** a rod or wand carried as a symbol of office or emblem of authority, as in the Church. ~*vb.* **6.** (*intr.;* foll. by *on*) to be near (to): *to verge on chaos.* **7.** (when *intr.,* sometimes foll. by *on*) to serve as the edge of (something): *this narrow strip verges the road.* [C15: < OF, < L *virga* rod]

verge[2] (vɜːdʒ) *vb.* (*intr.;* foll. by *to* or *towards*) to move or incline in a certain direction. [C17: < L *vergere*]

verger (ˈvɜːdʒə) *n. Chiefly Church of England.* **1.** a church official who acts as caretaker and attendant. **2.** an official who carries the verge or rod of office before a bishop or dean in ceremonies and processions. [C15: < OF, < *verge*, < L *virga* rod, twig]

verglas (ˈvɛəglɑː) *n., pl.* **-glases** (-glɑː, -glɑːz). a thin film of ice on rock. [< OF *verre-glaz*, < *verre* glass + *glaz* ice]

veridical (vɪˈrɪdɪkᵊl) *adj.* **1.** truthful. **2.** *Psychol.* of revelations in dreams, etc., that appear to be confirmed by subsequent events. [C17: < L, < *vērus* true + *dīcere* to say] —**veˌridiˈcality** *n.* —**veˈridically** *adv.*

veriest (ˈvɛrɪɪst) *adj. Arch.* (intensifier): *the veriest coward.*

verification (ˌvɛrɪfɪˈkeɪʃən) *n.* **1.** establishment of the correctness of a theory, fact, etc. **2.** evidence that provides proof of an assertion, theory, etc. —**ˈverifiˌcatory** *adj.*

verify (ˈvɛrɪˌfaɪ) *vb.* **-fying, -fied.** (*tr.*) **1.** to prove to be true; confirm. **2.** to check or determine the correctness or truth of by investigation, etc. **3.** *Law.* to substantiate or confirm (an oath). [C14: < OF, < Med. L *vērificāre,* < L *vērus* true + *facere* to make] —**ˈveriˌfiable** *adj.* —**ˈveriˌfiably** *adv.* —**ˈveriˌfier** *n.*

verily (ˈvɛrɪlɪ) *adv.* (*sentence modifier*) *Arch.* in truth; truly: *verily, thou art a man of God.* [C13: < VERY + -LY[2]]

verisimilar (ˌvɛrɪˈsɪmɪlə) *adj.* probable; likely. [C17: < L, < *vērus* true + *similis* like]

verisimilitude (ˌvɛrɪsɪˈmɪlɪˌtjuːd) *n.* **1.** the appearance or semblance of truth or reality. **2.** something that merely seems to be true or real, such as a doubtful statement. [C17: < L, < *vērus* true + *similitūdō* SIMILITUDE]

verism (ˈvɪərɪzəm) *n.* extreme naturalism in art or literature. [C19: < It. *verismo,* < *vero* true, < L *vērus*] —**ˈverist** *n., adj.* —**veˈristic** *adj.*

verismo (vɛˈrɪzməʊ) *n. Music.* a school of composition that originated in Italian opera towards the end of the 19th century, drawing its themes from real life. [C19: < It.; see VERISM]

veritable (ˈvɛrɪtəbᵊl) *adj.* (*prenominal*) (intensifier; *usually qualifying a word used metaphorically*): *he's a veritable swine!* [C15: < OF, < *vérité* truth; see VERITY] —**ˈveritableness** *n.* —**ˈveritably** *adv.*

verity (ˈvɛrɪtɪ) *n., pl.* **-ties.** **1.** the quality or state of being true, real, or correct. **2.** a true statement, idea, etc. [C14: < OF < L *vēritās,* < *vērus* true]

verjuice (ˈvɜːˌdʒuːs) *n.* **1.** the acid juice of unripe grapes, apples, or crab apples, formerly much used in making sauces, etc. **2.** *Rare.* sourness or sharpness of temper, looks, etc. [C14: < OF *vert jus* green (unripe) juice]

verkrampte (fəˈkramtə) *n.* (in South Africa) **a.** an Afrikaner Nationalist violently opposed to any liberal trends in government policy, particularly those related to race. **b.** (*as modifier*): *verkrampte politics.* [C20: < Afrik. (adj.), lit.: restricted]

verligte (fəˈləxtə) *n.* (in South Africa) **a.** a follower of any White political party who supports liberal trends in government policy. **b.** (*as modifier*): *verligte politics.* [C20: < Afrik. (adj.), lit.: enlightened]

vermeil (ˈvɜːmeɪl) *n.* **1.** gilded silver, bronze, or other metal, used esp. in the 19th century. **2. a.** vermilion. **b.** (*as adj.*): *vermeil shoes.* [C15: < OF, < LL *vermiculus* insect (of the genus *Kermes*) or the red dye prepared from it, < L: little worm]

vermi- *combining form.* worm: *vermicide; vermiform; vermifuge.* [< L *vermis* worm]

vermicelli (ˌvɜːmɪˈsɛlɪ, -ˈtʃɛlɪ) *n.* **1.** very fine strands of pasta, used in soups. **2.** tiny chocolate strands used to coat cakes, etc. [C17: < It.: little worms, < *verme,* < L *vermis*]

vermicide (ˈvɜːmɪˌsaɪd) *n.* any substance used to kill worms. —ˌ**vermiˈcidal** *adj.*

vermicular (vɜːˈmɪkjʊlə) *adj.* **1.** resembling the form, motion, or tracks of worms. **2.** of worms or wormlike animals. [C17: < Med. L, < L *vermiculus,* dim. of *vermis* worm] —**verˈmiculate** *adj.* —**verˌmicuˈlation** *n.*

vermiculite (vɜːˈmɪkjʊˌlaɪt) *n.* any of a group of micaceous minerals consisting mainly of hydrated silicate of magnesium, aluminium, and iron: on heating they expand and in this form are used in heat and sound insulation. [C19: < VERMICUL(AR) + -ITE[1]]

vermiform (ˈvɜːmɪˌfɔːm) *adj.* resembling a worm.

vermiform appendix *n.* a wormlike pouch extending from the lower end of the caecum in some mammals. Also called: **appendix.**

vermifuge (ˈvɜːmɪˌfjuːdʒ) *n.* any drug or agent able to destroy or expel intestinal worms. —**vermifugal** (ˌvɜːmɪˈfjuːgᵊl) *adj.*

vermilion (vəˈmɪljən) *n.* **1. a.** a bright red to reddish-orange colour. **b.** (*as adj.*): *a vermilion car.* **2.** mercuric sulphide, esp. when used as a bright red pigment; cinnabar. [C13: < OF *vermeillon,* < *vermeil,* < L *vermiculus,* dim. of *vermis* worm]

vermin (ˈvɜːmɪn) *n.* **1.** (*functioning as pl.*) small animals collectively, esp. insects and rodents, that are troublesome to man, domestic animals, etc. **2.** (*pl.* **-min**) an unpleasant person. [C13: < OF, < L *vermis* worm] —**ˈverminous** *adj.*

vermis (ˈvɜːmɪs) *n., pl.* **-mes** (-miːz). *Anat.* the middle lobe connecting the two halves of the cerebellum. [C19: via NL < L: worm]

vermouth (ˈvɜːməθ) *n.* any of several wines containing aromatic herbs. [C19: < F, < G *Wermut* WORMWOOD (absinthe)]

vernacular (vəˈnækjʊlə) *n.* **1. the.** the commonly spoken language or dialect of a particular people or place. **2.** a local style of architecture, in which ordinary houses are built: *a true English vernacular.* ~*adj.* **3.** relating to or in the vernacular. **4.** designating or relating to the common name of an animal or plant. **5.** built in the local style of ordinary houses. [C17: < L *vernāculus* belonging to a household slave, < *verna* household slave] —**verˈnacularly** *adv.*

vernal (ˈvɜːnᵊl) *adj.* **1.** of or occurring in spring. **2.** *Poetic.* of or characteristic of youth. [C16: < L, < *vēr* spring] —**ˈvernally** *adv.*

vernal equinox *n.* See at **equinox.**

vernal grass *n.* any of a genus of Eurasian grasses, such as **sweet vernal grass,** having the fragrant scent of coumarin.

vernalize *or* **-lise** (ˈvɜːnəˌlaɪz) *vb.* to shorten the period between sowing and flowering in (plants), esp. by subjection of the seeds to low temperatures before planting. —ˌ**vernaliˈzation** *or* **-liˈsation** *n.*

vernation (vɜːˈneɪʃən) *n.* the way in which leaves are arranged in the bud. [C18: < NL, < L *vernāre* to be springlike, < *vēr* spring]

vernier (ˈvɜːnɪə) *n.* **1.** a small movable scale running parallel to the main graduated scale in certain measuring instruments, such as theodolites, used to obtain a fractional reading of one of the divisions on the main scale. **2.** (*modifier*) relating to or fitted with a vernier: *a vernier scale.* [C18: after Paul *Vernier* (1580–1637), F mathematician, who described the scale]

vernissage (ˌvɜːnɪˈsɑːʒ) *n.* a preview or the opening or first day of an exhibition of paintings. [F, < *vernis* VARNISH]

Veronal (ˈvɛrənᵊl) *n.* a trademark for **barbitone.**

veronica[1] (vəˈrɒnɪkə) *n.* any plant of a genus, including the speedwells, of temperate and cold regions, having small blue, pink, or white flowers and flattened notched fruits. [C16: < Med. L, ? < the name *Veronica*]

veronica[2] (vəˈrɒnɪkə) *n. Bullfighting.* a pass in which the matador slowly swings the cape away from the charging bull. [< Sp., < the name *Veronica*]

verruca (vɛˈruːkə) *n., pl.* **-cae** (-siː) *or* **-cas.** **1.** *Pathol.* a wart, esp. one growing on the hand or foot. **2.** *Biol.* a wartlike outgrowth. [C16: < L: wart]

verrucose (ˈvɛrʊˌkəʊs) *or* **verrucous** (ˈvɛrʊkəs, vɛˈruːkəs) *adj. Bot.* covered with warty processes. [C17: < L *verrūcōsus* full of warts, < *verrūca* a wart] —**verrucosity** (ˌvɛrʊˈkɒsɪtɪ) *n.*

versant (ˈvɜːsᵊnt) *n.* **1.** the side or slope of a mountain or mountain range. **2.** the slope of a region. [C19: < F, < *verser* to turn, < L *versāre*]

versatile (ˈvɜːsəˌtaɪl) *adj.* **1.** capable of or adapted for many different uses, skills, etc. **2.** variable. **3.** *Bot.* (of an anther) attached to the filament by a small area so that it moves freely in the wind. **4.** *Zool.* able to turn forwards and backwards. [C17: < L *versātilis* moving around, < *versāre* to turn] —**ˈversaˌtilely** *adv.* —**versatility** (ˌvɜːsəˈtɪlɪtɪ) *n.*

verse (vɜːs) *n.* **1.** (not in technical usage) a stanza of a poem. **2.** poetry as distinct from prose. **3. a.** a series of metrical feet forming a rhythmical unit of one line. **b.** (*as modifier*): *verse line.* **4.** a specified type of metre or metrical structure: *iambic verse.* **5.** one of the series of short subsections into which most of the writings in the Bible are divided. **6.** a poem. ~*vb.* **7.** a rare word for **versify.** [OE *vers,* < L *versus* furrow, lit.: a turning (of the plough), < *vertere* to turn]

versed (vɜːst) *adj.* (*postpositive;* foll. by *in*) thoroughly knowledgeable (about), acquainted (with), or skilled (in).

versed sine *n.* a trigonometric function equal to one minus the cosine of the specified angle. [C16: < NL, < SINE[1] + *versus,* < *vertere* to turn]

versicle (ˈvɜːsɪkᵊl) *n.* **1.** a short verse. **2.** a short sentence recited or sung by a minister and responded to by his congregation. [C14: < L *versiculus* a little line, < *versus* VERSE]

versicolour *or U.S.* **versicolor** (ˈvɜːsɪˌkʌlə) *adj.* of variable or various colours. [C18: < L *versicolor,* < *versāre* to turn + *color* COLOUR]

versification (ˌvɜːsɪfɪˈkeɪʃən) *n.* **1.** the technique or art of versifying. **2.** the form or metrical composition of a poem. **3.** a metrical version of a prose text.

versify (ˈvɜːsɪˌfaɪ) *vb.* **-fying, -fied. 1.** (*tr.*) to render (something) into verse. **2.** (*intr.*) to write in verse. [C14: < OF, < L, < *versus* VERSE + *facere* to make] —ˈ**versiˌfier** *n.*

version (ˈvɜːʃən) *n.* **1.** an account of a matter from a certain point of view, as contrasted with others: *his version of the accident is different from the policeman's.* **2.** a translation, esp. of the Bible, from one language into another. **3.** a variant form of something. **4.** an adaptation, as of a book or play into a film. **5.** *Med.* manual turning of a fetus to correct an irregular position within the uterus. [C16: < Med. L *versiō* a turning, < L *vertere* to turn] —ˈ**versional** *adj.*

vers libre French. (vɛr librə) *n.* (in French poetry) another term for **free verse.**

verso (ˈvɜːsəʊ) *n., pl.* **-sos. 1. a.** the back of a sheet of printed paper. **b.** the left-hand pages of a book, bearing the even numbers. **2.** the side of a coin opposite to the obverse. [C19: < NL *versō foliō* the leaf having been turned, < L *vertere* to turn + *folium* leaf]

verst (vɛəst, vɜːst) *n.* a unit of length, used in Russia, equal to 1.067 kilometres (0.6629 miles). [C16: < F or G, < Russian *versta* line]

versus (ˈvɜːsəs) *prep.* **1.** (esp. in a competition or lawsuit) against. Abbrev.: **v.,** (esp. U.S.) **vs. 2.** in contrast with. [C15: < L: turned (in the direction of), opposite, < *vertere* to turn]

vertebra (ˈvɜːtɪbrə) *n., pl.* **-brae** (-briː) *or* **-bras.** one of the bony segments of the spinal column. [C17: < L: joint of the spine, < *vertere* to turn] —ˈ**vertebral** *adj.* —ˈ**vertebrally** *adv.*

vertebral column *n.* another name for **spinal column.**

vertebrate (ˈvɜːtɪˌbreɪt, -brɪt) *n.* **1.** any animal of a subphylum characterized by a bony skeleton and a well-developed brain: the group contains fishes, amphibians, reptiles, birds, and mammals. ~*adj.* **2.** of or belonging to this subphylum.

vertebration (ˌvɜːtɪˈbreɪʃən) *n.* the formation of vertebrae or segmentation resembling vertebrae.

vertex (ˈvɜːtɛks) *n., pl.* **-texes** *or* **-tices. 1.** the highest point. **2.** *Maths.* **a.** the point opposite the base of a figure. **b.** the point of intersection of two sides of a plane figure or angle. **c.** the point of intersection of a pencil of lines or three or more planes of a solid figure. **3.** *Anat.* the crown of the head. [C16: < L: whirlpool, < *vertere* to turn]

vertical (ˈvɜːtɪkᵊl) *adj.* **1.** at right angles to the horizon; upright: *a vertical wall.* **2.** extending in a perpendicular direction. **3.** directly overhead. **4.** *Econ.* of or relating to associated or consecutive, though not identical, stages of industrial activity: *vertical integration.* **5.** of or relating to the vertex. **6.** *Anat.* of or situated at the top of the head (vertex). ~*n.* **7.** a vertical plane, position, or line. **8.** a vertical post, pillar, etc. [C16: < LL *verticālis,* < L VERTEX] —ˌ**vertiˈcality** *n.* —ˈ**vertically** *adv.*

vertical angles *pl. n. Geom.* the pair of equal angles between a pair of intersecting lines.

vertical mobility *n. Sociol.* the movement of individuals or groups to positions in society that involve a change in class, status, and power.

vertices (ˈvɜːtɪˌsiːz) *n.* a plural of **vertex** (in technical and scientific senses only).

verticil (ˈvɜːtɪsɪl) *n. Biol.* a circular arrangement of parts about an axis, esp. leaves around a stem. [C18: < L *verticillus* whorl (of a spindle), < VERTEX] —**verˈticillate** *adj.*

vertiginous (vɜːˈtɪdʒɪnəs) *adj.* **1.** of, relating to, or having vertigo. **2.** producing dizziness. **3.** whirling. **4.** changeable; unstable. [C17: < L *vertīginōsus,* < VERTIGO] —**verˈtiginously** *adv.*

vertigo (ˈvɜːtɪgəʊ) *n., pl.* **vertigoes** *or* **vertigines** (vɜːˈtɪdʒɪˌniːz). *Pathol.* a sensation of dizziness resulting from a disorder of the sense of balance. [C16: < L: a whirling round, < *vertere* to turn]

vertu (vɜːˈtuː) *n.* a variant spelling of **virtu.**

vervain (ˈvɜːveɪn) *n.* any of several plants of the genus *Verbena,* having square stems and long slender spikes of purple, blue, or white flowers. [C14: < OF *verveine,* < L *verbēna* sacred bough]

verve (vɜːv) *n.* great vitality and liveliness. [C17: < OF: garrulity, < L *verba* words, chatter]

vervet (ˈvɜːvɪt) *n.* a variety of a South African guenon monkey having dark hair on the hands and feet and a reddish patch beneath the tail. [C19: < F, < *vert* green]

very (ˈvɛrɪ) *adv.* **1.** (intensifier) used to add emphasis to adjectives that are able to be graded: *very good; very tall.* ~*adj.* (*prenominal*) **2.** (intensifier) used with nouns preceded by a definite article or possessive determiner, in order to give emphasis to the significance or relevance of a noun in a particular context, or to give exaggerated intensity to certain nouns: *the very man I want to see; the very back of the room.* **3.** (intensifier) used in metaphors to emphasize the applicability of the image to the situation described: *he was a very lion in the fight.* **4.** *Arch.* genuine: *the very living God.* [C13: < OF *verai* true, < L *vērax,* < *vērus*]

▷ **Usage.** In strict usage adverbs of degree such as *very, too, quite, really,* and *extremely* are used only to qualify adjectives: *he is very happy; she is too sad.* By this rule, these words should not be used to qualify past participles that follow the verb *to be,* since they would then be technically qualifying verbs. With the exception of certain participles, such as *tired* or *disappointed,* that have come to be regarded as adjectives, all other past participles are qualified by adverbs such as *much, greatly, seriously,* or *excessively: he has been much* (not *very*) *inconvenienced.*

very high frequency *n.* a radio-frequency band or radio frequency lying between 300 and 30 megahertz. Abbrev.: **VHF.**

Very light (ˈvɛrɪ) *n.* a coloured flare fired from a special pistol (**Very pistol**) for signalling at night, esp. at sea. [C19: after Edward W. *Very* (1852–1910), U.S. naval ordnance officer]

very low frequency *n.* a radio-frequency band or radio frequency lying between 30 and 3 kilohertz. Abbrev.: **VLF.**

vesica (ˈvɛsɪkə) *n., pl.* **-cae** (-ˌsiː). *Anat.* a technical name for **bladder** (sense 1). [C17: < L: bladder, sac, blister] —ˈ**vesical** *adj.* —**vesiculate** (vɛˈsɪkjʊˌleɪt,-lɪt) *vb., adj.*

vesicant (ˈvɛsɪkənt) *or* **vesicatory** (ˈvɛsɪˌkeɪtərɪ) *n., pl.* **-cants** *or* **-catories. 1.** any substance that causes blisters. ~*adj.* **2.** acting as a vesicant. [C19: see VESICA]

vesicate (ˈvɛsɪˌkeɪt) *vb.* to blister. [C17: < NL *vēsīcāre* to blister; see VESICA] —ˌ**vesiˈcation** *n.*

vesicle (ˈvɛsɪkᵊl) *n.* **1.** *Pathol.* **a.** any small sac or cavity, esp. one containing serous fluid. **b.** a blister. **2.** *Geol.* a rounded cavity within a rock. **3.** *Bot.* a small bladder-like cavity occurring in certain seaweeds. **4.** any small cavity or cell.

[C16: < L *vēsīcula,* dim. of VESICA] —**vesicular** (vɛˈsɪkjʊlə) *adj.*

vesper (ˈvɛspə) *n.* **1.** an evening prayer, service, or hymn. **2.** *Arch.* evening. **3.** (*modifier*) of or relating to vespers. ~See also **vespers.** [C14: < L: evening, the evening star]

vespers (ˈvɛspəz) *n.* (*functioning as sing.*) **1.** *Chiefly R.C. Church.* the sixth of the seven canonical hours of the divine office. **2.** another word for **evensong** (sense 1).

vespertine (ˈvɛspəˌtaɪn) *adj.* **1.** *Bot., zool.* appearing, opening, or active in the evening: *vespertine flowers.* **2.** occurring in the evening or (esp. of stars) setting in the evening.

vespiary (ˈvɛspɪərɪ) *n., pl.* **-aries.** a nest or colony of social wasps or hornets. [C19: < L *vespa* a wasp, on the model of *apiary*]

vespid (ˈvɛspɪd) *n.* **1.** any of a family of hymenopterous insects, including the common wasp. ~*adj.* **2.** of or belonging to this family. [C19: < NL, < L *vespa* a wasp] —ˈ**vespine** *adj.*

vessel (ˈvɛsᵊl) *n.* **1.** any object used as a container, esp. for a liquid. **2.** a passenger or freight-carrying ship, boat, etc. **3.** *Anat.* a tubular structure that transports such body fluids as blood and lymph. **4.** *Bot.* a tubular element of xylem tissue transporting water. **5.** *Rare.* a person regarded as a vehicle for some purpose or quality. [C13: < OF, < LL *vascellum* urn, < L *vās* vessel]

vest (vɛst) *n.* **1.** an undergarment covering the body from the shoulders to the hips, made of cotton, nylon, etc. **2.** *U.S., Canad., & Austral.* a waistcoat. **3.** *Obs.* any form of dress. ~*vb.* **4.** (*tr.;* foll. by *in*) to place or settle (power, rights, etc., in): *power was vested in the committee.* **5.** (*tr.;* foll. by *with*) to bestow or confer (on): *the company was vested with authority.* **6.** (usually foll. by *in*) to confer (a right, title, etc., upon) or (of a right, title, etc.) to pass (to) or devolve (upon). **7.** (*tr.*) to clothe. **8.** (*intr.*) to put on clothes, ecclesiastical vestments, etc. [C15: < OF *vestir* to clothe, < L *vestīre,* < *vestis* clothing]

vesta (ˈvɛstə) *n.* a short friction match, usually of wood. [C19: after *Vesta,* Roman goddess of the hearth]

vestal (ˈvɛstᵊl) *adj.* **1.** chaste or pure. **2.** of or relating to the Roman goddess Vesta. ~*n.* **3.** a chaste woman, esp. a nun.

vestal virgin *n.* (in ancient Rome) one of the virgin priestesses whose lives were dedicated to Vesta and to maintaining the sacred fire in her temple.

vested (ˈvɛstɪd) *adj. Property law.* having a present right to the immediate or future possession and enjoyment of property.

vested interest *n.* **1.** *Property law.* an existing right to the immediate or future possession and enjoyment of property. **2.** a strong personal concern in a state of affairs, etc. **3.** a person or group that has such an interest.

vestiary (ˈvɛstɪərɪ) *n., pl.* **-aries.** *Obs.* a room for storing clothes or dressing in, such as a vestry. [C17: < LL *vestiārius,* < *vestis* clothing]

vestibule (ˈvɛstɪˌbjuːl) *n.* **1.** a small entrance hall or anteroom. **2.** any small bodily cavity at the entrance to a passage or canal. [C17: < L *vestibulum*]

vestige (ˈvɛstɪdʒ) *n.* **1.** a small trace; hint: *a vestige of truth.* **2.** *Biol.* an organ or part of an organism that is a small nonfunctioning remnant of a functional organ in an ancestor. [C17: via F < L *vestīgium* track] —**vesˈtigial** *adj.*

vestment (ˈvɛstmənt) *n.* **1.** a garment or robe, esp. one denoting office, authority, or rank. **2.** any of various ceremonial garments worn by the clergy at religious services, etc. [C13: < OF *vestiment,* < L *vestīmentum,* < *vestīre* to clothe] —**vestmental** (vɛstˈmɛntᵊl) *adj.*

vest-pocket *n.* (*modifier*) *Chiefly U.S.* small enough to fit into a waistcoat pocket.

vestry (ˈvɛstrɪ) *n., pl.* **-tries.** **1.** a room in or attached to a church in which vestments, sacred vessels, etc., are kept. **2.** a room in or attached to some churches, used for Sunday school, etc. **3. a.** *Church of England.* a meeting of all the members of a parish or their representatives, to transact the official and administrative business of the parish. **b.** the parish council. [C14: prob. < OF *vestiarie;* see VEST] —ˈ**vestral** *adj.*

vestryman (ˈvɛstrɪmən) *n., pl.* **-men.** a member of a church vestry.

vesture (ˈvɛstʃə) *Arch.* ~*n.* **1.** a garment or something that seems like a garment: *a vesture of cloud.* ~*vb.* **2.** (*tr.*) to clothe. [C14: < OF, < *vestir,* < L *vestīre,* < *vestis* clothing] —ˈ**vestural** *adj.*

vet[1] (vɛt) *n.* **1.** short for **veterinary surgeon.** ~*vb.* **vetting, vetted.** **2.** (*tr.*) *Chiefly Brit.* to make a prior examination and critical appraisal of (a person, document, etc.): *the candidates were well vetted.* **3.** to examine, treat, or cure (an animal).

vet[2] (vɛt) *n. U.S. & Canad.* short for **veteran** (senses 2, 3).

vet. *abbrev. for:* **1.** veteran. **2.** veterinarian. **3.** veterinary. ~Also (for senses 2, 3): **veter.**

vetch (vɛtʃ) *n.* **1.** any of various climbing plants having pinnate leaves, typically blue or purple flowers, and tendrils on the stems. **2.** any of various similar and related plants, such as the kidney vetch. **3.** the beanlike fruit of any of these plants. [C14 *fecche,* < OF *veche,* < L *vicia*]

vetchling (ˈvɛtʃlɪŋ) *n.* any of various tendril-climbing plants, mainly of N temperate regions, having winged or angled stems and showy flowers. See also **sweet pea.**

veteran (ˈvɛtərən) *n.* **1. a.** a person or thing that has given long service in some capacity. **b.** (*as modifier*): *veteran firemen.* **2.** a soldier who has seen considerable active service. **3.** *U.S. & Canad.* a person who has served in the military forces. [C16: < L, < *vetus* old]

veteran car *n. Brit.* a car constructed before 1919, esp. one constructed before 1905.

veterinary (ˈvɛtərɪnərɪ) *adj.* of or relating to veterinary science. [C18: < L *veterīnārius,* < *veterīnae* draught animals]

veterinary science *or* **medicine** *n.* the branch of medicine concerned with the health of animals and the treatment of injuries or diseases that affect them.

veterinary surgeon *n. Brit.* a person qualified to practise veterinary medicine. U.S. and Canad. term: **veterinarian.**

veto (ˈviːtəʊ) *n., pl.* **-toes.** **1.** the power to prevent legislation or action proposed by others: *the presidential veto.* **2.** the exercise of this power. ~*vb.* **-toing, -toed.** (*tr.*) **3.** to refuse consent to (a proposal, esp. a government bill). **4.** to prohibit, ban, or forbid: *her parents vetoed her trip.* [C17: < L: I forbid, < *vetāre* to forbid] —ˈ**vetoer** *n.*

vex (vɛks) *vb.* (*tr.*) **1.** to anger or annoy. **2.** to confuse; worry. **3.** *Arch.* to agitate. [C15: < OF *vexer,* < L *vexāre* to jolt (in carrying), < *vehere* to convey] —ˈ**vexer** *n.* —ˈ**vexing** *adj.*

vexation (vɛkˈseɪʃən) *n.* **1.** the act of vexing or the state of being vexed. **2.** something that vexes.

vexatious (vɛkˈseɪʃəs) *adj.* **1.** vexing or tending to vex. **2.** vexed. **3.** *Law.* (of a legal action or proceeding) instituted without sufficient grounds, esp. so as to cause annoyance to the defendant. —**vexˈatiously** *adv.*

vexed (vɛkst) *adj.* **1.** annoyed, confused, or agitated. **2.** much debated (esp. in **a vexed question**). —**vexedly** (ˈvɛksɪdlɪ) *adv.*

vexillology (ˌvɛksɪˈlɒlədʒɪ) *n.* the study and collection of information about flags. [C20: < L *vexillum* flag + -LOGY] —ˌ**vexilˈlologist** *n.*

vexillum (vɛkˈsɪləm) *n., pl.* **-la** (-lə). **1.** *Ornithol.* the vane of a feather. **2.** Also called: **standard.** *Bot.* the largest petal of a papilionaceous flower. [C18: < L: banner, ?< *vēlum* sail] —ˈ**vexillate** *adj.*

VF *abbrev. for* video frequency.

vg *abbrev. for* very good.

VG *abbrev. for* Vicar General.

VHF *or* **vhf** *Radio. abbrev. for* very high frequency.

VI *abbrev. for:* **1.** Vancouver Island. **2.** Virgin Islands.

v.i. *abbrev. for* vide infra.

via (ˈvaɪə) *prep.* by way of; by means of; through: *to London via Paris.* [C18: < L *viā*, < *via* way]

viable (ˈvaɪəbᵊl) *adj.* **1.** capable of becoming actual, etc.: *a viable proposition.* **2.** (of seeds, eggs, etc.) capable of normal growth and development. **3.** (of a fetus) having reached a stage of development at which further development can occur independently of the mother. [C19: < F, < *vie* life, < L *vīta*] —ˌ**viaˈbility** *n.*

Via Dolorosa (ˈviːə ˌdɒləˈrəʊsə) *n.* the route followed by Christ from the place of his condemnation to Calvary for his crucifixion. [L, lit.: sorrowful road]

viaduct (ˈvaɪəˌdʌkt) *n.* a bridge, esp. for carrying a road or railway across a valley, etc. [C19: < L *via* way + *dūcere* to bring, on the model of *aqueduct*]

vial (ˈvaɪəl) *n.* a less common variant of **phial.** [C14 *fiole*, < OF, ult. < Gk *phialē*; see PHIAL]

via media *Latin.* (ˈvaɪə ˈmiːdɪə) *n.* a compromise between two extremes.

viand (ˈviːənd) *n.* **1.** a type of food, esp. a delicacy. **2.** (*pl.*) provisions. [C14: < OF, ult. < L *vīvenda* things to be lived on, < *vīvere* to live]

viaticum (vaɪˈætɪkəm) *n., pl.* **-ca** (-kə) *or* **-cums. 1.** *Christianity.* Holy Communion as administered to a person dying or in danger of death. **2.** *Rare.* provisions or a travel allowance for a journey. [C16: < L, < *viāticus* belonging to a journey, < *via* way]

vibes (vaɪbz) *pl. n.* **1.** *Inf.* short for **vibraphone. 2.** *Sl.* short for **vibrations.**

vibraculum (vaɪˈbrækjʊləm) *n., pl.* **-la** (-lə). *Zool.* any of the specialized bristle-like polyps in certain bryozoans, the actions of which prevent parasites from settling on the colony. [C19: < NL, < L *vibrāre* to brandish]

vibrant (ˈvaɪbrənt) *adj.* **1.** characterized by or exhibiting vibration. **2.** giving an impression of vigour and activity. **3.** caused by vibration; resonant. [C16: < L *vibrāre* to agitate] —ˈ**vibrancy** *n.* —ˈ**vibrantly** *adv.*

vibraphone (ˈvaɪbrəˌfəʊn) *n.* a percussion instrument consisting of a set of metal bars placed over tubular metal resonators, which are made to vibrate electronically. —ˈ**vibraˌphonist** *n.*

vibrate (vaɪˈbreɪt) *vb.* **1.** to move or cause to move back and forth rapidly. **2.** (*intr.*) to oscillate. **3.** to resonate or cause to resonate. **4.** (*intr.*) to waver. **5.** *Physics.* to undergo or cause to undergo an oscillatory process, as of an alternating current. **6.** (*intr.*) *Rare.* to respond emotionally; thrill. [C17: < L *vibrāre*] —**vibratile** (ˈvaɪbrəˌtaɪl) *adj.* —**viˈbrating** *adj.* —**vibratory** (ˈvaɪbrətərɪ) *adj.*

vibration (vaɪˈbreɪʃən) *n.* **1.** the act or an instance of vibrating. **2.** *Physics.* **a.** a periodic motion about an equilibrium position, such as in the propagation of sound. **b.** a single cycle of such a motion. **3.** the process or state of vibrating or being vibrated. —**viˈbrational** *adj.*

vibrations (vaɪˈbreɪʃənz) *pl. n. Sl.* **1.** instinctive feelings supposedly influencing human communication. **2.** a characteristic atmosphere felt to be emanating from places or objects.

vibrato (vɪˈbrɑːtəʊ) *n., pl.* **-tos.** *Music.* **1.** a slight, rapid, and regular fluctuation in the pitch of a note produced on a stringed instrument by a shaking movement of the hand stopping the strings. **2.** an oscillatory effect produced in singing by fluctuation in breath pressure or pitch. [C19: < It., < L *vibrāre* to VIBRATE]

vibrator (vaɪˈbreɪtə) *n.* **a.** a device for producing a vibratory motion, such as one used in massage. **b.** such a device with a vibrating part or tip, used as a dildo.

vibrissa (vaɪˈbrɪsə) *n., pl.* **-sae** (-siː). (*usually pl.*) **1.** any of the bristle-like sensitive hairs on the face of many mammals; a whisker. **2.** any of the specialized bristle-like feathers around the beak in certain insectivorous birds. [C17: < L, prob. < *vibrāre* to shake] —**viˈbrissal** *adj.*

viburnum (vaɪˈbɜːnəm) *n.* **1.** any of various temperate and subtropical shrubs or trees having small white flowers and berry-like red or black fruits. **2.** the dried bark of several species of this tree, sometimes used in medicine. [C18: < L: wayfaring tree]

Vic. *Austral. abbrev. for* Victoria (the state).

vicar (ˈvɪkə) *n.* **1.** *Church of England.* **a.** (in Britain) a clergyman appointed to act as priest of a parish from which, formerly, he did not receive tithes but a stipend. **b.** a clergyman who acts as assistant to or substitute for the rector of a parish at Communion. **2.** *R.C. Church.* a bishop or priest representing the pope and exercising a limited jurisdiction. **3.** Also called: **lay vicar, vicar choral.** *Church of England.* a member of a cathedral choir appointed to sing certain parts of the services. [C13: < OF, < L *vicārius* (n.) a deputy, < *vicārius* (adj.) VICARIOUS] —**vicarial** (vɪˈkɛərɪəl) *adj.* —**viˈcariate** *n.* —ˈ**vicarly** *adj.*

vicarage (ˈvɪkərɪdʒ) *n.* the residence or benefice of a vicar.

vicar apostolic *n. R.C. Church.* a titular bishop having jurisdiction in missionary countries.

vicar general *n., pl.* **vicars general.** an official, usually a layman, appointed to assist the bishop of a diocese in discharging his administrative or judicial duties.

vicarious (vɪˈkɛərɪəs, vaɪ-) *adj.* **1.** undergone at second hand through sympathetic participation in another's experiences. **2.** undergone or done as the substitute for another: *vicarious punishment.* **3.** delegated: *vicarious authority.* **4.** taking the place of another. [C17: < L *vicārius* substituted, < *vicis* interchange] —**viˈcariously** *adv.* —**viˈcariousness** *n.*

Vicar of Christ *n. R.C. Church.* the pope when regarded as Christ's earthly representative.

vice[1] (vaɪs) *n.* **1.** an immoral, wicked, or evil habit, action, or trait. **2.** frequent indulgence in immoral or degrading practices. **3.** a specific form of pernicious conduct, esp. prostitution or sexual perversion. **4.** an imperfection in character, conduct, etc.: *smoking is his only vice.* **5.** a bad trick or disposition, as of horses, dogs, etc. [C13: via OF < L *vitium* a defect]

vice[2] *or U.S.* (*often*) **vise** (vaɪs) *n.* **1.** an appliance for holding an object while work is done on it, usually having a pair of jaws. ~*vb.* **2.** (*tr.*) to grip (something) with or as if with a vice. [C15: < OF *vis* a screw, < L *vītis* vine, plant with spiralling tendrils (hence the later meaning)]

vice[3] (vaɪs) *adj.* **1. a.** (*prenominal*) serving in the place of. **b.** (*in combination*): *viceroy.* ~*n.* **2.** *Inf.* a person who serves as a deputy to another. [C18: < L, < *vicis* interchange]

vice[4] (ˈvaɪsɪ) *prep.* instead of; as a substitute for. [C16: < L, ablative of *vicis* change]

vice admiral *n.* a commissioned officer of flag rank in certain navies, junior to an admiral and senior to a rear admiral.

vice-chairman *n., pl.* **-men.** a person who deputizes for a chairman and serves in his place during his absence. —ˌ**vice-ˈchairmanship** *n.*

vice chancellor *n.* **1.** the chief executive or administrator at some British universities. **2.** (in the U.S.) a judge in courts of equity subordinate to the chancellor. **3.** (formerly in England) a senior judge of the court of chancery who acted as assistant to the Lord Chancellor. **4.** a person serving as the deputy of a chancellor. —ˌ**vice-ˈchancellorship** *n.*

vicegerent (ˌvaɪsˈdʒɛrənt) *n.* **1.** a person appointed to exercise all or some of the authority of another. **2.** *R.C. Church.* the pope or any other representative of God or Christ on earth, such as a bishop. ~*adj.* **3.** invested with or characterized by delegated authority. [C16: < NL, < VICE[3] + L *gerere* to manage] —ˌ**viceˈgerency** *n.*

vicennial (vɪˈsɛnɪəl) *adj.* **1.** occurring every 20 years. **2.** lasting for a period of 20 years. [C18: < LL *vīcennium* period of twenty years, < L *vīciēs* twenty times + *-ennium*, < *annus* year]

vice president *n.* an officer ranking immediately below a president and serving as his deputy. A vice president takes the president's place during his absence or incapacity, after his death, and in certain other circumstances. Abbrev.: **VP.** —ˌ**vice-**ˈ**presidency** *n.*

viceregal (ˌvaɪsˈriːgᵊl) *adj.* **1.** of or relating to a viceroy. **2.** *Chiefly Austral. & N.Z.* of or relating to a governor or governor general. —ˌ**vice**ˈ**regally** *adv.*

vicereine (ˌvaɪsˈreɪn) *n.* **1.** the wife of a viceroy. **2.** a female viceroy. [C19: < F, < VICE[3] + *reine* queen, < L *rēgīna*]

viceroy (ˈvaɪsrɔɪ) *n.* a governor of a colony, country, or province who acts for and rules in the name of his sovereign or government. Related adj.: **viceregal.** [C16: < F, < VICE[3] + *roy* king, < L *rex*] —ˈ**viceroyship** *or* ˌ**vice**ˈ**royalty** *n.*

vice squad *n.* a police division to which is assigned the enforcement of gaming and prostitution laws.

vice versa (ˈvaɪsɪ ˈvɜːsə) *adv.* the other way around. [C17: < L: relations being reversed, < *vicis* change + *vertere* to turn]

vichyssoise (*French* viʃiswaz) *n.* a thick soup made from leeks, potatoes, chicken stock, and cream, usually served chilled. [F, < (*crème*) *vichyssoise* (*glacée*) (ice-cold cream) from Vichy]

vichy water (ˈviːʃiː) *n.* **1.** (*sometimes cap.*) a natural mineral water from springs at Vichy in France, reputed to be beneficial to the health. **2.** any sparkling mineral water resembling this.

vicinage (ˈvɪsənɪdʒ) *n. Now rare.* **1.** the residents of a particular neighbourhood. **2.** a less common word for **vicinity.** [C14: < OF *vicenage*, < *vicin* neighbouring, < L *vīcīnus*]

vicinal (ˈvɪsɪnᵊl) *adj.* **1.** neighbouring. **2.** (esp. of roads) of or relating to a locality or neighbourhood. [C17: < L *vīcīnālis* nearby, < *vīcīnus*, < *vīcus* a neighbourhood]

vicinity (vɪˈsɪnɪtɪ) *n., pl.* **-ties.** **1.** a surrounding area; neighbourhood. **2.** the fact or condition of being close in space or relationship. [C16: < L, < *vīcīnus* neighbouring, < *vīcus* village]

vicious (ˈvɪʃəs) *adj.* **1.** wicked or cruel: *a vicious thug.* **2.** characterized by violence or ferocity: *a vicious blow.* **3.** *Inf.* unpleasantly severe; harsh: *a vicious wind.* **4.** characterized by malice: *vicious lies.* **5.** (esp. of dogs, horses, etc.) ferocious or hostile. **6.** characterized by or leading to vice. **7.** invalidated by defects; unsound: *a vicious inference.* [C14: < OF, < L *vitiōsus* full of faults, < *vitium* defect] —ˈ**viciously** *adv.* —ˈ**viciousness** *n.*

vicious circle *n.* **1.** a situation in which an attempt to resolve one problem creates new problems that lead back to the original situation. **2.** *Logic.* **a.** a form of reasoning in which a conclusion is inferred from premises the truth of which cannot be established independently of that conclusion. **b.** an explanation given in terms that cannot be understood independently of that which was to be explained.

vicissitude (vɪˈsɪsɪˌtjuːd) *n.* **1.** variation or mutability in nature or life, esp. successive alternation from one condition or thing to another. **2.** a variation in circumstance, fortune, etc. [C16: < L *vicissitūdō*, < *vicis* change, alternation] —**vi**ˌ**cissi**ˈ**tudinous** *adj.*

victim (ˈvɪktɪm) *n.* **1.** a person or thing that suffers harm, death, etc.: *victims of tyranny.* **2.** a person who is tricked or swindled. **3.** a living person or animal sacrificed in a religious rite. [C15: < L *victima*]

victimize *or* **-mise** (ˈvɪktɪˌmaɪz) *vb.* (*tr.*) **1.** to punish or discriminate against selectively or unfairly. **2.** to make a victim of. —ˌ**victimi**ˈ**zation** *or* **-mi**ˈ**sation** *n.* —ˈ**victim**ˌ**izer** *or* **-m**ˌ**iser** *n.*

victor (ˈvɪktə) *n.* **1. a.** a person, nation, etc., that has defeated an adversary in war, etc. **b.** (*as modifier*): *the victor army.* **2.** the winner of any contest, conflict, or struggle. [C14: < L, < *vincere* to conquer]

victoria (vɪkˈtɔːrɪə) *n.* **1.** a light four-wheeled horse-drawn carriage with a folding hood, two passenger seats, and a seat in front for the driver. **2.** Also called: **victoria plum.** *Brit.* a large sweet variety of plum, red and yellow in colour. [C19: both after Queen *Victoria*]

Victoria Cross *n.* the highest decoration for gallantry in the face of the enemy awarded to the British and Commonwealth armed forces: instituted in 1856 by Queen Victoria.

Victoria Day *n.* the Monday preceding May 24: observed in Canada as a national holiday in commemoration of the birthday of Queen Victoria.

Victorian (vɪkˈtɔːrɪən) *adj.* **1.** of or characteristic of Victoria (1819–1901), queen of the United Kingdom, or the period of her reign. **2.** exhibiting the characteristics popularly attributed to the Victorians, esp. prudery, bigotry, or hypocrisy. Cf. **Victorian values.** **3.** of or relating to Victoria (the state in Australia or any of the cities). ~*n.* **4.** a person who lived during the reign of Queen Victoria. **5.** an inhabitant of Victoria (the state or any of the cities). —**Vic**ˈ**torian**ˌ**ism** *n.*

Victoriana (vɪkˌtɔːrɪˈɑːnə) *n.* objects, ornaments, etc., of the Victorian period.

Victorian values *pl. n.* the qualities of enterprise and initiative, the importance of the family, and the development of charitable voluntary work that are considered to characterize the Victorian period. Cf. **Victorian** (sense 2).

victorious (vɪkˈtɔːrɪəs) *adj.* **1.** having defeated an adversary: *the victorious nations.* **2.** of, indicative of, or characterized by victory: *a victorious conclusion.* —**vic**ˈ**toriously** *adv.*

victory (ˈvɪktərɪ) *n., pl.* **-ries.** **1.** final and complete superiority in a war. **2.** a successful military engagement. **3.** a success attained in a contest or struggle or over an opponent, obstacle, or problem. **4.** the act of triumphing or state of having triumphed. [C14: < OF *victorie*, < L *victōria*, < *vincere* to subdue]

victory roll *n.* a rolling aircraft manoeuvre made by a pilot to announce or celebrate the shooting down of an enemy plane.

victual (ˈvɪtᵊl) *vb.* **-ualling, -ualled** *or U.S.* **-ualing, -ualed.** to supply with or obtain victuals. ~See also **victuals.** [C14: < OF *vitaille*, < LL *victuālia* provisions, < L, < *victus* sustenance, < *vīvere* to live] —ˈ**victual-less** *adj.*

victualler (ˈvɪtələ) *n.* **1.** a supplier of victuals, as to an army. **2.** *Brit.* a licensed purveyor of spirits. **3.** a supply ship, esp. one carrying foodstuffs.

victuals (ˈvɪtᵊlz) *pl. n.* (*sometimes sing.*) food or provisions.

vicuña (vɪˈkuːnjə) *or* **vicuna** (vɪˈkjuːnə, -ˈkuːnjə) *n.* **1.** a tawny-coloured cud-chewing Andean mammal similar to the llama. **2.** the fine light wool obtained from this animal. [C17: < Sp., < Quechuan *wikúña*]

vide (ˈvaɪdɪ) (used to direct a reader to a specified place in a text, another book, etc.) refer to, see (often in **vide ante** (see before), **vide infra** (see below), **vide supra** (see above), etc.) Abbrev.: **v., vid.** [C16: < L]

videlicet (vɪˈdiːlɪˌsɛt) *adv.* namely: used to specify items, etc. Abbrev.: **viz.** [C15: < L]

video (ˈvɪdɪəʊ) *adj.* **1.** relating to or employed in the transmission or reception of a televised image. **2.** of, concerned with, or operating at video frequencies. ~*n., pl.* **-os.** **3.** the visual elements of a television broadcast. **4.** a film recorded on a video cassette. **5.** short for **video cassette, video cassette recorder.** **6.** *U.S.* an informal name for **television.** ~*vb.* **videoing, videoed.** **7.** to record (a television programme, etc.) on a video cassette recorder. [C20: < L *vidēre* to see, on the model of AUDIO]

video cassette *n.* a cassette containing video tape.

video cassette recorder *n.* a tape recorder for vision and sound signals using magnetic tape in closed plastic cassettes: used for recording and playing back television programmes and films. Often shortened to **video** or **video recorder.**

videodisc (ˈvɪdɪəʊˌdɪsk) *n.* a transparent plastic disc with a metal coating, carrying recorded video material for display on a television screen.

video frequency *n.* the frequency of a signal conveying the image and synchronizing pulses in a television broadcasting system. It lies in the range from about 50 hertz to 8 megahertz.

video game *n.* any of various games that can be played by using an electronic control to move points of light or graphical symbols on the screen of a visual display unit.

video jockey *n.* a person who introduces and plays videos, esp. of pop songs, on a television programme.

video nasty *n.* a film, usually specially made for video, that is explicitly horrific and pornographic.

videophone (ˈvɪdɪəˌfəʊn) *n.* a telephonic device in which there is both verbal and visual communication between parties.

video recorder *n.* short for **video cassette recorder.**

video tape *n.* **1.** magnetic tape used mainly for recording the video-frequency signals of a television programme or film for subsequent transmission. *~vb.* **video-tape. 2.** to record (a programme, etc.) on video tape.

video tape recorder *n.* a tape recorder for visual signals and sometimes accompanying sound, using magnetic tape on open spools: used in television broadcasting.

videotex (ˈvɪdɪəʊˌtɛks) *n.* another name for **viewdata.**

videotext (ˈvɪdɪəʊˌtɛkst) *n.* a means of providing a written or graphical representation of computerized information on a television screen.

vidicon (ˈvɪdɪˌkɒn) *n.* a small television camera tube, used in closed-circuit television and outside broadcasts, in which incident light forms an electric charge pattern on a photoconductive surface. [C20: < VID(EO) + ICON(OSCOPE)]

vie (vaɪ) *vb.* **vying, vied.** (*intr.*; foll. by *with* or *for*) to contend for superiority or victory (with) or strive in competition (for). [C15: prob. < OF *envier* to challenge, < L *invītāre* to INVITE] —ˈ**vier** *n.* —ˈ**vying** *adj., n.*

Viennese (ˌvɪəˈniːz) *adj.* **1.** of or relating to Vienna, capital of Austria. *~n., pl.* **-nese. 2.** a native or inhabitant of Vienna.

vies (fɪs) *adj. S. African sl.* angry. [< Afrik., < Du. *vies* nasty, loathsome]

Vietnamese (ˌvjɛtnəˈmiːz) *adj.* **1.** of or characteristic of Vietnam, in SE Asia, its people, or their language. *~n.* **2.** (*pl.* **-ese**) a native or inhabitant of Vietnam. **3.** the language of Vietnam.

vieux jeu *French.* (vjø ʒø) *adj.* old-fashioned. [lit.: old game]

view (vjuː) *n.* **1.** the act of seeing or observing. **2.** vision or sight, esp. range of vision: *the church is out of view.* **3.** a scene, esp. of a fine tract of countryside: *the view from the top was superb.* **4.** a pictorial representation of a scene, such as a photograph. **5.** (*sometimes pl.*) opinion: *my own view on the matter differs from yours.* **6.** (foll. by *to*) a desired end or intention: *he has a view to securing further qualifications.* **7.** a general survey of a topic, subject, etc. **8.** visual aspect or appearance: *they look the same in outward view.* **9.** a sight of a hunted animal before or during the chase. **10. in view of.** taking into consideration. **11. on view.** exhibited to the public gaze. **12. take a dim** *or* **poor view of.** to regard (something) with disfavour. **13. with a view to. a.** with the intention of. **b.** in anticipation or hope of. *~vb.* **14.** (*tr.*) to look at. **15.** (*tr.*) to consider in a specified manner: *they view the growth of Communism with horror.* **16.** (*tr.*) to examine or inspect carefully: *to view the accounts.* **17.** (*tr.*) to contemplate: *to view the difficulties.* **18.** to watch (television). **19.** (*tr.*) to sight (a hunted animal) before or during the chase. [C15: < OF, < *veoir* to see, < L *vidēre*] —ˈ**viewable** *adj.*

viewdata (ˈvjuːˌdeɪtə) *n.* an interactive videotext service in which the consumer is linked to a computer by telephone and is thus able to select the information required. Cf. **teletext.**

viewer (ˈvjuːə) *n.* **1.** a person who views something, esp. television. **2.** any optical device by means of which something is viewed, esp. one used for viewing photographic transparencies.

viewfinder (ˈvjuːˌfaɪndə) *n.* a device on a camera, consisting of a lens system, enabling the user to see what will be included in his photograph.

view halloo *interj.* a huntsman's cry uttered when the quarry is seen breaking cover or shortly afterwards.

viewing (ˈvjuːɪŋ) *n.* **1.** the act of watching television. **2.** television programmes collectively: *late-night viewing.*

viewless (ˈvjuːlɪs) *adj.* **1.** (of windows, etc.) not affording a view. **2.** having no opinions. **3.** *Poetic.* invisible.

viewpoint (ˈvjuːˌpɔɪnt) *n.* **1.** the mental attitude that determines a person's judgments. **2.** a place from which something can be viewed.

vigesimal (vaɪˈdʒɛsɪməl) *adj.* **1.** relating to or based on the number 20. **2.** taking place or proceeding in intervals of 20. **3.** twentieth. [C17: < L *vīgēsimus*, var. (infl. by *vīgintī* twenty) of *vīcēsimus* twentieth]

vigil (ˈvɪdʒɪl) *n.* **1.** a purposeful watch maintained, esp. at night, to guard, observe, pray, etc. **2.** the period of such a watch. **3.** *R.C. Church, Church of England.* the eve of certain major festivals, formerly observed as a night spent in prayer. [C13: < OF, < Med. L *vigilia* watch preceding a religious festival, < L, < *vigil* alert, < *vigēre* to be lively]

vigilance (ˈvɪdʒɪləns) *n.* **1.** the fact, quality, or condition of being vigilant. **2.** the abnormal state or condition of being unable to sleep.

vigilance committee *n.* (in the U.S.) a self-appointed body of citizens organized to maintain order, etc., where an efficient system of courts does not exist.

vigilant (ˈvɪdʒɪlənt) *adj.* keenly alert to or heedful of trouble or danger. [C15: < L *vigilāns*, < *vigilāre* to be watchful; see VIGIL] —ˈ**vigilantly** *adv.*

vigilante (ˌvɪdʒɪˈlæntɪ) *n.* **1.** a self-appointed protector of public order. **2.** *U.S.* a member of a vigilance committee. [C19: < Sp., < L *vigilāre* to keep watch]

vigilantism (ˌvɪdʒɪˈlæntɪzəm) *n.* *U.S.* the methods, conduct, attitudes, etc., associated with vigilantes, esp. militancy or bigotry.

vignette (vɪˈnjɛt) *n.* **1.** a small illustration placed at the beginning or end of a book or chapter. **2.** a short graceful literary essay or sketch. **3.** a photograph, drawing, etc., with edges that are shaded off. **4.** any small endearing scene, view, etc. *~vb.* (*tr.*) **5.** to finish (a photograph, etc.) with a fading border in the form of a vignette. **6.** to portray in or as in a vignette. [C18: < F, lit.: little vine; with reference to the vine motif frequently used in embellishments to a text] —**viˈgnettist** *n.*

vigoro (ˈvɪgəˌrəʊ) *n.* *Austral.* a ball game combining elements of cricket and baseball. [C20: < VIGOUR]

vigorous (ˈvɪgərəs) *adj.* **1.** endowed with bodily or mental strength or vitality. **2.** displaying, characterized by, or performed with vigour: *vigorous growth.* —ˈ**vigorously** *adv.*

vigour *or U.S.* **vigor** (ˈvɪgə) *n.* **1.** exuberant and resilient strength of body or mind. **2.** substantial effective energy or force: *the vigour of the tempest.* **3.** forcefulness: *I was surprised by the vigour of her complaints.* **4.** the capacity for survival or strong healthy growth in a plant or animal. **5.** the most active period or stage of life, manhood, etc. [C14: < OF, < L *vigor*, < *vigēre* to be lively]

Viking (ˈvaɪkɪŋ) *n.* (*sometimes not cap.*) **1.** Also called: **Norseman, Northman.** any of the Danes, Norwegians, and Swedes who raided by sea most of N and W Europe from the 8th to the 11th centuries. **2.** (*modifier*) of, relating to, or characteristic of a Viking or Vikings: *a Viking ship.* [C19: < ON *vīkingr*, prob. < *vīk* creek, sea inlet + *-ingr* (see -ING[3])]

vile (vaɪl) *adj.* **1.** abominably wicked; shameful or evil. **2.** morally despicable; ignoble: *vile accusations.* **3.** disgusting to the senses or emotions; foul:

a vile smell. **4.** tending to humiliate or degrade: *only slaves would perform such vile tasks.* **5.** unpleasant or bad: *vile weather.* [C13: < OF *vil,* < L *vīlis* cheap] —**'vilely** *adv.* —**'vileness** *n.*

vilify ('vɪlɪˌfaɪ) *vb.* **-fying, -fied.** (*tr.*) to revile with abusive language; malign. [C15: < LL, < L *vīlis* worthless + *facere* to make] —**vilification** (ˌvɪlɪfɪ'keɪʃən) *n.* —**'vili,fier** *n.*

vilipend ('vɪlɪˌpɛnd) *vb.* (*tr.*) *Rare.* **1.** to treat or regard with contempt. **2.** to speak slanderously of. [C15: < LL, < L *vīlis* worthless + *pendere* to esteem] —**'vili,pender** *n.*

villa ('vɪlə) *n.* **1.** (in ancient Rome) a country house, usually consisting of farm buildings and residential quarters around a courtyard. **2.** a large country residence. **3.** *Brit.* a detached or semidetached suburban house. [C17: via It. < L]

village ('vɪlɪdʒ) *n.* **1.** a small group of houses in a country area, larger than a hamlet. **2.** the inhabitants of such a community collectively. **3.** an incorporated municipality smaller than a town in various parts of the U.S. and Canada. **4.** (*modifier*) of or characteristic of a village: *a village green.* [C15: < OF, < *ville* farm, < L: VILLA] —**'villager** *n.*

villain ('vɪlən) *n.* **1.** a wicked or malevolent person. **2.** (in a novel, play, etc.) the main evil character and antagonist to the hero. **3.** *Often jocular.* a rogue. **4.** *Obs.* an uncouth person; boor. [C14: < OF *vilein* serf, < LL *villānus* worker on a country estate, < L: VILLA] —**'villainess** *fem. n.*

villainous ('vɪlənəs) *adj.* **1.** of, like, or appropriate to a villain. **2.** very bad or disagreeable: *a villainous climate.* —**'villainously** *adv.* —**'villainousness** *n.*

villainy ('vɪlənɪ) *n., pl.* **-lainies. 1.** vicious behaviour or action. **2.** an evil or criminal act or deed. **3.** the fact or condition of being villainous.

villanelle (ˌvɪlə'nɛl) *n.* a verse form of French origin consisting of 19 lines arranged in five tercets and a quatrain. [C16: < F, < It. *villanella,* < *villano* rustic]

-ville *n. and adj. combining form. Sl., chiefly U.S.* (denoting) a place, condition, or quality with a character as specified: *dragsville; squaresville.*

villein ('vɪlən) *n.* (in medieval Europe) a peasant personally bound to his lord, to whom he paid dues and services in return for his land. [C14: < OF *vilein* serf; see VILLAIN] —**'villeinage** *n.*

villiform ('vɪlɪˌfɔːm) *adj.* having the form of a villus or a series of villi. [C19: < NL *villiformis,* < L *villus* shaggy hair + -FORM]

villus ('vɪləs) *n., pl.* **villi** ('vɪlaɪ). (*usually pl.*) **1.** *Zool., anat.* any of the numerous finger-like projections of the mucous membrane lining the small intestine of many vertebrates. **2.** any similar membranous process. **3.** *Bot.* any of various hairlike outgrowths. [C18: < L: shaggy hair] —**villosity** (vɪ'lɒsɪtɪ) *n.* —**'villous** *adj.*

vim (vɪm) *n. Sl.* exuberant vigour and energy. [C19: < L, < *vīs;* rel. to Gk *is* strength]

vimineous (vɪ'mɪnɪəs) *adj. Bot.* having, producing, or resembling long flexible shoots. [C17: < L *vīmineus* made of osiers, < *vīmen* flexible shoot]

vina ('viːnə) *n.* a stringed musical instrument, esp. of India, related to the sitar. [C18: < Hindi *bīnā,* < Sansk. *vīṇā*]

vinaceous (vaɪ'neɪʃəs) *adj.* **1.** of, relating to, or containing wine. **2.** having a colour suggestive of red wine. [C17: < LL *vīnāceus,* < L *vīnum* wine]

vinaigrette (ˌvɪneɪ'grɛt) *n.* **1.** Also called: **vinegarette.** a small decorative bottle or box with a perforated top, used for holding smelling salts, etc. **2.** Also called: **vinaigrette sauce.** a salad dressing made from oil and vinegar with seasonings; French dressing. [C17: < F, < *vinaigre* VINEGAR]

Vincent's angina *or* **disease** ('vɪnsənts) *n.* an ulcerative bacterial infection of the mouth, esp. involving the throat and tonsils. [C20: after J. H. *Vincent* (died 1950), F bacteriologist]

vincible ('vɪnsɪbᵊl) *adj. Rare.* capable of being defeated or overcome. [C16: < L *vincibilis,* < *vincere* to conquer] —ˌ**vinci'bility** *n.*

vincristine (vɪn'krɪstiːn) *n.* an alkaloid used to treat leukaemia, derived from the tropical shrub Madagascar periwinkle. [C20: < NL *Vinca* genus name of the plant + L *crista* crest + -INE[2]]

vinculum ('vɪŋkjʊləm) *n., pl.* **-la** (-lə). **1.** a horizontal line drawn above a group of mathematical terms, used as an alternative to parentheses in mathematical expressions, as in $x + \overline{y - z}$ which is equivalent to $x + (y - z)$. **2.** *Anat.* any bandlike structure, esp. one uniting two or more parts. [C17: < L: bond, < *vincīre* to bind]

vindicable ('vɪndɪkəbᵊl) *adj.* capable of being vindicated; justifiable. —ˌ**vindica'bility** *n.*

vindicate ('vɪndɪˌkeɪt) *vb.* (*tr.*) **1.** to clear from guilt, blame, etc., as by evidence or argument. **2.** to provide justification for: *his promotion vindicated his unconventional attitude.* **3.** to uphold or defend (a cause, etc.): *to vindicate a claim.* [C17: < L *vindicāre,* < *vindex* claimant] —**'vindi,cator** *n.* —**'vindi,catory** *adj.*

vindication (ˌvɪndɪ'keɪʃən) *n.* **1.** the act of vindicating or the condition of being vindicated. **2.** a fact, evidence, etc., that serves to vindicate a claim.

vindictive (vɪn'dɪktɪv) *adj.* **1.** disposed to seek vengeance. **2.** characterized by spite or rancour. **3.** *English law.* (of damages) in excess of the compensation due to the plaintiff and imposed in punishment of the defendant. [C17: < L *vindicta* revenge, < *vindicāre* to VINDICATE] —**vin'dictively** *adv.* —**vin'dictiveness** *n.*

vin du pays *French.* (vɛ̃ du pei) *n., pl.* ***vins du pays.*** local wine.

vine (vaɪn) *n.* **1.** any of various plants, esp. the grapevine, having long flexible stems that creep along the ground or climb by clinging to a support by means of tendrils, leafstalks, etc. **2.** the stem of such a plant. [C13: < OF, < L *vīnea* vineyard, < *vīnum* wine] —**'viny** *adj.*

vinedresser ('vaɪnˌdrɛsə) *n.* a person who prunes, tends, or cultivates grapevines.

vinegar ('vɪnɪgə) *n.* **1.** a sour-tasting liquid consisting of impure dilute acetic acid, made by fermentation of beer, wine, or cider. It is used as a condiment or preservative. **2.** sourness or peevishness of temper, speech, etc. [C13: < OF, < *vin* WINE + *aigre* sour, < L *acer*] —**'vinegarish** *adj.* —**'vinegary** *adj.*

vinery ('vaɪnərɪ) *n., pl.* **-eries. 1.** a hothouse for growing grapes. **2.** another name for a **vineyard. 3.** vines collectively.

vineyard ('vɪnjəd) *n.* a plantation of grapevines, esp. where wine grapes are produced. [OE *wīngeard;* see VINE, YARD[2]]

vingt-et-un *French.* (vɛ̃teœ̃) *n.* another name for **pontoon**[2]. [lit.: twenty-one]

vini- *or before a vowel* **vin-** *combining form.* indicating wine: *viniculture.* [< L *vīnum*]

viniculture ('vɪnɪˌkʌltʃə) *n.* the process or business of growing grapes and making wine. —ˌ**vini'cultural** *adj.* —ˌ**vini'culturist** *n.*

viniferous (vɪ'nɪfərəs) *adj.* wine-producing.

vino ('viːnəʊ) *n., pl.* **-nos.** an informal word for **wine.** [jocular use of It. or Sp. *vino*]

vin ordinaire *French.* (vɛ̃n ɔrdinɛr) *n., pl.* ***vins ordinaires*** (vɛ̃z ɔrdinɛr). cheap table wine, esp. French.

vinosity (vɪ'nɒsɪtɪ) *n.* the distinctive and essential quality and flavour of wine. [C17: < LL *vīnōsitas,* < L *vīnōsus* VINOUS]

vinous ('vaɪnəs) *adj.* **1.** of or characteristic of wine. **2.** indulging in or indicative of indulgence in wine. [C17: < L, < *vīnum* WINE]

vintage ('vɪntɪdʒ) *n.* **1.** the wine obtained from a harvest of grapes, esp. in an outstandingly good year. **2.** the harvest from which such a wine is obtained. **3. a.** the harvesting of wine grapes. **b.** the season of harvesting these grapes or for making wine. **4.** a time of origin: *a car of Edwardian vintage.* **5.** *Inf.* a group of people or objects of the same period: *a fashion of last season's vintage.* ~*adj.* **6.** (of wine) of an outstandingly good year. **7.** representative of the best and most typical: *vintage Shakespeare.* **8.** of lasting interest and importance; classic: *vintage films.* **9.** old-fashioned; dated. [C15: < OF *vendage* (infl. by *vintener* VINTNER), < L *vindēmia*, < *vīnum* WINE, grape + *dēmere* to take away]

vintage car *n. Chiefly Brit.* an old car, esp. one constructed between 1919 and 1930.

vintager (ˈvɪntɪdʒə) *n.* a grape harvester.

vintner (ˈvɪntnə) *n.* a wine merchant. [C15: < OF *vinetier*, < Med. L, < L *vīnētum* vineyard]

vinyl (ˈvaɪnɪl) *n.* **1.** (*modifier*) of or containing the monovalent group of atoms CH_2CH^-: *vinyl chloride.* **2.** (*modifier*) of or made of a vinyl resin: *a vinyl raincoat.* **3.** any vinyl resin or plastic, esp. PVC. **4.** (collectively) conventional records made of vinyl as opposed to compact discs. [C19: < VINI- + -YL]

vinyl acetate *n.* a colourless volatile liquid unsaturated ester that polymerizes readily in light and is used for making polyvinyl acetate.

vinyl chloride *n.* a colourless flammable gaseous unsaturated compound made by the chlorination of ethylene and used as a refrigerant and in the manufacture of PVC.

vinyl resin *or* **polymer** *n.* any one of a class of thermoplastic materials, esp. PVC and polyvinyl acetate, made by polymerizing vinyl compounds.

viol (ˈvaɪəl) *n.* any of a family of stringed musical instruments that preceded the violin family, consisting of a fretted fingerboard, a body rather like that of a violin but having a flat back and six strings, played with a curved bow. [C15: < OF *viole*, < OProvençal *viola;* see VIOLA[1]]

viola[1] (vɪˈəʊlə) *n.* **1.** a bowed stringed instrument, the alto of the violin family; held beneath the chin when played. **2.** any of various instruments of the viol family, such as the viola da gamba. [C18: < It., prob. < OProvençal, <?]

viola[2] (ˈvaɪələ, vaɪˈəʊ-) *n.* any of various temperate perennial herbaceous plants, the flowers of which have showy irregular petals, white, yellow, blue, or mauve in colour. [C15: < L: violet]

viola clef (vɪˈəʊlə) *n.* another term for **alto clef.**

viola da gamba (vɪˈəʊlə də ˈgæmbə) *n.* the second largest and lowest member of the viol family. [C18: < It., lit.: viol for the leg]

viola d'amore (vɪˈəʊlə dæˈmɔːrɪ) *n.* an instrument of the viol family having no frets, seven strings, and a set of sympathetic strings. [C18: < It., lit.: viol of love]

violate (ˈvaɪəˌleɪt) *vb.* (*tr.*) **1.** to break, disregard, or infringe (a law, agreement, etc.). **2.** to rape or otherwise sexually assault. **3.** to disturb rudely or improperly. **4.** to treat irreverently or disrespectfully: *he violated a sanctuary.* [C15: < L *violāre* to do violence to, < *vīs* strength] —ˈ**violable** *adj.* —ˌ**vioˈlation** *n.* —ˈ**vioˌlator** *or* ˈ**vioˌlater** *n.*

violence (ˈvaɪələns) *n.* **1.** the exercise or an instance of physical force, usually effecting or intended to effect injuries, destruction, etc. **2.** powerful, untamed, or devastating force: *the violence of the sea.* **3.** great strength of feeling, as in language, etc. **4.** an unjust, unwarranted, or unlawful display of force. **5. do violence to. a.** to inflict harm upon: *they did violence to the prisoners.* **b.** to distort the sense or intention of: *the reporters did violence to my speech.* [C13: via OF < L *violentia* impetuosity, < *violentus* VIOLENT]

violent (ˈvaɪələnt) *adj.* **1.** marked or caused by great physical force or violence: *a violent stab.* **2.** (of a person) tending to the use of violence, esp. in order to injure or intimidate others. **3.** marked by intensity of any kind: *a violent clash of colours.* **4.** characterized by an undue use of force. **5.** caused by or displaying strong or undue mental or emotional force. [C14: < L *violentus*, prob. < *vīs* strength] —ˈ**violently** *adv.*

violent storm *n* a wind of force 11 on the Beaufort scale, reaching speeds of 64 to 72 mph.

violet (ˈvaɪəlɪt) *n.* **1.** any of various temperate perennial herbaceous plants of the genus *Viola*, such as the **sweet** (or **garden**) **violet**, having mauve or bluish flowers with irregular showy petals. **2.** any other plant of the genus *Viola*, such as the wild pansy. **3.** any of various similar but unrelated plants, such as the African violet. **4. a.** any of a group of colours that have a purplish-blue hue. They lie at one end of the visible spectrum. **b.** (*as adj.*): *a violet dress.* **5.** a dye or pigment of or producing these colours. **6.** violet clothing: *dressed in violet.* [C14: < OF *violete* a little violet, < L *viola* violet]

violin (ˌvaɪəˈlɪn) *n.* a bowed stringed instrument, the highest member of the violin family, consisting of a fingerboard, a hollow wooden body with waisted sides, and a sounding board connected to the back by means of a soundpost that also supports the bridge. It has two f-shaped sound holes cut in the belly. [C16: < It. *violino* a little viola, < VIOLA[1]]

violinist (ˌvaɪəˈlɪnɪst) *n.* a person who plays the violin.

violist (ˈvaɪəlɪst) *n.* a person who plays the viol.

violoncello (ˌvaɪələnˈtʃɛləʊ) *n., pl.* **-los.** the full name for **cello.** [C18: < It., < *violone* large viol + *-cello*, dim. suffix] —ˌ**violonˈcellist** *n.*

VIP *abbrev. for* very important person.

viper (ˈvaɪpə) *n.* **1.** any of a family of venomous Old World snakes having hollow fangs in the upper jaw that are used to inject venom. **2.** any of various other snakes, such as the horned viper. **3.** a malicious or treacherous person. [C16: < L *vīpera*, ? < *vīvus* living + *parere* to bear, referring to a tradition that the viper was viviparous]

viperous (ˈvaɪpərəs) *or* **viperish** *adj.* **1.** Also: **viperine** (ˈvaɪpəˌraɪn). of or resembling a viper. **2.** malicious.

viper's bugloss *n.* a Eurasian weed, having blue flowers and pink buds. Also called: (U.S.) **blueweed,** (Austral.) **Paterson's curse.**

virago (vɪˈrɑːgəʊ) *n., pl.* **-goes** *or* **-gos. 1.** a loud, violent, and ill-tempered woman. **2.** *Arch.* a strong or warlike woman. [OE, < L: a manlike maiden, < *vir* a man] —**viˈrago-ˌlike** *adj.*

viral (ˈvaɪrəl) *adj.* of or caused by a virus.

virelay (ˈvɪrɪˌleɪ) *n.* an old French verse form, rarely used in English, having stanzas of short lines with two rhymes throughout and two opening lines recurring at intervals. [C14: < OF *virelai*, prob. < *vireli* (associated with *lai* LAY[4]), word used as a refrain]

vireo (ˈvɪrɪəʊ) *n., pl.* **vireos.** any of a family of insectivorous American songbirds having an olive-grey back with pale underparts. [C19: < L: a bird, prob. a greenfinch; cf. *virēre* to be green]

vires (ˈvaɪriːz) *n.* the plural of ***vis.***

virescent (vɪˈrɛsᵊnt) *adj.* greenish or becoming green. [C19: < L *virescere*, < *virēre* to be green] —**viˈrescence** *n.*

virgate[1] (ˈvɜːgɪt, -geɪt) *adj.* long, straight, and thin; rod-shaped: *virgate stems.* [C19: < L *virgātus* made of twigs, < *virga* a rod]

virgate[2] (ˈvɜːgɪt, -geɪt) *n. Brit.* an obsolete measure of land area, usually taken as equivalent to 30 acres. [C17: < Med. L *virgāta* (*terrae*) a rod's measurement (of land), < L *virga* rod; translation of OE *gierd landes* a yard of land]

Virgilian *or* **Vergilian** (vɜːˈdʒɪlɪən) *adj.* of, relating to, or characteristic of Virgil (70–19 B.C.) Roman poet, or his style.

virgin (ˈvɜːdʒɪn) *n.* **1.** a person, esp. a woman, who has never had sexual intercourse. **2.** an unmarried woman who has taken a religious vow of chastity. **3.** any female animal that has never mated. **4.** a female insect that produces offspring by parthenogenesis. ~*adj.* (*usually prenominal*) **5.** of, suitable for, or characteristic of a virgin or virgins. **6.** pure and natural, uncorrupted or untouched: *virgin purity.* **7.** not yet cultivated, explored, exploited, etc., by man: *the virgin forests.* **8.** being the first or happening for the first time. **9.** (of a metal) made from an ore rather than from scrap. **10.** occurring naturally in a pure and uncombined form: *virgin silver.* [C13: < OF *virgine*, < L *virgō* virgin]

Virgin[1] (ˈvɜːdʒɪn) *n.* **1. the.** See **Virgin Mary. 2.** a statue or other artistic representation of the Virgin Mary.

Virgin[2] (ˈvɜːdʒɪn) *n.* **the.** the constellation Virgo, the sixth sign of the zodiac.

virginal[1] (ˈvɜːdʒɪnᵊl) *adj.* **1.** of, characterized by, or maintaining a state of virginity; chaste. **2.** extremely pure or fresh. [C15: < L *virginālis* maidenly, < *virgō* virgin] —ˈ**virginally** *adv.*

virginal[2] (ˈvɜːdʒɪnᵊl) *n.* (*often pl.*) a smaller version of the harpsichord, but oblong in shape, having one manual and no pedals. [C16: prob. < L *virginālis* VIRGINAL[1], ? because it was played largely by young ladies] —ˈ**virginalist** *n.*

Virgin Birth *n.* the doctrine that Jesus Christ was conceived solely by the direct intervention of the Holy Spirit so that Mary remained miraculously a virgin during and after his birth.

Virginia creeper (vəˈdʒɪnɪə) *n.* a woody vine of North America, having tendrils with adhesive tips, bluish-black berry-like fruits, and compound leaves that turn red in autumn: widely planted for ornament.

Virginia stock *n.* a Mediterranean plant cultivated for its white and pink flowers.

virginity (vəˈdʒɪnɪtɪ) *n.* **1.** the condition or fact of being a virgin. **2.** the condition of being untouched, unsullied, etc.

virginium (vəˈdʒɪnɪəm) *n. Chem.* a former name for **francium.**

Virgin Mary *n.* Mary, the mother of Christ. Also called: the **Virgin.**

virgin's-bower *n.* any of several American varieties of clematis.

virgin wool *n.* wool that is being processed or woven for the first time.

Virgo (ˈvɜːgəʊ) *n., Latin genitive* **Virginis** (ˈvɜːdʒɪnɪs). **1.** *Astron.* a large constellation on the celestial equator. **2.** *Astrol.* Also called: **the Virgin.** the sixth sign of the zodiac. The sun is in this sign between about Aug. 23 and Sept. 22. [C14: < L]

virgo intacta (ˈvɜːgəʊ ɪnˈtæktə) *n.* a girl or woman whose hymen is unbroken. [L, lit.: untouched virgin]

virgule (ˈvɜːgjuːl) *n. Printing.* another name for **solidus.** [C19: < F: comma, < L *virgula* dim. of *virga* rod]

viridescent (ˌvɪrɪˈdɛsᵊnt) *adj.* greenish or tending to become green. [C19: < LL *viridescere,* < L *viridis* green] —ˌ**viriˈdescence** *n.*

viridian (vɪˈrɪdɪən) *n.* a green pigment consisting of a hydrated form of chromic oxide. [C19: < L *viridis* green]

viridity (vɪˈrɪdɪtɪ) *n.* **1.** the quality or state of being green. **2.** innocence, youth, or freshness. [C15: < L *viriditās,* < *viridis* green]

virile (ˈvɪraɪl) *adj.* **1.** of or having the characteristics of an adult male. **2.** (of a male) possessing high sexual drive and capacity for sexual intercourse. **3.** of or capable of copulation or procreation. **4.** strong, forceful, or vigorous. [C15: < L *virīlis* manly, < *vir* a man; rel. to OE *wer* man] —**virility** (vɪˈrɪlɪtɪ) *n.*

virilism (ˈvɪrɪˌlɪzəm) *n. Med.* the abnormal development in a woman of male secondary sex characteristics.

virology (vaɪˈrɒlədʒɪ) *n.* the branch of medicine concerned with the study of viruses. —**virological** (ˌvaɪrəˈlɒdʒɪkᵊl) *adj.*

virtu *or* **vertu** (vɜːˈtuː) *n.* **1.** a taste or love for curios or works of fine art. **2.** such objects collectively. **3.** the quality of being appealing to a connoisseur (esp. in **articles of virtu; objects of virtu**). [C18: < It. *virtù;* see VIRTUE]

virtual (ˈvɜːtʃʊəl) *adj.* **1.** having the essence or effect but not the appearance or form of: *a virtual revolution.* **2.** *Physics.* being or involving a virtual image: *a virtual focus.* **3.** *Computers.* of or relating to virtual storage: *virtual memory.* [C14: < Med. L *virtuālis* effective, < L *virtūs* VIRTUE] —ˌ**virtuˈality** *n.*

virtual image *n.* an optical image formed by the apparent divergence of rays from a point, rather than their actual divergence from a point.

virtually (ˈvɜːtʃʊəlɪ) *adv.* in effect though not in fact; practically; nearly.

virtual storage *or* **memory** *n.* a computer system in which the size of the memory is increased by transferring sections of a program from a large capacity backing store, such as a disk, into the smaller core memory as they are required.

virtue (ˈvɜːtjuː) *n.* **1.** the quality or practice of moral excellence or righteousness. **2.** a particular moral excellence: *the virtue of tolerance.* **3.** any of the cardinal virtues (prudence, justice, fortitude, and temperance) or theological virtues (faith, hope, and charity). **4.** any admirable quality or trait. **5.** chastity, esp. in women. **6.** *Arch.* an effective, active, or inherent power. **7.** **by** *or* **in virtue of.** by reason of. **8.** **make a virtue of necessity.** to acquiesce in doing something unpleasant with a show of grace because one must do it in any case. [C13 *vertu,* < OF, < L *virtūs* manliness, courage]

virtuoso (ˌvɜːtjʊˈəʊzəʊ, -səʊ) *n., pl.* **-sos** *or* **-si** (-siː). **1.** a consummate master of musical technique and artistry. **2.** a person who has a masterly or dazzling skill or technique in any field of activity. **3.** a connoisseur or collector of art objects. **4.** (*modifier*) showing masterly skill or brilliance: *a virtuoso performance.* [C17: < It.: skilled, < LL *virtuōsus* good, virtuous] —**virtuosic** (ˌvɜːtjʊˈɒsɪk) *adj.* —ˌ**virtuˈosity** *n.*

virtuous (ˈvɜːtʃʊəs) *adj.* **1.** characterized by or possessing virtue or moral excellence. **2.** (of women) chaste or virginal. —ˈ**virtuously** *adv.*

virulent (ˈvɪrʊlənt) *adj.* **1. a.** (of a microorganism) extremely infective. **b.** (of a disease) having a violent effect. **2.** extremely poisonous, injurious, etc. **3.** extremely bitter, hostile, etc. [C14: < L *vīrulentus* full of poison, < *vīrus* poison] —ˈ**virulence** *or* ˈ**virulency** *n.* —ˈ**virulently** *adv.*

virus (ˈvaɪrəs) *n., pl.* **-ruses.** **1.** any of a group of submicroscopic entities consisting of a single nucleic acid surrounded by a protein coat and capable of replication only within the cells of animals and plants. **2.** *Inf.* a disease caused by a virus. **3.** any corrupting or infecting influence. [C16: < L: slime, poisonous liquid]

vis *Latin.* (vɪs) *n., pl.* ***vires.*** power, force, or strength.

visa (ˈviːzə) *n., pl.* **-sas.** **1.** an endorsement in a passport or similar document, signifying that the document is in order and permitting its bearer to travel into or through the country of the government issuing it. ~*vb.* **-saing, -saed.** **2.** (*tr.*) to enter a visa into (a passport). [C19: via F < L: things seen, < *vīsus,* p.p. of *vidēre* to see]

visage (ˈvɪzɪdʒ) *n. Chiefly literary.* **1.** face or countenance. **2.** appearance. [C13: < OF: aspect, < *vis* face, < L *vīsus* appearance]

-visaged *adj.* (*in combination*) having a visage as specified: *flat-visaged.*

vis-à-vis (ˌviːzɑːˈviː) *prep.* **1.** in relation to. **2.** face to face with. ~*adv., adj.* **3.** face to face; opposite. ~*n., pl.* **vis-à-vis.** **4.** a person or thing that is situated opposite to another. **5.** a person who corresponds to another in office, capacity, etc. [C18: F, < *vis* face]

Visc. *abbrev. for* Viscount *or* Viscountess.

viscacha (vɪsˈkætʃə) *n.* a gregarious burrowing rodent of southern South America, similar to but larger than the chinchillas. [C17: < Sp., < Quechuan *wiskácha*]

viscera (ˈvɪsərə) *pl. n., sing.* **viscus.** **1.** *Anat.* the large internal organs of the body collectively, esp. those in the abdominal cavity. **2.** (less formally) the intestines; guts. [C17: < L: entrails, pl. of *viscus* internal organ]

visceral (ˈvɪsərəl) *adj.* **1.** of or affecting the viscera. **2.** characterized by instinct rather than intellect. —ˈ**viscerally** *adv.*

viscid (ˈvɪsɪd) *adj.* **1.** cohesive and sticky. **2.** (esp. of a leaf) covered with a sticky substance. [C17: < LL *viscidus* sticky, < L *viscum* mistletoe, birdlime] —**visˈcidity** *n.*

viscose (ˈvɪskəʊs) *n.* **1. a.** a viscous orange-brown solution obtained by dissolving cellulose in sodium hydroxide and carbon disulphide. It can be converted back to cellulose by an acid, as in the manufacture of rayon and cellophane. **b.** (*as modifier*): *viscose rayon.* **2.** rayon made from this material. [C19: < LL *viscōsus* full of birdlime, sticky, < *viscum* birdlime]

viscosity (vɪsˈkɒsɪtɪ) *n., pl.* **-ties.** **1.** the state or property of being viscous. **2.** *Physics.* **a.** the extent to which a fluid resists a tendency to flow. **b.** Also called: **absolute viscosity.** a measure of this resistance, measured in newton seconds per metre squared. Symbol: η

viscount (ˈvaɪkaʊnt) *n.* **1.** (in the British Isles) a nobleman ranking below an earl and above a baron. **2.** (in various countries) a son or younger brother of a count. **3.** (in medieval Europe) the deputy of a count. [C14: < OF, < Med. L, < LL *vice-* VICE[3] + *comes* COUNT[2]] —ˈ**viscountcy** *or* ˈ**viscounty** *n.*

viscountess (ˈvaɪkaʊntɪs) *n.* **1.** the wife or widow of a viscount. **2.** a woman who holds the rank of viscount in her own right.

viscous (ˈvɪskəs) *adj.* **1.** (of liquids) thick and sticky. **2.** having or involving viscosity. [C14: < LL *viscōsus;* see VISCOSE] —ˈ**viscously** *adv.*

viscus (ˈvɪskəs) *n.* the singular of **viscera.**

vise (vaɪs) *n., vb. U.S.* a variant spelling of **vice**[2].

Vishnu (ˈvɪʃnuː) *n. Hinduism.* the Pervader or Sustainer, originally a solar deity occupying a secondary place in the Hindu pantheon, later the saviour appearing in many incarnations. [C17: < Sansk. *Viṣṇu,* lit.: the one who works everywhere] —ˈ**Vishnuism** *n.*

visibility (ˌvɪzɪˈbɪlɪtɪ) *n.* **1.** the condition or fact of being visible. **2.** clarity of vision or relative possibility of seeing. **3.** the range of vision: *visibility is 500 yards.*

visible (ˈvɪzɪbᵊl) *adj.* **1.** capable of being perceived by the eye. **2.** capable of being perceived by the mind: *no visible dangers.* **3.** available: *the visible resources.* **4.** of or relating to the balance of trade: *visible transactions.* [C14: < L *vīsibilis,* < *vidēre* to see] —ˈ**visibly** *adv.*

visible balance *n.* another name for **balance of trade.**

visible radiation *n.* electromagnetic radiation that causes the sensation of sight; light.

vision (ˈvɪʒən) *n.* **1.** the act, faculty, or manner of perceiving with the eye; sight. **2. a.** the image on a television screen. **b.** (*as modifier*): *vision control.* **3.** the ability or an instance of great perception, esp. of future developments: *a man of vision.* **4.** mystical or religious experience of seeing some supernatural event, person, etc.: *the vision of St John of the Cross.* **5.** that which is seen, esp. in such a mystical experience. **6.** (*sometimes pl.*) a vivid mental image produced by the imagination: *he had visions of becoming famous.* **7.** a person or thing of extraordinary beauty. [C13: < L *vīsiō* sight, < *vidēre* to see]

visionary (ˈvɪʒənərɪ) *adj.* **1.** marked by vision or foresight: *a visionary leader.* **2.** incapable of being realized or effected. **3.** (of people) characterized by idealistic or radical ideas, esp. impractical ones. **4.** given to having visions. **5.** of, of the nature of, or seen in visions. ~*n., pl.* **-aries.** **6.** a visionary person.

vison mixer *n. Television.* **1.** the person who selects and manipulates the television signals from cameras, film, etc., to make the composite programme. **2.** the equipment used for vision mixing.

visit (ˈvɪzɪt) *vb.* **1.** to go or come to see (a person, place, etc.). **2.** to stay with (someone) as a guest. **3.** to go or come to (an institution, place, etc.) for the purpose of inspecting or examining. **4.** (*tr.*) (of a disease, disaster, etc.) to afflict. **5.** (*tr.; foll. by upon* or *on*) to inflict (punishment, etc.). **6.** (often foll. by *with*) *U.S. & Canad. inf.* to chat (with someone). ~*n.* **7.** the act or an instance of visiting. **8.** a stay as a guest. **9.** a professional or official call. **10.** a formal call for the purpose of inspection or examination. **11.** *International law.* the right of an officer of a belligerent state to stop and search neutral ships in war to verify their nationality and ascertain whether they carry contraband. **12.** *U.S. & Canad. inf.* a chat. [C13: < L *vīsitāre* to go to see, < *vīsere* to examine, < *vidēre* to see] —ˈ**visitable** *adj.*

visitant (ˈvɪzɪtənt) *n.* **1.** a ghost; apparition. **2.** a visitor or guest, usually from far away. **3.** Also called: **visitor.** a migratory bird that is present in a particular region only at certain times: *a summer visitant.* [C16: < L *vīsitāns,* < *vīsitāre;* see VISIT]

visitation (ˌvɪzɪˈteɪʃən) *n.* **1.** an official call or visit for the purpose of inspecting or examining an institution. **2.** a visiting of punishment or reward from heaven. **3.** any disaster or catastrophe: *a visitation of the plague.* **4.** an appearance or arrival of a supernatural being. **5.** *Inf.* an unduly prolonged social call.

Visitation (ˌvɪzɪˈteɪʃən) *n.* **1. a.** the visit made by the Virgin Mary to her cousin Elizabeth (Luke 1:39–56). **b.** the Church festival commemorating this, held on July 2. **2.** a religious order of nuns, the **Order of the Visitation,** founded in 1610 and dedicated to contemplation.

visiting card *n. Brit.* a small card bearing the name and usually the address of a person, esp. for giving to business or social acquaintances.

visiting fireman *n. U.S. inf.* a visitor whose presence is noticed because he is an important figure, a lavish spender, etc.

visitor (ˈvɪzɪtə) *n.* **1.** a person who pays a visit. **2.** another name for **visitant** (sense 3).

visitor centre *n.* another term for **interpretive centre.**

visor *or* **vizor** (ˈvaɪzə) *n.* **1.** a piece of armour fixed or hinged to the helmet to protect the face and furnished with slits for the eyes. **2.** another name for **peak** (on a cap). **3.** a small movable screen used as protection against glare from the sun, esp. one attached above the windscreen of a motor vehicle. **4.** *Arch. or literary.* a mask or any other means of disguise. [C14: < Anglo-F *viser,* < OF *visiere,* < *vis* face; see VISAGE] —ˈ**visored** *or* ˈ**vizored** *adj.*

vista (ˈvɪstə) *n.* **1.** a view, esp. through a long narrow avenue of trees, buildings, etc., or such a passage or avenue itself. **2.** a comprehensive mental view of a distant time or a lengthy series of events. [C17: < It., < *vedere* to see, < L *vidēre*] —ˈ**vistaed** *adj.*

visual (ˈvɪʒʊəl, -zjʊ-) *adj.* **1.** of, done by, or used in seeing: *visual powers.* **2.** another word for **optical.** **3.** capable of being seen; visible. **4.** of, occurring as, or induced by a mental image. ~*n.* **5.** a sketch to show the proposed layout of an advertisement, as in a newspaper. **6.** (*often pl.*) a photograph, film, or other display material. [C15: < LL *vīsuālis,* < L *vīsus* sight, < *vidēre* to see] —ˈ**visually** *adv.*

visual aids *pl. n.* devices, such as films, slides, models, and blackboards, that display in visual form material to be understood or remembered.

visual display unit *n. Computers.* a device that displays characters or line drawings representing data in a computer memory. It usually has a keyboard for the input of information or inquiries. Abbrev.: **VDU.**

visual field *n.* the whole extent of the image falling on the retina when the eye is fixed on a given point.

visualize *or* **-lise** (ˈvɪʒʊəˌlaɪz) *vb.* to form a mental image of (something incapable of being viewed or not at that moment visible). —ˌ**visualiˈzation** *or* **-liˈsation** *n.*

visual magnitude *n. Astron.* the magnitude of a star as determined by visual observation.

visual purple *n.* another name for **rhodopsin.**

visual violet *n.* another name for **iodopsin.**

visual yellow *n.* another name for **retinene.**

vital (ˈvaɪtᵊl) *adj.* **1.** essential to maintain life: *the lungs perform a vital function.* **2.** forceful, energetic, or lively: *a vital person.* **3.** of, having, or displaying life: *a vital organism.* **4.** indispensable or essential: *books vital to this study.* **5.** of great importance: *a vital game.* ~*n.* **6.** (*pl.*) the bodily organs, such as the brain, liver, heart, lungs, etc., that are necessary to maintain life. **7.** (*pl.*) the essential elements of anything. [C14: via OF < L *vītālis,* < *vīta* life] —ˈ**vitally** *adv.*

vital capacity *n. Physiol.* the volume of air that can be exhaled from the lungs after the deepest possible breath has been taken.

vital force *n.* (esp. in early biological theory) a hypothetical force, independent of physical and chemical forces, regarded as being the causative factor of the evolution of living organisms.

vitalism ('vaɪtəˌlɪzəm) *n.* the philosophical doctrine that the phenomena of life cannot be explained in purely mechanical terms because there is something immaterial which distinguishes living from inanimate matter. —**'vitalist** *n., adj.* —ˌ**vital'istic** *adj.*

vitality (vaɪ'tælɪtɪ) *n., pl.* **-ties. 1.** physical or mental vigour, energy, etc. **2.** the power or ability to continue in existence, live, or grow: *the vitality of a movement.*

vitalize *or* **-lise** ('vaɪtəˌlaɪz) *vb.* (*tr.*) to make vital, living, or alive. —ˌ**vitali'zation** *or* **-li'sation** *n.*

vital staining *n.* the technique of treating living cells and tissues with dyes that do not immediately kill them, facilitating observation under a microscope.

vital statistics *pl. n.* **1.** quantitative data concerning human life or the conditions affecting it, such as the death rate. **2.** *Inf.* the measurements of a woman's bust, waist, and hips.

vitamin ('vɪtəmɪn, 'vaɪ-) *n.* any of a group of substances that are essential, in small quantities, for the normal functioning of metabolism in the body. They cannot usually be synthesized in the body but they occur naturally in certain foods. [C20 *vit-* < L *vīta* life + *-amin* < AMINE; so named by Casimir Funk (1884-1967), U.S. biochemist, who believed the substances to be amines] —ˌ**vita'minic** *adj.*

vitamin A *n.* **1.** Also called: **vitamin A_1, retinol.** a fat-soluble yellow unsaturated alcohol occurring in green and yellow vegetables, butter, egg yolk, and fish-liver oil. It is essential for the prevention of night blindness and the protection of epithelial tissue. **2.** Also called: **vitamin A_2.** a vitamin that occurs in the tissues of freshwater fish and has a function similar to that of vitamin A_1.

vitamin B *n., pl.* **B vitamins.** any of the vitamins in the vitamin B complex.

vitamin B complex *n.* a large group of water-soluble vitamins occurring esp. in liver and yeast: includes thiamine (**vitamin B_1**), riboflavin (**vitamin B_2**), nicotinic acid, pyridoxine (**vitamin B_6**), pantothenic acid, biotin, choline, folic acid, and cyanocobalamin (**vitamin B_{12}**). Sometimes shortened to **B complex.**

vitamin C *n.* another name for **ascorbic acid.**

vitamin D *n., pl.* **D vitamins.** any of the fat-soluble vitamins, including calciferol (**vitamin D_2**) and cholecalciferol (**vitamin D_3**), occurring in fish-liver oils, milk, butter, and eggs: used in the treatment of rickets.

vitamin D_1 *n.* the first isolated form of vitamin D, consisting of calciferol and its precursor, lumisterol.

vitamin E *n.* another name for **tocopherol.**

vitamin G *n.* another name (esp. U.S. and Canad.) for **riboflavin.**

vitamin H *n.* another name (esp. U.S. and Canad.) for **biotin.**

vitamin K *n., pl.* **K vitamins.** any of the fat-soluble vitamins, including phylloquinone (**vitamin K_1**) and the menaquinones (**vitamin K_2**), which are essential for the normal clotting of blood.

vitamin P *n., pl.* **P vitamins.** any of a group of water-soluble crystalline substances occurring mainly in citrus fruits, blackcurrants, and rose-hips: they regulate the permeability of the blood capillaries. Also called: **citrin, bioflavonoid.**

vitellin (vɪ'tɛlɪn) *n. Biochem.* a phosphoprotein that is the major protein in egg yolk. [C19: < VITELLUS + -IN]

vitelline membrane (vɪ'tɛlɪn) *n. Zool.* a membrane that surrounds a fertilized ovum and prevents the entry of other spermatozoa.

vitellus (vɪ'tɛləs) *n., pl.* **-luses** *or* **-li** (-laɪ). *Zool., rare.* the yolk of an egg. [C18: < L, lit.: little calf, later: yolk of an egg, < *vitulus* calf]

vitiate ('vɪʃɪˌeɪt) *vb.* (*tr.*) **1.** to make faulty or imperfect. **2.** to debase or corrupt. **3.** to destroy the force or legal effect of (a deed, etc.). [C16: < L *vitiāre* to injure, < *vitium* a fault] —ˌ**viti'ation** *n.* —**'vitiˌator** *n.*

viticulture ('vɪtɪˌkʌltʃə) *n.* **1.** the science, art, or process of cultivating grapevines. **2.** the study of grapes and the growing of grapes. [C19: *viti-*, < L *vītis* vine] —ˌ**viti'culturist** *n.*

vitreous ('vɪtrɪəs) *adj.* **1.** of or resembling glass. **2.** made of or containing glass. **3.** of or relating to the vitreous humour or vitreous body. [C17: < L *vitreus* made of glass, < *vitrum* glass] —**'vitreously** *adv.*

vitreous humour *or* **body** *n.* a transparent gelatinous substance that fills the interior of the eyeball between the lens and the retina.

vitrescence (vɪ'trɛsəns) *n.* **1.** the quality or condition of being or becoming vitreous. **2.** the process of producing a glass or turning a crystalline material into glass. —**vi'trescent** *adj.*

vitrify ('vɪtrɪˌfaɪ) *vb.* **-fying, -fied.** to convert or be converted into glass or a glassy substance. [C16: < F, < L *vitrum* glass] —**'vitriˌfiable** *adj.* —**vitrification** (ˌvɪtrɪfɪ'keɪʃən) *n.*

vitrine ('vɪtriːn) *n.* a glass display case or cabinet for works of art, curios, etc. [C19: < F, < *vitre* pane of glass, < L *vitrum* glass]

vitriol ('vɪtrɪˌɒl) *n.* **1.** another name for **sulphuric acid. 2.** any one of a number of sulphate salts, such as ferrous sulphate (**green vitriol**), copper sulphate (**blue vitriol**), or zinc sulphate (**white vitriol**). **3.** speech, writing, etc., displaying vituperation or bitterness. [C14: < Med. L *vitriolum*, < LL, < L *vitrum* glass, referring to the glossy appearance of the sulphates]

vitriolic (ˌvɪtrɪ'ɒlɪk) *adj.* **1.** (of a strong acid) highly corrosive. **2.** severely bitter or caustic.

vitriolize *or* **-lise** ('vɪtrɪəˌlaɪz) *vb.* (*tr.*) **1.** to convert into or treat with vitriol. **2.** to injure with vitriol. —ˌ**vitrioli'zation** *or* **-li'sation** *n.*

vittle ('vɪtᵊl) *n., vb.* an obsolete or dialect spelling of **victual.**

vituperate (vɪ'tjuːpəˌreɪt) *vb.* to berate or rail (against) abusively; revile. [C16: < L *vituperāre* to blame, < *vitium* a defect + *parāre* to make] —**vi**ˌ**tuper'ation** *n.* —**vi'tuperˌator** *n.*

viva[1] ('viːvə) *interj.* long live; up with (a specified person or thing). [C17: < It., lit.: may (he) live! < *vivere* to live, < L *vīvere*]

viva[2] ('vaɪvə) *Brit.* ~*n.* **1.** an oral examination. ~*vb.* **-vaing, -vaed.** (*tr.*) **2.** to examine orally. [shortened < VIVA VOCE]

vivace (vɪ'vɑːtʃɪ) *adj., adv. Music.* to be performed in a brisk lively manner. [C17: < It., < L *vīvax* vigorous, < *vīvere* to live]

vivacious (vɪ'veɪʃəs) *adj.* full of high spirits and animation. [C17: < L *vīvax* lively; see VIVACE] —**vi'vaciously** *adv.* —**vi'vaciousness** *n.*

vivacity (vɪ'væsɪtɪ) *n., pl.* **-ties.** the quality or condition of being vivacious.

vivarium (vaɪ'vɛərɪəm) *n., pl.* **-iums** *or* **-ia** (-ɪə). a place where live animals are kept under natural conditions for study, etc. [C16: < L: enclosure where live fish or game are kept, < *vīvus* alive]

viva voce ('vaɪvə 'vəʊtʃɪ) *adv., adj.* **1.** by word of mouth. ~*n., vb.* **2.** the full form of **viva**[2]. [C16: < Med. L, lit.: with living voice]

vive (viːv) *interj.* long live; up with (a specified person or thing). [< F]

vivid ('vɪvɪd) *adj.* **1.** (of a colour) very bright; intense. **2.** brilliantly coloured: *vivid plumage.* **3.** conveying to the mind striking realism, freshness, or trueness to life: *a vivid account.* **4.** (of a memory, etc.) remaining distinct in the mind. **5.** (of the imagination, etc.) prolific in the formation of lifelike images. **6.** uttered, operating, or acting with vigour: *vivid expostulations.* **7.** full of life or vitality: *a vivid personality.* [C17: < L *vīvidus* animated, < *vīvere* to live] —**'vividly** *adv.* —**'vividness** *n.*

vivify ('vɪvɪˌfaɪ) *vb.* **-fying, -fied.** (*tr.*) **1.** to bring to life; animate. **2.** to make more vivid or striking. [C16: < LL *vīvificāre*, < L *vīvus* alive + *facere* to make] —ˌ**vivifi'cation** *n.*

viviparous (vɪ'vɪpərəs) *adj.* **1.** (of most mammals) giving birth to living offspring that develop within the uterus of the mother. **2.** (of seeds) germinating before separating from the parent plant. **3.** (of plants) producing bulbils or young plants instead of flowers. [C17: < L, < *vīvus* alive + *parere* to bring forth] —**viviparity** (ˌvɪvɪˈpærɪtɪ) *or* **viˈviparousness** *n.* —**viˈviparously** *adv.*

vivisect (ˈvɪvɪˌsɛkt, ˌvɪvɪˈsɛkt) *vb.* to subject (an animal) to vivisection. [C19: back formation < VIVISECTION] —ˈ**viviˌsector** *n.*

vivisection (ˌvɪvɪˈsɛkʃən) *n.* the act or practice of performing experiments on living animals, involving cutting into or dissecting the body. [C18: < *vivi-*, < L *vivus* living + SECTION, as in DISSECTION] —ˌ**viviˈsectional** *adj.*

vivisectionist (ˌvɪvɪˈsɛkʃənɪst) *n.* a person who practises or advocates vivisection as being useful to science.

vivo (ˈviːvəʊ) *adj., adv. Music.* (*in combination*) with life and vigour: *allegro vivo.* [It.: lively]

vixen (ˈvɪksən) *n.* **1.** a female fox. **2.** a quarrelsome or spiteful woman. [C15 *fixen;* rel. to OE *fyxe,* fem. of FOX] —ˈ**vixenish** *adj.* —ˈ**vixenly** *adv., adj.*

Viyella (vaɪˈɛlə) *n. Trademark.* a soft fabric made of wool and cotton.

viz *abbrev. for* videlicet.

vizard (ˈvɪzəd) *n. Arch. or literary.* a means of disguise. [C16: var. of VISOR] —ˈ**vizarded** *adj.*

vizier (vɪˈzɪə) *n.* a high official in certain Muslim countries, esp. in the former Ottoman Empire. [C16: < Turkish *vezīr,* < Ar. *wazīr* porter, < *wazara* to bear a burden] —**viˈzierate** *n.* —**viˈzierial** *adj.* —**viˈziership** *n.*

vizor (ˈvaɪzə) *n.* a variant spelling of **visor.**

vizsla (ˈvɪʒlə) *n.* a breed of Hungarian hunting dog with a smooth rusty-gold coat. [C20: after *Vizsla,* town in Hungary]

VJ *abbrev. for* video jockey.

V-J Day *n.* the day marking the Allied victory over Japan in World War II (Aug. 15, 1945).

VL *abbrev. for* Vulgar Latin.

vlei (fleɪ, vleɪ) *n. S. African.* an area of low marshy ground, esp. one that feeds a stream. [C19: < Afrik.]

VLF *or* **vlf** *Radio. abbrev. for* very low frequency.

V neck *n.* **a.** a neck on a garment that comes down to a point, resembling the shape of the letter V. **b.** a sweater with such a neck. —ˈ**V-ˌneck** *or* ˈ**V-ˌnecked** *adj.*

voc. *or* **vocat.** *abbrev. for* vocative.

vocab (ˈvəʊkæb) *n.* short for **vocabulary.**

vocable (ˈvəʊkəbᵊl) *n.* any word, either written or spoken, regarded simply as a sequence of letters or spoken sounds. [C16: < L *vocābulum* a designation, < *vocāre* to call] —ˈ**vocably** *adv.*

vocabulary (vəˈkæbjʊlərɪ) *n., pl.* **-laries.** **1.** a listing, either selective or exhaustive, containing the words and phrases of a language, with meanings or translations into another language. **2.** the aggregate of words in the use or comprehension of a specified person, class, etc. **3.** all the words contained in a language. **4.** a range or system of symbols or techniques constituting a means of communication or expression, as any of the arts or crafts: *a wide vocabulary of textures and colours.* [C16: < Med. L *vocābulārium,* < L *vocābulum* VOCABLE]

vocal (ˈvəʊkᵊl) *adj.* **1.** of or designed for the voice: *vocal music.* **2.** produced or delivered by the voice: *vocal noises.* **3.** connected with the production of the voice: *vocal organs.* **4.** frequently disposed to outspoken speech, criticism, etc.: *a vocal minority.* **5.** full of sound or voices: *a vocal assembly.* **6.** endowed with a voice. **7.** *Phonetics.* **a.** of or relating to a speech sound. **b.** of or relating to a voiced speech sound, esp. a vowel. ~*n.* **8.** a piece of jazz or pop music that is sung. **9.** a performance of such a piece of music. [C14: < L *vōcālis* possessed of a voice, < *vōx* voice] —**vocality** (vəʊˈkælɪtɪ) *n.* —ˈ**vocally** *adv.*

vocal cords *pl. n.* either of two pairs of membranous folds in the larynx. The upper pair (**false vocal cords**) are not concerned with vocal production; the lower pair (**true vocal cords**) can be made to vibrate and produce sound when air from the lungs is forced over them.

vocalic (vəʊˈkælɪk) *adj. Phonetics.* of, relating to, or containing a vowel or vowels.

vocalise (ˌvəʊkəˈliːz) *n.* a musical passage sung upon one vowel usually as an exercise to develop flexibility and control of pitch and tone.

vocalism (ˈvəʊkəˌlɪzəm) *n.* **1.** the exercise of the voice, as in singing or speaking. **2.** *Phonetics.* **a.** a voiced speech sound, esp. a vowel. **b.** a system of vowels as used in a language.

vocalist (ˈvəʊkəlɪst) *n.* a singer, esp. one who regularly appears with a jazz band or pop group.

vocalize *or* **-ise** (ˈvəʊkəˌlaɪz) *vb.* **1.** to express with or use the voice. **2.** (*tr.*) to make vocal or articulate. **3.** (*tr.*) *Phonetics.* to articulate (a speech sound) with voice. **4.** another word for **vowelize.** **5.** (*intr.*) to sing a melody on a vowel, etc. —ˌ**vocaliˈzation** *or* **-iˈsation** *n.* —ˈ**vocalˌizer** *or* **-ˌiser** *n.*

vocal score *n.* a musical score that shows voice parts in full and orchestral parts in the form of a piano transcription.

vocation (vəʊˈkeɪʃən) *n.* **1.** a specified profession or trade. **2. a.** a special urge or predisposition to a particular calling or career, esp. a religious one. **b.** such a calling or career. [C15: < L *vocātiō,* < *vocāre* to call]

vocational (vəʊˈkeɪʃənᵊl) *adj.* **1.** of or relating to a vocation or vocations. **2.** of or relating to applied educational courses concerned with skills needed for an occupation, trade, or profession.

vocational guidance *n.* a guidance service based on psychological tests and interviews to find out what career may best suit a person.

vocative (ˈvɒkətɪv) *Grammar.* ~*adj.* **1.** denoting a case of nouns, in some inflected languages, used when the referent of the noun is being addressed. ~*n.* **2. a.** the vocative case. **b.** a vocative noun or speech element. [C15: < L *vocātīvus cāsus* the calling case, < *vocāre* to call]

voces (ˈvəʊsiːz) *n.* the plural of **vox.**

vociferate (vəʊˈsɪfəˌreɪt) *vb.* to exclaim or cry out about (something) clamorously or insistently. [C17: < L *vōciferārī,* < *vōx* voice + *ferre* to bear] —**voˌciferˈation** *n.*

vociferous (vəʊˈsɪfərəs) *adj.* **1.** characterized by vehemence or noisiness: *vociferous protests.* **2.** making an outcry: *a vociferous mob.* —**voˈciferously** *adv.* —**voˈciferousness** *n.*

vocoder (ˈvəʊˌkəʊdə) *n. Music.* a type of synthesizer that uses the human voice as an oscillator.

vodka (ˈvɒdkə) *n.* an alcoholic drink originating in Russia, made from grain, potatoes, etc., usually consisting only of rectified spirit and water. [C19: < Russian, dim. of *voda* water]

voe (vəʊ) *n.* (in Orkney and Shetland) a small bay or narrow creek. [C17: < ON *vagr*]

voetsek (ˈfʊtsɛk, ˈvʊt-) *sentence substitute. S. African sl.* an expletive used when chasing animals away: offensive when addressed to people. [< Afrik., < *voort se ek* away say I]

voetstoets *or* **voetstoots** (ˈfʊtstʊts, ˈvʊt-) *S. African.* ~*adj.* **1.** denoting a sale in which the vendor is freed from all responsibility for the condition of the goods being sold. ~*adv.* **2.** without responsibility for the condition of the goods sold. [Afrik., < Du.]

vogue (vəʊg) *n.* **1.** the popular style at a specified time (esp. in **in vogue**). **2.** a period of general or popular usage or favour: *the vogue for such dances is now over.* ~*adj.* **3.** (*usually prenominal*) fashionable: *a vogue word.* [C16: < F: a rowing, fashion, < OIt., < *vogare* to row, <?] —ˈ**voguish** *adj.*

voice (vɔɪs) *n.* **1.** the sound made by the vibration of the vocal cords, esp. when modified by the tongue and mouth. **2.** the natural and distinctive tone of the speech sounds characteristic of a particular person. **3.** the condition, quality, or tone of such sounds: *a hysterical voice.* **4.** the musical sound of a singing voice, with respect to its quality or tone: *she has a lovely voice.* **5.** the ability to speak, sing, etc.: *he has lost his voice.* **6.** a sound resembling or suggestive of vocal utterance: *the voice of hard experience.* **7.** written or spoken expression, as of feeling, opinion, etc. (esp. in **give voice to**). **8.** a stated choice, wish, or opinion: *to give someone a voice in a decision.* **9.** an agency through which is communicated another's purpose, etc.: *such groups are the voice of our enemies.* **10.** *Music.* **a.** musical notes produced by vibrations of the vocal chords at various frequencies and in certain registers: *a tenor voice.* **b.** (in harmony) an independent melodic line or part: *a fugue in five voices.* **11.** *Phonetics.* the sound characterizing the articulation of several speech sounds, including all vowels or sonants, that is produced when the vocal cords are set in vibration by the breath. **12.** *Grammar.* a category of the verb that expresses whether the relation between the subject and the verb is that of agent and action, action and recipient, or some other relation. **13. in voice.** in a condition to sing or speak well. **14. with one voice.** unanimously. ~*vb.* (*tr.*) **15.** to give expression to: *to voice a complaint.* **16.** to articulate (a speech sound) with voice. **17.** *Music.* to adjust (a wind instrument or organ pipe) so that it conforms to the correct standards of tone colour, pitch, etc. [C13: < OF *voiz,* < L *vōx*] —ˈ**voicer** *n.*

voice box *n.* **1.** another word for the **larynx. 2.** Also called: **talkbox.** an electronic guitar attachment with a tube into the player's mouth to modulate the sound vocally.

voiced (vɔɪst) *adj.* **1.** declared or expressed by the voice. **2.** (*in combination*) having a voice as specified: *loud-voiced.* **3.** *Phonetics.* articulated with accompanying vibration of the vocal cords: *in English* (b) *is a voiced consonant.*

voiceless (ˈvɔɪslɪs) *adj.* **1.** without a voice. **2.** not articulated: *voiceless misery.* **3.** silent. **4.** *Phonetics.* articulated without accompanying vibration of the vocal cords: *In English* (p) *is a voiceless consonant.* —ˈ**voicelessly** *adv.*

voice-over *n.* the voice of an unseen commentator heard during a film, etc.

voiceprint (ˈvɔɪsˌprɪnt) *n.* a graphic representation of a person's voice recorded electronically, usually having time plotted along the horizontal axis and the frequency of the speech on the vertical axis.

void (vɔɪd) *adj.* **1.** without contents. **2.** not legally binding: *null and void.* **3.** (of an office, house, etc.) unoccupied. **4.** (*postpositive;* foll. by *of*) destitute or devoid: *void of resources.* **5.** useless: *all his efforts were rendered void.* **6.** (of a card suit or player) having no cards in a particular suit: *his spades were void.* ~*n.* **7.** an empty space or area: *the huge desert voids of Asia.* **8.** a feeling or condition of loneliness or deprivation. **9.** a lack of any cards in one suit: *to have a void in spades.* ~*vb.* (*mainly tr.*) **10.** to make ineffective or invalid. **11.** to empty (contents, etc.) or make empty of contents. **12.** (*also intr.*) to discharge the contents of (the bowels or urinary bladder). [C13: < OF, < Vulgar L *vocītus* (unattested), < L *vacuus,* < *vacāre* to be empty] —ˈ**voidable** *adj.* —ˈ**voider** *n.*

voidance (ˈvɔɪdᵊns) *n.* **1.** an annulment, as of a contract. **2.** the condition of being vacant, as an office, benefice, etc. **3.** the act of voiding or evacuating. [C14: var. of AVOIDANCE]

voile (vɔɪl) *n.* a light semitransparent fabric of silk, rayon, cotton, etc., used for dresses, scarves, shirts, etc. [C19: < F: VEIL]

vol. *abbrev. for:* **1.** volcano. **2.** volume. **3.** volunteer.

volant (ˈvəʊlənt) *adj.* **1.** (*usually postpositive*) *Heraldry.* in a flying position. **2.** *Rare.* flying or capable of flight. [C16: < F, < *voler* to fly, < L *volāre*]

volar (ˈvəʊlə) *adj. Anat.* of or relating to the palm of the hand or the sole of the foot. [C19: < L *vola* hollow of the hand, palm, sole of the foot]

volatile (ˈvɒləˌtaɪl) *adj.* **1.** (of a substance) capable of readily changing from a solid or liquid form to a vapour. **2.** (of persons) disposed to caprice or inconstancy. **3.** (of circumstances) liable to sudden change. **4.** lasting only a short time: *volatile business interests.* **5.** *Computers.* (of a memory) not retaining stored information when the power supply is cut off. ~*n.* **6.** a volatile substance. [C17: < L *volātilis* flying, < *volāre* to fly] —ˈ**volatileness** *or* **volatility** (ˌvɒləˈtɪlɪtɪ) *n.*

volatilize *or* **-lise** (vɒˈlætɪˌlaɪz) *vb.* to change or cause to change from a solid or liquid to a vapour. —**voˈlatiˌlizable** *or* **-ˌlisable** *adj.* —**voˌlatilizˈation** *or* **-lisˈation** *n.*

vol-au-vent (*French* vɔlovɑ̃) *n.* a very light puff pastry case filled with a savoury mixture in a sauce. [C19: < F, lit.: flight in the wind]

volcanic (vɒlˈkænɪk) *adj.* **1.** of, produced by, or characterized by the presence of volcanoes: *a volcanic region.* **2.** suggestive of or resembling an erupting volcano: *a volcanic era.* —**volˈcanically** *adv.* —**volcanicity** (ˌvɒlkəˈnɪsɪtɪ) *n.*

volcanic glass *n.* any of several glassy volcanic igneous rocks, such as obsidian.

volcanism (ˈvɒlkəˌnɪzəm) *or* **vulcanism** *n.* those processes collectively that result in the formation of volcanoes and their products.

volcano (vɒlˈkeɪnəʊ) *n., pl.* **-noes** *or* **-nos. 1.** an opening in the earth's crust from which molten lava, rock fragments, ashes, dust, and gases are ejected from below the earth's surface. **2.** a mountain formed from volcanic material ejected from a vent in a central crater. [C17: < It., < L *Volcānus* Vulcan, Roman god of fire and metalworking, whose forges were believed to be responsible for volcanic rumblings]

volcanology (ˌvɒlkəˈnɒlədʒɪ) *or* **vulcanology** *n.* the study of volcanoes and volcanic phenomena. —**volcanological** (ˌvɒlkənəˈlɒdʒɪkᵊl) *or* ˌ**vulcanoˈlogical** *adj.*

vole (vəʊl) *n.* any of various small rodents, mostly of Eurasia and North America, having a stocky body, short tail, and inconspicuous ears. [C19: short for *volemouse,* < ON *vollr* field + *mus* MOUSE]

volitant (ˈvɒlɪtənt) *adj.* **1.** flying or moving about rapidly. **2.** capable of flying. [C19: < L *volitāre* to flit, < *volāre* to fly]

volition (vəˈlɪʃən) *n.* **1.** the act of exercising the will: *of one's own volition.* **2.** the faculty of conscious choice, decision, and intention. **3.** the resulting choice or resolution. [C17: < Med. L *volitiō,* < L *vol-* as in *volō* I will, present stem of *velle* to wish] —**voˈlitional** *adj.*

volitive (ˈvɒlɪtɪv) *adj.* of, relating to, or emanating from the will.

Volk (fɒlk) *n. S. African.* the Afrikaner people. [< Afrik., < Du.]

Volksraad (ˈfɒlksˌrɑːt) *n.* (in South Africa) the former Legislative Assemblies of the Transvaal and Orange Free State republics. [< Afrik., < Du. *volks* people's + *raad* council]

volley (ˈvɒlɪ) *n.* **1.** the simultaneous discharge of several weapons, esp. firearms. **2.** the projectiles or missiles so discharged. **3.** a burst of oaths, protests, etc., occurring simultaneously or in rapid succession. **4.** *Sport.* a stroke, shot, or kick at a moving ball before it hits the ground. **5.** *Cricket.* the flight of such a ball or the ball itself. ~*vb.* **6.** to discharge (weapons, etc.) in or as if in a volley or (of weapons, etc.) to be discharged. **7.** (*tr.*) to utter vehemently. **8.** (*tr.*) *Sport.* to strike or kick (a moving ball) before it hits the ground. [C16: < F *volée* a flight, < *voler* to fly, < L *volāre*] —ˈ**volleyer** *n.*

volleyball (ˈvɒlɪˌbɔːl) *n.* **1.** a game in which two teams hit a large ball back and forth over a high net with their hands. **2.** the ball used in this game.

volplane (ˈvɒlˌpleɪn) *vb.* **1.** (*intr.*) (of an aircraft) to glide without engine power. ~*n.* **2.** a glide by an aircraft. [C20: < F *vol plané* a gliding flight]

vols. *abbrev. for* volumes.

volt[1] (vəʊlt) *n.* the derived SI unit of electric

potential; the potential difference between two points on a conductor carrying a current of 1 ampere, when the power dissipated between these points is 1 watt. Symbol: V [C19: after Count Alessandro *Volta* (1745–1827), It. physicist]

volt[2] *or* **volte** (vɒlt) *n.* **1.** a small circle executed in dressage. **2.** a leap made in fencing to avoid an opponent's thrust. [C17: < F, < It. *volta* turn, ult. < L *volvere* to turn]

volta (ˈvɒltə; *Italian* ˈvɔlta) *n., pl.* **-te** (*Italian* -te). **1.** an Italian dance popular during the 16th and 17th centuries. **2.** a piece of music for or in the rhythm of this dance. [C17: < It.: turn; see VOLT[2]]

voltage (ˈvəʊltɪdʒ) *n.* an electromotive force or potential difference expressed in volts.

voltaic (vɒlˈteɪɪk) *adj.* another word for **galvanic** (sense 1).

voltaic cell *n.* another name for **primary cell.**

voltaic couple *n. Physics.* a pair of dissimilar metals in an electrolyte with a potential difference between the metals resulting from chemical action.

voltaic pile *n.* an early form of battery consisting of a pile of alternate dissimilar metals, such as zinc and copper, separated by pads moistened with an electrolyte.

voltameter (vɒlˈtæmɪtə) *n.* a device for measuring electric charge. —**voltametric** (ˌvɒltəˈmɛtrɪk) *adj.*

voltammeter (ˌvəʊltˈæmˌmiːtə) *n.* a dual-purpose instrument that can measure both potential difference and electric current, usually in volts and amperes respectively.

volt-ampere (ˈvəʊltˈæmpɛə) *n.* the product of the potential in volts across an electrical circuit and the resultant current in amperes.

volte-face (ˈvɒltˈfɑːs) *n., pl.* **volte-face.** **1.** a reversal, as in opinion. **2.** a change of position so as to look, lie, etc., in the opposite direction. [C19: < F, < It., < *volta* turn + *faccia* face]

voltmeter (ˈvəʊltˌmiːtə) *n.* an instrument for measuring potential difference or electromotive force.

voluble (ˈvɒljʊbᵊl) *adj.* **1.** talking easily and at length. **2.** *Arch.* easily turning or rotating. **3.** *Rare.* (of a plant) twining or twisting. [C16: < L *volūbilis* turning readily, < *volvere* to turn] —ˌ**voluˈbility** *or* ˈ**volubleness** *n.* —ˈ**volubly** *adv.*

volume (ˈvɒljuːm) *n.* **1.** the magnitude of the three-dimensional space enclosed within or occupied by an object, geometric solid, etc. **2.** a large mass or quantity: *the volume of protest.* **3.** an amount or total: *the volume of exports.* **4.** fullness of sound. **5.** the control on a radio, etc., for adjusting the intensity of sound. **6.** a bound collection of printed or written pages; book. **7.** any of several books either bound in an identical format or part of a series. **8.** the complete set of issues of a periodical over a specified period, esp. one year. **9.** *History.* a roll of parchment, etc. **10.** **speak volumes.** to convey much significant information. [C14: < OF, < L *volūmen* a roll, < *volvere* to roll up]

volumetric (ˌvɒljʊˈmɛtrɪk) *adj.* of, concerning, or using measurement by volume: *volumetric analysis.* —ˌ**voluˈmetrically** *adv.*

volumetric analysis *n. Chem.* quantitative analysis of liquids or solutions by comparing the volumes that react with known volumes of standard reagents, usually by titration.

voluminous (vəˈluːmɪnəs) *adj.* **1.** of great size, quantity, or extent. **2.** (of writing) consisting of or sufficient to fill volumes. [C17: < LL *volūminōsus* full of windings, < *volūmen* VOLUME] —**voluminosity** (vəˌluːmɪˈnɒsɪtɪ) *n.* —**voˈluminously** *adv.*

voluntarism (ˈvɒləntəˌrɪzəm) *n.* **1.** *Philosophy.* the theory that the will rather than the intellect is the ultimate principle of reality. **2.** a doctrine or system based on voluntary participation in a course of action. **3.** another name for **voluntaryism.** —ˈ**voluntarist** *n., adj.*

voluntary (ˈvɒləntərɪ) *adj.* **1.** performed, undertaken, or brought about by free choice or willingly: *a voluntary donation.* **2.** (of persons) serving or acting in a specified function without compulsion or promise of remuneration: *a voluntary social worker.* **3.** done by, composed of, or functioning with the aid of volunteers: *a voluntary association.* **4.** exercising or having the faculty of willing: *a voluntary agent.* **5.** spontaneous: *voluntary laughter.* **6.** *Law.* **a.** acting or done without legal obligation, compulsion, or persuasion. **b.** made without payment or recompense: *a voluntary conveyance.* **7.** (of the muscles of the limbs, neck, etc.) having their action controlled by the will. **8.** maintained by the voluntary actions or contributions of individuals and not by the state: *voluntary schools.* ~*n., pl.* **-taries.** **9.** *Music.* a composition or improvisation, usually for organ, played at the beginning or end of a church service. [C14: < L *voluntārius,* < *voluntās* will, < *velle* to wish] —ˈ**voluntarily** *adv.*

voluntaryism (ˈvɒləntərɪˌɪzəm) *or* **voluntarism** *n.* the principle of supporting churches, schools, and various other institutions by voluntary contributions rather than with state funds. —ˈ**voluntaryist** *or* ˈ**voluntarist** *n.*

volunteer (ˌvɒlənˈtɪə) *n.* **1. a.** a person who performs or offers to perform voluntary service. **b.** (*as modifier*): *a volunteer system.* **2.** a person who freely undertakes military service. **3. a.** a plant that grows from seed that has not been deliberately sown. **b.** (*as modifier*): *a volunteer plant.* ~*vb.* **4.** to offer (oneself or one's services) for an undertaking by choice and without request or obligation. **5.** (*tr.*) to perform, give, or communicate voluntarily: *to volunteer help.* **6.** (*intr.*) to enlist voluntarily for military service. [C17: < F, < L *voluntārius;* see VOLUNTARY]

voluptuary (vəˈlʌptjʊərɪ) *n., pl.* **-aries.** **1.** a person devoted to luxury and sensual pleasures. ~*adj.* **2.** of or furthering sensual gratification or luxury. [C17: < LL *voluptuārius* delightful, < L *voluptās* pleasure]

voluptuous (vəˈlʌptjʊəs) *adj.* **1.** relating to, characterized by, or consisting of pleasures of the body or senses. **2.** devoted or addicted to sensual indulgence or luxurious pleasures. **3.** sexually alluring, esp. through shapeliness or fullness: *a voluptuous woman.* [C14: < L *voluptuōsus* full of gratification, < *voluptās* pleasure] —**voˈluptuously** *adv.* —**voˈluptuousness** *n.*

volute (ˈvɒljuːt, vəˈluːt) *n.* **1.** a spiral or twisting turn, form, or object. **2.** Also called: **helix.** a carved ornament, esp. as used on an Ionic capital, that has the form of a spiral scroll. **3.** any of the whorls of the spirally coiled shell of a snail or similar gastropod mollusc. **4.** any of a family of tropical marine gastropod molluscs having a spiral shell with beautiful markings. ~*adj. also* **voluted** (vəˈluːtɪd). **5.** having the form of a volute; spiral. [C17: < L *volūta* spiral decoration, < *volūtus,* < *volvere* to roll up] —**voˈlution** *n.*

vomer (ˈvəʊmə) *n.* the thin flat bone forming part of the separation between the nasal passages in mammals. [C18: < L: ploughshare]

vomit (ˈvɒmɪt) *vb.* **1.** to eject (the contents of the stomach) through the mouth as the result of involuntary muscular spasms of the stomach and oesophagus. **2.** to eject or be ejected forcefully. ~*n.* **3.** the matter ejected in vomiting. **4.** the act of vomiting. **5.** an emetic. [C14: < L *vomitāre* to vomit repeatedly, < *vomere* to vomit] —ˈ**vomiter** *n.*

vomitory (ˈvɒmɪtərɪ) *adj.* **1.** Also: **vomitive** (ˈvɒmɪtɪv). causing vomiting; emetic. ~*n., pl.* **-ries.** **2.** a vomitory agent. **3.** Also called: **vomitorium** (ˌvɒmɪˈtɔːrɪəm). a passageway in an ancient Roman amphitheatre that connects an outside entrance to a tier of seats.

voodoo (ˈvuːduː) *n., pl.* **-doos.** **1.** Also called: **voodooism.** a religious cult involving witchcraft, common among Negroes in Haiti and other Caribbean islands. **2.** a person who practises voodoo. **3.** a charm, spell, or fetish involved in voodoo worship. ~*adj.* **4.** relating to or associated with voodoo. ~*vb.* **-dooing, -dooed.** **5.** (*tr.*) to affect by or as if by the power of voodoo. [C19: < Louisiana F *voudou,* ult. of West African origin] —ˈ**voodooist** *n.*

voorkamer (ˈfʊəˌkɑːmə) *n. S. African.* the front room of a house. [< Afrik., < Du. *voor* fore + *kamer* chamber]

voorlaaier (ˈfʊəˌlaɪə) *n. S. African.* a muzzle-loading gun. [< Afrik. *voor* front + *laai* load]

voorskot (ˈfʊəˌskɒt) *n.* (in South Africa) an advance payment made to a farmers' cooperative for a crop or wool clip. [< Afrik., < Du. *voorschieten* to lend, advance (money)]

Voortrekker (ˈfʊəˌtrɛkə) *n.* (in South Africa) **1.** one of the original Afrikaner settlers of the Transvaal and the Orange Free State who migrated from the Cape Colony in the 1830s. **2.** a member of the Afrikaner youth movement founded in 1931. [C19: < Du., < *voor-* FORE- + *trekken* to TREK]

voracious (vɒˈreɪʃəs) *adj.* **1.** devouring or craving food in great quantities. **2.** very eager or unremitting in some activity: *voracious reading.* [C17: < L *vorāx*, < *vorāre* to devour] —**voracity** (vɒˈræsɪtɪ) *or* **voˈraciousness** *n.*

-vorous *adj. combining form.* feeding on or devouring: *carnivorous.* [< L *-vorus;* rel. to *vorāre* to swallow up] —**-vore** *n. combining form.*

vortex (ˈvɔːtɛks) *n., pl.* **-texes** *or* **-tices** (-tɪˌsiːz). **1.** a whirling mass or motion of liquid, gas, flame, etc., such as the spiralling movement of water around a whirlpool. **2.** any activity or way of life regarded as irresistibly engulfing. [C17: < L: a whirlpool] —**vortical** (ˈvɔːtɪkᵊl) *adj.*

vorticella (ˌvɔːtɪˈsɛlə) *n., pl.* **-lae** (-liː). any of a genus of protozoans consisting of a goblet-shaped ciliated cell attached to the substratum by a long contractile stalk. [C18: < NL, lit.: a little eddy, < VORTEX]

vorticism (ˈvɔːtɪˌsɪzəm) *n.* an art movement in England combining the techniques of cubism with the concern for the problems of the machine age evinced in futurism. [C20: referring to the "vortices" of modern life on which the movement was based] —ˈ**vorticist** *n.*

votary (ˈvəʊtərɪ) *n., pl.* **-ries,** *also* **votarist. 1.** *R.C. Church, Eastern Churches.* a person, such as a monk or nun, who has dedicated himself or herself to religion by taking vows. **2.** a devoted adherent of a religion, cause, etc. ~*adj.* **3.** ardently devoted to the services or worship of God or a saint. [C16: < L *vōtum* a vow, < *vovēre* to vow] —ˈ**votaress** *fem. n.*

vote (vəʊt) *n.* **1.** an indication of choice, opinion, or will on a question, such as the choosing of a candidate: *10 votes for Jones.* **2.** the opinion of a group of persons as determined by voting: *it was put to the vote.* **3.** a body of votes or voters collectively: *the Jewish vote.* **4.** the total number of votes cast. **5.** the ticket, ballot, etc., by which a vote is expressed. **6. a.** the right to vote; franchise. **b.** a person regarded as the embodiment of this right. **7.** a means of voting, such as a ballot. **8.** *Chiefly Brit.* a grant or other proposition to be voted upon. ~*vb.* **9.** (when *tr., takes a clause as object or an infinitive*) to express or signify (one's preference or will) (for or against some question, etc.): *to vote by ballot.* **10.** (*intr.*) to declare oneself as being (something or in favour of something) by exercising one's vote: *to vote socialist.* **11.** (*tr.;* foll. by *into* or *out of,* etc.) to appoint or elect (a person to or from a particular post): *he was voted out of office.* **12.** (*tr.*) to determine the condition of in a specified way by voting: *the court voted itself out of existence.* **13.** (*tr.*) to authorize or allow by voting: *vote us a rise.* **14.** (*tr.*) *Inf.* to declare by common opinion: *the party was voted a failure.* [C15: < L *vōtum* a solemn promise, < *vovēre* to vow] —ˈ**votable** *or* ˈ**voteable** *adj.*

vote down *vb.* (*tr., adv.*) to decide against or defeat in a vote: *the bill was voted down.*

vote of no confidence *n. Parliament.* a vote on a motion put by the Opposition censuring an aspect of the Government's policy; if the motion is carried the Government is obliged to resign. Also called: **vote of censure.**

voter (ˈvəʊtə) *n.* a person who can or does vote.

voting machine *n.* (esp. in the U.S.) a machine at a polling station that voters operate to register their votes and that mechanically or electronically counts all votes cast.

votive (ˈvəʊtɪv) *adj.* **1.** given, undertaken, or dedicated in fulfilment of or in accordance with a vow. **2.** *R.C. Church.* having the nature of a voluntary offering: *a votive Mass.* [C16: < L *vōtīvus* promised by a vow, < *vōtum* a vow]

vouch (vaʊtʃ) *vb.* **1.** (*intr.;* usually foll. by *for*) to give personal assurance: *I'll vouch for his safety.* **2.** (when *tr., usually takes a clause as object;* when *intr.,* usually foll. by *for*) to furnish supporting evidence (for) or function as proof (of). **3.** (*tr.*) *Arch.* to cite (authors, principles, etc.) in support of something. [C14: < OF *vocher* to summon, ult. < L *vocāre* to call]

voucher (ˈvaʊtʃə) *n.* **1.** a document serving as evidence for some claimed transaction, as the receipt or expenditure of money. **2.** *Brit.* a ticket or card serving as a substitute for cash: *a gift voucher.* **3.** a person or thing that vouches for the truth of some statement, etc. [C16: < Anglo-F, noun use of OF *voucher* to summon; see VOUCH]

vouchsafe (ˌvaʊtʃˈseɪf) *vb.* (*tr.*) **1.** to give or grant or condescend to give or grant: *she vouchsafed no reply.* **2.** (*may take a clause as object or an infinitive*) to agree, promise, or permit, often graciously or condescendingly: *he vouchsafed to come yesterday.* [C14 *vouchen sauf;* see VOUCH, SAFE]

voussoir (vuːˈswɑː) *n.* a wedge-shaped stone or brick that is used with others to construct an arch or vault. [C18: < F, < Vulgar L *volsōrium* (unattested), ult. < L *volvere* to turn, roll]

vow (vaʊ) *n.* **1.** a solemn or earnest pledge or promise binding the person making it to perform a specified act or behave in a certain way. **2.** a solemn promise made to a deity or saint, by which the promiser pledges himself to some future act or way of life. **3. take vows.** to enter a religious order and commit oneself to its rule of life by the vows of poverty, chastity, and obedience. ~*vb.* **4.** (*tr.; may take a clause as object or an infinitive*) to pledge, promise, or undertake solemnly: *he vowed to return.* **5.** (*tr.*) to dedicate or consecrate to God or a saint. **6.** (*tr.; usually takes a clause as object*) to assert or swear emphatically. **7.** (*intr.*) *Arch.* to declare solemnly. [C13: < OF *vou,* < L *vōtum*; see VOTE] —ˈ**vower** *n.*

vowel (ˈvaʊəl) *n.* **1.** *Phonetics.* a voiced speech sound whose articulation is characterized by the absence of obstruction in the vocal tract, allowing the breath stream free passage. The timbre of a vowel is chiefly determined by the position of the tongue and the lips. **2.** a letter or character representing a vowel. [C14: < OF, < L *vocālis littera* vowel, < *vocālis,* < *vox* voice] —ˈ**vowel-**ˌ**like** *adj.*

vowel gradation *n.* another name for **ablaut.** See **gradation** (sense 5).

vowelize *or* **-lise** (ˈvaʊəˌlaɪz) *vb.* (*tr.*) to mark the vowel points in (a Hebrew word or text). —ˌ**voweliˈzation** *or* **-liˈsation** *n.*

vowel mutation *n.* another name for **umlaut.**

vowel point *n.* any of several marks or points placed above or below consonants, esp. those evolved for Hebrew or Arabic, in order to indicate vowel sounds.

vox (vɒks) *n., pl.* **voces.** a voice or sound. [L: voice]

vox pop *n.* interviews with members of the public on a radio or television programme. [C20: shortened < VOX POPULI]

vox populi (ˈpɒpjʊˌlaɪ) *n.* the voice of the people; popular or public opinion. [L]

voyage (ˈvɔɪɪdʒ) *n.* **1.** a journey, travel, or passage, esp. one to a distant land or by sea or air. ~*vb.* **2.** to travel over or traverse (something): *we will voyage to Africa.* [C13: < OF *veiage,* < L *viāticum* provision for travelling, < *viāticus,* < *via* way] —ˈ**voyager** *n.*

voyageur (ˌvɔɪəˈdʒɜː) *n.* (in Canada) a woodsman, guide, trapper, boatman, or explorer, esp. in the North. [C19: F: traveller, < *voyager* to VOYAGE]

voyeur (vwaɪˈɜː) *n.* a person who obtains sexual pleasure from the observation of people undressing, having intercourse, etc. [C20: F, lit.: one who sees, < *voir* to see, < L *vidēre*] —**voˈyeurism** *n.* —ˌ**voyeurˈistic** *adj.*

VP *abbrev. for:* **1.** verb phrase. **2.** Vice President.

VR *abbrev. for:* **1.** variant reading. **2.** Victoria Regina. [L: Queen Victoria]

V. Rev. *abbrev. for* Very Reverend.

vrou (frəʊ) *n. S. African.* an Afrikaner woman, esp. a married woman. [< Afrik., < Du.]

vrystater (ˈfreɪˌstɑːtə) *n. S. African.* a native inhabitant of the Free State, esp. one who is White. [< Afrik., < Du. *vrij* free + *staat* state]

vs *abbrev. for* versus.

VS *abbrev. for* Veterinary Surgeon.

v.s. *abbrev. for* vide supra (see **vide**).

V-sign *n.* **1.** (in Britain) an offensive gesture made by sticking up the index and middle fingers with the palm of the hand inwards. **2.** a similar gesture with the palm outwards meaning victory or peace.

VSO *abbrev. for:* **1.** very superior old: used to indicate that a brandy, port, etc., is between 12 and 17 years old. **2.** (in Britain) Voluntary Service Overseas: an organization that sends young volunteers to use and teach their skills in developing countries.

VSOP *abbrev. for* very special (*or* superior) old pale: used to indicate that a brandy, port, etc., is between 20 and 25 years old.

VTOL (ˈviːtɒl) *n.* vertical takeoff and landing; a system in which an aircraft can take off and land vertically. Cf. **STOL.**

VTR *abbrev. for* video tape recorder.

V-type engine *n.* a type of internal-combustion engine having two cylinder blocks attached to a single crankcase, the angle between the two blocks forming a V.

vug (vʌg) *n. Mining.* a small cavity in a rock or vein, usually lined with crystals. [C19: < Cornish *vooga* cave] —ˈ**vuggy** *adj.*

vulcanian (vʌlˈkeɪnɪən) *adj. Geol.* of or relating to a volcanic eruption characterized by the explosive discharge of gases, fine ash, and viscous lava that hardens in the crater. [C17: after *Vulcan,* Roman god of fire and metalworking]

vulcanism (ˈvʌlkəˌnɪzəm) *n.* a variant spelling of **volcanism.**

vulcanite (ˈvʌlkəˌnaɪt) *n.* a hard usually black rubber produced by vulcanizing natural rubber with sulphur. It is used for electrical insulators, etc. Also called: **ebonite.**

vulcanize *or* **-nise** (ˈvʌlkəˌnaɪz) *vb.* (*tr.*) **1.** to treat (rubber) with sulphur under heat and pressure to improve elasticity and strength or to produce a hard substance such as vulcanite. **2.** to treat (substances other than rubber) by a similar process in order to improve their properties. —ˌ**vulcaniˈzation** *or* **-niˈsation** *n.*

vulcanology (ˌvʌlkəˈnɒlədʒɪ) *n.* a variant spelling of **volcanology.**

Vulg. *abbrev. for* Vulgate.

vulgar (ˈvʌlgə) *adj.* **1.** marked by lack of taste, culture, delicacy, manners, etc.: *vulgar language.* **2.** (*often cap.; usually prenominal*) denoting a form of a language, esp. of Latin, current among common people, esp. at a period when the formal language is archaic. **3.** *Arch.* of or current among the great mass of common people. [C14: < L *vulgāris,* < *vulgus* the common people] —ˈ**vulgarly** *adv.*

vulgar fraction *n.* another name for **simple fraction.**

vulgarian (vʌlˈgɛərɪən) *n.* a vulgar person, esp. one who is rich or has pretensions to good taste.

vulgarism (ˈvʌlgəˌrɪzəm) *n.* **1.** a coarse, crude, or obscene expression. **2.** a word or phrase found only in the vulgar form of a language.

vulgarity (vʌlˈgærɪtɪ) *n., pl.* **-ties. 1.** the condition of being vulgar; lack of good manners. **2.** a vulgar action, phrase, etc.

vulgarize *or* **-rise** (ˈvʌlgəˌraɪz) *vb.* (*tr.*) **1.** to make commonplace or vulgar. **2.** to make (something little known or difficult to understand) widely known or popular among the public. —ˌ**vulgariˈzation** *or* **-riˈsation** *n.*

Vulgar Latin *n.* any of the dialects of Latin spoken in the Roman Empire other than classical Latin.

vulgate (ˈvʌlgeɪt, -gɪt) *n. Rare.* **1.** a commonly recognized text or version. **2.** the vernacular.

Vulgate (ˈvʌlgeɪt, -gɪt) *n.* **a.** (from the 13th century onwards) the fourth-century Latin version of the Bible produced by Jerome. **b.** (*as modifier*): *the Vulgate version.* [C17: < Med. L, < LL *vulgāta editiō* popular version (of the Bible), < L *vulgāre* to make common]

vulnerable (ˈvʌlnərəbᵊl) *adj.* **1.** capable of being physically or emotionally wounded or hurt. **2.** open to temptation, censure, etc. **3.** *Mil.* exposed to attack. **4.** *Bridge.* (of a side who have won one game towards rubber) subject to increased bonuses or penalties. [C17: < LL, < L *vulnerāre* to wound, < *vulnus* a wound] —ˌ**vulneraˈbility** *n.* —ˈ**vulnerably** *adv.*

vulnerary (ˈvʌlnərərɪ) *Med.* ~*adj.* **1.** of or used to heal a wound. ~*n., pl.* **-aries. 2.** a vulnerary drug or agent. [C16: < L *vulnerārius* < *vulnus* wound]

vulpine (ˈvʌlpaɪn) *adj.* **1.** of, relating to, or resembling a fox. **2.** crafty, clever, etc. [C17: < L *vulpīnus* foxlike, < *vulpēs* fox]

vulture (ˈvʌltʃə) *n.* **1.** any of various very large diurnal birds of prey of Africa, Asia, and warm parts of Europe, typically having broad wings and soaring flight and feeding on carrion. **2.** any similar bird of North, Central, and South America. **3.** a person or thing that preys greedily and ruthlessly on others, esp. the helpless. [C14: < OF *voltour,* < L *vultur*] —**vulturine** (ˈvʌltʃəˌraɪn) *or* ˈ**vulturous** *adj.*

vulva (ˈvʌlvə) *n., pl.* **-vae** (-viː) *or* **-vas.** the external genitals of human females, including the labia, mons pubis, clitoris, and the vaginal orifice. [C16: < L: covering, womb, matrix] —ˈ**vulvar** *adj.*

vulvitis (vʌlˈvaɪtɪs) *n.* inflammation of the vulva.

vv *abbrev. for* vice versa.

vv. *abbrev. for:* **1.** versus. **2.** *Music.* volumes.

w *or* **W** (ˈdʌbᵊlˌjuː) *n., pl.* **w's, W's,** *or* **Ws.** **1.** the 23rd letter of the English alphabet. **2.** a speech sound represented by this letter, usually a bilabial semivowel, as in *web.*

W *symbol for:* **1.** *Chem.* tungsten. [< NL *wolframium,* < G *Wolfram*] **2.** watt. **3.** West. **4.** women's (size). **5.** *Physics.* work.

w. *abbrev. for:* **1.** week. **2.** weight. **3.** *Cricket.* **a.** wide. **b.** wicket. **4.** width. **5.** wife. **6.** with.

W. *abbrev. for:* **1.** Wales. **2.** Welsh.

WA *abbrev. for:* **1.** Washington (state). **2.** Western Australia.

WAAAF *abbrev. for* Women's Auxiliary Australian Air Force.

WAAC (wæk) *n.* **1.** *acronym for* Women's Army Auxiliary Corps. **2.** Also called: **Waac.** a member of this corps.

WAAF (wæf) *n.* **1.** *acronym for* Women's Auxiliary Air Force. **2.** Also called: **Waaf.** a member of this force.

wabble (ˈwɒbᵊl) *vb., n.* a variant spelling of **wobble.**

wacke (ˈwækə) *n. Obs.* any of various soft earthy rocks derived from basalt. [C18: < G: rock, gravel, basalt]

wacky (ˈwækɪ) *adj.* **wackier, wackiest.** *Sl.* eccentric or unpredictable. [C19 (in dialect sense: a fool): < WHACK (hence, a *whacky,* a person who behaves as if he had been whacked on the head)] —ˈ**wackily** *adv.* —ˈ**wackiness** *n.*

wad (wɒd) *n.* **1.** a small mass or ball of fibrous or soft material, such as cotton wool, used esp. for packing or stuffing. **2. a.** a plug of paper, cloth, leather, etc., pressed against a charge to hold it in place in a muzzle-loading cannon. **b.** a disc of paper, felt, etc., used to hold in place the powder and shot in a shotgun cartridge. **3.** a roll or bundle of something, esp. of banknotes. ~*vb.* **wadding, wadded. 4.** to form (something) into a wad. **5.** (*tr.*) to roll into a wad or bundle. **6.** (*tr.*) **a.** to hold (a charge) in place with a wad. **b.** to insert a wad into (a gun). **7.** (*tr.*) to pack or stuff with wadding. [C14: < LL *wadda*]

wadding (ˈwɒdɪŋ) *n.* **1. a.** any fibrous or soft substance used as padding, stuffing, etc. **b.** a piece of this. **2.** material for wads used in cartridges or guns.

waddle (ˈwɒdᵊl) *vb.* (*intr.*) **1.** to walk with short steps, rocking slightly from side to side. ~*n.* **2.** a swaying gait or motion. [C16: prob. frequentative of WADE] —ˈ**waddler** *n.* —ˈ**waddling** *adj.*

waddy (ˈwɒdɪ) *n., pl.* **-dies. 1.** a heavy wooden club used as a weapon by Australian Aborigines. ~*vb.* **-dying, -died. 2.** (*tr.*) to hit with a waddy. [C19: < Abor., ? based on E WOOD]

wade (weɪd) *vb.* **1.** to walk with the feet immersed in (water, a stream, etc.). **2.** (*intr.;* often foll. by *through*) to proceed with difficulty: *to wade through a book.* **3.** (*intr.;* foll. by *in* or *into*) to attack energetically. ~*n.* **4.** the act or an instance of wading. [OE *wadan*] —ˈ**wadable** *or* ˈ**wadeable** *adj.*

wader (ˈweɪdə) *n.* **1.** a person or thing that wades. **2.** Also called: **wading bird.** any of various long-legged birds, esp. herons, storks, etc., that live near water and feed on fish, etc. **3.** a Brit. name for **shore bird.**

waders (ˈweɪdəz) *pl. n.* long waterproof boots, sometimes extending to the chest like trousers, worn by anglers.

wadi *or* **wady** (ˈwɒdɪ) *n., pl.* **-dies.** a watercourse in N Africa and Arabia, dry except in the rainy season. [C19: < Ar.]

wafer (ˈweɪfə) *n.* **1.** a thin crisp sweetened biscuit, served with ice cream, etc. **2.** *Christianity.* a thin disc of unleavened bread used in the Eucharist. **3.** *Pharmacol.* an envelope of rice paper enclosing a medicament. **4.** *Electronics.* a small thin slice of semiconductor material, such as silicon, that is separated into numerous individual components or circuits. **5.** a small thin disc of adhesive material used to seal letters, etc. ~*vb.* **6.** (*tr.*) to seal or fasten with a wafer. [C14: < OF *waufre,* < MLow G *wāfel*] —ˈ**wafery** *adj.*

waffle[1] (ˈwɒfᵊl) *n. Chiefly U.S. & Canad.* **a.** a crisp golden-brown pancake with deep indentations on both sides. **b.** (*as modifier*)*: waffle iron.* [C19: < Du. *wafel* (earlier *wæfel*), of Gmc origin]

waffle[2] (ˈwɒfᵊl) *Inf., chiefly Brit.* ~*vb.* **1.** (*intr.;* often foll. by *on*) to speak or write in a vague and wordy manner. ~*n.* **2.** vague and wordy speech or writing. [C19: <?] —ˈ**waffling** *adj., n.*

waft (wɑːft, wɒft) *vb.* **1.** to carry or be carried gently on or as if on the air or water. ~*n.* **2.** the act or an instance of wafting. **3.** something, such as a scent, carried on the air. **4.** *Naut.* (formerly) a signal flag hoisted furled to signify various messages depending on where it was flown. [C16 (in obs. sense: to convey by ship): back formation < C15 *wafter* a convoy vessel, < MDu. *wachter* guard]

wag[1] (wæg) *vb.* **wagging, wagged. 1.** to move or cause to move rapidly and repeatedly from side to side or up and down. **2.** to move (the tongue) or (of the tongue) to be moved rapidly in talking, esp. in gossip. **3.** to move (the finger) or (of the finger) to be moved from side to side, in or as in admonition. **4.** *Sl.* to play truant (esp. in **wag it**). ~*n.* **5.** the act or an instance of wagging. [C13: < OE *wagian* to shake]

wag[2] (wæg) *n.* a humorous or jocular person; wit. [C16: <?] —ˈ**waggish** *adj.*

wage (weɪdʒ) *n.* **1.** (*often pl.*) payment in return for work or services, esp. that made to workmen on a daily, hourly, weekly, or piecework basis. Cf. **salary. 2.** (*pl.*) *Econ.* the portion of the national income accruing to labour as earned income, as contrasted with the unearned income accruing to capital in the form of rent, interest, and dividends. **3.** (*often pl.*) recompense, return, or yield. ~*vb.* (*tr.*) **4.** to engage in. [C14: < OF *wagier* to pledge, < *wage,* of Gmc origin] —ˈ**wageless** *adj.*

wage earner *n.* **1.** a person who works for wages. **2.** the person who earns money to support a household by working.

wage freeze *n.* a statutory restriction on wage increases.

wage indexation *n.* a linking of wage rises to increases in the cost of living usually in order to maintain real wages during periods of high inflation.

wager (ˈweɪdʒə) *n.* **1.** an agreement to pay an amount of money as a result of the outcome of an unsettled matter. **2.** an amount staked on the outcome of such an event. **3. wager of battle.** (in medieval Britain) a pledge to do battle to decide guilt or innocence by single combat. **4. wager of law.** *English legal history.* a form of trial in which the accused offered to make oath of his innocence, supported by the oaths of 11 of his neighbours declaring their belief in his statements. ~*vb.* **5.** (when *tr., may take a clause as object*) to risk or bet (something) on the outcome of an unsettled matter. [C14: < Anglo-F *wageure* a pledge, < OF *wagier* to pledge; see WAGE] —ˈ**wagerer** *n.*

wage slave *n. Ironical.* a person dependent on a wage or salary.

wagga (ˈwɒgə) *n. Austral.* a blanket or bed covering made out of sacks stitched together. [C19: after *Wagga Wagga,* a city in SE Australia]

waggle (ˈwægᵊl) *vb.* **1.** to move or cause to move with a rapid shaking or wobbling motion. ~*n.* **2.** a rapid shaking or wobbling motion. [C16: < WAG[1]] —ˈ**waggly** *adj.*

waggon (ˈwægən) *n.* a variant spelling (esp. Brit.) of **wagon.**

wag-n-bietjie (ˈvɑːxᵊnˌbɪkɪ) *n. S. African.* any of

various thorn bushes or trees. [< Afrik. *wag* wait + *n* a + *bietjie* bit]

Wagnerian (vɑːɡˈnɪərɪən) *adj.* **1.** of or suggestive of the dramatic musical compositions of Richard Wagner (1813–83), German composer, their massive scale, dramatic and emotional intensity, etc. ~*n.* *also* **Wagnerite** (ˈvɑːɡnəˌraɪt). **2.** a follower or disciple of the music or theories of Richard Wagner.

wagon *or* **waggon** (ˈwæɡən) *n.* **1.** any of various types of wheeled vehicles, ranging from carts to lorries, esp. a vehicle with four wheels drawn by a horse, tractor, etc., and used for carrying heavy loads. **2.** *Brit.* a railway freight truck, esp. an open one. **3.** an obsolete word for **chariot**. **4. on** (*or* **off**) **the wagon.** *Inf.* abstaining (*or* no longer abstaining) from alcoholic drinks. [C16: < Du. *wagen* WAIN] —ˈ**wagonless** *or* ˈ**waggonless** *adj.*

wagoner *or* **waggoner** (ˈwæɡənə) *n.* a person who drives a wagon.

wagonette *or* **waggonette** (ˌwæɡəˈnɛt) *n.* a light four-wheeled horse-drawn vehicle with two lengthwise seats facing each other behind a crosswise driver's seat.

wagon-lit (*French* vaɡɔ̃li) *n., pl.* **wagons-lits** (vaɡɔ̃li). **1.** a sleeping car on a European railway. **2.** a compartment on such a car. [C19: < F, < *wagon* railway coach + *lit* bed]

wagonload *or* **waggonload** (ˈwæɡənˌləʊd) *n.* the load that is or can be carried by a wagon.

wagon train *n.* a supply train of horses and wagons, esp. one going over rough terrain.

wagon vault *n.* another name for **barrel vault**.

wagtail (ˈwæɡˌteɪl) *n.* any of various passerine songbirds of Eurasia and Africa, having a very long tail that wags when the bird walks.

Wahhabi *or* **Wahabi** (wəˈhɑːbɪ) *n., pl.* **-bis.** a member of a strictly conservative Muslim sect founded in the 18th century. —**Wah**ˈ**habism** *or* **Wa**ˈ**habism** *n.*

wahine (wɑːˈhiːnɪ) *n.* **1.** *N.Z.* a Maori woman. **2.** a Polynesian woman. [< Maori & Hawaiian]

wahoo (wɑːˈhuː, ˈwɑːhuː) *n., pl.* **-hoos.** a large fast-moving food and game fish of tropical seas. [<?]

wah-wah (ˈwɑːˌwɑː) *n.* **1.** the sound made by a trumpet, cornet, etc., when the bell is alternately covered and uncovered. **2.** an electronic attachment for an electric guitar, etc., that simulates this effect. [C20: imit.]

waif (weɪf) *n.* **1.** a person, esp. a child, who is homeless, friendless, or neglected. **2.** anything found and not claimed, the owner being unknown. [C14: < Anglo-Norman, var. of OF *gaif,* < ON] —ˈ**waif**ˌ**like** *adj.*

wail (weɪl) *vb.* **1.** (*intr.*) to utter a prolonged high-pitched cry, as of grief or misery. **2.** (*intr.*) to make a sound resembling such a cry: *the wind wailed in the trees.* **3.** (*tr.*) to lament, esp. with mournful sounds. ~*n.* **4.** a prolonged high-pitched mournful cry or sound. [C14: < ON] —ˈ**wailer** *n.*

Wailing Wall *n.* a wall in Jerusalem, a remnant of the temple of Herod, held sacred by Jews as a place of prayer and pilgrimage.

wain (weɪn) *n. Chiefly poetic.* a farm wagon or cart. [OE *wægn*]

wainscot (ˈweɪnskət) *n.* **1.** Also called: **wainscoting** *or* **wainscotting.** a lining applied to the walls of a room, esp. one of wood panelling. **2.** the lower part of the walls of a room, esp. when finished in a material different from the upper part. **3.** fine-quality oak used as wainscot. ~*vb.* **4.** (*tr.*) to line (a wall of a room) with a wainscot. [C14: < MLow G *wagenschot,* ? < *wagen* WAGON + *schot* planking]

wainwright (ˈweɪnˌraɪt) *n.* a person who makes wagons.

waist (weɪst) *n.* **1.** *Anat.* the constricted part of the trunk between the ribs and hips. **2.** the part of a garment covering the waist. **3.** the middle part of an object that resembles the waist in narrowness or position. **4.** the middle part of a ship. **5.** the middle section of an aircraft fuselage. **6.** the constriction between the thorax and abdomen in wasps and similar insects. [C14: <?] —ˈ**waistless** *adj.*

waistband (ˈweɪstˌbænd) *n.* an encircling band of material to finish and strengthen a skirt or trousers at the waist.

waistcoat (ˈweɪsˌkəʊt) *n.* **1.** a man's sleeveless waistlength garment worn under a suit jacket, usually buttoning up the front. **2.** a similar garment worn by women. ~U.S. and Canad. name: **vest.** —ˈ**waist**ˌ**coated** *adj.*

waistline (ˈweɪstˌlaɪn) *n.* **1.** a line around the body at the narrowest part of the waist. **2.** the intersection of the bodice and the skirt of a dress, etc., or the level of this.

wait (weɪt) *vb.* **1.** (when *intr.*, often foll. by *for, until,* or *to*) to stay in one place or remain inactive in expectation (of something). **2.** to delay temporarily or be temporarily delayed: *that work can wait.* **3.** (when *intr.*, usually foll. by *for*) (of things) to be ready or at hand; be in store (for a person): *supper was waiting for them when they got home.* **4.** (*intr.*) to act as a waiter or waitress. ~*n.* **5.** the act or an instance of waiting. **6.** a period of waiting. **7.** (*pl.*) *Rare.* a band of musicians who go around the streets, esp. at Christmas, singing and playing carols. **8. lie in wait.** to prepare an ambush (for someone). ~See also **wait on, wait up.** [C12: < OF *waitier*]

wait-a-bit *n.* any of various mainly tropical plants having sharp hooked thorns.

waiter (ˈweɪtə) *n.* **1.** a man whose occupation is to serve at table, as in a restaurant. **2.** a person who waits. **3.** a tray or salver.

waiting game *n.* the postponement of action or decision in order to gain the advantage.

waiting list *n.* a list of people waiting to obtain some object, treatment, status, etc.

waiting room *n.* a room in which people may wait, as at a railway station, doctor's or dentist's surgery, etc.

wait on *vb.* (*intr., prep.*) **1.** to serve at the table of. **2.** to act as an attendant to. ~*sentence substitute.* **3.** *N.Z.* stop! hold on! ~Also (for senses 1, 2): **wait upon.**

waitress (ˈweɪtrɪs) *n.* a woman who serves at table, as in a restaurant.

wait up *vb.* (*intr., adv.*) to delay going to bed in order to await some event.

waive (weɪv) *vb.* (*tr.*) **1.** to set aside or relinquish: *to waive one's right to something.* **2.** to refrain from enforcing or applying (a law, penalty, etc.). **3.** to defer. [C13: < OF *weyver,* < *waif* abandoned; see WAIF]

waiver (ˈweɪvə) *n.* **1.** the voluntary relinquishment, expressly or by implication, of some claim or right. **2.** the act or an instance of relinquishing a claim or right. **3.** a formal statement in writing of such relinquishment. [C17: < OF *weyver* to relinquish]

wake[1] (weɪk) *vb.* **waking, woke, woken. 1.** (often foll. by *up*) to rouse or become roused from sleep. **2.** (often foll. by *up*) to rouse or become roused from inactivity. **3.** (*intr.;* often foll. by *to* or *up to*) to become conscious or aware: *at last he woke up to the situation.* **4.** (*intr.*) to be or remain awake. ~*n.* **5.** a watch or vigil held over the body of a dead person during the night before burial. **6.** (in Ireland) festivities held after a funeral. **7.** the patronal or dedication festival of English parish churches. **8.** a solemn or ceremonial vigil. **9.** (*usually pl.*) an annual holiday in various towns in Northern England, when the local factories close. [OE *wacian*] —ˈ**waker** *n.*

▷ **Usage.** Where there is an object and the sense is the literal one *wake* (*up*) and *waken* are the commonest forms: *I wakened him; I woke him* (*up*). Both verbs are also commonly used without an object: *I woke up. Awake* and *awaken* are preferred to other forms of *wake* where the sense is a figurative one: *he awoke to the danger.*

wake[2] (weɪk) *n.* **1.** the waves or track left by a vessel or other object moving through water. **2.** the track or path left by anything that has passed: *wrecked houses in the wake of the hurricane.* [C16: of Scand. origin]

wakeful (ˈweɪkfʊl) *adj.* **1.** unable or unwilling to sleep. **2.** sleepless. **3.** alert. —ˈ**wakefully** *adv.* —ˈ**wakefulness** *n.*

wakeless (ˈweɪklɪs) *adj.* (of sleep) unbroken.

waken (ˈweɪkən) *vb.* to rouse or be roused from sleep or some other inactive state.

▷ **Usage.** See at **wake**[1].

wake-robin *n.* any of a genus of North American herbaceous plants having a whorl of three leaves and three-petalled solitary flowers.

wake-up *n.* **a wake-up to.** *Austral. sl.* fully alert to (a person, thing, action, etc.).

Waldenses (wɒlˈdɛnsiːz) *pl. n.* the members of a small sect founded as a reform movement within the Roman Catholic Church by Peter Waldo, a merchant of Lyons, in the late 12th century. —**Walˈdensian** *n., adj.*

Waldo (ˈwɔːldəʊ) *n., pl.* **-dos, -does.** a gadget for manipulating objects by remote control. [C20: after *Waldo* F. Jones, an inventor, in a science fiction story by Robert Heinlein]

wale (weɪl) *n.* **1.** the raised mark left on the skin after the stroke of a rod or whip. **2.** the weave or texture of a fabric, such as the ribs in corduroy. **3.** *Naut.* a ridge of planking along the rail of a ship. ~*vb.* **4.** (*tr.*) to raise a wale or wales on by striking. **5.** to weave with a wale. [OE *walu* weal]

walk (wɔːk) *vb.* **1.** (*intr.*) to move along or travel on foot at a moderate rate; advance in such a manner that at least one foot is always on the ground. **2.** (*tr.*) to pass through, on, or over on foot, esp. habitually. **3.** (*tr.*) to cause, assist, or force to move along at a moderate rate: *to walk a dog.* **4.** (*tr.*) to escort or conduct by walking: *to walk someone home.* **5.** (*intr.*) (of ghosts, spirits, etc.) to appear or move about in visible form. **6.** (*intr.*) to follow a certain course or way of life: *to walk in misery.* **7.** (*tr.*) to bring into a certain condition by walking: *I walked my shoes to shreds.* **8. walk it.** to win easily. **9. walk on air.** to be delighted or exhilarated. **10. walk tall.** *Chiefly U.S. & Canad. inf.* to have self-respect or pride. **11. walk the streets. a.** to be a prostitute. **b.** to wander round a town, esp. when looking for work or when homeless. ~*n.* **12.** the act or an instance of walking. **13.** the distance or extent walked. **14.** a manner of walking; gait. **15.** a place set aside for walking; promenade. **16.** a chosen profession or sphere of activity (esp. in **walk of life**). **17. a.** an arrangement of trees or shrubs in widely separated rows. **b.** the space between such rows. **18.** an enclosed ground for the exercise or feeding of domestic animals, esp. horses. **19.** *Chiefly Brit.* the route covered in the course of work, as by a tradesman or postman. **20.** a procession; march: *Orange walk.* **21.** *Obs.* the section of a forest controlled by a keeper. ~See also **walk away, walk into,** etc. [OE *wealcan*] —ˈ**walkable** *adj.*

walkabout (ˈwɔːkəˌbaʊt) *n.* **1.** a periodic nomadic excursion into the Australian bush made by an Aborigine. **2.** an occasion when celebrities, royalty, etc., walk among and meet the public.

walk away *vb.* (*intr., adv.*) **1.** to leave, esp. disregarding someone else's distress. **2. walk away with.** to achieve or win easily.

walker (ˈwɔːkə) *n.* **1.** a person who walks. **2.** Also called: **baby walker.** a tubular frame on wheels or casters to support a baby learning to walk. **3.** a similar support for walking, often with rubber feet, for use by disabled or infirm people.

walkie-talkie *or* **walky-talky** (ˌwɔːkɪˈtɔːkɪ) *n., pl.* **-talkies.** a small combined radio transmitter and receiver that can be carried around by one person: widely used by the police, medical services, etc.

walk-in *adj.* **1.** (of a cupboard) large enough to allow a person to enter and move about in. **2.** (of a flat or house) in a suitable condition for immediate occupation.

walking papers *pl. n. Sl., chiefly U.S. & Canad.* notice of dismissal.

walking stick *n.* **1.** a stick or cane carried in the hand to assist walking. **2.** the usual U.S. name for **stick insect.**

walk into *vb.* (*intr., prep.*) to meet with unwittingly: *to walk into a trap.*

Walkman (ˈwɔːkmən) *n., pl.* **-mans.** *Trademark.* a small portable cassette player with headphones.

walk off *vb.* **1.** (*intr.*) to depart suddenly. **2.** (*tr., adv.*) to get rid of by walking: *to walk off an attack of depression.* **3. walk (a person) off his feet.** to make (a person) walk so fast that he is exhausted. **4. walk off with. a.** to steal. **b.** to win, esp. easily.

walk-on *n.* **a.** a small part in a play or theatrical entertainment, esp. one without any lines. **b.** (*as modifier*): *a walk-on part.*

walk out *vb.* (*intr., adv.*) **1.** to leave without explanation, esp. in anger. **2.** to go on strike. **3. walk out on.** *Inf.* to abandon or desert. **4. walk out with.** *Brit., obs. or dialect.* to court or be courted by. ~*n.* **walkout. 5.** a strike by workers. **6.** the act of leaving a meeting, conference, etc., as a protest.

walkover (ˈwɔːkˌəʊvə) *n.* **1.** *Inf.* an easy or unopposed victory. **2.** *Horse racing.* **a.** the running or walking over the course by the only contestant entered in a race at the time of starting. **b.** a race won in this way. ~*vb.* **walk over.** (*intr., mainly prep.*) **3.** (*also adv.*) to win a race by a walkover. **4.** *Inf.* to beat (an opponent) conclusively or easily.

walk socks *pl. n.* the N.Z. name for **pop socks.**

walk through *Theatre.* ~*vb.* **1.** (*tr.*) to act or recite (a part) in a perfunctory manner, as at a first rehearsal. ~*n.* **walk-through. 2.** a rehearsal of a part.

walkway (ˈwɔːkˌweɪ) *n.* **1.** a path designed and sometimes landscaped for pedestrian use. **2.** a passage or path, esp. one for walking over machinery, connecting buildings, etc.

wall (wɔːl) *n.* **1. a.** a vertical construction made of stone, brick, wood, etc., with a length and height much greater than its thickness, used to enclose, divide, or support. **b.** (*as modifier*): *wall hangings.* Related adj.: **mural. 2.** (*often pl.*) a structure or rampart built to protect and surround a position or place for defensive purposes. **3.** *Anat.* any lining, membrane, or investing part that encloses or bounds a bodily cavity or structure: *abdominal wall.* Technical name: **paries.** Related adj.: **parietal. 4.** anything that suggests a wall in function or effect: *a wall of fire.* **5. drive** (*or* **push**) **to the wall.** to force into an awkward situation. **6. go to the wall.** *Inf.* to be ruined. **7. go** (*or* **drive**) **up the wall.** *Sl.* to become (*or* cause to become) crazy or furious. **8. have one's back to the wall.** to be in a very difficult situation. ~*vb.* (*tr.*) **9.** to protect, provide, or confine with or as if with a wall. **10.** (often foll. by *up*) to block (an opening) with a wall. **11.** (often foll. by *in* or *up*) to seal by or within a wall or walls. [OE *weall,* < L *vallum* palisade, < *vallus* stake] —**walled** *adj.* —ˈ**wall-less** *adj.*

wallaby (ˈwɒləbɪ) *n., pl.* **-bies** *or* **-by.** any of various herbivorous marsupials of Australia and New Guinea, similar to but smaller than kangaroos. [C19: < Abor. *wolabā*]

Wallaby (ˈwɒləbɪ) *n., pl.* **-bies.** a member of the international rugby union football team of Australia.

Wallace's line (ˈwɒlɪsɪz) *n.* the hypothetical boundary between the Oriental and Australasian zoogeographical regions, which runs through Indonesia and SE of the Philippines. [C20: after A. R. *Wallace* (1823–1913), Brit. naturalist]

wallah *or* **walla** (ˈwɒlə) *n.* (*usually in combination*) *Inf.* a person involved with or in charge of (a specified thing): *the book wallah.* [C18: < Hindi *-wālā* < Sansk. *pāla* protector]

wallaroo (ˌwɒləˈruː) *n., pl.* **-roos** *or* **-roo.** a large stocky Australian kangaroo of rocky or mountainous regions. [C19: < Abor. *wolarū*]

wall bars *pl. n.* a series of horizontal bars attached to a wall and used in gymnastics.

wallboard (ˈwɔːlˌbɔːd) *n.* a thin board made of materials, such as compressed wood fibres or gypsum plaster, between stiff paper, and used to cover walls, partitions, etc.

wall creeper *n.* a pink-and-grey woodpecker-like songbird of Eurasian mountain regions.

walled plain *n.* any of the largest of the lunar craters, having diameters between 50 and 300 kilometres.

wallet (ˈwɒlɪt) *n.* **1.** a small folding case, usually of leather, for holding paper money, documents, etc. **2.** *Arch., chiefly Brit.* a rucksack or knapsack. [C14: of Gmc origin]

walleye (ˈwɔːlˌaɪ) *n., pl.* **-eyes** *or* **-eye. 1.** a divergent squint. **2.** opacity of the cornea. **3.** an eye having a white or light-coloured iris. **4.** Also called: **walleyed pike.** a North American pikeperch valued as a food and game fish. [back formation < earlier *walleyed,* < ON *vagleygr,* < *vage* ? a film over the eye + *-eygr* -eyed, < *auga* eye; infl. by WALL] **—ˈwallˌeyed** *adj.*

wallflower (ˈwɔːlˌflaʊə) *n.* **1.** Also called: **gillyflower.** a cruciferous plant of S Europe, grown for its clusters of yellow, orange, brown, red, or purple fragrant flowers and naturalized on old walls, cliffs, etc. **2.** *Inf.* a person who stays on the fringes of a dance or party on account of lacking a partner or being shy.

wall of death *n.* (at a fairground) a giant cylinder round the inside vertical walls of which a motorcyclist rides.

Walloon (wɒˈluːn) *n.* **1.** a member of a French-speaking people living chiefly in S Belgium and adjacent parts of France. **2.** the French dialect of Belgium. *~adj.* **3.** of or characteristic of the Walloons or their dialect. [C16: < OF *Wallon,* < Med. L: foreigner, of Gmc origin]

wallop (ˈwɒləp) *vb.* **1.** (*tr.*) *Inf.* to beat soundly; strike hard. **2.** (*tr.*) *Inf.* to defeat utterly. **3.** (*intr.*) (of liquids) to boil violently. *~n.* **4.** *Inf.* a hard blow. **5.** *Inf.* the ability to hit powerfully, as of a boxer. **6.** *Inf.* a forceful impression. **7.** *Brit. sl.* beer. [C14: < OF *waloper* to gallop, < OF *galoper,* <?]

walloper (ˈwɒləpə) *n.* **1.** a person or thing that wallops. **2.** *Austral. sl.* a policeman.

walloping (ˈwɒləpɪŋ) *Inf.* *~n.* **1.** a thrashing. *~adj.* **2.** (intensifier): *a walloping drop in sales.*

wallow (ˈwɒləʊ) *vb.* (*intr.*) **1.** (esp. of certain animals) to roll about in mud, water, etc., for pleasure. **2.** to move about with difficulty. **3.** to indulge oneself in possessions, emotion, etc.: *to wallow in self-pity.* *~n.* **4.** the act or an instance of wallowing. **5.** a muddy place where animals wallow. [OE *wealwian* to roll (in mud)] **—ˈwallower** *n.*

wallpaper (ˈwɔːlˌpeɪpə) *n.* **1.** paper usually printed or embossed with designs for pasting onto walls and ceilings. *~vb.* **2.** to cover (a surface) with wallpaper.

wall pepper *n.* a small Eurasian plant having yellow flowers and acrid-tasting leaves.

wall plate *n.* a horizontal timber member placed along the top of a wall to support the ends of joists, rafters, etc., and distribute the load.

wallposter (ˈwɔːlˌpəʊstə) *n.* (in China) a bulletin or political message painted in large characters on a wall.

wall rocket *n.* any of several yellow-flowered European cruciferous plants that grow on old walls and in waste places.

wall rue *n.* a delicate fern that grows in rocky crevices and walls in North America and Eurasia.

Wall Street *n.* a street in lower Manhattan, New York, where the Stock Exchange and major banks are situated, regarded as the embodiment of American finance.

wall-to-wall *adj.* **1.** (esp. of carpeting) completely covering a floor. **2.** *Inf.* nonstop; widespread: *wall-to-wall sales.*

wally (ˈwɒlɪ) *n., pl.* **-lies.** *Sl.* a stupid person. [C20: shortened < the name *Walter*]

walnut (ˈwɔːlˌnʌt) *n.* **1.** any of a genus of deciduous trees of America, SE Europe, and Asia. They have aromatic leaves and flowers in catkins and are grown for their edible nuts and for their wood. **2.** the nut of any of these trees, having a wrinkled two-lobed seed and a hard wrinkled shell. **3.** the wood of any of these trees, used in making furniture, etc. **4.** a light yellowish-brown colour. *~adj.* **5.** made from the wood of a walnut tree: *a walnut table.* **6.** of the colour walnut. [OE *walh-hnutu,* lit.: foreign nut]

Walpurgis Night (vælˈpʊəgɪs) *n.* the eve of May 1, believed in German folklore to be the night of a witches' sabbath on the Brocken, in the Harz Mountains. [C19: translation of G *Walpurgisnacht,* the eve of the feast day of St Walpurga, 8th-cent. abbess in Germany]

walrus (ˈwɔːlrəs, ˈwɒl-) *n., pl.* **-ruses** *or* **-rus.** a mammal of northern seas, having a tough thick skin, upper canine teeth enlarged as tusks, and coarse whiskers, and feeding mainly on shellfish. [C17: prob. < Du., of Scand. origin]

walrus moustache *n.* a long thick moustache drooping at the ends.

waltz (wɔːls) *n.* **1.** a ballroom dance in triple time in which couples spin around as they progress round the room. **2.** a piece of music composed for or in the rhythm of this dance. *~vb.* **3.** to dance or lead (someone) in or as in a waltz. **4.** (*intr.*) to move in a sprightly and self-assured manner. **5.** (*intr.*) *Inf.* to succeed easily. **6. waltz Matilda** *Austral.* See **Matilda.** [C18: < G *Walzer,* < MHG *walzen* to roll]

waltzer (ˈwɔːlsə) *n.* **1.** a person who waltzes. **2.** a fairground roundabout on which people are spun round and moved up and down as it revolves.

wampum (ˈwɒmpəm) *n.* (formerly) money used by North American Indians, made of cylindrical shells strung or woven together. Also called: **peag, peage.** [C17: of Amerind origin, short for *wampumpeag,* < *wampompeag,* < *wampan* light + *api* string + *-ag* pl. suffix]

wan (wɒn) *adj.* **wanner, wannest. 1.** unnaturally pale, esp. from sickness, grief, etc. **2.** suggestive of ill health, unhappiness, etc. **3.** (of light, stars, etc.) faint or dim. [OE *wann* dark] **—ˈwanly** *adv.* **—ˈwanness** *n.*

wand (wɒnd) *n.* **1.** a slender supple stick or twig. **2.** a thin rod carried as a symbol of authority. **3.** a rod used by a magician, etc. **4.** *Inf.* a conductor's baton. **5.** *Archery.* a marker used to show the distance at which the archer stands from the target. [C12: < ON *vōndr*]

wander (ˈwɒndə) *vb.* (*mainly intr.*) **1.** (*also tr.*) to move or travel about, in, or through (a place) without any definite purpose or destination. **2.** to proceed in an irregular course. **3.** to go astray, as from a path or course. **4.** (of thoughts, etc.) to lose concentration. **5.** to think or speak incoherently or illogically. *~n.* **6.** the act or an instance of wandering. [OE *wandrian*] **—ˈwanderer** *n.* **—ˈwandering** *adj., n.*

wandering albatross *n.* a large albatross having a very wide wingspan and a white plumage with black wings.

wandering Jew *n.* any of several related creeping or trailing plants of tropical America, such as tradescantia.

Wandering Jew *n.* (in medieval legend) a character condemned to roam the world eternally because he mocked Christ on the day of the Crucifixion.

wanderlust (ˈwɒndəˌlʌst) *n.* a great desire to travel and rove about. [< G *Wanderlust,* lit.: wander desire]

wanderoo (ˌwɒndəˈruː) *n., pl.* **-deroos.** a macaque monkey of India and Sri Lanka, having black fur with a ruff of long greyish fur on each side of the face. [C17: < Sinhalese *vanduru* monkeys, lit.: forest-dwellers]

wandoo (wɒnˈduː) *n.* a eucalyptus tree of W Australia, having white bark and durable wood. [< Abor.]

wane (weɪn) *vb.* (*intr.*) **1.** (of the moon) to show a gradually decreasing portion of illuminated surface, between full moon and new moon. **2.** to decrease gradually in size, strength, power, etc. **3.** to draw to a close. *~n.* **4.** a decrease, as in size, strength, power, etc. **5.** the period during which the moon wanes. **6.** a drawing to a close.

7. a rounded surface or defective edge of a plank, where the bark was. **8. on the wane.** in a state of decline. [OE *wanian* (vb.)] —**'waney** *or* **'wany** *adj.*

wangle ('wæŋgᵊl) *Inf.* ~*vb.* **1.** (*tr.*) to use devious methods to get or achieve (something) for (oneself or another): *he wangled himself a salary increase.* **2.** to manipulate or falsify (a situation, etc.). ~*n.* **3.** the act or an instance of wangling. [C19: orig. printers' sl., ? a blend of WAGGLE & dialect *wankle* wavering, < OE *wancol*] —**'wangler** *n.*

wanigan *or* **wannigan** ('wɒnɪgən) *n. Canad.* **1.** a lumberjack's chest or box. **2.** a cabin, caboose, or houseboat. [C19: < Algonquian]

wank (wæŋk) *Taboo sl.* ~*vb.* **1.** (*intr.*) to masturbate. ~*n.* **2.** an instance of wanking. [<?]

wankel engine ('wæŋkᵊl) *n.* a type of rotary internal-combustion engine without reciprocating parts. It consists of a curved triangular-shaped piston rotating in an elliptical combustion chamber. [C20: after Felix *Wankel* (born 1902), G engineer who invented it]

wanker ('wæŋkə) *n. Sl.* **1.** *Taboo.* a person who wanks; masturbator. **2.** *Derog.* a worthless fellow.

want (wɒnt) *vb.* **1.** (*tr.*) to feel a need or longing for: *I want a new hat.* **2.** (when *tr., may take a clause as object or an infinitive*) to wish, need, or desire (something or to do something): *he wants to go home.* **3.** (*intr.;* usually used with a negative and often foll. by *for*) to be lacking or deficient (in something necessary or desirable): *the child wants for nothing.* **4.** (*tr.*) to feel the absence of: *lying on the ground makes me want my bed.* **5.** (*tr.*) to fall short by (a specified amount). **6.** (*tr.*) *Chiefly Brit.* to have need of or require (doing or being something): *your shoes want cleaning.* **7.** (*intr.*) to be destitute. **8.** (*tr.; often passive*) to seek or request the presence of: *you're wanted upstairs.* **9.** (*tr.; takes an infinitive*) *Inf.* should or ought (to do something): *you don't want to go out so late.* ~*n.* **10.** the act or an instance of wanting. **11.** anything that is needed, desired, or lacked: *to supply someone's wants.* **12.** a lack, shortage, or absence: *for want of common sense.* **13.** the state of being in need: *the state should help those in want.* **14.** a sense of lack; craving. [C12 (vb., in the sense: it is lacking), C13 (n.): < ON *vanta* to be deficient] —**'wanter** *n.*

want ad *n. Inf.* a classified advertisement in a newspaper, magazine, etc., for something wanted, such as property or employment.

wanting ('wɒntɪŋ) *adj.* (*postpositive*) **1.** lacking or absent. **2.** not meeting requirements or expectations: *you have been found wanting.*

wanton ('wɒntən) *adj.* **1.** dissolute, licentious, or immoral. **2.** without motive, provocation, or justification: *wanton destruction.* **3.** maliciously and unnecessarily cruel. **4.** unrestrained: *wanton spending.* **5.** *Arch. or poetic.* playful or capricious. **6.** *Arch.* (of vegetation, etc.) luxuriant. ~*n.* **7.** a licentious person, esp. a woman. ~*vb.* **8.** (*intr.*) to behave in a wanton manner. [C13 *wantowen* (in the obs. sense: unruly): < *wan-* (prefix equivalent to UN-[1]) + *-towen,* < OE *togen* brought up, < *tēon* to bring up] —**'wantonly** *adv.* —**'wantonness** *n.*

wapentake ('wɒpən,teɪk, 'wæp-) *n. English legal history.* a subdivision of certain shires or counties, esp. in the Midlands and North of England, corresponding to the hundred in other shires. [OE *wǣpen(ge)tæc*]

wapiti ('wɒpɪtɪ) *n., pl.* **-tis.** a large North American deer with large much-branched antlers, now also found in New Zealand. [C19: of Amerind origin, lit.: white deer, < *wap* (unattested) white; < the animal's white tail and rump]

war (wɔː) *n.* **1.** open armed conflict between two or more parties, nations, or states. Related adj.: **belligerent** (see sense 2). **2.** a particular armed conflict: *the 1973 war in the Middle East.* **3.** the techniques of armed conflict as a study, science, or profession. **4.** any conflict or contest: *the war against crime.* **5.** (*modifier*) of, resulting from, or characteristic of war: *war damage; a war story.* **6. in the wars.** *Inf.* (esp. of a child) hurt or knocked about, esp. as a result of quarrelling and fighting. ~*vb.* **warring, warred.** **7.** (*intr.*) to conduct a war. [C12: < ONorthern F *werre* (var. of OF *guerre*), of Gmc origin]

War. *abbrev. for* Warwickshire.

waratah ('wɒrətə) *n. Austral.* a shrub having dark green leaves and large clusters of crimson flowers. [< Abor.]

warble[1] ('wɔːbᵊl) *vb.* **1.** to sing (words, songs, etc.) with trills, runs, and other embellishments. **2.** (*tr.*) to utter in a song. ~*n.* **3.** the act or an instance of warbling. [C14: via OF *werbler,* of Gmc origin]

warble[2] ('wɔːbᵊl) *n. Vet. science.* **1.** a small lumpy abscess under the skin of cattle caused by the larvae of the warble fly. **2.** a hard lump of tissue on a horse's back, caused by prolonged friction of a saddle. [C16: <?]

warble fly *n.* any of a genus of hairy beelike dipterous flies, the larvae of which produce warbles in cattle.

warbler ('wɔːblə) *n.* **1.** a person or thing that warbles. **2.** a small active passerine songbird of the Old World having a cryptic plumage and slender bill, that is an arboreal insectivore. **3.** a small bird of an American family, similar to the Old World songbird but often brightly coloured.

war correspondent *n.* a journalist who reports on a war from the scene of action.

war crime *n.* a crime committed in wartime in violation of the accepted customs, such as ill-treatment of prisoners, etc. —**war criminal** *n.*

war cry *n.* **1.** a rallying cry used by combatants in battle. **2.** a cry, slogan, etc., used to rally support for a cause.

ward (wɔːd) *n.* **1.** (in many countries) one of the districts into which a city, town, parish, or other area is divided for administration, election of representatives, etc. **2. a.** a room in a hospital, esp. one for patients requiring similar kinds of care: *a maternity ward.* **b.** (*as modifier*): *ward maid.* **3.** one of the divisions of a prison. **4.** an open space enclosed within the walls of a castle. **5.** *Law.* Also called: **ward of court.** a person, esp. a minor or one legally incapable of managing his own affairs, placed under the control or protection of a guardian or of a court. **6.** the state of being under guard or in custody. **7.** a means of protection. **8. a.** an internal ridge or bar in a lock that prevents an incorrectly cut key from turning. **b.** a corresponding groove cut in a key. ~*vb.* **9.** (*tr.*) *Arch.* to guard or protect. ~See also **ward off.** [OE *weard* protector] —**'wardless** *adj.*

-ward *suffix.* **1.** (*forming adjectives*) indicating direction towards: *a backward step.* **2.** (*forming adverbs*) a variant and the usual U.S. and Canad. form of **-wards.** [OE *-weard* towards]

war dance *n.* a ceremonial dance performed before going to battle or after victory, esp. by certain North American Indian peoples.

warden ('wɔːdᵊn) *n.* **1.** a person who has the charge or care of something, esp. a building, or someone. **2.** a public official, esp. one responsible for the enforcement of certain regulations: *traffic warden.* **3.** a person employed to patrol a national park or a safari park. **4.** *Chiefly U.S. & Canad.* the chief officer in charge of a prison. **5.** *Brit.* the principal of any of various universities or colleges. **6.** See **churchwarden** (sense 1). [C13: < OF *wardein,* < *warder* to guard, of Gmc origin]

warder ('wɔːdə) *or* (*fem.*) **wardress** *n.* **1.** *Chiefly Brit.* an officer in charge of prisoners in a jail. **2.** a person who guards or has charge of something. [C14: < Anglo-F *wardere,* < OF *warder* to guard, of Gmc origin]

ward heeler *n. U.S. politics, disparaging.* a party worker who canvasses votes and performs chores for a political boss. Also called: **heeler.**

ward off *vb.* (*tr., adv.*) to turn aside or repel.

wardrobe ('wɔːdrəʊb) *n.* **1.** a tall closet or cupboard, with a rail or hooks on which to hang clothes. **2.** the total collection of articles of clothing belonging to one person. **3. a.** the collection of costumes belonging to a theatre or theatrical company. **b.** (*as modifier*): *wardrobe mistress.* [C14: < OF *warderobe,* < *warder* to guard + *robe* ROBE]

wardrobe trunk *n.* a large upright rectangular travelling case, usually opening longitudinally, with one side having a hanging rail, the other having drawers or compartments.

wardroom (ˈwɔːdˌruːm, -ˌrʊm) *n.* **1.** the quarters assigned to the officers (except the captain) of a warship. **2.** the officers of a warship collectively, excepting the captain.

-wards *or* **-ward** *suffix forming adverbs.* indicating direction towards: *a step backwards.* Cf. **-ward.** [OE *-weardes* towards]

wardship (ˈwɔːdʃɪp) *n.* the state of being a ward.

ware[1] (wɛə) *n.* (*often in combination*) **1.** (*functioning as sing.*) articles of the same kind or material: *silverware.* **2.** porcelain or pottery of a specified type: *jasper ware.* ~See also **wares.** [OE *waru*]

ware[2] (wɛə) *vb. Arch.* another word for **beware.** [OE *wær.* See AWARE, BEWARE]

warehouse *n.* (ˈwɛəˌhaʊs). **1.** a place where goods are stored prior to their use, distribution, or sale. **2.** See **bonded warehouse.** **3.** *Chiefly Brit.* a large commercial, esp. wholesale, establishment. ~*vb.* (ˈwɛəˌhaʊz, -ˌhaʊs). **4.** (*tr.*) to store or place in a warehouse, esp. a bonded warehouse. —ˈ**wareˌhouseman** *n.*

warehousing (ˈwɛəˌhaʊzɪŋ) *n. Business.* an attempt to maintain the price of a company's shares or to gain a significant stake in a company without revealing the identity of the purchaser.

wares (wɛəz) *pl. n.* **1.** articles of manufacture considered as being for sale. **2.** any talent or asset regarded as a saleable commodity.

warfare (ˈwɔːˌfɛə) *n.* **1.** the act, process, or an instance of waging war. **2.** conflict or strife.

warfarin (ˈwɔːfərɪn) *n.* a crystalline insoluble compound, used to kill rodents and, in the form of its sodium salt, as a medical anticoagulant. [C20: < the patent owners *W(isconsin) A(lumni) R(esearch) F(oundation)* + (COUM)ARIN]

war game *n.* **1.** a notional tactical exercise for training military commanders, in which no military units are actually deployed. **2.** a game in which model soldiers are used to create battles, esp. past battles, in order to study tactics.

warhead (ˈwɔːˌhɛd) *n.* the part of the fore end of a missile or projectile that contains explosives.

warhorse (ˈwɔːˌhɔːs) *n.* **1.** a horse used in battle. **2.** *Inf.* a veteran soldier or politician.

warlike (ˈwɔːˌlaɪk) *adj.* **1.** of, relating to, or used in war. **2.** hostile or belligerent. **3.** fit or ready for war.

warlock (ˈwɔːˌlɒk) *n.* a man who practises black magic. [OE *wǣrloga* oath breaker, < *wǣr* oath + *-loga* liar, < *lēogan* to lie]

warlord (ˈwɔːˌlɔːd) *n.* a military leader of a nation or part of a nation: *the Chinese warlords.*

warm (wɔːm) *adj.* **1.** characterized by or having a moderate degree of heat. **2.** maintaining or imparting heat: *a warm coat.* **3.** having or showing ready affection, kindliness, etc.: *a warm personality.* **4.** lively or passionate: *a warm debate.* **5.** cordial or enthusiastic: *warm support.* **6.** quickly or easily aroused: *a warm temper.* **7.** (of colours) predominantly red or yellow in tone. **8.** (of a scent, trail, etc.) recently made. **9.** near to finding a hidden object or guessing facts, as in children's games. **10.** *Inf.* uncomfortable or disagreeable, esp. because of the proximity of danger. ~*vb.* **11.** (sometimes foll. by *up*) to make or become warm or warmer. **12.** (when *intr.,* often foll. by *to*) to make or become excited, enthusiastic, etc. (about): *he warmed to the idea of buying a new car.* **13.** (*intr.;* often foll. by *to*) to feel affection, kindness, etc. (for someone): *I warmed to her mother from the start.* ~*n. Inf.* **14.** a warm place or area: *come into the warm.* **15.** the act or an instance of warming or being warmed. ~See also **warm up.** [OE *wearm*] —ˈ**warmer** *n.* —ˈ**warmish** *adj.* —ˈ**warmly** *adv.* —ˈ**warmness** *n.*

warm-blooded *adj.* **1.** ardent, impetuous, or passionate. **2.** *Zool.* the nontechnical term for **homoiothermic.** —ˌ**warm-ˈbloodedness** *n.*

war memorial *n.* a monument, usually an obelisk or cross, to those who die in a war, esp. those from a particular locality.

warm front *n. Meteorol.* the boundary between a warm air mass and the cold air above.

warm-hearted *adj.* kindly, generous, or readily sympathetic. —ˌ**warm-ˈheartedly** *adv.* —ˌ**warm-ˈheartedness** *n.*

warming pan *n.* a pan, often of copper and having a long handle, filled with hot coals and formerly drawn over the sheets to warm a bed.

warmonger (ˈwɔːˌmʌŋgə) *n.* a person who fosters warlike ideas or advocates war. —ˈ**warˌmongering** *n.*

warmth (wɔːmθ) *n.* **1.** the state, quality, or sensation of being warm. **2.** intensity of emotion: *he denied the accusation with some warmth.* **3.** affection or cordiality.

warm up *vb.* (*adv.*) **1.** to make or become warm or warmer. **2.** (*intr.*) to exercise immediately before a game, contest, or more vigorous exercise. **3.** (*intr.*) to get ready for something important; prepare. **4.** to run (an engine, etc.) until the working temperature is attained, or (of an engine, etc.) to undergo this process. **5.** to make or become more animated: *the party warmed up when Tom came.* **6.** to reheat (already cooked food) or (of such food) to be reheated. ~*n.* **warm-up.** **7.** the act or an instance of warming up. **8.** a preparatory exercise routine.

warn (wɔːn) *vb.* **1.** to notify or make (someone) aware of danger, harm, etc. **2.** (*tr.; often takes a negative and an infinitive*) to advise or admonish (someone) as to action, conduct, etc.: *I warn you not to do that again.* **3.** (*takes a clause as object or an infinitive*) to inform (someone) in advance: *he warned them that he would arrive late.* **4.** (*tr.;* usually foll. by *away, off,* etc.) to give notice to go away, be off, etc. [OE *wearnian*] —ˈ**warner** *n.*

warning (ˈwɔːnɪŋ) *n.* **1.** a hint, intimation, threat, etc., of harm or danger. **2.** advice to beware or desist. **3.** an archaic word for **notice** (sense 6). ~*adj.* **4.** (*prenominal*) intended or serving to warn: *a warning look.* —ˈ**warningly** *adv.*

warp (wɔːp) *vb.* **1.** to twist or cause to twist out of shape, as from heat, damp, etc. **2.** to turn or cause to turn from a true, correct, or proper course. **3.** *Naut.* to move (a vessel) by hauling on a rope fixed to a stationary object ashore or (of a vessel) to be moved thus. **4.** (*tr.*) to flood (land) with water from which alluvial matter is deposited. ~*n.* **5.** the state or condition of being twisted out of shape. **6.** a twist, distortion, or bias. **7.** a mental or moral deviation. **8.** the yarns arranged lengthways on a loom, forming the threads through which the weft yarns are woven. **9.** *Naut.* a rope used for warping a vessel. **10.** alluvial sediment deposited by water. [OE *wearp* a throw] —ˈ**warpage** *n.* —**warped** *adj.* —ˈ**warper** *n.*

war paint *n.* **1.** painted decoration of the face and body applied by certain North American Indians before battle. **2.** *Inf.* finery or regalia. **3.** *Inf.* cosmetics.

warpath (ˈwɔːˌpɑːθ) *n.* **1.** the route taken by North American Indians on a warlike expedition. **2. on the warpath. a.** preparing to engage in battle. **b.** *Inf.* in a state of anger.

warplane (ˈwɔːˌpleɪn) *n.* any aircraft designed for and used in warfare.

warrant (ˈwɒrənt) *n.* **1.** anything that gives authority for an action or decision; authorization. **2.** a document that certifies or guarantees, such as a receipt, licence, or commission. **3.** *Law.* an authorization issued by a magistrate allowing a constable or other officer to search or seize property, arrest a person, or perform some other specified act. **4.** (in certain armed services) the official authority for the appointment of warrant officers. ~*vb.* (*tr.*) **5.** to guarantee the quality, condition, etc., of (something). **6.** to give authority or power to. **7.** to attest to the character, worthiness, etc., of. **8.** to guarantee (a purchaser of merchandise) against loss of, damage to, or misrepresentation concerning the merchandise. **9.** *Law.* to guarantee (the title to an estate or other property). **10.** to declare confidently. [C13: < Anglo-F, var. of OF *guarant,* < *guarantir* to guarantee, of Gmc origin] —**'warrantable** *adj.* —ˌ**warranta'bility** *n.* —**'warrantably** *adv.* —**'warranter** *n.*

warrantee (ˌwɒrən'tiː) *n.* a person to whom a warranty is given.

warrant officer *n.* an officer in certain armed services who holds a rank between those of commissioned and noncommissioned officers. In the British army the rank has two classes: regimental sergeant major and company sergeant major.

Warrant of Fitness *n. N.Z.* a six-monthly certificate required for motor vehicles certifying mechanical soundness.

warrantor ('wɒrənˌtɔː) *n.* an individual or company that provides a warranty.

warranty ('wɒrəntɪ) *n., pl.* **-ties. 1.** *Property law.* a covenant, express or implied, by which the vendor of real property vouches for the security of the title conveyed. **2.** *Contract law.* an express or implied term in a contract collateral to the main purpose, such as an undertaking that goods contracted to be sold shall meet specified requirements as to quality, etc. **3.** *Insurance law.* an undertaking by the party insured that the facts given regarding the risk are as stated. [C14: < Anglo-F *warantie,* < *warantir* to warrant, var. of OF *guarantir;* see WARRANT]

warren ('wɒrən) *n.* **1.** a series of interconnected underground tunnels in which rabbits live. **2.** a colony of rabbits. **3.** an overcrowded area or dwelling. **4.** *Chiefly Brit.* an enclosed place where small game animals or birds are kept, esp. for breeding. [C14: < Anglo-F *warenne,* of Gmc origin]

warrigal ('wɒrɪgæl) *Austral.* ~*n.* **1.** a dingo. **2.** a wild horse or other wild creature. ~*adj.* **3.** untamed or wild. [C19: < Abor.]

warrior ('wɒrɪə) *n.* **a.** a person engaged in, experienced in, or devoted to war. **b.** (*as modifier*): *a warrior nation.* [C13: < OF *werreieor,* < *werre* WAR]

Warsaw Pact ('wɔːsɔː) *n.* a military treaty and association of E European countries, formed in 1955.

warship ('wɔːˌʃɪp) *n.* a vessel armed, armoured, and otherwise equipped for naval warfare.

Wars of the Roses *pl. n.* the struggle for the throne in England (1455-85) between the House of York (symbolized by the white rose) and the House of Lancaster (symbolized by the red rose).

wart (wɔːt) *n.* **1.** *Pathol.* any firm abnormal elevation of the skin caused by a virus. **2.** *Bot.* a small rounded outgrowth. **3. warts and all.** with all blemishes evident. [OE *weart*(*e*)] —**'warty** *adj.*

wart hog *n.* a wild pig of S and E Africa, having heavy tusks, wartlike protuberances on the face, and a mane of coarse hair.

wartime ('wɔːˌtaɪm) *n.* **a.** a period or time of war. **b.** (*as modifier*): *wartime conditions.*

war whoop *n.* the yell or howl uttered, esp. by North American Indians, while making an attack.

wary ('wɛərɪ) *adj.* **warier, wariest. 1.** watchful, cautious, or alert. **2.** characterized by caution or watchfulness. [C16: < WARE² + -Y¹] —**'warily** *adv.* —**'wariness** *n.*

was (wɒz; *unstressed* wəz) *vb.* (used with *I, he, she, it,* and with singular nouns) **1.** the past tense (indicative mood) of **be. 2.** *Not standard.* a form of the subjunctive mood used in place of *were,* esp. in conditional sentences: *if the film was to be with you, would you be able to process it?* [OE *wæs,* < *wesan* to be]

wash (wɒʃ) *vb.* **1.** to apply water or other liquid, usually with soap, to (oneself, clothes, etc.) in order to cleanse. **2.** (*tr.;* often foll. by *away, from, off,* etc.) to remove by the application of water or other liquid and usually soap: *she washed the dirt from her clothes.* **3.** (*intr.*) to be capable of being washed without damage or loss of colour. **4.** (of an animal such as a cat) to cleanse (itself or another animal) by licking. **5.** (*tr.*) to cleanse from pollution or defilement. **6.** (*tr.*) to make wet or moist. **7.** (often foll. by *away,* etc.) to move or be moved by water: *the flood washed away the bridge.* **8.** (esp. of waves) to flow or sweep against or over (a surface or object), often with a lapping sound. **9.** to form by erosion or be eroded: *the stream washed a ravine in the hill.* **10.** (*tr.*) to apply a thin coating of paint, metal, etc., to. **11.** (*tr.*) to separate (ore, etc.) from (gravel, etc.) by immersion in water. **12.** (*intr.; usually used with a negative*) *Inf., chiefly Brit.* to admit of testing or proof: *your excuses won't wash.* ~*n.* **13.** the act or process of washing. **14.** a quantity of articles washed together. **15.** a preparation or thin liquid used as a coating or in washing: *a thin wash of paint.* **16.** *Med.* **a.** any medicinal lotion for application to a part of the body. **b.** (*in combination*): *an eyewash.* **17. a.** the technique of making wash drawings. **b.** See **wash drawing. 18.** the erosion of soil by the action of flowing water. **19.** a mass of alluvial material transported and deposited by flowing water. **20.** land that is habitually washed by tidal or river waters. **21.** the disturbance in the air or water produced at the rear of an aircraft, boat, or other moving object. **22.** gravel, earth, etc., from which valuable minerals may be washed. **23.** waste liquid matter or liquid refuse, esp. as fed to pigs. **24.** an alcoholic liquid resembling strong beer, resulting from the fermentation of wort in the production of whisky. **25. come out in the wash.** *Inf.* to become known or apparent in the course of time. ~See also **wash down, wash out, wash up.** [OE *wæscan, waxan*]

washable ('wɒʃəbᵊl) *adj.* (esp. of fabrics or clothes) capable of being washed without deteriorating. —ˌ**washa'bility** *n.*

wash-and-wear *adj.* (of fabrics, garments, etc.) requiring only light washing, short drying time, and little or no ironing.

washbasin ('wɒʃˌbeɪsᵊn) *n.* **1.** Also called: **washbowl.** a basin or bowl for washing the face and hands. **2.** Also called: **wash-hand basin.** a bathroom fixture with taps, used for washing the face and hands.

washboard ('wɒʃˌbɔːd) *n.* **1.** a board having a surface, usually of corrugated metal, on which, esp. formerly, clothes were scrubbed. **2.** such a board used as a rhythm instrument played with the fingers in skiffle, country-and-western music, etc. **3.** *Naut.* a vertical planklike shield fastened to the gunwales of a boat to prevent water from splashing over the side.

washcloth ('wɒʃˌklɒθ) *n.* **1.** another term for **dishcloth. 2.** the U.S. and Canad. word for **face cloth.**

washday ('wɒʃˌdeɪ) *n.* a day on which clothes and linen are washed.

wash down *vb.* (*tr., adv.*) **1.** to wash completely, esp. from top to bottom. **2.** to take drink with or after (food or another drink).

wash drawing *n.* a pen-and-ink drawing that has been lightly brushed over with water to soften the lines.

washed out *adj.* (**washed-out** *when prenominal*). **1.** faded or colourless. **2.** exhausted, esp. when being pale in appearance.

washed up *adj.* (**washed-up** *when prenominal*). *Inf., chiefly U.S., Canad., & N.Z.* no longer hopeful, etc.: *our hopes for the new deal are all washed up.*

washer ('wɒʃə) *n.* **1.** a person or thing that washes. **2.** a flat ring or drilled disc of metal used under the head of a bolt or nut. **3.** any flat ring of rubber, felt, metal, etc., used to provide a seal under a nut or in a tap or valve seat. **4.** See **washing machine. 5.** *Austral.* a face cloth; flannel.

washerwoman ('wɒʃəˌwʊmən) *or* (*masc.*) **washerman** *n., pl.* **-women** *or* **-men.** a person who washes clothes for a living.

washery (ˈwɒʃərɪ) *n., pl.* **-eries.** a plant at a mine where water or other liquid is used to remove dirt from a mineral, esp. coal.

wash-hand basin *n.* another name for **washbasin** (sense 2).

wash house *n.* (formerly) an outbuilding in which clothes were washed.

washing (ˈwɒʃɪŋ) *n.* **1.** articles that have been or are to be washed together on a single occasion. **2.** something, such as gold dust, that has been obtained by washing. **3.** a thin coat of something applied in liquid form.

washing machine *n.* a mechanical apparatus, usually powered by electricity, for washing clothing, linens, etc.

washing powder *n.* powdered detergent for washing fabrics.

washing soda *n.* crystalline sodium carbonate, esp. when used as a cleansing agent.

washing-up *n. Brit.* **1.** the washing of dishes, cutlery, etc., after a meal. **2.** dishes and cutlery waiting to be washed up. **3.** (*as modifier*): *a washing-up machine.*

wash out *vb.* (*adv.*) **1.** (*tr.*) to wash (the inside of something) so as to remove (dirt). **2.** Also: **wash off.** to remove or be removed by washing: *grass stains don't wash out easily.* ~*n.* **washout. 3.** *Geol.* **a.** erosion of the earth's surface by the action of running water. **b.** a narrow channel produced by this. **4.** *Inf.* **a.** a total failure or disaster. **b.** an incompetent person.

washroom (ˈwɒʃˌruːm, -ˌrʊm) *n. U.S. & Canad.* a euphemism for **lavatory.**

washstand (ˈwɒʃˌstænd) *n.* a piece of furniture designed to hold a basin, etc., for washing the face and hands.

washtub (ˈwɒʃˌtʌb) *n.* a tub or large container used for washing anything, esp. clothes.

wash up *vb.* (*adv.*) **1.** *Chiefly Brit.* to wash (dishes, cutlery, etc.) after a meal. **2.** (*intr.*) *U.S.* to wash one's face and hands. ~*n.* **washup. 3.** *Austral.* the end, outcome of a process: *in the washup, three were elected.*

washy (ˈwɒʃɪ) *adj.* **washier, washiest. 1.** over-diluted, watery, or weak. **2.** lacking intensity or strength. —ˈ**washiness** *n.*

wasn't (ˈwɒzᵊnt) *contraction of* was not.

wasp (wɒsp) *n.* **1.** a social hymenopterous insect, such as the **common wasp,** having a black-and-yellow body and an ovipositor specialized for stinging. **2.** any of various solitary hymenopterans, such as the digger wasp and gall wasp. [OE *wæsp*] —ˈ**wasp**ˌ**like** *adj.* —ˈ**waspy** *adj.* —ˈ**waspily** *adv.* —ˈ**waspiness** *n.*

Wasp *or* **WASP** (wɒsp) *n. U.S. & Canad., usually derog.* a person descended from N European, usually Protestant, stock, forming a group often considered the most dominant, privileged, and influential in American society. [C20: *W(hite) A(nglo-)S(axon) P(rotestant)*]

waspish (ˈwɒspɪʃ) *adj.* **1.** relating to or suggestive of a wasp. **2.** easily annoyed or angered. —ˈ**waspishly** *adv.*

wasp waist *n.* a very slender waist, esp. one that is tightly corseted. —ˈ**wasp-**ˌ**waisted** *adj.*

wassail (ˈwɒseɪl) *n.* **1.** (formerly) a toast or salutation made to a person at festivities. **2.** a festivity when much drinking takes place. **3.** alcoholic drink drunk at such a festivity, esp. spiced beer or mulled wine. ~*vb.* **4.** to drink the health of (a person) at a wassail. **5.** (*intr.*) to go from house to house singing carols at Christmas. [C13: < ON *ves heill* be in good health] —ˈ**wassailer** *n.*

Wassermann test *or* **reaction** (ˈwæsəmən) *n. Med.* a diagnostic test for syphilis. [C20: after August von *Wassermann* (1866–1925), G bacteriologist]

wast (wɒst; *unstressed* wəst) *vb. Arch. or dialect.* (used with the pronoun *thou* or its relative equivalent) a singular form of the past tense (indicative mood) of **be.**

wastage (ˈweɪstɪdʒ) *n.* **1.** anything lost by wear or waste. **2.** the process of wasting. **3.** reduction in size of a workforce by retirement, etc. (esp. in **natural wastage**).

waste (weɪst) *vb.* **1.** (*tr.*) to use, consume, or expend thoughtlessly, carelessly, or to no avail. **2.** (*tr.*) to fail to take advantage of: *to waste an opportunity.* **3.** (when *intr.*, often foll. by *away*) to lose or cause to lose bodily strength, health, etc. **4.** to exhaust or become exhausted. **5.** (*tr.*) to ravage. **6.** (*tr.*) *Sl.* to murder or kill. ~*n.* **7.** the act of wasting or state of being wasted. **8.** a failure to take advantage of something. **9.** anything unused or not used to full advantage. **10.** anything or anyone rejected as useless, worthless, or in excess of what is required. **11.** garbage, rubbish, or trash. **12.** a land or region that is devastated or ruined. **13.** a land or region that is wild or uncultivated. **14.** *Physiol.* **a.** the useless products of metabolism. **b.** indigestible food residue. **15.** *Law.* reduction in the value of an estate caused by act or neglect, esp. by a life tenant. ~*adj.* **16.** rejected as useless, unwanted, or worthless. **17.** produced in excess of what is required. **18.** not cultivated, inhabited, or productive: *waste land.* **19. a.** of or denoting the useless products of metabolism. **b.** of or denoting indigestible food residue. **20.** destroyed, devastated, or ruined. **21. lay waste.** to devastate or destroy. [C13: < Anglo-F, < L *vastāre* to lay waste, < *vastus* empty]

wasted (ˈweɪstɪd) *adj.* **1.** not taken advantage of: *a wasted opportunity.* **2.** unprofitable: *wasted effort.* **3.** enfeebled and emaciated: *a thin wasted figure.* **4.** *Sl.* showing signs of habitual drug abuse.

wasteful (ˈweɪstfʊl) *adj.* **1.** tending to waste or squander. **2.** causing waste or devastation. —ˈ**wastefully** *adv.* —ˈ**wastefulness** *n.*

wasteland (ˈweɪstˌlænd) *n.* **1.** a barren or desolate area of land. **2.** a region, period in history, etc., that is considered spiritually, intellectually, or aesthetically barren or desolate.

wastepaper (ˈweɪstˌpeɪpə) *n.* paper discarded after use.

wastepaper basket *or* **bin** *n.* an open receptacle for paper and other dry litter. Usual U.S. and Canad. word: **wastebasket.**

waste pipe *n.* a pipe to take excess or used water away, as from a sink to a drain.

waster (ˈweɪstə) *n.* **1.** a person or thing that wastes. **2.** a ne'er-do-well; wastrel.

wasting (ˈweɪstɪŋ) *adj.* (*prenominal*) reducing the vitality, strength, or robustness of the body: *a wasting disease.* —ˈ**wastingly** *adv.*

wasting asset *n.* an unreplaceable business asset of limited life, such as an oil well.

wastrel (ˈweɪstrəl) *n.* **1.** a wasteful person; spendthrift; prodigal. **2.** an idler or vagabond.

wat (wɑːt) *n.* a Thai Buddhist monastery or temple. [Thai, < Sansk. *vāta* enclosure]

watap (wæˈtɑːp, wɑː-) *n.* a stringy thread made by North American Indians from the roots of various conifers and used for weaving and sewing. [C18: < Canad. F, < Cree *watapiy*]

watch (wɒtʃ) *vb.* **1.** to look at or observe closely or attentively. **2.** (*intr.;* foll. by *for*) to wait attentively. **3.** to guard or tend (something) closely or carefully. **4.** (*intr.*) to keep vigil. **5.** (*tr.*) to maintain an interest in: *to watch the progress of a child at school.* **6. watch it!** be careful! ~*n.* **7. a.** a small portable timepiece, usually worn strapped to the wrist (a **wristwatch**) or in a waistcoat pocket. **b.** (*as modifier*): *a watch spring.* **8.** a watching. **9.** a period of vigil, esp. during the night. **10.** (formerly) one of a set of periods into which the night was divided. **11.** *Naut.* **a.** any of the periods, usually of four hours, during which part of a ship's crew are on duty. **b.** those officers and crew on duty during a specified watch. **12.** the period during which a guard is on duty. **13.** (formerly) a watchman or band of watchmen. **14. on the watch.** on the lookout. ~See also **watch out.** [OE *wæccan* (vb.), *wæcce* (n.)] —ˈ**watcher** *n.*

-watch *suffix of nouns.* indicating a regular television programme or newspaper feature on the topic specified: *Crimewatch.*

watchcase (ˈwɒtʃˌkeɪs) *n.* a protective case for a watch, generally of metal such as gold or silver.

watch chain *n.* a chain used for fastening a pocket watch to the clothing. See also **fob**[1].

Watch Committee *n. Brit. history.* a local government committee responsible for the efficiency of the local police force.

watchdog (ˈwɒtʃˌdɒg) *n.* **1.** a dog kept to guard property. **2. a.** a person or group that acts as a protector against inefficiency, etc. **b.** (*as modifier*): *a watchdog committee.*

watch fire *n.* a fire kept burning at night as a signal or for warmth and light by a person keeping watch.

watchful (ˈwɒtʃfʊl) *adj.* **1.** vigilant or alert. **2.** *Arch.* not sleeping. —ˈ**watchfully** *adv.* —ˈ**watchfulness** *n.*

watch-glass *n.* **1.** a curved glass disc that covers the dial of a watch. **2.** a similarly shaped piece of glass used in laboratories for evaporating small samples of a solution, etc.

watchmaker (ˈwɒtʃˌmeɪkə) *n.* a person who makes or mends watches. —ˈ**watchˌmaking** *n.*

watchman (ˈwɒtʃmən) *n., pl.* **-men. 1.** a person employed to guard buildings or property. **2.** (formerly) a man employed to patrol or guard the streets at night.

watch night *n.* **1.** (in Protestant churches) the night of December 31, during which a service is held to mark the passing of the old year. **2.** the service held on this night.

watch out *vb.* (*intr., adv.*) to be careful or on one's guard.

watchstrap (ˈwɒtʃˌstræp) *n.* a strap of leather, cloth, etc., attached to a watch for fastening it around the wrist. Also called (U.S. and Canad.): **watchband.**

watchtower (ˈwɒtʃˌtaʊə) *n.* a tower on which a sentry keeps watch.

watchword (ˈwɒtʃˌwɜːd) *n.* **1.** another word for **password. 2.** a rallying cry or slogan.

water (ˈwɔːtə) *n.* **1.** a clear colourless tasteless odourless liquid that is essential for plant and animal life and constitutes, in impure form, rain, oceans, rivers, lakes, etc. Formula: H_2O. Related adj.: **aqueous. 2. a.** any body or area of this liquid, such as a sea, lake, river, etc. **b.** (*as modifier*): *water sports; a water plant.* Related adj.: **aquatic. 3.** the surface of such a body or area: *fish swam below the water.* **4.** any form or variety of this liquid, such as rain. **5.** See **high water, low water. 6.** any of various solutions of chemical substances in water: *ammonia water.* **7.** *Physiol.* **a.** any fluid secreted from the body, such as sweat, urine, or tears. **b.** (*usually pl.*) the amniotic fluid surrounding a fetus in the womb. **8.** a wavy lustrous finish on some fabrics, esp. silk. **9.** *Arch.* the degree of brilliance in a diamond. **10.** excellence, quality, or degree (in **of the first water**). **11.** *Finance.* capital stock issued without a corresponding increase in paid-up capital. **12.** (*modifier*) *Astrol.* of or relating to the three signs of the zodiac Cancer, Scorpio, and Pisces. **13. hold water.** to prove credible, logical, or consistent: *the alibi did not hold water.* **14. make water. a.** to urinate. **b.** (of a boat, etc.) to let in water. **15. pass water.** to urinate. **16. water under the bridge.** events that are past and done with. ~*vb.* **17.** (*tr.*) to sprinkle, moisten, or soak with water. **18.** (*tr.; often foll. by down*) to weaken by the addition of water. **19.** (*intr.*) (of the eyes) to fill with tears. **20.** (*intr.*) (of the mouth) to salivate, esp. in anticipation of food (esp. in **make one's mouth water**). **21.** (*tr.*) to irrigate or provide with water: *to water the land.* **22.** (*intr.*) to drink water. **23.** (*intr.*) (of a ship, etc.) to take in a supply of water. **24.** (*tr.*) *Finance.* to raise the par value of (issued capital stock) without a corresponding increase in the real value of assets. **25.** (*tr.*) to produce a wavy lustrous finish on (fabrics, esp. silk). ~See also **water down.** [OE *wæter*] —ˈ**waterer** *n.* —ˈ**waterless** *adj.*

water bag *n.* a bag, sometimes made of skin, leather, etc., but in Australia always canvas, for carrying water.

water bailiff *n.* an official responsible for enforcing laws on shipping and fishing.

water bear *n.* another name for a **tardigrade.**

water bed *n.* a waterproof mattress filled with water.

water beetle *n.* any of various beetles that live most of the time in freshwater ponds, rivers, etc.

water bird *n.* any aquatic bird, including the wading and swimming birds.

water biscuit *n.* a thin crisp plain biscuit, usually served with butter or cheese.

water blister *n.* a blister containing watery or serous fluid, without any blood or pus.

water boatman *n.* any of various aquatic bugs having a flattened body and oarlike hind legs, adapted for swimming.

waterborne (ˈwɔːtəˌbɔːn) *adj.* **1.** floating or travelling on water. **2.** (of a disease, etc.) transported or transmitted by water.

waterbuck (ˈwɔːtəˌbʌk) *n.* any of a genus of antelopes of swampy areas of Africa, having long curved ridged horns.

water buffalo *or* **ox** *n.* a member of the cattle tribe of swampy regions of S Asia, having widely spreading back-curving horns. Domesticated forms are used as draught animals.

water bug *n.* any of various heteropterous insects adapted to living in the water or on its surface, esp. any of the **giant water bugs** of North America, India, and southern Africa, which have flattened hairy legs.

water butt *n.* a barrel for collecting rainwater, esp. from a drainpipe.

water cannon *n.* an apparatus for pumping water through a nozzle at high pressure, used in quelling riots.

Water Carrier *or* **Bearer** *n.* **the.** the constellation Aquarius, the 11th sign of the zodiac.

water chestnut *n.* **1.** a floating aquatic plant of Asia, having four-pronged edible nutlike fruits. **2. Chinese water chestnut.** a Chinese plant with an edible succulent corm. **3.** the corm of the Chinese water chestnut, used in Oriental cookery.

water clock *or* **glass** *n.* any of various devices for measuring time that use the escape of water as the motive force.

water closet *n.* **1.** a lavatory flushed by water. **2.** a small room that has a lavatory. ~Usually abbreviated to **WC.**

watercolour *or U.S.* **watercolor** (ˈwɔːtəˌkʌlə) *n.* **1.** water-soluble pigment, applied in transparent washes and without the admixture of white pigment in the lighter tones. **2. a.** a painting done in watercolours. **b.** (*as modifier*): *a watercolour masterpiece.* **3.** the art or technique of painting with such pigments. —ˈ**waterˌcolourist** *or U.S.* ˈ**waterˌcolorist** *n.*

water-cool *vb.* (*tr.*) to cool (an engine, etc.) by a flow of water circulating in an enclosed jacket. —ˈ**water-ˌcooled** *adj.*

water cooler *n.* a device for cooling and dispensing drinking water.

watercourse (ˈwɔːtəˌkɔːs) *n.* **1.** a stream, river, or canal. **2.** the channel, bed, or route along which this flows.

watercraft (ˈwɔːtəˌkrɑːft) *n.* **1.** a boat or ship or such vessels collectively. **2.** skill in handling boats or in water sports.

watercress (ˈwɔːtəˌkrɛs) *n.* an Old World cruciferous plant of clear ponds and streams, having pungent leaves that are used in salads and as a garnish.

water cure *n. Med.* a nontechnical name for **hydropathy** or **hydrotherapy.**

water cycle *n.* the circulation of the earth's water, in which water evaporates from the sea into the atmosphere, where it condenses and falls as rain or snow, returning to the sea by rivers.

water diviner *n. Brit.* a person able to locate the presence of water, esp. underground, with a divining rod.

water down *vb.* (*tr., adv.*) **1.** to dilute or weaken with water. **2.** to modify, esp. so as to omit anything unpleasant or offensive: *to water down the truth.* —ˌ**watered-ˈdown** *adj.*

waterfall (ˈwɔːtəˌfɔːl) *n.* a cascade of falling water where there is a vertical or almost vertical step in a river.

water flea *n.* any of numerous minute freshwater crustaceans which swim by means of hairy branched antennae. See also **daphnia.**

waterfowl (ˈwɔːtəˌfaʊl) *n.* **1.** any aquatic freshwater bird, esp. any species of the family Anatidae (ducks, geese, and swans). **2.** such birds collectively.

waterfront (ˈwɔːtəˌfrʌnt) *n.* the area of a town or city alongside a body of water, such as a harbour or dockyard.

water gap *n.* a deep valley in a ridge, containing a stream.

water gas *n.* a mixture of hydrogen and carbon monoxide produced by passing steam over hot carbon, used as a fuel and raw material.

water gate *n.* **1.** a gate in a canal, etc., that can be opened or closed to control the flow of water. **2.** a gate through which access may be gained to a body of water.

Watergate (ˈwɔːtəˌgeɪt) *n.* **1.** an incident during the 1972 U.S. presidential campaign, when agents employed by the re-election organization of President Richard Nixon were caught breaking into the Democratic Party headquarters in the Watergate building, Washington, DC. The political scandal was exacerbated by attempts to conceal the fact that White House officials had approved the burglary. **2.** any similar public scandal, esp. involving politicians or a possible cover-up.

water gauge *n.* an instrument that indicates the presence or the quantity of water in a tank, reservoir, or boiler feed. Also called: **water glass.**

water glass *n.* **1.** a viscous syrupy solution of sodium silicate in water: used as a protective coating for cement and a preservative, esp. for eggs. **2.** another name for **water gauge.**

water gum *n.* any of several Australian gum trees that grow in swampy ground and beside creeks and rivers.

water hammer *n.* a sharp concussion produced when the flow of water in a pipe is suddenly blocked.

water hen *n.* another name for **gallinule.**

water hole *n.* **1.** a depression, such as a pond or pool, containing water, esp. one used by animals as a drinking place. **2.** a source of drinking water in a desert.

water hyacinth *n.* a floating aquatic plant of tropical America, having showy bluish-purple flowers and swollen leafstalks. It forms dense masses in rivers, ponds, etc.

water ice *n.* an ice cream made from a frozen sugar syrup flavoured with fruit juice or purée.

watering can *n.* a container with a handle and a spout with a perforated nozzle used to sprinkle water over plants.

watering hole *n.* **1.** a pool where animals drink; water hole. **2.** *Facetious sl.* a pub.

watering place *n.* **1.** a place where drinking water for people or animals may be obtained. **2.** *Brit.* a spa. **3.** *Brit.* a seaside resort.

water jacket *n.* a water-filled envelope surrounding a machine or part for cooling purposes, esp. the casing around the cylinder block of a pump or internal-combustion engine.

water jump *n.* a ditch or brook over which athletes or horses must jump in a steeplechase or similar contest.

water level *n.* **1.** the level reached by the surface of a body of water. **2.** the water line of a boat or ship.

water lily *n.* any of various aquatic plants of temperate and tropical regions, having large leaves and showy flowers that float on the surface of the water.

water line *n.* **1.** a line marked at the level around a vessel's hull to which the vessel will be immersed when afloat. **2.** a line marking the level reached by a body of water.

waterlogged (ˈwɔːtəˌlɒgd) *adj.* **1.** saturated with water. **2.** (of a vessel still afloat) having taken in so much water as to be unmanageable.

Waterloo (ˌwɔːtəˈluː) *n.* **1.** a small town in Belgium south of Brussels: battle (1815) fought nearby in which British and Prussian forces under the Duke of Wellington and Blücher routed the French under Napoleon. **2.** a total or crushing defeat (esp. in **meet one's Waterloo**).

water main *n.* a principal supply pipe in an arrangement of pipes for distributing water.

waterman (ˈwɔːtəmən) *n., pl.* **-men.** a skilled boatman. —ˈ**watermanˌship** *n.*

watermark (ˈwɔːtəˌmɑːk) *n.* **1.** a mark impressed on paper during manufacture, visible when the paper is held up to the light. **2.** another word for **water line.** ~*vb.* (*tr.*) **3.** to mark (paper) with a watermark.

water meadow *n.* a meadow that remains fertile by being periodically flooded by a stream.

watermelon (ˈwɔːtəˌmɛlən) *n.* **1.** an African melon widely cultivated for its large edible fruit. **2.** the fruit of this plant, which has a hard green rind and sweet watery reddish flesh.

water meter *n.* a device for measuring the quantity or rate of water flowing through a pipe.

water milfoil *n.* any of various pond plants having feathery underwater leaves and small inconspicuous flowers.

water mill *n.* a mill operated by a water wheel.

water moccasin *n.* a large dark grey venomous snake of swamps in the southern U.S. Also called: **cottonmouth.**

water nymph *n.* any fabled nymph of the water, such as the Naiad, Nereid, or Oceanid of Greek mythology.

water of crystallization *n.* water present in the crystals of certain compounds. It is chemically combined in a specific amount but can often be easily expelled.

water ouzel *n.* another name for **dipper** (the bird).

water pipe *n.* **1.** a pipe for water. **2.** another name for **hookah.**

water pistol *n.* a toy pistol that squirts a stream of water or other liquid.

water plantain *n.* any of a genus of marsh plants of N temperate regions and Australia, having clusters of small white or pinkish flowers and broad pointed leaves.

water polo *n.* a game played in water by two teams of seven swimmers in which each side tries to throw or propel an inflated ball into the opponents' goal.

water power *n.* **1.** the power latent in a dynamic or static head of water as used to drive machinery, esp. for generating electricity. **2.** a source of such power, such as a drop in the level of a river, etc.

waterproof (ˈwɔːtəˌpruːf) *adj.* **1.** not penetrable by water. Cf. **water-repellent, water-resistant.** ~*n.* **2.** *Chiefly Brit.* a waterproof garment, esp. a raincoat. ~*vb.* (*tr.*) **3.** to make (a fabric, etc.) waterproof.

water purslane *n.* a marsh plant of temperate and warm regions, having reddish stems and small reddish flowers.

water rail *n.* a large Eurasian rail of swamps, ponds, etc., having a long red bill.

water rat *n.* **1.** any of several small amphibious rodents, esp. the water vole or the muskrat. **2.** any of various amphibious rats of New Guinea, the Philippines, and Australia.

water rate *n.* a charge made for the public supply of water.

water-repellent *adj.* (of fabrics, garments, etc.) having a finish that resists the absorption of water.

water-resistant *adj.* (esp. of fabrics) designed to resist but not entirely prevent the penetration of water.

water scorpion *n.* a long-legged aquatic insect that breathes by means of a long spinelike tube that projects from the rear of the body and penetrates the surface of the water.

watershed (ˈwɔːtəˌʃɛd) *n.* **1.** the dividing line between two adjacent river systems, such as a ridge. **2.** an important period or factor that serves as a dividing line.

waterside (ˈwɔːtəˌsaɪd) *n.* **a.** the area of land beside a body of water. **b.** (*as modifier*): *waterside houses.*

watersider (ˈwɔːtəˌsaɪdə) *n. Austral. & N.Z.* a dock labourer.

water-ski *n.* **1.** a type of ski used for planing or gliding over water. ~*vb.* **-skiing, -skied** *or* **-ski'd. 2.** (*intr.*) to ride over water on water-skis while holding a rope towed by a speedboat. —ˈ**water-ˌskier** *n.* —ˈ**water-ˌskiing** *n.*

water snake *n.* any of various snakes that live in or near water, esp. any of a genus of harmless North American snakes.

water softener *n.* **1.** any substance that lessens the hardness of water, usually by precipitating calcium and magnesium ions. **2.** an apparatus that is used to remove chemicals that cause hardness.

water spaniel *n.* either of two large curly-coated breeds of spaniel (the Irish and the American), which are used for hunting waterfowl.

water splash *n.* a place where a stream runs over a road.

water sports *pl. n.* sports, such as swimming or windsurfing, that take place in or on water.

waterspout (ˈwɔːtəˌspaʊt) *n.* **1.** *Meteorol.* **a.** a tornado occurring over water that forms a column of water and mist. **b.** a sudden downpour of heavy rain. **2.** a pipe or channel through which water is discharged.

water table *n.* **1.** the level below which the ground is saturated with water. **2.** a string course that has a moulding designed to throw rainwater clear of the wall below.

water thrush *n.* either of two North American warblers having brownish backs and striped underparts and occurring near water.

watertight (ˈwɔːtəˌtaɪt) *adj.* **1.** not permitting the passage of water either in or out: *a watertight boat.* **2.** without loopholes: *a watertight argument.* **3.** kept separate from other subjects or influences.

water tower (ˈtaʊə) *n.* a reservoir or storage tank mounted on a tower-like structure so that water can be distributed at a uniform pressure.

water vapour *n.* water in the gaseous state, esp. when due to evaporation at a temperature below the boiling point.

water vole *n.* a large amphibious vole of Eurasian river banks. Also called: **water rat.**

water wagtail *n.* another name for **pied wagtail.**

waterway (ˈwɔːtəˌweɪ) *n.* a river, canal, or other navigable channel used as a means of travel or transport.

waterweed (ˈwɔːtəˌwiːd) *n.* any of various weedy aquatic plants.

water wheel *n.* **1.** a simple water-driven turbine consisting of a wheel having vanes set axially across its rim, used to drive machinery. **2.** a wheel with buckets attached to its rim for raising water from a stream, pond, etc.

water wings *pl. n.* an inflatable rubber device shaped like a pair of wings, which is placed under the arms of a person learning to swim.

waterworks (ˈwɔːtəˌwɜːks) *n.* **1.** (*functioning as sing.*) an establishment for storing, purifying, and distributing water for community supply. **2.** (*functioning as pl.*) a display of water in movement, as in fountains. **3.** (*functioning as pl.*) *Brit. inf., euphemistic.* the urinary system. **4.** (*functioning as pl.*) *Inf.* crying; tears.

waterworn (ˈwɔːtəˌwɔːn) *adj.* worn smooth by the action or passage of water.

watery (ˈwɔːtərɪ) *adj.* **1.** relating to, containing, or resembling water. **2.** discharging or secreting water or a water-like fluid. **3.** tearful; weepy. **4.** insipid, thin, or weak.

watt (wɒt) *n.* the derived SI unit of power, equal to 1 joule per second; the power dissipated by a current of 1 ampere flowing across a potential difference of 1 volt. Symbol: W [C19: after J. *Watt* (1736-1819), Scot. engineer & inventor]

wattage (ˈwɒtɪdʒ) *n.* **1.** power, esp. electric power, measured in watts. **2.** the power rating, measured in watts, of an electrical appliance.

watt-hour *n.* a unit of energy equal to a power of one watt operating for one hour.

wattle (ˈwɒtᵊl) *n.* **1.** a frame of rods or stakes interwoven with twigs, branches, etc., esp. when used to make fences. **2.** the material used in such a construction. **3.** a loose fold of skin, often brightly coloured, hanging from the neck or throat of certain birds, lizards, etc. **4.** any of various chiefly Australian acacia trees having spikes of small brightly coloured flowers and flexible branches. ~*vb.* (*tr.*) **5.** to construct from wattle. **6.** to bind or frame with wattle. **7.** to weave or twist (branches, twigs, etc.) into a frame. ~*adj.* **8.** made of, formed by, or covered with wattle. [OE *watol*] —ˈ**wattled** *adj.*

wattle and daub *n.* a form of wall construction consisting of interwoven twigs plastered with a mixture of clay, water, and sometimes chopped straw.

wattmeter (ˈwɒtˌmiːtə) *n.* a meter for measuring electric power in watts.

waul *or* **wawl** (wɔːl) *vb.* (*intr.*) to cry or wail plaintively like a cat. [C16: imit.]

wave (weɪv) *vb.* **1.** to move or cause to move freely to and fro: *the banner waved in the wind.* **2.** (*intr.*) to move the hand to and fro as a greeting. **3.** to signal or signify by or as if by waving something. **4.** (*tr.*) to direct to move by or as if by waving something: *he waved me on.* **5.** to form or be formed into curves, undulations, etc. **6.** (*tr.*) to set waves in (the hair). ~*n.* **7.** one of a sequence of ridges or undulations that moves across the surface of a body of a liquid, esp. the sea. **8. the waves.** the sea. **9.** any undulation on or at the edge of a surface reminiscent of a wave in the sea: *a wave across the field of corn.* **10.** anything that suggests the movement of a wave, as by a sudden rise: *a crime wave.* **11.** a widespread movement that advances in a body: *a wave of settlers.* **12.** the act or an instance of waving. **13.** *Physics.* an energy-carrying disturbance propagated through a medium or space by a progressive local displacement of the medium or a change in its physical properties, but without any overall movement of matter. **14.** *Physics.* a graphical representation of a wave obtained by plotting the magnitude of the disturbance against time at a particular point in the medium or space. **15.** a prolonged spell of some particular type of weather: *a heat wave.* **16.** an undulating curve or series of curves or loose curls in the hair. **17. make waves.** to cause trouble; disturb the status quo. [OE *wafian* (vb.); C16 (n.) changed < earlier *wāwe*, prob. < OE *wæg* motion] —ˈ**waveless** *adj.* —ˈ**waveˌlike** *adj.*

waveband (ˈweɪvˌbænd) *n.* a range of wavelengths or frequencies used for a particular type of radio transmission.

wave-cut platform *n.* a flat surface at the base of a cliff formed by erosion by waves.

wave down *vb.* (*tr., adv.*) to signal with a wave to (a driver or vehicle) to stop.

wave equation *n. Physics.* a partial differential equation describing wave motion.

waveform (ˈweɪvˌfɔːm) *n. Physics.* the shape of the graph of a wave or oscillation obtained by plotting the value of some changing quantity against time.

wave front *n. Physics.* a surface associated with a propagating wave and passing through all points in the wave that have the same phase.

wave function *n. Physics.* a mathematical function of position and sometimes time, used in wave mechanics to describe the state of a physical system. Symbol: ψ

waveguide (ˈweɪvˌgaɪd) *n. Electronics.* a solid rod of dielectric or a hollow metal tube, usually of rectangular cross section, used as a path to guide microwaves.

wavelength (ˈweɪvˌlɛŋθ) *n.* **1.** the distance, measured in the direction of propagation, between two points of the same phase in consecutive cycles of a wave. Symbol: λ **2.** the wavelength of the carrier wave used by a particular broadcasting station. **3. on someone's** (*or* **the same**) **wavelength.** *Inf.* having similar views, feelings, or thoughts (as someone else).

wavelet (ˈweɪvlɪt) *n.* a small wave.

wave mechanics *n.* (*functioning as sing.*) *Physics.* the formulation of quantum mechanics in which the behaviour of systems, such as atoms, is described in terms of their wave functions.

wave number *n. Physics.* the reciprocal of the wavelength of a wave.

waver (ˈweɪvə) *vb.* (*intr.*) **1.** to be irresolute; hesitate between two possibilities. **2.** to become unsteady. **3.** to fluctuate. **4.** to move back and forth or one way and another. **5.** (of light) to flicker or flash. ~*n.* **6.** the act or an instance of wavering. [C14: < ON *vafra* to flicker] —ˈ**waverer** *n.* —ˈ**wavering** *adj.* —ˈ**waveringly** *adv.*

wave theory *n.* **1.** the theory proposed by Huygens that light is transmitted by waves. **2.** any theory that light or other radiation is transmitted as waves. ~Cf. **corpuscular theory.**

wavey (ˈweɪvɪ) *n. Canad.* a snow goose or other wild goose. Also called: **wawa.** [via Canad. F < Algonquian (Cree *wehwew*)]

wavy (ˈweɪvɪ) *adj.* **wavier, waviest. 1.** abounding in or full of waves. **2.** moving or proceeding in waves. **3.** (of hair) set in or having waves. —ˈ**wavily** *adv.* —ˈ**waviness** *n.*

wax[1] (wæks) *n.* **1.** any of various viscous or solid materials of natural origin: characteristically lustrous, insoluble in water, and sensitive to heat, they consist largely of esters of fatty acids. **2.** any of various similar substances, such as paraffin wax, that have a mineral origin and consist largely of hydrocarbons. **3.** short for **beeswax** or **sealing wax. 4.** *Physiol.* another name for **cerumen. 5.** a resinous preparation used by shoemakers to rub on thread. **6.** any substance or object that is pliable or easily moulded: *he was wax in their hands.* **7.** (*modifier*) made of or resembling wax: *a wax figure.* **8. put on wax.** to make a gramophone record of. ~*vb.* **9.** (*tr.*) to coat, polish, etc., with wax. **10.** (*tr.*) *Inf.* to make a gramophone record of. [OE *weax*] —ˈ**waxer** *n.*

wax[2] (wæks) *vb.* (*intr.*) **1.** to become larger, more powerful, etc. **2.** (of the moon) to show a gradually increasing portion of illuminated surface, between new moon and full moon. **3.** to become: *to wax eloquent.* [OE *weaxan*]

wax[3] (wæks) *n. Inf., chiefly Brit.* a fit of rage or temper: *he's in a wax today.* [<?]

waxberry (ˈwæksbərɪ) *n., pl.* **-ries.** the waxy fruit of the wax myrtle or the snowberry.

waxbill (ˈwæksˌbɪl) *n.* any of various chiefly African finchlike weaverbirds having a brightly coloured bill and plumage.

wax cloth *n.* **1.** another name for **oilcloth. 2.** (formerly) another name for **linoleum.**

waxen (ˈwæksən) *adj.* **1.** made of, treated with, or covered with wax. **2.** resembling wax in colour or texture.

waxeye (ˈwæksˌaɪ) *n.* a small New Zealand bird with a white circle around its eye. Also called: **silver-eye, blighty.**

wax flower *n. Austral.* any of a genus of shrubs having waxy pink-white five-petalled flowers.

wax light *n.* a candle or taper of wax.

wax myrtle *n.* a shrub of SE North America, having evergreen leaves and a small berry-like fruit with a waxy coating. Also called: **bayberry, candleberry, waxberry.**

wax palm *n.* **1.** a tall Andean palm tree having pinnate leaves that yield a resinous wax used in making candles. **2.** another name for **carnauba** (sense 1).

wax paper *n.* paper treated or coated with wax or paraffin to make it waterproof.

waxplant (ˈwæksˌplɑːnt) *n.* a climbing shrub of E Asia and Australia, having fleshy leaves and clusters of small waxy white pink-centred flowers.

waxwing (ˈwæksˌwɪŋ) *n.* any of a genus of gregarious passerine songbirds having red waxy wing tips and crested heads.

waxwork (ˈwæksˌwɜːk) *n.* **1.** an object reproduced in wax, esp. as an ornament. **2.** a life-size lifelike figure, esp. of a famous person, reproduced in wax. **3.** (*pl.; functioning as sing. or pl.*) a museum or exhibition of wax figures.

waxy[1] (ˈwæksɪ) *adj.* **waxier, waxiest. 1.** resembling wax in colour, appearance, or texture. **2.** made of, covered with, or abounding in wax. —ˈ**waxily** *adv.* —ˈ**waxiness** *n.*

waxy[2] (ˈwæksɪ) *adj.* **waxier, waxiest.** *Brit. sl.* bad-tempered or irritable; angry.

way (weɪ) *n.* **1.** a manner, method, or means: *a way of life.* **2.** a route or direction: *the way home.* **3. a.** a means or line of passage, such as a path or track. **b.** (*in combination*): *waterway.* **4.** space or room for movement or activity (esp. in **make way, in the way, out of the way**). **5.** distance, usually distance in general: *you've come a long way.* **6.** a passage or journey: *on the way.* **7.** characteristic style or manner: *I did it my way.* **8.** (*often pl.*) habit: *he has some offensive ways.* **9.** an aspect of something; particular: *in many ways he was right.* **10. a.** a street in or leading out of a town. **b.** (*cap. when part of a street name*): *Icknield Way.* **11.** something that one wants in a determined manner (esp. in **get** *or* **have one's (own) way**). **12.** the experience or sphere in which one comes into contact with things (esp. in **come one's way**). **13.** *Inf.* a state or condition, usually financial or concerning health (esp. in **in a good** (*or* **bad**) **way**). **14.** *Inf.* the area or direction of one's home: *drop in if you're ever over my way.* **15.** movement of a ship or other vessel. **16.** a guide along which something can be moved, such as the surface of a lathe along which the tailstock slides. **17.** (*pl.*) the wooden or metal tracks down which a ship slides to be launched. **18.** a course of life including experiences, conduct, etc.: *the way of sin.* **19. by the way.** incidentally. **20. by way of. a.** via. **b.** serving as: *by way of introduction.* **c.** in the state or condition of: *by way of being an artist.* **21. each way.** (of a bet) laid on a horse, dog, etc., to win or gain a place. **22. give way. a.** to collapse or break down. **b.** to yield. **23. give way to. a.** to step aside for or stop for. **b.** to give full rein to (emotions, etc.). **24. go out of one's way.** to take considerable trouble or inconvenience oneself. **25. have a way with.** to have such a manner or skill as to handle successfully. **26. have it both ways.** to enjoy two things that would normally be mutually exclusive. **27. in a way.** in some respects. **28. in no way.** not at all. **29. lead the way. a.** to go first. **b.** to set an example. **30. make one's way. a.** to proceed or advance. **b.** to achieve success in life. **31. on the way out.** *Inf.* **a.** becoming unfashionable, etc. **b.** dying. **32. out of the way. a.** removed or dealt with so as to be no longer a hindrance. **b.** remote. **c.** unusual and sometimes improper. **33. see one's way (clear).** to find it possible and be willing (to do something). **34. under way.** having started moving or making progress. ~*adv.* **35.** *Inf.* **a.** at a considerable distance or extent: *way over yonder.* **b.** very far: *they're way up the mountain.* [OE *weg*]

▷ **Usage.** The use of *the way* for *as* in sentences such as *he does not write the way his father did* is well established in the U.S. and is common in British informal usage. Careful writers, however, prefer *as* in formal contexts.

waybill (ˈweɪˌbɪl) *n.* a document attached to goods in transit specifying their nature, point of origin, and destination as well as the route to be taken and the rate to be charged.

wayfarer (ˈweɪˌfɛərə) *n.* a person who goes on a journey. —ˈ**wayˌfaring** *n., adj.*

wayfaring tree *n.* a shrub of Europe and W Asia, having white flowers and berries that turn from red to black.

waylay (weɪˈleɪ) *vb.* **-laying, -laid.** (*tr.*) **1.** to lie in wait for and attack. **2.** to await and intercept unexpectedly. —**way'layer** *n.*

wayleave ('weɪˌliːv) *n.* access to property granted by a landowner for payment, for example to allow a contractor access to a building site.

waymark ('weɪˌmɑːk) *n.* a symbol or signpost marking the route of a footpath. —'**wayˌmarked** *adj.*

way-out *adj. Inf.* **1.** extremely unconventional or experimental. **2.** excellent or amazing.

-ways *suffix forming adverbs.* indicating direction or manner: *sideways.* [OE *weges*, lit.: of the way, < *weg* way]

ways and means *pl. n.* **1.** the revenues and methods of raising the revenues needed for the functioning of a state or other political unit. **2.** the methods and resources for accomplishing some purpose.

wayside ('weɪˌsaɪd) *n.* **1. a.** the side or edge of a road. **b.** (*modifier*) situated by the wayside: *a wayside inn.* **2. fall by the wayside.** to cease or fail to continue doing something: *of the nine starters, three fell by the wayside.*

wayward ('weɪwəd) *adj.* **1.** wanting to have one's own way regardless of others. **2.** capricious, erratic, or unpredictable. [C14: changed < *awayward* turned or turning away] —'**waywardly** *adv.* —'**waywardness** *n.*

wayworn ('weɪˌwɔːn) *adj. Rare.* worn or tired by travel.

wb *abbrev. for:* **1.** water ballast. **2.** Also: **W/B, WB.** waybill. **3.** westbound.

Wb *Physics. symbol for* weber.

WBA *abbrev. for* World Boxing Association.

WBC *abbrev. for* World Boxing Council.

WC *abbrev. for:* **1.** Also: **wc.** water closet. **2.** (in London postal code) West Central.

WD *abbrev. for:* **1.** War Department. **2.** Works Department.

we (wiː) *pron.* (*subjective*) **1.** refers to the speaker or writer and another person or other people: *we should go now.* **2.** refers to all people or people in general: *the planet on which we live.* **3.** a formal word for **I** used by editors or other writers, and formerly by monarchs. **4.** *Inf.* used instead of *you* with a tone of condescension or sarcasm: *how are we today?* [OE *wē*]

WEA (in Britain) *abbrev. for* Workers' Educational Association.

weak (wiːk) *adj.* **1.** lacking in physical or mental strength or force. **2.** liable to yield, break, or give way: *a weak link in a chain.* **3.** lacking in resolution or firmness of character. **4.** lacking strength, power, or intensity: *a weak voice.* **5.** lacking strength in a particular part: *a team weak in defence.* **6. a.** not functioning as well as is normal: *weak eyes.* **b.** easily upset: *a weak stomach.* **7.** lacking in conviction, persuasiveness, etc.: *a weak argument.* **8.** lacking in political or strategic strength: *a weak state.* **9.** lacking the usual, full, or desirable strength of flavour: *weak tea.* **10.** *Grammar.* **a.** denoting or belonging to a class of verbs, in Germanic languages, whose conjugation relies on inflectional endings rather than internal vowel gradation, as *look, looks, looking, looked.* **b.** belonging to any part-of-speech class, in any of various languages, whose inflections follow the more regular of two possible patterns. **11.** (of a syllable) not accented or stressed. **12.** (of an industry, market, securities, etc.) falling in price or characterized by falling prices. [OE *wāc* soft, miserable] —'**weakish** *adj.*

weaken ('wiːkən) *vb.* to become or cause to become weak or weaker. —'**weakener** *n.*

weak interaction *n. Physics.* an interaction between elementary particles that is responsible for certain decay processes, operates at distances less than about 10^{-15} metres, and is 10^{12} times weaker than the strong interaction.

weak-kneed *adj. Inf.* yielding readily to force, intimidation, etc. —ˌ**weak-'kneedly** *adv.*

weakling ('wiːklɪŋ) *n.* a person or animal that is lacking in strength or weak in constitution or character.

weakly ('wiːklɪ) *adj.* **-lier, -liest. 1.** sickly; feeble. ~*adv.* **2.** in a weak or feeble manner.

weak-minded *adj.* **1.** lacking in stability of mind or character. **2.** another word for **feeble-minded.** —ˌ**weak-'mindedly** *adv.* —ˌ**weak-'mindedness** *n.*

weakness ('wiːknɪs) *n.* **1.** a being weak. **2.** a failing, as in a person's character. **3.** a self-indulgent liking: *a weakness for chocolates.*

weal[1] (wiːl) *n.* a raised mark on the skin produced by a blow. [C19: var. of WALE, infl. in form by WHEAL]

weal[2] (wiːl) *n. Arch.* prosperity or wellbeing (now esp. in **the public weal, the common weal**). [OE *wela*]

weald (wiːld) *n. Brit. arch.* open or forested country. [OE]

Weald (wiːld) *n.* **the.** a region of SE England, in Kent, Surrey, and Sussex between the North Downs and the South Downs: formerly forested.

wealth (wɛlθ) *n.* **1.** a large amount of money and valuable material possessions. **2.** the state of being rich. **3.** a great profusion: *a wealth of gifts.* **4.** *Econ.* all goods and services with monetary or productive value. [C13 *welthe*, < WEAL[2]]

wealth tax *n.* a tax on personal property.

wealthy ('wɛlθɪ) *adj.* **wealthier, wealthiest. 1.** possessing wealth; rich. **2.** of or relating to wealth. **3.** abounding: *wealthy in friends.* —'**wealthily** *adv.* —'**wealthiness** *n.*

wean[1] (wiːn) *vb.* (*tr.*) **1.** to cause (a child or young mammal) to replace mother's milk by other nourishment. **2.** (usually foll. by *from*) to cause to desert former habits, pursuits, etc. [OE *wenian* to accustom]

wean[2] (weɪn) *n. Scot. & N English dialect.* a child. [? short form of WEANLING, or a contraction of *wee ane*]

weaner ('wiːnə) *n.* **1.** a person or thing that weans. **2.** a pig that has just been weaned and weighs less than 40 kg. **3.** *Austral. & N.Z.* a lamb, pig, or calf in the year in which it is weaned.

weanling ('wiːnlɪŋ) *n.* a child or young animal recently weaned. [C16: < WEAN[1] + -LING[1]]

weapon ('wɛpən) *n.* **1.** an object or instrument used in fighting. **2.** anything that serves to get the better of an opponent: *his power of speech was his best weapon.* **3.** any part of an animal that is used to defend itself, to attack prey, etc., such as claws or a sting. [OE *wǣpen*] —'**weaponed** *adj.* —'**weaponless** *adj.*

weaponry ('wɛpənrɪ) *n.* weapons regarded collectively.

wear[1] (wɛə) *vb.* **wearing, wore, worn. 1.** (*tr.*) to carry or have (a garment, etc.) on one's person as clothing, ornament, etc. **2.** (*tr.*) to carry or have on one's person habitually: *she wears a lot of red.* **3.** (*tr.*) to have in one's aspect: *to wear a smile.* **4.** (*tr.*) to display, show, or fly: *a ship wears its colours.* **5.** to deteriorate or cause to deteriorate by constant use or action. **6.** to produce or be produced by constant rubbing, scraping, etc.: *to wear a hole in one's trousers.* **7.** to bring or be brought to a specified condition by constant use or action: *to wear a tyre to shreds.* **8.** (*intr.*) to submit to constant use or action in a specified way: *his suit wears well.* **9.** (*tr.*) to harass or weaken. **10.** (when *intr.*, often foll. by *on*) (of time) to pass or be passed slowly. **11.** (*tr.*) *Brit. inf.* to accept: *Larry won't wear that argument.* ~*n.* **12.** the act of wearing or state of being worn. **13. a.** anything designed to be worn: *leisure wear.* **b.** (*in combination*): *nightwear.* **14.** deterioration from constant or normal use. **15.** the quality of resisting the effects of constant use. ~See also **wear down, wear off, wear out.** [OE *werian*] —'**wearer** *n.*

wear[2] (wɛə) *vb.* **wearing, wore, worn.** *Naut.* to tack by gybing instead of by going through stays. [C17: < earlier *weare*, <?]

wearable ('wɛərəbᵊl) *adj.* suitable for wear or able to be worn. —ˌ**weara'bility** *n.*

wear and tear *n.* damage, depreciation, or loss resulting from ordinary use.

wear down *vb.* (*adv.*) **1.** to consume or be

consumed by long or constant wearing, rubbing, etc. **2.** to overcome or be overcome gradually by persistent effort.

wearing (ˈwɛərɪŋ) *adj.* causing fatigue or exhaustion; tiring. —ˈ**wearingly** *adv.*

wearisome (ˈwɪərɪsəm) *adj.* causing fatigue or annoyance; tedious. —ˈ**wearisomely** *adv.*

wear off *vb.* (*adv.*) **1.** (*intr.*) to decrease in intensity gradually: *the pain will wear off in an hour.* **2.** to disappear or cause to disappear gradually through exposure, use, etc.

wear out *vb.* (*adv.*) **1.** to make or become unfit or useless through wear. **2.** (*tr.*) to exhaust or tire.

weary (ˈwɪərɪ) *adj.* **-rier, -riest. 1.** tired or exhausted. **2.** causing fatigue or exhaustion. **3.** caused by or suggestive of weariness: *a weary laugh.* **4.** (*postpositive;* often foll. by *of* or *with*) discontented or bored. ~*vb.* **-rying, -ried. 5.** to make or become weary. **6.** to make or become discontented or impatient. [OE *wērig*] —ˈ**weariless** *adj.* —ˈ**wearily** *adv.* —ˈ**weariness** *n.* —ˈ**wearying** *adj.* —ˈ**wearyingly** *adv.*

weasand (ˈwiːzənd) *n.* a former name for the **trachea.** [OE *wǣsend, wāsend*]

weasel (ˈwiːzˀl) *n., pl.* **-sel** *or* **-sels. 1.** any of various small predatory mammals, such as the **European weasel,** having reddish-brown fur, an elongated body and neck, and short legs. **2.** *Inf.* a sly or treacherous person. [OE *weosule, wesle*] —ˈ**weaselly** *adj.*

weasel out *vb.* **-selling, -selled** *or U.S.* **-seling, -seled.** (*intr., adv.*) *Inf., chiefly U.S. & Canad.* **1.** to go back on a commitment. **2.** to evade a responsibility, esp. in a despicable manner.

weasel words *pl. n. Inf.* intentionally evasive or misleading speech; equivocation. [C20: < the weasel's supposed ability to suck an egg out of its shell without seeming to break the shell]

weather (ˈwɛðə) *n.* **1. a.** the day-to-day meteorological conditions, esp. temperature, cloudiness, and rainfall, affecting a specific place. **b.** (*modifier*) relating to the forecasting of weather: *a weather ship.* **2. make heavy weather. a.** *Naut.* to roll and pitch in heavy seas. **b.** (foll. by *of*) *Inf.* to carry out with great difficulty or unnecessarily great effort. **3. under the weather.** *Inf.* not in good health. ~*adj.* **4.** (*prenominal*) on or at the side or part towards the wind: *the weather anchor.* Cf. **lee** (sense 2). ~*vb.* **5.** to expose or be exposed to the action of the weather. **6.** to undergo or cause to undergo changes, such as discoloration, due to the action of the weather. **7.** (*intr.*) to withstand the action of the weather. **8.** (when *intr.*, foll. by *through*) to endure (a crisis, danger, etc.). **9.** (*tr.*) to slope (a surface, such as a roof) so as to throw rainwater clear. **10.** (*tr.*) to sail to the windward of: *to weather a point.* [OE *weder*] —ˈ**weatherer** *n.*

weather-beaten *adj.* **1.** showing signs of exposure to the weather. **2.** tanned or hardened by exposure to the weather.

weatherboard (ˈwɛðəˌbɔːd) *n.* a timber board, with a groove (rabbet) along the front of its top edge and along the back of its lower edge, that is fixed horizontally with others to form an exterior cladding on a wall or roof. —ˈ**weatherˌboarding** *n.*

weather-bound *adj.* (of a vessel, aircraft, etc.) delayed by bad weather.

weathercock (ˈwɛðəˌkɒk) *n.* **1.** a weather vane in the form of a cock. **2.** a person who is fickle or changeable.

weathered (ˈwɛðəd) *adj.* **1.** affected by exposure to the action of the weather. **2.** (of rocks and rock formations) eroded, decomposed, or otherwise altered by the action of wind, frost, etc. **3.** (of a sill, roof, etc.) having a sloped surface so as to allow rainwater to run off.

weather eye *n.* **1.** the vision of a person trained to observe changes in the weather. **2.** *Inf.* an alert or observant gaze. **3. keep one's weather eye open.** to stay on the alert.

weatherglass (ˈwɛðəˌglɑːs) *n.* any of various instruments, esp. a barometer, that measure atmospheric conditions.

weather house *n.* a model house, usually with two human figures, one that comes out to foretell bad weather and one that comes out to foretell good weather.

weathering (ˈwɛðərɪŋ) *n.* the mechanical and chemical breakdown of rocks by the action of rain, snow, cold, etc.

weatherly (ˈwɛðəlɪ) *adj.* (of a sailing vessel) making very little leeway when close-hauled, even in a stiff breeze. —ˈ**weatherliness** *n.*

weatherman (ˈwɛðəˌmæn) *n., pl.* **-men.** *Inf.* a person who forecasts the weather, esp. one who works in a meteorological office.

weather map *or* **chart** *n.* a chart showing weather conditions, compiled from simultaneous observations taken at various weather stations.

weatherproof (ˈwɛðəˌpruːf) *adj.* **1.** designed or able to withstand exposure to weather without deterioration. ~*vb.* **2.** (*tr.*) to render (something) weatherproof.

weather station *n.* one of a network of meteorological observation posts where weather data is recorded.

weather strip *n.* a thin strip of compressible material, such as spring metal, felt, etc., that is fitted between the frame of a door or window and the opening part to exclude wind and rain. Also called: **weatherstripping.**

weather vane *n.* a vane designed to indicate the direction in which the wind is blowing.

weather window *n.* a limited interval when weather conditions can be expected to be suitable for a particular project.

weather-wise *adj.* **1.** skilful in predicting weather conditions. **2.** skilful in predicting trends in opinion, reactions, etc.

weatherworn (ˈwɛðəˌwɔːn) *adj.* another word for **weather-beaten.**

weave (wiːv) *vb.* **weaving, wove** *or* **weaved; woven** *or* **weaved. 1.** to form (a fabric) by interlacing (yarn, etc.), esp. on a loom. **2.** (*tr.*) to make or construct by such a process: *to weave a shawl.* **3.** to construct by interlacing (cane, twigs, etc.). **4.** (of a spider) to make (a web). **5.** (*tr.*) to construct by combining separate elements into a whole. **6.** (*tr.;* often foll. by *in, into, through,* etc.) to introduce: *to weave factual details into a fiction.* **7.** to create (a way, etc.) by moving from side to side: *to weave through a crowd.* **8. get weaving.** *Inf.* to hurry. ~*n.* **9.** the method or pattern of weaving or the structure of a woven fabric: *an open weave.* [OE *wefan*]

weaver (ˈwiːvə) *n.* **1.** a person who weaves, esp. as a means of livelihood. **2.** short for **weaverbird.**

weaverbird (ˈwiːvəˌbɜːd) *or* **weaver** *n.* any of a family of small Old World passerine songbirds, having a short thick bill and a dull plumage and building covered nests: includes the house sparrow and whydahs.

web (wɛb) *n.* **1.** any structure, fabric, etc., formed by or as if by weaving or interweaving. **2.** a mesh of fine tough threads built by a spider from a liquid secreted from its spinnerets and used to trap insects. **3.** a similar network of threads spun by certain insect larvae, such as the silkworm. **4.** a fabric, esp. one in the process of being woven. **5.** a membrane connecting the toes of some aquatic birds or the digits of such aquatic mammals as the otter. **6.** the vane of a bird's feather. **7.** a thin piece of metal, esp. one connecting two thicker parts as in an H-beam or an I-beam. **8. a.** a continuous strip of paper as formed on a paper machine or fed from a reel into some printing presses. **b.** (*as modifier*): *web offset.* **9.** any structure, construction, etc., that is intricately formed or complex: *a web of intrigue.* ~*vb.* **webbing, webbed. 10.** (*tr.*) to cover with or as if with a web. **11.** (*tr.*) to entangle or ensnare. **12.** (*intr.*) to construct a web. [OE *webb*] —ˈ**webless** *adj.*

webbed (wɛbd) *adj.* **1.** (of the feet of certain animals) having the digits connected by a thin fold of skin. **2.** having or resembling a web.

webbing (ˈwɛbɪŋ) *n.* **1.** a strong fabric of hemp, cotton, jute, etc., woven in strips and used under springs in upholstery or for straps, etc. **2.** the skin that unites the digits of a webbed foot.

webby (ˈwɛbɪ) *adj.* **-bier, -biest.** of, relating to, resembling, or consisting of a web.

weber (ˈveɪbə) *n.* the derived SI unit of magnetic flux; the flux that, when linking a circuit of one turn, produces in it an emf of 1 volt as it is reduced to zero at a uniform rate in one second. Symbol: Wb [C20: after W. E. *Weber* (1804–91), G physicist]

webfoot (ˈwɛbˌfʊt) *n.* **1.** *Zool.* a foot having the toes connected by folds of skin. **2.** *Anat.* a foot having an abnormal membrane connecting adjacent toes.

web-footed *or* **web-toed** *adj.* (of certain animals) having webbed feet that facilitate swimming.

webwheel (ˈwɛbˌwiːl) *n.* **1.** a wheel containing a plate or web instead of spokes. **2.** a wheel of which the rim, spokes, and centre are in one piece.

wed (wɛd) *vb.* **wedding, wedded** *or* **wed. 1.** to take (a person of the opposite sex) as a husband or wife; marry. **2.** (*tr.*) to join (two people) in matrimony. **3.** (*tr.*) to unite closely. [OE *weddian*] —ˈ**wedded** *adj.*

Wed. *abbrev. for* Wednesday.

we'd (wiːd; *unstressed* wɪd) *contraction of* we had *or* we would.

wedding (ˈwɛdɪŋ) *n.* **1. a.** the act of marrying or the celebration of a marriage. **b.** (*as modifier*): *wedding day.* **2.** the anniversary of a marriage (in such combinations as **silver wedding** or **diamond wedding**).

wedding breakfast *n.* the meal usually served after a wedding ceremony or just before the bride and bridegroom leave for their honeymoon.

wedding cake *n.* a rich fruit cake, with one, two, or more tiers, covered with almond paste and decorated with royal icing, which is served at a wedding reception.

wedding ring *n.* a band ring with parallel sides, typically of precious metal, worn to indicate married status.

wedge (wɛdʒ) *n.* **1.** a block of solid material, esp. wood or metal, that is shaped like a narrow V in cross section and can be pushed or driven between two objects or parts of an object in order to split or secure them. **2.** any formation, structure, or substance in the shape of a wedge: *a wedge of cheese.* **3.** something such as an idea, action, etc., that tends to cause division. **4.** a shoe with a wedge heel. **5.** *Golf.* a club, a No. 10 iron with a face angle of more than 50°, used for bunker or pitch shots. **6.** (formerly) a body of troops formed in a V-shape. **7. thin end of the wedge.** anything unimportant in itself that implies the start of something much larger. ~*vb.* **8.** (*tr.*) to secure with or as if with a wedge. **9.** to squeeze or be squeezed like a wedge into a narrow space. **10.** (*tr.*) to force apart or divide with or as if with a wedge. [OE *wecg*] —ˈ**wedgeˌlike** *adj.* —ˈ**wedgy** *adj.*

wedge heel *n.* a raised shoe heel with the heel and sole forming a solid block.

wedge-tailed eagle *n.* a large brown Australian eagle having a wedge-shaped tail. Also called: **eaglehawk**, (Inf.) **wedgie.**

Wedgwood (ˈwɛdʒwʊd) *Trademark.* ~*n.* **1. a.** pottery produced at the Wedgwood factory, near Stoke-on-Trent. **b.** such pottery having applied decoration in white on a coloured ground. ~*adj.* **2. a.** relating to pottery made at the Wedgwood factory. **b.** characteristic of such pottery: *Wedgwood blue.* [C18: after Josiah *Wedgwood* (1730–95), E potter]

wedlock (ˈwɛdlɒk) *n.* **1.** the state of being married. **2. born** *or* **conceived out of wedlock.** born or conceived when one's parents are not legally married. [OE *wedlāc*, < *wedd* pledge + *-lāc*, suffix denoting activity, ? < *lāc* game]

Wednesday (ˈwɛnzdɪ) *n.* the fourth day of the week; third day of the working week. [OE *Wōdnes dæg* Woden's day, translation of L *mercurii dies* Mercury's day]

wee[1] (wiː) *adj.* very small; tiny; minute. [C13: < OE *wǣg* weight]

wee[2] (wiː) *Inf., chiefly Brit.* ~*n.* **1. a.** the act or an instance of urinating. **b.** urine. ~*vb.* **2.** (*intr.*) to urinate. ~Also: **wee-wee.** [<?]

weed (wiːd) *n.* **1.** any plant that grows wild and profusely, esp. one that grows among cultivated plants, depriving them of space, food, etc. **2.** *Sl.* **a. the weed.** tobacco. **b.** marijuana. **3.** *Inf.* a thin or unprepossessing person. **4.** an inferior horse, esp. one showing signs of weakness. ~*vb.* **5.** to remove (useless or troublesome plants) from (a garden, etc.). [OE *weod*] —ˈ**weeder** *n.* —ˈ**weedless** *adj.*

weedkiller (ˈwiːdˌkɪlə) *n.* a substance, usually a chemical or hormone, used for killing weeds.

weed out *vb.* (*tr., adv.*) to separate out, remove, or eliminate (anything unwanted): *to weed out troublesome students.*

weeds (wiːdz) *pl. n.* a widow's black mourning clothes. Also called: **widow's weeds**. [C16: pl. of *weed* (OE *wǣd, wēd*) a band worn in mourning]

weedy (ˈwiːdɪ) *adj.* **weedier, weediest. 1.** full of or containing weeds: *weedy land.* **2.** (of a plant) resembling a weed in straggling growth. **3.** *Inf.* thin or weakly in appearance.

week (wiːk) *n.* **1.** a period of seven consecutive days, esp. one beginning with Sunday. Related adj.: **hebdomadal. 2.** a period of seven consecutive days beginning from or including a specified day: *a week from Wednesday.* **3.** the period of time within a week devoted to work. ~*adv.* **4.** *Chiefly Brit.* seven days before or after a specified day: *I'll visit you Wednesday week.* [OE *wice, wicu*]

weekday (ˈwiːkˌdeɪ) *n.* any day of the week other than Sunday and, often, Saturday.

weekend *n.* (ˌwiːkˈɛnd). **1. a.** the end of the week, esp. the period from Friday night until the end of Sunday. **b.** (*as modifier*): *a weekend party.* ~*vb.* (ˈwiːkˌɛnd). **2.** (*intr.*) *Inf.* to spend or pass a weekend.

weekends (ˌwiːkˈɛndz) *adv. Inf.* at the weekend, esp. regularly or during every weekend.

weekly (ˈwiːklɪ) *adj.* **1.** happening or taking place once a week or every week. **2.** determined or calculated by the week. ~*adv.* **3.** once a week or every week. ~*n., pl.* **-lies. 4.** a newspaper or magazine issued every week.

weeknight (ˈwiːkˌnaɪt) *n.* the evening or night of a weekday.

ween (wiːn) *vb. Arch.* to think or imagine (something). [OE *wēnan*]

weeny (ˈwiːnɪ) *adj.* **-nier, -niest.** *Inf.* very small; tiny. [C18: < WEE[1] with the ending *-ny* as in TINY]

weeny-bopper *n. Inf.* a child of 8 to 12 years who is a keen follower of pop music. [C20: formed on the model of TEENYBOPPER, < WEENY]

weep (wiːp) *vb.* **weeping, wept. 1.** to shed (tears). **2.** (*tr.;* foll. by *out*) to utter, shedding tears. **3.** (when *intr.*, foll. by *for*) to lament (for something). **4.** to exude (drops of liquid). **5.** (*intr.*) (of a wound, etc.) to exude a watery fluid. ~*n.* **6.** a spell of weeping. [OE *wēpan*]

weeper (ˈwiːpə) *n.* **1.** a person who weeps, esp. a hired mourner. **2.** something worn as a sign of mourning.

weeping (ˈwiːpɪŋ) *adj.* (of plants) having slender hanging branches. —ˈ**weepingly** *adv.*

weeping willow *n.* a Chinese willow tree having long hanging branches.

weepy (ˈwiːpɪ) *Inf.* ~*adj.* **weepier, weepiest. 1.** liable or tending to weep. ~*n., pl.* **weepies. 2.** a sentimental film or book. —ˈ**weepily** *adv.* —ˈ**weepiness** *n.*

weever (ˈwiːvə) *n.* a small marine fish having venomous spines around the gills and the dorsal fin. [C17: < OF *wivre* viper, ult. < L *vīpera* VIPER]

weevil (ˈwiːvɪl) *n.* any of numerous beetles, many having elongated snouts, that are pests, feeding on plants and plant products. [OE *wifel*] —ˈ**weevily** *adj.*

wee-wee *n., vb.* a variant of **wee**[2].

w.e.f. *abbrev. for* with effect from.

weft (wɛft) *n.* the yarn woven across the width of the fabric through the lengthways warp yarn. Also called: **filling, woof.** [OE]

weigela (waɪˈgiːlə, -ˈdʒiː-) *n.* a shrub of an Asian genus having clusters of showy bell-shaped flowers. [C19: < NL, after C. E. *Weigel* (1748–1831), G physician]

weigh[1] (weɪ) *vb.* **1.** (*tr.*) to measure the weight of. **2.** (*intr.*) to have weight: *she weighs more than her sister.* **3.** (*tr.;* often foll. by *out*) to apportion according to weight. **4.** (*tr.*) to consider carefully: *to weigh the facts of a case.* **5.** (*intr.*) to be influential: *his words weighed little with the jury.* **6.** (*intr.;* often foll. by *on*) to be oppressive (to). **7. weigh anchor.** to raise a vessel's anchor or (of a vessel) to have its anchor raised preparatory to departure. ~See also **weigh down, weigh in,** etc. [OE *wegan*] —ˈ**weighable** *adj.* —ˈ**weigher** *n.*

weigh[2] (weɪ) *n.* **under weigh.** a variant spelling of **under way.** [C18: var. due to the infl. of phrases such as *to weigh anchor*]

weighbridge (ˈweɪˌbrɪdʒ) *n.* a machine for weighing vehicles, etc., by means of a metal plate set into a road.

weigh down *vb.* (*adv.*) to press (a person, etc.) down by or as if by weight: *his troubles weighed him down.*

weigh in *vb.* (*intr., adv.*) **1. a.** (of a boxer or wrestler) to be weighed before a bout. **b.** (of a jockey) to be weighed after, or sometimes before, a race. **2.** *Inf.* to contribute, as in a discussion, etc.: *he weighed in with a few sharp comments.* ~*n.* **weigh-in. 3.** the act of checking a competitor's weight, as in boxing, racing, etc.

weight (weɪt) *n.* **1.** a measure of the heaviness of an object; the amount anything weighs. **2.** *Physics.* the vertical force experienced by a mass as a result of gravitation. **3.** a system of units used to express weight: *troy weight.* **4.** a unit used to measure weight: *the kilogram is the weight used in SI units.* **5.** any mass or heavy object used to exert pressure or weigh down. **6.** an oppressive force: *the weight of cares.* **7.** any heavy load: *the bag was such a weight.* **8.** the main force; preponderance: *the weight of evidence.* **9.** importance; influence: *his opinion carries weight.* **10.** *Statistics.* one of a set of coefficients assigned to items of a frequency distribution that are analysed in order to represent the relative importance of the different items. **11.** *Printing.* the apparent blackness of a printed typeface. **12. pull one's weight.** *Inf.* to do one's full or proper share of a task. **13. throw one's weight around.** *Inf.* to act in an overauthoritarian manner. ~*vb.* (*tr.*) **14.** to add weight to. **15.** to burden or oppress. **16.** to add importance, value, etc., to (one side rather than another). **17.** *Statistics.* to attach a weight or weights to. [OE *wiht*] —ˈ**weighter** *n.*

weighted average *n. Statistics.* a result produced by a technique designed to give recognition to the importance of certain factors when compiling the average of a group of values.

weighting (ˈweɪtɪŋ) *n.* **1.** a factor by which some quantity is multiplied in order to make it comparable with others. **2.** an allowance paid to compensate for higher living costs: *a London weighting.*

weightlessness (ˈweɪtlɪsnɪs) *n.* the condition of a person or apparatus in a spacecraft subject to no force except gravity. In this state the body is free from the stress normally experienced on earth where gravity is opposed by supporting forces acting on the surface of the body. —ˈ**weightless** *adj.*

weightlifting (ˈweɪtˌlɪftɪŋ) *n.* the sport of lifting barbells of specified weights in a prescribed manner. —ˈ**weightˌlifter** *n.*

weight training *n.* physical exercise involving lifting weights, either heavy or light weights, as a way of improving muscle performance.

weight watcher *n.* a person who tries to lose weight, esp. by dieting.

weighty (ˈweɪtɪ) *adj.* **weightier, weightiest. 1.** having great weight. **2.** important. **3.** causing worry. —ˈ**weightily** *adv.* —ˈ**weightiness** *n.*

weigh up *vb.* (*tr., adv.*) to make an assessment of (a person, situation, etc.); judge.

Weimaraner (ˈvaɪməˌrɑːnə, ˈwaɪməˌrɑː-) *n.* a breed of hunting dog, having a sleek short grey coat and short tail. [C20: after *Weimar,* city in East Germany, where the breed was developed]

weir (wɪə) *n.* **1.** a low dam that is built across a river to raise the water level, divert the water, or control its flow. **2.** a series of traps or enclosures placed in a stream to catch fish. [OE *wer*]

weird (wɪəd) *adj.* **1.** suggestive of or relating to the supernatural; eerie. **2.** strange or bizarre. **3.** *Arch.* of or relating to fate or the Fates. ~*n.* **4.** *Arch., chiefly Scot.* **a.** fate or destiny. **b.** one of the Fates. [OE (*ge*)*wyrd* destiny] —ˈ**weirdly** *adv.* —ˈ**weirdness** *n.*

weirdo (ˈwɪədəʊ) *or* **weirdie** (ˈwɪədɪ) *n., pl.* **-dos** *or* **-dies.** *Inf.* a person who behaves in a bizarre or eccentric manner.

Weismannism (ˈvaɪsmənˌɪzəm) *n.* the theory that all inheritable characteristics are transmitted by the reproductive cells and that characteristics acquired during the lifetime of the organism are not inherited. [C19: after August *Weismann* (1834–1914), G biologist]

weka (ˈwɛkə) *n.* a nocturnal flightless bird of New Zealand. Also called: **Maori hen, wood hen.** [< Maori]

welch (wɛlʃ) *vb.* a variant spelling of **welsh.**

Welch (wɛlʃ) *adj., n.* an archaic spelling of **Welsh.**

welcome (ˈwɛlkəm) *adj.* **1.** gladly and cordially received or admitted: *a welcome guest.* **2.** bringing pleasure: *a welcome gift.* **3.** freely permitted or invited: *you are welcome to call.* **4.** under no obligation (only in such phrases as **you're welcome,** as conventional responses to thanks). ~*sentence substitute.* **5.** an expression of cordial greeting. ~*n.* **6.** the act of greeting or receiving a person or thing; reception: *the new theory had a cool welcome.* **7. wear out** *or* **overstay one's welcome.** to come more often or stay longer than is pleasing. ~*vb.* (*tr.*) **8.** to greet the arrival of (guests, etc.) cordially. **9.** to receive or accept, esp. gladly. [C12: changed (through infl. of WELL[1]) < OE *wilcuma* (agent n. referring to a welcome guest), *wilcume* (a greeting of welcome), < *wil* WILL[2] + *cuman* to come] —ˈ**welcomely** *adv.* —ˈ**welcomer** *n.*

weld[1] (wɛld) *vb.* **1.** (*tr.*) to unite (pieces of metal or plastic), as by softening with heat and hammering or by fusion. **2.** to bring or admit of being brought into close union. ~*n.* **3.** a joint formed by welding. [C16: altered < obs. *well* to melt, weld] —ˈ**weldable** *adj.* —ˌ**weldaˈbility** *n.* —ˈ**welder** *or* ˈ**weldor** *n.*

weld[2] (wɛld), **wold,** *or* **woald** (wəʊld) *n.* a yellow dye obtained from the plant dyer's rocket. [C14: < Low G]

welfare (ˈwɛlˌfɛə) *n.* **1.** health, happiness, prosperity, and wellbeing in general. **2. a.** financial and other assistance given to people in need. **b.** (*as modifier*): *welfare services.* **3.** Also called: **welfare work.** plans or work to better the social or economic conditions of various underprivileged groups. **4. on welfare.** *Chiefly U.S. & Canad.* in receipt of financial aid from a government agency or other source. [C14: < *wel fare;* see WELL[1], FARE]

welfare state *n.* a system in which the government undertakes the chief responsibility for providing for the social and economic security of its population, usually through unemployment insurance, old age pensions, and other social-security measures.

welkin (ˈwɛlkɪn) *n. Arch.* the sky, heavens, or upper air. [OE *wolcen, welcen*]

well[1] (wɛl) *adv.* **better, best. 1.** (*often used in combination*) in a satisfactory manner: *the party went very well.* **2.** (*often used in combination*) in a skilful manner: *she plays the violin well; a well-chosen example.* **3.** in a correct or careful manner: *listen well to my words.* **4.** in a prosperous manner: *to live well.* **5.** (*usually used* *with auxiliaries*) suitably; fittingly: *you can't very well say that.* **6.** intimately: *I knew him well.* **7.** in a kind or favourable manner: *she speaks well of you.* **8.** fully: *to be well informed.* **9.** by a considerable margin: *let me know well in advance.* **10.** (preceded by *could, might,* or *may*) indeed: *you may well have to do it yourself.* **11. all very well.** used ironically to express discontent, dissent, etc. **12. as well. a.** in addition; too. **b.** (preceded by *may* or *might*) with equal effect: *you might as well come.* **13. as well as.** in addition to. **14. (just) as well.** preferable or advisable: *it would be just as well if you paid me now.* **15. leave well (enough) alone.** to refrain from interfering with something that is satisfactory. **16. well and good.** used to indicate calm acceptance, as of a decision. ~*adj.* (*usually postpositive*) **17.** (when *prenominal, usually used with a negative*) in good health: *I'm very well, thank you; he's not a well man.* **18.** satisfactory or pleasing. **19.** prudent; advisable: *it would be well to make no comment.* **20.** prosperous or comfortable. **21.** fortunate: *it is well that you agreed to go.* ~*interj.* **22. a.** an expression of surprise, indignation, or reproof. **b.** an expression of anticipation in waiting for an answer or remark. ~*sentence connector.* **23.** an expression used to preface a remark, gain time, etc.: *well, I don't think I will come.* [OE *wel*]

well[2] (wɛl) *n.* **1.** a hole or shaft bored into the earth to tap a supply of water, oil, gas, etc. **2.** a natural pool where ground water comes to the surface. **3. a.** a cavity, space, or vessel used to contain a liquid. **b.** (*in combination*): *an inkwell.* **4.** an open shaft through the floors of a building, such as one used for a staircase. **5.** a deep enclosed space in a building or between buildings that is open to the sky. **6.** a bulkheaded compartment built around a ship's pumps for protection and ease of access. **7.** (in England) the open space in the centre of a law court. **8.** an abundant source: *he is a well of knowledge.* ~*vb.* **9.** to flow or cause to flow upwards or outwards: *tears welled from her eyes.* [OE *wella*]

we'll (wiːl) *contraction of* we will *or* we shall.

well-advised *adj.* (**well advised** *when postpositive*). **1.** acting with deliberation or reason. **2.** well thought out: *a well-advised plan.*

well-affected *adj.* (**well affected** *when postpositive*). favourably disposed (towards); steadfast or loyal.

well-appointed *adj.* (**well appointed** *when postpositive*). well equipped or furnished.

wellaway (ˈwɛləˈweɪ) *interj. Arch.* woe! alas! [OE, < *wei lā wei,* var. of *wā lā wā,* lit.: woe! lo woe]

well-balanced *adj.* (**well balanced** *when postpositive*). **1.** having good balance or proportions. **2.** sane or sensible.

wellbeing (ˈwɛlˈbiːɪŋ) *n.* the condition of being contented, healthy, or successful; welfare.

well-bred *adj.* (**well bred** *when postpositive*). **1.** Also: **well-born.** of respected or noble lineage. **2.** indicating good breeding: *well-bred manners.* **3.** of good thoroughbred stock: *a well-bred spaniel.*

well-chosen *adj.* (**well chosen** *when postpositive*). carefully selected to produce a desired effect; apt: *a few well-chosen words.*

well-connected *adj.* (**well connected** *when postpositive*). having influential or important relatives or friends.

well-disposed *adj.* (**well disposed** *when postpositive*). inclined to be sympathetic, kindly, or friendly.

well-done *adj.* (**well done** *when postpositive*). **1.** (of food, esp. meat) cooked thoroughly. **2.** made or accomplished satisfactorily.

well dressing *n.* the decoration of wells with flowers, etc.: a traditional annual ceremony of great antiquity in some parts of Britain, originally associated with the cult of water deities.

well-favoured *adj.* (**well favoured** *when postpositive*). good-looking.

well-formed formula *n. Logic.* a group of logical symbols that makes sense; a logical sentence.

well-found *adj.* (**well found** *when postpositive*). furnished or supplied with all or most necessary things.

well-founded *adj.* (**well founded** *when postpositive*). having good grounds: *well-founded rumours.*

well-groomed *adj.* (**well groomed** *when postpositive*). having a tidy pleasing appearance.

well-grounded *adj.* (**well grounded** *when postpositive*). **1.** well instructed in the basic elements of a subject. **2.** another term for **well-founded.**

wellhead (ˈwɛlˌhɛd) *n.* **1.** the source of a well or stream. **2.** a source, fountainhead, or origin.

well-heeled *adj.* (**well heeled** *when postpositive*). *Inf.* rich; prosperous; wealthy.

wellies (ˈwɛlɪz) *pl. n. Brit. inf.* Wellington boots.

well-informed *adj.* (**well informed** *when postpositive*). **1.** having knowledge about a great variety of subjects: *he seems to be a well-informed person.* **2.** possessing reliable information on a particular subject.

Wellington boots (ˈwɛlɪŋtən) *pl. n.* **1.** Also called: **gumboots.** *Brit.* knee-length or calf-length rubber boots, worn esp. in wet conditions. Often shortened to **wellingtons, wellies. 2.** military leather boots covering the front of the knee but cut away at the back to allow easier bending of the knee. [C19: after the 1st Duke of *Wellington* (1769–1852), Brit. soldier & statesman]

wellingtonia (ˌwɛlɪŋˈtəʊnɪə) *n.* a giant Californian coniferous tree, often reaching 90 metres

---

ˈwell-acˈcustomed *adj.*
ˈwell-acˈquainted *adj.*
ˈwell-ˈacted *adj.*
ˈwell-aˈdapted *adj.*
ˈwell-adˈjusted *adj.*
ˈwell-adˈministered *adj.*
ˈwell-ˈadverˌtised *adj.*
ˈwell-ˈaimed *adj.*
ˈwell-ˈaired *adj.*
ˈwell-apˈplied *adj.*
ˈwell-ˈargued *adj.*
ˈwell-ˈarmed *adj.*
ˈwell-arˈranged *adj.*
ˈwell-asˈsorted *adj.*
ˈwell-asˈsured *adj.*
ˈwell-atˈtended *adj.*
ˈwell-atˈtested *adj.*
ˈwell-auˈthentiˌcated *adj.*
ˈwell-aˈware *adj.*
ˈwell-beˈhaved *adj.*
ˈwell-beˈloved *adj., n.*
ˈwell-ˈblessed *adj.*
ˈwell-ˈbuilt *adj.*
ˈwell-ˈcalcuˌlated *adj.*
ˈwell-ˈclothed *adj.*
ˈwell-ˈcoached *adj.*
ˈwell-ˈcompenˌsated *adj.*
ˈwell-conˈcealed *adj.*
ˈwell-conˈditioned *adj.*
ˈwell-conˈducted *adj.*
ˈwell-conˈfirmed *adj.*
ˈwell-conˈsidered *adj.*
ˈwell-conˈstructed *adj.*
ˈwell-conˈtented *adj.*
ˈwell-conˈtrolled *adj.*
ˈwell-ˈcooked *adj.*
ˈwell-ˈcovered *adj.*
ˈwell-ˈcultiˌvated *adj.*
ˈwell-deˈfended *adj.*
ˈwell-deˈfined *adj.*
ˈwell-ˈdemonˌstrated *adj.*
ˈwell-deˈscribed *adj.*
ˈwell-deˈserved *adj.*
ˈwell-deˈveloped *adj.*
ˈwell-deˈvised *adj.*
ˈwell-diˈgested *adj.*
ˈwell-ˈdisciplined *adj.*
ˈwell-ˈdocuˌmented *adj.*
ˈwell-ˈdressed *adj.*
ˈwell-ˈearned *adj.*
ˈwell-ˈeduˌcated *adj.*
ˈwell-emˈployed *adj.*
ˈwell-enˈdowed *adj.*
ˈwell-eˈquipped *adj.*
ˈwell-esˈtablished *adj.*
ˈwell-esˈteemed *adj.*
ˈwell-ˈfed *adj.*
ˈwell-fiˈnanced *adj.*
ˈwell-ˈfinished *adj.*
ˈwell-ˈfitted *adj.*
ˈwell-ˈformed *adj.*
ˈwell-ˈfought *adj.*
ˈwell-ˈfurnished *adj.*
ˈwell-ˈgoverned *adj.*
ˈwell-ˈguarded *adj.*
ˈwell-ˈhandled *adj.*
ˈwell-ˈhidden *adj.*
ˈwell-ˈhoused *adj.*
ˈwell-ˈillusˌtrated *adj.*
ˈwell-inˈclined *adj.*

high. Also called: **big tree, sequoia.** [C19: after the 1st Duke of *Wellington*]

well-intentioned *adj.* (**well intentioned** *when postpositive*). having benevolent intentions, usually with unfortunate results.

well-knit *adj.* (**well knit** *when postpositive*). strong, firm, or sturdy.

well-known *adj.* (**well known** *when postpositive*). **1.** widely known; famous; celebrated. **2.** known fully or clearly.

well-mannered *adj.* (**well mannered** *when postpositive*). having good manners; polite.

well-meaning *adj.* (**well meaning** *when postpositive*). having or indicating good intentions, usually with unfortunate results.

well-nigh *adv. Arch. or poetic.* nearly; almost: *it's well-nigh three o'clock.*

▷ **Usage.** In strict usage, *well-nigh* is an adverb meaning *nearly* or *almost* and not a preposition meaning *near: he well-nigh cried; he was near* (not *well-nigh*) *death.*

well-off *adj.* (**well off** *when postpositive*). **1.** in a comfortable or favourable position or state. **2.** financially well provided for; moderately rich.

well-oiled *adj.* (**well oiled** *when postpositive*). *Inf.* drunk.

well-preserved *adj.* (**well preserved** *when postpositive*). **1.** kept in a good condition. **2.** continuing to appear youthful: *she was a well-preserved old lady.*

well-read (ˈwɛlˈrɛd) *adj.* (**well read** *when postpositive*). having read widely and intelligently; erudite.

well-rounded *adj.* (**well rounded** *when postpositive*). **1.** rounded in shape or well developed: *a well-rounded figure.* **2.** full, varied, and satisfying: *a well-rounded life.*

well-spoken *adj.* (**well spoken** *when postpositive*). **1.** having a clear, articulate, and socially acceptable accent and way of speaking. **2.** spoken satisfactorily or pleasingly.

wellspring (ˈwɛlˌsprɪŋ) *n.* **1.** the source of a spring or stream. **2.** a source of abundant supply.

well-stacked *adj.* (**well stacked** *when postpositive*). *Brit. sl.* (of a woman) of voluptuous proportions.

well sweep *n.* a device for raising buckets from and lowering them into a well, consisting of a long pivoted pole, the bucket being attached to one end by a long rope.

well-tempered *adj.* (**well tempered** *when postpositive*). (of a musical scale or instrument) conforming to the system of equal temperament. See **temperament** (sense 4).

well-thought-of *adj.* respected.

well-thumbed *adj.* (**well thumbed** *when postpositive*). (of a book) having the pages marked from frequent turning.

well-to-do *adj.* moderately wealthy.

well-turned *adj.* (**well turned** *when postpositive*). **1.** (of a phrase, etc.) apt and pleasing. **2.** having a pleasing shape: *a well-turned leg.*

well-upholstered *adj.* (**well upholstered** *when postpositive*). *Inf.* (of a person) fat.

well-wisher *n.* a person who shows benevolence or sympathy towards a person, cause, etc. —ˈ**well-**ˌ**wishing** *adj., n.*

well-woman *n., pl.* **-women.** *Social welfare.* **a.** a woman who attends a health-service clinic for preventive monitoring, health education, etc. **b.** (*as modifier*): *well-woman clinic.*

well-worn *adj.* (**well worn** *when postpositive*). **1.** so much used as to be affected by wear: *a well-worn coat.* **2.** hackneyed: *a well-worn phrase.*

welsh *or* **welch** (wɛlʃ) *vb.* (*intr.*; often foll. by *on*) **1.** to fail to pay a gambling debt. **2.** to fail to fulfil an obligation. [C19: <?] —ˈ**welsher** *or* ˈ**welcher** *n.*

Welsh (wɛlʃ) *adj.* **1.** of, relating to, or characteristic of Wales, its people, their language, or their dialect of English. ~*n.* **2.** a language of Wales, belonging to the S Celtic branch of the Indo-European family. **3. the Welsh.** (*functioning as pl.*) the natives or inhabitants of Wales. [OE *Wēlisc, Wǣlisc*]

Welsh corgi *n.* another name for **corgi.**

Welsh dresser *n.* a sideboard with drawers and cupboards below and open shelves above.

Welsh harp *n.* a type of harp in which the strings are arranged in three rows.

Welshman (ˈwɛlʃmən) *or* (*fem.*) **Welshwoman** *n., pl.* **-men** *or* **-women.** a native or inhabitant of Wales.

Welsh poppy *n.* a perennial W European plant with large yellow flowers.

Welsh rabbit *n.* a savoury dish consisting of melted cheese sometimes mixed with milk, seasonings, etc., on hot buttered toast. Also called: **Welsh rarebit, rarebit.** [C18: a fanciful coinage; *rarebit* is a later folk-etymological var.]

Welsh terrier *n.* a wire-haired breed of terrier with a black-and-tan coat.

welt (wɛlt) *n.* **1.** a raised or strengthened seam in a garment. **2.** another word for **weal**[1]. **3.** (in shoemaking) a strip of leather, etc., put in between the outer sole and the inner sole and upper. ~*vb.* (*tr.*) **4.** to put a welt in (a garment, etc.). **5.** to beat soundly. [C15: <?]

welter (ˈwɛltə) *vb.* (*intr.*) **1.** to roll about, writhe, or wallow. **2.** (esp. of the sea) to surge, heave, or toss. **3.** to lie drenched in a liquid, esp. blood. ~*n.* **4.** a confused mass; jumble. [C13: < MLow G, MDu. *weltern*]

welterweight (ˈwɛltəˌweɪt) *n.* **1. a.** a professional boxer weighing 140–147 pounds (63.5–66.5 kg). **b.** an amateur boxer weighing 63.5–67 kg (140–148 pounds). **2. a.** a professional wrestler weighing 155–165 pounds (71–75 kg). **b.** an amateur wrestler weighing 69–74 kg (151–161 pounds).

wen[1] (wɛn) *n.* **1.** *Pathol.* a sebaceous cyst, esp. one occurring on the scalp. **2.** a large overcrowded city (esp. London, **the great wen**). [OE *wenn*]

wen[2] (wɛn) *n.* a rune having the sound of Modern English *w.* [OE *wen, wyn*]

ˈ**well-**ˈ**judged** *adj.*
ˈ**well-**ˈ**justi**ˌ**fied** *adj.*
ˈ**well-**ˈ**kept** *adj.*
ˈ**well-**ˈ**liked** *adj.*
ˈ**well-**ˈ**loved** *adj.*
ˈ**well-**ˈ**made** *adj.*
ˈ**well-**ˈ**managed** *adj.*
ˈ**well-**ˈ**marked** *adj.*
ˈ**well-**ˈ**matched** *adj.*
ˈ**well-**ˈ**merited** *adj.*
ˈ**well-**ˈ**mixed** *adj.*
ˈ**well-**ˈ**moti**ˌ**vated** *adj.*
ˈ**well-**ˈ**noted** *adj.*
ˈ**well-**ˈ**ordered** *adj.*
ˈ**well-**ˈ**organ**ˌ**ized** *or* **-**ˌ**ised** *adj.*
ˈ**well-**ˈ**paid** *adj.*
ˈ**well-**ˈ**phrased** *adj.*
ˈ**well-**ˈ**placed** *adj.*
ˈ**well-**ˈ**planned** *adj.*
ˈ**well-**ˈ**played** *adj.*
ˈ**well-**ˈ**pleased** *adj.*
ˈ**well-**ˈ**practised** *adj.*
ˈ**well-pre**ˈ**pared** *adj.*
ˈ**well-pro**ˈ**portioned** *adj.*
ˈ**well-pro**ˈ**tected** *adj.*
ˈ**well-pro**ˈ**vided** *adj.*
ˈ**well-**ˈ**quali**ˌ**fied** *adj.*
ˈ**well-**ˈ**reasoned** *adj.*
ˈ**well-re**ˈ**ceived** *adj.*
ˈ**well-**ˈ**recog**ˌ**nized** *or* **-**ˌ**nised** *adj.*
ˈ**well-**ˌ**recom**ˈ**mended** *adj.*
ˈ**well-re**ˈ**garded** *adj.*
ˈ**well-**ˈ**regu**ˌ**lated** *adj.*
ˈ**well-re**ˈ**hearsed** *adj.*
ˈ**well-re**ˈ**membered** *adj.*
ˈ**well-**ˌ**repre**ˈ**sented** *adj.*
ˈ**well-re**ˈ**spected** *adj.*
ˈ**well-re**ˈ**viewed** *adj.*
ˈ**well-**ˈ**ripened** *adj.*
ˈ**well-**ˈ**satis**ˌ**fied** *adj.*
ˈ**well-**ˈ**schooled** *adj.*
ˈ**well-**ˈ**seasoned** *adj.*
ˈ**well-se**ˈ**cured** *adj.*
ˈ**well-**ˈ**shaped** *adj.*
ˈ**well-**ˈ**situ**ˌ**ated** *adj.*
ˈ**well-**ˈ**spent** *adj.*
ˈ**well-**ˈ**stocked** *adj.*
ˈ**well-**ˈ**suited** *adj.*
ˈ**well-sup**ˈ**plied** *adj.*
ˈ**well-sup**ˈ**ported** *adj.*
ˈ**well-**ˈ**taught** *adj.*
ˈ**well-**ˈ**timed** *adj.*
ˈ**well-**ˈ**trained** *adj.*
ˈ**well-**ˈ**travelled** *adj.*
ˈ**well-**ˈ**treated** *adj.*
ˈ**well-**ˈ**tried** *adj.*
ˈ**well-**ˈ**trodden** *adj.*
ˈ**well-under**ˈ**stood** *adj.*
ˈ**well-**ˈ**used** *adj.*
ˈ**well-**ˈ**written** *adj.*

wench (wɛntʃ) *n.* **1.** a girl or young woman: now used facetiously. **2.** *Arch.* a female servant. **3.** *Arch.* a prostitute. ~*vb.* (*intr.*) **4.** *Arch.* to frequent the company of prostitutes. [OE *wencel* child, < *wancol* weak] —ˈ**wencher** *n.*

wend (wɛnd) *vb.* to direct (one's course or way); travel. [OE *wendan*]

Wend (wɛnd) *n.* (esp. in medieval European history) a member of the Slavonic people who inhabited the area between the Rivers Saale and Oder, in central Europe, in the early Middle Ages. Also called: **Sorb.**

wendigo (ˈwɛndɪˌgəʊ) *n. Canad.* **1.** (*pl.* **-gos**) (among Algonquian Indians) an evil spirit or cannibal. **2.** (*pl.* **-go** *or* **-gos**) another name for **splake.** [< Algonquian: evil spirit or cannibal]

Wendy house (ˈwɛndɪ) *n.* a small model house for children to play in. It is big enough for children, but not adults, to enter and use in comfort. [C20: after the house built for *Wendy*, the girl in J. M. Barrie's play *Peter Pan* (1904)]

wensleydale (ˈwɛnzlɪˌdeɪl) *n.* **1.** a type of white cheese with a flaky texture. **2.** a breed of sheep with long woolly fleece. [after *Wensleydale*, North Yorkshire]

went (wɛnt) *vb.* the past tense of **go.**

wentletrap (ˈwɛntᵊlˌtræp) *n.* a marine gastropod mollusc having a long pointed pale-coloured longitudinally ridged shell. [C18: < Du. *winteltrap* spiral shell, < *wintel*, earlier *windel*, < *wenden* to wind + *trap* a step]

wept (wɛpt) *vb.* the past tense and past participle of **weep.**

were (wɜː; *unstressed* wə) *vb.* the plural form of the past tense (indicative mood) of **be** and the singular form used with *you*. It is also used as a subjunctive, esp. in conditional sentences. [OE *wērun, wæron* p.t. pl. of *wesan* to be]

▷ **Usage.** *Were*, as a remnant of the past subjunctive in English, is used in formal contexts in clauses expressing hypotheses (*if he were to die, she would inherit everything*), suppositions contrary to fact (*if I were you, I would be careful*), and desire (*I wish he were there now*). In informal speech, however, *was* is often used instead.

we're (wɪə) *contraction of* we are.

weren't (wɜːnt) *contraction of* were not.

werewolf (ˈwɪəˌwʊlf, ˈwɛə-) *n., pl.* **-wolves.** a person fabled in folklore and superstition to have been changed into a wolf by being bewitched or said to be able to assume wolf form at will. [OE *werewulf*, < *wer* man + *wulf* wolf]

wergild, weregild (ˈwɜːˌgɪld, ˈwɛə-), *or* **wergeld** (ˈwɜːˌgɛld, ˈwɛə-) *n.* the price set on a man's life in Anglo-Saxon and Germanic law codes, to be paid as compensation by his slayer. [OE *wergeld*, < *wer* man + *gield* tribute]

wert (wɜːt; *unstressed* wət) *vb. Arch. or dialect.* (used with the pronoun *thou* or its relative equivalent) a singular form of the past tense (indicative mood) of **be.**

weskit (ˈwɛskɪt) *n.* an informal name for **waistcoat.**

Wesleyan (ˈwɛzlɪən) *adj.* **1.** of or deriving from John Wesley (1703-91), English preacher who founded Methodism. **2.** of or characterizing Methodism, esp. in its original form. ~*n.* **3.** a follower of John Wesley. **4.** a member of the Methodist Church. —ˈ**Wesleyanˌism** *n.*

west (wɛst) *n.* **1.** the direction along a parallel towards the sunset, at 270° clockwise from north. **2. the west.** (*often cap.*) any area lying in or towards the west. Related adjs.: **Hesperian, Occidental. 3.** (*usually cap.*) *Cards.* the player or position at the table corresponding to west on the compass. ~*adj.* **4.** situated in, moving towards, or facing the west. **5.** (esp. of the wind) from the west. ~*adv.* **6.** in, to, or towards the west. **7. go west.** *Inf.* **a.** to be lost or destroyed. **b.** to die. [OE]

West (wɛst) *n.* **the. 1.** the western part of the world contrasted historically and culturally with the East or Orient. **2.** the non-Communist countries of Europe and America contrasted with the Communist states of the East. **3.** (in the U.S.) that part of the U.S. lying approximately to the west of the Mississippi. **4.** (in the ancient and medieval world) the Western Roman Empire and, later, the Holy Roman Empire. ~*adj.* **5.** of or denoting the western part of a specified country, area, etc.

westbound (ˈwɛstˌbaʊnd) *adj.* going or leading towards the west.

west by north *n.* one point on the compass north of west.

west by south *n.* one point on the compass south of west.

West Country *n.* **the.** the southwest of England, esp. Cornwall, Devon, and Somerset.

West End *n.* **the.** a part of W central London containing the main shopping and entertainment areas.

westering (ˈwɛstərɪŋ) *adj. Poetic.* moving towards the west: *the westering star.*

Westerlies (ˈwɛstəlɪz) *pl. n. Meteorol.* the prevailing winds blowing from the west on the poleward sides of the horse latitudes, often bringing depressions and anticyclones.

westerly (ˈwɛstəlɪ) *adj.* **1.** of, relating to, or situated in the west. ~*adv., adj.* **2.** towards or in the direction of the west. **3.** (esp. of the wind) from the west. ~*n., pl.* **-lies. 4.** a wind blowing from the west. —ˈ**westerliness** *n.*

western (ˈwɛstən) *adj.* **1.** situated in or facing the west. **2.** going or directed to or towards the west. **3.** (of a wind, etc.) coming from the west. **4.** native to the west. **5.** *Music.* See **country-and-western.** —ˈ**westernˌmost** *adj.*

Western (ˈwɛstən) *adj.* **1.** of or characteristic of the Americas and the parts of Europe not under Communist rule. **2.** of or characteristic of the West as opposed to the Orient. **3.** of or characteristic of the western states of the U.S. ~*n.* **4.** (*often not cap.*) a film, book, etc., concerned with life in the western states of the U.S., esp. during the era of exploration.

Western Church *n.* **1.** the part of Christendom that derives its liturgy, discipline, and traditions principally from the patriarchate of Rome. **2.** the Roman Catholic Church, sometimes together with the Anglican Communion of Churches.

westerner (ˈwɛstənə) *n.* (*sometimes cap.*) a native or inhabitant of the west of any specific region.

western hemisphere *n.* (*often caps.*) **1.** that half of the globe containing the Americas, lying to the west of the Greenwich or another meridian. **2.** the lands contained in this, esp. the Americas.

westernize *or* **-ise** (ˈwɛstəˌnaɪz) *vb.* (*tr.*) to influence or make familiar with the customs, practices, etc., of the West. —ˌ**westerniˈzation** *or* **-iˈsation** *n.*

Western Roman Empire *n.* the westernmost of the two empires created by the division of the later Roman Empire, esp. after its final severance from the Eastern Roman Empire (395 A.D.). Also called: **Western Empire.**

westing (ˈwɛstɪŋ) *n. Navigation.* movement, deviation, or distance covered in a westerly direction, esp. as expressed in the resulting difference in longitude.

Westminster (ˈwɛstˌmɪnstə) *n.* **1.** Also called: **City of Westminster.** a borough of Greater London, on the River Thames. **2.** the Houses of Parliament at Westminster.

west-northwest *n.* **1.** the point on the compass or the direction midway between west and northwest, 292° 30′ clockwise from north. ~*adj., adv.* **2.** in, from, or towards this direction.

Weston standard cell (ˈwɛstən) *n.* a primary cell used as a standard of emf: consists of a mercury anode and a cadmium amalgam cathode in an electrolyte of saturated cadmium sulphate. [C20: < a trademark]

west-southwest *n.* **1.** the point on the compass or the direction midway between southwest and west, 247° 30′ clockwise from north. ~*adj., adv.* **2.** in, from, or towards this direction.

westward (ˈwɛstwəd) *adj.* **1.** moving, facing, or

situated in the west. ~*adv.* 2. Also: **westwards.** towards the west. ~*n.* 3. the westward part, direction, etc. —ˈ**westwardly** *adj., adv.*

wet (wɛt) *adj.* **wetter, wettest.** 1. moistened, covered, saturated, etc., with water or some other liquid. 2. not yet dry or solid: *wet varnish.* 3. rainy: *wet weather.* 4. employing a liquid, usually water: *a wet method of chemical analysis.* 5. *Chiefly U.S. & Canad.* permitting the free sale of alcoholic beverages: *a wet state.* 6. *Brit. inf.* feeble or foolish. 7. **wet behind the ears.** *Inf.* immature or inexperienced. ~*n.* 8. wetness or moisture. 9. rainy weather. 10. *Brit. inf.* a feeble or foolish person. 11. (*often cap.*) *Brit. inf.* a Conservative politician who is not a hardliner. 12. *Chiefly U.S. & Canad.* a person who advocates free sale of alcoholic beverages. 13. **the wet.** *Austral.* (in northern and central Australia) the rainy season. ~*vb.* **wetting, wet** *or* **wetted.** 14. to make or become wet. 15. to urinate on (something). [OE *wǣt*] —ˈ**wetly** *adv.* —ˈ**wetness** *n.* —ˈ**wettable** *adj.* —ˈ**wetter** *n.* —ˈ**wettish** *adj.*

wet-and-dry-bulb thermometer *n.* another name for **psychrometer.**

wet blanket *n. Inf.* a person whose low spirits or lack of enthusiasm have a depressing effect on others.

wet cell *n.* a primary cell in which the electrolyte is a liquid.

wet dream *n.* an erotic dream accompanied by an emission of semen.

wet fly *n. Angling.* an artificial fly designed to float or ride below the water surface.

wether (ˈwɛðə) *n.* a male sheep, esp. a castrated one. [OE *hwæther*]

wetland (ˈwɛtlənd) *n.* (*sometimes pl.*) **a.** an area of marshy land, esp. considered as part of an ecological system. **b.** (*as modifier*): *wetland species.*

wet look *n.* a shiny finish such as that given to certain clothing and footwear materials.

wet nurse *n.* 1. a woman hired to suckle the child of another. ~*vb.* **wet-nurse.** (*tr.*) 2. to act as a wet nurse to (a child). 3. *Inf.* to attend with great devotion.

wet pack *n. Med.* a hot or cold damp sheet or blanket for wrapping around a patient.

wet rot *n.* 1. a state of decay in timber caused by various fungi. The hyphal strands of the fungus are seldom visible, and affected timber turns dark brown. 2. any of the fungi causing this decay.

wet suit *n.* a close-fitting rubber suit used by skin-divers, yachtsmen, etc., to retain body heat.

wetting agent *n. Chem.* any substance added to a liquid to lower its surface tension and thus increase its ability to spread across or penetrate a solid.

we've (wiːv) *contraction of* we have.

wf *Printing. abbrev. for* wrong fount.

WFF *Logic. abbrev. for* well-formed formula.

WFTU *abbrev. for* World Federation of Trade Unions.

W. Glam. *abbrev. for* West Glamorgan.

whack (wæk) *vb.* (*tr.*) 1. to strike with a sharp resounding blow. 2. (*usually passive*) *Brit. inf.* to exhaust completely. ~*n.* 3. a sharp resounding blow or the noise made by such a blow. 4. *Inf.* a share or portion. 5. *Inf.* a try or attempt (esp. in **have a whack at**). [C18: ? var. of THWACK, ult. imit.] —ˈ**whacker** *n.*

whacking (ˈwækɪŋ) *Inf., chiefly Brit.* ~*adj.* 1. enormous. ~*adv.* 2. (intensifier): *a whacking big lie.*

whacky (ˈwækɪ) *adj.* **whackier, whackiest.** *U.S. sl.* a variant spelling of **wacky.**

whale[1] (weɪl) *n., pl.* **whales** *or* **whale.** 1. any of the larger cetacean mammals, excluding dolphins, porpoises, and narwhals. They have flippers, a streamlined body, and a horizontally flattened tail and breathe through a blowhole on the top of the head. 2. **a whale of a.** *Inf.* an exceptionally large, fine, etc., example of a (person or thing). [OE *hwæl*]

whale[2] (weɪl) *vb.* (*tr.*) to beat or thrash soundly. [C18: var. of WALE]

whaleboat (ˈweɪlˌbəʊt) *n.* a narrow boat from 20 to 30 feet long having a sharp prow and stern, formerly used in whaling. Also called: **whaler.**

whalebone (ˈweɪlˌbəʊn) *n.* 1. Also called: **baleen.** a horny elastic material forming numerous thin plates that hang from the upper jaw in the toothless (whalebone) whales and strain plankton from water entering the mouth. 2. a thin strip of this substance, used in stiffening corsets, bodices, etc.

whalebone whale *n.* any whale belonging to a cetacean suborder having a double blowhole and strips of whalebone between the jaws instead of teeth: includes the rorquals, right whales, and the blue whale.

whale oil *n.* oil obtained either from the blubber of whales (train oil) or the head of the sperm whale (sperm oil).

whaler (ˈweɪlə) *n.* 1. Also called (U.S.): **whaleman.** a person employed in whaling. 2. a vessel engaged in whaling. 3. *Austral. obs. sl.* a tramp or sundowner. 4. an aggressive shark of Australian coastal waters.

whale shark *n.* a large spotted whalelike shark of warm seas, that feeds on plankton and small animals.

whaling (ˈweɪlɪŋ) *n.* the work or industry of hunting and processing whales for food, oil, etc.

wham (wæm) *n.* 1. a forceful blow or impact or the sound produced by it. ~*vb.* **whamming, whammed.** 2. to strike or cause to strike with great force. [C20: imit.]

whang (wæŋ) *vb.* 1. to strike or be struck so as to cause a resounding noise. ~*n.* 2. the resounding noise produced by a heavy blow. 3. a heavy blow. [C19: imit.]

whangee (wæŋˈiː) *n.* 1. a tall woody grass of an Asian genus, grown for its stems. 2. a cane or walking stick made from the stem this plant. [C19: prob. < Chinese (Mandarin) *huangli,* < *huang* yellow + *li* bamboo cane]

whare (ˈwɔːrɪ; *Maori* ˈfɔrɛ) *n. N.Z.* 1. a Maori hut or dwelling place. 2. any simple dwelling place. [< Maori]

wharepuni (ˈfɔrɛˌpunɪ) *n. N.Z.* in a Maori community, a lofty carved building that is used as a guesthouse. [< Maori *whare* house + *puni* company]

wharf (wɔːf) *n., pl.* **wharves** (wɔːvz) *or* **wharfs.** 1. a platform built parallel to the waterfront at a harbour or navigable river for the docking, loading, and unloading of ships. ~*vb.* (*tr.*) 2. to moor or dock at a wharf. 3. to store or unload on a wharf. [OE *hwearf* heap]

wharfage (ˈwɔːfɪdʒ) *n.* 1. accommodation for ships at wharves. 2. a charge for use of a wharf. 3. wharves collectively.

wharfie (ˈwɔːfɪ) *n. Austral. & N.Z.* a wharf labourer; docker.

wharfinger (ˈwɔːfɪndʒə) *n.* an owner or manager of a wharf. [C16: prob. alteration of *wharfager*]

wharve (wɔːv) *n.* a wooden disc or wheel on a shaft serving as a flywheel or pulley. [OE *hweorfa,* < *hweorfan* to revolve]

what (wɒt; *unstressed* wət) *determiner.* 1. **a.** used with a noun in requesting further information about the identity or categorization of something: *what job does he do?* **b.** (*as pron.*): *what is her address?* **c.** (*used in indirect questions*): *tell me what he said.* 2. **a.** the (person, thing, persons, or things) that: *we photographed what animals we could see.* **b.** (*as pron.*): *bring me what you've written.* 3. (intensifier; used in exclamations): *what a good book!* ~*adv.* 4. in what respect? to what degree?: *what do you care?* 5. **what about.** what do you think, know, etc., concerning? 6. **what for. a.** for what purpose? why? **b.** *Inf.* a punishment or reprimand (esp. in **give (a person) what for**). 7. **what have you.** someone or something unknown or unspecified: *cars, motorcycles, or what have you.* 8. **what if. a.** what would happen if? **b.** what difference would it make if? 9. **what matter.** what does it matter? 10. **what's what.** *Inf.* the true state of affairs. [OE *hwæt*]

▷ **Usage.** In good usage, *what* is never used for *which*, as in *he gave me the letter what he had written. What* is used, however, for the things which and that or those which: *he saw what* (that which) *he had done.*

whatever (wɒtˈɛvə, wət-) *pron.* **1.** everything or anything that: *do whatever he asks you to.* **2.** no matter what: *whatever he does, he is forgiven.* **3.** *Inf.* an unknown or unspecified thing or things: *take a hammer, chisel, or whatever.* **4.** an intensive form of *what*, used in questions: *whatever can he have said to upset her so much?* ~*determiner.* **5.** an intensive form of *what*: *use whatever tools you can get hold of.* ~*adj.* **6.** (*postpositive*) absolutely; whatsoever: *I saw no point whatever in continuing.*

whatnot (ˈwɒtˌnɒt) *n.* **1.** Also called: **what-d'you-call-it.** *Inf.* a person or thing the name of which is unknown or forgotten. **2.** *Inf.* unspecified assorted material. **3.** a portable stand with shelves for displaying ornaments, etc.

whatsit (ˈwɒtsɪt), **whatsitsname,** (*masc.*) **whatshisname,** or (*fem.*) **whatshername** *n.* *Inf.* a person or thing the name of which is unknown or forgotten.

whatsoever (ˌwɒtsəʊˈɛvə) *adj.* **1.** (*postpositive*) at all: used as an intensifier with indefinite pronouns and determiners such as *none, anybody,* etc. ~*pron.* **2.** an archaic word for **whatever.**

whaup (hwɔːp) *n. Chiefly Scot.* a popular name for the **curlew.** [C16: rel. to OE *huilpe*, ult. imit. of the bird's cry]

wheal (wiːl) *n.* a variant spelling of **weal**[1].

wheat (wiːt) *n.* **1.** any of a genus of grasses, native to the Mediterranean region and W Asia but widely cultivated, having erect flower spikes and light brown grains. **2.** the grain of any of these grasses, used in making flour, pasta, etc. ~See also **durum.** [OE *hwǣte*]

wheatbelt (ˈwiːtˌbɛlt) *n.* an area in which wheat is the chief agricultural product.

wheatear (ˈwiːtˌɪə) *n.* a small northern songbird having a pale grey back, black wings and tail, white rump, and pale brown underparts. [C16: back formation < *wheatears* (wrongly taken as pl.), prob. < WHITE + ARSE]

wheaten (ˈwiːtᵊn) *adj.* **1.** made of the grain or flour of wheat. **2.** of a pale yellow colour.

wheat germ *n.* the vitamin-rich embryo of the wheat kernel.

wheatmeal (ˈwiːtˌmiːl) *n.* **a.** a brown flour intermediate between white flour and wholemeal flour. **b.** (*as modifier*): *a wheatmeal loaf.*

Wheatstone bridge (ˈwiːtstən) *n.* a device for determining the value of an unknown resistance by comparison with a known standard resistance. [C19: after Sir Charles *Wheatstone* (1802–75), E physicist & inventor]

whee (wiː) *interj.* an exclamation of joy, etc.

wheedle (ˈwiːdᵊl) *vb.* **1.** to persuade or try to persuade (someone) by coaxing words, flattery, etc. **2.** (*tr.*) to obtain thus: *she wheedled some money out of her father.* [C17: ? < G *wedeln* to wag one's tail, < OHG *wedil, wadil* tail] —ˈ**wheedler** *n.* —ˈ**wheedling** *adj.* —ˈ**wheedlingly** *adv.*

wheel (wiːl) *n.* **1.** a solid disc, or a circular rim joined to a hub by spokes, that is mounted on a shaft about which it can turn, as in vehicles. **2.** anything like a wheel in shape or function. **3.** a device consisting of or resembling a wheel: *a steering wheel; a water wheel.* **4.** (usually preceded by *the*) a medieval torture in which the victim was tied to a wheel and then had his limbs struck and broken by an iron bar. **5.** short for **wheel of fortune** or **potter's wheel.** **6.** the act of turning. **7.** a pivoting movement of troops, ships, etc. **8.** a type of firework coiled to make it rotate when let off. **9.** a set of short rhyming lines forming the concluding part of a stanza. **10.** *U.S. & Canad.* an informal word for **bicycle.** **11.** *Inf., chiefly U.S. & Canad.* a person of great influence (esp. in **big wheel**). **12. at the wheel. a.** driving or steering a vehicle or vessel. **b.** in charge. ~*vb.* **13.** to turn or cause to turn on or as if on an axis. **14.** (when *intr.*, sometimes foll. by *about* or *around*) to move or cause to move on or as if on wheels; roll. **15.** (*tr.*) to perform with or in a circular movement. **16.** (*tr.*) to provide with a wheel or wheels. **17.** (*intr.;* often foll. by *about*) to change direction. **18. wheel and deal.** *Inf.* to operate free of restraint, esp. to advance one's own interests. ~See also **wheels.** [OE *hweol, hweowol*]

wheel and axle *n.* a simple machine for raising weights in which a rope unwinding from a wheel is wound onto a cylindrical drum or shaft coaxial with or joined to the wheel to provide mechanical advantage.

wheel animalcule *n.* another name for **rotifer.**

wheelbarrow (ˈwiːlˌbærəʊ) *n.* a simple vehicle for carrying small loads, typically being an open container supported by a wheel at the front and two legs behind.

wheelbase (ˈwiːlˌbeɪs) *n.* the distance between the front and back axles of a motor vehicle.

wheelchair (ˈwiːlˌtʃɛə) *n.* special chair on large wheels, for use by invalids or others for whom walking is impossible or inadvisable.

wheel clamp *n.* a device fixed onto one wheel of an illegally parked car in order to immobilize it. The driver has to pay to have it removed.

wheeled (wiːld) *adj.* **a.** having a wheel or wheels. **b.** (*in combination*): *four-wheeled.*

wheeler (ˈwiːlə) *n.* **1.** Also called: **wheel horse.** a horse or other draught animal nearest the wheel. **2.** (*in combination*) something equipped with a specified sort or number of wheels: *a three-wheeler.* **3.** a person or thing that wheels.

wheeler-dealer *n. Inf.* a person who wheels and deals.

wheel horse *n.* **1.** another word for **wheeler** (sense 1). **2.** *U.S. & Canad.* a person who works steadily or hard.

wheelhouse (ˈwiːlˌhaʊs) *n.* another term for **pilot house.**

wheelie (ˈwiːlɪ) *n.* a manoeuvre on a bicycle or motorbike in which the front wheel is raised off the ground.

wheel lock *n.* **1.** a gunlock formerly in use in which the firing mechanism was activated by sparks produced by friction between a small steel wheel and a flint. **2.** a gun having such a lock.

wheel of fortune *n.* (in mythology and literature) a revolving device spun by a deity selecting random changes in the affairs of man.

wheels (wiːlz) *pl. n.* **1.** the main directing force behind an organization, movement, etc.: *the wheels of government.* **2.** an informal word for **car.** **3. wheels within wheels.** a series of intricately connected events, plots, etc.

wheel window *n.* another name for **rose window.**

wheelwright (ˈwiːlˌraɪt) *n.* a person who makes or mends wheels as a trade.

wheeze (wiːz) *vb.* **1.** to breathe or utter (something) with a rasping or whistling sound. **2.** (*intr.*) to make or move with a noise suggestive of wheezy breathing. ~*n.* **3.** a husky, rasping, or whistling sound or breathing. **4.** *Brit. sl.* a trick, idea, or plan. **5.** *Inf.* a hackneyed joke or anecdote. [C15: prob. < ON *hvǣsa* to hiss] —ˈ**wheezer** *n.* —ˈ**wheezy** *adj.* —ˈ**wheezily** *adv.* —ˈ**wheeziness** *n.*

whelk[1] (wɛlk) *n.* a marine gastropod mollusc of coastal waters and intertidal regions, having a strong snail-like shell. [OE *weoloc*]

whelk[2] (wɛlk) *n.* a raised lesion on the skin; wheal. [OE *hwylca,* <?] —ˈ**whelky** *adj.*

whelm (wɛlm) *vb.* (*tr.*) *Arch.* to engulf entirely; overwhelm. [C13 *whelmen* to turn over, <?]

whelp (wɛlp) *n.* **1.** a young offspring of certain animals, esp. of a wolf or dog. **2.** *Disparaging.* a youth. **3.** *Jocular.* a young child. **4.** *Naut.* any of the ridges, parallel to the axis, on the drum of a capstan to keep a rope, etc., from slipping. ~*vb.* **5.** (of an animal or, disparagingly, a woman) to give birth to (young). [OE *hwelp*(a)]

when (wɛn) *adv.* **1. a.** at what time? over what period?: *when is he due?* **b.** (*used in indirect questions*): *ask him when he's due.* **2. say when.**

to state when an action is to be stopped or begun, as when someone is pouring a drink. ~*conj.* **3.** (*subordinating*) at a time at which; just as; after: *I found it easy when I tried.* **4.** although: *he drives when he might walk.* **5.** considering the fact that: *how did you pass the exam when you hadn't worked for it?* ~*pron.* **6.** at which (time); over which (period): *an age when men were men.* ~*n.* **7.** a question as to the time of some occurrence. [OE *hwanne, hwænne*]

▷ **Usage.** Care should be taken so that *when* and *where* refer explicitly to time or place, and are not used loosely to substitute for *in which* after the verb *to be: paralysis is a condition in which* (not *when* or *where*) *parts of the body cannot be moved.*

whenas (wɛn'æz) *conj. Arch.* **1. a.** when; whenever. **b.** inasmuch as; while. **2.** although.

whence (wɛns) *Arch. or formal.* ~*adv.* **1.** from what place, cause, or origin? ~*pron.* **2.** (*subordinating*) from what place, cause, or origin. [C13 *whannes*, adv. genitive of OE *hwanon*]

▷ **Usage.** Careful users of English avoid the expression *from whence*, since *whence* already means from which place: *the tradition whence* (not *from whence*) *such ideas flow.*

whencesoever (ˌwɛnssəʊ'ɛvə) *conj.* (*subordinating*), *adv. Arch.* from whatever place, cause, or origin.

whenever (wɛn'ɛvə) *conj.* **1.** (*subordinating*) at every or any time that; when: *I laugh whenever I see that.* ~*adv. also* **when ever.** **2.** no matter when: *it'll be here, whenever you decide to come for it.* **3.** *Inf.* at an unknown or unspecified time: *I'll take it if it comes today, tomorrow, or whenever.* **4.** an intensive form of *when*, used in questions: *whenever did he escape?*

whensoever (ˌwɛnsəʊ'ɛvə) *conj., adv. Rare.* an intensive form of **whenever.**

where (wɛə) *adv.* **1. a.** in, at, or to what place, point, or position?: *where are you going?* **b.** (*used in indirect questions*): *I don't know where they are.* ~*pron.* **2.** in, at, or to which (place): *the hotel where we spent our honeymoon.* ~*conj.* **3.** (*subordinating*) in the place at which: *where we live it's always raining.* ~*n.* **4.** a question as to the position, direction, or destination of something. [OE *hwǣr, hwār*(*a*)]

▷ **Usage.** See at **when.**

whereabouts ('wɛərəˌbaʊts) *adv.* **1.** at what approximate place; where: *whereabouts are you?* ~*n.* **2.** (*functioning as sing. or pl.*) the place, esp. the approximate place, where a person or thing is.

whereas (wɛər'æz) *conj.* **1.** (*coordinating*) but on the other hand: *I like to go swimming whereas Sheila likes to sail.* ~*sentence connector.* **2.** (in formal documents) it being the case that; since.

whereat (wɛər'æt) *Arch.* ~*adv.* **1.** at or to which place. ~*sentence connector.* **2.** upon which occasion.

whereby (wɛə'baɪ) *pron.* by or because of which: *the means whereby he took his life.*

wherefore ('wɛəˌfɔː) *n.* **1.** (*usually pl.*) an explanation or reason (esp. in **the whys and wherefores**). ~*adv.* **2.** *Arch.* why? ~*sentence connector.* **3.** *Arch. or formal.* for which reason: used in legal preambles.

wherefrom (wɛə'frɒm) *Arch.* ~*adv.* **1.** from what or where? whence? ~*pron.* **2.** from which place; whence.

wherein (wɛər'ɪn) *Arch. or formal.* ~*adv.* **1.** in what place or respect? ~*pron.* **2.** in which place, thing, etc.

whereof (wɛər'ɒv) *Arch. or formal.* ~*adv.* **1.** of what or which person or thing? ~*pron.* **2.** of which (person or thing): *the man whereof I speak is no longer alive.*

whereon (wɛər'ɒn) *Arch.* ~*adv.* **1.** on what thing or place? ~*pron.* **2.** on which thing, place, etc.

wheresoever (ˌwɛəsəʊ'ɛvə) *conj.* (*subordinating*), *adv., pron. Rare.* an intensive form of **wherever.**

whereto (wɛə'tuː) *Arch. or formal.* ~*adv.* **1.** towards what (place, end, etc.)? ~*pron.* **2.** to which. ~Also (archaic): **whereunto.**

whereupon (ˌwɛərə'pɒn) *sentence connector.* at which; at which point; upon which.

wherever (wɛər'ɛvə) *pron.* **1.** at, in, or to every place or point which; where: *wherever she went, he would be there.* ~*conj.* **2.** (*subordinating*) in, to, or at whatever place: *wherever we go the weather is always bad.* ~*adv. also* **where ever.** **3.** no matter where: *I'll find you, wherever you are.* **4.** *Inf.* at, in, or to an unknown or unspecified place: *I'll go anywhere to escape: London, Paris, or wherever.* **5.** an intensive form of *where*, used in questions: *wherever can they be?*

wherewith (wɛə'wɪθ, -'wɪð) *Arch. or formal.* ~*pron.* **1.** (*often foll. by an infinitive*) with or by which: *the pen wherewith I write.* **2.** something with which: *I have not wherewith to buy my bread.* ~*adv.* **3.** with what? ~*sentence connector.* **4.** with or after that; whereupon.

wherewithal *n.* ('wɛəwɪðˌɔːl). **1. the wherewithal.** necessary funds, resources, or equipment: *these people lack the wherewithal for a decent existence.* ~*pron.* (ˌwɛəwɪð'ɔːl). **2.** a less common word for **wherewith.**

wherry ('wɛrɪ) *n., pl.* **-ries.** **1.** any of certain kinds of half-decked commercial boats. **2.** a light rowing boat. [C15: <?] —'**wherryman** *n.*

whet (wɛt) *vb.* **whetting, whetted.** (*tr.*) **1.** to sharpen, as by grinding or friction. **2.** to increase (the appetite, desire, etc.); stimulate. ~*n.* **3.** the act of whetting. **4.** a person or thing that whets. [OE *hwettan*] —'**whetter** *n.*

whether ('wɛðə) *conj.* **1.** (*subordinating*) used to introduce an indirect question or a clause after a verb expressing or implying doubt or choice: *he doesn't know whether she's in Britain or whether she's gone to France.* **2.** (*coordinating*) either: *any man, whether liberal or conservative, would agree with me.* **3. whether or no.** in any case: *he will be here tomorrow, whether or no.* **4. whether...or (whether).** if on the one hand...or even if on the other hand: *you'll eat that, whether you like it or not.* [OE *hwæther, hwether*]

whetstone ('wɛtˌstəʊn) *n.* **1.** a stone used for sharpening edged tools, knives, etc. **2.** something that sharpens.

whew (hwjuː) *interj.* an exclamation or sharply exhaled breath expressing relief, delight, etc.

whey (weɪ) *n.* the watery liquid that separates from the curd when milk is clotted, as in making cheese. [OE *hwǣg*]

wheyface ('weɪˌfeɪs) *n.* **1.** a pale bloodless face. **2.** a person with such a face. —'**wheyˌfaced** *adj.*

which (wɪtʃ) *determiner.* **1. a.** used with a noun in requesting that its referent be further specified, identified, or distinguished: *which house did you want to buy?* **b.** (*as pron.*): *which did you find?* **c.** (*used in indirect questions*): *I wondered which apples were cheaper.* **2. a.** whatever of a class; whichever: *bring which car you want.* **b.** (*as pron.*): *choose which of the cars suits you.* ~*pron.* **3.** used in relative clauses with inanimate antecedents: *the house, which is old, is in poor repair.* **4.** as; and that: used in relative clauses with verb phrases or sentences as their antecedents: *he died of cancer, which is what I predicted.* **5. the which.** an archaic form of **which** often used as a sentence connector. [OE *hwelc, hwilc*]

▷ **Usage.** See at **that.**

whichever (wɪtʃ'ɛvə) *determiner.* **1. a.** any (one, two, etc., out of several): *take whichever car you like.* **b.** (*as pron.*): *choose whichever appeals to you.* **2. a.** no matter which (one or ones): *whichever card you pick you'll still be making a mistake.* **b.** (*as pron.*): *it won't make any difference, whichever comes first.*

whichsoever (ˌwɪtʃsəʊ'ɛvə) *pron.* an archaic or formal word for **whichever.**

whicker ('wɪkə) *vb.* (*intr.*) (of a horse) to whinny or neigh; nicker. [C17: imit.]

whidah ('wɪdə) *n.* a variant spelling of **whydah.**

whiff (wɪf) *n.* **1.** a passing odour. **2.** a brief gentle gust of air. **3.** a single inhalation or exhalation from the mouth or nose. ~*vb.* **4.** to puff or waft. **5.** (*tr.*) to sniff or smell. **6.** (*intr.*) *Brit. sl.* to stink. [C16: imit.]

whiffle ('wɪfəl) *vb.* **1.** (*intr.*) to think or behave in an erratic or unpredictable way. **2.** to blow or be blown fitfully or in gusts. **3.** (*intr.*) to whistle softly. [C16: frequentative of WHIFF]

whiffletree ('wɪfəlˌtriː) *n. Chiefly U.S.* another word for **swingletree.** [C19: var. of WHIPPLETREE]

Whig (wɪg) *n.* **1.** a member of the English political party that opposed the succession to the throne of James, Duke of York (1679–80), on the grounds that he was a Catholic. Standing for a limited monarchy, the Whigs later represented the desires of industrialists and Dissenters for political and social reform, and provided the core of the Liberal Party. **2.** (in the U.S.) a supporter of the War of American Independence. Cf. **Tory. 3.** a member of the American political party that opposed the Democrats from about 1834 to 1855 and represented propertied and professional interests. **4.** *History.* a 17th-century Scottish Presbyterian, esp. one in rebellion against the Crown. ~*adj.* **5.** of, characteristic of, or relating to Whigs. [C17: prob. < *whiggamore,* one of a group of 17th-cent. Scottish rebels who joined in an attack on Edinburgh known as *the whiggamore raid;* prob. < Scot. *whig* to drive (<?) + *more* horse] —'**Whiggery** *or* '**Whiggism** *n.* —'**Whiggish** *adj.*

while (waɪl) *conj. also* **whilst. 1.** (*subordinating*) at the same time that: *please light the fire while I'm cooking.* **2.** (*subordinating*) all the time that: *I stay inside while it's raining.* **3.** (*subordinating*) in spite of the fact that: *while I agree about his brilliance I still think he's rude.* **4.** (*coordinating*) whereas; and in contrast: *houses are expensive, while flats are cheap.* ~*prep., conj.* **5.** *Scot. & N English dialect.* another word for **until:** *you'll have to wait while Monday.* ~*n.* **6.** (*usually used in adverbial phrases*) a period or interval of time: *once in a long while.* **7.** trouble or time (esp. in **worth one's while**): *it's hardly worth your while to begin work today.* [OE *hwīl*]

▷ **Usage.** The main sense of *while* is *during the time that.* However, many careful users of English would now accept as established the use of *while* to mean *although: while he disliked working, he was obliged to do so.* In careful usage, *while* is not used to mean *whereas* or *and: he thought that they were in Paris, whereas* (not *while*) *they had gone on to Rome; his friends went to Paris for their holiday, his brother to Rome, and* (not *while*) *his parents went to Berlin.* Careful writers try to avoid any ambiguity that may result from the possibility of two interpretations of *while* in context: *while* (*although* or *during the time that*) *his brother worked in the park, he refused to do any gardening at home.*

while away *vb.* (*tr., adv.*) to pass (time) idly and usually pleasantly.

whiles (waɪlz) *Arch. or dialect.* ~*adv.* **1.** at times; occasionally. ~*conj.* **2.** while; whilst.

whilom ('waɪləm) *Arch.* ~*adv.* **1.** formerly; once. ~*adj.* **2.** (*prenominal*) one-time; former. [OE *hwīlum,* dative pl. of *hwīl* while]

whilst (waɪlst) *conj. Chiefly Brit.* another word for **while** (senses 1–4). [C13: < WHILES + *-t* as in *amidst*]

whim (wɪm) *n.* **1.** a sudden, passing, and often fanciful idea; impulsive or irrational thought. **2.** a horse-drawn winch formerly used in mining to lift ore or water. [C17: < C16 *whim-wham,* <?]

whimbrel ('wɪmbrəl) *n.* a small European curlew with a striped head. [C16: < dialect *whimp* or < WHIMPER, < its cry]

whimper ('wɪmpə) *vb.* **1.** (*intr.*) to cry, sob, or whine softly or intermittently. **2.** to complain or say (something) in a whining plaintive way. ~*n.* **3.** a soft plaintive whine. [C16: < dialect *whimp,* imit.] —'**whimperer** *n.* —'**whimpering** *n., adj.* —'**whimperingly** *adv.*

whimsical ('wɪmzɪkəl) *adj.* **1.** spontaneously fanciful or playful. **2.** given to whims; capricious. **3.** quaint, unusual, or fantastic. —**whimsicality** (ˌwɪmzɪ'kælɪtɪ) *n.* —'**whimsically** *adv.*

whimsy *or* **whimsey** ('wɪmzɪ) *n., pl.* **-sies** *or* **-seys. 1.** a capricious idea or notion. **2.** light or fanciful humour. **3.** something quaint or unusual. ~*adj.* **-sier, -siest. 4.** quaint, comical, or unusual, often in a tasteless way. [C17: < WHIM]

whin[1] (wɪn) *n.* another name for **gorse.** [C11: < ON]

whin[2] (wɪn) *n.* short for **whinstone.** [C14 *quin,* <?]

whinchat ('wɪnˌtʃæt) *n.* an Old World songbird having a mottled brown-and-white plumage with pale cream underparts. [C17: < WHIN[1] + CHAT]

whine (waɪn) *n.* **1.** a long high-pitched plaintive cry or moan. **2.** a continuous high-pitched sound. **3.** a peevish complaint, esp. one repeated. ~*vb.* **4.** to make a whine or utter in a whine. [OE *hwīnan*] —'**whiner** *n.* —'**whining** *or* '**whiny** *adj.* —'**whiningly** *adv.*

whinge (wɪndʒ) *vb.* (*intr.*) **1.** to cry in a fretful way. **2.** to complain. ~*n.* **3.** a complaint. [< Northern var. of OE *hwinsian* to whine] —'**whingeing** *n., adj.*

whinny ('wɪnɪ) *vb.* **-nying, -nied.** (*intr.*) **1.** (of a horse) to neigh softly or gently. **2.** to make a sound resembling a neigh, such as a laugh. ~*n., pl.* **-nies. 3.** a gentle or low-pitched neigh. [C16: imit.]

whinstone ('wɪnˌstəʊn) *n.* any dark hard fine-grained rock, such as basalt. [C16: < WHIN[2] + STONE]

whip (wɪp) *vb.* **whipping, whipped. 1.** to strike (a person or thing) with several strokes of a strap, rod, etc. **2.** (*tr.*) to punish by striking in this manner. **3.** (*tr.;* foll. by *out, away,* etc.) to pull, remove, etc., with sudden rapid motion: *to whip out a gun.* **4.** (*intr.;* foll. by *down, into, out of,* etc.) *Inf.* to come, go, etc., in a rapid sudden manner: *they whipped into the bar for a drink.* **5.** to strike or be struck as if by whipping: *the tempest whipped the surface of the sea.* **6.** (*tr.*) to bring, train, etc., forcefully into a desired condition. **7.** (*tr.*) *Inf.* to overcome or outdo. **8.** (*tr.;* often foll. by *on, out,* or *off*) to drive, urge, compel, etc., by or as if by whipping. **9.** (*tr.*) to criticize virulently. **10.** (*tr.*) to wrap or wind (a cord, thread, etc.) around (a rope, cable, etc.) to prevent chafing or fraying. **11.** (*tr.*) (in fly-fishing) to cast the fly repeatedly onto (the water) in a whipping motion. **12.** (*tr.*) (in sewing) to join, finish, or gather with whipstitch. **13.** to beat (eggs, cream, etc.) with a whisk or similar utensil to incorporate air. **14.** (*tr.*) to spin (a top). **15.** (*tr.*) *Inf.* to steal: *he whipped her purse.* ~*n.* **16.** a device consisting of a lash or flexible rod attached at one end to a stiff handle and used for driving animals, inflicting corporal punishment, etc. **17.** a whipping stroke or motion. **18.** a person adept at handling a whip, as a coachman, etc. **19.** (in a legislative body) **a.** a member of a party chosen to organize and discipline the members of his faction. **b.** a call issued to members of a party, insisting with varying degrees of urgency upon their presence or loyal voting behaviour. **c.** (in the Brit. Parliament) a schedule of business sent to members of a party each week. Each item on it is underlined to indicate its importance: three lines means that the item is very important and every member must attend and vote according to the party line. **20.** an apparatus for hoisting, consisting of a rope, pulley, and snatch block. **21.** any of a variety of desserts made from egg whites or cream beaten stiff. **22.** See **whipper-in. 23.** flexibility, as in the shaft of a golf club, etc. ~See also **whip-round, whip up, whips.** [C13: ? < MDu. *wippen* to swing] —'**whipˌlike** *adj.* —'**whipper** *n.*

whip bird *n. Austral.* any of several birds having a whistle ending in a note sounding like the crack of a whip.

whipcord ('wɪpˌkɔːd) *n.* **1.** a strong worsted or cotton fabric with a diagonally ribbed surface. **2.** a closely twisted hard cord used for the lashes of whips, etc.

whip graft *n. Horticulture.* a graft made by

inserting a tongue cut on the sloping base of the scion into a slit on the sloping top of the stock.

whip hand *n.* (usually preceded by *the*) **1.** (in driving horses) the hand holding the whip. **2.** advantage or dominating position.

whiplash (ˈwɪpˌlæʃ) *n.* a quick lash or stroke of a whip or like that of a whip.

whiplash injury *n. Med. inf.* any injury to the neck resulting from a sudden thrusting forwards and snapping back of the unsupported head. Technical name: **hyperextension-hyperflexion injury.**

whipper-in *n., pl.* **whippers-in.** a person employed to assist the huntsman managing the hounds.

whippersnapper (ˈwɪpəˌsnæpə) *n.* an insignificant but pretentious or cheeky person, often a young one. Also called: **whipster.** [C17: prob. < *whipsnapper* a person who snaps whips, infl. by earlier *snippersnapper*, <?]

whippet (ˈwɪpɪt) *n.* a small slender breed of dog similar to a greyhound. [C16: <?; ? based on *whip it!* move quickly!]

whipping (ˈwɪpɪŋ) *n.* **1.** a thrashing or beating with a whip or similar implement. **2.** cord or twine used for binding or lashing. **3.** the binding formed by wrapping a rope, etc., with cord or twine.

whipping boy *n.* a person of little importance who is blamed for the errors, incompetence, etc., of others, esp. his superiors; scapegoat. [C17: orig. referring to a boy who was educated with a prince and who received punishment for any faults committed by the prince]

whippletree (ˈwɪpᵊlˌtriː) *n.* another name for **swingletree.** [C18: apparently < WHIP]

whippoorwill (ˈwɪpʊˌwɪl) *n.* a nightjar of North and Central America, having a dark plumage with white patches on the tail. [C18: imit. of its cry]

whip-round *Inf., chiefly Brit.* ~*n.* **1.** an impromptu collection of money. ~*vb.* **whip round. 2.** (*intr., adv.*) to make such a collection.

whips (wɪps) *pl. n.* (often foll. by *of*) *Austral. inf.* a large quantity: *I've got whips of cash at the moment.*

whipsaw (ˈwɪpˌsɔː) *n.* **1.** any saw with a flexible blade, such as a bandsaw. ~*vb.* **-sawing, -sawed, -sawed** *or* **-sawn.** (*tr.*) **2.** to saw with a whipsaw. **3.** *U.S.* to defeat in two ways at once.

whip scorpion *n.* any of an order of nonvenomous arachnids, typically resembling a scorpion but lacking a sting.

whip snake *n.* any of several long slender fast-moving nonvenomous snakes.

whipstitch (ˈwɪpˌstɪtʃ) *n.* a sewing stitch passing over an edge.

whipstock (ˈwɪpˌstɒk) *n.* a whip handle.

whip up *vb.* (*tr., adv.*) **1.** to excite; arouse: *to whip up a mob; to whip up discontent.* **2.** *Inf.* to prepare quickly: *to whip up a meal.*

whir *or* **whirr** (wɜː) *n.* **1.** a prolonged soft swish or buzz, as of a motor working or wings flapping. **2.** a bustle or rush. ~*vb.* **whirring, whirred. 3.** to make or cause to make a whir. [C14: prob. < ON; see WHIRL]

whirl (wɜːl) *vb.* **1.** to spin, turn, or revolve or cause to spin, turn, or revolve. **2.** (*intr.*) to turn around or away rapidly. **3.** (*intr.*) to have a spinning sensation, as from dizziness, etc. **4.** to move or drive or be moved or driven at high speed. ~*n.* **5.** the act or an instance of whirling; swift rotation or a rapid whirling movement. **6.** a condition of confusion or giddiness: *her accident left me in a whirl.* **7.** a swift round, as of events, meetings, etc. **8.** a tumult; stir. **9.** *Inf.* a brief trip, dance, etc. **10. give (something) a whirl.** *Inf.* to attempt or give a trial to (something). [C13: < ON *hvirfla* to turn about] —ˈ**whirler** *n.* —ˈ**whirling** *adj.* —ˈ**whirlingly** *adv.*

whirligig (ˈwɜːlɪˌgɪg) *n.* **1.** any spinning toy, such as a top. **2.** another name for **merry-go-round. 3.** anything that whirls about, spins, or moves in a circular or giddy way: *the whirligig of social life.* [C15 *whirlegigge,* < WHIRL + GIG[1]]

whirlpool (ˈwɜːlˌpuːl) *n.* **1.** a powerful circular current or vortex of water. **2.** something resembling a whirlpool in motion or the power to attract into its vortex.

whirlwind (ˈwɜːlˌwɪnd) *n.* **1.** a column of air whirling around and towards a more or less vertical axis of low pressure, which moves along the land or ocean surface. **2. a.** a motion or course resembling this, esp. in rapidity. **b.** (*as modifier*): *a whirlwind romance.* **3.** an impetuously active person.

whirlybird (ˈwɜːlɪˌbɜːd) *n.* an informal word for **helicopter.**

whish (wɪʃ) *n., vb.* a less common word for **swish.**

whisht (hwɪʃt) *or* **whist** (hwɪst) *Arch. or dialect, esp. Scot.* ~*interj.* **1.** hush! be quiet! ~*adj.* **2.** silent or still. [C14: cf. HIST]

whisk (wɪsk) *vb.* **1.** (*tr.;* often foll. by *away* or *off*) to brush, sweep, or wipe off lightly. **2.** (*tr.*) to move, carry, etc., with a light or rapid sweeping motion: *the taxi whisked us to the airport.* **3.** (*intr.*) to move, go, etc., quickly and nimbly: *to whisk downstairs for a drink.* **4.** (*tr.*) to whip (eggs, etc.) to a froth. ~*n.* **5.** the act of whisking. **6.** a light rapid sweeping movement. **7.** a utensil for whipping eggs, etc. **8.** a small brush or broom. **9.** a small bunch or bundle, as of grass, straw, etc. [C14: < ON *visk* wisp]

whisker (ˈwɪskə) *n.* **1.** any of the stiff sensory hairs growing on the face of a cat, rat, or other mammal. Technical name: **vibrissa. 2.** any of the hairs growing on a man's face, esp. on the cheeks or chin. **3.** (*pl.*) a beard or that part of it growing on the sides of the face. **4.** (*pl.*) *Inf.* a moustache. **5.** *Chem.* a very fine filamentary crystal having greater strength than the bulk material. **6.** a person or thing that whisks. **7.** a narrow margin or small distance: *he escaped death by a whisker.* —ˈ**whiskered** *or* ˈ**whiskery** *adj.*

whiskey (ˈwɪskɪ) *n.* the usual Irish and U.S. spelling of **whisky.**

whiskey sour *n. U.S.* a mixed drink of whisky and lime or lemon juice, sometimes sweetened.

whisky (ˈwɪskɪ) *n., pl.* **-kies.** a spirit made by distilling fermented cereals, which is matured and often blended. [C18: shortened < *whiskybae,* < Scot. Gaelic *uisge beatha,* lit.: water of life; see USQUEBAUGH]

whisky-jack *n. Canad.* another name for **Canada jay.**

whisky mac *n. Brit.* a drink consisting of whisky and ginger wine.

whisper (ˈwɪspə) *vb.* **1.** to speak or utter (something) in a soft hushed tone, esp. without vibration of the vocal cords. **2.** (*intr.*) to speak secretly or furtively, as in promoting intrigue, gossip, etc. **3.** (*intr.*) (of leaves, trees, etc.) to make a low soft rustling sound. **4.** (*tr.*) to utter or suggest secretly or privately: *to whisper treason.* ~*n.* **5.** a low soft voice: *to speak in a whisper.* **6.** something uttered in such a voice. **7.** a low soft rustling sound. **8.** a trace or suspicion. **9.** *Inf.* a rumour. [OE *hwisprian*] —ˈ**whisperer** *n.*

whispering campaign *n.* the organized diffusion of defamatory rumours designed to discredit a person, group, etc.

whispering gallery *n.* a gallery or dome with acoustic characteristics such that a sound made at one point is audible at distant points.

whist (wɪst) *n.* a card game for four in which the two sides try to win the balance of the 13 tricks: forerunner of bridge. [C17: ? changed < WHISK, referring to the sweeping up or whisking up of the tricks]

whist drive *n.* a social gathering where whist is played: the winners of each hand move to different tables to play the losers of the previous hand.

whistle (ˈwɪsᵊl) *vb.* **1.** to produce (shrill or flutelike sounds), as by passing breath through a narrow constriction most easily formed by the pursed lips. **2.** (*tr.*) to signal or command by whistling or blowing a whistle: *the referee whistled the end of the game.* **3.** (of a kettle, train, etc.) to produce (a shrill sound) caused by the emission of steam through a small aperture. **4.** (*intr.*) to move with a whistling sound caused by rapid passage through the air. **5.** (of animals, esp. birds) to emit (a shrill sound) resembling human whistling. **6. whistle in the dark.** to try to keep up one's confidence in spite of fear. ~*n.* **7.** a device for making a shrill high-pitched sound by means of air or steam under pressure. **8.** a shrill sound effected by whistling or blowing a whistle. **9.** a whistling sound, as of a bird, bullet, the wind, etc. **10.** a signal, etc., transmitted by or as if by a whistle. **11.** the act of whistling. **12.** an instrument, usually made of metal, that is blown down its end to produce a tune, signal, etc. **13. blow the whistle.** (usually foll. by *on*) *Inf.* **a.** to inform (on). **b.** to bring a stop (to). **14. clean as a whistle.** perfectly clean or clear. **15. wet one's whistle.** *Inf.* to take an alcoholic drink. ~See also **whistle for, whistle up.** [OE *hwistlian*]

whistle-blower *n. Inf.* a person who informs on someone or puts a stop to something.

whistle for *vb.* (*intr., prep.*) *Inf.* to seek or expect in vain.

whistler (ˈwɪslə) *n.* **1.** a person or thing that whistles. **2.** *Radio.* an atmospheric disturbance picked up by radio receivers, caused by the electromagnetic radiation produced by lightning. **3.** any of various birds having a whistling call, such as certain Australian flycatchers. **4.** any of various North American marmots.

whistle stop *n.* **1.** *U.S. & Canad.* **a.** a minor railway station where trains stop only on signal. **b.** a small town having such a station. **2. a.** a brief appearance in a town, esp. by a political candidate. **b.** (*as modifier*): *a whistle-stop tour.*

whistle up *vb.* (*tr., adv.*) to call or summon (a person or animal) by whistling.

whit (wɪt) *n.* (*usually used with a negative*) the smallest particle; iota; jot: *he has changed not a whit.* [C15: prob. var. of WIGHT]

Whit (wɪt) *n.* **1.** See **Whitsuntide.** ~*adj.* **2.** of or relating to Whitsuntide.

white (waɪt) *adj.* **1.** having no hue, owing to the reflection of all or almost all incident light. **2.** (of light, such as sunlight) consisting of all the colours of the spectrum or produced by certain mixtures of primary colours, as red, green, and blue. **3.** comparatively white or whitish-grey or having parts of this colour: *white clover.* **4.** (of an animal) having pale-coloured or white skin, fur, or feathers. **5.** bloodless or pale, as from pain, emotion, etc. **6.** (of hair, etc.) grey, usually from age. **7.** benevolent or without malicious intent: *white magic.* **8.** colourless or transparent: *white glass.* **9.** capped with or accompanied by snow: *a white Christmas.* **10.** blank, as an unprinted area of a page. **11.** (of coffee or tea) with milk or cream. **12.** denoting flour, or bread made from flour, that has had part of the grain removed. **13.** *Physics.* having or characterized by a continuous distribution of energy, wavelength, or frequency: *white noise.* **14.** *Inf.* honourable or generous. **15.** *Poetic or arch.* having a fair complexion; blond. **16. bleed white.** to deprive slowly of resources. ~*n.* **17.** a white colour. **18.** the condition of being white; whiteness. **19.** the white or lightly coloured part of something. **20.** (usually preceded by *the*) the viscous fluid that surrounds the yolk of a bird's egg, esp. a hen's egg; albumen. **21.** *Anat.* the white part (sclera) of the eyeball. **22.** any of various butterflies having white wings with scanty black markings. **23.** *Chess, draughts.* **a.** a white or light-coloured piece or square. **b.** the player playing with such pieces. **24.** anything that has or is characterized by a white colour, such as a white paint or white clothing. **25.** short for **white wine.** **26.** *Archery.* the outer ring of the target, having the lowest score. ~*vb.* **27.** *Obs.* to make or become white. ~See also **white out, whites.** [OE *hwīt*] —ˈ**whitely** *adv.* —ˈ**whiteness** *n.* —ˈ**whitish** *adj.*

White (waɪt) *n.* **1.** a member of the Caucasoid race. **2.** a person of European ancestry. ~*adj.* **3.** denoting or relating to a White or Whites.

white admiral *n.* a butterfly of Eurasia having brown wings with white markings.

white ant *n.* another name for **termite.**

whitebait (ˈwaɪtˌbeɪt) *n.* **1.** the young of herrings, sprats, etc., cooked and eaten whole as a delicacy. **2.** any of various small silvery fishes. [C18: < its formerly having been used as bait]

whitebeam (ˈwaɪtˌbiːm) *n.* a N temperate tree having leaves that are densely hairy on the undersurface and hard timber.

white blood cell *n.* a nontechnical name for **leucocyte.**

whitecap (ˈwaɪtˌkæp) *n.* a wave with a white broken crest.

white cedar *n.* either of two coniferous trees of North America, having scalelike leaves.

white clover *n.* a Eurasian clover plant with rounded white flower heads: cultivated as a forage plant.

white coal *n.* water, esp. when flowing and providing a potential source of usable power.

white-collar *adj.* of or designating nonmanual and usually salaried workers employed in professional and clerical occupations.

white currant *n.* a cultivated N temperate shrub having small rounded white edible berries.

whitedamp (ˈwaɪtˌdæmp) *n.* a mixture of poisonous gases, mainly carbon monoxide, occurring in coal mines.

whited sepulchre *n.* a hypocrite. [allusion to Matthew 23:27]

white dwarf *n.* one of a large class of small faint stars of enormous density, thought to mark the final stage in a star's evolution.

white elephant *n.* **1.** a rare albino variety of the Indian elephant, regarded as sacred in parts of S Asia. **2.** a possession that is unwanted by its owner. **3.** a rare or valuable possession the upkeep of which is very expensive.

White Ensign *n.* the ensign of the Royal Navy and the Royal Yacht Squadron, having a red cross on a white background with the Union Jack at the upper corner of the vertical edge alongside the hoist.

white-eye *n.* a songbird of Africa, Australia, New Zealand, and Asia, having a greenish plumage with a white ring around each eye.

white feather *n.* **1.** a symbol or mark of cowardice. **2. show the white feather.** to act in a cowardly manner. [< the belief that a white feather in a gamecock's tail was a sign of a poor fighter]

whitefish (ˈwaɪtˌfɪʃ) *n., pl.* **-fish** *or* **-fishes.** a food fish typically of deep cold lakes of the N hemisphere, having large silvery scales and a small head.

white fish *n.* (in the Brit. fishing industry) any edible marine fish or invertebrate excluding herrings but including trout, salmon, and all shellfish.

white flag *n.* a white flag or a piece of white cloth hoisted to signify surrender or request a truce.

white flour *n.* flour that consists substantially of the starchy endosperm of wheat, most of the bran and the germ having been removed by the milling process.

whitefly (ˈwaɪtˌflaɪ) *n., pl.* **-flies.** any of a family of insects typically having a body covered with powdery wax. Many are pests of greenhouse crops.

white friar *n.* a Carmelite friar, so called because of the white cloak that forms part of the habit of this order.

white gold *n.* any of various white lustrous hard-wearing alloys containing gold together with platinum and palladium and sometimes smaller amounts of silver, nickel, or copper.

white goods *pl. n.* **1.** household linen such as sheets, towels, tablecloths, etc. **2.** large household appliances, such as refrigerators or cookers.

Whitehall (ˌwaɪtˈhɔːl) *n.* **1.** a street in London stretching from Trafalgar Square to the Houses of Parliament: site of the main government offices. **2.** the British Government.

white heat *n.* **1.** intense heat characterized by emission of white light. **2.** *Inf.* a state of intense excitement or activity.
white hope *n. Inf.* a person who is expected to bring honour or glory to his group, team, etc.
white horse *n.* **1.** the outline of a horse carved into the side of a chalk hill, usually dating to the Neolithic, Bronze, or Iron Ages. **2.** (*usually pl.*) a wave with a white broken crest.
white-hot *adj.* **1.** at such a high temperature that white light is emitted. **2.** *Inf.* in a state of intense emotion.
White House *n.* **the. 1.** the official Washington residence of the president of the U.S. **2.** the U.S. presidency.
white lead (lɛd) *n.* **1.** a white solid usually regarded as a mixture of lead carbonate and lead hydroxide; basic lead carbonate: used in paint and in making putty and ointments for the treatment of burns. **2.** either of two similar white pigments based on lead sulphate or lead silicate.
white leg *n.* another name for **milk leg.**
white lie *n.* a minor or unimportant lie, esp. one uttered in the interests of tact or politeness.
white light *n.* light that contains all the wavelengths of visible light at approximately equal intensities, as in sunlight.
white-livered *adj.* **1.** lacking in spirit or courage. **2.** pallid and unhealthy in appearance.
White man's burden *n.* the supposed duty of the White race to bring education and Western culture to the non-White inhabitants of their colonies.
white matter *n.* the whitish tissue of the brain and spinal cord, consisting mainly of nerve fibres covered with a protective white fatlike substance.
white meat *n.* any meat that is light in colour, such as veal or the breast of turkey.
white metal *n.* any of various alloys, such as Babbitt metal, used for bearings.
white meter *n. Brit.* an electricity meter used to record the consumption of off-peak electricity.
whiten (ˈwaɪtᵊn) *vb.* to make or become white or whiter; bleach. —**ˈwhitener** *n.* —**ˈwhitening** *n.*
white noise *n.* sound or electrical noise that has a relatively wide continuous range of frequencies of uniform intensity.
white oak *n.* a large oak tree of E North America, having pale bark, leaves with rounded lobes, and heavy light-coloured wood.
white out *vb.* (*adv.*) **1.** (*intr.*) to lose or lack daylight visibility owing to snow or fog. **2.** (*tr.*) to create or leave white spaces in (printed or other matter). ~*n.* **whiteout. 3.** a polar atmospheric condition consisting of lack of visibility and sense of distance and direction due to a uniform whiteness of a heavy cloud cover and snow-covered ground, which reflects almost all the light it receives.
white paper *n.* (*often caps.*) an official government report in any of a number of countries, which sets out the government's policy on a matter that is or will come before Parliament.
white pepper *n.* a condiment, less pungent than black pepper, made from the husked dried beans of the pepper plant.
white pine *n.* a North American coniferous tree having blue-green needle-like leaves, hanging brown cones, and rough bark.
white poplar *n.* **1.** Also called: **abele.** a Eurasian tree having leaves covered with dense silvery-white hairs. **2.** another name for **tulipwood** (sense 1).
white rose *n. English history.* an emblem of the House of York.
White Russian *adj., n.* another term for **Byelorussian.**
whites (waɪts) *pl. n.* **1.** household linen or cotton goods, such as sheets. **2.** white or off-white clothing, such as that worn for playing cricket.
white sale *n.* a sale of household linens at reduced prices.
white sauce *n.* a thick sauce made from flour, butter, seasonings, and milk or stock.
white settler *n.* a well-off incomer to a district who takes advantage of what it has to offer without regard to the local inhabitants. [C20: < earlier colonial sense]
white slave *n.* a girl or woman forced or sold into prostitution. —**white slavery** *n.* —**ˌwhite-ˈslaver** *n.*
white spirit *n.* a colourless liquid obtained from petroleum and used as a substitute for turpentine.
white spruce *n.* a N North American spruce tree with grey bark.
white squall *n.* a violent highly localized weather disturbance at sea, in which the surface of the water is whipped to a white spray by the winds.
whitethorn (ˈwaɪtˌθɔːn) *n.* another name for **hawthorn.**
whitethroat (ˈwaɪtˌθrəʊt) *n.* either of two Old World warblers having a greyish-brown plumage with a white throat and underparts.
white tie *n.* **1.** a white bow tie worn as part of a man's formal evening dress. **2. a.** formal evening dress for men. **b.** (*as modifier*): *a white-tie occasion.*
whitewall (ˈwaɪtˌwɔːl) *n.* a pneumatic tyre having white sidewalls.
whitewash (ˈwaɪtˌwɒʃ) *n.* **1.** a substance used for whitening walls and other surfaces, consisting of a suspension of lime or whiting in water. **2.** *Inf.* deceptive or specious words or actions intended to conceal defects, gloss over failings, etc. **3.** *Inf.* a game in which the loser fails to score. ~*vb.* (*tr.*) **4.** to cover with whitewash. **5.** *Inf.* to conceal, gloss over, or suppress. **6.** *Inf.* to defeat (someone) in a game by preventing him from scoring. —**ˈwhiteˌwasher** *n.*
white water *n.* **1.** a stretch of water with a broken foamy surface, as in rapids. **2.** light-coloured sea water, esp. over shoals or shallows.
white whale *n.* a small white toothed whale of northern waters. Also called: **beluga.**
white wine *n.* wine made from pale grapes or from black grapes separated from their skins.
whitewood (ˈwaɪtˌwʊd) *n.* **1.** any of various trees with light-coloured wood, such as the tulip tree, basswood, and cottonwood. **2.** the wood of any of these trees.
whitey *or* **whity** (ˈwaɪtɪ) *n., pl.* **whities.** *Chiefly U.S.* (used contemptuously by Black people) a White man or White men collectively.
whither (ˈwɪðə) *Arch. or poetic.* ~*adv.* **1.** to what place? **2.** to what end or purpose? ~*conj.* **3.** to whatever place, purpose, etc. [OE *hwider, hwæder;* Mod. E form infl. by HITHER]
whithersoever (ˌwɪðəsəʊˈɛvə) *adv., conj. Arch. or poetic.* to whichever place.
whiting[1] (ˈwaɪtɪŋ) *n.* **1.** an important gadoid food fish of European seas, having a dark back with silvery sides and underparts. **2.** any of various similar fishes. [C15: ? < OE *hwītling*]
whiting[2] (ˈwaɪtɪŋ) *n.* white chalk that has been ground and washed, used in making whitewash, metal polish, etc. Also called: **whitening.**
whitlow (ˈwɪtləʊ) *n.* any pussy inflammation of the end of a finger or toe. [C14: changed < *whitflaw,* < WHITE + FLAW[1]]
Whitsun (ˈwɪtsᵊn) *n.* **1.** short for **Whitsuntide.** ~*adj.* **2.** of or relating to Whit Sunday or Whitsuntide.
Whit Sunday *n.* the seventh Sunday after Easter, observed as a feast in commemoration of the descent of the Holy Spirit on the apostles. Also called: **Pentecost.** [OE *hwīta sunnandæg* white Sunday, prob. after the ancient custom of wearing white robes at or after baptism]
Whitsuntide (ˈwɪtsᵊnˌtaɪd) *n.* the week that begins with Whit Sunday, esp. the first three days.
whittle (ˈwɪtᵊl) *vb.* **1.** to cut or shave strips or pieces from (wood, a stick, etc.), esp. with a knife. **2.** (*tr.*) to make or shape by paring or shaving. **3.** (*tr.;* often foll. by *away, down,* etc.) to reduce, destroy, or wear away gradually. [C16: var. of C15 *thwittle* large knife, ult. < OE *thwītan* to cut]
whity (ˈwaɪtɪ) *n., pl.* **whities. 1.** *Inf.* a variant

spelling of **whitey.** ~*adj.* **2. a.** whitish in colour. **b.** (*in combination*): *whity-brown.*

whiz *or* **whizz** (wɪz) *vb.* **whizzing, whizzed. 1.** to make or cause to make a loud humming or buzzing sound. **2.** to move or cause to move with such a sound. **3.** (*intr.*) *Inf.* to move or go rapidly. ~*n., pl.* **whizzes. 4.** a loud humming or buzzing sound. **5.** *Inf.* a person who is extremely skilful at some activity. [C16: imit.]

whiz-bang *or* **whizz-bang** *n* **1.** a World War I shell that travelled at such high velocity that the sound of its flight was heard only an instant before the sound of its explosion. **2.** a type of firework that jumps around emitting a whizzing sound and occasional bangs.

whiz kid, whizz kid, *or* **wiz kid** *n. Inf.* a person who is pushing, enthusiastic, and outstandingly successful for his or her age. [C20: < WHIZ, ? infl. by WIZARD]

who (huː) *pron.* **1.** which person? what person? used in direct and indirect questions: *he can't remember who did it; who met you?* **2.** used to introduce relative clauses with antecedents referring to human beings: *the people who lived here have left.* **3.** the one or ones who; whoever: *bring who you want.* **4. who's who. a.** the identity of individual, esp. important, people: *to know who's who.* **b.** a book or list containing the names and short biographies of prominent persons. [OE *hwā*]

▷ **Usage.** See at **whom.**

WHO *abbrev. for* World Health Organization.

whoa (wəʊ) *interj.* a command used esp. to horses to stop or slow down. [C19: var. of HO]

who-does-what *adj.* (of a dispute, strike, etc.) relating to the separation of kinds of work performed by different trade unions.

whodunit *or* **whodunnit** (huː'dʌnɪt) *n. Inf.* a novel, play, etc., concerned with a crime, usually murder.

whoever (huː'ɛvə) *pron.* **1.** any person who: *whoever wants it can have it.* **2.** no matter who: *I'll come round tomorrow, whoever may be here.* **3.** an intensive form of *who,* used in questions: *whoever could have thought that?* **4.** *Inf.* an unspecified person: *give those to Cathy or whoever.*

whole (həʊl) *adj.* **1.** containing all the component parts necessary to form a total; complete: *a whole apple.* **2.** constituting the full quantity, extent, etc. **3.** uninjured or undamaged. **4.** healthy. **5.** having no fractional or decimal part; integral: *a whole number.* **6.** designating a relationship by descent from the same parents; full: *whole brothers.* **7. out of whole cloth.** *U.S. & Canad. inf.* entirely without a factual basis. ~*adv.* **8.** in an undivided or unbroken piece: *to swallow a plum whole.* ~*n.* **9.** all the parts, elements, etc., of a thing. **10.** an assemblage of parts viewed together as a unit. **11.** a thing complete in itself. **12. as a whole.** considered altogether; completely. **13. on the whole. a.** taking all things into consideration. **b.** in general. [OE *hāl, hǣl*] —'**wholeness** *n.*

whole blood *n.* blood for transfusion from which none of the elements has been removed.

wholefood ('həʊlˌfuːd) *n.* (*sometimes pl.*) **a.** food that has been refined or processed as little as possible and is eaten in its natural state, such as brown rice, wholemeal flour, etc. **b.** (*as modifier*): *a wholefood restaurant.*

wholehearted (ˌhəʊl'hɑːtɪd) *adj.* done, acted, given, etc., with total sincerity, enthusiasm, or commitment. —ˌ**whole'heartedly** *adv.*

whole hog *n. Sl.* the whole or total extent (esp. in **go the whole hog**).

wholemeal ('həʊlˌmiːl) *adj. Brit.* (of flour, bread, etc.) made from the entire wheat kernel. Also called (esp. U.S. and Canad.): **whole-wheat.**

whole milk *n.* milk from which no constituent has been removed.

whole note *n.* the usual U.S. and Canad. name for **semibreve.**

whole number *n.* **1.** an integer. **2.** a natural number.

wholesale ('həʊlˌseɪl) *n.* **1.** the business of selling goods to retailers in larger quantities than they are sold to final consumers but in smaller quantities than they are purchased from manufacturers. Cf. **retail** (sense 1). ~*adj.* **2.** of or engaged in such business. **3.** made, done, etc., on a large scale or without discrimination. ~*adv.* **4.** on a large scale or without discrimination. ~*vb.* **5.** to sell (goods) at wholesale. —'**wholeˌsaler** *n.*

wholesale price index *n.* an indicator of price changes in the wholesale market.

wholesome ('həʊlsəm) *adj.* **1.** conducive to health or physical wellbeing. **2.** conducive to moral wellbeing. **3.** characteristic or suggestive of health or wellbeing, esp. in appearance. [C12: < WHOLE (healthy) + -SOME[1]] —'**wholesomely** *adv.* —'**wholesomeness** *n.*

whole tone *or U.S. & Canad.* **whole step** *n.* an interval of two semitones. Often shortened to **tone.**

whole-tone scale *n.* either of two scales produced by commencing on one of any two notes a chromatic semitone apart and proceeding upwards or downwards in whole tones for an octave.

whole-wheat *adj.* another term (esp. U.S. and Canad.) for **wholemeal.**

who'll (huːl) *contraction of* who will *or* who shall.

wholly ('həʊllɪ) *adv.* **1.** completely, totally, or entirely. **2.** without exception; exclusively.

whom (huːm) *pron.* the objective form of *who,* used when *who* is not the subject of its own clause: *whom did you say you had seen? he can't remember whom he saw.* [OE *hwām,* dative of *hwā* who]

▷ **Usage.** In formal English, careful writers always use *whom* when the objective form of *who* is required. In informal contexts, however, many careful speakers consider *whom* to be unnatural, esp. at the beginning of a sentence: *who were you looking for?* Careful speakers usually prefer *whom* where it closely follows a preposition: *to whom did you give it?* as contrasted with *who did you give it to?*

whomever (huːm'ɛvə) *pron.* the objective form of *whoever: I'll hire whomever I can find.*

whoop (wuːp) *vb.* **1.** to utter (speech) with loud cries, as of excitement. **2.** (huːp). *Med.* to cough convulsively with a crowing sound. **3.** (of certain birds) to utter (a hooting cry). **4.** (*tr.*) to urge on or call with or as if with whoops. **5.** (wʊp, wuːp). **whoop it up.** *Inf.* **a.** to indulge in a noisy celebration. **b.** *Chiefly U.S.* to arouse enthusiasm. ~*n.* **6.** a loud cry, esp. one expressing excitement. **7.** (huːp). *Med.* the convulsive crowing sound made during whooping cough. [C14: imit.]

whoopee *Inf.* ~*interj.* (wʊ'piː). **1.** an exclamation of joy, excitement, etc. ~*n.* ('wʊpiː). **2. make whoopee. a.** to engage in noisy merrymaking. **b.** to make love.

whoopee cushion *n.* a joke cushion that emits a sound like the breaking of wind when someone sits on it.

whooper *or* **whooper swan** ('wuːpə) *n.* a large Old World swan having a black bill with a yellow base and a noisy whooping cry.

whooping cough ('huːpɪŋ) *n.* an acute infectious disease characterized by coughing spasms that end with a shrill crowing sound on inspiration. Technical name: **pertussis.**

whoops (wʊps) *interj.* an exclamation of surprise or of apology.

whoosh *or* **woosh** (wʊʃ) *n.* **1.** a hissing or rushing sound. ~*vb.* **2.** (*intr.*) to make or move with such a sound.

whop (wɒp) *Inf.* ~*vb.* **whopping, whopped. 1.** (*tr.*) to strike, beat, or thrash. **2.** (*tr.*) to defeat utterly. **3.** (*intr.*) to drop or fall. ~*n.* **4.** a heavy blow or the sound made by such a blow. [C14: var. of *wap,* ? imit.]

whopper ('wɒpə) *n. Inf.* **1.** anything uncommonly large of its kind. **2.** a big lie. [C18: < WHOP]

whopping ('wɒpɪŋ) *adj. Inf.* uncommonly large.

whore (hɔː) *n.* **1.** a prostitute or promiscuous woman: often a term of abuse. ~*vb.* (*intr.*) **2.** to be or act as a prostitute. **3.** (of a man) to have promiscuous sexual relations, esp. with prostitutes. **4.** (often foll. by *after*) to seek that which is immoral, idolatrous, etc. [OE *hōre*] —**'whoredom** *n.* —**'whorish** *adj.*

whorehouse ('hɔːˌhaʊs) *n.* another word for **brothel.**

whoremonger ('hɔːˌmʌŋgə) *n.* a person who consorts with whores; lecher. Also called: **whoremaster.** —**'whoreˌmongery** *n.*

whoreson ('hɔːsən) *Arch.* ~*n.* **1.** a bastard. **2.** a scoundrel; wretch. ~*adj.* **3.** vile or hateful.

whorl (wɜːl) *n.* **1.** *Bot.* a radial arrangement of petals, stamens, leaves, etc., around a stem. **2.** *Zool.* a single turn in a spiral shell. **3.** anything shaped like a coil. [C15: prob. var. of *wherville* whirl, infl. by Du. *worvel*] —**whorled** *adj.*

whortleberry ('wɜːtᵊlˌbɛrɪ) *n., pl.* **-ries. 1.** Also called: **bilberry, blaeberry, huckleberry.** a small Eurasian ericaceous shrub with greenish-pink flowers and edible sweet blackish berries. **2.** the fruit of this shrub. **3. bog whortleberry.** a related plant of mountain regions, having pink flowers and black fruits. [C16: SW English dialect var. of *hurtleberry*, < ?]

who's (huːz) *contraction of* who is *or* who has.

whose (huːz) *determiner.* **1. a.** of who? belonging to who? used in direct and indirect questions: *I told him whose fault it was; whose car is this?* **b.** (*as pron.*): *whose is that?* **2.** of who; of which: used as a relative pronoun: *a house whose windows are broken; a man whose reputation has suffered.* [OE *hwæs*, genitive of *hwā* who & *hwæt* what]

▷ **Usage.** Since *whose* is the possessive of both *who* and *which*, it is quite acceptable to use *whose* of things as well as of people in careful usage: *these are the houses whose foundations are unsteady; this is the man whose leg was broken.*

whoso ('huːsəʊ) *pron.* an archaic word for **whoever.**

whosoever (ˌhuːsəʊ'ɛvə) *pron.* an archaic or formal word for **whoever.**

why (waɪ) *adv.* **1. a.** for what reason?: *why are you here?* **b.** (*used in indirect questions*): *tell me why you're here.* ~*pron.* **2.** for or because of which: *there is no reason why he shouldn't come.* ~*n., pl.* **whys. 3.** (*usually pl.*) the cause of something (esp. in **the whys and wherefores**). ~*interj.* **4.** an introductory expression of surprise, indignation, etc.: *why, don't be silly!* [OE *hwī*]

whydah *or* **whidah** ('wɪdə) *n.* any of various predominantly black African weaverbirds, the males of which grow very long tail feathers in the breeding season. Also called: **whydah bird, whidah bird, widow bird.** [C18: after a town in Benin in W Africa]

WI *abbrev. for:* **1.** West Indian. **2.** West Indies. **3.** Wisconsin. **4.** (in Britain) Women's Institute.

Wicca *or* **wicca** ('wɪkə) *n.* the cult or practice of witchcraft. [C20 revival of OE *wicca* witch]

wick[1] (wɪk) *n.* **1.** a cord or band of loosely twisted or woven fibres, as in a candle, that supplies fuel to a flame by capillary action. **2. get on (someone's) wick.** *Brit. sl.* to cause irritation to (someone). [OE *weoce*]

wick[2] (wɪk) *n. Arch.* a village or hamlet. [OE *wīc*; rel. to *-wich* in place names]

wicked ('wɪkɪd) *adj.* **1. a.** morally bad. **b.** (*as collective n.;* preceded by *the*): *the wicked.* **2.** mischievous or roguish, esp. in a playful way: *a wicked grin.* **3.** causing injury or harm. **4.** troublesome, unpleasant, or offensive. **5.** *Sl.* very good. [C13: < dialect *wick*, < OE *wicca* sorcerer, *wicce* witch] —**'wickedly** *adv.* —**'wickedness** *n.*

wicker ('wɪkə) *n.* **1.** a slender flexible twig or shoot, esp. of willow. **2.** short for **wickerwork.** ~*adj.* **3.** made of, consisting of, or constructed from wicker. [C14: < ON]

wickerwork ('wɪkəˌwɜːk) *n.* **a.** a material consisting of woven wicker. **b.** (*as modifier*): *a wickerwork chair.*

wicket ('wɪkɪt) *n.* **1.** a small door or gate, esp. one that is near to or part of a larger one. **2.** *Chiefly U.S.* a small window or opening in a door, esp. one fitted with a grating or glass pane. **3.** a small sluicegate. **4. a.** *Cricket.* either of two constructions, 22 yards apart, consisting of three stumps stuck in the ground with two wooden bails resting on top, at which the batsman stands. **b.** the strip of ground between these. **c.** a batsman's turn at batting or the period during which two batsmen bat: *a third-wicket partnership.* **d.** the act or instance of a batsman being got out: *the bowler took six wickets.* **5. keep wicket.** to act as a wicketkeeper. **6. on a good, sticky,** etc., **wicket.** *Inf.* in an advantageous, awkward, etc., situation. [C18: < OF *wiket*]

wicketkeeper ('wɪkɪtˌkiːpə) *n. Cricket.* the player on the fielding side positioned directly behind the wicket.

wickiup, wikiup, *or* **wickyup** ('wɪkɪˌʌp) *n. U.S. & Canad.* a crude shelter made of brushwood or grass and having an oval frame, esp. of a kind used by nomadic Indians now in the Oklahoma area. [C19: of Amerind origin]

widdershins ('wɪdəˌʃɪnz) *adv. Chiefly Scot.* a variant spelling of **withershins.**

wide (waɪd) *adj.* **1.** having a great extent from side to side. **2.** spacious or extensive. **3. a.** (*postpositive*) having a specified extent, esp. from side to side: *two yards wide.* **b.** (*in combination*): extending throughout: *nationwide.* **4.** remote from the desired point, mark, etc.: *your guess is wide of the mark.* **5.** (of eyes) opened fully. **6.** loose, full, or roomy: *wide trousers.* **7.** exhibiting a considerable spread: *a wide variation.* **8.** *Phonetics.* another word for **lax** (sense 4) or **open** (sense 32). **9.** *Brit. sl.* unscrupulous and astute: *a wide boy.* ~*adv.* **10.** over an extensive area: *to travel far and wide.* **11.** to the full extent: *he opened the door wide.* **12.** far from the desired point, mark, etc. ~*n.* **13.** (in cricket) a bowled ball that is outside the batsman's reach and scores a run for the batting side. [OE *wīd*] —**'widely** *adv.* —**'wideness** *n.* —**'widish** *adj.*

wide-angle lens *n.* a lens system on a camera that has a small focal length and therefore can cover an angle of view of 60° or more.

wide-awake *adj.* (**wide awake** *when postpositive*). **1.** fully awake. **2.** keen, alert, or observant. ~*n.* **3.** Also called: **wide-awake hat.** a hat with a low crown and very wide brim.

wide-body *adj.* (of an aircraft) having a wide fuselage, esp. wide enough to contain three rows of seats abreast.

wide-eyed *adj.* innocent or credulous.

widen ('waɪdᵊn) *vb.* to make or become wide or wider. —**'widener** *n.*

wide-open *adj.* (**wide open** *when postpositive*). **1.** open to the full extent. **2.** (*postpositive*) exposed to attack; vulnerable. **3.** uncertain as to outcome. **4.** *U.S. inf.* (of a town or city) lax in the enforcement of certain laws, esp. those relating to the sale of alcohol, gambling, etc.

widespread ('waɪdˌsprɛd) *adj.* **1.** extending over a wide area. **2.** accepted by or occurring among many people.

widgeon ('wɪdʒən) *n.* a variant spelling of **wigeon.**

widget ('wɪdʒɪt) *n. Inf.* any small mechanism or device, the name of which is unknown or temporarily forgotten. [C20: changed < GADGET]

widow ('wɪdəʊ) *n.* **1.** a woman whose husband has died, esp. one who has not remarried. **2.** (*with a modifier*) *Inf.* a woman whose husband frequently leaves her alone while he indulges in a sport, etc.: *a golf widow.* **3.** *Printing.* a short line at the end of a paragraph, esp. one that occurs as the top line of a page or column. **4.** (in some card games) an additional hand or set of cards exposed on the table. ~*vb.* (*tr.; usually passive*) **5.** to cause to become a widow. **6.** to deprive of something valued. [OE *widuwe*] —**'widowhood** *n.*

widow bird *n.* another name for **whydah.**

widower ('wɪdəʊə) *n.* a man whose wife has died and who has not remarried.

widow's cruse *n.* an endless or unfailing source of supply. [allusion to I Kings 17:16]

widow's mite *n.* a small contribution by a person who has very little. [allusion to Mark 12:43]

widow's peak *n.* a V-shaped point in the hairline in the middle of the forehead. [< the belief that it presaged early widowhood]

width (wɪdθ) *n.* **1.** the linear extent or measurement of something from side to side. **2.** the state or fact of being wide. **3.** a piece or section of something at its full extent from side to side: *a width of cloth.* **4.** the distance across a rectangular swimming bath, as opposed to its length. [C17: < WIDE + -TH[1], analogous to BREADTH]

wield (wiːld) *vb.* (*tr.*) **1.** to handle or use (a weapon, tool, etc.). **2.** to exert or maintain (power or authority). [OE *wieldan, wealdan*] —**ˈwieldable** *adj.* —**ˈwielder** *n.*

wieldy (ˈwiːldɪ) *adj.* **wieldier, wieldiest.** easily handled, used, or managed.

wiener (ˈwiːnə) *or* **wienerwurst** (ˈwiːnəˌwɜːst) *n. U.S. & Canad.* a kind of smoked sausage, similar to a frankfurter. [C20: shortened < G *Wiener Wurst* Viennese sausage]

Wiener schnitzel (ˈviːnə ˈʃnɪtsəl) *n.* a thin escalope of veal. [G: Viennese cutlet]

wife (waɪf) *n., pl.* **wives. 1.** a man's partner in marriage; a married woman. Related adj.: **uxorial. 2.** an archaic or dialect word for **woman. 3. take to wife.** to marry (a woman). [OE *wīf*] —**ˈwifehood** *n.* —**ˈwifely** *adj.*

wig (wɪg) *n.* **1.** an artificial head of hair, either human or synthetic, worn to disguise baldness, as part of a theatrical or ceremonial dress, as a disguise, or for adornment. ~*vb.* **wigging, wigged.** (*tr.*) **2.** *Brit. sl.* to berate severely. [C17: shortened < PERIWIG] —**wigged** *adj.* —**ˈwigless** *adj.*

wigeon *or* **widgeon** (ˈwɪdʒən) *n.* **1.** a Eurasian duck of marshes, swamps, etc., the male of which has a reddish-brown head and chest and grey-and-white back and wings. **2. American wigeon.** Also called: **baldpate.** a similar bird of North America, the male of which has a white crown. [C16: <?]

wigging (ˈwɪgɪŋ) *n. Brit. sl.* a reprimand.

wiggle (ˈwɪgᵊl) *vb.* **1.** to move or cause to move with jerky movements, esp. from side to side. ~*n.* **2.** the act of wiggling. [C13: < MLow G, MDu. *wiggelen*] —**ˈwiggler** *n.* —**ˈwiggly** *adj.*

wight (waɪt) *n. Arch.* a human being. [OE *wiht;* rel. to OFrisian *āwet* something]

wigwag (ˈwɪgˌwæg) *vb.* **-wagging, -wagged. 1.** to move (something) back and forth. **2.** to communicate with (someone) by means of a flag semaphore. ~*n.* **3. a.** a system of communication by flag semaphore. **b.** the message signalled. [C16: < obs. *wig,* prob. short for WIGGLE + WAG[1]] —**ˈwigˌwagger** *n.*

wigwam (ˈwɪgˌwæm) *n.* **1.** any dwelling of the North American Indians, esp. one made of bark, rushes, or skins spread over a set of arched poles lashed together. **2.** a similar structure for children. [< *wīkwām* (of Amerind origin), lit.: their abode]

wilco (ˈwɪlkəʊ) *interj.* an expression in signalling, telecommunications, etc., indicating that a message just received will be complied with. [C20: abbrev. for *I will comply*]

wild (waɪld) *adj.* **1.** (of animals) living independently of man; not domesticated or tame. **2.** (of plants) growing in a natural state; not cultivated. **3.** uninhabited; desolate: *a wild stretch of land.* **4.** living in a savage or uncivilized way: *wild tribes.* **5.** lacking restraint or control: *wild merriment.* **6.** of great violence: *a wild storm.* **7.** disorderly or chaotic: *wild talk.* **8.** dishevelled; untidy: *wild hair.* **9.** in a state of extreme emotional intensity: *wild with anger.* **10.** reckless: *wild speculations.* **11.** random: *a wild guess.* **12.** (*postpositive;* foll. by *about*) *Inf.* intensely enthusiastic: *I'm wild about my new boyfriend.* **13.** (of a card, such as a joker in some games) able to be given any value the holder pleases. **14. wild and woolly. a.** rough; barbarous. **b.** (of theories, plans, etc.) not fully thought out. ~*adv.* **15.** in a wild manner. **16. run wild. a.** to grow without cultivation or care: *the garden has run wild.* **b.** to behave without restraint: *he has let his children run wild.* ~*n.* **17.** (*often pl.*) a desolate or uninhabited region. **18. the wild. a.** a free natural state of living. **b.** the wilderness. [OE *wilde*] —**ˈwildish** *adj.* —**ˈwildly** *adv.* —**ˈwildness** *n.*

wild boar *n.* a wild pig of parts of Europe and central Asia, having a pale grey to black coat and prominent tusks.

wild brier *n.* another name for **wild rose.**

wild carrot *n.* an umbelliferous plant of temperate regions, having clusters of white flowers and hooked fruits. Also called: **Queen Anne's lace.**

wildcat (ˈwaɪldˌkæt) *n., pl.* **-cats** *or* **-cat. 1.** a wild European cat that resembles the domestic tabby but is larger and has a bushy tail. **2.** any of various other felines, such as the lynx and the caracal. **3.** *U.S. & Canad.* another name for **bobcat. 4.** *Inf.* a savage or aggressive person. **5.** *Chiefly U.S. & Canad.* an exploratory drilling for petroleum or natural gas. **6.** (*modifier*) *Chiefly U.S.* involving risk, esp. financially or commercially unsound: *a wildcat project.* ~*vb.* **-catting, -catted. 7.** (*intr.*) *Chiefly U.S. & Canad.* to drill for petroleum or natural gas in an area having no known reserves. —**ˈwildˌcatter** *n.* —**ˈwildˌcatting** *n., adj.*

wildcat strike *n.* a strike begun by workers spontaneously or without union approval.

wild cherry *n.* another name for **gean.**

wild dog *n.* another name for **dingo.**

wildebeest (ˈwɪldɪˌbiːst, ˈvɪl-) *n., pl.* **-beests** *or* **-beest.** another name for **gnu.** [C19: < Afrik., lit.: wild beast]

wilder (ˈwɪldə) *vb. Arch.* **1.** to lead or be led astray. **2.** to bewilder or become bewildered. [C17: <?]

wilderness (ˈwɪldənɪs) *n.* **1.** a wild uninhabited uncultivated region. **2.** any desolate area. **3.** a confused mass or collection. **4. a voice (crying) in the wilderness.** a person, group, etc., making a suggestion or plea that is ignored. [OE *wildēornes,* < *wildēor* wild beast + -NESS]

wild-eyed *adj.* glaring in an angry, distracted, or wild manner.

wildfire (ˈwaɪldˌfaɪə) *n.* **1.** a highly flammable material, such as Greek fire, formerly used in warfare. **2. a.** a raging and uncontrollable fire. **b.** anything that is disseminated quickly (esp. in **spread like wildfire**). **3.** another name for **will-o'-the-wisp.**

wild flower *n.* **1.** any flowering plant that grows in an uncultivated state. **2.** the flower of such a plant.

wildfowl (ˈwaɪldˌfaʊl) *n.* **1.** any bird that is hunted by man, esp. any duck or similar aquatic bird. **2.** such birds collectively. —**ˈwildˌfowler** *n.* —**ˈwildˌfowling** *adj., n.*

wild-goose chase *n.* an absurd or hopeless pursuit, as of something unattainable.

wilding (ˈwaɪldɪŋ) *n.* **1.** an uncultivated plant or a cultivated plant that has become wild. **2.** a wild animal. ~Also called: **wildling.**

wildlife (ˈwaɪldˌlaɪf) *n.* wild animals and plants collectively: a term used esp. of fauna.

wild pansy *n.* a Eurasian plant of the violet family having purple, yellow, and pale mauve spurred flowers. Also called: **heartsease, love-in-idleness.**

wild parsley *n.* any of various uncultivated umbelliferous plants that resemble parsley.

wild rice *n.* an aquatic North American grass with dark-coloured edible grain.

wild rose *n.* any of numerous roses, such as the dogrose and sweetbrier, that grow wild and have flowers with only one whorl of petals.

wild rubber *n.* rubber obtained from uncultivated rubber trees.

wild silk *n.* **1.** silk produced by wild silkworms. **2.** a fabric made from this, or from short fibres of silk designed to imitate it.

wild type *n. Biol.* the typical form of a species of

organism resulting from breeding under natural conditions.

Wild West *n.* the western U.S. during its settlement, esp. with reference to its frontier lawlessness.

wildwood (ˈwaɪldˌwʊd) *n. Arch.* a wood or forest growing in a natural uncultivated state.

wile (waɪl) *n.* **1.** trickery, cunning, or craftiness. **2.** (*usually pl.*) an artful or seductive trick or ploy. ~*vb.* **3.** (*tr.*) to lure, beguile, or entice. [C12: < ON *vel* craft]

wilful *or U.S.* **willful** (ˈwɪlfʊl) *adj.* **1.** intent on having one's own way; headstrong or obstinate. **2.** intentional: *wilful murder.* —ˈ**wilfully** *or U.S.* ˈ**willfully** *adv.* —ˈ**wilfulness** *or U.S.* ˈ**willfulness** *n.*

will[1] (wɪl) *vb. past* **would.** (takes an infinitive without *to* or an implied infinitive) used as an auxiliary. **1.** (esp. with *you, he, she, it, they,* or a noun as subject) to make the future tense. Cf. **shall** (sense 1). **2.** to express resolution on the part of the speaker: *I will buy that radio if it's the last thing I do.* **3.** to indicate willingness or desire: *will you help me with this problem?* **4.** to express commands: *you will report your findings to me tomorrow.* **5.** to express ability: *this rope will support a load.* **6.** to express probability or expectation: *that will be Jim telephoning.* **7.** to express customary practice or inevitability: *boys will be boys.* **8.** (*with the infinitive always implied*) to express desire: usually in polite requests: *stay if you will.* **9. what you will.** whatever you like. [OE *willan*]

▷ **Usage.** See at **shall.**

will[2] (wɪl) *n.* **1.** the faculty of conscious and deliberate choice of action. Related adj.: **voluntary. 2.** the act or an instance of asserting a choice. **3. a.** the declaration of a person's wishes regarding the disposal of his property after his death. **b.** a document in which such wishes are expressed. **4.** desire; wish. **5.** determined intention: *where there's a will there's a way.* **6.** disposition towards others: *he bears you no ill will.* **7. at will.** at one's own desire or choice. **8. with a will.** heartily; energetically. **9. with the best will in the world.** even with the best of intentions. ~*vb.* (*mainly tr.; often takes a clause as object or an infinitive*) **10.** (*also intr.*) to exercise the faculty of volition in an attempt to accomplish (something): *he willed his wife's recovery from her illness.* **11.** to give (property) by will to a person, society, etc.: *he willed his art collection to the nation.* **12.** (*also intr.*) to order or decree: *the king wills that you shall die.* **13.** to choose or prefer: *wander where you will.* [OE *willa*] —ˈ**willer** *n.*

willed (wɪld) *adj.* (*in combination*) having a will as specified: *weak-willed.*

willet (ˈwɪlɪt) *n.* a large American shore bird having a grey plumage with black-and-white wings. [C19: imit. of its call]

willful (ˈwɪlfʊl) *adj.* the U.S. spelling of **wilful.**

willie *or* **willy** (ˈwɪlɪ) *n. Brit. inf.* a childish or jocular term for **penis.**

willies (ˈwɪlɪz) *pl. n.* **the.** *Sl.* nervousness, jitters, or fright (esp. in **give** (*or* **get**) **the willies**). [C20: < ?]

willing (ˈwɪlɪŋ) *adj.* **1.** favourably disposed or inclined; ready. **2.** cheerfully compliant. **3.** done, given, accepted, etc., freely or voluntarily. —ˈ**willingly** *adv.* —ˈ**willingness** *n.*

williwaw (ˈwɪlɪˌwɔː) *n. U.S. & Canad.* **1.** a sudden strong gust of cold wind blowing offshore from a mountainous coast, as in the Strait of Magellan. **2.** a state of great turmoil. [C19: <?]

will-o'-the-wisp (ˌwɪləðəˈwɪsp) *n.* **1.** Also called: **friar's lantern, ignis fatuus, jack-o'-lantern.** a pale flame or phosphorescence sometimes seen over marshy ground at night. It is believed to be due to the spontaneous combustion of methane originating from decomposing organic matter. **2.** a person or thing that is elusive or allures and misleads. [C17: < *Will,* short for *William* + *wisp,* in former sense of a twist of hay burning as a torch]

willow (ˈwɪləʊ) *n.* **1.** any of a large genus of trees and shrubs, such as the weeping willow and osiers of N temperate regions, which have graceful flexible branches and flowers in catkins. **2.** the whitish wood of certain of these trees. **3.** something made of willow wood, such as a cricket bat. [OE *welig*]

willowherb (ˈwɪləʊˌhɜːb) *n.* **1.** any of various temperate and arctic plants having narrow leaves and terminal clusters of pink, purplish, or white flowers. **2.** short for **rosebay willowherb** (see **rosebay**).

willow pattern *n.* **a.** a pattern incorporating a willow tree, river, bridge, and figures, typically in blue on a white ground, used on porcelain, etc. **b.** (*as modifier*): *a willow-pattern plate.*

willowy (ˈwɪləʊɪ) *adj.* **1.** slender and graceful. **2.** flexible or pliant. **3.** covered or shaded with willows.

willpower (ˈwɪlˌpaʊə) *n.* **1.** the ability to control oneself and determine one's actions. **2.** firmness of will.

willy[1] (ˈwɪlɪ) *n., pl.* **-lies.** *Brit. inf.* a variant spelling of **willie.**

willy[2] (ˈwɪlɪ) *n. Austral. sl.* a sudden loss of temper; fit: *to throw a willy.*

willy-nilly (ˈwɪlɪˈnɪlɪ) *adv.* **1.** whether desired or not. ~*adj.* **2.** occurring or taking place whether desired or not. [OE *wile hē, nyle hē,* lit.: will he or will he not]

willy wagtail *n.* a black-and-white flycatcher found in Australasia and parts of Asia, having white feathers over the brows.

willy-willy (ˈwɪlɪˌwɪlɪ) *n., pl.* **-willies.** *Austral.* a small sometimes violent upward-spiralling cyclone or dust storm. [< Abor.]

wilt[1] (wɪlt) *vb.* **1.** to become or cause to become limp or drooping: *insufficient water makes plants wilt.* **2.** to lose or cause to lose courage, strength, etc. ~*n.* **3.** the act of wilting or state of becoming wilted. **4.** any of various plant diseases characterized by permanent wilting. [C17: ? var. of *wilk* to wither, < MDu. *welken*]

wilt[2] (wɪlt) *vb. Arch. or dialect.* (used with the pronoun *thou* or its relative equivalent) a singular form of the present tense (indicative mood) of **will**[1].

Wilton (ˈwɪltən) *n.* a kind of carpet with a close velvet pile of cut loops. [after *Wilton,* town in Wiltshire, where first made]

Wilts. (wɪlts) *abbrev. for* Wiltshire.

wily (ˈwaɪlɪ) *adj.* **wilier, wiliest.** sly or crafty. —ˈ**wiliness** *n.*

wimble (ˈwɪmbᵊl) *n.* **1.** any of a number of hand tools used for boring holes. ~*vb.* **2.** to bore (a hole) with a wimble. [C13: < MDu. *wimmel* auger]

wimp (wɪmp) *n. Inf.* a feeble ineffective person. [C20: <?] —ˈ**wimpish** *or* ˈ**wimpy** *adj.*

wimple (ˈwɪmpᵊl) *n.* **1.** a piece of cloth draped around the head to frame the face, worn by women in the Middle Ages and still worn by some nuns. ~*vb. Arch.* **2.** (*tr.*) to cover with or put a wimple on. **3.** (esp. of a veil) to lie or cause to lie in folds or pleats. [OE *wimpel*]

Wimpy (ˈwɪmpɪ) *n., pl.* **-pies.** *Trademark.* a hamburger served in a soft bread roll.

win (wɪn) *vb.* **winning, won. 1.** (*intr.*) to achieve first place in a competition. **2.** (*tr.*) to gain (a prize, first place, etc.) in a competition. **3.** (*tr.*) to succeed in or gain (something) with an effort: *we won recognition.* **4.** to gain victory or triumph in (a battle, argument, etc.). **5.** (*tr.*) to earn (a living, etc.) by work. **6.** (*tr.*) to capture: *the Germans never won Leningrad.* **7.** (when *intr.,* foll. by *out, through,* etc.) to reach with difficulty (a desired position) or become free, loose, etc., with effort: *the boat won the shore.* **8.** (*tr.*) to gain (the sympathy, loyalty, etc.) of someone. **9.** (*tr.*) to persuade (a woman, etc.) to marry one. **10.** (*tr.*) to extract (ore, coal, etc.) from a mine or (metal or other minerals) from ore. **11. you can't win.** *Inf.* an expression of resignation after an unsuccessful attempt to overcome difficulties. ~*n.* **12.** *Inf.* a success, victory, or triumph. **13.**

profit; winnings. ~See also **win over.** [OE *winnan*] —ˈ**winnable** *adj.*

▷ **Usage.** *Win* has become common in informal English as a noun meaning gain or victory. It is, however, regarded by careful users of English as inappropriate in formal contexts.

wince[1] (wɪns) *vb.* **1.** (*intr.*) to start slightly, as with sudden pain; flinch. ~*n.* **2.** the act of wincing. [C18 (earlier (C13) meaning: to kick): via OF *wencier, guenchir* to avoid, of Gmc origin] —ˈ**wincer** *n.* —ˈ**wincingly** *adv.*

wince[2] (wɪns) *n.* a roller for transferring pieces of cloth between dyeing vats. [C17: var. of WINCH[1]]

winceyette (ˌwɪnsɪˈɛt) *n. Brit.* a plain-weave cotton fabric with slightly raised two-sided nap. [< Scot. *wincey,* prob. altered < *woolsey* in *linsey-woolsey,* a fabric made of linen & wool]

winch[1] (wɪntʃ) *n.* **1.** a windlass driven by a hand- or power-operated crank. **2.** a hand- or power-operated crank by which a machine is driven. ~*vb.* **3.** (*tr.;* often foll. by *up* or *in*) to pull or lift using a winch. [OE *wince* pulley]

winch[2] (wɪntʃ) *vb.* (*intr.*) an obsolete word for **wince**[1].

Winchester rifle (ˈwɪntʃɪstə) *n. Trademark.* a breech-loading slide-action repeating rifle. Often shortened to **Winchester.** [C19: after O. F. *Winchester* (1810–80), U.S. manufacturer]

wind[1] (wɪnd) *n.* **1.** a current of air, sometimes of considerable force, moving generally horizontally from areas of high pressure to areas of low pressure. **2.** *Chiefly poetic.* the direction from which a wind blows, usually a cardinal point of the compass. **3.** air artificially moved, as by a fan, pump, etc. **4.** a trend, tendency, or force: *the winds of revolution.* **5.** *Inf.* a hint; suggestion: *we got wind that you were coming.* **6.** something deemed insubstantial: *his talk was all wind.* **7.** breath, as used in respiration or talk: *you're just wasting wind.* **8.** (often used in sports) the power to breathe normally: *his wind is weak.* **9.** *Music.* **a.** a wind instrument or wind instruments considered collectively. **b.** (*often pl.*) the musicians who play wind instruments in an orchestra. **c.** (*modifier*) of or composed of wind instruments: *a wind ensemble.* **10.** an informal name for **flatus. 11.** the air on which the scent of an animal is carried to hounds or on which the scent of a hunter is carried to his quarry. **12. between wind and water. a.** the part of a vessel's hull below the water line that is exposed by rolling or by wave action. **b.** any particularly susceptible point. **13. break wind.** to release intestinal gas through the anus. **14. get** *or* **have the wind up.** *Inf.* to become frightened. **15. how** *or* **which way the wind blows** *or* **lies.** what appears probable. **16. in the teeth** (*or* **eye**) **of the wind.** directly into the wind. **17. in the wind.** about to happen. **18. into the wind.** against the wind or upwind. **19. off the wind.** *Naut.* away from the direction from which the wind is blowing. **20. on the wind.** *Naut.* as near as possible to the direction from which the wind is blowing. **21. put the wind up.** *Inf.* to frighten or alarm. **22. raise the wind.** *Brit. inf.* to obtain the necessary funds. **23. sail close** *or* **near to the wind.** to come near the limits of danger or indecency. **24. take the wind out of someone's sails.** to disconcert or deflate someone. ~*vb.* (*tr.*) **25.** to cause (someone) to be short of breath: *the blow winded him.* **26. a.** to detect the scent of. **b.** to pursue (quarry) by following its scent. **27.** to cause (a baby) to bring up wind after feeding. **28.** to expose to air, as in drying, etc. [OE] —ˈ**windless** *adj.*

wind[2] (waɪnd) *vb.* **winding, wound. 1.** (often foll. by *around, about,* or *upon*) to turn or coil (string, cotton, etc.) around some object or point or (of string, etc.) to be turned, etc., around some object or point: *he wound a scarf around his head.* **2.** (*tr.*) to cover or wreathe by or as if by coiling, wrapping, etc.: *we wound the body in a shroud.* **3.** (*tr.;* often foll. by *up*) to tighten the spring of (a clockwork mechanism). **4.** (*tr.;* foll. by *off*) to remove by uncoiling or unwinding. **5.** (*usually intr.*) to move or cause to move in a sinuous, spiral, or circular course: *the river winds through the hills.* **6.** (*tr.*) to introduce indirectly or deviously: *he is winding his own opinions into the report.* **7.** (*tr.*) to cause to twist or revolve: *he wound the handle.* **8.** (*tr.;* usually foll. by *up* or *down*) to move by cranking: *please wind up the window.* ~*n.* **9.** the act of winding or state of being wound. **10.** a single turn, bend, etc.: *a wind in the river.* ~See also **wind down, wind up.** [OE *windan*] —ˈ**windable** *adj.*

wind[3] (waɪnd) *vb.* **winding, winded** *or* **wound.** (*tr.*) *Poetic.* to blow (a note or signal) on (a horn, bugle, etc.). [C16: special use of WIND[1]]

windage (ˈwɪndɪdʒ) *n.* **1. a.** a deflection of a projectile as a result of the effect of the wind. **b.** the degree of such deflection. **2.** the difference between a firearm's bore and the diameter of its projectile. **3.** *Naut.* the exposed part of the hull of a vessel responsible for wind resistance.

windbag (ˈwɪndˌbæg) *n.* **1.** *Sl.* a voluble person who has little of interest to communicate. **2.** the bag in a set of bagpipes, which provides a continuous flow of air to the pipes.

windblown (ˈwɪndˌbləʊn) *adj.* **1.** blown by the wind. **2.** (of trees, shrubs, etc.) growing in a shape determined by the prevailing winds.

wind-borne *adj.* (esp. of plant seeds or pollen) transported by wind.

windbound (ˈwɪndˌbaʊnd) *adj.* (of a sailing vessel) prevented from sailing by an unfavourable wind.

windbreak (ˈwɪndˌbreɪk) *n.* a fence, line of trees, etc., serving as a protection from the wind by breaking its force.

windburn (ˈwɪndˌbɜːn) *n.* irritation and redness of the skin caused by prolonged exposure to winds of high velocity.

windcheater (ˈwɪndˌtʃiːtə) *n.* a warm jacket, usually with a close-fitting knitted neck, cuffs, and waistband.

wind chest (wɪnd) *n.* a box in an organ in which air from the bellows is stored under pressure before being supplied to the pipes or reeds.

wind-chill (ˈwɪnd-) *n.* **a.** the serious chilling effect of wind and low temperature: measured on a scale that runs from hot to fatal to life. **b.** (*as modifier*): *wind-chill factor.*

wind cone (wɪnd) *n.* another name for **windsock.**

wind down (waɪnd) *vb.* (*adv.*) **1.** (*tr.*) to lower or move down by cranking. **2.** (*intr.*) (of a clock spring) to become slack. **3.** (*intr.*) to diminish gradually in force or power; relax.

winded (ˈwɪndɪd) *adj.* **1.** out of breath, as from strenuous exercise. **2.** (*in combination*) having breath or wind as specified: *broken-winded; short-winded.*

winder (ˈwaɪndə) *n.* **1.** a person or device that winds. **2.** an object, such as a bobbin, around which something is wound. **3.** a knob or key used to wind up a clock, watch, or similar mechanism. **4.** any plant that twists itself around a support. **5.** a step of a spiral staircase.

windfall (ˈwɪndˌfɔːl) *n.* **1.** a piece of unexpected good fortune, esp. financial gain. **2.** something blown down by the wind, esp. a piece of fruit.

windflower (ˈwɪndˌflaʊə) *n.* any of various anemone plants, such as the wood anemone.

wind gauge (wɪnd) *n.* **1.** another name for **anemometer. 2.** a scale on a gun sight indicating the amount of deflection necessary to allow for windage. **3.** *Music.* a device for measuring the wind pressure in the bellows of an organ.

wind harp (wɪnd) *n.* a less common name for **aeolian harp.**

windhover (ˈwɪndˌhɒvə) *n. Brit.* a dialect name for a **kestrel.**

winding (ˈwaɪndɪŋ) *n.* **1.** a curving or sinuous course or movement. **2.** anything that has been wound or wrapped around something. **3.** a particular manner or style in which something has been wound. **4.** a curve, bend, or complete turn in wound material, a road, etc. **5.** (*often pl.*) devious thoughts or behaviour: *the tortuous windings of political argumentation.* **6.** one or more turns of wire forming a continuous coil through which an electric current can pass, as used in transformers, generators, etc. ~*adj.* **7.** curving; sinuous: *a winding road.* —ˈ**windingly** *adv.*

winding sheet *n.* a sheet in which a corpse is wrapped for burial; shroud.

winding-up *n.* the process of finishing or closing something, esp. the process of closing down a business.

wind instrument (wɪnd) *n.* any musical instrument sounded by the breath, such as the woodwinds and brass instruments of an orchestra.

windjammer (ˈwɪndˌdʒæmə) *n.* a large merchant sailing ship.

windlass (ˈwɪndləs) *n.* **1.** a machine for raising weights by winding a rope or chain upon a barrel or drum driven by a crank, motor, etc. ~*vb.* **2.** (*tr.*) to raise or haul (a weight, etc.) by means of a windlass. [C14: < ON *vindáss*, < *vinda* to WIND² + *ass* pole]

windlestraw (ˈwɪndᵊlˌstrɔː) *n. Irish, Scot., & English dialect.* the dried stalk of any of various grasses. [OE *windelstrēaw*, < *windel* basket, < *windan* to wind + *strēaw* straw]

wind machine (wɪnd) *n.* a machine used, esp. in the theatre, to produce a wind or the sound of wind.

windmill (ˈwɪndˌmɪl, ˈwɪnˌmɪl) *n.* **1.** a machine for grinding or pumping driven by a set of adjustable vanes or sails that are caused to turn by the force of the wind. **2.** the set of vanes or sails that drives such a mill. **3.** Also called: **whirligig.** *Brit.* a toy consisting of plastic or paper vanes attached to a stick in such a manner that they revolve like the sails of a windmill. **4.** an imaginary opponent or evil (esp. in **tilt at** *or* **fight windmills**). ~*vb.* **5.** to move or cause to move like the arms of a windmill.

window (ˈwɪndəʊ) *n.* **1.** a light framework, made of timber, metal, or plastic, that contains glass or glazed opening frames and is placed in a wall or roof to let in light or air or to see through. Related adj.: **fenestral.** **2.** an opening in the wall or roof of a building that is provided to let in light or air or to see through. **3.** short for **windowpane.** **4.** the area behind a glass window in a shop used for display. **5.** any opening or structure resembling a window in function or appearance, such as the transparent area of an envelope revealing an address within. **6.** an opportunity to see or understand something usually unseen: *a window on the workings of Parliament.* **7.** short for **launch window** or **weather window.** **8.** *Physics.* a region of the spectrum in which a medium transmits electromagnetic radiation. **9.** (*modifier*) of or relating to a window or windows: *a window ledge.* ~*vb.* **10.** (*tr.*) to furnish with or as if with windows. [C13: < ON *vindauga*, < *vindr* WIND¹ + *auga* eye]

window box *n.* a long narrow box, placed on or outside a windowsill, in which plants are grown.

window-dresser *n.* a person employed to design and build up a display in a shop window.

window-dressing *n.* **1.** the ornamentation of shop windows, designed to attract customers. **2.** the pleasant aspect of an idea, etc., which is stressed to conceal the real nature.

windowpane (ˈwɪndəʊˌpeɪn) *n.* a sheet of glass in a window.

window sash *n.* a glazed window frame, esp. one that opens.

window seat *n.* **1.** a seat below a window, esp. in a bay window. **2.** a seat beside a window in a bus, train, etc.

window-shop *vb.* **-shopping, -shopped.** (*intr.*) to look at goods in shop windows without intending to buy. —ˈ**window-ˌshopper** *n.* —ˈ**window-ˌshopping** *n.*

windowsill (ˈwɪndəʊˌsɪl) *n.* a sill below a window.

windpipe (ˈwɪndˌpaɪp) *n.* a nontechnical name for **trachea** (sense 1).

wind rose (wɪnd) *n.* a diagram with radiating lines showing the frequency and strength of winds from each direction affecting a specific place.

windrow (ˈwɪndˌrəʊ, ˈwɪnˌrəʊ) *n.* **1.** a long low ridge or line of hay or a similar crop, designed to achieve the best conditions for drying or curing. **2.** a line of leaves, snow, dust, etc., swept together by the wind.

windscreen (ˈwɪndˌskriːn) *n. Brit.* the sheet of flat or curved glass that forms a window of a motor vehicle, esp. the front window. U.S. and Canad. name: **windshield.**

windscreen wiper *n. Brit.* an electrically operated blade with a rubber edge that wipes a windscreen clear of rain, snow, etc. U.S. and Canad. name: **windshield wiper.**

windshield (ˈwɪndˌʃiːld) *n.* the U.S. and Canad. name for **windscreen.**

windsock (ˈwɪndˌsɒk) *n.* a truncated cone of textile mounted on a mast so that it is free to rotate about a vertical axis: used, esp. at airports, to indicate the local wind direction. Also called: **air sock, drogue, wind sleeve, wind cone.**

Windsor (ˈwɪnzə) *adj.* of or relating to the British royal family, whose official name this has been from 1917.

Windsor chair *n.* a simple wooden chair, popular in England and America from the 18th century, usually having a shaped seat, splayed legs, and a back of many spindles.

Windsor knot *n.* a wide triangular knot, produced by making extra turns in tying a tie.

windstorm (ˈwɪndˌstɔːm) *n.* a storm consisting of violent winds.

wind-sucking *n.* a harmful habit of horses in which the animal arches its neck and swallows a gulp of air. —ˈ**windˌsucker** *n.*

windsurfing (ˈwɪndˌsɜːfɪŋ) *n.* the sport of riding on water using a surfboard steered and propelled by an attached sail.

windswept (ˈwɪndˌswɛpt) *adj.* open to or swept by the wind.

wind tunnel (wɪnd) *n.* a chamber for testing the aerodynamic properties of aircraft, aerofoils, etc., in which a current of air can be maintained at a constant velocity.

wind up (waɪnd) *vb.* (*adv.*) **1.** to bring to or reach a conclusion: *he wound up the proceedings.* **2.** (*tr.*) to tighten the spring of (a clockwork mechanism). **3.** (*tr.; usually passive*) *Inf.* to make nervous, tense, etc.: *he was all wound up before the big fight.* **4.** (*tr.*) to roll (thread, etc.) into a ball. **5.** an informal word for **liquidate** (sense 2). **6.** (*intr.*) *Inf.* to end up (in a specified state): *you'll wind up without any teeth.* **7.** (*tr.*) *Brit. sl.* to tease (someone). ~*n.* **wind-up.** **8.** the act of concluding. **9.** the end.

windward (ˈwɪndwəd) *Chiefly naut.* ~*adj.* **1.** of, in, or moving to the quarter from which the wind blows. ~*n.* **2.** the windward point. **3.** the side towards the wind. ~*adv.* **4.** towards the wind. ~Cf. **leeward.**

windy (ˈwɪndɪ) *adj.* **windier, windiest.** **1.** of, resembling, or relating to wind; stormy. **2.** swept by or open to powerful winds. **3.** marked by or given to prolonged and often boastful speech: *windy orations.* **4.** void of substance. **5.** an informal word for **flatulent.** **6.** *Sl.* frightened. —ˈ**windily** *adv.* —ˈ**windiness** *n.*

wine (waɪn) *n.* **1. a.** an alcoholic drink produced by the fermenting of grapes with water and sugar. **b.** (*as modifier*): *the wine harvest.* **c.** an alcoholic drink produced in this way from other fruits, flowers, etc.: *elderberry wine.* **2. a.** a dark red colour, sometimes with a purplish tinge. **b.** (*as adj.*): *wine-coloured.* **3.** anything resembling wine in its intoxicating or invigorating effect. **4. new wine in old bottles.** something new added to or imposed upon an old or established order. ~*vb.* **5.** (*intr.*) to drink wine. **6. wine and dine.** to entertain or be entertained with wine and fine food. [OE *wīn*, < L *vīnum*] —ˈ**wineless** *adj.*

wine bar *n.* a bar in a restaurant, etc., or an establishment that specializes in serving wine and usually food.

winebibber (ˈwaɪnˌbɪbə) *n.* a person who drinks a great deal of wine. —ˈ**wineˌbibbing** *n.*

wine box *n.* wine sold in a cubic carton with a tap for dispensing.

wine cellar *n.* **1.** a place, such as a dark cool cellar, where wine is stored. **2.** the stock of wines stored there.

wine cooler *n.* **1.** a bucket-like vessel containing ice in which a bottle of wine is placed to be cooled. **2.** the full name for **cooler** (sense 3).

wine gallon *n. Brit.* a former unit of capacity equal to 231 cubic inches.

wineglass (ˈwaɪnˌglɑːs) *n.* **1.** a glass drinking vessel, typically having a small bowl on a stem, with a flared foot. **2.** Also called: **wineglassful.** the amount that such a glass will hold.

wine grower *n.* a person engaged in cultivating vines in order to make wine. —**wine growing** *n.*

wine palm *n.* any of various palm trees, the sap of which is used, esp. when fermented, as a drink. Also called: **toddy palm.**

winepress (ˈwaɪnˌprɛs) *n.* any equipment used for squeezing the juice from grapes in order to make wine.

winery (ˈwaɪnərɪ) *n., pl.* **-eries.** *Chiefly U.S. & Canad.* a place where wine is made.

wineskin (ˈwaɪnˌskɪn) *n.* the skin of a sheep or goat sewn up and used as a holder for wine.

wing (wɪŋ) *n.* **1.** either of the modified forelimbs of a bird that are covered with large feathers and specialized for flight in most species. **2.** one of the organs of flight of an insect, consisting of a membranous outgrowth from the thorax containing a network of veins. **3.** either of the organs of flight in certain other animals, esp. the forelimb of a bat. **4. a.** a half of the main supporting surface on an aircraft, confined to one side of it. **b.** the full span of the main supporting surface on both sides of an aircraft. **5.** an organ, structure, or apparatus resembling a wing. **6.** anything suggesting a wing in form, function, or position, such as a sail of a windmill or a ship. **7.** *Bot.* **a.** either of the lateral petals of a sweetpea or related flower. **b.** any of various outgrowths of a plant part, esp. the process on a wind-dispersed fruit or seed. **8.** a means or cause of flight or rapid motion; flight: *fear gave wings to his feet.* **9.** *Brit.* the part of a car body that surrounds the wheels. U.S. and Canad. name: **fender. 10.** *Soccer, hockey, etc.* **a.** either of the two sides of the pitch near the touchline. **b.** a player stationed in such a position; winger. **11.** a faction or group within a political party or other organization. See also **left wing, right wing. 12.** a part of a building that is subordinate to the main part. **13.** the space offstage to the right or left of the acting area in a theatre. **14. in** *or* **on the wings.** ready to step in when needed. **15.** either of the two pieces that project forwards from the sides of some chair backs. **16.** (*pl.*) an insignia in the form of stylized wings worn by a qualified aircraft pilot. **17.** a tactical formation in some air forces, consisting of two or more squadrons. **18.** any of various flattened organs or extensions in lower animals, esp. when used in locomotion. **19. clip (someone's) wings. a.** to restrict (someone's) freedom. **b.** to thwart (someone's) ambitions. **20. on the wing. a.** flying. **b.** travelling. **21. on wings.** flying or as if flying. **22. spread** *or* **stretch one's wings.** to make full use of one's abilities. **23. take wing. a.** to lift off or fly away. **b.** to depart in haste. **c.** to become joyful. **24. under one's wing.** in one's care. ~*vb.* (*mainly tr.*) **25.** (*also intr.*) to make (one's way) swiftly on or as if on wings. **26.** to shoot or wound (a bird, person, etc.) superficially, in the wing or arm, etc. **27.** to cause to fly or move swiftly: *to wing an arrow.* **28.** to provide with wings. [C12: < ON] —**winged** *adj.* —ˈ**wingless** *adj.* —ˈ**wingˌlike** *adj.*

wing beat *or* **wing-beat** *n.* a complete cycle of moving the wing by a bird when flying.

wing-case *n.* the nontechnical name for **elytron.**

wing chair *n.* an easy chair having wings on each side of the back.

wing collar *n.* a stiff turned-up shirt collar worn with the points turned down over the tie.

wing commander *n.* an officer holding commissioned rank in certain air forces, such as the Royal Air Force: junior to a group captain and senior to a squadron leader.

wing covert *n.* any of the covert feathers of the wing of a bird, occurring in distinct rows.

wingding (ˈwɪŋˌdɪŋ) *n. Sl., chiefly U.S. & Canad.* **1.** a noisy lively party or festivity. **2.** a real or pretended fit or seizure. [C20: <?]

winge (wɪndʒ) *vb., n. Austral.* a variant spelling of **whinge.**

winger (ˈwɪŋə) *n. Soccer, hockey, etc.* a player stationed on the wing.

wing loading *n.* the total weight of an aircraft divided by its wing area.

wingman (ˈwɪŋmæn) *n. pl.* **-men.** a player in the wing position in Australian Rules.

wing nut *n.* a threaded nut tightened by hand by means of two flat lugs or wings projecting from the central body. Also called: **butterfly nut.**

wingspan (ˈwɪŋˌspæn) *or* **wingspread** (ˈwɪŋˌsprɛd) *n.* the distance between the wing tips of an aircraft, bird, etc.

wing tip *n.* the outermost edge of a wing.

wink (wɪŋk) *vb.* **1.** (*intr.*) to close and open one eye quickly, deliberately, or in an exaggerated fashion to convey friendliness, etc. **2.** to close and open (an eye or the eyes) momentarily. **3.** (*tr.; foll. by away, back,* etc.) to force away (tears, etc.) by winking. **4.** (*tr.*) to signal with a wink. **5.** (*intr.*) (of a light) to gleam or flash intermittently. ~*n.* **6.** a winking movement, esp. one conveying a signal, etc., or such a signal. **7.** an interrupted flashing of light. **8.** a brief moment of time. **9.** *Inf.* the smallest amount, esp. of sleep. **10. tip the wink.** *Brit. inf.* to give a hint. [OE *wincian*]

wink at *vb.* (*intr., prep.*) to connive at; disregard: *the authorities winked at corruption.*

winker (ˈwɪŋkə) *n.* **1.** a person or thing that winks. **2.** *Dialect or U.S. & Canad. sl.* an eye. **3.** another name for **blinker**[1] (sense 1).

winkle (ˈwɪŋkᵊl) *n.* **1.** See **periwinkle**[1]. ~*vb.* **2.** (*tr.; usually foll. by out, out of,* etc.) *Inf., chiefly Brit.* to extract or prise out. [C16: shortened < PERIWINKLE[1]]

winkle-pickers *pl. n.* shoes or boots with very pointed narrow toes.

winner (ˈwɪnə) *n.* **1.** a person or thing that wins. **2.** *Inf.* a person or thing that seems sure to win or succeed.

winning (ˈwɪnɪŋ) *adj.* **1.** (of a person, character, etc.) charming, engaging, or attractive: *a winning smile.* **2.** gaining victory: *the winning goal.* ~*n.* **3.** a shaft or seam of coal. **4.** (*pl.*) money, prizes, or valuables won, esp. in gambling. —ˈ**winningly** *adv.* —ˈ**winningness** *n.*

winning gallery *n. Real Tennis.* the gallery farthest from the net on either side of the court, into which any shot played wins a point.

winning opening *n. Real Tennis.* the grille or winning gallery, into which any shot played wins a point.

winning post *n.* the post marking the finishing line on a racecourse.

Winnipeg couch (ˈwɪnɪˌpɛg) *n. Canad.* a couch with no arms or back, opening out into a double bed. [after city in Canada]

winnow (ˈwɪnəʊ) *vb.* **1.** to separate (grain) from (chaff) by means of a wind or current of air. **2.** (*tr.*) to examine in order to select the desirable elements. **3.** (*tr.*) *Rare.* to blow upon; fan. ~*n.* **4. a.** a device for winnowing. **b.** the act or process of winnowing. [OE *windwian*] —ˈ**winnower** *n.*

wino (ˈwaɪnəʊ) *n., pl.* **winos.** *Inf.* a down-and-out who habitually drinks cheap wine.

win over *vb.* (*tr., adv.*) to gain the support or consent of (someone). Also: **win round.**

winsome (ˈwɪnsəm) *adj.* charming; winning; engaging: *a winsome smile.* [OE *wynsum,* < *wynn* joy + *-sum* -SOME[1]] —ˈ**winsomely** *adv.*

winter (ˈwɪntə) *n.* **1. a.** (*sometimes cap.*) the coldest season of the year, between autumn and spring, astronomically from the December solstice to the March equinox in the N hemisphere and at the opposite time of year in the S hemisphere. **b.** (*as modifier*): *winter pasture.* **2.** the period of cold weather associated with the winter. **3.** a time of decline, decay, etc. **4.** *Chiefly poetic.* a year represented by this season: *a man of 72 winters.* ~Related adj.: **hibernal.** ~*vb.* **5.** (*intr.*) to spend the winter in a specified place. **6.** to keep or feed (farm animals, etc.) during the winter or (of farm animals) to be kept or fed during the winter. [OE] —ˈ**winterer** *n.* —ˈ**winterless** *adj.*

winter aconite *n.* a small Old World herbaceous plant cultivated for its yellow flowers, which appear early in spring.

winter cherry *n.* **1.** a Eurasian plant cultivated for its ornamental inflated papery orange-red calyx. **2.** the calyx of this plant. ~See also **Chinese lantern.**

winter garden *n.* **1.** a garden of evergreen plants. **2.** a conservatory in which flowers are grown in winter.

wintergreen (ˈwɪntəˌgriːn) *n.* **1.** any of a genus of evergreen ericaceous shrubs, esp. a subshrub of E North America, which has white bell-shaped flowers and edible red berries. **2. oil of wintergreen.** an aromatic compound, formerly made from this and various other plants but now synthesized: used medicinally and for flavouring. **3.** any of a genus of plants, such as **common wintergreen,** of temperate and arctic regions, having rounded leaves and small pink globose flowers. **4. chickweed wintergreen.** a plant of N Europe and N Asia belonging to the primrose family, having white flowers and leaves arranged in a whorl. [C16: < Du. *wintergroen* or G *Wintergrün*]

winterize *or* **-rise** (ˈwɪntəˌraɪz) *vb.* (*tr.*) *U.S. & Canad.* to prepare (a house, car, etc.) to withstand winter conditions. —ˌ**winteriˈzation** *or* **-riˈsation** *n.*

winter jasmine *n.* a jasmine shrub widely cultivated for its winter-blooming yellow flowers.

winter solstice *n.* the time at which the sun is at its southernmost point in the sky (northernmost point in the S hemisphere) appearing at noon at its lowest altitude above the horizon. It occurs about December 22 (June 21 in the S hemisphere).

winter sports *pl. n.* sports held in the open air on snow or ice, esp. skiing.

wintertime (ˈwɪntəˌtaɪm) *n.* the winter season. Also (archaic): **wintertide.**

winterweight (ˈwɪntəˌweɪt) *adj.* (of clothes) suitably heavy and warm for wear in the winter.

winter wheat *n.* a type of wheat that is planted in the autumn and is harvested the following summer.

wintry (ˈwɪntrɪ) *or* **wintery** (ˈwɪntərɪ) *adj.* **-trier, -triest. 1.** (esp. of weather) of or characteristic of winter. **2.** lacking cheer or warmth; bleak. —ˈ**wintrily** *adv.* —ˈ**wintriness** *or* ˈ**winteriness** *n.*

winy (ˈwaɪnɪ) *adj.* **winier, winiest.** having the taste or qualities of wine; heady.

wipe (waɪp) *vb.* (*tr.*) **1.** to rub (a surface or object) lightly, esp., with a cloth, hand, etc., as in removing dust, water, etc. **2.** (usually foll. by *off, away, from, up,* etc.) to remove by or as if by rubbing lightly: *he wiped the dirt from his hands.* **3.** to eradicate or cancel (a thought, memory, etc.). **4.** to erase (a recording) from (a tape). **5.** to apply (oil, etc.) by wiping. **6.** *Austral. inf.* to abandon or reject (a person). **7. wipe the floor with (someone).** *Inf.* to defeat (someone) decisively. ~*n.* **8.** the act or an instance of wiping. **9.** *Dialect.* a sweeping blow. [OE *wīpian*]

wipe out *vb.* (*adv.*) **1.** (*tr.*) to destroy completely. **2.** (*tr.*) *Inf.* to kill. **3.** (*intr.*) to fall off a surfboard. ~*n.* **wipeout. 4.** an act or instance of wiping out. **5.** the interference of one radio signal by another so that reception is impossible.

wiper (ˈwaɪpə) *n.* **1.** any piece of cloth, such as a handkerchief, etc., used for wiping. **2.** a cam rotated to allow a part to fall under its own weight, as used in stamping machines, etc. **3.** See **windscreen wiper. 4.** *Electrical engineering.* a movable conducting arm that makes contact with a row or ring of contacts.

wire (ˈwaɪə) *n.* **1.** a slender flexible strand or rod of metal. **2.** a cable consisting of several metal strands twisted together. **3.** a flexible metallic conductor, esp. one made of copper, usually insulated, and used to carry electric current in a circuit. **4.** (*modifier*) of, relating to, or made of wire: *a wire fence.* **5.** anything made of wire, such as wire netting. **6.** a long continuous wire or cable connecting points in a telephone or telegraph system. **7.** *Old-fashioned.* an informal name for **telegram** or **telegraph. 8.** *U.S. & Canad. horse racing.* the finishing line on a racecourse. **9.** a snare made of wire for rabbits and similar animals. **10. get in under the wire.** *Inf., chiefly U.S. & Canad.* to accomplish something with little time to spare. **11. get one's wires crossed.** *Inf.* to misunderstand. **12. pull wires.** *Chiefly U.S. & Canad.* to exert influence behind the scenes; pull strings. ~*vb.* (*mainly tr.*) **13.** (*also intr.*) to send a telegram to (a person or place). **14.** to send (news, a message, etc.) by telegraph. **15.** to equip (an electrical system, circuit, or component) with wires. **16.** to fasten or furnish with wire. **17.** to snare with wire. **18. wire in.** *Inf.* to set about (something, esp. food) with enthusiasm. [OE *wīr*] —ˈ**wireˌlike** *adj.*

wire brush *n.* a brush having wire bristles, used for cleaning metal, esp. for removing rust, or for brushing against cymbals.

wire cloth *n.* a mesh or netting woven from fine wire, used in window screens, strainers, etc.

wiredraw (ˈwaɪəˌdrɔː) *vb.* **-drawing, -drew, -drawn.** to convert (metal) into wire by drawing through successively smaller dies.

wire-gauge *n.* **1.** a flat plate with slots in which standard wire sizes can be measured. **2.** a standard system of sizes for measuring the diameters of wires.

wire gauze *n.* a stiff meshed fabric woven of fine wires.

wire grass *n.* any of various grasses that have tough wiry roots or rhizomes.

wire-guided *adj.* (of a missile) able to be controlled in mid-flight by signals passed along a wire connecting the missile to the firer's control device.

wire-haired *adj.* (of an animal) having a rough wiry coat.

wireless (ˈwaɪəlɪs) *n., vb. Chiefly Brit.* another word for **radio.**

wireless telegraphy *n.* another name for **radiotelegraphy.**

wireless telephone *n.* another name for **radiotelephone. —wireless telephony** *n.*

wire netting *n.* a net made of wire, often galvanized, that is used for fencing, etc.

wirepuller (ˈwaɪəˌpʊlə) *n. Chiefly U.S. & Canad.* a person who uses private or secret influence for his own ends. —ˈ**wireˌpulling** *n.*

wire recorder *n.* an early type of magnetic recorder in which sounds were recorded on a thin steel wire magnetized by an electromagnet. **—wire recording** *n.*

wire service *n. Chiefly U.S. & Canad.* an agency supplying news, etc., to newspapers, radio, and television stations, etc.

wiretap (ˈwaɪəˌtæp) *vb.* **-tapping, -tapped. 1.** (*intr.*) to make a connection to a telegraph or telephone wire in order to obtain information secretly. **2.** (*tr.*) to tap (a telephone) or the telephone of (a person). —ˈ**wireˌtapper** *n.*

wire wheel *n.* a wheel in which the rim is held to the hub by wire spokes, esp. one used on a sports car.

wire wool *n.* a mass of fine wire, used esp. to clean kitchen articles.

wirework (ˈwaɪəˌwɜːk) *n.* **1.** functional or decorative work made of wire. **2.** objects made of wire, esp. netting.

wireworks (ˈwaɪəˌwɜːks) *n.* (*functioning as sing. or pl.*) a factory where wire or articles of wire are made.

wireworm (ˈwaɪəˌwɜːm) *n.* the wormlike larva of various beetles, which feeds on the roots of many plants and is a serious pest.

wiring (ˈwaɪərɪŋ) *n.* **1.** the network of wires used

in an electrical system, device, or circuit. ~*adj.* **2.** used in wiring.

wiry (ˈwaɪərɪ) *adj.* **wirier, wiriest. 1.** (of people or animals) slender but strong in constitution. **2.** made of or resembling wire, esp. in stiffness: *wiry hair.* **3.** (of a sound) produced by or as if by a vibrating wire. —ˈ**wirily** *adv.* —ˈ**wiriness** *n.*

wis (wɪs) *vb. Arch.* to know or suppose (something). [C17: a form derived < *iwis,* (< OE *gewiss* certain), mistakenly interpreted as *I wis* I know, as if from OE *witan* to know]

wisdom (ˈwɪzdəm) *n.* **1.** the ability or result of an ability to think and act utilizing knowledge, experience, understanding, common sense, and insight. **2.** accumulated knowledge or enlightenment. **3.** *Arch.* a wise saying or wise sayings. ~Related adj.: **sagacious.** [OE *wīsdōm*]

wisdom tooth *n.* **1.** any of the four molar teeth, one at the back of each side of the jaw, that are the last of the permanent teeth to erupt. Technical name: **third molar. 2. cut one's wisdom teeth.** to arrive at the age of discretion.

wise[1] (waɪz) *adj.* **1.** possessing, showing, or prompted by wisdom or discernment. **2.** prudent; sensible. **3.** shrewd; crafty: *a wise plan.* **4.** well-informed; erudite. **5.** informed or knowing (esp. in **none the wiser**). **6.** (*postpositive;* often foll. by *to*) *Sl.* in the know, esp. possessing inside information (about). **7.** *Arch.* possessing powers of magic. **8. be** *or* **get wise.** (often foll. by *to*) *Inf.* to be or become aware or informed (of something). **9. put wise.** (often foll. by *to*) *Sl.* to inform or warn (of). ~*vb.* **10.** See **wise up.** [OE *wīs*] —ˈ**wisely** *adv.* —ˈ**wiseness** *n.*

wise[2] (waɪz) *n. Arch.* way, manner, fashion, or respect (esp. in **any wise, in no wise**). [OE *wīse* manner]

-wise *adv. combining form.* **1.** indicating direction or manner: *clockwise; likewise.* **2.** with reference to: *businesswise.* [OE *-wisan;* see WISE[2]]

▷ **Usage.** The addition of *-wise* to a noun as a replacement for a lengthier phrase (such as *as far as ... is concerned*) is considered unacceptable by most careful speakers and writers: *talentwise, he's a little weak* (he's a little weak as regards talent).

wiseacre (ˈwaɪzˌeɪkə) *n.* **1.** a person who wishes to seem wise. **2.** a wise person: often used facetiously or contemptuously. [C16: < MDu. *wijsseggher* soothsayer. See WISE[1], SAY]

wisecrack (ˈwaɪzˌkræk) *Inf.* ~*n.* **1.** a flippant jibe or sardonic remark. ~*vb.* (*intr.*) **2.** to make a wisecrack. —ˈ**wiseˌcracker** *n.*

wise guy *n. Inf.* a person who is given to making conceited, sardonic, or insolent comments.

wisent (ˈwiːzᵊnt) *n.* another name for **European bison.** See **bison** (sense 2). [G, < OHG *wisunt* BISON]

wise up *vb.* (*adv.*) *Sl., chiefly U.S. & Canad.* (often foll. by *to*) to become or cause to become aware or informed (of).

wish (wɪʃ) *vb.* **1.** (when *tr., takes a clause as object or an infinitive;* when *intr.,* often foll. by *for*) to want or desire (something, often that which cannot be or is not the case): *I wish I lived in Italy.* **2.** (*tr.*) to feel or express a desire or hope concerning the future or fortune of: *I wish you well.* **3.** (*tr.*) to desire or prefer to be as specified. **4.** (*tr.*) to greet as specified: *he wished us good afternoon.* ~*n.* **5.** the expression of some desire or mental inclination: *to make a wish.* **6.** something desired or wished for: *he got his wish.* **7.** (*usually pl.*) expressed hopes or desire, esp. for someone's welfare, health, etc. **8.** (*often pl.*) *Formal.* a polite order or request. ~See also **wish on.** [OE *wȳscan*] —ˈ**wisher** *n.*

wishbone (ˈwɪʃˌbəʊn) *n.* the V-shaped bone above the breastbone in most birds consisting of the fused clavicles. [C17: < the custom of two people breaking apart the bone after eating: the person with the longer part makes a wish]

wishful (ˈwɪʃful) *adj.* having wishes or characterized by wishing. —ˈ**wishfully** *adv.* —ˈ**wishfulness** *n.*

wish fulfilment *n.* (in Freudian psychology) any successful attempt to fulfil a wish stemming from the unconscious mind, whether in fact, in fantasy, or by disguised means.

wishful thinking *n.* the erroneous belief that one's wishes are in accordance with reality. —**wishful thinker** *n.*

wish on *vb.* (*tr., prep.*) to hope that (someone or something) should be imposed (on someone); foist: *I wouldn't wish my cold on anyone.*

wishy-washy (ˈwɪʃɪˌwɒʃɪ) *adj. Inf.* **1.** lacking in substance, force, colour, etc. **2.** watery; thin.

wisp (wɪsp) *n.* **1.** a thin, light, delicate, or fibrous piece or strand, such as a streak of smoke or a lock of hair. **2.** a small bundle, as of hay or straw. **3.** anything slender and delicate: *a wisp of a girl.* **4.** a mere suggestion or hint. **5.** a flock of birds, esp. snipe. [C14: var. of *wips,* <?] —ˈ**wispˌlike** *adj.* —ˈ**wispy** *adj.*

wist (wɪst) *vb. Arch.* the past tense and past participle of **wit**[2].

wisteria (wɪˈstɪərɪə) *n.* any twining woody climbing plant of the genus *Wisteria,* of E Asia and North America, having blue, purple, or white flowers in large drooping clusters. [C19: < NL, after Caspar *Wistar* (1761–1818), U.S. anatomist]

wistful (ˈwɪstful) *adj.* sadly pensive, esp. about something yearned for. —ˈ**wistfully** *adv.* —ˈ**wistfulness** *n.*

wit[1] (wɪt) *n.* **1.** the talent or quality of using unexpected associations between contrasting or disparate words or ideas to make a clever humorous effect. **2.** speech or writing showing this quality. **3.** a person possessing, showing, or noted for such an ability. **4.** practical intelligence (esp. in **have the wit to**). **5.** *Arch.* mental capacity or a person possessing it. ~See also **wits.** [OE *witt*]

wit[2] (wɪt) *vb.* **wot, wist. 1.** *Arch.* to be or become aware of (something). **2. to wit.** that is to say; namely (used to introduce statements, as in legal documents). [OE *witan*]

witan (ˈwɪtᵊn) *n.* (in Anglo-Saxon England) **1.** an assembly of higher ecclesiastics and important laymen that met to counsel the king on matters such as judicial problems. **2.** the members of this assembly. ~Also called: **witenagemot.** [OE *witan,* pl. of *wita* wise man]

witblitz (ˈvɪtˌblɪts) *n. S. African.* alcoholic drink illegally distilled. [< Afrik. *wit* white + *blits* lightning]

witch[1] (wɪtʃ) *n.* **1.** a person, usually female, who practises or professes to practise magic or sorcery, esp. black magic, or is believed to have dealings with the devil. **2.** an ugly or wicked old woman. **3.** a fascinating or enchanting woman. ~*vb.* (*tr.*) **4.** a less common word for **bewitch.** [OE *wicca*] —ˈ**witchˌlike** *adj.*

witch[2] (wɪtʃ) *n.* a flatfish of N Atlantic coastal waters, having a narrow greyish-brown body marked with tiny black spots: related to the plaice, flounder, etc. [C19: ? < WITCH[1], < the appearance of the fish]

witchcraft (ˈwɪtʃˌkrɑːft) *n.* **1.** the art or power of bringing magical or preternatural power to bear or the act or practice of attempting to do so. **2.** the influence of magic or sorcery. **3.** fascinating or bewitching influence or charm.

witch doctor *n.* a man in certain societies, esp. preliterate ones, who appears to possess magical powers, used esp. to cure sickness but also to harm people. Also called: **shaman, medicine man.**

witch-elm *n.* a variant spelling of **wych-elm.**

witchery (ˈwɪtʃərɪ) *n., pl.* **-eries. 1.** the practice of witchcraft. **2.** magical or bewitching influence or charm.

witches'-broom *n.* a dense abnormal growth of shoots on a tree or other woody plant, usually caused by parasitic fungi.

witchetty grub (ˈwɪtʃɪtɪ) *n.* the wood-boring edible caterpillar of an Australian moth. Also: **witchetty, witchety.** [C19 *witchetty,* < Abor.]

witch hazel *or* **wych-hazel** *n.* **1.** any of a genus of trees and shrubs of North America, having ornamental yellow flowers and medicinal properties. **2.** an astringent medicinal solution containing an extract of the bark and leaves of one of these shrubs, applied to treat bruises, inflammation, etc.

witch-hunt *n.* a rigorous campaign to expose dissenters on the pretext of safeguarding the public welfare. —**ˈwitch-ˌhunting** *n., adj.*

witching (ˈwɪtʃɪŋ) *adj.* **1.** relating to or appropriate for witchcraft. **2.** *Now rare.* bewitching. —**ˈwitchingly** *adv.*

witching hour *n.* **the.** the hour at which witches are supposed to appear, usually midnight.

witenagemot (ˌwɪtɪnəgɪˈməʊt) *n.* another word for **witan.** [OE *witena,* genitive pl. of *wita* councillor + *gemōt* meeting]

with (wɪð, wɪθ) *prep.* **1.** using; by means of: *he killed her with an axe.* **2.** accompanying; in the company of: *the lady you were with.* **3.** possessing; having: *a man with a red moustache.* **4.** concerning or regarding: *be patient with her.* **5.** in spite of: *with all his talents, he was still humble.* **6.** used to indicate a time or distance by which something is away from something else: *with three miles to go, he collapsed.* **7.** in a manner characterized by: *writing with abandon.* **8.** caused or prompted by: *shaking with rage.* **9.** often used with a verb indicating a reciprocal action or relation between the subject and the preposition's object: *agreeing with me.* **10. with it.** *Inf.* **a.** fashionable; in style. **b.** comprehending what is happening or being said. **11. with that.** after that. [OE]

withal (wɪˈðɔːl) *adv.* **1.** *Literary.* as well. **2.** *Arch.* therewith. ~*prep.* **3.** (*postpositive*) an archaic word for **with.** [C12: < WITH + ALL]

withdraw (wɪðˈdrɔː) *vb.* **-drawing, -drew, -drawn.** **1.** (*tr.*) to take or draw back or away; remove. **2.** (*tr.*) to remove from deposit or investment in a bank, etc. **3.** (*tr.*) to retract or recall (a promise, etc.). **4.** (*intr.*) to retire or retreat: *the troops withdrew.* **5.** (*intr.;* often foll. by *from*) to depart (from): *he withdrew from public life.* **6.** (*intr.*) to detach oneself socially, emotionally, or mentally. [C13: < WITH (in the sense: away from) + DRAW] —**withˈdrawer** *n.*

withdrawal (wɪðˈdrɔːəl) *n.* **1.** an act or process of withdrawing. **2.** the period a drug addict goes through following abrupt termination in the use of narcotics, usually characterized by physical and mental symptoms (**withdrawal symptoms**). **3.** Also called: **withdrawal method, coitus interruptus.** the deliberate withdrawing of the penis from the vagina before ejaculation, as a method of contraception.

withdrawing room *n.* an archaic term for **drawing room.**

withdrawn (wɪðˈdrɔːn) *vb.* **1.** the past participle of **withdraw.** ~*adj.* **2.** unusually reserved or shy. **3.** secluded or remote.

withe (wɪθ, wɪð, waɪð) *n.* **1.** a strong flexible twig, esp. of willow, suitable for binding things together; withy. **2.** a band or rope of twisted twigs or stems. ~*vb.* **3.** (*tr.*) to bind with withes. [OE *withthe*]

wither (ˈwɪðə) *vb.* **1.** (*intr.*) (esp. of a plant) to droop, wilt, or shrivel up. **2.** (*intr.;* often foll. by *away*) to fade or waste: *all hope withered away.* **3.** (*intr.*) to decay or disintegrate. **4.** (*tr.*) to cause to wilt or lose vitality. **5.** (*tr.*) to abash, esp. with a scornful look. [C14: ? var. of WEATHER (vb.)] —**ˈwitherer** *n.* —**ˈwithering** *adj.* —**ˈwitheringly** *adv.*

withers (ˈwɪðəz) *pl. n.* the highest part of the back of a horse, behind the neck between the shoulders. [C16: short for *widersones,* < *wider* with + *-sones,* ? var. of SINEW]

withershins (ˈwɪðəˌʃɪnz) *or* **widdershins** *adv. Chiefly Scot.* in the direction contrary to the apparent course of the sun; anticlockwise. [C16: < MLow G *weddersinnes,* < MHG, lit.: opposite course, < *wider* against + *sinnes,* genitive of *sin* course]

withhold (wɪðˈhəʊld) *vb.* **-holding, -held.** **1.** (*tr.*) to keep back: *he withheld his permission.* **2.** (*tr.*) to hold back; restrain. **3.** (*intr.;* usually foll. by *from*) to refrain or forbear. —**withˈholder** *n.*

within (wɪˈðɪn) *prep.* **1.** in; inside; enclosed or encased by. **2.** before (a period of time) has elapsed: *within a week.* **3.** not differing by more than (a specified amount) from: *live within your means.* ~*adv.* **4.** *Formal.* inside; internally.

without (wɪˈðaʊt) *prep.* **1.** not having: *a traveller without much money.* **2.** not accompanied by: *he came without his wife.* **3.** not making use of: *it is not easy to undo screws without a screwdriver.* **4.** (*foll. by a present participle*) not, while not, or after not: *she can sing for two minutes without drawing breath.* **5.** *Arch.* on the outside of: *without the city walls.* ~*adv.* **6.** *Formal.* outside.

withstand (wɪðˈstænd) *vb.* **-standing, -stood.** **1.** (*tr.*) to resist. **2.** (*intr.*) to remain firm in endurance or opposition. —**withˈstander** *n.*

withy (ˈwɪðɪ) *n., pl.* **withies.** a variant spelling of **withe** (senses 1, 2). [OE *wīdig(e)*]

witless (ˈwɪtlɪs) *adj.* lacking wit, intelligence, or sense. —**ˈwitlessly** *adv.* —**ˈwitlessness** *n.*

witling (ˈwɪtlɪŋ) *n. Arch.* a person who thinks himself witty.

witness (ˈwɪtnɪs) *n.* **1.** a person who has seen or can give first-hand evidence of some event. **2.** a person or thing giving or serving as evidence. **3.** a person who testifies, esp. in a court of law, to events or facts within his own knowledge. **4.** a person who attests to the genuineness of a document, signature, etc., by adding his own signature. **5. bear witness to. a.** to give written or oral testimony to. **b.** to be evidence or proof of. ~Related adj.: **testimonial.** ~*vb.* **6.** (*tr.*) to see, be present at, or know at first hand. **7.** (*tr.*) to give evidence of. **8.** (*tr.*) to be the scene or setting of: *this field has witnessed a battle.* **9.** (*intr.*) to testify, esp. in a court of law, to events within a person's own knowledge. **10.** (*tr.*) to attest to the genuineness of (a document, etc.) by adding one's own signature. [OE *witnes,* < *witan* to know + -NESS] —**ˈwitnesser** *n.*

witness box *or esp. U.S.* **witness stand** *n.* the place in a court of law in which witnesses stand to give evidence.

wits (wɪts) *pl. n.* **1.** (*sometimes sing.*) the ability to reason and act, esp. quickly (esp. in **have one's wits about one**). **2.** (*sometimes sing.*) right mind, sanity (esp. in **out of one's wits**). **3. at one's wits' end.** at a loss to know how to proceed. **4. live by one's wits.** to gain a livelihood by craftiness rather than by hard work.

-witted *adj.* (*in combination*) having wits or intelligence as specified: *slow-witted; dim-witted.*

witter (ˈwɪtə) *vb.* (*intr.;* often foll. by *on*) *Inf.* to chatter or babble pointlessly or at unnecessary length. [C20: ? < obs. *whitter* to warble, twitter]

witticism (ˈwɪtɪˌsɪzəm) *n.* a clever or witty remark. [C17: < WITTY; coined by Dryden (1677) by analogy with *criticism*]

witting (ˈwɪtɪŋ) *adj. Rare.* **1.** deliberate; intentional. **2.** aware. —**ˈwittingly** *adv.*

witty (ˈwɪtɪ) *adj.* **-tier, -tiest.** **1.** characterized by clever humour or wit. **2.** *Arch. or dialect.* intelligent. —**ˈwittily** *adv.* —**ˈwittiness** *n.*

wive (waɪv) *vb. Arch.* **1.** to marry (a woman). **2.** (*tr.*) to supply with a wife. [OE *gewīfian,* < *wīf* wife]

wivern (ˈwaɪvən) *n.* a less common spelling of **wyvern.**

wives (waɪvz) *n.* **1.** the plural of **wife.** **2. old wives' tale.** a superstitious tradition, occasionally one that contains an element of truth.

wiz (wɪz) *n., pl.* **wizzes.** *Inf.* a variant spelling of **whiz** (sense 5).

wizard (ˈwɪzəd) *n.* **1.** a male witch or a man who practises or professes to practise magic or sorcery. **2.** a person who is outstandingly clever in some specified field. ~*adj.* **3.** *Inf., chiefly Brit.* superb; outstanding. **4.** of or relating to a wizard or wizardry. [C15: var. of *wissard,* < WISE¹ + -ARD] —**ˈwizardly** *adj.*

wizardry (ˈwɪzədrɪ) *n.* the art, skills, and practices of a wizard, sorcerer, or magician.

wizen (ˈwɪzᵊn) *vb.* **1.** to make or become shrivelled. ~*adj.* **2.** a variant of **wizened.** [OE *wisnian*]

wizened (ˈwɪzᵊnd) *or* **wizen** *adj.* shrivelled, wrinkled, or dried up, esp. with age.

wk *abbrev. for:* 1. (*pl.* **wks**) week. 2. work.

wkly *abbrev. for* weekly.

w.l. *or* **WL** *abbrev. for* water line.

WMO *abbrev. for* World Meteorological Organization.

WNW *symbol for* west-northwest.

WO *abbrev. for:* 1. War Office. 2. Warrant Officer. 3. wireless operator.

woad (wəʊd) *n.* 1. a European cruciferous plant, formerly cultivated for its leaves, which yield a blue dye. 2. the dye obtained from this plant, used esp. by the ancient Britons as a body dye. [OE *wād*]

wobbegong (ˈwɒbɪˌgɒŋ) *n.* any of various sharks of Australian waters, having a richly patterned brown-and-white skin. [< Abor.]

wobble (ˈwɒbᵊl) *vb.* 1. (*intr.*) to move or sway unsteadily. 2. (*intr.*) to shake: *her voice wobbled with emotion.* 3. (*intr.*) to vacillate with indecision. 4. (*tr.*) to cause to wobble. ~*n.* 5. a wobbling movement or sound. [C17: var. of *wabble*, < Low G *wabbeln*] —ˈ**wobbler** *n.*

wobble board *n. Austral.* a piece of fibreboard used as a rhythmical musical instrument, producing a characteristic sound when flexed.

wobbly (ˈwɒblɪ) *adj.* **-blier, -bliest.** 1. shaky, unstable, or unsteady. ~*n.* 2. **throw a wobbly.** *Sl.* to become suddenly very agitated or angry. —ˈ**wobbliness** *n.*

wodge (wɒdʒ) *n. Brit. inf.* a thick lump or chunk cut or broken off something. [C20: alteration of WEDGE]

woe (wəʊ) *n.* 1. *Literary.* intense grief. 2. (*often pl.*) affliction or misfortune. 3. **woe betide (someone).** misfortune will befall (someone): *woe betide you if you arrive late.* ~*interj.* 4. Also: **woe is me.** *Arch.* an exclamation of sorrow or distress. [OE *wā, wǣ*]

woebegone (ˈwəʊbɪˌgɒn) *adj.* sorrowful or sad in appearance. [C14: < a phrase such as *me is wo begon* woe has beset me]

woeful (ˈwəʊfᵊl) *adj.* 1. expressing or characterized by sorrow. 2. bringing or causing woe. 3. pitiful; miserable: *a woeful standard of work.* —ˈ**woefully** *adv.* —ˈ**woefulness** *n.*

WOF (in New Zealand) *abbrev. for* Warrant of Fitness.

wog[1] (wɒg) *n. Brit. sl., derog.* a person who is not White. [prob. < GOLLIWOG]

wog[2] (wɒg) *n. Austral. sl.* any ailment or disease, such as influenza, a virus infection, etc. [C20: <?]

woggle (ˈwɒgᵊl) *n.* the ring of leather through which a Scout neckerchief is threaded. [C20: <?]

wok (wɒk) *n.* a large metal Chinese cooking pot having a curved base like a bowl: used esp. for stir-frying. [< Chinese (Cantonese)]

woke (wəʊk) *vb.* the past tense of **wake**[1].

woken (ˈwəʊkən) *vb.* the past participle of **wake**[1].

wold[1] (wəʊld) *n. Chiefly literary.* a tract of open rolling country, esp. upland. [OE *weald* bush]

wold[2] (wəʊld) *n.* a variant of **weld**[2].

Wolds (wəʊldz) *pl. n.* **the.** a range of chalk hills in NE England: consists of the **Yorkshire Wolds** to the north, separated from the **Lincolnshire Wolds** by the Humber estuary.

wolf (wʊlf) *n., pl.* **wolves.** 1. a predatory canine mammal which hunts in packs and was formerly widespread in North America and Eurasia but is now less common. Related adj.: **lupine.** 2. any of several similar and related canines, such as the red wolf and the coyote (**prairie wolf**). 3. the fur of any such animal. 4. a voracious or fiercely cruel person or thing. 5. *Inf.* a man who habitually tries to seduce women. 6. Also called: **wolf note.** *Music.* **a.** an unpleasant sound produced in some notes played on the violin, etc., owing to resonant vibrations of the belly. **b.** an out-of-tune effect produced on keyboard instruments accommodated esp. to the system of mean-tone temperament. 7. **cry wolf.** to give a false alarm. 8. **have** *or* **hold a wolf by the ears.** to be in a desperate situation. 9. **keep the wolf from the door.** to ward off starvation or privation. 10. **lone wolf.** a person or animal who prefers to be alone. 11. **wolf in sheep's clothing.** a malicious person in a harmless or benevolent disguise. ~*vb.* 12. (*tr.*; often foll. by *down*) to gulp (down). 13. (*intr.*) to hunt wolves. [OE *wulf*] —ˈ**wolfish** *adj.* —ˈ**wolf**ˌ**like** *adj.*

Wolf Cub *n. Brit.* the former name for **Cub Scout.**

wolffish (ˈwʊlfˌfɪʃ) *n., pl.* **-fish** *or* **-fishes.** a large northern deep-sea fish. It has large sharp teeth and no pelvic fins and is used as a food fish. Also called: **catfish.**

wolfhound (ˈwʊlfˌhaʊnd) *n.* the largest breed of dog, used formerly to hunt wolves.

wolfram (ˈwʊlfrəm) *n.* another name for **tungsten.** [C18: < G, orig. ? < the proper name *Wolfram*, used pejoratively of tungsten because it was thought inferior to tin]

wolframite (ˈwʊlfrəˌmaɪt) *n.* a black to reddish-brown mineral, a compound of tungsten, iron, and manganese: it is the chief ore of tungsten.

wolfsbane (ˈwʊlfsˌbeɪn) *or* **wolf's bane** *n.* any of several poisonous N temperate plants of the ranunculaceous genus *Aconitum* having hoodlike flowers.

wolf spider *n.* a spider which chases its prey to catch it. Also called: **hunting spider.**

wolf whistle *n.* 1. a whistle made by a man to express admiration of a woman's appearance. ~*vb.* **wolf-whistle.** 2. (when *intr.*, sometimes foll. by *at*) to make such a whistle (at someone).

Wolof (ˈwɒlɒf) *n.* 1. (*pl.* **-of** *or* **-ofs**) a member of a Negroid people of W Africa living chiefly in Senegal. 2. the language of this people, belonging to the Niger-Congo family.

wolverine (ˈwʊlvəˌriːn) *n.* a large musteline mammal of northern forests of Eurasia and North America having dark very thick water-resistant fur. Also called: **glutton.** [C16 *wolvering*, < WOLF + -ING[3] (later altered to *-ine*)]

wolves (wʊlvz) *n.* the plural of **wolf.**

woman (ˈwʊmən) *n., pl.* **women.** 1. an adult female human being. 2. (*modifier*) female or feminine: *a woman politician.* 3. women collectively. 4. (usually preceded by *the*) feminine nature or feelings: *babies bring out the woman in him.* 5. a female servant or domestic help. 6. a man considered as having female characteristics, such as meekness. 7. *Inf.* a wife or girlfriend. 8. **the little woman.** *Brit. inf., old-fashioned.* one's wife. 9. **woman of the streets.** a prostitute. ~*vb.* (*tr.*) 10. *Obs.* to make effeminate. [OE *wīfmann, wimman*] —ˈ**womanless** *adj.* —ˈ**woman-**ˌ**like** *adj.*

womanhood (ˈwʊmənˌhʊd) *n.* 1. the state or quality of being a woman or being womanly. 2. women collectively.

womanish (ˈwʊmənɪʃ) *adj.* 1. having qualities regarded as unsuitable to a man. 2. characteristic of or suitable for a woman. —ˈ**womanishly** *adv.* —ˈ**womanishness** *n.*

womanize *or* **-ise** (ˈwʊməˌnaɪz) *vb.* 1. (*intr.*) (of a man) to indulge in casual affairs with women. 2. (*tr.*) to make effeminate. —ˈ**woman**ˌ**izer** *or* **-**ˌ**iser** *n.*

womankind (ˈwʊmənˌkaɪnd) *n.* the female members of the human race; women collectively.

womanly (ˈwʊmənlɪ) *adj.* 1. possessing qualities, such as warmth, attractiveness, etc., generally regarded as typical of a woman. 2. characteristic of or belonging to a woman.

womb (wuːm) *n.* 1. the nontechnical name for **uterus.** 2. a hollow space enclosing something. 3. a place where something is conceived: *the Near East is the womb of western civilization.* 4. *Obs.* the belly. [OE *wamb*] —**wombed** *adj.* —ˈ**womb**ˌ**like** *adj.*

wombat (ˈwɒmbæt) *n.* a burrowing herbivorous Australian marsupial having short limbs, a heavy body, and coarse dense fur. [C18: < Abor.]

women (ˈwɪmɪn) *n.* the plural of **woman.**

womenfolk (ˈwɪmɪnˌfəʊk) *pl. n.* 1. women collectively. 2. a group of women, esp. the female members of one's family.

Women's Institute *n.* (in Britain and Commonwealth countries) a society for women interested in engaging in craft and cultural activities.

Women's Liberation *n.* a movement directed towards the removal of attitudes and practices that preserve inequalities based upon the assumption that men are superior to women. Also called: **women's lib.**

Women's Movement *n.* a grass-roots movement of women concerned with women's liberation. See **Women's Liberation.**

won (wʌn) *vb.* the past tense and past participle of **win.**

wonder (ˈwʌndə) *n.* **1.** the feeling excited by something strange; a mixture of surprise, curiosity, and sometimes awe. **2.** something that causes such a feeling, such as a miracle. **3.** (*modifier*) exciting wonder by virtue of spectacular results achieved, feats performed, etc.: *a wonder drug.* **4. do** *or* **work wonders.** to achieve spectacularly fine results. **5. nine days' wonder.** a subject that arouses general surprise or public interest for a short time. **6. no wonder.** (*sentence connector*) (I am) not surprised at all (that): *no wonder he couldn't come.* **7. small wonder.** (*sentence connector*) (I am) hardly surprised (that): *small wonder he couldn't make it tonight.* ~*vb.* (when *tr., may take a clause as object*) **8.** (when *intr.*, often foll. by *about*) to indulge in speculative inquiry: *I wondered about what she said.* **9.** (when *intr.*, often foll. by *at*) to be amazed (at something): *I wonder at your impudence.* [OE *wundor*] —ˈ**wonderer** *n.*

wonderful (ˈwʌndəfʊl) *adj.* **1.** exciting a feeling of wonder. **2.** extremely fine; excellent. —ˈ**wonderfully** *adv.*

wonderland (ˈwʌndəˌlænd) *n.* **1.** an imaginary land of marvels or wonders. **2.** an actual place or scene of great or strange beauty or wonder.

wonderment (ˈwʌndəmənt) *n.* **1.** rapt surprise; awe. **2.** puzzled interest. **3.** something that excites wonder.

wonderwork (ˈwʌndəˌwɜːk) *n.* something done or made that excites wonder. —ˈ**wonderˌworker** *n.* —ˈ**wonder-ˌworking** *n., adj.*

wondrous (ˈwʌndrəs) *Arch. or literary.* ~*adj.* **1.** exciting wonder; marvellous. ~*adv.* **2.** (intensifier): *it is wondrous cold.* —ˈ**wondrously** *adv.* —ˈ**wondrousness** *n.*

wonky (ˈwɒŋkɪ) *adj.* **-kier, -kiest.** *Brit. sl.* **1.** unsteady. **2.** askew. **3.** liable to break down. [C20: var. of dialect *wanky*, < OE *wancol*]

wont (wəʊnt) *adj.* **1.** (*postpositive*) accustomed (to doing something): *he was wont to come early.* ~*n.* **2.** a manner or action habitually employed by or associated with someone (often in **as is my wont, as is his wont,** etc.). ~*vb.* **3.** (when *tr., usually passive*) to become or cause to become accustomed. [OE *gewunod*, p.p. of *wunian* to be accustomed to]

won't (wəʊnt) *contraction of* will not.

wonted (ˈwəʊntɪd) *adj.* **1.** (*postpositive*) accustomed (to doing something). **2.** (*prenominal*) usual: *she is in her wonted place.*

woo (wuː) *vb.* **wooing, wooed. 1.** to seek the affection, favour, or love of (a woman) with a view to marriage. **2.** (*tr.*) to seek after zealously: *to woo fame.* **3.** (*tr.*) to beg or importune (someone). [OE *wōgian*, <?] —ˈ**wooer** *n.* —ˈ**wooing** *n.*

wood (wʊd) *n.* **1.** the hard fibrous substance consisting of xylem tissue that occurs beneath the bark in trees, shrubs, and similar plants. **2.** the trunks of trees that have been cut and prepared for use as a building material. **3.** a collection of trees, shrubs, grasses, etc., usually dominated by one or a few species of tree: usually smaller than a forest: *an oak wood.* Related adj.: **sylvan. 4.** fuel; firewood. **5.** *Golf.* **a.** a long-shafted club with a wooden head, used for driving. **b.** (*as modifier*): *a wood shot.* **6.** *Tennis, etc.* the frame of a racket: *he hit a winning shot off the wood.* **7.** one of the biased wooden bowls used in the game of bowls. **8.** *Music.* short for **woodwind. 9. from the wood.** (of a beverage) from a wooden container rather than a metal or glass one. **10. out of the wood** *or* **woods.** clear of or safe from dangers or doubts: *we're not out of the wood yet.* **11. see the wood for the trees.** (*used with a negative*) to obtain a general view of a situation without allowing details to cloud one's analysis: *he can't see the wood for the trees.* **12.** (*modifier*) made of, employing, or handling wood: *a wood fire.* **13.** (*modifier*) dwelling in or situated in a wood: *a wood nymph.* ~*vb.* **14.** (*tr.*) to plant a wood upon. **15.** to supply or be supplied with firewood. ~See also **woods.** [OE *widu, wudu*]

wood alcohol *n.* another name for **methanol.**

wood anemone *n.* any of several woodland anemone plants having finely divided leaves and solitary white flowers. Also called: **windflower.**

wood avens *n.* another name for **herb bennet.**

woodbine (ˈwuːdˌbaɪn) *n.* **1.** a honeysuckle of Europe, SW Asia, and N Africa, having fragrant yellow flowers. **2.** *U.S.* another name for **Virginia creeper. 3.** *Austral. sl.* an Englishman.

wood block *n.* a small rectangular flat block of wood that is laid with others as a floor surface.

woodcarving (ˈwʊdˌkɑːvɪŋ) *n.* **1.** the act of carving wood. **2.** a work of art produced by carving wood. —ˈ**woodˌcarver** *n.*

woodchuck (ˈwʊdˌtʃʌk) *n.* a North American marmot having coarse reddish-brown fur. Also called: **groundhog.** [C17: by folk etymology < Cree *otcheck* fisher, marten]

woodcock (ˈwʊdˌkɒk) *n.* an Old World game bird resembling the snipe but larger and having shorter legs and neck.

woodcraft (ˈwʊdˌkrɑːft) *n. Chiefly U.S. & Canad.* **1.** ability and experience in matters concerned with living in a wood or forest. **2.** ability or skill at woodwork, carving, etc.

woodcut (ˈwʊdˌkʌt) *n.* **1.** a block of wood with a design, illustration, etc., from which prints are made. **2.** a print from a woodcut.

woodcutter (ˈwʊdˌkʌtə) *n.* **1.** a person who fells trees or chops wood. **2.** a person who makes woodcuts. —ˈ**woodˌcutting** *n.*

wooded (ˈwʊdɪd) *adj.* **a.** covered with or abounding in woods or trees. **b.** (*in combination*): *a soft-wooded tree.*

wooden (ˈwʊdᵊn) *adj.* **1.** made from or consisting of wood. **2.** awkward or clumsy. **3.** bereft of spirit or animation: *a wooden expression.* **4.** obstinately unyielding: *a wooden attitude.* **5.** mentally slow or dull. **6.** not highly resonant: *a wooden thud.* —ˈ**woodenly** *adv.*

wood engraving *n.* **1.** the art of engraving pictures or designs on wood by incising them with a burn. **2.** a block of wood so engraved or a print taken from it. —**wood engraver** *n.*

woodenhead (ˈwʊdᵊnˌhɛd) *n. Inf.* a dull, foolish, or unintelligent person. —ˌ**woodenˈheaded** *adj.* —ˌ**woodenˈheadedness** *n.*

wooden spoon *n.* a booby prize, esp. in sporting contests.

woodgrouse (ˈwʊdˌgraʊs) *n.* another name for **capercaillie.**

woodland (ˈwʊdlənd) *n.* **a.** land that is mostly covered with woods or dense growths of trees and shrubs. **b.** (*as modifier*): *woodland fauna.* —ˈ**woodlander** *n.*

woodlark (ˈwʊdˌlɑːk) *n.* an Old World lark similar to but slightly smaller than the skylark.

woodlouse (ˈwʊdˌlaʊs) *n., pl.* **-lice** (-ˌlaɪs). any of various small terrestrial isopod crustaceans having a flattened segmented body and occurring in damp habitats.

woodman (ˈwʊdmən) *n., pl.* **-men. 1.** a person who looks after and fells trees used for timber. **2.** another word for **woodsman.**

woodnote (ˈwʊdˌnəʊt) *n.* a natural musical note or song, like that of a wild bird.

wood nymph *n.* one of a class of nymphs fabled to inhabit the woods, such as a dryad.

woodpecker (ˈwʊdˌpɛkə) *n.* a climbing bird, such as the **green woodpecker,** having a brightly coloured plumage and strong chisel-like bill with which it bores into trees for insects.

wood pigeon *n.* a large Eurasian pigeon having

white patches on the wings and neck. Also called: **ringdove, cushat.**

woodpile (ˈwʊdˌpaɪl) *n.* a pile or heap of firewood.

wood pulp *n.* **1.** wood that has been ground to a fine pulp for use in making newsprint and other cheap forms of paper. **2.** finely pulped wood that has been digested by a chemical, such as caustic soda: used in making paper.

woodruff (ˈwʊdrʌf) *n.* any of several plants, esp. the sweet woodruff of Eurasia, which has small sweet-scented white flowers and whorls of narrow fragrant leaves used to flavour wine and liqueurs and in perfumery. [OE *wudurofe,* < WOOD + *rōfe*]

woods (wʊdz) *pl. n.* **1.** closely packed trees forming a forest or wood, esp. a specific one. **2.** another word for **backwoods** (sense 2). **3.** the woodwind instruments in an orchestra.

woodscrew (ˈwʊdˌskruː) *n.* a metal screw that tapers to a point so that it can be driven into wood by a screwdriver.

woodshed (ˈwʊdˌʃɛd) *n.* a small outbuilding where firewood, garden tools, etc., are stored.

woodsman (ˈwʊdzmən) *n., pl.* **-men.** a person who lives in a wood or who is skilled in woodcraft. Also called: **woodman.**

wood sorrel *n.* a Eurasian plant having trifoliate leaves, an underground creeping stem, and white purple-veined flowers.

wood spirit *n. Chem.* another name for **methanol.**

wood tar *n.* any tar produced by the destructive distillation of wood.

wood warbler *n.* **1.** a European woodland warbler with a dull yellow plumage. **2.** another name for the **American warbler.** See **warbler** (sense 3).

woodwind (ˈwʊdˌwɪnd) *Music.* ~*adj.* **1.** of, relating to, or denoting a type of wind instrument, formerly made of wood but now often made of metal, such as the flute. ~*n.* **2.** (*functioning as pl.*) woodwind instruments collectively.

woodwork (ˈwʊdˌwɜːk) *n.* **1.** the art or craft of making things in wood. **2.** components made of wood, such as doors, staircases, etc.

woodworking (ˈwʊdˌwɜːkɪŋ) *n.* **1.** the process of working wood. ~*adj.* **2.** of, relating to, or used in woodworking. —ˈ**wood**ˌ**worker** *n.*

woodworm (ˈwʊdˌwɜːm) *n.* **1.** any of various insect larvae that bore into wooden furniture, beams, etc., esp. the larvae of the furniture beetle and the deathwatch beetle. **2.** the condition caused in wood by any of these larvae.

woody (ˈwʊdɪ) *adj.* **woodier, woodiest. 1.** abounding in or covered with forest or woods. **2.** connected with, belonging to, or situated in a wood. **3.** consisting of or containing wood or lignin: *woody tissue; woody stems.* **4.** resembling wood in hardness or texture. —ˈ**woodiness** *n.*

woodyard (ˈwʊdˌjɑːd) *n.* a place where timber is cut and stored.

woody nightshade *n.* a scrambling woody Eurasian plant, having purple flowers and producing poisonous red berry-like fruits. Also called: **bittersweet.**

woof[1] (wuːf) *n.* **1.** the crosswise yarns that fill the warp yarns in weaving; weft. **2.** a woven fabric or its texture. [OE *ōwef,* < *ō-,* ? < ON, + *wef* web (see WEAVE); modern form infl. by WARP]

woof[2] (wʊf) *interj.* **1.** an imitation of the bark or growl of a dog. ~*vb.* **2.** (*intr.*) (of dogs) to bark.

woofer (ˈwuːfə) *n.* a loudspeaker used in high-fidelity systems for the reproduction of low audio frequencies.

wool (wʊl) *n.* **1.** the outer coat of sheep, yaks, etc., which consists of short curly hairs. **2.** yarn spun from the coat of sheep, etc., used in weaving, knitting, etc. **3. a.** cloth or a garment made from this yarn. **b.** (*as modifier*): *a wool dress.* **4.** any of certain fibrous materials: *glass wool; steel wool.* **5.** *Inf.* short thick curly hair. **6.** a tangled mass of soft fine hairs that occurs in certain plants. **7. keep one's wool on.** *Brit. inf.* to keep one's temper. **8. pull the wool over someone's eyes.** to deceive or delude someone. [OE *wull*] —ˈ**wool-**ˌ**like** *adj.*

wool clip *n.* the total amount of wool shorn from a particular flock in one year.

wool fat *or* **grease** *n.* another name for **lanolin.**

woolfell (ˈwʊlˌfɛl) *n. Obs.* the skin of a sheep or similar animal with the fleece still attached.

woolgathering (ˈwʊlˌgæðərɪŋ) *n.* idle or absent-minded daydreaming.

woolgrower (ˈwʊlˌgrəʊə) *n.* a person who keeps sheep for their wool. —ˈ**wool**ˌ**growing** *n.*

woollen *or U.S.* **woolen** (ˈwʊlən) *adj.* **1.** relating to or consisting partly or wholly of wool. ~*n.* **2.** (*often pl.*) a garment or piece of cloth made wholly or partly of wool, esp. a knitted one.

woolly *or U.S.* (*often*) **wooly** (ˈwʊlɪ) *adj.* **-lier, -liest. 1.** consisting of, resembling, or having the nature of wool. **2.** covered or clothed in wool or something resembling it. **3.** lacking clarity or substance: *woolly thinking.* **4.** *Bot.* covered with long soft whitish hairs: *woolly stems.* ~*n., pl.* **-lies. 5.** (*often pl.*) a garment, such as a sweater, made of wool or something similar. —ˈ**woollily** *adv.* —ˈ**woolliness** *n.*

woolly bear *n.* the caterpillar of any of various tiger moths, having a dense covering of soft hairs.

woolpack (ˈwʊlˌpæk) *n.* **1.** the cloth wrapping used to pack a bale of wool. **2.** a bale of wool.

woolsack (ˈwʊlˌsæk) *n.* **1.** a sack containing or intended to contain wool. **2.** (in Britain) the seat of the Lord Chancellor in the House of Lords, formerly made of a large square sack of wool.

woolshed (ˈwʊlˌʃɛd) *n. Austral. & N.Z.* a large building in which sheepshearing takes place.

wool stapler *n.* a person who sorts wool into different grades or classifications.

woomera *or* **womera** (ˈwʊmərə) *n. Austral.* a type of notched stick used by Australian Aborigines to increase leverage and propulsion in the throwing of a spear. [< Abor.]

Woop Woop (ˈwuːp ˌwuːp) *n. Austral. sl.* a jocular name for any backward or remote town or district.

woozy (ˈwuːzɪ) *adj.* **woozier, wooziest.** *Inf.* **1.** dazed or confused. **2.** experiencing dizziness, nausea, etc. [C19: ? a blend of *woolly* + *muzzy* or *dizzy*] —ˈ**woozily** *adv.* —ˈ**wooziness** *n.*

wop (wɒp) *n. Sl., derog.* a member of a Latin people, esp. an Italian. [C20: prob. < It. dialect *guappo* dandy, < Sp. *guapo*]

Worcester sauce (ˈwʊstə) *or* **Worcestershire sauce** *n.* a commercially prepared piquant sauce, made from a basis of soy sauce, with vinegar, spices, etc.

Worcs. *abbrev. for* Worcestershire.

word (wɜːd) *n.* **1.** one of the units of speech or writing that is the smallest isolable meaningful element of the language, although linguists would analyse these further into morphemes. **2.** an instance of vocal intercourse; chat, talk, or discussion: *to have a word with someone.* **3.** an utterance or expression, esp. a brief one: *a word of greeting.* **4.** news or information: *he sent word that he would be late.* **5.** a verbal signal for action; command: *when I give the word, fire!* **6.** an undertaking or promise: *he kept his word.* **7.** an autocratic decree; order: *his word must be obeyed.* **8.** a watchword or slogan, as of a political party: *the word now is "freedom".* **9.** *Computers.* a set of bits used to store, transmit, or operate upon an item of information in a computer. **10. as good as one's word.** doing what one has undertaken to do. **11. at a word.** at once. **12. by word of mouth.** orally rather than by written means. **13. in a word.** briefly or in short. **14. my word! a.** an exclamation of surprise, annoyance, etc. **b.** *Austral.* an exclamation of agreement. **15. of one's word.** given to or noted for keeping one's promises: *I am a man of my word.* **16. put in a word** *or* **good word for.** to make favourable mention of (someone); recommend. **17. take someone at his** *or* **her word.** to assume that someone means, or will do, what he or she says: *when he told her to go, she took him at his word and left.* **18. take someone's word for**

it. to accept or believe what someone says. **19. the last word. a.** the closing remark of a conversation or argument, esp. a remark that supposedly settles an issue. **b.** the latest or most fashionable design, make, or model: *the last word in bikinis.* **c.** the finest example (of some quality, condition, etc.): *the last word in luxury.* **20. the word.** the proper or most fitting expression: *cold is not the word for it, it's freezing!* **21. upon my word! a.** *Arch.* on my honour. **b.** an exclamation of surprise, annoyance, etc. **22. word for word.** (of a report, etc.) using exactly the same words as those employed in the situation being reported; verbatim. **23. word of honour.** a promise; oath. **24.** (*modifier*) of, relating to, or consisting of words: *a word list.* ~*vb.* **25.** (*tr.*) to state in words, usually specially selected ones; phrase. ~See also **words.** [OE] —**'wordless** *adj.* —**'wordlessly** *adv.*

Word (wɜːd) *n.* **the. 1.** *Christianity.* the 2nd person of the Trinity. **2.** Scripture, the Bible, or the Gospels as embodying or representing divine revelation. Often called: **the Word of God.** [translation of Gk *logos,* as in John 1:1]

wordage ('wɜːdɪdʒ) *n.* words considered collectively, esp. a quantity of words.

word association *n.* an early method of psychoanalysis in which the patient thinks of the first word that comes into consciousness on hearing a given word. In this way it was claimed that aspects of the unconscious could be revealed before defence mechanisms intervene.

word blindness *n.* the nontechnical name for **alexia** and **dyslexia.** —**'word-ˌblind** *adj.*

wordbook ('wɜːdˌbʊk) *n.* a book containing words, usually with their meanings.

word deafness *n.* loss of ability to understand spoken words, esp. as the result of a cerebral lesion. Also called: **auditory aphasia.**

word game *n.* any game involving the formation, discovery, or alteration of a word or words.

wording ('wɜːdɪŋ) *n.* **1.** the way in which words are used to express a statement, report, etc., esp. a written one. **2.** the words themselves.

word order *n.* the arrangement of words in a phrase, clause, or sentence.

word-perfect *or U.S.* **letter-perfect** *adj.* **1.** correct in every detail. **2.** (of a speaker, actor, etc.) knowing one's speech, role, etc., perfectly.

wordplay ('wɜːdˌpleɪ) *n.* verbal wit based on the meanings of words; puns, repartee, etc.

word processing *n.* the storage and organization of written text by electronic means, esp. for business purposes.

word processor *n.* an installation for word processing, typically consisting of a keyboard and a VDU incorporating a microprocessor, with storage and processing capabilities.

words (wɜːdz) *pl. n.* **1.** the text of a part of an actor, etc. **2.** the text of a song, as opposed to the music. **3.** angry speech (esp. in **have words with someone**). **4. eat** *or* **swallow one's words.** to retract a statement. **5. for words.** (preceded by *too* and an adj. or adv.) indescribably; extremely: *the play was too funny for words.* **6. have no words for.** to be incapable of describing. **7. in other words.** expressing the same idea but differently. **8. in so many words.** explicitly or precisely. **9. of many** (*or* **few**) **words.** (not) talkative. **10. put into words.** to express in speech or writing. **11. say a few words.** to give a brief speech. **12. take the words out of someone's mouth.** to say exactly what someone else was about to say. **13. words fail me.** I am too happy, sad, amazed, etc., to express my thoughts.

word square *n.* a puzzle in which the player must fill a square grid with words that read the same across as down.

word wrapping *n. Computers.* the automatic shifting of a word at the end of a line to a new line in order to keep within preset margins.

wordy ('wɜːdɪ) *adj.* **wordier, wordiest.** using or containing an excess of words: *a wordy document.* —**'wordily** *adv.* —**'wordiness** *n.*

wore (wɔː) *vb.* the past tense of **wear**[1] and **wear**[2].

work (wɜːk) *n.* **1.** physical or mental effort directed towards doing or making something. **2.** paid employment at a job or a trade, occupation, or profession. **3.** a duty, task, or undertaking. **4.** something done, made, etc., as a result of effort or exertion: *a work of art.* **5.** another word for **workmanship** (sense 3). **6.** the place, office, etc., where a person is employed. **7. a.** decoration, esp. of a specified kind. **b.** (*in combination*): *wirework.* **8.** an engineering structure such as a bridge, building, etc. **9.** *Physics.* the transfer of energy expressed as the product of a force and the distance through which its point of application moves in the direction of the force. **10.** a structure, wall, etc., built or used as part of a fortification system. **11. at work. a.** at one's job or place of employment. **b.** in action; operating. **12. make short work of.** *Inf.* to dispose of very quickly. **13.** (*modifier*) of, relating to, or used for work: *work clothes; a work permit; a work song.* ~*vb.* **14.** (*intr.*) to exert effort in order to do, make, or perform something. **15.** (*intr.*) to be employed. **16.** (*tr.*) to carry on operations, activity, etc., in (a place or area): *that salesman works Yorkshire.* **17.** (*tr.*) to cause to labour or toil: *he works his men hard.* **18.** to operate or cause to operate, esp. properly or effectively: *to work a lathe; that clock doesn't work.* **19.** (*tr.*) to till or cultivate (land). **20.** to handle or manipulate or be handled or manipulated: *to work dough.* **21.** to shape or process or be shaped or processed: *to work copper.* **22.** to reach or cause to reach a specific condition, esp. gradually: *the rope worked loose.* **23.** (*intr.*) to move in agitation: *his face worked with anger.* **24.** (*tr.; often foll. by* up) to provoke or arouse: *to work someone into a frenzy.* **25.** (*tr.*) to effect or accomplish: *to work one's revenge.* **26.** to make (one's way) with effort: *he worked his way through the crowd.* **27.** (*tr.*) to make or decorate by hand in embroidery, tapestry, etc.: *she was working a sampler.* **28.** (*intr.*) (of liquids) to ferment, as in brewing. **29.** (*tr.*) *Inf.* to manipulate or exploit to one's own advantage. ~See also **work in, work off,** etc., **works.** [OE *weorc* (n.), *wircan, wyrcan* (vb.)] —**'workless** *adj.*

workable ('wɜːkəbᵊl) *adj.* **1.** practicable or feasible. **2.** able to be worked. —**ˌworka'bility** *or* **'workableness** *n.*

workaday ('wɜːkəˌdeɪ) *adj.* (*usually prenominal*) **1.** being a part of general human experience; ordinary. **2.** suitable for working days; everyday or practical.

workaholic (ˌwɜːkə'hɒlɪk) *n.* a person obsessively addicted to work. [C20: < WORK + -HOLIC, coined in 1971 by U.S. author Wayne Oates]

workbag ('wɜːkˌbæg) *n.* a container for implements, tools, or materials, esp. sewing equipment. Also called: **work basket, workbox.**

workbench ('wɜːkˌbɛntʃ) *n.* a heavy table at which work is done by a carpenter, mechanic, toolmaker, etc.

workbook ('wɜːkˌbʊk) *n.* **1.** an exercise book used for study, esp. with spaces for answers. **2.** a book of instructions for some process. **3.** a book in which is recorded all work done or planned.

work camp *n.* a camp set up for young people who voluntarily do manual work on a worthwhile project.

workday ('wɜːkˌdeɪ) *n.* **1.** the usual U.S. and Canad. term for **working day.** ~*adj.* **2.** another word for **workaday.**

worked (wɜːkt) *adj.* made or decorated with evidence of workmanship; wrought, as with embroidery or tracery.

worked up *adj.* excited or agitated.

worker ('wɜːkə) *n.* **1.** a person or thing that works, usually at a specific job: *a research worker.* **2.** an employee, as opposed to an employer or manager. **3.** a manual labourer working in a manufacturing industry. **4.** any other member of the working class. **5.** a sterile female member of a colony of bees, ants, or wasps that forages for food, cares for the larvae, etc.

worker director *n.* (in certain British companies) an employee of a company chosen by his or her fellow workers to represent their interests on the board of directors. Also called: **employee director.**

worker-priest *n.* a Roman Catholic priest who has employment in a secular job to be more in touch with the problems of the laity.

work ethic *n.* a belief in the moral value of work.

workforce (ˈwɜːkˌfɔːs) *n.* **1.** the total number of workers employed by a company on a specific job, project, etc. **2.** the total number of people who could be employed: *the country's workforce is growing.*

work function *n. Physics.* the minimum energy required to transfer an electron from a point within a solid to a point just outside its surface. Symbol: ϕ or Φ

work-harden *vb.* (*tr.*) to increase the strength or hardness of (a metal) by a mechanical process, such as tension, compression, or torsion.

workhorse (ˈwɜːkˌhɔːs) *n.* **1.** a horse used for nonrecreational activities. **2.** *Inf.* a person who takes on the greatest amount of work in a project.

workhouse (ˈwɜːkˌhaʊs) *n.* **1.** (formerly in England) an institution maintained at public expense where able-bodied paupers did unpaid work in return for food and accommodation. **2.** (in the U.S.) a prison for petty offenders serving short sentences at manual labour.

work in *vb.* (*adv.*) **1.** to insert or become inserted: *she worked the patch in carefully.* **2.** (*tr.*) to find space for: *I'll work this job in during the day.* ~*n.* **work-in. 3.** a form of industrial action in which a factory that is to be closed down is occupied and run by its workers.

working (ˈwɜːkɪŋ) *n.* **1.** the operation or mode of operation of something. **2.** the act or process of moulding something pliable. **3.** a convulsive or jerking motion, as from excitement. **4.** (*often pl.*) a part of a mine or quarry that is being or has been worked. **5.** a record of the steps by which the solution of a problem, calculation, etc., is obtained: *all working is to be submitted to the examiners.* ~*adj.* (*prenominal*) **6.** relating to or concerned with a person or thing that works: *a working man.* **7.** concerned with, used in, or suitable for work: *working clothes.* **8.** (of a meal or occasion) during which business discussions are carried on: *a working lunch.* **9.** capable of being operated or used: *a working model; in working order.* **10.** adequate for normal purposes: *a working majority; a working knowledge of German.* **11.** (of a theory, etc.) providing a basis, usually a temporary one, on which operations or procedures may be carried out.

working bee *n. N.Z.* a voluntary group doing a job for charity.

working capital *n.* **1.** *Accounting.* current assets minus current liabilities. **2.** current or liquid assets. **3.** that part of the capital of a business enterprise available for operations.

working class *n.* **1.** Also called: **proletariat.** the social stratum, usually of low status, that consists of those who earn wages, esp. as manual workers. ~*adj.* **working-class. 2.** of, relating to, or characteristic of the working class.

working day *or esp. U.S. & Canad.* **workday** *n.* **1.** a day on which work is done, esp. for an agreed or stipulated number of hours in return for a salary or wage. **2.** the part of the day allocated to work.

working drawing *n.* a scale drawing of a part that provides a guide for manufacture.

working party *n.* **1.** a committee established to investigate a problem, question, etc. **2.** a group of soldiers or prisoners assigned to perform some manual task or duty.

working week *or esp. U.S. & Canad.* **workweek** *n.* the number of hours or days in a week allocated to work.

workload (ˈwɜːkˌləʊd) *n.* the amount of work to be done, esp. in a specified period.

workman (ˈwɜːkmən) *n., pl.* **-men. 1.** a man who is employed in manual labour or who works an industrial machine. **2.** a craftsman of skill as specified: *a bad workman.*

workmanlike (ˈwɜːkmənˌlaɪk) *or* (*less commonly*) **workmanly** *adj.* appropriate to or befitting a good workman.

workmanship (ˈwɜːkmənʃɪp) *n.* **1.** the art or skill of a workman. **2.** the art or skill with which something is made or executed. **3.** the degree of art or skill exhibited in the finished product. **4.** the piece of work so produced.

workmate (ˈwɜːkˌmeɪt) *n.* a person who works with another; fellow worker.

work of art *n.* **1.** a piece of fine art, such as a painting or sculpture. **2.** something that may be likened to a piece of fine art, esp. in beauty, intricacy, etc.

work off *vb.* (*tr., adv.*) **1.** to get rid of or dissipate, as by effort: *he worked off some of his energy by digging the garden.* **2.** to discharge (a debt) by labour rather than payment.

work on *vb.* (*intr., prep.*) to persuade or influence or attempt to persuade or influence.

work out *vb.* (*adv.*) **1.** (*tr.*) to achieve or accomplish by effort. **2.** (*tr.*) to solve or find out by reasoning or calculation: *to work out an answer; to work out a sum.* **3.** (*tr.*) to devise or formulate: *to work out a plan.* **4.** (*intr.*) to prove satisfactory: *did your plan work out?* **5.** (*intr.*) to happen as specified: *it all worked out well.* **6.** (*intr.*) to take part in physical exercise, as in training. **7.** (*tr.*) to remove all the mineral in (a mine, etc.) that can be profitably exploited. **8.** (*intr.*; often foll. by *to* or *at*) to reach a total: *your bill works out at a pound.* ~*n.* **workout. 9.** a session of physical exercise, esp. for training or to keep onself fit.

work over *vb.* **1.** (*tr., adv.*) to do again; repeat. **2.** (*intr., prep.*) to examine closely and thoroughly. **3.** (*tr., adv.*) *Sl.* to assault or thrash.

workpeople (ˈwɜːkˌpiːpᵊl) *pl. n.* the working members of a population.

workroom (ˈwɜːkˌruːm, -ˌrʊm) *n.* **1.** a room in which work, usually manual labour, is done. **2.** a room in a house set aside for a hobby.

works (wɜːks) *pl. n.* **1.** (*often functioning as sing.*) a place where a number of people are employed, such as a factory. **2.** the sum total of a writer's or artist's achievements, esp. when considered together: *the works of Shakespeare.* **3.** the deeds of a person, esp. virtuous or moral deeds: *works of charity.* **4.** the interior parts of the mechanism of a machine, etc.: *the works of a clock.* **5. the works.** *Sl.* **a.** full or extreme treatment. **b.** a very violent physical beating: *to give someone the works.*

works council *n. Chiefly Brit.* **1.** a council composed of both employer and employees convened to discuss matters of common interest concerning a factory, plant, business policy, etc. **2.** a body representing the workers of a plant, factory, etc., elected to negotiate with the management about working conditions, wages, etc. ~Also called: **works committee.**

work sheet *n.* **1.** a sheet of paper used for the rough draft of a problem, design, etc. **2.** a piece of paper recording work in progress.

workshop (ˈwɜːkˌʃɒp) *n.* **1.** a room or building in which manufacturing or other forms of manual work are carried on. **2.** a room in a private dwelling, school, etc., set aside for crafts. **3.** a group of people engaged in study or work on a creative project or subject: *a music workshop.*

workshy (ˈwɜːkˌʃaɪ) *adj.* not inclined to work.

work station *n.* an area in an office where one person works.

work-study *n.* an examination of ways of finding the most efficient method of doing a job.

worktable (ˈwɜːkˌteɪbᵊl) *n.* **a.** any table at which writing, sewing, or other work may be done. **b.** (in English cabinetwork) a small elegant table fitted with sewing accessories.

worktop (ˈwɜːkˌtɒp) *n.* a surface in a kitchen,

often of heat-resistant plastic, used for food preparation.

work-to-rule *n.* **1.** a form of industrial action in which employees adhere strictly to all the working rules laid down by their employers, with the deliberate intention of reducing the rate of working. *~vb.* **work to rule. 2.** (*intr.*) to decrease the rate of working by this means.

work up *vb.* **1.** (*tr., adv.*) to arouse the feelings of; excite. **2.** (*tr., adv.*) to cause to grow or develop: *to work up a hunger.* **3.** to move or cause to move gradually upwards. **4.** (*tr., adv.*) to manipulate or mix into a specified object or shape. **5.** (*tr., adv.*) to gain skill at (a subject). **6.** (*adv.*) (foll. by *to*) to develop gradually or progress (towards): *working up to a climax.*

world (wɜːld) *n.* **1.** the earth as a planet, esp. including its inhabitants. **2.** mankind; the human race. **3.** people generally; the public: *in the eyes of the world.* **4.** social or public life: *to go out into the world.* **5.** the universe or cosmos; everything in existence. **6.** a complex united whole regarded as resembling the universe. **7.** any star or planet, esp. one that might be inhabited. **8.** (*often cap.*) a division or section of the earth, its history, or its inhabitants: *the Ancient World; the Third World.* **9.** an area, sphere, or realm considered as a complete environment: *the animal world.* **10.** any field of human activity or way of life or those involved in it: *the world of television.* **11.** a period or state of existence: *the next world.* **12.** the total circumstances and experience of an individual that make up his life: *you have shattered my world.* **13.** a large amount, number, or distance: *worlds apart.* **14.** worldly or secular life, ways, or people. **15. bring into the world. a.** (of a midwife, doctor, etc.) to deliver (a baby). **b.** to give birth to. **16. come into the world.** to be born. **17. for all the world.** in every way; exactly. **18. for the world.** (*used with a negative*) for any inducement, however great. **19. in the world.** (intensifier; *usually used with a negative*): *no-one in the world can change things.* **20. man** (*or* **woman**) **of the world.** a man (or woman) experienced in social or public life. **21. not long for this world.** nearing death. **22. on top of the world.** *Inf.* elated or very happy. **23. out of this world.** *Inf.* wonderful; excellent. **24. set the world on fire.** to be exceptionally or sensationally successful. **25. the best of both worlds.** the benefits from two different ways of life, philosophies, etc. **26. think the world of.** to be extremely fond of or hold in very high esteem. **27. world of one's own.** a state of mental detachment from other people. **28. world without end.** for ever. **29.** (*modifier*) of or concerning most or all countries; worldwide: *world politics; a world record.* **30.** (*in combination*) throughout the world: *world-famous.* [OE *w(e)orold,* < *wer* man + *ald* age, life]

World Bank *n.* an international cooperative organization established in 1945 to assist economic development, esp. of backward nations, by the advance of loans guaranteed by member governments. Officially called: **International Bank for Reconstruction and Development.**

world-beater *n.* a person or thing that surpasses all others in its category; champion.

World Court *n.* another name for **International Court of Justice.**

World Cup *n.* an international association football championship competition held every four years between national teams selected through preliminary tournaments.

worldling (ˈwɜːldlɪŋ) *n.* a person who is primarily concerned with worldly matters.

worldly (ˈwɜːldlɪ) *adj.* **-lier, -liest. 1.** not spiritual; mundane or temporal. **2.** Also: **worldly-minded.** absorbed in or concerned with material things. **3.** Also: **worldly-wise.** versed in the ways of the world; sophisticated. —ˈ**worldliness** *n.*

world power *n.* a state that possesses sufficient power to influence events throughout the world.

world-shaking *adj.* of enormous significance; momentous.

World War I *n.* the war (1914–18), fought mainly in Europe and the Middle East, in which the Allies (principally France, Russia, Britain, Italy after 1915, and the U.S. after 1917) defeated the Central Powers (principally Germany, Austria-Hungary, and Turkey). Also called: **First World War, Great War.**

World War II *n.* the war (1939–45) in which the Allies (Britain and France) declared war on Germany (Sept. 3, 1939) as a result of the German invasion of Poland (Sept. 1, 1939). Italy entered the war on the side of Germany (forming the Axis) on June 10, 1940. On June 22, 1941 the Axis powers attacked the Soviet Union and on Dec. 7, 1941 the Japanese attacked the U.S. at Pearl Harbor. On Sept. 8, 1943 Italy surrendered, the war in Europe ending on May 7, 1945 with the unconditional surrender of the Germans. The Japanese capitulated on Aug. 14, 1945. Also called: **Second World War.**

world-weary *adj.* no longer finding pleasure in living. —ˈ**world-ˌweariness** *n.*

worldwide (ˈwɜːldˈwaɪd) *adj.* applying or extending throughout the world; universal.

worm (wɜːm) *n.* **1.** any of various invertebrates, esp. the annelids (earthworms, etc.), nematodes (roundworms), and flatworms, having a slender elongated body. **2.** any of various insect larvae having an elongated body, such as the silkworm and wireworm. **3.** any of various unrelated animals that resemble annelids, nematodes, etc., such as the glow-worm and shipworm. **4.** a gnawing or insinuating force or agent that torments or slowly eats away. **5.** a wretched or spineless person. **6.** anything that resembles a worm in appearance or movement. **7.** a shaft on which a helical groove has been cut, as in a gear arrangement in which such a shaft meshes with a toothed wheel. **8.** a spiral pipe cooled by air or flowing water, used as a condenser in a still. *~vb.* **9.** to move, act, or cause to move or act with the slow sinuous movement of a worm. **10.** (foll. by *in, into, out of,* etc.) to make (one's way) slowly and stealthily; insinuate (oneself). **11.** (*tr.; often foll. by out of or from*) to extract (information, etc.) from by persistent questioning. **12.** (*tr.*) to free from or purge of worms. ~See also **worms.** [OE *wyrm*] —ˈ**wormer** *n.* —ˈ**wormˌlike** *adj.*

WORM (wɜːm) *n. Computers. acronym for* write once read many times: an optical disk which enables users to store their own data.

wormcast (ˈwɜːmˌkɑːst) *n.* a coil of earth or sand that has been excreted by a burrowing earthworm or lugworm.

worm-eaten *adj.* **1.** eaten into by worms: *a worm-eaten table.* **2.** decayed; rotten. **3.** old-fashioned; antiquated.

worm gear *n.* **1.** a device consisting of a threaded shaft (**worm**) that mates with a gear-wheel (**worm wheel**) so that rotary motion can be transferred between two shafts at right angles to each other. **2.** Also called: **worm wheel.** a gear-wheel driven by a threaded shaft or worm.

wormhole (ˈwɜːmˌhəʊl) *n.* a hole made by a worm in timber, plants, etc. —ˈ**wormˌholed** *adj.*

worms (wɜːmz) *n.* (*functioning as sing.*) any disease or disorder, usually of the intestine, characterized by infestation with parasitic worms.

worm's eye view *n.* a view seen from below or from a more lowly or humble point.

wormwood (ˈwɜːmˌwʊd) *n.* **1.** Also called: **absinthe.** any of various plants of a chiefly N temperate genus, esp. a European plant yielding a bitter extract used in making absinthe. **2.** something that embitters, such as a painful experience. [C15: changed (through infl. of WORM & WOOD) < OE *wormōd, wermōd*]

wormy (ˈwɜːmɪ) *adj.* **wormier, wormiest. 1.** worm-infested or worm-eaten. **2.** resembling a worm in appearance, ways, or condition. **3.** (of wood) having irregular small tunnels bored into it and tracked over its surface, made by worms. **4.** low or grovelling. —ˈ**worminess** *n.*

worn (wɔːn) *vb.* **1.** the past participle of **wear**[1] and **wear**[2]. *~adj.* **2.** affected, esp. adversely, by long use or action: *a worn suit.* **3.** haggard; drawn. **4.** exhausted; spent. —**'wornness** *n.*

worn-out *adj.* (**worn out** *when postpositive*). **1.** worn or used until threadbare, valueless, or useless. **2.** exhausted; very weary.

worriment ('wʌrɪmənt) *n. Inf., chiefly U.S.* anxiety or the trouble that causes it; worry.

worrisome ('wʌrɪsəm) *adj.* **1.** causing worry; vexing. **2.** tending to worry. —**'worrisomely** *adv.*

worrit ('wʌrɪt) *vb.* (*tr.*) *Dialect.* to tease or worry. [prob. var. of WORRY]

worry ('wʌrɪ) *vb.* **-rying, -ried. 1.** to be or cause to be anxious or uneasy, esp. about something uncertain or potentially dangerous. **2.** (*tr.*) to disturb the peace of mind of; bother: *don't worry me with trivialities.* **3.** (*intr.;* often foll. by *along* or *through*) to proceed despite difficulties. **4.** (*intr.;* often foll. by *away*) to struggle or work: *to worry away at a problem.* **5.** (*tr.*) (of a dog, wolf, etc.) to lacerate or kill by biting, shaking, etc. **6.** (when *intr.*, foll. by *at*) to bite, tear, or gnaw (at) with the teeth: *a dog worrying a bone.* **7.** (*tr.*) to touch or poke repeatedly and idly. **8. not to worry.** *Inf.* you need not worry. ~*n., pl.* **-ries. 9.** a state or feeling of anxiety. **10.** a person or thing that causes anxiety. **11.** an act of worrying. [OE *wyrgan*] —**'worried** *adj.* —**'worriedly** *adv.* —**'worrying** *adj.* —**'worryingly** *adv.*

worry beads *pl. n.* a string of beads that when fingered or played with supposedly relieves nervous tension.

worryguts ('wʌrɪˌgʌts) *n.* (*functioning as sing.*) *Inf.* a person who tends to worry, esp. about insignificant matters.

worse (wɜːs) *adj.* **1.** the comparative of **bad**[1]. **2. none the worse for.** not harmed by (adverse events or circumstances). **3. the worse for wear. a.** shabby or worn. **b.** a slang term for **drunk. 4. worse luck!** *Inf.* unhappily; unfortunately. **5. worse off.** (*postpositive*) in a worse, esp. a worse financial, condition. ~*n.* **6.** something that is worse. **7. for the worse.** into a less desirable or inferior state or condition: *a change for the worse.* ~*adv.* **8.** in a more severe or unpleasant manner. **9.** in a less effective or successful manner. [OE *wiersa*]

worsen ('wɜːsᵊn) *vb.* to grow or cause to grow worse.

worship ('wɜːʃɪp) *vb.* **-shipping, -shipped** *or U.S.* **-shiping, -shiped. 1.** (*tr.*) to show profound religious devotion and respect to; adore or venerate (God or any person or thing considered divine). **2.** (*tr.*) to be devoted to and full of admiration for. **3.** (*intr.*) to have or express feelings of profound adoration. **4.** (*intr.*) to attend services for worship. ~*n.* **5.** religious adoration or devotion. **6.** the formal expression of religious adoration; rites, prayers, etc. **7.** admiring love or devotion. [OE *weorthscipe*] —**'worshipper** *n.*

Worship ('wɜːʃɪp) *n. Chiefly Brit.* (preceded by *Your, His,* or *Her*) a title used to address or refer to a mayor, magistrate, etc.

worshipful ('wɜːʃɪpfʊl) *adj.* **1.** feeling or showing reverence or adoration. **2.** (*often cap.*) *Chiefly Brit.* a title used to address or refer to various people or bodies of distinguished rank. —**'worshipfully** *adv.* —**'worshipfulness** *n.*

worst (wɜːst) *adj.* **1.** the superlative of **bad**[1]. ~*adv.* **2.** in the most extreme or bad manner or degree. **3.** least well, suitably, or acceptably. **4.** (*in combination*) in or to the smallest degree or extent; least: *worst-loved.* ~*n.* **5. the worst.** the least good or most inferior person, thing, or part in a group, narrative, etc. **6.** (often preceded by *at*) the most poor, unpleasant, or unskilled quality or condition: *television is at its worst these days.* **7.** the greatest amount of damage or wickedness of which a person or group is capable: *the invaders came and did their worst.* **8.** the weakest effort or poorest achievement that a person or group is capable of making: *the applicant did his worst at the test because he did not want the job.* **9. at worst. a.** in the least favourable interpretation or view. **b.** under the least favourable conditions. **10. come off worst** *or* **get the worst of it.** to enjoy the least benefit from an issue or be defeated in it. **11. if the worst comes to the worst.** if all the more desirable alternatives become impossible or if the worst possible thing happens. ~*vb.* **12.** (*tr.*) to get the advantage over; defeat or beat. [OE *wierrest*]

worsted ('wʊstɪd) *n.* **1.** a closely twisted yarn or thread made from combed long-staple wool. **2.** a fabric made from this, with a hard smooth close-textured surface and no nap. **3.** (*modifier*) made of this yarn or fabric: *a worsted suit.* [C13: after *Worstead,* a district in Norfolk]

wort (wɜːt) *n.* **1.** (*in combination*) any of various unrelated plants, esp. ones formerly used to cure diseases: *liverwort.* **2.** the sweet liquid from the soaked mixture of warm water and ground malt, used to make a malt liquor. [OE *wyrt* root]

worth (wɜːθ) *adj.* (governing a noun with prepositional force) **1.** worthy of; meriting or justifying: *it's not worth discussing.* **2.** having a value of: *the book is worth £30.* **3. for all one is worth.** to the utmost. **4. worth one's weight in gold.** extremely helpful, kind, etc. ~*n.* **5.** high quality; excellence. **6.** value; price. **7.** the amount of something of a specified value: *five pounds' worth of petrol.* [OE *weorth*]

worthless ('wɜːθlɪs) *adj.* **1.** without value or usefulness. **2.** without merit; good-for-nothing. —**'worthlessly** *adv.* —**'worthlessness** *n.*

worthwhile ('wɜːθ'waɪl) *adj.* sufficiently important, rewarding, or valuable to justify time or effort spent.

worthy ('wɜːðɪ) *adj.* **-thier, -thiest. 1.** (*postpositive;* often foll. by *of* or an infinitive) having sufficient merit or value (for something or someone specified); deserving. **2.** having worth, value, or merit. ~*n., pl.* **-thies. 3.** *Often facetious.* a person of merit or importance. —**'worthily** *adv.* —**'worthiness** *n.*

wot (wɒt) *vb. Arch. or dialect.* (used with *I, she, he, it,* or a singular noun) a form of the present tense (indicative mood) of **wit**[2].

would (wʊd; *unstressed* wəd) *vb.* (takes an infinitive without *to* or an implied infinitive) used as an auxiliary: **1.** to form the past tense or subjunctive mood of **will**[1]. **2.** (with *you, he, she, it, they,* or a noun as subject) to indicate willingness or desire in a polite manner: *would you help me, please?* **3.** to describe a past action as being accustomed or habitual: *every day we would go for walks.* **4.** I wish: *would that he were here.*

▷ **Usage.** See at **should.**

would-be *adj.* (*prenominal*) **1.** *Usually derog.* wanting or professing to be: *a would-be politician.* **2.** intended to be: *would-be generosity.*

wouldn't ('wʊdᵊnt) *contraction of* would not.

wouldst (wʊdst) *vb. Arch. or dialect.* (used with the pronoun *thou* or its relative equivalent) a singular form of the past tense of **will**[1].

Woulfe bottle (wʊlf) *n. Chem.* a bottle with more than one neck, used for passing gases through liquids. [C18: after Peter *Woulfe* (?1727–1803), E chemist]

wound[1] (wuːnd) *n.* **1.** any break in the skin or an organ or part as the result of violence or a surgical incision. **2.** any injury or slight to the feelings or reputation. ~*vb.* **3.** to inflict a wound or wounds upon (someone or something). [OE *wund*] —**'wounding** *adj.* —**'woundingly** *adv.*

wound[2] (waʊnd) *vb.* the past tense and past participle of **wind**[2] and **wind**[3].

wounded ('wuːndɪd) *adj.* **1. a.** suffering from wounds; injured, esp. in a battle or fight. **b.** (as *collective n.;* preceded by *the*): *the wounded.* **2.** (of feelings) damaged or hurt.

woundwort ('wuːndˌwɜːt) *n.* **1.** any of various plants, such as field woundwort, having purple, scarlet, yellow, or white flowers and formerly used for dressing wounds. **2.** any of various other plants used in this way.

wove (wəʊv) *vb.* a past tense of **weave.**

woven ('wəʊvᵊn) *vb.* a past participle of **weave.**

wove paper *n.* paper with a very faint mesh impressed on it by the paper-making machine.

wow[1] (waʊ) *interj.* **1.** an exclamation of admiration, amazement, etc. ~*n.* **2.** *Sl.* a person or thing that is amazingly successful, attractive, etc. ~*vb.* **3.** (*tr.*) *Sl.* to arouse great enthusiasm in. [C16: orig. Scot.]

wow[2] (waʊ, wəʊ) *n.* a slow variation or distortion in pitch that occurs at very low audio frequencies in sound-reproducing systems. See also **flutter** (sense 12). [C20: imit.]

wowser (ˈwaʊzə) *n. Austral. & N.Z. sl.* **1.** a fanatically puritanical person. **2.** a teetotaller. [C20: < E dialect *wow* to complain]

wp *abbrev. for* word processor.

wpb *abbrev. for* wastepaper basket.

WPC (in Britain) *abbrev. for* woman police constable.

wpm *abbrev. for* words per minute.

WRAAC *abbrev. for* Women's Royal Australian Army Corps.

WRAAF *abbrev. for* Women's Royal Australian Air Force.

WRAC (in Britain) *abbrev. for* Women's Royal Army Corps.

wrack[1] *or* **rack** (ræk) *n.* **1.** collapse or destruction (esp. in **wrack and ruin**). **2.** something destroyed or a remnant of such. [OE *wræc* persecution, misery]

wrack[2] (ræk) *n.* **1.** seaweed or other marine vegetation that is floating in the sea or has been cast ashore. **2.** any of various seaweeds, such as serrated wrack. [C14 (in the sense: a wrecked ship, hence later applied to marine vegetation washed ashore): ? < MDu. *wrak* wreckage; the term corresponds to OE *wræc* WRACK[1]]

WRAF (in Britain) *abbrev. for* Women's Royal Air Force.

wraith (reɪθ) *n.* **1.** the apparition of a person living or thought to be alive, supposed to appear around the time of his death. **2.** a ghost or any apparition. [C16: Scot., <?] —ˈ**wraith,like** *adj.*

Wran (ræn) *n.* a member of the Women's Royal Australian Naval Service.

wrangle (ˈræŋgᵊl) *vb.* **1.** (*intr.*) to argue, esp. noisily or angrily. **2.** (*tr.*) to encourage, persuade, or obtain by argument. **3.** (*tr.*) *Western U.S. & Canad.* to herd (cattle or horses). ~*n.* **4.** a noisy or angry argument. [C14: < Low G *wrangeln*]

wrangler (ˈræŋglə) *n.* **1.** one who wrangles. **2.** *Western U.S. & Canad.* a herder; cowboy. **3.** *Brit.* (at Cambridge University) a candidate who has obtained first-class honours in part II of the mathematics tripos. Formerly, the wrangler with the highest marks was called the **senior wrangler.**

WRANS *abbrev. for* Women's Royal Australian Naval Service. See also **Wran.**

wrap (ræp) *vb.* **wrapping, wrapped.** (*mainly tr.*) **1.** to fold or wind (paper, cloth, etc.) around (a person or thing) so as to cover. **2.** (often foll. by *up*) to fold paper, etc., around to fasten securely. **3.** to surround or conceal by surrounding. **4.** to enclose, immerse, or absorb: *wrapped in sorrow.* **5.** to fold, wind, or roll up. **6.** (*intr.;* often foll. by *about, around,* etc.) to be or become wound or extended. **7.** (often foll. by *up*) Also: **rap.** *Austral. inf.* to praise (someone). ~*n.* **8.** a garment worn wrapped around the body, esp. the shoulders, such as a shawl or cloak. **9.** *Chiefly U.S.* wrapping or a wrapper. **10. keep under wraps.** to keep secret. **11. take the wraps off.** to reveal. **12.** Also: **rap.** *Austral. inf.* a commendation. [C14: <?]

wrapover (ˈræp,əʊvə) *or* **wrapround** *adj.* **1.** (of a garment, esp. a skirt) not sewn up at one side, but worn wrapped round the body and fastened so that the open edges overlap. ~*n.* **2.** such a garment.

wrapped (ræpt) *vb.* **1.** the past participle of **wrap. 2. wrapped up in.** *Inf.* **a.** completely absorbed or engrossed in. **b.** implicated or involved in. ~*adj.* **3.** Also: **rapt.** *Austral. inf.* very pleased; delighted.

wrapper (ˈræpə) *n.* **1.** the cover, usually of paper or cellophane, in which something is wrapped. **2.** a dust jacket of a book. **3.** the ripe firm tobacco leaf forming the outermost portion of a cigar. **4.** a loose negligee or dressing gown.

wrapping (ˈræpɪŋ) *n.* the material used to wrap something.

wrapround (ˈræp,raʊnd) *or* **wraparound** *adj.* **1.** made so as to be wrapped round something: *a wrapround skirt.* **2.** surrounding, curving round, or overlapping. **3.** curving round in one continuous piece: *a wrapround windscreen.* ~*n.* **4.** *Printing.* a flexible plate of plastic, metal, or rubber that is made flat but used wrapped round the plate cylinder of a rotary press. **5.** another name for **wrapover.**

wrap up *vb.* (*adv.*) **1.** (*tr.*) to fold paper around. **2.** to put warm clothes on. **3.** (*intr.; usually imperative*) *Sl.* to be silent. **4.** (*tr.*) *Inf.* **a.** to settle the final details of. **b.** to make a summary of.

wrasse (ræs) *n.* a marine fish of tropical and temperate seas, having thick lips, strong teeth, and usually a bright coloration: many are used as food fishes. [C17: < Cornish *wrach*]

wrath (rɒθ) *n.* **1.** angry, violent, or stern indignation. **2.** divine vengeance or retribution. **3.** *Arch.* a fit of anger or an act resulting from anger. [OE *wrǣththu*]

wrathful (ˈrɒθfʊl) *adj.* **1.** full of wrath; raging or furious. **2.** resulting from or expressing wrath. —ˈ**wrathfully** *adv.* —ˈ**wrathfulness** *n.*

wreak (ri:k) *vb.* (*tr.*) **1.** to inflict (vengeance, etc.) or to cause (chaos, etc.): *to wreak havoc on the enemy.* **2.** to express or gratify (anger, hatred, etc.). **3.** *Arch.* to take vengeance for. [OE *wrecan*] —ˈ**wreaker** *n.*

wreath (ri:θ) *n., pl.* **wreaths** (ri:ðz, ri:θs). **1.** a band of flowers or foliage intertwined into a ring, usually placed on a grave as a memorial or worn on the head as a garland or a mark of honour. **2.** any circular or spiral band or formation. **3.** (loosely) any floral design placed on a grave as a memorial. [OE *wrǣth, wrǣd*] —ˈ**wreath,like** *adj.*

wreathe (ri:ð) *vb.* **1.** to form into or take the form of a wreath by intertwining or twisting together. **2.** (*tr.*) to decorate, crown, or encircle with wreaths. **3.** to move or cause to move in a twisting way: *smoke wreathed up to the ceiling.* [C16: ? back formation < *wrēthen,* < OE *writhen,* p.p. of *wrīthan* to writhe]

wreck (rɛk) *vb.* **1.** to involve in or suffer disaster or destruction. **2.** (*tr.*) to cause the wreck of (a ship). ~*n.* **3. a.** the accidental destruction of a ship at sea. **b.** the ship so destroyed. **4.** *Maritime law.* goods cast ashore from a wrecked vessel. **5.** a person or thing that has suffered ruin or dilapidation. **6.** Also called: **wreckage.** the remains of something that has been destroyed. **7.** Also called: **wreckage.** the act of wrecking or the state of being wrecked. [C13: < ON] —ˈ**wrecking** *n., adj.*

wrecked (rɛkt) *adj. Sl.* in a state of intoxication, stupor, or euphoria, induced by drugs or alcohol.

wrecker (ˈrɛkə) *n.* **1.** a person or thing that ruins or destroys. **2.** *Chiefly U.S. & Canad.* a person whose job is to demolish buildings or dismantle cars. **3.** (formerly) a person who lures ships to destruction to plunder the wreckage. **4.** a U.S. and Canad. name for a breakdown van.

wrecking bar *n.* a short crowbar, forked at one end and slightly angled at the other to make a fulcrum.

wren (rɛn) *n.* **1.** any small brown passerine songbird of a chiefly American family (in Britain **wren,** in the U.S. and Canada **winter wren**). They have a slender bill and feed on insects. **2.** any of various similar birds, such as the Australian warblers, New Zealand wrens, etc. [OE *wrenna, werna*]

Wren (rɛn) *n. Inf.* (in Britain and certain other nations) a member of the Women's Royal Naval Service. [C20: < the abbrev. WRNS]

wrench (rɛntʃ) *vb.* **1.** to give (something) a sudden or violent twist or pull, esp. so as to remove (something) from that to which it is attached: *to wrench a door off its hinges.* **2.** (*tr.*) to twist suddenly so as to sprain (a limb): *to wrench one's ankle.* **3.** (*tr.*) to give pain to. **4.**

(*tr.*) to twist from the original meaning or purpose. **5.** (*intr.*) to make a sudden twisting motion. ~*n.* **6.** a forceful twist or pull. **7.** an injury to a limb, caused by twisting. **8.** sudden pain caused esp. by parting. **9.** a parting that is difficult or painful to make. **10.** a distorting of the original meaning or purpose. **11.** a spanner, esp. one with adjustable jaws. See also **torque wrench.** [OE *wrencan*]

wrest (rɛst) *vb.* (*tr.*) **1.** to take or force away by violent pulling or twisting. **2.** to seize forcibly by violent or unlawful means. **3.** to obtain by laborious effort. **4.** to distort in meaning, purpose, etc. ~*n.* **5.** the act or an instance of wresting. **6.** *Arch.* a small key used to tune a piano or harp. [OE *wrǣstan*] —ˈ**wrester** *n.*

wrestle (ˈrɛsᵊl) *vb.* **1.** to fight (another person) by holding, throwing, etc., without punching with the closed fist. **2.** (*intr.*) to participate in wrestling. **3.** (when *intr.*, foll. by *with* or *against*) to fight with (a person, problem, or thing): *wrestle with one's conscience.* **4.** (*tr.*) to move laboriously, as with wrestling movements. ~*n.* **5.** the act of wrestling. **6.** a struggle or tussle. [OE *wrǣstlian*] —ˈ**wrestler** *n.*

wrestling (ˈrɛslɪŋ) *n.* any of certain sports in which the contestants fight each other according to various rules governing holds and usually forbidding blows with the closed fist. The principal object is to overcome the opponent either by throwing or pinning him to the ground or by causing him to submit.

wrest pin *n.* (on a piano, harp, etc.) a pin, embedded in the **wrest plank,** around which one end of a string is wound: it may be turned by means of a tuning key to alter the tension of the string.

wretch (rɛtʃ) *n.* **1.** a despicable person. **2.** a person pitied for his misfortune. [OE *wrecca*]

wretched (ˈrɛtʃɪd) *adj.* **1.** in poor or pitiful circumstances. **2.** characterized by or causing misery. **3.** despicable; base. **4.** poor, inferior, or paltry. **5.** (*prenominal*) (intensifier qualifying something undesirable): *a wretched nuisance.* —ˈ**wretchedly** *adv.* —ˈ**wretchedness** *n.*

wrick (rɪk) *n.* **1.** a sprain or strain. ~*vb.* **2.** (*tr.*) to sprain or strain.

wrier *or* **wryer** (ˈraɪə) *adj.* the comparative of **wry.**

wriest *or* **wryest** (ˈraɪɪst) *adj.* the superlative of **wry.**

wriggle (ˈrɪgᵊl) *vb.* **1.** to make or cause to make twisting movements. **2.** (*intr.*) to progress by twisting and turning. **3.** (*intr.;* foll. by *into* or *out of*) to manoeuvre oneself by clever or devious means: *wriggle out of an embarrassing situation.* ~*n.* **4.** a wriggling movement or action. **5.** a sinuous marking or course. [C15: < MLow G] —ˈ**wriggler** *n.* —ˈ**wriggly** *adj.*

wright (raɪt) *n.* (*now chiefly in combination*) a person who creates, builds, or repairs something specified: *a playwright; a shipwright.* [OE *wryhta, wyrhta*]

wring (rɪŋ) *vb.* **wringing, wrung. 1.** (often foll. by *out*) to twist and compress to squeeze (a liquid) from (cloth, etc.). **2.** (*tr.*) to twist forcibly: *wring its neck.* **3.** (*tr.*) to clasp and twist (one's hands), esp. in anguish. **4.** (*tr.*) to distress: *wring one's heart.* **5.** (*tr.*) to grip (someone's hand) vigorously in greeting. **6.** (*tr.*) to obtain as by forceful means: *wring information out of.* **7. wringing wet.** soaking; drenched. ~*n.* **8.** an act or the process of wringing. [OE *wringan*]

wringer (ˈrɪŋə) *n.* another name for **mangle**[2] (sense 1).

wrinkle[1] (ˈrɪŋkᵊl) *n.* **1.** a slight ridge in the smoothness of a surface, such as a crease in the skin as a result of age. ~*vb.* **2.** to make or become wrinkled, as by crumpling, creasing, or puckering. [C15: back formation < *wrinkled,* < OE *gewrinclod,* p.p. of *wrinclian* to wind around] —ˈ**wrinkly** *adj.*

wrinkle[2] (ˈrɪŋkᵊl) *n. Inf.* a clever or useful trick, hint, or dodge. [OE *wrenc* trick]

wrinklies (ˈrɪŋklɪz) *pl. n. Inf., derog.* old people.

wrist (rɪst) *n.* **1.** *Anat.* the joint between the forearm and the hand. Technical name: **carpus. 2.** the part of a sleeve or glove that covers the wrist. **3.** *Machinery.* **a.** See **wrist pin. b.** a joint in which a wrist pin forms the pivot. [OE]

wristband (ˈrɪstˌbænd) *n.* **1.** a band around the wrist, esp. one attached to a watch or forming part of a long sleeve. **2.** a sweatband around the wrist.

wristlet (ˈrɪstlɪt) *n.* a band or bracelet worn around the wrist.

wrist pin *n.* **1.** a cylindrical boss or pin attached to the side of a wheel parallel with the axis, esp. one forming a bearing for a crank. **2.** the U.S. and Canad. name for **gudgeon pin.**

wristwatch (ˈrɪstˌwɒtʃ) *n.* a watch worn strapped around the wrist.

wristy (ˈrɪstɪ) *adj.* (of a player's style of hitting the ball in cricket, tennis, etc.) characterized by considerable movement of the wrist.

writ (rɪt) *n.* **1.** a document under seal, issued in the name of the Crown or a court, commanding the person to whom it is addressed to do or refrain from doing some specified act. **2.** *Arch.* a piece or body of writing: *Holy Writ.* [OE]

write (raɪt) *vb.* **writing, wrote, written. 1.** to draw or mark (symbols, words, etc.) on a surface, usually paper, with a pen, pencil, or other instrument. **2.** to describe or record (ideas, experiences, etc.) in writing. **3.** to compose (a letter) to or correspond regularly with (a person, organization, etc.). **4.** (*tr.; may take a clause as object*) to say or communicate by letter: *he wrote that he was on his way.* **5.** (*tr.*) *Inf., chiefly U.S. & Canad.* to send a letter to (a person, etc.). **6.** to write (words) in cursive as opposed to printed style. **7.** (*tr.*) to be sufficiently familiar with (a specified style, language, etc.) to use it in writing. **8.** to be the author or composer of (books, music, etc.). **9.** (*tr.*) to fill in the details for (a document, form, etc.). **10.** (*tr.*) to draw up or draft. **11.** (*tr.*) to produce by writing: *he wrote ten pages.* **12.** (*tr.*) to show clearly: *envy was written all over his face.* **13.** (*tr.*) to spell, inscribe, or entitle. **14.** (*tr.*) to ordain or prophesy: *it is written.* **15.** (*intr.*) to produce writing as specified. **16.** *Computers.* to record (data) in a location in a storage device. **17.** (*tr.*) See **underwrite** (sense 3a). ~See also **write down, write in,** etc. [OE *wrītan* (orig.: to scratch runes into bark)] —ˈ**writable** *adj.*

▷ **Usage.** Careful writers and speakers avoid the omission of *to* after the verb *write* in clauses without a direct object: *I'll write to you* (not *I'll write you*). This omission of *to* is very common in informal English in the U.S., but is nevertheless not accepted as good formal usage.

write down *vb.* (*adv.*) **1.** (*tr.*) to set down in writing. **2.** (*tr.*) to harm or belittle by writing about (a person) in derogatory terms. **3.** (*intr.;* foll. by *to* or *for*) to write in a simplified way (to a supposedly less cultured readership). **4.** (*tr.*) *Accounting.* to decrease the book value of (an asset). ~*n.* **write-down. 5.** *Accounting.* a reduction made in the book value of an asset.

write in *vb.* (*tr.*) **1.** to insert in (a document, form, etc.) in writing. **2.** (*adv.*) to write a letter to a company, institution, etc. **3.** (*adv.*) *U.S.* to vote for (a person not on a ballot) by inserting his name.

write off *vb.* (*tr., adv.*) **1.** *Accounting.* **a.** to cancel (a bad debt or obsolete asset) from the accounts. **b.** to consider (a transaction, etc.) as a loss or set off (a loss) against revenues. **c.** to depreciate (an asset) by periodic charges. **d.** to charge (a specified amount) against gross profits as depreciation of an asset. **2.** to cause or acknowledge the complete loss of. **3.** to dismiss from consideration. **4.** to send a written order (for something): *she wrote off for a brochure.* **5.** *Inf.* to damage (something, esp. a car) beyond repair. ~*n.* **write-off. 6.** *Accounting.* **a.** the act of cancelling a bad debt or obsolete asset from the accounts. **b.** the bad debt or obsolete asset cancelled. **c.** the amount cancelled against gross profits, corresponding to the book value of the bad debt or obsolete asset. **7.** *Inf.* something damaged beyond repair, esp. a car.

write out *vb.* (*tr., adv.*) **1.** to put into writing or reproduce in full form in writing. **2.** to exhaust (oneself or one's creativity) by excessive writing. **3.** to remove (a character) from a television or radio series.

writer (ˈraɪtə) *n.* **1.** a person who writes books, articles, etc., esp. as an occupation. **2.** the person who has written something specified. **3.** a person who is able to write or write well. **4.** a scribe or clerk. **5.** a composer of music. **6. Writer to the Signet.** (in Scotland) a member of an ancient society of solicitors, now having the exclusive privilege of preparing crown writs.

writer's cramp *n.* a muscular spasm or temporary paralysis of the muscles of the thumb and first two fingers caused by prolonged writing.

write up *vb.* (*tr., adv.*) **1.** to describe fully, complete, or bring up to date in writing: *write up a diary.* **2.** to praise or bring to public notice in writing. **3.** *Accounting.* **a.** to place an excessively high value on (an asset). **b.** to increase the book value of (an asset) in order to reflect more accurately its current worth in the market. ~*n.* **write-up. 4.** a published account of something, such as a review in a newspaper or magazine.

writhe (raɪð) *vb.* **1.** to twist or squirm in or as if in pain. **2.** (*intr.*) to move with such motions. **3.** (*intr.*) to suffer acutely from embarrassment, revulsion, etc. ~*n.* **4.** the act or an instance of writhing. [OE *wrīthan*] —ˈ**writher** *n.*

writing (ˈraɪtɪŋ) *n.* **1.** a group of letters or symbols written or marked on a surface as a means of communicating. **2.** short for **handwriting. 3.** anything expressed in letters, esp. a literary composition. **4.** the work of a writer. **5.** literary style, art, or practice. **6.** written form: *give it to me in writing.* **7.** (*modifier*) related to or used in writing: *writing ink.* **8. writing on the wall.** a sign or signs of approaching disaster. [sense 8: allusion to Daniel 5:5]

writing desk *n.* a piece of furniture with a writing surface and drawers and compartments for papers, writing materials, etc.

writing paper *n.* paper sized to take writing ink and used for letters and other manuscripts.

writ of execution *n. Law.* a writ ordering that a judgment be enforced.

written (ˈrɪtᵊn) *vb.* **1.** the past participle of **write.** ~*adj.* **2.** taken down in writing; transcribed: *written evidence; the written word.*

WRNS *abbrev. for* Women's Royal Naval Service. See also **Wren.**

wrong (rɒŋ) *adj.* **1.** not correct or truthful: *the wrong answer.* **2.** acting or judging in error: *you are wrong to think that.* **3.** (*postpositive*) immoral; bad: *it is wrong to cheat.* **4.** deviating from or unacceptable to correct or conventional laws, usage, etc. **5.** not intended or wanted: *the wrong road.* **6.** (*postpositive*) not working properly; amiss: *something is wrong with the engine.* **7.** (of a side, esp. of a fabric) intended to face the inside so as not to be seen. **8. get on the wrong side of.** *Inf.* to come into disfavour with. **9. go down the wrong way.** (of food) to pass into the windpipe instead of the gullet. ~*adv.* **10.** in the wrong direction or manner. **11. get wrong. a.** to fail to understand properly. **b.** to fail to provide the correct answer to. **12. go wrong. a.** to turn out other than intended. **b.** to make a mistake. **c.** (of a machine, etc.) to cease to function properly. **d.** to go astray morally. ~*n.* **13.** a bad, immoral, or unjust thing or action. **14.** *Law.* **a.** an infringement of another person's rights, rendering the offender liable to a civil action: *a private wrong.* **b.** a violation of public rights and duties, affecting the community as a whole and actionable at the instance of the Crown: *a public wrong.* **15. in the wrong.** mistaken or guilty. ~*vb.* (*tr.*) **16.** to treat unjustly. **17.** to discredit, malign, or misrepresent. [OE *wrang* injustice] —ˈ**wronger** *n.* —ˈ**wrongly** *adv.* —ˈ**wrongness** *n.*

wrongdoer (ˈrɒŋˌduːə) *n.* a person who acts immorally or illegally. —ˈ**wrongˌdoing** *n.*

wrong-foot *vb.* (*tr.*) **1.** *Tennis, etc.* to play a shot in such a way as to cause (one's opponent) to be off balance. **2.** to take by surprise so as to place in an embarrassing or disadvantageous situation.

wrongful (ˈrɒŋfʊl) *adj.* unjust or illegal. —ˈ**wrongfully** *adv.* —ˈ**wrongfulness** *n.*

wrong-headed *adj.* **1.** constantly wrong in judgment. **2.** foolishly stubborn; obstinate. —ˌ**wrong-ˈheadedly** *adv.* —ˌ**wrong-ˈheadedness** *n.*

wrong number *n.* a telephone number wrongly connected or dialled in error, or the person so contacted.

wrote (rəʊt) *vb.* the past tense of **write.**

wroth (rəʊθ, rɒθ) *adj. Arch. or literary.* angry; irate. [OE *wrāth*]

wrought (rɔːt) *vb.* **1.** *Arch.* a past tense and past participle of **work.** ~*adj.* **2.** *Metallurgy.* shaped by hammering or beating. **3.** (*often in combination*) formed, fashioned, or worked as specified: *well-wrought.* **4.** decorated or made with delicate care. [C16: var. of *worht*, < OE *geworht*, p.p. of (*ge*)*wyrcan* to work]

wrought iron *n.* **a.** a pure form of iron having a low carbon content: often used for decorative work. **b.** (*as modifier*): *wrought-iron gates.*

wrought-up *adj.* agitated or excited.

wrung (rʌŋ) *vb.* the past tense and past participle of **wring.**

WRVS *abbrev. for* Women's Royal Voluntary Service.

wry (raɪ) *adj.* **wrier, wriest** *or* **wryer, wryest. 1.** twisted, contorted, or askew. **2.** (of a facial expression) produced or characterized by contorting of the features. **3.** dryly humorous; sardonic. **4.** warped, misdirected, or perverse. ~*vb.* **wrying, wried. 5.** (*tr.*) to twist or contort. [C16: < dialect *wry* to twist, < OE *wrīgian* to turn] —ˈ**wryly** *adv.* —ˈ**wryness** *n.*

wrybill (ˈraɪˌbɪl) *n.* a New Zealand plover, having its bill deflected to one side enabling it to search for food beneath stones.

wryneck (ˈraɪˌnɛk) *n.* **1.** either of two cryptically coloured Old World woodpeckers, which do not drum on trees. **2.** another name for **torticollis. 3.** *Inf.* a person who has a twisted neck.

WSW *symbol for* west-southwest.

wt. *abbrev. for* weight.

wunderkind (ˈwʌndəˌkɪnd; *German* ˈvʊndərˌkɪnt) *n., pl.* **-kinds** *or* **-kinder** (*German* -ˌkɪndər). **1.** a child prodigy. **2.** a person who is exceptionally successful in his field while still young. [C20: < G *Wunderkind*, lit.: wonder child]

wurst (wɜːst, wʊəst, vʊəst) *n.* a large sausage, esp. of a type made in Germany, Austria, etc. [< G *Wurst*, lit.: something rolled]

wuthering (ˈwʌðərɪŋ) *adj. N English dialect.* **1.** (of a wind) blowing strongly with a roaring sound. **2.** (of a place) characterized by such a sound. [var. of *whitherin*, < *whither* blow, < ON *hvithra*]

wych-elm *or* **witch-elm** (ˈwɪtʃˌɛlm) *n.* **1.** a Eurasian elm tree, having a rounded shape, longish pointed leaves, clusters of small flowers, and winged fruits. **2.** the wood of this tree. [C17: < OE *wice*]

wynd (waɪnd) *n. Scot.* a narrow lane or alley. [C15: < the stem of WIND[2]]

WYSIWYG (ˈwɪzɪˌwɪg) *n., adj. Computers. acronym for* what you see is what you get: referring to what is displayed on the screen being the same as what will be printed out.

wyvern *or* **wivern** (ˈwaɪvən) *n.* a heraldic beast having a serpent's tail and a dragon's head and a body with wings and two legs. [C17: var. of earlier *wyver*, < OF, < L *vīpera* VIPER]

X

x *or* **X** (ɛks) *n., pl.* **x's, X's,** *or* **Xs.** **1.** the 24th letter of the English alphabet. **2.** a speech sound sequence represented by this letter, pronounced as *ks* or *gz* or, in initial position, *z*, as in *xylophone*.

x *symbol for:* **1.** *Commerce, finance, etc.* ex. **2.** *Maths.* the *x*-axis or a coordinate measured along the *x*-axis in a Cartesian coordinate system. **3.** *Maths.* an algebraic variable. **4.** multiplication.

X *symbol:* **1. a.** (formerly) indicating a film that may not be publicly shown to anyone under 18. Since 1982 replaced by symbol 18. **b.** (*as modifier*): *an X film.* **2.** denoting any unknown, unspecified, or variable factor, number, person, or thing. **3.** (on letters, cards, etc.) denoting a kiss. **4.** (on ballot papers, etc.) indicating choice. **5.** (on examination papers, etc.) indicating error. **6.** for Christ; Christian. [< the Gk letter khi (X), first letter of *Khristos* Christ] ~**7.** *the Roman numeral for* ten. See **Roman numerals.**

xanthein (ˈzænθiːn) *n.* the soluble part of the yellow pigment that is found in the cell sap of some flowers.

xanthene (ˈzænθiːn) *n.* a yellowish crystalline compound used as a fungicide.

xanthic (ˈzænθɪk) *adj.* **1.** of, containing, or derived from xanthic acid. **2.** *Bot., rare.* having a yellow colour.

xanthic acid *n.* any of a class of sulphur-containing acids.

xanthine (ˈzænθiːn, -θaɪn) *n.* **1.** a crystalline compound found in urine, blood, certain plants, and certain animal tissues. Formula: $C_5H_4N_4O_2$. **2.** any of three substituted derivatives of xanthine, which act as stimulants and diuretics.

Xanthippe (zænˈθɪpɪ) *or* **Xantippe** (zænˈtɪpɪ) *n.* **1.** the wife of Socrates, proverbial as a scolding and quarrelsome woman. **2.** any nagging, peevish, or irritable woman.

xantho- *or before a vowel* **xanth-** *combining form.* indicating yellow: *xanthophyll.* [< Gk *xanthos* yellow]

xanthochroism (zænˈθɒkrəʊˌɪzəm) *n.* a condition in certain animals, esp. aquarium goldfish, in which all skin pigments other than yellow and orange disappear. [C19: < Gk *xanthokhro(os)* yellow-skinned + -ISM]

xanthoma (zænˈθəʊmə) *n. Pathol.* the presence in the skin of fatty yellow or brownish plaques or nodules, esp. on the eyelids, caused by a disorder of lipid metabolism.

xanthophyll *or esp. U.S.* **xanthophyl** (ˈzænθəʊfɪl) *n.* any of a group of yellow carotenoid pigments occurring in plant and animal tissue. —ˌ**xanthoˈphyllous** *adj.*

xanthous (ˈzænθəs) *adj.* of, relating to, or designating races with yellowish hair and a light complexion.

x-axis *n.* a reference axis, usually horizontal, of a graph or two- or three-dimensional Cartesian coordinate system along which the *x*-coordinate is measured.

X-chromosome *n.* the sex chromosome that occurs in pairs in the diploid cells of the females of many animals, including humans, and as one of a pair with the Y-chromosome in those of males. Cf. **Y-chromosome.**

Xe *the chemical symbol for* xenon.

xebec, zebec, *or* **zebeck** (ˈziːbɛk) *n.* a small three-masted Mediterranean vessel with both square and lateen sails, formerly used by Algerian pirates and later used for commerce. [C18: earlier *chebec* < F, ult. < Ar. *shabbāk;* present spelling infl. by Catalan *xabec*, Sp. *xabeque* (now *jabeque*)]

xeno- *or before a vowel* **xen-** *combining form.* indicating something strange, different, or foreign: *xenogamy.* [< Gk *xenos* strange]

xenogamy (zɛˈnɒgəmɪ) *n. Bot.* another name for **cross-fertilization.** —**xeˈnogamous** *adj.*

xenoglossia (ˌzɛnəˈglɒsɪə) *n.* an ability claimed by some mediums, clairvoyants, etc., to speak a language with which they are unfamiliar. [C20: < Gk, < XENO- + *glossa* language]

xenolith (ˈzɛnəlɪθ) *n.* a fragment of rock differing in origin, composition, structure, etc., from the igneous rock enclosing it. —ˌ**xenoˈlithic** *adj.*

xenon (ˈzɛnɒn) *n.* a colourless odourless gaseous element occurring in trace amounts in air; formerly considered inert, it is now known to form compounds and is used in radio valves, stroboscopic and bactericidal lamps, and bubble chambers. Symbol: Xe; atomic no.: 54; atomic wt.: 131.30. [C19: < Gk: something strange]

xenophile (ˈzɛnəˌfaɪl) *n.* a person who likes foreigners or things foreign. [C19: < Gk, < XENO- + -PHILE]

xenophobia (ˌzɛnəˈfəʊbɪə) *n.* hatred or fear of foreigners or strangers or of their politics or culture. [C20: < Gk, < XENO- + -PHOBIA] —ˈ**xenoˌphobe** *n.* —ˌ**xenoˈphobic** *adj.*

xeric (ˈzɪərɪk) *adj. Ecology.* of, relating to, or growing in dry conditions. —ˈ**xerically** *adv.*

xero- *or before a vowel* **xer-** *combining form.* indicating dryness: *xeroderma.* [< Gk *xēros* dry]

xeroderma (ˌzɪərəʊˈdɜːmə) *or* **xerodermia** (ˌzɪərəʊˈdɜːmɪə) *n. Pathol.* **1.** any abnormal dryness of the skin as the result of diminished secretions from the sweat or sebaceous glands. **2.** another name for **ichthyosis.** —**xerodermatic** (ˌzɪərəʊdəˈmætɪk) *or* ˌ**xeroˈdermatous** *adj.*

xerography (zɪˈrɒgrəfɪ) *n.* a photocopying process in which an electrostatic image is formed on a selenium plate or cylinder. The plate or cylinder is dusted with a resinous powder, which adheres to the charged regions, and the image is then transferred to a sheet of paper on which it is fixed by heating. —**xeˈrographer** *n.* —**xerographic** (ˌzɪərəˈgræfɪk) *adj.* —ˌ**xeroˈgraphically** *adv.*

xerophilous (zɪˈrɒfɪləs) *adj.* (of plants or animals) adapted for growing or living in dry surroundings. —**xerophile** (ˈzɪərəʊˌfaɪl) *n.* —**xeˈrophily** *n.*

xerophthalmia (ˌzɪərɒfˈθælmɪə) *n. Pathol.* excessive dryness of the cornea and conjunctiva, caused by a deficiency of vitamin A. Also called: **xeroma** (zɪˈrəʊmə). —ˌ**xerophˈthalmic** *adj.*

xerophyte (ˈzɪərəˌfaɪt) *n.* a xerophilous plant, such as a cactus. —**xerophytic** (ˌzɪərəˈfɪtɪk) *adj.* —ˌ**xeroˈphytically** *adv.* —ˈ**xeroˌphytism** *n.*

Xerox (ˈzɪərɒks) *n.* **1.** *Trademark.* **a.** a xerographic copying process. **b.** a machine employing this process. **c.** a copy produced by this process. ~*vb.* **2.** to produce a copy of (a document, illustration, etc.) by this process.

Xhosa (ˈkɔːsə) *n.* **1.** (*pl.* **-sa** *or* **-sas**) a member of a cattle-rearing Negroid people of southern Africa, living chiefly in Cape Province of the Republic of South Africa. **2.** the language of this people, belonging to the Bantu group and characterized by several clicks in its sound system. —ˈ**Xhosan** *adj.*

xi (zaɪ, saɪ, ksaɪ, ksiː) *n., pl.* **xis.** the 14th letter in the Greek alphabet (Ξ, ξ).

xiphisternum (ˌzɪfɪˈstɜːnəm) *n., pl.* **-na** (-nə). *Anat., zool.* the cartilaginous process forming the lowermost part of the breastbone (sternum). Also called: **xiphoid, xiphoid process.** [C19: < Gk *xiphos* sword + STERNUM]

xiphoid (ˈzɪfɔɪd) *adj.* **1.** *Biol.* shaped like a sword. **2.** of or relating to the xiphisternum. ~*n.* **3.** Also called: **xiphoid process.** another name for **xiphisternum.** [C18: < NL, < Gk, < *xiphos* sword + *eidos* form]

Xmas (ˈɛksməs, ˈkrɪsməs) *n. Inf.* short for **Christmas.** [C18: < symbol X for Christ + -MAS]

x-ray *or* **X-ray** *n.* **1. a.** electromagnetic radiation emitted when matter is bombarded with fast electrons. X-rays have wavelengths shorter than that of ultraviolet radiation, that is less than about 1×10^{-8} metres. Below about 1×10^{-11} metres they are often called gamma radiation or bremsstrahlung. **b.** (*as modifier*): *x-ray astronomy.* **2.** a picture produced by exposing photographic film to x-rays: used in medicine as a diagnostic aid as parts of the body, such as bones, absorb x-rays and so appear as opaque areas on the picture. ~*vb.* (*tr.*) **3.** to photograph (part of the body, etc.) using x-rays. **4.** to treat or examine by means of x-rays. [C19: partial translation of G *X-Strahlen* (< *Strahl* ray), coined by W. K. Roentgen, G physicist who discovered it in 1895]

x-ray astronomy *n.* the branch of astronomy concerned with the detection and measurement of x-rays emitted by certain celestial bodies, such as x-ray stars.

x-ray crystallography *n.* the study and practice of determining the structure of a crystal by passing a beam of x-rays through it and observing and analysing the diffraction pattern produced.

x-ray star *n.* a star that emits x-rays, as well as other types of radiation. The x-rays are detected and measured by instruments carried in satellites and space probes.

x-ray tube *n.* an evacuated tube containing a metal target onto which is directed a beam of electrons at high energy for the generation of x-rays.

xylem (ˈzaɪləm, -lɛm) *n.* a plant tissue that conducts water and mineral salts from the roots to all other parts, provides mechanical support, and forms the wood of trees and shrubs. [C19: < Gk *xulon* wood]

xylene (ˈzaɪliːn) *n.* an aromatic hydrocarbon existing in three isomeric forms, all three being colourless flammable volatile liquids used as solvents and in the manufacture of synthetic resins, dyes, and insecticides; dimethylbenzene.

xylo- *or before a vowel* **xyl-** *combining form.* **1.** indicating wood: *xylophone.* **2.** indicating xylene: *xylidine.* [< Gk *xulon* wood]

xylocarp (ˈzaɪləˌkɑːp) *n. Bot.* a fruit, such as a coconut, having a hard woody pericarp. —ˌ**xylo**ˈ**carpous** *adj.*

xylograph (ˈzaɪləˌgrɑːf) *n.* **1.** an engraving in wood. **2.** a print taken from a wood block. ~*vb.* **3.** (*tr.*) to print (a design, illustration, etc.) from a wood engraving. —**xylography** (zaɪˈlɒgrəfɪ) *n.*

Xylonite (ˈzaɪlənaɪt) *n. Trademark.* a thermoplastic of the cellulose nitrate type.

xylophagous (zaɪˈlɒfəgəs) *adj.* (of certain insects, crustaceans, etc.) feeding on or living within wood.

xylophone (ˈzaɪləˌfəʊn) *n. Music.* a percussion instrument consisting of a set of wooden bars of graduated length. It is played with hard-headed hammers. —**xylophonic** (ˌzaɪləˈfɒnɪk) *adj.* —**xylophonist** (zaɪˈlɒfənɪst) *n.*

xylose (ˈzaɪləʊz, -ləʊs) *n.* a white crystalline sugar found in wood and straw. It is extracted by hydrolysis with acids and used in dyeing, tanning, and in foods for diabetics.

xyster (ˈzɪstə) *n.* a surgical instrument for scraping bone; surgical rasp or file. [C17: via NL < Gk: tool for scraping, < *xuein* to scrape]

Y

y *or* **Y** (waɪ) *n., pl.* **y's, Y's,** *or* **Ys.** **1.** the 25th letter of the English alphabet. **2.** a speech sound represented by this letter, usually a semivowel, as in *yawn,* or a vowel, as in *symbol* or *shy.* **3.** something shaped like a Y.

y *Maths. symbol for:* **1.** the *y*-axis or a coordinate measured along the *y*-axis in a Cartesian coordinate system. **2.** an algebraic variable.

Y *symbol for:* **1.** any unknown or variable factor, number, or thing. **2.** *Chem.* yttrium.

y. *abbrev. for* year.

-y[1] *or* **-ey** *suffix forming adjectives.* **1.** (*from nouns*) characterized by; consisting of; filled with; resembling: *sunny; sandy; smoky; classy.* **2.** (*from verbs*) tending to; acting or existing as specified: *leaky; shiny.* [< OE *-ig, -ǣg*]

-y[2], **-ie,** *or* **-ey** *suffix of nouns. Inf.* **1.** denoting smallness and expressing affection and familiarity: *a doggy; Jamie.* **2.** a person or thing concerned with or characterized by being: *a groupie; a goalie; a fatty.* [C14: < Scot. *-ie, -y,* familiar suffix orig. in names]

-y[3] *suffix forming nouns.* **1.** (*from verbs*) indicating the act of doing what is indicated by the verbal element: *inquiry.* **2.** (*esp. with combining forms of Greek, Latin, or French origin*) indicating state, condition, or quality: *geography; jealousy.* [< OF *-ie,* < L *-ia*]

yabby *or* **yabbie** (ˈjæbɪ) *Austral.* ~*n., pl.* **-bies.** **1.** a small edible freshwater crayfish. **2.** a saltwater prawn used as bait; nipper. ~*vb.* **-bying, -bied.** **3.** (*intr.*) to go out to catch yabbies. [< Abor.]

yacht (jɒt) *n.* **1.** a vessel propelled by sail or power, used esp. for pleasure cruising, racing, etc. ~*vb.* **2.** (*intr.*) to sail or cruise in a yacht. [C16: < obs. Du. *jaghte,* short for *jahtschip,* < *jagen* to chase + *schip* ship] —**ˈyachting** *n., adj.*

yachtie (ˈjɒtɪ) *n. Austral. & N.Z. inf.* a yachtsman; sailing enthusiast.

yachtsman (ˈjɒtsmən) *or* (*fem.*) **yachtswoman** *n., pl.* **-men** *or* **-women.** a person who sails a yacht or yachts. —**ˈyachtsmanship** *n.*

yack (jæk) *n., vb.* a variant spelling of **yak**[2].

yackety-yak (ˈjækɪtɪˈjæk) *n. Sl.* noisy, continuous, and trivial talk or conversation. [imit.]

yaffle (ˈjæfᵊl) *n.* another name for **green woodpecker** (see **woodpecker**). [C18: imit. of its cry]

yah (jɑː, jɛə) *sentence substitute.* **1.** an informal word for **yes.** ~*interj.* **2.** an exclamation of derision or disgust.

yahoo (jəˈhuː) *n., pl.* **-hoos.** a crude, brutish, or obscenely coarse person. [C18: < a race of brutish creatures resembling men in Jonathan Swift's *Gulliver's Travels* (1726)] —**yaˈhooism** *n.*

Yahweh (ˈjɑːweɪ) *or* **Yahveh** (ˈjɑːveɪ) *n. Old Testament.* a vocalization of the Tetragrammaton. [< Heb., < YHVH, with conjectural vowels; see also JEHOVAH]

Yahwism (ˈjɑːwɪzəm) *or* **Yahvism** (ˈjɑːvɪzəm) *n.* the use of the name Yahweh, esp. in parts of the Old Testament, as the personal name of God.

Yahwist (ˈjɑːwɪst) *or* **Yahvist** (ˈjɑːvɪst) *n. Bible.* **the.** the conjectured author or authors of the earliest sources of the Pentateuch in which God is called *Yahweh* throughout. —**Yahˈwistic** *or* **Yahˈvistic** *adj.*

yak[1] (jæk) *n.* an ox of Tibet having long shaggy hair. [C19: < Tibetan *gyag*]

yak[2] (jæk) *Sl.* ~*n.* **1.** noisy, continuous, and trivial talk. ~*vb.* **yakking, yakked.** **2.** (*intr.*) to chatter or talk in this way. [C20: imit.]

yakka, yakker, *or* **yacker** (ˈjækə) *n. Austral. & N.Z. inf.* work. [C19: < Abor.]

Yale lock (jeɪl) *n. Trademark.* a type of cylinder lock using a flat serrated key. [C19: after L. *Yale* (1821–68), U.S. inventor]

yam (jæm) *n.* **1.** any of various twining plants of tropical and subtropical regions, cultivated for their edible tubers. **2.** the starchy tuber of any of these plants, eaten as a vegetable. **3.** *Southern U.S.* the sweet potato. [C17: < Port. *inhame,* ult. of W African origin]

yammer (ˈjæmə) *Inf.* ~*vb.* **1.** to utter or whine in a complaining manner. **2.** to make (a complaint) loudly or persistently. ~*n.* **3.** a yammering sound. **4.** nonsense; jabber. [OE *geōmrian* to grumble] —**ˈyammerer** *n.*

Yang (jæŋ) *n.* See **Yin and Yang.**

yank (jæŋk) *vb.* **1.** to pull with a sharp movement; tug. ~*n.* **2.** a jerk. [C19: <?]

Yank (jæŋk) *n.* **1.** a slang word for an **American.** **2.** *U.S. inf.* short for **Yankee.**

Yankee (ˈjæŋkɪ) *or* (*inf.*) **Yank** *n.* **1.** *Often disparaging.* a native or inhabitant of the U.S.; American. **2.** a native or inhabitant of New England. **3.** a native or inhabitant of the Northern U.S., esp. a Northern soldier in the Civil War. ~*adj.* **4.** of, relating to, or characteristic of Yankees. [C18: ? < Du. *Jan Kees* John Cheese, nickname used derisively by Du. settlers for English colonists in Connecticut]

Yankee Doodle *n.* **1.** an American song, popularly regarded as a characteristically national melody. **2.** another name for **Yankee.**

yap (jæp) *vb.* **yapping, yapped.** (*intr.*) **1.** (of a dog) to bark in quick sharp bursts; yelp. **2.** *Inf.* to talk at length in an annoying or stupid way; jabber. ~*n.* **3.** a high-pitched or sharp bark; yelp. **4.** *Sl.* annoying or stupid speech; jabber. **5.** *Sl., chiefly U.S.* a derogatory word for **mouth.** [C17: imit.] —**ˈyapper** *n.* —**ˈyappy** *adj.*

yapok (jəˈpɒk) *n.* an amphibious nocturnal opossum of Central and South America. Also called: **water opossum.** [C19: after *Oyapok,* a river flowing between French Guiana & Brazil]

yarborough (ˈjɑːbərə, -brə) *n. Bridge, whist.* a hand of 13 cards in which no card is higher than nine. [C19: supposedly after the second Earl of *Yarborough* (died 1897), said to have bet a thousand to one against its occurrence]

yard[1] (jɑːd) *n.* **1.** a unit of length equal to 3 feet and defined in 1963 as exactly 0.9144 metre. **2.** a cylindrical wooden or hollow metal spar, slung from a mast of a vessel, and used for suspending a sail. [OE *gierd* rod, twig]

yard[2] (jɑːd) *n.* **1.** a piece of enclosed ground, often adjoining or surrounded by a building or buildings. **2. a.** an enclosed or open area used for some commercial activity, for storage, etc.: *a builder's yard.* **b.** (*in combination*): *a shipyard.* **3.** a U.S. and Canad. word for **garden** (sense 1). **4.** an area having a network of railway tracks and sidings, used for storing rolling stock, making up trains, etc. **5.** *U.S. & Canad.* the winter pasture of deer, moose, and similar animals. **6.** *N.Z.* short for **stockyard.** [OE *geard*]

Yard (jɑːd) *n.* **the.** *Brit. inf.* short for **Scotland Yard.**

yardage[1] (ˈjɑːdɪdʒ) *n.* a length measured in yards.

yardage[2] (ˈjɑːdɪdʒ) *n.* **1.** the use of a railway yard for cattle. **2.** the charge for this.

yardarm (ˈjɑːdˌɑːm) *n. Naut.* the outer end of a yard, outside the sheave holes.

yard grass *n.* an Old World perennial grass with prostrate leaves, growing as a troublesome weed on open ground, yards, etc.

yard of ale *n.* **1.** the beer or ale contained in a narrow horn-shaped drinking glass. **2.** such a drinking glass itself.

yardstick (ˈjɑːdˌstɪk) *n.* **1.** a measure or standard used for comparison. **2.** a graduated stick, one yard long, used for measurement.

yarmulke (ˈjɑːməlkə) *n. Judaism.* a skullcap worn by Orthodox male Jews at all times and by others during prayer. [< Yiddish, < Ukrainian &

Polish *yarmulka* cap, prob. < Turkish *yağmurluk* raincoat, < *yağmur* rain]

yarn (jɑːn) *n.* **1.** a continuous twisted strand of natural or synthetic fibres, used in weaving, knitting, etc. **2.** *Inf.* a long and often involved story, usually of incredible or fantastic events. **3. spin a yarn.** *Inf.* **a.** to tell such a story. **b.** to make up a series of excuses. ~*vb.* **4.** (*intr.*) to tell such a story or stories. [OE *gearn*]

yarn-dyed *adj.* (of fabric) dyed while still in yarn form, before being woven.

yarran (ˈjærən) *n.* a small hardy tree of inland Australia: useful as fodder and for firewood. [< Abor.]

yarrow (ˈjærəʊ) *n.* any of several plants of the composite family of Eurasia, having finely dissected leaves and flat clusters of white flower heads. Also called: **milfoil.** [OE *gearwe*]

yashmak *or* **yashmac** (ˈjæʃmæk) *n.* the face veil worn by Muslim women when in public. [C19: < Ar.]

yataghan (ˈjætəgən) *n.* a Turkish sword with a curved blade. [C19: < Turkish *yatağan*]

yaup (jɔːp) *vb., n.* a variant spelling of **yawp.** —ˈ**yauper** *n.*

yaw (jɔː) *vb.* **1.** (*intr.*) (of an aircraft, etc.) to turn about its vertical axis. **2.** (*intr.*) (of a ship, etc.) to deviate temporarily from a straight course. **3.** (*tr.*) to cause (an aircraft, ship, etc.) to yaw. ~*n.* **4.** the movement of an aircraft, etc., about its vertical axis. **5.** the deviation of a vessel from a straight course. [C16: <?]

yawl (jɔːl) *n.* **1.** a two-masted sailing vessel with a small mizzenmast aft of the rudderpost. **2.** a ship's small boat, usually rowed by four or six oars. [C17: < Du. *jol* or MLow G *jolle,* <?]

yawn (jɔːn) *vb.* **1.** (*intr.*) to open the mouth wide and take in air deeply, often as in involuntary reaction to sleepiness or boredom. **2.** (*tr.*) to express or utter while yawning. **3.** (*intr.*) to be open wide as if threatening to engulf (someone or something): *the mine shaft yawned below.* ~*n.* **4.** the act or an instance of yawning. [OE *gionian*] —ˈ**yawner** *n.* —ˈ**yawning** *adj.* —ˈ**yawningly** *adv.*

yawp (jɔːp) *Dialect U.S. & Canad. inf.* ~*vb.* (*intr.*) **1.** to yawn, esp. audibly. **2.** to shout, cry, or talk noisily. **3.** to bark or yowl. ~*n.* **4.** a shout, bark, or cry. **5.** a noisy, foolish, or raucous utterance. [C15 *yolpen,* prob. imit.] —ˈ**yawper** *n.*

yaws (jɔːz) *n.* (*usually functioning as sing.*) an infectious disease of tropical climates characterized by red skin eruptions. [C17: of Carib origin]

***y*-axis** *n.* a reference axis of a graph or two- or three-dimensional Cartesian coordinate system along which the *y*-coordinate is measured.

Yb *the chemical symbol for* ytterbium.

Y-chromosome *n.* the sex chromosome that occurs as one of a pair with the X-chromosome in the diploid cells of the males of many animals, including humans. Cf. **X-chromosome.**

yclept (ɪˈklɛpt) *adj. Obs.* having the name of; called. [OE *gecleopod,* p.p. of *cleopian* to call]

Y connection *n. Electrical engineering.* a three-phase star connection.

yd *or* **yd.** *abbrev. for* yard (measure).

YDT (in Canada) *abbrev. for* Yukon Daylight Time.

ye[1] (jiː, *unstressed* jɪ) *pron.* **1.** *Arch. or dialect.* refers to more than one person including the person addressed. **2.** Also: **ee** (iː). *Dialect.* refers to one person addressed: *I tell ye.* [OE *gē*]

ye[2] (ðiː, *spelling pron.* jiː) *determiner.* a form of **the**[1], used as a supposed archaism: *ye olde oake.* [< a misinterpretation of *the* as written in some ME texts. The runic letter thorn (þ, representing *th*) was incorrectly transcribed as *y* because of a resemblance in their shapes]

yea (jeɪ) *sentence substitute.* **1.** a less common word for **aye** (yes). ~*adv.* **2.** (*sentence modifier*) *Arch. or literary.* indeed; truly: *yea, though they spurn me, I shall prevail.* [OE *gēa*]

yeah (jɛə) *sentence substitute.* an informal word for **yes.**

yean (jiːn) *vb.* (of a sheep or goat) to give birth to (offspring). [OE *geēanian*]

yeanling (ˈjiːnlɪŋ) *n.* the young of a goat or sheep.

year (jɪə) *n.* **1.** the period of time, the **calendar year,** containing 365 days or in a **leap year** 366 days. It is divided into 12 calendar months, and reckoned from January 1 to December 31. **2.** a period of twelve months from any specified date. **3.** a specific period of time, usually occupying a definite part or parts of a twelve-month period, used for some particular activity: *a school year.* **4.** Also called: **astronomical year, tropical year, equinoctial year.** the period of time, the **solar year,** during which the earth makes one revolution around the sun, measured between two successive vernal equinoxes: equal to 365.242 19 days. **5.** the period of time, the **sidereal year,** during which the earth makes one revolution around the sun, measured between two successive conjunctions of a particular star: equal to 365.256 36 days. **6.** the period of time, the **lunar year,** containing 12 lunar months and equal to 354.3671 days. **7.** the period of time taken by a specified planet to complete one revolution around the sun. **8.** (*pl.*) age, esp. old age: *a man of his years should be more careful.* **9.** (*pl.*) time: *in years to come.* **10.** a group of pupils or students, who are taught or study together. **11. the year dot.** *Inf.* as long ago as can be remembered. **12. year in, year out.** regularly or monotonously, over a long period. ~Related adj.: **annual.** [OE *gear*]

▷ **Usage.** In writing spans of years, it is important to choose a style that avoids ambiguity. The practice adopted in this dictionary is, in four-figure dates, to specify the last two digits of the second date if it falls within the same century as the first: *1801–08; 1850–51; 1899–1901.* In writing three-figure B.C. dates, it is advisable to give both dates in full: *159–156* B.C., not *159–56* B.C. unless of course the span referred to consists of 103 years rather than three years. It is also advisable to specify B.C. or A.D. in years under 1000 unless the context makes this self-evident.

yearbook (ˈjɪəˌbʊk) *n.* an almanac or other reference book published annually and containing details of events of the previous year.

yearling (ˈjɪəlɪŋ) *n.* **1.** the young of any of various animals, including the antelope and buffalo, between one and two years of age. **2.** a thoroughbred racehorse counted as being one year old until the second January 1 following its birth. **3. a.** a bond that is intended to mature after one year. **b.** (*as modifier*): *yearling bonds.* ~*adj.* **4.** being a year old.

yearlong (ˈjɪəˈlɒŋ) *adj.* throughout a whole year.

yearly (ˈjɪəlɪ) *adj.* **1.** occurring, done, appearing, etc., once a year or every year; annual. **2.** lasting or valid for a year; annual: *a yearly subscription.* ~*adv.* **3.** once a year; annually.

yearn (jɜːn) *vb.* (*intr.*) **1.** (usually foll. by *for* or *after* or an infinitive) to have an intense desire or longing (for). **2.** to feel tenderness or affection. [OE *giernan*] —ˈ**yearner** *n.* —ˈ**yearning** *n., adj.* —ˈ**yearningly** *adv.*

year of grace *n.* any year of the Christian era, as from the presumed date of Christ's birth.

year-round *adj.* open, in use, operating, etc., throughout the year.

yeast (jiːst) *n.* **1.** any of various single-celled fungi which reproduce by budding and are able to ferment sugars: a rich source of vitamins of the B complex. **2.** a commercial preparation containing yeast cells and inert material such as meal, used in raising dough for bread or for fermenting beer, whisky, etc. **3.** a preparation containing yeast cells, used to treat diseases caused by vitamin B deficiency. **4.** froth or foam, esp. on beer. ~*vb.* **5.** (*intr.*) to froth or foam. [OE *giest*] —ˈ**yeastless** *adj.* —ˈ**yeastˌlike** *adj.*

yeasty (ˈjiːstɪ) *adj.* **yeastier, yeastiest. 1.** of, resembling, or containing yeast. **2.** fermenting or causing fermentation. **3.** tasting of or like yeast. **4.** insubstantial or frivolous. **5.** restless, agitated, or unsettled. **6.** covered with or containing froth or foam. —ˈ**yeastily** *adv.* —ˈ**yeastiness** *n.*

yegg (jɛg) *n. Sl., chiefly U.S.* a burglar or safe-breaker. [C20: ? < the surname of a burglar]

yell (jɛl) *vb.* **1.** to shout, scream, cheer, or utter in a loud or piercing way. ~*n.* **2.** a loud piercing inarticulate cry, as of pain, anger, or fear. **3.** *U.S. & Canad.* a rhythmic cry, used in cheering in unison. [OE *giellan*] —ˈ**yeller** *n.*

yellow (ˈjɛləʊ) *n.* **1.** any of a group of colours such as that of a lemon or of gold, that vary in saturation but have the same hue. Yellow is the complementary colour of blue. Related adj.: **xanthous.** **2.** a pigment or dye of or producing these colours. **3.** yellow cloth or clothing: *dressed in yellow.* **4.** the yolk of an egg. **5.** a yellow ball in snooker, etc. ~*adj.* **6.** of the colour yellow. **7.** yellowish in colour or having parts or marks that are yellowish. **8.** having a yellowish skin; Mongoloid. **9.** *Inf.* cowardly or afraid. **10.** offensively sensational, as a cheap newspaper (esp. in **yellow press**). ~*vb.* **11.** to make or become yellow. ~See also **yellows.** [OE *geolu*] —ˈ**yellowish** *adj.* —ˈ**yellowly** *adv.* —ˈ**yellowness** *n.* —ˈ**yellowy** *adj.*

yellow belly *n. Austral.* any of several freshwater food fishes with yellow underparts.

yellow-belly *n., pl.* **-lies.** a slang word for **coward.** —ˈ**yellow-ˌbellied** *adj.*

yellow bile *n. Arch.* one of the four bodily humours, choler.

yellow card *n. Soccer.* a card of a yellow colour raised by a referee in international competitions to warn a player who has violated a rule.

yellow fever *n.* an acute infectious disease of tropical and subtropical climates, characterized by fever, haemorrhages, vomiting, and jaundice: caused by a virus transmitted by the bite of a certain mosquito. Also called: **yellow jack.**

yellowhammer (ˈjɛləʊˌhæmə) *n.* a European bunting, having a yellowish head and body and brown-streaked wings and tail. [C16: < ?]

yellow jack *n.* **1.** *Pathol.* another name for **yellow fever.** **2.** another name for **quarantine flag.** **3.** any of certain large yellowish food fishes of warm and tropical Atlantic waters.

yellow journalism *n.* the type of journalism that relies on sensationalism to attract readers. [C19: ? shortened < *Yellow Kid journalism,* referring to the *Yellow Kid,* a cartoon (1895) in the *New York World,* a newspaper having a reputation for sensationalism]

yellow line *n. Brit.* a yellow line painted along the edge of a road indicating vehicle waiting restrictions.

yellow metal *n.* **1.** a type of brass having about 60 per cent copper and 40 per cent zinc. **2.** another name for **gold.**

yellow pages *pl. n.* a classified telephone directory or section of a directory that lists subscribers by the business or service provided.

yellow peril *n.* the power or alleged power of Asiatic peoples, esp. the Chinese, to threaten or destroy White or Western civilization.

yellows (ˈjɛləʊz) *n.* (*functioning as sing.*) **1.** any of various fungal or viral diseases of plants, characterized by yellowish discoloration and stunting. **2.** *Vet. science.* another name for **jaundice.**

yellow spot *n. Anat.* another name for **macula lutea.**

yellow streak *n. Inf.* a cowardly or weak trait.

yellow underwing *n.* any of several species of noctuid moths, the hind wings of which are yellow with a black bar.

yellowwood (ˈjɛləʊˌwʊd) *n.* **1.** any of several leguminous trees of the southeastern U.S., having clusters of white flowers and yellow wood yielding a yellow dye. **2.** Also called: **West Indian satinwood.** a rutaceous tree of the West Indies, with smooth hard wood. **3.** any of several other trees with yellow wood, esp. a conifer of southern Africa the wood of which is used for furniture and building. **4.** the wood of any of these trees.

yelp (jɛlp) *vb.* (*intr.*) **1.** (esp. of a dog) to utter a sharp or high-pitched cry or bark, often indicating pain. ~*n.* **2.** a sharp or high-pitched cry or bark. [OE *gielpan* to boast] —ˈ**yelper** *n.*

yen[1] (jɛn) *n., pl.* **yen.** the standard monetary unit of Japan. [C19: < Japanese *en,* < Chinese *yüan* dollar]

yen[2] (jɛn) *Inf.* ~*n.* **1.** a longing or desire. ~*vb.* **yenning, yenned.** **2.** (*intr.*) to yearn. [? < Chinese *yan* a craving]

yeoman (ˈjəʊmən) *n., pl.* **-men.** **1.** *History.* **a.** a member of a class of small freeholders who cultivated their own land. **b.** an attendant or lesser official in a royal or noble household. **2.** (in Britain) another name for **yeoman of the guard.** **3.** (*modifier*) characteristic of or relating to a yeoman. **4.** a petty officer or noncommissioned officer in the Royal Navy or Marines in charge of signals. [C15: ? < *yongman* young man]

yeomanly (ˈjəʊmənlɪ) *adj.* **1.** of, relating to, or like a yeoman. **2.** having the virtues attributed to yeomen, such as staunchness, loyalty, and courage. ~*adv.* **3.** in a yeomanly manner.

yeoman of the guard *n.* a member of the ceremonial bodyguard (**Yeomen of the Guard**) of the British monarch.

yeomanry (ˈjəʊmənrɪ) *n.* **1.** yeomen collectively. **2.** (in Britain) a volunteer cavalry force, organized in 1761 for home defence: merged into the Territorial Army in 1907.

yep (jɛp) *sentence substitute.* an informal word for **yes.**

yerba *or* **yerba maté** (ˈjɜːbə) *n.* another name for **maté.** [< Sp. *yerba maté* herb maté]

yes (jɛs) *sentence substitute.* **1.** used to express affirmation, consent, agreement, or approval or to answer when one is addressed. **2.** used to signal someone to speak or keep speaking, enter a room, or do something. ~*n.* **3.** an answer or vote of *yes.* **4.** (*often pl.*) a person who votes in the affirmative. [OE *gēse,* < *iā sīe* may it be]

yeshiva (jəˈʃiːvə; *Hebrew* jəˈʃiːva) *n., pl.* **-vahs** *or* **-voth** (*Hebrew* -vɔt). **1.** a traditional Jewish school devoted chiefly to the study of the Talmud. **2.** a school run by Orthodox Jews for children of elementary school age, providing both religious and secular instruction. [< Heb. *yĕshībhāh* a seat, hence, an academy]

yes man *n.* a servile, submissive, or acquiescent subordinate, assistant, or associate.

yester (ˈjɛstə) *adj. Arch.* of or relating to yesterday: *yester sun.* [OE *geostror*]

yester- *prefix.* indicating a period of time before the present one: *yesteryear.* [OE *geostran*]

yesterday (ˈjɛstədɪ, -ˌdeɪ) *n.* **1.** the day immediately preceding today. **2.** (*often pl.*) the recent past. ~*adv.* **3.** on or during the day before today. **4.** in the recent past.

yesteryear (ˈjɛstəˌjɪə) *Formal or literary.* ~*n.* **1.** last year or the past in general. ~*adv.* **2.** during last year or the past in general.

yestreen (jɛˈstriːn) *adv. Scot.* yesterday evening. [C14: < YEST(E)R- + E(V)EN[2]]

yet (jɛt) *sentence connector.* **1.** nevertheless; still; in spite of that: *I want to and yet I haven't the courage.* ~*adv.* **2.** (*usually used with a negative or interrogative*) so far; up until then or now: *they're not home yet; is it teatime yet?* **3.** (often preceded by *just; usually used with a negative*) now (as contrasted with later): *we can't stop yet.* **4.** (*often used with a comparative*) even; still: *yet more potatoes for sale.* **5.** eventually in spite of everything: *we'll convince him yet.* **6. as yet.** so far; up until then or now. [OE *gēta*]

yeti (ˈjɛtɪ) *n.* another term for **abominable snowman.** [C20: < Tibetan]

yew (juː) *n.* **1.** any coniferous tree of the Old World and North America having flattened needle-like leaves, fine-grained elastic wood, and cuplike red waxy cones resembling berries. **2.** the wood of any of these trees, used to make bows for archery. **3.** *Archery.* a bow made of yew. [OE *īw*]

Y-fronts *pl. n. Trademark.* boys' or men's underpants having a front opening within an inverted Y shape.

Yggdrasil *or* **Ygdrasil** (ˈɪgdrəsɪl) *n. Norse myth.* the ash tree that was thought to bind together earth, heaven, and hell with its roots and branches. [ON (prob. meaning: Uggr's horse), <

Uggr a name of Odin, < *yggr, uggr* frightful + *drasill* horse, <?]

YHA (in Britain) *abbrev. for* Youth Hostels Association.

YHVH *or* **YHWH** *Bible.* the letters of the **Tetragrammaton.**

yid (jɪd) *n. Sl.* a derogatory word for a **Jew.** [C20: prob. < *Yiddish,* < MHG *Jude* JEW]

Yiddish (ˈjɪdɪʃ) *n.* **1.** a language spoken as a vernacular by Jews in Europe and elsewhere by Jewish emigrants, usually written in the Hebrew alphabet. It is a dialect of High German with an admixture of words of Hebrew, Romance, and Slavonic origin. *~adj.* **2.** in or relating to this language. [C19: < G *jüdisch,* < *Jude* JEW]

Yiddisher (ˈjɪdɪʃə) *adj.* **1.** in or relating to Yiddish. **2.** Jewish. *~n.* **3.** a speaker of Yiddish; Jew.

yield (jiːld) *vb.* **1.** to give forth or supply (a product, result, etc.), esp. by cultivation, labour, etc.; produce or bear. **2.** (*tr.*) to furnish as a return: *the shares yielded three per cent.* **3.** (*tr.*; often foll. by *up*) to surrender or relinquish, esp. as a result of force, persuasion, etc. **4.** (*intr.*; sometimes foll. by *to*) to give way, submit, or surrender, as through force or persuasion: *she yielded to his superior knowledge.* **5.** (*intr.*; often foll. by *to*) to agree; comply; assent: *he eventually yielded to their request for money.* **6.** (*tr.*) to grant or allow; concede: *to yield right of way.* *~n.* **7.** the result, product, or amount yielded. **8.** the profit or return, as from an investment or tax. **9.** the annual income provided by an investment. **10.** the energy released by the explosion of a nuclear weapon expressed in terms of the amount of TNT necessary to produce the same energy. **11.** *Chem.* the quantity of a specified product obtained in a reaction or series of reactions. [OE *gieldan*] —ˈ**yieldable** *adj.* —ˈ**yielder** *n.*

yielding (ˈjiːldɪŋ) *adj.* **1.** compliant, submissive, or flexible. **2.** pliable or soft: *a yielding material.*

yield point *n.* the stress at which an elastic material under increasing stress ceases to behave elastically; the elongation becomes greater than the increase in stress.

Yin and Yang (jɪn) *n.* two complementary principles of Chinese philosophy: Yin is negative, dark, and feminine, Yang is positive, bright, and masculine. [< Chinese *yin* dark + *yang* bright]

yippee (jɪˈpiː) *interj.* an exclamation of joy, pleasure, anticipation, etc.

yips (jɪps) *pl. n.* **the.** *Inf.* (in sport) nervous twitching or tension that destroys concentration. [C20: <?]

-yl *suffix forming nouns.* (in chemistry) indicating a group or radical: *methyl.* [< Gk *hulē* wood]

ylang-ylang (ˈiːlæŋˈiːlæŋ) *n.* **1.** an aromatic Asian tree with fragrant greenish-yellow flowers yielding a volatile oil. **2.** the oil obtained from this tree, used in perfumery. [C19: < Tagalog *ilang-ilang*]

ylem (ˈaɪləm) *n.* the original matter from which the basic elements are said to have been formed following the explosion postulated in the big-bang theory of cosmology. [ME, < OF *ilem,* < L *hȳlē* stuff, < Gk *hulē* wood]

YMCA *abbrev. for* Young Men's Christian Association.

-yne *suffix forming nouns.* denoting an organic chemical containing a triple bond: *alkyne.* [alteration of -INE[2]]

yob (jɒb) *or* **yobbo** (ˈjɒbəʊ) *n., pl.* **yobs** *or* **yobbos.** *Brit. sl.* an aggressive and surly youth, esp. a teenager. [C19: ? back sl. for BOY] —ˈ**yobbery** *n.* —ˈ**yobbish** *adj.*

yodel (ˈjəʊdᵊl) *n.* **1.** an effect produced in singing by an abrupt change of register from the chest voice to falsetto, esp. in folk songs of the Swiss Alps. *~vb.* **-delling, -delled** *or U.S.* **-deling, -deled. 2.** to sing (a song) in which a yodel is used. [C19: < G *jodeln,* imit.] —ˈ**yodeller** *n.*

yoga (ˈjəʊgə) *n.* (*often cap.*) **1.** a Hindu system of philosophy aiming at the mystical union of the self with the Supreme Being in a state of complete awareness and tranquillity through certain physical and mental exercises. **2.** any method by which such awareness and tranquillity are attained, esp. a course of related exercises and postures. [C19: < Sansk.: a yoking, < *yunakti* he yokes] —**yogic** (ˈjəʊgɪk) *adj.*

yogh (jɒg) *n.* **1.** a character (ʒ) used in Old and Middle English to represent a palatal fricative very close to the semivowel sound of Modern English *y.* **2.** this same character as used in Middle English for both the voiced and voiceless palatal fricatives; when final or in a closed syllable in medial position the sound approached that of German *ch* in *ich,* as in *knyʒt* (knight). [C14: ? < *yok* yoke, from the letter's shape]

yoghurt, yogurt, *or* **yoghourt** (ˈjəʊgət, ˈjɒg-) *n.* a thick custard-like food prepared from milk curdled by bacteria, often sweetened and flavoured with fruit. [C19: < Turkish *yogurt*]

yogi (ˈjəʊgɪ) *n., pl.* **-gis** *or* **-gin** (-gɪn). a person who is a master of yoga.

yo-heave-ho (ˌjəʊhiːvˈhəʊ) *interj.* a cry formerly used by sailors while pulling or lifting together in rhythm.

yohimbine (jəʊˈhɪmbiːn) *n.* an alkaloid found in the bark of a West African tree and used in medicine. [C19: < Bantu *yohimbé* a tropical African tree + -INE[1]]

yo-ho-ho *interj.* **1.** an exclamation to call attention. **2.** another word for **yo-heave-ho.**

yoicks (haɪk; *spelling pron.* jɔɪks) *interj.* a cry used by fox-hunters to urge on the hounds.

yoke (jəʊk) *n., pl.* **yokes** *or* **yoke. 1.** a wooden frame, usually consisting of a bar with an oxbow at either end, for attaching to the necks of a pair of draught animals, esp. oxen, so that they can be worked as a team. **2.** something resembling a yoke in form or function, such as a frame fitting over a person's shoulders for carrying buckets. **3.** a fitted part of a garment, esp. around the neck, shoulders, and chest or around the hips, to which a gathered, pleated, flared, or unfitted part is attached. **4.** an oppressive force or burden: *under the yoke of a tyrant.* **5.** a pair of oxen or other draught animals joined by a yoke. **6.** a part that secures two or more components so that they move together. **7.** (in the ancient world) a symbolic yoke, consisting of two upright spears with a third lashed across them, under which conquered enemies were compelled to march, esp. in Rome. **8.** a mark, token, or symbol of slavery, subjection, or suffering. **9.** *Now rare.* a link, tie, or bond: *the yoke of love.* *~vb.* **10.** (*tr.*) to secure or harness (a draught animal) to (a plough, vehicle, etc.) by means of a yoke. **11.** to join or be joined by means of a yoke; couple, unite, or link. [OE *geoc*]

yokel (ˈjəʊkᵊl) *n. Disparaging.* (used chiefly by townspeople) a person who lives in the country, esp. one who is simple and old-fashioned. [C19: ? < dialect *yokel* green woodpecker]

yolk (jəʊk) *n.* **1.** the substance in an animal ovum that nourishes the developing embryo. **2.** a greasy substance in the fleece of sheep. [OE *geoloca,* < *geolu* yellow] —ˈ**yolky** *adj.*

yolk sac *n. Zool.* the membranous sac that is attached to the surface of the embryos of birds, reptiles, and some fishes, and contains yolk.

Yom Kippur (jɒm ˈkɪpə; *Hebrew* jɔm kiˈpur) *n.* an annual Jewish holiday celebrated as a day of fasting, on which prayers of penitence are recited in the synagogue. Also called: **Day of Atonement.** [< Heb., < *yōm* day + *kippūr* atonement]

yomp (jɒmp) *vb.* (*intr.*) to walk or trek laboriously, esp. over difficult terrain. [C20: mil. sl., <?]

yon (jɒn) *determiner.* **1.** *Chiefly Scot. & N English.* **a.** an archaic or dialect word for **that:** *yon man.* **b.** (*as pronoun*): *yon's a fool.* **2.** a variant of **yonder.** [OE *geon*]

yond (jɒnd) *Obs. or dialect.* *~adj.* **1.** the farther, more distant. *~determiner.* **2.** a variant of **yon.**

yonder (ˈjɒndə) *adv.* **1.** at, in, or to that relatively distant place; over there. *~determiner.* **2.** being at a distance, either within view or as if within view: *yonder valleys.* [C13: < OE *geond* yond]

yoni (ˈjəʊnɪ) *n. Hinduism.* **1.** the female genitalia, regarded as a divine symbol of sexual pleasure and matrix of generation. **2.** an image of these as an object of worship. [C18: < Sansk., lit.: vulva]

yonks (jɒŋks) *pl. n. Inf.* a very long time; ages: *I haven't seen him for yonks.* [C20: <?]

yoo-hoo (ˈjuːˌhuː) *interj.* a call to attract a person's attention.

YOP (jɒp) *n.* (formerly, in Britain) **a.** *acronym for* Youth Opportunities Programme. **b.** (*as modifier*): *a YOP scheme.*

yore (jɔː) *n.* **1.** time long past (now only in **of yore**). *~adv.* **2.** *Obs.* in the past; long ago. [OE *gēara*, genitive pl. of *gēar* year]

york (jɔːk) *vb.* (*tr.*) *Cricket.* to bowl (a batsman) by pitching the ball under or just beyond the bat. [C19: back formation < YORKER]

yorker (ˈjɔːkə) *n. Cricket.* a ball bowled so as to pitch just under or just beyond the bat. [C19: prob. after the *Yorkshire* County Cricket Club]

yorkie (ˈjɔːkɪ) *n.* short for **Yorkshire terrier.**

Yorkist (ˈjɔːkɪst) *English history.* *~n.* **1.** a member or adherent of the royal House of York, esp. during the wars of the Roses. *~adj.* **2.** of, belonging to, or relating to the supporters or members of the House of York.

Yorks. (jɔːks) *abbrev. for* Yorkshire.

Yorkshire pudding (ˈjɔːkʃɪə) *n. Chiefly Brit.* a light puffy baked pudding made from a batter of flour, eggs, and milk, traditionally served with roast beef.

Yorkshire terrier *n.* a very small breed of terrier with a long straight glossy coat of steel-blue and tan.

Yoruba (ˈjɒrʊbə) *n.* **1.** (*pl.* **-bas** *or* **-ba**) a member of a Negroid people of W Africa, living chiefly in the coastal regions of SW Nigeria. **2.** the language of this people. —ˈ**Yoruban** *adj.*

you (juː; *unstressed* jʊ) *pron.* (*subjective or objective*) **1.** refers to the person addressed or to more than one person including the person or persons addressed: *you know better; the culprit is among you.* **2.** refers to an unspecified person or people in general: *you can't tell the boys from the girls.* *~n.* **3.** *Inf.* the personality of the person being addressed: *that hat isn't really you.* **4. you know what** *or* **who.** a thing or person that the speaker does not want to specify. [OE *ēow*, dative & accusative of *gē* ye]

▷ **Usage.** See at **me.**

you'd (juːd; *unstressed* jʊd) *contraction of* you had *or* you would.

you'll (juːl; *unstressed* jʊl) *contraction of* you will *or* you shall.

young (jʌŋ) *adj.* **younger** (ˈjʌŋgə), **youngest** (ˈjʌŋgɪst). **1. a.** having lived, existed, or been made or known for a relatively short time: *a young man; a young movement; a young country.* **b.** (*as collective n.;* preceded by *the*): *the young.* **2.** youthful or having qualities associated with youth; vigorous or lively. **3.** of or relating to youth: *in my young days.* **4.** having been established or introduced for a relatively short time: *a young member.* **5.** in an early stage of progress or development; not far advanced: *the day was young.* **6.** (*often cap.*) of or relating to a rejuvenated group or movement or one claiming to represent the younger members of the population: *Young Socialists.* *~n.* **7.** (*functioning as pl.*) offspring, esp. young animals: *a rabbit with her young.* **8. with young.** (of animals) pregnant. [OE *geong*] —ˈ**youngish** *adj.*

young blood *n.* young, fresh, or vigorous new people, ideas, attitudes, etc.

Young Fogey *n.* a young person who adopts the conservative values of an older generation.

young lady *n.* a girlfriend; sweetheart.

youngling (ˈjʌŋlɪŋ) *n. Literary.* **a.** a young person, animal, or plant. **b.** (*as modifier*): *a youngling brood.* [OE *geongling*]

young man *n.* a boyfriend; sweetheart.

Young Pretender *n.* Charles Edward Stuart (1720–88), son of James Edward Stuart (see **Old Pretender**). He led the Jacobite Rebellion (1745–46) in an attempt to re-establish the Stuart succession to the British throne. Also known as **Bonnie Prince Charlie.**

Young's modulus (jʌŋz) *n.* a modulus of elasticity, applicable to the stretching of a wire, etc., equal to the ratio of the applied load per unit area of cross section to the increase in length per unit length. [after Thomas *Young* (1773–1829), E physicist]

youngster (ˈjʌŋstə) *n.* **1.** a young person; child or youth. **2.** a young animal, esp. a horse.

Young Turk *n.* **1.** a progressive, revolutionary, or rebellious member of an organization, political party, etc. **2.** a member of an abortive reform movement in the Ottoman Empire.

younker (ˈjʌŋkə) *n.* **1.** *Arch. or literary.* a young man; lad. **2.** *Obs.* a young gentleman or knight. [C16: < Du. *jonker*, < MDu. *jonc* young]

your (jɔː, jʊə; *unstressed* jə) *determiner.* **1.** of, belonging to, or associated with you: *your nose; your house.* **2.** belonging to or associated with an unspecified person or people in general: *the path is on your left heading north.* **3.** *Inf.* used to indicate all things or people of a certain type: *your part-time worker is a problem.* [OE *eower*, genitive of *gē* ye]

you're (jɔː; *unstressed* jə) *contraction of* you are.

yours (jɔːz, jʊəz) *pron.* **1.** something or someone belonging to or associated with you. **2.** your family: *greetings to you and yours.* **3.** used in conventional closing phrases at the end of a letter: *yours sincerely; yours faithfully.* **4. of yours.** belonging to or associated with you.

yourself (jɔːˈsɛlf, jʊə-) *pron., pl.* **-selves. 1. a.** the reflexive form of *you.* **b.** (intensifier): *you yourself control your destiny.* **2.** (*preceded by a copula*) your usual self: *you're not yourself.*

▷ **Usage.** See at **myself.**

yours truly *pron.* an informal term for *I* or *me.* [< the closing phrase of letters]

youth (juːθ) *n., pl.* **youths** (juːðz). **1.** the quality or condition of being young, immature, or inexperienced: *his youth told against him in the contest.* **2.** the period between childhood and maturity. **3.** the freshness, vigour, or vitality characteristic of young people. **4.** any period of early development. **5.** a young person, esp. a young man or boy. **6.** young people collectively: *youth everywhere is rising in revolt.* [OE *geogoth*]

youth club *n.* a centre providing leisure activities for young people.

youthful (ˈjuːθfʊl) *adj.* **1.** of, relating to, possessing, or characteristic of youth. **2.** fresh, vigorous, or active: *he's surprisingly youthful for his age.* **3.** in an early stage of development: *a youthful culture.* **4.** Also: **young.** (of a river, valley, or land surface) in the early stage of the cycle of erosion, characterized by steep slopes, lack of flood plains, and V-shaped valleys. —ˈ**youthfully** *adv.* —ˈ**youthfulness** *n.*

youth hostel *n.* one of an organization of inexpensive lodging places for young people travelling cheaply. Often shortened to **hostel.**

you've (juːv; *unstressed* jʊv) *contraction of* you have.

yowl (jaʊl) *vb.* **1.** to express with or produce a loud mournful wail or cry; howl. *~n.* **2.** a wail or howl. [C13: < ON *gaula*] —ˈ**yowler** *n.*

yo-yo (ˈjəʊjəʊ) *n., pl.* **-yos. 1.** a toy consisting of a spool attached to a string, the end of which is held while it is repeatedly spun out and reeled in. *~vb.* **yo-yoing, yo-yoed.** (*intr.*) **2.** to change repeatedly from one position to another; fluctuate. [C20: orig. a trademark for this type of toy]

yr *abbrev. for:* **1.** (*pl.* **yrs**) year. **2.** younger. **3.** your.

yrs *abbrev. for:* **1.** years. **2.** yours.

YST (in Canada) *abbrev. for* Yukon Standard Time.

YT *abbrev. for* Yukon Territory.

YTS (in Britain) *abbrev. for* Youth Training Scheme.

ytterbia (ɪˈtɜːbɪə) *n.* another name for **ytterbium oxide.** [C19: NL; see YTTERBIUM]

ytterbium (ɪˈtɜːbɪəm) *n.* a soft malleable silvery element of the lanthanide series of metals that is used to improve the mechanical properties of steel. Symbol: Yb; atomic no.: 70; atomic wt.: 173.04. [C19: NL, after *Ytterby*, Swedish quarry where discovered]

ytterbium oxide *n.* a weakly basic hygroscopic substance used in certain alloys and ceramics.

yttria (ˈɪtrɪə) *n.* another name for **yttrium oxide.** [C19: NL; see YTTERBIUM]

yttrium (ˈɪtrɪəm) *n.* a silvery metallic element used in various alloys, in lasers, and as a catalyst. Symbol: Y; atomic no.: 39; atomic wt.: 88.90. [C19: NL; see YTTERBIUM]

yttrium metal *n. Chem.* any one of a group of elements including yttrium and the related lanthanides.

yttrium oxide *n.* a colourless or white insoluble solid used in incandescent mantles.

yuan (ˈjuːˈæn) *n., pl.* **-an.** the standard monetary unit of the People's Republic of China. [< Chinese *yüan* round object; see YEN[1]]

yucca (ˈjʌkə) *n.* any of a genus of liliaceous plants of tropical and subtropical America, having stiff lancelike leaves and spikes of white flowers. [C16: < American Sp. *yuca*, ult. < Amerind]

yuck *or* **yuk** (jʌk) *interj. Sl.* an exclamation indicating contempt, dislike, or disgust.

yucky *or* **yukky** (ˈjʌkɪ) *adj.* **yuckier, yuckiest** *or* **yukkier, yukkiest.** *Sl.* disgusting; nasty.

Yugoslav *or* **Jugoslav** (ˈjuːgəʊˌslɑːv) *n.* **1.** a native or inhabitant of Yugoslavia, a federal republic in SE Europe, on the Adriatic. **2.** (not in technical use) another name for **Serbo-Croatian** (the language). ~*adj.* **3.** of, relating to, or characteristic of Yugoslavia or its people.

yulan (ˈjuːlæn) *n.* a Chinese magnolia that is often cultivated for its showy white flowers. [C19: < Chinese, < *yu* a gem + *lan* plant]

yule (juːl) *n.* (*sometimes cap.*) *Literary, arch., or dialect.* **a.** Christmas or the Christmas season. **b.** (*in combination*): *yuletide.* [OE *geōla*, orig. a pagan feast lasting 12 days]

yule log *n.* a large log of wood traditionally used as the foundation of a fire at Christmas.

yummy (ˈjʌmɪ) *Sl.* ~*interj.* **1.** Also: **yum-yum.** an exclamation indicating pleasure or delight, as in anticipation of delicious food. ~*adj.* **-mier, -miest.** **2.** delicious, delightful, or attractive. [C20: < *yum-yum*, imit.]

Yuppie (ˈjʌpɪ) (*sometimes not cap.*) ~*n.* **1.** *acronym for* young urban (*or* upwardly mobile) professional. ~*adj.* **2.** designed for or appealing to Yuppies.

yurt (jʊət) *n.* a circular tent consisting of a framework of poles covered with felt or skins, used by Mongolian and Turkic nomads of E and central Asia. [< Russian *yurta*, of Turkic origin]

YWCA *abbrev. for* Young Women's Christian Association.

Z

z *or* **Z** (zɛd; *U.S.* ziː) *n., pl.* **z's, Z's,** *or* **Zs. 1.** the 26th and last letter of the English alphabet. **2.** a speech sound represented by this letter. **3. a.** something shaped like a Z. **b.** (*in combination*): *a Z-bend in a road.*

z *Maths. symbol for:* **1.** the *z*-axis or a coordinate measured along the *z*-axis in a Cartesian or cylindrical coordinate system. **2.** an algebraic variable.

Z *symbol for:* **1.** any unknown, variable, or unspecified factor, number, person, or thing. **2.** *Chem.* atomic number. **3.** *Physics.* impedance. **4.** zone.

z. *abbrev. for:* **1.** zero. **2.** zone.

zabaglione (ˌzæbəˈljəʊnɪ) *n.* a light foamy dessert made of egg yolks, sugar, and marsala, whipped together and served warm in a glass. [It.]

zaffer *or* **zaffre** (ˈzæfə) *n.* impure cobalt oxide, used to impart a blue colour to enamels. [C17: < It. *zaffera*]

zaibatsu (ˈzaɪbætˈsuː) *n.* (*functioning as sing. or pl.*) the group or combine comprising a few wealthy families that controls industry, business, and finance in Japan. [< Japanese, < *zai* wealth + *batsu* family, person of influence]

zakuski *or* **zakouski** (zæˈkʊskɪ) *pl. n., sing.* **-ka** (-kə). *Russian cookery.* hors d'oeuvres, consisting of tiny open sandwiches spread with caviar, smoked sausage, etc., or a cold dish such as radishes in sour cream, all usually served with vodka. [Russian, < *zakusit'* to have a snack]

Zambian (ˈzæmbɪən) *adj.* **1.** of or relating to Zambia, a republic in central Africa. ~*n.* **2.** a native or inhabitant of Zambia.

zambuck *or* **zambuk** (ˈzæmbʌk) *n. Austral. & N.Z. inf.* a first-aid attendant at a sports event. [< name of a proprietary ointment]

ZANU (ˈzɑːnuː) *n. acronym for* Zimbabwe African National Union.

zany (ˈzeɪnɪ) *adj.* **zanier, zaniest. 1.** comical in an endearing way; imaginatively funny or comical, esp. in behaviour. ~*n., pl.* **-nies. 2.** a clown or buffoon, esp. one in old comedies who imitated other performers with ludicrous effect. **3.** a ludicrous or foolish person. [C16: < It. *zanni,* < dialect *Zanni,* nickname for *Giovanni* John; one of the traditional names for a clown] —ˈ**zanily** *adv.* —ˈ**zaniness** *n.*

zap (zæp) *Sl.* ~*vb.* **zapping, zapped. 1.** (*tr.*) to attack, kill, or destroy, as with a sudden bombardment. **2.** (*intr.*) to move quickly. **3.** (*tr.*) *Computers.* **a.** to clear from the screen. **b.** to erase. **4.** (*intr.*) *Television.* to change channels rapidly by remote control. ~*n.* **5.** energy, vigour, or pep. ~*interj.* **6.** an exclamation used to express sudden or swift action. [imit.]

zapateado *Spanish.* (ˌθapateˈaðo) *n., pl.* **-dos** (-ðos). a Spanish dance with stamping and very fast footwork. [< *zapatear* to tap with the shoe, < *zapato* shoe]

zappy (ˈzæpɪ) *adj.* **-pier, -piest.** *Sl.* full of energy; zippy.

ZAPU (ˈzæpuː) *n. acronym for* Zimbabwe African People's Union.

Zarathustrian (ˌzærəˈθuːstrɪən) *adj., n.* another name for **Zoroastrian.** [C19: < *Zarathustra* the Old Iranian form of Zoroaster]

zareba *or* **zareeba** (zəˈriːbə) *n.* (in northern E Africa, esp. formerly) **1.** a stockade or enclosure of thorn bushes around a village or camp site. **2.** the area so protected or enclosed. [C19: < Ar. *zarībah* cattlepen, < *zarb* sheepfold]

zarf (zɑːf) *n.* (esp. in the Middle East) a holder, usually ornamental, for a hot coffee cup. [< Ar.: container]

zarzuela (zɑːˈzweɪlə) *n.* **1.** a type of Spanish vaudeville or operetta, usually satirical in nature. **2.** a seafood stew. [< Sp., after *La Zarzuela,* the palace near Madrid where such vaudeville was first performed (1629)]

z-axis *n.* a reference axis of a three-dimensional Cartesian coordinate system along which the *z*-coordinate is measured.

ZB station *n.* (in New Zealand) a radio station of a commercial network.

Z chart *n. Statistics.* a chart often used in industry and constructed by plotting on it three series: monthly, weekly, or daily data, the moving annual total, and the cumulative total dating from the beginning of the current year.

zeal (ziːl) *n.* fervent or enthusiastic devotion, often extreme or fanatical in nature, as to a religious movement, political cause, ideal, or aspiration. [C14: < LL *zēlus,* < Gk *zēlos*]

zealot (ˈzɛlət) *n.* an immoderate, fanatical, or extremely zealous adherent to a cause, esp. a religious one. [C16: < LL *zēlōtēs,* < Gk, < *zēloun* to be zealous, < *zēlos* zeal] —ˈ**zealotry** *n.*

Zealot (ˈzɛlət) *n.* any of the members of an extreme Jewish sect or political party that resisted all aspects of Roman rule in Palestine in the 1st century A.D.

zealous (ˈzɛləs) *adj.* filled with or inspired by intense enthusiasm or zeal; ardent; fervent. —ˈ**zealously** *adv.* —ˈ**zealousness** *n.*

zebec *or* **zebeck** (ˈziːbɛk) *n.* variant spellings of **xebec.**

zebra (ˈziːbrə, ˈzɛbrə) *n., pl.* **-ras** *or* **-ra.** any of several mammals of the horse family, such as the common zebra of southern and eastern Africa, having distinctive black-and-white striped hides. [C16: via It. < OSp.: wild ass, prob. < Vulgar L *eciferus* (unattested) wild horse, < L *equiferus,* < *equus* horse + *ferus* wild] —**zebrine** (ˈziːbraɪn, ˈzɛb-) *or* ˈ**zebroid** *adj.*

zebra crossing *n. Brit.* a pedestrian crossing marked on a road by broad alternate black and white stripes. Once on the crossing the pedestrian has right of way.

zebra finch *n.* any of various Australasian songbirds with zebra-like markings.

zebrawood (ˈzɛbrəˌwʊd, ˈziː-) *n.* **1.** a tree of tropical America, Asia, and Africa, yielding striped hardwood used in cabinetwork. **2.** any of various other trees or shrubs having striped wood. **3.** the wood of any of these trees.

zebu (ˈziːbuː) *n.* a domesticated ox having a humped back, long horns, and a large dewlap: used in India and E Asia as a draught animal. [C18: < F *zébu,* ? of Tibetan origin]

Zech. *Bible. abbrev. for* Zechariah.

zed (zɛd) *n.* the British spoken form of the letter *z.* [C15: < OF *zede,* via LL < Gk *zēta*]

zedoary (ˈzɛdəʊərɪ) *n.* the dried rhizome of a tropical Asian plant, used as a stimulant and a condiment. [C15: < Med. L *zedoaria,* < Ar. *zadwār,* of Persian origin]

zee (ziː) *n.* the U.S. word for **zed** (letter *z*).

Zeeman effect (ˈziːmən) *n.* the splitting of a spectral line of a substance into several closely spaced lines when the substance is placed in a magnetic field. [C20: after Pieter *Zeeman* (1865–1943), Du. physicist]

zein (ˈziːɪn) *n.* a protein occurring in maize and used in the manufacture of plastics, paper coatings, adhesives, etc. [C19: < NL *zēa* maize, < L: a kind of grain, < Gk *zeia* barley]

Zeitgeist *German.* (ˈtsaɪtˌgaɪst) *n.* the spirit, attitude, or general outlook of a specific time or period, esp. as it is reflected in literature, philosophy, etc. [G, lit.: time spirit]

Zen (zɛn) *Buddhism. n.* **1.** a Japanese school, of 12th-century Chinese origin, teaching that contemplation of one's essential nature to the exclusion of all else is the only way of achieving pure enlightenment. **2.** (*modifier*) of or relating to this school: *Zen Buddhism.* [< Japanese, < Chinese *ch'an* religious meditation, < Pali *jhāna,* < Sansk. *dhyāna*] —ˈ**Zenic** *adj.* —ˈ**Zenist** *n.*

zenana (zɛˈnɑːnə) *n.* (in the East, esp. in Muslim and Hindu homes) part of a house reserved for the women and girls of a household. [C18: < Hindi *zanāna,* < Persian, < *zan* woman]

Zend (zɛnd) *n.* **1.** a former name for **Avestan.** **2.** short for **Zend-Avesta.** **3.** an exposition of the Avesta in the Middle Persian language (Pahlavi). [C18: < Persian *zand* commentary, exposition; used specifically of the MPersian commentary on the Avesta, hence of the language of the Avesta itself] —ˈ**Zendic** *adj.*

Zend-Avesta (ˌzɛndəˈvɛstə) *n.* the Avesta together with the traditional interpretive commentary known as the Zend, esp. as preserved in the Avestan language among the Parsees. [< Avestan, representing *Avesta'-va-zend* Avesta with interpretation]

Zener diode (ˈziːnə) *n.* a semiconductor diode that exhibits a sharp increase in reverse current at a well-defined reverse voltage: used as a voltage regulator. [C20: after C. M. *Zener* (b. 1905), U.S. physicist]

zenith (ˈzɛnɪθ) *n.* **1.** *Astron.* the point on the celestial sphere vertically above an observer. **2.** the highest point; peak; acme: *the zenith of someone's achievements.* [C17: < F *cenith,* < Med. L, < OSp. *zenit,* based on Ar. *samt,* as in *samt arrās* path over one's head] —ˈ**zenithal** *adj.*

zenithal projection *n.* a type of map projection in which part of the earth's surface is projected onto a plane tangential to it, either at one of the poles (**polar zenithal**), at the equator (**equatorial zenithal**), or between (**oblique zenithal**).

zeolite (ˈziːəˌlaɪt) *n.* **1.** any of a large group of glassy secondary minerals consisting of hydrated aluminium silicates of calcium, sodium, or potassium: formed in cavities in lava flows and plutonic rocks. **2.** any of a class of similar synthetic materials used in ion exchange and as selective absorbents. [C18: *zeo-,* < Gk *zein* to boil + -LITE; < the swelling up that occurs under the blowpipe] —**zeolitic** (ˌziːəˈlɪtɪk) *adj.*

Zeph. *Bible. abbrev. for* Zephaniah.

zephyr (ˈzɛfə) *n.* **1.** a soft or gentle breeze. **2.** any of several delicate soft yarns, fabrics, or garments, usually of wool. [C16: < L *zephyrus,* < Gk *zephuros* the west wind]

zeppelin (ˈzɛpəlɪn) *n.* (*sometimes cap.*) a large cylindrical rigid airship built from 1900 to carry passengers and used in World War I for bombing and reconnaissance. [C20: after Count von *Zeppelin* (1838-1917), its G designer]

zero (ˈzɪərəʊ) *n., pl.* **-ros** *or* **-roes. 1.** the symbol 0, indicating an absence of quantity or magnitude; nought. Former name: **cipher. 2.** the integer denoted by the symbol 0; nought. **3.** the ordinal number between +1 and -1. **4.** nothing; nil. **5.** a person or thing of no significance; nonentity. **6.** the lowest point or degree: *his prospects were put at zero.* **7.** the line or point on a scale of measurement from which the graduations commence. **8. a.** the temperature, pressure, etc., that registers a reading of zero on a scale. **b.** the value of a variable, such as temperature, obtained under specified conditions. **9.** *Maths.* **a.** the cardinal number of a set with no members. **b.** the identity element of addition. ~*adj.* **10.** having no measurable quantity, magnitude, etc. **11.** *Meteorol.* **a.** (of a cloud ceiling) limiting visibility to 15 metres (50 feet) or less. **b.** (of horizontal visibility) limited to 50 metres (165 feet) or less. ~*vb.* **-roing, -roed. 12.** (*tr.*) to adjust (an instrument, apparatus, etc.) so as to read zero or a position taken as zero. ~*determiner.* **13.** *Inf., chiefly U.S.* no (thing) at all: *this job has zero interest.* ~See also **zero in.** [C17: < It., < Med. L *zephirum,* < Ar. *sifr* empty]

zero gravity *n.* the state or condition of weightlessness.

zero hour *n.* **1.** *Mil.* the time set for the start of an attack or the initial stage of an operation. **2.** *Inf.* a critical time, esp. at the commencement of an action.

zero in *vb.* (*adv.*) **1.** (often foll. by *on*) to bring (a weapon) to bear (on a target), as while firing repeatedly. **2.** (*intr.;* foll. by *on*) *Inf.* to bring one's attention to bear (on a problem, etc.). **3.** (*intr.;* foll. by *on*) *Inf.* to converge (upon): *the police zeroed in on the site of the crime.*

zero option *n.* (in international nuclear arms negotiations) an offer to remove all shorter-range nuclear missiles or, in the case of the **zero-zero option** all intermediate-range nuclear missiles, if the other side will do the same.

zero-rated *adj.* denoting goods on which the buyer pays no value-added tax although the seller can claim back any tax he has paid.

zero stage *n.* a solid-propellant rocket attached to a liquid-propellant rocket to provide greater thrust at liftoff.

zeroth (ˈzɪərəʊð) *adj.* denoting a term in a series that precedes the term otherwise regarded as the first term. [C20: < ZERO + -TH[2]]

zest (zɛst) *n.* **1.** invigorating or keen excitement or enjoyment: *a zest for living.* **2.** added interest, flavour, or charm; piquancy: *her presence gave zest to the occasion.* **3.** something added to give flavour or relish. **4.** the peel or skin of an orange or lemon, used as flavouring in drinks, etc. ~*vb.* **5.** (*tr.*) to give flavour, interest, or piquancy to. [C17: < F *zeste* peel of citrus fruits used as flavouring, <?] —ˈ**zestful** *adj.* —ˈ**zestfully** *adv.* —ˈ**zestfulness** *n.* —ˈ**zesty** *adj.*

zeta (ˈziːtə) *n.* the sixth letter in the Greek alphabet (Z, ζ). [< Gk]

ZETA (ˈziːtə) *n.* a torus-shaped apparatus used for research on controlled thermonuclear reactions and plasma physics. [C20: < *z*(*ero-*)*e*(*nergy*) *t*(*hermonuclear*) *a*(*pparatus*)]

zeugma (ˈzjuːgmə) *n.* a figure of speech in which a word is used to modify or govern two or more words although appropriate to only one of them or making a different sense with each, as in *Mr Pickwick took his hat and his leave* (Charles Dickens). [C16: via L < Gk: a yoking, < *zeugnunai* to yoke] —**zeugmatic** (zjuːgˈmætɪk) *adj.*

zho (zəʊ) *n.* a variant spelling of **zo.**

zibeline (ˈzɪbəˌlaɪn, -lɪn) *n.* **1.** a sable or the fur of this animal. **2.** a thick cloth made of wool or other animal hair, having a long nap and a dull sheen. ~*adj.* **3.** of, relating to, or resembling a sable. [C16: < F, < OIt. *zibellino,* ult. of Slavonic origin]

zibet (ˈzɪbɪt) *n.* a large civet of S and SE Asia, having tawny fur marked with black spots and stripes. [C16: < Med. L *zibethum,* < Ar. *zabād* civet]

ziff (zɪf) *n. Austral. inf.* a beard. [C20: <?]

ziggurat (ˈzɪgʊˌræt) *n.* a type of rectangular temple tower or tiered mound erected by the Sumerians, Akkadians, and Babylonians in Mesopotamia. [C19: < Assyrian *ziqqurati* summit]

zigzag (ˈzɪgˌzæg) *n.* **1.** a line or course characterized by sharp turns in alternating directions. **2.** one of the series of such turns. **3.** something having the form of a zigzag. ~*adj.* **4.** (*usually prenominal*) formed in or proceeding in a zigzag. **5.** (of a sewing machine) capable of producing stitches in a zigzag. ~*adv.* **6.** in a zigzag manner. ~*vb.* **-zagging, -zagged. 7.** to proceed or cause to proceed in a zigzag. **8.** (*tr.*) to form into a zigzag. [C18: < F, < G *zickzack,* < *Zacke* point]

zigzagger (ˈzɪgˌzægə) *n.* **1.** a person or thing that zigzags. **2.** an attachment on a sewing machine for sewing zigzag stitches, as for joining two pieces of material.

zilch (zɪltʃ) *n. Sl., chiefly U.S. & Canad.* nothing. [C20: <?]

zillion (ˈzɪljən) *Inf.* ~*n., pl.* **-lions** *or* **-lion. 1.** (*often pl.*) an extremely large but unspecified number, quantity, or amount: *zillions of flies in this camp.* ~*determiner.* **2.** amounting to a zillion: *a zillion different problems.* [C20: coinage after MILLION]

Zimbabwean (zɪmˈbɑːbwɪən) *adj.* **1.** of or relating to Zimbabwe, a republic in southern Africa. ~*n.* **2.** a native or inhabitant of Zimbabwe.

Zimmer (ˈzɪmə) *n. Trademark.* Also: **Zimmer aid.** another name for **walker** (sense 3).

zinc (zɪŋk) *n.* **1.** a brittle bluish-white metallic element that is a constituent of several alloys, esp. brass and nickel-silver, and is used in die-casting, galvanizing metals, and in battery electrodes. Symbol: Zn; atomic no.: 30; atomic wt.: 65.37. **2.** *Inf.* corrugated galvanized iron. [C17: < G *Zink*, ? < *Zinke* prong, < its jagged appearance in the furnace] —ˈ**zincic** *adj.* —ˈ**zincky**, ˈ**zincy**, *or* ˈ**zinky** *adj.*

zinc blende *n.* another name for **sphalerite.**

zinc chloride *n.* a white soluble poisonous granular solid used in manufacturing parchment paper and vulcanized fibre and in preserving wood. It is also a soldering flux, embalming agent, and medical astringent and antiseptic.

zincite (ˈzɪŋkaɪt) *n.* a red or yellow mineral consisting of zinc oxide in hexagonal crystalline form. It occurs in metamorphosed limestone.

zincography (zɪŋˈkɒgrəfɪ) *n.* the art or process of etching on zinc to form a printing plate. —**zincograph** (ˈzɪŋkəˌgrɑːf) *n.* —**zin**ˈ**cographer** *n.*

zinc ointment *n.* a medicinal ointment consisting of zinc oxide, petrolatum, and paraffin.

zinc oxide *n.* a white insoluble powder used as a pigment in paints (**zinc white** or **Chinese white**), cosmetics, glass, and printing inks. It is an antiseptic and astringent and is used in making zinc ointment. Formula: ZnO. Also called: **flowers of zinc.**

zinc sulphate *n.* a colourless soluble crystalline substance used as a mordant, in preserving wood and skins, and in the electrodeposition of zinc.

zing (zɪŋ) *n. Inf.* **1.** a short high-pitched buzzing sound, as of a bullet or vibrating string. **2.** vitality; zest. ~*vb.* **3.** (*intr.*) to make or move with or as if with a high-pitched buzzing sound. [C20: imit.] —ˈ**zingy** *adj.*

zinjanthropus (zɪnˈdʒænθrəpəs) *n.* a type of australopithecine, remains of which were discovered in the Olduvai Gorge in Tanzania in 1959. [C20: NL, < Ar. *Zinj* East Africa + Gk *anthrōpos* man]

zinnia (ˈzɪnɪə) *n.* any of a genus of annual or perennial plants of the composite family, of tropical and subtropical America, having solitary heads of brightly coloured flowers. [C18: named after J. G. Zinn (d. 1759), G botanist]

Zion (ˈzaɪən) *or* **Sion** *n.* **1.** the hill on which the city of Jerusalem stands. **2.** *Judaism.* **a.** the ancient Israelites of the Bible. **b.** the modern Jewish nation. **c.** Israel as the national home of the Jewish people. **3.** *Christianity.* heaven regarded as the city of God and the final abode of his elect.

Zionism (ˈzaɪəˌnɪzəm) *n.* **1.** a political movement for the establishment and support of a national homeland for Jews in Palestine, now concerned chiefly with the development of the modern state of Israel. **2.** a policy or movement for Jews to return to Palestine from the Diaspora. —ˈ**Zionist** *n., adj.* —ˌ**Zion**ˈ**istic** *adj.*

zip (zɪp) *n.* **1. a.** Also called: **zip fastener.** a fastening device operating by means of two parallel rows of metal or plastic teeth on either side of a closure that are interlocked by a sliding tab. U.S. and Canad. term: **zipper. b.** (*modifier*) having such a device: *a zip bag.* **2.** a short sharp whizzing sound, as of a passing bullet. **3.** *Inf.* energy; vigour; vitality. ~*vb.* **zipping, zipped. 4.** (*tr.;* often foll. by *up*) to fasten (clothing, etc.) with a zip. **5.** (*intr.*) to move with a zip: *the bullet zipped past.* **6.** (*intr.;* often foll. by *along, through,* etc.) to hurry; rush. [C19: imit.]

zip code *n.* the U.S. equivalent of **postcode.** [C20: < *z*(*one*) *i*(*mprovement*) *p*(*lan*)]

zip gun *n. U.S. & Canad. sl.* a crude home-made pistol, esp. one powered by a spring or rubber band.

zipper (ˈzɪpə) *n.* the U.S. & Canad. word for **zip** (sense 1a).

zippy (ˈzɪpɪ) *adj.* **-pier, -piest.** *Inf.* full of energy; lively.

zircalloy (zɜːkˈælɔɪ) *n.* an alloy of zirconium containing small amounts of tin, chromium, and nickel. It is used in pressurized-water reactors.

zircon (ˈzɜːkɒn) *n.* a reddish-brown, grey, green, blue, or colourless hard mineral consisting of zirconium silicate: it is used as a gemstone and a refractory. [C18: < G *Zirkon,* < F *jargon,* via It. & Ar., < Persian *zargūn* golden]

zirconium (zɜːˈkəʊnɪəm) *n.* a greyish-white metallic element, occurring chiefly in zircon, that is exceptionally corrosion-resistant and has low neutron absorption. It is used as a coating in nuclear and chemical plants, as a deoxidizer in steel, and alloyed with niobium in superconductive magnets. Symbol: Zr; atomic no.: 40; atomic wt.: 91.22. [C19: < NL; see ZIRCON] —**zirconic** (zɜːˈkɒnɪk) *adj.*

zirconium oxide *n.* a white amorphous powder that is insoluble in water and highly refractory, used as a pigment for paints, a catalyst, and an abrasive.

zit (zɪt) *n. U.S. sl.* a pimple. [<?]

zither (ˈzɪðə) *n.* a plucked musical instrument consisting of numerous strings stretched over a resonating box, a few of which may be stopped on a fretted fingerboard. [C19: < G, < L *cithara,* < Gk *kithara*] —ˈ**zitherist** *n.*

zloty (ˈzlɒtɪ) *n., pl.* **-tys** *or* **-ty.** the standard monetary unit of Poland. [< Polish: golden, < *zlyoto* gold]

Zn *the chemical symbol for* zinc.

zo, zho, *or* **dzo** (zəʊ) *n., pl.* **zos, zhos, dzos** *or* **zo, zho, dzo.** a Tibetan breed of cattle, developed by crossing the yak with common cattle. [C20: < Tibetan]

zo- *combining form.* a variant of **zoo-** before a vowel.

-zoa *suffix forming plural proper nouns.* indicating groups of animal organisms: *Protozoa.* [< NL, < Gk *zōia,* pl. of *zōion* animal]

zodiac (ˈzəʊdɪˌæk) *n.* **1.** an imaginary belt extending 8° either side of the ecliptic, which contains the 12 **zodiacal constellations** and within which the moon and planets appear to move. It is divided into 12 equal areas, called **signs of the zodiac,** each named after the constellation which once lay in it. **2.** *Astrol.* a diagram, usually circular, representing this belt and showing the symbols, illustrations, etc., associated with each of the 12 signs of the zodiac, used to predict the future. [C14: < OF *zodiaque,* < L *zōdiacus,* < Gk *zōidiakos* (*kuklos*) (circle) of signs, < *zōidion* animal sign, < *zōion* animal] —**zodiacal** (zəʊˈdaɪəkəl) *adj.*

zodiacal constellation *n.* any of the 12 constellations after which the signs of the zodiac are named: Aries, Taurus, Gemini, Cancer, Leo, Virgo, Libra, Scorpio, Sagittarius, Capricorn, Aquarius, or Pisces.

zodiacal light *n.* a very faint cone of light in the sky, visible in the east just before sunrise and in the west just after sunset.

zoic (ˈzəʊɪk) *adj.* **1.** relating to or having animal life. **2.** *Geol.* (of rocks, etc.) containing fossilized animals. [C19: < NL, < Gk *zōion* animal]

-zoic *adj. and n. combining form.* indicating a geological era: *Palaeozoic.* [< Gk *zōē* life + -IC]

Zollverein *German.* (ˈtsɔlfɛrˌain) *n.* the customs union of German states organized in the early 1830s under Prussian auspices. [C19: < *Zoll* tax + *Verein* union]

zombie *or* **zombi** (ˈzɒmbɪ) *n., pl.* **-bies** *or* **-bis. 1.** a person who is or appears to be lifeless, apathetic, or totally lacking in independent judgment; automaton. **2.** a supernatural spirit that reanimates a dead body. **3.** a corpse brought to life in this manner. [< W African *zumbi* good-luck fetish]

zonation (zəʊˈneɪʃən) *n.* arrangement in zones.

zone (zəʊn) *n.* **1.** a region, area, or section characterized by some distinctive feature or quality. **2.** an area subject to a particular political, military, or government function, use, or jurisdiction: *a demilitarized zone.* **3.** (*often cap.*) *Geog.* one of the divisions of the earth's surface, esp. divided into latitudinal belts according to temperature. See **Torrid Zone, Frigid Zone, Temperate Zone.** **4.** *Geol.* a distinctive layer or region of rock, characterized by particular fossils, etc. **5.** *Ecology.* an area, esp. a belt of land, having a particular flora and fauna determined by the prevailing environmental conditions. **6.** *Maths.* a portion of a sphere between two parallel planes intersecting the sphere. **7.** *Arch. or literary.* a girdle or belt. **8.** *N.Z.* a section on a transport route; fare stage. **9.** *N.Z.* a catchment area for a specific school. ~*vb.* (*tr.*) **10.** to divide into zones, as for different use, jurisdiction, activities, etc. **11.** to designate as a zone. **12.** to mark with or divide into zones. [C15: < L *zōna* girdle, climatic zone, < Gk *zōnē*] —**ˈzonal** *adj.* —**ˈzonated** *adj.* —**ˈzoning** *n.*

zone refining *n.* a technique for producing solids of extreme purity, esp. for use in semiconductors. The material, in the form of a bar, is melted in one small region that is passed along the solid. Impurities concentrate in the melt and are moved to the end of the bar.

zonetime (ˈzəʊnˌtaɪm) *n.* the standard time of the time zone in which a ship is located at sea, each zone extending 7½° to each side of a meridian.

zonked (zɒŋkt) *adj. Sl.* **1.** highly intoxicated from drugs or alcohol. **2.** exhausted. [C20: imit.]

zoo (zuː) *n., pl.* **zoos.** a place where live animals are kept, studied, bred, and exhibited to the public. Formal term: **zoological garden.** [C19: shortened < *zoological gardens* (orig. those in London)]

zoo- *or before a vowel* **zo-** *combining form.* indicating animals: *zooplankton.* [< Gk *zōion* animal]

zoogeography (ˌzəʊədʒɪˈɒgrəfɪ) *n.* the branch of zoology concerned with the geographical distribution of animals. —ˌ**zoogeˈographer** *n.* —**zoogeographic** (ˌzəʊəˌdʒɪəˈgræfɪk) *or* ˌ**zooˌgeoˈgraphical** *adj.* —ˌ**zooˌgeoˈgraphically** *adv.*

zoography (zəʊˈɒgrəfɪ) *n.* the branch of zoology concerned with the description of animals. —**zoˈographer** *n.* —**zoographic** (ˌzəʊəˈgræfɪk) *or* ˌ**zooˈgraphical** *adj.*

zooid (ˈzəʊɔɪd) *n.* **1.** any independent animal body, such as an individual of a coelenterate colony. **2.** a motile cell or body, such as a gamete, produced by an organism. —**zoˈoidal** *adj.*

zool. *abbrev. for:* **1.** zoological. **2.** zoology.

zoolatry (zəʊˈɒlətrɪ) *n.* **1.** (esp. in ancient or primitive religions) the worship of animals as the incarnations of certain deities, etc. **2.** extreme or excessive devotion to animals, particularly domestic pets. —**zoˈolatrous** *adj.*

zoological garden *n.* the formal term for **zoo.**

zoology (zəʊˈɒlədʒɪ, zuː-) *n., pl.* **-gies. 1.** the study of animals, including their classification, structure, physiology, and history. **2.** the biological characteristics of a particular animal or animal group. **3.** the fauna characteristic of a particular region. —**zoological** (ˌzəʊəˈlɒdʒɪkᵊl, ˌzuːə-) *adj.* —**zoˈologist** *n.*

zoom (zuːm) *vb.* **1.** to make or cause to make a continuous buzzing or humming sound. **2.** to move or cause to move with such a sound. **3.** (*intr.*) to move very rapidly; rush: *we zoomed through town.* **4.** to cause (an aircraft) to climb briefly at an unusually steep angle, or (of an aircraft) to climb in this way. **5.** (*intr.*) (of prices) to rise rapidly. ~*n.* **6.** the sound or act of zooming. **7.** See **zoom lens.** [C19: imit.]

zoom in *or* **out** *vb.* (*intr., adv.*) *Photog., films, television.* to increase or decrease rapidly the magnification of the image of a distant object by means of a zoom lens.

zoom lens *n.* a lens system that allows the focal length of a camera lens to be varied continuously without altering the sharpness of the image.

zoomorphism (ˌzəʊəˈmɔːfɪzəm) *n.* **1.** the conception or representation of deities in the form of animals. **2.** the use of animal forms or symbols in art, etc. —ˌ**zooˈmorphic** *adj.*

-zoon *n. combining form.* indicating an individual animal or an independently moving entity derived from an animal: *spermatozoon.* [< Gk *zōion* animal]

zoophilism (zəʊˈɒfɪˌlɪzəm) *n.* the tendency to be emotionally attached to animals. —**zoophile** (ˈzəʊəˌfaɪl) *n.*

zoophobia (ˌzəʊəˈfəʊbɪə) *n.* an unusual or morbid dread of animals. —**zoophobous** (zəʊˈɒfəbəs) *adj.*

zoophyte (ˈzəʊəˌfaɪt) *n.* any animal resembling a plant, such as a sea anemone. —**zoophytic** (ˌzəʊəˈfɪtɪk) *or* ˌ**zooˈphytical** *adj.*

zooplankton (ˌzəʊəˈplæŋktən) *n.* the animal constituent of plankton, which consists mainly of small crustaceans and fish larvae.

zoospore (ˈzəʊəˌspɔː) *n.* an asexual spore of some algae and fungi that moves by means of flagella. —ˌ**zooˈsporic** *or* **zoosporous** (zəʊˈɒspərəs, ˌzəʊəˈspɔːrəs) *adj.*

zoosterol (zəʊˈɒstəˌrɒl) *n.* any of a group of animal sterols, such as cholesterol.

zootechnics (ˌzəʊəˈtɛknɪks) *n.* (*functioning as sing.*) the science concerned with the domestication and breeding of animals.

zootomy (zəʊˈɒtəmɪ) *n.* the branch of zoology concerned with the dissection and anatomy of animals. —**zootomic** (ˌzəʊəˈtɒmɪk) *or* ˌ**zooˈtomical** *adj.* —ˌ**zooˈtomically** *adv.* —**zoˈotomist** *n.*

zootoxin (ˌzəʊəˈtɒksɪn) *n.* a toxin, such as snake venom, that is produced by an animal.

zoot suit (zuːt) *n. Sl.* a man's suit consisting of baggy tapered trousers and a long jacket with wide padded shoulders, popular esp. in the 1940s. [C20: <?]

zoril *or* **zorille** (zəˈrɪl) *n.* a skunklike African mammal, having a long black-and-white coat. [C18: < F, < Sp. *zorrillo* a little fox, < *zorro* fox]

Zoroastrian (ˌzɒrəʊˈæstrɪən) *adj.* **1.** of or relating to Zoroastrianism. ~*n.* **2.** an adherent of Zoroastrianism.

Zoroastrianism (ˌzɒrəʊˈæstrɪənˌɪzəm) *or* **Zoroastrism** *n.* the dualistic religion founded by the Persian prophet Zoroaster in the late 7th or early 6th century B.C. and set forth in the sacred writings of the Zend-Avesta. It is based on the concept of a continuous struggle between Ormazd (or Ahura Mazda), the god of creation, light, and goodness, and his archenemy, Ahriman, the spirit of evil and darkness.

zoster (ˈzɒstə) *n. Pathol.* short for **herpes zoster.** [C18: < L: shingles, < Gk *zōster* girdle]

Zouave (zuːˈɑːv, zwɑːv) *n.* **1.** (formerly) a member of a body of French infantry composed of Algerian recruits noted for their dash, hardiness, and colourful uniforms. **2.** a member of any body of soldiers wearing a similar uniform, esp. a volunteer in such a unit of the Union Army in the American Civil War. [C19: < F, < *Zwāwa*, tribal name in Algeria]

zounds (zaʊndz) *or* **swounds** (zwaʊndz, zaʊndz) *interj. Arch.* a mild oath indicating surprise, indignation, etc. [C16: euphemistic shortening of *God's wounds*]

Zr *the chemical symbol for* zirconium.

zucchetto (tsuːˈkɛtəʊ, suː-, zuː-) *n., pl.* **-tos.** *R.C. Church.* a small round skullcap worn by certain ecclesiastics and varying in colour according to the rank of the wearer, the Pope wearing white, cardinals red, bishops violet, and others black. [C19: < It., < *zucca* a gourd, < LL *cucutia*, prob. < L *cucurbita*]

zucchini (tsuːˈkiːnɪ, zuː-) *n., pl.* **-ni** *or* **-nis.** *Chiefly U.S., Canad., & Austral.* another name for **courgette.** [It., pl. of *zucchino* a little gourd, < *zucca* gourd; see ZUCCHETTO]

zugzwang (*German* ˈtsuːktsvaŋ) *Chess.* ~*n.* **1.** a position in which one player can move only with loss or severe disadvantage. ~*vb.* **2.** (*tr.*) to manoeuvre (one's opponent) into a zugzwang. [< G, < *Zug* a pull + *Zwang* force]

Zulu (ˈzuːluː, -luː) *n.* **1.** (*pl.* **-lus** *or* **-lu**) a member of a tall Negroid people of SE Africa, living chiefly in N Natal, who became dominant during the 19th century due to a warrior-clan system organized by the powerful leader, Shaka. **2.** the language of this people.

Zuñi (ˈzuːnjiː, ˈsuː-) *n.* **1.** (*pl.* **-ñis** *or* **-ñi**) a member of a North American Indian people of W New Mexico. **2.** the language of this people. —**ˈZuñian** *adj., n.*

zwieback (ˈzwiːˌbæk; *German* ˈtsviːbak) *n.* a small type of rusk, which has been baked first as a loaf, then sliced and toasted. [G: twice-baked]

Zwinglian (ˈzwɪŋglɪən, ˈtsvɪŋ-) *n.* **1.** an upholder of the religious doctrines or movement of Zwingli (1484-1531), Swiss leader of the Reformation. ~*adj.* **2.** of or relating to Zwingli, his religious movement, or his doctrines.

zwitterion (ˈtsvɪtərˌaɪən) *n. Chem.* an ion that carries both a positive and a negative charge. [C20: < G *Zwitter* bisexual + ION]

zygapophysis (ˌzɪgəˈpɒfɪsɪs, ˌzaɪgə-) *n., pl.* **-ses** (-ˌsiːz). *Anat., zool.* one of several processes on a vertebra that articulates with the corresponding process on an adjacent vertebra. [< Gk ZYG- + *apophusis* a sideshoot]

zygo- *or before a vowel* **zyg-** *combining form.* indicating a pair or a union: *zygodactyl; zygospore.* [< Gk *zugon* yoke]

zygodactyl (ˌzaɪgəʊˈdæktɪl, ˌzɪgə-) *adj. also* **zygodactylous. 1.** (of the feet of certain birds) having the first and fourth toes directed backwards and the second and third forwards. ~*n.* **2.** a zygodactyl bird.

zygoma (zaɪˈgəʊmə, zɪ-) *n., pl.* **-mata** (-mətə). another name for **zygomatic arch.** [C17: via NL < Gk, < *zugon* yoke] —**zygomatic** (ˌzaɪgəʊˈmætɪk, ˌzɪg-) *adj.*

zygomatic arch *n.* the slender arch of bone that forms a bridge between the cheekbone and the temporal bone on each side of the skull of mammals. Also called: **zygoma.**

zygomatic bone *n.* either of two bones, one on each side of the skull, that form part of the side wall of the eye socket and part of the zygomatic arch; cheekbone.

zygomorphic (ˌzaɪgəʊˈmɔːfɪk, ˌzɪg-) *or* **zygomorphous** *adj.* (of a flower) capable of being cut in only one plane so that the two halves are mirror images.

zygophyte (ˈzaɪgəʊˌfaɪt, ˈzɪg-) *n.* a plant, such as an alga, that reproduces by means of zygospores.

zygospore (ˈzaɪgəʊˌspɔː, ˈzɪg-) *n.* a thick-walled sexual spore formed from the zygote of some fungi and algae. —ˌ**zygoˈsporic** *adj.*

zygote (ˈzaɪgəʊt, ˈzɪg-) *n.* **1.** the cell resulting from the union of an ovum and a spermatozoon. **2.** the organism that develops from such a cell. [C19: < Gk *zugōtos* yoked, < *zugoun* to yoke] —**zygotic** (zaɪˈgɒtɪk, zɪ-) *adj.* —**zyˈgotically** *adv.*

zymase (ˈzaɪmeɪs) *n.* a mixture of enzymes that is obtained as an extract from yeast and ferments sugars.

zymo- *or before a vowel* **zym-** *combining form.* indicating fermentation: *zymology.* [< Gk *zumē* leaven]

zymogen (ˈzaɪməʊˌdʒɛn) *n. Biochem.* any of a group of compounds that are inactive precursors of enzymes.

zymology (zaɪˈmɒlədʒɪ) *n.* the chemistry of fermentation. —**zymologic** (ˌzaɪməʊˈlɒdʒɪk) *or* ˌ**zymoˈlogical** *adj.* —**zyˈmologist** *n.*

zymolysis (zaɪˈmɒlɪsɪs) *n.* the process of fermentation. Also called: **zymosis.**

zymosis (zaɪˈməʊsɪs) *n., pl.* **-ses** (-siːz). **1.** *Med.* **a.** any infectious disease. **b.** the developmental process or spread of such a disease. **2.** another name for **zymolysis.**

zymotic (zaɪˈmɒtɪk) *adj.* **1.** of, relating to, or causing fermentation. **2.** relating to or caused by infection; denoting or relating to an infectious disease. —**zyˈmotically** *adv.*

zymurgy (ˈzaɪmɜːdʒɪ) *n.* the branch of chemistry concerned with fermentation processes in brewing, etc.